The

EUROPA WORLD OF LEARNING

2015

The

EUROPA WORLD OF LEARNING 2015

65th Edition

VOLUME I

INTRODUCTORY ESSAYS
INTERNATIONAL ORGANIZATIONS
AFGHANISTAN–MYANMAR

Routledge
Taylor & Francis Group
LONDON AND NEW YORK

Sixty-fifth edition published 2014
by Routledge
2 Park Square, Milton Park, Abingdon, Oxfordshire, OX14 4RN, United Kingdom

and by Routledge
711 Third Avenue, New York, NY 10017

www.worldoflearning.com

Routledge is an imprint of the Taylor & Francis Group, an Informa business

First published 1947

Library of Congress Catalog Card Number 47-30172

ISBN: 978-1-85743-723-2 (The Set)
ISBN: 978-1-85743-724-9 (Vol. I)
ISSN: 0084-2117

Typeset in New Century Schoolbook
by Data Standards Limited, Frome, Somerset

Senior Editor: Anthony Gladman

Editorial Researchers: Denize Rodricks (*Editorial Research Team Leader*), Nimisha Chaurasia, Shikha Garg, Anindita Mondal, Robinson Raju, Minkushree Saikia

Editorial Assistant: Lydia de Cruz

Editorial Director: Paul Kelly

FSC
www.fsc.org
MIX
Paper from responsible sources
FSC® C020872

FOREWORD

It gives us great pleasure to introduce the 2015 edition of THE EUROPA WORLD OF LEARNING. First published in 1947, it has since become established as an authoritative reference work on academic institutions all over the world.

THE EUROPA WORLD OF LEARNING is unique in offering information over the entire spectrum of academic activity. Our listings cover not only universities and colleges, but also research institutes, libraries and archives, museums and art galleries and learned societies. Further to this, regulatory and representative bodies are covered in a section which also has details of relevant ministries, accrediting bodies and funding organizations. Each chapter has an introductory survey outlining the country's higher education system.

Each year we invite entrants to review and update their entries. Entrants may do so by email to wol@routledge.co.uk or online at updates.worldoflearning.com. We are, as ever, grateful to those who help bring our information up to date with their prompt replies. Continuous research on the internet and in the world's press, as well as contact with official sources worldwide, supplements this method of revision.

In addition to the regular updating of our entries, this edition has expanded coverage of institutions in a number of areas. Special projects to update and expand our listings were undertaken in chapters covering South and Central America (Argentina, Belize, Bolivia, Brazil, Chile, Colombia, Costa Rica, Ecuador, El Salvador, French Guiana, Guatemala, Guyana, Honduras, Mexico, Nicaragua, Panama, Paraguay, Peru, Puerto Rico, Suriname, Uruguay, and Venezuela), and chapters covering Ireland, New Zealand, South Africa, and the United Kingdom.

This edition of THE EUROPA WORLD OF LEARNING features essays commissioned by its editorial board. For each edition the board chooses a theme pertinent to international higher education, and guides the commissioning of about five essays to address it. The board's remit is to approve essays that are lively, panoramic, and engaging; that argue a proposition rather than summarize an issue. The theme for this edition is academic freedom. The board also appoints guest editors to oversee each set of thematically linked essays and to write an accompanying introduction to the issue. For details of the editorial board members, and the guest editors and authors contributing to this edition, please see page 3.

In the sections on Universities and Colleges, our classification follows the practice of the country concerned. This in no way implies any official evaluation on our part. Readers who are interested in the matter of the equivalence of institutions, degrees or diplomas should correspond directly with the institutions concerned, or with the national or international bodies set up for this purpose. Further information on these can be found in the Regulatory and Representative Bodies section of each chapter under the subheading Accreditation.

An online version of THE EUROPA WORLD OF LEARNING offers regular updates of content and an unprecedented level of access to institutions of higher education and learning worldwide, and to the people who work within them. Please see page vi or visit www.worldoflearning.com for further details.

August 2014

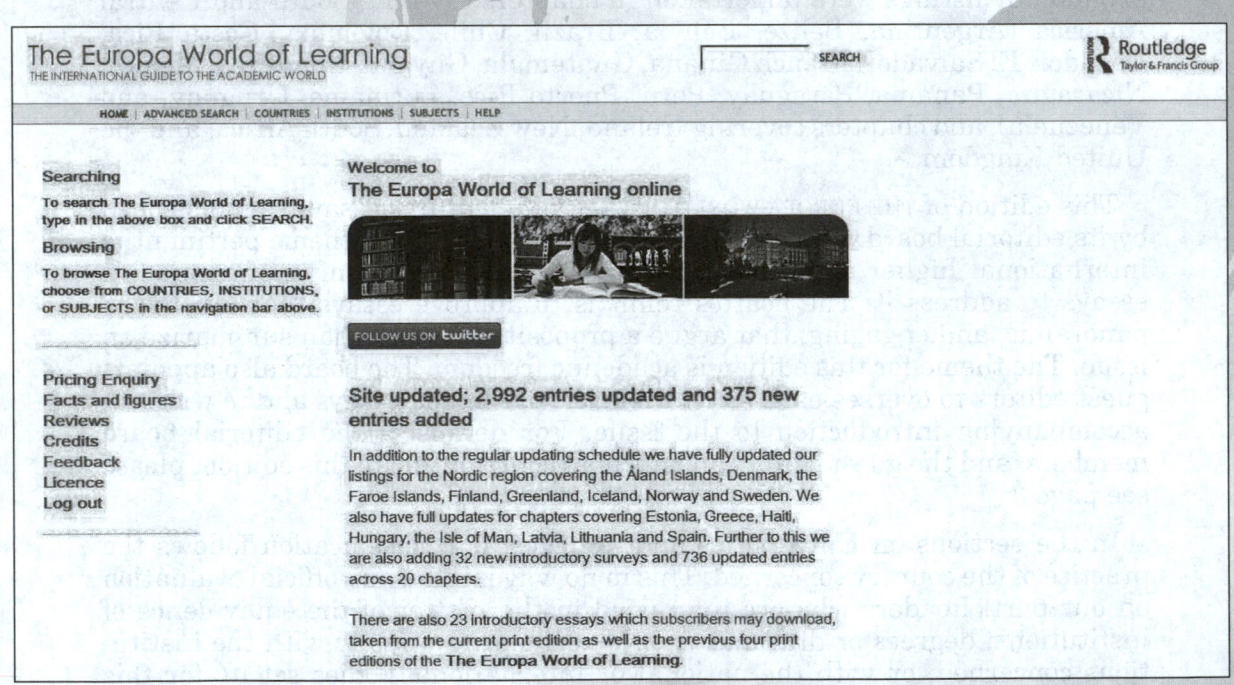

CONTENTS

• An Index of Institutions is to be found at the end of Volume II

ABBREVIATIONS

AB	Aktiebolag, Aktiebolaget (stock company); Alberta
Abog.	Abogado (lawyer)
Acad.	Academician; Academy
ACT	Australian Capital Territory
Admin.	Administration; Administrative
AGS	Aguascalientes
AIDS	acquired immunodeficiency syndrome
AK	Alaska
AL	Alabama
Apdo	Apartado (post box)
approx.	approximately
AR	Arkansas
Arq.	Arquitecto; Arquiteto
AS	Aksjeselskap (stock company)
AS CR	Academcy of Sciences of the Czech Republic
Asscn	Association; Associate
Asst	Assistant
Atty	Attorney
AV ČR	Akademie věd České republiky (Academcy of Sciences of the Czech Republic)
Av.	Avenida (avenue)
Avda	Avenida (avenue)
Ave	Avenue
Avv.	Avvocato (Advocate)
AZ	Arizona
BA	Bachelor of Arts
BC	Baja California; British Columbia
BCS	Baja California Sur
Bd	Bulevard (boulevard)
Bdul	Bulevardul (boulevard)
Beng	Bachelor of Engineering
BiH	Bosne i Hercegovine (Bosnia and Herzegovina)
Bldg	Building
Blvd	Boulevard
Blvr	Bulevar (boulevard)
BP	Boîte postale (post box)
Br.	Branch
Brig.	Brigadier
Bro.	Brother
Brs	Branches
BSc	Bachelor of Science
Bul.	Bulvar (boulevard)
bulv.	bulvāris (boulevard)
c.	circa (approximately)
c/o	care of
CA	California
CAM	Campeche
Capt.	Captain
CAR	Central African Republic
Ccl	Council
Cdra	cuadra (block)
CD-ROM	compact disc read-only memory
CEA	Commissariat à l'Energie Atomique
CEO	Chief Executive Officer
Chair.	Chairman; Chairperson; Chairwoman
CHIH	Chihuahua
CHIS	Chiapas
Cmdr	Commander
CNR	Consiglio Nazionale delle Ricerche
cnr	corner
CNRS	Centre National de la Recherche Scientifique
CO	Colorado
Co	Company; County
COAH	Coahuila
COL	Colima
Col	Colonel
Col.	Colonia (district)
colln	collection
Comm.	Commission
Commr	Commissioner
Conf.	Conference
Corp.	Corporation
Corresp.	Correspondent; Corresponding
CP	Caixa postal, Case postale, Casella postale (post box)
Cr	Contador
CRC	Cooperative Research Centre
CT	Connecticut
Ctra	carretera (highway)
Cttee	Committee
cu	cubic
DC	District of Colombia
DE	Delaware
Del.	Delegación (borough); Delegate; Delegation
Dept	Department
Deptl	Departmental
devt	development
DF	Distrito Federal
DGO	Durango
Dipl.	Diploma
Dir	Director
Dist.	District
Div.	Division
Divs	Divisions
Doc.	Docent
Dott.	Dottore; Dottoressa
Doz.	Dozent (lecturer)
Dr Hab.	Doktor Habilitowany (Assistant Professor)
Dr	Doctor
Dr.	Drive
Dra	Doctora
Drs	Doctorandus
DVD	digital versatile disc
E	East, Eastern
e.g.	exempli gratia
Edif.	Edificio (building)
edn	edition
Eng.	Engineer
EngD	Doctor of Engineering
esp.	especially
Esq.	Esquina (corner)
Est.	Established
etc.	et cetera
EU	European Union
eV	Eingetragener Verein (non-profit society/association)
Exec.	Executive
f.	founded
f.t.e.	Full-time equivalent
FAO	Food and Agriculture Organization
Fed.	Federal; Federation
FL	Florida
Fl.	Floor
fmr	former
fmrly	formerly
Fr	Father
ft	feet
GA	Georgia
Gdns	Gardens
Gen.	general
GmbH	Gesellschaft mit beschränkter Haftung (limited liability company)
Gov.	Governor
Govt	Government
GPOB	Government Post Office Box
GRO	Guerrero
GTO	Guanajuato
HE	His (Her) Excellency; His Eminence
HEI	Higher Education Institution
HGO	Hidalgo
HI	Hawaii
HIV	human immunodeficiency virus
HM	His (Her) Majesty
HND	Higher National Diploma
Hon.	Honorary; Honourable
HQ	Headquarters
HRH	His (Her) Royal Highness
IA	Iowa
ID	Idaho
IL	Illinois
ILO	International Labour Organization
IN	Indiana
Inc.	Incorporated
incl.	include; includes; including
Ind.	Independent
Ing.	Ingénieur (Engineer)
Instn	Institution
Int.	International
Ir	Insinyur (Engineer)
IT	information technology
JAL	Jalisco
Jl	Jalan (street)
Jr	Junior
Jr.	Jirón (street)
JSC	joint Stock Company
jt	joint
jtly	jointly
Kft	korlátolt felelösségû társaság (limited liability company)
km	kilometre; kilometres
korp.	korpus (building)
KS	Kansas
küç.	küçasi (street)
kv.	kvartal (apartment block); kvartira (apartment)
KY	Kentucky
LA	Louisiana
Lic.	Licenciado
Licda	Licenciada
Lt	Lieutenant
Ltd.	Limited
m	metre; metres
m.	million
MA	Massachusetts; Master of Arts
Mag.	Magister (Masters degree)
Man.	Manager; Managing
MB	Manitoba
MBA	Master of Business Administration
MD	Maryland
ME	Maine

Mem.	Member
Mems	Members
MEng	Master of Engineering
MEX	Mexico
Mgr	Monseigneur; Monsignor
MI	Michigan
MICH	Michoacan
Min.	Minister; Ministry
misc.	miscellaneous
mm	millimetre; millimetres
MN	Minnesota
MO	Missouri
MOR	Morelos
MRC	Medical Research Council
MS	Mississippi
MSc	Master of Science
MSS	Manuscripts
MT	Montana
N	North, Northern
N°	Número (number)
nám.	náměstí (square)
NASA	National Aeronautics and Space Administration
Nat.	National
NAY	Nayarit
NB	New Brunswick
NC	North Carolina
ND	North Dakota
NE	Nebraska; Northeast; Northeastern
NGO	Non-Governmental Organization
NH	New Hampshire
NJ	New Jersey
NL	Newfoundland and Labrador; Nuevo Leon
NM	New Mexico
No	Número (number)
NS	Nova Scotia
NSW	New South Wales
NT	Northern Territory; Northwest Territories
NU	Nunavut Territory
NV	Nevada
NW	Northwest, Northwestern
NY	New York
NZ	New Zealand
OAX	Oaxaca
obl.	oblast
Of.	Oficina
OH	Ohio
OK	Oklahoma
ON	Ontario
OR	Oregon
Org.	Organization
PA	Pennsylvania
PAN	Polska Akademia Nauk (Polish Academy of Sciences)
PE	Prince Edward Island
PEN	Poets, Playwrights, Essayists, Editors and Novelists (Club)
PhD	Doctor of Philosophy
pl.	place, platz, ploshchad (square)
PMB	private Mail Bag
POB	Post Office Box
pr.	prospekt (avenue)
Pres.	President
Prin.	Principal
Prof.	Professor
Profa	Professora
Psje	Pasaje (passage)
Publ.	publication
Publs	publications
PUE	Puebla
Q ROO	Quintana Roo
QC	Québec
QLD	Queensland
QRO	Queretaro
q.v.	quod vide (to which refer)
Rd	Road
Rep.	Representative
retd	retired
Rev.	Reverend
RI	Rhode Island
RP	Révérend Père
Rr.	Rruga
Rt Hon.	Right Honourable
Rt Rev.	Right Reverend
ry	rekisteröity yhdistys (registered association)
S	South, Southern
s/n	sin número (without number)
SA	South Africa(n); South Australia
SAR	Special Administrative Region
SC	South Carolina
SD	South Dakota
SDI	Selective Dissemination of Information
SE	Southeast, Southeastern
Sec.	Secretary
SIN	Sinaloa
Sis.	Sister
SK	Saskatchewan
SLP	San Luis Potosi
Soc.	Society
SON	Sonora
spec.	special
Sq.	Square
Sr	Senior
St	Saint, Sint; Street
Sta	Santa
Ste	Sainte
str.	stradă, strada, Strasse (street)
SW	Southwest; Southwestern
TAB	Tabasco
TAMPS	Tamaulipas
TAS	Tasmania
tel.	telephone
TLAX	Tlaxcala
TN	Tennessee
Treas.	Treasurer
TX	Texas
u.	utca (street)
UK	United Kingdom
ul.	ulica, ulitsa (street)
UN	United Nations
UNESCO	United Nations Educational, Scientific and Cultural Organization
Univ.	Universidad, Universidade, Università, Universität, Université, Universitas, Universitat, Universitatea, Universiteit, Universitet, Universiteti, Universiti, University, Univerza, Univerzita, Univerzitet, Uniwersytet (University)
Urb.	Urbanización (neighbourhood)
USA	United States of America
UT	Utah
VA	Virginia
VER	Veracruz
VIC	Victoria
Vols	Volumes
VT	Vermont
vul.	vulitsa, vulytsa (street)
W	West, Western
WA	Washington (State); Western Australia
WI	Wisconsin
WV	West Virginia
WY	Wyoming
YT	Yukon Territory
YUC	Yucatan
ZAC	Zacatecas
ZRC SAZU	Znanstvenoraziskovalni center Slovenske akademije znanosti in umetnosti (Research Centre of the Slovenian Academy of Sciences and Arts)

INTERNATIONAL TELEPHONE CODES

To make international calls to telephone and fax numbers listed in *The Europa World of Learning*, dial the international access code of the country from which you are calling, followed by the appropriate country code for the organization you wish to call (listed below), followed by the area code (if applicable) and telephone or fax number listed in the entry.

	Country code	+ or – GMT*
Afghanistan	93	+4½
Åland Islands	358	+2
Albania	355	+1
Algeria	213	+1
Andorra	376	+1
Angola	244	+1
Antigua and Barbuda	1 268	–4
Argentina	54	–3
Armenia	374	+4
Aruba	297	–4
Australia	61	+8 to +10
Austria	43	+1
Azerbaijan	994	+5
Bahamas	1 242	–5
Bahrain	973	+3
Bangladesh	880	+6
Barbados	1 246	–4
Belarus	375	+2
Belgium	32	+1
Belize	501	–6
Benin	229	+1
Bermuda	1 441	–4
Bhutan	975	+6
Bolivia	591	–4
Bonaire	599	–4
Bosnia and Herzegovina	387	+1
Botswana	267	+2
Brazil	55	–3 to –4
Brunei	673	+8
Bulgaria	359	+2
Burkina Faso	226	0
Burundi	257	+2
Cambodia	855	+7
Cameroon	237	+1
Canada	1	–3 to –8
Cabo Verde	238	–1
Cayman Islands	1 345	–5
Central African Republic	236	+1
Chad	235	+1
Chile	56	–4
China, People's Republic	86	+8
Christmas Island	61	+7
Cocos (Keeling) Islands	61	+6½
Colombia	57	–5
Comoros	269	+3
Congo, Democratic Republic	243	+1
Congo, Republic	242	+1
Cook Islands	682	–10
Costa Rica	506	–6
Côte d'Ivoire	225	0
Croatia	385	+1
Cuba	53	–5
Curaçao	599	–4
Cyprus	357	+2
Czech Republic	420	+1
Denmark	45	+1
Djibouti	253	+3
Dominica	1 767	–4
Dominican Republic	1 809	–4
Ecuador	593	–5
Egypt	20	+2
El Salvador	503	–6
Equatorial Guinea	240	+1
Eritrea	291	+3
Estonia	372	+2
Ethiopia	251	+3
Faroe Islands	298	0
Fiji	679	+12
Finland	358	+2
France	33	+1
French Guiana	594	–3
French Polynesia	689	–9 to –10
Gabon	241	+1
Gambia	220	0
Georgia	995	+4
Germany	49	+1
Ghana	233	0
Gibraltar	350	+1
Greece	30	+2
Greenland	299	–1 to –4
Grenada	1 473	–4
Guadeloupe	590	–4
Guam	1 671	+10
Guatemala	502	–6
Guernsey	44	0
Guinea	224	0
Guinea-Bissau	245	0
Guyana	592	–4
Haiti	509	–5
Honduras	504	–6
Hong Kong	852	+8
Hungary	36	+1
Iceland	354	0
India	91	+5½
Indonesia	62	+7 to +9
Iran	98	+3½
Iraq	964	+3
Ireland	353	0
Isle of Man	44	0
Israel	972	+2
Italy	39	+1
Jamaica	1 876	–5
Japan	81	+9
Jersey	44	0
Jordan	962	+2
Kazakhstan	7	+6
Kenya	254	+3
Kiribati	686	+12 to +13
Korea, Democratic People's Republic (North Korea)	850	+9
Korea, Republic (South Korea)	82	+9
Kosovo	381†	+3

	Country code	+ or – GMT*
Kuwait	965	+3
Kyrgyzstan	996	+5
Laos	856	+7
Latvia	371	+2
Lebanon	961	+2
Lesotho	266	+2
Liberia	231	0
Libya	218	+1
Liechtenstein	423	+1
Lithuania	370	+2
Luxembourg	352	+1
Macao	853	+8
Macedonia, former Yugoslav republic	389	+1
Madagascar	261	+3
Malawi	265	+2
Malaysia	60	+8
Maldives	960	+5
Mali	223	0
Malta	356	+1
Marshall Islands	692	+12
Martinique	596	–4
Mauritania	222	0
Mauritius	230	+4
Mayotte	262	+3
Mexico	52	–6 to –7
Micronesia, Federated States	691	+10 to +11
Moldova	373	+2
Monaco	377	+1
Mongolia	976	+7 to +9
Montenegro	382	+1
Morocco	212	0
Mozambique	258	+2
Myanmar	95	+6½
Namibia	264	+2
Nauru	674	+12
Nepal	977	+5¾
Netherlands	31	+1
New Caledonia	687	+11
New Zealand	64	+12
Nicaragua	505	–6
Niger	227	+1
Nigeria	234	+1
Norway	47	+1
Oman	968	+4
Pakistan	92	+5
Palau	680	+9
Palestinian Territories	970 or 972	+2
Panama	507	–5
Papua New Guinea	675	+10
Paraguay	595	–4
Peru	51	–5
Philippines	63	+8
Poland	48	+1
Portugal	351	0
Puerto Rico	1 787	–4
Qatar	974	+3
Réunion	262	+4
Romania	40	+2
Russia	7	+3 to +12
Rwanda	250	+2
Saba	599	–4
Saint Christopher and Nevis	1 869	–4
Saint Lucia	1 758	–4
Saint Vincent and the Grenadines	1 784	–4
Samoa	685	+13

	Country code	+ or – GMT*
San Marino	378	+1
São Tomé and Príncipe	239	0
Saudi Arabia	966	+3
Senegal	221	0
Serbia	381	+1
Seychelles	248	+4
Sierra Leone	232	0
Singapore	65	+8
Sint Eustatius	1721	–4
Sint Maarten	1721	–4
Slovakia	421	+1
Slovenia	386	+1
Solomon Islands	677	+11
Somalia	252	+3
South Africa	27	+2
South Sudan	211	+2
Spain	34	+1
Sri Lanka	94	+5½
Sudan	249	+2
Suriname	597	–3
Swaziland	268	+2
Sweden	46	+1
Switzerland	41	+1
Syria	963	+2
Taiwan	886	+8
Tajikistan	992	+5
Tanzania	255	+3
Thailand	66	+7
Timor-Leste	670	+9
Togo	228	0
Tonga	676	+13
Trinidad and Tobago	1 868	–4
Tunisia	216	+1
Turkey	90	+2
'Turkish Republic of Northern Cyprus'	90 392	+2
Turkmenistan	993	+5
Turks and Caicos Islands	1 649	–5
Tuvalu	688	+12
Uganda	256	+3
Ukraine	380	+2
United Arab Emirates	971	+4
United Kingdom	44	0
United States of America	1	–5 to –10
United States Virgin Islands	1 340	–4
Uruguay	598	–3
Uzbekistan	998	+5
Vanuatu	678	+11
Vatican City	39	+1
Venezuela	58	–4½
Viet Nam	84	+7
Yemen	967	+3
Zambia	260	+2
Zimbabwe	263	+2

* The times listed compare the standard (winter) times in the various countries. Some countries adopt Summer (Daylight Saving) Time—i.e. +1 hour—for part of the year.

† Mobile telephone numbers for Kosovo use either the country code for Monaco (377) or the country code for Slovenia (386).

Note: Telephone and fax numbers using the Inmarsat ocean region code 870 are listed in full. No country or area code is required, but it is necessary to precede the number with the international access code of the country from which the call is made.

PART ONE

Introductory Essays

CONTRIBUTORS

EDITORIAL BOARD

Prof. Ronald Barnett

Ronald Barnett is Emeritus Professor of Higher Education at the Institute of Education, London (United Kingdom), and his work focuses on the conceptual and theoretical understanding of the university and higher education. His books include *Realizing the University in an Age of Supercomplexity* (2000), *A Will to Learn: Being a Student in an Age of Uncertainty* (2007) and *Beyond All Reason: Living with Ideology in the University* (2003). In 2014 he was working on completing a trilogy, with *Being a University* (2011) and *Imagining the University* (2013) already published. He is a former Chair of the Society for Research into Higher Education, has been awarded the inaugural prize by the European Association for Educational Research for his 'outstanding contribution to Higher Education Research, Policy and Practice' and has been an invited speaker in around 35 countries.

Dr John Aubrey Douglass

John Aubrey Douglass is Senior Research Fellow—Public Policy and Higher Education at the Center for Studies in Higher Education (CSHE) at the University of California—Berkeley. He is the co-editor of *Globalization's Muse: Universities and Higher Education Systems in a Changing World* (Bristol, Public Policy Press, 2009), and the author of *The Conditions for Admissions* (Redwood City, CA, Stanford Press, 2007) and *The California Idea and American Higher Education* (Redwood City, CA, Stanford University Press, 2000 and 2007; published in Chinese in 2008 and in Japanese 2012).

Among the research projects he has co-founded, and of which he remains the Berkeley Principle Investigator, is the Student Experience in the Research University (SERU) Consortium—a group of major research universities in the US and internationally, with members in China, Brazil, South Africa, the Netherlands and Russia. He is also the editor of the Center's Research and Occasional Paper Series (ROPS), sits on the editorial board of international higher education journals in the UK, China, and Russia, and serves on the international advisory boards of a number of higher education institutes.

His recent publications include *China Futurisms: Research Universities and Leaders or Followers?* translated into Chinese and published by University Education Science, Hunan University, May 2014; originally published in *Social Research: An International Quarterly*, vol. 79, no. 3, 2012; *Profiling the Flagship University Model: An Exploratory Proposal for Changing the Paradigm From Ranking to Relevancy*, CSHE.5.14 (April 2014); editorial version published in *University World News*, "The Flagship University: A Response to the World Class University Paradigm,"25 April 2014: http://www.universityworldnews.com/article.php?story=20140423113704590; a version translated into Vietnamese; and Douglass, J. A., Edelstein, and Hoareau, C. (2014). *Bring the world to California: A global hub for higher education*, in *BOOM: A Journal of California*, 4(1).

David Palfreyman

David Palfreyman, FRSA MA MBA LLB, is the Bursar of and a Fellow of New College, Oxford University; and is also the Director of the Oxford Centre for Higher Education Policy Studies (OxCHEPS). His latest books include: *Reshaping the University: The Rise of the Regulated Market in Higher Education* (2014, Oxford University Press), *The Law of Higher Education* (2012, Oxford University Press), *London's Inns of Court* (2011, Oracle), *London's Livery Companies* (2010, Oracle), and *The Oxford Tutorial* (2008, OxCHEPS and in Chinese, 2010, Peking University Press). He is a co-editor of the projected 25-volume Routledge comparative *International Studies in Higher Education* series, in which he has contributed *Structuring Mass Higher Education: The Role of Elite Institutions* (2009). David is also the Honorary Treasurer of the Society for Research into Higher Education (SRHE).

Assoc. Prof. Leesa Wheelahan

Leesa Wheelahan is an associate professor at the Ontario Institute of Studies in Education (OISE) at the University of Toronto where she holds the William G. Davis Chair in Community College Leadership. She has recently joined OISE from the LH Martin Institute for Tertiary Education Leadership and Management, and at the Melbourne Graduate School of Education at the University of Melbourne (Australia). She is a leading Australian and international researcher on the relationship between the vocational education and training and the higher education sectors, and has published widely on lifelong learning, tertiary education policy, student equity and the role of theoretical knowledge in curriculum. Indicative recent publications include: 'Babies and Bathwater: revaluing the role of the academy in knowledge' in Ron Barnett's and Paul Gibb's *Thinking about higher education* (Springer: New York);*Accessing Knowledge in the University of the Future: Lessons from Australia*, in Ron Barnett's *The Future University: Ideas and Possibilities* (New York, Routledge, 2012); *Why Knowledge Matters in Curriculum: A Social Realist Argument* (London, Routledge, 2012); and (with Gavin Moodie) *Rethinking Skills in Vocational Education and Training: from Competencies to Capabilities* (Sydney, Board of Vocational Education and Training, 2011).

GUEST EDITORS

Prof. James G. Jackson

Professor Jim Jackson is an Emeritus Professor at Southern Cross University (Australia), having been founding Dean of the Law Faculty there.

He has a BCom (UNSW), LLB (UNSW), LLM (Hons)(Sydney), Grad Dip in Education (Tertiary) and a PhD (Sydney). His PhD thesis was in the area of academic freedom and he has written widely in the field of higher education law, including papers on governance, dismissal processes, compulsory student unionism, marketing law, academic freedom, legal rights of international students, speech rights and the fiduciary obligations of university governing bodies. In addition to work on education law, his research includes monographs on corporation law and articles on commercial law and trade practices law. From 2010 to 2011 he was College Director for Kaplan Singapore. Before that he was Chair of the Academic Board at Southern Cross University and Professor of Law, and a member of senior committees of that University, including its Council and Finance Committees. He has also held positions at Darling Downs Institute of Advanced Education (DDIAE) and at Wollongong and Bond Universities.

He is a trained Australian Universities Quality Agency (AUQA)/Tertiary Education Quality and Standards Agency (TEQSA) auditor and was on the first TEQSA panel to review an Australian university.

With Sally Varnham (*q.v.*), he has jointly written *Law for Educators: School and University Law in Australia* (Chatswood, LexisNexis Butterworths, 2007). He was also co-leader of a team that gained an Australian Learning and Teaching Council grant to examine student grievance issues in Australian universities.

Prof. Sally Varnham

Dr Sally Varnham is a Professor with the Faculty of Law at the University of Technology, Sydney (Australia). Since 2010 she has been Chair of the University's Academic Board. She was admitted to the New Zealand Bar and practised law in Wellington and then in London, United Kingdom, before beginning her teaching career. Her main research interest is in legal issues arising in compulsory and higher education, and her theses for LLM (VUW) and PhD (UNSW) are in this area. She is widely published in Australia, New Zealand, the United Kingdom and Europe and she regularly presents at national and international conferences. Until recently she was a Student Ombudsman at the University of Technology, Sydney. Together with Professor Jackson, she is the author of *Law for*

Educators: School and University Law in Australia (Chatswood, LexisNexis Butterworths, 2007). She is currently completing co-editing *Higher Education and the Law* (due for publication with Federation Press in late 2014).

CONTRIBUTING AUTHORS

Prof. Dennis Hayes

Dennis Hayes is the Professor of Education at the University of Derby (United Kingdom) and the Director of the influential campaign group Academics for Academic Freedom (AFAF), which he founded in 2006. He was a columnist for the *Times Educational Supplement* and is a member of the editorial board of the *Times Higher Education* magazine. In 2009 he edited and contributed to a special edition of the *British Journal of Educational Studies* (vol. 57) on Academic Freedom and he writes regularly in the national and international press on free speech and academic freedom. His latest book is *The 'Limits' of Academic Freedom* (2013).He is in constant demand around the world as a speaker on academic freedom and, in 2010, he took part in the 50th Doha Debate alongside Professor Tariq Ramadan, defending the proposition that 'Education is worthless without freedom of speech', for a programme with a potential audience of 350 million people. In the educational world he is well-known for his controversial co-authored book, *The Dangerous Rise of Therapeutic Education* (2008), which has been described as 'one of the most important books to have been written in at least the last twenty years in that crucial area where philosophy, policy and practice coincide'.

Prof. Michael Fraser

Michael Fraser, AM, is a Professor of Law at the University of Technology, Sydney (Australia), and Director of its Communications Law Centre (CLC), which is Australia's independent, non-profit, public-interest centre specializing in communications, media and online law and policy.

He was a founder and the chief executive of Copyright Agency Limited (CAL) for 21 years and he was a founding director of Australian, foreign and international copyright management organizations. He is Chairman of the Australian Copyright Council, Chairman of the Stolen Generations Testimonies Foundation, President of International PEN—Sydney Centre, a Director of the Dictionary of Sydney Trust and a member of the Australian Communications Consumer Action Network (ACCAN) Expert Advisory Committee.

Dr Petra Butler

Petra Butler is an Associate Professor at Victoria University of Wellington and an Associate Director of the New Zealand Centre of Public Law, specializing in human rights and international commercial law. She has written extensively in both areas, *inter alia*, *The New Zealand Bill of Rights Act 1990: A Commentary* (2006—soon available in its 2nd edition), with Andrew Butler; and *UN Law on International Sales* (2009), with Professor Peter Schlechtriem. She has held visiting positions around the world, including at the University of Melbourne (Australia), Universidad de Navarra (Spain), Bucerius Law School (Germany) and Northwestern University Law School (USA). She has been admitted as a barrister and solicitor of the High Court of New Zealand. She has advised the New Zealand Government and private clients on both human rights and international commercial law issues. She is New Zealand's CLOUT (Case Law on UNCITRAL Texts) correspondent for the CISG (UN Convention on Contracts for the International Sale of Goods—Vienna Convention) and the Model Law on Electronic Commerce.

Prof. John Higgins

John Higgins holds the Arderne Chair in Literature at the University of Cape Town (South Africa). One of the first in the humanities to be awarded an A-rating by the National Research Foundation, he was elected a Fellow of UCT in 2003, a member of the Academy of Science of South Africa in 2009 and a Fellow of the Stellenbosch Institute of Advanced Study in 2011. His monograph *Raymond Williams: Literature, Marxism and Cultural Materialism* (Routledge, 1999) won both the Altron National Book Award and the UCT Book Prize; and Blackwell published his *Raymond Williams Reader* in 2001. He was founding editor of the influential journal, *Pretexts: literary and cultural studies* (1989–2003), and was granted an Award of Excellence by the Cape Tercentenary Foundation for his services to literature and culture in South Africa in 2000. His main research interests are in contemporary literary and cultural theory, and debates in and around the politics of higher education. *Academic Freedom in the New South Africa* was published by Wits University Press in 2013, with a US edition due to appear from Bucknell University Press in 2014.

PREFACE[1]

The idea and ideal of 'academic freedom' or 'faculty freedom of expression' is much discussed but little understood. Its presence—along with that of 'tenure' for academic staff (or faculty) and the rather fuzzy concept of 'collegiality'—is usually considered as the essence of 'the University' in terms of protecting both institutional autonomy and that of its academics in order that both may better fulfil the duty of speaking truth to power, of being the constructive critic of the national society within which the university is located and its academics operate. Especially for the individual academic, there is also the professional duty to engage fearlessly with the research task of pushing the boundaries of knowledge and then of disseminating the results through teaching, and occasionally even dismantling paradigms that form the parameters of the current accepted orthodoxy of thinking.

There can, of course, be tension and confusion where the academic freedom and autonomy of the university qua institution comes into conflict with the academic freedom of the individual faculty member as an employee of that corporation: where academic freedom for the faculty and the collegial tradition within university governance conflict with the growing trend towards campus corporatism and managerialism—and indeed this may be just a somewhat sordid dispute over who owns what intellectual property in teaching materials used for digital- and distance-learning. There can also be conflict when academic freedom as an element in the university-academic contract of employment (as, in effect, an aspect of the academic profession's terms and conditions) conflicts with wider concepts of free speech that may be a right enjoyed by any citizen, as well as merging with any protected rights as a whistle-blowing employee. And, sadly, there can be strife, even bloodshed, where the university and its members become the focus of the defence not only of academic freedom within a politically hostile society but also of wider rights to freedom of speech.

Pure academic freedom of expression undoubtedly and most simply or obviously applies when academic X speaks out, utilizing the measured professional language of academe, about topic Y as something in which he or she can claim research and scholarship expertise. But what if X is trespassing into other academic areas, and what if X is just generally sounding off on a broad political issue just as any citizen might? What if X is simply criticizing the university's governance or strategy from the stance of being a member and employee of the institution and where his or her professional expertise in, say, Philosophy or Sociology may have no obvious link to the expression of doubts about the competence of the university's management of its finances, of its building projects, of its catering operations? And what if academic X under the asserted protection of academic freedom is using provocative, strident, and 'un-academic' or un-professional' language? Do academics ever abuse the immense privilege and protection of academic freedom simply to play politics or to avoid the reasonable requirements of their employers?

We are pleased to have persuaded Sally Varnham and Jim Jackson not only to gather together a collection of interesting contributors covering the wide political, professional, and organizational contexts within which academic freedom of expression is needed and invoked, but also themselves to contribute one of these six stimulating essays. The Editorial Board is grateful to them and to the other contributors for deploying their academic expertise and freedom of expression to provide us with an interesting exploration of this important theme of the 2015 edition of *The Europa World of Learning*.

David Palfreyman
June 2014, Oxford

[1] For a general discussion of the law relating to academic freedom, see: (in a USA context) Kaplin, W. A. and Lee, B. A. (2013, fifth edition) *The Law of Higher Education* (San Francisco, CA, Jossey-Bass)—Chapter 7 on 'Faculty Academic Freedom and Freedom of Expression'; and (in a UK context) Farrington, D. and Palfreyman, D. (2012, second edition) *The Law of Higher Education* (Oxford, Oxford University Press)—Chapter 13, 'Academic Freedom and HEI Autonomy'. For a comparative USA/UK/German study, see Barendt, E. (2010) *Academic Freedom and the Law* (Oxford, Hart). On the concept of collegiality as, arguably, a key feature of the university's organisational culture, see Tapper, T. and Palfreyman, D. (2010) *The Collegial Tradition in the Age of Mass Higher Education* (Dordrecht and London, Springer). On the potential conflict between faculty collegiality and freedom of expression and the university as an increasingly managed and commercialized corporate entity operating within a commercialized marketplace (sliding downhill from acropolis to agora!), see: Palfreyman, D. and Tapper, T. (2014) *Reshaping the University: The Rise of the Regulated Market in Higher Education* (Oxford, Oxford University Press).

UNIVERSITIES AS THE 'CRITICS AND CONSCIENCE OF SOCIETY'[2]: THE CHALLENGES AND THREATS TO ACADEMIC FREEDOM AND UNIVERSITY AUTONOMY IN TODAY'S HIGHER EDUCATION SECTOR

SALLY VARNHAM and JIM JACKSON

The defining characteristic of the university is its commitment to open and independent inquiry. This characteristic also distinguishes the nature of university research, which, unlike partisan research, seeks knowledge and understanding in a completely unrestricted manner. The same principles of unfettered inquiry apply to teaching and the dissemination of knowledge. This commitment to the pursuit of truth gives universities all over the world their universal values and enables them to embark on the important paths of regional and international co-operation, which are so important to the vitality of the modern university.

(UNESCO-CEPES, European Centre for Higher Education, Sinaia Statement on Academic Freedom)

Socrates, it is said, chose to die by eating hemlock rather than to compromise his deep commitment to free intellectual enquiry and open and fearless debate. While not exhorting modern academics to similar action, this essay collection draws attention to many issues that question the standing of the intellectual freedom of academics and universities in modern, liberal, Western democracies. We explore threats to these ideals posed by a commercialized and internationalized higher education system, subject to a plethora of national and global constraints and dilemmas, and in many instances 'cash strapped' and subject to the whim of successive governments. The writers raise, analyse and question issues relating to academic freedom within the current global scenario, such as its practical effect and its future in a very different world from that in which it was first conceived. Unchanged is the sentiment and rationale that spawned the concept in 16th-century Europe from a need to protect academics and universities from religious and political interference, and that is shown by the UNESCO statement above, which resulted from a conference at Sinaia in Romania in 1992. However, the notions of what a university is, and what a university education is, are shifting.

Globally, much rhetoric surrounds the concept of academic freedom. Most people emphasize the common good, the community of scholars and the national importance of the freedom of universities to have unfettered pursuit of truth and knowledge. A powerful statement on the meaning of academic freedom and the conditions necessary for its protection emerged in 1940, from a meeting between the American Association of University Professors (AAUP) and the Association of American Colleges (AAC, now the Association of American Colleges and Universities):

> Institutions of higher education are conducted for the common good and not to further the interest of either the individual teacher or the institution as a whole. The common good depends upon the free search for truth and its free exposition.
>
> Academic freedom is essential to these purposes and applies to both teaching and research. Freedom in research is fundamental to the advancement of truth. Academic freedom in its teaching aspect is fundamental for the protection of the rights of the teacher in teaching and of the student to freedom in learning. It carries with it duties correlative with rights.
>
> Tenure is a means to certain ends; specifically: (1) freedom of teaching and research and of extramural activities, and (2) a sufficient degree of economic security to make the profession attractive to men and women of ability. Freedom and economic security, hence, tenure, are indispensable to the success of an institution in fulfilling its obligations to its students and to society.
>
> (AAUP and AAC, 1940 Statement of Principles on Academic Freedom and Tenure)

One of the strongest international statements on academic freedom comes from UNESCO:

> Institutions of higher education, and more particularly universities, are communities of scholars preserving, disseminating and expressing freely their opinions on traditional knowledge and culture, and pursuing new knowledge without constriction by prescribed doctrines. The pursuit of new knowledge and its application lie at the heart of the mandate of such institutions of higher education.
>
> (UNESCO, 1997 Recommendation concerning the Status of Higher-Education Teaching Personnel)

The strength of this UNESCO statement is that is neatly picks up on the connection between what is at the heart of a university—pursuit of new knowledge and the notion of a community of scholars free to disseminate and express themselves—and the concept of mandate. In other words, academic freedom is a two-way street; it goes as much as to the role of the university as it does to the right of a particular academic or student to speak out. Once this fundamental point is understood, other matters flow. The university must put in place conditions within itself such that it will meet the requirements of the statute under which it is incorporated. The university will have to act in ways that enable academics to meet their teaching and research obligations, so that the university can do likewise. To put it simply, if you deny academic freedom to an academic, you deny at least partly the capacity of the university to meet its research and teaching objects. If an academic denies academic freedom to a fellow academic, that person impinges on the capacity of the university to meet its objects. This also takes us to the related but separate concept of institutional autonomy. As a creature of statute, a university must be allowed to meet its statutory objects. If it is not, that university has had its autonomy weakened.

The principle of academic freedom has widened and become intermingled with concomitant principles of freedom of speech and freedom of expression, and it is embodied generally and specifically in the constitutions, legislation and university acts of most Western, liberal democracies. It has long been affirmed by the judiciary, for example in the USA, where it is typified in the much quoted statement of Justice Felix Frankfurter of the US Supreme Court: 'The essentiality of freedom in the community of American universities is almost self-evident. No one should underestimate the vital role in a democracy that is played by those who guide and train our youth. To impose any strait jacket upon the intellectual leaders in our colleges and universities would imperil the future of our Nation' (US Supreme Court, 1957, *Sweezy v. New Hampshire*, 354 US 235).

In Europe, the architecture of the Bologna Process continues to embrace the principles of academic freedom by restating the principles in its communiqués, as cited by Jan De Groof (2013),

[2] New Zealand Education Act 1989, section 162(4)(a).

following conferences in Bergen, Norway, in 2005, London, United Kingdom, in 2007, Leuven/Louvain-la-Neuve, Belgium, in 2009 and Bucharest, Romania, in 2012.

In Australia, there is no general constitutional guarantee of academic freedom. Other countries, such as South Africa (in the 1996 Constitution), New Zealand (Education Act 1989, section 161), the United Kingdom (Education Reform Act 1988, s. 202) and Ireland (Universities Act 1997, s. 14), gained academic freedom protection during the late 1980s and the early 1990s, but at that time the Australian Vice-Chancellors' Committee did not support the introduction of such measures (as recorded in a copy of an undated letter from Professor Brian Wilson, Vice-Chancellor of the University of Queensland, when Chairman of the Committee, to the Minister for Higher Education—contained in University of Queensland Archives S435). Academic freedom in Australia was accorded Commonwealth legislative recognition only in 2011, when the Higher Education Support Act 2003 was amended to insert a requirement stating that universities 'have a policy that upholds free intellectual inquiry in relation to learning, teaching and research' (section 19-115). Further provision has also recently been made in the Higher Education Standards Framework (Threshold Standards) 2011 (discussed by Jim Jackson in his essay, *q.v.*).

Academic freedom and university autonomy are concepts long held dear in democratic, liberal jurisdictions as fundamental precepts for the provision and pursuit of higher education. They are terms that are used frequently in relation to universities, usually together with constitutionally protected freedom of speech (particularly in the USA under the First Amendment to the Constitution), with institutional self-governance and freedom from state and political interference. They are also accepted as preconditions for the pursuit of institutional excellence and the advancement of knowledge through teaching and research activities by universities and their academics.

While seemingly simple and self-evident, academic freedom is fragile and, over the decades, it has proved notoriously difficult to define. It has been said: 'The concept is both omnipresent and elusive. It is called self-evident but seems, at the same time, in many aspects, miles away from any evidence. Academics often pretentiously claim academic freedom but, unfortunately, for reasons of expediency, often betray it in practice' (De Groof, 2013: 156). Is it merely, in the words of one commentator, 'a woolly blanket'? Or is the concept not only tangible, but increasingly essential as the key to the higher education systems of the world being the seekers and disseminators of truth and wisdom? Can the principles withstand the counteracting forces they face in the stresses and strains that characterize today's world of higher education? Are they stealthily being sacrificed or severely limited by economic, social and political expediency?

The higher education sector globally is now being called upon to respond to phenomena variously referred to as 'massification', 'commodification', 'corporatization' and 'managerialism', accompanied and assisted by the rapidly accelerating impact of technology. In Western countries, this has led to an ever-increasing reliance on the international student dollar, on private philanthropy and on commercially sponsored research. In turn, universities have had to develop a much greater sensitivity to the market and to market image, perceiving themselves increasingly as pursuing the business of higher education. A new suspicion has crept into the traditional relationship between universities and the state, which was hitherto founded on strong principles of autonomy and respect for the preserve of the former to decide how, what and where they would deliver education. Governments require of universities 'more for less', in terms of accountability for the public dollar spent on teaching and learning and on research.

As perhaps an inevitable outcome of the application of the market model to higher education, it has become fashionable in recent years to apply the supplier–consumer analogy to the university–student relationship (Kamvounias and Varnham, 2006, and 2010; Farringdon and Palfreyman, 2012). It is easy to see how this perception has taken hold: through the increasingly higher fees able to be charged by universities and the downgrading of liberal arts studies, compared with the popularity of courses such as law, medicine and accounting, which lead to higher income and status (Norton, 2012); through the application of 'managerialism' and 'corporatization' in and to higher education, and the entry into the 'marketplace' of large numbers of private providers, some of which are 'for-profit'; through the reliance worldwide on the overseas student full-fee-paying dollar; and through many other social, economic and cultural factors now surrounding the sector. The market-driven environment, with the accompanying acceptance of the student–consumer model, has significant implications for academic freedom and university autonomy. It requires academics to pursue safety, often at the expense of innovation, and slavish adherence to market surveys and factors driven by market competition, where teaching and research based on exciting intellectual enquiry may take second place to efficiency.

Universities both are creatures of and help to shape their environments, and they operate on the shifting sands of the social, political, cultural and economic imperatives that surround them. These essays focus on the threats and proselytize that, in the face of such forces, there is ever more a need for universities to hold fast to their academics' freedoms, their autonomy and their integrity, while demonstrating flexibility in their way forward. It is not easy. Universities, academics and their students are confronted now with many challenges that go to the very core of their existence and their role in society. A plethora of competing interests and factors not seen by our forefathers have questionably led to a reconceptualization of universities as institutions providing simply a 'private benefit', leading to individual advancement in terms of economic and social status, rather than the historical concept of the promotion of the public good of education for the betterment of society.

Considered here are the implications of these changes on the long-held and historically sacrosanct concept of academic freedom and university autonomy from the perspective of threats posed by prevailing factors within various jurisdictions, but with global relevance. Rather than considering requests by individuals for recognition of rights, we take a wider view to question the strength of the principles in the face of the countervailing circumstances within which they stand. While the essays consider the situations in the United Kingdom and Europe, Australia, New Zealand and South Africa, the discussions and arguments are of universal applicability and may be viewed in a wide context.

The themes are developed through two interrelated strands. The first strand makes the argument that academic freedom is curtailed or limited by the demands of the commercialization of higher education and that the demands of marketization lead to a need for 'safety' of the academic and their university and the protection of the supposedly vulnerable student. The focus is also on the freedom of academics in relation to ownership of the works generated by their research, as commercialization leads to 'creep' by the universities to assert ownership over the material generated by academics in both their research and their teaching. It is argued that copyright law provides the means to guarantee the freedom of academics to deal with the materials that they have created as they wish.

In his essay 'Free speech, academic freedom and human being', Dennis Hayes argues that the freedoms of enquiry and of expression have been restricted by notions of 'professionalism', which limit academics to speaking out on matters relating to their research alone. He argues that they have been sacrificed to the need to protect students. He posits that, while historically academics' freedom included the freedom to venture views however and on whatever they chose, limiting the concept to professionalism has divorced their freedom from its relationship with the right to freedom of speech. Marketization and its by-product, the professionalism of free academic thought, have led to the 'therapeutic university' (a phrase used by Hayes and others he cites). He discusses an institutional discouragement of open debate, which is based on the fear that it may cause offence or fail to protect the vulnerable. He stresses that market concepts such as customer satisfaction have overtaken the exposure of students to intellectual enquiry and the challenge to beliefs and opinion. This trend is put down to the wider social, political and cultural changes that have occurred as a result of not only the commodification and marketization of universities and the sector generally, but also 'the war on terror' and a perceived need to counter 'extremism' in, for example, UK universities.

Michael Fraser argues for academic copyright as 'a pillar of academic freedom' and suggests a solution to the university's grab for the academic's research product. He approaches academic freedom from the perspective of the common law and contractual relationship between academics and their institutions and the freedom of academics to deal with the materials that they create, counterbalanced against the rights and duties contained in copyright legislation (he uses the Australian Copyright Act 1968). He considers the assertion of rights by universities over academic material created for teaching and learning, and that arising from research. In his argument, as universities face increasing financial pressures and seek wider sources of revenue in this era of the commercialization and marketization of higher education, ownership of a wider range of materials created by academics will become ever more attractive. While acknowledging the public role of universities and their institutional uniqueness in the pursuit of knowledge and the creation and dissemination of critical and original research essential to the furtherance of society, Fraser argues strongly for the protection of the ownership rights of academics and that, in order to flourish, those academics need the ability to 'deal with their copyright content without fear or favour'. He suggests uniform terms providing for academic ownership of copyright should be introduced at an institutional level, overriding copyright legislation provisions on employer ownership in the specific context of the academic creation of copyright works.

The second strand explores the demands of state regulation and accountability and the effect of political and economic considerations on universities. In terms of funding and of the freedom of research of individual academics, it is argued that the output-based funding schemes prevailing in many countries restrict experimentation and innovation by encouraging academics to engage only in 'safe' research. Within this framework, Petra Butler considers compromises to the freedom of academics posed by performance-based research funding schemes (PBRS). She argues that these schemes are central to the market-driven agenda and that they sit alongside and are integral to the other commercial agendas of governments for higher education, such as 'user pays' and partnerships with industry for research. While she speaks from a New Zealand perspective, she uses comparative examples, and her views have universality, because such schemes have been instituted by many governments, including that of the United Kingdom, to provide the framework for the allocation of government funding to universities. She contends that the system of peer review, which forms the basis of such schemes, limits research freedom by encouraging conventionality at the expense of innovation. She cites many examples of how peer review favours orthodoxy and "mainstream", disciplinary-based, basic, "safe" research at the expense of applied, interdisciplinary or speculative research' (quoting Linda Butler in a 2010 report from the Organisation for Economic Co-operation and Development). In her essay, Petra Butler contends that the PBRS is a flawed funding system, because it infringes and places unjustifiable limitations on the autonomy of university researchers to apply their knowledge and expertise in the pursuit of research of their own determination. While acknowledging the right of the state to allocate funds to public universities, and the legitimacy of its establishment of systems to do so, she suggests alternatives that, in her view, would promote greater research excellence by creating an environment in which academics could follow their instincts, driven by their knowledge, to pursue innovative new research areas.

Jackson, in his paper, discusses transnational education (TNE), quality assurance and academic freedom. He notes that there are many Western universities that are major players in TNE. These universities may have international stand-alone campuses, but in many countries, such as in Singapore and the People's Republic of China, this model is not allowed, or very few foreign universities are allowed to operate on a completely independent basis. Therefore, in most cases, the foreign university will have a collaborative arrangement with a local provider and will contract some or all of the teaching to that institution. Invariably, that organization will rely extensively on casual academic staff to teach. On occasion, there is no culture of free speech in the overseas country and no real culture of that among the teachers or the students. This places teaching and learning, and especially critical enquiry in the classroom, in complete jeopardy. Questioning is already a difficult concept to teach and practise in many international classrooms where language difficulties and polite deference to the teacher are the norm, and unquestioned, paternalistic, one-party government the rule. Jackson concludes by suggesting that, to date, there is no evidence that quality assurance agencies have done anything about this in the past. He surmises that this is because they are ultimately arms of government, with clear briefs to protect TNE and other international student income.

In relief, John Higgins's essay provides crucial insight into the place of higher education and the part played by academic freedom in the fraught path to democracy in South Africa, 'caught as it is between the rock of global higher education policy and the hard place of local political pressures'. He discusses the immense pressures relating to the transition of higher education from the opposing ideas of academic freedom and the relationship between state and university that are held by Afrikaans universities and those instituted to train Blacks, Coloureds and Indians for more subordinate roles. He traces the path from the 1980s, with the mounting challenges inside and outside universities to the state and its apartheid system, and describes the part played by academics in the disruption. He argues that, although the Constitution of democratic South Africa asserts academic freedom, it does so within the context of freedom of speech and expression generally, and it does little in practice to establish boundaries between universities and the state. In fact, it leaves open the potential for 'hegemony' to be asserted by government for economic, social or political imperatives. Higgins points to new legislation that leaves university autonomy at the whim of the current sociopolitical climate, driven in the interests of 'public accountability', as providing a disturbing reminder of the fragility of the principles surrounding the freedom of academics and universities.

As stated at the beginning of this introduction, these essays do not aim to canvass the effect of constraints on the freedom of academics specifically in terms of security of academic employment. One of the authors, Jackson, has conducted a major study on academic freedom in Australian universities and the detail will not be repeated here (Jackson, 2002, 2005 (a), 2005 (b) and 2006). Suffice it to say that his conclusion, like that of others around the world, is that the single most important factor in the protection of academic freedom is sturdy protection of academics against arbitrary dismissal, a point strongly recognized in the AAUP-ACP 1940 Statement. Such protection generally does exist for full-time and, on occasion, part-time and casual staff through individual university-staff collective bargaining agreements. Many countries, however, including Australia and Singapore, have a growing 'for profit', private, non-university college system not renowned for cherishing tenure or other protections against arbitrary dismissal. In any case, such institutions rely extensively on part-time and casual staff whose contract may last only for the length of the immediate teaching term. Rather than dismissing an academic for what they may have had to say, and therefore attracting litigation and unwanted attention, it is far simpler to let the contract expire through effluxion of time. Even in that bastion of tenure, the USA, the numbers of the workforce on the non-tenure track are increasing rapidly:

> Between 1993 and 2003 the proportion of all new full-time faculty appointments employed on short-term contracts and without prospect of tenure increased from 50 percent to 58.6 percent of those hired. This "restructuring" has been going on since the mid-1970s and shows no sign of slowing down: between 1976 and 2005 the full-time con-

tingent academic workforce grew by 223 percent, the part-time contingent workforce grew by 214 percent, while the tenured and tenure-track workforce grew by just 17 percent.

(Head, 2011: 323)

The commonality of these essays is their focus on the new 'commercialization' and its counterbalance with the forces that create the trust that society must have in its academics to apply their intellect and ability with integrity. The issues raised are underpinned by the tension between the place of individual academics, as the creators and purveyors of knowledge and intellectual enquiry, to follow their own conscience and their self-determination in relation to their creations, and what are seen as political, social and economic imperatives towards the market good.

CONCLUSION: GATHERING CLOUDS?

Free intellectual enquiry and the freedom of universities to pursue their teaching and research proceeds are unquestioned until political, social or economic factors throw a spotlight on their parameters. It is only then that attention is focusedon the need for re-examination and protection of the principles. Many instances are outlined in these essays. In Australia in recent times this has been within the context of the debate relating to climate change and the science of global warming. In 2011 'hate campaigns' were waged against a number of university academics speaking publicly about the results of their research, requiring an affirmation from Universities Australia in a statement that stressed the importance of free intellectual enquiry and open debate. In early 2014 there was the very public controversy faced by the University of Sydney in criticism of its failure to discipline academics for their publicly held views on the situation in the Middle East. In a troubling response, the Federal Minister for Education, Christopher Pyne, was quoted in *The Australian* national newspaper, on 14 January 2014, as saying that 'each university is responsible for its own governance, but universities should avoid needless controversies that damage their reputation [and] also make Australia look less respectable to our potential student market'. He also stated: 'Obviously, many members of parliament are concerned to ensure that the reputation for high quality that Australian universities have earned over decades is not threatened in any way'.

Here it is suggested that many prevailing factors in the vortex of today's world conspire to mount an assault on or, at the very least, to water down academic freedom and university autonomy.This leads us to the most dangerous enemy of academic freedom and academics, the one inside their head. This is often described as the chilling effect: real or imagined constraints on academic freedom from within the academic; the risk avoidance of controversial topics; the fear of bullying or disfavour from their colleagues or senior management; or the concern that controversy may affect their university's funding. This leads to the making of research funding applications to maximize chances of success, while minimizing critique and heterodoxy; the tailoring of articles for the traditional and prestigious, but often bland, journals with high rankings, because this will carry more status or better suit the research 'ethos' of their academic department; or the emphasis on numerical outputs and ranking scores, gained via the safe and secure, without proper expression of the true critic within the academic. The list is as long as that of the inner demons of the academic.

While it is axiomatic that a right is not dependent upon being earned, it is also true that if academics and universities are to withstand the pressures and to be respected as the 'critics and conscience of society', they must adhere to the highest standards of ethical and professional conduct in their teaching, research and related activities within and outside the university. That is not to urge that academics succumb (in the words of Hayes) to the 'narrowing' of academic freedom by 'professionalism', to commenting only on specific research or teaching matters, and to the fear of stepping out of the box, of causing offence or of inciting 'extremism'. Factors such as the need for external funding of research, the tension between the old orthodoxy and the new, the need for political correctness and the role of the media all play a part in the warps and wefts of what we simply call 'academic freedom'. There has been discussion here, within different contexts, of the threats posed by increasing managerialism of the sector, commercial imperatives and the need for funding to be met either by government on certain conditions, such as in the PBRS, or by private industry, which has its own, potentially conflicting agenda.

What is not discussed to any significant extent is the impact of the internationalization of universities or the globalization of the sector with enrolment of students from 'sanctioned' regimes (in Australia, for example, that is provided for in federal legislation, the Autonomous Sanctions Act 2011) and the prohibition on export, which could includedissemination of research, that may be used for purposes counter to the 'war on terror' (as provided for in Australia by the enacted, but yet to be implemented, Defence Trade Controls Act 2012). What of the freedom of academics to speak in or engage with, or of universities to teach in, societies whose principles run counter to ours, particularly those with less robust systems and respect for human rights or standards of state control? How can strong principles be maintained while weaving through the ethical minefield created by the need for the dollar and the maintenance of the highest academic standards expected of universities in a free and liberal society? In this era of global mobility and interaction of universities, academics and students, the maintenance of vigilance in protecting and promoting the principles that underpin Western democracies is of the utmost importance. The world of higher education is becoming borderless, in physical terms, but far behind is a commitment to the ethos of academic freedoms and university autonomy. Jackson has considered these questions within the framework of regulatory regimes in partner jurisdictions. Many Western universities are now setting up campuses in less liberal jurisdictions; academics are engaging in collaborative research and teaching on articulated degrees in countries with strongly restrictive regimes; and international universities are establishing campuses and articulations in all jurisdictions. In discussing the internationalization of faculty in the USA, William Kaplin points to recent controversies involving US academics wishing to travel to teach and research abroad and, conversely, foreign academics seeking to pursue their intellectual endeavours in the USA. He cites as an example the case of *Faculty Senate of Florida International University v. Roberts* (574 F. Supp.2d 1331) and *Faculty Senate of Florida International University v. Winn* (616 F.3d 1206, 11th Circuit, 2010), in which academics claimed that a state ban on US scholars travelling abroad to certain countries violated their academic freedom (Kaplin and Lee, 2013). Not far removed is the recent media publicity and criticism faced by the University of Sydney (mentioned above) following a visit by one of its academics to meet with Bashar al-Assad and members of the Syrian regime (reported by C. Kerr, in *The Australian*, 4 January 2014). In response, while stating that universities 'do not and should not' endorse the views of any particular academic, Professor Stephen Garton, Provost and Acting Vice-Chancellor of the University of Sydney, made a statement:

> The mandate of universities in modern democracies is to provide an environment for the development of ideas, rigorous experimentation, the testing of hypotheses, and critical analysis of existing knowledge.
>
> Universities are here to encourage open and rigorous discussions designed to advance knowledge, not rubber-stamp some ideas as good and others as bad based on the personal views we may hold.
>
> (*The Australian*, 10 January 2014)

Finally, we return to the place of academics as 'the critic and conscience of society' and conclude with words from the New Zealand media that are both deeply disturbing and a call to arms for the freedom and integrity of academics worldwide. The item appeared in response to a suggestion made by Craig

Prichard, a management academic at Massey University in New Zealand, that the sale of TradeMe (an online competitor to the US eBay) was 'an opportunity lost for New Zealand'. The academic suggested that, rather than the founder pocketing the millions made from the sale, there could have been a profit-distribution scheme involving the traders (the worth of TradeMe having been generated by their activity). A columnist at *The Dominion Post* said:

> I am not sure whether to be appalled that we pay academics to inculcate impressionable students with their mad-cap ideas, or grateful to Dr Prichard for coming forward and revealing himself. It's useful to know what's going on in the universities.
>
> (Karl du Fresne, *The Dominion Post*, 21 March 2006)

REFERENCES

De Groof, J. 'In Bluebeard's Castle? Some Musings on Academic Freedom and Academic Integrity', in Alen, A., Joosten, V., Leysen, R., and Verrijdt, W. (eds). *Liberae Cogitationes: Liber amicorum Marc Bossuyt*. Cambridge and Antwerp, Intersentia, 2013.

Farringdon, D., and Palfreyman, D. *The Law of Higher Education* (2nd edn). Oxford, Oxford University Press, 2012.

Head, S. 'The Grim Threat to UK Universities' (citing Schuster and Finkelstein, *The American Faculty*, p. 323), in *The New York Review of Books*. 13 January 2011 (www.nybooks.com/articles/archives/2011/jan/13/grim-threat-british-universities/?page=3).

Jackson, J. 'Legal Rights to Academic Freedom in Australian Universities', PhD thesis. University of Sydney, 2002.

'When Can Speech Lead to Dismissal in a University?', in *Australia and New Zealand Journal of Law and Education*, vol. 10, no. 23. 2005 (a).

'Express Rights to Academic Freedom in Australian Public University Employment', in *Southern Cross University Law Review*, vol. 9, no. 107. 2005 (b).

'Implied Contractual Rights to Academic Freedom', in *Southern Cross University Law Review*, vol. 10, no. 139. 2006.

Kamvounias, P., and Varnham, S. 'Getting What They Paid For: Consumer Rights of Students in Higher Education', in *Griffith Law Review* (Special Issue), vol. 15(2), pp. 306–32, 2006.

'Legal Challenges to University Decisions Affecting Students in Australian Courts and Tribunals', in *Melbourne University Law Review*, vol. 34(1), pp. 140–80, 2010.

Kaplin, W., and Lee, B. *The Law of Higher Education* (5th edn), Hoboken, NJ, John Wiley & Sons, 2013.

Norton, A. 'Graduate Winners: Assessing the public and private benefits of higher education', Grattan Institute Report No. 2012-7, 2012.

FREE SPEECH, ACADEMIC FREEDOM AND HUMAN BEING

DENNIS HAYES

Free speech is not simply an aspect of the educational enterprise to be weighed against other desirable ends. It is the very precondition of the academic enterprise itself.

(American Association of University Professors—AAUP, 'On Freedom of Expression and Campus Speech Codes', November 1994)

Eric Hobsbawm famously remarked when reviewing the 'short' 20th century that 'The historical memory was no longer alive' and that most young people now 'grow up in a sort of permanent present' (Hobsbawm, 1994: 3). Whether old or young, the loss of an historical perspective is a problem for all academics and not merely for historians. It means that academics can be particularly blind to recent historical differences, and academic freedom needs to be seen from the perspective of an historical shift in the idea of a university. That shift is from a university whose purpose was the pursuit of knowledge and understanding without fear or favour to what I have called the 'therapeutic university' (Hayes and Wynyard, 2002; Hayes, 2004; Ecclestone and Hayes, 2008; Barnett, 2011).

The concept of academic freedom is determined by the idea we have of the university in wider social culture. If the cultural concept of the university shifts, so will our concept of academic freedom. This cultural contextualization of the idea of a university is not determined in the abstract, but is contingent on the idea that we have of ourselves as human beings, and central to this vision will be an understanding of freedom of speech (Hayes, 2009, 2011 and 2014 (c); Pupavac, 2012).

THE NARROWING OF THE CONCEPT OF ACADEMIC FREEDOM

This is not an historical account of the many changes to our idea of academic freedom. I wish to point out recent but significant shifts as reminders of how much has changed. In the early 1970s capitalism and class loyalty were part of mainstream discussions of academic freedom (Fisk, 1972 (a) and 1972 (b); Jones, 1972; Schmitt, 1972). Academic workers were held to be functionaries of the capitalist system and true academic freedom would be possible only in a future communist society, and then not confined to academics alone. The debates were confused in not recognizing the progressive tendencies of capitalist educational structures, which might take truth-seeking so far and then thwart it, because of the contradictions in the academic workplace. They also made the related mistake of seeing the academic workplace as a unitary and functional whole, rather than as a plurality of conflicting and contradictory tendencies. It is tempting and quaint to re-engage with these debates, but it is enough to recall how different debates about the university were in the decades before 1989 and the collapse of communism. In the period since then, which Francis Fukuyama called the 'end of history', discussions of the 'bourgeois' university are rarely found even among residual left-wing groupuscules. Whether we see it or not, we are now in the period defined by the outlook that can be expressed though Mrs Thatcher's slogan, 'There is no alternative' (TINA).

In the liberal 1960s and early 1970s there was an easy equation of 'academic freedom' with 'free speech' and 'free expression', and a desire to extend them because of faith in human potential, whether that led to socialism or to a better form of capitalism. Anthony Arblaster, writing in Penguin Education's special, *Academic Freedom* (pp. 13–14), in 1974, argues:

The freedom that matters is the openness of education; that is, the tolerance of a great range and diversity of opinions, not only in relation to specific subjects, but also in relation to education itself, its purposes and methods. . . . In education the freedom to hold opinions, especially unorthodox opinions, and to advocate them openly and without any fear of reprisal, is supremely important . . . It is not the business of teachers or educational administrators to set themselves up as arbiters of the politics or the morality of either staff or students—although they frequently attempt to do so.

For Arblaster, 'academic freedom' was 'rather a pompous term for freedom of, and within education' (p. 9) and there was little interest in attempting to differentiate it from freedom of expression.

This equation of 'academic freedom' with free speech and a wide range of freedoms was unproblematic to many and not just to radicals. The Free Speech Movement (FSM) at the University of California, Berkeley, involved many hundreds of students and academics (see Searle, 1971). These were confident times in the academy. To some, however, and particularly to lawyers and First Amendment scholars in the USA, it seemed that academic freedom had lost its meaning. The use of the term was so promiscuous and so wide in its application that, according to *The Encyclopaedia of Higher Education* (cited in Van Alstyne, 1972 (a): 141–42), it '(in its modern conception, though not in the past) includes the right of the academic individual to engage in political activity'.

This was too much for the law professors and, in 1972, William Van Alstyne declared, at a symposium on academic freedom, that the usage had to regain its ties with the profession or vocation of the academic: 'It is the seemingly small and reactionary purpose of this essay to suggest that this development in the usage of academic freedom was never sound and that it ought now to be abandoned' (Van Alstyne, 1972 (a): 142).

By separating 'academic freedom' from the 'civil liberty' that every citizen under the US Constitution has to freedom of speech, Van Alstyne intended to re-professionalize the notion of freedom of speech and to tie it down to the academic's job and the core duties of the profession (Van Alstyne, 1972 (b): 73). This, he believed, would protect that freedom without giving ground to the demand that academics have to meet higher, more academic standards in their private exercise of freedom of speech than the ordinary citizen.

Van Alstyne's project has been entirely successful. The first piece in the first edition of the AAUP *Journal of Academic Freedom*, tellingly entitled 'Professionalization as the Basis for Academic Freedom and Faculty Governance', refers to his article:

The concept of academic freedom was not simply another term to describe 'freedom of speech' as guaranteed under the First Amendment, which in a limited way protected the speech of all citizens from direct government suppression, but rather a more specific safeguard of the right of faculty at both public and private colleges and universities freely to teach in a manner they thought appropriate, to engage in research of their own choosing, and to publicize the results of that research.

(Gerber, 2010: 6)

This distinction is therefore now commonplace (see Levinson, 2007).

The process of professionalization, while narrowing the concept of academic freedom, also widens it to cover much that is disconnected from freedom of speech. In the United Kingdom, in 2009, the University and College Union (UCU) published a

Statement on Academic Freedom, which adds a democratic argument to the professionalization of academic freedom:

> Academic freedom requires the development of open, democratic and collegial forms of institutional governance, including access to proper whistleblowing procedures. ... academic and academic-related staff must play the pre-eminent role in determining the curriculum, assessment standards and research priorities. Academic freedom means that academic and academic-related staff should also have the right to elect a majority of representatives to academic bodies (Senates, Academic Boards, etc.) ... as well as inclusion on governing bodies. Collegial decision-making should encompass decisions regarding curricula, research, administration, outreach and community work, the allocation of resources and other related activities.
>
> (UCU Statement on Academic Freedom, June 2009)

The UCU did not have any First Amendment-type qualms about freedom of speech and added a section about the 'responsibilities' that follow from academic freedom. It expects members to refrain from all forms of harassment, prejudice and unfair discrimination, whether on the grounds of sex, race, ethnic or national origin, religion, colour, class, caring responsibilities, marital status, sexuality, disability, age or other status or personal characteristic (National Rule 6.1). The ever-growing list of things about which one might be even 'prejudiced' is a serious undermining of academic freedom. It is ironic that one of the major drivers to the production of this statement was the founding of Academics for Academic Freedom (AFAF), which in 2006 had issued a Millian statement of academic freedom in order to counter the increasing range of issues that people found 'offensive' and that academics were not allowed to be 'prejudiced' about (see below).

This widening of professional interests was a consequence of restricting academic freedom to the academic job. Even Terence Kealey, one of the most liberal of British vice-chancellors, feels that he can protect academic freedom by defending the professional role: 'universities exist to foster the ideals of scholarship, so if an academic employs the apparatus of scholarship to defend an idea, then that academic should be free to do so. But an academic otherwise enjoys no particular licence to speak his or her mind saloon bar-wise' (Kealey, 2013).

Whether stated or unstated, the most common view of academic freedom is now the professional one. It is about your area of expertise or, worse still, your 'research'. As an example of how this professionalization limits academic freedom, consider this statement from Regent's University, that:

> Academic freedom must be applied carefully and has limitations in practice. Academic staff should never make statements that are at variance with the institutional values of the university, which they have contractually agreed to support. In particular staff must be careful to ensure that they apply mutual respect to colleagues and opponents in debate and not promote views which can be interpreted as discriminatory in terms of gender, racial background, sexual orientation, age or any other personal characteristics. They are encouraged to avoid controversial issues not related directly to their fields of study and if communicating in public they should indicate clearly that they are not speaking for Regent's University London unless they are authorized to do so.
>
> (Regent's University, 'Academic Freedom and Collegiality' policy statement, 2013)

Compare this approach with the situation in the 1960s and 1970s when there was a defence of open debate on social and political matters and a rejection of university management imposing any political, moral or other restriction on academic freedom. Now academics not only must avoid giving offence and expressing opinions that might be 'interpreted as discriminatory', but must not challenge the values of the institution that employs them. They must avoid controversial issues and not use the university's name without permission if they speak about topics outside of their professional expertise.

University websites contain many similar statements and most academics have accepted their role as professional employees. It is only a few academic oddballs, political activists or libertarians that have any problem with what we might call the 'Van Alstyne settlement'. The Van Alstyne settlement has its champion in the United Kingdom, Eric Barendt, but, above all others, it is Stanley Fish in the USA who promotes the view that academic freedom is just about the job, and he wants academics to regain a 'narrow sense of vocation' (Fish, 2008 (a): 8). Fish believes that he is a lone fighter: 'Academic freedom is a spectrum at one end of which is the "It's Just a Job" school—identifying himself as likely its only member—which treats academics as employees hired to perform a specific job, with freedom limited to that scope' (reported in Walker, 2012; see also Fish, 2008 (b) and 2014). The contention in this essay is, first, that Fish is wrong and, secondly, that most academics are members of his school.

ACADEMIC FREEDOM UNDER ATTACK

Perhaps the most concerning feature of the contemporary university is the silence of academics and the lack of public collegial support for dissident opinions and academic freedom. It is hard to understand this silence, given that the roll call of high-profile British and Irish academics who have had their 'academic freedom' attacked continues to grow: Chris Brand, Frank Ellis, Simon Davies, Edzard Ernst, David Coleman, Sal Fiore, David Colquhoun, Hicham Yezza, Rizwaan Sabir, Chris Knight, David Nutt, Dylan Evans and Rod Thornton. All these cases are different and there are many lesser 'stars' whose academic freedom is quietly suppressed. These cases and their merits will not be discussed here (see the Academics for Academic Freedom website, www.afaf.org.uk, *Times Higher Education* and the relevant case studies in Barendt, 2010).

Looked at 'ahistorically', it might appear that these are just the usual cases of individuals up against the system. They strayed beyond their professional role and were mostly disciplined but not sacked. In the case of Evans, therapy was suggested even though he was found not guilty. The message to academics was clear: keep quiet; hold your tongue; do your research; and do not speak unless it is on the basis of your research findings. A climate has developed in which academics are afraid to speak about any topic without having a research project to back up what they say. This puts the academic cart before the horse. Free speech and debate are necessary before research can begin.

The professional turn was not the result of a few academic papers and the pontifications of legal scholars. It was made possible by wider social, political and cultural changes. The usual suspects are 9/11 and the 'war on terror', culture wars and the 'commodification' or 'marketization' of universities (Downs, 2005; Doumani, 2006; Gerstmann and Streb, 2006; O'Neil, 2008; Brown and Carasso, 2013; Williams, 2013). David Palfreyman, the Director of the Oxford Centre for Higher Education Policy Studies (OxCHEPS), argues for keeping these changes in proportion: 'The threat to academic freedom within UK higher education, albeit minimally protected in law at present, from anti-terrorism legislation and its ramifications is probably not significant and is somewhat exaggerated' (Palfreyman, 2007). Palfreyman's balanced and sanguine perspective was possible only by looking too narrowly at legal issues and not considering wider cultural factors. He may be less sanguine today, as many of the high-profile cases listed above came after his balanced assessment. One example was the international furore over the 'Nottingham Two' (Yezza and Sabir) and the academic 'whistleblower' Rod Thornton (see http://nottinghamwhistleblower.wordpress.com/2011/05/04/rod-thorton-university-of-nottingham-whistle-blower-suspended/). The case involved the May 2008 arrest instigated by the University of Nottingham of Sabir, a student, and Yezza, an administrator, after a copy of the so-called al-Qa'ida'Training Manual' was found on a computer.

Thornton wrote a 112-page account of the case in 2011, which was published on the British International Studies Association (BISA) website before being removed. Thornton was suspended and ultimately left the university. The case raised many issues: who was an academic (Yezza being an administrator); what was acceptable for students to read; whether reading lists should be vetted; and what was or was not 'academic freedom'. The arrest changed the academic climate at the university and there were many unpleasant incidents, conflicts between staff and fears about academic freedom, whether well-founded or not. This and other cases in which an individual's academic freedom has allegedly been challenged need to be publicized, because most academics do not know about them. The professionalization of academic freedom means that there is a loss of interest in broader academic issues.

This lack of interest was politically problematic for a time, as it was a challenge to the British state's concern with countering 'extremism' in universities. It needed the Minister of State for Innovation, Universities and Skills, Bill Rammell, to give a powerful speech to the Fabian Society in 2007 arguing that academics must tackle extremism through the exercise of academic freedom, to:

> Give people the chance to challenge their views through free debate. Not the criminals, but those whose words remain within the law, whether they come from extreme religious groups, the BNP, the Animal Liberation Front or elsewhere. And let their views be exposed and challenged for the falsehoods they are. By not allowing them to be heard, we undermine the unsaid, but more important message, to students: that we value tolerance and open debate. And let history judge them.

Today the situation could not be more different. Using the 'Prevent' strategy, the police are inviting themselves on to campus to ensure that 'vulnerable' young people are not radicalized and that safe spaces can be found for discussion (Hayes, 2012).

To understand the shift from open debate to protecting the vulnerable, it is necessary to look at the major cultural change. Writing this paper at the time of the 25th anniversary of the fatwa against Salman Rushdie by Iran's Ayatollah Khomeini on St Valentine's Day, 14 February 1989, I want to suggest that the 'Rushdie Affair' more than any other single factor shifted attitudes to both freedom of speech and academic freedom.

Societal turning from support for freedom of speech to quietude through fear of offence is largely a result of the Rushdie Affair (Malik, 2009; Hayes, 2013; Winston, 2014). Malik puts the consequence bluntly: 'From the Enlightenment onwards, freedom of expression had come to be seen not just as an important liberty but as the very foundation of liberty ... No longer. Today, in liberal eyes, free speech is as likely to be seen as a threat to liberty as its shield' (Malik, 2009: 155–56). Discussing the effect of the fatwa on freedom of speech and academic freedom at the time of the 25th anniversary of the publication of *The Satanic Verses*, he said:

> The critics of... Rushdie lost the battle but they have largely won the war. They never managed to prevent the publication of *The Satanic Verses*. But the claim at the heart of the anti-Rushdie campaign—that it is morally wrong to offend deeply held cultural or religious sensibilities—has become incorporated into mainstream liberal thinking. From publishing to academia, from broadcasting to theatre, there is a great reluctance to give offence. In effect we have internalised the fatwa.
> (Kenan Malik, quoted in Hayes, 2013)

This internalization leads to self-censorship and fear of speaking up, not just about Islam and controversial issues, but generally. The legacy of the fatwa is that if you do not like something, you cry 'offence' and it is enough to silence anyone, particularly timid academics. It has transformed academic consciousness.

A puzzle remains. If there are so many attacks on academic freedom, with universities demanding that academics accept their 'corporate' values, including taking responsibility for customer satisfaction; and when academics are criticized, or disciplined or dismissed for their views on a wide range of issues; when the police think they have a quasi-academic role on campus; and when academics self-censor and fear offending anyone; why does it not seem that bad?

The retreat into professionalism is part of the explanation, but the fundamental reason is the dominance of therapy culture in the university. It is not only the police who see students as 'vulnerable', but universities, which have promoted the idea of the 'vulnerable' student through making up the non-academic and empty concept of the 'student experience' and filling it with counselling sessions, stress workshops, 'Bibliotherapy' areas in libraries and wacky ideas like 'therapy dogs' to comfort anxious students in class (Ecclestone and Hayes, 2008; Hayes, 2014—b).

These may seem like incidental matters, outsidethe university proper, which consists, as ever, of academics teaching their subjects to students. The therapeutic culture is, however, beginning to extend to more academic matters by suggesting that young people are not merely emotionally vulnerable, but that they are intellectually vulnerable. I have discovered a course in a top university on 'Overcoming Perfectionism', which aims to save students from damaging their emotional and mental health by wanting to be the very best; a leaflet suggesting that students might find their subjects of study disturbing and need counselling; and, depressingly, that 'Trigger Warnings' on curricula are being mooted to keep students mentally safe. Such warnings may be widely adopted in the next few years (Hayes, 2014—b). Even the 'No Platform' policies adopted by student unions in the United Kingdom have shifted from concern about 'fascist' and 'racist' speakers to ensuring that students feel safe (Hayes, 2008; Hayes and Reynolds, 2008; Hayes 2014—a). The message is that young people today can no longer cope with the rigours of academia, in which their deepest beliefs and opinions might be and should be challenged. They are seen as vulnerable, diminished human beings.

The therapeutic turn produces a seemingly kindly, diminished idea of human being, but, in the intellectual background, there are harsher criticisms of humanity's Enlightenment hubris about reason, truth and progress. This stronger misanthropic viewpoint is clearly expressed in the writings of John Gray, particularly in his 2002 best seller *Straw Dogs: Thoughts on Humans and Other Animals*, which presents 'a view of things in which humans are not central' and is anti-rational: 'Humanists like to think they have a rational view of the world; but their core belief in progress is a superstition, further from the truth about the human animal than any of the world's religions' (Gray, 2002: ix–xi). Fortunately, this misanthropic philosophy has been countered by some powerful defences of the human spirit (Bookchin, 1995; Guldberg, 2010; Tallis, 2011). For most anti-humanists, a diminished idea of human being is very difficult to express except through therapeutic approaches. This is particularly true when referring to young people and students.

Caring about students' intellectual safety is the strongest pointer to the dangers of the anti-human therapeutic turn in the academy. When fear of offence or of lowering student self-esteem replace intellectual challenge, free speech is increasingly curtailed and there is a decline in academic discussion and debate. The therapeutic university, once a tendency, has become real.

FREEDOM OF SPEECH AND ACADEMIC FREEDOM

In 2005 Professor Roy Harris and I were writing and commenting on free speech issues (see Harris, 2005; and Hayes, 2005) and wondered what could be done. The eventual outcome of our thinking was the AFAF Statement of Academic Freedom, inspired by the Hillhead amendment to the Education Reform Bill 1988 (see Russell, 1993). The statement asks academics to stand up for the right to put forward ideas that might be offensive and to challenge the therapeutic culture of 'niceness' that was supporting the corporate culture of conformism on campus. The statement has two principles: first, that academics, both inside and outside the classroom, have unrestricted liberty to question and test received wisdom and to put forward controversial and unpopular opinions, whether or not these are deemed offensive; and, secondly, that academic institutions have no right to curb the exercise of this freedom by members of their staff, or to use it as grounds for disciplinary action or dismissal.

The AFAF statement is a challenge to Van Alstyne, Fish and Barendt. Barendt, the author of a major work on freedom of speech (originally published in 1985, but cited here in a later edition as Barendt, 2007) understood that the AFAF statement 'really means an unrestricted freedom for academic staff to put forward their views on any topic of public concern, no matter how offensive they are to the community and irrespective of any limits imposed by academic institutions', but which he claimed was 'too simple' (Barendt, 2010: 3).

There is a virtue in simplicity and the statement was an attempt to restore unfettered freedom of speech and, with it, faith in human being. We saw no issues with academics or ordinary people arguing about anything and everything. That is what freedom of speech means. Barendt has lost faith in the power and importance of free speech and he makes a curious remark that 'it is hard to find a single justification for freedom of speech' (Barendt, 2010: 72).

We value freedom of speech because it is the foundational freedom on which all our other freedoms depend and without which they have no meaning. Free speech is usually seen as just one freedom among many and as something that sometimes must be traded off in the interest of other freedoms or values. This position is often summarized with the statement that freedom of speech is not an 'absolute' (Lee, 1990: 25). I have addressed the many objections to this in arguing elsewhere for academic freedom 'No Ifs, No Buts' (Hayes, 2011 and 2014—c). Here I want to give an *a priori* argument to show why free speech is an absolute, and then supplement this with an empirical argument.

The *a priori* argument

What academics have forgotten in their preoccupation with the research and scholarship in their academic jobs is that free speech is a prerequisite for all other freedoms, including theirs. Roy Harris has argued convincingly that 'freedom is, in the first instance, freedom of speech. Freedom of speech is the archetypal freedom' (Harris, 2009: 125), and:

> The general rationale for giving priority to freedom of speech can be stated very succinctly. For any proposed freedom F, being free may turn out to be an illusion if there has been no opportunity to test the freedom claimed against contrary opinions. In short, we cannot know that we enjoy freedom F—we cannot even know what exercising that freedom would be—until F itself has been subjected to and survived unrestricted critical scrutiny. And that in turn requires freedom of speech. For if we rely on anything short of that, the freedom we had imagined we were exercising may be illusory.
>
> (Harris, 2009: 126)

To take Harris's argument a step further we can say that we do not understand our own opinions unless we present them for criticism. This argument does away with Barendt's claim that 'it is hard to find a single justification for freedom of speech'.

The empirical argument

The 'empirical' argument derived from the radical philosopher, Tony Skillen, is based on 'claims of "very general facts" about how minds work and the role of discourse in that working' (Skillen, 1982: 149).

In an impressive attempt to provide a defence of freedom of speech 'on socialist terms', Skillen says this about challenging beliefs:

> One's beliefs are close to the centre of 'who one is' and criticism of them can cut deep and meet protective resistance. But it is of the essence of human rationality that beliefs are held as valid, as justified by their correspondence to what is the case. The mind expresses itself and thus exposes itself to change through criticism. Criticism and discussion respect these dimensions of rationality, whereas silencing smashes at them, practically denying the capacity, not only to have reached views through some process of experience and reflection, but to go beyond them through further formative activity. This contempt applies also to your status as 'hearer' of speech, denying your capacity to reason and reflect on what you hear. You are treated as if words could actually causally affect you in an almost physical way rather than through their according with your grasp of things and thus their being 'acceptable' to you.
>
> (Skillen, 1982: 145)

The perception we have of a young person, a student and of humanity is exemplified by the attitude that Skillen castigates as 'contempt', but in its therapeutic expression it is a 'caring contempt'. It expresses a profoundly diminished sense of human potential, but with compassion.

Vanessa Pupavac has documented in a detailed historical and global survey how we have moved from the Enlightenment view of a common humanity seeking rational understanding through communication, and replaced it with 'linguistic governance'. Linguistic governance expresses a view of humanity as constituted by vulnerable citizens who must be protected: 'the concept of vulnerability involves anticipatory victimhood and the imperative to take preventative action' (Pupavac, 2012: 227). The result is restrictive legislation, speech codes, no-platform policies and censorship. These restrictions have gathered strength in the last few years in the name of victims and the vulnerable. The Leveson proposals for press regulation in the United Kingdom are the starkest example of this new illiberality, which has gained support from hundreds of once liberal academics, writers and actors (Hume, 2012 and 2014).

The loss of the Enlightenment vision of humanity's potential and its replacement by a diminished idea of human being has led to a decline in the support intellectuals and politicians give to free speech. This decline is paralleled by a decline in academic freedom.

Academic freedom is best seen as part of a continuum (Fish calls it a spectrum). A society that values freedom of speech will support the university as a place where academics may take freedom of speech to its fullest expression, not just in giving opinions, but in research and scholarship to test those opinions. If a society ceases to value freedom of speech, it will cease to value the university and academic freedom. This is not to commit the 'naturalistic fallacy' as it merely records a shift of value along a continuum of values.

It is the collapse in support for free speech that has led to the lack of confidence of academics in academic freedom, fostered by their turn to professionalism. This is why we find Barendt (2010: 5) arguing that: 'However persuasive the case for academic freedom may be, it is unlikely to enjoy widespread popular support'. This is also why he can talk about the 'puzzle' that is 'academic freedom' and ask: 'How can academic freedom be justified, granted that it appears to confer special freedoms or rights on certain individuals and institutions?'

If we believe in freedom of speech we can see that there is nothing elitist or special about academics having freedom of speech above citizen rights, because there is something special about academics, as the Australian philosopher John Anderson wrote in 1960 (republished in a 1980 publication, so cited as Anderson, 1980):

> The work of the academic, qua academic, is criticism; and, whatever his special field may be, his development of independent views will bring him into conflict with prevailing opinions and customary attitudes in the public arena and not merely among his fellow professionals.

This is a confident view of the academic as a social critic stepping beyond the area of his special expertise. We have lost this confidence (Dworkin, 1996: 197). To regain it requires a defence of freedom of speech. If academics make the case for freedom of speech, academic freedom is likely to enjoy widespread popular support.

BRINGING ACADEMIC FREEDOM BACK IN

Academics need to be aware of the quietism produced by the therapeutic culture of safety in universities. They need to be reminded of their duty to question and test received wisdom and to be the societal models of autonomous individuals exercising free speech. They can be uniquely critical human beings, because criticism is their work. All that academics need to do is to speak up. Not to speak up about their research for purposes of evidencing 'impact', but to engage with wider issues and not to be afraid to come into conflict with prevailing attitudes and ideas. The first step in regaining academic confidence is for academics to speak up for freedom of speech, even offensive, hateful and crazy speech and, of course, the right to respond to it with more speech. They should take inspiration from the concurring opinion of US Supreme Court Justice Louis Brandeis: 'If there be time to expose through discussion the falsehood and fallacies, to avert the evil by the processes of education, the remedy to be applied is more speech, not enforced silence' in the judgment of *Whitney v. California*, 274 US 357 (1927). To paraphrase Larry Flint: defending the lowest speech will defend academic freedom.

When Van Alstyne's paper with its 'small and reactionary purpose' was written in the 1970s, free speech was an unquestioned good because of belief in human beings, in the potential of ordinary people. In the 21st century freedom of speech is restricted everywhere, because of distrust and caring contempt for ordinary people. In the current climate of conformism and censorship, restoring free speech is the duty of every academic. What is the alternative? At my University of Derby inaugural lecture on 'The "Limits" of Academic Freedom' (Hayes, 2011; Reisz, 2011), one of the questions asked was: 'Does an academic have the right not to be critical, not to defend freedom of speech?' The eristic questioner raised a valid point, to which the answer is 'Yes! They do have that choice.' We can choose to be an intellectual slave. It is a real choice, but not one most human beings would or should make.

REFERENCES

Anderson, J. 'The Place of the Academic in Modern Society', in Phillips, D. Z. (Ed.). *Education and Inquiry*, pp. 214–21, Oxford, Basil Blackwell, 1980.

Arblaster, A. *Academic Freedom*. Harmondsworth, Penguin Education, 1974.

Barendt, E. *Freedom of Speech*, 2nd edn (1st edn, 1985). Oxford, Oxford University Press, 2007.

Academic Freedom and the Law: A Comparative Study. Oxford and Portland, OR, Hart Publishing, 2010.

Barnett, R. *Being a University*. London and New York, Routledge, 2011.

Bookchin, M. *Re-enchanting Humanity: A defense of the human spirit against anti-humanism, misanthropy, mysticism and primitivism*. London and New York, Cassell, 1995.

Brown, R., and Carasso, H. *Everything for Sale? The Marketisation of UK Higher Education*. London and New York, Routledge/Society for Research into Higher Education, 2013.

Doumani, B. *Academic Freedom after September 11*. Cambridge, MA, MIT Press, 2006.

Downs, A. D. *Restoring Free Speech and Liberty on Campus*. Cambridge, The Independent Institute/Cambridge University Press, 2005.

Dworkin, R. 'We Need a New Interpretation of Academic Freedom', in Menand, L. (Ed.). *The Future of Academic Freedom*, pp. 187–98, Chicago, IL, and London,University of Chicago Press, 1996.

Ecclestone, K., and Hayes, D. *The Dangerous Rise of Therapeutic Education*. London and New York, Routledge, 2008.

Fish, S. *Save the World on Your Own Time*. Oxford, Oxford University Press, 2008 (a).

'Academic Freedom is not a divine right', in *The Chronicle of Higher Education*, 5 September 2008 (b) (http://chronicle.com/article/Academic-Freedom-Is-Not-a/10461 (subscription), accessed 14 April 2014).

Fish, S. *Versions of Academic Freedom: From Professionalism to Revolution*. Chicago, IL, University of Chicago Press, 2014.

Fisk, M. 'Academic Freedom in Class Society', in Pincoffs, E. L. (Ed.). *The Concept of Academic Freedom*, pp. 5–26, Austin, TX, and London, University of Texas Press, 1972 (a).

'Comments on Hardy Jones and Bertram Davis', in Pincoffs, E. L. (Ed.). *The Concept of Academic Freedom*, pp. 52–55, Austin, TX, and London, University of Texas Press, 1972 (b).

Gerber, L. G. 'Professionalization as the Basis for Academic Freedom and Faculty Governance', in *Journal of Academic Freedom*, vol. 1. AAUP, 2010 (www.aaup.org/sites/default/files/files/JAF/2010%20JAF/Gerber.pdf, accessed 14 April 2014).

Gerstmann, E., and Streb, M. J. (Eds). *Academic Freedom at the Dawn of a New Century: How Terrorism, Governments and Culture Wars Impact Free Speech*. Stanford, CA, Stanford University Press, 2006.

Gray, J. *Straw Dogs: Thoughts on Humans and Other Animals*. London, Granta Books, 2002.

Guldberg, H. *Just Another Ape?* Exeter, Imprint Academic, 2010.

Harris, R. 'Speaking out for the right to speak evil', in the *Times Higher Education Supplement*. 9 December 2005 (www.timeshighereducation.co.uk/story.asp?sectioncode=26&storycode=200263, accessed 14 April 2014).

'Freedom of Speech and Philosophy of Education', in *British Journal of Educational Studies*, vol. 57, no. 2, pp. 111–26, June 2009.

Hayes, D. 'The Therapeutic Turn in Education', in Hayes, D. (Ed.), *The Routledge Guide to Key Debates in Education*, pp. 180–85, London and New York, Routledge, 2004.

Hayes, D. 'The touchy-feely brigade: coming your way soon', in the *Times Higher Education Supplement*. 4 November 2005 (www.timeshighereducation.co.uk/story.asp?storyCode=199536&sectioncode=26, accessed 14 April 2014).

Hayes, D. 'Verbal brawling is just what the academy needs' in the *Times Higher Education Supplement*. 22 December 2006 (www.timeshighereducation.co.uk/story.asp?sectioncode=26&storycode=207259, accessed 14 April 2014).

Hayes, D. 'Academic freedom means free speech and no "buts"', in *The Free Society*. 4 March 2008 (www.thefreesociety.org/Issues/Free-Speech/academic-freedom-means-free-speech-and-no-buts, accessed 14 April 2014).

'Freedom and the diminished subject', in *British Journal of Educational Studies*, vol. 57, no. 2, pp. 127–45, June 2009.

'The "Limits" of Academic Freedom', inaugural lecture. University of Derby, 30 March 2011.

Hayes, D. 'Stop policing the university', in *Spiked*. 1 November 2012 (www.spiked-online.com/newsite/article/13044#.U1ZyyfldWM5).

'Rushdie fatwa, 25 years on: fear casts long shadow', in *Times Higher Education*. 26 September 2013 (www.timeshighereducation.co.uk/comment/opinion/rushdie-fatwa-25-years-on-fear-casts-long-shadow/2007653, accessed 14 April 2014).

'Now is the time to challenge no platform', in *The Free Society*. 13 March 2014 (a) (www.thefreesociety.org/Columnists/Dennis-Hayes/now-is-the-time-to-challenge-no-platform, accessed 24 April 2014).

'How trigger warnings shoot down free debate', in *Spiked*. 20 March 2014 (b) (www.spiked-online.com/newsite/article/how-trigger-warnings-shoot-down-free-debate/14816#.U1T2kfldWM4, accessed 21 April 2014).

The 'Limits' of Academic Freedom. London, Academics for Academic Freedom, 2014 (c).

Hayes, D., and Reynolds, R. 'Time to No Platform "No Platform"', in *The Free Society*. 31 October 2008 (www.thefreesociety.org/Issues/Free-Speech/time-to-no-platform-no-platform, accessed 14 April 2014).

Hayes, D., and Wynyard, R. (Eds). *The McDonaldization of Higher Education*. Westport, CT, and London, Bergin & Garvey, 2008.

Hobsbawm, E. *Age of Extremes: The Short Twentieth Century 1914-1991*. London, Michael Joseph, 1994.

Hume, M. *There is No Such Thing As a Free Press ... and we need one more than ever*. Exeter, Imprint Academic, 2012.

'Liberal UK signs its own death warrant', in *Spiked*. 24 March 2014 (www.spiked-online.com/freespeechnow/fsn_article/leveson-liberal-uk-signs-its-own-death-warrant#.U1jdzPldWM4, accessed 24 April 2014).

Jones, H. E. 'Academic Freedom as a Moral Right', in Pincoffs, E. L. (Ed.). *The Concept of Academic Freedom*, pp. 37–51, Austin, TX, and London, University of Texas Press, 1972.

Kealey, T. 'Academic Freedom exists to protect academics from each other', in *Times Higher Education*. 7 November 2013 (www.timeshighereducation.co.uk/comment/opinion/academic-freedom-protects-academics-from-each-other/2008812.article, accessed 14 April 2014).

Lee, S. *The Cost of Free Speech*. London, Faber & Faber, 1990.

Levinson, R. 'Academic Freedom and the First Amendment', presentation to the AAUP Summer Institute. 2007 (www.aaup.org/our-work/protecting-academic-freedom/academic-freedom-and-first-amendment-2007, accessed 14 April 2014).

Malik, K. *From Fatwa to Jihad: The Rushdie Affair and Its Legacy*. London, Atlantic Books, 2009.

Menand, L. (Ed.). *The Future of Academic Freedom*. Chicago, IL, and London, University of Chicago Press, 1996.

O'Neil, R. M. *Academic Freedom in the Wired World: Political Extremism, Corporate Power, and the University*. Cambridge, MA, Harvard University Press, 2008.

Palfreyman, D. 'Is academic freedom under threat in UK and US higher education?', OxCHEPS Occasional Paper No 23. 2007 (http://oxcheps.new.ox.ac.uk/MainSite%20pages/Resources/OxCHEPS_OP23.pdf, accessed 23 April 2014).

Pincoffs, E. L. (Ed.). *The Concept of Academic Freedom*. Austin, TX, and London, University of Texas Press, 1972.

Pupavac, V. *Language Rights: From Free Speech to Linguistic Governance*. London and New York, Palgrave Macmillan, 2012.

Rammell, B. 'The last shadow of liberty? Academic Freedom in the 21st Century', speech to the Fabian Society. 27 November 2007 (; e-mail online at National Archives, www.dius.gov.uk/speeches/rammell_fabiansociety_271107.html, accessed 14 April 2014).

Reisz, M. 'More ferrets, fewer sponges', in *Times Higher Education*. 31 March 2011 (www.timeshighereducation.co.uk/news/more-ferrets-fewer-sponges/415669, accessed 24 April 2014).

Russell, C. *Academic Freedom*. London and New York, Routledge, 1993.

Schmitt, R. 'Academic Freedom: The Future of a Confusion', in Pincoffs, E. L. (Ed.). *The Concept of Academic Freedom*, pp. 111–24, Austin, TX, and London, University of Texas Press, 1972.

Searle, J. R. *The Campus War: A Sympathetic Look at the University in Agony*. New York, World Publishing Co, 1971 (online at www.ditext.com/searle/campus/campus.html).

Skillen, T. 'Freedom of Speech', in Graham, K. (Ed.). *Contemporary Political Philosophy: Radical Studies*, pp. 139–59, Cambridge, Cambridge University Press, 1982.

Tallis, R. *Aping Mankind: Neuromania, Darwinitis and the Misrepresentation of Humanity*. Durham, Acumen, 2011.

Van Alstyne, W. W. 'The Specific Theory of Academic Freedom and the General Issue of Civil Liberties', *Annals of the American Academy of Political and Social Science*, vol. 404, pp. 140–56, 1972 (a) (online as Faculty Publications, Paper 792, http://scholarship.law.wm.edu/facpubs/792, accessed 14 April 2014).

'The Specific Theory of Academic Freedom and the General Issue of Civil Liberty', in Pincoffs, E. L. (Ed.). *The Concept of Academic Freedom*, pp. 59–85, Austin, TX, and London, University of Texas Press, 1972 (b).

Walker, T. 'Defining the boundaries of academic freedom with scholar Stanley Fish', 2012 Campbell Lecture, Rice University, in *Rice News*. 19 April 2012 (http://news.rice.edu/2012/04/19/defining-the-boundaries-of-academic-freedom-with-scholar-stanley-fish/, accessed 21 April 2014).

Williams, J. *Consuming Higher Education: Why Learning Can't Be Bought*. London and New York, Bloomsbury Academic, 2013.

Winston, B. *A Right to Offend*. London, Bloomsbury, 2012.

The Rushdie Fatwa and After: A Lesson to the Circumspect. London and New York, Palgrave Macmillan, 2014.

ACADEMICS' COPYRIGHT: A PILLAR OF ACADEMIC FREEDOM

MICHAEL FRASER

INTRODUCTION

In Australia, research and teaching may still be perceived as the primary objects of universities, notwithstanding that the modern Australian university engages in a range of activities beyond those traditionally undertaken[3]. Indeed, the public purposes of research and teaching are still recognized in the enabling Acts of some higher education institutions (the University of Western Australia—UWA, or the University of Adelaide, for example).

Academic freedom ensures that the activities of universities, and of university academics, may be conducted in a manner that is of public benefit. Through independent and full enquiry, knowledge is advanced. University staff enjoying academic freedom may freely exchange knowledge with colleagues, and may transfer knowledge to students and the public at large. These processes enhance public discourse, serving democracy. They may—but need not necessarily—result in useful and commercially successful innovations.

Australia's Copyright Act 1968 vests ownership of copyright in all works created by an employee during the course of their employment in their employer—at section 35(6). Given that many academics are in an employment relationship with the university at which they conduct research and teach, the employment provisions of the Act are relevant to the copyright materials created by academics while conducting work duties.

This essay considers how copyright materials created by academics are treated in the employment contracts and intellectual property policies of Australian universities. As the Copyright Act's provisions on employer copyright may be overridden by private agreement, under section 35(3), university contracts (and documents incorporated by reference into them) may modify the position on copyright ownership that would otherwise apply under the Act. In many cases, university contracts and policies reflect the statutory position on ownership of copyright in works, allowing university ownership of copyright materials created during the course of employment. However, they often go further, to provide universities with rights that they would not obtain under the Act. In addition, other clauses of university contracts and policies often further limit academics' rights to deal with copyright materials created by them.

At common law, long-standing practices exist in recognition of the university and the academic's particular societal roles (see below). Unless contradicted by express agreement, these practices mean that universities and employed academics are taken to have agreed certain terms with respect to copyright materials. In particular, academics are by implication understood to own copyright in scholarly materials (such as journal articles) created by them. However, due to recent developments in the higher education sector, it is possible that these practices will be eroded. Universities may seek to rely on their statutory rights to academic-created materials, or to expand these even further. Any such limitation on academic control and exploitation of copyright materials risks constraining scholarly expression and academic discourse. Of greatest concern is that university copyright owners could prevent publication of research results (perhaps for commercial reasons), thereby restricting the timely exchange and transfer of new knowledge.

[3] For example, the Full Federal Court decision in *University of Western Australia v. Gray* [2009] FCAFC 116 (3 September 2009) noted that UWA, similar to other Australian universities, now engages in commercial activities—at [184]. None the less, the Court held that there was no evidence 'to suggest that those commercial activities have displaced . . . UWA's traditional public function as an institution of higher education in favour of the pursuit of commercial purposes'—at [184].

Here it is argued that academic copyright is essential to academic freedom. University employment contracts and policies should be modified to offer greater copyright protection to academics. In particular, academics should expressly own copyright in all materials created by them, including scholarly works and teaching materials, subject to a licence and shared revenue return to their employing university. This would allow academics to control the publication and to ensure proper management of their original works, and to receive rents from exploitation of their materials. Such contractual arrangements would provide academics with improved incentives to create original works, and would enhance academic freedom.

INTRODUCTION TO THE ROLE OF THE UNIVERSITY AND ACADEMIC FREEDOM

Universities in the Western European tradition have always had a 'crucial role in society at large' (Monotti and Ricketson, 2003: 9). While their principal functions are teaching and research, these activities typically result in the communication of new (potentially competing) ideas to the public. In this way, universities provide 'some kind of community or external service'[4]. Indeed, universities in Australia (and in comparable nations, such as the United Kingdom and the USA) were long 'financed as a public service' in recognition of the role that they play in the creation of public knowledge (Cornish, 1992).

In addition to the communication of ideas, the activities of university scholars may result in socially useful innovations—although, as William Cornish comments, the practical application of research results has traditionally been a by-product, rather than the object, of scholarly endeavours. Indeed, he notes that, in the latter half of the 20th century, 'resources were concentrated on work at the pure, fundamental end of the spectrum', with 'a certain disdain being shown towards mere practical applications' (he further notes that in line 'with this attitude, universities showed no undue concern for the commercial potential of academic ideas').

The enduring concept of academic freedom reflects the four essential freedoms of a university, as outlined, in the USA, by Justice Felix Frankfurter: '[t]o determine for itself on academic grounds who may be taught, what may be taught, how it should be taught, and who may be admitted to study' (I emphasize, 'on academic grounds'—*Sweezy v. New Hampshire*, 1957; see also Pila, 2010—a). The concept also encompasses freedoms (characterized as aspects of 'individual academic freedom' in Pila, for example) in the conduct of research, both as a precursor to teaching and as an end in itself. It requires the 'liberty to choose the subjects to research and the means of pursuing them', as well as to 'decide when to make the fruits of that research public and how (if at all) to exploit them' (Cornish, 1992). Chris Triggs (2005) notes that the ability to 'control publication' is 'an important component of academic freedom'.

Academic freedom exists only without undue interference, whether institutional, governmental or commercial; it relies on independence and objectivity (Triggs, 2005; Monotti and Ricketson, 2003). In this way, it encourages the rigorous pursuit of truth and fact. It also allows the pursuit of research, and the dissemination of views, without fear of reprisal or in anticipation of favourable treatment (Pila, 2010—a). Pila also notes that academic freedoms (both institutional and individual) 'share a basis in the liberal ideal of the pursuit of truth through teaching, discussion and scholarly research'.

[4] Monotti and Ricketson, 2003: 17. They also note that 'community service' is one of the 'traditional functions' of the university, together with teaching and research: at 45.

Academic freedom thereby ensures that academic teaching and research may be conducted in a manner that is of public benefit. By encouraging the publication of the results of research and informed, unbiased views, it improves the quality of public discourse, which in turn heightens culture and enhances democracy. It also provides indirect public benefit, by allowing the free flow of ideas between institutions, and between colleagues at the same institution, fostering knowledge which is ultimately communicated to the public through teaching or public comment.

In Australia, the concept of academic freedom receives some support in the federal Higher Education Support Act 2003, section 19 of which requires institutions to have a policy ensuring 'free intellectual inquiry'. Institutional policies are occasionally more explicit in their recognition of the freedom—for example, the University of Melbourne's 'Freedom of Expression Policy' commits to preserving, defending and promoting the 'traditional principles of academic freedom', so that 'all scholars at the University are free to engage in critical enquiry, scholarly endeavour and public discourse without fear or favour'.

However, in Australia there is no general right to freedom of expression that provides support to the notion of academic freedom. In this respect, the USA, with its free speech right enshrined in the First Amendment to the nation's Constitution, provides a more solid basis on which to rest the concept of academic freedom. The absence of a broad free speech right may go some way to explaining why the existence and scope of academic freedom may be considered 'contested' in Australia (*UWA v. Gray*, 2009), notwithstanding the concept's long pedigree in the Western liberal tradition (an implied right to freedom of expression has been read into the Australian Constitution, but the guarantee is for freedom of communication in relation to government or political matters, and bears certain limitations).

INTRODUCTION TO COPYRIGHT IN THE UNIVERSITY CONTEXT

A. Copyright under statute

In Australia, copyright is regulated at a federal level by the Copyright Act 1968. This statute extends copyright protection to categories of 'original' works and subject matter. As a general rule in relation to original works, the first owner of copyright in a work is its author. In derogation from the general rule, the Act vests copyright ownership of all works created by an employee, in the course of their employment, in his or her employer. This provision may be overridden by agreement.

Where copyright subsists in an original work, the copyright owner is granted exclusive rights to do certain acts in relation to, and make certain uses of, the work. For example, the owner of copyright in a literary work has the exclusive right to reproduce that work. This has the effect that others may not reproduce the work without the permission of the copyright owner. An unauthorized reproduction is an infringement actionable by the copyright owner.

B. Copyright under university employment contracts and policies

As discussed above, the provisions of Australia's Copyright Act on employer ownership have effect unless 'excluded or modified by agreement', according to section 35(3). Such an agreement may be express, or (as considered further below) implied. In the United Kingdom, under a similar legislative provision ('subject to any agreement to the contrary') in section 11(2) of the Copyright, Designs and Patents Act 1988, it has been questioned whether parties are left free only to displace the statutory presumption of employer ownership (to the benefit of the employee), or may privately agree further to diminish the employee author's rights (Pila, 2010 (b); Monotti and Ricketson, 2003). Whatever the correct reading of the legislation in the United Kingdom and Australia, in practice, university employment contracts and policies often contemplate university ownership of a broad scope of materials.

Australian universities frequently assert, in employment contracts and associated policies, their ownership of all intellectual property created by academics during the course of their employment, with limited exceptions. To this extent, the terms privately agreed by employer and employee reflect the statutory position under the Copyright Act in respect of 'works' (similarly in the UK, according to Pila, 2010—b). However, some university documents assert university copyright ownership extending beyond that which would otherwise result from application of the Act's provisions.

The University of Queensland 'Intellectual Property Policy' deems certain categories of intellectual property to have been created 'in or during the course of employment' (University of Queensland Policy 4.10.13, 'Intellectual Property for Staff, Students and Visitors'). For example, where the creation of intellectual property (Foreground IP) by academics results from the 'use of', or 'incorporates', intellectual property already owned by the university (Background IP), the policy deems the Foreground IP to have been created in the course of employment. This has the effect that the university owns the Foreground IP. Clauses such as this have the potential to operate broadly, potentially extending university ownership of academic-created copyright materials.

Furthermore, some university policies refer to materials created 'in the course of or in connection with' or 'in the course of or incidental to' employment (University of Melbourne Statute 14.1, 'Intellectual Property', as an example). They thereby have the potential to capture some expressions of academic activity with a merely tangential connection with work duties.

Finally, some universities extend the categories of materials in which they assert copyright ownership to those created using, or with the substantial contribution of, university resources (respectively, for example, under the University of Queensland policy already cited and the University of Technology Sydney's 'Intellectual Property Policy'). The provision of resources is not a matter into which the Copyright Act enquires when determining the proper owner of copyright in an original work. Rather, the author—being the person who reduces the work into 'material form' (under sections 22(1) and 32(1) of the Act)—is recognized as the work's first owner.

In addition to the above-mentioned contractual provisions, which have the effect of diminishing academics' rights of ownership in materials created by them, university policies often require academic employees to keep confidential all intellectual property created in the course of their employment (at least, academic-created intellectual property with 'potential for commercialisation', as in the University of Adelaide 'Intellectual Property Policy Procedure'; the University of Technology Sydney policy also recognizes that publication and commercialization objectives may be in conflict).

Likewise, in institutional policies, universities often provide themselves with rights in respect of intellectual property commercialization. For example, it is often expressly provided that the university may decide, in its sole discretion, whether or not to proceed with the commercialization of intellectual property, such as copyright materials. Upon any commercialization, the university determines and distributes revenue shares. Together, these measures restrict academics' freedom to deal with the materials that they create.

C. Implied terms and the 'teacher exception'

At common law, there has long been recognition that the circumstances of academic employment are unlike other employment contexts[5]. The distinction results principally from the particular role of the university, as outlined earlier, and of the traditional role of the academic within the university. While universities now operate 'in the market' (which practice will be described further below), they are still not entirely 'of the market' (Pila, 2010—b). They have purposes beyond immediate commercial purposes, and their employees are required to advance these. In addition, academic freedom dictates that employed academics have latitude in choosing

[5] Triggs (2005) remarks that there is a 'long history of treating academics differently than other employees'. This comment, made in the Canadian context, is reflected in practices adopted in the USA (Cooper Dreyfuss, 2000; Gorman, 2000), the UK (Pila, 2010—b) and Australia (Monotti and Ricketson, 2003).

how to discharge their duties. In this sense, they are unlike 'typical' employees.

In light of these circumstances, practices developed in Australia, and in comparable jurisdictions, recognize in academics an entitlement to deal freely with their copyright materials in certain contexts. For example, there is a long-standing international practice of letting academics deal freely with their scholarly works (including journal articles and research in progress). Similarly, academics have traditionally been allowed to take their teaching materials to new workplaces, to use as their 'stock in trade' (for example, there is US case law holding that academics own common law copyright in their lectures, as they require 'portability' in order to do their job and to seek jobs elsewhere—Gorman, 2000).

In the USA and Canada, these practices have been characterized as a 'teacher exception' or 'academic exception' to the statutory rule that an employer takes copyright ownership of materials created by an employee within the course of employment (Sandler, 2001; Triggs, 1995). In Australia, the practices may be viewed as giving rise to terms implicitlyimplicitly agreed between a university and an employed academic. Monotti and Ricketson (2003) posit that ownership of academics' scholarly works vests by implication in their academic authors. They further argue that there exists an implied licence of teaching materials to their creators, which licence allows academics to continue using these materials, for certain purposes, even after they leave the employment of the institution for which they were created.

In some cases, the traditional practices described above have come to be reflected in the express terms of university policies. For example, universities sometimes expressly refrain from asserting ownership of copyright in the scholarly works created by academics (such as the University of Technology Sydney, the University of Melbourne, the University of Queensland or the University of Adelaide), and recognize that academics have a perpetual licence to continue using their teaching materials for limited purposes (such as the University of Sydney or the University of Queensland).

RECENT DEVELOPMENTS AND THEIR POTENTIAL EFFECT ON ACADEMIC FREEDOM

Despite being well-established and sound in rationale, the practices founding the 'teacher exception' are increasingly at risk (Monotti and Ricketson, 2003; Triggs, 2005—the latter notes that recently 'the academic exception has been shifted from a norm of practice to a legal question'). It has been suggested that, as universities search for new sources of revenue and as copyright materials become of greater value, the universities will likely seek to assert ownership of a broader range of academic-created copyright materials (Pila, 2010 (b); Gorman, 2000). This places at risk the traditional practice of allowing academics to deal freely with certain materials, and with it, academic freedom itself.

A. Recent developments

Globally, the universities of today are subjected to a 'questioning attitude' that now accompanies public funding (Cornish, 1992, who suggests that this 'questioning' has its genesis in the 1980s). Not only has public funding for universities decreased in many jurisdictions, but universities bear a heightened responsibility to account to government for the use of public funds.

In Australia, as in other nations, universities must increasingly run as businesses, which report on the 'outputs' and 'outcomes' of specific grants (PhillipsKPA, 2012), whose 'Vice-Chancellors are . . . chief executive officers and presidents', and whose 'deans and department heads are middle managers' with budgetary and reporting responsibilities (Monotti and Ricketson, 2003). According to consultants PhillipsKPA's 2012 report, universities' increased accountability with respect to funding, together with other regulatory compliance obligations, create burdens of both time and cost. The consultancy service's report concluded that, in 2011, the 'typical' Australian university required approximately 2,000 days of staff time, and spent between $A800,000 and $A900,000, in meeting the reporting requirements of the Department of Education (formerly the Department of Industry, Innovation, Science, Research and Tertiary Education).

In this context, Australian universities are constrained to seek new sources of revenue. Fee-paying students constitute one such source. Private contract work provides another. In addition, there is the 'relatively recent phenomenon' (Pila, 2010—b) of turning academic knowledge and ideas to account (Cornish, 1992). In particular, the copyright creations of faculty members—which previously held little promise of generating revenue, relative to patentable inventions—are of increasing interest to universities, due to their growing potential as a source of income (Monotti and Ricketson, 2003; Cooper Dreyfuss, 2000; Gorman, 2000; moreover, Cornish notes that the 'liveliest commercial potential in university research currently lies in computer programs', which are protected as copyright literary works, as well as through patent). In addition, copyright materials now represent an important source of income to universities through their centrality to Massive Open Online Courses (MOOCs), a form of online distance learning.

B. Potential effect on academic freedom

This corporate climate places at risk the essential liberties comprised in academic freedom. First, the increasing level of government oversight and the growing necessity to form partnerships with private enterprise risk a culture in which research is directed by government policy priorities or short-term commercial interests, rather than by long-term need or merit. A 'utilitarian concept of value' (Pila, 2010—b), measured according to funders' desired 'outputs' and 'outcomes', compromises the liberty to pursue freely lines of questioning (and particularly those with no immediately apparent commercial application). Likewise, government involvement in the content of university courses, through the setting of universal standards and quality requirements, might usefully serve other purposes, but it restricts academic freedom to determine what and how subject matter is taught. Time and funds spent maintaining compliance with, and reporting on, universal standards also potentially affect the resources that can be devoted to research and teaching.

Of particular concern, as universities become subject to increasing funding pressure and seek to protect their investment in academic-created copyright materials, is the risk that universities will more frequently seek to rely on their statutory rights to copyright in works created during the course of employment. As discussed above, institutional agreements and policies already provide universities with extensive rights in academic-created copyright materials, which are bolstered by obligations of confidentiality on the part of academics, and exclusive commercialization rights on the part of the university. Expansive university rights are often tempered by recognition (either implied, or through express terms in institutional agreements and policies) of the long-standing practices of the 'teacher exception'. However, these conventional practices may easily be abandoned.

The most worrying aspect of advancing university copyright ownership is that the choice to publish is taken out of the hands of the academic creator. As noted above, the owner of copyright in a literary work has the exclusive right to reproduce that work. The copyright owner also has the exclusive right to publish the work. Therefore, if universities choose to invoke their statutory rights to all copyright materials created by academics during the course of employment, the decision whether to publish will lie in the hands of the university, which may 'prevent publication altogether' (Cornish, 1992). In particular, it may decide to withhold or suppress content that is inconsistent with the institutional agenda.

As Monotti and Ricketson (2003) contend, this would 'sit uncomfortably with the academic's right to freedom of expression'. A further possible result is that academics may choose to conduct research, and produce content, which they know will find favour with the institution and therefore receive exposure (a necessity for academics, whose career performance is measured in part according to the frequency and prominence of their publications). This would clearly affect the independence and objectivity that are the hallmarks of academic freedom.

The current trend towards open access in academic publishing (Working Group or Finch Report, 2012—see below) provides another cause for concern. The open access movement aims to achieve increased access to scholarly materials, as the cost of access approaches a zero point (Swan, 2006). However, the model of open access recommended by the UK's 2012 Report of the Working Group on Expanding Access to Published Research Findings (the 'Finch Report') has 'turn[ed] the subscription-based model on its head'. In many cases, the open access model imposes charges on authors to publish, rather than on readers to read. As reported by journalist Daniel Boffey in *The Guardian* newspaper in January 2013, universities have already moved to pay the levied Article Processing Charges on behalf of academic authors, yet this raises concern as it enlarges universities' control over if, how, and where to publish academics' works. The proposal has already rung alarm bells among scholars.

C. Consequences of curtailing academic freedom

It can be seen that the current higher education environment raises concerns for liberty in the conduct of research, liberty in teaching and the freedom to decide whether, when and how to publish research results. The intrusion of external interests means academic independence is compromised, to the extent that decisions can no longer be made in the absence of fear or favour.

While academic freedom has its basis in the 'liberal ideal of the pursuit of truth [and knowledge] through teaching, discussion and scholarly research' (Pila, 2010—b), this ideal is placed at risk when teaching and research must be directed towards other outcomes, and when discussion is potentially limited by institutional commercialization objectives. If research, in particular, cannot be conducted freely, with the 'systematic investigation' and 'scientific rigour' that are aspects of academic freedom (Monotti and Ricketson, 2003), then society will not realize the full possibilities of increases in knowledge and innovation. That, in turn, would limit the original content that may be shared between colleagues and, ultimately, taught to students.

If academics' freedom to publish and otherwise disseminate ideas is restricted, then the university's role as a transferor of knowledge cannot be fully realized. Accordingly, in such conditions, we cannot hope to achieve what Monotti and Ricketson describe as the 'heightening of ... general culture', 'improvements in public debate and civic affairs' and resultant improvement in 'economic and social well-being' that might otherwise be attained[6].

ACADEMIC COPYRIGHT AS A PILLAR OF ACADEMIC FREEDOM

It seems unlikely that the university—now, in the words of Cornish (1992), a 'Technopolis'—will ever return to the days of the pure 'Academe'. The Australian Government, according to its official responses of December 2013, is set to implement the recommendations of the 2013 Report on the Review of Higher Education Regulation and the 2012 Report on the Review of Reporting Requirements for Universities, but corporate-style university reporting requirements appear likely to remain, even as an attempt is made to reduce 'red tape'. Likewise, as government funding for Australian universities is unlikely to increase significantly, the pressure to seek alternative sources of income—and the possibilities offered by exploitation of copyright materials to generate revenue—will remain as features of the higher education landscape.

A. Towards a solution: academic copyright

To defend against the greatest risks of the present landscape, academics should be the first owners of copyright in their lectures and research output. This is necessary to return the control of copyright materials to their academic creators, thereby promoting academic freedom; the 'essential point', according to the contention of Cornish (1992), is to guard the 'freedom to publish' of academics, avoiding the intolerable incursion on academic freedom that results if universities have the power to prevent publication of research and associated materials.

Academic ownership of copyright would also have the benefit of providing academics with additional incentive to produce copyright materials[7]. This is particularly important in the university environment, for two reasons. First, the copyright materials created by academics (whether scholarly works or teaching materials) tend to have high social utility. Secondly, academics have freedom to determine how to fulfil their work duties, and are not commonly given directions to create specific copyright materials (Cornish, 1992). Therefore, it is in the public interest that they should be provided with additional encouragement to do so. Thirdly, copyright ownership—and the rights to revenue that usually follow from ownership—may well incentivize the production of high-quality materials, and may attract higher-quality staff to universities, which would also ultimately benefit society at large (Monotti and Ricketson, 2003; Triggs, 2005).

B. Uniform private terms to implement the solution

The proposed change, allowing for ownership by academics of all materials created by them, would need to be supported by uniform private terms overriding copyright legislation. The 'Intellectual Property Ordinance' of the University of Cambridge, in the United Kingdom, provides a precedent. It states that:

> Intellectual property rights [other than patent and trade mark rights], arising from the activities of University staff in the course of their employment by the University ... belong to the University staff member who creates the results subject to any third party rights which he or she may have previously agreed.

It can be noted that the Ordinance anticipates that staff members may negotiate away their rights when dealing with third parties—it is important, however, that the starting position is one of academic ownership (see Cornish, 1992).

A feature of the Cambridge solution is a licence to the university to use teaching materials created by its employed academics. Such a licence should be a feature of the solution proposed here, so that each university retains rights to use materials for teaching. Academics might further agree to share with their employing universities the revenue received from exploitation of their copyright materials. This would ensure a return on investment to universities, safeguarding their interest in increasingly valuable copyright materials.

It may be queried, as Triggs (2005) does, why the starting position might not equally be one of university ownership, with a licence to each academic creator to use materials for a set of defined purposes. Aside from the fact that universities generally have a superior ability to bargain favourable licence terms, a licence to use copyright materials (plus a guaranteed share in exploitation revenue) would sufficiently safeguard universities' legitimate interests. In contrast, a licence from the university to academics to use copyright materials for limited purposes does not provide academics with that essential aspect of academic freedom, which is the liberty to decide whether and how to make the results of research public.

While academic claims to copyright ownership are theoretically stronger in respect of scholarly works, as distinct from teaching materials, academics should own copyright in their teaching materials as well as scholarly and research works. The benefits of a consistent approach are multiple. It would reduce uncertainty (and therefore inefficiency), limit practical difficulties of academic career mobility and provide incentive to create high-quality teaching materials (as well as high-quality scholarly works). As scholarly works and teaching materials tend to cross-fertilize (Monotti and Ricketson, 2003), it is in fact difficult, as well as undesirable, to maintain a distinction between the two categories of material.

[6] Triggs (2005) also recognizes that 'the freedom to disseminate ensures that the public domain has the full benefit of the knowledge produced by universities': at 74.

[7] Copyright, similar to other intellectual property rights, is 'said to provide an incentive for the production of intellectual goods that are of cultural or practical value to society' (Van Caenegem, 2009: 10).

C. Considering the alternatives

A solution of academic copyright ownership, effected through uniform private terms overriding the provisions of the Copyright Act, is recommended here. This is not to suggest that reliance be placed on the unspoken practices of the international scholarly community, described above as giving rise to a 'teacher exception'. As discussed, these long-standing practices of allowing academics to deal freely with their copyright materials in certain instances give rise in Australia to implied terms that function as a private 'agreement' for the purposes of the Copyright Act—specifically, section 35(3).

These conventions have operated effectively, so much so that journal publishers frequently deal with academics as though they were the owners of their journal articles, even though, on the face of the legislation, they may often not be. However, as academic copyright materials become more valuable and universities take an increasing interest in them, it would be unwise to rely upon terms of implied agreement. By virtue of their nature, implied terms create uncertainty. They are of uncertain scope and create potential inconsistency with the terms that employers and employees put in writing. For this reason, in order to reduce uncertainty, academic copyright ownership should be reflected in express contractual terms (Monotti and Ricketson, 2003).

In addition, the implied terms recognized in the Australian context do not go far enough: currently, while it is implicitly agreed that an academic author owns copyright in his or her scholarly works, the law goes only so far as recognizing a licence to use teaching materials for limited purposes. For the reasons described above, this is insufficient.

Likewise, there should not be continued reliance on existing university polices. First, none of the Australian university policies discussed above provides for academic ownership of all copyright materials created in the course of employment. Some provide for academic ownership of scholarly works (with a limited licence to the university) and university ownership of teaching works (with a limited licence to the academic creator). In this sense, they reflect the implied terms discussed above, and are subject to the same limitations of scope.

Furthermore, as discussed earlier, some university agreements and policies in fact extend university ownership of academic-created copyright beyond that which would be obtained under the Copyright Act. For example, some universities extend the categories of materials in which they assert copyright to those created using, or with the substantial contribution of, university resources (whether or not in the course of an academic's employment).

Accordingly, existing university agreements and policies dealing with copyright should be amended to include uniform terms of the nature described above. These would recognize academics' ownership of copyright in all materials created by them, in the manner of the Cambridge ordinance. Any inconsistent terms, which in practice derogate from the rights vesting in academics as copyright owners, should be removed.

CONCLUSION

This essay has argued that academic copyright is necessary for academic freedom. For academic freedom to flourish, academics need the ability to deal with their copyright content without fear or favour. Copyright ownership means academics have the initial right to seek revenue from exploitation of their copyright materials (if desired). This provides an incentive to create materials of high quality, and fortifies academics' independence against the wishes of external funders.

Academics require the ability to control publication of their works, and the ability to share freely research results with colleagues, students and the public at large. It is only by maintaining these liberties that academics can maintain their independence and a university may fulfil its important role in public life. Allowing universities copyright ownership of scholarly works, and thereby the ability to control publication, constitutes an impermissible restriction on academic freedom, in an environment in which this ideal is already under threat from various quarters.

A proposed contribution to the defence of academic freedom is that uniform private terms recognizing academic ownership should be included in university employment agreements and policies. Such documents should also provide for a licence and revenue return to the employing university, to protect the university's investment in the creation of copyright materials by academics. This solution is preferable to a starting position of university copyright ownership, with a licence to academics for limited purposes. The latter alternative would not sufficiently protect academic freedom or independence.

The solution proposed here is also preferable to reliance on existing implied terms, which have grown out of standard practices and are uncertain in both scope and status. While some Australian university agreements and policies already recognize academic copyright ownership of some materials created by them during their employment, university terms are not uniform, are limited in providing for academic copyright and tend concurrently to extend university rights. Accordingly, in order to preserve academic freedom and the public role of the university, uniform terms providing for academic ownership of copyright should be introduced at institutional level, overriding the Copyright Act's provisions on employer ownership in the specific context of academic creation of copyright works.

REFERENCES

Boffey, D. 'Historians warn minister: hands off our academic freedoms', in *The Guardian* (online). 27 January 2013 (www.theguardian.com/education/2013/jan/26/historians-warn-minister-over-academic-freedom).

Cooper Dreyfuss, R. 'Collaborative Research: Conflicts on Authorship, Ownership, and Accountability', in *Vanderbilt Law Review*, vol. 53, no. 4, 2000

Cornish, W. R. 'Rights in University Innovations: The Herchel Smith Lecture for 1991', in *European Intellectual Property Review*, vol. 14(1), 1992.

Gorman, R. A. 'Copyright Conflicts on the University Campus: The First Annual Christopher A. Meyer Memorial Lecture', in *Journal of the Copyright Society of the USA*, 47, 2000.

Government of Australia, Department of Education. *Government Response to the Review of Reporting Requirements for Universities*. 11 December 2013 (https://education.gov.au/government-response-review-reporting-requirements-universities).

Review of Higher Education Regulation. 14 November 2013 (https://education.gov.au/review-higher-education-regulation-1).

Monotti, A., and Ricketson, S. *Universities and Intellectual Property: Ownership and Exploitation*. Oxford, Oxford University Press, 2003.

PhillipsKPA Pty Ltd. *Review of Reporting Requirements for Universities*. Cremorne, PhillipsKPA, 2012.

Pila, J. 'Academic Freedom and the Courts', in *Law Quarterly Review*, vol. 126, 2010 (a).

'Who owns the intellectual property rights in academic work?', in *European Intellectual Property Review*, vol. 32(12), 2010 (b).

Sandler, C. 'Copyright Ownership: A Fundamental of "Academic Freedom"', in *Albany Law Journal of Science and Technology*, vol. 12, 2001.

Swan, A. 'Overview of scholarly communication', in Jacobs, N.(Ed.). *Open Access: Key Strategic, Technical and Economic Aspects*. Oxford, Chandos Publishing, 2006.

Triggs, C. 'Academic Freedom, Copyright and the Academic Exception', in *Workplace: A Journal for Academic Labor*, vol. 7(1), November 2005.

Van Caenegem, W. *Intellectual and Industrial Property in Australia*. Chatswood, LexisNexis Butterworths, 2009.

Working Group on Expanding Access to Published Research Findings. *Accessibility, sustainability, excellence: how to expand access to research publication* ('Finch Report'), June 2012.

PERFORMANCE-BASED RESEARCH FUNDING AND ACADEMIC FREEDOM: AN OXYMORON?

PETRA BUTLER[8]

No [one] ought to meddle with the universities, who does not know them well and love them well.

(Thomas Arnold, 'Letter to George Pryme', in A. Stanley, *The Life and Correspondence of Thomas Arnold, DD*, vol. 2 (12th edn): 69. London, J. Murray, 1881)

INTRODUCTION

Plato, in *Republic*, proposed that philosophers who devote their lives to obtaining insights that benefit their fellow citizens can be trusted to be wise and good, and should govern not only themselves, but the rest of society, to optimize the benefit to all. Modern administrators are more demanding. In most countries, universities are government funded, reflecting the public good of academic enquiry and higher education. Due to the immense growth of student numbers after the Second World War, and more recently a considerable decrease in available public funds, many governments have asserted a need to manage public money with sophisticated funding regimes, to ensure the best value for what they spend (Genua, 2001). Many have adopted variations of the United Kingdom's model, which attaches government funding for university research to peer review of academic output (for example, Spain, the Slovak Republic, Hong Kong, Australia, Poland, Portugal, Italy, Belgium, Norway, Sweden, Denmark and Finland—see Hicks, 2012).

Output-based university research funding systems are all versions of the same basic model that ties future government funding to assessment of research already completed. Most commentators characterize them as part of a modern neoliberal imperative that emphasizes accountability and efficiency, delivered through market mechanisms (Curtis, 2008). They sit alongside other elements of that agenda, such as 'user pays' student fees and partnerships with industry. Others express concern that these imperatives erode the traditional ethos of a university, emphasizing higher learning as an end in itself rather than education as a public good (Shore and Taitz, 2012)[9].

This essay argues that output-based peer review funding systems emphasize the contemporary usefulness of research, and inveigles researchers to favour conventional and well accepted lines of enquiry, placing less value on innovative and controversial contributions and potentially threatening academic freedom. History reveals that insights arise in novel ways, often rejected by the establishment (including the academic establishment) in the first instance. Also, new insights may not prove valuable until they fall into place with other findings, possibly years after they are first described. One of academic freedom's utilitarian justifications is the value of qualified people pursuing knowledge that lacks immediate justification for these reasons. That is why academia has historically stood apart from commercial imperatives and the need for economic returns. It is the academic researcher's raison d'être and one of the building blocks necessary for social progress. Only recently the German Constitutional Court emphasized the significance of academia for society, the centrality of academia for the knowledge society and the responsibility of academia (Bundesverfassungsgericht 2 BvL 4/10, 14 February 2012).

Output-based peer review systems threaten academic freedom, in particular the freedom to research. If new knowledge has to demonstrate its worth at the time of its creation, knowledge that does not make the grade on this criterion will not be pursued. Focus on the present risks losing the larger view. This chilling effect is an infringement of academic freedom. Unless limitations can be justified, there are implications for the long-term quality of research.

This essay briefly considers the parameters of academic freedom. It then sets out the essential features of output-driven funding systems, such as New Zealand's Performance-Based Research Fund, and outlines the way in which such regimes can infringe the researcher's academic freedom, or at least pose a serious risk of doing so. It then argues that this infringement imposes an unjustified limitation on the right of academic freedom.

PROTECTION OF THE UNIVERSITY RESEARCHER'S ACADEMIC FREEDOM

While institutions recognizable as universities have existed since the 12th century in Europe, it is only in relatively modern times that they have embraced the concept of academic freedom. Medieval universities were created to prepare students for the professions of law, medicine and holy orders (Bhattacharya, 2012), which they did by transmitting a received body of knowledge (Karran, 2009). Learning for its own sake was not a major consideration (Brockliss, 2000), nor was research. The body of knowledge was static and widely accepted (Brockliss—law, for instance, meant learning the *Corpus Iuris Civilis*) and teachers were expected to remain within the boundaries of orthodoxy.

The idea that knowledge was not fixed first emerged as a significant consideration in Germany in the 1800s. The educationalist, Wilhelm von Humboldt, emphasized research and the freedom to pursue it as a core principle of university life. He and other academics and philosophers, such as Immanuel Kant, argued that knowledge was open to permanent increase (Ricken, 2007). The idea spread to the rest of Europe after 1850 (Brockliss, 2000). A professor was accorded almost absolute freedom when researching and teaching within his field of expertise, even though in his personal sphere, such as political opinions, he was subject to the same censorship as everyone else (Altbach, 2001).

Comparative research paints a universally agreed core of the researcher's right to academic freedom. Interestingly, as far as the author can establish, while contemporary research has established a universally agreed concept of the researcher's right to academic freedom, jurisprudence on the freedom of research is not vast (for the USA, see Sinder, 1990)[10] and extensive legal commentary is predominantly—though not exclusively—confined to the USA and Germany (with the caveat that the author was limited by accessibility of foreign material).

The right to academic freedom is widely recognized in the modern world and 82 nations have constitutions that protect it explicitly (see Committee on Freedom and Responsibility in the conduct of Science at www.icsu.org, the International Council for Science). The Charter of Fundamental Rights of the European Union (EU) states: 'The arts and scientific research shall be free of constraint. Academic freedom shall be respected'. The UN Educational, Scientific and Cultural

[8] This essay is a shorter and revised version of P. Butler and R. Mulgan's 'Can Academic Freedom Survive Performance Based Research Funding?', in *Victoria University of Wellington Law Review*, vol. 44(3), 2013. I am grateful to Roderick Mulgan for his immense input.

[9] For extensive research relating to this funding system, see Codd (2004), Bourke (1997), Dalziel (2005), Davies, Craig and Robertson (2005), Hobbs and Stewart (2006), House of Commons Science and Technology Committee (2002), McNay (1999), Talib (2002), Coryn et al. (2007), Hicks (2012), European Centre for Strategic Management of Universities (2010) and Butler/OECD (2010).

[10] Compare Scholz (2012), Article 5(III) with an overview of the literature existing in Germany, and Alber-Malchow and Steigleder (2000).

Organization (UNESCO) General Conference in 1997 adopted the following recommendation:

> The right to education, teaching and research can only be fully enjoyed in an atmosphere of academic freedom...the open communication of findings, hypotheses and opinions lies at the very heart of higher education and provides the strongest guarantee of accuracy and objectivity of scholarship and research.

Courts and commentators throughout the world recognize that academic freedom encompasses the utility of discovering and disseminating knowledge. Academic freedom includes the freedom of research and the freedom to choose the methods and subject matter of what is taught.

Comparative research establishes that freedom of research includes the right to pursue any research using any methodology that the researcher thinks fit, as long as it is comprehensible and reproducible. The freedom of research is the freedom of the individual scholar in his/her research to pursue truth wherever it seems to lead, without fear or punishment or termination of employment for having offended some political, religious or social orthodoxy (for example, Berdahl, 1990, and Jarass, 2004).

It is also uncontroversial that the freedom of research encompasses the freedom not to undertake a certain enquiry or not pursue research at any given time (Robertson, 1978). Academic freedom can best flourish in an environment that contains both a subjective right of researchers to be free from any state interference and an objective value system. The latter compels the state to foster and guarantee research and scholarship through the provision of an organizational framework in which research and scholarship can flourish unhindered (the debate in the USA is slightly obscured by the First Amendment discussion—Post, 2012).

The general observations about the scope of the right to freedom of academia hold true for its core scope under national constitutions. Freedom of academia is either protected directly by the constitutions (as mentioned above) or as part of the right to freedom of expression. This essay is founded on an understanding of the ambit of freedom of academia gained through comparative analysis advanced above.

This analysis rests on four broad paradigms of independence: economic, institutional, social and professional, and subject matter. First, freedom of research means freedom from economic pressures that direct a researcher's choices and/or steer him or her towards certain enquiry. The researcher's funding has to allow for independent decision-making in the search for truth. This independence could be likened to that of the judiciary.

Secondly, it is the business of a university to provide an atmosphere that is most conducive to speculation, experimentation and creation. The well-known 1940 Statement of Principles on Academic Freedom and Tenure from the American Association of University Professors, widely endorsed in the USA (O'Neil, 2004), asserted that:

> Teachers are entitled to full freedom in research and in the publication of the results, subject to adequate performance of their other academic duties.

The reference to 'other academic duties' implies that this freedom has particular relevance to the researcher's relationship with their employing institution, to whom such duties are owed. It implies that if a researcher discharges his or her obligations to teach and otherwise contribute to the life of the university, as required by their employment contract, 'full freedom' can be enjoyed with regard to research. This can only be taken to mean the employing institution cannot dictate research methods and agendas, or the dissemination of results (for the recent criticism of the insufficient protection in the USA, see Lee, 2014). This differentiates university researchers from those in the private sphere, who must take directions from corporate employers.

Employing institutions can hold researchers to certain basic criteria, such as complying with ethical requirements, pursuing ideas that have some reasonable basis for justifying enquiry, and demonstrating progress and results over time. However, the institution cannot dictate the research agenda.

Thirdly, academic enquiry may not sit well with popular sentiment, but academic freedom must encompass social and professional independence (Scholz, 2012). Ideas that are popular may have little merit when examined critically, and unreasonable beliefs may likewise prove to have justification. It was once seriously argued that homosexuality was a psychiatric condition, and that smoking was 'positive and pleasurable'[11]. If research were confined to social consensus, these ideas might be with us yet.

Empirical science is a process of observation and argument, not a democratic election. The humanities likewise expect a substantial scope of autonomy for those who devote their careers to a subject and attain a level of understanding well beyond the layperson. It follows that research will be truly free, reflective (including critically reflective) and innovative only if it is not required to conform to social expectations.

Pressures of consensus do not arise only from the masses. The academic community can also entertain accepted principles, and the same objections apply to allowing a professional consensus to stifle research into opposing views (Tinsley, 2013).

In the USA, some have argued that the greatest threat to academic freedom comes from within the academy. Critics claim that the dominant forces in the professoriate, mainly in the social sciences and humanities, seek to enforce 'political correctness'—imposing academic orthodoxy, usually from a liberal or radical perspective, and seeking to silence those with opposing viewpoints (Altbach, 2001). Yet freedom of research means the ability to proceed without a social consensus, and even the ability to proceed against opposition, including the opposition of research peers. The state, therefore, is required to create room within its developed structures for the unobstructed, free exercise of research and scholarship through adequate organizational measures. The academic framework in which research and scholarship is conducted must be organized in such a way that it neither endangers the functioning of research and scholarship nor affects the sphere of freedom necessary for scientific endeavour. Freedom of academia demands that the organization of universities and therewith also the organizational decision-making processes must be regulated in such a way that unhindered research is possible.

Finally, independence of subject matter must be preserved. The progress of knowledge values what is called 'blue sky' or 'curiosity-driven' research. Such research is not amenable to commercial imperatives. First, knowledge is produced in ignorance of the end uses to which it might one day be put. Many lines of enquiry might prove unhelpful, but the fruitful ones unfold in ways that simply cannot be known ahead of time. DNA, for instance, was discovered through a chain of discoveries over a period of 100 years, from 1869, when Swiss chemist Friedrich Miescher isolated 'nuclein' inside white blood cells, to the final insights of James Watson and Francis Crick in the 1950s, who put the pieces of the puzzle together (Portugal and Cohen, 1980). None of the prior steps held promise of the final discovery, or its implications, but were pursued in a spirit of open-ended enquiry (to compare the evolution of scientific research in general, see Kuhn, 2012).

Furthermore, new insights often fail to impress knowledgeable people at the time of their creation. Charles Darwin's theory of evolution, one of the most important insights in the whole of the natural sciences, was first presented to a scientific audience on 1 July 1858, at a meeting of the Linnean Society in

[11] For example, Ronald Bayer's *Homosexuality and American Psychiatry* (Princeton, NJ, Princeton University Press, 1987) or Allan Brandt's 'The cigarette, risk and American culture', in Judith Leavitt and Ronald Numbers (Eds), *Sickness and Health In America: Readings in the history of medicine and public health* (Madison, WI, University of Wisconsin Press, 1997).

London, United Kingdom. It made no lasting impression on the 50 or so men of medicine and science who heard it[12].

Darwin himself wrote later, in his autobiography:

> Nevertheless, our joint productions excited very little attention, and the only published notice of them which I can remember was by Professor Haughton of Dublin, whose verdict was that all that was new in them was false, and what was true was old.
>
> (N. Barlow (Ed.). *The Autobiography of Charles Darwin, 1809–1882*. London, Collins, 1958)

Ignaz Semmelweis was a 19th-century Hungarian physician who proposed that the incidence of maternal infection after childbirth (a leading cause of female mortality) could be greatly reduced if the attending doctors disinfected their hands. He was able to demonstrate the benefit in practical trials, but there was no scientific explanation for his theory, and he was widely ridiculed by his colleagues. He was vindicated only years after his death when Louis Pasteur demonstrated the existence of bacteria (Carter, 2005).

Arguably, it is such ground that is most sensitive to funding systems that require researchers to show the benefit of their work, and it is this type of research that will be most affected by any 'chilling' influence of over-managed funding systems.

Private researchers who work for companies seeking commercial returns may also advance society, as with new drugs, but no voices are raised that they enjoy unique rights, such as the ability to dictate their own research agenda. Academic freedom requires something more. It acknowledges that universities and their staff have a particular role in finding out truth, free of commercial constraints. Much of what enriches society, such as basic research (*Grundlagenforschung*), does not have a commercial application that will pay for people to investigate. Much of what advances science in the medium term are discoveries born from a spirit of enquiry, whose applications cannot be known ahead of time.

In summary, for academic freedom, and in particular the freedom to research, to be fully protected, the state has to allow and foster research and scholarship through the allocation of personal, financial and organizational means. This is the reason for the practice of funding university research without tying it to any externally imposed conditions. This practice is not a source of inefficiency to be resolved by better governmental scrutiny; it is the system's strength and purpose. It is at the heart of what research is about and for. The focus of this essay is that an output evaluation-orientated funding system poses a threat to academic freedom, particularly in its potential to curtail a researcher's choices in research activity.

Research is a different kind of endeavour from most other businesses—by definition it cannot be purchased off-the-shelf from a supplier (Gluckman, 2012). Academic research and scholarship in its widest sense constitutes a macroeconomic productivity force of the first order. Its economic, social and political significance is self-evident (European Commission, 2010; Scholz, 2012). It is a condition of progress. As discussed, freedom of research requires researchers to be 'truly' free. That means, the researcher has to be able to be free to decide the subject matter, the methodology, the timing and the mode of dissemination of his or her research (Robertson, 1978).

Peer review-driven evaluation systems (performance-based funding systems—PBFS) are not glaringly arbitrary. They have checks and balances, and undoubtedly their creators and executors operate with the best of intentions. They do not necessarily prevent the researcher from conducting the research he or she wants to conduct or publish. However, that does not mean these systems cannot infringe the freedom of research indirectly.

PERFORMANCE-BASED FUNDING SYSTEMS

According to Diana Hicks (2012), PBFS are relatively recent, and are still in the process of development. Around a dozen countries have implemented them, starting with the United Kingdom in the mid-1980s (subsequently, Spain, Slovak Republic, Hong Kong, Australia, Poland, Portugal, Italy, Belgium, Norway, Sweden, Denmark and Finland). They are subject to substantial ongoing revision. They have the following characteristics: they evaluate completed research outputs only (not research proposals); they direct the allocation of state funding; and they are national in scope.

PBFS have been created to deliver various goals, particularly those stated by governments as enhancing research excellence. A number of these systems are based on peer review, although there is no obvious reason that peer review should be preferred—it is not part of the definition of a PBFS. While substantial state funds are distributed on the basis of these systems, the amount that is redistributed from one institution to another is often not significant, particularly among the top tier of recipients. The influence of these systems seems to be primarily through the reputation associated with a high ranking, and not necessarily through the money that the rankings attract (Butler/OECD, 2010; Hicks, 2012). PBFS are generally structured to deliver a single grant to each tertiary institution, with the institution retaining control over how the money is spent within its own needs. There is no guarantee that extra funding will be made to the researchers who created the grade that attracted it (Hicks, 2012).

The New Zealand authorities, after considering various models of targeted research funding (the British system in particular—see Barnard, 1998, and Watt, 2012), opted for performance-based funding, the Performance-Based Research Fund (PBRF), for the research component of tertiary education activity (Boston et al., 2005; Butler and Mulgan, 2013). New Zealand's model uses both peer review and performance indicators and is based on three components (Cole, 2012): measurement of external research income (15%), the measurement of research degree completion (25%) and a periodic quality evaluation, which determines the main portion of the funding (60%). Furthermore, peer review applies to individual academics, not a school or university department. The New Zealand model is probably the most all-encompassing indicator model. Other models use only one or the other of performance-based indicators, such as that of the United Kingdom (institutional peer review) or of Australia (performance indicators). As Boston and his co-authors (2005) further point out, most countries have followed the United Kingdom—where the concept of funding based on peer assessment was pioneered—and evaluate at the collective level, such as research unit, department or institution.

While the requirement to have a PBFS is dictated by government, universities are actively involved in implementing it. The membership of the peer-review and moderation panels, for instance, is under their control. This essay does not question the fair and robust nature of the system as created, and as evidenced by a considerable body of scholarship. Rather it asks whether such systems have the potential to limit the researcher's freedom to research as protected by most constitutions and the so-called International Bill of Rights. The essay contends that the protection of academic freedom may not be adequately taken into account in the design of such systems.

Under a PBFS, researchers may well be able to conduct the research they want to conduct and disseminate the results as they see fit in many instances, but this is not enough. Given the importance of freedom of research for society and the state, even a minor infringement by the state requires justification. The potential infringement of freedom of research by a peer-reviewed system imposed by the state lies in the indirect influence that it exerts on researchers to enforce conformity with mainstream thinking. This is a function of the operation of peer review, as discussed in the next section. It could be argued that the pressure on a researcher to conform is ultim-

[12] Professor Thomas Bell, who chaired the meeting, remarked, 'The year which has passed has not, indeed, been marked by any of those striking discoveries'—cited in J. E. Browne's *Charles Darwin: Volume 2—The Power of Place* (London, Jonathan Cape, 2002).

ately exerted by university management, which wants to maximize their status and funding. Even if this is true, the imperative still arises from the state in the first place, and it is the state that is responsible for it.[13]

PEER REVIEW

As set out above, peer review is at the heart of the performance-based funding system. If research is to be evaluated by an outside agency, freedom from undue influence will be assured only if the measure used is objective and apolitical. It is far from assured that peer review meets these criteria.

A recent report commissioned by the Organisation for Economic Co-operation and Development (OECD) found that the whole concept of measuring performance with the help of peer review is problematic (Hicks, 2012). Another recent article examined the peer review procedure used by the National Health and Research Council of Australia to allocate research grants. It found that random variation affected the success of many proposals, and successful applicants were often those who knew the right tactics (Graves et al., 2011). It appeared that panellist bias was greatest where proposals were innovative. Scores on such applications were likely to be controversial, the more innovative and edgy ideas often getting disparate scores, rendering them less likely to be funded (Gluckman, 2012).

According to Dieter Hart (1998), that peer review promotes the orthodox is evidenced in to the field of medical research, where (orthodox) peer review is deliberately used to evaluate research to safeguard patients' safety and well-being. The levels of existing scientific knowledge and of medical experience are paramount considerations before allowing medical research that involves the 'use of' patients. Recognition of the profession is a cornerstone of patient safety. Medical research that involves patients is deliberately researched in small steps to safeguard patients. The problem is also particularly marked in small countries, where academics are more likely to know each other, and a reviewer can be influenced by personality and reputation, often unconsciously (Pouris, 1988).

PBFS are liable to the general factors that produce bias in peer review, but also have some specialized factors of their own. Bias may arise in a PBFS where the academic elite had a significant hand in its design and implementation. Richard Whitley (2007) suggests that novelty, innovation and intellectual diversity may be suppressed because 'elites' judge proposals on their relevance to paradigms that they themselves have established. Where elites seek research excellence at the international level (that is, published in English), contributions of value to national and cultural identity may be lost (Butler/OECD, 2010).

Evidence suggests that, at least in some disciplines, researchers have changed their research pattern and produced research more aligned with the perceived relevant quality assurance criteria (the same claim has been made about the tenure process in the USA—Byrne, 1989). McNay's (1999) survey of the British system found that nearly one-half of the research managers surveyed felt that the United Kingdom's Research Assessment Exercise (RAE) hindered the pursuit of new research areas or risky 'blue skies' research. Around one-quarter of staff also reported that they avoided new lines of research and speculative topics because they believed that quality outputs could not be achieved by RAE submissions deadlines. This was corroborated by Evaluation Associates' study of the 1996 RAE, which found that 63% of researchers felt pressure to get results published early to meet cut-off points, and a small minority felt that there was little incentive to focus on longer-term research at all (Butler/OECD, 2010; Talib, 2002).

It is widely recognized that these systems risk disadvantaging novel and speculative research. One author observed that:

> Strong evaluation systems will reinforce the influence of conservative scientific elders, thereby suppressing novelty, new fields, diversity and pluralism. This problem will be exacerbated if a country's scientific elite is cohesive and if they also control project-based funding through peer review.

(Whitley, 2007)[14]

An OECD report (Butler/OECD, 2010) observed:

> A general concern of all PRFSs...is that they favour 'mainstream', disciplinary-based, basic, 'safe' research at the expense of applied, interdisciplinary or speculative research.

THE INFLUENCE OF PBFS ON RESEARCH: DOES IT LIMIT THE FREEDOM OF ACADEMIA?

The influence of a PBFS on research may well be subtle. The full effects of PBFS on researchers' decisions to avoid certain directions or focus on others, or to disseminate their research in a particular way, are impossible to identify, and their significance may not be felt for decades. An infringement of freedom of research does not require that all researchers are influenced by peer review. The importance of research freedom, as outlined above, means that even a subtle infringement of the researcher's freedom constitutes a prima facie infringement of academic freedom and must be justified by the state. So, is the limitation that the PBFS places on the researcher's freedom justified?

It is axiomatic that there is no right without limits. Every state has to balance the rights of others or legitimate interests of the community against the right in question.

In general, courts are able to review whether the legislature's limitation of a right is justifiable, but they are not able to substitute their own views (Wolff, 2000). The legislature is afforded a margin in regulating a matter, which is wider when it concerns political, social or economic issues. When determining whether limitation of a right is justifiable, courts generally undertake a balancing exercise with the help of a proportionality analysis.[15]The German jurisprudence in this regard has been the cornerstone of the development of proportionality in Europe (Lord Hoffmann, in Ellis, 1999: 107). It will be used here to determine whether PBRS pose an unjustified limit on freedom of academia. The principle of proportionality requires: (1) suitability: an administrative or legal power must be exercised in a way that is suitable to achieve the purpose intended for which the power was conferred; (2) necessity: the exercise of the power must be necessary to achieve the relevant purpose; and (3) proportionality in the narrower sense: the exercise of the power must not impose burdens, or cause harm to other legitimate interests, that are disproportionate to the importance of the objective to be achieved.

The first issue to determine is whether performance-based research funding is suitable to achieve a fairer distribution of

[13] For New Zealand's Performance-Based Research Fund (PBRF), see Curtis, 2008: 190. At the same time, senior management at the institutional level signalled their wish to pick winners and to develop a range of initiatives to improve results across all the components of the PBRF. Much of this is infuriating to academics; after all, the 'crisis' facing universities is one of funding and not of scholarship, but the PBRF and the managerial initiatives that flow from it threaten to convert the decline in state funding into a problem of research quality. In the subsequent rush of managerial initiatives to enhance research activity, research degree completions and externally funded research, the ongoing stagnation in funding—in particular the creation of the PBRF from equivalent full-time student (EFTS) funding—is being overlooked or crowded out by managerial pronouncements on research excellence.

[14] See also Corsi, D'Ippoliti and Lucidi, 2010, who point out that the problems generated by cohesive intellectual elites in control of a performance-based quality evaluation system may be particularly visible in the area of economics, with its striking division between neoclassical scholars and everybody else; Harley and Lee, 1997; and Lee, 2006.

[15] With regard to common law and the history of proportionality in general: Eric Engle (2012) and Jeremy McBride in Ellis (1999): 23.

government funding for tertiary institutions and the fostering of research excellence. The standard must be high to ensure that trivial objectives or those discordant with the principles of a free and democratic society do not gain protection (Wolff, 2000). As set out earlier, the university researcher fulfils an important role in regard to the state's social, political, and economic innovation. Due to its importance, academic freedom confers on the individual researcher the right to be 'left alone', but it also has an objective value. This mandates that, to make freedom of research an effective right, the state has to provide the organizational framework in which research and scholarship can flourish unhindered. That includes at least a minimum of funding so that the researcher can conduct his or her research. However, the state has finite funds to support the researcher. The aim of targeting finite funding to its best use via an unbiased and non-arbitrary funding model is arguably sufficiently important to justify the curtailment of freedom of research.

It can be argued, however, that the use of PBFS is not suitable to foster research excellence, because of the considerable limitations of peer review, in particular its emphasis on orthodoxy. Innovation is a hard measure to capture—the utility of innovative research often shows its worth only years after it was made. A study in 2009 (Himanen et al.) comparing five European university funding models revealed that the Dutch higher education institutions showed the most constant increase in both publication output and citation of all five European states. The Dutch funding system does not use a PBFS. In the Netherlands, universities assess their own activities, and the results are used for developing the internal policies and strategies of universities, not for allocating research funding. In comparison, growth in the United Kingdom with regard to publications and citations was very modest, despite the peer review-driven research assessment exercises carried out by the funding councils. Is the use of performance-based research funding necessary to achieve a distribution of government tertiary funding?

The state is entitled to promote and encourage research and science based on evaluating, selecting or prioritizing decisions and methods. These aims can be achieved by more than one means, and Government and Parliament must be able to choose the most cost-effective measure. However, it is doubtful whether PFBS are the most cost-effective measures. High transaction and compliance costs were identified by Jonathan Boston as one of the negative features of New Zealand's PBRF (Boston, 2013).

The aim of PBFS is to distribute government funding and to improve research quality. However, the paradigm within which the state can promote and encourage research is limited by allowing a maximum of scientific expertise to unfold and absolute autonomy of the researcher. Research, and especially innovative research, is a vital engine for the state's well-being and of great public importance. A limitation on freedom of research can be justified only if it infringes the right as necessary and as little as possible.

As outlined above, the PBFS have a direct effect on research behaviour. The PBFS lead researchers to abandon certain research endeavours in favour of research more fitting to perceived criteria promulgated by the state through the peer review process. The change in behaviour is particularly marked the less established (generally younger) the researcher is. It can, for example, lead to risk-avoiding behaviour that means that the only outputs produced are easily attainable and perceived as 'safe'—they are within the orthodoxy. It threatens long-term research projects that use uncharted research methodology and venture into new research areas.

Are there any alternatives, which fairly distribute state funds without infringing academic freedom, or which infringe academic freedom less than the PBFS, but still guarantee research quality? The literature recognizes a considerable variety of funding models, which fall into several broad categories. First, there is strictly no need to evaluate research at all. Akin to the Dutch funding model, universities would still carry out their core functions if they received bulk funds from the Government to spend as they saw fit, with some basic measure to determine their relative allocations, such as student numbers or the size of their catchment areas. Research activity is motivated by curiosity and academic prestige, not financial reward. Similarly, the Norwegian funding model relies on a dialogue between universities and the state, but with the emphasis on the autonomy of the universities on how to distribute funding (Himanen et al., 2009).

If money is tied to evaluation, the first choice is between ex ante (research proposals) and ex post (research completed). To allocate on ex-ante principles, the Government could call for tenders on projects in which it had an interest, or put up a pool of contestable funding and make decisions on proposals received. The problem for present purposes is that ex-ante evaluations also rely on peer review. They are likely to impact on academic freedom as much as peer review-based output evaluations (criticism and discussion about peer review is mostly related to ex-ante research bidding processes).

There are various measures for determining research quality. Hanne Foss Hansen (2010) has divided these measures into three orders of indicators. First-order indicators measure inputs, structures and results. They include factors such as the amount of external research funding an institution secures; the attraction and retention of academic staff and doctorate students; seminar and conference activity; the number of occasions staff are asked to give keynote addresses; the number of visiting research appointments; the number of staff active in research; the number of prestige appointments (for example, editorships); reputation and esteem; facilities (for example, library and laboratories); the amount of published work; and the number of times published work is cited. Some of those indicators also rely on peer review, such as external research funding or prestige appointments.

Second-order indicators are a more sophisticated take on the same sort of data. The Journal Impact Factor, for instance, measures the average number of citations an article achieves within a given time. The H index gives the number of articles a researcher has published that have been cited more than the number of H. For instance, an H index of 20 means a researcher has published 20 articles with more than 20 citations.[16]The advantage of an H index is that it measures consistency over time, not occasional 'big hits'.

Both first- and second-order indicators are proxies of research performance. They have their strengths and weaknesses. Citation analysis approximates most closely to peer review as a means of identifying areas of particular research achievement. It is less subjective, being based on numerical formulas, but arguably reflects mainstream thinking in a similar way. However, it allows for the opportunity to recognize publications in non-'mainstream' and foreign journals without attaching any value to those publications, as might be the case in a peer review process.

Third-order indicators are peer review. It is acknowledged that peer review is currently more popular than proxy measures. A system of proxy measures was considered and rejected in New Zealand. However, popularity does not necessarily determine the best way forward. A system in vogue does not deserve to persist if its flaws cannot be addressed. The effect on research freedom is of fundamental importance, and the option of limited or no outside research evaluation should be reconsidered.

To safeguard freedom of research to its fullest extent, funding decisions should not belong to the state, but rather to the individual universities and its community of researchers. The importance of research demands a state funding system that is blind to the (at the time of assessment) 'quality' of the individual researcher's research. To allow the flourishing of research, the state should regulate research to a minimum via funding, but leave it to the community of researchers, as organized through the universities, to distribute funding (akin to the Dutch model). The management structure of universities is, however, not a topic of this essay. Self-governed funding would allow the special circumstances of research to be taken into

[16]The formula is actually: 'Index is h if researcher's Np papers have at least h citations each, and the other (Np-h) papers have no more than h citations each'.

account. The author acknowledges that this has its own problems and that peer opinion would most likely still play a role in distributing funding. Arguably peer review within the confines of the same institution brings researcher and decision-makers closer together, which allows ideas to be discussed directly and eliminates the fear of the evaluation by an external committee. Fringe, unconventional ideas would have more chance of getting heard under such a system. A reconstructable methodology and the comprehensiveness of the research would be the criteria that decide upon its value.

CONCLUSION

No research funding system is perfect and free from legitimate criticism. It is not disputed that the state has the right to ration the funds provided for university research. It follows that the state can also devise a system to allocate funds to best use if desired. Freedom of research, however, is crucial and any funding allocation system has to limit this as little as possible. The author contends that, in the first instance, the PBFS is not suitable for the goal of allocating money to achieve research excellence. For reasons discussed here, PBFS favours conventional lines of enquiry at the expense of innovation. The PBFS also fails on the requirement of necessity, i.e. limiting the right as little as possible. Other, non-peer review methods of allocating funding are available, which allow for more research freedom.[17]

Peer review-based evaluation systems unjustifiably limit freedom of research in the absence of particular safeguards. Whether and which part of the research community might be affected is unpredictable. Research suggests that early-career academics are particularly affected in the choice and the conduct of their research by PBFS. The influence may be subtle and take years to have any effect; it may be limited to a change in the tone and emphasis within the research community. The argument concerns what did not happen (research that did not occur, or was influenced in a different direction), however, so empirical evidence is difficult to obtain, although the article by Himanen and others (2009) is an intriguing indication that the chilling effect is more than speculative.

Although there is no uncontroversial research funding system, and although governments undoubtedly have the right to limit the pool of research funds and impose rationing systems, the limit on academic freedom imposed by the PBFS is unjustified. The limit is unjustified because of the importance of academic freedom, both in its practical benefits and its constitutional standing, and because alternative systems are available, which do not limit academic freedom to the same degree as PBFS do.

If the use of PBFS continues, its effect on academic freedom should be acknowledged and addressed as far as possible. Alternative measures for evaluating research should be considered—those that emphasize purely objective criteria. The evaluation panels should include young and mid-career academics, as well as long-established ones. A diverse panel of experts from the civil law and common law world would challenge each others' orthodoxies. The importance of academic freedom demands no less.

REFERENCES

Alber-Malchow, C., and Steigleder, T. 'Definition der Begriffe Wissenschaft und Forschung-Eigengesetzlichkeit von Wissenschaft und Forschung', in Wagner, H. (Ed.). *Rechtliche Rahmenbedingunen fuer Wissenschaft und Forschung*, vol. 1, Baden Baden, Nomos, 2000.

Altbach, P. G. 'Academic freedom: International realities and challenges', in *Higher Education*, vol. 41, 2001.

Barlow, N. (Ed.). *The Autobiography of Charles Darwin, 1809–1882*. London, Collins, 1958.

Barnard, J. W. 'Reflections on Britain's Research Assessment Exercise', in *Journal of Legal Education*, vol. 48(4), 1998.

Berdahl, R. 'Academic freedom, autonomy and accountability in British universities', in *Studies in Higher Education*, vol. 15, 1990.

Bhattacharya, N. 'The Evolution of Knowledge in the University', in *The Information Society: An International Journal*, vol. 28, 2012.

Boston, J. 'Will PBRF Go One Round Too Many?' in *Tertiary Update*, vol. 16, no. 17 (Tertiary Education Union), 2013.

Boston, J., Mischewski, B., and Smyth, R. 'Performance-based Research Fund—Implications for Research in the Social Sciences and Social Policy', in *Social Policy Journal of New Zealand*, issue 24, April 2005.

Bourke, P. *Evaluating University Research*, Report No. 56. Australian Research Council, 1997.

Brockliss, L. 'Gown and Town: The University and the City in Europe, 1200–2000', in *Minerva*, vol. 38, 2000.

Browne, J. E. *Charles Darwin: Volume 2—The Power of Place*. London, Jonathan Cape, 2002.

Butler, L./Organisation for Economic Co-operation and Development. *Performance-based Funding for Public Research in Tertiary Education Institutions*, Workshop Proceedings (Norway). Paris, OECD Publishing, 2010.

Butler, P., and Mulgan, R. 'Can Academic Freedom Survive Performance Based Research Funding?', in *Victoria University of Wellington Law Review*, vol. 44, 2013.

Byrne, J. P. 'Academic Freedom: "A Special Concern of the First Amendment"', in *Yale Law Journal*, vol. 99, 1989.

Carter, B. R. *Childbed Fever: A Scientific Biography of Ignaz Semmelweis*. Piscataway, NJ, Transaction Publishers, 2005.

Codd, J. 'The Performance-Based Research Fund: Fallacies, Flaws and Failings', paper presented to the annual conference, New Zealand Association for Research in Education, December 2004.

Cole, D. *Performance-Based Research Fund*. Wellington, Parliamentary Library, April 2012.

Corsi, M., D'Ippoliti, C., and Lucidi, F. 'Pluralism at risk? Heterodox economic approaches and the evaluation of economic research in Italy', in *American Journal of Economics and Sociology*, vol. 69(5), November 2010.

Coryn, C., et al. 'Models and Mechanisms for Evaluating Government-Funded Research: An International Comparison', in *American Journal of Evaluation*, vol. 28, 2007.

Curtis, B. 'The Performance Based Research Fund: research assessment and funding in New Zealand', in *Globalisation, Societies and Education*, vol. 6, 2008.

Dalziel, P. 'Rewarding Individual Research Excellence in the PBRF', in *New Zealand Journal of Tertiary Education Policy*, vol. 1, 2005.

Davies, E., Craig, D., and Robertson, N. 'Is the Performance Based Research Fund in the public interest?', in *New Zealand Journal of Tertiary Education Policy*, vol. 1, 2005.

Ellis, E. (Ed.). *The Principle of Proportionality in the Laws of Europe*. Oxford, Hart Publishers, 1999.

Engle, E. 'The History of the General Principle of Proportionality: An Overview', in *Dartmouth Law Journal*, vol. 10, 2012.

European Centre for Strategic Management of Universities (ESMU). *Funding Higher Education: A View Across Europe*. Brussels, ESMU, 2010.

European Commission. *Assessing Europe's University Based Research*. Luxembourg, Publications Office of the European Union, 2010.

Genua, A. 'The Changing Rationale for European University Research Funding: Are there negative consequences?', in *Journal of Economic Issues*, vol. 35, 2001.

Gluckman, P. *Which science to fund: time to review peer review?* Wellington, Office of the Prime Minister's Science Advisory Committee, 2012.

[17] Since, in the author's view, the PBFS fails on the first two requirements of the proportionality principle, it was not opportune in the limited space of this article to discuss the third requirement of the proportionality principle.

Graves, A., et al. 'Funding grant proposals for scientific research: retrospective analysis of scores by members of grant review panel', in *British Medical Journal*, vol. 343, issue 4,797, 27 September 2011.

Hansen, H. F./Organisation for Economic Co-operation and Development. *Performance-based Funding for Public Research in Tertiary Education Institutions*, Workshop Proceedings (Norway). Paris, OECD Publishing, 2010.

Harley, S., and Lee, F. S. 'Research Selectivity, Managerialism, and the Academic Labor Process: The Future of Nonmainstream Economics in UK Universities', in *Human Relations*, vol. 50(11), 1997.

Hart, D. 'Ärztliche Leitlinien—Definitionen, Funktionen, rechtliche Bewertungen', in *Medizinrecht (MedR)*, vol. 16(1), January 1998.

Hicks, D. 'Performance-based university funding systems' in *Research Policy*, vol. 41, 2012.

Himanen, L., et al. 'Effectiveness of research funding and science policy on university research performance: a comparison of five countries', in *Science and Public Policy*, vol. 36, 2009.

Hobbs, F., and Stewart, P. 'How should we rate research?', in *British Medical Journal*, vol. 332, 2006.

Hoffmann, Lord. 'The Influence of the European Principle of Proportionality upon UK Law', in Ellis, E. (Ed.). *The Principle of Proportionality in the Laws of Europe*. Oxford, Hart Publishers, 1999.

House of Commons, Select Committee for Science and Technology. *The Research Assessment Exercise*, 2nd Report of Session 2001/02, London, Science and Technology Committee, 2002.

Jarass, H., in Jarass, H., and Pieroth, B. (Eds). *Grundgesetz für die Bundesrepublik Deutschland*, 7th edn. Munich, Beck, 2004.

Karran, T. 'Academic freedom in Europe: Reviewing UNESCO's recommendation', in *British Journal of Educational Studies*, vol. 57, 2009.

Kuhn, T. *The Structure of Scientific Revolutions*, 50th edn. Chicago, IL, University of Chicago Press, 2012.

Lee, F. S. 'The Research Assessment Exercise, the state and the dominance of mainstream economics in British universities', in *Cambridge Journal of Economics*, vol. 31(2), 2006.

Lee, P. 'A Contract Theory of Academic Freedom.' 13 March 2014 (available at SSRN: http://ssrn.com/abstract=2408530 or http://dx.doi.org/10.2139/ssrn.2408530).

McBride, J. 'Proportionality and the European Convention on Human Rights', in Ellis, E. (Ed.). *The Principle of Proportionality in the Laws of Europe*. Oxford, Hart Publishers, 1999.

McNay, I. 'The Paradoxes of Research Assessment and Funding', in Henkel, M., and Little, B. (Eds). *Changing Relationships between Higher Education and the State*. London, J. Kingsley Publishers, 1999.

O'Neil, R. 'University governance and academic freedom', in Tierney, W. G. (Ed.). *Competing conceptions of academic governance: negotiating the perfect storm*. Baltimore, MD, Johns Hopkins University Press, 2004.

Portugal, F. H., and Cohen, J. S. *A Century of DNA: A History of the Discovery of the Structure and Function of the Genetic Substance*, Cambridge, MA, MIT Press, 1980.

Post, R. 'Discipline and Freedom in the Academy', in *Arkansas Law Review*, vol. 65, 2012.

Pouris, A. 'Peer review in scientifically small countries', in *R&D Management*, vol. 18(4), October 1988.

Ricken, N. 'The deliberate university: remarks on the "idea of the university" from a perspective of knowledge', in *Studies in Philosophy and Education*, vol. 26. 2007.

Robertson, J. A. 'The scientist's right to research: a constitutional analysis', in *Southern California Law Review*, vol. 51, 1978.

Scholz, R., in Scholz, R., and Herzog, R. (Eds). *Theodor Maunz-Günter Dürig: Grundgesetz Kommentar* (updated). Munich, Beck, 2012.

Shore, C., and Taitz, M. 'Who "owns" the university? Institutional autonomy and academic freedom in an age of knowledge capitalism', in *Globalisation, Societies and Education*, vol. 10, 2012.

Sinder, J. 'Academic Freedom: A Bibliography', in *Law and Contemporary Problems*, vol. 53, 1990.

Talib, A. A. 'Performance Measures and Resource Allocation: The Behavioural Consequences of the University Research Assessment Exercise', PhD thesis. University of Warwick, 2002.

Tinsley, Y. 'Science in the Criminal Courts: Tool in Service, Challenge to Legal Authority or Indispensable Ally?', in *New Zealand Universities Law Review*, vol. 25, 2013.

Watt, G. 'The UK's Research Excellence Framework 2014', in *British Medical Journal*, vol. 345, issue 7,885, 1 December 2012.

Whitley, R. 'Changing governance of the public science', in Whitley, R., and Gläser, J. (Eds). *The Changing Governance of the Sciences: The Advent of Research Evaluation Systems*, Sociology of the Sciences Yearbook, vol. 26, Dordrecht, Springer, 2007.

Wolff, H. *Ungeschriebenes Verfassungsrecht unter dem Grundgesetz*. Tübingen, Mohr Siebeck, 2000.

QUALITY ASSURANCE AND ACADEMIC FREEDOM WITH EMPHASIS ON TRANSNATIONAL EDUCATION

JIM JACKSON

INTRODUCTION

I see academic freedom as a reciprocal duty of both the university to provide and the academic to use. Neither the university nor the academic may act so as to damage the knowledge discovery obligations of others, for example by disseminating that which is false or poorly researched. Similarly, a university has to act in accordance with what is true. It is in the truth business; it cannot be untruthful or deceptive in its dealings and still meet its mission. Managers and governors of the university have a legal obligation to give effect to its objects. It follows that the university community must act in ways that enable academics to meet their teaching and research obligations.

Accordingly, universities must provide the conditions for knowledge discovery and transmission, and academics should use that power professionally so to discover and teach. A university that removes or does not provide that power will always struggle to meet the definition of a university. Academics who do not use the power are not teaching properly; they are no better than the texts from which they plagiarize, regurgitate and transfer existing knowledge. Note that academic freedom is not the same as an ordinary citizen's freedom of speech. The latter flows from the particular human rights set in the state the citizen is in, and indeed might not exist at law at all. Academic freedom in the context of university academics is merely a day-to-day tool, which must be exercised to meet their truth-hunting role and that of their employer; William Van Alstyne (1990) claims: 'universities are licensed truth-hunters defined and bound by academic freedom.' This description suggests that academic freedom goes to the very heart of what a university is, and becomes a defining characteristic. The Canadian Association of University Teachers (CAUT) would agree:

> The common good of society depends upon the search for knowledge and its free exposition. Academic freedom in universities is essential to both these purposes in the teaching function of the university as well as in its scholarship and research.
>
> (CAUT Council, 'Policy Statement on Academic Freedom', May 1973)

So where does this leave those agencies charged with assurance and regulation of universities and other higher education providers? Their first task should be to test the very existence of academic freedom in the institution. If they cannot find it, or at least the conditions under which it may arise, they have to ask the most fundamental question: should this institution be in the business of higher education?

There is one other theme that needs brief exploration: do quality agencies inhibit academic freedom? This was the topic of the Magna Charta Observatory in 2011 (see References) and, accordingly, will be dealt with only briefly here. My view is that the agencies should enhance, not limit academic freedom, if they are performing their tasks properly. As Hans van Ginkel (2011) said in his address to the Magna Charta Observatory conference, the 'ultimate aim of quality assessments and accreditation should not be to establish conformity to some standard, but rather to promote excellence, creativity and innovation'.

There is, however, little doubt that institutional autonomy is challenged by quality agencies. Indeed, so much so that in Germany, litigation has been launched against an accreditation agency because its refusal to accredit a programme was seen as violating freedom of teaching (*Lehrfreiheit*), as described in the German Constitution, article 5: 'Art and science, research and teaching are free. Freedom of teaching does not absolve from loyalty to the constitution'. The matter was referred by the court to the Federal Constitutional Court of Germany; to date, a decision has not been delivered (Jungblut, 2011).

ACADEMIC FREEDOM IN AUSTRALIA AND THE TERTIARY EDUCATION QUALITY AND STANDARDS AGENCY (TEQSA)

All public universities in Australia are established by statute. Even private universities have enabling statutes. Academic freedom is mentioned in the statutes establishing some universities, especially those in New South Wales or Victoria.

The University of Sydney Act 1989 (NSW), in common with all university statutes in New South Wales (as amended by 2001 legislation), provides *inter alia* for 'free inquiry' as an object. Section 6(2) goes on to describe principal functions as including 'the encouragement of the dissemination, advancement, development and application of knowledge informed by free inquiry', 'the participation in public discourse' and 'the provision of teaching and learning that engage with advanced knowledge and inquiry'. Similarly, Victorian university statutes include an object to serve the Victorian, Australian and international communities and the public interest by 'promoting critical and free enquiry, informed intellectual discourse and public debate within the University and in the wider society'.

If one wants to judge or quality-assure a university, here is the starting point: is the university meetings its objectives? In the language of quality agencies, is the university fit for purpose? This represents a nice merger of a legal concept based around the *ultra vires* doctrine with a quality concept. It also follows, however, that a quality agency cannot decide to ignore the university statute or whether the university is meeting its objectives, expressed around knowledge discovery, free enquiry, critical engagement with students and the like.

The above conclusions work reasonably well in a public university setting, but there are many providers in Australia that are not universities. What of academic freedom in such institutions? Again, the constitution of the entity, often a corporation established under the federal Corporations Act 2001, may be useful to enable similar arguments to those cited above, although it should be noted that Australian corporation law does not require corporations to have objectives. Nevertheless, the provider must have a 'clearly articulated higher education purpose' under the Provider Registration Standards discussed below.

The Tertiary Education Quality and Standards Agency (TEQSA) has now replaced the previous quality agency, the Australian Universities Quality Agency (AUQA), under legislation passed in 2011. An institution with non-self-accrediting status must apply to TEQSA to approve the introduction of new courses or the re-accreditation of existing courses. TEQSA may conduct quality or compliance assessments. A compliance assessment has to be conducted to see whether an organization can be registered as a higher education provider. Quality assessments can be of individual providers or a group, or of the whole sector.

Under the TEQSA legislation, there exists a standards framework, the Higher Education Standards Framework (Threshold Standards) 2011. If a provider (be that, for example, a university, university college, bible college, or a large, listed for-profit education company) gains registration from TEQSA by meeting these Threshold Standards it will become a Higher Education Provider (HEP). If it does not meet, or continue to meet, the standards, it can lose its status as an HEP.

These threshold standards embrace provider registration standards, provider category standards (covering type of provider, such as higher education provider, university, university college, overseas university), course accreditation standards and qualification standards. The standards have quite a bit to say about intellectual enquiry, and this may well flow from a submission made by AUQA to a Senate inquiry in 2008:

> Academic freedom is a necessary pre-condition in the development of a knowledge society and in the foundation of knowledge institutions such as universities. Institutional autonomy should be used to create the conditions to protect academic freedom both within the institution and to protect staff from pressure on academic freedom from the external environment. This includes protecting the academic staff from external government, public or private sector interference.
> (AUQA, 'Submission to Enquiry into Academic Freedom', August 2008)

Importantly, AUQA then argued for a strengthening of protocols:

> AUQA recommends that the National Protocols and Quality Audit Factors be strengthened in relation to the requirement for institutions to display academic freedom. Then AUQA's audits will provide a check on the health of academic freedom within our society.

The protocols referred to have been replaced by the Threshold Standards. Under chapter 2, section 1.2, an HEP must have a 'clearly articulated higher education purpose that includes a commitment to and support for free intellectual inquiry in its academic endeavours'.

The teaching and learning it delivers must engage with advanced knowledge and inquiry (section 1.3) and its academic staff must be active in scholarship (section 1.4). Under chapter 3, curriculum must provide appropriate engagement by students in intellectual enquiry consistent with the nature and level of the units being taught and the course learning outcomes (section 1.7). The provider has to ensure that teachers must be capable of so engaging students (section 4.2).

Under chapter 1, section 4 of the Provider Registration Standards, an HEP must maintain 'academic quality and integrity in its higher education operations'. These provisions are not common in a standards document, accordingly they are quoted in full:

> 4.1 The higher education provider's objectives for its higher education operations include the cultivation in students of critical and independent thought and the capacity for learning throughout life.
>
> 4.2 The higher education provider promotes and protects free intellectual inquiry and expression in its higher education learning, teaching, and research activities.
>
> 4.3 The higher education provider protects academic integrity in higher education through effective policies and measures to:
>
> - ensure the integrity of student assessment;
> - ensure the integrity of research and research activity;
> - prevent, detect and address academic misconduct by students or staff, including cheating and plagiarism;
> - ensure that academic staff are free to make public comment on issues that lie within their area of expertise; and,
> - ensure that the awarding of multiple awards, including higher education awards offered in conjunction with another entity, protects the integrity of the higher education awards offered by the higher education provider.
>
> 4.4 Research carried out under the higher education provider's auspices meets appropriate codes of conduct, safety, and ethics clearance requirements, and is consistent with legislative or other regulatory requirements and any applicable national guidelines.
>
> 4.5 Where the higher education provider has an arrangement in place with another entity to manage or deliver some or all of a course of study on its behalf, the higher education provider has effective mechanisms to manage and quality-assure all aspects of the arrangement, including admission and support of students and delivery of the course of study to ensure student learning outcomes equivalent to those for the same or a cognate course of study when delivered by the higher education provider.

The standards are thorough and embrace fundamental principles of academic freedom. They cannot be ignored by an HEP, and certainly not by TEQSA.

If TEQSA is performing an audit on an organization, it must *inter alia* test quality against what the organization itself stands for under its constitution, through its objectives, or, in the language of section 1.2, 'a clearly articulated higher education purpose that includes a commitment to and support for free intellectual inquiry in its academic endeavours'. If the organization was demonstrably ignoring its constitution or, worse, acting against it, it is difficult to see how it could pass an audit; its registration must be in jeopardy.

ACADEMIC FREEDOM IN THE UNITED KINGDOM AND THE UK QAA

Other essays in this collection have considered this issue in more detail. Suffice it to say that much of what has been said in relation to Australian law and principles applies to the United Kingdom, or indeed had its origins in the United Kingdom. Academic freedom will be found in university constitutions or policy. It may also be found in tradition and custom and industrial agreements. There are other potential sources, including the Human Rights Act 1998, which applies the European Convention on Human Rights into British law. Furthermore, the Education Act (No. 2) 1986 secures speech rights in universities for members, employees, students and visiting speakers, and requires universities to maintain codes of practice relating to speech rights. It has been noted that the oft-quoted section 202 of the Education Reform Act 1988 imposes academic freedom obligations on university commissioners who no longer exist. Nevertheless, that legislation has been seen as entrenching the principle of academic freedom enunciated in the legislation in university statutes and articles of government (see Annexure C: 'The law: a summary of the legal framework' to Universities UK, 'Freedom of Speech on Campus: rights and responsibilities in UK Universities').

The Quality Assurance Agency for Higher Education (QAA) assures quality and standards in the United Kingdom. Its main tool for doing this is the UK Quality Code for Higher Education. Unlike the Australian Threshold Standards, there is no mention of academic freedom in the document. The closest is the 'Expectation' in Chapter B3, 'Learning and Teaching':

> The Quality Code sets out the following expectation about learning and teaching, which higher education providers are required to meet: Higher education providers, working with their staff, students and other stake holders, articulate and systematically review and enhance the provision of learning opportunities and teaching practices, so that every student is enabled to develop as an independent learner, study their chosen subject(s) in depth and enhance their capacity for analytical, critical and creative thinking.
>
> (QAA, UK Quality Code for Higher Education)

This, however, is a long way from the concept of academic freedom as described in this collection, or in the Australian threshold standards. Some, including myself, would argue that academic freedom should be included in the UK Quality Code, perhaps in similar terms to what Australia or Malaysia has (see below).

Geoffrey Alderman (2006) notes:

> This year, I plucked up the courage to suggest that the Quality Assurance Agency extend its code of practice to include a section on academic freedom. At present, the code is completely silent on the matter, and its inspectors are not encouraged—and are certainly under no obligation—to inquire whether an institution undergoing review even has a policy on this most fundamental principle.

Alderman then describes an obvious link between quality and academic freedom, suggesting that unless a university was to guarantee a right to freedom of expression in its staff and students, it could never make a claim to be of good quality. He also suggests that audits of collaborative partners should also test whether the same academic freedom is given as in the awarding institution.

TRANSNATIONAL EDUCATION

Many Australian and British universities operate in transnational education (TNE), which, as described by the QAA, 'typically refers to higher education provision of a UK degree-awarding body which is delivered in a country outside the United Kingdom and often by delivery organisations other than the degree awarding body' (according to the wording of a consultation on British TNE by the QAA and the UK Higher Education International Unit, December 2013).

Data from the UK Higher Education Statistics Agency (HESA) suggest that, in 2012/13, 598,925 students were studying for British qualifications wholly overseas. Just under half of these were in Asia, (281,775); the top three countries were Malaysia, with approximately 68,000 students, followed by Singapore, with 50,000, and the People's Republic of China, with 42,000. Business education is the dominant field. To put that in context, more than 2.3m. students were studying in higher education institutions within the United Kingdom in 2012/13. Of these, over 425,000 were international students studying in the United Kingdom. More than 25% of students of British universities were therefore studying outside the United Kingdom itself. It should be noted that a proportion of these students are enrolled in distance programmes with British institutions, but even so, what remains is a surprisingly high percentage. In a UK analysis for 2011, Nick Clark (2012) put the number of those in TNE at one-sixth of all students. He concluded that the market in both the United Kingdom and Australia is significant and growing.

In Australia, the number of higher education TNE students (approximately 108,000) is just under 10% of the total of all students, although this number includes distance students studying outside Australia. According to Australian Education International ('Research Snapshot' for 2012), approximately 65% of these are in management and commerce (57.2%) and information technology (7.7%). The main countries in which this TNE are Singapore, China and Malaysia, in that order. There is therefore much in common between the sectors in the United Kingdom and Australia. The main teaching discipline is business, and the three major markets are China, Malaysia and Singapore.

Malaysia and Singapore

To date, broad quality assurance (QA) mechanisms in the United Kingdom and Australia have been examined. I now move to a more specific examination of this theme in the context of two major TNE receiving markets: Singapore and Malaysia. A question that must be addressed is whether those countries have their own QA mechanisms to protect their side of the TNE relationship. While Australian and British universities are doing well out of these relationships, so does the host country. In particular, Malaysia and Singapore host many thousands of students from other countries studying with foreign universities.

In a typical example, a student might come to Singapore from China and undertake their study programme entirely in that country in what, under Singapore's Private Education Act 2009, is termed a 'Private Education Institution' (PEI). If this PEI is in collaboration with a British university, the student is ultimately issued with a degree from that university, and not with an award from the PEI. This brings very significant revenue into Singapore and the market is strongly protected as part of the Singaporean 'brand'. PEIs cannot usually issue their own degrees, so these international students are gaining an international degree, but not from a Singaporean university.

The other major market for these PEIs and their foreign collaborating universities is from local part-time students who have already completed a diploma from a Singaporean polytechnic, and from local full-time students who were not able to gain a place in one of the Singaporean universities. This represents another win for the Singaporean Government; they are burdened only with the cost of educating the strongest academically of their citizens, while the balance have to pay their own way, but may go on to obtain an international qualification without ever having left the country.

This model is administered by the Council for Private Education (CPE), established in 2009 by the Private Education Act. It emerged as Singapore's answer to some serious quality issues arising out of a small number of fraudulent activities involving private educators at an earlier time in that country. The CPE applies standards contained in the Edutrust Certification Scheme Guidance Document to determine whether a PEI should be given the 'Edutrust' ranking, which is necessary if it wishes to enrol international students. The Guidance Document contains many fine provisions, in particular its standards relating to agents, management commitment, corporate governance, student protection and insurance, academic processes, and QA monitoring. Like the British Quality Code, however, it has nothing to say about academic freedom or critical engagement.

For example, the Guidance Document has rules about staff recruitment, including minimum qualifications to be held to teach at a certain level (criterion 2.3.1), but no standards relating to the capacity of the staff member to teach critically or to engage so with the students. The standards require a curriculum development process, but do not attempt to define the attributes of the curriculum. The nearest the Guidance Document gets is criterion 5.2.2, note 2:

> For courses offered in conjunction with a partner organisation, the PEI shall have procedures to ensure that the delivery process meets the quality and rigour stipulated by the partner organisation. These shall include academic staff qualification, course delivery modes, assessment modes and frequency and criteria for award of achievement upon course completion.
>
> (Council for Private Education, Edutrust Certification Scheme Guidance Document)

This is a useful Singaporean standard that a foreign university (or their quality agency) could seize on to ensure that its collaborative partner gives full effect to degree rules and outcomes, but it does not go to notions of academic freedom or critique. The message is clear: if such things are important, the university itself must provide for them.

Malaysia established the Malaysian Qualifications Agency (MQA) under the Malaysian Qualifications Agency Act 2007. It both quality-assures and accredits providers. It applies a Code of Practice for Programme Accreditation, as well as the Code of Practice for Institutional Audit. These codes are quite sophisticated and recognize academic freedom, without using that term (Benchmark standards 2.1.1):

> The academic staff must be given sufficient autonomy to focus on areas of his expertise, such as curriculum development and implementation, academic supervision of students, research and writing, scholarly activities, and academically-related administrative duties and community engagement.
> (MQA, Code of Practice for Programme Accreditation, December 2008)

Later in the same Code, Benchmark standards 2.1.2 states:

The boundaries of academic autonomy for the department and the academic staff should continue to expand, reflecting the intellectual maturity of the HEP.

In addition, the document routinely describes critique, development of the quest for knowledge and describes as a general goal: 'the nurturing of the ability to analyse and solve problems, as well as to evaluate and make decisions critically and creatively based on evidence and experience'. It deserves praise for what it requires in terms of teaching, research and academic freedom, although at no stage does it use that last term. The MQA documentation is more thorough than the Singaporean Edutrust literature generally, and decidedly more embracing of academic freedom concepts than either the British or Singaporean examples.

QUALITY ASSURANCE AND ACADEMIC FREEDOM IN TNE

The QAA is very aware of the income and student number imperatives in the context of TNE. This is an export that must be protected:

> The UK is a leading TNE exporter with 75 per cent of UK awarding institutions now engaged in TNE in over 200 countries. In 2011-12, some 570,000 students were studying overseas on programmes leading to UK awards—more than the number of international students (including those from the European Union) studying in the UK (435,000). The growth in demand for UK TNE is predicted to continue.
>
> (QAA and UK Higher Education International Unit, consultation document, December 2013)

Similarly, Australian commentators as long ago as 2000 had described the economic imperative to establish AUQA, saying that:

> Two overriding factors were difficult to ignore if Australia were to maintain its position as the world's third largest English-speaking provider of international HE programs and services...First, there was overwhelming demand for accountability concerning public investment in HE by a world that had already decided quality could best be managed by national external audit agencies and by networks of these agencies at the global level. Secondly, the fear of repercussions from non-compliance in the worldwide QA industry would have meant Australian HE being excluded from lucrative markets and ultimately reduced to irrelevance.
>
> (Julie Hayford, 2004—at the Australian Universities Quality Forum 2003)

What was said back in 2003 is even more critical in 2014, as the international competition for international students steps up. Many more nations are competing for their share, and at the same time they have set up their own QA agencies.

While the AUQA institutional audits did not describe academic freedom issues in any depth, they certainly raised other and related issues, many of which were described in the 2003 report that reviewed AUQA institutional reports, including Australian TNE operations (Martin, 2003). Issues involving international matters included a lack of consistency across offshore and local campus activities, insufficient data on student performance generally, inconsistent implementation of accreditation policies and practices, and a lack of external review procedures.

In the United Kingdom, the QAA and the Higher Education International Unit engaged in a recent major consultation with British higher education providers to review TNE quality assurance. They identified three key drivers for so doing: first, the growth in demand for TNE, with the QAA immediately linking this to the quality of its education exports; secondly, increasing assurance complexity and risk, which was linked to compliance with local regulatory frameworks; and, thirdly, the failure of TNE quality in one individual institution having the 'potential to impact negatively on every institution'.

It is not surprising that none of the questions in the consultation related to academic freedom, even in the most general terms. After all, the UK Quality Code itself does not use the term 'academic freedom' or 'intellectual freedom'. From the perspective of survival of UK TNE in some countries (but not academic freedom), this may be a good thing. It seems that the QAA is not going to ask the difficult academic freedom questions, since it does not have to under its own code. However, it cannot always control the answers it gets when conducting TNE audits, and these could prompt a further exploration of whether a university is acting in accordance with its own charter or articles of association in the foreign classroom.

The Quality Code teaching-and-learning expectation was described above. Where the QAA has serious doubts about an institution's capacity to deliver on that expectation—the key and only expectation in Chapter B3—one would envisage that the institution will fail any audit and ultimately be forced out of the collaboration. The QAA would be forced to test the Expectation where it was abundantly clear that teaching and learning were suffering because the absence of classroom academic freedom was detracting from and not enhancing the 'student's capacity for analytical, critical and creative thinking'.

In 2012 the QAA conducted a survey of UK TNE in China and noted that 70 UK institutions (over 40%) were teaching there in 2010/11. While this QAA review (published in 2013) did mention the importance of the UK brand, it did not mention academic freedom at all. Furthermore, to complete the circle, a recent Universities UK study of freedom of speech in British universities does not mention quality assurance at all. The closest that the QAA review got was on teaching of the so-called 'soft skills':

> One of the aims of Chinese–foreign cooperation in higher education appears to be to extend the skills of graduates beyond those needed to build a large technical knowledge base. However, the development of these so-called soft skills—which include leadership, problem-solving, team working, communication, innovation, critical thinking and entrepreneurship—also implies a greater adoption in China of Western approaches to teaching and learning. These approaches are characterized by: independent learning and research projects; academic discussion between students and tutors as peers; analysis and problem-solving through the use of case studies; oral presentations on topics to students and tutors; and the use of personal development planning. The implementation of such approaches is not as easy as stating them as an objective, since they are often at odds with the conventional Chinese approach, which involves heavily timetabled class teaching, a deference of students to their tutors, and an emphasis on knowledge acquisition.
>
> (QAA, *Review of UK transnational education in China 2012*. Gloucester, QAA, 2013)

Those of us who have attempted to teach these 'soft skills' in Asia would immediately relate to what the QAA is saying. Part of the difficulty, especially in teaching communication and critical thinking, is that this requires high levels of academic freedom in the classroom, and the teaching of these skills and values in the same way as back at their home university is not without its risks for both teacher and student. It is far safer and easier for fly-in/fly-out teachers to stick to the technical skills and basic knowledge transfer acquisition, especially where student English-language skills are elementary. Accordingly, the visiting lecturer, not entirely sure of themselves, with a classroom of students with only average language skills who will, on occasion misunderstand the subtleties, could well be inclined to takes the safe political and cultural ground. If the class is being offered by a local lecturer the issues become more problematic. If this was the subject of an Australian audit, TEQSA should consider whether the provider has ensured that teachers are capable of engaging students, but the QAA is faced with no such imperative.

There are real issues here for standards; the students are not receiving the same experience or acquiring the same skills as students in the United Kingdom (or in Australia, for that matter). Lecturers may have imposed their own 'chilling effect' on academic freedom, real or imagined. Of course we know that there are safe ways to teach critique that will not bring the secret police through the door, but this requires a great deal of the most careful thinking, which may not be required back in the home classroom. The classroom difficulties described above therefore raise issues under Indicator 11 of the UK Quality Code:

> Degree-awarding bodies are responsible for the academic standards of all credit and qualifications granted in their name. This responsibility is never delegated. Therefore, degree-awarding bodies ensure that the standards of any of their awards involving learning opportunities delivered by others are equivalent to the standards set for other awards that they confer at the same level. They are also consistent with UK national requirements.

Quality assurance agencies may be presented with somewhat of a dilemma in relation to academic freedom in a TNE context. When conducting their audits, do they ask the difficult questions of the local staff or university academics: have they ever felt constrained as to the issues they talk about in class for fear of upsetting the local people or government? Moreover, what will the agency do if an academic or a number of academics are no longer welcome to teach in the foreign country, and this can be linked to what they said or have been accused of saying on a previous visit? What will an agency do when they realize that the language difficulties of students are preventing any real possible critique in the classroom? Or when it realizes that TNE students are simply refusing to engage with the subject content in the classroom out of fear of offending fellow classmates or of stirring racial issues?

What is the agency to do with a yes answer to the above questions? In an Australian context, can the higher education provider be said to be meeting the Threshold Standards previously described in the events described above? The answer is no; the intellectual freedom tests are clearly failed. Another chilling effect will be in course selection for the overseas campus; it is unlikely that the university will offer 'controversial' programmes in overseas jurisdictions, which essentially amounts to another form of self-censorship. Would an agency ask why a particular programme was not offered overseas?

CONCLUSIONS

The existence of QA agencies that have a brief to test, *inter alia*, academic freedom as it relates to universities and their teaching or research partners has the potential to create some embarrassment for the universities in their TNE operations. The teaching that occurs in an overseas country will be from the domestic faculty of the university, the so called fly-in/fly-out model; staff employed by the international partner; or some combination of both. Whichever way the particular staffing arrangement works, however, there is the risk that the teacher may speak in such a way as to give offence to the Government.

More worrying is another outcome: being aware that something could create a furore, the lecturer tempers their remarks—the self-imposed chilling effect. So, in teaching the same class, one domestically and one internationally, the teacher does not teach the same material, or, far worse, leaves significant topics out, because that material might cause offence in the second instance. In addition, where a local teacher is used in the international classroom, using teaching materials supplied by the university, that local teacher may be inclined to censor such materials to avoid trouble in his/her own country; or the materials might previously have been censored by the academic back at the university, knowing that they were just too radical for the overseas operation. Again, we see the chilling effect. Most academics are simply not that brave, and will avoid trouble, especially when they feel they are, and should be respectful as, guests in another country.

The issues become even more pronounced in some countries, because all teachers, including foreign academics, have to be notified to a government agency before they may teach. For example, in Singapore, the names and prescribed particulars of teachers in PEIs must be notified to the Council for Private Education (under section 44 of the Private Education Act 2009). The Council interprets this to include fly-in/fly-out staff of universities associated with the PEIs.

TNE does not exist now, if it ever did, with noble objectives of reaching out to bring mass education to the poor in Asia or other parts of the world, or to create graduates steeped in critique, engorged with the spirit of new-found democratic principles and liberated by their new voices. The Western drivers are unashamedly economic, and university managers know that it is best, if possible, to leave difficult issues such as the existence of conditions under which academic freedom may be exercised, or not, in these offshore ventures, firmly buried. There is simply too much money at stake here for the universities to stand too highly on what are, in fact, some very fundamental principles, which go to the heart of their now entirely corporatized university beings. One can only hope that this decidedly short-term thinking does not fundamentally weaken their respective higher education sectors in the long term. Quality assurance agencies have a fundamental role here to protect the universities and other higher education providers from themselves, but will they take academic freedom seriously?

REFERENCES

Alderman, G. 'Too Timid to make a Stand for Freedom', in *Times Higher Education*, 17 November 2006 (www.timeshighereducation.co.uk/news/too-timid-to-make-a-stand-for-free dom/206791, article accessed 5 May 2014).

Clark, N. 'Understanding Transnational Education, Its Growth and Implications', in *World Education News and Reviews*, 1 August 2012.

Hayford, J. 'Does Being Last Give You the Advantage?', in Nair, C. S., and Harris, R. (Eds). *National Quality in a Global Context*, Proceedings of the Australian Universities Quality Forum 2003, Melbourne, 11–13 June 2003, Melbourne, AUQA, 2004.

Jungblut, J. 'Can Quality Assurance Harm Academic Freedom? A Short Case Study from Germany', in Proceedings of the Conference of the Magna Charta Observatory, 15–16 September 2011 (see below), Bologna, Bononia University Press, 2011.

Magna Charta Observatory. *Contemporary Threats and Opportunities: Academic Freedom and Institutional Autonomy within the Context of Accreditation, Quality Assurance and Rankings*, Proceedings of the Conference of the Magna Charta Observatory, 15–16 September 2011, Bologna, Bononia University Press/Magna Charta Observatory for Fundamental University Values and Rights, 2011 (www.magna-charta.org/observatoryPublication.aspx?uid=%7Bee752d70-7afe-484a-89a9-f3e76d7006d2%7D, accessed 6 May 2014).

Martin, A. '2002 Institutional Audit Reports Analysis and Comment', AUQA Occasional Publication No. 1, Melbourne, AUQA, June 2003.

Van Alstyne, W. W. 'Academic Freedom and the First Amendment in the Supreme Court of the United States: An Unhurried Historical Review', Symposium on Academic Freedom, in *Law and Contemporary Problems*, vol. 53(3), 1990.

van Ginkel, H. 'Keynote Address of the Conference', in Proceedings of the Conference of the Magna Charta Observatory, 15–16 September 2011 (see above), Bologna, Bononia University Press, 2011.

THE CONSTITUTIONAL IMPERATIVE FOR ACADEMIC FREEDOM IN SOUTH AFRICA

JOHN HIGGINS

This essay examines the tensions around the idea and practice of academic freedom in South Africa in the 20 years since the advent of democracy. In part, these tensions are doubtless generated by the highly specific circumstances of South Africa's ongoing transition from apartheid state to democratic society. At the same time, they reflect the particular pressures on academic freedom generated in the global rethinking and restructuring of the contemporary university, associated for many with the new constraints and directives promoted by Margaret Thatcher's 1988 Higher Education Act (Russell, 1993; Head, 2011). Caught as it is between the rock of global higher education policy and the hard place of local political pressures, thinking about academic freedom from the particular South African perspective raises or reinvigorates important issues around the understanding of academic freedom and the place of the university in the contemporary world.

My starting point for this essay is the unusually privileged place given to academic freedom in the new Constitution adopted by South Africa in 1996 (Barendt, 2010). The new Constitution—widely regarded as one of the most progressive in the world—is one of the few that seeks to give an explicit place to, and pledge formal defence for, academic freedom in a democratic society. In so doing, it makes the defence of academic freedom a constitutional imperative. Yet the place it gives—as I shall argue below—is, in some crucial respects, an ambivalent and perhaps ultimately a contradictory and self-defeating one.

My argument here is that, while this ambivalence doubtless embodies and reflects some of the complexities of South Africa's troubled and violent history of racial segregation, it also embodies the pressures imposed on higher education policy in general by what Roger King (2010) has called 'policy internationalism'. Let us first examine some of the political and conceptual tensions around academic freedom in South Africa generated in and by the apartheid period (1948–94), as these form part of the necessary background to understanding the ambivalences in the constitutional imperative.

HISTORICAL BACKGROUND: 'EVERYONE AGREED THAT UNIVERSITIES SHOULD HAVE ACADEMIC FREEDOM'

The clearest account and embodiment of the tensions around academic freedom in the apartheid period is to be found in the *Main Report of the Commission of Inquiry into Universities*, by what is generally known as the van Wyk de Vries Commission (van Wyk de Vries Commission, 1974). The Commission's task was to report back to the Government on the state of the universities in South Africa, in particular responding to the charges from the 'open' liberal universities that their academic freedom had been compromised or even destroyed by the apartheid Government's higher education policies, notably the 1959 Extension of University Education Act (Act 45 of 1959).

Under the provisions of that Act, no black person would be allowed to register as a student at a traditionally white university without express permission from the relevant minister. The Act elicited a barrage of criticism from the English-speaking liberal universities, with many of these instigating an annual academic freedom lecture to keep protest against government policy alive in the public mind (see *The Open Universities in South Africa*, 1957).

T. B. Davie, Vice-Chancellor of the University of Cape Town, formulated the key principles of the South African defence and assertion of academic freedom in a series of lectures and interventions that he gave through the 1950s, while the National Party Government was putting in place the legal structures for the apartheid state. Davie identified the practice of academic freedom as:

> Our freedom from external interference in (a) who shall teach, (b) what we teach, (c) how we teach, and (d) whom we teach.
>
> (T. B. Davie definition, in van der Sandt Centlivres, 1959).

The T. B. Davie definition (as it became known) was powerful enough to gain international recognition, and was notably cited by Felix Frankfurter in an 'enormously influential' Supreme Court judgment in the USA in 1957, and continues to form a reference point—although a contested one, as we shall see below—for much current local analysis and debate (cited by Barendt, 2010: 174-75; Gauntlett, 2013; Higgins, 2013; Nzimande, 2013; Pillay, 2013; Kistner, 2013).

For the van Wyk de Vries report, the idea of academic freedom was at once absolutely central and absolutely controversial. The report sought at one and the same time to maintain that '[E]veryone agreed that universities should have academic freedom' (van Wyk de Vries Commission, 1974: 27), but also insisted that 'there is no room in any country for more than one conception of the university' (cited in du Toit, 2013: 31). In reality, much of the ideological and conceptual work of the Commission was to seek to annul Davie's powerful formulations (for a thorough analysis, see 'Academic Freedom in the New South Africa', in Higgins, 2013: 43).

In the eyes of the apartheid state, the correct perspective on academic freedom is only possible through a prior understanding of, and commitment to, the 'university's coherence with the nation, and, in a narrower sense, its interwovenness with a particular community' (van Wyk de Vries Commission, 1974: 19). In a classic instance of Freudian negation—in which strong conscious denial implies unconscious acceptance of an unpalatable truth—the Commission emphasized (though without providing any argument or evidence in this regard) that this *volksgebondenheit* or 'national bond' by no means entailed 'subordination to the nation or a kind of twentieth-century national totalitarianism', insisting that 'the freedom of the university is in no way curtailed by its bond with the nation' (34). All that acknowledgement of the 'national bond' demanded, according to the Commission, was the necessary respect for the 'realities of the situation' (27). Paramount was the need to preserve and maintain apartheid, or, in the words of the report, to 'ensure that respective language groups will be free to determine the character and direction of the university in the light of their cultural backgrounds and principles' (27). According to the Commission, once due respect to these principles—the principles of apartheid segregation—was granted, considerable degrees of freedom and autonomy for the universities were then permissible. The central point was that university—its staff and its students—should not engage (as the 'open' universities insisted on doing) in 'political ideology and public action that would bring it into conflict with society or the state' (Moja and Cloete, 1995: 51).

In this regard, there were two contrasting and mutually exclusive ideas of the definition of the university at work in the apartheid period. The first and dominant one was the Afrikaaner definition, in which the university is understood as a direct instrument of the state, and academic freedom is no more than (in Friedrich Nietzsche's phrase) 'service to the state'; the six historically Afrikaans universities fully accepted their role as '"creatures of the state"... acting in the service of government' (Bunting, 2002: 66). Against this entirely instrumental and authoritarian role, the four historically English-speaking universities insisted on asserting their standing as 'part of an international community of scholars which was dedicated to the advancement and propagation of all human knowledge' (Bunting, 2002: 71), and they repeatedly stressed that their 'commitment to the universal values of academic freedom made it impossible for them to act as the servants of the apartheid state' (70).

By the late 1980s, as the whole apartheid system began to come apart at the seams, both the liberal universities and students and staff at some of the historically non-white universities began to challenge the state through marches, demonstrations and both intra- and extra-mural speech. A defining moment came in the inaugural address of the new Vice-Chancellor of the ('coloured') University of the Western Cape in June 1987: Jakes Gerwel declared that the university faced 'the historical imperative to respond to the democratic left, to be an intellectual home of the left' and to refuse the 'reproduction and maintenance of a social order which is undemocratic, discriminatory, exploitative and repressive' (cited in Badat, 2013; see in Higgins, 2013, Chapter 8, 'Living Out Our Differences: interview with Jakes Gerwel': 227–53).

In a desperate measure, the state promulgated new regulations concerning the state funding of education in October 1987. These regulations—known as the de Klerk regulations after their prime architect, F. W. de Klerk, then Minister of Education—claimed to have as their aim the safeguarding of academic freedom on campuses in the face of revolutionary disruption. Protests against the new regulations included staff and students not only from the 'open' universities of Cape Town, Natal and the Witwatersrand, but also from the University of the North and the University of the Western Cape. These protests were the high point of popular support for academic freedom as a point of resistance to apartheid rule (Higgins, 2013: 11–41).

THE CONSTITUTIONAL IMPERATIVE

Given this dynamic and troubled history, and the active role of some students and staff in engaging the regime, particularly in the dying days of apartheid, is it not surprising that the body tasked with drawing up a new Constitution for South Africa, the Constitutional Assembly, had to pay 'special attention' in the new Constitution to the defence of academic freedom (Kruger, 2013). The End Conscription Campaign, for instance, drew a great deal of support from the National Union of South African Students, and its banning in August 1988 led to significant protests at the University of Cape Town and on other campuses.

This special attention was deemed necessary in the light of the severe restrictions on academic freedom placed by the apartheid regime, and a strong sense that the right to individual freedom of expression—so strongly constrained by the apartheid state—included or contained in some way an individual's right to academic freedom (Kruger, 2013). Moreover, in 1990 at least, the African National Congress (ANC) saw the 'open' universities' stance in defence of academic freedom as to be 'commended' as, in the words of ANC Deputy President, Walter Sisulu, in a T. B. Davie Memorial Lecture at the University of Cape Town, a 'stand against the [apartheid] government's effort to deny black people their fundamental right to a decent education' (Sisulu, 1991).

At the same time, though, some hesitation was expressed about specific constitutional support for academic freedom, particularly if twinned—as it was in T. B. Davie's four principles—with support for institutional autonomy from government interference. Generally, the fear at the time was that 'constitutional protection of academic freedom in the form of institutional autonomy could justify resistance to transformation' (Kruger, 2013), with particular concern that the cluster of Afrikaans-medium universities might use the principle of institutional autonomy to insist on maintaining the principles of racial segregation. As André du Toit later put it, 'the defenders of academic freedom may turn out to have their own ulterior motives and hidden agendas' (du Toit, 2000).

From this perspective, the constitutive link for which Davie argued, between institutional autonomy and academic freedom, as a way of countering the Government's forced racial segregation of the universities, had to be broken as it was felt that it could be turned, if granted, in the new democracy, into legally justifiable resistance to democratic transformation. Legal advisers at the time did argue that such fears were 'groundless', noting: 'If a university resists transformation ... it will be possible for Parliament to intervene in terms of the limitation clause [of the Bill of Rights] to remedy the position' (Theme Committee 4, in 1995, cited in Kruger, 2013). The constitutional imperative was in this sense two-sided: it brought the individual's academic freedom under the protection of the Constitution, but placed the question of institutional autonomy deliberately outside it.

The South African Constitution recognizes and asserts academic freedom in two ways: as academic freedom proper and as a related freedom of 'scientific research'. The 1994 interim Constitution, among the fundamental rights, under the heading, 'Religion, belief and opinion', reads at section 14(1): 'Every person shall have the right to freedom of conscience, religion, thought, belief and opinion, which shall include academic freedom in institutions of higher learning', while section 15(1), under 'Freedom of Expression', has it: 'Every person shall have the right to freedom of speech and expression, which shall include freedom of the press and other media, and the freedom of artistic creativity and scientific research'. The 1997 final Constitution includes similar provisions in the Bill of Rights (Chapter 2). Under the title 'Freedom of religion, belief and opinion', section 15(1) simply reads: 'Everyone has the right to freedom of conscience, religion, thought, belief and opinion', but section 16(1), under 'Freedom of expression', states: 'Everyone has the right to freedom of expression, which includes ... freedom of the press and other media ... freedom to receive or impart information or ideas ... freedom of artistic creativity; and ... academic freedom and freedom of scientific research'.

The South African Constitution undoubtedly valorizes academic freedom by placing it alongside such core human rights as freedom of religion and freedom of association. It took centuries of democratic struggle to gain recognition for these individual rights; indeed, they are still notably absent on many parts of the continent and in many parts of the world. Placing academic freedom alongside them suggests that it, too, has a crucial role in the development and maintenance of a vital and living democracy, and this constitutional emphasis is to be welcomed.

The problem, though, is that by placing academic freedom (and viewing freedom of scientific research as equivalent to academic freedom) squarely under the rubrics of freedom of religion, belief and opinion, and freedom of expression, the Constitution tends to individualize this right, and so in effect marginalizes, or even puts out of the picture altogether, the complex institutional setting in which alone the practice of academic freedom makes sense. Any right to academic freedom must in reality depend upon how far the institutions in which it is practised observe their constitutive duty to enable it and make it possible (for an illuminating discussion on this point, see Barendt, 2010: 45–46).

The Constitution's idea of academic freedom as the right of any individual, akin to, and on the model of, the freedom of creative expression, distracts attention from the real dimensions in which academic freedom operates, and in which local and global forces interact: the complex and politically charged exchanges within institutions between academics and the new managerial class of administrators; the struggles between universities and the state in relation to the control of teaching and research priorities; and the all-encompassing ideological battle between liberal and neoliberal ideas about the very purpose of higher education, which many commentators and policy advisers prefer to pretend is not happening. A significant amount of counter-commentary is, however, beginning to emerge (Nussbaum, 2010; Collini, 2012).

These struggles and the real dimensions in which the ideal of academic freedom comes into the world became more visible in the two translations of the constitutional imperative that have followed. In each of these, we shall see at work the uneasy conjunction of the pressures of local political transformation with the new global policy templates. The first translation is that of the constitutional imperative into formal policy, with the publication in 1996 of the report of the National Commission on Higher Education, *A Framework for Transformation* (NCHE, 1996); the second, the translation, in turn, of policy into practice in the decade following the resulting Higher Education Act 1997 (Act 101 of 1997). In and through each translation we shall see how the original constitutional imperative for academic freedom is effectively undermined as (to put it in linguistic terms) the original imperative mode is modified to a conditional or concessive form.

TRANSLATING THE CONSTITUTIONAL IMPERATIVE INTO POLICY

The constitutional imperative, as we have seen above, seeks to valorize and respect academic freedom by placing it alongside other core democratic principles such as freedom of speech and freedom of religious belief. However, in this placing, academic freedom is framed above all as an individual right, thus severing it from its usual and perhaps indeed constitutive connections with university autonomy. How this severing threatens to restrict severely or undermine any actual possibilities for the real practice of academic freedom becomes clearer in the translation or exposition of the constitutional imperative in the policy framework proposed by the NCHE report of 1996.

It becomes particularly clear in the Framework (NCHE, 1996) that, while the content of apartheid higher education policy is fundamentally altered, its form is not. What is retained from the apartheid period is the instrumental form of the university's relation to the state, with a consequent undermining of academic freedom as an institutionally-bound practice. At the same time, and in somewhat complex and contradictory fashion, this undermining of academic freedom is also heightened by the state's general encouragement of and reward for the application of the new managerial authoritarianism drawn from global policy templates. The report as a whole is torn between two very different attitudes towards higher education: the first generated by the strong democratic impulse of the post-apartheid moment, which sees 'the task of higher education [as] to support a healthy public opinion and vibrant public debate by developing a culture of critical discourse in society'; the second by the narrowing down of the goals of higher education to the 'provision of person-power for the changing labour market', as demanded by the new global policy templates.

As for the van Wyk de Vries report before it, the Framework report maintains that academic freedom and institutional autonomy stand 'at the heart of the debate about governance in higher education' (NCHE, 1996). The NCHE report distinguishes between three 'incompatible' positions on academic freedom and university autonomy. The first 'privileges the pursuit of knowledge for its own sake (academicism)' and 'asserts the autonomy of higher education institutions against any form of state interference'—as we have seen, the position maintained by the English 'liberal' campuses under apartheid. The second 'privileges knowledge in the service of socioeconomic development' and recommends that the university 'should therefore accept the hegemony of government'. In the third, 'higher education is seen as a key agent of social change and mobility that must play an important role in promoting equity'.

Conceptually, there are really only two views at odds with one another here: the first position, described in somewhat pejorative terms as, in inverted commas, academicism, and the second, which maintains the need for 'the hegemony of government', whether for purposes of the vision of socioeconomic development championed by what Olsen and Maasen (2007) refer to as 'Reform' policy, or the urgent calls for social change, mobility and equity essential to correct the devastating heritage of apartheid.

Thus, in a key paragraph, the Commission both 'proposes that the principles of academic freedom and institutional autonomy be maintained as key conditions for a vibrant higher education system' and insists that its 'proposals on co-operative governance therefore preclude any form of state control over, or arbitrary interference in the affairs of institutions'. None the less, despite this insistence, it is made increasingly clear that state control is a central feature of the White Paper's vision, however sugared that pill may be. 'However', the paragraph continues, 'co-operative governance does not mean government indifference to higher education. On the contrary, it rests on the assumption that both government and higher education institutions are committed to the same societal goals' (NCHE, 1996: 194).

In the first flush of rainbow nation democracy, such an assumption was, perhaps, not unlikely; but this was an assumption in which, over time, there was likely to be increased recognition of the difference between 'societal goals' understood as the consensual goals expressed by a whole society, and 'societal goals' determined for a society. Indeed, the document goes on anticipate potential dissent when it adds, in a warning note, that 'the new developments will have an impact on the scope of institutional autonomy in the sense that they will necessitate a culture of co-operation and will lead to increased accountability' (NCHE, 1996: 195). Finally, academic freedom takes place 'within the context of the increased accountability implied by the principle and the system of co-operative governance' (NCHE, 1996: 197). What, in the end, is most notable in the Framework report is the way in which the imperative for academic freedom is effectively translated into a subordinate and conditional form, as the university is held to embody (as for the earlier van Wyk de Vries report) a merely instrumental relation to the state. Thus, while the Constitution protects the academic freedom of individuals, the 'Framework' does not work to protect the autonomy of the university necessary to the full practice of academic freedom.

TRANSLATING POLICY INTO PRACTICE, 1997–2008

We have seen above that higher education policy made explicit the disconnect between academic freedom and institutional autonomy operated in the constitutional imperative. By narrowing down the scope of academic freedom to a subset of an individual's right to freedom of expression or belief, *A Framework for Transformation* sought to assert scope for state intervention, presented in the guise of a democratically sanctioned notion of co-operative governance with some moments of uneasiness in the formulations. Despite these misgivings, the general attitude of the Framework report was perhaps best summed up in the frustrated call that it was high time for 'indiscriminate reference to academic freedom' to 'stop' (Moodie, 1997).

In the decade following the Framework and the Higher Education Act that accompanied it, reference to academic freedom did not stop. The translation of policy into practice raised a number of concerns, notable among these the simple fact that the constitutionally protected individual right of academic freedom somehow did not appear to provide any actual protection to academics or the institutions that housed them.

To get a sense of these concerns, I will draw here on the summary and survey of the changing ways in which policy was put into practice in 1997–2007 as presented in a Council on Higher Education (CHE) task team report, *Academic Freedom, Institutional Autonomy and Public Accountability in South African Higher Education* (CHE, 2008). The Council notes that the occasion for its report is the continued uncertainty and agitation around the related ideas of academic freedom and institutional autonomy, despite the proposal, in *A Framework for Transformation* and in the new Higher Education Act and its various amendments around the idea of co-operative governance. The report was driven primarily 'by concerns and claims that government steering of higher education risked becoming "interference"' (CHE, 2008: vii).

Unlike the 1996 Framework and van Wyk de Vries reports before it, rather than seeking an impossible consensus, the CHE document is more overtly dissensual, and more open to the expression of differences and disagreements around questions of academic freedom. Perhaps this is in part due to the ways in which the translation of policy into practice in the decade following 1997 had shown that there were emerging grounds for the misgivings that came through, despite some of the Framework's apotropaic formulations. What makes the 2008 CHE report is its open quality of dissension, and particularly the ways in which it is more open to the expression of differences and disagreements around questions of academic freedom.

On the one hand, the report shares and appears to endorse the Constitution's definition of academic freedom as a purely individual right when it repeatedly rejects the too-easy conflation of academic freedom with institutional autonomy (du Toit, 2013). On the other, the report is forthright in all its criticisms of the decade-long translation of policy into practice: the ways in which, for all the rhetoric of 'co-operative governance', the state finds it easier to command universities than to consult with them; that the application of 'growth and development' imperatives to teaching and research provision may be 'reckless'; and that, all in all, the Government, in its calls for the accountability of higher education, may, ironically enough, not itself be exercising its own democratic accountability 'for developing the higher education system' (CHE, 2008). For a useful analysis of many of these features, see one of the referenced sources for the report, the 41st T. B. Davie Memorial Lecture, 'Accounting for Autonomy', delivered by Jonathan Jansen (2004). Indeed, in at least one strand of its thinking, the CHE report comes around to asserting the values of an academic freedom that it seems at first to abjure, an academic freedom rooted in, rather than separated out from, its context as a highly mediated institutional practice, caught betwixt and between the interests of commerce and society, the state and the university, the managerial and the academic.

In the end, the key finding or recommendation of the 2008 CHE report may well be its insistence in dissent on the recognition that:

> No one party can know how, or should have the sole power, to draw a fixed boundary between higher education and society, or between academic freedom and institutional autonomy and accountability. It believes that any party claiming to know how to do this—or vested with unilateral power to do this—may in practice suppress necessary engagement and free expression of difference.
>
> (CHE, 2008: 26)

PRESENT CONCERNS

In its 2008 report on academic freedom, the Council on Higher Education concluded that it was essential to recognize 'government's right to and responsibility to lead system-level change' (CHE, 2008), but that it was equally essential to reject the view that 'government has the only authoritative grasp of what is required of higher education'. Given the inevitable tensions, the Council advised the need for a 'constant alertness to the implications of policy and implementation for academic freedom, institutional autonomy and accountability' and suggested that the Council itself needed to play a central role in monitoring 'potential violations'.

Are there grounds for continued concern about academic freedom in South Africa since the 2008 report? A number of events suggest that there are. In particular, two pieces of higher education legislation have provoked considerable controversy, and (in the very words of Minister of Higher Education and Training, Blade Nzimande) raised the 'spectre of state interference in the work of universities, generating fears of political interference by a minister bent on extending his control and crushing any opposition to it' (Nzimande, 2013). The minister goes on to reassure the public, although in terms which, on closer analysis, are hardly reassuring at all: 'If there are any extraordinary interventions by government in the work of universities, it will be for the sake of ensuring that universities are able to carry out their functions and do not misuse the trust that the government puts in them'. The first piece of legislation is the Higher Education and Training Laws Amendment Act (Act 23 of 2012); the second is the establishment in 2013 of a new oversight committee, tasked with overseeing transformation at South African universities and chaired by Professor Malegapuru William Makgoba, Vice-Chancellor of the University of KwaZulu-Natal (UKZN). Certainly, the common thread of the initiatives is cause for concern for anyone interested in asserting the constitutional protection of academic freedom, as the effect of each initiative is to centralize authority over various aspects of higher education in the hands of the minister or those appointed directly by him.

With regard to the new higher education Act, Barney Pityana, former Vice-Chancellor of the University of South Africa (UNISA), argues that 'rather as in apartheid-style legislating', the new Nzimande regulations 'give the minister open-ended and ill-defined powers to intervene in higher education institutions well beyond the powers already available to him'. Ihron Rensburg, Vice-Chancellor at the University of Johannesburg, emphasizes that the new legislation—although at the moment of writing, still to be signed into law by President Zuma—'undermines the careful balance struck between university autonomy and public accountability crafted by the Constitution and the initial Higher Education Act'. The new Act not only gives 'one individual enormous power over the higher education system', but, he warns, 'also confuses the "public" with the "state"' (Barney Pityana, 'Free our universities from Nzimande's blade', in *The Sunday Independent* of 4 November 2012; Ihron Rensburg, 'Regulatory overkill threatens academic autonomy in South Africa', in *Business Day* of 31 January 2013; Jeremy Gauntlett, 'Minister given a blue light to ride roughshod over academic rights', in *Mail and Guardian* of 17 May 2013).

In line with Rensburg's analysis of the anti-democratic authoritarianism at work in the new legislation is the simple fact that it was developed without following any of the usual processes of consultation with stakeholders and interested parties established in higher education to encourage democratic participation and accountability since 1994. Neither the statutory Council on Higher Education, which exists precisely to advise the minister on higher education matters, nor Higher Education in South Africa (HESA), the body that represents all 23 vice-chancellors at South African universities, was consulted before the introduction of the new Act. The summary of the HESA and CHE positions may be seen in 'Universities round on Nzimande and his Higher Education Bill', an article by Bongani Nkosi (2012) in the *Mail and Guardian* of 9 November 2012. In it, the HESA Chair, Ahmed Bawa, is cited as noting that, 'Under normal circumstances ... the minister would have consulted us on his intentions to introduce new amendments'.

Similarly, for the CHE, the establishment of the new Transformation Committee appears to contradict and override the role of university councils in monitoring transformation at their universities, noting that 'an oversight committee of the sort proposed could erode the authority of these councils' (cited in Jeffrey Mabelebele's article of 15 February 2013, in the *Mail and Guardian*, 'Blade's new committee risks undermining university councils'). Confidence in the committee is not deepened by its issuing—with considerable fanfare—of a new 'seminal' study, 'An Equity Index for South Africa' (Govinder and Makgoba, 2013), which was soon found to be open to a series of flaws in methodology and argument (Cloete, 2014; Dunne, 2014; Moultrie and Dorrington, 2014).

CONCLUSION

What are we to make of the continued tensions around academic freedom and institutional autonomy in post-apartheid South Africa? The constitutional imperative for the defence of academic freedom does not seem to be met in practice, as successive waves of its translation into policy and practice have shown. It seems as if the constitutional imperative embodies the ways in which academic freedom has perhaps always been an inconvenient ideal, one that it is easier and more comfortable to support in theory than to observe in practice.

Yet the continued agitation around and appeal to notions of academic freedom also reveal that South Africa, and doubtless other systems of higher education, know that at some level they benefit from free and open-ended enquiry, at the same time as they often fear it. The fear is that the capacity for reflective thought and criticism developed by university education might turn out, instead of being in simple service to the state and the economy, to turn against state interests and economic ideologies. In this regard, what Jacques Derrida wrote of the university is perhaps particularly appropriate to the current moment of tension in South Africa:

> For more than eight hundred years, 'university' has been the name given by a society to a sort of supplementary body that at one and the same time it wanted to project outside itself and to keep jealously to itself, to emancipate and control.
>
> (Derrida, 1983: 19)

'To emancipate and to control': surely the ambivalence we have traced out here as the constitutional imperative is to emancipate, but the counter-imperative is for control. Paradoxically enough, it is the challenges to the constitutional imperative that keep questions of academic freedom alive in South Africa.

REFERENCES

Badat, S. 'Jakes Gerwel (1946–2012): Humble intellectual, scholar and leader', in *South African Journal of Science*, vol. 109 (1/2), 2013.

Barendt, E. *Academic Freedom and the Law: A Comparative Study*. Portland, OR, and Oxford, Hart Publishing, 2010.

Bunting, I. 'The Higher Education Landscape under Apartheid', in Cloete, N., et al. (Eds). *Transformation in Higher Education: Global pressures and local realities in South Africa*. Sunnyside, Centre for Higher Education Transformation, 2002.

Cloete, N. 'A new look at demographic transformation: Comments on Govinder et al. (2013)', in *South African Journal of Science*, vol. 110 (1/2), 5 February 2014.

Collini, S. *What are Universities for?* Harmondsworth, Penguin, 2012.

Council on Higher Education (CHE). *Academic Freedom, Institutional Autonomy and Public Accountability in South African Higher Education*, report of the independent task team on Higher Education, Institutional Autonomy and Academic Freedom (HEIAAF). Pretoria, CHE, 2008.

Derrida, J. 'The Principle of Reason: The university in the eyes of its pupils', in *Diacritics*, vol. 13 (3), 1983.

du Toit, A. 'From Autonomy to Accountability: Academic freedom under threat in South Africa?' in *Social Dynamics*, vol. 26 (1), 2000.

'Losing the Academic Freedom Plot? The CHE and the debate on institutional autonomy and public accountability', in *Kagisano No. 8: Academic Freedom*. Pretoria, CHE, March 2013.

Dunne, T. 'Mathematical errors, smoke and mirrors in pursuit of an illusion: Comment on Govinder et al. (2013)', in *South African Journal of Science*, vol. 110 (1/2), 5 February 2014.

Gauntlett, J. 'Minister given a blue light to ride roughshod over academic rights', in *Mail and Guardian* (Johannesburg), 17 May 2013.

Govinder, K. S., and Makgoba, M. W. 'An Equity Index for South Africa', in *South African Journal of Science*, vol. 109 (5/6), 23 May 2013.

Head, S. 'The Grim Threat to British Universities', in *The New York Review of Books*, 13 January 2011.

Higgins, J. *Academic Freedom in a Democratic South Africa: Essays and Interviews on Higher Education and the Humanities*. Johannesburg, Witwatersrand University Press, 2013.

Jansen, J. D. 'Accounting for Autonomy', 41st T. B. Davie Memorial Lecture at the University of Cape Town, 26 August 2004

King, R. 'Governing Knowledge Globally: policy internationalism and higher education in the age of globalisation', in Brennan, J., et al. *Higher Education and Society: A Research Report*. London, Centre for Higher Education and Research and Information (Open University), 2010.

Kistner, U. 'Humanities row displays bad "form"', in *Mail and Guardian* (Johannesburg), 10 May 2013.

Kruger, R. 'The Genesis and Scope of Academic Freedom in the South African Constitution', in *Kagisano No. 8: Academic Freedom*. Pretoria, CHE, March 2013.

Mabelebele, J. 'Blade's new committee risks undermining university councils', in *Mail and Guardian* (Johannesburg), 15 February 2013.

Moja, T., and Cloete, N. 'Academic Freedom in South Africa', in Daniel, J., et al. (Eds). *Academic Freedom 3: Education and Human Rights*, London, Zed Books, 1995.

Moodie, G. C. 'Academic Freedom and the Transformation of Higher Education', in *English Academy Review: Southern African Journal of English Studies*, vol. 14 (1), 1997.

Moultrie, T. A., and Dorrington, R. E. 'Flaws in the approach and application of the Equity Index: Comments on Govinder et al. (2013)', in *South African Journal of Science*, vol. 110 (1/2), 5 February 2014.

National Commission on Higher Education (NCHE). *A Framework for Transformation*, NCHE report. Pretoria, Human Sciences Research Council, 1996.

Nkosi, B. 'Universities round on Nzimande and his Higher Education Bill', in *Mail and Guardian* (Johannesburg), 9 November 2012.

Nussbaum, M. *Not for Profit: Why democracy needs the humanities*. Princeton, NJ, and Oxford, Princeton University Press, 2010.

Nzimande, B. 'Nzimande: we will not uphold the status quo', in *Mail and Guardian* (Johannesburg), 5 July 2013.

Olsen, J. P., and Maasen, P. 'European debates on the knowledge institution: The modernization of the university at the European level', in Maasen, P., and Olsen, J. P. (Eds). *University Dynamics and European Integration*, Dordrecht, Springer, 2007.

The Open Universities in South Africa, proceedings of the Conference of Representatives of the University of Cape Town and the University of the Witwatersrand, 1957, Johannesburg, University of Witwatersrand Press, 1957.

Pillay, S. 'Is institutional autonomy a myth?', in *Mail and Guardian* (Johannesburg), 7 June 2013.

Pityana, B. 'Free our universities from Nzimande's blade', in *The Sunday Independent* (South Africa), 4 November 2012.

Rensburg, I. 'Regulatory overkill threatens academic autonomy in South Africa', in *Business Day* (Johannesburg), 31 January 2013.

Sisulu, W. 'Academic Freedom and Intellectual Empowerment', in *Pretexts: studies in writing and culture*, vol. 3 (1/2), 1991.

Spivak, G. 'Academic Freedom', in *Pretexts: studies in writing and culture*, vol. 5 (1/2), 1995.

van der Sandt Centlivres, A. *Blundering into University Apartheid*. Cape Town, University of Cape Town (Academic Freedom Committee), 1959.

van Wyk de Vries Commission. *Main Report of the Commission of Inquiry into Universities*. Pretoria, Department of National Education, 1974.

Russell, C. *Academic Freedom*. London, Routledge, 1993.

PART TWO

International Organizations

INTERNATIONAL ORGANIZATIONS

UNITED NATIONS EDUCATIONAL, SCIENTIFIC AND CULTURAL ORGANIZATION (UNESCO)

7 pl. de Fontenoy, 75352 Paris 07 SP, France
Telephone: 145681000
E-mail: bpi@unesco.org
Internet: www.unesco.org

Founded 1945

'For the purpose of advancing, through the educational, scientific and cultural relations of the peoples of the world, the objectives of international peace and the common welfare of mankind'; 195 mems and 8 assoc. mems

Functions

UNESCO's activities are funded through a budget provided by member states and also through other sources, particularly the UNDP.

International Intellectual Cooperation

UNESCO assists the interchange of experience, knowledge and ideas through a world network of specialists. Apart from the work of its professional staff, UNESCO cooperates regularly with the national associations and international federations of scientists, artists, writers and educators, some of which it helped to establish.

UNESCO convenes conferences and meetings, and coordinates international scientific efforts; it helps to standardize procedures of documentation and provides clearing house services; it offers fellowships; and it publishes a wide range of specialized works, including source books and works of reference.

UNESCO promotes various international agreements, including the Universal Copyright Convention and the World Cultural and Natural Heritage Convention, which member states are invited to accept.

Operational Assistance

UNESCO has established missions that advise governments, particularly in the developing member countries, in the planning of projects; and it appoints experts to assist in carrying them out. The projects are concerned with the teaching of functional literacy to workers in development undertakings; teacher training; establishing of libraries and documentation centres; provision of training for journalists, radio, television and film workers; improvement of scientific and technical education; training of planners in cultural development; and the international exchange of persons and information.

Promotion of Peace

UNESCO organizes various research efforts on racial problems, and is particularly concerned with prevention of discrimination in education, and improving access for women to education. It also promotes studies and research on conflicts and peace, violence and obstacles to disarmament, and the role of international law and organizations in building peace. It is stressed that human rights, peace and disarmament cannot be dealt with separately, as the observance of human rights is a prerequisite to peace and not vice versa.

Member States

(July 2014)

Afghanistan
Albania
Algeria
Andorra
Angola
Anguilla (Associate Member)
Antigua and Barbuda
Argentina
Armenia
Aruba (Associate Member)
Australia
Austria
Azerbaijan
Bahamas
Bahrain
Bangladesh
Barbados
Belarus
Belgium
Belize
Benin
Bhutan
Bolivia
Bosnia and Herzegovina
Botswana
Brazil
British Virgin Islands (Associate Member)
Brunei
Bulgaria
Burkina Faso
Burundi
Cambodia
Cameroon
Canada
Cape Verde
Cayman Islands (Associate Member)
Central African Republic
Chad
Chile
China, People's Republic
Colombia
Comoros
Congo, Democratic Republic
Congo, Republic
Cook Islands
Costa Rica
Côte d'Ivoire
Croatia
Cuba
Cyprus
Czech Republic
Denmark
Djibouti
Dominica
Dominican Republic
Ecuador
Egypt
El Salvador
Equatorial Guinea
Eritrea
Estonia
Ethiopia
Faroe Islands (Associate Member)
Fiji
Finland
France
Gabon
Gambia
Georgia
Germany
Ghana
Greece
Grenada
Guatemala
Guinea
Guinea-Bissau
Guyana
Haiti
Honduras
Hungary
Iceland
India
Indonesia
Iran
Iraq
Ireland
Israel
Italy
Jamaica
Japan
Jordan
Kazakhstan
Kenya
Kiribati
Korea, Democratic People's Republic
Korea, Republic
Kuwait
Kyrgyzstan
Laos
Latvia
Lebanon
Lesotho
Liberia
Libya
Lithuania
Luxembourg
Macao (Associate Member)
Macedonia, former Yugoslav Republic
Madagascar
Malawi
Malaysia
Maldives
Mali
Malta
Marshall Islands
Mauritania
Mauritius
Mexico
Micronesia, Federated States
Moldova
Monaco
Mongolia
Montenegro
Morocco
Mozambique
Myanmar
Namibia
Nauru
Nepal
Netherlands

New Zealand
Nicaragua
Niger
Nigeria
Niue
Norway
Oman
Pakistan
Palau
Panama
Papua New Guinea
Paraguay
Peru
Philippines
Poland
Portugal
Qatar
Romania
Russia
Rwanda
St Christopher and Nevis
St Lucia
St Vincent and the Grenadines
Samoa
San Marino
São Tomé e Príncipe
Saudi Arabia
Senegal
Serbia
Seychelles
Sierra Leone
Sint Maarten (Associate Member)
Slovakia
Slovenia
Solomon Islands
Somalia
South Africa
South Sudan
Spain
Sri Lanka
Sudan
Suriname
Swaziland
Sweden
Switzerland
Syria
Tajikistan
Tanzania
Thailand
Timor-Leste
Togo
Tokelau (Associate Member)
Tonga
Trinidad and Tobago
Tunisia
Turkey
Turkmenistan
Tuvalu
Uganda
Ukraine
United Arab Emirates
United Kingdom
United States of America
Uruguay
Uzbekistan
Vanuatu
Venezuela
Viet Nam
Yemen
Zambia
Zimbabwe

Organization

GENERAL CONFERENCE

The supreme governing body of the Organization. Meets in ordinary session once in two years and is composed of representatives of the member states and associate members.

EXECUTIVE BOARD

Consists of 58 member states with a four-year term of office. Prepares the programme to be submitted to the Conference and supervises its execution. Meets twice or three times a year.

SECRETARIAT

Director-General IRINA BOKOVA.

The Director-General has an international staff of some 2,000 civil servants. Of the professional staff (specialists in various disciplines and administrators), about two-thirds are on technical assistance missions in member states.

COOPERATING BODIES

In accordance with UNESCO's constitution, national commissions have been set up in most member states. These help to integrate work within the member states and the work of UNESCO.

UNESCO LIAISON OFFICES

UNESCO Liaison Office Addis Ababa: ECA New Building, Menelik Avenue, Addis Ababa, Ethiopia; tel. 115513953; fax 115511414; e-mail addis@unesco.org; Dir FIRMIN MATOKO

UNESCO Liaison Office Brussels: UN House, Fifth floor, 14 Rue Montoyer, 1000 Brussels, Belgium; tel. (2) 290-89-60; e-mail brussels@unesco.org; Head MARIE-PAULE ROUDIL

UNESCO Liaison Office Geneva: 15 route des Morillons, 1218 Grand-Saconnex Geneva, Switzerland; tel. 229177880; fax 229177805; e-mail geneva@unesco.org; Officer-in-Charge KERSTIN HOLST.

UNESCO Liaison Office New York: Suite 900, 2 United Nations Plaza, New York, NY 10017, USA; tel. (212) 963-5995; fax (212) 963-8014; e-mail newyork@unesco.org; Dir PHILIPPE KRIDELKA

UNESCO FIELD OFFICES

(See also under relevant country)

Africa: Bujumbura (Burundi), Kinshasa (Democratic Republic of Congo), Brazzaville (Republic of the Congo), Maputo (Mozambique), Abuja (Nigeria).

Arab States: Iraq (Iraq), Amman (Jordan), Ramallah (Palestinian Authority), Khartoum (Sudan).

Asia and the Pacific: Kabul (Afghanistan), Dhaka (Bangladesh), Phnom Penh (Cambodia), Kathmandu (Nepal), Islamabad (Pakistan), Tashkent (Uzbekistan), Hanoi (Viet Nam).

Latin America and the Caribbean: Brasilia (Brazil), Santiago (Chile), Guatemala (Guatemala), Port-au-Prince (Haiti), México (Mexico), Lima (Peru).

Activities

EDUCATION

UNESCO has an overall policy of regarding education as a lifelong process. As an example, one implication is the increasing priority given to basic education for all, including early childhood care and development, primary education and adult education. This approach has been the guideline for many of the projects recently planned.

Each year, expert missions are sent to member states on request to advise on all matters concerning education. They also help with programmes for training abroad, and UNESCO provides study fellowships; in these forms of assistance, priority is given to the rural regions of developing member countries. The issues and problems involved in human resources development have been at the forefront of UNESCO's education programme since the Organization's foundation. Objectives include the eradication of illiteracy, universal primary education, secondary education reform, technical and vocational education, higher education, adult, non-formal and permanent education, population education, and education of women and girls. In addition to its regular programme budget, UNESCO's extra-budgetary sources include the UN Development Programme (UNDP), the UN Children's Fund (UNICEF), the UN Population Fund (UNFPA) and the World Bank.

NATURAL SCIENCES

UNESCO promotes science for peace, sustainable development and human security and well-being, in close collaboration with its Member States and partners. It has established scientific unions and bodies and initiated programmes like the Man and the Biosphere Programme, the International Hydrological Programme, and the International Oceanographic Commission. Giving priority to developing countries, in particular to Africa, UNESCO hosts major international programmes in the freshwater, marine, ecological, earth and basic sciences.

The Natural Sciences sector of UNESCO has field offices with a regional mandate in Nairobi (Africa), Jakarta (Asia and the Pacific), Venice (Europe and North America), Cairo (Arab States), and Montevideo (Latin America and the Caribbean).

It adopted the Medium-Term Strategy for 2008 to 2013 in its 34th session of the UNESCO General Conference (in 2007), setting Africa and gender equality as its two priorities for this six-year period. The following themes are of particular focus: biodiversity, natural disaster reduction, engineering, science education, climate change and sustainable development in small island developing states.

At the international level, UNESCO has over the years set up various forms of intergovernmental cooperation concerned with the environmental sciences and research on natural resources.

The Man and Biosphere Programme (MAB) gives emphasis to the reinforcement of the World Network of Biosphere Reserves, which aims to reconcile the conservation of biodiversity, the quest for social and economic development, and the maintenance of associated cultural values. The MAB also promotes an interdisciplinary approach to solving land-use problems through research and training, covering topics such as arid-land crops, sacred sites, coastal regions, the Sahel-Sahara observatories, and the biology and fertility of tropical soils.

The International Basic Sciences Programme (IBSP) strengthens national capacities in the basic sciences and science education with intergovernmental cooperation among member states and partner organizations.

The International Geoscience Programme (IGCP) is a cooperative initiative of UNESCO and the International Union of Geological Sciences (IUGS) and stimulates comparative studies in the Earth Sciences. Projects focused on building safer environment, the relationship between natural geological factors and health problems, biodiversity, climate change, and mineral and groundwater resources extraction.

The International Hydrological Programme deals with the scientific aspects of water resources assessment and management; and the Intergovernmental Oceanographic Commission (*q.v.*) promotes scientific investigation into the nature and resources of the oceans through the concerted action of its member states.

SOCIAL AND HUMAN SCIENCES

UNESCO's Social and Human Sciences Sector acts as a think tank for the nations regarding their policy formulation and implementation. The sector advances knowledge, standards and intellectual cooperation in order to facilitate social transformations conducive to the universal values of justice, freedom and human dignity.

In its 35th General Conference held in 2009, the organization has fixed two priorities: to develop and implement standards in the field of ethics and human rights, and to reinforce the link between social sciences research and public policy by developing the opportunities for discussion between researchers and political decision-makers and creating new venues to reflect on meaningful topics such as gender equality, international migration, social inclusion, youth and poverty eradication issues, giving priority to Africa and the small island developing States (SIDS) and the most vulnerable populations.

With these two priorities, the sector is focused on four main fields. Promotes human rights, with focus on democracy and peace. Provides support for the formulation of policies on regional integration, migration, SIDS, urban development and youth. Promotes policies on physical education and sport and the fight against drug addiction, with focus on the implementation of the International Convention against Doping in Sport, adopted in 2005. Encourages programmes and infrastructure to support the formulation of policies on the ethics of science and technology and bioethics.

CULTURE

In the field of cultural heritage, the programme concentrates on six major lines of action: protecting and conserving cultural and natural heritage through the effective implementation of the 1972 Convention; enhancing the protection of cultural property and fighting against traffic in cultural property through the effective implementation of the 1954, 1970 and 2001 Conventions; safeguarding the intangible cultural heritage through the effective implementation of the 2003 Convention; sustaining and promoting the diversity of cultural expressions through the effective implementation of the 2005 Convention; promoting the role of culture in development at the global, regional and national levels; promoting intercultural dialogue, social cohesion and a culture of peace and non-violence.

UNESCO has Africa and Gender Equality in cultural heritage policies as its main global priorities.

The focus is on capacity-building for a better conservation of cultural and natural heritage of Africa. The sector promotes cooperation between African countries through sharing of best practices, and the development of transnational World Heritage nominations, as well as activities linking heritage conservation to sustainable development, in cooperation with African World Heritage Fund (AWHF).

UNESCO addresses the global gender equality issue through its work in the domains of tangible and intangible cultural heritage, museums, creative industries and cultural policies, HIV and AIDS prevention, intercultural dialogue and indigenous issues.

COMMUNICATION AND INFORMATION

The Communication and Information Sector (CI) came into its present form in 1990 and has 27 UNESCO field offices. It consists of two divisions: Freedom of Expression and Media Development, and Knowledge Societies Division.

The Freedom of Expression and Media Development (FEM) Division implements activities to promote the free flow of information, the freedom of expression, and freedom of the press. It creates awareness among governments, public institutions and civil society on freedom of expression and freedom of the press, and celebrates World Press Freedom Day. The Division assists UNESCO's Member States in developing standards and legal instruments for press freedom and freedom of information in accordance with internationally recognized standards, and monitors the state of the safety of journalists, including impunity as regards violence against journalists. It mobilizes international support for the International Programme for the Development of Communication (IPDC).

The Knowledge Societies Division (KSD) promotes the application of Information and Communication Technologies (ICTs) to enhance the quality of and access to education, build scientific knowledge, promote open access to scientific research results, and empower local communities. It coordinates UNESCO's overall contribution to the follow-up to the World Summit on the Information Society (WSIS).

Moreover, the sector runs two intergovernmental programmes: the International Programme for the Development of Communication (IPDC), and the Information for All Programme (IFAP).

The sector has adopted the Medium-term Strategy, 2008-2013 in its 34th session; and adopted the approved programme and budget, 2012-2013 in its 36th session, based on 'Overarching objective 5: Building inclusive knowledge societies through information and communication' of the and the 'Major Programme V: Communication and information' of the Approved programme and budget, 2012-2013.

UNESCO's CI encourages the establishment of Category 2 Institutes and Centres to conduct research, facilitate workshops, and facilitate the development of creative solutions for many of the development challenges facing countries around the world.

PUBLICATIONS

(Mostly in English, French and Spanish editions; Arabic, Chinese and Russian versions are also available in many cases.)

Atlas of the World's Languages in Danger of Disappearing (online).

Copyright Bulletin (4 a year).

Education for All Global Monitoring Report

Encyclopedia of Life Support Systems (online).

International Review of Education (4 a year).

International Social Science Journal (4 a year).

Museum International (4 a year).

Nature and Resources (4 a year).

Prospects (review on education, 4 a year).

The New Courier (4 a year).

UNESCO Sources (12 a year).

UNESCO Statistical Yearbook.

UNESCO World Atlas of Gender Equality in Education

World Communication Report.

World Educational Report (every 2 years).

World Heritage Review (4 a year).

World Information Report.

World Science Report (every 2 years).

INTERNATIONAL BUREAU OF EDUCATION (IBE)

CP 199, 1211 Geneva 20, Switzerland
15 route des Morillons, 1218 Grand-Saconnex GE, Switzerland
Telephone: 229177800
E-mail: ibe.administration@unesco.org
Internet: www.ibe.unesco.org

Founded 1925, became an intergovernmental org. in July 1929 and was incorporated into UNESCO in January 1969 as an int. centre of comparative education.

COUNCIL

The Council of the IBE is composed of representatives of 28 member states designated by the General Conference of UNESCO. The Council meets once a year.

Dir: CLEMENTINA ACEDO (Switzerland).

FUNCTIONS

International Conference on Education (irregular).

IBE Documentation Centre: 100,000 vols; 100 current journals; 500,000 research reports on microfiche; 650 titles of archived periodicals from 87 countries.

BUDGET

Financed from the budget of UNESCO.

PUBLICATIONS

Educational Innovation and Information (4 a year, newsletter).

Prospects, international comparative education review (4 a year).

INTERNATIONAL INSTITUTE FOR EDUCATIONAL PLANNING (IIEP)

7–9 rue Eugène Delacroix, 75116 Paris, France
Telephone: 145037700
E-mail: info@iiep.unesco.org
Internet: www.iiep.unesco.org
Regional Office: Agüero 2071, 1425 Buenos Aires, Argentina
Telephone: (11) 4806-9366
E-mail: info@iipe-buenosaires.org.ar

Founded 1963

serves as a world centre for advanced training and research in educational planning. Its purpose is to help all member states of UNESCO in their social and economic development efforts, by enlarging the fund of knowledge about educational planning and the supply of competent experts in this field. Legally and administratively a part of UNESCO, the Institute enjoys intellectual autonomy, and its policies and programme are controlled by its own Governing Board, under special statutes voted by the General Conference of UNESCO.

Chair. of Governing Board: RAYMOND E. WANNER (USA)

Dir: KHALIL MAHSHI (Palestinian Autonomous Area)

Publication: A catalogue of publications, listing 440 titles, is available on request.

UNITED NATIONS UNIVERSITY (UNU)

5–53–70, Jingumae 5-chome, Shibuya-ku, Tokyo 150-8925, Japan
Telephone: (3) 54671212
E-mail: mbox@hq.unu.edu
Internet: www.unu.edu
Office in Europe: c/o UNESCO Bureau 7B 4.06, 1 rue Miollis, 75732 Paris Cedex 15, France
Telephone: 145684642
E-mail: unuoe@unesco.org*Office in North America*: Room DC2-2060, New York, NY 10017, USA
Telephone: (212) 963-6387

The University is an autonomous institution within the UN framework and is sponsored jointly by the UN and UNESCO. It is guaranteed academic freedom by a charter approved by the General Assembly in 1973. Its work began in September 1975. The UNU is governed by a 24-mem. Council who are appointed by the Sec.-Gen. of the UN and the Dir-Gen. of UNESCO to serve for six years. They come from various regions of the world and have diverse academic backgrounds.

The UNU is funded by voluntary contributions from the govts of many countries, bilateral and multilateral development assistance agencies, foundations, and other public and private sources. The UNU receives no funds from the budget of the UN; contributions are made to the UNU Endowment Fund, which yields investment income, and to its operating funds, as well as to specific programmes and projects.

The UNU undertakes problem-oriented, multidisciplinary research on the problems of human survival, development and welfare that are the concern of the UN and its agencies, and works to strengthen research and training capabilities in developing countries. The programme covers the areas of peace and governance, development, environment, and science and technology. Although the UNU has no students or degree courses, it conducts various training activities in association with its programme and provides fellowships for postgraduate scientists and scholars from developing countries.

The research, training and dissemination activities of the UNU are carried out mainly through networks of collaborating institutions and individual scientists and scholars. These include associated institutions, which are universities and research institutes linked with the University under general agreements of cooperation. The programme is coordinated by the University Centre in Tokyo, Japan, and by research and training centres and programmes that are being established by the UNU to deal with long-term problems and needs. The UNU's research and training centres and programmes include: the Maastricht Economic and Social Research Institute on Innovation and Technology in Maastricht, Netherlands; the UNU Food and Nutrition Programme for Human and Social Development, based at Cornell University, USA; the UNU Geothermal Training Programme and UNU fisheries Training Programme, both based in Iceland; the UNU Institute for Environment and Human Security in Bonn, Germany; the UNU Institute for Integrated Management of Material Fluxes and of Resources in Dresden, Germany; the UNU Institute for Natural Resources in Africa in Accra, Ghana, with a mineral resources unit in Lusaka, Zambia; the UNU Institute for Sustainability and Peace in Tokyo, Japan; the UNU Institute for Water, Environment and Health in Ontario, Canada; the UNU Institute of Advanced Studies in Yokohama, Japan; the UNU International Institute for Global Health in Kuala Lumpur, Malaysia; the UNU International Institute for Software Technology in Macao; the UNU International Institute for the Alliance of Civilizations in Barcelona, Spain; the UNU Programme for Biotechnology in Latin America and the Caribbean in Caracas, Venezuela; the UNU Programme on Comparative Regional Integration Studies in Bruges, Belgium; the UNU World Institute for Development Economics Research in Helsinki, Finland.

Rector: Prof. Dr KONRAD OSTERWALDER (Switzerland)
Vice-Rector: Prof. KAZUHIKO TAKEUCHI (Japan)
Vice-Rector: Dr GOVINDAN PARAYIL (Japan)
Vice-Rector in Europe: Dr JAKOB RHYNER (Germany)

UNIVERSITY FOR PEACE

San José, Costa Rica
Telephone: 2205-9000
E-mail: info@upeace.org
Internet: www.upeace.org

Founded 1980

Organisation of UN but financially independent; conducts academic research on all aspects of peace, including disarmament, conflict resolution and mediation, the relation between peace and development, and the effects on peace of migration and refugees; various international and governmental institutions are collaborating with the University; initiated a programme of extensive reforms and expansion in 1999; World Centre for Research and Training in Conflict Resolution established in Bogotá, Colombia, in 2001. First students were admitted in 1985.

Chancellor: Hon. RUTH DREIFUSS (Switzerland)
Rector: JOHN J. MARESCA (Italy/USA)

Library of 20,000 vols
Number of teachers: 71
Number of students: 159

Publications: *Africa Peace and Conflict Review* (online, www.apcj.upeace.org), *Peace and Conflict Monitor* (12 a year, in English, online, www.monitor.upeace.org), *Peace and Conflict Review* (online, www.review.upeace.org).

INTERNATIONAL COUNCIL FOR SCIENCE

International Council for Science (ICSU): 5 rue Auguste Vacquerie, 75116 Paris, France; tel. 145250329; e-mail secretariat@icsu.org; internet www.icsu.org; f. 1931, present name 1998; 3 regional offices in Africa, Asia and the Pacific, Latin America and the Caribbean; 17 interdisciplinary bodies est. with strategic partners; identifies and addresses major issues of importance to science and soc.; promotes participation and interaction among scientists across all disciplines and countries; provides advice to scientific community and govts, civil soc., private sector; organizes confs and a scientific forum; 120 nat. scientific bodies in 140 countries, 31 int. scientific union mems; Pres. Prof. Dr YUAN TSEH LEE (Taiwan); Sec.-Gen. Prof. Dr DAVID BLACK (Australia).

UNIONS FEDERATED TO THE ICSU

International Astronomical Union/ Union Astronomique Internationale: 98 bis blvd Arago, 75014 Paris, France; tel. 143258358; e-mail iau@iap.fr; internet www.iau.org; f. 1919; internationally recognized authority for assigning designations to celestial bodies and surface features on them; defines fundamental astronomical and physical constants; unambiguous astronomical nomenclature; promotes astronomical education and research; organizes scientific meetings, 9 annual int. symposia; 10,894 individual mems in 92 countries, 73 nat. mems; Pres. NORIO KAIFU (Japan); Gen. Sec. Dr THIERRY MONTMERLE (France); publs *Highlights of Astronomy* (every 3 years), *IAU Symposium Proceedings*, *Transactions of the IAU—B*.

International Brain Research Organization (IBRO): c/o Stephanie de La Rochefoucauld, 255 rue St Honoré, 75001 Paris, France; tel. 146479292; e-mail ibro@wanadoo.fr; internet www.ibro.org; f. 1961; promotes and supports neuroscience training and collaborative research around the world; 6 regional cttees; promotes int. collaboration and interchange of scientific information; 56 nat. mem. socs, 12 academic mem. socs, 14 regional and int. mem. socs; Pres. Prof. Dr CARLOS BELMONTE (Spain); Sec.-Gen. Prof. STEN GRILLNER (Sweden); publ. *Neuroscience* (28 a year).

International Geographical Union/ Union Géographique Internationale: c/o Michael Meadows, Private Bag X3, Dept of Environmental and Geographical Science, Univ. of Cape Town, South Lane, Upper Campus, Cape Town, Rondebosch 7701, S Africa; tel. (21) 650-2873; e-mail mmeadows@mweb.co.za; internet www.igu-online.org; f. 1922; encourages study of problems relating to geography; promotes and coordinates research requiring int. cooperation; organizes int. congresses and commissions; 83 mem. countries; Pres. RONALD F. ABLER (USA); Sec.-Gen. and Treas. MICHAEL E. MEADOWS (South Africa); publ. *Bulletin* (1 a year).

International Mathematical Union: Secretariat, Markgrafenstr. 32, 10117 Berlin, Germany; tel. (30) 20372430; e-mail office@mathunion.org; internet www.mathunion.org; f. 1950; promotes int. cooperation in mathematics; supports and assists the Int.

Congress of Mathematicians and other int. scientific meetings or confs; encourages and supports int. activities for devt of mathematical science; 80 mem. countries; Pres. Prof. Dr INGRID DAUBECHIES (USA); Sec. Prof. Dr MARTIN GRÖTSCHEL (Germany).

International Society for Photogrammetry and Remote Sensing/Société Internationale de Photogrammétrie et de Télédétection: c/o Christian Heipke, Leibniz Univ. Hannover, Institute of Photogrammetry and GeoInformation, Nienburger Str. 1, 30167 Hannover, Germany; tel. (511) 7622486; e-mail isprs-sg@ipi.uni-hannover.de; internet www.isprs.org; f. 1910 as Int. Soc. for Photogrammetry, current name adopted 1980; devt of int. cooperation for the advancement of photogrammetry and remote sensing and their applications by initiating and coordinating research; 90 nat. mem. orgs, 11 assoc. mem. socs, 14 regional mem. assocs, 78 sustaining mems; Pres. CHEN JUN (People's Republic of China); Sec.-Gen. CHRISTIAN HEIPKE (Germany); publs *ISPRS International Journal of Geo-Information* (4 a year, online, www.mdpi.com/journal/ijgi), *ISPRS Journal of Photogrammetry and Remote Sensing* (12 a year, online, www.itc.nl/isprsjournal).

International Sociological Association/Asociación Internacional de Sociología/Association Internationale de Sociologie: see under Associations Federated to the ISSC.

International Union for Physical and Engineering Sciences in Medicine: c/o Prof. James Goh, Div. of Bioengineering, Faculty of Engineering, Nat. Univ. of Singapore, Block E3A, 04–15, Seven Engineering Dr., Singapore 117574, Singapore; tel. 65165259; e-mail dosgohj@nus.edu.sg; internet www.iupesm.org; f. 1982; organizes and coordinates the triennial World Congress for Medical Physics and Biomedical Engineering; organizes and coordinates int. meetings or confs for constituent orgs; represents interests of mems in the Int. Council for Science; disseminates, promotes and develops standards of practice in the fields of medical physics and biomedical engineering; 40,000 individual mems, 100 nat. mems; Pres. Prof. HERBERT VOIGT (USA); Sec.-Gen. Prof. JAMES GOH (Singapore); publ. *Health and Technology*.

International Union for Quaternary Research (INQUA): c/o Dr Julius Lejju, Dept of Biology, Mbarara Univ. of Science and Technology, POB 1410, Mbarara, Uganda; tel. (782) 809814; e-mail lejju2002@yahoo.co.uk; internet www.inqua.tcd.ie; f. 1928; 5 comms: coastal and marine processes, humans and the biosphere, palaeoclimates, stratigraphy and chronography, terrestrial processes, deposits and history; provides leadership in different spheres of research; promotes communication and int. collaboration in basic and applied aspects of quaternary research; awards grants; 35 mem. countries; Pres. Dr MARGARET AVERY (South Africa); Sec.-Gen. Dr JULIUS LEJJU (Uganda); publ. *Quaternary International*.

International Union of Anthropological and Ethnological Sciences (IUAES)/Union Internationale des Sciences Anthropologiques et Ethnologiques: see under Associations Federated to the ISSC.

International Union of Basic and Clinical Pharmacology: c/o Dr S. J. Enna, Univ. of Kansas Medical Centre, 3901 Rainbow Blvd, Mail Stop 4016, Kansas City, KS 66160, USA; tel. (913) 588-7533; e-mail iuphar@kumc.edu; internet www.iuphar.org; f. 1959 as Int. Union of Pharmacology (as section of Int. Union of Physiological Sciences), present status 1966, present name 2006; works for devt and public awareness on pharmacological issues; promotes cooperation among socs that represent pharmacology and related disciplines internationally; sponsors and assists int. and regional congresses and meetings; organizes a jt congress of basic and clinical pharmacology every 4 years; 50 nat. mem. socs, 7 regional mem. socs; Pres. Dr PATRICK DU SOUICH (Canada); Sec.-Gen. Prof. Dr S. J. ENNA (USA).

International Union of Biochemistry and Molecular Biology: c/o Prof. Michael P. Walsh, Dept of Biochemistry and Molecular Biology, Univ. of Calgary, 3330 Hospital Dr. NW, Calgary, AB, T2N 4N1, Canada; tel. (403) 220-3021; internet www.iubmb.org; f. 1955; seeks to advance int. molecular life sciences community by promoting interactions; creates networks across all levels; opportunities for young scientists; provides evidence-based advice on public policy; promotes values, standards and ethics of science; sponsors Int. Congress of Biochemistry and Molecular Biology, workshops and holds confs and congresses; 78 mem. adhering bodies, 29 assoc. adhering bodies, 4 assoc. orgs; Pres. Prof. GREG PETSKO (USA); Gen. Sec Prof. MICHAEL P. WALSH (Canada); Treas. Prof. FRANCO BONOMI (Italy); publs *Biochemistry and Molecular Biology Education* (12 a year), *Biofactors* (4 a year), *Biotechnology and Applied Biochemistry* (6 a year), *IUBMB Life* (12 a year), *Molecular Aspects of Medicine* (6 a year), *Trends in Biochemical Sciences* (12 a year).

International Union of Biological Sciences/Union Internationale des Sciences Biologiques: Bâtiment 442, Université Paris-Sud 11, 91405 Orsay Cedex, France; tel. 169155027; e-mail secretariat@iubs.org; internet www.iubs.org; f. 1919; promotes study of biological sciences; initiates, facilitates and coordinates research and other scientific activities for int. interdisciplinary cooperation; ensures discussion and dissemination of the results of cooperative research; supports org. of int. confs and assists in the publication of their reports; 44 ordinary mems, 80 scientific mems; Pres. NILS CHR. STENSETH (Norway); Sec.-Gen. HIROYUKI TAKEDA (Japan); publ. *Biology International* (2 a year).

International Union of Crystallography/Union Internationale de Cristallographie: 2 Abbey Sq., Chester CH1 2HU, UK; tel. (1244) 345431; e-mail execsec@iucr.org; internet www.iucr.org; f. 1947; promotes int. cooperation in crystallography; contributes to the advancement of crystallography in all its aspects, incl. related topics concerning the non-crystalline states; facilitates int. standardization of methods, of units, of nomenclature and of symbols used in crystallography; draws focus to the relations of crystallography to other sciences; 20 comms; maintains online World Directory/Database of Crystallographers; awards the Ewald Prize; 40 mem. countries; Pres. Prof. G. R. DESIRAJU (India); Gen. Sec. and Treas. Prof. L. VAN MEERVELT (Belgium); publs *Acta Crystallographica* (Sections A and B, 6 a year; Sections C, D, E and F, 12 a year), *Journal of Applied Crystallography* (6 a year), *Journal of Synchrotron Radiation* (6 a year).

International Union of Food Science and Technology (IUFoST): POB 61021, Ste 19, 511 Maple Grove Dr., Oakville, ON L6J 6X0, Canada; tel. (905) 815-1926; e-mail secretariat@iufost.org; internet www.iufost.org; f. 1970; encourages int. cooperation and exchange of scientific and technical information among scientists, food technologists and specialists of mem. nations; supporting int. progress in both theoretical and applied areas of food science; advances technology in the processing, manufacturing, preservation, storage and distribution of food products; encourages appropriate education and training in food science and technology; fostering professionalism and professional organization among food scientists and technologists; 65 mem. countries; Pres. Dr RICKEY YADA (Canada); Sec.-Gen. and Treas. JUDITH MEECH (Canada); publs *Food Science and Technology* (6 a year), *The International Review of Food Science and Technology* (1 a year), *Trends in Food Science and Technology* (12 a year), *World of Food Science* (online, www.worldfoodscience.org, jtly with Institute of Food Technologists).

International Union of Forest Research Organizations/Union Internationale des Instituts de Recherches Forestières/Internationaler Verband Forstlicher Forschungsanstalten: Marxergasse 2, 1030 Vienna, Austria; tel. (1) 87701510; e-mail office@iufro.org; internet www.iufro.org; f. 1892; promotes global cooperation in forest-related research; disseminates scientific knowledge to stakeholders and decision-makers; contributes to forest policy and on-the-ground forest management; 700 mem. orgs in 110 countries; Pres. Prof. NIELS ELERS KOCH (Denmark); Exec. Dir ALEXANDER BUCK (Austria); publs *IUFRO Spotlight*, *IUFRO World Series*.

International Union of Geodesy and Geophysics/Union Géodésique et Géophysique Internationale: c/o Karlsruhe Institute of Technology, Geophysical Institute, Hertzstr. 16, Karlsruhe 76187, Germany; tel. (721) 60844494; e-mail secretariat@iugg.org; internet www.iugg.org; f. 1919; promotes and coordinates physical, chemical and mathematical studies of the Earth and its environment in space; initiates, facilitates and coordinates research into those problems of geodesy and geophysics that require int. cooperation; fed. of 8 asscns representing Cryospheric Sciences, Geodesy, Geomagnetism and Aeronomy, Hydrological Sciences, Meteorology and Atmospheric Physics, Physical Sciences of the Oceans, Seismology and Physics of the Earth's Interior, Volcanology and Chemistry of the Earth's Interior, which meet at the Gen. Assemblies of the Union; jt cttees of the various asscns either among themselves or with other unions; organizes scientific meetings and sponsors various permanent services to collect, analyse and publish geophysical data; 69 mem. countries; Pres. HARSH GUPTA (India); Sec.-Gen. ALIK ISMAIL-ZADEH (Germany); publs *IUGG E-Journal*, *IUGG Yearbook*, *Proceedings of Assemblies*.

International Union of Geological Sciences (IUGS)/Union Internationale des Sciences Géologiques: IUGS Secretariat, MS-917, US Geological Survey, Reston, VA 20192, USA; tel. (703) 648-6050; e-mail iugs@usgs.gov; internet www.iugs.org; f. 1961; promotes and encourages study of geological problems of worldwide significance; supports and facilitates int. and interdisciplinary cooperation in the earth sciences; encourages formulation and testing of new geological concepts, models and methodologies; stimulates education and research in geology; improves publ., dissemination and use of geological information internationally; 121 nat. mems; Pres. Prof. Dr ROLAND OBERHANSLI (Germany); Sec.-Gen. Dr IAN LAMBERT (Australia); publ. *Episodes* (4 a year).

International Union of Immunological Societies/Union Internationale des Soci-

étés d'Immunologie: c/o Gerlinde M. Jahn, Vienna Medical Academy, Alser Str. 4, 1090 Vienna, Austria; tel. (1) 40513830; e-mail iuis-central-office@medacad.org; internet www.iuisonline.org; f. 1969; contributes to advancement of immunology in all its aspects; organizes int. cooperation in immunology; promotes communication between brs of immunology and allied subjects; organizes Int. Congresses of Immunology every 3 years; 65 mem. socs; Pres. Prof. Dr STEFEN H. E. KAUFFMANN (Germany); Sec.-Gen. Prof. Dr SEPPO MERI (Finland).

International Union of Microbiological Societies (IUMS)/Union Internationale des Sociétés de Microbiologie: c/o Dr Robert A. Samson, CBS-KNAW Fungal Biodiversity Centre Uppsalalaan 8, 3584 CT Utrecht, Netherlands; tel. (30) 2122600; internet www.iums.org; f. 1927 as Int. Soc. of Microbiology, present status 1982; promotes study of microbiological sciences internationally; initiates and supports research and scientific activities involving int. cooperation; promotes publication of int. study and research; 3 divs: bacteriology and applied microbiology, mycology, virology; organizes int. confs, symposia and meetings; 96 nat. mem. socs, 26 assoc. mem. socs; Pres. GEOFFREY L. SMITH (UK); Sec.-Gen. Dr ROBERT A. SAMSON (Netherlands); publs *Archives of Virology* (12 a year), *Biologicals* (4 a year), *International Journal of Food Microbiology* (26 a year), *International Journal of Systematic and Evolutionary Microbiology* (12 a year, online, ijs.sgmjournals.org), *Journal of Medical and Veterinary Mycology*.

International Union of Nutritional Sciences/Union Internationale des Sciences de la Nutrition: c/o Institute of Nutritional Sciences, Univ. of Vienna, Althanstr. 14/Ebene 5/Spange F, 1090 Vienna, Austria; e-mail info@iuns.org; internet www.iunsweb.org; f. 1946; promotes advancement in nutrition science through int. cooperation; encourages research and devt on nature and determinants of child devt and their implications for programmatic interventions with young children and issues of obesity; encourages communication and collaboration among nutrition scientists; disseminates information in nutritional sciences; addresses issues on food and nutrition problems in developing countries and food safety training for nutritionists; 80 adhering bodies, 15 affiliated bodies; Pres. Prof. Dr IBRAHIM ELMADFA (Austria); Sec.-Gen. Prof. REKIA BELAHSEN (Morocco).

International Union of Physiological Sciences/Union Internationale des Sciences Physiologiques: c/o Walter Boron, David and Inez Myers/Antonio Scarpa Professor of Physiology and Biophysics, Dept of Physiology & Biophysics, Case Western Univ., 10900 Euclid Ave, Cleveland, OH 44106, USA; tel. (216) 368-3400; e-mail iups@case.edu; internet www.iups.org; f. 1953; encourages advancement of physiological sciences; facilitates dissemination of knowledge in the field of physiology; promotes the Int. Congresses of Physiological Sciences; creates awareness about physiology of animals and humans in gen. public; 8 comms dealing with locomotion, circulation/respiration, endocrinology, reproduction and devt, senses, secretion and absorption, neural control, comparative physiology, genomics and biodiversity; 51 nat. mems, 14 assoc. mems, 4 regional mems, 2 affiliated mems; Pres. Prof. DENIS NOBLE (UK); Sec.-Gen. Prof. WALTER BORON (USA); publ. *Physiology* (4 a year, online, physiologyonline.physiology.org).

International Union of Psychological Science: c/o Dr Michel Sabourin, Dept of Psychology, Univ. of Montreal, POB 6128, Downtown Station, Montreal QC H3C 3J7, Canada; tel. (31) 2618288; e-mail info@iupsys.org; internet www.iupsys.net; f. 1889; organizes Int. Congresses of Psychology and other meetings; encourages exchange of ideas and scientific information between psychologists of different countries; assists publication of psychological knowledge; encourages education, training, research and applications of psychology; 82 nat. mems and 20 affiliated org.; Pres. Dr SATHS COOPER (South Africa); Sec.-Gen. Dr ANN WATTS (South Africa); publ. *International Journal of Psychology* (6 a year).

International Union of Pure and Applied Chemistry/Union Internationale de Chimie Pure et Appliquée: POB 13757, Research Triangle Park, NC 27709-3757, USA;104 T. W. Alexander Dr., Bldg 19, Research Triangle Park, NC 27709, USA; tel. (919) 485-8700; e-mail secretariat@iupac.org; internet www.iupac.org; f. 1919; cooperates with other int. orgs that deal with topics of a chemical nature; contributes to the advancement of pure and applied chemistry in all its aspects; authority on chemical nomenclature, terminology, standardized methods for measurement, atomic weights and other critically evaluated data; sponsors int. meetings; 83 mem. countries; Pres. Prof. KAZUYUKI TATSUMI (Japan); Sec.-Gen. Prof. RENÉ DEPLANQUE (Germany); publs *Chemistry International* (6 a year, online, www.iupac.org/publications/ci/index.html), *Pure and Applied Chemistry* (12 a year, online, www.iupac.org/publications/pac).

International Union of Pure and Applied Physics: c/o Institute of Physics, 76 Portland Pl., London, W1B 1NT, UK; tel. (20) 74704849; e-mail admin.iupap@iop.org; internet www.iupap.org; f. 1922; stimulates and fosters int. cooperation in physics; sponsors suitable int. meetings and assists organizing cttees; publishes abstracts of papers and tables of physical constants; promotes int. agreements on use of symbols, units, nomenclature and standards; encourages research and education; 60 affiliated mems, 18 int. commissions, 4 int. assoc. commissions; Pres. CECILIA JARLSKOG (Sweden); Sec.-Gen. STUART PALMER (UK); publ. *Quarterly Reviews of Biophysics*.

International Union of Radio Science/Union Radio-Scientifique Internationale: c/o INTEC, Ghent Univ., Sint-Pietersnieuwstraat 41, 9000 Ghent, Belgium; tel. (9) 2643320; e-mail info@ursi.org; internet www.ursi.org; f. 1919; encourages and coordinates research in the field of radio, telecommunication and electronic sciences; facilitates establishment of common radio measurement techniques and standards; 42 mem. cttees; Pres. Prof. Dr PHIL WILKINSON (Australia); Sec.-Gen. Prof. PAUL LAGASSE (Belgium); publs *Records of General Assemblies* (every 3 years), *The Radio Science Bulletin* (4 a year).

International Union of Soil Science (IUSS)/Association Internationale de la Science du Sol/Internationale Bodenkundliche Gesellschaft: c/o Prof. Alfred Hartemink, Dept of Soil Science, Univ. of Wisconsin, 1525 Observatory Dr., Madison, WI 53706-1299, USA; tel. (118) 378-6559; e-mail hartemink@wisc.edu; internet www.iuss.org; f. 1924 as Int. Soc. of Soil Science, current name adopted 1993; fosters all brs of soil sciences and their applications; supports soil scientists in the research; organizes meetings, confs and the World Congress of Soil Sciences; 55,000 mems in 70 countries; Pres. JAE YANG (Korea); Sec.-Gen. Prof. ALFRED HARTEMINK (Netherlands).

International Union of the History and Philosophy of Science: c/o Div. of the History of Science and Technology, Nat. Hellenic Research Foundation, 48 Vas. Constantinou av, 11635 Athens, Greece; f. 1956; establishes and promotes int. contacts among historians and philosophers of science and scientists who are interested in the history and problems of discipline; collects documents useful for devt of history and philosophy of science; encourages and sustains research and study of problems in these fields; organizes and supports int. confs, symposia and scientific exchange; organizes int. congress every 4 years; 49 nat. mems, 22 scientific commissions, 5 inter-union commissions, 3 scientific sections; Pres. EFTHYMIOS NICOLAIDIS; Sec.-Gen. CATHERINE JAMI.

International Union of Theoretical and Applied Mechanics/Union Internationale de Mécanique Théorique et Appliquée: c/o Centre de Mathématiques et de Leurs Applications, Ecole Normale Supérieure de Cachan, 94235 Cachan, France; tel. 147405900; e-mail sg@iutam.net; internet www.iutam.net; f. 1946; promotes devt of mechanics, theoretical and applied, as br. of science; works to form link between persons and orgs engaged in scientific work in all brs of theoretical and applied mechanics and related sciences; organizes int. congresses of theoretical and applied mechanics and other int. meetings; 450 mems representing 55 countries and 18 affiliated orgs; Pres. Prof. TIMOTHY J. PEDLEY (UK); Sec.-Gen. Prof. FREDERIC DIAS (France); publs *Proceedings of IUTAM World Congress* (every 4 years), *Proceedings of the International Congresses on Theoretical and Applied Mechanics (ICTAM)*.

International Union of Toxicology: 1821 Michael Faraday Dr., Suite 300, Reston, VA 20190, USA; tel. (703) 438-3103; e-mail iutoxhq@iutox.org; internet www.iutox.org; f. 1980; fosters int. scientific cooperation among toxicologists and promotes global acquisition, dissemination and use of knowledge in the science of toxicology; ensures continued training and devt of toxicologists worldwide; organizes Int. Congress on Toxicology every 3 years; sponsors Congresses on Toxicology in developing countries every 3 years; 20,000 individual mems, 51 affiliated socs; Pres. Dr DANIEL ACOSTA, Jr (USA); Sec.-Gen. Prof. Dr ELAINE FAUSTMAN (USA).

INTERDISCIPLINARY BODIES

To plan and organize international scientific initiatives and offer advice in a policy context on specific themes, ICSU has set up following interdisciplinary bodies:

Committee on Data for Science and Technology: 5 rue Auguste Vacquerie, 75016 Paris, France; tel. 145250496; e-mail codata@dial.oleane.com; internet www.codata.org; f. 1966; promotes improvement in quality, reliability, management and accessibility of scientific data, incl. quantitative information on the properties and behaviour of matter, and other experimental and observational data; considers data access and intellectual property issues; sponsors biennial CODATA Int. Conf. on data and task groups, working groups, comms and other groups addressing specific data issues; organizes specialist meetings and publications; 18 nat. mems, 2 assoc. mems, 16 scientific union mems; Pres. Prof. HUADONG GUO (China); Sec.-Gen. Dr ROBERT CHEN (USA); publs *Biological Sciences Bulletin*, *Computer Data Handling Bulletin*, *Data Science Journal*, *Directory Chapters Bulletin*, *Environmental*

Science Bulletin, Geological Sciences Bulletin, International Compendium of Numerical Data Projects, International Conference Proceedings, Materials Properties Bulletin, Physical Constants and Properties Bulletin, Thermodynamics Bulletin.

Committee on Space Research: c/o CNES, 2 pl. Maurice Quentin, 75039 Paris Cedex 01, France; tel. 144767510; e-mail cospar@cosparhq.cnes.fr; internet cosparhq.cnes.fr; f. 1958; promotes scientific research in space on int. level, with emphasis on exchange of results, information and opinions; organizes scientific assemblies every 2 years; capacity building workshops; advises the UN and other int. orgs on space research matters and on the assessment of scientific issues; prepares scientific and technical standards related to space research; 46 mem. countries, 13 int. scientific unions; Pres. Prof. G. F. BIGNANI (Italy); Exec. Dir Dr J.-L. FELLOUS; publs *Advances in Space Research, Space Research Today* (3 a year).

ICSU World Data System: c/o NICT, 4-2-1 Nukui-kitamachi, Koganei, Tokyo 184-8795, Japan; tel. (4) 23276395; e-mail ipo@icsu-wds.org; internet www.icsu-wds.org; f. 2008 by merger of ICSU World Data Centres and Fed. of Astronomical and Geophysical Data Analysis Service; enables universal and equitable access to scientific data, data services, products and information; ensures long-term data stewardship; fosters compliance to agreed-upon data standards and conventions; provides mechanisms to facilitate and improve access to data and data products; 49 mem. orgs; Chair. Prof. Dr BERNARD MINSTER (USA); Exec. Dir Dr MUSTAPHA MOKRANE.

Scientific Committee on Antarctic Research: Scott Polar Research Institute, Lensfield Rd, Cambridge CB2 1ER, UK; tel. (1223) 336550; e-mail info@scar.org; internet www.scar.org; f. 1958; initiates, promotes and coordinates scientific research in Antarctica; promotes int. cooperation in scientific research and education in the Antarctic; holds biennial conf.; facilitates free and unrestricted access to Antarctic scientific data and information; provides scientific advice to the Antarctic Treaty Consultative Meetings and other orgs on issues of science and conservation affecting management of Antarctica and the Southern Ocean; 31 full mems (nat. acads of science and scientific unions), 9 union mems, 6 assoc. mems; Pres. Prof. JERÓNIMO LÓPEZ-MARTÍNEZ (Spain); Exec. Dir Dr MICHAEL SPARROW (UK); publ. *SCAR Report* (irregular).

Scientific Committee on Frequency Allocations for Radio Astronomy and Space Science/Comité Scientifique pour l'Allocation des Fréquences à la Radio Astronomie et la Recherche Spatiale: c/o Observatoire de Paris, GEPI, 5 place Jules Janssen, 92195 Meudon, France; tel. 145077731; e-mail iucafchair@iucaf.org; internet www.iucaf.org; f. 1960, fmrly Inter-Union Commission on the Allocation of Frequencies for Space Research and Radio Astronomy (IUCAF); sponsored by Int. Astronomical Union, Int. Union of Radio Science, Cttee on Space Research; studies and coordinates requirements for frequency bands and radio frequency protection for research in the fields of radio astronomy, earth exploration and space science and make their requirements known to the appropriate frequency-allocation authorities; 10 mems; Chair. MASATOSHI OHISHI (Japan); Vice-Chair. HARVEY S. LISZT (USA).

Scientific Committee on Oceanic Research: Robinson Hall, College of Earth, Ocean, and Environment, Univ. of Delaware, Newark, DE 19716, USA; tel. (302) 831-7011; e-mail secretariat@scor-int.org; internet www.scor-int.org; f. 1957; promotes int. cooperation in planning and conducting oceanographic research; advances int. scientific activity in all brs of oceanic research; library of 300 vols; Pres. Prof. PETER BURKILL (UK); Exec. Dir Dr ED URBAN; Sec. Dr MARY H. FEELEY (USA); publ. *SCOR Proceedings* (1 a year).

Scientific Committee on Problems of the Environment: c/o UNESCO, Bât. 7, Room 3.16, 1 rue Miollis, 75015 Paris, Cedex 15, France; tel. 145684571; e-mail secretariat@scopenvironment.org; internet www.scopenvironment.org; f. 1969; identifies and provides scientific analyses of emerging environmental challenges and opportunities caused by or impacting on humans and environment; 40 nat. cttees, 22 int. unions; Pres. Prof. JON SAMSETH (Norway); Sec.-Gen. Prof. JACK SADDLER (Canada); publs *Environmental Development* (4 a year), *UNESCO-SCOPE-UNEP Policy Briefs Series*.

Scientific Committee on Solar-Terrestrial Physics: c/o Centre for Research in Earth and Space Science, York Univ., Petrie Science and Engineering Bldg, 4700 Keele St, Toronto, ON M3J 1P3, Canada; tel. (416) 736-2100; internet www.yorku.ca/scostep; f. 1966 as an Inter-Union Comm. on Solar-Terrestrial Physics, present status 1978; organizes and conducts int. solar-terrestrial physics programmes in cooperation with other ICSU bodies; promotes int. interdisciplinary programmes; provides advice and defines data relating to these programmes to be exchanged through the World Data Centres; 400 mems; Pres. Prof. Dr NATCHIMUTHUK GOPALSWAMY (USA); Scientific Sec. Dr MARIANNA G. SHEPHERD (Canada).

INTERNATIONAL COUNCIL FOR PHILOSOPHY AND HUMANISTIC STUDIES

International Council for Philosophy and Humanistic Studies (ICPHS)/Conseil International de la Philosophie et des Sciences Humaines: Maison de l'UNESCO, 1 rue Miollis, 75732 Paris, Cedex 15, France; tel. 145684885; e-mail cipsh@unesco.org; internet www.cipsh.org; f. 1949; coordinates works of researchers and intellectuals in fields of philosophy, human sciences and related disciplines; strengthens endogenous capacities of scientific research and cultural devt in least developed countries; sustains int. mobility of researchers and dissemination of leading int. instruments of scientific information; protects tangible and intangible heritage of mankind; 1,600 federated scientific asscns through 15 int. bodies; Pres. CHA IN-SUK (Korea); Sec.-Gen. MAURICE AYMARD (France); publ. *Diogene* (4 a year, in Arabic, English, French, Spanish).

UNIONS FEDERATED TO THE ICPHS

International Academic Union/Union Académique Internationale: Palace of Academy, 1 rue Ducale, 1000 Brussels, Belgium; tel. (2) 5502200; e-mail info@uai-iua.org; internet www.uai-iua.org; f. 1919; promotes cooperation between nat. acads and instns concerned with the field of human and social sciences; safeguards and advances human and social sciences at nat. and int. level; promotes int. cooperation through collective research in philology, archaeology, history, social sciences and humanities in general; nat. acads from 60 countries; Pres. JANUSZ K. KOZLOWSKI (Poland); Gen. Sec. HERVÉ HASQUIN (Belgium); publs *Archivum Latinitatis Medii Aevi* (every 2 years), *Compte rendu (de la session annuelle) du Comité* (1 a year), *Novum Glossarium* (every 2 years).

International Association for the History of Religions/Association Internationale pour l'Histoire des Religions: c/o Prof. Tim Jensen, Study of Religions, Univ. of Southern Denmark, Campusvej 55, 5230 Odense M, Denmark; tel. 65-50-33-15; e-mail t.jensen@sdu.dk; internet www.iahr.dk; f. 1950; promotes study of the history of religions through int. collaboration of scholars; encourages production of publs; holds world congresses every 5 years; sponsors regional and spec. confs; 40 nat. mems, 5 regional mem. assocs and socs, 4 affiliated socs; Pres. Prof. ROSALIND I. J. HACKETT (USA); Gen. Sec. Prof. TIM JENSEN (Denmark); publs *IAHR E-Bulletin, NVMEN: International Review for the History of Religions* (5 a year).

International Committee for the History of Art/Comité International d'Histoire de l'Art: c/o Thierry Dufrêne, Institut national d'histoire de l'art, 2 rue Vivienne, 75084 Paris Cedex 02, France; tel. 147038584; e-mail ciha@inha.fr; internet www.ciha-arthistory.org; f. 1930; develops historical and methodological study of artistic activities and productions; ensures permanent links between art historians of all countries; stimulates and coordinates dissemination of information about research; organizes confs, publications, research projects; studies means of improving methods of teaching and research and of increasing research resources for art historians; mems in 34 countries; Pres. ULRICH GROSSMANN (Germany); Scientific Sec. Prof. THIERRY DUFRÊNE (France); Treas. and Admin. Sec. Prof. PETER SCHNEEMANN (Switzerland); publ. *Bibliography of the History of Art* (CD-ROM, 4 a year).

International Committee of Historical Sciences/Comité International des Sci-

ences Historiques: c/o Pascal Cauchy, Centre d'histoire-Sciences Po, 27 rue St Guillaume, 75005 Paris, France; tel. 140462790; e-mail pascal.cauchy@sciences-po.fr; internet www.cish.org; f. 1926; encourages advancement of historical sciences through int. coordination; organizes int. congress every 5 years; 91 mems in 53 countries (incl. 50 nat. cttees, 32 int. affiliated orgs, 9 internal cttees); Pres. Prof. MARJATTA HIETALA (Finland); Sec.-Gen. Prof. ROBERT FRANK (France); publs *Bibliographie Internationale des Sciences Historiques*, *Bulletin d'Information*.

International Federation for Modern Languages and Literatures/Fédération Internationale des Langues et Littératures Modernes: c/o Anders Pettersson, Gröna Gatan 37, 414 54 Göteborg, Sweden; tel. (90) 786-5797; e-mail anders.pettersson@littvet.umu.se; internet www.fillm.ulg.ac.be; f. 1928 as Comm. Internationale d'Histoire Littéraire Moderne, current name and status 1951; promotes, develops and encourages scholarly study of modern languages and literatures; organizes triennial int. congress; rep. of mem. asscns on int. platform; promotes establishment of permanent contact between historians of literature; develops facilities for work of historians; 9 mem. asscns in 85 countries; Pres. Prof. ROGER D. SELL (Finland); Sec.-Gen. Prof. ANDERS PETTERSSON (Sweden).

International Federation of Philosophical Societies/Fédération Internationale des Sociétés de Philosophie: c/o Dermot Moran, Pres. School of Philosophy, Univ. College Dublin, Dublin, 4, Ireland; tel. (765) 494-4285(01) 7168123; e-mail dermot.moran@ucd.ie; internet www.fisp.org; f. 1948; develops professional relations between philosophers of all countries; fosters contacts between instns, socs and periodical publs dedicated to philosophy; collects documentation useful for devt of philosophical studies; sponsors World Congress every 5 years, int. confs and other philosophical meetings; 90 nat. mem. socs, 35 int. mem. socs; Pres. DERMOT MORAN (Ireland); Sec.-Gen. LUCA MARIA SCARANTINO (Italy); Admin. Sec. EMILIYA IVANOVA.

International Federation of the Societies of Classical Studies/Fédération Internationale des Associations d'Études Classiques: c/o Prof. Paul Schubert, 7 rue des Beaux-Arts, 2000 Neuchatel, Switzerland; e-mail paul.schubert@unige.ch; internet www.fiecnet.org; f. 1948; promotes education of all types on the ancient civilizations of Greece and Rome; groups main asscns proposing advancement of education in Latin or Greek studies; organizes int. congresses; 81 mem. asscns; Pres. Prof. AVERIL CAMERON (UK); Sec.-Gen. Prof. PAUL SCHUBERT (Switzerland); publ. *L'Année Philologique* (bibliography, 1 a year).

International Musicological Society/Internationale Gesellschaft für Musikwissenschaft/Sociedad Internacional de Musicología/Société Internationale de Musicologie: POB 1561, 4001 Basel, Switzerland; tel. 449231022; e-mail dorothea.baumann@ims-online.ch; internet www.ims-online.ch; f. 1927; promotes musicological research, encourages study and coordinates work of musicologists worldwide; organizes int. congress every 5 years, intercongressional symposia, int. study groups, regional asscns; 52 mem. countries, 1,000 individual mems; Pres. Prof. Dr DINKO FABRIS (Italy); Sec.-Gen. Dr DOROTHEA BAUMANN (Switzerland); publs *Acta Musicologica* (2 a year, online, www.acta-musicologica.net), *Catalogus Musicus* (irregular), *Documenta Musicologica* (irregular), *International Inventory of Musical Sources* (RISM, print and online, www.rism.info), *International Repertory of Musical Iconography* (RIDIM, online, www.ridim.org), *International Repertory of Music Literature* (RILM, online, www.rilm.org), *Répertoire International de la Presse Musicale* (RIPM, print and online, www.ripm.org).

International Union of Anthropological and Ethnological Sciences (IUAES)/Union Internationale des Sciences Anthropologiques et Ethnologiques: see under Unions Federated to the ISSC.

International Union of the History and Philosophy of Science: see under Unions Federated to the ICSU.

International Union of the Prehistoric and Protohistoric Sciences/Union Internationale des Sciences Préhistoriques et Protohistoriques: c/o Prof. Luiz Oosterbeek, Instituto Politécnico de Tomar, Ave Dr Cândido Madureira 13, 2300-531 Tomar, Portugal; tel. 249346363; e-mail secretary@uispp.org; internet www.uispp.org; f. 1931; promotes congresses and scientific work in the fields of pre- and protohistory; promotes pluri-disciplinary and inter-institutional collaborations through the regional and thematic scientific comms, affiliated orgs and scientific instns; 40,000 mems, 120 mem. countries; Pres. Prof. JEAN BOURGEOIS (Belgium); Sec.-Gen. Prof. LUIZ OOSTERBEEK (Portugal); publs *Prähistorische Bronzefunde*, *Proceedings of the XV World Congress, Lisbon*.

Permanent International Committee of Linguists/Comité International Permanent des Linguistes: c/o Prof. Dr P. G. J. van Sterkenburg, POB 3023, 2301 DA Leiden, Netherlands; tel. (71) 5211552; e-mail pvansterkenburg@planet.nl; internet www.ciplnet.com; f. 1928; assists in devt of linguistic science; furthers linguistic research and encourages int. cooperation; organizes quintannual int. congresses; 39 mem. countries; Pres. Prof. N. VINCENT (UK); Sec.-Gen. Prof. P. G. J. VAN STERKENBURG (Netherlands); publ. *Linguistic Bibliography* (1 a year, online, www.linguisticbibliography.com/public).

INTERNATIONAL SOCIAL SCIENCE COUNCIL

International Social Science Council (ISSC)/Conseil International des Sciences Sociales/Consejo Internacional de las Ciencias Sociales: UNESCO House, 1 rue Miollis, 75732 Paris Cedex 15, France; tel. 145684860; e-mail issc@worldsocialscience.org; internet www.worldsocialscience.org; f. 1952; advances social sciences worldwide and their application to the major problems of the world; encourages cooperation at int. level between specialists in the social sciences; provides central clearing house for collection, interpretation, analysis and dissemination of data on social science resources, their availability for research and their impact on soc.; broadens interdisciplinary collaboration; works to link social science knowledge effectively to public policies and local needs; 14 mem. asscns and unions, 34 mem. orgs, 13 assoc. mems; Pres. Dr OLIVE SHISANA (South Africa); Exec. Dir Dr HEIDE HACKMANN (Netherlands); publ. *e-bulletin*.

ASSOCIATIONS FEDERATED TO THE ISSC

International Association of Legal Sciences/Association Internationale des Sciences Juridiques: c/o CISS/UNESCO, 1 rue Miollis, 75015 Paris, France; tel. 145684858; e-mail info@aisj-ials.org; internet aisj-ials.org; f. 1950 as Int. Cttee of Comparative Law, present name 1955; promotes mutual knowledge and understanding of nations; increases learning by encouraging worldwide study of foreign legal systems and comparative method in legal science; governed by Int. Cttee of Comparative Law; 30 nat. cttees, 10 assoc. mems; Pres. Prof. ERGUN ÖZSUNAY (Turkey); Sec.-Gen. MEIR LEKER (France).

International Economic Association/Association Internationale des Sciences Economiques: c/o Institut de Anàlisis Econòmico-CSIC, Campus de la UAB, 08193 Barcelona, Spain; tel. 935806612; e-mail iea@iea-world.org; internet www.iea-world.com; f. 1950; promotes int. collaboration for advancement of economic knowledge; develops personal contacts between economists; encourages provision of means for dissemination of economic knowledge; 62 mem. asscns; Pres. JOSEPH STIGLITZ (USA); Sec.-Gen. JOAN ESTEBAN (Spain).

International Geographical Union/Union Géographique Internationale: see under Unions Federated to the ICSU.

International Institute of Administrative Sciences/Institut International des Sciences Administratives: 1 rue Defacqz, Bte 11, 1000 Brussels, Belgium; tel. (2) 5360880; e-mail info@iias-iisa.org; internet www.iias-iisa.org; f. 1930; research and programmes for improving admin. law and practices and for technical assistance; consultative status with ECOSOC, ILO and UNESCO; provides worldwide platform for exchanges between practitioners and academics; improves organization and operation of public admin.; develops effective admin. methods and techniques; contributes to governance progress within the nat. and int. admins; holds int. congresses; 130 mems, 36 mem. states, 29 nat. sections, 4 int. govt orgs, 61 corporate mems; Pres. Prof. Dr GEERT BOUCKAERT (Belgium); Dir-Gen. ROLET LORETAN (Switzerland); publ. *International Review of Administrative Sciences/Revue internationale des sciences administratives* (4 a year, in Chinese, English, French, Spanish).

International Peace Research Association/Association Internationale de Recherche pour la Paix: c/o Katuya Kodama, Mie Univ., 1577 Kurimamachiya-cho, Tsu City Mie Prefecture, 514-8507, Japan; tel. (59) 2315588; e-mail kodama@kni.biglobe.ne.jp; internet ipra-peace.com; f. 1964; advances interdisciplinary research into conditions of peace and causes of war and other forms of violence; promotes nat. and int. studies and teaching relating to the pursuit of world peace; facilitates contacts between scholars and educators throughout the world; encourages int. dissemination of results of research in the field and of information on significant devt of peace research; organizes int. and interdisciplinary confs; 5 regional peace research orgs; 1,300 mems in 90 countries, 400 corporate, 10 nat. and regional asscns; Sec.-Gen. JAKE LYNCH (Australia); Sec.-Gen. KATUYA KODAMA (Japan); publs *International Journal of Peace Studies*, *Journal of Peace Education*.

International Political Science Association (IPSA)/Association Internationale de Science Politique: 1590 ave Docteur-Penfield, Bureau 331, Montreal, QC H3G 1C5, Canada; tel. (514) 848-8717; e-mail info@ipsa.org; internet www.ipsa.org; f. 1949; promotes internationally planned research and scholarly collaboration, organizes int. confs, symposia, triennial world congresses; provides documentary and reference services; holds World Congresses of Political Science every second year; 3,500 individual mems, nat. asscns in 53 countries, 120 assoc. mems, 50 affiliated asscns; Pres. Prof. Dr HELEN V. MILNER (USA); Sec.-Gen. Prof. Dr GUY LACHAPELLE (Canada); publs *International Political Science Abstracts* (6 a year), *International Political Science Review* (5 a year), *Participation* (irregular).

International Sociological Association/Asociación Internacional de Sociología/Association Internationale de Sociologie: Faculty of Political Sciences and Sociology, Univ. Complutense, 28223 Madrid, Spain; tel. 913527650; e-mail isa@isa-sociology.org; internet www.isa-sociology.org; f. 1949; promotes sociological research; develops personal contacts among the sociologists of all countries and ensures the exchange of sociological information; 53 research cttees on variety of sociological topics; holds World Congresses every 4 years; ISA Forum every 4 years; 5,000 individual mems from 167 countries, 150 collective mems; Pres. Prof. Dr MICHAEL BURAWOY (USA); Exec. Sec. Dr IZABELA BARLINSKA (Poland); publs *Current Sociology / Sociologie Contemporaine* (6 a year), *e-Bulletin* (3 a year), *International Sociology* (6 a year).

International Union for the Scientific Study of Population/Unión Internacional para el Estudio Científico de la Población/Union Internationale pour l'Étude Scientifique de la Population: 3–5 rue Nicolas, 75980, Paris Cedex 20, France; tel. 156062173; e-mail iussp@iussp.org; internet www.iussp.org; f. 1928, reconstituted 1947; promotes science of demography; organizes scientific meetings, confs and training activities; advances the progress of quantitative and qualitative demography as a science; 1,730 mems, 622 student assocs from 128 countries; Pres. Dr PETER MCDONALD (Australia); Exec. Dir MARY ELLEN ZUPPAN (France); Sec.-Gen. and Treas. Dr EMILY GRUNDY (UK); publ. *Genus* (3 a year).

International Union of Anthropological and Ethnological Sciences (IUAES)/Union Internationale des Sciences Anthropologiques et Ethnologiques: c/o Junji Koizumi, Dept of Anthropology, Faculty of Human Sciences, Osaka Univ., 1–2 Yamadaoka, Suita, Osaka 565-0871, Japan; tel. (6) 68798085; e-mail iuaes@glocol.osaka-u.ac.jp; internet www.iuaes.org; f. 1948; develops int. scientific and professional cooperation in the fields of anthropology and ethnology; fosters devt of scientific and professional instns at int. and regional level; develops appropriate roles for anthropology and ethnology in int. interdisciplinary scientific endeavours; organizes World Congress every 5 years; sponsors Inter-Congresses, seminars and symposia; 20 nat., 80 institutional, 200 individuals worldwide, 20 honorary mems; Pres. Prof. Dr PETER J. M. NAS (Netherlands); Sec.-Gen. Prof. Dr JUNJI KOIZUMI (Japan).

International Union of Psychological Science (IUPsyS): see under Unions Federated to the ICSU.

World Association for Public Opinion Research: c/o UNL Gallup Research Center, Univ. of Nebraska-Lincoln, 201 N 13th St, Lincoln, NE 68588-0242, USA; tel. (402) 472-7720; internet wapor.org; f. 1947; establishes and promotes contacts between persons in the field of survey research on opinions, attitudes and behaviour of people worldwide; advances the use of scientific survey research in nat. and int. affairs; 450 mems in 60 countries; Pres. Dr ALEJANDRO MORENO (Mexico); Gen. Sec. Prof. Dr ALLAN L. MCCUTCHEON; publ. *International Journal of Public Opinion Research* (4 a year).

World Federation for Mental Health/Fédération Mondiale pour la Santé Mentale: POB 807, Occoquan, VA 22125, USA; tel. (703) 494-6515; e-mail info@wfmh.com; internet www.wfmh.org; f. 1948; promotes advancement of mental health awareness, prevention of mental disorders, advocacy and best practice recovery focused interventions worldwide; works with ECOSOC, UNESCO, WHO and other agencies of the UN to promote mental health; helps other voluntary asscns in the improvement of mental health services; 1,000 individual mems, affiliated orgs, voting orgs; Pres. DEBORAH WAN (Hong Kong); Dir for Admin. Dr DEBORAH MAGUIRE (USA).

INTERNATIONAL ASSOCIATION OF UNIVERSITIES (IAU)

UNESCO House, 1 rue Miollis, 75732 Paris Cedex 15, France; tel. 145684800; e-mail iau@iau-aiu.net; internet www.iau-aiu.net; f. 1950; provides centre of cooperation at int. level among univs and similar instns of higher education of all countries; 628 mems (incl. 601 mem. instns and 27 mem. orgs), 12 affiliates, 11 assocs

Organization

GENERAL CONFERENCE

Composed of the full and assoc. mems. Meets every 5 years. Discusses topics of importance for the future of univ. education, determines gen. policy and elects the Pres. and mems of the Admin. Board. Fourteenth Gen. Conference was held in San Juan, Puerto Rico, in 2012.

ADMINISTRATIVE BOARD

Chaired by the Pres. of the IAU, and composed of 20 elected and 2 ex officio members as follows: 18 executive heads of member institutions and two heads of member organizations, the immediate past President and the Secretary-General. Meets annually, ensures that decisions of the Gen. Conference are implemented and guides the work of the Int. Univs Bureau.

Pres.: JUAN RAMÓN DE LA FUENTE (Former Rector, National Autonomous University of Mexico).

Sec.-Gen. and Exec. Dir EVA EGRON-POLAK

INTERNATIONAL UNIVERSITIES BUREAU (IUB)

The IUB, created in 1949, provides the Permanent Secretariat for the IAU. It is the principal instrument for the execution of the activities of the IAU. Its main tasks include monitoring and analysing trends in higher education and research at global level, and facilitating and promoting the exchange of information, experience and ideas, of students, teachers, researchers and administrators, and of publications and material for teaching and research.

Exec. Dir (Ex-Officio) EVA EGRON-POLAK.

Principal Activities

Information

Under a formal Agreement with UNESCO, the IAU operates a joint IAU/UNESCO Information Centre on Higher Education at its Int. Univs Bureau. The Centre holds 40,000 vols and a large colln of unpublished materials; it has subscriptions to 300 current specialized periodicals and maintains a colln of 4,000 prospectuses of higher education instns, as well as conference reports, occasional papers, CD-ROMs, etc. The Centre was fully computerized in 1989, and all holdings were subsequently catalogued in the Centre's own database (IAUDOC). All references can be found in the int. bibliographical database (HEDBIB), accessible via the IAU website. The database links to nat. and int. information centres and data networks. The IAU acts as the coordinating agency for the World Academic Database (WAD).

Studies, Research and Meetings

The IAU coordinates and carries out studies and research on issues of higher education and higher education policies that are either common to instns and systems worldwide, or where a comparative analysis between different situations and approaches is of particular benefit to higher education instns. Conferences, symposia, colloquia, seminars, round tables and workshops provide an int. forum for the discussion of topics of common concern to higher education leaders and specialists.

Cooperation

The IAU provides an important clearing-house function to its mems for academic exchange and cooperation. The IAU has adopted the *Kyoto Declaration and Agenda for Sustainable Development 1993*, to promote and support univ. cooperation; the *Durban Declaration on Internationalization 2000* to ensure that higher education instns seize the initiative in the process of internationalization rather than reacting to the forces of globalization and the market; and the *São Paolo Declaration on Information and Communication Technologies (ICTs) 2004*, to act as a platform for information-sharing in regard to the use of ICTs in higher education.

SELECTED PUBLICATIONS

Guide to Higher Education in Africa (irregular).

Higher Education Policy (4 a year, English).

IAU Horizons (3 a year)

International Bibliographic Database on Higher Education (HEDBIB)

International Handbook of Universities (every 2 years, English).

Issues in Higher Education (3 or 4 a year, English).

World Academic Database (WAD)(CD-ROM; 1 a year, English and French).

World List of Universities and Other Institutions of Higher Education (every 2 years, English and French).

OTHER INTERNATIONAL ORGANIZATIONS

General

Academy of Europe/Academia Europaea: 4th Fl., 21 Albemarle St, London W1S 4HS, UK; tel. (20) 74953717; internet www.acadeuro.org; f. 1988; encourages European activities in scholarship and the undertaking of ind. studies on matters of European importance; makes recommendations to nat. govts and int. agencies concerning matters affecting science, scholarship and academic life in Europe; encourages interdisciplinary and int. research in all areas of learning; holds meetings, symposia, study groups; 3,000 mems; Pres. Prof. LARS WALLOE (Norway); Exec. Sec. Dr DAVID COATES; publs *Academia Europaea, Year Book, European Review* (4 a year).

European Academy of Sciences and Arts/Academia Scientiarum et Artium Europaea: St Peter-Bezirk 10, 5020 Salzburg, Austria; tel. (662) 841345; e-mail office@euro-acad.eu; internet www.euro-acad.eu; f. 1990; promotes interdisciplinary discussion across specialist areas, ideologies and scientific cultures; encourages transnational dialogue and visionary devts of new scientific knowledge and academic thinking; disseminates scientific information; implements major multinational projects; 1,200 mems; Pres. Prof. Dr FELIX UNGER; Sec. MARIA ANNA EDER.

International Studies Association: 324 Social Sciences, Univ. of Arizona, Tucson, AZ 85721, USA; tel. (520) 477-2050; e-mail isa@isanet.org; internet www.isanet.org; f. 1959; promotes research and cooperation into int. studies; provides opportunities for communications among educators, researchers and practitioners to share intellectual interests; improves teaching and dissemination of ideas, concepts, methods, information in the field of int. studies; assoc. mem. of Int. Social Science Council; 5,800 mems in 80 countries; Pres. ETEL SOLINGEN (USA); Exec. Dir Dr THOMAS J. VOLGY (USA); publs *Foreign Policy Analysis* (4 a year), *International Interactions* (4 a year), *International Political Sociology* (4 a year), *International Studies Perspectives* (4 a year), *International Studies Quarterly* (4 a year), *International Studies Review* (4 a year).

Agriculture and Veterinary Science

Food and Agriculture Organization of the United Nations/Organisation des Nations Unies pour l'Alimentation et l'Agriculture: Viale delle Terme di Caracalla, 00153 Rome RM, Italy; tel. 657051; e-mail fao-hq@fao.org; internet www.fao.org; f. 1945; raises level of nutrition and living standards, improves production and distribution of food and agricultural products, and improves the conditions of rural population; improves production in all areas of agriculture, forestry and fisheries; promotes conservation and management of plant and animal genetic resources; increases investment in agriculture through irrigation, fertilizer, seed and other rural devt schemes; collects, analyses and disseminates information needed by govts and int. bodies; making available technical data; works towards greater world food security by ensuring production of adequate food supplies, maximizing stability in the flow of supplies, and securing access to available supplies for those who need them; composed of 7 depts: agriculture and consumer protection, economic and social devt, fisheries and aquaculture, forestry, corporate services, human resources and finance, natural resources management and environment, technical cooperation; regional offices in 130 countries; 191 mem. nations, 2 assoc. mems, 1 mem. org. (EU); library: FAO David Lubin Memorial Library of 1m. vols and 13,000 journals, 1,450 ejournals; Chair. LUC GUYAU (France); Dir-Gen. Dr JOSÉ GRAZIANO DA SILVA (Brazil); publs *Animal Health and Fertilizers, Commodity Review and Outlook, FAO Quarterly Bulletin of Statistics, Food and Agricultural Legislation* (2 a year), *Forestry and Fisheries, Plant Protection Bulletin, Rural Development* (1 a year), *State of the World's Forests* (every 2 years), *The State of Agricultural Commodity Markets* (every 2 years), *The State of Food and Agriculture* (1 a year), *The State of Food Insecurity in the World, The State of World Fisheries and Aquaculture* (online), *Unasylva* (4 a year), *World Animal Review* (4 a year), *Yearbooks of Trade and Production in Agriculture.*

OTHER ORGANIZATIONS

Africa Rice Centre/Centre du Riz pour l'Afrique (ADRAO): 01 B.P. 2551 Bouaké 01, Côte d'Ivoire; tel. 64-18-13-13; internet www.africarice.org; f. 1971 as West Africa Rice Devt Asscn (WARDA), current name adopted 2009; intergovernmental asscn of African mem. countries; promotes research, devt and partnership activities to increase productivity and profitability of the rice sector in ways that ensure sustainability of the farming environment; supported by Consultative Group on Int. Agricultural Research (CGIAR); 25 mem. countries; library of 16,442 monographs, 1,523 periodicals; Chair. PETER MATLON (USA); Dir-Gen. Dr ADAMA TRAORE.

Bioversity International: Via dei Tre Denari 472/a, 00057 Maccarese, Rome RM, Italy; tel. 661181; e-mail bioversity@cgiar.org; internet www.bioversityinternational.org; f. 1974 as Int. Board for Plant Genetic Resources, current name and status 2006; investigates conservation and use of agricultural biodiversity in order to achieve better nutrition, improve smallholders' livelihoods and enhance agricultural sustainability; supported by Consultative Group on Int. Agricultural Research (CGIAR); library of 6,000 vols; Chair. Dr CRISTIAN SAMPER (USA); Dir-Gen. Dr ANN TUTWILER (Italy).

CAB International (CABI): Nosworthy Way, Wallingford, OX10 8DE, UK; tel. (1491) 832111; e-mail enquiries@cabi.org; internet www.cabi.org; f. 1910 as Entomological Research Cttee, current name adopted 1986; researches and finds solutions to agricultural and environmental problems; manages genetic resource colns; conducts microbiological identifications, provides cultures for sale and offers preservation and consultancy services; 46 mem. countries; Chair. JOHN RIPLEY (UK); CEO Dr TREVOR NICHOLLS (UK); publs *Animal Health Research Reviews* (2 a year), *Aquatic Resources, Culture and Development* (4 a year), *Bibliography of Systematic Mycology* (2 a year), *British Journal of Nutrition* (12 a year), *Bulletin of Entomological Research* (6 a year), *Chinese Journal of Agricultural Biotechnology* (3 a year), *Equine and Comparative Exercise Physiology* (4 a year), *For-*

estry Abstracts (12 a year), *Horticultural Science Abstracts* (12 a year), *International Journal of Tropical Insect Science* (4 a year), *Journal of Helmintology* (4 a year), *Leisure, Recreation and Tourism Abstracts* (4 a year), *Pig News and Information* (4 a year), *Plant Breeding Abstracts* (12 a year), *Plant Genetics Resources* (3 a year), *Renewable Agriculture and Food Systems* (4 a year), *Rural Development Abstracts* (4 a year), *Seed Science Research* (4 a year), *Soil Use and Management* (4 a year), *World Poultry Science* (4 a year).

Centre for International Forestry Research (CIFOR): POB 0113 BOCBD, Bogor 10065, Indonesia; Jl. CIFOR, Situ Gede, Sindangbarang, Bogor Barat 16115, Indonesia; tel. (251) 8622622; e-mail cifor@cgiar.org; internet www.cifor.org; f. 1993; seeks balanced management of forests and forest lands through collaborative strategic and applied research and related activities; regional offices in Burkina Faso, Cameroon and Kenya; supported by Consultative Group on Int. Agricultural Research (CGIAR); Chair. Dr M. HOSNY EL-LAKANY (Canada); Dir-Gen. PETER HOLMGREN.

Centro Internacional de Agricultura Tropical (CIAT) (International Centre for Tropical Agriculture (CIAT)): Km 17, Recta Cali-Palmira, Apdo aéreo 6713, Cali, Colombia; tel. (2) 4450000; e-mail ciat@cgiar.org; internet www.ciat.cgiar.org; f. 1967; research on cultivation of beans, cassava, rice, tropical fruit and fodder, combined with applied social sciences; conducts interdisciplinary and applied research through partnerships with nat. programmes, civil soc. orgs and the private sector; produces improved germplasm, technologies, methodologies, knowledge; regional offices in Kenya and Viet Nam; supported by Consultative Group on Int. Agricultural Research (CGIAR); 1,300 mems; library of 100,000 records and documents; Chair. WANDA COLLINS (USA); Dir-Gen. RUBEN G. ECHEVERRÍA (Uruguay); publ. *Pasturas Tropicales* (3 a year).

Commonwealth Forestry Association: The Crib, Dinchope, Craven Arms, SY7 9JJ, UK; tel. (1588) 672868; e-mail cfa@cfa-international.org; internet www.cfa-international.org; f. 1921; facilitates networking of professional mems and orgs and exchange of knowledge; promotes capacity building by helping to organize training courses, workshops, confs; gives the Queen's Award for Forestry, the Young Forester Award, the Young Scientist Research Award; 1,500 mems; Pres. JIM BALL; Chair. JOHN INNES; publ. *International Forestry Review* (4 a year).

Consultative Group on International Agricultural Research (CGIAR): 900 19th St, NW, Sixth Fl., Washington, DC 20433, USA; tel. (202) 473-8951; e-mail cgiar@cgiar.org; internet www.cgiar.org; f. 1971; promotes agricultural research to reduce rural poverty, increase food security, improve human health and nutrition and ensure sustainable management of natural resources; consortium of 15 centres; 58 mems incl. govts, int. orgs and private foundations; Chair. CARLOS PÉREZ DEL CASTILLO; CEO Dr FRANK RIJSBERMAN.

Inter-American Institute for Cooperation on Agriculture/Instituto Interamericano de Cooperación para la Agricultura: Apdo 55–2200, San Isidro de Coronado, San José, Costa Rica; tel. 2216-0222; e-mail iicahq@iica.ac.cr; internet www.iica.int; f. 1942 as Inter-American Institute of Agricultural Sciences; encourages, promotes and supports the efforts of the mem. states to achieve agricultural devt and rural well-being; 34 mem. states; library of 50,000 vols; Dir-Gen. Dr VÍCTOR M. VILLALOBOS (Mexico); publs *Communica*, *Turrialba* (4 a year).

International Association of Agricultural Economists/Conférence Internationale des Economistes Agricoles: 555 E Wells St, Suite 1100, Milwaukee, WI 53202, USA; tel. (414) 918-3199; e-mail iaae@execinc.com; internet www.iaae-agecon.org; f. 1929; advances knowledge of agricultural processes and the economic organization of agriculture; facilitates communication and exchange of information among those concerned with rural welfare worldwide; 1,700 mems in 95 countries; Pres. Prof. Dr KEIJIRO OTSUKA (Japan); Sec. and Treas. Dr WALTER J. ARMBRUSTER (USA); publ. *Agricultural Economics*.

International Association of Horticultural Producers/Association Internationale des Producteurs de l'Horticulture: Horticulture House, 19 High St, Theale, RG7 5AH Reading, UK; tel. (118) 930-8956; e-mail sg@aiph.org; internet www.aiph.org; f. 1948; rep. of horticultural producers' orgs; organizes meetings, publs, press notices, resolutions and addresses to govts and int. authorities; approves int. horticultural exhibitions; 25 mem. orgs, 19 mem. countries; Pres. VIC KRAHN; Sec.-Gen. TIM BRIERCLIFFE; publ. *Statistical Yearbook*.

International Centre for Advanced Mediterranean Agronomic Studies/ Centre International de Hautes Études Agronomiques Méditerranéennes: 11 rue Newton, 75116 Paris, France; tel. 153239100; e-mail secretariat@ciheam.org; internet www.ciheam.org; f. 1962; encourages networked research and regional debate on Mediterranean agriculture, food and rural devt; provides a supplementary technical, economic and social education for graduates of the higher schools, faculties of agriculture in Mediterranean countries at postgraduate level; examines the int. problems posed by rural devt and regional planning; develops methods of investigation in ecological topics; contributes to the devt of int. cooperation among agronomists and economists in Mediterranean countries; grants scholarships; 14 mems: Albania, Algeria, Egypt, France, Greece, Italy, Lebanon, Malta, Morocco, Portugal, Spain, Tunisia, Turkey, Yugoslavia; Pres. Prof. Dr ADEL EL-BELTAGY (Egypt); Sec.-Gen. Dr FRANCISCO MOMBIELA MURUZABAL (France); publs *New Medit* (4 a year), *Options Méditerranéennes*, *Watch Letter* (4 a year).

Constituent Institutes:

CIHEAM-Mediterranean Agronomic Institute of Bari/CIHEAM-Istituto Agronomico Mediterraneo di Bari: Via Ceglie 9, 70010 Valenzano, Bari BA, Italy; tel. 804606207; e-mail iamdir@iamb.it; internet www.iamb.it; f. 1962; courses on land and water resources management, integrated pest management of Mediterranean fruit and vegetable crops, Mediterranean organic agriculture, sustainable agriculture, food and rural devt; collaborates with int. and nat. orgs involved in cooperation for devt; library of 6,500 vols; Dir Dr COSIMO LACIRIGNOLA; publ. *New Medit*.

Mediterranean Agronomic Institute of Chania: Alsyllio Agrokepiou, POB 85, Chania, 73 100 Crete, Greece; tel. (28) 21035000; e-mail info@maich.gr; internet www.maich.gr; f. 1985; courses on business economics and management, food quality and chemistry of natural products, geoinformation in environmental management, horticultural genetics and biotechnology, sustainable agriculture; coordinates research networks; library of 7,000 vols, 11,000 papers, 467 serial titles; Dir Dr GEORGE BAOURAKIS.

Mediterranean Agronomic Institute of Montpellier/Institut Agronomique Méditerranéen de Montpellier: 3191 route de Mende, 34093 Montpellier Cedex 5, France; tel. 467046000; e-mail cfle@iamm.fr; internet www.iamm.fr; f. 1962; courses on economics and politics of the agricultural sector and food supplies, economics and agricultural policies, rural devt and popularization; Dir PASCAL BERGERET.

Mediterranean Agronomic Institute of Zaragoza: Ave Montañana, 1005, 50059 Zaragoza, Spain; tel. 976716000; e-mail iamz@iamz.ciheam.org; internet www.iamz.ciheam.org; f. 1969; courses on animal nutrition, animal genetics and reproduction, rural devt, environment, plant breeding and genetics, agricultural systems, agricultural technologies, agricultural and food products, agro-food technology and marketing, aquaculture, fisheries; Dir IGNACIO ROMAGOSA

International Centre for Agricultural Research in the Dry Areas (ICARDA): POB 5466, Aleppo, Syria; Aleppo-Damascus Highway, Tel Hadya, Aleppo, Syria; tel. (21) 2213433; e-mail icarda@cgiar.org; internet www.icarda.cgiar.org; f. 1975; works for improvement of lentil, barley and fava bean production; serves dry-area developing countries for improvement of on-farm water-use efficiency, rangeland and small ruminant production; in W and Central Asia and N Africa, works for improvement of bread, durum wheat and chickpea production and farming systems; promotes improved land management, diversification of production systems, and value-added crop and livestock products; supported by Consultative Group on Int. Agricultural Research (CGIAR); library of 16,129 vols, 958 periodicals; Dir-Gen. Dr MAHMOUD SOLH (Syria); publ. *ICARDA Caravan* (2 a year).

International Commission for Food Industries/Comisión Internacional de las Industrias Agroalimentarias/Commission Internationale des Industries Agricoles et Alimentaires: 42 rue Scheffer, 75116 Paris, France; tel. 153702246; e-mail ciia@wanadoo.fr; internet www.ciia-c.com; f. 1934; develops int. cooperation in promoting agricultural and food industries; organizes int. congresses, annual study sessions and advanced training courses for executives and high-level technicians in the scientific, technical, management and economic fields; promotes general study of scientific, technical, economic and social questions relating to agricultural and food industries; Sec.-Gen. MICHEL FOUCAULT (France); publ. *Industries Alimentaires et Agricoles* (6 a year, online, www.revue-iaa.fr).

International Commission of Agricultural and Biosystems Engineering: see under Other International Organizations—Engineering and Technology

International Committee on Veterinary Gross Anatomical Nomenclature (ICVGAN)/Commission Internationale de la Nomenclature Macroanatomique Vétérinaire: Dept of Veterinary Anatomy, Bischofsholer Damm 15, 30173 Hanover, Germany; tel. (511) 8567211; f. 1957; 40 mems; Chair. Prof. H. GASSE (Germany); Sec. Prof. W. VAN DEN BROECK (Belgium); publ. *Nomina Anatomica Veterinaria*.

International Crops Research Institute for the Semi-Arid Tropics (ICRISAT): Patancheru, Andhra Pradesh 502324, India;

tel. (40) 30713071; e-mail icrisat@cgiar.org; internet www.icrisat.org; f. 1972; research covers all physical and socioeconomic aspects of improving farming systems on unirrigated land; world centre for genetic improvement of sorghum, millets, pigeonpea, chickpea and groundnut production, and for research on management of resources in semi-arid tropics; supported by Consultative Group on Int. Agricultural Research (CGIAR); Chair. Prof. Dr NIGEL POOLE (UK); Dir-Gen. Dr WILLIAM D. DAR (Philippines); publs *Journal of SAT Agricultural Research* (online, ejournal.icrisat.org), *Research and Information Bulletins*, *Workshop Proceedings*.

International Dairy Federation/Fédération Internationale du Lait: 70/B, Blvd Auguste Reyers, 1030 Brussels, Belgium; tel. (2) 733-98-88; e-mail info@fil-idf.org; internet www.fil-idf.org; f. 1903; links all dairy asscns in order to encourage the solution of scientific, technical and economic problems affecting the dairy industry; rep. of dairy farmers, dairy processing industry, dairy suppliers, academics and govts and food control authorities at int. level; nat. cttees in 35 countries; Pres. RICHARD DOYLE; Dir-Gen. CHRISTIAN ROBERT; publs *Bulletin* (online), *International Standards* (online).

International Federation of Agricultural Producers/Federación Internacional de Productores Agropecuarios/Fédération International des Producteurs Agricoles: 60 rue Saint-Lazare, 75009 Paris, France; tel. 145260553; e-mail ifap@ifap.org; internet www.ifap.org; f. 1946; acts as a forum for leaders of nat. farmers' orgs to meet and exchange information, experiences and ideas; rep. of farmers' concerns on int. platform; promotes creation and strengthening of ind., rep. orgs of farmers; organizes World Farmers Congress every 2 years; 112 nat. orgs in 87 countries; Pres. AJAY VASHEE (Zambia); Sec.-Gen. DAVID KING; publ. *General Conference Reports* (every 2 years).

International Food Policy Research Institute: 2033 K St, NW, Washington, DC 20006-1002, USA; tel. (202) 862-5600; e-mail ifpri@cgiar.org; internet www.ifpri.org; f. 1975; identifies and analyses alternative nat. and int. strategies for improving the food situation of low-income countries; encourages people and instns in developing countries that conduct research on food, agriculture, and nutrition policies; 6 divs: environment and production technology, food consumption and nutrition, markets, trade and institutions, int. service for nat. agricultural research, devt strategy and governance, communications and 2020 vision initiative; supported by Consultative Group on Int. Agricultural Research (CGIAR); library of 4,200 research reports, 3,000 monographs, 175 periodicals; Chair. FAWZI AL-SULTAN (Kuwait); Dir-Gen. Dr SHENGGEN FAN (China).

International Institute of Tropical Agriculture: Carolyn House, 26 Dingwall Rd, Croydon, CR9 3EE, UK; PMB 5320, Ibadan, Oyo State, Nigeria; tel. (2) 7517472; e-mail iita@cgiar.org; internet www.iita.org; f. 1967; conducts research in areas of biotechnology and genetic improvement, natural resource management, social sciences and agribusiness, plant production and plant health; involved in 8 Consortium Research Programmes: integrated systems for the humid tropics, policies, instns and markets, maize, roots, tubers and bananas, grain legumes, agriculture for improved nutrition and health, water, land and ecosystems, climate change, agriculture and food security; supported by Consultative Group on Int. Agricultural Research (CGIAR); library of 76,500 vols and in-house database of 105,500 records; Chair. Prof. BRUCE COULMAN (Canada); Dir-Gen. Dr NTERANYA SANGINGA (Democratic Republic of the Congo).

International Livestock Research Institute: POB 30709, Nairobi 00100, Kenya; tel. (20) 4223000; e-mail ilri-kenya@cgiar.org; internet www.ilri.cgiar.org; f. 1995; interdisciplinary research, training and information centre that promotes and improves livestock production worldwide; conducts research through 3 themes: biotechnology, markets, gender and livelihoods, people, livestock and the environment; principal site in Addis Ababa and field programmes in Ethiopia, Kenya, Niger and Nigeria; supported by Consultative Group on Int. Agricultural Research (CGIAR); library of 37,500 vols, 32,000 microfiches, 1,800 periodicals; Chair. Dr KNUT HOVE (Norway); Dir-Gen. Dr JIMMY SMITH; publ. *Bulletin*.

International Maize and Wheat Improvement Centre/Centro Internacional de Mejoramiento de Maíz y Trigo: Apdo 6–641, 06600 México, DF, Mexico; Km 45, Carretera Mexico-Veracruz, El Batan, Texcoco, CP, Mexico; tel. (55) 58042004; e-mail cimmyt@cgiar.org; internet www.cimmyt.org; f. 1943; improves maize and wheat varieties; promotes productivity-enhancing, resource-conserving farming practices; regional offices in Africa, Asia and S and Central America; supported by Consultative Group on Int. Agricultural Research (CGIAR); library of 44,000 vols (incl. monographs, journals, annual reports, theses, reprints, publs, microfiches, video cassettes, maps, CD-ROM databases); Chair. Dr SARA BOETTIGER (USA); Dir-Gen. THOMAS A. LUMPKIN.

International Organization for Biological Control of Noxious Animals and Plants (IOBC)/Organisation Internationale de Lutte Biologique contre les Animaux et les Plantes Nuisibles: c/o Dr Russell Messing, Univ. of Hawaii at Manoa, Kauai Agricultural Research Center, 7370 Kuamoo Rd, Kapaa, HI 96746, USA; tel. (808) 822-4984; e-mail messing@hawaii.edu; internet www.iobc-global.org; f. 1955; promotes environmentally safe methods of pest and disease control; collects, evaluates and disseminates information about biological control; promotes nat. and int. research; arranges confs, meetings and symposia; 6 regional sections; affiliated to Int. Council of Scientific Unions; public or private from 50 countries; Pres. Dr BARBARA BARRATT (New Zealand); Sec.-Gen. Dr RUSSELL MESSING (USA); Treas. JOSEP JACAS MIRET (Spain); publ. *BioControl*.

International Potato Centre/Centro Internacional de la Papa: Avda La Molina 1895, La Molina, POB 1558, Lima 12, Peru; tel. (1) 3496017; e-mail cip@cgiar.org; internet www.cipotato.org; f. 1971; encourages research, innovation in science and technology, capacity strengthening regarding root and tuber farming and food systems; supported by Consultative Group on Int. Agricultural Research (CGIAR); library of 14,700 vols of monographs or theses, 80 journals subscription, 15,800 reprints, 65,000 references; Chair. Dr RODNEY D. COOKE (UK); Dir-Gen. Dr PAMELA K. ANDERSON; publ. *Program Report* (every 2 years).

International Rice Research Institute (IRRI): POB 7777, 1301 Metro Manila, Philippines; Los Baños, Philippines; tel. (2) 580-5600; e-mail info@irri.org; internet www.irri.org; f. 1960; research on rice and rice-based cropping systems; works with public and private sector partners in nat. agricultural research and extension systems in major rice-growing countries; informs govts to help them to formulate policy to improve the supply of rice; supported by Consultative Group on Int. Agricultural Research (CGIAR); library of 158,000 vols; Chair. Dr EMERLINDA R. ROMAN (Philippines); Dir-Gen. Dr ROBERT S. ZEIGLER; publs *Facts about Cooperation* (1 a year), *IRRI Hotline* (4 a year), *IRRI Technical Bulletin*, *International Rice Research Notes* (2 a year), *Rice Literature Update* (2 a year), *Rice Today Magazine* (1 a year).

International Seed Testing Association: Zuerichstr. 50, 8303 Bassersdorf, Switzerland; tel. 448386000; e-mail ista.office@ista.ch; internet www.seedtest.org; f. 1924; promotes uniformity in seed quality evaluation, through research and by organizing triennial congresses, annual ordinary meetings and periodic training courses; produces internationally agreed rules for seed sampling and testing; accredits laboratories; promotes research; provides int. seed analysis certificates and training; disseminates knowledge in seed science and technology; 211 mem. laboratories, 45 personal mems, 50 assoc. mems from 80 countries; Pres. Dr JOËL LÉCHAPPÉ (France); Sec.-Gen. Dr BENJAMIN KAUFMAN (Switzerland); publs *ISTA International Rules for Seed Testing* (1 a year), *Seed Science and Technology* (3 a year).

International Society for Horticultural Science/Société Internationale de la Science Horticole: POB 500, 3001 Leuven 1, Belgium; Corbeekhoeve, Pastoriestraat 2, 3360 Korbeek-Lo, Belgium; tel. (16) 22-94-27; e-mail info@ishs.org; internet www.ishs.org; f. 1959; promotes and encourages research and education in all brs of horticultural science; facilitates cooperation and knowledge transfer on global scale through its symposia and congresses, publs and scientific structure; 7,000 individiual mems, 50 mem. states and countries; Pres. Prof. Dr ANTÓNIO A. MONTEIRO (Portugal); Exec. Dir Ir. JOZEF VAN ASSCHE (Belgium); publs *Acta Horticulturae* (about 35 a year), *Chronica Horticulturae* (4 a year).

International Society for Tropical Crop Research and Development (ISTCRAD): c/o Prof. N. K. Nayar (Assoc. Director of Research (Planning), Kerala Agricultural University, Thrissur 680656, Kerala, India; tel. (487) 370497; e-mail dr@kau.in; f. 1990; provides a forum for interaction among scientists, progressive farmers and entrepreneurs; Dir Dr D. ALEXANDER; publs *News Bulletin* (4 a year), *Scientific Journal* (4 a year).

International Society for Tropical Root Crops (ISTRC): c/o Prof. Keith Tomlins, Natural Resources Institute, Univ. of Greenwich, Central Ave, Chatham Maritime, Kent ME4 4TB, UK; tel. (1634) 883460; e-mail k.i.tomlins@gre.ac.uk; internet www.istrc.org; f. 1964; sponsors regional, int. meetings, workshops, study groups and training courses related to tropical root crop production and utilization; encourages cooperation between nat., regional and int. research centres and orgs through involvement in jtly planned research and training programmes; facilitates exchange of personnel and germplasm materials; provides financial assistance to mems; organizes triennial symposia; 300 mems; Pres. Prof. KEITH TOMLINS (UK); Sec. and Treas. Prof. LATEEF SANNI (Nigeria).

International Water Management Institute (IWMI): POB 2075, Colombo, Sri Lanka; 127 Sunil Mawatha, Pelawatte, Battaramulla, Sri Lanka; tel. (11) 2880000; e-mail iwmi@cgiar.org; internet www.iwmi.cgiar.org; f. 1985; works for sustainable management of water and land resources for food, livelihood and nature; supported by Consultative Group on Int. Agricultural Research (CGIAR); Chair. Prof. JOHN SKERRITT (Australia); Dir-Gen. Dr JEREMY BIRD (UK).

World Agroforestry Centre: United Nations Ave, Gigiri, POB 30677, Nairobi 00100, Kenya; tel. (20) 7224000; e-mail worldagroforestry@cgiar.org; internet www.worldagroforestry.org; f. 1978 as Int. Ccl for Research in Agroforestry, current name adopted 2002; conducts collaborative research on sustainable forestry and its impact on farming, to alleviate poverty and protect the environment; research sites in 23 tropical countries; supported by Consultative Group on Int. Agricultural Research (CGIAR); library of 8,000 vols, 30,000 reprints, 80 journal titles, colln of maps; Chair. Prof. Dr ERIC TOLLENS (Belgium); Dir-Gen. TONY SIMONS.

World Association for Animal Production: Via Tomassetti 3–1/A, 00161 Rome RM, Italy; tel. 644202639; e-mail waap@waap.it; internet www.waap.it; f. 1965; promotes high standards in research, devt and application of technology, education and science-based public policy in animal science; encourages exchange of scientific and educational information among its mems; arranges World Conf. on Animal Production every 5 years; 17 mem. orgs; Pres. NORMAN H. CASEY (South Africa); Sec.-Gen. ANDREA ROSATI (Italy).

World Fish Centre: POB 500, 10670 Penang, Malaysia; Jl Batu Maung, Batu Maung, 11960 Bayan Lepas, Penang, Malaysia; tel. (4) 6261606; e-mail worldfishcenter@cgiar.org; internet www.worldfishcenter.org; f. 1977; conducts collaborative research in developing countries to promote the sustainable use of living aquatic resources based on environmentally sound management; supported by Consultative Group on Int. Agricultural Research (CGIAR); library of 32,000 vols; Chair. REMO GAUTSCHI (Switzerland); Dir-Gen. Dr STEPHEN HALL (Australia); publ. *NAGA—WorldFish Centre Quarterly*.

World Veterinary Association/Association Mondiale Vétérinaire: Rue Defacqz 1, 1000 Brussels, Belgium; tel. (2) 533-70-22; e-mail secretariat@worldvet.org; internet www.worldvet.org; f. 1863; promotes animal health, public health and animal welfare at global level; organizes congress every 3 years; 80 nat. mem. asscns, 13 assoc. mems; Pres. Dr FAOUZI KECHRID (Tunisia); Exec. Sec. JAN VAARTEN (Belgium); publs *Bulletin* (2 a year), *World Veterinary Directory*.

Arts

Asociación de Lingüística y Filología de América Latina/Associação de Lingüística e Filologia da América Latina (Latin American Association of Linguistics and Philology): c/o Adolfo Elizaincín, Universidad de la República, CP 1410, 11000 Montevideo, Uruguay; e-mail elizaincin.alfal@gmail.com; internet www.mundoalfal.org; f. 1964; promotes progress of theoretical and applied linguistics and philology in Latin America; 1,009 mems; Pres. ADOLFO ELIZAINCÍN (Uruguay); Sec.-Gen. DIANA LUZ PESSOA DE BARROS (Brazil); publs *Atas dos Congressos, Cuadernos de la ALFAL, Cuadernos de Lingüística, Lingüística*.

Association for Commonwealth Literature and Language Studies: Private Bag X01, c/o Michael Wessels, English Studies, OMB, Univ. of KwaZulu-Natal, Scottsville, Pietermaritzburg, South Africa; tel. (33) 260-5747; e-mail wesselsm@ukzn.ac.za; internet www.aclals.ulg.ac.be; f. 1964; encourages study on Commonwealth literatures and languages, incl. comparative studies between literatures in English and indigenous literatures and languages, new kinds of English and use of mass media; holds triennial confs; organizes seminars, workshops, lectures, regional meetings, visits and exchanges; collects source material and publishes creative, critical, historical and bibliographical material; 1,600 mems; Chair. Dr MICHAEL WESSELS (South Africa); Vice-Chair. and Sec. JEAN ROSSMANN (South Africa).

Commonwealth Association of Museums: 10023 93 St, Edmonton, AB T5H 1W6, Canada; tel. (780) 424-2229; e-mail catherinec.cole@telus.net; internet www.maltwood.uvic.ca/cam; f. 1974; maintains and strengthens links between mems of the museum profession; promotes professional excellence; collaborates with nat. and regional museum asscns; organizes symposia and workshops, internships, distance-learning programme in basic museum studies; 350 mems, 53 mem. states; Pres. ROOKSANA OMAR (South Africa); Sec.-Gen. CATHERINE C. COLE (Canada); publ. *Online Journal* (irregular).

Communauté Africaine de Culture: c/o Présence africaine, 25 bis, rue des Ecoles, 75005 Paris, France; tel. 143541374; e-mail presaf@club-internet.fr; f. 2005, fmrly Société africaine de culture (f. 1956); promotes solidarity among intellectuals, writers and artists; enhances cultural, artistic and intellectual production in Africa and its diaspora; promotes cooperation and intercultural dialogue to promote peace; nat. asscns and individuals in 44 countries and territories, assoc. mems in 4 countries; Pres. WOLE SOYINKA; Sec.-Gen. Mme YZNDE CHRISTIANE DIOP; publ. *Présence Africaine* (2 a year).

Europa Nostra: Lange Voorhout 35, 2514 EC The Hague, Netherlands; tel. (70) 3024050; e-mail info@europanostra.org; internet www.europanostra.org; f. 1963 merged with Int. Castles Institute (IBI) 1991; works for protection of Europe's architectural and natural heritage; promotes high standards in architecture and in town and country planning; undertakes campaigns, confs, research, exhibitions and an annual award scheme; 1,500 individual mems, 250 mem. orgs, 150 associated orgs; Pres. Prof. GIANNI PERBELLINI (Italy); Sec. Dr MURIEL JOYEUX (France); publs *Awards Review* (1 a year), *Europa Nostra Scientific Bulletin* (1 a year), *European Cultural Heritage Review* (1 a year).

European Cultural Foundation/Fondation Européenne de la Culture: Jan van Goyenkade 5, 1075 HN Amsterdam, Netherlands; tel. (20) 5733868; e-mail ask@culturalfoundation.eu; internet www.culturalfoundation.eu; f. 1954; initiates and manages its own projects and programmes and gives grants to other bodies for European-level cultural activities; emphasizes the importance of developing a pluralistic civil soc. in Europe by encouraging the linkage of cultural activity and social responsibility; supports a network of nat. cttees based in 23 European countries; Pres. HRH Princess LAURENTIEN OF THE NETHERLANDS; Chair. WOLFGANG PETRITSCH (Austria); Dir KATHERINE WATSON (Canada/Finland); publ. *Beyond Borders* (3 a year).

European Society of Culture/Società Europea di Cultura/Société Européenne de Culture: Villa Hériot, Giudecca 54 P, 30133 Venice VE, Italy; tel. 415230210; e-mail info@societaeuropeacultura.it; internet www.societaeuropeacultura.it; f. 1950; unites artists, poets, scientists, philosophers and others through mutual interests and friendship to safeguard and improve the conditions required for creative activity; enhances int. collaboration and peace; 1,600 mems in 60 countries; library of 5,500 vols, 360 periodicals; Pres. VINCENZO CAPPELLETTI (Italy); Int. Gen. Sec. COSIMA CAMPAGNOLO (Italy); publ. *Comprendre* (irregular).

Fédération Internationale des Ecrivains de Langue Française (FIDELF): 3492 ave Laval, Montreal, QC H2X 3C8, Canada; tel. (515) 849-6239; f. 1982; 18 mem. asscns; Pres. ALIOUNE BADARA BEYE (Senegal); Sec.-Gen. MAMADOU TRAORÉ DIOP (Senegal).

International Amateur Theatre Association/Asociación Internacional del Teatro de Arte/Association Internationale du Théâtre Amateur: c/o Office of the BDAT, Postfach 14 06, 49784 Lingen, Germany; tel. (591) 61002888; e-mail office@amateurtheatre.net; internet www.aitaiata.org; f. 1952; promotes understanding and education through theatre; composed of nat. centres; organizes int. confs, colloquia, seminars, workshops, festivals incl. world festival of amateur theatre every 4 years; mems in 65 countries; Pres. MERJA LAAKSOVIRTA (Finland); publ. *Bulletin AITA/IATA*.

International Association for Caribbean Archaeology/Asociación Internacional de Arqueología del Caribe/Association Internationale d'Archéologie de la Caraïbe: Impasse Majoute, 97100 Basse Terre, Guadeloupe, France; internet museum-server.archanth.cam.ac.uk/iaca/www/iaca.htm; f. 1962 as Int. Assoc. for the Study of Pre-Columbian Cultures of the Lesser Antilles, present name 1985; ensures conservation of archaeological, historical and cultural heritage of the French Caribbean; promotes devt of archaeological and historical research on Caribbean civilization and culture; maintains and promotes free professional contacts among archaeologists interested in the study, history, civilization and culture of the Caribbean; organizes congresses every 2 years; 59 mems; Pres. A. REG MURPHY (Antigua); Sec. QUETTA KAYE (UK); publ. *Proceedings*.

International Association of Applied Linguistics/Association Internationale de Linguistique Appliquée: c/o Prof. Dr Daniel Perrin, ZHAW Zurich Univ. of Applied Sciences, School of Applied Linguistics, 8401 Winterthur, Switzerland; tel. 589346060; e-mail secretariat@aila.info; internet www.aila.info; f. 1964; contributes to devt of all subject areas of applied linguistics; promotes the exchange of scientific knowledge and practical experience; stimulates int. cooperation; fosters language pluralism; supports applied linguistics in developing countries; holds triennial world congress; 8,000 individual mems; Pres. Prof. Dr BERND RÜSCHOFF (Germany); Sec.-Gen. Prof. Dr DANIEL PERRIN (Switzerland); publs *AILA Applied Linguistics Series* (3 a year), *AILA Review* (1 a year).

International Association of Art Critics/Association Internationale des Critiques d'Art: 32 rue Yves Toudic, 75010 Paris, France; tel. 147701742; e-mail aica.office@gmail.com; internet www.aica-int.org; f. 1950; promotes art criticism as a discipline and contributes to its methodology; defends freedom of expression and thought and opposes arbitrary censorship; protects ethical and professional interests of its mems; contributes to mutual understanding of visual arts and aesthetics in all cultures; consultative status with UNESCO; 4,600 mems from 95 countries; Pres. MAREK BARTELIK (USA); Gen. Sec. BRANE KOVIC (Slovenia); publ. *Annuaire AiCA*.

International Association of Arts/Association Internationale des Arts Plastiques: UNESCO, 1 rue Miollis, 75015 Paris, France; tel. 145684454; e-mail iaaaiapunesco@gmail.com; internet www.aiap-iaa.org; f. 1954; stimulates int. cooperation among artists worldwide; improve the economic and social position of artists at nat. and int. level; defends artists' material and moral rights; Pres. ROSA-MARIA BURILLO (Mexico); Exec. Sec. MARTINE PASQUET.

International Association of Literary Critics/Association Internationale des Critiques Littéraires: 38 rue du Faubourg-St-Jacques, 75014 Paris, France; tel. 153101200; e-mail aicl.org@tiscalinet.it; internet www.aicl.org; f. 1969; fosters links between cultures in the field of literary criticism; promotes cultural devt in the contemporary world by encouraging exchanges between literature through the translations; organizes congresses; 32 nat. centres and individual mems; Pres. NERIA DE GIOVANNI (Italy); publs *L'Année Littéraire* (2 a year), *Revue* (1 a year).

International Center of Films for Children and Young People/Centre International du Film pour l'Enfance et la Jeunesse: End of Seif St, Phase 3, Shahrak-e Gharb-Sanaat Sq., 1466893311 Tehran, Iran; tel. (21) 88087870; e-mail info@cifej.com; internet www.cifej.com; f. 1955; research centre and clearing-house of information about entertainment films (cinema and television) for children; 80 mems from 37 countries; Pres. FIRDOZE BULBULIA (South Africa); Sec.-Gen. MOHSEN CHINIFOROUSHAN (Iran); Exec. Dir ELHAM SHIRVANI; publ. *CIFEJ Info* (4 a year).

International Centre for the Study of the Preservation and Restoration of Cultural Property (ICCROM)/Centre International d'Études pour la Conservation et la Restauration des Biens Culturels: Via di San Michele 13, 00153 Rome RM, Italy; tel. 6585531; e-mail iccrom@iccrom.org; internet www.iccrom.org; f. 1959; works for conservation of cultural heritage; assembles documentation and disseminates knowledge by way of publs and meetings; coordinates research, organizes training of specialists and short courses; offers technical advice; int. documentation centre; 133 mem. states; library of 100,000 vols (incl. 1,800 journal titles and 17,000 images); Chair. GRELLAN ROURKE; Dir-Gen. STEFANO DE CARO (Italy).

International Committee of Museums and Collections of Arms and Military History (ICOMAM): c/o Mathieu Willemsen, Curator Firearms—Conservateur Armes à feu Legermuseum, Legermuseum, Korte Geer 1, 2611 CA Delft, Netherlands; tel. (15) 2152622; e-mail m.willemsen@legermuseum.nl; internet www.klm-mra.be/icomam; f. 1957; encourages scientific research about arms and armour and military collns; stimulates professional standards of colln care, management, conservation and use in line with internationally recognized good practice and guidelines; promotes highest standards in display and interpretation; encourages networking and partnerships between museums and research worldwide; organizes triennial congresses and annual symposia; 260 mems in 50 countries; Chair. PIET DE GRYSE (Belgium); Sec. MATHIEU WILLEMSEN (acting) (Netherlands); publs *Glossarium Armourum: Arma Defensiva, Repertory of Museums of Arms and Military History, Triennial Reports*.

International Comparative Literature Association/Association Internationale de Littérature Comparée: c/o Prof. Steven P. Sondrup, 3168 JFSB, Brigham Young Univ., Provo, UT 84602-6702, USA; tel. (801) 422-5598; e-mail ailc.icla@gmail.com; internet www.ailc-icla.org; f. 1954; promotes study of literature undertaken from an int. point of view through int. cooperation; organizes int. congresses every 3 or 4 years; 5,000 mems (socs and individuals) in 65 countries; Pres. Prof. STEVEN P. SONDRUP (USA); Sec. Prof. JOHN BURT FOSTER (USA); Sec. Prof. MARC MAUFORT (Belgium); publs *ICLA Bulletin, Recherche Littéraire / Literary Research* (1 a year).

International Confederation of Societies of Authors and Composers/Confederación Internacional de Sociedades de Autores y Compositores/Confédération Internationale des Sociétés d'Auteurs et Compositeurs: 20–26 blvd du Parc, 92200 Neuilly sur Seine, France; tel. 155620850; e-mail cisac@cisac.org; internet www.cisac.org; f. 1926; strengthens and develops int. network of copyright socs; ensures effective protection of the rights of authors and composers; improves legislation on literary and artistic rights; organizes research on problems concerning the rights of authors on the internet; participates in preparatory work for intergovernmental confs on authors' rights; regional offices in Budapest, Santiago de Chile, Johannesburg and Singapore; 232 mem. socs in 121 countries; Pres. HERVÉ DI ROSA (France); Dir-Gen. OLIVIER HINNEWINKEL; publ. *CISAC News* (4 a year).

International Council for Film, Television and Audiovisual Communication/Conseil International du Cinéma, de la Télévision et de la Communication audiovisuelle: UNESCO, 1 rue Miollis, 75732 Paris Cedex 15, France; tel. 145684855; e-mail secretariat@cict-iftc.org; f. 1958; advises int. orgs and states for the implementation of artistic, educational and industrial policies; encourages training and research in all areas of broadcasting by offering a space for reflection on the devt of technologies for education and culture; seeks to provide a link of information and jt action between mem. orgs and assists them in their int. work in film and television; organizes confs, seminars and int. symposia; develops and supports festivals and exhibitions; 44 int. and regional mem. asscns, 12 assoc. mems; Pres. HISANORI ISOMURA; Sec.-Gen. LOLA POGGI-GOUJON.

International Council of Communication Design (Icograda): 455 Saint Antoine Ouest, Suite SS 10, Montreal, QC H2Z 1J1, Canada; tel. (514) 448-4949; e-mail info@icograda.org; internet www.icograda.org; f. 1963; collects and exchanges information relating to graphic design; organizes exhibitions and congresses and issues reports and surveys; raises the standards of graphic design and professional practice and the professional status of graphic designers; supports the devt of communication design education; poster and records archives at Brighton Univ., UK; 200 mem. orgs in 67 countries; Pres. LEIMEI JULIA CHIU (Japan); Sec.-Gen. IVA BABAJA (Croatia); publ. *Iridescent: Icograda Journal of Design Research*.

International Council of Museums (ICOM)/Conseil International des Musees/Consejo Internacional de Museos: Maison de l'UNESCO, 1 rue Miollis, 75732 Paris Cedex 15, France; tel. 147340500; e-mail secretariat@icom.museum; internet icom.museum; f. 1946; establishes minimum standards for professional practices and achievements for museums and their employees; 31 int. cttees conduct advanced research in their respective fields for the benefit of museum community; fights illicit traffic of cultural goods; encourages protection of tangible and intangible heritage; 30,000 individual and institutional mems in 137 countries; Pres. Dr HANS-MARTIN HINZ (Germany); Dir-Gen. HANNA PENNOCK (acting) (France); publs *ICOM News / Nouvelles de l'ICOM / Noticias del ICOM* (4 a year, in English, French, Spanish), *Study Series / Cahier d'Étude* (1 a year).

International Council on Monuments and Sites (ICOMOS)/Conseil International des Monuments et des Sites: 49–51 rue de la Fédération, 75015 Paris, France; tel. 145676770; e-mail secretariat@icomos.org; internet www.icomos.org; f. 1965; promotes application of theory, methodology and scientific techniques to the conservation of the architectural and archaeological heritage; 11,088 individual mems, 95 nat. cttees, 27 int. scientific cttees; library: Documentation Centre on preservation and restoration of monuments and sites: 30,000 vols, 350 periodicals, 25,000 slides; Pres. GUSTAVO ARAOZ (USA); Sec.-Gen. KIRSTI KOVANEN (Finland); publ. *Icomos Scientific Journal*.

International Federation for Theatre Research/Fédération Internationale pour la Recherche Théâtrale: c/o Prof. Jan Clarke, School of Modern Languages and Cultures, Durham Univ., Elvet Riverside, Durham DH1 3JT, UK; e-mail jan.clarke@durham.ac.uk; internet www.firt-iftr.org; f. 1957; facilitates communication and exchange between scholars of theatre and performance research; attached research institute Istituto Internazionale per la Ricerca Teatrale: see under Italy; organizes World Congress every 4 years, annual int. confs, regional confs, research working group symposia; 900 mems in 44 countries; Pres. Prof. CHRISTOPHER BALME (Germany); Sec.-Gen. for Admin. Prof. JAN CLARKE (UK); Sec.-Gen. for Communications PAUL MURPHY (UK); publ. *Theatre Research International* (4 a year).

International Institute for Conservation of Historic and Artistic Works/Institut International pour la Conservation des Objets d'Art et d'Histoire: 3 Birdcage Walk, Westminster, London SW1H 9JJ, UK; tel. (20) 77995500; e-mail iic@iiconservation.org; internet www.iiconservation.org; f. 1950 as Int. Institute for the Conservation of Museum Objects, current name adopted 1959; coordinates and improves knowledge, methods and working standards needed to protect and preserve cultural heritage; publishes information on research into all processes connected with conservation, both scientific, practical and technical, and on the devt of those processes; holds congress every 2 years; regional groups in Austria, France, Greece, Japan, Scandinavia (the Nordisk Konservatorforbund), Spain, Netherlands; offers awards, hon. fellowship of the Institute, sponsored lectures, bursaries for students and mems from developing countries; 2,000 mems from 40 countries; Pres. SARAH STANIFORTH (USA); Sec.-Gen. JO KIRBY ATKINSON (UK); publs *Studies in Conservation* (6 a year), *News in Conservation* (6 a year, online).

International Literary and Artistic Association/Association Littéraire et Artistique Internationale: c/o Kimbrough and Associés, 51 ave Raymond Poincaré, 75116 Paris, France; tel. 153302424; e-mail yves.gaubiac@kimbroughlaw.com; internet alai.org; f. 1878; promotes int. recognition of legal protection of authors for their intellectual work; plays role in preparation of int. legal instruments related to copyright and performers' rights; organizes congresses and study days; nat. mem. groups in 28 countries;

Pres. VICTOR NABHAN (France); Sec.-Gen. YVES GAUBIAC (France).

International Numismatic Council/Conseil International de Numismatique: c/o Carmen Arnold-Biucchi, Harvard Univ. Art Museums, 32 Quincy St, Cambridge, MA 02138, USA; e-mail carmen_arnold-biucchi@harvard.edu; internet www.inc-cin.org; f. 1927; facilitates cooperation among individuals and instns in the field of numismatics; organizes Int. Numismatic Congresses; 160 mems in 38 countries; Pres. Dr CARMEN ARNOLD-BIUCCHI (USA); Sec. Dr MICHAEL ALRAM (Austria); publ. *INeN*.

International Pragmatics Association (IPrA): POB 33, 2018 Antwerp 11, Belgium; Univ. of Antwerp, Stadscampus, Prinsstraat 13, 2000 Antwerp, Belgium; tel. (3) 265-45-63; e-mail info@ipra.be; internet ipra.ua.ac.be; f. 1986; aims to create a framework for the discussion and comparison of results of research in all aspects of language use or functions of language; disseminates knowledge about pragmatic aspects of language; incorporates a research centre; organizes meetings; 1,200 individual mems in 60 countries; Pres. JAN-OLA ÖSTMAN (Finland); Sec.-Gen. JEF VERSCHUEREN (Belgium); publ. *Pragmatics* (4 a year).

International Robert Musil Society/Internationale Robert-Musil-Gesellschaft: c/o Robert Musil-Institut für Literaturforschung der Universität Klagenfurt/Kärntner Literaturarchiv, Bahnhofstr. 50, 1, Stock, 9020 Klagenfurt, Austria; tel. (463) 27002921; e-mail walter.fanta@uni-klu.ac.at; internet www.musilgesellschaft.at; f. 1974; promotes int. cooperation in research and publs on Musil and edns of his writings; organizes colloquia; 267 mems; Pres. Prof. Dr KLAUS AMANN; Sec.-Gen. Dr WALTER FANTA; publ. *Musil-Forum* (every 2 years).

International Theatre Institute/Institut International du Théâtre: UNESCO, 1 rue Miollis, 75732 Paris Cedex 15, France; tel. 145684880; e-mail info@iti-worldwide.org; internet www.iti-worldwide.org; f. 1948; facilitates cultural exchanges and int. understanding in the domain of the performing arts; encourages transfer of knowledge and research in the performing arts; holds confs, workshops, publs; education and training in performing arts; protection and promotion of cultural diversity; 102 mem. nations; Pres. RAMENDU MAJUMDAR (Bangladesh); Sec. MOHAMMED SAIF AL-AFKHAM (UAE); Dir-Gen. TOBIAS BIANCONE (Switzerland); publs *The World of Theatre* (every 2 years, in Arabic, English, French), *World Theatre Directory* (online).

International Union of Architects/Union Internationale des Architectes: Tour Maine Montparnasse, BP 158, 33 ave du Maine, 75755 Paris Cedex 15, France; tel. 145243688; e-mail uia@uia-architectes.org; internet www.uia-architectes.org; f. 1948; holds triennial congress; rep. of architects on int. level; 1m. mems in 124 countries and territories; Pres. ALBERT DUBLER (France); Sec.-Gen. MICHEL BARMAKI (Lebanon).

International Union of Cinema/Union Internationale du Cinéma: c/o Jan P. Essing, Lente 33, 8251 NT Dronten, Netherlands; tel. (321) 319529; e-mail essing.jan@hetnet.nl; internet www.unica-web.com; f. 1937; promotes video and film-making as means of int. communication; achieves recognition of independence and freedom of expression for mem. feds; supports int. cultural cooperation; represents its mem. feds in UNESCO; organizes congresses, int. film and video competitions and exchanges, int. seminars, debates on new concepts and theories about art and culture; nat. feds in 34 countries; library of 1,100 films and video cassettes; Pres. GEORGES FONDEUR (Luxembourg); Sec.-Gen. JAN ESSING (Netherlands); publ. *UNICA News*.

Organization for Museums, Monuments and Sites of Africa/Organisation pour les Musées, les Monuments et les Sites d'Afrique: POB 3343, Accra, Ghana; f. 1975; aims to foster the collection, study and conservation of the natural and cultural heritage of Africa; cooperation between mem. countries through seminars, workshops, confs; exchange of personnel, developing training facilities, drawing up legislative and admin. measures; mems from 30 countries; Pres. Dr J. M. ESSOMBA (Cameroon); Dir-Gen. Dr CLAUDE MARTIN (Ghana).

PEN International: Brownlow House, 50/51 High Holborn, London, WC1V 6ER, UK; tel. (20) 74050338; e-mail info@pen-international.org; internet www.pen-international.org; f. 1921 as PEN, present name 2010; promotes cooperation between writers worldwide in the interests of literature, freedom of expression and int. goodwill; 4 cttees: writers for peace, writers in prison, women writers, translation and linguistic rights; 145 autonomous centres worldwide; 20,000 mems; Int. Pres. Dr JOHN RALSTON SAUL (Canada); Int. Sec. HORI TAKEAKI (Japan); publs *PEN International* (2 a year, in English, French and Spanish, in asscn with UNESCO), *The Magazine* (4 a year).

World Academy of Art and Science: see under Other International Organizations—Science.

World Crafts Council: Auras Corporate Centre, Third Fl., 98-A Dr Radhakrishnan Salai, Chennai 600004, Tamil Nadu India; tel. (44) 28478500; e-mail wcc.sect.in@gmail.com; internet www.worldcraftscouncil.org; f. 1964; maintains the status of crafts as a vital part of cultural life; promotes fellowship among the world's craftsmen; offers help and advice to craftsmen, consults with govts, nat. and int. instns; mems in 90 countries; Pres. USHA KRISHNA (India); Sec.-Gen. SANGEET CHOPRA (India); publ. *World Crafts Council—Asia Pacific* (2 a year).

Bibliography

Association for Health Information and Libraries in Africa: c/o Nasra Gathoni, POB 30270-00100, Aga Khan Univ., Nairobi, Kenya; tel. 203662039; e-mail president@ahila.org; internet www.ahila.org; f. 1984 as Asscn of African Medical Librarians Asscn, present name 1988; promotes cooperation among African health information centres and libraries, to enhance health information services; encourages professional devt of health librarians; develops an African *Index Medicus*; 46 mem. countries; Pres. NASRA GATHONI (Kenya); Sec.-Gen. CECILE COULIBALY (Côte d'Ivoire).

Association of Caribbean University, Research and Institutional Libraries/Asociacion de Bibliotecas Universitarias, de Investigacion e Institucionales del Caribe/Association des Bibliothèques Universitaires, de Recherche et Institutionnelles de la Caraibe: POB 23317, UPR Station, San Juan, PR 00931-3317, Puerto Rico; c/o Caribbean Regional Library and Latin American Studies, José M. Lázaro Library, Univ. of Puerto Rico, Río Piedras Campus, Puerto Rico; tel. (787) 790-8054; e-mail acuril@gmail.com; internet acuril.uprrp.edu; f. 1969; facilitates devt and use of libraries, archives and information services; identification, collection and preservation of information resources in support of intellectual and educational endeavours in the area; strengthens archival, library and information professions; 200 mems; Pres. FRANÇOISE BEAULIEU THYBULLE (Haiti); Exec. Sec. LUISA VIGO-CEPEDA; publs *ACURILEANA* (online), *Conference Proceedings*.

Association of European Research Libraries/Ligue des Bibliothèques Européennes de Recherche (LIBER): Koninklijke Bibliotheek, Nat. Library of the Netherlands, POB 90407, 2509 LK The Hague, Netherlands; e-mail liber@kb.nl; internet www.libereurope.eu; f. 1971; represents and promotes interests of research libraries in Europe to assist them to create a functional research network across nat. boundaries; promotes preservation of cultural heritage; 430 mems from 40 European countries; Pres. Dr PAUL AYRIS; Sec.-Gen. Dr ANN MATHESON; Exec. Dir Dr IZASKUN LACUNZA; publ. *LIBER Quarterly* (online, liber.library.uu.nl/index.php/lq).

Commonwealth Library Association: POB 144, Mona, Kingston 7, Jamaica; tel. 9270083; e-mail nkpodo@uwimona.edu.jm; f. 1972; creates and strengthens professional relationships between librarians; promotes the status and education of librarians and the reciprocal recognition of qualifications; improves libraries; initiates research projects designed to promote library provision and to advance technical devt of libraries in the Commonwealth; 52 mems incl. 40 nat. asscns, 130 affiliated mems; Pres. (vacant); publ. *COMLA Bulletin* (3 a year).

European Association for Health Information and Libraries: POB 1393, 3600 BJ Maarssen, Netherlands; e-mail eahil-secr@list.ecompass.nl; internet www.eahil.eu; f. 1987; improves cooperation among health care libraries throughout Europe; strengthens links with medical and health libraries in Eastern and Central Europe; raises standards of provision and practice in health care and medical research libraries; encourages mobility and continuing education, esp. with regard to new technologies; represents health librarians at European level, in particular at European instns and at WHO; 1,400 mems; Pres. MARSHALL DOZIER (UK); Hon. Sec. KAREN BUSET (Norway); Treas. GHISLAINE DECLEVE; publ. *Journal of the European Association for Health Information and Libraries* (4 a year).

European Theological Libraries/Europäische Bibliotheken für Theologie/Bibliothèques Européennes de Théologie: c/o Veronique Verspeurt, Meerbeekhof 11, 3190 Boortmeerbeek, Belgium; e-mail veronique.verspeurt@theo.kuleuven.be; internet theo.kuleuven.be/beth; f. 1970 as Conseil Int. des Associations de Bibliothèques de Théologie, fmrly Int. Ccl of Asscn of Theological Libraries, present name 1999; promotes cooperation among the theological and ecclesiastical libraries in Europe; stimulates devt of theological libraries through shared knowledge and experience and through training theological librarians; serves interests of European theological libraries in the scientific and academic sphere and on int. level; 37 mems (12 ordinary, 16 extraordinary, 9 individuals); Pres. GEERT HARMANNY; Sec. CAROL REEKIE.

International Association for Media and Communication Research (IAMCR)/Associacion Internacional des Estudios de Communicacion Social (AIECS)/Association Internationale des Études et Recherches sur l'Information et la Communication (AIERI): c/o Janet Wasko, Univ. of Oregon, Eugene, OR, USA; internet iamcr.org; f. 1957; encourages research and systematic study, esp. in areas of media production and consumption and structure and transformation of media and communication markets in the wake of social and technological transformation; provides forum for exchange of information; works to bring about improvements in communication practice, policy and research; encourages improvement of training for journalism; runs the Schiller and Smythe awards for outstanding papers in critical media research; 1,000 mems in 100 countries; Pres. JANET WASKO (USA); Sec.-Gen. MARIA MICHALIS (UK).

International Association of Agricultural Information Specialists/Asociación Internacional de Especialistas en Información Agrícola/Association Internationale des Spécialistes de l'Information Agricole: POB 63, Lexington, KY 40588-0063, USA; tel. (859) 254-0752; e-mail info@iaald.org; internet www.iaald.org; f. 1955; unites agricultural information specialists worldwide; organizes meetings and educational programmes, workshops and annual confs in various parts of the world; communicates and advocates value of knowledge and information through social networks; collaborates with partner orgs; 300 mems representing 80 countries; Pres. FEDERICO SANCHO GUEVARA (Costa Rica); Sec. and Treas. TONI GREIDER (USA); publ. *Agricultural Information Worldwide* (online, journals.sfu.ca/iaald/index.php/aginfo).

International Association of Bibliophiles/Association Internationale de Bibliophilie: c/o Bibliothèque Nationale de France, Réserve des livres rares, Quai François Mauriac, 75706 Paris Cedex 13, France; tel. 153795476; f. 1963; forms a meeting point for bibliophiles from different countries; organizes int. congresses every 2 years; 450 mems; Pres. T. KIMBALL BROOKER (USA); Sec.-Gen. JEAN-MARC CHATELAIN (France); publ. *Le Bulletin du Bibliophile* (2 a year).

International Association of Law Libraries (IALL)/Association Internationale des Bibliothèques de Droit: c/o Barbara Garavaglia, Univ. of Michigan Law Library, Ann Arbor, MI 48109-12103, USA; tel. (734) 764-9338; e-mail bvaccaro@umich.edu; internet www.iall.org; f. 1959; offers worldwide cooperation in the devt of law libraries and the collection of legal documentation; promotes education of law librarians and other legal information professionals by providing educational programs on foreign and int. legal systems; grants bursaries and scholarships to legal information professionals, esp. those from developing nations to support educational and professional opportunities; holds annual conf.; 400 mems in 50 countries; Pres. PETAL KINDER (Australia); Sec. BARBARA GARAVAGLIA (USA); publ. *International Journal of Legal Information* (3 a year).

International Association of Scientific and Technological University Libraries (IATUL)/Association Internationale des Bibliothèques d'Universités Polytechniques: c/o Dr Elisha Chiware, Cape Peninsula Univ. of Technology Library, POB 1906, Bellville, 7535, South Africa; tel. (21) 959-6322; e-mail chiwaree@cput.ac.za; internet www.iatul.org; f. 1955 as Int. Asscn of Technological Univ. Libraries, current name adopted 2009; promotes cooperation between mem. libraries and conducts research on library problems; provides forum for discussion matters and problems of current significance; 220 univ. libraries in 41 countries; Pres. Dr REINER KALLENBORN (Germany); Sec. Dr ELISHA CHIWARE (South Africa); publ. *IATUL Proceedings* (1 a year).

International Board on Books for Young People (IBBY): Nonnenweg 12, Postfach, 4003 Basel, Switzerland; tel. 612722917; e-mail ibby@ibby.org; internet www.ibby.org; f. 1953; promotes int. understanding through children's books; encourages the production and distribution of quality children's books esp. in developing countries; promotes scientific investigation into problems of juvenile books; organizes Int. Children's Book Day and a biennial int. congress; presents the Hans Christian Andersen Award every 2 years to a living author and illustrator for outstanding contribution to children's literature and the IBBY-Asahi Reading Promotion Award annually to an org. that has made a significant contribution to children's literature; makes a biennial selection of outstanding books to form the IBBY Honour List; 70 nat. sections, individual mems in 77 countries; Pres. AHMAD REDZA AHMAD KHAIRUDDIN (Malaysia); Exec. Dir LIZ PAGE (Switzerland); publ. *Bookbird: A Journal of International Children's Literature* (4 a year).

International Committee for Social Science Information and Documentation/Comité International pour l'Information et la Documentation des Sciences Sociales: c/o Clacso, Callao 875 (3° piso), 1023 Buenos Aires, Argentina; e-mail saugy@clacso.edu.ar; internet www.unesco.org/most/icssd.htm; f. 1950; collects and disseminates information on documentation services in social sciences; helps to improve documentation; advises socs on problems of documentation and to draw up rules likely to improve the presentation of all documents; reinforces social science's nat., regional and global infrastructure; works for capacity-building through workshops and seminars; promotes availability of secondary and primary scientific information in less privileged countries and regions; mems from int. asscns specializing in social sciences or in documentation; assoc. mem. of Int. Social Science Ccl; Pres. KRISHANA G. TYAGI (India); Sec.-Gen. CATALINA SAUGY (Argentina); publ. *International Bibliography of the Social Sciences* (1 a year, 4 series).

International Council on Archives/Conseil International des Archives: 60 rue des Francs-Bourgeois, 75003 Paris, France; tel. 140276306; e-mail ica@ica.org; internet www.ica.org; f. 1948; works for effective management of records and the preservation, care and use of the world's archival heritage through its representation of records and archive professionals across the globe; 13 regional brs; 1,500 mems from 195 countries and territories; Pres. MARTIN BERENDSE (Netherlands); Sec.-Gen. DAVID A. LEITCH (France); publs *COMMA International Journal on Archives* (2 a year), *FLASH* (2 a year).

International Federation of Film Archives/Federacion Internacional de Archivos Filmicos/Fédération Internationale des Archives du Film: 1 rue Defacqz, 1000 Brussels, Belgium; tel. (2) 538-30-65; e-mail info@fiafnet.org; internet www.fiafnet.org; f. 1938; encourages creation of archives worldwide for the collection and conservation of the film heritage; facilitates cooperation and exchanges between mem. film archives; promotes public interest in the art of cinema; aids and conducts research in this field and to compile new documentation; holds annual congresses; offers FIAF Award to contributors to the cause of film preservation from around the world; 150 mem. instns in 77 countries; Pres. ERIC LE ROY (France); Sec.-Gen. MEG LABRUM (Australia); publ. *Journal of Film Preservation* (2 a year).

International Federation of Library Associations and Institutions (IFLA)/Fédération Internationale des Associations de Bibliothécaires et des Bibliothèques: POB 95312, 2509 CH, The Hague, Netherlands; Prins Willem-Alexanderhof 5, 2595 BE The Hague, Netherlands; tel. (70) 3140884; e-mail ifla@ifla.org; internet www.ifla.org; f. 1927; promotes high standards of provision and delivery of library and information services; encourages understanding of value of library and information services; promotes int. library cooperation in all fields of library activity; provides a rep. body in matters of int. interest; 1,500 mems in 150 countries; Pres. SINIKKA SIPILÄ (Finland); Sec.-Gen. JENNEFER NICHOLSON (Netherlands); publs *IFLA Journal* (4 a year), *IFLA Professional Reports*, *IFLA Publication Series* (6 a year).

International Institute for Children's Literature and Reading Research/Institut für Jugendliteratur/Institut International de Littérature pour Enfants et de Recherches sur la Lecture: Mayerhofgasse 6, 1040 Vienna, Austria; tel. (1) 5050359; e-mail office@jugendliteratur.net; internet www.jugendliteratur.net; f. 1965; serves as service and communication centre for children and youth literary field; promotes int. research; arranges confs and exhibitions; compiles recommendation lists; individual and group mems in 26 countries; library of 60,000 vols of children's literature, 7,000 trade books; Dir Mag. KARIN HALLER (Austria); publs *1000 und 1 Buch* (4 a year, online, www.1001buch.at), *Bookbird* (4 a year).

International Society for Knowledge Organization (ISKO): c/o Vivien Petras, Humboldt-Universität zu Berlin, Institut für Bibliotheks- und Informationswissenschaft, Unter den Linden 6, 10099 Berlin, Germany; tel. (30) 20934325; e-mail secr@isko.org; internet www.isko.org; f. 1989; promotes research, devt and applications of knowledge organization systems that advance the philosophical, psychological and semantic approaches for ordering knowledge; provides means of communication and networking on knowledge organization for its mems; advises on the construction, perfection and application of classification systems, thesauri, terminologies, etc.; organizes int. conf. every 2 years; 400 mems; Pres. H. PETER OHLY (Germany); Sec. and Treas. Prof. VIVIEN PETRAS (Germany); publs *Advances in Knowledge Organization, Ergon* (irregular, proceedings in English), *Fortschritte in der Wissensorganisation, Ergon* (irregular, proceedings in German), *Knowledge Organization* (24 a year), *Knowledge Organization in Subject Areas 1994–* (irregular).

International Youth Library/Internationale Jugendbibliothek: Schloss Blutenburg, 81247 Munich, Germany; tel. (89) 8912110; e-mail info@ijb.de; internet www.ijb.de; f. 1949; associated project of UNESCO since 1953; encourages int. exchange and cooperation in children's book publishing, research and promotion of reading; provides information and advice to students, teachers, publishers; organizes exhibitions; library of 600,000 vols in 130 languages; Chair. Dr FREIHERR DOMINIK VON KÖNIG; Dir Dr CHRISTIANE RAABE; publs *Das Bücherschloss* (1 a year), *White Ravens* (1 a year).

Economics, Political Science and Sociology

International Labour Organization (ILO): 4 route des Morillons, 1211 Geneva 22, Switzerland; tel. 227996111; e-mail ilo@ilo.org; internet www.ilo.org; f. 1919; promotes and realizes standards and fundamental principles and rights at work; is concerned with the safety, health and social security of workers and provides technical expertise where required by mem. countries; seeks to improve labour conditions, raise living standards and promote productive employment in all countries; strengthens tripartism and social dialogue; enhances coverage and effectiveness of social protection for all; 185 mem. countries; library: see under Switzerland; Dir-Gen. GUY RYDER (UK); publs *Bulletin of Labour Statistics* (12 a year), *International Labour Documentation*, *International Labour Review*, *Official Bulletin*, *World of Work*, *Yearbook of Labour Statistics*.

Associated Institutions:

International Institute for Labour Studies: POB 6, 1211 Geneva 22, Switzerland; tel. 227996128; e-mail inst@ilo.org; internet www.ilo.org/public/english/bureau/inst; f. 1960; provides global forum for interaction between business, labour, policy-makers and academics on emerging labour policy issues; promotes research networks on policy implications of changing relationships between labour, business and the state; develops the research capacities of ministries of labour and employers' and workers' orgs; Chair. JUAN SOMAVIA; Dir RAYMOND TORRES.

International Training Centre of the ILO/Centre International de Formation de l'OIT: Viale Maestri del Lavoro 10, 10127 Turin TO, Italy; tel. 116936111; e-mail communications@itcilo.org; internet www.itcilo.org; f. 1964; offers advanced training facilities for managers, trainers and social partners and technical specialists from ILO mem. states; Exec. Dir PATRICIA O'DONOVAN

OTHER ORGANIZATIONS

African Training and Research Centre in Administration for Development/ Centre Africain de Formation et de Recherche Administratives pour le Développement (CAFRAD): Pavillon International, Blvd Mohammed V, POB 1796, 90001 Tangier, Morocco; tel. 539322707; e-mail cafrad@cafrad.org; internet www.cafrad.org; f. 1964; supports govts' actions and those of related bodies in capacity devt, innovation in public admin. for improved service delivery to the citizens; promote inter-African cooperation and serve as a think-tank framework for knowledge devt and exchange of experiences between experts, practitioners and policy-makers and instns; research into admin. problems in Africa, documentation of results and the provision of a consultation service for govts and orgs in Africa; organizes seminars, confs and workshops; 37 mem. states; library of 35,000 vols; Chair. ABDELAÂDIM GUERROUJ; Dir-Gen. Dr SIMON MAMOSI LELO; publs *African Administrative Studies* (2 a year, in English and French), *African Public Service Charter*, *Directory of African Consultants*, *Directory of African Training and Research Institutions in Public Administration and Management*, *Juelles Verifier et Expedia*, *Proceedings of Pan-African Conference of Ministers of the Civil Service* (every 2 years), *Studies and Documents (Series)* (irregular).

American Society for Political and Legal Philosophy: c/o Dr Alex Zakaras, Univ. of Vermont, 522 Old Mill, 94 University Pl., Burlington, VT 05405, USA; tel. (802) 656-8229; e-mail theasplp@gmail.com; internet www.political-theory.org; f. 1955; brings together a group of political scientists, philosophers and law scholars interested in exploring legal and political philosophy outside of their home disciplines; organizes annual meeting; 500 mems; Pres. Prof. Dr NANCY ROSENBLUM (USA); Sec. and Treas. Dr ALEX ZAKARAS (USA); publ. *NOMOS* (yearbook).

Association of International Accountants: Staithes 3, The Watermark, Metro Riverside, Newcastle upon Tyne, NE11 9SN, UK; tel. (191) 4930277; e-mail aia@aiaworldwide.com; internet www.aiaworldwide.com; f. 1928; promotes and supports the advancement of the accountancy profession worldwide; offers a professional qualification for accountants and statutory auditors; 7,000 mems; Pres. ANDREW LAMB (UK); Chief Exec. PHILIP TURNBULL; publ. *International Accountant* (6 a year).

Association of Social Anthropologists of the UK and Commonwealth: c/o RAI, 50 Fitzroy St, London W1T 5BT, UK; e-mail admin@theasa.org; internet www.theasa.org; f. 1946; promotes study and teaching of social anthropology; rep. of interests of social anthropology and maintains its professional status; holds annual conf.; 530 mems; Chair. Prof. VERONICA STRANG; Hon. Sec. Dr ZEMIRAH MOFFAT; publs *ASA Annals* (online), *ASA Essays* (online), *ASA Annual Monograph*, *ASA Online*.

Centre for Democracy and Development/Centre pour la Démocratie et le Développement: Unit 2L Leroy House, 436 Essex Rd, London, N1 3QP, UK; tel. (20) 73597775; internet www.cddwestafrica.org; f. 1997; encourages research, information and exchange of ideas on questions of democratic devt and peace-building in West Africa; offers strategic training in promoting democracy and devt; regional offices in Abuja and Lagos, Nigeria; Dir Dr JIBRIN IBRAHIM; publ. *Democracy and Development: Journal of West African Affairs* (2 a year).

Econometric Society: c/o Claire Sashi, Dept of Economics, New York Univ., 19 West Fourth St, Sixth Fl., New York, NY 10012, USA; tel. (212) 998-3820; e-mail sashi@econometricsociety.org; internet www.econometricsociety.org; f. 1930; promotes studies on the unification of the theoretical-quantitative and the empirical-quantitative approach to economic problems; organizes scientific meetings; 656 mems; Pres. JEAN CHARLES ROCHET (Switzerland); Gen. Man. CLAIRE SASHI (USA); publs *Econometrica* (24 a year), *Quantitative Economics* (online (www.qeconomics.org)), *Theoretical Economics* (3 a year, online (econtheory.org)).

European Association for Population Studies/Association Européenne pour l'Étude de la Population: POB 11676, 2502 AR The Hague, Netherlands; Lange Houtstraat 19, 2511 CV The Hague, Netherlands; tel. (70) 3565200; e-mail contact@eaps.nl; internet www.eaps.nl; f. 1983; promotes study of population in Europe through cooperation between persons interested or engaged in European demographics; organizes scientific confs every 2 years, seminars, symposia and working groups; publishes and disseminates information dealing with population questions; demographers and other population scientists from all European countries; Pres. FRANCESO BILLARI (Italy); Sec.-Gen. and Treas. MARC LUY (Austria); publ. *European Journal of Population / Revue Européenne de Démographie* (4 a year).

European Centre for Social Welfare Policy and Research: Berggasse 17, 1090 Vienna, Austria; tel. (1) 3194505-0; e-mail ec@euro.centre.org; internet www.euro.centre.org; f. 1974 as European Centre for Social Welfare Training and Research, present name 1989; conducts applied social science and comparative empirical research on social policy and welfare; serves as information and knowledge centre providing social science-supported social policy intelligence through a think-net; library of 8,000 vols; Chair. YURY FEDOTOV; Exec. Dir Prof. Dr BERND MARIN (Austria); publ. *Eurosocial Reports Series* (in English, French and German).

European Economic Association: c/o Prof. Piero Tedeschi, Universita Cattolicá, Instituto di Economia dell'Impresa e del Lavoro, Via P. Necchi 5, 20123 Milan MI, Italy; tel. 272343050; e-mail admin@eeassoc.org; internet www.eeassoc.org; f. 1985; contributes to devt and application of economics as a science in Europe; improves communication and exchange between teachers, researchers and students in economics in different European countries; develops and sponsors cooperation between teaching instns of univ. level and research instns in Europe; organizes annual congress; standing cttees on teaching/research and cttee for women in economics; 3,100 mems; Pres. Prof. ORAZIO ATTANASIO (UK); Exec. Vice-Pres. Prof. GUGLIELMO WEBER (Italy); publ. *Journal of the European Economic Association (JEEA)* (6 a year).

European Foundation for Management Development (EFMD): 88 rue Gachard, POB 3, 1050 Brussels, Belgium; tel. (2) 629-08-10; e-mail info@efmd.org; internet www.efmd.be; f. 1971; provides forum for worldwide cooperation in management devt; European Quality Initiative (EQUAL) project seeks int. cooperation in assessing quality in management education; coordinates projects and activities to foster an active dialogue and exchange between companies and academic instns; generates new ideas for enhancement of management thinking and practices; manages int. projects in Asia, CIS and the Arab World; 780 mem. orgs in 80 countries; Pres. ALAIN DOMINIQUE PERRIN (France); Dir-Gen. and CEO ERIC CORNUEL; publ. *Forum* (3 a year).

Futuribles International: 47 rue de Babylone, 75007 Paris, France; tel. 153633770; e-mail diffusion@futuribles.com; internet www.futuribles.com; f. 1960, fmrly Assn Internationale Futuribles; identifies and analyses emerging trends and devts in the medium- and long-term strategic environment orgs and territories; training concepts and methods for monitoring, forecasting and strategy; encourages discussion and debate on key issues of the contemporary world and the future, through confs, round tables, workshops, publs and symposia; 65 mems; Hon. Pres. JACQUES LESOURNE; Pres. HUGUES DE JOUVENEL (France); publs *Bibliographie Prospective* (11 a year), *Futuribles* (6 a year).

Inter-American Statistical Institute/ Instituto Interamericano de Estadística: c/o INEC, Contraloría General de la República, POB 0816-01521, 0816 Panama, Panama; tel. 510-4890; e-mail fabpan@cwpanama.net; internet www.contraloria.gob.pa/inec/iasi; f. 1940; works for devt and strengthening of the statistical profession; promotes and disseminates advances in statistical theory and methods; improves methodology for production of governmental and non-governmental statistics; promotes measures aimed at improving the comparability and availability of economic and social statistics among the nations of the region; holds seminars, courses and meetings; 267 mems (218 individual, 34 ex officio, 15 affiliated (institutional)); Pres. Dr PEDRO A. MORETTIN (Brazil); Exec. Dir Prof. EVELIO O. FABBRONI; publ. *Estadística* (2 a year).

International African Institute (IAI)/ Institut Africain International: c/o School of Oriental and African Studies, Thornhaugh St, Russell Sq., London WC1H 0XG, UK; tel. (20) 78984420; e-mail iai@soas.ac.uk; internet www.internationalafricaninstitute .org; f. 1926 as Int. Institute of African Languages and Cultures; promotes scholarly study of African history, socs, cultures and political systems and disseminates the results of research; hosts Lugard Lecture every 2 years; Chair. Prof. V. Y. MUDIMBE; Hon. Dir Prof. PHILIP BURNHAM; publs *Africa* (4 a year), *Africa Bibliography* (1 a year).

International Association for South-East European Studies/Association Internationale d'Études du Sud-Est Européen (AIESEE): Ap. 18, Nicolae Racota 12–14, 011393 Bucharest, Romania; tel. 212242965; internet www.aiesee.org; f. 1963; promotes study on the civilizations spread over the Balkan and SE European spaces, on their relationship with the other civilizations of Europe or of the rest of the world, on their share to the world's cultural patrimony, thus turning this study into a means for reaching peace and friendship, rising above the variety of ideologies and political regimes; organizes int. congress; 24 mem. countries; Pres. Prof. ANDRÉ GUILLOU (France); Sec.-Gen. Prof. RĂZVAN THEODORESCU (Romania); publs *Bulletin d'archéologie sud-est européenne*, *Bulletin de l'AIESEE* (1 a year).

International Association for the Study of Insurance Economics/Geneva Association: 53 route de Malagnou, 1208 Geneva, Switzerland; tel. 227076600; e-mail secretariat@genevaassociation.org; internet www.genevaassociation.org; f. 1973; detects early ideas and emerging debates on political, economic and societal issues concerning the industry; develops research programmes, regular publs and int. meetings; serves as a catalyst for progress in understanding risk and insurance matters; acts as an information creator and disseminator; organizes int. expert networks and manages discussion platforms for insurance execs, specialists, policy-makers, regulators and multilateral orgs; int. insurance think tank for insurance and risk management issues; 90 mem. CEOs from the world's insurance companies; Chair. NIKOLAUS VON BOMHARD (Germany); Sec.-Gen. and Man. Dir of Geneva Assn JOHN H. FITZPATRICK (USA/Ireland); publs *The Geneva Papers on Risk and Insurance* (4 a year), *The Geneva Reports* (irregular), *The Geneva Risk and Insurance Review* (2 a year).

International Association of Schools of Social Work (IASSW)/Asociacion Internacional de Escuelas de Trabajo Social/ Association Internationale des Ecoles de Travail Social: c/o Prof. Vimla Nadkarni, School of Social Work, Tata Institute of Social Sciences, Maharashtra, India; e-mail iassw.secretary@gmail.com; internet www.iassw-aiets.org; f. 1928; promotes devt of social work education throughout the world; develops standards to enhance quality of social work education; encourages international exchange, provides forums for sharing social work research and scholarship; promotes human rights and social devt through policy and advocacy activities; organizes conf. of social work educators every 2 years; 1,700 mem. schools of social work in 90 countries and 35 nat. asscns of schools; Pres. Prof. Dr VIMLA NADKARNI (India); Sec. TETYANA SEMIGINA (Ukraine); publs *International Social Work*, *Social Dialogue* (online, social-dialogue.com).

International Center for Monetary and Banking Studies/Centre International d'Études Monétaires et Bancaires: 11A ave de la Paix, 1202 Geneva, Switzerland; tel. 227349548; e-mail secretariat@cimb.ch; internet www.icmb.org; f. 1972; associated with the Graduate Institute of Int. and Devt Studies; facilitates exchange of ideas and information, research and scientific study of int. monetary, financial and banking issues; organizes yearly int. confs, public lectures; Pres. THOMAS JORDAN (Switzerland); Dir Prof. CHARLES WYPLOSZ (Switzerland); publ. *Geneva Reports on the World Economy*.

International Centre for Ethnic Studies: 554/6A, Peradeniya Rd, Mulgampola, Kandy, Sri Lanka; tel. (81) 2232381; e-mail icesresch@sltnet.lk; internet ices.lk; f. 1982; encourages cross-national comparative research in ethnic policy studies; provides an institutional focus and identity for the study and management of ethnic conflict; cultivates understanding of ethnicity, identity politics and conflict; fosters conditions for an inclusive, just and peaceful soc. nationally, regionally and globally, through research, publication, dialogue, creative expression and knowledge transfer; library of 14,000 vols, spec. collns on ethnicity and women's issues; Chair. Dr DEEPIKA UDAGAMA (Sri Lanka); Exec. Dir Dr DHAMMIKA HERATH (acting) (Sri Lanka); publs *International Journal of Ethnic and Social Studies* (2 a year), *Nethra Review* (2 a year).

International Centre of Bantu Civilization/Centre International des Civilisations Bantu: BP 770, Libreville, Gabon; tel. 775084; e-mail ciciba@caramail.com; internet www.ciciba.net; f. 1983; research and documentation centre for the conservation and promotion of the cultural heritage of the Bantu civilization; activities in all fields of culture, science and education; 10 mem. states; library of 4,000 vols, and spec. colln of univ. theses (microfiche) on mem. states; Dir-Gen. VATOMENE KUKANDA; publs *CICIBA-Informations* (4 a year), *Muntu* (2 a year).

International Commission for the History of Representative and Parliamentary Institutions/Commission Internationale pour l'Histoire des Assemblées d'Etats: c/o Prof. Dr Lothar Höbelt, Universität Wien, Institut für Geschichte, Dr-Karl-Lueger-Ring 1, 1010 Vienna, Austria; e-mail lothar.hoebelt@univie.ac.at; internet www.ichrpi.com; f. 1936; affiliated to the Int. Cttee of Historical Sciences; encourages research on origin and history of rep. and parliamentary instns; encourages study of devt of rep. instns in a wide and comparative way; facilitates int. exchange of bibliographical information; organizes annual confs; publishes monographs; 200 mems from 30 countries; Pres. Prof. MARIA SOFIA CORCIULO (Italy); Sec. LOTHAS HÖBELT (Austria); publ. *Parliaments, Estates and Representation* (2 a year).

International Council on Social Welfare/ Conseil International d'Action Sociale/ Consejo Internacional del Bienestar Social: POB 28957, Kampala, Uganda; tel. (414) 321150; e-mail icsw@icsw.org; internet www.icsw.org; f. 1928; promotes forms of social and economic devt that aim to reduce poverty, hardship and vulnerability worldwide, esp. in developing countries; prepares statements on positions collated from membership to present at UN level; conducts training forums for NGOs in ICSW regions on the Social Protection Fl. Initiative; centres in 9 regions; 97 mem. orgs in 84 countries; Pres. MICHAEL CICHON; Exec. Dir SERGEI ZELENEV; publs *International Social Work*, *Proceedings of International Conferences on Social Welfare* (every 2 years).

International Federation of Business and Professional Women (BPW International)/Federación Internacional de Mujeres de Negocios y Profesionales: Rue de Saint-Jean 26, 1203, Geneva, Switzerland; e-mail presidents.office@bpw-international.org; internet www.bpw-international.org; f. 1930; develops the professional and leadership potential of women at all levels; promotes interests of business and professional women to bring their specialized knowledge and skills to play more effective part in int. governmental orgs; 25,000 mems; Pres. FREDA MIRIKLIS (Australia); Exec. Sec. Dr YASMIN DARWICH (Mexico).

International Federation of Social Science Organizations/Fédération Internationale des Organisations de Science Sociale: Room 209, Palma Hall, Univ. of the Philippines, Diliman, 1101 Quezon City, Philippines; tel. (2) 926-2511; e-mail ifsso_secretariat@yahoo.com; internet ifsso.net; f. 1973 as a Standing Cttee for Cooperation with Nat. Ccls, current name and status 1979; stimulates and promotes social science research; advances exchange of information, ideas and experiences among its mems; encourage int. cooperation in social sciences; organizes a gen. conf. every 2 years; 19 mems, 13 full mem. orgs, 6 assoc. mem. orgs; Pres. Dr NESTOR T. CASTRO (Philippines); Sec.-Gen. HAKAN GULERCE (Turkey).

International Fiscal Association: World Trade Center, Beursplein 37, POB 30215, 3001 DE Rotterdam, Netherlands; tel. (10) 4052990; e-mail a.gensecr@ifa.nl; internet www.ifa.nl; f. 1938; studies and advances int. and comparative law with regard to public finance and esp. int. and comparative fiscal law and the financial and economic aspects of taxation; nat. brs in 66 countries; 12,500 mems in 111 countries; Pres. PORUS F. KAKA (India); Sec.-Gen. Prof. Dr H. A. KOGELS (Netherlands); publ. *Cahiers de Droit Fiscal International* (Studies on International Fiscal Law, 2 a year).

International Institute for Ligurian Studies/Istituto Internazionale di Studi Liguri: Via Romana 39, 18012 Bordighera IM, Italy; tel. 184263601; e-mail iisl@istitutostudi.191.it; internet www.iisl.it; f. 1947; encourages study and promotion of the history and archaeology, ancient monuments and the regional tradition in the NW Mediterranean originally inhabited by the Ligurians; mems in France, Italy, Spain, Switzerland; library of 90,000 vols; Pres. COSIMO COSTA; Dir Prof. CARLO VARALDO (Italy); publs *Bollettino IISL*, *Rivista di Studi Liguri*.

International Institute of Philosophy (IIP)/Institut International de Philosophie: 96 Blvd Raspail, 75006 Paris, France; tel. 143363911; e-mail inst.intern.philo@wanadoo.fr; internet www.i-i-p.org; f. 1937; clarifies fundamental issues of contemporary philosophy in annual meetings and by several series of publs; promotes mutual understanding among thinkers of different traditions and cultural backgrounds; 106 mems in 45 countries; Pres. ENRICO BERTI (Italy); Sec.-Gen. Prof. BERNARD BOURGEOIS (France); publs *Actes des congrès internationaux* (1 a year), *Bibliography of Philosophy* (online), *Philosophy of Education*, *Surveys (Chroniques) of Philosophy*.

International Institute of Sociology/ Institut International de Sociologie: c/o The Swedish Collegium for Advanced Study, Linneanum, Thunbergsvägen 2, 752 38 Uppsala, Sweden; tel. (18) 557-085; e-mail info@iisoc.org; internet www.iisoc.org; f. 1893; stimulates and facilitates devt, exchange and application of scientific knowledge to questions of sociological relevance; organizes congress every 2 years; 300 mems in 45 countries; Pres. BJÖRN WITTROCK (Sweden); Sec.-Gen. PETER HEDSTRÖM (UK); publs *Annales de l'Institut International de Sociologie/The Annals of the International Institute of Sociology*, *The International Review of Sociology/Revue Internationale de Sociologie*.

International Monetary Fund Institute: c/o Int. Monetary Fund, 700 19th St, NW, Washington, DC 20431, USA; tel. (202) 623-6660; e-mail insinfo@imf.org; internet www.imf.org/external/np/ins/english/about.htm; f. 1964; provides specialist training in economic analysis and policy, statistics, public finance, and bank supervision, for officials of mem. countries; 7 regional training centres; organizes seminars and confs; courses and seminars in Arabic, English, French and Spanish; library; 188 mem. countries; Dir Dr SHARMINI COOREY (Sri Lanka); publ. *Courier* (2 a year).

International Peace Institute: 777 United Nations Plaza, New York, NY 10017-3521, USA; tel. (212) 687-4300; e-mail ipi@ipinst.org; internet www.ipinst.org; f. 1970 as Int. Peace Acad., present name 2008; works closely with the UN and other governmental and non-governmental orgs to promote the prevention and settlement of armed conflicts between and within states by strengthening int. peace and security instns; employs policy research, convening, publishing and outreach; Pres. TERJE RØD-LARSEN (Norway); Sec. and Treas. MORTIMER B. ZUCKERMAN (USA); publs *International Peacekeeping* (4 a year, co-edited by IPI), *IPI Working Papers*.

International Society for Ethnology and Folklore/Internationale Gesellschaft für Ethnologie und Folklore/Société Internationale d'Ethnologie et de Folklore: c/o Meertens Institute, Joan Muyskenweg 25, 1096 CJ Amsterdam, Netherlands; tel. (20) 4628500; e-mail sief@meertens.knaw.nl; internet www.siefhome.org; f. 1964; attached to World Ccl of Anthropological Assns (WCAA), American Folklore Soc. (AFS) and European Asscn of Social Anthropologists (EASA): collaboration with UNESCO; organizes comms, symposia, congresses; establishes and maintains collaboration between specialists in European ethnology, folklore studies and adjoining fields; organizes int. congress every 2 years; 500 mems; Pres. ULLRICH KOCKEL (UK).

International Society for the Study of Medieval Philosophy/Société Internationale pour l'Étude de la Philosophie Médiévale: c/o Prof. Dr Maarten J. F. M. Hoenen, Albert-Ludwigs-Universität Freiburg, Philosophisches Seminar, Pl. der Universität 3, 79085 Freiburg im Breisgau, Germany; tel. (761) 2032440; e-mail siepm.membership@philosophie.uni-freiburg.de; internet www.siepm.uni-freiburg.de; f. 1958; promotes study of medieval thought and the collaboration between individuals and instns engaged in this field; provides representation for those institutions and scholars on nat. and int. bodies that give academic and financial support for philosophical study and research; organizes int. congresses every 5 years and annual colloquium between congresses; 800 mems in 45 countries; Chair. LORIS STURLESE (Italy); Sec.-Gen. Prof. Dr MAARTEN J. F. M. HOENEN (Germany); publs *Bulletin de Philosophie Médiévale* (1 a year), *Rencontres de philosophie médiévale*.

International Society for Third-Sector Research (ISTR): Room 578, Wyman Park Bldg, 3400 N Charles St, Baltimore, MD 21218-2688, USA; tel. (410) 516-4678; e-mail istr_secretariat@jhu.edu; internet www.istr.org; f. 1992; encourages research and education internationally on Third Sector related issues, theories and politics; enhances dissemination and application of knowledge about the Third Sector; regional research networks in Africa, Asia, Europe, Latin America and the Caribbean, Middle East; organizes conf. every 2 years; offers Emerging Scholar Dissertation Award, Best Paper Award, Best Poster Award every 2 years; 875 mems; Pres. WENDY EARLES (Australia); Exec. Dir MARGERY B. DANIELS; publ. *Voluntas* (4 a year).

International Society of Criminology/Sociedad Internacional de Criminología/Société Internationale de Criminologie: Hooverplein 10, 3000 Leuven, Belgium; tel. (16) 32-51-15; e-mail crim.sic@gmail.com; internet www.isc-sic.org; f. 1938; promotes scientific study of criminal phenomena at int. level; organizes World Congresses of Criminology every 3 years and Int. Courses in Criminology; observatory on academic criminology programmes; 800 mems; Pres. Prof. TONY PETERS (Belgium); Sec.-Gen. Prof. STEPHAN PARMENTIER (Belgium); publ. *International Annals of Criminology* (1 a year, online (www.isc-sic.org/web/index.php/en/international-annals)).

International Society of Social Defence and Humane Criminal Policy/Société Internationale de Défense Sociale pour une Politique Criminelle Humaniste: c/o Centro nazionale di prevenzione e difesa sociale, Palazzo comunale delle scienze sociali, Piazza Castello 3, 20121 Milan MI, Italy; tel. 286460714; e-mail cnpds.ispac@cnpds.it; f. 1946; consultative status with UN Economic and Social Ccl; studies crime-related problems in the perspective of a system of reactions, which through prevention and resocialization of deviants, aims to protect the individuals and soc. at large; 350 mems; Pres. LUIS ARROYO ZAPATERO (Spain); Sec.-Gen. EDMONDO BRUTI LIBERATI (Italy); publ. *Cahiers de défense sociale* (1 a year, in English, French and Spanish).

Inter-Parliamentary Union/Union Interparlementaire: 5 chemin du Pommier, CP 330, 1218 Le Grand-Saconnex GE, Switzerland; tel. 229194150; e-mail postbox@ipu.org; internet www.ipu.org; f. 1889; fosters contacts, coordination and exchange of experience among parliaments and parliamentarians of all countries; promotes democracy by strengthening and developing the means of action of rep. instns; organizes confs to study political, economic, social, juridical, cultural and environmental problems of int. significance; promotes free and fair elections and provides assistance to rep. assemblies; helps to solve cases of violation of parliamentarians' rights; promotes status of women in political life; gathers and disseminates information on parliamentary matters; 163 mems and 10 assoc. mems; Pres. Dr ABDELWAHAD RADI (Morocco); Sec.-Gen. ANDERS B. JOHNSSON (Sweden); publs *IPU Review* (4 a year), *Panorama of Parliamentary Elections* (1 a year), *Summary Records of the Proceedings of IPU Assemblies* (2 a year, in English and French), *World Directory of Parliaments* (1 a year).

Italian–Latin American Institute/Istituto Italo-Latino Americano: Via Giovanni Paisiello, 24, 00198 Rome RM, Italy; tel. 6684921; e-mail info@iila.org; internet www.iila.org; f. 1966; develops and coordinates research and documentation on the problems, achievements and prospects of mem. countries in cultural, scientific, economic, technical and social fields; organizes meetings and promotes activities to create awareness of Latin America in Italy; cooperates with intergovernmental bodies, instns and orgs specializing in dealing with Latin America; 21 mem. countries; library of 90,000 vols, 4,500 periodicals; Dir-Gen. SIMONETTA CAVALIERI; Sec.-Gen. GIORGIO MALFATTI DI MONTE TRETTO; publs *Quaderni IILA* (series *Economia, Scienza, Cooperazione*), *Revista IILA-SICA*.

Nordic Institute of Asian Studies/Nordisk Institut for Asienstudier: Univ. of Copenhagen, City Campus, Øster Farimagsgade 5, 1353 Copenhagen K, Denmark; tel. 35-32-95-00; e-mail sec@nias.ku.dk; internet www.nias.ku.dk; f. 1968; funded through Nordic Ccl of Mins; research and documentation centre for modern Asian studies within humanities and social sciences to promote research and publish books on Asia; organizes confs and workshops, accessible information resources, commentary on current affairs; 23 Nordic univs and research instns; library of 38,000 vols; Chair. Prof. Dr LARS BO KASPERSEN (Denmark); Sec. to the Board and Dir Dr GEIR HELGESEN.

Organisation for Economic Co-operation and Development (OECD)/Organisation de Coopération et de Développement Économiques (OCDE): 2 rue André-Pascal, 75775 Paris Cedex 16, France; tel. 145248200; internet www.oecd.org; f. 1961; works with govts to understand economic, social and environmental change; measures productivity and global flows of trade and investment; analyses and compares data to predict future trends; works with businesses, labour and other civil soc. orgs; 34 mem. countries; Sec.-Gen. ANGEL GURRÍA (Mexico); publs *CELE Exchange* (3 a year), *Creditor Reporting System on Aid Activities* (6 a year), *Energy Prices and Taxes* (4 a year), *Financial Market Trends* (3 a year), *Higher Education Management and Policy* (3 a year), *Indicators of Industry and Services* (4 a year), *International Trade by Commodity Statistics* (5 a year), *Journal of Business Cycle Measurement and Analysis* (3 a year), *Main Economic Indicators* (12 a year), *Main Science and Technology Indicators* (2 a year), *Monthly Statistics of International Trade* (12 a year), *NEA News* (2 a year), *Nuclear Law Bulletin* (2 a year), *OECD Economic Outlook* (2 a year), *OECD Economic Surveys* (every 2 years), *OECD Journal: Economic Studies* (2 a year), *OECD Journal of Competition Law and Policy* (4 a year), *OECD Journal on Budgeting* (3 a year), *OECD Papers* (12 a year), *Oil, Gas, Coal and Electricity—Quarterly Statistics* (4 a year), *Quarterly Labour Force Statistics*, *Quarterly National Accounts*, *The DAC Journal* (4 a year), *The OECD Observer* (6 a year, online, www.oecdobserver.org), *Yearbook*.

Pan African Institute for Development/Institut Panafricain pour le Développement: POB 35527, Bastos, Yaoundé, Cameroon; tel. 22208235; e-mail sg-paid-ipd@hotmail.ch; internet www.paidafrica.org; f. 1965; implements, organizes and supports training institutes, research and support projects working for social and economic devt; seeks ways economic, moral or material of any nature to solve the problem of training for devt of Africa; 5 regional brs; Sec.-Gen. Dr MBUKI V. MWAMUFIYA; publs *PAID Report* (2 a year), *Yearly Progress Report*.

Society for International Development/Société Internationale pour le Développement: 1101 15th St, NW, Third Fl., Washington, DC 20005, USA; tel. (202) 331-1317; e-mail generalinquiries@sidw.org; internet www.sidw.org; f. 1957; mobilizes and strengthens civil soc. groups by building partnerships among them and with other sectors; fosters local initiatives and new forms of social experimentation; organizes regional and topical workgroup events, monthly chapter events and special programmes; 3,000 mems in 80 countries, with 45 local chapters, 1,200 individual mems and 55 institutional mems; Pres. DANIEL F. RUNDE; Sec. MELISSA LOGAN; Exec. Dir DAYNA CADE; publ. *Development* (4 a year).

Statistical Institute for Asia and the Pacific: JETRO-IDE Bldg, 2–2, Wakaba 3-chome, Mihama-ku, Chiba-shi, Chiba 261-8787, Japan; tel. (43) 2999782; e-mail staff@unsiap.or.jp; internet www.unsiap.or.jp; f. 1970 as Asian Statistical Institute (ASI), present name 1977; subsidiary body of UN Economic and Social Comm. for Asia and the Pacific (ESCAP); provides training in official statistics to govt statisticians in the Asia-Pacific region as recommended by resolution 75 (XXIII) of ESCAP; assists mems and economies in transition in establishing or strengthening their statistical training capability; 20 Fellows (Production and Devt of Official Statistics course), 19 Fellows (ICT course), 22 Fellows (Analysis, Interpretation and Use of Official Statistics course), 5 Fellows (Central Asian Countries course); library of 20,000 vols, 200 series of periodicals, 300 types of documents; Dir MARGARITA F. GUERRERO.

Stockholm International Peace Research Institute (SIPRI): Signalistgatan 9, 169 70 Solna, Sweden; tel. (8) 655-9700; e-mail director@sipri.org; internet www.sipri.org; f. 1966; research into problems of peace and conflict with particular attention to the problems of disarmament and arms control; provides data, analysis and recommendations to policy-makers, researchers, media and the interested public; library of 52,000 vols; Chair. GÖRAN LENNMARKER (Sweden); Dir Prof. Dr TILMAN BRÜCK (Germany); publs *SIPRI Insights on Peace and Security*, *SIPRI Policy Papers*, *SIPRI Research Reports*, *SIPRI Yearbook*.

UNESCO Institute for Statistics: CP 6128, Succursale Centre-Ville, Montreal, QC H3C 3J7, Canada; 5255 ave Decelles, Seventh Fl., Montreal, QC H3T 2B1, Canada; tel. (514) 343-6880; e-mail uis.information@unesco.org; internet www.uis.unesco.org; f. 1999; primary data source of education and literacy data for leading publs and databases: Education For All Global Monitoring Report, World Devt Indicators, Human Devt Report, State of World's Children; collects and disseminates statistics in education, science and technology, culture and communication; designs new indicators to better reflect policy needs of developing countries; promotes wider use of data for policy-making; Chair. GRACE BEDIAKO (Ghana); Dir HENDRIK VAN DER POL; publ. *Global Education Digest* (1 a year, in Arabic, English, French and Spanish).

United Nations Institute for Training and Research (UNITAR)/Institut des Nations Unies pour la Formation et la Recherche/Instituto de las Naciones Unidas para Formación Profesional e Investigaciones: Palais des Nations, 1211 Geneva 10, Switzerland; International Environment House, 11–13 chemin des Anémones, 1219 Chatelaine Geneva, Switzerland; tel. 229178400; e-mail info@unitar.org; internet www.unitar.org; f. 1965 as an autonomous body within the framework of the UN; enhances the effectiveness of the UN in achieving the major objectives of the org., in particular the maintenance of peace and security and the promotion of economic and social devt through training and research; conducts capacity devt and research activities around the world; conducts seminars for diplomats and others who work in the UN system and carries out training, either at UN HQ or in the field, which has spec. relevance for developing countries; conducts research into problems of concern to the UN system; Chair. HE HENRI LOPES; Dir SALLY FEGAN-WYLES (Ireland).

United Nations University World Institute for Development Economics Research (UNU-WIDER): Katajanokanlaituri 6B, 00160 Helsinki, Finland; tel. (9) 6159911; e-mail wider@wider.unu.edu; internet www.wider.unu.edu; f. 1985; conducts policy-oriented research into inequality and poverty, global economic devt and related issues; provides a forum for professional interaction and advocacy of policies leading to robust, equitable and environmentally sustainable growth; promotes capacity strengthening and training for scholars and govt officials in the fields of economic and social policy-making; library of 10,000 vols; Chair. Prof. ERNEST ARYEETEY (Ghana); Dir Prof. Dr FINN TARP (Finland).

Vienna Institute for International Dialogue and Cooperation/Wiener Institut für Internationalen Dialog und Zusammenarbeit: Moellwaldpl. 5/3, 1040 Vienna, Austria; tel. (1) 7133594; e-mail office@vidc.org; internet www.vidc.org; f. 1962, present status 1987; disseminates information on problems and achievements of developing countries by all possible means in order to convince the public or industrialized nations of the necessity to increase devt aid and to strengthen int. cooperation; research programmes; organizes cultural exchanges between South and North; engages in anti-racism and anti-discrimination activities in sports at nat. and European level; Pres. Mag. BARBARA PRAMMER (Austria); Dir Mag. WALTER POSCH (Austria).

World Bank Institute: 1818 H St, NW, Washington, DC 20433, USA; tel. (202) 473-6436; e-mail wbi_infoline@worldbank.org; internet wbi.worldbank.org/wbi; f. 1955; provides learning programmes and policy advice in the areas of climate change, fragile and conflict-affected states, governance, growth and competitiveness, health systems, public-private partnerships, urban devt; delivers training activities for policy-makers in 149 countries through direct and distance learning; has formal partnerships with 130 academic and training instns in developed nations and client countries; Vice-Pres. Dr SANJAY PRADHAN; publ. *Development Outreach* (4 a year).

World Intellectual Property Organization (WIPO)/Organisation Mondiale de la Propriété Intellectuelle/Organización Mundial de la Propiedad Intelectual: 34 chemin des Colombettes, 1211 Geneva 20, Switzerland; tel. 223389111; e-mail wipo.mail@wipo.int; internet www.wipo.int; f. 1967; promotes use of intellectual property as a means of stimulating innovation and creativity; promotes the protection of intellectual property rights worldwide; extends benefits of the int. intellectual property system to all mem. states; progressive devt of int. intellectual property law, assisting developing countries and providing services to facilitate the process of obtaining intellectual property rights in multiple countries; 185 mem. states; library of 35,000 references; Dir-Gen. FRANCIS GURRY; publs *International Designs Bulletin* (12 a year), *WIPO Gazette of International Marks* (52 a year), *WIPO Magazine* (24 a year, in English, French and Spanish).

World Society for Ekistics: 23 Strat. Syndesmou St, 106 73 Athens, Greece; tel. (210) 3623216; e-mail ekistics@otenet.gr; internet www.ekistics.org; f. 1965, current status 1970; promotes devt of knowledge and ideas concerning human settlements by research and through publs and confs; encourages devt and expansion of education in ekistics; educates public opinion concerning ekistics; promotes recognition of benefits and necessity of an interdisciplinary approach to the needs of human settlements; 223 mems; Pres. Prof. CALOGERO MUSCARA (Italy); Sec.-Gen. and Treas. PANAYIS PSOMOPOULOS (Greece); publ. *EKISTICS—The Journal* (12 a year).

Education

Academic Cooperation Association (ACA): 15 rue d'Egmontstraat, 1000 Brussels, Belgium; tel. (2) 513-22-41; e-mail info@aca-secretariat.be; internet www.aca-secretariat.be; f. 1993; promotes innovation and internationalization in higher education and training; enhances contacts, networking and cooperation between its mem. orgs and third parties; expert centre; produces studies and evaluations; organizes int. seminars and confs; provides information on new devts in European and global higher education; 24 mem orgs (21 European and 3 non-European); Pres. Dr SIJBOLT NOORDA; Dir BERND WÄCHTER.

African and Malagasy Council for Higher Education/Conseil Africain et Malgache pour l'Enseignement Supérieur (CAMES): 01 BP 134, Ouagadougou 01, Burkina Faso; tel. 50368146; e-mail cames@bf.refer.org; internet www.lecames.org; f. 1968; ensures coordination between mem. states in fields of higher education and research; gathers and disseminates academic papers and research; develops and promotes dialogue to coordinate systems of higher education and research in order to harmonize programs and staffing levels in different HEIs; 19 mem. countries, 12 institutional mems; Sec.-Gen. Prof. Dr BERTRAND MBATCHI (Gabon); publs *CAMES info* (4 a year), *Revue CAMES*.

Agence Universitaire de la Francophonie: Case postale du Musée, CP 49714, Montreal, QC H3T 2A5, Canada; 3034 Blvd Edouard-Montpetit, Montreal, QC H3T 1J7, Canada; tel. (514) 343-6630; e-mail rectorat@auf.org; internet www.auf.org; f. 1961, present name 1998; supports devt strategies of mem. instns; aims to establish a French-language int. academic community that produces and transmits knowledge; 70 instns in 40 countries; 786 mem. instns in 98 countries; Chair. YVON FONTAINE (Canada); Exec. Dir Prof. BERNARD CERQUIGLINI.

Arab Bureau of Education for the Gulf States: POB 94693, Diplomatic Quarters, Jabir Ibn Hayyan Sq., Riyadh 11614, Saudi Arabia; tel. (1) 4800555; e-mail abegs@abegs.org; internet www.abegs.org; f. 1975; coordinates and integrates efforts of mem. states (Bahrain, Kuwait, Oman, Qatar, Saudi Arabia and the UAE) in fields of education, science and culture; Gulf Arab States Educational Research Center: see Kuwait chapter; established Arabian Gulf Univ. in Bahrain; Dir-Gen. Dr ALI BIN ABDUL KHALIQ AL-KARNI; publ. *Rissalat al-Khaleej al Araby* (Message of the Arabian Gulf, 4 a year).

Asian Association of Open Universities: c/o Wawasan Open Univ., 54 Jalan Sultan Ahmad Shah, 10050, Penang, Malaysia; tel. (4) 2180333; e-mail secretariat@aaou.net; internet www.aaou.net; f. 1987; promotes education by distance teaching systems and develops its potentialities; promotes professional and ethical standards among distance educators; facilitates cooperation with other similar regional and int. bodies; 48 full mems, 22 assoc. mems, 2 individual supporting mems; Pres. Prof. Dr WONG TAT MENG (Malaysia); Sec.-Gen. Prof. Dr HO SINN CHYE (Malaysia); publ. *Asian Association of Open Universities Journal* (2 a year).

Asociación Iberoamericana de Educación Superior a Distancia (AIESAD)/ Ibero-American Association for Open University Education: Calle Bravo Murillo 38 (9A), 28015 Madrid, Spain; tel. 913986549; e-mail secretaria.ejecutiva@aiesad.org; internet www.aiesad.org; f. 1980; promotes research and application of new methods and techniques in the field of higher distance education and facilitates their use; facilitates cooperation and exchange of teachers, researchers, administrators and students among mems; develops educational and cultural programs of common interest to all mem. countries; 27 mem. from 14 Ibero-American countries; Pres. Dr CARLOS BIELSCHOWSKY (Brazil); Sec. and Treas. Dr ROSARIO DOMINGO NAVAS (Spain); publ. *Revista Iberoamericana de Educación a Distancia (RIED)* (print and online, ried.utpl.edu.ec).

Associação das Universidades de Língua Portuguesa (AULP) (Association of Portuguese Language Universities): Ave Santos Dumont, 67, 2°, 1050-203 Lisbon, Portugal; tel. 217816360; e-mail aulp@aulp.org; internet www.aulp.org; f. 1986; promotes cooperation and research between univs and educational instns of Portuguese-speaking countries through the exchange of researchers and students; 120 mem. instns in Angola, Brazil, Cape Verde, Guinea-Bissau, Macao, Mozambique, Portugal, São Tomé e Príncipe and Timor-Leste; Pres. JORGE FERRÃO (Mozambique); Exec. Sec. TERESA BOTELHEIRO (Portugal); publs *Actas dos Encontros*, *Revista Internacional em Língua Portuguesa (RILP)*.

Association for Teacher Education in Europe (ATEE): 67 Rue Hobbema, 1000 Brussels, Belgium; tel. (479) 40-61-19; e-mail ateesecretariat@gmail.com; internet www.atee1.org; f. 1976; enhances quality of teacher education in Europe; supports professional devt of teachers and teacher educators at all levels; establishes contacts between instns for teacher education and those responsible for that education; arranges working groups, annual conf.; undertakes consultancy work for European orgs; 120 mems; Pres. Dr JUSTINA ERCULJ (Slovenia); Vice-Pres. Dr JOANA SALAZAR NOGUERA (Spain); publ. *European Journal of Teacher Education* (4 a year).

Association Internationale de Pédagogie Universitaire: c/o Michel Delhaxhe, Service Guidance Etude, Administration de l'Enseignement et des Etudiants, Université de Liège, Etude Bâtiment B3E, Traverse des architectes 3, 4000 Liège, Belgium; tel. (4) 366-20-73; e-mail mdelhaxhe@ulg.ac.be; internet www.aipu-assos.org; f. 1980; Francophone org. promoting research and devt in teaching and higher education; encourages inter-university cooperation through the exchange of information and experiences in univ. teaching; 800 mems; Pres. Prof. SYLVIE DORE (Canada); Vice-Pres. Prof. AZIZ ETTAHIR (Morocco); Sec.-Gen. MICHEL DELHAXHE (Belgium); publ. *RIPES* (2 a year, online, ripes.revues.org).

Association Montessori Internationale: Koninginneweg 161, 1075 CN Amsterdam, Netherlands; tel. (20) 6798932; e-mail info@montessori-ami.org; internet www.montessori-ami.org; f. 1929; propagates ideals and educational methods of Dr Maria Montessori and spreads knowledge on child devt without racial, religious or political prejudice; supervises affiliated training courses for teachers; sponsors int. congresses and study confs on Montessori education; creates new training centres and offers affiliation to Montessori socs; Pres. ANDRÉ ROBERFROID; Exec. Dir LYNNE LAWRENCE; publs *Communications* (2 a year), *The AMI Bulletin* (3 a year).

Association of African Universities/ Association des Universités Africaines: POB AN5744, Accra-North, Ghana; African Univs House, 11 Aviation Rd Extension, Airport Residential Area, Accra, Ghana; tel. (302) 774495; e-mail info@aau.org; internet www.aau.org; f. 1967; promotes cooperation among African higher education instns in training, research, community services and higher education policy, curriculum devt and determination of equivalence in academic degrees; collects, classifies and disseminates information on higher education and research, particularly in Africa; facilitates cooperation between its mems and the int. academic world; encourages devt and wide use of African languages and supports training of univ. teachers and administrators to deal with problems in African education in general; studies, publicizes and advocates the educational and related needs of African higher education instns; 265 mems from 46 African countries; Pres. Prof. GEORGE ALBERT MAGOHA (acting) (Kenya); Sec.-Gen. Prof. ETIENNE EHOUN EHILE (Côte d'Ivoire); publ. *Handbook* (every 2 years).

Association of Amazonian Universities/ Associação de Universidades Amazônicas (UNAMAZ)/Asociación de Universidades Amazónicas: Ave Tancredo Neves, 2501 Bairro Montese Campos da UFRA, 66077-530 Belém, PA, Brazil; tel. (91) 32105230; e-mail unamaz@amazon.com.br; f. 1987; promotes mutual understanding among mem. instns and identifes needs, capabilities and common opportunities; addresses common regional problems and promotes solutions through information, communication and scientific cooperation; encourages and supports training and qualification of human resources at all levels for sustainable devt in the Amazon; 66 mem. univs in Bolivia, Brazil, Colombia, Ecuador, Guyana, Peru, Suriname and Venezuela; Pres. ALFREDO QUINTEROS GARCÍA; Sec. MAXIMILIAN STEINBRENNER.

Association of American International Colleges and Universities: c/o Dr Joseph G. Jabbra, Lebanese American Univ., POB 36, Byblos, Lebanon; e-mail president.aaicu@lau.edu.lb; internet www.aaicu.org; f. 1971 as Asscn of Int. Colleges and Univs, present name 1988; promotes cooperation among ind. instns offering int. education in Europe and the Near E; 18 regular mem. univs and colleges, 8 assoc. mem. univs and colleges; Pres. Dr JOSEPH G. JABBRA (Lebanon).

Association of Arab Universities: POB 401, Jubeyha, Amman, Jordan; tel. (6) 5062048; e-mail secgen@aaru.edu.jo; internet www.aaru.edu.jo; f. 1964; consolidates cooperation and coordinates efforts among Arab univs and instns of higher education in terms of student activities, teaching methods and facilities; promotes jt research projects and quality assurance and accreditation in the Arab univs; 240 Arab univ. mems; Sec.-Gen. Prof. Dr SULTAN ABU-ORABI; publs *Bulletin* (6 a year), *Directory of Arab Universities*, *Directory of Teaching Staff of Arab Universities*, *Journal of the Association of Arab University* (4 a year).

Association of Caribbean Universities and Research Institutes (UNICA): c/o Annette Insanally, Latin American-Caribbean Centre, Regional HQs, Univ. of the West Indies, Mona, Kingston 7, Jamaica; tel. 7024721; e-mail unica@uwimona.edu.jm; internet www.uwi.edu/unica; f. 1967; fosters contact and collaboration between mem. univs and institutes; organizes confs, meetings, seminars; disseminates information through newsletters, bulletins; facilitates cooperation and the pooling of resources in research; encourages exchanges of staff and students; mems: 37 mem. univs and instns; Pres. Prof. E. NIGEL HARRIS (Jamaica); Sec.-Gen. ANNETTE INSANALLY (Jamaica); publ. *Caribbean Educational Bulletin* (4 a year).

Association of Commonwealth Universities (ACU): Woburn House, 20–24 Tavistock Sq., London, WC1H 9HF, UK; tel. (20) 73806700; e-mail info@acu.ac.uk; internet www.acu.ac.uk; f. 1913 as Univs Bureau of the British Empire, present name 1963; promotes contact and cooperation in higher education throughout the Commonwealth; provides assistance with staff and student mobility and devt programmes; researches and disseminates information about univs and relevant policy issues; organizes major meetings of Commonwealth univs and their reps; provides the secretariats for, and administers, various scholarship and fellowship schemes (incl. the Commonwealth Scholarship Comm. in the UK, the Marshall Aid Commemoration Comm. and the Commonwealth Univs Study Abroad Consortium; also administers the Commonwealth Foundation Medical Electives Bursaries, the ACU Devt Fellowships, the DFID Shared Scholarship Scheme, the T. H. B. Symons Fellowship, the Canada Memorial Foundation Scholarships); operates various subject specialist networks for higher education staff; provides an appointments, advertising and publicity service; operates a policy research unit; addresses the gender imbalance in higher education leadership through its women's programme; organizes various training workshops; hosts the Observatory on Borderless Higher Education; provides the secretariat for the Staff and Educational Devt Asscn; hosts an Africa Unit; 500 mem. instns; library of 18,500 vols; Sec.-Gen. Prof. Dr JOHN WOOD; publ. *Bulletin*.

Association of Southeast Asian Institutions of Higher Learning: c/o Dr Ninnat Olanvoravuth, Jamjuree 1 Bldg, Chulalongkorn Univ., Phayathai Rd, Bangkok, 10330, Thailand; tel. (2) 251-6966; e-mail ninnat.o@chula.ac.th; internet www.seameo.org/asaihl; f. 1956; promotes economic, cultural and social welfare of people of SE Asia by means of educational cooperation and research programmes; serves as a clearing-house for information, provides opportunities for discussion and recognizes distinctive academic achievements; 183 mem. instns from 22 countries; Sec.-Gen. Dr NINNAT OLANVORAVUTH; publ. *Seminar Proceedings*.

Association of the Carpathian Region Universities (ACRU): c/o Prof. Paul-Serban Agachi, Universitatea Babes-Bolyai of Cluj-Napoca, M. Kogalniceanu Str. Nr. 1, 400084 Cluj Napoca, Romania; tel. 264405300; e-mail serban.agachi@ubbcluj.ro; internet acru.uvlf.sk; f. 1994; fosters mobility of univ. community as a support of increased knowledge of languages and cultures; facilitates exchange of experience and learning; organizes forums to study and debate questions of regional nature; cooperates with local authorities, NGOs, int. instns to promote devt of the Carpathian region; 24 higher education mem. instns in Hungary, Poland, Romania, Serbia, Slovakia, Ukraine; Pres. Prof. Dr PAUL-SERBAN AGACHI (Romania); Sec.-Gen. Prof. Dr JANA MOJŽIŠOVÁ (Slovakia).

Association of Universities of Asia and the Pacific (AUAP): c/o Centre for Int.

Affairs, Suranaree Univ. of Technology, 111 University Ave, Muang, Nakhon Ratchasima 30000, Thailand; tel. (44) 224-143; e-mail auap@sut.ac.th; internet auap.sut.ac.th; f. 1995; sub-HQ in China, Philippines and Thailand; organizes confs every 2 years; 210 regular mems in 19 countries, 2 assoc. mems; Pres. Prof. Dr PRASART SUEBKA (Thailand); Sec. Prof. Dr RUBEN C. UMALY (Philippines); publ. *Gazette* (4 a year).

Association of Universities of Latin America and the Caribbean/Unión de Universidades de América Latina y el Caribe: Circuito Norponiente del Estadio Olímpico, Ciudad Universitaria, Apdo 70232, Del. Coyoacán, 04510 México, DF, Mexico; tel. (55) 56162383; e-mail contacto@udual.org; internet www.udual.org; f. 1949; links Latin American univs and other instns and cultural orgs; promotes programmes for institutional strengthening of univs in structural aspects of academic and admin. management to determine their quality; organizes general assemblies and confs; permanent statistical work; 230 affiliated mem. univs in 22 Latin American countries; library of 12,000 vols, 300 serials, records, microforms; Pres. Dr JOSÉ TADEU JORGE (Brazil); Sec.-Gen. Dr ROBERTO ESCALANTE SEMERENA (Mexico); publs *Gaceta UDUAL* (4 a year), *Proceedings of Latin American Universities Conferences*, *Revista Universidades* (4 a year), *Window* (4 a year).

Caribbean Network of Educational Innovation for Development (CARNEID): The Towers, 25 Dominica Dr., Third Fl., Kingston 5, Jamaica; tel. 4274771; e-mail kingston@unesco.org; internet www.unesco.org/carneid; f. 1981; 1 of 5 regional networks est. by UNESCO to promote systematic contact among educational instns of Caribbean mem. states in order to promote educational innovation and change; promotes cooperative efforts through exchange of information, documentation, experiences; facilitates understanding of processes and practices of educational change and experimentation; publs *Caribbean Education Annual*, *The Caribbean Teacher*.

Caribbean Regional Council for Adult Education: c/o Azad Hosein, Adult Education Unit, 51 Frederick St, Port-of-Spain, Trinidad and Tobago; tel. 625-4091; e-mail carcae@usa.net; internet carcae.tripod.com; f. 1978; promotes and facilitates cooperation among nat. adult education orgs and agencies in non-Spanish-speaking territories of the region; advocates awareness and recognition of the importance of adult education and seeks funding from govts and other sources; holds confs, seminars, training courses; advises govts and other bodies on adult education; library of 5,000 vols; Chair. VILMA MCCLENAN (Jamaica); Exec. Sec. and Treas. AZAD HOSEIN (Trinidad and Tobago).

CEMS—The Global Alliance in Management Education: 1 rue de la Libération, 78350 Jouy-en-Josas, France; tel. 139677457; e-mail info@cems.org; internet www.cems.org; f. 1988; offers masters in int. management, provides education and professional experience for multilingual, multicultural postgraduate students; involves academic and corporate partners in the definition and teaching of curriculum, implementation of a series of jt research projects; 28 mem. business schools, 70 corporate partners, 4 social partners (NGOs); Chair. Prof. Dr THOMAS BIEGER (Switzerland); Exec. Dir ROLAND SIEGERS; publs *CEMS Magazine* (2 a year, print and online), *European Business Forum* (4 a year; print and online, in asscn with PricewaterhouseCoopers).

Commonwealth Association of Polytechnics in Africa: c/o Technical Univ. of Kenya, POB 52428, Nairobi, Kenya; tel. (2) 338232; e-mail capa@kenpoly.ac.ke; internet www.capa-sec.org; f. 1978; provides forum for exchange of professional ideas and practices in technical and business education and training; improves content and methods of polytechnic teaching; policy analysis and advocacy of skills devt; disseminates information through publs and workshops; has a data centre and reference library; mem. of World Fed. of Colleges and Polytechnics; mem. of Commonwealth Consortium for Education; 177 mem. technical univs, polytechnics, vocational training instns; library of 1,200 vols; Sec.-Gen. Dr OLUBUNMI OWOSO; publ. *CAPA Scientific Journal (CAPA-SJ)* (2 a year).

Commonwealth of Learning: 1055 W Hasting St, Suite 1200, Vancouver, BC V6E 2E9, Canada; tel. (604) 775-8200; e-mail info@col.org; internet www.col.org; f. 1988; works with mins of education, schools, colleges, univs and NGOs to increase access to opportunities for learning; promotes cooperation among Commonwealth countries, utilizing distance education techniques, incl. communications technologies, to strengthen mem. countries' capacities in human resources devt; helps developing nations improve access to quality education and training; 54 mem. countries; library of 7,800 vols; Chair. Hon. BURCHELL WHITEMAN (Jamaica); Pres. and CEO Prof. ASHA KANWAR (India); publs *Connections/EdTech News* (3 a year), *Three-Year Plan*.

Commonwealth Secretariat, Education Section, Social Transformation Programmes Division: Marlborough House, Pall Mall, London, SW1Y 5HX, UK; tel. (20) 7747-6460; e-mail education@commonwealth.int; internet www.thecommonwealth.org/internal/151476/stpd; encourages and supports educational consultation and cooperation between Commonwealth countries through confs, seminars, workshops, meetings of experts, training courses for educational personnel (with assistance from the Commonwealth Fund for Technical Cooperation); contributes to nat. educational devt through studies of particular problems, handbooks, directories and training manuals, and by providing information on educational subjects; undertakes consultancies for govts on request; holds triennial conf. of Ministers of Education; Dir Dr SYLVIA ANIE; publ. *LinkIn* (4 a year).

Conference of Baltic University Rectors (CBUR): c/o Prof. Jaak Aaviksoo, Univ. of Tartu, Ülikooli 18, 51014 Tartu, Estonia; e-mail cbur@ut.ee; internet www.ut.ee/cbur; f. 1990; promotes inter-univ. cooperation in the Baltic Sea area; engages in jt research; shares didactic experience; creates and develops mutual contacts of academic staff and students of its mem. univs; holds conf. every second year; 82 full mems, 6 affiliate mem.univs; Pres. Prof. JAAK AAVIKSOO (Estonia); publ. *Universities in the Age of Information Technology* (proceedings).

Congregazione per l'Educazione Cattolica/Congregacion Para la Educacion Catolica (Congregation for Catholic Education): Palazzo delle Congregazioni, Piazza Pio XII 3, 00193 Rome RM, Italy; tel. 669884167; e-mail cec@cec.va; internet www.vatican.va/roman_curia/congregations/ccatheduc; f. 1588, present name 1988; concerned with the direction, temporal admin. and studies of Catholic univs, seminaries, schools and colleges; fosters nomination of rectors and the erection of seminaries; 31 mem. cardinals, archbishops and bishops; Prefect Cardinal ZENON GROCHOLEWSKI; Sec. Archbisop ANGELO VINCENZO ZANI; publ. *Seminarium*.

Consejo Superior Universitario Centroamericano (CSUCA) (Higher Council of Central American Universities): Avda Las Américas, 1–03 zona 14, Int. Club Los Arcos, 01014 Guatemala City, Guatemala; tel. 23671833; e-mail sg@csuca.org; internet www.csuca.org; f. 1948; exec. body of the Confederación Universitaria Centroamericana; promotes Central American integration and the strengthening of higher education in the region; fosters devt of univs through cooperation and jt work with soc. and the state; encourages devt of scientific, technological and humanistic knowledge and its application in the training of professionals for sustainable devt in the region; 20 mem. univs in Belize, Costa Rica, Dominican Republic, El Salvador, Guatemala, Honduras, Nicaragua, Panama; Sec.-Gen. Dr JUAN ALFONSO FUENTES SORIA; publ. *Boletines*.

Consortium for North American Higher Education Collaboration (CONAHEC)/Consortium pour la Collaboration dans l'Enseignement Supérieur en Amérique du Nord/Consorcio para la Colaboración en la Educación Superior en América del Norte: Univ. of Arizona, POB 210300, Tucson, AZ 85721-0300, USA; Univ. of Arizona, 220 W Sixth St, University Services Annex Bldg 300A, Room 108, Tucson, AZ 85701, USA; tel. (520) 621-7761; e-mail fmarmole@email.arizona.edu; internet www.conahec.org; f. 1994; fosters academic collaboration among instns, orgs and agencies of higher education in Canada, Mexico and the USA; promotes linkages between N America and higher education entities around the world; 165 mem. instns (incl. 16 in Canada, 73 in Mexico, 45 in the USA and 31 affiliate mems); Pres. FERNANDO LEÓN (Mexico); Exec. Dir FRANCISCO J. MARMOLEJO.

Coordinación Educativa y Cultural Centroamericana (CECC) (Coordinating Body for Education and Culture in Central America): De la Nunciatura, 100 m al norte, casa N° 8815, Rohmoser, San José, Costa Rica; tel. 2283-7630; e-mail sgcecc@racsa.co.cr; internet www.sica.int/cecc; f. 1982; promotes and works for integration in the areas of education and culture in Central America through process of decentralization and respect for cultural and natural diversity of soc. of its mem. countries; promotes exchanges between the leaders and officials of the Mins of Education and Culture; 7 mem. countries (Belize, Costa Rica, El Salvador, Guatemala, Honduras, Nicaragua, Panama), 1 assoc. country (Dominican Republic); Sec.-Gen. MARÍA EUGENIA PANIAGUA PADILLA (Costa Rica).

Danube Rectors' Conference (DRC)/Donau Rektoren Konferenz: DRC Secretariat—operated by IDM, Hahngasse 6/24, 1090 Vienna, Austria; tel. (1) 3197258; e-mail info@drc-danube.org; internet www.drc-danube.org; f. 1983; improves higher education in teaching and research; coordinates ideas and actions of its mems through the exchange of information on issues of common interest; est. working groups to address the issues of univ. legislation, curricula and evaluation of teaching and research; 70 mem. HEIs in the Danube region; Pres. Prof. Dr JIRI BALIK (Czech Republic).

Education International (EI)/Internacional de la Educación/Internationale de l'Education (IE): 5 blvd du Roi Albert II, 1210 Brussels, Belgium; tel. (2) 224-0611; e-mail headoffice@ei-ie.org; internet www.ei-ie.org; f. 1993 from the merger of the

World Confederation of Orgs of the Teaching Profession (WCOTP/CMOPE) and the Int Fed. of Free Teachers' Unions (IFFTU/SPIE); advances the cause of orgs of teachers and education employees; promotes status, interests and welfare of mems and defends their trade union and professional rights on int. level; promotes free, quality, public education for all; promotes peace, democracy, social justice, equality and the application of the Universal Declaration on Human Rights through the devt of education and the collective strength of teachers and education employees; builds solidarity and mutual cooperation among mem. orgs; 400 mem. nat. orgs in 170 countries; Pres. SUSAN HOPGOOD (Australia); Gen. Sec. FRED VAN LEEUWEN (Netherlands); publs *Monitor* (in English, French and Spanish), *The Education International Quarterly Magazine* (in English, French and Spanish).

ERASMUS (European Community Action Scheme for the Mobility of University Students): c/o Education Audiovisual and Culture Exec. Agency, 1 Ave du Bourget, 1140 Brussels, Belgium; tel. (2) 296-16-55; e-mail eac-info@ec.europa.eu; internet ec.europa.eu/education/lifelong-learning-programme/doc80_en.htm; f. 1987; aims to encourage greater student and staff mobility throughout the EU and EFTA (European Free Trade Asscn) countries by means of the creation of a European Univ. Network, the awarding of 'mobility' grants to students, arrangements for mutual recognition of qualifications and courses, and other supporting measures; offers opportunity for student placements in enterprises, univ. staff teaching and training; funds cooperation projects between HEIs across Europe; 33 participatory mem. countries; Head MONIKA HOLIK; publ. *ERASMUS and Lingua Action II Directory* (1 a year).

EuroAsian Universities Association: B-106, GSP-1, Moscow State Univ. 'M. V. Lomonosov', Leninskie Gory, Moscow, Russia, 119991; tel. (495) 9392769; e-mail eau_msu@rector.msu.ru; internet www.eau.msu.ru; f. 1989 as Univs Asscn of the Union of Soviet Socialist Republics, present name 1992; promotes implementation of the Eurasianism ideas in the sphere of education and science; fosters maintenance and devt of common educational environment and humanitarian collaboration, learning of int. practices on reformation of higher education under specific conditions of new states' establishment in the former Soviet Union; organizes confs, forums, inter-university cooperation; 128 mem. univs in 13 countries; Pres. Acad. VIKTOR A. SADOVNICHIY.

European Association for International Education: POB 11189, 1001 GD Amsterdam, Netherlands; Herengracht 487, 1017 BT Amsterdam, Netherlands; tel. (20) 3445100; e-mail info@eaie.org; internet www.eaie.org; f. 1989; stimulates and facilitates the internationalization of higher education in Europe and around the world; helps to professionalize mems and serve all those involved in the internationalization of higher education; organizes training, confs, knowledge acquisition and sharing; 2,000 mems; Pres. HANS-GEORG VAN LIEMPD (Netherlands); Exec. Dir LEONARD ENGEL (Netherlands); publs *Forum* (3 a year), *Journal of Studies in International Education*, *Occasional Papers*, *Professional Development Series*.

European Association for the Education of Adults/Asociación Europea para la Educación de Adultos/Association Européenne pour l'Education des Adultes/Europäischer Verband für Erwachsenenbildung: 40 Rue d' Arlon, 1000 Brussels, Belgium; tel. (2) 234-37-63; e-mail eaea-info@eaea.org; internet www.eaea.org; f. 1953, fmrly European Bureau of Adult Education; policy advocacy for lifelong learning at European level; encourages cooperation between adult education orgs on questions of methods, materials and exchange of individuals; arranges study sessions and tours; also has offices in Girona (Spain) and Helsinki (Finland); 127 mem. orgs in 43 countries; Pres. SUE WADDINGTON (UK); Sec.-Gen. GINA EBNER.

European Association of Distance Teaching Universities: POB 2960, 6401 DL Heerlen, Netherlands; Valkenburgerweg 177, 6419 AT Heerlen, Netherlands; tel. (45) 5762214; e-mail secretariat@eadtu.eu; internet www.eadtu.eu; f. 1987; promotes lifelong, open and flexible learning by means of higher distance education; supports bilateral and multilateral contacts between academic staff; supports cooperation in research, course devt, course transfer and credit transfer; develops new methods for higher distance education; organizes common projects in cooperation with European authorities; European Open Univ. Network (f. 1995) acts as exec. arm; 200 mem. univs; Pres. WILL SWANN; Sec.-Gen. PIET HENDERIKX (Belgium).

European Association of Institutions in Higher Education (EURASHE): Ravensteingalerij 27/3, 1000 Brussels, Belgium; tel. (2) 211-41-97; e-mail eurashe@eurashe.eu; internet www.eurashe.eu; f. 1990; promotes interests of professional higher education in the mem. countries of the EU and in other European countries, in instns that are public or recognized and/or financed by the public authorities of an EU mem. country or another European country; encourages applied and profession-related research and its technological applications; organizes annual confs, thematic seminars and tailor-made events; 1,400 higher education mem. instns in 40 countries; Pres. Prof. ANDREAS G. ORPHANIDES (Cyprus); Sec.-Gen. STEFAN DELPLACE (Belgium).

European Distance and E-Learning Network (EDEN): c/o Budapest Univ. of Technology and Economics, Budapest, Egry J.u. 1, 1111, Hungary; tel. (1) 463-1628; e-mail secretariat@eden-online.org; internet www.eden-online.org; f. 1991; fosters devts in flexible, distance and e-learning; shares knowledge and improves understanding among professionals in distance and e-learning; 1,175 mems (incl. 175 instns, 1,000 individuals in the Network of Academics and Professionals); Pres. Prof. Dr MORTEN FLATE PAULSEN (Norway); Sec.-Gen. Dr ANDRÁS SZŰCS; publs *Conference Proceedings* (1 a year), *European Journal of Open and Distance Learning* (online, www.eurodl.org).

European Institute of Education and Social Policy/Institut Européen d'Éducation et de Politique Sociale: c/o J. Gordon, 84 rue Vergniaud, 75013 Paris, France; c/o ESCP Europe, 81 ave de la République, 75543 Paris Cedex 11, France; tel. 149235830; e-mail ieeps@eiesp.org; internet www.eiesp.org; f. 1975 by the European Cultural Foundation, the European Comm., the Int. Ccl for Educational Devt; studies specific issues in education, employment and social policy; policy-oriented, research programmes and seminars undertaken for European govts, int. orgs, univs, regional and local bodies; develops systems, approaches, tools and practices for learning process; Chair. Dr JEAN-CLAUDE RUANO-BORBALAN; Dir JEAN GORDON; publ. *European Journal of Education* (4 a year, in English).

European University Association/Association Européenne de l'Université: Ave de l'Yser, 24, 1040 Brussels, Belgium; tel. (2) 230-55-44; e-mail info@eua.be; internet www.eua.be; f. 2001 by merger of Asscn of European Univs and Confederation of European Union Rectors' Confs; represents and supports univs and nat. rectors' confs in 47 European countries; influences EU policies on higher education, research and innovation; acts as a forum for exchange of ideas and good practice among univs; disseminates knowledge through confs, seminars, website and publs; 850 individual, collective mems and affiliate mems in 47 countries; Pres. Prof. MARIA HELENA NAZARÉ (Portugal); Sec.-Gen. LESLEY WILSON (Belgium); publ. *EUA News* (online, www.eua.be).

Fédération Internationale des Professeurs de Français (International Federation of Teachers of French): 1 ave Léon Journault, 92318 Sèvres Cedex, France; tel. 146265316; e-mail ieeps@eiesp.org; internet www.fipf.org; f. 1969; contributes to the dissemination and optimization of the teaching of the French language in the world; unites asscns of French teachers and those involved in the teaching of French worldwide; encourages sharing of experiences and educational research to promote the teaching of French; 186 mem. asscns in 140 countries; Pres. JEAN-PIERRE CUQ (France); Sec.-Gen. and Treas. MADELINE ROLLE-BOUMLIC (France); publs *Dialogues et Cultures* (1 a year), *Echanges: Lettre FIPF* (4 a year), *Le Français dans le Monde* (6 a year, online, nathan-cms.customers.artful.net/fdlm-v2), *Recherches et applications* (2 a year).

Federation of the Universities of the Islamic World (FUIW)/Fédération des Universités du monde Islamique (FUMI): ISESCO, Ave des F.A.R., Hay Ryad, POB 2275, 10104 Rabat, Morocco; tel. 537566052; e-mail fumi@isesco.org.ma; internet www.fuiw.org; part of Islamic Educational, Scientific and Cultural Organization (*q.v.*); supports univs and higher education instns of comparable level in the Islamic world and encourages cooperation between them; encourages scientific researches in fields, exchanging their findings, and linking them with the developmental and civilizational requirements of the Islamic Ummah; 193 mem. univs; Chair. Prof. Dr SULEIMAN BIN ABDULLAH ABA AL-KHAIL; Sec.-Gen. Dr ABDULAZIZ OTHMAN ALTWIJRI; publ. *Journal of the Federation of the Universities of the Islamic World*.

Institut für den Donauraum und Mitteleuropa (IDM) (Institute for the Danube Region and Central Europe): Hahngasse 6/1/24, 1090 Vienna, Austria; tel. (1) 3197258; e-mail idm@idm.at; internet www.idm.at; f. 1953 as Research Institute for Issues of the Danube Region, present name 1993; extramural research think tank working in the fields of politics, education, research, culture and business; supports the work of embassies, trade missions, cultural institutes and nat. tourist offices in the countries of the Danube region and Central and SE Europe; organizes seminars, lectures, symposiums, trips and excursions; Chair. Dr ERHARD BUSEK (Austria); Gen. Sec. Prof. Dr ANDREAS BREINBAUER (Austria); publs *Das Magazin für den Donauraum und Mitteleuropa*, *Der Donauraum* (scientific journal, 4 a year), *IDM-Studien*, *Info Europa* (5 a year).

Instituto Internacional para la Educación Superior en América Latina y el Caribe (IESALC) (UNESCO International Institute for Higher Education in Latin America and the Caribbean): Avda Los Chorros con Calle Acueducto, Edif. Asovincar, Altos de Sebucán, Caracas D. F., Venezuela; tel. (212) 286-1020; internet www.iesalc.unesco.org.ve; autonomous body operating as part of UNESCO; contributes to the devt of higher education in the region and its nat. higher education instns and systems; promotes nat. and regional mechanisms aimed to strengthen the quality of higher education by means of processes of evaluation and accreditation; promotes use of new information and communication technologies in higher education instns; Dir PEDRO HENRÍQUEZ GUAJARDO.

Inter-American Distance Education Consortium/Consorcio-red de Educación a Distancia/Consorcio-rede de Educação a Distância: c/o Dr Armando Villarroel, Fischler School of Education and Human Services, Nova Southeastern Univ., 1750 NE 167th St, N Miami Beach, FL 33162-3017, USA; tel. (954) 262-7829; e-mail cread@nsu.nova.edu; internet www.cread.org; f. 1990, present status 1994; promotes improvement of distance education and the diffusion of knowledge about its practice throughout the Americas; plays leadership role as a coordinating mechanism for inter-American distance education and training; holds confs, seminars, professional devt sessions; promotes applied research and scholarly inquiry in distance education; assists in the devt and strengthening of regional and nat. distance education asscns; Pres. Dr HÉCTOR ALEJANDRO BARCELÓ (Argentina); Exec. Dir Dr ARMANDO VILLARROEL (USA).

Inter-American Organization for Higher Education/Organisation Universitaire Interaméricaine/Organização Universitária Interamericana/Organización Universitaria Interamericana: Université de Montréal, 3744, rue Jean-Brillant, bureau 592, Montreal, QC H3T 1P1, Canada; tel. (514) 343-6111; e-mail secretariat@oui-iohe.qc.ca; internet www.oui-iohe.org; f. 1980; promotes academic collaboration among higher education institutes in the Americas; improves quality of information; awards the Inter-American Prize to univ., political and socio-economic figures for contribution to devt of higher education and the strengthening of scientific and cultural ties in the Americas; 300 instns and nat. univ. asscn mems; library of 500 vols; Pres. Dr MARCIAL RUBIO CORREA (Peru); Exec. Dir PATRICIA GUDIÑO (Canada).

Inter-University Council for East Africa: East African Development Bank Bldg, Third Fl., Plot 4, Nile Ave, POB 7110, Kampala, Uganda; tel. (41) 256251; e-mail info@iucea.org; internet www.iucea.org; f. 1984 as Asscn of Eastern and Southern African Universities; encourages and develops mutually beneficial collaboration between mem. univs, and between them and nat. govts and other orgs in E Africa and other regions; provides forum for discussion on a wide range of academic and other matters relating to higher education; facilitates maintenance of internationally comparable education standards in E Africa to promote the region's competitiveness in higher education; 86 public and private mem. univs in Kenya, Tanzania, Uganda, Rwanda and Burundi; Chair. Prof. FREDERICK I. B. KAYANJA (Uganda); Exec. Sec. Prof. Dr MAYUNGA H. H. NKUNYA (Tanzania).

International Association for Educational and Vocational Guidance/Asociación Internacional para la Orientación Educativa y Profesional/aAssociation Internationale d'Orientation Scolaire et Professionnelle/Internationale Vereinigung für Schul- und Berufsberatung: c/o IAEVG/Canadian Career Devt Foundation, 119 Ross Ave, Suite 202, Ottawa, ON K1Y 0N6, Canada; tel. (613) 729-6164; e-mail lester.oakes@clear.net.nz; internet www.iaevg.org; f. 1951; advocates professional and recognized educational and vocational guidance and counselling; contributes to career devt, vocational guidance practice and promotes contact between mems across the world; assists in areas of research, practice and policy devt for the preparation of appropriate and effective methods and materials for guidance; works towards addressing diversity and social justice issues in education and work; organizes int. seminars, colloquial, symposia, confs, congresses, workshops and study tours; promotes professional training of staff and initiates internationally agreed accreditation standards and procedures; 16,000 mems in 53 countries; Pres. LESTER OAKES (New Zealand); Sec.-Gen. SUZANNE BULTHEEL (France); publ. *International Journal for Educational and Vocation Guidance* (3 a year).

International Association for the Exchange of Students for Technical Experience (IAESTE): Rue Albert Ier, 51, 1117, Luxembourg, Luxembourg; e-mail board@iaeste.org; internet www.iaeste.org; f. 1948; operates practical training exchange programme between mems to enhance technical and professional devt; provides students in higher education with technical experience relevant to studies; source of cultural enrichment for trainees and their host communities; 5,000 mems; Gen. Sec. GORAN RADNOVIC (Serbia); publ. *Friends* (4 a year).

International Association of Dental Students: c/o FDI World Dental Federation, Tour de Cointrin, Ave Louis Casaï 84, CP 3, Cointrin, 1216 Geneva, Swizerland; tel. 22-560-81-50; e-mail secretary@iads-web.org; internet www.iads-web.org; f. 1951; promotes int. contact between dental students; advances and encourages their interest in the science and art of dentistry; promotes exchanges and int. congresses; serves as platform for exchange of knowledge and experiences about dentistry at int. level; 200,000 mems; Pres. PAVEL SCARLAT (Romania); Gen. Sec. NADA UNCIANSCHI (Romania); publ. *Bulletin* (2 a year).

International Association of University Presidents (IAUP): 809 United Nations Pl., New York, NY 10017-3580, USA; e-mail secretary-general@iaup.org; internet iaup.org; f. 1964; encourages exchange of experiences, levels of collaboration and networking between univ. leaders; strengthens quality of education in HEIs; promotes global awareness, competence, peace and int. understanding through education; facilitates exchange of professional experience through confs, seminars, publs and comms; 600 mems from 100 countries; Pres. Prof. Dr NEAL KING (USA); Sec.-Gen. Prof. Dr JASON SCORZA (USA); publ. *Academe*.

International Baccalaureate Organization (IBO)/Organisation du Baccalauréat International/Organización del Bachillerato Internacional: 15 route des Morillons, Grand-Saconnex, 1218 Geneva, Switzerland; tel. 223092540; e-mail ibhq@ibo.org; internet www.ibo.org; f. 1968; works with schools, govts and int. orgs to develop programmes of int. education and assessment; organizes workshops and confs; offers 3 programmes of int. education and a certificate; provides short-term grants for schools; 3,480 mem. schools in 143 countries; Dir-Gen. JEFFREY R. BEARD (USA); publs *IB World* (3 a year), *Journal of Research in International Education* (3 a year).

International Bureau of Education: see under UNESCO.

International Centre for Agricultural Education (CIEA)/Internationales Studienzentrum für landwirtschaftliches Bildungswesen: c/o HAFL, Länggasse 85, 3052 Zollikofen, Switzerland; tel. 319102111; e-mail info@ciea.ch; internet www.ciea.ch; f. 1956; organizes seminars and int. courses on vocational education and teaching in agriculture every 2 years; Dir ROLAND STÄHLI.

International Council for Adult Education/Conseil International d'Education des Adultes/Consejo Internacional de Educación de Persons Adultas: Avda 18 de Julio 2095, apt 301, 11200 Montevideo, Uruguay; tel. 2409 7982; e-mail secretariat@icae.org.uy; internet www.icae2.org; f. 1973; global network of NGOs promoting adult and lifelong learning; areas of activities incl. adult literacy, primary health care reform, adult education in prison, global citizenship and gender justice, peace education and conflict resolution, globalization, Adult Learners' Week, education and transformative capacity of work spaces; organizes annual int. training course for lifelong learning advocacy leaders; 800 mems in 75 countries; Pres. ALAN TUCKETT (UK); Sec.-Gen. CELIA ECCHER (Uruguay).

International Council for Open and Distance Education: Lilleakerveien 23, 0283 Oslo, Norway; tel. 22-06-26-30; e-mail icde@icde.org; internet www.icde.org; f. 1938 as Int. Ccl for Correspondence Education, current name adopted 1982; fosters int. collaboration in open and distance education; promotes intercultural cooperation and understanding; supports and develops networks at nat., regional, global and linguistic affinity groups level; contributes to devt of new methodologies and technologies to improve lifelong learning; organizes confs and workshops; supported by the Norwegian Min. of Education and Research; consultative partner status with UNESCO; affiliate mem. of the SE Asian Min. of Education Org.; 162 mems in 60 countries; Pres. Prof. TIAN BELAWATI (Indonesia); Sec.-Gen. GARD TITLESTAD (Norway); publ. *Open Praxis* (4 a year, online, www.openpraxis.org).

International Federation of Catholic Universities/Fédération Internationale des Universités Catholiques (FIUC)/Federación Internacional de Universidades Católicas: c/o Institut Catholique, 21 rue d'Assas, 75270 Paris Cedex 06, France; tel. 144395226; e-mail sgfiuc@bureau.fiuc.org; internet www.fiuc.org; f. 1924, officially recognized by the Holy See in 1949; contributes to devt of Catholic higher education and its Catholic character; represents mems at the int. orgs and asscns; cooperates with other int. orgs; develops networks of knowledge to foster effective collaboration between its mems; 211 mem. catholic univs in 56 countries; Pres. PEDRO RUBENS FERREIRA OLIVEIRA (Brazil); Sec.-Gen. Prof. Mgr GUY-RÉAL THIVIERGE (France); publs *Idem Aliter* (12 a year), *Journal / Cahiers / Cuadernos*, *PIPER Journal* (in English, French and Spanish, online, www.fiuc.org/PIPER), *Revista Análisis* (online).

International Federation of Language Teacher Associations/Fédération Internationale des Professeurs de Langues Vivantes: POB 216, Belgrave VIC, 3160, Australia; c/o European Centre for Modern Languages, Nikolaipl. 4, 8020, Graz, Austria; tel. (3) 9754-4714; e-mail djc@netspace.net.au; internet www.fiplv.org; f. 1931; supports devt and promotion of world languages through professional asscn; professional devt of language teachers; organizes world congress every 3 years; Pres. TERRY LAMB (UK); Vice-Pres. PAOLO BALBONI (Italy); Sec.-Gen. DENIS CUNNINGHAM (Australia); Treas.-Gen. KIRSTI SANTAHOLMA (Finland).

International Federation of University Women/Fédération Internationale des Femmes Diplômées des Universités: 10 rue du Lac, 1207 Geneva, Switzerland; tel. 227312380; e-mail ifuw@ifuw.org; internet www.ifuw.org; f. 1919; promotes lifelong education for women and girls; offers fellowships and study grants; undertakes studies dealing with the status of women; encourages int. cooperation, advances the devt of education, represents univ. women in int. orgs; organizes confs, seminars and workshops; affiliate mems in 61 countries, individual mems in 40 countries; Pres. CATHERINE BELL (South Africa); Exec. Dir DANIÈLE CASTLE (Switzerland).

International Federation of Workers' Education Associations: c/o Labour Research Service, POB 376, Woodstock, Cape Town, 7915, South Africa; tel. (21) 447-1677; e-mail ifweasecretariat@lrs.org.za; internet www.ifwea.org; f. 1945; promotes devt of workers' education; encourages cooperation among nat. and int. trade unions, workers' education assns, NGOs and foundations engaged in the provision of adult education opportunities for workers and the communities; 105 affiliated mem. orgs in 65 countries; Pres. SUSAN SCHURMAN (USA); Gen. Sec. SAHRA RYKLIEF (South Africa); publs *E-bulletins*, *Workers' Education* (4 a year, in English).

International Institute for Educational Planning: see under UNESCO.

International Phonetic Association (IPA): c/o Prof. Patricia Keating, Dept of Linguistics, UCLA, 3125 Campbell Hall, Los Angeles, CA 90095-1543, USA; tel. (310) 794-6316; e-mail keating@humnet.ucla.edu; internet www.langsci.ucl.ac.uk/ipa; f. 1886; promotes scientific study of phonetics and its applications; hosts Int. Congress of Phonetic Sciences every 4 years; offers examinations in phonetics; 400 mems; Pres. Prof. JOHN H. ESLING (Canada); Sec. Prof. Dr PATRICIA KEATING (USA); publ. *Journal of the International Phonetic Association* (3 a year).

International Reading Association: 800 Barksdale Rd, POB 8139, Newark, DE 19714-8139, USA; tel. (302) 731-1600; e-mail pubinfo@reading.org; internet www.reading.org; f. 1956; sets standards for effective reading instruction; advances quality of literacy instruction and research worldwide through the study of the reading process and teaching techniques; promotes lifelong reading habit and public awareness of global literacy; organizes annual convention, regional confs, biennial World Congress; 60,000 mems; library of 6,000 vols; Pres. Prof. Dr CARRICE C. CUMMINS (USA); Exec. Dir MARCIE CRAIG POST (USA); publs *Journal of Adolescent and Adult Literature* (8 a year), *Reading Research Quarterly* (4 a year), *The Reading Teacher* (8 a year).

International Schools Association (ISA): c/o Luis Martinez,10333 Diego Dr. S, Boca Raton, FL 33428, USA; tel. (561) 883-3854; e-mail info@isaschools.org; internet www.isaschools.org; f. 1951; merged in 1968 with the Conf. of Internationally-minded Schools (CIS); encourages creation of new int. schools; encourages cooperation among int. schools through consultation on teaching and admin. questions; facilitates study of educational problems of interest to schools; nurtures interest in nat. schools of int. matters to improve int. understanding; organizes int. conf. every 2 years; 43 mem. schools worldwide; Chair. LUIS MARTINEZ-ZORZO (Spain); Sec.-Gen. ANDREW MCEWEN (UK).

International Society for Business Education/Société Internationale pour l'Enseignement Commercial: c/o Dr Judy Olson Sutton, 6302 Mineral Point Rd, Ste 100, Madison, WI 53705, USA; tel. (608) 273-8467; e-mail secretary@siec-isbe.org; internet www.siecisbe.org; f. 1901; provides opportunities to observe, interact and exchange ideas on educational strategies with multinational participants; encourages and maintains networking opportunities with business and educational leaders worldwide; encourages dissemination of information; focuses on int. business topics; encourages research and partnerships in int. projects; organizes annual int. conf.; 1,600 mems organized in 19 nat. groups; Pres. Dr TAMRA S. DAVIS (USA); Gen. Sec. Dr JUDITH OLSON-SUTTON (USA); publ. *The Review* (1 a year).

International Society for Education through Art (InSEA)/Société Internationale pour l'Education Artistique: James H. Sanders III, c/o Dept of Admin., Education and Policy, Ohio State Univ., 1813 N. High St., Room 135D (1st Fl.), Columbus, OH 43210, USA; e-mail insea.treasurer@gmail.com; internet www.insea.org; f. 1951; advocates and advances research in art education; unites art educators worldwide; encourages exchange of information; organizes int. congresses, projects and exhibitions; 1,500 mems (1000 active mems); Pres. TERESA ECA (Portugal); Sec. VEDAT ÖZSOY (Turkey); Treas. Assoc. Prof. JAMES H. SANDERS, III (USA); publ. *International Journal of Education through Art* (3 a year).

International Union of Students/Union Internationale des Etudiants: POB 58, 17th November St, 110 01 Prague 01, Czech Republic; tel. (2) 71731257; e-mail ius@cfs-fcee.ca; internet www.stud.uni-hannover.de/gruppen/ius; f. 1946 as Int. Student Ccl; works towards education for all, through the universal establishment of free compulsory primary and secondary education; defends rights and interests of students; encourages implementation of the reform and democratization of education, achievement of academic freedom and univ. autonomy; mobilizes students for peace and disarmament; strives for peace, nat. independence; promotes and defends nat. culture, equal possibilities for women, unity of student movements; organizes meetings, relief projects, cultural and sports activities, student tourism, travel and exchange; 152 nat. unions of students of 114 countries; Pres. MANISH TEWARI (India); Sec.-Gen. FRAGE SHERIF; publs *Democratization of Education*, various regional and other bulletins (4 a year), *World Student News*.

International Young Christian Workers/Jeunesse Ouvrière Chrétienne Internationale: 6 rue Rodenbach, 1030 Brussels, Belgium; tel. (2) 242-18-11; e-mail joci@jociycw.net; internet www.joci.org; f. 1912, present name and status 1957; promotes inter-religious dialogue among the young workers and creates an intercultural soc.; trains, organizes and defends the rights of young workers; develops analysis and action on areas such as informal work, the conditions for young female workers, unemployment, apprenticeships, temporary and dangerous employment; holds int. ccls and training sessions at local, nat. and int. level; nat. orgs in 60 countries; Pres. GEETHANI PERIES (Sri Lanka); Sec.-Gen. BRIDGET RAUCH; Treas. ARLINDO DE OLIVEIRA (Brazil).

Islamic Educational, Scientific and Cultural Organization (ISESCO)/Organisation Islamique pour l'Education, les Sciences et la Culture: Ave des F. A. R., Hay Ryad, POB 2275, 10104 Rabat, Morocco; tel. 537566052; e-mail scgce@isesco.org.ma; internet www.isesco.org.ma; f. 1982; promotes and consolidates cooperation and devt among mem. states in the fields of education, science, culture and communication within the framework of the human Islamic values and ideals; furthers interest in Islamic culture, highlights its specifications and publicizes its landmarks in intellectual studies, scientific researches and educational curricula; supports efforts of the educational, scientific and cultural instns for Muslims in non mem. states; encourages research, studies and training for the devt and upgrading of education in mem. states; holds educational, scientific and cultural competitions and forums; Islamic Data Bank service (BIDI); 50 mem states; Dir-Gen. Dr ABDULAZIZ OTHMAN ALTWAIJRI; publs *ISESCO Bulletin* (4 a year), *ISESCO Triennial*, *ISESCO Yearbook*, *Islam Today* (2 a year, in Arabic, English and French).

Latin American Institute for Educational Communication/Instituto Latinoamericano de la Comunicación Educativa: Calle del Puente 45, Col. Ejidos de Huipulco, Delegación Tlalpan, 14380 México, DF, Mexico; tel. (55) 50206500; e-mail contacto@ilce.edu.mx; internet www.ilce.edu.mx; f. 1956; promotes educational technology; provides leadership in educational communication and technical assistance to mems; regional cooperation in research, experimentation, production and distribution of audiovisual materials; produces and broadcasts educational television programmes; offers online educational services; training at the Center for Training and Advanced Studies on Educational Communication (CETEC); operates Center of AV Documentation for Latin America (CEDAL); 14 mem. countries; library of 34,000 vols; Pres. Dr JOSÉ ÁNGEL CÓRDOVA VILLALOBOS; Dir-Gen. Lic. JOSE LUIS ESPINOSA PIÑA; publ. *Tecnología y Comunicación Educativas (TyCE)* (4 a year).

OECD Centre for Educational Research and Innovation (CERI): c/o Dirk van Damme, 2 rue André Pascal, 75775 Paris Cedex 16, France; tel. 145247901; e-mail ceri.contact@oecd.org; internet www.oecd.org/edu/ceri; f. 1968; promotes educational research; projects incl.: future thinking in education, univ. future, evidence-based policy research in education, nat. reviews on educational research and devt, learning sciences and brain research, formative assessment, systemic innovation; vocational education and training; open educational resources, measuring the social outcomes of learning; globalization and linguistic competencies; promotes generation of forward-looking research analyses and syntheses; identifies and stimulates educational innovation; encourages int. exchange of knowledge and experience; 33 mem. countries; Head Prof. Dr DIRK VAN DAMME (Belgium).

Organization of Ibero-American States for Education, Science and Culture/Organização dos Estados Ibero-americanos para a Educação a Ciência e a Cultura/Organización de Estados Iberoamericanos para la Educación, la Ciencia y la Cultura (OEI): Bravo Murillo 38, 28015 Madrid, Spain; tel. 915944382; e-mail oeiba@oei.org.ar; internet www.oei.es; f. 1949 as Ibero-American Bureau of Education, present name 1985; encourages educational, scientific and cultural cooperation within the Ibero-American countries; provides technical assistance to Ibero-American devt systems in the above areas; provides information and documentation on the devt of education, science and culture; encourages exchanges in these fields; organizes training courses; govts of 23 Ibero-American countries; library of 8,000 vols, 500 periodicals; Sec.-Gen. ALVARO MARCHESI ULLASTRES; publ. *Boletín*.

Southeast Asian Ministers of Education Organization (SEAMEO): Mom Luang Pin Malakul Centenary Bldg, Fourth Fl., 920 Sukhumvit Rd, Klongtoey, Prakanong, Bangkok 10110, Thailand; tel. (23) 910-144; e-mail secretariat@seameo.org; internet www.seameo.org; f. 1965; promotes regional cooperation in education, science and culture in SE Asian countries; 19 regional centres; 20 specialist instns; 11 mem. countries, 7 assoc. mem. countries, 3 affiliate mems; library of 2,000 vols of SEAMEO docs; Pres. HE PEHIN ABU BAKAR APONG (Brunei); Dir Dr WITAYA JERADECHAKUL (Thailand); publs *SEAMEO Accomplishments Report* (1 a year), *SEAMEO Directory* (1 a year), *SEAMEO Education Agenda* (2 a year).

Steering Committee for Culture, Heritage and Landscape (CDCPP): c/o Council of Europe, 67075 Strasbourg Cedex, France; tel. 390214998; e-mail culturedoc@coe.int; internet www.coe.int/t/dg4/cultureheritage/cdcpp; f. 2012; oversees Ccl of Europe's work in the field of culture and intercultural dialogue, heritage and landscape; advises Cttee of Mins on questions within its area of competence, in particular the promotion of democracy; 50 mem. states; Chair. DEIANA DANILOVA (Bulgaria); publs *EUDISED European Educational Research Yearbook*, *European Heritage*.

Steering Committee for Higher Education and Research (CDESR): c/o Council of Europe, Div. for Higher Education and Research, Directorate of Education and Languages, Directorate General IV-Education, Culture and Cultural Heritage, Youth and Sport, 67075 Strasbourg Cedex, France; tel. 388412000; e-mail katia.dolgova-dreyer@coe.int; internet www.coe.int/t/dg4/highereducation/cdesr; f. 1978; steering cttee under the Committee of Ministers of the Council of Europe; promotes cooperation among European countries in the field of higher education and research; work programmes for univ. policy, academic mobility (esp. jt Ccl of Europe-UNESCO network of information centres on equivalences and mobility and a new jt convention on recognition); main contributor to the Bologna Process; projects on higher education as a public responsibility, higher education governance, the heritage of European univs, intercultural dialogue; assistance in higher education reform in countries of SE Europe and newly ind. states; 96 mem. delegates from 48 countries; Chair. LUC WEBER (Switzerland); Sec. KATIA DOLGOVA-DREYER.

UNESCO European Centre for Higher Education/Centre Européen pour l'Enseignement Supérieur (CEPES): Str. Stirbei Voda 39, 010102 Bucharest, Romania; tel. 13130839; e-mail info@cepes.ro; f. 1972; centre for policy devt and the promotion of int. higher education cooperation in Europe, N America and Israel; Secretariat of Jt UNESCO/Council of Europe European Recognition Convention and of the ENIC Network of Information Centres on Recognition and Mobility in Europe; library of 6,000 vols (incl. books and monographs), 135 periodicals, 3,200 documents, 2,000 UNESCO documents and publs; Dir Dr JAN SADLAK; publ. *Higher Education in Europe* (4 a year, in English, online in French and Russian).

UNESCO Institute for Information Technologies in Education: 8 Kedrova St, Bldg 3, Moscow, Russia, 117292; tel. (499) 1292990; e-mail liste.info.iite@unesco.org; internet iite.unesco.org; f. 1997; contributes to the design and implementation of programmes in regard to application of information and communication technologies in education; monitors and supports use of ICTs in education; provides training for those working in education; assist UNESCO member states in problems relating to ICTs; Chair. Prof. BERNARD CORNU (France); Dir DENDEV BADARCH (acting); publ. *Proceedings*.

UNESCO Institute for Lifelong Learning/Institut de l'UNESCO pour l'Apprentissage tout au Long de la Vie/UNESCO-Institut für Lebenslanges Lernen: Feldbrunnenstr. 58, 20148 Hamburg, Germany; tel. (40) 4480410; e-mail uil@unesco.org; internet www.uil.unesco.org; f. 1951; int. research institute of UNESCO; main concern is content and quality of education in the framework of lifelong learning, with an emphasis on adult learning, non-formal education and adult literacy; provides technical support to mem. states, incl. consulting services and programme monitoring and evaluation; enhances literacy and non-formal education, adult and lifelong learning through advocacy and networking, research, dissemination, promotion, research-based training and documentation; a worldwide network for exchange of information on literacy; a research-oriented training programme; library of 58,000 vols, 80 periodicals; spec. collns: sample learning materials on literacy, post-literacy and continuing education from 120 countries; Dir ARNE CARLSEN; publ. *International Review of Education* (6 a year, in English, French and German).

UNESCO International Institute for Capacity Building in Africa: POB 2305, Addis Ababa, Ethiopia; tel. 115445284; e-mail info@unesco-iicba.org; internet www.unesco-iicba.org; f. 1999; develops capacity of instns in Africa in the fields of teacher education, curriculum devt, educational policy, planning and management, and distance education; addresses educational, technical and professional needs of mem. states; provides a forum for sharing experiences; brings the latest research and devt to instns in Africa; 2 regional offices in Senegal and South Africa; Officer in Charge Dr JULIEN DABOUE; publ. *Proceedings*.

UNESCO International Institute for Higher Education in Latin America and the Caribbean/Instituto Internacional de la UNESCO para la Educación en América Latina y el Caribe/Instituto Internacional para la Educación Superior en América Latina y el Caribe (IESALC): Edificio Asovincar, Avda Los Chorros con Calle Acueducto, Altos de Sebucán, Apdo Postal 68.394, Caracas, Venezuela; tel. (212) 286-1020; e-mail iesalc@unesco.org.ve; internet www.iesalc.unesco.org.ve; fosters cooperation between mem. states of the region, their instns and specialists in the field of higher education; contributes in the improvement of the mutual knowledge of the tertiary education systems; provides assistance to mem. states to improve and develop its tertiary education systems and instns; promotes nat. and regional mechanisms aimed at strengthening the quality of higher education by means of processes of evaluation and accreditation; encourages and supports in the context of regional integration greater mobility of higher education professionals; library: 13,315 bibliographies, 2,500 abstracts, 900 digital monographs and occasional papers; Dir PEDRO HENRÍQUEZ GUAJARDO; publ. *Revista Educación Superior y Sociedad* (2 a year).

UNESCO-UNEVOC International Centre for Technical and Vocational Education and Training: UN Campus, Platz der Vereinten Nationen 1, 53113 Bonn, Germany; tel. (228) 8150100; e-mail unevoc@unesco.org; internet www.unevoc.unesco.org; f. 2002; assists UNESCO's 195 mem. states to strengthen and upgrade their technical and vocational education and training (TVET) systems; offers online services such as highly frequented e-Forum, knowledge-sharing platform TVETipedia and the UNEVOC Network Portal; 285 UNEVOC centres in more than 165 countries; links and fosters interaction and learning among diverse instns of TVET stakeholders around the world; conducts training, consultations and confs in the different areas of TVET and advocates for global TVET devt; Head of Office Prof. Dr SHYAMAL MAJUMDAR (India).

University of the Arctic: POB 122, 96101 Rovaniemi, Finland; tel. (16) 341341; e-mail secretariat@uarctic.org; internet www.uarctic.org; f. 2001; cooperative network of univs, colleges and other orgs committed to higher education and research in the N; works for education, research and the promotion of indigenous and local capacities and sustainable devt in the circumpolar N; 142 mem. instns; Pres. LARS KULLERUD (Norway); Vice-Pres. for Admin. OUTI SNELLMAN (Finland); Sec. PIRKKO PULKKANEN; publ. *Shared Voices Magazine*.

World Association for Educational Research (WAER)/Asociación Mundial de Ciencias de la Educación (AMCE)/Association Mondiale des Sciences de l'Education (AMSE): c/o Yves Lenoir, Faculté d'Education, Université de Sherbrooke, 2500 blvd de l'Université, Sherbrooke, QC J1K 2R1, Canada; tel. (819) 821-8000 ext. 61339; e-mail amseamcewaer@usherbrooke.ca; f. 1953, present name 2004; encourages research in educational sciences by organizing congresses, issuing publs, the exchange of information; promotes teaching of the sciences of education at univ. level and internationally; 500 individual mems in 32 countries; Pres. YVES LENOIR; Gen. Sec. FOUAD CHAFIQI (Morocco); publs *Bulletin* (3 or 4 a year, in English, French and Spanish), *Proceedings of WAER Congresses*, *Recherche en Education autour du Monde* (2 a year).

World Education Fellowship-International (WEF): c/o Guadalupe G. de Turner, 54 Fox Lane, Palmers Green, London, N13 4AL, UK; tel. (20) 8245-4561; e-mail generalsecretary@wef-international.org; internet www.wef-international.org; f. 1921; promotes exchange and practice of progressive educational ideas worldwide; promotes social and economic justice and equality through high standard of education; fosters educational contacts between people worldwide to further int. understanding and peace; organizes workshops, meetings and biennial confs; sections and groups in 22 countries; Chair. CHRISTINE WYKES (UK); Pres. Prof. SHINJO OKUDA (Japan); Gen. Sec. GUADALUPE G. DE TURNER (UK); publ. *New Era in Education* (3 a year).

World Maritime University: Citadellsvägen 29, POB 500, 201 24 Malmö, Sweden; tel. (40) 356-300; e-mail info@wmu.se; internet www.wmu.se; f. 1983; language of instruction English; offers postgraduate and doctoral programmes in maritime affairs for students from around the world; Chancellor KOJI SEKIMIZU (Japan); Pres. Prof. Dr BJÖRN KJERFVE (USA); Vice-Pres. for Academics Prof. NEIL BELLEFONTAINE (Canada); Vice-Pres. for Int. Affairs Prof. Dr SHUO MA (China); Dir for Research and Doctoral Programme Prof. Dr OLOF LINDÉN (Sweden); Librarian CHRISTOPHER HOEBEKE (USA); library of 18,000 vols; spec. colln: IMO depository; 100 teachers; 300 students; publ. *Journal of Maritime Affairs* (2 a year).

World Student Christian Federation (WSCF)/Federación Universal de Movimientos Estudiantiles Cristianos/Fédération Universelle des Associations

Chrétiennes d'Etudiants: WSCF Inter-Regional Office, Ecumenical Centre, POB 2100, 5 route des Morillons, 1211 Geneva 2, Switzerland; tel. 227916358; e-mail wscf@wscf.ch; internet www.wscfglobal.org; f. 1895; an ecumenical student, univ. and secondary school org. with participants from all major Christian confessions; consultative status with the UN and UNESCO; promotes Christian witness within the academic community; rep. in 6 regions: Africa, Asia-Pacific, Europe, Latin America and Caribbean, Middle East and N America; 100 affiliated nat. movements; Chair. HORACIO MESONES (Uruguay); Hon. Treas. YOUHANNA KAMAL SHAWKY (Egypt); Gen. Sec. CHRISTINE HOUSEL (USA/Switzerland); publs *Federation News* (2 a year), *Student World* (1 a year).

World Union of Jewish Students: POB 39359, 61392 Tel Aviv, Israel; tel. (2) 6251682; e-mail office@wujs.org.il; internet wujs.org.il; f. 1924; acts as global org. for nat. Jewish student bodies; sponsors and organizes educational programmes, leadership training seminars, women's seminars, Project Areivim, a service programme for Diaspora communities; divided into 6 regions; organizes Congress every 3 years; youth affiliate of World Jewish Congress, mem. org. of World Zionist Org.; 48 nat. mem. unions; Chair. OLIVER WORTH; Dir YONI FORSYTH; publs *Heritage and History* (Jewish student activist yearbook), *WUJS Leads*.

ACCREDITATION AND QUALITY ASSURANCE

Arab Network for Quality Assurance in Higher Education (ANQAHE): POB 533, Maadi, Egypt; 13 Bergas St, Garden City, Cairo, Egypt; tel. (2) 25240113; e-mail secretariat@anqahe.org; internet www.anqahe.org; f. 2007; aims to create a mechanism between the Arab countries to exchange information about quality assurance; constructs and supports new quality assurance orgs; develops standards and disseminates good practice; strengthens liaison between quality assurance bodies in the different countries; works in association with the International Network for Quality Assurance Agencies in Higher Education (*q.v.*) and the Asscn of Arab Univs (*q.v.*); Pres. Dr NADIA BADRAWI (Egypt); Sec.-Gen. Dr TARIQ ALSINDI (Bahrain).

Asia Pacific Accreditation and Certification Commission (APACC): CPSC, Bldg Blk C, DepEd Complex, Meralco Ave, 1600 Pasig City, Metro Manila, Philippines; tel. (2) 633-8413; e-mail cpsc@cpsctech.org; internet www.apacc4hrd.org; f. 2004; attached to Int. Network for Quality Assurance Agencies in Higher Education (INQAAHE); conducts accreditation and certification of Technical and Vocational Education and Training (TVET) instns in its mem. countries; guides TVET instns in equipping themselves with internationally recognized standards and systems; 16 mem. countries; Pres. Dr MOHAMMAD NAIM YAAKUB; Jt Coordinator Prof. THEODORA GAYONDATO; Projects and Consultancy Officer ADRIENNE ABRIL.

Asia-Pacific Quality Network (APQN): c/o Dr Li Yaogang, Shanghai Education Evaluation Institute, 202 S Shaan Xi Rd, 200031, Shanghai, People's Republic of China; tel. (21) 54041392; e-mail rsclyg@dhu.edu.cn; internet www.apqn.org; f. 2003; promotes good practice in maintenance and improvement of quality in higher education in the Asia-Pacific region; facilitates research into the practice of quality management and its effectiveness in improving the quality of higher education; provides advice and expertise to assist devt of new quality assurance agencies; 117 mems (30 full, 17 intermediate, 7 assoc., 63 institutional); Pres. Dr JAGANNATH PATIL (India); Sec. and Treas. Prof. Dr LI YAOGANG (People's Republic of China).

Caribbean Area Network for Quality Assurance in Tertiary Education (CANQATE): c/o Dr Yvonnette Marshall, Univ. Ccl of Jamaica, 6B Oxford Rd, Kingston 5, St Andrew, Jamaica; tel. 9297299; e-mail info@canqate.org; internet www.canqate.org; f. 2004; attached to Int. Network for Quality Assurance Agencies in Higher Education (INQAAHE); promotes cooperation and exchange of information among mems about the maintenance, evaluation, accreditation and improvement of higher education in the Caribbean; disseminates good practices in the field of quality assurance; 135 mems; Pres. Dr YVONNETTE MARSHALL (Jamaica); Sec. NICOLE MANNING (Jamaica).

Central and Eastern European Network of Quality Assurance Agencies in Higher Education (CEENQA): Budapest, Krisztina krt. 39/B, Fourth Fl., 1013, Hungary; tel. (1) 344-0134; e-mail rozsnyai@mab.hu; internet www.ceenetwork.hu; f. 2001, constituted 2011; provides information and best practice examples in quality assurance and quality devt in higher education; participates in int. projects; organizes events, seminars, workshops and confs; maintains relations with other European and non-European orgs; shares experiences and fosters cooperation among mem. agencies; 27 mem. agencies; Pres. IRING WASSER (Germany); Sec.-Gen. CHRISTINA ROZSNYAI (Hungary); Project Man. MILA ZARKH.

Consejo Centroamericano de Acreditación de la Educación Superior (CCA) (Central American Council for Accreditation in Higher Education): 100 m norte y 75 m este de Office Depot, Avda Central, San Pedro, Montes de Oca, San José, Costa Rica; tel. 2511-6133; e-mail cca@ucr.ac.cr; internet www.cca.ucr.ac.cr; f. 2003; creates system of evaluation and accreditation to promote and strengthen Caribbean higher education; aims to contribute to improve socio-political conditions, quality of democracy, peace and freedom in the region for the improvement of quality in education; Pres. LEA AZUCENA CRUZ CRUZ; Exec. Dir Licda MARIANELA AGUILAR ARCE; publ. *CCAlidad*.

European Association for Quality Assurance in Higher Education (ENQA): Ave de Tervuren 38, boîte 4, 1040 Brussels, Belgium; tel. (2) 735-56-59; e-mail secretariat@enqa.eu; internet www.enqa.eu; f. 2000 as European Network for Quality Assurance in Higher Education, present name and status 2004; disseminates information, experiences and good practices in the field of quality assurance in higher education to European quality assurance agencies, public authorities and higher education instns; contributes to devt of quality assurance across all the Bologna signatory countries; financed by the European Comm.; 89 full mem. agencies (39 nat., 2 European) in 24 countries; affiliate mems (33 nat., 10 European, 4 non-European, 1 regional) in 26 countries; Pres. Dr PADRAIG WALSH (Ireland); Dir Dr MARIA KELO (Belgium).

European Consortium for Accreditation: NVAO, POB 85498, 2508 CD The Hague, Netherlands; tel. (70) 3122352; e-mail secretariat@ecaconsortium.net; internet www.ecaconsortium.net; f. 2003; aims to achieve the mutual recognition of accreditation decisions among the participants; encourages mutual learning and disseminating best practices in accreditation; provides information on quality and supports internationalization of instns and students; 16 mem. orgs in 12 countries; Chair. ROLF HEUSSER; Coordinator MARK FREDERIKS.

International Network for Quality Assurance Agencies in Higher Education (INQAAHE): AQU Catalunya, C. dels Vergós 36-42, 08017 Barcelona, Spain; tel. 932688950; e-mail secretariat@inqaahe.org; internet www.inqaahe.org; f. 1991; collects and disseminates information on theory and practice in the assessment, improvement and maintenance of quality in higher education; undertakes research in areas relevant to quality in higher education; provides advice and expertise to assist existing and emerging quality assurance agencies; organizes seminars, workshops and confs; 277 mems (incl. 172 full mems, 70 assoc. mems, 35 affiliates); Pres. Dr CAROL BOBBY (USA); Sec. Dr MARTÍ CASADESÚS (Spain); publ. *Quality in Higher Education* (3 a year).

Red Iberoamericana para la Acreditación de la Calidad de la Educación Superior (RIACES) (Ibero—American Network for Higher Education Accreditation): CONEAU, Av. Santa Fe 1385, Piso 4, C1059ABH, Buenos Aires, Argentina; tel. (11) 4815-1767; e-mail coordinacion@riaces.net; internet www.riaces.net; f. 2003; promotes cooperation and the exchange of information and experiences between Iberoamerican instns concerned with the evaluation and accreditation of quality in higher education; 35 mem. agencies; Pres. GUILLERMO VARGAS SALAZAR; Sec.-Gen. HORACIO O'DONNELL.

Engineering and Technology

International Union of Technical and Engineering Associations/Union Internationale des Associations et Organismes Techniques (UATI): 1 rue Miollis, 75732 Paris Cedex 15, France; tel. 145684829; e-mail uati@uati.info; internet uati.uisf.fr; f. 1951; promotes and coordinates education, training and scientific, technical, technological, social and cultural exchanges, in particular with the developing or emerging countries; supports sustainable devt to eradicate poverty and to improve the quality of life; conducts studies, seminars, confs, theme days; working groups and cttees to identify, promote and coordinate actions of mem. asscns in areas of common interest; facilitates relations with int. bodies, in particular UNESCO, UNIDO and ECOSOC; mems (see under Member Organizations) also incl. Académie Internationale de Génie Génétique, Académie des Sciences Minières de la Russie, Agence Nationale pour la Rénovation Urbaine, Asscn des Ingénieurs Territoriaux de France, Asscn Tunisienne de Génie Sismique, Comité Transnat. de Géotechnique d'Afrique, Institut de la Gestion Déléguée, Institut de Prévention et de Gestion des Risques Urbains, Int. Ccl for Education, Science and Technology; 12 mem. orgs; Pres. PHILIPPE AUSSOURD; Vice-Pres. ELIE ABSI.

MEMBER ORGANIZATIONS

Alliance of European Cultural Cities/Alliance des Villes Européennes de Culture: Service patrimoine, Mairie d'Arles, BP 193, 13637 Arles Cedex, France; e-mail amandine@avecnet.net; internet www.avecnet.net; f. 1997, present status 2000; encourages and facilitates exchange of experiences and good practices in the field of heritage devt; offers scholarships; promotes sustainable devt of historical and cultural cities and territories in Europe; maintains local heritage; 30 mems (incl. 27 active mem. cities, 3 assoc. mem. orgs); Pres. JOSE ERNESTO D'OLIVEIRA (Portugal); publ. *Proceedings of the International Workshop*.

Union Internationale des Ingénieurs et des Scientifiques utilisant la langue Française (UISF): c/o UATI, Maison de l'UNESCO, 1 rue Miollis, 75732 Paris Cedex 15, France; tel. 145684827; e-mail eabsi@uisf.fr; internet www.uisf.fr; encourages and facilitates cooperation and exchange of information among mems; establishes working groups on topical issues; Pres. Prof. ELIE ABSI; Sec.-Gen. MARC LEVILION; publ. *Proceedings*.

World Road Association/Association mondiale de la Route: La Grande Arche, Paroi Nord, Niveau 2, 92055 Paris-La Défense Cedex, France; tel. 147968121; e-mail info@piarc.org; internet www.piarc.org; f. 1909; serves as forum for analysis and discussion of the full spectrum of transport issues, related to roads and road transport; identifies, develops and disseminates best practice and gives better access to int. information; develops and promotes efficient tools for decision-making on matters related to roads and road transport; organizes congresses every 4 years, technical seminars, publs; has nat. cttees in 37 mem. countries; 118 mem. govts; Pres. ANNE-MARIE LECLERC (Canada); Sec.-Gen. JEAN-FRANÇOIS CORTÉ (France); publs *CD-Route* (technical reports, every 2 years), *Congress proceedings*, *Reports to International Winter Road Congress* (every 4 years), *Reports to World Road Congress* (every 4 years), *Routes/Roads* (4 a year).

OTHER ORGANIZATIONS

Arab Petroleum Training Institute: POB 6037, Al Tajeyat, Baghdad, Iraq; tel. (1) 5234100; f. 1979; conducts research on training needs in the oil sector in mem. states; training of high-level personnel in all aspects of the oil industry; 11 mem. states; library of 5,000 vols, bibliographic and non-bibliographic databases; Dir-Gen. Dr TAL'AT NAJEEB HATTAB.

European Organization for Civil Aviation Equipment (EUROCAE)/Organisation Européenne pour l'Equipement de l'Aviation Civile: 102 rue Etienne Dolet, 92240 Malakoff, France; tel. 140927930; e-mail eurocae@eurocae.net; internet www.eurocae.net; f. 1963; studies and advises on technical problems related to the application of equipment to aviation and prepares minimum performance specifications that admins in Europe may use for approving equipment; organizes annual symposium, training activities; 132 mems; Pres. JEAN-PAUL PLATZER; Sec.-Gen. ABDOULAYE N'DIAYE.

European Society for Engineering Education (SEFI)/Société Européenne pour la Formation des Ingénieurs/Europäische Gesellschaft für Ingenieur-Ausbildung: 39 rue des Deux Eglises, 1000 Brussels, Belgium; tel. (2) 502-36-09; e-mail info@sefi.be; internet www.sefi.be; f. 1973; serves as European Forum for higher engineering education actors and policy-makers; provides services and information about engineering education to European instns, academic staff and industry; supports European devt in higher engineering education; encourages exchanges between teachers, researchers and students of engineering; organizes confs, deans' conventions; 410 mems; Pres. Prof. Dr KAMEL HAWWASH (UK); Sec.-Gen. FRANÇOISE CÔME (Belgium); publ. *European Journal for Engineering Education* (6 a year).

ICHCA International Ltd: Suite 2, 85 Western Rd, Romford, RM1 3LS, UK; tel. (1708) 735295; e-mail info@ichca.com; internet www.ichca.com; f. 1952, inc. 2002; provides management information and exchange of technical data relating to methods and techniques in the industry keeping account of future trends and training needs; rep. of mems and industry at int. level; organizes confs, symposia, meetings, workshops for exchange of information; studies technical questions relating to cargo-handling matters; disseminates information on topical trends, devts and technical matters; contributes to debates on industry issues around the world and has direct effect on the formation of int. regulations and legislation; promotes safety and efficiency in the handling and movement of goods; 900 mems from more than 80 countries; Chair. DAVID BENDALL (Australia); Sec. and Exec. Dir ROSEMARY NEILSON (UK); publ. *Cargo World* (1 a year).

International Academy for Production Engineering/Collège International pour la Recherche en Productique/Internationale Akaddemie fur Produktionstechnik: 9 rue Mayran, 75009 Paris, France; tel. 145262180; e-mail cirp@cirp.net; internet www.cirp.net; f. 1951 as Int. Instn for Production Engineering Research; promotes scientific research, related to manufacturing processes, production equipment and automation, manufacturing systems, product design and manufacturing; encourages industrial application of the fundamental research work; 600 mems and research affiliates from 50 countries; Pres. Prof. LASZLO MONOSTORI (Hungary); Sec.-Gen. Treas. Prof. DIDIER DUMUR (France); publs *CIRP Annals—Manufacturing Technology* (2 vols, 1 a year), *CIRP Journal of Manufacturing Science & Technology* (4 a year).

International Association for Bridge and Structural Engineering (IABSE)/Association Internationale des Ponts et Charpentes/Internationale Vereinigung für Brückenbau und Hochbau: c/o ETH-Zurich, Hoenggerberg HIL E21.3, 8093 Zurich, Switzerland; tel. 446332647; e-mail secretariat@iabse.org; internet www.iabse.org; f. 1929; promotes int. cooperation among scientists, engineers, researchers and manufacturers; facilitates interchange of knowledge, ideas and the results of research work in the sphere of bridge and structural engineering; organizes confs, publs, technical working groups, awards; 4,000 mems from 100 countries; Pres. PREDRAG POPOVIC (USA); Exec. Dir UELI BRUNNER; publs *Bulletin*, *Conference Report* (irregular), *Structural Engineering Document* (1 a year), *Structural Engineering International* (4 a year).

International Association for Hydro-Environment Engineering and Research: Paseo Bajo Virgen del Puerto 3, 28005 Madrid, Spain; tel. 913357908; e-mail iahr@iahr.org; internet www.iahr.org; f. 1935; organizes confs and workshops; publishes technical and scientific journals, magazines and books; forum for engineers and water specialists working in fields related to the hydro-environmental sciences and their practical application; stimulates and promotes research and its application to contribute to sustainable devt, optimization of world water resources management and industrial flow processes; 2,300 individual mems, 100 mem. institutes; Pres. Prof. ROGER FALCONER (UK); Sec.-Gen. Dr RAMÓN M. GUTIÉRREZ SERRET (New Zealand); Exec. Dir Dr CHRISTOPHER B. GEORGE; publs *Journal of Hydraulic Research* (6 a year), *Journal of Hydroenvironment Research*, *Journal of River Basin Management* (4 a year), *Hydrolink magazine* (6 a year).

International Association of Public Transport/Union Internationale des Transports Publics (UITP)/Internationaler Verband für Öffentliches Verkehrswesen: 6 rue Ste Marie (Quai des Charbonnages), 1080 Brussels, Belgium; tel. (2) 673-61-00; e-mail info@uitp.org; internet www.uitp.org; f. 1885; studies problems related to the operation of public transportation; provides platform for worldwide cooperation, business devt and the sharing of information and experiences; organizes exhibitions, workshops, world and regional congresses, confs, training sessions and study tours; 3,400 mems from 92 countries; library of 25,000 vols, 200 journals; online library; Pres. OUSMANE M. THIAM (Senegal); Sec.-Gen. ALAIN FLAUSCH (Belgium); publ. *Public Transport International Magazine* (6 a year, in English, French, German, Russian, Italian and Spanish).

International Centre for Science and High Technology (ICS): AREA Science Park, Padriciano 99, 34149 Trieste TS, Italy; tel. 409228111; e-mail info@ics.trieste.it; internet www.ics.trieste.it; f. 1988; an int. centre of the United Nations Industrial Devt Org. (UNIDO); promotes transfer and application of scientific knowledge and eco-friendly technologies in support of sustainable industrial devt for the benefit of developing countries and countries in economic transition; promotes and stimulates research in applied science; organizes workshops, expert group meetings and training courses, networking and e-learning activities; works on 3 thematic fields: utilization and valorization of biomass, knowledge-based food valorization, renewable energy technologies; Man. Dir STEFANO BOLOGNA.

International Commission of Agricultural and Biosystems Engineering (CIGR): c/o Research Group of Bioproduction Engineering, Research Faculty of Agriculture, Hokkaido Univ., N-9, W-9, Kita-ku, Sapporo, Hokkaido, 060-8589, Japan; tel. (11) 7063885; e-mail cigr_gs2010@bpe.agr.hokudai.ac.jp; internet www.cigr.org; f. 1930 as Int. Comm. of Agricultural Engineering, current name adopted 2008; stimulates devt and application of science and technology in the field of agricultural engineering; encourages education, training and mobility of young professionals; encourages interregional mobility to facilitate exchange of research results and technology; conservation, irrigation, land improvement and reclamation; rural construction and equipment; agricultural machinery; distribution of electricity in rural areas and its application in the general energy context; 34 mems (7 regional mems, 19 nat. mems, 6 corporate mems, 2 individual mems); Pres. Prof. DA-WEN SUN (Ireland); Sec.-Gen. Prof. TOSHINORI KIMURA (Japan); publs *CIGR Journal* (online, www.cigrjournal.org), *CIGR Proceedings*.

International Commission on Glass (ICG): c/o Instituto de Cerámica y Vidrio (CSIC), Kelsen 5, Campus de Cantoblanco, 28049 Madrid, Spain; tel. 903221678; e-mail psimurka@gmail.com; internet www.icglass.org; f. 1933; promotes and stimulates understanding and cooperation between glass experts in the fields of science and technology, art, history and education; promotes dissemination of information on the art, history, science and technology of glass; holds congress; 37 mem. orgs; Pres. Prof. SHOU PENG (China); Exec. Sec. Dr PETER SIMURKA (Slovakia).

International Commission on Illumination (CIE)/Commission Internationale de l'Éclairage/Internationale Beleuchtungskommission: Kegelgasse 27, 1030 Vienna, Austria; tel. (1) 71431870; e-mail ciecb@cie.co.at; internet www.cie.co.at; f. 1900 as Int. Commission on Photometry, present name and status 1913; provides an int. forum for the discussion of all matters relating to science, technology and art in the fields of light and lighting; develops basic standards and procedures of metrology; provides guidance in the application of basic principles and procedures to the devt of int. standards; prepares and publishes reports and standards; maintains liaison and technical interaction with relevant int. orgs; 71 mem. cttees (incl. 37 nat. cttees, 3 assoc. nat. cttees, 15 assoc. mems, 16 supportive mems); Pres. ANN WEBB (UK); Sec. YOSHIKI NAKAMURA (Japan); publ. *Proceedings of Conferences and Symposia*.

International Commission on Irrigation and Drainage/Commission Internationale des Irrigations et du Drainage/Comisión Internacional de Riegos y Drenajes: 48 Nyaya Marg, Chanakyapuri, New Delhi 110021, India; tel. (11) 26116837; e-mail icid@icid.org; internet www.icid.org; f. 1950; stimulates and promotes devt of the arts, sciences and techniques of engineering, agriculture, economics, ecology and social sciences in managing water and land resources for irrigation, drainage, flood control and river training applications, incl. research and devt and capacity-building by adopting comprehensive approaches and up-to-date techniques for sustainable agriculture in the world; 65 active mem. countries, 110 nat. mem. cttees; Pres. Prof. Dr GAO ZHANYI (China); Sec.-Gen. AVINASH C. TYAGI (India); Exec. Sec. S. A. KULKARNI (India); publ. *Irrigation and Drainage* (5 a year).

International Commission on Large Dams/Commission Internationale des Grands Barrages: 61 ave Kléber, 75116 Paris, France; tel. 147041780; e-mail secretaire.general@icold-cigb.org; internet www.icold-cigb.org; f. 1928; sets standards and guidelines to ensure that dams are built and operated safely, efficiently, economically, and are environmentally sustainable and socially equitable; encourages advances in planning, design, construction, operation and maintenance of large dams and their associated civil works; collects and disseminates relevant information and studies related technical questions; organizes capacity-building sessions for engineers; 95 mem. countries; Pres. A. NOMBRE (Burkina Faso); Sec.-Gen. M. DE VIVO; publs *ICOLD Congress Proceedings and Transactions* (every 3 years), *World Register of Dams*.

International Congress on Fracture (ICF): c/o A. T. Yokobori, Jr, Dept of Nano Mechanics, Graduate School of Engineering, Tohoku Univ., Aobayama 01, Aobaku, Sendai, 980-8579, Japan; tel. (22) 795-6894; e-mail yokobori@md.mech.tuhoku.ac.jp; internet www.icf-wasi.org; f. 1965; fosters research in the mechanics and phenomena of fracture, fatigue and strength of materials; promotes cooperation among scientists in the field; holds Int. Conf. every 4 years; 30 mem. orgs; Founder Pres. Prof. T. YOKOBORI (Japan); Pres. Prof. ALBERTO CARPINTERI (Italy); Sec.-Gen. A. TOSHIMITSU YOKOBORI, Jr (Japan); publ. *Proceedings* (every 4 years).

International Council for Research and Innovation in Building and Construction (CIB): Kruisplein 25G, 3014 DB Rotterdam, Netherlands; tel. (10) 4110240; e-mail secretariat@cibworld.nl; internet www.cibworld.nl; f. 1953 as Conseil International du Bâtiment, current name adopted 1998; facilitates int. cooperation and information exchange between orgs with research, univ., industry or govt background active in all aspects of research and innovation for building and construction; source of information for research and innovation worldwide in the field of building and construction; has 7 regional offices; 350 mem. orgs; Pres. Dr SHYAN SUNDER (USA); Sec.-Gen. Dr WIM BAKENS (Netherlands); publ. *CIB Congress and Symposium Proceedings*.

International Council for Scientific and Technical Information (ICSTI)/Conseil International pour l'Information Scientifique et Technique: 5 rue Ambroise Thomas, 75009 Paris, France; tel. 614651657; e-mail icsti@icsti.org; internet www.icsti.org; f. 1952 as ICSU Abstracting Board, present name 1984; aims to increase accessibility to and awareness of scientific and technical information; fosters communication and interaction among participants to improve effectiveness of scientific research; scientific assoc. of Int. Council for Science (ICSU); 61 mem. orgs; Pres. ROBERTA SHAFFER (USA); Gen. Sec. WENDY WARR (UK); Treas. PAM BJORNSON (Canada); publ. *ICSTI Insights* (4 a year).

International Council of Academies of Engineering and Technological Sciences, Inc. (CAETS): c/o William C. Salmon, 112 Pleasant Grove Rd, Locust Grove, VA 22508, USA; tel. (703) 527-5782; e-mail caets@nae.edu; internet www.caets.org; f. 1978, present name and status 2000; promotes devt of engineering and technology worldwide and to provide an int. forum for the discussion of technological and engineering issues; encourages int. engineering efforts to promote economic growth and social welfare; advises govts and int. orgs on technical and policy issues related to its areas of expertise; encourages improvement of engineering education and practice internationally; 26 nat. mem. acads; Pres. RENE DANDLIKER (Switzerland); Sec. and Treas. WILLIAM C. SALMON (USA).

International Council on Large Electric Systems/Conseil International des Grands Réseaux Électriques (CIGRE): 21 rue d'Artois, 75008 Paris, France; tel. 153891295; e-mail secretary-general@cigre.org; internet www.cigre.org; f. 1921; encourages engineers and specialists to exchange information related to power systems; works on issues related to planning and operation of power systems, design, construction, maintenance and disposal of HV equipment and plants; conducts studies and research and makes work available to the decision-makers of the industry; 16 study cttees and 1 technical cttee; organizes symposia; 6,360 individual mems, 1,137 collective mems; library of 6,800 references of publs; Pres. KLAUS FRÖHLICH (Switzerland); Sec.-Gen. FRANÇOIS MESLIER (France); publs *Electra* (6 a year, in English and French), *Session Papers and Proceedings* (every 2 years), *Symposium Papers (CD)* (irregular).

International Dairy Federation: see under Agriculture and Veterinary Science.

International Electrotechnical Commission (IEC)/Commission Electrotechnique Internationale: 3 rue de Varembé, POB 131, 1211 Geneva 20, Switzerland; tel. 229190211; e-mail info@iec.ch; internet www.iec.ch; f. 1906; promotes int. cooperation in the electrotechnical industry; administers int. conformity assessment schemes in the areas of electrical equipment and components testing and certification (IECEE), quality of electronic components, materials and processes (IECQ), certification of electrical equipment operated in explosive atmospheres (IECEx); prepares and publishes int. standards for all electrical, electronic and related technologies; creator of the International System (SI) of units of measurement; compiled a multi-language electronic vocabulary; 82 nat. cttee mems (60 full mems and 22 assoc. mems); library of 6,000 vols; Pres. Dr KLAUS WUCHERER (Germany); Gen. Sec. and CEO FRANS VREESWIJK; publ. *e-tech* (online).

International Federation for Housing and Planning (IFHP)/Fédération Internationale pour l'Habitation, l'Urbanisme et l'Aménagement des Territoires (FIHUAT)/Internationaler Verband für Wohnungswesen, Städtebau und Raumordnung (IVWSR): Binckhorstlaan 36, 2516 BE The Hague, Netherlands; tel. (70) 3244557; e-mail info@ifhp.org; internet www.ifhp.org; f. 1913; global network of professionals from the field of housing and planning; corporate and individual mems; holds annual congress; promotes understanding of urban devt issues; Pres. FLEMMING BORRESKOV (Denmark); CEO DEREK MARTIN (Netherlands).

International Federation for Information Processing: Hofstr. 3, 2361 Laxenburg, Austria; tel. (2236) 73616; e-mail ifip@ifip.org; internet www.ifip.org; f. 1960; promotes information science and technology by fostering int. cooperation in this field, stimulating research, devt and application of information processing in science and human activity, furthering dissemination and exchange of information about subject, and encouraging education in information processing; sponsors confs; 53 mem. orgs (incl. 4 affiliate mems); library of 700 vols; Pres. LEON STROUS (Netherlands); Sec. MARIA RAFFAI (Hungary); publs *Computers and Security*, *Computers in Industry*, *Education and Information Technologies*, *Entertainment Computing*, *International Journal of Critical Infrastructure Protection*.

International Federation of Automatic Control (IFAC)/Fédération Internationale de l'Automatique: Schlosspl. 12, 2361 Laxenburg, Austria; tel. (2236) 71447; e-mail secretariat@ifac-control.org; internet www.ifac-control.org; f. 1957; promotes science and technology of control in all systems, in theory and application; maintains working relationships with other nat. or int. orgs, esp. with other non-governmental professional feds; provides framework for collaboration between those working in automatic control and systems engineering; promotes exchange of ideas and experts within its professional fields; organizes int. world congresses every 3 years; sponsors symposia, confs and workshops; 52 nat. mem. orgs; Pres. IAN K. CRAIG (South Africa); Sec. KURT SCHLACHER (Austria); publs *Annual Reviews in Control* (2 a year), *Automatica* (12 a year, in English, online, www.autsubmit.com), *Control Engineering Practice* (12 a year), *Engineering Applications of Artificial Intelligence* (6 a year), *Journal of Process Control* (8 a year), *Mechatronics* (10 a year).

International Federation of Automotive Engineering Societies/Fédération Internationale des Sociétés d'Ingénieurs des Techniques de l'Automobile (FISITA): 30 Percy St, London, W1T 2DB, UK; tel. (20) 72996630; e-mail info@fisita.com; internet www.fisita.com; f. 1948; promotes active cooperation and exchange of information between mem. socs; supports professional devt of automotive engineers; supports education, training and int. experience of students and young engineers; 199,065 mems, nat. automotive mem. socs in 37 countries; Pres. J. E. ROBERTSON (USA); Chief Exec. IAN DICKIE (UK).

International Federation of Operational Research Societies (IFORS): c/o Mary Thomas Magrogan, 5521 Research Park Dr., Suite 200, Catonsville, MD 21228, USA; tel. (443) 757-3534; e-mail secretary@ifors.org; internet www.ifors.org; f. 1959; encourages devt of operational research as a unified science and its advancement worldwide; sponsors int. meetings; provides means for exchanging information on operational research; encourages establishment of new operational research socs; promotes operational research education; comprises nat. Operations Research socs of over 50 countries from 4 geographical regions: Asia Pacific, Europe, N America, S America; organizes confs; 50 nat. socs, 1 kindred soc.; Pres. Nelson Maculan (Brazil); Sec. Mary Thomas Magrogan (USA); publs *International Abstracts in Operations Research* (8 a year), *International Transactions in Operational Research*.

International Federation of Robotics: c/o VDMA R and A, Lyoner Str. 18, 60528 Frankfurt am Main, Germany; tel. (69) 66031697; e-mail secretariat@ifr.org; internet www.ifr.org; f. 1987; promotes research, devt, use and int. cooperation in the entire field of robotics to act as a focal point for orgs, manufacturers and integrators in activities related to robotics; organizes Int. Symposium on Robotics annually with an int. robot exhibition; 50 asscns, research and devt institutes; Pres. Arturo Baroncelli (Italy); Gen. Sec. Gudrun Litzenberger (Germany); publs *World Robotics-Industrial Robots* (1 a year, online, www.worldrobotics.org), *World Robotics-Service Robots* (1 a year, online, www.worldrobotics.org).

International Federation of Surveyors/ Fédération Internationale des Géomètres/Internationale Vereinigung der Vermessungsingenieure: Kalvebod Brygge 31–33, 1780 Copenhagen V, Denmark; tel. 38-86-10-81; e-mail fig@fig.net; internet www.fig.net; f. 1878; provides int. forum for discussion and devt to promote professional practice and standards; promotes knowledge and best practices in surveying; 10 technical comms; organizes int. congresses every 4 years and annual working weeks; 106 mem. asscns from 88 countries, 41 affiliates from 38 countries, 25 corporate mems, 85 academic mems from 56 countries, 14 correspondents, 32 honorary mems; Pres. Teo CheeHai (Malaysia); Dir Markku Villikka (Denmark).

International Gas Union/Union Internationale du Gaz: c/o Statoil, 0246 Oslo, Norway; Kjoerboveien 18, Sandvika, Norway; tel. 51-99-00-00; e-mail secrigu@statoil.com; internet www.igu.org; f. 1931; advocates for gas as an integral part of sustainable global energy system; promotes political, technical and economic progress of the gas industry; promotes devt of technologies which add to the environmental benefits of gas and enhance safe production, transmission, distribution and utilisation of gas; 79 charter mems and 38 assoc. mems in 78 countries; Pres. Dr Rahim Hashim (Malaysia); Sec.-Gen. Torstein Indreboe (Norway).

International Information Centre for Terminology (Infoterm)/Centre International d'Information pour la Terminologie/Internationales Informationszentrum für Terminologie: Gymnasiumstr. 50, 1190 Vienna, Austria; tel. (1) 427758026; e-mail infopoint@infoterm.org; internet www.infoterm.info; f. 1971, present status 1996; associated with DPI and ISONETl; consultative status with ECOSOC and UNESCO; operates the secretariat of ISO/TC 37 'Terminology and Other Language and Content Resources'; facilitates research and devt in creating terminologies; disseminates information on terminological activities and raising awareness of importance of terminology; provide teaching and training; promotes and supports cooperation of existing and establishment of new terminology centres and networks; 51 mem. asscns; library of 5,600 vols, 15,000 vols of specialized dictionaries, vocabulary standards at Cologne Univ. of Applied Sciences; Pres. Dr Albina Auksoriūtė (Lithuania); Dir Dr Christian Galinski (Austria).

International Institute of Communications: 2 Printers Yard, 90a Broadway, London, SW19 1RD, UK; tel. (20) 84170600; e-mail enquiries@iicom.org; internet www.iicom.org; f. 1969 as Int. Broadcast Institute; worldwide research and education on trends and devts relevant to the telecommunications, content, media and internet industries; hosts seminars, Media Forum meetings, and annual conf.; mems in 70 countries; library of 15,000 vols, 200 periodicals; Pres. Fabio Colasanti; Dir-Gen. Andrea Millwood Hargrave; publ. *Intermedia* (5 a year).

International Institute of Refrigeration/ Institut International du Froid: 177 blvd Malesherbes, 75017 Paris, France; tel. 142273235; e-mail orders@iifiir.org; internet www.iifiir.org; f. 1908; promotes knowledge of refrigeration and associated technologies; studies and disseminates latest devts in all technical, scientific and industrial issues concerning refrigeration systems, cryogenics, air conditioning, heat pumps and their applications; organizes congresses and confs; has a library, abstract database; provides bibliographical searches; 60 mem. countries; Dir Didier Coulomb (France); publs *Bulletin of the IIR* (bibliographical, in English and French), *International Journal of Refrigeration* (8 a year), *Proceedings of Conferences*.

International Institute of Welding/Institut International de la Soudure: BP 51362, Villepinte, 95942 Roissy ch de Gaulle Cedex, France; Zone Industrielle Paris Nord II, 90 rue des Vanesses, 93420 Villepinte, France; tel. 1-49-90-36-08; e-mail iiw@iiwelding.org; internet www.iiwelding.org; f. 1948; promotes science and application of joining technology; provides forum for networking and knowledge exchange among scientists, researchers and industry; identifies, develops and implements the IIW education, training, qualification and certification programmes on global basis; 56 mem. countries; Pres. Baldev Raj (India); CEO Dr Cécile Mayer (France); publ. *Welding in the World* (6 a year).

International Measurement Confederation (IMEKO)/Confédération Internationale de la Mesure: Dalszínház utca 10, 1 stock No 3, Budapest, 1061, Hungary; tel. (1) 353-1562; e-mail imeko@t-online.hu; internet www.imeko.org; f. 1958; promotes int. exchange of scientific and technical information relating to devts in measuring techniques, instrument design and manufacture and in application of instrumentation in scientific research and industry; promotes cooperation among scientists and engineers and with other int. orgs; organizes congresses every 3 years, confs, symposia, workshops; 38 mem. orgs, 24 technical cttees; Pres. Prof. Pasquale Daponte (Italy); Sec.-Gen. Dr Zoltan Zelenka (Austria); publs *Acta IMEKO* (proceedings of World Congresses, online, acta.imeko.org/index.php/acta-imeko), *Measurement* (10 a year).

International Organization for Standardization/Organisation Internationale de Normalisation: 1 rue de Varembé, CP 56, 1211 Geneva 20, Switzerland; tel. 227490111; e-mail central@iso.org; internet www.iso.org; f. 1947; develops int. standards for all aspects of technology and business; promotes devt of standardization and related activities in the world with a view to facilitating the int. exchange of goods and services and to developing mutual cooperation in the spheres of intellectual, scientific, technological and economic activity; has reference library holding full collns of ISO and IEC standards; 164 mems (incl. 111 mem. bodies, 49 correspondent mems, 4 subscriber mems); Pres. Dr Boris Aleshin (Russia); Sec.-Gen. Rob Steele (New Zealand); publs *ISO Focus+* (12 a year), *ISO International Standards*, *ISO Management Systems* (6 a year).

International Society for Soil Mechanics and Geotechnical Engineering/Société Internationale de Mécanique des Sols et de la Géotechnique: City Univ. London, Northampton Sq., London, EC1V 0HB, UK; tel. (20) 70408154; e-mail secretariat@issmge.org; internet www.issmge.org; f. 1936, current name adopted 1997; promotes int. cooperation among engineers and scientists for the advancement and dissemination of knowledge in the field of geotechnics and its engineering and environmental applications; organizes int. and regional confs, symposia and workshops; affiliated mem. of Int. Union of Geological Sciences (IUGS); 86 mem. socs, 19,600 individual mems; Pres. Prof. Dr Roger Frank (France); Sec.-Gen. Prof. Dr R. Neil Taylor (UK).

International Union of Laboratories and Experts in Construction Materials, Systems and Structures/Réunion Internationale des Laboratoires d'Essais et Experts des Matériaux, systèmes de constructions et ouvrages (RILEM): 157 rue des Blains, 92220 Bagneux, France; tel. 145361020; e-mail dg@rilem.net; internet www.rilem.net; f. 1947; advances scientific knowledge related to construction materials, systems and structures; encourages transfer and application of related knowledge worldwide; promotes sustainable and safe construction, improved performance and cost benefit for society; stimulates new directions of research and its applications to promote excellence in construction; fosters cooperation at int. scale by general access to advanced knowledge; 1,248 mems; Pres. Prof. Mark Richner (Switzerland); Gen. Sec. Pascale Ducornet; publs *Concrete Science and Engineering Journal* (4 a year), *Materials and Structures / Matériaux et Constructions* (10 a year), *RILEM Proceedings*.

International Water Association: Alliance House, 12 Caxton St, London, SW1H 0QS, UK; tel. (20) 76545500; e-mail water@iwahq.org; internet www.iwahq.org; f. 1999 by the merger of the Int. Asscn on Water Quality and the Int. Water Supply Asscn; develops effective and sustainable approaches to global water management through research, collaboration, practice and publs; mems incl. academic researchers, research centres, energy utilities, consultants, water industry regulators, industrial water users and water equipment manufacturers; 10,000 individual mems, 500 corporate mems in 130 countries; Pres. and Chair. Dr Glen Daigger; Exec. Dir Paul Reiter; publs *Hydrology Research* (5 a year, print and online, www.iwaponline.com/nh), *Journal of Hydroinformatics* (4 a year, print and online, www.iwaponline.com/jh), *Journal of Water and Climate Change* (4 a year, print and online, www.iwaponline.com/jwc), *Journal of Water and Health* (4 a year, print and online, www.iwaponline.com/jwh), *Journal of Water Reuse and Desalination* (4 a year, print and online, www.iwaponline.com/jwrd), *Journal of Water, Sanitation and Hygiene for*

Development (online, www.iwaponline.com/washdev), *Journal of Water Supply: Research and Technology—AQUA* (8 a year, print and online, www.iwaponline.com/jws), *Water21* (6 a year, print and online, www.iwaponline.com/w21), *Water Intelligence Online* (12 a year), *Water Practice and Technology* (4 a year, online, www.iwaponline.com/wpt), *Water Research* (20 a year, print and online), *Water Science and Technology* (24 a year, print and online, www.iwaponline.com/wst), *Water Science and Technology: Water Supply* (6 a year, print and online, www.iwaponline.com/ws), *Water Utility Management International* (4 a year, print and online, www.iwaponline.com/wumi).

ITRI Ltd: Unit 3, Curo Park, Frogmore, St Albans, AL2 2DD, UK; tel. (1727) 875544; e-mail info@itri.co.uk; internet www.itri.co.uk; f. 1932; involved in statistics, market surveys, environmental affairs, sustainability work and technology networks; hosts seminars, confs and industry-specific group meetings; operates commercial testing and contract research laboratories; provides information on new tin uses and opportunities for innovation; provides regular market reports as a basis for sound investment decisions and policy-making; has office in China; 200 mems in 35 countries; Man. Dir David Bishop (UK).

PIANC—World Association for Waterborne Transport Infrastructure/Association Internationale de Navigation: Bâtiment Graaf de Ferraris, 11ème étage, Boîte 3, blvd du Roi Albert II 20, 1000 Brussels, Belgium; tel. (2) 553-71-61; e-mail info@pianc.org; internet www.pianc.org; f. 1885; promotes inland and ocean navigation by fostering and encouraging progress in the design, construction, improvement, maintenance and operation of inland and maritime waterways, ports and coastal areas for the benefit of mankind; promotes cooperation among int. experts on technical, economic and environmental issues pertaining to waterborne transport infrastructure; organizes int. congresses, confs; 2,488 mems (incl. 2,000 individual mems, 450 corporate mems, 36 qualifying mems, 2 int. river comms); Pres. Geoffroy Caude (France); Sec.-Gen. Louis van Schel (Belgium); publ. *PIANC 'On Course'* (3 a year, online).

Textile Institute: First Fl., St James's Bldgs, Oxford St, Manchester, M1 6FQ, UK; tel. (161) 2371188; e-mail tiihq@textileinst.org.uk; internet www.texi.org; f. 1910, Royal Charter 1925 and 1955; facilitates education and training, professional standards and exchange of information within the industry by means of publs, confs, meetings and information services; 60 nat. and regional brs; 8,000 mems in 85 countries; library of 1,500 vols, 120 journals; Chair. John R. Wilson; Hon. Sec. Elizabeth Fox; publs *Textiles* (4 a year), *The Journal of the Textile Institute* (4 a year).

World Energy Council (WEC)/Conseil Mondial de l'Energie (CME): 5th Fl., Regency House, 1–4 Warwick St, London, W1B 5LT, UK; tel. (20) 77345996; e-mail info@worldenergy.org; internet www.worldenergy.org; f. 1924 as World Power Conf., current name adopted 1992; collates data about and undertakes and promotes research into the means of supplying and using energy and impact on natural environment; disseminates results of research by publishing data; holds triennial congress; promotes regional symposia and technical studies; 93 autonomous mem. cttees; Chair. Pierre Gadonneix (France); Sec.-Gen. Prof. Dr Christoph Frei (London); publs *Energy Efficiency Policies and Indicators* (every 3 years), *Performance of Generating Plant* (every 3 years), *World Survey of Energy Resources* (every 3 years).

World Foundrymen Organization: Winton House, Lyonshall, Kington, HR5 3JP, UK; tel. (121) 6016976; e-mail secretary@thewfo.com; internet www.thewfo.com; f. 1927; promotes int. cooperation between mem. asscns and other orgs; centre of strategic foundry knowledge, designed to develop, enhance and improve the production of metal castings; organizes congress every 2 years to disseminate information of latest research and devts in the cast metals industry; 31 nat. technical asscns; Pres. Xabier Gonzalez Azpiri (Spain); Sec.-Gen. Ing. Andrew Turner (UK); publ. *International Foundry Research* (4 a year).

World Steel Association: 120 rue Colonel Bourg, 1140 Brussels, Belgium; tel. (2) 702-89-00; e-mail steel@worldsteel.org; internet www.worldsteel.org; f. 1967 as Int. Iron and Steel Institute, present name 2008; also has office in China; promotes interests of the world's steel industries; serves as a forum for exchange of knowledge and discussion of problems relating to steel industries; collects, disseminates and maintains statistics and information; serves as a liaison body between int. and nat. steel orgs; 180 mem. steel companies; Chair. Xiaogang Zhang (China); Dir-Gen. Dr Edwin Basson (South Africa); publs *Crude Steel Production Monthly*, *Iron Production Monthly*.

World Wide Web Consortium (W3C): c/o Massachusetts Institute of Technology, Computer Science and Artificial Intelligence Laboratory (CSAIL), 32 Vassar St, Cambridge, MA 02139, USA; tel. (617) 253-2613; e-mail team-liaisons@w3.org; internet www.w3.org; f. 1994; provides an open forum for discussing the technical evolution of the World Wide Web; develops protocols and guidelines to ensure long-term growth of the Web; makes standards that define key parts of what makes the World Wide Web work; 386 mem. orgs; CEO Dr Jeffrey Jaffe; Dir Tim Berners-Lee.

Law

Hague Academy of International Law/Académie de Droit International de La Haye: Peace Palace, Carnegieplein 2, 2517 KJ The Hague, Netherlands; tel. (70) 3024242; e-mail communication@hagueacademy.nl; internet www.hagueacademy.nl; f. 1923; centre for research and teaching in public and private int. law; furthers scientific and advanced studies of the legal aspects of int. relations; Pres. Boutros Boutros-Ghali (Egypt); Sec.-Gen. Prof. Yves Daudet (France); publ. *Collected Courses of the Hague Academy of International Law*.

Associated Centre:

Centre for Studies and Research in International Law and International Relations: Peace Palace, Carnegieplein 2, 2517 KJ The Hague, Netherlands; tel. (70) 3024242; e-mail s.deseze@hagueacademy.nl; internet www.hagueacademy.nl/centre-for-studies-and-research-in-international-law-and-international-relations; f. 1957; postdoctoral 4-week research courses in August and September after courses held by Academy; participants to undertake original research on common general theme determined each year by the Academy; 12 English-speaking, 12 French-speaking participants; Dir for studies for English-speaking section Maarit Jantera-Jareborg; Dir for studies for French-speaking section Prof. Hélène Tigroudja.

Hague Conference on Private International Law/Conférence de La Haye de droit International Privé: Scheveningseweg 6, 2517 KT The Hague, Netherlands; tel. (70) 3633303; e-mail secretariat@hcch.net; internet www.hcch.net; f. 1893; works for the unification of the rules of private int. law; assists in organizing and participates in confs and seminars at int., regional and nat. level to educate personnel and mems of the legal system; 72 mems (incl. 71 states and 1 regional economic integration); Sec.-Gen. J. H. A. van Loon; publ. *Proceedings of the Conference's Diplomatic Sessions/Actes et documents des Sessions diplomatiques de la Conférence*.

Institute of International Law/Institut de Droit International: c/o Joe Verhoeven, 24 rue de Morsaint, 1390, Grez-Doiceau, Belgium; tel. 229085720; e-mail isabelle.gerardi@gmail.com; internet www.idi-iil.org; f. 1873; promotes devt of int. law by endeavouring to formulate gen. principles in accordance with civilized ethical standards and by giving assistance to achieve gradual and progressive codification of int. law; 101 mems, 50 assocs worldwide; Pres. Hisashi Owada; Sec.-Gen. Prof. Joe Verhoeven; publs *Annuaire de l'Institut de droit International*, *Tableau général des Résolutions*.

Inter-American Bar Association/Federación Interamericana de Abogados/Federação Interamericana de Advogados/Fédération Inter-Américaine des Avocats: 1211 Connecticut Ave NW, Suite 202, Washington, DC 20036, USA; tel. (202) 466-5944; e-mail iaba@iaba.org; internet www.iaba.org; f. 1940; establishes and maintains relations among nat. and local orgs of lawyers in the Americas; provides forum for exchange of views; advances the science of jurisprudence, particularly study of comparative law; disseminates knowledge of the laws of the Americas; promotes the Rule of Law and admin. of justice, encouraging the establishment and maintenance of ind. judicial systems in all countries of the Americas; holds annual int. conf.; 40 affiliate mem. bar asscns; Pres. Rafael A. Veloz (Venezuela); Sec.-Gen. Dante Figueroa (USA); publs *Conference Proceedings* (1 a year), *Inter-American Journal of International and Comparative Law* (1 a year).

Intergovernmental Committee of the Universal Copyright Convention: UNESCO, 7 pl. de Fontenoy, 75700 Paris, France; tel. 145684711; f. 1952; studies problems concerning the application and operation of the Universal Copyright Convention; makes preparation for periodic revisions of this Convention; 17 mem. states (Algeria, Argentina, Austria, Cameroon, China, Croatia, France, Greece, Guatemala, India, Israel, Japan, Morocco, Portugal, Russia, Ukraine and USA); Chair. Abdullah Ouadrhiri (Morocco); publ. *Copyright Bulletin* (4 a year).

International Association for Philosophy of Law and Social Philosophy (IVR)/Internationale Vereinigung für Rechts- und Sozialphilosophie/Association Internationale de Philosophie du Droit et de Philosophie Sociale: Wiesbaden, Germany; e-mail l.schulz@jur.uni-frankfurt.de; internet ivronline.org; f. 1909; cultivates and promotes legal and social philosophy at nat. and int. level through scientific research; holds int. congresses every 2 years and lectures; 44 nat. sections; 2,300 mems; Pres. Prof. Dr Ulfrid Neumann (Germany); Sec.-Gen. Prof. Dr Lorenz Schulz (Germany); publ. *Archiv für Rechts- und Sozialphilosophie* (Archives for the Philosophy of Law and Social Philosophy, 4 a year).

International Association of Democratic Lawyers (IADL)/Association Internationale des Juristes Démocrates: 21 rue Brialmont, 1210 Brussels, Belgium; tel. (2) 223-33-10; e-mail oniikura@als.aoyama.ac.jp; internet www.iadllaw.org; f. 1946; aims to facilitate contacts and exchanges of view between lawyers and lawyers' assocs and to foster understanding and goodwill; works together to achieve the aims of the Charter of the UN; restores, defends and develops democratic rights and liberties in legislation and practice; mems in 102 countries; in consultative status with UN Economic and Social Council and UNESCO; Pres. JEANNE MIRER (USA); Sec.-Gen. OSAMU NIIKURA (Japan); publ. *Revue Internationale de Droit Contemporain* (International Review of Contemporary Law, 2 a year, in English, French and Spanish).

International Association of Lawyers/Union Internationale des Avocats (UIA)/Unión Internacional de Abogados: 25 rue du Jour, 75001 Paris, France; tel. 144885566; e-mail uiacentre@uianet.org; internet www.uianet.org; f. 1927; promotes independence and freedom of lawyers and defends their ethical and material interests on an int. level; contributes to devt of an int. order based on law; offers congresses, seminars, training sessions for education purposes; 2,000 individual mems, 200 bar, fed. and asscn mems from 110 countries; Pres. DRISS CHATER; Sec.-Gen. MARY-DAPHNÉ FISHELSON (France); Exec. Dir MARIE-PIERRE RICHARD (France); publ. *Juriste International* (4 a year).

International Association of Penal Law/Association Internationale de Droit Pénal/Asociación Internacional de Derecho Penal: POB 60118, 33008 Bordeaux Cedex, France; tel. 556066673; e-mail secretariat@penal.org; internet www.penal.org; f. 1924, successor of the Int. Union of Penal Law; promotes cooperation between bodies and individuals engaged in the study or practice of criminal law; studies crime, its causes and the means of preventing it; advances the theoretical and practical devt of int. penal law; holds congress, int. and regional confs, prizes and working groups; 2,000 mems; Pres. Prof. JOSÉ LUIS DE LA CUESTA (Spain); Sec.-Gen. KATALIN LIGETI (Luxembourg); publ. *Revue Internationale de Droit Pénal* (International Review of Penal Law, 2 a year).

International Bar Association: Fourth Fl., 10 Saint Bride St, London, EC4A 4AD, UK; tel. (20) 78420090; e-mail iba@int-bar.org; internet www.ibanet.org; f. 1947; influences devt of int. law reform and shapes future of the legal profession throughout the world; enables interchange of information and views among its mems about laws, practices and professional responsibilities relating to the practice of business law around the globe; supports independence of the judiciary and the right of lawyers; organizes annual conf.; 45,000 individual mem. lawyers, 200 mem. bar asscns and law socs; Pres. AKIRA KAWAMURA; Sec.-Gen. DAVID W. RIVKIN; Exec. Dir MARK ELLIS; publs *Business Law International* (3 a year), *Competition Law International* (2 a year, print and online), *Construction Law International* (4 a year), *Convergence* (online, www.ibanet.org/Publications/Convergence/contents.aspx), *Dispute Resolution International* (2 a year), *IBA Global Insight* (fmrly Int. Bar News, 6 a year), *Insolvency and Restructuring International* (2 a year), *Journal of Energy and Natural Resources Law* (4 a year), *The In-House Perspective* (4 a year).

International Bureau of Fiscal Documentation (IBFD): H. J. E. Wenckebachweg 210, 1096 AS Amsterdam, Netherlands; tel. (20) 5540100; e-mail info@ibfd.org; internet www.ibfd.org; f. 1938; ind. tax research; provides education and information on fiscal law and its application; tax treaties database, European taxation database and OECD database, on CD-ROM; promotes and disseminates understanding of cross-border taxation; offices in China, Malaysia and the USA; library of 19,000 vols, 1,100 journals, official gazettes, loose-leaf services, CD-ROMs and online databases, 8,000 law texts and official documents; Chair. S. VAN DER FELTZ; publs *Asia-Pacific Tax Bulletin* (6 a year), *Bulletin for International Taxation* (12 a year), *Derivatives and Financial Instruments* (6 a year), *European Taxation* (12 a year), *International Transfer Pricing* (6 a year), *International VAT Monitor* (6 a year), *World Tax Journal* (3 a year).

Attached Academy:

IBFD International Tax Training: POB 20237, 1000 HE Amsterdam, Netherlands; Rietlandpark 301, 1019 DW Amsterdam, Netherlands; tel. (20) 5540157; e-mail taxcourses@ibfd.org; internet www.ibfd.org/training; f. 1989; provides education and training on int. and comparative tax law

International Commission of Jurists/Commission Internationale de Juristes: POB 91, 33 rue des Bains, 1211 Geneva 8, Switzerland; tel. 229793800; e-mail info@icj.org; internet www.icj.org; f. 1952; promotes and protects human rights; advances independence of judiciary and legal profession and administration of justice according to int. law; promotes global adoption and implementation of int. human rights standards; encourages establishment and enforcement of legal system protecting against violation of human rights; library of 2,000 vols; Pres. Prof. PEDRO NIKKEN (Venezuela); Sec.-Gen. WILDER TAYLER; publ. *Attacks on Justice* (online).

International Development Law Organization/Organisation Internationale de Droit du Développement: Viale Vaticano 106, 00165 Rome RM, Italy; tel. 640403200; e-mail idlo@idlo.int; internet www.idlo.int; f. 1983; offers legal expertise, resources, tools and professional support to govts, multilateral partners and civil society orgs; carries out research and advocacy at nat. and int. level; br. office in The Hague, country offices in Afghanistan, Kenya, Kyrgyzstan, S Sudan, Somalia (based in Nairobi) and Tajikistan; 27 mem. countries; Dir-Gen. IRENE KHAN.

International Federation for European Law/Fédération Internationale pour le Droit Européen (FIDE): Via Nicolò Tartaglia 5, 00197 Rome RM, Italy; e-mail info@fide2012.eu; internet www.fide-europe.eu; f. 1961; advances studies on European law among mems of the European Community by coordinating activities of mem. socs and by organizing regular colloquies on topical problems of European law; organizes congress every 2 years; 28 nat. mem. asscns; Pres. Prof. Dr JULIA LAFFRANQUE (Estonia); Sec.-Gen. PATRICK MCCANN.

International Institute for the Unification of Private Law/Institut International pour l'Unification du Droit Privé (Unidroit): Via Panisperna 28, 00184 Rome RM, Italy; tel. 6696211; e-mail info@unidroit.org; internet www.unidroit.org; f. 1926 as an auxiliary organ of the League of Nations, present status 1940; studies needs and methods for modernizing, harmonizing and coordinating private and commercial law between states and groups of states; formulates uniform law instruments, principles and rules; organizes confs, int. congresses and publishes works on such subjects; meetings of orgs concerned with the unification of law; 63 mem. states; library of 270,000 vols, 430 current periodicals; Pres. Prof. BERARDINO LIBONATI (Italy); Sec.-Gen. Prof. HERBERT KRONKE (Germany); publs *Digest of Legal Activities of International Organizations*, *UNIDROIT Proceedings and Papers*, *Uniform Law Review* (4 a year, online, www.unidroit.org/english/publications/review/main.htm).

International Institute of Space Law (IISL)/Institut International de Droit de l'Espace: 94 bis, Ave de Suffren, 75015 Paris, France; e-mail cmj@advancingspace.com; internet www.iislweb.org; f. 1960; promotes cooperation with int. orgs and nat. instns in the field of space law; fosters devt of space law; studies legal and social science aspects of the exploration and use of outer space; holds meetings, colloquia and competitions on juridical and social science aspects of space activities; publishes reports; makes awards; holds an annual Colloquium; 386 individual mems elected for life; Pres. TANJA L. MASSON-ZWAAN (Netherlands); Exec. Sec. CORINNE M. JORGENSON (USA); publ. *Proceedings of Colloquia* (1 a year).

International Law Association/Association de Droit International: Charles Clore House, 17 Russell Sq., London WC1B 5DR, UK; tel. (20) 7323-2978; e-mail info@ila-hq.org; internet www.ila-hq.org; f. 1873; studies and advances public and private int. law; promotes int. understanding and respect for int. law; promotes and carries out research, surveys and investigations and publish useful results; holds exhibitions, meetings, lectures, classes, seminars and training courses; 22 cttees, 6 study groups and 50 regional brs worldwide; 3,500 mems; Pres. Prof. ALEXANDER YANKOV; Sec.-Gen. DAVID J. C. WYLD.

International Legal Institute/Internationaal Juridisch Instituut: R. J. Schimmelpennincklaan 20–22, 2517 JN, The Hague, Netherlands; tel. (70) 3460974; e-mail info@iji.nl; internet www.iji.nl; f. 1918 as Institut Intermédiaire Int.; provides information in the field of private int. law and foreign law to professionals working within the legal sector; Chair. E. M. WESSEL-ING-VAN GENT (Netherlands); Sec. Drs A. C. OLLAND (Netherlands); Dir J. M. J. KELTJENS.

International Maritime Committee/Comité Maritime International (CMI): Everdijstraat 43, 2000 Antwerp, Belgium; tel. (3) 227-35-26; e-mail admini@cmi-imc.org; internet www.comitemaritime.org; f. 1897; contributes to unification of maritime and commercial law, maritime customs, usages and practices; promotes establishment of nat. asscns of maritime law and cooperates with other int. asscns or orgs having the same object; work incl. drafting of conventions on collisions at sea, salvage and assistance at sea, limitation of shipowners' liability, maritime mortgages; mem. asscns in 51 countries; Pres. KARL-JOHAN GOMBRII (Norway); Sec.-Gen. NIGEL FRAWLEY (acting) (Canada); publ. *Yearbook*.

World Jurist Association (WJA): 7910 Woodmont Ave, Suite 1440, Bethesda, MD 20814, USA; tel. (202) 466-5428; e-mail wja@worldjurist.org; internet www.worldjurist.org; f. 1963; promotes continued devt of int. law and world order; provides open forum to judges, lawyers, law professors and other professionals from around the world to strengthen and expand the Rule of Law and its instns; fosters cooperative dialogue on world peace; holds biennial world confs, World Law Day, demonstration trials, research programmes and publs; has 4 affiliated orgs: World Asscn of Lawyers, World Asscn of Judges, World Asscn of Law Professors, World Business Assocs; lawyers, jurists and legal scholars in 140 countries; Pres. ALEXANDER BĚLOHLÁVEK (Czech Republic); Exec. Vice-Pres. SONA PANCHOLY (USA); publs *Law/Technology* (4 a year), *World Jurist* (Bulletin, 6 a year).

Medicine and Public Health

World Health Organization/Organisation Mondiale de la Santé: Ave Appia 20, 1211 Geneva 27, Switzerland; tel. 227912111; e-mail mediainquiries@who.int; internet www.who.int; f. 1948; provides leadership on matters critical to health and engages in partnerships where jt action is needed; shapes research agenda and stimulates generation, translation and dissemination of knowledge; sets norms and standards and promotes and monitors their implementation; articulates ethical and evidence-based policy options; provides technical support, catalysing change and building sustainable institutional capacity; monitors health situation and assesses health trends; 194 mem. states; library: see in Switzerland chapter; Dir-Gen. Dr MARGARET CHAN (Switzerland); publs *Bulletin of WHO* (12 a year, in English with multilingual abstracts in Arabic, Chinese, French, Russian and Spanish, print and online, www.who.int/bulletin), *Eastern Mediterranean Health Journal* (12 a year, in Arabic, English and French, print and online, www.emro.who.int/emh-journal/eastern-mediterranean-health-journal), *Weekly Epidemiological Record* (51 a year, in English and French, online), *WHO Drug Information* (4 a year, print and online, www.who.int/medicines/publications/druginformation), *WHO South-East Asia Journal of Public Health*, *World Health Report* (1 a year, online).

CIOMS

Council for International Organizations of Medical Sciences (CIOMS)/Conseil des Organisations Internationales des Sciences Médicales: c/o WHO, 20 ave Appia, 1211 Geneva 27, Switzerland; c/o WHO, Bldg V, Offices 117–121, ave Appia, 1211 Geneva 27, Switzerland; tel. 227913413; e-mail cioms@who.int; internet www.cioms.ch; f. 1949; facilitates and coordinates the activities of its mems; acts as coordinating centre between mems and the nat. instns; maintains collaboration with the UN; facilitates and promotes int. activities in the field of biomedical sciences; serves the scientific interests of the int. biomedical community; assoc. mems (see under Assoc. mems of CIOMS) also incl. American Soc. for Bioethics and Humanities, Academy of Medical, Dental and Pharmaceutical Sciences of Japan, Consulta di Bioetica, Fed. of Polish Medical Orgs Abroad, Fed. of Polish Medical Socs, Good Clinical Practice Alliance, Group for the Respect of Ethics and Excellence in Science, Nat. Fund for Scientific Research; 66 int. assoc., nat. academic and research ccls in 30 countries; Pres. Prof. JOHANNES J. M. VAN DELDEN; Sec.-Gen. Dr GUNILLA SJÖIN-FORSBERG; publs *International Ethical Guidelines for Biomedical Research Involving Human Subjects*, *International Guidelines for Ethical Review of Epidemiological Studies*, *International Nomenclature of Diseases*.

INTERNATIONAL MEMBERS OF CIOMS

International Association of Bioethics: POB 280, Univ. of the Philippines, Diliman, 1101 Quezon City, Philippines; e-mail secretariat@bioethics-international.org; internet bioethics-international.org; f. 1992; facilitates contacts and exchange of information between those working in bioethics worldwide; organizes int. confs; encourages devt of research and teaching in bioethics; 1,000 individual and instn mems; Pres. ANGUS J. DAWSON (UK); Sec. ANGELA BALLANTYNE (New Zealand); publs *Bioethics*, *Developing World Bioethics*.

International College of Angiology: 161 Morin Dr., Jay, VT 05859, USA; tel. (802) 988-4065; e-mail denisemrossignol@cs.com; internet www.intlcollegeofangiology.org; f. 1958; provides structure for research scientists in the field of angiology to carry out their ind. research and shortens interval between the translation of research findings into clinical practice; disseminates evolving medical knowledge of the vascular system to physicians; provides forum for interchange of clinical experiences and technical research associated with circulatory diseases; organizes clinical, diagnostic and therapeutic symposia, seminars, workshops and teaching confs; Pres. Prof. Dr TAKAO OHKI (Japan); Sec.-Gen. Prof. Dr VICTOR A. FERRARIS (USA); publ. *International Journal of Angiology*.

International College of Surgeons/Collège International de Chirurgiens: 1516 N Lakeshore Dr., Chicago, IL 60610, USA; tel. (312) 642-3555; e-mail info@icsglobal.org; internet www.icsglobal.org; f. 1935; improves devt and education of mems and advancement of the medical field; organizes surgical congresses, research and scholarship project and surgical teams project of volunteers to developing countries; encourages exchange of surgical knowledge; also operates the Int. Museum of Surgical Science located at HQ; 8,000 mems from 100 countries; World Pres. Dr SAID A. DAEE (USA); Exec. Dir MAX C. DOWNHAM; publ. *International Surgery* (6 a year).

International Federation of Clinical Neurophysiology/Fédération Internationale de Neurophysiologie Clinique: c/o Stephanie Stevenson, Venue West Conference Services Ltd, 100–873 Beatty St, Vancouver, BC V6B 2M6, Canada; tel. (604) 681-5226; e-mail sstevenson@venuewest.com; internet www.ifcn.info; f. 1949; fosters and encourages scientific research, investigation and demonstration in the field of clinical neurophysiology; improves quality of instruction in the professions dealing with these sciences; proposes standards, agreements and regulations and gives advice concerning criteria for the best apparatus, methods, techniques and for the interpretation of results; establishes and maintains collaboration with int. and nat. learned socs, govt orgs, professional asscns, socs, instns and individuals contributing to the field of clinical neurophysiology; mem. orgs in 58 countries; Pres. Prof. PAOLO ROSSINI (Italy); Sec. Prof. Dr DANIEL M. CIBILS (Uruguay); publs *Clinical Neurophysiology* (12 a year), *EMG and Motor Control* (6 a year), *Evoked Potentials* (6 a year).

International Federation of Oto-Rhino-Laryngological Societies/Fédération Internationale des Sociétés Oto-rhino-laryngologiques: c/o Dr Milan Profant, Antolská 11, 85107 Bratislava, Slovakia; e-mail info@ifosworld.org; internet www.ifosworld.org; f. 1965; promotes scientific and clinical research into oto-rhino-laryngology; works to improve aural health in developing countries; plays continuing medical educational role and has developed undergraduate curricula; organizes confs and world congresses; 120 mem. countries; Pres. Dr PAULO PONTES (Brazil); Gen. Sec. Prof. Dr MILAN PROFANT (Slovakia).

International Rhinologic Society: c/o Prof. M. Onerci, Ankara, Turkey; e-mail metin@tr.net; f. 1965; affiliates nat. and regional socs of rhinology; organizes int. congresses and courses of instruction; encourages study, research and scientific advancement in the field of rhinology and related sciences; nat. and regional soc. mems in 31 countries; Pres. D. PASSALI (Italy); Sec.-Gen. and Treas. M. ONERCI (Turkey); publs *American Journal of Rhinology*, *Rhinology* (4 year, online, www.rhinologyjournal.com).

International Society for Pharmacoepidemiology: 5272 River Rd, Suite 630, Bethesda, MD 20816, USA; tel. (301) 718-6500; e-mail ispe@paimgmt.com; internet www.pharmacoepi.org; provides forum for exchange of scientific information; promotes devt of policy, education and advocacy for the field of pharmacoepidemiology, incl. areas such as pharmacovigilance, drug utilization research, comparative effectiveness research, therapeutic risk management; organizes int. conf.; mems in 53 countries; Pres. STELLA BLACKBURN (UK); Exec. Sec. Dr MARK H. EPSTEIN (USA); publ. *Pharmacoepidemiology and Drug Safety*.

International Society of Audiology/Société Internationale d'Audiologie: c/o Dr G. Mencher, Dalhousie Univ., 121 Anchor Dr., Halifax NS B3N 3B9, Canada; tel. (902) 477-5360; e-mail info@isa-audiology.org; internet www.isa-audiology.org; f. 1952; facilitates knowledge, protection and rehabilitation of human hearing; coordinates and disseminates information to and from its mems and mem. socs; holds courses and int. congresses; 500 individual mems, 27 affiliated socs; Pres. Prof. Dr BOB COWAN (Australia); Sec.-Gen. Prof. Dr GEORGE A. TAVARTKILADZE (Russia); publ. *International Journal of Audiology* (1 a year).

International Society of Internal Medicine/Société Internationale de Médecine Interne: c/o Prof. Hans P. Kohler, Dept of Internal Medicine, RSZ-Bern Hospitals, Zieglerspital, Morillonstr. 75–91, 3001 Bern, Switzerland; tel. 319707178; e-mail hanspeter.kohler@spitalnetzbern.ch; internet www.isim-online.org; f. 1948; promotes scientific knowledge and unity in internal medicine; encourage research and education of internists; organizes postgraduate meetings in internal medicine; sponsors and organizes Int. Congress of Internal Medicine every 2 years; 61 nat. mem. socs; Pres. Prof. WILLIAM J. HALL (USA); Sec.-Gen. Prof. HANS-PETER KOHLER (Switzerland).

International Society of Pharmacovigilance (ISoP): 140 Emmanuel Rd, London, SW12 0HS, UK; tel. (203) 2560027; e-mail administration@isoponline.org; internet www.isoponline.org; encourages and extends research in the field of pharmacovigilance; promotes exchange of information on pharmacovigilance by organising meetings, symposia, workshops, bulletins, congresses and annual meeting; encourages pharmacovigilance education at all levels; mems in 63 countries; Pres. ALEX DODOO (Ghana); Sec.-Gen. EUGENE VAN PUIJENBROEK (Netherlands); publ. *Drug Safety* (12 a year).

International Union of Basic and Clinical Pharmacology: see under Unions Federated to the ICSU.

Medical Women's International Association (MWIA): c/o Dr Shelley Ross, 7555 Morley Dr., Burnaby BC V5E 3Y2, Canada; tel. (604) 522-1960; e-mail secretariat@mwia

.net; internet mwia.net; f. 1919; organizes MWIA Congresses every 3 years; facilitates contacts between medical women and encourages their cooperation in matters connected with int. health problems; works against gender-related inequalities in the medical profession between female and male doctors incl. career opportunities and economical aspects; 20,000 nat. asscn mems in 48 countries; Pres. Prof. KYUNG AH PARK (Korea); Sec.-Gen. Dr SHELLEY ROSS (Canada); publs *Congress Report* (every 3 years), *MWIA Update* (3 a year).

World Allergy Organization (WAO): 555 East Wells St, Suite 1100, Milwaukee, WI 53202-3823, USA; tel. (414) 276-1791; e-mail info@worldallergy.org; internet www.worldallergy.org; f. 1951; advances work in the educational, research and practical medical aspects of allergy diseases; sponsors scientific symposia in developing countries and postgraduate programs on allergy and clinical immunology; 89 regional and nat. socs; Pres. RUBY PAWANKAR (Japan); Sec.-Gen. MARIO SÁNCHEZ BORGES (Venezuela); publ. *Allergy & Clinical Immunology International* (6 a year, online).

World Association of Societies of Pathology and Laboratory Medicine (WASPaLM): c/o Japanese Society of Laboratory Medicine, 2F UI Bldg, 2–2 Kanda Ogawamachi, Chiyoda-ku, Tokyo 101-0052, Japan; tel. (3) 32950353; e-mail info@waspalm.org; internet www.waspalm.org; f. 1947 as Int. Soc. of Clinical Pathology, present name 1999; promotes education, research and int. quality standards; promotes high-quality, cost-effective medical laboratory services; promotes exchange of information between pathologists and laboratory scientists throughout the world; encourages formation of and cooperation between, socs of pathology and laboratory medicine; fosters cooperation with other int. health orgs; organizes int. congress every 2 years; 33 mem. socs, colleges and asscns in 18 countries; Pres. GAMZE MOCAN KUZEY (Turkey); Sec. and Treas. JAGDISH BUTANY (Canada); Exec. Dir Prof. MASAMI MURAKAMI.

World Federation for Ultrasound in Medicine and Biology (WFUMB): 14750 Sweitzer Lane, Suite 100, Laurel, MD 20707-5906, USA; tel. (301) 498-4100; e-mail admin@wfumb.org; internet www.wfumb.org; f. 1969; encourages research in the field of ultrasound in medicine and biology; promotes int. cooperation; disseminates scientific information; sponsors meetings and awards prizes and distinctions; promotes coordination of bibliographic and informational services and improvement of standards in terminology, equipment, methods and safety practices; organizes world congress; 49,073 mems; Pres. Dr MASATOSHI KUDO (Japan); Sec. Dr DAVID EVANS (UK); publ. *Ultrasound in Medicine & Biology*.

World Medical Association/Association Médicale Mondiale: 13 chemin du Levant, CIB-Bâtiment A, 01210 Ferney-Voltaire, France; tel. 450407575; e-mail wma@wma.net; internet www.wma.net; f. 1947; promotes high standards of medical ethics; provides ethical guidance to physicians through its declarations, resolutions and statements; promotes and defends basic rights of patients and physicians; provides medical education to physicians; 797 constituent and assoc. mems; Pres. Dr CECIL B. WILSON (USA); Sec.-Gen. Dr OTMAR KLOIBER (Germany); publ. *World Medical Journal* (6 a year).

World Psychiatric Association/Association Mondiale de Psychiatrie/Asociación Mundial de Psiquiatría: Geneva Univ. Psychiatric Hospital, Bâtiment Les Voirons 2, chemin du Petit-Bel-Air, 1225 Chêne-Bourg, Geneva, Switzerland; tel. 223055737; e-mail wpasecretariat@wpanet.org; internet www.wpanet.org; f. 1950; encourages raising of standards of clinical practice; enhances work of the mem. socs to fight stigma and advocate the human right to mental health; supports psychiatrists and other mental health professionals; disseminates knowledge of the effect of mass violence on mental health; encourages multi-centre research and enhances standards of training; promotes non-discrimination (parity) in the provision of care of the mentally ill; organizes the World Congress every 3 years and Int. Congresses; works with WHO and other governmental agencies to advance public health; 135 mem. socs in 117 countries; Pres. Prof. PEDRO RUIZ (USA); Sec.-Gen. LEVENT KUEY (Turkey); publ. *World Psychiatry* (3 a year, in 10 languages).

ASSOCIATE MEMBERS OF CIOMS

American College of Chest Physicians: 3300 Dundee Rd, Northbrook, IL 60062-2348, USA; tel. (847) 498-1400; e-mail accp@chestnet.org; internet www.chestnet.org; f. 1935; medical org. raising awareness about dangers of tobacco use and importance of lung health, promotes prevention, diagnosis and treatment of chest diseases through education, communication and research; provides key courses and resources to help mem. physicians prepare for their board examinations in pulmonary, critical care, sleep and paediatric pulmonary medicine; 18,500 mems in 100 countries; Pres. Dr SUHAIL RAOOF; Exec. Vice-Pres. and CEO PAUL A. MARKOWSKI; publs *Chest* (12 a year, online, journal.publications.chestnet.org), *CHEST Physician* (12 a year, online, www.chestnet.org/accp/chest-physician).

Asia Pacific Academy of Ophthalmology: c/o Chinese Univ. of Hong Kong, Dept of Ophthalmology and Visual Sciences, Hong Kong Eye Hospital, 4/F, 147K Argyle St, Kowloon, Hong Kong; tel. 39435827; e-mail secretariat@apaophth.org; internet www.apaophth.org; f. 1958; promotes prevention of blindness and restoration of sight through service, research and teaching; encourages exchange of ophthalmic knowledge and advancement of the standard of eye care through hosting of regional congresses or other confs; 19 mem. orgs; Pres. FRANK MARTIN (Australia and New Zealand); Sec.-Gen. and CEO DENNIS LAM (Hong Kong).

International Association of Oral Pathologists: c/o Prof Sonja Boy, Dept of Oral Pathology and Oral Biology, Faculty of Health Sciences, Medunsa Campus, Univ. of Limpopo, Pretoria, South Africa; tel. (12) 5214869; e-mail sonja.iaop@gmail.com; internet www.iaop.com; f. 1976; advances knowledge in clinical aspects, laboratory diagnosis and research in oral pathology; holds congress every 2 years; Pres. MICHAEL ALDRED; Sec. Prof. SONJA BOY (South Africa); publs *Head and Neck Pathology*, *Journal of Oral Pathology*.

International Council for Laboratory Animal Science: Washington St 40, 1050, Brussels, Belgium; e-mail info@iclas.org; internet iclas.org; f. 1956; promotes quality definition and monitoring of laboratory animals; collects and disseminates information on laboratory animal science; acts as worldwide resource for laboratory animal science knowledge; 96 mems (incl. 32 nat. mems, 33 scientific mems, 5 union mems, 1 institutional mem., 24 assoc. mems, 1 affiliate mem.); Pres. PATRI VERGARA (Spain); Sec.-Gen. CYNTHIA PEKOW (acting) (USA).

International Federation of Clinical Chemistry and Laboratory Medicine: Via Carlo Farini 81, 20159 Milan MI, Italy; tel. 266809912; e-mail ifcc@ifcc.org; internet www.ifcc.org; f. 1952 as Int. Asscn of Clinical Biochemists; fosters educational activities and managerial skills; promotes expansion of scientific, educational and managerial services within laboratory medicine; holds confs, scientific meetings and publs; offers scientific exchange scholarships, travel scholarships and visiting lecturer programmes; 87 full mem. socs, 52 corporate mems, 10 affiliate mem. socs (48,000 individuals); Pres. Dr GRAHAM BEASTALL (UK); Sec. Prof. Dr SERGIO BERNARDINI (Italy); Treas. Prof. Dr BERNARD GOUGET; publ. *eJIFCC* (4 a year).

International Federation of Medical Students' Associations: c/o World Medical Asscn, 13 ch. du Levant, CIB-Bâtiment A, 01210 Ferney-Voltaire, France; e-mail gs@ifmsa.org; internet www.ifmsa.org; f. 1951; provides opportunities for medical students to take part in clinical and research exchanges around the world; provides int. framework for medical student projects; organizes professional exchanges in pre-clinical and clinical fields of medicine; 114 mem. orgs in 108 countries; Pres. CHRISTOPHER PLEYER (Austria); Sec.-Gen. MIRJANA SPASOJEVIC (Serbia).

International Medical Sciences Academy: Second Fl., National Medical Library Bldg, Ansari Nagar, Ring Rd, New Delhi 110029, India; tel. (11) 26589660; e-mail imsawhq06@gmail.com; internet www.imsaonline.com; undertakes, organizes and facilitates research, study courses, confs, lectures in matters relating to different health sciences and health care systems of the world; develops, establishes and prescribes int. standards with respect to medical education, medical and health care and medical research; Pres. Dr K. JAGADEESAN; Sec.-Gen. Dr R. K. THUKRAL; publ. *JIMSA* (4 a year).

International Society for Hepatic Encephalopathy and Nitrogen Metabolism: Upper 3rd Fl., UCL Medical School, Rowland Hill St, NW3 2PF London, UK; tel. (20) 7433-2785; e-mail r.jalan@ucl.ac.uk; internet www.ishen.org; f. 1971; promotes scientific and clinical research on nitrogen metabolism and brain disorders associated with liver disease; supports research in neuroscience, hepatology, metabolism, nutrition contributing to understanding of nitrogen metabolism and the pathophysiology, diagnosis or management of liver-related brain disorders; organizes, holds and facilitates nat. and int. meetings, symposia, congresses, workshops; provides forum for dissemination of experiences and knowledge; Pres. Prof. RAJIV JALAN (UK); Exec. Sec. JUAN CORDOBA (Spain).

International Union of Microbiological Societies: see under Unions Federated to the ICSU.

International Union of Nutritional Sciences: see under Unions Federated to the ICSU.

International Union of Physiological Sciences: see under Unions Federated to the ICSU.

World Association for Medical Law: e-mail worldassocmedlaw@gmail.com; internet wafml.memberlodge.org; f. 1967; encourages study and discussion of medical law; promotes study of consequences of new devts in medicine and related sciences; provides political leadership and advocacy for medical law professionals and encourages research and devt in medical law and related fields; Pres. THOMAS NOGUCHI; Sec.-Gen. ROY BERAN; publ. *Medicine and Law* (4 a year).

World Federation of Chiropractic: 1246 Yonge St, Suite 203, Toronto, ON M4T 1W5, Canada; tel. (416) 484-9978; e-mail info@wfc.org; internet www.wfc.org; f. 1988; encourages improved standards of chiropractic education and practice; encouraging research through int. congresses; promotes ethical practice; nat. asscns in 88 countries; Pres. DENNIS RICHARDS (Australia); Sec.-Gen. DAVID CHAPMAN-SMITH (Canada).

World Organization of National Colleges, Academies and Academic Associations of General Practitioners/Family Physicians (WONCA)/World Organization of Family Doctors: 12A-05 Chartered Square Bldg, 152 N Sathon Rd, Silom, Bangrak, Bangkok, 10500, Thailand; tel. (2) 637-9010; e-mail admin@wonca.net; internet www.globalfamilydoctor.com; f. 1972; provides forum for exchange of knowledge and information between mem. orgs and between gen. practitioners/family physicians; encourages and supports devt of academic orgs of gen. practitioners/family physicians; 126 mem. orgs in 102 countries; Pres. Prof. Dr RICHARD ROBERTS (USA); CEO Dr GARTH MANNING (UK).

World Veterinary Association: see under Agriculture and Veterinary Science.

OTHER ORGANIZATIONS

African Medical and Research Foundation (AMREF): Langata Rd, POB 27691, 00506, Nairobi, Kenya; tel. (20) 6993000; e-mail info@amref.org; internet www.amref.org; f. 1957 as Flying Doctor Service of East Africa; works to improve the health of people in E Africa; facilitates primary health care, training, teaching aids, health behaviour and education, airborne medicine, flying doctor service, medical radio communication, ground mobile medicine, emergency intervention in famine and other crises, research, consultancies; library of 6,000 vols, 122 periodicals; Chair. Dr PASCOAL MANUEL MOCUMBI (Mozambique); Dir-Gen. Dr TEGUEST GUERMA (Ethiopia); publs *AFYA* (4 a year), *AMREF News* (4 a year), *COBASHECA* (4 a year), *Defender* (4 a year), *Helper* (4 a year), *HEN* (4 a year).

Asociación Latinoamericana de Análisis y Modificación del Comportamiento y Terapia Cognitivo Conductual (Latin American Association of Analysis, Modification and Cognitive Behavioural Therapy): Caracas, Venezuela; internet www.alamoc.net; f. 1975; facilitates, conducts and promotes scientific research and dissemination in various areas of human devt and its relation to context; organizes confs, symposia, seminars, courses, publs and events; 22 mem. countries; Pres. GUILLERMO RODRÍGUEZ (Venezuela); Sec.-Gen. EDGARD PACHECO (Peru); publ. *Learning and Behavior* (2 a year).

Cystic Fibrosis Worldwide: c/o Christine Noke, 210 Park Ave Suite 267, Worcester, MA 01609, USA; tel. (508) 762-4232; e-mail information@cfww.org; internet www.cfww.org; f. 2003 by merger of Int. Asscn of Cystic Fibrosis Adults and Int. Cystic Fibrosis (Mucoviscidosis) Asscn; promotes access to knowledge and appropriate care to those people living with cystic fibrosis and among medical health professionals and govts worldwide; organizes educational confs, capacity building programs, clinical devt, int. lobbying efforts; 60 mem. countries; Pres. MITCH MESSER (Australia); Exec. Dir CHRISTINE NOKE (USA).

European Federation of Internal Medicine: c/o Aneta Trajkovska, 287 Ave Louise, Fourth Fl., 1050 Brussels, Belgium; tel. (2) 643-20-40; e-mail info@efim.org; internet www.efim.org; f. 1996; facilitates research and publishes outcome of its research and resolutions; organizes annual scientific congress and meetings; facilitates communication among European specialists in internal medicine; 33 nat. mem. socs; Pres. Prof. RAMON PUJOL FARRIOLS (Spain); Sec.-Gen. Dr JAN WILLEM F. ELTE (Netherlands); publ. *European Journal of Internal Medicine* (4 a year, online, www.ejinme.com).

European Society of Anaesthesiology (ESA): 24 Rue des Comédiens, 1000 Brussels, Belgium; tel. (2) 743-32-90; e-mail info@esahq.org; internet www.euroanaesthesia.org; f. 2005 by merger of European Soc. of Anaesthesiologists (ESA), European Academy of Anaesthesiology (EAA) and Confederation of European Nat. Socs of Anaesthesiologists (CENSA); promotes exchange of information between European anaesthesiologists; disseminates information in regard to anaesthesiology; fosters and encourages education, research, scientific progress and exchange of information to raise standards of the speciality; promotes and protects interest of its mems; promotes improvements in safety and quality of care of patients by facilitating and harmonizing the activities of nat. and int. socs of anaesthesiologists in Europe; organizes annual Euroanaesthesia congress; 5,000 full mems; Pres. EBERHARD KOCHS (Germany); Sec. ANDREAS HOEFT (Germany); publ. *European Journal of Anaesthesiology* (12 a year).

European Society of Cardiology: c/o The European Heart House, 2035 Route des Colles, Les Templiers, BP 179, 06903 Sophia Antipolis, France; tel. 492947600; e-mail cfoulis@escardio.org; internet www.escardio.org; f. 1950; aims to bring together socs of cardiology in all European countries; provides a forum for working groups on subjects of common interest; organizes congress; comprises 6 asscns, 5 ccls, 18 working groups, 55 nat. socs; 70,000 mems; Pres. PANAGIOTIS E. VARDAS (Greece); Sec. and Treas. STEEN DALBY KRISTENSEN (Denmark); CEO I. BARDINET (France); publs *Cardiovascular Nursing* (4 a year), *Cardiovascular Research* (14 a year), *EP Europace* (12 a year), *European Heart Journal—Acute Cardiovascular Care*, *European Heart Journal—Cardiovascular Imaging* (6 a year), *European Journal of Cardiovascular Nursing*, *European Journal of Heart Failure* (12 a year), *European Journal of Preventive Cardiology* (24 a year), *The European Heart Journal* (24 a year).

FDI World Dental Federation: Tour de Cointrin, Ave Louis Casaï 84, CP 3, 1216 Cointrin GE, Switzerland; tel. 225608150; e-mail info@fdiworldental.org; internet www.fdiworldental.org; f. 1900 as Fédération Dentaire Internationale; rep. of dental profession on int. level; promote optimal oral and general health; supports mem. asscns in enhancing the ability provide oral health care to the public and to advance and promote the ethics, art, science and practice of dentistry; stimulates and facilitates exchange of information; 200 nat. mem. asscns from 130 countries; Pres. Dr ORLANDO MONTEIRO DA SILVA; Exec. Dir JEAN-LUC EISELÉ; publs *Community Dental Health* (4 a year), *Developing Dentistry* (2 a year), *European Journal of Prosthodontics and Restorative Dentistry* (4 a year), *International Dental Journal* (6 a year), *Journal of the International Academy of Periodontology* (4 a year), *Worldental Communiqué* (6 a year).

Inclusion International: KD.2.03, Univ. of East London, Docklands Campus, 4–6 University Way, London, E16 2RD, UK; tel. (20) 82237709; e-mail info@inclusion-international.org; internet www.inclusion-international.org; f. 1960; advocates for human rights of persons with intellectual disabilities and their families worldwide; furthers cooperation between nat. bodies, organizes congresses and symposia; collects and disseminates information on all aspects of intellectual disability; consultative status with UNESCO, UNICEF, WHO, ILO, ECOSOC and the Council of Europe; official relations with IIN, the Comm. of the European Communities and various other orgs; 200 mem. feds in 115 countries; Pres. KLAUS LACHWITZ; Sec.-Gen. RALPH JONES; publ. *Proceedings*.

International Academy of Cytology/Academia Internacional de Citología/Academie Internationale de Cytologie/ Internationale Akademie für Zytologie: c/o Dr Fernando Schmitt, POB 1347, 79013 Freiburg, Germany; tel. (761) 2923801; e-mail centraloffice@cytology-iac.org; internet www.cytology-iac.org; f. 1957; encourages cooperation among persons engaged in the practice of clinical cytology; fosters and facilitates int. exchange of knowledge and information on specialized problems of clinical cytology; standardizes terminology; encourages research and stimulates devt of all phases of clinical cytology; organizes congresses, Int. Board of Cytopathology examinations; Pres. Dr DIANE SOLOMON (USA); Sec. and Treas. Prof. Dr FERNANDO SCHMITT (Portugal); publ. *Acta Cytologica—Journal of Clinical Cytology and Cytopathology* (6 a year, online).

International Agency for Research on Cancer/Centre International de Recherche sur le Cancer: 150 cours Albert-Thomas, 69372, Lyon Cedex 08, France; tel. 472738485; internet www.iarc.fr; f. 1965 as an Agency of the World Health Organization; promotes int. collaboration in cancer research; coordinates research across countries and orgs; conducts research in low- and middle-income countries through partnerships and collaborations with researchers in these regions; 22 mem. countries; library of 8,200 vols, 211 journals; Chair. Dr P. PUSKA (Finland); Dir Dr CHRISTOPHER P. WILD; publ. *Report* (every 2 years).

International Agency for the Prevention of Blindness/Organisation Mondiale Contre la Cécité: London School of Hygiene and Tropical Medicine, Keppel St, London, WC1E 7HT, UK; e-mail packland@iapb.org; internet www.iapb.org; f. 1975; umbrella org. in official relationship with WHO; promotes the formation of national cttees and programmes on prevention of blindness; disseminates ideas and information on approaches to eye care delivery; unites govts and non-governmental agencies to facilitate planning, devt and implementation of sustainable nat. eye care programmes based on 3 core strategies of disease control, human resource devt and infrastructure devt, incorporating principles of primary health care; 115 mem. orgs; Chair. and Pres. CHRISTIAN G. GARMS; CEO PETER ACKLAND; publ. *IAPB News* (2 a year).

International Association for Child and Adolescent Psychiatry and Allied Professions/Association Internationale de Psychiatrie de l'Enfant et de l'Adolescent et de Professions Associées: c/o Dr Daniel Fung, Institute of Mental Health, Duke-NUS Graduate Medical School and Yong Loo Lin Medical School, Nat. Univ. of Singapore, Singapore; tel. 63892851; e-mail daniel_fung@imh.com.sg; internet iacapap.org; f. 1948; disseminates information and fosters training through multidisciplinary study groups, congresses, publs and educational initiatives; 73 mems (incl. 57 nat. mem. orgs, 7 affiliate mem. orgs and 9 individual mems); Pres. Prof. Dr Olayinka Omigbodun (Nigeria); Sec.-Gen. Dr Daniel Fung (Singapore).

International Association for Humanitarian Medicine (IAHM): Divisione Chirurgia Plastica, MBC, Ospedale Civico, 90127, Palermo PA, Italy; tel. 916663631; e-mail contact@iahm.org; internet www.iahm.org; f. 1984; promotes and delivers health care on the principles of humanitarian medicine through the provision of equitable medical, surgical, nursing and rehabilitation care to patients in or from developing countries; brings relief to disaster victims where health aid is lacking; mobilizes hospitals and health specialists in developed countries to receive and treat such patients free of charge; advocates humanitarian practice of medicine, on the principle of health as a human right; membership limited to 100 on invitation; Pres. Prof. Dr S. William A. Gunn (Switzerland); Sec.-Gen. Prof. Dr Leo Klein (Czech Republic); Dir Dr M. Masellis (Italy); publ. *Journal of Humanitarian Medicine* (4 a year).

International Association for Radiation Research: c/o Gianfranco Grossi, Dept of Physics, Univ. of Naples Federico II, Complesso Universitario Monte Sant'Angelo, 80126 Napoli NA, Italy; tel. 81676277; e-mail gianfranco.grossi@unina.it; internet timssnet2.allenpress.com/ecomiarr; f. 1962; advances radiation research in the fields of physics, chemistry, biology and medicine; fosters and maintains scientific cooperation and communication between nat. and regional socs, groups and individual scientists; organizes quadrennial int. congress; 3,246 mems, 14 mem. orgs; Pres. Marco Durante (Germany); Sec. and Treas. Gianfranco Grossi (Italy); publ. *Proceedings of International Congresses of Radiation Research.*

International Association for the Study of the Liver: c/o Dr K. Rajender Reddy, Hospital of the Univ. of Pennsylvania, Second Fl., Dulles Bldg, 3400 Spruce St, Philadelphia, PA 19104, USA; tel. (215) 662-4276; e-mail iasloffice2010@gmail.com; internet www.iaslonline.com; f. 1958; encourages research on the liver and its diseases and helps to facilitate prevention, recognition and treatment of liver and biliary tract diseases in the int. community; Pres. Federico Villamil; Sec. and Treas. Dr K. Rajender Reddy (USA); publ. *Liver International.*

International Association of Agricultural Medicine and Rural Health/Association Internationale de Médecine Agricole et de Santé Rurale: c/o Yuko Kunugi, J. A. Toride Medical Center, Hongo 2–1–1, Toride, Ibaraki, 302-0022, Japan; tel. (297) 745551; e-mail iarm@live.jp; internet www.iaamrh.org; f. 1961 as Int. Asscn of Agricultural Medicine, present name and status 1978; improves status of health of rural communities and protects health of agricultural workers; helps mem. orgs adopt scientific approach in the field of agricultural medicine and rural health and assists in its practical application; studies issues of agricultural and rural health in association with other sciences and provides scientific information and advises mems and mem. orgs; organizes congresses, meetings, exchange and collaborative programmes; 14 country divs; 500 mems in 51 countries; Pres. Dr Ashok Patil (India); Sec.-Gen. Dr Shuzo Shintani (acting) (Japan); publ. *Journal of International Agricultural Medicine and Rural Health* (4 a year).

International Association of Applied Psychology/Association Internationale de Psychologie Appliquée: c/o Janel Gauthier, Dept of Psychology, Laval Univ., Pavillion Fa Savard, Sainte Foy, QC G1K7P4, Canada; tel. (418) 6562-592; e-mail iaap@psy.ulaval.ca; internet www.iaapsy.org; f. 1920 as Association Internationale de Psychotechnique, present name 1955; establishes contacts between those carrying out scientific work on applied psychology; promotes science and practice of applied psychology; sponsors and organizes int. and regional congresses; 18 divs; 2,500 mems in 80 countries; Pres. José M. Peiró (Spain); Sec.-Gen. Janel Gauthier (Canada); publs *Applied Psychology: An International Review* (4 a year), *Applied Psychology: Health and Wellbeing* (4 a year), *IAAP Bulletin.*

International Association of Asthmology/Association Internationale d'Asthmologie (INTERASMA): internet www.interasma.org; f. 1954; unites efforts of interns, paediatricians, allergologists and chest physicians to provide better standard of care for asthmatic patients; advances medical knowledge of bronchial asthma and allied disorders; disseminates asthma education among specialists, non-asthma specialists and allied health professionals; organizes world congress every 3 years; 1,000 mems in 52 countries; Pres. Dr You-Young Kim (Korea); Sec.-Gen. Carlos Nunes (Portugal); publ. *Journal of Investigational Allergology and Clinical Immunology* (7 a year).

International Association of Environmental Mutagen Societies (IAEMS): 1821 Michael Faraday Dr., Suite 300, Reston, VA 20190-5348, USA; tel. (703) 438-3103; e-mail beidemiller@aim-hq.com; internet www.iaems.net; f. 1973; promotes science-based risk assessment activities and regulatory policies on issues of environmental and human health; facilitates int. agreement on acceptable methodologies and technologies in these fields; provides education and training to scientists and promotes informed public awareness and understanding on issues of the mutational basis of human disease and risk; promotes collaborative research at int. level on mutational basis of human disease, new methodologies and technologies in the field and application of new information to the risk assessment process; organizes world conf. every 4 years; 12 mem. socs (12,000 individuals); Pres. Dr Stefano Bonassi (Italy); Sec. Dr Hester F. Vismer (South Africa); Exec. Dir Dr Betty J. Eidemiller (USA).

International Association of Gerontology and Geriatrics (IAGG): c/o Faculté de Médecine, Institut du Vieillissement, 37 Allées Jules Guesde, 31000 Toulouse, France; tel. 561145639; e-mail contact@iagg.info; internet www.iagg.info; f. 1950; promotes research and training in gerontology and geriatrics; collaborates with other int., intergovernmental and non-governmental orgs to promote gerontological interests globally and on behalf of its mem. asscns; 45,100 mems in 73 nat. mem. orgs in 65 countries; Pres. Prof. Dr Bruno Vellas (France); Vice-Pres. and Sec.-Gen. Prof. Alain Franco (France); Treas. Prof. Athanase Benetos (Greece); publ. *Journal of Nutrition, Health and Aging.*

International Association of Hydatidology/Asociación Internacional de Hidatidología: Florida 460, 3° piso, 1005 Buenos Aires, Argentina; tel. (11) 4322-3431; f. 1941; has specialized library; 650 mems in 40 countries; Pres. António Menezes da Silva (Portugal); Sec.-Gen. Eduardo Guarnera (Argentina); publs *Archivos Internacionales de la Hidatidosis* (every 4 years), *Boletín de Hidatidosis* (4 a year).

International Association of Oral and Maxillofacial Surgeons: 17 West 220 22nd St, Suite 420, Oakbrook Terrace, IL 60181, USA; tel. (630) 833-0945; e-mail info@iaoms.org; internet www.iaoms.org; f. 1962; improves quality and safety of health care worldwide through the advancement of patient care, education and research in oral and maxillofacial surgery; organizes int. conf. every 2 years; promotes collaborative research, educational programmes in developing countries; 5,800 mems in 78 countries; Pres. Dr Kishore Nayak (India); Exec. Dir Barbara Morrison (USA); publ. *International Journal of Oral and Maxillofacial Surgery* (12 a year).

International Cell Research Organization/Organisation Internationale de Recherche sur la Cellule: c/o UNESCO, SC/BES/LSC, 1 rue Miollis, 75732 Paris Cedex 15, France; tel. 145685818; f. 1962; creates, encourages and promotes cooperation between scientists of different disciplines worldwide for the advancement of fundamental knowledge of the cell; organizes int. training courses and exchange of scientists; 400 mems; Chair. Prof. Q. S. Lin (China); Exec. Sec. Prof. G. N. Cohen (France).

International Center of Information on Antibiotics: c/o Prof. M. Welsch, Inst. de Pathologie, Université de Liège, Sart-Tilman, 4000 Liège, Belgium; f. 1961; gathers information on antibiotics and strains producing them; establishes contact with discoverers of antibiotics with a view to obtaining samples and filing information; Dir Prof. M. Welsch; Senior Scientist in Charge Dr L. Delcambe.

International Commission on Occupational Health/Commission Internationale de la Santé au Travail: c/o INAIL, Italian Workers' Compensation Authority, Dept of Occupational Medicine (fmrly ISPESL), Via Fontana Candida 1, 00040 Monteporzio Catone, Rome RM, Italy; tel. 694181506; e-mail icoh@inail.it; internet www.icohweb.org; f. 1906; studies new findings in the field of occupational health; publicizes results of study and investigation in occupational health; organizes meetings and world congress every 3 years on nat. or int. problems in this field; 33 scientific cttees; 2,000 mems in 93 countries; Pres. Dr Kazutaka Kogi (Japan); Sec.-Gen. Dr Sergio Iavicoli (Italy).

International Committee of Military Medicine/Comité International de Médecine Militaire: Hôpital Militaire Reine Astrid, 1120 Brussels, Belgium; tel. (2) 264-43-48; e-mail info@cimm-icmm.org; internet www.cimm-icmm.org; f. 1921, current name 1990; promotes world cooperation on questions of military medicine; fosters its int. and humanitarian character; organizes int. study sessions and courses on subjects of interest to military medicine, in particular int. advanced courses for young officers of the Armed Forces Medical Services; holds int. congress every 2 years; awards prizes for books, articles or reports describing work of innovative nature in military medicine or in the medico-legal field; 110 mem. states; Chair. Major Gen. Dr Saeed Mohammed Al-Asmary (Saudi Arabia); Sec.-Gen. Major Gen. Dr Roger van Hoof (Belgium); publ. *International Review of the Armed Forces Medical Services* (4 a year, in English and French).

International Council of Nurses (ICN)/Conseil International des Infirmières (CII)/Consejo Internacional de Enfermeras(CIE): 3 pl. Jean-Marteau, 1201 Geneva, Switzerland; tel. 229080100; e-mail icn@icn.ch; internet www.icn.ch; f. 1899; works to ensure universal quality nursing care, sound health policies worldwide and advancement of nursing knowledge; organizes congress every 4 years; standards, guidelines and policies for nursing practice, education, management, research and socio-economic welfare are accepted globally as the basis of nursing policy; 130 nat. nurses asscn mems; Pres. JUDITH SHAMIAN (Canada); CEO DAVID A. BENTON; publ. *International Nursing Review*.

International Council of Ophthalmology: c/o Dr Bruce E. Spivey, 945 Green St 10, San Francisco, CA 94133, USA; e-mail info@icoph.org; internet www.icoph.org; f. 1927; enhances ophthalmic education and improves access to quality eye care; organizes biannual World Ophthalmology Congress; 120 mem. socs; Pres. Dr BRUCE E. SPIVEY; CEO WILLIAM C. FELCH, JR.

International Council on Alcohol and Addictions/Conseil International sur les Problèmes de l'Alcoolisme et des Toxicomanies: c/o Addiction-Info Suisse, Ave Louis-Ruchonnet 14, CP 870, 1001 Lausanne, Switzerland; tel. 213209865; e-mail secretariat@icaa.ch; internet www.icaa.ch; f. 1907 as Int. Bureau Against Alcoholism, present name 1968; reduces and prevents harmful effects of the use of alcohol and other drugs by the study of addiction problems and the devt of programmes in this field; studies concepts and methods of prevention, treatment and rehabilitation; disseminates knowledge in the interests of public health and personal and social well-being; holds Int. Institute annually and Int. Congress every 3 or 4 years, symposia, study courses, training courses on substance abuse in developing countries; 135 orgs, 500 individuals from 85 countries; library: spec. colln of 6,000 vols on drug dependence, 12,000 pamphlets, reprints, 120 periodicals; Pres. Dr PETER A. VAMOS (Canada); Exec. Dir Dr SHARAFUDDIN MALIK; publ. *ICAA News* (4 a year).

International Diabetes Federation/Fédération Internationale du Diabète: 166 Chaussée de la Hulpe, 1170 Brussels, Belgium; tel. (2) 538-55-11; e-mail info@idf.org; internet www.idf.org; f. 1949; influences policy; increases public awareness and encourages health improvement; promotes exchange of high-quality information about diabetes; provides education for people with diabetes and their health care providers; produces tools and resources for health professional education and training; 200 nat. asscns in 160 countries; Pres. Prof. JEAN CLAUDE MBANYA (Cameroon); Exec. Dir LUC HENDRICKX; publs *Diabetes Atlas* (1 a year), *Diabetes Research and Clinical Practice (DRCP)* (online, www.diabetesresearchclinicalpractice.com), *Diabetes Voice* (4 a year, in English, French, Spanish and Russian), *Triennial Report*.

International Epidemiological Association/Association Internationale d'Épidémiologie: c/o Prof. Matthias Egger, Finkenhubelweg 11, 3012 Bern, Switzerland; e-mail ieasecretariat@ispm.unibe.ch; internet www.ieaweb.org; f. 1954; facilitates communication among those engaged in research and teaching in epidemiology; engages in devt and use of epidemiological methods in all fields of health incl. social, community and preventive medicine and health services admin.; holds int. meetings every 3 years and regional meetings throughout the world; 1,500 mems in 100 countries; Pres. Prof. CESAR VICTORA; Sec. Prof. MATTHIAS EGGER (Switzerland); Treas. Prof. AHMED MANDIL (Egypt); publ. *International Journal of Epidemiology* (6 a year, online, ije.oxfordjournals.org).

International Federation for Medical and Biological Engineering/Fédération Internationale du Génie Médical et Biologique: c/o Ian Wolstencroft, Institute of Physics and Engineering in Medicine, UK; e-mail office@ifmbe.org; internet www.ifmbe.org; f. 1959 as Int. Fed. for Medical Electronics and Biological Engineering; represents int. community of medical and biological engineering; fosters creation, dissemination and application of medical and biological engineering knowledge and management of technology; promotes devt, recognition and awareness of the medical and biological engineering profession; advances collaboration between nat. and transnational socs, industry, govt and non-governmental orgs engaged in health care and in biomedical research and its applications; recommends policies and provide guidelines in professional, educational and ethical areas; organizes world congress every 3 years; 62 mem. orgs; Pres. Prof. RATKO MAGJAREVIC (Croatia); Sec.-Gen. Prof. SHANKHAR KRISHNAN (USA); publs *Medical and Biological Engineering and Computing* (6 a year), *Proceedings of International Conference on Medical and Biological Engineering* (irregular).

International Federation of Associations of Anatomists (IFAA)/Fédération Internationale des Associations d'Anatomistes: c/o Friedrich Paulsen, Universitätsstr. 19, 91054, Erlangen, Germany; e-mail friedrich.paulsen@medizin.uni-halle.de; internet www.ifaa.net; f. 1903; promotes progress of all anatomical or biomorphological sciences; encourages and increases scientific, technological, educational and admin. exchanges among anatomists worldwide; provides gen. guidelines for educational, technological and scientific purposes and issues of gen. interest to anatomical sciences; coordinates and supports preparation, revision and publication of documents on the terminology of the anatomical sciences and biomorphology; organizes int. scientific congresses, symposia and other meetings; 52 mem. asscns; Pres. BERNARD MOXHAM (UK); Sec.-Gen. Prof. Dr FRIEDRICH PAULSEN (Germany); publs *Directory*, Proceedings of each Federative International Congress of Anatomy (every 4 or 5 years).

International Federation of Gynecology and Obstetrics/Fédération Internationale de Gynécologie et d'Obstétrique: FIGO House, Suite 3, Waterloo Court, 10 Theed St, London, SE1 8ST, UK; tel. (20) 79281166; e-mail figo@figo.org; internet www.figo.org; f. 1954; assists and contributes to research in gynaecology and obstetrics; promotes wellbeing of women and raising standards of practice in obstetrics and gynaecology; aims to facilitate exchange of information and perfect methods of teaching; organizes int. congress every 3 years; 124 nat. mem. socs; Pres. Prof. SABARATNAM ARULKUMARAN (UK); Chief Exec. Prof. HAMID RUSHWAN (Sudan/UK); publ. *International Journal of Gynecology and Obstetrics* (12 a year).

International Federation of Physical Education/Fédération Internationale d'Éducation Physique (FIEP): c/o Comenius Univ., Faculty of Physical Education and Sport, L. Svobodu 9, 814 69 Bratislava, Slovakia; e-mail antala@fsport.uniba.sk; internet www.fiepeurope.eu; f. 1923, current name adopted 1935; promotes physical education science and its practical applications; aims to develop nat. and int. physical education and sport-for-all; organizes congresses and courses; mems in 134 countries; Pres. ALMIR ADOLFO GRUHN (Brazil); Gen. Sec. Prof. CLAUDIO BOSHI (Brazil).

International Federation of Surgical Colleges/Fédération Internationale des Collèges de Chirurgie: c/o Royal College of Surgeons in Ireland, 123 St Stephen's Green, Dublin 2, Ireland; tel. (1) 4022707; e-mail ifsc@rcsi.ie; internet www.ifsc-net.org; f. 1958; promotes improvement and maintenance of the standards of surgery worldwide, by establishment and maintenance of cooperation and interchange of medical and surgical information; encourages high standards of education, training and research in surgery and its allied sciences; assists developing countries in surgical advancement; 70 nat. colleges or socs and 500 assocs; Pres. PETER MCLEAN (Ireland); Sec.-Gen. Prof. S. W. A. GUNN (Switzerland).

International Hospital Federation/Fédération Internationale des Hôpitaux: PA Hospital de Loex, Route de Loex 151, 1233 Bernex, Switzerland; tel. 228509420; e-mail info@ihf-fih.org; internet www.ihf-fih.org; f. 1929 as Int. Hospital Asscn, present name and status 1947; aims to promote improvements in the planning and management of hospitals and health services through int. confs, field study courses, training courses, information services, publs and research projects; contributes to devt of effective health care management; 110 nat. hospital and health service mem. orgs (37 full mems and 73 assoc. mems); Pres. THOMAS C. DOLAN (USA); CEO ERIC DE ROODENBEKE (France); publs *Building Quality in Health* (jtly with Methodist Int., 2 a year), *Care Journal* (2 a year), *International Hospital Federation Reference Yearbook* (1 a year), *World Hospitals and Health Services* (4 a year).

International Institute on Ageing, United Nations—Malta (INIA): 117 St Paul St, Valletta, VLT 1216, Malta; tel. 21243044; e-mail info@inia.org.mt; internet www.inia.org.mt; f. 1988; offers int. training programmes in social gerontology, economic and financial aspects of ageing, health promotion, quality of life and well-being; policy formulation, planning, implementation and monitoring of the Madrid Int. Plan of Action on Ageing; demographic aspects of population ageing, its implications for socioeconomic devt policies and plans; in-situ training programmes in developing countries, research and data collection; technical cooperation (advisory services, project design, planning and implementation of training programmes); library of 800 vols; Chair. SHA ZUKANG; Dir Prof. DU PENG (China); publ. *BOLD* (4 a year).

International League Against Epilepsy/Ligue Internationale contre l'Epilepsie: 342 N Main St, West Hartford, CT 06117-2507, USA; tel. (860) 586-7547; e-mail pshisler@ilae.org; internet www.ilae.org; f. 1909; collects and disseminates information concerning epilepsy and encourages research on it; promotes prevention, diagnosis, treatment, advocacy and care for all persons suffering from these disorders; fosters cooperation with other org. in similar fields; improves education and training in the field of the epilepsies; holds scientific congress every 2 years in conjunction with Int. Bureau for Epilepsy, regional congresses every 2 years and nat. congresses annually by each nat. chapter; 15,000 mems, 114 nat. chapters; Pres. Dr EMILIO PERUCCA; Sec.-Gen. Dr HELEN CROSS; Admin. Dir PRISCILLA SHISLER; publs *Epilepsia* (12 a year), *Epileptic Disorders* (4 a year, in English, online, www.epilepticdisorders.com).

International Leprosy Association/Asociación Internacional de la Lepra/Association Internationale contre la Lèpre: POB 3021, Bauru-SP, 17034-971, Brazil; tel. (14) 31035855; e-mail ila@ilsl.br; internet www.leprosy-ila.org; f. 1931; provides latest, medically and scientifically accurate information about leprosy to all professionals; promotes int. cooperation into research on and treatment of leprosy; organizes int. congress every 5 years; 1,200 mems; Pres. Dr MARCOS VIRMOND (Brazil); Sec. Prof. INDIRA NATH (India).

International Organization Against Trachoma/Organisation Internationale contre le Trachome: c/o Prof. Georges Cornand, La Bergère, Route de Grenoble, 05140 Aspres-sur-Buëch, France; f. 1923; promotes research and study of trachomatous conjunctivitis and ophthalmological tropical and sub-tropical diseases; organizes int. meetings; Pres. Prof. GABRIEL COSCAS (France); Sec.-Gen. Dr PIERRE HUGUET; publ. *Revue Internationale du Trachome* (4 a year).

International Pediatric Association/Asociación Internacional de Pediatría/Association Internationale de Pédiatrie: 141 Northwest Point Blvd, Elk Grove Village, IL 60007-1098, USA; e-mail adminoffice@ipa-world.org; internet www.ipa-world.org; f. 1910; promotes education on child health issues; encourages training and research in all aspects of paediatrics; holds regional and int. seminars and symposia; organizes int. paediatric congresses every 3 years; 167 mem. socs (incl. 144 nat. paediatric socs from 139 countries, 10 regional paediatric socs, 13 int. paediatric speciality socs); Pres. Prof. SERGIO CABRAL (Brazil); Exec. Dir Prof. Dr WILLIAM J. KEENAN (USA); publ. *IPA News* (4 a year).

International Psychoanalytical Association/Asociación Psicoanalítica Internacional/Association Psychanalytique Internationale/Internationale Psychoanalytische Vereinigung: Broomhills, Woodside Lane, London, N12 8UD, UK; tel. (20) 84468324; e-mail ipa@ipa.org.uk; internet www.ipa.org.uk; f. 1910; accrediting and regulatory body for psychoanalysis; devt of psychoanalysis for benefit of psychoanalytic patients; organizes research, public activities, devt of new psychoanalytic groups, professional and scientific activities; 12,000 mems in 74 constituent orgs in 35 countries; Pres. CHARLES M. T. HANLY; Sec.-Gen. H. GUNTHER PERDIGÃO; Exec. Dir PAUL CRAKE.

International Radiation Protection Association: c/o EDF Cap Ampère, 1 Place Pleyel, 93282 St Denis Cedex, France; tel. 143694093; e-mail bernard.le-guen@edf.fr; internet www.irpa.net; f. 1965; holds and supports int. meetings to provide for discussion of the scientific and practical aspects of the protection of mankind and his environment from the hazards caused by ionizing and non-ionizing radiation, facilitating the exploitation of radiation and nuclear energy; encourages establishment of radiation protection socs throughout the world as means of achieving int. cooperation; scientific assoc. of ICSU, official relations with WHO, ILO, IAEA, ICRP; 48 mem. socs, 60 mem. countries; Pres. RENATE CZARWINSKI (Germany); Exec. Officer Dr BERNARD LE GUEN (France); publ. *International Congress Proceedings*.

International Scientific Council for Trypanosomiasis Research and Control (ISCTRC)/Conseil Scientifique International pour la Recherche et la Lutte contre les Trypanosomoses: c/o AU-IBAR, Kenindia Business Park, Museum Hill, Westlands Rd, POB 30786, Nairobi, 00100, Kenya; tel. (20) 3674000; f. 1949; collaborates with other agencies engaged in the field of trypanosomiasis to stimulate the progress, coordination and encouragement of research into the problems of tsetse and trypanosomiasis in Africa and promotes coordination between research workers and orgs in African countries; provides opportunity for the discussion of related problems and their resolution; exchanges and disseminates information through meetings and publs; provides scientific and technical support to African countries; organizes biennial scientific conf.; Sec. Dr JAMES WABACHA.

International Society for Clinical Electrophysiology of Vision: c/o Ruth Hamilton, Dept of Clinical Physics, c/o X-Ray, Royal Hospital for Sick Children, Dalnair St, Glasgow, G3 8SJ, UK; tel. (141) 2016953; e-mail secretary-general@iscev.org; internet www.iscev.org; f. 1958; promotes and extends knowledge of clinical electrophysiology of vision; promotes cooperation and communication among workers in the field of clinical and basic electrophysiology of vision; organizes int. symposia and regional meetings; 300 mems; Pres. Prof. A. PATRIZIA TORMENE (Italy); Sec.-Gen. Dr RUTH HAMILTON (UK); publ. *Documenta Ophthalmologica* (6 a year).

International Society for the Psychopathology of Expression and Art Therapy/Société Internationale de Psychopathologie de l'Expression et d'Art-Thérapie: c/o Hôpital La Grave-Casselardit, Service Universitaire de Psychiatrie et de Psychologie Médicale, 170 ave de Casselardit, TSA 40031, 31059 Toulouse Cedex 9, France; tel. 559326610; e-mail contact@sipe-art-therapy.com; internet www.sipe-art-therapy.com; f. 1959; establishes and maintains links between specialists interested in the relationships between expression, creation and art; fosters nat. and int. research in the field of psychiatry and art therapy, psychoanalysis, psychology and sociology; 625 mems; Chair. Prof. LAURENT SCHMITT (France); Sec.-Gen. JEAN-LUC SUDRES (France).

International Society of Blood Transfusion/Société Internationale de Transfusion Sanguine: Marnixstraat 317, 1016 TB Amsterdam, Netherlands; tel. (20) 7601760; e-mail office@isbtweb.org; internet www.isbt-web.org; f. 1935; recognizes and promotes science and education related to blood, cells and transplantation; provides opportunities for knowledge and information exchange on science, clinical and technical practice and research and devt; promotes, enables and maintains high level of ethical medical and scientific standards in blood transfusion science and medicine; hosts and supports educational activities, workshops, int. symposiums through ISBT academy; awards fellowships and prizes; organizes int. and regional congresses; 2,000 mems in 97 countries; Exec. Dir JUDITH CHAPMAN; publs *Transfusion Today* (4 a year), *Vox Sanguinis* (8 a year).

International Society of Hematology/Société Internationale d'Hématologie: c/o Dr Sabri Kehmali, Div. of Pediatric Hematology, Dept of Pediatrics, Faculty of Medicine, Ankara Univ., Ankara, Turkey; tel. (532) 264-55-02; e-mail sabri.kemahli@medicine.ankara.edu.tr; internet www.ishworld.org; f. 1946; provides forum for discussion of haematologic problems on int. scale and encourages scientific investigation of these problems; promotes advancement of haematology and its recognition as a br. of the biological sciences; attempts to standardize on int. scale haematological methods and nomenclature; promotes better understanding of the scientific basic principles of haematology among practitioners of haematology and physicians in general; fosters better understanding and interest in clinical haematological problems among scientific investigators; 4,000 mems; Pres. ZHI-XIANG SHEN (China); publ. *Hematology* (6 a year).

International Society of Hypnosis: 269 Viale Regina Margherita, 00198, Rome RM, Italy; tel. 68548205; e-mail contact@ish-hypnosis.org; internet www.ish-hypnosis.org; f. 1959 as Int. Soc. for Clinical and Experimental Hypnosis, present name and status 1973; encourages and improves professional research, cooperative relations among scientific disciplines with regard to the study and application of hypnosis; brings together persons using hypnosis and sets up standards for professional training and adequacy; organizes int. congress; 26 int. mem. socs; Pres. Dr CAMILLO LORIEDO (Italy); Sec. and Treas. Dr CONSUELO CASULA (Italy); publ. *International Journal of Clinical and Experimental Hypnosis* (4 a year).

International Society of Lymphology: c/o Prof. M. H. Witte, Dept of Surgery, Room 4406, Univ. of Arizona College of Medicine, 1501 N Campbell Ave, POB 245200, Tucson, AZ 85724-5200, USA; tel. (520) 626-6118; e-mail grace@medcenter.arizona.edu; internet www.u.arizona.edu/~witte/isl.htm; f. 1966; advances and disseminates knowledge progress in lymphology and related subjects; stimulates and strengthens experimental and clinical investigation; organizes int. working groups and regional chapters; cooperates with other nat. and int. orgs; organizes int. congresses and postgraduate courses; 400 mems; Pres. R. BAUMEISTER (Germany); Sec.-Gen. Prof. MARLYS H. WITTE (USA); publs *Lymphology* (4 a year), *Progress in Lymphology* (every 2 years).

International Society of Neuropathology: c/o Dr David Hilton, Dept of Cellular and Anatomical Pathology, Derriford Hospital, Plymouth, PL6 8DH, UK; e-mail davidhilton@nhs.net; internet www.intsocneuropathol.com; f. 1950 as Int. Cttee of Neuropathology, current name and status 1967; initiates and maintains permanent cooperation between nat. and regional socs of neuropathology; fosters links with other int. orgs in the same field; encourages formation of nat. and regional socs of neuropathology; organizes int. congresses, symposia, meetings, colloquia and research projects; 2,500 mems; Pres. Prof. Dr HERBERT BUDKA (Austria/Switzerland); Sec.-Gen. Dr DAVID HILTON (UK); publ. *Brain Pathology* (4 a year).

International Society of Orthopaedic Surgery and Traumatology (SICOT)/Société Internationale de Chirurgie Orthopédique et de Traumatologie: Rue Washington 40-b.9, 1050 Brussels, Belgium; tel. (2) 648-68-23; e-mail hq@sicot.org; internet www.sicot.org; f. 1929; advances science and art of orthopaedics and traumatology at int. level for enhancement of patient care; fosters and develops teaching, research and education; facilitates and encourages interchange of professional experience; holds yearly conf. and triennial world congress; awards fellowships to students; 113 mem. countries, 20,000 individual mems; Pres. Prof. MAURICE HINSENKAMP (Belgium); Sec.-Gen. Prof. JOCHEN EULERT (Germany); Treas. Prof. SHANMUGANATHAN RAJASEKARAN; publ. *International Orthopaedics* (12 a year).

International Society of Physical and Rehabilitation Medicine (ISPRM): c/o Kenes Asscns Worldwide, Rue de Chantepoulet 1–3, POB 1726, 1211 Geneva 1, Switzerland; tel. 229080483; e-mail sbobinet@kenes.com; internet www.isprm.org; f. 1999 by merger of Int. Rehabilitation Medicine Assn (IRMA) and Int. Fed. of Physical and Rehabilitation Medicine; improves knowledge, skills and attitudes of physicians in the understanding of the pathodynamics and management of impairments and disabilities; provides mechanism to facilitate physical and rehabilitation medicine input to int. health orgs; organizes world congress; Pres. Prof. Dr GEROLD STUCKI; Sec. JORGE LAINS; publs *Journal of Rehabilitation Medicine, News and Views* (1 a year).

International Society of Radiology/Société Internationale de Radiologie: Preston White Dr. 1891, Reston, VA 20191, USA; tel. (703) 648-8360; e-mail director@isradiology.org; internet www.isradiology.org; f. 1925, present status 1995; promotes education in radiology; advances practice, radiation science and protection; encourages exchange and discussion of ideas and experiences among radiologists worldwide; 3 permanent Int. Comms on: Radiological Protection (ICRP), Radiation Units and Measurements (ICRU), Radiological Education (ICRE); 86 nat. radiological soc. mems; Pres. Dr JAN LABUSCAGNE (Australia); Sec.-Gen. Dr LUIS DONOSO BACH (Spain); Exec. Dir THOMAS M. CALDWELL (USA).

International Society of Surgery (ISS)/Société Internationale de Chirurgie (SIC): c/o Allveco AG, Seltisbergerstr. 16, 4419 Lupsingen, Switzerland; tel. 618159666; e-mail surgery@iss-sic.ch; internet www.iss-sic.com; f. 1902; advances science and art of surgery by research, education and nurturing of surgical practice throughout the world; organizes congresses; 3,500 mems; Pres. Prof. GÖRAN ÅKERSTRÖM (Sweden); Sec.-Gen. Prof. Dr JEAN-CLAUDE GIVEL (Switzerland); publ. *World Journal of Surgery* (12 a year).

International Union against Sexually Transmitted Infections: c/o Dr Janet Wilson, Dept of Genito Urinary Medicine, Leeds General Infirmary, Great George St, Leeds, LS1 3EX, UK; tel. (11) 33926762; e-mail secretary@iusti.org; internet www.iusti.org; f. 1923; organizes and sponsors regional and int. meetings and congresses for information exchange; admin. and educational activities, public health and technical aspects of sexually transmitted diseases, esp. HIV/AIDS; 800 individual mems, 50 nat. and soc. mems; Pres. Dr RAJ PATEL (UK); Sec.-Gen. Dr JANET WILSON (UK); publs *International Journal of STD & AIDS* (12 a year, online, www.ij-sa.rsmjournals.com), *Sexual Health* (6 a year, online, www.publish.csiro.au/nid/164.htm).

International Union against Tuberculosis and Lung Disease/Union Internationale contre la Tuberculose et les Maladies Respiratoires: 68 blvd Saint-Michel, 75006 Paris, France; tel. 144320360; e-mail union@iuatld.org; internet www.theunion.org; f. 1920; coordinates efforts of anti-tuberculosis asscns; promotes programmes and research in tuberculosis control, chest diseases and community health and cooperates in these respects with WHO; promotes int. and regional confs; collects and disseminates relevant information; assists in developing nat. programmes in cooperation with nat. asscns; 13 regional and country offices; 3,000 orgs and individual mems in 75 countries; Pres. Dr JANE CARTER (USA); Exec. Dir Dr NILS E. BILLO (Switzerland); Sec.-Gen. Dr CAMILO ROA, Jr (Philippines); publs *International Journal of Tuberculosis and Lung Disease* (12 a year, in English), *Public Health Action* (online, ingentaconnect.com/journals/browse/iuatld/pha).

International Union for Health Promotion and Education/Union Internationale de Promotion de la Santé et d'Education pour la Santé/Unión Internacional de Promoción de la Salud y Educación para la Salud: 42 blvd de la Libération, 93203 St Denis Cedex, France; tel. 148137120; e-mail iuhpe@iuhpe.org; internet www.iuhpe.org; f. 1951; advocates investment in health promotion and health education by govts, intergovernmental orgs, NGOs and private sector of soc.; contributes to devt of knowledge and practice to further the field of health promotion and health education; disseminates evidence-based knowledge and practical experience; provides mechanisms for exchange of ideas, knowledge and experiences and devt of relevant collaborative projects; organizes world confs; orgs in 21 countries, groups and individuals in 90 countries; Pres. MICHAEL SPARKS (Australia); Exec. Dir MARIE-CLAUDE LAMARRE (France); publs *Critical Public Health, Global Health Promotion, Health Education Research, Health Promotion International* (4 a year, in a trilingual edition in English, French and Spanish); special supplement issues throughout the year), *International Journal of Mental Health Promotion, International Journal of Public Health.*

International Vaccine Institute: SNU Research Park, San 4–8, Nakseongdae-dong, Gwanak-gu, Seoul 151-919, Republic of Korea; tel. (2) 872-2801; e-mail iviinfo@ivi.int; internet www.ivi.org; f. 1997; established by the UN Development Programme (UNDP); develops and deploys new vaccines for the poor in countries worldwide through programs in vaccine research, training, technical assistance and policy implementation; 32 mem. countries; Chair. Prof. RAGNAR NORRBY (Sweden); Dir-Gen. Dr CHRISTIAN LOUCQ (France).

Multiple Sclerosis International Federation: Third Fl., Skyline House, 200 Union St, London, SE1 0LX, UK; tel. (20) 76201911; e-mail info@msif.org; internet www.msif.org; f. 1967; coordinates and advances work of nat. multiple sclerosis orgs worldwide; encourages scientific research in the field and related neurological diseases; collects and disseminates information; advises and helps in advancing the devt of voluntary nat. multiple sclerosis orgs; 42 mem. socs; Pres. WEYMAN T. JOHNSON (USA); CEO PEER BANEKE; publs *MSIF Annual Review, MS in Focus* (2 a year, in English, French, German and Spanish).

Organisation Ouest Africaine de la Santé (OOAS)/Organização Oeste Africana da Saúde (WAHO) (West African Health Organization): 01 BP 153, Bobo-Dioulasso 01, Burkina Faso; tel. 20975772; e-mail wahooas@wahooas.org; internet www.wahooas.org; f. 1987 by merger of OCCGE (Organisation de Coordination et de Coopération pour la Lutte contre les Grandes Endémies in Bobo-Dioulaso Burkina Faso) and WAHC (West African Health Community/Communauté Ouest Africaine de la Santé) in Lagos, Nigeria; proactive instrument of regional health integration that enables high-impact and cost-effective interventions; conducts research and trains medical workers; collects, interprets and disseminates information; 15 mem. states: Benin, Burkina Faso, Cape Verde, Côte d'Ivoire, Gambia, Ghana, Guinea, Guinea-Bissau, Liberia, Mali, Niger, Nigeria, Senegal, Sierra Leone, Togo; library of 4,072 vols, 21 current serials, 3,196 technical documents; Dir-Gen. Dr PLACIDO M. CARDOSO; publs *Bulletin bibliographique mensuel* (4 a year), *Profil OOAS* (4 a year).

Rehabilitation International: 25 E 21st St, Fourth Fl., New York, NY 10010, USA; tel. (212) 420-1500; e-mail ri@riglobal.org; internet www.riglobal.org; f. 1922, current name adopted 1972; protects the rights of people with disabilities, incl. ensuring access to and improvement of crucial services for persons with disabilities and their families; advocates for strong policies and legislation at int., regional and nat. level to promote these rights; organizes world congress and regional confs every 4 years; mem. orgs in 100 countries; Pres. JAN A. MONSBAKKEN (Norway); Sec.-Gen. VENUS ILAGAN (USA); publ. *International Rehabilitation Review.*

Société de Neurochirurgie de Langue Française (Society of French-Speaking Neurosurgeons): Service de neurochirurgie, Ave de Vaudagne 4, 1217 Meyrin, Switzerland; tel. 149958146; e-mail bernard.george@lrb.aphp.fr; internet www.snclf.com; f. 1948; provides platform to neurosurgeons working in French language to share knowledge and disseminate worldwide neurosurgical culture of Western Europe; organizes 2 int. meetings every year; organizes an annual course in int. neurosurgery; 450 mems; Pres. CHRISTIAN RAFTOPOULOS (Belgium); Sec.-Gen. DANIEL MAY (Switzerland); publs *Bulletin, Neurochirurgie* (6 a year).

Union for International Cancer Control (UICC)/Union Internationale contre le Cancer: 62 route de Frontenex, 1207 Geneva, Switzerland; tel. 228091811; e-mail info@uicc.org; internet www.uicc.org; f. 1933; promotes on int. level the campaign against cancer in its research, therapeutic and preventive aspects; organizes congress every 2 years; 760 mem orgs in 155 countries; Pres. Prof. MARY GOSPODAROWICZ (Canada); CEO CARY ADAMS (Switzerland); publs *International Journal of Cancer* (24 a year), *TNM Classification of Malignant Tumours.*

World Association of Veterinary Microbiologists, Immunologists and Specialists in Infectious Diseases/Association Mondiale des Vétérinaires Microbiologistes, Immunologistes et Spécialistes des Maladies Infectieuses: Ecole Nationale Vétérinaire d'Alfort, 7 ave du Général de Gaulle, 94704 Maisons-Alfort Cedex, France; tel. 143967021; f. 1967; facilitates int. contacts in the field of veterinary microbiologists, immunologists and specialists in infectious diseases; Pres. Prof. CH. PILET (France).

World Confederation for Physical Therapy: Victoria Charity Centre, 11 Belgrave Rd, London, SW1V 1RB, UK; tel. (20) 79316465; e-mail info@wcpt.org; internet www.wcpt.org; f. 1951; encourages high standards of physical therapy education, practice and research; develops and promotes strength of nat. orgs of physical therapists; organizes int. congresses of physical therapists; represents physical therapy internationally; 106 mem. orgs; Pres. MARILYN MOFFAT; Sec.-Gen. BRENDA J. MYERS (UK).

World Council of Optometry: 42 Craven St, London, WC2N 5NG, UK; tel. (20) 78394385; e-mail enquiries@worldoptometry.org; internet www.worldoptometry.org; f. 1927; aims to coordinate efforts to provide a high standard of ophthalmic optical (optometric) care worldwide; provides forum for the exchange of ideas between different countries; concerned with optometric education and advice upon standards of qualification; involved in getting legislation approved in relation to optometry worldwide; provides financial assistance to optometrists and students of optometry around the world; 150 mem. orgs; Pres. TONE GARAAS-MAURDALEN (Norway); Treas. Dr RICHARD WALLINGFORD (USA); publ. *World Focus.*

World Federation for Medical Education: c/o Univ. of Copenhagen, Faculty of Health Sciences, Blegdamsvej 3, 2200 Copenhagen N, Denmark; tel. 35-32-71-03; e-mail wfme@wfme.org; internet www.wfme.org; f.

1972; promotes and integrates study and implementation of medical education worldwide; facilitates exchange of information among its mems and their constituencies; conducts and supports comparative studies of medical education; engaged on programme for worldwide reorientation of medical training; non-governmental relations with WHO, UNICEF, UNESCO, UNDP and the World Bank; organizes confs, publs and seminars; 6 regional mem. asscns at global level; Pres. Prof. Dr STEFAN LINDGREN (Sweden); Sec. ANNA IVERSEN.

World Federation of Associations of Paediatric Surgeons: c/o Prof. J. Boix-Ochoa, Apatado de Correos 3, 08490 Tordera (Barcelona), Spain; tel. 937643958; e-mail jboix99@hotmail.com; internet www.wofaps.org; f. 1974; promotes high standard of paediatric surgery; encourages ethical practice of paediatric surgery; improves standards of education for the training of paediatric surgeons; promotes and encourages paediatric surgical research; organizes world congress; 100 mem. countries; Pres. Prof. RICHARD G. AZIZKHAN (USA); Sec.-Gen. and Treas. Prof. JOSÉ BOIX-OCHOA.

World Federation of Neurology: Hill House, Heron Sq, Richmond, TW9 1EP, UK; tel. (208) 4399556; e-mail info@wfneurology.org; internet www.wfneurology.org; f. 1957; promotes education and research in neurology and prevention and treatment of disorders of the nervous system; organizes world congress and int. meetings; 114 mem. socs in 113 countries; Pres. Dr VLADIMIR HACHINSKI (Canada); Sec.- and Treas.-Gen. Dr RAAD SHAKIR (UK); publ. *Journal of the Neurological Sciences*.

World Federation of Neurosurgical Societies/Fédération Mondiale des Sociétés de Neurochirurgie: c/o Hsiao-Hui Chen, 5 rue du Marché, 1260 Nyon VD, Switzerland; tel. 223624303; e-mail teresachen@wfns.ch; internet www.wfns.org; f. 1955; promotes global improvement in neurosurgical care; improves worldwide neurosurgical care, training and research to benefit patients of mem. socs; provides help in the education and training of neurosurgeons all over the world; organizes Int. Congress of Neurological Surgery every 4 years; 124 mems (incl. 5 continental asscns, 115 nat. neurosurgical socs, 7 affiliate socs); Pres. Prof. YONG-KWANG TU (Taiwan); Sec. Prof. BASANT MISRA (India).

World Federation of Societies of Anaesthesiologists (WFSA)/Federación Mundial de Sociedades de Anestesiólogos/ Weltverband der Anaesthesisten-Gesellschaften: 21 Portland Pl., London, W1B 1YP, UK; tel. (20) 76318880; e-mail wfsahq@anaesthesiologists.org; internet www.anaesthesiologists.org; f. 1955; assists and encourages formation of nat. socs of anaesthesiologists; promotes education, research and dissemination of scientific information; recommends desirable standards for training in anaesthesiology; provides information regarding opportunities for postgraduate training and research; encourages establishment of safety measures incl. standardization of equipment; organizes world congress and sponsors regional congresses; offers fellowship training programmes for young anaesthetists from low income countries; 125 nat. mem. socs; Pres. Dr DAVID WILKINSON (UK); Hon. Sec. Dr GONZALO BARREIRO (Uruguay); publs *Update in Anaesthesia* (2 a year, in English, French, Mandarin, Russian and Spanish), *World Anaesthesia* (3 a year, in 3 languages).

World Gastroenterology Organisation: 555 East Wells St, Suite 1100, Milwaukee, WI 53202, USA; tel. (414) 918-9798; e-mail info@worldgastroenterology.org; internet www.worldgastroenterology.org; f. 1935; raises awareness of the worldwide prevalence and optimal care of digestive disorders through the provision of high-quality, accessible and ind. education and training; promotes formation of nat. gastroenterological orgs; organizes workshops, global training centres network, global guidelines, World Digestive Health Day research support, int. digestive cancer alliance; 108 nat. and regional socs and 4 regional asscns; Pres. Prof. HENRY COHEN (Uruguay); Sec.-Gen. Prof. CIHAN YURDAYDIN (Turkey); publs *Journal of Clinical Gastroenterology*, *World Gastroenterology News* (online).

World Heart Federation: 7 rue des Battoirs, CP 155, 1211, Geneva 4, Switzerland; 7 rue des Battoirs, 1211 Geneva, Switzerland; tel. 228070320; e-mail admin@worldheart.org; internet www.worldheart.org; f. 1978 as Int. Soc. and Fed. of Cardiology by merger of Int. Soc. of Cardiology (ISC) and Int. Cardiology Fed. (ICF), present name 1998; promotes study, prevention and relief of cardiovascular diseases and strokes through scientific and public education programmes, particularly in low- and middle-income countries; organizes the exchange of materials between its affiliated socs and foundations and with related agencies; organizes world congress every 2 years; 200 nat., continental and assoc. mem. orgs from 100 countries; Pres. Prof. SRINATH REDDY (India); Sec. Dr NOOSHIN BAZARGANI (UAE); CEO JOHANNA RALSTON (Switzerland); publs *Global Heart*, *Nature Reviews Cardiology*.

Music

International Music Council (IMC)/Conseil International de la Musique (CIM): c/o Maison de l'UNESCO, 1 rue Miollis, 75732 Paris Cedex 15, France; tel. 145684850; e-mail info@imc-cim.org; internet www.imc-cim.org; f. 1949; fosters exchange of musicians, music (written and recorded) and information; supports contemporary composers, traditional music and young professional musicians; fosters appreciation of music by the public; promotes diverse music; advancement of music rights; 129 mems (incl. 62 nat. music ccls, 48 int. and regional music orgs, 19 mems of honour); Pres. PAUL DUJARDIN (Belgium); Sec.-Gen. SILJA FISCHER (Germany).

MEMBERS OF IMC

European Festivals Association/Association Européenne des Festivals: Kleine Gentstraat 46, 9051 Ghent, Belgium; tel. (9) 241-80-80; e-mail info@efa-aef.eu; internet www.efa-aef.eu; f. 1952; maintains high artistic standards in festivals, widens the field of operation; organizes information and publicity; represents festivals in the int. cultural debate; provides training and education opportunities through the European Atelier for Young Festival Managers; stimulates researches on festivals; 107 mems; Pres. DARKO BRLEK (Slovenia); Sec.-Gen. KATHRIN DEVENTER.

Foundation Adkins Chiti—Women in Music/Fondazione Adkins Chiti—Donne in Musica: Teatro Comunale, Piazza Trento e Trieste, 03014 Fiuggi Città FR, Italy; tel. 7751685635; e-mail forum@donneinmusica.org; internet www.donneinmusica.org; f. 1978; promotes and presents music composed and created by women worldwide; encourages formation of orgs for documentation and information regarding women composers; research and publ. of books on music by women; 27,000 affiliated mem. orgs in 108 countries; library of 12,000 vols, 43,000 scores of music by women composers; Pres. PATRICIA ADKINS CHITI; Vice-Pres. GIGLIOLA ZECCHI BALSAMO.

International Association of Music Information Centres (IAMIC): Steenstraat/Rue des pierres 25, 1000 Brussels, Belgium; tel. (2) 504-90-99; e-mail iamic@iamic.net; internet www.iamic.net; f. 1958 as Nat. Music Centre Reps, current name adopted 1986, current status 1991; promotes and documents music; raises public profile of key cultural operators and increases access to their resources; facilitates exchange of knowledge and expertise in the field of music documentation, promotion and information; organizes int. congress; mem. orgs in 35 countries; Pres. OLGA SMETANOVÁ (Slovakia); Sec. STEF CONINX (Belgium).

International Association of Music Libraries, Archives and Documentation Centres (IAML)/Die Internationale Vereinigung der Musikbibliotheken, Musikarchive und Musikdokumentationszentren/L'Association Internationale des Bibliothèques, Archives et Centres de Documentation Musicaux: c/o Pia Shekhter, Gothenburg Univ. Library, Music and Drama Library Box 210, 405 30 Gothenburg, Sweden; tel. (31) 786-4057; e-mail secretary@iaml.info; internet www.iaml.info; f. 1951 as Int. Asscn of Music Libraries; promotes better understanding of the cultural importance of music libraries, facilitates cooperation between music libraries and information centres; compiles music bibliographies; promotes professional training of music librarians and documentalists; annual confs, large-scale documentation projects; nat. brs in 22 countries, 5 professional brs, 4 subject comms; 1,800 individual and institutional mems in 50 countries; Pres. ROGER FLURY (New Zealand); Sec.-Gen. PIA SHEKHTER (Sweden); publ. *Fontes artis musicae* (4 a year).

International Association of Schools of Jazz: Juliana van Stolberglaan 1, 2595 CA The Hague, Netherlands; tel. (70) 3151484; e-mail info@iasj.com; internet www.iasj.com; f. 1989; facilitates int. collaboration for jazz teachers and exchange of knowledge and experiences; organizes meetings and confs; disseminates information about major events in jazz education; 80 mems from 40 countries; Chair. JARI PERKIOMAKI (Finland); Sec. DIMOS DIMITRIADIS (Greece).

International Council of Organizations of Folklore Festivals and Folk Arts/Conseil International des Organisations de Festivals de Folklore et d'Arts Traditionnels/Consejo Internacional de Organizaciones de Festivales de Folklore y de las Artes Tradicionales: c/o Philippe Beaussant, 3 pl. Emile Roux, 16500 Confolens, France; tel. 545290707; e-mail info@cioff.org; internet www.cioff.org; f. 1970; promotes intangible heritage, through forms of expression such as dance, music, games, rituals, customs and other arts; supports mems and non-governmental orgs working in the areas of folklore and cultural heritage; compiling Directory of Experts in Folklore; organizes int. folklore festivals, seminars, confs; holds workshops in traditional dance, music, singing and crafts; 93 mems (incl. 69 nat. sections, 3 assoc. mems and 21 corresponding mems); Pres. Dr UDOMSAK SAKMUNGVONG; Sec.-Gen. PHILIPPE BEAUSSANT.

International Federation for Choral Music/Fédération Internationale pour la Musique Chorale/Federación Internacional de Música Coral/Internationale Föderation für Chormusik: c/o Michael J.

Anderson, Dept of Performing Arts, Univ. of Illinois at Chicago, 1040 West Harrison St, Room L018, MC255, Chicago, IL 60607-7130, USA; e-mail office@ifcm.net; internet www.ifcm.net; f. 1982; facilitates communication and exchange between choral musicians throughout the world; holds world and regional symposia, master classes, World Youth Choir, Choral Music Database; 2,000 mems in 83 countries; Pres. MICHAEL J. ANDERSON (USA); First Vice-Pres. LEON TONG SHIU-WAI (Hong Kong); publ. *International Choral Bulletin* (4 a year, in English, French, German and Spanish).

International Federation of Chopin Societies/Międzynarodowa Federacja Towarzystw Chopinowskich: Tamka 43, 00-355 Warszawa, Poland; tel. (22) 4416196; e-mail chopin@post.pl; internet www.ifcs.pl; f. 1985; disseminates and expands knowledge about Fryderyk Chopin and his artistic works; supports int. artistic and scholarly endeavours related to Fryderyk Chopin; organizes concerts, festivals, competitions, exhibitions, lectures, seminars and confs; facilitates int. exchanges of artists and scholars; 36 socs from 26 countries; Pres. THEODOR KANITZER (Austria); Gen. Sec. ELŻBIETA ARTYSZ (Poland); publ. *Chopin in the World* (1 a year).

International Federation of Musicians/Fédération Internationale des Musiciens: 21 bis, rue Victor Massé, 75009 Paris, France; tel. 145263123; e-mail office@fim-musicians.org; internet www.fim-musicians.org; f. 1948; protects and furthers economic, social and artistic interests of musicians of mem. unions; promotes int. exchange of musicians; makes agreements with other int. orgs in the interest of mem. unions and of the profession; obtains and compiles statistical and other information referring to the music profession and provides such information to mem. unions; holds int. congresses and confs; 72 mem. unions; Pres. JOHN F. SMITH (UK); Gen. Sec. BENOÎT MACHUEL.

International Music and Media Centre/Internationales Musikzentrum und Medienzentrum: Stiftgasse 29, 1070 Vienna, Austria; tel. (1) 8890315; e-mail office@imz.at; internet www.imz.at; f. 1961; develops and promotes all forms of classical, jazz, world and contemporary music and classical and contemporary dance through audiovisual media; organizes congresses, seminars and screenings on music in the audiovisual media; organizes competitions to strengthen relations between composers, interpreters and directors, with particular emphasis on the promotion of the younger generation; 180 mems from 35 countries; Pres. CHRIS HUNT (UK); Sec.-Gen. FRANZ PATAY.

International Music Managers' Forum: 61 Moriatry Close, London, N7 0EF, UK; e-mail info@immf.com; internet immf.com; safeguards, respects and protects moral and professional interests of mems and worldwide community of music managers; fosters awareness of importance of the rights of artists as the creators of copyright; supports formation of nat. and regional orgs; facilitates exchange of information and knowledge; 16 mem. nat. feds in 15 countries; Chair. BRIAN HETHERMAN; Exec. Dir JAKE BEAUMONT-NESBITT.

International Society for Contemporary Music/Société Internationale pour la Musique Contemporaine: c/o Gaudeamus Muziekweek, Loevenhoutsedijk 301, 3552 XE, Utrecht, Netherlands; tel. (6) 29069173; e-mail info@iscm.org; internet www.iscm.org; f. 1922; promotes devt of contemporary music; organizes annual World Music Days; 124 mems (incl. 47 nat. sections, 9 assoc. mems, 1 allied assoc. mem., 67 hon. mems); Pres. JOHN DAVIS (Australia); Sec.-Gen. ARTHUR VAN DER DRIFT (Netherlands); publ. *World New Music Magazine* (1 a year).

International Society for Music Education: Suite 148, 45 Glenferrie Rd, Malvern, Vic 3144, Australia; tel. (8) 9386-2654; e-mail isme@isme.org; internet www.isme.org; f. 1953; promotes music education as a part of gen. education and community life; organizes int. confs. and seminars; cooperates with other int. music orgs; acts as an advisory body to UNESCO; cooperates with orgs representing other fields of education; 1,900 individual mems, 100,000 assoc. mems; Pres. Prof. MARGARET BARRETT; Sec.-Gen. ANGELA RUGGLES; publs *International Journal of Music Education (IJME)* (4 a year), *ISME World Conference Proceedings*.

Jeunesses Musicales International (JMI): Rue Defacqz 1, 1000 Brussels, Belgium; tel. (2) 513-97-74; e-mail mail@jmi.net; internet www.jmi.net; f. 1945; provides musical opportunities for young people; helps young musicians to interact internationally; creates cultural understanding by conducting musical events; 63 mems; Pres. PER EKEDAHL; Sec.-Gen. BLASKO SMILEVSKI (acting).

World Federation of International Music Competitions/Fédération Mondiale des Concours Internationaux de Musique: 104 rue de Carouge, 1205 Geneva, Switzerland; tel. 223213620; e-mail fmcim@fmcim.org; internet www.wfimc.org; f. 1957; generates and communicates positive image and high profile for int. music competitions; identifies and deals with potential opportunities and challenges to the world of int. music competitions; coordinates activities of mems and maintains links between them, arranges the calendar of competitions; creates forum for sharing interests and concerns; 120 mem. competitions; Pres. GLEN KWOK (USA); Sec.-Gen. MARIANNE GRANVIG (Denmark); publ. *Yearbook*.

OTHER ORGANIZATIONS

International Council for Traditional Music/Conseil International de la Musique Traditionelle: c/o Dept of Musicology, Faculty of Arts, Univ. of Ljubljana, Aškerčeva 2, 1000, Ljubljana, Slovenia; tel. (410) 501-55-59; e-mail secretariat@ictmusic.org; internet www.ictmusic.org; f. 1947 as Int. Folk Music Ccl, present name 1981; affiliated to UNESCO; furthers study, practice, documentation, preservation and dissemination of traditional music and dance of all countries; organizes world confs, symposia and colloquia; 1,600 mems; Pres. Dr ADRIENNE L. KAEPPLER (USA); Sec.-Gen. SVANIBOR PETTAN (Slovenia); publs *Bulletin of the ICTM* (2 a year), *Directory of Traditional Music* (online for mems), *Yearbook for Traditional Music* (1 a year).

International Repertory of Music Literature (RILM)/Répertoire International de Littérature Musicale (RILM)/Internationales Repertorium der Musikliteratur: RILM International Center, City Univ. of New York, 365 Fifth Ave, Suite 3108, New York, NY 10016-4309, USA; tel. (212) 817-1990; e-mail questions@rilm.org; internet www.rilm.org; f. 1966; sponsored by Int. Assn of Music Libraries, Archives and Documentation Centers, Int. Musicological Soc. and Int. Ccl for Traditional Music; research and gathering of bibliographic references of all significant writings on music, from all nations, for online, 770,000 records in 151 languages; 50 nat. mem. cttees; library of 1,200 vols, 10,000 music journals; Editor-in-Chief BARBARA DOBBS MACKENZIE; Exec. Editor ZDRAVKO BLAZEKOVIC.

International Research Institute for Media, Communication and Cultural Development (MEDIACULT)/Internationales Forschungsinstitut für Medien, Kommunikation und kulturelle Entwicklung: Marxergasse 48/8, 1030 Vienna, Austria; tel. (1) 2363923; e-mail office@mediacult.at; internet www.mediacult.at; f. 1969; carries out research in the areas of media and culture using theories and methodologies; cooperates with nat. and int. instns; 8 mems; library of 1,200 vols; Pres. Prof. RAYMOND WEBER (Luxembourg); Sec.-Gen. Prof. Dr ALFRED SMUDITS (Austria).

Science

Abdus Salam International Centre for Theoretical Physics (ICTP): Strada Costiera 11, 34151 Trieste TS, Italy; tel. 402240111; e-mail sci_info@ictp.it; internet www.ictp.it; f. 1964; administered under a tripartite agreement between UNESCO, the Int. Atomic Energy Agency and the Italian Govt; training and research into high-energy physics, cosmology and astroparticle physics, condensed matter and statistical physics, Earth system physics, mathematics and applied physics; library of 68,500 vols, 320 journals, 4,200 ejournals, 1,200 ebooks, 1,500 theses; Dir Prof. Dr FERNANDO QUEVEDO (Costa Rica).

African Academy of Sciences: POB 24916, Nairobi, Kenya; off Ngong Rd, Miotoni Rd, Miotoni Lane, House No. 8 Karen, Nairobi, Kenya; tel. (2) 8060674; e-mail aas@aasciences.org; internet www.aasciences.org; f. 1985; promotes, supports and fosters growth of research and technology base in Africa; works for mobilization and strengthening of the African scientific community (includes the Network of African Scientific Institutions, profiles and data bank of African scientists and instns, African Dissertation Internship Programme, assistance to regional orgs); research devt and public policy; capacity building in science and technology; facilitates, coordinates and undertakes publication and dissemination of scientific and technological achievements in Africa; 209 mem. fellows incl. 8 assoc. fellows; library of 2,000 vols; Pres. Prof. AHMADOU LAMINE NDIAYE (Senegal); Sec.-Gen. Dr Eng. SHEM ARUNGU-OLENDE (Kenya); Exec. Dir Prof. BERHANU ABEGAZ (Kenya); publs *Discovery and Innovation* (4 a year), *Whydah* (4 a year).

African Association for the Advancement of Science and Technology: c/o Prof. C. Kamala, KNAAS, POB 47288, Nairobi, Kenya; f. 1978; Sec. Prof. C. KAMALA.

African Organization for Cartography and Remote Sensing/Organisation Africaine de Cartographie et Télédétection: BP 102, Hussein Dey, 16040 Algiers, Algeria; tel. (21) 231717; e-mail tpn4@oact.dz; f. 1988; encourages devt of cartography and of remote sensing by satellite; organizes confs and other meetings; promotes establishment of training instns; coordinates 4 regional training centres in Burkina Faso, Kenya, Nigeria and Tunisia; 24 mem. countries; Contact MOHAMED SAFAR ZITOUN.

Association for the Taxonomic Study of Tropical African Flora/Association pour l'Étude Taxonomique de la Flore d'Afrique Tropicale: c/o Prof. Dr Sebsebe Demissew, Faculty of Science, Addis Ababa Univ., POB 3434, Addis Ababa, Ethiopia; tel. (1) 114323; e-mail sebsebed@bio.aau.edu.et; f.

1951; 800 mems from 70 countries; Gen. Sec. Prof. Dr SEBSEBE DEMISSEW; publ. *Bulletin* (1 a year).

BirdLife International: 1 Wellbrook Court, Girton Rd, Girton, Cambridge, CB3 0NA, UK; tel. (1223) 277-318; e-mail birdlife@birdlife.org; internet www.birdlife.org; f. 1922; determines status of bird species worldwide and compiles data on all endangered species; identifies conservation problems and priorities and runs a programme of related field projects; partners and reps in over 100 countries; collaborates on regional work programmes; 2,500,000 mems; Chair. KHALID IRANI (Jordan); Managing Dir Dr HAZELL SHOKELLU THOMPSON (UK); publs *Bird Conservation International* (4 a year), *World Birdwatch* (4 a year).

Charles Darwin Foundation for the Galapagos Islands/Fundación Charles Darwin para las Islas Galápagos: Puerto Ayora, Santa Cruz Island, Galapagos, Ecuador; Avda 6 de Diciembre N 36–109 y Pasaje California, POB 17–01–3891, Quito, Ecuador; tel. (5) 2526146; e-mail cdrs@fcdarwin.org.ec; internet www.darwinfoundation.org; f. 1959; provides scientific research, technical information and assistance for preservation of biological diversity and natural resources of the Galapagos Islands; library of 10,000 vols; Pres. Prof. Dr DENNIS GEIST; Exec. Dir Dr GABRIEL LOPEZ; publ. *Galapagos Research* (2 a year).

Circum-Pacific Council: c/o Michele Redner, 12201 Sunrise Valley Dr., MS-917, Reston, VA 20192, USA; tel. (703) 648-5042; e-mail mredner@usgs.gov; internet www.circum-pacificcouncil.org; f. 1972 as Circum-Pacific Council for Energy and Mineral Resources; non-profit int. org. of earth scientists and engineers; develops and promotes research and cooperation among industry, govt and academics, for the sustainable use of natural resources in the Pacific region; facilitates exchange of Pacific Basin geologic information in regard to resources, economies, environment, habitats; cooperation of 46 int. geoscience orgs; sponsors confs, meetings, workshops and research incl. the Circum-Pacific Map Project, and int. training schools; Pres. H. GARY GREENE (USA); Chair. EDWARD SAADE (USA); Sec. ERICK MACK (USA).

Commonwealth Geographical Bureau: c/o Prof. Tony Binns, Dept of Geography, Univ. of Otago, POB 56, Dunedin, New Zealand; tel. (3) 4798774; e-mail j.a.binns@geography.otago.ac.nz; internet www.commonwealthgeography.org; f. 1968; encourages devt of geographical research and study, particularly in developing Commonwealth countries, through assistance to the profession; regional seminars, assistance for study visits; disseminates information of interest to Commonwealth geographers; 300 mem. depts, units, sections in 58 commonwealth countries; Pres. Prof. TONY BINNS (New Zealand); Hon. Sec. Prof. ELIZABETH THOMAS-HOPE (Jamaica).

Council for International Congresses of Entomology/Comité Permanent des Congrès Internationaux d'Entomologie: c/o Dr James Ridsdill-Smith, 75A Birdwood Circus E, Birdwood, WA 6157, Australia; tel. (8) 9339-0762; e-mail president@int-cong-ent.org; internet www.int-cong-ent.org; f. 1910; acts as link between periodic congresses and arranges the venue for each congress; the cttee is also the entomology section of the Int. Union of Biological Sciences; 23 mems; Chair. Dr HARI C. SHARMA (India); Sec. and Treas. Dr JAMES T. RIDSDILL-SMITH (Australia).

Council of Managers of National Antarctic Programs (COMNAP): c/o Gateway Antarctica, Univ. of Canterbury, Private Bag 4800, Christchurch 8140, New Zealand; Ground Fl. (First Fl.), Geography Bldg, cnr of Arts and Forestry Rd, Univ. of Canterbury, Ilam, Christchurch 8140, New Zealand; tel. 33642273; e-mail info@comnap.aq; internet www.comnap.aq; f. 1988; brings together National Antarctic Programmes from around the world to develop and promote best practice in managing the support of scientific research in Antarctica; serves as forum to develop practices that improve effectiveness of activities in an environmentally responsible manner; facilitates and promotes int. partnerships; advises Antarctic Treaty System from the National Antarctic Programs' pool of expertise; 28 mem. countries; Chair. HEINZ MILLER (Germany); Exec. Sec. MICHELLE ROGAN-FINNEMORE.

European Atomic Energy Community (Euratom): c/o European Comm., EUFO 2161, Rue Alcide de Gasperi, 2920 Luxembourg, Luxembourg; Complexe Euroforum, 10 rue Robert Stumper, 2557 Luxembourg, Luxembourg; tel. 430136738; e-mail esa-aae@ec.europa.eu; internet ec.europa.eu/energy/nuclear/euratom/euratom_en.htm; based on a formal treaty signed in Rome, Italy in March 1957, at the same time as the treaty establishing the EEC; aims to integrate the programmes of mem. states for the peaceful uses of atomic energy; ensures security of atomic energy supply within the framework of centralized monitoring system; created Euratom Supply Agency to ensure regular and equitable supply of ores, source materials and special fissile materials in the EU; since 1967 combined with the ECSC and EEC; Dir-Gen. of Euratom Supply Agency STAMATIOS TSALAS.

European Centre for Medium-Range Weather Forecasts: Shinfield Park, Reading, RG2 9AX, UK; tel. (118) 9499000; e-mail dg@ecmwf.int; internet www.ecmwf.int; f. 1975 as COST (European Co-operation in Science and Technology) project, present status 1979; devt of numerical methods for medium-range weather forecasting; collection and storage of data and products, providing operational forecasts to the mem. states and cooperating states, providing advanced training in numerical weather prediction; 19 mem. states; library of 4,000 vols of monographs, 8,000 reports, journals, films, video cassettes and CD-ROMs; Dir-Gen. Prof. ALAN THORPE (UK).

European Geosciences Union: Philippe Courtial, Luisenstr. 37, 80333 Munich, Germany; tel. (89) 21806549; e-mail info@egu.eu; internet www.egu.eu; f. 2002 by merger of the European Geophysical Soc. and the European Union of Geosciences; promotes the sciences of the Earth and its environment and of planetary and space sciences; encourages cooperation and discussion in Europe among scientists; organizes topical confs and short courses; 12,500 mems; Pres. DONALD BRUCE DINGWELL; Exec. Sec. PHILIPPE COURTIAL; publs *Annales Geophysicae (ANGEO)* (12 a year, online, www.annales-geophysicae.net), *Atmospheric Chemistry and Physics (ACP)* (online, www.atmospheric-chemistry-and-physics.net), *Atmospheric Chemistry and Physics Discussions (ACPD)* (online, www.atmospheric-chemistry-and-physics.-net), *Atmospheric Measurement Techniques (AMT)* (online, www.atmospheric-measurement-techniques.net), *Atmospheric Measurement Techniques Discussions (AMTD)* (online, www.atmospheric-measurement-techniques.net), *Biogeosciences (BG)* (online, www.biogeosciences.net), *Biogeosciences Discussions (BGD)* (online, www.biogeosciences-discuss.net), *Climate of the Past (CP)* (online, www.climate-of-the-past.net), *Climate of the Past Discussions (CPD)* (online, www.climate-of-the-past.net), *Earth System Dynamics (ESD)* (online, www.earth-system-dynamics.net), *Earth System Dynamics Discussions (ESDD)* (online, www.earth-system-dynamics.net), *Geoscientific Instrumentation, Methods and Data Systems (GI)* (online, www.geoscientific-instrumentation-methods-and-data-systems.net), *Geoscientific Instrumentation, Methods and Data Systems Discussions (GID)* (online, www.geoscientific-instrumentation-methods-and-data-systems.net), *Geoscientific Model Development (GMD)* (online, www.geoscientific-model-development.net), *Geoscientific Model Development Discussions (GMDD)* (online, www.geoscientific-model-development.net), *Hydrology and Earth System Sciences* (online, www.hydrology-and-earth-system-sciences.net), *Hydrology and Earth System Sciences Discussions* (online, www.hydrology-and-earth-system-sciences.net), *Natural Hazards and Earth System Sciences (NHESS)* (online, www.natural-hazards-and-earth-system-sciences.net), *Nonlinear Processes in Geophysics (NPG)* (online, www.nonlinear-processes-in-geophysics.net), *Ocean Science (OS)* (online, www.ocean-science.net), *Ocean Science Discussions (OSD)* (online, www.ocean-sci-discuss.net/volumes_and_issues.html), *Solid Earth (SE)* (online, www.solid-earth.net), *Solid Earth Discussions (SED)* (online, www.solid-earth-discuss.net/volumes_and_issues.html), *The Cryosphere (TC)* (online, www.the-cryosphere.net), *The Cryosphere Discussions (TCD)* (online, www.the-cryosphere-discuss.net/volumes_and_issues.html).

European Institute of Environmental Medicine: Odos Kerasundos 2, 162 32 Athens, Greece; tel. 2107628460; e-mail eiem@otonet.gr; f. 1970; brings together scientists and scholars with cross-sectional background and research interests; conducts multidisciplinary educational and research activities studying the interactions between man and his environment (natural and technical); Dir Prof. C. K. KYRILOV.

European Molecular Biology Laboratory: Meyerhofstr. 1, 69117 Heidelberg, Germany; tel. (6221) 3870; e-mail info@embl.de; internet www.embl.de; f. 1974; financed by 15 European states and Israel; basic research in molecular biology; outstations in Hinxton, UK, Grenoble, France, Hamburg, Germany, Monterotondo, Italy; performs basic research in molecular biology; trains scientists, students and visitors at all levels; develops new instruments and methods; engages in technology transfer; organizes seminars; 20 mem. states and 1 assoc. mem.; library of 11,000 monographic titles, 250 journals, 70 active series; Chair. Prof. EERO VUORIO (Finland); Dir-Gen. Prof. Dr IAIN MATTAJ; publs *Handbook of Statistics* (1 a year), *Research Report* (1 a year).

European Molecular Biology Organization (EMBO)/Organisation Européenne de Biologie Moléculaire: Postfach 1022.40, 69012 Heidelberg, Germany; Meyerhofstr. 1, 69117 Heidelberg, Germany; tel. (6221) 88910; e-mail embo@embo.org; internet www.embo.org; f. 1964; promotes excellence in the molecular life sciences in Europe; awards research fellowships; sponsors scientific meetings; awards installation grants to build scientific capacity in selected countries; provides opportunities for career devt to young group leaders in the EMBO Young Investigator Programme; offers fellowships and training for scientists outside Europe; offers scientific advice on European science policy; provides quality reviews of nat. science programmes, information and online services for life sciences communities; annual life sciences conf.; 1,500 mems; Chair. ARI HELENIUS (Switzerland); Dir Prof. MARIA LEPTIN; publs *EMBO Journal* (24 a year, online, www.nature.com/emboj/index.html), *EMBO Molecular Medicine* (12 a year), *EMBO Reports* (12 a year, online, www.nature.com/embor/index.html), *Molecular Systems Biology* (26 a year, online, www.nature.com/msb/index.html).

European Organization for Nuclear Research (CERN)/Organisation Européenne pour la Recherche Nucléaire: 1211 Geneva 23, Switzerland; tel. 227676111; e-mail cern.reception@cern.ch; internet public.web.cern.ch; f. 1954; carries out and coordinates research on fundamental particles; research is undertaken mostly by teams of visiting scientists who remain based at their parent instns; research is carried out with the aid of a proton synchrotron of 28 GeV (the PS), the super proton synchrotron (SPS) of 450 GeV and the 27-km LEP electron-positron collider; 20 mem. states; Pres. of the Council MICHEL SPIRO; Dir-Gen. ROLF-DIETER HEUER; publs *CERN Bulletin* (online), *CERN Courier* (12 a year, in English and French, online, cerncourier.com/cws/latest/cern).

European Physical Society: 6 rue des Frères Lumière, 68200 Mulhouse, France; tel. 389329440; e-mail secretariat@eps.org; internet www.eps.org; f. 1968; promotes advancement of physics in Europe and neighbouring countries by all suitable means; develops and organizes activities in fields of education, policy, publ., public outreach; 6,621 mems (incl. 41 nat. mem. orgs, 6,500 individual mems, 80 assoc. mems); Sec.-Gen. DAVID LEE; publs *Annual Reviews, ECA and Conference Proceedings, EPL* (24 a year, print and online), *European Journal of Physics* (6 a year), *Europhysics News* (6 a year, online, www.europhysicsnews.org), *Physics Publishing Alliance*.

European Research Council: c/o European Comm., ERC Exec. Agency, COV2, 1049 Brussels, Belgium; Covent Garden, Pl. Charles Rogier 16, 1210 Saint-Josse-ten-Noode Brussels, Belgium; tel. (2) 298-76-31; e-mail rtd-erc@ec.europa.eu; internet erc.europa.eu; f. 2007; supports investigator-driven frontier research; complements funding activities in Europe; directs scientific strategy, establishes methodologies and procedures; evaluates proposals, scientific reporting and monitoring; Pres. Prof. JEAN-PIERRE BOURGUIGNON (Austria); Sec.-Gen. Prof. Dr DONALD B. DINGWELL (Canada); Dir PABLO AMOR.

European Science Foundation: 1 quai Lezay-Marnésia, BP 90015, 67080 Strasbourg Cedex, France; tel. 388767100; internet www.esf.org; f. 1974; advances European research collaboration and explores new directions for research; incl. research funding, research performing orgs and acads from 29 countries; peer review, evaluation services; 66 mem. orgs in 29 countries; Pres. Prof. PÄR OMLING (Sweden); Chief Exec. MARTIN HYNES.

European Southern Observatory/ Organisation Européenne pour des Recherches Astronomiques dans l'Hémisphère Austral: Karl-Schwarzschild-Str. 2, 85748 Garching bei München, Germany; tel. (89) 320060; e-mail information@eso.org; internet www.eso.org; f. 1962; astronomical research in the southern hemisphere; construction and operation of an int. observatory in Chile (see under Chile); fosters European cooperation in astronomy; 15 mem. states; Dir-Gen. Prof. TIM DE ZEEUW (Netherlands); publ. *The Messenger*.

European Space Agency (ESA): 8–10 rue Mario Nikis, 75738 Paris Cedex 15, France; tel. 153697654; e-mail contact@esa.int; internet www.esa.int; f. 1964, current name adopted 1975, following merger of ELDO and ESRO; promotes cooperation among European states in space research and technology for peaceful purposes, with a view to their being used for scientific purposes and for operational space applications systems; elaborates and implements a long-term European space policy by recommending space objectives to its mems and by concerting their nat. policies with respect to other nat. and int. orgs and instns; implements activities and programmes in the space field by coordinating the European space programme and nat. programmes; major establishments: ESTEC in Noordwijk (Netherlands), ESOC in Darmstadt (Germany), ESRIN in Frascati (Italy), ESAC in Madrid (Spain); 20 mem. countries; library of 48,000 vols, 1m. microfiches, 42,000 reports and standards; Dir-Gen. JEAN-JACQUES DORDAIN (France); publs *Connect* (2 a year), *ESA Bulletin* (4 a year), *Eurocomp* (1 a year), scientific and technical reports.

Federation of Arab Scientific Research Councils: Alawayh, POB 13027, Baghdad, Iraq; tel. (1) 5372832; e-mail fasrc@uruklink.net; f. 1976; strengthens scientific and technological cooperation and coordination between Arab countries; holds confs, seminars, workshops and training courses; publishes Directory of Arab Scientific Research Institutions; 15 mem. countries; Sec.-Gen. Prof. MUBARAK MOHAMED ALI MAGZOUB; publs *Computer Research, Proceedings of Scientific Activities*.

Federation of Asian Scientific Academies and Societies (FASAS): c/o Australian Academy of Science, GPOB 783, Canberra ACT 2601, Australia; tel. (2) 6201-9456; e-mail fasas@science.org.au; internet www.fasas.org.au; f. 1984; promotes advancement of science and technology for devt in Asia; promotes integration of science and technology into national devt planning and policy-making processes; enhances contribution and impact of academies and socs in nat. and regional devt; collects, collates and disseminates scientific information; 16 mems; Pres. Acad. Dr OMAR ABDUL RAHMAN (Malaysia); Sec.-Gen. Acad. Ir LEE YEE CHEONG (Malaysia).

Foundation for International Scientific Coordination/Fondation 'Pour la Science', Centre international de Synthèse: ENS-45, rue d'Ulm, 75005 Paris, France; tel. 144322655; e-mail revuedesynthese@ens.fr; internet www.revue-de-synthese.eu; f. 1924; Founder HENRI BERR; Co-Dir ERIC BRIAN; Co-Dir MICHEL BLAY; publs *Revue de Synthèse* (4 a year), *Revue d'Histoire des Sciences* (4 a year), *Semaines de Synthèse, L'Evolution de l'Humanité*.

Institute of Mathematical Statistics: POB 22718, Beachwood, OH 44122, USA; tel. (216) 295-2340; e-mail ims@imstat.org; internet www.imstat.org; f. 1935; gives awards; holds lectures and meetings; 4,500 mems; Pres. HANS RUDOLF KÜNSCH (Switzerland); Exec. Sec. AURORE DELAIGLE (Australia); publs *Annals of Applied Probability* (4 a year), *Annals of Applied Statistics, Annals of Probability, Annals of Statistics* (6 a year), *CBMS Regional Conference Series in Probability and Statistics, IMS Bulletin* (6 a year), *IMS Lecture Notes—Monograph Series, Statistical Science*.

Intergovernmental Oceanographic Commission (IOC) of UNESCO/Commission Océanographique Intergouvernementale de l'UNESCO: c/o UNESCO, 1 rue Miollis, 75732 Paris Cedex 15, France; tel. 145683984; e-mail ioc.secretariat@unesco.org; internet ioc-unesco.org; f. 1960; promotes int. cooperation and coordinates programmes in research, services and capacity building to learn more about the nature and resources of the oceans and coastal areas and applies this knowledge to improved management, sustainable devt and protection of the marine environment and the decision-making processes of states; 144 mem. states; Chair. Dr SANG-KYUNG BYUN (Republic of Korea); Exec. Sec. Dr WENDY WATSON-WRIGHT (Canada); publ. *IOC Technical Series*.

International Academy of Astronautics (IAA)/Académie Internationale d'Astronautique: BP 1268–16, 75766 Paris Cedex 16, France; 6 rue Galilée, 75116 Paris, France; tel. 147238215; e-mail sgeneral@iaamail.org; internet www.iaaweb.org; f. 1960; fosters devt of astronautics for peaceful purposes; recognizes individuals who have distinguished themselves in the field and provides a programme through which mems can contribute to int. cooperation; liaises with nat. academies of science; developing a multilingual (20 languages) Database; maintains the following cttees: Space Sciences, Int. Space Plans and Policies, Life Sciences, Benefits to Soc. from Space Activities, Economics of Space Operations, Interstellar Space Exploration, Search for Extraterrestrial Intelligence, Safety and Rescue, Space and Environmental Change, History of Astronautics, Scientific Legal Liaison; 975 mems in 56 countries; Pres. Dr MADHAVAN NAIR (India); Sec.-Gen. Dr JEAN-MICHEL CONTANT (France); publs *Acta Astronautica* (12 a year), *Proceedings of Symposia*.

International Association for Mathematics and Computers in Simulation/ Association Internationale pour les Mathématiques et Calculateurs en Simulation: c/o Dept of Computer Science, Hill Center, Busch Campus, Rutgers Univ., New Brunswick, NJ 08903, USA; internet www.research.rutgers.edu/~imacs; f. 1955; advances study of general methods for modelling and computer simulation of dynamic systems; Pres. ROBERT BEAUWENS (Belgium); Treas. ERNEST H. MUND (Belgium); publs *Applied Numerical Mathematics* (6 a year), *Journal of Computational Acoustics, Mathematics and Computers in Simulation*.

International Association for Plant Taxonomy/Association Internationale pour la Taxonomie Végétale: c/o Institute of Botany, Slovak Acad. of Sciences, Dubravska cesta 9, 845 23 Bratislava, Slovakia; Chemin de l'Impératrice 1, 1292, Chambésy, Switzerland; tel. (2) 59-42-61-51; e-mail office@iapt-taxon.org; internet www.iapt-taxon.org; f. 1950; promotes all aspects of botanical systematics; encourages relationships and communication among plant taxonomists and systematists and their institutes worldwide; encourages devt and maintenance of stable and effective botanical nomenclature; institutes and individuals in 87 countries; Pres. VICKI FUNK (USA); Sec.-Gen. KAROL MARHOLD (Slovakia); publs *Regnum vegetabile* (irregular), *Taxon* (6 a year).

International Association for the Physical Sciences of the Ocean (IAPSO)/ Association Internationale des Sciences Physiques de l'Océan: c/o Johan Rodhe, Dept of Earth Science, Univ. of Gothenburg, POB 460, 405 30 Gothenburg, Sweden; tel. (31) 786-2876; e-mail johan.rodhe@gu.se; internet iapso.iugg.org; f. 1919; promotes study of scientific problems relating to oceans, chiefly by the aid of mathematics, physics and chemistry; initiates, facilitates and coordinates research; organizes, sponsors, co-sponsors formal and informal int. forums for communication among ocean scientists throughout the world; provides basic services significant to the conduct of physical oceanography; 81 mem. states; Pres. Prof. Dr EUGENE G. MOROZOV (Russia); Sec.-Gen. Prof. JOHAN RODHE (Sweden); publs *Procès-verbaux* (every 2–4 years), *Publications Scientifiques* (irregular).

International Association for Vegetation Science/Association Internationale pour l'Étude de la Végétation: c/o Nina A. C. Smits, Wes Beekhuizenweg 3, 6871 VJ Renkum, Netherlands; e-mail admin@iavs.org; internet www.iavs.org; f. 1939 as Int. Phytosociological Soc., present name and status 1981–82; promotes research, education and publ. of research results in vegetation science; facilitates scientific and personal contacts among vegetation scientists worldwide; promotes applications of vegetation science; holds symposium every year and sponsors a phytogeographical field-study excursion every 1–2 years; 1,490 mems; Pres. MARTIN DIEKMANN (Germany); Sec. SUSAN WISER (New Zealand); publs *Applied Vegetation Science*, *Journal of Vegetation Science*.

International Association of Biological Oceanography: c/o Dr Mark Costello, Leigh Marine Laboratory, Univ. of Auckland, POB 349, Warkworth, New Zealand; tel. (9) 3737599; e-mail m.costello@auckland.ac.nz; internet www.iabo.org; f. 1966; attached to Int. Union of Biological Sciences; organizes meetings and discussions to facilitate communication between marine biologists; Pres. Dr MARK J. COSTELLO (New Zealand).

International Association of Geodesy/Association Internationale de Géodésie: Alfons-Goppel-Str. 11, 80539 Munich, Germany; tel. (89) 230311107; e-mail iag@dgfi.badw.de; internet www.iag-aig.org; f. 1862 as Mitteleuropäische Gradmessung, current name adopted 1886; furthers geodetic theory through research and teaching; collects, analyses, models and interprets observational data; stimulates technological devt and provides consistent representation of the figure, rotation, and gravity field of the Earth and planets and their temporal variations; promotes and coordinates int. cooperation in this field; publishes results; a mem. asscn of IUGG; nat. cttees in 78 countries; Pres. CHRIS RIZOS (Australia); Sec.-Gen. Hon. Prof. Dr Ing. HERMANN DREWES (Germany); publs *IAG Reports* (every 4 years), *Journal of Geodesy* (12 a year).

International Association of Geomagnetism and Aeronomy (IAGA)/Association Internationale de Géomagnétisme et d'Aéronomie: c/o Prof. Mioara Mandea, Earth Observation/Directorate for Strategy and Programmes, CNES-Centre National d'Etudes Spatiales, 2 Pl. Maurice Quentin, 75001. Paris, France; tel. 144767948; e-mail iaga_sg@gfz-potsdam.de; internet www.iugg.org/iaga; f. 1919; study of magnetism and aeronomy of the earth and other bodies of the solar system and of the interplanetary medium and its interaction with these bodies; encourages exchange of scientific information, facilitates int. collaboration in research; sponsors meetings and workshops; mems: countries that adhere to the Int. Union of Geodesy and Geophysics are eligible; 5,000 mems; Pres. Prof. KATHRYN WHALER (UK); Sec.-Gen. Prof. MIOARA MANDEA (France); publs *IAGA News* (1 a year), *IAGA Proceedings*.

International Association of Hydrological Sciences/Association Internationale des Sciences Hydrologiques: c/o Christophe Cudennec, Agrocampus Ouest, CS 84215, 35042 Rennes, France; tel. 223485558; e-mail cudennec@agrocampus-ouest.fr; internet iahs.info; f. 1922; part of IUGG; organizes gen. assemblies, symposia; 84 nat. cttees; awards Int. Hydrology Prize and Tison Award; Pres. Prof. GORDON YOUNG (Canada); Sec.-Gen. Prof. CHRISTOPHE CUDENNEC (France); publ. *Hydrological Sciences Journal* (8 a year, online).

International Association of Meteorology and Atmospheric Sciences (IAMAS)/Association Internationale de Météorologie et de Sciences de l'Atmosphère: c/o Dr Hans Volkert, Deutsches Zentrum für Luft und Raumfahrt e.V., Institut für Physik der Atmosphäre, Münchner Str. 20, 82234 Oberpfaffenhofen, Germany; tel. (8153) 282570; e-mail hans.volkert@dlr.de; internet www.iamas.org; f. 1919; an asscn of the Int. Union of Geodesy and Geophysics; coordinates research in atmospheric science fields within 10 int. comms; facilitates education, devt and participation of early career scientists and atmospheric scientists from resource-limited countries in int. scientific assemblies and confs; Pres. Dr ATHENA COUSTENIS (France); Vice-Pres. Prof. JOHN TURNER (UK); Vice-Pres. Prof. JOYCE PENNER (USA); Sec.-Gen. Dr HANS VOLKERT (Germany); publ. *IAMAP Assembly Proceedings* (every 2 years).

International Association of Sedimentologists: c/o Marc De Batist, Dept of Geology and Soil Science, Ghent Univ., Krijgslaan 281/S8, 9000 Ghent, Belgium; e-mail marc.debatist@ugent.be; internet www.sedimentologists.org; f. 1952; promotes study of Sedimentology by encouraging interchange of research, promoting integration with other disciplines and publs, discussion and comparison of research results; 2,000 mems; Pres. POPPE DE BOER (Netherlands); Gen. Sec. VINCENZO PASCUCCI (Italy); Treas. MARC DE BATIST (Belgium); publ. *Sedimentology* (6 a year).

International Association of Volcanology and Chemistry of the Earth's Interior (IAVCEI)/Association Internationale de Volcanologie et de Chimie de l'Intérieur de la Terre: c/o Joan Marti, Institute of Earth Sciences Jaume Almer, CSIC, Luis Sole Sabaris s/n, 08028, Barcelona, Spain; tel. 934095410; e-mail joan.marti@ictja.csic.es; internet www.iavcei.org; f. 1919 as Int. Asscn of Volcanology; studies scientific problems related to volcanoes and volcanic processes, and to the chemistry of the Earth's interior; promotes int. cooperation in these studies; holds scientific gen. assemblies; sponsors workshops; participates in IUGG gen. assemblies; 1,500 individual mems and nat. correspondents; Pres. Dr RAY CAS (Australia); Sec.-Gen. Dr JOAN MARTI (Spain); publ. *Catalogue of the Active Volcanoes of the World*.

International Association of Wood Anatomists/Association Internationale des Anatomistes du Bois: c/o Naturalis Biodiversity Center, POB 9517, 2300 RA Leiden, Netherlands; e-mail eevn@euronet.nl; internet www.iawa-website.org; f. 1931; facilitates collection, storage and exchange of research materials and information; encourages and assists study and teaching of wood anatomy and related fields; 600 mems in 60 countries; Exec. Sec. Dr FREDERIC LENS (Netherlands); publ. *IAWA Journal* (4 a year).

International Astronautical Federation (IAF)/Fédération Internationale d'Astronautique: 94 bis ave de Suffren, 75015 Paris, France; tel. 145674260; e-mail info@iafastro.org; internet www.iafastro.com; f. 1951; fosters devt of astronautics for peaceful purposes at nat. and int. level; created the Int. Academy of Astronautics (IAA), the Int. Institute of Space Law (IISL) (for information on these bodies, see elsewhere in this chapter) and cttees on activities and membership; organizes Allan D. Emil Award, finances, publs, liaison with int. orgs and developing nations, education, student activities, SYRE, Solar Sail, astrodynamics, Earth observations, satellite communications, natural disaster reduction, life sciences, microgravity science and processes, space exploration, space power, space propulsion, space transportation, space stations, space systems, materials and structures; annual student awards; 226 mems in 59 countries; Pres. KIYOSHI HIGUCHI (Japan); Hon. Sec. HANS HOFFMANN (Germany); Exec. Dir Dr CHRISTIAN FEICHTINGER; publ. *Proceedings* (of Annual Congresses).

International Atomic Energy Agency (IAEA): Vienna International Centre, POB 100, 1400 Vienna, Austria; tel. (1) 2600-0; e-mail official.mail@iaea.org; internet www.iaea.org; f. 1957; serves as global focal point for nuclear cooperation; assists its mem. states, in context of social and economic goals, in planning for and using nuclear science and technology for various peaceful purposes, incl. generation of electricity and facilitates transfer of such technology and knowledge in a sustainable manner to developing mem. states; develops nuclear safety standards and based on these standards promotes achievement and maintenance of high levels of safety in applications of nuclear energy and protection of human health and environment against ionizing radiation; verifies through its inspection system that states comply with their commitments, under Non-Proliferation Treaty and other non-proliferation agreements, to use nuclear material and facilities only for peaceful purposes; 158 mem. states; library of 55,000 vols, 50,000 technical reports, 32,000 electronic resources, 990 audiovisual items, 1,350 journals, 1m. IAEA, UN and Specialised Agencies documents; Dir-Gen. YUKIYA AMANO (Japan); publs *Atomic Energy Review (AER)* (4 a year), *IAEA Bulletin* (2 a year, printed and online), *INIS Atomindex* (24 a year), *INIS Database* (online), *Meetings on Atomic Energy* (4 a year, online, www.iaea.org/cgi-bin/maeps.page.pl/tableofcontents.htm), *Nuclear Fusion* (12 a year), *Nuclear Safety Review* (1 a year), *Nuclear Technology Review* (every 2 years).

International Biometric Society (IBS)/Société Internationale de Biométrie: 1444 I St, NW, Suite 700, Washington, DC 20005, USA; tel. (202) 712-9049; e-mail ibs@tibs.org; internet www.biometricsociety.org; f. 1947; promotes devt and application of statistical and mathematical theory and methods in the biosciences; 19 regional orgs and 19 nat. groups; affiliated to the Int. Statistical Institute and the World Health Organization, constitutes the section of Biometry of the Int. Union of Biological Sciences; sponsors int. conf. every 2 years; 6,000 mems in 80 countries; Pres. CLARICE DEMÉTRIO (Brazil); Sec. and Treas. LINDA YOUNG (USA); Exec. Dir DEE ANN WALKER (USA); publs *Biometrics* (4 a year), *Journal of Agricultural, Biological and Environmental Statistics (JABES)* (4 a year, jtly with American Statistical Asscn).

International Bureau of Weights and Measures/Bureau International des

Poids et Pesures: Pavillon de Breteuil, 92312 Sèvres Cedex, France; tel. 145077070; e-mail fjoly@bipm.org; internet www.bipm.org; f. 1875; determination of nat. standards; precision measurements in physics; establishment of the int. atomic time scale; preserves standards of the Int. System of Units (SI) and worldwide unification of the units of measurement; 54 mem. states; Pres. Dr B. INGLIS (Australia); Sec. Dr R. KAARLS (Netherlands); Dir Prof. Dr MICHAEL KÜHNE; publs *Comptes Rendus des Conférences Générales* (every 4 years), *Metrologia*, *Procès-verbaux* (1 a year), *Sessions des dix Comités consultatifs auprès du Comité International* (irregular).

International Centre of Insect Physiology and Ecology: POB 30772-00100, Nairobi, Kenya; tel. (20) 8632000; e-mail icipe@icipe.org; internet www.icipe.org; f. 1970; aims to serve as the regional focus for bioscience and technology information and knowledge; develops, through research, plant-borne, human and animal disease management and control strategies; library of 8,000 vols, 3,500 vols bound periodicals, 200 periodicals; Chair. Prof. Dr JOHN A. PICKETT (UK); Dir-Gen. and CEO Dr SEGENET KELEMU (Ethiopia); publ. *International Journal of Tropical Insect Science* (4 a year).

International Commission for Optics (ICO)/Commission Internationale d'Optique: c/o Angela M. Guzman, CREOL, College of Optics and Photonics, Univ. of Central Florida, POB 162700, 4000 Central Florida Blvd, Orlando, FL 32816-2700, USA; tel. (561) 948-4204; e-mail angela.guzman@creol.ucf.edu; internet e-ico.org; f. 1947; contributes on int. basis to the progress of theoretical and instrumental optics and its application, through confs, colloquia, summer schools; 53 mem. territories (incl. 13 assoc. mems), 6 int. mem. orgs; Pres. Prof. DUNCAN T. MOORE (USA); Sec. Prof. ANGELA M. GUZMAN (USA); publs *International Trends in Optics*, *Proceedings of ETOP* (online, spie.org/x95260.xml).

International Commission for the Scientific Exploration of the Mediterranean Sea/Commission Internationale pour l'Exploration Scientifique de la Mer Méditerranée (CIESM): 16 blvd de Suisse, 98000 Monaco, Monaco; tel. 93303879; e-mail ciesm@ciesm.org; internet www.ciesm.org; f. 1919; organizes research workshops, biodiversity atlases, high-resolution digital maps of the sea bottom, congresses; 6 cttees in fields of marine geosciences, physics and climate of the ocean, marine biogeochemistry, marine microbiology and biotechnology, living resources and marine ecosystems, coastal systems and marine policy; 23 mem. states; Pres. HSH The Prince ALBERT II OF MONACO; Dir-Gen. Prof. Dr FRÉDÉRIC BRIAND; publ. *Congress Proceedings* (every 3 years).

International Commission on Zoological Nomenclature/Commission Internationale de Nomenclature Zoologique: c/o Natural History Museum, Cromwell Rd, London, SW7 5BD, UK; tel. (20) 7942-5653; e-mail iczn-em@nhm.ac.uk; internet iczn.org; f. 1895; fmrly a standing organ of the Int. Zoological Congresses, now reports to the Gen. Assembly of IUBS; the Commission has judicial powers to determine all matters relating to the interpretation of the *International Code of Zoological Nomenclature* and also plenary powers to suspend the operation of the *Code* where strict application would lead to confusion and instability of nomenclature; responsible also for maintaining and developing the *Official Lists of Names in Zoology* and the *Official Indexes of Rejected and Invalid Names in Zoology*; Pres. Dr JAN VAN TOL (Netherlands); Exec. Sec. Dr ELLINOR MICHEL (UK); publ. *Bulletin of Zoological Nomenclature* (1 a year).

International Confederation for Thermal Analysis and Calorimetry (ICTAC): c/o Prof. Ranjit K. Verma, Univ. Dept of Chemistry, Magadh Univ., Bodh Gaya, Bihar 824234, India; tel. (631) 2222469; e-mail profrkverma@gmail.com; internet www.ictac.org; f. 1968 as Int. Confederation for Thermal Analysis, present name 1992; promotes int. understanding and cooperation in thermal analysis and calorimetry through the organization of int. congresses and work of its scientific cttees; supports nat. and regional seminars and symposia; organizes quadrennial int. conf.; 500 individual mems, 24 affiliated nat. or regional socs; Pres. Prof. Dr ANDRZEJ MALECKI (Poland); Sec. Prof. Dr RANJIT K. VERMA (India); publ. *ICTAC NEWS* (2 a year).

International Council for the Exploration of the Sea (ICES)/Conseil International pour l'Exploration de la Mer: H. C. Andersens Blvd 44–46, 1553 Copenhagen V, Denmark; tel. 33-38-67-00; e-mail info@ices.dk; internet www.ices.dk; f. 1902; provides scientific advice on the marine ecosystem to govts and int. regulatory bodies that manage the N Atlantic Ocean and adjacent seas; maintains Data Centre on marine fisheries, oceanography and the marine environment; 20 mem. countries; Pres. Dr PAUL CONNOLLY (Ireland); Gen. Sec. ANNE CHRISTINE BRUSENDORFF; publs *ICES Advice*, *ICES Cooperative Research Reports*, *ICES Fisheries Statistics*, *ICES Identification Leaflets for Diseases and Parasites of Fish and Shellfish*, *ICES Identification Leaflets for Plankton*, *ICES Insight*, *ICES Journal of Marine Science*, *ICES Marine Science Symposia*, *ICES Techniques in Marine Environmental Sciences*.

International Earth Rotation and Reference Systems Service (IERS): Bundesamt für Kartographie und Geodäsie, Referat G1, Richard-Strauss-Allee 11, 60598 Frankfurt am Main, Germany; tel. (69) 6333273; e-mail central_bureau@iers.org; internet www.iers.org; f. 1988 as Int. Earth Rotation Service, current name adopted 2003; organized jtly by IAU and IUGG; responsible for defining and maintaining a conventional terrestrial reference system based on observing stations using high-precision techniques of space geodesy; defines and maintains conventional celestial reference system based on extragalactic radio sources and relates it to other celestial reference systems; determines earth orientation parameters connecting these systems; organizes operational activities for observation and data analysis; collects and archives appropriate data and results and disseminates the results; Dir of Central Bureau Dr DANIELA THALLER; Chair. of Directing Board Dr BRIAN LUZUM; publ. *IERS Technical Notes*.

International Federation for Cell Biology/Fédération Internationale de Biologie Cellulaire: c/o Hernandes F. Carvalho, Dept of Cell Biology, Institute of Biology, UNICAMP, Campinas SP, 13083-863, Brazil; e-mail hern@unicamp.br; internet www.ifcbiol.org; f. 1972; sponsors an int. congress every 2 years, workshops and symposia; 5 regional orgs; 34 mems (incl. 15 full mems and 19 assoc. mems), 3 affiliated socs; Pres. Dr NOBUTAKA HIROKAWA (Japan); Sec.-Gen. HERNANDES F. CARVALHO (Brazil); publ. *Cell Biology International* (online).

International Federation of Societies for Microscopy/Fédération Internationale des Sociétés de Microscopie: c/o Prof. Brendan Griffin, Centre for Microscopy, Characterisation and Analysis (M010), Univ. of Western Australia, First Fl., Physics Bldg, 35 Stirling Highway, Crawley WA 6009, Australia; tel. (8) 6488-2739; e-mail brendan.griffin@uwa.edu.au; internet www.ifsm.info; f. 1955; contributes to advancement of microscopy in all its aspects; sponsors meetings, int. confs; supports students to attend meetings of regional mems; awards John M. Cowley Medal and Wolf Prize for physics; 46 mems (incl. 7 assoc. mems and 3 regional mems); Pres. Prof. C. BARRY CARTER (USA); Gen. Sec. Prof. BRENDAN GRIFFIN (Australia).

International Food Information Service (IFIS): Lane End House, Shinfield Rd, Shinfield, Reading, RG2 9BB, UK; tel. (118) 9883895; e-mail ifis@ifis.org; internet www.ifis.org; f. 1968; governed by CAB International (UK), Institute of Food Technologists (USA), the Centrum voor Landbouwpublikaties en Landbouwdocumentatie (Netherlands) and the Bundesministerium für Landwirtschaft Ernährung und Forsten (represented by Deutsche Landwirtschafts-Gesellschaft eV) in Germany; promotes education and research in food science and technology; evaluates, collates, manages and distributes food- and drink-related information to industry professionals around the world, incl. scientists, technologists and nutritionists; Chair. BARBARA BYRD-KEENAN; Man. Dir RICHARD HOLLINGSWORTH; publ. *Food Science and Technology Abstracts* (12 a year, in print, online, CD-ROM).

International Foundation of the High-Altitude Research Stations, Jungfraujoch and Gornergrat/Fondation Internationale des Stations Scientifiques du Jungfraujoch et du Gornergrat: Sidlerstr. 5, 3012 Bern, Switzerland; tel. 316314052; e-mail claudine.frieden@space.unibe.ch; internet www.ifjungo.ch; f. 1930; provides infrastructure and support for scientific research of int. significance carried out at an altitude of 3,000–3,500 m above sea level or for which a high alpine climate and environment are necessary; 2 astronomical observatories: Gornergrat S and Gornergrat N; Pres. Prof. Dr ERWIN O. FLÜCKIGER; Dir Prof. Dr MARKUS LEUENBERGER (Switzerland).

International Genetics Federation: c/o Prof. Charles H. Langley, Dept of Evolution and Ecology, Univ. of California-Davis, 1 Shield Ave, Davis, CA 95616-8554, USA; tel. (530) 752-4085; e-mail info@meiosis.org; internet www.meiosis.org; f. 1968; encourages understanding and cooperation among geneticists worldwide; plans and supports int. and regional congresses of genetics; encourages and supports specialized symposia, confs and workshops in genetics; disseminates scientific information; promotes teaching of genetics; supports programs for the preservation of genetic stocks and resources; 37 mem. countries; Pres. Prof. ALFRED NORDHEIM (Germany); Sec.-Gen. Prof. CHARLES H. LANGLEY (USA).

International Glaciological Society: Scott Polar Research Institute, Lensfield Rd, Cambridge, CB2 1ER, UK; tel. (1223) 355974; e-mail igsoc@igsoc.org; internet www.igsoc.org; f. 1936; encourages interest in and research into scientific and technical problems of snow and ice in all countries; facilitates dissemination of ideas and information; sponsors int. symposia, lectures and field meetings; awards Seligman Crystal and the Richardson Medal; 950 mems; Pres. DOUGLAS R. MACAYEAL; Sec.-Gen. MAGNÚS MÁR MAGNÚSSON; publs *Annals of Glaciology* (4 a year, online), *Journal of Glaciology* (6 a year, online).

International Hydrographic Organization (IHO)/Organisation Hydrographique Internationale: BP 445, 4B quai Antoine 1er, Monte Carlo, 98011 MonacoCedex, Monaco; tel. 93108100; e-mail info@iho.int; internet www.iho.int; f. 1921 as Int. Hydrographic Bureau, present name and status 1970; coordinates the activities of the nat. hydrographic offices of mem. states in order to render maritime navigation easier and safer; obtains uniformity in nautical charts and documents; encourages the adoption of the best methods of conducting hydrographic surveys and improvement in the theory and practice of hydrography; encourages surveying in those areas where accurate charts are lacking; encourages coordination of hydrographic surveys with relevant oceanographic activities and provides for cooperation between the IHO and int. orgs in the fields of maritime safety and oceanography; extends and facilitates the application of oceanographic knowledge for the benefit of navigators; 80 mem. states; library of 750 vols, 100 periodicals, 26,000 charts published by mem. states; Pres. ROBERT WARD (Australia); Dir GILLES BESSERO (France); Dir MUSTAFA IPTES (Turkey).

International Institute for Applied Systems Analysis (IIASA): Schlossplatz 1, 2361 Laxenburg, Austria; tel. (2236) 8070; e-mail inf@iiasa.ac.at; internet www.iiasa.ac.at; f. 1972; non-governmental research org.; research into issues of global environmental, economic, technological and social change in the 21st century; 19 mem. orgs; Chair. Prof. Dr PETER LEMKE (Germany); Dir and CEO Prof. Dr PAVEL KABAT; publ. *Options* (2 a year).

International Institute of Seismology and Earthquake Engineering: Building Research Institute, 1 Tatehara, Tsukuba, Ibaraki 305-0802, Japan; tel. (298) 79-0680; e-mail iisee@kenken.go.jp; internet iisee.kenken.go.jp; f. 1962; attached to Building Research Institute, Japan; carries out training and research works on seismology and earthquake engineering for the purpose of fostering these research activities in the developing countries; undertakes survey, research, guidance and analysis of information on earthquakes and their related matters; organizes int. symposium; 58 mem. countries; Dir Dr SHOICHI ANDO; publs *Bulletin of IISEE* (1 a year), *Individual Studies by Participants at the IISEE* (1 a year), *Year Book*.

International Masonry Society: c/o Dr K. Fisher, Shermanbury, 6 Church Rd, Whyteleafe, CR3 0AR, UK; tel. (20) 8660-3633; e-mail secretary@masonry.org.uk; internet www.masonry.org.uk; f. 1986 as British Masonry Soc., current name and status 2008; promotes discussion and advancement of the science and practice of masonry as allied to its constituent materials and to all aspects of the design and use of masonry and the construction process; disseminates research and current thinking; organizes meetings, seminars and symposia; 300 mems in 31 countries; Sec. Dr K. FISHER; publs *Masonry International* (3 a year), *Proceedings of Conferences*.

International Mineralogical Association (IMA): c/o Hon. Prof. Dr Richard Goed, Dept für Lithosphärenforschung, Univ. of Vienna, Althanstr. 14, 1090 Vienna, Austria; tel. (1) 427753362; e-mail richard.goed@univie.ac.at; internet www.ima-mineralogy.org; f. 1958; organizes meetings and field excursions; maintains 8 comms and 5 working groups; Comm. on New Minerals, Nomenclature and Classification regularly reports on the acceptance of new minerals and on mineral classification; 38 mem. mineralogical socs or groups in 38 countries; Pres. Prof. EKKEHART TILMANNS (Austria); Sec. Hon. Prof. Dr RICHARD GOED (Austria); Treas. Prof. ROBERT T. DOWNS (USA); publ. *World Directories* (mineralogists; mineral collns).

International Organization of Legal Metrology/Organisation Internationale de Métrologie Légale: 11 rue Turgot, 75009 Paris, France; tel. 148781282; e-mail stephen.patoray@oiml.org; internet www.oiml.org; f. 1955; documentation and information centre on methods of verifying and checking legal measurements; studies ways of harmonization; determines general principles of legal metrology; develops model regulations, Int. Recommendations to help mems with an internationally agreed-upon basis for the establishment of nat. legislation on various categories of measuring instruments; organizes technical seminars; 57 mem. states, 64 corresponding mems; Pres. P. MASON (acting); Dir STEPHEN PATORAY; publs *Bulletin* (4 a year), *International Recommendations and Documents*.

International Ornithologists' Union: c/o Prof. Dr Dominique G. Homberger, Dept of Biological Sciences, 202 Life Sciences Bldg, Louisiana State Univ., Baton Rouge, LA 70803-1715, USA; tel. (225) 578-1747; e-mail secretary@int-ornith-union.org; internet int-ornith-union.org; f. 1884; supports, promotes and advances avian biology; disseminates ornithological knowledge; interacts with other scientific orgs, foundations and instns; stimulates and strengthens locally based research that incl. the participation of amateur ornithologists; fosters knowledge transfer between basic research and applied sciences; organizes int. congress every 4 years; 260 mems; Pres. FRANZ BAIRLEIN (Germany); Sec. Prof. Dr DOMINIQUE G. HOMBERGER (USA); publ. *IOC Proceedings*.

International Palaeontological Association: Palaeontological Institute, 1475 Jayhawk Blvd., Room 121, Lindley Hall, Univ. of Kansas, Lawrence, KS 66045, USA; tel. (785) 864-3338; e-mail roger.thomas@fandm.edu; internet ipa.geo.ku.edu; f. 1933; promotes and coordinates int. cooperation in palaeontology, incl. palaeobotany and palaeozoology of all geological periods; encourages integration and synthesis of all palaeontological knowledge; organizes int. congress and meetings; publishes world directory of palaeontologists; affiliated to the Int. Union of Geological Sciences and the Int. Union of Biological Sciences; Pres. MICHAEL BENTON (UK); Sec.-Gen. ROGER THOMAS (USA); publs *Directory of Palaeontologists of the World*, *IPA Fossil Collections of the World*, *Lethaia*.

International Permafrost Association: c/o Dr Hugues Lantuit, Alfred Wegener Institute for Polar and Marine Research, Telefrafenberg A43, 14473 Potsdam, Germany; tel. (331) 2882162; e-mail contact@ipa-permafrost.org; internet ipa.arcticportal.org; f. 1983; promotes cooperation among people, nat. and int. orgs engaged in scientific investigation and engineering work on permafrost; outreach activities incl. coordinating int. networks e.g. Global Terrestrial Network for Permafrost (GTN-P) and Int. Network of Permafrost Observatories (INPO) and Permafrost Young Researchers Network; working groups; organizes int. confs with field excursions; 26 mem. countries; Pres. Prof. ANTONI G. LEWKOWICZ (Canada); Vice-Pres. Prof. HANNE H. CHRISTIANSEN (Norway); Vice-Pres. Prof. VLADIMIR E. ROMANOVSKY (USA); publs *Frozen Ground* (Bulletin, 1 a year), *Permafrost and Periglacial Processes* (2 a year), *Proceedings of the International Conferences on Permafrost*.

International Society for Human and Animal Mycology (ISHAM)/Société Internationale de Mycologie Humaine et Animale: c/o Dr J. Peter Donnelly, Dept of Haematology, Radboud Univ. Nijmegen Medical Centre and Nijmegen Institute for Infection, Inflammation and Immunity, Geert Grooteplein Zuid 8, 6525 GA Nijmegen, Netherlands; tel. (24) 3619987; internet www.isham.org; f. 1954; encourages practice and study of all aspects of medical and veterinary mycology; facilitates exchange of ideas and information and provides assistance pertaining to medical and veterinary mycology on int. level; organizes int. congress every 3 years; 1,000 mems, 23 affiliated asscns; Pres. Prof. DAVID ELLIS (Australia); Gen. Sec. Dr J. PETER DONNELLY (Netherlands); publ. *Medical Mycology* (1 a year, in 6 parts).

International Society for Tropical Ecology: c/o Dept of Botany, Banaras Hindu Univ., Varanasi, Uttar Pradesh 221005, India; tel. (542) 2368399; e-mail iste@tropecol.com; internet www.tropecol.com; f. 1960; promotes and develops the science of ecology in the tropics; holds meetings, excursions, symposia and seminars at nat. and int. level; organizes training courses in ecology; 500 mems; Pres. Dr SKIP J. VAN BLOEM (USA); Sec. Prof. J. S. SINGH (India); publ. *Tropical Ecology* (2 a year, in English, French, Spanish and Portuguese, online, www.tropecol.com/journal/online).

International Society of Biometeorology: c/o Dr Jonathan M. Hanes, Dept of Geography, Bolton 410, POB 413, Univ. of Wisconsin-Milwaukee, Milwaukee, WI 53201-0413, USA; tel. (414) 229-6611; e-mail jmhanes@uwm.edu; internet www.biometeorology.org; f. 1956; aims to unite biometeorologists working in fields of agricultural, botanical, cosmic, entomological, forestry, human, veterinary, zoological and other brs of biometeorology; organizes int. congress; 243 individual mems in 44 countries, 7 mem. orgs; Pres. GLENN MCGREGOR (New Zealand); Sec. Dr JONATHAN HANES (USA); publs *International Journal of Biometeorology* (6 a year), *Progress in Biometeorology*.

International Society of Developmental Biologists: c/o Prof. Marianne Bronner-Fraser, Beckman Institute 234, M/C 139–74, California Institute of Technology, Pasadena, CA 91125, USA; tel. (626) 395-3355; e-mail mbronner@caltech.edu; internet www.developmental-biology.org; f. 1911 as Int. Institute of Embryology, present name 1968; promotes study of developmental biology; promotes int. cooperation among researchers in this field; Developmental Biology Section of the Int. Union of Biological Sciences (*q.v.*); organizes scientific meetings, workshops and congress every 4 years; awards Ross Harrison Prize to scientists; 900 individual mems and 7 corporate mems; Pres. CLAUDIO STERN (UK); Sec. Prof. MARIANNE BRONNER-FRASER (USA); publs *Gene Expression Patterns* (6 a year), *Mechanisms of Development* (12 a year).

International Society of Electrochemistry: rue de Sebeillon 9B, 1004 Lausanne, Switzerland; tel. 216483974; e-mail info@ise-online.org; internet www.ise-online.org; f. 1949; serves worldwide electrochemical community and that of related disciplines through advancement of electrochemical science and technology; disseminates scientific and technological knowledge; promotes int. cooperation; 2,700 mems in 70 countries; Pres. Prof. Dr M. ORAZEM (USA); Sec.-Gen. M. RUEDA (Spain); publ. *Electrochimica Acta*.

International Society of Exposure Science: c/o Infinity Conf. Group Inc., 1035 Sterling Rd, Suite 202, Herndon, VA 20170, USA; tel. (703) 925-9455; e-mail ises@isesweb.org; internet www.isesweb.org; f. 1989 as Int. Soc. of Exposure Analysis; holds annual confs; fosters and advances science of exposure analysis related to environmental contamination in human population and ecosystems; promotes communication among exposure analysts, epidemiologists, toxicologists, and other scientists; recommends approaches to substantive or methodological concerns; 500 mems; Pres. Dr RICHARD FENSKE; Sec. DEBRA KADEN; publ. *Journal of Exposure Science and Environmental Epidemiology* (6 a year).

International Society of Limnology (SIL)/Association Internationale de Limnologie Théorique et Appliquée: c/o Prof. Dr Morten Søndergaard, Freshwater Biological Laboratory, Univ. of Copenhagen. 51 Helsingørsgade, 3400 Hillerød, Denmark; e-mail msondergaard@bi.ku.dk; internet www.limnology.org; f. 1922; promotes study and understanding of all aspects of limnology; organizes congress every 3 years to promote scientific intercourse among those pursuing fundamental research and those concerned with practical fishery, pollution, water-supply problems; sponsors int. symposia and workshops on research subjects of theoretical and applied limnology; 3,000 mems; Pres. Prof. Dr BRIAN MOSS (UK); Gen. Sec. and Treas. Prof. Dr MORTEN SØNDERGAARD (Denmark); publ. *Inland Waters* (4 a year, print and online).

International Statistical Institute/Institut International de Statistique: POB 24070, 2490 AB The Hague, Netherlands; Henri Faasdreef 312, 2492 JP The Hague-Leidschenveen, Netherlands; tel. (70) 3375737; e-mail isi@cbs.nl; internet isi.cbs.nl; f. 1885; promotes and disseminates research and best practice in statistical sciences and education; works to broaden the range of areas of application; promotes public awareness of good statistical practice and its value to the community; enhances support for statistical community in developing countries; Pres. VIJAY NAIR (USA); Sec., Treas. and Dir Permanent Office ADA VAN KRIMPEN; publs *International Statistical Review / Book Reviews* (3 a year), *Stat* (online).

International Union for the Study of Social Insects/Union Internationale pour l'Étude des Insectes Sociaux: c/o Joan M. Herbers, EEOB Dept, 381 W 12th, Ohio State Univ., Columbus OH 43210, USA; e-mail herbers.4@osu.edu; internet www.iussi.org; f. 1951; organizes congress and symposium; comprises 7 regional and nat. sections; 500 mems from 24 countries; Pres. BEN OLDROYD; Sec.-Gen. JOAN HERBERS; publs *Congress Proceedings*, *Insectes sociaux* (4 a year).

International Union of Speleology (UIS)/Union Internationale de Spéléologie: c/o Institute of Karst Research, Titov trg 2, Postojna, Slovenia; e-mail secretary@uis-speleo.org; internet www.uis-speleo.org; f. 1965; encourages cooperation between speleologists of all nations and coordination of their activities internationally; 60 mem. countries; Pres. ANDREW JAMES EAVIS (UK); Gen. Sec. Dr FADI NADER (Lebanon); publs *Bulletin* (1 or 2 a year), *Bulletin Bibliographique Spéléologique / Speleological Abstracts* (1 a year, online, www.ssslib.ch/bbs), *International Journal of Speleology* (1 a year).

Islamic World Academy of Sciences (IAS)/l'Académie des Sciences du Monde Islamique: POB 830036, Amman 11183, Jordan; 17th Djibouti St, Sixth Circle, Amman, Jordan; tel. (6) 5522104; e-mail ias@go.com.jo; internet www.iasworld.org; f. 1986, current name adopted 2005; promotes modern science, technology and devt in the Islamic and developing worlds; organizes confs and seminars; supervises training workshops; encourages research; acts as the scientific adviser to the OIC (Org. of the Islamic Conf.) and developing countries; acts as an academic repository of the history of science in the context of the Islamic civilization; 108 fellows and 13 hon. fellows from 57 mem. countries; Pres. Prof. Dr ABDEL-SALAM MAJALI (Jordan); Sec.-Gen. Prof. Dr MOHAMED HAG ALI HASSAN (Sudan); Dir-Gen. Dr MONEEF R. ZOU'BI; publ. *Medical Journal* (4 a year).

IUCN, International Union for Conservation of Nature/UICN, l'Union Internationale pour la Conservation de la Nature/La UICN, la Unión Internacional para la Conservacion de la Naturaleza: Rue Mauverney 28, 1196 Gland, Switzerland; tel. 229990000; e-mail mail@iucn.org; internet www.iucn.org; f. 1948; offices in 45 countries; influences int. environmental conventions, policies and laws through govt and NGO orgs; runs conservation projects worldwide for sustainable management of biodiversity and natural resource; sets definitive int. standards in the fields of biodiversity; 1,200 mem. orgs; Pres. XINSHENG ZHANG (China); Dir-Gen. JULIA MARTON-LEFÈVRE (Switzerland); publs *Best Policy Guidelines*, *IUCN's Science Bulletin*, *Red Lists: Environmental Policy and Law Papers*, *World Conservation* (in English, French and Spanish).

Nordita (Nordic Institute for Theoretical Physics)/Nordiska Institutet för Teoretisk Fysik/Nordisk Institut for Teoretisk Fysik/Nordisk Institutt for Teoretisk Fysikk/Norræna Stofnunin í Kennilegri Eðlisfræði/Teoreettisen Fysiikan Pohjoismainen Laitos: Roslagstullsbacken 23, 106 91 Stockholm, Sweden; tel. (8) 5537-8444; e-mail info@nordita.org; internet www.nordita.org; f. 1957 as the Nordic Institute for Theoretical Atomic Physics in Copenhagen, Denmark, under the Nordic Council of Ministers, moved to Stockholm, Sweden, in 2007; intergovernmental research institute of Denmark, Finland, Iceland, Norway and Sweden; run jtly by the Royal Institute of Technology (KTH) and Stockholm Univ.; research in astrophysics, biophysics, condensed matter physics, cosmology, gravitational physics, high energy physics, statistical physics; Dir Prof. LÁRUS THORLACIUS.

OECD Nuclear Energy Agency (NEA)/Agence de l'OCDE pour l'Energie Nucléaire: Le Seine St-Germain, 12 blvd des Îles, 92130 Issy-les-Moulineaux, France; tel. 145241015; e-mail nea@oecd-nea.org; internet www.oecd-nea.org; f. 1958 as European Nuclear Energy Agency (ENEA), present name 1972; assists mem. countries to maintain and further develop, through int. cooperation, the scientific, technological and legal bases required for a safe, environmentally friendly and economical use of nuclear energy for peaceful purposes, as input to govt decisions on nuclear energy policy and to broader OECD policy analyses in areas such as energy and sustainable devt; source of information, data and analyses, drawing on int. networks of technical experts; 30 mem. countries; Dir-Gen. LUIS ECHÁVARRI (Spain); publs *NEA News* (2 a year), *Nuclear Law Bulletin* (2 a year).

Pacific Science Association/Association Scientifique du Pacifique: Bishop Museum, 1525 Bernice St, Honolulu, HI 96817, USA; tel. (808) 848-4124; e-mail psa@pacificscience.org; internet www.pacificscience.org; f. 1920; facilitates interdisciplinary and int. research and collaboration in the Asia-Pacific region; facilitates science that focuses on key issues and problems in the region; sponsors congresses and inter-congresses; 18 nat. mems; Pres. Dr NANCY D. LEWIS (USA); Sec.-Gen. and Treas. Dr MAKOTO TSUCHIYA (Japan); publ. *Pacific Science* (4 a year, online, www.uhpress.hawaii.edu/t-pacific-science.aspx).

Pan-American Institute of Geography and History/Instituto Panamericano de Geografía e Historia: Apdo 18879, 11870 México DF, Mexico; c/o Sec.-Gen. Ex-Arzobispado 29, Col. Observatorio, 11860 México, DF, Mexico; tel. (55) 52775888; e-mail secretariageneral@ipgh.org; internet www.ipgh.org; f. 1928; encourages, coordinates and promotes study of cartography, geophysics, geography, history, anthropology, archaeology and other related scientific studies; conducts studies, work and training in these disciplines; 21 mem. countries, 3 permanent observer countries; library of 229,062 vols; Pres. Prof. HÉCTOR O. J. PENA (Argentina); Sec.-Gen. SANTIAGO BORRERO MUTIS (Colombia); publs *Boletín de Antropología Americana* (1 a year), *Revista Cartográfica* (1 a year), *Revista de Arqueología Americana* (1 a year), *Revista de Historia de América* (2 a year), *Revista Geofísica*, *Revista Geográfica* (2 a year).

Wetlands International: POB 471, 6700 AL Wageningen, Netherlands; Horapark 9, Second Fl., 6700 LZ Ede, Netherlands; tel. (318) 660910; e-mail post@wetlands.org; internet www.wetlands.org; f. 1954; sustains and restores wetlands, their resources and biodiversity through worldwide research, information exchange and conservation activities; 18 offices around the world; 58 mem. countries; CEO JANE MADGWICK (Australia).

World Academy of Art and Science: 4225 Solano Ave, Suite 631, Napa CA, 94558, USA; e-mail president@worldacademy.org; internet www.worldacademy.org; f. 1960; forum for reflective scientists, artists and scholars to discuss the social consequences and policy implications of knowledge; 650 fellows from 86 countries; Pres. IVO SLAUS (Croatia); Sec.-Gen. ZBIGNIEW BOCHNIARZ (USA); Chair. of the Board of Trustees and CEO GARRY JACOBS; publs *CADMUS* (online, www.cadmusjournal.org), *ERUDITIO* (online, www.eruditio.worldacademy.org).

World Academy of Sciences (TWAS): ICTP Campus, Via Beirut 6, 34151 Trieste TS, Italy; ICTP Enrico Fermi Bldg, First Fl., Via Beirut 6, 34151 Trieste TS, Italy; tel. 402240327; e-mail edoffice@twas.org; internet twas.ictp.it; f. 1983, fmrly Third World Acad. of Sciences, present name 2012; recognizes, supports and promotes excellence in scientific research in the developing world; promotes worldwide cooperation in science, technology and innovation; encourages scientific research and sharing of experiences in solving major problems facing developing countries; awards prizes, research grants, fellowships and associateships to scientists working and living in developing countries; regional offices in Rio de Janeiro, Brazil, Beijing, China, Alexandria, Egypt, Bangalore, India, Nairobi, Kenya; 1,073 mems; Pres. CHUNLI BAI (Brazil); Sec.-Gen. A.K. SOOD (India); Exec. Dir ROMAIN MURENZI (Italy); publs *Excellence in Science: Profiles of Research Institutions in Developing Countries*, *TWAS Newsletter* (4 a year).

World Meteorological Organization/Organisation Météorologique Mondiale:

7 bis, ave de la Paix, CP 2300, 1211 Geneva 2, Switzerland; tel. 227308111; e-mail wmo@wmo.int; internet www.wmo.int; f. 1950; worldwide cooperation in making and standardizing meteorological, climatological, hydrological and related geophysical observations and their exchange and publication; assists in training, research and technology transfer; furthers the application of meteorology to aviation, shipping, water problems, agriculture, environmental problems (incl. climate and climate change) and to sustainable devt; 191 mem. states and territories; Pres. DAVID GRIMES (Canada); Sec.-Gen. MICHEL JARRAUD (France); publ. *WMO Bulletin* (2 a year, online, www.wmo.int/pages/publications/bulletin_en)

World Organisation of Systems and Cybernetics/Organisation Mondiale pour la Systémique et la Cybernétique: c/o Prof. Raul Espejo, Flat 3, North Pl., 30 Nettleham Rd, Lincoln LN2 1RE, UK; tel. (1522) 589252; e-mail r.espejo@syncho.org; internet www.wosc.co; f. 1969; acts as focal point for all socs concerned with cybernetics, systems and allied subjects; aims for the recognition of cybernetics as a bona fide science; maintains liaison with other int. bodies; holds int. congresses every 3 years; awards Norbert Wiener Memorial Gold Medal; 41 hon. fellows, nat. orgs in more than 20 countries; Pres. Prof. ROBERT VALLÉE; Dir-Gen. Prof RAUL ESPEJO; publ. *Kybernetes* (10 a year, online).

PART THREE
Afghanistan–Myanmar

AFGHANISTAN

The Higher Education System

The higher education system in Afghanistan, which is overseen by the Ministry of Higher Education, was established with the foundation of Kabul University in 1932. However, during more than 20 years of civil war from 1979 higher education was disrupted by the departure of many teaching staff from Afghanistan and the destruction of educational buildings and infrastructure. In 1991 there were six institutions of higher education with a total enrolment of 17,000 students. In September 1996 the Islamist Taliban movement gained control of Kabul and issued decrees enforcing their fundamentalist interpretation of Islam, which included banning women from receiving education. In late 2001 a US-led military coalition ousted the Taliban regime following the 11 September terrorist attacks on the USA, which were blamed on the al-Qa'ida organization of Osama bin Laden, a Saudi dissident based in Afghanistan. In March 2002 Kabul University (which has 14 faculties) was re-opened for men and women. In 2009 there were 22 universities in operation with some 62,000 students enrolled at the higher education level. In 2011, according to the Afghan Ministry of Higher Education, 17 institutes of higher education were operating under its supervision; in 2012 the UK National Recognition Information Centre (NARIC) gave the number as 19. Over the last 10 years or so the Afghan Government has received substantial amounts of international aid (in the form of finance, books, computers, technical equipment, etc.) to rehabilitate the country's education sector. The American University of Afghanistan (the country's first private, not-for-profit institution of higher education) was inaugurated in Kabul in 2006 and a number of other universities—including those in Qandahar, Khost, Herat, Nangarhar and Balkh—have been renovated or rebuilt. The American University of Afghanistan, which is funded by the US Agency for International Development (USAID) and had 1,700 full- and part-time students enrolled in 2012, offers three undergraduate degrees—in business administration, information technology and computer science, and political science and public administration—and a postgraduate Masters course in Business Administration which was scheduled to begin in 2014. The limited funding within the education sector is exacerbated by the government policy that forbids educational institutions from charging tuition fees. In 2009 the Afghan Government launched a US $560m. five-year national higher education plan to redirect universities towards producing graduates relevant to the employment market (particularly within sectors such as engineering, accountancy, agriculture and business) as well as providing scientific solutions for key economic and social problems.

In order to be admitted to higher education students must complete the Baccalauria and pass an entrance examination (Concours) . In 2004 the Ministry of Higher Education, in co-operation with UNESCO, put forward a plan for a four-tier structure of academic institutions: universities with degree-conferring rights at Bachelors, Masters and doctoral levels; technological and pedagogical institutes providing the same degrees as universities but within their particular field of specialization; colleges operating Bachelor degree-level programmes; and community colleges offering courses of up to two years leading to the award of a certificate or diploma. The reform is ongoing. There are also plans to implement a national qualifications framework (NQF) following the Bologna Process of a three-year Bachelor degree, a two-year Masters degree and a four-year Doctorate.

In 2006 the USAID-funded four-year Higher Education Project (HEP) was launched to rebuild and strengthen the 18 institutions offering teacher education programmes. By 2010 professional development centres had been established in 11 institutions and a Masters Degree in Education established at Kabul Educational University, which follows strict parity regulations. (In 2011 there were 11 female and 11 male graduates.) The Afghanistan Higher Education Portal (available in English, Dari and Pashto) was introduced in 2008 to provide education providers with an internet platform to access and share learning resources and to participate in an online network to support professional development. The portal included a digital library, a discussion board, a news page and web pages to support HEP activities. Over the course of two years, 80% of Afghanistan's various educators had registered to use the portal, the library had rapidly expanded and the discussion boards had become increasingly active. The issue of poor quality within the Afghan higher education sector can be illustrated by the fact that in 2011 it was estimated that only around 20% of university academics had a postgraduate degree and fewer than 5% held a Doctorate. In mid-2011 the Afghan Government allocated US $5m. to send exceptional students to other countries to continue their higher education in the fields of engineering, pharmaceutical studies, mining and agriculture.

There are currently three post-secondary technicums (technical colleges) in Afghanistan: the Auto-Mechanic Technicum in Kabul, the Petroleum and Gas Technicum in Balkh and the Electro-Mechanical Technicum in Qandahar. These three institutions admit students who have completed middle school and train them for six years. Upon completion of their studies, the students receive a technical certificate that represents two years of study beyond Baccalauria level.

Responsibility for quality assurance at tertiary level rests with the Ministry of Higher Education, although, in practice, little monitoring is actually carried out and a number of study programmes are known to be substandard. However, there are plans to establish an Afghan Accreditation Agency, the assessment operations of which would be mainly programme-based.

Regulatory and Representative Bodies

GOVERNMENT

Ministry of Education: Mohammad Jan Khan Watt, Deh Afghanan, Kabul; internet moe.gov.af; Minister Dr GHULAM FAROOQ WARDAK.

Ministry of Higher Education: Karte Char, Kabul; tel. (20) 2500324; e-mail info@mohe.gov.af; internet www.mohe.gov.af; f. 1356; Minister SARWAR DANISH (acting).

Ministry of Information & Culture: Mohammad Jan Khan Watt, Kabul; tel. (20) 2101301; internet www.moic.gov.af; Minister Dr SAYED MAKHDOOM RAHEEN.

NATIONAL BODIES

Afghan Rectors' Conference: c/o Kabul Univ., Kabul; e-mail rida_azimi2004@yahoo.com; Pres. Dr DAUD RAWOSH; Sec.-Gen. RIDA AZIMI.

UNESCO Office Kabul: House KB 647, Behind Esmat Muslim St, PD 10, Shahr-e-Naw, Kabul; tel. (20) 214522; e-mail kabul@unesco.org; internet www.unesco.org/new/en/kabul; promotes peace through culture, education and communication and information on interventions; Dir SHIGERU AOYAGI; Public Information Officer MOHAMMAD AMIN SADIQI.

Learned Societies

GENERAL

Academy of Sciences of Afghanistan: POB 894, Central Post Office, Kabul; Char Rahi Shirpur, Shahr-e-Naw, Dist. 10, Kabul; tel. (20) 2102919; e-mail afghanistan_as@yahoo.com; f. 1937 as Pashtu Academy, current name adopted 1979; research in science, technology, humanities and culture, Islamic studies; 4 main divs: Centre of Natural Sciences (*q.v.*), Institute of Social Sciences (*q.v.*), Institute of Languages and Literature (*q.v.*), Int. Centre for Pashtu Studies (*q.v.*); Islamic Studies Centre added 2000; further units incl. Int. Research Centre of Kushan Studies and Archaeology, Publication and Literature Dept, Encyclopedia and Dictionaries Dept; 300 mems; library of 50,000 vols; Pres. Dr ABDUL BARI RASHID; Sec. SAYED AMIN MUJAHID; publs *Ariana, Afghanistan, Kushani* (archaeology (Humanities)), *Khurasan, Pashtu, Kabul, Zeray* (Language and Literature), *Tabiat* (Natural Sciences), *Tafeker, Science and Technology, Tebion* (Islamic Studies).

Afghan Cultural House: House 582, St 9, Karte se, Kabul; tel. (20) 2500480; e-mail info@ach.af; internet www.ach.af; f. 2010; promotes culture of reading, writing, citizen journalism; organizes workshops, seminars, competitions; library of 2,000 vols; Gen. Dir MASUMA IBRAHIMI; Librarian PARYIA IBRAHIMI.

LANGUAGE AND LITERATURE

Goethe-Institut: c/o Embassy of the Federal Republic of Germany, POB 83, Kabul; Shah Mahmood St, Wazir Akbar Khan, Kabul; tel. (20) 2105200; e-mail info@kabul.goethe.org; internet www.goethe.de/ins/af/kab; f. 1965; promotes cultural exchange with Germany, and contributes to reconstruction of cultural and educational instns in Afghanistan; Dir ANNE EBERHARD.

Research Institutes

GENERAL

Afghanistan Research and Evaluation Unit (AREU): POB 3169, Shahr-e-Naw Post Office, Min. of Interior Rd, Shahr-e-Naw, Kabul; Flower St (cnr of St 2), Shahr-e-Naw, Kabul; e-mail areu@areu.org.af; internet www.areu.org.af; f. 2002; promotes research and learning by strengthening analytical capacity in Afghanistan and facilitating reflection and debate; library of 13,000 vols, periodicals, maps, CDs and DVDs; Dir Dr PAULA KANTOR.

Institute of Social Sciences: Kabul; attached to Acad. of Sciences of Afghanistan; archaeology, economics, history, philosophy; Pres. Dr HAKIM HELALI; publs *Afghanistan* (4 a year, in English, French and German), *Ariana* (4 a year, in Pashtu and Dari).

ECONOMICS, LAW AND POLITICS

Centre for Conflict and Peace Studies: Kabul; e-mail director@caps.af; internet www.caps.af; research, training and knowledge exchanges on conflicts, people and cultures, violent groups in Afghanistan and region; Dir HEKMAT KHALIL KARZAI; Deputy Dir MARIAM SAFI.

National Centre for Policy Research: Kabul Univ., Kabul; tel. (20) 2500390; e-mail admin@ncpr.af; internet www.ncpr.af; f. 2003; attached to Kabul Univ.; depts of economics, law and political sciences, peace and conflict studies and social science; provides research services in regard to the related fields and conducts capacity building programs; holds seminars, symposiums, roundtables and nat. confs; conducts surveys/public polls in reference to important interior issues of the country; Dir Dr HAMIDULLAH NOOR EBAD.

HISTORY, GEOGRAPHY AND ARCHAEOLOGY

Afghan Institute of Archaeology: Medina Bazaar, Qala-e-Fatullah, Dist. 10, Kabul; tel. (20) 2202651; e-mail archaeology_review@yahoo.com; f. 1966; attached to Min. of Information and Culture; promotes archaeological research and field work; Dir NADIR RASOULI.

LANGUAGE AND LITERATURE

International Centre for Pashtu Studies: Kabul; attached to Acad. of Sciences of Afghanistan; research, compilation and translation; publ. *Pashtu Quarterly*.

MEDICINE

Afghan National Public Health Institute: Min. of Public Health, 3rd Microrsyon, Block No 12B, H No 16, Kabul; f. 1963, officially revived 2006; attached to Min. of Public Health; public health training and research; govt reference laboratory; Gen. Dir BASHIR NOORMAL.

NATURAL SCIENCES

Physical Sciences

Afghanistan Geological Survey: Afghanistan Geological Survey Bldg, Jalalabad Rd, Dist. 9, Kabul; internet www.bgs.ac.uk/afghanminerals/index.htm; f. 1955; attached to Min. of Mines and Petroleum; research, mapping, prospecting, exploration; library of 8,300 vols; Pres. Dr ATIQ SEDIQI; publ. *Journal of Mines and Industries* (4 a year).

Libraries and Archives

Badakhshan

Badakhshan Provincial Library: Faizabad, Dist. 5, Badakhshan; f. 1967; attached to Min. of Information and Culture; 1,235 vols; Librarian MOHAMMAD OSMAN.

Badghis

Badghis Provincial Library: Municipality Bldg, Qala-e-Naw, Dist. 2, Badghis; f. 1973; attached to Min. of Information and Culture; 1,677 vols; Librarian ABDUL QUDOS.

Baghlan

Baghlan Provincial Library: Pul-e-Khumri, Dist. 3, Baghlan; attached to Min. of Information and Culture; Dir HAMIDA.

Balkh

Balkh Provincial Mowlana Khasta Library: Mowlana Khasta, Bagh-e-Huzur, Dist. 5, Mazar-i-Sharif, Balkh; f. 1963; Dir JAMILA QASEMI.

Balkh University Library: Masoud Shahid St, Mazar-i-Sharif, Balkh; e-mail balkh_university@yahoo.com; 30,000 vols, 10,000 periodicals; Dir VIANA WAZIRI.

Bamyan

Bamyan Provincial Library: Dist. 1, Bamyan; tel. (79) 5803412; f. 1973; attached to Min. of Information and Culture; 3,068 vols; Library Man. SAFAR ALI; publ. *Reading Books Culture* (online).

Daykundi

Daykundi Provincial Library: Sare Nili Petab, Nili, Daykundi; f. 2004; attached to Min. of Information and Culture; Dir BAKHT MOHAMMAD HAIDARI.

Farah

Farah Provincial Library: Jada Qasabi Dist., Farah; f. 1967; attached to Min. of Information and Culture; 2,674 vols; Dir FAZEL AHMAD.

Faryab

Faryab Provincial Library: Woloswali Bldg, Andkhoi, Faryab; f. 1966; attached to Min. of Information and Culture; 1,323 vols; Dir MOHAMMAD RAUF.

Faryab Provincial Library: Dist. 3, Maymana, Faryab; f. 1966; attached to Min. of Information and Culture; Dir HAJI ABDUL QADER.

Ghazni

Ghazni Provincial Library: Dist. 1, Ghazni; f. 2001; attached to Min. of Information and Culture; Dir BESMELLA.

Herat

Herat Provincial Library: Dist. 2, Park Farhang, Shahr-e-Naw, Herat; tel. (40) 223471; f. 1960; 30,000 vols; Dir SAYYED GHULAM FARROKH HASHIMI.

Herat University Library: Dist. 6, Sarak Baghi Azadi, Herat; tel. (40) 253471; 30,000 vols; Librarian AZIZULLAH MOJADIDI.

Jowzjan

Jowzjan Provincial Library: Dist. 1, Sheberghan, Jowzjan; f. 1966; attached to Min. of Information and Culture; Dir AHBEDA HANAN.

Kabul

Kabul Public Library: c/o Min. of Information and Culture, Mohammad Jan Khan Watt, Kabul; Char Rahi Malik Asghar, Dist. 2, Kabul; tel. (20) 2103289; f. 1957; attached to Min. of Information and Culture; 200,000 vols, 433 MSS, 30 current periodicals; Dir ABDUL HAMID NABIZADA.

Kabul University Library: Jamal Mina, Dist. 3, Kabul; tel. (20) 2500236; internet www.ku.edu.af/en/page/9146/9150; f. 1932; Dir SARAJUDDIN ALIMI.

Library of the National Bank: c/o Min. of Information and Culture, Mohammad Jan Khan Watt, Kabul; Bank Millie Afghan, Ibn Sina Watt, Kabul; f. 1941; 5,600 vols; Dir A. AZIZ.

Library of the Press and Information Department: c/o Min. of Information and Culture, Mohammad Jan Khan Watt, Kabul; Sanaii Watt, Kabul; f. 1931; 28,000 vols and 800 MSS; Dir MOHAMMED SARWAR RONA.

National Archives: Salang Watt St, De Afghanan, Dist. 2, Kabul; tel. (20) 2202975; e-mail sakhimuneer@yahoo.com; f. 1978; attached to Min. of Information and Culture; 150,000 items incl. old books, newspapers, journals, bank notes and coins, postage stamps, treaties, official documents, deeds, licences and seals, personal letters and diaries, maps, family trees, historic photographs of Afghanistan, Afghan royal family members and Afghan politicians, music recordings, Treaty of 1919; Head GHULAM SAKHI MUNEER.

National Film Archives: Ansari Watt, Wazir Akbar Khan, Dist. 10, Kabul; tel. (20) 2102845; e-mail eng_latif_film@yahoo.com; f. 1968; films made by Afghans, foreign film colln incl. 35 mm films from the Soviet Union, Iran and many Western countries, travelling film colln comprising 16 mm films; Dir SULTAN MOHAMMAD ISTALIFI.

Nazo Annah Library: Karte 3, Pul-e-Surkh, Dist. 6, St 4, House 259, Kabul; e-mail friba.farid07@gmail.com; internet www.necdo.org.af; f. 2004, fmrly Women's Welfare Soc. Library; attached to Noor Educational and Capacity Devt Org.; 680 vols; Librarian FRIBA HAMIDI.

Kandahar

Kandahar Provincial Library: Habibi Watt, Chowk Shuhada, Dist. 1, Kandahar; f. 1973; attached to Min. of Information and Culture; 1,352 vols; Dir HABIBULLAH.

Kapisa

Kapisa Provincial Library: Dist. 1, Mahmud-e-Raqi, Kapisa; f. 1976; attached to Min. of Information and Culture; 2,870 vols; Dir MOHAMMAD AZIM.

Kunar

Kunar Provincial Library: Dist. 1, Asadabad, Kunar; f. 1973; attached to Min. of Information and Culture; 1,059 vols; Dir RAHMATULLAH.

Kunduz

Kunduz Provincial Library: Spinzar Tasadi Bldg, Dist. 1, Kunduz; e-mail informationculturekunduz@yahoo.com; f. 1973; attached to Min. of Information and Culture; 2,880 vols; Librarian ABDUL SALIM.

Nangarhar

Nangarhar Provincial Library: Dist. 1, Jalalabad, Nangarhar; f. 1966; attached to Min. of Information and Culture; 2,597 vols; Librarian SHAH MAHMOOD.

Takhar

Takhar Provincial Library: Sahr-e-Chowk, Dist. 1, Taloqan, Takhar; f. 1972; attached to Min. of Information and Culture; 3,500 vols; Dir PAYENDA MOHAMMAD.

Museums and Art Galleries

Bamyan

Bamyan Museum: Afghanistan- Bamyan Province, Directorship of Bamyan Information and Culture, Bamyan; e-mail aliravi .bamyan@gmail.com.

Ghazni

Ghazni Museum of Islamic Art: Rauza, Ghazni; f. 1966; 16th-century Timurid architecture, objects from Ghazanvid period, bronze articles, ceramic tiles and glassware.

Herat

Herat Provincial Museum and Archive: c/o Min. of Information and Culture, Mohammad Jan Khan Watt, Kabul; Qala Ikhtyaruddin, Darb-e-Maik, Dist. 7, Herat; tel. (40) 111310; f. 1966; items from Timurid period; undergoing restoration; Dir of Museum and Archives GHULAM YAHYA KHOSHBIN; Dir of Archives BAHAUDDIN BAHA TIMURI.

Kabul

National Museum of Afghanistan: Opposite Darulaman Palace, Darulaman Rd, Kabul; tel. (20) 25001426; e-mail o .masoudi@nationalmuseum.af; internet www .nationalmuseum.af; f. 1922, present bldg 2004; attached to Min. of Information and Culture; archaeology; exhibits 3,000 pieces in stone, terracotta, metal; Gen. Dir OMARA KHAN MASOUDI; Gen. Deputy Dir MOHAMMAD YAHYA MOHIBZADA.

Kandahar

Kandahar Museum: c/o Min. of Information and Culture, Mohammad Jan Khan Watt, Kabul; Kandahar.

Mazar-i-Sharif

Mazar-i-Sharif Museum: c/o Min. of Information and Culture, Mohammad Jan Khan Watt, Kabul; Mazar-i-Sharif; closed temporarily; colln destroyed or stolen during the 1992–1996 civil war and subsequent 1996–2001 Taliban regime.

Universities

ALBERONI UNIVERSITY

Kapisa
Internet: www.au.edu.af

Founded 2000
State control

Faculties of agriculture, education, engineering, law, medical science, Sharia

Chancellor: RASHID KHAN AZIZ KOHISTANI

Number of teachers: 61
Number of students: 1,643

AMERICAN UNIVERSITY OF AFGHANISTAN

POB 458, Central Post Office, Darulaman Rd, Kabul
E-mail: library@auaf.edu.af
Internet: www.auaf.edu.af

Founded 2006
Private control

Depts of business and economics, information technology and computer science, science and mathematics, social sciences and humanities

Chair.: Dr AKRAM FAZEL
Pres.: Dr C. MICHAEL SMITH
Chief Academic Officer: Dr SHARIF FAYEZ
Vice-Pres for Finance and Admin.: Dr GORDON ANDERSON
Provost: Dr DAWN DEKLE
Registrar: PAUL REVEERE
Library Dir: ANN E. MARSH

Number of teachers: 46
Number of students: 789

BAGHLAN UNIVERSITY

Hussain Khel, Baghlan
Internet: www.baghlan.edu.af

Founded 1993 as Hakim Naser Khesraw Univ., reopened in 2003

Faculties of agriculture, education

Chancellor: Prof. ZIAYEE

Number of teachers: 43
Number of students: 1,468

BAKHTAR INSTITUTE OF HIGHER EDUCATION/BAKHTAR UNIVERSITY

Karte–Char, Kabul
E-mail: info@bakhtar.edu.af
Internet: bakhtar.edu.af

Founded 2005
Private control

Depts of civil engineering, commerce, computer science, economics, English, health management, journalism, law, political science, public administration, sociology

Chancellor: ABDUL LATIF ROSHAN

BALKH UNIVERSITY

Masoud Shahid St, Mazar-i-Sharif, Balkh
E-mail: info@balkh-university.edu.af
Internet: www.balkh-university.edu.af

Founded 1988
State control

Faculties of agriculture, economics, engineering, Islamic law, journalism, law and political science, literature and human science, medicine and science, theology

Chancellor: Prof. HABIBUALLAH HABIB

Library: see under Libraries and Archives
Number of teachers: 242
Number of students: 6,500

BAMYAN UNIVERSITY

Bamyan
Internet: www.bu.edu.af

Founded 1996, re-established 2004
State control

Depts of biology, chemistry, Dari, English, history, mathematics, physics, psychology, sociology

Chancellor: HAMIDULLAH ADINA

Number of teachers: 45
Number of students: 719

HERAT UNIVERSITY

Herat
E-mail: info@hu.edu.af
Internet: www.hu.edu.af

Founded 1988
State control

Faculties of agriculture, art, computer science, economics, education, engineering, law, literature, medicine, science, theology and Islamic law

Pres.: Prof. MIR GHULAM OSMAN BAREZ HUSSAINY
Vice-Chancellor: SAYED FARHAD SHAHIDZADA
Dir for Academic Affairs: MOHAMMAD NASER RAHYAB
Dir for Student Affairs: Dr ABDUL ZAHER O
Librarian: AZIZULLAH MOJADIDI

Library: see under Libraries and Archives
Number of teachers: 247
Number of students: 5,285

KABUL EDUCATIONAL UNIVERSITY

Kabul

Founded 2002 as Kabul Institute of Pedagogy, current name and status 2003
State control

Chancellor: AMANULLAH HAMIDZAI

Number of teachers: 164
Number of students: 4,139

KABUL MEDICAL UNIVERSITY

Kabul

Telephone: (20) 2500327
E-mail: dryousufmw@yahoo.com
Internet: www.kmu.edu.af

Founded 1932 as Kabul Medical Faculty, current name and status 2005
State control
Languages of instruction: Dari, English
Academic year: April to December

Faculties of allied health, curative medicine, nursing, stomatology; affiliated teaching hospitals at Aliabad and Maiwand

Chancellor: Prof. SHERIN AQA ZARIF
Dean: Dr ABDUL SAMAD OMAR

Library of 20,000 vols
Number of teachers: 312
Number of students: 3,445

Publication: *Afghan Medical Journal*

KABUL UNIVERSITY

Jamal Mina, Kabul

Telephone: (20) 2500238
E-mail: hamedullahamin@ku.edu.af
Internet: www.ku.edu.af

Founded 1932
State control
Academic year: March to January
Language of instruction: Dari

Chancellor: Prof. HAMIDULLAH AMIN

Vice-Chancellor for Academic Affairs: Prof. MOHAMMAD SALIM RAHIMI
Vice-Chancellor for Admin. Affairs: Prof. MUKAMEL ALAKOZAI
Vice-Chancellor for Student Affairs: Prof. Dr ABDUL RAOOF GOHARI
Librarian: REYHANA POPALZAI

Library of 200,000 vols
Number of teachers: 450
Number of students: 7,000

Publication: *Natural Science and Social Science* (4 a year)

DEANS

Faculty of Computer Science: Prof. HOMAYON NASERI
Faculty of Education: Prof. GUL RAHMAN HAKIM
Faculty of Fine Arts: Prof. MOHAMMAD ALEM
Faculty of Law and Political Science: Prof. IQRAL WASIL
Faculty of Pharmacy: Prof. MOHAMMAD NASIM SEDIQI
Faculty of Psychology: Prof. MIR AKRAM MIRZAD
Faculty of Sharia: Prof. DIN MOHAMMAD GRAN
Faculty of Social Sciences: Prof. M. DAUD RAWOSH

KANDAHAR UNIVERSITY

Kandahar
Internet: kan.edu.af

Founded 1990
State control

Faculties of agriculture, economics, education, engineering, Islamic studies, medicine, Sharia

Chancellor: HAZRATMEER TOTAKHIL
Vice-Chancellor: SHAH MAHMOUD BARAK

Number of teachers: 162
Number of students: 2,850

NANGARHAR UNIVERSITY

Jalalabad, Nangarhar
E-mail: info@nu.edu.af
Internet: nu.edu.af

Founded 1962
State control

Language of instruction: Pashtu

Chancellor: Dr MOHAMMAD SABER
Vice-Chancellor: NAEAM JAN SARWARI
Dean: Prof. ABDUL QADIR FAZLI

Number of teachers: 300
Number of students: 7,000

DEANS

Faculty of Medicine: Prof. ASSADULLAH SHINWARI
Faculty of Political Science: MIRWAIS AHMADZAI

PAKTIA UNIVERSITY

Gardez, Paktia
Telephone: (79) 9883747
Internet: www.pu.edu.af

Founded 2004
State control

Faculties of agriculture, education

Number of teachers: 45
Number of students: 4,000

POLYTECHNICAL UNIVERSITY OF KABUL

Kabul
E-mail: arzomand@polytechnic-kabul.org
Internet: www.polytechnic-kabul.org

Founded 1963
State control

Faculties of construction, electromechanics, geology and mining

Pres.: Prof. Dr EZATULLAH AMED
Vice-Pres. for Admin. Affairs: Prof. AKBAR JAN ARZOMAND
Vice-Chancellor for Research and Scientific Affairs: Prof. Dr ABDUL QAYUOM KARIMZADA
Vice-Chancellor for Students Affairs: Prof. ABDULBAQI RAHMANI

Number of teachers: 161
Number of students: 2,900

SHAIKH ZAYED UNIVERSITY/KHOST UNIVERSITY

Khost
E-mail: dr.gulnawaz@szu.edu.af
Internet: szu.edu.af

Founded 1992 as Khost Univ. in Peshawar, Pakistan; current name and location 2001
State control

Chancellor: Prof. Dr GUL HASSAN WALIZEI
Vice-Chancellor: Dr GUL NAWAZ
Vice-Chancellor for Academic Affairs: Dr MUHAMMAD HUSSAIN HUSSAINI

Number of teachers: 118
Number of students: 3,000

DEANS

Faculty of Agriculture: Asst Prof. ABDUL KHALIL AFGHANI
Faculty of Journalism: Asst Prof. MATER WAHIDI
Faculty of Law and Political Science: MOHAMMADULLAH MANDOZAI
Faculty of Medical Science: Dr JAHAN SHA TANI

TAKHAR UNIVERSITY

Takhar
Internet: www.tu.edu.af

Founded 1995
State control

Number of teachers: 47
Number of students: 1,572

Colleges

Afghanistan Technical Vocational Institute: Karta-e Char, POB 1969, Kabul; tel. (20) 2504157; e-mail info@atvi.edu.af; internet www.atvi.edu.af; f. 2007; offers undergraduate vocational courses in agriculture and horticulture, business admin., construction, information and communications technology, vehicle maintenance; 2,000 students; Pres. SARDAR ROSHAN.

Badakhshan Institute of Higher Education: Badakhshan; f. 1961, present status 2003; faculty of education; 18 teachers; 369 students.

Faryab Higher Education Institution: Faryab; f. 1977, present status 1987; teacher training; faculties of agriculture, education; 36 teachers; 637 students.

Institute of Higher Education, Jowzjan: Jowzjan; f. 2001; faculties of engineering, sciences, social sciences; 700 students; Rector GUL AHMAD FAZLI.

Kaboora Institute of Higher Education: Qala-e-Fatullah, Dist. 10–St 4, Kabul; e-mail info@kaboora.edu.af; internet www.kaboora.edu.af; f. 2001; anaesthesia, banking, business, civil engineering, computer science, dentistry, economics, finance, journalism, management, medical technology, midwifery, nursing, pharmacy, physiotherapy, radiology; Chancellor HABIBULLAH PEERZADA; Vice-Chancellor Prof. SULTAN M. GARDIWAL.

Kabul Art School: Bibi Mahro, Kabul; music, painting and sculpture courses.

Kabul Health Sciences Institute: Qala-e-Fatullah, Dist. 10–St 4, Kabul; e-mail info@kaboora.edu.af; internet www.kabuli.edu.af; f. 2004; anaesthesia, advanced nursing, dentistry, medical technology, midwifery, pharmacy, physiotherapy, radiology; Chancellor Prof. AQA MUHAMMAD LOUDIN; Exec. Dir HABIBULLAH PEERZADA.

Kunduz Higher Education Institution: Kunduz; f. 1967, present status 1994; faculties of agriculture, education; 30 teachers; 990 students.

Parwan Higher Education Institution: Parwan; f. 1961, present status 1999; 35 teachers; 1,312 students.

ALBANIA

The Higher Education System

Higher education is offered through universities and higher schools and is governed by legislation enacted in 1999, 2003, 2007 and 2010. In 2012 there were 14 public sector higher education institutions, including 11 universities, the oldest of which is the Aleksandër Xhuvani University of Elbasan, founded (as a teacher training establishment) in 1909. The number of private providers of higher education has escalated substantially in recent years, and in 2012 there were 47 officially accredited private sector higher education institutions. The Law on Higher Education of 1999 introduced and guaranteed state funding for public higher education. The funding of public universities is now regulated through the provision of a 'block grant' to each institution rather than through three separate budget headings (as practised formerly). Albania joined the Bologna Process in 2003, and in the same year implemented a new higher education act that introduced a two-tier (Bachelors and Masters level) degree structure. The Law on Higher Education of 2007 governs not only the institutions but also the structure, study programmes and cycles, supervision, students' rights and the financial aspects of higher education. Its enactment marked the official start of the implementation of three-cycle Bologna Process degrees. In 2010 the law was amended to regulate the types of programmes and qualifications provided by the institutions.

In 2008/09 a total of 116,292 students were enrolled at Albania's institutions of higher education.

University Rectors and Higher School Directors and Headmasters belong to the Conference of Rectors, the highest decision-making body in Albania's higher education system. All universities consist of faculties, which are governed by faculty councils, and sometimes of higher schools; the highest decision-making body in a higher school is the school council. Both faculties and higher schools consist of departments, in which the department council is the highest decision-making body.

Admission to higher education is conducted according to quotas and is subject to main and secondary fees. Main admission fees are proposed by the Ministry of Education and Science, following recommendations from the universities and higher schools, and are approved by the Council of Ministers. Secondary fees are levied for specialist education and can equate to a maximum of 10% of the main fees. Admission to public universities and higher schools is based on competitive examinations which are organized by the Ministry of Education and Science on the advice of the Conference of Rectors. Successful students are then admitted subject to the established fees.

Pre-Bologna (until 2007), there were three levels of university qualifications: Diplomë (Diploma), Kandidat í Shkencave (Candidate of Sciences) and Doktor í Shkencave (Doctor of Sciences). The Diplomë was usually a four-year undergraduate degree; however, degrees in engineering, technology and dentistry lasted five years, and courses in medicine lasted six years. The Kandidat í Shkencave was a first postgraduate degree of two to three years. The Doktor í Shkencave was based on a significant period of research. There was no grading system for this level of study. Qualifications from the three military institutions (the Higher Military Academies in Tiranë and Vlora, and the Higher Unified Military School in Tirana) had the same equivalency as civilian qualifications.

Post-Bologna there are six levels of qualification: in the first cycle are the Diplomë Jo-Universitare (Non-University Diploma), which is a higher education award consisting of a study programme of 120 European Credit Transfer and Accumulation System credits (ECTS), in applied subjects, offered at universities and professional colleges (credits can be transferred to a First Level Diploma programme) and the Diplomë í Nivelit te Pare (First Level Diploma), which is a degree awarded after at least three years, of no less than 180 ECTS, and can be issued by universities, academies or professional colleges providing access to second cycle awards. In the second cycle are the Master í Nivelit te Pare (First Level Master), a degree which is an essential requirement for teachers whose first cycle degree is not sufficient, consisting of no less than 60 ECTS, but is not recognized as completion of the second cycle and therefore does not allow access to the third level, and the Diplomë e Nivelit te Dyte (Second Level Diploma), which is a degree awarded after two years' study, involving the attainment of 120 ECTS, allowing entry to the third cycle. In the third cycle are the Master í Nivelit te Dyte (Second Level Master), which is a degree awarded after another one to two years' study and represents the entry requirement to become a university professor, and Doktor í Shkencave (Doctor of Sciences), which takes three to five years and requires completion of 60 ECTS in the first year (although holders of the Second Level Master are exempt), followed by research and defence of a doctoral thesis.

Quality assessment of public and private universities and higher schools and academic accreditation is carried out by the independent Albanian Public Agency for Accreditation of Higher Education and the Accrediting Council, under the authority of the Council of Ministers. Recent positive developments include the formal establishment of a Quality Assurance Unit at each university in conformity with the 2007 Law on Higher Education. In addition, Bologna Follow-up Groups have been set up at a number of universities.

Regulatory and Representative Bodies

GOVERNMENT

Ministry of Education and Science: Rruga Durrësit 23, Tiranë; tel. (4) 2230289; e-mail ministri@mash.gov.al; internet www.mash.gov.al; Minister LINDITA NIKOLLA.

Ministry of Culture: Rr. e Kavajës, Tiranë; tel. (4) 2222508; e-mail informacion@mtkrs.gov.al; internet www.mtkrs.gov.al; Minister MIRELA KUMBARO-FURXHI.

ACCREDITATION

ENIC/NARIC Albania: Drejtoria e Arsimit të Lartë dhe Njohjes së Diplomave, Rr. Durrësit 23, Tiranë; tel. (4) 2227975; e-mail ecane@mash.gov.al; internet www.mash.gov.al; Specialist EDMOND CANE.

Public Agency for Accreditation of Higher Education: Blvd Zhan 'D' Ark, Pallatet e Lanës, no. 2, Shk 2, Ap. 17, Tiranë; tel. (4) 2266302; e-mail infoaal@gmail.com; internet www.aaal.edu.al; f. 1999; attached to Min. of Education and Science; state-funded instn for evaluation of HEIs; conducts evaluations, ranking, preparation of evaluation criteria, procedures, performance indicators and standards, documentation for the ccl of accreditation; Dir Prof. AVNI MESHI.

NATIONAL BODIES

Albanian Rectors' Conference: c/o Ministry of Education and Science, Rr. e Durrësit 23, Tiranë.

Department of Higher Education and Recognition of Diplomas: c/o Ministry of Education and Science, Rr. e Durrësit 23, Tiranë; tel. (4) 226307; e-mail amucaj@mash.gov.al; internet www.mash.gov.al; Dir of Higher Education Dr AGIM MUÇAJ.

Learned Societies

GENERAL

Academy of Sciences of Albania: Fan. S. Noli Sq., 1000 Tiranë; tel. (42) 230305; e-mail ecane@akad.edu.al; internet www.akad.edu.al; f. 1972; theoretical and practical research in social, natural and technical sciences; facilitates the application of these studies; attached research institutes: see Research Institutes; 29 mems; library of 65,000 vols; Pres. Acad. MYZAFER KORKUTI; Vice-Pres. Acad. GUDAR BEQIRAJ; Scientific Sec. Acad. VASIL TOLE; publs *Albanian Journal of Natural and Technical Sciences* (2 a year), *Studia Albanica* (2 a year).

Komiteti Shqiptar për Marrëdhënie Kulturore me botën e jashtme (Albanian Committee for Cultural Relations Abroad): Tiranë; Pres. JORGO MELIKA.

LANGUAGE AND LITERATURE

Alliance Française: Rr. e Barrikadave 122, Tiranë; tel. (4) 2274841; e-mail info@aftirana.org; internet www.aftirana.org; f. 1991; offers courses and examinations in French language and culture; promotes cultural exchange with France; attached teaching centres in Elbasan, Korçë and Shkodra; Dir DRITA HADAJ; Sec.-Gen. GENT BEGA; Head of Treasury IRENA CACI.

British Council: Rr. 'Perlat Rexhepi', Pall 197, Ana, Tiranë; tel. (4) 2240856; e-mail info@britishcouncil.org.al; internet www.britishcouncil.org/albania; offers courses and examinations in English language and British culture; promotes cultural exchange with the UK; library of 4,000 vols; Dir CLARE SEARS.

Lidhja e Shkrimtarëve dhe e Artistëve të Shqipërisë (Union of Writers and Artists of Albania): Tiranë; f. 1957; 1,750 mems; Pres. DRITËRO AGOLLI; Secs FEIM IBRAHIMI, PETRO KOKUSHTA, NASI LERA; publs *Drita* (journal, 52 a year), *Les Lettres Albanaises* (4 a year), *Nëntori* (Review, 12 a year).

PEN Centre of Albania: Rr. 'Ded Gjo Luli', Pallati 5, shk. 3/4, Tiranë; internet www.pen-international.org/centres/albanian-centre; Pres. BESNIK MUSTAFAJ.

NATURAL SCIENCES

Physical Sciences

Shoqata e Gjeologëve te Shqipërisë (Geologists' Association of Albania): Blloku 'Vasil Shanto', Tiranë; tel. (4) 2226597; f. 1989; 450 mems; Chair. ALEKSANDËR ÇINA; Sec.-Gen. ILIR ALLIU; publ. *Buletini i Shkencave Gjeologjike.*

Research Institutes

AGRICULTURE, FISHERIES AND VETERINARY SCIENCE

Instituti i Duhanit (Tobacco Institute): Lagja 2, Pallati 51/2, Cërrik; tel. (67) 4062508; e-mail arqileamato@gmail.com; f. 1956; library of 1,000 vols; Dir ARQILEA MATO; publ. *Bulletin des sciences de l'agriculture* (4 a year).

Instituti i Kërkimeve Bujqësore Lushnje (Lushnje Institute of Agricultural Research): Lushnje; tel. (65) 224498; f. 1952; focuses on cultivating new varieties of bread and durum wheat, cotton, sunflower and dry bean; library of 8,000 vols; Dir VLADIMIR MALO.

Instituti i Kërkimeve Pyjore dhe Kullotave (Forest and Pasture Research Institute): Rr. Halil Bego 23, Tiranë; tel. (4) 371242; e-mail ikpk@albaniaonline.net; f. 1992; Dir SPIRO KARADUMI.

Instituti i Kërkimeve të Foragjere (Forage Research Institute): Fushë-Krujë; tel. (4) 233354; f. 1973; Dir VASILLAQ DHIMA.

Instituti i Kërkimeve të Pemëve Frutore dhe Vreshtave (Institute of Fruit Growing and Vineyard Research): Tiranë; tel. (4) 2229704; f. 1984; library of 70 vols; Dir STEFAN GJOKA; publs *Pemëtaria*, *Bulletini i Shkencave Bujqësore*.

Instituti i Kërkimeve të Zooteknisë (Institute of Animal Husbandry Research): Laprake, Tiranë; tel. (4) 2223135; f. 1955; library of 1,900 vols; Dir MINA SPIRU.

Instituti i Kërkimeve Veterinare (Institute of Veterinary Research): 'Aleksander Moisiu' St 10, Tiranë; tel. (4) 2372912; f. 1928; Dir Prof. Dr KRISTAQ BERXHOLI; publ. *Veterinaria* (3 a year).

Instituti i Kerkimit te Bimeve te Arave, Stacioni Eksperimental (Experimental Station of the Research Institute for Arable Farming): Rr. Voskopojës, Korçë; e-mail stacionieksperimental@yahoo.com; f. 1953; attached to Min. of Agriculture, Food and Consumer Protection; library of 600 vols; Dir Dr EQREM MEÇOLLARI.

Instituti i Mbrojtjes Bimeve (Institute of Plant Protection Research): Shkozet, Durrës; tel. (52) 22182; e-mail imb@anep.al.eu.org; f. 1971; library of 2,410 vols; Dir Dr SKENDER VARRAKU.

Instituti i Perimeve dhe i Patates (Institute of Vegetables and Potatoes): Rr. Skënder Kosturi, Tiranë; tel. (4) 2228422; f. 1980; library of 6,000 vols; Dir XHEVAT SHIMA; publs *Bulletin of Agricultural Sciences*, *Bulletin of Vegetables*, *Bulletin of Vegetables and Potatoes*.

Instituti i Studimeve dhe i Projektimeve të Veprave të Kullimit dhe Ujitjes (Institute of Irrigation and Drainage Studies and Designs): Tiranë; f. 1970; Dir DHIMITËR VOGLI.

Instituti i Studimit të Tokave (Institute of Soil Studies): Tiranë; tel. (4) 2223278; f. 1971; library of 5,000 vols; Dir ALBERT DUBALI.

Instituti i Ullirit dhe i Agrumeve (Institute of Olives and Citrus Plants): 'Uji i Jtohtë', Vlorë; tel. (33) 23225; f. 1971; library of 500 vols; Dir Dr HAIRI ISMAILI.

Qendra e Transferimit te Teknologjive Bujqesore (Agriculture Technologies Transfer Centre (ATTC)): Shkodër; tel. (225) 1200; e-mail qttb_shkoder@yahoo.com; f. 1971 as Institute of Maize and Rice, present name 2006; applied research activity and technology devt; identification, testing, introduction of new methods and materials into agriculture practices; identification, preservation, collection, multiplication of high value authentic genetic resources; preparing of technological package for maize culture and other priority cultures of the region (arboriculture, horticulture, vegetable, etc.); production of pre-basic and basic certified seeds and seedlings; activities of technology transfer; laboratory analysis (chemical and biochemical laboratory wide range analysis) of both agriculture and cattle products; 15 mems; library of 4,900 vols; Dir ISMET LLOSHI; publs *Agriculture Science Bulletin* (4 a year), *Albanian Agriculture* (12 a year).

Stacioni i Studimeve dhe i Kërkimeve të Peshkimit (Research Station and Fisheries Research): Rr. 'Skenderbeg', L. Teuta, Durrës; tel. (52) 22552; f. 1960; Dir KASTRIOT OSMANI.

ARCHITECTURE AND TOWN PLANNING

Instituti i Monumenteve të Kulturës (Institute of Cultural Monuments): Rr. Aleksandër Moisiu 76, Tiranë; tel. (4) 2340348; e-mail imk@albmail.com; f. 1965; attached to Min. of Culture; research and restoration of ancient and medieval architecture, cultural bldgs and artistic monuments; library of 9,000 vols; Dir FATJON DAUTI; publ. *Monumentet* (Monuments, 2 a year).

Instituti i Studimeve e Projektimeve Urbanistikë (Institute of Urban Planning and Design): Rr. M. Gjollesha Istn, Tiranë; tel. (4) 2223361; f. 1991; library of 400 vols; Dir GJERGJ KOTMILO.

ECONOMICS, LAW AND POLITICS

Albanian Institute for International Studies: Rr. Andon Z, Cajupi 20, Tiranë; tel. (4) 4400084; e-mail aiis@aiis-albania.org; internet www.aiis-albania.org; f. 1997; non-profit research and policy institute; areas of research incl. issues in Euro-Atlantic integration, democracy, security and transition, regional security and cooperation; Chair. BESNIK MUSTAFAJ; Exec. Dir ALBERT RAKIPI.

Instituti i Studimeve të Marrëdhënieve Ndërkombëtare (Institute of International Relations): Tiranë; tel. (4) 2229521; f. 1981; Dir SOKRAT PLAKA; publ. *Politika ndërkombëtare* (International Politics, 4 a year).

EDUCATION

Instituti i Zhvillimit të Arsimit (Institute of Education Development): Rr. Naim Frashëri 37, Tiranë; tel. (4) 2256440; e-mail sekretaria@izha.edu.al; internet www.izha.edu.al; f. 1970; Dir GERTI JANAQI; publs *Albanian Language and Literature in School* (2 a year), *Chemistry and Biology in School* (2 a year), *Elementary School* (1 a year), *Foreign Languages in School* (1 a year), *Mathematics and Physics in School* (2 a year), *Nursery School 3–6* (1 a year), *Revista Pedagogjike* (4 a year), *Social Materials in School* (2 a year), *Vocational Schools* (2 a year), *Yllkat* (12 a year).

FINE AND PERFORMING ARTS

Qendra e Studimeve të Artit (Centre for Art Studies): Rr. Don Bosko 60, Tiranë; tel. (4) 2259667; e-mail qsa@akad.edu; f. 1984; attached to Acad. of Sciences of Albania; research in fine arts, music, choreography, theatre, cinema, art and culture instns; Dir Prof. JOSIF PAPAGJONI; publ. *Studime për Artin* (Studies for Art, 2 a year).

HISTORY, GEOGRAPHY AND ARCHAEOLOGY

Instituti i Arkeologjisë (Institute of Archaeology): Bulevardi Dëshmorët e Kombit, Sheshi Nënë Tereza, Tiranë; tel. (4) 2271822; e-mail instark@albmail.com; f. 1976; attached to Centre of Albanological Studies; Dir Prof. ILIRIAN GJIPALI; publs *Candavia* (in Albanian, publ. of the Late Antique and Medieval Dept of the Institute of Archaeology), *Iliria* (1 a year, in Albanian, English and French).

Instituti i Historisë (Institute of History): Rr. Naim Frashëri 7, Tiranë; tel. (4) 2225869; e-mail ihistorise@albaniaonline.net; f. 1972; attached to Acad. of Sciences of Albania; study of ancient and modern Albanian history and people; library of 52,000 vols, 10,000 periodicals; Dir Prof. Dr ANA LALAJ; publ. *Studime Historike* (Historical Studies, 4 a year).

Qendra e Kërkimeve Gjeografike (Centre for Geographical Research): Qendri e Studimeve Hidraulike, Sheshi Fan S. Noli, Tiranë; tel. (4) 2227985; e-mail geography_albania2003@yahooo.com; f. 1986; attached to Acad. of Sciences of Albania; library of 3,200 vols; Dir Prof. Dr ARQILE BERXHOLI; publ. *Studime Gjeografike* (Geographical Studies, 1 a year).

LANGUAGE AND LITERATURE

Instituti i Gjuhësisë dhe i Letërsisë (Institute of Linguistics and Literature): Rr. Naim Frashëri 7, Tiranë; tel. (4) 2240461; e-mail enver_muhametaj@yahoo.com; f. 1972; attached to Acad. of Sciences of Albania; Dir Prof. Dr ENVER MUHAMETAJ; publs *Gjuha Jonë* (Our Language, 1 a year), *Studime Filologjike* (Philological Studies, 2 a year).

Qendra e Enciklopedisë Shqiptare (Centre for the Albanian Encyclopedical Dictionary): Sheshi Fan S. Noli 7, Tiranë; tel. (4) 2250369; e-mail encikloped@yahoo.com; f. 1988 to prepare revised edn of the *Albanian Encyclopedical Dictionary*; attached to Centre for Albanological Studies; sections of social sciences, natural and technical sciences; Dir Prof. Dr MUHARREM DEZHGIU.

MEDICINE

Instituti i Mjekësisë Popullore (Institute of Folk Medicine): Tiranë; tel. (4) 2223493; f. 1977; Dir Dr GËZIM BOCARI; publ. *Përmbledhje Studimesh* (Collections of Studies, irregular).

Instituti i Shëndetit Publik (Institute of Public Health): Aleksander Moisiu St 80, Tiranë; tel. (4) 2374756; f. 1969 as Research Institute of Hygiene, Epidemiology and Immunobiological Products, current name adopted 1995; Dir Prof. EDUARD KAKARRIQI; publ. *Revista Mjekesore* (Albanian Medical Journal, 4 a year).

NATURAL SCIENCES

Biological Sciences

Instituti i Kërkimeve Biologjike (Institute of Biological Research): Rr. Sami Frasheri 5, Tiranë; tel. (4) 222638; e-mail ikbiol@albmail.com; f. 1978; attached to Acad. of Sciences of Albania; Dir Prof. EFIGJENI KONGJIKA.

Mathematical Sciences

Instituti i Informatikës dhe i Matematikës së Aplikuar (Institute of Informatics and Applied Mathematics): Rr. Lek Dukagjini 3, Tiranë; tel. (4) 2362968; e-mail inima@inima.al; f. 1971; attached to Acad. of Sciences of Albania; Dir Prof. Dr GUDAR BEQIRAJ.

Physical Sciences

Instituti i Energjetikës (Institute of Energetics): Tiranë; f. 1982; Dir LLAZAR PAPAJORGJI.

Instituti i Fizikës Bërthamore (Institute of Nuclear Physics): POB 85, Tiranë; tel. (4) 2376341; e-mail inp@albaniaonline.net; f. 1970; attached to Acad. of Sciences of Albania; Dir Prof. Dr FATOS YLLI.

Instituti i Hidrometeorologjisë (Institute of Hydrometeorology): Rr. e Durrësit 219, Tiranë; tel. (4) 2223518; e-mail a.selenica@voila.fr; f. 1962, replaced Hydrometeorological Service f. 1949; attached to Acad. of Sciences of Albania; comprises 2 divs: dept of meteorology and dept of hydrology; Dir Prof. Dr AGIM SELENICA; publ. *Hydrometeorological Reports* (periodic review).

Instituti i Sizmologjise (Institute of Seismology): Tiranë; tel. (4) 2228274; e-mail sizmo@akad.edu.al; f. 1993; attached to Acad. of Sciences of Albania; Dir Prof. Dr SHYQYRI ALIAJ.

Instituti i Studimeve dhe Projektimeve të Gjeologjisë (Geological Research Institute): Blloku 'Vasil Shanto', Tiranë; tel. (4) 2226597; f. 1962; library of 20,000 vols; Dir ALAUDIN KODRA; publ. *Buletini i Shkencave Gjeologjike* (4 a year).

RELIGION, SOCIOLOGY AND ANTHROPOLOGY

Instituti i Kulturës Popullore (Institute of Folk Culture): Rr. Kont Urani 3, Tiranë; tel. (4) 2222323; e-mail ikp.alb@icc.al.org; f. 1961, present status 1979; attached to Acad. of Sciences of Albania; depts of ethnology, ethnomusicology and ethnochoreography, prose and poetry; library of 10,000 vols, 1.5m. verses of poetry; Dir Asst Prof. AFËRDITA ONUZI; publ. *Folk Culture* (2 a year).

TECHNOLOGY

Infraproject Consulting SH.p.K.: Rr. Sami Frasheri, Tiranë; tel. (4) 2225206; road, railway and waterway engineering; library of 900 vols; Dir-Gen. VEHIP GURI.

Instituti i Kerkimeve të Ushqimit (Food Research Institute): Rr. 'Muhamed Gjollesha' 56, Tiranë; tel. (4) 2226770; e-mail iku@anep.al.eu.org; f. 1961; Dir MAKSIM DELIANA; publ. *Përmbledhje Studimesh* (Collections of Studies, irregular).

Instituti i Studimeve dhe i Projektimeve të Hidrocentraleve (Institute of Hydraulic Studies and Design): Tiranë; f. 1966; Dir EGON GJADRI.

Instituti i Studimeve dhe i Projektimeve të Minierave (Mining Research Institute): Blloku 'Vasil Shanto', Tiranë; tel. (4) 2229445; f. 1983; library of 10,000 vols; Dir ENGJELL HOXHAJ; publ. *Buletini i Shkencave Minerare* (2 a year, summaries in English).

Instituti i Studimeve dhe i Projektimeve të Teknologjisë Kimike (Institute of Chemical Studies and Technological Design): Tiranë; f. 1981; Dir GASTOR AGALLIU.

Instituti i Studimeve dhe i Projektimeve të Teknologjisë Mekanike (Institute of Mechanical Technology Studies and Design): Tiranë; f. 1969; Dir ROBERT LAPERI.

Instituti i Studimeve dhe i Projektimeve Teknologjike të Mineraleve (Institute for Studies and Technology of Minerals): Tiranë; tel. (4) 2225582; f. 1979; mineral-processing research; library of 1,480 vols; Dir JLIR LAKRORI.

Instituti i Studimeve dhe i Projektimeve Teknologjike të Naftës e të Gazit (Institute for Studies and Design of Oil and Gas Technology): Tiranë; f. 1981; Dir PERPARIM HOXHA; publ. *Nafta dhe Gazi* (Oil and Gas, 6 a year).

Instituti i Studimeve dhe i Teknologjisë Ndërtimit (Institute of Building Technology Studies): Rr. 'Muhamet Gjollesha', Tiranë; tel. (4) 2273449; e-mail info@institutindertimit.com; internet www.institutindertimit.com; f. 1979; library of 1,500 vols; Dir Ing. MUHANEM DELIU.

Instituti i Studimeve dhe Projektimeve Mekanike (Mechanics Research Institute): Rr. 'Ferit Xajko', Tiranë; tel. (4) 2228543; f. 1970; library of 3,000 vols; Dir NEDIM KAMBO.

Qendra e Kerkimeve Hidraulike (Centre of Hydraulic Research): Rr. Sami Frasheri 5, Tiranë; tel. (4) 2227322; e-mail qekehid@albmail.com; f. 1957; attached to Acad. of Sciences of Albania; Dir Prof. Dr STAVRI LAMI.

Libraries and Archives

Durrës

Durrës Public Library: Durrës; tel. (52) 22281; f. 1945; 265,000 vols; Dir MIRELA YLLI.

Elbasan

Elbasan Public Library: Elbasan; f. 1934; 284,000 vols.

Gjirokastër

Gjirokastër Public Library: Gjirokastër; 90,000 vols.

Korçë

Korçë Public Library: Korçë; f. 1938; 139,000 vols.

Shkodër

Shkodër Public Library: Shkodër; tel. (2) 2242307; e-mail biboigjo@yahoo.co.uk; internet www.library-shkodra.com; f. 1931; 260,000 vols from the 15th and 16th centuries printed in Germany, Italy, France, Switzerland; collns incl. MSS, Albans-Balkanology, maps and incunabula; Dir GJOVALIN ÇUNI.

Tiranë

Centre for Scientific and Technical Information and Documentation: Rr. Lek Dukagjini 5, Tiranë; tel. (4) 222491; f. 1981; attached to Min. of Education and Science; Dir HYDAI MYFTIU; publ. *Buletin Analitik Fushor* (Disciplinary Analytical Bulletin, 12 a year).

National Library: Sheshi Skenderbej, Tiranë; tel. (4) 223843; e-mail a_plasari@hotmail.com; internet www.bksh.al; f. 1922; 1m. vols; Dir Dr AUREL PLASARI; publs *National Bibliography of Albanian Books* (4 a year), *National Bibliography of Albanian Periodicals* (12 a year).

Scientific Library: Tiranë; f. 1972; attached to Acad. of Sciences of Albania; Dir NATASHA PANO.

State Archives: Rr. 'Jordan Misja', Tiranë; tel. (4) 227959; e-mail dpa@albarchive.gov.al; internet www.albarchive.gov.al; document conservation and research; Dir NIKA NEVILA.

Museums and Art Galleries

Berat

District Historical Museum: Berat; tel. (32) 32595; f. 1948; Dir ARBEM JANPAJ.

Ethnographic Museum: Lagja 13, Shtatori, Berat; tel. (32) 32224; e-mail info@beratmuseum.net; internet www.beratmuseum.net; f. 1979; folk ethnographic culture from Berat and southern Albanian region; Dir KASTRIOT DERVISHI.

'Onufri' Iconographic Museum: Lagja Kala, Berat; tel. (32) 32248; e-mail info@beratmuseum.net; internet www.beratmuseum.net; f. 1986; located in the town's castle; exhibits incl. icons by the medieval painter Onufri; Dir KASTRIOT DERVISHI.

Durrës

Archaeological Museum: 1st Quartier, Talantia St, Durrës; tel. (52) 22253; f. 1951; exhibits representing life in ancient Durrës; artefacts from ancient Greek, Roman and medieval periods.

Elbasan

Kristoforidhi, K., House-Museum: Elbasan; birthplace of the patriot and linguist; Dir LIMAN VAROSHI.

Fier

Apollonia Archaeological Museum: Fier; f. 1958; exhibits incl. archaeological items from the fmr town of Apollonia.

District Historical Museum: Fier; tel. (34) 2583; e-mail informacion@bashkiafier.gov.al; f. 1948; Dir PETRIT MALUSHI.

Korçë

Mio, V., House-Museum: Korçë; house where the painter worked; contains works of art by Mio.

Museum of Education: L 12, Blvd Shen Gjergji, Korçë; tel. (824) 3022; f. 1887 as the first Albanian school of language, converted to museum 1960; displays the history of the Albanian alphabet and devt of education in Albania.

Museum of the Struggle for National Liberation: Blvd Repuplika, Korçë; tel. (824) 2888; f. 1977; library of 400 vols.

Muzeu Kombetar i Artit Mesjetar (National Museum of Medieval Art): Korçë; tel. (824) 3022; internet www.muzeumesjetar.al; f. 1980; attached to Min. of Culture; 7,000 items; colln of icons by Onufri and Onufer Qiprioti and other anonymous artists of 13th and 14th centuries; Dir LORENC GLOZHENI.

Kruja

National Ethnographic Museum: Fortress of Kruja, Kruja; tel. (53) 22225; e-mail info@muzeukombetarskenderbeukruje.com; f. 1989; objects on display depict the Albanian way of living over 300 years; collns incl. ceramics, cotton, silk, wool; various embroideries.

National Museum 'George Kastriot Skenderbeu': Krujë Castle, Kruja; tel. (53) 22225; f. 1982; memorabilia of the nat. hero; items depicting history of 15th-century Albania.

Përmet

Frashëri Brothers Museum: Përmet; birthplace of the brothers Frashëri.

Shkodër

Gurakuqi, Luigi, House-Museum: Shkodër; house where the patriot lived.

Migjeni House-Museum: Shkodër; where the writer Migjeni lived.

Pascha, Vaso, House-Museum: Shkodër; house where the patriot lived.

Tiranë

Albanian National Culture Museum: Tiranë; e-mail nnati@akad.edu.al; attached to Institute of Nat. Culture; exhibits incl. agricultural tools of all periods, stock-breeding equipment, interiors and exteriors, household objects, textiles and customs, local crafts and ceramics up to the present day.

Galeria Kombetare e Arteve: Blvd Dëshmorët e Kombit, Tiranë; tel. (4) 2233976; e-mail info@gka.al; internet www.gka.al; f. 1954; Dir ARTAN SHABANI.

National Historic Museum: Blvd Dëshmorët e Kombit, sheshi Skenderbej, Tiranë; tel. (4) 2228389; f. 1981; displays 4,750 objects in pavilions representing different periods in Albanian history, heraldic emblems of Albanian princes, cathedral columns, icons by Onufri, Illyrian and Greco-Roman artefacts, history of modern Albania; Dir VILSON KURI.

National Museum of Archaeology: Tiranë; tel. (4) 2226541; e-mail nnati@akad.edu.al; f. 1948; attached to the Institute of Archaeology of the Acad. of Sciences of Albania; exhibits from prehistoric and historic times up to Middle Ages; responsible for archaeological museums at Durrës, Apollonia and Butrinti; library of 7,200 vols, film and photograph libraries; Curator ILIR GJIPALI; publ. *Illyria* (2 a year).

Natural Science Museum: Tiranë; tel. (4) 22908; e-mail info@unitir.edu.al; internet www.fshn.edu.al; attached to Univ. of Tiranë; f. 1948; zoology, botany, geology; Head ELTJO HALIMI.

Vlorë

District Historical Museum: Vlorë; tel. (63) 2646; f. 1953; archaeology, history of art, history.

Muzeu Etnografik i Vlorës (Ethnographic Museum): Vlorë; tel. (33) 23514.

Muzeu i Pavarësisë (Independence Museum): Vlorë; tel. (33) 2229419; f. 1936; museum bldg was the site of the Ismail Qemali govt and drafting of the declaration of independence; exhibits incl. objects and documents from the Nat. Renaissance period of Albania, rooms where the first Albanian prime min. worked, the meeting room, a camera from 1912; Chief Officer AGRON SKEHU.

Universities

ALEKSANDËR MOISIU UNIVERSITY OF DURRËS

Rr. Currilave 1, Durrës
Telephone: (52) 239162
E-mail: info@uamd.edu.al
Internet: www.uamd.edu.al

Founded 2005
State control
Languages of instruction: Albanian, English
Academic year: October to July

Rector: Prof. Dr MITHAT MEMA
Deputy Rector: Dr SOFOKLI GARO
Deputy Rector: Dr ARBEN DUSHI
Chancellor: Dr ULPIAN HOTI
Head of Int. Relations and Projects Office: BELINA BEDINI
Library Dir: VENERA ALIAJ

Library of 5,000 vols, foreign scientific periodicals, 26 Albanian periodicals from 1945 to 2003
Number of teachers: 225
Number of students: 6,000
Publication: *Journal of Studies on Economics and Society*

DEANS

Faculty of Business: Prof. Dr BARDHYL CEKU
Faculty of Education: Dr EDI PUKA
Faculty of Information and Technology: Doc. LINDITA MUKLI
Faculty of Integrated Studies with Practice: Dr VLADIMIR MUKA (acting)
Faculty of Juridical and Political Sciences: Dr ALKET HYSENI
Faculty of Professional Studies: KSEANELA SOTIROFSKI (Dir)

UNIVERSITETI 'ALEKSANDËR XHUVANI' ELBASAN

Rinia, Elbasan
Telephone: (54) 52782
E-mail: info@uniel.edu.al
Internet: www.uniel.edu.al

Founded 1909
State control
Academic year: October to July

Rector: Prof. Dr JANI DODE

Library of 100,000 vols
Number of teachers: 245
Number of students: 11,000
Publications: *Scientific Bulletin* (4 a year), *Studenti* (magazine)

DEANS

Faculty of Economics: Dr ALBERT DELIMETA
Faculty of Human Sciences: Prof. Dr ROLAND GJINI
Faculty of Natural Sciences: Prof. Dr PEÇI NAQELLARI
Faculty of Social Sciences: Prof. Dr VILSON KURI

UNIVERSITETI BUJQËSOR I TIRANËS (Agricultural University of Tiranë)

Kodër-Kamëz, Tiranë
Telephone: (47) 200873
E-mail: iroaut@yahoo.com
Internet: www.ubt.edu.al

Founded 1951 as Instituti i Lartë Bujqësor (Higher Agricultural Institute), present status 1991
State control
Language of instruction: Albanian
Academic year: October to September

Rector: Prof. Dr FATOS HARIZAJ
Vice-Rector for Education: Prof. Dr BIZENA BIJO
Vice-Rector for Research: Prof. Dr VELESIN PEÇULI
Head of Int. Relations office: Prof. Dr ARBEN VERÇUNI
Head of Research and Scientific Cooperation: Prof. Dr ANILA HODA
Library Dir: ERMIRA TOZAJ

Library of 15,000 vols
Number of teachers: 290
Number of students: 13,450
Publication: *Albanian Review of Agricultural Sciences*

DEANS

Faculty of Agriculture and Environment: Prof. Dr ARDIAN MAÇI
Faculty of Biotechnology and Food: Prof. Dr VLASH MARA
Faculty of Economy and Agribusiness: Prof. Dr BAHRI MUSABELLIU
Faculty of Forestry Sciences: Assoc. Prof. VATH TABAKU
Faculty of Veterinary Medicine: Assoc. Prof. DHIMITËR RAPTI

UNIVERSITETI EQREM ÇABEJ

Rr. Shtatori 18, Gjirokastër
Telephone: (84) 263408
E-mail: rektori@uogj.edu.al
Internet: www.uogj.edu.al

Founded 1971
State control
Language of instruction: Albanian
Academic year: October to July

Rector: GËZIM SALA

DEANS

Faculty of Education and Social Sciences: ROLAND ZISI
Faculty of Natural Sciences: Prof. Dr LAVDI HASANI

UNIVERSITETI FAN S. NOLI

Rr. Gjergj Kastrioti, Korçë
Telephone: (82) 42230
E-mail: info@unkorce.edu.al
Internet: www.unkorce.edu.al

Founded 1971 as Higher Agricultural Institute, present name and title 1992

State control
Languages of instruction: Albanian, English
Academic year: October to July

Rector: Asst Prof. Dr GJERGJI MERO
Vice-Rector for Tuition: Prof. Dr ALI JASHARI
Vice-Rector for Research: Prof. Dr GJERGJI PENDAVINJI
Chancellor: ILIR SOSOLI
Librarian: EDMOND TOLE

Library of 40,000 books
Number of teachers: 124 full-time and 139 part-time
Number of students: 5,447 (incl. part-time and full-time)
Publication: *Buletin Shkencor* (Scientific Research Bulletin)

DEANS

Faculty of Agriculture: Prof. Dr IRENA KALLÇO
Faculty of Economy: Prof. Dr ELFRIDA ZEFI
Faculty of Education: Asst Prof. Dr ALEKSANDRA PILURI
Br. of Nursing: EDA STASA

PROFESSORS

JASHARI, A., Education
MANOKU, Y., Economics
PENDAVINJI, G., Education
TENEQEXHIU, K., Agriculture
ZEFI, E., Economics

UNIVERSITETI I ARTEVE, TIRANË
(University of Arts, Tiranë)

Blvd Dëshmorët e Kombit, Sheshi Nen Tereza, Tiranë
Telephone: (4) 2225488
Internet: www.uart.edu.al

Founded 1966 as Instituti i Lartë i Arteve (Higher Institute of Arts), present status 1990, current name adopted 2011
State control
Language of instruction: Albanian

Rector: Prof. PETRIT MALAJ
Deputy Rector: Assoc. Prof. ARBEN LLOZI
Deputy Rector: Assoc. Prof. ERALD BAKALLI
Library Dir: MIRANDA BAKIASI

Library of 50,000 vols
Number of teachers: 386
Number of students: 947

DEANS

Faculty of Fine Arts: Assoc. Prof. ARTAN PEQINI
Faculty of Music: Prof. SOKOL SHUPO
Faculty of Scenic Arts, Drama: Prof. KASTRIOT ÇAUSHI

UNIVERSITETI I SHKODRËS 'LUIGJ GURAKUQI'
(University of Shkodra 'Luigj Gurakuqi')

Rektorati, Sheshi 2 Prilli, Shkodër
Telephone: (22) 42235
E-mail: iroshkoder@unishk.edu.al
Internet: www.unishk.edu.al

Founded 1991, based on fmr Instituti i Lartë Pedagogjik (Higher Pedagogical Institute), Shkodër (f. 1957)
State control
Languages of instruction: Albanian, English, French, German, Italian
Academic year: October to July

Chancellor: FLORIAN BJANKU
Rector: Prof. Dr ARTAN HAXHI
Vice-Rector: Prof. Dr FATMIR VADAHI
Librarian: ALIDA LUKA

Library of 1,000 vols in Albanian, catalogue of Albanologist and Balkanologist, 32 rare books dating to the beginning of 16th century
Number of teachers: 635 (incl. 183 full-time, 452 part-time)
Number of students: 13,750 (incl. 8,051 full-time, 5,699 part-time)
Publication: *Scientific Bulletin* (1 a year)

DEANS

Faculty of Economics: Prof. Dr ARJETA TROSHANI
Faculty of Education: Prof. Dr GEZIM DIBRA
Faculty of Foreign Languages: Dr RAJMONDA KËÇIRA
Faculty of Law: GASPËR KOKAJ
Faculty of Natural Sciences: Prof. Dr ADEM BEKTESHI
Faculty of Social Sciences: Prof. Dr MIMOZA PRIKU

UNIVERSITETI I SPORTEVE TE TIRANËS
(Sports University of Tiranë)

Rr. Muhamet Gjollesha, Tiranë
Telephone: (4) 2226652
E-mail: contact@ust.edu.al
Internet: www.ust.edu.al

Founded 1958 as Higher Institute of Physical Education
State control
Language of instruction: Albanian
Academic year: October to July

Rector: Prof. Dr VEJSEL RIZVANOLLI
Vice-Rector: Dr ARBEN KACURRI

Library of 2,835
Number of teachers: 68
Number of students: 835
Publications: *Focus* (2 a year), *Journal of Sport Science* (2 a year)

DEANS

Faculty of Movement Science: Prof. Dr MEHMET SPAHIU
Faculty of Physical Activity and Recreation: Prof. Assoc. Dr AGRON KASA
Sports Research Institute: Dr ARTAN SHYTAJ

UNIVERSITETI I TIRANËS
(University of Tiranë)

Blvr Dëshmorët e Kombit, Sheshi Nen Tereza, POB 183, Tiranë
Telephone: (4) 2228402
E-mail: info@unitir.edu.al
Internet: www.unitir.edu.al

Founded 1957
State control
Academic year: September to June

Rector: Prof. Dr DHORI KULE
Vice-Rector: Prof. Dr ELSA KONE
Sec.: MAKLENA ÇABEJ
Library Dir: ARJANA KITA

Library of 700,000 vols
Number of teachers: 750
Number of students: 27,745
Publications: *Buletini i Shkencave Mjekësore* (Medicine, 4 a year), *Buletini i Shkencave të Natyrës* (Natural Sciences, 4 a year), *Përmbledhje studimesh* (Colln of Studies, 4 a year, with Institute of Geological Research)

DEANS

Faculty of Economics: Dr KADRI XHULALI
Faculty of Foreign Languages: Doc. AVNI XHELILI
Faculty of History and Linguistics: Dr PASKAL MILO
Faculty of Law: ZEF BROZI
Faculty of Mechanics and Electronics: Dr GËZIM KARAPICI
Faculty of Medicine: Doc. KRISTO PANO
Faculty of Natural Science: Prof. Dr LLUKAN PUKA
Faculty of Philosophy and Sociology: Doc. LUAN PIRDENI

UNIVERSITETI POLITEKNIK I TIRANËS
(Polytechnic University of Tiranë)

Blvd Dëshmorët e Kombit, Sheshi Nen Tereza, Nr 4, Tiranë
Telephone: (4) 2227996
E-mail: enkjaho@yahoo.com
Internet: www.upt.al

Founded 1951 as Polytechnic Institute, present status 1991
State control

Rector: JORGAQ KACANI
Vice-Rector: AKLI FUNDO

Library of 250,000 vols, 20,000 periodicals
Number of teachers: 470
Number of students: 6,297

DEANS

Faculty of Construction Engineering: ANDREA MALIQARI
Faculty of Electrical Engineering: AIDA SPAHIU
Faculty of Geology and Mining: PERPARIM HOXHA
Faculty of Mechanical Engineering: ANDONAQ LONDO

UNIVERSITETI TEKNOLOGJIK 'ISMAIL QEMAL' VLORË
('Ismail Qemal' Technological University of Vlorë)

Lagija 'Pavaresia', Skele Vlore, Vlorë
Telephone: (63) 24952
E-mail: kancelar@univlora.edu.al
Internet: www.univlora.edu.al

Founded 1994 as a Technological University
State control

Rector: EUSTRAT ZHUPA
Chancellor: MIMOZA XHELADINI

Library of 10,100 vols
Number of teachers: 195
Number of students: 15,000

DEANS

Faculty of Economics: Dr ALBERT QARRI
Faculty of Humanities: Dr ENGJELL LICAJ
Faculty of Public Health: Asst Prof. HAJDAR KICAJ
Faculty of Technical Sciences: (vacant)

UNIVERSITY OF NEW YORK TIRANË

Rr. 'Medar Shtylla' prane Kopshtit Botanik, POB 2301, Tiranë
Telephone: (42) 273056
E-mail: admissions@unyt.edu.al
Internet: www.unyt.edu.al

Founded 2002, accredited by Min. of Education and Science 2006
Private control
Language of instruction: English
Academic year: September to August

Rector: Dr DIONYSIOS MENTZENIOTIS
Deputy Rector: KONSTANTINOS GIAKOUMIS
Pres. and Founder: ELIAS FOUTSIS

Library of 4,000 vols
Number of teachers: 82
Number of students: 524

DEANS

Faculty of Computer Science: Dr MARENGLEN BIBA
Faculty of Economics and Business: Prof. AGIM KUKELI
Faculty of English: Dr MIMOZA RISTA-DEMA
Faculty of Humanities and Social Sciences: Dr ADAM EHRLICH
Faculty of Mathematics and Natural Sciences: Prof. FEJZI KOLANECI

ALGERIA

The Higher Education System

Only the Université d'Alger, which was founded on the French model in 1879 (and reorganized in 1909), pre-dates independence in 1962. From this date the number of higher education establishments in the newly independent Algeria and the number of students enrolled increased considerably. The system of tertiary education was reformed in 1971 and in 1985/86 (when students were encouraged to specialize in vocational subjects and exact sciences), with further major reforms following in 1988. The higher education system in Algeria falls under the authority of the Ministry of Higher Education and Scientific Research. In 2009/10 the number of students receiving higher education (including postgraduate students) was 1,144,271, and several thousand students also go abroad to study. In September 2011 the Government reported that the capacity of the higher education system for 2011/12 was 1,404,700 students, an increase of more than 150,000 compared with the previous academic year. In addition to the 47 main accredited universities, there are 10 Centres universitaires, 19 Écoles nationales supérieures, five Écoles normales supérieures (teacher training institutes) and a number of technical colleges.

Students are admitted to higher education on the basis of either the Baccalauréat de l'enseignement secondaire or the Baccalauréat de technicien. The three levels of higher education qualifications are the Diplôme or Licence, Maîtrise and Doctorat d'état. Both the Diplôme d'études universitaires appliquées (DEUA) and the Licence are awarded after three years of study, while the Diplôme d'études supérieures (covering scientific fields only) is awarded after four to six years. Engineering, medicine, dentistry and pharmacy degrees and other professional courses within the first level last for five years, while the Docteur en médecine is awarded after seven years. The second degree level (and first postgraduate) is the Maîtrise. This is a two-year taught course including a thesis. Finally, following a Maîtrise awarded with a grade of at least assez bien, a Doctorat d'état is awarded after three to five years of additional study.

Students may also undertake technical or vocational training at university level. On completion of basic education, vocational training is offered by Centres de formation professionnelle, and on completion of the three-year course a student is awarded the Certificat d'aptitude professionelle (also called the Certificat de technicien), whilst completion of a four-year course leads to the Brevet de maîtrise.

Instituts de technologie (technological institutes) are educational establishments operated by other ministries or national corporations. Degrees offered include the DEUA, the Diplôme de technicien supérieur (two-and-a-half or three years) and the Diplôme d'ingénieur (five years). These institutes are regulated by the ministry or national corporation responsible, and programmes are not standardized.

Higher education in Algeria, which was traditionally based on the French system, is currently undergoing reform. The new system, known as LMD (Licence, Masters, Doctorate) aims to bring Algerian higher education into line with other international education systems, such as the European Bologna model. The first stage, a three-year 180-credit Licence began to be phased in from 2004 and has since been implemented as a pilot project at 10 universities. The second stage, a two-year 120-credit Masters (or Maîtrise) was phased in from 2007/08. Any university that intends to offer the new-style three-tier courses has first to undergo quality assurance and a validation process undertaken by the Ministry of Higher Education and Scientific Research. The implementation of the LMD system is ongoing and, in the mean time, traditional degrees are still being offered alongside the new degrees. At the end of 2011 the European Union entered into an agreement on scientific and technological cooperation with Algerian universities and a number of reforms were being carried out in postgraduate medical and pharmaceutical courses, adding a further year of study to allow a six-year programme leading to a Doctorate. Decrees were issued in 2012 by the Ministry of Higher Education and Scientific Research naming those establishments authorized to offer Masters and Doctorates and fixing the number of students on each of the courses over the next three years. Admissions were to be made on the basis of a national 'concours'.

Regulatory and Representative Bodies

GOVERNMENT

Ministry of Culture: BP 100, Palais de la Culture 'Moufdi Zakaria', Plateau des Annassers, Kouba, Algiers; tel. (21) 291010; e-mail contact@m-culture.gov.dz; internet www.m-culture.gov.dz; Minister KHALIDA TOUMI.

Ministry of Higher Education and Scientific Research: 11, chemin Doudou Mokhtar, Ben Aknoun, 16422, Algiers; tel. (21) 912323; e-mail info@mesrs.dz; internet www.mesrs.dz; Minister MOHAMED MEBARKI.

Ministry of National Education: 8, rue de Pékin, el-Mouradia, Algiers; tel. (21) 605560; e-mail men@education.gov.dz; internet www.education.gov.dz; Minister Prof. ABDELLATIF BABA AHMED.

Ministry of Training and Vocational Education: rue des Frères Aîssou, Ben Aknoun, Algiers; tel. (21) 911503; e-mail contact@mfep.gov.dz; internet www.mfep.gov.dz; Minister NOUREDINE BEDOUI.

ACCREDITATION

Direction de la Formation Supérieure Graduée (Directorate of Higher Education Qualifications): 11, chemin Doudou Mokhtar, Ben Aknoun, 16422 Algiers; tel. (21) 911796; e-mail dfsg@mesrs.dz; attached to Min. of Higher Education and Scientific Research; central admin. body that regulates, assesses and accredits HEIs; Dir MUSTAPHA HAOUCHINE.

Sub-Directorates:

Sous Directeur des Agréments, du Contrôle et des Equivalences (Sub-Directorate of Skills Assessment and Credential Recognition): tel. (21) 914408; e-mail sdsace@mesrs.dz; Dir HADDA WAHIDA SAÏL.

Sous Directeur des Sciences Exactes, des Technologies et des Sciences de la Nature et de la Vie (Sub-Directorate of Applied Science and Technology, and Natural and Life Sciences): tel. (21) 912354; e-mail sdsetnv@mesrs.dz; Dir ASSIA ABABOU.

Sous Directeur des Sciences Sociales et Humaines, des Lettres et des Langues (Sub-Directorate of Social and Human Sciences, Arts and Languages): tel. (21) 912880; e-mail sdsshll@mesrs.dz; Dir DJAMEL BOUKEZZATA.

Sous Directeur du Suivi Pédagogique et de l'Evaluation (Sub-Directorate of Educational Conformity and Evaluation): tel. (21) 911030; e-mail sdspe@mesrs.dz; Dir ABDERAHMANE BOUHENNA.

NATIONAL BODIES

Agence Nationale de Développement et de la Recherche Universitaire (National Development Agency for University Research): ave Pasteur Hacène Badi, El Harrach, 16200 Algiers; tel. (21) 526801; e-mail andru@wissal.dz; attached to Min. of Higher Education and Scientific Research.

Agence Nationale de Valorisation des Résultats de la Recherche et du Développement Technologique (National Agency for Valuation of Results of Research and Technological Development): 23, ave Slimane Asselah, Telemly, Algiers; tel. (21) 639007; e-mail info@anvredet.org.dz; internet www.anvredet.org.dz; attached to

Min. of Higher Education and Scientific Research; Dir HALLICHE DJAMILA.

Agence Nationale pour le Développement de la Recherche en Santé (National Agency for the Development of Health Research): BP 1801/08, Oran; tel. (41) 581404; e-mail info@andrs-dz.org; internet www.andrs-dz.org; Dir Prof. KAOUEL MEGUENNI; publ. *Journal Algérien de Médicine*.

Learned Societies

GENERAL

El-Djazairia el-Mossilia: 1, rue Hamitouche, Algiers; f. 1930; cultural soc., particularly concerned with Arab classical music; 452 mems; Pres. NACEREDDINE BENMERABET; Sec. Gen. ABDELHADI MERAOUBI.

AGRICULTURE, FISHERIES AND VETERINARY SCIENCE

Société Algérienne de Médecine Vétérinaire (Algerian Society for Veterinary Medicine): 21, rue Didouche Mourad, Algiers; tel. (21) 386232; Pres. Dr TRIKI YAMANI.

HISTORY, GEOGRAPHY AND ARCHAEOLOGY

Société Archéologique du Département de Constantine (Constantine Archaeological Society): Musée Gustave Mercier, Constantine; f. 1852; 250 mems; library of 10,000 vols; Pres. Dr BAGHLI (acting); publ. *Recueil des Notices et Mémoires*.

Société Historique Algérienne (Algerian Historical Society): c/o Faculté des Lettres, Univ. d'Alger, Algiers; f. 1963; 600 mems; publ. *Revue d'Histoire et Civilisation du Maghreb*.

LANGUAGE AND LITERATURE

British Council: British Embassy, 3, chemin Captain Hocine Slimane, Algiers; tel. (21) 480947; e-mail john.mitchell@britishcouncil.org; internet www.britishcouncil.org/algeria.htm; offers courses and examinations in English language and British culture and promotes cultural exchange with the UK; Dir JOHN MITCHELL.

Goethe Institut: 165, chemin de Sfindja, 16000 Algiers; tel. (21) 742559; e-mail spr@algier.goethe.org; f. closed in 1994; reopened in 2003; offers courses and examinations in German language and culture and promotes cultural exchange; Dir ANDREAS ZÜRN.

Instituto Cervantes: 9, rue Khelifa Boukhalfa, 16000 Algiers; tel. (21) 633802; e-mail cenarg@cervantes.es; internet argel.cervantes.es; f. 1992; offers courses and examinations in Spanish language and culture and promotes cultural exchange with Spain and Spanish-speaking Latin and Central America; Dir RAQUEL ROMERO GUILLEMAS; Academic Head JUAN VICENTE PIQUERAS SALINAS; Administrator MARÍA JOSÉ ARTÉS RODRÍGUEZ.

MEDICINE

Société Algérienne de Cardiologie (Algerian Society of Cardiology): CHU Mustapha, 16024 Algiers; tel. (21) 236381; f. 1998; Pres. Prof. YASSIN BOUHOUITA; publ. *Journal de la Société Algérienne de Cardiologie*.

Société Algérienne de Médecine Générale (SAMG) (Algerian Society of General Medicine): 21, rue des chouhadas hassi-Mameche, 27004 Mostaganem; tel. (45) 220369; e-mail contact@samgdz.org; internet samgdz.org; f. 2012; promotes primary care and general medicine; Dir Dr HADJIDJ REDOUANE.

Société Algérienne de Neurochirurgie (Algerian Society for Neurosurgery): CHU Bab El Oued, blvd Said Touati, Algiers; tel. (21) 964470; internet www.sanc-dz.com; Pres. Dr ABDERRAHMANE SIDI SAID; publ. *Journal de Neurochirurgie*.

Société Algérienne de Psychiatrie (Algerian Psychiatric Society): EHS Chéraga, rue Souidani Boudjemaa, Chéraga, Algiers; tel. (21) 372330; e-mail contact@sapsy-dz.com; internet www.sapsy-dz.com; f. 1998; Pres. Prof. F. KACHA; publ. *Revue* (irregular).

Union Médicale Algérienne (Algerian Medical Association): POB 8, Aadun St, Algiers; tel. (31) 525304; e-mail saidkhaled11@yahoo.fr; publ. *Algérie Médicale*.

NATURAL SCIENCES

Société Algérienne de Chimie (Algerian Society of Chemistry): BP 63, El Alia, Bab Ezzouar, 16111 Algiers; publ. *Journal de la Société Algérienne de Chimie* (2 a year; in English, French and Arabic).

Research Institutes

GENERAL

Direction Générale de la Recherche Scientifique et du Développement Technologique (Directorate General of Scientific Research and Technological Development): 11, chemin Doudou Mokhtar Ben Aknoun, Algiers; tel. (21) 278620; e-mail h.aourag@dgrsdt.dz; internet www.nasr.dz; f. 1998; main executive body for govt policy; Dir-Gen. Prof. HAFID AOURAG; Dir for Research Programming, Evaluation and Prospection Prof. MOLHTAR SELLAMI; Dir for Admin. and Financing of Scientific Research Prof. MOHAMED BOUHICHA; Dir for Devt and Scientific and Technical Services Prof. YAHIA RACHEDI.

AGRICULTURE, FISHERIES AND VETERINARY SCIENCE

Institut National de la Recherche Agronomique (INRAA) (National Institute of Agronomic Research): BP 200, 2, rue des Frères Ouadak, Belfort, El Harrach, 16200 Algiers; tel. (21) 521283; e-mail inraa@inraa.dz; internet www.inraa.dz; f. 1966; attached to Min. of Agriculture and Rural Devt; library of 6,500 vols; Dir M. BEKKOUCHE; publ. *Recherche Agronomique*.

Institut National de Recherche Forestière (INRF) (National Institute of Forestry Research): BP 37, Chéraga, Algiers; tel. (21) 901026; e-mail info@inrf.dz; internet www.inrf.dz; f. 1981; attached to Min. of Agriculture and Rural Devt; library of 4,000 vols; Dir ABDELLAH DEDJAHI; publ. *Annale de la recherche forestière*.

BIBLIOGRAPHY, LIBRARY SCIENCE AND MUSEOLOGY

Centre de Recherche sur l'Information Scientifique et Technique (Centre for Research into Scientific and Technical Information): 5, rue des 3 Fréres Aissou, Ben Aknoun, Algiers; tel. (21) 912136; e-mail ceristdir@cerist.dz; internet www.cerist.dz; f. 1985.

Institut de Bibliothéconomie et des Sciences Documentaires (Institute of Library Economics and Documentation): Univ. d'Alger, 2, rue Didouche Mourad, Algiers; tel. (21) 777108; e-mail allahoum@yahoo.fr; f. 1975; Dir Prof. RABAH ALLAHOUM.

ECONOMICS, LAW AND POLITICS

Centre de Recherche en Economie Appliquée pour le Développement (CREAD) (Centre for Research in Applied Economics for Development): Algiers; tel. (21) 942367; internet www.cread-dz.org; divs of agriculture, territory and environment, human development and social economics, industrial economics, macroeconomics; Dir MOHAMED YASSINE FERFERA; publ. *Les Cahiers du CREAD* (4 a year).

Institut National du Travail (National Work Institute): Algiers; tel. (21) 310314; e-mail intalgerie@int.dz; internet www.int.dz; publ. *Revue Algérienne du Travail*.

EDUCATION

Institut National de Recherche en Education (INRE) (National Institute for Research into Education): BP 193, Oued Romane El Achour, Algiers; tel. (21) 300448; internet www.inre-dz.org; f. 1996; Dir MOHAMMED IDER; publ. *Les Cahiers de l'INRE* (1 a year).

HISTORY, GEOGRAPHY AND ARCHAEOLOGY

Centre National de Recherche en Anthropologie Sociale et Culturelle (National Research Centre for Social and Cultural Anthropology): BP 1955, El-M'Naouer, Technopôle de l'USTO, Bir El Djir, 31000 Oran; tel. (41) 560475; e-mail crasc@crasc.org; internet www.crasc-dz.org; f. 1992 as a research unit; present status 2003; Dir NOURIA BENGHABRIT-REMAOUN; publ. *Insaniyat*.

Centre National de Recherches Préhistoriques Anthropologiques et Historiques (National Centre for Prehistorical, Anthropological and Historical Research): 3, rue Franklin Roosevelt, 16500 Algiers; tel. (21) 747929; e-mail contact@cnrpah.org; internet www.cnrpah.org; f. 1955 as Centre Algérien de Recherches Anthropologiques, Préhistoriques et Ethnographiques; 1964 Centre de Recherche Anthropologiques, Préhistoriques et Ethnographiques; present status 2003; attached to Min. of Culture; library of 35,000 vols; Dir SLIMANE HACHI; publs *El Insan, Lybica* (1 a year), *Madjallat et Tarikh, Travaux, Mémoires et Documents du CNRPAH*.

Institut National de Cartographie et de Télédétection (National Institute of Cartography and Remote Detection): Palais de Expositions, Pins Maritimes, Algiers; tel. (21) 219107; e-mail contact@inct.dz; internet www.inct.mdn.dz; f. 1967; under trusteeship of Min. of Defence; Dir NADIR SAADI; publs maps (100 to 150 a year), *Bulletin des Sciences Géographiques* (2 a year).

MEDICINE

Institut National d'Hygiène et de Sécurité (National Institute of Hygiene and Safety): Lotissement Meridja, BP 07, 42395 Saoula; tel. (21) 307701; f. 1972; library of 8,000 vols, 110 periodicals, 45,000 microfiches; Dir-Gen. CHÉRIF SOUAMI; publ. *Revue Algérienne de Prévention* (4 a year).

Institut National de Santé Publique (National Institute for Public Health): 4, chemin El Bakr, El Biar, Algiers; tel. (21) 945297; internet www.ands.dz/insp/insp-accueil.htm; f. 1993; attached to Min. of Health; to promulgate health information, disease control, protection and promotion of public health.

Institut Pasteur d'Algérie (Pasteur Institute in Algeria): route du Petit Staouéli, Dély-Brahim, Algiers; tel. (21) 372674; e-mail contact@pasteur.dz; internet www.pasteur.dz; f. 1910; research and higher studies in microbiology, parasitology and immunology; preparation of vaccines and sera in conjunction with the health services of Algeria; library of 47,000 vols, 500 periodicals; Dir Prof. KAMAL KEZZAL; publ. *Archives* (12 a year).

NATURAL SCIENCES

Centre de Recherche en Astronomie, Astrophysique et Géophysique CRAAG (Astronomy, Astrophysics and Geophysics Research Centre): BP 63, route de l'Observatoire, Bouzareah, Algiers; tel. (21) 904454; internet www.craag.dz; f. 1890 l'Observatoire d'Alger; present status 1991; attached to Min. of the Interior; Dir KAMEL TOUMADJ.

TECHNOLOGY

Centre de Développement des Energies Renouvelables (CDER) (Centre for the Development of Renewable Energies): BP 62, route de l'Observatoire Bouzaréah, Algiers; tel. (21) 901503; e-mail sdirection@cder.dz; internet www.cder.dz; f. 1988; Dir Dr NACHIDA KASBADJI MERZOUK; publ. *Revue des Energies Renouvelables*.

Research Units:

Unité de Développement des Equipements Solaires (Solar Energy Development Unit): BP 386, route Nationale 11, Bou-Ismail, 42415 Tipaza; tel. (24) 410200; internet www.udes.dz; Dir SALAH BOUHOUCHE.

Unité de Recherche Appliquée en Energies Renouvelables (Applied Research Unit for Renewable Energies): BP 88, Gart Taam, ZI Bounoura, Ghardaia; tel. (29) 870126; e-mail direction@uraer.dz; internet www.uraer.dz; Dir Dr SAMIRA CHADER KERDJOU.

Unité de Recherche en Energies Renouvelables en Milieu Saharien (Renewable Energies in the Sahara Research Unit): BP 478, route de Reggane, Adrar; tel. (49) 965168; e-mail urerms@urerms.dz; internet www.urerms.dz; Dir Dr MESSAOUD HAMOUDA.

Centre de Développement des Technologies Avancées (Centre for the Development of Advanced Technologies): Cité 20 Aout 1956 Baba Hassen, Algiers; tel. (21) 351018; internet www.cdta.dz; f. 1988; laboratories for robotics, plasma, lasers, thermonuclear fusion, cybernetics, ionization, microelectronics, nanotechnology, informatics and telecommunication; Dir B. BOUZOUIA; publ. *Technologies Avancées*.

Centre de Recherche en Biotechnologie (Biotechnology Research Centre): BP E73, Ali Mendjli Nouvelle Ville UV 03, Constantine; tel. (31) 672203; e-mail webmaster@crbt-dz.org; internet www.crbt-dz.org; f. 2010; divs of agriculture, biotechnology industries, environment, food-processing, health.

Centre de Recherche en Technologie des Semi-conducteurs pour l'Energétique (CRTSE) (Technological Research Centre on Semi-conductors for Energy Systems): BP 140, 2, blvd Frantz Fanon, 16027 Algiers; tel. (21) 433511; internet www.crtse.dz; f. 2012.

Centre de Recherche Scientifique et Technique sur les Régions Aride (Scientific and Technical Research Centre for Arid Regions): Univ. Mohamed Khider de Biskra, Algiers; tel. (33) 734214; e-mail crstra@crstra.dz; internet www.crstra.dz; f. 1991.

Centre National de Recherche en Soudage et Contrôle (National Research Centre for Welding and Testing): BP 64 Chéraga, route de Dély-Ibrahim, Algiers; tel. (21) 361850; e-mail m.yahi@csc.dz; internet www.csc.dz; Dir M. YAHI.

Research Units:

Unité de Recherche en Technologies Industrielles (URTI) (Industrial Technologies Research Unit): Dir HAZEM MERRADI.

Unité des Recherches Appliquées en Sidérurgie Métalliurgie (URASM) (Steel and Metalworks Applied Research Unit): Dir SALAH BOUHOUCHE.

Commissariat à l'Energie Atomique (Atomic Energy Commissariat): BP 1017, Algiers Gare; tel. (21) 434444; e-mail bibl-crna@crna.dz; f. 1983; attached to Min. of Energy and Mines; research and devt in the field of renewable sources of energy, incl. atomic, solar, wind and geothermal energy; incl. centres for energy conversion and for nuclear and solar studies; Librarian AIDA BAHLOUL.

Office National de la Recherche Géologique et Minière/Service Géologique de l'Algérie (National Office of Geological and Mining Research): BP 102, Cité Ib Khaldoun, 35000 Boumerdès; tel. (24) 817599; e-mail orgm-dg@orgm.com.dz; internet www.orgm.com.dz; f. 1883; attached to Min. of Energy and Mines; 5 regional divs: E (located in Tebessa), Central (Tizi Ouzou), W (Sidi Bel Abbes), SW (Béchar) and S (Tamanrasset); library of 50,000 vols, periodicals, maps and aerial photographs; Gen. Man. ABDELKADER SEMIANI; publs *Bulletins du Service Géologique d'Algérie* (2 a year), *Mémoires du Service Géologique de l'Algérie* (1 a year).

Libraries and Archives

Algiers

Archives Nationale d'Algérie (National Archives of Algeria): BP 38, Algiers; 20, rue Hassan Bennamane, Birkhadem, Algiers; tel. (21) 541620; internet www.archives-dgan.gov.dz; f. 1971; Dir ABDELMADJID CHIKHI.

Bibliothèque de l'Université d'Alger (Library of the University of Algiers): 2, rue Didouche Mourad, 16000 Algiers; tel. (21) 637101; e-mail bu@univ-alger.dz; internet bu.univ-alger.dz; f. 1880; 800,000 vols; Dir ABDALLAH ABDI.

Bibliothèque du Centre de Recherche sur l'Information Scientifique et Technique (CERIST) (Library of the Centre for Scientific and Technical Information): 5, rue des 3 Frères Aissou-Ben Aknoun, Algiers; tel. (21) 916205; e-mail cerist.bib@mail.cerist.dz; internet biblio.cerist.dz; 7,900 monographs, proceedings of conferences.

Bibliothèque Nationale (National Library): BP 127, El Hamma, 16200 Algiers; tel. (21) 675781; e-mail contact@biblionat.dz; internet www.biblionat.dz; f. 1835; spec. collns incl. Africa and the Maghreb; 950,000 vols; Dir MUHAMMAD AÏSSA-MOUSSA; publs *Bibliographie de l'Algérie* (2 a year), *Publications*, several collns in Arabic and French.

Centre d'Information et de Documentation sur les Droits de l'Enfant et de la Femme (CIDDEF) (Information and Documentation Centre for Women's and Children's Rights): 5, rue Ibn Hazm, Sacré Coeur, Algiers; tel. (21) 743447; e-mail ciddefenfant@yahoo.fr; internet www.ciddef-dz.com; f. 2002; 2,000 documents on women's and children's rights, legal advice; Dir NADIA AÏT-ZAÏ; publ. *CIDDEF Revue*.

Constantine

Bibliothèque Municipale (Municipal Library): Hôtel de Ville, Constantine; f. 1895; 15,060 ancient texts on medicine, philosophy, law; 25,000 vols; Librarian LYNDA GASMI.

Museums and Art Galleries

Algiers

Direction de la Conservatoin et la Restauration du Patrimoine Culturel (Office of the Conservation and Restoration of Cultural Heritage): Ministère de la Culture et du Tourisme, Kouba, Algiers; e-mail dcrpc@m-culture.gov.dz; f. 1901; gen. admin. of museums, restoration, conservation and archaeological excavations; library of 8,000 vols, 300 periodicals; Dir MOURAD BOUTEFLIKA; publ. *Bulletin d'Archéologie Algérienne* (1 a year).

Musée National d'Art Moderne et Contemporain (National Museum of Modern and Contemporary Art): 25, rue Larbi Ben M'hidi, 16002 Algiers; tel. (21) 717252; e-mail contact@mama-dz.com; internet mama-dz.com; f. 2006; industrial design since 1905, modern art since 1945, plastic arts, graphical and photographic arts, new media.

Musée National des Antiquités (National Museum of Antiquities): 177, blvd Krim Belkacem, Parc de la Liberté, 16000 Algiers; tel. (21) 681129; e-mail museemna@musee-antiquites.art.dz; internet www.musee-antiquites.art.dz; f. 1897; library of 3,100 vols, 102 periodicals; Dir DRIAS LAKHDAR; publ. *Annales du Musée National des Antiquités*.

Musée National des Arts et Traditions Populaires (National Museum of Arts and Popular Tradition): 9, rue Mohamed Akli Malek, Algiers; tel. (21) 439908; e-mail contact@mnatp-algerie.org; internet www.mnatp-algerie.org; f. 1987; colln of 20,000 photographs.

Musée National des Beaux Arts (National Fine Arts Museum): pl. Dar-el-Salem, El-Hamma, Algiers; tel. (21) 664916; e-mail directrice@musee-beauxarts.dz; internet www.musee-beauxarts.dz; f. 1930; library of 17,000 vols, 300 periodicals; Dir DALILA ORFALI; publ. *Revue* (1 a year).

Musée National du Bardo (National Museum of Bardo): 3, blvd Franklin Roosevelt, Algiers; tel. (21) 747641; f. 1930; prehistory, ethnography; library of 3,000 vols; Dir FATIMA AZZOUG.

Musée National du Djihad (National Museum of Djihad): El Madania, Algiers; tel. (21) 653488; f. 1983; contemporary history; publ. *Actes du Musée*.

Constantine

Musée National Cirta (National Museum Cirta): Coudiat Aty, 25000 Constantine; tel. (31) 923895; e-mail museecirta@gmail.com; internet www.cirtamuseum.org.dz; f. 1853; archaeology, art; library of 20,000 vols; Dir AHMED GUEDDOUDA; publ. *Recueil et Mémoires de la Société Archéologique de Constantine*.

Oran

Musée National Zabana (National Museum Zabana): 19, ave Ahmed Zabana, Oran; tel. (41) 403781; e-mail info@museenationalzabana.dz; f. 1935; prehistory, Roman and Punic archaeology, ethnography, zoology, geology, botany, sculpture and painting; Dir Dr MALKI NORDINE.

Sétif

Musée Public National de Sétif: rue de l'A.L.N., 19000 Sétif; tel. (36) 514670; e-mail setifmuseum@gmail.com; internet www.setif-musee.net; f. 1992; prehistoric, Roman, Byzantine and medieval Islamic antiquities; Curator CHERIF RIACHE; Translator SEKHERI KHEMISSI.

Skikda

Musée de Skikda (Museum of Skikda): Skikda; Punic and Roman antiquities, modern art.

Tipaza

Musée de Tipaza (Museum of Tipaza): rue du Musée, Tipaza; tel. (24) 478938; f. 1955; ceramics and mosaics from pre-Roman necropolise.

Tlemcen

Musée de Tlemcen (Museum of Tlemcen): rue des Frères Abdeldjebba, 13000 Tlemcen; tel. (43) 204620; f. 1901; islamic art, minerals, botany, Numidian and Roman archaeology and ethnography.

Musée Moudjahid (Moudjahid Museum): plateau de Lalla Setti, 13000 Tlemcen; f. 2011; artefacts from the war of occupation to independence.

Musée National d'Art et d'Histoire (National Museum of Art and History): rue du 20 Août, 13000 Tlemcen; tel. (43) 204620; f. 2009; Islamic art and history.

Universities

UNIVERSITÉ 8 MAI 1945 DE GUELMA
(University 8 May 1945 of Guelma)

BP 401, 24000 Guelma
Telephone: (37) 204980
E-mail: recteur@univ-guelma.dz
Internet: www.univ-guelma.dz

Founded 2001
State control

Faculties of economics and management, humanities and social sciences, law, science and engineering

Rector: Prof. MOHAMED NEMAMCHA
Vice-Rector for Devt: Prof. MOHAMED ABDAOUI
Vice-Rector for Graduate Education: Dr SALAH ELLAGOUNE
Vice-Rector for Scientific Research and External Relations: Dr MOHAMED ZINE AISSAOUI

Number of teachers: 137
Number of students: 6,716

UNIVERSITÉ ABBES LAGHROUR KHENCHELA
(Abbes Laghrour University Khenchela)

Route de Constantine, BP 1252, El Houria, 40004 Khenchela
Telephone: (32) 331966
Internet: www.univ-khenchela.dz

Founded 2001 as Centre Universitaire de Khenchela; present status 2012
State control

Faculties of economic, business and management sciences, law and political sciences, literature and languages, nature and life sciences, social and human sciences, science and technology

UNIVERSITÉ ABDELHAK BENHAMOUDA DE JIJEL
(Abdelhak Benhamouda of Jijel University)

BP 98, Ouled Aissa, 18000 Jijel
Telephone: (34) 501400
E-mail: webmaster@univ-jijel.dz
Internet: www.univ-jijel.dz

Founded 1998
State control

Number of teachers: 137
Number of students: 3,757

DEANS

Faculty of Economic, Business and Management Sciences: MOHAMED BACHIR MIBIROUK
Faculty of Exact and Natural Sciences: ESSAID LEGHOUCHI
Faculty of Languages, Literature and Social Sciences: TAHAR BELAIOUAR
Faculty of Law and Political Sciences
Faculty of Science and Technology: MOHAMED RACHID MEKIDECHE

UNIVERSITÉ ABDELHAMID IBN BADIS DE MOSTAGANEM
(Abdelhamid Ibn Badis of Mostaganem University)

POB 227, 27000 Mostaganem
Telephone: (45) 265455
E-mail: amina.benbernou@univ-mosta.dz
Internet: www.univ-mosta.dz

Founded 1978
State control

Rector: Prof. M'HAMED MOHAMED SALAH EDDINE SEDDIKI
Vice-Rector for Devt: Prof. AHMED HEBBAR
Vice-Rector for External Relations: Dr AHMED CHAALAL
Vice-Rector for Graduate and Continuing Education: Prof. BERRABAH BENDOUKHA
Vice-Rector for Postgraduate Affairs and Scientific Research: Prof. NOOR EDDINE BENDERDOUCHE
Gen. Sec.: CHAREF OUNASSA ABID

Publication: *Annales du Patrimoine* (Arabic and French, 2 a year)

DEANS

Faculty of Arts and Letters: Dr SAADANE BRAIK
Faculty of Exact and Information Sciences: Dr HOUARI BELMEKKI
Faculty of Law and Political Sciences: Dr BENNAZZOUZ
Faculty of Nature and Life Sciences: Prof. ABDELLAH BERKANI
Faculty of Sciences and Technology: Prof. SAMIR BENTATA
Faculty of Social Sciences: Dr DJILALI HADJ SMAHA
Institute of Sports and Physical Education: Dr BENKAZDAALI

UNIVERSITÉ ABOU BEKR BELKAID DE TLEMCEN
(Abou Bekr Belkaid de Tlemcen University)

BP 119, 22, rue Abi Ayad Abdelkrim, Faubourg Pasteur, 13000 Tlemcen
Telephone: (43) 203189
E-mail: webcri@univ-tlemcen.dz
Internet: www.univ-tlemcen.dz

Founded 1974 as Centre Universitaire de Tlemcen
State control
Languages of instruction: Arabic, French
Academic year: September to July

Rector: ZOUBIR CHAOUCHE-RAMDANE
Vice-Rector for Devt: BOUCHERIT ROUISSET
Vice-Rector for External Relations: MUSTAFA DJAFOUR
Vice-Rector for Graduate and Continuing Education: FARID LAHFA
Vice-Rector for Postgraduate Affairs and Scientific Research: ABDESLAM TALEB
Librarian: NOUREDDINE HADJI

Library of 66,000 vols
Number of teachers: 1,130
Number of students: 30,036

PROFESSORS

Medicine:

ALLAL, M. R., Radiology
BENKALFAT, F. Z., Cardiology
BENKALFAT, M., General Surgery
HADJ ALLAL, F., Otorhinolaryngology

Science:

BABA AHMED, A., Physical Chemistry
BENMOUANA, M., Nuclear Engineering
BENYOUCEF, B., Energy Physics
BOUAMOUD, M., Atomic Physics
BOUCHERIF, A., Applied Mathematics
HADJIAT, M., Mathematics
TALEB BENDIAB, S. A., Chemistry

Social Sciences and Humanities:

BELMOKADEM, M., Quantitative Technology
BENDIABDALLAH, A., Management
BOUCHENAK KHELLADI, S. M., Management
DENDOUNI, H., Civil Law
DERRAGUI, Z., Literature
KAHLOULA, M., Private Law
KALFAT, C., Criminology
SOUTI, M., Finance

UNIVERSITÉ AMAR TELIDJI DE LAGHOUAT
(Amar Telidji of Laghouat University)

Route de Ghardaia, BP 37G, 03000 Laghouat
Telephone: (29) 932698
E-mail: rectorat@mail.lagh-univ.dz
Internet: www.lagh-univ.dz

Founded 1986 as École Normale Supérieure de l'Enseignement Technique; univ. status 2001
State control
Languages of instruction: Arabic, French
Academic year: October to July

Faculties of arts and letters, economic, business and management sciences, human and social sciences, law and political sciences, sciences, technology; institute of technical and applied sports sciences

Rector: Dr AZIB MAKHLOUF
Vice-Rector for Undergraduate, Graduate and Continuing Education: Prof. SAYAH GOUAL
Librarian: NOUIOUA HADJIRA

Library of 65,427 vols, 10 periodicals
Number of teachers: 312
Number of students: 9,417, 41 foreign students

UNIVERSITÉ BADJI MOKHTAR DE ANNABA
(University Badji Mokhtar of Annaba)

BP 12, 23000 Annaba
Telephone: (38) 875399
E-mail: abdelkrim.kadi@univ-annaba.org
Internet: www.univ-annaba.dz

Founded 1975
State control
Languages of instruction: Arabic, French
Academic year: September to June

Rector: Prof. ABDELKRIM KADI
Vice-Rector for External Relations: Prof. ABDELMADJID HANOUN
Vice-Rector for Graduate Studies: Prof. MOHAMED MANAA

Vice-Rector for Planning: Prof. MOUSSA OUCHEFOUN
Vice-Rector for Postgraduate Studies and Research: Prof. LOUISA ZOUIOUÉCHE ARIBI
Chief Admin. Officer: AHMED HAMDAOUI
Librarian: HADJ JAHEL

Library of 16,400 vols, 205 journals
Number of teachers: 2,278
Number of students: 42,446

Publications: *El-Tawassol* (humanities and social sciences, 2 a year), *Synthese* (science and technology, 2 a year)

DEANS

Faculty of Earth Sciences: NACER KHÉRICI
Faculty of Economics and Management: BELGACEM MADI
Faculty of Engineering: Prof. KAMEL CHAOUI
Faculty of Law: DJAMEL ABDELNASSER MANAA
Faculty of Letters, Humanities and Social Sciences: FOUAD BOUGUETTA
Faculty of Medicine: RACHID BENALI
Faculty of Science: ABDELAZIZ DOGHMANE

UNIVERSITÉ COLONEL AHMED DRAIA D'ADRAR
(Colonel Ahmed Draia of Adrar University)

Rue 11 Décembre 1960, 01960 Adrar
Telephone: (49) 965907
E-mail: cssi@univ-adrar.dz
Internet: www.univ-adrar.dz

Founded 2001
State control

Rector: A. ABBASSI
Vice-Rector for Devt: A. BAHAMAOUI
Vice-Rector for External Relations: D. BENABDEKFATTAH
Vice-Rector for Graduate and Continuing Education: S. HAMLIL
Vice-Rector for Research Devt and Communication: L. BOUKEMICHE

Number of teachers: 35
Number of students: 1,030

DEANS

Faculty of Arts and Humanities: M. ELMESSERI
Faculty of Science and Engineering: M. ABDELLAOUI
Faculty of Social Sciences and Islamic Studies: R. DEFROUR

UNIVERSITÉ D'ALGER
(University of Algiers)

2, rue Didouche Mourad, Algiers
Telephone: (21) 646970
E-mail: contact@univ-alger.dz
Internet: www.univ-alger.dz

Founded 1879 (reorganized 1909)
Languages of instruction: Arabic, French
State control
Academic year: September to June

Pres.: Prof. TAHAR HADJAR
Deputy-Pres. for Pedagogy: S. BABA-AMEUR
Deputy-Pres. for Planning: RABAH KHIMA
Deputy-Pres. for Postgraduates and Scientific Research: A. E. R. AZZI
Librarian: ABDELLAH ABDI

Number of teachers: 1,400
Number of students: 32,000.

FACULTIES

Faculty of Islamic Sciences: Annexe du Caroubier Hussein Dey, Algiers; tel. (21) 497027; internet www.fac-islamique-alger.dz.

Faculty of Law: Campus de Ben Aknoun II, Algiers; tel. (21) 912343; internet www.fac-droit-alger.dz; publ. *Revue Algérienne des Sciences Juridiques Economiques et Politiques* (2 a year).

Faculty of Medicine: 18, ave Pasteur, 16000 Algiers; tel. (21) 636874; e-mail fac-med.alger@yahoo.fr; internet www.faculte-medecine-alger.dz

UNIVERSITÉ D'ALGER 2
(University of Algiers 2)

Bouzaréah, 16032 Algiers
Telephone: (21) 909578
E-mail: contact@univ-alger2.dz
Internet: www.univ-alger2.dz

Founded 2009
State control

Faculties of Arabic language and literature, foreign languages, human sciences, social sciences

UNIVERSITÉ DE BÉCHAR
(University of Béchar)

BP 417, route de Kenadsa, 08000 Béchar
Telephone: (49) 815581
E-mail: webmaster@univ-bechar.dz
Internet: www.univ-bechar.dz

Founded 1986 as Institut National d'Etude Supérieure, present name 2009

Faculties of arts, human and social sciences, economics, business and administration sciences, languages, law and politics, science and technology

Rector: SLIMANI ABD AL-KADER

Library of 103,589 vols
Number of teachers: 371
Number of students: 8,461

UNIVERSITÉ DE BEJAIA
(University of Bejaia)

Route de Terga Ouzemour, 06000 Bejaia
Telephone: (34) 214333
E-mail: rectorat@univ-bejaia.dz
Internet: www.univ-bejaia.dz

Founded 1983
State control

Rector: Prof. BOUALEM SAIDANI

Library of 146,000 vols
Number of teachers: 1,197
Number of students: 30,600

DEANS

Faculty of Arts and Languages: MOUHAND MAHRAZI
Faculty of Economic, Business and Management Sciences: KHELLOUDJA ARABI
Faculty of Exact Sciences: YOUCEF KHALFAOUI
Faculty of Human and Social Sciences: NOUARA KAÏD TLILANE
Faculty of Law: ABDELKARIM BOUDRIOUA
Faculty of Medicine: A. OUDAI
Faculty of Natural and Life Sciences: DJEBBAR ATMANI
Faculty of Technology: BOUALEM SAIDANI

UNIVERSITÉ DE GHARDAIA
(University of Ghardaia)

Alnoumrat, 47000 Ghardaia
Telephone: (29) 870187
E-mail: siteuniv47@gmail.com
Internet: www.univ-ghardaia.dz
State control

Founded 2006 as centre universitaire

Faculties of humanities and social sciences, natural and life sciences, trade
Number of students: 1,187

UNIVERSITÉ DE KHEMIS MILIANA
(University of Khemis Miliana)

Route de Theniet El-Had, 44225 Khemis Miliana
Telephone: (27) 664232
E-mail: contact@univ-km.dz
Internet: www.cu-km.dz

Founded 2001 as centre universitaire
State control

Faculties of economics, business and management sciences, language and literature, law and political sciences, science and technology, social and human sciences, nature and earth sciences; institute of sports science

Rector: Prof. MOHAMED BEZZINI

UNIVERSITÉ DE LA FORMATION CONTINUE
(University of Continuous Education)

BP 43, rue Ahmed Ouaked, Dely Ibrahim, Algiers
Telephone: (21) 910681
E-mail: recteur@ufc.dz
Internet: www.ufc.dz

Founded 1990
State control

Rector: ABDELDJEBAR LEMNOUAR
Vice-Rector for Communication: BRAHIM BOUKRAA
Vice-Rector for Teaching: ABDELKADER NACERI
Gen. Sec.: ABDELKARIM SENIANE

UNIVERSITÉ D'EL TARF
(El Tarf University)

BP 73, 36000 El Tarf
Telephone: (38) 600943
E-mail: admin@univ-eltarf.dz
Internet: www.univ-eltarf.dz

Founded 1992 as centre universitaire
State control

Faculties of economic, business and management sciences, law and political sciences, literature and languages, nature and life sciences, social and human sciences, science and technology

Dir: Prof. RACHID SIAB

UNIVERSITÉ D'EL OUED
(El Oued University)

POB 789, Central Valley, 39000 El Oued
Telephone: (32) 223003
E-mail: sg@univ-eloued.dz
Internet: www.univ-eloued.dz

Founded 1995 as centre universitaire
State control

Faculties of arts and languages, commerce, economics and management, law and administration, science and technology, social and human sciences
Number of students: 11,435

UNIVERSITÉ DE MASCARA
(University of Mascara)

BP 305, route de Mamounia, 29000 Mascara
Telephone: (45) 804169
E-mail: rectorat@univ-mascara.dz
Internet: www.univ-mascara.dz

Faculties of economic, business and management sciences, human and social sciences, law and political science, natural and life sciences, science and technology

UNIVERSITÉ DE M'SILA
(University of M'sila)

BP 166, Ichebilia, 28000 M'sila
Telephone: (35) 550609

Internet: www.univ-msila.dz
Founded 2001
State control
Academic year: September to July
Rector: Prof. ABBAOUI LYAZID
Vice-Rector for Devt: Dr ZINELABIDINE RAHMOUNI
Vice-Rector for External Relations: Prof. LAHCÈNE MEZRAG
Vice-Rector for Graduate and Continuing Education: Prof. DEHIMI OUALI
Vice-Rector for Postgraduate Affairs and Scientific Research: Dr ALI DEBBI
Gen. Sec.: DJAMEL KHALDOUNE
Librarian: ALAOUA KADRI
Number of teachers: 1,230
Number of students: 28,000

DEANS
Faculty of Law and Political Sciences: Dr KHERBACHI AKILA
Faculty of Management and Economics: Prof. BOUGUERA RABAH
Institute of STAPS: Dr BOUSKERA AHMED

UNIVERSITÉ DES SCIENCES ET DE LA TECHNOLOGIE HOUARI BOUMEDIENE
(Houari Boumediene University of Science and Technology)

BP 32, El Alia, Bab Ezzouar, 16111 Algiers
Telephone: (21) 247950
E-mail: recteur@usthb.dz
Internet: www.usthb.dz
Founded 1974
Languages of instruction: Arabic, French
Academic year: September to July
Rector: Prof. BENALI BENZAGHOU
Vice-Rector for Communications: Prof. FAWZAI CHAFA-MEKIDECHE
Vice-Rector for Devt: Prof. MALEK BOUHADEF
Vice-Rector for Graduate and Continuing Studies: Prof. MOHAMED SAIDI
Vice-Rector for Postgraduate Studies and Scientific Affairs: Prof. DJAMEL EDDINE AKRETCHE
Sec. Gen.: M. RABAH SIAD
Librarian: SOUHILA BENRABAH
Number of teachers: 1,509
Number of students: 24,819
Publication: *Annales des Sciences et de la Technologie*

DEANS
Faculty of Biological Sciences: FATIMA LARABA-DJEBARI
Faculty of Chemistry: MOHAMED CHATER
Faculty of Civil Engineering: FARID KAOUA
Faculty of Earth Science, Geography and Management Territory: AZIOUZ OUABADI
Faculty of Electronics and Computer Science: ZAIA ALIMAZIGHI
Faculty of Mathematics: KAMEL BOUKHETALA
Faculty of Mechanical Engineering and Chemical Engineering: RACHIDA MAACHI
Faculty of Physics: Prof. AKILA FRAHI-AMROUN

UNIVERSITÉ DES SCIENCES ET DE LA TECHNOLOGIE MOHAMED BOUDIAF D'ORAN
(Mohamed Boudiaf of Oran University of Science and Technology)

BP 1505, El M'naouer, Oran
Telephone: (41) 560333
E-mail: webmaster@univ-usto.dz
Internet: www.univ-usto.dz
Founded 1975
Languages of instruction: Arabic, French
Academic year: September to July
Rector: Prof. M. BENSAFI
Vice-Rector for Planning and Orientation: MOHAMED TEBBAL
Vice-Rector for Graduate and Continuing Education: MAAMAR BOUDIA
Vice-Rector for Postgraduate Studies, Research and External Relations: BENYOUNES MAZART
Sec.-Gen.: ELOUADI DORGHAM
Librarian: BACHIR YAKOUBI
Number of teachers: 582
Number of students: 11,491

DEANS
Faculty of Architecture and Civil Engineering: MABROUH HAMANE
Faculty of Electrical Engineering: AZEDINE HAMID
Faculty of Mechanical Engineering: BENAMEUR HAMOUDI
Faculty of Sciences: MOSTEFA KAMECHE

UNIVERSITÉ DES SCIENCES ISLAMIQUES EMIR ABDELKADER DE CONSTANTINE
(Science University of Islamiques Emir Abdelkader of Constantine)

BP 137, Al Kaddour Bumdus, 25000 Constantine
Telephone: (31) 922694
E-mail: a.boukhalkhal@univ-emir.dz
Internet: www.univ-emir.dz
Founded 1984
State control
Academic year: September to June
Faculties of arts and humanities, culture and sharia, fundamentals of Islam, fundamentals of religion
Rector: Dr ABDULLAH BOUKHALKHAL
Vice-Rector for Devt: BOUBAKER AOUATI
Vice-Rector for Research: HAMIDA AMIRAOUI
Vice-Rector for Studies: ISMAIL SAMAI
Gen. Sec.: ABDELAZIZ KERADA
Library of 16,000 vols
Number of teachers: 205
Number of students: 3,934

UNIVERSITÉ DE TÉBESSA
(University of Tébessa)

12002 Tébessa
Telephone: (37) 490248
E-mail: cutebessa@ist.cerist.dz
Internet: www.univ-tebessa.dz
Founded 2009
Rector: Prof. SAID FIKRA
Vice-Rector for Devt: LAID HEMILA
Vice-Rector for Graduate and Continuing Studies: MOHAMMED KARA
Vice-Rector for Scientific Research and Communications: LOUIZA BOUDIBA
Gen. Sec.: BACHIR KARDI
Library of 120,000 vols
Number of students: 12,879

DEANS
Faculty of Economic, Business and Management Sciences: LAID BOUZENADA
Faculty of Exact Sciences, Nature and Life Sciences: MOHAMMED LOTFI BENKHEDIR
Faculty of Law and Political Sciences: DJALEL DIB
Faculty of Letters, Humanities and Social Sciences: (vacant)
Faculty of Science and Technology: FAÏÇAL CHEMAM

UNIVERSITÉ DJILLALI LIABES DE SIDI BEL ABBÈS
(University Djillali Liabes of Sidi Bel Abbès)

BP 89, 22000 Sidi Bel Abbès
Telephone: (48) 549888
E-mail: rectorat@univ-sba.dz
Internet: www.univ-sba.dz
Founded 1978 as centre universitaire; present status 1989
State control
Rector: ABDEL NACER TOU
Library of 70,000 vols
Number of teachers: 1,580
Number of students: 52,069

DEANS
Faculty of Economics: M. DANI ELKBIR
Faculty of Engineering: A. KHALFI
Faculty of Humanities: N. SEBBAR
Faculty of Law: B. MEKELKEL
Faculty of Medicine: A. DJADEL
Faculty of Science: M. BENYAHYA

UNIVERSITÉ D'ORAN
(Oran University)

BP 1524, El-M'Naouer, 31000 Oran
Telephone: (41) 581947
E-mail: contact@univ-oran.dz
Internet: www.univ-oran.dz
Founded 1967
State control
Languages of instruction: Arabic, French
Academic year: September to July (2 semesters)
Rector: Prof. LARBI CHAHED
Vice-Rector for Devt: MOHAMMED DELLIL
Vice-Rector for External Relations: Prof. A. Z. FOUATIH
Vice-Rector for Graduate and Continuing Education: AHMED BENAYED
Vice-Rector for Postgraduate Studies and Research: Prof. SAÏDI
Sec.-Gen.: MABROUK IKHLEF
Librarian: S. CHAIB DRAA
Library of 800,000 vols
Number of teachers: 1,200
Number of students: 45,000
Publications: *Applied Biology and Biotechnology*, *Resolang*

DEANS
Faculty of Economic, Business and Management Sciences: Prof. BACHIR BOULANDUAR
Faculty of Geography and Land Management: Prof. LARBI MEKAHLI
Faculty of Law: Prof. BACHIR YELLES CHAOUCH
Faculty of Letters and Arts: Prof. SAFIA MITAHRI
Faculty of Medical Studies: Prof. ZOUBIR FOUATIH
Faculty of Sciences: Prof. YAGOUBI BELABBAS
Faculty of Social Sciences: Prof. MOHAMMED MEZIANE

UNIVERSITÉ DR YAHIA FARÈS DE MÉDÉA
(Dr Yahia Farès de Médéa University)

Ain d'Heb, 26000 Médéa
Telephone: (25) 581687
E-mail: infos@univ-medea.dz
Internet: www.univ-medea.dz
Founded 1989
Faculties of arts, commerce and management, economics, languages, law, science and technology, social sciences and humanities
Dir: Dr CHAABAIKI MONKEY
Publication: *Revue de Recherche et Etude Scientifique*

UNIVERSITÉ DU 20 AOÛT 1955 DE SKIKDA
(University of 20 August 1955 of Skikda)

BP 26, Route d'El-Hadaiek, 21000 Skikda
Telephone: (38) 701032
E-mail: rectorat@univ-skikda.dz
Internet: www.univ-skikda.dz

Founded 2001
State control
Languages of instruction: English, French
Academic year: September to July

Rector: Prof. ALI KOUADRIA
Vice-Rector for Devt: Dr SALIM HADDAD
Vice-Rector for External Relations: Dr NARDJES BOUGHRARA
Vice-Rector for Graduate and Continuing Education: Prof. MOULOUD BELACHIA
Vice-Rector for Postgraduate Affairs and Scientific Research: Prof. OTMANI AMARA
Gen. Sec.: KHALED BOUDJELLAL

Number of teachers: 1,205
Number of students: 22,000

UNIVERSITÉ FERHAT ABBAS DE SÉTIF
(Ferhat Abbas de Sétif University)

Route de Scipion, 19000 Sétif
Telephone: (36) 620224
E-mail: sg@univ-setif.dz
Internet: www.univ-setif.dz

Founded 1978
State control
Languages of instruction: Arabic, French
Academic year: September to June

Rector: Prof. CHEKIB-ARSLANE BAKI
Vice-Pres. for Devt: Dr LARBI MOKRANI
Vice-Pres. for External Relations and Cooperation: BELKACEM NOUICER
Vice-Pres. for Graduate and Continuing Education: Prof. DAOUD HARZALLAH
Vice-Pres. for Research and Postgraduate Studies: Prof. MOHAMMED MOSTEFAI
Vice-Pres. for Undergraduate Studies: Prof. NABIL NANCIB
Gen. Sec.: NOUREDDINE BENHENNI
Librarian: CHÉRIF CHIDEKH

Number of teachers: 594
Number of students: 12,700

Publication: *Annales* (4 a year)

DEANS

Faculty of Arts and Languages: KAMEL KADRI
Faculty of Economics, Business and Management Sciences: SALAH SALHI
Faculty of Human and Social Sciences: MILOUD SEFFARI
Faculty of Law and Political Sciences: EL KHIER GUECHI
Faculty of Medicine: ABDEREZZAK TOUABTI
Faculty of Nature and Life Sciences: ALI CHOUGHUI
Faculty of Sciences: MUSTAPHA MAAMACHE
Faculty of Technology: RAHMANI LAZHER
Institute of Optometric and Precision Sciences: ABDELKRIM BENAICHE

UNIVERSITÉ HADJI LAKHDAR DE BATNA
(University Hadji Lakhdar of Batna)

5, ave Chahid Boukhlouf, 05000 Batna
Telephone: (33) 860602
E-mail: recteur@univ-batna.dz
Internet: www.univ-batna.dz

Founded 1977 as Centre Universitaire de Batna

Faculties of agronomic and veterinary sciences, economics, humanities and social sciences, hydraulic and civil engineering, law and political sciences, medicine, science and technology

Rector: Prof. TAHAR BENABID
Vice-Rector for Devt: Dr HACENE CHAABANE
Vice-Rector for External Relations: Dr TAYEB BOUZID
Vice-Rector for Graduate and Continuing Education: Prof. MED EL HADI RAHAL GHARBI
Vice-Rector for Postgraduate Students and Research: Prof. LAMINE MELKEMI
Sec.-Gen.: ALI LABOUEL

Library of 60,000 vols

Publications: *Revue Algérienne de Physique*, *Revue des Sciences et de la Technologie*

UNIVERSITÉ HASSIBA BENBOUALI DE CHLEF
(University Hassiba Benbouali of Chlef)

Hay Salam, route nationale 19, 02000 Chlef
Telephone: (27) 721067
E-mail: info@univ-chlef.dz
Internet: www.univ-chlef.dz

Founded 1983; present status 2001
State control

Faculties of arts and languages, civil engineering and architecture, economic, business and management sciences, human and social sciences, law and political sciences, sciences, technology; institutes of sport and physical sciences, agronomy sciences

Rector: A. OUAGUED
Vice-Rector for Communication and External Relations: BACHIR BELMADANI
Vice-Rector for Devt: LAMRI BELKACEM
Vice-Rector for Postgraduate and Research Studies: SOUMIA KOUADRI MOSTEFAI
Vice-Rector for Undergraduate, Graduate and Continuing Education: MOHAMMED F. FEKAOUNI

Library of 10,220 vols, 127 periodicals
Number of teachers: 275
Number of students: 12,522

Publication: *Nature et Technologie* (2 a year)

UNIVERSITÉ IBN KHALDOUN DE TIARET
(Ibn Khaldoun de Tiaret University)

BP 78, 14000 Tiaret
Telephone: (46) 425688
E-mail: univ-tiaret@mail.univ-tiaret.dz
Internet: www.univ-tiaret.dz

Founded 1980 as Institut National d'Enseignement Supérieur de Tiaret, became Centre Universitaire de Tiaret 1992, present name and status 2001
Languages of instruction: Arabic, French
Academic year: October to July

Faculties of arts and languages, economics, business and management sciences, human and social sciences, law and political science, nature and life sciences, technology and material sciences; institute of veterinary science

Rector: MUSTAPHA RAHMOUN
Vice-Rector for Devt: KAMEL HADOUCHE
Vice-Rector for External Relations: KOULA DOUKANI
Vice-Rector for Graduate and Continuing Education: BACHIR MAHMOUDI
Librarian: ABED MAKHLOUFI

Library of 150,000 vols
Number of teachers: 229
Number of students: 20,000

UNIVERSITÉ KASDI MERBAH D'OUARGLA
(Kasdi Merbah d'Ouargla)

BP 511, route de Ghardaïa, Ouargla
Telephone: (29) 711936
E-mail: info@univ-ouargla.dz
Internet: www.univ-ouargla.dz

Founded 1987 as École Nationale Supérieure; present status 2001
State control
Academic year: September to June

Rector: Prof. AHMED BOUTARFAIA
Vice-Rector for Devt: Prof. AMAR MESSAITFA
Vice-Rector for Graduate and Continuing Education: Prof. ABDELHAKIM SENOUSSI
Vice-Rector for Scientific Research and External Relations: Prof. FOUDIL DAHOU
Gen. Sec.: MESSAOUD SEGUEI

Number of teachers: 1,016
Number of students: 25,000

DEANS

Faculty of Economic, Business and Management Sciences: Dr AISSA BAHADI
Faculty of Human and Social Sciences: Dr MHAMED ELMAHDI BENAISSA
Faculty of Law and Political Sciences: Dr BOUHANIA GOUI
Faculty of Letters and Languages: Prof. MECHRI BENKHALIFA
Faculty of Nature, Life and Earth Sciences: Dr SAMIA BISSATL
Faculty of Technology and Material Sciences: Dr MOURAD KORICHI

UNIVERSITÉ LARBI BEN M'HIDI D'OUM EL-BOUAGHI
(University Larbi Ben M'hidi of Oum El-Bouaghi)

BP 358, 04000 Oum El-Bouaghi
Telephone: (32) 421036
E-mail: a.bouras@univ-oeb.dz
Internet: www.univ-oeb.dz

Founded 1983 as l'École Nationale Supérieure; 1997 became centre universitaire; present status 2009
State control
Languages of instruction: Arabic, French
Academic year: September to July

Rector: Prof. AHMED BOURAS
Vice-Rector for Devt, Strategic Planning and Orientation: Dr KHELLIL LATROUS
Vice-Rector for Graduate and Continuing Education: Prof. NOUREDDINE GHERRAF
Vice-Rector for Research Devt and External Relations: Dr ABDEL HAKIM HADDOUN
Gen. Sec.: BOUDJEMAA BELFRAIKH

Library of 160,592 vols
Number of teachers: 792
Number of students: 21,149

Publication: *Journal of New Technology and Materials*

DEANS

Faculty of Economics, Business and Management: SAID BRIKA
Faculty of Exact, Nature and Life Sciences: CHERIFA AZIZI
Faculty of Languages and Literatures: LAALMI LARAOUI
Faculty of Law and Political Science: MOKHTAR BOUABDELLAH
Faculty of Science and Applied Sciences: Dr ABDERRAHMANE DIB
Faculty of Social and Human Sciences: AHMED ZERZOUR
Institute of Earth Sciences and Architecture: MOHAMED CHERIF
Institute of Science and Technology of Physical and Sporting Activities: Prof. MOURAD BOUTEBBA

Institute of Urban Management Techniques: Dr AHMED GHENOUCHI

UNIVERSITÉ MENTOURI DE CONSTANTINE
(University Mentouri of Constantine)

BP 325, route Ain El Bey, 25017 Constantine
Telephone: (31) 818705
E-mail: vice-rect-relex@umc.edu.dz
Internet: www.umc.edu.dz

Founded 1969
Languages of instruction: Arabic, French
Faculties of earth sciences, economic sciences, engineering sciences, exact sciences, humanities and languages, medicine, nature and life sciences; institute of nutrition and food technology

Rector: Prof. ABDELHAMID DJEKOUN
Vice-Rector for External Relations: Prof. FARIDA HOBAR
Vice-Rector for Orientation, Planning and Information: Dr EMBARK FERKOUS
Vice-Rector for Postgraduate and Scientific Research: Prof. SAID CHEKROUD
Vice-Rector for Teaching: Dr MED EL HADI LATRECHE
Sec.-Gen.: FOUDIL BELAOUIRA
Librarian: TEBOURA BENKAID-KESBA

Library of 240,000 vols
Number of teachers: 2,467
Number of students: 78,782

Publications: *Sciences et Technologies* (12 a year), *Sciences Humaines* (2 a year)

UNIVERSITÉ M'HAMED BOUGARA DE BOUMERDÈS
(University M'hamed Bougara of Boumerdes)

Ave de l'indépendance, 35000 Boumerdès
Telephone: (24) 816901
E-mail: recteur@umbb.dz
Internet: www.umbb.dz

Founded 1981
Faculties of economics, business and management sciences, electrical engineering and electronics, engineering sciences, hydrocarbons and chemistry, law, sciences

Rector: OUIZA CHERIFI
Vice-Rector for Communication and External Relations: ABDEL AZZIZ TAIRI
Vice-Rector for Devt: MOHAMED ZAOUI
Vice-Rector for Postgraduate and Research Studies: MOHAND KESSAL
Vice-Rector for Undergraduate, Graduate and Continuing Education: ABDEL AZZIZ BENAISSA
Gen. Sec.: AHMED BOUFELLAH

Number of teachers: 1,214
Number of students: 25,538

UNIVERSITÉ MOHAMED CHÉRIF MESSAADIA DE SOUK AHRAS
(Mohamed Chérif Messaadia University of Souk Ahras)

BP 1553, route de Aannaba, 41000 Souk-Ahras
Telephone: (37) 351901
Internet: www.cu-soukahras.dz

Founded 2001 as centre universitaire
State control
Faculties of language and literature, economic, business and management sciences, law and administration, natural and life sciences, science and technology

Rector: YOUCEF BERRICHE

Number of teachers: 285
Number of students: 8,000

UNIVERSITÉ MOHAMED EL BACHIR EL IBRAHIMI DE BORDJ BOU ARRÉRIDJ
(Mohamed El Bachir El Ibrahimi University of Bordj Bou Arréridj)

Bordj Bou Arréridj
Telephone: (35) 666301
E-mail: direction@univ-bba.dz
Internet: www.univ-bba.dz

Founded 2000 as centre universitaire; present status 2012
State control
Faculties of economic, business and management sciences, law and political sciences, literature and languages, mathematics and information sciences, natural, earth and life sciences, social and human sciences, science and technology

UNIVERSITÉ MOHAND AKLI OUELHADJ BOUIRA
(Mohand Akli Ouelhadj University Bouira)

Bouira
Telephone: (26) 938843
Internet: www.univ-bouira.dz

Founded 2005 as Centre Universitaire de Bouira; present status 2012
State control
Academic year: September to July
Faculties of Arabic language and literature, Berber language and culture, economics and management, human and social sciences, law

Number of teachers: 145
Number of students: 12,600

UNIVERSITÉ MOULOUD MAMMERI DE TIZI-OUZOU
(University Mouloud Mammeri of Tizi-Ouzou)

BP 17, Oued-Aissi, Tizi-Ouzou
Telephone: (26) 215314
E-mail: univ_tizi@mail.ummto.dz
Internet: www.ummto.dz

Founded 1977; present status 2001
State control
Faculties of arts and humanities, biology and agronomy, construction engineering, economics and management, electrical and computer engineering, law, medicine and science

Rector: Prof. NACEUR EDDINE HANNACHI

Library of 24,472 monographs, 3,623 theses, 208 journals
Number of students: 45,000

Publication: *Research Review of Sciences and Technologies*

UNIVERSITÉ SAAD DAHLAB DE BLIDA
(University Saad Dahlab of Blida)

Route de Soumaa, BP 270, 09000 Blida
Telephone: (25) 433625
E-mail: contact@univ-blida.dz
Internet: www.univ-blida.dz

Founded 1981 as Centre Universitaire de Blida
Faculties of economic, business and management sciences, law and political sciences, literature and languages, medicine, sciences, technology, veterinary and biological sciences

Rector: MED TAHAR ABADLIA
Vice-Rector for Communication Relations: SALIHA OUKID KHOUAS
Vice-Rector for Devt: DJAMEL BOUKERCH
Vice-Rector for External Relations: KARIMA MENOUERI
Vice-Rector for Graduate Studies: SI LAKEHAL BAHIA
Vice-Rector for Postgraduate Affairs and Scientific Research: MOHAMMED MEGHATRIA

Number of teachers: 644
Number of students: 12,318

Publication: *Revue de l'Université*

UNIVERSITÉ TAHAR MOULAY DE SAIDA
(Tahar Moulay of Saida University)

BP 138, Cité Ennasr, 20000 Saida
Telephone: (48) 477729
E-mail: webmaster@univ-saida.dz
Internet: www.univ-saida.dz

Rector: Prof. BELGOUMÈNE BERREZOUG

Number of teachers: 538
Number of students: 11,000

UNIVERSITÉ MOHAMED KHIDER DE BISKRA
(University Mohamed Khider of Biskra)

BP 145, 07000 Biskra
Telephone: (33) 746160
E-mail: rectorat@univ-biskra.dz
Internet: www.univ-biskra.dz

Founded 1998
State control

Rector: Prof. BELKACEM SELATNIA
Vice-Rector for External Relations: Prof. BRAHIM MEZERDI
Vice-Rector for Graduate Education: Prof. ABDELOUHAD CHALA
Vice-Rector for Postgraduate Affairs and Scientific Research: Prof. ABDELHAMID GUETTALA
Gen. Sec.: NACER GHAMRI

Number of teachers: 800
Number of students: 28,000

Publication: *Courrier du Savoir*

DEANS

Faculty of Arts: Prof. MOHAMED KHAN
Faculty of Human and Social Sciences: Prof. ABDERRAHMANE BERKOUK
Faculty of Law and Political Sciences: Dr ZINE AZRI
Faculty of Management and Economy: Dr ABDELOUAHAB BENBRAIKA
Faculty of Sciences: Dr MEKKI MELLAS

ATTACHED RESEARCH UNIT

Laboratoire de Recherche en Hydraulique Souterraine et de Surface: tel. (33) 745090; e-mail info@larhyss.net; internet www.larhyss.net

UNIVERSITÉ ZIANE ACHOUR DE DJELFA
(University Ziane Achour of Djelfa)

Route Moudjbara, BP 3117, 17000 Djelfa
Telephone: (27) 900203
E-mail: recteur@univ-djelfa.dz
Internet: www.univ-djelfa.dz

Founded 1990

Rector: ALI CHOUKRI
Vice-Rector for Postgraduate and Continuing Education: AMEUR KADDOURI
Vice-Rector for Scientific Research and Public Relations: MOKHTAR FODHILI
Vice-Rector for Student Devt: BRAHIM LEHRACH
Sec.: MOHAMED TETA
Dir of Distance Learning: MESSAOUD KARBOUA
Librarian: MOHAMED DIF

Number of students: 17,406

DEANS

Faculty of Economic, Business and Management Sciences: AHMED TAIBA

Faculty of Law and Political Sciences: A. HAMMADI

Faculty of Literature, Languages, Social and Human Sciences: HICHEM HASSAN

Faculty of Natural and Life Sciences: MOKHTAR LAHRECH

Faculty of Science and Technology: BOUBKEUR BENCHEIKH

University Centres

CENTRE UNIVERSITAIRE DE AÏN TÉMOUCHENT
(University Centre of Aïn Témouchent)

BP 284, route de Sidi Bellabes, 46000 Aïn Témouchent
Telephone: (43) 603431
Internet: www.cuniv-aintemouchent.dz
State control

Institutes of Arabic literature and language, economic, business and management sciences, foreign languages, information technology, law and political sciences, material science, science and technology

CENTRE UNIVERSITAIRE D'EL BAYADH
(University Centre of El Bayadh)

BP 900 route d'Aflou, Géryville, 3200 El Badayh

Founded 2011
State control

Institutes of economics and management, technology, natural and life sciences

Dir: Dr ABDELOUAHAB EL ACHBI

CENTRE UNIVERSITAIRE DE MILA
(University Centre of Mila)

Mila
Telephone: (31) 570123
E-mail: directeur@centre-univ-mila.dz
Internet: www.centre-univ-mila.dz

Founded 2008
State control

Dir: Prof. ALI BOUKAROURA

Number of teachers: 120
Number of students: 5,700

CENTRE UNIVERSITAIRE DE NAAMA
(University Centre of Naama)

Naama
Internet: www.cuniv-naama.dz

Founded 2010
State control

Institutes of administration and languages and literature

Dir: BOUCHRIT KÉBIR

Number of teachers: 33
Number of students: 237

CENTRE UNIVERSITAIRE DE RÉLIZANE
(University Centre of Rélizane)

Rélizane
E-mail: cur48@cu-relizane.dz
Internet: www.cu-relizane.dz

Founded 2008
State control

Institutes of agronomy, hydraulic science, science and technology

Dir: BENAÏSSA BEKKOUCHE

CENTRE UNIVERSITAIRE DE TAMANRASSET
(University Centre of Tamanrasset)

Tamanrasset
Telephone: (29) 347744
Internet: www.cu-tamanrasset.dz
State control

Institutes of economic and business sciences, human and social sciences, law and political sciences, literature and languages, science and technology

Dir: ISMAIL RUIN

CENTRE UNIVERSITAIRE DE TINDOUF
(University Centre of Tindouf)

Tindouf

Founded 2012
State control

Institutes of Arabic Language and literature, earth sciences, economic, business and management sciences, law

Dir: ABDELHAMID TOUHAMI

CENTRE UNIVERSITAIRE DE TIPAZA
(University Centre of Tipaza)

Tipaza

Founded 2012

Institutes of economic and business sciences, human and social sciences, science

Dir: FADILA HARTITI
Number of students: 2,000

National Schools and Institutes

ÉCOLE DES HAUTES ÉTUDES COMMERCIALES
(School of Commerce Studies)

11, chemin Doudou Mokhtar, Ben Aknoun, Algiers
Telephone: (21) 911176
E-mail: contact@hec.dz
Internet: www.hec.dz

Founded 1970 as Institut de Technologie du Commerce; current status 2009
State control

Dir: Prof. ABDESSELAM SAADI

ÉCOLE NATIONALE D'ADMINISTRATION
(National College of Administration)

13 chemin Abdelkader Gadouche, Hydra, Algiers
Telephone: (21) 601350
E-mail: ena@wissal.dz
Internet: www.ena.dz

Founded 1964
State control

Provides training for entry into the civil service

Dir: HOCINE CHERHABIL

Library of 30,000 vols, 120 periodicals

Publication: *Idara* (2 a year)

ÉCOLE NATIONALE POLYTECHNIQUE
(National College of Polytechnic)

Ave Hassen Badi El Harrach, 16200 Algiers
Telephone: (21) 521027
E-mail: enp@enp.edu.dz
Internet: www.enp.edu.dz

Founded 1962
State control
Language of instruction: French
Academic year: September to July

Dir: Prof. MOHAMED DEBYECHE
Deputy Dir for External Relations and Continuous Education: Prof. AHMED BOUBAKEUR
Deputy Dir for Postgraduate Studies and Scientific Research: Prof. DJAMAL BOUKHETALA
Deputy Dir for Undergraduate Studies: Dr REDOUAN TAHMI

Library of 45,000 vols
Number of teachers: 200
Number of students: 1,500 (1,000 undergraduate, 500 graduate/doctorate)

DEANS

Faculty of Automatic Engineering: Prof. FARES BOUDJEMA

Faculty of Chemical Engineering: Dr FAROUDJA MOHELLEBI

Faculty of Civil Engineering: Dr RATIBA KETTAB-MITICHE

Faculty of Electronics: Dr SALAH AIT CHEIKH

Faculty of Electrotechnique: Prof. RACHID IBTIOUEN

Faculty of Environmental Engineering: Dr RABAH BOUARAB

Faculty of Hydraulics: Dr ABDELMALEK BERMAD

Faculty of Industrial Engineering (Industrial Management–Innovation Management): Prof. NACÉRA ABOUN

Faculty of Mechanical Engineering: Prof. SAID RECHAK

Faculty of Metallurgy: Prof. MOHAMED CHITROUB

Faculty of Mining Engineering: Dr MALEK OULD HAMOU

Faculty of Quality–Hygiene–Security–Environment and Risk Management: Dr SALIHA ZEBOUDJ

ÉCOLE NATIONALE POLYTECHNIQUE D'ORAN
(National Polytechnic College of Oran)

BP 1523, El-M'naouer, 31000 Oran
Telephone: (41) 290776
E-mail: benziane_baki@yahoo.fr
Internet: www.enset-oran.dz

Founded 1970

Depts of chemistry, civil engineering, electrical engineering, languages, management, mathematics–computing, mechanical engineering, physics–chemistry

Dir: Prof. ABDELBAKI BENZIANE

Library of 34,917 vols

Publication: *COST*

ÉCOLE NATIONALE SUPÉRIEURE AGRONOMIQUE (ENSA)
(National College of Agronomics)

ave Hacène Badi, El Harrach, 16200 Algiers
Telephone: (21) 521987
E-mail: f.mekemeche@ensa.dz
Internet: www.ensa.dz

Founded 1905
State control

Dir: ROSA ISSOLAH

Library of 22,848 vols, 122 periodicals
Number of teachers: 165
Number of students: 1,400

Publication: *Annales* (1 a year)

ÉCOLE NATIONALE SUPÉRIEURE D'HYDRAULIQUE
(National College of Hydraulics)

BP 31, 29, route de Soumaa, 09000 Blida
Telephone: (25) 399447
E-mail: contact@ensh.dz
Internet: www.ensh.dz
Founded 1972
State control
Depts of continuing education, core courses, research and postgraduate studies, specialized subjects, training and education
Dir: MOHAMED SAÏD BENHAFID
Publication: *Journal de l'Eau et de l'Environnement* (12 a year)

ÉCOLE NATIONALE SUPÉRIEURE D'INFORMATIQUE (ESI)
(National College of Informatics (ESI))

BP 68M, Oued Smar, El Harrach, 16309 Algiers
Telephone: (21) 516077
E-mail: de@esi.dz
Internet: www.esi.dz
Founded 2008
Training and research in information science
Dir-Gen.: MOULOUD KOUDIL
Dir for Studies: NACERA CHERID
Gen. Sec.: MOHAMED DARTERKI
Librarian: ABD RAHMAN HAMRI

ÉCOLE NATIONALE SUPÉRIEURE DE JOURNALISME ET DES SCIENCES DE L'INFORMATION
(National College of Journalism and Information Science)

11, rue Doudou Mokhtar, Ben Aknoun, 16058 Algiers
Telephone: (21) 230113
E-mail: contact@ensjsi.com
Internet: www.ensjsi.com
Founded 2010
State control
Dir: BRAHIM BRAHIMI

ÉCOLE NATIONALE SUPÉRIEURE DE MANAGEMENT
(National College of Management)

37, rue Ben M'Hidi, Algiers
Telephone: (21) 749776
E-mail: contact@ensm.dz
Internet: www.ensm.dz
Founded 2008
State control
Dir: CHERIF BELMIHOUB

ÉCOLE NATIONALE SUPÉRIEURE DE SCIENCES POLITIQUES (ENSSP)
(National College of Political Science)

Algiers
Internet: enssp.net
Founded 2009
State control

ÉCOLE NATIONALE SUPÉRIEURE DE STATISTIQUE ET D'ÉCONOMIE APPLIQUÉE (ENSSEA)
(National College of Statistics and Applied Economics)

11, chemin Doudou Mokhtar Benaknoun, Algiers
Telephone: (21) 912133
E-mail: contact@enssea.dz
Internet: www.enssea.dz
Founded 1970 as Institut des Techniques de Planification, renamed 1983, current status 2010
State control
Dir: Prof. AHMED ZAKANE
Number of teachers: 99
Number of students: 1,703

ÉCOLE NATIONALE SUPÉRIEURE DE TECHNOLOGIE
(National College of Technology)

route nationale 5, Z.I. Rouiba, Algiers
Telephone: (21) 815674
Internet: www.enst.dz
Founded 2009
State control
Dir: DJAMAL DINE BARAMA

ÉCOLE NATIONALE SUPÉRIEURE DES MINES ET DE LA MÉTALLURGIE
(National College of Mines and Metallurgy)

BP 233, Annaba
Telephone: (30) 822368
E-mail: contact@ensmm-annaba.org
Internet: ensmm-annaba.dz
Founded 2009
State control
Dir: HACÈNE CHADLI

ÉCOLE NATIONALE SUPÉRIEURE DES SCIENCES DE LA MER ET DE L'AMÉNAGEMENT DU LITTORAL (ENSSMAL)
(National High School of Marine Sciences and Coastal Management)

Campus Universitaire, BP 19, Bois des Cars Dély Ibrahim, 16320 Algiers
Telephone: (21) 918908
E-mail: enssmal@enssmal.dz
Internet: www.enssmal.dz
Founded 1882
Language of instruction: French
Academic year: September to July
Dir: Dr DJAMEL EDDINE ZOUAKH
Library of 11,500 vols
Number of teachers: 62
Number of students: 1,001 (971 graduates, 30 postgraduates)
Publication: *Pelagos* (irregular)

ÉCOLE NATIONALE SUPÉRIEURE DES SCIENCES DE LA MER ET DE L'AMENAGEMENT DU LITTERAL
(Higher National School of Science of the Sea and of the Literal Development)

BP 19, Campus Universitaire de Dely Ibrahim, Bois des Cars, 16320 Algiers
Telephone: (21) 917774
E-mail: dir@enssmal.dz
Internet: www.enssmal.dz
Founded 1882; 1964 Institut Oceanographie d'Alger; 1975 Centre de Recherches Océanographiques et des Pêches (CROP); 1983 Institut des Sciences de la Mer et de l'Amenagement du Litteral (ISMAL); present status 2008
State control
Five-year degree courses in marine engineering
Dir: DJAMEL EDDINE ZOUAKH
Librarian: WAHIBA BESSAOU

ÉCOLE NATIONALE SUPÉRIEURE DES TRAVAUX PUBLICS (ENSTP)
(National College of Public Works (ENSTP))

BP 32, rue Sidi Garidi, 16051 Algiers
Telephone: (21) 286838
E-mail: entp@wissal.dz
Internet: www.entp.edu.dz
Founded 1966
State control
Publication: *Algérie Équipement*

ÉCOLE NATIONALE SUPÉRIEURE EN INFORMATIQUE
(National College in Computer Science)

BP 68, Oued Smar, El Harrach, 16270 Algiers
Telephone: (21) 516077
E-mail: adg@esi.dz
Internet: www.esi.dz
State control
Dir: M. KOUDIL

ÉCOLE NATIONALE SUPÉRIEURE VÉTÉRINAIRE (ENSV)
(National Veterinary College)

BP 161, Hacène Badi, El Harrach, Algiers
Telephone: (21) 525132
Internet: www.ensv.dz
Founded 1970
State control
Dir: Prof. YOUCEF HAMDI-PACHA
Library of 8,000 vols, 40 periodicals
Number of teachers: 77
Number of students: 1,139
Publication: *Revue des Sciences Vétérinaires*

ÉCOLE POLYTECHNIQUE D'ARCHITECTURE ET D'URBANISME
(Polytechnic School of Architecture and Planning)

BP 177, route de Beaulieu, El Harrach, 16200 Algiers
Telephone: (21) 52-53-83
E-mail: zeroualа54@yahoo.com
Internet: www.epau-alger.edu.dz
Founded 1970
State control
Language of instruction: French
Academic year: September to July
Dir: Prof. MOHAMED SALAH ZEROUALA
Library of 43,000 vols, 8,767,320 periodicals
Number of students: 1,152
Number of teachers: 152

ÉCOLE SUPÉRIEURE DE COMMERCE
(Higher School of Commerce)

1, rampe Salah Gharbi, Agha, Algiers
Telephone: (21) 423231
E-mail: contact@esc-alger.com
Internet: www.esc-alger.com
Founded 1900
State control
4-Year first degree courses, 2-year Masters course
Number of teachers: 89
Number of students: 663

Colleges

Conservatoire de Musique et de Déclamation (Conservatory of Music and Recitation): 2 blvd Ché Guévara, Algiers; f. 1920; library: 6,800 vols; 600 students; Dir-Gen.

BACHETARZI MOHIEDDINE; Sec.-Gen. KADDOUR GUECHOUD.

École Supérieure des Beaux-Arts (Higher School of Fine Arts): Blvd Krim Belkacem, Parc Zyriab, 16200 Algiers; tel. (21) 239090; e-mail esba@m-culture.gov.dz; f. 1881; painting, sculpture, ceramics, design; library: 9,000 vols; 65 teachers; 350 students; Dir NACER EDDINE KASSAB.

Institut Hydrométéorologique de Formation et de Recherches (IHFR): BP 7019, Séddikia, 31025 Oran; tel. (41) 422801; e-mail ihfr@djazair-connect.com; internet www.ihfr.edu.dz; f. 1970; library: 15,000 vols; 200 students; Dir A. LAGHA.

Institut National Supérieur de Musique (Higher National Institute of Music): ave du 1er Novembre, Algiers; tel. (21) 738957; e-mail insm.alger@gmail.com; 4-year courses in musicology.

Institut Supérieur des Métiers des Arts du Spectacle et de l'Audiovisuel (Professional Higher Institute of the Performing Arts and of the Audiovisual): 3, rue Larbi Tebessi, Bordj el Kiffan, Algiers; tel. (21) 202790; e-mail direction@ismas-dz.org; internet www.ismas-dz.org; f. 1970 as Institut National des Arts Dramatique et Chorégraphique; current name and status 2004.

ANDORRA

The Higher Education System

University-level education is generally undertaken abroad, although there is one state university, the Universitat d'Andorra. The University, which was established in 1997, maintains two centres for vocational training, the School of Nursing and the School of Information Technology and Management, and a Centre of Virtual Learning for distance education. The University has adapted all of its courses to conform with the European Higher Education Area, in accordance with the three-tier Bologna Process (Bachelors/Masters/Doctorate). Approximately 75% of the University's funding is provided by the Andorran Government. The Ministry of Education and Youth oversees higher education. In 2005/06 1,065 students were enrolled in universities; 431 students were studying in Andorra, 131 in France and 503 in Spain. In 2006/07 a total of 245 students were in non-university higher education: 68 were in Andorran institutions, 166 in French institutions and 11 in Spanish institutions. By 2010/11 the number of students in non-university higher education had risen to 370. In September 2012 the first private university, L'Universitat de les Valls, opened a Dentistry Faculty offering a Masters course to a maximum of thirty students. Another private university, Universitat Oberta la Salle, offers Masters distance qualifications in business and computing.

A new baccalaureate examination, which was intended to facilitate direct access for students in the Andorran education system to universities in other European countries, was introduced in 2008.

The Law of Higher Education 12/2008 was passed in June 2008 and a Decree of recognition of foreign qualifications was published in March 2009. With these new regulations, Andorra recognizes levels of qualifications according to the Bologna Process and the Lisbon Convention.

An accreditation body for higher education—the Agència de qualitat del'ensenyament superior d'Andorra—was established in 2006 to oversee the degrees offered by the Universitat d'Andorra.

Regulatory and Representative Bodies

GOVERNMENT

Ministry of Culture: Edifici administratiu del Govern, C. Prat de la Creu, 62–64, 1r pis, AD500 Andorra la Vella; tel. 875700; e-mail cultura.gov@andorra.ad; internet www.cultura.ad; Minister ALBERT ESTEVE GARCIA.

Ministry of Education and Youth: Edif. el Molí, 21–23 Avda Rocafort, AD600 Sant Julià de Lòria; tel. 743300; e-mail educacio@govern.ad; internet www.educacio.ad; Minister ROSER SUÑÉ PASCUET.

ACCREDITATION

ENIC/NARIC Andorra: Ministra d'Educació, Formació Professional, Joventut i Esports, Edif. el Molí, 4a Planta, 21–23 Avda Rocafort, AD600 Sant Julià de Lòria; tel. 743300; e-mail portal@govern.ad; internet www.govern.ad; Assessor MERITXELL GALLO YANES.

Learned Societies

GENERAL

Amics de la Cultura (Friends of Culture): Plaça Co-Prínceps 4 bis, Despatx No 1, AD700 Escaldes-Engordany.

Associació Cultural i Artística Els Esquirols (Els Esquirols Cultural and Arts Association): Sala Parroquial, Plaça de l'Església, AD400 La Massana.

Centre de Trobada de les Cultures Pirenenques (Centre for the Understanding of Pyrenean Culture): Edif. Prada Casadet, C/ Prat de la Creu, AD500 Andorra la Vella; tel. 860768; f. 1983; attached to Comunitat de Treball dels Pirineus; database on the Pyrenees; Dir ELISENDA VIVES BALMAÑA.

Cercle de les Arts i de les Lletres (Arts and Letters Circle): 24 Avda Carlemany, AD700 Escaldes-Engordany; tel. 824815; e-mail cercleartslletres@gmail.com; internet www.cercleartsilletres.net; f. 1968; Pres. JOAN BURGUÉS MARTISELLA.

BIBLIOGRAPHY, LIBRARY SCIENCE AND MUSEOLOGY

International Council of Museums, Andorran National Committee: Patrimoni Cultural d'Andorra, Carretera de Bixessarri s/n Aixovall, AD600 Sant Julià de Lòria; tel. 844141; e-mail icom@andorra.ad; internet www.icomandorra.ad; f. 1988; 48 mems and 5 institutional mems; Pres. MARTA PLANAS; Sec. LOURDES LÓPEZ MONTANYA.

LANGUAGE AND LITERATURE

Alliance Française: Centre Cultural la Llacuna, Mossèn Cinto Verdaguer 4, AD500 Andorra la Vella; tel. 342852; e-mail alianca-af@andorra.ad; internet www.alliance-francaise-andorre.org; offers courses and examinations in French language and culture and promotes cultural exchange with France.

NATURAL SCIENCES

General

Societat Andorrana de Ciències (Andorra Scientific Society): Centre Cultural la Llacuna, C/ M. C. Verdaguer 4, AD500 Andorra la Vella; tel. 829729; e-mail sac@andorra.ad; internet www.sac.ad; f. 1983; carries out research; organizes talks, conferences and symposiums; 292 mems; Pres. ANGELS MACH; Sec. PERE MUNOZ; Treas. CONXITA NAUDI; publs *Diada Andorrana a la UCE* (1 a year), *El Sac* (12 a year), *Jornades* (1 a year), *Papers de Recerca Històrica* (1 a year), *Recull de Conferències* (1 a year), *Trobades Culturals Pirenenques* (1 a year).

Biological Sciences

Associació per a la Defensa de la Natura (Association for Nature Conservation): Apdo Correus Espanyols 96, AD500 Andorra la Vella; tel. 866086; e-mail adn@andorra.ad; internet www.adn-andorra.org; f. 1986; disseminates information and organizes courses, conferences, school lectures, awareness campaigns about nature and wildlife in Andorra; 300 mems; Pres. ÁNGELS CODINA FARRÁS; Sec. JORDI PALAUI PUIGVERT; publ. *Aigüerola*.

Research Institutes

GENERAL

Institut d'Estudis Andorrans (Institute of Andorran Studies): Edif. el Molí, 3r pis, 21–23 Avda Rocafort, AD600 Sant Julià de Lòria; tel. 7[illegible]; e-mail iea@iea.ad; internet www.iea.ad; f. 1976; centres in Barcelona (Spain) and Toulouse (France); Dir JORDI GUILLAMET.

Attached institutes:

Centre de Biodiversitat (Centre for Biodiversity): Edif. el Molí, 3r pis, 21–23 Avda Rocafort, AD600 Sant Julià de Lòria; tel. 742630; e-mail cbdiea@andorra.ad; f. 1998; study and monitoring of Andorra's biological diversity; library of 450 vols; Dir MARTA DOMÈNECH FERRÉS; publ. *Hàbitats* (2 a year).

Centre d'Estudis de la Neu i de la Muntanya d'Andorra: Edif. el Molí, 3r pis, 21–23 Avda Rocafort, AD600 Sant Julià de Lòria; tel. 742630; e-mail cenma@iea.ad.

Centre de Recerca en Ciències de la Terra (Centre for Earth Sciences Research): Edif. el Molí, 3r pis, 21–23 Avda Rocafort, AD600 Sant Julià de Lòria; tel. 742630; e-mail crecit@andorra.ad; internet www.iea.ad/crecit/index2.html; f. 2001.

Centre de Recerca Sociològica (Centre for Sociological Research): Edif. el Molí, 3r pis, 21–23 Avda Rocafort, AD600 Sant Julià de Lòria; tel. 742630; e-mail cres@iea.ad; internet www.iea.ad/cres/noticies; f. 2000.

Libraries and Archives

Andorra la Vella

Arxiu Nacional d'Andorra (National Archive of Andorra): Edif. Prada Casadet, C/ Prada Casadet, 8–12, AD500 Andorra la Vella; tel. 802288; e-mail ana.gov@andorra.ad; internet www.arxius.ad; f. 1975; 280,000 vols; Head of Nat. Archives SUSANNA VELA PALOMARES.

Biblioteca Nacional d'Andorra (National Library of Andorra): Placeta de Saint Esteve, Casa Bauró, AD500 Andorra la Vella; tel. 826445; e-mail bncultura.gov@andorra.ad; internet www.bibliotecanacional.ad; f. 1974; legal deposit, Andorran standard book number agency (ISBN); 13,000 vols, 120 periodicals; Chief Librarian PILAR BURGUES MONSERRAT.

Biblioteca Publica del Govern (Government Public Library): Edif. Prada Casadet 2, C/ Prat de la Creu, AD500 Andorra la Vella; tel. 828750; e-mail bibliopublica@andorra.ad; internet www.catalegbiblioteques.ad; f. 1930; 57,758 vols; Head INÉS DOMINGO SANCHEZ.

Canillo

Biblioteca Comunal de Canillo (Canillo Community Library): Edif. Telecabina, 3er pis, AD100 Canillo; tel. 753623; e-mail bibliocanillo@andorra.ad; internet www.biblioteques.ad/bibliocanillo; f. 1988; 7,643 items; Librarian DOLORS CALVÓ.

Encamp

Biblioteca Comunal d'Encamp (Encamp Community Library): Complex Esportiu i Sociocultural, AD200 Encamp; tel. 832830; e-mail biblioteca@encamp.ad; internet www.biblioteques.ad/biblioencamp; f. 1930; 40,000 vols; Librarian CODINA ALFONS.

Escaldes-Engordany

Biblioteca Comunal d'Escaldes-Engordany (Escaldes-Engordany Community Library): Centre Neuràlgic, Parc de la Mola 6, AD700 Escaldes-Engordany; tel. 890875; internet www.biblioteques.ad/biblioescaldes; f. 1971; 33,500 vols; Librarian ALEXIA CARRERAS SIRES.

La Massana

Biblioteca Comunal de la Massana (La Massana Community Library): Avda St Antoni 2, Edif. Telecabina, Plaça del Quart, AD400 La Massana; tel. 838910; e-mail biblioteca@lamassana.ad; internet www.catalegbiblioteques.ad; f. 1990; 18,367 vols, 45 periodicals; Librarian PAINO GABRIELA; Man. Librarian JOSEFA DIÉGUEZ.

Ordino

Biblioteca Comunal d'Ordino (Ordino Community Library): Edif. la Font, 3a pl., AD300 Ordino; tel. 878136; e-mail bibliotecacomunal@ordino.ad; internet www.biblioteques.ad/biblioordino; f. 1995; 11,000 vols.

Sant Julià de Lòria

Biblioteca Communal de Sant Julià de Lòria (Sant Julià de Lòria Community Library): Centre Cultural i de Congressos Lauredià, Plaça de la Germandat, AD600 Sant Julià de Lòria; tel. 744044; e-mail biblioteca@comusantjulia.ad; internet www.biblioteques.ad/bibliostjulia; f. 1993; 15,522 vols.

Museums and Art Galleries

Andorra la Vella

Casa de la Vall: C/ de la Vall, AD500 Andorra la Vella; tel. 829129; e-mail guies_casa_de_la_vall@govern.ad; f. 1580.

Canillo

Le Sanctuaire de Meritxell (Meritxell Sanctuary): Meritxell, AD100 Canillo; tel. 851253; historical record of the Andorran people's devotion to their patron saint, the Virgin of Meritxell.

Museu de Les Dues Rodes (Museum of Two Wheels): Ctra. General de Canillo s/n, Al Costat de St Joan de Caselles, AD100 Canillo; tel. 853444; e-mail m2r@canillo.ad; internet www.m2r.ad; motorcycles from the early 20th century to the present day.

Encamp

Electricity Museum: Edif. FEDA, Avda de la Bartra s/n, Sortida d'Escaldes en Direcció a Encamp per la CG2, AD200 Encamp; tel. 739111; e-mail museumw@feda.ad.

Museu d'Art Sacre (Sacred Art Museum): Placeta de Santa Eulàlia, AD200 Encamp; tel. 833551; e-mail casacristo@encamp.ad; colln of liturgical objects from the town's churches, exhibits from 14th century to date.

Museu Nacional de l'Automòbil (National Motor Car Museum): Avda Co-Princep Episcopal 64, AD200 Encamp; tel. 839760; e-mail museusandorra@gmail.com; f. 1988; cars, motorbikes and bicycles from 1898 to 1950, components, miniature cars in porcelain and iron.

Escaldes-Engordany

Andorran Model Museum: Avda de Pessebre 16, AD700 Escaldes-Engordany; tel. 861506; models of prominent Andorran monuments and structures.

Escaldes-Engordany Arts Centre: Avda Carlemany 30, AD700 Escaldes-Engordany; tel. 802255; e-mail centreart@e-e.ad; internet www.e-e.ad; f. 1934; collns of Josep Viladomat and Andorra Romanesque art.

Museu del Perfum (Perfume Museum): 1era Planta, Avda Carlemany 115, AD700 Escaldes-Engordany; tel. 801926; e-mail museudelperfum@julia.ad; internet www.museudelperfum.ad.

Museu Viladomat d'Escultura (Municipal Cultural Museum): Avda Parc de la Mola 5, Les Escaldes, AD700 Escaldes-Engordany; tel. 829340; e-mail museuviladomat@andorra.ad; f. 1987; Curator GLORIA PUJOL.

La Massana

Casa Rull de Sispony (Rull House of Sispony): C/ Major, Sispony, AD400 La Massana; tel. 836919; e-mail casarull@andorra.ad; family and heritage.

Farga Rossell (Rossell Forge): Avda del Través s/n, AD400 La Massana; tel. 839760; e-mail fargarosell@andorra.ad; internet www.fargarossell.ad; f. 2002.

Ordino

Badge Museum: Ansalonga la Cortinada, AD300 Ordino; tel. 749000; 108,000 different badges relating to significant historical events.

Centre d'Interpretació de la Natura de les Valls d'Ordino (Ordino Valley Nature Interpretation Centre): AD300 Ordino; tel. 837939; e-mail cinvo@andorra.ad; interprets the cultural landscape (nature and culture) of Ordino.

Museu Casa d'Areny-Plandolit (Areny-Plandolit House Museum): C/ Major s/n, AD300 Ordino; tel. 839760; e-mail casa.areny-plandolit@andorra.ad; internet www.patrimonicultural.ad; f. 1987; typical 17th-century house, with later alterations; furniture, porcelain, costumes; museum portrays 19th- and 20th-century Andorra; houses Andorra Nat. Auditorium; Chief of Nat. Museums MARTA PLANAS.

Museu Postal d'Andorra (Andorra Postal Museum): Borda del Raser, C/ Major, AD300 Ordino; tel. 839760; f. 1986, refounded 1998.

Nicolaï Siadristy's Microminiature Museum: Edif. Coma, AD300 Ordino; tel. 838376; e-mail azorzano@andornet.ad.

Sant Jordi Iconography and Christianity Museum: Edif. Maragda, AD300 Ordino; tel. 838338; e-mail azorzano@andornet.ad; Christian and Orthodox icons from the main schools in the Ukraine, Russia, Greece and Bulgaria from the 14th to the 19th centuries; 70 polychrome wood statues of Christ from Spanish schools from the 11th to 19th centuries.

Sant Julià de Lòria

Museu del Tabac (Tobacco Museum): Doctor Palau 17, AD600 Sant Julià de Lòria; tel. 741545; e-mail info@museudeltabac.com; internet www.museudeltabac.com; tools, machines, fittings and aromas used in tobacco factories from the 17th century to date; on site of former Reig tobacco factory (1909 to 1957); Dir MARIA MARTÍ.

University

UNIVERSITAT D'ANDORRA

Plaça de la Germandat 7, AD600 Sant Julià de Lòria

Telephone: 743000

E-mail: uda@uda.ad

Internet: www.uda.ad

Founded 1997

Language of instruction: Catalan

Vice-Chancellor: DANIEL BASTIDA OBIOLS

DIRECTORS

School of Information Technology and Management: FLORENCI PLA ALTISENT

School of Nursing: ROSA MARI MANDICÓ ALCOBÉ

Centre of Virtual Learning and Univ. Extension: MONTSERRAT CASALPRIM RAMONET

ANGOLA

The Higher Education System

Higher education was established when Angola was still a Portuguese colony, initially with the foundation in 1958 of institutes for training Catholic priests. In 1962 the Estudos Gerais Universitários de Angola was established in Luanda and became the Universidade de Luanda in 1968; a branch was also set up in Huíla. Following independence in 1975 all non-state institutions were closed, and in 1979 the Universidade de Luanda was renamed Universidade de Angola, which in turn became the Universidade Agostinho Neto in 1985; it remains Angola's only public university and has around 9,000 student places. The state university has seven faculties covering: arts and social sciences, agriculture sciences, economics, engineering, law, medicineand sciences. In May 2011 the Government announced plans to establish, within the Universidade Agostinho Neto, Africa's first centre for sustainable development—the Excellence Centre for Sciences Applied to Sustainability—which would provide earth science education and research opportunities for scientists in sub-Saharan Africa. Independent Angola's first private university, the Universidade Católica de Angola, was founded in 1992. Currently there are nine private universities operating, one private non-university institution (which offers courses in international relations) and 30 post-secondary vocational institutes. A teacher training establishment, the Instituto Superior de Ciências e Educação in Lubango, is part of the Universidade Agostinho Neto. In 2009/10 there were 66,251 students in higher education.

Under legislation passed in 1995 full autonomy was conferred on Universidade Agostinho Neto, and staff were empowered to elect organs and officials. Financing for higher education depends on the status of the university: Universidade Agostinho Neto is heavily reliant on state funding, while the private universities rely on students' fees and donations from individuals and non-governmental organizations. In February 2009 the Angolan Government approved the reorganization of the higher education system; this involved the creation of seven academic regions to define the operations and expansion of institutions.

To attend university students must hold the Habilitação Literárias (secondary school leaving certificate), pass the entrance examinations and complete either a period of state employment or pre-university education.

The first undergraduate qualification is the Bacharel, study for which lasts for four years. Students may continue for a further two years, after which the Licenciado is awarded. The Licenciado may also be awarded on completion of a five-year university course, or a six-year course for medical students. A doctorate requires a further two or three years' research following the award of the Licenciado.

The accreditation body for tertiary education in Angola is entitled the National Institute of Evaluation and Accreditation of Higher Education in Angola and is overseen by the Ministry of Science and Technology.

Regulatory Bodies

GOVERNMENT

Ministry of Culture: Edif. Ministerial, 1° andar, Largo António Jacinto, Luanda; tel. 222322070; e-mail geral@mincult.gov.ao; internet www.mincult.gov.ao; Minister ROSA MARIA MARTINS DA CRUZ E SILVA.

Ministry of Education: Largo António Jacinto, CP 1281, Luanda; tel. 222321236; e-mail geral@med.gov.ao; internet www.med.gov.ao; Minister PINDA SIMÃO.

Ministry of Science and Technology: Ave Lenine 106/108, Maianga, Luanda; tel. 222330218; e-mail geral@mct.gov.ao; internet www.mct.gov.ao; Minister MARIA CANDIDA PEREIRA TEIXEIRA.

Learned Societies

LANGUAGE AND LITERATURE

Alliance Française: Largo da Sagrada Familia, Traversa Barbosa do Bocage 12, CP 1578, Luanda; tel. 222321993; e-mail afluanda@ebonet.net; offers courses and examinations in French language and culture and promotes cultural exchange with France; attached teaching centres in Benguela, Cabinda and Lubango.

União dos Escritores Angolanos (Association of Angolan Writers): Avda Ho-Chi-Min, Largo das Escolas 1° de Maio, CP 2767-C, Luanda; tel. 222322421; e-mail contacto@ueangola.com; internet www.ueangola.com; f. 1975; 75 mems; library of 2,000 vols; Sec.-Gen. LUANDINO VIEIRA; publs *Criar* (4 a year), *Lavra & Oficina* (12 a year).

Research Institutes

AGRICULTURE, FISHERIES AND VETERINARY SCIENCE

Instituto de Investigação Agronómica (Agronomic Research Institute): CP 406, Estação Experimental Agrícola da Chianga, Huambo; f. 1962; agrarian documentation centre; publs *Comunicações*, *Série Divulgação*.

Instituto de Investigação Veterinária (Institute for Veterinary Research): CP 405, Lubango; tel. 222322094; f. 1965; Dir Dr A. M. POMBAL; publ. *Acta Veterinaria-separatas* (1 a year).

NATURAL SCIENCES

Physical Sciences

Direcção Provincial da Indústria, Geologia e Minas (Provincial Directorate of Industry, Geology and Mining): Rua Comandante Hoji Ya Henda, Luanda; tel. 2612222837; e-mail dpindgeominas@live.com; f. 1914; attached to Provincial Govt of Huíla; geology, geological mapping and exploration of mineral deposits; library of 40,000 vols; Dir J. TRIGO MIRA; publs *Carta Geológica de Angola*, *Memória*.

Libraries and Archives

Luanda

Arquivo Histórico Nacional (National Historical Archive): Rua Pedro Félix Machado 49, Luanda; tel. 222333512; e-mail ahadg@nexus.ao; f. 1977; 20,000 vols, 3,000 periodicals; Dir ROSA CRUZ E SILVA; publ. *Guias de Informação Documental para o Estudo da História de Angola*.

Biblioteca Municipal (Municipal Library): CP 1227, Luanda; tel. 222392297; f. 1873; 31,470 vols; Dir CUSTA GANHAR FILIPE.

Biblioteca Nacional de Angola (National Library of Angola): Largo António Jacinto, CP 2915, Luanda; tel. 222326331; e-mail bibliotecanacional@netangola.com; f. 1969; IFLA colln legal deposit, nat. deposit for UNESCO and FAO publs; 84,000 vols; Dir MARIA JOSÉ F. RAMOS.

Museums and Art Galleries

Luanda

Instituto Nacional do Patrimonio Cultural (National Institute for Cultural Heritage): CP 1267, Luanda; tel. 222332575; e-mail mincultura@mincultura.gv.ao; nat. antiquities dept; Dir FRANCISCO XAVIER YAMBO.

Affiliated Museums:

Museu Central das Forças Armadas (Central Museum of the Armed Forces): CP 1267, Luanda; e-mail mincultura@mincultura.gv.ao; Dir SILVESTRE A. FRANCISCO.

Museu do Dundo (Dundo Museum): CP 14, Chitato, Lunda Norte; e-mail mincultura@mincultura.gv.ao; f. 1948; reopened 2012; archaeology, ethnography and natural history; library of 35,000 vols; Dir MAZAMBI VUVU.

Museu Nacional da Escravatura (Museum of Slavery): CP 1267, Luanda; e-mail mincultura@mincultura.gv.ao; f. 1977; Dir ANICETE DO AMARAL GOURGEL.

Museu Nacional de Antropologia (National Anthropology Museum): Avda de Portugal 61° (Coqueiros), CP 2159, Luanda; tel. 222337024; e-mail antropologia@angoladigital.net; internet www.museuantropologia.angoladigital.net; f. 1976; collns incl. 6,000 objects on ethnography; Dir AMÉRICO KWONONOKA.

Museu Nacional de Arqueologia (National Archaeology Museum): CP 79, Benguela; e-mail mincultura@mincultura.gv.ao; Dir PAULO VALONGO.

Museu Nacional de História Natural (National Museum of Natural History): CP 1267, Luanda; tel. 222334054; e-mail contactos@museunhn-angola.org; internet www.museunhn-angola.org; f. 1956; Dir ANA PAULA DOS SANTOS C. VICTOR.

Museu Regional de Cabinda (Cabinda Regional Museum): CP 283, Cabinda; e-mail mincultura@mincultura.gv.ao; ethnography; Dir TADEU DOMINGOS.

Museu Regional da Huíla (Huíla Regional Museum): CP 445, Lubango; e-mail mincultura@mincultura.gv.ao; f. 1957; 1,526 ethnographic colln and 1,995 photographs; Dir SORAIA SANTOS.

Universities

UNIVERSIDADE AGOSTINHO NETO
(Agostinho Neto University)

CP 815, Av. 4 de Fevereiro 7, 2º andar, Luanda

Telephone: 222330517
E-mail: info@uan-angola.org
Internet: www.agostinhoneto.co.ao

Founded 1962
Language of instruction: Portuguese
Academic year: October to June

Rector: JOÃO SEBASTIÃO TETA

Number of teachers: 700
Number of students: 9,000

DEANS

Faculty of Agriculture Sciences: Dr AMILCAR MATEUS DE OLIVEIRA SALUMBO
Faculty of Arts and Social Sciences: (vacant)
Faculty of Economics: Dr LAURINDA DE JESUS FERNANDES HOYGAARD
Faculty of Engineering: CARLOS ALBERTO ABREU SERENO
Faculty of Law: Dr ADERITO CORREIA
Faculty of Medicine: Dr PAULO ADÃO CAMPOS
Faculty of Sciences: Dr ABILO ALVES FERNANDES

AFFILIATED INSTITUTES

Centro Nacional de Investigação Científica: Av. Revolução de Outubro, Luanda; tel. 222350762; Coordinator Dr NANIZEYI KINDUDI ANDRÉ.

Instituto Superior de Ciências da Educação: Rua Salvador Allende, 12, CP 10609, Luanda; tel. 222394979; Dean Dr DANIEL MINGAS

UNIVERSIDADE CATÓLICA DE ANGOLA
(Catholic University of Angola)

Rua N. Sra da Muxima 29, CP 2064, Luanda

Telephone: 222331973
E-mail: info@ucan.edu
Internet: www.ucan.edu

Founded 1992

controlled by Episcopal Conf. of Angola and São Tomé
Academic year: May to December

Faculties of economics, informatics, law, management

Chancellor and Rector: Archbishop DAMIÃO FRANKLIN
Vice-Rector: Fr Dr FILOMENO VIEIRA DIAS
Head of Admin.: Fr Dr MANUEL S. GONÇALVES
Head of Library and Documentation: Fr Dr JOSÉ CACHADINHA

Number of teachers: 99
Number of students: 1,800

Publications: *Revista Academica*, *UCAN Boletim Informativo*

UNIVERSIDADE JEAN PIAGET DE ANGOLA
(Jean Piaget University of Angola)

Campus Universitário de Viana, Bairro Capalanka, Viana 10365, Brito Godins

Telephone: 222301148
E-mail: info@unipiaget-angola.org

Founded 1998

Courses offered in social sciences and education, science and technology and health

College

Instituto Médio Industrial de Luanda (Medium Industrial Institute of Luanda): Largo de Soweto, CP 2513, Luanda; tel. 222343200; e-mail imil@netangola.com; f. 1956 as Escola Industrial de Luanda; courses in civil engineering, mechanics, chemistry.

ANTIGUA AND BARBUDA

The Higher Education System

Higher education is provided by an extramural department of the University of the West Indies, which offers several foundation courses leading to higher study at branches elsewhere, and at several other institutes and colleges. Teacher training and technical training are available at the Antigua State College in St John's, which was founded in 1977 (following the merger of the teacher training college and the technical college) and which absorbed the Antigua and Barbuda School of Nursing in 2000. There is also an International Institute of Technology (f. 2001), a Hospitality Training Institute (as the Hotel Training Center was renamed in 2003) and a private University of Health Sciences, which was established in 1982 and which offers a four-year Doctor of Medicine programme and a three-year course at the Macedonia School of Nursing. The Hospitality Training Institute, which is a statutory body of the Ministry of Tourism, Civil Aviation and Culture, offers one-year certificate programmes and two-year diplomas, and has developed links with the University of the West Indies for accreditation of the courses in hospitality management and culinary arts. The American University of Antigua (AUA), which was established in 2004, is a private institution of higher education located near St John's. The AUA comprises a College of Medicine, which in 2010 adopted the US-style two-year academic programme and in 2011 was recognized by the Medical Board of California, and the Kasturba Medical College International Center which offers a six-year programme with two years of premedical training in India, two years of basic science training at the AUA, followed by two further years in a teaching hospital in either the USA, Canada or India. Although in 2008/09 official figures gave a total of 1,037 students enrolled in tertiary education in Antigua and Barbuda, by 2011 there was a total enrolment in the AUA alone of 1,950 students.

Admission to tertiary education is usually dependent upon award of the Caribbean Advanced Proficiency Examination (CAPE). Grading in higher education is based on the system used by the University of the West Indies.

Regulatory Bodies

GOVERNMENT

Ministry of Education, Sports, Youth and Gender Affairs: Govt Office Complex, Queen Elizabeth Highway, St John's; tel. 462-0192; e-mail mineduc@ab.gov.ag; internet www.education.gov.ag; Minister MERVYN RICHARDS.

Ministry of Tourism, Civil Aviation and Culture: Govt Office Complex, Bldg 1, Queen Elizabeth Highway, St John's; tel. 462-0480; e-mail mblackman@tourism.gov.ag; Minister JOHN HERBERT MAGINLEY.

Learned Societies

BIBLIOGRAPHY, LIBRARY SCIENCE AND MUSEOLOGY

Library Association of Antigua and Barbuda: POB 822, St John's; tel. 462-3500; f. 1983; 40 mems; Pres. MOLIVAR SPENCER; Sec. TRACY SAMUEL.

LANGUAGE AND LITERATURE

Alliance Française: POB 2086, St John's; tel. 462-3625; offers courses and examinations in French language and culture and promotes cultural exchange with France.

Archives

St John's

Antigua and Barbuda National Archives: Victoria Park, Factory Rd, St John's; tel. 462-4959; e-mail archives@antigua.gov.ag; f. 1982; Dir Dr MARION BLAIR.

University

UNIVERSITY OF HEALTH SCIENCES ANTIGUA

Dowhill Campus, Piccadilly, POB 510, St John's

Telephone: 460-1391

E-mail: admissions@uhsa.edu.ag

Internet: www.uhsa.ag

Founded 1982

Schools of liberal arts and sciences, medicine, nursing, veterinary medicine, postgraduate medical education

Pres.: Dr AKIN OMITOWOJU

Registrar: IVORY TAYLOR

Librarian: (vacant)

Dean for School of Medicine: Dr N. OLOWOPOPO

Number of teachers: 32

Number of students: 203

Colleges

Antigua and Barbuda International Institute of Technology (ABIIT): POB 736, St John's; tel. 480-2400; e-mail info@abiit.edu.ag; internet www.abiit.edu.ag; f. 2001; Pres. GLADWIN HENRY; Dean of Academics EUSTACE HILL.

Antigua State College: POB 193, Golden Grove, St John's; tel. 462-1434; f. 1977 by merger of Leeward Islands Teachers' Training College and Golden Grove Technical College, absorbed Antigua and Barbuda School of Nursing in 2000; hospitality and tourism management, teacher training, technical training.

University of the West Indies School of Continuing Studies (Antigua and Barbuda): POB 142, St John's; tel. 462-1355; e-mail university@candw.ag; f. 1949; adult education courses, spec. programmes for women, summer courses for children, occasional seminars and workshops; library: 10,000 vols; 23 part-time tutors; 350 students; Resident Tutor Dr ERMINA OSOBA.

ARGENTINA

The Higher Education System

The Federal Law of Education of 1993 decentralized the education system, with administration devolving to each of the 23 individual provinces and to the Municipality of Buenos Aires. The federal Ministry of Education is responsible for the provision of university education, while each provincial ministry of education is responsible for education provision at post-secondary, non-university level. Technical education is supervised by the Consejo Nacional de Educación Técnica (National Council for Technical Education). The first university established in Argentina, and one of the first in the entire Americas region, was the Universidad Nacional de Córdoba (UNCNational University of Córdoba) founded in 1613. The private sector in the country's higher education system began in 1958 with the establishment of Argentina's first private university, the Universidad del Salvador. According to the federal Ministry of Education, in 2013 there were 47 public/national universities, 49 private universities, seven public/national university institutes (run by the police and the armed forces), 14 private university institutes, one provincial university, one overseas university, one international university and numerous teacher training establishments throughout the country. More than 80% of the student population attend public/national universities and these establishments account for more than 50% of the scientific research carried out in the country. The public and private university institutes are essentially single-faculty establishments, offering Licenciatura qualifications in academic and professional areas. There are, in addition, more than 1,600 recognized tertiary non-university institutions in both the public and private sectors. These establishments are not authorized to offer Licenciatura or postgraduate qualifications but may award short-cycle degrees and technical programmes in professional and vocational areas.

Between 2003 and 2007 a number of laws were passed that defined education as a national priority and laid the foundation for developing a state policy. Among these were: the National Education Law (Law No. 26.206, 2007), the Education Finance Act (Law No. 26.075, 2005), the Vocational Technical Education Act (Law No. 26.058, 2005), the Law on National Comprehensive Sex Education (Law No. 26.150, 2006), the Teaching Salary Guarantee Act and 180 days of school (Law No. 25.864, 2003), the Law on the National Teaching Incentive Fund (Law No. 25.919, 2004) and the Law on the Protection of the Rights of Children and Adolescents (Act No. 26.061, 2005). Between 2003 and 2011 nine state universities were created, five in the Greater Buenos Aires area and four in the provinces. Enrolment in the five new universities in the Buenos Aires area increased by 13% compared to an increase of 2% in other traditional universities, according to the Minister of Education in 2011. A majority of the 3,000 students who enrolled in Florencio Varela University, one of the most recent to open, live in areas of poverty with limited transport infrastructure and come from socio-economic groups which have traditionally not had ready access to higher education.

Unlike several other Latin American countries, there is no national entrance examination for access to higher education in Argentina. By law, admission to higher education is dependent upon successful completion of the secondary qualification (the Título de Bachillerato—High School Certificate), although many universities set their own admissions procedures which may take the form of an examination or completion of an access course. The Universidad de Buenos Aires, for example, requires that all applicants complete a one-year Ciclo Básico Común (Basic Common Cycle) prior to commencing degree courses. There are two types of undergraduate degree offered at Argentinian universities: the intermediate short-cycle Carreras Pregrado/Títulos Intermedios, study for which lasts for between two and three years, and the long-cycle Carreras de Grado, study for which lasts for between four and six years (depending on the subject) and leads to the award of a Licenciatura or professional title. Some Carreras de Grado degree programmes in professional areas, such as medicine, engineering and architecture, are regulated by the state under ministerial resolutions, which determine the length and content of study and the professional rights conferred on graduates. There are three types of postgraduate qualification available: Especialización/Especialista (involving specialization programmes of a professional nature), Maestría (Masters degree) and Doctorado (Doctorate). As well as being offered at some universities, vocational and professional post-secondary education and training is available at higher technical schools or institutes of technology, also known as polytechnic institutes, and at higher commercial schools. Courses at these institutions are usually two years in length, and successful students are awarded a title such as Técnico Superior or Técnico Universitario in their area of specialization.

Public universities in Argentina are entirely state-funded and do not charge tuition fees for undergraduate studies, although many postgraduate courses require some form of private funding. Some 14% of total government expenditure is allocated for education, of which about 18% is spent on higher education. Private universities are dependent on student fees for their funding. Structural changes to the higher education system, following the reforms of the mid-1990s, were implemented with US $240m. of financial assistance from the World Bank.

Argentina is a member state of the Mercado Común del Sur (Mercosur—Southern Common Market) and as such is a participant in its accreditation programme: El Mecanismo Experimental de Acreditación de Carreras del Mercosur. This programme has so far accredited Argentinian degrees in agronomy, medicine and engineering. The national accreditation body for the higher education sector (at both undergraduate and postgraduate level), the Comisión Nacional de Evaluación y Acreditación Universitaria (CONEAUNational Commission of University Evaluation and Accreditation), was established in 1995 by the Organic Law on Education as an autonomous body affiliated to the Ministry of Education. Its aim is to maintain high levels of quality in tertiary education, by means of institutional assessment and the implementation of its recommendations for the sector.

According to World Bank figures, some 75% of those in the relevant age group (defined as up to five years following secondary education) were enrolled in tertiary education in 2010. This figure represents one of the highest higher education enrolment rates in Latin America. According to UNESCO, a total of 2,520,985 students were enrolled in higher education in 2010, of whom 1,838,367 were enrolled in public institutions. By 2010 the number of students enrolled at general non-university institutions had increased to 691,007 (from 512,000 in 2004) and by 2011 to 727,444.

Regulatory and Representative Bodies

GOVERNMENT

Ministry of Education: Pizzurno 935, C1020ACA, Buenos Aires; tel. (11) 4129-1000; e-mail prensa@me.gov.ar; internet www.me.gov.ar; Minister Prof. ALBERTO ESTANISLAO SILEONI.

Ministry of Science, Technology and Productive Innovation: Godoy Cruz 2320, C1425FQD, Buenos Aires; tel. (11) 4899-5000; e-mail info@mincyt.gob.ar; internet www.mincyt.gov.ar; Minister Dr LINO BARAÑAO.

ACCREDITATION

Comisión Nacional de Evaluación y Acreditación Universitaria (CONEAU) (National Commission of University Evaluation and Accreditation): Avda Santa Fe 1385,4°, C1059ABH, Buenos Aires; tel. (11) 4819-9050; e-mail consulta@coneau.gob.ar; internet www.coneau.gov.ar; f. 1996; govt agency under Min. of Education; evaluates projects submitted by new public and private univs; performs external evaluation of univs; conducts evaluation processes for accreditation of private evaluation and accreditation orgs; serves as Secretariat of Red Iberoamericana para la Acreditación de la Calidad de la Educación Superior (RIACES); 12 mems; Pres. NÉSTOR RAÚL PAN; Vice-Pres. LUIS MARIA FERNANDEZ.

NATIONAL BODIES

Academia Nacional de Educación (National Academy of Education): Pacheco de Melo 2084, C1126AAF Buenos Aires; tel. (11) 4806-2818; e-mail ane@acaedu.edu.ar; internet www.acaedu.edu.ar; f. 1984 as Argentina Academy of Education; current name adopted 1989); promotes educational creativity and innovation; Pres. PEDRO LUIS BARCIA; First Vice-Pres ANTONIO FRANCISCO SALONIA; Second Vice-Pres. HORACIO SANGUINETTI; Sec. JORGE ADOLFO RATTO.

Consejo de Rectores de las Universidades Privadas (CRUP) (Council of Rectors of Private Universities): Montevideo 1910 PB, C1021AAH, Buenos Aires; tel. (11) 4811-6435; internet www.crup.org.ar; representative and consultative org.; coordinates teaching in private univs in conjunction with Min. of Education and the Provincial Ccls of Rectors; fosters collaboration between mem. univs; Pres. Dr JUAN CARLOS MENA; Vice-Pres. Dr HÉCTOR CÉSAR SAURET; Vice-Pres. Dr OSVALDO AGUSTÍN BLANCO; Sec. RODOLFO DE VINCENZI.

Consejo Interuniversitario Nacional (CIN) (National Inter-University Council): Pacheco de Melo 2084, C1126AAF, Buenos Aires; tel. (11) 4806-2269; e-mail info@cin.edu.ar; internet www.cin.edu.ar; f. 1985; proposes and coordinates policy for mem. univs; consults on creation or closure of nat. univs; generates and supports self-evaluation and external evaluation policies for mems; promotes compatibility and quality assurance of study programmes; Pres. Ing. ARTURO SOMOZA; Vice-Pres. Lic. FRANCISCO MOREA; publ. *Revista CIN, print and online, www.cin.edu.ar/archivo-revista*.

Learned Societies

AGRICULTURE, FISHERIES AND VETERINARY SCIENCE

Academia Nacional de Agronomía y Veterinaria (Academy of Agronomy and Veterinary Science): Avda Alvear 1711, 2°, 1014 Buenos Aires; tel. (11) 4812-4168; e-mail acadagrovet@anav.org.ar; internet www.anav.org.ar; f. 1909; 98 mems; library of 4,000 vols; Pres. Dr CARLOS O. SCOPPA; Sec.-Gen. Ing. Agr. RODOLFO G. FRANK; publ. *Anales* (1 a year).

Asociación Argentina de la Ciencia del Suelo (Argentine Association of Soil Science): Pabellón INGEIS, Ciudad Universitaria, 1428 Buenos Aires; tel. (11) 4783-3021; e-mail cosenti@agro.uba.ar; internet www.suelos.org.ar; f. 1958; organizes Nat. and Latin American Congress of Soil Science every 2 years and cultural and scientific activities related with soil; 800 mems; Pres. Dr JOSÉ LUIS PANIGATTI; Vice-Pres. Dr DIEGO COSENTINO; publ. *Ciencia del Suelo* (2 a year).

Sociedad Rural Argentina (Argentine Agricultural Society): Florida 460, 1005 Buenos Aires; tel. (11) 4322-0468; internet www.sra.org.ar; f. 1866; 10,000 mems; library: see under Libraries and Archives; Pres. Dr LUIS MIGUEL ETCHEVEHERE.

ARCHITECTURE AND TOWN PLANNING

Sociedad Central de Arquitectos (Central Society of Architects): Montevideo 938, C1019ABT Buenos Aires; tel. (11) 4812-3644; e-mail contacto@socearq.org; internet www.socearq.org; f. 1886; represents architects and deals with their rights, works for the planned construction of cities, their devt and preservation; 8,500 mems; library of 9,200 vols, 90 periodicals; Pres. Arq. ENRIQUE GARCÍA ESPIL; Sec.-Gen. Arq. ROBERTO R. BUSNELLI; publ. *Revista de Arquitectura*.

BIBLIOGRAPHY, LIBRARY SCIENCE AND MUSEOLOGY

Asociación de Bibliotecarios Graduados de la República Argentina (ABGRA) (Association of Librarian Graduates of the Argentine Republic): Paraná 918, 2°, C1017AAT Buenos Aires; tel. (11) 4816-3422; e-mail info@abgra.org.ar; internet www.abgra.org.ar; f. 1953; 1,650 mems; Pres. GRACIELA AYOS; Sec.-Gen. MIRTA VILLALBA; publ. *Revista Referencias* (3 a year).

Comisión Nacional de Museos y de Monumentos y Lugares Históricos (National Commission for Museums and Historic Monuments and Sites): Avda de Mayo 556, C1084AAN Buenos Aires; tel. (11) 4343-5835; e-mail info@comisionmonumentos.gov.ar; internet www.monumentosysitios.gov.ar; f. 1938; supervises museums and protects the nat. historical heritage; library; Pres. Dr RICARDO LEVENE.

Comisión Nacional Protectora de Bibliotecas Populares (National Commission for the Protection of Public Libraries): Ayacucho 1578, C1112AAB Buenos Aires; tel. (11) 4511-6275; e-mail me@conabip.gov.ar; internet www.conabip.gob.ar; f. 1870; Pres. ÁNGELA SIGNES; Sec. Lic. MARTÍN CÁNEVA; publ. *Revista BePé*.

ECONOMICS, LAW AND POLITICS

Academia Nacional de Ciencias Económicas (National Academy of Economic Sciences): Avda Alvear 1790, C1014AAR Buenos Aires; tel. (11) 4813-2078; e-mail ance@anceargentina.org; internet www.anceargentina.org; f. 1914; studies questions related to political economy, philosophy and economic methodology, economic policy and economic history; 144 mems; library of 13,500 vols; Pres. Dr LUISA MONTUSCHI; Sec. Dr RINALDO ANTONIO COLOMÉ; publ. *Anales*.

Academia Nacional de Ciencias Morales y Políticas (National Academy of Moral and Political Sciences): Avda Alvear 1711, PB, 1014 Buenos Aires; tel. (11) 4811-2049; e-mail ancmyp@ancmyp.org.ar; internet www.ancmyp.org.ar; f. 1938; 35 mems; library of 15,000 vols; Pres. Dr MANUEL SOLANET; Vice-Pres. SANTIAGO KOVADLOFF; Sec. LEONARDO MC LEAN; publ. *Anales* (1 a year).

Academia Nacional de Derecho y Ciencias Sociales de Buenos Aires (National Academy of Law and Social Sciences of Buenos Aires): Avda Alvear 1711 (1°), C1014AAE Buenos Aires; tel. (11) 4815-6976; internet www.academiadederecho.org.ar; f. 1874; 25 mems; Pres. Dr GREGORIO BADENI; Sec. Dr ROBERTO E. LUQUI; Sec. Dr EMILIO P. MANÓVIL; publ. *Anales*.

Academia Nacional de Derecho y Ciencias Sociales de Córdoba (National Academy of Law and Social Sciences of Córdoba): Gral. Artigas 74, 5000 Córdoba; tel. (351) 421-4929; e-mail secretaria@acaderc.org.ar; internet www.acaderc.org.ar; f. 1941; promotes and disseminates knowledge of law and social sciences, encourages improvement of legislation; 172 mems; library of 5,000 vols, 200 periodicals; Pres. Dr JUAN CARLOS PALMERO; Sec. Dr JORGE DE LA RÚA; publ. *Anales*.

Colegio de Abogados de la Ciudad de Buenos Aires (Buenos Aires City Bar Association): Montevideo 640, C1019ABN Buenos Aires; tel. (11) 4371-1110; e-mail info@colabogados.org.ar; internet www.colabogados.org.ar; f. 1913; 1,600 mems; library of 30,000 vols; Pres. Dr MAXIMO J. FONROUGE; Exec. Dir FERNANDO R. FRÁVEGA; publ. *Revista* (2 a year).

FINE AND PERFORMING ARTS

Academia Nacional de Bellas Artes (National Academy of Fine Arts): Sánchez de Bustamante 2663, 2°, C1425DVA Buenos Aires; tel. (11) 4802-2469; e-mail info@anba.org.ar; internet www.anba.org.ar; f. 1936; promotes conservation and enhancement of property; 30 mems, 30 foreign corresp. mems; library of 6,000 vols; Pres. RICARDO BLANCO; Gen. Sec. MATILDE MARÍN; publs *Cuaderno Especial: 'Escenas del Campo Argentino' 1885–1900*, *Documentos de Arte Argentino*, *Documentos de Arte Colonial Sudamericano*, *Serie Estudios de Arte en la Argentina*.

Fondo Nacional de las Artes (National Arts Foundation): Alsina 673, C1087AAI Buenos Aires; tel. (11) 4343-1590; e-mail fnartes@fnartes.gov.ar; internet www.fnartes.gov.ar; f. 1958; 15 mems; library of 13,000 vols; Pres. VIRGILIO TEDIN URIBURU; publs *Anuario del Teatro Argentino*, *Bibliografía Argentina de Artes y Letras*.

HISTORY, GEOGRAPHY AND ARCHAEOLOGY

Academia Nacional de Geografía (National Academy of Geography): Avda Cabildo 381, 7°, C1426AAD Buenos Aires; tel. (11) 4771-3043; e-mail secretaria@an-geografia.org.ar; internet www.an-geografia.org.ar; f. 1956; 40 mems; Pres. Prof. ANTONIO CORNEJO; Sec. CARLOS EDUARDO EREÑO; publ. *Anales*.

Academia Nacional de la Historia de la República Argentina (National Academy of History of Argentina): Balcarce 139, C1064AAC Buenos Aires; tel. (11) 4331-5147; e-mail admite@an-historia.org.ar; internet www.an-historia.org.ar; f. 1893; study of Argentine and American history; 255 mems (32 ordinary, 223 foreign corresp.); Pres. Dr MIGUEL ANGEL DE MARCO; Sec. Dra NILDA GUGLIELMI; publ. *Investigaciones y Ensayos*.

Instituto Bonaerense de Numismática y Antigüedades (Buenos Aires Institute of Numismatics and Antiquities): San Martín 336, C1004AAH Buenos Aires; tel. (11) 449-2659; internet www.ibna.com.ar; f. 1872; 192 mems; Pres. Dr EDUARDO A. SADOUS; Sec. ROBERTO A. BOTTERO.

Junta de Historia Eclesiástica Argentina (Council of Argentine Ecclesiastical History): Reconquista 269, C1003ABE Buenos Aires; tel. (11) 4343-4397; e-mail info@jhea.org.ar; internet www.jhea.org.ar; f. 1942; 100 mems; Pres. Dr ERNESTO R. SALVIA; Sec. Profa ANA MARÍA WOITES; publ. *Revista Archivum* (1 a year).

Sociedad Argentina de Estudios Geográficos (Argentina Society of Geographical Studies): Rodríguez Peña 158, 4° Dpto 7, C1020ADD Buenos Aires; tel. (11) 4373-0588; e-mail informes@gaea.org.ar; internet www.gaea.org.ar; f. 1922; 7,415 mems; library of 12,000 vols; Pres. Dr DARIO CESAR SANCHEZ; Sec. Lic. GRACIELA B. JAUREGUI; publ. *Contribuciones Científicas* (1 a year).

LANGUAGE AND LITERATURE

Academia Argentina de Letras (Argentine Academy of Letters): Sánchez de Bustamante 2663, C1425DVA Buenos Aires; tel. (11) 4802-3814; e-mail administracion@aal.edu.ar; internet www.aal.edu.ar; f. 1931; 77 mems (24 ordinary, 53 corresp.); library of 15,000 vols; Pres. JOSE LUIS MOURE; Sec.-Gen. NORMA CARRICABURO.

Alliance Française: Avda Córdoba 936–946, C1054AAV Buenos Aires; tel. (11) 4322-0068; e-mail info@alianzafrancesa.org.ar; internet www.alianzafrancesa.org.ar; f. 1893; offers courses and examinations in French language and culture; promotes cultural exchange with France; Dir Gen., Argentina BRUNO SIMONIN.

British Council: Marcelo T. de Alvear 590, C1058AAF Buenos Aires; tel. (11) 4114-8600; e-mail info@britishcouncil.org.ar; internet www.britishcouncil.org/argentina; offers courses and examinations in English language and British culture and promotes cultural exchange with the UK; Dir JAMES SHIPTON.

Goethe-Institut: Avda Corrientes 319, C1043AAD Buenos Aires; tel. (11) 4318-5600; e-mail info@buenosaires.goethe.org; internet www.goethe.de/buenosaires; offers courses and examinations in German language and culture and promotes cultural exchange with Germany; library of 15,000 vols, 37 periodicals; Admin. Dir BARBARA SCHULZ.

PEN Club Argentino—Centro Internacional de la Asociación PEN (International PEN Centre): Coronel Diaz 2089, Buenos Aires; tel. (11) 4825-8548; f. 1930; 100 mems; Pres. TERESITA FRUGONI DE FRITZSCHE; Sec. ALICIA BERMOLEN.

Sociedad Argentina de Autores y Compositores de Música (SADAIC) (Argentine Society of Authors and Music Composers): Lavalle 1547, C1048AAK Buenos Aires; tel. (11) 4379-8600; internet www.sadaic.org.ar; f. 1936; library of 4,000 vols, 13,000 music scores; Pres. ATILIO STAMPONE; Sec. VICTOR HUGO YUNES.

Sociedad General de Autores de la Argentina (Argentores) (Argentine Society of Authors): Pacheco de Melo 1820, C1126AAB Buenos Aires; tel. (11) 4811-2582; e-mail info@argentores.org.ar; internet www.argentores.org.ar; f. 1910; legal protection and management of copyright; 2,000 mems; library of 60,000 vols; Pres. MIGUEL ANGEL SPLENDIANI; Sec. GUILLERMO HARDWICK; publ. *Florencio* (4 a year, print and online, www.argentores.org.ar/11_servicios_online/01_florencio/index.html).

MEDICINE

Academia Argentina de Cirugía (Argentine Academy of Surgery): Marcelo T. de Alvear 2416, 1122 Buenos Aires; tel. (11) 4822-2905; e-mail academia@aac.org.ar; internet www.academiadecirugia.org.ar; f. 1911; Pres. Dr NORBERTO A. MEZZADRI; Gen. Sec. Dr JUAN PEKOLJ.

Academia de Ciencias Médicas de Córdoba (Academy of Medical Sciences of Córdoba): Ambrosio Olmos 820, X5000JGQ Córdoba; tel. (351) 460-9194; e-mail info@academiadecienciasmedicas.org; internet www.academiadecienciasmedicas.org; f. 1975; promotes the progress of biology, chemistry, dentistry, medicine and related sciences; 350 mems; Pres. ZENÓN M. SFAELLO; Sec. MIGUEL A. DAHBAR.

Academia Nacional de Medicina (National Academy of Medicine): Avda Gral. Las Heras 3092, C1425ASU Buenos Aires; tel. (11) 4805-5759; e-mail acamedbai@acamedbai.org.ar; internet www.acamedbai.org.ar; f. 1822; 35 mems; library of 50,000 vols; Pres. Dr ROBERTO N. PRADIER; publ. *Boletín de la Academia de Medicina de Buenos Aires* (2 a year).

Asociación Argentina de Biología y Medicina Nuclear (Argentine Association of Biology and Nuclear Medicine): Luis Sáenz Peña 250, 6° piso, 1110 Buenos Aires; tel. (11) 4382-0583; e-mail aabymn_1@ciudad.com.ar; internet www.aabymn.org.ar; f. 1963; 190 mems; Pres. Dr ARTURO J. SAN MARTÍN; Sec. Dra MARÍA DEL CARMEN ALAK.

Asociación Argentina de Cirugía (Argentine Association of Surgery): Marcelo T. de Alvear 2415, C1122AAM Buenos Aires; tel. (11) 4822-2905; e-mail info@aac.org.ar; internet www.aac.org.ar; f. 1930; promotes professional devt of surgeons; 3,700 mems; Pres. Dr NORBERTO A. MEZZADRI; publ. *Revista Argentina de Cirugía* (8 a year).

Asociación Argentina de Farmacia y Bioquímica Industrial (Argentine Association of Pharmacy and Industrial Biochemistry): Uruguay 469, 2° B, C1015ABI Buenos Aires; tel. (11) 4373-8900; e-mail info@safybi.org; internet www.safybi.org.ar; f. 1952; 1,100 mems; library of 500 vols; Pres. Dr FEDERICO E. MONTES DE OCA; Sec. Dra MIRTA B. FARIÑA; publ. *Revista SAFYBI*.

Asociación Argentina de Ortopedia y Traumatología (Argentine Association of Orthopaedia and Traumatology): Vicente López 1878, C1128ABC Buenos Aires; tel. (11) 4801-2320; e-mail informes@aaot.org.ar; internet www.aaot.org.ar; f. 1936, current name adopted 1982; 2,944 mems; library of 1,500 vols, 116 periodicals; Pres. Dr MARIO LAMPRÓPULOS; Sec.-Gen. Dr RICARDO G. DENARI; publ. *Revista AAOT* (4 a year).

Asociación Médica Argentina (Argentine Medical Association): Avda Santa Fe 1171, C1059ABF Buenos Aires; tel. (11) 5276-1040; e-mail info@ama-med.org.ar; internet www.ama-med.org.ar; f. 1891; 3,520 mems; library of 32,000 vols, 1,200 periodical titles; Pres. Prof. Dr ELÍAS HURTADO HOYO; Sec.-Gen. MIGUEL A. GALMÉS; publ. *Revista AMA* (4 a year).

Asociación Odontológica Argentina (Argentine Dental Association): Junín 959, C1113AAC Buenos Aires; tel. (11) 4961-6141; e-mail aoa@aoa.org.ar; internet www.aoa.org.ar; f. 1896; incl. postgraduate school for dentists; 11,500 mems; library of 8,000 vols, 25,000 periodicals; Pres. DAMIÁN BASRANI; Sec. GLADYS FOL; publ. *Revista AOA*.

Asociación para la Lucha Contra la Parálisis Infantil (ALPI) (Association for Combating Infantile Paralysis): Soler 3945, C1425BWO Buenos Aires; tel. (11) 4821-1200; e-mail comunicacion@alpi.org.ar; internet www.alpi.org.ar; f. 1943; 30 mems; library of 3,000 vols; Pres. ALEJANDRO ALLENDE; Sec. Dr JORGE SAUCEDO; publ. *Memoria y Balance Anual*.

Federación Argentina de Asociaciones de Anestesia, Analgesia y Reanimación (Argentine Federation of Associations of Anaesthesia, Analgesia and Resuscitation): Olazabal 1515, Piso 10, C1428DGG Buenos Aires; tel. (11) 4782-9691; e-mail faaaar@anestesia.org.ar; internet www.anestesia.org.ar; f. 1970; conducts courses, workshops, symposia and confs; 1,113 mems; Pres. Dr LUIS PARRILE; Gen. Sec. Dr MARTÍN SEGALOTTI; publ. *Revista Argentina de Anestesiología*.

Liga Argentina Contra la Tuberculosis (Argentine League Against Tuberculosis): Uriarte 2477, C1425FNI, Buenos Aires; tel. (11) 4777-4447; e-mail lalat1901@yahoo.com.ar; internet www.lalat.org.ar; f. 1901; library of 140 series of periodicals; Medical Dir Dr VICENTE DONATO; publ. *Revista Argentina del Tórax*.

Sociedad Argentina de Dermatología (Argentine Society of Dermatology): Avda Callao 852, 2° piso, C1023AAO Buenos Aires; tel. (11) 4814-4916; e-mail sad@sad.org.ar; internet www.sad.org.ar; f. 1934; 2,100 mems; Pres. MIGUEL ANGEL J. ALLEVATO; Sec.-Gen. JULIO GIL; publ. *Dermatología Argentina* (5 a year).

Sociedad Argentina de Endocrinología y Metabolismo (Argentine Society of Endocrinology and Metabolism): Avda Díaz Vélez 3889, C1200AAF Buenos Aires; tel. (11) 4983-9800; e-mail info@saem.org.ar; internet www.saem.org.ar; f. 1941; develops intellectual and cultural links with similar societies; 600 mems; Pres. Dr HUGO BOQUETE; Sec. Dr N. MARCELO VITALE; publ. *Revista* (4 a year).

Sociedad Argentina de Farmacología y Terapéutica (Argentine Society of Pharmacology and Therapeutics): Avda Santa Fe 1171, C1059ABF Buenos Aires; tel. (11) 4811-3580; e-mail safyt_2003@hotmail.com; f. 1929; 100 mems; Pres. Dr ALFREDO VITALE; Sec. Dr RICARDO CERDA.

Sociedad Argentina de Fisiológia (Argentine Society of Physiology): Solís 453, C1078AAI Buenos Aires; tel. (11) 4378-1151; e-mail safis@safisiol.org.ar; internet www.safisiol.org.ar; f. 1950; 330 mems; library of 600 vols; Pres. Dr RAÚL A. MARINELLI; Gen. Sec. CRISTINA CARNOVALE; publ. *Physiological Mini-Reviews* (12 a year).

Sociedad Argentina de Gastroenterología (Argentine Society of Gastroenterology): Marcelo T. de Alvear 1381, 9°, C1058AAU Buenos Aires; tel. (11) 4816-9391; e-mail sagesecretaria@gmail.com; internet www.sage.org.ar; f. 1927; 900 mems; Pres. Dr ALFREDO GARCIA; Gen. Sec. Dr SERGIO HUERNOS; publ. *Acta Gastroenterológica Latinoamericana*.

Sociedad Argentina de Gerontología y Geriatría (Argentine Society of Gerontology and Geriatrics): San Luis 2538, C1056AAD Buenos Aires; tel. (11) 4961-0070; e-mail info@sagg.org.ar; internet www.sagg.org.ar; f. 1951; 1,500 mems; Pres. Dr HUGO ALBERTO SCHIFIS; Sec.-Gen. Prof. Dra ADRIANA M. A. ALFANO; publs *Revista Argentina de Gerontología y Geriatría* (6 a year), *Vivir en Plenitud* (6 a year).

Sociedad Argentina de Hematología (Argentine Society of Haematology): Julian

Álvarez 146, C1414DRD Buenos Aires; tel. (11) 4855-2452; e-mail sah@sah.org.ar; internet www.sah.org.ar; f. 1945; 800 mems; Pres. Dr Gustavo Kusminsky; Sec. Dr Gustavo Chiappe; publ. *Revista Argentina de Hematologia* (3 a year, print and online, www.sah.org.ar/revista).

Sociedad Argentina de Investigación Clínica (Argentine Society of Clinical Research): Combatientes de Malvinas 3150, C1427ARO Buenos Aires; tel. (11) 4523-4963; e-mail saic@saic.org.ar; internet www.saic.org.ar; f. 1960; 567 mems; Pres. Carlos Alberto Davio; Sec. Liliana Graciela Bianciotti; publ. *Medicina* (4 a year).

Sociedad Argentina de Oftalmología (Argentine Ophthalmological Society): Viamonte 1465 7°, C1055ABA Buenos Aires; tel. (11) 4373-8826; e-mail info@sao.org.ar; internet www.sao.org.ar; f. 1921; promotes scientific knowledge and research in ophthalmology; 2,700 mems; Pres. Dr Fabian Lerner; Sec. Dr Andres Bastien; publ. *Archivos de Oftalmología de Buenos Aires* (12 a year).

Sociedad Argentina de Patología (Argentine Society of Pathology): Pte. Gral. Perón 2234, C1040AAJ Buenos Aires; tel. (11) 4951-2152; e-mail infosap@patologia.org.ar; internet www.patologia.org.ar; f. 1933; 220 mems; Pres. Dr Martin Paradelo; Gen. Sec. Dra Laura Jufe.

Sociedad Argentina de Pediatría (Argentine Society of Paediatrics): Avda Coronel Díaz 1971/75, C1425DQF Buenos Aires; tel. (11) 4821-8612; e-mail cdsap@sap.org.ar; internet www.sap.org.ar; f. 1911; 7,500 mems; library of 5,000 vols; Pres. Dr Gustavo Cardigni; Gen. Sec. Dra Stella Maris Gil; publ. *Archivos Argentinos de Pediatría* (6 a year).

Sociedad de Psicología Médica, Psicoanálisis y Medicina Psicosomática (Society of Medical Psychology, Psychoanalysis and Psychosomatic Medicine): Avda Santa Fe 1171, C1059ABF Buenos Aires; tel. (11) 4814-2182; e-mail amalia.racciatti@gmail.com; internet www.psicoama.com.ar; f. 1939; 80 mems; Pres. Dra Amalia Racciatti de Messuti; Sec. Lic. Dora Birgin.

NATURAL SCIENCES

General

Academia Nacional de Ciencias (National Academy of Sciences): Avda Vélez Sarsfield 229, 5000 Córdoba; tel. (351) 433-2089; e-mail info@anc-argentina.org.ar; internet www.anc-argentina.org.ar; f. 1869; 79 mems; library of 12,000 vols, 3,800 periodicals; Pres. Dr Juan Tirao; Academic Sec. Dr Roberto Rossi.

Academia Nacional de Ciencias de Buenos Aires (National Academy of Sciences of Buenos Aires): Avda Alvear 1711, 3°, C1014AAE Buenos Aires; tel. (11) 4811-3066; e-mail info@ciencias.org.ar; internet www.ciencias.org.ar; f. 1935; 35 mems; library of 7,500 vols of journals, 10,000 monographs; Pres. Dr Marcelo Urbano Salerno; Sec. Ing. Juan Carlos Ferreri; publs *Anales*, *Escritos de Filosofía* (4 a year).

Academia Nacional de Ciencias Exactas, Físicas y Naturales (National Academy of Exact, Physical and Natural Sciences): Avda Alvear 1711, 4°, C1014AAE Buenos Aires; tel. (11) 4811-2998; e-mail acad@ancefn.org.ar; internet www.ancefn.org.ar; f. 1874; 155 mems (29 full voting, 32 nat. corresp., 86 foreign corresp., 8 hon.); library of 400 vols; Pres. Dr Roberto L. O. Cignoli; Sec.-Gen. Dr Enrique J. Baran; publ. *Anales* (1 a year).

Asociación Argentina de Ciencias Naturales (Argentine Association of Natural Sciences): Avda Angel Gallardo 470, C1405DJR Buenos Aires; tel. (11) 4982-8370; f. 1912; 450 mems; Pres. Juan Carlos Giacchi; Sec. Dra Cristina Marinone; publ. *Physis* (2 a year).

Asociación Argentina para el Progreso de las Ciencias (Argentine Association for the Advancement of Science): Avda Alvear 1711, 4°, C1014AAE Buenos Aires; tel. (11) 4811-6951; e-mail secretaria@aargentinapciencias.org; internet www.aargentinapciencias.org; f. 1933; education and training of researchers and scientists; 215 mems (200 ordinary, 15 assoc.); Pres. Dr Miguel Ángel Blesa; Sec. Dra Alicia Sarce; publ. *Revista Ciencia e Investigación*.

Sociedad Científica Argentina (Argentine Scientific Society): Avda Santa Fe 1145, C1059ABF Buenos Aires; tel. (11) 4816-4745; e-mail sociedad@cientifica.org.ar; internet www.cientifica.org.ar; f. 1872; affiliations in Santa Fe, La Plata, San Juan; 698 mems; library of 38,000 vols and 1,600 publs; Pres. Dr Eduardo Castro; Sec. Lic. Ernesto O. Celman; publ. *Anales* (1 a year).

Biological Sciences

Asociación Argentina de Micología (Argentine Association of Mycology): Suipacha 531, S2000LRK Rosario; tel. (341) 480-4592; internet www.asam.org.ar; f. 1960; studies in medical and veterinary mycology, and mycotoxins; 150 mems; Pres. Dra Laura Ramos; Sec. Marisa Biasoli; publ. *Revista Argentina de Micología* (3 a year).

Asociación Paleontológica Argentina (Argentine Association of Palaeontology): Maipú 645, 1°, C1006ACG Buenos Aires; tel. (11) 4326-7463; e-mail secretaria@apaleontologica.org.ar; internet www.apaleontologica.org.ar; f. 1955; 500 mems; Pres. Dr Emilio Vaccari; Sec. Dr Javier N. Gelfo; publ. *Ameghiniana* (4 a year).

Sociedad Argentina de Biología (Argentine Society of Biology): Vuelta de Obligado 2490, C1428ADN Buenos Aires; tel. (11) 4783-2869; e-mail info@biologia.org.ar; internet www.biologia.org.ar; f. 1919; 140 mems; Pres. Dr Gustavo M. Somoza; Sec. Dra Griselda Irusta; publ. *Revista* (1 a year).

Sociedad Argentina de Fisiología Vegetal (Argentine Society of Plant Physiology): Facultad de Agronomía, Universidad de Buenos Aires, Avda San Martin 4453, C1417DSE Buenos Aires; tel. (11) 4524-8000; e-mail presidencia@safv.com.ar; internet www.safv.com.ar; f. 1958; 260 mems; Pres. Dr Roberto Benech Arnold; publs *Agricultural Sciences*, *Microbiome*, *Plant Methods* (online), *Rice*.

Sociedad Entomológica Argentina (Argentine Entomological Society): Paseo del Bosque s/n, B1900FWA La Plata; tel. (221) 425-7744; e-mail novedadessea@gmail.com; internet www.sea.org.ar; f. 1925; promotes activities related to the knowledge and research of insects and arachnids; 350 mems; library of 950 vols, 600 periodicals; Pres. Dr Analía A. Lanteri; Sec. Dr María Cecilia Melo; publs *Publicación Especial de la Sociedad Entomológica Argentina* (irregular), *Revista de la Sociedad Entomológica Argentina* (2 a year).

Mathematical Sciences

Unión Matemática Argentina (Argentine Mathematical Union): Instituto de Matemática Aplicada del Litoral, CONICET, Güemes 3450, S3000GLN Santa Fe; tel. (342) 455-9175; e-mail contacto@union-matematica.org.ar; internet www.union-matematica.org.ar; f. 1936; 600 mems; Pres. Hugo Aimar; Sec. Pedro Morin; publs *Revista de Educación Matemática* (1 a year), *Revista de la Unión Matemática Argentina*.

Physical Sciences

Asociación Argentina Amigos de la Astronomía (Argentine Association for the Friends of Astronomy): Avda Patricias Argentinas 550, C1405BWS Buenos Aires; tel. (11) 4863-3366; internet www.amigosdelaastronomia.org; f. 1929; maintains an observatory and museum; 1,000 mems; library of 6,600 vols and 138 periodicals; Pres. Luis Manterola Rivero; Sec. Matías Jones; publ. *Revista Astronómica* (4 a year).

Asociación Argentina de Astronomía (Argentine Association of Astronomy): Laprida 854, X5000BGR Córdoba; tel. (351) 433-1066; e-mail aaacd@fcaglp.unlp.edu.ar; internet www.astronomiaargentina.org.ar; f. 1958; promotes advancement of astronomy, astrophysics and related activities; 312 mems; Pres. Dr Cristina H. Mandrini; Sec. Dra Elsa Giacani.

Asociación Argentina de Geofísicos y Geodestas (Argentine Association of Geophysicists and Geodesists): Facultad de Ciencias Exactas y Naturales, Universidad de Buenos Aires, Güiraldes 2160, C1428EGA Buenos Aires; e-mail lmburgues@hotmail.com; internet www.aagg.org.ar; f. 1959; Pres. Luís Lenzano; Sec. Leticia Burgués; publ. *Geoacta* (1 a year).

Asociación Bioquímica Argentina (Argentine Biochemical Association): Venezuela 1823, 3°, C1096ABE Buenos Aires; tel. (11) 4381-2907; e-mail info@aba-online.org.ar; internet www.aba-online.org.ar; f. 1934; Pres. Dr Alberto Villagra; Sec. Aníbal Bagnarelli; publ. *Revista Bioquímica y Patología Clínica*.

Asociación Geológica Argentina (Argentine Geological Association): Maipú 645, C1006ACG Buenos Aires; tel. (11) 4325-3104; e-mail secretaria@geologica.org.ar; internet www.geologica.org.ar; f. 1945; 1,750 mems; Pres. Martín Gozalvez; Sec. Mariela Etcheverría.

Asociación Química Argentina (Argentine Chemical Association): Sánchez de Bustamante 1749, C1425DUI Buenos Aires; tel. (11) 4822-4886; e-mail aqa@aqa.org.ar; internet www.aqa.org.ar; f. 1912; 1,000 mems; library of 10,000 vols, 500 periodicals; Pres. Dr Eduardo A. Castro; Sec. Dr Raúl F. Laba; publs *Anales de la Asociación Química Argentina* (Scientific), *Industria y Química* (Technical).

Centro Argentino de Espeleología (Argentine Centre of Speleology): Avda de Mayo 651, 1° piso, 1428 Buenos Aires; tel. (11) 4331-6798; e-mail caespeleo@hotmail.com; internet caespeleo.tripod.com; f. 1970; 60 mems; library of 250 vols; Pres. Eduardo Zappettini; Sec. Pablo Puig; publ. *Las Brujas* (1 a year).

Grupo Argentino del Color (Argentine Colour Group): Universidad de Buenos Aires, Pab. 3, 4°, C1428BFA Buenos Aires; tel. (11) 4789-6289; e-mail eugeniabravo@ymail.com; internet www.fadu.uba.ar/sitios/sicyt/color/gac.htm; f. 1980; promotes research and studies on colours; 159 mems; Pres. María Paula Giglio; Sec. María Eugenia Bravo.

PHILOSOPHY AND PSYCHOLOGY

Sociedad Argentina de Psicología (Buenos Aires Psychological Society): Callao 435, 1°, C1022AAE Buenos Aires; tel. (11) 4432-3760; f. 1930; Pres. Juan Cuatrecasas.

RELIGION, SOCIOLOGY AND ANTHROPOLOGY

Asociación Argentina de Estudios Americanos (Argentine Association of American Studies): Maipú 672, 1424 Buenos Aires; tel. (11) 4392-4971; e-mail estudiosamericanos@starmedia.com.

Sociedad Argentina de Antropología (Argentine Society of Anthropology): Moreno 350, C1091AAH Buenos Aires; e-mail saantropologia@saantropologia.org.ar; internet www.saantropologia.com.ar; f. 1936; 600 mems; Pres. VERÓNICA WILLIAMS; Sec. SONIA LANZELOTTI; publ. *Relaciones* (1 a year).

Sociedad Argentina de Sociología (Argentine Society of Sociology): Trejo 241, 5000 Córdoba; tel. (351) 44-5901; f. 1950; Pres. Prof. ALFREDO POVIÑA; Sec.-Gen. Prof. ODORICO PIRES PINTO.

TECHNOLOGY

Asociación Argentina del Frío (Argentine Association for Refrigeration): Avda Belgrano, 3° Piso, Oficina K, C1092AAF Buenos Aires; tel. (11) 4343-1560; e-mail aafrio@aafrio.org.ar; internet www.aafrio.org.ar; f. 1932; 178 mems; Pres. Ing. ROBERTO RICARDO AGUILO; Sec. Ing. CARLOS MITROGA; publ. *Clima* (12 a year).

Asociación Electrotécnica Argentina (Argentine Association of Electrotechnology): Posadas 1659, C1112ADC Buenos Aires; tel. (11) 4804-3454; e-mail info@aea.org.ar; internet www.aea.org.ar; f. 1913; 2,000 mems; library of 2,500 vols; Pres. Ing. ERNESTO O. VIGNAROLI; Sec.-Gen. Ing. ABEL JORGE CRESTA; publ. *Revista Electrotécnica*.

Centro Argentino de Ingenieros (Argentine Centre of Engineers): Cerrito 1250, C1010AAZ Buenos Aires; tel. (11) 4811-0570; e-mail informes@cai.org.ar; internet www.cai.org.ar; f. 1895; 10,231 mems; library of 11,000 vols; Pres. CARLOS BACHER; Sec. HORACIO CRISTIANI; publ. *Revista la Ingeniería*.

Federación Lanera Argentina (Argentine Wool Federation): 25 de Mayo 516, 4° Piso, C1002ABL Buenos Aires; tel. (11) 5199-5618; e-mail info@flasite.com; f. 1929; concerned with all aspects of wool trade, from breeding to sales; 50 mems; Pres. JULIO E. AISENSTEIN; Sec. RAÚL ERNESTO ZAMBONI; publ. *Argentine Wool Statistics* (12 a year).

Research Institutes

GENERAL

Instituto de Matemática de Bahía Blanca (INMABB) (Institute of Mathematics of Bahía Blanca): Avda Alem 1253, B8000CPB Bahía Blanca; tel. (291) 459-5116; e-mail sinmabb@inmabb-conicet.gob.ar; internet inmabb-conicet.gob.ar; f. 1980; attached to CONICET and Universidad Nacional del Sur; Dir MARÍA INÉS PLATZECK; Vice-Dir MARÍA JULIA REDONDO.

Instituto Torcuato Di Tella (Torcuato Di Tella Institute): Miñones 2159/77, 1°, 1428 Buenos Aires; tel. (11) 5169-7000; e-mail salvadororsini@fibertel.com.ar; internet www.itdt.edu; f. 1958; promotes scientific research and artistic creativity on a nat. and int. scale; administers research centres and HEIs; postgraduate courses in economics, sociology and administration; library of 85,000 vols; Pres. ANDRÉS LAUTARO DI TELLA.

AGRICULTURE, FISHERIES AND VETERINARY SCIENCE

Estación Experimental Agro-Industrial 'Obispo Colombres' ('Obispo Colombres' Agro-Industrial Experimental Research Station): Avda William Cross 3150, Las Talitas, T4101XAC Tucumán; tel. (381) 452-1000; e-mail dt@eeaoc.org.ar; internet www.eeaoc.org.ar; f. 1909 as Agricultural Experiment Station of Tucumán (EEAT), current name adopted 1978; autonomous unit of the Tucumán provincial govt; research, technological devts and services for agri-industrial business of NW Argentina; library of 60,000 vols, 7,000 periodicals; Pres. and Chair. JUAN JOSÉ BUDEGUER; Technical Dir and CEO Dr LEONARDO DANIEL PLOPER; publs *Avance Agroindustrial* (4 a year), *Informe Annual EEAOC* (1 a year), *Publicación Especial EEAOC* (irregular), *Revista Industrial y Agrícola de Tucumán* (2 a year).

Instituto Nacional de Investigación y Desarrollo Pesquero (National Institute for Fisheries Research and Development): Paseo Victoria Ocampo n°1, Escollera Norte, B7602HSA Mar del Plata; tel. (223) 486-2586; e-mail biblio@inidep.edu.ar; internet www.inidep.edu.ar; f. 1977 from fmr Mar del Plata Marine Biology Institute; attached to Min. of Agriculture, Livestock and Fisheries; devt and colln of growing technologies for raising marine and commercial-interest freshwater organisms, as well as the valorization of fishing crops and marine biodiversity; 300 researchers and assts; library of 4,600 vols, 763 periodicals, 350 theses/dissertations; Dir Dr OTTO WÖHLER; publs *INIDEP Informe Técnico* (irregular), *Revista de Investigación y Desarrollo Pesquero* (irregular).

Instituto Nacional de Tecnología Agropecuaria (INTA) (National Institute for Agricultural Technology): Rivadavia 1439, C1033AAE Buenos Aires; tel. (11) 4338-4600; e-mail revista_ria@correo.inta.gov.ar; internet www.inta.gob.ar; f. 1956; attached to Ministry of Agriculture, Livestock and Fisheries; 50 experimental stations, 16 research institutes; Pres. Ing. Agr. CARLOS CASAMIQUELA; Nat. Dir Ing. Agr. ELISEO MONTI; publs *Idia XXI* (3 a year), *Revista de Investigaciones Agropecuarias (RIA)* (3 a year), *Revista Voces y Ecos*.

Instituto Nacional de Vitivinicultura (National Vine Institute): San Martín 430, 5500 Mendoza; tel. (261) 521-6600; e-mail prensa@inv.gov.ar; internet www.inv.gov.ar; f. 1959; library of 15,000 vols, 690 journals; Pres. GUILLERMO DANIEL GARCIA; publs *Estadística Vitivinícola* (1 a year), *Exportaciones Argentinas de Productos Vitivinícolas* (1 a year), *Revista Vinifera*, *Superficie de Vinos por Variedades Implatada en la República Argentina*.

ARCHITECTURE AND TOWN PLANNING

Instituto de Planeamiento Regional y Urbano (IPRU) (Regional and Urban Planning Institute): Calle Posadas 1265 (7°), 1011 Buenos Aires; f. 1952; Dir FERNANDO PASTOR; publs *Cuadernos de IPRU*, *Plan*.

BIBLIOGRAPHY, LIBRARY SCIENCE AND MUSEOLOGY

Centro de Documentación Bibliotecológica (Centre for Library Science Documentation): Universidad Nacional del Sur, Avda Alem 1253, 8000 Bahía Blanca; tel. (291) 42-8035; f. 1962; teaching and research in library science; library of 2,980 vols, 332 periodicals; Chief Librarian MARTA IBARLUCEA DE RUIZ; publs *Bibliografía Bibliotecológica Argentina 1978–81*, *Documentación Bibliotecológica*, *Revista de Revistas*.

Instituto de Bibliografía del Ministerio de Educación de la Provincia de Buenos Aires (Bibliographical Institute of the Ministry of Education of the Province of Buenos Aires): Calle 47 No 510 (6°), 1900 La Plata; tel. (221) 43-5915; Dir MARÍA DEL CARMEN CRESPI DE BUSTOS; publ. *Bibliografía Argentina de Historia*.

ECONOMICS, LAW AND POLITICS

Centro de Investigaciones Económicas (Economic Research Centre): Instituto Torcuato Di Tella, Miñones 2159/77, 1°, 1428 Buenos Aires; tel. (11) 5169-7000; e-mail salvadororsini@fibertel.com.ar; internet www.itdt.edu; f. 1960; library of 85,000 vols; Pres. ANDRÉS LAUTARO DI TELLA.

Instituto de Desarrollo Económico y Social (Institute of Economic and Social Development): Aráoz 2838, C1425DGT Buenos Aires; tel. (11) 4804-4949; e-mail ides@ides.org.ar; internet www.ides.org.ar; f. 1960; promotes research in social sciences, provides a forum for discussing ideas, disseminates scientific production through its publs programme; library of 15,000 vols; Pres. ALEJANDRO DUJOVNE; publ. *Desarrollo Económico—Revista de Ciencias Sociales* (4 a year).

Instituto Nacional de Estadística y Censos (National Institute of Statistics and Censuses): Avda Julio A. Roca 615, C1067ABB Buenos Aires; tel. (11) 4349-9200; e-mail ces@indec.mecon.gov.ar; internet www.indec.gov.ar; f. 1968; coordinates all public statistical activities; library of 30,000 vols; Dir ANA MARÍA EDWIN; publs *Anuario Estadístico de la República Argentina* (1 a year), *Comercio Exterior Argentino* (1 a year), *INDEC Informa* (12 a year).

Instituto para el Desarrollo Empresarial de la Argentina (Institute for Business Development): Moreno 1850, C1094ABB Buenos Aires; tel. (11) 5861-4300; e-mail info@ideamail.com.ar; internet www.ideared.org; f. 1960; library of 10,000 vols, 50 periodicals; Exec. Dir Ing. ERNESTO J. FERRER; publ. *Revista IDEA* (2 a year).

Instituto para la Integración de América Latina y el Caribe (Institute for the Integration of Latin America and the Caribbean): Esmeralda 130 (pisos 16 y 17), C1035ABD Buenos Aires; tel. (11) 4323-2350; e-mail intal@iadb.org; internet www.iadb.org/intal; f. 1965 following an agreement between the Inter-American Devt Bank and the Govt of Argentina; undertakes research and provides support in all aspects of regional integration and cooperation; provides technical support for hemispheric integration processes agreed during Summit of the Americas 1994; library: Documentation Centre of 100,000 documents, 12,000 vols, 400 periodicals; Dir GRACIELA SCHAMIS; publ. *Integración & Comercio* (Integration & Trade, 2 a year).

FINE AND PERFORMING ARTS

Instituto Nacional de Estudios de Teatro (National Institute for the Study of Theatre): Avda Córdoba 1199, 1055 Buenos Aires; tel. (11) 4815-8885; e-mail estudiosdeteatro@inet.gov.ar; f. 1936; also nat. theatre museum; library of 16,000 vols, archives; Dir Profa CRISTINA LASTRA BELGRANO.

HISTORY, GEOGRAPHY AND ARCHAEOLOGY

Departamento de Estudios Históricos Navales (Department of Naval History Studies): Avda Almirante Brown 401, 1155 Buenos Aires; tel. (11) 4362-1248; e-mail estudioshistoricosnavales@yahoo.com.ar; internet www.ara.mil.ar/pag.asp?iditem=440; f. 1957; large number of publs, also paintings and medals; Dir Capt. GUILLERMO ANDRÉS OYARZABAL.

Dirección Nacional del Antártico (National Antarctic Office): Balcarce 290, C1064AAF Buenos Aires; tel. (11) 4331-2900; e-mail dna@dna.gov.ar; internet www.dna.gov.ar; f. 1970; plans, directs, coordinates and controls scientific and technical Antarctic tasks of Argentina; scientific colln; maintains Yubany station at King George Island, Antarctica; library of 15,000 vols; Dir Dr MARIANO ARNALDO MEMOLLI; publs *Boletín del SCAR* (3 a year, Spanish edn of SCAR Bulletin), *Contribuciones Científicas* (irregular), *Revista Antártica*.

Attached Institute:

Instituto Antártico Argentino (Argentine Antarctic Institute): Cerrito 1248, C1010AAZ Buenos Aires; tel. (11) 4331-2911; e-mail diriaa@dna.gov.ar; internet www.antartida.gov.ar; f. 1951; Dir Dr NESTOR CORIA.

Instituto Argentino de Oceanografía (Argentine Institute of Oceanography): Camino La Carrindanga, Km 7.5), B8000FWB Bahía Blanca; tel. (291) 486-1112; internet www.iado-conicet.gob.ar; f. 1969; attached to CONICET and Universidad Nacional del Sur; promotes the devt of scientific research on the Argentine Sea and its resources; library of 1,893 vols; Dir Dr RUBÉN JOSÉ LARA; Vice-Dir Dr EDUARDO ALBERTO GÓMEZ.

Instituto Geográfico Nacional (National Geographical Institute): Avda Cabildo 381, C1426AAD Buenos Aires; tel. (11) 4576-5576; e-mail contacto@ign.gob.ar; internet www.ign.gob.ar; f. 1879 as Instituto Geográfico Militar, current name adopted 2009; topographic survey of Argentina; Dir SERGIO RUBEN CIMBARO; publ. *Revista el Ojo del Cóndor* (4 a year).

MEDICINE

Administración Nacional de Laboratorios e Institutos de Salud 'Dr Carlos G. Malbran' (National Administration of Laboratories and Institutes of Health 'Dr. Carlos G. Malbrán'): Avda Vélez Sarsfield 563, 1281 Buenos Aires; tel. (11) 4303-1804; e-mail direccion@anlis.gov.ar; internet www.anlis.gov.ar; f. 1996; library of 6,500 vols; Dir Dr JAIME LAZOVSKI.

Centro de Investigaciones Neurobiológicas 'Prof. Dr Christfried Jakob' (Christfried Jakob Centre for Neurobiological Research): Avda Amancio Alcorta 1602, 1283 Buenos Aires; tel. (11) 4306-7314; f. 1899; attached to Min. of Public Health and Welfare; neuroscience research; Dir Prof. Dr MARIO-FERNANDO CROCCO; publ. *Folia Neurobiológica Argentina*.

Instituto de Biología y Medicina Experimental (Institute of Biology and Experimental Medicine): Vuelta de Obligado 2490, Belgrano, 1428 Buenos Aires; tel. (11) 4783-2869; e-mail ibyme@ibyme.org.ar; internet www.ibyme.org.ar; f. 1944; basic and applied research, training of pre- and post-doctoral fellows, contributes to the improvement of human health, quality of life and socio-economic devt; library of 15,000 vols; Dir Dra DAMASIA BECU-VILLALOBOS; publ. *Memoria* (1 a year).

Instituto de Investigaciones Médicas 'Alfredo Lanari' (Alfredo Lanari Institute of Medical Research): Avda Combatientes de Malvinas 3150, C1427ARO Buenos Aires; tel. (11) 4514-8701; e-mail director@lanari.fmed.uba.ar; internet www.lanari.fmed.uba.ar; f. 1957; clinical and basic medical research, teaching; library of 4,185 vols, 6,738 periodicals; Dir Prof. Dr EDUARDO LUIS DE VITO; publ. *Medicina* (4 a year).

NATURAL SCIENCES

General

Consejo Nacional de Investigaciones Científicas y Técnicas (CONICET) (National Scientific and Technical Research Council): Avda Rivadavia 1917, C1033AAJ Buenos Aires; tel. (11) 5983-1420; e-mail info@conicet.gov.ar; internet www.conicet.gov.ar; f. 1958; agrarian, engineering and material sciences; biological and health sciences; exact and natural sciences; social science and humanities; Pres. ROBERTO CARLOS SALVAREZZA.

Fundación Miguel Lillo (Miguel Lillo Foundation): Miguel Lillo 251, T4000JFE San Miguel de Tucumán; tel. (381) 433-0868; e-mail direccion@lillo.org.ar; internet www.lillo.org.ar; f. 1947; scientific research in natural sciences and history; incl. institutes of botany, geology and zoology; maintains Geobiological Information Centre of NOA, Cultural Centre 'Alberto Rouges', Study Centre 'Juan Dalma', Lillo Museum of Natural Sciences; library of 132,900 vols and 4,250 periodicals; Pres. Dr EDUARDO GARCÍA HAMILTON; Sec. FRANCISCO SASSI COLOMBRES; publs *Acta Geologica Lilloana* (2 a year), *Actas Jornadas la Generación del Centenario* (2 a year), *Acta Zoologica Lilloana* (2 a year), *Extensión Científica y Cultural* (irregular), *Genera et Species Animalium Argentinorum* (2 a year), *Genera et Species Plantarum Argentinarum* (2 a year), *Lilloa* (botanical, 2 a year), *Miscelánea* (2 a year), *Opera Lilloana* (2 a year).

Biological Sciences

Estación Hidrobiológica de Puerto Quequén (Hydrobiology Station of Puerto Quequén): Avda Alte. Brown s/n, esq. calle 520, 7630 Puerto Quequén, Buenos Aires; e-mail ehpq@yahoo.com.ar; f. 1928; attached to 'B. Rivadavia' Argentine Museum of Natural Sciences; scientific research on the marine ecosystem; Dir Lic. GUSTAVO CHIARAMONTE; publ. *Trabajos de la Estación Hidrobiológica* (irregular).

Instituto de Botánica 'Carlos Spegazzini' ('Carlos Spegazzini' Botanical Institute): Calle 53 No. 477, B1900AVJ La Plata; tel. (221) 421-9845; internet www.fcnym.unlp.edu.ar/museo/institutos/spegazzini/indexibs.html; f. 1930; affiliated to Museo de La Plata; mycological research, biodiversity of saprotrophic and biotrophic fungi; mycological collns from Argentina and S America; germplasm bank of arbuscular mycorrhizal fungi; library of 526 526 vols, 5,000 speciality publs; Dir Dra ANGELICA M. ARAMBARRI.

Instituto de Botánica 'Darwinion' (Darwinian Botanical Institute): Labardén 200, Estanislao del Campo, B1642HYD San Isidro; tel. 4743-4800; e-mail secretaria@darwin.edu.ar; internet www2.darwin.edu.ar; f. 1911; attached to the Academia Nacional de Ciencias Exactas, Físicas y Naturales and CONICET; fields of research: systematic botany, phytogeography, plant anatomy and cytogenetics, palynology, ethnobotany, archaeobotany; library of 160,000 vols, 12,000 books and 2,100 periodicals; Dir Dr FERNANDO O. ZULOAGA; publs *Hickenia* (irregular), *Revista Darwiniana* (2 a year).

Instituto de Investigaciones Bioquímicas (INIBIBB) (Biochemical Research Institute): Camino La Carrindanga Km 7, B8000FWB Bahía Blanca; tel. (291) 486-1201; internet www.inibibb-conicet.gob.ar; f. 1970; attached to CONICET and Universidad Nacional del Sur; Dir Dra MARTA I. AVELDAÑO; Vice-Dir Dra CECILIA BOUZAT.

Instituto Municipal de Botánica, Jardín Botánico 'Carlos Thays' (Municipal Institute of Botany, Botanical Garden Carlos Thays): Sante Fe 3951, 1425 Buenos Aires; tel. (11) 469-3954; f. 1898; library of 10,000 vols, 1,000 books; Dir-Gen. Ing. DANIEL GARCIA MANSILLA; publs *Index Seminum*, *Revista del Instituto de Botánica*.

Instituto Nacional de Limnología (National Institute of Limnology): Paraje 'El Pozo', 3000 Santa Fe; tel. (342) 451-1645; e-mail secretaria@inali.unl.edu.ar; internet www.inali.santafe-conicet.gov.ar; f. 1962; scientific investigations dedicated to the study of aquatic ecosystems within the Argentine continent, especially those related to the Paraná river; library of 3,000 vols, 385 periodicals; Dir Dr PABLO A. COLLINS.

Physical Sciences

Centro de Recursos Naturales Renovables de la Zona Semiárida (CERZOS) (Renewable Natural Resource Center of the Semi-Arid): Camino La Carrindanga, Km 7, B8000FWB Bahía Blanca; tel. (291) 486-1124; internet www.cerzos-conicet.gov.ar; f. 1980; attached to CONICET and Universidad Nacional del Sur; agricultural research; Dir Dr NÉSTOR R. CURVETTO; Vice-Dir Dr JUAN A. GALANTINI.

Comisión Nacional de Actividades Espaciales (CONAE) (National Commission on Space Activities): Avda Paseo Colón 751, C1063ACH Buenos Aires; tel. (11) 4331-0074; e-mail si@conae.gov.ar; internet www.conae.gov.ar; f. 1991; develops Argentina's Nat. Space Programme; Exec. and Technical Dir Dr CONRADO FRANCO VAROTTO.

Comisión Nacional de Energía Atómica (National Atomic Energy Commission): Avda Del Libertador 8250, C1429BNP Buenos Aires; tel. (11) 4704-1000; e-mail comunicacion@cnea.gov.ar; internet www.cnea.gov.ar; f. 1950; govt agency; promotes and undertakes scientific and industrial research and applications of nuclear transmutations and reactions; research centres in Buenos Aires, Constituyentes, Ezeiza and Bariloche; library: see under Libraries and Archives; Pres. Lic. NORMA LUISA BOERO; Vice-Pres. Ing. MAURICIO BISAUTA; publ. *Revista CNEA*.

Observatorio Astronómico (Astronomical Observatory): Laprida 854, X5000BGR Córdoba; tel. (351) 433-1064; e-mail dgl@oac.uncor.edu; internet www.oac.uncor.edu; f. 1871; attached to the Nat. Univ. of Córdoba; research and undergraduate and postgraduate teaching; library of 5,000 vols; Dir Dr DIEGO GARCIA LAMBAS; publ. *Resultados*.

Observatorio Astronómico (Astronomical Observatory): Paseo del Bosque s/n, B1900FWA La Plata; tel. (221) 423-6593; e-mail academic@fcaglp.fcaglp.unlp.edu.ar; internet www.fcaglp.unlp.edu.ar; f. 1883; library of 25,000 vols, 500 periodicals; Dean Dr ADRIÁN BRUNINI.

Planta Piloto de Ingeniería Química (PLAPIQUI) (Chemical Engineering Pilot Plant): Camino La Carrindanga, Km 7, 8000 Bahía Blanca; tel. (291) 486-1700; e-mail plapiqui@plapiqui.edu.ar; internet www.plapiqui.edu.ar; f. 1963; attached to CONICET and Universidad Nacional del Sur; research, education and technology devt; Dir Dra ADRIANA BRANDOLIN; Vice-Dir Dra LIDIA M. QUINZANI.

Servicio Geológico Minero Argentino (Argentine Geological and Mining Service): Avda Julio Argentino Roca 651, C1067ABB Buenos Aires; tel. (11) 4349-3200; e-mail mjanit@mecon.gov.ar; internet www

.segemar.gov.ar; f. 1904; attached to the State Secretariat of Mining of the Min. of Economy and Public Works; Pres. Ing. JORGE OMAR MAYORAL; publ. *Estadística Minera de la República Argentina* (1 a year).

Servicio Meteorológico Nacional (National Meteorological Service): 25 de Mayo 658, C1002ABN Buenos Aires; tel. (11) 5167-6767; e-mail smn@smn.gov.ar; internet www.smn.gov.ar; f. 1872; library of 45,000 vols; Dir Dr HÉCTOR HORACIO CIAPPESONI; publ. *Boletin Climatológico*.

RELIGION, SOCIOLOGY AND ANTHROPOLOGY

Departamento de Estudios Etnográficos y Coloniales (Department of Ethnographical and Colonial Studies): Calle 25 de Mayo 1470, 3000 Santa Fe; tel. (342) 457-3550; e-mail etnosfe@santafe.gov.ar; internet www2.ceride.gov.ar/wxis/etnografico/inicio .htm; f. 1940; Dir Arq. LUIS MARIA CALVO; publ. *America* (1 a year).

Instituto Nacional de Antropología y Pensamiento Latinoamericano (National Institute of Anthropology and Latin American Thought): Calle 3 de Febrero 1378, C1426BJN Buenos Aires; tel. (11) 4782-7251; internet www.inapl.gov.ar; f. 1943; attached to the Secretariat for Culture at the President's Office; library of 25,000 vols; Dir Dra DIANA ROLANDI; publ. *Cuadernos*.

TECHNOLOGY

Instituto Argentino de Normalización y Certificación (IRAM) (Argentine Standards and Certification Institute): Perú 552/556, C1068AAB Buenos Aires; tel. (11) 4346-0600; e-mail iram-iso@iram.org.ar; internet www.iram.org.ar; f. 1935; library of 350,000 standards; Dir-Gen. Ing. LUIS TRAMA.

Instituto de Mecánica Aplicada y Estructuras (Institute of Applied Mechanics and Structures): Riobamba y Berutti, Rosario; tel. (341) 480-8538; e-mail imaesecr@eie.fceia.unr.edu.ar; internet web .fceia.unr.edu.ar/en/institutional/institutes/37-instituto-de-mecanica-aplicada-y-estructuras-imae.html; f. 1963; attached to Faculty of Exact Sciences, Engineering and Surveying, Universidad Nacional de Rosario; performs applied research, participates in academic activities and provides technical assistance and technology transfer specialists; library of 1,000 vols, 3,000 periodicals; Dir Ing. JORGE CARLOS ADUE.

Instituto Nacional de Tecnología Industrial (INTI) (National Institute of Industrial Technology): Parque Tecnológico Miguelete, Colectora de Avda General Paz 5445 entre Albarellos y Avda de los Constituyentes, Casilla de correo 157, B1650KNA San Martín; tel. (11) 4724-6200; e-mail consultas@inti .gob.ar; internet www.inti.gob.ar; f. 1957; library of 32,000 vols, 2,216 periodicals, 105,000 standards; Pres. Ing. RICARDO HORACIO DEL VALLE; publs *Dendroenergía* (2 a year), *Noticiteca* (4 a year).

Libraries and Archives

Bahía Blanca

Asociación Bernardino Rivadavia—Biblioteca Popular (People's Library of the Bernardino Rivadavia Association): Avda Colón 31, B8000FTA Bahía Blanca; tel. (291) 455-4055; e-mail abr@abr.org.ar; internet www.abr.org.ar; f. 1882; 158,319 vols, 1,000 periodicals, 1,000 video cassettes and archive of newspapers; Dir Lic. NORMA E. BISIGNANO.

Biblioteca Central de la Universidad Nacional del Sur (Central Library of the National University of the South): Avda Alem 1253, B8000CPB Bahía Blanca; tel. (291) 459-5111; e-mail unsbc@uns.edu.ar; internet bc.uns.edu.ar; f. 1948; 164,000 vols, 7,293 periodicals; Chief Librarian LUIS A. HERRERA; publs *Memoria Anual, Ultimas Adquisiciones*.

Buenos Aires

Archivo General de la Nación (National Archives): Avda Leandro N. Alem 246, C1003AAP Buenos Aires; tel. (11) 4331-5531; e-mail archivo@mininterior.gov.ar; internet www.mininterior.gov.ar; f. 1821; collects and preserves the written documentation, photographic, filmic, videographic, sonic and machine readable items of interest to the country; 100,000 vols; Supervisor ENRIQUE TANDETER.

Biblioteca Argentina para Ciegos (Argentine Library for the Blind): Lezica 3909, C1202AAA Buenos Aires; tel. (11) 4981-0137; e-mail bac@bac.org.ar; internet www.bac.org.ar; f. 1924; 14,000 vols in Braille, talking books; Pres. TANIA GARCIA; publs *Burbujas* (in Braille, for children), *Con Fundamento* (in Braille, for young people), *Hacia La Luz* (in Braille, for adults).

Biblioteca Central de la Armada (Central Library of the Navy): Avda Comodoro Py 2055, C1104BEA Buenos Aires; tel. (11) 4317-2000; e-mail esgnbib@ara.mil.ar; f. 1914; 160,000 vols; 50 brs; Dir ALICIA PEREZ; publ. *Revista de Publicaciones Navales*.

Biblioteca Central de la Universidad del Salvador 'Padre Guillermo Furlong' (Fr Guillermo Furlong Central Library of the University of Salvador): Tte. Gral. Perón 1818, Subsuelo, C1040AAB Buenos Aires; tel. (11) 4371-0422; e-mail uds-bibl@salvador .edu.ar; f. 1956; 55,000 vols; Dir LILIANA LAURA REGA; publ. *Boletín Bibliográfico*.

Biblioteca de la Sociedad Rural Argentina (Library of Argentine Rural Society): Florida 460, C1005AAJ Buenos Aires; tel. (11) 4322-3431; f. 1866; 50,000 vols; Dir Dr VÍCTOR LUIS FUNES; publs *Anales de la Sociedad Rural Argentina* (4 a year), *Memoria* (1 a year).

Biblioteca de Leprología 'Dr Enrique P. Fidanza' (Dr Enrique P. Fidanza Library of Leprosy): Federación del Patronato del Enfermo de Lepra de la República Argentina, Beruti 2373/77, 1106 Buenos Aires; tel. (11) 483-1815; f. 1930; 4,000 vols, 35,000 cards in its catalogues; museum of histopathology of skin; publ. *Temas de Leprología*.

Biblioteca del Bibliotecario 'Dr Augusto Raúl Cortazar' (Library of the Librarian Dr Augusto Raúl Cortazar): México 564, C1097AAL Buenos Aires; f. 1944; attached to Escuela Nacional de Bibliotecarios (Instituto Superior de Enseñanza); 2,500 vols; Dir RUBY A. ESCANDE.

Biblioteca del Colegio de Escribanos 'José A. Negri' (José A. Negri Library of the College of Notaries): Avda Callao 1542, C1024CAA Buenos Aires; tel. (11) 4807-1637; e-mail bibnegri@colegio-escribanos.org.ar; internet www.colegio-escribanos.org.ar; f. 1866; law and social sciences; 32,500 vols; Librarian ANA MARÍA DANZA; publs *Boletín de Legislación, Revista del Notariado*.

Biblioteca del Congreso de la Nación (Library of the National Congress): Hipólito Yrigoyen 1750, C1089AAH Buenos Aires; tel. (11) 4010-3000; e-mail coordinacion@bcn.gob .ar; internet www.bcnbib.gov.ar; f. 1859; 3m. vols; Pres. ROXANA ITATÍ LATORRE; Gen. Coordinating Dir ALEJANDRO LORENZO CESAR SANTA; publ. *Revista Nexo*.

Biblioteca del Ministerio de Relaciones Exteriores y Culto (Library of the Ministry of Foreign Affairs and Religion): Arenales 761, C1061AAA Buenos Aires; tel. (11) 441-1498; 50,000 vols; Dir HORACIO R. PIÑEYRO.

Biblioteca del Museo Nacional de Bellas Artes 'Raquel Edelman' (Raquel Edelman Library of the National Museum of Fine Arts): Avda Libertador 1473, C1425AAA Buenos Aires; tel. (11) 5288-9972; e-mail bibliotecamnba@yahoo.com.ar; f. 1910; visual arts; 150,000 vols.

Biblioteca del Servicio Geológico Minero Argentino (Library of the Argentine Mining Geology Service): Avda Julio Argentino Roca 651, C1067ABB Buenos Aires; tel. (11) 4349-3198; e-mail mjanit@ secind.mecon.gov.ar; internet www.segemar .gov.ar; f. 1904; 150,000 vols, 45,000 pamphlets, 15,000 maps; Dir Lic. MARA JANITENS; publ. *Anales*.

Biblioteca Nacional (National Library): Calle Agüero 2502, C1425EID Buenos Aires; tel. (11) 4808-6000; e-mail contacto@bn.gov .ar; internet www.bn.gov.ar; f. 1810; 2m. vols, 46, 177 MSS; Dir Dr HORACIO GONZÁLEZ.

Biblioteca Nacional de Aeronáutica (National Library of Aeronautics): Casilla de Correo 3389, C1000WBH Buenos Aires; Paraguay 748, C1057AAH Buenos Aires; tel. (11) 4514-4233; e-mail info@binae.org.ar; internet www.binae.org.ar; f. 1927; aeronautics, astronautics, aeronautical law; 60,000 vols; Dir Brig. PEDRO IRAIZOZ; Chief Librarian Lic. ANGÉLICA A. LLORCA; publ. *Aeroespacio* (6 a year).

Biblioteca Nacional de Maestros (National Library for Teachers): Pizzurno 953, C1020ACA Buenos Aires; tel. (11) 4129-1272; e-mail bnminfo@me.gov.ar; internet www.bnm.me.gov.ar; f. 1870; 150,000 vols; general reference and education; Dir Lic. GRACIELA TERESA PERRONE.

Biblioteca Nacional Militar 'Agustín P. Justo' (Agustín P. Justo National Military Library): Avda Santa Fe 750, C1059ABO Buenos Aires; tel. (11) 4311-1071; e-mail biblioteca@circulomilitar.org; f. 1938; 150,000 vols; Dir Col CARLOS ALBERTO OZARÁN.

Biblioteca Prebisch (Prebisch Library): Reconquista 250, C1003ABF Buenos Aires; tel. (11) 4348-3772; e-mail biblio@bcra.gov .ar; internet www.bcra.gov.ar/institucional/in050100.asp; f. 1935; 120,000 vols; Dir LILIANA MARÍA COVA.

Biblioteca Tornquist (Tornquist Library): Reconquista 266, Hall San Martín–Planta Baja, C1003ABF Buenos Aires; tel. (11) 4348-3500; e-mail biblio@bcra.gov.ar; internet www.bcra.gov.ar/institucional/in050200.asp; f. 1916; economics and social sciences; 35,842 vols, 1,155 periodicals; Dir Lic. LILIANA MARIA COVA.

Centro Argentino de Información Científica y Tecnológica (CAICYT) (Argentine Centre of Scientific and Technological Information): Saavedra 15, C1083ACA Buenos Aires; tel. (11) 4951-7310; e-mail info@caicyt .gov.ar; internet www.caicyt.gov.ar; f. 1958; attached to Consejo Nacional de Investigaciones Científicas y Técnicas; organizes information for research and innovation; Dir Prof. MARÍA ANGELINA BOSCH.

Centro de Documentación e Información Internacional (International Centre of Documentation and Information): Dirección Nacional General de Cooperación Internacional, Ministerio de Educación, Agüero 2502 (3°), 1425 Buenos Aires; f. 1959; publs by UN, Organization of American States, etc.; 5,000 vols; Dir FRANCISCO PIÑÓN.

Centro de Información de la Comisión Nacional de Energía Atómica (Information Centre of the National Atomic Energy Commission): Avda General Paz 1499, B1650KNA Buenos Aires; tel. (11) 6772-7163; e-mail referencia@cnea.gov.ar; internet www.cnea.gov.ar/cac/ci/default.htm; f. 1950; 36,700 vols, 450 current periodicals, 450,000 microcards and reports; Dir GABRIELA PUGLIA; publs *Informes CNEA*, *Memoría CNEA*.

Centro de Información y Estadística Industrial (Centre for Industrial Information and Statistics): c/o INTI, Avda Leandro N. Alem 1067 (1°), 1101 Buenos Aires; attached to Instituto Nacional de Tecnología Industrial; Dir Ing. ALFREDO P. GALLIANO.

Dirección General de Bibliotecas Municipales (General Directorate of Municipal Libraries): Calle Talcahuano 1261, C1014ADA Buenos Aires; tel. (11) 4811-9027; f. 1928; comprises 25 public municipal libraries in Buenos Aires with an aggregate of 350,000 vols; Dir-Gen. Profa JOSEFINA DELGADO; publs *Cuadernos de Buenos Aires*, *Guía Cultural de Buenos Aires*.

Sistema de Bibliotecas y de Información, Universidad de Buenos Aires (Library and Information System of the University of Buenos Aires): Avda Corrientes 2052, C1045AAP Buenos Aires; tel. (11) 4952-6557; e-mail bib@sisbi.uba.ar; internet www.sisbi.uba.ar; f. 1985; 17 constituent faculty libraries; Dir Gen. ELSA ELENA ELIZALDE (acting).

Córdoba

Biblioteca Mayor de la Universidad Nacional de Córdoba (Main Library of Córdoba National University): Calle Obispo Trejo 242, 1°, 5000 Córdoba; tel. (351) 433-1072; e-mail biblio@bmayor.unc.edu.ar; internet www.bmayor.unc.edu.ar; f. 1613; 150,000 vols, 3,890 periodicals and pre-1860 newspapers; partial depository for UN publs; Dir Lic. ROSA M. BESTANI.

Sistema de Bibliotecas de la Universidad Católica de Córdoba (Library of Córdoba Catholic University): Obispo Trejo 323, 5000 Córdoba; tel. (351) 428-6125; e-mail bibdir@uccor.edu.ar; internet www.ucc.edu.ar/biblioteca; f. 1956; 100,000 vols, 3,600 periodicals; Dir Mag. SANDRA GISELA MARTÍN; publs *Contabilidad y Decisiones*, *Diálogos Pedagógicos* (2 a year), *Studia Politicae* (2 a year).

La Plata

Biblioteca del Ministerio de Gobierno de la Provincia de Buenos Aires (Library of the Interior Ministry of the Province of Buenos Aires): Casa de Gobierno, 1900 La Plata; law, politics and economics; 20,000 vols.

Biblioteca Publica de la Universidad Nacional de La Plata (Public Library of the National University of La Plata): Plaza Rocha 137, 1900 La Plata; tel. (221) 423-6607; e-mail secretaria@biblio.unlp.edu.ar; internet www.biblio.unlp.edu.ar; f. 1884; spec. collns incl. S American newspapers relating to the Independence movement, S American history and geography and first travels in S America; 60 br. libraries within the univ.; 600,000 vols, 3,600 periodicals; Dir Bibl. NORMA MANGIATERRA; publ. *Informaciones*.

Biblioteca y Centro de Documentación del Ministerio de Economía de la Provincia de Buenos Aires (Library and Documentation Centre of the Ministry of the Economy of the Province of Buenos Aires): Calle 8 entre 45 y 46, 1900 La Plata; tel. (221) 429-4400; 13,800 vols; Dir (vacant); publs *Cuadernos de Economia* (6 a year), *Noticias de Economia* (6 a year).

Mendoza

Biblioteca Central de la Universidad Nacional de Cuyo (Central Library of the National University of Cuyo): Parque Gral San Martín, 5500 Mendoza; tel. (261) 413-5203; e-mail sid-comunicacion@uncu.edu.ar; f. 1939; 120,000 vols; Dir HORACIO DEGIORGI; publs *Boletín Bibliográfico* (irregular), *Cuadernos de la Biblioteca* (irregular).

Biblioteca Pública General San Martín (General San Martín Public Library): Remedios Escalada de San Martín 1843, 5500 Mendoza; tel. (261) 423-1674; e-mail bibliotecapublicasanmartin@gmail.com; f. 1822; 130,000 vols; spec. collns: local authors, children's books; Dir LUCIA BOURGUET.

Pergamino (Buenos Aires)

Biblioteca Pública Municipal 'Dr Joaquín Menéndez' (Dr Joaquín Menéndez Municipal Public Library): San Martín 838, 2700 Pergamino, Buenos Aires; tel. (2477) 417-327; e-mail bibliotecamenendez@yahoo.com.ar; f. 1900; 58,000 vols; Librarian ALICIA D. PARODI.

Resistencia

Centro de Información Bioagropecuaria y Forestal (CIBAGRO) (Bio-Farming and Forestry Information Centre): Dirección de Bibliotecas, Universidad Nacional del Nordeste, Avda Las Heras 727, 3500 Resistencia, Chaco; tel. (3722) 44-3742; e-mail cibagro@bib.unne.edu.ar; f. 1976; 2,500 books, 2,800 pamphlets, 1,000 periodicals; spec. collns: FAO and other int. agricultural orgs; Dir Lic. ILDA CONESA; publs *Agronea*, *Bibliografía Forestal Nacional*, *Bibliografía sobre El Picudo del Algodonero*, *Bibliografía sobre El Quebracho*, *Ciencias Forestales—Bibliografía*.

Red de Información Forestal para América Latina y el Caribe (RIFALC) (Forest Information Network for Latin America and the Caribbean): CIBAGRO, Dirección de Bibliotecas, Universidad Nacional del Nordeste, Avda Las Heras 727, 3500 Resistencia, Chaco; tel. (3722) 44-3742; e-mail jencinas@bib.unne.edu.ar; f. 1985; coordinates and integrates at regional level the efforts made by individual networks, and makes accessible in each country all the information available; mems: 19 orgs in 12 countries; publ. *Boletín Informativo*.

Rosario

Biblioteca Argentina 'Dr Juan Alvarez' de la Municipalidad de Rosario (Dr Juan Alvarez Argentine Library of the Municipality of Rosario): Pte Roca 731, 2000 Rosario; tel. (341) 480-2538; e-mail bib-novedades@rosario.gov.ar; internet www.biblioargentina.org.ar; f. 1912; 190,000 vols; Dir MARÍA DEL CARMEN D'ANGELO.

Biblioteca Pública 'Estanislao S. Zeballos' (Estanislao S. Zeballos Public Library): Blvd Oroño 1261, 2000 Rosario; tel. (341) 480-2793; e-mail biblioteca@fcecon.unr.edu.ar; internet www.fcecon.unr.edu.ar/web-nueva/?q=biblioteca; f. 1915; attached to Faculty of Economics and Statistics, Nat. Univ. of Rosario; accountancy, business studies, economics, statistics; 111,000 vols; Dir BEATRIZ LODEZANO; publs *Ciudad y Región* (3 a year), *Revista de la Facultad de Ciencias Económicas y Estadística* (irregular).

San Miguel (Buenos Aires)

Biblioteca de las Facultades de Filosofía y Teología de San Miguel (Library of the Faculties of Philosophy and Theology of San Miguel): Avda Ricardo Balbín 3226, 1663 San Miguel, Buenos Aires; tel. (11) 4455-7992; e-mail gerardo@bibusv.edu.ar; internet www.facultades-smiguel.org.ar/biblioteca; f. 1931; central deposit library; 127,000 vols, 714 periodicals; Librarian Prof. GERARDO LOSADA; publ. *Stromata* (4 a year).

Tucumán

Biblioteca Central de la Universidad Nacional de Tucumán (Central Library of the National University of Tucumán): Lamadrid 817, T4000BEQ San Miguel de Tucumán; tel. (381) 410-7292; e-mail biblio@rectorado.unt.edu.ar; internet biblio.unt.edu.ar/b_central; f. 1917; 48,000 vols; Dir-Gen. JUAN RICARDO ACOSTA; publ. *Boletín Bibliográfico*.

Museums and Art Galleries

Buenos Aires

Museo Argentino de Ciencias Naturales 'Bernardino Rivadavia' (Bernardino Rivadavia Argentine Museum of Natural Sciences): Avda Angel Gallardo 470, C1405DJR Buenos Aires; tel. (11) 4982-4494; e-mail info@macn.gov.ar; internet www.macn.gov.ar; f. 1812; zoology, botany, palaeontology, geology and ecology; library of 500,000 vols; Dir Dr PABLO L. TUBARO; publ. *La Revista del Museo* (irregular).

Museo de Armas de la Nación (National Arms Museum): Santa Fe 702, C1059ABO Buenos Aires; tel. (11) 4311-1070; e-mail museo@circulomilitar.org; internet www.museodearmas.com.ar; f. 1904; library of 1,000 vols; Dir JULIO E. SOLDAINI.

Museo de Arte Español 'Enrique Larreta' (Enrique Larreta Museum of Spanish Art): Juramento 2291, C1428DNK Buenos Aires; tel. (11) 4784-4040; e-mail museolarreta@ibuenosaires.gob.ar; internet www.museos.buenosaires.gob.ar/museos.htm; f. 1962; 13th to 18th-century wood carvings, gilt objects and painted panels, paintings of Spanish School from 16th to 20th centuries, tapestries, furniture; library of 12,000 vols; Dir MERCEDES DI PAOLA DE PICOT.

Museo de Arte Hispanoamericano 'Isaac Fernández Blanco' (Isaac Fernández Blanco Museum of Spanish-American Art): Suipacha 1422, C1011ACF Buenos Aires; tel. (11) 4327-0228; e-mail mifb_prensa@buenosaires.gob.ar; f. 1947; 16th to 19th-century Spanish and Portuguese-American art, silver, furniture; library of 5,000 vols; Dir Lic. JORGE COMETTI.

Museo de Arte Moderno de Buenos Aires (Museum of Modern Art): Avda San Juan 350, C1143AAO Buenos Aires; tel. (11) 4342-3001; e-mail mambamail@gmail.com; f. 1956; modern and contemporary art exhibitions; video art screenings; experimental music concerts; Dir VICTORIA NOORTHOORN.

Museo de Bellas Artes de la Boca (Boca Fine Arts Museum): Avda Pedro de Mendoza 1835, C1169AAC Buenos Aires; tel. (11) 4301-1080; f. 1933; paintings, sculpture, engravings, and maritime museum; Dir Dr GUILLERMO C. DE LA CANAL.

Museo de la Policía Federal Argentina (Argentine Federal Police Museum): San Martín 353, 7, C1004AAG Buenos Aires; tel. (11) 4394-6857; f. 1899; Dir JOSÉ A. GUTIÉRREZ.

Museo Etnográfico 'Juan B. Ambrosetti' (Juan B. Ambrosetti Ethnographical Museum): Moreno 350, C1091AAH Buenos Aires; tel. (11) 4345-8196; e-mail info.museo@

filo.uba.ar; internet museoetnografico.filo.uba.ar; f. 1904; attached to Faculty of Philosophy and Letters of the Univ. of Buenos Aires; ethnography and archaeology of Argentina, the Americas, Africa, Asia and Oceania; library of 80,000 vols; Dir MYRIAM TARRAGÓ; publ. *Runa* (1 a year).

Museo Histórico Buenos Aires 'Cornelio de Saavedra' (Brig.-Gen. Cornelio de Saavedra Historical Museum of the City of Buenos Aires): Calle Crisólogo Larralde 6309, C1431AQG Buenos Aires; tel. (11) 4572-0746; e-mail museosaavedra_ecultural@buenosaires.gob.ar; f. 1921; 10 permanent exhibitions: 19th century urban and rural silver, furniture, iconography and decorative arts from first and second half of 19th century, independence hall, clothing, accessories and jewellery of 19th century, coins, firearms and weapons; library of 5,000 vols; Dir Lic. ALBERTO GABRIEL PIÑEIRO.

Museo Histórico Nacional (National History Museum): Defensa 1600, C1143AAD Buenos Aires; tel. (11) 4307-1182; e-mail informes@mhn.gov.ar; f. 1889 as City Historical Museum, current name adopted 1891; library of 15,000 vols, 46,000 artefacts; Dir Dr JOSÉ ANTONIO PÉREZ GOLLÁN; publ. *El Museo Histórico Nacional* (1 a year).

Museo Histórico Sarmiento (Sarmiento History Museum): Juramento 2180, C1428DNJ Buenos Aires; tel. (11) 4781-2989; e-mail info@museosarmiento.gov.ar; internet www.museosarmiento.gov.ar; f. 1938; library of 13,000 vols; Dir MARTA GERMANI.

Museo Mitre (Mitre Museum): San Martín 336, C1004AAH Buenos Aires; tel. (11) 4394-8240; e-mail biblioteca@museomitre.gov.ar; internet www.museomitre.gov.ar; f. 1907; preserves the household of Gen. Bartolomé Mitre; antique books and maps, rare books, coins, medals; library of 70,000 vols, 5,000 maps, 100,000 historical documents; Dir Lic. MARÍA GOWLAND.

Museo Nacional de Aeronáutica (National Museum of Aeronautics): Avda Eva Perón 2700, Morón, B1708FEZ Buenos Aires; tel. (11) 4697-9769; e-mail mna@uolsinectis.com.ar; internet www.fuerzaaerea.mil.ar/historia/museo_aeronautico.html; f. 1960; Dir Brig. D. EDMUNDO CIVATTI BERNASCONI.

Museo Nacional de Arte Decorativo (National Museum of Decorative Art): Avda del Libertador 1902, C1425AAS Buenos Aires; tel. (11) 4801-8248; e-mail museo@mnad.org; internet www.mnad.org; f. 1937; furniture, sculpture, tapestries, European and S American works; library of 2,000 vols; Dir Arq. ALBERTO GUILLERMO BELLUCCI.

Museo Nacional de Arte Oriental (National Museum of Oriental Art): Avda del Libertador 1902, 1°, C1425AAS Buenos Aires; tel. (11) 4801-5988; e-mail mnao@mnao.gov.ar; f. 1965; Asian and African art; library of 1,500 vols, 2,500 periodicals; Dir Lic. MARÍA DEL VALLE GUERRA.

Museo Nacional de Bellas Artes (National Museum of Fine Arts): Avda del Libertador 1473, C1425AAA Buenos Aires; tel. (11) 5288-9900; e-mail prensa@mnba.gob.ar; internet www.mnba.gob.ar; f. 1896; Argentine, American and European paintings since 14th century, classical painting and sculpture, pre-Columbian art; library of 50,000 vols, 200,000 booklets; Dir Dra MARCELA CARDILLO.

Museo Naval de la Nación (National Museum of Naval History): Paseo Victorica 602, Tigre, 1648 Buenos Aires; tel. (11) 4749-0608; e-mail museonaval@ara.mil.ar; f. 1892; preserves, researches, exhibits and communicates cultural heritage; photo archive; shows history, culture and tradition of naval maritime nation, its evolution, technology and tasks in maritime field; library of 3,000 vols; Dir Capt. ALBERTO JULIO MONGES.

Museo Numismático 'Dr José Evaristo Uriburu' ('Dr José Evaristo Uriburu' Numismatics Museum): Banco Central de la República Argentina, San Martin 216, C1004AAF Buenos Aires; tel. (11) 4348-3882; e-mail museo@bcra.gov.ar; internet www.bcra.gov.ar/institucional/in040200.asp; f. 1935; attached to Central Bank of Argentina; Dir DANIEL ANTONIO REY.

Córdoba

Museo Botánico (Botanical Museum): Avda Vélez Sársfield 299, 5000 Córdoba; tel. (351) 433-2104; e-mail museo@imbiv.unc.edu.ar; f. 1870; conducts research as a unit of Instituto Multidisciplinario de Biología Vegetal (run by CONICET and Universidad Nacional de Córdoba); library of 8,000 vols; Dir Dr ANA M. ANTON; publ. *Kurtziana* (1 a year).

Museo Provincial de Bellas Artes 'Emilio A. Caraffa' (Emilio A. Caraffa Provincial Museum of Fine Arts): Avda Poeta Lugones 411, X5000HZE Córdoba; tel. (351) 434-3348; e-mail comunicacion@museocaraffa.org.ar; internet www.museocaraffa.org.ar; f. 1916; Argentine and foreign paintings, sculptures, drawings and engravings; library of 1,500 vols; Dir Prof. JORGE TORRES.

Museo Provincial de Ciencias Naturales 'Bartolomé Mitre' (Bartolomé Mitre Provincial Museum of Natural Sciences): Avda Hipólito Yrigoyen 115, Córdoba; tel. (351) 422-1428; f. 1919; geology, zoology, botany; library of 3,400 vols and periodicals; Dir MARTA CANO DE MARTIN.

Corrientes

Museo Histórico de Corrientes (Corrientes Historical Museum): Calle 9 de Julio 1044, Corrientes; tel. (3783) 475-916; f. 1929; history of Corrientes Province; library of 2,000 vols; Dir MIGUEL FERNANDO GONZÁLEZ AZCOAGA; publ. *Boletín de Extensión Cultural* (4 a year).

La Plata

Museo de La Plata (La Plata Museum): Paseo del Bosque s/n, B1900FWA La Plata; tel. (221) 425-7744; e-mail museo@fcnym.unlp.edu.ar; internet www.museo.fcnym.unlp.edu.ar; f. 1884; anthropology, archaeology, geology, natural history (incl. palaeontological colln of Patagonian mammalia); library of 60,000 vols, 5,000 periodicals; Dir Dra SILVIA AMETRANO; publs *Anales*, *Revista*, *Serie Técnica y Didáctica*.

Luján

Complejo Museografico 'Enrique Udaondo' (Enrique Udaondo Museographic Complex): Lezica y Torrezuri 917, 6700 Luján; tel. (2323) 42-0245; e-mail museo_lujan@ic.gba.gov.ar; internet www.ic.gba.gov.ar/patrimoniocultural/udaondo; f. 1923; comprises 4 museums: Museo Colonial e Histórico (history, archaeology, silver, paintings, furniture), Museo de Transportes (transport), Museo del Automóvil and Pabellón 'Belgrano' y Depósitos (vintage cars); Dir ARACELLI BELLOTA.

Mendoza

Museo de Ciencias Naturales y Antropológicas 'Juan Cornelio Moyano' (Juan Cornelio Moyano Museum of Anthropology and Natural Sciences): Extremo Sur del Lago, Parque General San Martín, Mendoza; tel. (261) 428-7666; e-mail museomoyano@mendoza.gov.ar; f. 1911; library of 18,900 vols on American and Argentine history; Asst Dir Profa CLARA ABAL DE RUSSO.

Paraná

Museo de Ciencias Naturales y Antropológicas 'Prof. Antonio Serrano' ('Prof. Antonio Serrano' Museum of Anthropology and Natural Sciences): Carlos Gardel 62, E3100FWB Paraná; tel. (343) 420-8894; e-mail museoserrano@gmail.com; f. 1917; scientific investigations; papers; editions; exhibitions; library of 35,000 vols; Dir Profa GISELA BAHLER; publs *Catalogos*, *Memorias*.

Museo Histórico de Entre Rios 'Martiniano Leguizamón' ('Martiniano Leguizamón' Historical Museum of Entre Rios): Laprida y Buenos Aires, 3100 Paraná; tel. (343) 420-7869; e-mail museohistorico_er@hotmail.com; f. 1948; library of 27,000 vols; Dir MARIA ANGELA MATHIEU MAYA.

Rosario

Museo Histórico Provincial de Rosario 'Dr Julio Marc' (Dr Julio Marc Provincial History Museum of Rosario): Avda del Museo, Parque de la Independencia, 2000 Rosario; tel. (341) 472-1457; e-mail museomarc@santafe.gov.ar; f. 1939; preserves, researches and disseminates various aspects of local history; library of 33,000 vols; Dir Profa IRMA B. MONTALVAN.

Museo Municipal de Arte Decorativo 'Firma y Odilo Estevez' (Firma y Odilo Estevez Municipal Museum of Decorative Arts): Santa Fe 748, S2000ATH Rosario; tel. (341) 480-2547; e-mail museo@museoestevez.gov.ar; internet www.museoestevez.gov.ar; f. 1968; Curator P. A. SINOPOLI.

Museo Municipal de Bellas Artes 'Juan B. Castagnino' (Juan B. Castagnino Municipal Museum of Fine Arts): Avda Pellegrini 2202, Rosario; tel. (341) 480-2542; e-mail comunicacion@macromuseo.org.ar; internet www.museocastagnino.org.ar; f. 1937; library of 2,500 vols; Dir MARCELA RÖMER.

San Carlos de Bariloche

Museo de la Patagonia 'Dr Francisco P. Moreno' (Dr Francisco P. Moreno Museum of Patagonia): Centro Cívico, San Carlos de Bariloche, Río Negro; tel. (294) 442-2309; e-mail museodelapatagonia@apn.gov.ar; internet www.museodelapatagonia.nahuelhuapi.gov.ar; f. 1940; social and political history of Patagonia, ethnology, natural sciences, archaeology; library of 3,500 vols; Dir Lic. EDUARDO MIGUEL BESSERA; publs *Antropología e. Historia*, *Diversidad Cultural de la Argentina*, *La Conquista del Desierto*.

Santa Fé

Museo Histórico Provincial de Santa Fe (Santa Fe Provincial Museum of History): San Martín 1490, S3000FRH Santa Fe; tel. (342) 457-3529; e-mail info@museohistorico-sfe.gov.ar; internet www.museohistorico-sfe.gov.ar; f. 1943; Dir Prof. ALICIA TALSKY DE RONCHI.

Museo Provincial de Bellas Artes 'Rosa Galisteo de Rodriguez' (Rosa Galisteo de Rodriguez Museum of Fine Arts): 4 de Enero 1510, S3000XAC Santa Fe; tel. (342) 457-3577; internet www.museorosagalisteo.gob.ar; f. 1922; contemporary Argentine and modern art; library of 5,000 vols, 2,000 periodicals and 3,000 slides; Dir Arq. MARCELO OLMOS.

Museo Provincial de Ciencias Naturales 'Florentino Ameghino' (Provincial Museum of Natural Sciences 'Florentino Ameghino'): 1° Junta 2859, 3000 Santa Fe; tel. (342) 457-3770; e-mail ameghino@santafe-conicet.gov.ar; internet www.unl.edu

.ar/santafe/museocn.htm; f. 1914; zoology, botany, geology, palaeobiology; library of 5,136 vols, 1,090 journals; Dir Lic. CARLOS A. VIRASORO.

Santiago del Estero

Museo Provincial de Arqueología 'Wagner' (Wagner Provincial Museum of Archaeology): Calle Avellaneda 355, G4200XAG Santiago del Estero; tel. (385) 421-1380; e-mail museowagnersgo@gmail.com; f. 1917; archaeology of Chaco-Santiagueno and later cultures; Dir ANDRÉS A. CHAZARRETA RUIZ.

Tandil

Museo Municipal de Bellas Artes de Tandil (Tandil Municipal Museum of Fine Arts): Chacabuco 357, 7000 Tandil; tel. (249) 443-2067; e-mail direccionmuseo@tandil.gov.ar; internet www.mumbat.com; f. 1920; paintings of Classical, Impressionist, Cubist and Modern schools, 20th-century Argentine art, small statues, furniture, engravings; small library; Dir CRISTIAN SEGURA.

Ushuaia

Museo del Fin del Mundo (The End of the World Museum): Maipú 173, V9410BJC Ushuaia, Tierra del Fuego; tel. (2901) 42-1863; e-mail museo@tierradelfuego.ml.org; f. 1979; history and natural sciences; library of 5,000 vols; Dir OSCAR PABLO ZANOLA; publs *Arqueología de la Isla Grande de Tierra del Fuego*, *Museo Territorial*, *Raíces del Fin del Mundo* (3 a year).

Universities

There are three main categories of Universities in Argentina: National (or Federal), which are supported by the Federal Budget; Provincial (or State), supported by the Provincial Budgets; and Private Universities, created and supported entirely by private initiative, but authorized to function by the Ministry of Education.

PONTIFICIA UNIVERSIDAD CATÓLICA ARGENTINA 'SANTA MARÍA DE LOS BUENOS AIRES'
(Pontifical Catholic University of Argentina 'Santa María de Los Buenos Aires')

Avda Alicia Moreau de Justo 1300, C1107AAZ Buenos Aires
Telephone: (11) 4349-0200
E-mail: info@uca.com.ar
Internet: www.uca.edu.ar

Founded 1958
Private control
Language of instruction: Spanish
Academic year: March to November

Grand Chancellor: MARIO A. POLI
Rector: Dr VICTOR MANUEL FERNÁNDEZ
Vice-Rector for Academic and Institutional Affairs: Dr GABRIEL LIMODIO
Vice-Rector for Economic Affairs: Dr HORACIO RODRÍGUEZ PENELAS
Vice-Rector for Research: Dra BEATRIZ BALIAN DE TAGTACHIAN
Number of teachers: 3,200
Number of students: 16,800

Publications: *Boletín de Ciencias Económicas* (6 a year), *Colección* (2 a year, political science), *Letras* (2 a year, Argentinian and comparative literature), *Prudentia Juris* (2 a year), *Sapientia* (2 a year), *Teología* (2 a year), *Valores* (3 a year, economics and social ethics), *UCActualidad* (irregular, print and online)

DEANS

Faculty of Agriculture: Dr JORGE GALOTTA
Faculty of Arts and Music: Dra DIANA FERNÁNDEZ CALVO
Faculty of Canon Law: Dr MAURICIO LANDRA
Faculty of Chemistry and Engineering (Rosario): Dr FRANCISCO A. CASIELLO
Faculty of Economic Sciences: Dr CARLOS GARAVENTA
Faculty of Economics (Mendoza): ALEJANDRO BARTOLOMEO
Faculty of Economic Sciences (Rosario): GUILLERMO BOGGINO
Faculty of Humanities and Education (Mendoza): Lic. AUGUSTO JORGE BARACCHINI
Faculty of Humanities 'Teresa de Avila' (Paraná): Dr LUIS ALFREDO ANAYA
Faculty of Law: Dr DANIEL A. HERRERA
Faculty of Law and Social Sciences (Rosario): NELSON COSSARI
Faculty of Medical Sciences: Dr MIGUEL ÁNGEL SCHIAVONE
Faculty of Philosophy and Letters: Dr JAVIER ROBERTO GONZÁLEZ
Faculty of Physical Sciences, Mathematics and Engineering: Ing. ROBERTO ACOSTA
Faculty of Psychology and Educational Psychology: Dr MARCELO NOËL
Faculty of Social Sciences and Communication Policy: Dr ENRIQUE AGUILAR
Faculty of Theology: Dr FERNANDO JOSÉ ORTEGA

UNIVERSIDAD ARGENTINA DE LA EMPRESA
(Argentine University of Administration Sciences)

Lima 775, C1073AAO Buenos Aires
Telephone: (11) 4000-7600
E-mail: contactouade@uade.edu.ar
Internet: www.uade.edu.ar

Founded 1963
Private control
Language of instruction: Spanish
Academic year: March to December

Rector: Dr RICARDO OROSCO
Academic and Legal Sec.: Dr EDUARDO J. FASULINO
Librarian: RODOLFO LÖHE
Library of 69,177 vols, 15,288 ejournals
Number of teachers: 750
Number of students: 15,581

Publications: @ *UADE* (12 a year), *El Graduado de UADE*

DEANS

Faculty of Business and Management: RICARDO FELIPE SMURRA
Faculty of Communication and Design: CLAUDIA CORTEZ
Faculty of Economics: RICARDO FELIPE SMURRA
Faculty of Engineering and Exact Sciences: SEBASTIÁN ODDONE
Faculty of Law and Social Sciences: SILVIA SUSANA TOSCANA

UNIVERSIDAD ARGENTINA 'JOHN F. KENNEDY'
(John F. Kennedy University of Argentina)

Calle Bartolomé Mitre 1411, Buenos Aires
Telephone: (11) 4476-4338
E-mail: info@kennedy.edu.ar
Internet: www.kennedy.edu.ar

Founded 1964
Private control
Language of instruction: Spanish

Rector: Dra MARÍA ELISA HERREN DE DAVID
Vice-Rector: Dr OSCAR ANTONIO CÁMPOLI
Sec. for Academic Affairs: Dr MARIO ALBERTO COSCIO
Library of 50,000 vols
Number of teachers: 1,800
Number of students: 17,500

Publications: *Revista Borromeo* (1 a year), *Revista Realidad*, *Universidad Kennedy Revista* (3 a year)

UNIVERSIDAD AUTÓNOMA DE ENTRE RÍOS
(Autonomous University of Entre Ríos)

Avda Ramírez 1143, Paraná, Entre Ríos
Telephone: (343) 423-2369
E-mail: rectorado@uader.edu.ar
Internet: www.uader.edu.ar

Founded 2000
State control
Language of instruction: Spanish

Rector: ANÍBAL SATTLER
Vice-Rector: Ing. JUAN BOZZOLO
Sec.-Gen.: LUCIANO FILIPUZZI

Publication: *Revista ExtendER*

DEANS

Faculty of Humanities, Arts and Social Sciences: MARÍA DEL ROSARIO BADANO
Faculty of Life Sciences and Health: Lic. ESTELA GROSS
Faculty of Management Science: Prof. LILIANA PATRICIA BATTAUZ
Faculty of Science and Technology: Prof. MARINO SCHNEEBERGER

UNIVERSIDAD CAECE
(University CAECE)

Avda de Mayo 866, Buenos Aires
Telephone: (11) 5217-7878
E-mail: informes@caece.edu.ar
Internet: www.ucaece.edu.ar

Founded 1967
Private control
Language of instruction: Spanish

Depts of admin., biological sciences, humanities and social sciences, mathematics, systems and psychology and educational sciences

Rector: Dr EDGARDO BOSCH
Academic Vice-Rector: Dr CARLOS A. LAC PRUGENT
Academic Sec.: Lic. MARÍA ALEJANDRA CORMONS
Library Dir: PAULA SADIER
Library of 9,000 vols
Number of teachers: 300
Number of students: 2,600

Publication: *Elementos de Matemática* (4 a year)

UNIVERSIDAD CATÓLICA DE CÓRDOBA
(Catholic University of Córdoba)

Obispo Trejo 323, X5000IYG Córdoba
Telephone: (351) 421-9000
E-mail: info@uccor.edu.ar
Internet: www.ucc.edu.ar

Founded 1956
Private control
Academic year: February to December

Chancellor: Mgr CARLOS JOSÉ ÑANEZ (Archbishop of Córdoba)
Vice-Chancellor: R. P. ALVARO RESTREPO
Rector: Lic. RAFAEL VELASCO
Vice-Rector for Academics: Dr DIEGO OSVALDO FONTI
Vice-Rector for Economics: HUGO LORENZO GIMÉNEZ
Vice-Rector for Univ. Community: ARTURO EDUARDO SANDIANO
Academic Sec.: CLAUDIO JAVIER SENTANA

Dir for Library System: Mag. SANDRA GISELA MARTÍN
Library: see under Libraries and Archives
Number of teachers: 1,575
Number of students: 9,810
Publication: *Studia Politicae*

DEANS

Faculty of Agriculture: Ing. Agr. GUSTAVO DARIO GUERRA
Faculty of Architecture: Arq. SANTIAGO IAN DUTARI
Faculty of Chemical Sciences: Mag. GRACIELA INES ASCAR
Faculty of Economics and Administration: TERESA BEATRIZ OLIVI
Faculty of Education: OLGA CONCEPCIÓN BONETTI
Faculty of Engineering: Mag. LUIS EDUARDO TOLEDO
Faculty of Law and Social Sciences: Abog. CARLOS FRANCISCO FERRER
Faculty of Medicine: Dra ANALÍA ESTER CUDOLA
Faculty of Philosophy and Humanities: Dra CECILIA PADVALSKIS-SIMKUS
Faculty of Political Sciences and International Relations: Dr ALEJANDRO JOSE GROPPO
Institute of Administrative Sciences: Mag. GONZALO JAVIER GARCÍA ESPECHE (Dir)

UNIVERSIDAD CATÓLICA DE CUYO
(Catholic University of Cuyo)

Avda José Ignacio de la Roza 1516, Oeste Rivadavia, 5400 San Juan
Telephone: (264) 429-2300
E-mail: secretariaextension@uccuyo.edu.ar
Internet: www.uccuyo.edu.ar
Founded 1953
Private control
Language of instruction: Spanish
Academic year: April to March
Grand Chancellor: ALFONSO DELGADO EVERS
Rector: Dra MARÍA ISABEL LARRAURI
Vice-Rector: Prof. CECILIA TRINCADO DE MURÚA
Sec.-Gen. for Academics: ANA SÁNCHEZ
Dir for Library: EUGENIA CARRASCOSA DE YUNES
Library of 35,850 vols
Number of teachers: 900
Number of students: 6,100
Publication: *Revista Cuadernos*

DEANS

Faculty of Economics and Business: Lic. ALEJANDRO LARGACHA
Faculty of Education: Lic. LUCIA GHILARDI DE CARRIZO
Faculty of Food Sciences: Dr CLAUDIO LARREA
Faculty of Law and Social Sciences: Dr JAVIER VERA
Faculty of Medical Sciences: Dra MERCEDES GÓMEZ DE HERRERA
Faculty of Philosophy and Humanities: Lic. JORGE BERNAT GIGANTINO

UNIVERSIDAD CATÓLICA DE LA PLATA
(Catholic University of La Plata)

Calle 13 No. 1227, 1900 La Plata
Telephone: (221) 422-7100
E-mail: info@ucalp.edu.ar
Internet: www.ucalp.edu.ar
Founded 1964
Private control
Academic year: March to November
Grand Chancellor: Mgr HÉCTOR RUBÉN AGUER
Rector: Dr HERNÁN MATHIEU
Vice-Rector for Academic Affairs: Dr EDUARDO VENTURA
Vice-Rector for Admin.: Dr MARIO VIVINO
Librarian: ROBERTO JAVIER IRAZU
Library of 26,535 books and pamphlets, 7,200 periodicals
Number of teachers: 650
Number of students: 3,800
Publications: *Link, Revista el Guía* (irregular)

DEANS

Faculty of Architecture and Design: Arq. RAÚL MEDA
Faculty of Dentistry: Dr CARLOS CONESA ALEGRE
Faculty of Economic and Social Sciences: Dr EDUARDO VENTURA
Faculty of Health Sciences: Dr FERMÍN GARCÍA MARCOS
Faculty of Humanities: AMELIA URRUTIBEHEITY
Faculty of Law and Political Science: Dr CLAUDIA A. CASTAGNET
Faculty of Sciences and Engineering: Ing. ALEJANDRO CARLOS ROCCA

UNIVERSIDAD CATÓLICA DE SALTA
(Catholic University of Salta)

Campo Castañares, 4400 Salta
Telephone: (387) 426-8524
E-mail: rectorado@ucasal.net
Internet: www.ucasal.net
Founded 1963
Private control
Language of instruction: Castellano
Academic year: March to December
Grand Chancellor: Mgr MARIO ANTONIO CARGNELLO
Rector: Lic. JORGE ANTONIO MANZARAZ
Academic Vice-Rector: Dra MARÍA ISABEL VIRGILI DE RODRIGUEZ
Admin. Vice-Rector: Lic. GRACIELA MARIA PINAL
Vice-Rector for Training: Prof. FRANCISCO NUÑEZ
Sec.-Gen.: Dra ADRIANA IBARGUREN
Library Dir: Lic. BEATRIZ KESSLER
Library of 44,000 vols
Number of students: 26,700

DEANS

Faculty of Agricultural and Veterinary Sciences: Dra. JAVIER BINDA
Faculty of Architecture and Urban Planning: Arq. PABLO ANDRÉS PRONE
Faculty of Art and Sciences: Lic. OSVALDO GARCIA LÓPEZ
Faculty of Economics and Administration: JUAN CARLOS RAMPULLA
Faculty of Engineering: Ing. NÉSTOR EUGENIO LESSER
Faculty of Law: Dr BENJAMIN PEREZ RUIZ
School of Business: Ing. DESIRE D'AMBROSIO

UNIVERSIDAD CATÓLICA DE SANTA FE
(Catholic University of Santa Fe)

Echagüe 7151, S3004JBS Santa Fe
Telephone: (342) 460-3030
E-mail: ucsf@ucsf.edu.ar
Internet: www.ucsf.edu.ar
Founded 1957
Private control
Academic year: February to December
Grand Chancellor: Dr JOSÉ MARÍA ARANCEDO
Rector: Arq. RICARDO MARIO ROCCHETTI
Vice-Rector for Academic Affairs: Lic. EUGENIO MARTIN DE PALMA
Vice-Rector for Training: Lic. CARLOS HUGO SCATIZZA
Sec.-Gen.: Arq. CARLOS LUIS BORRA
Library Dir: Lic. ANA MARIA ALBERDI
Number of teachers: 480
Number of students: 3,864
Publications: *Revista Krinein, Revista Politikos, Revista Universidad HOY*

DEANS

Faculty of Architecture: Arq. CARLOS GUSTAVO GIOBANDO
Faculty of Economic Sciences: PABLO BARTOLOMÉ OGGERO
Faculty of Earth Sciences and Environment: Dr ESTEBAN PASSEGGI (Academic Sec.)
Faculty of Health Sciences: Ing. MARÍA ALEJANDRA DE LOS MILAGROS SAUX (Sec.)
Faculty of Humanities: Dra ANABEL VERONICA GAITAN
Faculty of Law and Political Science: Dra ZULLY MARÍA DEGANO
Faculty of Philosophy: Lic. FERNANDO J. FAVA (acting) (Academic Sec.)
Faculty of Psychology: Lic. SILVIA TORNIMBENI

UNIVERSIDAD CATÓLICA DE SANTIAGO DEL ESTERO

Avda Alsina y Dalmacio Vélez Sársfield, 4200 Santiago del Estero
Telephone: (385) 421-1777
E-mail: postmaster@ucse.edu.ar
Internet: www.ucse.edu.ar
Founded 1960
Language of instruction: Spanish
Academic year: April to November
Grand Chancellor: Mgr GERARDO EUSEBIO SUELDO
Rector: LUIS LUCENA
Admin. Dir: Lic. MARÍA ÉLIDA CERRO DE ÁBALOS
Librarian: Prof. Dr MATIAS ZUZEC
Library of 19,000 vols
Number of teachers: 450
Number of students: 4,000
Publication: *Nuevas Propuestas*

DEANS

Faculty of Applied Mathematics: Ing. OCTAVIO JOSÉ MÉDICI
Faculty of Economics: Lic. VÍCTOR MANUEL FEIJÓO
Faculty of Education: Hna Lic. LILIANA BADALONI
Faculty of Politics, Social Sciences and Law: Abog. MARIA TERESA TENTI DE VOLTA

PROFESSORS

Faculty of Applied Mathematics:
- CORONEL, J. C., Introduction to Mathematical Analysis
- KORSTANJE, A. P., Operational Research
- MARTÍNEZ, E., Systems Evaluation
- PASTORINO, M. I., Numerical Methods
- TRAJTENBERG, J. O., Introduction to Data Processing

Faculty of Economics:
- ALEGRE, J. C., Bankruptcy Law
- BRAVO, W., Auditing
- CHAYA, H. N., Administration and Personnel
- CORONEL, J. C., Budgeting
- FERRERO DE AZAR, A. M., Company Law
- MARIGLIANO, M., Business Organization
- MARTELEUR, R., Introduction to Economics
- MORELLINI, P. A., Accounting, Budget Sheet Analysis
- OSTENGO, H., Accounting
- PASTORINO, M. I., Statistics
- TERUEL, R., General Administration

Faculty of Education:
- CASTIGLIONE, J. C., Theology
- GELID, T., General Sociology and Sociology of Education

MUHN, G., Vocational Orientation
RIERA DE LUCENA, E., Philosophical Anthropology, Basic Epistemology
SGOIFO, M. DEL V., Psychology

Faculty of Politics, Social Sciences and Law:
ALEGRE, J. C., Agricultural and Mining Law
ARGAÑARAZ ORGAZ, C., Administrative Law
ARGUELLO, L. R., Roman Law
ARNEDO, E., Private International Law
AUAD, A., Social Philosophy
BENEVOLE DE GAUNA, T., Legal Consultation
BONACINA, R. A., Introduction to Economics
BRIZUELA, N., General and Social Psychology
BRUNELLO DE ZURITA, A., Civil Law
CASTIGLIONE, J. C., Philosophy of Law
CERRO, F. E., Theory of the State
CHRISTENSEN, E., Finance and Financial Law
HARO DE SURIAN, E., Economic Geography
LEDESMA, A. E., Civil and Penal Procedural Law
NAVARRO, J. V., Penal Law
PAZ, G. M., Civil Law
PAZ, M. J., Commercial Law
RETAMOSA, J. R., History of Ideas and Political Institutions, History of the World, History of Argentina
RIGOURD, C., Public Law
RIMINI, J. C., Commercial Law
SALERA, J. B., Sociology
VICTORIA, M. A., Agricultural and Mining Law
ZURITA DE GONZÁLEZ, M., Civil Law

UNIVERSIDAD DE BELGRANO
(University of Belgrano)

Zabala 1837, C1426DQG Buenos Aires
Telephone: (11) 4788-5400
E-mail: ingresos@ub.edu.ar
Internet: www.ub.edu.ar

Founded 1964
Private control
Language of instruction: Spanish
Academic year: March to November

Rector: Dr AVELINO JOSÉ PORTO
Vice-Rector for Institutional Affairs: Prof. ALDO J. PÉREZ
Vice-Rector for Legal and Technical Admin.: Dr EUSTAQUIO CASTRO
Librarian: MERCEDES PATALANO

Library of 70,043 vols, 2,500 periodicals
Number of teachers: 1,100
Number of students: 10,500

Publications: *Académicos* (12 a year), *Postcátedra* (4 a year), *UB News* (52 a year)

DEANS

Faculty of Agriculture: Ing. LEONARDO GALABURRI
Faculty of Architecture and Town Planning: Arq. MÓNICA FERNÁNDEZ
Faculty of Distance Learning Education: Dra CLARA BONFILL
Faculty of Economics: Dra PATRICIA BONATTI
Faculty of Engineering and Computer Technology: Ing. ALBERTO GUERCI
Faculty of Exact and Natural Sciences: Dr HERNAN JAVIER ALDANA MARCOS
Faculty of Graduate Studies: Dr LUIS MARIA PALMA
Faculty of Health Sciences: Dr HERNÁN JAVIER ALDANA MARCOS
Faculty of Humanities: Dra SUSANA SEIDMANN
Faculty of Languages and Foreign Studies: Prof. RAQUEL ALBORNOZ
Faculty of Law and Social Sciences: Dr DINO BELLORIO CLABOT
Graduate School of Business: Dr ALBERTO RUBIO
Graduate School of Law: Dra MARÍA BLANCA NOODT TAQUELA

UNIVERSIDAD DE BUENOS AIRES
(University of Buenos Aires)

Calle Viamonte 430/444, C1053ABJ Buenos Aires
Telephone: (11) 4510-1100
E-mail: secprivada@rec.uba.ar
Internet: www.uba.ar

Founded 1821
State control
Language of instruction: Spanish
Academic year: March to November

Rector: Dr RUBÉN HALLÚ
Vice-Rector: Prof. Dr ALBERTO EDGARDO BARBIERI
Sec.-Gen.: CARLOS ESTEBAN MAS VELEZ

Number of teachers: 6,650
Number of students: 100,800

Library: see under Libraries and Archives

Publications: *Encrucijadas* (4 a year), *Oikos* (4 a year)

DEANS

Faculty of Agriculture: Ing. Agr. RODOLFO ANGEL GOLLUSCIO
Faculty of Architecture, Design and Town Planning: Arq. EDUARDO CAJIDE
Faculty of Dentistry: Prof. Dra MARÍA BEATRIZ GUGLIELMOTTI
Faculty of Economic Sciences: Prof. Dr ALBERTO EDGARDO BARBIERI
Faculty of Engineering: Dr Ing. CARLOS ALBERTO ROSITO
Faculty of Exact and Natural Sciences: Dr JORGE ALIAGA
Faculty of Law: Dra MÓNICA PINTO
Faculty of Letters and Philosophy: Dr HÉCTOR HUGO TRINCHERO
Faculty of Medicine: Prof. Dr MARCELO L. TORINO
Faculty of Pharmacy and Biochemistry: Prof. Dr ALBERTO BOVERIS
Faculty of Psychology: Prof. Lic. NELIDA CARMEN CERVONE
Faculty of Social Sciences: Prof. SERGIO CALETTI
Faculty of Veterinary Sciences: Med. Vet. MARCELO SERGIO MIGUEZ

SELECTED AFFILIATED SCHOOLS

Colegio Nacional de Buenos Aires: Bolívar 263, C1066AAE Buenos Aires; tel. (11) 4331-6777; e-mail rector@cnba.uba.ar; internet www.cnba.uba.ar; Rector GUSTAVO FABIÁN ZORZOLI.

Escuela Superior de Comercio 'Carlos Pellegrini': Marcelo T. de Alvear 1851, C1122AAA Buenos Aires; tel. (11) 4815-4001; e-mail info@cpel.uba.ar; internet www.cpel.uba.ar; f. 1890, inc. in the Univ. of Buenos Aires 1913; 6-year course in commercial education; Rector Dr MARCELO RICARDO ROITBARG

UNIVERSIDAD DE CONCEPCIÓN DEL URUGUAY
(University of Concepción del Uruguay)

8 de Junio 522, E3260ANJ Concepción del Uruguay, Entre Ríos
Telephone: (3442) 425-606
E-mail: info@ucu.edu.ar
Internet: www.ucu.edu.ar

Founded 1971
Private control
Language of instruction: Spanish
Academic year: February to December

Rector: Dr HÉCTOR CÉSAR SAURET
Vice-Rector: Dra GEORGINA VIERCI
Sec. Gen.: Lic. JUAN VELAZQUEZ
Academic Sec.: Dr MAURICIO A. LÓPEZ
Library Dir: ROSA M. MURILLO

Library of 4,300 vols
Number of teachers: 230
Number of students: 2,600

Publication: *Revista Comunic@r*

DEANS

Faculty of Agronomy: Ing. Agr MARÍA DEL CARMEN BLÁZQUEZ
Faculty of Architecture and Town Planning: Arq. CRISTINA BONUS
Faculty of Communication Sciences and Education: Prof. LUIS A. CERRUDO
Faculty of Economic Sciences: Cr MARCELO GRANILLO
Faculty of Judicial and Social Sciences: Dr JORGE SANTINI
Faculty of Medical Sciences 'Dr Bartolomé Vasallo': Dr RICARDO MASRAMÓN

UNIVERSIDAD DE LA MARINA MERCANTE
(University of the Merchant Navy)

Avda Rivadavia 2258, C1034ACO Buenos Aires
Telephone: (11) 4953-9000
E-mail: info@udemm.edu.ar
Internet: www.udemm.edu.ar

Founded 1974
Private control
Language of instruction: Spanish
Academic year: March to December

Pres.: Ing. GUSTAVO C. ZOPATTI
Rector: Dr NORBERTO FRAGA
Gen. Sec.: Lic. MIRKO E. MAYER
Sec. for Research and Technological Devt: Dr EDMUNDO DANTE RAMOS

Number of teachers: 290
Number of students: 2,200

Publications: *Atenea*, *Novedades*

DEANS

Faculty of Administration and Economics: Dra SILVIA ISABEL GÓMEZ MEANA
Faculty of Engineering: Ing. VICENTE GIMENEZ
Faculty of Humanities: Lic. CLAUDIA ETKIN (acting)
Faculty of Law, Social Sciences and Communication: Lic. HECTOR NAREDO

UNIVERSIDAD DE MENDOZA
(University of Mendoza)

Avda Boulogne-sur-Mer 683, 5500 Mendoza
Telephone: (261) 420-2017
E-mail: rectorado@um.edu.ar
Internet: www.um.edu.ar

Founded 1960
Private control
Language of instruction: Spanish
Academic year: March to November

Rector: Dr Ing. SALVADOR B. NAVARRÍA
Vice-Rector: Ing. CARLOS PALACIO
Vice-Rector: Dr EMILIO VÁZQUEZ VIERA
Admin. Sec.: CARLOS PICIGHELLI
Librarian: DANIEL SERRANO

Number of teachers: 790
Number of students: 6,250

Publications: *Idearium*, *Ideas*, *Revista*

DEANS

Faculty of Architecture and Town Planning: Arq. ALICIA BRAVERMAN
Faculty of Economic Sciences: Dr EMILIO VÁZQUEZ VIERA
Faculty of Engineering: Ing. ALFREDO IGLESIAS
Faculty of Health Sciences: Dr JUAN CARLOS BEHLER

Faculty of Law and Social Sciences: Dr EMILIO VÁZQUEZ VIERA

UNIVERSIDAD DE MORÓN
(University of Morón)

Cabildo 134, B1708JPD Morón, Buenos Aires
Telephone: (11) 5627-2000
Internet: www.unimoron.edu.ar

Founded 1960
Private control
Academic year: March to December

Rector: Dr HÉCTOR NORBERTO PORTO LEMMA
Sec.-Gen.: Dr WALTER OSCAR FERNÁNDEZ
Sec. for Academic Affairs: Dr EDUARDO NÉSTOR COZZA
Sec. for Admin.: Dr JORGE EDUARDO MARCOS
Library Dir: MARIANA TUROLLA

Library of 59,000 vols
Number of teachers: 2,200
Number of students: 16,000

Publications: *Paradigma*, *Revista Integraciòn*, *UM Saber* (24 a year)

DEANS

Faculty of Agronomy and Food Sciences: Ing. Agr. ANTONIO RAMÓN ANGRISANI
Faculty of Architecture, Design, Art and Town Planning: Arq. OSCAR ANIBAL BORRACHIA
Faculty of Computer Sciences, Communication Sciences and Special Technology: Ing. HUGO RENE PADOVANI
Faculty of Economic and Business Sciences: Dr JORGE RAÚL LEMOS
Faculty of Engineering: Ing. ENRIQUE LUIS OTERO
Faculty of Exact, Chemical and Natural Sciences: Dr AQUILES CARLOS FERRANTI
Faculty of Law, Political and Social Sciences: Dr BRUNO OSCAR CORBO
Faculty of Medicine: Dr DOMINGO LIOTTA
Faculty of Philosophy, Education and Humanities: Dr ROBERTO MARIO PATERNO
Faculty of Sciences applied to Tourism and Population: Lic. ALEJANDRO GAVRIC

UNIVERSIDAD DEL ACONCAGUA
(University of Aconcagua)

Catamarca 147, 5500 Mendoza
Telephone: (261) 520-1600
E-mail: informes@uda.edu.ar
Internet: www.uda.edu.ar

Founded 1965 as Instituto Superior de la Empresa, univ. status 1973
Private control
Language of instruction: Spanish
Academic year: April to October

Rector: Prof. Dr OSVALDO S. CABALLERO
Sec.-Gen.: OSCAR DAVID CERUTTI
Academic Sec.: Lic. MARIA ESTER GIBBS
Librarian: BEATRIZ C. CONSTANTINO

Number of teachers: 450
Number of students: 4,800

DEANS

Faculty of Economics and Commerce: Dr ROLANDO GALLI REY
Faculty of Medical Sciences: Dr GUSTAVO L. MAURICIO
Faculty of Psychology: Lic. HUGO ALBERTO LUPIAÑEZ
Faculty of Social Sciences and Administration: Dr OSCAR E. LAMATTINA

UNIVERSIDAD DEL CEMA
(University of CEMA)

Avda Córdoba 374, C1054AAP Buenos Aires
Telephone: (11) 6314-3000
E-mail: admisiones@ucema.edu.ar
Internet: www.ucema.edu.ar

Founded 1978
Private control
Language of instruction: Spanish

Rector: Dr CARLOS ALFREDO RODRÍGUEZ
Vice-Rector: Dr EDGARDO ZABLOTSKY
Sec.-Gen.: TRACY MINCEY
Academic Sec.: Dr MARCOS GALLACHER
Library Coordinator: Lic. PATRICIA MÓNICA ALLENDEZ SULLIVAN

Library of 43,434 vols
Number of teachers: 180
Number of students: 1,180

Publications: *Journal of Applied Economics* (2 a year), *Revista UCEMA* (4 a year)

UNIVERSIDAD DEL CENTRO EDUCATIVO LATINOAMERICANO
(University of the Latin American Educational Centre)

Avda Pellegrini 1332, S2000BUN Rosario
Telephone: (341) 449-9292
Internet: www.ucel.edu.ar

Founded 1993
Private control
Language of instruction: Spanish
Academic year: March to February

Rector: STELLA REQUENA
Vice-Rector: Abog. EFRAIM TORRES
Sec. for Academic Affairs: Lic. NOEMI LAGRECA
Sec. for Admin.: LORENA SARASOLA
Sec. for Int. Relations: Prof. FANNY GODFRID
Sec. for Research and Devt: Dr WILLIAM DAROS

Publication: *Invenio* (print and online, www.ucel.edu.ar/seccion.php?id=39)

DEANS

Faculty of Chemistry: Dr DANIEL CORIA
Faculty of Economics and Business: ROGELIO PONTÓN
Faculty of Law and Social Sciences: Abog. EFRAIM TORRES

UNIVERSIDAD DEL CINE
(Film University)

Pasaje J. M. Giuffra 330, San Telmo, C1064ADD Buenos Aires
Telephone: (11) 4300-1413
E-mail: info@ucine.edu.ar
Internet: www.ucine.edu.ar

Founded 1991
Private control

Faculties of cinematography and communication

Rector: MANUEL ANTIN
Vice-Rector: Arq. MARIO A. SANTOS
Academic Sec.: Prof. GRACIELA B. FERNÁNDEZ TOLEDO

UNIVERSIDAD DEL MUSEO SOCIAL ARGENTINO
(University of the Argentine Museum of Sociology)

Avda Corrientes 1723, C1042AAD Buenos Aires
Telephone: (11) 5530-7600
E-mail: informes@umsa.edu.ar
Internet: www.umsa.edu.ar

Founded 1928
Private control
Language of instruction: Spanish

Rector: Dr GUILLERMO E. GARBARINI ISLAS
Academic Vice-Rector: M. ALEJANDRA GARBARINI ISLAS
Vice-Rector for Research and Graduate Studies: Dr EDUARDO E. SISCO
Sec.-Gen.: Dr PATRICIO M. ASENSIO VIVES
Librarian: Lic. MARIANO QUIÑONES

Library of 17,000 books, 500 periodicals and 444 video cassettes
Number of students: 3,600

DEANS

Faculty of Arts: Arq. CLAUDIO BARRERA
Faculty of Economic Sciences: CLAUDIA DE BONIS
Faculty of Human Sciences: Lic. GUSTAVO A. MÄUSEL
Faculty of Law and Social Sciences: Dr FEDERICO POLAK
Faculty of Modern Languages: MARÍA CRISTINA DE ORTÚZAR

UNIVERSIDAD DEL NORTE SANTO TOMÁS DE AQUINO
(North University of St Thomas Aquinas)

9 de Julio 165, T4000IHC San Miguel de Tucumán
Telephone: (381) 410-1141
E-mail: ciu@unsta.edu.ar
Internet: www.unsta.edu.ar

Founded 1965
Private control
Academic year: March to November

Grand Chancellor: Dr FRAY PABLO C. SICOULY
Rector: Ing. LUIS RAÚL ALCAIDE
Sec.: MIGUEL RIVADENEIRA
Academic Sec.: Prof. LILIANA DEL V. OTERINO
Dir for Library: LILIAN GARTNER

Number of teachers: 700
Number of students: 6,300

Publication: *Itinerantes*

DEANS

Faculty of Economics and Administration: GUILLERMO JORGE DI LELLA
Faculty of Engineering: Ing. JOSE FEDERICO FANJUL
Faculty of Health Sciences: Dra GRACIELA DI BENEDETTO PUERTO
Faculty of Humanities: Dr RAFAEL ROBERTO CUNSOLO
Faculty of Law and Political Sciences: Dr CARLOS EDUARDO SALTOR
Faculty of Philosophy: Dr HECTOR JOSE DEL BOSCO

UNIVERSIDAD DEL SALVADOR
(University of Salvador)

Avda Callao y Córdoba, C1023AAB Buenos Aires
Telephone: (11) 4813-9630
E-mail: info@usal.edu.ar
Internet: www.usal.edu.ar

Founded 1956
Private control
Language of instruction: Spanish
Academic year: January to December

Rector: Dr JUAN ALEJANDRO TOBIAS
Academic Vice-Rector: Dr PABLO GABRIEL VARELA
Vice-Rector for Economics: Dr FERNANDO LUCERO SCHMIDT
Vice-Rector for Research and Devt: PAULA ORTIZ
Vice-Rector for Training: Dr JUAN ALEJANDRO TOBIAS (acting)
Sec.-Gen.: Lic. LILIANA ELIZABETH MARTINEZ
Library: see under Libraries and Archives
Number of teachers: 2,500
Number of students: 16,000

Publications: *Anales*, *Signos*

DEANS

Faculty of Administration: Lic. HECTOR F. DAMA
Faculty of Economic Sciences: Dr SERGIO OMAR GARCIA

Faculty of Educational Sciences and Social Communication: Lic. MÁXIMO PAZ
Faculty of History, Geography and Tourism: Prof. PABLO MAERSK NIELSEN
Faculty of Law: CARLOS SALVADORES DE ARZUAGA
Faculty of Medicine: Dr JORGE CESAR MARTINEZ
Faculty of Philosophy and Letters: Dra ANA MARIA ZAGARI
Faculty of Psychology and Psychopedagogy: Dra GABRIELA MARIA RENAULT
Faculty of Science and Technology: Ing. MIGUEL GUERRERO
Faculty of Social Sciences: Lic. EDUARDO SUÁREZ

UNIVERSIDAD NACIONAL DE CATAMARCA
(National University of Catamarca)

Esquiú 799, Catamarca
Telephone: (3833) 442-4099
E-mail: protocolo@unca.edu.ar
Internet: www2.unca.edu.ar

Founded 1972
State control
Language of instruction: Spanish
Academic year: February to December

Rector: Ing. FLAVIO SERGIO FAMA
Vice-Rector: Ing. OSCAR ARELLANO
Sec.-Gen.: Ing. MARCELO FABIÁN VERA
Library Dir: LUISA GUERRERO

Number of teachers: 304
Number of students: 15,000

Publication: *Aportes*

DEANS
Faculty of Agricultural Sciences: Ing. Agr. OSCAR ARELLANO
Faculty of Economics and Administration: CPN MARIA BEATIZ MAZA
Faculty of Exact and Natural Sciences: Lic. ELINA SILVERA DE BUENADER
Faculty of Health Sciences: OMAR TEODULFO BARRIONUEVO
Faculty of Humanities: Esp. LETICIA DEL VALLE VARGAS
Faculty of Technology and Applied Sciences: Ing. Agrim. CARLOS HUMBERTO SAVIO

UNIVERSIDAD NACIONAL DE CHILECITO
(National University of Chilecito)

9 de Julio 22, F5360CKB Chilecito
Telephone: (3825) 427-200
E-mail: infoinstitucional@undec.edu.ar
Internet: www.undec.edu.ar

Founded 2003
State control
Language of instruction: Spanish
Academic year: February to November

Rector: Ing. NORBERTO RAUL CAMINOA
Gen. Sec.: FRANCISCO PEREDA

Publication: *Ciencia, Público y Sociedad* (2 a year)

UNIVERSIDAD NACIONAL DE CÓRDOBA
(National University of Córdoba)

Avda Haya de la Torre s/n, Pabellón Argentina, Ciudad Universitaria, Córdoba
E-mail: informes@comunicacion.unc.edu.ar
Telephone: (351) 433-4081
Internet: www.uncor.edu

Founded 1613, charter received from Philip III of Spain 1622, fully est. by Pope Urban VIII 1634, nationalized 1856
State control
Language of instruction: Spanish
Academic year: February to December

Rector: Dr FRANCISCO TAMARIT
Vice-Rector: Dra SILVIA BAREI
Sec.-Gen.: Dr ALBERTO E. LEÓN
Librarian: Lic. ROSA M. BESTANI

Library: see under Libraries and Archives
Number of teachers: 6,900
Number of students: 107,000 (100,000 undergraduate and 7,000 postgraduate students)

Publication: *Revista*

DEANS
Faculty of Agricultural Sciences: Ing. Agr. DANIEL PEIRETTI
Faculty of Architecture, Planning and Design: Arq. ELVIRA FERNÁNDEZ
Faculty of Arts: Prof. ANA GUILLERMINA YUKELSON
Faculty of Chemistry: Dra MIRIAM CRISTINA STRUMIA
Faculty of Dentistry: Dra MARÍA R. DEL CARMEN VISVISIAN
Faculty of Economics: Lic. FRANCISCO A. ECHEGARAY
Faculty of Exact, Physical and Natural Sciences: Ing. ROBERTO TERZARIOL
Faculty of Languages: Dra MIRIAM ALICIA CARBALLO
Faculty of Law and Social Sciences: Dra MARCELA ASPELL
Faculty of Mathematics, Astronomy and Physics: Dra ESTHER GALINA
Faculty of Medical Sciences: Dr GUSTAVO IRICO
Faculty of Philosophy and Humanities: Dr DIEGO TATIÁN
Faculty of Psychology: Prof. CLAUDIA TORCOMIAN

UNIVERSIDAD NACIONAL DE CUYO
(National University of Cuyo)

Centro Universitario, M5502JMA Mendoza
Telephone: (261) 413-5000
Internet: www.uncu.edu.ar

Founded 1939
State control
Language of instruction: Spanish
Academic year: March to November

Rector: Prof. Ing. Agr. ARTURO ROBERTO SOMOZA
Vice-Rector: Prof. Ing. Agr. JOSÉ GUILLERMO RODRÍGUEZ
Academic Sec.: Prof. CLAUDIA HILDA PAPARINI
Library Dir: HORACIO DEGIORGI

Library: see under Libraries and Archives
Number of teachers: 4,500
Number of students: 40,000

Publication: *Boletín Oficial*

DEANS
Faculty of Agricultural Sciences: Prof. Ing. Agr. CONCEPCIÓN ARJONA
Faculty of Applied Sciences: Ing. ROBERTO RAMON BATTISTON
Faculty of Arts and Design: Prof. CARLOS BRAJAK KRALJ
Faculty of Dentistry: Dr ALBERTO JOSE MARTIN
Faculty of Economics: JORGE ANTONIO LOPEZ
Faculty of Engineering: Ing. MARCELO GUSTAVO ESTRELLA
Faculty of Law: Dr EDUARDO EMILI
Faculty of Medical Sciences: Dr ROBERTO VALLES
Faculty of Philosophy and Letters: Prof. ADRIANA AIDA GARCIA
Faculty of Political and Social Sciences: GRACIELA COUSINET
Specialty and Elementary Education: Dra MONICA ELISABETH CASTILLA

UNIVERSIDAD NACIONAL DE ENTRE RÍOS
(National University of Entre Ríos)

Eva Perón 24, Concepción del Uruguay, Entre Ríos
Telephone: (3442) 42-1500
E-mail: sacademica@uner.edu.ar
Internet: www.uner.edu.ar

Founded 1973
State control
Language of instruction: Spanish
Academic year: April to March

Rector: Ing. JORGE GERARD
Vice-Rector: Lic. ELOÍSA DE JONG
Gen. Sec.: MARLENE LILIAN LEIVA
Academic Sec.: Lic. ROXANA PUIG
Library Dir: Prof. JORGE TITO MARTÍNEZ

Number of teachers: 1,219
Number of students: 13,204

Publication: *Ciencia, Docencia y Tecnología* (2 a year)

DEANS
Faculty of Administrative Science: HIPÓLITO BUENAVENTURA FINK
Faculty of Agricultural Sciences: Dr Ing. Agr. SERGIO LUIS LASSAGA
Faculty of Bromatology: MARÍA CLARA MELCHIORI
Faculty of Economics: ANDRES SABELLA
Faculty of Education: MARCELA REYNOSO
Faculty of Engineering: GERARDO GABRIEL GENTILETTI
Faculty of Health Sciences: Lic. MARIA CRISTINA SOSA MONTENEGRO
Faculty of Nutritional Sciences: Dr HUGO CIVES
Faculty of Social Services: SANDRA MARCELA ARITO

UNIVERSIDAD NACIONAL DE FORMOSA
(National University of Formosa)

Don Bosco 1082, Formosa
Telephone: (0370) 443-0485
E-mail: rectorado@unf.edu.ar
Internet: www.unf.edu.ar

Founded 1988
State control
Language of instruction: Spanish

Rector: Ing. MARTÍN RENÉ ROMANO
Vice-Rector: Dr ROQUE SILGUERO
Sec.-Gen. for Academics: Lic. OFELIA INÉS FANTÍN
Sec.-Gen. for Science and Technology: Ing. DARVIN CÁCERES
Sec. for Management and Devt: MARISA ALBARRACIN (acting)
Sec. for Student Affairs and Univ. Extension: RAFAEL OLMEDO

Library of 12,000 vols
Number of students: 11,937

DEANS
Faculty of Economics and Business Administration: Dr EMILIO GRIPPALDI
Faculty of Health Sciences: Dr RAFAEL TRINIDAD PORTOCARRERO
Faculty of Humanities: Prof. CESAR AUGUSTO PALMETLER
Faculty of Natural Resources: Ing. VICENTE SANCHEZ
Faculty of Production and Environment: Ing. MIGUEL ALONSO TORRES (Dir)

Faculty of Engineering: Ing. OSCAR RENÉ MIURA
Faculty of Humanities and Social Sciences: Lic. CLAUDIA COICAUD
Faculty of Law: Dr DARDO RUBÉN PETROLI
Faculty of Natural Sciences: Mag. LIDIA BLANCO

UNIVERSIDAD NACIONAL DE LA PLATA
(National University of La Plata)

Avda 7 No. 776, La Plata
Telephone: (221) 423-6804
E-mail: portal@presi.unlp.edu.ar
Internet: www.unlp.edu.ar

Founded 1905
State control
Language of instruction: Spanish
Academic year: March to December

Pres.: Dr FERNANDO ALFREDO TAUBER
Vice-Pres. for Academic Area: Ing. ARMANDO DE GIUSTI
Vice-Pres. for Institutional Area: Lic. RAÚL ANIBAL PERDOMO
Gen. Sec.: Lic. CARLOS ARMANDO GUERRERO
Library Dir: NORMA MANGIATERRA

Library: see under Libraries and Archives
Number of teachers: 12,056
Number of students: 108,934

Publication: *Revista de la Universidad*

DEANS
Faculty of Agriculture and Forestry: Ing. PABLO YAPURA
Faculty of Architecture and Town Planning: Arq. GUSTAVO AZPIAZU
Faculty of Astronomy and Geophysics: Dr ADRIÁN BRUNINI
Faculty of Dentistry: Dra MARIA MERCEDES MEDINA
Faculty of Economic Sciences
Lic. MARTÍN LÓPEZ ARMENGOL
Faculty of EngineeringDr Ing. MARCOS ACTIS
Faculty of Exact SciencesDra GRACIELA DE ANTONI
Faculty of Fine ArtsProf. MARIEL CIAFARDO
Faculty of Humanities and EducationDr ANÍBAL VIGUERA
Faculty of InformaticsLic. FRANCISCO JAVIER DIAZ
Faculty of Juridical and Social SciencesHERNÁN GÓMEZ
Faculty of Medical SciencesDr JORGE MARTÍNEZ
Faculty of Natural SciencesDra ALEJANDRA RUMMI MACCHI ZUBIAURRE
Faculty of Veterinary SciencesEDUARDO PONS
School of Journalism and Social CommunicationDra FLORENCIA SAINTOUT
School of PsychologyEDITH PEREZ
School of Social WorkVERONICA CRUZ

UNIVERSIDAD NACIONAL DE LA RIOJA
(National University of Rioja)

Avda Dr Rene Favaloro s/n, 5300 La Rioja
Telephone: (380) 445-7003
E-mail: rector@unlar.edu.ar
Internet: www.unlar.edu.ar

Founded 1973
State control
Language of instruction: Spanish
Academic year: February to December

Rector: Prof. Dr ENRIQUE DANIEL NICOLAS TELLO ROLDAN
Vice-Rector: Prof. Dra VALERIA SARA QUINTEROS
Sec.-Gen. and Admin. Sec.: Prof. EDUARDO ALBERTO VIDAL

Library of 23,000 vols
Number of teachers: 1,200
Number of students: 16,500

Publication: *Revista UNLaR Ciencia*

DEANS
Department of Economics, Law and Social Studies: Prof. Dra CAROLINA ROMANA CASCO
Department of Exact, Physical and Natural Sciences: Prof. Ing. CAROLINA PEÑA POLLASTRI
Department of Health Science and Education: Prof. Lic. ROSA BEATRIZ MORALES
Department of Humanities: Prof. SANDRA ROMAN
Department of Science and Technology: Prof. Ing. FRANCISCO ASÍS FILONZI

UNIVERSIDAD NACIONAL DE LANÚS
(National University of Lanús)

29 de Septiembre 3901, Lanús, Buenos Aires
Telephone: (11)5533-5600
E-mail: info@unla.edu.ar
Internet: www.unla.edu.ar

Founded 1995
State control
Language of instruction: Spanish
Academic year: March to December (2 semesters)

Depts of community health, humanities and arts, planning and public policy, and production, productivity and technology

Rector: Dra ANA MARÍA JARAMILLO
Vice-Rector: Dr NERIO NEIROTTI
Sec. for Academic Affairs: Lic. ANA CLEMENT
Sec. for Admin.: GUILLERMO GROSSKOPF
Sec. for Public Service and Cooperation: Lic. GEORGINA HERNÁNDEZ
Sec. for Science and Technology: HERALDO ROBERTO DE ROSE
Librarian: Lic. ELVIRA LOFIEGO
Number of students: 7,079

UNIVERSIDAD NACIONAL DE LOMAS DE ZAMORA
(National University of Lomas de Zamora)

Camino de Cintura y Juan XXIII, Buenos Aires
Telephone: (11) 4282-8045
E-mail: rector@unlz.edu.ar
Internet: www.unlz.edu.ar

Founded 1972
State control

Rector: DIEGO MOLEA
Academic Vice-Rector: HORACIO DAVID CASABE
Admin. Vice-Rector: HORACIO GEGUNDE
Sec.-Gen.: MARÍA VICTORIA LORENCES
Librarian: HORACIO INCAURGARAT

Number of teachers: 3,800
Number of students: 45,000

DEANS
Faculty of Agrarian Science: Ing. CARLOS ALBERTO ROSSI
Faculty of Economics: ALEJANDRO KURUC
Faculty of Engineering: Ing. OSCAR MANUEL PASCAL
Faculty of Law: Dr LUCAS LIENDRO KAPUSTIK
Faculty of Social Sciences: Lic. SANTIAGO ARAGON

UNIVERSIDAD NACIONAL DE LUJÁN
(National University of Luján)

Ruta 5 y Avda Constitución, Luján, Buenos Aires
Telephone: (2323) 42-3171
E-mail: informes@unlu.edu.ar
Internet: www.unlu.edu.ar

Founded 1972
State control
Language of instruction: Spanish
Academic year: February to December

Rector: Dr ORESTE CARLOS CANSANELLO
Vice-Rector: HERNAN ALBERTO BACARINI
Sec.-Gen.: MARÍA ESTHER LEGUIZAMON
Librarian: MARÍA GRACIELA CORTABARRÍA

Number of teachers: 1,000
Number of students: 19,000

Publications: *Cuadernos de Antropología, Cuadernos de Economía, Cuadernos de Historia Regional, Cuadernos de Trabajo*

DEANS
Department of Basic Sciences: JORGE DOMINGO MUFATO
Department of Education: Lic. MARIA EUGENIA CABRERA
Department of Social Sciences: Dra ALICIA ELSA REY
Department of Technology: Dra Ing. SUSANA LEONTINA VIDALES

UNIVERSIDAD NACIONAL DE MAR DEL PLATA
(National University of Mar del Plata)

Diagonal J. B. Alberdi 2695, Mar del Plata, Buenos Aires
Telephone: (223) 492-1705
E-mail: cecom@mdp.edu.ar
Internet: www.mdp.edu.ar

Founded 1961
State control
Language of instruction: Spanish
Academic year: March to November

Rector: Lic. FRANCISCO MOREA
Vice-Rector: Ing. RAÚL CONDE
Academic Sec.: Lic. PAULA MESCHINI
Librarian: Lic. OSCAR ALBERTO FERNÁNDEZ

Number of teachers: 1,600
Number of students: 27,000

Publications: *Revista de Letras* (3 a year), *Revista Jurídica*

DEANS
Faculty of Agricultural Sciences: VIRGINIA HAMDAM
Faculty of Architecture and Town Planning: Arq. ROBERTO OSCAR GUADAGNA
Faculty of Economics and Social Sciences: MONICA MABEL BIASONE
Faculty of Engineering: Dr Ing. GUILLERMO A. LOMBERA
Faculty of Exact and Natural Sciences: Dra SONIA E. TREPODE
Faculty of Health Sciences and Social Services: PAULA CRISTINA MANTERO
Faculty of Humanities: Dra MARÍA DEL CARMEN COIRA
Faculty of Law: MARÍA DEL CARMEN ORTEGA
Faculty of Psychology: Lic. ANA MARÍA HERMOSILLA

UNIVERSIDAD NACIONAL DE MISIONES
(National University of Misiones)

Ruta Nacional No. 12, Km $7^1/_2$, Miguel Lanús, Misiones
Telephone: (3752) 48-0916
E-mail: info@unam.edu.ar
Internet: www.unam.edu.ar

Founded 1973
State control
Language of instruction: Spanish
Academic year: February to December

Rector: Mag. JAVIER GORTARI
Vice-Rector: Lic. CARLOS ALBERTO TREVISAN
Sec.: Prof. GRACIELA INES ARBELAIZ

Number of teachers: 900
Number of students: 8,800

Publications: *Revista, Tekne*

DEANS

Faculty of Arts: JORGE SENN
Faculty of Economic Sciences: MARÍA ALEJANDRA BEATRÍZ YURKEVICH
Faculty of Engineering: Ing. SERGIO ALBERTO GARASSINO
Faculty of Forestry Sciences: Ing. OSCAR GAUTO
Faculty of Humanities and Social Sciences: LUIS ÁNGEL NELLI
Faculty of Sciences: Ing. FERNANDO LUIS KRAMER

UNIVERSIDAD NACIONAL DE QUILMES
(National University of Quilmes)

Roque Sáenz Peña 352, B1876BXD Bernal, Buenos Aires
Telephone: (11) 4365-7100
E-mail: info@unq.edu.ar
Internet: www.unq.edu.ar

Founded 1989
State control
Language of instruction: Spanish
Depts of finance and admin., science and technology and social sciences

Rector: Dr MARIO LOZANO
Vice-Rector: Dr ALEJANDRO VILLAR
Sec.-Gen.: ALFREDO ALFONSO
Sec. for Academics: Dra SARA PEREZ
Sec. for Admin.: CARMEN CHIARADONNA
Sec. for Postgraduate Affairs: NANCY DIAZ LARRAÑAGA
Sec. for Research: Dra LILIANA SEMORILE

Library of 16,000 vols
Number of students: 11,000
Publications: *Prismas, Revista de Historía Intelectual* (1 a year), *Redes* (irregular, online), *Revista de Ciencias Sociales*

UNIVERSIDAD NACIONAL DE RÍO CUARTO
(National University of Río Cuarto)

Ruta Nacional 36 km 601, X5804BYA Río Cuarto, Córdoba
Telephone: (358) 467-6200
E-mail: postmaster@unrc.edu.ar
Internet: www.unrc.edu.ar

Founded 1971
State control
Language of instruction: Spanish
Academic year: February to December

Rector: Prof. MARCELO RUIZ
Vice-Rector: Prof. JAVIER SALMINIS
Gen. Sec.: Prof. PABLO GALIMBERTI
Academic Sec.: Prof. CLAUDIO ASAAD
Economic Sec.: Prof. LUIS BAROVERO
Extension and Devt Sec.: Prof. SILVINA BAIGORRIA
Science and Technology Sec.: Prof. ALEJANDRO LARRIESTRA
Welfare Sec.: Prof. MARÍA NIDIA ZILETTI
Librarian: CRISTINA CH. DE FAUDA

Number of teachers: 1,800
Number of students: 20,000
Publications: *Contextos de Educación* (2 a year), *Crónia* (2 a year), *Fundamentos* (2 a year), *Interciencia* (2 a year, print and online, www.unrc.edu.ar/publicar/intercien), *Revista* (2 a year), *Voces de la Universidad* (2 a year, print and online, www.unrc.edu.ar/publicar/presen.htm)

DEANS

Faculty of Agriculture and Veterinary Science: Prof. ELENA MERCEDES FERNANDEZ
Faculty of Economics: Dr ROBERTO TAFANI
Faculty of Engineering: Ing. PEDRO ENRIQUE DUCANTO
Faculty of Exact, Physical, Chemical and Natural Sciences: Lic. ROSA CATTANA
Faculty of Humanities: Prof. GISELA VÉLEZ

UNIVERSIDAD NACIONAL DE RÍO NEGRO
(National University of Río Negro)

Belgrano 526, Viedma, Río Negro
Telephone: (2920) 428-601
E-mail: info@unrn.edu.ar
Internet: www.unrn.edu.ar

Founded 2007
State control
Language of instruction: Spanish
Rector: Lic. JUAN CARLOS DEL BELLO
Number of teachers: 300
Number of students: 6,000

UNIVERSIDAD NACIONAL DE ROSARIO
(Rosario National University)

Córdoba 1814, S2000AXD Rosario
Telephone: (341) 480-2620
E-mail: rector@unr.edu.ar
Internet: www.unr.edu.ar

Founded 1968
State control
Language of instruction: Spanish
Academic year: April to November

Rector: Prof. DARIO MAIORANA
Vice-Rector: Lic. EDUARDO SEMINARA
Sec.-Gen.: Prof. Dr HECTOR DARIO MASIO

Number of teachers: 5,800
Number of students: 76,000
Publication: *e-Universitas*

DEANS

Faculty of Agricultural Sciences: Ing. GUILLERMO MONTERO
Faculty of Architecture, Planning and Design: Dr ISABEL MARTÍNEZ DE SAN VICENTE
Faculty of Biochemistry and Pharmacy: Dr ESTEBAN CARLOS SERRA
Faculty of Dentistry: Prof. GUILLERMO J. FRANCHELLA
Faculty of Economic Sciences and Statistics: JAVIER EDUARDO GANEM
Faculty of Exact Sciences, Engineering and Surveying: Ing. OSCAR ENRIQUE PEIRE
Faculty of Humanities and Arts: Prof. JOSE GOITY
Faculty of Law: Dr ERNESTO IGNACIO JOSE GRANADOS
Faculty of Medical Sciences: Prof. Dr MIGUEL ANGEL FARRONI
Faculty of Political Science and International Relations: Lic. FRANCO BARTOLACCI
Faculty of Psychology: LAURA MANAVELLA
Faculty of Veterinary Sciences: GUSTAVO ADOLFO SANMIGUEL

UNIVERSIDAD NACIONAL DE SALTA
(National University of Salta)

Avda Bolivia 5150, Salta
Telephone: (387) 425-8671
E-mail: rector@unsa.edu.ar
Internet: www.unsa.edu.ar

Founded 1972
State control
Language of instruction: Spanish
Academic year: March to December

Rector: VICTOR HUGO CLAROS
Vice-Rector: Dr MIGUEL ANGEL BOSO
Sec.-Gen.: Ing. RICARDO FALÚ
Sec. for Academic Affairs: Dra MARTA ELENA TORINO
Sec. for Administrative Affairs: MIGUEL MARTIN NINA

Library of 57,633 vols, 42,300 periodicals
Number of teachers: 1,400
Number of students: 23,000

DEANS

Faculty of Economics, Juridical and Social Sciences: ANTONIO FERNANDEZ
Faculty of Engineering: Ing. EDGARDO LING SHAM
Faculty of Exact Sciences: Ing. CARLOS EUGENIO PUGA
Faculty of Health Sciences: Lic. MARIA INMACULADA PASSAMAI
Faculty of Humanities: Lic. LILIANA AIDA FORTUNY GASSER
Faculty of Natural Sciences: Ing. ADRIANA ORTIN VUJOVICH

UNIVERSIDAD NACIONAL DE SAN JUAN
(National University of San Juan)

Mitre 396 (E), J5402CWH San Juan
Telephone: (264) 429-5000
E-mail: academica@unsj.edu.ar
Internet: www.unsj.edu.ar

Founded 1973
State control
Language of instruction: Spanish
Academic year: April to March

Rector: Dr Ing. OSCAR NASISI
Vice-Rector: MONICA COCA
Sec. for Academic Affairs: Ing. RUBEN MARCELO BELLINI
Sec. for Science and Technology: Dr MARIO ERNESTO GIMÉNEZ
Librarian: RAÚL I. LOZADA

Number of teachers: 2,000
Number of students: 20,000

DEANS

Faculty of Architecture, Town Planning and Design: Arq. GUSTAVO ROBERTO GOMEZ
Faculty of Engineering: Ing. ROBERTO ROMUALDO GÓMEZ GUIRADO
Faculty of Exact, Physical and Natural Sciences: Lic. NÉSTOR EUGENIO WEIDMANN
Faculty of Humanities, Philosophy and Arts: ROSA ANA GARBARINO
Faculty of Social Sciences: Lic. RICARDO MARCELO COCA

UNIVERSIDAD NACIONAL DE SAN LUIS
(National University of San Luis)

Ejército de los Andes 950, D5700HHW San Luis
Telephone: (266) 442-4027
E-mail: prensa@unsl.edu.ar
Internet: www.unsl.edu.ar

Founded 1974
State control
Language of instruction: Spanish
Academic year: March to December

Rector: Dr FÉLIX DANIEL NIETO QUINTAS
Vice-Rector: JORGE RAUL OLGUÍN
Sec.-Gen.: JOSÉ LUIS MARTINEZ
Librarian: MIGUEL A. LUCERO

Number of teachers: 260
Number of students: 14,000

DEANS

Faculty of Chemistry, Biochemistry and Pharmacy: Dr JULIO RABA
Faculty of Engineering and Social Sciences: Ing. SERGIO RIBOTTA
Faculty of Health Sciences: Lic. FOURCADE MARIA BEATRIZ
Faculty of Human Sciences: Lic. VIVIANA RETA
Faculty of Physical, Mathematical and Natural Sciences: Dr FELIX DANIEL NIETO QUINTAS
Faculty of Tourism and Urbanism: Lic. NORMA G. PEREYRA

UNIVERSIDAD NACIONAL DE SANTIAGO DEL ESTERO
(National University of Santiago del Estero)

Avda Belgrano (s) 1912, Santiago del Estero
Telephone: (385) 450-9500
E-mail: info@unse.edu.ar
Internet: www.unse.edu.ar

Founded 1973
State control
Language of instruction: Spanish
Academic year: February to December

Rector: Lic. NATIVIDAD NASSIF
Vice-Rector: Dr CARLOS RAUL LOPEZ
Gen. Sec.: LUIS ALBERTO MIGUEL
Librarian: JORGE LUJAN GEREZ

Library of 20,000 vols
Number of teachers: 900
Number of students: 12,000

Publications: *Cuadernos de la UNSE*, *Revista de Ciencia y Técnica* (1 a year), *Revista 'Quebracho'* (forestry, 1 a year), *Revista 'Unase'* (6 a year)

DEANS

Faculty of Agriculture and Agricultural Industry: Ing. JOSÉ MANUEL SALGADO
Faculty of Exact Sciences and Technology: Ing. HECTOR RUBEN PAZ
Faculty of Forestry: Ing. MARTA ROSALIA GULOTTA
Faculty of Humanities, Social Sciences and Health: Lic. MARÍA MERCEDES ARCE

UNIVERSIDAD NACIONAL DE TRES DE FEBRERO
(National University of Tres de Febrero)

Mosconi 2736, B1674AHF Sáenz Peña, Buenos Aires
Telephone: (11) 4519-6010
E-mail: info@untref.edu.ar
Internet: www.untref.edu.ar

Founded 1995
State control
Language of instruction: Spanish
Academic year: March to December

Depts of administration and economics, engineering, health sciences and social security, mathematics, statistics and methodology, social sciences

Rector: ANÍBAL Y. JOZAMI
Vice-Rector: MARTÍN KAUFMANN
Sec.-Gen.: Dr JOSÉ MARÍA BERRAONDO
Sec. for Academics: Ing. CARLOS MUNDT
Sec. for Extension: Prof. GABRIEL ASPRELLA
Sec. for Research and Devt: Dr PABLO JACOVKIS

Number of teachers: 700
Number of students: 9,300

Publications: *Cibertronic: Revista de Artes Mediáticas* (www.untref.edu.ar/cibertronic), *Estudios Curatoriales*, *Infountref* (www.untref.edu.ar/contenido/infountref), *RAES—Revista Argentina de Educación Superior* (www.raes.org.ar)

UNIVERSIDAD NACIONAL DE TUCUMÁN
(National University of Tucumán)

Ayacucho 491, T4000INI San Miguel de Tucumán, Tucumán
Telephone: (381) 424-7752
E-mail: postmaster@unt.edu.ar
Internet: www.unt.edu.ar

Founded 1914
State control
Language of instruction: Spanish
Academic year: April to December

Rector: JUAN ALBERTO CERISOLA
Vice-Rector: Dra ALICIA BARDÓN
Sec. for Academic Affairs: Dr EDGARDO CUTÍN
Sec. for Admin. and Management Policy: MAURO FELDMAN
Sec. for Planning, Works and Services: CARLOS PRIETO
Sec. for Postgraduate Affairs: Dra MARÍA LAURA DE ARRIBA
Sec. for Science and Technology: Dra DORA MICELI
Sec. for Student Welfare: RODRIGO ALDERETE
Sec. for Univ. Extension: Dr MARIO LEAL
Sec. for Univ. Welfare: MAURICIO ARGIRÓ

Library: see under Libraries and Archives
Number of teachers: 4,500
Number of students: 60,000

DEANS

Faculty of Agriculture and Animal Husbandry: Prof. Ing. JOSÉ RAMÓN GARCÍA
Faculty of Architecture and Town Planning: EDUARDO JOSÉ COLETTI
Faculty of Arts: Dra RAQUEL PASTOR DE LA SILVA
Faculty of Biochemistry, Chemistry and Pharmacy: Dra SILVIA NELINA GONZÁLEZ DE ELÍAS
Faculty of Dentistry: Prof. DANIEL ANTONIO GARCIA
Faculty of Economics: SANTIAGO MARIO DI LULLO
Faculty of Exact Sciences and Technology: Ing. SERGIO JOSE PAGANI
Faculty of Law and Social Sciences: Dr JOSÉ LUIS VÁZQUEZ
Faculty of Medicine: Prof. Lic. ROSSANA LINA MOYANA (Dir)
Faculty of Natural Sciences and Miguel Lillo Institute: Dr RICARDO MON
Faculty of Philosophy and Letters: Dra JUDITH Y. CASALI DE BABOT
Faculty of Physical Education: Prof. NÉLIDA SUSANA VILLARRUEL
Faculty of Psychology: Lic. ADELA DEL VALLE ESTOFÁN DE TERRAF

UNIVERSIDAD NACIONAL DE VILLA MARÍA
(National University of Villa María)

Avda Arturo Jauretche 1555, Villa María, Córdoba
Telephone: (353) 453-9103
E-mail: comunica@unvm.edu.ar
Internet: www.unvm.edu.ar

Founded 1995
State control
Language of instruction: Spanish
Academic year: March to November (2 semesters)

Rector: MARTÍN RODRIGO GILL
Vice-Rector: MARIA CECILIA ANA CONCI
Academic Sec.: Dra LUISA MARGARITA SCHWEIZER
Sec.-Gen.: GERMÁN BLAS CARIGNANO
Number of students: 3,000

Publication: *Revista Senderos* (1 a year)

DEANS

Institute of Basic and Applied Sciences: HUGO EMILIO TRAVERSO
Institute of Human Sciences: LUIS ALBERTO NEGRETTI
Institute of Social Sciences: ALDO MANUEL PAREDES

UNIVERSIDAD NACIONAL DEL CENTRO DE LA PROVINCIA DE BUENOS AIRES
(National University Centre of Buenos Aires Province)

Gen. Pinto 399, B7000GHG Tandil, Buenos Aires
Telephone: (249) 442-2000
E-mail: informes@rec.unicen.edu.ar
Internet: www.unicen.edu.ar

Founded 1974
State control
Academic year: February to December

Rector: Cr ROBERTO M. TASSARA
Vice-Rector: Ing. Agr. OMAR LOSARDO
Gen. Sec.: Ing. GUILLERMO CORRES
Academic Sec.: Prof. MABEL PACHECO
Admin. Sec.: Cr JOSÉ LUIS BIANCHINI
Library Dir: Prof. ZULEMA GRANDINETTI DE CAGLIOLO

Library of 96,500 books and 876 periodicals
Number of teachers: 1,600
Number of students: 13,500

Publications: *Alternativas*, *Revista 'Espacios en Blanco'* (online, www.cartapacio.edu.ar), *Revista Intersecciones en Antropología* (1 a year)

DEANS

Faculty of Agronomy: Ing. Agr. LILIANA MONTERROSO
Faculty of Art: Lic. MARIO LORENZO VALIENTE
Faculty of Economic Sciences: Dr ALFREDO RÉBORI
Faculty of Engineering: Ing. MARCELO ALBERTO SPINA
Faculty of Exact Sciences: Dr SERGIO CELANI
Faculty of Human Sciences: Prof. ALICIA SPINELLO
Faculty of Law: Prof. LAURA MARIA GIOSA
Faculty of Social Sciences: Dr RAFAEL CURTONI
Faculty of Veterinary Sciences: Dr MARCELO ABA

UNIVERSIDAD NACIONAL DEL CHACO AUSTRAL
(National University of Southern Chaco)

Comandante Fernández 755, Presidencia Roque Sáenz Peña, Chaco
Telephone: (364) 442-0137
E-mail: rector@uncaus.edu.ar
Internet: www.uncaus.edu.ar

Founded 2007
State control
Language of instruction: Spanish
Academic year: February to December

Depts of basic and applied sciences, and humanities and social sciences

Rector: Ing. OMAR VICENTE JUDIS
Vice-Rector: Ing. WALTER GUSTAVO LOPEZ
Academic Sec.: Prof. PEDRO DANIEL LEGUIZA
Admin. Sec.: Ing. LUIS SEBASTIÁN PUGACZ

Number of teachers: 60
Number of students: 1,900

UNIVERSIDAD NACIONAL DEL COMAHUE
(National University of Comahue)

Buenos Aires 1400, Q8300BCX Neuquén, Patagonia
Telephone: (299) 449-0363
E-mail: webinfo@dti.uncoma.edu.ar
Internet: www.uncoma.edu.ar

Founded 1972
State control
Language of instruction: Spanish
Academic year: March to March

Rector: Profa TERESA PETRONA VEGA
Vice-Rector: Ing. Agr. MIGUEL ANGEL SILVA
Sec.-Gen.: Lic. NELSON FABIAN FERNANDEZ
Academic Sec.: Lic. MARINA BARBABELLA
Sec. for Research: Lic. LUIS BERTANI
Librarian: EUGENIA CARLOTA LUQUE

Number of teachers: 1,700
Number of students: 30,000

DEANS

Bariloche Regional University Centre: Prof. VICTOR HUMBERTO BAEZ
Faculty of Agricultural Sciences: Prof. SERGIO JORGE BRAMARDI
Faculty of Computer Science: Prof. CLAUDIO ALEJANDRO VAUCHERET
Faculty of Economics and Administration: Prof. CORA BERNARDI
Faculty of Educational Sciences: Prof. DIANA MARTIN
Faculty of Engineering: Ing. DANIEL RODOLFO BOCCANERA
Faculty of Environment and Health: Dr CARLOS CALDERÓN
Faculty of Humanities: Prof. PEDRO BARREIRO
Faculty of Law and Social Sciences: OMAR RUBÉN JURGEIT
Faculty of Medical Sciences: Prof. ALVARO FERNANDO OLIVA
Faculty of Science and Technology of Food: Dra ADRIANA CATALINA CABALLERO
Faculty of Tourism: Prof. MARCELO MANCINI
School of Languages: Profa MARIA ALEJANDRA OLIVARES
Zona Atlantica Regional University Centre: Prof. OSVALDO AGUSTIN ALONSO

UNIVERSIDAD NACIONAL DEL LITORAL
(National University of Litoral)

Blvd Pellegrini 2750, S3000ADQ Santa Fe
Telephone: (342) 457-1110
E-mail: informes@unl.edu.ar
Internet: www.unl.edu.ar

Founded 1919
State control
Language of instruction: Spanish
Academic year: March to December

Rector: Ing. ALBOR CANTARD
Vice-Rector: Dr MARIO T. CADIOTI
Gen. Sec.: Dr PEDRO SÁNCHEZ IZQUIERDO
Academic Sec.: Arq. CARLOS SASTRE
Sec. for Economic and Financial Affairs: GERMÁN BONINO
Sec. for Science and Technology: Dra ERICA HYNES
Librarian: MARISA PULIOTTI DE FERRARI

Number of teachers: 2,200
Number of students: 42,000

Publications: *ConCiencia*, *Science and Technology, Society and Culture*

DEANS

Faculty of Agrarian Sciences: Ing. Agr. LUIS RISTA
Faculty of Architecture, Design and Town Planning: Arq. MIGUEL IRIGOYEN
Faculty of Biochemistry and Biological Sciences: Dr JAVIER LOTTERSBERGER
Faculty of Chemical Engineering: Ing. ENRIQUE MAMMARELLA
Faculty of Economics: Lic. CARLOS BELTRÁN
Faculty of Humanities and Sciences: Prof. CLAUDIO LIZÁRRAGA
Faculty of Law and Social Sciences: Dr JOSÉ MANUEL BENVENUTI
Faculty of Medical Sciences: Dr SAMUEL SEIREF
Faculty of Veterinary Sciences: Med. Vet. JOSÉ LUIS PERALTA
Faculty of Water Resources Engineering and Sciences: Ing. MARIO SCHREIDER

UNIVERSIDAD NACIONAL DEL NORDESTE
(National University of Nordeste)

25 de Mayo 868, 3400 Corrientes
Telephone: (3783) 42-5064
E-mail: eluniversitario@unne.edu.ar
Internet: www.unne.edu.ar

Founded 1956
State control
Language of instruction: Spanish
Academic year: March to December

Rector: Ing. EDUARDO E. DEL VALLE
Vice-Rector: Prof. MARÍA DELFINA VEIRAVE
Sec.-Gen. for Admin.: SUSANA CORREU DE DUSEK
Sec.-Gen. for Planning: Dr CESAR HORACIO DELLAMEA
Sec.-Gen. for Science and Technology: Dra SILVIA MAZZA
Sec.-Gen. for Univ. Extension: Cr ARIEL FRETE
Library Dir: Lic. MARÍA C. MARCOS DE CABALLERO

Number of teachers: 4,541
Number of students: 49,875

Publications: *Cuadernos Serie Agro*, *Revista de la Facultad de Ciencias Veterinarias*, *Revista de la Facultad de Derecho*, *Revista Nordeste*, *Serie Medicina*, *Serie Planeamiento*

DEANS

Faculty of Agricultural Sciences: Dra SARA VAZQUEZ
Faculty of Architecture and Town Planning: Arq. GUSTAVO ORLANDO CÁCERES
Faculty of Arts, Design and Cultural Sciences: FEDERICO A. VEIRAVÉ
Faculty of Dentistry: Prof. ROQUE OSCAR ROSENDE
Faculty of Economics: BEATRIZ DEL CARMEN MONFARDINI DE FRANCHINI
Faculty of Engineering: Dr Ing. JORGE VICTOR PILAR
Faculty of Humanities: Prof. MARÍA DELFINA VEIRAVÉ
Faculty of Law and Social and Political Sciences: Dra VERÓNICA TORRES DE BREARD
Faculty of Medicine: Prof. SAMUEL BLUVSTEIN
Faculty of Natural Sciences and Surveying: Dra LIDIA ITATÍ FERRARO DE CORONA
Faculty of Veterinary Sciences: Dr ELVIO EDUARDO RIOS

UNIVERSIDAD NACIONAL DEL NOROESTE DE LA PROVINCIA DE BUENOS AIRES
(National University of Northwestern Buenos Aires)

Roque Saenz Peña 456, Junín, Buenos Aires
Telephone: (236) 440-7750
E-mail: secretariaprivada@unnoba.edu.ar
Internet: www.unnoba.edu.ar

Founded 2002
State control
Academic year: February to December

Schools of agricultural, natural and environment sciences, economics and law, technology

Rector: Dr GUILLERMO R. TAMARIT
Vice-Rector: DANYA V. TAVELA
Sec.-Gen.: PABLO G. PETRAGLIA
Academic Sec.: MARÍA FLORENCIA CASTRO
Economic and Financial Sec.: MARIELA GARCIA
Legal and Technical Sec.: CARLOS PÉREZ

UNIVERSIDAD NACIONAL DEL SUR
(National University of the South)

Avda Colón 80, B8000FTN Bahía Blanca
Telephone: (291) 459-5015
E-mail: rector@uns.edu.ar
Internet: www.uns.edu.ar

Founded 1956
Academic year: February to December

Rector: Dr GUILLERMO HÉCTOR CRAPISTE
Vice-Rector: Dr MARÍA DEL CARMEN VAQUERO
Gen. Sec. for Academic Affairs: Mg. GRACIELA BRIZUELA
Gen. Sec. for Culture and Univ. Extension: Abog. CLAUDIO CARUCCI
Gen. Sec. for Institutional Relations and Planning: Dr GASTÓN MILANESI
Gen. Sec. for Science and Technology: Dra CINTIA PICCOLO
Gen. Sec. for Student Affairs: Ing. ROLANDO SCUDELATI
Gen. Sec. for Technical-Admin.: Lic. CLAUDIA LEGNINI
Gen. Sec. for Univ. Superior Ccl: Abog. DIEGO DUPRAT
Library: see under Libraries and Archives

Number of teachers: 2,069
Number of students: 22,571

Publications: *Agro UNS* (3 a year), *Cuadernos del sur-Filosofía* (1 a year), *Cuadernos del sur-Historia* (1 a year), *Cuadernos del sur-Letras* (1 a year), *Escritos Contables y Administración* (2 a year), *Estudios Económicos* (2 a year), *Latin American Applied Research* (3 a year), *Programma* (1 a year), *Revista de la Unión Matemática Argentina* (2 a year), *Revista Universitaria de Geografía* (1 a year)

UNIVERSIDAD NOTARIAL ARGENTINA
(Argentine University for Lawyers)

Avda 51 No. 435, B1900AVI La Plata
Telephone: (221) 421-9283
E-mail: uninotlp@universidadnotarial.edu.ar
Internet: www.universidadnotarial.edu.ar

Founded 1964
Private control
Academic year: March to November

Rector: CRISTINA NOEMI ARMELLA
Vice-Rector: ADRIANA N. ABELLA
Sec.-Gen.: MALVINA ZALABARDO
Librarian: Dra DORA C. TÁLICE DE SECO VILLALBA

Number of teachers: 150
Number of students: 2,300

Publication: *Cuadernos Notariales*

UNIVERSIDAD TECNOLÓGICA NACIONAL
(National Technological University)

Sarmiento 440, C1041AAJ Buenos Aires
Telephone: (11) 5371-5600
E-mail: seu@frro.utn.edu.ar
Internet: www.utn.edu.ar

Founded 1959
State control
Academic year: April to November

29 Regional colleges located in Chaco, Entre Rios, Santa Fe, La Rioja, Tucumán, Buenos Aires, Córdoba, Mendoza, Chubut, Neuquén, Santa Cruz and Tierra del Fuego

Rector: Ing. HECTOR CARLOS BROTTO
Vice-Rector: Ing. CARLOS EDUARDO FANTINI
Academic Sec.: Ing. JOSÉ MARÍA VIRGILI
Admin. Sec.: Dr ROGELIO ANTONIO GOMEZ
Sec. for Culture and Univ. Extension: Lic. SEBASTIÁN E. PUIG
Sec. for Science, Technology and Graduate Studies: Dr WALTER E. LEGNANI
Sec. for Institutional Relations: Ing. MARIO ROBERTO GOS
Sec. for Student Affairs: ALBERTO ATILIO VIARENGO

Number of teachers: 16,185
Number of students: 70,000

Publications: *Technología y Sciencia* (1 a year), *Boletín Informativo*

UNIVERSIDAD TORCUATO DI TELLA (Torcuato di Tella University)

Avda Figueroa Alcorta 7350, C1428BCW Buenos Aires
Telephone: (11) 5169-7000
E-mail: eschargr@utdt.edu
Internet: www.utdt.edu

Founded 1991
Private control

Schools of architecture and urban studies, business, law; depts of art, economics, history, mathematics and statistics and political science and international studies

Rector: Ernesto Schargrodsky
Vice-Rector: Catalina Smulovitz
Sec.: Pablo Guidotti
Library Dir: María Alejandra Plaza

Library of 95,000 vols, 2,500 print journals and 35,000 electronic journals
Number of teachers: 70
Number of students: 2,500

Publication: *Revista Argentina de Teoría Jurídica* (2 a year)

University Institutes

Instituto de Enseñanza Superior del Ejército (Institute of Higher Military Education): Avda Cabildo 65, 1° piso, Buenos Aires; tel. (11) 4576-5648; e-mail informes@iese.edu.ar; internet www.iese.edu.ar; f. 1990; depts of distance learning, information technology and modern languages; National Military College, Technical College and War College; Rector Bari del Valle Sosa; Academic Sec. Guillermo Horacio Eduardo Lafferriere.

Instituto Tecnológico de Buenos Aires (Buenos Aires Institute of Technology): Avda Eduardo Madero 399, C1106ACD Buenos Aires; tel. (11) 6393-4822; e-mail informes@itba.edu.ar; internet www.itba.edu.ar; f. 1959; 520 teachers; 2,450 students; Rector Dr Ing. Germán Guido Lavalle; Academic Sec. Dr Ing. Arturo T. de Zan; publs *Acontecer*, *Boletín General*, *Revista del Instituto Tecnológico de Buenos Aires*.

Instituto Universitario Aeronáutico (Aeronautical Institute): Avda Fuerza Aérea 6500, X5010JMX, Córdoba; tel. (351) 443-5000; e-mail informes@iua.edu.ar; internet www.iua.edu.ar; f. 1947 as Escuela de Ingeniería Aeronáutica, joined Nat. Univ. System 1971; faculty of administration and engineering; Rector Ing. Edgar Mario Karpowicz; Sec.-Gen. Armando Jose Gutierrez.

Instituto Universitario de Ciencias de la Salud Fundación 'H.A. Barceló' (University Institute of Health Sciences Foundation 'H.A. Barceló'): Avda Las Heras 2191, C1127AAD Buenos Aires; tel. (11) 4800-0200; e-mail informesba@barcelo.edu.ar; internet www.barcelo.edu.ar; f. 1991; Rector Prof. Dr Héctor A. Barceló; Vice-Rector Lic. Axel Barceló; Sec.-Gen. Dr Guillermo Lojo; Library Dir Lic. Leandro Rodriguez Ares.

Instituto Universitario de Gendarmería Nacional (Institute of National Gendarmerie): Paseo Colón 533, C1063ACF Buenos Aires; tel. (11) 5169-3326; e-mail info@iugna.edu.ar; internet www.iugna.edu.ar; f. 2007; Rector José Miguel Martin; Vice-Rector José Alfredo Aparicio.

Instituto Universitario de La Policía Federal Argentina (University Institute of the Federal Police Argentina): Rosario 532, Caballito, C1424CCL Buenos Aires; tel. (11) 4905-5001; e-mail informes@iupfa.edu.ar; internet www.universidad-policial.edu.ar; f. 1974 as Academia Federal de Estudios Policiales, present name and status 1995; faculties of biomedical sciences, criminal sciences, law and social sciences and security sciences; library: 25,000 vols; Rector Lic. Alejandro Salomón; Vice-Rector Lic. Liliana Velázquez.

Instituto Universitario de Seguridad Marítima (University Institute of Maritime Safety): Avda Eduardo Madero 235, C1106ACC Buenos Aires; tel. (11) 4314-2434; e-mail arl@arnet.com.ar; internet www.prefecturanaval.edu.ar/iupna; f. 2002; Rector Prefecto Gen. Osvaldo Daniel Tourn.

Instituto Universitario del Gran Rosario (University Institute of Gran Rosario): Corrientes 1254, Rosaria Santa Fe; tel. (341) 411-0506; e-mail info@iugr.edu.ar; internet www.iugr.edu.ar; f. 2008; Rector Ing. Javier Machhi; Academic Vice-Rector Lic. Arturo Forcher; Admin. Vice-Rector Dr Gerardo Strada Sáenz; Library Dir Marta E. Barrera.

Instituto Universitario Escuela Argentina de Negocios (Argentina School of Business): Avda Córdoba 1690, Buenos Aires; tel. (11) 5032-3900; e-mail informes@iuean.edu.ar; internet www.iuean.edu.ar; f. 1992; Rector Ariana de Vincenzi; Academic Vice-Rector Dra Bettina Checchia; Admin. Vice-Rector Patricia Prieto.

Instituto Universitario ESEADE (ESEADE University Institute): Uriarte 2472, C1425FNJ Buenos Aires; tel. (11) 4773-5825; e-mail info@eseade.edu.ar; internet www.eseade.edu.ar; f. 1978; schools of admin. corporate and training, art and design, economics and social sciences and humanities; Rector Dr Alfredo Enrique Blousson; Academic Sec. Adrian Pin; Library Dir Pablo Ruiz.

Instituto Universitario ISEDET (University Institute ISEDET): Camacuá 282, DOF1406C Buenos Aires; tel. (11) 4632-5030; e-mail info@isedet.edu.ar; internet www.isedet.edu.ar; f. 2001; depts of Bible studies, history, practical theology, social sciences and theology correlation, systematic theology; library: 105,000 vols; Rector Mgr. Elsa Beatriz Agüero; Library Dir Lic. Guillermo Steinfeld; publ. *Cuadernos de Teología* (1 a year).

Instituto Universitario Italiano de Rosario (Italian University Institute of Rosario): Virasoro 1249, S2001ODA Rosario; tel. (341) 482-0363; e-mail iunir@iunir.edu.ar; internet www.iunir.edu.ar; f. 2001; schools of dentistry, medicine, nursing, psychology; Rector Dr Mario A. Secchi; Vice-Rector Dr Enrique Daniel Coscarelli; Academic Sec. Dr Walter Bordino; Librarian Miriam Testero.

Instituto Universitario Nacional del Arte (National Institute of Art): Azcuénaga 1129, C1115AAG Buenos Aires; tel. (11) 5777-1300; internet www.iuna.edu.ar; f. 1996; Rector Lic. Raúl Osvaldo Moneta; Sec.-Gen. Prof. Roberto De Rose.

Instituto Universitario Naval (Naval Institute): Avda del Libertador 8209, C1429BNC Buenos Aires; tel. (11) 4704-8200; e-mail administra@inun.edu.ar; internet www.inun.edu.ar; f. 1978 as Instituto Universitario de Estudios Navales y Marítimos; current name and status 1991; Rector Ing. Julio Marcelo Pérez; Academic Sec. Lic. Julio E. Grosso.

Schools of Art and Music

Conservatorio Superior de Música 'Manuel de Falla' (Conservatory of Music 'Manuel de Falla'): Gallo 238, 2º, C1172ABF Buenos Aires; tel. (11) 4865-9005; internet cmfalla.caba.infd.edu.ar; f. 1919; library: 8,000 scores and vols; 300 teachers; 2,500 students; Dir Prof. Susana Galimberti.

Escuela de Danzas 'Aída V. Mastrazzi' (Dance School 'Aída V. Mastrazzi'): Esmeralda 285, C1035ABE Buenos Aires; tel. (11) 4326-5478; internet art300de1.buenosaires.edu.ar; f. 1924 as Conservatorio Nacional de Música, Arte Escénico y Declamación, present name 2003; Dir Profa Eleonara Ferraro.

Escuela Nacional de Arte Dramático (National School of Dramatic Arts): French 3614, C1425AXD Buenos Aires; tel. (11) 4804-7970; f. 1924; library: 4,200 vols; 300 students; Rector Carlos Albarenga.

Escuela Nacional de Bellas Artes 'Prilidiano Pueyrredón' (National School of Fine Arts 'Prilidiano Pueyrredón'): Las Heras 1749, C1018AAB Buenos Aires; tel. (11) 442-0657; f. 1878; depts of painting, engraving and sculpture; library: 5,923 vols; 373 students; Dir Domingo Mazzone.

Escuela Superior de Bellas Artes 'Ernesto de la Cárcova' (College of Fine Arts 'Ernesto de la Cárcova'): Tristán Achaval Rodríguez 1701, 1107 Buenos Aires; tel. (11) 4361-5144; f. 1923; painting, sculpture, engraving and decor; museum of tracings; library: 4,500 vols; Rector Prof. Eduardo A. Audivert.

ARMENIA

The Higher Education System

The oldest university in Armenia is the Yerevan State University, which was founded in 1919. Most institutions of higher education were founded while Armenia was a full Union Republic of the Union of Soviet Socialist Republics (USSR). Armenia declared independence from the USSR in 1991. Higher education is overseen by the Ministry of Education and Science, and is governed by the Constitution (1995), which states that all citizens have the right to receive an education, and by the Law on Education (1999), which outlines the system's structure. In 2000 the National Assembly approved the State Programme for Education Sector Development 2001–05, which outlined a five-year programme of reforms aimed at rationalizing and modernizing the entire education system. The Law on Higher and Postgraduate Professional Education (2004) outlined the reforms to prepare Armenia for the Bologna Process, which it joined in 2005. The private Eurasia International University (which was established in Yerevan in 1997) has fully conformed to the requirements of the Bologna Process since 2007. The Educational Development National Programme 2008–15 further outlined the measures needed to reform the system. In 2011, there were 22 state-run higher education institutes and 31 private ones. In 2011, some 111,000 students were enrolled in higher education, including universities.

To enter higher education students must hold the Mijnakarg Yndhanur Krtoutian Attestat (Certificate of Completed Secondary Education) and pass the unified state secondary examinations (introduced in 2007).

There are three levels of higher education degrees in Armenia, one undergraduate and two postgraduate. The main undergraduate degree is the Bakalavr (Bachelors), which is usually a four-year programme. In line with the reforms of the Bologna Process, the Government has been introducing the European Credit Transfer System (ECTS) since the 2002/03 academic year and most degree courses are now based on this system. The Specialist Diploma, a Soviet-style five-year degree was no longer available after 2010; as in other former Soviet countries, the Specialist Diploma had been equated to a Masters degree. From 2007/08 higher education institutions issued the Diploma Supplement to students graduating from first- and second-cycle programmes (Bachelors and Masters, respectively). The first postgraduate degree is the Magistros (Masters), a one- or two-year course, admission to which is by examination in the student's chosen field of specialization. The second and final level of postgraduate education comprises the two-year course to become a Researcher and the course to attain the Aspirantura (Doctorate), which is split into two stages: the Candidate of Science and the Doctor of Science. The first stage lasts for two years and consists of taught and research components, while the second stage is purely research and necessary only for those who wish to pursue a career in higher education.

The first level of non-university technical and vocational education is Preliminary Professional (Vocational) Education and is open to holders of the Himnakan Yndhanur Krtutyan Attestat (Certificate of Basic Education) or the Certificate of Completed Secondary Education. Courses generally run for between one and three years and are offered at upper secondary vocational schools and middle professional schools. The second level of technical and vocational education is known as Intermediate Level Professional (Vocational) Education and is open to holders of the Certificate of Completed Secondary Education. The principal aim is to train specialists in fields such as the arts, finance, health, the humanities, pedagogy and technology. Training may last between 22 months and 58 months and is undertaken at middle professional schools. Upon qualification students gain the title Junior Specialist. Courses in technical and vocational subjects are also offered at undergraduate and postgraduate levels, leading to the award of a Bachelors, Certified Specialist or Masters. Programmes at this level aim to prepare highly qualified specialists as leaders in their chosen fields of specialization. There are also two levels of teacher training: Junior Specialist for primary and basic school teaching; and Bachelors or Specialist Diploma for secondary school teaching.

In 2009 the National Centre for Professional Education Quality Assurance (ANQA) was established to replace the Licensing and Accreditation Service. The Centre's main responsibility is to verify the quality of education and to implement the accreditation process of higher education institutions and their programmes according to European and state standards and guidelines for quality assurance. The accreditation process was scheduled to be carried out during 2011–15. The first stakeholder conference on quality assurance was held in 2010 and in 2011 site visits were made to the Armenian State Pedagogical University and the Yerevan State University of Architecture and Construction under the pilot accreditation process supported by a World Bank grant project.

Regulatory and Representative Bodies

GOVERNMENT

Ministry of Culture: Republic Sq. 1, Govt Bldg 3, 0010 Yerevan; tel. (10) 54-40-27; e-mail info@mincult.am; internet www.mincult.am; Minister HASMIK POGHOSYAN.

Ministry of Education and Science: Main Ave, Govt Bldg 3, 0010 Yerevan; tel. (10) 52-73-43; e-mail info@edu.am; internet www.edu.am; Minister ARMEN ASHOTYAN.

ACCREDITATION

ENIC/NARIC Armenia: Nat. Information Centre for Academic Recognition and Mobility, 0070 Yerevan, Vratsyan 73; tel. (10) 57-84-56; e-mail armenic@cornet.am; internet www.armenic.am; f. 2006; provides information, advice and formal decision on recognition of int. qualifications; information centre for recognition and internationalization of education; facilitates int. integration of the nat. education system into worldwide educational services; promotes mobility; supports devt of int. cooperation between educational instns and other sectors; Exec. Dir Dr GAYANE HARUTYUNYAN.

Learned Societies

GENERAL

National Academy of Sciences of Armenia: Marshal Baghramyan Ave 24, 0019 Yerevan; tel. (10) 52-70-31; e-mail academy@sci.am; internet www.sci.am; f. 1943; depts of physical, mathematical and technological sciences, natural sciences, humanities; research institutes attached to depts: see under Research Institutes; 119 mems; Pres. F. T. SARGASIAN; Acad.-Sec. and Vice-Pres. V. B. BARKHUDARIAN; publs *Astrofizika* (Astrophysics), *Biologicheskii Zhurnal Armenii* (Biological Journal of Armenia), *Doklady* (Reports), *Istoriko-Filologicheskii Zhurnal* (Historical and Philological Journal), *Izvestiya* (Bulletins: Mathematics, Mechanics, Physics, Engineering Sciences, Earth Sciences), *Khimicheskii Zhurnal Armenii* (Chemical Journal of Armenia), *Meditsinskaya Nauka Armenii* (Medical Science of Armenia), *Neirokhimiya* (Neurochemistry), *Soobshcheniya Byurakanskoi Observatorii* (Reports of the Byurakan Astrophysical Observatory), *Vestnik Khirurgii Armenii* (Herald of Armenian Surgery), *Vestnik Obshchestvennykh Nauk* (Herald of Social Sciences).

LANGUAGE AND LITERATURE

Alliance Française: Univ. Acharyan, Moskovyan 3, 3rd Fl., 0001 Yerevan; tel. (10) 58-66-99; e-mail secretariat@alliancefr.am; internet www.alliancefr.am; offers courses and examinations in French language and culture and promotes cultural exchange with France; Dir SUSAN YE. GHARAMYAN.

British Council: 9 Alex Manoogian, 0070 Yerevan; tel. (10) 55-29-45; e-mail info@britishcouncil.am; internet www.britishcouncil.am; offers courses and examinations in English language and British culture and promotes cultural exchange with the UK; Dir AREVIK SARIBEKYAN.

Research Institutes

GENERAL

Institute of the Arts: Pr. Marshala Bagramyana 24G, 0019 Yerevan; tel. (10) 58-37-02; e-mail instart@sci.am; f. 1958; attached to Nat. Acad. of Sciences of Armenia; depts of architecture, fine arts, folk arts, music, theatre and cinema; Dir A. AGHASYAN.

AGRICULTURE, FISHERIES AND VETERINARY SCIENCE

Institute of Hydroponics Problems: Noragyugh 108, 0082 Yerevan; tel. (10) 56-51-62; e-mail hydrop@netsys.am; internet www.sci.am; f. 1947; attached to Nat. Acad. of Sciences of Armenia; devt of technologies for hydroponic cultivation of valuable, rare and endangered medicinal, aromatic and dye-bearing plants, trees and shrubs; library of 10,000 vols; Dir Dr KHACHATUR MAIRAPETYAN; publ. *Communications of IHP* (every 3 years).

Scientific Centre of Agriculture and Plant Protection: Armavir Marz, St Isy le Moulino St 1, 1110 Echmiadzin; tel. (23) 15-34-54; attached to Min. of Agriculture; 6 depts, 11 laboratories; Dir H. HOVSEPIAN.

ECONOMICS, LAW AND POLITICS

Armenian Centre for National and International Studies: Yerznkian St 75, 0033 Yerevan; tel. (10) 52-87-80; e-mail root@acnis.am; internet www.acnis.am; f. 1994; covers 5 main areas: public policy, economics, int. and regional studies, nat. security studies, and global and regional trends; holds confs, seminars and meetings; library of 4,200 vols; Founder and Pres. Dr RAFFI HOVANNISIAN; publ. *The Changing World: Viewpoints from Yerevan* (4 a year).

Institute of Economics: ul. Abovyana 15, 0001 Yerevan; tel. (10) 58-19-71; e-mail nas_ie@sci.am; f. 1955; attached to Nat. Acad. of Sciences of Armenia; Dir V. E. KHOJABEKYAN.

HISTORY, GEOGRAPHY AND ARCHAEOLOGY

Armenian Genocide Museum–Institute: Tsitsernakaberd Memorial Complex, 0028 Yerevan; tel. (10) 39-09-81; e-mail info@genocide-museum.am; internet www.genocide-museum.am; f. 1995; attached to Nat. Acad. of Sciences of Armenia; Dir HAYK DEMOYAN.

Institute of Archaeology and Ethnography: Charents 15, 0025 Yerevan; tel. (10) 55-68-96; e-mail pavetisyan@sci.am; f. 1959; attached to Nat. Acad. of Sciences of Armenia; library of 15,000 vols; Dir A. A. KALANTARYAN.

Institute of History: Pr. Marshala Bagramyana 24G, 0019 Yerevan; tel. (10) 52-92-63; e-mail history@sci.am; f. 1943; attached to Nat. Acad. of Sciences of Armenia; Dir A. MELKONYAN.

Institute of Oriental Studies of National Academy of Sciences of Armenia: Marshala Bagramyana 24/4, 0019 Yerevan; tel. (10) 58-33-82; e-mail info@orient.sci.am; internet www.orient.sci.am; f. 1971; history, sociopolitical, int. and regional relations, culture, religion, problems of nat. minorities and ethnic groups of Middle East, Caucasus and E Asia from antiquity to present; library of 60,000 vols; Dir Dr RUBEN A. SAFRASTYAN; Deputy Dir Dr ROBERT P. GHAZARYAN; publs *Near East: History, Politics, Culture*, *The Countries and Peoples of the Near and Middle East, Turcic and Ottoman Studies*.

Shirak Armenology Research Centre: Gorky St 62, 3101 Gyumri; tel. (241) 33-173; e-mail hkentron@mail.ru; f. 1997; attached to Nat. Acad. of Sciences of Armenia; Dir SERGEY A. HAYRAPETYAN.

LANGUAGE AND LITERATURE

Abegyan Institute of Literature: ul. Grikora Lusavoricha 15, 0015 Yerevan; tel. (10) 56-32-54; f. 1943; attached to Nat. Acad. of Sciences of Armenia; Dir A. K. EGHIAZARYAN.

Atcharian Institute of Linguistics: ul. Abovyana 15, 0001 Yerevan; tel. (10) 56-53-37; e-mail inslang@sci.am; f. 1943; attached to Nat. Acad. of Sciences of Armenia; Dir G. B. DJAUKYAN.

MEDICINE

Armenian Institute of Spa Treatment and Physiotherapy: ul. Bratev Orbeli 41, 0028 Yerevan; internet www.medlib.am/spa; f. 1930; library of 30,000 vols; Dir Prof. G. AGADJANIAN.

Armenian Research Centre of Maternal and Child Health Care: Mesrop Mashtots Ave 22, 0002 Yerevan; tel. (10) 53-01-72; internet www.armobgyn.com; f. 1931; library of 25,000 vols; Dir Prof. G. OKOYEV.

Centre of Medical Genetics and Primary Health Care: Tigran Mets Ave 4, 0010 Yerevan; tel. (10) 54-43-67; e-mail inform@cmg.am; internet www.cmg.am; f. 1998; attached to Nat. Acad. of Sciences of Armenia; Dir Dr TAMARA F. SARKISIAN.

Centre of Traumatology, Orthopaedics, Burns and Radiology: Marash 9th St, 0047 Yerevan; tel. (10) 65-00-40; internet www.ctooir.narod.ru; f. 1945; fmrly Yerevan Scientific Research Institute of Orthopaedics and Traumatology; depts of acute trauma, polytrauma, post-traumatic complications, infection complication, bone pathology, adult orthopaedics, paediatric orthopaedics, morphology, experimental biology; research depts: bone defect reconstruction, joint replacement, vertebral surgery, bone matrix preparation, bone tumour surgery, complex burns treatment; Dir AIVAZYAN VACHAGAN; publ. *Abstracts of Annual Congress of Traumatologists & Orthopaedic Surgeons of Armenia* (1 a year).

Mikaelian Research Institute of Surgery: Hasratyan 9, Yerevan; tel. (10) 28-19-90; e-mail surgery@netsys.am; f. 1974; library of 5,000 vols; Dir H. S. TAMAZIAN.

Research Centre for Epidemiology, Virology and Medical Parasitology: Marshal Khudyavkovi St 1, 0009 Yerevan; tel. (10) 62-99-24; e-mail melikandreasyan@mail.ru; internet www.epidinstitute.info.am; Dir GAYANE G. MELIK-ANDREASYAN.

NATURAL SCIENCES

Biological Sciences

Buniatian, H. Institute of Biochemistry NAS RA: Paruyra Sevak Str. 5/1, 0014 Yerevan; tel. (10) 28-18-40; e-mail schailyan@sci.am; f. 1961; attached to Nat. Acad. of Sciences of Armenia; Dir Prof. Dr SAMVEL CHAILIAN; publ. *Neurokhimija* (4 a year).

Centre for Ecological–Noosphere Studies: Abovian 68, 0025 Yerevan; tel. (10) 57-29-24; e-mail ecocentr@sci.am; internet www.ecocentre.am; f. 1989; attached to Nat. Acad. of Sciences of Armenia; research areas: environment, assessment of natural resources, food chain risk assessment; library of 1,686 vols; Dir ARMEN SAGHATELYAN.

Institute of Botany: Avan, 0063 Yerevan; tel. (10) 62-17-81; e-mail academy@sci.am; f. 1939; attached to Nat. Acad. of Sciences of Armenia; Dir A. A. CHARCHOGLYAN.

Institute of Microbiology: 2201 Abovian; tel. (222) 2-00-73; e-mail microbio@sci.am; f. 1961; attached to Nat. Acad. of Sciences of Armenia; library of 5,000 vols; Dir L. S. MARKOSYAN.

Institute of Molecular Biology: Hasratyan 7, 0014 Yerevan; tel. (10) 28-16-26; e-mail aboyajyan@sci.am; internet molbiol.sci.am; f. 1966; attached to Nat. Acad. of Sciences of Armenia; Dir Prof. ANNA BOYAJYAN; Deputy Dir ARSEN ARAKELYAN.

Institute of Zoology: ul. Paruyra Sevaka 7, 0044 Yerevan; tel. (10) 28-14-70; e-mail zool@sci.am; f. 1943; attached to Nat. Acad. of Sciences of Armenia; Dir S. H. MOVSESIAN.

Orbeli Institute of Physiology: Orbeli Bros St 22, 375028 Yerevan; tel. (10) 27-38-61; e-mail vsargsyan@neuroscience.am; f. 1943; attached to Nat. Acad. of Sciences of Armenia; library of 4,000 vols; Dir V. V. FANARDJIAN.

Sevan Institute of Hydroecology and Ichthyology: ul. Kirova 186, 1510 Sevan; tel. (10) 56-85-54; e-mail rhovan@sci.am; f. 1923; attached to Nat. Acad. of Sciences of Armenia; Dir R. HOVHANNISYAN.

State Microbial Depository Centre: 2201 Abovian; tel. (222) 2-32-40; e-mail microbio@sci.am; internet www.rcdm.am; f. 1993; attached to Nat. Acad. of Sciences of Armenia; library of 22,000 vols; Dir E. G. AFRIKIAN.

Mathematical Sciences

Institute of Mathematics: Marshala Bagramyana 24/5, 0019 Yerevan; tel. (10) 52-47-91; e-mail rafayel@instmath.sci.am; internet math.sci.am; f. 1971; attached to Nat. Acad. of Sciences of Armenia; Dir Dr RAFAYEL BARKHUDARYAN (acting); Scientific Sec. Dr ARPI STEPANYAN; publs *Armenian Journal of Mathematics* (2 a year), *Journal of Contemporary Mathematical Analysis* (6 a year).

Physical Sciences

Byurakan Astrophysical Observatory: Ashtarak raion, 0213 Byurakan; tel. (10) 24-85-75; e-mail ekhach@bao.sci.am; internet www.sci.am/ac/bao.html; f. 1946; attached to Nat. Acad. of Sciences of Armenia; Dir E. KHACHIKIAN.

Garni Geophysical Observatory: Pr. Marshal Baghramyana 24A, 0019 Yerevan; tel. (10) 52-54-61; e-mail romella.pashayan@geology.am; f. 1982; attached to Nat. Acad. of Sciences of Armenia; Dir L. A. HAKHVERDYAN.

Garni Space Astronomy Institute: Kotayk, 2215 Garni; tel. (10) 64-90-01; f. 1982; attached to Nat. Acad. of Sciences of Armenia; Dir G. A. GURZADYAN.

Institute of Chemical Physics: ul. Paruyra Sevak 5/2, 0014 Yerevan; tel. (10) 28-14-81; e-mail tavadyan@ichph.sci.am; internet www.chph.sci.am; f. 1975; attached to Nat. Acad. of Sciences of Armenia; library of 33,410 vols; Dir Prof. LEVOM TAVADYAN.

Institute of Fine Organic Chemistry: Pr. Azatutyana 26, 0014 Yerevan; tel. (10) 28-83-34; e-mail ifoc@msrc.am; f. 1955; attached to

Nat. Acad. of Sciences of Armenia; Dir B. T. GHARIBJANIAN.

Institute of General and Inorganic Chemistry: ul. Fioletova 11110, 0051 Yerevan; tel. (10) 23-07-38; f. 1957; attached to Nat. Acad. of Sciences of Armenia; Dir S. S. KARAKHANIAN.

Institute of Geological Sciences: Pr. Marshala Bagramyana 24A, 0019 Yerevan; tel. (10) 52-44-26; e-mail hrshah@sci.am; internet www.geology.am; f. 1935; attached to Nat. Acad. of Sciences of Armenia; conducts research on engineering geology and hydrogeology, general and regional geology, geochemistry and mineralogy of hydrothermal ore formations, geological informatics, geology and petrology of magmatic and metamorphic formations, lithogenesis of sedimentary and volcanic-sedimentary formations, seismic hazard assessment, seismic tectonics, volcanic hazard assessment, volcanology; Dir Prof. Dr ARKADY KARAKHANYAN; Scientific Deputy Dir Dr KHACHATUR MELIKSETIAN.

Institute of Geophysics and Engineering Seismology: Pr. Leningradyana 5, 3115 Gjumry; tel. (312) 3-12-61; e-mail as_iges@shirak.am; f. 1961; attached to Nat. Acad. of Sciences of Armenia; Dir S. M. HOVHANNISYAN.

Institute of Organic Chemistry: ul. Zakaria Kanakertsy 167A, 0091 Yerevan; tel. (10) 28-35-21; internet www.stcopc.sci.am; f. 1935; attached to Nat. Acad. of Sciences of Armenia; Dir SH. H. BADANYAN.

Research Institute of Radiophysical Measurements: ul. Komitasa 49/4, 0014 Yerevan; tel. (10) 23-49-90; Dir P. M. GERUNI.

Yerevan Physics Institute: ul. Bratev Alikhanyan 2, 0036 Yerevan; tel. (10) 34-15-00; e-mail asnl@yerphi.am; internet www.yerphi.am; f. 1942; particle and nuclear physics; library of 10,000 vols; Dir ASHOT CHINGARIAN.

PHILOSOPHY AND PSYCHOLOGY

Institute of Philosophy, Sociology and Law: Aram St 44, 0010 Yerevan; tel. (10) 53-05-71; e-mail gevork@sci.am; internet www.ipsol.sci.am; f. 1969; attached to Nat. Acad. of Sciences of Armenia; scientific research on philosophy, history of Armenian philosophy, aesthetics, Armenian law and history, sociology and political science; library of 7,000 vols; Dir Prof. Dr GEVORG POGHOYSAN.

TECHNOLOGY

Institute for Physical Research: 0210 Ashtarak; tel. (232) 31172; e-mail ifi@ipr.sci.am; f. 1968; attached to Nat. Acad. of Sciences of Armenia; Dir Prof. ARAM PAPOYAN.

Institute of Applied Problems of Physics: Str. Hr. Nersesian 25, 0014 Yerevan; tel. (10) 24-11-10; e-mail amkrtchyan@sci.am; internet www.sci.am/ac/iapp.html; f. 1980; attached to Nat. Acad. of Sciences of the Republic of Armenia; Dir Dr A. H. MKRTCHYAN; Scientific Sec. VARDAN V. MARGARYAN.

Institute of Mechanics: Pr. Marshala Bagramyana 24B, 0019 Yerevan; tel. (10) 52-48-90; e-mail mechins@sci.am; f. 1955; attached to Nat. Acad. of Sciences of Armenia; Dir L. A. AGHALOVIAN.

Institute of Problems in Informatics and Automation: ul. Paruyra Sevaka 1, 0014 Yerevan; tel. (10) 28-58-12; e-mail shouk@sci.am; internet ipia.sci.am; f. 1957; attached to Nat. Acad. of Sciences of Armenia; Dir YU. H. SHOUKOURIAN.

Institute of Radiophysics and Electronics: Alikhanyan Brothers St 1, 0203 Ashtarak; tel. (10) 28-78-50; e-mail office@irphe.am; internet www.irphe.am; f. 1960; attached to Nat. Acad. of Sciences of Armenia; library of 12,000 vols; Dir Dr ARSEN HAKHOUMIAN; Deputy Dir Dr EMIL ASMARYAN.

Special Experimental Design Technological Institute: Sarkisyana 5A, 3101 Gjumry; tel. (312) 4-56-63; e-mail academy@sci.am; f. 1976; attached to Nat. Acad. of Sciences of Armenia; Dir R. Y. SARKISSYAN.

Yerevan Automated Control Systems Scientific Research Institute: ul. A. Akopyana 3, 0003 Yerevan; tel. (10) 27-77-79; e-mail atoyan@yercsi.am; internet www.yercsi.am; f. 1992; Dir R. ATOIAN.

Yerevan Computer Research and Development Institute: Hagop Hagopyan 3, 0033 Yerevan; tel. (10) 27-77-79; e-mail ghovhan@ycrdi.am; internet www.ycrdi.am; f. 1956; Dir G. T. HOVHANNISIAN.

Yerevan Telecommunications Research Institute: Dzorapy 26, 0015 Yerevan; tel. (10) 56-60-61; e-mail mark@yetri.am; internet www.yetri.am; f. 1978.

Libraries and Archives

Yerevan

Fundamental Scientific Library of the National Academy of Sciences of Armenia: Baghramyana Ave 24D, 0019 Yerevan; tel. (10) 52-47-50; e-mail tigran@flib.sci.am; internet www.flib.sci.am; f. 1935; 3m. vols; Dir Dr TIGRAN ZARGARYAN.

Matenadaran Institute of Ancient Armenian Manuscripts: Mashtots Ave 53, Yerevan; tel. (10) 56-25-78; e-mail contacts@matenadaran.am; internet www.matenadaran.am; f. 1959; incorporates research institute of Armenian textology and codicology; 17,000 Armenian MSS dating from 5th to 18th centuries, miniature paintings, 100,000 archival documents and works by Greek, Syrian, Persian, Arabic, Latin, Georgian and Ethiopian authors; Dir S. AREVSHATIAN; publ. *Banber Matenadarani*.

National Centre of Innovation and Entrepreneurship: Komitas 49/3, 0051 Yerevan; tel. (10) 23-67-74; e-mail info@innovcentre.am; internet www.innovcentre.am; f. 1961 as Armenian Centre for Scientific and Technical Information, current name adopted 2009; 22m. vols; Dir H. E. MARGARYAN; publ. *Gitutyun ev Tekhnika* (Science and Technology, online).

National Library of Armenia: Teryan 72, 0009 Yerevan; tel. (10) 58-42-59; e-mail compdpt@nla.am; internet www.nla.am; f. 1919; 6.2m. vols; Dir DAVIT SARGSYAN.

Republican Scientific Medical Library: Roubinyants St 29/3, 0035 Yerevan; tel. (10) 24-96-77; e-mail info@medlib.am; internet www.medlib.am; f. 1939; attached to Nat. Acad. of Sciences of Armenia; 500,000 vols, theses, serials, microfiche and audiovisual items; Dir ANNA SHIRINYAN.

Yerevan State University Library: ul. Mravyana 1, 0049 Yerevan; internet lib.ysu.am; 1.5m. vols; Dir V. S. ARSLANIAN.

Museums and Art Galleries

Yerevan

Armenian State Historical Museum: Republic Sq. 4, 0010 Yerevan; tel. (10) 58-27-61; e-mail museum@cln.am; internet www.historymuseum.am; f. 1919; archaeological, ethnographical, documentary and other evidence charting history and culture of Armenia from prehistoric times; Dir ANELKA GRIGORIAN.

Geological Museum of the Institute of Geology: ul. Aboviana 10, Yerevan; tel. (10) 58-06-63; f. 1937; Dir G. B. MEZHLUMYAN.

National Gallery of Armenia: Arami 1, 0010 Yerevan; tel. (10) 58-08-12; e-mail galleryarmenia@yahoo.com; internet www.gallery.am; f. 1921; W European, Armenian, Russian and Oriental art; library of 10,330 vols; Dir FARAON MIRZOYAN.

Yegishe Charents State Museum of Literature and Art: Mashtots St 17, Yerevan; tel. (10) 53-55-94; f. 1921; Armenian literature (since 18th century), theatre, cinema and music; library of 84,526 vols, 862,252 MSS; Dir H. BAKHCHINYAN.

Yerevan Children's Picture Gallery: ul. Aboviana 13, Yerevan; tel. (10) 52-78-93; f. 1970; works of art by children of Armenian and other nationalities; Dir H. IKITIAN.

Universities

ARMENIAN–RUSSIAN (SLAVONIC) STATE UNIVERSITY

Hovsep Emin Str. 123, 0051 Yerevan
Telephone: (10) 28-97-00
E-mail: rector@rau.am
Internet: www.rau.am
Founded 1998 by govts of Russia and Armenia
State control
Languages of instruction: Armenian, Russian
Academic year: September to June
Rector: Prof. Dr ARMEN DARBINYAN
Library of 71,000 vols, 2,000 journals
Number of teachers: 290
Number of students: 2,482
Publication: *Vestnik* (2 a year)

DEANS

Faculty of Applied Mathematics and Information Technologies: Dr VLADIMIR YEGIAZARYAN
Faculty of Biomedical Sciences: Prof. Dr HRACHIK VARDAPETYAN
Faculty of Economics: ALBERT VARDANYAN
Faculty of Foreign Languages and Area Studies: Assoc. Prof. ARMINE SIMONYAN
Faculty of Journalism: RAFAEL AIRAPETYAN
Faculty of Law: Dr KAREN SARDARYAN
Faculty of Philology: Prof. ANAID KHACHIKYAN
Faculty of Physics and Technology: Dr HAYK SARKISYAN
Faculty of Politology: Dr VAHAN MELIKYAN
Faculty of Psychology: Dr ASYA BERBERYAN
Faculty of Tourism and Advertisement: Dr NINA KEVORKOVA

ARMENIAN STATE PEDAGOGICAL UNIVERSITY

Khandyjan 5, 0070 Yerevan
Telephone: (10) 52-26-04
E-mail: armped@netsys.am
Founded 1922, present status 2000
State control
Academic year: September to July
Rector: MISAK DAVTYAN
Number of teachers: 620
Number of students: 4,200
Publication: *Mankavarzh* (12 a year)

DEANS

Armenian Language and Literature: MARTIN GILAVIAN
Art and Aesthetic Education: ARKADIY SHEKUNTS
Biology and Chemistry: MEZHLUM YERITSIAN
Culture: RUBEN MIRZAKHANIAN
History and Geography: POGHOS SIMONIAN
Industrial Pedagogy: KLEMENT ANANIAN
Mathematics and Physics: ALEXANDER GHUSHCHIAN
Primary Education and Defectology: DIMITRIY NAZARIAN
Psychology and Pedagogics: ROBERT DASHIAN
Public Professions: KAMO MKRYTCHIAN

FRENCH UNIVERSITY OF ARMENIA

Aigestan 8, 0067 Yerevan
Telephone: (10) 57-16-04
E-mail: ufa@arminco.com
Internet: www.ufa.am
Founded 2000
State control
Rector: PAUL ROUSSET
Sec.-Gen. and Dir for Studies: LUCIE HUCHOT

DEANS

Faculty of Business: NORAYR SAFARIAN
Faculty of Commerce: ARTAK MELKONIAN
Faculty of Law: GRIGOR BADIRIAN

GAVAR STATE UNIVERSITY

Azatutian 1, 1201 Gavar
Telephone: (264) 25775
E-mail: infogsu@mail.ru
Internet: www.gsu.am
Founded 1993; attached to RA Min. of Education and Science
State control
Languages of instruction: Armenian, English, German, Russian
Academic year: September to June
Rector: RUZANNA HAKOBYAN
Vice-Rector: ARSEN APROYAN
Vice-Rector: NELLI KUTUZYAN
Librarian: YELENA HAKOBYAN
Library of 40,000 vols, yearly collns of the Materials of GSU Scientific Confs
Number of teachers: 200
Number of students: 3,000

DEANS

Faculty of Economics: SAMVEL AMIRKHANYAN
Faculty of Humanities: HAMLET GHAJOYAN
Faculty of Natural Sciences: MARTIN AVAGIAN
Faculty of Part-Time Education: NELLI KUTUZYAN
Faculty of Philology: VIKTOR KATVALYAN

STATE ENGINEERING UNIVERSITY OF ARMENIA (POLYTECHNIC)

ul. Teryana 105, 0009 Yerevan
Telephone: (10) 56-79-68
E-mail: info@seua.am
Internet: www.seua.am
Founded 1933
State control
Languages of instruction: Armenian, English, Russian
Academic year: September to July
Faculties of applied mathematics, chemical technologies and environmental engineering, computer systems and informatics, correspondence education, cybernetics, electrical engineering, machine building, mechanics and machine study, mining and metallurgy, power engineering, radio engineering and communication systems, transportation systems
Rector: ARA S. AVETISYAN
Library of 950,000 vols
Number of teachers: 900
Number of students: 10,000

YEREVAN STATE MEDICAL UNIVERSITY AFTER MKHITAR HERATSI

Koryun Str. 2, 0025 Yerevan
Telephone: (10) 58-25-32
E-mail: info@ysmu.am
Internet: www.ysmu.am
Founded 1920
State control
Languages of instruction: Armenian, English, Russian
Academic year: September to June
Rector: Prof. Dr MIKAYEL NARIMANYAN
Vice-Rector for Academic Affairs: Prof. Dr SAMVEL AVETISYAN
Vice-Rector for Clinical Affairs: Prof. Dr ARMEN MINASYAN
Vice-Rector for Financial and Business Affairs: ASHOT ZALINYAN
Vice-Rector for Int. Relations: Dr YERVAND SAHAKYAN
Vice-Rector for Postgraduate and Continuing Medical Education: Prof. Dr ARMEN HAMBARDZUMYAN
Library of 524,980 vols
Number of teachers: 1,052
Number of students: 5,008
Publications: *Apaga Bzhishk* (Future Doctor), *Medicine, Science and Education*, *New Armenian Medical Journal*

DEANS

Department of International Students' Education Affairs: ANNA SARGSYAN
Faculty of General Medicine: NUNE SHAHVERDYAN
Faculty of Military Medicine: SAMVEL GALSTYAN
Faculty of Pharmacy: BAGRAT YENOKYAN
Faculty of Postgraduate and Continuing Education: ARMEN HAMBARDZUMYAN
Faculty of Stomatology: LAZAR YESAYAN

YEREVAN STATE UNIVERSITY

Alex Manoogian 1, 0025 Yerevan
Telephone: (10) 55-46-29
E-mail: rector@ysu.am
Internet: www.ysu.am
Founded 1919
State control
Language of instruction: Armenian
Academic year: September to June
Rector: ARAM H. SIMONYAN
Vice-Rector for Academic Affairs: ALEKSANDR K. GRIGORYAN
Vice-Rector for Admin.-Economic Issues: ARARAT TS. MALKHASYAN
Vice-Rector for Scientific Policy and Int. Cooperation: GEGHAM G. GEVORGYAN
Vice-Rector for Students, Alumni and Public Relations: RUBEN L. MARKOSYAN
Dir for Library: ASHOT S. ALEKSANYAN
Library of 2,010,960 vols
Number of teachers: 1,571
Number of students: 18,000
Publications: *Physical and Mathematical Sciences* (3 a year), *Proceedings of Yerevan State University*, *Scientific Bulletins* (geology and geography, biology and chemistry, 3 a year)

DEANS

Faculty of Armenian Philology: ARTSRUN AVAGYAN
Faculty of Biology: EMIL GEVORGYAN
Faculty of Chemistry: TARIEL V. GHOCHIKYAN
Faculty of Economics: HAYK L. SARGSYAN
Faculty of Geology and Geography: MARAT A. GRIGORYAN
Faculty of History: EDIK G. MINASYAN
Faculty of Informatics and Applied Mathematics: VAHRAM ZH. DUMANYAN
Faculty of International Relations: GEGHAM H. PETROSYAN
Faculty of Journalism: NAGHASH N. MARTIROSYAN
Faculty of Law: GAGIK S. GHAZINYAN
Faculty of Mathematics and Mechanics: ARTHUR A. SAHAKYAN
Faculty of Oriental Studies: GURGEN V. MELIKIAN
Faculty of Philosophy and Psychology: ALEXANDER S. BAGHDASARYAN
Faculty of Physics: ROLAND M. AVAGYAN
Faculty of Radiophysics: YURI L. VARDANIAN
Faculty of Romanic-Germanic Philology: SAMVEL A. ABRAHAMYAN
Faculty of Russian Philology: PAVEL B. BALAYAN
Faculty of Sociology: ARTHUR E. MKRTICHYAN
Faculty of Theology: ANUSHAVAN BISHOP ZHAMKOCHYAN

YEREVAN STATE UNIVERSITY OF LINGUISTICS, 'V. BRUSOV'

Toumanian 42, 0002 Yerevan
Telephone: (10) 53-05-52
E-mail: yslu@brusov.am
Internet: www.brusov.am
Founded 1935
State control
Faculties of foreign languages, linguistics and inter-cultural communication, Romance and Germanic languages, Russian language and literature
Rector: SUREN ZOLYAN
Number of teachers: 409
Number of students: 4,371

Other Higher Educational Institutes

Armenian Agricultural Academy: ul. Teryana 74, 0009 Yerevan; tel. (10) 52-45-41; e-mail agacad@arminco.com; internet www.arminco.com/homepages/usdaes/acad/acad.htm; f. 1994 from merger of Armenian Agricultural Institute (f. 1930) and Yerevan Zootechnical and Veterinary Institute (f. 1928); faculties of advanced studies, agrarian studies, economics, engineering, technology, zootechnical and veterinary studies; library: 563,389 vols; 419 teachers; 4,322 students; Rector A. KHACHATRIAN; publs *Agronews* (52 a year), *Agroscience* (12 a year), *News* (52 a year).

Armenian State Institute of Physical Education: Alex Manoogian 11, 0070 Yerevan; tel. (10) 55-24-31; f. 1945; faculties of education, sports; Rector VAHRAM ARAKELIAN.

Gyumri M. Nalbandian State Pedagogical Institute: Paruir Sevak 4, 3126 Gyumri; tel. (312) 3-77-32; e-mail postmaster@shirak.am; f. 1935; faculties of foreign languages, history and philology, natural sciences and geography, pedagogy, physical education, physics and mathematics; Rector HOURIK HARUTUNIAN.

Vanadzor State Pedagogical Institute: Tigran Mets 36, 2000 Vanadzor; tel. (322) 4-63-87; e-mail mankocol@hragir.aua.am; f. 1969; faculties of biology, history and geography, mathematics and physics, philology and pre-school education, psychology; 310

teachers; 1,900 students; Rector RAFIK YEDOVAN; Vice-Rector SHVAITS SAHAKIAN.

Yerevan Institute of Architecture and Construction: ul. Teryana 105, 0009 Yerevan; tel. (10) 58-01-77; internet yeriac.iatp .irex.am; f. 1989; faculties of architecture, construction and urban economy, hydrotechnical studies, industrial and civil construction, technology, transport construction; library: 1.4m. vols; 262 teachers; 1,624 students; Rector A. G. BEGLARIAN.

Yerevan Komitas State Conservatoire: Sayat-Nova 1A, 0001 Yerevan; tel. (10) 58-11-64; e-mail ysc@edu.am; f. 1920; orchestral, chamber, choral, folk music; library: 130,000 vols; 386 teachers; 1,045 students; Rector Prof. ARMEN SMHATYAN.

Yerevan State Academy of Fine Arts: Isahakian 36, 0009 Yerevan; tel. (10) 56-07-26; e-mail ysifa@edu.am; internet www.iatp .am/yafa; f. 1945; faculties of art, decorative arts, design; brs in Gjumri and Dilijan; library: 25,000 vols; 98 teachers; 428 students; Rector Prof. ARAM ISABEKIAN.

AUSTRALIA

The Higher Education System

In 2010 there were 39 public universities and two private universities, one Australian branch of an overseas university and three other self-accrediting higher education institutions as well as over 150 non-self-accrediting higher education providers (including several that are registered in more than one state or territory) approved by state/territory to offer specific higher education programmes. In 2011/12 more than 1.2m. students (including 335,000 foreign students) were enrolled in higher education, with 93.7% of students going to the public universities. Under the federal system of government in Australia, the six states and two territories are responsible for providing education services for their own residents. The Australian Constitution, however, empowers the Federal Government to make special-purpose financial grants to the states for education in both government and non-government schools. Responsibility for educational policy rests with the Minister for Higher Education and Skills. An education department headed by a Director-General deals with all aspects of education within each state. In November 2011 the Federal Government announced the establishment of the Office for Learning and Teaching, which was to support and promote excellence in higher education with funding of $A50m. over four years for a Grants and Awards Programme.

The Commonwealth (through the Federal Government) is the most important source of funding for universities; in 2003 the Government contributed 41% of accounted funding. Under the Higher Education Support Act 2003, an education provider has to be approved by the Federal Government before it can receive grants or its students be eligible for government assistance. Most Australian students contribute to the cost of their courses under the Higher Education Loan Programme (HELP), with the amount of the student's contribution (in the form of a deferred payment through an interest-free loan) depending on the cost of the course and likely future earnings. HELP is jointly administered by the Department of Education and the Australian Taxation Office. Financial assistance is available to certain students subject to a means and assets test. In addition, there are a limited number of equity and merit scholarships which exempt students from the HELP charge.

Universities are administered by a Governing Body such as a Council, Senate or Board of Governors, chaired by a Chancellor. A Chief Executive, usually a Vice-Chancellor or President, oversees the day-to-day running of the university and reports to the Governing Body.

In 1990 a Unified National System was established, replacing the previously existing binary system of universities and non-university institutions. The Australian Qualifications Framework (AQF) was introduced in 1995 and implemented by 1999, leading to the development of a comprehensive national framework for post-secondary education and training. The AQF identifies six post-secondary levels of qualification: Diploma, Advanced Diploma, Bachelors degree, Graduate Certificate and Graduate Diploma, Masters degree and doctoral degree. In July 2011 a new independent national regulatory and quality agency, the Tertiary Education Quality and Standards Agency, was established. In 2012 the Education Services for Overseas Students (ESOS) Act gave the Agency regulatory responsibility for full registration, compliance and enforcement powers over higher education providers; it was also charged with creating a national register of higher education to provide an authoritative source of information on the status of registered institutes.

Universities administer their own admissions processes. Admission is usually based on a combination of completion of Year 12, leading to the award of the Senior Secondary Certificate of Education (the name may vary in each state or territory), and entrance test scores. Applicants who have not completed a recent or standard Year 12 qualification may take the Special Tertiary Admissions Test (STAT), which assesses skills rather than knowledge of the curriculum. The Diploma and Advanced Diploma, requiring two and three years of study respectively, are sub-degree qualifications that may in certain circumstances allow entry to the second year of a Bachelors degree. The Bachelors degree may be rated either Ordinary/Pass after three years of study or Honours after at least four years of study. The Graduate Certificate and Graduate Diploma require one or two semesters of full-time study respectively following a Bachelors degree. The Masters degree is awarded after two years of study following an Ordinary/Pass Bachelors or after one year of study following an Honours Bachelors. Finally, the doctoral degree (mainly Doctor of Philosophy—PhD) requires three years of full-time study and research plus submission of a thesis. Other, more recent, doctoral-level awards include the Professional Doctorate and the Higher Doctorate.

Vocational education and training (VET) is supervised by the Australian National Training Authority, established in 1994. The Australian Recognition Framework approves VET qualifications. VET programmes are offered at upper-secondary schools, Technical and Further Education colleges and state- or territory-accredited private providers. VET programmes require between one and three years' study depending upon the requirements of the course and the level of qualification sought. The range of VET qualifications is as follows: Certificates I, II, III, IV; Diploma; Advanced Diploma. Teacher training usually requires either a three-year Bachelors degree in the subject to be taught, followed by a one- to two-year (Graduate) Diploma in Education, or the four-year Bachelor of Education.

Regulatory and Representative Bodies

GOVERNMENT

Department of Education: GPOB 9880, Canberra, ACT 2601; 50 Marcus Clarke St, Canberra, ACT 2601; tel. (3) 5454-5345; e-mail planningandperformance@deewr.gov.au; internet education.gov.au; Minister for School Education CHRISTOPHER PYNE.

ACCREDITATION

AEI-NOOSR: Australian Govt, Dept of Education, GPOB 1407, Canberra, ACT 2601; tel. 354-545-245; e-mail educational.noosr@education.gov.au; internet www.aei.gov.au/services-and-resources/pages/aeinoosr.aspx; provides official information and advice on the comparability of overseas qualifications with Australian qualifications; Dir of AEI-NOOSR LIZ CAMPBELL-DORNING.

Australian Qualifications Framework: GPOB 9839, Adelaide, SA 5001; Level 9, 63 Pirie St, Adelaide, SA 5000; tel. (8) 8406-4735; e-mail aqfc@aqf.edu.au; internet www.aqf.edu.au; f. 1995; nat. policy for regulated qualifications in Australian education and training; incorporates the qualifications from each education and training sector into a single nat. qualifications framework; Chair. JOHN DAWKINS; Exec. Dir LYNDAL GROOM.

Tertiary Education Quality and Standards Agency: GPOB 1672, Melbourne, VIC 3001; tel. (3) 8306-2400; e-mail enquiries@teqsa.gov.au; internet www.teqsa.gov.au; f. 2011; all Australian Univ. Quality Agency operations transferred to the Tertiary Education Quality and Standards Agency; nat. regulator of Australia's higher education sector incl. both public and private univs; Chief Commr Dr CAROL NICOLL.

NATIONAL BODIES

Adult Learning Australia Inc: POB 298, Flinders Lane, Melbourne, VIC 8009; CAE Bldg, Level 4, 253 Flinders Lane, Melbourne, VIC, 8009; tel. (3) 9652-0861; e-mail info@ala.asn.au; internet www.ala.asn.au; f. 1960 as Australian Asscn of Adult Education, present name 1998; coordinates and encourages adult and community education at nat. level; publishes educational books; lobbies govts and appropriate depts; holds nat. confs; 500 mems, also corporate mems; Pres. DOROTHY LUCARDIE; Sec. RON CURRIE; Treas. GEORGE PAPALLO; publs *Australian Journal of Adult Learning* (3 a year), *Quest* (4 a year, online, www.ala.asn.au/quest-online).

Australian Research Council: GPOB 2702, Canberra, ACT 2601; Level 2, 11 Lancaster Pl., Majura Park, ACT 2609; tel. (2) 6287-6600; e-mail info@arc.gov.au; internet www.arc.gov.au; f. 1965, present name 1988; attached to Industry, Innovation, Science, Research and Tertiary Education (IISRTE) portfolio, Govt of Australia; advises the Govt on research matters; manages the Nat. Competitive Grants Program and Excellence in Research for Australia (ERA); research and research training in fields of science, social sciences and humanities; 135 mems; Minister for Climate Change, Industry and Innovation GREG COMBET.

Centre for Adult Education (CAE): Level 2, 253 Flinders Lane, Melbourne, VIC 3000; tel. (3) 9652-0611; e-mail international@cae.edu.au; internet www.cae.edu.au; f. 1947; statutory body engaged in providing adult education and business training in VIC; library of 120,000 vols; Chair. FRANK KING; CEO DENISE O'BRIEN; publs *Dialogue* (every 3 years, catalogue of book, film and music titles available for self-directed learning groups), *Program Guide* (5 a year).

Universities Australia: GPOB 1142, Canberra, ACT 2601; 1 Geils Court, Deakin, ACT 2600; tel. (2) 6285-8100; e-mail contact@universitiesaustralia.edu.au; internet www.universitiesaustralia.edu.au; f. 1920 as Australian Vice-Chancellors' Cttee, present status 2007; acts as a consultative and advisory body for all univ. affairs; provides information about Australian univs; Chair. Prof. SANDRA HARDING; CEO BELINDA ROBINSON.

Learned Societies

GENERAL

Academy of the Social Sciences in Australia: GPOB 1956, Canberra, ACT 2601; 26 Balmain Crescent, Acton, ACT 2601; tel. (2) 6249-1788; e-mail assa.secretariat@assa.edu.au; internet www.assa.edu.au; f. 1943 as Social Science Research Cttee, current name adopted 1970; 540 fellows; Pres. Prof. DEBORAH TERRY; Exec. Dir Dr JOHN BEATON; publs *Dialogue* (3 a year), *Occasional Paper* (irregular).

Australian Academy of the Humanities: GPOB 93, Canberra, ACT 2601; 3 Liversidge St, Acton, Canberra, ACT 2601; tel. (2) 6125-9860; e-mail enquiries@humanities.org.au; internet www.humanities.org.au; f. 1969; archaeology, European languages and cultures, classical studies, history, fine arts, Asian studies, English, linguistics, philosophy and the history of ideas, religion, cultural and communication studies; 575 mems; Pres. Prof. LESLEY JOHNSON; Vice-Pres. Prof. DEIRDRE COLEMAN; Vice-Pres. and Int. Sec. Prof. JOHN FITZGERALD; Treas. Prof. RICHARD WATERHOUSE; Exec. Dir, Secretariat Dr CHRISTINA PAROLIN; Hon. Sec. Prof. GRAEME CLARKE; publ. *Humanities Australia* (1 a year).

AGRICULTURE, FISHERIES AND VETERINARY SCIENCE

Australian Institute of Agricultural Science and Technology: POB 130, Curtin, ACT 2605; Suite Three, 22 Strangways St, Curtin, ACT 2605; tel. (2) 6163-8122; e-mail members@aiast.com.au; internet www.aiast.com.au; f. 1935; 2,500 mems; Nat. Pres. MIKE STEPHENS; Dir and Company Sec. WILLIAM LEWIS; Dir and Treas. ROBERT A. PATTERSON; publ. *Agricultural Science* (4 a year).

Australian Veterinary Association: Unit 40, 6 Herbert St, St Leonards, NSW 2065; tel. (2) 9431-5000; e-mail members@ava.com.au; internet www.ava.com.au; f. 1921; 5,500 mems; Pres. Dr BARRY SMYTH; Treas. Dr BEN GARDINER; publ. *Australian Veterinary Journal* (12 a year).

Dairy Industry Association of Australia Inc.: PMB 16, Werribee, VIC 3030; 671 Sneydes Rd, Werribee, VIC 3030; tel. (3) 8742-6600; e-mail info@diaa.asn.au; internet www.diaa.asn.au; f. 1946; divs in each State; 1,600 mems; Pres. WAYNE AUSTIN; Sec. KRISTINE MANSER; publ. *Australian Dairy Foods* (6 a year).

Primary Industries Ministerial Council: GPOB 858, Canberra, ACT 2601; tel. (2) 6272-5216; e-mail scopi@daff.gov.au; internet www.mincos.gov.au; f. 2001; facilitates the implementation of plans and proposals; works with Australian/state/territory and New Zealand govt ministers responsible for agriculture, food, fibre, forestry, fisheries and aquaculture industries; Exec. Dir Dr MAXINE COOPER; Sec. CONALL O'CONNELL.

ARCHITECTURE AND TOWN PLANNING

Australian Council of National Trusts: POB 413, Campbell, ACT 2612; 14/71 Constitution Ave, Campbell, ACT 2612; tel. (2) 6247-6766; e-mail admin@nationaltrust.org.au; internet www.nationaltrust.org.au; f. 1965; Federal Ccl of the State and Territory Nat. Trusts est. for the conservation of lands and bldgs of beauty or of nat., historic, scientific, architectural or cultural interest and Aboriginal relics and wildlife; 80,000 mems; Chair. Dr GRAEME L. BLACKMAN.

Australian Institute of Architects: POB 3373, Manuka, Canberra, ACT 2603; Level 2/7, Nat. Circuit, Barton, ACT 2600; tel. (2) 6121-2000; e-mail national@architecture.com.au; internet www.architecture.com.au; f. 1930; 10,000 mems; Nat. Pres. SHELLEY PENN; CEO DAVID PARKEN; publ. *Architecture Australia* (6 a year).

Australian Institute of Quantity Surveyors: Level 6, 65 York St, Sydney, NSW 2000; tel. (2) 9262-1822; e-mail education@aiqs.com.au; internet www.aiqs.com.au; f. 1971; 4,326 mems; Pres. PETER COX; Gen. Man. TREVOR SANDERS; publs *Australian Journal of Construction Economics and Building* (2 a year), *The Building Economist* (4 a year).

Planning Institute of Australia: POB 5427, Kingston, ACT 2604; tel. (2) 6262-5933; e-mail ea@planning.org.au; internet www.planning.org.au; f. 1951; 3,444 mems; CEO KIRSTY KELLY; Nat. Pres. DYAN CURRIE; Hon. Treas. MAX FRAGAR; publ. *Australian Planner* (4 a year).

BIBLIOGRAPHY, LIBRARY SCIENCE AND MUSEOLOGY

Australian Library and Information Association: POB 6335, Kingston, ACT 2604; ALIA House, 9–11 Napier Close, Deakin, ACT 2600; tel. (2) 6215-8222; e-mail enquiry@alia.org.au; internet alia.org.au; f. 1937; 6,000 mems; Pres. ROXANNE MISSINGHAM; Exec. Dir SUE HUTLEY; publs *Australian Academic and Research Libraries* (4 a year), *Australian Library Journal* (4 a year).

Bibliographical Society of Australia and New Zealand: c/o Dr Chris Tiffin, Hon. Sec. BSANZ, School of EMSAH, Univ. of Queensland, Brisbane, QLD 4072; tel. (7) 3369-1783; internet www.bsanz.org; f. 1969; publishes a journal and occasional publs, holds confs; 200 mems; Pres. Dr DONALD KERR; Treas. ANDREW SERGEANT; publ. *Script & Print* (4 a year).

Museums Australia: POB 266, Civic Sq., ACT 2608; c/o National Museum of Australia, Acton, ACT 2601; tel. (2) 6230-0346; e-mail ma@museumsaustralia.org.au; internet www.museumsaustralia.org.au; f. 1993; provides devt services and coordination of specialist networks across the museums and galleries in Australia; advocacy of museums to all levels of govt and community; ensuring museums and cultural heritage instns provide primary content and learning materials for the Australian nat. curriculum; and to foster high standards in all aspects of museum operations through nat. advocacy, professional devt, training, research, policy formulation, publs, collaborative facilitation and partnerships; 2,000 mems (instns and individuals); Nat. Pres. ANDREW SAYERS; Nat. Dir BERNICE MURPHY; publ. *Museums Australia Magazine* (4 a year).

ECONOMICS, LAW AND POLITICS

Australian Bar Association: Ground Fl., Inns of Court N Quay, Brisbane, QLD 4001; tel. (7) 3238-5100; e-mail mail@austbar.asn.au; internet www.austbar.asn.au; f. 1962; 3,440 mems; Pres. CRAIG COLVIN; Hon. Treas. RAELENE WEBB; Hon. Sec. DAN O'CONNOR.

Australian Institute of Credit Management: Level 3, 619 Pacific Highway, St Leonards, NSW 2065; tel. (2) 9906-4563; e-mail aicm@aicm.com.au; internet www.aicm.com.au; f. 1937; 3,000 mems; undertakes research and makes submissions to govts on credit related issues; CEO TERRY COLLINS; Nat. Training Man. DEL CSETI; publs *AICM Journal* (5 a year), *Credit Management in Australia* (5 a year).

Australian Institute of International Affairs: 32 Thesiger Court, Deakin, ACT 2600; tel. (2) 6282-2133; e-mail ceo@aiia.asn.au; internet www.aiia.asn.au; f. 1924, formed as a nat. body in 1933; ind., non-profit org. seeking to promote interest in and understanding of int. affairs in Australia; 1,600 mems; Nat. Pres. JOHN MCCARTHY; Nat. Vice-Pres. ZARA KIMPTON; Nat. Exec. Dir MELISSA H. CONLEY TYLER; Treas. DAYLE REDDEN; publs *Australia in World Affairs* (every 5 years), *Australian Journal of International Affairs* (5 a year).

Australian Institute of Management: see under Libraries and Archives.

Australian Political Studies Association: The Univ. of Melbourne, School of Social and Political Science, Parkville, VIC 3010; tel. (3) 8344-8550; e-mail georgina.cahill@unimelb.edu.au; internet www.auspsa.org.au; f. 1952; sponsors nat. political science projects; int. exchange programmes with similar asscns; organizes an annual conf.; workshops; 312 mems; Pres. Assoc. Prof. ADRIAN LITTLE; Sec. and Treas.

Prof. JASON SHARMAN; publ. *Australian Journal of Political Science* (4 a year).

Australian Property Institute: 6 Campion St, Deakin, ACT 2600; POB 145, Curtin, ACT 2605; tel. (2) 6282-2411; e-mail national@api.org.au; internet www.api.org.au; f. 1926; 8,600 mems; Pres. BARRY BRAKEY; Dir GRANT WARNER; publs *Australian & New Zealand Valuation Principles & Standards Manual*, *Australian Property Journal* (4 a year), *Professional Practice* (1 a year), *Valuation Principles and Practices*.

Committee for Economic Development of Australia: Level 13, 440 Collins St, Melbourne, VIC 3000; tel. (3) 9662-3544; e-mail info@ceda.com.au; internet www.ceda.com.au; f. 1960; facilitates discussion, research and interdisciplinary communication in the interests of the devt of the nat. economy and the future of Australia; holds more than 250 events, seminars and exec. round tables each year; 1,000 orgs; Nat. Chair. GEOFF ALLEN; Chief Exec. Prof. STEPHEN MARTIN; publs *Australian Chief Executive* (4 a year), *Growth Reports*, *Information Papers*.

Economic Society of Australia: POB 937, St Ives, NSW 2075; tel. (2) 9440-0241; e-mail ecosoc@ecosoc.org.au; internet www.ecosoc.org.au; f. 1925; 7 brs across Australia; 1,400 mems; Pres. Prof. BRUCE CHAPMAN; Sec. Assoc. Prof. RUSSELL ROSS; Treas. BRENT TUCKER; publs *Economic Papers* (4 a year), *The Economic Record* (4 a year).

Institute of Public Affairs: Level 2, 410 Collins St, Melbourne, VIC 3000; tel. (3) 9600-4744; e-mail ipa@ipa.org.au; internet www.ipa.org.au; f. 1943; non-profit educational org. to study economic and industrial problems and to advance the cause of free enterprise in Australia; supported by 550 companies and 3,500 individuals; Chair. ROD KEMP; Exec. Dir JOHN ROSKAM; publs *Backgrounder* (10 a year), *Current Issues* (5 a year), *IPA Review* (4 a year).

Law Council of Australia: GPOB 1989, Canberra, ACT 2601; 19 Torrens St, Braddon, ACT 2612; tel. (2) 6246-3788; e-mail mail@lawcouncil.asn.au; internet www.lawcouncil.asn.au; f. 1933; advises govts, courts and federal agencies on ways in which the law and justice system can be improved for the benefit of the community; 56,000 mems; Pres. CATHERINE GALE; Sec. Gen. (vacant); Treas. MICHAEL COLBRAN; publ. *Australian Law Management Journal* (4 a year).

Law Society of New South Wales: 170 Phillip St, Sydney, NSW 2000; tel. (2) 9926-0333; e-mail lawsociety@lawsociety.com.au; internet www.lawsocnsw.asn.au; f. 1884; 21,000 mems; library of 32,000 vols; Pres. JUSTIN DOWD; Sec. C. CAWLEY; Treas. JOHN EADES; publs *Caveat* (irregular), *Law Society Journal* (12 a year).

Local Government Managers Australia: POB 5175, S Melbourne, VIC 3205; Level 2, 153–161 Park St, S Melbourne, VIC 3205; tel. (3) 9682-9222; e-mail national@lgma.org.au; internet www.lgma.org.au; f. 1936; professional local govt assoc. for gen. managers, chief execs and officers employed in management; 2,500 mems; Chief Exec. JOHN RAVLIC; publ. *Local Government Manager* (6 a year).

EDUCATION

Australian College of Educators: POB 73, Carlton, VIC 3053; tel. (3) 9035-5473; e-mail ace@austcolled.com.au; internet austcolled.com.au; f. 1959; an ind. professional asscn of educators from every field of education throughout Australia; encourages professional advancement of its mems and the nat. devt of education; brs and regional groups in each state and territory; conducts nat. and state confs, surveys and studies; 6,000 mems; CEO DEBRA GOLDFINCH; Nat. Pres. Dr LYNDSAY CONNORS; publ. *Professional Educator* (4 a year).

IDP Education Australia Ltd: Level 8, 535 Bourke St, Melbourne, VIC 3000; tel. (3) 9612-4400; e-mail info@idp.com; internet www.idp.com; f. 1969 as the Int. Devt Program of Australian Univs and Colleges Ltd, current name adopted 1994; placement and support service for people pursuing an int. education experience; provides English language proficiency services; 38 mem. Australian univs; CEO ANDREW THOMPSON.

Open and Distance Learning Association of Australia Inc.: POB 176, Bathurst, NSW 2795; tel. (2) 6332-3782; e-mail executive@odlaa.org; internet www.odlaa.org; f. 1974; professional asscn for teachers, educational developers and designers, researchers, consultants and administrators from Australia and overseas involved in open and distance learning; 85 mems; Pres. Dr SOM NAIDU; Sec. Dr MUTUOTA KIGOTHO; Treas. STEPHEN RELF; publ. *Distance Education* (3 a year).

FINE AND PERFORMING ARTS

Australia Council for the Arts: POB 788, Strawberry Hills, NSW 2012; 372 Elizabeth St, Cnr of Cooper St, Surry Hills, NSW 2010; tel. (2) 9215-9000; e-mail mail@australiacouncil.gov.au; internet www.australiacouncil.gov.au; f. 1968; aims to foster the devt of the arts through the programmes of 8 boards: music, dance, theatre, interdisciplinary/new media arts, literature, visual arts, community partnerships and Aboriginal and Torres Straits Islander Arts; library of 6,500 vols; Chair. RUPERT MEYER; Deputy Chair. ROBYN ARCHER; CEO TONY GRYBOWSKI.

Musicological Society of Australia: GPOB 2404, Canberra, ACT 2601; e-mail secretary@msa.org.au; internet www.msa.org.au; f. 1963; 290 mems; Pres. JANE DAVIDSON; National Sec. Dr JONATHAN MACINTOSH; Treas. Dr ROBERT FAULKNER; publ. *Musicology Australia* (2 a year).

Royal Art Society of New South Wales: 25–27 Walker St, N Sydney, NSW 2060; tel. (2) 9955-5752; e-mail lavender@royalart.com.au; internet www.royalart.com.au; f. 1880; school for painting (beginners to Diploma RAS of NSW); 400 mems; Pres. JUDY PENNEFATHER; Sec. and Gallery Man. CHRISTINE FEHER.

Royal Queensland Art Society Inc.: Unit 3, 162 Petrie Terrace, Brisbane, QLD 4000; tel. (7) 3367-1977; e-mail rqasi@oznetcom.com.au; internet www.rqas.com.au; f. 1887; encourages and promotes the cultivation and appreciation of the fine arts of painting, sculpture, architecture and the artistic crafts; 500 mems; Sec. VASHTI BARDSLEY.

Royal South Australian Society of Arts: POB 8154 Station Arcade, Adelaide, SA 5000; Cnr N Terrace and Kintore Ave, Adelaide, SA 5000; tel. (8) 8232-0450; e-mail rsasarts@bigpond.net.au; internet rsasarts.com.au; f. 1856; 702 mems; Pres. BEVERLY M. BILLS; Hon. Sec. JAMES E. G. RAGGATT; publ. *Kalori* (irregular).

Victorian Artists' Society: 430 Albert St, East Melbourne, VIC 3002; tel. (3) 9662-1484; e-mail admin@victorianartistssociety.com.au; internet www.victorianartistssociety.com.au; f. 1870; 4 galleries and a studio; 1,000 mems; Pres. GREGORY R. SMITH; Sec. TED DANSEY; Treas. CAROL PAGNON; publ. *Gallery on Eastern Hill*.

HISTORY, GEOGRAPHY AND ARCHAEOLOGY

Australian and New Zealand Association for Medieval and Early Modern Studies (Inc.): School of Humanities, M208, Univ. of Western Australia, 35 Stirling Highway, Crawley, WA 6009; e-mail lesley.obrien@uwa.edu.au; internet www.anzamems.arts.uwa.edu.au; f. 1996 by merger of ANZAMRS (Australian and New Zealand Asscn of Medieval and Renaissance Studies) and AHMEME (Australian Historians of Medieval and Early Modern Europe); supports research network; promotes all aspects of medieval, and early modern studies in Australia and New Zealand; 270 mems; Pres. Prof. CONSTANT MEWS (Monash Univ.); Sec. Dr MEGAN CASSIDY-WELCH (Monash Univ.); Treas. Dr DOLLY MACKINNON (Univ. of Queensland); publ. *Parergon* (2 a year).

Australian Numismatic Society: POB 366, Brookvale, NSW 2100; tel. (2) 9223-4578; e-mail anseditor@hotmail.com; internet www.the-ans.com; f. 1913; promotes the study of coins, banknotes and medals with particular reference to Australasia and the Pacific region; monthly meetings in Sydney and Brisbane; 199 mems (incl. overseas); Pres. JOHN VELTMEYER; Sec. MICHAEL TICHY; publs *ANS Journal*, *NAA Journal* (1 a year), *Report* (2 a year).

Geographical Society of New South Wales Inc.: Locked Bag 1797, Penrith, NSW 2751; tel. (2) 4736-0959; e-mail office@gsnsw.org.au; internet www.gsnsw.org.au; f. 1927; professional org. dedicated to the promotion, support and defence of geographical research, scholarship and education; management of environmental and social issues in Australia; expansion of geographical literacy among the public of NSW; 300 mems; Pres. Prof. KEVIN DUNN; Hon. Sec. MARTIN PLÜSS; Hon. Treas. JIM FORREST; publ. *Australian Geographer* (3 a year).

Mapping Sciences Institute, Australia: GPOB 1817, Brisbane, QLD 4000; tel. (7) 3343-7706; e-mail msiau@gil.com.au; internet www.mappingsciences.org.au; f. 1952; professional, NGO; Nat. Council and Divisions based on the Australian states and territories; holds biennial confs; 1,250 mems; Nat. Pres. DAVID FRASER; Hon. Sec. KEITH SMITH; Nat. Treas. JOHN MCCORMACK; publ. *Cartography* (2 a year).

Royal Australian Historical Society: History House, 133 Macquarie St, Sydney, NSW 2000; tel. (2) 9247-8001; e-mail history@rahs.org.au; internet www.rahs.org.au; f. 1901; 2,280 mems; library of 30,000 items; Pres. Dr ANNE-MAREE WHITAKER; Treas. Dr KATHRINE REYNOLDS; publs *History Magazine* (4 a year), *Journal of the Royal Australian Historical Society* (2 a year).

Royal Geographical Society of Queensland Inc.: 237 Milton Rd, Milton, QLD 4064; tel. (7) 3368-2066; e-mail info@rgsq.org.au; internet www.rgsq.org.au; f. 1885; monthly lectures, geographical trips, organizes Australian Geography Competition; 400 mems; library of 2,500 monographs, 320 periodicals, maps; Pres. DAVID CARSTENS; Vice-Pres. Prof. JAMIE SHULMEISTER; Administrator KATHRYN BERG; Sec. CHRIS SPRIGGS; Treas. JOHN NOWILL.

Royal Historical Society of Queensland: POB 12057, George St, Brisbane, QLD 4003; 115 William St, Brisbane, QLD; tel. (7) 3221-4198; e-mail info@queenslandhistory.org.au; internet queenslandhistory.org.au; f. 1913; Welsby library; research; historical documents preserved and filed; photographic colln; social history; museum; 600 mems; Pres. Dr IAN HADWEN; Man. CHRISTINA

MICHIE; publ. *Queensland History Journal* (4 a year).

Royal Historical Society of Victoria: 239 A'Beckett St, Melbourne, VIC 3000; tel. (3) 9326-9288; e-mail office@historyvictoria.org.au; internet www.historyvictoria.org.au; f. 1909; research; colln of historical material; exhibitions; mem. of the Federation of Australian Historical Societies; 1,600 mems; library of 8,000 vols, MSS, photographs, paintings and prints; Pres. Dr ANDREW LEMON; Treas. JOHN HULSKAMP; publ. *Victorian Historical Journal* (2 a year).

Royal Western Australian Historical Society: Stirling House, 49 Broadway, Nedlands, WA 6009; tel. (8) 9386-3841; e-mail histwest@git.com.au; internet www.histwest.org.au; f. 1926; runs museum, research library and bookshop specializing in W Australian history and archival products; 1,000 mems; Pres. Dr LENORE LAYMAN; Vice-Pres. JACK HONNIBALL; Treas. JULIA HEDLEY; publ. *Early Days* (1 a year).

Society of Australian Genealogists: Richmond Villa, 120 Kent St, Sydney, NSW 2000; tel. (2) 9247-3953; e-mail info@sag.org.au; internet www.sag.org.au; f. 1932; 5,500 mems; library of 20,000 vols, 1,000 microfilm reels, 1m. names on microfiche, 40,000 photographs, 30,000 MSS; Pres. and Hon. Treas. IAN JOHNSON; Hon. Sec. and Vice-Pres. MARTYN KILLION; publ. *Descent* (4 a year).

LANGUAGE AND LITERATURE

Alliance Française: POB 6125, O'Connor, ACT 2602; 66 McCaughey St, Turner, Canberra, ACT 2612; tel. (2) 6247-5027; e-mail director@alliancefrancaise.com.au; internet www.alliancefrancaise.com.au; offers courses and examinations in French language and culture and promotes cultural exchange with France; attached teaching centres in Adelaide, Albury, Armidale, Atherton, Ballarat, Blue Mountains, Brisbane, Canberra, Darwin, Davenport, Esperance, Eurobodolla, Geelong, Gold Coast, Gosford, Hobart, Illawarra, Launceston, Lismore, Melbourne, Merimbula, Milton/Ulladulla, Newcastle, Perth, Port Macquerie, Rockhampton, Sunshine Coast, Sydney, Toowoomba, Townsville, Wagga Wagga; Dir PHILIPPE MILLOUX.

Australasian and Pacific Society for Eighteenth-Century Studies: c/o Humanities Research Centre, Australian National University, ACT 0200; f. 1970; a sponsoring body of the David Nichol Smith Seminars; 80 mems; Pres. NICOLAS PELLETIER.

Australian Society of Authors Ltd: Suite C1.06, 22–36 Mountain St, Ultimo, NSW 2007; tel. (2) 9211-1004; e-mail asa@asauthors.org; internet www.asauthors.org; f. 1963; 3,000 mems; Chair. SUSAN HAYES; Exec. Dir ANGELO LOUKAKIS; Gen. Man. STEVE WIMMER; publ. *The Australian Author* (4 a year).

British Council: POB 88, Edgecliff, NSW 2027; tel. (2) 9326-2022; e-mail enquiries@britishcouncil.org.au; internet www.britishcouncil.org/au.htm; f. 1934; offers courses and examinations in English language and British culture and promotes cultural exchange with the UK; Dir NICK MARCHAND; Deputy Dir KIRSTEN FREEMAN.

English Association Sydney Inc.: POB 91, Wentworth Bldg, Univ. of Sydney, Sydney, NSW 2006; e-mail melissa.hardie@sydney.edu.au; internet www.englishassociation.org; f. 1923; organizes confs for teachers and study days for students; 70 mems; Pres. MELISSA JANE HARDIE; Vice-Pres. KATE LILLEY; Sec. Dr ROB JACKSON; Treas. CERIDWEN LEE; publ. *Southerly* (3 a year).

Fellowship of Australian Writers NSW Inc.: POB 488, Rozelle, NSW 2039; tel. (2) 9810-1307; e-mail honsecretary@fawnsw.org.au; internet www.fawnsw.org.au; f. 1928; brs in all states and territories; 4,000 nat. mems; State Pres. TREVAR LANGLANDS; Hon. Sec. COLLEEN PARKER; Treas. KAY BAKON; publ. *Writers' Voice* (4 a year).

Goethe-Institut: 90 Ocean St, Woollahra, Sydney, NSW 2025; tel. (2) 8356-8333; e-mail info@sydney.goethe.org; internet www.goethe.de/sydney; offers courses and examinations in the German language and promotes German culture and cultural exchange with Germany; Dir Dr ARPAD A. SÖLTER.

PEN International (Sydney Centre): c/o Faculty of Arts and Social Sciences, Univ. of Technology, POB 123 Broadway, Sydney, NSW 2007; tel. (2) 9514-2738; e-mail sydney@pen.org.au; internet pen.org.au; f. 1931; promotes friendship and intellectual cooperation among writers; 170 mems; Pres. Prof. MICHAEL FRASER; publ. *PEN Magazine* (2 a year).

MEDICINE

Australasian Association of Clinical Biochemists: POB 7336, Alexandria, NSW 2015; Unit 5, 85 Bourke Rd, Alexandria, NSW 2015; tel. (2) 9669-6600; e-mail office@aacb.asn.au; internet www.aacb.asn.au; f. 1961; professional soc. for practising clinical biochemists in Australia and New Zealand; full mem. of the Int. Federation of Clinical Chemistry and Laboratory Medicine (IFCC) and Asia-Pacific Federation for Clinical Biochemistry and Laboratory Medicine (APFCB); provides both professional and individual benefits; 1,400 mems; Chair. MARY CONROY; Pres. ANDREW ST JOHN; Sec. CONCHITA KUEK.

Australasian Chapter of Sexual Health Medicine: 145 Macquarie St, Sydney, NSW 2000; tel. (2) 9256-9643; e-mail shmed@racp.edu.au; internet www.racp.edu.au; f. 1988; aims to further the professional devt of medical practitioners in the discipline of sexual health medicine; est. within the Adult Medicine Division of the Royal Australasian College of Physicians (RACP); 190 mems; Pres. Prof. RICHARD HILLMAN; Exec. Officer Dr MARILENA SALVO.

Australasian College of Dermatologists: POB 3785, Rhodes, NSW 2138; tel. (2) 8765-0242; e-mail admin@dermcoll.asn.au; internet www.dermcoll.asn.au; f. 1966; 510 mems; Pres. STEPHEN SHUMACK; Hon. Sec. Dr PATRICIA LOWE; Hon. Treas. Dr JEREMY HORTON; publ. *The Australasian Journal of Dermatology* (3 a year).

Australian and New Zealand Association of Neurologists: Royal Australasian College of Physicians, 145 Macquarie St, Sydney, NSW 2000; tel. (2) 9256-5443; e-mail anzan@anzan.org.au; internet www.anzan.org.au; f. 1950; 450 mems; Pres. Prof. GEOFFREY DONNAN; Hon. Sec. Assoc. Prof. RICHARD MACDONNELL; publs *Clinical and Experimental Neurology* (1 a year), *Journal of Clinical Neuroscience*.

Australian Dental Association: POB 520, St Leonards, NSW 1590; 14-16 Chandos St, St Leonards, NSW 2065; tel. (2) 9906-4412; e-mail adainc@ada.org.au; internet www.ada.org.au; f. 1928; 9,500 mems; Chief Exec. ROBERT N. BOYD-BOLAND; Pres. K. ALEXANDER; Treas. R. OLIVE; Vice-Pres. C. BONANNO; publ. *Australian Dental Journal* (4 a year).

Australian Institute of Holistic Medicine: POB 3079, Success, WA 6964; tel. (8) 9417-3553; internet www.aihm.wa.edu.au; f. 1946; Dean of Studies Dr S. JAYAWARDANA.

Australian Medical Association: POB 6090, Kingston, ACT 2604; 42 Macquarie St, Barton, ACT 2600; tel. (2) 6270-5400; e-mail ama@ama.com.au; internet ama.com.au; f. 1962; represents the registered medical practitioners (doctors) and medical students of Australia; Pres. Dr STEVE HAMBLETON; Vice-Pres. Prof. GEOFFREY DOBB; publs *Australian Medicine* (12 a year), *Medical Journal of Australia*.

Australian Physiological Society: School of Medical Sciences, Univ. of Sydney, NSW 2006; tel. (2) 9351-4602; e-mail president@aups.org.au; internet aups.org.au; f. 1960; assists and encourages the professional devt of tertiary education in physiology; 350 mems; Pres. Prof. DAVID ALLEN; Nat. Sec. Dr ROBYN MURPHY; Treas. Assoc. Prof. PETER THORN; publ. *Proceedings* (2 a year).

Australian Physiotherapy Association: POB 437, Hawthorn, VIC 3122; Level 1, 1175 Toorak Rd, Camberwell, VIC 3124; tel. (3) 9092-0888; e-mail national.office@physiotherapy.asn.au; internet www.physiotherapy.asn.au; f. 1905; 14,000 mems; Nat. Pres. MARCUS DRIPPS; CEO CRIS MASSIS; publ. *Journal of Physiotherapy* (4 a year).

Australian Society of Clinical Hypnotherapists: 65 Hume St, Crows Nest, NSW 2065; tel. (3) 0085-1176; e-mail secretary@asch.com.au; internet www.asch.com.au; f. 1974; advances knowledge and practice of hypnosis and to maintain the highest ethical standards in its use; 374 mems; Pres. LYNDALL BRIGGS; Sec. EDWARD ZWICKI; publ. *The Australian Journal of Clinical Hypnotherapy and Hypnosis* (2 a year).

Optometrists Association Australia: POB 185, Carlton S, VIC 3053; tel. (3) 9668-8500; e-mail oaanat@optometrists.asn.au; internet www.optometrists.asn.au; f. 1918; 4,400 mems; Pres. ANDREW HARRIS; Dir and Treas. GAVIN O'CALLAGHAN; publ. *Clinical and Experimental Optometry* (6 a year).

Royal Australasian College of Dental Surgeons: Level 13, 37 York St, Sydney, NSW 2000; tel. (2) 9262-6044; e-mail registrar@racds.org; internet www.racds.org; f. 1965; holds scientific meetings and administers examinations; 1,233 fellows; Pres. Assoc. Prof. WERNER H. BISCHOF; Hon. Sec. STEPHEN C. DAYMOND; Hon. Treas. S. HANLIN; publs *Annals* (2 a year), *Lecture Notes in Anatomy* (1 a year), *Lecture Notes in Biochemistry* (1 a year), *Lecture Notes in Histology* (1 a year), *Lecture Notes in Microbiology* (1 a year), *Lecture Notes in Pathology* (1 a year), *Lecture Notes in Physiology* (1 a year), *Sedation Guidelines* (irregular).

Royal Australasian College of Physicians: 145 Macquarie St, Sydney, NSW 2000; tel. (2) 9256-5444; e-mail racp@racp.edu.au; internet www.racp.edu.au; f. 1938; charitable, educational and scientific activities; 13,500 physicians and paediatricians; library of 40,000 vols; History of Medicine library containing Ford Colln of rare Australiana; Pres. Dr JILL SEWELL (Vic.); CEO CRAIG PATTERSON; publs *Internal Medicine Journal* (12 a year), *Journal of Paediatrics and Child Health* (6 a year).

Royal Australasian College of Surgeons: College of Surgeons' Gardens, 250–290 Spring St, East Melbourne, VIC 3002; tel. (3) 9249-1200; e-mail college.sec@surgeons.org; internet www.surgeons.org; f. 1927 present name 1930; Pres. and Chair. of Ccl and Exec. IAN CIVIL; Treas. MICHAEL HOLLANDS; publ. *Australian and New Zealand Journal of Surgery* (12 a year).

Royal Australian and New Zealand College of Ophthalmologists: 94–98 Chalmers St, Surry Hills, Sydney, NSW 2010;

UNIVERSIDAD NACIONAL DE GENERAL SAN MARTÍN
(National University of General San Martín)

Avda 25 de Mayo y Francia, CP 1650, San Martín, Buenos Aires
Telephone: (11) 4006-1500
E-mail: rectorado@unsam.edu.ar
Internet: www.unsam.edu.ar

Founded 1992
State control
Language of instruction: Spanish

Rector: CARLOS RAFAEL RUTA
Vice-Rector: DANIEL DI GREGORIO
Sec.-Gen.: CARLOS GRECO
Academic Sec.: ALEXANDRE ROIG
Admin. Sec.: HÉCTOR FERNÁNDEZ (acting)
Library Dir Gen.: Lic. MARIELA L. FRÍAS
Number of students: 7,942

Library of 4,700 vols, 350 periodicals

Publications: *Educación en Ciencias, Educación en Ciencias Sociales, Política y Gestión, Revista de la Escuela de Economía y Negocios*

DEANS

Dan Beninson Institute of Technology: CARLA NOTARI
Institute of Biotechnical Research: ALBERTO FRASCH
Institute of Higher Social Studies: ALEJANDRO GRIMSON
Institute of Industrial Quality: JOAQUÍN VALDÉS
Institute of Rehabilitation Sciences and Movement: HUGO RODRÍGUEZ ISARN
Institute of Research and Environment Engineering: JORGE FERNANDEZ NIELLO
Prof. Jorge A. Sabato Institute of Technology: ANA MARÍA MONTI
School of Economics and Business: MARCELO PAZ
School of Government and Politics: MARÍA MATILDE OLLIER
School of Humanities: ENRIQUE CORTI
School of Science and Technology: FRANCISCO PARISI

UNIVERSIDAD NACIONAL DE GENERAL SARMIENTO
(National University of General Sarmiento)

Juan María Gutiérrez 1150, entre José León Suarez y Verdi, B1613GSX Buenos Aires
Telephone: (11) 4469-7500
E-mail: info@ungs.edu.ar
Internet: www.ungs.edu.ar

Founded 1993
State control
Language of instruction: Spanish
Academic year: October to April

Institutes of human devt, industry, science and suburbs,

Rector: Dr EDUARDO RINESI
Vice-Rector: Lic. GUSTAVO KOHAN
Sec.-Gen.: Prof. JOSÉ GUSTAVO RUGGIERO
Academic Sec.: Dra GABRIELA DIKER
Admin. Sec.: DANIELA LETICIA GUARDADO
Legal and Technical Sec.: Dr JAIME GONZÁLEZ
Research Sec.: Lic. PABLO BONALDI

Library of 18,000 vols, 121 periodicals
Number of students: 5,547

UNIVERSIDAD NACIONAL DE JUJUY
(National University of Jujuy)

Avda Bolivia 1239, 4600 San Salvador de Jujuy
Telephone: (388) 422-1515
E-mail: consultas@unju.edu.ar
Internet: www.unju.edu.ar

Founded 1972
State control
Language of instruction: Spanish
Academic year: March to December

Rector: Dr Ing. ENRIQUE MATEO ARNAU
Vice-Rector: Lic. ANGELICA MERCEDES GARAY DE FUMAGALLI
Sec. for Academic Affairs: Ing. GUSTAVO LORES
Sec. for Admin. Affairs: PATRICIA CUELLAR DE COMAS
Sec. for Science and Technology: Dr LILIANA LUPO
Sec. for Student Welfare: MARIO PEREZ
Sec. for Univ. Extension: Ing. LILIAN ABRAHAM DE MENDEZ
Librarian: MARÍA ESTHER CENTENO DE MARTÍNEZ

Library of 18,000 vols
Number of teachers: 700
Number of students: 13,000

DEANS

Faculty of Agricultural Sciences: Ing. Agr. MARIO CESAR BONILLO
Faculty of Economic Sciences: OSCAR ALBERTO FERNANDEZ
Faculty of Engineering: Ing. JOSE LUCAS SANCHEZ MERA
Faculty of Humanities: Dr RICARDO ENRIQUE GREGORIO SLAVUTSKY

UNIVERSIDAD NACIONAL DE LA MATANZA
(National University of La Matanza)

Florencio Varela 1903, B1754JEC San Justo, Buenos Aires
Telephone: (11) 4480-8900
E-mail: webgestion@unlam.edu.ar
Internet: www.unlam.edu.ar

Founded 1989
State control
Language of instruction: Spanish
Academic year: March to December (2 semesters)

Rector: Prof. Dr DANIEL EDUARDO MARTÍNEZ
Vice-Rector: Prof. Dr VICTOR RENÉ NICOLETTI
Sec.-Gen.: Dr LUIS ENRIQUE BUSNELLI
Sec. for Academic Affairs: Lic. GUSTAVO DUEK
Sec. for Admin. Affairs: Cdor. ADRIAN SANCCI
Sec. for Information Technology and Communications: Lic. MARCELO PÉREZ GUNTIN
Sec. for Legal and Technical Affairs: Dr JAVIER LORENZUTTI
Sec. for Management and Planning: Dr JORGE LUIS NARVAÉZ
Sec. for Univ. Public Relations: Lic. ROBERTO LUIS AYUB
Number of students: 19,368

DEANS

Economics: Dr ALBERTO LONGO
Engineering and Technological Research: Ing. OSVALDO SPOSITTO
Health Sciences: Dr MARIO ROBERTO ROVERE
Humanities and Social Sciences: Dr FERNANDO LUJÁN ACOSTA
Law and Political Science: Dr EDUARDO ROLLERI

UNIVERSIDAD NACIONAL DE LA PAMPA
(National University of Pampa)

Cnel. Gil 353 Santa Rosa, La Pampa
Telephone: (2954) 451-600
E-mail: info@unlpam.edu.ar
Internet: www.unlpam.edu.ar

Founded 1958
State control
Academic year: April to November

Rector: SERGIO A. BAUDINO
Vice-Rector: HUGO ALFREDO ALFONSO
Academic Sec.: Prof. MARÍA ESTELA TORROBA
Librarian: NORMA LAURNAGARAY

Number of teachers: 640
Number of students: 11,000

DEANS

College of Engineering: Ing. CARLOS D'AMICO
Faculty of Agronomy: Dr GUSTAVO DANIEL FERNANDEZ
Faculty of Economics and Law: OSCAR DANIEL ALPA
Faculty of Exact and Natural Sciences: Dra GRACIELA BEATRIZ ROSTON
Faculty of Human Sciences: Lic. SERGIO D. MALUENDRES
Faculty of Veterinary Science: Dr JOSÉ MARÍA ROMERO

UNIVERSIDAD NACIONAL DE LA PATAGONIA AUSTRAL
(National University of Southern Patagonia)

Lisandro de la Torre 860, Río Gallegos, Santa Cruz
Telephone: (2966) 442-376
E-mail: rectorad@unpa.edu.ar
Internet: www.unpa.edu.ar

Founded 1994
State control
Language of instruction: Spanish

Rector: Ing. ADES EUGENIA MÁRQUEZ
Vice-Rector: Ing. HUGO SANTOS ROJAS
Sec.-Gen. for Academic Affairs: Lic. MARÍA JOSÉ LENO
Sec. for Admin. and Finance: Lic. MARCELO MILJAK
Sec. for Science and Technology: Dra SANDRA CASAS
Sec. for Univ. Public Relations: Profa VIRGINIA BARBIERI
Dean for Caleta Olivia Campus: DANIEL PANDOLFI
Dean for Río Gallegos Campus: Dr ALEJANDRO SÚNICO
Dean for Río Turbio Campus: MARCELA VILLA
Dean for San Julian Campus: CLAUDIA MALIK DE TCHARA
Number of students: 7,000

UNIVERSIDAD NACIONAL DE LA PATAGONIA SAN JUAN BOSCO
(National University of Patagonia San Juan Bosco)

Ciudad Universitaria, Km 4, Comodoro Rivadavia, Chubut
Telephone: (297) 455-7856
E-mail: cup@unpata.edu.ar
Internet: www.unp.edu.ar

Founded 1980 by merger of Universidad de la Patagonia San Juan Bosco and Universidad Nacional de la Patagonia
State control
Language of instruction: Spanish
Academic year: February to December

Rector: Lic. ADOLFO DOMINGO GENINI
Vice-Rector: Dra ALICIA BORASO
Sec.-Gen.: Prof. NIDIA SILVIA LEON
Academic Sec.: Mag. SUSANA PERALES
Science and Technology Sec.: Dra ADRIANA MÓNICA NILLNI
Librarian: Lic. HAYDEE MURGA

Number of teachers: 850
Number of students: 16,000

Library of 40,000 vols

Publications: *Naturalia Patagónica* (4 a year), *Panorama Universitario* (irregular)

DEANS

Faculty of Economic Sciences: RICARDO MARIO BARRERA

tel. (2) 9690-1001; e-mail ranzco@ranzco.edu; internet www.ranzco.edu; f. 1969 (fmrly Ophthalmological Soc. of Australia); organizes the examination system and sets the curriculum; maintains a Continuing Professional Development (CPD) system; 1,550 mems; Pres. Dr STEPHEN BEST; Hon. Treas. Dr BRADLEY HORSBURGH; publ. *Clinical and Experimental Ophthalmology* (9 a year).

Royal Australian and New Zealand College of Psychiatrists: 309 La Trobe St, Melbourne, VIC 3000; tel. (3) 9640-0646; e-mail ranzcp@ranzcp.org; internet www.ranzcp.org; f. 1963, present name 1976; provides accreditation and representation for psychiatry and psychiatrists in Australia and New Zealand; 3,000 fellows, 1,000 trainees; CEO and Sec. Dr ANDREW PETERS; publs *Australian and New Zealand Journal of Psychiatry*, *Australasian Psychiatry*.

Royal Australian and New Zealand College of Radiologists: Level 9, 51 Druitt St, Sydney, NSW 2000; tel. (2) 9268-9777; e-mail ranzcr@ranzcr.edu.au; internet www.ranzcr.edu.au; f. 1935 as the Australian and New Zealand Association of Radiology, current name adopted 1998; promotes and improves the standards of training and practice in radiology and radiation oncology for the people of Australia and New Zealand; 2,301 mems; Pres. DINESH VARMA; Chair. for New Zealand Branch Dr LANCE LAWLER; publs *Australasian Radiology*, *The Journal of Medical Imaging and Radiation Oncology (JMIRO)* (1 a year).

Royal Australian College of General Practitioners: 1 Palmerston Crescent, S Melbourne, VIC 3205; tel. (3) 8699-0414; e-mail racgp@racgp.org.au; internet www.racgp.org.au; f. 1958; Pres. CLAIRE LOUISE JACKSON; CEO Dr ZENA BURGESS.

Royal College of Nursing, Australia: POB 219, Deakin West, ACT 2600; 1 Napier Close, Deakin West, ACT 2600; tel. (2) 6283-3400; e-mail canberra@rcna.org.au; internet www.rcna.org.au; f. 1949; grants membership to graduates of approved courses; administers nat. scholarships and research grants; conducts policy and devt programme, distance education programme; 10,000 mems; CEO DEBRA CERASA; Pres. STEPHANIE FOX-YOUNG; publs *Collegian* (4 a year), *Connections* (4 a year).

Royal College of Pathologists of Australasia: Durham Hall, 207 Albion St, Surry Hills, NSW 2010; tel. (2) 8356-5858; e-mail rcpa@rcpa.edu.au; internet www.rcpa.edu.au; f. 1956; 2,700 mems; CEO Dr DEBRA GRAVES; Pres. Prof. YEE KHONG; publ. *Pathology*.

Sydney Medical School Foundation: Rm 212, Edward Ford Bldg A27, Univ. of Sydney, Sydney, NSW 2006; tel. (2) 9351-7315; e-mail sue.merrilees@sydney.edu.au; internet sydney.edu.au/medicine/foundation; f. 1958 fmrly known as the Medical Foundation; supports all areas of medical research within the Faculty of Medicine at the Univ. of Sydney; focuses on the translation of research knowledge to health outcomes through improved treatment options and prevention of disease; funds research; Pres. ROBERT SALTERI; Treas. SCOTT FURBY (acting).

NATURAL SCIENCES

General

Australian Academy of Science: GPOB 783, Canberra, ACT 2601; tel. (2) 6201-9400; e-mail aas@science.org.au; internet www.science.org.au; f. 1954; recognizes research excellence, advises govt, organizes scientific conferences, publishes scientific books and journals; administers int. exchange programmes; 420 fellows; Pres. Prof. Dr SUZANNE CORY; Chief Exec. SUE MEEK; publ. *Records*.

Australian and New Zealand Association for the Advancement of Science (ANZAAS): POB 788, Northcote, VIC 3070; tel. (8) 8303-4965; e-mail chair@anzaas.org.au; internet anzaas.org.au; f. 1888; 1,000 mems; divs in NSW, VIC, SA, WA, TAS, ACT and NT, also overseas mems; Sec. ROBERT PERRIN; publ. *ANZAAS Mercury* (4 a year).

Australian Conservation Foundation: 1st Fl., 60 Leicester St, Carlton, VIC 3053; tel. (3) 9345-1111; e-mail acf@acfonline.org.au; internet www.acfonline.org.au; f. 1965; 60,000 mems and supporters; library of 15,000 vols; Pres. Prof. IAN LOWE; Hon. Sec. GAVIN WIGGINTON; Treas. TODD DAVIES; publs *Bilby Bulletin*, *Habitat* (6 a year).

Science & Technology Australia: POB 259, Canberra, ACT 2601; Unit 4, 7 Napier Close, Deakin, ACT 2600; tel. (2) 6257-2891; e-mail accounts@sta.org.au; internet scienceandtechnologyaustralia.org.au; f. 1985; promotes views on a wide range of policy issues to Govt, industry and the community; 60,000 mems; Pres. Prof. MICHAEL HOLLAND; Sec. Dr JEREMY C. BROWNLIE.

Royal Society of New South Wales: Bldg H47, Univ. of Sydney, Sydney, NSW 2006; tel. (2) 9036-5282; e-mail info@royalsoc.org.au; internet nsw.royalsoc.org.au; f. 1821; colln of monographs and periodicals relating to the history of Australian science, MSS of original research results; 305 mems; Pres. JOHN R. HARDIE; Hon. Treas. DAVID BEALE; publ. *Journal and Proceedings* (2 a year).

Royal Society of Queensland: POB 6021, St Lucia, QLD 4067; e-mail rsocqld@gmail.com; internet www.royalsocietyqld.org; f. 1884; natural and applied sciences; 100 mems; library of 20,000 vols; Pres. Dr GEOFF EDWARDS; publ. *Proceedings of the Royal Society of Queensland* (1 a year).

Royal Society of South Australia Inc.: c/o South Australian Museum, N Terrace, Adelaide, SA 5000; tel. (8) 8207-7590; e-mail roysocsa@gmail.com; internet www.adelaide.edu.au/rssa; f. 1853; natural sciences; 222 mems; library of 750 vols; Pres. Dr CRAIG WILLIAMS; Hon. Sec. Dr KIM CRITCHLEY; Treas. D. PAGE; publs *Regional Natural Histories* (irregular), *Transactions of the Royal Society of South Australia* (2 a year).

Royal Society of Tasmania: GPOB 1166, Hobart, TAS 7001; 19 Davey St, Hobart, TAS 7001; tel. (3) 6211-4177; e-mail info@rst.org.au; internet www.rst.org.au; f. 1843; lectures, panel discussions, symposia and excursions and publs; 360 mems; library of 40,000 vols; Pres. Prof. SUE JONES; Hon. Sec. TONY CULBERG; Hon. Treas. PETER MEYER; publ. *Papers and Proceedings* (1 a year).

Royal Society of Victoria: 9 Victoria St, Melbourne, VIC 3000; tel. (3) 9663-5259; e-mail rsv@sciencevictoria.org.au; internet www.sciencevictoria.org.au; f. 1854; works for the advancement of science through discussions and publs; 750 mems; library: large colln of scientific periodicals since 1854; Pres. Prof. LYNNE SELWOOD; Hon. Sec. Dr. WILLIAM D. BIRCH; Hon. Treas. NORMAN P. KENNEDY; publ. *Proceedings* (2 a year).

Royal Society of Western Australia: POB 7026, Karawara, WA 6152; tel. (8) 9212-3771; e-mail secretary@rswa.org.au; internet www.rswa.org.au; f. 1913; promotes and assists in the advancement of science within the community; fosters and facilitates interdisciplinary interaction in physical and natural sciences; organizes monthly meetings, public lectures and symposia; promotes interdisciplinary interaction among postgraduate students from various univs; awards medals of honour; 250 mems; library of 95 vols; Pres. and Tres. Dr PHILIP O'BRIEN; Sec. Dr LYNNE MILNE; publ. *Journal of the Royal Society of Western Australia* (2 a year).

Biological Sciences

Australian Society for Fish Biology: School of Earth and Environmental Sciences, Univ. of Adelaide, 5005; tel. (8) 8303-7036; e-mail c.izzo@adelaide.edu.au; internet www.asfb.org.au; f. 1971; 530 mems; Pres. Dr BRONWYN GILLANDERS; Sec. CHARLES TODDS; Treas. CHRISTOPHER IZZO.

Australian Society for Limnology: Museum of Victoria, GPOB 666, Melbourne, VIC 3001; tel. (3) 8341-7433; e-mail rmarch@museum.vic.gov.au; internet www.asl.org.au; f. 1961; study and management of inland waters, maintenance of biodiversity, restoration of water quality and wise use of aquatic resources; 400 mems, incl. researchers, managers, engineers, teachers and tertiary-level students; Pres. BELINDA ROBSON; Sec. Dr RICHARD MARCHANT; Treas. REBECCA LESTER.

Australian Society for Microbiology Inc.: 210/55 Flemington Rd, N Melbourne, VIC 3051; tel. (3) 1300-656-423; e-mail admin@theasm.com.au; internet www.theasm.org.au; f. 1959; 2,000 mems; Pres. Assoc. Prof. JOHN TURNIDGE; Sec. Dr J. LANSER; publs *Microbiology Australia* (5 a year), *Recent Advances in Microbiology* (1 a year).

Australian Society for Parasitology: c/o Heather Koch, Secretary, PO Royal Brisbane Hospital, Brisbane, QLD 4029; tel. (2) 6257-9022; e-mail heather.koch@animalhealthalliance.org.au; internet parasite.org.au; f. 1964; all aspects of parasitology, incl. immunology and vaccinology; 450 mems; Pres. DENISE DOOLAN; Exec. Sec. ROBERT ADLARD; Treas. KATHY ANDREWS; publ. *International Journal for Parasitology* (12 a year).

BirdLife Australia: Suite 2-05, 60 Leicester St, Carlton, VIC 3053; tel. (3) 9347-0757; e-mail info@birdlife.org.au; internet www.birdlife.org.au; f. 2012, by merger of Birds Australia with Bird Observation and Conservation Australia (BOCA); conserves, studies and appreciates native Australasian birds and their habitats; extensive library and database; 10,000 mems; CEO PAUL SULIVAN; Sec. PETER DANN; Treas. ROBERT DUNN; publs *Australian Birdlife* (4 a year), *Australian Field Ornithology* (4 a year), *Emu—Austral Ornithology* (4 a year), *State of Australia's Birds* (4 a year).

Ecological Society of Australia Inc.: POB 2187, Windsor, QLD 4030; tel. (7) 3162-0901; e-mail executiveofficer@ecolsoc.org.au; internet www.ecolsoc.org.au; f. 1960; promotes the application of ecological principles to the devt, utilization and conservation of Australian natural resources; advises govt and other agencies; fosters the reservation of natural areas for scientific and recreational purposes; 1,564 mems; Pres. Prof. KRIS FRENCH; Hon. Sec. MATT PEARSON; Hon. Treas. NIGEL ANDREW; publs *Austral Ecology* (8 a year), *Environmental Management and Restoration* (3 a year).

Entomological Society of New South Wales Inc.: c/o Australian Museum, 6 College St, Sydney, NSW 2000; tel. (2) 9981-3749; e-mail contact@entsocnsw.org.au; internet www.entsocnsw.org.au; f. 1953; 180 mems; Pres. MARTIN HORWOOD; Hon. Sec. TANYA JAMES; publ. *General and Applied Entomology* (irregular).

Entomological Society of Queensland: POB 537, Indooroopilly, Brisbane, QLD 4068; tel. (7) 3202-7507; e-mail k.ebert@uq.edu.au;

internet www.esq.org.au; f. 1923; 280 mems; Pres. BILL PALMER; Sec. KATHY EBERT; publ. *The Australian Entomologist* (4 a year).

Field Naturalists Club of Victoria: 1 Gardenia St, Locked Bag 3, Blackburn, VIC 3130; tel. (3) 9877-9860; e-mail admin@fncv.org.au; internet www.fncv.org.au; f. 1880; 900 mems; Pres. JOHN HARRIS; Hon. Sec. VICTORIA AITKEN; Hon. Treas. BARBARA BURNS; publ. *The Victorian Naturalist* (6 a year).

Malacological Society of Australasia: c/o Dept of Malacology, Australian Museum, 6 College St, Sydney, NSW 2010; tel. (2) 9320-6052; e-mail info@malsocaus.org; internet www.malsocaus.org; f. 1955; promotes the study of molluscs; 170 mems; Pres. Dr RACHEL PRZESLAWSKI; Treas. Dr DON COLGAN; publ. *Molluscan Research* (3 a year).

Royal Zoological Society of New South Wales: POB 20, Mosman, NSW 2088; tel. (2) 9969-7336; e-mail office@rzsnsw.org.au; internet www.rzsnsw.org.au; f. 1879; 1,000 mems; Pres. Assoc. Prof. PETER BANKS; Exec. Officer HAYLEY BATES; publ. *Australian Zoologist* (2 a year).

Royal Zoological Society of South Australia Inc.: Frome Rd, Adelaide, SA 5000; tel. (8) 8267-3255; e-mail pr@zoossa.com.au; internet www.zoossa.com.au; f. 1878; maintains public zoo and open-range park; plays an active role in the conservation of endangered species, conservation education and in conservation research; 30,360 mems; library of 5,200 catalogued items; books, audiovisual and digital media, journal articles, photographs; CEO Prof. E. BENSTED; publ. *Zoo Times* (3 a year).

Wildlife Preservation Society of Australia Limited: POB 42, Brighton Le Sands, NSW 2216; tel. (2) 9556-1537; e-mail info@wpsa.org.au; internet www.wpsa.org.au; f. 1909; provides advice to govt agencies and instns regarding environmental and conservation issues; nat. environmental education programmes, political lobbying, advocacy and practical conservation work; 1,000 mems; Pres. Dr DAVID MURRAY; Hon. Sec. and CEO PATRICK W. MEDWAY; publ. *Australian Wildlife* (4 a year).

Zoological Parks and Gardens Board: POB 74, Parkville, VIC 3052; tel. (3) 9285-9300; e-mail zpgb@zoo.org.au; internet www.zoo.org.au; f. 1937 as successor to Royal Zoological and Acclimatization Soc. of Victoria (f. 1857); responsible for the management of the Royal Melbourne Zoological Gardens, Healesville Sanctuary and Victoria's Open Range Zoo at Werribee; 9 mems; Chair. ANDREW E. J. FAIRLEY.

Mathematical Sciences

Australian Mathematical Society: Australian Mathematical Society Inc Dept of Mathematics, Australian Nat. Univ., ACT 0200; tel. (2) 6125-8922; e-mail office@austms.org.au; internet www.austms.org.au; f. 1956; 1,000 mems; fosters communication among its mems, and organizes and supports mathematical confs in Australasia; makes grants to promote mathematical investigations; awards prizes; Pres. Prof. PETER FORRESTER; Sec. Dr PETER STACEY; Treas. Dr ALGY HOWE; publs *ANZIAM Journal* (4 a year), *Journal of the Australian Mathematical Society* (6 a year).

Statistical Society of Australia, Inc.: POB 213, Belconnen, ACT 2616; tel. (2) 6251-3647; e-mail eo@statsoc.org.au; internet www.statsoc.org.au; f. 1962; 700 mems; Pres. JOHN HENSTRIDGE; Sec. Dr DOUGLAS SHAW; publ. *The Australian and New Zealand Journal of Statistics* (4 a year).

Physical Sciences

Astronomical Society of Australia: c/o School of Physics, Univ. of Sydney, Sydney, NSW 2006; tel. (2) 9351-3184; e-mail john.obyrne@sydney.edu.au; internet asa.astronomy.org.au; f. 1966 as the Org. of Professional Astronomers in Australia; trustee of the Foundation for the Advancement of Astronomy (FAA); 500 mems; Pres. Dr KATE BROOKS; Vice-Pres. Prof. ANDREW HOPKINS; Sec. Prof. JOHN O'BYRNE; Sec. Dr. MARC DULDIG; Treas. Dr KATRINA SEALEY; publ. *Publications of the Astronomical Society of Australia* (online).

Astronomical Society of South Australia Inc.: GPOB 199, Adelaide, SA 5001; tel. (8) 8270-3631; e-mail info@assa.org.au; internet www.assa.org.au; f. 1892; 500 mems; library of 400 vols; Pres. ROBERT JENKINS; Sec. IAN ANDERSON; Treas. LYNETTE O'BORN.

Astronomical Society of Tasmania Inc.: c/o The Secretary, GPOB 1654, Hobart, TAS 7001; tel. (3) 6323-3777; internet ast.freehostia.com; f. 1934; 100 mems; Pres. PHIL WATKINS; Sec. JOY. COGHLAN; Treas. BOB COGHLAN; publs *Annual Ephemeris for Tasmania, Bulletin* (6 a year).

Astronomical Society of Victoria Inc.: GPOB 1059, Melbourne, VIC 3001; tel. (3) 9888-7130; e-mail president@asv.org.au; internet www.asv.org.au; f. 1922; 18 sections: Astrophotography, Computing, Comet, Cosmology and Astrophysics, Deep Sky, Demonstrators, Historical, Instrument Making, Lunar and Planetary, Outdoor Lighting Improvement, Meteors, Radio Astronomy, Solar, Variable Stars and Nova Search, Club, Diurnals (day group), Junior (for children aged 17 and under) and New Astronomers' Group; 1,000 mems; library of 2,600 vols incl. 700 texts, over 200 printed articles, 60 antique books and 130 DVDs; Pres. BARRY ADCOCK; Gen. Sec. ANNE WILLIAMS; publ. *Crux Magazine* (6 a year).

Australasian College of Physical Scientists and Engineers in Medicine: Suite 3.13 Aero, 247 Coward St, Mascot, NSW 2020; tel. (2) 9700-8522; e-mail admin@acpsem.org.au; internet www.acpsem.org.au; f. 1977; 600 mems; Pres. Dr STEFAN EBERL; Hon. Sec. Dr JOHN R. COLES; Hon. Treas. RICHARD DOVE; publ. *Australasian Physical and Engineering Sciences in Medicine* (4 a year).

Australian Acoustical Society: POB 1843, Toowong, QLD. 4066; tel. (7) 3122 2605; e-mail generalsecretary@acoustics.asn.au; internet www.acoustics.asn.au; f. 1964, inc. 1971; aims to promote and advance the science and practice of acoustics in all its brs to the wider community and provide support to acousticians; 600 mems; Pres. Dr N. BRONER; Gen. Sec. RICHARD BOOKER; Treas. G. A. BARNES; publ. *Acoustics Australia* (3 a year).

Australian Institute of Physics: 119 Buckhurst St, S Melbourne, VIC 3205; tel. (3) 9646-9515; e-mail aip@aip.org.au; internet www.aip.org.au; f. 1963; 2,500 mems; Pres. Dr MARC DULDIG; Hon. Sec. ANDREW GREENTREE; Hon. Treas. JUDITH POLLARD; publ. *Australian Physics* (6 a year).

Geological Society of Australia: Suite 61, 104 Bathurst St, Sydney, NSW 2000; tel. (2) 9290-2194; e-mail info@gsa.org.au; internet www.gsa.org.au; f. 1952; 2,314 mems; Exec. Dir SUE FLETCHER; publs *Alcheringa* (4 a year), *Australian Journal of Earth Sciences* (8 a year), *The Australian Geologist* (4 a year).

Royal Australian Chemical Institute: 1/21 Vale St, N Melbourne, VIC 3051; tel. (3) 9328-2033; e-mail member@raci.org.au; internet www.raci.org.au; f. 1917, inc. by Royal Charter 1932; 6,000 mems; Pres. Prof. DAVID EDMONDS; Hon. Gen. Sec. Prof. Dr MARTINA STENZEL; Hon. Gen. Treas. Prof. MUTHUPANDIAN ASHOKKUMAR; publ. *Chemistry in Australia* (12 a year).

PHILOSOPHY AND PSYCHOLOGY

Australasian Association of Philosophy: GPOB 1978, Hobart, TAS 7001; tel. (3) 6294-6319; e-mail elizagoddard@aap.org.au; internet www.aap.org.au; f. 1923; professional org. of academic philosophers in Australia, New Zealand and Singapore; 400 mems; Pres. Prof. GARRETT CULLITY; Sec. Dr TIM OAKLEY; Treas. Dr STUART BROCK; publ. *Australasian Journal of Philosophy* (4 a year).

Australian Psychological Society: POB 38, Flinders Lane, VIC 8009; Level 11, 257 Collins St, Melbourne, VIC 3000; tel. (3) 8662-3300; e-mail contactus@psychology.org.au; internet www.psychology.org.au; f. 1944, inc. as The Australian Psychological Society Ltd. in 1966; committed to advancing psychology as a discipline and profession; 21,000 mems; Pres. Assoc. Prof. TIM HANNAN; Exec. Dir Prof. LYN LITTLEFIELD; publs *Australian Journal of Psychology* (4 a year), *Australian Psychologist* (6 a year).

RELIGION, SOCIOLOGY AND ANTHROPOLOGY

The Australian Sociological Association: Swinburne Institute for Social Research, Swinburne Univ. of Technology, POB 218, Mailbag H98, Hawthorn, VIC 3122; tel. (3) 9214-5283; e-mail admin@tasa.org.au; internet www.tasa.org.au; f. 1963 as Sociological Assen of Australia and New Zealand, current name adopted 1988; aims to promote devt of sociology in Australia, facilitate sociology teaching and research, and enhance the professional devt of mems; holds annual confs, gives awards and publishes journals; 725 mems; Pres. Assoc. Prof. JO LINDSAY; Sec. Dr THERESA PETRAY; Exec. Officer SALLY DALY; publs *Health Sociology Review* (4 a year), *Journal of Sociology* (4 a year).

TECHNOLOGY

Australasian Institute of Mining and Metallurgy: POB 660, Carlton S, VIC 3053; tel. (3) 9658-6100; e-mail publications@ausimm.com.au; internet www.ausimm.com; f. 1893; 11,000 mems; Pres. ALICE CLARK; publ. *International Transactions*.

Australian Academy of Technological Sciences and Engineering: GPOB 4055, Melbourne, VIC 3001; Level 1, 1 Bowen Crescent, Melbourne, VIC 3004; tel. (3) 9864-0900; e-mail info@atse.org.au; internet www.atse.org.au; f. 1976; 670 fellows (incl. 8 hon., 9 foreign, 1 Royal); Pres. and Chair. Dr ROBIN BATTERHAM; CEO and Dir Dr MARGARET HARTLEY; publs *Annual Symposia Proceedings, ATSE Focus* (4 a year).

Australian Ceramic Society: c/o Dept of Applied Physics, Curtin Univ. of Technology, GPOB U1987, Perth, WA 6845; tel. (8) 9266-7544; e-mail j.low@curtin.edu.au; internet www.austceram.com; f. 1961; promotes ceramic science and technology and its applications for Australian ceramic industry and art; 300 mems; Fed. Pres. Dr JEFF SELLARS; Fed. Sec. Prof. JIM LOW; Treas. MARTIN STEWART; publ. *Journal of the Australian Ceramic Society* (2 a year).

Australian Institute of Energy: POB 193, Surrey Hills, VIC 3127; tel. (2) 4393-1114; e-mail aie@aie.org.au; internet www.aie.org

.au; f. 1978; 1,500 mems; Pres. Dr TONY VASSALLO; Hon. Sec. PAUL MCGREGOR; Hon. Treas. Dr GLEN CURRIE.

Australian Institute of Food Science and Technology Inc.: POB 6436, Alexandria, NSW 2015; Suite 2, Level 2, 191 Botany Rd, Waterloo, NSW 2017; tel. (2) 8399-3996; e-mail aifst@aifst.asn.au; internet www.aifst.asn.au; f. 1967; Pres. Prof. JO DAVEY; Treas. Dr JEFF FAIRBROTHER; publ. *Food Australia* (11 a year).

Australian Institute of Nuclear Science and Engineering: Locked Bag 2001, Kirrawee, NSW 2232; tel. (2) 9717-3376; e-mail ainse@ainse.edu.au; internet www.ainse.edu.au; f. 1958; consortium of Australian univs and the Univ. of Auckland, New Zealand, in partnership with the Australian Nuclear Science and Technology Org.; make the facilities of the Lucas Heights Research Laboratories available to research staff and students from mem. institutions; organizes Australian Numerical Simulation and Modelling Services and Australian Radioisotope Services; organizes confs, awards postgraduate studentships and research grants; 49 mems; Pres. Prof. BRENDAN KENNEDY; Scientific Sec. Dr DENNIS MATHER; publ. *AINSE Conference Books*.

Australian Robotics and Automation Association Inc.: GPOB 1527, Sydney, NSW 2001; tel. (2) 9959-3239; internet www.araa.asn.au; f. 1981; Pres. MATTHEW DUNBABIN; Sec. STEFAN WILLIAMS; Treas. BEN UPCROFT.

Chartered Institute of Logistics and Transport Australia: POB 4594, Robina, QLD 4230; tel. (61) 459-363-271; e-mail admin@cilta.com.au; internet www.cilta.com.au; f. 1935; 1,600 mems in Australia; Chair. ANDREW STEWART; Exec. Officer HANNA LUCAS.

Institution of Engineers, Australia trading as Engineers Australia: 11 National Circuit, Barton, ACT 2600; tel. (2) 6270-6555; e-mail memberservices@engineersaustralia.org.au; internet www.engineersaustralia.org.au; f. 1919; incorporates colleges of Biomedical Engineers, Chemical Engineers, Civil Engineers, Electrical Engineers, Environmental Engineers, Information Telecommunications and Electronics Engineers, Mechanical Engineers, and Structural Engineers; 90,000 mems; Chief Exec. PETER TAYLOR; publs *Australian Journal of Civil Engineering*, *Australian Journal of Electrical and Electronics Engineering*, *Australian Journal of Mechanical Engineering*, *Australian Journal of Multidisciplinary Engineering*, *Australian Journal of Water Resources*, *Chemical Engineering in Australia*, *Civil Engineers Australia* (12 a year), *Engineering World* (6 a year), *Engineers Australia* (12 a year), *Transport Engineering in Australia*.

Royal Aeronautical Society, Australian Division: POB 573, Mascot, NSW 2020; tel. (2) 9523-4332; e-mail austdivision@raes.org.au; internet www.raes.org.au; f. 1927; brs in Adelaide, Brisbane, Canberra, Melbourne, Perth, Sydney; Div. Pres. ANDREW DRYSDALE; Hon. Sec. ROSS D. BARKLA; Hon. Treas. BOB STEVENS; publ. *Australian Aeronautics* (every 2 years).

Surveying and Spatial Sciences Institute: POB 307, Deakin W, ACT 2600; 27–29 Napier Close, Deakin, Canberra, ACT 2600; tel. (2) 6282-2282; e-mail support@sssi.org.au; internet www.sssi.org.au; f. 1952; CEO and Company Sec. ROGER BUCKLEY; Pres. GARY MAGUIRE; Treas. JONATHAN SAXON.

Research Institutes

AGRICULTURE, FISHERIES AND VETERINARY SCIENCE

Australian Centre for Intellectual Property in Agriculture: Griffith Law School, Griffith Univ., Nathan, QLD 4111; tel. (7) 3735-7772; e-mail acipa@griffith.edu.au; internet www.acipa.edu.au; attached to Griffith Univ.; aims to engage in innovative, ind. and critical research; remains focused on the devt of workable solutions; Dir BRAD SHERMAN.

ARCHITECTURE AND TOWN PLANNING

Department of Planning & Infrastructure: GPOB 39, Sydney, NSW 2001; 23–33 Bridge St, Sydney, NSW 2000; tel. (2) 9228-6333; e-mail information@planning.nsw.gov.au; internet www.planning.nsw.gov.au; supports sustainable growth in NSW; effective management of natural, environmental and cultural resources and values; implements frameworks that support infrastructure; Dir-Gen. SAM HADDAD.

BIBLIOGRAPHY, LIBRARY SCIENCE AND MUSEOLOGY

Elda Vaccari Collection of Multicultural Studies: Victoria Univ. Library, Footscray Park Campus, POB 14428, Melbourne City Mail Centre, Melbourne, VIC 8001; tel. (3) 9919-4809; e-mail mark.armstrong-roper@vu.edu.au; internet www.vu.edu.au/library/researcher-support/special-collections-archives/elda-vaccari-collection; f. 1982; research on immigrant and minority groups in Australia; supported by Vaccari Italian Historical Trust; library of 4,000 vols; Spec. Collns Librarian MARK ARMSTRONG-ROPER.

EDUCATION

Australian Council for Educational Research: POB 55, Camberwell, Vic. 3124; 19 Prospect Hill Rd, Camberwell, VIC 3124; tel. (3) 9277-5555; e-mail sales@acer.edu.au; internet www.acer.edu.au; f. 1930; offices in Melbourne, Sydney, Brisbane, Perth, Adelaide, Dubai and New Delhi; library of 50,000 vols incl. journals, govt reports and conference proceedings, bibliographic database of educational theses, audio, video and CD-ROM material; CEO Prof. GEOFFREY MASTERS; publs *Australian Journal of Career Development* (3 a year), *Australian Journal of Education* (3 a year), *Education Research Theses* (subscription database), *Professional Educator* (4 a year), *Recent Developments* (2 a year), *Teacher* (12 a year).

National Centre for Vocational Education Research (NCVER): POB 8288 Station Arcade, Adelaide, SA 5000; Level 11, 33 King William St, Adelaide, SA 5000; tel. (8) 8230-8400; e-mail ncver@ncver.edu.au; internet www.ncver.edu.au; f. 1981; ind. org. established by the Fed., state and territory ministers; responsible for collecting, managing, analysing and communicating research and statistics about vocational education and training (VET); collects and manages nat. VET and New Apprenticeship statistics; provides VET research findings from Australian and int. sources through its VOCEDplus research database; library of 36,000 vols, 20,000 full-text, 55,000 English language records, 280 journals, research reports, policy documents, survey results, conference proceedings and theses; Chair. PETER SHERGOLD; Man. Dir Dr TOM KARMEL; publ. *Insight* (4 a year).

HISTORY, GEOGRAPHY AND ARCHAEOLOGY

Tasmanian Historical Research Association: 81 Salamanca Pl., Hobart, TAS 7000; tel. (3) 6260-2604; e-mail info@thra.org.au; internet www.thra.org.au; f. 1951; Pres. CAROLINE HOMER; Sec. ANDREW MCKINLEY; Treas. ROSS KELLY; publ. *Papers and Proceedings* (3 a year).

MEDICINE

Australian Institute for Suicide Research and Prevention: Rm 1.48 Psychology Bldg (M24), Griffith Univ. Messines Ridge Rd, Mt Gravatt, QLD 4122; tel. (7) 3735-3382; e-mail aisrap@griffith.edu.au; internet www.griffith.edu.au/health/australian-institute-suicide-research-prevention; attached to Griffith Univ.; nat. and int. suicide research; works for suicide prevention and manages the Queensland Suicide Register; Dir Prof. DIEGO DE LEO.

Australian Radiation Protection and Nuclear Safety Agency: 619 Lower Plenty Rd, Yallambie, VIC 3085; tel. (3) 9433-2211; e-mail info@arpansa.gov.au; internet www.arpansa.gov.au; f. 1929; attached to Australian Dept of Health and Ageing; library of 10,000 vols; CEO Dr CARL-MAGNUS LARSSON; publ. *Radiation Protection Series*.

Australian Society for Medical Research: 145 Macquarie St, Sydney, NSW 2000; tel. (2) 9256-5450; e-mail asmr@alwaysonline.net.au; internet www.asmr.org.au; f. 1961; holds Nat. Scientific Conf. and Australian Health and Medical Research Congress; Pres. Dr EMMA PARKINSON-LAWRENCE; Sr Exec. Officer CATHERINE WEST; publ. *Proceedings*.

Baker IDI Heart and Diabetes Institute: POB 6492, St Kilda Rd Central, Melbourne, VIC 8008; 75 Commercial Rd, Melbourne, VIC 3004; tel. (3) 8532-1111; e-mail reception@bakeridi.edu.au; internet www.bakeridi.edu.au; f. 2008 by merger of Baker Heart Research Institute and Int. Diabetes Institute; researches on cardiovascular disease, diabetic complications, physiology, pharmacology, endocrinology, molecular and cell biology and vascular biology and hypertension; offers postgraduate and doctoral programmes; library of 15,000 vols; Chair. ROBERT STEWART; Pres. GARRY JENNINGS.

Eskitis Institute for Cell and Molecular Therapies: Eskitis Two Bldg (N75) Griffith Univ., Brisbane Innovation Park, Don Young Rd, Nathan, QLD 4111; tel. (7) 3735-6000; e-mail eskitis@griffith.edu.au; internet www.griffith.edu.au/science-aviation/eskitis-institute-cell-molecular-therapies; attached to Griffith Univ.; works towards the devt of new strategies to prevent and treat disease with an emphasis on multi-disciplinary research and collaboration; Dir Prof. RONALD J. QUINN.

Institute of Dental Research: POB 412, Westmead, NSW 2145; Darcy Rd, Westmead, NSW 2145; tel. (2) 9845-9000; internet www.wmi.org.au/ourresearch; f. 1946; attached to Westmead Millennium Institute for Medical Research; focuses on oral infections, incl. dental caries and periodontal disease, which have complex aetiologies; Dir Prof. NEIL HUNTER (acting).

Kolling Institute of Medical Research: Royal North Shore Hospital, Pacific Highway, St Leonards, NSW 2065; tel. (2) 9926-4500; e-mail kolling@sydney.edu.au; internet www.kolling.usyd.edu.au; f. 1920 as the Institute of Pathological Research of NSW, current name adopted 1931; attached to The Univ. of Sydney; research focus on lifespan conditions incl. pregnancy and childbirth, cancer and genetics, kidney and heart disease, pain and neurological disorders, diseases of bones and joints and tissue regeneration; offers Masters and doctoral programmes; Dir Prof. JONATHAN MORRIS; Operations Man. Dr VIC DANIS.

MacFarlane Burnet Institute for Medical Research and Public Health Ltd (Burnet Institute): Commercial Rd, Melbourne, VIC 3004; tel. (3) 9282-2113; e-mail prathbone@burnet.edu.au; internet www.burnet.edu.au; aims to achieve better health for poor and vulnerable communities in Australia and internationally through research, education and public health; Dir and CEO Prof. Dr BRENDAN CRABB.

Mental Health Research Institute: POB 11, Parkville, VIC 3052; POB 11, Parkville, VIC 3052; Kenneth Myer Bldg, 30 Royal Parade (corner Genetics Lane), Parkville, Vic. 3052; tel. (3) 9035-6789; e-mail enquiries@mhri.edu.au; internet www.mhri.edu.au; f. 1956 as part of the Victorian Hygiene Dept, current name adopted 1987; attached to Univ. of Melbourne, Melbourne Health and Monash Univ.; studies aspects of the nature and treatment of psychiatric illnesses with a particular emphasis on a neuroscience approach to Alzheimer's, Parkinson's and schizophrenia; Exec. Dir Prof. COLIN MASTERS; COO and Sec. LISA KEAM.

National Health and Medical Research Council: GPOB 1421, Canberra, ACT 2601; Level 1, 16 Marcus Clarke St, Canberra, ACT 2601; tel. (2) 6217-9000; e-mail nhmrc@nhmrc.gov.au; internet www.nhmrc.gov.au; f. 1926 as the Federal Health Council, current name adopted 1937; CEO Prof. WARWICK ANDERSON.

National Vision Research Institute of Australia: Conr Keppel and Cardigan Sts, Carlton, Melbourne, VIC 3053; tel. (3) 9349-7519; e-mail info@nvri.org.au; internet www.nvri.org.au; f. 1972; attached to Australian College of Optometry; basic, applied and clinical research into vision and visual dysfunction; Dir Prof. MICHAEL ROBERT IBBOTSON.

Prince Henry's Institute of Medical Research: Monash Medical Centre, Level 4, Block E, 246 Clayton Rd, Clayton, VIC 3168; tel. (3) 9594-4372; internet www.princehenrys.org; f. 1960; attached to Monash University; works to improve quality of life through investigation of hormones in the fields of reproductive health, cancer, diabetes, obesity, bone health and cardiovascular disease; Dir MATTHEW GILLESPIE.

QIMR Berghofer Medical Research Institute: Locked Bag 2000, Royal Brisbane Hospital, Herston, QLD 4029; 300 Herston Rd, Herston, QLD 4006; tel. (7) 3362-0222; e-mail enquiries@qimrberghofer.edu.au; internet www.qimrberghofer.edu.au; f. 1945; Chair. PAUL DE JERSEY; Dir and CEO Prof. FRANK GANNON.

SA Pathology: POB 14, Rundle Mall, Adelaide, SA 5000; 28 Frome Rd, Adelaide, SA 5000; tel. (8) 8222-3000; e-mail sapathology@health.sa.gov.au; internet www.imvs.sa.gov.au; f. 1938; researches on diseases and disorders ranging from blood, breast and colon cancer, bone fractures, rheumatoid arthritis, asthma, hepatitis, infectious diseases and inherited (genetic) disorders; Exec. Dir KEN BARR.

Walter and Eliza Hall Institute of Medical Research: 1G Royal Parade, Parkville, VIC 3052; tel. (3) 9345-2555; e-mail information@wehi.edu.au; internet www.wehi.edu.au; f. 1915; attached to Univ. of Melbourne and The Royal Melbourne Hospital; research into cellular and molecular immunology, cancer, chronic inflammatory diseases, infectious diseases, immunopathology and immunoparasitology, genome science and bioinformatics; postgraduate training; library of 20,000 vols; Dir Prof. DOUGLAS HILTON.

NATURAL SCIENCES

General

Commonwealth Scientific and Industrial Research Organisation (CSIRO): Locked Bag 10, Clayton S, VIC 3169; tel. (3) 9545-2176; e-mail enquiries@csiro.au; internet www.csiro.au; f. 1926; researches all fields of the physical and biological sciences except defence science, nuclear energy and clinical medicine; sectors: field crops; food processing; forestry, wood and paper industries; horticulture; meat, dairy and aquaculture; wool and textiles; biodiversity; climate and atmosphere; land and water; marine; information technology and telecommunications; built environment; measurement standards; radio astronomy; services; chemicals and plastics; integrated manufactured products; pharmaceuticals and human health; energy; mineral exploration and mining; mineral processing and metal production; petroleum; library: see under Libraries and Archives; Chief Exec. Dr MEGAN CLARK; publs *Animal Production Science* (12 a year), *Australian Journal of Botany* (6 a year), *Australian Journal of Chemistry* (12 a year), *Australian Mammalogy* (2 a year), *Australian Journal of Physics* (6 a year), *Australian Journal of Plant Physiology* (8 a year), *Australian Journal of Zoology* (6 a year), *Australian Systematic Botany* (6 a year), *ECOS* (4 a year, online (www.ecosmagazine.com)), *Invertebrate Systematics* (6 a year), *Marine and Freshwater Research* (12 a year), *Reproduction, Fertility and Development* (6 a year), *Soil Research* (8 a year), *Wildlife Research* (8 a year), *Crop & Pasture Science* (12 a year), *CSIRO Solve* (4 a year), *Emu-Austral Ornithology* (4 a year), *Environmental Chemistry* (6 a year), *Functional Plant Biology* (12 a year), *Historical Records of Australian Science* (2 a year), *Process, Resourceful* (3 a year), *Sexual Health* (6 a year).

National Facility Within CSIRO:

CSIRO–Australia Telescope National Facility: POB 76, Epping, NSW 1710; tel. (2) 9372-4100; e-mail atnf-enquiries@csiro.au; internet www.atnf.csiro.au; f. 1988; a radio telescope array consisting of 6 22-m antennas at the Paul Wild Observatory, Narrabri, NSW, a 22-m antenna at Mopra, west of Coonabarabran, NSW, and a 64-m antenna near Parkes, NSW; Chair. Prof. LISTER STAVELEY-SMITH; Dir Prof. BRIAN BOYLE.

Biological Sciences

Australian Institute of Marine Science: PMB 3, Townsville, QLD 4810; tel. (7) 4753-4444; e-mail web@aims.gov.au; internet www.aims.gov.au; f. 1972; focus areas incl. Great Barrier Reef World Heritage Area, Ningaloo Marine Park in Western Australia and NW Australia; library of 12,000 vols, 3,500 journals; Chair. WAYNE OSBORNE; CEO JOHN GUNN.

Australian National Botanic Gardens: GPOB 1777, Canberra, ACT 2601; Clunies Ross St, Black Mountain, Canberra, ACT; tel. (2) 6250-9450; e-mail anbg-info@anbg.gov.au; internet www.anbg.gov.au; f. 1970 as Canberra Botanic Gardens, current name adopted 1984; living colln of 74,000 individual plants incl. 6,200 species of Australian native plants; scientific identification of plant species represented in the living colln and scientific information on Australian plants; contributes scientific data to the Global Biodiversity Information Facility and other int. biodiversity projects; library of 18,500 vols, 400 journals and 5,000 maps; Exec. Dir Dr JUDY WEST; Gen. Man. PETER BYRON.

Genomics Research Centre: Institute of Health and Biomedical Innovation, Queensland Univ. of Technology, Q Block, 60 Musk Ave, Kelvin Grove, QLD 4059; tel. (7) 3138-0970; e-mail grcclinic@qut.edu.au; internet www.genomicsresearchcentre.org; attached to Queensland Univ. of Technology; investigates the genetic basis of disease; focuses on common chronic human disorders; Dir Prof. L. GRIFFITHS.

Royal Botanic Gardens: Mrs Macquaries Rd, Sydney, NSW 2000; tel. (2) 9231-8111; e-mail botanical.is@rbgsyd.nsw.gov.au; internet www.rbgsyd.nsw.gov.au; f. 1816; 470-ha living plant colln in 3 botanic gardens and herbarium of 1.2m. specimens; research on Australian native plants; library of 50,000 vols; Exec. Dir Prof. DAVID MABBERLEY; publs *Cunninghamia*, *Telopea* (2 a year).

Royal Botanic Gardens Melbourne: PMB 2000, Birdwood Ave, S Yarra, VIC 3141; tel. (3) 9252-2300; e-mail rbg@rbg.vic.gov.au; internet www.rbg.vic.gov.au; f. 1846; more than 50,000 different species and cultivars of Australian and exotic plants; herbarium of 1m. specimens; library of 50,000 vols; Dir and Chief Exec. Dr PHILIP MOORS; publ. *Muelleria*.

Mathematical Sciences

Australian Bureau of Statistics: Locked Bag 10, Belconnen, ACT 2616; ABS House, 45 Benjamin Way, Belconnen, ACT 2617; tel. (2) 9268-4909; internet www.abs.gov.au; f. 1905; library of 38,000 vols, 9,600 periodicals; Australian Statistician BRIAN PINK.

Physical Sciences

Australian Nuclear Science and Technology Organisation (ANSTO): Locked Bag 2001, Kirrawee DC, NSW 2232; New Illawarra Rd, Lucas Heights, NSW 2234; tel. (2) 9717-3111; e-mail media@ansto.gov.au; internet www.ansto.gov.au; f. 1949, present status 1987; attached to Dept of Innovation, Industry, Science and Research; aims to bring the benefits of atomic science and technology to industry, medicine and the community; research and devt programmes focusing on industrial and other applications of atomic science, environmental science, advanced materials, biomedicine and health; operates nat. facilities; provides technical advice and training; library: 50,000 monographs, 6,500 ejournals, 1,700 print journals and 200 databases; CEO Dr ADRIAN PATERSON.

Commonwealth Bureau of Meteorology: GPOB 1289, Melbourne, VIC 3001; tel. (3) 9669-4000; e-mail webops@bom.gov.au; internet www.bom.gov.au; f. 1908; regional offices in Perth, Adelaide, Brisbane, Sydney, Hobart, Darwin and Melbourne; contributes to nat. social, economic, cultural and environmental goals; provides observational, meteorological, hydrological and oceanographic services; undertakes research in science and environment related issues; library of 80,000 vols; Dir Dr ROB VERTESSY; publ. *Australian Meteorological and Oceanographic Journal* (4 a year).

Geological Survey of New South Wales: POB 344, Hunter Region Mail Centre, Maitland, NSW 2310; 516 High St, Maitland, NSW 2320; tel. (2) 4931-6666; internet www.resources.nsw.gov.au/geological; f. 1875; attached to Div. of Mineral Resources and Energy, NSW Trade and Investment; advises on geology and mineral resources of NSW, incl. preparation of standard series geological, geophysical and metallogenic maps; research studies in tectonics, palaeontology, petrology and selected mineral commodities; library of 1,000 vols; Dir-Gen. MARK PATERSON; publs *Memoirs, Mineral Industry, Mineral Resources, Palaeontological Memoirs, Quarterly Notes, Records of the Geological Survey of New South Wales*.

Geological Survey of Western Australia: Mineral House, 100 Plain St, East Perth, WA 6004; tel. (8) 9222-3222; e-mail geological .survey@dmp.wa.gov.au; internet www.dmp .wa.gov.au/gswa; attached to Dept of Mines and Petroleum; Exec. Dir Dr RICK ROGERSON; publ. *Fieldnotes* (4 a year).

Geoscience Australia (GA): GPOB 378, Canberra, ACT 2601; Cnr Jerrabomberra Ave and Hindmarsh Dr., Symonston, ACT 2609; tel. (2) 6249-9111; e-mail feedback@ga .gov.au; internet www.ga.gov.au; f. 1946 as Bureau of Mineral Resources; attached to Dept of Resources, Energy and Tourism; Geology and Geophysics (BMR) to develop a comprehensive, scientific understanding of the geology of Australia, its offshore area, and the Australian Antarctic Territory; develops a sustainable energy supply for Australia's future; library of 43,000 vols, 653 serial titles; CEO Dr CHRIS PIGRAM; publ. *AusGeo News*.

GeoScience Victoria: Dept of Primary Industries, GPOB 4440, Melbourne, VIC 3002; 1 Spring St, Melbourne, VIC; tel. (3) 5332 5000; e-mail information.centre@dpi.vic .gov.au; internet www.dpi.vic.gov.au/ earth-resources/about-earth-resources/ branches/geoscience; f. 2004, by merger of Geological Survey of Victoria and the Petroleum Br.; attached to Earth Resources Div., Dept of Primary Industries; collects, enhances and provides geoscientific information to increase investment in and understanding of minerals and petroleum resources; Dir PAUL McDONALD (acting); Library Man. KEN SHERRY.

Mineral Resources Tasmania: POB 56, Rosny Park, TAS 7018; 30 Gordons Hill Rd, Rosny Park, TAS 7018; tel. (3) 6233-8377; e-mail info@mrt.tas.gov.au; internet www .mrt.tas.gov.au; f. 1885; produces and promotes up-to-date geoscientific information on Tasmania; library of 10,000 books, 300 periodicals; Chief Geologist CAROL BACON.

Perth Observatory: 337 Walnut Rd, Bickley, WA 6076; tel. (8) 9293-8255; e-mail perth .observatory@dec.wa.gov.au; internet www .perthobservatory.wa.gov.au; f. 1896; astronomy research, education and outreach and information provision; research areas incl. optical astronomy, variable and transient monitoring, photometry, planetary observations, microlens monitoring and minor body tracking; public star-viewing, guided tours and museum; library of 20,000 vols; Govt Astronomer RALPH MARTIN (acting).

Primary Industries and Regions South Australia (PIRSA): GPOB 1671, Adelaide, SA 5001; Level 14, 25 Grenfell St, Adelaide, SA; tel. (8) 8226-0222; e-mail pirsaforestry@ sa.gov.au; internet www.pir.sa.gov.au; f. 1892; sustainable use of the state's agriculture, wine, seafood, forestry and food industries; assoc. research; regulation, policy devt and biosecurity imperatives; library of 25,000 vols (spec. colln on early S Australian mining); Chief Exec. IAN NIGHTINGALE; publs *PIRSA Milestones, Prime Time* (12 a year).

Queensland Department of Environment and Resource Management: GPOB 2454, Brisbane, QLD 4001; 41 George St, Brisbane, QLD 4000; tel. (7) 3224-8790; e-mail info@derm.qld.gov.au; internet www .derm.qld.gov.au; f. 1874; library of 8,800 monographs, 27,000 reports, 1,000 serials, records, maps, map commentaries, guidebooks; Dir-Gen. JIM REEVES; publs *DME Reviews, Minerals and Energy Review, Queensland Geology, Queensland Government Mining Journal* (12 a year), *Records*.

Research School of Astronomy and Astrophysics—Mount Stromlo and Siding Spring Observatories: Cotter Rd, Weston Creek, ACT 2611; tel. (2) 6125-0230; e-mail director.rsaa@anu.edu.au; internet rsaa.anu.edu.au; f. 1924 as Commonwealth Solar Observatory; attached to Australian Nat. Univ.; operates 2.3m Advanced Technology Telescope at Sliding Spring Observatory; Mount Stromlo Observatory damaged by fire in 2003; currently under reconstruction; library of 17,000 vols; Dir Prof. MATTHEW COLLESS.

Riverview Observatory: Lane Cove, NSW 2066; tel. (2) 9882-8296; e-mail bwmarsh@ riverview.nsw.edu.au; f. 1905; meteorological observations, worldwide standard seismograph network station (1962); Dir R. W. MARSH.

RELIGION, SOCIOLOGY AND ANTHROPOLOGY

Australian Institute of Aboriginal and Torres Strait Islander Studies: GPOB 553, Canberra, ACT 2601; tel. (2) 6246-1111; e-mail research@aiatsis.gov.au; internet www.aiatsis.gov.au; f. 1961; library of 102,000 vols, 10,800 MSS, 3,800 titles in 200 languages, 1,930 rare books; audiovisual colln incl. 45,000 hours of recorded sound, 650,000 photographic images and 1,000 artefacts; Chair. Prof. MICHAEL DODSON; Prin. RUSSELL TAYLOR; publ. *Australian Aboriginal Studies* (2 a year).

Australian Institute of Archaeology: La Trobe Univ., Bundoora, VIC 3086; tel. (3) 9455-2882; e-mail director@aiarch.org.au; internet www.aiarch.org.au; f. 1946; teaching programmes and exhibitions on the ancient Near East and Biblical archaeology; arranges public lectures, sponsors exhibitions, promotes research and produces occasional publs; library of 10,000 vols, spec. colln on Palestinian, Egyptian and Mesopotamian archaeology; Dir CHRISTOPHER DAVEY; Registrar MARGARET MAHER; publ. *Buried History* (1 a year).

Australian Institute of Criminology: GPOB 2944, Canberra, ACT 2601; 74 Leichhardt St, Griffith, ACT 2603; tel. (2) 6260-9200; e-mail front.desk@aic.gov.au; internet www.aic.gov.au; f. 1973; conducts criminology research, confs and seminars; provides policy-relevant research to the Australian govt and other key stakeholders; library: see under Libraries and Archives; Dir Dr ADAM TOMISON; Library Man. JANINE CHANDLER; publ. *Trends and Issues in Crime and Criminal Justice* (20 a year).

TECHNOLOGY

AMDEL: Unit 3, 435 Williamstown Rd, Port Melbourne, Melbourne, VIC 3207; tel. (3) 9922 0700; internet www.amdel.com; f. 1960, present status 2008; attached to Bureau Veritas Group; analysis, testing, services in mineral engineering, chemical metallurgy, materials technology, mineralogy and petrology, process control instrument devt, petroleum, geoanalysis, chemical analysis; offices and laboratories around Australia and New Zealand and representatives worldwide; 900 offices across 140 countries; Chair. and CEO FRANK PIEDELIÈVRE.

ARRB Group Ltd: 500 Burwood Highway, Vermont S, VIC 3133; tel. (3) 9881-1555; e-mail info@arrb.com.au; internet www.arrb .com.au; f. 1960 as the Australian Road Research Board, current name adopted 1965; provides advice, technical expertise and solutions to transport and road authorities across the world; mem. agencies incl. federal, state and local govt bodies; library of 170,000 vols and journals on land transport, 1m. records on land transport available online; National Interest Services (NIS); Man. Dir GERARD WALDRON; Company Sec. SUE ROLLAND; publs *ARRB Research Reports* (irregular), *Proceedings of Biennial Conference, Road & Transport Research* (4 a year), *Transport and Road Update* (12 a year).

Defence Science and Technology Organisation: F2-2-008, 24 Fairbairn Ave, Canberra BC, ACT 2600; tel. (2) 6265-9111; e-mail information@dsto.defence.gov.au; internet www.dsto.defence.gov.au; f. 1910 as the Chemical Adviser's Laboratory; attached to Dept of Defence; provides scientific advice and support to the Australian Defence Org; conducts fatigue tests on military and civilian air structures and engine components; awards scholarships in engineering and telecommunications; library: Site libraries in Edinburgh (Adelaide, SA), Fishermans Bend (Melbourne, Vic.), Scottsdale (Tas.), Stirling (WA) and Sydney (NSW); Chief Defence Scientist Dr ALEXANDER ZELINSKY; publ. *Defence Science Australia* (4 a year).

Associated Research Laboratory:

Defence Science and Technology Organisation, Fishermens Bend: 506 Lorimer St, Fishermens Bend, VIC 3207; tel. (3) 9626-7000; f. 1939; incl. divs of Airframes and Engines, Air Operations and Guided Weapons.

Libraries and Archives

Australian Capital Territory

Australian Institute of Criminology, J. V. Barry Library: GPOB 2944, Canberra, ACT 2601; 74 Leichhardt St, Griffith, ACT 2603; tel. (2) 6260-9264; e-mail jvbarry@aic .gov.au; internet www.aic.gov.au/en/library .aspx; f. 1974; provides information services to researchers at the Institute; 35,000 monographs, 800 periodicals; articles and monographs of Australian criminological interest are indexed for CINCH—The Australian Criminology Database, publicly available on the Informit network; Library Man. JANINE CHANDLER.

Australian National University Library: J. B. Chifley Bldg (15), Canberra, ACT 0200; tel. (2) 6125-2003; e-mail librarian@anu.edu .au; internet anulib.anu.edu.au; f. 1948; 2.5m. vols incl. ANU doctoral theses, audiovisual material, books, journals, microforms, music scores and rare books; Librarian ROXANNE MISSINGHAM (acting).

High Court of Australia Library: POB 6309, Kingston, ACT 2604; Parkes Pl., Parkes, ACT 2600; tel. (2) 6270-6922; e-mail library@hcourt.gov.au; internet www.hcourt .gov.au/library; f. 1903; private library of the Justices of the Court and barristers; 160,000 vols incl. law reports, US state reports and historical texts; Court Librarian PETAL KINDER.

IP Australia Library: POB 200, Woden, 2606; Discovery House, Ground Fl., 47 Bowes St, Phillip, ACT 2606; tel. (2) 6283-2058; e-mail assist@ipaustralia.gov.au; internet www.ipaustralia.gov.au; f. 1904 as The Australian Patent Office; affiliated with Australian Law Librarians Association; 15,000 vols, 300 periodicals; Australian and foreign patent specifications from all patent countries, science and technology and intellectual property; Dir-Gen. PHILIP NOONAN; publs *Australian Official Journal of Patents*, *Australian Official Journal of Trade Marks*, *Australian Official Journal of Designs*, *Plant Varieties Journal*.

Library and Information Service, Shared Service Centre, Department of Education and Employment: GPOB 9880, Canberra, ACT 2601; tel. (2) 6240-8848; e-mail library@ssc.gov.au; f. 1945; 40,000 vols; Dir KYM HOLDEN (acting).

National Archives of Australia: POB 7425, Canberra Business Centre, Canberra, ACT 2600; Queen Victoria Terrace, Parkes, ACT 2610; tel. (2) 6212-3600; e-mail archives@naa.gov.au; internet www.naa.gov .au; f. 1946 as the Commonwealth Archives Cttee; archival authority of the Commonwealth since 1952; responsible for the management of Commonwealth records: survey, storage, preservation, retention or destruction, retrieval and access; provides information to the public on nature and location of Commonwealth records and on agencies and persons responsible for them; collns of documents, maps, plans, films, photographs, records, paintings, models, microforms and electronic records (487,522 shelf m); holdings date from the early 19th century, but most date from Federation (1901), derived from a variety of sources; offices in Canberra, Darwin and all state capitals; Dir-Gen. DAVID FRICKER; publ. *Your Memento* (1 a year).

National Library of Australia: Parkes Pl., Canberra, ACT 2600; tel. (2) 6262-1111; e-mail www@nla.gov.au; internet www.nla .gov.au; f. 1901; maintains nat. colln of Australian library materials and provides a gateway to nat. and int. sources of information; 2.9m. vols, 41,031 current serial titles, 643,792 maps, 12,895 m of MSS material, 16,297 oral history recordings, 189,031 music scores, 64,373 pictures and prints, 750,299 photographs, 860,187 aerial photographs, 3,812 electronic media; Dir-Gen. ANNE-MARIE SCHWIRTLICH; publs *APAIS* (online), *Gateways* (online, 6 a year), *The National Library Magazine* (4 a year).

University of Canberra Library: Bldg 8 Univ. of Canberra, ACT 2601; tel. (2) 6201-2282; e-mail askalibrarian@canberra.edu.au; internet www.canberra.edu.au/library; f. 1968; 480,000 vols, 39,000 electronic journals; Univ. Librarian and Library Man. ANITA CROTTY.

New South Wales

Charles Sturt University—Division of Library Services: Charles Sturt Univ. Locked Bag 7003, Bathurst, NSW 2795; tel. (2) 6338-4732; e-mail kjohnson@csu.edu.au; internet www.csu.edu.au/division/library; f. 1989 by amalgamation of Mitchell College of Advanced Education and Riverina-Murray Institute of Higher Education; libraries at Albury-Wodonga, Bathurst, Dubbo, Orange, Wagga Wagga; Burlington (Ontario, Canada); 619,171 vols, 2013 Aleph EOY report; Exec. Dir KAREN JOHNSON.

City of Sydney Library: 31 Alfred St, Sydney, NSW 2000; tel. (2) 9242-8555; e-mail library@cityofsydney.nsw.gov.au; internet www.cityofsydney.nsw.gov.au; f. 1909; 9 brs, 2 library links; 500,000 vols, incl. books, CDs, DVDs, audio-books, magazines, 50 newspaper titles; 1,250 items on Australian Koori Aboriginal colln; spec. collns: Australiana, local govt; Library Man. JEFFERY CRUZ; Librarian LYDIE BACOT.

Macquarie University Library: Bldg C3C, Macquarie Univ., Macquarie Dr., NSW 2109; tel. (2) 9850-7500; e-mail maxine.brodie@mq .edu.au; internet www.mq.edu.au/ on_campus/library; f. 1964; provides books, journals, newspapers, reports, conference proceedings, working papers, maps, Macquarie postgraduate theses, computer software, multimedia, microfilm, microfiche, posters, toys, games and additional non-print resources; 1.8m. vols; Univ. Librarian MAXINE BRODIE; Deputy Univ. Librarian JENNIFER PEASLEY.

Newcastle Region Library: War Memorial Cultural Centre, Laman St, Newcastle, NSW 2300; tel. (2) 4974-5300; e-mail library@ncc .nsw.gov.au; internet www.newcastle.nsw .gov.au/services/newcastle_library; f. 1938; 9 brs; spec. facilities: information works, local studies, hunter photo bank, earthquake database; 406,242 vols incl. colln of 100,000 reference works, 2,663 periodicals; 121 newspaper titles, demographic statistics for the Hunter region, parliamentary papers, motor manuals, classic and out of print Australian fiction, colln of rare books; Man. for Library Services DAVID JENKINS.

Parliamentary Library of New South Wales: Parliament House, Sydney, NSW 2000; tel. (2) 9230-2383; e-mail libreq@ parliament.nsw.gov.au; internet www .parliament.nsw.gov.au; f. 1840; 200,000 vols incl. colln of Australian state and federal legislation, parliamentary papers, parliamentary debates (Hansard) and proceedings, in addition to strong holdings of British parliamentary publications; rare books incl. accounts of the early years of the colony written by David Collins, Watkin Tench and John Hunter, books of exploration by James Cook and Matthew Flinders, 1800 Settlers' Muster Book and Gould's Birds of Australia; Man. for Parliamentary Research Dr GARETH GRIFFITH; Parliamentary Librarian ANNETTE MCNICOL.

State Library of New South Wales: Macquarie St, Sydney, NSW 2000; tel. (2) 9273-1414; e-mail library@sl.nsw.gov.au; internet www.sl.nsw.gov.au; f. 1826; state legal deposit privileges; special collns: Australian, historical pictures, maps, MSS, of Australia and the Pacific; 2 public reading rooms, specialist client-focused information services; 5m. items incl. 1.1m. photographs; 11.2 linear km of MSS; 234,000 prints, drawings, paintings, maps and oral histories; NSW State Librarian and Chief Exec. Dr ALEX BYRNE.

State Records Authority of New South Wales: POB 516, Kingswood, NSW 2747; tel. (2) 9673-1788; e-mail info@records.nsw.gov .au; internet www.records.nsw.gov.au; f. 1961; NSW govt's archives and records management authority; incl. Univ. Archives and Heritage Centre; records and archives strategy for the broader public sector; preservation of the State Archives colln; reference services; reading rooms, online access, enquiry and copying services, exhibitions, publs, talks and tours; 10,000 vols; Dir ALAN VENTRESS.

University of New England Library: Dixson Library, Univ. of New England, Armidale, NSW 2351; tel. (2) 6773-2165; e-mail unilib@une.edu.au; internet www .une.edu.au/library; f. 1954 Univ. College of Univ. of Sydney, 1938-1954; supports teaching and research in agricultural sciences, arts, Australian law, education, humanities and social sciences, health, medicine and sciences; spec. collns: Campbell Howard (Australian plays in MSS), Gordon Athol Anderson (music), New England, Royal Soc. of NSW, Australian League of Rights, Saunders Colln in War and Peace; incl. Dixson Library, Law Library and the UNE Archives and Heritage Centre; 1,153,593 vols incl. 266,315 ebooks, 675,890 books, 65,032 current serial titles and 211,388 serial vols; Univ. Librarian BARBARA PATON.

University of New South Wales Library: Sydney, NSW 2052; tel. (2) 9385-2650; internet www.library.unsw.edu.au; f. 1949; 2.9m. items at Kensington and other centres; Univ. Librarian ANDREW WELLS; Dir for Information Services JANET FLETCHER.

University of Newcastle Library: Callaghan Campus, Univ. Dr., Callaghan, NSW 2308; tel. (2) 4921-5851; internet www .newcastle.edu.au/services/library; f. 1965; 6 brs and a campus library in Singapore; 1.3m. vols; Librarian GREGORY ANDERSON.

University of Sydney Library: Univ. of Sydney, NSW 2006; tel. (2) 9351-2993; e-mail loanenq@library.usyd.edu.au; internet sydney.edu.au/library; f. 1852; 10 brs, Curriculum Resource Colln, East Asian Colln and Archive of Australian Judaica; 5.2m. vols, 281,600 ebooks, 68,130 ejournals; Univ. Librarian ANNE BELL.

Northern Territory

Northern Territory Library: Parliament House, POB 42, Darwin, NT 0801; tel. (8) 8999-7177; e-mail ntl.info@nt.gov.au; internet www.artsandmuseums.nt.gov.au/ northern-territory-library; f. 1950 as Darwin Public Library; principal documentary heritage colln for the Northern Territory; incl. historical and contemporary material; 140,000 vols, 4,132 periodicals, 80,000 photographs, 3,000 maps, 2,500 films and video cassettes, 7,000 microforms; incl. the Northern Territory Colln (1 copy of all types of library material dealing with North and Central Australia, and NT in particular); Dir PATRICK GREGORY; publ. *Occasional Papers*.

Queensland

Queensland Parliamentary Library and Research Service: Parliamentary Annex, Alice St, Brisbane, QLD 4000; tel. (7) 3406-7219; e-mail library.inquiries@parliament .qld.gov.au; internet www.parliament.qld .gov.au; f. 1860; research and information service to mems of state legislature; statistics, economics, politics, law and education; 120,000 vols; spec. collns incl. 32,000 colonial O'Donovan Collns, 19th-century parliamentary library; news and audiovisual clippings; Queensland political history; Librarian KATHERINE BRENNAN.

Queensland University of Technology, Library Services: Gardens Point, Level 3, V Block, 2 George St, Brisbane, Qld 4000; tel. (7) 3138-2083; e-mail c2.davies@qut.edu.au; internet www.library.qut.edu.au; f. 1989; 73,000 vols, 5,000 print and microform periodicals, 36,000 electronic periodicals; spec. colln incl. the Cilento Gift, QUT Community colln for grantseekers, fundraisers and philanthropists, Library Store colln, QUT ePrints, QUT Theses, Sugar Industry colln, Ozcase Queensland Historical Legal colln (QHLC) and Construction Innovation colln; Dir of Library Services JUDY STOKKER.

State Library of Queensland: POB 3488, South Brisbane, QLD 4101; tel. (7) 3840-7666; e-mail info@slq.qld.gov.au; internet www.slq.qld.gov.au; f. 1896 as Brisbane Public Library, current name adopted 1971; incl. John Oxley Library of Queensland History, James Hardie Library of Australian Fine Arts and Australian Library of Art colln; has library deposit privileges, exhibitions, events; CEO and State Librarian JANETTE WRIGHT.

Supreme Court of Queensland Library: POB 15019, City East, Brisbane, QLD 4002; Fourth Fl., Law Courts Bldg, cnr George and Adelaide Sts, Brisbane; tel. (7) 3247-4373;

e-mail librarian@sclqld.org.au; internet www.sclqld.org.au; f. 1862; primary legal information provider in Queensland for courts, mems of the legal profession, researchers, schools and public; 150,000 vols; Supreme Court Librarian ALADIN RAHEMTULA; publs *Qld Legal Indexes, Supreme Court History Program Yearbook*.

University of Queensland Library: QLD 4072; tel. (7) 3346-4312; e-mail universitylibrarian@library.uq.edu.au; internet www.library.uq.edu.au; f. 1910; 15 br libraries; works in partnership with the academic community to provide access to quality information; manages and provides access to Univ. of Queensland scholarship; 2m. vols, 116,000 journal titles, 1,000 databases, 500,000 ebooks, 38,000 DVDs and video cassettes; MSS, microform and pictorial collns; Univ. Librarian ROBERT GERRITY.

South Australia

Flinders University Library: Flinders Univ. Library, The Flinders Univ., GPOB 2100, Adelaide, SA 5001; The Flinders Univ., Sturt Rd, Bedford Park, SA 5042; tel. (8) 8201-2131; e-mail library@flinders.edu.au; internet www.flinders.edu.au/library; f. 1966; 1.5m. vols; Univ. Librarian IAN MCBAIN.

State Library of South Australia: GPOB 419, Adelaide, SA 5001; Corner North Terrace and Kintore Ave, Adelaide, SA 5000; tel. (8) 8207-7250; e-mail info@slsa.sa.gov.au; internet www.slsa.sa.gov.au; f. 1884; state general reference library and legal depository; online services incl. networked CD-ROMs; supports 138 public libraries (1.5m. vols); 1,500,000 vols incl. Bray Reference Colln (400,000 vols, 21,000 serial titles, 6,000 current, 109,000 maps); South Australiana Colln (62,000 vols, 12,000 serial titles, 8,000 current, Archival Collns of 4,500 m); spec. collns incl. Children's Literature Research Colln (55,000 vols), Edwardes Colln of Shipping Photographs (8,000), Arbon-Le Maistre Colln of Shipping Photographs (70,000), Mountford-Sheard Colln of Aboriginal Ethnology, Thomas Hardy Wine Library (1,000 vols), Paul McGuire Maritime Library (3,000 vols), Rare Books Colln (92,000 vols), Royal Geographical Soc. of South Australia Inc. Library, J. D. Somerville Oral History Colln (1,500 cassette tapes), Pictorial Colln (350,000 images), Bradman Colln of Cricketing Memorabilia; Dir ALAN SMITH; publ. *Extra Extra* (2 a year).

University of Adelaide Library: Univ. of Adelaide, Adelaide, SA 5005; tel. (8) 8313-5759; e-mail library@adelaide.edu.au; internet www.adelaide.edu.au/library; f. 1876; 2.1m. items; rare books, spec. collns incl. univ. archives, arts and heritage, press; 2,400,000 vols; Univ. Librarian RAY CHOATE.

University of South Australia Library: GPOB 2471, Adelaide, SA 5001; Mawson Lakes Blvd, Mawson Lakes, SA 5095; e-mail library-web@unisa.edu.au; internet www.library.unisa.edu.au; f. 1856 as School of Art, present name 1991; 6 brs; special collns incl. Oregon Colln of Theses in Physical Education and Sport, Doris Taylor Colln on Ageing, Gavin Walkley colln on Architectural History; Clearing house in Australia for Adult Basic Education and Literacy, Aboriginal and Torres Strait Islander Special Colln, Australian Bureau of Statistics Colln and HOPE Colln; 1m. vols, 700,000 monographs and print journals, 100,000 e-books, 50,000 journals and 420 databases; Univ. Librarian HELEN LIVINGSTON.

Tasmania

LINC Tasmania: LINC Tasmania, 91 Murray St, Hobart, TAS 7000; tel. (3) 6165-5559; e-mail linc@education.tas.gov.au; internet www.linc.tas.gov.au; f. 1850; state legal deposit privileges; 46 brs, 4 reference and spec. collns; links adult education, state library of Tasmania, online access centres and the Tasmanian archive and heritage office combining learning, information and literacy; 913,032 vols; Dir JENNY RAYNER.

University of Tasmania Library: PMB 25, GPO, Hobart, TAS 7001; tel. (3) 6226-1818; e-mail library.queries@utas.edu.au; internet www.library.utas.edu.au; f. 1892; Sandy Bay Campus libraries: Law, Morris Miller (social sciences and humanities) and Science; Centre for the Arts Library, Hunter St, Hobart; Clinical Library, 43 Collins St, Hobart; Launceston Campus Library, Newnham, Launceston; spec. collns on Quakerism; houses the Royal Soc. of Tasmania Library; 996,832 vols; Univ. Librarian KARMEN PEMBERTON.

Victoria

Commonwealth Scientific and Industrial Research Organisation, Library Network: Bag 10, Clayton S, Vic. 3169; tel. (2) 6246-5675; e-mail thomas.girke@csiro.au; internet www.csiro.au/libraries; publishes and communicates science information in print, video and multimedia, and electronic databases; disseminates science and research information through CSIRO Library Network, search and inquiry services SEARCH PARTY; archival services for CSIRO research and records; Sr Man. CAROL MURRAY.

La Trobe University Library: Bundoora, VIC 3086; tel. (3) 9479-2922; e-mail library@latrobe.edu.au; internet www.lib.latrobe.edu.au; f. 1964; spec. emphasis on humanities and social sciences, allied health sciences; area studies: Latin America, India and Canada; 1.5m. vols; Univ. Librarian JENNIFER PEASLEY.

Monash University Library: POB 4, Monash Univ., VIC 3800; tel. (3) 9905-5054; e-mail libweb@monash.edu; internet monash.edu/library; f. 1960; 7 brs; 4m. vols, 450,000 ebooks, 140,000 print and electronic journals; Univ. Librarian CATHRINE HARBOE-REE.

Public Record Office Victoria: 99 Shiel St, North Melbourne, VIC 3051; tel. (3) 9348-5600; e-mail enquiries@prov.vic.gov.au; internet www.prov.vic.gov.au; f. 1973; 80,000 linear m of public records; Dir and Keeper of Public Records JUSTINE HEAZLEWOOD; publs *Journal* (1 a year, online), *Profile* (4 a year).

State Library of Victoria: 328 Swanston St, Melbourne, VIC 3000; tel. (3) 8664-7000; e-mail info@slv.vic.gov.au; internet www.slv.vic.gov.au; f. 1854; legal deposit library responsible for collecting, preserving and making available all published materials and associated material relating to the heritage of the state of Victoria; offers community outreach and learning programmes; works with other library sectors, cultural instns and the education sector to provide access to information and promote Victorian cultural heritage; 2m. vols and periodicals, spec. collns incl. La Trobe Colln (Australiana), art, newspapers, music and performing arts, Anderson Chess Colln, maps, MSS and pictures; digitization of 200,000 items from the Pictures Colln and a broader range of formats incl. text, audio and music are available online; CEO and State Librarian SUE ROBERTS; publ. *La Trobe Journal* (2 a year).

University of Melbourne Library: VIC 3010; tel. (3) 8344-9590; e-mail library-feedback@unimelb.edu.au; internet www.lib.unimelb.edu.au; f. 1855; provides research material and information services for the univ.; 3.5m. vols; spec. collns incl. Australiana, E Asia; responsible for Univ. Archives and Grainger Museum; 63,000 gen. and specialist journals; Librarian PHILIP G. KENT; publ. *Ex Libris* (4 a year).

Victorian Parliamentary Library & Information Service: Parliament of Victoria, Spring St, Melbourne, VIC 3002; tel. (3) 9651-8911; e-mail info@parliament.vic.gov.au; internet www.parliament.vic.gov.au; f. 1851; reference and research service for MPs and associated staff; media monitoring; statistics, economics, politics, law, govt publs; Parliamentary Librarian CAROLYN MACVEAN; Coordinator for Research and Enquiries JON BREUKEL; publ. *Victorian Parliamentary Handbook* (every 4 years).

Western Australia

Curtin University Library: POB U1987, Perth, WA 6845; tel. (8) 9266-7166; e-mail i.garner@curtin.edu.au; internet library.curtin.edu.au; f. 1966; colln reflects the current and past research and teaching interests of Curtin; 669,445 vols, 186,905 current serial titles, 200,253 ebooks; Univ. Librarian IMOGEN GARNER.

State Library of Western Australia: 25 Francis St, Perth Cultural Centre, Perth, WA 6000; tel. (8) 9427-3111; e-mail info@slwa.wa.gov.au; internet www.slwa.wa.gov.au; f. 1889 as the Victoria Public Library; enables access to resources for information, learning, enterprise and recreation; collects and preserves social and documentary heritage; offers James Sykes Battye Memorial Fellowship; 1,500,400 vols, 138,000 vols in the J. S. Battye Library of W Australian History, 18,000 serial and newspaper titles, 17,500 microfilm reels, 32,600 cartographic items, 110,000 ephemeral items, 572,000 pictorial images, 12,000 film and video reels, 16,000 oral history hours, 3,900 m of private archives; gen. reference services: 306,000 vols, 1,100 serial and newspaper titles, 55,500 music scores, 13,200 music recordings, 14,900 microfilm reels, 23,000 cartographic items; spec. collns of music business genealogy and Australian children's literature; CEO and State Librarian MARGARET ALLEN.

University of Western Australia Library: 35 Stirling Highway, Crawley, WA 6009; tel. (8) 6488-1777; e-mail askuwa-lib@uwa.edu.au; internet www.is.uwa.edu.au; f. 1913; 6 libraries; IT infrastructure and services, telephone and audiovisual services; research and learning support services and special collns; 1m. vols, incl. 850,000 books, 230,000 MSS and electronic databases; 480,000 vols of journals, magazines and newspapers; Univ. Librarian and Dir Dr MARY DAVIES.

Museums and Art Galleries

Australian Capital Territory

Australian War Memorial: GPOB 345, Canberra, ACT 2601; Treloar Crescent, Campbell, ACT 2612; tel. (2) 6243-4211; e-mail info@awm.gov.au; internet www.awm.gov.au; f. 1917; museum, research centre and art gallery illustrating and recording aspects of all wars in which the Armed Forces of Australia have been engaged; dioramas of historical battles, and a total colln of over 3.5m. items; works of art, relics, documentary and audiovisual records; library: books, serials, pamphlets, photographs, maps, film and sound recordings on military history; repository of operational records of Australian fighting units; Ccl Chair. KEN DOOLAN; Dir BRENDAN NELSON; publs *Journal of the Australian War Memorial* (2 a year), *Wartime* (4 a year).

National Gallery of Australia: GPOB 1150, Canberra, ACT 2601; Parkes Pl., Parkes, Canberra, ACT 2600; tel. (2) 6240-6411; e-mail information@nga.gov.au; internet www.nga.gov.au; f. 1975; Nat. Colln has 160,000 works of Australian and int. art; Australian colln incl. fine and decorative arts, folk art, commercial art, architecture and design; other collns incl. arts of Asia and SE Asia, Oceania, Africa and Pre-Columbian America, European art, also prints, drawings, illustrated books since 1800, photography; colln of Australian archives, colln of oral histories, access to digital publs on the visual arts; library of 160,000 vols, 35,000 auction sales catalogues, 1,200 current serials, 47,000 microfiches, 1m. ephemeral materials; Exec. Dir MARYANNE VOYAZIS; publ. *Artonview* (4 a year).

National Museum of Australia: GPOB 1901, Canberra, ACT 2601; Lawson Crescent, Acton Peninsula, Canberra, ACT 2601; tel. (2) 6208-5000; e-mail information@nma.gov.au; internet www.nma.gov.au; f. 1980; Australian history, Aboriginal and Torres Strait Island cultures, social history and environment; library of 45,000 vols, incl. personal and professional papers and rare books; Dir MATHEW TRINCA (acting); publ. *reCollections* (2 a year, print and online, recollections.nma.gov.au).

New South Wales

Art Gallery of New South Wales: Art Gallery Rd, The Domain, Sydney, NSW 2000; tel. (2) 9225-1700; e-mail artmail@ag.nsw.gov.au; internet www.artgallery.nsw.gov.au; f. 1874; representative colln of Australian art, Aboriginal and Melanesian art; collns of British art since 18th century; European painting and sculpture (since 15th century); Asian art, particularly Chinese and Japanese ceramics and Japanese painting; Australian, British and European prints and drawings, contemporary Australian and foreign art; photography; Pres., Board of Trustees GUIDO BELGIORNO-NETTIS; Vice-Pres. Dr MARK NELSON; Dir Dr MICHAEL BRAND.

Australian Museum: 6 College St, Sydney, NSW 2010; tel. (2) 9320-6000; e-mail library@austmus.gov.au; internet www.australianmuseum.net.au; f. 1827; natural history, museology, anthropology, palaeontology, mineralogy, biodiversity; library of 120,000 vols, 12,000 serial titles and 70,000 monographs; Dir KIM MCKAY; Man. for Devt TEHMI SUKHLA; publ. *Records of the Australian Museum* (4 a year).

Australian National Maritime Museum: POB 5131, Sydney, NSW 2001; 2 Murray St, Sydney, NSW 2000; tel. (2) 9298-3777; e-mail info@anmm.gov.au; internet www.anmm.gov.au; f. 1991; illustrates maritime history as exemplified by the colonial navies, the Royal Australian Navy, merchant shipping and trade, whaling and the fishing industry, explorers and cartographers, immigration, the design and use of leisure and sporting craft and int. competition, surfing, surf life saving and the culture of the beach, and the maritime activities of the Aborigines; models, prints and drawings, glass plate negatives, uniforms, relics, full-size vessels; library of 27,000 vols, 750 periodicals; Chair. PETER DEXTER; Dir MARY-LOUISE WILLIAMS; publ. *Signals* (4 a year).

J. T. Wilson, Museum of Human Anatomy: Rm S421, Anderson Stuart Bldg, Dept of Anatomy, Sydney, NSW 2006; tel. (2) 9351-2816; e-mail marcusr@anatomy.usyd.edu.au; internet sydney.edu.au/medicine/anatomy/museums; f. 1886; attached to Univ. of Sydney; incl. 1,000 dissected parts and cross-sections of the human body; 660 specimens covering all regions of the body; Museum Curator MARCUS ROBINSON.

Macleay Museum: Gosper Lane, off Science Rd, Univ. of Sydney, Sydney, NSW 2006; tel. (2) 9351-2274; e-mail university.museums@sydney.edu.au; internet sydney.edu.au/museums/collections/macleay.shtml; f. 1888 based on colln begun in 1790; attached to Univ. of Sydney; entomology, zoology, ethnology, 19th-century scientific instruments; Australian photographs since 1850s; Dir DAVID ELLIS.

Museum of Applied Arts and Sciences: 500 Harris St, Ultimo, POB K346 Haymarket, Sydney, NSW 1238; tel. (2) 9217-0111; e-mail info@phm.gov.au; internet www.powerhousemuseum.com; f. 1880, present name 1945, present location 1979; public museum operated by the state Govt; comprises Powerhouse Museum (decorative arts, history, science and technology), Sydney Observatory astronomical museum, Powerhouse Discovery Centre; colln stored at Castle Hill; Dir Dr DAWN CASEY.

Museum of Contemporary Art: POB R1286, Royal Exchange, NSW 1223; Level 5, 140 George St, Sydney, NSW 2000; tel. (2) 9245 2400; e-mail mail@mca.com.au; internet www.mca.com.au; f. 1991; promotes creativity and education in the arts; supports and promotes Australian and int. artists; Dir ELIZABETH ANN MACGREGOR.

Nicholson Museum: Univ. of Sydney, Sydney, NSW 2006; tel. (2) 9351-2812; e-mail nicholsonmuseum@usyd.edu.au; internet sydney.edu.au/museums/collections/nicholson.shtml; f. 1860; attached to Univ. of Sydney; colln of Egyptian, Near East, Cypriot, European, Greek and Roman antiquities; Dir DAVID ELLIS; Sr Curator MICHAEL TURNER.

Northern Territory

Museum and Art Gallery of the Northern Territory: GPOB 4646, Darwin, NT 0801; Conacher St, Bullocky Point, Darwin, NT 0820; tel. (8) 8999 8264; e-mail museum.magnt@nt.gov.au; internet www.nretas.nt.gov.au/arts-and-museums; f. 1969; art, history, culture, and natural history of the N Territory, particularly Aboriginal visual arts and material culture; SE Asian and Oceanic art and material culture; maritime archaeology; 5 major permanent galleries; touring gallery; educational facilities for students; library of 10,000 vols, 1,000 serials; Dir ANNA MALGORZEWICZ.

Queensland

Queensland Art Gallery: POB 3686, S Brisbane, QLD 4101; Stanley St, S Brisbane, QLD 4101; tel. (7) 3840-7333; e-mail gallery@qag.qld.gov.au; f. 1895, opened 2nd site, Gallery of Modern Art (GoMA) in 2006, incl. Australian Cinematheque and Children's Art Centre; state colln of Australian and int. paintings, prints, drawings and photographs, sculpture and decorative arts; education and advisory services; holds Asia Pacific Triennial of contemporary art; library of 35,000 books, 500 periodicals, photographs, catalogues, Asia Pacific research colln; Dir TONY ELLWOOD; publ. *Artlines*.

Queensland Herbarium: Brisbane Botanic Gardens Mt Coot-tha, Mt Coot-tha Rd, Toowong, QLD 4066; tel. (7) 3896-9326; e-mail info@ehp.qld.gov.au; internet http://www.qld.gov.au/environment/plants-animals/plants/herbarium/; f. 1874 as Botanic Museum and Herbarium; research and information on the flora, ecology and vegetation of Queensland, rare and threatened plant species and ecosystems, weeds, poisonous plants and economic botany; 811,000 specimens of plants, algae, lichens and fungi; library of 10,000 vols; Queensland Minister for Environment and Heritage Protection ANDREW POWELL; publ. *Austrobaileya* (1 a year).

Queensland Museum: POB 3300, Cultural Centre, South Bank, BC, South Brisbane, QLD 4101; tel. (7) 3840-7555; e-mail discoverycentre@qm.qld.gov.au; internet www.qm.qld.gov.au; f. 1862; anthropology, geology, history, palaeontology, technology, zoology; library of 95,000 vols incl. 5,000 serial titles, 900 rare books, 2,000 maps; special colln incl. Library of the Royal Society of Queensland, Parnell Colln on the Anthropology, History and Natural History of New Guinea, Australian Patents colln and Thomas Macleod Queensland Aviation Colln; Chief Exec. Officer Dr IAN GALLOWAY; Dir Dr GRAEME POTTER; publs *Memoirs of the Queensland Museum*, *Memoirs of the Queensland Museum: Cultural Heritage Series*.

South Australia

Art Gallery of South Australia: N Terrace, Adelaide, SA 5000; tel. (8) 8207-7000; e-mail agsainformation@artgallery.sa.gov.au; internet www.artgallery.sa.gov.au; f. 1881, present status 1967; comprehensive colln of Australian works of art, British and European painting, prints, drawings and sculpture 16th century to present; British, European and Asian decorative arts; Indian and Indonesian textiles and Japanese art, early S Australian pictures; public programmes; guided tours; education services; library of 37,000 vols; journals, ephemera colln; Dir NICK MITZEVICH; publ. *Articulate* (4 a year).

South Australian Museum: N Terrace, Adelaide, SA 5000; tel. (8) 8207-7500; e-mail marketing@samuseum.sa.gov.au; internet www.samuseum.sa.gov.au; f. 1856; anthropological, geological and zoological material mainly related to SA; Australian ethnological colln; education and advisory services; school holiday programme; public exhibitions; Waterhouse art prize; ANZANG nature photography competition; information centre; library of 45,000 vols, 7,000 monographs, 2,300 rare books, 30,000 journals and 21,200 photographic images; Dir BRIAN OLDMAN; Librarian JILL EVANS; publ. *Transactions of the Royal Society of South Australia (incorporating Records of the South Australian Museum)*.

Tasmania

Queen Victoria Museum and Art Gallery: POB 403, Launceston, TAS 7250; Two Invermay Rd, Launceston, TAS 7248; tel. (3) 6323-3777; e-mail enquiries@qvmag.tas.gov.au; internet www.qvmag.tas.gov.au; f. 1891; collns comprise pure and applied art, Tasmanian history, Tasmanian and gen. anthropology, Tasmanian botany, geology, palaeontology and zoology; library of 11,000 vols; Dir RICHARD MULVANEY; publ. *Occasional Papers*.

Tasmanian Museum and Art Gallery: GPOB 1164, Hobart, TAS 7001; 5 Argyle St, Hobart, TAS 7001; tel. (3) 6211-4177; e-mail tmagmail@tmag.tas.gov.au; internet www.tmag.tas.gov.au; f. 1852; applied science, art and natural and human history, with emphasis on Tasmania and Australia generally; incl. Tasmanian Herbarium, coin collns, early photography, collns relating to the Aboriginal people of Tasmania; collns also at the W Coast Pioneers' Museum at Zeehan (mining, local history and minerals); and the Australasian Golf Museum at Bothwell (golfing memorabilia); Chair. GUY GREEN; Dir BILL BLEATHMAN; publ. *Research Journal—Kanunnah* (1 a year).

Victoria

Museum Victoria: GPOB 666, Melbourne, VIC 3001; tel. (3) 8341-7777; internet museumvictoria.com.au; f. 1854 as Nat. Museum of Victoria, present name 1983; takes responsibility for the state's scientific and cultural collns; provides public access through three museums; CEO Dr J. PATRICK GREENE; Pres. Prof. MARGARET GARDNER; Treas. MICHAEL PERRY; publ. *Memoirs of Museum Victoria* (1 a year).

Constituent Museums:

Immigration Museum: Old Customs House, 400 Flinders St, Melbourne, VIC 3000; tel. (3) 9927-2700; internet museumvictoria.com.au/immigrationmuseum; f. 1998; recreates the real-life stories of coming to Australia with moving images, personal and community voices, memories and memorabilia.

Melbourne Museum: 11 Nicholson St, Carlton Gardens, Carlton, VIC 3053; tel. (3) 8341-7777; internet museumvictoria.com.au/melbournemuseum; f. 2000; science, technology, Australian soc., environment, indigenous cultures and human mind and body; incl. Aboriginal Centre, Children's Museum, living forest gallery, IMAX theatre and Royal Exhibition Building.

Scienceworks Museum: POB 666, Melbourne, VIC 3001; 2 Booker St, Spotswood, VIC 3015; tel. (3) 9392-4800; internet museumvictoria.com.au/scienceworks; f. 1992; science and technology, Melbourne Planetarium, Spotswood Pumping Station.

National Gallery of Victoria: POB 7259, St Kilda Rd, Melbourne, VIC 8004; tel. (3) 8620-2222; e-mail enquiries@ngv.vic.gov.au; internet www.ngv.vic.gov.au; f. 1861; old masters and depts of prints and drawings, modern European art, Australian art, aboriginal and Oceanic art, decorative art and design, Asian art, antiquities, photography, pre-Columbian art, costume and textiles; library of 45,000 vols, and 50,000 monographs, serials and auction catalogues; Dir TONY ELLWOOD; publs *Art Journal of the National Gallery of Victoria* (1 a year), *Gallery* (6 a year).

Western Australia

Art Gallery of Western Australia: POB 8363, Perth Business Centre, Perth, WA 6849; Perth Cultural Centre, Perth, WA 6000; tel. (8) 9492-6600; e-mail admin@artgallery.wa.gov.au; internet www.artgallery.wa.gov.au; f. 1895; develops the art colln in WA by acquiring, preserving, displaying and interpreting the visual arts from the past and present; aboriginal art, Australian and foreign paintings, sculpture, decorative arts and crafts; free guided tours; public and educational programmes; library of 17,000 vols; Dir Dr STEFANO CARBONI.

Western Australian Museum: Locked Bag 49, Welshpool DC, Perth, WA 6986; 49 Kew St, Welshpool, Perth, WA 6106; tel. (8) 9212-3700; e-mail reception@museum.wa.gov.au; internet www.museum.wa.gov.au; f. 1891 as the Geological Museum; present name adopted 1897; 4.6m. objects and artefacts; anthropology and archaeology, aquatic zoology, earth and planetary sciences, maritime archaeology, maritime history, materials conservation, social history, terrestrial zoology; library of 20,000 vols, 1,500 journal titles, 750 old and rare books; Chair. Investment Committee JUSTIN MANNOLINI.

Universities

AUSTRALIAN CAPITAL TERRITORY

AUSTRALIAN NATIONAL UNIVERSITY

Canberra, ACT 0200
Telephone: (2) 6125-5111
E-mail: admiss.enq@anu.edu.au
Internet: www.anu.edu.au
Founded 1946
Academic year: March to December
Chancellor: Prof. GARETH EVANS
Pro-Chancellor: ILANA ATLAS
Vice-Chancellor, CEO and Pres.: Prof. IAN YOUNG
Deputy Vice-Chancellor for Academic Affairs: Prof. MARNIE HUGHES-WARRINGTON
Deputy Vice-Chancellor for Research and Vice-Pres.: Prof. LAWRENCE CRAM
Pro-Vice-Chancellor for E-Strategies: Prof. ROBIN STANTON
Pro-Vice-Chancellor for Innovation and Advancement: Prof. MICHAEL CARDEW-HALL
Pro-Vice-Chancellor for Int. and Outreach: (vacant)
Pro-Vice-Chancellor for Research and Research Training: Prof. MANDY THOMAS
Pro-Vice-Chancellor for Students: Prof. ELIZABETH DEANE
Exec. Dir for Admin. and Planning: Dr BROK GLENN
Univ. Librarian: MAGGIE SHAPLEY (acting)
Library: see under Libraries and Archives
Number of teachers: 1,578
Number of students: 16,715

DEANS

ANU College of Arts and Social Sciences: Prof. TONI MAKKAI
ANU College of Asia and the Pacific: Prof. ANDREW MACINTYRE
ANU College of Business and Economics: Prof. JAYNE GODFREY
ANU College of Engineering and Computer Science: Prof. JOHN HOSKING
ANU College of Law: MICHAEL COPER
ANU College of Medicine, Biology and Environment: Prof. NICHOLAS GLASGOW
ANU College of Physical and Mathematical Sciences: Prof. AIDAN BYRNE
Australian National Institute for Public Policy: Prof. ADAM GRAYCAR

UNIVERSITY OF CANBERRA

ACT 2601
Univ. Dr., Bruce, ACT 2617
Telephone: (2) 6201-5111
E-mail: international@canberra.edu.au
Internet: www.canberra.edu.au
Founded 1990 from fmr Canberra CAE
State control
Academic year: February to December (3 semesters)
Chancellor: JOHN MACKAY
Vice-Chancellor and Pres.: Dr Prof. STEPHEN PARKER
Deputy Vice-Chancellor and Vice-Pres. for Education: Prof. NICHOLAS KLOMP
Deputy Vice-Chancellor for Research: Prof. FRANCES SHANNON
Pro-Vice-Chancellor for Int. and Major Projects: Prof. MONIQUE SKIDMORE
Group Chief Operating Officer: MARIA STORTI
Registrar: BRUCE LINES
Univ. Librarian: ANITA R. M. CROTTY
Library: see under Libraries and Archives
Number of teachers: 449 (full-time)
Number of students: 14,113

DEANS

Faculty of Applied Science: Prof. ARTHUR GEORGES
Faculty of Arts and Design: Prof. LYNDON ANDERSON
Faculty of Business, Govt and Law: Prof. LAWRENCE PRATCHETT
Faculty of Education, Science, Technology and Mathematics: Prof. GEOFFREY RIORDAN
Faculty of Health: Prof. DIANE GIBSON
Faculty of Information Sciences and Engineering: Prof. DHARMENDRA SHARMA

PROFESSORS

AKERLIND, G., Teaching & Learning
AULICH, C., Public Administration
BATTYE, G., Media Arts
BERRY, H., Public Health
BLACKMAN, D.
BLOOD, R. W., Professional Communication
BOER, D., Clinical Psychology
BOTTERILL, L., Australian Public Policy
CAMPBELL, J., Information Systems
CAPON, T., Public Health
CHO, G., Geoinformatics and the Law
COCHRANE, T., Public Health
CREAGH, D., Physics
CRUICKSHANK, M., Nursing
DALY, A., Economics
DAVEY, R., Public Health
DAVIS, D., Nursing & Midwifery
DUNCAN, A.
EASTEAL, P., Law
EVANS, M.
FITZGERALD, R., Education
GEORGES, A., Applied Ecology
HALLIGAN, J., Public Administration
HARTOONIAN, G., Architecture
HONE, J., Wildlife Management
KEATING, B., Management Studies
LEAHY, P.
LENNARD, C., Forensic Studies
LEWIS, P., Economics
MAHER, B., Environmental Chemistry
MAK, A., Psychology
MCDONALD, C., Informatics
MCQUEEN, K., Earth Science
MIR, M., Accounting, Banking & Finance
NORMAN, B., Urban Planning
PAMPHILON, B., Development & International
PUTNIS, P., Communication
QUAZI, A., Communication
RAFF, M., Law
RICKETSON, M., Journalism
RICKWOOD, D., Psychology
ROBERTSON, J., Forensic Studies
SARRE, S., Wildlife Genetics
SATHYE, M., Public Administration
SHARMA, D., Software Engineering
SOFO, F., Community Education
SPRIGGS, J., Community Education
THOMPSON, K., Sports Studies
TURNER, M., Public Administration
WADDINGTON, G., Physiotherapy
WAGNER, M., Software Engineering
WATSON, L., Secondary Education
WEBB, J., Writing
WILLIAMS, L., Nutrition & Dietetics
ZOU, P., Building & Construction Management

NEW SOUTH WALES

AUSTRALIAN CATHOLIC UNIVERSITY

POB 968, N Sydney, NSW 2059
40 Edward St, N Sydney, NSW 2060
Telephone: (2) 9739-2368
E-mail: studentcentre@mackillop.acu.edu.au
Internet: www.acu.edu.au

Founded 1991 by amalgamation of Catholic College of Education, Sydney, Institute of Catholic Education, Victoria, McAuley College, Brisbane, and Signadou College, Canberra
Academic year: February to December
Chancellor: Gen. PETER COSGROVE
Pro-Chancellor: EDWARD EXELL
Vice-Chancellor: Prof. GREG CRAVEN
Deputy Vice-Chancellor for Academic Affairs: Prof. PAULINE NUGENT
Deputy Vice-Chancellor for Admin. and Resources: JOHN CAMERON
Deputy Vice-Chancellor for Research: Prof. THOMAS MARTIN
Deputy Vice-Chancellor for Students, Learning and Teaching: Prof. ANNE CUMMINS
Exec. Dir for Univ. Services: JOHN CAMERON
Dir for Libraries: FIDES LAWTON
Library of 460,903 vols, 2,296 periodicals, 5,415 online journals
Number of teachers: 784
Number of students: 20,446
Publications: *ACU Insight* (4 a year), *Interlogue* (2 a year), *Journal of Religious Education* (4 a year)

DEANS

Faculty of Arts and Sciences: Prof. Dr GAIL CROSSLEY
Faculty of Business: Prof. ELIZABETH MORE
Faculty of Education: Prof. MARIE EMMITT
Faculty of Health Sciences: Prof. MICHELLE CAMPBELL
Faculty of Theology and Philosophy: Prof. ANNE HUNT

AUSTRALIAN COLLEGE OF THEOLOGY

Suite 4, Level 6, 51 Druitt St, Sydney, NSW 2000
Telephone: (2) 9262-7890
E-mail: info@actheology.edu.au
Internet: www.actheology.edu.au
Founded 1891
Private control
Bachelors and Masters degrees in divinity and ministry; doctoral degrees in ministry, philosophy and theology
CEO and Dean: Rev. Dr MARK HARDING
Dir for Academic Services: SIMON DAVIES
Assoc. Dean for Learning, Teaching and Research: Rev. GRAEME CHATFIELD
Finance Officer: VICKI CHEN
Number of students: 2,400

CHARLES STURT UNIVERSITY

Chancellery, Panorama Ave, Bathurst, NSW 2795
Telephone: (2) 6338-4000
E-mail: inquiry@csu.edu.au
Internet: www.csu.edu.au
Founded 1989 by merger of Mitchell College of Advanced Education (f. 1951) with Riverina-Murray Institute of Higher Education (f. 1947)
State control
Academic year: January to December
Chancellor: LAWRENCE WILLETT
Vice-Chancellor and Pres.: Prof. ANDREW VANN
Deputy Vice-Chancellor: SHIRLEY OAKLEY
Deputy Vice-Chancellor for Academic Affairs: Prof. GARRY MARCHANT
Deputy Vice-Chancellor for Research: Prof. SUE THOMAS
Deputy Vice-Chancellor for Admin. Services: Prof. KEN DILLON
Univ. Sec. and Dir Corporate Affairs: MARK BURDACK
Exec. Dir for Finance: PAUL DOWLER
Exec. Dir for Library Services: KAREN JOHNSON
Library of 619,171 vols
Number of teachers: 850
Number of students: 39,379

DEANS

Faculty of Arts: Assoc. Prof. TRACEY GREEN
Faculty of Business: Prof. LESLEY WHITE
Faculty of Education: Prof. TONI DOWNES
Faculty of Science: Prof. TIM WESS

CONSTITUENT CAMPUSES

Albury–Wodonga Campus

POB 789, Albury, NSW 2640
Telephone: (2) 6051-9000
E-mail: inquiry@csu.edu.au
Internet: www.csu.edu.au
Founded 1989
Head of Campus: Prof. SUE MOLONEY

Bathurst Campus

Panorama Ave, Bathurst, NSW 2795
Telephone: (2) 6338-4000
E-mail: inquiry@csu.edu.au
Internet: www.csu.edu.au
Founded 1989
Head of Campus: COLIN SHARP

Canberra Campus

15 Blackall St, Barton, ACT 2600
Telephone: (2) 6272-6252
E-mail: inquiry@csu.edu.au
Internet: www.csu.edu.au
Founded 1998

Dubbo Campus

Locked Bag 49, Dubbo E, NSW 2830
Telephone: (2) 6885-7300
E-mail: inquiry@csu.edu.au
Internet: www.csu.edu.au
Founded 1995
Head of Campus: Dr BEVERLEY MORIARTY

Goulburn Campus

Locked Bag 2005, Goulburn, NSW 2580
Telephone: (2) 4824-2521
E-mail: inquiry@csu.edu.au
Internet: www.csu.edu.au
Founded 1970

Manly Campus

POB 168, Manly, NSW 1655
Telephone: (2) 9934-4828
E-mail: inquiry@csu.edu.au
Internet: www.csu.edu.au
Founded 1992

Ontario Campus/CSU Ontario School of Education

860 Harrington Court, Burlington, ON Canada L7N 3N4
Telephone: (5) 333-4955
E-mail: canada@csu.edu.au
Internet: www.charlessturt.ca
State control
Language of instruction: English
Academic year: September to May
Head of Campus: Prof. WILLIAM LETTS
Dean of Faculty of Education: Dr TONI DOWNES

Orange Campus

POB 883, Orange, NSW 2800
Telephone: (2) 6365-7500
E-mail: inquiry@csu.edu.au
Internet: www.csu.edu.au
Head of Campus: Prof. Dr HEATHER ROBINSON

Port Macquarie Campus

POB 2136, Port Macquarie, NSW 2444
Telephone: (2) 6582-9334
E-mail: inquiry@csu.edu.au
Internet: www.csu.edu.au
Founded 2012
Head of Campus: Prof. ROSS CHAMBERS

Wagga Wagga Campus

Locked Bag 588, Wagga Wagga, NSW 2678
Telephone: (2) 6933-2000
E-mail: inquiry@csu.edu.au
Internet: www.csu.edu.au
Founded 1989
Head of Campus: ADRIAN LINDNER

MACQUARIE UNIVERSITY

Balaclava Rd, North Ryde, NSW 2109
Telephone: (2) 9850-7111
E-mail: mqinfo@mq.edu.au
Internet: www.mq.edu.au
Founded 1964, opened 1967
State control
Academic year: January to December
Chancellor: Hon. MICHAEL RUEBEN EGAN
Chief Operating Officer: Dr PAUL SCHREIER
Deputy Chancellor: ELIZABETH CROUCH
Vice-Chancellor: Prof. BRUCE DOWTON
Deputy Vice-Chancellor and Provost: Prof. JUDYTH SACHS
Deputy Vice-Chancellor for Research: Prof. SAKKIE PRETORIUS
Deputy Vice-Chancellor for Students and Registrar: DEIDRE ANDERSON
Deputy Vice-Chancellor for Corporate Engagement and Advancement: Prof. DAVID WILKINSON
Chief Financial Officer: JOHN GORMAN
Gen. Counsel: PAUL LUTTRELL
Univ. Librarian: JOANNE SPARKS
Library: 1.8m. vols
Number of teachers: 1,158
Number of students: 37,921
Publications: *Quest* (4 a year), *Research Report* (1 a year)

DEANS

Faculty of Arts: Prof. JOHN SIMONS (Exec. Dean)
Faculty of Business and Economics: Prof. MARK GABBOTT (Exec. Dean)
Faculty of Human Sciences: Prof. JANET GREELEY (Exec. Dean)
Faculty of Science: Prof. PETER NELSON (acting) (Exec. Dean)
Macquarie Graduate School of Management: Dr GUY FORD (Dir)
Sydney Institute of Business and Technology: SONIA JEFFARES (Dir)

SOUTHERN CROSS UNIVERSITY

POB 157, Lismore, NSW 2480
Military Rd E, Lismore, NSW 2480
Telephone: (2) 6620-3000
E-mail: enquiry@scu.edu.au
Internet: www.scu.edu.au

Founded 1970 as Lismore Teachers College, current name adopted 1994
Academic year: February to November (2 semesters)
Campuses at Lismore, Coffs Harbour and Tweed Heads
Chancellor: JOHN DOWD
Vice-Chancellor: Prof. PETER LEE
Pro Vice-Chancellor for Academics: ANDREW MCAULEY
Pro Vice-Chancellor for Int. and Enterprise: CHRIS PATTON
Library: incl. Australian Baptist heritage colln
Number of teachers: 350
Number of students: 14,631
Publication: *Research Report* (1 a year)

DEANS

Gnibi College of Indigenous Australian Peoples: Prof. ADRIAN MILLER
Hotel School Sydney: PAUL WEEKS (Dir)
School of Arts and Social Sciences: Prof. MIKE EVANS
School of Education: Prof. MARTIN HAYDEN (Head)
School of Environmental Science and Management: Prof. JERRY VANCLAY (Head)
School of Health and Human Sciences: Prof. IAIN GRAHAM
School of Law and Justice: Prof. ROCQUE REYNOLDS
School of Tourism and Hospitality Management: Prof. SANDRA SPEEDY (acting) (Head)
Southern Cross Business School: Prof. STEPHEN KELLY (Head)

PROFESSORS

ATKINSON, J., Indigenous Australian Peoples
BAVERSTOCK, P., Graduate Research College (and PVC Research)
BRAITHWAITE, R., Tourism and Hospitality Management
DELVES, A., University Enterprise and International Activities (PVC)
GARTSIDE, D. F., Resource Science and Management
GRAHAM, J., Health and Applied Sciences Division (Executive Dean)
HAYDEN, M., Teaching and Learning Unit
HENRY, R. J., Plant Conservation Genetics
JACKSON, J. G., Law and Justice
KLICH, Z., University Academic and Quality Matters (PVC)
KOUZMIN, A., Graduate College of Management
LEIPER, N., Tourism and Hospitality Management
MCCONCHIE, D., Environmental Science and Management
MEREDITH, G., Business Administration
MURUGESAN, S., Multimedia and Information Technology
NECK, P., Business Administration
ROTHWELL, B., Manager, Tweed Gold Coast Campus
SAENGER, P., Environmental Science and Management
SAVERY, L., Business Division (Executive Dean)
SCOTT, D., Commerce and Management
SIMPSON, R., National Marine Science Centre
SPECHT, R., Environmental Science and Management
SPEEDY, G., Teaching and Learning Centre
TAYLOR, B., Nursing and Health Care Practices
THOM, P., Arts Division (Executive Dean)
VANCLAY, J., Environmental Science and Management
WILSON, P., Psychology
YEO, S. M. H., Law and Justice
ZANN, L. P., Environmental Science and Management

UNIVERSITY OF NEW ENGLAND

Armidale, NSW 2351
Telephone: (2) 6773-3333
E-mail: admissions@une.edu.au
Internet: www.une.edu.au

Founded 1954; previously New England Univ. College (f. 1938); Armidale College of Advanced Education merged with the Univ. in 1989
commonwealth govt control
Academic year: February to November (2 semesters)
Chancellor: RICHARD TORBAY
Deputy Chancellor: SCOTT WILLIAMS
Deputy Vice-Chancellor for Research: Prof. ANNABELLE DUNCAN
Vice-Chancellor and CEO: Prof. Dr JIM BARBER
Chair. to the Academic Board: Prof. EILIS MAGNER
Pro-Vice-Chancellor: Prof. JENNIE SHAW
Pro-Vice-Chancellor: Prof. Dr VICTOR MINICHIELLO
Pro-Vice-Chancellor for Students and Social Inclusion: Prof. EVELYN WOODBERRY
Exec. Dir for Business and Admin.: G. DENNEHY
Sec. to Academic Board: CAROLINE GIRVIN
Librarian: BARBARA PATON (acting)
Library: see under Libraries and Archives
Number of teachers: 484
Number of students: 18,863
Publications: *Australasian Victorian Studies Journal* (1 a year), *Australian Folklore: A Yearly Journal of Folklore Studies*, *Journal of Australian Colonial History* (2 a year), *South Asia* (1 a year), *TalentEd* (3 a year), *The University of New England Law Journal* (2 a year), *Wool Technology and Sheep Breeding* (4 a year)

DEANS

Faculty of Arts and Sciences: Prof. JENNIE SHAW
Faculty of the Professions: Prof. Dr VICTOR MINICHIELLO

PROFESSORS

BINDON, B., CRC for Cattle and Beef Quality
BOULTON, A. J., Environmental Sciences and Natural Resources Management
BRASTED, H. V., Classics, History and Religion
BRUNCKHORST, D., Institute for Rural Futures/UNESCO Centre for Bioregional Resource Management
BYRNE, B. J., Psychology
CARRINGTON, K. L., Social Sciences
CHOCT, M., Rural Science and Agriculture
COLBRAN, S., Law
COOKSEY, R. W., New England Business School
COTTLE, D., Rural Science and Agriculture
DAVIDSON, I., Human and Environmental Studies
DOLLERY, B. E., Economics
ECKERMAN, A.-K., Professional Development and Leadership
FORD, H. A., Environmental Sciences and Natural Resources Management
FORREST, P. R. H., Social Sciences
FRANZMANN, M., Classics, History and Religion
GEISER, F., Environmental Sciences and Natural Resources Management
GIBSON, J., Rural Science and Agriculture
GODDARD, C. W., Languages, Cultures and Linguistics
GOSSIP, C. J., Languages, Cultures and Linguistics
GUNTER, M. J., Biological and Molecular Sciences
HORSLEY, G. H. R., Classics, History and Religion
HUTCHINSON, P. J., New England Business School
KAUR, A., Economics
KENT, D. A., Classics, History and Religion
KIERNANDER, A. R. D., English, Communication and Theatre
KINGHORN, B. P., Rural Science and Agriculture
LLOYD, C., Economics
MAGNER, E. S., Law
MEEK, V. L., Professional Development and Leadership
NOBLE, W., Psychology
NOLAN, J. V., Rural Science and Agriculture
PEGG, J. E., Education
ROGERS, L. J., Biological, Biomedical and Molecular Sciences
ROWE, J. B., Rural Science and Agriculture
RUVINSKY, A., Rural Science and Agriculture
SAJEEV, A. S. M., Mathematics, Statistics and Computing Science
SCOTT, J. M., Rural Science and Agriculture
SIMPSON, R. D., Environmental Sciences and Natural Resources Management
TAJI, A., Rural Science and Agriculture
THOMPSON, J. M., Rural Science and Agriculture
TREADGOLD, M. L., Economics
UNSWORTH, L., Education
WALMSLEY, D. J., Human and Environmental Studies
WARE, H. R., Professional Development and Leadership
WATSON, K., Biological, Biomedical and Molecular Sciences

UNIVERSITY OF NEW SOUTH WALES

Sydney, NSW 2052
Telephone: (2) 9385-1000
E-mail: studentcentral@unsw.edu.au
Internet: www.unsw.edu.au

Founded 1949
Academic year: February to November (2 sessions)
Chancellor: DAVID GONSKI
Pres. and Vice-Chancellor: Professor FRED HILMER
Deputy Vice-Chancellor for Academic Affairs: Prof. RICHARD HENRY
Deputy Vice-Chancellor for Research: Prof. LES FIELD
Pro-Vice-Chancellor for Research: Prof. MARGARET HARDING
Pro-Vice-Chancellor for Students: Prof. WAI FONG CHUA
Pro-Vice-Chancellor UNSW Int.: JENNIE LANG
Pres. of the Academic Board: Prof. PREM RAMBURUTH

Exec. Dir of Finance and Operations: JONATHAN BLAKEMAN
Chief Exec., UNSW Foundation: JENNIFER BOTT
Exec. Dir for Univ. Services: NEIL MORRIS
Univ. Librarian: ANDREW WELLS

Number of teachers: 2,497 (f.t.e.)
Number of students: 46,000

DEANS

Australian School of Business: Prof. Dr ALEC CAMERON
College of Fine Arts: Prof. IAN HOWARD
Faculty of Arts and Social Sciences: Prof. Dr JAMES DONALD
Faculty of Engineering: Prof. Dr GRAHAM DAVIES
Faculty of Law: Prof. Dr DAVID DIXON
Faculty of Medicine: Prof. PETER SMITH
Faculty of Science: Prof. Dr MERLIN CROSSLEY
Faculty of the Built Environment: Prof. ALEC TZANNES
Graduate Research: Prof. Dr LAURA POOLE-WARREN
UNSW at the Australian Defence Force Academy: Prof. MICHAEL FRATER (Rector)

PROFESSORS

Faculty of Arts and Social Sciences:

ALEXANDER, C., English
ALEXANDER, P., English
ASHCROFT, W., English
BELL, P., History and Philosophy of Science
BELL, R., History
BENNETT, B., Humanities
CAHILL, D., History
CASS, B., Social Policy
CHAN, J., Social Sciences and Policy
CHANDLER, P., Education
CONDREN, C., Politics and International Politics
COOPER, M., Education
COTTON, J., Humanities
DANIEL, A., Sociology
DENNIS, P., Humanities
DONALD, J., Media, Film and Theatre
EGGERT, P., Humanities
GASCOIGNE, J., History
GREY, J., Humanities
GROSS, M., Education
HALL, R., Social Sciences and Policy
HUGMAN, R., Social Work
HUMPHREY, M., Sociology
JOHNSON, R., History
KATZ, I., Social Policy
KITCHING, G., Politics and International Relations
LYONS, M., History
OLDROYD, D., History and Philosophy of Science
PATTON, P., Philosophy
PEARSON, M., History
SAUNDERS, P., Social Policy
SCHUSTER, J., Media and Communications
SWELLER, J., Education
THAYER, C., Humanities
TYRRELL, I., History
WILLIAMS, M., Politics and International Relations
WOODMAN, S., Humanities

Faculty of Commerce and Economics:

ANDERSON, E., Economics
BALZER, L., Banking and Finance
BROWN, R., Accounting
DWYER, L., Accounting
FELDMAN, D., Banking and Finance
FIEBIG, D., Economics
FOSTER, F., Banking and Finance
FOX, K., Economics
HILL, R., Economics
KOHN, R., Economics
LAYTON, R., Marketing
MORRISON, P., Marketing
MOSHIRIAN, F., Banking and Finance
UNCLES, M., Marketing

Faculty of Engineering:

ACWORTH, R., Civil Engineering
ADESINA, A., Chemical Engineering
ASHBOLT, N., Civil and Environmental Engineering
BRADFORD, M., Civil and Environmental Engineering
CARMICHAEL, D., Civil and Environmental Engineering
CELLER, B., Electrical Engineering
CHATTOPADHYAY, G., Civil and Environmental Engineering
COMPTON, P. J., Computer Science
CROSKY, A., Materials Science and Engineering
DAVIS, T., Chemical Engineering
DOCTORS, L., Mechanical Engineering
DZURAK, A., Electronic Engineering and Telecommunications
FANE, A., Chemical Engineering
FELL, R., Civil and Environmental Engineering
FLEET, G., Chemical Engineering
FOO, N., Computer Science
FORSTER, B., Surveying and Spatial Information Systems
FOSTER, N., Chemical Engineering
GALVIN, J., Mining Engineering
GILBERT, R., Civil and Environmental Engineering
HEBBLEWHITE, B., Mining Engineering
HEISER, G., Computer Science
HOUGH, R., Engineering
JEFFERY, R., Computer Science
KAEBERNICK, H., Mechanical Engineering
KELLY, D., Mechanical Engineering
LEONARDI, E., Mechanical Engineering
MAROSSZEKY, M., Civil and Environmental Engineering
MORRISON, G., Mechanical Engineering
NOWOTNY, J., Materials Science and Engineering
OSTROVSKI, O., Materials Science and Engineering
PINCZEWSKI, W., Petroleum Engineering
RANDALL, R., Mechanical Engineering
RIZOS, C., Surveying and Spatial Information Systems
SAHAJWALLA, V., Materials Science and Engineering
SAMMUT, C., Computer Science
SAVKIN, A., Electrical Engineering
SCHINDHELM, K., Biomedical Engineering
SENEVIRATNE, A., Electrical Engineering
SHARMA, A., Civil and Environmental Engineering
SHAW, J., Computer Science
SKYLLAS-KAZACOS, M., Chemical Engineering
SOLO, V., Electrical Engineering
SORRELL, C., Materials Science and Engineering
TIN LOI, F., Civil and Environmental Engineering
TRIMM, D., Chemical Engineering
TRINDER, J., Surveying and Spatial Information Systems
VALLIAPPAN, S., Civil and Environmental Engineering
WAITE, D., Civil and Environmental Engineering
WENHAM, S., Photovoltaic Engineering
YU, A., Materials Science and Engineering

Faculty of Law:

ARONSON, M., Law
BROWN, D., Law
BYRNES, A., Law
CUNNEEN, C., Law
DISNEY, J., Law
DIXON, D., Law
GREENLEAF, G., Law
KINGSFORD-SMITH, D., Law
KRYGIER, M., Law
REDMOND, P., Law
WILLIAMS, G., Law

Faculty of Medicine:

ANDERSON, D., Medicine
ANDREWS, J., Psychiatry
BARRY, P., Physiology
BENNETT, M., Obstetrics and Gynaecology
BRODATY, H., Psychiatry
CALVERT, G., Medicine
CAMPBELL, T., Medicine
CHESTERMAN, C., Medicine, Pathology
CHISHOLM, D., Medicine, Metabolic Research
CHONG, B., Medicine
COIERA, E., Medical Sciences
COOPER, D., Medicine
CORONEO, M., Ophthalmology
DAY, R., Medicine, Clinical Pharmacology
DEANE, S., Surgery
DICKSON, H., Rehabilitation, Aged and Extended Care
EISENBUCH, I., Medicine
EISMAN, J., Medicine, Bone and Mineral Research
GANDEVIA, S., Medicine
GECZY, C., Pathology
GRAHAM, R., Medicine
HALL, B., Medicine
HARRIS, M., Medicine
HARRISON, G., Anaesthetics
HARVEY, R., Medicine
HENRY, R., Paediatrics
HILLMAN, K., Anaesthetics and Intensive Care
HOGG, P., Pathology
HOLDEN, B. A., Optometry
HOWES, L., Medicine, Physiology
KALDOR, J., Epidemiology
KEARSLEY, J., Surgery
KHACHIGIAN, L., Pathology
KIPPAX, S., HIV Social Research Centre
KRILIS, S., Medicine
KUMAR, R., Pathology
LAWSON, J., Health Services Management
LEE, A., Medical Microbiology
LLOYD, A., Pathology
LORD, R., Surgery
LUMBERS, E., Physiology
MACDONALD, G., Medicine
MCLACHLAN, E., Physiology, Medical Research
MORRIS, D., Surgery
O'ROURKE, M., Medicine
O'SULLIVAN, W., Medical Biochemistry
PARKER, G., Psychiatry
POOLE, M., Surgery
RICHMOND, R., Medicine
ROTEM, A., Medical Education
ROWE, M., Physiology
RUSSELL, P., Medicine
SCHINDHELM, K., Biomedical Engineering
SILOVE, D., Psychiatry
TARANTOLA, D., Medicine
TORDA, T. A., Anaesthetics and Intensive Care
WAKEFIELD, D., Pathology
WHITE, L., Paediatrics
ZWAR, N., Paediatrics
ZWI, A., Paediatrics

Faculty of Science:

ADAMS, M., Biological, Earth and Environmental Science
BALLARD, J., Biotechnology and Biomolecular Science
BISHOP, R., Chemical Sciences
BLACK, D. ST C., Chemical Sciences
BRYANT, R., Psychology
CADOGAN, M., Physics
CAMPBELL, S., Physical, Environmental and Mathematical Sciences
CLARK, R., Physics
COOPER, D., Biological, Earth and Environmental Science
COUCH, W., Physics
COWLING, M., Mathematics
DADDS, M., Psychology
DAIN, S., Optometry

DAWES, W., Biotechnology and Biomolecular Science
DORAN, P., Biotechnology and Biomolecular Science
DUNSMUIR, W., Mathematics
ENGLAND, M., Mathematics
FLAMBAUM, V., Physics
FORGAS, J., Psychology
GAL, M., Physics
GILLAM, B., Psychology
GRAY, P., Biotechnology and Biomolecular Science
HIBBERT, D., Chemical Sciences
HUON, G., Psychology
JACKSON, W., Physical, Environmental and Mathematical Sciences
KEHOE, J., Psychology
KINGSFORD, R., Biological, Earth and Environmental Science
KJELLEBERG, S., Biotechnology and Biomolecular Science
LAMB, R., Chemical Sciences
LESLIE, L., Mathematics
LITTLE, F., Biotechnology and Biomolecular Science
LOVIBOND, P., Psychology
MCCONKEY, K., Psychology
MCLEAN, R., Physical, Environmental and Mathematical Sciences
MCMURTRIE, R., Biological, Earth and Environmental Science
MIDDLETON, J., Mathematics
NEILAN, B., Biotechnology and Biomolecular Science
NEILSON, D., Physics
PASK, C., Physical, Environmental and Mathematical Sciences
ROGERS, C., Mathematics
SAMMUT, R., Physical, Environmental and Mathematical Sciences
SIMMONS, M., Physics
SLOAN, I., Mathematics
STEINBERG, P., Biological, Earth and Environmental Science
STOREY, J., Physics
SUSHKOV, O., Physics
SUTHERLAND, C., Mathematics
SUTHERLAND, P., Mathematics
TAFT, M., Psychology
WAND, M., Mathematics
WARD, C., Biological, Earth and Environmental Science
WEBB, J., Physics
WILKINS, M., Biotechnology and Biomolecular Science
WOLFE, J., Physics

Faculty of the Built Environment:

CUTHBERT, A., Architecture
LANG, J., Architecture
LOOSEMORE, M., Built Environment
RUAN, X., Architecture
WEIRICK, J., Landscape Architecture

ASSOCIATE COLLEGES

Faculty of the College of Fine Arts: Selwyn St, Paddington, NSW 2021; tel. (2) 9385-0888; e-mail cofa@unsw.edu.au; f. 1990 following merger of the City Art Institute and the Univ.; Dean and Dir IAN HOWARD.

University College, Australian Defence Force Academy: Northcott Dr., Campbell, ACT 2601; tel. (2) 6268-8111; e-mail sas@adfa.edu.au; f. 1981 by agreement between the Commonwealth of Australia and the Univ. of NSW; degree courses started 1986; Rector Prof. ROBERT KING; Exec. Officer T. HODSON.

ASSOCIATED INSTITUTE

Australian Graduate School of Management: Sydney, NSW 2052; tel. (2) 9931-9200; e-mail admissions@agsm.edu.au; f. 1975; postgraduate MBA and PhD courses, residential courses for execs; 42 faculty mems; library of 25,000 vols; Dir Prof. ROBERT MCLEAN; publ. *Australian Journal of Management*, *AGSM Working Paper Series*

UNIVERSITY OF NEWCASTLE

Univ. Dr., Callaghan, NSW 2308
Telephone: (2) 4921-5000
E-mail: enquirycentre@newcastle.edu.au
Internet: www.newcastle.edu.au
Founded 1965
State control
Academic year: March to November (2 semesters)
Chancellor: Prof. TREVOR WARING
Vice-Chancellor and Pres.: Prof. CAROLINE MCMILLEN
Deputy Vice-Chancellor for Academic and Global Relations: Prof. KEVIN MCCONKEY
Deputy Vice-Chancellor for Research: Prof. MIKE CALFORD
Deputy Vice-Chancellor for Univ. Services: Dr SUE GOULD
Pro-Vice-Chancellor for External Relations: Prof. STEPHEN CRUMP
Pro-Vice-Chancellor, Central Coast Campus: Dr STEPHEN CRUMP
Pro-Vice-Chancellor for Teaching and Learning: Prof. BILL HOGARTH
Dean for Students: Assoc. Prof. STEWART FRANKS
Univ. Librarian: GREG ANDERSON
Library: see under Libraries and Archives
Number of teachers: 800
Number of students: 30,000
Publication: *Cetus* (1 a year)

PRO-VICE-CHANCELLORS

English Language and Foundation Studies Centre: Assoc. Prof. SEAMUS FAGAN (Dir)
Faculty of Business and Law: Prof. AMIR MAHMOOD (acting)
Faculty of Education and Arts: Prof. JOHN GERMOV
Faculty of Engineering and Built Environment: Prof. JOHN CARTER
Faculty of Health: Prof. NICK TALLEY
Faculty of Science and Information Technology: Prof. BILL HOGARTH

PROFESSORS

Faculty of Business and Law (internet www.newcastle.edu.au/faculty/bus-law):

BATES, F., Law
BOYCE, G.
BRAY, M., Employment Studies
BURGESS, K.
CATLEY, B., Management
EASTON, S., Finance
MITCHELL, W., Economics
NICHOLAS, S., International Business Strategy
O'CASS, A., Marketing
WINSEN, J., Commerce
WRIGHT, T., Law

Faculty of Education and Arts (internet www.newcastle.edu.au/faculty/educ-arts):

ALBRIGHT, J., Education
ALLEN, M., Sociology and Anthropology
BOURKE, S., Education
CAREY, H., History
CRAIG, H., English
EMELJANOW, V., Drama
EWANS, M., Drama
FOLEY, D.
FOREMAN, P., Education
FUERY, P., Film, Media and Cultural Studies
GORE, J., Curriculum Teaching and Learning
GRAHAM, A., Fine Art
GRAY, M., Social Work
HOLBROOK, A.
LAURA, R., Education
LOVAT, T., Education
MCDOWELL, J., Theology
MAYNARD, J., Indigenous History
PLOTNIKOFF, R.
SCOTT, J.
TARRANT, H., Classics
VELLA, R., Music
WEBB, S.

Faculty of Engineering and Built Environment (internet www.eng.newcastle.edu.au):

BETZ, R., Electrical and Computer Engineering
CARTER, J., Geotechnical Engineering
DLUGOGORSKI, B., Chemical Engineering
EVANS, G., Chemical Engineering
FU, M., Electrical Engineering
GALVIN, K., Chemical Engineering
GOODWIN, G., Electrical Engineering
JAMESON, G., Chemical Engineering
JONES, M., Bulk Solids
KENNEDY, E., Chemical Engineering
KISI, E., Mechanical Engineering
LEHMANN, S., Architecture
MELCHERS, R., Civil Engineering
MIDDLETON, R., Electrical Engineering
MILLER, M., Computer Science and Software Engineering
MOGHTADERI, B., Chemical Engineering
MOHEIMANI, S., Electrical and Computer Engineering
MURCH, G., Materials Engineering
NINNESS, B., Electrical and Computer Engineering
OSTWALD, M., Architecture
ROBERTS, A., Mechanical Engineering
SHENG, D., Civil Engineering
SLOAN, S., Civil Engineering
STEWART, M., Civil Engineering
WALL, T., Fuels and Combustion Engineering

Faculty of Health (internet www.newcastle.edu.au/faculty/health):

ASHMAN, L., Medical Biochemistry
ATTIA, J.
BAKER, A.
BURNS, G., Medical Biochemistry
BYLES, J.
CALFORD, M., Human Physiology
CALLISTER, R., Anatomy
DAY, T., Anatomy
DEANE, S.
D'ESTE, C., Public Health
DUNKLEY, P., Medical Biochemistry
FAHY, K., Nursing and Midwifery
FORBES, J.
FOSTER, P., Immunology and Microbiology
GARG, M., Pharmacy and Experimental Pharmacology
GLEESON, M., Immunology
HAZELTON, M., Nursing
HENSLEY, M., Medicine
HIGGINS, I., Nursing
JONES, A.
JONES, K., Human Physiology
KEATINGE, D., Paediatrics
KELLY, B., Public Health
LI, S., Pharmacy and Experimental Pharmacology
LUMBERS, E., Pharmacy and Experimental Pharmacology
POND, D., Medical Practice and Population Health
RIVETT, D., Physiotherapy
ROSTAS, J.
RYAN, S., Occupational Therapy
SANSON-FISHER, R., Public Health
SCOTT, R., Medical Genetics
SMITH, D., Occupational Health and Safety
SMITH, R.
ZARDAWI, I.

Faculty of Science and Information Technology (internet www.newcastle.edu.au/faculty/science-it):

AITKEN, J., Biological Sciences
BOLAND, N., Mathematics

BORWEIN, J., Mathematics
DASTOOR, P., Physics
ERSKINE, W., Applied Sciences
GROF, C., Biological Sciences
HEATHCOTE, A., Psychology
HOGARTH, B.
JIN, J., Information Technology
KING, B., Physics
LAWRANCE, G., Chemistry
MCCLUSKEY, A., Chemistry
MCGUIRK, P., Geography and Environmental Studies
MENK, F., Physics
O'CONNOR, J., Physics
RAYNER, J., Statistics
RODGER, J., Biological Sciences
ROSE, R., Biological Sciences
STARTUP, M., Psychology
WILLIS, G., Mathematics

UNIVERSITY OF SYDNEY

Sydney, NSW 2006
Telephone: (2) 9351-2222
E-mail: info.centre@sydney.edu.au
Internet: sydney.edu.au
Founded 1850
Private control
Academic year: February to December

Chancellor: HE Prof. MARIE BASHIR
Deputy Chancellor: ALAN CAMERON
Vice-Chancellor and Principal: Dr MICHAEL SPENCE
Provost and Deputy Vice-Chancellor: Prof. STEPHEN GARTON
Deputy Vice-Chancellor for Education and Registrar: Prof. DERRICK ARMSTRONG
Deputy Vice-Chancellor for Indigenous Strategy and Services: Dr Prof. SHANE HOUSTON
Deputy Vice-Chancellor for Int. Affairs: Prof. JOHN HEARN
Deputy Vice-Chancellor for Research: Prof. JILL TREWHELLA
Deputy Vice-Chancellor Strategic Management: Prof. ANN BREWER
Gen. Counsel: RICHARD FISHER
Univ. Librarian: ANNE BELL
Chair. of Academic Bd: Assoc. Prof. PETER MCCALLUM

Library: see under Libraries and Archives
Number of teachers: 3,431
Number of students: 49,020

DEANS

Faculty of Agriculture, Food and Natural Resources: Prof. MARK ADAMS
Faculty of Architecture, Design and Planning: Prof. JOHN REDMOND (acting)
Faculty of Arts and Social Sciences: Prof. DUNCAN IVISON
Faculty of Dentistry: Prof. CHRIS PECK
Faculty of Education and Social Work: Prof. ROBERT J. TIERNEY
Faculty of Engineering and Information Technologies: Prof. ARCHIE JOHNSTON
Faculty of Health Sciences: (vacant)
Faculty of Pharmacy: Prof. IQBAL RAMZAN
Faculty of Science: Prof. TREVOR HAMBLEY (acting)
Sydney Business School: Prof. TYRONE CARLIN (acting)
Sydney College of the Arts: Prof. COLIN RHODES
Sydney Conservatorium of Music: Prof. KARL KRAMER
Sydney Law School: Prof. GILLIAN TRIGGS
Sydney Medical School: Prof. BRUCE ROBINSON
Sydney Nursing School: Prof. JILL WHITE

PROFESSORS

Faculty of Agriculture, Food and Natural Resources (Suite 401, Biomedical Bldg, One Central Ave, Australian Technology Park, Eveleigh, NSW 2015; tel. (2) 9351-2935; e-mail agriculture.dean@sydney.edu.au; internet sydney.edu.au/agriculture):

COPELAND, L., Agriculture
GUEST, D., Horticulture
KENNEDY, I., Agricultural and Environmental Chemistry
MCBRATNEY, A., Soil Science
PARK, R., Cereal Rust Research
SHARP, P., Molecular Plant Breeding
SUTTON, B.
TRETHOWAN, R., Plant Breeding

Faculty of Architecture, Design and Planning (Wilkinson Bldg, G04 148 City Rd, NSW 2006; tel. (2) 9351-2686; e-mail architecture@sydney.edu.au):

BLAKELY, E., Urban and Regional Planning
GERO, J., Design Science
HENEGHAN, T., Architecture
HYDE, R., Architectural Science
MAHER, M., Design Computing

Faculty of Arts and Social Sciences (Lobby H, Main Quadrangle A14, NSW 2006; tel. (2) 9351-3129; e-mail arts.undergraduate@sydney.edu.au):

School of Languages and Cultures:

DUNSTAN, H., Chinese Studies
EBIED, R., Arabic and Islamic Studies
NEWBIGIN, N., Italian Studies
RIEGEL, J., Languages and Cultures
SANKEY, M., French Studies
VICKERS, A., South East Asian Studies
YANG, M., Asian Studies

School of Letters, Art and Media:

BARNES, G., Medieval Literature
BENJAMIN, R., Art History and Aboriginal Art
CLARK, J., Asian Art History
CLUNIES-ROSS, M., English Language and Early English Literature
DIXON, R., Australian Literature
FOLEY, W., Linguistics
GAY, P., English Literature and Drama
MARTIN, J., Linguistics

School of Philosophical and Historical Inquiry:

ALDRICH, R., European History
CSAPO, E., Classics and Ancient History
FLETCHER, R., Theoretical and World Archaeology
GARTON, S., History
GATENS, M., Philosophy
GAUKROGER, S., History of Philosophy and History of Science
IVISON, D., Political Philosophy
MILLER, M., Classical Archaeology
POTTS, D., Middle Eastern Archaeology
PRICE, H., Philosophy
PROBYN, E., Gender and Cultural Studies
REDDING, P., Philosophy
SLUGA, G., International History
WATERHOUSE, R., Australian History
WHITE, S., American History
WILSON, P., Classics

School of Social and Political Sciences:

AUSTIN-BROOS, D., Anthropology
GILL, G., Government and Public Administration
HAGE, G., Anthropology
HUMPHREY, M., Sociology and Social Policy
JACKSON, M., Government and Public Administration
STILWELL, F., Political Economy
TIFFIN, R., Government and International Relations
WEISS, L., Government and International Relations

Faculty of Dentistry (NSW 2006; tel. (2) 9351-8334; e-mail dentistry.dean@sydney.edu.au):

BLINKHORN, A., Dentistry
BRYANT, R., Conservative Dentistry
DARENDELILER, M., Orthodontics
KLINEBERG, I., Prosthodontics
MURRAY, G., Dentistry
SWAIN, M., Biomaterials Science

Faculty of Education and Social Work (Education Bldg A35 Univ. of Sydney NSW 2006; tel. (2) 9351-2422):

ARMSTRONG, D., Education and Social Work
CONNELL, R., Education and Social Work
FAWCETT, B., Education and Social Work
FREEBODY, P., Education and Social Work
GOODYEAR, P., Education and Social Work
JONES, P., Education and Social Work
MEAGHER, G., Education and Social Work
PALTRIDGE, B., Education and Social Work
REIMANN, P., Education and Social Work
SHERRINGTON, G., History of Education
WELCH, A., Education and Social Work

Faculty of Engineering and Information Technologies (Level 3 Peter Nicol Russell Bldg (PNR), J02; tel. (2) 9351-2534; e-mail engineering.undergraduate@sydney.edu.au):

School of Aerospace, Mechanical and Mechatronic Engineering:

ARMFIELD, S., Aerospace, Mechanical and Mechatronic Engineering
DURRANT-WHYTE, H., Aerospace, Mechanical and Mechatronic Engineering
MAI, Y., Aerospace, Mechanical and Mechatronic Engineering
MASRI, A., Aerospace, Mechanical and Mechatronic Engineering
NEBOT, E., Aerospace, Mechanical and Mechatronic Engineering
TANNER, R., Mechanical Engineering
TONG, L., Aerospace, Mechanical and Mechatronic Engineering
YE, L., Aerospace, Mechanical and Mechatronic Engineering
ZHANG, L., Aerospace, Mechanical and Mechatronic Engineering

School of Chemical and Biomolecular Engineering:

BARTON, G., Chemical and Biomolecular Engineering
COSTER, H., Chemical and Biomolecular Engineering
HAYNES, B., Chemical and Biomolecular Engineering
PETRIE, J., Chemical and Biomolecular Engineering

School of Civil Engineering:

HANCOCK, G., Steel Structures
RASMUSSEN, K., Civil Engineering
SMALL, J., Civil Engineering

School of Electrical and Information Engineering:

AGELIDIS, V., Power Engineering
EADES, P., Software Technology
FENG, D., Electrical and Information Engineering
JOHNSTON, R., Electrical and Information Engineering
MINASIAN, R., Electrical and Information Engineering
PATRICK, J., Language Technologies
VUCETIC, B., Electrical and Information Engineering
YAN, H., Electrical and Information Engineering
ZOMAYA, A., High Performance Computing, Networking and Internetworking

Faculty of Health Sciences (tel. (2) 9351-9161):

BANATI, R., Medical Radiation Sciences
BOHIE, P., Work and Health
BUNDY, A., Occupational Therapy
EINFELD, S., Mental Health
FIATARONE SINGH, M., Exercise and Sport Science
KENDIG, H., Ageing and Health
KENNY, D., Psychology and Music

LLEWELLYN, G., Occupation and Leisure Sciences
MADDEN, R., Classification in Health
MAHER, C., Physiotherapy
MATHEWS, M., Ageing, Health and Disability
ONSLOW, M., Stuttering Research
REFSHAUGE, K., Physiotherapy
VEITCH, C., Community Health
WESTBROOK, J., Health Informatics

Faculty of Pharmacy (Pharmacy Bldg (A15) Camperdown Campus, Univ. of Sydney, Sydney, NSW, 2006; tel. (2) 9351-2320; e-mail pharmacy.enquiries@sydney.edu.au):

ARMOUR, C., Pharmacy
BENRIMOJ, S., Pharmacy Practice
BRIEN, J., Clinical Pharmacy
CHAN, H., Pharmaceutics (Advanced Drug Delivery)
MCLACHLAN, A., Pharmacy (Aged Care)
MURRAY, M., Pharmacogenomics (Pharmaceutics)
RAMZAN, I., Pharmaceutics
ROUFOGALIS, B., Pharmaceutical Chemistry
WHITE, L., Pharmacy Management

Faculty of Science (Faculty of Science Office Level 2, Carslaw Bldg (F07), Univ. of Sydney, NSW 2006; tel. (2) 9351 3021; e-mail science.information@sydney.edu.au):

School of Biological Sciences:

CHAPMAN, G., Marine Ecology
DICKMAN, C., Terrestrial Ecology
OLDROYD, B., Behavioural Genetics
OVERALL, R., Plant Cell Biology
PARKER, A., Biological Sciences
SHINE, R., Biological Sciences
SIMPSON, S., Biological Sciences
SKURRAY, R., Biology (Genetics)
THOMPSON, M., Zoology
UNDERWOOD, A., Experimental Ecology
WATERHOUSE, P., Biological Sciences

School of Chemistry:

CROSSLEY, M., Chemistry (Organic Chemistry)
HAMBLEY, T., Chemistry
HARROWELL, P., Chemistry
KABLE, S., Chemistry
LAY, P., Chemistry (Inorganic Chemistry)
WARR, G., Chemistry

School of Geosciences:

CLARKE, G., Geosciences
CONNELL, J., Geosciences
HATHERLY, P., Mining Geophysics
HIRSCH, P., Geosciences

School of Mathematics and Statistics:

CANNON, J., Mathematical Statistics
DANCER, E., Pure Mathematics
JOSHI, N., Applied Mathematics
ROBINSON, J., Mathematical Statistics
WEBER, N., Mathematical Statistics

School of Molecular and Microbial Biosciences:

BRAND-MILLER, J., Molecular and Microbial Biosciences
CAMPBELL, I., Molecular Biology
CATERSON, I., Human Nutrition
CHRISTOPHERSON, R., Molecular and Microbial Biosciences
CROSSLEY, M., Molecular and Microbial Biosciences
KUCHEL, P., Molecular and Microbial Biosciences
REEVES, P., Molecular and Microbial Biosciences
WEISS, A., Molecular and Microbial Biosciences

School of Physics:

BALDOCK, C., Medical Physics
BEDDING, T., Astrophysics
CAIRNS, I., Physics
DE STERKE, M., Theoretical Physics
GREEN, A., Physics
HUNSTEAD, R., Astrophysics
LENZEN, M., Astrophysics
MCKENZIE, D., Physics (Material Physics)
MCPHEDRAN, R., Physics (Electromagnetic Physics)
MELROSE, D., Physics
SADLER, E., Physics
VLADIMIROV, S., Physics

School of Psychology:

ANDREWS, S., Psychology
BLASZCZYNSKI, A., Psychology
BUTOW, P., Psychology
MCGREGOR, I., Psychology
TOUYZ, S., Clinical Psychology

Faculty of Veterinary Science (JD Stewart Bdg (B01), Univ. of Sydney, NSW 2006; tel. (2) 9351-8783; e-mail vet.science@sydney.edu.au):

CANFIELD, P., Veterinary Science
EVANS, G., Veterinary Science
FULKERSON, W., Veterinary Science
HUSBAND, A., Veterinary Science
JEFFCOTT, L., Veterinary Science
MAXWELL, C., Veterinary Science
MORAN, C., Veterinary Science
RAADSMA, H., Veterinary Science
WARD, M., Veterinary Science
WHITTINGTON, R., Veterinary Science

Sydney College of the Arts (Rozelle Campus Balmain Rd, Locked Bag 15 Rozelle, Sydney, NSW 2039; tel. (2) 9351-1104):

DUNN, R., Contemporary Visual Art
RHODES, C., Art

Sydney Conservatorium of Music (Univ. of Sydney, Cnr Bridge and Macquarie St., Sydney, NSW 2000; tel. (2) 9351-1222; e-mail con.info@sydney.edu.au):

BOYD, A., Music
CHARTERIS, R., Historical Musicology
MARETT, A., Music
PALLÓ, I., Conducting
WALKER, K., Music

Sydney Law School (Level 3, Law School Bldg (F10), E Ave, Camperdown Campus, NSW 2006; tel. (2) 9351-0351):

ALLARS, M., Law
APPS, P., Public Economics in Law
ASTOR, H., Law
BENNETT, B., Health and Medical Law
BOER, B., Environmental Law
BURNS, L., Taxation Law
BUTT, P., Law
CARNEY, T., Law
CARTER, J., Commercial Law
COOPER, G., Taxation Law
CROCK, M., Public Law
FINDLAY, M., Law
GRAYCAR, R., Law
HILL, J., Law
KINLEY, D., Human Rights Law
MCCALLUM, R., Industrial Law
O'MALLEY, P., Law
PARKINSON, P., Law
SADURSKI, W., Legal Philosophy
STUBBS, J., Criminology
TRIGGS, G., Law
VANN, R., Law

Sydney Medical School (Edward Ford Bldg A27, The Univ. of Sydney, NSW 2006; tel. (2) 9351-3132; e-mail medicine.info@sydney.edu.au):

ALLEN, D., Physiology
ALLEN, R., Transplantation Surgery
ANDERSON, C., Stroke Medicine and Clinical Neuroscience
ARMSTRONG, B., Medicine
BANDLER, R., Anatomy and Pain Research
BARTER, P., Medicine
BAUMAN, A., Public Health (Behavioural Epidemiology and Health Promotion)
BAUR, L., Medicine
BAXTER, R., Medicine
BENNETT, M., Physiology
BEREND, N., Respiratory Medicine
BILLSON, F., Clinical Ophthalmology and Eye Health
BISHOP, J., Cancer Medicine
BLACK, J., Medicine
BOKEY, E., Colorectal Surgery
BOOY, R., Medicine
BOYCE, P., Psychological Medicine
BRAITHWAITE, A., Medicine
BRAND-MILLER, J., Medicine
BRITTON, W., Medicine
BURKE, D., Medicine
BYRNE, M., Developmental and Marine Biology
CAMERON, I., Rehabilitation Medicine
CAMPBELL, I., Molecular Biology
CARTER, J., Gynaecological Oncology
CASS, D., Paediatric Surgery
CATERSON, I., Human Nutrition
CELERMAJER, D., Scandrett Cardiology
CHAPMAN, S., Medicine
CHRISTIE, M., Medicine
CHRISTODOULOU, J., Medicine
CHRISTOPHERSON, R., Medicine
CISTULLI, P., Respiratory Medicine
CLARKE, S., Medicine
COATS, A., Medicine
COLAGIURI, S., Metabolic Health
COOK, D., Cellular Physiology
COUSINS, M., Anaesthesia and Pain Management
CRAIG, J., Clinical Epidemiology
CROSSLEY, M., Molecular Genetics
CUMMING, R., Epidemiology and Geriatric Medicine
CUNNINGHAM, A., Medicine
DAMPNEY, R., Cardiovascular Neuroscience
DANDONA, L., International Public Health
DAVIES, M., Medicine
DELBRIDGE, L., Surgery
DOS REMEDIOS, C., Medicine
DREHER, B., Visual Neuroscience
DUNN, S., Psychological Medicine
ELLIOTT, E., Paediatrics and Child Health
FAZEKAS, B., Medicine
FIELD, M., Medicine
FINFER, S., Medicine
FLETCHER, J., Surgery
FRASER, I., Reproductive Medicine
FREEDMAN, S., Cardiology
GAMBLE, J., Vascular Biology
GASKIN, K., Paediatric Nutrition
GEORGE, J., Gastroenterology and Hepatic Medicine
GIBSON, W., Otolaryngology
GILES, W., Medicine
GOTTLIEB, D., Haematology
GÖTZ, J., Molecular Biology
GRAU, G., Vascular Immunology
GUNNING, P., Medicine
GUSS, M., Structural Biology
HABER, P., Medicine
HALL, R., Medicine
HALLIDAY, G., Medicine
HANDELSMAN, D., Reproductive Endocrinology and Andrology
HARPER, C., Neuropathology
HARRIS, D., Medicine
HARRIS, J., Vascular Surgery
HAWKE, S., Medicine
HAZELL, P., Medicine
HEARN, J., Medicine
HICKIE, I., Psychiatry
HORVATH, J., Medicine
HUNT, N., Pathology
HUNYOR, S., Medicine
IRWIG, L., Epidemiology
JEREMY, R., Medicine
JOHNSTON, G., Pharmacology
KAM, C., Anaesthetics
KEECH, A., Medicine, Cardiology and Epidemiology
KEFFORD, R., Medicine
KEMP, A., Paediatric Allergy and Clinical Immunology
KIDD, M., General Practice

KING, N., Medicine
KUCHEL, P., Biochemistry
LAMBERT, T., Psychiatry
LE COUTER, D., Geriatric Medicine
LEEDER, S., Public Health and Community Medicine
LIDDLE, C., Clinical Pharmacology and Hepatology
LINDLEY, R., Geriatric Medicine
LUSBY, R., Surgery
LYLE, D., Rural Health
MCCAUGHAN, G., Gastroenterology and Hepatology
MCINTYRE, P., Medicine
MACINTYRE, R., Medicine
MACMAHON, S., Cardiovascular Medicine and Epidemiology
MCMINN, P., Infectious Diseases
MASON, R., Endocrine Physiology
MAY, J., Surgery
MELLIS, C., Medicine
MINDEL, A., Sexual Health Medicine
MITCHELL, R., Medicine
MITROFANIS, J., Medicine
MORRIS, B., Physiology (Molecular Hypertension)
MORRIS, J., Obstetrics and Gynaecology
MURPHY, C., Histology and Embryology
NANAN, R., Paediatrics
NICHOLSON, G., Medicine
NORTH, K., Paediatrics and Child Health
NORTON, R., Public Health
NUTBEAM, D., Medicine
O'BRIEN, C., Medicine
OUVRIER, R., Paediatric Neurology
PARMENTER, T., Developmental Disability
PEEK, M., Medicine
POLLARD, J., Neurology
POLLOCK, C., Medicine
RASKO, J., Medicine
RASMUSSEN, H., Cardiology
REDDEL, R.
REEVES, P., Microbiology
REICHARDT, J., Molecular Biology (Molecular Medicine)
RICHARDSON, D., Medicine
ROBINSON, B., Medicine (Endocrinology)
ROBINSON, P., Medicine
RUSSELL, P., Medicine
RUSSELL, R., Medical Entomology
RYE, K., Medicine
SALKELD, G., Public Health
SAMBROOK, P., Rheumatology
SEALE, J., Clinical Pharmacology
SEIBEL, M., Endocrinology
SILINK, M., Medicine
SILLENCE, D., Medical Genetics
SIMES, J., Medicine
SIMPSON, J., Biostatistics
SMITH, R., Medicine
SONNABEND, D., Orthopaedic and Traumatic Surgery
SORRELL, T., Clinical Infectious Diseases
STEVENSON, M., Injury Prevention
STOCKER, R., Biochemistry in Vascular Medicine
STONE, J., Retinal and Cerebral Neurobiology
SULLIVAN, C., Medicine
TAM, P., Medicine
TARNOW-MORDI, W., Neonatal Medicine
TATTERSALL, M., Cancer Medicine
THOMPSON, J., Melanoma and Surgical Oncology
TOFLER, G., Preventive Cardiology
TONKIN, M., Hand Surgery
TRENT, R., Medical Molecular Genetics
TREWHELLA, J., Medicine
TRUDINGER, B., Obstetrics and Gynaecology
TRUSCOTT, R., Medicine
USHERWOOD, T., General Practice
VADAS, M., Cancer Medicine and Cell Biology
VAN ASPEREN, P., Paediatric Respiratory Medicine
VAN ZANDWIJK, N., Asbestos Disease
WALL, J., Medicine
WALTER, G., Child and Adolescent Psychiatry
WANG, S., Radiology
WATERHOUSE, P., Medicine
WEBSTER, W., Medicine
WEISS, A., Medicine
WENINGER, W., Dermatology
WILEY, J., Medicine (Haematology)
WILLIAMS, L., Cognitive Neuropsychiatry
YUE, D., Kellion Endocrinology

Sydney Nursing School (Univ. of Sydney 88 Mallett St, Camperdown, NSW 2050; tel. (2) 9351-0693; e-mail nursing.info@sydney.edu.au):

LAWLER, J., Nursing
RUDGE, T., Nursing
WHITE, J., Nursing
WHITE, K., Nursing

ATTACHED COLLEGES

Sydney College of the Arts: e-mail info.centre@sydney.edu.au; Dir Prof. RON NEWMAN.

Sydney Conservatorium of Music: e-mail con.reception@sydney.edu.au; Prin. Prof. S. E. PRETTY

UNIVERSITY OF TECHNOLOGY, SYDNEY

POB 123, Broadway, Sydney, NSW 2007
Telephone: (2) 9514-2000
E-mail: info.office@uts.edu.au
Internet: www.uts.edu.au

Founded 1965 as NSW Institute of Technology; univ. status 1988
Academic year: March to December

Chancellor: Prof. VICKI SARA
Deputy Chancellor: BRIAN WILSON
Vice-Chancellor and Pres.: Prof. ROSS MILBOURNE
Sr Deputy Vice-Chancellor and Sr Vice-Pres.: Prof. PETER BOOTH
Deputy Vice-Chancellor and Vice-Pres. for Corporate Services: ANNE DWYER
Deputy Vice-Chancellor and Vice-Pres. for Int. and Devt: Prof. WILLIAM PURCELL
Deputy Vice-Chancellor and Vice-Pres. for Research: Prof. ATTILA BRUNGS
Deputy Vice-Chancellor and Vice-Pres. for Resources: PATRICK WOODS
Deputy Vice-Chancellor and Vice-Pres. for Teaching, Learning and Equity: Prof. SHIRLEY ALEXANDER
Registrar: JOHN HARTIGAN
Librarian: MAL BOOTH

Library of 626,983 vols, 37,929 ejournals, 3,775 print journals
Number of teachers: 2,460 (full-time)
Number of students: 36,300

Publications: *African Journal of Information and Communication Technology* (4 a year), *Australasian Journal of Construction Economics and Building* (4 a year), *Commonwealth Journal of Local Governance* (2 a year), *Cosmopolitan Civil Societies: An Interdisciplinary Journal* (4 a year), *CREArTA* (2 a year, research and education in the arts), *Cultural Studies Review* (2 a year, published jtly with Univ. of Melbourne), *Form/Work* (irregular), *Gateways: International Journal of Community Research and Engagement* (1 a year), *Journal of Project, Program and Portfolio Management* (2 a year), *Literacy and Numeracy Studies* (2 a year, education and training of adults), *Locality* (3 a year), *Pacific Rim Property Research Journal* (4 a year), *PORTAL Journal of Multidisciplinary International Studies* (2 a year), *Provincial China* (1 a year), *Public Communication Review* (1 a year), *Public History Review* (1 a year), *Public Space: The Journal of Law and Social Justice*, *Sydney Journal* (1 a year), *UTS Law Review* (1 a year), *UTS Writer's Anthology* (1 a year)

DEANS

Faculty of Arts and Social Sciences: Prof. MARY SPONGBERG
Faculty of Business: Prof. ROY GREEN
Faculty of Design, Architecture and Building: Prof. DESLEY LUSCOMBE
Faculty of Engineering and Information Technology: Prof. HUNG NGUYEN
Faculty of Law: Prof. LESLEY HITCHENS
Faculty of Nursing, Midwifery and Health: Prof. JOHN DALY
Faculty of Science: Prof. BRUCE MILTHORPE

UNIVERSITY OF WESTERN SYDNEY

Locked Bag 1797, Penrith, NSW 2751
Telephone: (2) 9852-5222
E-mail: internationalstudy@uws.edu.au
Internet: www.uws.edu.au

Founded 1989
State control
Academic year: March to December

Chancellor: Prof. PETER SHERGOLD
Vice-Chancellor: Prof. BARNEY GLOVER
Deputy Vice-Chancellor for Education: Prof. KERRI-LEE KRAUSE
Deputy-Vice-Chancellor for Research and Devt: Prof. SCOTT HOLMES
Assoc. Vice-Chancellor for Engagement and Int. Affairs: JULIE LANTZ
Pro-Vice-Chancellor for Students: ANGELO KOURTIS
Deputy Vice-Chancellor for Corporate Strategy and Services: RHONDA HAWKINS
Chief Financial Officer: PETER PICKERING
Academic Registrar: SHANEEN MCGLINCHEY
Univ. Librarian: SUE CRAIG

Library: 1m. vols
Number of teachers: 1,435
Number of students: 40,257

Publication: *GradLife Alumni magazine*

DEANS

School of Business: Prof. CLIVE SMALLMAN
School of Computing, Engineering and Mathematics: Prof. SIMEON SIMOFF
School of Education: Prof. MICHELE SIMONS
School of Humanities and Communication Arts: Prof. PETER HUTCHINGS
School of Law: Prof. MICHAEL ADAMS
School of Medicine: Prof. ANNEMARIE HENNESSY
School of Nursing and Midwifery: Prof. RHONDA GRIFFITHS
School of Science and Health: Prof. GREGORY KOLT
School of Social Sciences and Psychology: Prof. KEVIN DUNN

UNIVERSITY OF WOLLONGONG

Northfields Ave, Wollongong, NSW 2522
Telephone: (2) 4221-3555
E-mail: askuow@uow.edu.au
Internet: www.uow.edu.au

Founded 1951 as a College of the Univ. of New South Wales; merged with Wollongong Institute of Education 1982
public control
Academic year: March to November (2 sessions), and a summer session from December to February

Chancellor: JILLIAN BROADBENT
Deputy Chancellor: Dr STEPHEN ANDERSEN
Vice-Chancellor: Prof. PAUL WELLINGS
Sr Deputy Vice-Chancellor: Prof. JOHN PATTERSON
Vice-Prin. for Admin.: CHRIS GRANGE

Deputy Vice-Chancellor for Academic and Int. Affairs: Prof. ROB CASTLE
Deputy Vice-Chancellor Int.: Prof. JOE F. CHICHARO
Deputy Vice-Chancellor for Operations: Prof. JOHN PATTERSON
Deputy Vice-Chancellor for Research: Prof. JUDY RAPER
Pro-Vice-Chancellor for Health: Prof. DON IVERSO
Pro-Vice-Chancellor for Research: Prof. MARGARET SHEIL
Deputy Vice-Prin. for Finance and IT: DAMIEN ISRAEL
Pres. of the Dubai Campus: Prof. GHASSAN AOUAD
Vice-Prin. for Overseas Operations: JAMES LANGRIDGE
Exec. Dean Business and Faculty of Commerce: Prof. JOHN J. GLYNN
Dean for Research: Prof. TIMOTHY MARCHANT
Dean for Students: YVONNE KERR
Registrar: Dr DAVID CHRISTIE (acting)
Librarian: MARGIE JANTTI

Library of 708,248 vols, 190,191 journals, 7,063 ebooks, 510,944 monographs
Number of teachers: 865
Number of students: 28,904
Publications: *Australian Journal of Information Systems*, *Australian Journal of Natural Resources Law and Policy*, *Boxkite* (creative arts), *Illawarra Unity* (labour history), *International Journal of Forensic Psychology*, *Journal of University Teaching and Learning Practice*, *Rhizome* (2 a year)

DEANS

Faculty of Arts: Prof. WENCHE OMMUNDSEN
Faculty of Commerce: Prof. TREVOR SPEDDING
Faculty of Creative Arts: Prof. AMANDA LAWSON
Faculty of Education: Prof. PAUL CHANDLER
Faculty of Engineering: Prof. CHRIS COOK (acting)
Faculty of Health and Behavioural Sciences: Prof. PATRICK CROOKES
Faculty of Informatics: Prof. PHILIP OGUNBONA
Faculty of Law: Prof. LUKE MCNAMARA
Faculty of Science: Prof. WILLIAM E. PRICE
Graduate School of Medicine: Prof. ALISON JONES
Sydney Business School: Prof. JOHN L GLYNN

PROFESSORS

Faculty of Arts:
- BEDER, S., Social Sciences, Media and Communication
- DODDS, S., English Literature, Philosophy and Languages
- HAGAN, J., Arts
- KITLEY, P., Social Sciences, Media and Communication
- MARSHALL, D., Social Sciences, Media and Communication
- MARTIN, B., Social Sciences, Media and Communication
- OMMUNDSEN, W., English Literature, Philosophy and Languages
- WOLFERS, E., History and Politics

Faculty of Commerce:
- BARRETT, M., Management and Marketing
- DAWSON, P., Management and Marketing
- DOLNICAR, S., Management and Marketing
- GAFFIKIN, M., Accounting and Finance
- LEWIS, D., Economics and Information Systems
- METWALLY, M., Economics
- ROSSITER, J., Management and Marketing
- SPEDDING, T., Management and Marketing
- VILLE, S., Economics

Faculty of Creative Arts:
- LAWSON, J., Arts and Design
- MILLER, S., Music and Drama
- WOOD CONROY, D., Arts and Design

Faculty of Education:
- DINHAM, S., Educational Leadership and Pedagogy
- FERRY, B., Education
- RUSSELL, T., Education
- THOMAS, R., Education

Faculty of Engineering:
- ARNDT, G., Mechanical Materials and Mechatronics
- ARNOLD, P., Mechanical Materials and Mechatronics
- BRINSON, G., Mechanical Materials and Mechatronics
- BROWN, H., Coating Technology
- CHIU, C., Engineering
- CHOWDURY, R., Civil Mining and Environmental Engineering
- DIPPENAAR, R., Mechanical Materials and Mechatronics
- DOU, S., Mechanical Materials and Mechatronics
- DUNNE, D., Mechanical Materials and Mechatronics
- INDRARATNA, B., Civil Mining and Environmental Engineering
- LEWIS, R., Engineering Physics
- LIU, H., ISEM
- MCCARTHY, G., Civil Mining and Environmental Engineering
- METCALFE, P., Engineering Physics
- NORRISH, J., Materials Welding and Joining
- PERELOMA, E., Mechanical Materials and Mechatronics
- PIGHATEL, G., Engineering Physics
- ROBINSON, P., Engineering
- ROZENFELD, A., Engineering Physics
- SEN, G., Civil Mining and Environmental Engineering
- SPINKS, G., Mechanical Materials and Mechatronics
- TIEU, A., Mechanical Materials and Mechatronics
- VARIN, R. A., Mechanical Materials and Mechatronics
- ZHANG, C., Engineering Physics

Faculty of Health and Behavioural Sciences:
- BARRY, R., Psychology
- BUSHNELL, J., Graduate School of Medicine
- CALVERT, D., Health Sciences
- CARR, N., Graduate School of Medicine
- CROOKES, P., Nursing, Midwifery and Indigenous Health
- DEANE, F., Psychology
- ELSE, P., Health Sciences
- FARMER, E., Graduate School of Medicine
- HEAVEN, P., Psychology
- HOGG, J., Medicine
- HUANG, X., Health Sciences
- JONES, S., Centre for Health Initiatives
- LILLIOJA, S., Health and Behavioural Sciences
- MANOHARAN, A., Medicine
- STEELE, J., Health Sciences
- TAIT, N., Graduate School of Medicine
- TAPSELL, L., Biomedical Sciences
- WALSH, K., Nursing, Midwifery and Indigenous Health
- YEO, W., Graduate School of Medicine

Faculty of Informatics:
- BOUZERDOUM, S., Electrical, Computer and Telecommunications Engineering
- BUNDER, M., Mathematics and Applied Statistics
- CHAMBERS, R., Mathematics and Applied Statistics
- DUTKIEWICZ, E., Electrical, Computer and Telecommunications Engineering
- EKLUND, P., Information Systems and Technology
- FULCHER, J., Computer Science and Software Engineering
- GHOSE, A., Computer Science and Software Engineering
- GOSBELL, V., Electrical, Computer and Telecommunications Engineering
- GRIFFITHS, D. A., Mathematics and Applied Statistics
- HILL, J., Mathematics and Applied Statistics
- LANDSTAD, M., Mathematics and Applied Statistics
- NAGHDY, F., Electrical, Computer and Telecommunications Engineering
- OGUNBONA, P., Information Technology and Computer Science
- RAEBURN, I., Mathematics and Applied Statistics
- SAFAEI, F., Electrical, Computer and Telecommunications Engineering
- SEBERRY, J., Information Technology and Computer Science
- SOETANTO, D., Electrical, Computer and Telecommunications Engineering
- STEEL, D., Mathematics and Applied Statistics
- WAND, M., Mathematics and Applied Statistics
- ZHU, S., Mathematics and Applied Statistics

Faculty of Law:
- ANTONS, C., Comparative Law
- CHAPPELL, D., Centre for Transnational Crime Prevention
- CHURCHILL, R., ANCORS
- FARRIER, M., Natural Resources Law and Policy
- TSAMENYI, M., Centre for Maritime Policy

Faculty of Science:
- AYRE, D., Biological Sciences
- BRADSTOCK, R., Chemistry
- BREMNER, J., Chemistry
- BUTTEMER, B., Biological Sciences
- CHAPPELL, B., Earth and Environmental Sciences
- CHIVAS, A., Geosciences
- DIXON, N., Chemistry
- GRIFFITH, D., Chemistry
- HEAD, L., Earth and Environmental Sciences
- HULBERT, T., Biological Sciences
- KANE-MAGUIRE, L., Chemistry
- MORRISION, J., Earth and Environmental Science
- MURRAY-WALLACE, C., Earth and Environmental Science
- NANSON, G., Geosciences
- NE'EMAN, G., Biological Sciences
- OFFICER, D., Intelligent Polymer Research Institute
- OLSSEN, M., Biological Sciences
- PRICE, W., Chemistry
- PYNE, S., Chemistry
- WALKER, M., Biological Sciences
- WALLACE, G., Intelligent Polymer Research Institute
- WILSON, M., Biological Sciences
- WOODROFFE, C., Earth and Environmental Sciences

NORTHERN TERRITORY

BATCHELOR INSTITUTE OF INDIGENOUS TERTIARY EDUCATION

c/o Post Office, Batchelor, NT 0845
Telephone: (8) 8939-7111
E-mail: enquiries@batchelor.edu.au
Internet: www.batchelor.edu.au

Founded 1974, present status 1999

2 Campuses: Batchelor campus and Central Australian campus; faculties of education, arts and social sciences, health, business, science; research div.

Academic year: February to December (2 semesters)

Dir: Adrian Mitchell
Registrar and Head of Corporate Services: Karl Ashton
Head of Research: Dr Peter Stephenson
Library and Information Services Man.: Ann Williams
Number of teachers: 118
Number of students: 2,728

CHARLES DARWIN UNIVERSITY

Darwin, NT 0909
Telephone: (8) 8946-6666
E-mail: international@cdu.edu.au
Internet: www.cdu.edu.au
Founded 2003 by the merger of N Territory Univ. and Centralian College
federal control
Academic year: February to November
Chancellor: Sally Thomas
Vice-Chancellor: Prof. Simon Maddocks
Pro-Vice-Chancellor for Academic Affairs: Assoc. Prof. Martin Carroll
Pro-Vice-Chancellor Indigenous Leadership: Prof. Steven Larkin
Pro-Vice-Chancellor for Vocational Education and Training: John Hassed
Deputy Vice-Chancellor for Research and Int. Affairs: Prof. Sharon Bell
Deputy Vice-Chancellor for Teaching and Learning: Prof. C. Webb
Exec. Dir of Corporate Services: Dr Debra Farrelly
Exec. Dir Finance and Asset Services: Rob Brelsford-Smith
Number of teachers: 500
Number of students: 21,000

PRO-VICE-CHANCELLORS
Faculty of Engineering, Health, Science and the Environment: Prof. Sue Carthew
Faculty of Law, Education, Business and Arts: Prof. Giselle Byrnes (acting)

QUEENSLAND

BOND UNIVERSITY

Gold Coast, QLD 4229
Telephone: (7) 5595-1024
E-mail: information@bond.edu.au
Internet: www.bond.edu.au
Founded 1987
Private control
Academic year: January to December
Chancellor: Dr Helen Nugent
Vice-Chancellor and Pres.: Prof. Dr Tim Brailsford
Deputy Vice-Chancellor and Provost: Prof. Garry Marchant
Pro-Vice-Chancellor for Students and Academic Support: Alan Finch
Pro-Vice-Chancellor for Research: Prof Geraldine Mackenzie
Pro-Vice-Chancellor for Spec. Projects: Prof. Raoul Mortley
Pro-Vice-Chancellor for Quality, Teaching and Learning: Prof. Richard Hays
Dir for Finance: John Le Lievre
Dir for Information Services: Grace Saw
Dir for Marketing and Admissions: Valerie Runyan
Registrar: Alan Finch
Number of teachers: 461
Number of students: 5,370
Publication: *Revenue Law Journal*

DEANS
Faculty of Business, Technology and Sustainable Devt: Prof. Dr Mark Hirst
Faculty of Health Sciences and Medicine: Prof. Richard Hays
Faculty of Humanities and Social Sciences: Prof. Raoul Mortley
Faculty of Law: Prof. Geraldine Mackenzie
Institute of Sustainable Devt and Architecture: Prof. George Earl (Dir)

PROFESSORS
Faculty of Business, Technology and Sustainable Devt:
Ariff, M., Finance
Bertin, W., Finance
Earl, G., Sustainable Devt
Fisher, C., Management
Gaston, N., Economics
Gordon, R., Business
Iselin, E., Accounting
Kent, P., Accounting
Moores, K., Family Business
Morrison, I., Information Technology
Roberts, E., Hotel, Resort and Tourism Management
Shaw, J. B., Human Resource Management
Williams, B., Finance

Faculty of Health Sciences and Medicine:
Chess-Williams, R., Biomedical Sciences
Gass, G., Exercise and Sports Science
Henly, D., Biomedical Sciences
Quick, S., Sport Management
van Daal, A., Forensic Sciences

Faculty of Humanities and Social Sciences:
Hicks, R., Psychology
Molloy, B., Film and Television
Mortley, R., Philosophy
Pearson, M., Communication and Media
Webb, S., Australian Studies
Wilson, P., Criminology

Faculty of Law:
Boulle, L., Medication, Alternative Dispute Resolution
Carney, G., Constitutional and Administrative Law
Colvin, E., Criminal Law
Corkery, J., Corporate and Taxation Law
Field, D., Criminal Law
Forder, J., Contract Law, Information Technology and Electric Commerce Law
Gerrard, A., Constitutional Law, Admin. Law, Taxation of Business Entities
Hiscock, M., Contract Law, Int. Law
Lessing, J., Corporations Law, Partnerships
Lupton, M., Law and Medicine
Marshall, B., Restrictive Trade Practices
Ong, D., Equity, Securities Law
Spencer, L., Franchise Law
Svantesson, D., eCommerce, Private Int. Law
Wade, J., Mediation, Negotiation, Family Law

School of Information Technology:
Finnie, G., Information Systems
Krishnan, P., Software Systems

CQ UNIVERSITY

Bldg 5, Bruce Highway, Rockhampton, QLD 4702
Telephone: (7) 4930-9000
E-mail: publicrelations@cqu.edu.au
Internet: www.cqu.edu.au
Founded 1967 as Queensland Institute of Technology (Capricornia), current name adopted 2008
Campuses at Adelaide, Brisbane, Bundaberg, Emerald, Gladstone, Mackay, Melbourne, Noosa, Rockhampton and Sydney
Chancellor: Rennie Fritschy
Vice-Chancellor and Pres.: Prof. Scott Bowman
Deputy Vice-Chancellor for Academic and Research: Prof. Hilary Winchester
Deputy Vice-Chancellor for Univ. Services: Alastair Dawson
Deputy Vice-Chancellor for Industry and Vocational Education and Training: Nikola Babovic
Pro-Vice-Chancellor for Engagement and Campuses: Prof. Pierre Viljoen
Chief Financial Officer: Narelle Pearse
Univ. Sec: Jenny Roberts
Number of teachers: 365
Number of students: 19,569

GRIFFITH UNIVERSITY

Nathan campus, Griffith Univ. 170 Kessels Rd, Nathan, QLD 4111
Telephone: (7) 3735-7111
E-mail: international@griffith.edu.au
Internet: www.griffith.edu.au
Founded 1971, opened 1975
Has campuses in Gold Coast, Meadowbrook, Mt Gravatt and S Brisbane
State control
Academic year: February to November
Chancellor: Leneen Forde
Vice-Chancellor and Pres.: Prof. Ian O'Connor
Deputy Vice-Chancellor for Research and Provost Gold Coast: Prof. Ned Pankhurst
Deputy Vice-Chancellor for Academic Affairs: Prof. Susan H. Spence
Deputy Vice-Chancellor and Provost: Prof. Marilyn McMeniman
Pro-Vice-Chancellor for Admin.: Colin McAndrew
Pro-Vice-Chancellor for Community Partnerships: Prof. M. Standage
Pro-Vice-Chancellor for Health: Prof. Allan Cripps
Pro-Vice-Chancellor for Information Services: Janice Rickards
Pro-Vice-Chancellor for Int. Affairs: Linda O'Brien
Academic Registrar: Kathy Grgic
Dir for Queensland College of Art: Prof. Paul Cleveland
Dir for Queensland Conservatorium: Prof. Huib Schippers
Library of 933,959 vols
Number of teachers: 2,966 (full-time)
Number of students: 43,000

PRO-VICE-CHANCELLORS
Arts, Education and Law: Prof. Dr Paul Mazerolle
Griffith Business School: Prof. Michael Powell
Griffith Health: Prof. Allan Cripps
Science, Environment, Engineering and Technology: Prof. Sue Berners-Price

PROFESSORS
Aitken, L., Nursing
Arthington, A. H., Environmental Science
Auld, C., Tourism, Leisure, Hotel and Sports Management
Bagnall, R., Education
Balasubramaniam, A. B., Engineering
Balfour, M., Education
Bamber, G., Business
Barker, M., Management
Beacham, I., Medical Science
Berns, S., Law
Borbasi, S., Nursing
Braddock, R., Environmental Sciences
Bramley-Moore, M., Queensland College of Art
Brown, L., Environmental Sciences
Brown, P., Leisure Studies
Buckley, R., Engineering
Bunn, S., Environmental Studies
Burch, D., Science
Burton, B., Education
Bushell, G., Science
Chaboyer, W., Nursing
Chenoweth, L., Human Services

CHU, C., Public Health
CLARKE, F., Biomolecular and Physical Sciences
COUCHMAN, P., Management
CREED, P., Psychology
CREEDY, D., Health
CRIPPS, A., Health
CUMMING, J., Education
DALY, K., Criminology and Criminal Justice
DAVIDSON, M. C., Tourism, Leisure, Hotel and Sports Management
DE LEO, D., Suicide Research and Prevention
DEHNE, F., Information and Communication Technology
DEMPSTER, N., Education
DEWAR, J. K., Law
DIMITRIJEV, S., Microelectronic Engineering
DOBSON, J., Science
DRAPER, P., Music
DREW, R., Biomolecular and Physical Sciences
DREW, R., Environmental Studies
DROMEY, R. G., Computing and Information Technology
DYCK, M. J., Business
ELKINS, J., Education
ESTIVILL-CASTRO, V., Information and Communication Technology
FARQHAR, M., International Business and Asian Studies
FERRES, K., Arts
FINNANE, M. J., Arts, Postgraduate Studies
FRAZER, L., Marketing
FULOP, E., Marketing and Management
GAMMACK, J., Management
GIDDINGS, J., Law
GLEESON, B., Environmental Planning
GRIFFITHS, L., Medical Science
GUEST, R., Graduate School of Management
GUILDING, C., Tourism, Leisure, Hotel and Sports Management
HALFORD, G., Psychology
HALFORD, W. K., Health and Applied Psychology
HARRISON, H. B., Microelectronic Engineering
HEAD, B., Law
HEADRICK, J., Medical Science
HEALY, P., Science
HOMEL, R. J., Criminology and Criminal Justice
HOPE, G., Science
HUDSON, C. W., Humanities
HUGHES, J., Environmental Sciences
HUNTER, R., Law
HYDE, M. B., Education
ISLAM, Y., International Business and Asian Studies
IVANOVSKI, S., Dentistry and Oral Health
JENKINS, I., Science
JOHNSON, L., Research
JOHNSON, N. W., Dentistry and Oral Health
JOHNSTONE, R., Law
KANE, J., Politics and Public Policy
KEITH, R., International Business and Asian Studies
KITCHING, R. L., Environmental Science
KNIGHT, A. E., Science
KNIGHT, K., International Business and Asian Studies
KWON, O. Y., International Business and Asian Studies
LAM, A. K., Medicine
LEE, S., Environmental Studies
LISNER, P., Microelectronic Engineering
LOO, Y.-C., Engineering
MCDONALD, J., Law
MACKAY-SIM, A., Biomolecular and Biomedical Sciences
MACKERRAS, C. P., International Business and Asian Studies
MCLURE, R. J., Medicine
MCMENIMAN, M., Education
MCQUEEN, R. I., Law
MCROBBIE, C., Education
MCTAINSH, G., Environmental Studies
MAKIN, A., Accounting, Finance and Economics
MERRILEES, W., Marketing and Management
MIA, L., Accounting and Finance
MORAN, A., Arts
MOYLE, W., Nursing
MUIRHEAD, B. D., Education
NESDALE, A. R., Commerce, Management and Applied Psychology
NG, A. C., Accounting
NGUYEN, D. T.
O'CONNOR, I., Economics
O'FAIRCHEALLAIGH, C. S., Politics and Public Policy
O'TOOLE, J., Education
PALIWAL, K., Microelectronic Engineering
PARRY, K., Management
PATEL, B., Biomolecular and Physical Sciences
PEETZ, D., Industrial Relations
PEGG, D. T., Science
POWELL, M. J., Business
QUINN, R. J., Science
RICKARD, C., Nursing
RICKSON, R., Environmental Studies
ROEMFELDT, P. J., Music
SADLER, D. R., Education
SAMPFORD, C. J., Criminology and Criminal Justice
SATTAR, A., Information Technology
SCHULTZ, J., Public Culture
SCHUMAN, A. D., Business
SCUFFHAM, P., Medicine
SEARLE, J., Medicine
SELVANATHAN, A., International Business and Asian Studies
SELVANATHAN, S., Accounting, Finance and Economics
SHEPHERD, W., International Business and Asian Studies
SHORT, S. D., Public Health
SMITH, C., Accounting, Finance and Economics
SPARKS, B., Tourism and Hotel Management
STANDAGE, M., Science and Health
STEVENSON, J. C., Education
STRACHAN, G., Commerce and Business
SUN, C., Computing and Information Technology
TACON, P., Arts
THIEL, D. V., Microelectronic Engineering
TOH, S. H., Multi-faith Centre
TOMLINSON, R., Environmental Engineering
TOPOR, R. W., Computing and Information Technology
TURNBULL, P. G., Arts
VLACIC, L., Microelectronic Engineering
VON ITZTEIN, M., Biomolecular Science
WALLIS, M., Nursing
WANNA, J., Politics and Public Policy
WELLER, P. M., Politics and Public Policy
WISEMAN, H. M., Science
XU, Z., Environmental Studies
YEO, R., Humanities
ZEVENBERGEN, R., Education

ACADEMIC CENTRES AND INSTITUTES

Centre for Applied Linguistics and Languages: tel. (7) 3735-7089; e-mail call@griffith.edu.au; internet www.griffith.edu.au/centre/call; Dir MARGARET CASEY.

Centre for Applied Studies in Deafness: tel. (7) 5552-8619; e-mail m.hyde@griffith.edu.au; internet www.griffith.edu.au/centre/casd; Dir Prof. MERVYN HYDE.

Centre for Credit and Consumer Law: tel. (7) 3735-4211; e-mail n.howell@griffith.edu.au; internet www.griffith.edu.au/centre/cccl; Dir NICOLA HOWELL.

Centre for Environmental and Population Health: tel. (7) 3735-7458; e-mail c.chu@griffith.edu.au; internet www.griffith.edu.au/centre/ceph; Dir Prof. CORDIA CHU.

Centre for Leadership and Management in Education: tel. (7) 3735-5626; e-mail clme@griffith.edu.au; internet www.griffith.edu.au/centre/clme; Dir (vacant).

Griffith Graduate Research School: tel. (7) 3735-5958; e-mail j.cumming@griffith.edu.au; internet www.griffith.edu.au/ggrs; Dir Prof. JOY CUMMING.

Griffith Institute for Higher Education: tel. (7) 3735-5982; e-mail c.birch@griffith.edu.au; internet www.griffith.edu.au/centre/gihe; Dir Prof. KERRI-LEE KRAUSE.

GUMURRII Student Support Centre: tel. (7) 3735-7676; e-mail kerryn.brown@griffith.edu.au; internet www.griffith.edu.au/centre/gumurrii; Dir Prof. B. ROBERTSON.

Institute for Educational Research, Policy and Evaluation: e-mail gier@griffith.edu.au; Dir (vacant).

Unit for Italian Studies: Dir C. KENNEDY

JAMES COOK UNIVERSITY

Townsville, QLD 4811
Telephone: (7) 4781-5601
E-mail: jcu.enquiries@jcu.edu.au
Internet: www.jcu.edu.au
Founded 1970
Private control
Academic year: February to November
Chancellor: Lt-Gen. JOHN GREY
Vice-Chancellor: Prof. SANDRA HARDING
Deputy Vice-Chancellor: Prof. SALLY KIFT
Pro-Vice-Chancellors: Prof. IAN WRONSKI, Prof. JEFFREY LOUGHRAN
Registrar: M. KERN
Librarian: ALICE LUETCHFORD
Librarian: LYN CLARK
Librarian: MARK COLLINS
Number of teachers: 4,425
Number of students: 18,968
Publication: *JCU Outlook* (12 a year)

EXECUTIVE DEANS

Faculty of Arts, Education and Social Sciences: Prof. NOLA ALLOWAY
Faculty of Law, Business and the Creative Arts: Prof. ROBYN MCGUIGGAN
Faculty of Medicine, Health and Molecular Sciences: Prof. IAN WRONSKI
Faculty of Science and Engineering: Prof. JEFFREY LOUGHRAN

PROFESSORS

BAXTER, A. G., Biochemistry
BELL, T. H., Earth Sciences
BURNELL, J. N., Biochemistry
CARTER, R. M., Earth Sciences
CLARK, G., Law
COLLINS, B., Tropical Environment
CROZIER, R., Zoology
DAVIS, D. F., Creative Arts
GADEK, P., Tropical Biology
GILBERT, R., Education
GILLIESON, D., Tropical Environment
GLASS, B., Pharmacy
GRAW, S. B., Law
HASSALL, A. J., English
HAVEMANN, P., Law
HAYES, B. A., Nursing
HELMES, E., Psychology
HENDERSON, R. A., Earth Sciences
HERBERT, H. J., Indigenous Australian Studies
HERON, M. L., Physics
HO, Y. H., Medicine
HUGHES, T. P., Marine Biology
KEENE, F. R., Chemistry
KENNEDY, L., Medicine
KINGSFORD, M., Marine Biology
LANKSHEAR, C., Education
LAVERY, B., Information Technology
LAWN, R. J., Tropical Crop Science and CRC for Sustainable Sugar Production
LEAKEY, R., Tropical Biology

LOUGHRAN, J., Engineering
MARSH, H. D., Environmental Science
MILLER, D., Biochemistry and Molecular Biology
NOTT, J., Tropical Environment
OLIVER, N. H. S., Economic Geology
PATTERSON, J. C., Environmental Engineering
PEARCE, P. L., Tourism
PEARSON, R. G., Biological Science
PIERCE, P. F., Australian Literature
PORTER, R., Medicine
PRIDEAUX, B., Business
RANE, A., Medicine
REICHELT, R., CRC Reef Research
SPEARE, R., Public Health and Tropical Medicine
STORK, N. E., CRC Rainforest
SUMMERS, P. M., Tropical Veterinary Science
THORPE, R. M., Social Work
WHITTINGHAM, I., Mathematics and Physics
YELLOWLEES, D., Pharmacy

QUEENSLAND UNIVERSITY OF TECHNOLOGY

GPOB 2434, Brisbane, QLD 4001
Telephone: (7) 3138-2000
E-mail: askqut@qut.edu.au
Internet: www.qut.edu.au
Founded 1965, present status 1990
State control
Campuses in Gardens Point, Kelvin Grove, Caboolture
Chancellor: Major Gen. PETER ARNISON
Vice-Chancellor: Prof. PETER COALDRAKE
Deputy Vice-Chancellor: KEN BOWMAN
Deputy Vice-Chancellor for Academic Affairs: Prof. CAROL DICKENSON
Deputy Vice-Chancellor for Int. and Devt: SCOTT SHEPPARD
Deputy Vice-Chancellor for Learning and Teaching: Prof. SUZI VAUGHAN
Deputy Vice-Chancellor for Research and Commercialisation: Prof. ARUN SHARMA
Deputy Vice-Chancellor for Technology, Information and Learning Support: Prof. TOM COCHRANE
Exec. Dir of Finance and Resource Planning: STEPHEN PINCUS (acting)
Registrar: JANE BANNEY (acting)
Dir for Library Services: JUDY STOKKER
Library of 672,000 vols
Number of students: 40,563 (30,193 full-time)

DEANS

Creative Industries: Prof. ROD WISSLER
Faculty of Education: Prof. WENDY PATTON
Faculty of Health: Prof. ANDREW WILSON
QUT Business School: Prof. PETER LITTLE
School of Law: Prof. MICHAEL LAVARCH
Science and Engineering: Prof. MARTIN BETTS

PROFESSORS

ABBEY, J., Nursing
ARMSTRONG, H., Design and Built Environment
ARNOLD, N., Advertising, Marketing and Public Relations
ARTHURS, A., Music
BETTS, M., Faculty Office (Built Environment and Engineering)
BOASHASH, B., Electrical and Electronic Systems
BOULTON-LEWIS, G., Learning and Professional Studies
BOWMAN, K., Faculty Office (Health)
BOYCE, G., International Business
BOYD, T., Construction Management and Property
BROMLEY, M., Journalism
CAELLI, W., Data Communications
CARNEY, L., Optometry
CHANG, A., Nursing
CLEMENTS, J., Life Science
COALDRAKE, P., Chancellery
COLLIER, B., Law
COOPER, T., Mathematics, Science and Technology Education
COPE, M., Faculty Office (Law)
CORONES, S., Law Research
COURTNEY, M., Nursing
CRAWFORD, R., Mechanical, Manufacturing and Medical Engineering
CUNNINGHAM, S., Creative Industries Research and Applications Centre
DALE, J., Faculty Office (Science and Technology)
DAWSON, E., Data Communications
DOUGLAS, E., Brisbane Graduate School of Business
DUNCAN, W., Law
EDWARDS, H., Nursing
ENGLISH, L., Mathematics, Science and Technology Education
FERREIRA, L., Civil Engineering
FISHER, D., Law
FITZGERALD, B., Law School
GABLE, G., Information Systems
GARDINER, D., Chancellery
GARDNER, I., Life Science
GEORGE, G., Faculty Office (Science and Technology)
GIBSON, D., Chancellery
GOUGH, J., Research and Advancement
GRIFFIN, M., Faculty Office (Business)
HAMPSON, K., Cooperative Research Centre for Construction
HARDING, S., Faculty Office (Business)
HARTLEY, J., Faculty Office (Creative Industries)
HERINGTON, A., Life Science
HOCKINGS, J., Design and Built Environment
HUDSON, P., Life Science
HURN, A., Economics and Finance
JONES, J., Creative Industries Research and Applications Centre
KABANOFF, B., Management
LANE, W., Law School
LAVERY, P., Creative Industries Faculty Advancement
LAYTON, A., Economics and Finance
LEDWICH, G., Electrical and Electronic Systems
LEHMANN, S., Design and Built Environment
LITTLE, P., Accountancy
MCELWAIN, D., Mathematics
MCGREGOR-LOWNDES, M., Centre of Philanthropy and Non-profit Studies
MCLEAN, V., Faculty Office (Education)
MCROBBIE, C., Mathematics, Science and Technology Education
MCWILLIAM, E., Cultural and Language Studies in Education
MAEDER, A., Electrical and Electronic Systems
MAHENDRAN, M., Civil Engineering
MATCHETT, R., QUT Carseldine
MATHEW, J., Mechanical, Manufacturing and Medical Engineering
MOODY, M., Electrical and Electronic Systems Engineering
NEWMAN, B., Public Health
OLDENBURG, B., Public Health
PARKER, A., Human Movement Studies
PATTI, C., Advertising, Marketing and Public Relations
PATTON, W., Learning and Professional Studies
PEARCY, M., Mechanical, Manufacturing and Medical Engineering
PETTITT, A., Mathematics
PHAM, B., Information Technology
POPE, J., Physical Sciences
RENFORTH, W., Business
RYAN, N., Management
SARA, V., Life Science
SHEEHAN, M., Psychology and Counselling
SIDWELL, A., Construction Management and Property
SKITMORE, R., Construction Management and Property
SRIDHARAN, S., Electrical and Electronic Systems
TAYLER, C., Early Childhood
THAMBIRATNAM, D., Civil Engineering
TOWERS, S., Creative Industries Faculty Academic Programs
TROCKI, C., Humanities and Human Services
TROUTBECK, R., Civil Engineering
WALDERSEE, R., Business
WILLETT, R., Accountancy
WISSLER, R., Research and Advancement
YOUNG, R., Psychology and Counselling

UNIVERSITY OF QUEENSLAND

QLD 4072
Brisbane, St Lucia, QLD 4072
Telephone: (7) 3365-1111
E-mail: admissionsenquiries@admin.uq.edu.au
Internet: www.uq.edu.au
Founded 1910
public control
Academic year: January to December (2 semesters, and summer semester)
Chancellor: JOHN STORY
Deputy Chancellor: Dr JANE WILSON
Vice-Chancellor and Pres.: Prof. PETER HØJ
Provost: Prof. MAX LU
Deputy Vice-Chancellor for Academic Affairs: Prof. JOANNE WRIGHT
Deputy Vice-Chancellor for Int. Affairs: Prof. MONIQUE SKIDMORE
Deputy Vice-Chancellor for Research: Prof. ANTON MIDDELBERG (acting)
Pro-Vice-Chancellor: Prof. ALAN RIX
Pro-Vice-Chancellor for Advancement: CLARE PULLAR
Pro-Vice-Chancellor for Indigenous Education: Prof. CINDY SHANNON
Pro-Vice-Chancellor for Research and Int. Affairs: Prof. ALASTAIR MCEWAN (acting)
Chief Operating Officer: MAURIE MCNARN
Pres. of Academic Board: Prof. KAYE BASFORD
Univ. Librarian: ROBERT GERRITY
Library: see under Libraries and Archives
Number of teachers: 2,836
Number of students: 46,826

EXECUTIVE DEANS

Faculty of Business, Economics and Law: Prof. IAIN WATSON
Faculty of Engineering, Architecture and Information Technology: Prof. CAROLINE CROSTHWAITE (acting)
Faculty of Health and Behavioural Sciences: Prof. BRUCE ABERNETHY
Faculty of Humanities and Social Sciences: Prof. TIM DUNNE
Faculty of Medicine and Biomedical Sciences: Prof. NICHOLAS FISK
Faculty of Science: Prof. STEPHEN WALKER

PROFESSORS

Faculty of Business, Economics and Law (Level 3, GPN 3 Bldg, Campbell Rd, St Lucia Campus, QLD 4072; tel. (7) 3365-7111; e-mail bel@uq.edu.au; internet www.bel.eu.edu.au):

ALLAN, J., Law
ANDERSON, D., Business
ARONEY, N., Law
ASHKANASY, N., Business
BALLANTYNE, R., Tourism
BARKER, K., Law
BURTON-JONES, A., Business
CALLAN, V., Business
CAMPBELL, H., Economics
CLARKSON, P., Business
CORRIN, J., Law

DERRINGTON, S., Law
DEVEREUX, J., Law
DODGSON, M., Business
DOLNICAR, S., Tourism
DOUGLAS, H., Law
FAFF, R., Business
FOSTER, J., Economics
FRIJTERS, P., Economics
GASKELL, N., Law
GETZ, D., Tourism
GRANT, S., Economics
GRANTHAM, R., Law
GRAY, S., Business
GRIFFITHS, A., Business
HÄRTEL, C., Business
HAYWARD, M., Business
HODGSON, A., Business
LIESCH, P., Business
MCCOLL-KENNEDY, J., Business
MCLENNAN, A., Economics
MENEZES, F., Economics
O'DONNELL, C., Economics
ORR, G., Law
QUIGGIN, J., Economics
RAO, P., Economics
RATNAPALA, S., Law
ROHDE, F., Business
SANDBERG, J., Business
SCHLOENHARDT, A., Law
SMITH, T., Business
STRACHAN, R., Economics
TRIVEDI, P., Economics
VESSEY, I., Business
WILTSHITE, K., Business
WYATT, A., Business

Faculty of Engineering, Architecture and Information Technology (Room S204, Level 2, Hawken Eng. Bldg, St Lucia Campus, QLD 4072; tel. (7) 3365-4777; e-mail enquiries@eait.uq.edu.au; internet www.eait.uq.edu.au):

ATRENS, A., Mechanical and Mining Engineering
BAILES, P., Information Technology and Electrical Engineering
BALDOCK, T., Civil Engineering
BERGMANN, N., Information Technology and Electrical Engineering
BHATIA, S., Chemical Engineering
BRADLEY, A., Information Technology and Electrical Engineering
CAMERON, I., Chemical Engineering
CHANSON, H., Civil Engineering
CHARLES, P., Civil Engineering
CLARKE, W., Chemical and Civil Engineering
COOPER-WHITE, J., Chemical Engineering
CROSTHWAITE, C., Engineering
CROZIER, S., Information Technology and Electrical Engineering
DA COSTA, J., Chemical Engineering
DO, D., Chemical Engineering
FERREIRA, L., Civil Engineering
GURGENCI, H., Mechanical and Mining Engineering
HALLEY, P., Chemical Engineering
HAYES, P., Chemical Engineering
HAYES, I., Information Technology and Electrical Engineering
HICKMAN, M., Civil Engineering
HUANG, H., Mechanical and Mining Engineering
INDULSKA, J., Information Technology and Electrical Engineering
JAK, E., Chemical Engineering
KAJI-O'GRADY, S., Architecture
KELLER, J., Advanced Water Management
KITIPORNCHAI, S., Civil Engineering
KNIGHTS, P., Mechanical and Mining Engineering
LANT, P., Chemical Engineering
LEVER, P., Mechanical and Mining Engineering
LI, L., Civil Engineering
LINDSAY, P., Information Technology and Electrical Engineering
LOCKINGTON, D., Civil Engineering
LOVELL, B., Information Technology and Electrical Engineering
MCAREE, R., Mechanical and Mining Engineering
MACARTHUR, J., Architecture
MARTIN, D., Chemical Engineering
MEE, D., Mechanical and Mining Engineering
MEMMOTT, P., Architecture
MORGAN, R., Mechanical and Mining Engineering
NGUYEN, A., Chemical Engineering
NIELSEN, L., Chemical Engineering
RUDOLPH, V., Chemical Engineering
SADIQ, S., Information Technology and Electrical Engineering
SAHA, T., Information Technology and Electrical Engineering
ST JOHN, D., Mechanical and Mining Engineering
SANDERSON, P., Information Technology and Electrical Engineering
SCHAFFER, G., Mechanical and Mining Engineering
SHEN, H., Information Technology and Electrical Engineering
SKINNER, P., Architecture
SMART, M., Mechanical and Mining Engineering
STROOPER, P., Information Technology and Electrical Engineering
TORERO, J., Civil Engineering
WANG, L., Chemical Engineering
WILES, J., Information Technology and Electrical Engineering
WILLIAMS, D., Civil Engineering
WILSON, S., Information Technology and Electrical Engineering
YUAN, Z., Advanced Water Management
ZHANG, M., Mechanical and Mining Engineering
ZHAO, X., Chemical Engineering
ZHOU, X., Information Technology and Electrical Engineering
ZHU, J., Chemical Engineering
ZOU, J., Mechanical and Mining Engineering

Faculty of Health and Behavioural Sciences (Room S423, Level 4, Social Sciences Bldg, St Lucia Campus, QLD 4072; tel. (7) 3365-7487; e-mail habs@uq.edu.au; internet www.health.uq.edu.au):

BLAND, R., Social Work and Human Services
BRAUER, S., Health and Rehabilitation Sciences
BROWN, W., Human Movement Studies
BURGESS-LIMERICK, R., Human Movement Studies
CAPRA, S., Human Movement Studies
COOMBES, J., Human Movement Studies
GONDA, T., Pharmacy
HALFORD, K., Psychology
HASLAM, A., Psychology
HASLAN, C., Psychology
HEALY, K., Social Work and Human Services
HICKSON, L., Health and Rehabilitation Sciences
HODGES, P., Health and Rehabilitation Sciences
HORNSEY, M., Psychology
JETTEN, J., Psychology
KARGER, H., Social Work and Human Services
KENARDY, J., Psychology
KRUSKE, S., Psychology
MACDONALD, D., Human Movement Studies
MATTINGLEY, J., Psychology
MEREDITH, N., Dentistry
MONSOUR, P., Dentistry
MONTEITH, G., Pharmacy
NEAL, A., Psychology
PACHANA, N., Psychology
REMINGTON, R., Psychology
RIEK, S., Human Movement Studies
RODGER, S., Health and Rehabilitation Sciences
ROSENMAN, L., Social Work and Human Services
SAMARANAYAKE, L., Dentistry
SANDERS, M., Psychology
SANDERSON, P., Psychology
SEOW, W., Dentistry
SHAW, N., Pharmacy
SLAUGHTER, V., Psychology
STRONG, J., Health and Rehabilitation Sciences
SUDDENDORF, T., Psychology
THEODOROS, D., Health and Rehabilitation Sciences
TINNING, R., Human Movement Studies
TROST, S., Human Movement Studies
VICENZINO, B., Health and Rehabilitation Sciences
VON HIPPEL, B., Psychology
WALSH, L., Dentistry
WARD, L., Health and Rehabilitation Sciences
WILSON, J., Social Work and Human Services
WORRALL, L., Health and Rehabilitation Sciences
ZIVIANI, J., Health and Rehabilitation Sciences

Faculty of Humanities and Social Sciences (Room E207, Level 2, Forgan Smith Bldg, St Lucia Campus, QLD 4072; tel. (7) 3365-1333; e-mail hass@uq.edu.au; internet www.hass.uq.edu.au):

ALMOND, P., History of European Discourses
BALDAUF, D., Education
BARRETT, M., Music
BAXTER, J., Social Science
BELL, S., Political Science and International Studies
BLANSHARD, A., History, Philosophy, Religion and Classics
BLEIKER, R., Political Science and International Studies
CARTER, D., English, Media Studies and Art History
CHEN, P., Languages and Comparative Cultural Studies
CLARK, I., Political Science and International Studies
COCHRANE, G., Social Science
CRYLE, P., History of European Discourses
DUNNE, T., Political Science and International Studies
DURING, S., History of European Discourses
FERRIER, C., English, Media Studies and Art History
GELBER, K., Political Science and International Studies
GILLIES, R., Education
GOOS, M., Education
HARRISON, P., History of European Discourses
HAWKINS, G., Critical and Cultural Studies
HOLDAWAY, S., Social Science
HUNTER, I., History of European Discourses
KHAN, A., Social Science
LAWRENCE, G., Social Science
LEVY, M., Languages and Comparative Cultural Studies
LINGARD, B., Education
MEHIGAN, T., Languages and Comparative Cultural Studies
MILLS, M., Education
MOORE, C., History, Philosophy, Religion and Classics
NAJMAN, J., Social Science

O'REGAN, T., English, Media Studies and Art History
RENSHAW, P., Education
REUS-SMIT, C., Political Science and International Studies
RIGSBY, B., Social Science
SKRBIS, Z., Social Science
SPEARRITT, P., History, Philosophy, Religion and Classics
SUMMERHAYES, G., Social Science
TOMPKINS, J., English, Media Studies and Art History
TRIGGER, D., Social Science
TURNER, G., Critical and Cultural Studies
WALTER, R., Social Science
WEISLER, M., Social Science
WHITEHOUSE, G., Political Science and International Studies
WHITLOCK, E., English, Media Studies and Art History

Faculty of Medicine and Biomedical Sciences (Level 5, Centre for Clinical Research, Bldg 71/918, Royal Brisbane and Women's Hospital, Herston, QLD 4029; tel. (7) 3365-5342; e-mail mabs.reception@uq.edu.au; internet www.mabs.uq.edu.au):

BENNETT, M., Biomedical Sciences
BURGESS, P., Population Health
BYRNE, G., Medicine
CALLAWAY, L., Medicine
CAPRA, M., Biomedical Sciences
CHEN, C., Biomedical Sciences
CLEMENTS, A., Population Health
COULTHARD, A., Medicine
CRAWFORD, D., Medicine
DAVIES, P., Population Health
DOBSON, A., Population Health
EAKIN, E., Population Health
KEY, B., Biomedical Sciences
KHOO, S., Medicine
KISELY, S., Population Health
LAKHANI, S., Medicine
LIPMAN, J., Medicine
MCINTYRE, D., Medicine
MARTIN, J., Medicine
MCCOMBE, P., Medicine
MINCHIN, R., Biomedical Sciences
MISHRA, G., Population Health
MITCHELL, G., Medicine
NAJMAN, J., Population Health
NICHOLSON, G., Medicine
PARKER, M., Medicine
PINSKY, W., Medicine
SOYER, P., Medicine
TAYLOR, S., Biomedical Sciences
THOMAS, W., Biomedical Sciences
THORN, P., Biomedical Sciences
VAN DRIEL, M., Medicine
WALKER, P., Medicine
WHITBY, M., Medicine
WHITEFORD, H., Population Health
WHITTAKER, M., Population Health
WILLIAMS, G., Population Health

Faculty of Science (Bldg 69, Level 2, The Univ. of Queensland, St Lucia Campus, QLD 4072; tel. (7) 3365-1888; e-mail science.enquiries@uq.edu.au; internet www.science.uq.edu.au):

ADAMS, P., Mathematics and Physics
ADKINS, S., Agriculture and Food Sciences
BARKER, S., Chemistry and Molecular Biosciences
BARNARD, R., Chemistry and Molecular Biosciences
BASFORD, K., Agriculture and Food Sciences
BELL, M., Geography, Planning and Environmental Management
BERNHARDT, D., Chemistry and Molecular Biosciences
BERNHARDT, P., Chemistry and Molecular Biosciences
BEVERIDGE, C., Biological Sciences
BHANDARI, B., Agriculture and Food Sciences
BLOWS, M., Biological Sciences
BOTELLA, J., Agriculture and Food Sciences
BROWN, M., Chemistry and Molecular Biosciences
BRYANT, D., Mathematics and Physics
BRYDEN, W., Agriculture and Food Sciences
BURN, P., Chemistry and Molecular Biosciences
CARROLL, B., Chemistry and Molecular Biosciences
CAVES, C., Mathematics and Physics
COLEMAN, G., Veterinary Science
COLLINS, R., Agriculture and Food Sciences
CRAMB, R., Agriculture and Food Sciences
DAVIS, M., Mathematics and Physics
DE VOSS, J., Chemistry and Molecular Biosciences
DEGNAN, B., Biological Sciences
DRENNAN, J., Centre for Microscopy and Microanalysis
DRINKWATER, M., Mathematics and Physics
ESTERLE, J., Earth Sciences
FRANKLIN, C., Biological Sciences
FUKAI, S., Agriculture and Food Sciences
GAHAN, L., Chemistry and Molecular Biosciences
GARSON, M., Chemistry and Molecular Biosciences
GENTLE, I., Chemistry and Molecular Biosciences
GILLAM, E., Chemistry and Molecular Biosciences
GODWIN, I., Agriculture and Food Sciences
GOLDING, S., Earth Sciences
GOODHILL, G., Mathematics and Physics
GOULD, G., Mathematics and Physics
GRESSHOFF, P., Agriculture and Food Sciences
GROTOWSKI, J., Mathematics and Physics
HALL, R., Chemistry and Molecular Biosciences
HAYNES, D., Agriculture and Food Sciences
HILL, J., Veterinary Science
HOCKINGS, M., Geography, Planning and Environmental Management
HOEGH-GULDBERG, O., Biological Sciences
HOLLAND, M., Veterinary Science
HUGENHOLTZ, P., Chemistry and Molecular Biosciences
JOYCE, D., Agriculture and Food Sciences
KHROMYKH, A., Chemistry and Molecular Biosciences
KOBE, B., Chemistry and Molecular Biosciences
KROESE, D., Mathematics and Physics
LOVELOCK, C., Biological Sciences
MCALPINE, C., Geography, Planning and Environmental Management
MCEWAN, A., Chemistry and Molecular Biosciences
MCGOWAN, M., Veterinary Science
MCKENZIE, R., Mathematics and Physics
MCLACHLAN, G., Mathematics and Physics
MARK, A., Chemistry and Molecular Biosciences
MENZIES, N., Agriculture and Food Sciences
MEREDITH, P., Mathematics and Physics
MILBURN, G., Mathematics and Physics
MILLS, P., Veterinary Science
MONTEIRO, M., Chemistry and Molecular Biosciences
MUMBY, P., Biological Sciences
O'DONOGHUE, P., Chemistry and Molecular Biosciences
PANDOLFI, J., Biological Sciences
PARTON, R., Centre for Microscopy and Microanalysis
PHILLIPS, C., Veterinary Science
PHINN, S., Geography, Planning and Environmental Management
POLLETT, P., Mathematics and Physics
POPPI, D., Agriculture and Food Sciences, Veterinary Science
POSSINGHAM, H., Biological Sciences, Mathematics and Physics
RALPH, T., Mathematics and Physics
RAND, J., Veterinary Science
ROSS, H., Agriculture and Food Sciences
RUBINSZTEIN-DUNLOP, H., Mathematics and Physics
SCHEMBRI, M., Chemistry and Molecular Biosciences
SCHENK, P., Agriculture and Food Sciences
SCHMIDT, S., Agriculture and Food Sciences
SHULMEISTER, J., Geography, Planning and Environmental Management
SMITH, M., Integrated Preclinical Drug Development
SMITH, R., Chemistry and Molecular Biosciences
SOUTHAM, G., Earth Sciences
TOTH, I., Chemistry and Molecular Biosciences
TRAU, M., Chemistry and Molecular Biosciences
TYSON, S., Earth Sciences
VASCONCELOS, P., Earth Sciences
WALKER, M., Chemistry and Molecular Biosciences
WANG, Y., Mathematics and Physics
WARNAAR, O., Mathematics and Physics
WEBB, G., Earth Sciences
WHITE, A., Mathematics and Physics
WISEMAN, H., Mathematics and Physics
YOUNG, P., Chemistry and Molecular Biosciences
ZALUCKI, M., Biological Sciences
ZHAO, J., Earth Sciences

UNIVERSITY OF SOUTHERN QUEENSLAND

W St, Toowoomba, QLD 4350
Telephone: (7) 4631-5315
E-mail: international@usq.edu.au
Internet: www.usq.edu.au

Founded 1992 (fmrly the Univ. College of Southern Queensland, founded 1991 from the Darling Downs Institute of Advanced Education)
State control
Academic year: January to December

Chancellor: BOBBIE BRAZIL
Vice-Chancellor and Pres.: Prof. JAN THOMAS
Deputy Vice-Chancellor for Scholarship: Prof. GRAHAM BAKER
Deputy Vice-Chancellor for Global Learning: Prof. PHILIP C. CANDY
Deputy Vice-Chancellor for Global Learning and Pro-Vice-Chancellor for Academic Enterprise: Prof. JANET VERBYLA (acting)
Pro-Vice-Chancellor for Student Management: CARL RALLINGS
Pro-Vice-Chancellor for Social Justice: Prof. PETER GOODALL
Pro-Vice-Chancellor for Research Devt: Prof. ALLAN LAYTON
Pro-Vice-Chancellor for Partnerships: Prof. NITA TEMMERMAN
Pro-Vice-Chancellor for Research Training: Prof. FRANK BULLEN
Pro-Vice-Chancellor for Learning, Teaching and Quality: Prof. BELINDA TYNAN
Gen. Man. for Univ. Services: STEVE TANZER
Librarian: KERRIE MCLAREN

Library of 40,000 vols and 60,000 full-text electronic books
Number of teachers: 480
Number of students: 24,756

DEANS

Faculty of Arts: Prof. PETER GOODALL
Faculty of Business and Law: Prof. ALLAN LAYTON
Faculty of Education: Prof. NITA TEMMERMAN
Faculty of Engineering and Surveying: Prof. FRANK BULLEN
Faculty of Sciences: Prof. JANET VERBYLA

PROFESSORS

BILLINGSLEY, J., Engineering and Surveying
ERWEE, R., Business
FOGARTY, G., Sciences
HEGNEY, D., Sciences
HORSFIELD, B., Arts
MCMILLEN, D., Arts
ROBERTS, A., Sciences
ROSS, D., Engineering and Surveying
SMITH, R., Engineering and Surveying
TERRY, P., Sciences
TRAN-CONG, T., Engineering and Surveying
VAN ERP, G., Engineering and Surveying

UNIVERSITY OF THE SUNSHINE COAST

Locked Bag 4, Maroochydore D.C., QLD 4558
Sippy Downs Dr., Sippy Downs, QLD 4556
Telephone: (7) 5430-1234
E-mail: information@usc.edu.au
Internet: www.usc.edu.au

Founded 1994, univ. status granted and present name 1998
public control
Academic year: February to December

Chancellor: JOHN M. DOBSON
Vice-Chancellor and Pres.: Prof. GREG HILL
Deputy Vice-Chancellor: Prof. BIRGIT LOHMANN
Pro-Vice-Chancellor for Int. and Quality: Prof. ROBERT ELLIOT
Pro-Vice-Chancellor for Corporate Services and Chief Financial Officer: PETER SULLIVAN
Pro-Vice-Chancellor for Engagement: Prof. MIKE HEFFERAN
Pro-Vice-Chancellor for Research: Prof. ROLAND DE MARCO
Dir for Information Services: SANDRA JEFFRIES
Dir for Student Admin.: PATRICIA ALLEN
Dir for Student Services: EVA-MARIE SEETO
Library Man.: SHARON LENORD

Number of teachers: 212 full-time
Number of students: 8,000

DEANS

Faculty of Arts and Business: Prof. JOANNE SCOTT
Faculty of Science, Health, Education and Engineering: Prof. JOHN BARTLETT

PROFESSORS

Faculty of Arts and Social Sciences:
- ELLIOT, R.
- LAMBLE, S.
- SCOTT, J.

Faculty of Business:
- DOUGLAS, E. J.
- HEDE, A.
- RALSTON, D.

Faculty of Science, Health and Education:
- LOWE, J.
- MEYERS, N.
- SIMPSON, R.

SOUTH AUSTRALIA

FLINDERS UNIVERSITY

GPOB 2100, Adelaide, SA 5001
Sturt Rd, Bedford Park, Adelaide, SA
Telephone: (8) 8201-3911
E-mail: web@flinders.edu.au
Internet: www.flinders.edu.au

Founded 1966, merged in 1991 with Sturt Campus of South Australian College of Advanced Education
Academic year: March to November (2 semesters)

Chancellor: Sir STEPHEN GERLACH
Vice-Chancellor and Pres.: Prof. Dr MICHAEL N. BARBER
Pro-Vice-Chancellor for Information and Communication Technology Services: Prof. RICHARD P. CONSTANTINE
Deputy Chancellor: LEONIE J. CLYNE
Deputy Vice-Chancellor for Academic Affairs: Prof. Dr ANDREW W. PARKIN
Deputy Vice-Chancellor for Int. Relations and Communities: Prof. Dr DEAN K. FORBES
Deputy Vice-Chancellor for Research: Prof. DAVID DAY
Vice-Pres. for Strategic Finance and Resources: SHANE MCGREGOR
Vice-Pres. for Strategy and Planning: (vacant)
Dir for Admin.: B. FERGUSSON
Registrar: B. SIMONDSON
Librarian: IAN MCBAIN

Library: see under Libraries and Archives
Number of teachers: 768
Number of students: 20,187

Publications: *Australian Economic Papers* (with Univ. of Adelaide), *Australian Journal of Political Science*

EXECUTIVE DEANS

Faculty of Education, Humanities, Law and Theology: Prof. RICHARD MALTBY
Faculty of Health Sciences: Prof. MICHAEL KIDD
Faculty of Science and Engineering: Prof. WARREN LAWRANCE
Faculty of Social and Behavioural Sciences: Prof. PHYLLIS THARENOU

PROFESSORS

ABRAHAMSON, B., Computer Science, Engineering and Mathematics
ADCOCK, W., Chemical and Physical Sciences
AFNAN, I., Physics
ANDERSON, J., Education
AYLWARD, P., Medicine
AYLWARD, P., Public Health
BARRITT, G. T., Medical Biochemistry
BAUM, F., Public Health
BERSTEN, A. A., Medicine
BEVAN, D.J., Chemical and Physical Sciences
BLANDY, R., Business
BLESSING, W. W., Medicine
BLEVIN, H., Chemical and Physical Sciences
BLEWETT, N., Politics and Public Policy
BOND, M., Medicine
BRADLEY, E., Immunology, Allergy and Arthritis
BRENNAN, M., Chemical and Physical Sciences
BRUGGEMANN, R., Disability Studies
BULL, M., Biological Sciences
BURGOYNE, L., Biological Sciences
BUTCHER, A. R., Communication Disorders
CARATI, C., Medicine
CARSON, D., Rural Health
CATCHESIDE, D. E. A., Biological Sciences
CATCHESIDE, P., Medicine
CAVAYE, A., Business
CLARK, D. J., Law
CLARK, N., Chemical and Physical Sciences
CONDON, J., Psychiatry
CONSTANTINE, R., Information Services M. Cook International Studies
COOPER, L. L., Social Administration and Social Work
COSTA, M., Neurophysiology
COSTER, D. J., Ophthalmology
COX, K., Biological Sciences
CRAMOND, W., Psychiatry
CROCKER, A. D., Psychiatry
CROTTY, M., Rehabilitation, Aged and Extended Care
CURROW, D. C., Palliative Care
DARROCH, J., Computer Science, Engineering and Mathematics
DE LACEY, S., Nursing
DEBATS, D. A., American Studies
DODDS, P. G., Mathematics and Statistics
DUNBAR, J., Rural Health
ECKERMANN, S., Medicine
FAIRWEATHER, P. G., Biological Sciences
FILAR, J., Mathematics
FINLAY-JONES, J., Microbiology and Infectious Diseases
FISHER, G., Business
FORBES, D. K., Geography
FORSYTH, K. D., Paediatrics and Child Health
FULLER, J., Nursing
GIBBINS, I. L., Anatomy and Histology
GILLHAM, G., Nursing
GLEADLE, J., Medicine
GOODMAN, A. E., Biology
GORDON, T. P., Immunology, Allergy and Arthritis
GORE, C., Education
GRANTHAM, H., Paramedics
GRBICH, C., Social Health Sciences
GUERIN, P., Psychology
HABERBERGER, R., Anatomy and Histology
HANCOCK, K., Labour Studies
HASSAN, R. U., Sociology
HAY, I. M., Geography
HENDERSON, D. W., Medicine
HOLLEDGE, J., Drama
JAARSMA, R., Surgery
JAMES, J., Tourism
JANUS, E., Rural Health
KALUCY, R. S., Psychiatry
KEIRSE, M., Obstetrics and Gynaecology
KIDD, M., Medicine
KNIGHTS, K., Clinical Pharmacology
KNOWLES, G. P., Computer Systems Engineering
KRISHNAN, J., Surgery
LAATIKAINEN, T., Rural Health
LAWRANCE, W., Chemistry
LAWSON, M. J., Education
LENNON, G., Environment
LEONARD, D., Economics
LINACRE, A., Forensics
LLEWELLYN-SMITH, I., Cardiology
LUSZCZ, M. A., Psychology
MCCARLEY, J., Psychology
MCDONALD, J. M., Economics
MCDONALD, P., Microbiology and Infectious Diseases
MACDOUGALL, C., Public Health
MCEVOY, D., Medicine
MACKENZIE, P. I., Clinical Pharmacology
MACKINNON, A., Medicine
MCKINNON, R., Cancer Research
MCMILLAN, J., Ethics Law and Professionalism
MALTBY, R. G., Screen Studies
MARLIN, C. D., Computer Science
MARTIN, E., Biological Sciences
MAVROMARAS, K., Labour Studies
MEGAW, V., Archaeology
MINERS, J. O., Clinical Pharmacology
MORLEY, A. A., Haematology
MORLEY, M., Drama
MURRAY, A., Biological Sciences
NEILD, T., Human Physiology
NEL, D., Business
NICHOLAS, T., Business
NICHOLLS, M., Psychology
OLIVER, J., Human Physiology
OWEN, H., Anaesthesia and Pain Medicine
OWENS, L., Education
PARKIN, A., Political and International Studies
PATERSON, J., Nursing
PETERSON, P., Chemical and Physical Sciences
PHILLIPS, P., Medicine
PILLER, N. B., Public Health
PRIDEAUX, D. J., Health Professional Education
RANN, M., Politics and Public Policy
RATCLIFFE, J., Health Economics
REED, R., General Practice

REYNOLDS, K., Computer Science, Engineering and Mathematics
RICHARDS, E. S., History
RICHARDSON, S., National Institute of Labour Studies
ROACH ANLEU, S. L., Sociology
ROCHE, A. M., National Centre for Education and Training on Addiction
RODDICK, J. F., Computer Science
RUSH, R. A., Human Physiology
RUSSEL, A., Education
RYALL, R. L., Surgery
SAGE, M. R., Medical Imaging
SCHOO, A., Physiotherapy
SCHUWIRTH, L., Medical Education
SCHWERDTFEGER, P., Airborne Research
SEET, P., Business
SHERIDAN, D., Nursing
SHERIDAN, S. M., Women's Studies
SIMMONS, C. T., Groundwater
SIMS, N., Medical Biochemistry
SMITH, C., Archaeology
SMITH, D., Rehabilitation Medicine
SMITH, J, Ophthalmology
SMITH, M. D., Medicine
SMYTH, J., Education
STORER, R., Physics
SYKES, P., Haematology
TAYLOR, M., Biomedical Engineering
TEUBNER, P. J. O., Physics
THARENOU, P., Social and Behavioural Sciences
TIGGEMANN, M., Psychology
TILT, C., Accounting
TOMCZAK, M., Earth Sciences
TONKIN, A. M., Medicine
TOOULI, J., Surgery
TRENT, F. H., Education
TULLOCH, G. J., English
VARTIAINEN RURAL, E., Health
VERED, K., Screen and Media
VON DER BORCH, C., Environment
WATSON, D., Surgery
WEBB, G., Physiotherapy
WEIGOLD, E., Chemical and Physical Sciences
WILLIAMS, K., Ophthalmology
WILLOUGHBY, J. O., Medicine
WILSON, B., Nursing
WING, L. M. H., Medicine
WOLFF, A., Rural Health
WORLEY, P. S., Rural and Remote Health
YOUNG, G. P., Gastroenterology
YOUNG, R., Psychology

UNIVERSITY OF ADELAIDE

Adelaide, SA 5005
Telephone: (8) 8313-4455
E-mail: council.secretary@adelaide.edu.au
Internet: www.adelaide.edu.au

Founded 1874
Private control
Language of instruction: English
Academic year: March to November

Chancellor: The Hon. ROBERT HILL
Vice-Chancellor and Pres. and CEO: Prof. JAMES MCWHA
Deputy Vice-Chancellor and Vice-Pres. for Academic Affairs: Prof. PASCALE QUESTER
Deputy Vice-Chancellor and Vice-Pres. for Research: Prof. MIKE BROOKS
Vice-Pres. for Services and Resources: PAUL DULDIG
Pro-Vice-Chancellor for Int. Affairs: Prof. KENT ANDERSON
Pro-Vice-Chancellor for Research Operations: Prof. RICHARD RUSSELL
Pro-Vice-Chancellor for Research Strategy: (vacant)
Pro-Vice-Chancellor for Student Engagement: Prof. DENISE KIRKPATRICK
Univ. Librarian: RAY C. CHOATE

Library of 2,400,000 vols
Number of teachers: 1,600
Number of students: 25,000

Publications: *Australian Economic Papers* (2 a year), *Australian Feminist Studies* (2 a year), *Australian Journal of Legal History* (2 a year), *Australian Journal of Social Research* (4 a year), *Australian Women's Studies* (1 a year), *Corporate and Business Law Journal* (2 a year), *Economic Briefings* (3 a year), *Research Report* (1 a year), *Social Analysis* (2 a year), *The Joseph Fisher Lecture in Commerce* (irregular)

EXECUTIVE DEANS

Faculty of Animal and Veterinary Science: Prof. IAIN REID
Faculty of Engineering, Computer and Mathematical Sciences: Prof. JOHN BEYNON
Faculty of Health Sciences: Prof. JUSTIN BEILBY
Faculty of Humanities and Social Sciences: Prof. NICK HARVEY
Faculty of Sciences: Prof. BOB HILL
Faculty of the Professions: Prof. Dr CHRISTOPHER FINDLAY

PROFESSORS

Faculty of Engineering, Computer and Mathematical Sciences (Level 1, Ingkarni Wardli, The Univ.of Adelaide, SA 5005; tel. (8) 8313-4148; e-mail ecms_office@adelaide.edu.au; internet www.ecms.adelaide.edu.au):

BARTER, C. J., Computer Science
BEGG, S. H., Petroleum Engineering and Management
BEHRBRUCH, P., Petroleum Engineering and Management
BRATVOLD, R. B., Petroleum Engineering and Management
BROOKS, M. J., Computer Science
COLE, P. H., Electrical and Electronic Engineering
COUTTS, R. P., Telecommunications
DANDY, G. D., Civil Engineering
GRAY, D. A., Sensor Signal Processing
HANSEN, C. H., Mechanical Engineering
IRELAND, V., Education Centre for Innovation and Commercialisation
KHURANA, A. K., Petroleum Engineering and Management
KING, K. D., Chemical Engineering
LINTON, V. M., Welded Structures (Cooperative Research Centre)
MCLEAN, A. J., Road Accident Research
SARMA, H. K., Petroleum Engineering and Management
WHITE, L. B., Electrical and Electronic Engineering

Faculty of Health Sciences (Level Two, N Terrace Campus, The Univ. of Adelaide, Adelaide, SA 5005; tel. (8) 8303-5336; e-mail health.sciences@adelaide.edu.au; internet www.health.adelaide.edu.au):

BARRETT, R. J., Psychiatry
BARTOLD, P. M., Dentistry
BEILBY, J. J., General Practice
BOCHNER, F., Clinical and Experimental Pharmacology
DEKKER, G., Obstetrics and Gynaecology
FREWIN, D. B., Clinical and Experimental Pharmacology
GOLDNEY, R. D., Psychiatry
GOSS, A. N., Dentistry
HENNENBERG, M., Anatomical Sciences
HILLER, J. E., Public Health
HOROWITZ, J. D., Medicine
HOROWITZ, M., Medicine
HOWIE, D. W., Orthopaedics, Trauma
JAMIESON, G. G., Surgery
JONES, N., Surgery
KOTLARSKI, I., Health Sciences Faculty Office
LUDBROOK, G. L., Anaesthesia and Intensive Care
MCFARLANE, A. C., Psychiatry
MACLENNAN, A. H., Obstetrics and Gynaecology
MADDERN, G. J., Surgery
MOYES, D. G., Anaesthesia and Intensive Care
NETTELBECK, T. J., Psychology
NORMAN, R. J., Obstetrics and Gynaecology
ROBERTON, D. M., Paediatrics
ROBINSON, J. S., Obstetrics and Gynaecology
RUFFIN, R. E., Medicine
RUNCIMAN, W. B., Anaesthesia and Intensive Care
SAMPSON, W. J., Dentistry
SAWYER, M. G., Paediatrics
SLADE, G. D., Dentistry
SOMOGYI, A. A., Clinical and Experimental Pharmacology
SPENCER, A. J., Dentistry
TAN, H. L., Paediatrics
TAPLIN, J. E., Psychology
THOMPSON, P. D., Medicine
TIERNEY, A. J., Clinical Nursing
TILLEY, W. D., Medicine
TOWNSEND, G. C., Dentistry
VERNON-ROBERTS, B., Pathology
WHITE, J. M., Clinical and Experimental Pharmacology
WORMALD, P. J., Surgery

Faculty of Humanities and Social Sciences (Ground Fl., Napier Bldg, N Terrace Campus, Adelaide, SA 5005; tel. (8) 8313-5245; e-mail humss.office@adelaide.edu.au; internet www.hss.adelaide.edu.au):

BODMAN RAE, C., Music
BOUMELHA, P. A., English
BULBECK, C., Social Inquiry
HARVEY, N., Geographical and Environmental Studies
HUGO, G. J., Social Applications of Geographical Information Systems
JAIN, P. C., Asian Studies
MORTENSEN, C. E., Philosophy
MUHLHAUSLER, P., European Studies, General Linguistics
PREST, W. R., History
SHAPCOTT, T. W., English
WILLIAMS, M. A., Geographical and Environmental Studies

Faculty of the Professions (Level 11 Nexus, 10 Bldg, Adelaide, SA 5005; tel. (8) 8303-8131; e-mail asktheprof@adelaide.edu.au; internet www.adelaide.edu.au/professions):

ANDERSON, K., Economics
BRADBROOK, A. J., Law
DETMOLD, M. J., Law
FAIRALL, P. A., Law
MCDOUGALL, F. M., Graduate School of Business
MARJORIBANKS, K. M., Graduate School of Education
NAFFINE, N. M., Law
PARKER, L. D., Commerce
POMFRET, R. W., Economics
QUESTER, P. G., Commerce
RADFORD, A. D., Architecture, Landscape and Urban Design
SHERIDAN, K., Graduate School of Business
SMOLICZ, J. J., Graduate School of Education
TAYLOR, D. W., Commerce

Faculty of Sciences (Ground Fl., Darling Bldg, N Terrace Campus, Adelaide, SA 5005; tel. (8) 8313-5673; e-mail faculty .sciences@adelaide.edu.au; internet www .sciences.adelaide.edu.au):

AUSTIN, A. D., School of Earth and Environmental Sciences
BOWIE, J. H., School of Chemistry and Physics
BRUCE, M. I., School of Chemistry and Physics
BURRELL, C. J., School of Molecular and Biomedical Sciences
COVENTRY, D. R., School of Earth and Environmental Sciences

FINCHER, G. B., School of Agriculture and Wine
GREENHALGH, S. A., School of Earth and Environmental Sciences
HILLIS, R. R., Petroleum Geology and Geophysics (National Centre)
HYND, P. I., School of Agriculture and Wine
KALDI, J. G., Petroleum Geology and Geophysics (National Centre)
LANGRIDGE, P., School of Agriculture and Wine
LINCOLN, S. F., School of Chemistry and Physics
MCMILLEN, I. C., School of Molecular and Biomedical Sciences
MILES, T. S., School of Molecular and Biomedical Sciences
MUNCH, J., School of Chemistry and Physics
OWENS, J. A., School of Molecular and Biomedical Sciences
PATON, J. C., School of Molecular and Biomedical Sciences
RANDLES, J. W., School of Agriculture and Wine
RATHJEN, P. D., School of Molecular and Biomedical Sciences
SCHMIDT, O., School of Agriculture and Wine
SEDGLEY, M., School of Agriculture and Wine
SEYMOUR, R. S., School of Earth and Environmental Sciences
SMITH, S. E., School of Earth and Environmental Sciences
TYERMAN, S. D., School of Agriculture and Wine
VINCENT, R. A., School of Chemistry and Physics
WALLACE, J. C., School of Molecular and Biomedical Sciences
WHAN, B., Molecular Plant Breeding (Cooperative Research Centre)

UNIVERSITY OF SOUTH AUSTRALIA

GPOB 2471, Adelaide, SA 5001
Telephone: (8) 8302-6611
E-mail: study@unisa.edu.au
Internet: www.unisa.edu.au

Founded 1991 by the merger of the South Australian Institute of Technology and three campuses of the South Australian College of Advanced Education; campuses at City East, City West, Magill, Mawson Lakes, Underdale and Whyalla

Autonomous (est. by Act of Parliament)
Academic year: January to December

Chancellor: Dr IAN GOULD
Vice-Chancellor and Pres.: Prof. DAVID LLOYD
Deputy Vice-Chancellor and Vice-Pres. for Research and Innovation: Prof. SAKKIE PRETORIUS
Deputy Vice-Chancellor and Vice-Pres for Int. and Advancement: NIGEL RELPH
Exec. Dir and Vice-Pres. for Finance and Resources: PAUL BEARD
Dir of Student and Academic Services: ALLAN TABOR
Univ. Librarian: HELEN LIVINGSTON

Library: 1m. vols, and research colln incl. 700,000 monographs and print journals and 420 databases
Number of teachers: 983
Number of students: 37,000

Publication: *UniSA Researcher* (online, 6 a year)

PRO-VICE-CHANCELLORS

Division of Business: Prof. GERRY GRIFFIN
Division of Education, Arts and Social Sciences: Prof. PAL AHLUWALIA
Division of Health Sciences: Prof. ALLAN EVANS
Division of Information Technology, Engineering and the Environment: Prof. ROBERT SHORT

TASMANIA

AUSTRALIAN MARITIME COLLEGE

Locked Bag 1399, Launceston, TAS 7250
Maritime Way, Newnham, TAS 7250
Telephone: (3) 6324-3775
E-mail: amcinfo@amc.edu.au
Internet: www.amc.edu.au

Founded 2008; attached to Univ. of Tas.

2 Campuses: Newnham Campus and Beauty Point Campus; 3 nat. centres: Nat. Centre for Maritime Engineering and Hydrodynamics, Nat. Centre for Ports and Shipping and Nat. Centre for Marine Conservation and Resource Sustainability

Prin.: Prof. NEIL BOSE (acting)
Chair.: BOB RUDDICK (acting)

UNIVERSITY OF TASMANIA

Hobart campus: POB 51 Hobart, TAS 7001
Telephone: (3) 6226-2999
Burnie (Cradle Coast) campus: POB 3501, Burnie, TAS 7320
Telephone: (3) 6430-4999
Launceston campus: POB 1345 Launceston, TAS 7250
Telephone: (3) 6324-3999
E-mail: course.info@utas.edu.au
Internet: www.utas.edu.au

Founded 1991 through merger of the Univ. of Tasmania (f. 1890) and the Tasmanian State Institute of Technology
Academic year: February to October (2 terms)

Chancellor: Dr DAMIAN BUGG
Vice-Chancellor and Pres.: Prof. PETER RATHJEN
Deputy Vice-Chancellor: ROD ROBERTS
Deputy Vice-Chancellor for Research: Prof. PADDY NIXON
Deputy Vice-Chancellor for Students and Education: Prof. DAVID SADLER
Provost: Prof. DAVID RICH
Pro-Vice-Chancellor for Regional Devt: Prof. JANELLE ALLISON
Exec. Dir for Finance and Admin.: A. FERRALL
Exec. Dir for Strategy: PAUL BARNETT
Academic Registrar: C. P. CARSTENS
Librarian: JANE LONG

Library: see under Libraries and Archives
Number of teachers: 800
Number of students: 18,108

DEANS

Board of Graduate Research: Prof. PETER FRAPPELL
Faculty of Arts: Prof. SUSAN DODDS
Faculty of Business: Prof. GARY. O'DONOVAN
Faculty of Education: Prof. IAN HAY
Faculty of Health Science: Prof. RAYMOND PLAYFORD
Faculty of Law: Prof. Dr MARGARET OTLOWSKI
Faculty of Science, Engineering and Technology: Prof. MARGARET BRITZ
Institute for Marine and Antarctic Studies: Prof. MIKE COFFIN (Exec. Dir)

PROFESSORS

at Hobart campus:

Faculty of Arts (PMB 44, Hobart, TAS 7001; tel. (3) 6226-7814; e-mail arts.faculty@utas.edu.au; internet fcms.its.utas.edu.au/arts):

BENNETT, M. J., History and Classics
BLAND, R., Sociology
FRANKHAM, N. H., Fine Art
KELLOW, A. J., Government
KNEHANS, D., Music
MALPAS, J. E., Philosophy
PAKULSKI, J., Sociology
REYNOLDS, H., History and Classics
WHITE, R., Sociology and Social Work

Faculty of Commerce (PMB 84, Hobart, TAS 7001; tel. (3) 6226-2160; e-mail course.info@utas.edu.au; internet www.utas.edu.au/commerce):

CARROLL, P. G. H., Accounting and Finance
GODFREY, J., Accounting and Finance
KEEN, C. D., Information Systems
RAY, R., Economics

Faculty of Education (PMB 66, Hobart, TAS 7001; tel. (3) 6226-2546; e-mail www@educ.utas.edu.au; internet www.utas.edu.au/educ):

ARNOLD, R. M., Empathic Intelligence and Pedagogy
HOGAN, D. J., Sociology of Education
MULFORD, W. R., Educational Leadership
WILLIAMSON, J. C., Teaching Studies and Teacher Education

Faculty of Health Science (PMB 99, Hobart, TAS 7001; tel. (3) 6226-4281; e-mail faculty.secretary@healthsci.utas.edu.au; internet www.utas.edu.au/healthsci):

CARMICHAEL, A., Paediatrics and Child Health
CLARK, M. G., Biochemistry
CLEMENT, C., Obstetrics and Gynaecology
DWYER, T., Population Health
KIRKBY, K. C., Psychiatry
MUDGE, P., General Practice
PETERSON, G., Pharmacy
STANTON, P. D., Surgery
VICKERS, J. C., Pathology
WALTERS, H., Medicine

Faculty of Law (PMB 89, Hobart, TAS 7001; tel. (3) 6226-2066; e-mail secretary@law.utas.edu.au; internet www.law.utas.edu.au):

CHALMERS, D. R. C., Law
WARNER, C. A., Law

Faculty of Science, Engineering and Technology (PMB 50, Hobart, TAS 7001; tel. (3) 6226-2125; e-mail set.enquiries@utas.edu.au; internet ww.utas.edu.au/set):

BUDD, W. F., Antarctic and Southern Ocean Environment
BULLEN, F., Engineering
BUXTON, C. D., Aquaculture and Fisheries
CANTY, A. J., Chemistry
CLARK, R. J., Agricultural Science
CRAWFORD, A., Earth Sciences
DAVIS, M. R., Civil and Mechanical Engineering
FORBES, L., Mathematics
GRIFFIN, R., Cooperative Research Centre for Sustainable Production Forestry
HADDAD, P. R., Chemistry
JOHNSON, C., Zoology
KIRKPATRICK, J. B., Geography and Environmental Studies
LARGE, R. R., Earth Sciences
MCMEEKIN, T. A., Agricultural Science
NGUYEN, D. T., Electrical Engineering and Computer Science
REID, J. B., Plant Science
SALE, A., Computing
SUMMERS, J. J., Psychology
VANCLAY, F., Agricultural Science

at Launceston campus:

Faculty of Arts (Locked Bag 1340, Launceston, TAS 7250; tel. (3) 6324-3223; e-mail arts.faculty@utas.edu.au; internet www.utas.edu.au/arts):

BLAND, R., Sociology and Social Work
HATLEY, B., Asian Languages and Studies
MCGRATH, V. F., Visual and Performing Arts

Faculty of Education (Locked Bag 1307, Launceston, TAS 7250; tel. (3) 6324-3446;

e-mail www@educ.utas.edu.au; internet www.utas.edu.au/educ):

MULFORD, W. R., Educational Leadership
WILLIAMSON, J. C., Secondary and Post-compulsory Education

Faculty of Health Science (PMB 99, Hobart, TAS 7001; tel. (3) 6226-4757; e-mail shssec@utas.edu.au; internet www.healthsci.utas.edu.au):

BALL, M., Biomedical Science
FARRELL, G., Nursing
WALKER, J. H., Rural Health

Faculty of Science, Engineering and Technology (PMB 50, Hobart, TAS 7001; tel. (3) 6226-2125; e-mail alex.hamiltonsmith@utas.edu.au; internet www.utas.edu.au/scieng):

CHOI, Y. J., Computing
FAY, R., Architecture and Urban Design
PANKHURST, N. W., Aquaculture

VICTORIA

DEAKIN UNIVERSITY

1 Gheringhap St, Geelong, VIC 3220
Telephone: (3) 5227-1100
E-mail: enquire@deakin.edu.au
Internet: www.deakin.edu.au

Founded 1974
Academic year: February to November

Campuses at Melbourne (Burwood), Geelong, Warrnambool and Geelong Waterfront

Chancellor: DAVID M. MORGAN
Vice-Chancellor: Prof. JANE DEN HOLLANDER
Vice-Pres. for Enterprise: KEAN J. SELWAY
Deputy Vice-Chancellor for Academic Affairs and Vice-Pres.: Prof. JOHN CATFORD
Deputy Vice-Chancellor for Int. and Devt: ROBIN BUCKHAM
Deputy Vice-Chancellor for Research: Prof. LEE ASTHEIMER
Univ. Librarian: ANNE HORN

Library of 1,600,823 vols (print and electronic books), 93,990 serials
Number of teachers: 1,562
Number of students: 41,635
Publication: *Deakin at a Glance* (1 a year)

PRO-VICE-CHANCELLORS

Faculty of Arts and Education: Prof. BRENDA CHEREDNICHENKO
Faculty of Business and Law: Prof. GAEL McDONALD
Faculty of Health: Prof. BRENDAN CROTTY
Faculty of Science and Technology: Prof. TREVOR DAY (acting)

LA TROBE UNIVERSITY

Melbourne, VIC 3086
Telephone: (3) 9479-1111
E-mail: international@latrobe.edu.au
Internet: www.latrobe.edu.au

Founded 1967
Private control
Academic year: March to November

Campuses in Albury-Wodonga, Bendigo, Mildura, Melbourne City and Shepparton

Chancellor: ADRIENNE E. CLARKE
Deputy Chancellor: Prof. JOHN McKENZIE
Vice-Chancellor: Prof. JOHN DEWAR
Senior Deputy Vice-Chancellor and Vice-Pres. for Global Relations: Prof. JOHN ROSENBERG
Deputy Vice-Chancellor for Research: Prof. KEITH NUGENT
Pro-Vice-Chancellor for Equity and Student Services: Prof. K. FERGUSON
Pro-Vice-Chancellor for Educational Partnerships and Quality: Dr J. JACKSON
Pro-Vice-Chancellor for Graduate Research: Prof. A. BRENNAN
Pro Vice-Chancellor for Future Learning: C. MACKEN
Vice-Pres. for Admin.: NATALIE MACDONALD
Univ. Librarian: JENNIFER PEASLEY

Number of teachers: 1,600
Number of students: 34,492
Publication: *Synergy* (2 a year)

DEANS

Faculty of Business, Economics and Law: Prof. LEIGH DRAKE
Faculty of Education: Prof. LORRAINE LING
Faculty of Health Sciences: Prof. KAREN DODD
Faculty of Humanities and Social Sciences: Prof. TIM MURRAY
Faculty of Science, Technology and Engineering: Prof. BRIAN McGAW

PROFESSORS

AIKHENVALD, A., Research Centre for Linguistics Typology
ALTMAN, D., Politics
ARNASON, J. P., Sociology and Anthropology
BEILHARZ, D. M., Sociology and Anthropology
BERNARD, C., Psychology
BLAKE, B. J., Linguistics
BOLAND, R. C., European Studies
BRANSON, J. E., Education
BROWN, D. F., Accounting and Management
CAHILL, L. W., Electronics Engineering
CAMILLERI, J., Politics
CHANOCK, M., Law and Legal Studies
CROUCH, G., Tourism and Hospitality
DILLON, T. S., Computer Science and Computer Engineering
DIXON, R. M. W., Research Centre for Linguistics Typology
DYSON, P., Physics
ENDACOTT, R., Mental Health
FITZGERALD, J. J., Asian Languages
FOOK, J., Health Sciences
FREADMAN, R. B., English
FROST, A. J., History
GATT-RUTTER, J. A., Italian Studies
GAUNTLETT, E., Hellenic Studies
HANDLEY, C., Human Biosciences
HARBRIDGE, R. J., Management
HOFFMAN, A., Genetics and Human Variation
HOOGENRAAD, N. J., Biochemistry
JEFFREY, R., Politics
KAHN, J., Sociology and Anthropology
KELLEHEAR, S., Public Health
KING, J. E., Economics and Finance
LAKE, M., History
LECKEY, R. C. G., Physics
LEDER, G., Education
LIN, V., Health
LINDQUIST, B. I., Occupational Therapy
LUMLEY, J. M., Mothers' and Children's Health
McDONALD, S. J., Midwifery
McDOWELL, G. H., Agriculture
MILLS, T. M., Mathematics
MOOSA, I. A., Economics and Finance
MORRIS, M. E., Physiotherapy
MURPHY, P., Tourism and Hospitality
MURRAY, T. A., Archaeology
NAY, R. M., Nursing
O'MALLEY, P., Law and Legal Studies
PARISH, R. W., Botany
PEARSON, A., Nursing
PERRY, A. R., Human Communication Science
PITTS, M. K., Health and Sexuality
PORTER, R. S., Business
PRATT, C., Psychological Sciences
RAYMOND, K., Pharmacy
REILLY, S., Human Communication Sciences
ROSENTHAL, D. A., Health Sciences
SALMOND, J. A., History
STEPHENSON, D., Zoology
STREET, A. F., Nursing
SUGIMOTO, Y., Sociology and Anthropology
SULLIVAN, P. A., Education
TAMIS, A., Hellenic Studies
THORNTON, M. R., Law and Legal Studies
TORRANCE, C., Nursing
WALKER, G. R., Law and Legal Studies
WHITE, C. M., Graduate School of Management
WILLIS, E. M., Humanities

MCD UNIVERSITY OF DIVINITY

21 Highbury Grove, Kew, VIC. 3101
Telephone: (3) 9853-3177
E-mail: directorofadminfin@mcd.edu.au
Internet: www.mcd.edu.au

Founded 1910 as Melbourne College of Divinity, present status 2012
Academic year: February to October (2 semesters)

Comprises 11 colleges in Adelaide, Melbourne and Sydney; Masters degrees in divinity, arts and theological studies; doctoral degrees in philosophy and theology

Chancellor: Dr GRAEME L. BLACKMAN
Vice-Chancellor: Dr PETER SHERLOCK
Deputy Chancellor: Dr ANDREW MENZIES
Dean: Prof. PAUL BEIRNE
Dir for Coursework: JOHN BARTHOLOMEUSZ
Dir for Finance and Admin. and Registrar: JEFF REANEY
Dir for Research: Dr MARK LINDSAY

MONASH UNIVERSITY

Wellington Rd, Clayton, VIC 3800
Telephone: (3) 9902-6000
E-mail: study@monash.edu
Internet: www.monash.edu

Founded 1958 (opened 1961); merged with Chisholm Institute of Technology and Gippsland Institute of Advanced Education 1990, and with Victorian College of Pharmacy 1992
Academic year: March to November

Chancellor: Dr ALAN FINKEL
Vice-Chancellor and Pres.: Prof. ED BYRNE
Provost and Sr Vice-Pres.: Prof. EDWINA CORNISH
Chief Operating Officer and Sr Vice-Pres.: PETER MARSHALL
Academic Pres., Monash S Africa: Prof. ALWYN LOUW
Academic Vice-Pres., Campus Transition and Partnerships: Prof. ROBIN POLLARD
Academic Vice-Pres., China and India: Prof. TAM SRIDHAR
Academic Vice-Pres., Monash-Warwick Alliance: Prof. ANDREW COATS
Vice-Pres. for Finance and Chief Financial Officer: DAVID PITT
Vice-Pres. for Information and Chief Information Officer: Dr IAN TEBBETT
Vice-Pres. for Marketing and Communication: DAVID BUCKINGHAM
Vice-Pres. for Services: RUSSELL ELLIOTT
Pro-Vice-Chancellor, Office of the Provost: Prof. MERRAN EVANS
Pro-Vice-Chancellor and Pres., Sunway campus, Malaysia: Prof. HELEN BARTLETT
Pro-Vice-Chancellor, Berwick and Peninsula: Prof. LEON PITERMAN
Pro-Vice-Chancellor for Major Campuses and Student Engagement: Prof. DAVID COPOLOV
Librarian: CATHRINE HARBOE-REE

Library: see under Libraries and Archives
Number of teachers: 8,162 (f.t.e.)
Number of students: 63,022

DEANS

Faculty of Art Design and Architecture: Prof. SHANE MURRAY
Faculty of Arts: Prof. RAE FRANCES
Faculty of Business and Economics: Prof. COLM KEARNEY
Faculty of Education: Prof. JOHN LOUGHRAN

Faculty of Engineering: Prof. FRIEDER SEIBLE
Faculty of Information Technology: Prof. FRIEDER SEIBLE
Faculty of Law: Prof. BRYAN HORRIGAN
Faculty of Medicine, Nursing and Health Sciences: Prof. CHRISTINA MITCHELL
Faculty of Pharmacy and Pharmaceutical Sciences: Prof. WILLIAM CHARMAN
Faculty of Science: Prof. SCOTT O'NEILL

PROFESSORS

Faculty of Art Design and Architecture (900 Dandenong Rd, Caulfield East, VIC 3145; tel. (3) 9903-2494; e-mail mada@monash.edu; internet www.monash.edu/mada):

ARMSTRONG, M., Design
BERTRAM, N., Architecture
DE BONO, A., Design
MORTON, C., Fine Arts
RAMIREZ, D., Architecture
TERSTAPPEN, C., Photography
WARWICKER, J., Design

Faculty of Arts (Bldg 11, Clayton Campus, Monash Univ., Clayton, VIC 3800; tel. (3) 9902-6011; e-mail arts-student-services@monash.edu; internet artsonline.monash.edu.au):

ATTWOOD, B., Philosophy, History and International Studies
BARTON, G., Political and Social Inquiry
BENJAMIN, A., English, Communications and Performance Studies
BOSWORTH, M., Political and Social Inquiry
BROWN, R., Geography and Environment Science
BURKE, R., Music
BURRIDGE, K., Languages, Cultures and Linguistics
DAVIES, G., Languages, Literatures, Cultures and Linguistics/Chinese Studies
GARRETT, L., Jewish Civilisation
GARRIOCH, D., History
GERSTER, R., Communications and Media Studies
GOULD, A., Music
HOCKING, J., Journalism and Australian Studies
IWABUCHI, K., Arts
KARTOMI, M., Music
KOSSEW, S., English
LINDGREN, M., Journalism, Australian and Indigenous Studies
MCCULLOCH, J., Political and Social Inquiry/Criminology
MCNIVEN, I., Geography and Environment Science
MARKUS, A., Jewish Civilisation
MEWS, C., Religion and Theology
NASH, C., Journalism and Australian Studies
O'CONNOR, J., Communications and Media Studies
OPPY, G., Philosophical, Historical and International Studies
PAVLYSHYN, M., Mykola Zerov Ukranian Studies
PICKERING, S., Criminology
RANGAN, P., Geography and Environment Science
RIGBY, K., Comparative Literature and Cultural Studies
RUSSELL, L., National Australian Studies
SCATES, B., History and Australian Studies
SELGELID, M., Political and Social Inquiry/Human Bioethics
SHARIFIAN, F., Language and Society Centre
SNOW, P., Theatre Performance
STEVENS, C., Languages, Literatures, Cultures and Linguistics/Japanese Studies
TAPPER, N., Environmental Science
THOMSON, A., Philosophical, Historical and International Studies
TRUE, J., Behavioural Studies
TWOMEY, C., Philosophy, History and International Studies/History
WALTER, J., Politics/Anthropology
WILSON, R., Languages, Cultures and Linguistics
WINAND, P., European Studies

Faculty of Business and Economics (POB 197, Caulfield East, VIC 3145; tel. (3) 9903-1400; e-mail enquiries.caulfield@monash.edu; internet www.buseco.monash.edu.au):

BROOKS, D., Econometrics and Business Statistics
BROWN, C., Accounting and Finance
CHALMERS, K., Accounting and Finance
HARRIS, A., Health Economics
KREVER, R., Business Law and Taxation
MAGEE, G., Economics
OPPEWEL, H., Marketing
SMYTH, R., Economics
VAHID, F., Econometrics and Business Statistics
WOLFRAM-COX, J., Management

Faculty of Education (Bldg 6, Clayton Campus, Monash Univ., Clayton, VIC 3800; tel. (3) 9905-2800; e-mail education.clayton@monash.edu; internet www.monash.edu/education):

FLEER, M., Education
FORGASZ, H., Education
KENWAY, J., Education
MOORE, D., Education
PENNEY, D., Education
SELWYN, N., Education
SNYDER, I., Education
SULLIVAN, P., Education
WEBB, S., Education
WHITE, S., Education

Faculty of Engineering (Bldg 82, New Horizons, Clayton Campus, Monash Univ., Clayton, VIC 3800; tel. (3) 9905-3419; e-mail eng-it.dean.pa@monash.edu; internet www.eng.monash.edu.au):

ARMSTRONG, J., Electrical and Computer Systems Engineering
BACH, U., Materials Engineering
BHATTACHARYA, S., Chemical Engineering
BIRBILIS, N., Materials Engineering
BLACKBURN, H., Mechanical and Aerospace Engineering
BOGER, D., Chemical Engineering
BOUAZZA, A., Civil Engineering (Geomechanics Engineering)
CAMERON, N., Materials Engineering
CHAUHAN, S., Mechanical and Aerospace Engineering
CHENG, Y., Materials Engineering
CHIU, W., Mechanical and Aerospace Engineering
CODNER, G., Civil Engineering
CURRIE, G., Civil Engineering
DAVIES, C., Mechanical Engineering
DELETIC, A., Sustainable Water Resources
DRUMMOND, T., Electrical and Computer Systems Engineering
DUENWEG, B., Chemical Engineering
ESTRIN, J., Materials Engineering
EVANS, J., Electrical and Computer Systems Engineering
GARNIER, G., Australian Pulp and Paper Studies
HAPGOOD, K., Chemical Engineering
HOURIGAN, K., Biological Engineering
JAGADEESHAN, R., Chemical Engineering
JIANG, L., Chemical Engineering
JONES, R., Mechanical and Aerospace Engineering
KODIKARA, J., Civil Engineering (Geomechanics Engineering)
KRISHNAMOORTHY, M., Mechanical and Aerospace Engineering
LI, D., Materials Engineering
LOWERY, A., Electrical and Computer Systems Engineering
NIE, J., Materials Engineering
PATHEGAMA GAMAGE, R., Civil Engineering (Geomechanics Engineering)
PREMARATNE, M., Electrical and Computer Systems Engineering
ROSE, G., Civil Engineering (Transport Engineering)
RUDMAN, M., Mechanical and Aerospace Engineering
SAWFORD, B., Mechanical and Aerospace Engineering
SHEN, W., Chemical Engineering
SHERIDAN, J., Mechanical Engineering
SHIRINZADEH, B., Mechanical and Aerospace Engineering
SIMON, G., Materials Engineering
SINGH, R., Mechanical and Aerospace Engineering
SMITS, A., Mechanical Engineering
SORIA, J., Mechanical and Aerospace Engineering
SUZUKI, K., Materials Engineering
THOMPSON, M., Mechanical and Aerospace Engineering
TIEN, J., Civil Engineering
TURNEY, T., Materials Engineering
VITERBO, E., Electrical and Computer Systems Engineering
WALKER, J., Civil Engineering
WANG, H., Chemical Engineering
WU, X., Design in Light Materials
YOUNG, W., Civil Engineering
ZHAO, D., Chemical Engineering
ZHAO, X., Civil Engineering

Faculty of Information Technology (Bldg 82, New Horizons, Clayton Campus, Monash Univ., Clayton, VIC 3800; tel. (3) 9905-3419; e-mail eng-it.dean.pa@monash.edu; internet www.infotech.monash.edu):

BUNTINE, W., Artificial Intelligence
BURSTEIN, F., Information Systems/Decision Support Systems
FARR, G., Computation Theory and Mathematics
FISHER, J., Information Systems Management
GARCIA DE LA BANDA, M., Artificial Intelligence/Bioinformatics/Computation Theory and Mathematics
GREEN, D., Artificial Intelligence
MCKEMMISH, S., Library and Information Systems/Archival Studies
MARRIOTT, K., Artificial Intelligence
MEYER, B., Artificial Intelligence/Computation Theory and Mathematics
NICHOLSON, A., Artificial Intelligence
SCHRIEBER, F., Artificial Intelligence
SRINIVASAN, B., Distributed Computing
WALLACE, M., Computation Theory and Mathematics/Information Systems
WEBB, G., Artificial Intelligence
ZUKERMAN, I., Artificial Intelligence

Faculty of Law (Bldg 12, Clayton Campus, Monash Univ., Clayton, VIC 3800; tel. (3) 9905-3357; e-mail law-undergraduate@monash.edu; internet www.law.monash.edu):

BARKOCZY, S.
CLOUGH, J.
DAVISON, M.
EVANS, A.
GOLDSWORTHY, J.
HODGE, G.
JOSEPH, S.
KNEEBONE, S.
LEE, H. P.
MALBON, J.
MONOTTI, A.
PARKER, C.
PITTARD, M.
SOURDIN, T.
WAINCYMER, J.

Faculty of Medicine, Nursing and Health Sciences (Bldg 64, Clayton Campus, Monash Univ., Clayton, VIC 3800; tel. (3) 9905-4301;

e-mail enquiries@med.monash.edu; internet www.med.monash.edu.au):

ALSTON, M., Social Work
BAIRD, M., Medical Imaging and Radiation Sciences
BERTRAM, J., Anatomy and Developmental Biology
BOYD, L., Emergency Health and Paramedic Practice
BOYD, R., Anatomy and Developmental Biology
CARROLL, J., Biomedical Sciences
CLARKE, I., Physiology
CORNISH, K., Psychology
CROSS, W., Nursing and Midwifery
DALY, R., Biochemistry and Molecular Biology
DAVIS, I., Eastern Clinical School
DOERIG, C., Microbiology
DRUMMER, O., Forensic Medicine
EBELING, P., Medicine
FARNWORTH, L., Occupational Therapy
FREEZER, N., Paediatrics
GIBSON, P., Gastroeterology
JANE, S., Medicine
KEATING, J., Physiotherapy
KISSANE, D., Psychiatry
LEWIN, S., Infectious Diseases
MACKAY, F., Immunology
MCNEIL, J., Public Health and Preventative Medicine
MAZZA, D., General Practice
MORAND, E., Southern Clinical School
MORGAN, P., Physiotherapy
MYLES, P., Anaesthesia and Perioperative Medicine
O'HEHIR, R., Allergy, Immunology, Respiratory Medicine
OLDENBURG, B., Global Health Improvement
ROSENFELD, J., Surgery
RUSSELL, G., Primary Health Care
SMITH, J., Surgery
TRUBY, H., Nutrition and Dietetics
WALKER, J., Rural Health
WALLACE, E., Obstetrics and Gynaecology
WIDDOP, R., Pharmacology
WILLIAMS, B., Community Emergency and Paramedic Practice
ZAUBU, A., Jeffrey Cheah School of Medicine and Health

Faculty of Pharmacy and Pharmaceutical Sciences (381 Royal Parade, Parkville, VIC 3052; tel. (3) 9903-9635; e-mail pharmacy.info@monash.edu; internet monash.edu/pharm):

BAELL, J., Medicinal Chemistry
BUNNETT, N., Drug Discovery Biology
CHARMAN, S., Drug Candidate Optimization
CHRISTOPOLOUS, A., Drug Discovery Biology
KIRKPATRICK, C., Pharmaceutics
LI, J., Drug Delivery, Disposition and Dynamics
NORTON, R., Medicinal Chemistry
PORTER, C., Drug Delivery, Disposition and Dynamics
POUTON, C. W., Pharmaceutics
SCAMMELLS, P., Biopharmaceutics
SEXTON, P., Drug Discovery Biology
SUMMERS, R., Drug Discovery Biology

Faculty of Science (Bldg 26, Level 1, Clayton Campus, Monash Univ., Clayton, VIC 3800; tel. (3) 9902-0274; e-mail sci-enquiries@monash.edu; internet www.monash.edu/science):

ANDREWS, P., Chemistry
ASTEN, M., Geosciences
BATTEN, S., Chemistry
BEARDALL, J., Biological Sciences
BOWMAN, J., Biological Sciences
BRUGGER, J., Geosciences
CALLY, P., Mathematical Sciences
CARTWRIGHT, I., Geosciences
CAS, R., Geosciences
CHAFFEE, A., Chemistry
CHOWN, S., Biological Sciences
CLAYTON, M., Biological Sciences
CRUDEN, S., Geosciences
DAVIS, J., Biological Sciences
FUHRER, M., Physics
HALL, P., Mathematical Sciences
HEARN, M., Chemistry
HEGER, A., Mathematical Sciences
HELMERSON, K., Physics
HOLLOWAY, B., Biological Sciences
JAKOB, C., Mathematical Sciences
JONES, C., Chemistry
KEAYS, R., Geosciences
KLEBANER, F., Mathematical Sciences
LAKE, S., Biological Sciences
LATTANZIO, J., Mathematical Sciences
MACFARLANE, D., Chemistry
MCNAUGHTON, D., Chemistry
MARRIOTT, P., Chemistry
MORGAN, M., Physics
PERLMUTTER, P., Chemistry
REEDER, M., Mathematical Sciences
SMITH-MILES, K., Mathematical Sciences
SMYTH, D., Biological Sciences
SPICCIA, L., Chemistry
VICKERS-RICH, P., Geosciences
WANLESS, I., Mathematical Sciences
WARREN, J., Biological Sciences
WEINBERG, R., Geosciences
WORMALD, N., Mathematical Sciences

AFFILIATED INSTITUTION

Mannix College: Wellington Rd, Monash Univ., Clayton, VIC 3800; tel. (3) 9544-8895; e-mail enquiries.mannix@general.monash.edu.au; internet www.mannix.monash.edu.au; Prin. SEAN BRITO-BABAPULLE

ROYAL MELBOURNE INSTITUTE OF TECHNOLOGY

GPOB 2476, Melbourne, VIC 3001
Locked Bag 10, A'Beckett St, Melbourne, VIC 8006
Telephone: (3) 9925-2260
E-mail: study@rmit.edu.au
Internet: www.rmit.edu.au
Founded 1887; univ. status 1992
Academic year: February to November
Campuses in Melbourne, Bundoora and Brunswick; int. campuses in Hanoi and Saigon (Ho Chi Minh City), Viet Nam
Chancellor: Dr ZIGGY SWITKOWSKI
Vice-Chancellor and Pres.: Prof. MARGARET GARDENER
Vice-Chancellor for Research and Innovation and Vice-Pres.: Prof. DAINE ALCORN
Deputy Vice-Chancellor for Academics and Vice-Pres.: Prof. GILL PALMER
Deputy Vice-Chancellor for Int. and Devt and Vice-Pres.: STEPHEN CONNELLY
Chief Operating Officer and Vice-Pres. for Resources: STEPHEN SOMOGY
Univ. Sec. and Vice-Pres.: Dr JULIE WELL
Dean for Learning and Teaching: Prof. GEOFFREY CRISP
Dean for Students: Prof. OWEN HUGHES
Dir, TAFE and Vice-Pres.: ALLAN BALLAGH
Academic Registrar: MADDY MCMASTER
Univ. Librarian: CRAIG ANDERSON
Library of 704,322 vols
Number of students: 74,000
Publication: *Research Highlights* (1 a year)

PRO-VICE-CHANCELLORS

College of Business: Prof. IAN PALMER
College of Design and Social Context: Prof. COLIN FUDGE
College of Science, Engineering and Health: Prof. PETER COLOE

SWINBURNE UNIVERSITY OF TECHNOLOGY

POB 218, Hawthorn, VIC 3122
Telephone: (3) 9214-8000
E-mail: study@swinburne.edu.au
Internet: www.swinburne.edu.au
Founded 1908 as Eastern Suburbs Technical College; present name and status 1992
Academic year: March to November
Campuses at Croydon, Hawthorn, Lilydale, Prahran, Wantirna and one in Sarawak, E Malaysia
Chancellor: Dr BILL SCALES
Vice-Chancellor: Prof. LINDA KRISTJANSON
Deputy Vice-Chancellor for Research: (vacant)
Deputy Vice-Chancellor for Academic Affairs: Prof. SHIRLEY LEITCH
Deputy Vice-Chancellor for TAFE: LINDA BROWN
Pro-Vice-Chancellor and Chief Exec. Sarawak campus: Prof. HELMUT LUECKENHAUSEN
Pro-Vice-Chancellor for Learning Transformations: Prof. GILLY SALMON
Pro-Vice-Chancellor for Research: Prof. MATTHEW BAILES
Pro-Vice-Chancellor for Research Quality: Prof. MICHAEL GILDING
Vice-Pres. for Int. and Devt: JEFFREY SMART
Vice-Pres. for Student and Corporate Services: STEPHEN BEALL
Librarian: DEREK WHITEHEAD
Library of 250,000 vols
Number of teachers: 657 (362 Higher Education, 295 Technical and Further Education—TAFE)
Number of students: 31,920 (18,134 Higher Education, 13,786 Technical and Further Education—TAFE)
Publication: *Research Report*

DEANS

Faculty of Business and Enterprise: Prof. MIKE DONNELLY
Faculty of Design: Prof. KEN FREIDMAN
Faculty of Engineering and Industrial Sciences: Prof. JOHN BEYNON
Faculty of Higher Education, Lilydale: Prof. BRUCE CALWAY (acting)
Faculty of Information and Communication Technologies: LEON STERLING
Faculty of Life and Social Sciences: Prof. RUSSELL CRAWFORD

UNIVERSITY OF BALLARAT

POB 663, Ballarat, VIC 3353
Telephone: (3) 5327-9018
E-mail: info@ballarat.edu.au
Internet: www.ballarat.edu.au
Founded 1976 as Ballarat College of Advanced Education; Univ. status 1994
Vice-Chancellor: Prof. DAVID BATTERSBY
Deputy Vice-Chancellor: Prof. TERRY LLOYD
Deputy Vice-Chancellor for Corporate Services: ROWENA COUTTS
Pro-Vice-Chancellor for Learning and Quality: Prof. TODD WALKER
Pro-Vice-Chancellor for Research: Prof. FRANK STAGNITTI
Pro-Vice-Chancellor for Schools and Programs: Prof. ANDREW SMITH
Vice-Pres. for Student Support and Services: DARREN HOLLAND
Number of students: 22,000 (higher education and Technical and Further Education—TAFE)

DEANS

School of Business: Assoc Prof. MIKE WILLIS
School of Human Services: Assoc. Prof. SHIRLEY FRASER (acting)

UNIVERSITY OF MELBOURNE

Melbourne, VIC 3010
Telephone: (3) 8344-4000
E-mail: vc@unimelb.edu.au
Internet: www.unimelb.edu.au

Founded 1853 (opened 1855)
autonomous institution est. by Act of Parliament (State of Victoria) and financed mainly by Commonwealth Govt.
Academic year: February to December

Chancellor: The Hon. ELIZABETH A. ALEXANDER
Vice-Chancellor and Prin.: Prof. GLYN DAVIS
Sr Vice-Prin.: IAN MARSHMAN
Provost: Prof. MARGARET SHEIL
Deputy Vice-Chancellor for Research: Prof. JAMES MCCLUSKEY
Deputy Vice-Chancellor for Global Engagement: Prof. SUSAN ELLIOTT
Deputy Vice-Chancellor for Univ. Affairs: Prof. WARREN BEBBINGTON
Deputy Vice-Chancellor for Academic Affairs: Prof. PIP PATTISON
Pro-Vice-Chancellor for Graduate Research: Prof. RICHARD STRUGNELL
Pro-Vice-Chancellor for Research: Prof. LYN YATES
Pro-Vice-Chancellor for Research Partnerships: Prof. JAMES MCCLUSKEY
Pro-Vice-Chancellor for Research Collaborations: Prof. LIZ SONENBERG
Pro-Vice-Chancellors: Prof. GEOFFREY STEVENS, Prof. RON SLOCOMBE
Pres. for Academic Board: Prof. RON SLOCOMBE
Sr Vice-Prin.: IAN MARSHMAN
Head of Univ. Services: LINLEY MARTIN
Chief Financial Officer: ALLAN TAIT
Gen. Counsel: CHRIS PENMAN
Exec. Dir for Human Resources: NIGEL WAUGH
Exec. Dir for Student Services and Academic Registrar: NEIL ROBINSON
Exec. Dir for Property and Campus Services: CHRIS WHITE
Exec. Dir for Research: DAVID COOKSON
Univ. Sec.: CHRISTOPHER STEWARDSON

Number of teachers: 3,347
Number of students: 36,626

DEANS

Faculty of Architecture, Building and Planning: Prof. TOM KVAN
Faculty of Arts: Prof. MARK CONSIDINE
Faculty of Business and Economics: Prof. MARGARET ABERNETHY
Faculty of Medicine, Dentistry and Health Sciences: Prof. JAMES ANGUS
Faculty of Science: Prof. ROBERT SAINT
Faculty of VCA and Music: Prof. BARRY CONYNGHAM
Faculty of Veterinary Science: Prof. KEN HINCHCLIFF
Melbourne Business School: Prof. JENNIFER GEORGE (Dir)
Melbourne Consulting and Custom Programs: Prof. MARIANN FEE (Exec. Dean)
Melbourne Graduate School of Education: Prof. FIELD RICKARDS
Melbourne School of Engineering: Prof. IVEN MAREELS
Melbourne School of Graduate Research: Prof. DICK STRUGNELL (Pro-Vice-Chancellor)
Melbourne School of Land and Environment: Prof. RICHARD ROUSH
Melbourne Law School: Prof. CAROLYN EVANS
School of Graduate Studies: Prof. RICHARD STRUGNELL

PROFESSORS

Faculty of Architecture, Building and Planning (tel. (3) 8344-6429; e-mail msd-courseadvice@unimelb.edu.au; internet www.abp.unimelb.edu.au):

BRAWN, G. W., Architecture
BULL, C., Landscape Architecture
DOVEY, K. G., Architecture and Urban Design
FINCHER, R., Urban Planning
GOAD, P., Architecture, Building and Planning
GREEN, R., Landscape Architecture
HUTSON, A., Architecture
KING, R. J., Environmental Planning
LEWIS, M. B.
ROBINSON, J. R. W., Property and Construction
RODGER, A., Architecture, Building and Planning
YENCKEN, D., Architecture, Building and Planning

Faculty of Arts (tel. (3) 8344-6395; e-mail arts-enquiries@unimelb.edu.au; internet www.arts.unimelb.edu.au):

ANDERSON, J., Fine Arts, Classical Studies and Archaeology
AUSTIN, P. K., Linguistics and Applied Linguistics
BUDIMAN, A., Indonesian
CLARKE, A. F., Equine Studies
COALDRAKE, W. H., Japanese
DURING, S., English
ENRIGHT, N. J., Anthropology, Geography and Environmental Studies
FINLAYSON, B., Anthropology, Geography and Environmental Studies
FREIBERG, A., Criminology
GALLIGAN, B. J., Political Science
GELDER, K., English
GRIMSHAW, P. A., History
HAJEK, J., French and Italian Studies
HOLM, D., Chinese
HOLMES, L. T., Political Science
HOME, R. W., History and Philosophy of Science
HURST, A., School of French
JACKSON, A. C., Social Work
LANGTON, M. L., Australian Indigenous Studies
MCINNES, C. V., Higher Education
MACINTYRE, S. F., History
MCPHEE, P. B., History
MALCOLM, E. L., Irish Studies
NETTELBECK, C., School of Languages
O'BRIEN, A., Creative Arts
PIKE, K., Criminology
PRIEST, P. G., Philosophy
RICKLEFS, M., Melbourne Institute of Asian Languages and Societies
RIDLEY, R., History
SEAR, F. B., Classics and Archaeology
STEELE, P. D., English
WALLACE-CRABBE, C. K., English
WEBBER, M. J., Geography

Faculty of Business and Economics (198 Berkeley St, Bldg 110, The Univ. of Melbourne, Parkville, VIC 3010; tel. (3) 8344-5317; e-mail commerce-courseadvice@unimelb.edu.au; internet www.fbe.unimelb.edu.au):

ABERNETHY, M. A., Accounting and Business Information Systems
BARDSLEY, P., Economics
BORLAND, J., Economics
BROWN, R., Finance
CREEDY, J., Economics
DAVIS, K. T., Finance
DAWKINS, P. J., Melbourne Institute of Applied Economic and Social Research
DICKSON, D., Economics
FREEBAIRN, J. W., Economics
GRIFFITHS, B., Economics
HARDY, C., Management
HOUGHTON, K. A., Accounting
KING, S. P., Economics
KOFMAN, P., Finance
KULIK, C., Management
LEECH, S., Accounting and Business Information Systems
LLOYD, P. J., Economics
MCDONALD, I. M., Economics
MARCHANT, G., Accounting and Business Information Systems
MARTIN, V., Economics
NASSER, S., Accounting and Business Information Systems
NICHOLAS, S., Management
PERKINS, E. J., Economics
SAMSON, D., Management
SHAPIRO, P., Economics
TOURKY, R., Economics
WHEATLEY, S., Finance
WIDING, R. E., Management
WILLIAMS, R. A., Econometrics
WOODEN, M., Melbourne Institute of Applied Economics and Social Research

Faculty of Education (234 Queensberry St, Univ. of Melbourne, VIC 3010; tel. (3) 8344-8285; e-mail enquiries@edfac.unimelb.edu.au; internet www.education.unimelb.edu.au):

CALDWELL, B. J., Education (Leadership and Management)
CHRISTIE, F., Language, Literacy and Arts Education
EVANS, G., Learning and Educational Development
GRIFFIN, P. E., Assessment
HILL, P., Education (Leadership and Management)
LAKOMSKI, G., Education
LEE DOW, K., Education
MAGLEN, L. R., Asian Pacific Economics of Education and Training
RABAN-BISBY, B., Early Childhood Studies
RICKARDS, F. W., Education (Learning, Assessment and Special Education)
STACEY, K. C., Science and Mathematics Education
START, B., Learning and Educational Development

Faculty of Medicine, Dentistry and Health Sciences (The Univ. of Melbourne, VIC 3010; tel. (3) 8344-5890; e-mail sc-mdhs@unimelb.edu.au; internet www.sc.mdhs.unimelb.edu.au):

ADAMS, J. M., Medical Biology
ALCORN, D., Anatomy
ANDERSON, I. P., Public Health
ANDERSON, J. N., Public Health
ANDERSON, V., Psychology
BERK, M., Psychiatry
BERKOVIC, S. F., Medicine
BEST, J. D., Medicine
BHATHAL, P. S., Pathology
BLOCH, S., Psychiatry
BOWES, G., Paediatrics
BREARLEY-MESER, L., Paediatrics
BRENNECKE, S. P., Obstetrics and Gynaecology
BROWN, G. V., Medicine
BYRNE, E., Experimental Neurology
CARLIN, J. B., Public Health
CHAN, S. T. F., Surgery
CHIU, E., Psychiatry
CLEMENT, J. G., Forensic Odontology
CORY, S., Medical Biology
CREAMER, M., Psychiatry
DENNERSTEIN, L., Psychiatry
DOHERTY, P., Microbiology and Immunology
DONNAN, G., Medicine
DOWELL, R. C., Otolaryngology
DUNNING, T., Nursing
FAIRLEY, C. K., Sexual Health
FUNDER, J., Medicine
FURNESS, J. B., Anatomy
GALEA, M. P., Physiotherapy

GAYLER, K. R., Biochemistry and Molecular Biology
GETHING, M. J., Biochemistry and Molecular Biology
GIBSON, R. M., Radiology
GOODWIN, A. W., Anatomy
GRAHAM, H. K., Orthopaedic Surgery
GRAVES, S. E., Orthopaedic Surgery
HARRAP, S. B., Physiology
HARRIS, P. J., Physiology
HARRISON, L. C., Medical Biology
HOPPER, J. L., Public Health
JACKSON, H. J., Psychology
KAYE, A. H., Surgery
LOUIS, W. J., Clinical Pharmacology and Therapeutics
MCCALMAN, J. S., Public Health
MCCLUSKEY, J., Microbiology and Immunology
MCMEEKEN, J., Physiotherapy
MANDERSON, L. H., Women's Health
MASTERS, C. L., Pathology
MESSER, H. H., Restorative Dentistry
MESSER, L. J. B., Child Dental Health
MILLGROM, J., Psychology
MORGAN, T. O., Physiology
MORRISON, W. A., Surgery
MULHOLLAND, E. K., Paediatrics
NELSON, S., Nursing
NICHOLSON, G. C., Medicine
NICOLA, N., Medical Biology
NOLAN, T. M., Public Health
O'BOYLE, M. W., Psychology
OLEKALNS, M., Psychology
PARKER, J. M., Postgraduate Nursing
PATTISON, P. E., Psychology
PERMEZEL, J. M. H., Obstetrics and Gynaecology
PIERCE, R., Medicine
PRIOR, M., Psychology
PROIETTO, J., Medicine
REYNOLDS, E. C., Dental Science
ROBINS-BROWN, R. M., Microbiology and Immunology
SCHWEITZER, I., Psychiatry
SHORTMAN, K. D., Medical Biology and Developmental Immunology
SINGH, B. S., Psychiatry
SMALLWOOD, R. A., Medicine
SPEED, T. P., Medical Biology
STRUGNELL, R. A., Microbiology and Immunology
TAYLOR, H. R., Ophthalmology
TILLER, J. W. G., Psychiatry
TRESS, B. M., Radiology
TRINDER, J. A., Psychology
TYAS, M. J., Dental Science
VADJA, F., Medicine
WARD, T., Psychology
WARK, J. D., Medicine
WATTERS, D. A. K., Surgery
WEARING, A. J., Psychology
WETTENHALL, R. E. H., Biochemistry
WICKS, I. P., Medical Biology
WILLIAMS, D. A., Physiology
YEOMANS, N. D., Medicine
YOUNG, D., General Practice
ZAJAC, J. D., Medicine

Faculty of Science (Ground Fl., Old Geology Bldg, Univ. of Melbourne, VIC 3010; tel. (3) 8344-6404; e-mail science-queries@unimelb.edu.au; internet www.science.unimelb.edu.au):

BACIC, A., Botany
BAKER, A. J. M., Botany
CAMPBELL, G. D., Zoology
CHAN, D. Y. C., Mathematics
CLARKE, A. E., Botany
COLE, B. L., Optometry
FERGUSON, I. S., Forest Science
GHIGGINO, K. P., Chemistry
GRIESER, F., Chemistry
GUTTMANN, A. J., Mathematics
HYNES, M. J., Genetics
KOTAGIRI, R., Computer Science
KLEIN, A. G., Physics
LADIGES, P. Y., Botany
MCBRIEN, N. A., Optometry
MCKELLAR, B. H. J., Theoretical Physics
MCKENZIE, J. A., Genetics
MILLER, C. F., Mathematics
MORRISON, I., Information Systems
NUGENT, K. A., Physics
PICKETT-HEAPS, J. D., Botany
PLIMER, I. R., Geology
RENFREE, M. B., Zoology
RUBINSTEIN, J. H., Mathematics
SCHIESSER, C., Chemistry
SONENBERG, E. A., Information Systems
STERLING, L. S., Computer Science
TAYLOR, G. N., Physics
THOMPSON, C. J., Mathematics
WEDD, A. G., Chemistry

Faculty of VCA and Music (tel. (3) 9035-9495; e-mail vcam-info@unimelb.edu.au; internet www.vcam.unimelb.edu.au):

BEBBINGTON, W. A., Music
BROADSTOCK, B., Music
GRIFFITHS, J. A., Music

Faculty of Veterinary Science (Cnr Park Dr. and Flemington Rd, Parkville, VIC 3052; tel. (3) 8344-7357; e-mail vet-info@unimelb.edu.au; internet www.vet.unimelb.edu.au):

CAHILL, R. N. P., Veterinary Biology
CAPLE, I. W., Veterinary Medicine
CLARKE, A. F., Equine Studies
SLOCOMBE, R. F., Veterinary Pathology

Melbourne Business School (Leicester St, Carlton, VIC 3053; tel. (3) 9349-8403; e-mail mbs@unimelb.edu.au; internet www.mbs.unimelb.edu.au):

ALFORD, J. L., Public Sector Management
DAINTY, P., Human Resources Management and Employee Relations
GANS, J. S., Management
GRUNDY, B., Finance
HARPER, I. R., Commerce and Business Administration
KING, S., Economics
LEWIS, G., Strategy
MANN, L., Organizational Behaviour and Decision-Making
MISHRA, D., Marketing
OLEKALNS, M., Leadership and Decision-Making
RIZZO, P., Finance and Management
SAMSON, D. A., Manufacturing Management
SINCLAIR, A. M. A., Management (Diversity and Change)
SPEED, R., Marketing Management and Advanced Marketing Strategy
WILLIAMS, P. L., Management (Law and Economics)

Melbourne Law School (Univ. Sq 185 Pelham St., Carlton, VIC 3053; tel. (3) 8344-4475; e-mail post@law.unimelb.edu.au; internet www.law.unimelb.edu.au):

BRYAN, M., Law
CHRISTIE, A. F., Intellectual Property
COLMAN, P. M., Medical Biology
COWMAN, A. F., Medical Biology
CROMMELIN, B. M. L., Law
MCCORMACK, T. L. H., International Humanitarian Law
MITCHELL, R. J., Law
MORGAN, J. J., Law
RAMSAY, I. M., Commercial Law
RICKETSON, S., Law
SAUNDERS, C. A., Law
SKENE, L., Law
SMITH, M. D. H., Asian Law
TRIGGS, G., Law

Melbourne School of Engineering (Bldg 173 The Univ. of Melbourne, Parkville, VIC 3010; tel. (3) 8344-6619; e-mail officeofthedean@eng.unimelb.edu.au; internet www.eng.unimelb.edu.au):

BISHOP, I. D., Geomatics
BOGER, D. V., Chemical Engineering
CHING, M. S., Mechanical and Manufacturing Engineering
EVANS, R. J., Electrical Engineering
FENTON, J. D., Civil and Environmental Engineering
FRASER, C. S., Geomatics
GOOD, M. C., Mechanical and Manufacturing Engineering
HUTCHINSON, G. L., Civil and Environmental Engineering
KOTAGIRI, R., Computer Science and Software Engineering
KRISHNAMURTHY, V., Electrical and Electronic Engineering
MCMAHON, T. A., Environmental Hydrology
MAREELS, I. M. V., Electrical Engineering
MOFFAT, A. M., Computer Science and Software Engineering
MORAN, W., Electronic and Electrical Engineering
STERLING, L. S., Computer Science and Software Engineering
STEVENS, G. W., Chemical Engineering
STUCKLEY, P. J., Computer Science and Software Engineering
TUCKER, R. S., Electrical Engineering
VAN DEVENTER, J., Mineral and Process Engineering
WATSON, H. C., Mechanical and Manufacturing Engineering
WILLIAMSON, I. P., Surveying and Land Information
WOOD, D. G., Engineering
YOUNG, D. M., Engineering Construction Management
ZUCKERMAN, M., Electronic and Electrical Engineering

Melbourne School of Land and Environment (Univ. of Melbourne, Parkville, VIC 3010; tel. (3) 8344-0276; e-mail enquiries@landfood.unimelb.edu.au; internet www.land-environment.unimelb.edu.au):

BRITZ, M., Food Science
CHAPMAN, D. F., Pasture Science
COUSENS, R. D., Crop Science
EGAN, A. R., Agriculture (Animal Science)
FALVEY, J. L., Agriculture
FERGUSON, I. S., Forest Science
GODDARD, M., Agriculture
HEMSWORTH, P., Agriculture
HILLIER, A. J., Agriculture
KOLLMORGEN, J. F., Agriculture
MACMILLAN, K. L., Agriculture
RICHARDSON, R. A., Land and Food Resources
ROSS, E. W., Agriculture
VINDEN, P., Forest Industries

Victorian College of the Arts (234 St Kilda Rd, Southbank, VIC 3010; tel. (3) 9685-9300; internet www.vca.unimelb.edu.au):

HULL, A. (Dir)

VICTORIA UNIVERSITY

POB 14428, Melbourne, VIC 8001
Telephone: (3) 9919-4000
E-mail: graduate@vu.edu.au
Internet: www.vu.edu.au

Founded 1916 as Footscray Technical School; after various mergers established as Victoria Univ. of Technology in 1990, present name 2005

Academic year: March to November

Chancellor: GEORGE PAPPAS
Pres. and Vice-Chancellor: Prof. PETER DAWKINS
Deputy Vice-Chancellor for Academic and Students: Dr ANNE JONES
Deputy Vice-Chancellor for Planning, Marketing and External Affairs: Prof. DUNCAN BENTLEY

Deputy Vice-Chancellor for Research and Knowledge Exchange: Prof. LINDA ROSENMAN
Pro-Vice-Chancellor for Academic and Student: Prof. GREG BAXTER
Pro-Vice-Chancellor for External Affairs: Dr ROB BROWN
Pro-Vice-Chancellor for Learning and Teaching: Prof. MARGARET MAZZOLINI
Pro-Vice-Chancellor and Chief Information Officer: Prof. PETER CREAMER
Pro-Vice-Chancellor for Research and Research Training: Prof. WARREN PAYNE
Vice-Pres. for Int. Affairs: ANDREW HOLLOWAY
Univ. Gen. Counsel: Dr STEVEN STERN
Univ. Librarian: RALPH KIEL
Library of 561,341 vols
Number of teachers: 2,607
Number of students: 53,935
Publications: *Connections* (2 a year), *Journal of Business Systems, Governance and Ethics*

DEANS

Faculty of Arts, Education and Human Devt: Prof. DIANE MAYER
Faculty of Business and Law: Prof. DAVID LAMOND
Faculty of Health, Engineering and Science: Prof. Dr MICHELLE TOWSTOLESS
Faculty of Technical and Trades Innovation: CORALIE MORRISSEY
Faculty of Workforce Devt: GRANT DREHER
VU College: SUSAN YOUNG

PROFESSORS

ANDERSON, R., Accounting
ANDREWS, N., Law
ARMSTRONG, A., School of Management
ARUP, C., Law
BAKER, H., Nursing
BROCK, D., Psychology
CARLSON, J., Centre for Ageing, Rehabilitation, Exercise and Sport
CARY, J., Key Research Area of Integrated Food Value Chain
CLARK, C., Accounting
DAVIDSON, J., History
DEERY, P., Dept of Asian and Int. Studies
DRAGOMIR, S., Engineering
EADE, R., Arts
FAULKNER, M., Telecommunications
GABB, R., Centre for Educational Devt and Support
GEORGE, G., Accounting
GLASBEEK, H., Business and Law
GREWAL, B., Centre for Strategic Economic Studies
HOUGHTON, J., Centre for Strategic Economic Studies
JAGO, L., Tourism and Hospitality Studies
KALAM, A., Engineering
KING, B., School of Hospitality, Tourism and Marketing
LEUNG, C., Computer Science
MCGRATH, M., Information Systems
MCQUEEN, R., Law
MORRIS, A., Human Devt, Health, Engineering and Science
PATIENCE, A., Arts
POLONSKY, M., Marketing
PRIESTLY, I., Accounting
PRILLELTENSKY, I., Psychology
ROBERTS, T., School of Human Movement, Recreation and Performance
RYAN, M., Education
SEEDSMAN, T., Human Devt, Health, Engineering and Science
SHEEHAN, P., Centre for Strategic Economic Studies
SINCLAIR, J., Arts
THOMAS, I., Centre for Environmental Safety and Risk Engineering
THORPE, G., School of the Built Environment
TURNER, L., School of Applied Economics
WILSON, K., Economics
XIE, M., Engineering
ZHANG, Y., Computer Science

WESTERN AUSTRALIA

CURTIN UNIVERSITY

GPOB U1987, Perth, WA 6845
Telephone: (8) 9266-9266
Internet: www.curtin.edu.au
Founded 1966 as Western Australian Institute of Technology, present name and status 1987
Academic year: February to November (2 semesters)
Chancellor: Dr JIM GILL (acting)
Vice-Chancellor: Prof. JEANETTE HACKET
Deputy Vice-Chancellor for Academic Services: Prof. COLIN STIRLING
Deputy Vice-Chancellor for Education: Prof. ROBYN QUIN
Deputy Vice-Chancellor for Int.: Prof. DAVID WOOD
Deputy Vice-Chancellor for Research and Devt: Prof. GRAEME WRIGHT
Vice-Pres. for Corporate Relations and Devt: VAL RAUBENHEIMER
Chief Financial Officer: DAVID MENARRY
Academic Registrar: JOHN ROWE
Univ. Librarian: IMOGEN GARNER
Number of teachers: 1,200
Number of students: 46,634

PRO-VICE-CHANCELLORS

Curtin Business School: Prof. TONY TRAVAGLIONE
Health Sciences: Prof. JILL DOWNIE
Humanities: Prof. MAJELLA FRANZMANN
Science and Engineering: Prof. ANDRIS STELBOVICS

EDITH COWAN UNIVERSITY

270 Joondalup Dr., Joondalup, WA 6027
Telephone: (8) 6304-0000
E-mail: enquiries@ecu.edu.au
Internet: www.ecu.edu.au
Founded 1991
State control
Academic year: February to November (2 semesters)
Chancellor: Hon. Dr HENDY COWAN
Vice-Chancellor: Prof. Dr KERRY O. COX
Deputy Vice-Chancellor for Academic Affairs: Prof. ARSHAD OMARI
Deputy Vice-Chancellor for Research and Advancement and Vice-Pres.: Prof. JOHN FINLAY-JONES
Deputy Vice-Chancellor for Int. Affairs: Prof. TONY WATSON
Pro-Vice-Chancellor: Prof. ATIQUE ISLAM
Pro-Vice-Chancellor: Prof. LYNNE COHEN
Pro-Vice-Chancellor Equity and Engagement: Prof. COLLEEN HAYWARD
Pro-Vice-Chancellor for Equity and Indigenous Affairs: Prof. BRENDA CHEREDNICHENKO
Pro-Vice-Chancellor for Health Advancement: Prof. COBIE RUDD
Pro-Vice-Chancellor for Teaching and Learning: Prof. RON OLIVER
Vice-Pres. for Corporate Services: SCOTT HENDERSON
Vice-Pres. for Resources and Chief Financial Officer: WARREN SNELL
Dean for ECU Int.: Prof. GENSHENG SHEN
Univ. Librarian: DAVID HOWARD
Number of teachers: 693
Number of students: 22,511
Publications: *Alumination*, *HD Magazine* (1 a year), *Inside WAAPA*

DEANS

Faculty of Business and Law: Prof. ATIQUE ISLAM
Faculty of Computing, Health and Science: Prof. TONY WATSON
Faculty of Education and Arts: Prof. LYNNE COHENN
Faculty of Regional Professional Studies: ROBERT IRVINE

MURDOCH UNIVERSITY

90 S St, Murdoch, WA 6150
Telephone: (8) 9360-6000
E-mail: study@murdoch.edu.au
Internet: www.murdoch.edu.au
Founded 1973; postgraduate courses began 1974; undergraduate courses began 1975
State control
Academic year: February to November
Chancellor: The Hon. TERRY C. BUDGE
Deputy Chancellor: EVA SKIRA
Vice-Chancellor: Prof. RICHARD HIGGOTT
Sr Deputy Vice-Chancellor: Prof. GARY R. MARTIN
Deputy Vice-Chancellor for Academic Affairs: Assoc. Prof. BEV THIELE
Deputy Vice-Chancellor for Education: Prof. ANN CAPLING
Deputy Vice-Chancellor for Research: Prof. JOHN PLUSK (acting)
Head of Admin.: JON BALDWIN
Dir of Library Services: LIZ BURKE
Library: 2m. vols incl. books and journals (print and electronic), DVDs and specific collns for researchers
Number of teachers: 455
Number of students: 18,000

DEANS

Murdoch Business School: Prof. MALCOLM TULL
School of Biological Sciences and Biotechnology: Assoc. Prof. CAROLYN JONES
School of Chemical and Mathematical Sciences: Prof. PETER MAY
School of Chiropractic and Sports Science: Dr BRIAN NOOK
School of Education: Assoc. Prof. JUDY MACCALLUM
School of Engineering and Energy: Prof. PARISA ARABZADEH BAHRI
School of Environmental Science: Assoc. Prof. JOHN BAILEY
School of Information Technology: Assoc. Prof. PETER COLE
School of Law: Prof. JÜRGEN BRÖHMER
School of Media Communication and Culture: Assoc. Prof. CHRIS SMYTH
School of Nursing and Midwifery: Prof. PAUL MORRISON
School of Psychology: Dr MAX SULLY
School of Social Sciences and Humanities: Assoc. Prof. ANDREW WEBSTER
School of Veterinary and Biomedical Sciences: DAVID HAMPSON

NOTRE DAME UNIVERSITY

19 Mouat St, POB 1225, Fremantle, WA 6959
Telephone: (8) 9433-0555
E-mail: international@nd.edu.au
Internet: www.nd.edu.au
Founded 1989 by Act of Parliament
Private control (Archdiocese of Perth)
Language of instruction: English
Academic year: February to December
Campuses at Broome, Fremantle and Sydney (Broadway and Darlinghurst)
Chancellor: TERENCE TOBIN
Vice-Chancellor: Dr CELIA HAMMOND
Deputy Chancellor: PETER PRENDIVILLE
Deputy Vice-Chancellor, Broome: Prof. LYNETTE HENDERSON-YATES

Deputy Vice-Chancellor, Fremantle and Pro-Vice-Chancellor Int.: Prof. PETA SANDERSON (acting)
Sr Deputy Vice-Chancellor and Provost, Sydney Campus: Prof. HAYDEN RAMSEY
Pro-Vice-Chancellor for Research: Prof. RICHARD BERLACH (acting)
Pro-Vice-Chancellor for Sydney and Academic: Prof. MARGOT KEARNS
Pro-Vice-Chancellor, Fremantle: Assoc. Prof. MARK TANNOCK
Exec. Dir for Admissions and Student Services, Fremantle: ROMMIE MASAREI
Exec. Dir for Admissions and Student Services, Sydney: MARK TANNOCK
Exec. Dir for Resources and Devt: WAYNE MCGRISKIN
Chief Finance Officer and Univ. Sec.: DARREN CUTRI
Univ. Registrar: MURRAY ALESSANDRINI
Exec. Dir for Academic Services and Univ. Librarian: STEPHEN MCVEY

Number of teachers: 170
Number of students: 3,500

DEANS

Broome and Fremantle Campuses:

School of Arts and Sciences: Prof. DYLAN KORCZYNSKYJ
School of Business: Assoc. Prof. CHRIS DOEPEL
School of Education: Prof. MICHAEL O'NEILL
School of Health Sciences: Prof. NAOMI TRENGOVE
School of Law: Assoc. Prof. CHRIS DOEPEL
School of Medicine: Prof. GAVIN FROST
School of Nursing: Assoc. Prof. SELMA ALLIEX
School of Philosophy and Theology: Prof. MATTHEW C. OGILVIE
School of Physiotherapy: Prof. PETER HAMER

UNIVERSITY OF WESTERN AUSTRALIA

35 Stirling Highway, Crawley, WA 6009
Telephone: (8) 6488-6000
E-mail: general.enquiries@uwa.edu.au
Internet: www.uwa.edu.au

Founded 1911
Academic year: February to October

Chancellor: Dr MICHAEL CHANEY
Pro-Chancellor: Dr PENNY FLETT
Vice-Chancellor: Prof. PAUL JOHNSON
Sr. Deputy Vice-Chancellor: Prof. DAWN FRESHWATER
Deputy Vice-Chancellor for Education: Prof. ALEC CAMERON
Deputy Vice-Chancellor for Research: Prof. ROBYN OWENS
Pro-Vice-Chancellor for Health and Medical Research: Prof. JOHN CHALLIS
Pro-Vice-Chancellor for Research: Prof. PETER DAVIES
Exec. Dir for Corporate Services and Registrar: PETER CURTIS
Chief Operating Officer: GAYE MCMATH
Univ. Librarian and Dir for Information Management: (vacant)

Library of 850,000 vols, incl. 230,000 non-print items, 480,000 vols of serials (journals, magazines, newspapers); MS of A. B. Facey's *A Fortunate Life* and a selection of medieval MSS; Australian literature, maritime history and shipping, theatre, medieval European history and theology, early modern European literature and Indian history
Number of teachers: 1,534
Number of students: 25,047

Publications: *Research Expertise* (1 a year), *Uniview* (3 a year)

DEANS

Faculty of Architecture, Landscape and Visual Arts: Prof. SIMON ANDERSON
Faculty of Arts: Prof. KRISHNA SEN
Faculty of Education: Prof. HELEN WILDY
Faculty of Engineering, Computing and Mathematics: Prof. JOHN DELL
Faculty of Law: Prof. ERIKA TECHERA
Faculty of Medicine, Dentistry and Health Sciences: Prof. IAN PUDDEY
Faculty of Science: Prof. TONY O'DONNELL
Graduate Research School: Prof. ALAN DENCH
School of Indigenous Studies: Prof. JILL MILROY
UWA Business School: Prof. PHILLIP DOLAN

PROFESSORS

Faculty of Architecture, Landscape and Visual Arts:

ANDERSON, S., Architecture
BLACKWELL, T., Landscape Architecture
LONDON, G. L., Architecture
TAYLOR, W. M., Architecture

Faculty of Arts:

BROOMHALL, S., History
DENCH, A., Linguistics
GREGORY, J., History
HONG, F., Asian Studies
KENNEDY, D. L., Classics and Ancient History
LEVINE, M., Philosophy
LYDON, J., Archaeology
MADDERN, P. C., History
POLIZZOTTO, L., European Languages and Studies
SEN, K., Arts
SMITH, B., Archaeology
VETH, P., Archaeology
WALKER, B., English and Cultural Studies
WATLING, J., Archaeology
WHITE, R. S., English and Cultural Studies
WRIGHT, P., Music

Faculty of Education:

ANDRICH, D. CHAPMAN, A. HOUGHTON, S. J. O'DONOGHUE, T. A. VENVILLE, G. VIDOVICH, L. WILDY, H.

Faculty of Engineering, Computing and Mathematics:

BAILLIE, C., Civil, Environmental and Mining Engineering
BASSOM, A., Mathematics and Statistics
BENNAMOUN, M., Computer Science and Software Engineering
CANTONI, A., Electrical, Electronic and Computer Engineering
CASSIDY, M., Offshore Foundation Systems
CHENG, L., Civil, Environmental and Mining Engineering
CHUA, H. T., Mechanical and Chemical Engineering
DELL, J., Electrical, Electronic and Computer Engineering
DIGHT, P., Geotechnical Engineering
DYSKIN, A., Civil, Environmental and Mining Engineering
EFTHYMIOU, M., Offshore Foundation Systems
FARAONE, L., Electrical, Electronic and Computer Engineering
FOURIE, A., Civil, Environmental and Mining Engineering
HU, X. Z., Mechanical and Chemical Engineering
IVEY, G. N., Civil, Environmental and Mining Engineering
JOHNS, M., Mechanical and Chemical Engineering
LEHANE, B. M., Civil, Environmental and Mining Engineering
LI, C. H., Mathematics and Statistics
LIU, Y., Mechanical and Chemical Engineering
MAY, E., Gas Processing Engineering
MILLER, K., Mechanical and Chemical Engineering
MILNE, G. J., Computer Science and Software Engineering
NOAKES, J. L., Mathematics and Statistics
OLDHAM, C., Civil, Environmental and Mining Engineering
PAN, J., Mechanical and Chemical Engineering
PATTIARATCHI, C., Civil, Environmental and Mining Engineering
PRAEGER, C. E., Mathematics and Statistics
RANDOLPH, M., Offshore Foundation Systems
SAMPSON, D. D., Electrical, Electronic and Computer Engineering
SMALL, M., Mathematics and Statistics
SMETTEM, K. R., Civil, Environmental and Mining Engineering
TREVELYAN, J. P., Mechanical and Chemical Engineering
WAITE, A., Civil, Environmental and Mining Engineering
WANG, S., Mathematics and Statistics
WHITE, D., Offshore Foundation Systems
WONG, K. P., Electrical, Electronic and Computer Engineering
ZHANG, D., Mechanical and Chemical Engineering

Faculty of Law:

BARTLETT, R. H.
BLAGG, H.
BURRELL, R.
CULLEN, H.
HANDFORD, P. R.
ISRAEL, M.
SHARKEY, N.
TECHERA, E.

Faculty of Medicine, Dentistry and Health Sciences:

ABBOTT, P. V., Dentistry
ALMEIDA, O. P., Psychiatry
ATLAS, M. D., Otolaryngology
BOWER, C., Epidemiology
BRUCE, D. G., Medicine and Pharmacology
CARAPETIS, J., Child Health
CELENZA, T., Emergency Medicine
COLE, C., Paediatrics and Child Health
CROSS, D., Child Health
DAVIS, T. M. E., Medicine and Pharmacology
DE KLERK, N., Child Health
DESSARAB, D., Aboriginal Medical and Dental Health
EDMOND, K., Paediatrics and Child Health
ERBER, W., Pathology and Laboratory Medicine
EVERARD, M., Paediatrics and Child Health
FLETCHER, D. R., Surgery
FLICKER, L., Geriatric Medicine
FRENCH, M., Pathology and Laboratory Medicine
FRITSCHI, L., Epidemiology
HAMDORF, J., Surgery
HANKEY, G., Medicine and Pharmacology
HARVEY, J., Pathology and Laboratory Medicine
HOLMAN, D., Population Health
HULSE, G. K., Psychiatry
HUNG, J., Medicine and Pharmacology
IACOPETTA, B., Surgery
JABLENSKY, A. V., Psychiatry
JACOBS, I., Emergency Medicine
JANCA, A., Psychiatry
JEFFREY, G. P., Medicine and Pharmacology
JOYCE, D., Medicine and Pharmacology
KING, N., Dentistry
KLINKEN, S. P., Clinical Biochemistry
KNUIMAN, M. W., Population Health
LAKE, F., Medicine and Pharmacology
LAURENT, G., Cell Therapy and Regenerative Medicine
LE SOUËF, P. N., Paediatrics and Child Health

LEE, Y. C. G., Respiratory Medicine
LEEDMAN, P. J., Cancer Medicine
LIM, L. Y., Medicine and Pharmacology
LUCAS, R., Child Health
MACKEY, D., Ophthalmology and Visual Science
MILLWARD, M., Clinical Cancer Care
MILROY, H., Aboriginal Medical and Dental Health
MORAHAN, G., Diabetes Research
MOSES, E., Genetic Origins of Health and Disease
NEWNHAM, J. P., Maternal-Foetal Medicine
NIVBRANT, B., Surgery
NORMAN, P. E., Vascular Surgery
PAECH, M., Anaesthesia
PLATELL, C. F., Surgery
PRESCOTT, S. L., Paediatrics and Child Health
PUDDEY, I., Medicine, Dentistry and Health Sciences
RAKOCZY, P. E., Ophthalmology and Visual Science
RAVINE, D., Medical Genetics
REGLI-VON UNGERN-STERNBERG, B., Medicine and Pharmacology
RILEY, G., Primary, Aboriginal and Rural Health Care
ROBINSON, B., Medicine and Pharmacology
SAUNDERS, C., Surgery
SHELLAM, G. R., Pathology and Laboratory Medicine
SIMMER, K., Paediatrics and Child Health
SINGER, K. P., Surgery
STACEY, M. C., Vascular Surgery
STARKSTEIN, S. E., Psychiatry
STEWART, G. A., Pathology and Laboratory Medicine
THOMPSON, P., Respiratory Medicine
THOMPSON, S., Rural Health
WATTS, F. G., Medicine and Pharmacology
WOOD, F., Surgery
WOOD, D. J., Orthopaedic Surgery
XU, J., Pathology and Laboratory Medicine
YU, D. Y., Ophthalmology and Visual Science
ZHENG, M. H., Orthopaedic Surgery
ZUBRICK, S., Child Health

Faculty of Science:
ABRAHAM, L., Chemistry and Biochemistry
ACKLAND, T. R., Occupational Biomechanics and Ergonomics
BADCOCK, D. R., Psychology
BARBETTI, M., Plant Biology
BLAIR, D. G., Physics
CAWOOD, P., Earth and Environment
COLLIN, S., Animal Biology
COLMER, T., Plant Biology
COWLING, W., Plant Biology
DADOUR, I., Forensic Science
DAWSON, B. T., Exercise Physiology and Biochemistry
DENTITH, M., Petroleum Geoscience
DUARTE, C., Plant Biology
DUNLOP, S., Animal Biology
EASTWOOD, P., Anatomy, Physiology and Human Biology
GREEN, D. J., Exercise Physiology and Biochemistry
GRIFFIN, M., Psychology
GROVE, B., Exercise, Health and Sport Psychology
HARTMANN, P. E., Chemistry and Biochemistry
HARVEY, A. R., Anatomy, Physiology and Human Biology
HOPPER, S., Plant Biology
HUNT, D., Animal Biology
JESSELL, M., Earth and Environment
KENDRICK, G., Plant Biology
KUZENKO, S., Physics
LAMBERS, H., Plant Biology
LAWRENCE, C., Psychology
LEE, G., Forensic Science
LEWANDOWSKY, S., Psychology
LOW, P., Chemistry and Biochemistry
LUMLEY, D., Petroleum Geoscience
MCARTHUR, I., Physics
MACLEOD, C., Psychology
MARTIN, G. B., Animal Biology
MILAR, H., Chemistry and Biochemistry
MITCHELL, H. W., Physiology
MUCINA, L., Plant Biology
O'DONNELL, T., Science
PAGE, A., Psychology
PANNEL, D. J., Agricultural and Resource Economics
POWLES, S., Plant Biology
REGENAUER-LIEB, K., Earth and Environment
RENGEL, Z., Earth and Environment
ROBERTS, D., Animal Biology
SCHMITT, L. H., Anatomy, Physiology and Human Biology
SIDDIQUE, K., Agriculture
SIMMONS, L., Animal Biology
SMITH, S., Chemistry and Biochemistry
SPACKMAN, M. A., Chemistry and Biochemistry
TENNANT, M., Anatomy, Physiology and Human Biology
TOBAR, M., Physics
VAN KANN, F., Physics
VRIELINK, A., Chemistry and Biochemistry
WADDELL, B. J., Anatomy, Physiology and Human Biology
WATLING, J., Forensic Science
WILLIAMS, J. F., Physics
WITHERS, P. C., Animal Biology

UWA Business School:
CLEMEMTS, K. W., Economics
CORDERY, J. L., Management and Organizations
DA SILVA ROSA, R., Accounting and Finance
DAY, D., Management and Organizations
DOLAN, P., Business
HANCOCK, P., Accounting and Finance
HEANEY, R., Accounting and Finance
IZAN, H. Y., Accounting and Finance
GIBSON, C., Management and Organizations
LAMBERT, R. V., Management and Organizations
LEE, J. A., Marketing
MCSHANE, S., Management and Organizations
MAZZAROL, T., Marketing
PARKER, S., Management and Organizations
PRESTON, A., Business
ROBERTSON, P., Economics
SOUTAR, G. N., Marketing
STOCKPORT, G., Management and Organizations
SWEENEY, J., Marketing
TARCA, A., Accounting and Finance
TURKINGTON, D., Economics
TYERS, R., Economics
WATSON, J., Accounting and Finance

Colleges

AUSTRALIAN CAPITAL TERRITORY

Canberra Institute of Technology: GPOB 826, Canberra, ACT 2601; tel. (2) 6207-3100; e-mail infoline@cit.edu.au; internet cit.edu.au; f. 1988, current name adopted 1992; campuses at Bruce, Fyshwick, Reid and Woden; Bachelors degrees in business studies, design, games and virtual worlds, photography and forensic science; 34,000 students; Chief Exec. ADRIAN MARRON; Exec. Dir for Students TRACEY CAPPIE-WOOD; Librarian JACI GANENDRAN.

Institute of Chartered Accountants in Australia: GPOB 9985, Canberra, ACT 2601; Level 10, 60 Marcus Clarke St, Canberra, ACT 2601; tel. (2) 6122-6100; e-mail service@charteredaccountants.com.au; internet www.charteredaccountants.com.au; f. 1928; professional body for chartered accountants in Australia and mems operating in more than 100 countries; offers postgraduate chartered accountants programme; library: 13,000 vols; 12,000 students; Pres. CRAIG FARROW; CEO LEE WHITE; Gen. Man. for Learning and Business Solutions ANNE MCCOTTER; publ. *Charter Magazine* (12 a year).

NEW SOUTH WALES

Academy of Information Technology: POB K913, Haymarket, NSW 1240; Level 2, 7 Kelly St, Ultimo, ACT 2007; tel. (2) 9211-8399; e-mail info@ait.nsw.edu.au; internet www.ait.nsw.edu.au; f. 1999; offers Bachelors courses in interactive media; Dean for Studies Dr ADRIAN BENNETT; Academic Dir FRANCES BERTRAND; Gen. Man. ADAM STEPICH.

APM College of Business and Communication: 171 Pacific Highway, Level 5, 213 Miller St, N Sydney, NSW 2060; tel. (2) 9492-3203; e-mail enquiries@apm.edu; internet www.apm.edu.au; f. 1987; campuses in Sydney and Brisbane; Bachelors courses in business, marketing, event management, public relations, advertising and journalism; Gen. Man. JENNY JENKINS; Head of College JEFF LAURIE.

Asia Pacific International College: Level 11, 53 Walker St, N Sydney, NSW 2060; tel. (2) 8920-9688; e-mail admin@apicollege.edu.au; internet www.apicollege.edu.au; f. 2004; offers postgraduate degree courses in business and project management; Pres. ALI JAAFARI.

Australian College of Applied Psychology: Level 5, Wynyard Green, 11 York St, Sydney, NSW 2000; tel. (2) 9964-6174; e-mail info.acap@navitas.com; internet www.acap.edu.au; campuses in Adelaide, Brisbane, Melbourne and Sydney; Bachelors degrees in applied social science and psychological science; Gen. Man. ANDREW LITTLE; Dean Dr ED GREEN; Dir for Student Admin. and Registrar Services RUTH FREEMAN.

Australian College of Physical Education: 1 Figtree Dr., Sydney Olympic Park, Sydney, NSW 2127; tel. (2) 9739-3303; e-mail dean@acpe.edu.au; internet www.acpe.edu.au; f. 1917; Bachelors degrees in applied fitness, applied dance, dance education, health and movement, sports business, sports coaching and administration; CEO DAVID MCDONALD; Dean Dr SCOTT DICKSON; Dir for Finance RICHARD ROGERS; Registrar CHRISTINE HAQUE; Library Man. MARILYN WAGSTAFF.

Australian Film, Television and Radio School: POB 2286, Strawberry Hills, NSW 2012; tel. (2) 9805-6611; e-mail foi@aftrs.edu.au; internet www.aftrs.edu.au; f. 1973; library: 15,000 vols incl. books and reports; 8,000 feature films, documentaries, television programmes and short films; 300 journal titles; 3,100 students (100 full-time and 3,000 part-time); Dir for Corporate Services ANN BROWNE; Library Man. ELISABETH MCDONALD.

Australian Institute of Higher Education: Level 4, 451 Pitt St, Sydney, NSW 2000; tel. (2) 8917-6850; e-mail enquiries@aih.nsw.edu.au; internet aih.nsw.edu.au; offers Bachelors degrees in accounting and business; library: 100,000 journals; Dean and Chief Operating Officer JOO-GIM HEANEY.

Australian Institute of Music: 1–51 Foveaux St, Surry Hills, NSW 2010; tel. (2) 9219-5444; e-mail enquiries@aim.edu.au;

internet www.aim.edu.au; f. 1968 as Sydney Guitar School; library: 4,000 vols, 90 journals, 6,000 printed music items, 1,900 CDs and DVDs; 1,000 students; Dean Dr IAN BOFINGER; Chief Operating Officer MUKESH CHANDER; Registrar NARA KRUM; Librarian JULIA MITFORD.

Australian International Conservatorium of Music: 114 Victoria Rd, Rozelle, Sydney, NSW 2039; tel. (2) 9637-0777; e-mail admin@aicm.edu.au; internet www.aicm.edu.au; offers Bachelors degree in music; focus areas incl. jazz, composition, classical, musical theatre and production; Pres. Prof. KYUNGHEE LEE; Dean IAN BROOKS.

Australian Nuclear Science and Technology Organisation (ANSTO)—Training: Locked Bag 2001, Kirrawee, NSW 2232; New Illawarra Rd, Lucas Heights, NSW 2234; tel. (2) 9717-3111; internet www.ansto.gov.au; f. 1949; training arm of the Univ. of NSW and the Australian Nuclear Science and Technology Organisation; short courses in use of radioisotopes, radionuclides in medicine, radiation protection and occupational health and safety; responsible for delivering specialized advice, scientific services and products to govt, industry, academia and other research orgs; CEO Dr ADRIAN PATERSON; Exec. Dir Dr IAN SMITH.

Avondale College: POB 19, Cooranbong, NSW 2265; 582 Freemans Dr., Cooranbong, NSW 2265; tel. (2) 4980-2277; e-mail enquiries@avondale.edu.au; internet www.avondale.edu.au; f. 1892 present location 1897; campuses in Cooranbong and Sydney; offers courses through school of humanities and creative arts; faculty of business, school of education, faculty of nursing and health, school of science and mathematics and school of ministry and theology; library: 24,000 vols, 220 journals, 1,300 DVDs and other audiovisual items (Sydney campus); Pres. RAY ROENNFELDT; Vice-Pres. for Admin. and Research Dr VIVIENNE J WATTS; Vice-Pres. for Finance PAUL HATTINGH; Vice-Pres. for Learning and Teaching Dr JANE FERNANDEZ-GOLDBOROUGH; Chief Information Officer SIMON N. SHORT; Registrar Dr GWEN WILKINSON; Head Librarian GANE MARILYN.

Billy Blue College of Design: 171 Pacific Highway, N Sydney, NSW 2060; internet www.billyblue.edu.au; f. 1987; campuses in Melbourne, Sydney and Brisbane; graduate courses offered in communication design and applied design; Head of College ANDREW BARNUM.

Blue Mountains International Hotel Management School: POB A256, Sydney S, NSW 1235; tel. (2) 9307-4600; e-mail enquiry@bluemountains.edu.au; internet www.bluemountains.edu.au; f. 1991; campuses in Sydney and Leura in NSW; offers Bachelors in business and Masters in hotel management; CEO GUY BENTLEY.

Campion College: POB 3052, Toongabbie East, NSW 2146; 8–14 Austin Woodbury Pl., Old Toongabbie, NSW 2146; tel. (2) 9896-9300; e-mail info@campion.edu.au; internet www.campion.edu.au; f. 2006; offers BA in liberal arts; library: 25,000 vols; 73 students; Pres. Dr DAVID DAINTREE; Deputy Pres. and Registrar TONY HEYWOOD; Librarian ANGELA KOLAR.

Carrick Higher Education: Level 9, 540 George St, Sydney, NSW 2000; tel. (2) 8236-6877; e-mail admissions@carrickeducation.edu.au; internet www.carrickeducation.edu.au; f. 1987, present status 2011; attached to Kaplan Professional; campuses in Adelaide, Brisbane, Melbourne and Sydney; int. campus in Beijing, China; offers Bachelors degrees in accounting and business; Nat. Academic Dir Prof. JIM JACKSON.

Chartered Secretaries Australia: POB 1594, Sydney, NSW 2001; Level 10, 5 Hunter St, Sydney, NSW 2000; tel. (2) 9223-5744; e-mail info@csaust.com; internet www.csaust.com; f. 1909, present status 1947, current name adopted 2000; offers postgraduate course in governance; gateway to membership of CSA and the Institute of Chartered Secretaries and Administrators; Chief Exec. TIM SHEEHY; Dir for Finance and Admin. CHERYL BIGENI; Dir for Education and Training STEPHEN WRIGHT; publ. *Journal* (12 a year).

College of Law: POB 2, St Leonards, NSW 1590; 2 Chandos St, St Leonards, NSW 2065; tel. (2) 9965-7000; e-mail support@collaw.edu.au; internet www.collaw.edu.au; f. 1973; comprises colleges in NSW, VIC, QLD, WA and New Zealand; Masters of applied law programmes; CEO and Prin. NEVILLE CARTER; Deputy CEO and Gen. Man. for Education LEWIS PATRICK.

College of Nursing: Locked Bag 3030, Burwood, NSW 1805; 14 Railway Parade, Burwood, NSW 2134; tel. (2) 9745-7500; e-mail ssc@nursing.edu.au; internet www.nursing.edu.au; f. 1949; postgraduate nursing education programmes; 250 teachers; 3,816 students; Pres. KATHY BAKER; Chief Exec. TRACEY OSMOND; Dir for Education Services JOHN KEMSLEY; Dir for Finance and Business NICK WOOD; Library Man. GRAHAM SPOONER; publ. *Nursing.Aust* (4 a year).

Institute for Emotionally Focused Therapy: POB 97, Annandale, NSW 2038; 83 Johnston St, Annandale, NSW 2038; tel. (2) 9552-2977; e-mail admin@eftherapy.com; internet www.eftherapy.com; f. 1987 as Counselling Training Centre; Dir Dr MICHELLE WEBSTER.

International College of Management: 151 Darley Rd, Manly, NSW 2095; tel. (2) 9977-0333; e-mail info@icms.edu.au; internet www.icms.edu.au; f. 1885 as St Patrick's Seminary, current name adopted 2003; Bachelors and Masters degrees in hospitality management, event management, international tourism, retail services management, sport management and property services management; library: 2,000 vols, 100 journals; Exec. Chair. DARRYL COURTNEY-O'CONNOR; Executive Dean ROGER ALEXANDER; Man. Dir FRANK PRESTIPINO; Academic Dir Dr ROGER ALEXANDER; Head of Student Services and Registrar DEREK MARTIN.

Jansen Newman Institute: POB 1222, Crows Nest, NSW 1585; Levels 1 and 2, 575 Pacific Highway, St Leonards, NSW 2065; tel. (2) 9436-3055; e-mail jni@jni.edu.au; internet www.jni.edu.au; f. 1978 as Relationship Devt Centre, current name adopted 1981; Bachelors degree in applied science; Head of College and Nat. Academic Dir Prof. Dr CAROLYN NOBLE.

JMC Academy: 41 Holt St, Surry Hills, NSW 2010; tel. (02) 9281-8899; internet www.jmcacademy.edu.au; f. 1982; campuses in Brisbane, Sydney and Melbourne; offers courses in music, film and television; Bachelors degree in creative technology; Man. Dir JOHN MARTIN CASS.

Kaplan Professional: GPOB 9995, Sydney, NSW 2001; Level 4, 45 Clarence St, Sydney, NSW 2000; tel. (2) 9908-0200; e-mail info@kaplan.edu.au; internet www.kaplanprofessional.edu.au; f. 1938; attached to Washington Post Co; courses offered through Kaplan Professional, Kaplan Business School Australia, Bradford College, Murdoch Institute of Technology and Franklyn Scholar and Carrick Education Group; offers graduate and postgraduate finance courses; 600 locations in more than 30 countries1m. students; CEO MARK COGGINS.

Kent Institute of Business and Technology: Level 5, 70–72 Bathurst St, WEA House, Sydney, NSW 2000; tel. (2) 9267-9284; e-mail info@kent.edu.au; internet www.kentinstitute.nsw.edu.au; f. 1989; offers Bachelors degree in business; CEO KELVIN CHU.

King's Own Institute: Level 1, 545 Kent St, Sydney, NSW 2000; tel. (2) 9283-3583; e-mail ask@koi.edu.au; internet www.koi.edu.au; offers Bachelors of business in accounting and management and finance; CEO and Dean Dr DOUG HINCHLIFFE; Chair. Prof. JOHN LOXTON.

Le Cordon Bleu Australia: Level 4, Bldg A, 250 Blaxland Rd, Ryde, NSW 2112; tel. (2) 8878-3100; e-mail australia@cordonbleu.edu; internet www.lecordonbleu.com.au; f. 1895; campuses in Adelaide, Sydney and Melbourne; Masters in business administration, international hospitality management and Bachelors of business; Pres. ANDRÉ J. COINTREAU.

Macleay College: 28 Foveaux St, Surry Hills, NSW 2010; tel. (2) 9267-3311; e-mail study@macleay.edu.au; internet www.macleay.edu.au; f. 1989; offers Bachelors of arts with specialization in journalism and advertising; Chair. Prof. BOB ROBERTSON; Dean Dr RAFFAELE MARCELLINO; Registrar LEE BUCKLEY.

Moore College: 1 King St, Newtown, NSW 2042; tel. (2) 9577-9999; e-mail info@moore.edu.au; internet www.moore.edu.au; f. 1856; Bachelors and Masters degrees in theology and divinity; library: 215,000 vols, 800 journals; 7,000 students; Prin. JOHN WOODHOUSE; Chief Financial Officer MARTIN SUMPTER; Dean for Quality and Planning ALAN HOHNE; Registrar RHONDA BERRY; Library Man. JULIE A. OLSTON.

Morling College: 120 Herring Rd, Macquarie Park, NSW 2113; tel. (2) 9878-0201; e-mail enquiries@morling.edu.au; internet www.morling.nsw.edu.au; f. 1916 as Baptist Theological College, current name adopted 1985; Bachelors, Masters and doctoral degrees in ministry and theology; library: 45,000 vols, 180 journals; Prin. Rev. Dr ROSS CLIFFORD; Vice-Prin. for Admin. Rev. Dr BRIAN POWELL; Registrar ANDREW LANE; Librarian KAREN ROACH; publ. *Summa Supremo*.

Nan Tien Institute: POB 1336, Unanderra, NSW 2526; 180 Berkeley Rd, Berkeley, NSW 2506; tel. (2) 4272-0618; e-mail info@nantien.edu.au; internet www.nantien.edu.au; f. 2001; offers postgraduate courses in Buddhist studies; Dean JOHN LOXTON.

National Art School: Forbes St, Darlinghurst, NSW 2010; tel. (2) 9339-8744; e-mail enquiries@nas.edu.au; internet www.nas.edu.au; f. 1843 as Sydney Mechanics' School of Arts, current name adopted 1926; honours and Masters courses offered in ceramics, painting, photography, printmaking, sculpture with painting and art history and art theory; organizes a visual arts public programme; 100 teachers; 400 students; CEO SIMON COOPER.

National Institute of Dramatic Art: UNSW, Sydney, NSW 2052; 215 Anzac Parade, Kensington, NSW 2033; tel. (2) 9697-7600; e-mail info@nida.edu.au; internet www.nida.edu.au; f. 1958; degree, graduate diploma and advanced diploma courses in acting, design, stage management, event management, lighting, sound, costume making, wardrobe management, scenery construction, properties and special effects; library: 45,000 vols, 26,500 plays, 50 journals, 6,000 video cassettes and 3,400 sound recordings; archives NIDA performances in form of prompt copies, programs, show tapes and video cassettes; 150 full-time students, 5,000 part-time students in Open Program; Dir and CEO LYNNE WILLIAMS.

New South Wales and Institute of Psychiatry: Locked Bag 7118, Parramatta BC, NSW 2124; Cumberland Hospital Campus, 5 Fleet St, N Parramatta, NSW 2151; tel. (2) 9840-3833; e-mail institute@nswiop.nsw.edu.au; internet www.nswiop.nsw.edu.au; f. 1964; graduate and postgraduate degrees in mental health; Dir Dr ROS MONTAGUE; Librarian DAVID WONG-SEE.

Raffles College of Design and Commerce: 99 Mount St, N Sydney, NSW 2060; tel. (2) 9922-4278; e-mail contact@raffles.edu.au; internet www.raffles.edu.au; specializes in design, visual communication, commerce and accountancy; int. campuses in Auckland, New Zealand, Beijing, Shanghai and Guangzhou in China, Hanoi and Ho Chi Minh City in Viet Nam, Wanchai in Hong Kong, Kuala Lumpur in Malaysia, Ulaanbaatar in Mongolia, Mumbai in India and Singapore; 700 full-time students; CEO ISAAC NG; Finance Man. DENNIS LAI; Academic Dir Prof. PATRICK BERNARD; Registrar Dr GREG COOPER; Library Man. ORIANA MITCHELL.

SAE Institute, Qantm College: Level 2, 74–78 Wentworth Ave, Surry Hills, NSW 2010; tel. (2) 8241-5300; e-mail infosydney@qantm.com.au; internet www.qantm.com; f. 1996, present status 2004; campuses in Sydney, Brisbane, Melbourne, Adelaide and Perth; int. campuses in Amsterdam in Netherlands, Berlin, Cologne, Hamburg and Munich in Germany, Paris in France, Singapore, Vienna in Austria and Zurich in Switzerland; courses incl. game design, web design and graphic design; CEO and Founder Dr THOMAS MISNER; CEO, Australia and New Zealand JOSEPH ANTHONYSZ.

Sydney College of Divinity: POB 1882, Macquarie Centre, N Ryde, NSW 2113; Suite G5, 64 Talavera Rd, Macquarie Park, N Ryde, NSW 2113; tel. (2) 9889-1969; e-mail scd@scd.edu.au; internet www.scd.edu.au; f. 1983; postgraduate and doctoral degrees in arts, divinity and theology; 8 mem. instns; 2,300 students; Dean Prof. Dr DIANE SPEED; Dir for Admin. Dr LES GAINER; Dir for Finance DAVID CHEETHAM; Dir for Research Dr MARGARET BEIRNE; Registrar HEIDI WRIGHT.

Top Education Institute: 1 Central Ave, Australian Technology Park, Eveleigh, Sydney, NSW 2015; tel. (2) 9209-4888; e-mail info@top.edu.au; internet www.top.edu.au; Masters in professional accounting and business; Chair. Prof. BRIAN STODDART; Prin. Dr MINSHEN ZHU; Provost Prof. PETER FLOOD; Dir for Research and Curriculum Devt Prof. BRIAN GIBSON.

UIC Sydney: Locked Bag 7, Redfern, Sydney, NSW 2016; Tower 2, 1 Lawson Sq., Redfern, Sydney, NSW 2016; e-mail info@uic.edu.au; internet www.uic.edu.au; incl. Metro English College and Central College; offers Bachelors courses in accounting and business; 11 teachers; Man. Dir ALAN MANLY; Dean DAVID KNIGHT.

Wesley Institute: POB 534, Drummoyne, NSW 1470; 5 Mary St, Drummoyne, NSW 2047; tel. (2) 9819-8888; e-mail info@wi.edu.au; internet www.wi.edu.au; f. 1983; Masters in counselling, teaching, theology and theological studies; Man. Dir Dr GREG ROUGH; Academic Dir Dr MARTIN DOWSON; Dean for Quality HILDA CAINE.

Whitehouse Institute of Design: 2 Short St, Surry Hills, NSW 2010; tel. (2) 9267-8799; e-mail enquiry@whitehouse-design.edu.au; internet www.whitehouse-design.edu.au; campuses in Sydney and Melbourne; offers Bachelors of design; library: 2,500 items; CEO IAN TUDOR; Chair. Prof. ANDREW GONCZI; Academic Dir Dr MELISSA LAIRD.

William Blue College of Hospitality Management: Northpoint, 171 Pacific Highway, N Sydney, NSW 2060; e-mail info@williamblue.edu.au; internet www.williamblue.edu.au; f. 1990; offers Bachelors degrees in business, event management, hospitality and management; Head of College JENNY JENKINS; Man. Dir PETER EVERINGHAM; Academic Dir Dr GEORGE BROWN.

NORTHERN TERRITORY

Australian Institute of Management: GPOB 2971, Darwin, NT 0801; tel. (8) 8941-7051; e-mail enquiry@aim.com.au; internet www.aim.com.au; f. 1941 as Foremanship Asscn, present name 1949; offers management and leadership devt programmes; 5 divisional offices; library: 8,000 vols, incl. books, journals and audiovisual resources; Pres. JIM WALKER; CEO VIVIENNE ANTHON; publs *Agenda* (12 a year), *Management Today* (12 a year).

Campuses:

Australian Institute of Management—NSW and ACT: 215 Pacific Highway, N Sydney, NSW 2060; tel. (2) 9956-3030; e-mail info@aimnsw.com.au; internet www.aim-nsw-act.com.au; library of 7,000 vols; CEO DAVID WAKELEY.

Australian Institute of Management—South Australia: 180 Port Rd, Hindmarsh, SA 5007; tel. (8) 8241-8000; e-mail aimsa@aimsa.com.au; internet www.aimsa.com.au; CEO JOHN STOKES.

Australian Institute of Management—Victoria and Tasmania: 181 Fitzroy St, St Kilda, VIC 3182; tel. (3) 9534-8181; e-mail enquiry@aimvic.com.au; internet www.aimvic.com.au; CEO SUSAN HERON.

Australian Institute of Management—Western Australia: POB 195, Wembley, WA 6913;76 Birkdale St, Floreat, WA 6014; tel. (8) 9383-8088; e-mail webenquiries@aimwa.com; internet www.aimwa.com; CEO PATRICK CULLEN.

QUEENSLAND

Alphacrucis College: POB 1147, Oxley, QLD 4075; Metro Church, 308 Seventeen Mile Rocks Rd, Seventeen Mile Rocks, QLD 4073; e-mail info@alphacrucis.edu.au; internet ac.edu.au; f. 1948; affiliated to Australian Christian Churches, Assemblies of God and Sydney College of Divinity; campuses in Sydney, Brisbane and Auckland, New Zealand; Pres. Pastor JOHN IULIANO; Prin. Pastor STEPHEN FOGARTY; Acad. Dean Dr JACQUELINE GREY (acting); Dean of Acad. Advancement Dr MARK HUTCHINSON.

Australian Institute of Professional Counsellors: Locked Bag 15, Fortitude Valley, QLD 4006; tel. (7) 3112-2000; e-mail headoffice@aipc.net.au; internet www.aipc.net.au; campuses in Adelaide, Melbourne, Perth, Port Macquarie and Sydney; int. campuses in New Zealand and Singapore; CEO SANDRA POLETTO; Head of School Dr CLIVE JONES; publ. *Institute Inbrief* (online, www.aipc.net.au/ezine).

Australian Institute of Psychology: Level 2, 140 Brunswick St, Fortitude Valley, QLD 4006; e-mail info@aip.edu.au; internet www.aip.edu.au; offers Bachelors of psychology science; conducts research on psychosocial health, growth, devt and well-being of individuals and interpersonal relationships; campuses in Adelaide, Brisbane, Melbourne, Perth, Queensland and Sydney; Head of School Dr CLIVE JONES; Head of Research and Academic Programme Devt Prof. DAVID FRYER.

Christian Heritage College: POB 2246, Mansfield, Brisbane, QLD 4122; 322 Wecker Rd, Carindale, QLD 4152; tel. (7) 3347-7900; e-mail sadmin@chc.edu.au; internet www.chc.edu.au; f. 1986; offers undergraduate and postgraduate courses through school of business, education and humanities, ministries and social sciences; 800 students; Prin. Prof. BRIAN MILLIS; Registrar FAYE CRANE; Librarian PATTY OVEREND.

Cromwell College: Walcott St, St Lucia, QLD 4067; tel. (7) 3377-1300; e-mail stay@cromwell.uq.edu.au; internet www.cromwell.uq.edu.au; f. 1950, opened in 1954; attached to Univ. of Queensland; 250 students; Chair. BEN DE JONG; Prin. ROSS A. SWITZER.

Duchesne College: College Rd, St Lucia, QLD 4067; tel. (7) 3377-2333; e-mail duchesne.college@duchesne.uq.edu.au; internet www.uq.edu.au/duchesne; f. 1937, present status 1959; attached to Univ. of Queensland; 154 students; Prin. NANETTE KAY; Vice-Prin. Sr KATHLEEN MUIRHEAD; Dean for Students MATTHEW DOWNEY.

Endeavour College of Natural Health: 362 Water St, Fortitude Valley, Brisbane, QLD 4006; tel. (7) 3257-1883; e-mail info@endeavour.edu.au; internet www.endeavour.edu.au; f. 1975, fmrly Australian College of Natural Medicine; attached to Endeavour Learning Group; 6 campuses: Adelaide, Brisbane, Gold Coast, Melbourne, Perth and Sydney; Bachelors courses in acupuncture, homeopathy, musculoskeletal therapy, naturopathy, nutritional medicine, Western herbal medicine; CEO CAROLYN BARKER; Dir for Education Dr NICK VARDAXIS; Head of School and Assoc. Dir for Education Dr SEROYA CROUCH.

Gestalt Therapy Brisbane: POB 116, Holland Park West, QLD 4121; 847 Logan Rd, Holland Park, QLD 4121; tel. (7) 3324-2435; e-mail contact@gestaltinstitute.com.au; internet www.gestaltinstitute.com.au; f. 2007 by merger of Brisbane Gestalt Institute and Gestalt Asscn of Queensland Inc; offers Masters degree in gestalt therapy; Man. Dir Dr GREER WHITE.

Grace College: Walcott St, St Lucia, QLD 4067; tel. (7) 3842-4000; e-mail graceadmin@grace.uq.edu.au; internet www.grace.uq.edu.au; f. 1970; attached to Univ. of Queensland; Chair. Rev. RAY HERRMANN; Deputy Chair. DENIS BROSNAN; Prin. Dr SUE FAIRLEY.

Harvest Bible College: POB 4838, Robina Town Centre, QLD 4230; 2 Mieke Court, Burleigh Heads, QLD 4220; tel. (7) 5522-4066; e-mail info.qld@harvest.edu.au; internet www.harvest.edu.au; f. 1985; campuses in Queensland and Melbourne; graduate and postgraduate degrees in biblical studies and ministry; library: 55,000 vols, 100 journals; Pres. Dr BRENDAN ROACH; Dir for Academic Affairs Dr DAVID MORGAN; Dir for Student Services CAROL ROACH; Dir for Training Rev. IAN GRANT.

International House: 5 Rock St, St Lucia, QLD 4067; tel. (7) 3721-2480; e-mail ihadmissions@inthouse.uq.edu.au; internet www.internationalhouse.uq.edu.au; f. 1965; attached to Univ. of Queensland; Pres. Dr JOHN MORRISON; Dir Dr CARLA TROMANS.

Jazz Music Institute: POB 2215, Fortitude Valley, Brisbane, QLD 4006; 1/47 Brookes St, Bowen Hills, QLD 4006; tel. (7) 3216-1110; e-mail play@jazz.qld.edu.au; internet www.jazz.qld.edu.au; f. 1997; Bachelors of music in jazz and performance; Chair. Dr MARILYN

HEALY; Head of School DANIEL QUIGLEY; Registrar PAULA GIRVAN.

King's College: Upland Rd, St Lucia, QLD 4067; tel. (7) 3871-9600; e-mail kings .college@uq.edu.au; internet www.kings.uq .edu.au; f. 1913 at Kangaroo point, present location and present status 1954; attached to Univ. of Queensland; Pres. Hon. Justice MARTIN DAUBNEY; Master and Chief Exec. GREGORY C. EDDY; Deputy Master JAMIE SMITH; publ. *Kingsman Magazine*.

St Leo's College: College Rd, St Lucia, QLD 4067; tel. (7) 3878-0600; internet www.stleos .uq.edu.au; f. 1917 at Wickham Terrace, present location 1961; attached to Univ. of Queensland; Chair. JOAN SHELDON; Rector Bro. VINCE SKELLY; Vice-Rector for Students STEPHEN FOLEY; Vice-Rector for Admin. Bro. GERRY BURKE.

Southbank Institute of Technology: Level 1, C Block, 66 Ernest St, S Brisbane, QLD 4101; tel. (7) 3244-5000; internet www .southbank.edu.au; f. 1863 as South Brisbane Mechanical Institute, present status 2008; courses offered to univ. qualified students; 114 courses; 29,600 students; Chief Exec. Dr PIM BORREN; Dir for Corporate Services and Chief Financial Officer SUE WHIDBORNE; Dir for Business and Community Education JOHN MARTIN.

The Women's College: College Rd, St Lucia, QLD 4067; tel. (7) 3377-4500; e-mail administration@womens.uq.edu.au; internet www.womens.uq.edu.au; f. 1914 at Kangaroo Point, present location 1958; attached to Univ. of Queensland; Pres. Dr SALLYANNE ATKINSON; Head and CEO Adjunct Prof. IYLA DAVIES; Dean of Students LIZA ALLEN.

Union College: Upland Rd, St Lucia, QLD 4067; tel. (7) 3377-1500; e-mail union .college@uq.edu.au; internet www.uq.edu.au/ union; f. 1965; attached to Univ. of Queensland; residential college for undergraduate and postgraduate studies; Chair. CHRIS BURGESS; Head of College JILL HEWITT.

SOUTH AUSTRALIA

Acelin Institute of Business: POB 89, Kent Town DC, SA 5071; Level 3, 14 Grenfell St, Adelaide, SA 5000; tel. (8) 8212-0184; e-mail acelin@acelin.edu.au; internet www .acelin.edu.au; f. 2005; offers business and management programmes to both undergraduate and postgraduate levels; Chief Exec. MICHAEL LIN.

Adelaide Central School of Art: 45 Osmond Terr., Norwood, SA 5067; tel. (8) 8364-5075; e-mail info@acsa.sa.edu.au; internet www.acsa.sa.edu.au; f. 1982; attached to Flinders Univ.; offers Bachelors degrees in visual art; conducts workshops with practitioners; CEO INGRID KELLENBACH; Head of Academic Affairs KEN ORCHARD; Librarian CATHERINE KERRIGAN.

Adelaide College of Divinity: 34 Lipsett Terrace, Brooklyn Park, SA 5032; tel. (8) 8416-8400; e-mail college.divinity@flinders .edu.au; internet www.acd.edu.au; f. 1979; attached to Flinders Univ.; offers Bachelors, Masters and doctoral degrees in ministry; library: 60,000 vols; Pres. Rev. Prof. ANDREW DUTNEY; Exec. Officer JANET BUCHAN; Librarian ROSEMARY HOCKING.

Adelaide College of Ministries: POB 5, Klemzig, SA 5087; 18A, Fourth Ave, Klemzig, SA 5087; tel. (8) 8369-1414; e-mail acm@acm .sa.edu.au; internet www.acm.sa.edu.au; f. 1982 present location 1994; offers Bachelors degree in ministry; library: 12,000 vols and 300 journals; Prin. Dr TOM GOLDING; Academic Dean LESLIE CRAWFORD.

Aquinas College: 1 Palmer Pl., N Adelaide, SA 5006; tel. (8) 8334-5000; e-mail admin@ aquinas.edu.au; internet www.aquinas.edu .au; f. 1950; attached to Univ. of Adelaide; Head Dr COLIN MACMULLIN; College Sec. JUDITH KIRBY; Dean of Studies Bro. JOHN FURLONG.

Australian Institute of Business: 82 Flinders St, Adelaide, SA 5000; tel. (8) 8212-8111; e-mail enquiries@aib.edu.au; internet www .aib.edu.au; f. 1985 present status 1995; offers postgraduate and doctoral courses in management; overseas teaching centres in Egypt, Guyana, Ireland, St Lucia, Singapore, Sri Lanka and Trinidad and Tobago; Chair. Prof. Dr SELVA ABRAHAM; publ. *Gibaran Journal of Applied Management*.

Australian Lutheran College: 104 Jeffcott St, N Adelaide, SA 5006; tel. (8) 8267-7400; e-mail alc@alc.edu.au; internet www.alc.edu .au; f. 1892, present name 2004, present status 2010; attached to Melbourne College of Divinity; offers courses through schools of educational theology, pastoral theology and theological studies; library: 90,000 vols, 13,400 periodicals, 255 periodicals; Prin. JOHN HENDERSON; Vice-Prin. DEAN ZWECK; Dean STEPHEN HAAR; Dean of Chapel LINARDS JANSONS; Library Man. BLAN MACDONAGH; publ. *Lutheran Theological Journal* (3 a year).

Bible College SA: 176 Wattle, St Malvern, SA 5061; tel. (8) 8291-8188; e-mail admin@ biblecollege.sa.edu.au; internet www .biblecollege.sa.edu.au; f. 1924 as Adelaide Bible Institute, present name 1973, present location 1980; offers Bachelors degrees in Christian studies, ministry, theology; postgraduate degrees in ministry and theology; library: 27,000 vols, 70 journals; Pres. BILL DICKSON; Prin. Rev. PETER LOCKERY; Dean for College MARK KULIKOVSKY; Treas. SCOTT TILLEY; Librarian BARBARA COOPER; Registrar JAN WHITFORD.

Carnegie Mellon University, Heinz College—Australia: Torrens Bldg, 220 Victoria Sq., Adelaide, SA 5000; tel. (8) 8110-9900; e-mail admissions@cmu.edu.au; internet www.heinz.cmu.edu/australia; f. 2006; courses incl. Masters of science in information technology and public policy management; Exec. Dir Dr TERRY F. BUSS; Dean RAMAYYA KRISHNAN; Admissions Man. MONICA RUSTON; publ. *Heinz Journal*.

International College of Hotel Management: Days Rd, Regency Park, SA 5010; tel. (8) 8228-3636; e-mail admissions@ichm.edu .au; internet www.ichm.edu.au; offers Bachelors degrees in hospitality management and international hotel management; Chief Exec. GERALD LIPMAN; Prin. Dr IAN WHYTE.

Kathleen Lumley College: 51 Finniss St, N Adelaide, SA 5006; tel. (8) 8267-3270; e-mail klc@adelaide.edu.au; internet www .adelaide.edu.au/klc; f. 1967; attached to Univ. of Adelaide; Master Assoc. Prof. FELIX PATRIKEEFF.

Law Society of South Australia: POB 2066, Adelaide, SA 5001; 124 Waymouth St, Adelaide, SA 5000; tel. (8) 8229-0222; e-mail email@lawsocietysa.asn.au; internet www .lawsocietysa.asn.au; f. 1879; provides practical legal training to law students of local and interstate univs; Pres. RALPH BÖNIG; Exec. Dir JAN MARTIN; Gen. Man. STEPHEN HODDER; Man. of Finance CIRO PIPOLO; Man. of Education GRAHAM JOBLING.

Lincoln College: 45 Brougham Pl., N Adelaide, SA 5006; tel. (8) 8290-6000; e-mail admin@lincoln.edu.au; internet www.lincoln .edu.au; f. 1952; attached to Univ. of Adelaide; Prin. BEC PANNELL; Dean JORDAN BELL.

Roseworthy Residential College: Roseworthy, SA 5371; tel. (8) 8303-7888; e-mail roseworthycollege@adelaide.edu.au; f. 1991; attached to Univ. of Adelaide; library: 33,000 books, 700 journal titles; 250 students; Prin. Dr D. TAPLIN.

St Ann's College Inc.: 187 Brougham Pl., N Adelaide, SA 5006; tel. (8) 8267-1478; e-mail info@stannscollege.edu.au; internet www .stannscollege.edu.au; f. 1939; attached to Univ. of Adelaide; Prin. Dr ROSEMARY H. S. BROOKS.

St Mark's College: 46 Pennington Terrace, N Adelaide, SA 5006; tel. (8) 8334-5600; e-mail stmarks@stmarkscollege.com.au; internet www.stmarkscollege.com.au; f. 1925; attached to Univ. of Adelaide; library: 22,000 vols; Master and CEO ROSE S. ALWYN; Dean LESLEY PETRIE.

Tabor Adelaide: POB 1777, Unley, SA 5061; 181 Goodwood Rd, Millswood, SA 5034; tel. (8) 8373-8777; e-mail enquiry@ adelaide.tabor.edu.au; internet www .taboradelaide.edu.au; graduate and postgraduate courses in counselling, education, humanities, ministry, theology and culture; library: 70,000 vols, incl. journals and audiovisual items; Prin. DON OWERS; Library Man. JAN BARWICK.

UCL School of Energy and Resources: Torrens Bldg, 220 Victoria Sq., Adelaide, SA 5000; tel. (8) 8110-9960; e-mail australia@ucl .ac.uk; internet www.ucl.ac.uk/australia; attached to Univ. College London (United Kingdom); offers Masters and doctoral degrees in energy and resources; 4 teachers; 51 students (48 graduate and 3 research students); CEO DAVID TRAVERS; Chief Financial Officer BRONTE TRELOAR; Vice-Provost for Academic Affairs Prof. MICHAEL WORTON; Academic Dir Prof. TONY OWEN.

TASMANIA

Australian Maritime College: Locked Bag 1399, Launceston, TAS 7250; Maritime Way, Newnham, TAS 7250; tel. (3) 6324-3775; e-mail searchinfo@search.amc.edu.au; internet www.amc.edu.au; f. 1978; attached to Univ. of Tasmania; 2 campuses, Newnham and Beauty Point; library: 36,800 vols AMC-wide policies, procedures and related documents; 75 teachers; 1,300 students; Prin. Prof. NEIL BOSE (acting); Asst Registrar ELIZABETH VAGG; Dir of Faculty of Fisheries and Marine Environment Dr PAUL MCSHANE; Research Dir, Maritime Transport Policy Centre Dr BARRIE LEWARN; Library Officer MICHELLE STEVENS.

Tabor College Tasmania: 45 Melville St Hobart, TAS 7000; tel. (3) 6231-5889; e-mail registrar@tabor.tas.edu.au; internet www .tabor.tas.edu.au; offers Bachelors degree courses in min. and social sciences; Pres. DERMOT COTTULI; Registrar JAN NORTON; Librarian RUTH JONES.

Worldview Centre for Intercultural Studies: POB 21, St Leonards, TAS 7250; 41 Station Rd, St Leonards, TAS 7250; tel. (3) 6337-0444; e-mail enquiry@worldview.edu .au; internet www.worldview.edu.au; f. 1956; offers Bachelors of cross-cultural ministry; library: 19,000 vols, 150 magazines; Team Leader ROD VARDY; Academic Dean DENISE JARMAN.

VICTORIA

Australian Academy of Design: 220 Ingles St, Port Melbourne, VIC, 3207; tel. (3) 9676-9000; e-mail info@designacademy.edu.au; internet www.designacademy.edu.au; f. 1998; Bachelors of design arts with emphasis on advertising, fashion design, graphic design, photographic media and visual arts.

Australian Guild of Music Education System: 451 Glenferrie Rd, Kooyong, VIC 3144; tel. (3) 9822-3111; e-mail guild@hotkey.net.au; internet www.guildmusic.edu.au; f. 1969 as a continuation of London Guild of Music and Speech; offers Bachelors of music; holds public examinations for music and speech; CEO BERNADETTE NORTON; Dean Dr ERN KNOOP.

Box Hill Institute: POB 2014, Box Hill, VIC 3128; e-mail courseinfo@bhtafe.edu.au; internet www.bhtafe.edu.au; f. 1924 as Box Hill Technical School for Girls and Women, present status and name 1984; offers Bachelors degrees in commerce, fashion, hospitality management and sustainable built environments; campuses in Elgar Rd, Nelson, Whitehorse and Ceylon; 39,668 students; CEO and Pres. JOHN MADDOCK; Deputy CEO and Chief Operating Officer DARRELL CAIN; Vice-Pres. for Int. Enterprises NOEL LYONS; Chief Finance Officer JOANNE JAMES; Chief Information Officer JOHN ITALIANO; Sr Exec. Dir of Education and Training JENNIFER OLIVER; Exec. Dir of Learning and Academic Affairs SANDRA WALLS; Exec. Dir of Org. Devt DELIA MCLVER.

Cairnmillar Institute—School of Psychology Counselling and Psychotherapy: 993 Burke Rd, Camberwell, VIC 3124; tel. (3) 9813-3400; e-mail education@cairnmillar.edu.au; internet www.cairnmillar.edu.au; f. 1961; postgraduate courses in psychology and psychotherapy; Exec. Dir Dr FRANCIS MACNAB.

Cambridge International College, Australia: 422 Lt Collins St, Melbourne, VIC 3000; tel. (3) 9663-4933; e-mail info@cambridgecollege.com.au; internet www.cambridgecollege.com.au; f. 1995; campuses in Adelaide, Melbourne and Perth; Bachelors degrees in accounting, management and marketing; CEO PHIL HONEYWOOD; Man. Dir ROGER FERRETT.

Centre for Pavement Engineering Education Inc.: Suite 6, 935 Station St, Box Hill N, VIC 3129; tel. (3) 9890-5155; e-mail admin@pavementeducation.edu.au; internet www.pavementeducation.edu.au; postgraduate distance courses; incl. Masters courses in pavement technology.

Chifley Business School: POB 1272, Melbourne, VIC 3001; Level 4, 163 East Rd, S Melbourne, VIC 3205; tel. (3) 9695-8855; e-mail mba@chifley.edu.au; internet www.chifley.edu.au; f. 1989; postgraduate programmes in business administration, technology management and project management; campuses in Sydney and Brisbane; 800 students; CEO SIMON CHRISTENSEN; Operations Man. TONY HOLLAND; Postgraduate Programmes Man. NARELLE LEECH; Academic Dean Prof. DANNY SAMSON.

Chisholm Institute: POB 684, Dandenong, VIC 3175; tel. (3) 9212-5000; e-mail enquiries@chisholm.edu.au; internet www.chisholm.edu.au; f. 1998; campuses in Bass Coast, Berwick, Cranbourne, Dandenong, Frankston, Mornington Peninsula, offers Bachelors degrees in accounting, community mental health, engineering and interactive media design; Dir and CEO MARIA PETERS; Deputy CEO PETER HARRISON.

Holmes Institute: 185 Spring St, Melbourne, VIC 3000; tel. (3) 9662-2055; e-mail melbourne@holmes.edu.au; internet www.holmes.edu.au; f. 1963; campuses in Melbourne, Sydney, Brisbane, Cairns and Gold Coast in Australia; int. campus in Hong Kong; Bachelors and Masters degrees in business and professional accounting; Exec. Dean Prof. MIKE BERRELL.

Holmesglen Institute: POB 42, Holmesglen, VIC 3148; tel. (3) 9564-1555; e-mail info@holmesglen.edu.au; internet www.holmesglen.edu.au; f. 1982; 4 campuses in Chadstone, City, Moorabbin and Waverley; Bachelors courses in building and construction, business and finance, education and languages, hospitality management and nursing; faculties: language and vocational pathways, design, arts and science, engineering, electrical and information technology, health science and community studies, education, service skills and environment, business and finance and building, construction and architectural design; 50,000 students; Chief Exec. BRUCE MACKENZIE; Exec. Dir for Educational Devt and Design MARY FARAONE; Exec. Dir for Information Services FRANK VIRIK.

John Paul II Institute for Marriage & Family: 278 Victoria Parade, East Melbourne, VIC 3002; tel. (3) 9417-4349; e-mail info@jp2institute.org; internet www.jp2institute.org; f. 2001; courses incl. Masters in bioethics, theological studies and sacred theology; doctoral programmes; Pres. DENIS HART; Deputy Pres. FERGUS RYAN; Dir for Admin. Rev. PETER J. ELLIOTT; Dean Prof. TRACEY ROWLAND; Registrar Lt Col TOBY HUNTER.

Kollel Beth HaTalmud Yehuda Fishman Institute: 362A Carlisle St, Balaclava, VIC 3183; tel. (3) 9527-6156; e-mail office@kollel.com.au; internet www.kollelbht.com; offers Bachelors degrees in Talmud and Rabbinic thought.

Marcus Oldham College: POB 116, Geelong MC, VIC 3221; 145 Pigdons Rd, Waurn Ponds, Geelong, VIC 3216; tel. (3) 5243 3533; internet www.marcusoldham.vic.edu.au; Bachelors degrees in agribusiness, farm management and horse business management; library: 7,000 vols, 130 journals; Prin. Dr SIMON LIVINGSTONE; Chief Financial Officer TONY MCMEEL; Librarian MARG FREWIN.

Mayfield Education: 2–10 Camberwell Rd, Hawthorn, East Victoria, VIC 3123; tel. (3) 9882-7644; internet www.mayfield.edu.au; f. 1963; areas of study incl. hospitality, management and leadership and nursing; CEO MAVIS E. SMITH; Deputy CEO and Dir of Education MICHAEL BROWNING; Finance Man. NATALIA ZALOMSKI.

Melbourne Institute of Technology (MIT): 388–392 Lonsdale St, Melbourne, VIC 3000; tel. (3) 8600-6700; e-mail enquiries@mit.edu.au; internet www.mit.edu.au; f. 1996; attached to Univ. of Ballarat; postgraduate degrees in engineering, networking and professional accounting; campuses in Melbourne and Sydney; CEO SHESH GHALE; Provost (vacant); Man. Dir JAMUNA GURUNG.

MIECAT: 15–17 Victoria St, Fitzroy, VIC 3065; tel. (3) 9486-9081; e-mail admin@miecat.org.au; internet www.miecat.org.au; f. 1997; MA by supervision and MA by research in experiential and creative arts therapy; professional doctorate in experiential arts practice; Dir Dr JAN ALLEN.

Navitas College of Public Safety: POB 12302, A'Beckett St, Melbourne, VIC 8006; 400 Queen St, Melbourne, Vic. 3000; tel. (3) 8327-2600; e-mail degrees@ncps.edu.au; internet www.ncps.edu.au; f. 1990; offers Bachelors degree in criminal justice with emphasis on criminology, criminal psychology, criminal law and procedure law enforcement, corrections and justice related issues.

Oceania Polytechnic Institute of Education: Level 3, 446 Collins St, Melbourne, VIC 3000; tel. (3) 9663-3129; e-mail info@opie.vic.edu.au; internet www.opie.vic.edu.au; f. 1988; Bachelors degrees offered in areas of architecture, bldg design, drafting interior design and interior decoration; Head of Institute Prof. NICODEMOS CHARALAMBOUS.

Phoenix Institute of Australia: 314 Queen St, Melbourne, VIC 3000; tel. (3) 9510-4264; e-mail info@phoenixinstitute.com.au; internet www.phoenixinstitute.com.au; f. 1997; offers Bachelors of holistic counselling; CEO JANICE CRITTENDEN; Head of School MARTIN PEAKE; Strategic Operations and Chief Financial Man. LLOYD VOLKWYN; Librarian KIRSTY NEEDHAM.

Southern School of Natural Therapies: Level 1, 25 Victoria St, Fitzroy, VIC 3065; tel. (3) 9415-3333; e-mail sservices@ssnt.com.au; internet www.ssnt.edu.au; f. 1961 as Victorian br. of Australian Nat. Assen of Naturopaths, Osteopaths and Chiropractors, current name adopted 1981; Bachelors degrees in Chinese medicine, health science and naturopathy.

Stott's Colleges: 252 Lygon St, Carlton, Melbourne, VIC 3053; tel. (3) 9663-3399; e-mail study@stotts.vic.edu.au; internet stotts.vic.edu.au; f. 1883; offers Bachelors courses in accounting, business and community services; Registrar MANDY SIMONS.

Tabor College Victoria: 44–60 Jacksons Rd, Mulgrave, VIC 3170; tel. (3) 9790-9200; internet www.tabor.vic.edu.au; f. 1988; Bachelors degrees in general studies and theology; Masters of arts in vocational practice; library: 70,000 vols incl. books, audio cassettes and video cassettes; 25 teachers; 450 students; Prin. Dr WYNAND DE KOCK; Exec. Dir of Operations CHERYL OSMENT; Dean of Learning, Teaching and Research JOHN CAPPER; Dean of Quality and Registrar PETER DOBSON; publ. *Tabor Life* (1 a year).

Turning Point Alcohol and Drug Centre: 54–62 Gertrude St, Fitzroy, VIC 3065; tel. (3) 8413-8413; e-mail info@turningpoint.org.au; internet www.turningpoint.org.au; f. 1994; attached to Monash Univ.; offers graduate courses in alcohol and drug studies; Dir Prof. DAN LUBMAN.

William Angliss Institute: 555 La Trobe St, Melbourne, VIC 3000; tel. (3) 9606-2111; e-mail info@angliss.edu.au; internet www.angliss.edu.au; f. 1940; campuses in Cranbourne, Melbourne and Sydney in Australia; int. campus in Singapore; provides Bachelors degree courses for culinary management, foods and tourism and hospitality; 21,900 students; CEO NICHOLAS HUNT; Dir for Teaching and Learning ROBYN JACKSON.

WESTERN AUSTRALIA

Australian School of Management: Level 1, 641 Wellington St, Perth, WA 6000; tel. (8) 9211-3222; e-mail info@asm.edu.au; internet www.asm.edu.au; Bachelors degrees in business and hotel management; Man. Dir ALAN WILLIAMS; Finance Man. PEGGY CHAN; Student Services Man. NANA YAMAUCHI.

Harvest West Bible College Inc.: POB 128, Belmont, WA 6984; 79A Robinson Ave, Belmont, WA; tel. (8) 9479-3443; e-mail info@harvestwest.edu.au; internet www.harvestwest.edu.au; attached to Assemblies of God of W Australia; offers Bachelors degrees in arts, min. and biblical studies; Prin. Dr ASHLEY CRANE; Dean for Men MURRAY PATCHETT; Registrar and Dean for Women JESSICA DONALD.

Paramount College of Natural Medicine: POB 2039, Malaga, WA 6090; 11/15 Bonner Dr., Malaga, WA 6090; tel. (8) 9209-3335; e-mail info@paramountcollege.edu.au; internet www.paramountcollege.edu.au; f. 2003; campuses in Perth and Albany; Bachelors degrees in naturopathy, nutritional medicine, Western herbal medicine, homeopathy and mind body medicine; Prin. GILLIANE BURFORD.

Perth Bible College: 1 College Court, Karrinyup, WA 6018; tel. (8) 9243-2000; e-mail college@pbc.wa.edu.au; internet www.pbc.wa.edu.au; f. 1928; Bachelors of ministry and postgraduate courses either by course work or research; library: 25,000 vols; Prin. DAVID SMITH; Dean of Academic Affairs Dr ANDRE VAN OUDTSHOORN; Dean of Student Affairs GILLIAN DIXON; Dean of Studies ADAM NIVEN.

Polytechnic West: POB 1336, Midland, WA 6936; tel. (8) 9267-7777; e-mail info.centre@polytechnic.wa.edu.au; internet www.polytechnic.wa.edu.au; campuses in Armadale, Balga, Bentley, Carlisle, Midland, Thornlie; courses in aerospace, animals and horticulture, automotive, business and finance, engineering and information technology; 30,000 students; Man. Dir WAYNE COLLYER; publ. *TechTalk*.

SAE Institute: Level 1, 3–5 Bennett St E, Perth, WA 6004; tel. (8) 9325-4533; e-mail infoperth@sae.edu; internet www.sae.edu; f. 1976; hq in Oxford, UK; 50 institutes around the world; offers courses in media studies, audio engineering, film making, electronic music production, multimedia and web design, games programming, animation and music business; CEO Dr THOMAS MISNER; CEO Australia and New Zealand JOSEPH ANTHONYSZ; publ. *SAE Magazine*.

AUSTRIA

The Higher Education System

Austria's oldest (and largest) higher education institution is the University of Vienna, established in 1365. Institutes of adult education (Volkshochschulen) are found in all provinces, as are other centres operated by public authorities, church organizations and the Austrian Trade Union Federation. The central controlling and funding body of the higher education sector is the Federal Ministry of Science, Research and Economy. University-level education is free (although proposals were made in 2011 to reintroduce tuition fees—fees had been charged between 2001 and 2008), and the guiding framework is based on the General Law for University Education (1966) and the University Organization Law (1975). Since 2003 extensive reforms of the higher education system have been enacted. Universities have become quasi-autonomous institutions, independent of state control. A more 'top-down' form of management has been introduced, with university councils responsible for appointing senior managers (Rektorat). In 2012 the Private Universities Act came into force, accompanied by a comprehensive amendment of the University of Applied Sciences Studies Act, as well as a raft of reforms concerning nursing, health sciences and midwifery.

In 2010/11 there were 308,895 students enrolled on degree programmes in universities and Fachhochschulen. In 2010/11 there were 13 accredited private universities with 6,300 students. Admission to higher education is based on award of the Reifeprüfung (the certificate received upon successful completion of secondary education). In addition, all Austrian citizens over the age of 24 years, and with professional experience, may attend certain university courses in connection with their professional career or trade. However, for certain courses of study offered at Fachhochschulen (Universities of Applied Sciences—see below) students may be required to take extra examinations. Students without the Reifeprüfung can gain admission to university study by completing a preparatory course and the Studienberechtigungsprüfung examination. Successful completion of this course gives access to study in the fields in which the examinations were taken. In 2012 the Austrian Agency for Quality Assurance, the Austrian Accreditation Council and the Fachhochschulrat, which had hitherto been responsible for overseeing the public and private universities and the Fachhochschulen (Universities of Applied Sciences) Board, respectively, merged into a single Agency for Quality Assurance and Accreditation, in order to centralize the quality and access to courses, following a number of reforms covering higher and medical education.

As one of the original signatories to the Bologna Process, from 2002 Austria gradually implemented the two-tier system of undergraduate and graduate Bachelor and Masters level degrees alongside the traditional degrees, with a view to phasing the latter out entirely. The majority of degree programmes had changed to the Bologna format by 2007. However, medical degree programmes and upper-secondary teaching qualifications are exempt from the new system. The following degrees are available: Bakkalaureat, Diplomstudium/Magister, Fachhochschule Bakkalaureat and Kurzstudium (all undergraduate); Magisterstudium (Bologna), Aufbaustudium and Doktoratstudium (all postgraduate). The traditional undergraduate degree is the Diplomstudium, leading to the title Magister or Diplom (according to the field of study) and lasting four to six years. The Bologna equivalent is the Bakkalaureat, lasting three to four years. Students with the Diplom or Magister traditionally proceeded directly to Doctoral studies, which usually lasted between one and three years and required the writing of a thesis and the passing of final examinations, known as Rigorosum. Under the Bologna Process students are now expected to study for up to two years after the Bakkalaureat and earn the Magisterstudium before undertaking Doctoral studies (lasting a minimum of three years).

Non-university higher education is offered in Hochschulen for students, graduates and those who do not have the Reifeprüfung. Fachhochschulen, entry into which requires the Reifeprüfung, were launched in 1993. These establishments, of which there were 27 in 2010, offer professional training in technology, economics, and social affairs and society (media, law, and training of teachers and educators) which lasts for three to four years (leading to a Bakkalaureat) and allows admission to doctoral studies. Akademien and Kollegs also offer vocational training. In 2010 there were 20 Konservatorium, which are operated by the provinces and offer post-secondary courses in musical training leading to a diploma.

Regulatory and Representative Bodies

GOVERNMENT

Federal Ministry of Education and Women's Affairs: Minoritenpl. 5, 1014 Vienna; tel. (1) 531200; e-mail ministerium@bmukk.gv.at; internet www.bmukk.gv.at; Federal Minister Gabriele Heinisch-Hosek.

Federal Ministry of Science, Research and Economy: Minoritenpl. 5, 1014 Vienna; tel. (1) 5312000; e-mail infoservice@bmwf.gv.at; internet www.bmwf.gv.at; Federal Minister Dr Reinhold Mitterlehner.

ACCREDITATION

Agency for Quality Assurance and Accreditation Austria: Renngasse 5, 1010 Vienna; tel. (1) 53202200; e-mail office@aq.ac.at; internet www.aq.ac.at; f. 2012 by merger of Austrian Accreditation Council and Fachhochschulrat; accredits higher education instns and degree programmes; Man. Dir. Dr Achim Hopbach; Deputy Man. Dir Anita Kruisz.

ENIC-NARIC Austria: Bundesministerium für Wissenschaft und Forschung, Abteilung III/7, Teinfaltstr. 8, 1014 Vienna; tel. (1) 531205921; e-mail naric@bmwf.gv.at; internet www.naric.at; f. 1981; assessment and recognition of academic qualifications; counselling services for institutions and persons; 8 mems; Dir Dr Heinz Kasparovsky; Deputy Dir Mag. Ingrid Wadsack-Köchl; publs *Austria. Institutions of Post-secondary Education, Führung akademischer Grade, The Austrian Higher Education System.*

Österreichische Fachhochschul-Konferenz (Austrian Association of Universities of Applied Sciences): Bösendorferstr. 4/11, 1010 Vienna; tel. (1) 890634520; e-mail kurt.koleznik@fhk.ac.at; internet www.fhk.ac.at; f. 1995; assn of Austrian Fachhochschulen (Universities of Applied Sciences); supports Fachhochschulen in achieving common educational goals; Pres. Dr Helmut Holzinger; Sec.-Gen. Kurt Koleznik.

FUNDING

Fonds zur Förderung der wissenschaftlichen Forschung (Austrian Science Fund): Haus der Forschung, Sensengasse 1, 1090 Vienna; tel. (1) 5056740; e-mail office@fwf.ac.at; internet www.fwf.ac.at; f. 1967; all Austrian univs with their faculties, the art schools and the Austrian Academy of Sciences are represented, also delegates of non-univ. research instns and professional asscns; Austria's central funding org. for basic research; Pres. Prof. Dr Pascale Ehrenfreund; Man. Dir Dr Dorothea Sturn; publ. *Info Magazine* (German, online, www.fwf.ac.at/de/public_relations/printprodukte/info-archiv.html).

NATIONAL BODY

OeAD (Österreichische Austauschdienst) GmbH (Austrian Agency for International Cooperation in Education and Research): Ebendorferstr. 7, 1010 Vienna; tel. (1) 534080; e-mail info@oead.at; internet www.oead.at; f. 1961 as asscn of the Austrian

Rectors' Conf., present name 2009; CEO Prof. Dr HUBERT DÜRRSTEIN; publ. *OeADnews*.

Learned Societies

GENERAL

Österreichische Akademie der Wissenschaften (ÖAW) (Austrian Academy of Sciences (AAS)): Dr Ignaz Seipel-Pl. 2, 1010 Vienna; tel. (1) 515810; e-mail office@ricam.oeaw.ac.at; internet www.oeaw.ac.at; f. 1847; consists of sections of mathematics and natural sciences and humanities and social sciences; attached institutes: see under Research Institutes; 673 mems; library: see under Libraries and Archives; Pres. Prof. Dr HELMUT DENK; Vice-Pres. Prof. Dr SIGRID JALKOTZY-DEGER; Sec.-Gen. Prof. Dr ARNOLD SUPPAN; Sec. Prof. Dr GEORG STINGL; publs *Almanach, Anzeiger math.-nat. Klasse, Anzeiger phil.-hist. Klasse, Denkschriften der Gesamtakademie, Denkschriften math.-nat. Klasse, Denkschriften phil.-hist. Klasse, Monatshefte für Chemie, Sitzungsberichte math.-nat. Klasse Abt. I, II, Sitzungsberichte phil.-hist. Klasse, Thema: The Magazine* (3 a year).

AGRICULTURE, FISHERIES AND VETERINARY SCIENCE

Österreichische Gesellschaft der Tierärzte (Austrian Society of Veterinary Medicine): Veterinärpl. 1, 1210 Vienna; tel. (1) 25077-1800; e-mail oegt@vetmeduni.ac.at; internet www.oegt.at; f. 1914; 1,000 mems; Pres. Dr HARALD POTHMANN-REICHL; Vice-Pres. Dr DETLEF BIBL; Sec. Mag. BEATRIX GRÜNBERGER; publ. *Wiener Tierärztliche Monatsschrift* (6 a year).

ARCHITECTURE AND TOWN PLANNING

Österreichische Gesellschaft für Raumplanung (Austrian Society for Regional Planning): Technical Univ. of Vienna, Karlspl. 13, 1040 Vienna; tel. (1) 58801280233; e-mail oegr@oegr.at; internet www.oegr.at; Pres. Prof. Mag. Dr RUDOLF GIFFINGER; Sec. Dipl.-Ing. JOHN BOCKSTEFL; publs *FORUM Raumplanung* (2 a year), *Schriftenreihe* (irregular).

Österreichischer Ingenieur- und Architekten-Verein (Austrian Society of Engineers and Architects): Eschenbachgasse 9, 1010 Vienna; tel. (1) 5873536; e-mail office@oiav.at; internet www.oiav.at; f. 1848; 4,000 mems; Pres. Dipl.-Ing. Dr HEINZ BRANDL; Gen. Sec. Dipl.-Ing. PETER REICHEL; publ. *Österreichische Ingenieur- und Architekten-Zeitschrift* (6 a year).

Zentralvereinigung der Architekten Österreichs-ZV (Central Association of Austrian Architects): Salvatorgasse 10, 1010 Vienna; tel. (1) 5334429; e-mail zv@aaf.or.at; internet www.zv-architekten.at; f. 1907; 700 mems; Pres. HANS HOLLEIN.

BIBLIOGRAPHY, LIBRARY SCIENCE AND MUSEOLOGY

Gesellschaft für Landeskunde von Oberösterreich (Upper Austrian Cultural Heritage Association): Haus der Volkskultur, Promenade 33/103–104, 4020 Linz; tel. (732) 770218; e-mail office@ooelandeskunde.at; internet www.ooelandeskunde.at; f. 1833; offers cultural heritage by publs, reports, excursions; visit of exhibitions and museums; 700 mems; Chair. Dr GEORG SPIEGELFELD; Sec. Dr STEFAN TRAXLER; publs *Beiträge zur Landeskunde von Oberösterreich, Jahrbuch, Mitteilungen* (3 a year), *Schriftenreihe*.

Österreichische Gesellschaft für Dokumentation und Information (Austrian Society for Documentation and Information): c/o TermNet, Mooslackengasse 17, 1190 Vienna; Wollzeile 1–3, 1010 Vienna; e-mail office@oegdi.at; internet www.oegdi.at; f. 1951; organizes vocational training for information professionals, workshops, conferences and lectures in the field of information and library science; 80 mems; Pres. Dr GABRIELE SAUBERER; Exec. Sec. Dr HERMANN HUEMER.

Vereinigung Österreichischer Bibliothekarinnen und Bibliothekare (Austrian Librarians Association): Fluher str. 4, 6900 Bregenz; tel. (5574) 51144010; e-mail voeb@uibk.ac.at; internet www.univie.ac.at/voeb; f. 1945; represents the professional interests and concerns of member librarians; organizes central training event of the academic library system every 2 years; 1,200 mems; Pres. Dr HARALD WEIGEL; Sec. Dr ORTWIN HEIM; publ. *Mitteilungen* (4 a year).

ECONOMICS, LAW AND POLITICS

Nationalökonomische Gesellschaft (Austrian Economics Association): c/o Univ. of Linz, Dept of Economics, Altenberger Str. 69, 4040 Linz; tel. (2) 24688213; e-mail noeg@jku.at; internet www.noeg.ac.at; f. 1918; promotes scientific progress in theoretical and applied economic sciences; 240 mems; Pres. Prof. Dr JOHANN K. BRUNNER; Vice-Pres. Prof. Dr FRITZ BREUSS; Vice-Pres. Prof. Dr MANFRED NERMUTH; Gen. Sec. Prof. Dr GERALD J. PRUCKNER; publ. *Empirica* (5 a year, applied economics and economic policy).

Österreichische Gesellschaft für Aussenpolitik und die Vereinten Nationen (Foreign Policy and United Nations Association of Austria): Hofburg/Stallburg, Reitschulg, 2/2, OG 1010 Vienna; tel. (1) 5354627; e-mail office@oegavn.org; internet www.oegavn.org; f. 1945; 700 mems; Pres. Dr WOLFGANG SCHUESSEL; Vice-Pres. Dr GREGOR WOSCHNAGG; Sec.-Gen. MICHAEL F. PFEIFER; publ. *Global View* (4 a year).

Österreichische Gesellschaft für Kirchenrecht (Austrian Society for Ecclesiastical Law): c/o Institut für Rechtsphilosophie, Religions- und Kulturrecht, Rechtswissenschaftliche Fakultät der Universität Wien, Schenkenstr. 8–10, 1010 Vienna; tel. (1) 427735813; e-mail harald.baumgartner@univie.ac.at; internet www.univie.ac.at/recht-religion/ogk; f. 1949; promotes research and practice in religion and law; conducts 8 lectures and book presentations in a year; 200 mems; Pres. Mag. ANDREAS LOTZ; Vice-Pres. Hon. Prof. Dr RAOUL KNEUCKER; Sec. Dr HARALD BAUMGARTNER; publ. *Österreichisches Archiv für Recht und Religion*.

Österreichische Statistische Gesellschaft (Austrian Statistical Society): c/o Statistik Austria, Guglgasse 13, 1110 Vienna; tel. (1) 711287269; e-mail osg@statistik.gv.at; internet www.osg.or.at; f. 1951; promotes statistical science in all its forms and applications; awards annual scholarships for Masters and diploma theses and dissertations in statistics; 600 mems; Pres. Mag. MARGIT EPLER; publ. *Austrian Journal of Statistics* (3 or 4 a year).

Wiener Juristische Gesellschaft (Vienna Legal Association): Österreichisches Normungsinstitut, Heinestr. 38, 1020 Vienna; tel. (1) 21300605; e-mail office@wjg.at; internet www.wjg.at; f. 1867; promotes and develops law in theory and practice; 600 mems; Pres. Prof. Dr WALTER BARFUSS; Vice-Pres. Prof. Dr CLEMENS JABLONER; Vice-Pres. Prof. Dr KARL KORINEK; Gen. Sec. Mag. WOLFGANG MÜLLER.

EDUCATION

Österreichische Universitätenkonferenz (Universities Austria): Floragasse 7/7, 1040 Vienna; tel. (1) 31056560; e-mail office@uniko.ac.at; internet www.uniko.ac.at; f. 1911 as Austrian Rectors' Conf., current name adopted 2008; handles internal coordination of 21 Austrian public univs.; represents the univs in nat. and int. orgs and provides administrative and organizational support to the Nat. Univ. Federation; 21 mems; Pres. Prof. Dr HEINRICH SCHMIDINGER; Sec.-Gen. ELISABETH FIORIOLI.

Verband der Akademikerinnen Österreichs (Austrian Association of Women Academics): Reitschulgasse 2, 1010 Vienna; tel. (1) 5339080; e-mail office.vaoe-wien@aon.at; internet www.vaoe.at; f. 1922; promotes scientific and professional advancement of univ. women graduates; 650 mems; Pres. Dr INGRID NOWOTNY; Vice-Pres. Mag. ELISABETH GYÖRFY; publ. *VAÖ-Mitteilungen* (4 a year).

FINE AND PERFORMING ARTS

Bundesdenkmalamt (Federal Office for the Care and Protection of Monuments): Hofburg, Säulenstiege, 1010 Vienna; tel. (1) 534159; e-mail kontakt@bda.at; internet www.bda.at; f. 1850; protection and restoration of historical, artistic and cultural monuments; 200 mems; library of 70,000 vols; Pres. Dr BARBARA NEUBAUER; publs *Österreichische-Kunsttopographie, Österreichische Zeitschrift für Kunst und Denkmalpflege*.

Gesellschaft der Musikfreunde in Wien (Society of Friends of Music in Vienna): Bösendorferstr. 12, 1010 Vienna; tel. (1) 5058190; e-mail office@musikverein.at; internet www.musikverein.at; f. 1812; organizes more than 700 concerts a year; 11,000 mems; choir of 300 mems; library: see under Libraries and Archives; Exec. and Artistic Dir Dr THOMAS ANGYAN; publ. *Musikverein* (12 a year).

Internationale Franz Lehár-Gesellschaft (International Franz Lehár Society): Lothringerstr. 20, 1030 Vienna; tel. (1) 7132761; e-mail alleslehar@aon.at; internet www.franz-lehar-gesellschaft.com; f. 1949; Pres. HELGA PAPOUSCHEK; Gen. Sec. Prof. HARALD SERAFIN.

Johann Strauss-Gesellschaft Wien (Johann Strauss Society of Vienna): Hetzgasse 19/9, 1030 Vienna; tel. (1) 5339194; e-mail office@johann-strauss-gesellschaft.at; internet www.johann-strauss-gesellschaft.at; f. 1936; 300 mems; Pres. Prof. Mag. PETER WIDHOLZ; Vice-Pres. Prof. WERNER RESEL; Sec.-Gen. Brig. FRIEDRICH FALTUS; publ. *Wiener Bonbons* (4 a year).

Kunsthistorische Gesellschaft (Art History Society): c/o Institut für Kunstgeschichte der Universität Wien, Universitätscampus Hof 9, Spitalgasse 2 (Eingang Garnisongasse 13), 1090 Vienna; tel. (1) 427741410; f. 1953; 385 mems; Chair. Prof. Dr MICHAEL VIKTOR SCHWARZ; Deputy Chair. Doz. Dr WERNER TELESKO; Sec. Prof. Dr INGEBORG SCHEMPER.

Künstlerhaus (Gesellschaft Bildender Künstler Österreichs) (Austrian Artists Association): Karlspl. 5, 1010 Vienna; tel. (1) 5879663; e-mail office@k-haus.at; internet www.k-haus.at; f. 1861; 460 mems; Pres. MICHAEL PILZ; Dir PETER ZAWREL; Sec. NICOLA SCHENK.

Österreichische Gesellschaft für Kommunikationswissenschaft (Austrian Society of Communications): Institut für Kommunikationswissenschaft, Universität Salzburg, Rudolfskai 42, 5020 Salzburg; tel. (662) 80444150; e-mail oegk@sbg.ac.at;

internet www.ogk.at; f. 1976 as Austrian Society for Communication Issues, merged with Austrian Society for Media and Communication Studies in 1999 for present name; 140 mems; CEO Dr MICHAEL MANFÉ; Sec. Mag. PETRA STROHMAIER; publ. *Medien Journal* (4 a year).

Österreichische Gesellschaft für Musik (Austrian Music Society): Hanuschgasse 3, 1010 Vienna; tel. (1) 5123143; e-mail office@oegm.org; f. 1964; lectures, symposia, composer and artist profiles, publications; 1,000 mems; library of 1,000 vols mainly on contemporary music and records; Pres. Dr WALBURGA LITSCHAUER; Exec. Dir Dr CARMEN OTTNER; publ. *Beiträge* (every 2 years).

Österreichischer Komponistenbund (Association of Austrian Composers): Baumannstr. 8–10, 1031 Vienna; tel. (1) 7147233; e-mail info@komponistenbund.at; internet www.komponistenbund.at; f. 1913; represents and lobbies for contemporary music composers; initiates musical and artistic projects, concerts, CD and video productions of contests, calls and seminars to int. confs and exchanges; 500 mems; Pres. Prof. KLAUS AGER; Sec. JOHANNES KRETZ.

Wiener Beethoven-Gesellschaft (Vienna Beethoven Society): Heiligenstadt, Probusgasse 6, 1190 Vienna; tel. (1) 3188215; e-mail office@beethovengesellschaft.at; e-mail bjelik@mdw.ac.at; f. 1954; 260 mems; Pres. Prof. ERWIN ORTNER; Gen. Sec. Mag. CHRISTIAN KIRCHER; publ. *Mitteilungsblatt* (4 a year).

Wiener Konzerthausgesellschaft (Vienna Concert Hall Society): Lothringerstr. 20, 1030 Vienna; tel. (1) 24200333; e-mail wiener@konzerthaus.at; internet www.konzerthaus.at; f. 1913; 6,700 mems; Pres. Dr THERESA JORDIS; Vice-Pres. Dr BURKHARD GANTENBEIN; Vice-Pres. Dr CHRISTOPH KRAUS; publ. *Konzerthaus Nachrichten* (8 a year).

Wiener Secession (Vienna Secession Association of Visual Artists): Friedrichstr. 12, 1010 Vienna; tel. (1) 5875307; e-mail office@secession.at; internet www.secession.at; f. 1897; promotes exhibitions of contemporary art in its own gallery; 357 mems; Pres. Prof. ANDRAS PALFFY; Vice-Pres. CHRISTINA ZURFLUH; Vice-Pres. ANITA WITEK; Sec. MICHAEL KIENZER.

HISTORY, GEOGRAPHY AND ARCHAEOLOGY

Geschichtsverein für Kärnten (Historical Association of Carinthia): Museumgasse 2, 9020 Klagenfurt; tel. (463) 53630573; e-mail geschichtsverein@landesmuseum.ktn.gv.at; internet www.geschichtsverein.ktn.gv.at; f. 1844; 3,000 mems; Dir Prof. Dr CLAUDIA FRÄSS-EHRFELD; Sec. Prof. Dr GERNOT PICCOTTINI; publs *Archiv für Vaterländische Geschichte und Topographie* (irregular), *Aus Forschung und Kunst* (irregular), *Carinthia I* (1 a year).

Heraldisch-Genealogische Gesellschaft 'Adler' ('Eagle' Heraldry and Genealogy Society): Universitätstr. 6/9B, 1096 Vienna; e-mail office@adler-wien.at; internet www.adler-wien.at; f. 1870; 700 mems; library of 40,000 vols, 180 journals; Pres. Dr GEORG KUGLER; Sec.-Gen. Dr ANDREAS CORNARO; publs *Jahrbuch*, *Zeitschrift* (4 a year).

Historische Landeskommission für Steiermark (Historical Commission for Styria): Karmeliterpl. 3/II, 8010 Graz; tel. (316) 8773013; e-mail office@hlkstmk.at; internet www.hlkstmk.at; f. 1892; 44 mems; Pres. Mag. FRANZ VOVES; Sec. Prof. Dr ALFRED ABLEITINGER; publs *Forschungen und Darstellungen zur Geschichte des Steiermärkischen Landtages*, *Forschungen zur geschichtlichen Landeskunde der Steiermark*, *Geschichte der Steiermark*, *Mitteilungen der Korrespondentinnen und Korrespondenten der Historischen Landeskommission für Steiermark*, *Quellen zur geschichtlichen Landeskunde der Steiermark*, *Veröffentlichungen der Historischen Landeskommission für Steiermark*.

Historischer Verein für Steiermark (Styrian Historical Association): Karmeliterpl. 3, 8010 Graz; tel. (316) 8772366; e-mail info@historischerverein.li; internet www.historischerverein.li; f. 1850; 1,360 mems; Chair. Prof. Dr GERHARD PFERSCHY; Sec. MARCO SCHAEDLER; publs *Beiträge zur Erforschung Steirischer Geschichtsquellen*, *Blätter für Heimatkunde*, *Zeitschrift*.

Kommission für Neuere Geschichte Österreichs (Commission for Modern Austrian History): Neustiftgasse 47/7, 1070 Vienna; tel. (1) 515817313; e-mail kfngoe@chello.at; internet www.oesterreichische-geschichte.at; f. 1900; 29 mems; Chair. Prof. BRIGITTE MAZOHL; Sec. Dr KARIN SCHNEIDER; publ. *Veröffentlichungen der Kommission für Neuere Geschichte Österreichs*.

Österreichische Byzantinische Gesellschaft (Austrian Byzantine Society): c/o Institut für Byzantinistik und Neogräzistik, Universität Wien, Postgasse 7/1/3, 1010 Vienna; tel. (1) 427741001; e-mail byz-neo@univie.ac.at; internet www.byzneo.univie.ac.at/oebg; f. 1946; attached to Institute for Byzantine and Modern Greek Studies, Faculty of Historical and Cultural Studies, Univ. of Vienna; studies in Byzantine history and philology, culture and art; organization of lectures and int. confs; 145 mems; Pres. Prof. Dr JOHANNES KODER; Vice-Pres. Mag. Dr PETER K. SOUSTAL; Sec. Prof. Dr. ANDREAS KÜLZER; publ. *Mitteilungen aus der österreichischen Byzantinistik und Neogräzistik* (1 a year).

Österreichische Geographische Gesellschaft (Austrian Geographical Society): Karl Schweighofer-Gasse 3, 1071 Vienna; tel. (1) 5237974; e-mail kanzlei@oegg.info; internet www.oegg.info; f. 1856; represents and supports interests of Austrian geographers in all professional fields; promotes geography education; organizes lectures, discussions, excursions; 1,400 mems; library: see under Libraries and Archives; Pres. Dr CHRISTIAN STAUDACHER; Sec.-Gen. ROBERT MUSIL; publ. *Mitteilungen der Österreichischen Geographischen Gesellschaft* (1 a year).

Österreichische Gesellschaft für Archäologie (Austrian Archaeological Society): c/o Institut für Alte Geschichte, Altertumskunde und Epigraphik, Universität Wien, Dr Karl Lueger-Ring I, 1010 Vienna; e-mail oega@univie.ac.at; internet www.univie.ac.at/oega; f. 1972; 190 mems; Pres. Doz. Dr PETER SCHERRER; Vice-Pres. Dr GUNTER FITZ; Sec. REINHARD LANG; publs *Althistorisch-epigraphische Studien* (irregular), *Austria Antiqua* (irregular), *Römisches Österreich* (1 a year).

Österreichische Gesellschaft für Ur- und Frühgeschichte (Austrian Society for Pre- and Early History): c/o Institut für Ur- und Frühgeschichte, Franz-Klein-Gasse 1, 1190 Vienna; tel. (1) 427740473; e-mail alexandra.krenn-leeb@univie.ac.at; internet www.oeguf.ac.at; f. 1950; 1,050 mems; Gen. Sec. Mag. Dr ALEXANDRA KRENN-LEEB; publ. *Archäologie Österreichs* (2 a year).

Österreichische Numismatische Gesellschaft (Austrian Numismatic Society): c/o Münze Österreich, Am Heumarkt 1, 1010 Vienna; tel. (1) 525244203; e-mail office@oeng.at; internet www.oeng.at; f. 1870; organizes exhibitions, lectures, excursions related to numismatics; 400 mems; library of 5,000 vols; Pres. Dr GÜNTHER DEMBSKI; Vice-Pres. DIETMAR SPRANZ; Sec. Dr MICHAEL ALRAM; publ. *Numismatische Zeitschrift* (irregular).

Österreichische Orient-Gesellschaft Hammer-Purgstall (Austrian Orient Society Hammer-Purgstall): Dominikanerbastei 6/6, 1010 Vienna; tel. (1) 5128936; e-mail office@orient-gesellschaft.at; internet www.orient-gesellschaft.at; f. 1952; offers courses in oriental languages, talks, lectures, seminars, symposia, cultural evenings and workshops on education, but also on topical issues; Pres. Prof. Dr BERT FRAGNER; Gen. Sec. Dr SIEGFRIED HAAS.

Verband Österreichischer Historiker und Geschichtsvereine (Union of Austrian Historians and Historical Associations): Österreichisches Staatsarchiv Nottendorfergasse 2, 1030 Vienna; tel. (1) 79540254; e-mail lorenz.mikoletzky@oesta.gv.at; f. 1949; 130 mem. socs; Pres. WILLIBALD ROSNER; Vice-Pres. Prof. Dr LORENZ MIKOLETZKY; Gen. Sec. Dr ERWIN A. SCHMIDL; publ. *Veröffentlichungen des Verbands Österreichischer Historiker und Geschichtsvereine* (irregular).

Verein für Geschichte der Stadt Wien (Association for the History of the City of Vienna): Wiener Stadt- und Landesarchiv, Rathaus, 1082 Vienna; Wiener Stadt- und Landesarchiv, 11, Guglgasse 14, Gasometer D, 5. Stock, Zimmer 506, 1082 Vienna; tel. (1) 400084815; e-mail post@geschichte-wien.at; internet www.geschichte-wien.at; f. 1853; based in Vienna Municipal and Provincial Archives; researches and publishes on Vienna's history; 1,592 mems; Pres. Dr KARL FISCHER; Vice-Pres. Dr HELMUT KRETSCHMER; Sec. Dr SUSANNE CLAUDINE PILS; publs *Forschungen und Beiträge zur Wiener Stadtgeschichte* (irregular), *Studien zur Wiener Geschichte* (1 a year), *Wiener Geschichtsblätter* (4 a year).

LANGUAGE AND LITERATURE

Austria Esperantista Federacio (Austrian Esperanto Society): POB 39, 1014 Vienna; tel. (1) 8934196; e-mail aef@esperanto.at; internet www.esperanto.at; f. 1935; promotes the Esperanto language by serving as a contact, exchanging and disseminating information, operating the website, producing and distributing information material, working with int. or nat. Esperanto orgs, maintaining and sharing experience and contacts; 500 mems; library of 1,500 vols, 1,000 pamphlets; Hon. Pres. Prof. Dr HANS MICHAEL MAITZEN; Chair. BERNHARD TUIDER; Deputy Chair. KATALIN FETES-TOSEGI; publs *Austria-Esperanto-Revuo*, *Esperanto—Aktuell* (6 a year), *Esperanto-Servo* (4 a year).

British Council: Siebensterngasse 21, 1070 Vienna; tel. (1) 533261677; e-mail exams@britishcouncil.at; internet www.britishcouncil.at; f. 1946; offers IELTS and Cambridge ESOL English language examinations; promotes cultural exchange with the UK; library contains large colln of modern British fiction, titles on British studies and English-language learning materials; access to British websites, databases and learning software; Dir WILL TODD.

Eranos Vindobonensis: Institut für Klassische Philologie, Mittel- und Neulatein, Universität Wien, Dr Karl Lueger-Ring 1, 1010 Vienna; tel. (1) 4277419; e-mail andrea.duchac@univie.ac.at; internet kphil.ned.univie.ac.at/node/124629; f. 1876; promotes devt of classical archaeology by specialized lectures and presentations, knowledge and experience; 90 mems; Pres. Prof. Dr MARION

MEYER; Vice-Pres. Prof. Dr FAROUK F. GREWAL; Sec. and Treas. Prof. Dr PAUL RAIMUND LORENZ.

Gesellschaft für Klassische Philologie in Innsbruck (Classical Philological Society of Innsbruck): Institut für Klassische Philologie, Universität Innsbruck, Innrain 52, 6020 Innsbruck; tel. (512) 5074082; e-mail klassphil@uibk.ac.at; internet www.uibk.ac.at/sci-org/klassphil; f. 1958; offers lectures, readings productions and travels; 200 mems; Chair. SIMON ZUENELLI; Chair. Dr LAV SUBARIC; Chair. Prof. Dr KARL HEINZ TÖCHTERLE; Sec. KATHY ZIPSER; publ. *Acta philologica Aenipontiana*.

Gesellschaft zur Förderung Slawistischer Studien (Society for Slavic Studies): Teschnergasse 4/17, 1180 Vienna; f. 1983; Dir AAGE HANSEN-LÖVE; publs *Journal* (2 a year), *Wiener Slawistischer Almanach*, monograph series (4 a year).

Instituto Cervantes: Schwarzenbergpl. 2, 1010 Vienna; tel. (1) 5052535; e-mail cenvie@cervantes.es; internet viena.cervantes.es; f. 1991; offers courses and examinations in Spanish language and culture and promotes cultural exchanges with Spain and Spanish-speaking Latin and Central America; library of 27,000 vols, 70 periodicals, 920 music CDs, 2,000 video cassettes and DVDs; Dir JUAN MANUEL CASADO RAMOS; Asst Dir BARBARA STURZEIS.

Österreichische Gesellschaft für Literatur (Austrian Literary Society): Herrengasse 5, 1010 Vienna; tel. (1) 5338159; e-mail office@ogl.at; internet www.ogl.at; f. 1961; promotes and propagates Austrian literature; presentations, discussions, translations; builds cultural connections; Pres. MARIANNE GRUBER.

Österreichische Goethe-Gesellschaft (Austrian Goethe Society): Prof. Dr. Herbert Zeman, Peterspl. 10/2A, 1010 Vienna; tel. (1) 5336728; e-mail goethe.germanistik@univie.ac.at; internet www.univie.ac.at/goethe/html; f. 1878 as Wiener Goethen-Verein, present name 2004; conducts readings, lectures, concerts, recitations, symposia, tours, excursions to promote life and work of Johann Wolfgang von Goethe; 300 mems; library of 2,000 vols; Pres. Prof. Dr HERBERT ZEMAN; Vice-Pres. Prof. Dr HEINZ KREJCI; Sec. Mag. EMMERICH MAZAKARINI; publ. *Jahrbuch*.

Wiener Humanistische Gesellschaft: Institut für Klassische Philologie, Mittel- und Neulatein, Univ. Wien, Universitaetsring 1, 1010 Vienna; tel. (1) 427741901; e-mail kurt.smolak@univie.ac.at; internet www.univie.ac.at/klassphil; f. 1947; 600 mems; Jt Pres. Prof. HEINRICH STREMITZER; Jt Pres. Prof. KURT SMOLAK; Sec. ANDREA DUCHAC; publ. *Wiener Humanistische Blätter*.

Wiener Sprachgesellschaft (Vienna Language Society): Universität Wien, Institut für Sprachwissenschaft, Sensengasse 3A, 1090 Vienna; e-mail wsg.sprachwissenschaft@univie.ac.at; internet www.univie.ac.at/indogermanistik/wsg; f. 1947; promotes academic study of language in all its forms; 120 mems; Pres. Prof. Dr ALEXANDRA N. LENZ; Exec. Sec. Dr HANS CHRISTIAN LUSCHÜTZKY; publ. *Die Sprache* (1 a year).

MEDICINE

Gesellschaft der Ärzte in Wien (College of Physicians in Vienna): Frankgasse 8, 1090 Vienna; tel. (1) 4054777; e-mail info@billrothhaus.at; internet www.billrothhaus.at; f. 1837; training, presentation of new medical research findings; organizes scientific events; 2,500 mems; library of 200,000 vols, 25,900 monographs; Pres. Prof. Dr FRANZ KAINBERGER; Sec. Prof. Dr PAUL AIGINGER; Sec. Prof. Dr HELMUT SINZINGER; publ. *Wiener Klinische Wochenschrift*.

Gesellschaft der Chirurgen in Wien (Vienna Society of Surgeons): c/o Universitätsklinik für Chirurgie, Klin. Abteilung für Allgemeinchirurgie, Währinger Gürtel 18–20, 1090 Vienna; tel. (1) 404006566; e-mail chirurgie@billrothhaus.at; internet www.chirurgie-ges.at; f. 1935; 171 mems; Pres. Prof. Dr ADELHEID END; Sec.-Gen. Prof. Dr BÉLA TELEKY.

Internationale Paracelsus Gesellschaft: Duerlingerstr. 23, 5020 Salzburg; tel. (662) 826773; e-mail info@paracelsusgesellschaft.at; internet www.paracelsusgesellschaft.at; f. 1951; 315 mems, 27 mem. asscns; Pres. Prof. Dr HEINZ DOPSCH; Gen. Sec. GERTRAUD WEISS; publ. *Salzburger Beiträge zur Paracelsusforschung* (irregular).

Österreichische Gesellschaft für Anästhesiologie, Reanimation und Intensivmedizin (Austrian Society of Anaesthesiology, Resuscitation and Intensive Care Medicine): Höfergasse 13, 1090 Vienna; tel. (1) 4064810; e-mail office@oegari.at; internet www.oegari.at; f. 1951; promotes and develops anaesthesiology, resuscitation, intensive care, pain management, emergency medicine and disaster medicine; organizes meetings, lectures, scientific meetings, demonstrations, discussions, training programmes; 1,431 mems; Pres. Prof. Dr HELFRIED METZLER; Sec. Dr MANFRED GREHER; publ. *A + IC News* (4 a year).

Österreichische Gesellschaft für Arbeitsmedizin (Austrian Society for Occupational Health): Kaplanhofstr. 1, 4020 Linz; tel. (732) 7815600; internet www.gamed.at; f. 1954; research and identification of work-related health hazards; promotion and devt of workplace health; training programmes for medical and non-medical audiences; 350 mems; Pres. Dr CHRISTINE KLIEN.

Österreichische Gesellschaft für Chirurgie (Austrian Society for Surgery): Frankgasse 8, POB 80, 1096 Vienna; tel. (1) 4087920; e-mail chirurgie@billrothhaus.at; internet www.chirurgie-ges.at; f. 1958; incl. the associated Austrian socs for traumatology, orthopaedic, thoracic and cardiac surgery, vascular surgery, neurosurgery, obesity surgery, paediatric surgery, plastic, aesthetic and reconstructive surgery, surgical oncology, osteosynthesis, coloproctology, hand surgery, surgical research, maxillofacial surgery, surgical endocrinology, keyhole surgery, medical videography, surgical endoscopy, hernia surgery, implantology and tissue-integrated prosthesis, Austrian Section of the Int. Soc. for Digestive Surgery; 5,290 mems; Pres. Prof. Dr FREYJA-MARIA SMOLLE-JÜTTNER; publs *Chirurgie* (4 a year), *European Surgery/Acta Chirurgica Austriaca* (6 a year).

Österreichische Gesellschaft für Dermatologie und Venereologie (Austrian Dermatological and Venereological Society): c/o Wiener Medizinische Akademie, Alser str. 4, 1090 Vienna; tel. (1) 405138320; e-mail kknob@medacad.org; internet www.oegdv.at/cms; f. 1890; organizes annual scientific and educational confs and operates a special working group for dermatological training; 876 mems; Pres. Prof. Dr JOSEF AUBÖCK; Vice-Pres. Prof. Dr BEATRIX VOLC-PLATZER.

Österreichische Gesellschaft für Geriatrie und Gerontologie (Austrian Society for Geriatrics and Gerontology): Sozialmedizinisches Zentrum, Apollogasse 19, 1070 Vienna; tel. (1) 521035770; e-mail ilse.howanietz@wextern.wienkav.at; internet www.geriatrie-online.at; f. 1955; researches into ageing process, geriatric and gerontologic knowledge; organizes scientific meetings and int. asscns in the same field; 3 sections: geriatric, biogerontology and social gerontology; 400 mems; library of 2,000 vols; Pres. Prof. Dr KATHARINA PILS; Vice-Pres. Dr HANNES PLANK; Vice-Pres. Dr THOMAS FRÜHWALD; Sec. ILSE HOWANIETZ; publs *Aktuelle Gerontologie* (12 a year), *European Journal of Geriatrics*, *Geriatrie Praxis Österreich* (6 a year), *Scriptum Geriatricum* (1 a year).

Österreichische Gesellschaft für Hals-, Nasen-, Ohrenheilkunde Kopf- und Halsschirurgie (Austrian Society of Otorhinolaryngology, Head and Neck Surgery): Frau Mag. Andrea BALCAR, c/o Mondial Congress & Events Operngasse 20, 1040 Vienna; tel. (1) 58804800; e-mail sekretariat@hno.at; internet www.hno.at; f. 1892; 900 mems; Pres. Prof. Dr MARTIN BURIAN; Gen. Sec. Prof. Dr HANS EDMUND ECKEL.

Österreichische Gesellschaft für Innere Medizin (Austrian Society for Internal Medicine): c/o MAW Freyung 6/3, 1010 Vienna; tel. (1) 5366316; e-mail oegim@oegim.at; internet www.oegim.at; f. 1901; science and research, education and training in the entire field of internal medicine; promotes and improves the field based on latest medical care; lobbies public instns on matters regarding internal medicine; 400 mems; Pres. Prof. Dr ERNST PILGER; Sec.-Gen. Prof. Dr MARKUS PECK-RADOSAVLJEVIĆ; publ. *Education (Wiener klinische Wochenschrift)*.

Österreichische Gesellschaft für Kinder- und Jugendheilkunde (Austrian Society for Paediatrics and Adolescent Medicine): Landes-Frauen- und Kinderklinik Linz Krankenhausstr. 26–30, 4020 Linz; tel. (5055) 46322002; e-mail monika.matzinger@gespag.at; internet www.docs4you.at; f. 1962; scientific org. representing interests of its members and providing professional-oriented information; raises awareness, consults on policy-making in the field; 805 mems; Pres. Prof. Dr KLAUS SCHMITT; Vice-Pres. Prof. Dr REINHOLD KERBL; Exec. Sec. MONIKA MATZINGER; publs *Monatsschrift Kinderheilkunde* (online), *Pädiatrie und Pädologie* (6 a year).

Österreichische Gesellschaft für Klinische Neurophysiologie (Austrian Clinical Neurophysiological Society): Institut für Neurophysiologie der Universität Wien, Währingerstr. 18–20, 1090 Vienna; e-mail mcgraf@aon.at; internet www.oegkn.at; f. 1956; promotes cooperation in fields of electroencephalography and clinical neurophysiology (research and area of application of neurobioelectric appearances); 250 mems; Pres Prof. Dr CHRISTOPH BAUMGARTNER; Pres. Prof. Dr EUGEN TRINKA; Sec. Prof. Dr IRIS UNTERBERGER; publs *EEG/EMG*, *Thieme* (4 a year).

Österreichische Gesellschaft für Reproduktionsmedizin und Endokrinologie (Austrian Society of Reproductive Medicine and Endocrinology): Kaiser Franz Josef Kai 46/1, 8010 Graz; tel. (316) 831650; e-mail wolfgang.urdl@ivf-institut.at; internet www.oegrm.at; f. 1983 as Austrian Soc. for In Vitro Fertilization and Assisted Reproduction, current name adopted 1997; Pres. Prof. Dr WOLFGANG URDL; Vice-Pres. Prof. Dr LUDWIG WILDT; Sec. Prof. Dr HERBERT ZECH BREGENZ; Sec. Doz. Dr DIETMAR SPITZER; publ. *Journal für Reproduktionsmedizin und Endokrinologie*.

Österreichische Gesellschaft für Urologie und Andrologie (Austrian Society for Urology and Andrology): Landesklinikum Weinviertel Mistelbach, Liechtensteinstr. 67, 2130 Mistelbach; tel. (2572) 33419600;

e-mail walter.albrecht@mistelbach.lknoe.at; internet www.uro.at; organizes annual training conf., seminars, teaching and training sessions, conducts scientific research and publishes study results; represents interests of the urologists and andrologists in relations with public bodies and instns; 511 mems; Pres. Dr KLAUS JESCHKE; Sec. Doz. Dr WALTER ALBRECHT; publ. *NÖGU* (2 a year).

Österreichische Ophthalmologische Gesellschaft (Austrian Ophthalmological Society): Schlüsselgasse 9, 1080 Vienna; tel. (1) 4028540; e-mail oeog@augen.at; internet www.augen.at; f. 1955; promotes ophthalmology and represents the interests of ophthalmologists in Austria and internationally; 730 mems; library of 2,100 vols; Pres. Prof. Dr GÜNTHER GRABNER; Sec. Dr MATTHIAS BOLZ; publ. *Spectrum der Augenheilkunde* (6 a year).

Österreichische Röntgengesellschaft—Gesellschaft für Medizinische Radiologie und Nuklearmedizin (Austrian Radiological Society—Society for Medical Radiology and Nuclear Medicine): Neutorgasse 9/2, 1010 Vienna; tel. (1) 5320507; e-mail office@oerg.at; internet www.oerg.at; f. 1946; 800 mems; Pres. Prof. Dr WERNER JASCHKE; Sec. Dr GERLIG WIDMANN; publ. *ÖRG—Mitteilungen* (4 a year).

Verein für Psychiatrie und Neurologie (Society for Psychiatry and Neurology): Kundratstr. 3, 1100 Vienna; tel. (1) 404003514; e-mail julia.ferrari@bbwien.at; internet www.verein-psychiatrie-neurologie.at; f. 1867; promotes the scientific and medical communication between psychiatrists and neurologists; holds regular meetings; bestows research support awards; Pres. Prof. Dr KENNETH THAU; Sec. Prof. Dr ANDREAS ERFURTH.

Wiener Medizinische Akademie für Ärztliche Fortbildung und Forschung (Vienna Academy of Postgraduate Medical Education and Research): Alser str. 4, 1090 Vienna; Spitalgasse 2, Entrance 'Freud Tor 1', Hof, Ehem. Direktionsgebäude, 2nd. Fl., 1090 Vienna; tel. (1) 40513830; e-mail office@medacad.org; internet www.medacad.org; f. 1924; conf. and asscn management instn for medical non-profit community, providing leadership, organizational guidance, headquarters facilities and staff resources; Pres. Prof. Dr H. GRÜBER; Secs Prof. Dr W. GRISOLD; Sec. Prof. Dr R. DUDCZAK.

NATURAL SCIENCES

General

Naturwissenschaftlicher Verein für Kärnten (Carinthian Association of Natural Sciences): Museumgasse 2, Landesmuseum, 9021 Klagenfurt; tel. (463) 53630574; e-mail nwv@naturwissenschaft-ktn.at; internet www.naturwissenschaft-ktn.at; f. 1848; 1,300 mems; Pres. Dr HELMUT ZWANDER; publ. *Carinthia II* (1 a year, with special issues).

Biological Sciences

Österreichische Mykologische (Pilzkundliche) Gesellschaft (Austrian Mycological Society): Rennweg 14, 1030 Vienna; tel. (1) 427754050; e-mail irmgard.greilhuber@univie.ac.at; internet www.myk.univie.ac.at; f. 1919; mycological herbarium colln, fungal records online database, excursions, lectures, newsletter; 320 mems; library of 1,000 vols; Pres. IRMGARD KRISAI-GREILHUBER; Vice-Pres. HEINZ PRELICZ; Vice-Pres. FRIEDRICH EHRENDORFER; publ. *Österreichische Zeitschrift für Pilzkunde* (1 a year).

Zoologisch-Botanische Gesellschaft in Österreich (Austrian Zoological-Botanical Society): Althanstr. 14, POB 45, 1091 Vienna; e-mail barbara-amina.gereben@univie.ac.at; internet www.univie.ac.at/zoobot; f. 1851; lectures; excursions; library; publs; exchange of publs; nature conservation; botanical illustration courses; confers Walter Fiedler Promotion award; 510 mems; library of 60,000 vols; spec. library for zoology, botany and ecology; 2,800 periodicals, 4,500 monographs and 8,700 reprints; Pres. Dr FRIEDRICH SCHIEMER; Sec.-Gen. Dr BARBARA-AMINA GEREBEN-KRENN; publs *Abhandlungen* (irregular), *Koleopterologische Rundschau* (1 a year), *Verhandlungen* (1 a year).

Mathematical Sciences

Mathematisch-Physikalische Gesellschaft in Innsbruck (Mathematics and Physics Society of Innsbruck): c/o Manfred P. Leubner, Institut für Astrophysik, Universität Innsbruck, Technikerstr. 25, 6020 Innsbruck; tel. (512) 5126060; e-mail math-phys-ges@uibk.ac.at; f. 1936; 126 mems; Chair. MANFRED P. LEUBNER.

Österreichische Mathematische Gesellschaft (Austrian Mathematical Society): Technische Univ., E104, Wiedner Hauptstr. 8–10, 1040 Vienna; tel. (1) 5880110423; e-mail oemg@oemg.ac.at; internet www.oemg.ac.at; f. 1903; 537 mems; Chair. M. DRMOTA; Sec. F. URBANEK; publs *International Mathematical News* (3 a year), *Monatshefte für Mathematik* (12 a year).

Physical Sciences

Chemisch-Physikalische Gesellschaft in Wien (Vienna Chemical-Physical Society): Universität Wien, Fakultät für Physik, Strudlhofgasse 4/Boltzmanngasse 5, 1090 Vienna; tel. (1) 4277-51108; e-mail christl.langstadlinger@univie.ac.at; internet www.cpg.univie.ac.at; f. 1869; holds meetings, promotes research papers to encourage the spread of skills in chemistry and physics; awards the Loschmidt Prize to support graduates in chemistry or physics; 260 mems; Pres. Prof. Dr CHRISTOPH DELLAGO; Sec.-Gen. CHRISTL LANGSTADLINGER.

Gesellschaft Österreichischer Chemiker (Austrian Chemical Society): Nibelungengasse 11/6, 1010 Vienna; tel. (1) 5874249; e-mail office@goech.at; internet www.goech.at; f. 1897; 1,900 mems; Pres. Prof. Dr HERBERT IPSER; Vice-Pres. Dr PETER JAITNER; Man. Dir Dr ERICH LEITNER; publs *Chemiereport.at* (online (www.chemiereport.at)), *Chemistry—A European Journal* (co-author), *Monatshefte für Chemie* (Chemical Monthly).

Österreichische Geologische Gesellschaft (Austrian Geological Society): Geologische Bundesanstalt, Neulinggasse 38, 1030 Vienna; tel. (1) 71256740; e-mail oegg@geologie.ac.at; internet www.geol-ges.at; f. 1907; promotes the science of geology theoretical and practical, especially of the Austrian Alps and surrounding areas; affiliated to American Association of Petroleum Geologists (AAPG); 714 mems; Pres. CHRISTIAN SPÖTL; Vice-Pres. WOLFGANG NACHTMANN; Sec. GERHARD SCHUBERT; publ. *Austrian Journal of Earth Sciences*.

Österreichische Gesellschaft für Analytische Chemie (Austrian Society for Analytical Chemistry): Institut für Analytische Chemie, Universität Wien, Wachringer Str. 38, 1090 Vienna; tel. (1) 427752300; e-mail wolfgang.lindner@univie.ac.at; internet www.asac.at; f. 1948; provides support to research, teaching and application of microchemistry and analytical chemistry; gives awards, scholarships; holds training programmes, confs and seminars; 400 mems; Pres. Prof. Dr WOLFGANG LINDNER; Sec. Prof. Dr R. KRSKA; Sec. Prof. Dr M. LÄMMERHOFER.

Österreichische Gesellschaft für Erdölwissenschaften (Austrian Society for Petroleum Sciences): c/o Wirtschaftskammer Österreich, Wiedner Hauptstr. 63, Zimmer 4208, 1045 Vienna; tel. (5) 909004891; e-mail oegew@oil-gas.at; internet www.oegew.org; f. 1960; promotes science, research, technology and training in exploration, production and storage of petroleum and natural gas; processing and use of petroleum, natural gas and derived products; 502 mems; Pres. REINHART SAMHAT; Sec. SABINE JEHOTEK.

Österreichische Gesellschaft für Laboratoriumsmedizin und Klinische Chemie (Austrian Society of Laboratory Medicine and Clinical Chemistry): Tullnertalgasse 72, 1230 Vienna; tel. (1) 8896238; e-mail office@oeglmkc.at; internet www.oeglmkc.at; f. 2004; 29 mems; Pres. Doz. Dr ALEXANDER C. HAUSHOFER; Vice-Pres. Dr GEORG MUSTAFA.

Österreichische Gesellschaft für Meteorologie (Austrian Meteorological Society): Hohe Warte 38, 1190 Vienna; tel. (1) 360262202; internet www.meteorologie.at; f. 1865; organizes meetings, lectures, confs; 270 mems; Pres. Dr FRITZ NEUWIRTH; Sec.-Gen. Dr ERNEST RUDEL; publ. *Meteorologische Zeitschrift* (6 a year).

Österreichische Gesellschaft für Molekulare Biowissenschaften und Biotechnologie (ÖGMBT) (Austrian Association for Molecular Life Sciences and Biotechnology): c/o Univ. of Natural Resources and Applied Life Sciences, Muthgasse 18, 1190 Vienna; tel. (1) 476546394; e-mail alexandra.khassidov@oegmbt.at; internet www.oegmbt.at; f. 2008; attached to ÖGBT (Austrian Soc. for Biotechnology), ÖGGGT (Austrian Asscn for Genetics and Genetic Engineering) and ÖGBM (Austrian Asscn for Biochemistry and Molecular Biology); promotes research and education in biochemistry, molecular biology and cell biology; organizes scientific events; 1,000 mems; Pres. JOSEF GLOESSL; Vice-Pres. ANGELA SESSITSCH; Vice-Pres. LUKAS A. HUBER; Gen. Sec. ALEXANDRA KHASSIDOV; publ. *ÖGBM Nachrichten* (4 a year).

Österreichische Physikalische Gesellschaft (Austrian Physical Society): c/o Dr Karl Riedling, Institute of Sensor and Actuator Systems, TU Vienna, Gusshausstrasse 27/366 1040 Vienna; tel. (1) 5880136658; e-mail karl.riedling@tuwien.ac.at; internet www.oepg.at; f. 1950; promotes physical sciences in research, devt and teaching; 534 mems; Pres. Prof. Dr WOLFGANG ERNST; Vice-Pres. Prof. Dr ERICH GORNIK; Man. Dir Prof. Dr KARL RIEDLING.

Österreichischer Astronomischer Verein (Austrian Astronomical Association): Hasenwartgasse 32, 1230 Vienna; tel. (1) 88935410; e-mail astbuero@astronomisches-buero-wien.or.at; internet www.astronomisches-buero-wien.or.at; f. 1924; organizes lectures and guided tours; runs a fully automatic fireball station at Martinsberg, Lower Austria and an open-air planetarium in Vienna, Georgenberg; 1,500 mems; Pres. Prof. Dr ROBERT WEBER; Sec. Prof. HERMANN MUCKE; publs *Astronomische Buero: Der Sternenbote* (12 a year), *Der Sternenbote* (12 a year), *Österreichischer Himmelskalender* (1 a year).

PHILOSOPHY AND PSYCHOLOGY

Österreichische Gesellschaft für Parapsychologie und Grenzbereiche der Wissenschaften (Austrian Society for Parapsychology and Frontier Areas of Science): c/o Prof. Peter Mulacz, Hernalser Hauptstrasse 38/13, 1170 Vienna; tel. (43) 6603609550; e-mail office@parapsychologie.ac.at; internet parapsychologie.ac.at; f. 1927;

150 mems; library of 1,200 vols; Vice-Pres. and Sec.-Gen. Prof. W. PETER MULACZ.

Philosophische Gesellschaft Wien (Philosophical Society of Vienna): Universitätsstr. 7/2/2, 1010 Vienna; tel. (1) 427747402; f. 1954; 100 mems; Dir Prof. Dr HANS-DIETER KLEIN.

Sigmund Freud Privatstiftung (Sigmund Freud Foundation): Berggasse 19, 1090 Vienna; tel. (1) 3191596; e-mail office@freud-museum.at; internet www.freud-museum.at; f. 2003; history and application of psychoanalysis; archives; Sigmund Freud museum; 1,000 mems; library of 38,000 vols, 15,000 offprints, 45 journals; Chair. INGE SCHOLZ-STRASSER.

Wiener Psychoanalytische Vereinigung (Vienna Psychoanalytic Society): Salzgries 16/3, 1010 Vienna; tel. (1) 5330767; e-mail office@wpv.at; internet www.wpv.at; f. 1908; 202 mems; Pres. Dr CHRISTINE DIERCKS; Sec. VIOLA SEIBERT.

RELIGION, SOCIOLOGY AND ANTHROPOLOGY

Anthropologische Gesellschaft in Wien (Vienna Anthropological Society): Burgring 7, 1010 Vienna; tel. (1) 52177569; e-mail ag@nhm-wien.ac.at; internet www.ag-wien.org; f. 1870; 300 mems; Pres. Prof. Mag. Dr HERMANN MÜCKLER; Sec. Dr ANTON KERN; publs *Anthropologische Forschungen* (irregular), *Mitteilungen der Anthropologischen Gesellschaft in Wien* (1 a year), *Prähistorische Forschungen* (irregular), *Völkerkundliche Veröffentlichungen* (irregular).

Evangelische Akademie Wien (Evangelical Academy in Vienna): Schwarzspanierstr. 13, 1090 Vienna; tel. (1) 4080695; e-mail akademie@evang.at; internet www.evang-akademie.at; f. 1955; Dir WALTRAUT KOVACIC.

Gesellschaft für die Geschichte des Protestantismus in Österreich (Society for History of Protestantism in Austria): c/o Univ. Prof. Dr Rudolf Leeb, Room 6OG009, Schenkenstr. 8–10, 1010 Vienna; e-mail rudolf.leeb@univie.ac.at; f. 1879; 300 mems; Pres. Prof. Dr RUDOLF LEEB.

Österreichische Gesellschaft für Soziologie (Austrian Sociological Society): Fachbereich Soziologie Technische Universität Wien Paniglgasse 16, 1040 Vienna; tel. (1) 5880127312; e-mail kontakt@oegs.ac.at; internet www.oegs.ac.at; f. 1950; 500 mems; Pres. Prof. Dr JENS DANGSCHAT; publ. *Österreichische Zeitschrift für Soziologie* (4 a year).

Verein für Landeskunde von Niederösterreich (Association for Regional Studies of Lower Austria): Landhauspl. 1, Haus Kulturbezirk 4, 3109 St Pölten; tel. (2742) 900512059; e-mail verein.k2@noel.gv.at; internet www.noel.gv.at/bildung/landeskundliche-forschung/verein-fuer-landeskunde.html; f. 1864; 1,300 mems; Pres. Dr ANTON EGGENDORFER; Gen. Sec. Mag. Dr WILLIBALD ROSNER; publs *Forschungen zur Landeskunde von Niederösterreich*, *Jahrbuch für Landeskunde von Niederösterreich*, *Unsere Heimat* (4 a year).

Verein für Volkskunde (Society of Ethnography and Popular Culture): Gartenpalais Schönborn, Laudongasse 15–19, 1080 Vienna; tel. (1) 4068905; e-mail verein@volkskundemuseum.at; internet www.volkskunde.org/index_verein_vk.htm; f. 1894; promotes Austrian and European folklore; legal representative of Österreichischen Museums für Volkskunde; 900 mems; Pres. Dr WOLFGANG MADERTHANER; Sec. Mag. MATTHIAS BEITL; publs *Österreichische Zeitschrift für Volkskunde* (4 a year), *Volkskunde in Österreich* (12 a year).

Wiener Katholische Akademie (Vienna Catholic Academy): Edith-Stein-Haus, Ebendorferstr. 8/10, 1010 Vienna; tel. (1) 4023917; e-mail wka@edw.or.at; internet www.kath-akademie.at; f. 1945; seminars and lectures, symposia, publs on significant ideological issues; 110 mems; library of 7,000 vols; Protector Erzbischof Cardinal Dr CHRISTOPH SCHÖNBORN; Gen. Sec. Mag. Dr ELISABETH MAIER; publ. *Schriften der Wiener Katholischen Akademie*.

TECHNOLOGY

Österreichische Gesellschaft für Artificial Intelligence (ÖGAI) (Austrian Association for Artificial Intelligence): POB 177, 1014 Vienna; tel. (1) 4016036317; e-mail anfrage@oegai.at; internet www.oegai.at; f. 1981; promotes exploration of principles, methods and applications in the field of artificial intelligence; represents interests of its members in nat. and int. bodies; awards ÖGAI Prize to young scientists; 100 mems; Pres. Dr ERNST BUCHBERGER; Vice-Pres. Dr SILVIA MIKSCH; Sec. Dr HARALD TROST.

Österreichische Gesellschaft für Vermessung und Geoinformation (Austrian Society for Surveying and Geoinformation): Schiffamtsgasse 1–3, 1020 Vienna; tel. (1) 2167551; e-mail office@ovg.at; internet www.ovg.at; f. 1973; 600 mems; library of 3,000 vols; Pres. Dipl.-Ing. GERT STEINKELLNER; Sec. Dipl.-Ing. KARL HAUSSTEINER; publ. *Österreichische Zeitschrift für Vermessung und Geoinformation* (4 a year).

Österreichische Studiengesellschaft für Kybernetik (Austrian Society for Cybernetic Studies): Freyung 6/6, 1010 Vienna; tel. (1) 5336112; e-mail sec@ofai.at; internet www.osgk.ac.at; f. 1969; 1,238 mems (38 ordinary, 1,200 corresp.); Pres. Prof. Dr ROBERT TRAPPL; Sec. Prof. Dr HARALD TROST; publs *Applied Artificial Intelligence: An International Journal* (10 a year), *Cybernetics and Systems: An International Journal* (8 a year), *Reports* (irregular).

Research Institutes

AGRICULTURE, FISHERIES AND VETERINARY SCIENCE

Bundesamt und Forschungszentrum für Landwirtschaft, Wien (Federal Office and Research Centre for Agriculture, Vienna): Straudorfer Str. 1, 2286 Haringsee; tel. (2214) 7100; f. 1995; library of 100,000 vols; Dir-Gen. Hofrat Dipl.-Ing. A. KÖCHL; publs *Die Bodenkultur* (4 a year), *Pflanzenschutz* (4 a year), *Pflanzenschutzberichte* (2 a year).

Bundesamt und Forschungszentrum für Wald (Federal Office and Research Centre for Forests): Seckendorff-Gudent-Weg 8, 1131 Vienna; tel. (1) 878380; e-mail direktion@bfw.gv.at; internet bfw.ac.at; f. 1874; 6 depts, 2 forestry training centres; research focuses on sustainable multi-functional use, management and protection of forest ecosystems and catchment areas for drinking water supply, long-term changes in ecosystems and biodiversity conservation and enhancement and protection against natural hazards and geo-risk management; library of 1,712,731,805 vols of books and journals; Chair. Dipl.-Forstwirt Dr HUBERT DÜRRSTEIN; Vice-Chair. Dr JOHANNES SCHIMA; publ. *BFW-Berichte* (irregular).

Bundesanstalt für Agrarwirtschaft (Federal Institute of Agricultural Economics): Marxergasse 2, 1030 Vienna; tel. (1) 8773651; e-mail office@awi.bmlfuw.gv.at; internet www.awi.bmlfuw.gv.at; f. 1960; socioeconomic research on issues of agricultural policy, food economics, agricultural enterprises and rural areas; library of 52,193 vols, 442 periodicals; Dir Dipl.-Ing. Dr HUBERT PFINGSTNER; Librarian Mag. HUBERT SCHLIEBER; publs *Agrarpolitische Arbeitsbehelfe* (irregular), *Schriftenreihe der Bundesanstalt* (irregular).

Bundesanstalt für Alpenländische Landwirtschaft, Gumpenstein (Federal Research Institute for Agriculture in Alpine Regions, Gumpenstein): Raumberg 38, 8952 Irdning; tel. (3682) 224510; e-mail office@raumberg-gumpenstein.at; internet www.gumpenstein.at/c; f. 1947; research and education facility; research in areas of livestock, animal husbandry, organic farming, plant production and cultural landscape; library of 21,000 vols; Dir Prof. Mag. Dr ALBERT SONNLEITNER; publs *BAL-Berichte*, *BAL-Veröffentlichungen*.

ARCHITECTURE AND TOWN PLANNING

Institut für Angewandte Mechanik (Institute of Applied Mechanics): Technikerstr. 4/II, 8010 Graz; tel. (316) 8737640; e-mail gundula.anger@tugraz.at; internet www.mech.tugraz.at; attached to Graz Univ. of Technology; research and teaching in mechanics regarding civil engineering; research focused on simulation of wave propagation phenomena, modelling of porous and granular media, dynamics with friction; Dir Prof. Dr-Ing. MARTIN SCHANZ.

Institut für Architektur und Landschaft (Institute of Architecture and Landscape): Technikerstraße 4/V, 8010 Graz; tel. (316) 8736311; e-mail ial@tugraz.at; internet www.ial.tugraz.at; attached to Graz Univ. of Technology; Chair. Prof. Dipl.-Ing. KLAUS K. LOENHART.

Institut für Architektur und Medien (Institute of Architecture and Media): Inffeldgasse 10/II, 8010 Graz; tel. (316) 8734721; e-mail barbara.rauch@tugraz.at; internet iam.tugraz.at; attached to Graz Univ. of Technology; Dir Prof. URS LEONHAND HIRSCHBERG.

Institut für Architekturtechnologie (Institute of Architecture Technology): Rechbauerstr. 12/I, 8010 Graz; tel. (316) 8736301; e-mail office@at.tugraz.at; internet at.tugraz.at; attached to Graz Univ. of Technology; Dir Prof. Dipl.-Ing. ROGER RIEWE.

Institut für Architekturtheorie, Kunst- und Kulturwissenschaften (Institute of Architectural Theory, History of Art and Cultural Studies): Technikerstr. 4/3, 8010 Graz; tel. (316) 8736276; e-mail christine.leitgeb@tugraz.at; internet www.kunstundkultur.tugraz.at; attached to Graz Univ. of Technology; conveys knowledge of culture, history and theory of visual arts in the field of architecture; research areas lie in the analysis of architectural and artistic production in culture, media and social sciences; Dir Prof. Mag. Dr ANSELM WAGNER.

Institut für Baubetrieb und Bauwirtschaft (Institute of Construction Management and Economics): Lessingstr. 25/II, 8010 Graz; tel. (316) 8736251; e-mail sekretariat.bbw@tugraz.at; internet www.bbw.tugraz.at; attached to Graz Univ. of Technology; Dir Prof. Dipl.-Ing. HANS LECHNER.

Institut für Eisenbahnwesen und Verkehrswirtschaft (Institute of Railway Engineering and Transport Economy): Rechbauerstr. 12/II, 8010 Graz; tel. (316) 8736216; e-mail office.ebw@tugraz.at; internet www.ebw.tugraz.at; attached to Graz Univ. of Technology; overall railway system focusing on alignment, feasibility studies of new railway connections, public transport systems and solutions of the logistic problems arising; vehicles under spec. view of the wheel-rail-contact, basic research in the range of the ballast bed; studies on transport economics; Dir Prof. Dipl.-Ing. Dr PETER VEIT.

Institut für Gebäude und Energie (Institute of Buildings and Energy): Rechbauerstr. 12, 8010 Graz; tel. (316) 8734751; e-mail ige@tugraz.at; internet www.ige.tugraz.at; attached to Graz Univ. of Technology; pursues the goal of energy-efficient architecture; maximizing the energy performance of buildings by optimization of the form and construction; Dir Prof. BRIAN CODY.

Institut für Gebäudelehre (Institute of Architectural Typologies): Lessingstr. 25/IV, 8010 Graz; tel. (316) 8736291; e-mail r.lenz@tugraz.at; internet www.gl.tugraz.at; attached to Graz Univ. of Technology; Dir Prof. Dipl.-Ing. HANS GANGOLY.

Institut für Hochbau und Bauphysik (Institute of Building Construction and Building Physics): Lessingstr. 25/III, 8010 Graz; tel. (316) 8736241; e-mail office@ihb.tugraz.at; internet www.ihb.tugraz.at; attached to Graz Univ. of Technology; Dir Prof. Mag. Dr Dipl.-Ing. PETER KAUSCH.

Institut für Ingenieurgeodäsie und Messsysteme (Institute of Engineering Geodesy and Measurement Systems): Steyrergasse 30, 8010 Graz; tel. (316) 8736321; e-mail sandra.reinbacher@tugraz.at; internet www.igms.tugraz.at; attached to Graz Univ. of Technology; methodology of engineering geodesy, foundation of the measurement methods in civil engineering, measurement of the geometry and the deformation of objects, monitoring and guidance of processes in civil and geotechnical engineering, measurement systems and sensors, experimental methods and modelling; Head Prof. Dipl.-Ing. Dr FRITZ K. BRUNNER.

Institut für Raumgestaltung (Institute for Spatial Design): Rechbauerstr. 12/II, 8010 Graz; tel. (316) 8736481; e-mail r.krueger@tugraz.at; internet www.raumgestaltung.tugraz.at; attached to Graz Univ. of Technology; focuses on teaching and research; causal analysis of architectural space, perception of space and light; Dir Prof. Mag. IRMGARD FRANK.

Institut für Städtebau (Institute for Urbanism): Rechbauerstr. 12, 8010 Graz; tel. (316) 8736286; e-mail m.haselbacher-berner@tugraz.at; internet www.staedtebau.tugraz.at; attached to Graz Univ. of Technology; architectural research focused on city and energy, urban devt and information technology, epistemology; Dir Prof. Dipl.-Ing. Dr JEAN MARIE CORNEILLE MEUWISSEN.

Institut für Strassen- und Verkehrswesen (Institute of Highway Engineering and Transport Planning): Rechbauerstr. 12/II, 8010 Graz; tel. (316) 8736221; e-mail isv@tugraz.at; internet www.isv.tugraz.at; attached to Graz Univ. of Technology; focuses on GIS-based modelling of transport networks of motorized and non-motorized trips in private, public and freight transport; also research in environment-related traffic issues; Dir Prof. Dr-Ing. MARTIN FELLENDORF.

Institut für Tragwerksentwurf (Institute of Structural Design): Technikerstr. 4/IV, 8010 Graz; tel. (316) 8736211; e-mail tragwerksentwurf@tugraz.at; internet www.ite.tugraz.at; attached to Graz Univ. of Technology; principles of mechanics for bldg constructions and relevant topics; Dir Prof. Dr-Ing. STEFAN PETERS.

Institut für Wasserbau und Wasserwirtschaft (Institute of Hydraulic Engineering and Water Resources Management): Stremayrgasse 10/II, 8010 Graz; tel. (316) 8738861; e-mail hydro@tugraz.at; internet www.hydro.tugraz.at; f. 1865; attached to Graz Univ. of Technology; study of hydraulic structures and their optimization in engineering, fluid engineering, construction and economy, in conjunction with relevant subject areas (esp. geotechnical), and with the quantitative water management principles in accordance with environmental requirements; Dir Prof. GERALD ZENZ.

Österreichisches Institut für Raumplanung (Austrian Institute for Regional Studies and Spatial Planning): Franz Josefs Kai 27, 1010 Vienna; tel. (1) 53387470; e-mail oir@oir.at; internet www.oir.at; f. 1957; planning and consulting services for interaction of economic, social, ecological and technical issues in spatial, urban and regional planning; library of 38,000 vols; Chair. BERND SCHUH; CEO ERICH DALLHAMMER; publ. *RAUM* (4 a year, online (www.raum-on.at)).

ECONOMICS, LAW AND POLITICS

Bundesanstalt Statistik Österreich/Statistik Austria (Statistics Austria): Guglgasse 13, 1110 Vienna; tel. (1) 711280; e-mail info@statistik.gv.at; internet www.statistik.at; f. 1829, ind. federal instn since 2000; provides data on economic, demographic, social, ecological and cultural situation in Austria; library of 170,000 vols; Dir-Gen. Dr KONRAD PESENDORFER; Dir-Gen. Dr GABRIELE PETROVIĆ; publs *Österreichischer Zahlenspiegel* (12 a year), *Statistisches Jahrbuch für Österreich* (1 a year), *Statistische Nachrichten* (12 a year), *Statistische Übersichten* (4 a year).

Dr Karl Kummer Institut für Sozialreform, Sozial- und Wirtschaftspolitik (Institute for Social Reform and Social Politics): Laudongasse 16, 1080 Vienna; tel. (1) 4052674; e-mail office@kummer-institut.at; internet www.kummer-institut.at; f. 1953; consolidates social and welfare policy supported by Christian ideals; emphasizes on corporate social responsibility, work and social partnership, home ownership and middle-sized capital formation, social and health policy, youth and education policy, family and generation politics; Chair. Dr NORBERT SCHNEDL; Exec. Dir Mag. ALEXANDER RAUNER; publ. *Gesellschaft und Politik* (4 a year).

Forschungsinstitut für Altersökonomie (Research Institute for Economics of Ageing): Nordbergstr. 15, Annexe D, 7th Fl., 1090 Vienna; tel. (1) 313365398; e-mail aging@wu-wien.ac.at; internet www.wu.ac.at/altersoekonomie; f. 2006; attached to Vienna Univ. of Economics and Business; Dir Prof. ULRIKE SCHNEIDER.

Forschungsinstitut für Familienunternehmen (Research Institute for Family Business): Augasse 2–6, 1090 Vienna; tel. (1) 313365416; e-mail fofu@wu.ac.at; internet www.wu.ac.at/fofu; attached to Vienna Univ. of Economics and Business; basic and applied research on family businesses; completed projects incl. strategic behaviour and success factors of family; current projects are market orientation in family, success factors and good case studies; Dir Dr HERMANN FRANK.

Forschungsinstitut für Gesundheitsmanagement und Gesundheitsökonomie (Research Institute for Health Care Management and Health Economics): Althanstr. 51, 1090 Vienna; tel. (1) 313364548; e-mail healthcare@wu-wien.ac.at; internet www.wu.ac.at/healthcare; attached to Vienna Univ. of Economics and Business; research on health care facilities as social orgs; effects of management and leadership decisions on staff, business performance indicators and patient outcomes; trains management personnel for health care orgs; Dirs Prof. Dr AUGUST ÖSTERLE; Dir Prof. Dr JOHANNES STEYRER.

Forschungsinstitut für Kooperationen und Genossenschaften (Research Institute for Cooperation and Cooperatives): Augasse 2–6, Upper level 3A, 1090 Vienna; tel. (1) 313364332; e-mail ricc@wu-wien.ac.at; internet www.wu.ac.at/ricc; attached to Vienna Univ. of Economics and Business; Austrian cooperatives' research unit for business admin; deals with intercompany cooperation, cooperatives and their management; Dir Prof. Dr DIETMAR RÖSSL.

Forschungsinstitut Rechenintensive Methoden (Research Institute for Computational Methods): Augasse 2–6, 1090 Vienna; tel. (1) 313365057; e-mail firm-office@wu.ac.at; internet www.wu.ac.at/firm; attached to Vienna Univ. of Economics and Business; devt of advanced computational methods in the areas of finance, information systems; Dir Prof. Dr KURT HORNIK.

Institut für Europäische Integrationsforschung (EIF) (Institute for European Integration Research): Strohgasse 45/DG, 1030 Vienna; tel. (1) 427722401; e-mail eif@univie.ac.at; internet eif.univie.ac.at; f. 1998; attached to Univ. of Vienna; research on EU and its policies across multiple levels; research incl. internal EU policies, EU as externally oriented global actor in policy areas, implementation of the various forms of EU law and the resulting effects; Head Prof. Dr GERDA FALKNER; publs *European Integration online Papers* (irregular, online), *Living Reviews in European Governance* (irregular, online).

Institut für Europäisches Schadenersatzrecht (Institute of European Tort Law): Reichsratsstr. 17/2, 1010 Vienna; tel. (1) 427729651; e-mail etl@oeaw.ac.at; internet www.etl.oeaw.ac.at; f. 2002, present status 2008; attached to Austrian Acad. of Sciences; comparative legal research in tort law; primary focus European law; examines other jurisdictions like USA, S Africa, Israel, Japan and Korea; library of 11,000 vols; Dir Prof. Dr KEN OLIPHANT; publ. *Journal of European Tort Law* (3 a year).

Institut für Höhere Studien (Institute for Advanced Studies): Stumpergasse 56, 1060 Vienna; tel. (1) 59991-122; e-mail communication@ihs.ac.at; internet www.ihs.ac.at; f. 1963; postgraduate training and research in economics and finance, sociology and political science; combines theoretical and empirical research in economics and other social science disciplines; library of 23,500 vols, 500 current periodicals; Dir Prof. Dr CHRISTIAN KEUSCHNIGG; publs *Economics, Sociological and Political Science Series*, *Empirical Economics* (4 a year), *European Societies* (4 a year), *German Economic Revue* (4 a year), *Soziale Sicherheit* (12 a year), *Health System Watch* (4 a year).

Österreichische Forschungsstiftung für Internationale Entwicklung (Austrian Foundation for Development Research): Sensengasse 3, 1090 Vienna; tel. (1) 3174010; e-mail office@oefse.at; internet www.oefse.at; f. 1967; documentation and information on devt aid, developing countries and int. devt, particularly relating to Austria; library of 70,000 vols, 170 periodicals; Dir Dr WERNER RAZA; publs *ÖFSE-Edition* (irregular), *ÖFSE-Forum* (irregular), *Österreichische Entwicklungspolitik Analysen-Berichte-Informationen* (1 a year).

Österreichisches Institut für Wirtschaftsforschung (Austrian Institute of Economic Research): Arsenal, Objekt 20, 1030 Vienna; tel. (1) 7982601; e-mail office@wifo.ac.at; internet www.wifo.ac.at; f. 1927; analyses economic devts in Austria and internationally; 5 research groups: macroeconomics and European economic policy, labour market, income and social security, industrial economics, innovation and int. competition, structural change and regional devts, environment, agriculture and energy; Dir Prof. Dr KARL AIGINGER; publs *Austrian Economic Quarterly*, *Empirica* (3 a year, with Austrian Economic Assen), *Monatsberichte* (12 a year).

Spezialforschungsbereich International Tax Coordination (Special Research Program on International Tax Coordination): Nordbergstr. 15, 1090 Vienna; tel. (1) 313364890; internet www.sfb-itc.at; f. 2003; attached to Vienna Univ. of Business and Economics.

FINE AND PERFORMING ARTS

Abteilung für Inventarisation und Denkmalforschung des Bundesdenkmalamtes (Department of Art Research and Inventory of the Federal Office for the Protection of Monuments): Hofburg, Schweizerhof, Säulenstiege, 1010 Vienna; tel. (1) 53415121; e-mail denkmalforschung@bda.at; internet www.bda.at; f. 1911; research and documentation on works of art in Austria; library of 22,000 vols; Chief Officer Dr ANDREAS LEHNE; publs *Denkmal Heute*, *Österreichische Zeitschrift für Kunst und Denkmalpflege*.

Gesellschaft für vergleichende Kunstforschung (Society of Comparative Art Research): c/o Mag. Paul Mahringer Bundesdenkmalamt, Abteilung für Inventarisation und Denkmalforschung, Hofburg Säulenstiege, 1010 Vienna; tel. (1) 53415192; e-mail paul.mahringer@vergleichende.at; internet www.vergleichende.at/home.html; f. 1934; conducts research, lectures, courses and excursions related to art and publishes the results; Pres. Dr VERONIKA BIRKE; Sec.-Gen. Mag. PAUL MAHRINGER; publ. *Mitteilungen* (3 a year).

Institut für Zeitgenössische Kunst (Institute of Contemporary Art): Inffeldgasse 10/II, 8010 Graz; tel. (316) 8734721; e-mail ikg@tugraz.at; internet izk.tugraz.at; attached to Graz Univ. of Technology; research and practice in the aesthetic field; learning artistic skills and collection of personal experiences in dealing with materials, machines and media with an emphasis on contemporary ways of working; Dir Prof. HANS KUPELWIESER.

Wiener Gesellschaft für Theaterforschung (Viennese Society for Theatre Research): Hofburg, Batthyanystiege, 1010 Vienna; tel. (1) 427748401; e-mail otto.schindler@univie.ac.at; f. 1944; Pres. Prof. Dr WOLFGANG GREISENEGGER; Gen. Sec. Dr OTTO G. SCHINDLER; publs *Jahrbuch*, *Theater in Österreich* (1 a year).

HISTORY, GEOGRAPHY AND ARCHAEOLOGY

Center for Geosciences: Wohllebengasse 12–14, E.04, 1040 Vienna; tel. (1) 515813630; e-mail andrea.berger@oeaw.ac.at; internet www.oeaw.ac.at/gwz; f. 2007; attached to Austrian Academy for Sciences; coordinates 4 commissions that focus on the earth sciences; initiates interdisciplinary geoscientific research projects; acts as liaison between geoscience research and public; Dir Prof. Dr HANS PETER SCHÖNLAUB.

Forschungsgesellschaft Wiener Stadtarchäologie (Research Unit for Archaeology in Vienna): Apollogasse 7, 1070 Vienna; tel. (676) 7215105; internet www.archaeologie-wien.at; Chair. Doz. Dr ORTOLF HARL; publ. *Onomasticon Provinciarum Europae Latinarum*.

Institut für Angewandte Geowissenschaften (Institute of Applied Geosciences): Rechbauerstr. 12, 8010 Graz; tel. (316) 8736361; e-mail geomin@egam.tugraz.at; internet www.egam.tugraz.at; attached to Graz Univ. of Technology; institute of engineering geology, mineralogy and hydrochemistry; engineering geology ensures that geological factors that influence the design, construction and operation of engineering structures are correctly identified, interpreted and presented; mineralogy and hydrochemistry includes the devt and use of natural and synthetic mineral materials, water-rock interaction and the genesis and contamination of natural waters; Dir DANIEL SCOTT KIEFFER.

Institut für Demographie (Institute of Demography): Wohllebengasse 12–14, 1040 Vienna; tel. (1) 515817702; e-mail vid@oeaw.ac.at; internet www.oeaw.ac.at/vid; attached to Austrian Acad. of Sciences; Dir Dr WOLFGANG LUTZ.

Institut für Interdisziplinäre Gebirgsforschung (Institute for Interdisciplinary Mountain Research): Technikerstr. 21A, Otto Hittmair-Pl. 1, 6020 Innsbruck; tel. (512) 50749410; e-mail igf-office@oeaw.ac.at; internet www.mountainresearch.at; f. 2006; attached to Austrian Academy of Sciences; inter- and transdisciplinary research in mountain areas across the world with int. group of scientists; focuses on regional sustainability, global change adaptation; interdependence of man and environment in European mountain regions; Dir Prof. Dr AXEL BORSDORF; publ. *eco.mont* (2 a year).

Institut für Kulturgeschichte der Antike (IKAnt) (Institute for the Study of Ancient Culture): Bäckerstr. 13, 1010 Vienna; tel. (1) 515813483; e-mail antike@oeaw.ac.at; internet www.oeaw.ac.at/antike; f. 2000; attached to Austrian Academy of Sciences; comprehensive cultural-historical problems within a supra-regional range; emphasis on living and residing in antiquity and the early middle ages, sepulchral context and collective ideals, urbanism and settlement-historical transformation processes; library of 2,000 vols; Dir Doz. Mag Dr ANDREAS PÜLZ.

Institut für Realienkunde des Mittelalters und der Frühen Neuzeit (Institute for Medieval and Early Modern Material Culture): Körnermarkt 13, 3500 Krems an der Donau; tel. (2732) 84793; e-mail sekretariat.imareal@sbg.ac.at; internet www.imareal.sbg.ac.at; f. 1969; attached to Univ. of Salzburg; Dir Dr ELISABETH VAVRA; publs *Forschungen* (every 2 years), *Medium Aevum Quotidianum* (3 or 4 a year), *Veröffentlichungen* (every 2 years).

Institute for Geographic Information Science: Schillerstr. 30, 5020 Salzburg; tel. (662) 80447510; e-mail office.giscience@oeaw.ac.at; internet www.oeaw.ac.at/giscience; attached to Austrian Academy of Sciences; researches the concepts and methods for modelling, organizing, analysis and communication of geospatial information; Dir JOSEF STROBL.

LANGUAGE AND LITERATURE

Institut für Österreichische Dialekt- und Namenlexika (Institute for Lexicography of Austrian Dialects and Names): Wohllebengasse 12–14, 1040 Vienna; tel. (1) 5158172707292; e-mail dinamlex@oeaw.ac.at; internet www.oeaw.ac.at/dinamlex; attached to Austrian Acad. of Sciences; f. 1911 as Kommission zur Schaffung des Bayerisch-Österreichischen Wörterbuches und zur Erforschung unserer Mundarten; research in lexicography of dialects and onomastics; major publs written by 7 linguists; has collected a dialect database; Man. Dir Dr INGEBORG GEYER.

MEDICINE

CeMM Research Centre for Molecular Medicine: Lazarettgasse 14, AKH BT 25.3, 1090 Vienna; tel. (1) 4016070011; e-mail office@cemm.oeaw.ac.at; internet www.cemm.oeaw.ac.at; attached to Austrian Academy of Sciences; interdisciplinary research centre in molecular medicine; research focus on cancer, inflammation and immune disorders; Man. Dir Dr GERHARD SCHADLER.

Forschungsinstitut für Biomedizinische Alternsforschung, Universität Innsbruck (Institute for Biomedical Ageing Research, University of Innsbruck): Rennweg 10, 6020 Innsbruck; tel. (512) 50750801; e-mail iba@uibk.ac.at; internet www.uibk.ac.at/iba; f. 1992; attached to Univ. of Innsbruck; aims to study ageing processes at the cellular/molecular level and to define measures to postpone/prevent age-related impairments; researches ageing through immunology, endocrinology, molecular and cell biology; Dir BEATRIX GRUBECK-LOEBENSTEIN.

Institut für Atemgasanalytik (Breath Research Institute): Rathauspl. 4, 6850 Dornbirn; tel. (664) 8051560000; e-mail office-aa@oeaw.ac.at; internet www.oeaw.ac.at/aa; research in the upcoming field of breath analysis enabled diagnosis; Scientific Dir Prof. Dr ANTON AMANN.

NATURAL SCIENCES

General

Institut für Wissenschaft und Kunst (Institute for Science and Art): Berggasse 17/1, 1090 Vienna; tel. (1) 3174342; e-mail iwk.institut@aon.at; internet www.univie.ac.at/iwk; f. 1946; research on women's studies and emigration research; library of 7,000 vols, 100 magazines and newspapers; Pres. Doz. Dr JOHANN DVORAK; publ. *Mitteilungen*.

Institut für Wissenschaftstheorie (Institute for the Philosophy of Science): Linzergasse 16, 5020 Salzburg; tel. (662) 909627; e-mail wissenschaftstheorie@sbg.ac.at; internet www.philosophy-of-science.org; f. 1961; philosophy of science, foundations of logic, mathematics and ethics, philosophy of religion; library of 12,000 vols; Dir Prof. Dr PAUL WEINGARTNER; publ. *Forschungsgespräche* (irregular).

Biological Sciences

Biologische Station Neusiedler See (Biological Station Neusiedler See): Amt d. Burgenl. Landesregierung, Abt. 5, 7142 Illmitz; tel. (2175) 23280; e-mail post.bs-illmitz@speed.at; f. 1971; environmental research, nature conservation, limnology, ornithology, botany, water analysis; Dir Prof. Dr ALOIS HERZIG; publ. *BFB (Biologisches Forschungsinstitut Burgenland)–Berichte* (irregular).

Department für Botanik und Biodiversitätsforschung (Department of Botany and Biodiversity Research): Rennweg 14, 1030 Vienna; tel. (1) 4277-54100; e-mail botanik@univie.ac.at; internet www.botanik.univie.ac.at; f. 1754 (Garden) and 1844 (Institute), current name adopted 2008; library of 61,000 vols, 161 periodicals; Dir Prof. Dr JÜRG SCHÖNENBERGER; publs *Neilreichia* (1 a year), *Österreichische Zeitschrift für Pilzkunde* (1 a year).

Forschungsinstitut für Limnologie, Mondsee (Research Institute for Limnology, Mondsee): Mondseestr. 9, 5310 Mondsee; tel. (43) 512507; internet www.uibk.ac.at/limno; f. 1972; attached to Univ. of Innsbruck; performs basic and applied ecological research on inland waters; Head Dr RAINER KURMAYER.

Gregor Mendel Institute of Molecular Plant Biology GmbH: Dr Bohr-Gasse 3, 1030 Vienna; tel. (1) 790449000; e-mail office@gmi.oeaw.ac.at; internet www.gmi.oeaw.ac.at; f. 2000; attached to Austrian Acad. of Sciences; research in plant molecular biology; covers molecular genetics, basic mechanisms of epigenetics, population genetics, chromosome biology, developmental biology and stress signal transduction; Science Dir Dr MAGNUS NORDBORG.

Institute of Molecular Biotechnology: Dr Bohr-Gasse 3, 1030 Vienna; tel. (1) 79044; internet www.imba.oeaw.ac.at; attached to Austrian Acad. of Sciences; f. 1999; conducts research on basic biological questions at the molecular level; uses cell biology, structural biology, biochemistry, genomics and genetics to tackle these questions; Scientific Dir Prof. Dr JOSEF PENNINGER; Admin. Dir MICHAEL KREBS.

Physical Sciences

Atominstitut der Österreichischen Universitäten (Atomic Institute of the Austrian Universities): Stadion Allee 2, 1020 Vienna; tel. (1) 58801141202; e-mail office@ati.ac.at; internet www.ati.ac.at; f. 1958; research and training in the areas of atomic, nuclear and reactor physics, radiation physics, radiation protection, environmental analytics and radiochemistry, nuclear measurement technology and solid state physics, with quantum physics, quantum optics, low temperature physics and superconductivity as additional focus points of research; Dir Prof. Dipl.-Ing. Dr HANNES-JÖRG SCHMIEDMAYER.

BMLFUW Abteilung VII/3–Wasserhaushalt (Federal Ministry of Agriculture, Forestry, Environment and Water Management Sub-Dept VII/3–Water Balance): Marxergasse 2, 1030 Vienna; tel. (1) 711006942; e-mail wasserhaushalt@bmlfuw.gv.at; internet www.lebensministerium.at; f. 1893; library of 8,000 vols; Head of Div. VII/3 Dr-Ing. REINHOLD GODINA; publs *Hydrographisches Jahrbuch von Österreich* (1 a year), *Hydrological Atlas of Austria*, *Mitteilungsblatt des Hydrographischen Dienstes von Österreich* (irregular).

Geologische Bundesanstalt (Geological Survey of Austria): Neulinggasse 38, Postfach 127, 1031 Vienna; tel. (1) 7125674-0; e-mail office@geologie.ac.at; internet www.geologie.ac.at; f. 1849; represents geo-management in Austria's public sector; conducts geoscientific mapping of Austrian territory, manages databases and publishes results; library of 270,270 vols, 2,897 periodicals, 46,575 geological maps, 9,942 aerial photographs, 16,178 archive items, 14,039 microforms; Dir Dr PETER SEIFERT; publ. *Jahrbuch*.

Institut für Astron- und Teilchenphysik, Universität Innsbruck (Institute of Astro- and Particle Physics, University of Innsbruck): Technikerstr. 25, 6020 Innsbruck; tel. (512) 5076061; e-mail astro@uibk.ac.at; internet astro.uibk.ac.at; f. 1904; attached to Faculty of Mathematics, Computer Science and Physics, Univ. Innsbruck; conducts research on astrophysics, astroparticle physics and particle physics; talks, seminars, public outreach activities; library of 4,598 vols; Dir Prof. Dr SABINE SCHINDLER; publ. *Mitteilungen* (irregular).

Institut für Astronomie der Universität Wien (Vienna University Observatory): Türkenschanzstr. 17, 1180 Vienna; tel. (1) 427753801; e-mail astronomie@univie.ac.at; internet www.astro.univie.ac.at; f. 1755; attached to Faculty of Earth Sciences, Geography and Astronomy, Univ. of Vienna; researches into the history of astronomy, various aspects of stars and planets, galaxies and cosmic matter circuit; library of 21,655 vols; Pres. Prof. Mag Dr FRANZ KERSCHBAUM; publ. *Communications in Asteroseismology*.

Associated Body:

Leopold Figl Observatorium für Astrophysik (Leopold Figl Observatory for Astrophysics): Türkenschanzstr. 17, 1180 Vienna; Mitterschöpfl, Altenmarkt an der Triesting, 2571 Vienna; tel. (1) 427751801; e-mail admin@astro.univie.ac.at; internet astro.univie.ac.at/foa; f. 1969; astronomical research; lab courses for astronomy programme at Univ of Vienna; public outreach; Head of Science Operations Prof. Dr WERNER W. ZEILINGER.

Institut für Hochenergiephysik (Institute of High Energy Physics): Nikolsdorfer Gasse 18, 1050 Vienna; tel. (1) 5447328; e-mail ess@hephy.oeaw.ac.at; internet www.hephy.at; f. 1966; attached to Austrian Acad. of Sciences; Dir Doz. Dr MANFRED KRAMMER.

Institut für Schallforschung (Acoustics Research Institute): Wohllebengasse 12–14/1st Fl., 1040 Vienna; tel. (1) 51582501; e-mail konrad.antonicek@oeaw.ac.at; internet www.kfs.oeaw.ac.at; f. 1972; attached to Austrian Acad. of Sciences; active in 5 major areas: computational acoustics, computational hearing, psychoacoustics, acoustic phonetics, audiological acoustics and mathematics and signal processing in acoustics; Dir Dr PETER BALAZS.

Institut für Weltraumforschung (Space Research Institute): Schmiedlstr. 6, 8042 Graz; tel. (316) 4120400; e-mail office.iwf@oeaw.ac.at; internet www.iwf.oeaw.ac.at; f. 1970; attached to Austrian Acad. of Sciences; covers Austrian activities in solar-system exploration, near-earth space plasma physics and satellite geodesy; involved in int. space projects and nat. space agencies in USA, Japan, France and China; 3 depts: experimental space research, extraterrestrial physics, satellite geodesy; Exec. Dir Prof. Dr WOLFGANG BAUMJOHANN.

Kuffner-Sternwarte (Kuffner Observatory): Johann-Staud-Str. 10, 1160 Vienna; tel. (1) 7295494; e-mail service.astronomie@vhs.at; internet www.kuffner.ac.at; f. 1883; astronomical observatory; incl. instruments such as the great refractor, the heliometre, the meridian circle and the vertical circle; library of 500 vols; Dir Dr PETER HABISON.

Ludwig Boltzmann Institut für Festkörperphysik (Ludwig Boltzmann Institute for Solid State Physics): Nussdorfer Str. 64, 6th Fl., 1090 Vienna; tel. (1) 5132750; e-mail office@lbg.ac.at; internet www.lbg.ac.at; f. 1965; research into semiconductors, conducting polymers and high-temperature superconductors; Gen. Man. Mag. CLAUDIA LINGNER.

Österreichische Geodätische Kommission (Austrian Geodetic Commission): c/o Norbert Höggerl, Bundesamt für Eich unfd Vermessungswesen, Schiffamtsgasse 1–3, 1020 Vienna; tel. (1) 211103201; e-mail norbert.hoeggerl@bev.gv.at; internet www.oegk-geodesy.at; f. 1863; library of 2,000 vols; Pres. Prof. Dr HARALD SCHUH; Sec. NORBERT HÖGGERL; publ. *Österreichische Zeitschrift für Vermessung und Geoinformation*.

Sonnenobservatorium Kanzelhöhe der Universität Graz (Kanzelhöhe Solar Observatory of the University of Graz): Kanzelhöhe 19, 9521 Treffen; tel. (4248) 2717; internet www.solobskh.ac.at; f. 1943; attached to Institute of Physics, Univ. of Graz; conducts systematic observations of the sun and the climate; develops instruments; Dir Prof. Dr ARNOLD HANSLMEIER.

Stefan Meyer Institut für Mittelenergiephysik (Stefan Meyer Institute of Medium Energy Physics): Boltzmanngasse 3, 1090 Vienna; tel. (1) 427729701; e-mail smi@oeaw.ac.at; internet www.oeaw.ac.at/imep; f. 1910, current name adopted 2004; attached to Austrian Acad. of Sciences; conducts research in subatomic physics; focuses on study of fundamental symmetries and interactions; specializes in precision spectroscopy of exotic atoms and exotic meson-nucleus bound states as part of int. collaborations at large-scale research facilities; Dir Prof. Dr EBERHARD WIDMANN.

Umweltbundesamt (Environment Agency Austria): Spittelauer Lände 5, 1090 Vienna; tel. (1) 31304; e-mail office@umweltbundesamt.at; internet www.umweltbundesamt.at; f. 1985; elaboration of scientific studies and basic data for environmental protection policy in Austria; elaboration of recommendations for decision-makers in politics, business and admin. and devt of strategic perspectives and scenarios for the achievement of environmental policy targets in Austria and Europe; library of 20,000 vols, 300 periodicals; Man. Dir GEORGE REBELO.

Zentralanstalt für Meteorologie und Geodynamik (Central Institute for Meteorology and Geodynamics): Hohe Warte 38, 1191 Vienna; tel. (1) 36026; e-mail dion@zamg.ac.at; internet www.zamg.ac.at; f. 1851; provides nat. weather service; acts in all fields of meteorology except aeronautical field; nat. body responsible for geophysics; library of 80,000 vols; Dir Dr MICHAEL STAUDINGER; Sec. HERMI FUERST; publ. *Österreichische Beiträge zu Meteorologie und Geophysik* (irregular).

PHILOSOPHY AND PSYCHOLOGY

Institut für Kultur- und Geistesgeschichte Asiens (Institute for the Cultural and Intellectual History of Asia): Apostelgasse 23, 1030 Vienna; tel. (1) 51581-6400; e-mail office.ias@oeaw.ac.at; internet ikga.oeaw.ac.at; attached to Austrian Acad. of Sciences; Dir Doz. Dr HELMUT KRASSER.

Konrad-Lorenz-Institut für Vergleichende Verhaltensforschung (Konrad Lorenz Institute of Comparative Behavioural Research): Savoyenstr. 1A, 1160 Vienna; tel. (1) 4515812700; e-mail initial.name@klivv.oeaw.ac.at; internet www.oeaw.ac.at/klivv; f. 1945; attached to Austrian Acad. of Sciences; Dir Dr DUSTIN PENN.

Psychotechnisches Institut (Psychotechnical Institute): Augasse 9, 2103 Langenzersdorf; tel. (2244) 30996-0; e-mail psychotech@utanet.at; internet www.psychotech.at; f. 1926; conducts psychological group discussions, questionnaire analysis, business interviews, seminars and lectures; Dir Dr HANS-RICHARD GRÜMM; Dir Dr SUSANNE HACKL-GRÜMM.

RELIGION, SOCIOLOGY AND ANTHROPOLOGY

Institut für Kirchliche Zeitgeschichte (Institute for Contemporary Ecclesiastical History): Mönchsberg 2A, 5020 Salzburg; tel. (662) 842521161; e-mail kirchliche-zeitgeschichte@ifz.kirchen.net; f.

1961; library of 8,500 vols; Dir Doz. Dr ALFRED RINNERTHALER; publs *Hirtenbriefe aus Deutschland, Österreich und der Schweiz* (1 a year), *Publikationen des Instituts für Kirchliche Zeitgeschichte*.

Institut für Realienkunde des Mittelalters und der frühen Neuzeit (Institute for Medieval and Early Modern Material Culture): Körnermarkt 13, 3500 Krems an der Donau; tel. (662) 80444980; e-mail sekretariat.imareal@sbg.ac.at; internet www.imareal.sbg.ac.at; f. 1969; attached to Univ. of Salzburg; research into the diversity of human lifestyles, based on the material culture; basic research in systematic devt of traces of life in the past; in applied research cultural studies are evaluated on the basis of processed material; Dir Dr ELISABETH VAVRA.

Institut für Stadt- und Regionalforschung (Institute for Urban and Regional Research): Postgasse 7/4/2, 1010 Vienna; tel. (1) 515813520; e-mail isr@oeaw.ac.at; internet www.oeaw.ac.at/isr; f. 1946 as Commission for Spatial Research and Reconstruction; current name adopted 1988; attached to Austrian Acad. of Sciences; focuses on interdisciplinary urban and regional devt on nat. and European scale; Dir Prof. Dr HEINZ FASSMANN.

Institut für vergleichende Medien- und Kommunikationsforschung (Institute for Comparative Media and Communication Studies): Postgasse 7/4/1, 1010 Vienna; tel. (1) 515813110; e-mail cmc@oeaw.ac.at; internet www.oeaw.ac.at/cmc; f. 1994 as Commission for Mass Communication History; current name adopted 2013; attached to Austrian Acad. of Sciences and Alpen-Adria-Univ. of Klagenfurt; research on role of media in political communication; participates in numerous nat. and int. cooperative ventures; Dir Prof. Dr Dr MATTHIAS KARMASIN; Sec. Mag. INGRID SERINI.

Mayr-Melnhof Institut für den Christlichen Osten (Mayr-Melnhof Institute of Eastern Christian Studies): Mönchsberg 2A 5020, Salzburg; tel. (662) 842521141; e-mail salzburg@ro-oriente.at; internet www.kirchen.net/mmico; f. 1961; research on Christianity in Middle East, India and (S) Eastern Europe through knowledge of cultural characteristics and religious traditions; library of 15,000 vols; Dir Prof. Dr DIETMAR W. WINKLER.

Vienna Institute of Demography (VID): Wohllebengasse 12–14, 6th Fl., 1040 Vienna; tel. (1) 515817702; e-mail vid@oeaw.ac.at; internet www.oeaw.ac.at/vid; f. 1975; attached to Austrian Acad. of Sciences; demographic research in comparative European demography; focuses on fertility, fertility intentions and family; demography of Austria; population dynamics and forecasting; population economics and health and mortality incl. population ageing and labour, differential health and mortality, and human capital and migration; Dir Prof. Dr WOLFGANG LUTZ.

TECHNOLOGY

Austrian Standards Institute (Österreichisches Normungsinstitut): Heinestr. 38, 1020 Vienna; tel. (1) 21300; e-mail office@as-institute.at; internet www.as-institute.at; f. 1920; library of 236,000 documents (standards) online, 23,000 Austrian, European, int. standards; Pres. Prof. Dr WALTER BARFUß; Man. Dir Ing. Dr GERHARD HARTMANN; publs *AS+ top news* (24 a year), *CONNEX* (6 a year, in German).

Erich-Schmid-Institut für Materialwissenschaft (Erich Schmid Institute of Solid Material Sciences): Jahnstr. 12, 8700 Leoben; tel. (3842) 804112; e-mail maria.fliesser@mu-leoben.at; internet www.oeaw.ac.at/esi; f. 1971; attached to Austrian Acad. of Sciences; performs research on new materials concepts; educates students and scientists; collaborates with industrial and scientific partners; Dir Prof. Dr GERHARD DEHM.

Holzforschung Austria (Wood Research Austria): Arsenal, Franz Grillstr. 7, 1030 Vienna; tel. (1) 79826230; e-mail hfa@holzforschung.at; internet www.holzforschung.at; f. 1948; conducts seminars, confs, workshops, training courses, in-house training; library of 35,000 vols; Dir Dipl.-Ing. Dr MANFRED BRANDSTÄTTER; publs *Literature Database of the Austrian Wood Research Society* (24 a year), *Magazin für den Holzbereich* (4 a year).

Institut für Baustatik (Institute for Structural Analysis): Lessingstr. 25/II, 8010 Graz; tel. (316) 8736181; e-mail ifb@tugraz.at; internet www.ifb.tugraz.at; attached to Graz Univ. of Technology; research in computational mechanics, main research in boundary element method and finite element method; other research priorities are numerical simulation in tunnelling, numerical simulation in physics and computational biomechanics; Dir Prof. Dr -Ing. THOMAS-PETER FRIES.

Institut für Betonbau (Institute of Structural Concrete): Lessingstr. 25, 8010 Graz; tel. (316) 8736191; e-mail betonbau@tugraz.at; internet www.ibb.tugraz.at; attached to Graz Univ. of Technology; teaching and research in the field of structural concrete construction; static and dynamic analysis of un-reinforced, reinforced and prestressed concrete flaccid structures and their structural perfection; composite structures with a dominant share of concrete and masonry structures; library of 1,700 books and magazines; Dir Prof. Dr-Ing. VIET TUE NGUYEN.

Institut für Bodenmechanik und Grundbau (Institute of Soil Mechanics and Foundation Engineering): Rechbauerstr. 12, 8010 Graz; tel. (316) 8736231; e-mail margit.rueckert@tugraz.at; internet soil.tugraz.at; attached to Graz Univ. of Technology; research in soil mechanics and foundation engineering; aims to provide a basis for new technologies and methods in design and construction; research activities include laboratory and in situ tests, devt of constitutive laws for soils and calculations based on numerical methods; Dir Prof. Dipl.-Ing. Dr STEPHAN SEMPRICH.

Institut für Diskrete Mathematik und Geometrie (Institute of Discrete Mathematics and Geometry): Wiedner Hauptstr. 8–10/104, 1040 Vienna; tel. (1) 5880110400; e-mail michael.drmota@tuwien.ac.at; internet www.dmg.tuwien.ac.at; f. 1999; attached to Austrian Acad. of Sciences; Head Dr MICHAEL DRMOTA.

Institut für Felsmechanik und Tunnelbau (Institute of Rock Mechanics and Tunnelling): Rechbauerstr. 12, 8010 Graz; tel. (316) 8738114; e-mail tunnel@tugraz.at; internet www.tunnel.tugraz.at; attached to Graz Univ. of Technology; education and research in the field of rock mechanics and tunnelling; partner to contractors, clients, and consultants in questions of rock engineering; emphasises interdisciplinary cooperation; Dir Prof. Dipl.-Ing. Dr WULF SCHUBERT.

Institut für Holzbau und Holztechnologie (Institute of Timber Engineering and Wood Technology): Inffeldgasse 24/I, 8010 Graz; tel. (316) 8734601; e-mail lignum@tugraz.at; internet www.lignum.at; attached to Graz Univ. of Technology; research in core competencies in the disciplines of timber engineering and wood technology; design and construction sciences in timber engineering and material and structure sciences in wood technology; Dir Prof. Dipl.-Ing. Dr GERHARD SCHICKHOFER.

Institut für Materialprüfung und Baustofftechnologie mit ang TVFA (TVFA, the Institute for Testing and Research in Materials Technology): Stremayrgasse 11, 8010 Graz; tel. (316) 8737151; e-mail office@tvfa.tugraz.at; internet www.tvfa.tugraz.at; attached to Graz Univ. of Technology; research comprises the whole field of the building materials of building construction, engineering and infrastructure; focus on sustainable construction, structural renovation and properties of mineral binders; Dir Prof. Dipl.-Ing. Dr PETER MAYDL.

Institut für Quantenoptik und Quanteninformation (Institute for Quantum Optics and Quantum Information): Boltzmanngasse 3, 1090 Vienna; tel. (1) 427729571; e-mail iqoqi-vienna@oeaw.ac.at; internet iqoqi.at; f. 2003; attached to Austrian Academy of Sciences; 2 brs; theoretical and basic research in quantum optics and quantum information; also focuses on theoretical concepts for realization and implementation of quantum computers, quantum protocols; experimental work is concerned with quantum-optical experiments, realization of quantum computers on basis of individual stored ions; Man. Dir Dr PETER ZOLLER.

Institut für Siedlungswasserwirtschaft und Landschaftswasserbau (Institute of Urban Water Management and Landscape Water Engineering): Stremayrgasse 10/I, 8010 Graz; tel. (316) 8738371; e-mail office@sww.tugraz.at; internet www.sww.tugraz.at; f. 1975; attached to Graz Univ. of Technology; research focuses on management of sewage water systems, sustainable optimization of water infrastructure, hydrological test areas and urban hydrology and hydraulic optimization of sewer systems and treatment plants; Dir Prof. Dipl.-Ing. Dr HARALD KAINZ.

Institut für Stahlbau und Flächentragwerke (Institute for Steel Structures and Shell Structures): Lessingstr. 25/III, 8010 Graz; tel. (316) 8736201; e-mail s.pammer@tugraz.at; internet www.stahlbau.tugraz.at; f. 1988; attached to Graz Univ. of Technology; computer oriented design of steel structures, fatigue design of bridges and their components, stability of thin-walled cylindrical structures and the limit load design of beam-columns of steel; Dir Prof. Dipl.-Ing. Dr RICHARD GREINER.

Institut für Technikfolgen-Abschätzung (Institute of Technology Assessment): Strohgasse 45/5, 1030 Vienna; tel. (1) 515816582; e-mail tamail@oeaw.ac.at; internet www.oeaw.ac.at/ita; f. 1994; attached to Austrian Acad. of Sciences; scientific research at the interface of technology and society; focuses on devt trends, societal consequences and options for shaping technological change; Dir Doz. Dr MICHAEL NENTWICH.

Institut für Wasserbau und Hydrometrische Prüfung (Institute for Hydraulic Engineering and Calibration of Hydrometrical Current-Meters): Severingasse 7, 1090 Vienna; tel. (1) 40268020; e-mail office.iwb@baw.bmlfuw.gv.at; internet www.iwbhp.at; f. 1913; attached to Federal Agency for Water Management; calculation and implementation of measures concerning the protection and maintenance of waters and flood protection; physical model tests and mathematical models for studies in the field of hydraulic engineering; consulting in hydraulic engineering; devt of ecological bed stabilization methods; library of 5,845 vols; Dir Dr MICHAEL HENGL.

Institute for Integrated Sensor Systems: Viktor Kaplan Str. 2, 2700 Wiener Neustadt; tel. (2622) 23420; e-mail office.iiss@oeaw.ac.at; internet www.iiss.oeaw.ac.at; f. 2004; attached to Austrian Academy of Sciences; investigates concepts and methodologies for smart sensors, their design, interconnection, and application; interdisciplinary research in medical technology, electrochemistry, tribology, and micro systems; Head Dipl.-Ing. Dr THILO SAUTER.

Johann Radon Institute for Computational and Applied Mathematics: Altenbergerstr. 69, 4040 Linz; tel. (732) 24685211; e-mail annette.weihs@oeaw.ac.at; internet www.ricam.oeaw.ac.at; attached to Austrian Academy of Sciences; basic research in computational and applied mathematics; research groups in computational mathematics for direct field problems, inverse problems, symbolic computation, analysis of partial differential equations, optimization and control, mathematical imaging; Dir Prof. Dr HEINZ W. ENGL.

KMU Forschung Austria (Austrian Institute for SME Research): Gusshausstr. 8, 1040 Vienna; tel. (1) 5059761; e-mail office@kmuforschung.ac.at; internet www.kmuforschung.ac.at; f. 1954 as Österreichisches Institut für Gewerbeforschung; conducts social and economic research with focus on small and medium-sized enterprises; library of 3,200 vols; Pres. Prof. Dr J. HANNS PICHLER; Dir Dr WALTER BORNETT; Dir Mag. PETER VOITHOFER.

Labor für konstruktiven Ingenieurbau (Laboratory for Structural Engineering): Inffeldgasse 24, 8010 Graz; tel. (316) 8737051; e-mail lki@tugraz.at; internet www.lki.tugraz.at; attached to Graz Univ. of Technology; experimental research on the entire field of structural engineering in cooperation with the theoretically working groups of the constructive institute; Dir Dipl.-Ing. Dr BERNHARD FREYTAG.

Österreichisches Forschungsinstitut für Artificial Intelligence (Austrian Research Institute for Artificial Intelligence): Freyung 6/6, 1010 Vienna; tel. (1) 533611260; e-mail sec@ofai.at; internet www.ofai.at; f. 1984; basic and applied research in language technology, interaction technologies, neural computation and robotics, intelligent music processing and machine learning, intelligent software agents and new media and artificial intelligence and society; library of 3,000 vols; Dir Prof. Dr ROBERT TRAPPL; publs *Applied Artificial Intelligence: An International Journal* (10 a year), *Technical Reports* (irregular).

Österreichisches Forschungsinstitut für Technikgeschichte (ÖFiT) am Technischen Museum in Wien (Austrian Research Institute for the History of Technology at the Museum of Technology in Vienna): Mariahilfer Str. 212, 1140 Vienna; tel. (1) 89998-2500; e-mail helmut.lackner@tmw.at; internet www.tmw.at; f. 1931; Pres. Prof. Dr REINHOLD REITH; publ. *Blätter für Technikgeschichte* (1 a year).

Österreichisches Forschungszentrum Seibersdorf GmbH (Austrian Research Centre, Seibersdorf): 2444 Seibersdorf; tel. (2254) 7800; e-mail seibersdorf@zdfzs.arcs.ac.at; f. 1956; contract research and devt in instrumentation and information technology, process and environmental technologies, engineering, life sciences and systems research; library of 15,500 vols; Dir KONRAD FREYBORN; publ. *OEFSZ Reports*.

Österreichisches Giesserei-Institut (Austrian Foundry Research Institute): Parkstr. 21, 8700 Leoben; tel. (3842) 431010; e-mail office@ogi.at; internet www.ogi.at; f. 1952; services include research and devt, technical advice, material testing, material and component analysis, computed tomography, numerical simulation and seminars and training; library of 2,140 vols; Man. and Tech. Dir Prof. Dr PETER SCHUMACHER; publ. *Giesserei Rundschau* (6 a year).

ÖTI—Institut für Ökologie, Technik und Innovation GmbH (Institute of Ecology, Technology and Innovation GmbH): Spengergasse 20, 1050 Vienna; tel. (1) 54425430; e-mail office@oeti.at; internet www.oeti.at; f. 1967 as Austrian Carpet Research Institute, present name 2009; accredited testing, inspection and certification institute and notified body in textiles, toys and comforters; int. br. offices; Man. Dir DI Dr ERICH ZIPPEL.

Physikalisch-Technische Versuchsanstalt für Wärme- und Schalltechnik am Technologischen Gewerbemuseum (Physical-technical Institute for Research on Heat and Noise Technology at the Technological Industrial Museum): Währingerstr. 59, 1090 Vienna; tel. (1) 33126411; research in heat and refrigeration technology, testing of vibrations, indoor acoustics, noise nuisances, absorption and suppression measurement; Dir F. BRUCKMAYER.

Zentrum für Elektronenmikroskopie Graz (Graz Centre for Electron Microscopy): Steyrergasse 17, 8010 Graz; tel. (316) 8738320; e-mail office@felmi-zfe.at; internet www.felmi-zfe.tugraz.at; f. 1959; attached to Austrian Centre for Electron Microscopy and Nanoanalysis at Graz Univ. of Technology; research centre for electron microscopy and nanocharacterization of materials; facilitates interaction between industry and research; provides results from est. and emerging new methods in the field; library of 2,000 vols; Head Prof. Dipl.-Ing. Dr HOFER FERDINAND.

Libraries and Archives

Admont

Bibliothek der Benediktinerabtei (Library of the Benedictine Abbey): 8911 Admont; tel. (3613) 2312602; e-mail tomaschek@stiftadmont.at; internet www.stiftadmont.at; f. 1074; library within Admont Benedictine Monastery; has 3-vol. giant Bible and Book of Gospels from 1070; 200,000 vols, 1,400 MSS, 530 incunabula; Librarian Mag. Dr JOHANN TOMASCHEK.

Bregenz

Vorarlberger Landesarchiv (Vorarlberg State Archives): Kirchstr. 28, 6900 Bregenz; tel. (5574) 51145005; e-mail landesarchiv@vorarlberg.at; internet www.landesarchiv.at; f. 1898; 25,000 vols; Dir Prof. Dr ALOIS NIEDERSTÄTTER; publ. *Zeitschrift Montfort* (2 a year).

Vorarlberger Landesbibliothek (Vorarlberg State Library): Fluher Str. 4, 6900 Bregenz; tel. (5574) 51144100; e-mail info.vlb@vorarlberg.at; internet www.vorarlberg.at/vlb; f. 1904; 570,000 vols, 1,632 current periodicals incl. depositary copies, 1,632 e-journals, 15,000 postcards, 920 maps, 220,000 photographs; spec. collns incl. late Baroque prayer book MSS, 100 vol. of incunabula; Dir Dr HARALD WEIGEL.

Eisenstadt

Burgenländische Landesbibliothek (Burgenland Provincial Library): Europapl. 1, Landhaus, 7000 Eisenstadt; tel. (2682) 6002358; e-mail post.bibliothek@bgld.gv.at; internet www.burgenland.at/kultur/landesbibliothek; f. 1922; 135,000 vols, 235 periodicals; Dir Dr JAKOB MICHAEL PERSCHY; publs *Burgenländische Forschungen* (2 or 3 a year), *Burgenländische Heimatblätter* (4 a year), *Burgenländische Landesbibliographie* (1 a year).

Burgenländisches Landesarchiv (Burgenland Provincial Archives): Europapl. 1, 7000 Eisenstadt; tel. (2682) 6002358; e-mail post.archiv@bgld.gv.at; f. 1922; Head Dr ROLAND ARIES; publs *Burgenländische Forschungen* (2 a year), *Burgenländische Heimatblätter* (4 a year).

Graz

Steiermärkische Landesbibliothek (Styrian Federal State Library): Kalchberggasse 2, Graz; tel. (316) 8774600; e-mail stlbib@stmk.gv.at; internet www.landesbibliothek.steiermark.at; f. 1811; 750,000 vols, 2,800 periodicals, 2,300 MSS; Dir Mag. KATHARINA KOCHER-LICHEM; publs *Arbeiten aus der Steiermärkischen Landesbibliothek* (irregular), *Steirische Bibliographie* (irregular), *Steirische Zeitungsdokumentation* (irregular).

Steiermärkisches Landesarchiv (Styrian Provincial Archives): Karmeliterpl. 3, 8010 Graz; tel. (316) 8772361; e-mail fald@stmk.gv.at; internet www.landesarchiv.steiermark.at; f. 1811; 100,000 vols; Dir Prof. Dr JOSEF RIEGLER; publs *Ausstellungsbegleiter* (irregular), *Mitteilungen* (1 a year), *Quellen aus steirischen Archiven* (irregular), *Styriaca* (irregular), *Veröffentlichungen* (irregular).

Universitätsbibliothek der Technischen Universität Graz (University Library of Graz University of Technology): Technikerstr. 4, 8010 Graz; tel. (316) 8736151; e-mail service.bibliothek@tugraz.at; internet www.ub.tugraz.at; f. 1875; 650,000 vols, 1,680 journals; Dir EVA BERTHA.

Universitätsbibliothek Graz (University Library, Graz): Universitätspl. 3A, 8010 Graz; tel. (316) 3803100; e-mail ubgraz@uni-graz.at; internet www.uni-graz.at/en/ubwww.htm; f. 1573; 3.6m. vols, 14,000 electronic journals, 2,203 MSS, 1,150 incunabula; mem. of IFLA, LIBER; spec. colln incl. 300,000 objects before 1900; Dir Dr WERNER SCHLACHER.

Heiligenkreuz bei Baden

Stiftsarchiv des Zisterzienserstiftes (Cistercian Abbey Archives): 2532 Heiligenkreuz; tel. (2258) 8703; e-mail information@stift-heiligenkreuz.at; internet www.stift-heiligenkreuz.at; archives since foundation of the monastery in 1133; Archivist Dr FR ALCUIN SCHACHENMAYR; publs *Analecta Cisterciensia*, *Sancta Crux*.

Innsbruck

Tiroler Landesarchiv (Tyrolese Provincial Archives): Michael-Gaismair-Str. 1, 6020 Innsbruck; tel. (512) 5083502; e-mail landesarchiv@tirol.gv.at; internet www.tirol.gv.at/landesarchiv; f. 13th century; 30,000 archival units; Dir Dr WILFRIED BEIMROHR; publs *Tiroler Erbhöfe* (irregular), *Tiroler Geschichtsquellen* (irregular), *Veröffentlichungen des Tiroler Landesarchivs* (irregular).

Universitätsbibliothek Innsbruck (University Library, Innsbruck): Innrain 50, 6010 Innsbruck; tel. (512) 5072401; e-mail ub-hb@uibk.ac.at; internet www.uibk.ac.at/ub; f. 1746; 3.5m. vols, 6,139 print journals, 1,100 MSS, 2,000 incunabula; Dir Dr MARTIN WIESER.

Klagenfurt

Kärntner Landesarchiv (Carinthian Provincial Archives): St Ruprechter Str. 7, 9020 Klagenfurt; tel. (463) 56234; e-mail post

.landesarchiv@ktn.gv.at; internet www .landesarchiv.ktn.gv.at; f. 1904; Dir Dr WILHELM WADL; publ. *Das Kärntner Landesarchiv* (1 a year).

Universitätsbibliothek Klagenfurt (University Library, Klagenfurt): Universitätsstr. 65–67, 9020 Klagenfurt; tel. (463) 2700-9580; e-mail info.bibliothek@uni-klu.ac.at; internet ub.aau.at; f. 1775; 820,000 vols; Dir Mag. LYDIA ZELLACHER (acting).

Klosterneuburg

Bibliothek des Augustiner-Chorherrenstiftes (Library of the Augustine Abbey): Stiftspl. 1, 3400 Klosterneuburg; tel. (2243) 411-151; e-mail info@stift-klosterneuburg.at; internet www.stift-klosterneuburg.at; f. 1114; 260,000 vols, 1,250 MSS, 836 incunabula; Dir Dr HEINZ RISTORY.

Leoben

Universitätsbibliothek Leoben (University Library, Leoben): Franz-Josef-Str. 18, 8700 Leoben; tel. (3842) 402; e-mail office@unileoben.ac.at; internet www.unileoben.ac .at/bibliothek; f. 1840; 265,000 vols, 665 current journals, 4,800 magazine titles; Librarian FRANZ JUREK; Librarian Dr CHRISTIAN HASENHÜTTL.

Linz

Bibliothek der Oberösterreichischen Landesmuseen (Library of the Upper Austrian Provincial Museums): Museumstr. 14, 4010 Linz; tel. (732) 774482-41; e-mail bibliothek@landesmuseum.at; internet www .landesmuseum.at; f. 1836; 160,000 vols; Chief Librarian WALTRAUD FAISSNER.

Oberösterreichische Landesbibliothek (State Library of Upper Austria): Schillerpl. 2, 4021 Linz; tel. (732) 664071-0; e-mail landesbibliothek@ooe.gv.at; internet www .landesbibliothek.at; f. 1774; 450,000 vols; Dir Dr CHRISTIAN ENICHLMAYR; Dir Dr RUDOLF LINDPOINTNER.

Oberösterreichisches Landesarchiv (Provincial Archives of Upper Austria): Anzengruberstr. 19, 4020 Linz; tel. (732) 772014601; e-mail landesarchiv@ooe.gv.at; internet www.landesarchiv-ooe.at; f. 1896; Dir Dr GERHART MARCKHGOTT; publs *Beiträge zur Zeitgeschichte Oberösterreichs* (irregular), *Forschungen zur Geschichte Oberösterreichs* (irregular), *Mitteilungen* (irregular), *Quellen zur Geschichte Oberösterreichs* (irregular).

Universitätsbibliothek der Johannes Kepler Universität Linz: Altenberger Str. 69, 4040 Linz; tel. (732) 2468 9380; e-mail bibliothek@jku.at; internet www.jku.at/ub/content; f. 1965; 1,106,616 vols, 22,704 periodicals; Dir Dr SUSANNE CASAGRANDA.

Melk

Bibliothek des Benediktinerklosters Melk in Niederösterreich (Library of the Melk Benedictine Monastery in Lower Austria): 3390 Stift Melk; tel. (2752) 555; e-mail bibliothek@stiftmelk.at; internet www .stiftmelk.at; 80,000 vols (mostly pre-20th-century), 1,800 codices, 750 incunabula; Librarian Dr GOTTFRIED GLASSNER; Librarian Mag. BERNADETTE KALTEIS; publ. *Thesaurus Mellicensis* (irregular).

Salzburg

Bibliothek der Benediktiner Erzabtei St Peter (Library of the Benedictine Abbey of St Peter): St. Peter-Bezirk 1/Postfach 113, 5010 Salzburg; tel. (662) 844576141; e-mail bibliothek@erzabtei.at; internet www .stift-stpeter.at; f. 700; 120,000 vols, 1,300 MSS, 899 incunabula, 2,000 journals; Dir Mag. SONJA FÜHRER.

Salzburger Landesarchiv (Salzburg Provincial Archives): Michael Pacher Str. 40, 5020 Salzburg; tel. (662) 80424527; e-mail landesarchiv@salzburg.gv.at; internet www .salzburg.gv.at/archive.htm; f. 1875; 35,000 photographs, 811 furniture, paintings, crests and seals; 1,000 leaves of graphic arts colln, 1,156 posters and 334 modern calendars; Dir Dr OSKAR DOHLE.

Universitätsbibliothek Salzburg (Salzburg University Library): Hofstallgasse 2–4, 5020 Salzburg; tel. (662) 804477550; e-mail info.hb@sbg.ac.at; internet www .uni-salzburg.at/bibliothek; f. 1623; 2m. vols, 1,100 MSS, 2,400 incunabula, 564 drawings, 1,546 prints; spec. collns incl. 5,600 rare books; Dir Mag. Dr URSULA SCHACHL-RABER.

Sankt Florian

Bibliothek des Augustiner-Chorherrenstiftes (Library of the Augustine Canonical Foundation): Stiftstr. 1, 4490 St Florian; tel. (7224) 890254; e-mail bibliothek@stift-st-florian.at; internet www .stift-st-florian.at; f. 1071; 150,000 vols, 920 MSS, 952 incunabula; Dir Prof. Dr KARL REHBERGER.

Sankt Pölten

Bundesstaatliche Paedagogische Bibliothek beim Landesschulrat für Niederösterreich (Library of the Lower Austrian Education Authority): Rennbahnstr. 29, 3109 St Pölten; tel. (2742) 2801482; e-mail pbn@lsr-noe.gv.at; internet pbn.lsr-noe.gv.at; f. 1923; 173,000 vols, 374 periodicals; Dir Mag. ERNST CHORHERR.

Niederösterreichische Landesbibliothek (Lower Austrian Provincial Library): Landhauspl. 1, Haus Kulturbezirk 3, 3109 St Pölten; tel. (2742) 900512847; e-mail post.k3@noel.gv.at; internet www.noe .gv.at/landesbibliothek; f. 1813; 300,000 vols, 4,000 newspapers and periodicals, 20,000 maps; Dir Dr GEBHARD KÖNIG.

Niederösterreichisches Landesarchiv (Lower Austrian Provincial Archives): Landhauspl. 1, Haus Kulturbezirk 4, 3109 St Pölten; tel. (2742) 9005-12059; e-mail post .k2archiv@noel.gv.at; internet www.noe.gv .at/bildung/landesarchiv-.html; f. 1513; archives of the province of Lower Austria; preserves state representation, documents, files, MSS since its inception; 31,000 vols; Dir Mag. Dr WILLIBALD ROSNER; publs *Mitteilungen*, *NÖLA*.

Seckau

Bibliothek der Benediktinerabtei (Library of the Benedictine Abbey): 8732 Seckau; f. 1883; 160,000 vols; Dir Dr P. BENNO ROTH.

Vienna

AK Bibliothek Wien für Sozialwissenschaften (Chamber of Labour Library for Social Sciences): Prinz Eugenstr. 20–22, 1040 Vienna; tel. (1) 501652452; e-mail bibliothek@akwien.at; internet wien .arbeiterkammer.at/bibliothek; f. 1922; 470,000 vols, 850 periodicals; Dir Dr HERWIG JOBST; Vice-Dir INGE NEUBÖCK; publ. *Jahrbuch der AK Biboiothek Wien für Sozialwissenschaften*.

Archiv, Bibliothek und Sammlungen der Gesellschaft der Musikfreunde in Wien (Archives, Library and Collections of the Society of Friends of Music in Vienna): Bösendorferstr. 12, 1010 Vienna; tel. (1) 505868144; e-mail office@a-wgm.com; internet www.a-wgm.com; f. 1812; consists of music and letters autographs, music MSS, file archive of the history of society and the conservatory; handwritten and printed books, medieval MSS and tablatures, song books, magazines and other periodicals, libretti, printed documents; historical and non-European musical instruments, music memorabilia, portrait, picture collns, busts, statuettes, reliefs and medals; 23,000 vols; 73,000 scores, historical material; Dir Prof. Dr Dr OTTO BIBA.

Archiv der Universität Wien (Archives of the University of Vienna): Postgasse 9, 1010 Vienna; tel. (1) 427717201; e-mail archiv@univie.ac.at; internet bibliothek.univie.ac.at/archiv; f. 1365; preserving records of the Univ. of Vienna from 14th to 20th century; Archivist THOMAS MAISEL.

Archiv des Schottenstiftes (Schotten Abbey Archives): Schottenstift Wien, Freyung 6, 1010 Vienna; tel. (1) 53498140; e-mail archiv@schottenstift.at; internet www .schottenstift.at; f. 1155; 200,000 vols, 750 MSS, 442 incunabula, 2,500 handwritten church music compositions, 600 printed music scores; Archivist MAXIMILIAN A. TROFAIER; Librarian P. AUGUSTINUS ZEMAN.

Bibliothek, Archiv, Sammlungen: Information & Service Österreichische Akademie der Wissenschaften (Library, Archive, Collections: Information & Service of Austrian Academy of Sciences): Dr-Ignaz-Seipel-Pl. 2, 1010 Vienna; tel. (1) 515811600; e-mail bibliothek@oeaw.ac.at; internet www .oeaw.ac.at/biblio; f. 1847; 376,779 vols; Dir Prof. Dr CHRISTINE OTTNER-DIESENBEGRER; Librarian IRMTRAUD SCHÖRG.

Bibliothek der Bundesanstalt Statistik Österreich (Library of Statistics Austria): Guglgasse 13, 1110 Vienna; tel. (1) 71128-7814; e-mail alois.gehart@statistik.gv.at; f. 1829; 175,000 vols; Dir and Chief Librarian Dr ALOIS GEHART.

Bibliothek der Mechitharisten-Congregation (Library of the Mechitharisten-Congregation): Mechitaristengasse 4, 1070 Vienna; tel. (1) 5236417; e-mail vahanhov58@hotmail.com; internet www .mechitaristen.org; f. 1773; 150,000 vols, 3,000 Armenian MSS, all current Armenian newspapers and periodicals; Dir P. VAHAN HOVAGIMIAN; publ. *Handes Amsorya* (1 a year).

Bibliothek der Österreichischen Geographischen Gesellschaft (Library of the Austrian Geographical Society): Nottendorfer Gasse 2, 1030 Vienna; tel. (1) 5237974; e-mail kanzlei@oegg.info; internet arcims.isr .oeaw.ac.at/website/oegg/oegg.htm; f. 1856; 22,000 vols of monographs, 41,000 maps and globes; Librarian Dr PETER FRITZ.

Bibliothek der Wirtschaftskammer Wien (Vienna Chamber of Commerce Library): Stubenring 8–10, 1010 Vienna; tel. (1) 514501370; e-mail bibliothek@wkw.at; internet portal.wko.at; f. 1849; 200,000 vols.

Bibliothek des Bundesministeriums für Finanzen (Library of the Ministry of Finance): Johannesgasse 5, 1010 Vienna; tel. (1) 51433501143; e-mail bibliothek@bmf .gv.at; internet www.bmf.gv.at; f. 1810; 200,000 vols; Head of Library Mag. PATRIZIA RABA.

Bibliothek des Bundesministeriums für Land- und Forstwirtschaft, Umwelt und Wasserwirtschaft (Library of the Federal Ministry of Agriculture, Forestry, the Environment and Water Management): Stubenring 1, 1012 Vienna; tel. (1) 71100; e-mail ingrid.saberi@lebensministerium.at; f. 1868; 127,500 vols; Librarian Mag. INGRID SABERI.

Bibliothek des Bundesministeriums für Soziale Sicherheit, Generationen und Konsumentenschutz (Library of the Federal Ministry for Social Security and Consumer Protection): Stubenring 1, 1010 Vienna; tel. (1) 711006143; e-mail ilga

.kubela@bmsg.gv.at; f. 1917; 150,000 vols; Dir ILGA ANNA KUBELA.

Bibliothek des Instituts für Österreichische Geschichtsforschung (Library of the Institute of Austrian Historical Research): Dr Karl Lueger Ring 1, 1010 Vienna; tel. (1) 427727205; e-mail paul .herold@univie.ac.at; internet www.univie.ac .at/geschichtsforschung/biblio.htm; f. 1854; collns based on the teaching and research environment and the tasks of the institute; institute files since 1854; 75,000 vols, 200 periodicals; Librarian Mag. Dr PAUL HEROLD.

Bibliothek des Österreichischen Patentamtes (Library of the Austrian Patent Office): Dresdner Str. 87, 1200 Vienna; tel. (1) 53424153; e-mail bibliothek@patentamt .at; internet www.patentamt.at; f. 1899; 26,000,000 vols; Dir Dr INGRID WEIDINGER; Librarian WILHELM KORINEK; publs *Österreichischer Markenanzeiger*, *Österreichischer Musteranzeiger*, *Österreichisches Gebrauchsmusterblatt*, *Österreichisches Patentblatt*.

Bibliothek des Österreichischen Staatsarchivs (Library of the Austrian State Archives): Nottendorfer Gasse. 2, 1030 Vienna; tel. (1) 79540115; e-mail stabpost@ oesta.gv.at; internet www.oesta.gv.at; f. 1984 by combining all libraries in the state archives; 800,000 vols; Dir Dr GERHARD ARTL.

Büchereien Wien (Vienna Public Libraries): Urban-Loritz-Pl. 2A, 1070 Vienna; tel. (1) 400084510; e-mail post@buechereien .wien.at; internet www.buechereien.wien.at; f. 1945; 1.5m. vols, 270,000 audio media items; Chief Librarian MARKUS FEIGL.

Clusterbibliothek (Cluster Library): Bundesministerium für Wissenschaft, Forschung und Wirtschaft, Stubenring 1, 1011 Vienna; tel. (1) 711005483; e-mail clusterbibliothek@ bmwfw.gv.at; internet www.bmwfw.gv.at; 550,000 vols, 850 journals, 300 loose-leaf editions; Dir Dr BRIGITTA KOHLERT-WINDISCH.

Diözesanarchiv Wien (Vienna Diocesan Archives): Wollzeile 2/3, 1010 Vienna; tel. (1) 51552; e-mail daw@edw.or.at; internet www.erzdioezese-wien.at; f. 1936; history of archdiocese of Vienna and of parishes and convents in Vienna and the E part of lower Austria; 75,000 vols, 800 periodicals, 9,000 documents and files; Dir JOHANN WEIẞENSTEINER.

Fachbereichsbibliothek Rechtswissenschaften (Faculty Library of Legal Studies): Schottenbastei 10–16, 1010 Vienna; tel. (1) 427716311; e-mail fb-recht@univie.ac.at; internet bibliothek.univie.ac.at/fb-rewi; f. 1922; 365,000 vols, 800 periodicals; Dir Dr THOMAS LUZER.

Österreichische Nationalbibliothek (Austrian National Library): Josefspl. 1, POB 308, 1015 Vienna; tel. (1) 53410444; e-mail information@onb.ac.at; internet www .onb.ac.at; picture archives and graphics dept, map dept, dept of music, literary archives, dept of papyri, dept of planned languages, dept of MSS and rare books, archives of the Austrian folk song institute; 8 spec. collns and main library; 9,808,728 vols, 3,768,728 books and periodicals, 8,030 incunabula, 18,379 microforms, 296,850 maps, 708 globes, 135,288 vols of printed music, 40,053 audiovisual items, 3,085,129 pictures, 141,065 papyri and 378,876 other materials (ex libris and other collns); Dir-Gen. Dr JOHANNA RACHINGER; publs *Ausstellungskataloge* (irregular), *Biblios. Beiträge zu Buch, Bibliothek und Schrift* (every 2 years), *Corpus Papyrorum Raineri*, *Mitteilungen aus der Papyrussammlung* (irregular), *NILUS* (irregular), *Profile. Magazin des Literaturarchivs der Österreichischen Nationalbibliothek* (irregular), *Sichtungen* (1 a year).

Österreichische Zentralbibliothek für Physik & Fachbereichsbibliothek Chemie (Austrian Central Library for Physics and Chemistry Library): Boltzmanngasse 5, 1090 Vienna; tel. (1) 427727600; e-mail infophysik.ub@univie.ac.at; internet www .zbp.univie.ac.at; f. 1980 as Central Library for Physics in Vienna; current name adopted 2000; attached to Vienna Univ. Library; Austrian National INIS Centre; depository library for USAEC/USDOE report colln; acquires, develops physics-related literature and information sources; 380,000 vols, 2,890 periodicals, 1,175,000 microfiches; Dir Mag. BRIGITTE KROMP.

Österreichisches Staatsarchiv (Austrian State Archives): Nottendorfer Gasse 2, 1030 Vienna; tel. (1) 795400; e-mail gdpost@oesta .gv.at; internet www.oesta.gv.at; f. 1945; 177,700 linear m of shelves; Dir-Gen. Prof. Dr LORENZ MIKOLETZKY; publ. *Mitteilungen des österreichischen Staatsarchivs*.

Parlamentsbibliothek (Library of Parliament): Dr Karl Renner-Ring 3, 1017 Vienna; tel. (1) 401100; e-mail bibliothek@parlament .gv.at; internet www.parlament.gv.at/ bibliothek; f. 1869; 347,000 vols, 270 journals and newspapers; Dir Dr ELISABETH DIETRICH-SCHULZ; Deputy Dir Dr SIEGLINDE OSIEBE.

Universitätsbibliothek der Akademie der bildenden Künste Wien (Library of the Academy of Fine Arts): Schillerpl. 3, 1010 Vienna; tel. (1) 588162300; e-mail b.bastl@ akbild.ac.at; internet www.akbild.ac.at/ portal/einrichtungen/universitatsbibliothek; f. 1773; attached to Academy of Fine Arts Vienna; exhibitions, lectures, presentation of new books; main collecting areas: architecture, art history, conservation and restoration, contemporary art, cultural studies, education in the arts, visual arts; 200,000 vols, 130 periodicals, spec. collns incl. 10,000 historical holdings with 5 incunabula; Dir Dr BEATRIX BASTL.

Universitätsbibliothek der Technischen Universität Wien (Vienna University of Technology Library): Resselgasse 4, 1040 Vienna; tel. (1) 58801-44001; e-mail info@ub .tuwien.ac.at; internet www.ub.tuwien.ac.at; f. 1815; 1,325,500 vols; Head EVA RAMMINGER; Deputy Head FRIEDRICH NEUMAYER.

Universitätsbibliothek der Universität für Musik und darstellende Kunst Wien (Library of the Vienna University for Music and Dramatic Art): Lothringerstr. 18, 1030 Vienna; tel. (1) 711558101; e-mail infobib@ mdw.ac.at; internet www.ub.mdw.ac.at; f. 1909; 250,000 vols, 52,000 audiovisual media items; Dir MICHAEL STAUDINGER.

Universitätsbibliothek der Veterinärmedizinischen Universität Wien (University Library of Vetmeduni Vienna): Veterinärpl. 1, 1210 Vienna; tel. (1) 250771414; e-mail bibliothekinfo@ vetmeduni.ac.at; internet www.vu-wien.ac .at/bibl; f. 1777; 218,380 vols, 692 periodicals; Head of Library CLAUDIA HAUSBERGER.

Universitätsbibliothek der Wirtschaftsuniversität Wien (Library of the Vienna University of Economics and Business): Augasse 2–6, 1090 Vienna; tel. (1) 313364990; e-mail library@wu.ac.at; internet www.wu.ac.at/library; f. 1898; 800,000 vols; Dir NIKOLAUS BERGER.

Universitätsbibliothek und Universitätsarchiv der Universität für Bodenkultur Wien (Library and Archives of the University of Natural Resources and Applied Life Sciences, Vienna): Peter-Jordanstr. 82, 1190 Vienna; tel. (1) 476542060; e-mail ub .support@boku.ac.at; internet www.boku.ac .at/bib.html; f. 1872; 570,000 vols, 1,300 periodicals, 14,900 dissertations, 3,000 e-journals; Dir Mag. MARTINA HÖRL.

Universitätsbibliothek Wien (Vienna University Library): Dr Karl Lueger Ring 1, 1010 Vienna; tel. (1) 427715001; e-mail direktion@univie.ac.at; internet bibliothek .univie.ac.at; f. 1365; attached to Univ. of Vienna; 6.6m. vols; Dir Hofrätin Mag. MARIA SEISSL.

Wiener Stadt- und Landesarchiv (Municipal and Provincial Archives of Vienna): Rathaus, 1082 Vienna; Guglgasse 14, Gasometer D, 11 Vienna; tel. (1) 400084808; e-mail post@m08.magwien.gv.at; internet www.wien.gv.at/kultur/archiv; f. 1889; 35,000 m of archives; cartographic colln of 50,000 plans, 20,000 photos, 439 MSS, 550 pieces of commemorative sheets; Dir Mag. Dr BRIGITTE RIGELE; publ. *Veröffentlichungen*.

Wiener Stadt- und Landesbibliothek (Vienna City and Provincial Library): Rathaus, 1082 Vienna; tel. (1) 400084920; e-mail post@wienbibliothek.at; internet www .stadtbibliothek.wien.at; f. 1856; 550,000 vols, 250,000 MSS, 100,000 musical items, 100,000 MSS musical items, 300,000 posters; Dir Dr SYLVIA MATTL-WURM.

Zentralarchiv des Deutschen Ordens (Central Archive of the Teutonic Order): Singerstr. 7, 1010 Vienna; tel. (1) 5121065261; e-mail zentralarchiv@ deutscher-orden.at; internet www .deutscher-orden.at; f. 1852; 11,668 vols, 12,000 documents; Archivist Mag. Dipl. FRANK BAYARD.

Zentralbibliothek im Justizpalast (Central Library of the Palace of Justice): Schmerlingpl. 11, 1011 Vienna; tel. (1) 521520; e-mail ogh.bibliothek@justiz.gv.at; internet www.ogh.gv.at/zentralbibliothek; f. 1829; attached to Supreme Court of Justice; 145,000 vols, 199 legal journals (Austria, Germany, Switzerland and Liechtenstein); Dir GABRIELE SVIRAK.

Museums and Art Galleries

Bad Deutsch-Altenburg

Archäologisches Museum Carnuntinum (Carnuntinum Archaeological Museum): Badgasse 40–46, 2405 Bad Deutsch-Altenburg; tel. (2165) 216333770; internet www .carnuntum.co.at/park/archaeologisches-museum-carnuntinum; f. 1904; attached to Archaeological Park Carnuntinum; library of 12,000 vols; Curator Mag. FRANZ HUMER.

Bregenz

Vorarlberger Landesmuseum (Vorarlberg Provincial Museum): Kornmarktpl 1, 6900 Bregenz; tel. (5574) 46050; e-mail info@vlm .at; internet www.vlm.at; f. 1857; archaeology, art and folklore of the region; 150,000 objects from the Mesolithic period to the present, 24 oil paintings, 350 graphics; reopened 2013 after major renovation; Dir Dr ANDREAS RUDIGIER; publ. *Jahrbuch*.

Eggenburg

Krahuletz Museum Eggenburg: Krahuletzpl. 1, 3730 Eggenburg; tel. (2984) 34003; e-mail gesellschaft@krahuletzmuseum.at; internet www.krahuletzmuseum.at; f. 1902; Dir Dr JOHANNES M. TUZAR; publ. *Katalogreihe Krahuletz-Museum*.

Eisenstadt

Burgenländisches Landesmuseum (Burgenland Provincial Museum): Museumgasse 1–5, 7000 Eisenstadt; tel. (2682) 6001234; e-mail landesmuseum@bgld.gv.at; internet www.burgenland.at/landesmuseum; f. 1926; archaeology, geology, history of art, natural history, ethnology, numismatics, history of music, economic history of Burgenland; library of 31,000 vols; Dir Dr JOSEF TIEFENBACH; publ. *Wissenschaftliche Arbeiten aus dem Burgenland*.

Furth bei Göttweig

Graphische Sammlung und Kunstsammlungen Stift Göttweig (Göttweig Abbey Graphic Art Collection): Stift Göttweig, 3511 Furth bei Göttweig; tel. (2732) 85581226; e-mail graph.kabinett@stiftgoettweig.at; internet www.stiftgoettweig.at; f. 1714; graphic art from the 16th century to the present, music, coins and medals; 32,000 engravings; library of 280,000 vols (history, law, theology, history of art, sciences), 1,110 MSS, 1,120 incunabula, 2,750 archives (1054–1900); Curator Prof. Dr GREGOR MARTIN LECHNER; Deputy Curator Mag. BERNHARD RAMEDER.

Graz

Universalmuseum Joanneum: Mariahilferstr. 2–4, 8020 Graz; tel. (316) 80170; e-mail welcome@museum-joanneum.at; internet www.museum-joanneum.at; f. 1811; 4.5m. objects related to history, archaeology; natural history, art (exhibits housed on several sites); picture and sound archives, incl. Styrian armoury colln, coin cabinet, hunting museum, sculpture park, agriculture museum, etc.; Dir PETER PAKESCH; Dir Dr WOLFGANG MUCHITSCH.

Innsbruck

Kaiserliche Hofburg (Imperial Palace): Rennweg 1, 6020 Innsbruck; tel. (512) 587186; e-mail hofburg.ibk@burghauptmannschaft.at; internet www.hofburg-innsbruck.at; built as residence of the Tyrolean provincial rulers under Archduke Sigismund the Rich and extended under Emperor Maximilian I (1459–1519); Maria Theresia (1717–80) rebuilt the Palace in the late Viennese baroque style; spec. exhibitions throughout the year; Dir WALTRAUD SCHREILECHNER.

Kunsthistorisches Museum Sammlungen Schloss Ambras (Museum of Fine Art Collections, Ambras Castle): Schloss str. 20, 6020 Innsbruck; tel. (1) 525244802; e-mail info.ambras@khm.at; internet www.schlossambras-innsbruck.at; f. 1580; Dir Mag. Dr VERONIKA SANDBICHLER; Asst EVELYN TAURER.

Museum im Zeughaus (Zeughaus Museum): Zeughausgasse, 6020 Innsbruck; tel. (512) 59489-313; e-mail zeughaus@tiroler-landesmuseen.at; internet www.tiroler-landesmuseen.at; f. 1973; Dir WOLFGANG MEIGHÖRNER; Curator for Historical Collns Dr CLAUDIA SPORER-HEIS.

Tiroler Landesmuseum Ferdinandeum (Tyrol Provincial Museum): Museumstr. 15, 6020 Innsbruck; tel. (512) 59489; e-mail sekretariat@tiroler-landesmuseum.at; internet www.tiroler-landesmuseum.at; f. 1823; ind. graphics colln established in 1976; historical colln; art history colln divided into older art history and modern; ancient musical instruments, music supplies and materials to Tyrolean music history; natural sciences colln consisting of colln of earth science, botanical, zoological and spec. collns; early provincial Roman collns; library of 240,000 vols; Dir Dr WOLFGANG MEIGHÖRNER; publs *Ferdinandea* (4 a year), *Veröffentlichungen des Tiroler Landesmuseums Ferdinandeum* (1 a year).

Tiroler Volkskunstmuseum (Tyrol Folk Art Museum): Universitätsstr. 2, 6020 Innsbruck; tel. (512) 59489510; e-mail volkskunstmuseum@tirol.gv.at; internet www.tiroler-volkskunstmuseum.at; f. 1929; local folk arts and crafts; focus on arts and crafts, cottage industries, popular religiosity, masks and costumes of the area; library of 2,940 vols; Dir Dr HERLINDE MENARDI.

Klagenfurt

Landesmuseum für Kärnten (Provincial Museum of Carinthia): Museumgasse 2, 9021 Klagenfurt; tel. (50) 53630599; e-mail willkommen@landesmuseum.ktn.gv.at; internet www.landesmuseum-ktn.at; f. 1844; history, natural history, archaeology, art, folk arts and crafts; library of 130,000 vols; Dir Mag. ERICH WAPPIS; publs *Archiv für Vaterländische Geschichte und Topographie*, *Carinthia I* (archaeology, history, history of art, and folklore), *Carinthia II* (science), *Kärntner Heimatleben*.

Landesmuseum für Kärnten, Kärntner Botanikzentrum (Carinthian Botanic Centre): Prof.-Dr-Kahler-Pl. 1, 9020 Klagenfurt am Woerthersee; tel. (463) 53630531; e-mail kbz@landesmuseum.ktn.gv.at; internet www.landesmuseum.ktn.gv.at; f. 1862, current location 1958; cultivation of central and southern Alpine flora; school and adult education in botany and nature conservation; collns of bromeliads, succulents, poisonous and medicinal herbs, spices and useful plants, fossils (6,000 specimens); ethnobotanical and carpological collns; herbarium of 160,000 phanerogams and 50,000 cryptogams; garden for the blind; library of 15,000 vols, 20,000 offprints, slides, biographical and bibliographical collns; Curator Mag. Dr ROLAND K. EBERWEIN; Curator Dr HELENE RIEGLER-HAGER; Librarian SONJA KUSS; publs *Index Seminum Klagenfurt* (1 a year), *Wulfenia* (1 a year).

Krems

WEINSTADT Museum (Museum of the Wine City): Körnermarkt 14, 3500 Krems; tel. (2732) 801567; e-mail museum@krems.gv.at; internet www.weinstadtmuseum.at; f. 1996; Dir Dr FRANZ SCHÖNFELLNER.

Kremsmünster

Sternwarte Kremsmünster (Kremsmünster Observatory): Benediktinerstift 4550 Kremsmünster; tel. (7583) 5275; e-mail sternwarte.kremsmuenster@telecom.at; internet members.nextra.at/stewar; f. 1748; geological, palaeontological and prehistoric collns; focus on folklore, ethnology, history of civilization; also museum of astronomy; showcases devt of scientific research for quarter of a millennium; library of 25,000 vols; Dir Mag. Dr P. AMAND KRAML; publ. *Naturwissenschaftliche Sammlungen Kremsmünster* (irregular).

Linz

Lentos Kunstmuseum Linz: Ernst-Koref-Promenade 1, 4020 Linz; tel. (732) 70703600; e-mail info@lentos.at; internet www.lentos.at; f. 1948 as Neue Galerie der Stadt Linz; current name adopted 2003; gallery of contemporary art with paintings (ranging from Klimt, Schiele and Kokoschka to Arnulf Rainter, Karel Appel and Hermann Nitsch), drawings, prints, posters and sculptures since 19th century; 1,600 works of painting, 450 sculpture and art objects; 10,000 graphics, incl. 1,100 photo exhibits; library of 30,000 vols, 25 magazines of visual art; Dir for Art STELLA ROLLIG.

Oberösterreichische Landesmuseen (State Museums for Upper Austria): Museumstr. 14, 4010 Linz; tel. (732) 7744820; e-mail info@landesmuseum.at; internet www.landesmuseum.at; f. 1833; library of 130,000 vols; Dir Mag. Dr PETER ASSMANN; publs *Beiträge zur Naturkunde Oberösterreichs*, *Denisia*, *Linzer biologische Beiträge*, *Neues Museum*, *Stapfia*, *Studien zur Kulturgeschichte von Oberösterreich*, *Vogelkundliche Nachrichten aus Oberösterreich*.

St Pölten

Niederösterreichisches Landesmuseum (Provincial Museum of Lower Austria): Kulturbezirk 5, 3109 St Pölten; tel. (2742) 908090; e-mail info@landesmuseum.net; internet www.landesmuseum.net; f. 1907; natural history, history of art (since the medieval period); many attached deptl museums located in lower Austria, incl. Haydn's birthplace at Rohrau; information centre; Dir BRIGITTE SCHLÖGL; Dir CORNELIA LAMPRECHTER.

Salzburg

Haus der Natur/Museum für Natur und Technik (Natural History Museum): Museumpl. 5, 5020 Salzburg; tel. (662) 8426530; e-mail office@hausdernatur.at; internet www.hausdernatur.at; f. 1924; zoology, botany, anthropology, geology; science centre, reptile zoo, aquarium, space hall; Dir Dr NORBERT WINDING.

Mozarteum: Schwarzstr. 26, 5020 Salzburg; tel. (662) 889400; internet www.mozarteum.at; f. 1914 by 'Internationale Stiftung Mozarteum'; concert rooms; 2 museums dedicated to life and work of Mozart; autographs, first editions, early prints of selected works and portraits; library of 35,000 vols., 6,000 music sheets, 22,000 sound recordings, 2,800 video cassettes; Man. Dir Dr STEPHAN PAULY.

Mozarts Wohnhaus (Mozart Residence): Makartpl. 8, 5020 Salzburg; tel. (662) 87422740; e-mail museum.service@mozarteum.at; internet www.mozarteum.at; biographies of the family members of Mozart; Dir Dr GABRIELE RAMSAUER.

Residenzgalerie Salzburg: Residenzpl. 1, 5010 Salzburg; tel. (662) 8404510; e-mail office@residenzgalerie.at; internet www.residenzgalerie.at; f. 1923; 16th to 19th century European paintings; focus on 17th century Dutch paintings, 17th and 18th century Italian, French and Austrian paintings; works by 19th century Austrian masters; Dir Dr GABRIELE GROSCHNER.

Salzburg Museum: Neue Residenz, Mozartpl. 1, 5010 Salzburg; tel. (662) 6208080; e-mail office@salzburgmuseum.at; internet www.salzburgmuseum.at; f. 1834, reopened in 2007; prehistoric and Roman remains, art, coins, musical instruments, costumes, toys; library of 130,000 vols, archives; Dir Mag. PETER HUSTY.

Schloss Hellbrunn (Hellbrunn Palace and Trick Fountains): 5020 Salzburg; tel. (662) 8203720; e-mail info@hellbrunn.at; internet www.hellbrunn.at; f. 1612; Dir INGRID SONVILLA.

Stillfried/March

STILLFRIED–Zentrum der Urzeit Museum für Ur- und Frühgeschichte (Stillfried–Prehistoric Centre, Museum for Pre- and Early History): Museumsverein Stillfried, Hauptstr. 23, 2262 Stillfried/March (Niederösterreich); tel. (676) 6113979; e-mail stillfried@aon.at; internet www.museumstillfried.at; f. 1914; local archaeology and palaeontology from late Palaeolithic to Middle Ages; Dir Dr WALPURGA ANTL; publ. *Museumsnachrichten* (1 a year).

Vienna

Albertina: Albertinapl. 1, 1010 Vienna; tel. (1) 534830; e-mail info@albertina.at; internet www.albertina.at; f. 1805; prints, drawings, posters; classical modern art; 50,000 drawings, 900,000 graphic art works; 50,000 architectural objects; 100,000 objects in photographic colln; library of 100,000 vols; Dir Dr KLAUS ALBRECHT SCHRÖDER.

Department und Sammlungen für Geschichte der Medizin (Department and Collections for the History of Medicine): Währingerstr. 25, 1090 Vienna; tel. (1) 4016026000; e-mail sammlungen@meduniwien.ac.at; internet www.meduniwien.ac.at/josephinum; f. 1785 as acad. for military surgeons; 18th-century wax anatomical colln, museum of the Vienna Medical Schools, museum of medical endoscopy and anaesthesia, colln of instruments and pictures; library of 80,000 historical medical books; Co-Head of Dept Mag. Assoc. Prof. Dr SONIA HORN.

Erzbischöfliches Dom- und Diözesanmuseum (Archiepiscopal Cathedral and Diocesan Museum): Stephanspl. 6, 1010 Vienna; tel. (1) 515523300; e-mail dommuseum@edw.or.at; internet www.dommuseum.at; f. 1933; ecclesiastical art incl. sculpture and painting; fine art with accent on sacral works from St Stephen's Cathedral; 3,000 works of modern art; Dir Dr BERNHARD A. BÖHLER.

Gemäldegalerie der Akademie der Bildenden Künste Wien (Vienna Academy of Fine Arts Gallery): Schillerpl. 3, 1010 Vienna; tel. (1) 588162222; e-mail gemgal@akbild.ac.at; internet www.akademiegalerie.at; f. 1822; paintings since 14th century; Deputy Dir MARTINA FLEISCHER.

Heeresgeschichtliches Museum (Military History Museum): Arsenal Objekt 1 Vienna; tel. (1) 795610; e-mail contact@hgm.or.at; internet www.hgm.or.at; f. 1891; exhibits dating from Thirty Years War to Second World War; library of 70,000 vols; Dir Dr MANFRIED RAUCHENSTEINER.

Kunsthistorisches Museum (Museum of Fine Arts): Maria Theresien-Pl., 1010 Vienna; tel. (1) 525244025; e-mail info@khm.at; internet www.khm.at; f. 1891 from Hapsburg Imperial collns; paintings, Egyptian and other antiquities, numismatics, armour, historical costume, plastics and handicrafts, musical instruments, secular and ecclesiastical relics of the Holy Roman Empire and the Hapsburg dynasty, state carriages (at Schönbrunn Palace); library of 256,000 vols; Dir-Gen. Dr SABINE HAAG.

Kupferstichkabinett der Akademie der Bildenden Künste (Graphic Art Collection of the Academy of Fine Arts): Schillerpl. 3, Raum 113, 1010 Vienna; tel. (1) 588162400; e-mail m.knofler@akbild.ac.at; internet www.akbild.ac.at/kuka; f. 1689; drawings, prints, photographs, architecture, sculpture gallery; 40,000 drawings, 100,000 prints, 20,000 photographs; reflects central European art education; library: see under Libraries and Archives; Dir Dr MONIKA KNOFLER.

Leopold Museum: Museumspl. 1, 1070 Vienna; tel. (1) 52570-0; e-mail office@leopoldmuseum.org; internet www.leopoldmuseum.org; f. 2001; fmrly private art colln of Rudolf and Elisabeth Leopold; works by Schiele, Klimt, Kokoschka and others; Man. Dir PETER WEINHÄUPL.

MAK—Österreichisches Museum für angewandte Kunst/Gegenwartskunst (MAK—Austrian Museum of Applied Arts/Contemporary Art): Stubenring 5, 1010 Vienna; tel. (1) 711360; e-mail office@mak.at; internet www.mak.at; f. 1864; applied arts from Roman to modern times, incl. furniture and woodwork, textiles and carpets, glass and ceramics, metalworks, the Wiener Werkstätte Archive and contemporary art; library of 200,000 vols, 3,700 magazines, 500,000 prints; Dir CHRISTOPH THUN-HOHENSTEIN.

Museum für Völkerkunde (Museum of Ethnology): Neue Burg, 1010 Vienna; tel. (1) 525245052; e-mail info@ethno-museum.ac.at; internet www.ethno-museum.ac.at; f. 1928; attached to Kunsthistorisches Museum; colln of 200,000 ethnographic objects and works of art, 75,000 historical photographs; library of 144,000 vols on history, culture, art and everyday life of predominantly non-European people; Dir Dr STEVEN ENGELSMAN; Deputy Dir Dr BARBARA PLANKENSTEINER; publs *Archiv für Völkerkunde* (1 a year), *Veröffentlichungen zum Archiv für Völkerkunde*.

Museum Moderner Kunst Stiftung Ludwig Wien (Museum of Modern Art Ludwig Foundation Vienna): Museumspl. 1, 1070 Vienna; tel. (1) 52500; e-mail info@mumok.at; internet www.mumok.at; f. 1962 as Museum des 20 Jahrhunderts; current name adopted 1991; modern and contemporary art, incl. American Pop Art and concurrent European movements; 9,000 works in paintings, sculptures, installations, drawings, graphic works, photographs, video cassettes and films; library of 30,000 vols; Dir KAROLA KRAUS.

Naturhistorisches Museum (Natural History Museum): I, Burgring 7, 1010 Vienna; tel. (1) 521770; e-mail info@hm-wien.ac.at; internet www.nhm-wien.ac.at; f. 1889; 25m. natural objects; ecology, geology, palaeontology, zoology, botany, anthropology, prehistory, speleology; library of 400,000 vols; Dir-Gen. Prof. Dr CHRISTIAN KÖBERL; publ. *Annalen*.

Österreichische Galerie Belvedere (Austrian Gallery): Oberes Belvedere, Prinz Eugenstr. 27, 1030 Vienna; tel. (1) 795570; e-mail info@belvedere.at; internet www.belvedere.at; Austrian painting and sculpture from Middle Ages to present, foreign painting and sculpture since 19th century, spec. colln of sculpture by G. Ambrosi; world's largest Gustav Klimt painting colln; library of 80,000 media units; Dir Dr AGNES HUSSLEIN-ARCO; publ. *Belvedere*.

Österreichisches Gesellschafts- und Wirtschafts-Museum (Austrian Museum for Economics and Social Affairs): Vogelsanggasse 36, 1050 Vienna; tel. (1) 5452551; e-mail wirtschaftsmuseum@oegwm.ac.at; internet www.wirtschaftsmuseum.at; f. 1925; archives, maps, photographs; public library on 'Austria Yesterday and Today'; Dir Mag. HANS HARTWEGER; Librarian GERHARD HALUSA; publ. *Österreichs Wirtschaft im Überblick* (1 a year; also in English).

Österreichisches Museum für Volkskunde (Austrian Museum of Folk Life and Folk Art): Laudongasse 15–19, 1080 Vienna; tel. (1) 4068905; e-mail office@volkskundemuseum.at; internet www.volkskundemuseum.at; f. 1895; historical folk art and folk culture; historical and contemporary lifestyles, cultural expressions of European social and ethnic groups; incl. nat. furniture colln and other spec. collns (housed on separate sites); library of 130,000 vols; Dir Mag. MATTHIAS BEITL; publ. *Österreichische Zeitschrift für Volkskunde* (4 a year).

Österreichisches Theatermuseum (Austrian Theatre Museum): Lobkowitzpl. 2, 1010 Vienna; tel. (1) 525243460; e-mail info@theatermuseum.at; internet www.theatermuseum.at; f. 1975; 100,000 hand drawings, 1,000 stage design and architectural models, 700,000 photographs, 600 portraits, role, and scene pictures; 600 original costumes with accessories; library of 80,000 vols; Dir Dr THOMAS TRABITSCH.

Schloss Schönbrunn Kultur- und Betriebsges. m.b.H. (Schönbrunn Palace): Schönbrunn Palace, 1130, Vienna; tel. (1) 811130; e-mail info@schoenbrunn.at; internet www.schoenbrunn.at; f. 1992; mid-18th-century fmr Imperial summer residence of the Habsburg dynasty; baroque and botanical gardens; zoological garden opened 1752; placed on UNESCO World Cultural Heritage List in 1996; Dir Dipl.-Ing. WOLFGANG KIPPES; Dir Dr FRANZ SATTLECKER.

Technisches Museum Wien (Museum of Technology in Vienna): Mariahilferstr. 212, 1140 Vienna; tel. (1) 899980; e-mail museumsbox@tmw.at; internet www.tmw.at; f. 1909; colln of scientific and technological instruments from 18th century to present; library of 100,000 vols, 750 magazines; Dir Dr GABRIELE ZUNA-KRATKY; publ. *Blätter für Technikgeschichte* (1 a year).

Wien Museum (Vienna Museum): Karlspl., 1040 Vienna; tel. (1) 50587470; e-mail office@wienmuseum.at; internet www.wienmuseum.at; f. 1887; local history from prehistoric times to the present; among many associated museums are premises once occupied by Beethoven, Haydn, Mozart, Schubert and Johann Strauss; Dir Dr WOLFGANG KOS.

Universities

All institutions of higher education have university status.

AKADEMIE DER BILDENDEN KÜNSTE WIEN
(Academy of Fine Arts Vienna)

Schillerpl. 3, 1010 Vienna
Telephone: (1) 588160
E-mail: info@akbild.ac.at
Internet: www.akbild.ac.at

Founded 1692
State control
Languages of instruction: English, German
Academic year: October to June

Rector: Prof. Dr STEPHAN SCHMIDT-WULFFEN
Pro-Rector: Mag. ANDREAS SPIEGL
Pro-Rector: Mag. ANNA STEIGER
Librarian: BEATRIX BASTL

Library: see under Libraries and Archives

PROFESSORS

ALLIEZ, E., Aesthetics and Sociology of Art
BAATZ, W., Conservation and Restoration
BAUER, U. M., Theory, Practice and Transfer of Contemporary Art
BISCHOF, E., Textile Art
DAMISCH, G., Drawing and Graphic Techniques
GIRONCOLI, B., Sculpture
GRAF, F., Expanded Artistic Environment
GRAF, O., Art History
GREEN, R., Conceptual Art
HASPEL, F., Textile Art
KOGLER, P., Computer and Video Art
LAINER, R., Architectural Design
OBHOLZER, W., Abstract Art
PRUSCHA, C., Architectural Design and Habitat, Environment and Conservation
ROSENBLUM, A., Representational Painting and Drawing
SAMSONOW, E., Philosophical and Historical Anthropology of the Arts
SCHLEGEL, E., Photography and Art
SCHMALIX, H., Art in Public Space
SCHREINER, M., Natural Science and Technology in Art
SCHULZ, J., Textile Arts and Crafts, Tapestry
SLOTERDIJK, P., Cultural Philosophy and Media Theory
WAGNER, K., Construction and Technology
WONDER, E., Stage Design

ZENS, H., Education and Science of Art
ZOBERNIG, H., Sculpture

ALPEN-ADRIA-UNIVERSITÄT KLAGENFURT
(University of Klagenfurt)

Universitätsstr. 65–67, 9020 Klagenfurt
Telephone: (463) 27009200
E-mail: uni@aau.at
Internet: www.aau.at

Founded 1970
State control
Academic year: October to June (2 semesters)
Rector: Prof. Dr OLIVER VITOUCH
Vice-Rector for Human Resources: Prof. Dr MARTIN HITZ
Vice-Rector for Int. Relations and Studies: Prof. Dr CRISTINA BERETTA
Vice-Rector for Research: Prof. Dr FRIEDERIKE WALL
Library Dir: Mag. LYDIA ZELLACHER
Library of 75,000 vols
Number of teachers: 1,200
Number of students: 10,000

DEANS

Faculty of Humanities: Prof. Dr STEPHAN STING
Faculty of Interdisciplinary Studies: Prof. Dr VERENA WINIWARTER
Faculty of Management and Economics: Prof. Dr ERICH SCHWARZ
Faculty of Technical Sciences: Prof. Dr GERHARD FRIEDRICH
School of Education: Prof. Dr KONRAD KRAINER

PROFESSORS

Faculty of Humanities (tel. (463) 27001002):
AYAß, R., Cultural Studies
AYDIN, N., Psychology
BERGHOLD, J., Psychology
BILALIC, M., Psychology
DOLESCHAL, U., Slavonic Studies
FLAMM, C., Musicology
GLÜCK, J., Psychology
GRUBER, E., Educational Sciences
HAUSER, B., Cultural Studies
HELBIG, J., English and American Studies
HESSE, P., Slavonic Studies
JAMES, A., English and American Studies
KARMASIN, M., Media and Communication Science
MAYRING, P., Psychology
MEIER, J., German studies
NEYMEYR, B., German Studies
PECHRIGGL, A., Philosophy
POHL, D., Contemporary History
POPP, U., Educational Sciences
RENNER, W., Psychology
RENZ, U., Philosophy
SCHACHTNER, C., Media and Communication Science
SEELBACH, S., German Studies
SOBOLEVA, M., Philosophy
STAUBER, R., Modern and Austrian History
STING, S., Educational Sciences
STROBEL, K., Ancient History and Archaeology
TAUBNER, S., Psychology
VITOUCH, O., Psychology
WILHELM, R., Romance Studies
WINTER, R., Media and Communication Science

Faculty of Interdisciplinary Studies:
FISCHER, M., Social Ecology
FISCHER, R., Mathematics
GROSSMANN, R., Organizational Development
HELLER, A., Palliative Care
KRAUSMANN, F., Social Ecology
WINIWARTER, V., Environmental History

Faculty of Management and Economics:
BAUMGARTNER, G., Law
BÖGENHOLD, D., Sociology
EGNER, H., Geography and Regional Studies
HEINRICH, J., Law
KANDUTH-KRISTEN, S., Financial Management
KRAUSE, D., Business Management
NADVORNIK, W., Financial Management
NECK, R., Economics
PERNER, S., Law
REINER, G., Production Management and Business Logistics
RONDO-BROVETTO, P., Business Administration
SCHWARZ, E., Business Administration
STARK, O., Economics
TERLUTTER, R., Business Management
WALL, F., Business Management

Faculty of Technical Sciences (tel. (463) 27005003):
BETTSTETTER, C., Computer Science
BÖSZÖRMENYI, L., Computer Science
EDER, J., Computer Science
ELMENREICH, W., Computer Science
FRIEDRICH, G., Computer Science
HELLWAGNER, H., Computer Science
HEUBERGER, C., Mathematics
HITZ, M., Computer Science
HORSTER, P., Computer Science
KALTENBACHER, B., Mathematics
KYAMAKYA, K., Computer Science
MAYR, H., Computer Science
PILZ, J., Statistics
PINZGER, M., Computer Science
PÖTZSCHE, C., Mathematics
RENDL, F., Mathematics
RINNER, B., Computer Science
ZANGL, H., Computer Science

School of Education:
AMANN, K., Literary Studies
BÖCK, M., German Didactics
GAIDOSCHIK, M., Mathematics Education
KRAINER, K., Instructional and School Development
MAYR, J., Instructional and School Development
WINTERSTEINER, W., Peace Research, German Didactics

ANTON BRUCKNER PRIVATUNIVERSITÄT
(Anton Bruckner Private University)

Wildbergstr. 18, 4040 Linz
Telephone: (732) 7010000
E-mail: information@bruckneruni.at
Internet: www.bruckneruni.at

Founded 1863
Private control
Academic year: October to September (2 semesters)
Rector: Prof. Dr URSULA BRANDSTÄTTER
Vice-Rector for Art: JOSEF EIDENBERGER
Univ. Dir: Mag. BRIGITTE MÖSSENBÖCK
Dean for Art Studies: THOMAS KERBL
Library Dir: Mag. JOHN LACKINGER
Library of 10,000 vols, 40,000 notes and 2,000 audiovisual media
Number of teachers: 200
Number of students: 850

DONAU-UNIVERSITÄT KREMS/ UNIVERSITÄT FÜR WEITERBILDUNG
(Danube University Krems/University of Continuing Education)

Dr-Karl-Dorrek-Str. 30, 3500 Krems
Telephone: (2732) 8930
E-mail: info@donau-uni.ac.at
Internet: www.donau-uni.ac.at

Founded 1994
State control
Languages of instruction: English, German
Academic year: October to June
Rector: Prof. Dr JÜRGEN WILLER
Vice-Rector: Prof. Dr VIKTORIA WEBER
Library of 79,312 vols, 24,698 electronic journals
Number of teachers: 1,590
Number of students: 5,692
Publication: *Upgrade* (4 a year)

PROFESSORS

BAHLI, B., Management and Economics
BAUMGARTNER, P., Interactive Media and Educational Technology
BIFFL, G., Migration, Integration and Security
BRAININ, M., Clinical Medicine and Preventive Medicine
FALKENHAGEN, D., Environmental and Medical Sciences
FILZMAIER, P., Political Communication
FINA, S., European Integration
GARTLEHNER, G., Evidence-based Medicine and Clinical Epidemiology
GENSCH, G., Arts and Management
GRAU, O., Applied Cultural Studies
LEITNER, A., Psychosocial Medicine and Psychotherapy
LEITNER, C., New Public Management and E-Governance
MIKSCH, S., Information and Knowledge Engineering
NEHRER, S., Regenerative Medicine
RISKU, H., Knowledge and Communication Management
STELZEL, M., Interdisciplinary Dentistry and Technology
WAGNER, M., Technology Enhanced Learning and Multimedia
WILLER, J., Interdisciplinary Dentistry and Technology

JOHANNES KEPLER UNIVERSITÄT LINZ
(Johannes Kepler University, Linz)

Altenberger Str. 69, 4040 Linz
Telephone: (732) 24680
E-mail: rektor@jku.at
Internet: www.jku.at

Founded 1966 as Acad. for Social and Economic Sciences, present name and status 1975
State control
Languages of instruction: English, German
Academic year: October to June
Rector: Prof. Dr RICHARD HAGELAUER
Vice-Rector for Acad. Affairs: Prof. Dr HERBERT KALB
Vice-Rector for Int. Affairs: Prof. Dr FRIEDRICH ROITHMAYR
Vice-Rector for Finance: Dr BARBARA ROMAUER
Vice-Rector for Research: Prof. Dr GABRIELE KOTSIS
Admin. Dir: Dr JOSEF SCHMIED
Library Dir: Dr SUSANNE CASAGRANDA
Library: see under Libraries and Archives
Number of teachers: 1,400
Number of students: 18,000
Publication: *UNIVATIONEN—Forschungsmedienservice der Johannes Kepler Universität Linz* (4 a year)

DEANS

Faculty of Engineering and Natural Sciences: Prof. Dr ERICH PETER KLEMENT
Faculty of Law: Prof. Dr MEINHARD LUKAS
Faculty of Social Sciences, Economics and Business: Prof. Dr TEODORO D. COCCA

PROFESSORS

Faculty of Engineering and Natural Sciences (Altenberger Str. 69, 4040 Linz; tel. (732) 2468-3220; e-mail tnf-dekanat@jku.at; internet www.tn.jku.at):

AMRHEIN, W., Electrical Drives and Power Electronics
BAUER, G., Semiconductor Physics
BAUER, S., Soft Matter Physics
BÄUERLE, D., Applied Physics
BIERE, A., Formal Models and Verification
BREMER, H., Robotics
BUCHBERGER, W., Analytical Chemistry
CHROUST, G., Systems Engineering and Automation
COOPER, J. B., Functional Analysis
DEL RE, L., Design and Control of Mechatronical Systems
ENGL, H., Industrial Mathematics
FALK, H., Organic Chemistry
FERSCHA, A., Pervasive Computing
GITTLER, P., Fluid Mechanics and Heat Transfer
GRITZNER, G., Chemical Technology of Inorganic Materials
HAGELAUER, R., Integrated Circuits
HOCHREITER, S., Bioinformatics
IRSCHIK, H., Technical Mechanics
JAKOBY, B., Microelectronics
JANTSCH, W., Solid State Physics
JÜTTLER, B., Applied Geometry
KLEMENT, E. P., Fuzzy Logic
KNÖR, G., Inorganic Chemistry
KOTSIS, G., Telecooperation
KROTSCHECK, E., Many Particle Systems
LANGER, U., Computational Mathematics
LARCHER, G., Financial Mathematics
MÖSSENBÖCK, H., System Software
MÜHLBACHER, J., Information Processing and Microprocessor Technology
PAULE, P., Symbolic Computation
PILZ, G., Algebra
POHL, P., Biophysics
SAMHABER, W., Process Engineering
SARICIFTCI, N. S., Physical Chemistry
SCHÄFFLER, F., Semiconductor Physics
SCHEIDL, R., Machine Design and Hydraulic Drives
SCHLACHER, K., Automatic Control and Control Systems Technology
SCHLÖGLMANN, W., Mathematics Education
SCHMIDT, H., Chemical Technology of Organic Materials
SOBCZAK, R., Polymer Science
SPRINGER, A., Communications and Information Engineering
TITULAER, U. M., Condensed Matter Theory
VOLKERT, J., Graphics and Parallel Processing
WAGNER, R., Applied Knowledge Processing
WEIß, P., Stochastics
WIDMER, G., Computational Perception
WINKLER, F., Symbolic Computation
ZAGAR, B., Electrical Measurement Technology
ZEMAN, K., Computer-aided Methods in Mechanical Engineering
ZEPPENFELD, P., Atomic Physics and Surface Science

Faculty of Law (tel. (732) 2468-3201; e-mail re-dekanat@jku.at; internet www.re.jku.at):

ACHATZ, M., Administrative Law and Management
ACHATZ, M., Research Department for Tax Law and Tax Management
APATHY, P., Roman Law
BINDER, B., Administrative Law and Administrative Sciences
BURGSTALLER, A., European and Austrian Civil Procedure Law
DOLINAR, H., Civil Procedure
FLOSZMANN, U., History of Austrian and German Law
FUNK, B.-C., University Law
HAUER, A., Public Law with Special Reference to Austrian Administrative Law
HENGSTSCHLÄGER, J., Constitutional Law and Political Science
JABORNEGG, P., Labour Law and Social Security
KALB, H., Canon Law
KAROLLUS, M., Commercial and Securities Law
KEINERT, H., Commercial and Securities Law
KERSCHNER, F., Civil Law and Environmental Law
KLINGENBERG, G., Roman Law
KÖCK, H., Public International Law and European Law
LEITL, B., Correspondence Course
OBERNDORFER, P., Administrative Law and Administrative Sciences
REISCHAUER, R., Civil Law
RIEDLER, A., Correspondence Course
RUMMEL, P., Civil Law
SPIELBUECHLER, K., Civil Law
WEGSCHEIDER, H., Criminal Law and Procedure
WIDDER, H., Constitutional Law and Political Science
VELTEN, P., Criminal Law and Procedure

Faculty of Social Sciences, Economics and Business (tel. (732) 2468-3211; e-mail sowi-dekanat@jku.at; internet www.sowi.jku.at):

ALTRICHTER, H., Education and Educational Psychology
BACHER, J., Sociology
BATINIC, B., E-learning
BECKER, P., Modern and Contemporary History
BÖHNISCH, W., Business Administration (Management), Human Resources Management
BRUNNER, J., Economics
COCCA, T., Asset Management
DULLECK, U., Economics
DYK, I., Socio-politics
EULER, H. P., Sociology
FELDBAUER-DURSTMÜLLER, B., Business Administration (Accountancy, Auditing, Business Taxation and Controllership)
FRÜHWIRTH-SCHNATTER, S., Applied Statistics and Econometrics
GADENNE, V., Philosophy and Theory of Science
HAUCH, G., Modern and Contemporary History, Gender Studies
KAILER, N., Entrepreneurship and Business Development
LANDESMANN, M., National Economy
MALINSKY, A. H., Environmental Management in Business and Regional Policy
MATZLER, K., Business Administration
MÜLLER, W. G., Applied Statistics
PERNSTEINER, H., Corporate Finance
PILS, M., Data Processing
PÖLL, G., Economics
POMBERGER, G., Software Engineering
ROHATSCHEK, R., Business Administration, Accountancy, Auditing, Business Taxation and Controllership
ROITHMAYR, F., Information Engineering
SANDGRUBER, R., Social and Economic History
SCHAUER, R., Business Administration (Public Administration and Non-Profit Organizations)
SCHNEIDER, F., Economics, Public Economics, Public Choice
SCHREFL, M., Data and Knowledge Engineering
SCHURER, B., Economic and Business Education
SCHUSTER, H., Economics
STARY, C., Communications Engineering
STREHL, F., Business Administration
TUMPEL, M., Business Administration, Accountancy, Auditing, Business Taxation and Controllership
WEIDENHOLZER, J., Social Policy
WINTER-EBMER, R., Economics
WÜHRER, G., Business Administration (Marketing)

KARL-FRANZENS-UNIVERSITÄT GRAZ
(Graz University)

Universitätspl. 3, 8010 Graz
Telephone: (316) 3800
E-mail: info@uni-graz.at
Internet: www.uni-graz.at

Founded 1585
State control
Academic year: October to September (2 terms)

Rector: Prof. Dr ALFRED GUTSCHELHOFER
Vice-Rector for Human Resources Management: Prof. Dr RENATE DWORCZAK
Vice-Rector for Int. Relations and Interdisciplinary Cooperation: Prof. Dr ROBERTA MAIERHOFER
Vice-Rector for Research and Continuing Education: Prof. Dr IRMTRAUD FISCHER
Vice-Rector for Studies and Teaching: Prof. Dr MARTIN POLASCHEK
Chief Admin. Officer: Dr MARIA EDLINGER
Librarian: Dr WERNER SCHLACHER

Library: see under Libraries and Archives
Number of teachers: 2,563
Number of students: 27,000

Publication: *UNIZEIT* (4 a year)

DEANS

Faculty of Arts and Humanities: Mag. THERES HINTERLEITNER
Faculty of Environmental and Regional Sciences and Education: Prof. Dr WERNER LENZ
Faculty of Law: Prof. Dr WILLIBALD POSCH
Faculty of Natural Sciences: Prof. Dr KARL CRAILSHEIM
Faculty of Social and Economic Sciences: Prof. Dr WOLF RAUCH
Faculty of Theology: Prof. Dr ANGEL HANS-FERDINAND

PROFESSORS

Faculty of Arts and Humanities (Universitätspl. 3, 8010 Graz; tel. (316) 380-2288; e-mail geisteswiss.dekanat@uni-graz.at; internet www.uni-graz.at/en/gewi.htm):

EISMANN, W., Slavic Studies
ERTLER, K.-D., Romance Studies
GOLTSCHNIGG, D., German Studies
GÖPFERICH, S., Translation and Interpreting Studies
HÄRTEL, R., History
HAUG-MORITZ, G., History
HEINEMANN, S., Romance Studies
HELMICH, W., Romance Studies
HIEBEL, H.-H., German Studies
HÖFLECHNER, W., History
HÖLBLING, W., American Studies
HUMMEL, M., Romance Studies
HURCH, B., Linguistics
KASER, K., History
KONRAD, H., History
MAHLER, A., English Studies
MEYER, L., Philosophy
PARNCUTT, R., Music
PIEPER, R., History
PORTMANN, P., German Studies
PRUNC, E., Translation and Interpreting Studies
TOSOVIC, B., Slavic Studies
WALTER, M., Music
WOLF, W., English Studies
ZIEGLER, A., German Studies

Faculty of Environmental and Regional Sciences and Education (Universitätspl. 3, 8010 Graz; tel. (316) 380-8020; e-mail urbi.dekan@uni-graz.at; internet www.uni-graz.at/en/brek3www.htm):

HACKL, B., Teacher Training
HOPFNER, J., Education
LENZ, W., Education
SCHEIPL, J., Education
STRASSER, U., Geography and Regional Sciences
SUST, M., Sport Science
ZIMMERMANN, F., Geography and Regional Sciences

Faculty of Law (Universitätsstr. 15/A, 8010 Graz; tel. (316) 380-3260; e-mail rewi.dekanat@uni-graz.at; internet www.uni-graz.at/en/enredwww):

BENEDEK, W., International Law and International Relations
KOLLER, P., Legal Philosophy, Sociology and Informatics
MARHOLD, F., Labour Law and Social Security Law
MEDIGOVIC, U., Criminology and Criminal Justice
SCHICK, P., Criminology and Criminal Justice
SCHMALENBACH, K., International Law and International Relations
SCHMÖLZER, G., Criminology and Criminal Justice
SOYER, R., Criminology and Criminal Justice
THÜR, G., Roman Law, Ancient Legal History and Modern Legal History

Faculty of Natural Sciences (Universitätspl. 3, 8010 Graz; tel. (316) 380-5000; e-mail nawi.dekanat@uni-graz.at; internet www.uni-graz.at/nawi):

ALBERT, D., Psychology
ALKOFER, R., Physics
ARENDASY, M., Psychology
BAUER, R., Pharmacognosy
BLANZ, P., Botany
CRAILSHEIM, K., Zoology
FISCHER, P., Psychology
FRÖHLICH, K.-U., Molecular Biosciences
GATTRINGER, C., Physics
GRUBER, K., Molecular Biosciences
HAASE, G., Mathematics and Scientific Computing
HANSLMEIER, A., Physics
KALLUS, K. W., Psychology
KAPPEL, F., Mathematics
KIRCHENGAST, G., Physics
KOHLWEIN, S.-D., Molecular Biosciences
KRATKY, C., Molecular Biosciences
KRENN, H., Physics
KUNISCH, K., Mathematics and Scientific Computing
LANG, C., Physics
MADEO, F., Molecular Biosciences
MAYER, B. M., Pharmacology and Toxicology
NETZER, F., Physics
NEUBAUER, A., Psychology
NEUPER, C., Psychology
PAECHTER, M., Psychology
PÖTZ, W., Physics
REIDL, J., Molecular Biosciences
RINDERMANN, H., Psychology
ROITSCH, T., Plant Sciences
RÖMER, H., Zoology
SCHAPPACHER, W., Mathematics and Scientific Computing
SCHIENLE, A., Psychology
SCHULTER, G., Psychology
SPAHN-LANGGUTH, H., Pharmaceutical Sciences
STURMBAUER, CH., Zoology
UHLIG, T., Psychology
ZECHNER, R., Molecular Biosciences
ZIMMER, A., Pharmaceutical Sciences

Faculty of Social and Economic Sciences (Universitätsstr. 15/A, 8010 Graz; tel. (316) 380-6813; e-mail sowi.dekanat@uni-graz.at; internet sowi.uni-graz.at):

BAIGENT, N., Public Economics
FISCHER, E., Finance
FOSCHT, T., Marketing
HALLER, M., Sociology
LEOPOLD-WILDBURGER, U., Statistics and Operations Research
ORTLIEB, R., Human Resource Management
RAUCH, W., Information Science and Information Systems
REIMANN, M., Production and Operations Management
WETTERER, A., Sociology

Faculty of Theology (Universitätspl. 3, 8010 Graz; tel. (316) 380-3150; e-mail theologisches.dekanat@uni-graz.at; internet www-theol.uni-graz.at):

BECHMANN, U., World Religions
BUCHER, R.-M., Psychology and Pastoral Theology
ESTERBAUER, R., Theology and Philosophy
FISCHER, I., Old Testament Studies
GROEN, B., Liturgics, Church Music and Christian Art
HEIL, C., New Testament Studies
LARCHER, G., Fundamental Theology

KATHOLISCH-THEOLOGISCHE PRIVATUNIVERSITÄT LINZ (Private Catholic Theological University of Linz)

Bethlehemstr. 20, 4020 Linz
Telephone: (732) 784293
E-mail: rektorat@ktu-linz.ac.at
Internet: www.ktu-linz.ac.at

Founded 1978
Private control

Rector: Prof. Dr EWALD VOLGGER
Pro-Rector: Prof. Dr MICHAEL ROSENBERGER
Admin. Dir: Mag. MONIKA HOLLER
Library Dir: INGO GLÜCKLER

Library of 180,000 vols, 500 periodicals, 20 MSS, 126 incunabula
Number of teachers: 41

Publications: *Kunst und Kirche* (4 a year), *Theologisch-praktische Quartalschrift (ThPQ)* (4 a year)

LEOPOLD-FRANZENS UNIVERSITÄT INNSBRUCK (Innsbruck University)

Christoph-Probst-Pl., Innrain 52, 6020 Innsbruck
Telephone: (512) 5070
E-mail: international-relations@uibk.ac.at
Internet: www.uibk.ac.at

Founded 1669
State control
Languages of instruction: English, German
Academic year: October to July (2 semesters)

Rector: Prof. Dr TILMANN MÄRK
Vice-Rector for Infrastructure: Prof. Dipl.-Ing. ANKE BOCKREIS
Vice-Rector for Research: Prof. Dr SABINE SCHINDLER
Vice-Rector for Staff and Faculty: Asst Prof. Mag. Dr WOLFGANG MEIXNER
Vice-Rector for Teaching and Students: Prof. Dr ROLAND PSENNER
Librarian: Dr MARTIN WIESER

Library: see under Libraries and Archives
Number of teachers: 3,117
Number of students: 28,000

Publication: *Veröffentlichungen* (irregular)

DEANS

Faculty of Architecture: Prof. MARTIN COY
Faculty of Biology: Prof. Dr ULRIKE TAPPEINER
Faculty of Catholic Theology: Prof. Dr WOLFGANG PALAVER
Faculty of Chemistry and Pharmacy: Prof. Dr HUBERT HUPPERTZ
Faculty of Economics and Statistics: Prof. Dr HANNELORE WECK-HANNEMANN
Faculty of Education: MICHAEL SCHRATZ
Faculty of Engineering Science: Prof. Dr GÜNTER HOFSTETTER
Faculty of Geo- and Atmospheric Sciences: Prof. Dr BERNHARD FÜGENSCHUH
Faculty of Humanities I: Prof. Mag. Dr KLAUS EISTERER
Faculty of Humanities II: Prof. Mag. Dr SEBASTIAN DONAT
Faculty of Law: Prof. Dr BERNHARD ECCHER
Faculty of Mathematics, Computer Sciences and Physics: Prof. Mag. Dr GÜNTHER SPECHT
Faculty of Psychology and Sport Science: Prof. Dr PIERRE SACHSE
School of Management: Prof. MATTHIAS BANK
School of Political Science and Sociology: Prof. Dr HELMUT STAUBMANN

AFFILIATED INSTITUTES

Arbeitskreis für Gleichbehandlungsfragen: Technikerstrasse 13, 6020 Innsbruck; e-mail gleichbehandlung@uibk.ac.at.

Forschungsinstitut 'Brenner-Archiv': Innrain 52, Neubau/VIII, 6020 Innsbruck; e-mail brenner-archiv@uibk.ac.at; f. 1979.

Forschungsinstitut für Alpenländische Land- und Forstwirtschaft (Dept of Alpine Agriculture and Forestry): Technikerstr. 13, 6020 Innsbruck; f. 1977.

Forschungsinstitut für Alpine Vorzeit: Kaiser-Franz-Josef-Str. 12, 6020 Innsbruck.

Forschungsinstitut für Hochgebirgsforschung in Obergurgl (Alpine Research Department of the University of Innsbruck in Obergurgl): Innrain 52, 6020 Innsbruck; f. 1951.

Forschungsinstitut für Prophylaxe der Suchtkrankheiten: Krankenhaus Maria Ebene Frastanz, Vorarlberg; f. 1990.

Forschungsinstitut für Textilchemie und Textilphysik: Höchsterstr. 73, 6850 Dornbirn; e-mail textilchemie@uibk.ac.at; f. 1982.

Senatsinstitut für Zwischenmenschliche Kommunikation: Sillgasse 8, 6020 Innsbruck; f. 1991.

Sportinstitut: Fürstenweg 185, 6020 Innsbruck; e-mail usi@uibk.ac.at; f. 1959.

Universitätsarchiv: Innrain 52, 6020 Innsbruck; f. 1950

MEDIZINISCHE UNIVERSITÄT GRAZ (Medical University of Graz)

Auenbruggerpl. 2, 8036 Graz
Telephone: (316) 3850
E-mail: rektor@medunigraz.at
Internet: www.medunigraz.at

Founded 1863 as Medical Faculty of Graz Univ.; univ. status 2004
State control
Language of instruction: German
Academic year: October to September (2 semesters)

Rector: Prof. Dr JOSEF SMOLLE
Vice-Rector for Financial Management and Org.: Mag. OLIVER SZMEJ
Vice-Rector for Human Resources and Gender Equality: Prof. Dr ANDREA LANGMANN
Vice-Rector for Research: Prof. Dr IRMGARD THERESIA LIPPE
Vice-Rector for Teaching and Studies: Prof. Dr GILBERT REIBNEGGER
Librarian: Dr ULRIKE KORTSCHAK

Library of 370 textbooks, 60,000 vols of journals
Number of teachers: 741
Number of students: 4,058

MEDIZINISCHE UNIVERSITÄT INNSBRUCK
(Medical University, Innsbruck)

Christoph-Probst-Pl., Innrain 52, 6020 Innsbruck
Telephone: (512) 5070
E-mail: i-master@i-med.ac.at
Internet: www.i-med.ac.at

Founded 2004 from the medical faculty of the Univ. of Innsbruck
State control
Language of instruction: German
Academic year: October to July

Rector: Prof. Dr HERBERT LOCHS
Vice-Rector for Finance: Dr GABRIELE DÖLLER
Vice-Rector for Human Resources, Human Resources Devt and Gender Equality: Prof. Dr DORIS BALOGH
Vice-Rector for Research: Prof. Dr GÜNTHER SPERK
Vice-Rector for Teaching and Studies: Prof. Dr NORBERT MUTZ
Librarian: Dr MARION BREITSCHOPF

Library of 30,000 vols of journals, 350 current journals
Number of teachers: 1,700
Number of students: 3,500

MEDIZINISCHE UNIVERSITÄT WIEN
(Medical University, Vienna)

Spitalgasse 23, 1090 Vienna
Telephone: (1) 401600
E-mail: infopoint-meduni@meduniwien.ac.at
Internet: www.meduniwien.ac.at

Founded 1365 as Medical Faculty, Univ. of Vienna; autonomous univ. since 2004
State control
Language of instruction: German
Academic year: October to July (2 semesters)

Rector: Prof. Dr WOLFGANG SCHÜTZ
Vice-Rector for Clinical Affairs: Prof. OSWALD WAGNER
Vice-Rector for Education: Prof. Dr RUDOLF MALLINGER
Vice-Rector for Finance: Mag. PETER SOSWINSKI
Vice-Rector for Human Resource Devt and Women's Issues: Prof. Dr KARIN GUTIÉRREZ-LOBOS
Library Dir: Mag. BRUNO BAUER

Library of 520,000 vols, 2,400 periodicals
Number of teachers: 1,200
Number of students: 7,500

MODUL UNIVERSITY VIENNA

Am Kahlenberg 1, 1190 Vienna
Telephone: (1) 3203555101
E-mail: office@modul.ac.at
Internet: www.modul.ac.at

Founded 1908
Private control

Pres.: Dr KARL WÖBER
Vice-Pres.: Dr ARNO SCHARL
Man. Dir: Mag. CHRISTIAN HOFFMANN
Librarian: JOHANNA HUBWEBER
Number of students: 250

MONTANUNIVERSITÄT LEOBEN
(University of Leoben)

Franz-Josef Str. 18, 8700 Leoben
Telephone: (3842) 4020
E-mail: office@unileoben.ac.at
Internet: www.unileoben.ac.at

Founded 1840
Languages of instruction: English, German
Academic year: October to July

Rector: Prof. Dr WOLFHARD WEGSCHEIDER
Vice-Rector for Admin.: Dr MARTHA MÜHLBURGER
Vice-Rector for Finance and Auditing: Prof. Dr HUBERT BIEDERMAN
Librarian: Dr CHRISTIAN HASENHÜTTEL

Library: see under Libraries and Archives
Number of students: 2,338

Publications: *BHM Berg- und Hüttenmannische Monatshefte* (12 a year), *Triple M* (4 a year)

PROFESSORS

BIEDERMANN, H., Economics, Industrial Management and Industrial Engineering
DANZER, R., Ceramics
EBNER, F., Geology and Mineral Resources
EICHLSEDER, W., Mechanical Engineering
ENGELHARDT, C., Industrial Logistics
FISCHER, D., Mechanics
GALLER, R., Subsurface Engineering
HARMUTH, H., Refractory Materials, Ceramics, Glass and Cement
HEINEMANN, Z., Reservoir Engineering
IMRICH, W., Applied Mathematics
JEGLITSCH, F., Physical Metallurgy and Material Testing
KEPPLINGER, W., Industrial Environmental Protection
KESSLER, F., Conveying Technology
KIRSCHENHOFER, P., Mathematics
KNEISSL, A., Metallography
KRIEGER, W., Ferrous Metallurgy
KUCHAR, F., Physics
LANG, R., Plastics
LANGECKER, G., Plastics Technology
LEDERER, K., Chemistry of Plastics
LORBER, K., Decontamination
MAURITSCH, H., Geophysics
MEISEL, T., Gen. and Analytical Chemistry
MILLAHN, K., Applied Geophysics
O'LEARY, P., Automation
PASCHEN, P., Nonferrous Metallurgy
RUTHAMMER, G., Petroleum Engineering
SACHS, H., Applied Geometry
SITTE, W., Physical Chemistry
STEINER, H., Mineral Processing
VORTISCH, W., Applied Sedimentology
WAGNER, H., Mining Engineering
WEISS, G., Electrical Engineering
WOERNDLE, R., Plastics
WOLFBAUER, J., Business Economics

PARACELSUS MEDIZINISCHE PRIVATUNIVERSITÄT
(Paracelsus Medical University)

Strubergasse 21, 5020 Salzburg
Telephone: (662) 4420020
E-mail: herbert.resch@pmu.ac.at
Internet: www.pmu.ac.at

Founded 2002
Private control

Rector: Prof. Dr HERBERT RESCH
Hon. Rector: Dr JULIAN FRICK
Vice-Rector: Prof. Dr FELIX SEDLMAYER
Chancellor: Dr MICHAEL NAKE
Dean for Academic Affairs: Prof. Dr MICHAEL STUDNICKA
Dean for Curriculum: Prof. Dr HEINRICH MAGOMETSCHNIGG
Dean for Research: Prof. Dr CHRISTOPH STUPPACK
Dean for Student Affairs: Doz. Dr ROSEMARIE FORSTNER
Library Man.: Mag. CVETKA FLORENTINA LIPUS

Library of 2,000 medical journals, medical databases

PEF PRIVATUNIVERSITÄT FÜR MANAGEMENT
(PEF Private University of Management)

Brahmspl. 3, 1040 Vienna
Telephone: (1) 534390
E-mail: pef@pef.co.at
Internet: www.pef.at
Private control
Man. Dir: Mag. ANDREA KOBLMÜLLER

PRIVATUNIVERSITÄT DER KREATIVWIRTSCHAFT—NEW DESIGN UNIVERSITY
(Private University of the Creative Industries—New Design University)

Maria Zeller Str. 97, 3100 St Pölten
Telephone: (2742) 8902418
E-mail: office@ndu.ac.at
Internet: www.ndu.ac.at

Founded 2004
Private control

DEANS

Faculty of Design: Mag. Dr THOMAS GRONEGGER
Faculty of Engineering: Dipl.-Ing. Dr ANDREAS HASENZAGL

PRIVATUNIVERSITÄT SCHLOSS SEEBURG
(Castle Seeburg Private University)

Seeburgstrasse 8, 5201 Salzburg
Telephone: (6212) 2626
E-mail: info@uni-seeburg.at
Internet: www.uni-seeburg.at

Founded 2007
Private control

Rector: Prof. Dr CHRISTIAN WERNER
Vice-Rector: Prof. Dr FLORIAN KAINZ
Vice-Rector: Prof. Dr WALTER EMBERGER

Number of teachers: 76

DEANS

Faculty of Business Administration: Prof. Dr BIRGIT RENZL
Faculty of Economic Psychology: Prof. Dr JÜRGEN KASCHUBE
Faculty of Sports and Event Management: Prof. Dr PETER KAPUSTIN

SIGMUND FREUD PRIVATUNIVERSITÄT WIEN
(Sigmund Freud Private University Vienna)

Schnirchgasse 9A 1030 Vienna
Telephone: (1) 7984098
E-mail: rektorat@sfu.ac.at
Internet: www.sfu.ac.at

Founded 2003
Private control
Languages of instruction: English, German
Academic year: October to June

Rector: Prof. Dr ALFRED PRITZ
Vice-Rector: Dr JUTTA FIEGL
Vice-Rector for Research: Dr BRIGITTE SINDELAR
Vice-Rector for Teaching: Mag. STEFAN HAMPL
Registrar: HEINZ LAUBREUTER
Number of students: 650

TECHNISCHE UNIVERSITÄT GRAZ
(Graz University of Technology)

Rechbauerstr. 12, 8010 Graz
Telephone: (316) 8730
E-mail: info@tugraz.at
Internet: www.tugraz.at

Founded 1811
State control
Academic year: October to July
Rector: Prof. Dr HARALD KAINZ
Vice-Rector for Acad. Affairs: Prof. Dr BERNHARD HOFMANN-WELLENHOF
Vice-Rector for Finances and Infrastructure: Dr ANDREA HOFFMANN
Vice-Rector for Research: Prof. Dr HORST BISCHOF
Librarian: Dr WERNER SCHLACHER
Library: see under Libraries and Archives
Number of teachers: 1,402
Number of students: 12,105
Publications: *TU Graz People* (4 a year), *TU Graz Research* (2 a year, in English and German)

DEANS

Faculty of Architecture: Prof. Dr LEONARD HIRSCHBERG
Faculty of Civil Engineering: Prof. Dr MARTIN FELLENDORF
Faculty of Computer Science: Prof. Dr FRANZ WOTAWA
Faculty of Electrical and Information Engineering: Prof. Dr HEINRICH STIGLER
Faculty of Mathematical and Physical Engineering: Prof. Dr ROBERT TICHY
Faculty of Mechanical Engineering and Economic Sciences: Prof. Dr CHRISTOF SOMMITSCH
Faculty of Technical Chemistry, Chemical and Process Engineering, Biotechnology: Prof. Dr FRANK UHLIG
Faculty of Technical Mathematics and Technical Physics: WOLFGANG ERNST

PROFESSORS

ARRIGONI, E., Theoretical Physics
AURENHAMMER, F., Basics of Information Processing
BAUER, U., Industrial Management
BEER, G., Building Statics
BERKES, I., Probability Theory and Statistics
BESENHARD, O. J., Inorganic Chemical Technology
BRASSEUR, G., Electrical Measurement and Measurement Signals Processing
BRENN, G., Fluid Mechanics
BRUNNER, F. K., Geodesy
BURKARD, R., Mathematics
CELIGOJ, CH., Strength of Materials
CERJAK, H., Materials Science and Welding
DOURDOUMAS, N., Automatic Control
EICHLSEDER, H., Combustion Engines
ERNST, W., Experimental Physics
FICKERT, L., Electrical Installations
FRANK, A., Manufacturing Technology
FRANK, I., Interior Design
GAMERITH, H., Building and Design
GESCHEIDT-DEMNER, G., Material Testing
GRAMPP, G., Physical Chemistry
GREINER, R., Timberwork and Elevation
GRIENGL, H., Organic Chemistry
HABERFELLNER, R., Management
HEIGERTH, G., Hydraulic Design and Water Resources Management
HEITMEIR, F., Thermo Turbo-Machinery
HIRSCHBERG, W., Automotive Engineering
HOFMANN-WELLENHOF, B., Theoretical Geodesy
JABERG, H., Hydraulic Turbo-machinery
JÜRGENS, G., Machine Principles
KAHLERT, H., Solid State Physics
KAINZ, H., Hydraulics, Agricultural and Industrial Hydraulic Engineering
KERN, G., Analysis and Applications
KNAPP, G., Analytical Chemistry
KOUDELKA, O., Telecommunications
KUBIN, G., Non-linear Signals Processing
KUPELWIESER, H., Artistic Forms
LEBERL, F., Computer-aided Geometry and Graphics
LECHNER, H., Project Envelopment and Project Management
LEITGEB, N., Hospital Technology
MAASS, W., Information Processing
MACHEROUX, P., Biochemistry
MARR, R. J., Process Engineering
MAURER, H., Information Processing
MEUWISSEN, J. M. C., Building and Town Planning
MORITZ, H., Geodesy
MUHR, H. M., Electrical Power Systems and High Voltage Engineering
NIDETSKY, B., Biotechnology
OSER, J., Materials Handling and Mechanical Engineering Design
PFANNHAUSER, W., Food Chemistry
POSCH, R., Applied Information Processing and Communications Technology
RENTMEISTER, M., Electrical Engineering
RIESSBERGER, K., Railways
RÖSCHEL, O., Geometry
SCHUBERT, W., Rock Mechanics and Tunnelling
SCHWAB, H., Biotechnology
SEMPRICH, S., Soil Mechanics and Foundation Engineering
SPAROWITZ, L., Concrete Construction
STADLER, G., Building
STADLOBER, E., Probability Theory and Statistics
STAUDINGER, G., Instrument Construction and Mechanical Techniques
STELZER, F., Chemical Technology of Organic Materials
STIGLER, H., Electricity Economy and Energy Innovation
SÜNKEL, H., Theoretical Geodesy
TICHY, R., Mathematics
TSCHOM, H., Domestic Architecture
VON DER LINDEN, W., Theoretical Physics
VÖSSNER, S., Mechanical Engineering and Industrial Informatics
WACH, P., Theoretical Methods in Mechanical Engineering and Industrial Informatics
WEISS, R., Computer Engineering
WOESS, W., Mathematics
WOHINZ, J., Industrial Management
WOLFBAUER, O., Chemical and Process Engineering
WÜRSCHUM, R., Materials Science and Physical Methods

TECHNISCHE UNIVERSITÄT WIEN
(Vienna University of Technology)

Karlspl. 13, 1040 Vienna
Telephone: (1) 588010
E-mail: pr@tuwien.ac.at
Internet: www.tuwien.ac.at
Founded 1815
State control
Language of instruction: German
Academic year: October to June (2 semesters)
Rector: Prof. Dr PETER SKALICKY
Vice-Rector: Prof. Dr GERHARD SCHIMAK
Vice-Rector for Academic Affairs: Prof. Dr ADALBERT PRECHTL
Vice-Rector for Finance and Controlling: Dr PAUL JANKOWITSCH
Vice-Rector for Infrastructure and Devt: Prof. Dr GERHARD SCHIMAK
Vice-Rector for Research: Prof. Dr SABINE SEIDLER
Dir: Mag. EVELINE URBAN
Librarian: Dr PETER KUBALEK
Library: see under Libraries and Archives
Number of teachers: 3,020
Number of students: 23,452
Publication: *ZID-Line*

DEANS

Faculty of Architecture and Planning: Prof. Dr KLAUS SEMSROTH
Faculty of Civil Engineering: Prof. Dr JOSEF EBERHARDSTEINER
Faculty of Electrical Engineering and Information Technology: Prof. Dr GOTTFRIED MAGERL
Faculty of Informatics: Prof. Dr GERALD STEINHARDT
Faculty of Mathematics and Geoinformation: Prof. Dr DIETMAR DORNINGER
Faculty of Mechanical Engineering: Prof. Dr BERNHARD GERINGER
Faculty of Physics: Prof. Dr GERALD BADUREK
Faculty of Technical Chemistry: Prof. Dr JOHANNES FRÖHLICH

PROFESSORS

Faculty of Architecture and Planning (Karlspl. 13, 1040 Vienna; tel. (1) 5880125001; e-mail e250@tuwien.ac.at; internet www.rpl-arch.tuwien.ac.at):

ALSOP, W., Building Construction and Building Systems for Architects
BÖKEMANN, D., Town and Country Planning
BRÜLLMANN, K., Residential Building
CERWENKA, P., Transport Systems Planning
DANGSCHAT, J., Urban and Regional Research
FRANCK-OBERASPACH, G., Computer-aided Design and Planning Methods
HIERZEGGER, H., Local Area Planning
JORMAKKA, K. J., Architectural History and Historic Building Survey
JOURDA, F. H., Spatial Design
LESAK, F., Model Construction
MAHDAVI, A., Building Physics and Human Ecology
RICHTER, H., Structural Engineering for Architects
SCHÖNBÄCK, W., Public Finance and Infrastructure Policy
SEMSROTH, K., Urban Design and Planning
STILES, R., Landscape Planning and Garden Architecture
STRAUBE, M., Banking and Securities Law
WEBER, G., History of Art and Cultural Conservation
WEHDORN, M., History of Art, Architectural Conservation, and Industrial Archaeology
WINTER, W., Studies of Structural Design and Timber Construction
WOLFF-PLOTTEGG, M., Building Design and Theory
ZEHETNER, F., Public Law

Faculty of Civil Engineering (Karlspl. 13, 1040 Vienna; tel. (1) 5880120001; e-mail info@bauwesen.tuwien.ac.at; internet www.bauwesen.tuwien.ac.at):

BRANDL, H., Foundations
BRUNNER, P. H., Waste Management
DREYER, J., Building Material Sciences, Building Physics and Fire Protection
DROBIR, H., Water Plant Construction, Navigable Waterways and Environmental Hydraulics
GUTKNECHT, D., Hydraulics, Hydrology and Water Supply
JODL, H. G., Construction Practice and Methods
KNOFLACHER, H., Traffic Planning and Engineering
KOLBITSCH, A., Building Construction and Industrial Buildings
KOLLEGGER, J., Reinforced Concrete Construction and Massive Construction
KROISS, H., Water Supply, Sewage Purification and Prevention of Water Pollution
LITZKA, J., Road Engineering and Maintenance
MANG, H., Elasticity and Strength
MATSCHE, N., Water Quality and Waste Management

OBERNDORFER, W. J., Construction and Planning
OGRIS, H., Experimental Hydraulics
RAMBERGER, G., Steel Girder Construction
RUBIN, H., Structural Analysis
SCHIMMERL, J., Rational Mechanics
SCHNEIDER, U., Building Materials
TENTSCHERT, E. H., Geology
ZIEGLER, F., Applied Mechanics

Faculty of Electrical Engineering and Information Technology (Gusshausstr. 25–29, 1040 Vienna; tel. (1) 5880135001; e-mail goppenhe@pop.tuwien.ac.at; internet www.info.tuwien.ac.at/et):

BERTAGNOLLI, E., Solid State Electronics
BONEK, E., High Frequency and Communications Technology
BRAUNER, G., Power Systems
CHABICOVSKY, R., Industrial Electronics and Materials Science
DETTER, H., Precision Engineering
DIETRICH, D., Computer Technology
EIER, R., Data Processing
FALLMANN, W., Industrial Electronics and Materials Science
GORNIK, E., Solid State Electronics
HAAS, H., Fundamentals and Theory of Electrical Engineering
KRAUSZ, F., Photonics
LEEB, W., Communications and Radio-Frequency Engineering
MAGERL, G., Electrical Measurement Technology
MECKLENBRÄUKER, W., Low Frequency Technology
PFUNDNER, P., Industrial Electronics and Materials Science
PRECHTL, A., Theory of Electrical Engineering
RUMMICH, E., Electrical Drives and Machines
RUPP, M., Communications and Radio-Frequency Engineering
SCHMIDT, A., Quantum Electronics and Lasers
SCHRÖDL, M., Electrical Machines and Drives
SELBERHERR, S., Software Technology for Microelectronic Systems
VAN AS, H. R., Communication Networks
VELLEKOOP, M., Industrial Electronics and Materials Science
WEINMANN, A., Electrical Control, Navigation and Power Engineering
WEINRICHTER, J., Communications and Radio-Frequency Engineering
ZACH, F., Electrical Drives and Machines
ZEICHEN, G., Flexible Automation
ZIMMERMANN, H., Electrical Measurements and Circuit Design

Faculty of Informatics (Getreidemarkt 9, 1060 Vienna; tel. (1) 5880110000; e-mail dek100@mail.zserv.tuwien.ac.at; internet www.cs.tuwien.ac.at):

BREITENEDER, C., Software
BROCKHAUS, M., Information Technology
EITER, T., Information Systems
FLEISSNER, P., Design and Assessment/Social Cybernetics
GOTTLOB, G., Applied Informatics
GRÜNBACHER, H., Computer Engineering (VLSI-Design)
JAZAYERI, M., Information Systems
KAPPEL, G., Software Technology and Interactive Systems
KOPETZ, H., Software Technology
KROPATSCH, W., Design and Manufacturing
KUICH, W., Mathematical Logic and Computer Languages
LEITSCH, A., Computer Languages
MUTZEL, P., Computer Graphics and Algorithms
PURGATHOFER, W., Computer Graphics and Algorithms
SCHILDT, G.-H., Automation Systems
TJOA, A. M., Software Engineering
VIERTL, R., Applied Statistics and Information Science
WAGNER, I., Design and Assessment of Technology

Faculty of Mathematics and Geoinformation (Getreidemarkt 9, 1060 Vienna; tel. (1) 5880110000; e-mail dekmug@mail.zserv.tuwien.ac.at; internet www.math.tuwien.ac.at):

BARON, G., Geometry
CARSTENSEN, C., Applied and Numerical Mathematics
DIRSCHMID, H., Analysis and Technical Mathematics
DORNINGER, D., Algebra and Computational Mathematics
DUTTER, R., Technical Statistics
EBEL, H., Technical Physics
FRANK, A., Surveying and Geoinformation
GRUBER, P., Mathematical Analysis
HERTLING, J., Applied and Numerical Mathematics
KAHMEN, H., General Geodesy
KAISER, H., Algebra and Computational Mathematics
KELNHOFER, F., Cartography and Reproduction Technology
KUICH, W., Mathematical Logic and Computer Languages
LANGER, H., Applied Analysis
MLITZ, R., Applied and Numerical Mathematics
POTTMANN, A., Geometry
SCHACHERMAYER, W., Statistics and Probability Theory
SCHNABL, R., Analysis and Technical Mathematics
SCHUH, H., Geodesy and Geophysics
STACHEL, H., Geometry
TROCH, I., Analysis and Technical Mathematics
VANA, N., Dosimetry
VIERTL, R., Applied Statistics and Information Science
WERTZ, W., Financial and Actuarial Mathematics

Faculty of Mechanical Engineering (Karlspl. 13, 1040 Vienna; tel. (1) 5880130001; e-mail mrosen@pop.tuwien.ac.at; internet www.tuwien.ac.at/maschinenbau):

BIBERSCHICK, D., Industrial Engineering, Ergonomics and Business Economics
DEGISCHER, H. P., Materials Science and Testing
GAMER, U., Mechanics
GRÖSEL, B., Handling and Transport Technology and General Design Engineering
HASELBACHER, H., Thermal Turbo-Machinery and Power Plants
JÖRGL, H. P., Machine- and Process-Engineering
KLUWICK, A., Hydrodynamics
KOPACEK, P., Handling Devices and Robotics
LENZ, H. P., Internal Combustion Vehicles
LINZER, W., Theory of Heat
LUGNER, P., Mechanics
MATTHIAS, H. B., Water-powered Machines and Pumps
PATZAK, G., Industrial Engineering, Ergonomics and Business Economics
RAMMERSTORFER, F., Light Engineering, Aeroplane Engineering
RINDER, L., Machine Parts
SCHNEIDER, W., Gas and Thermodynamics
SCHUÖCKER, D., Non-conventional Processing, Forming and Laser Technology
SCHWAIGER, W., Accounting and Controlling
SEIDLER, S., Materials Science and Testing
SPRINGER, H., Machine Dynamics and Measurement
STEPAN, A., Industrial Business Management
TROGER, H., Mechanics
UHLIR, H., Industrial Engineering, Ergonomics and Business Economics
VARGA, T., Welding
WESESLINDTNER, H., Computer Integrated Manufacturing
WOJDA, F., Business Management
ZEMAN, J., Pressure Vessel and Plant Technology

Faculty of Physics (Wiedner Hauptstr. 8–10, 1040 Vienna; tel. (1) 5880110000; internet www.physik.tuwien.ac.at):

AIGINGER, J., Ionizing Radiation
BADUREK, G., Nuclear Solid State Physics
BALCAR, E., Neutron and Solid State Physics
BENES, E., General Physics
BRÜCKL, E., Geophysics
BURGDÖRFER, J., Theoretical Physics
EBEL, H., Technical Physics
FLECK, M. C., Neutron Physics
KIRCHMAYR, H., Experimental Physics
KRAUS, K., Photogrammetry
KUMMER, W., Theoretical Physics
RAUCH, H., Experimental Nuclear Physics
SCHUH, H., Geodesy and Geophysics
SCHWEDA, M., Theoretical Physics
SKALICKY, P., Applied Physics
WEBER, H. W., Low Temperature Physics
WINTER, H., General Physics

Faculty of Technical Chemistry (Getreidemarkt 9, 1060 Vienna; tel. (1) 5880110000; e-mail johannes.froehlich@tuwien.ac.at; internet www.chemie.tuwien.ac.at):

FABJAN, C., Technical Electrochemistry and Solid State Chemistry
GRASSERBAUER, M., Analytical Chemistry
GRUBER, H., Chemical Technology of Organic Materials
HAMPEL, W., Biochemical Technology
HOFBAUER, H., Chemical Engineering, Fuel Technology and Environmental Technology
KNÖZINGER, E., Physical Chemistry
KUBEL, F., Mineralogy, Crystallography and Structural Chemistry
MARINI, I., Chemical Engineering, Fuel Technology and Environmental Technology
SCHMID, R., Inorganic Chemistry
SCHUBERT, U., Inorganic Chemistry
SCHWARZ, K., Physical and Theoretical Chemistry
STACHELBERGER, H., Botany, Technical Microscopy and Organic Raw Materials
WEINBERGER, P., Technical Electrochemistry and Solid State Chemistry
WRUSS, W., Chemical Technology of Inorganic Materials
WURST, F., Applied Botany, Technical Microscopy, and Organic Raw Materials Science

UMIT—PRIVATE UNIVERSITÄT FÜR GESUNDHEITSWISSENSCHAFTEN, MEDIZINISCHE INFORMATIK UND TECHNIK
(Health and Life Sciences University)

Eduard Wallnöfer-Zentrum 1, 6060 Hall
Telephone: (50) 86483000
E-mail: lehre@umit.at
Internet: www.umit.at

Founded 2002
Private control

Rector: Prof. Dr CHRISTA THEM
Vice-Rector for Finance and Human Resources: PHILIPP UNTERHOLZNER

Library of 7,750 vols, 30 journals, 500 CDs, DVDs and video cassettes
Number of teachers: 270
Number of students: 1,370

UNIVERSITÄT FÜR ANGEWANDTE KUNST IN WIEN
(University of Applied Arts in Vienna)

Oskar Kokoschkapl. 2, 1010 Vienna
Telephone: (1) 711330
E-mail: pr@uni-ak.ac.at
Internet: www.dieangewandte.at

Founded 1867
State control
Academic year: October to September (2 semesters)

Rector: Dr GERALD BAST
Vice-Rector for Facilities Devt and Publication Issues: Prof. Dipl.-Ing Dr WOLF D. PRIX
Vice-Rector for Quality Assurance, Education Issues, Mediation and Communication: Prof. Mag. BARBARA PUTZ-PLECKO
Vice-Rector for Teaching: Prof. Mag. JOSEF KAISER
Chair. of the Academic Senate: Mag. Dr RUTH MATEUS-BERR
Univ. Dir: Dr HEINZ ADAMEK
Head Librarian: Dr GABRIELE JURJEVEC-KOLLER

Library: 400 periodicals, 100,000 monographs, 2,500 video cassettes
Number of teachers: 380
Number of students: 1,800

Publication: *Prospect* (2 a year)

UNIVERSITÄT FÜR BODENKULTUR WIEN
(University of Natural Resources and Applied Life Sciences, Vienna)

Gregor Mendelstr. 33, 1180 Vienna
Telephone: (1) 476540
E-mail: office.rektorat@boku.ac.at
Internet: www.boku.ac.at

Founded 1872
State control
Academic year: October to June

Rector: Prof. Dr MARTIN H. GERZABEK
Vice-Rector for Finances: ANDREA REITHMAYER
Vice-Rector for Research and Int. Research Collaboration: Prof. Dr JOSEF GLÖßL
Vice-Rector for Strategic Devt: Dr GEORG HABERHAUER
Vice-Rector for Teaching and Int. Affairs: Prof. Dr BARBARA HINTERSTOISSER
Librarian: Mag. MARTINA HÖRL

Library: see under Libraries and Archives
Number of teachers: 1,000
Number of students: 11,350

Publications: *Blick ins Land* (12 a year), *Die Bodenkultur*, *Ökoenergie* (6 a year), *Zentralblatt für das gesamte Forstwesen* (4 a year)

PROFESSORS

ATZBERGER, C.
BERGMEISTER, K.
BERNHARDT, K.
BÜRSTMAYR, H.
DÜRRSTEIN, H.
FIEBIG, M.
FLORINETH, F.
FORNECK, A.
FRANK, T.
FREYER, B.
GERIKE, R.
GERZABEK, M.
GIERUS, M.
GINDL-ALTMUTTER, W.
GLÖßL, J.
GODBOLD, D.
GRONALT, M.
GRONAUER, A.
GÜBITZ, G.
HABERSACK, H.
HACKLÄNDER, K.
HALTRICH, D.
HASENAUER, H.
HIETZ, P.
HOFREITHER, M.
HOGL, K.
HUBER-HUMER, M.
HÜBL, J.
JUNGWIRTH, M.
KANTELHARDT, J.
KASPER, C.
KAUL, H.
KNEIFEL, W.
KOSMA, P.
KROMP-KOLB, H.
KRSKA, R.
KUNERT, R.
LEISCH, F.
LICHTENEGGER, H.
LICKA, L.
LIEBERT, W.
LOISKANDL, W.
MATTANOVICH, D.
MEIMBERG, H.
NOWAK, W. G.
OBINGER, C.
OOSTENBRINK, C.
PFEIFER, C.
PRÖBSTL-HAIDER, U.
PRÖLL, T.
REIMHULT, E.
RENNEBERG, W.
ROSENAU, T.
SCHIEBEL, W.
SCHMID, E.
SCHNEIDER, G.
SCHOPF, A.
SCHULEV-STEINDL, E.
SCHULZ, K.
SEKOT, W.
SINNER, E.-K.
SÖLKNER, J.
STAMPFER, K.
STEINKELLNER, S.
STINGEDER, G. J.
STÖGER, E.
STRAUSS, J.
TEISCHINGER, A.
TOCA-HERRERA, J. L.
TREBERSPURG, M.
WENZEL, W.
WINCKLER, C.
WU, W.
ZANGERL, C.
ZECHMEISTER-BOLTENSTERN, S.

UNIVERSITÄT FÜR KÜNSTLERISCHE UND INDUSTRIELLE GESTALTUNG LINZ
(University of Art and Industrial Design, Linz)

Hauptpl. 8, 4010 Linz
Telephone: (732) 78980
E-mail: international.office@ufg.ac.at
Internet: www.ufg.ac.at

Founded 1947, present status 1998
State control
Academic year: October to June (2 semesters)

Rector: Prof. Dr RICHARD KANNONIER
Vice-Rector for Central Services: Dr CHRISTINE WINDSTEIGER
Vice-Rector for Research: Dr MANFRED LECHNER
Vice-Rector for Studies and Teaching: Prof. Mag. RAINER ZENDRON
Librarian: Dr MANFRED LECHNER

Library: 200 journals

UNIVERSITÄT FÜR MUSIK UND DARSTELLENDE KUNST GRAZ
(University of Music and Performing Arts, Graz)

Leonhardstr. 15, Palais Meran, 8010 Graz
Telephone: (316) 3890
E-mail: info@kug.ac.at
Internet: www.kug.ac.at

Founded 1816, conservatory 1920, academy 1963, present status 1998
State control
Language of instruction: German
Academic year: October to June

Rector: Prof. Mag. Dr GEORG SCHULZ
Vice-Rector for Arts and Research: Prof. Mag. Dr ROBERT HÖLDRICH
Vice-Rector for Quality Management, Human Resource Devt, Gender Mainstreaming: Mag. DORIS CARSTENSEN
Vice-Rector for Study: Prof. Mag. EIKE STRAUB
Univ. Dir: Mag. ASTRID WEDENIG
Library Dir: Mag. ROBERT SCHILLER

Library of 210,000 vols incl. books, journals, sheets, records, audio cassettes and other media
Number of teachers: 424
Number of students: 2,000

HEADS OF INSTITUTES

Institute of Aesthetics of Music: Prof. Dr ANDREAS DORSCHEL
Institute of Church Music and Organ: Prof. Dr GUNTHER MICHAEL ROST
Institute of Composition, Music Theory, Music History and Conducting: Prof. Dr PETER REVERS
Institute of Drama: Prof. Dr EVELYN DEUTSCH-SCHREINER
Institute of Early Music and Performance Practice: Prof. Dr KLAUS HUBMANN
Institute of Electronic Music and Acoustics: Dr ALOIS SONTACCHI
Institute of Ethnomusicology: Prof. Dr GERD GRUPE
Institute of Jazz: Prof. ANTHONY PARTYKA
Institute of Jazz Research: Prof. Dr FRANZ KERSCHBAUMER
Institute of Music Education: Prof. Mag. GERHARD WANKER
Institute of Opera: Prof. FRANK CRAMER
Institute of Piano: Prof. EUGEN JAKAB
Institute of Stage Design: Prof. HANS SCHAVERNOCH
Institute of Strings: Prof. Dr KERSTIN FELTZ
Institute of the Oberschützen Campus: Prof. Dr KLAUS ARINGER
Institute of Voice, Lied and Oratorio: Prof. MARTIN KLIETMANN
Institute of Wind and Percussion Instruments: Prof. Mag. THOMAS EIBINGER

UNIVERSITÄT FÜR MUSIK UND DARSTELLENDE KUNST WIEN (MDW)
(University of Music and Performing Arts Vienna)

Anton-von-Webern-Pl. 1, 1030 Vienna
Telephone: (1) 71155
E-mail: rektor@mdw.ac.at
Internet: www.mdw.ac.at

Founded 1817 as Conservatorium der Gesellschaft der Musikfreunde, nationalized 1909
Language of instruction: German
Academic year: October to June

Rector: Prof. Mag. Dr WERNER HASITSCHKA
Vice-Rector: Prof. Mag. WOLFGANG HEIßLER
Vice-Rector: ANDREA KLEIBE
Vice-Rector: ULRIKE SYCH
Library Dir: Mag. MICHAEL STAUDINGER

Number of teachers: 862
Number of students: 3,188

DEANS

Office for Instrumental Studies: Prof. AVEDIS KOUYOUMDJIAN
Office for Music Education Programmes: Prof. Mag. PAUL STEJSKAL

HEADS OF INSTITUTES

Bruckner Institute (Theory, Aural Training and Conducting): ALOIS GLASSNER
Film Academy: CLAUDIA WALKENSTEINER-PRESCHL
Hellmesberger Institute (Stringed Instruments): WOLFGANG AICHINGER
Institute of Chamber Music and Special Ensembles: JOHANNES MEISSL
Institute of Composition and Sound Technology: JOHANNES KRETZ
Institute of Conducting: THOMAS KREUZBERGER
Institute of Cultural Management: FRANZ-OTTO HOFECKER
Institute of Folk Music Research and Ethnomusicology: URSULA HEMETEK
Institute of Keyboard Instruments: MARTIN HUGHES
Institute of Music and Movement Education and Music Therapy: ANGELIKA HAUSER-DELLEFANT
Institute of Music Teaching: PETER RÖBKE
Institute of Organ, Organ Research and Church Music: ERWIN ORTNER
Institute of Research into Musical Style: MARIA HELFGOTT
Institute of Song and Musicals: KARLHEINZ HANSER
Institute of Stringed Instruments: STEFAN KROPFITSCH
Institute of the Analysis, Theory and History of Music: CORNELIA SZABO-KNOTIK
Institute of the Sociology of Music: ALFRED SMUDITS
Institute of Wind and Percussion Instruments: BARBARA GISLER
Ludwig van Beethoven Institute (Keyboard Instruments): JOHANNES MARIAN
Max Reinhardt Seminar: HANS HOFFER
Popular Music: WOLFGANG PUSCHNIG
Salieri Institute (Song): MARIA BAYER
Schubert Institute (Wind and Percussion Instruments): WALTER WRETSCHITSCH
Vienna Institute of Sound: WILFRIED KAUSEL

UNIVERSITÄT MOZARTEUM SALZBURG
(Mozarteum University Salzburg)

Schrannengasse 10A, 5020 Salzburg
Telephone: (662) 61980
E-mail: info@moz.ac.at
Internet: www.uni-mozarteum.at

Founded 1841
State control
Academic year: October to June

Depts of art and craft education, brass, composition and music theory, conducting, drama, fine arts, keyboard studies, music and dance education, music education (Innsbruck), music education (Salzburg), musicology, music theatre, stage design, string studies, vocal studies, wind and percussion studies

Rector: Prof. REINHART VON GUTZEIT
Vice-Rector for Research and Devt: Prof. Dr WOLFGANG GRATZER
Vice-Rector for Resources: Mag. BRIGITTE HÜTTER
Vice-Rector for Teaching: Prof. BRIGITTE ENGELHARD
Librarian: Dr MANFRED KAMMERER

Number of teachers: 500
Number of students: 1,650

Publications: *International Summer Academy Mozarteum Brochure* (1 a year), *Uni-Art* (8 a year)

UNIVERSITÄT SALZBURG
(Salzburg University)

Kapitelgasse 4–6, 5020 Salzburg
Telephone: (662) 80440
E-mail: uni.service@sbg.ac.at
Internet: www.uni-salzburg.at

Founded 1622, closed 1810, College 1810–50, ind. faculty of Catholic Theology 1850–1962, reconstituted 1962
State control
Languages of instruction: English, German
Academic year: October to June (2 semesters)

Rector: Prof. Dr HEINRICH SCHMIDINGER
Vice-Rector for Education: Prof. Dr RUDOLF MOSLER
Vice-Rector for Int. Relations and Communications: Prof. Dr SONJA PUNTSCHER-RIEKMANN
Vice-Rector for Research: Prof. Dr ALBERT DUSCHL
Librarian: Dr URSULA SCHACHL-RABER

Library: see under Libraries and Archives
Number of teachers: 750
Number of students: 14,000

DEANS

Faculty of Catholic Theology: Prof. Dr WOLBERT WERNER
Faculty of Cultural and Social Sciences: Prof. Dr SYLVIA HAHN
Faculty of Law: Prof. Dr FRIEDRICH HARRER
Faculty of Natural Science: Prof. Dr ULRIKE-GABRIELE BERNINGER

PROFESSORS

Faculty of Arts:

BETTEN, A., German
BOTZ, G., History
BRUCHER, G., History of Austrian Art
DALFEN, J., Classical Philology
DOPSCH, H., History
EHMER, J., Modern History
FABRIS, H., Journalism and Communications
FELTEN, F., Classical Archaeology
GOEBL, H., Romance Languages
GRASSL, H., Ancient History
GRÖSSING, S., Sport
HAAS, H., Austrian History
HAIDER, H., Linguistics
HASLINGER, A., German
JALKOTZY, S., Ancient History
KLEIN, H. M., English
KNOCHE, M., Journalism and Communications
KOLMER, L., Medieval History and Historic Auxiliary Sciences
KRONSTEINER, O., Slavic Languages
KRUMM, V., Education
KUON, P., Romance Philology
MAYER, G., Slavic Languages
MESSNER, D., Romance Languages
MORSCHER, E., Philosophy
MÜLLER, E., Physical Education
MÜLLER, U., German
PANAGL, O., Linguistics
PATRY, J. L., Education
PETERSMANN, G., Classical Philology
PIEL, F., Medieval and Modern History of Art
ROSSBACHER, K., German
SCHMOLKE, M., Journalism and Communications
STAGL, J., Sociology
STENZL, J., Music Science
TRUCHLAR, L., English
WEINGARTNER, P., Philosophy
ZAIC, F., English

Faculty of Catholic Theology:

BACHL, G., Dogmatics
BEILNER, W., New Testament Studies
BUCHER, A., Catechism and Religious Education
KÖHLER, W., Christian Philosophy and Psychology
MÖDLHAMMER, J., Ecumenical Theology
NIKOLASCH, F., Liturgy
PAARHAMMER, J., Church Law
PAUS, A., Epistemology and Religious Studies
SCHLEINZER, F., Pastoral Theology
SCHMIDINGER, H., Christian Philosophy
WINKLER, G. B., Church History
WOLBERT, W., Moral Theology

Faculty of Law:

BERKA, W., General Theory of the State, Theory of Administration, Constitutional and Administrative Law
BUSCHMANN, A., German Legal History, German Private and Civil Law
GRILLBERGER, K., Industrial Law
HACKL, K., Roman and Civil Law
HAGEN, J., Sociology of Law
HAMMER, R., Management
HARRER, F., Civil and Commercial Law
KARL, W., International Law
KOJA, F., General Constitutional Law
KOPPENSTEINER, H.-G., Austrian and International Commercial Law
KYRER, A., Economics
MAYER-MALY, TH., German and Austrian Private Law
MIGSCH, E., Civil Law
RAINER, J., Roman and Modern Private Law
SCHÄFFER, H., Public Law
SCHMOLLER, K., Austrian Criminal Law
SCHUMACHER, W., International Commercial Law and Civil Law
SCHWIMANN, M., International Civil Law
STOLZLECHNER, H., Public Law
TRIFFTERER, O., Austrian and International Criminal Law

Faculty of Natural Sciences:

AMTHAUER, G., Geology
BAUMANN, U., Psychology
BENTRUP, F. W., Plant Physiology and Anatomy
BREITENBACH, M., Molecular Genetics
CLAUSEN, H., Systems Analysis
CZIHAK, G., Genetics
FÜRNKRANZ, D., Botany
GERL, P., Mathematics
HERMANN, A., Zoology
NEUBAUER, F., Geology
PERNER, J., Psychology
PFALZGRAF, J., Computer Science
RIEDL, H., Geography
SCHWEIGER, F., Mathematics
STADEL, CH., Geography
STEINHÄUSLER, F., Biophysics
STRACK, H.-B., Biochemistry
WALLBOTT, H., Psychology
WERNER, H., Sciences Education
ZINTERHOF, P., Mathematics

Inter-faculty Institutes:

CROLL, G., Music History of Salzburg
FAUPEL, K., Political Science
GACHOWETZ, H., Organizational Psychology
HAUPTMANN, W., Criminal Psychology
KOPPENSTEINER, H. G., European Law
LAUBER, V., Political Science
MAYER-MALY, TH., Energy Law, Law of Liechtenstein
MIGSCH, E., Private Insurance Law
MORSCHER, E., Philosophy, Technology, Economics
ZINTERHOF, P., Software Technology

UNIVERSITÄT WIEN
(University of Vienna)

Dr Karl Lueger-Ring 1, 1010 Vienna
Telephone: (1) 42770
E-mail: public@univie.ac.at
Internet: www.univie.ac.at

Founded 1365
State control
Academic year: October to June (2 semesters)

Rector: Prof. Dr HEINZ W. ENGL

Vice-Rector for Educational Program Devt and Internationalization: Prof. Dr ARTHUR METTINGER
Vice-Rector for Infrastructure, Resources and Library Affairs: Prof. Dr JOHANN JURENITSCH
Vice-Rector for Research and Career Devt: Prof. Dr HEINZ W. ENGL
Vice-Rector for Student Affairs and Continuing Education: Prof. Dr CHRISTA SCHNABL
Librarian: Mag. MARIA SEISSL

Library: see under Libraries and Archives
Number of teachers: 6,747
Number of students: 88,000

DEANS

Centre for Molecular Biology: Prof. Dr GRAHAM WARREN (Head)
Centre for Sports Sciences and University Sports: Prof. Dr ARNOLD BACA (Head)
Centre for Translation Studies: Prof. Dr NORBERT GREINER (Head)
Faculty of Business, Economics and Statistics: Prof. Dr GERHARD SORGER
Faculty of Catholic Theology: Prof. Dr MARTIN JÄGGLE
Faculty of Chemistry: Prof. Dr BERNHARD KEPPLER
Faculty of Computer Science: Prof. Dr WOLFGANG KLAS
Faculty of Earth Sciences, Geography and Astronomy: Prof. Dr HEINZ FAßMANN
Faculty of Historical and Cultural Studies: Prof. Dr MICHAEL VIKTOR SCHWARZ
Faculty of Law: Prof. Dr HEINZ MAYER
Faculty of Life Sciences: Prof. Dr HORST SEIDLER
Faculty of Mathematics: Prof. Dr HARALD RINDLER
Faculty of Philological and Cultural Studies: Prof. Dr SUSANNE WEIGELIN-SCHWIEDRZIK
Faculty of Philosophy and Educational Sciences: Prof. Dr INES MARIA BREINBAUER
Faculty of Physics: Prof. Dr CHRISTOPH DELLAGO
Faculty of Protestant Theology: Prof. Dr CHRISTIAN DANZ
Faculty of Psychology: Prof. Dr GERMAIN WEBER
Faculty of Social Sciences: Prof. Dr RUDOLF RICHTER

PROFESSORS

Centre for Sports Sciences and University Sports (tel. (1) 427759001; e-mail sportwissenschaft@univie.ac.at; internet www.univie.ac.at/sportwissenschaft):

ANKNER, P.
BACHL, N.
BENDA, F.
HACKL-JAGENBREIN, S.
KELLNER, A.
KOLB, M.
MUNZAR, S.
WEIß, O.

Centre for Translation Studies (tel. (1) 427758001; e-mail translation@univie.ac.at; internet www.univie.ac.at/transvienna):

BUDIN, G.
FRANK, G.
KASTOVSKY, D.
KLAMBAUER, E.
LEIMEIER, C.
MOLDAU, S.
RESCH, R.
SCHÄTTLE, M.
SNELL-HORNBY, M.
WILDMANN, D.

Faculty of Business, Economics and Statistics (tel. (1) 427737030; e-mail dekanat-win@univie.ac.at; internet www.univie.ac.at/wirtschaftswissenschaften):

ALTENBERGER, O., Business Studies
BONZE, I., Economics
CLEMENZ, G., Economics
DIAMANTOPOULOS, A., Business Studies
DOCKNER, E., Business Studies
FINSINGER, J., Business Studies
FITZSIMONS, C. O., Business Languages
HARTL, R., Business Studies
HEIDENBERGER, K., Business Studies
KUNST, R., Computer Science and Business Informatics
LECHNER, E., Commercial Law
MUELLER, D., Economics
NERMUTH, M., Economics
OROSEL, G., Economics
PFEIFFER, T., Business Studies
PFLUG, G., Statistics and Decision Support Systems
PÖTSCHER, B., Statistics and Decision Support Systems
SORGER, G., Economics
TRAXLER, F., Government
VAN DER BELLEN, A., Economics
WAGENER, A., Economics
WAGNER, U., Business Studies
WEILINGER, A., Commercial Law
WINCKLER, G., Economics
WIRL, F., Business Studies
ZECHNER, J., Business Studies

Faculty of Catholic Theology (tel. (1) 42773001; internet www.univie.ac.at/ktf):

FEULNER, H.-J., Liturgical Studies
FIGL, J., Study of Religion
GABRIEL, I., Social Ethics
JÄGGLE, M., Religious Education
KÜHSCHELM, R., Ethics and Social Sciences
LANGTHALER, R., Christian Philosophy
MÜLLER, L., Canon Law
PROKSCHI, R., Theology and History of Eastern Churches
REIKERSTORFER, J., Fundamental Theology and Apologetics
SCHLOSSER, M., Theology of Spirituality
STUBENRAUCH, B., Dogmatics
VIRT, G., Moral Theology

Faculty of Chemistry (tel. (1) 427751001; e-mail chemie.dekanat@univie.ac.at; internet chemie.univie.ac.at):

BRINKER, U., Organic Chemistry
DICKERT, F., Analytical Chemistry and Food Chemistry
DJINOVIĆ-CARUGO, K., Biomolecular Structural Chemistry
FRINGELI, U. P., Biophysical Chemistry
IPSER, H., Inorganic Chemistry
KEPPLER, B., Inorganic Chemistry
KONRAT, R., Biomolecular Structural Chemistry
LINDNER, W., Analytical Chemistry and Food Chemistry
LISCHKA, H., Theoretical Chemistry
MULZER, J., Organic Chemistry
SCHMID, W., Organic Chemistry
SCHUSTER, P., Theoretical Chemistry
SONTAG, G., Analytical Chemistry and Food Chemistry
STEINHAUSER, O., Biomolecular Structural Chemistry

Faculty of Computer Science (tel. (1) 427739001; internet www.cs.univie.ac.at):

EDER, J., Knowledge and Business Engineering
GROSSMANN, W., Computer Science
HARING, G., Faculty of Computer Science
KARAGIANNIS, D., Knowledge and Business Engineering
KLAS, W., Computer Science
QUIRCHMAYR, G., Distributed and Multimedia Systems
ZIMA, H., Department of Scientific Computing

Faculty of Earth Sciences, Geography and Astronomy (tel. (1) 427753001; internet www.univie.ac.at/geowissenschaften):

BREGER, M., Astronomy
FAßMANN, H., Geography and Regional Research
FERGUSON, D. K., Palaeontology
HANTEL, M., Meteorology and Geophysics
HENSLER, G., Astronomy
HOFMANN, T., Environmental Geosciences
KAINZ, W., Geography and Regional Research
RABEDER, G., Palaeontology
RICHTER, W., Lithospheric Sciences
STEINACKER, R., Meteorology and Geophysics
STEINHAUSER, P., Meteorology and Geophysics
TILLMANNS, E., Mineralogy and Crystallography
WEICHHART, P., Geography and Regional Research
WOHLSCHLÄGL, H., Geography and Regional Research

Faculty of Historical and Cultural Studies (tel. (1) 427740001; e-mail guntram.schneider@univie.ac.at; internet www.univie.ac.at/dekanat-hist-kult):

ASH, M., History
BACH, F. T., Art History
BIETAK, M., Egyptology
BOTZ, G., Contemporary History
BRUCKMÜLLER, E., Social and Economic History
BRUNNER, K., History
DIENST, H., History
DOBESCH, G., Ancient History, Papyrology and Epigraphy
DONNERMAIR, C., Social and Economic History
DREKONJA, G., History
EHMER, J., Social and Economic History
FRIESINGER, H., Prehistoric and Medieval Archaeology
HAHN, W., Numismatics and Monetary History
HASELSTEINER, H., East and Southern European History
KAPPELER, A., East and Southern European History
KLIMBURG-SALTER, D., Art History
KODER, J., Byzantine and Modern Greek Studies
KOHLER, A., History
KÖSTLIN, K., European Ethnology
KRESTEN, O., Byzantine and Modern Greek Studies
KRINZINGER, F., Classical Archaeology
LANGE, A., Jewish Studies
LIPPERT, A., Prehistoric and Medieval Archaeology
LORENZ, H., Art History
MALECZEK, W., History
MEYER, M., Classical Archaeology
PALME, B., Ancient History, Papyrology and Epigraphy
PILLINGER, R., Classical Archaeology
ROSENAUER, A., Art History
SACHSE, C., Contemporary History
SAURER, E., History
SCHMALE, W., History
SCHMIDT-COLINET, A., Classical Archaeology
SCHMITT, O., Eastern and Southern European History
SCHWARZ, M., Art History
SIEWERT, P., Institute of Ancient History, Papyrology and Epigraphy
STELZER, W., History
STEMBERGER, G., Jewish Studies
STERN, F., Contemporary History
STIEFEL, D., Social and Economic History
SUPPAN, A., Eastern and Southern European History
THEIS, L., Art History
WERNER, F., Jewish Studies

Faculty of Law (Schottenbastei 10–16, 1010 Vienna; tel. (1) 427734001; e-mail dekanat-jur@univie.ac.at; internet www.juridicum.at):

AICHER, J., Commercial Law
BAJONS, E. M., Procedural Law
BENKE, N., Roman Law and Ancient Legal History
BÖHM, P., Civil Procedural Law
BRANDSTETTER, W., Criminal Law and Criminology
BRAUNEDER, W., Austrian and European Legal History
BURGSTALLER, M., Criminal Law and Criminology
DORALT, W., Financial Law
FENYVES, A., Civil Law
FISCHER-CZERMAK, C., Civil Law
FUCHS, H., Criminal Law and Criminology
FUNK, B. CHR., State and Administrative Law
HAFNER, G., International Law and International Relations
HÖPFEL, F., Criminal Law and Criminology
IRO, G., Civil Law
KONECNY, A., Procedural Law
KOPETZKI, C., Commercial and Business Law
KREJCI, H., Commercial Law
LUF, G., Legal Philosophy and Legal Theory
MAYER, H., State and Administrative Law
MAZAL, W., Labour Law and Social Law
MEISSEL, F. S., Roman Law and Antique Legal History
NEUHOLD, H. P., International Law and International Relations
OFNER, H., European, International and Comparative Law
ÖHLINGER, T., State and Administrative Law
PIELER, P. E., Roman Law and History of Ancient Law
POTZ, R., Cultural and Religious Law
RASCHAUER, B., State and Administrative Law
REBHAHN, R., Labour Law and Law of Social Security
RECHBERGER, W., Civil Procedural Law
RIEDL, K., Civil Law
SCHAUER, M., Civil Law
SCHRAMMEL, W., Labour Law and Social Law
SCHREUER, CHR., International Law and International Relations
SIMON, T., Legal and Constitutional History
STELZER, M., State and Administrative Law
TANZER, M., Financial Law
THIENEL, R., State and Administrative Law
VERSCHRÄGEN, B., Comparative Law
WELSER, R., Civil Law
WILHELM, G., Civil Law
WILLVONSEDER, R., Roman Law and Ancient Legal History

Faculty of Mathematics (tel. (1) 427756001; e-mail dekanat.mathematik@univie.ac.at; internet www.mat.univie.ac.at):

FRIEDMAN, S.-D., Mathematics
GRÖCHENIG, K.-H., Mathematics
KOTH, M., Mathematics
LOSERT, V., Mathematics
MARKOWICH, P., Mathematics
MITSCH, H., Mathematics
MUTHSAM, H., Mathematics
NEUMAIER, A., Mathematics
RINDLER, H., Mathematics
SCHMIDT, K., Mathematics
SCHWERMER, J., Mathematics
SIGMUND, K., Mathematics

Faculty of Philological and Cultural Studies (tel. (1) 427745001; internet www.univie.ac.at/dekanat-phil-kult):

ALLGAYER-KAUFMANN, R., Musicology
BESTERS-DILGER, J., Slavonic Studies
BIRKHAN, H., German Studies
CAVIC-PODGORNIK, N. A., Slavonic Studies
CYFFER, N., African Studies
DÖNT, E., Classical Philology, Medieval and Neo-Latin Studies
DORMELS, R., East Asian Studies
DRESSLER, W., Linguistics
EBENBAUER, A., German Studies
EICHNER, H., Linguistics
FAISTAUER, R., German Studies
FROSCH, F., Romance Studies
GREISENEGGER, W., Theatre Arts
GRUBER, G., Musicology
HAIDER, H., Theatre Arts
HARRAUER, C., Classical Philology, Medieval and Neo-Latin Studies
HASSAUER, F., Romance Studies
HOLUBOWSKY, E., East Asian Studies
HUBER, W., English and American Studies
HUNGER, H., Near Eastern Studies
HÜTTNER, J., Theatre Arts
KASPER, C., European and Comparative Literature and Language Studies
KASTOVSKY, D., English and American Studies
KÖHBACH, M., Near Eastern Studies
KREMNITZ, G., Romance Studies
KRUMM, H.-J., German Studies
LAAKSO, J., European and Comparative Literature and Language Studies
LINHART, S., East Asian Studies
LIPOLD-STEVENS, I., English and American Studies
LOHLKER, R., Musicology
MARTINO, A., European and Comparative Literature and Language Studies
MEHLMAUER-LARCHER, B., English and American Studies
MENGEL, E., English and American Studies
METZELTIN, M., Romance Studies
MIKLAS, H., Slavonic Studies
NEWEKLOWSKY, G., Slavonic Studies
NEWERKLA, S. M., Slavonic Studies
POLJAKOV, F., Slavonic Studies
PREISENDANZ, K., South Asian, Tibetan and Buddhist Studies
ROHRWASSER, M., German Studies
RÖMER, F., Classical Philology, Medieval and Neo-Latin Studies
ROSSEL, S. H., European and Comparative Literature and Language Studies
RUBIK, M., English and American Studies
SCHENDL, H., English and American Studies
SCHICHO, W., African Studies
SCHJERVE-RINDLER, R., Romance Studies
SCHMIDT-DENGLER, W., German Studies
SEIDLHOFER, B., English and American Studies
SELZ, G., Near Eastern Studies
SMOLAK, K., Classical Philology, Medieval and Neo-Latin Studies
SODEYFI, H., Slavonic Studies
SOOMAN, I., European and Comparative Literature and Language Studies
STEINKELLNER, E., South Asian, Tibetan and Buddhist Studies
VAN UFFELEN, H., European and Comparative Literature and Language Studies
WAGNER, B., Romance Studies
WEIGELIN-SCHWIEDRZIK, S., East Asian Studies
WIESINGER, P., German Studies
WOLDAN, A., Slavonic Studies
WOYTEK, E., Classical Philology, Medieval and Neo-Latin Studies
ZEMAN, H., German Studies

Faculty of Philosophy and Educational Sciences (tel. (1) 427746001; internet homehobel.phl.univie.ac.at):

BIEWER, G., Educational Sciences
BREINBAUER, I. M., Educational Sciences
GIAMPIERI-DEUTSCH, P., Philosophy
HÄMMERLE, M., Educational Sciences
HOPMANN, S., Educational Sciences
KAMPITS, P., Philosophy
KLEIN, H.-D., Philosophy
NAGL, H., Philosophy
OESER, E., Philosophy of Science
PIAS, C., Philosophy
POLLMEISTER, K., Educational Sciences
PÖLTNER, G., Philosophy
SWERTZ, C., Educational Sciences
WALLNER, F., Philosophy

Faculty of Physics (tel. (1) 427751001; e-mail dekanat.physik@univie.ac.at; internet physics.univie.ac.at):

AICHELBURG, P. C., Theoretical Physics
BARTL, A., Theoretical Physics
DELLAGO, C., Experimental Physics
HAFNER, J., Materials Physics
HORVATH, H., Experimental Physics
KARNTHALER, H.-P., Materials Physics
KUTSCHERA, W., Isotope Research and Nuclear Physics
RUPP, R., Experimental Physics
VOGL, G., Materials Physics
YNGVASON, J., Theoretical Physics
ZEILINGER, A., Experimental Physics

Faculty of Protestant Theology (Rooseveltplatz 10, 1090 Vienna; tel. (1) 427732001; internet www.univie.ac.at/etf):

ADAM, G., Religious Education
DANZ, C., Systematic Theology
DEEG, M., Systematic Theology
HEINE, S., Pastoral Theology and Psychology of Religion
KÖRTNER, U., Systematic Theology
LEEB, R., Christian History, Art and Archaeology
LOADER, J., Old Testament and Biblical Archaeology
PRATSCHER, W., New Testament Studies
WISCHMEYER, W., Christian History, Art and Archaeology

Faculty of Psychology (tel. (1) 427747001; internet www.univie.ac.at/psychologie):

BAUER, H., Clinical, Biological and Differential Psychology
FORMANN, A., Psychological Basic Research
HERKNER, W., Psychological Basic Research
KIRCHLER, E., Economic Psychology, Educational Psychology and Evaluation
KRYSPIN-EXNER, I., Clinical, Biological and Differential Psychology
KUBINGER, K., Developmental Psychology and Psychological Assessment
LEDER, H., Psychological Basic Research
SPIEL, C., Economic Psychology, Educational Psychology and Evaluation
VORACEK, M., Psychological Basic Research

Faculty of Social Sciences (tel. (1) 427749001; internet www.univie.ac.at/sowi):

AMANN, A., Sociology
BAUER, T. A., Communication
DUCHKOWITSCH, W., Communication
FELT, U., Vienna Interdisciplinary Research Unit for the Study of (Techno) Science and Society
GERLICH, P., Government
GINGRICH, A., Social and Cultural Anthropology
GOTTSCHLICH, M., Communication
GOTTWEIS, H., Political Science
GRIMM, J., Communication
KRAMER, H., Political Science
KREISKY, H. E., Political Science
LANGENBUCHER, W., Communication
RICHTER, R., Sociology

ROSENBERGER, S., Political Science
SAUER, B., Political Science
SCHULZ, W., Sociology
SEGERT, D., Political Science
SEIDL, E., Nursing Science
TÁLOS, E., Government
UCAKAR, K., Government
VITOUCH, P., Communication

VETERINÄRMEDIZINISCHE UNIVERSITÄT WIEN
(University of Veterinary Medicine, Vienna)

Veterinärpl. 1, 1210 Vienna
Telephone: (1) 250770
E-mail: rektor@vu-wien.ac.at
Internet: www.vu-wien.ac.at
Founded 1765
State control
Academic year: October to June (2 semesters)
Rector: Dr SONJA HAMMERSCHMID
Vice-Rector for Acad. Affairs and Clinical Veterinary Medicine: Prof. Dr PETRA WINTER
Vice-Rector for Resources: Prof. Dr JOSEF EBENBICHLER
Librarian: Mag. DORIS REINITZER
Library: see under Libraries and Archives
Number of teachers: 206
Number of students: 2,300
Publications: *Uni Vet Wien Report* (4 a year), *Wiener Tierärztliche Monatsschrift* (12 a year)

PROFESSORS
ARNOLD, W., Wildlife Biology
AURICH, J. E., Obstetrics, Gynaecology and Andrology
BAMBERG, E., Biochemistry
BAUMGARTNER, W., Internal Medicine and Contagious Diseases of Ruminants and Swine
BÖCK, P., Histology and Embryology
FRANZ, C., Applied Botany
GEMEINER, M., Medical Chemistry
GÜNZBURG, W., Virology
HOFECKER, G., Physiology
KÖNIG, H., Anatomy
MAYRHOFER, E., Radiology
MÜLLER, M., Stock Breeding, Genetics
NIEBAUER, G., Surgery and Ophthalmology
NOHL, H., Pharmacology and Toxicology
ROSENGARTEN, R., Bacteriology, Mycology, Hygiene
SCHMIDT, P., Pathology, Forensic Medicine
SMULDERS, F., Meat Hygiene, Meat Technology, Food Science
STANEK, CH., Orthopaedics in Ungulates
THALHAMMER, J. G., Small Animals and Horses
TROXLER, J., Animal Husbandry, Animal Welfare
WINDISCHBAUER, G., Medical Physics, Biostatistics
ZENTEK, J., Nutrition

WEBSTER UNIVERSITY, VIENNA

Berchtoldgasse 1, 1220 Vienna
Telephone: (1) 26992930
E-mail: info@webster.ac.at
Internet: www.webster.ac.at
Founded 1981
Private control
Academic year: August to July (2 semesters)
Dir: Dr ARTHUR HIRSCH
Library Dir: BENJAMIN FASCHING-GRAY
Library of 10,000 vols
Number of teachers: 84
Number of students: 500

WIRTSCHAFTSUNIVERSITÄT WIEN
(Vienna University of Economics and Business)

Augasse 2–6, 1090 Vienna
Telephone: (1) 313360
E-mail: lehre@wu.ac.at
Internet: www.wu.ac.at
Founded 1898
State control
Languages of instruction: German, English
Academic year: October to June (2 semesters)
Rector: Prof. Dr CHRISTOPH BADELT
Vice-Rector for Acad. Programs and Student Affairs: Prof. Dr KARL SANDNER
Vice-Rector for Financial Affairs: Prof. Dr EVA EBERHARTINGER
Vice-Rector for Infrastructure and Human Resources: Dr MICHAEL HOLOUBEK
Vice-Rector for Research, Int. Affairs and External Relations: Prof. Dr BARBARA SPORN
Librarian: Dr NIKOLAUS BERGER
Library: see under Libraries and Archives
Number of teachers: 72
Number of students: 26,800
Publication: *Journal für Betriebswirtschaft* (Journal for Business Administration, 6 a year)

PROFESSORS
ABELE, H., Economic Theory and Policy
AFF, J., Economics
ALEXANDER, R. J., English Business Communication
AMBOS, B., International Marketing and Management
BERTL, R., Auditing, Accounting and International Accounting
BOGNER, ST., Department of Corporate Finance
EBERHARTINGER, E., Tax-oriented Business Management
FISCHER, M., Economic and Social Geography
FRANKE, N., Entrepreneurship and Foundation Research
GAREIS, R., Project Management
GRILLER, S., Research Institute for European Affairs
GRÜN, O., Business Organization and Materials Management
HANAPPI-EGGER, E., Gender and Diversity in Organizations
HOLOUBEK, M., Constitutional and Administrative Law
HORNIK, K., Mathematical and Statistical Methods
JAMMERNEGG, W., Industrial Information Processing
JANKO, W., Information Processing and Information Economics
KALSS, S., Business Law
KASPER, H., Management and Management Development
KUBIN, I., International Economics and Development Planning
KUMMER, S., Transportation
LANG, M., International Tax Law
LAURER, H. R., Constitutional and Administrative Law
LIENBACHER, G., Austrian and European Public Law
LUPTÁČIK, M., Economic Theory and Policy
MAUTNER, G., English Business Communication
MAYRHOFER, W., Business and Government Management
MAZANEC, J., Tourism
MEYER, M., Non-profit Management
MOSER, R., International Business
MUGLER, J., Small Business
NEUMANN, G., Business Informatics and New Media
NOWOTNY, C., Commercial Law
NOWOTNY, E., Financial Politics
OBENAUS, W., English Business Communication
OBERMANN, G., Public Finance
PANNY, W., Applied Computer Science
PFEIFFLE, H, Theory of Education
PICHLER, J. H., Economic Theory and Policy
PICHLER, S., Economic Theory and Policy
RAINER, F., Romance Languages
RATHMAYR, R., Slavonic Languages
RIEGLER, C., Integrated Business Accounting
RUNGGALDIER, U., Labour Law, Social Law
SANDNER, K., General Management
SCHEUCH, F., Marketing
SCHLEGELMILCH, B., International Marketing and Management
SCHNEDLITZ, P., Retail Management
SCHNEIDER, U., General Sociology and Economic Sociology
SCHNEIDER, U., Social Policy
SCHUCH, J., International Tax Law
SCHÜLEIN, J. A., General and Economic Sociology
SCHWEIGER, G., Advertising and Market Research
SEICHT, G., Industrial Management
SPECKBACHER, G., Business Management
STEGU, M., Romance Languages
STIASSNY, A., Quantitative Political Economy
STRASSER, H., Experimental Methods of Mathematics and Statistics
TAUDES, A., Industrial Information Processing
VOGEL, G., Technology and Commodity Economics
WALTHER, H., Employment Theory and Policy
WENTGES, P., Business Management

Schools of Applied Science

CAMPUS 02 Fachhochschule der Wirtschaft (CAMPUS 02 University for Applied Sciences): Körblergasse 126, 8021 Graz; tel. (316) 6002177; e-mail info@campus02.at; internet www.campus02.at; f. 2001; degree programmes in automation technology, information technologies and business informatics, innovation management, international marketing and sales management, financial accounting and management accounting; library: 7,800 printed media; 1,792 students; Man. Dir Mag Dr. ERIC BRUGGER; Man. Dir Dr ANNETTE ZIMMER.

Fachhochschul-Studiengang Bauingenieurwesen-Baumanagement (School of Applied Construction Engineering and Management): Daumegasse 1, 2nd Fl., 1100 Vienna; tel. (1) 60668772120; e-mail bau@fh-campuswien.ac.at; f. 1996; BA and MA courses in construction engineering and management; Dir Dr DORIS LINK.

Fachhochschul-Studiengang Burgenland GmbH (School of Applied Sciences Burgenland): Campus 1, 7000 Burgenland; tel. (5) 90106090; e-mail officefh@burgenland.at; internet www.fh-burgenland.at; f. 1994; 2 campuses; BA and MA courses in economics, environmental and energy management, health studies, information technology and management; Dir Mag. INGRID SCHWAB-MATKOVITS.

Fachhochschul-Studiengang Oberösterreich (School of Applied Sciences of Upper Austria): Franz-Fritsch-Str. 11, 4600 Wels; tel. (7242) 448080; e-mail info@fh-ooe.at; internet www.fh-ooe.at; f. 1994; Bachelors and Masters courses; campuses in Hagenberg (software, information technology and media), Linz (health and social welfare), Steyr (business and management studies) and Wels (engineering and environment and energy studies); Dir Dr GERALD REISINGER.

Fachhochschul-Studiengang Salzburg (School of Applied Sciences Salzburg): Urstein Süd 1, 5412 Puch/Salzburg; tel. (662) 5022110; e-mail press@fh-salzburg.ac.at; internet www.fh-salzburg.ac.at; f. 1995, present status 2004; campuses in Kuchl and Urstein; Bachelors and Masters courses in information technologies, wood and biogene technologies, business and tourism, media and design; library: 27,800 vols, 170 subscriptions; 100 teachers; 2,262 students; Man. Dirs RAIMUND RIBITSCH, Mag. DORIS WALTER.

Fachhochschul-Studiengänge bfi Wien (School of Applied Science bfi Vienna): Wohlmutstr. 22, 1020 Vienna; tel. (1) 7201286; e-mail info@fh-vie.at; internet www.fh-vie.ac.at; f. 1996, present status 2002; Bachelors programmes in work design and HR management, banking and finance, European economy and business management, logistics and transport management, project management and information technology, technical sales and distribution management; Masters programmes in banking and finance, European economy and business management, logistics and transport management, project management and organization and quantitative asset and risk management; library: 10,000 media; Man. Dir Dr HELMUT HOLZINGER.

Fachhochschul-Studiengänge Campus Wien (School of Applied Sciences Vienna Campus): Daumegasse 3, 1100 Vienna; tel. (1) 6066877-100; e-mail office@fh-campuswien.ac.at; internet www.fh-campuswien.ac.at; f. 1999; language of instruction: German; diploma courses in bioengineering, biotechnology, information technology and telecommunications, social work, and technical project and process management; Bachelors courses in construction engineering and management; Masters courses in local management and economics, and social management; Dir Ing. WILHELM BEHENSKY; publ. *Aktuell* (12 a year).

Fachhochschul-Studiengänge der Wiener Neustadt (School of Applied Sciences Wiener Neustadt): Johannes Gutenberg Str. 3, 2700 Vienna-Neustadt; tel. (2622) 890840; e-mail office@fhwn.ac.at; internet www.fhwn.ac.at; f. 1994, official status in 1999; BA in business consultancy, business and engineering, information technologies, mechatronics and microsystems engineering, aerospace engineering, biomedical analytics, occupational therapy, speech therapy and radiological technology; 200 teachers; 3,200 students; CEO Prof. Dipl.-Ing. Dr GERHARD PRAMHAS; CEO Mag. SUSANNE SCHARNHORST.

Fachhochschul-Studiengänge Kufstein (School of Applied Sciences Kufstein): Andreas Hofer Str. 7, 6330 Kufstein; tel. (5372) 71819; e-mail info@fh-kufstein.ac.at; internet www.fh-kufstein.ac.at; f. 1997, present status in 2005; diploma course in property economics and facility management; Bachelors courses in business information technology, sport, culture and event management, European energy economics, facility management and property economics and int. economics and management; Masters courses in crisis management and corporate restructuring, facility and real estate management, int. business studies, European energy, sports, culture and event management; library: 14,000 publs, incl. 80 professional journals, 15 newspapers; 120 teachers; 1,200 students; Exec. Dir Mag. WOLFGANG RICHTER.

Fachhochschul-Studiengänge St Pölten (School of Applied Sciences St Pölten): Matthias Corvinus-Str. 15, 3100 St. Pölten; tel. (2742) 313228333; e-mail office@fhstp.ac.at; internet www.fhstp.ac.at; f. 1993 as Society for holding of higher education courses St Pölten; present status in 2004; 9 Bachelors degree programmes in dietetics, railway infrastructure technology, industrial simulation, IT security, media and communications consulting, media management, media technology, physiotherapy and social work, 5 Masters programmes in digital media technologies, industrial simulation, information security, media management and social work; 9 training courses in event management, event equipment, photography, IT security, clinical dietetics and nutritional management, MBA programmes in media management, pre-production management and addiction treatment and prevention; library: 16,000 books, DVDs, CD-ROMs, 150 magazine subscriptions; 260 teachers; 1,800 students; Man. Dir Dr GABRIELA FERNANDES; Man. Dir Dipl.-Ing. GERNOT KOHL; publ. *FACTS* (2 a year).

Fachhochschul-Studiengänge Technikum Joanneum (School of Applied Sciences Technikum Joanneum): Alte Poststr. 147–154, Eggenberger Allee 9–13, 8020 Graz; tel. (316) 54530; e-mail info@fh-joanneum.at; internet www.fh-joanneum.at; f. 1995; 3 campuses; 24 BA programmes, 18 MA programmes in information, design and technologies, int. business, and life, building, environment; language of instruction: German; library: 48,000 books, journals, theses, CD-ROMs, video cassettes and DVDs; Man. Dir Prof. Dipl.-Ing. Dr KARL PETER PFEIFFER.

Fachhochschul-Studiengänge WIFI Steiermark (School of Applied Sciences WIFI Styria): Körblergasse 111–113, 8021 Graz; tel. (316) 6021234; e-mail info@stmk.wifi.at; internet www.stmk.wifi.at; campuses in Graz, Niklasdorf and Unterpremstätten; courses in business management, business studies, modern languages, information technology, civil and mechanical engineering, energy technology, health and welfare, environmental management, tourism and gastronomy, traffic and security systems, personality devt; Pres. Ing. Mag. PETER HOCHEGGER.

Fachhochschule IMC Krems (IMC University of Applied Sciences): Piaristengasse 1, 3500 Krems; tel. (2732) 8020; e-mail information@fh-krems.ac.at; internet www.fh-krems.ac.at; f. 1994; BA and MA programmes in business studies, life sciences and health studies; library: 50,000 items; 425 teachers; 1,800 students; Rector Prof. EVA WERNER.

Fachhochschule Technikum Kärnten (School of Applied Science Carinthia): Villacher Str. 1, 9800 Spittal; tel. (4762) 905000; e-mail info@fh-kaernten.at; internet www.fh-kaernten.at; f. 1995; courses in civil engineering, electronic engineering, geoinformation, healthcare management, medical information technology, public management, social work, network engineering; int. MA programmes in communication engineering for information technology, healthcare information technology, integrated systems and circuit design and spatial information management; 5 campuses; library: 40,000 media units in 4 libraries; 2,000 students; Exec. Dir Dipl.-Ing. SIEGFRIED SPANZ.

Fachhochschule Technikum Wien (School of Applied Science Vienna): Mariahilfer Str. 37–39, 1060 Vienna; tel. (1) 588390; e-mail info@technikum-wien.at; internet www.technikum-wien.at; f. 1994, present status 2000; 11 BA and 17 MA programmes in communication technologies and electronic engineering, information technologies and business solutions, engineering and environmental technologies and life science technologies; courses are offered as full-time and/or part-time degree programmes; library: 10,000 books, theses, magazines and CDs; 2,500 students; Dir Dr MICHAEL WÜRDINGER.

Fachhochschule Vorarlberg (School of Applied Sciences Vorarlberg): Hochschulstr. 1, 6850 Dornbirn; tel. (5572) 7920; e-mail info@fhv.at; internet www.fhv.at; f. 1997; 7 BA, 7 MA courses in technology, business and commerce, design and social work; 6 of these are part-time; library: 48,000 vols, 260 magazines, 2,200 CDs, 2,000 DVDs; 1,027 students; Man. Dir Dr HEDWIG NATTER.

FH Gesundheitsberufe OÖ GmbH (Upper Austria University of Applied Sciences Health Professions): Semmelweisstr. 34/D3, 4020 Linz; tel. (50) 34420000; e-mail office@fhgooe.ac.at; internet www.fh-gesundheitsberufe.at; f. 2010; Bachelors degrees in biomedical science, dietetics, occupational therapy, midwifery, physical therapy and radiography; Masters degree in management for health professionals and an MA course in university teaching and learning for health professions; 800 students; Man. Mag. BETTINA SCHNEEBAUER.

FH—Wien-Studiengänge der WKW (FH—Wien University of Applied Sciences): Währinger Gürtel 97, 1180 Vienna; tel. (1) 476775744; e-mail studienzentrum@fh-wien.ac.at; internet www.fh-wien.ac.at; f. 1994; 16 BA and MA courses in finance, real estate, journalism, communications, marketing, human resources, tourism, organizational and personal devt; 737 teachers; 2,363 students; Dir Mag. MICHAEL HERITSCH.

FHG—Zentrum für Gesundheitsberufe Tirol GmbH (FHG—Centre for Health Sciences, Tirol GmbH): Innrain 98, 6020 Innsbruck; tel. (50) 86484700; e-mail info@fhg-tirol.ac.at; internet www.fhg-tirol.ac.at; f. 2006; BA and MA in biomedical science, dietetics, midwifery, occupational therapy, speech therapy, physiotherapy, osteopathy and radiography; Man. Dir WALTER DRAXL.

Holztechnikum Kuchl: Markt 136, 5431 Salzburg; tel. (662) 62445372; e-mail office@holztechnikum.at; internet www.holztechnikum.at; f. 1943; Pres. WIESNER MARKUS.

Lauder Business School: Hofzeile 18–20, 1190 Vienna; tel. (1) 3691818; e-mail office@lbs.ac.at; internet www.lbs.ac.at; f. 2003; BA programme in intercultural business admin. and MA programme in intercultural management and leadership; also offers Jewish learning programme for Jewish students; Dean Prof. Dr SILVIA KUCERA.

MCI Management Centre Innsbruck—Internationale Hochschule GmbH (MCI Management Centre Innsbruck–International Academy GmbH): Universitaetsstr. 15, 6020 Innsbruck; tel. (512) 20700; e-mail office@mci.edu; internet www.mci.edu; f. 1996; graduate, non-graduate and post-graduate educational programmes to senior and junior managers from all management levels and brs; 200 teachers; Exec. Dir Prof. Dr ANDREAS ALTMANN.

Other Colleges

Diplomatische Akademie Wien (Diplomatic Academy of Vienna): Favoritenstr. 15A, 1040 Vienna; tel. (1) 5057272; e-mail info@da-vienna.ac.at; internet www.da-vienna.ac.at; f. 1964; Diploma and MA of advanced int. studies programmes prepare Austrian and foreign graduates for careers in diplomacy, int. business and finance, int. orgs and public admin.; library: 35,000 vols,

330 newspapers in German, English, French, Spanish, Italian and Russian; 82 teachers; 80 students; Dir Dr HANS WINKLER.

Hochschule für Agrar- und Umweltpädagogik Wien (College of Agricultural and Environmental Education Vienna): Angermayergasse 1, 1130 Vienna; tel. (1) 87722660; e-mail info@agrarumweltpaedagogik.ac.at; internet www.agrarumweltpaedagogik.ac.at; f. 2007; BA in agricultural education, environmental education; MA in management education in rural areas; library: 11,000 books and periodicals; 58 teachers; Rector Mag. Dr THOMAS HAASE.

Institut für Psychosoziale Intervention und Kommunikationsforschung (Institute for Psychosocial Intervention and Communication Research): Schöpfstr. 3, 6020 Innsbruck; tel. (512) 5070; e-mail psyko@uibk.ac.at; internet www.uibk.ac.at/psyko; f. 2010; attached to Univ. of Innsbruck; dipl, BA, MA, PhD, training and research in professional intervention methods in psychotherapy; Dir Prof. Dr JOSEF CHRISTIAN AIGNER.

International College for Tourism and Management: Johann Strauss Str. 2, 2540 Bad Vöslau; tel. (2252) 790260; e-mail office@itm-college.eu; internet www.itm-college.eu; f. 1986; BA programmes in business admin., int. management and hospitality management with tourism; 20 teachers; Dir for Studies CLAUDIA ROTHWANGL.

Schools of Art and Music

Anton Bruckner Privatuniversität (Anton Bruckner Private University): see under Universities.

Joseph Haydn Konservatorium des Landes Burgenland (Joseph Haydn Conservatory of Burgenland): Glorietteallee 2, 7000 Eisenstadt; tel. (2682) 63734; e-mail office@haydnkons.at; internet www.haydnkons.at; f. 1929; BMus in instrumental studies, singing, music theory and composition; 40 teachers; 400 students; Dir Prof. Mag WALTER BURIAN.

Kärntner Landeskonservatorium (Carinthian Conservatory of Music): Miesstalerstr. 8, 9020 Klagenfurt; tel. (50) 53640510; e-mail info@konse.at; internet www.konse.at; f. 1827; BA, MA courses and doctorates in musicology in cooperation with Alpa Adria Klagenfurt Univ., 75 teachers; 900 students; Dir Mag. ROLAND STEINER.

Konservatorium Wien Privatuniversität (Conservatory Vienna University): Johannesgasse 4A, 1010 Vienna; tel. (1) 5127747; e-mail office@konswien.at; internet www.konservatorium-wien.ac.at; f. 1938; 30 BA and MA courses in music and dramatic arts; library: 36,000 media, 17,800 songs; 250 teachers; 860 students; Dir GOTTFRIED EISL; Dir RANKO MARKOVIĆ; publ. *Fidelio* (5 a year).

Tiroler Landeskonservatorium (Tirol Conservatory of Music): Paul-Hofhaimer-Gasse 6, 6020 Innsbruck; tel. (512) 508-6850; internet www.tirol.gv.at/konservatorium; f. 1818; 75 teachers; 500 students; library: 100,000 vols and musical notes; Dir Dr THOMAS JUEN; Librarian FRANZ BAUER.

Vienna Konservatorium (Vienna Conservatory): Stiegergasse 15–17, Fenzlgasse 26, 1150 Vienna; tel. (1) 9858112; e-mail office@viennaconservatory.at; internet www.viennaconservatory.at; BA and MA programmes in music theory and performance, music theory and composition, classical instruments, classical-vocal, jazz instruments, jazz-vocal; 109 teachers; Dir ROBERT BRANDSTÖTTER.

Vorarlberger Landeskonservatorium GmbH (Vorarlberg State Conservatory GmbH): Reichenfeldgasse 9, 6800 Feldkirch; tel. (5522) 711100; e-mail sekretariat@vlk.ac.at; internet www.vlk.ac.at; f. 1856; BA in music from Univ. Mozart Salzburg in instrumental, vocal training; library: 4,000 vols, 17,000 notes, 3,800 CDs, 15,000 records, 25 periodicals; 58 teachers; CEO Dr PETER SCHMID.

AZERBAIJAN

The Higher Education System

The higher education system was established when Azerbaijan was a full Union Republic of the Union of Soviet Socialist Republics (USSR). The main language of instruction is Azerbaijani, but there are also Russian-language schools and some teaching in Georgian and Armenian. From 1992 a Turkic version of the Latin alphabet was used in Azerbaijani-language schools (replacing the Cyrillic script). In June 1999 legislation entitled The Programme of Education Reforms of the Republic of Azerbaijan was passed by presidential decree, affecting reforms at all levels of education. In 2005 Azerbaijan signed up to the Bologna Process, under which all European countries were to endeavour to adopt a universal three-tier Bachelors–Masters–Doctorate degree structure. The Bologna Process, including a new credit system as well as the issuing of the Diploma Supplement, was implemented from 2006/07 onwards. After the passing of the Education Act in 2009 a state programme of reforms of the higher education system was put into place for the years 2009 to 2013 in order to coordinate the normative and legal aspects of the Act. In 2010/11 there were 51 state-supported institutions of higher education, including the Azerbaijan State Oil Academy, which was founded in 1920 and trains engineers for the oil industry, and around 15 private universities. In that year a total of 140,241 students were enrolled in higher education.

The state oversees educational policy, dispenses funding and lays down guidelines for quality assurance. By law, individual institutions are responsible for employing teaching staff and establishing curricula. In 2006 the Ministry of Education established the Standing Commission on Accreditation to act as the main quality assurance body for higher education institutions and secondary specialized institutions. Institutions are subject to inspection every four years. Since 2004/05 entrance examinations for state institutions have been organized by a central body, the Talaba Qabulu üzre Dövlat Komissiyasi (TQDK—State Students Admission Commission). There are four examinations, each one of which covers a specialist group of subjects: the first group deals with physics, applied chemistry, mathematics, engineering and other technical subjects; the second covers economics, business studies, sociology and geography; the third group involves the arts and humanitarian subjects, including journalism and psychology; and the fourth covers medicine, chemistry, biology and agriculture. An estimated 20% of school-leavers enter higher education through this process.

The three levels of higher education qualifications are Bachelors, Masters and Doctorates. Study for the Bachelors degree lasts for three to four years, while the Soviet-style Specialist Diploma, which is still offered in some professionally orientated disciplines (such as engineering, law and medicine), lasts for five to six years. The Masters degree was introduced in 1997/98 and lasts for up to two years. By 2006 Masters degrees had been introduced in 39 higher institutions throughout Azerbaijan, with approximately 10,000 students enrolled. Doctoral studies, which are available to holders of Masters degrees or equivalent qualifications, last a minimum of three years and end with the defence of a thesis. Successful graduates are awarded the title Doctor of Philosophy (Falsafa doktoru).

Vocational and technical education in Azerbaijan is currently undergoing reform following the approval of the state programme for the development of vocational education covering the period 2007–12. In 2010 there were 108 vocational establishments in the country, all of which were overseen by the Ministry of Education. Gabala Vocational Education Centre for Tourism and Hotel Management was inaugurated in 2008 as part of a pilot project by the British Council and European Commission to improve the competitiveness of non-oil sector vocational studies. Vocational and technical education is offered at two levels: vocational schools/lyceums, and vocational and technical colleges. Students can enter vocational schools and lyceums after having completed basic (nine years) or full (11 years) secondary education. For those who have completed only nine years at secondary school, vocational lyceums incorporate general education modules into their curriculum alongside the subject-specific modules, while vocational schools provide purely vocational education. The duration of study lasts from two to three years in vocational schools and from three to four years in vocational lyceums. Students who enrol at vocational schools and lyceums after having completed full secondary education normally require one to two years to complete their study programmes. On the successful completion of their studies, students are awarded a Diploma confirming their professional rights. Admission into vocational and technical colleges, which provide advanced vocational training, is based on the attainment of the level of either Grade 9 or Grade 11 in secondary education. Courses at these institutions last from two to four years, depending on the student's previous education and field of study. The content of the courses is developed in cooperation with relevant undergraduate programmes; this means that graduates of vocational and technical colleges may continue their education at tertiary level. High-achieving students may be accepted into the second year of the appropriate Bachelors degree.

Regulatory and Representative Bodies

GOVERNMENT

Ministry of Culture and Tourism: 1000 Baku, 40 U. Hajibayov st, House of Govt; tel. (12) 493-43-98; e-mail mct@mct.gov.az; internet www.mct.gov.az; Minister Äbülfäz Qarayev.

Ministry of Education: 1008 Baku, 49 Khatai Ave; tel. (12) 496-06-47; e-mail office@edu.gov.az; internet www.edu.gov.az; Minister Mikayil Cabbarov.

ACCREDITATION

ENIC/NARIC Azerbaijan: Min. of Education, 1008 Baku, Khatai Ave 49; tel. (12) 96-34-14; e-mail a_akhundov@yahoo.com; internet www.min.edu.az; Sr Expert Azad Akhundov.

NATIONAL BODY

Council of University Presidents: 370096 Baku, Mehseti 11; tel. (12) 21-79-27; e-mail contact@khazar.org; internet www.khazar.org; Pres. Prof. Hamlet Isaxanli.

Talaba Qabulu üzre Dövlat Komissiyasi (TQDK) (State Students Admission Commission): Academician H. Aliev st 17, 1078 Baku; tel. (12) 4413747; e-mail info@tqdk.gov.az; internet www.tqdk.gov.az; f. 1992; directly subordinate to Pres.; centralized org. for management of student admissions; develops regulations for admission to higher and secondary spec. schools; conducts examinations; prepares and implements organizational, scientific and methodical and planning activities; develops proposals for improvement of higher and secondary spec. education on the basis of systemic analysis of admission campaign results; Chair. Abbaszade Maleyka Mehdi; publ. *Abiturient* (www.abiturient.az).

Learned Societies

GENERAL

Azerbaijan National Academy of Sciences: 1141 Baku, F. Ağayev küç. 9; tel. (12) 441-72-81; e-mail secretary@iit.ab.az; internet www.science.az; f. 1945; depts of physical, mathematical and technical sciences (Acad.-Sec. A. J. Hajiyev), chemical sciences (Acad.-Sec. A. A. EFENDIYEV), earth sciences (Acad.-Sec. A. M. ALIZADEH), biological sciences (Acad.-Sec. M. A. MUSAYEV), humanities and social sciences (Acad.-Sec. A. A. AKHUNDOV); attached research institutes: see under Research Institutes; Pres. M. K. KERIMOV; Acad.-Sec. T. N. SHAKHTAKHTINSKIY; publs *Applied and Computational Mathematics* (2 a year), *Azerbaijan and Azerbaijanists* (12 a year, in English and Russian), *Azerbaijan Journal of Chemistry* (4 a year, in Azeri and Russian), *Azerbaijan Journal of Physics* (4 a year, in Azeri, English and Russian), *Journal of Physics* (4 a year, in Azeri, English and Russian), *Journal of Problems of Eastern Philosophy* (2 a year, in Arabic, Azeri, English, Farsi, French, German and Turkish), *Journal of Turkology* (1 a year, in Azeri and Russian), *Proceedings* (4 a year, in Azeri and Russian), *Processes of Petrochemistry and Oil Refining Journal* (6 a year, in English and Russian), *Transactions* (series: physical, mathematical and technical sciences, biological sciences, historical, philosophical and judicial, economics, literature, philology and art, geological).

LANGUAGE AND LITERATURE

British Council: 1010 Baku, 8th Fl., The Landmark III Bldg, 90A Nizami St; tel. (12) 497-20-13; e-mail enquiries@britishcouncil.az; internet www.britishcouncil.org/azerbaijan.htm; office opened 1993; offers courses and examinations in English language and British culture and promotes cultural exchange with the UK; Dir MARGARET JACK.

Research Institutes

AGRICULTURE, FISHERIES AND VETERINARY SCIENCE

Agricultural Research Institute: 1016 Baku, U. Hadjibeyov küç. 40; tel. (12) 497-49-31; f. 1950; attached to Min. of Agriculture; Dir A. MUSAYEV.

A. I. Karaev Institute of Physiology (IPh): Sharif-Zade küç. 2, 1100 Baku; tel. (12) 4321520; e-mail azinphys@science.az; f. 1968; attached to Azerbaijan Nat. Acad. of Sciences; conducts research studies on animals and partially on humans; neurochemistry and neurophysiology of ontogenesis, biochemistry and neurophysiology of learning and memory, studies of impact of adverse environmental factors on animals, cytochemical changes in brain cells during sleep and food deprivation, physiological correlates of longevity in humans, studies of brain-specific proteins in memory and visual analysis processes, biophysics of brain cells under impact of environmental factors and pharmacological studies of plant-derived physiologically active substances; Dir TELMAN AQAYEV; publ. *Transactions* (1 a year, in Azeri and Russian).

Institute of Genetic Resources: 1106 Baku, Azadlyg Ave; tel. (12) 462-94-62; e-mail akparov@yahoo.com; f. 2003; attached to Azerbaijan Nat. Acad. of Sciences; Dir Z. I. AKPAROV; publ. *Transactions* (irregular, in Azeri and Russian).

Institute of Soil Science and Agrochemistry: 1073 Baku, M. Arif küç. 5; e-mail soiman@dcacs.ab.az; tel. (12) 438-32-40; f. 1945; attached to Azerbaijan Nat. Acad. of Sciences; Dir M. P. BABAYEV; publ. *Transactions* (1 a year, in Azeri and Russian).

Rajably Scientific Research Institute of Horticulture and Sub-Tropical Plants: 4035 Quba, Zardabi; tel. (169) 45-37-17; f. 1926; Dir D. BAYRAMOVA.

ARCHITECTURE AND TOWN PLANNING

Institute of Architecture and Art: 1143 Baku, H. Javid Ave 31; tel. (12) 439-34-94; e-mail ertegin@baku.ab.az; internet www.artandculture.com; f. 1945; attached to Azerbaijan Nat. Acad. of Sciences; research in history and theory of architecture; art of Azerbaijan and Turkic culture; Dir Prof. Dr ARTEGIN SALAMZADE; publs *International Scientific Journal*, *Problems of Art and Culture*.

BIBLIOGRAPHY, LIBRARY SCIENCE AND MUSEOLOGY

'Mähämmäd Füzuli' Institute of Manuscripts (IMANAS): 1001 Baku, Istiglaliyyat küç. 8; tel. (12) 492-31-97; e-mail elyazmalarinstitutu@mail.ru; internet www.elyazmalarinstitutu.com; f. 1950; attached to Azerbaijan Nat. Acad. of Sciences; library of 40,000 MSS, documents and vols; Dir Dr PASHA KARIMOV; publs *Älyazmalar khäzinäsinda* (irregular), *Kechmishimizdän gälän säslär* (irregular), *Orta äsr älyazmalari vä Azärbaycan mädäniyyäti problemläri* (every 2 years).

ECONOMICS, LAW AND POLITICS

Institute of Economics: 1143 Baku, Pr. H. Javid 31; tel. (12) 439-37-28; e-mail economy@eco.ab.az; f. 1958; attached to Azerbaijan Nat. Acad. of Sciences; Dir S. M. MURADOV.

Institute of Philosophy and Law: 1143 Baku, Pr. H. Javid 31; tel. (12) 439-37-28; e-mail phillaw@lan.ab.az; f. 1945; attached to Azerbaijan Nat. Acad. of Sciences; Dir A. ABASOV; publ. *Qendershunaslig* (11 a year, in Azeri and English).

HISTORY, GEOGRAPHY AND ARCHAEOLOGY

Institute of Archaeology and Ethnography: 370143 Baku, Pr. H. Javid 31; tel. (12) 539-36-49; e-mail parvin@arch.ab.az; internet www.science.az/en/archaeology; attached to Azerbaijan Nat. Acad. of Sciences; Dir MAISA NURBALA GIZI RAGIMOVA.

Institute of Geography: Pr. H. Javid 31, 1143 Baku; tel. (12) 5382900; e-mail ramiz.mamedov@geo.ab.az; f. 1945; attached to Azerbaijan Nat. Acad. of Sciences; research into climatology, desertification, ecology, geomorphology, hydrometeorology of the Caspian Sea and its coastal dynamics, industrial and infrastructural problems, landscape and landscape planning, palaeogeography, natural resources; library of 53,000 vols; Dir Acad. BUDAG BUDAGOV; Deputy Dir RAMIZ MAMMADOV; publ. *Khabarlar* (2 a year).

Institute of History: 1143 Baku, Pr. H. Javid 31; tel. (12) 439-36-15; f. 1940; attached to Azerbaijan Nat. Acad. of Sciences; Dep. Dir J. A. BAHRAMOV.

Institute of Oriental Studies: 1143 Baku, Pr. H. Javid 31; tel. (12) 439-23-51; e-mail sharq@lan.ab.az; f. 1958; attached to Azerbaijan Nat. Acad. of Sciences; Dir G. B. BAKHSHALIYEVA.

LANGUAGE AND LITERATURE

Nasimi Institute of Linguistics: 1143 Baku, Pr. H. Javid 31; tel. (12) 439-35-71; f. 1932; attached to Azerbaijan Nat. Acad. of Sciences; library of 6,000 vols, 50 periodicals; Dir Prof. A. A. AKHUNDOV; publ. *Turkology* (4 a year).

Nizami Institute of Literature: 1143 Baku, 5th Fl., H. Javid 31; tel. (12) 441-74-25; e-mail adib@aas.ab.az; internet www.science.az/en/literature; f. 1932; attached to Azerbaijan Nat. Acad. of Sciences; Dir B. A. NABIYEV.

MEDICINE

Azerbaijan Institute of Traumatology and Orthopaedics: Abbas Sakhat st 32, 1007 Baku; tel. (12) 4401000; e-mail azettoi@yahoo.com; f. 1946; researches in orthopaedics, traumatology and emergency medicine; library of 5,000 vols; publ. *Azerbaijan Orthopaedics and Traumatology Journal* (2 a year).

Azerbaijan Institute of Tuberculosis and Pulmonology: 1001 Baku, 2514 kv., 8 km settlement; tel. (12) 421-22-62.

Azerbaijan Medical Association: 1000 Baku, POB 16; tel. (12) 492-80-92; e-mail info@azmed.az; internet www.azmed.az; f. 1999; 2,600 mems; Dir Dr NARIMAN SAFARLI.

Azerbaijan Research Institute of Haematology and Blood Transfusion: 1007 Baku, M. Kaskkay 87; tel. (12) 440-53-18; e-mail hajiev_azad@yahoo.com; f. 1943; Dir AZAD HAJIYEV; publ. *Azerbaijan Medical Journal* (4 a year).

Azerbaijan Research Institute of Ophthalmology: 1065 Baku, 6-ya Kommunisticheskaya küç. 5; tel. (12) 421-22-62.

Research Institute of Gastroenterology: 1110 Baku, Leningradsky pr. 111; tel. (12) 464-45-09; f. 1988; Dir B. A. AGAYEV; publ. *Actual Questions of Gastroenterology* (1 a year).

Research Institute of Medical Rehabilitation and Natural Therapeutic Factors: 1008 Baku, Khatai Ave 3; tel. (12) 466-31-93; f. 1936; Dir Prof. Dr A. V. MUSAYEV.

NATURAL SCIENCES

Biological Sciences

Botanical Garden: 1073 Baku, Patamdartskoe shosse 40; e-mail cbg@lan.ab.az; f. 1934; attached to Azerbaijan Nat. Acad. of Sciences; Dir O. V. IBADLI.

Institute of Botany: 1073 Baku, Patamdartskoe shosse 40; tel. (12) 439-32-30; e-mail botanica@baku.ab.az; f. 1936; attached to Azerbaijan Nat. Acad. of Sciences; Dir V. H. HAJIYEV.

Institute of Microbiology: 1340 Baku, Patamdart Ave 40; tel. (12) 539-23-59; internet www.science.gov.az/en/microbiology/index.htm; f. 1972; attached to Azerbaijan Nat. Acad. of Sciences; Dir M. A. SALMANOV; publ. *Transactions* (1 a year, in Azeri and Russian).

Institute of Zoology: 1073 Baku, Proezd 1128, kv. 504, A. Abbasov; tel. (12) 439-73-71; e-mail izb@dcacs.ab.az; f. 1936; attached to Azerbaijan Nat. Acad. of Sciences; Dir I. KH. ALAKBAROV; publ. *Transactions* (irregular, in Azeri and Russian).

Mardakan Arboretum: 1044 Baku; tel. (12) 454-30-12; e-mail dendrary@mail.az; f. 1926; attached to Azerbaijan Nat. Acad. of Sciences; Dir T. S. MAMEDOV.

Mathematical Sciences

Institute of Mathematics and Mechanics: 1141 Baku, Agaeva küç. 9; tel. (12) 439-39-24; e-mail frteb@aas.ab.az; attached to Azerbaijan Acad. of Sciences; Dir AKIF GADJIEV; publ. *Proceedings* (4 a year, in Azeri, English and Russian).

Physical Sciences

Azerbaijan National Aerospace Agency: 1115 Baku, S. S.Akhundov str. 1; tel. (12) 5629387; e-mail a.shirin-zadeh@box.az; f. 1975; Dir-Gen. Prof. ALCHIN SHIRIN-ZADA.

Institute of Chemical Problems: 1143 Baku, Pr. H. Javid 29; tel. (12) 439-29-08; e-mail itpcht@lan.ab.az; f. 1935; attached to Azerbaijan Nat. Acad. of Sciences; Dir T. N. SHASKHTAKHTINSKI.

Institute of Geology: 1143 Baku, Pr. H. Javid 29A; tel. (412) 497-52-86; e-mail gia@azdata.net; internet www.gia.az; f. 1938; attached to Azerbaijan Nat. Acad. of Sciences; 250 mems; library of 24,000 vols, 70,000 periodicals; Dir A. A. ALI-ZADEH; publs *Proceedings* (1 a year), *Sciences of the Earth* (4 a year).

Institute of Physics: 1143 Baku, Javid Ave, 33; tel. (12) 439-41-51; e-mail director@physics.ab.az; f. 1945; attached to Azerbaijan Nat. Acad. of Sciences; scientific research in the different brs of theoretical and experimental physics; Dir Prof. ARIF GASHIMOV.

Institute of Radiation Problems: 1143 Baku, B. Vaxabzade 9; tel. (12) 539-33-91; e-mail nukl@box.az; internet www.irp.science.az; f. 1969; attached to Azerbaijan Nat. Acad. of Sciences; Dir A. A. GARIBOV.

Şamaxı Astro-Physical Observatory: 5600 Şamaxı, Pos. Mamedalieva; tel. (12) 497-52-68; e-mail shao@lan.ab.az; f. 1960; attached to Azerbaijan Nat. Acad. of Sciences; Dir A. S. GULUYEV; publ. *The Azerbaijan Astronomical Journal* (4 a year, in Azeri, English and Russian).

TECHNOLOGY

Azerbaijan Petroleum Machinery Research and Design Institute (Azinmash): 1029 Baku, 4 Araz küç.; tel. (12) 467-08-88; e-mail office@azinmash.azeri.com; internet www.azinmash.com; f. 1930; Dir R. DJABBAROV.

Azerbaijan Scientific Gas Research and Projects Institute: 1025 Baku, Yusif Safarov küç. 23; tel. (12) 490-43-59.

Azerbaijan Scientific-Research and Design-Prospecting Power Engineering Institute: 1012 Baku, Pr. H. Zardabi 94; tel. (12) 432-80-76; e-mail energy_institut@mail.ru; internet www.pei.az; f. 1933; research into power potential and effective use of water resources, power systems, power and automation issues of oil industry, thermodynamics, research of gases less distinctive than ideal gases and committing the generalized case equations of the oil hydrocarbons and their fractions, etc.; library of 59,000 vols; Dir Prof. NURALI ADIL YUSIFBAYLI; publ. *Electroenergetics, Electrotechnics, Electromechanics + Control* (1 a year).

Guliyev, A.M., Institute of Additive Chemistry: 1603 Baku, Beyukshorskoe shosse, kv. 2062; tel. (12) 467-65-33; e-mail aki@lan.ab.az; f. 1965; attached to Azerbaijan Nat. Acad. of Sciences; lubricant and fuel additives, cutting fluids and erosion inhibitors; library of 9,000 vols; Dir Dr V. M. FARZALIYEV.

Institute of Cybernetics: 9, B.Vahabzade St, 1141 Baku; tel. (12) 4390151; e-mail director@cyber.az; internet www.telmanaliev.az; f. 1965; attached to Azerbaijan Nat. Acad. of Sciences; Dir Prof. TELMAN ALIEV; publ. *Transactions of National Academy of Sciences* (2 a year).

Institute of Deep Oil and Gas Deposits: 1143 Baku, Pr. H. Javid 33; tel. (12) 439-21-40; e-mail arif.guliyev@lan.ab.az; attached to Azerbaijan Nat. Acad. of Sciences; Dir A. M. GULIYEV.

Institute of Information Technology: 1141 Baku, B.Vahabzade st 9; tel. (12) 539-01-67; e-mail secretary@iit.ab.az; internet www.ict.az; f. 2003; attached to Azerbaijan Nat. Acad. of Sciences; Dir R. M. ALGULIYEV.

Institute of Polymer Materials: 5004 Sumqayıt, Samed Vargun küç. 124; tel. (12) 497-60-38; e-mail ipoma@dcacs.ab.az; f. 1966; attached to Azerbaijan Nat. Acad. of Sciences; Dir ABASGULU MAMED GULIYEV.

Mamedaliev, Yu. G., Institute of Petrochemical Processes: 1025 Baku, N. Rafiyev 30; tel. (12) 490-24-76; e-mail ipcp@baku-az.net; internet www.science.az/en/oilchemistry; f. 1929; attached to Azerbaijan Nat. Acad. of Sciences; Dir M. I. RUSTAMOV; publ. *Process of Petrochemistry and Oil Refining* (6 a year, in English and Russian).

Oil Research and Design Institute (AzNIPIneft): 1033 Baku, Aga Neymatully küç. 39; tel. (12) 493-64-29.

Research and Design Institute for Oil Engineering: 1000 Baku, Aga Neymatully küç. 39; tel. (12) 466-21-69.

Research Institute of Photoelectronics: 1000 Baku, Block 555, Agaeva küç; tel. (12) 439-13-08; f. 1972; library of 1,095 vols; Dir Prof. S. E. YUNISOGLU.

Libraries and Archives

Baku

Azarbaycan Milli Kitabxanasi (Azerbaijan National Library): 1000 Baku, Khagani str. 29; tel. (12) 493-40-03; e-mail contact@anl.az; internet www.anl.az; f. 1923, Azerbaijan Nat. Library named after M. F. Akhundov 1939, present status 2005; 4,545,478 vols, 31,574 audiovisual items; Dir Dr TAHIROV KARIM MAHAMMAD OĞLU; Scientific Sec. AMINA DJAFAROVA; publs *Azerbaijan Bibliography* (1 a year), *New Books, New Literature on Culture, Art and Tourism, The Calendar of Significant and Historical Days*.

Central Scientific Library: 370143 Baku, Pr. Narimanova 31; tel. (12) 438-60-17; e-mail mail@csl-az.com; internet www.csl-az.com; f. 1925; attached to Azerbaijan Nat. Acad. of Sciences; 2.5m. vols, periodicals and serials; Dir M. M. CASANOVA.

Scientific Library of Baku State University: 1148 Baku, Z. Khalilova küç. 23; tel. (12) 439-06-21; e-mail sara_ibragimova@yahoo.com; f. 1919; 2,458,991 vols; Librarian SARA IBRAGIMOVA; publs *Estestvennikh nauk* (4 a year), *Gumanitarnikh nauk* (4 a year), *Sotsialno-politicheskikh nauk* (4 a year), *Vestnik Bakinskogo Universiteta: Fiziko-Matematicheskikh nauk* (4 a year).

Museums and Art Galleries

Baku

Azerbaijan State Museum of Art: 1001 Baku, Niyazi 9–11; tel. (12) 492-57-89; f. 1920; library of 11,000 vols; Dir A. R. ASRAFILOV.

Baku Museum of Education: 370001 Baku, Niazi küç. 11; tel. (8922) 92-04-53; f. 1940; library of 52,000 vols; Dir T. Z. AHMEDZADE.

Huseyn Javid Memorial Flat—Museum: 1000 Baku, Istiglaliyat 8; tel. (12) 492-06-57; e-mail muzey@huseyncavid.com; internet huseyncavid.com; f. 1981; attached to Azerbaijan Nat. Acad. of Sciences; Dir Dr GÜLBENIZ BABAXANLI.

Museum of the History of Azerbaijan: 1005 Baku, H. Z. Tagiyev 4; tel. (12) 493-36-48; e-mail aztarmuzey@azhistorymuseum.az; internet www.azhistorymuseum.az; f. 1920; attached to Azerbaijan Nat. Acad. of Sciences; history of the Azerbaijani people since ancient times; Dir N. M. VALIKHANLI.

Nizami Gandjavi State Museum of Azerbaijan Literature: 1001 Baku, Isteglal küç. 53; tel. (12) 492-18-64; internet www.nizamimuseum.az; f. 1939; history of Azerbaijani literature since ancient times; Dir R. B. HUSEYNOV.

State Museum Palace of Shirvan-Shakh: 1004 Baku, Zamkovski pereulok 76; tel. (12) 492-95-73; e-mail shirvanshah@bakililar.az; internet www.culture.az:8101/museums/shirv/titlerus.htm; f. 1964; historical and architectural museum; Dir SEVDA DADASHEVA.

Stepano-Kert

Stepanakert Museum of the History of Nagornyi-Karabakh: 2600 Xankandi (Stepanakert), Gorkogo küç. 4; history of the Armenian people of Arthakh (Nagornyi Karabakh).

Universities

AZERBAIJAN MEDICAL UNIVERSITY

1022 Baku, Bakizkhanov küç. 23
Telephone: (12) 495-43-13
E-mail: info@amu.edu.az
Internet: amu.edu.az

Founded 1930
State control

Rector: AHLIMAN TAPDIQ AMIRASLANOV

Library of 600,000 vols
Number of teachers: 1,620
Number of students: 8,000

DEANS

Admin. for Foreign Students: Assoc. Prof. SEYIDOVA GULER MIR CAFAR
Faculty of Medicine: Assoc. Prof. ISMAYILOV TARIYEL MUSTAFA
Faculty of Pharmacology: AKHMED ŞIXEMMEDOV NURMAMMED
Faculty of Stomatology: Asst Prof. MAMMADOV RIZVAN MOHSUM OGHLU
Medico Preventive and Biology: Assoc. Prof. AYDIN M. MAMEDOV

AZERBAIJAN STATE PEDAGOGICAL UNIVERSITY 'NASREDDIN TUSI'

1000 Baku, U. Hacjibeyov St 34
Telephone: (12) 493-00-32
E-mail: adpu@azeri.com

Founded 1921
State control
Languages of instruction: Azeri, Russian

Faculties of Azeri language and literature, chemistry and biology, drawing and imitation arts, elementary military education and physical training, geography, history, mathematics, pedagogy and psychology, physics

Pres.: BAHLUL AGAJEV
Number of students: 7,975

AZERBAIJAN STATE UNIVERSITY OF CULTURE AND ART

1065 Baku, Inshaatchilar küç. 9
Telephone: (12) 438-43-10
E-mail: info@admiu.edu.az
Internet: www.admiu.edu.az

Founded 1922 as Baku State Turkish School, current name adopted 1945
State control
Academic year: September to July

Rector: TIMUCHIN AFENDIYEV
Vice-Rector: RAFIQ SADIQOV

Library of 80,384 vols

Number of teachers: 190
Number of students: 2,865

DEANS

Faculty of Cultural Studies: ALEKPER MAMMADOV
Faculty of Fine Arts: VEFA ALIYEV
Faculty of Management: BAYRAM HADJIYEV
Faculty of Music: VAMIG MAMMEDALIYEV
Faculty of Painting: DJABBAR HASSANOV
Faculty of Theatre and Cinema: MAMMEDSHAH ATAYEV

AZERBAIJAN STATE UNIVERSITY OF ECONOMICS

1001 Baku, Istiqlaliyyat 6
Telephone: (12) 437-10-86
E-mail: aseu@aseu.az
Internet: www.aseu.az
Founded 1930, current name adopted and status 2000
State control
Languages of instruction: Azeri, English, Russian, Turkish
Academic year: September to June
Faculties of accountancy, commerce, economics, finance, informatics, management, world economy
Rector: Prof. Dr ADALET MURADOV
Dean for World Economy: Asst Prof. MUZAFFAR MAMMADLI
Number of teachers: 1,200
Number of students: 18,000

AZERBAIJAN TECHNICAL UNIVERSITY

1073 Baku, Hussein Javid Ave 25
Telephone: (12) 538-33-43
E-mail: aztu@aztukm.baku.az
Internet: www.aztu.edu.az
Founded 1950
State control
Languages of instruction: Azeri, Russian
Academic year: September to July
Rector: Prof. Dr HAVAR AMIR OGLU MAMMADOV
Vice-Rector for Admin.–Economic Affairs: ABUZAR AGAVERDI OGLU MIRZALIYEV
Vice-Rector for Education Work: Assoc. Prof. KHALIG MADJID OGLU YAHUDOV
Vice-Rector for Educational Affairs: Assoc. Prof. ISA ALI OGLU KHALILOV
Vice-Rector for General Affairs: Assoc. Prof. NAMIG ZIYADDIN OGLU MAMMADOV
Vice-Rector for Int. Relations: Assoc. Prof. MUSTAFA BABA OGLU BABANLI
Vice-Rector for Research and Devt: Prof. Dr ELSHAD GULAM OGLU ISMIBEYLI
Registrar and Chief Admin. Officer: AZIZA B. GASIMLI
Librarian: NARINGUL KHALAFOVA
Library of 700,000 vols
Number of teachers: 620
Number of students: 7,778
Publications: *Research Works* (4 a year), *Ziya* (12 a year)

DEANS

Faculty of Automation and Computing Techniques: Asst Prof. RAUF ALESKER OGLU HASANOV
Faculty of Electrotechnics and Energetics: Dr MAHIR MADJNUN OGLU BASHIROV
Faculty of Engineering Business and Management: Asst Prof. ILHAM ALIDJI OGLU ASLANZADEH
Faculty of Machine-Building: Assoc. Prof. ARASTUN SALMAN OGLU MAMMADOV
Faculty of Metallurgy: Prof. Dr AQIL ISA OGLU BABAYEV
Faculty of Radio-Engineering and Communications: Prof. Dr BAYRAM GANIMAT OGLU IBRAHIMOV
Faculty of Special Equipment and Technology: Assoc. Prof. RAMIZ AHMAD OGLU HUSSEINOV
Faculty of Technological and Light Industry Machines: Assoc. Prof. FARIZ GACHAY OGLU AMIROV
Faculty of Transport: Asst Prof. FAZIL ABDULAZIM OGLU HASANOV
Foreign Students Department: Assoc. Prof. ELCHIN RAMIZ OGLU MUSTAFAYEV

PROFESSORS

Faculty of Automation and Computing Techniques (tel. (12) 438-94-06):
ALIYEV, A. B., Higher Mathematics
DUNYAMALIEV, M. A., Applied Mathematics
MAMMADOV, H. A., Automation and Control
MUSAYEV, V. H., Informatics and Information Technologies
RZAYEV, T. G., Automation

Faculty of Electrotechnics and Energetics (tel. (12) 439-12-47):
BASHIROV, M. M., Thermal Engineering and Heating Mechanisms
GURBANOV, M. A., Physics
GURBANOV, T. B., Automation
LAZIMOV, T. M., Automation
SHAKHVERDIYEV, A. H., Thermal Engineering and Heating Mechanisms

Faculty of Engineering Business and Management (tel. (12) 439-13-96):
ALIYEV, A. H., Philosophy and Political Science
ALIYEV, R. Z., Physical Education and Sport
GASIMOV, SH. M., History
GULIYEV, R. I., Theory of Economics
HUSEYNOV, S. Y., Philosophy and Political Science
ISMAYILOV, R. A., French
ISKENDEROV, R. K., Economy and Management
JUMSHUDOV, S. Q., Economy and Management of Transportation
KARIMOV, E. S., Philosophy and Politology
NACAFOV, B. I., History

Faculty of Machine-Building (tel. (12) 439-13-56):
ABBASOV, V. A., Metal-cutting Machines and Tools
GODJAYEV, E. M., Physics
HUSEYNOV, S. O., Hydraulics
MOVLAZADE, V. Z., Machine-building Technology
RUSTAMOV, M. I., Metal-cutting Machines and Tools
SADYKHOV, A. H., Repair Technology of Machines
YUSUBOV, N. D., Repair Technology of Machines

Faculty of Machine Sciences (tel. (12) 438-94-70):
ABDULLAYEV, A. H., Lift Transport Machines
HUSEYNOV, H. A., Automated Design Systems in Machine-building
KENGERLI, A. M., Mechanical Theory
NAJAFOV, A. M., Machine-Building Technology
RASULOV, N. M., Machine-Building Technology

Faculty of Metallurgy (tel. (12) 438-34-69):
AKHMADOV, SH. A., Ecology
AMIROV, S. T., Construction Materials Technology, Powder Metallurgy and Corrosion
BABANLI, M. B., Construction Materials Technology, Powder Metallurgy and Corrosion
BABAYEV, F. R., Chemistry
HUSEYNOV, R. G., Construction Materials Technology, Powder Metallurgy and Corrosion
MAMMADOV, A. T., Metallurgy and Science of Metals
MAMMADOV, Z. G., Metallurgy and Science of Metals
NAMAZOV, S., Metallurgy and Science of Metals
NOVRUZOV, H. D., Powder Metallurgy and Corrosion
RUSTAMOV, M. A., Chemistry
SHUKUROV, R. I., Metallurgy and Science of Metals

Faculty of Radio-Engineering and Communications (tel. (12) 438-50-13):
ABILOV, C. I., Automation
EFENDIYEV, C. A., Television and Radio Systems
HASANOV, A. N., Telecommunications
IBRAHIMOV, B. G., Electronic Communications
IMAMVERDIYEV, G. M., Electronic Communications
ISKENDERZADE, Z. A., Applied Physics and Microelectronics
ISMIBEYLI, E. G., Electrodynamics and High Frequency Instruments
KENGERLI, U. S., General Theoretical Radio-Engineering
MAGARRAMOV, V. A., General Theoretical Radio-Engineering
MAMMADOV, F. H., Telecommunications
MAMMADOV, I. R., General Theoretical Radio-Engineering
MANSUROV, T. M., Telecommunications
ORUCOV, H. S., Physics
RAHIMOV, A. T., Television and Radio Systems

Faculty of Transport (tel. (12) 439-12-51):
AKHMADOV, H. M., Road Transport and Road Safety
BAKSHALIYEV, V. I., Road Transport and Road Safety
HASANOV, SH. H., Road Transport and Road Safety
HEYDAROV, SH. H., Road Transport and Road Safety
KARIMOV, Z. X., Theoretical Mechanics
MIRSALIMOV, V. M., Automechanics of Materials Resistance
NASIBOV, N. E., Theoretical Mechanics
TAGIZADE, A. G., Road Transport and Road Safety

AZERBAIJAN TECHNOLOGICAL UNIVERSITY

2011 Ganja, Heydar Aliyev Ave. 103
Telephone: (22) 57-56-29
E-mail: info@aztu-ganja.ws
Internet: aztu-ganja.ws
Founded 1980 as Azerbaijan Technological Institute, present name and status 2000
State control
Rector: Prof. Dr MALIKOV TELMAN GULU OGLU
Dir of Library: GASANOV UMID IMRAN OQLU
Number of students: 1,713
Publications: *Scientific Messages*, *Technologist*

DEANS

Faculty of Economy and Management: Asst Prof. AGAYEVA KHALIDA MEHDI QIZI
Faculty of Foodstuff and Tourism: Asst Prof. HASANOV ARZU NAJAF OQLU
Faculty of Standardization and Technological Machines: Asst Prof. ASKAROV NAMIQ RZA OQLU
Faculty of Technology of Consumer Goods and Examination: Asst Prof. ABBASOV GARAY SURKHAI OQLU

AZERBAIJAN UNIVERSITY

1141 Baku, S. Dadashov, 84
Telephone: (12) 434-76-89
E-mail: office@au.edu.az
Internet: www.au.edu.az
Founded 1991
Private control
Pres.: Prof. AKIF MUSAYEV
Vice-Rector for Gen. Affairs: AGAMALIYEV AGAMALI GULU
Vice-Rector for Scientific Works: Prof. IBRAHIMLI XALEDDIN JALAL
Vice-Rector for Teaching Affairs: BAĞIROV MAJID HEYDAR
Library of 40,603 vols
Number of teachers: 133
Number of students: 895

DEANS
Faculty of Economy and Management: ALIZADEH AKIF VALI
Faculty of Humanities: TALISHLI MAHIR IBRAHIM

AZERBAIJAN UNIVERSITY OF ARCHITECTURE AND CONSTRUCTION

1073 Baku, 5 A. Sultanova str., Yasamal dis.
Telephone: (12) 439-15-97
E-mail: info@azmiu.edu.az
Internet: www.azmiu.edu.az
Founded 1975 as construction faculty in Baku State Univ., present status 1992, current name adopted 2000
State control
Languages of instruction: Azeri, English, Russian
Academic year: September to June (2 semesters)
Rector: Prof. Dr GULCHOHRA MAMMADOVA
Number of teachers: 632
Number of students: 6,000
Publications: *Ecology and Water Economics*, *Scientific Articles*, *Theoretical and Applied Mechanics*, *Urbanism*

DEANS
Architecture: Prof. TOFIQ ABDULLAYEV
Construction: Prof. HIKMAT MAMMADOV
Construction Economics: Prof. NAZIMA MAMMADOVA
Construction Technology: Prof. NAMIG AGHABAYLI
Mechanization and Automation: Prof. ARIF HAJIYEV
Transportation: Prof. YAGUB PIRIYEV
Water Economics and Engineering Communication Systems: Prof. ZAKIR MUSAYEV

AZERBAIJAN UNIVERSITY OF LANGUAGES

1014 Baku, R. Behbudov küç. 60
Telephone: (12) 421-22-31
E-mail: mail@adu.edu.az
Internet: www.adu.edu.az
Founded 1937 as School of Foreign Languages, present name and status 2000
State control
Faculties of English, French, German, international relations and regional studies, Italian, Korean, philology, Russian, Spanish, translation; 3 campuses
Chancellor: SAMAD I. SEYIDOV
Library of 532,268 vols, 24,303 ebooks
Number of teachers: 700
Number of students: 4,573

BAKU BUSINESS UNIVERSITY

Baku, H. Zardabi St 88A
Telephone: (12) 431-91-18
E-mail: info@bbu.edu.az
Internet: www.bbu.edu.az
Founded 1993
Private control
Languages of instruction: Azeri, English, Russian
Academic year: September to June
Rector: Dr IBAD MUSA OGLU ABBASOV
Vice-Rector for Education: SABIR ABUZAR OGLU AMIRKHANOV
Vice-Rector for Gen. Affairs: Dr KHATIRA CINAYIDDIN GIZI AZIZOVA
Vice-Rector for Scientific Works: AGASALIM KARIM OGLU ALASGAROV
Vice-Rector for Teaching: RAHIM FARAHIM OGLU SADIGOV
Number of students: 2,000
Publication: *Audit* (4 a year)

DEANS
School of Business and Management: Dr ANAR ALI OGLU AZIZOV
School of Economy and Management: Dr AFIDA IBRAHIM GIZI HASANOVA

BAKU ISLAMIC UNIVERSITY

1000 Baku, Mirza Fatali 7
Telephone: (12) 492-82-23
E-mail: biu_qafqaz@hotmail.com
State control
Rector: Haji SABIR HASANLI

BAKU SLAVIC UNIVERSITY

1014 Baku, Suleyman Rustam St 25
Telephone: (12) 440-27-70
E-mail: bakslavuniver@hotmail.com
Internet: www.bsu-edu.org
Founded 1946 as M. F. Akhundov Azerbaijan State Teacher Training Institute, current name adopted and status 2000
State control
Academic year: September to August
Rector: Prof. Dr KAMAL M. ABDULLAYEV
Vice-Rector for Education: Prof. Dr ASIF A. HAJIEV
Vice-Rector for Educational Work: Dr OKTAY A. SAMEDOV
Vice-Rector for Int. Relations: Prof. Dr SAHIBA A. GAFAROVA
Vice-Rector for Research: Prof. MAMED A. ALIYEV
Library of 500,000 vols
Number of teachers: 576
Number of students: 3,500
Publications: *BSU Scientific Works*, *Mutarjim*, *Russian Language and Literature in Azerbaijan* (4 a year)

DEANS
International Relations and Regional Studies Faculty: ADIL RAJABLI
Philological Faculty: Assoc. Prof. IBRAHIMPASHA A. BABAYEV
Translation Faculty: Asst Prof. SEYFEL HASANOV

BAKU STATE UNIVERSITY

1148 Baku, Academic Zahid Xalilov St 23
Telephone: (12) 430-32-45
E-mail: info@bsu.az
Founded 1919
Academic year: September to July
Depts of applied mathematics, biology, chemistry, commerce, geology and geography, Hebrew studies, international law and international relations, journalism, law, library sciences, mathematics, Oriental studies, philology, philosophy and psychology, physics, preparatory studies, religion
Rector: ABEL MAMMADALI MAHARRAMOV
Pro-Rector: BAKHRAM MEKHRALI ASKEROV
Pro-Rector: IZZAT ASHRAF RUSTAMOV
Pro-Rector: SHAHVALAD BINNAT KHALILOV
Pro-Rector: VUSAT AMIR EFENDIYEV
Librarian: SARA IBRAGIMOVA
Library: see under Libraries and Archives
Number of teachers: 1,380
Number of students: 15,300
Publications: *Estestvennikh nauk* (4 a year), *Gumanitarnikh nauk* (4 a year), *Sotsialno-politicheskikh nauk* (4 a year), *Vestnik Bakinskogo Universiteta: Fiziko–Matematicheskikh nauk* (4 a year)

GANJA STATE UNIVERSITY

Haydar Aliev Ave 187, 2000 Ganja
Telephone: (22) 56-73-10
E-mail: info@gsu.az
Internet: www.gsu.az
Founded 1938, current name adopted and status 2000
State control
Languages of instruction: English, Russian
Academic year: September to June
Faculties of chemistry and biology, educational psychology, engineering education, foreign languages, history, mathematics and computer science, philology
Rector: Prof. ELMAN MAMMADOV
Pro-Rector: Dr ASIF CAVADOV
Pro-Rector: FAKRADDIN HASANOV
Pro-Rector: Dr NADIR IBADOV
Pro-Rector: Prof. YUSIF YUSIFOV
Library of 2,000 vols
Number of teachers: 554
Number of students: 5,000
Publication: *Scientific Journal of GSU* (3 a year)

KHAZAR UNIVERSITY

370096 Baku, Mehseti St 11
Telephone: (12) 421-10-93
E-mail: ashadlinskaya@khazar.org
Internet: www.khazar.org
Founded 1991
Private control
Languages of instruction: Azeri, English, Russian
Academic year: September to June
Pres.: Prof. Dr HAMLET ISAKHANLI
Vice-Pres.: Prof. MOHAMMAD NOURIYEV
Library of 60,000 vols, 87 periodicals
Number of teachers: 200
Number of students: 1,700
Publications: *Azerbaijani Archaeology* (4 a year), *Journal of Azerbaijani Studies* (4 a year), *Khazar Journal of Mathematics*, *Khazar View* (literary and scientific, 24 a year)

DEANS
School of Architecture, Engineering and Applied Science: Assoc. Prof. RAFIG M. AHMADOV
School of Economics and Management: Prof. MAHAMMAD N. NURIYEV
School of Education: ELZA SAMADOVA
School of Humanities and Social Sciences: (vacant)
School of Law: Prof. JABIR Z. KHALILOV
School of Medicine, Dentistry and Public Health: Assoc. Prof. NIGAR ILYASOVNA

BAGIROVA

LANKARAN STATE UNIVERSITY

4200 Lankaran, Pr. Azi Aslanov 50

Telephone: (171) 5-25-88
E-mail: office@lsu.edu.az
Internet: www.lsu.edu.az

Founded 1991
State control

Faculties of economics, humanities, natural sciences

Rector: ASAF ISKENDEROV
Number of students: 1,369

NAKHCHIVAN STATE UNIVERSITY

7012 Nakhchivan, Mardanov Gardashlari 99

Telephone: (12) 94-99-97
E-mail: rector@ndu.edu.az
Internet: www.ndu.edu.az

Founded 1967 as Nakhchivan br. of Azerbaijan State Pedagogical Institute
State control
Language of instruction: Azerbaijani
Academic year: September to July

Rector: Prof. Dr ISA HABBIBBEYLI
Vice-Rector for Admin. and Economy Affairs: ARAZ IBRAHIM ZALOV
Vice-Rector for Educational Affairs: Prof. Dr MAMMAD HUSEYN OGLU RZAYEV
Vice-Rector for Scientific Affairs: Prof. Dr ANAR ALTAY KAZIMOV
Vice-Rector for Teaching Affairs: Prof. HUSEYN MAMMAD OGLU HASHIMLI
Head of Library: PARVIN YAGUB GIZI ALIYEVA

Library of 151,000 vols
Number of teachers: 450
Number of students: 4,000

Publication: *Scientific Works*

DEANS

Architecture: Dr MUBARIZ NURIYEV
Art: Dr ISMAYIL MURSELOV
Economy: Prof. Dr ASIF SHIRALIYEV
History and Philology: Dr IMAN JAFAROV
International Relations and Foreign Languages: Dr GURBAN GURBANLI
Law: Dr GARIB ALLAHVERDIYEV
Medical: Dr BAHRUZ MAMMADOV
Nature Study: Dr AKIF MARDANLI
Pedagogy: Dr IBRAHIM RUSTEMOV
Physics and Mathematics: Dr TOFIG NAJAFOV

ODLAR YURDU UNIVERSITY

1072 Baku, Koroglu Rahimov St 13

Telephone: (12) 465-82-00
E-mail: fuadhud@yahoo.com
Internet: www.oyu.edu.az

Founded 1995
Private control

Depts of business and management, engineering ecology, medicine, pedagogics, translations

Rector: Dr SAMIR VALIYEV
Vice-Rector for Academic Affairs: VAQIF SADIGZADEH
Vice-Rector for Financial Issues: MUNIR VALIYEV
Vice-Rector for Int. Relations: RUSLAN SADIRKHANOV
Vice-Rector for Medical Qualifications: AKIF SALEHOV

Library of 50,000 vols

QAFQAZ UNIVERSITY

Baku-Sumqayıt Rd 16-km Xirdalan, 0101 Baku

Telephone: (12) 448-28-62
E-mail: iro@qu.edu.az
Internet: www.qu.edu.az

Founded 1993
Private control
Languages of instruction: Azerbaijani, English
Academic year: October to June

Rector: Prof. Dr AHMET SANIÇ
Vice-Rector for Academic Discipline and Behaviour: Dr. SHAIG NABIYEV
Vice Rector for Admin. Issues: Dr SAHIN DURMAZ
Vice-Rector for Education: Assoc. Prof CIHAN BULUT
Vice-Rector for External Affairs: SANNUR ALIYEV
Vice-Rector for Scientific Research: Dr. NIFATLI GOJAYEV
Dir for Library: MEHMET ALI CEYHAN

Library of 80,000 vols, 20,000 ebooks
Number of teachers: 260 (180 full-time, 80 part-time)
Number of students: 3,200 (2,800 undergraduate, 400 graduate)

Publication: *Journal of Qafqaz University*

DEANS

Faculty of Economic and Administrative Sciences: Assoc. Prof. HEZI EYNALOV
Faculty of Engineering: YADULLAH BABAYEV
Faculty of Pedagogy: Assoc. Prof. ERDAL KARAMAN

Other Higher Educational Institutes

Azerbaijan State Academy for Physical Training and Sports: 1072 Baku, 98 Fatali Khan Khoyski; tel. (12) 498-47-31; e-mail agacanbox@mail.ru; f. 1930; faculties of physical education, sports; 3,589 students; Rector AGADJAN ABIYEV.

Azerbaijan State Marine Academy: 1000 Baku, Zarifa Aliyeva st; tel. (12) 493-09-19; e-mail akademiya@adda.edu.az; internet adda.edu.az; f. 1881; library: 90,000 vols; 55 doctoral staff; 350 students; Rector Prof. BASHIROV RASIM JAVAD OGLU; Vice-Rector for Training and Education Prof. SULEYMANOV ASADULLAH MAHMUD OGLU; Vice-Rector for Scientific Works AKHUNDOV MAHAMMAD BAGIR OGLU; Vice-Rector for International Relations NASIROV VUGAR VOROSHIL OGLU.

Azerbaijan State Oil Academy: 1010 Baku, Pr. Azadlyg 20; tel. (12) 493-45-57; e-mail ihm@adna.baku.az; internet www.adna.baku.az; f. 1920; faculties of automation of production, chemical technology, engineering economics, oil and gas exploitation, oil mechanical engineering, power engineering; brs in Sumqayıt and Mingaçevir; library: 860,000 vols; 870 teachers; 6,232 students; Rector S. QARAYEV.

Uzeir Hajibeyov Baku Academy of Music: 370014 Baku, Shamsi Badalbeyli 98; tel. (12) 493-22-48; e-mail info@musigi-dunya.az; internet musakademiya.musigi-dunya.az/mus_academy_en.html; f. 1920; courses in choral conducting, composition, folk instruments, musicology, orchestral instruments, piano, singing; library: 220,000 vols and 25,000 scores; 290 lecturers; 630 students; Rector F. SH. BADALBEYLI.

BAHAMAS

The Higher Education System

The Bahamas is a contributing country to the University of the West Indies (UWI). The UWI Centre for Hotel and Tourism Management is located in Nassau. Other institutions of higher education include the College of the Bahamas (a community college transitioning to a university) and the Eugene Dupuch Law School (founded in 1998). The Ministry of Education is responsible for education and in 2004 it created the Department of Higher Education and Lifelong Learning, which is responsible for tertiary education and quality assurance. To gain admission to degree programmes students must have at least two GCE A-level subjects or equivalent. Available degrees include Associates, Bachelors, Masters and Doctorates. In addition, the College of the Bahamas offers the UWI's undergraduate law degree as well as a pharmacy degree in conjunction with the University of Technology, Jamaica. Associate degrees are taken after GCE O-levels and last for two years. Bachelors degrees last for three years, and Masters degrees last for two years after the Bachelors. A Doctorate takes a further two years after the Masters degree. Associate degrees are mostly available at the College of the Bahamas.

The College of the Bahamas was established in 1974 by an act of Parliament and in 2011 had a total enrolment of 4,936 students studying at four academic campuses (the main one of which is located in the capital, Nassau). The College offers degrees through eight academic units, comprising an institute and seven schools (six of which are organized into faculties headed by an academic dean). In 2011 there were plans for the College to be granted university status in the near future as the national University of the Bahamas. In that year a third campus—the Northern Campus, situated near Freeport on Grand Bahama—was opened as part of a planned university community. A new large library (the Henry C. Moore Library) was also opened, the historical archives of which were to serve as the de facto national library of the Bahamas. The Gerace Research Centre which specializes in marine science research, archaeology and geology is housed on the island of San Salvador.

Aside from the vocational and technical courses available at the College of the Bahamas, the Princess Margaret Hospital offers a nursing course and trade-skills courses are offered by the Bahamas Technical and Vocational Institute, which was founded in 1980 and which has two campuses—the main campus in Nassau and a satellite campus (the Freeport Campus) on Grand Bahama; in 2011 the Institute hosted some 1,900 full- and part-time students.

Regulatory Body

GOVERNMENT

Ministry of Education: Thompson Blvd, POB N-3913, Nassau; tel. 502-2700; e-mail info@bahamaseducation.com; internet www.bahamaseducation.com; Minister Hon. JEROME K. FITZGERALD.

Ministry of Youth, Sports and Culture: Thompson Blvd, POB N-3913, Nassau; tel. 502-0600; e-mail culturemysc@bahamas.gov.bs; internet www.bahamas.gov.bs/mysc; Minister DANIEL JOHNSON.

Learned Societies

GENERAL

Bahamas National Trust: POB N-4105, Nassau; tel. 393-1317; e-mail bnt@bnt.bs; internet www.bnt.bs; f. 1959; preservation of bldgs, wildlife and areas of beauty or historic interest; manages 27 nat. parks and protected areas; 2,500 mems; Exec. Dir ERIC CAREY; publ. *Trust Notes* (6 a year).

HISTORY, GEOGRAPHY AND ARCHAEOLOGY

Bahamas Historical Society: POB SS-6833, Nassau-New Providence; tel. 322-4231; e-mail info@bahamashistoricalsociety.com; internet www.bahamashistoricalsociety.com; f. 1959; 400 mems; collection and preservation of material relating to the history of the Bahamas; Pres. JIM LAWLOR; Corresp. Sec. JOAN CLARKE; publ. *Bahamas Historical Journal* (1 a year).

LANGUAGE AND LITERATURE

Alliance Française: POB SP-61476, Ocean Pl., West Bay St, Nassau; tel. 356-0961; e-mail admin@afbahamas.org; internet afbahamas.org; offers courses and examinations in French language and culture and promotes cultural exchange with France; Dir ITALIA WATKINS-JAN.

Libraries and Archives

Freeport

Sir Charles Hayward Public Lending Library: POB F-40040, Freeport, Grand Bahama; tel. 352-7048; e-mail sircharleshaywardpubliclibrary@google.com; f. 1966; 40,000 vols; Librarian SHANREIKAH S. GARDINER.

Nassau

College of the Bahamas–Libraries and Instructional Media Services: POB N-4912, Nassau; tel. 302-4552; e-mail library@cob.edu.bs; f. 1974; 75,000 vols; spec. collns incl. Bahamiana, Caribbean dissertations; document delivery and interlibrary loans; deposit collns of the UN, WHO and Pan-American Health Organization; Dir WILLAMAE M. JOHNSON; publ. *Library Informer*.

Department of Archives: POB SS-6341, Nassau; tel. 393-2175; e-mail archives@batelnet.bs; internet www.bahamasnationalarchives.bs; f. 1971; nat. archival depository; 2,689 linear ft of records; Govt record centre records management, research centre appraisals, conservation and preservation microfilming information technology; Dir M. ELAINE TOOTE; Asst Dir PATRICE MARIA WILLIAMS; Chief Archivist SHERRILEY E. STRACHAN; publ. *Preservum* (every 2 years).

Nassau Public Library: POB N-3210, Nassau; tel. 322-4907; f. 1837; 80,000 vols; Library Supervisor WINNIFRED MURPHY.

Museum

Nassau

National Museum of The Bahamas: POB EE 15082, Nassau; tel. 326-2566; e-mail info@ammcbahamas.com; internet www.ammcbahamas.com; collns incl. artefacts from shipwrecks, historic bldgs, furniture; Dir Dr KEITH TINKER.

Colleges

College of the Bahamas: Thompson Blvd, POB N-4912, Nassau; tel. 323-8550; internet www.cob.edu.bs; f. 1974; 4-year college; assoc. degrees in arts, business, natural and social sciences, nursing, teaching, technology; BA degrees in accounting, banking and finance, education, management, nursing; continuing education; library: 68,000 vols; 160 teachers; 4,836 students; Pres. Dr LEON HIGGS; publs *At Random* (1 a year), *COBLA Journal* (2 a year), *College Forum* (2 a year).

University of the West Indies (Bahamas Office): POB N-1184, Nassau; tel. 323-6593; e-mail matwilliam@hotmail.com; f. 1965; Representative MATTHEW WILLIAM.

BAHRAIN

The Higher Education System

The University of Bahrain was founded in 1986 by Amiri decree as a merger between University College of Arts, Science and Education and Gulf Polytechnic. It comprises 10 Colleges: of Arts, Business Administration, Engineering, Health Sciences, Information Technology, Law, Science, Applied Studies, Teaching (the Bahrain Teachers College) and the Academy of Physical Education and Physiotherapy. The other main institution of higher education ais the Bahrain Polytechnic, founded in 2008. The Arabian Gulf University, founded in 1980 as a joint venture between six (now seven) Arab governments comprises the College of Medicine and Medical Sciences, the College of Graduate Studies and (from 2007) the French Arabian School of Management and Finance. Some 32,327 students were enrolled in higher education in 2011/12 and in 2010/11 12,709 students were enrolled at the University of Bahrain alone.

In 2011 there were 12 private tertiary education providers registered with the Higher Education Council (HEC). These are a combination of institutions that are wholly owned locally, institutions that have international partners, and institutions that are campuses of universities located in other countries. Following poor reviews from the Higher Education Review Unit in 2011 two of these—the New York Institute of Technology and the Birla Institute of Technology—announced their intention to withdraw from Bahrain and they subsequently put in place teaching-out plans.

Admission to higher education is based on a test score of 70% or higher in the Tawjihiya examinations. The main undergraduate qualifications are the Associate and Bachelors degrees, whilest the main postgraduate qualifications are the Masters degree, Doctorate, and Postgraduate Diploma. The undergraduate degrees are based on the US credits system: Associate degrees last for two years and require 65–80 credits, and Bachelors degrees are generally four years in length and require 130–140 credits. The Masters degree and Postgraduate Diploma are based on the British Masters degree, and last for two to four years, with an equal division between taught classes and research. Finally, the Doctorate, usually PhD, requires three to five years of full-time study and research. All Bahraini students studying abroad are required to have their degrees submitted for recognition by the Commission for the Evaluation of Academic Degrees. A Quality Assurance Authority for Education and Training (QAAET), which is affiliated to the HEC, was established by Amiri decree in 2008. The QAAET is composed of four units, including a Vocational Review Unit, which monitors the quality of vocational education offered at providers licensed by the Ministry of Labour, and a Higher Education Review Unit, which conducts reviews of private universities at programme and institutional level. The units report back to the Ministry of Education. The Higher Education Review Unit does not itself have the authority to license or accredit university programmes. Rather, decisions on the licensing and accreditation of new programmes are made by the HEC based on the quality review reports submitted by the Unit.

Non-university level education is offered at the University of Bahrain in the form of two-year diploma courses in a number of subjects. The admissions criteria are the same as those for a full degree course. The College of Health Sciences offers Certificates, Associate degrees, Post-basic diplomas and Bachelors degrees in mostly medical-related subjects. Vocational and technical training is also offered at the Bahrain Training Institute (founded in 1992 to offer courses in the manufacturing, process, construction, commercial and services industries), Bahrain Polytechnic (established in Isa Town in 2008), the Hotel and Catering Training Centre and the Vocational and Training Centre (the latter being run by the Ministry for Labour).

Plans to establish a 'Higher Education City' (a regional hub for ICT research and training) were put into place in 2006. From the mid-2000s the implantation of branches of foreign universities gathered pace in Bahrain. For example, construction of the Royal College of Surgeons, within Ireland Medical University of Bahrain at Muharraq, was completed in 2008.

The QAAET is one of the key measures of the National Education Reform Initiatives, a programme which was launched in 2008 as part of Bahrain's Vision 2030 and which aimed to develop the education system at all levels. The Initiatives also included the establishment of Bahrain Teachers College and of Bahrain Polytechnic and the creation of a School Improvement Programme. A joint two-year project in partnership with the Scottish Qualifications Authority has been put in place to create a National Qualification Framework.

Regulatory Body

GOVERNMENT

Ministry of Culture: POB 2199, Manama; tel. 17298777; e-mail info@moc.gov.bh; internet www.moc.gov.bh; Minister SHEIKA MAI BINT MUHAMMAD AL KHALIFA.

Ministry of Education: POB 43, Manama; tel. 17278999; e-mail moe@moe.gov.bh; internet www.moe.gov.bh; Minister Dr MAJID BIN ALI AL-NAIMI.

ACCREDITATION

Quality Assurance Authority for Education and Training: Bahrain; tel. 17583330; e-mail talsindi@batelco.com.bh; f. 2008; affiliated to Higher Education Ccl; Dir TARIQ ALSINDI.

Learned Societies

ECONOMICS, LAW AND POLITICS

Bahrain Bar Society: POB 5025, Manama; tel. 17720566; f. 1977; 65 mems; Pres. HASSAN ALI RADHI; publ. *Al Muhami*.

FINE AND PERFORMING ARTS

Bahrain Arts Society: POB 26264, Manama; tel. 17590551; e-mail info@bahrainartssociety.net; internet www.bahrainartssociety.com; f. 1983; promotes fine arts of Bahrain nationally and internationally; incl. a school of fine arts and art gallery, and the official photography club; 184 mems; Pres. ALI AL-MAHMEED.

Bahrain Contemporary Art Association: POB 26232, Manama; tel. 17728046; e-mail alsaariart@hotmail.com; f. 1970; 60 mems; library of 250 vols; Pres. RASHID AL-ORAFI; Dir ABDUL KARIM AL-ORRAYED; Information Officer SAYED HASSAN AL SAARI.

HISTORY, GEOGRAPHY AND ARCHAEOLOGY

Bahrain Historical and Archaeological Society: POB 5087, Manama; tel. 17727895; f. 1953; 143 mems; library: reference library; Pres. Dr ESSA AMIN; Hon. Sec. Dr KHALID KHALIFA; publ. *Dilmun* (2 a year).

LANGUAGE AND LITERATURE

Alliance Française: POB 840, Manama; tel. 17683295; e-mail info@afbahrain.com; internet www.afbahrain.com; f. 1969; offers courses and exams in French language and culture and promotes cultural exchange with France; library of 5,000 French books, CDs and DVDs.

Bahrain Writers and Literature Association: POB 1010, Manama; tel. 17274866; f. 1969; 40 mems; library of 700 vols; Pres. ALI AL-SHARGAWI; Sec. FAREED RAMADAN.

British Council: AMA Centre, 146, Shaikh Salman Highway, Manama 356, POB 452; tel. 17261555; e-mail bc.enquiries@britishcouncil.org.bh; internet www

.britishcouncil.org/me-bahrain.htm; office opened 1959; attached teaching centre; offers courses and exams in English language and British culture and promotes cultural exchange with the UK; library of 9,000 vols; Dir AMANDA BURRELL.

MEDICINE

Bahrain Medical Society: POB 26136, Adliya; tel. 17827818; e-mail bahrainmedical1@gmail.com; f. 1972; 350 mems; library of 300 vols; Pres. Dr ALI MOHD MATAR; Gen. Sec. Dr FAISAL A. ALNASIR; publ. *Journal* (4 a year).

RELIGION, SOCIOLOGY AND ANTHROPOLOGY

Bahrain Society of Sociologists: POB 26488, Manama; tel. 17826309; f. 1979; 65 mems; library of 423 vols; Pres. Dr AHMED AL-SHARYAN; Sec. Gen. EBRAHIM ALALAWI.

Islamic Association: POB 22484, Manama; tel. 17671788; e-mail islamyia@islamyia.org; internet www.islamyia.net; f. 1979; teaches the Koran, Fiqh, Hadith, Sunnah; distributes zakat and donations; 200 mems; Pres. Dr ABDULATIF MAHMOUD AL-MAHMOUD.

TECHNOLOGY

Bahrain Information Technology Society: POB 26089, Manama; Villa 6, Gate 1334, Rd 3729, Manama 337; tel. 17741770; e-mail bits@batelco.com.bh; internet www.bits.org.bh; f. 1981; 260 mems; Pres. ABDULNABI A. KAL AWADH.

Bahrain Society of Engineers: POB 835, Manama; tel. 17727100; e-mail mohandis@batelco.com.bh; internet www.mohandis.org; f. 1972; 1,502 mems; Pres. A. MAJEED AL GASSAB; Exec. Man. JAFFAR Y. ALSAMEIKH; publ. *Al-Mohandis* (4 a year).

Research Institute

NATURAL SCIENCES

General

Bahrain Centre for Studies and Research: POB 496, Manama; tel. 17754757; internet www.bcsr.gov.bh; f. 1981; scientific study and research in economics, politics and strategy, marketing and consumer behaviour, social, educational and tourism studies, int. and inter-civilization studies; library of 6,000 vols, 40 periodicals; Sec. Gen. Dr HASAN MAHMOOD AL-BASTAKI; publs *Arab Magazine for Food and Nutrition* (2 a year), *Journal of Strategic Research* (irregular).

Libraries and Archives

Isa Town

University of Bahrain Libraries and Information Services: POB 32038, Isa Town; tel. 17838808; e-mail library@admin.uob.bh; internet libwebserver.uob.edu.bh/assets; f. 1986; 150,000 vols, 700 periodicals; Dir HEDI TALBI.

Manama

Ahmed Al-Farsi Library (College of Health Sciences): POB 12, Manama; tel. 17255555; internet www.chs.edu.bh/library; f. 1976; 29,000 vols, 545 periodicals, 375 audiovisual items; Librarian ABBAS AL-KHATEM.

Educational Documentation Library: POB 43, Manama; tel. 17710599; e-mail edudoc@batelco.com.bh; internet www.education.gov.bh/english/edu-library; f. 1976; attached to Min. of Education; 22,000 vols, 197 periodicals, 300 files of documents; Chief Officer FAIQA SAEED AL-SALEH; publs *Acquisitions List* (12 a year), *Bibliographical Lists* (1 a year), *Educational Index of Arabic Periodicals*, *Educational Index of Foreign Periodicals*, *Educational Indicative Abstracts* (3 a year), *Educational Information Abstracts* (3 a year), *Educational Legislation Index*, *Educational Selective Articles* (6 a year).

Historical Documents Centre: POB 28882, Manama; tel. 17664454; f. 1978; attached to Crown Prince's Court; maintains historical documents and MSS on the history of Bahrain and the Gulf; 4,000 vols; Pres. SHAIKH ABDULLAH BIN KHALID AL-KHALIFA; Dir Dr ALI ABA-HUSSAIN; publ. *Al-Watheeka* (2 a year).

Manama Central Library: c/o Ministry of Education, POB 43, Manama; tel. 17231105; e-mail libman@batelco.com.bh; f. 1946; 171,622 vols, 734 periodicals; Dir for Public Libraries MANSOOR MOHAMED SARHAN; publ. *Bahrain National Bibliography* (every 4 years).

Museum

Manama

Bahrain National Museum: Min. of Culture, Museum Directorate, POB 2199, Manama; tel. 17298777; e-mail musbah@batelco.com.bh; internet www.moc.gov.bh/en/visitingbahrain/destinations/bahrainnationalmuseum; f. 1970; attached to Min. of Culture; archaeology, ethnography, natural history, art; Dir ABDUL RAHMAN MUSAMAH.

Universities

AHLIA UNIVERSITY

POB 10878, Manama
Telephone: 17298999
E-mail: info@ahlia.edu.bh
Internet: www.ahlia.edu.bh

Founded 2001
Private control

Colleges of arts, science and education; business and finance; engineering; graduate studies and research; information technology; medical and health sciences

Pres.: Prof. ABDULLA Y. AL-HAWAJ
Vice-Pres. for Admin. and Finance: Prof. WAJEEH EL-ALI
Number of students: 1,836

APPLIED SCIENCE UNIVERSITY

POB 5055, Jufair
Telephone: 17728777
E-mail: info@asu.edu.bh
Internet: www.asu.edu.bh

Founded 2004
Private control

Pres.: Prof. WAHEEB AHMED AL-KHAJAH

ARABIAN GULF UNIVERSITY

POB 26671, Manama
Telephone: 17239999
Internet: www.agu.edu.bh

Founded 1980 by the 7 Gulf States
Languages of instruction: Arabic, English
Academic year: September to June

Pres.: Dr KHALID BIN ABDUL-RAHMAN AL-OHALY
Dir for Admin. and Financial Affairs: HISHAM ALI AL-ANSARI
Dean for Student Affairs: Prof. ABDULRAHMAN YOSIF ISMAEEL
Head of Personnel Affairs: GHADA ABDULLA AL-BUFLASA
Head of Student Affairs: MONA ABDUL AZIZ AL-KHALIFA
Registrar: ABDUL HAMEED MARHOON
Librarian: SUAD ALI AL-KHALIFA

Library of 33,000 vols, 50 periodicals and 2,000 online periodicals
Number of teachers: 90
Number of students: 1,294

Publications: *AGU Annual Catalogue*, *Journal of Scientific Research* (3 a year)

DEANS

College of Graduate Studies: Prof. WALEED KHALIL ZUBARI
College of Medicine and Medical Sciences: Prof. FAZAL KARIM DAR

PROFESSORS

AD-DIN, M. N., Microbiology
AKBAR, M. M.
AL-AAQIB, AR-R., Water Engineering, Energy
AL-ABADIN, M. Z., Physiology
AL-ANSARI, M. J.
AL-DIN, N. A.
AL-KHOLY, U.
AL-QAISI, K. A., Botany, Algae
ASH-SHAZALI, H., Paediatrics
BANDARANAYAKE, R. C.
BOTTA, G.
FULEIHAN, F., Internal Medicine
GRANGULY, P. K.
GRANT, N. I.
GREALLY, J.
HAMDY, H.
ISSA, A. A.
KHADER, M. H. A., Organic Chemistry
MATHUR, V., Pharmacology
MATHUR, V. S.
NASSER, A. I., Mechanical Engineering
NAYAR, U.
PRASAD, K.
RAHIM, F. AS-A. A., Education and Psychology
RAKHA, I., General Surgery, Orthopaedics
SACHDEVA, U.
SATIR, A. A.
SKERMAN, J. H.

BAHRAIN AMA INTERNATIONAL UNIVERSITY

POB 18041, Salmabad
Telephone: 17787978
E-mail: amaiu@batelco.com.bh
Internet: www.amaiu.edu.bh

Founded 2002
Private control

Dir: Dr MARIE REDINA VICTORIA
Registrar: NOLY MANZANO
Librarian: RICHELLE AFINIDAD

DEANS

College of Business Administration: MANOLO ANTO
College of Computer Studies and Engineering: Dr RAMON J. CABIGAO
College of International Studies: Dr ROY TUMANENG

DELMON UNIVERSITY FOR SCIENCE AND TECHNOLOGY

POB 2469, Manama
Telephone: 17294400
E-mail: info@delmon.bh
Internet: www.delmonuniversity.com

Founded 2004
Private control

Faculties of economics and administrative sciences, information technology and computer science, law

Pres.: Dr HASSAN M. AL-QUADHI
Vice-Pres. for Academic Affairs: Prof. Dr SAAD Z. DARWISH
Dean for Student Affairs: Dr HISHAM OBAIDA

GULF UNIVERSITY

POB 26489, Sanad
Telephone: 17620092
E-mail: info@gulfuniversity.net
Internet: www.gulfuniversity.net

Founded 2001
Private control

Colleges of business, management and finance, computer engineering sciences, education, engineering, law

Pres.: Dr MONA RASHID AL-ZAYANI
Vice-Pres. for Admin. and Finance: MOHAMMED AL-ANNI

KINGDOM UNIVERSITY

POB 40434, Manama
Telephone: 17238899
E-mail: info@ku.edu.bh
Internet: www.ku.edu.bh

Founded 2001
Private control
Languages of instruction: Arabic, English
Academic year: September to August

Pres.: Dr YOUSEF ABDUL GHAFFAR
Librarian: MOHAMMED AZAHIM SALDEEN
Librarian: HAMDY GHONAIM

Library of 3,250 vols, 20 periodicals
Number of teachers: 62 (35 full-time, 15 part-time, 12 visiting)
Number of students: 1,200

DEANS

College of Arts: Dr REDA ABDULWAJED AMEEN
College of Business Sciences and Finance: Dr WALEED ABDUL AZIZ
College of Computing and Information Technology: Prof. MUSTAFA ABDUL ATHEEM
College of Engineering: Dr SAMI ALI KAMEL
College of Law: Dr MOHAMMED AL-HITI

ROYAL COLLEGE OF SURGEONS IN IRELAND MEDICAL UNIVERSITY OF BAHRAIN

POB 15503, Adliya
Telephone: 17351450
E-mail: info@rcsi-mub.com
Internet: www.rcsi-mub.com

Founded 2004
State control

Pres.: Prof. KEVIN O'MALLEY

ROYAL UNIVERSITY FOR WOMEN

POB 37400, West Riffa
Telephone: 17764444
E-mail: info@ruw.edu.bh
Internet: www.ruw.edu.bh

Founded 2005
Private control

Pres.: Prof. MAZIN JUMAH
Librarian: BINDHU NAIR

Library of 10,000 print vols, 21,000 electronic vols, 5,000 periodicals, 100,000 art images

DEANS

Faculty of Art, Design and Computing Science: Dr Z. HADDAD
Faculty of Business Studies: Dr Q. ALI
Faculty of Education: (vacant)

UNIVERSITY OF BAHRAIN

POB 32038, Isa Town
Telephone: 17439996
E-mail: admreg@uob.edu.bh
Internet: www.uob.edu.bh

Founded 1986 by merger of Univ. College of Arts, Science and Education, and Gulf Polytechnic
autonomous control
Language of instruction: Arabic
Academic year: October to August

Chair. of Board of Trustees: THE MINISTER OF EDUCATION
Pres.: Dr IBRAHIM MOHAMMED JANAHI
Vice-Pres. for Academic Programmes and Research: Dr NIZAR AL-BAHARNA
Vice-Pres. for Admin. and Finance: Dr SAMIR FAKHRO
Vice-Pres. for Planning and Community Service: Dr GEORGE NAJJAR
Registrar: Dr ISA AL-KHAYAT
Dir for Library and Information Services: WARWICK PRICE

Library: see under Libraries and Archives
Number of teachers: 320
Number of students: 12,000

DEANS

Bahrain Teacher's College: HANADA TAHA (acting)
College of Applied Studies: SADIQ MAHDI AL-ALAWI
College of Arts: Dr ALAWI HASHIM AL HASHIMI
College of Business Administration: Prof. MINWIR AL-SHAMMARI
College of Education: KHALIL YOUSIF SULAIMAN ALKHALILI
College of Engineering: Prof. NADER AL-BASTAKI
College of Health Sciences: Dr ANEESA AL-SINDI
College of Information Technology: Dr HESHAM MOHMED AL-AMMAL
College of Law: Prof. MOHAMMAD YOUSEF AL-ZUBI
College of Physical Education and Physiotherapy: (vacant)
College of Science: Dr HASHIM AHMAD YOUSIF AL-SAYED

Colleges

College of Health Sciences: POB 12, Ministry of Health, Bahrain; tel. 17279664; e-mail ayousif1@health.gov.bh; internet www.chs.edu.bh; f. 1976; divs of allied health, English, integrated science, nursing; Educational Devt Centre; library: see under Libraries and Archives; 111 teachers; Dean Dr SHAWKI ABDULLA AMEEN; Head of Registration and Student Affairs ALI EBRAHIM AL-SAEED; Librarian (Ahmed Al-Farsi Library) ABBAS A. AL-KHATEM.

Gulf College of Hospitality and Tourism: POB 22088, Muharraq; tel. 17320191; e-mail mancat5@batelco.com.bh; internet www.gulf-college.com; f. 1976; higher nat. diploma and degree courses in hospitality management and travel and tourism; library: 10,000 vols; Dean TONY SPICER; Dir DAVID PATTERSON.

University College of Bahrain: POB 55040, Manama; tel. 17790828; e-mail ealkhalifa@ucb.edu.bh; internet www.ucb.edu.bh; schools of business, information technology, media and communication; Pres. Dr KHALID BIN MOHAMMED AL-KHALIFA; Exec. Dir Dr EBRAHIM BIN KHALID AL-KHALIFA; Registrar ISAM AHMED AL-SARAF; Librarian MOUSSA HARB.

BANGLADESH

The Higher Education System

The University of Dhaka, which was established in 1921 when the area now comprising Bangladesh was still part of India, is the oldest university in the country. The provision of higher education has expanded greatly in recent years, particularly at private institutions following the implementation of the Private Universities Act of 1992. However, there are huge variances in the quality of education provided by the private universities (in 2006, following an official assessment in 2004 of the quality of teaching provided by the private sector in tertiary education, the Government ordered the immediate closure of three under-performing institutions—a ruling that is the subject of an ongoing legal battle). In 2011 there were 31 public universities, 58 private universities (incl. three with Court Stay Orders), and three international universities recognized by the University Grants Commission (UGC). In 2011 the Government reiterated its commitment to establishing a public university in each of the country's 64 districts. In 2010 there were 2,848 technical colleges, vocational institutes and colleges offering general education with a total enrolment of 447,927 students of whom 23% were girls. In 2008 some 160,447 students were enrolled in public universities and 226,986 in private universities. Both public and private universities are governed by the UGC, founded by an Act of Parliament in 1973; private universities are also subject to the Private Universities Act (2010, see below). The Government accounts for 95% of public university funding, with the rest coming from students' tuition fees and other compulsory fees. A World Bank-funded initiative entitled the Higher Education Quality Enhancement Project (2009–13) is currently being implemented at an estimated cost of US $81m. The aim of the project is to encourage innovation and accountability in universities and to enhance technical and institutional capacity in the higher education sector in general. There are four categories of university: General, Special, Open and Affiliating. The President or Prime Minister of Bangladesh acts as the Chancellor of a university and appoints the Vice-Chancellors and the academic and executive heads of the universities. The Syndicate is the university's executive body. Its decisions are ratified by the Senate, a board that also approves the accounts. The Academic Council of a university consists of professors and other teaching representatives. Deans of Faculty are either elected by the faculty or appointed by the Academic Council, depending on the institution in question. Most public universities are modelled on the University of London (United Kingdom), consisting of a central department with affiliated colleges and institutions.

Admission is based on completion of 12 years' general education, receipt of the Higher Secondary Certificate, or equivalent, and success in entrance examinations. The main university degrees are the Bachelors, Masters and Doctor of Philosophy. Bachelors degrees from affiliated colleges of public universities are known as 'Pass' degrees and are three years in length; Bachelors degrees from public universities are known as 'Honours' degrees and last four years. Most private universities have adopted the US-style 'major' and 'minor' subject system with a Grade Point Average grading system. A Masters degree requires two years of further study after a 'Pass' degree, and one year after an 'Honours' degree. The Doctorate requires at least three years of further study and research.

There is a formal system of Islamic education, consisting of a two-year Fazil, roughly equivalent to the Bachelors, and the two-year Kamil, equivalent to the Masters. Under the supervision of the Bangladesh Madrasah Education Board, students are examined in fields such as Arabic, Hadith and Tafsir (Koranic interpretation). Technical and vocational education is overseen by the Bangladesh Technical Education Board (BTEB). There are three levels of technician award: Secondary School Certificate (SSC), Higher Secondary Certificate (HSC) and a four-year Diploma.

In July 2010 the Private Universities Act 2010 was passed by Parliament (replacing the Private Universities Act 1992); the new legislation aimed to ensure the provision of consistently high standards of education within the private sector through effective management and the establishment of an independent National Accreditation Council. However, as of late 2012 the Council had not yet been set up.

Regulatory and Representative Bodies

GOVERNMENT

Ministry of Cultural Affairs: Bangladesh Secretariat, Bhaban 6, Dhaka 1000; tel. (2) 9513677; e-mail sas-moca@mailcity.com; internet www.moca.gov.bd; Minister HASANUL HAQ INU.

Ministry of Education: Bangladesh Secretariat, Bldg 6, Fl. No 17th–18th, Dhaka 1000; tel. (2) 9576679; e-mail info@moedu.gov.bd; internet www.moedu.gov.bd; Minister NURUL ISLAM NAHID.

Ministry of Science and Technology: Bangladesh Secretariat, Bhaban 6, 9th Fl., Dhaka 1000; tel. (2) 7170840; e-mail section16@most.gov.bd; internet www.mosict.gov.bd; Minister ABDUL LATIF SIDDIQUI.

FUNDING

University Grants Commission of Bangladesh: Agargaon, Dhaka 1207; tel. (2) 8112629; e-mail chairmanugc@yahoo.com; internet www.ugc.gov.bd; f. 1973; supervises, maintains, promotes and coordinates univ. education; also responsible for maintaining standard and quality in all public and private univs in Bangladesh; assesses needs of public univs in terms of funding and advises Govt on various issues related to higher education; Chair. Prof. A. K. AZAD CHOWDHURY.

NATIONAL BODIES

Association of Universities of Bangladesh (AUB): House 47, Rd 10/A, Dhanmondi R/A, Dhaka 1209; tel. (2) 8126101; coordinates activities of public univs in Bangladesh and liaises with the Govt and the Univ. Grants Comm. in admin. and financial matters; Chair. MUHAMMAD MUSTAFIZUR RAHMAN; Exec. Sec. S. M. SAIFUDDIN.

Bangladesh Bureau of Educational Information and Statistics (BANBEIS): 1 Sonargaon Rd (Palashi-Nilkhet), Dhaka 1205; tel. (2) 9665457; e-mail banbeis@banbeis.gov.bd; internet www.banbeis.gov.bd; f. 1977; attached to Min. of Education; central depository of Bangladesh govt for collection, compilation and dissemination of information and statistics relating to post primary stages of education in Bangladesh; act as coordinator in the UNESCO Institute for Statistics activities.

Bangladesh Medical and Dental Council: 203 Shaheed Sayed Nazrul Islam Sarani (86, Bijoy Nagar), Dhaka 1000; tel. (2) 9555538; e-mail info@bmdc.org.bd; internet www.bmdc.org.bd; f. 1973 as Bangladesh Medical Council; custodian of medical and dental basic and higher education in Bangladesh; regulates undergraduate and postgraduate medical and dental education in Bangladesh; approves journals published by different orgs and asscns; Pres. Prof. ABU SHAFI AHMED AMIN.

Bangladesh Technical Education Board: Sher-e-Bangla Nagar Agargaon, Dhaka; e-mail info@bteb.gov.bd; internet www.bteb.gov.bd; f. 1960 as Directorate of Technical Education, current name adopted and status 1969; regulates technical education in Bangladesh; grants recognition to education instns offering its courses; Chair. Prof. MD ABUL KASHEM; Sec. Dr MD ABDUL HOQUE TALUKDER; Dir of Curriculum MD ABDUR REZZAK.

Learned Societies

GENERAL

Indira Gandhi Cultural Centre: House 24, Rd 2 High Commission of India, Dhanmondi, Dhaka; tel. (2) 9612324; e-mail iccdhaka@gmail.com; internet www.iccrindia.net/dhaka.html; f. 2010; br in Gulshan; head office in India; activities incl. exchange visits between scholars, artists and people of eminence in the field of art and culture; exchange of exhibitions; int. confs and seminars; library of 21,000 vols; Dir ANKAN BANERJEE.

Society of Arts, Literature and Welfare: Society Park, K. C. Dey Rd, Chittagong; f. 1942; 500 mems; Gen. Sec. NESAR AHMED CHOWDHURY.

UNESCO Office Dhaka: House 122, Rd 1, Block F, Banani, Dhaka 1213; tel. (2) 9873210; e-mail dhaka@unesco.org; internet www.unesco.org/dhaka; f. 1996; contributes to building of peace, alleviation of poverty, sustainable devt and intercultural dialogue through its mandates in education, sciences, culture, communication and information; 25 mems; library of 3,500 vols; Officer in Charge DEREK ELIAS.

BIBLIOGRAPHY, LIBRARY SCIENCE AND MUSEOLOGY

Bangladesh Association of Librarians, Information Scientists and Documentalists: CDL, House 67/B, Rd 9/A, Dhanmondi, Dhaka 1209; tel. (2) 8856000; e-mail mmr@northsouth.edu; internet www.balid.org; f. 1986; library professional devt; runs courses in library and information sciences; organizes seminar, workshop; 600 mems; library of 2,500 vols; Chair. Dr MD. MOSTAFIZUR RAHMAN; Sec.-Gen. Dr HANIF UDDIN AHMED; publ. *Informatics* (4 a year).

Library Association of Bangladesh: Dhaka University Library, Shahbagh Dhaka 1000; tel. (2) 9661900; internet www.lab.org.bd; f. 1956; provides leadership for devt, promotion, and improvement of library and information services and profession of librarianship; Pres. Prof. Dr NASIR UDDIN MUSHI.

ECONOMICS, LAW AND POLITICS

Bangladesh Bureau of Statistics: Parishankhyan Bhaban, E-27/A, Agargaon, Sher-e-Bangla Nagar, Dhaka 1207; tel. (2) 9112589; e-mail dg@bbs.gov.bd; internet www.bbs.gov.bd; f. 1974 by merger of Agriculture Census Commission, Bureau of Agriculture Statistics, Bureau of Statistics, Population Census Commission; collection, analysis and publ. of statistics covering all sectors of soc. and the economy; Dir-Gen. MD SHAHJAHAN ALI MOLLAH; publs *Child Nutrition Survey* (1 a year), *Foreign Trade Statistics* (1 a year), *Labour Force Survey* (1 a year), *Statistical Bulletin* (12 a year), *Statistical Pocket Book* (1 a year), *Statistical Yearbook* (1 a year), *Yearbook of Agricultural Statistics* (1 a year).

Bangladesh Economic Association: 4/C Eskaton Garden Rd, Dhaka 1000; tel. (2) 9345996; e-mail bea.dhaka@gmail.com; f. 1958; Pres. Dr ABUL BARKAT.

LANGUAGE AND LITERATURE

Alliance Française de Dhaka: GPOB 405, Dhaka 1205; 26 Mirpur Rd, Dhanmondi, Dhaka 1205; tel. (2) 9675249; e-mail administration@afdhaka.org; internet www.afdhaka.org; offers courses and exams in French language and culture; promotes cultural exchange with France; brs in Baridhara, Uttara; f. 1959; library of 7,500 vols; Pres. M. ABDUL MUYEED CHOWDHURY; Dir SALIHA LEFEVRE; Deputy Dir for Training and Courses JÉRÔME CHARBONNEAU.

Bangla Academy: Burdwan House 3, Kazi Nazrul Islam Ave, Ramna, Dhaka 1000; tel. (2) 8619577; e-mail bacademy@citechco.net; f. 1955; promotes culture and devt of the Bengali language and literature; produces dictionaries, translates scientific and reference works into Bangla; library of 102,000 vols; Dir-Gen. SHAMSUZZAMAN KHAN; publs *Bangla Academy Patrika* (4 a year), *Dhanshaliker Desh* (2 a year, juvenile), *Journal* (2 a year, in English), *Research Journal*, *Science Journal* (4 a year, in Bangla), *Uttaradhikar* (12 a year, literary).

British Council: POB 161, Dhaka 1000; 5 Fuller Rd, Dhaka 1000; tel. (2) 8618905; e-mail dhaka.enquiries@bd.britishcouncil.org; internet www.britishcouncil.org/bangladesh; teaching centre; offers courses and exams in English language and British culture and promotes cultural exchange with the UK; attached teaching centres in Chittagong and Dhaka; Dir Dr CHARLES NATTALL.

Goethe-Institut: GPOB 903, Dhaka 1000; House 10, Rd 9 (new), Dhanmondi R/A, Dhaka 1205; tel. (2) 9126525; e-mail info@dhaka.goethe.org; internet www.goethe.de/dhaka; offers courses and exams in German language and culture, and promotes cultural exchange with Germany; library of 4,000 vols, 20 periodicals; Dir JUDITH MIRSCHBERGER.

MEDICINE

Bangladesh Medical Association: BMA Bhaban, 15/2 Topkhana Rd, Dhaka 1000; tel. (2) 9555522; e-mail info@bma.org.bd; internet www.bma.org.bd; f. 1971; provides a forum for doctors; arranges lectures, discussions, demonstrations concerning medical and allied sciences; organizes volunteer corps for medical relief during epidemics and in time of emergency in Bangladesh or anywhere outside Bangladesh; 34,000 mems; library of 8,000 vols; Pres. Dr MAHMUD HASAN; Sec.-Gen. Dr MD SHARFUDDIN AHMED; publ. *Bangladesh Medical Journal* (4 a year).

Bangladesh Pharmaceutical Society: Rd 2, 22 Dhanmondi, Dhaka 1205; tel. (2) 8611370; e-mail bps@agni.com; internet www.bps-bd.org; f. 1968; advancement of Pharmacy incl. its application to practical problems; Pres. MD NASSER SHAHREAR ZAHEDEE; Vice-Pres. Prof. Dr ANWAR UL ISLAM; Vice-Pres. M. AZIZUL HUQ; publs *Bangladesh Pharmaceutical Journal* (2 a year), *National Formulary of Bangladesh*, *Pharmachronicle*.

NATURAL SCIENCES

General

Bangladesh Academy of Sciences: c/o Nat. Science and Technology Museum Bhaban, Agargaon, Dhaka 1207; tel. (2) 9110425; e-mail office@bas.org.bd; internet www.bas.org.bd; f. 1973; promotes research in pure and applied science; disseminates scientific knowledge among people through symposia, seminars, publs; 59 mems (41 fellows, 9 foreign fellows, 9 expatriate fellows); Pres. Prof. Dr M. SHAMSHER ALI; Vice-Pres. Prof. Dr A. K. M. AMINUL HAQUE; Vice-Pres. Prof. Dr MESBAHUDDIN AHMAD; Sec. Prof. Dr NAIYYUM CHOUDHURY; publs *Journal of the Bangladesh Academy of Sciences* (2 a year), *Year Book of the Bangladesh Academy of Sciences*.

Biological Sciences

Zoological Society of Bangladesh: c/o Dept of Zoology, Univ. of Dhaka, Dhaka 1000; tel. (2) 7168321; e-mail contact@zsbd.org; internet www.zsbd.org; f. 1972; 1,500 mems; Pres. Prof. MD SOHRAB ALI; Vice-Pres. Prof. Dr GULSHAN ARA LATIFA; Vice-Pres. Prof. Dr NOOR JAHAN SARKER; Vice-Pres. Prof. BADRUL AMIN BHUIYAN; Gen. Sec. ABDUR RAHMAN; publs *Bangladesh Journal of Zoology* (2 a year), *Proceedings of National Conference* (every 2 years).

RELIGION, SOCIOLOGY AND ANTHROPOLOGY

Asiatic Society of Bangladesh: 5 Old Secretariat Rd (Nimtali), Ramna, Dhaka 1000; tel. (2) 7168940; e-mail info@asiaticsociety.org.bd; internet www.asiaticsociety.org.bd; f. 1952 as Asiatic Society of Pakistan, present name 1972; study of man and nature of Asia; 1,034 mems; library of 10,000 vols, 500 Urdu and Persian MSS; Pres. Prof. SIRAJUL ISLAM; Vice-Pres. Prof. HARUN-OR-RASHID; Vice-Pres. Prof. NAZRUL ISLAM; Vice-Pres. Prof. PERWEEN HASAN; Gen. Sec. Prof. MAHFUZA KHANAM; publs *Journal of the Asiatic Society of Bangladesh—Humanities* (2 a year), *Journal of the Asiatic Society of Bangladesh—Science* (2 a year).

TECHNOLOGY

Institution of Engineers, Bangladesh: Ramna, Dhaka 1000; tel. (2) 9566336; e-mail info.iebhq@gmail.com; internet www.iebbd.org; f. 1948; promotes and disseminates knowledge and practice of engineering and science; 25,000 mems; library of 4,050 vols; Pres. Eng. MD NURUL HUDA; Vice-Pres. for Academic and International Affairs Eng. MD HABIBUR RAHMAN; Vice-Pres. for Administration and Finance Eng. MESBAHUR RAHMAN TUTUL; Vice-Pres. for Human Resources Development Eng. MD KABIR AHMED BHUIYAN; Hon. Gen. Sec. Eng. MD ABDUS SABUR; publs *Journal of Agricultural Engineering*, *Journal of Chemical Engineering*, *Journal of Civil Engineering*, *Journal of Electrical Engineering*, *Journal of Mechanical Engineering*, *Multidisciplinary Journal*.

Research Institutes

GENERAL

Accident Research Centre: Bangladesh University of Engineering and Technology, Dhaka 1000; tel. (2) 9669368; e-mail dirarc@arc.buet.ac.bd; internet www.buet.ac.bd/ari; f. 2002; attached to Bangladesh Univ. of Engineering and Technology; advancement of safety research in Bangladesh; scientific research and investigation into causes of accidents on roads, railways and waterways; creating awareness on transport safety; Dir Prof. Dr HASIB MOHAMMED AHSAN.

Bangladesh Council of Scientific and Industrial Research: Dr Qudrat-I-Khuda Rd, Dhanmondi, Dhaka 1205; tel. (2) 8620020; e-mail info@bcsir.gov.bd; internet www.bcsir.gov.bd; f. 1973; initiates, promotes and guides scientific, industrial and technological research on problems connected with establishment and devt of industries; library of 15,000 vols, 25,000 journals; Chair. Prof. Dr A. K. M. ASADUZZAMAN; publs *Bangladesh Journal of Scientific and Industrial Research*, *Bigganer Joyjattra*, *Purogami Bijnan*, *Science, Technology & Development*, *Scientific & Technological Contributions of BCSIR*.

Attached Research Institutes:

BCSIR Laboratory, Chittagong: Chittagong Cantonment, Chittagong 4220; e-mail ctglab@bcsir.gov.bd; f. 1965 as Natural Drug Research and Development Institute; 8 research divs: chemical; drugs and toxins; fruit and vegetables; industrial botany; industrial microbiology; marine biology and aquatics; medicinal and aromatic plants; soil management and agronomical; Dir Dr M. MANZUR-I-KHUDA.

BCSIR Laboratory, Dhaka: Dr Qudrat-i-Khuda Rd, Dhanmondi, Dhaka 1205; tel. (2) 8617924; e-mail dhakalab@bcsir.gov.bd; f. 1955 as East Regional Laboratories; 7 divs: analytical; biological; chemical; fibre and polymer; industrial physics; physical instrumentation; pulp and paper; Dir Dr MD TOFAZZAL HOSSAIN.

BCSIR Laboratory, Rajshahi: Binodpur Bazar, Rajshahi 6206; tel. (721) 750757; e-mail rajshahilab@bcsir.gov.bd; 7 divs: applied botany; applied zoology; drugs and toxins; fibre and polymer; fruits and food processing and preservation; natural products; oils, fats and waxes; Dir Dr HUSNA PARVIN NOOR.

Institute of Food Science and Technology, Dhaka: Dr Qudrat-i-Khuda Rd, Dhanmondi, Dhaka 1205; tel. (2) 8621148; e-mail ifst@bcsir.gov.bd; f. 1955, present name and status 1983; research in brs of food science and technology; 7 divs: animal food products; biochemistry and applied nutrition; food science and quality control; industrial development; microbiology; plant food products; technology of food-grains; Dir MAJEDA BEGUM.

Institute of Fuel Research and Development, Dhaka: Dr Qudrat-i-Khuda Rd, Dhanmondi, Dhaka 1205; tel. (2) 8622908; e-mail ifrd@bcsir.gov.bd; f. 1955, present name and status 1980; research and devt activities on renewable energy like biomass, solar, wind, mini and micro-hydro sources; 2 divs: research; application; Dir SUDHANGSHU KUMAR ROY.

Institute of Glass and Ceramic Research and Testing: Dr Qudrat-i-Khuda Rd, Dhanmondi, Dhaka 1205; tel. (2) 9669677; e-mail igcrt@bcsir.gov.bd; f. 2001; 6 divs: ceramic raw materials and ceramic material testing; ceramic; enamel; glass; inorganic pigment and chemical; refractories and structural ceramic; Dir MAINUL AHSAN.

Leather Research Institute: Nayerhat, Savar, Dhaka; tel. (2) 7708754; e-mail ictcell@bcsir.gov.bd; 6 divs: animal by-products; chemical; leather processing; leather products; pilot plant; tanning material.

Pilot Plant and Process Development Centre: Dr Qudrat-i-Khuda Rd, Dhanmondi, Dhaka 1205; tel. (2) 8622809; e-mail pppdc@bcsir.gov.bd; f. 1983; conducts techno-economic feasibility study of processes developed in laboratories; Dir MD ABU ANIS JAHANGIR.

AGRICULTURE, FISHERIES AND VETERINARY SCIENCE

Animal Husbandry Research Institute: Comilla; f. 1947; Prin. Scientific Officer SALIL KUMAR DHAR.

Bangladesh Agricultural Research Institute: Joydebpur, Gazipur 1701; tel. (2) 9252715; e-mail dg.bari@bari.gov.bd; internet www.bari.gov.bd; f. 1976; conducts research on crops, such as cereals, tubers, pulses, oilseeds, vegetables, fruits, spices, flowers, etc.; carries out research on non-commodity areas, such as soil and crop management, disease and insect management, irrigation and water management, devt of farm machinery, improvement of cropping and farming system management, post-harvest handling and processing, and socio-economics studies related to production, marketing, and consumption; library of 28,092 vols, 150 periodicals; Dir-Gen. Dr RAFIQUL ISLAM MONDAL; Dir of Research Dr MD SHIRAZUL ISLAM; Dir of Training and Communication Dr MD MUKHLESUR RAHMAN; Sr Librarian A. B. M. FAZLUR RAHMAN; publ. *Bangladesh Journal of Agricultural Research* (4 a year).

Bangladesh Jute Research Institute: Manik Miah Ave, Dhaka 1207; tel. (2) 8121929; e-mail info@bjri.gov.bd; internet www.bjri.gov.bd; f. 1951; oldest mono-crop research institute; constitutes 3 main brs: agricultural, technological, marketing and economic research on Jute; Dir-Gen. Dr M. FIROZE SHAH SIKDER; Dir of Agriculture M. ASADUZZAMAN; Dir of Technology M. KAMALUDDIN.

Bangladesh Livestock Research Institute: Savar, Dhaka 1341; tel. (2) 7791676; e-mail dgblri09@yahoo.com; internet www.blri.gov.bd; f. 1984; research related to livestock, poultry; Dir-Gen. Dr KHAN SHAHIDUL HUQUE; publ. *Bangladesh Journal of Livestock Research* (2 a year).

Poultry Research and Training Centre: Khulshi, Chittagong 4202; tel. (31) 2566372; e-mail kazikm54@yahoo.com; internet www.cvasu.ac.bd; f. 2008; attached to Chittagong Veterinary and Animal Sciences Univ.; research related to poultry nutrition, disease diagnosis and control, poultry production, marketing and management; Dir Dr KAZI M. KAMARUDDIN.

BIBLIOGRAPHY, LIBRARY SCIENCE AND MUSEOLOGY

Varendra Research Museum: Univ. of Rajshahi, Aksaya Kumar Maitra Rd, Rajshahi; tel. (721) 752752; internet www.ru.ac.bd; f. 1910; attached to Univ. of Rajshahi; museum-based research instn; exhibits from the Indus Valley Civilization, Buddhist and Hindu stone sculptures, Sanskrit, Arabic and Persian scripts and stone inscriptions, indigenous, tribal culture of Rajshahi region; museum colln; library of 14,060 vols, 5,500 MSS; Dir Prof. Dr SULTAN AHMAD; publ. *Journal* (1 a year).

ECONOMICS, LAW AND POLITICS

Bangladesh Unnayan Gobeshona Protishthan (Bangladesh Institute of Development Studies): GPOB 3854, Dhaka 1207; E-17 Agargaon, Sher-e-Bangla Nagar, Dhaka 1207; tel. (2) 9143441; e-mail dg_bids@bids.org.bd; internet www.bids.org.bd; f. 1957 as Pakistan Institute of Devt Economics (PIDE), current name adopted 1974; divs of agriculture and rural devt, general economics, human resources, industries and physical infrastructures, population studies; provides training in socioeconomic analysis and research methodology; library: see under Libraries and Archives; Dir-Gen. and CEO Dr MUSTAFA K. MUJERI; Sec. and Head of Admin. SUBASH C. SAHA; publs *Bangladesh Development Studies* (4 a year), *Bangladesh Unnayan Samikhha* (1 a year, in Bengali).

Institute of Health Economics: University of Dhaka, Dhaka 1000; tel. (2) 8620952; e-mail duregstr@bangla.net; f. 1998; attached to Univ. of Dhaka; offers postgraduate degrees, conducts training programmes, carries out research in health economics; Dir Dr SHAMSUDDIN AHMAD.

EDUCATION

Directorate of Continuing Education: Bangladesh University of Engineering and Technology, Dhaka 1000; tel. (2) 9665650; e-mail dirdce@dce.buet.ac.bd; internet www.buet.ac.bd/dce; f. 1995; attached to Bangladesh Univ. of Engineering and Technology; promotes professional devt of engineers in Bangladesh to cope with the intense global devt of Science and Technology; Dir Prof. Dr MUHAMMAD ABDUR RASHID SARKAR.

Institute of Education and Research: University of Rajshahi, Syed Ismail Hossain Seraji Bhaban, First Fl., Rajshahi 6205; tel. (2) 711168; e-mail ier@udhaka.net; internet inst.ru.ac.bd/ier; f. 1960; attached to Univ. of Dhaka; conducts advanced research studies and provides extension services in education; library of 38,000 vols; Dir Prof. GOLAM KABIR.

LANGUAGE AND LITERATURE

Institute of Modern Languages: University of Dhaka, Dhaka 1000; tel. (2) 9661900; e-mail duregstr@bangla.net; f. 1974; attached to Univ. of Dhaka; promotes and provides facilities for study of modern languages; offers Arabic, Bangla, Chinese, English, French, German, Italian, Japanese, Korean, Persian, Russian, Spanish, Turkish language courses; Dir MD ABDUR RAHIM; publ. *Journal of the Institute of Modern Languages* (1 a year).

MEDICINE

Bio-Medical Engineering Centre: Bangladesh University of Engineering and Technology, Dhaka 1000; tel. (2) 9665650; e-mail dirbmec@bmec.buet.ac.bd; attached to Bangladesh Univ. of Engineering and Technology; provides higher training in maintenance, operation, management and devt of medical equipment; Dir Prof. Dr MD AYNAL HAQUE.

Centre for Medical Education (CME): National Health Library Bldg, 3rd Fl., Mohakhali, Dhaka 1212; tel. (2) 8821809; e-mail director@cmedhaka.gov.bd; internet www.cmedhaka.gov.bd; f. 1983; conducts research related to health care services, health manpower devt and education of health professionals; library of 2,000 vols, 15,000 journals; Dir Prof. Dr A. B. M. ABDUL HANNAN.

ICDDR,B: International Centre for Diarrhoeal Disease Research, Bangladesh: GPOB 128, Dhaka 1000; 68 Shahid Tajuddin Ahmed Sharani, Mohakhali, Dhaka 1212; tel. (2) 8860523; e-mail info@icddrb.org; internet www.icddrb.org; f. 1960; funded by 55 countries and NGOs; library of 40,611 vols, 14,600 documents; Exec. Dir Prof. ALEJANDRO CRAVIOTO; publs *Health and Science Bulletin* (4 a year), *Journal of Health, Population and Nutrition* (4 a year).

Institute of Epidemiology, Disease Control and Research and National Influenza Centre (IEDCR): Mohakhali, Dhaka 1212; tel. (2) 9898796; e-mail info@iedcr.org; internet www.iedcr.org; f. 1978; depts of biostatistics, epidemiology, medical entomology and vector bionomics, medical social science, microbiology, parasitology, virology, zoonosis; activities incl. disease surveillance, investigation of known and unknown disease outbreaks with rapid response, management of disease outbreak, training and research for the Nat. Influenza Centre of Bangladesh; library of 6,000 vols; Dir Prof. MAHMUDUR RAHMAN.

NATURAL SCIENCES

Biological Sciences

Institute of Biological Sciences: Univ. of Rajshahi, 3rd Science Bldg, 3rd Fl., Rajshahi 6205; tel. (721) 750928; e-mail director_ibsc@ru.ac.bd; internet www.ru.ac.bd/ibsc; f. 1989; attached to Univ. of Rajshahi; pursues research and capacity devt in biological sciences and agriculture; library of 3,389 vols; Dir Prof. TANZIMA YEASMIN; publ. *Journal of Bio-Science*.

Institute of Nutrition and Food Sciences: Univ. of Dhaka, Dhaka 1000; tel. (2) 9661900; e-mail duregstr@bangla.net; f.

1969; attached to Univ. of Dhaka; basic and applied research in different aspects and fields of nutrition and food science incl. evaluation of interventions, food and nutrition policy, food sciences, health sciences, laboratory experiments, microbiology, nutrition survey and surveillance, research in nutrition, technical advisory services, training; Dir Prof. Dr SAGARMOY BARUA.

Mathematical Sciences

Institute of Statistical Research and Training: Univ. of Dhaka, Dhaka 1000; tel. (2) 9661900; e-mail duregstr@bangla.net; internet www.isrt.ac.bd; f. 1964; attached to Univ. of Dhaka; offers Bachelors, Masters and doctorate degree in applied statistics; library of 15,000 vols; Dir Dr MD AMIR HOSSAIN; publ. *Journal of Statistical Research* (2 a year).

Physical Sciences

Centre for Energy Studies: Bangladesh Univ. of Engineering and Technology, Dhaka 1000; tel. (2) 9665650; e-mail dirces@buet.ac.bd; internet www.buet.ac.bd/ces; f. 1984; attached to Bangladesh Univ. of Engineering and Technology; promotes education and research, organizes seminars, symposia, training workshops, short courses and outreach programs, and publishes journal, monographs and books on energy-related interdisciplinary matters; Dir Prof. MD ZAHURUL HAQ; publ. *Journal of Energy and Environment*.

Centre for Environmental and Resource Management: Bangladesh Univ. of Engineering and Technology, Dhaka 1000; tel. (2) 9663693; e-mail dircerm@cerm.buet.ac.bd; internet www.buet.ac.bd; attached to Bangladesh Univ. of Engineering and Technology; improves capability of professionals in the field of environmental management; develops local environmental manpower and expertise; Dir Prof. Dr MUHAMMAD DELWAR HOSSAIN.

Geological Survey of Bangladesh: 153 Pioneer Rd, Segunbagicha, Dhaka 1000; tel. (2) 9333858; e-mail geologicalsurveybd@gmail.com; internet www.gsb.gov.bd; f. 1971; attached to Min. of Energy and Mineral Resources; conducts geoscientific activities and systematic geological mapping within Bangladesh; conducts research and assessment of natural hazards; library of 7,688 vols, 16,657 periodicals; Dir-Gen. MOONIRA AKHTER CHOWDHURY; publ. *Records of the Geological Survey of Bangladesh* (irregular).

Institute of Environmental Science: Fourth Science Bldg, Univ. of Rajshahi, Ground Fl., Rajshahi 6205; tel. (721) 750930; e-mail ies_ru_2004@lycos.com; internet www.ru.ac.bd/ies; f. 1999; attached to Univ. of Rajshahi; library of 1,436 vols; Dir Prof. Dr MD. AZIZUL ISLAM; publ. *Rajshahi University Journal of Environmental Science* (1 a year).

Institute of Renewable Energy: Science Library Campus, Univ. of Dhaka, Dhaka 1000; tel. (2) 9677125; e-mail rerc@univdhaka.edu; attached to Univ. of Dhaka; research and devt activities in areas of renewable energy technology; Dir Prof. Dr REZAUL KARIM MAZUMDER.

Institute of Water and Flood Management: Bangladesh Univ. of Engineering and Technology, Dhaka 1000; tel. (2) 9665601; e-mail diriwfm@iwfm.buet.ac.bd; internet teacher.buet.ac.bd/diriwfm; f. 1974 as Institute of Flood Control and Drainage Research, present name 2002; attached to Bangladesh Univ. of Engineering and Technology; research and capacity devt in the field of water and flood management; Dir Prof. ANISUL HAQUE; Asst Dir MD NURUZZAMAN SHEIKH.

RELIGION, SOCIOLOGY AND ANTHROPOLOGY

Institute of Bangladesh Studies: Univ. of Rajshahi, Rajshahi 6205; tel. (721) 750753; e-mail ibsru@yahoo.com; internet www.ru.ac.bd/ibs; f. 1973; attached to Univ. of Rajshahi; conducts inter-disciplinary study and research on various aspects of Bangladesh culture, life, society; library of 23,788 vols; Dir Prof. MD SHAHIDULLAH; publ. *Journal of the Institute of Bangladesh Studies* (in Bengali and English).

TECHNOLOGY

Bangladesh Atomic Energy Commission: Paramanu Bhaban, E-12/A, Agargaon, Sher-e-Bangla Nagar, Dhaka 1207; tel. (2) 8130469; e-mail baec@agni.com; internet www.baec.org.bd; f. 1973; promotes nuclear science, technology for peaceful uses of atomic energy in the fields of agriculture, environment, food, health, industry; library of 25,375 vols, 192 periodicals; Chair. Eng. MD MUZAMMEL HAQUE; publ. *Nuclear Science & Applications* (Series A: Biological Sciences; Series B: Physical Sciences).

Attached Institutes:

Atomic Energy Centre: POB 164, Ramna, Dhaka 1000; 4 Kazi Nazrul Islam Ave, Ramna, Dhaka 1000; tel. (2) 9675367; e-mail aliaecd@yahoo.com; f. 1961; basic and applied research in physics, electronics and chemistry; library of 10,728 vols, 100 periodicals; Dir Dr MUHAMMAD ALI.

Atomic Energy Research Establishment: POB 3787, Dhaka 1000; Ganakbari, Savar, Dhaka 1000; tel. (2) 7789252; e-mail dg@baec.org.bd; internet www.aere.org.bd; f. 1975; library of 10,000 vols of books; consists of 10 separate institutes: Central Engineering Facilities (CEF), Institute of Computer Sciences (ICS), Institute of Electronics (IE), Institute of Food and Radiation Biology (IFRB), Institute of Nuclear Science and Technology (INST), Nuclear Mineral Unit (NMU), Reactor Operation and Maintenance Unit (ROMU), Scientific Information Unit (SIU), Tissue Banking and Biomaterial Research Unit (TBBRU) and Energy Institute (EI); Dir-Gen. MD ALI ZULQUARNAIN; Sr Librarian SHAMSUL ISLAM.

Beach Sand Minerals Exploitation Centre: GPOB 15, Kalatoli, Cox's bazar; tel. (341) 63320; e-mail bsmec_cox@baec.org.bd; explores, exploits, processes heavy minerals in the beach sands of coastal areas and off-shore islands of Bangladesh; Dir MOHAMMAD ZAFRUL KABIR.

Radioactivity Testing and Monitoring Laboratory: GPOB 1352, Chittagong; Chittagong Medical College Hospital Campus, Chittagong; tel. (31) 632147; e-mail rtml.baec@gmail.com; f. 1987; tests imported and exportable food stuffs entering through Chittagong Port and gives clearance certificate on the basis of their acceptable radioactivity limits; workplace radiation monitoring; checking of scrap metals for radioactive contamination; Dir MASUD KAMAL.

Rooppur Nuclear Power Project: Diar Shahapur, Pabna; tel. (7326) 63643; e-mail rrpp@bttb.net.bd; Officer-in-Charge K. B. M. RUHUL KUDDUS; publ. *AERE Annual Technical Report* (1 a year).

Institute of Appropriate Technology: Bangladesh Univ. of Engineering and Technology, Dhaka 1000; tel. (2) 9662365; e-mail iatdir@iat.buet.ac.bd; internet www.buet.ac.bd/iat; attached to Bangladesh Univ. of Engineering and Technology; conducts postgraduate academic program in specialized fields; initiates, promotes, conducts research on technology policies, technology assessment, technology transfer, technology devt and technology dissemination; Dir Prof. Dr MUHAMMAD KAMAL UDDIN.

Institute of Energy Technology: Chittagong 4349; tel. (31) 714920; e-mail iet@cuet.ac.bd; internet www.cuet.ac.bd/iet; f. as Centre for Energy Technology, current status adopted 2003; attached to Chittagong Univ. of Engineering and Technology; advanced studies, research work on energy and environmental system; Dir Prof. Dr M. SHAMSUL ALAM; Sec. Eng. MD NAZMUDDUZA.

Institute of Information and Communication Technology: Bokshi Bazar, Bangladesh Univ. of Engineering and Technology, Dhaka 1000; tel. (2) 9665602; e-mail lutfulkabir@iict.buet.ac.bd; internet www.buet.ac.bd/iict; f. 2001; attached to Bangladesh Univ. of Engineering and Technology; contributes to industrial and infrastructural devt, economic growth, social prosperity by providing a platform for teaching, learning and research in information and communication technology; Dir Prof. Dr S. M. LUTFUL KABIR; Assoc. Dir Prof. Dr ABUL KASHEM MIA.

Institute of Information Technology: Univ. of Dhaka, Dhaka 1000; tel. (2) 9675215; e-mail joarder@univdhaka.edu; internet iit.univdhaka.edu; f. 1985 as Computer Centre, present name and status 2001; attached to Univ. of Dhaka; offers market oriented programmes based on Communication and Information Technology; Dir Prof. Dr MD. MAHBUBUL ALAM JOARDER.

Libraries and Archives

Chittagong

Divisional Government Public Library: POB 771, K. C. Dey Rd, Chittagong; tel. (31) 611578; f. 1963; 74,505 vols, 35 periodicals; Sr Librarian A. D. M. ALI AHAMMED.

Dhaka

AIUB Library: 58/B, Rd 21 Kemal Ataturk Ave, Banani, Dhaka; tel. (2) 9894641; e-mail library@aiub.edu; internet www.aiub.edu/library; f. 1994; attached to American International Univ. Bangladesh; 40,000 vols; Asst Librarian MD NAZIMUDDIN AHMED.

Ayesha Abed Library: 66 Mohakhali, Dhaka 1212; tel. (2) 8824051; e-mail librarian@bracu.ac.bd; internet library.bracu.ac.bd; attached to BRAC Univ.; 17,000 vols; Librarian HASINA AFROZ.

Bangladesh Institute of Development Studies Library: GPOB 3854, Dhaka 1207; E-17, Agargaon, Sher-e-Bangla Nagar, Dhaka 1207; tel. (2) 8110759; e-mail secy10bids@bids.org.bd; internet www.bids-bd.org; f. 1957; depository of publs of Asian Development Bank, International Monetary Fund, UN, World Bank; 140,000 vols, 600 periodicals; Chief Librarian Dr MD ANWARUL ISLAM (acting).

Bangladesh National Scientific and Technical Documentation Centre (BANSDOC): E-14/Y, Agargaon, Sher-e-Bangla Nagar, Dhaka 1207; tel. (2) 8127744; e-mail docu@bansdoc.gov.bd; internet www.bansdoc.gov.bd; f. 1963; nat. apex body in the field of scientific and technological library, information and documentation services in Bangladesh; 20,035 vols, 147 nat. periodicals, 295 foreign periodicals; Dir MIJANUR RAHMAN; publs *Bangladesh Science and Technology Abstracts* (1 a year), *Current Scientific and Technological*

Research Projects of Bangladesh (every 2 years), *National Catalogue of Scientific and Technological Periodicals of Bangladesh* (every 2 years), *Report of the Survey of Research and Development Activities in Bangladesh* (every 2 years).

Central Public Library Dhaka: 3 Liaquat Ave, Dhaka 1000; tel. (2) 8500819; internet www.centralpubliclibrarydhaka.org; f. 1958; colln of 40 to 50 MSS titles for research and reference services; 119,750 vols; Librarian AHMAD HUSAIN.

Department of Public Libraries: 10 Kazi Nazrul Islam Ave, Shahbagh Dhaka 1000; tel. (2) 8610422; e-mail centrallibrary_58@yahoo.com; internet www.publiclibrary.org.bd; f. 1958; 1m. vols, 2,300 periodicals; spec. colln: depository for UNESCO publs; controls 68 govt public libraries incl. Bangladesh Central Public Library, 5 divisional govt public libraries, 58 dist. govt public libraries, 4 br libraries in Bangladesh; Dir MD NUR HOSSAIN TALUKDER.

Directorate of Archives and Libraries: 32 Justice S. M. Murshed Sarani, Agargaon, Sher-e-Bangla Nagar, Dhaka 1207; tel. (2) 9129992; e-mail nanldirector@gmail.com; internet www.nanl.gov.bd; f. 1971; attached to Min. of Cultural Affairs; coordinating centre for archives and libraries at nat. level; 500,000 vols, 105 Bengali periodicals, 10 foreign periodicals, 20 maps, 3,000 microfilms, 60 rolls of microfiche, 235 issues of National Bibliography (1972–1991); Head Prof. Dr TAIBUL HASAN KHAN.

Institutions under the control of the Directorate:

National Archives of Bangladesh: Nat. Archives Bldg, Sher-e-Bangla Nagar, Agargaon, Dhaka 1207; e-mail nanldirector@gmail.com; f. 1972; 225,000 vols of records and documents, 3,500 books, 58 rolls of microfilm, 10,000 press clippings; Head Prof. Dr MD TAIBUL HASAN KHAN; publs *Annual Reports 1973–84*, *Bulletin of Dissertations and Theses by Bangladeshi Scholars 1947–73*, *SWARBICA Journal Vol III*.

National Library of Bangladesh: Nat. Library Bldg, Sher-e-Bangla Nagar, Agargaon, Dhaka 1207; e-mail nanldirector@gmail.com; f. 1972; 550,000 vols, 3,000 maps; Head Prof. Dr TAIBUL HASAN KHAN; publs *Articles Index*, *Bangladesh National Bibliography*.

North South University Library: Plot 15 Block B, Bashundhara, Dhaka 1229; tel. (2) 8852000; e-mail library@northsouth.edu; internet library.northsouth.edu; f. 1992; attached to North South Univ.; 39,500 vols, 64 journals; Librarian Dr MD MOSTAFIZUR RAHMAN; Asst Librarian M. M. SHOEB.

University of Dhaka Library: Ramna, Dhaka 1000; tel. (2) 9661920; e-mail dulap@univdhaka.edu; internet www.univdhaka.edu/du_library.php; f. 1921; 6.8m. vols, 30,000 rare MSS and a large number of tracts (booklets, leaflets, pamphlets and puthis) in microfilm format; rare books and reports, puthis, Bengali Tracts and private colln of Buchanan on Bengal have been acquired from the British Museum, UK; Librarian Prof. Dr M. NASIRUDDIN MUNSHI.

Rajshahi

University of Rajshahi Library: Rajshahi 6205; tel. (721) 750666; e-mail ad_rucl@ru.ac.bd; internet www.ru.ac.bd/rulib/library.htm; f. 1953, present location 1964; 351,686 vols incl. 309,659 books and 42,027 journals; Administrator Prof. Dr SHAFIQUNNABI SAMADEE.

Museums and Art Galleries

Dhaka

Ahsan Manzil Museum: Nawab Ahsanulla Rd, Shadarghat, Dhaka; tel. (2) 7391122; fmr home of the Nawab of Dhaka; 23 galleries displaying portraits, furniture and other objects used by the Nawab.

Balda Museum: Dhaka; f. 1927; Bengali art and ancient artefacts; Superintendent MUHAMMAD HANNAN.

Bangabandhu Memorial Museum: House 10 Rd 32, Dhanmondi Residential Area, Dhaka; tel. (2) 8110046; residence of the father of the nation, Bangabandhu Sheikh Mujibur Rahman (1920–75); colln of personal effects and photographs of his lifetime; Convener Prof. A. F. SALAHUDDIN; Curator SYED SIDDIQUR RAHMAN.

Bangladesh National Museum: POB 355, Shahbag, Dhaka 1000; tel. (2) 8619396; e-mail dgmuseum@yahoo.com; internet bangladeshmuseum.gov.bd; f. 1913, present status 1983; history and classical art, ethnography and decorative art, natural history, contemporary art and world civilization; conservation, public education; 85,000 objects representing Hindu–Buddhist civilization, Islamic heritage of Bengal, and life, culture and society of contemporary Bangladesh; library of 35,816 vols; Chair. Dr M. AZIZUR RAHMAN; Dir-Gen. PROKASH CHANDRA DAS; publ. *Bangladesh Jadughar Samachar* (Journal of Bangladesh National Museum, 4 a year).

Dhaka Zoo: Mirpur-1, Dhaka; tel. (2) 9002020; e-mail info@bforest.gov.bd; internet www.bforest.gov.bd; f. 1964; attached to Min. of Fisheries and Livestock; colln of more than 2,150 native and non-native animals and wildlife; Curator A. B. M. SHAHID ULLAH.

Liberation War Museum: 5 Segun Bagicha, Dhaka 1000; tel. (2) 9559091; e-mail mukti@citechco.net; internet www.liberationwarmuseum.org; f. 1996; concerns Bangladesh's Liberation War (1971); ancient Bengali artefacts, and items from the British Raj period and the Pakistani period, photographs of the war and items used by the freedom fighters during the period; exhibits 10,732 objects; Gen. Man. MAHBUBUL ALAM.

National Art Gallery: Shilpakala Academy, Segun Bagicha, Dhaka 1000; tel. (2) 9562801; e-mail info@bdshilpakala.org; internet www.shilpakala.gov.bd; f. 1965; colln of folk art and paintings by Bangladeshi artists.

National Botanical Garden: Mirpur, 16 Km NW of city, Dhaka; tel. (2) 8018092; e-mail info@bforest.gov.bd; internet www.bforest.gov.bd; f. 1961; attached to Min. of Environment and Forests; colln of 50,000 plants, herbs, shrubs and trees on a 200-acre site.

National Museum of Science & Technology: Agargaon, Sher-e-Bangla Nagar, Dhaka 1207; tel. (2) 9112084; e-mail info@nmst.gov.bd; internet www.nmst.gov.bd; f. 1965; attached to Min. of Science and Technology; popularizes science and technology through display of scientific exhibits; encourages young and non-professional scientists for their innovative activities; library of 4,064 vols, 400 journals; Dir SADARUDDIN AHMED; publ. *Nabin Biggani* (4 a year).

Universities

AHSANULLAH UNIVERSITY OF SCIENCE AND TECHNOLOGY

141–142 Love Rd, Tejgaon Industrial Area, Dhaka 1208
Telephone: (2) 9897311
E-mail: vc@aust.edu
Internet: www.aust.edu
Private control, sponsored by Dhaka Ahsania Mission
Founded 1995
Chancellor: PRES. OF THE PEOPLE'S REPUBLIC OF BANGLADESH
Chair.: KAZI RAFIQUL ALAM
Vice-Chancellor: Prof. A. M. M. SAFIULLAH
Registrar: MUHAMMAD ABDUL GAFUR
Proctor: Prof. Dr M. SHAHABUDDIN
Librarian: MUHAMMAD MOSHARRAF HOSSAIN
Library of 16,000 vols
Number of teachers: 374 (284 full-time, 90 part-time)
Number of students: 6,500
Publication: *AUST Journal of Science and Technology* (2 a year)

DEANS

Faculty of Architecture and Planning: Prof. Dr M. A. MUKTADIR
Faculty of Business and Social Science: Prof. SIRAJUDDAULA SHAHEEN
Faculty of Education: FATEMA KHATUN
Faculty of Engineering: Prof. Dr A. F. M. ANWARUL HAQUE

ATTACHED INSTITUTE

Institute of Technical and Vocational Education and Training: ITVET Campus, 20 West Testuri Bazar Rd, Tejgaon, Dhaka 1215; tel. (2) 9130613; e-mail info@aust.edu; f. 1995; offers mid-level programmes in architecture technology, chemical technology, civil technology, computer technology, electrical technology, electronic technology, textile engineering; Dir A. K. MD WAHIDUL HAQUE

AMERICAN INTERNATIONAL UNIVERSITY BANGLADESH

House 83/B Rd 4, Kemal Ataturk Ave, Banani, Dhaka 1213
Telephone: (2) 9890415
E-mail: info@aiub.edu
Internet: www.aiub.edu
Founded 1994
Private control
Academic year: January to December
Vice-Chancellor: CARMEN Z. LAMAGNA
Chair.: Dr ANWARUL ABEDIN
Pro-Vice-Chancellor: Prof. Dr ANWAR HOSSAIN
Vice-Pres. for Academics: Prof. Dr TAFAZZAL HOSSAIN
Vice-Pres. for International Affairs and Public Relations: ISHTIAQUE ABEDIN
Vice-Pres. for Student Affairs: NADIA ANWAR
Registrar: Prof. M. A. QUAIYUM
Library: see Libraries and Archives
Number of teachers: 100
Number of students: 8,690
Publications: *AIUB Journal of Business and Economics* (2 a year), *AIUB Journal of Science and Engineering* (1 a year)

DEANS

Faculty of Arts and Social Science: Dr CHARLES CARILLO VILLANUEVA
Faculty of Business Administration: Prof. Dr CHARLES CARILLO VILLANUEVA (acting)
Faculty of Engineering: Dr A. B. M. SIDDIQUE HOSSAIN

Faculty of Science and Information Technology: Prof. Dr TAFAZZAL HOSSAIN

ASA UNIVERSITY BANGLADESH

23/3 Khilji Rd, Shyamoli, Mohammadpur, Dhaka 1207
Telephone: (2) 8122555
E-mail: info@asaub.edu.bd
Internet: www.asaub.edu.bd
Founded 2006
Private control
Academic year: 2 semesters
Chancellor: PRES. OF THE PEOPLE'S REPUBLIC OF BANGLADESH
Chair.: MD SHAFIQUAL HAQUE CHOUDHURY
Vice-Chancellor: Prof. MD MUINUDDIN KHAN
Registrar: MD SHAHJAHAN
Number of teachers: 90
Number of students: 5,600

DEANS

Faculty of Arts and Social Science: Prof. Dr MOHAMMAD SIRAJUL ISLAM
Faculty of Business Studies: Prof. Dr ABDUL HYE
Faculty of Law: Prof. Dr A. B. M. MAHBUBUL ISLAM

ASIAN UNIVERSITY FOR WOMEN

20/A M. M. Ali Rd, Chittagong
Telephone: (31) 2854980
E-mail: info@asian-university.org
Internet: www.asian-university.org
Private control
Chancellor: CHERIE BLAIR
Vice-Chancellor: Dr FAHIMA AZIZ
Number of students: 3,000

DEANS

Faculty of Physical and Environmental Sciences: Prof. ASHOK KESHARI
Faculty of Public Health Studies: Assoc. Prof. GEORGIA GULDAN (acting)

ASIAN UNIVERSITY OF BANGLADESH

Uttara Campus: House 9 Rd 5, Sector 7, Uttara Model Town, Dhaka 1230
Telephone: (2) 8916116
E-mail: info@aub-bd.org
Internet: www.aub-bd.org
Founded 1996
Private control
Academic year: 3 semesters
Campuses in Dhanmondi, Motijheel, Khulna, Rajshahi, Uttara
Vice-Chancellor: Prof. Dr ABULHASAN M SADEQ
Pro-Vice-Chancellor: Prof. Dr MD KAYSAR HUSSAIN
Dir for Academic Affairs: Dr A. N. M. ABDUR RAHMAN
Dir for Admission and Records: Prof. MD FAZLUL HAQUE
Dir for Planning and Devt: MD JAHIRUL HAQUE
Registrar: MD QUDDUS KHAN
Library of 96,000 vols, 1,350 journals, 350 audiovisual materials
Number of students: 7,000

DEANS

School of Arts: Prof. S. M. GAZIUR RAHMAN
School of Business: Prof. MD ASHRAF HOSSAIN
School of Science and Engineering: Prof. Dr S. M. AZHARUL ISLAM
School of Social Sciences: Prof. MD SHARIFUDDIN KHAN

ATISH DIPANKAR UNIVERSITY OF SCIENCE AND TECHNOLOGY

House 83, Rd 4 Block B, Banani, Dhaka
Telephone: (2) 8816762
E-mail: info@atishdipankaruniversity.edu.bd
Internet: www.atishdipankaruniversity.edu.bd
Private control
Vice-Chancellor: Prof. Dr ANWARA BEGUM

DEANS

Department of Business Administration: Prof. Dr AZHAR-UD-DIN
Faculty of Agriculture, Biological Science, Biotechnology and Textile: Prof. Dr KABIR HOSSAIN TALUKDER

BANGABANDHU SHEIKH MUJIB MEDICAL UNIVERSITY

POB 3048, Dhaka 1000
Telephone: (2) 9661065
E-mail: info@bsmmu.org
Founded 1965 as Institute of Postgraduate Medicine and Research; present name and status 1998
Academic year: July to June
Chancellor: PRES. OF THE PEOPLE'S REPUBLIC OF BANGLADESH
Vice-Chancellor: Prof. PRAN GOPAL DATTA
Chair.: Prof. MOHAMMAD AMANULLAH
Pro-Vice-Chancellor for Academics: Prof. A. K. M. ANISUL HAQUE
Pro-Vice-Chancellor for Admin.: Prof. MD SHAHIDULLAH
Registrar: MUHAMMAD ABDUL GAFUR
Chief Librarian: Prof. TAIMUR A.K. MAHMUD
Colleges and Postgraduate Institutes Inspector: Prof. ABU SHAFI AHMED AMIN
Founded 1965
Library of 23,000 vols, 100 periodicals
Number of teachers: 200
Number of students: 704
Publications: *Bangladesh Journal of Neurology* (2 a year), *Bangladesh Journal of Psychiatry* (2 a year), *Journal of the Institute of Postgraduate Medicine and Research* (2 a year)

DEANS

Faculty of Basic Science: Prof. M. IQBAL ARSLAN
Faculty of Dentistry: Prof. SAMSUL ALAM
Faculty of Medicine: Prof. K. M. H. S. SIRAJUL HAQUE
Faculty of Surgery: Prof. MOHAMMAD SAIFUL ISLAM

BANGABANDHU SHEIKH MUJIBUR RAHMAN AGRICULTURAL UNIVERSITY

Salna, Gazipur 1706
Telephone: (2) 9205323
E-mail: info@bsmrau.edu.bd
Internet: bsmrau.edu.bd
Founded 1983 as Bangladesh College of Agricultural Sciences; became Institute of Postgraduate Studies in Agriculture 1994; current name adopted and status 1998
State control
Academic year: November to October
Chancellor: PRES. OF THE PEOPLE'S REPUBLIC OF BANGLADESH
Vice-Chancellor: Prof. Dr ABDUL MANNAN AKANDA
Registrar: MOHAMMAD ABUL KALAM AZAD
Proctor: MD. NASIMUL BARI
Deputy Librarian: ABDUR ROUF MIAN
Library of 19,400 vols
Number of teachers: 104
Number of students: 757
Publication: *Annals of Bangladesh Agriculture* (every 2 years)

DEANS

Faculty of Agriculture: Prof. Dr A. J. M. SIRAJUL KARIM
Faculty of Fisheries: Prof. Dr MD AMZAD HOSSAIN
Faculty of Graduate Studies: Prof. Dr MD MIZANUR RAHMAN
Faculty of Veterinary Medicine and Animal Science: Prof. Dr ABU NASAR MD AMINOOR RAHMAN

BANGLADESH AGRICULTURAL UNIVERSITY

Mymensingh 2202
Telephone: (91) 67401
E-mail: registrar@bau.edu.bd
Internet: www.bau.edu.bd
Founded 1961
Autonomous control
Languages of instruction: Bengali, English
Academic year: July to June (2 semesters)
Chancellor: PRES. OF THE PEOPLE'S REPUBLIC OF BANGLADESH
Vice-Chancellor: Prof. Dr MD RAFIQUL HOQUE
Registrar: MUHAMMAD NAZIBUR RAHMAN
Public Relations and Publs Dir: DIWAN RASHIDUL HASSAN
Cttee for Advanced Studies and Research Coordinator: Prof. Dr SULTAN UDDIN BHUIYA
Librarian: PRABIR KUMAR MITRA BISWAS
Library of 193,614 vols, 2,083 periodicals, 152 current journals
Number of teachers: 534
Number of students: 4,663
Publications: *Bangladesh Journal of Agricultural Economics*, *Bangladesh Journal of Agricultural Engineering*, *Bangladesh Journal of Agricultural Science*, *Bangladesh Journal of Animal Science*, *Bangladesh Journal of Aquaculture*, *Bangladesh Journal of Crop Science*, *Bangladesh Journal of Environmental Science* (1 a year), *Bangladesh Journal of Extension Education*, *Bangladesh Journal of Fisheries* (4 a year), *Bangladesh Journal of Horticulture* (2 a year), *Bangladesh Journal of Plant Pathology*, *Bangladesh Journal of Seed Science and Technology* (2 a year), *Bangladesh Journal of Training and Development*, *Bangladesh Veterinary Journal*, *Journal of Veterinary Medicine*, *Progressive Agriculture*, *The Bangladeshi Veterinarian*

DEANS

Faculty of Agricultural Economics and Rural Sociology: Prof. TOFAZZAL HOSSAIN MIAH
Faculty of Agricultural Engineering and Technology: Prof. Dr M. BURHAN-UD-DIN
Faculty of Agriculture: Prof. Dr MOHAMMAD ABDUL KARIM
Faculty of Animal Husbandry: Prof. Dr M. ALI AKBAR
Faculty of Fisheries: Prof. Dr MUHAMMAD ABDUL WAHAB
Faculty of Veterinary Science: Prof. Dr MUHAMMAD MOTAHAR HUSSAIN MONDAL

PROFESSORS

Faculty of Agricultural Economics and Rural Sociology:

AKBAR, M., Agribusiness and Marketing
AKTERUZZAMAN, M., Agricultural Economics
ALAM, S., Agribusiness & Marketing
ALI, M., Rural Sociology
BASHAR, M., Agricultural Finance
BEGUM, R., Agricultural Statistics
DEBNATH, S., Agricultural Statistics

HAQUE, M., Agricultural Statistics
HOSSAIN, M., Agricultural Statistics
ISLAM, M., Agricultural Economics
JABBAR, M., Agricultural Finance
JAIM, W., Agricultural Economics
MANDAL, M., Agricultural Economics
MIA, M., Agribusiness and Marketing
MIAH, M., Agricultural Economics
MIAH, T., Agricultural Finance
MODAK, P., Agricultural Statistics
MOLLA, A., Agricultural Economics
QUDDUS, M., Agricultural Statistics
RAHA, S., Agribusiness and Marketing
RAHMAN, K., Agricultural Statistics
RAHMAN, M., Agricultural Economics
RASHID, M., Agricultural Economics
SABUR, S., Agribusiness and Marketing

Faculty of Agricultural Engineering and Technology:

ABEDIN, M., Farm Structure
AHMED, M., Irrigation and Water Management
AKHTARUZZAMAN, M., Farm Power and Machinery
ALAM, M., Farm Power and Machinery
ALI, M., Computer Science and Mathematics
ASHRAF, M., Farm Structure
AWAL, A., Farm Structure
BALA, B., Farm Power and Machinery
BASAK, N., Computer Science and Mathematics
BASUNIA, M., Farm Power and Machinery
HAQUE, M., Farm Power and Machinery
HASSNUZZAMAN, K., Irrigation and Water Management
HOQUE, M., Farm Structure
HOQUE, M., Irrigation and Water Management
HOSSAIN, M., Farm Power and Machinery
HUQ, M., Computer Science and Mathematics
HUSSAIN, M., Farm Power and Machinery
HYE, M., Computer Science and Mathematics
ISLAM, M., Food Technology and Rural Industries
ISLAM, M., Irrigation and Water Management
KHAIR, A., Irrigation and Water Management
KHAN, L., Irrigation and Water Management
MOJID, M., Irrigation and Water Management
RAHMAN, K., Farm Structure
RASHID, M., Farm Structure
SARKER, M., Farm Power and Machinery
SATTAR, M., Farm Power and Machinery
SHAMS-UD-DIN, M., Food Technology and Rural Industries
TALUKDER, M., Irrigation and Water Management
UDDIN, M., Food Technology and Rural Industries
ZIAUDDIN, A., Farm Power and Machinery

Faculty of Agriculture:

AHMAD, M., Entomology
AHMAD, M., Plant Pathology
AHMED, K., Entomology
AHMED, Q., Genetics and Plant Breeding
ALAM, M., Genetics and Plant Breeding
ALI, M., Plant Pathology
ASHRAFUZZAMAN, M., Crop Botany
ASHRAFUZZAMAN, M., Plant Pathology
AWAL, M., Crop Botany
BATEN, M., Environmental Science
BEGUM, M., Agronomy
BHUIYA, M., Agronomy
CHOUDHURY, M., Horticulture
CHOWDHURY, A., Agronomy
CHOWDHURY, B., Biochemistry
CHOWDHURY, M., Agricultural Chemistry
FAKIR, M., Crop Botany
FAROOQUE, A., Horticulture
HAQUE, M., Biotechnology
HAQUE, M., Entomology
HAQUE, M.
HASHEM, M., Soil Science
HASSAN, L., Genetics and Plant Breeding
HOSSAIN, A., Soil Science
HOSSAIN, I., Plant Pathology
HOSSAIN, M., Agricultural Extension Education
HOSSAIN, M., Agroforestry
HOSSAIN, M., Biochemistry
HOSSAIN, M., Plant Pathology
HOSSAIN, M., Plant Pathology
HUQUE, M., Agricultural Extension Education
ISLAM, K., Entomology
ISLAM, M., Agricultural Extension Education
ISLAM, M., Crop Botany
ISLAM, M., Genetics and Plant Breeding
ISLAM, M., Soil Science
ISLAM, N., Agronomy
JAHAN, M., Entomology
JAHIRUDDIN, M., Soil Science
KARIM, A., Agricultural Extension Education
KARIM, M., Crop Botany
KARIM, S., Agronomy
KASHEM, M., Agricultural Extension Education
KHAN, A., Entomology
KHAN, M., Crop Botany
MATIN, M., Soil Science
MEAH, M., Plant Pathology
MIAH, M., Agricultural Extension Education
MIAN, M., Soil Science
MIAN, M., Soil Science
MONDAL, M., Horticulture
MOSLEHUDDIN, A., Soil Science
NASIRUDDIN, K., Biotechnology
NEWAZ, M., Biochemistry
NEWAZ, M., Genetics and Plant Breeding
PATWARY, M., Genetics and Plant Breeding
PRAMANIK, M., Crop Botany
PRODHAN, A., Crop Botany
QUDDUS, M., Genetics and Plant Breeding
RABBANI, M., Horticulture
RAHIM, M., Horticulture
RAHMAN, G., Agroforestry
RAHMAN, M., Agricultural Chemistry
RAHMAN, M., Agricultural Extension Education
RAHMAN, M., Agronomy
RAHMAN, M., Crop Botany
RAHMAN, M., Horticulture
RAHMAN, M., Soil Science
RASHID, A., Plant Pathology
RASHID, M., Agricultural Extension Education
RASHID, M., Biochemistry
REZA, M., Biochemistry
ROY, P., Biochemistry
SAHA, K., Physics and Chemistry
SALIM, M., Agronomy
SAMAD, M., Agronomy
SARKAR, M., Agronomy
SATTAR, M., Environmental Science
SEAL, H., Physics and Chemistry
SHAHJAHAN, M., Entomology
SHAMSUDDIN, A., Genetics and Plant Breeding
SIDDIQUA, M., Biochemistry
SIDDQUE, M., Horticulture
WAZUDDIN, M., Genetics and Plant Breeding
ZAMAN, M., Agricultural Chemistry

Faculty of Animal Husbandry:

AKBAR, M., Animal Nutrition
AKHTER, S., Animal Science
ALAM, M., Animal Science
ALI, A., Animal Breeding and Genetics
ALI, M., Poultry Science
AMIN, M., Animal Breeding and Genetics
AMIN, M., Animal Science
BHUIYAN, A., Animal Breeding and Genetics
CHOWDHURY, S., Poultry Science
FARUQUE, M., Animal Breeding and Genetics
HASHEM, M., Animal Science
HASSAN, M., Dairy Science
HOSSAIN, M., Animal Science
HOWLIDER, M., Poultry Science
HUSAIN, S., Animal Breeding and Genetics
ISLAM, M., Dairy Science
KHAN, M., Animal Nutrition
KHAN, M., Animal Science
KHAN, M., Dairy Science
KHANDAKER, M., Animal Breeding and Genetics
KHANDAKER, Z., Animal Nutrition
MOKHTARUZZAMAN, M., Dairy Science
WADUD, A., Dairy Science

Faculty of Fisheries:

AHMED, G., Aquaculture
AHMED, N., Fisheries Management
AHMED, Z., Fisheries Management
ALAM, A., Fisheries Technology
ALAM, M., Fisheries Biology and Genetics
ALI, M., Aquaculture
AMIN, M., Aquaculture
CHAKRABORTY, S., Fisheries Technology
CHANDRA, K., Aquaculture
CHOWDHURY, M., Aquaculture
DAS, M., Aquaculture
FARUK, A., Aquaculture
HABIB, M., Aquaculture
HAQ, M., Fisheries Management
HAQUE, A., National Professor
HAQUE, M., Fisheries Management
HAQUE, S., Fisheries Management
HOSEN, M., Aquaculture
HOSSAIN, M., Fisheries Biology and Genetics
HOSSAIN, M., Fisheries Technology
ISLAM, M., Fisheries Technology
KAMAL, M., Fisheries Technology
KHAN, M., Fisheries Biology and Genetics
KHAN, S., Fisheries Management
MANSUR, M., Fisheries Technology
MIAH, M., Aquaculture
MIAH, M., Fisheries Management
MOLLAH, M., Fisheries Biology and Genetics
RAHMAN, M., Fisheries Management
RAHMATULLAH, S., Aquaculture
RASHID, M., Aquaculture
SALAM, M., Aquaculture
SARDER, M., Fisheries Biology and Genetics
UDDIN, M., Fisheries Technology
WAHAB, M., Fisheries Management

Faculty of Veterinary Science:

AHMAD, N., Physiology
AHMED, J., Surgery and Obstetrics
AHMED, M., Anatomy and Histology
ALAM, M., Surgery and Obstetrics
ASADUZZAMAN, M., Anatomy and Histology
AWAL, M., Anatomy and Histology
AWAL, M., Pharmacology
BAKI, M., Pathology
BARI, A., Pathology
BARI, F., Surgery and Obstetrics
BEGUM, M., Parasitology
BHUIYAN, M., Surgery and Obstetrics
CHOWDHURY, E., Pathology
DAS, P., Pathology
HASHIM, M., Surgery and Obstetrics
HOSSAIN, M., Pathology
HOSSAIN, M., Surgery and Obstetrics
ISLAM, M., Microbiology and Hygiene
ISLAM, M., Pathology
KHAN, M., Anatomy and Histology
KHAN, M., Microbiology and Hygiene
KHAN, M., Pathology
MONDAL, M., Parasitology
MOSTOFA, M., Pharmacology
RAHMAN, M., Medicine
RAHMAN, M., Microbiology and Hygiene
RAHMAN, M., Pathology

RAHMAN, M., Physiology
SAMAD, M., Medicine
SEN, M., Medicine
SHAMSUDDIN, M., Surgery and Obstetrics
UDDIN, M., Physiology

BANGLADESH ISLAMI UNIVERSITY

89/12 R. K. Mission Rd, Maniknagar, Biswa Rd, Dhaka 1203
Internet: www.biu.ac.bd
Private control

Depts of business administration, English, Islamic studies, law

Chancellor: PRES. OF THE PEOPLE'S REPUBLIC OF BANGLADESH
Chair.: Dr ABDULLAH OMER NASEEF
Vice-Chair.: Dr ABDULLAH ABDUL AZIZ AL-MOSLEH
Sec.-Gen.: Prof. KAMALUDDIN ABDULLAH ZAFREE
Vice-Chancellor: Prof. Dr MD ANWARUL ISLAM
Deputy Registrar: MD MORSHEDUR RAHMAN
Asst Librarian: MOHAMMAD ARIFUR RAHMAN

BANGLADESH OPEN UNIVERSITY

Board Bazar, Gazipur 1705
Telephone: (2) 9291112
E-mail: regi@bou.edu.bd
Internet: www.bou.edu.bd
Founded 1992
State control

Chancellor: PRES. OF THE PEOPLE'S REPUBLIC OF BANGLADESH
Vice-Chancellor: Prof. Dr R. I. M. AMINUR RASHID
Pro-Vice-Chancellor: Prof. R. I. SHARIF
Registrar: MUHAMMAD MONJUR-E-KHODA TARAFDAR
Librarian: MUHAMMAD SAADAT ALI

Library of 11,000 vols
Number of teachers: 62
Number of students: 308,682

DEANS

Open School: MD ALINOOR RAHMAN
School of Agriculture and Rural Development: Dr MD ABU TALEB
School of Business: Prof. ABDUL AWAL KHAN
School of Education: Prof. MONIRA BEGUM HOSSAIN
School of Science and Technology: Prof. Dr MOFIZ UDDIN AHMED
School of Social Science, Humanities and Languages: Prof. Dr ABUL HOSSAIN AHMED BHUIYAN

REGIONAL RESOURCE CENTRES

Regional Resource Centre, Barishal: Bangladesh Open University, Rupatali, Post Jagua, Barishal; tel. (431) 71322; e-mail rrcbrisal@bou.bangla.net.

Regional Resource Centre, Bogra: Bangladesh Open University, Bishwa Rd, Banani, Bogra; tel. (51) 72974; e-mail rrcbogra@bou.bangla.net.

Regional Resource Centre, Chittagong: Bangladesh Open University, C. R. B. Rd (Chittagong Stadium), Cothwali, Chittagong; tel. (31) 619633; e-mail rrcctg@bou.bangla.net.

Regional Resource Centre, Comilla: Bangladesh Open University, Dhaka-Chittagong Trunk Rd, Noapara, Durgapur, Comilla; tel. (81) 77557; e-mail rrccom@bou.bangla.net.

Regional Resource Centre, Dhaka: Government Laboratory, School Rd, Dhanmondi, Dhaka 1205; tel. (2) 8616065; e-mail rrcdhaka@bou.bangla.net.

Regional Resource Centre, Faridpur: Beside Nadigabashana Institute, Harokandi, Barishal Rd, Faridpur; tel. (631) 62081; e-mail rrcfarid@bou.bangla.net.

Regional Resource Centre, Jessore: Jessore Upa-Shahar (Dhaka Rd), Jessore; tel. (421) 73250; e-mail rrcjes@bou.bangla.net.

Regional Resource Centre, Khulna: Rd 5, House 51, Sonadanga Residential Area, Khulna 9000; tel. (41) 731795; e-mail rrckhul@bou.bangla.net.

Regional Resource Centre, Mymensingh: Mashkanda (Dhaka–Mymensingh Highway), Mymensingh; tel. (91) 52408; e-mail rrcmyn@bou.bangla.net.

Regional Resource Centre, Rajshahi: Bangladesh Open University, Nohata, Paba, Rajshahi; tel. (721) 761607; e-mail rrcraj@bou.bangla.net.

Regional Resource Centre, Rangpur: Bangladesh Open University, R. K. Rd, Rangpur; tel. (521) 63593; e-mail rrcrnp@bou.bangla.net.

Regional Resource Centre, Sylhet: Bangladesh Open University, Pirijpur, S Surma, Sylhet; tel. (821) 719523; e-mail rrcsyl@bou.bangla.net

BANGLADESH UNIVERSITY

15/1 Asad Ave, Mohammadpur, Dhaka 1207
Telephone: (2) 9136061
E-mail: info@bu.edu.bd
Internet: www.bu.edu.bd
Founded 2001
Private control
Language of instruction: English
Academic year: 2 semesters

Faculties of arts, business, and science and engineering; 2 campuses

Pres.: QUAZI JAMIL AZHER
Vice-Chancellor: Prof. Dr MD GOLAM ALI FAKIR (acting)

BANGLADESH UNIVERSITY OF BUSINESS AND TECHNOLOGY

Dhaka Commerce College Rd, Mirpur, Dhaka 1216
Telephone: (2) 8057581
E-mail: info@bubt.edu.bd
Internet: www.bubt.edu.bd
Founded 2003
Private control
Academic year: October to September (3 semesters)

Faculties of arts and humanities, business, engineering and applied sciences, law, mathematical and physical science, social sciences

Chair.: Prof. Dr SHAFIQUE AHMED SIDDIQUE
Vice-Chancellor: Prof. Dr ABU SALEH
Pro-Vice-Chancellor: Prof. MD ALI AZAM

BANGLADESH UNIVERSITY OF ENGINEERING AND TECHNOLOGY

Palassy, Ramna, Dhaka 1000
Telephone: (2) 9665650
E-mail: vcoffice@vc.buet.ac.bd
Internet: www.buet.ac.bd
Founded 1947 as Ahsanullah Engineering College, present name and status 1962
State control
Language of instruction: English
Academic year: January to December

Chancellor: PRES. OF THE PEOPLE'S REPUBLIC OF BANGLADESH
Vice-Chancellor: Prof. Dr S. M. NAZRUL ISLAM
Pro-Vice-Chancellor: Prof. Dr M. HABIBUR RAHMAN
Registrar: Prof. Dr ABU SIDDIQUE
Librarian: SURAIYA BEGUM (acting)

Library of 132,586 vols
Number of teachers: 501
Number of students: 7,773

Publications: *Bangladesh Journal of Water Resource Research, Chemical Engineering Research Bulletin, Electrical and Electronic Engineering Research Bulletin, Industrial and Production Engineering Research Bulletin, Journal of Energy and Environment, Journal of Mechanical Engineering Research and Development, Protibesh Journal of the Dept of Architecture*

DEANS

Faculty of Architecture and Planning: Prof. ROXANA HAFIZ
Faculty of Civil Engineering: Prof. Dr MUHAMMAD ZAKARIA
Faculty of Electrical and Electronic Engineering: Prof. Dr SATYA PRASAD MAJUMDER
Faculty of Engineering: Prof. Dr MD NASRUL HAQUE
Faculty of Mechanical Engineering: Prof. Dr SADIQUL BAREE

BANGLADESH UNIVERSITY OF PROFESSIONALS

Mirpur Cantonment, Dhaka 1216
Telephone: (2) 8035997
E-mail: info@bup.edu.bd
Internet: www.bup.edu.bd
Founded 2008
State control

Vice-Chancellor: ABUL KALAM MOHAMMAD HUMAYUN KABIR
Registrar: MD SHA ALAM CHOUDHURY
Asst Librarian: YASMIN ARA

DEANS

Faculty of Business Studies: MD FARUQUE-UL-HAQUE
Faculty of General Studies: SAYEED MD GOLAM YEAZDANI
Faculty of Medical Studies: MD EUNUS ALI MONDOL
Faculty of Securities and Strategic Studies: M M JASIMUDDIN BHUIYAN
Faculty of Technology and Engineering Studies: MIRZA IQBAL HAYAT

BANGLADESH UNIVERSITY OF TEXTILES

92 Shaheed Tajuddin Ahmed Sarani, Tejgaon, Dhaka 1208
Telephone: (2) 9114260
E-mail: butexedubd@yahoo.com
Internet: ww.butex.edu.bd
Founded 2010
State control

Chancellor: PRES. OF THE PEOPLE'S REPUBLIC OF BANGLADESH
Vice-Chancellor: Prof. Dr NITAI CHANDRA SUTRADHAR

Library of 8,188 vols, 657 journals

DEANS

Faculty of Textile Chemical Processing Engineering and Applied Science: Prof. Dr MD ZULHASH UDDIN
Faculty of Textile Clothing, Fashion and Business Studies: Assoc. Prof. MD MONIRUL ISLAM
Faculty of Textile Manufacturing Engineering: Prof. MASUD AHMED

BEGUM ROKEYA UNIVERSITY

House 14 Rd 2, Lalkuthi, Dhap, Rangpur
Telephone: (521) 66731
Internet: www.brur.ac.bd
Founded 2008 as Rangpur University

State control
Academic year: 2 semesters
Faculties of administration, arts and social science, science and engineering
Vice-Chancellor: Prof. Dr M. A. JALIL MIAH
Number of students: 890

BGC TRUST UNIVERSITY BANGLADESH

BGC Biddyanagar, Chandanaish, Chittagong
Telephone: (31) 656841
E-mail: bgctub@yahoo.com
Internet: www.bgctub-edu.com
Private control
Academic year: July to December
Chair.: Eng. AFSAR UDDIN AHMAD
Vice-Chancellor: Prof. Dr SAROJ KANTI SINGH
Registrar: Prof. FARID AHMAD
Library of 8,000 vols

DEANS

Faculty of Business Administration: Prof. Dr RANJIT KUMAR CHOWDHURY

BRAC UNIVERSITY

66 Mohakhali, Dhaka 1212
Telephone: (2) 8824051
E-mail: info@bracu.ac.bd
Internet: www.bracuniversity.net
Founded 2001
Private control, under BRAC non-governmental devt org.
Chair.: Sir FAZLE HASAN ABED
Vice-Chancellor: Prof. AINUN NISHAT
Pro-Vice-Chancellor: Dr MD GOLAM SAMDANI FAKIR
Registrar: ISHFAQ ILAHI CHOUDHURY
Librarian: HASINA AFROZ
Library: see under Libraries and Archives
Number of students: 1,659

DEANS

Faculty of Architecture: Prof. FUAD H. MALLICK
Faculty of Computer Science and Engineering: Prof. SAYEED SALAM
Faculty of Economics and Social Sciences: Dr ANWARUL HOQUE
Faculty of English and Humanities: Prof. FIRDOUS AZIM
Faculty of Mathematics and Natural Sciences: Prof. MOFIZ UDDIN AHMED

ATTACHED SCHOOLS AND INSTITUTES

BRAC Business School: Head Dr MD GOLAM SAMDANI (acting).

BRAC Development Institute: Dir Prof. SYED M. HASHEMI.

Centre for Languages: 66 Mohakhali, Dhaka 1212; tel. (2) 8824051; e-mail nsabera@bracu.ac.bd; internet www.bracuniversity.net/cfl; offers language courses in Bangla, Chinese, English, French, Spanish; Dir SYEDA SARWAT ABED.

Institute of Educational Development: House 113, Block A, Rd 2, Niketon, Gulshan 1, Dhaka 1212; tel. (2) 8824180; e-mail bu-ied@brac.net; internet www.bracuniversity.net/ied; promotes professional capacity building; provides technical support for improving quality in the public education system esp. at primary and secondary levels; Dir Dr ERUM MARIAM.

Institute of Governance Studies: 40/6 North Ave, Gulshan 2, Dhaka 1212; tel. (2) 8810306; e-mail igs-info@bracu.ac.bd; internet www.igs-bracu.ac.bd; f. 2005 as Centre for Governance Studies, present name 2007; offers postgraduate degree, professional training, undertakes research in areas of governance and devt; Dir Dr RIZWAN KHAIR (acting).

James P. Grant School of Public Health: BRAC University, 66 Shaheed Tajuddin Ahmed Sharani, Mohakhali ICDDR, B ED's Bldg, 5th Fl., Dhaka 1212; tel. (2) 8824051; e-mail mrityunjoy@bracu.ac.bd; internet sph.bracu.ac.bd; f. 2005; promotes and practices innovative higher public health education; Dean TIMOTHY G. EVANS.

School of Law: Dir Dr SHAHDEEN MALIK

CHITTAGONG UNIVERSITY OF ENGINEERING AND TECHNOLOGY

Chittagong 4349
Telephone: (31) 714946
E-mail: registrar@cuet.ac.bd
Internet: www.cuet.ac.bd
Founded 1968 as Engineering College, Chittagong; renamed Bangladesh Institute of Technology, Chittagong 1986; present name and status 2003
State control
Language of instruction: English
Chancellor: PRES. OF THE PEOPLE'S REPUBLIC OF BANGLADESH
Vice-Chancellor: Prof. Dr SHYAMAL KANTI BISWAS
Registrar: Eng. MD SHAFIQUL ISLAM
Librarian: MD ABUL HOSSAIN SHAIKH
Number of teachers: 112
Number of students: 1,800

DEANS

Faculty of Architecture and Planning: Prof. Dr MD JAHANGIR ALAM
Faculty of Electrical and Computer Engineering: Prof. MD RAFIQUL ALAM
Faculty of Engineering: Prof. Dr SHYAMAL KANTI BISWAS

CHITTAGONG VETERINARY AND ANIMAL SCIENCES UNIVERSITY

Khulshi, Chittagong 4202
Telephone: (31) 659492
E-mail: khalilcvasu@yahoo.com
Internet: www.cvasu.ac.bd
Founded 1996 as Chittagong Govt Veterinary College, present name and status 2006
State control
Vice-Chancellor: Prof. Dr A. S. MAHFUZUL BARI
Registrar: Prof. Dr MD KABIRUL ISLAM KHAN
Dir for External Affairs: MD ASHRAF ALI BISWAS
Dir for Research and Extension: Prof. Dr MD KABIRUL ISLAM KHAN
Dir for Student Welfare: GOUTAM KUMAR DEBNATH
Librarian: MD HABIBUR RAHMAN KHAN (acting)
Library of 10,000 vols

DEANS

Faculty of Food Science and Technology: Prof. GOUTAM BUDDHA DAS
Faculty of Veterinary Medicine: Prof. Dr MD MASUDUZZAMAN

CITY UNIVERSITY

Bulu Ocean Tower, 40 Kemal Ataturk Ave, Banani, Dhaka 1213
Telephone: (2) 9893983
E-mail: admission_city@yahoo.com
Internet: www.cityuniversity.edu.bd
Founded 2002
Private control
Academic year: June to May (2 semesters)
Depts of business administration, computer science and engineering, English, law, social science, textile engineering
Chair.: ALHAJ MOCKBUL HOSSAIN
Vice-Chancellor: Prof. Dr N. R. M. BORHAN UDDIN
Registrar: R. A. M. OBAIDUL MUKTADIR CHOWDHURY
Librarian: MD KABIRUL ISLAM
Number of students: 1,800

COMILLA UNIVERSITY

Comilla
Telephone: (181) 9945318
E-mail: kubhiyan@yahoo.com
Internet: www.cou.ac.bd
Founded 2007
State control
Faculties of arts, business studies, social science, science
Chancellor: PRES. OF THE PEOPLE'S REPUBLIC OF BANGLADESH
Vice-Chancellor: Prof. Dr AMIR HUSSAIN KHAN
Registrar: KAMAL UDDIN BHIYAN
Number of teachers: 85
Number of students: 2,000

DAFFODIL INTERNATIONAL UNIVERSITY

102 Shukrabad, Mirpur Rd, Dhanmondi, Dhaka 1207
Telephone: (2) 9138234
E-mail: vcoffice@daffodilvarsity.edu
Internet: www.daffodilvarsity.edu.bd
Founded 2002
Private control
Academic year: January to May (2 semesters)
Faculties of allied health sciences, business and economics, humanities and social sciences, science and information technology
Vice-Chancellor: ADNANUZZAMAN CHOWDHURY
Registrar: SURANJIT MONDAL
Librarian: MD MILAN KHAN
Number of teachers: 195 (155 full-time, 40 part-time)
Number of students: 1,324

DARUL IHSAN UNIVERSITY

House No. 21, Rd No. 9/A, Dhanmondi R/A, Dhaka 1209
Telephone: (2) 9127841
E-mail: info@diu.ac.bd
Internet: www.diu.ac.bd
Founded 1989
Private control
Language of instruction: English
Academic year: January to December (3 semesters)
Faculties of human sciences, natural sciences, religious sciences
Vice-Chancellor: Prof. Dr ANWAR ISLAM
Library of 21,564 vols

DHAKA INTERNATIONAL UNIVERSITY

House 6, Rd 1 Block F, Banani, Dhaka 1213
Telephone: (2) 8858734
E-mail: info@diu.net.bd
Internet: www.diu.net.bd
Founded 1995
Private control
Vice-Chancellor: Prof. Dr NURUL MOMEN
Chair.: Dr S. QUADIR PATWARI
Registrar: S. H. PATWERY
Sr Asst Librarian: MD ISMAIL HOSSAIN

DEANS

Faculty of Arts and Social Science: Prof. Dr K. M. MOHSIN
Faculty of Law: Prof. Dr AZIZUR RAHMAN CHOWDHURY
Faculty of Pharmacy: Assoc. Prof. HASAN KAWSER
Faculty of Science and Engineering: Prof. Dr MD SANA ULLAH

DHAKA UNIVERSITY OF ENGINEERING AND TECHNOLOGY

Gazipur 1700
Telephone: (2) 9204703
E-mail: reg_duet@duet.ac.bd
Internet: www.duet.ac.bd
Founded 1980, current name adopted and status 2003
State control
Language of instruction: English
Chancellor: PRES. OF THE PEOPLE'S REPUBLIC OF BANGLADESH
Vice-Chancellor: Prof. Dr M. SABDER ALI
Registrar: M. S. DOHA (acting)
Deputy Librarian: MD ANISUR RAHMAN
Library of 25,000 vols
Number of students: 1,519
Publication: *DUET Journal*

DEANS

Faculty of Civil Engineering: Prof. Dr MD SHOWKAT OSMAN
Faculty of Electrical and Electronic Engineering: Prof. Dr MOHAMMAD ABDUL MANNAN
Faculty of Mechanical Engineering: Prof. MD ABDUL HANNAN MIAH

EAST DELTA UNIVERSITY

1267/A Goshaildanga, Agrabad, Chittagong
Telephone: (1) 2514441
E-mail: enquiry@eastdelta.edu.bd
Internet: www.eastdelta.edu.bd
Private control
Language of instruction: English
Academic year: September to August (3 semesters)
Chair.: Prof. Dr DEBASISH CHAKRABORTY
Vice-Chancellor: Prof. MUHAMMAD SEKANDAR KHAN
Registrar: A. QAIYUM CHOWDHURY (acting)
Number of teachers: 41 (full-time)

DEANS

School of Business: Prof. Dr MOHAMMAD ABUL HOSSAIN

EAST WEST UNIVERSITY

43 Mohakhali C/A, Dhaka 1212
Telephone: (2) 8811381
E-mail: info@ewubd.edu
Internet: www.ewubd.edu
Founded 1996
Private control
Academic year: 3 semesters
Chair.: JALALUDDIN AHMED
Vice-Chancellor: Prof. Dr MUNIRUDDIN AHMED (acting)
Pro-Vice-Chancellor: Prof. Dr MUNIRUDDIN AHMED
Registrar: SHAH MURTOZA ALI
Librarian: DILARA BEGUM
Library of 23,740 vols, 1,400 CDs
Number of teachers: 187
Number of students: 5,000
Publications: *East West Journal of Business & Social Studies* (in English, 1 a year), *East West Journal Of Humanities*

DEANS

Faculty of Business and Economics: Prof. Dr MUHAMMAD SIRAJUL HAQUE
Faculty of Liberal Arts and Social Science: Dr BIJOY P. BARUA
Faculty of Science and Engineering: Prof. Dr CHOWDHURY FAIZ HOSSAIN

GONO BISHWABIDYALAY

P.O. Mirzanagar via Savar Cantonment, Dhaka 1344
Telephone: (2) 7708230
E-mail: gbidyala@bdonline.com
Internet: www.gonouniversity-bd.com
Founded 1998
Private control
Chancellor: PRES. OF THE PEOPLE'S REPUBLIC OF BANGLADESH
Chair.: TAHERUNNESA ABDULLAH
Vice-Chancellor: Prof. MESBAHUDDIN AHMAD
Registrar: MD DELOWER HOSSAIN
Library of 20,000 vols

DEANS

Faculty of Basic and Social Sciences: Prof. MAHMUD SHAH QURESHI
Faculty of Health Science: Prof. MD SHAHIDULLAH

GREEN UNIVERSITY OF BANGLADESH

220/D Begum Rokeya Sarani, West Kafrul, Dhaka 1207
Telephone: (2) 9014725
E-mail: admission@green.edu.bd
Internet: green.edu.bd/gub
Founded 2003
Private control
Academic year: 3 semesters
Chair.: TAFAZZAL HOSSAIN DHALI
Vice-Chancellor: Prof. Dr ANWARULLAH CHOWDHURY
Registrar: MD SHAHID ULLAH

DEANS

Faculty of Arts and Social Science: Prof. Dr AHMED FAZLE HASAN CHOWDHURY
Faculty of Business Studies: Prof. MD OMAR ALI
Faculty of Science and Engineering: Prof. KHAWJA JAKARIA AHMAD CHISTY

HAJEE MOHAMMAD DANESH UNIVERSITY OF SCIENCE AND TECHNOLOGY

Rangpur, Dhaka Highway, Dinajpur 5200
Telephone: (531) 65429
E-mail: vcmdstu@dhaka.net
Internet: www.hstu.ac.bd
Founded 1979 as Agricultural Extension Training Institute; present name and status 1999
State control
Chancellor: PRES. OF THE PEOPLE'S REPUBLIC OF BANGLADESH
Vice-Chancellor: Prof. Dr M. AFZAL HOSSAIN
Registrar: Prof. Dr BALARAM ROY
Librarian: MOHAMED ALAUDDIN KHAN
Library of 20,000 vols
Number of students: 903
Publication: *HSTU Journal*

DEANS

Faculty of Agriculture: Prof. MD MIJANUR RAHAMAN
Faculty of Agro-Industrial and Food Processing Engineering: Prof. Dr MD KAMAL UDDIN SARKER
Faculty of Business Studies: Prof. Dr FAHIMA KHANAM
Faculty of Computer Science and Engineering: Prof. MD RUHUL AMIN
Faculty of Fisheries: Prof. MD ANIS KHAN
Faculty of Veterinary and Animal Science: Prof. Dr MD ABDUL HAMID

INDEPENDENT UNIVERSITY, BANGLADESH

Plot 16, Block B, Aftabuddin Ahmed Rd, Bashundhara Residential Area, Dhaka 1229
Telephone: (2) 8401645
E-mail: info@iub.edu.bd
Founded 1993
Private control
Language of instruction: English
Academic year: August to July
Chancellor: PRES. OF THE PEOPLE'S REPUBLIC OF BANGLADESH
Vice-Chancellor: Prof. M OMAR EZAZ RAHMAN
Dir for Admin.: A. B. M. BAZLUR RAHMAN
Dir for Finance and Accounts: MUHAMMED SAIDUZZAMAN
Dir for Planning and Development: Eng CHOWDHURY ALAMGIR KABIR
Registrar: Dr TANVIR AHMED KHAN
Librarian: MUHAMMAD HOSSAM HAIDER CHOWDHURY
Library of 25,300 vols, 72 journal subscriptions
Number of teachers: 205 (160 full-time, 45 part-time)
Number of students: 4,100
Publication: *Independent Business Review* (2 a year)

DEANS

School of Business: NADIM JAHANGIR
School of Engineering and Computer Science: MOHAMMED ANWER
School of Environmental Science and Management: HAROUN-ER RASHID
School of Liberal Arts and Social Sciences: ZAKIR HOSSAIN RAJU
School of Life Sciences: Dr RITA YUSUF
School of Public Health: Prof. OMAR EZAZ RAHMAN

PROFESSORS

School of Business:
KUMAR SEN, D.
MOHAMMAD ABDUR, R.

School of Engineering and Computer Science:
ANWER, M.
KHODADAT KHAN, A. F. M.
NURUZZAMAN, M.
SUFDERUL HUQ, S.

School of Environmental Science and Management:
HOSSAIN, M. A.
KAMAL, N.
KARIM, Z.
RAHMAN, M. L.
RAHMAN, O.

School of Liberal Arts and Social Sciences:
ISLAM, N.

INTERNATIONAL ISLAMIC UNIVERSITY CHITTAGONG

154/A, College Rd, Chittagong 4203
Telephone: (31) 610085
E-mail: info@iiuc.ac.bd
Internet: www.iiuc.ac.bd
Founded 1995
Private control
Chancellor: PRES. OF THE PEOPLE'S REPUBLIC OF BANGLADESH
Vice-Chancellor: Prof. Dr M. MAHBUB ULLAH

Pro-Vice-Chancellor: Prof. Dr ABU BAKR RAFIQUE
Dir of Academic Affairs: MURTAZA AHMED (acting)
Registrar: MUHAMMAD NURUL ISLAM
Library Dir: MD NURUL KABIR KHAN (acting)

Library of 148,432 vols

DEANS

Faculty of Arts and Humanities: Prof. CHOWDHURY MOHAMMAD ALI
Faculty of Business Studies: Prof. Dr ABUL KALAM AZAD
Faculty of Laws: Prof. MORSHED MAHMUD KHAN
Faculty of Science and Engineering: Prof. Dr DELAWER HOSSAIN
Faculty of Shari'ah and Islamic Studies: Prof. Dr A. K. M. QUADER

ISLAMIC UNIVERSITY

Shantidanga-Dulalpur, Kushtia 7003
Telephone: (71) 62201
E-mail: vc@iubd.net
Internet: www.iubd.net

Founded 1985
State control
Chancellor: PRES. OF THE PEOPLE'S REPUBLIC OF BANGLADESH
Vice-Chancellor: Prof. Dr M. ALAUDDIN
Pro-Vice-Chancellor: Prof. Dr MD KAMAL UDDIN
Treas.: Prof. Dr MD SHAHJAHAN ALI
Registrar: MUHAMMAD MOSLEM UDDIN
Librarian: (vacant)

Library of 22,000 vols
Number of teachers: 65
Number of students: 10,000

DEANS

Faculty of Social Sciences: Dr M. MAMUN
Faculty of Theology and Islamic Studies: Prof. M. A. HAMID (acting)

ISLAMIC UNIVERSITY OF TECHNOLOGY

Board Bazar, Gazipur 1704
Telephone: (2) 9291250
E-mail: regstrar@iut-dhaka.edu
Internet: www.iutoic-dhaka.edu

Founded 1986 as Islamic Centre for Technical and Vocational Training and Research, became Islamic Institute of Technology 1994, present name and status 2001
Academic year: December to September
Chancellor: Prof. Dr EKMELEDDIN IHSANOGLU
Vice-Chancellor: Prof. Dr M. IMTIAZ HOSSAIN
Registrar: MOHAMMAD AHSAN HABIB
Dir for Library: Dr MIRZA MOHAMMAD REZAUL ISLAM

Library of 37,000 vols, 17 periodicals, 600 projects and thesis, 5,000 titles of online journals
Number of teachers: 110
Number of students: 1,135

Publication: *Journal of Engineering and Technology* (2 a year)

PROFESSORS

ABSAR CHOWDHURY, M. N., Mechanical Engineering
AMIN, M. R., Electrical and Electronic Engineering
CLEMENT, C. K., Technical and Vocational Education
HOQUE, M. A., Electrical and Electronic Engineering
IQBAL HUSSAIN, A. K. M., Mechanical Engineering
ISLAM, K. K., Electrical and Electronic Engineering
ISLAM, M. R., Electrical and Electronic Engineering
KARIM, M. R., Civil and Environmental Engineering
MOTTALIB, M. A., Computer Science and Information Technology
RAZZAQ AKHANDA, M. A., Mechanical Engineering
SADRUL ISLAM, A. K. M., Mechanical Engineering
ULLAH, M. S., Electrical and Electronic Engineering

IUBAT—INTERNATIONAL UNIVERSITY OF BUSINESS, AGRICULTURE AND TECHNOLOGY

4 Embankment Drive Rd, Sector 10, Uttara Model Town, Dhaka 1230
Telephone: (2) 8923471
E-mail: info@iubat.edu
Internet: www.iubat.edu

Founded 1991
Private control
Language of instruction: English
Academic year: January to December
Chancellor: PRES. OF THE PEOPLE'S REPUBLIC OF BANGLADESH
Vice-Chancellor: Prof. Dr M. ALIMULLAH MIYAN
Pro-Vice-Chancellor: Prof. MAHMUDA KHANUM
Treas.: SELINA NARGIS
Registrar: Prof. Dr M. A. HANNAN
Dir for Int. Programmes: TANVIR H. DEWAN
Librarian: MONOWARA SARWAR (acting)

Library of 14,510 vols, 375 journals, 100 periodicals
Number of teachers: 250
Number of students: 7,700

DEANS

Centre for Global Environmental Culture: Dr MOHAMMAD ATAUR RAHMAN
Centre for Management Development: MOKSUD AHMED
Centre for Policy Research: Dr M. A. JABBER
Centre for Technology Research Training and Consultancy: Prof. Dr JAVED BARI
College of Agricultural Sciences: Prof. Dr SHOHIDULLAH MIAH
College of Arts and Sciences: Prof. ABUL KHAIR
College of Business Administration: Prof. Dr M. ALIMULLAH MIYAN
College of Engineering and Technology: Prof. Dr MONIRUL ISLAM
College of Health Sciences and Medical Education: Dr A. S. A. MASUD
College of Nursing: Dr KAREN LUND
College of Tourism and Hospitality Management: Prof. AMAN ULLAH
Computer Education and Training Centre: Dr UTPAL KANTI DAS
Counselling and Guidance Centre: Prof. MAHMUDA KHANUM
Dept of Accounting: Prof. M. A. MANNAN
Dept of Civil Engineering: Prof. Dr MONIRUL ISLAM
Dept of Computer Sciences and Engineering: Dr UTPAL KANTI DAS
Dept of Economics: Dr M. A. JABBER
Dept of Electrical and Electronics Engineering: ABUL BASHAR
Dept of Mechanical Engineering: Prof. Dr A. Z. A. SAIFULLAH
Dept of Physics: Dr MAHBUBUR RAHMAN
English Language Centre: Prof. MOMTAZUR RAHMAN
Health and Population Centre: Dr KAREN LUND
South Asian Disaster Management Centre: Prof. Dr M ALIMULLAH MIYAN

PROFESSORS

ALAM, K. M. T., Economics
ALAM, M. S., Psychology
AL YOUSUF KHAN, A., Finance
AMAN ULLAH, M., Mathematics
AMAN ULLAH, M., Tourism and Hospitality
AZAD, M. A. K., English
AZAM, M. S., Civil Engineering
AZIZUL HUQ, M., Physics
BANERJEE, S. K., Tourism and Hospitality
BARI, J., Civil Engineering
BISWAS, S. K., Chemistry
CHISTY, K. K. S., Marketing
DAS, U. K., Computer Science and Engineering
DEY, N. K., Chemistry
FARJANA, S., Agriculture
FAROOQUE, A. M., Agriculture
HANNAN, M. A., Agriculture
HUDA, S. N., Nursing
IQBAL, K. S., Mechanical Engineering
ISLAM, M. M., Civil Engineering
ISLAM, M. S., Electrical and Electronics Engineering
JABBER, M. A., Economics
KARIM, M. A., Chemistry
KARIM, M. R., Agriculture
KHAIR, A., Chemistry
KHAN, M. R., Agriculture
KHANUM, M., Psychology
LUND, K., Nursing
MAHBUBUR RAHMAN, M., Physics
MANNAN, M., Accounting
MASUD, A., Nursing
MIYAN, M. A., Marketing
MOTTALIB, M., History
NARGIS, S., Psychology
RAHMAN, M. A., Environment
RAHMAN, M. M., English
RASUL, M. T., Civil Engineering
REHAN, D., Environment
SAIFULLAH, A., Mechanical Engineering
SALAH UDDIN, M., Agriculture
SARKER, C. K., Economics
SHAHJAHAN, M., Statistics
SHARMIN, S., Agriculture
SHOHIDULLAH MIAH, M., Agriculture
SULTANA, K. A., Psychology
UR RASHID, M. H., Chemistry
VERMA, G., Nursing

JAGANNATH UNIVERSITY

Dhaka 1100
E-mail: exambdinfo@gmail.com
Internet: www.jnu.ac.bd

Founded 1858 as Dhaka Brahma School, present status 1968
State control

Faculties of arts, business studies, science, social science

Chancellor: PRES. OF THE PEOPLE'S REPUBLIC OF BANGLADESH
Vice-Chancellor: Prof. Dr MESBAHUDDIN AHMED
Registrar: Eng. MD OHIDUZZAMAN

Library of 19,000 vols
Number of teachers: 271
Number of students: 27,000

Publications: *General Journal*, *Jagannath University Journal of Arts*, *Jagannath University Journal of Business Studies*, *Jagannath University Journal of Science*, *Jagannath University Journal of Social Sciences*

JAHANGIRNAGAR UNIVERSITY

Savar, Dhaka 1342
Telephone: (2) 7791045
E-mail: vc@juniv.edu
Internet: www.juniv.edu

Founded 1970
State control

Languages of instruction: Bengali, English
Academic year: July to June (3 terms)

Chancellor: PRES. OF THE PEOPLE'S REPUBLIC
Vice-Chancellor: Prof. Dr SHARIFF ENAMUL KABIR
Pro-Vice-Chancellor for Academics: Prof. Dr MOHAMMED MUNIRUZZAMAN
Pro-Vice-Chancellor for Admin.: Prof. Dr MD FORHAD HOSSAIN
Registrar: ABU BAKR SIDDIQUE (acting)
Librarian: Prof. SUBASH CHANDRA DAS

Library of 103,000 vols, 193 periodicals
Number of teachers: 423
Number of students: 8,105

Publications: *Asian Studies*, *Bangladesh Geoscience Journal*, *Bangladesh Journal of Life Sciences* (Biological and Life Sciences), *Clio* (History), *Copula* (Philosophy), *Harvest* (English Studies), *Jahangirnagar Economic Review*, *Jahangirnagar Physics Studies*, *Jahangirnagar Planning Review*, *Jahangirnagar Review* (Arts and Humanities), *Jahangirnagar Review* (Social Sciences), *Jahangirnagar University Chemical Review*, *Jahangirnagar University Journal of Sciences* (Mathematical and Physical Sciences), *Journal of Business Research*, *Journal of Electronic and Computer Science*, *Journal of Mathematics and Mathematical Sciences*, *Journal of Statistical Studies*, *Nre Baggan Patrica* (Anthropology), *Pratnatattva* (Archaeology), *Theatre Studies*, *Vhasa Shahitta Patra* (Bengali Studies), *Vogal Patrica* (Geography)

DEANS

Faculty of Arts and Humanities: Prof. MUHAMMAD NASIRUDDIN
Faculty of Biological Sciences: Prof. SHAHABUDDIN KABIR CHOWDHURY (Dir)
Faculty of Mathematical and Physical Sciences: Prof. MAHMOODA GHANI AHMED
Faculty of Social Sciences: Prof. AMIN MUHAMMAD ALI

JATIYA KABI KAZI NAZRUL ISLAM UNIVERSITY

Trishal, Mymensingh 2220
Telephone: (9032) 56272
E-mail: aminul_regknu@yahoo.com
Internet: www.jkkniu.edu.bd

Founded 2005
State control

Chancellor: PRES. OF THE PEOPLE'S REPUBLIC OF BANGLADESH
Vice-Chancellor: Prof. Dr SYED GIASUDDIN AHMED
Registrar: MD AMINUL ISLAM
Librarian: NURUL AMIN

Library of 27,800 vols, 40 journals

DEANS

Faculty of Arts: Prof. Dr SYED GIASUDDIN AHMED (acting)
Faculty of Business Administration: Prof. Dr SUBRATA KUMAR DEY
Faculty of Science and Engineering: Prof. Dr ABUL BASHAR (acting)
Faculty of Social Science: Dr HABIBUR RAHMAN

KHULNA UNIVERSITY

Gollamari, Khulna 9208
Telephone: (41) 720663
E-mail: registrar@ku.ac.bd
Internet: www.ku.ac.bd

Founded 1991
State control
Language of instruction: English
Academic year: July to June

Vice-Chancellor: Prof. Dr MOHAMAD FAYEK UZZAMAN
Registrar: Dr MOLLA AMIR HOSSEN (acting)
Librarian: Dr KAZI MOKLESUR RAHMAN (acting)

Library of 38,000 vols, 6,000 journals
Number of teachers: 310
Number of students: 5,000

Publications: *Business Review* (2 a year), *Khulna University Studies* (2 a year), *Plan Plas* (1 a year), *South Asian Journal of Agriculture* (1 a year)

DEANS

Institute of Fine Arts: Prof. Dr AFROZA PARVIN (Dir)
School of Arts and Humanities: Prof. Dr AHMED AHSANUZZAMAN (acting)
School of Life Science: Prof. Dr SAMIR KUMAR SADHU
School of Management and Business Administration: Prof. Dr A. T. M. JAHIRUDDIN
School of Science, Engineering and Technology: Prof. MD RAFIQUL ISLAM
School of Social Science: Prof. MOHAMMED ZIAUL HAIDER (acting)

KHULNA UNIVERSITY OF ENGINEERING AND TECHNOLOGY

Fulbarigate, Khulna 9203
Telephone: (41) 769468
E-mail: info@kuet.ac.bd
Internet: www.kuet.ac.bd

Founded 1967 as Khulna Engineering College; became Bangladesh Institute of Technology, Khulna 1986; present name and status 2003
State control

Chancellor: PRES. OF THE PEOPLE'S REPUBLIC OF BANGLADESH
Vice-Chancellor: Prof. Dr MUHAMMED ALAMGIR
Registrar: MD ABDUR ROUF
Librarian: MD AKKAS UDDIN PATHAN (acting)

Library of 30,000 vols
Number of teachers: 202
Number of students: 3,111

DEANS

Faculty of Civil Engineering: Prof. Dr MD ABUL BASHAR
Faculty of Electrical and Electronic Engineering: Prof. Dr MD RAFIQUL ISLAM
Faculty of Mechanical Engineering: Prof. Dr KH. AFTAB HOSSAIN

LEADING UNIVERSITY

Sylhet Campus: Modhuban, Sylhet 3100
Telephone: (2) 1720303
Dhaka Campus: 83 Siddeshwari, Dhaka
Telephone: (2) 8353468
E-mail: info@lus.ac.bd
Internet: www.lus.ac.bd

Founded 2002
Private control
Academic year: 2 semesters

Vice-Chancellor: Prof. Dr MD KABIR HOSSAIN (acting)
Pro-Vice-Chancellor: Prof. Dr M. R. KABIR
Pro-Vice-Chancellor: Dr A. N. M. MESHQUAT UDDIN

DEANS

Faculty of Modern Science: Prof. Dr M. WASHIM BARI

MAWLANA BHASHANI UNIVERSITY OF SCIENCE AND TECHNOLOGY

Santosh, Tangail 1902
Telephone: (921) 55399
E-mail: registrar@mbstu.ac.bd
Internet: mbstu.ac.bd

Founded 1999
State control

Chancellor: PRES. OF THE PEOPLE'S REPUBLIC OF BANGLADESH
Pro-Vice-Chancellor: Prof. Dr MONIRUZZAMAN
Vice-Chancellor: Prof. Dr M. NURUL ISLAM
Registrar: MD SHAHADAT HOSSAIN

DEANS

Faculty of Business Studies: Prof. Dr MONIRUZZAMAN
Faculty of Computer Science and Engineering: Prof. Dr M. NURUL ISLAM
Faculty of Life Sciences: Prof. Dr A. K. M. MOHIUDDIN
Faculty of Science: Prof. Dr M. NURUL ISLAM

METROPOLITAN UNIVERSITY

Al-Hamra 7th fl., Zindabazar, Sylhet 3100
Telephone: (821) 713077
E-mail: info@metrouni.edu.bd
Internet: www.metrouni.edu.bd

Founded 2003
Private control
Academic year: May to August, September to December, January to April (3 semesters)

Chair.: Dr TOUFIQUE RAHMAN CHOWDHURY
Vice-Chancellor: Prof. MD ABDUL AZIZ
Registrar: Prof. KHANDKER MAHMUDUR RAHMAN
Librarian: DILIP KUMAR DEB (acting)

Publication: *Metropolitan University Journal*

DEANS

School of Business: MD ABUL KALAM CHOWDHURY
School of Humanities and Social Sciences: Dr SURESH RANJAN BASAK
School of Law: M. AROSH ALI
School of Science and Technology: Prof. Dr ABDUL ROB

PROFESSORS

Department of Business Administration:
CHOWDHURY, A. K.
KHALIFA, T.
RAHMAN, K.

Department of Computer Science and Engineering:
ROB, A.
TALUKDER, R.

Department of Economics:
AZIZ, M. A.
CHOWDHURY, T.
SEN, S.

Department of English:
BASAK, S.

Department of Law and Justice:
ALI, M. A.

MILLENNIUM UNIVERSITY

Momenbagh, Shantinagar, Motijhil, Dhaka 1217
Telephone: (2) 9360836
E-mail: khanfoun@bdonline.com
Internet: themillenniumuniversity.edu.bd

Founded 2003
Private control

Faculties of business administration, computer science and technology, humanities, law

Vice-Chancellor: Prof. ABU AYUB MOHAMMAD BAQUER

Number of teachers: 32
Number of students: 1,086

NATIONAL UNIVERSITY

Board Bazar, Gazipur 1704
Telephone: (2) 9291018
E-mail: vc@nu.edu.bd
Internet: www.nu.edu.bd

Founded 1992
State control
Chancellor: PRES. OF THE PEOPLE'S REPUBLIC OF BANGLADESH
Vice-Chancellor: Prof. Dr KAZI SHAHIDULLAH
Pro-Vice-Chancellor: Prof. Dr M. ABU SAEED KHAN
Pro-Vice-Chancellor: Prof. Dr TOFAIL AHMAD CHOWDHURY
Dean of the School of Undergraduate Studies: Prof. FAKIR RAFIQUL ALAM
Dean of Graduate Education, Training and Research: Dr S. M. ABU RAIHAN
Number of students: 100,000
Publications: *Jatiya Bishawvidalaya Patrika* (4 a year), *Journal* (4 a year)

NOAKHALI SCIENCE AND TECHNOLOGY UNIVERSITY

Noakhali
Telephone: (1720) 197824
E-mail: info@nstu.edu.bd
Internet: www.nstu.edu.bd

Founded 2005
State control
Depts of applied chemistry and chemical engineering, computer science and telecommunication, engineering, English, fisheries and marine science, mathematics, microbiology, pharmacy
Vice-Chancellor: Prof. A. K. M. SAYEDUL HAQUE CHOWDHURY
Registrar: Prof. MD MOMINUL HUQ
Deputy Librarian: MD JAHANGIR HOSSAIN
Library of 3,270 vols, 500 journals
Number of teachers: 29
Number of students: 695

NORTH SOUTH UNIVERSITY

1 plot 15 Block B, Bashundhara, Dhaka 1229
Telephone: (2) 8852000
E-mail: registrar@northsouth.edu
Internet: www.northsouth.edu

Founded 1992
Private control
Academic year: January to December (3 semesters)
Chancellor: PRES. OF THE PEOPLE'S REPUBLIC OF BANGLADESH
Vice-Chancellor: Dr HAFIZ G. A. SIDDIQI
Pro-Vice-Chancellor: Dr S. A. M. KHAIRUL BASHAR
Registrar: B. M. ISA (acting)
Librarian: Dr MUHAMMAD MOSTAFIZUR RAHMAN
Library: see under Libraries and Archives
Number of teachers: 383 (234 full-time, 149 part-time)
Number of students: 15,000
Publications: *North South Business Review* (2 a year, in English), *Panini: NSU Studies in Language and Literature* (1 a year)

DEANS

School of Arts and Social Sciences: Prof. Dr A. K. M. ATIQUR RAHMAN
School of Business: Prof. Dr ABDUL HANNAN CHOWDHURY
School of Engineering and Applied Sciences: Prof. Dr A. T. M. NURUL AMIN
School of Life Sciences: Dr DONALD JAMES GOMES

NORTHERN UNIVERSITY BANGLADESH

93 Kazi Nazrul Islam Ave, Dhaka 1215
Telephone: (2) 9110293
E-mail: admission@nub.ac.bd
Internet: www.nub.ac.bd

Founded 2002
Private control
Academic year: January to December (3 semesters)
Chair.: Prof. Dr ABU YOUSUF MD ABDULLAH
Vice-Chancellor: Prof. Dr M. SHAMSUL HAQUE
Pro-Vice-Chancellor: (vacant)
Registrar: Prof. Dr MD NURUL ISLAM
Librarian: SHAHIDA BEGUM (acting)

DEANS

Faculty of Arts and Humanities: Prof. Dr SADRUDDIN AHMED
Faculty of Business Administration: Prof. Dr ABDUL AWAL KHAN
Faculty of Law: Prof. Dr A. W. M. ABDUL HUQ
Faculty of Science and Engineering: Prof. Dr MD NURUL ISLAM

PATUAKHALI UNIVERSITY OF SCIENCE AND TECHNOLOGY

Dumki, Patuakhali 8602
Telephone: (4427) 56011
E-mail: admission@pstu.ac.bd
Internet: www.pstu.ac.bd

Founded 2002
State control
Vice-Chancellor: Prof. Dr SYED SAKHAWAT HUSAIN
Librarian: MOHAMED ANWAR HOSSEIN
Number of students: 578

DEANS

Faculty of Agriculture: Prof. Dr A. K. M. MOSTAFA ZAMAN
Faculty of Computer Science and Engineering: Prof. ALI AZGOR BHUIYA
Faculty of Doctor in Veterinary Medicine: Prof. Dr SYED SAKHAWAT HUSAIN (acting)
Faculty of Fisheries: Prof. Dr SYED SAKHAWAT HUSAIN (acting)
Faculty of Postgraduate Studies: Prof. Dr ABUL KASHEM CHOWDHURY

PROFESSORS

BASHIR, M.
BISWAS, A.
HASAN, K.
HOSEN, Z.
HOSSEN, B.
HOSSEN, J.
ISLAM, M.
ISLAM, T.
MAHMUD, S.
PARVEZ, A.
RAHAMAN, A.
RAHAMAN, J.
RAHMAN, T.
ZAMAN, M.

PEOPLE'S UNIVERSITY OF BANGLADESH

3/2 Block A, Asad Ave, Mohammadpur, Dhaka 1207
Telephone: (2) 9127807
E-mail: infoadmission.uc@pub.ac.bd
Internet: www.pub.ac.bd

Founded 1996
Private control
Academic year: January to December (3 semesters)
Chancellor: PRES. OF THE PEOPLE'S REPUBLIC OF BANGLADESH
Chair.: MOHAMMAD ABDUL BATEN
Vice-Chancellor: Prof. MUSTAFIZUR RAHMAN
Registrar: HARUNOR RASHID BHUIYAN
Librarian: DILRUBA BAGUM

DEANS

School of Applied Science and Engineering: Prof. Dr M. EKIN UDDIN
School of Arts: Prof. Dr AHSANUL HAQUE

PREMIER UNIVERSITY

1/A O.R. Nizam Rd, Prabartak Circle, Panchlaish, Chittagong
Telephone: (31) 656917
E-mail: info@puc.ac.bd
Internet: www.puc.ac.bd

Founded 2001
Private control
Faculties of arts and social science, business studies, engineering, law
Chair.: ALHAJ. MOHAMMAD MANJUR ALAM
Vice-Chancellor: Prof. Dr ANUPAM SEN
Registrar: SK MOHAMMED IBRAHIM (acting)
Asst Librarian: KOWSAR ALAM

PRESIDENCY UNIVERSITY

11/A Rd 92, Gulshan, Dhaka 1212
Telephone: (2) 8857617
E-mail: info@presidency.edu.bd
Internet: www.presidency.edu.bd

Founded 2003
Private control
Schools of business, engineering, liberal arts and social science; campus in Banani
Chair.: MOAZZAM HOSSAIN
Vice-Chancellor: Prof. ANWAR HOSSAIN (acting)
Registrar: RASHIDA AKHTER (acting)

PRIME UNIVERSITY

2A/1, N E of Darus Salam Rd, Mirpur, Section-1, Dhaka 1216
Telephone: (2) 8014045
E-mail: info@primeuniversity.edu.bd
Internet: www.primeuniversity.edu.bd

Founded 2002
Private control
Academic year: January to December (3 semesters)
Faculties of arts and social science, business studies, engineering, information technology; campus in Uttara
Chair.: SAJJATUZ JUMMA
Vice-Chancellor: Prof. Dr PROFULLA C. SARKER
Registrar: Prof. MOHAMMAD ARSHAD ALI
Deputy Librarian: MD MUHIUDDIN ALAM
Library of 20,000 vols

PRIMEASIA UNIVERSITY

12 Kemal Ataturk Ave, Banani, Dhaka 1213
Telephone: (2) 8853386
E-mail: admission@primeasia.edu.bd
Internet: test.primeasia.edu.bd

Founded 2003
Private control
Academic year: 3 semesters
Schools of business, engineering and technology, law, science
Chair.: M. A. WAHHAB
Vice-Chancellor: Prof. Dr GIAS UDDIN AHMAD
Number of teachers: 200 (150 full-time)
Number of students: 3,750

PUNDRA UNIVERSITY OF SCIENCE AND TECHNOLOGY

Gokul, Bogra
Telephone: (51) 73563

Founded 2001, present status 2002
Private control
Vice-Chancellor: Prof. LUTFOR RAHMAN

RAJSHAHI UNIVERSITY OF ENGINEERING AND TECHNOLOGY

Rajshahi Natore Dhaka Rd, Kazla, Rajshahi 6204
Telephone: (721) 750742
E-mail: registrar@ruet.ac.bd
Internet: www.ruet.ac.bd
Founded 1964 as faculty of Engineering under Univ. of Rajshahi; present name and status 2002
State control
Vice-Chancellor: Prof. Dr SIRAJUL KARIM CHOUDHURY
Pro-Vice-Chancellor: Prof. Dr MD MORTUZA ALI
Number of students: 1,763

DEANS
Faculty of Civil Engineering: Prof. Dr TARIF UDDIN AHMED
Faculty of Electrical and Computer Engineering: Prof. Dr MUHAMMAD ABDUL GOFFAR KHAN
Faculty of Mechanical Engineering: MD SHAMIM AKHTER

ROYAL UNIVERSITY OF DHAKA

House 02, Rd 10, Block B, Banani, Dhaka 1213
Telephone: (2) 9886150
Internet: www.royal.edu.bd
Founded 2003
Private control
Chancellor: PRES. OF THE PEOPLE'S REPUBLIC OF BANGLADESH
Chair.: Dr MOMTAZ BEGUM
Vice-Chancellor: Prof. Dr M. BADIUL ALAM
Faculties of arts and social science, business, science
Number of teachers: 50
Number of students: 680

SHAHJALAL UNIVERSITY OF SCIENCE AND TECHNOLOGY

Kumargaon, Sylhet 3114
Telephone: (821) 713491
E-mail: registrar@sust.edu
Internet: www.sust.edu
Founded 1987
State control
Languages of instruction: English, Bengali
Academic year: July to June
6 Affiliated medical colleges
Chancellor: PRES. OF THE PEOPLE'S REPUBLIC OF BANGLADESH
Vice-Chancellor: Prof. Dr MD SALEH UDDIN
Registrar: MOHD ISHFAQUL HUSSAIN
Librarian: MD ABDUL HAYEE SAMENI
Library of 54,000 vols, 6,000 journals
Number of teachers: 424
Number of students: 12,006
Publication: *SUST Studies* (1 a year)

DEANS
School of Agriculture and Mineral Science: Prof. Dr KABIR HUSSAIN (acting)
School of Applied Sciences and Technology: Prof. Dr AKTARUL ISLAM
School of Business Administration: Prof. Dr MUHAMMAD NAZRUL ISLAM (acting)
School of Life Sciences: Prof. Dr M. HABIBUL AHSAN
School of Medical Science: Prof. Dr REZAUL KARIM
School of Physical Sciences: Prof. Dr SYED SAMSUL ALAM
School of Social Sciences: Prof. Dr TULSHI KUMAR DAS

PROFESSORS
AHMED, M., Physics
AHSAN, H., Physics
ALAM, A., Chemistry
ALAM, J., Civil and Environmental Engineering
ALAM, S., Chemistry
ALAM, S., Physics
ALI, R., Statistics
ASHRAF UDDIN, M., Mathematics
BATEN, A., Statistics
BEGUM, S., Physics
BISWAS, A., Anthropology
BISWAS, E., Mathematics
CHAWDHURY, N., Physics
CHOUDHURY, E., Statistics
CHOWDHURY, A., Civil and Environmental Engineering
CHOWDHURY, A., Statistics
CHOWDHURY, G., Mathematics
CHOWDHURY, H., Physics
CHOWDHURY, K., Sociology
DAS, S., Geography and Environment
DAS, S., Physics
DAS, T., Social Work
FARUQUE, B., Physics
GHANI, A., Sociology
HANNAN, A., Physics
HAQUE, Y., Physics
HASAN, M., Social Work
HOSSAIN, I., Physics
HOSSAIN, K., Statistics
HOSSAIN, Z., Statistics
IQBAL, M., Industrial and Production Engineering
IQBAL, Z., Computer Science and Engineering
IQBAL, Z., Electrical and Electronic Engineering
ISLAM, A., Chemical Engineering and Polymer Science
ISLAM, A., Mathematics
ISLAM, N., Business Administration
ISLAM, S., Biochemistry and Molecular Biology
ISLAM, S., Chemistry
ISLAM, S., Statistics
KABIR, A., Statistics
KARIM, S., Mathematics
KAZAL, M., Economics
KHONDKER, R., Economics
MAHBUBUZZAMAN, A., Social Work
NIZAM UDDIN, M., Chemistry
RAHIM, A., Bangla
RAHMAN, M., Chemistry
SAHA, N., Forestry and Environmental Science
SHARAFUDDIN, S., Physics
SUBHAN, A., Chemistry
TALUKDER, R., Mathematics
YOUNUS, M., Chemistry

SHANTO-MARIAM UNIVERSITY OF CREATIVE TECHNOLOGY

House 01, Rd 14, Sector 13, Uttara, Dhaka 1230
Telephone: (2) 8918932
E-mail: smuctbd@yahoo.com
Internet: www.smuct.edu.bd
Private control
Vice-Chancellor: Prof. Dr SHAMSUL HAQ
Registrar: HOSNE ARA RAHMAN

DEANS
Faculty of Design and Technology: Prof. Dr MUHAMMAD ABDUL HALIM SHAIKH
Faculty of Fine and Performing Arts: Prof. MIZANUR RAHIM
Faculty of Management and General Studies: Prof. QUAZI MD MAFIZUR RAHMAN

SHER-E-BANGLA AGRICULTURAL UNIVERSITY

Sher-e-Bangla Nagar, Dhaka 1207
Telephone: (2) 9144270
E-mail: vcsau@dhaka.net
Internet: www.sau.ac.bd
Founded 2001
State control
Vice-Chancellor: Prof. Dr MD SHAH-E-ALAM
Registrar: Prof. Dr A. M. M. SHAMSUZZAMAN (acting)
Librarian: MOHAMED ALI (acting)
Library of 45,700 vols
Number of teachers: 20
Number of students: 1,536
Publications: *Journal of Agricultural Education and Technology*, *Journal of Agricultural Science and Technology*, *Journal of Sher-e-Bangla Agricultural University*

DEANS
Faculty of Agribusiness Management: Prof. M. ZAKIR HOSSAIN
Faculty of Agriculture: Prof. Dr M. SERAJUL ISLAM BHUIYAN

PROFESSORS
ABEDIN, M.
AHMED REZA, Z.
AKBAR MIA, A.
AKHTAR, N.
ALI, M.
ALI, M.
BEGUM, J.
BEGUM, R.
CHANDRA SUTRADHAR, G.
FAZLUL KARIM, M.
HAQUE BEG, M.
HOSSAIN, M.
HOSSAIN BHUIYAN, M.
ISLAM BHUIYAN, M.
JAFAR ULLAH, M.
JALIL, G.
KANTI BISWAS, P.
KUMAR PAUL, A.
MAHTABUDDIN, A.
MANDAL, G.
MANNAN MIAH, M.
NAZRUL ISLAM, M.
NURUL ISLAM, M.
RAFIQUEL ISLAM, M.
RAFIQUL ISLAM, M.
RAHMAN MAZUMDER, M.
RASHID BHUIYAN, M.
RUHUL AMIN, A.
RUHUL AMIN, M.
SADRUL ANAM SARDAR, M.
SAROWAR HOSSAIN, M.
SHADAT ULLA, M.
SHAHJAHAN MIAH, M.
SHAMSUL HOQUE, M.
SHAMSUZZAMAN, A.
UDDIN AHMED, K.
ZAHIDUL HAQUE, M.

SOUTHEAST UNIVERSITY

House 64, Rd 18, Block B, Banani, Dhaka
Telephone: (2) 8860456
E-mail: info@seu.ac.bd
Internet: www.seu.ac.bd
Founded 2002
Private control
Academic year: January to January (3 semesters)
Vice-Chancellor: Prof. Dr A. N. M. MESHQUAT UDDIN (acting)
Registrar: MD ALI AMBIAL HAQUE KHAN
Deputy Librarian: ABDULLAH AL-MODABBER
Library of 10,793 vols, 98 periodicals

DEANS

School of Arts and Social Sciences: Prof. MD ABDUL BATEN MIAH (acting)
School of Business Studies: Dr HELAL UDDIN AHMED (acting)
School of Science and Engineering: Prof. Dr RAFIQUL ISLAM SHARIF

SOUTHERN UNIVERSITY

739/A Mehedibagh Rd, Chittagong
Telephone: (31) 626744
E-mail: southern_u@mail.com
Internet: www.southern-bd.info
Founded 1998 as Institute of Management and Information Technology, present name and status 2002
Private control
Academic year: January to December (3 semesters)
Faculties of arts, social science and law, business administration, science and engineering
Chair.: ALHAJ. KHALILUR RAHMAN
Vice-Chancellor: Prof. MOHAMMAD ALI
Publications: *Journal of Business and Society* (1 a year), *Journal of Engineering and Science* (1 a year), *Journal of General Education* (1 a year)

STAMFORD UNIVERSITY BANGLADESH

744 Satmosjid Rd, Dhanmondi, Dhaka 1209
Telephone: (2) 8153168
E-mail: admission@stamforduniversity.edu.bd
Internet: www.stamforduniversity.edu.bd
Founded 1994, present status 2002
Private control
Academic year: January to December (3 semesters)
Depts of architecture, business administration, civil engineering, computer science, economics, electrical and electronic engineering, environmental science, film and media, journalism and media studies, law, microbiology, pharmacy, public administration
Pres.: Prof. M. A. HANNAN FEROZ
Vice-Chancellor: Prof. Dr M. MAJIBUR RAHMAN
Pro-Vice-Chancellor: Prof. Dr MOUDOOD ELAHI
Registrar: S. M. IKRAMUL HAQUE
Deputy Librarian: MD AMIRUZZAMAN MIA
Number of students: 9,100

STATE UNIVERSITY OF BANGLADESH

77 Satmasjid Rd, Dhanmondi, Dhaka 1205
Telephone: (2) 8151783
E-mail: info@sub.edu.bd
Internet: www.sub.edu.bd
Founded 2002
Private control
Chancellor: PRES. OF THE PEOPLE'S REPUBLIC OF BANGLADESH
Pres.: Dr A. M. SHAMIM
Vice-Chancellor: Prof. Dr IFTEKHAR GHANI CHOWDHURY
Registrar: Prof. A. Y. M. EKRAM-UD-DAULAH
Library of 11,000 vols
Publications: *Eduvista, Journal of SUB* (2 a year), *SUB Journal of Public Health* (2 a year)

DEANS

School of Science and Technology: Prof. A. A. K. M. LUTFUZZAMAN

SYLHET AGRICULTURAL UNIVERSITY

Shamimabad, Bagbari, Sylhet
Telephone: (821) 760930
E-mail: siu_syl@yahoo.com
Internet: www.sylhetagrivarsity.edu.bd
Founded 2006
State control
Faculties of agricultural economics and business studies, agriculture, fisheries, veterinary and animal science
Vice-Chancellor: Dr MD SHAHID ULLAH TALUKDAR
Number of teachers: 84
Number of students: 1,250

SYLHET INTERNATIONAL UNIVERSITY

Shamimabad, Kanishail Rd, Bagbari, Sylhet 3100
Telephone: (821) 720771
E-mail: info@siu.edu.bd
Internet: www.siu.edu.bd
Founded 2001
Private control
Academic year: March to September (2 semesters)
Faculties of business administration, electronics and communication engineering, engineering, humanities and social science, law
Chair.: SHAMIM AHMED
Vice-Chancellor: Prof. SYED AKMAL MAHMOOD (acting)
Registrar: MD ABDUL LATIF
Deputy Librarian: MOSTAFA KAMAL
Library of 10,000 vols

UNITED INTERNATIONAL UNIVERSITY

House 80, Rd 8/A, Mirza Golam Hafiz Rd, Dhanmondi, Dhaka 1209
Telephone: (2) 9125912
E-mail: info@uiu.ac.bd
Internet: www.uiubd.com
Founded 2003
Private control
Academic year: February to January (3 semesters)
Chair.: HASAN MAHMOOD RAJA
Vice-Chancellor: Prof. Dr M. REZWAN KHAN
Pro-Vice-Chancellor: Prof. Dr CHOWDHURY MOFIZUR RAHMAN
Registrar: Prof. A. S. M. SALAHUDDIN
Asst Librarian: MD MANJURUL HAQUE KHAN

DEAN

School of Business: Prof. Dr HABIBUR RAHMAN

UNIVERSITY OF ASIA PACIFIC

House 73, Rd 5A, Dhanmondi, Dhaka 1209
Telephone: (2) 9664953
E-mail: admission@uap-bd.edu
Internet: www.uap-bd.edu
Founded 1996
Private control
Academic year: April to September
Chair.: Eng. M. ABU TAHER
Vice-Chancellor: Prof. Dr ABDUL MATIN PATWARI
Pro-Vice-Chancellor: Prof. Dr M. R. KABIR
Registrar: KAZI ASHFAQ AHMED
Deputy Librarian: SHEIKH MD JALAL UDDIN (acting)
Publication: *International Journal of Computer and Information Technology* (2 a year)

DEANS

School of Design: Prof. SHAMSUL WARES
School of Engineering: Dr M. R. KABIR

UNIVERSITY OF CHITTAGONG

University Post Office, Chittagong 4331
Telephone: (31) 651287
Internet: www.cu.ac.bd
Founded 1966
Languages of instruction: Bengali, English
Academic year: July to June
Chancellor: PRES. OF THE PEOPLE'S REPUBLIC OF BANGLADESH
Vice-Chancellor: Prof. MD ANWARUL AZIM ARIF
Pro-Vice-Chancellor: Prof. Dr MD ALAUDDIN
Registrar: Prof. Dr MOHAMMED SHAFIUL ALAM (acting)
Librarian: SYED MOHAMED ABU TAHER
Library of 201,514 vols
Number of teachers: 690
Number of students: 19,134

DEANS

Faculty of Arts: Prof. Dr GOLAM KIBRIYA BHUIYAN
Faculty of Commerce: Prof. Dr K. M. GOLAM MOHIUDDIN
Faculty of Law: Prof. MD JAKIR HOSSAIN
Faculty of Medicine: Prof. MUHAMMED GOFRANUL HAQUE
Faculty of Science: Prof. Dr MD ABUL KALAM AZAD
Faculty of Social Science: Prof. Dr JYOTI PRAKASH DUTTA

PROFESSORS

Faculty of Arts

Arabic and Islamic Studies:

AHMAD, R.
CHOWDHURY, A. S. M
DOZA, H. M. B
HAQUE, A. F. M. A.
KHATIBI, M. A. H.
QUADER, A. K. M. A.
RASHID, M.

Bengali:

ALAM, M. S.
AMIN, M. N.
AZIM, A.
AZIZ, M. M.
BISWAS, S. N.
CHOWDHURY, A. U. M. Z. H.
DASTIDAR, S. R.
IQBAL, B. M.
ISLAM, A. K. M. N.
MANIRUZZAMAN, M.
QUASEM, M. A.
SHAHJAHAN
ZAMAN, A. L.

English:

ALAM, M. U.
BARUA, T. J.
BILLA, Q. M.
CHOWDHURY, G. S.
DUTTA, S. K.
ISLAM, M. S.
MOHMOOD, A. B. M. M.

Fine Arts:

ALI, S. M. A.
AZIM, F.
BANU, N.
ISLAM, M. S.
KARIM, M. M.
KHALED, S. A.
MANSUR, A.
RAHIM, M.
ROY, A.

History:

CHOWDHURY, M. A.
HOQUE, M.

HOSSAIN, E.
HOSSAIN, H.
KABIR, E.
KHALED, A. M. M. S.
SAYED, A.
SHAH, M.

Islamic History and Culture:

AHMED, A.
AHMED, S.
ALAM, A. Q. M. S.
BHUIYAN, G. K.
CHOWDHURY, M. T. H.
HUQ, M. I.
SHAFIQ ULLAH, S. M.
YUSUF, A.

Oriental Languages:

BARUA, D. S.
BARUA, R. K.
HALDER, S. R.

Philosophy:

AHMED, R.
ALAM, M. S.
ALI, M. A.
ANWAR, A. J.
CHOWDHURY, M. A.
KHALEQUE, A. S. M. A.
RAHMAN, A. K. M. S.
RAHMAN, A. M. M. W.
RAHMAN, M. B.
RAHMAN, M. L.

Faculty of Commerce

Accounting and Information Systems:

AHMED, S.
BHATTACHARJEE, M. K.
CHOWDHURY, R. K.
DAS, S. R.
DATTA, D. K.
MAHMUD, M. M.
MOHIUDDIN, K. M. G.
NAG, A. B.
PURAHIT, K. K.
RASHID, H.
SALAUDDIN, A.
SHARMA, B. K.

Finance and Banking:

HOQUE, M. J.
LOQMAN, M.
MOQTADIR, A. N. M. A.
NABI, K. A.
RASHID, M. H.

Management:

ALAM, M. F.
ALI, A. F. M. A.
ARIF, M. A. A.
ATHER, S. M.
MAMUN, M. A.
MANNAN, M. A.
SIKDER, Z. H.
TAHER, M. A.

Marketing:

BHUIYAN, S. M. S. U.
CHOWDHURY, A. J. M.
KARIM, A. N. M. N.
MEHER, M. S.
SHAHIN, S.
SOLAIMAN, M.

Faculty of Law

Law:

ALAM, M. S.

Faculty of Science

Applied Physics and Electronics:

BHUIYAN, M. A. S.
HOSSAIN, A.
KHAN, M. R. H.
SAHA, S. L.

Biochemistry and Molecular Biology:

ALAUDDIN, M.

Botany:

AHMED, M.
ALAMGIR, A. N. M.
BASET, Q. A.
BHADRA, S. K.
CHOWDHURY, A. M.
GAFUR, M. A.
MRIDHA, M. A.
PASHA, M. K.
RAHMAN, M. A.

Chemistry:

AHMED, M. J.
AHMED, M. S. U.
AKHTAR, S.
BEGUM, S. A.
CHOWDHURY, D. A.
CHOWDHURY, M. Z. A.
DEY, B. K.
HABIB ULLAH, M.
HAZARI, S. K. S.
ISLAM, M.
KABIR, A. K. M. S.
NAZIMUDDIN, M.
PALIT, D.
RAHMAN, K. M. M.
ROY, T. G.
SALAM, M. A.
SALEH, M. A.
UDDIN, M. H.

Computer Science:

MOSTAFA, M. N.

Mathematics:

AHMED, M.
AZAD, A. K.
BHATTACHARJEE, N. R.
ISLAM, M. A.
ISLAM, M. N.
MOHIUDDIN, M.
RAHMAN, M. M.

Microbiology:

ANWAR, M. N.
HAKIM, M. A.

Physics:

AHMED, F. K.
AHMED, M.
BANU, H.
BARUA, B. P.
BEGUM, D. A.
DEB, A. K.
ISLAM, M. N.
MIYA, M. M. H.
NABI, S. R.
PAUL, D. P.
ROY, M. K.
SAFIULLAH, M. A.
SAHA, S. K.
SIDDIQA, N.

Soil Science:

OSMAN, K. T.

Statistics:

ISLAM, S. M. S.
PAUL, J. C.
RAHMAN, M. M.
RASUL, M. A.
ROY, M. K.
SHAMSUDDIN, M.
SHIL, R. N.
YAHYA, N. S. M.

Zoology:

AHMED, B.
AHSAN, M. F.
ALAM, M. S.
ASMAT, G. S. M.
AZADI, M. A.
BANU, Q.
BHUIYAN, A. M.
BHUIYAN, M. A.
HAFIZUDDIN, A. K. M.
ISLAM, M. A.
KHAN, M. A. G.
MEAH, M. I.
NASIRUDDIN, M.
ULLAH, G. M. R.

Faculty of Social Science

Anthropology:

CHOWDHURY, A. F. H.

Economics:

ASHRAF, M. A.
AZAD, A. K.
CHOWDHURY, M. A. M.
DEY, H. K.
DUTTA, J. P.
HOQ, M.
HOQUE, M. S.
HOSSAIN, B.
ISLAM, M.
KHAN, I. K.
KHAN, M. S.
MAHBUB, U.
NAG, N. C.
SALEHUDDIN, M.
TAHERA, B. S.

Political Science:

AHMED, A. N. M. M.
AHMED, S. Z.
AKHTER, M. Y.
ALAM, M. B.
CHOWDHURY, M. H.
CHOWDHURY, S. A.
HAKIM, M. A.
HASSAN, M.
HOQUE, M. E.
KABIR, B. M. M.
KHAN, Z. N.
KHANAM, J.
KHANAM, R.
MUSHRAFI, M. E. M.
SHAMSUDDIN, M.

Public Administration:

AHMED, N. U.
AHMED, T.
AMIN, M. R.
BEGUM, A.
ISLAM, M. N.
MASHREQUE, M. S.
NOOR, A.
WAHHAB, M. A.

Sociology:

ALI, A. F. I.
BHUIYAN, M. A.
CHOWDHURY, A. Q.
CHOWDHURY, H. Z.
CHOWDHURY, I. U.
HUSSAIN, M.
KARIM, M. O.
MAHABUBULLAH, M.
QUDDUS, A. H. G.
SALEHUDDIN, G.
SEN, A.

UNIVERSITY OF DEVELOPMENT ALTERNATIVE

80 Satmasjid Rd, Dhanmondi, Dhaka
Telephone: (2) 9145741
E-mail: registrar@uoda.edu.bd
Internet: www.uoda.edu.bd

Founded 2002
Private control
Academic year: 3 semesters

Vice-Chancellor: Prof. Dr EMAJUDDIN AHAMED
Registrar: Dr IFFAT CHOWDHURY

DEANS

Faculty of Arts: Prof. M. MOSTFIZUR RAHMAN
Faculty of Business Administration: Prof. MD LATIFUR RAHMAN
Faculty of Engineering: Prof. Dr MD OSMAN GANI TALUKDER
Faculty of Life Science: Prof. Dr MOHAMMED RAHMATULLAH
Faculty of Social Sciences: Prof. Dr AHMADULLAH MIA

UNIVERSITY OF DHAKA

Ramna, Dhaka 1000
Telephone: (2) 8614150
E-mail: duregstr@bangla.net
Internet: www.univdhaka.edu

Founded 1921
Private control
Languages of instruction: Bengali, English
Academic year: July to June (3 terms)

Chancellor: PRES. OF THE PEOPLE'S REPUBLIC OF BANGLADESH
Vice-Chancellor: Prof. Dr A. A. M. S. AREFIN SIDDIQUE
Pro-Vice-Chancellor: Prof. Dr HARUN OR RASHID
Treas.: Prof. Dr MIZANUR RAHMAN
Registrar: SYED REZAUR RAHMAN (acting)
Librarian: Dr M. S. ISLAM (acting)

Library: see under Libraries and Archives
Number of teachers: 1,805
Number of students: 33,112

Publications: *Dhaka University Studies* (2 a year), *Dhaka Viswa Vidyalaya Bartra* (4 a year), *Dhaka Viswa Vidyalaya Patrika* (3 a year), *Sahitya Patrika* (3 a year), *Social Science Newsletter* (4 a year)

DEANS

Faculty of Arts: Prof. Dr SADRUL AMIN
Faculty of Biological Sciences: Prof. Dr SHAHID AKTHER HOSSAIN
Faculty of Business Studies: Dr JAMAL UDDIN AHMED
Faculty of Earth and Environmental Sciences: Prof. Dr NASREEN AHMAD
Faculty of Education: Prof. Dr MD IDRIS ALI
Faculty of Engineering and Technology: Prof. Dr REZAUL KARIM MAZUMDER
Faculty of Fine Art: Prof. Dr EMDADUL HAQUE MD MATLUB ALI
Faculty of Law: Prof. Dr TASLIMA MONSOOR
Faculty of Medicine: Prof. Dr ISMAIL KHAN
Faculty of Pharmacy: Prof. M. A. B. M. FAROQUE
Faculty of Postgraduate Medical Sciences and Research: Prof. MAGRUB HUSSAIN
Faculty of Science: Dr MD YOUSUF ALI MOLLAH
Faculty of Social Sciences: Prof. FARID UDDIN AHMED

PROFESSORS

ABDULLAH, A. S. A., Accounting and Information Systems
ABEDIN, K. M., Physics
ABRAR, C. R., International Relations
ABULULAYEE, S. K. M., Philosophy
ADEEB, K., Nutrition and Food Science
ADITYA, S. K., Applied Physics and Electronics
AFROEZ, D., Psychology
AFTABUDDIN, M., Biochemistry and Molecular Biology
AHAD, S. A., Soil, Water and the Environment
AHMAD, N., Arabic
AHMED, A., Economics
AHMED, A., Political Science
AHMED, A. F., Public Administration
AHMED, A. I. M. U., Sociology
AHMED, A. K. M. U., Economics
AHMED, A. T. A., Zoology
AHMED, A. U., Nutrition and Food Science
AHMED, E., Chemistry
AHMED, E., International Relations
AHMED, F., Applied Physics and Electronics
AHMED, F., Economics
AHMED, I., Business Administration
AHMED, J. U., Finance
AHMED, K. U., Political Science
AHMED, M., Accounting and Information Systems
AHMED, M., Clinical Pharmacy and Pharmacology
AHMED, M., Economics
AHMED, M., Physics
AHMED, M., Public Administration
AHMED, M. F., Finance
AHMED, M. G., Chemistry
AHMED, N., Geography and the Environment
AHMED, S., Anthropology
AHMED, S., Economics
AHMED, S., Economics
AHMED, S., Management Studies
AHMED, S. A., Chemistry
AHMED, S. G., Public Administration
AHMED, S. J., Theatre and Music
AHMED, S. U., History
AHMED, S. U., Management Studies
AHMED, W., Bengali
AHMED, Z., History
AHMED MAJIB, U., Accounting and Information Systems
AHMED MAMATAJ, U., Accounting and Information Systems
AHSAN, A., Management Studies
AHSAN, C. R., Microbiology
AHSAN, M., Pharmaceutical Chemistry
AHSAN, M. A., Education and Research
AHSAN, M. Q., Chemistry
AHSAN, R. M., Geography and the Environment
AKHTER, N., Botany
AKHTER, R., Philosophy
AKHTER, S. H., Geology
AKHTERUZZAMAN, M., Islamic History and Culture
AKKAS, M. A., Management Studies
AKTER, S., Education and Research
ALAM, A. F., Marketing
ALAM, A. M. S., Chemistry
ALAM, B., Physics
ALAM, F., English
ALAM, H. A., Philosophy
ALAM, K. M. U., Geology
ALAM, K. S., Marketing
ALAM, M., Geology
ALAM, M. D., Soil, Water and the Environment
ALAM, M. K., Soil, Water and the Environment
ALAM, M. M., Economics
ALAM, M. M., Geology
ALAM, M. R., Fine Arts
ALAM, S. S., Botany
ALI, A. H. M. M., Fine Arts
ALI, A. K. M. I., Islamic History and Culture
ALI, A. M., Mass Communication and Journalism
ALI, M. A., Education and Research
ALI, M. S., Physics
ALI, M. S., Zoology
ALI, R., Psychology
ALI, S. M. K., Nutrition and Food Science
ALVI, S. A. B., Fine Arts
AMIN, M. R., Islamic Studies
AMIN, S., English
AMIN, S. N., History
AMINUZZAMAN, S. M., Development Studies
ANISUZZAMAN, Philosophy
ANOWAR, A. J., Philosophy
ANOWAR, S. F., Business Administration
ANSARUDDIN, M., Islamic Studies
ARA, R., Philosophy
AREFEEN, H. K. S., Anthropology
ASADUZZAMAN, M., Public Administration
AWAL, A. Z. M. I., History
AZAD, S. A. K., Marketing
AZIM, F., English
AZIZ, A., Botany
BANOO, R., Pharmaceutical Chemistry
BANU, K., Statistics
BANU, N., Zoology
BANU, R., Modern Languages
BANU, S., Mathematics
BANU, S., Psychology
BANU, U. A. B. R. A., Political Science
BAPARY, M. N. A., Political Science
BAQI, A., Islamic Studies
BAQUEE, A. H. M. A., Geography and the Environment
BARI, M. E., Law
BARKAT, M. A., Economics
BARMAN, D. C., Peace and Conflict Studies
BARUA, S., Nutrition and Food Science
BASHAR, M. H., Chemistry
BASHER, A., Zoology
BEGUM, A., Islamic History and Culture
BEGUM, A., Physics
BEGUM, F., Sanskrit and Pali
BEGUM, H. A., Education and Research
BEGUM, H. A., Psychology
BEGUM, H. J., Physics
BEGUM, K., Education and Research
BEGUM, L., Philosophy
BEGUM, M., Botany
BEGUM, N., Economics
BEGUM, N., Islamic History and Culture
BEGUM, R., Botany
BEGUM, R., Clinical Psychology
BEGUM, R., Education and Research
BEGUM, R., Marketing
BEGUM, S., Zoology
BEGUM, S. F., Social Welfare and Research
BEGUM, Z. N. T., Botany
BHATTACHARJEE, D. D., Management Studies
BHATTACHARJEE, H., Marketing
BHOWMIK, D. K., Sanskrit and Pali
BHOWMIK, N. C., Applied Physics and Electronics
BHUIYAN, G. M., Physics
BHUIYAN, M. A. H., Nutrition and Food Science
BHUIYAN, M. M. R., Statistics
BHUIYAN, M. S., Management Studies
BHUIYAN, M. S., Political Science
BHUIYAN, M. Z. H., Marketing
BHUIYAN, S., History
BILLAH, M. M., Statistics
BISWAS, N. C., Sanskrit and Pali
BORHANUDDIN, Geography and the Environment
BSAHAR, M. A., Botany
CHAKMA, N. K., Philosophy
CHOWDHURY, A., Zoology
CHOWDHURY, A. A. M. U., Finance
CHOWDHURY, A. B. M. H., Islamic Studies
CHOWDHURY, A. K. A., Clinical Psychology
CHOWDHURY, A. M., History
CHOWDHURY, A. M. S. U., Applied Chemistry and Chemical Technology
CHOWDHURY, A. R., Law
CHOWDHURY, A. U., Anthropology
CHOWDHURY, B., Bengali
CHOWDHURY, D. K., Accounting and Information Systems
CHOWDHURY, F., Mathematics
CHOWDHURY, G. M., Business Administration
CHOWDHURY, H. U., Political Science
CHOWDHURY, I. G., Business Administration
CHOWDHURY, L. H., Public Administration
CHOWDHURY, M. A., Economics
CHOWDHURY, M. A. I., Marketing
CHOWDHURY, M. A. M., Management Studies
CHOWDHURY, M. H., Social Welfare and Research
CHOWDHURY, M. M., Political Science
CHOWDHURY, M. M. R., Sociology
CHOWDHURY, M. R., Biochemistry and Molecular Biology
CHOWDHURY, M. R., Mathematics
CHOWDHURY, M. S., Physics
CHOWDHURY, M. S., Soil, Water and the Environment
CHOWDHURY, N., Statistics
CHOWDHURY, N., Women's Studies
CHOWDHURY, P. B., Management Studies
CHOWDHURY, Q. A., Sociology
CHOWDHURY, R. R., Accounting and Information Systems
CHOWDHURY, S., Physics
CHOWDHURY, S. Q., Geology
CHOWDHURY, T. A., Chemistry
DAS, A. K., Chemistry
DATTA, B. K., Pharmaceutical Chemistry

ELAHI, S. F., Soil, Water and the Environment
EUSUF, A. Z., Geography and the Environment
FAIZ, B., Soil, Water and the Environment
FAIZ, S. M. A., Soil, Water and the Environment
FAROUK, A. B. M., Pharmaceutical Technology
FERDAUSI, N., Physics
FERDAUSI, R. R., Mathematics
GHOSH, B., Bengali
GHOSH, S. N., Accounting and Information Systems
GOMES, D. J., Microbiology
HADIUZZAM, S., Botany
HAIDER, A. F. M. Y., Physics
HAIDER, A. R. M. A., Islamic Studies
HAKIM, M. A., Accounting and Information Systems
HALDER, A. K., Mathematics
HALIM, M. A., International Relations
HANNAN, F., Sociology
HAQ, M., Fine Arts
HAQ, M., Psychology
HAQ, M. M., Microbiology
HAQ, M. R., International Relations
HAQ, P., Psychology
HAQUE, A. N. M. S., Marketing
HAQUE, I., Sociology
HAQUE, K. B., Management Studies
HAQUE, M., Geology
HAQUE, M. A., Geology
HAQUE, M. E., Biochemistry and Molecular Biology
HAQUE, M. M. N., Education and Research
HAQUE, S. A., Bengali
HAROON, S. M. I., Mass Communication and Journalism
HASAN, C. M., Pharmaceutical Chemistry
HASAN, M. A., Botany
HASAN, M. N., Nutrition and Food Science
HASAN, M. S., Population Sciences
HASAN, P., Islamic History and Culture
HASAN, S. R., Marketing
HASHEM, A., Accounting and Information Systems
HASSAN, S. A., Political Science
HAYE, A. H. M. A., Modern Languages
HOSSAIN, A., Chemistry
HOSSAIN, A., International Relations
HOSSAIN, A., Public Administration
HOSSAIN, A. H. M. M., Islamic Studies
HOSSAIN, A. M. M. M., Nutrition and Food Science
HOSSAIN, B., Marketing
HOSSAIN, K. M., Sociology
HOSSAIN, K. M. A., English
HOSSAIN, M., Bengali
HOSSAIN, M. A., Biochemistry and Molecular Biology
HOSSAIN, M. A., Marketing
HOSSAIN, M. A., Mathematics
HOSSAIN, M. A., Pharmaceutical Chemistry
HOSSAIN, M. F., Political Science
HOSSAIN, M. H., Education and Research
HOSSAIN, M. I., Zoology
HOSSAIN, M. K., Finance
HOSSAIN, M. M., Botany
HOSSAIN, M. M., Mathematics
HOSSAIN, M. N., Arabic
HOSSAIN, M. Q., Geology
HOSSAIN, M. S., Geology
HOSSAIN, M. S., Geology
HOSSAIN, M. S., Physics
HOSSAIN, M. S., Soil, Water and the Environment
HOSSAIN, M. T., Physics
HOSSAIN, M. Z., Business Administration
HOSSAIN, N. M., Microbiology
HOSSAIN, S., English
HOSSAIN, S. A., Bengali
HOSSAIN, S. A., Soil, Water and the Environment
HOSSAIN, S. H., Geography and the Environment
HOSSAIN, S. M., Accounting and Information Systems
HOSSAIN, S. S., Statistical Research and Training
HOWLADER, M. M. A., Zoology
HOWLADER, S. R., Health Economics
HUDA, S. N., Nutrition and Food Science
HUQ, A. K. M. M. S., Political Science
HUQ, A. Q. M. F., Bengali
HUQ, D., Applied Chemistry and Chemical Technology
HUQ, K. M. H., English
HUQ, M. I., Botany
HUQ, R., English
HUQ, S., Soil, Water and the Environment
HUQ, S. A., English
HUQ, S. A., History
HUQ, S. M. F., English
HUQ, S. M. I., Soil, Water and the Environment
HUQ, Z. S. M. M., Geography and the Environment
IBRAHIM, M., Islamic History and Culture
IBRAHIM, M., Physics
ILYAS, K. S. M., Psychology
IMAM, M. B., Geology
IMAM, M. O., Finance
ISLAM, A., Philosophy
ISLAM, A. F. M. M., Business Administration
ISLAM, A. K. M. N., Botany
ISLAM, A. N., Philosophy
ISLAM, K., Nutrition and Food Science
ISLAM, K. M. S., Information Science and Library Management
ISLAM, L. N., Biochemistry and Molecular Biology
ISLAM, M. A., Chemistry
ISLAM, M. A., Marketing
ISLAM, M. A., Mathematics
ISLAM, M. A., Statistics
ISLAM, M. A., Zoology
ISLAM, M. M., History
ISLAM, M. M., Statistics
ISLAM, M. N., Mathematics
ISLAM, M. N., Political Science
ISLAM, M. N., Social Welfare and Research
ISLAM, M. N., Statistics
ISLAM, M. NAZRUL, Sociology
ISLAM, M. NURAL, Sociology
ISLAM, M. S., Applied Physics and Electronics
ISLAM, M. S., Biochemistry and Molecular Biology
ISLAM, M. S., Clinical Pharmacy and Pharmacology
ISLAM, M. S., English
ISLAM, M. S., Management Studies
ISLAM, N., Geography and the Environment
ISLAM, N., Psychology
ISLAM, R., Applied Chemistry and Chemical Technology
ISLAM, S. N., Nutrition and Food Science
ISLAM, T. S. A., Chemistry
ISLAM, Z., Anthropology
JAHAN, K., Nutrition and Food Science
JAHAN, N., Botany
JAHANGIR, M., Modern Languages
JALIL, R., Pharmaceutical Technology
JINNAH, M. A., Public Administration
KABIR, A., Bengali
KABIR, K. A., Physics
KABIR, M. H., Statistical Research and Training
KABIR, Y., Biochemistry and Molecular Biology
KADER, D. A., Modern Languages
KALAM, A., Microbiology
KALIMULLAH, N. A., Public Administration
KAMAL, A. H. A., History
KAMAL, B. A., Bengali
KAMAL, M. M. U., Marketing
KARIM, M. N., Management Studies
KARIM, N., Sociology
KARIM, R., Nutrition and Food Science
KARIM, S. F., Psychology
KARMAKER, J. L., Botany
KARMAKER, S. S., Management Studies
KHAIR, A., Chemistry
KHALEQUE, M. A., Physics
KHALILY, M. A. B., Finance
KHAN, A. A., Geology
KHAN, A. A., Management Studies
KHAN, A. K. M. S. I., Microbiology
KHAN, A. M. M. A. U., Geography and the Environment
KHAN, A. N. M. A. M., Arabic
KHAN, A. T. M. N. R., Bengali
KHAN, A. Z. M. N. A., Botany
KHAN, G. A., Philosophy
KHAN, H., Genetic Engineering and Biotechnology
KHAN, H. R., Zoology
KHAN, M. A. A., Education and Research
KHAN, M. A. H., Fine Arts
KHAN, M. A. H., Soil, Water and the Environment
KHAN, M. A. R., Banking
KHAN, M. A. R., Microbiology
KHAN, M. H., Fine Arts
KHAN, M. H. R., Economics
KHAN, M. H. R., Soil, Water and the Environment
KHAN, M. M., Accounting and Information Systems
KHAN, M. M., Public Administration
KHAN, M. M. I., Sociology
KHAN, M. N. I., Nutrition and Food Science
KHAN, M. S. H., Statistical Research and Training
KHAN, R. U., Bengali
KHAN, S., Public Administration
KHAN, S. A., Mass Communication and Journalism
KHAN, T. H., Soil, Water and the Environment
KHAN, Z. R., Public Administration
KHANAM, B. K., Fine Arts
KHANAM, H., Zoology
KHANAM, M., Psychology
KHANDAKER, M., Botany
KHANDAKER, M., Marketing
KHANDAKER, N., Economics
KHATUN, H., Geography and the Environment
KHATUN, H., Islamic History and Culture
KHATUN, K., Statistical Research and Training
KHATUN, M., Botany
KHATUN, R., Sociology
KHATUN, S., Arabic
KHUDA, B. A., Economics
KIBRIA, R., International Relations
KOWSER, F., Bengali
LATIFA, G. A., Zoology
MABUD, M. A., Arabic
MAHBUB, A. Q. M., Geography and the Environment
MAHMUD, A. H. W. U., Economics
MAHMUD, A. J., Chemistry
MAHMUD, S., Biochemistry and Molecular Biology
MAHMUD, S. H., Psychology
MAHMUDA, S., Bengali
MAHTAB, N., Women's Studies
MAJID, A. K. M. S., Business Administration
MAJUMDER, A. R., Physics
MALEK, M. A., Islamic Studies
MALEK, M. A., Microbiology
MALEK, M. A., Nutrition and Food Science
MALLICK, S. A., Statistics
MAMUM, M. K., History
MAMUN, M. A. A., Chemistry
MAMUN, M. Z., Business Administration
MANNAN, K. A., Mass Communication and Journalism
MANNAN, K. A. I. F. M., Physics
MANNAN, M. A., Management Studies
MANNAN, S. M., Information Science and Library Management
MATIN, A., Botany
MATIN, K. A., Statistical Research and Training
MATIN, M. A., Mathematics

MAWLA, A., Nutrition and Food Science
MAWLA, G., Nutrition and Food Science
MAZUMDAR, M. A. R., Soil, Water and the Environment
MAZUMDER, K. A. B., Persian and Urdu
MAZUMDER, R. K., Applied Physics and Electronics
MAZUMDER, T. I. M. A., Botany
MIAH, M. S., Bengali
MIAH, M. S., Education and Research
MIAH, M. S., Philosophy
MINA, M. S., Finance
MOHIUDDIN, M., Management Studies
MOHSIN, A., International Relations
MOKADDEM, M., Economics
MOLLAH, M. G., Political Science
MOLLAH, M. Y. A., Chemistry
MONDAL, A. C., Mathematics
MONDAL, R., Soil, Water and the Environment
MONSUR, M. H., Geology
MORSHED, A. J. M. H., Finance
MORSHED, M. S., Botany
MOSHIHUZZAMAN, M., Chemistry
MOWLA, S. G., Management Studies
MOYEEN, M. A., Management Studies
MUNSHI, M. S. H., Political Science
MUSA, A. M. M. A., Modern Languages
MUSTAFA, A. I., Applied Chemistry and Chemical Technology
MUTTAQUI, M. I. A., Education and Research
NABI, A. K. M. N., Population Sciences
NABI, M. R., Fine Arts
NAHAR, B., Nutrition and Food Science
NAHAR, L., Nutrition and Food Science
NAHAR, N., Chemistry
NASIRUDDIN, M., Finance
NASREEN, G. A., Mass Communication and Journalism
NAZNEEN, D. R. Z. A., Peace and Conflict Studies
NIZAMI, A. B. M. S. R., Arabic
OSMAN, B., Fine Arts
OSMANY, S. H., History
PAHA, N. A., Chemistry
PARVEEN, K. N., Political Science
PARVEEN, Z., Soil, Water and the Environment
PERVIN, S., Mathematics
QADRI, S. S., Biochemistry and Molecular Biology
QAIS, N., Clinical Pharmacy and Pharmacology
QUADER, M. A., Chemistry
QUASEM, M. A., Philosophy
QUDDUS, M. A., Marketing
QUDDUS, M. A., Mathematics
QUDDUS, M. M. A., Zoology
QUYYUM, M. A., Applied Chemistry and Chemical Technology
RAB, M. A., Geography and the Environment
RABBANI, K. S. E., Physics
RAFIQ, S., Applied Physics and Electronics
RAHIM, K. A., Biochemistry and Molecular Biology
RAHIM, T., Botany
RAHMA, P. K. M. M., Statistical Research and Training
RAHMAN, A., Health Economics
RAHMAN, A., Information Science and Library Management
RAHMAN, A., Modern Languages
RAHMAN, A. H. M. A., Political Science
RAHMAN, A. H. M. H., Finance
RAHMAN, A. H. M. M., Applied Chemistry and Chemical Technology
RAHMAN, A. H. M. M., Soil, Water and the Environment
RAHMAN, A. K. M. M., Information Technology
RAHMAN, A. M. M. H., Modern Languages
RAHMAN, A. S. M. A., Social Welfare and Research
RAHMAN, A. Z. M. A., Accounting and Information Systems
RAHMAN, B. W., Education and Research
RAHMAN, J., Applied Physics and Electronics
RAHMAN, K. M., Nutrition and Food Science
RAHMAN, K. M. M., Statistical Research and Training
RAHMAN, K. R., English
RAHMAN, M., Accounting and Information Systems
RAHMAN, M., Biochemistry and Molecular Biology
RAHMAN, M., Marketing
RAHMAN, M., Public Administration
RAHMAN, M. A., Chemistry
RAHMAN, M. A., Clinical Psychology
RAHMAN, M. A., Law
RAHMAN, M. A., Marketing
RAHMAN, M. A., Mathematics
RAHMAN, M. A., Physics
RAHMAN, M. A., Political Science
RAHMAN, M. F., Arabic
RAHMAN, M. F., Zoology
RAHMAN, M. G., Mass Communication and Journalism
RAHMAN, M. H., Pharmaceutical Technology
RAHMAN, M. H., Sociology
RAHMAN, M. K., Biochemistry and Molecular Biology
RAHMAN, M. K., Soil, Water and the Environment
RAHMAN, M. K., Zoology
RAHMAN, M. L., Computer Science and Engineering
RAHMAN, M. M., Arabic
RAHMAN, M. M., Chemistry
RAHMAN, M. M., Clinical Psychology
RAHMAN, M. M., Marketing
RAHMAN, M. M., Mathematics
RAHMAN, M. M., Microbiology
RAHMAN, M. M., Nutrition and Food Science
RAHMAN, M. M., Philosophy
RAHMAN, M. M., Physics
RAHMAN, M. M., Soil, Water and the Environment
RAHMAN, M. M., Statistics
RAHMAN, M. S., Bengali
RAHMAN, M. S., Education and Research
RAHMAN, M. S., Soil, Water and the Environment
RAHMAN, M. S., Statistics
RAHMAN, M. T., Mathematics
RAHMAN, N., Business Administration
RAHMAN, N., Sociology
RAHMAN, N. N., Pharmaceutical Chemistry
RAHMAN, R., Biochemistry and Molecular Biology
RAHMAN, S. M. L., Bengali
RAHMAN, S. M. M., Banking
RAISUDDIN, A. N. M., Islamic Studies
RASHED, K. B. S., Geography and the Environment
RASHID, A. H. M. H., Philosophy
RASHID, G. H., Soil, Water and the Environment
RASHID, H., Management Studies
RASHID, M. A., Pharmaceutical Chemistry
RASHID, M. H., Accounting and Information Systems
RASHID, M. H., Political Science
RASHID, M. H., Soil, Water and the Environment
RASHID, P., Botany
RASHID, R. I. M. A., Physics
ROY, K. N., English
ROY, P. K., Philosophy
SAHA, M., Applied Chemistry and Chemical Technology
SAHA, M. L., Botany
SAHA, P. K., Education and Research
SAHA, S. K., Accounting and Information Systems
SALAM, S. A., Mass Communication and Journalism
SALAMATULLAH, K., Nutrition and Food Science
SALEH, M. A., Management Studies
SALMA, U., Persian and Urdu
SAMAD, A., Biochemistry and Molecular Biology
SAMAD, M., Social Welfare and Research
SARKER, A. H., Social Welfare and Research
SARKER, A. M., Fine Arts
SARKER, N., Fisheries
SARKER, N. R., Psychology
SARKER, R. H., Botany
SATTER, M. A., Fine Arts
SATTER, M. A., Physics
SEN, K., Statistics
SERAJ, Z. I., Biochemistry and Molecular Biology
SHAFEE, A., Physics
SHAFEE, S., Physics
SHAFI, M., Geology
SHAH, A. K. F. H., Marketing
SHAH, A. S., Fine Arts
SHAHED, S. M., Bengali
SHAHED, S. N., Bengali
SHAHEEN, N., Nutrition and Food Science
SHAHIDULLAH, A. K. M., Political Science
SHAHIDULLAH, K., History
SHAHIDULLAH, S. M., Psychology
SHAHIDUZZAMAN, M., International Relations
SHAMIM, I., Sociology
SHAMSI, S., Botany
SHARIF, M. R. I., Applied Physics and Electronics
SHEIKH, M. D. H., Education and Research
SIDDIQ, A. F. M. A. B., Arabic
SIDDIQ, M. A. B., Arabic
SIDDIQUE, A. A. M. S. A., Mass Communication and Journalism
SIDDIQUE, A. H., Management Studies
SIDDIQUE, S. A., Accounting and Information Systems
SIDDIQUE, T. A., Political Science
SIKDER, S. A., Fine Arts
SUFI, G. B., Zoology
SUKLADAS, J. C., Accounting and Information Systems
SULTANA, A., Mass Communication and Journalism
SULTANA, A., Philosophy
SYED, S., Nutrition and Food Science
TAHER, M. A., Social Welfare and Research
TALUKDER, A. S., Marketing
TASLIM, M. A., Economics
THAKURATA, M. G., International Relations
UDDIN, M. J., Education and Research
ULLAH, A. S. M. O., Geology
ULLAH, S. M., Soil, Water and Environment
WADUD, N., Psychology
WAHID, A. Q. F., Philosophy
YUSUF, H. K. M., Biochemistry and Molecular Biology
ZAFAR, M. A., Bengali
ZAMAN, F., Fine Arts
ZAMAN, N., English
ZAMAN, S. U., Economics

ATTACHED INSTITUTES

Institute of Business Administration: University of Dhaka, Dhaka 1000; tel. (2) 9661900; e-mail iba@univdhaka.edu; internet www.iba-du.edu; f. 1966; attached to Univ. of Dhaka; promotes business education in Bangladesh; Dir Prof. G. M. CHOWDHURY.

Institute of Social Welfare and Research: University of Dhaka, Dhaka 1000; tel. (2) 8622860; e-mail duregstr@bangla.net; f. 1973; attached to Univ. of Dhaka; Dir Dr MUHAMMAD SAMAD.

BUREAUX AND RESEARCH CENTRES

Bureau of Economic Research: University of Dhaka, Dhaka 1000; tel. (2) 9661900; f. 1956; attached to Univ. of Dhaka; research in the field of economics and related subjects; Dir Prof. FARID UDDIN AHMED.

Biotechnology Research Centre: University of Dhaka, Dhaka 1000; tel. (2) 9661900; e-mail lailanislam@yahoo.com; f. 1985;

attached to Univ. of Dhaka; research in the fields of health and agriculture applying biotechnology; Dir Prof. Dr LAYLA NUR ISLAM.

Bose Centre for Advanced Studies and Research in Natural Sciences: University of Dhaka, Dhaka 1000; tel. (2) 9661900; f. 1974; attached to Univ. of Dhaka; undertakes research projects in faculty of science; Dir Prof. SHAMIMA K. CHOUDHURY.

Bureau of Business Research: University of Dhaka, Dhaka 1000; tel. (2) 9661900; f. 1974; attached to Univ. of Dhaka; research in areas of commerce, industry, trade; Dir Prof. Dr MAHMOD OSMAN IMAM.

Centre for Advanced Research in Arts and Social Sciences: University of Dhaka, Dhaka 1000; tel. (2) 9661900; f. 2005; attached to Univ. of Dhaka; research in Arts and Social Sciences; Dir Prof. Dr A. H. AHMED KAMAL.

Centre for Advanced Research in Social Sciences: University of Dhaka, Dhaka 1000; tel. (2) 9661900; f. 1974; attached to Univ. of Dhaka; conducts research on key policy management issues affecting Bangladesh's economic, social, admin., and political devt; Dir Prof. Dr MAMTAZ UDDIN AHMED.

Centre for Advanced Studies and Research in Biological Sciences: University of Dhaka, Dhaka 1000; tel. (2) 9661900; e-mail coe@univdhaka.edu; f. 1975; attached to Univ. of Dhaka; research activities in the faculty of biological sciences; Dir Prof. KHONDOKER MONIRUZZAMAN.

Centre for Advanced Studies in Humanities: University of Dhaka, Dhaka 1000; tel. (2) 9661900; f. 1984; attached to Univ. of Dhaka; encourages and creates interdepartmental research works and research facilities; arranges discussions, meetings and lectures in various subjects; publishes research articles, books; gives research scholarships; library of 250 vols; Dir Prof. Dr NURUR RAHMAN KHAN.

Centre for Development and Policy Research: University of Dhaka, Dhaka 1000; tel. (2) 9661900; f. 1928; attached to Univ. of Dhaka; promotes free market economy and democratic, political culture; Dir Prof. Dr FAZLUL HAQUE SHAH.

Delta Research Centre: University of Dhaka, Dhaka 1000; tel. (2) 9661900; e-mail dsc@univdhaka.edu; f. 1990; attached to Univ. of Dhaka; geological studies of Bengal delta region; Dir Prof. Dr MOSTAFA ALAM.

Development Centre of Philosophical Research: University of Dhaka, Dhaka 1000; tel. (2) 9661900; f. 1980; attached to Univ. of Dhaka; research in philosophy esp. in areas of human welfare, social progress, world brotherhood; Dir Prof. Dr AZIZUNNAHAR ISLAM; publ. *Darshan O Progati* (in Bengali), *Philosophy and Progress* (in English).

Disaster Research Training and Management Centre: University of Dhaka, Dhaka 1000; tel. (2) 9661900; e-mail drtmc.du@gmail.com; f. 1989; attached to Univ. of Dhaka; conducts scientific research, professional training in the field of disaster management; disseminates knowledge through published materials and seminars; assists govt to develop disaster related curriculum and manpower; Dir Prof. Dr A. M. M. AMANAT ULLAH KHAN; publ. *Duryogbarta* (2 a year).

Semiconductor Technology Research Centre: University of Dhaka, Dhaka 1000; tel. (2) 9661900; f. 1985; attached to Univ. of Dhaka; research in the field of semiconductor materials, semiconductor device fabrication; thin film technology; Dir Prof. A. K. M. MAKBULUR RAHMAN

UNIVERSITY OF INFORMATION TECHNOLOGY AND SCIENCES

Jamalpur Twin Tower (Tower 2), Baridhara View, GA–37/1 Pragati Sharani, Baridhara J-Block, Dhaka 1212
Telephone: (2) 8899751
E-mail: vc@uits.edu.bd
Internet: www.uits.edu.bd

Founded 2003
Private control
Academic year: 3 semesters

Faculties of business, liberal arts, science and engineering

Chancellor: PRES. OF THE PEOPLE'S REPUBLIC OF BANGLADESH
Chair.: AL HAJ SUFI MOHAMED MIZANUR RAHMAN CHOWDHURY
Vice-Chancellor: Prof. MOHAMMED ABDUL AZIZ
Librarian: MD KAMRUZZAMAN

UNIVERSITY OF LIBERAL ARTS BANGLADESH

House 56, Rd 4/A Satmasjid Rd, Dhanmondi, Dhaka 1209
Telephone: (2) 9661255
E-mail: communications@ulab.edu.bd
Internet: www.ulab.edu.bd

Founded 2004
Private control
Academic year: May to May (3 semesters)

Faculties of arts and humanities, business, science and engineering, social science

Chancellor: PRES. OF THE PEOPLE'S REPUBLIC OF BANGLADESH
Pres.: KAZI SHAHID AHMED
Vice-Chancellor: Prof. RAFIQUL ISLAM
Pro-Vice-Chancellor: Prof. IMRAN RAHMAN
Registrar: KHALED MAHMOOD KHAN
Deputy Librarian: K. M. HASAN EMAM

Publications: *Crossings: ULAB Journal of English Studies* (1 a year), *ULAB Journal of Science and Engineering* (2 a year)

UNIVERSITY OF RAJSHAHI

Motihar, Rajshahi 6205
Telephone: (721) 711011
E-mail: registrar@ru.ac.bd
Internet: www.ru.ac.bd

Founded 1953
Languages of instruction: Bengali, English
Academic year: July to June (3 terms)

Chancellor: PRES. OF THE PEOPLE'S REPUBLIC OF BANGLADESH
Vice-Chancellor: Prof. MUHAMMAD MIZANUDDIN
Pro-Vice-Chancellor: Prof. CHOWDHURY SARWAR JAHAN
Registrar: Prof. MUHAMMAD ENTAZUL HUQUE
Librarian: (vacant)

Library: see under Libraries and Archives
Number of teachers: 1,225
Number of students: 26,000

Publications: *Calendar* (every 2 years), *Rajshahi University Studies* (1 a year)

DEANS

Faculty of Agriculture: Dr SHAHANA QAIS
Faculty of Arts: Prof. KHANDAKER FORHAD HOSSAIN
Faculty of Business Studies: Prof. M. AMJAD HOSSAIN
Faculty of Engineering: Prof. ABU BAKAR MD ISMAIL
Faculty of Law: BISWAJIT CHANDA
Faculty of Life and Earth Science: Prof. M. ABDUL LATIF
Faculty of Medicine: Prof. SYED GOLAM KIBRIA
Faculty of Science: Prof. M. HABIBUR RAHMAN
Faculty of Social Science: Prof. NILUFAR SULTANA

PROFESSORS

Faculty of Agriculture:

ALAM, A. M. S., Agronomy and Agricultural Extension
ALAM, M. N., Crop Science and Technology
ALI, M. K., Crop Science and Technology
ALIM, M. A., Agronomy and Agricultural Extension
ASGAR, M. A., Crop Science and Technology
AZAD, M. A. K., Crop Science and Technology
BAREE, M. A., Crop Science and Technology
BORKATULLAH, M. A., Crop Science and Technology
CHOWDHURY, F., Agronomy and Agricultural Extension
HOQUE, M., Agronomy and Agricultural Extension
HOSSAIN, M. A., Agronomy and Agricultural Extension
IQBAL, M. T., Fisheries
ISLAM, M. K., Crop Science and Technology
ISLAM, M. S., Crop Science and Technology
MOSLEH-UDDIN, M., Crop Science and Technology
RAHMAN, M. A., Agronomy and Agricultural Extension
RAHMAN, M. M., Agronomy and Agricultural Extension
SARDER, M. J., Animal Husbandry and Veterinary Science
TARIQUE, M. H., Agronomy and Agricultural Extension

Faculty of Arts:

AHMAD, S., Islamic History and Culture
AHMED, I., Islamic History and Culture
AHMED, L., Languages
AKHTARA, B., Arabic
AKTER, M. S., Islamic History and Culture
ALAM, A. K. M. S., Arabic
ALAM, M. S., History
AL-GALIB, M. A., Arabic
ALI, M. A., English
ALI, M. A., Philosophy
AMIN, M. R., Islamic Studies
ANOWAR, M. S., Fine Arts
ASADUZZAMAN, M., Islamic Studies
ASHRAF-UZ-ZAMAN, M., Islamic Studies
BAKR, S. M. A., Philosophy
BALA, A., Bengali
BARI, M., Islamic History and Culture
BEGUM, G. N., Fine Arts
BISWAS, N. R., Languages
BULU, D. A., Islamic History and Culture
CHOWDHURY, M., Fine Arts
CHOWDHURY, M. A. M., Languages
DAS, A. K., English
FARUK-UZZAMAN, M., History
FARUQUE, M. G., Fine Arts
HAMID, S., Bengali
HAQ, M. M., Islamic History and Culture
HAQUE, M. A., Islamic History and Culture
HAQUE, M. F., Islamic History and Culture
HARUN-OR-RASHID, M., Bengali
HOSSAIN, K. F., Bengali
HOSSAIN, M. B., Islamic Studies
HOSSAIN, S. M. Z., Fine Arts
HOUDA, M. N., Languages
HOWLADER, M. S., Arabic
IQBAL, M. S., Bengali
ISLAM, M. J., English
ISLAM, M. M., History
ISLAM, M. R., Islamic Studies
ISLAM, M. S., Islamic Studies
ISLAM, P. M. S., Bengali
JAHANGIR, A. W. K. M., Arabic
KAMALI, H. A., Languages
KAMALUDDIN, M., Languages
KASHEM, M. A., History
KHALED, M., History
KHAN, M. S., Languages
KHATUN, F., History

KHATUN, M., History
KHATUN, S. N. K., Islamic History and Culture
KUMAR, S. S., Bengali
LATIF, A. K. M. A., Islamic Studies
MIAN, M. A. S., Arabic
MISRA, C. R., History
NAKIBULLAH, M., Arabic
NIZAMUDDIN, M., Arabic
QAIS, M., Bengali
QAIYUM, M. N., History
RAHMAN, K. M. M., Islamic History and Culture
RAHMAN, M. M., Fine Arts
RAHMAN, M. M., History
RAHMAN, M. M., Islamic Studies
RAZA, A. K. M. M., Bengali
SALAM, M. A., Arabic
SALAM, S. M. A., Arabic
SAMADI, S., Bengali
SARKER, J. N., Philosophy
SARKER, M. S. H., Philosophy
SHAHJAHAN, A. B. M., Islamic History and Culture
SHEREZZAMAN, M., History
SIDDIQUE, M. A. B., Arabic
SIDDIQUEE, A. F. M. R. K., English
SIDDIQUEE, M. M., Islamic History and Culture
TAHER, A., Fine Arts
TALUKDAR, S. S., Fine Arts
TALUKDER, A. H., Philospohy
TALUKDER, A. M., Fine Arts
TAQUI, F. M. A. H., Islamic Studies

Faculty of Business Studies:

ABDULLAH-AL-HAROON, M., Accounting and Information Systems
ABEDIN, M. M. M., Accounting and Information Systems
AHMED, R. A., Finance and Banking
ALAM, M. S., Accounting and Information Systems
ALI, M. A., Management Studies
ALI, M. S. N., Management Studies
ALI, M. B., Marketing
ANSARI, R., Finance and Banking
AZAD, M. R., Marketing
BANU, S., Accounting and Information Systems
BHOWMICK, M. K., Management Studies
CHOWDHURY, A. Z. K., Finance and Banking
CHOWDHURY, M. A. M., Accounting and Information Systems
DEY, M. M., Accounting and Information Systems
HAQUE, A. H. M. Z., Finance and Banking
HENA, H., Management Studies
HOSSAIN, D. A., Accounting and Information Systems
HOSSAIN, M. A., Finance and Banking
HOSSAIN, M. E., Marketing
HOSSAIN, M. Z., Finance and Banking
HOSSAIN, S. Z., Accounting and Information Systems
ISLAM, M. A., Accounting and Information Systems
ISLAM, M. F., Marketing
ISLAM, M. N., Finance and Banking
ISLAM, M. O., Management Studies
ISLAM, M. R., Management Studies
ISLAM, M. R., Marketing
ISLAM, M. S., Management Studies
ISLAM, M. T., Accounting and Information Systems
KABIR, M. H., Accounting and Information Systems
KABIR, S. M., Marketing
KHAN, A. B. M. M., Management Studies
KHAN, M. M. I., Finance and Banking
KHATUN, M. F., Accounting and Information Systems
MAINUDDIN, M., Accounting and Information Systems
MAJID, A. K. M. A., Finance and Banking
MONDAL, A. K. M., Marketing
MOSTAFA, M. G., Management Studies
NURULLAH, S. M., Management Studies
NURUZZAMAN, M., Marketing
PRAMANIK, M. A. R., Accounting and Information Systems
QUDDUS, A., Finance and Banking
RAHMAN, A. K., Marketing
RAHMAN, M. H., Finance and Banking
RAHMAN, M. M., Finance and Banking
RAHMAN, M. N., Marketing
REZA, M. S., Marketing
SADIQUE, M. Z., Finance and Banking
SAHA, S. K., Marketing
SAYADUZZAMAN, M., Accounting and Information Systems
SHAMSUDDIN, M., Marketing
SHIL, S. C., Accounting and Information Systems

Faculty of Engineering:

AHMAD, S., Computer Science and Engineering
AHSAN, M. S., Applied Chemistry and Chemical Engineering
ALAM, M. T., Applied Chemistry and Chemical Engineering
ALI, M. R., Applied Chemistry and Chemical Engineering
ALI, S. M. M., Applied Chemistry and Chemical Engineering
AZAD, M. A. K., Applied Chemistry and Chemical Engineering
AZAD, M. A. K., Applied Chemistry and Chemical Engineering
BAKR, M. A., Applied Chemistry and Chemical Engineering
BEGUM, D. A., Applied Chemistry and Chemical Engineering
BISWAS, R. K., Applied Chemistry and Chemical Engineering
ENAYETULLAH, S., Applied Physics and Electronics Engineering
HABIB, M. A., Applied Chemistry and Chemical Engineering
HASHEM, M. A., Applied Physics and Electronics Engineering
HOSSAIN, M. M., Applied Physics and Electronics Engineering
ISLAM, M. J., Applied Physics and Electronic Engineering
ISLAM, M. R., Applied Physics and Electronics Engineering
ISMAIL, A. B. M., Applied Physics and Electronics Engineering
KERAMAT, M., Applied Physics and Electronics Engineering
KHANKER, M. M., Applied Physics and Electronic Engineering
MIAH, M. A. A., Applied Physics and Electronics Engineering
MOLLA, M. A. H., Applied Chemistry and Chemical Engineering
MOLLA, M. K. I., Computer Science and Engineering
MONDAL, M. I. H., Applied Chemistry and Chemical Engineering
MOSTAFA, C. M., Applied Chemistry and Chemical Engineering
NAHID, M. A. I., Applied Physics and Electronic Engineering
RAHMAN, M. S., Applied Chemistry and Chemical Engineering
RAKIBUZZAMAN, M., Applied Chemistry and Chemical Engineering
SALAM, S. M. A., Applied Chemistry and Chemical Engineering
SALAM, S. M. A., Applied Physics and Electronic Engineering
SAYEED, M. A., Applied Chemistry and Chemical Engineering
SHEIKH, M. R. K., Applied Physics and Electronic Engineering
SOBHAN, M. A., Applied Physics and Electronics Engineering
TALUKDER, M. M. R., Applied Physics and Electronics Engineering

Faculty of Law:

HANNAN, M. A., Law
HOSSAIN, M. A., Law
KABIR, M. A., Law
SIDDIQUA, B. A., Law

Faculty of Life and Earth Science:

AFROZ, N., Psychology
AHMED, M., Geology and Mining
AHMED, R., Geography and Environmental Studies
AHMED, S. S., Geology and Mining
ALAM, M. F., Botany
ALAM, M. S., Botany
ALAM, M. S., Geology and Mining
ALAM, M. S. A., Geography and Environmental Studies
ALAM, M. Z., Geology and Mining
ALI, I. A., Zoology
ALI, M., Zoology
AMIN, M. N., Botany
ANISUZZAMAN, M., Botany
BEGUM, M. F., Botany
DAS, B. C., Zoology
DEB, A. C., Genetic Engineering and Biotechnology
ELIAS, M. S., Psychology
ENAM, S., Psychology
FARUKI, M. S. I., Zoology
FERDOUSI, Z., Genetic Engineering and Biotechnology
HAIDER, S. A., Botany
HAQUE, K. E., Geology and Mining
HAQUE, M. M., Zoology
HASAN, M. M., Zoology
HASSAN, M. Z., Geography and Environmental Studies
HOSSAIN, M. M., Botany
HOSSAIN, M. S., Genetic Engineering and Biotechnology
HOSSAIN, N., Botany
HUQ, M. E., Psychology
ISLAM, A. K., Botany
ISLAM, M. B., Geology and Mining
ISLAM, M., Zoology
ISLAM, M., Zoology
ISLAM, M. S., Zoology
KABIR, S., Geology and Mining
KEYA, M. K., Psychology
KHALEKUZZAMAN, M., Genetic Engineering and Biotechnology
KHALEKUZZAMAN, M., Zoology
KHAN, M. A. R., Zoology
KHAN, M. M., Psychology
KHAN, Y. A., Geology and Mining
LATIF, M. A., Psychology
LAZ, R., Zoology
MANNAN, M. A., Zoology
MAZUMDER, Q. H., Geology and Mining
MOHAMMAD, N., Geography and Environmental Studies
NAHAR, S., Botany
NAZ, S., Botany
NURULLAH, M., Psychology
PARVEEN, S., Zoology
PAUL, N. K., Botany
RAHMAN, A. S., Zoology
RAHMAN, M. A., Geography and Environmental Studies
RAHMAN, M. H., Geography and Environmental Studies
RAHMAN, M. H., Zoology
RAHMAN, M. H., Geology and Mining
RAHMAN, M. R., Geography and Environmental Studies
RAHMAN, S. M., Zoology
REZA, A. M. S., Zoology
ROY, M. K., Geology and Mining
RUMI, S. R., Geography and Environmental Studies
SAHA, A. K., Zoology
SALAM, M. A., Zoology
SARKER, M. A., Botany

SHAIKH, M. A., Geography and Environmental Studies
SHOEB, A. Z. M., Geography and Environmental Studies
SIKDAR, B., Genetic Engineering and Biotechnology
SUFI, A. H., Psychology
SULTAN-UL-ISLAM, M., Geology and Mining
ZAMAN, S., Genetic Engineering and Biotechnology
ZIAUDDIN, S. M., Psychology

Faculty of Science:
AHMAD, H., Chemistry
AHSAN, M. R., Physics
AKHTER, M. N., Mathematics
ALAM, S. M., Chemistry
ALFAZ UDDIN, M., Physics
ALI, D. M., Mathematics
ALI, M. A., Applied Mathematics
ALI, M. A., Chemistry
ALI, M. H., Chemistry
ALI, M. U., Mathematics
ANSARI, M. A., Mathematics
ANWAR-UL-ISLAM, M., Pharmacy
ASADUZZAMAN, M., Mathematics
BEGUM, A. A., Statistics
BELALUDDIN, M., Biochemistry and Molecular Biology
BHATTACHARJEE, S., Physics
BHATTACHARJEE, S. K., Statistics
BISWAS, K. K., Biochemistry and Molecular Biology
DEY, K. K., Mathematics
FAROOQUE, M. A., Chemistry
GAFUR, M. A., Pharmacy
GONI, M. A., Physics
HAKIM, M. O., Physics
HAQUE, A. B., Chemistry
HAQUE, A. K., Physics
HAQUE, M. E., Physics
HAQUE, M. E., Physics
HAQUE, M. S., Biochemistry and Molecular Biology
HASSAN, M. T., Chemistry
HOQUE, M. A., Mathematics
HOQUE, M. A., Statistics
HOSSAIN, M. A., Mathematics
HOSSAIN, M. G., Statistics
HOSSAIN, M. K., Biochemistry and Molecular Biology
HOSSAIN, M. R., Statistics
HOSSAIN, M. T., Biochemistry and Molecular Biology
HOWLADER, M. B., Chemistry
HUQUE, M. E., Chemistry
ISLAM, F. N., Physics
ISLAM, M. A., Biochemistry and Molecular Biology
ISLAM, M. A., Chemistry
ISLAM, M. N., Chemistry
ISLAM, M. N., Chemistry
ISLAM, M. N., Statistics
ISLAM, M. R., Population Science and Human Resource Development
ISLAM, M. S., Physics
ISLAM, M. S., Chemistry
ISLAM, M. S., Chemistry
JASMINE, H. A., Mathematics
KARIM, M. R., Biochemistry and Molecular Biology
KARIM, M. R., Statistics
KARMOKAR, P. K., Statistics
KHAN, M. K., Physics
KHANAM, J. A., Biochemistry and Molecular Biology
LATIF, M. A., Mathematics
LUCY, I. B., Physics
MIAH, M. A. J., Chemistry
MIAN, M. A., Statistics
MOLLAH, M. N., Statistics
MORTUZA, M. G., Physics
MOSADDIK, M. A., Pharmacy
MOSTAFA, M. G., Population Science and Human Resource Development
NASSER, M., Statistics
NIKKON, F., Biochemistry and Molecular Biology
PAUL, A. C., Mathematics
PAUL, G. C., Mathematics
PERVEEN, F., Biochemistry and Molecular Biology
PRAMANIK, J. N., Mathematics
PRAMANIK, M. W., Mathematics
RAHMAN, J. A., Population Science and Human Resource Development
RAHMAN, M. H., Biochemistry and Molecular Biology
RAHMAN, M. H., Chemistry
RAHMAN, M. L., Mathematics
RAHMAN, M. M., Physics
RAHMAN, M. M., Statistics
RAHMAN, M. S., Statistics
RAZZAQUE, M. A., Statistics
REZA, M. Y., Chemistry
ROY, D. C., Statistics
ROY, H. N., Chemistry
ROY, N., Biochemistry and Molecular Biology
SADIQUE, M. G., Pharmacy
SANA, N. K., Biochemistry and Molecular Biology
SARKAR, M. J., Physics
SARKAR, S. K., Statistics
SARKER, M. S., Applied Mathematics
SAUD, M. Z., Biochemistry and Molecular Biology
SHAH, M. A., Statistics
SHAHA, R. K., Biochemistry and Molecular Biology
SHAHJAHAN, M., Biochemistry and Molecular Biology
SHANTA, S. S., Mathematics
SULTANA, N., Mathematics
SULTANA, Q. S., Mathematics
TARIQ, A. S., Physics
WAHED, M. I., Pharmacy
ZAKARIA, C., Chemistry
ZAMAN, M., Chemistry

Faculty of Social Science:
AHMED, M. K., Political Science
AHSAN, M. T., Folklore
AKMAM, W., Sociology
ALI, M., Economics
AMIN, M. R., Political Science
ANSARUDDIN, M., Political Science
AREFIN, M. S., Social Work
ASHRAFUZZAMAN, M., Social Work
BHUIYAN, M. A., Social Work
CHOWDHURY, M. A., Social Work
CHOWDHURY, S., Folklore
EMAJUDDIN, M., Social Work
HAIDER, S. K., Social Work
HOSSAIN, M. A., Folklore
HOSSAIN, M. E., Economics
IMAM, M. H., Sociology
ISLAM, A. K., Sociology
ISLAM, M. F., Social Work
ISLAM, M. R., Economics
ISLAM, M. Z., Sociology
JALALUDDIN, M., Social Work
KARIM, K. M., Social Work
KHAN, M. M., Economics
KHANAM, S. M., Sociology
MAMUN, S. A., Social Work
MIAH, M. N., Political Science
NOMAN, A. N., Economics
OBAIDULLAH, A. T., Public Administration
PANDAY, P. K., Public Administration
QUASEM, M. A., Political Science
QUAYUM, M. A., Economics
RAHMAN, A. H., Sociology
RAHMAN, K. B., Economics
RAHMAN, M. A., Folklore
RAHMAN, M. M., Political Science
RAHMAN, M. S., Political Science
RAZY, S. M., Political Science
SIDDIQUA, M., Folklore
SIDDIQUEE, M. A., Sociology
SULTANA, N., Sociology
WADUD, M. A., Economics
ZAMAN, N., Political Science

UNIVERSITY OF SCIENCE AND TECHNOLOGY CHITTAGONG

Foy's Lake, Chittagong 4202
Telephone: (31) 659069
E-mail: info@ustc.ac.bd
Internet: www.ustc.ac.bd

Founded 1989 as Institute of Applied Health Sciences
Private control

Vice-Chancellor: Prof. Dr NURUL ISLAM
Pro-Vice-Chancellor: Prof. Dr M. JAFAR ALAM
Registrar: Prof. SHAMS-UD-DOHA
Librarian: M. JASIMUDDIN

Publication: *University of Science and Technology Annual (USTA)*

DEANS

Faculty of Basic Medical and Pharmaceutical Sciences: Prof. Dr SAHADAT HOSSAIN
Faculty of Business Administration: Assoc. Prof. SURAJIT SARBABIDYA
Faculty of Medicine: Prof. Dr M. REZAUL KARIM
Faculty of Science, Engineering and Technology: Prof. Dr M. ABDUS SAMAD
Faculty of Social Sciences and Humanities: TOFAIL AHMED

UNIVERSITY OF SOUTH ASIA

House 76–78, Rd 14, Block B, Banani, Dhaka 1213
Telephone: (2) 8857073
E-mail: info@unisa.ac.bd
Internet: www.unisa.ac.bd
Private control
Academic year: January to December (3 semesters)

Faculties of arts, business administration, public health and life sciences, science and information technology

Chancellor: PRES. OF THE PEOPLE'S REPUBLIC OF BANGLADESH
Vice-Chancellor: Prof. M. A. MATIN
Pro-Vice-Chancellor: Prof. Dr M. A. MUHIT
Registrar: Prof. Dr NASER AHMED

UTTARA UNIVERSITY

House 04 Rd 15, Sector 06, Uttara, Dhaka 1230
Telephone: (2) 8919794
E-mail: uumain_edu@yahoo.com
Internet: www.uttarauniversity.edu.bd

Founded 2003
Private control

Faculties of arts and social science, business, education and physical education, science and engineering

Chair.: Dr M. FAZLUL HAQUE
Vice-Chancellor: Dr M. AZIZUR RAHMAN
Library Officer: MUHAMMAD SARWAR HOSSAIN
Library of 30,000 vols

VICTORIA UNIVERSITY OF BANGLADESH

69/K Panthapath, Dhaka 1205
Telephone: (2) 8622634
E-mail: info@vub.edu.bd
Internet: www.vub.edu.bd

Founded 2003
Private control

Depts of business administration, English, tourism and hospitality management

Vice-Chancellor: Prof. Dr CURTIS R. DOYLE
Registrar: A. K. MONSUR AHMED

WORLD UNIVERSITY OF BANGLADESH

Unit-1, Main Campus House 3/A, Rd 4, Dhanmondi, Dhaka 1205
Telephone: (2) 9611410
E-mail: info@wub.edu.bd
Internet: www.wub.edu.bd
Founded 2003
Private control
Faculties of arts, business, engineering, pharmacy
Chancellor: Pres. of the People's Republic of Bangladesh
Vice-Chancellor: Prof. Dr Abdul Mannan Choudhury

Colleges

Armed Forces Medical College: Dhaka Cantonment, Dhaka; e-mail info@afmcbd.com; internet www.afmcbd.com; f. 1999; depts of anaesthesiology, anatomy, biochemistry, community medicine, dermatology and venereology, forensic medicine, medicine with allied subject, microbiology, obstetrics and gynaecology, ophthalmology, orthopaedic surgery, otorhinolarygnology and head neck surgery, paediatrics, pathology, pharmacology, physiology, psychiatry, radiology and imaging, surgery with allied subjects, transfusion medicine; Chair. Md Jahangir Hossain Mollik; Dir of Training Md Shahadat Hossain Sharif; publ. *Journal of AFMC*.

Bangladesh College of Leather Technology: 44–50 Hazaribagh, Dhaka 1209; tel. (2) 8617439; e-mail bclt47@yahoo.com; internet www.bclt.com.bd; f. 1949; constituent college of Univ. of Dhaka under the faculty of engineering and technology; graduate courses in footwear technology, leather technology, leather product technology; library: 10,689 vols, 2,343 journals; 22 teachers; 1,000 students; Prin. Prof. Dr Md Fazlul Karim.

Bangladesh College of Physicians and Surgeons: 67 Shaheed Tajuddin Ahmed Sarani, Mohakhali, Dhaka 1212; tel. (2) 8825005; e-mail bcps@bcps-bd.org; internet www.bcpsbd.org; f. 1972; offers postgraduate medical education; faculties of anaesthesiology, basic sciences, family medicine, gynaecology and obstetrics, haematology, medicine, ophthalmology, otolaryngology, paediatrics, physical medicine and rehabilitation, psychiatry, radiology-imaging and radiotherapy, surgery incl. dentistry; library: 5,130 vols, 5,200 dissertations, 125 periodicals; Pres. Prof. Dr Mahmud Hasan; Sr Vice-Pres. Prof. Dr Md Sanawar Hossain; Vice-Pres. Prof. Dr Abdul Kader Khan; publ. *Journal of Bangladesh College of Physicians and Surgeons*.

Begumgonj Textile Engineering College: Begumgonj, Noakhali; tel. (321) 51758; f. 1918, current name adopted 2007; offers BSc in textile engineering; Prin. Md Abdul Mannan.

BGC Trust Medical College: BGC Biddyanagar, Chandanaish, Chittagong; tel. (443) 4482197; e-mail bgctmc@yahoo.com; f. 2002; depts of anatomy, biochemistry, community medicine, physiology; 630 students; Prin. Prof. Dr Mohammad Faridul Islam.

Chattagram International Dental College: 206/1 Haji Chand Meah Rd, Shamserpara, Chandgaon, Chittagong; tel. (31) 672062; e-mail info.cidchbd@gmail.com; internet www.cidch.org; f. 2003; offers Bachelors degree in dental surgery; Chair. Prof. Kazi Deen Mohammad; Prin. Prof. Dr Kazi Mehdih ul Alam; Academic Dir Dr Md Muslim Uddin.

Chittagong Medical College: 57 K. B. Fazlul Kader Rd, P. S.–Panchlaish, P. O. Chawkbazar, Chittagong; tel. (31) 619400; e-mail info@cmc.edu.bd; internet www.cmc.edu.bd; f. 1957; offers dental and medical undergraduate courses; medical postgraduate courses; Prin. Prof. Dr Selim Mohammed Jahangir; Vice-Chancellor Prof. Dr Aminuddin A. Khan.

City Dental College: 1085/1, Malibagh Chowdhury Para, Dhaka 1219; tel. (2) 8331307; e-mail citydentalcollege@gmail.com; internet citydentalcollege.googlepages.com; f. 1996; offers Bachelor of dental surgery courses; library: 5,863 vols, 855 journals; 112 teachers; 342 students; Chair. Dr A. S. M. Badruddoza; Rector Prof. N. I. Khan; Prin. Prof. Dr Aziza Begum; publ. *City Dental College Journal*.

Dhaka College: Mirpur Rd, P.O. New Market, Dhanmondi, Dhaka 1205; tel. (2) 8611354; e-mail info@dhakacollege.edu.bd; internet www.dhakacollege.edu.bd; f. 1835, college status 1841, present status 1858; depts of accounting, Arabic and Islamic studies, Bengali, botany, chemistry, economics, English, geography, history, Islamic history and culture, management, mathematics, philosophy, physics, political science, psychology, social science, statistics, zoology; library: 30,000 vols; Prin. Dr Ayesha Begum; Vice-Prin. Dr Md Ashraf Ali Khan; Librarian Kaniz Mouluda Akhter.

Dhaka Medical College: Near Shahbagh, Dhaka 1000; tel. (2) 9669340; e-mail dmc_principal@yahoo.com; internet www.dmc.edu.bd; f. 1946; Prin. Prof. Dr Quazi Deen Mohammad; Vice-Prin. Prof. Md Margub Hussain.

Dhaka National Medical College: 53/1, Johnson Rd, Dhaka 1100; tel. (2) 7118272; e-mail info@dnmc.edu.bd; internet www.dnmc.edu.bd; f. 1925 as Dhaka National Medical Institute, current name adopted and status 1994; depts of anaesthesiology, anatomy, biochemistry, cardiology, community medicine, dentistry, forensic medicine and toxicology, medicine, microbiology, obstetrics and gynaecology, ophthalmology, orthopaedics, otolaryngology, paediatrics, pathology, pharmacology and therapeutics, physiology, radiology and imaging, skin and VD, surgery; Chair. Md Mizanur Rahman Khan; Prin. Prof. Md Aref Rahman (acting).

Dinajpur Medical College: New Town, Dinajpur; tel. (531) 61787; e-mail dinajmc@ac.dghs.gov.bd; internet www.dinajmc.org; f. 1992; Prin. Prof. Dr Md Hamidul Hoque Khandker; publ. *Dinajpur Medical College Journal (DjMCJ)* (2 a year).

East West Medical College: Aichi Nagar, JBCS Sarani, Horirampur, Turag, Uttara, Dhaka 1230; tel. (2) 8982123; e-mail info@ewmch.com; internet www.ewmch.com; f. 2000; depts of anatomy, anaesthesiology, biochemistry, blood transfusion, cardiology, community medicine, dermatology, ENT, eye, forensic medicine, gynaecology, medicine, microbiology, orthopaedics, pathology, paediatrics, pharmacology, physical medicine, physiology, radiology and imaging, surgery; Prin. Prof. Dr Md Zaforullah Chowdhury; Academic Dir Dr Miah Md Zakir Hossain.

Enam Medical College: 9/3 Parboti Nagar, Thana Rd, Savar, Dhaka; tel. (2) 7743778; e-mail abu_shamim@yahoo.com; f. 2003; offers 5 years MBBS course and 1 year internship training in Enam Medical College and Hospital; Prin. Prof. Dr Abdul Mannan Sikder.

Faridpur Medical College: Faridpur 7800; tel. (631) 62744; internet fmcbd.org; f. 1992; depts of anatomy, anaesthesiology, biochemistry, community medicine, dermatology, ENT, forensic medicine, medicine, microbiology, obstetrics and gynaecology, ophthalmology, orthopaedics, paediatrics, pathology, pharmacology, physiology, psychiatry, radiology, radiotherapy, surgery.

Holy Family Red Crescent Medical College: GPOB 81, Dhaka; 1 Eskaton Garden Rd, Dhaka; tel. (2) 8313234; internet www.hfrcmc.edu.bd; f. 2000; Chair. Prof. Dr Mohammad Abdur Rob; publ. *Journal of Medical Science and Research* (2 a year).

Ibrahim Medical College: 122 Kazi Nazrul Islam Ave, Shahabag, Dhaka 1000; tel. (2) 9663560; e-mail info@imc-bd.net; internet www.imc-bd.net; f. 2002; depts of anatomy, biochemistry, community medicine, forensic medicine, microbiology, pathology, pharmacology, physiology; 194 teachers; Chair. Prof. Pran Gopal Datta; Prin. Prof. A. K. M. Nurul Anwar; Librarian Idris Ali Momen; publ. *Ibrahim Medical College Journal* (2 a year).

International Medical College: Gushulia, Sataish, Tongi, Gazipur; tel. (2) 9814713; e-mail info@imc-bd.com; internet www.imc-bd.com; f. 2000; 554 students; Chair. Prof. Dr Shahla Khatun; Man. Dir M. Abdur Rab; Prin. Prof. Dr A. T. M. Mahbubul Alam.

Islami Bank Medical College: Airport Rd, Nawdapara, Sopura, Rajshahi; tel. (721) 862240; e-mail ibmcr_bd@yahoo.com; internet ibmedicalcollege.com; f. 2003; Chair. Shah Abdul Hannan; Prin. Prof. Dr Md Nazrul Islam.

Jahurul Islam Medical College: Bhagalpur, Bajitpur, Kishoregonj; tel. (9423) 64202; e-mail principal@jimedcol.org; internet www.jimedcol.org; f. 1992; offers 5-year course in Bachelor of medicine and surgery; Prin. Prof. Syed Mahmudul Aziz; Vice-Prin. Prof. Md Sayeed Hasan.

Jalalabad Ragib—Rabeya Medical College: Ragib-Rabeya Medical College Rd, Pathantula, Sylhet; tel. (821) 719090; e-mail jrrmc@btsnet.net; internet www.jrrmc.edu.bd; f. 1995; depts of anatomy, biochemistry, community medicine, forensic medicine and toxicology, gynaecology and obstetrics, medicine, microbiology, pathology, pharmacology and therapeutics, physiology, surgery; Chair. Ragib Ali; Prin. Prof. Md Nazmul Islam; Vice-Prin. Prof. A. T. M. A. Jalil; publs *Annual Magazine*, *College Journal*, *Hat Patra*.

Khwaja Yunus Ali Medical College: Enayetpur Sharif, Sirajgonj; tel. (751) 63761; e-mail education@kyamch.org; internet www.kyamch.org; Chair. Dr M. M. Amjad Hussain.

MAG Osmani Medical College: Sylhet; tel. (821) 713667; e-mail osmanimedical@gmail.com; internet www.magosmanimedical.com; f. 1962, current name adopted 1986; offers graduate and postgraduate courses in medical sciences; library: 25,000 vols; Prin. Prof. Dr Osul Ahmed Chowdhury.

Medical College for Women: Plot 4, Rd 8/9 Sector 1, Uttara Model Town, Dhaka 1230; tel. (2) 8913939; e-mail info@mcwh.org; internet www.mcwh.org; library: 3,523 vols, 1,420 journals; Chair. Prof. A. Q. M. Badruddoza Choudhury; Prin. Prof. Dr Majibur Rahman; Vice-Prin. Prof. Dr Gulshan Ara; Librarian Ireen Begum; publ. *Journal of the Medical College for Women and Hospital*.

Mymensingh Medical College: Mymensingh 2206; tel. (91) 66063; e-mail mmc@ac.dghs.gov.bd; internet www.mmc.gov.bd; f. 1924 as Lytton Medical School, present name 1962; offers graduate and postgraduate courses in medical sciences; library: 25,000 vols; Prin. Dr Md Motiur Rahman (acting);

publ. *Mymensingh Medical Journal* (4 a year).

North East Medical College: South Surma, Sylhet 3100; tel. (821) 2832829; e-mail info@nemc.edu.bd; internet www.nemc.edu.bd; f. 1948; offers 5-year graduate course of study in medical science; library: 1,700 vols, 1,200 journals; Chair. Prof. Dr M. A. RAQUIB.

Notre Dame College: GPOB 5, Dhaka 1000; Motijheel Circular Rd, Motijheel, Dhaka 1000; tel. (2) 7192325; e-mail info@notredame.ac.bd; internet www.notredame.ac.bd; f. 1949 as St. Gregory College, present name 1955; offers degree courses in arts, social sciences; Prin. FR BENJAMIN COSTA; Vice-Prin. FR STANISLAUS BAKUL ROZARIO.

Pioneer Dental College: Plot:-Ka 40/1, Lichu Bagan Rd Joar Sahara, Baridhara, Dhaka; tel. (2) 9891035; e-mail info@piodcol.com; internet www.pioneerdentalcollegeandhospital.com; f. 1995; offers Bachelor of dental surgery; Chair. Dr MD RAQUIBUL HOSSAIN; Prin. Prof. Dr REZAUL HUQ.

Rajshahi Medical College: Rajshahi 6000; tel. (721) 772150; e-mail info@rmc.ac.bd; internet www.rmc.ac.bd; f. 1954; offers graduate and postgraduate courses in medical sciences; graduate course in dental science; library: 16,000 vols, 1,800 journals; Prin. Prof. A. B. M. ABDUL HANNAN; Vice-Prin. Dr S. R. TARAFDAR; publ. *Journal of Teachers Association*.

Rangpur Medical College: Dhap, Jail Rd, Rangpur; tel. (521) 62288; e-mail rangmc@ac.dghs.gov.bd; internet www.rangpurmedical.webs.com; f. 1970; offers graduate and postgraduate courses in medical sciences; library: 20,000 vols; Prin. Prof. M. A. ROUF; publ. *Northern Medical Journal* (2 a year).

Sapparo Dental College: Plot 24, Court Bari Rd, Sector 08 Uttara Model Town, Dhaka 1230; tel. (2) 8358404; e-mail sdch@bol-online.com; internet www.sapporodentalcollege.com.bd; f. 1993 as Sapporo Dental Care, current name adopted and status 2000; offers undergraduate course in dental science; Prin. Prof. Dr M. A. HANNAN.

Sher-e-Bangla Medical College: Shagoedi, Band Rd, Barisal; tel. (431) 52151; internet www.sbmc.edu.bd; f. 1969 as Barisal Medical College; Prin. Dr ABRAR AHMED.

Sylhet Women's Medical College: Mirboxtola, Sylhet; tel. (821) 28300040; e-mail college@swmc.edu.bd; internet www.swmc.edu.bd; f. 2007; provides medical education; Prin. Prof. Dr MOHAMMED REZAUL KARIN.

Tairunnessa Memorial Medical College: Targach, Konia, Gazipur, Dhaka; tel. (2) 9291423; e-mail tmmch@citechco.net; internet www.tmmch.com; f. 1998; offers graduate course in medical sciences; Prin. Prof. Dr DILRUBA RAHMAN (acting); Vice-Prin. Dr A. B. M. OMAR FARUQUE.

University Dental College: 120/A, Siddeshwari Outer Circular Rd, Century Arcade, Moghbazar, Dhaka 1217; tel. (2) 8332632; e-mail udchedu@yahoo.com; internet udchedu.150m.com; f. 1995; offers graduate course in dental science.

Uttara Adhunik Medical College: House 34 Rd 4, Sector 9, Sonargaon Janapath, Uttara Model Town, Dhaka 1230; tel. (2) 8911600; e-mail uamcoffice08@yahoo.com; internet www.uamc-edu.com; f. 2007; offers graduate course in medical sciences; 100 teachers; Chair. Prof. ABU AHMED CHOWDHURY; Prin. Prof. Dr QUAZI SHAFIQUR RAHMAN; publ. *Journal of Uttara Adhunik Medical College*.

Z. H. Sikder Women's Medical College: Monica Estate, Western Dhanmondi, Dhaka 1209; tel. (2) 8115951; e-mail admission@sikderhospital.com; internet www.sikderhospital.com; f. 1992; offers pre-clinical and clinical medical disciplines required for undergraduate course in medical sciences; 600 students; Chair. ZAINUL HAQUE SIKDER; Rector Prof. M. A. T. SIDDIQUE.

BARBADOS

The Higher Education System

The main institution of higher education on the island is the Cave Hill branch campus of the University of the West Indies (UWI). Non-university post-secondary education is offered by the Samuel Jackman Prescod Polytechnic and the Barbados Community College. In 2008/09 there were 14,324 students enrolled in tertiary education. Higher education in Barbados is overseen by the Tertiary Unit of the Ministry of Education, Science, Technology and Innovation.

Admission to the University is based on satisfactory performance in secondary school examinations (the Caribbean Advanced Proficiency examinations, the General Certificate of Education examinations and the Caribbean Secondary Education Certificate examinations). The University offers Associate, Bachelors, Masters and Doctoral degree programmes. The Associate degree lasts for two years, the Bachelors three to five years, the Masters one to two years after the Bachelors and the Doctorate three more years after the Masters.

Provision of vocational training at post-secondary level (both public and private) is diverse with a wide range of qualifications and certification. The Barbados Vocational Training Board was established in 1980 to ensure an adequate provision of technical and vocational training in Barbados. The Board provides different types of occupational training, including apprenticeships (usually lasting three years), skills training programmes and evening programmes. In order to promote coherency and high standards of achievement the Technical and Vocational Education and Training Council (founded in 1993) has developed a system of National Vocational Qualifications (NVQs) which is closely based on the British education system and comprises five levels. The first NVQs were awarded by the Samuel Jackman Prescod Polytechnic in 2009.

The Samuel Jackman Prescod Polytechnic, which was established in 1969, offers trade and craft programmes that require one or two years of full-time study. The certificates and diplomas awarded to successful students include City and Guilds qualifications, NVQs and Royal Society of Arts qualifications. Certificates, diplomas, two-year Associate degrees and Bachelors degrees are also available from the Barbados Community College (founded in 1968).

Erdiston Teachers' College, which was established in 1948, offers non-graduate teachers a two-year course in primary education, while graduate teachers can pursue further study in collaboration with the UWI.

The Barbados Accreditation Council (BAC) was established in 2004 and is responsible for the registration of post-secondary and tertiary institutions, the accreditation of these institutions and their programmes, and the verification and recognition of overseas qualifications. Registration with the BAC is compulsory for all providers of post-secondary and tertiary education who want to operate legally in Barbados and is subject to annual renewal. Accreditation, however, is a voluntary process, which involves assessment of the standards of study programmes by independent consultants.

Regulatory Body

GOVERNMENT

Ministry of Culture, Sports and Youth: Constitution Rd, Sky Mall, Haggatt Hall, St Michael; tel. 621-2700; e-mail psculture@barbados.gov.bb; Minister STEPHEN LASHLEY.

Ministry of Education, Science, Technology and Innovation: Elsie Payne Complex, St Michael; tel. 430-2700; e-mail mined1@caribsurf.com; internet www.mes.gov.bb; Minister RONALD D. JONES.

Learned Societies

GENERAL

Caribbean Conservation Association: The Garrison, St Michael; tel. 426-5373; e-mail execdirector@ccanet.net; f. 1967; ind., non-profit-making; preservation and devt of the environment, conservation of the cultural heritage in the Caribbean as a whole; 200 mems; Pres. ATHERTON MARTIN; Exec. Dir Dr JOTH SINGH.

BIBLIOGRAPHY, LIBRARY SCIENCE AND MUSEOLOGY

Library Association of Barbados: POB 827E, Bridgetown; f. 1968; 60 mems; Pres. SHIRLEY YEARWOOD; Sec. HAZELYN DEVONISH; publ. *Update* (irregular).

HISTORY, GEOGRAPHY AND ARCHAEOLOGY

Barbados Museum and Historical Society: see Museum.

LANGUAGE AND LITERATURE

Alliance Française: POB 357, GPO, Cheapside, Bridgetown; tel. 233-3234; e-mail info@afbridgetown.org; internet afbridgetown.unblog.fr; offers courses and examinations in French language and culture and promotes cultural exchange with France; Pres. DENISE HAYNES.

MEDICINE

Barbados Association of Medical Practitioners: BAMP Complex, Spring Garden, St Michael; tel. 429-7569; e-mail bamp@sunbeach.net; internet www.bamp.org.bb; f. 1973; 348 mems; Pres. Dr JEROME WALCOTT; Gen. Sec. RANDOLPH CARRINGTON.

Barbados Pharmaceutical Society: c/o BCSI, 14 Pine Plantation Rd, St Michael; tel. 429-5357; e-mail secretarypsoc@barbadospharmacy.org; internet www.barbadospharmacy.org; f. 1948, inc. 1961; 155 mems; Pres. DELORES MORRIS; Sec. GEORGE ALLEYNE; publ. *Pharmacy in Progress*.

Research Institute

GENERAL

Bellairs Research Institute: Holetown, St James; tel. 422-2087; e-mail bellairs@caribsurf.com; internet www.mcgill.ca/bellairs; f. 1954; affiliated with McGill University, Canada; field courses, workshops, research and teaching in all aspects of tropical environments; library of 200 vols; Dir Dr BRUCE R. DOWNEY.

Libraries and Archives

Bridgetown

Public Library: Coleridge St, Bridgetown; tel. 436-6081; f. 1847; 7 brs, 6 centres, and a mobile service to 66 primary schools; acts as a nat. repository for legal deposit printed materials; spec. Barbadian and West Indian research colln; 165,000 vols; Dir JUDY BLACKMAN; publ. *National Bibliography of Barbados* (2 a year with annual cumulations).

University of the West Indies Main Library: POB 1334, Bridgetown; tel. 417-4444; e-mail barbara.chase@cavehill.uwi.edu; internet mainlibrary.uwichill.edu.bb; f. 1963; 155,000 vols, spec. West Indies colln, OAS, UN, UNESCO and World Bank depository library; Librarian BARBARA CHASE.

St James

Department of Archives: Black Rock, St James; tel. 425-5150; e-mail archives@sunbeach.net; f. 1963; part of the Prime Minister's Office; 990 linear m of archives, 2,366 vols and pamphlets, 922 serials, 391 microfilm reels, 2,747 fiches, 220 sound recordings; Chief Archivist DAVID WILLIAMS.

Museum

St Ann's Garrison

Barbados Museum and Historical Society: St Ann's Garrison, St Michael; tel. 427-0201; e-mail museum@caribsurf.com; internet www.barbmuse.org.bb; f. 1933; collns illustrating the island's geology, prehistory, history, natural history and marine life; European decorative arts, militaria, furniture; library of 5,000 vols; Pres. Dr TREVOR

CARMICHAEL; Dir ALISSANDRA CUMMINS; publ. *Journal* (1 a year).

University

THE UNIVERSITY OF THE WEST INDIES, CAVE HILL CAMPUS

POB 64, Bridgetown 11000
Telephone: 417-4000
E-mail: cregoffice@cavehill.uwi.edu
Internet: www.cavehill.uwi.edu
Founded 1963
Language of instruction: English
Academic year: August to May (2 semesters)
Private control
Chancellor: Sir GEORGE ALLEYNE
Vice-Chancellor: Prof. E. NIGEL HARRIS
Pro-Vice-Chancellor and Prin.: Prof. HILARY M. BECKLES
Registrar: JACQUELINE E. WADE
Campus Librarian: ELIZABETH WATSON
Library of 190,000 vols, 2,346 serial titles
Number of teachers: 528 (incl. 363 part-time)
Number of students: 8,342
Publications: *Caribbean Journal of Mathematics* (1 a year), *Caribbean Journal of Science, Economic and Financial Review, Caribbean Law Review* (2 a year), *Current Awareness Bulletin, Journal of Eastern Caribbean Studies* (4 a year), *The Journal of Carribean Literatures*

DEANS

Faculty of Humanities and Education: Dr PEDRO WELCH
Faculty of Law: Hon. Prof. VELMA NEWTON
Faculty of Pure and Applied Sciences: PETER GIBBS
Faculty of Social Sciences: Dr GEORGE A. V. BELLE
School of Clinical Medicine and Research: Prof. HENRY FRASER

PROFESSORS

ANDERSON, W., Int. and Off-shore Law
ANTOINE, R., Labour Law and Off-shore Law
BARRITEAU, E., Gender and Public Policy
BARROW, C., Sociology
BRYCE, J., Literature
CARNEGIE, A., Law
CARRINGTON, S., Plant Biology
COBLEY, A., South African and Comparative History
CRAIGWELL, R., Financial Economics
FAIDJOE, A., Law
FRASER, H., Medicine and Clinical Pharmacology
HAMBLETON, I., Research
HENNIS, A., Research
HORROCKS, J., Conservation Ecology
HOWARD, M., Economics
IYARE, O., Financial Economics
JOLLIFFE, L., Tourism
KACZOROWSKA, A., European Law
KHAN, J., Public Sector Management
KODILYNE, A., Property Law
LANDIS, C., Research
LAVOIE, M., Microbiology
MCDOWELL, S., Theoretical and Computational Chemistry
MCINTOSH, S., Jurisprudence
MAHDI, S., Mathematical Statistics
MAHON, R., Marine Affairs
MAMINGI, N., Economics
O'CALLAGHAN, E., West Indian Literature
OXENFORD, H., Marine Ecology and Fisheries
PUNNETT, B. J., International Business
RAY, T., Theoretical Physics
ROBERTS, P., Creole Linguistics
ROSIN, R. D., Surgery
SAVOLAINEN, H., Surgery
SINGH, U., Condensed Matter Physics
TINTO, W., Organic Chemistry

ATTACHED RESEARCH INSTITUTES

Caribbean Law Institute Centre: POB 64, Bridgetown 11000; tel. 417-4560; e-mail clic@cavehill.uwi.edu; Exec. Dir Prof. RALPH CARNEIGE (acting).

Cave Hill School of Business: POB 64, Bridgetown 11000; tel. 424-7731; e-mail chsb@uwichill.uwi.edu; internet www.uwichsb.org; Dir Dr JENNINE COMMA.

Centre for Gender and Development Studies: POB 64, Bridgetown 11000; tel. 417-4490; e-mail gender@uwichill.edu.bb; internet www.cavehill.uwi.edu/gender; Head JOAN CUFFIE.

Shridath Ramphal Centre for International Trade Law, Policy and Services: tel. 417-4533; e-mail src@cavehill.uwi.edu; internet www.shridathramphalcentre.org; Dir Dr KEITH NURSE.

Sir Arthur Lewis Institute of Social and Economic Studies (SALISES): POB 64, Bridgetown 11000; tel. 417-4478; e-mail salises@cavehill.uwi.edu; internet www.cavehill.uwi.edu/salises; Dir Dr JUDY WHITEHEAD.

Tertiary Level Institutions Unit: tel. 417-4506; e-mail eriic@cavehill.uwi.edu; internet www.cavehill.uwi.edu/tliu; Dir Dr LOUIS. WHITTINGTON

Colleges

Barbados Community College: 'The Eyrie', Howell's Cross Rd, St Michael; tel. 426-2858; e-mail eyrie@bcc.edu.bb; internet www.bcc.edu.bb; f. 1968; commerce, liberal arts, health sciences, fine arts, science, technology, Barbados Language Centre, Hospitality Institute, general and continuing education, computer studies, physical education; library: 35,000 vols; 449 teachers (149 full-time, 300 part-time); 3,697 students; Prin. NORMA J. I. HOLDER; Registrar SYDNEY O. ARTHUR.

Samuel Jackman Prescod Polytechnic: Wildey, St Michael; tel. 426-1920; e-mail info@sjpp.edu.bb; internet www.sjpp.edu.bb; f. 1969 in Bridgetown; merged with Barbados Technical Institute in 1972; div. of Agriculture est. at Eckstein Village and main br. relocated in 1975; relocation to present site 1982; attached to Min. of Education, Science, Technology and Innovation; divs of building, electrical engineering, mechanical engineering and printing, human ecology, business studies, general studies, agriculture, motor vehicles and welding, distance and continuing education, open and flexible learning centre.

BELARUS

The Higher Education System

Until its independence in 1991 Belarus was part of the Union of Soviet Socialist Republics (USSR), and its education system was based on the Soviet model. Following independence the Government began to introduce greater provision for education in the Belarusian language and more emphasis on Belarusian, rather than Soviet or Russian, history and literature. Higher education is the responsibility of the Ministry of Education, while research is coordinated by the National Academy of Sciences of Belarus. All Belarusians have the right to free higher education. By 2012 there were 45 state-operated and 10 private higher education institutions, including 32 universities (most of which were in the public sector), 11 institutes and three higher colleges. In 2010/11 442,900 students were enrolled in higher education.

The Ministry of Education administers admission to higher education on the joint basis of the Certificate of General Secondary Education (or equivalent) and competitive university entrance examinations. The introduction of centralized testing (an externally assessed examination which is organized and conducted by the Republican Institute for Knowledge Control) in the early 2000s partly replaced entrance examinations to universities. The main undergraduate degree is the Bachelors, which is usually taken in conjunction with the Specialist Diploma. The attainment of these two qualifications takes a combined five years. The first level of postgraduate study is the Magister (Masters), requiring one to two years' study, culminating in research and presentation of a thesis. Entry into postgraduate education is based on the successful completion of a Specialist Diploma or Bachelors degree as well as an entrance examination. The final level of postgraduate education includes the Aspirantura, leading to the Kandidat Nauk (Candidate of Sciences), and Doctorantura (Doctorate), leading to the title Doctor of Sciences; both of these qualifications are based on the defence of a scientific thesis.

Non-university post-secondary education is provided by technical and vocational schools, sometimes known as technicums. Courses vary in length from one to four years, depending on the level of specialization. There are currently 174 technicums, 26 colleges, 49 intermediate occupational education institutions, four higher colleges and eight private secondary specialized establishments. In 2009/10 105,700 students were enrolled in technical and vocational education.

Reform of the higher education system began in 1993, including the introduction of a standardized syllabus and increased institutional autonomy. In 2001 a number of laws were passed to this effect, culminating in 2007 with 'On Higher Education', which brought the country in line with the Bologna Process, including adoption of the European Credit Transfer System (ECTS) and recognition of foreign degrees. The law also introduced a Department of Quality Control within the Ministry of Education. In mid-2012, however, it was reported that the subject of Belarus's accession to the Bologna Process had been removed from the agenda of the Summit of Ministers of Education of the European Higher Education Area, and that any question about the possibility of joining had been postponed until 2015.

Regulatory and Representative Bodies

GOVERNMENT

Ministry of Culture: 220004 Minsk, pr. Pobeditelei 11; tel. (17) 203-75-74; e-mail ministerstvo@kultura.by; internet kultura.by; Minister BARYS U. SVYATLOU.

Ministry of Education: 220010 Minsk, 9 Sovetskaya St; tel. (17) 227-47-36; e-mail root@minedu.unibel.by; internet edu.gov.by; Minister SERGEY ALEKSANDROVICH MASKEVICH.

ACCREDITATION

Department of Quality Control in Education of the Ministry of Education: 220037 Minsk, 28 Kozlov St; tel. (17) 237-30-18; e-mail gnikon@rambler.ru; Dir VALERIY STEPANOVICH OVSYANIKOV.

ENIC/NARIC Belarus: Foreign Credentials Assessment Dept (Belarusian ENIC), 220007 Minsk, vul. Moskovskaya 15; tel. (17) 228-13-13; e-mail rector@nihe.by; internet www.nihe.bsu.by; Head INA MITSKEVICH.

NATIONAL BODIES

Academy of Postgraduate Education: 220040 Minsk, vul. Nekrasova 20; tel. (17) 285-78-28; e-mail tavgen@academy.edu.by; internet www.academy.edu.by; f. 1955; attached to Min. of Education; Rector Dr ANDREI MANASTYRNY.

National Institute for Higher Education: 220007 Minsk, vul. Moskovskaya 15; tel. (17) 222-83-15; e-mail mitskevich@nihe.by; internet www.nihe.bsu.by; f. 1973; organizes qualification improving courses, personnel retraining programs, postgraduate studies; participates in the creation and devt of the continuous professional educational system; scientific and methodological support of the educational system modernization process aimed at higher education quality improvement to comply with the nat. and int. standards; Rector Prof. Dr MIKHAIL I. DEMCHUK; Exec. Dir of Belarusian ENIC INA MITSKEVICH.

Learned Societies

GENERAL

National Academy of Sciences of Belarus: 220072 Minsk, pr. Nezavisimosti 66; tel. (17) 284-18-01; e-mail nasb@presidium.bas-net.by; internet www.ac.by; f. 1929; depts of biological sciences, chemical and earth sciences, humanities and arts, medical sciences, physical and technical sciences, physics, mathematics and information science; also research institutes; 243 mems (94 academicians, 129 corresps, 17 foreign mems, 3 hon. mems); library: see under Libraries and Archives; Chair. MIKHAIL V. MYASNIKOVICH (acting); Chief Scientific Sec. NIKOLAI S. KAZAK; publs *Computational Methods in Applied Mathematics* (4 a year), *Doklady* (Reports, 6 a year), *Inzhenerno-Fizicheskii Zhurnal* (Journal of Engineering Physics and Thermophysics, 6 a year), *Litasfera* (Lithosphere, 12 a year), *Materialy, Technologii, Instrumenty* (Materials, Technologies, Tools, 4 a year), *Nonlinear Phenomena in Complex Systems* (4 a year), *Prirodnye Resurcy* (Natural Resources, 4 a year), *Trenie i Iznos* (Friction and Wear, 6 a year), *Vestsi* (Bulletins: Physical-Technical Sciences, Biological Sciences, Biomedical Sciences, Physical-Mathematical Sciences, Humanities, Chemistry, 4 a year), *Zhurnal Prikladnoi Spektroskopii* (Journal of Applied Spectroscopy, 6 a year).

AGRICULTURE, FISHERIES AND VETERINARY SCIENCE

Department of Agricultural Sciences of the National Academy of Sciences of Belarus: 220049 Minsk, vul. Nezavisimosti 1; tel. (17) 284-18-12; attached to Nat. Acad. of Sciences; comprises 16 research institutes and 8 experimental stations; 32 mems (13 academicians, 19 corresp. mems); library: see under Libraries and Archives; Pres. VLADIMIR G. GUSAKOV; Scientific Sec. SVETLANA A. KASYANCHIK.

HISTORY, GEOGRAPHY AND ARCHAEOLOGY

Department of Humanitarian Sciences and Arts of the National Academy of Sciences of Belarus: 220072 Minsk, pr. Nezavisimosti 66; tel. (17) 284-07-74; internet www.ac.by/organizations/departments/ogum.html; fields of study include: history; historical geography and cartography; comparative historical and structural-typological studies of Belarusian and other languages; Belarusian literature, poetry and folklore; history of philosophy and politics in Belarus; sociolinguistic and psycholinguistic investigation; Acad. Sec. Acad. PYOTR G. NIKITENKO.

LANGUAGE AND LITERATURE

Goethe-Institut: 220034 Minsk, vul. Frunze 5; tel. (17) 236-34-33; e-mail info@minsk.goethe.org; internet www.goethe.de/minsk; offers courses and exams in German language and culture and promotes cultural exchange with Germany; library of 8,840 vols; Dir BARBARA FRAENKEL-THONET.

MEDICINE

Department of Medical Sciences of the National Academy of Sciences of Belarus: 220072 Minsk, pr. Nezavisimosti 66; tel. (17) 284-07-78; e-mail medicine@presidium.bas-net.by; internet www.ac.by/organizations/departments/omed.html; develops and coordinates research in the fields of: physiology of self-regulation; devt of theoretical basis for management of compensatory-recombinatory processes; modern ecosystems and their effects on the physiological state and health of humans; and the devt of medical-biological problems connected with the consequences of the Chornobyl (Chernobyl) nuclear accident in 1986; Acad. Sec. Acad. EVGENIY D. BELOYENKO.

NATURAL SCIENCES

Department of Biological Sciences of the National Academy of Sciences of Belarus: 220072 Minsk, pr. Nezavisimosti 66; tel. (17) 284-03-79; e-mail biology@presidium.bas-net.by; internet www.ac.by/organizations/departments/obio.html; f. 1946; fields of study incl.: biophysics, genetics, molecular biology, plant physiology and biochemistry, microbiology, genomics and proteomics, biodiversity of plants and animals in Belarus; devt of methods of protection of flora and fauna; reproduction and rational use of biological resources in conditions of anthropogenic pressure; 24 mems (9 academicians and 15 corresp.); Acad. Sec. Acad. IGOR D. VOLOTOVSKI.

Department of Chemistry and Earth Sciences of the National Academy of Sciences of Belarus: 220072 Minsk, pr. Nezavisimosti 66; tel. (17) 284-03-71; e-mail chemistry@presidium.bas-net.by; internet www.ac.by/organizations/departments/ochi.html; develops and coordinates research in the fields of: chemistry of polymers and their application; organic synthesis of substances with valuable properties; chemistry of inorganic materials; physical chemistry; chemistry of proteins, nucleic acids and low-molecular bioregulators; Acad. Sec. Acad. NIKOLAI P. KRUTKO.

Department of Physical and Engineering Sciences of the National Academy of Sciences of Belarus: 220072 Minsk, pr. Nezavisimosti 66; tel. (17) 284-03-77; e-mail engine@presidium.bas-net.by; internet www.ac.by/organizations/departments/ochi.html; develops and coordinates research and applied scientific investigations in the fields of: power engineering; conservation of energy and resources; materials and high-energy technologies; and machine building, modelling and diagnostics; Acad. Sec. Acad. SERGEI A. ZHDANOK.

Department of Physics, Mathematics and Informatics of the National Academy of Sciences of Belarus: 220072 Minsk, pr. Nezavisimosti 66; tel. (17) 284-03-76; e-mail physics@presidium.bas-net.by; internet www.ac.by/organizations/departments/ochi.html; develops and coordinates research in the fields of: optics, spectroscopy, laser and plasma physics; atomic and molecular analysis and diagnostics; study and control of the natural environment (incl. laser-sensing and airspace spectrometry); development of materials with electrical, magnetic, optical, and physical-mechanical properties; advanced information technologies (incl. fibre optics, design of automated technical systems); image processing (digital cartography, processing of space images), modelling of intelligent processes (incl. voice-recognition and neurocomputing); Acad. Sec. Prof. SERGEI V. ABLAMEYKO.

Research Institutes

AGRICULTURE, FISHERIES AND VETERINARY SCIENCE

Belarus Research and Technological Institute of the Meat and Dairy Industry: 220075 Minsk, pr. Partizansky 72; tel. (17) 244-38-52; attached to Acad. of Agricultural Sciences of the Republic of Belarus; Dir NIKOLAY A. PROKOPEV.

Belarus Research Institute for Potato Cultivation: 223013 Minsk obl., pos. Samokhvalovichi, vul. Kovaleva 2A; tel. (17) 506-61-45; internet mshp.minsk.by/science/kartof; f. 1957; attached to Nat. Acad. of Sciences of Belarus; Dir SERGEI A. BANADYSEV; publ. *Potato Growing* (1 a year).

Belarus Research Institute for Soil Science and Agrochemistry: 220108 Minsk, vul. Kazintsa 62; tel. (17) 277-08-21; e-mail brissa@mail.belpak.by; internet mshp.minsk.by/science/niiagrhru.htm; f. 1931; attached to Acad. of Agricultural Sciences of the Republic of Belarus; Dir Prof. IOSIF M. BOGDEVICH; publs *Soil Investigation and Fertilizer Application* (every 2 years), *Soil Science and Agrochemistry* (1 a year).

Belarus Research Institute of Power Engineering for Agro-industrial Complex: 220024 Minsk, vul. Stebeneva 20; tel. (17) 275-19-07; e-mail energetika@forenet.by; f. 1994; attached to Acad. of Agricultural Sciences of the Republic of Belarus; Dir Prof. VIKENTIY I. RUSAN; publs *Problems in the Development of Power Engineering and Electrification for Agro-industrial Complex, Use of Renewable Energy*.

Forest Institute: 246001 Gomel, Proletarskaya St 71; tel. (232) 74-73-73; e-mail forinstnanb@gmail.com; internet www.forinst.basnet.by; f. 1930; attached to Nat. Acad. of Sciences of Belarus; research and devt activities in the natural and engineering sciences; library of 22,227 vols; Dir Dr ALEXANDER I. KOVALEVICH; publ. *Questions in Silvics and Silviculture* (1 a year).

Grodno Zonal Planting Institute: 231510 Grodno raion, Shchuchin, Akademicheskaya 21; tel. (1514) 2-36-90; e-mail gznii@tut.by; f. 1910; attached to Nat. Acad. of Sciences of Belarus; 87 mems; library of 22,000 vols; Dir VLADIMIR KURILOVICH.

Institute for Fruit Growing: 223013 Minsk raion, pos. Samokhvalovichi, Kovaleva 2; tel. (17) 506-61-40; e-mail belhort@it.org.by; internet belsad.by; f. 1925; attached to Nat. Acad. of Sciences of Belarus; breeding and introduction of fruit, small fruit, nut bearing and vine crops and their rootstocks for practical use in breeding; genetic resources bank; production and intergovernmental exchange; developing and improving technologies of fruit and small fruit production, storage and processing; diagnostics of virus, virus-like and bacterial pathogens, and basic colln and creation of virus-free plants; Dir Dr VYACHESLAV A. SAMUS; publ. *Collected articles 'Fruit Growing'* (1 a year).

Institute for Land Reclamation: 220040 Minsk, vul. M. Bogdanovicha 153; tel. (17) 232-49-41; e-mail niimel@mail.ru; internet www.niimelio.niks.by; f. 1910; attached to Nat. Acad. of Sciences of Belarus; Dir NIKOLAI VAKHONIN; publ. *Reclamation* (2 a year).

Institute of Agricultural Economics: 220108 Minsk, vul. Kazintsa 103; tel. (17) 277-04-11; e-mail agrecinst@mail.belpak.by; f. 1958; attached to Acad. of Agricultural Sciences of the Republic of Belarus; library of 20,000 vols; Dir Dr VLADIMIR G. GUSAKOV; publ. *Agricultural Economics* (12 a year).

Institute of Animal Production: 222160 Minsk obl., Zhodino, vul. Frunze 11; tel. (1775) 3-34-26; e-mail belniig@tut.by; f. 1949; attached to Nat. Acad. of Sciences of Belarus; library of 68,000 vols; Dir Prof. IVAN P. SHEYKO; publ. *Zootechnic Science of Belarus* (1 a year).

Institute of Experimental Veterinary Medicine 'S. N. Wyshelesski': 223020 Minsk raion, pos. Kuntsevshchina, Vyshelessky 2; tel. (17) 508-81-31; f. 1930; attached to Acad. of Agricultural Sciences of the Republic of Belarus; Dir ALIAKSANDR P. LYSENKA; publ. *Veterinarnaya Nauka-Proisvodstvu* (1 a year).

Institute of Plant Protection: 223011 Minsk raion, pos. Priluki, vul. Mira 2; tel. (17) 509-23-39; e-mail entom@izr.belpak.minsk.by; attached to Acad. of Agricultural Sciences of the Republic of Belarus; Dir SERGEY V. SOROKA.

Institute of Vegetable Crops: 220028 Minsk, vul. Mayakovskogo 127A; tel. (17) 221-37-11; e-mail inst@belniio.belpak.minsk.by; internet mshp.minsk.by/science/niiov.htm; attached to Acad. of Agricultural Sciences of the Republic of Belarus; Dir GENNADY I. GANUSH.

Research and Practical Centre of NAS of Belarus for Arable Farming: 222160 Minsk raion, Zhodino, vul. Timiryazeva 1; tel. (1775) 3-25-68; e-mail izis@tut.by; internet www.izis.by; f. 1928 as Institute of Socialist Agriculture; present name 2006; attached to Nat. Acad. of Sciences of the Republic of Belarus; conducts applied and basic research in arable farming, plant growing, selection, genetics and crop protection; devt of highly productive varieties of agricultural crops, working with resource-saving technologies; library of 46,000 vols; Gen. Dir Dr FEDOR PRIVALOV; publs *Farming and Plant Protection* (6 a year), *Transactions on Arable Farming and Plant Growing in Belarus* (1 a year).

Research Institute of Radiology (RIR): 246000 Belarus, Feduninski St 16; tel. (23) 251-68-21; e-mail office@rir.by; internet www.rir.by; f. 1986; attached to Acad. of Agricultural Sciences of the Republic of Belarus; brs in Minsk, Brest, Mogilev; research projects and devts in field of nuclear and radiological response and recovery related to consequences of Chernobyl NPP catastrophe of 1986; devt of countermeasures for rehabilitation of affected population and contaminated territories, i.e. affected agricultural sector; recommendations and guidelines for farming on territories affected; scientific supervision of practical application of developed recommendations, and other types of activity; offers laboratory services and postgraduate courses in radiobiology; Dir Dr VIKTOR S. AVERIN; Sec. VICTORIA V. DROBYSHEVSKAYA.

RUE 'Fish Industries Institute: Scientific and Practical Centre of the National Academy of Sciences of Belarus for Animal Husbandry': 220024 Minsk, vul. Stebeneva 22; tel. (17) 275-36-46; e-mail belniirh@tut.by; internet www.belniirh.by; f. 1957; attached to Nat. Acad. of Sciences of Belarus; Dir Dr M. M. RADZKO;

publ. *Belarus Fish Industry Problems* (1 a year, in Russian with summary in English).

RUE 'Scientific and Practical Centre of the National Academy of Sciences of Belarus for Agriculture Mechanization': 220049 Minsk, vul. Knorina 1; tel. (17) 266-02-91; e-mail belagromech@tut.by; f. 1947; attached to Nat. Acad. of Sciences of Belarus; devt and implementation of new equipment for crop production and livestock farming, engineering and construction of vegetable storage facilities, creation of technological systems of machinery and equipment for agriculture mechanization; Dir-Gen. VLADIMIR G. SAMOSYUK.

ARCHITECTURE AND TOWN PLANNING

Research and Design Institute of Construction Materials 'BelNIIS': 220114 Minsk, Staroborisovsky tr.; tel. (17) 264-10-01; e-mail lmdp@nsys.by; Dir NADEZHDA N. TSYBULKO.

ECONOMICS, LAW AND POLITICS

Institute for Economic Research of the Ministry of Economics of the Republic of Belarus: 220086 Minsk; tel. (17) 200-64-65; e-mail d.niei@mail.by; f. 1962; strategic research, elaboration of medium and long-term forecasts and programs, social policy, human potential and social sphere devt, scientific, innovation and investment devt, regional research and devt, economic and mathematic simulation and informatization, world economy research; library of 51,425 vols; Dir AALEXANDER CHERVIAKOV.

Institute for State and Law: 220072 Minsk, vul. Surganava 1, korp. 2; tel. (17) 284-18-64; e-mail philos@bas-net.by; f. 1999; attached to Nat. Acad. of Sciences of Belarus; Dir Dr VLADIMIR P. IZOTKO.

Institute of Economics: 220072 Minsk, vul. Surganava 1–2, korp. 2; tel. (17) 284-24-43; e-mail director@economics.basnet.by; internet economics.bas-net.by; f. 1931; attached to Nat. Acad. of Sciences of Belarus; Dir Prof. ALEKSEJ DAJNEKO; publ. *Organizatsiya i upravleniye* (Organization and Management, 4 a year, in Russian).

Research Institute of Criminalistics and Forensic Expertise: 220073 Minsk, vul. Kalvariiskaya 43; tel. (17) 226-72-79; e-mail sudexpertiza@adsl.by; internet www.sudexpertiza.by; f. 1929; attached to Min. of Justice; library of 10,000 vols; Dir Dr ALEXANDER RUBIS; publ. *Issues of Criminalistics, Criminology and Forensic Expertise* (1 a year).

EDUCATION

National Institute of Education: 220004 Minsk vul. Korolja 16; tel. (17) 200-56-35; internet www.adu.by; f. 1990; library of 20,000 vols; Dir Dr BORIS KRAIKO; publ. *Adulcatsia i Wychawanne*.

HISTORY, GEOGRAPHY AND ARCHAEOLOGY

Institute of History: 220072 Minsk, vul. Akademicheskaya 1; tel. (17) 284-02-19; f. 1929; attached to Nat. Acad. of Sciences of Belarus; Dir Prof. ALEKSANDR A. KOVALENYA (acting).

LANGUAGE AND LITERATURE

Institute of Linguistics 'Ya. Kolas': 220072 Minsk, vul. Surganava 1, korp. 2; tel. (17) 268-48-84; e-mail inlinasbel@tut.by; f. 1929; attached to Nat. Acad. of Sciences of Belarus; Dir ALEKSANDR A. LUKASHANETS.

Institute of Literature: 220072 Minsk, pr. Nezavisimosti 66; tel. (17) 268-58-86; e-mail inlit@bas-net.by; f. 1931; attached to Nat. Acad. of Sciences of Belarus; Dir VLADIMIR V. GNILOMEDOV.

MEDICINE

Institute of Pulmonology and Phthisiology: 223059 Minsk raion, pos. Novinki; tel. (17) 289-87-95; e-mail niipulm@users.med.by; f. 1923; library of 7,000 vols; Dir VALENTIN V. BORSHCHEVSKIY; publ. *Research Report* (1 a year).

N. N. Alexandrov National Cancer Centre of Belarus: 223040 Minsk, p.o. Lesnoy-2; tel. (17) 287-95-05; e-mail oncobel@omr.med.by; internet omr.med.by; f. 1960 as N. N. Alexandrov Research Institute of Oncology and Medical Radiology, current name adopted 2008; library of 15,000 vols, 55 periodicals; Dir Prof. OLEG G. SUKONKO; publs *Oncological Journal* (4 a year), *Topical Problems in Oncology and Medical Radiology* (1 a year).

Republican Research and Practical Centre for Epidemiology and Microbiology: 220114 Minsk, vul. Filimonova 23; tel. (17) 267-30-50; e-mail belriem@gmail.com; internet www.belriem.by; f. 1924 as Belarusian Pasteur Institute; research to improve surveillance of infectious diseases, study of molecular mechanisms of pathogenicity of main infectious and immune diseases, devt of immuno- and molecular biologic diagnostic preparations against the agents of main infections, elaboration and implementation into medical practice of up-to-date diagnostic, medical and vaccine preparations, quality controls of immunobiological products, medical information support in the control of infectious and immune diseases; library of 10,000 vols; Dir Dr VLADIMIR A. GORBUNOV.

Republican Scientific Practical Centre of Hygiene: 220012 Minsk, Akademicheskaya 8; tel. (17) 284-13-70; e-mail rspch@rspch.by; internet www.rspch.by; f. 1927; library of 11,982 vols; Dir SERGEY SOKOLOV.

Research Institute of Neurology, Neurosurgery and Physiotherapy: 220061 Minsk vul. Filatova 9; tel. (17) 295-43-48; Head VLADIMIR PONOMAREV.

Research Institute of Traumatology and Orthopaedics: Minsk vul. Gorkogo 2.

Scientific Practical Centre 'Cardiology': 220036 Minsk, R. Luxemburg St 110; tel. (17) 286-14-66; e-mail info@cardio.by; internet www.cardio.by; f. 1977; Dir ALEXANDR MROCHEK.

Skin and Venereological Research Institute: Minsk, vul. Prilukskaya 46A.

NATURAL SCIENCES

Biological Sciences

Central Botanical Garden: 220012 Minsk, vul. Surganava 2A; tel. (17) 284-14-84; e-mail cbg@it.org.by; internet hbc.bas-net.by/cbg; f. 1932; attached to Nat. Acad. of Sciences of Belarus; Dir Acad. VLADIMIR N. RESHETNIKOV.

Institute for Nature Management: 220114 Minsk, 10 F. Skariny Str.; tel. (17) 267-26-32; e-mail nature@ecology.basnet.by; internet www.ecology.basnet.by; f. 1932; attached to Nat. Acad. of Sciences of Belarus; nature management, environment protection, geotechnology, geoecology, geography and palaeogeography, climatology and hydrogeochemistry; library of 235,500 vols; Dir ALEXANDER KARABANOV; publ. *Nature Management* (2 a year).

Institute of Biochemistry: 230017 Grodno, bul. Leninskogo Komsomola 50; tel. (15) 233-41-61; e-mail val@biochem.unibel.by; f. 1985; attached to Nat. Acad. of Sciences of Belarus; library of 40,000 vols; Dir Prof. PAVEL S. PRONKO.

Institute of Bio-organic Chemistry: 220141 Minsk, vul. Akad. V. F. Kuprevicha 5; tel. (17) 264-87-61; e-mail info@iboch.bas-net.by; internet iboch.bas-net.by; f. 1974; attached to Nat. Acad. of Sciences of Belarus; Dir Acad. FYODOR A. LAKHVICH.

Institute of Biophysics and Cell Engineering: 220072 Minsk, vul. Akademicheskaya 27; tel. (17) 284-17-49; e-mail ipb@biobel.bas-net.by; internet biobel.bas-net.by/biophys; f. 1973; attached to Nat. Acad. of Sciences of Belarus; Dir Acad. IGOR D. VOLOTOVSKIY; publ. *Godnev's Lectures: Plant Photobiology and Photosynthesis* (1 a year).

Institute of Genetics and Cytology: 220072 Minsk, vul. Akademicheskaya 27; tel. (17) 284-18-48; e-mail dromash@biobel.bas-net.by; internet biobel.bas-net.by/igc; f. 1965; attached to Nat. Acad. of Sciences of Belarus; Dir ALEKSANDR V. KILCHEVSKIY.

Institute of Microbiology: 220141 Minsk, vul. Akad. V. F. Kuprevicha 2; tel. (17) 202-99-46; e-mail microbio@mbio.bas-net.by; internet www.mbio.bas-net.by; f. 1975; attached to Nat. Acad. of Sciences of Belarus; Dir EMILIYA I. KOLOMETS.

Institute of Physiology: 220072 Minsk, vul. Akademichnaya 28; tel. (17) 284-24-61; e-mail biblio@fizio.bas-net.by; internet www.physiology.by; f. 1953; attached to Nat. Acad. of Sciences of Belarus; Dir JOSEPH ZALUTSKY.

Institute of Radiobiology: 246007 Gomel, Fedyuninskogo Str. 4; tel. (232) 57-07-06; e-mail irb@mail.gomel.by; internet irb.basnet.by; f. 1987; attached to Nat. Acad. of Sciences of Belarus; monitors and forecasts radioactive contamination level of environment; creates new technologies for prophylaxis of diseases with use of bioactive additives and other medical agents; develops protective measures for overcoming the long-term radioecological consequences of Chernobyl accident; researches adaptation mechanisms in organisms, incl. ionizing radiation; offers postgraduate courses in radiation biology and radioecology; Dir Dr ALIAKSANDR NAVUMAV; Scientific Sec. ALEKSANDER NIKITIN.

Institute of Zoology: 220072 Minsk, vul. Akademichnaya 27; tel. (17) 284-22-75; e-mail zoo@biobel.bas-net.by; internet biobel.bas-net.by/zoo; f. 1958; attached to Nat. Acad. of Sciences of Belarus; Dir MIKHAIL E. NIKIFOROV.

V. F. Kuprevich Institute of Experimental Botany: 220072 Minsk, Academicheskaya str. 27; tel. (17) 284-15-64; e-mail nan.botany@yandex.by; internet botany-institute.bas-net.by; f. 1931; attached to Nat. Acad. of Sciences of Belarus; Dir ALEKSANDR V. PUHACHEUSKI.

Mathematical Sciences

Institute of Mathematics: 220072 Minsk, vul. Surganava 11; tel. (17) 284-17-01; internet im.bas-net.by; f. 1959; attached to Nat. Acad. of Sciences of Belarus; Dir Acad. IVAN V. GAISHUN.

Physical Sciences

Institute of Applied Optics: 212793 Mogilev, vul. Bialynitskaga-Biruli 11; tel. (22) 226-46-49; f. 1970; attached to Nat. Acad. of Sciences of Belarus; Dir V. P. REDKO.

Institute of General and Inorganic Chemistry: 220072 Minsk, vul. Surganava 9; tel. (17) 284-27-23; e-mail secretar@igic.bas-net.by; f. 1959; attached to Nat. Acad. of Sciences of Belarus; Dir NIKOLAI P. KRUTKO.

Institute of Molecular and Atomic Physics: 220072 Minsk, pr. Nezavisimosti 70; tel. (17) 284-16-35; e-mail imafbel@imaph.bas-net.by; internet imaph.bas-net.by; f. 1992; attached to Nat. Acad. of Sciences of Belarus; Dir Dr SERGEY V. GAPONENKO; publ. *Journal of Applied Spectroscopy*.

Institute of Physical Organic Chemistry: 220072 Minsk, vul. Surganava 13; tel. (17) 284-23-38; e-mail ifoch@ifoch.bas-net.by; internet ifoch.bas-net.by; f. 1929; attached to Nat. Acad. of Sciences of Belarus; Dir Prof. ALEKSANDR V. BILDYUKEVICH (acting).

Institute of Physics 'B. I. Stepanov': 220072 Minsk, pr. Nezavisimosti 68; tel. (17) 284-17-55; internet ifanbel.bas-net.by; f. 1955; attached to Nat. Acad. of Sciences of Belarus; Dir Prof. VLADIMIR V. KABANOV (acting).

Institute of Solid State and Semiconductor Physics: 220072 Minsk, vul. P. Brovki 17; tel. (17) 284-28-14; e-mail ifttpanb@iftt.basnet.minsk.by; f. 1963; attached to Nat. Acad. of Sciences of Belarus; library of 72,000 items; Dir Prof. VALERY M. FEDOSYUK.

PHILOSOPHY AND PSYCHOLOGY

Institute of Philosophy: 220072 Minsk, vul. Surganava 1, korp. 2; tel. (17) 284-18-63; e-mail institute@philosophy.by; internet www.philosophy.by; f. 1931; attached to Nat. Acad. of Sciences of Belarus; research in the field of theory and methodology of natural scientific and socio-humanitarian cognition, philosophical anthropology, social ecology, ethics and aesthetics; elaboration of innovative strategies of social, spiritual, cultural and scientific progress; study of the actual problems of contemporary socio-political and cultural devt; study and summary of the achievements of the world and nat. philosophical thought; strategic European studies and research in the field of int. humanitarian collaboration; Dir Dr ANATOLY A. LAZAREVICH.

RELIGION, SOCIOLOGY AND ANTHROPOLOGY

Institute of Arts, Ethnography and Folklore: 220072 Minsk, vul. Surganava 1, korp. 2; tel. (17) 239-59-21; e-mail secr@bas-net.by; f. 1957; attached to Nat. Acad. of Sciences of Belarus; Dir Prof. VALERY I. ZHUK.

Institute of Sociology: 220072 Minsk, vul. Surganava 1, korp. 2; tel. (17) 239-48-65; e-mail isst@socio.bas-net.by; f. 1990; attached to Nat. Acad. of Sciences of Belarus; Dir E. M. BABOSOV.

TECHNOLOGY

A. V. Luikov Heat and Mass Transfer Institute: 220072 Minsk, P. Brovki St 15; tel. (17) 284-21-36; e-mail office@hmti.ac.by; internet www.itmo.by; f. 1952; attached to Nat. Acad. of Sciences of Belarus; research and devt on problems of heat and mass transfer in capillary-porous bodies, dispersal systems, rheological and non-equilibrium media, turbulent non-uniform flows, aerothermo-optical devices and low-temperature generators, laser technologies, hydrogen power engineering, nanomaterials and nanotechnologies, plasma and waste treatment, energy and resources saving computer modelling and simulation of heat and mass transfer processes; Dir Prof. OLEG G. PENYAZKOV.

Belarusian Institute of System Analysis and Information Support for Scientific and Technical Sphere (BELISA): 220004 Minsk, pr. Pobeditelei 7; tel. (17) 203-14-87; internet www.belisa.org.by; operated by the State Cttee on Science and Technologies of Belarus; Dir VALERJY E. KRATENOK.

Institute of Applied Physics: 220072 Minsk, vul. Akademicheskaya 16; tel. (17) 284-17-94; e-mail admcom@iaph.bas-net.by; internet iaph.bas-net.by; f. 1963; attached to Nat. Acad. of Sciences of Belarus; physics of non-destructive testing; Dir Prof. Dr NIKOLAI P. MIGUN.

Institute of Chemistry of New Materials: 220141 Minsk, F. Skorina St 36; tel. (17) 237-68-28; e-mail mixa@ichnm.basnet.by; internet ichnm.by; f. 1998; attached to Nat. Acad. of Sciences of Belarus; Dir Acad. VLADIMIR E. AGABEKOV.

Institute of Electronics: 220090 Minsk, Logoiskiy trakt 22; tel. (17) 265-34-13; e-mail inel@inel.bas-net.by; f. 1973; attached to Nat. Acad. of Sciences of Belarus; Dir YURIY V. TROFIMOV.

Institute of Energetics Problems: 220109 Minsk, vul. Akad. Krasina; tel. (17) 246-70-55; f. 1991; attached to Nat. Acad. of Sciences of Belarus; Dir Dr YURIY V. KLIMENKOV.

Institute of Engineering Cybernetics: 220012 Minsk, vul. Surganava 6; tel. (17) 268-51-71; e-mail cic@newman.basnet.minsk.by; f. 1965; attached to Nat. Acad. of Sciences of Belarus; Dir Prof. VYACHESLAV S. TANAYEV.

Institute of Machine Mechanics and Reliability: 220072 Minsk, vul. Akademicheskaya 12; tel. (17) 210-07-48; e-mail admin@inmash.bas-net.by; f. 1971; attached to Nat. Acad. of Sciences of Belarus; Dir Dr YURIY V. KLIMENKOV.

Institute of Radiation Physical-Chemical Problems: 220109 Minsk, Akad. Krasina 99; tel. (17) 246-77-50; e-mail fokov@sosny.bas-net.by; f. 1991; attached to Nat. Acad. of Sciences of Belarus; Dir SERGEY E. CHIGRINOV.

Institute of Technical Acoustics: 210023 Vitebsk, ave Lyudnikova 13; tel. (212) 24-39-53; e-mail ita@vitebsk.by; internet www.belpak.vitebsk.by/ita; f. 1995; attached to Nat. Acad. of Sciences of Belarus; library of 43,000 vols; Dir Prof. VASILIY V. RUBANIK.

Institute of Technology of Metals: 212030 Mogilev, vul. Bialynitskaga-Biruli 11; tel. (222) 26-46-43; e-mail inmet@mogilev.unibel.by; internet www.ussr.to/belarus/itm; f. 1992; attached to Nat. Acad. of Sciences of Belarus; Dir Dr EVGENIY MARUKOVICH.

Medical Biotechnological Institute: 220029 Minsk, vul. Varvasheny 17; tel. (17) 234-32-06; e-mail mbirb@mail.bn.by; internet www.medbiotech.bn.by; f. 1972; Dir VICTOR N. TERECHOV; Dir for Scientific Research K. M. BELIAVSKY.

Metal Polymer Research Institute 'V. A. Belyi': 246050 Gomel, vul. Kirova 32A; tel. (232) 77-52-12; e-mail mpri@mail.ru; internet mpri.org.by; f. 1969; attached to Nat. Acad. of Sciences of Belarus; library of 19,519 vols; Dir Prof. NIKOLAI K. MYSHKIN; publs *Friction and Wear* (6 a year), *Materials, Technologies and Tools* (4 a year).

Non-Traditional Energetics and Energy-Saving Scientific and Engineering Centre: 220109 Minsk, Sosny; tel. (17) 246-76-61; f. 1992; attached to Nat. Acad. of Sciences of Belarus; Dir V. N. YERMASHKEVICH.

Physical-Technical Institute: 220141 Minsk, vul. Akad. V. F. Kuprevicha 10; tel. (17) 267-60-10; e-mail phti@belhost.by; internet www.phti.belhost.by; f. 1931; attached to Nat. Acad. of Sciences of Belarus; Dir ANATOLIY I. GORDIENKO.

PLASMOTEG Scientific Engineering Centre of the Physical Technical Institute: 220141 Minsk, 10 Kuprevich St; tel. (17) 211-83-71; e-mail pec@bas-net.by; internet www.plasmoteg.org.by; f. 1990; attached to Nat. Acad. of Sciences of Belarus; plasma technology devt for obtaining of super hard coatings for vehicle parts, cutting tolls and dies, as well as biocompatible coating for medical implants, decorative coatings etc.; plasma electrolytic polishing and high voltage hart anodizing; plasma sources and ion sources design and manufacturing; Head of Laboratory Dr MIKALAI CHEKAN.

Republican Scientific and Engineering Centre for Environmental Remote Sensing 'Ecomir': 220012 Minsk, vul. Surganava 2; tel. (17) 284-00-49; e-mail ecomir@open.by; internet www.ecomir-eeica.com; f. 1990; attached to Nat. Acad. of Sciences of Belarus; Dir Prof. A. A. KOVALEV.

Scientific and Practical Center for Foodstuffs: 220037 Minsk, Kozlova 29; tel. (17) 285-39-70; e-mail info@belproduct.com; f. 2006; attached to Nat. Acad. of Sciences of Belarus; library of 20,000 vols; Dir ZENON LOVKIS.

Libraries and Archives

Brest

Brest Oblast Library 'M. Gorky': 210601 Brest, vul. Kosmanavtov 48; tel. (162) 22-22-01; e-mail brl@tut.by; internet grl.brest.by; f. 1940; regional centre for 19 central libraries and 818 brs; 740,000 vols; Dir TAMARA P. DANILYUK; publ. *Bibliopanorama* (irregular).

Gomel

Gomel Oblast Universal Library 'V. I. Lenin': 246000 Gomel, pl. Pobedy 2A; tel. (232) 77-36-51; e-mail goub@it.org.by; Dir VALENTINA P. DUBROVA.

Minsk

Belarus Agricultural Library: 220108 Minsk, vul. Kazintsa 86/2; tel. (17) 212-15-61; e-mail belal@belal.by; internet belal.by; f. 1960; attached to Nat. Acad. of Sciences of Belarus; 500,000 vols; Dir VALENTINA YURCHENKO.

Belarusian State University Library: 220030 Minsk, pr. Nezavisimosti 4; tel. (17) 209-52-47; e-mail lapo@bsu.by; internet www.library.bsu.by; f. 1921; 2m. vols; Dir PETR M. LAPO.

Central Scientific Archive of the National Academy of Sciences of Belarus: 220072 Minsk, pr. Nezavisimosti 66; tel. (17) 284-22-87; f. 1931; Head MARYNA HLEB.

Central Scientific Library of the National Academy of Sciences of Belarus 'Ya. Kolas': 220072 Minsk, vul. Surganava 15; tel. (17) 284-14-28; internet www.csl.bas-net.by; f. 1925; 3.1m. vols; Dir NATALIYA YU. BEREZKINA.

National Library of Belarus: 220114 Minsk, pr. Nezavisimosti 116; tel. (17) 266-37-00; e-mail inbox@nlb.by; internet nlb.by; f. 1922; 8.9m. vols; Dir Prof. ROMAN MOTULSKI; publs *Chernobyl: Bibliographical Index* (2 a year), *New Literature on the Culture and Art of Belarus* (12 a year), *Novyja Knigi* (12 a year), *Social Sciences* (12 a year).

Republican Library for Science and Technology of Belarus: 220004 Minsk, pr. Pobediteley 7; tel. (17) 203-31-38; e-mail rlst@rlst.org.by; internet www.rlst.org.by; f. 1977; 2.0m. vols (excl. patents); Dir RAISA SUKHORUKOVA.

Republican Scientific Medical Library: 220007 Minsk, vul. Fabritsiusa 28; tel. (17) 226-21-52; e-mail rsml@rsml.med.by;

internet www.rsml.med.by; f. 1941; 860,000 vols; Dir VLADIMIR N. SOROKO.

Mogilev

Mogilev Oblast Library 'V. I. Lenin': 212030 Mogilev, vul. Krylenko 8; tel. (222) 22-51-14; e-mail adm@library.mogilev.by; internet www.library.mogilev.by; f. 1935; Dir ILONA V. SOROKINA; publ. *Bibliographic Indices* (irregular).

Vitebsk

Vitebsk Oblast Library 'V. I. Lenin': 210601 Vitebsk, vul. Lenina 8A; tel. (212) 37-45-21; f. 1921; Dir ALEKSANDR SEMKIN.

Museums and Art Galleries

Belovezhskaya Pushcha

'Belovezhskaya Pushcha' National Park Museum: 225063 Brestskaya oblast, Kamenetzky raion; tel. (1631) 5-63-96; e-mail box@npbprom.belpak.brest.by; internet www.npbp.cis.by; f. 1960; displays flora and fauna of the Belovezhskaya Pushcha Primeval Forest, and shows work being done to preserve the biological diversity in the primeval forest, particularly with respect to the European Bison; Dir NIKOLAI N. BAMBIZA.

Grodno

Grodno State Historical and Archaeological Museum: 230023 Grodno, vul. Zamkovaya 22; tel. (152) 74-08-33; e-mail grodno_museum@tut.by; internet www.history.grodno.museum.by; f. 1920; museum colln contains 190,000 items; library of 35,000 vols; Dir Dr YURY KITURKA; publ. *Krayaznauchya zapiski* (Journal of Regional Studies, every 2 years).

Minsk

Great Patriotic War Museum: 220030 Minsk, pr. Nezavisimosti 25A; tel. (17) 227-11-66; e-mail museumww2@tut.by; internet nacbibl.org.by/war_museum; f. 1943; Soviet Army and partisans' war history 1941–1945; library of 14,000 vols; Dir GENNADIY I. BARKUN.

National Art Museum of the Republic of Belarus: 220030 Minsk, Lenin St. 20; tel. (17) 227-71-63; e-mail nmmrb@bk.ru; internet www.artmuseum.by; f. 1939 as State Art Gallery; current name adopted 1993; Belarusian art from 11th century to early 20th century; European art from 16th century to early 20th century; Russian art from 18th century to early 20th century; Oriental Art of the 14th to 20th centuries; temporary exhibitions; Dir VLADIMIR I. PROKOPTSOV.

National History Museum of the Republic of Belarus: 220030 Minsk, vul. K. Marksa 12; tel. (17) 328-63-75; e-mail histmuseum@tut.by; internet histmuseum.by; f. 1957; archaeological, ethnographical and coin colins; library of 20,000 vols; Dir SERGEJ VECHER.

Universities

BARANOVICHI STATE UNIVERSITY

225404 Baranovichi, Voikov Str. 21
Telephone: (163) 45-78-60
E-mail: barsu@brest.by
Internet: www.barsu.by
Founded 2004
State control
Languages of instruction: Belarusian, English, German, Russian
Academic year: September to July
Rector: Prof. Dr VASILIY KOCHURKO
First Vice-Rector: Dr GALINA ZHITKEVICH
Vice-Rector: BORIS BOGDANOV
Vice-Rector: VITALIY ZHERKO
Vice-Rector for Academic Work: Dr TATYANA YAKUBOVICH
Vice-Rector for Scientific Work: Dr ALLA NIKISHOVA
Library of 287,934 vols, incl. 25,862 periodicals
Number of teachers: 447
Number of students: 9,960

DEANS

Faculty of Economy and Law: VICTORIA BEZUGLAYA
Faculty of Education by Correspondence: NATALYA SHLYAGO
Faculty of Engineering: ALEXANDR AKULOV
Faculty of Pedagogy and Psychology: ZOYA KOZLOVA
Faculty of Pre-University Training: IGOR DUBEN
Faculty of Refresher Training: ELENA VASHCHILKO
Faculty of Re-Training: IRINA VYSOTENKO
Faculty of Slavic and German Languages: NATALIA KRUGLJAKOVA

BELARUS STATE ECONOMIC UNIVERSITY

220070 Minsk, Partizanski pr. 26
Telephone: (17) 249-40-32
E-mail: umoms@bseu.by
Internet: www.bseu.by
Founded 1933
Language of instruction: Russian
State control
Academic year: September to June
Rector: Prof. Dr VLADIMIR SHIMOV
Dean's Office for Int. Students: Dr NATALIA SKRIBA
Library: 1.5m. vols
Number of teachers: 1,200
Number of students: 27,000
Publications: *Belarusian Economic Journal*, *Bookkeeping, Accounting and Analysis*

DEANS

Faculty of Accounting and Economics: VLADIMIR BEREZOVSKY
Faculty of Commerce, Economics and Management: LEXANDER YARTSEV
Faculty of Finance and Banking: NATALIA LESNEVSKAYA
Faculty of International Business Communication: NATALIA POPOK
Faculty of International Economics Relations: GALINA SHMARLOVSKAYA
Faculty of Law: A. SHKLYAREVSKY
Faculty of Management: VALENTINA SIMKHOVICH
Faculty of Marketing: VALERY BORODENYA
Faculty of Pre-University Training: SERGEY KUCHUK
Higher School of Business and Management: SERGEY KRYCHEVSKIY
Higher School of Tourism: NIKOLAY KABUSHKIN
Special Faculty of Psychology and Pedagogy for Teachers of Economics: BORIS KRAYKO

BELARUS STATE TECHNOLOGICAL UNIVERSITY

220050 Minsk, vul. Sverdlova 13A
Telephone: (17) 226-14-32
E-mail: root@belstu.by
Internet: www.belstu.by
Founded 1930
Academic year: September to June
Rector: IVAN M. ZHARSKIY
Pro-Rector for Academic Affairs: ALEKSANDR S. FEDORENCHIK
Pro-Rector for Admin. Affairs: BORIS V. ALDANOV
Pro-Rector for Economic Affairs: ALEKSANDR I. KUPTSOV
Pro-Rector for Education: GENNADY M. KVESKO
Pro-Rector for Research: PETR A. LYSHCHIK
Library of 1,200,000 vols
Number of teachers: 630
Number of students: 11,500

DEANS

Faculty of Chemical Technology and Engineering: SVETLANA E. OREKHOVA
Faculty of Engineering Economics: MIKHAIL I. BARANOV
Faculty of External Studies: ANDREY R. GORONOVSKIY
Faculty of Forestry: VALERIY K. GVOZDEV
Faculty of Forestry Technology: NIKOLAY P. VYRKO
Faculty of Organic Substance Technology: VALERIY N. FARAFONTOV
Faculty of Publishing and Printing: LEONID M. DAVIDOVICH
Faculty of Qualifications Improvement and Retraining of Specialists: ANDREY I. ROVKACH

BELARUSIAN NATIONAL TECHNICAL UNIVERSITY

220027 Minsk, pr. Nezavisimosti 65
Telephone: (17) 232-74-26
E-mail: bntu@bntu.by
Internet: www.bntu.by
Founded 1920
Faculties of architecture, construction, economics and management, instrument-making, mechanics and technology, motor vehicles and tractors, power engineering, road construction, robots and robot systems
Rector: Prof. BORIS M. KHRUSTALEV
Library: 2m. vols
Number of teachers: 2,643
Number of students: 15,000
Publications: *Energetica* (4 a year), *Mir Technologij* (4 a year), *Vestnik BNTU* (4 a year)

BELARUSIAN-RUSSIAN UNIVERSITY

212005 Mogilev, pr. Mira 43
Telephone: (222) 23-61-00
E-mail: bru@bru.mogilev.by
Internet: www.bru.mogilev.by
Founded 1961
Rector: IGOR S. SAZONOV
First Pro-Rector: FEDOR G. LOVSHENKO
Pro-Rector for Academic Affairs: ALEKSANDR A. KATKALO
Pro-Rector for Academic Affairs: ALEKSANDR A. ZHOLOBOV
Pro-Rector for Academic, Economic and Int. Affairs: GRIGORIY P. KOSYACHENKO
Library: 1.5 m. vols
Number of teachers: 1,100
Number of students: 6,300

DEANS

Faculty of Automotive and Mechanical Engineering: STANISLAV B. PARTNOV
Faculty of Construction: SERGEY D. GALYUZHIN
Faculty of Economics: NIKOLAY S. ZHELTOK
Faculty of Electrotechnology: ALEKSANDR S. KOVAL
Faculty of Machine Building: VIKTOR A. POPKOVSKY

BELARUSIAN STATE AGRARIAN TECHNICAL UNIVERSITY

220023 Minsk, pr. Nezavisimosti 99
Telephone: (17) 264-47-71
E-mail: rektorat@batu.edu.by
Internet: www.batu.edu.by

Founded 1954

Faculties of agroenergy, agromechanics, business and management, humanities and ecology in social work, pre-university training and technical service, qualifications improvement and personnel retraining and vocational guidance

Rector: Prof. NIKOLAY V. KAZAROVETS

Library of 381,968 vols
Number of teachers: 519
Number of students: 8,783

BELARUSIAN STATE PEDAGOGICAL UNIVERSITY 'M. TANK'

220050 Minsk, ul. Sovetskaya 18
Telephone: (17) 226-40-20
E-mail: rector@bspu.unibel.by
Internet: www.bspu.unibel.by

Founded 1922
Language of instruction: Russian

Rector: PETR D. KUKHARCHUK
First Pro-Rector: ALEKSANDR I. ANDARALO
Pro-Rector for Academic Affairs: (vacant)
Pro-Rector for Admin. Affairs: VLADIMIR V. YADLOVSKIY
Pro-Rector for Education and Social Affairs: SVETLANA I. KOPTEVA
Pro-Rector for Information and Analytical Affairs: VALERIY M. ZELENKEVICH
Pro-Rector for Research: VASILIY V. BUSHCHIK
Librarian: NADEZHDA P. SYATKOVSKAYA

Library: 1.5m. vols
Number of teachers: 1,380
Number of students: 18,000

DEANS

Faculty of Aesthetic Education: TATYANA S. BOGDANOVA
Faculty of Belarusian and Russian Philology: VASILIY D. STARICHENOK
Faculty of History: NIKOLAY N. ZABAVSKIY
Faculty of Mathematics: VLADIMIR V. SHLYKOV
Faculty of Natural Science: NATALYA V. NAYMENKO
Faculty of Physical Education: MIKHAIL M. KRYTALEVICH
Faculty of Physics: IVAN I. DYADULYA
Faculty of Pre-School Training: LIYDMILA N. VORONETSKAYA
Faculty of Pre-University Training: SERGEY V. YAKOVENKO
Faculty of Primary Education: NATALYA V. ZHDANOVICH
Faculty of Psychology: LEONID A. PERGAMENSHCHIK
Faculty of Social Pedagogical Technologies: ALEKSANDR V. KASOVICH
Faculty of Special Education: SVETLANA E. GAIDYKEVICH

BELARUSIAN STATE UNIVERSITY

220030 Minsk, pr. Nezavisimosti 4
Telephone: (17) 209-52-03
E-mail: bsu@bsu.by
Internet: www.bsu.by

Founded 1921
State control
Languages of instruction: Belarusian, Russian
Academic year: September to June

Rector: Acad. Prof. Dr SERGEY V. ABLAMEYKO
Vice-Rector for Research: Acad. Prof. Dr OLEG A. IVASHKEVICH
First Pro-Rector: Prof. Dr MICHAEL A. ZHURAVKOV
Pro-Rector for Admin. and Finance: VLADIMIR V. ROGOVITSKIY
Pro-Rector for Economic and Commercial Affairs: IGOR V. VOYTOV
Pro-Rector for Education and Social Affairs: VLADIMIR V. SUVOROV
Pro-Rector for Int. Affairs: VLADIMIR A. ASTAPENKO

Library: 2m. vols
Number of teachers: 2,500
Number of students: 35,000

Publications: *Belarusskiy Universitet* (24 a year), *Higher School* (6 a year), *Sociology* (4 a year), *Vestnik BGU* (12 a year)

DEANS

Faculty of Applied Mathematics and Informatics: P. A. MANDRIK
Faculty of Biology: V. V. LYSAK
Faculty of Chemistry: D. V. SVIRIDOV
Faculty of Economics: M. M. KOVALEV
Faculty of Geography: I. I. PIROZHNIK
Faculty of History: S. N. KHODZIN
Faculty of International Relations: V. G. SHADURSKY
Faculty of Law: S. A. BALASHENKO
Faculty of Mechanics and Mathematics: D. G. MEDVEDEV
Faculty of Philology: I. S. ROVDO
Faculty of Philosophy and Social Studies: A. V. RUBANOV
Faculty of Physics: V. M. ANISCHIK
Faculty of Radiophysics and Computer Technologies: S. G. MULIARCHIK
Institute of Business and Management Technologies: V. V. APANASOVICH
Institute of Journalism: S. V. DUBOVIK
State Institute of Management and Social Technologies: P. I. BRIGADIN

BELARUSIAN STATE UNIVERSITY OF INFORMATICS AND RADIOELECTRONICS

220013 Minsk, ul. Brovska 6
Telephone: (17) 293-89-17
E-mail: oms@bsuir.by
Internet: www.bsuir.by

Founded 1964
State control
Languages of instruction: Belarusian, English, Russian
Academic year: September to May

Rector: Prof. MIKHAIL P. BATURA
First Vice-Rector: Dr ANATOLY OSIPOV
Vice-Rector for Admin.: VLADIMIR I. TARASEVITCH
Vice-Rector for Education: Prof. ALEXANDER A. KHMYL
Vice-Rector for Education: Dr BORIS NIKULSHIN
Vice-Rector for Education: Dr HELENA ZHIVITSKAYA
Vice-Rector for Research and Devt: Prof. ALEXANDER P. KUZNETSOV
Chief Librarian: LUDMILA SIZOVA

Library: 1.5m. vols, 300 periodicals
Number of teachers: 1,000
Number of students: 15,000

Publication: *Doklady Bguir*

DEANS

Continuous and Distance Education: Dr VASILY BONDARIK
Faculty of Computer-Aided Design: Dr SERGEY DICK
Faculty of Computer Systems and Networks: Dr VALERY PRITKOV
Faculty of Engineering Economics: Dr LUDMILA KNYAZEVA
Faculty of Extramural Training: Dr ALEXANDER V. LOMAKO
Faculty of Information Technologies and Control Systems: Dr ARTUR BUDNIK
Faculty of Military Studies: Col. ALEXANDER DMITRIUK
Faculty of Pre-University Preparation and Occupational Guidance: Dr GALINA F. SMIRNOVA
Faculty of Radioengineering and Electronics: Dr ALEXANDER KOROTKEVICH
Faculty of Telecommunications: Dr OLEG D. TCHERNUKHO

PROFESSORS

ABRAMOV, I., Quantum Mechanics and Statistical Physics
AKSENCHIK, A., Probability Theory
ASAYONOK, I., Psychophysiology
BAKHTIZIN, V., Software Design and Programming Language
BELAYEV, B., Information Protection and Intellectual Property Management
BOBOV, M., Protection of Databases and Software
BORBOTKO, T., Information Protection in Bank Technologies
BORISENKO, V., Nanoelectronics
BRIGIDIN, A., Methods and Devices for Signal Shaping
DASHENKOV, V., Radiotechnical Circuits and Signals
DROBOT, S., Radioelectronics
DVORNIKOV, O., Designing of Integrated Circuits Topology
GAPONENKO, N., Nanophotonics
GASENKOVA, I., Information Protection and Intellectual Property Management
GOLENKOV, V., Mathematical Framework for Artificial Intelligence
GOLIKOV, V., Cryptoprotection of Information in Telecommunications
GULYAKINA, N., General Systems Theory
GURSKY, A., Digital and Microprocessor Units of Gauge Devices
KATKOVSKY, V., Information Protection and Intellectual Property Management
KHATKO, V., General Systems Theory
KIRILLOV, V., Metrological Support
KIRVEL, I., Ecology and Energy Saving, Environmental Economics
KLIUEV, L., Electrical Communication Theory
KOBRINSKY, G., Labour Management
KOLOSOV, S., Algorithmization and Programming
KOMLICHENKO, V., Computer Networks
KONOPELKO, V., Coding Theory
KRIVONOSOVA, T., Programming
KUREYCHIK, K., Computer Architecture
KUZNETSOV, A., Control System Calculation against Random Input
LISTOPAD, N., Transmitter-Receivers, Computer Systems for Data Transfer
LOSIK, G., Cognitive Graphics
LUKIYANETS, S., Automated Control Theory
LYNKOV, L., Information Protection and Intellectual Property Management
MALYKHINA, G., Logics
MUKHA, V., Statistical Methods for Data Processing
MUKHUROV, N., Information Protection and Intellectual Property Management
MURAVYOV, V., Satellite and Radio-Relay Communication Systems
NELAEV, V., Computer-Aided Design Systems in Micro- and Nanoelectronics
NOVIK, E., History of Belarus
PASHUTO, V., Foreign Economic Activities, Labour Management and Rating
PETROV, N., Theory and Methodology of Athletic Training
PRISCHEPA, S., Systems for CAD of Digital Devices
RESHETILOV, A., Electronics and Microcircuitry
SADYKHOV, R., Digital Processing of Signals and Images
SAK, A., Economic Forecasting and Planning

SHILIN, L., Theory of Electrical Circuits
SINITSYN, A., Algorithmization and Programming
SMIRNOV, A., Devices Based on Quantum and Magnetic Effects and Sensors
STOLER, V., Descriptive Geometry and Engineering Graphics
SURIN, V., Engineering Mechanics
TARCHENKO, N., Communication Systems
VILKOTSKY, M., EMC of Radioelectronic Appliances
YARMOLIK, V., Control and Diagnostics of Computer Equipment
YASHIN, K., Novel Production Equipment, Innovative Technologies, Labour Safety
ZABRODSKI, E., Political Science, Human Rights, Ideology of the Belarusian State

BELARUSIAN STATE UNIVERSITY OF PHYSICAL CULTURE

220020 Minsk, Pieramozhcau Ave 105
Telephone: (17) 250-39-36
E-mail: interdepbsupc@gmail.com
Internet: www.sportedu.by

Founded 1937
State control
Languages of instruction: Belarusian, Russian
Academic year: September to July

Rector: Prof. Dr RYHOR KASIACHENKA
First Vice-Rector: Prof. Dr ALEXEY GATATULLIN
Vice-Rector for Education: ALENA FILGINA
Vice-Rector for Science: TATSIANA PALIAKOVA

Number of teachers: 388
Number of students: 6,000 (3,000 full-time, 3,000 part-time)

Publication: *The World of Sport* (Scientific Journal)

DEANS

Faculty of Health-Oriented Physical Training and Tourism: NATALYA MASHARSKAYA
Faculty of Mass Sports: IRYNA GUSLISTOVA
Faculty of Pre-University Education: VLADIMIR LITVINOVICH
Faculty of Sports Games and Combative Sport: ALEXANDR SHAKHLAY
Institute of Tourism: LIUDMILA SAKUN

BELARUSIAN STATE UNIVERSITY OF TRANSPORT

246653 Gomel, ul. Kirova 34
Telephone: (232) 95-20-96
E-mail: belsut@belsut.gomel.by

Founded 1953

Rector: Prof. VENIAMIN I. SENKO
First Pro-Rector and Pro-Rector for Academic Affairs: Prof. VIKTOR YA. NEGREY
Pro-Rector for Academic Affairs: SERGEY I. SUKHOPAROV
Pro-Rector for Admin. Affairs: VALERIY V. BABIY
Pro-Rector for Economics: GALINA M. BYCHKOVA
Pro-Rector for Education: GALINA M. CHAYANKOVA
Pro-Rector for Research: Prof. KONSTANTIN A. BOCHKOV

Library of 650,000 vols
Number of teachers: 358
Number of students: 3,390

Publication: *Vestnik BelGUTa: Nauka i Transport* (4 a year)

DEANS

Faculty of Continuing Education: VLADIMIR V. PIGUNOV
Faculty of Electrical Engineering: ALEKSANDR V. GRAPOV
Faculty of Engineering: VIKTOR A. BERBILO
Faculty of Foreign Students: IRINA G. PASHKO
Faculty of Humanities and Economics: YURI P. LYCH
Faculty of Industrial and Civil Construction: ANATOLIY G. TASHNIKOV
Faculty of Mechanical Engineering: YURI G. SAMODUM
Faculty of Military Transportation: Col VLADIMIR V. LEVTRINSKIY
Faculty of Transport Management: NIKOLAY P. BERLIN
Faculty of Vocational Guidance and Pre-University Training: OLEG P. GORAEV

BELARUSIAN TRADE AND ECONOMIC UNIVERSITY OF CONSUMER COOPERATIVES

246029 Gomel, pr. Oktyabrya 50
Telephone: (232) 47-23-71
E-mail: priem@bteu.by
Internet: www.i-bteu.by

Founded 1964
Private control

Rector: Dr SVIATLANA N. LEBEDZEVA
First Vice-Rector: Dr LYUDMILA V. MISNIKOVA
Vice-Rector for Academic Affairs: Dr VASILIY V. BOGUSH
Vice-Rector for Academic Affairs: Dr LYUBOMIR M. SKORIK
Vice-Rector for Admin. Affairs: SIARHEI V. KARPOVITCH
Vice-Rector for Scientific Research: Dr GEORGE S. MITYURICH
Vice-Rector for Scientific Studies and Innovations: Dr NATALIA A. SNYTKOVA
Pro-Rector for Ideological and Educational Work: Dr ALEKSANDR I. KAPSHTYK

Library of 500,000 vols
Number of teachers: 330
Number of students: 10,000

DEANS

Correspondence Faculty of Commerce and Management: NIKOLAY V. MAKSIMENKO
Correspondence Faculty of Economics and Accounting: NIKOLAY V. OKSENCHUK
Faculty of Accounting and Finance: VALENTINA A. ASTAFYEVA
Faculty of Commerce: KLAVDIYA I. LOKTEVA
Faculty of Economics and Management: TATYANA V. EMELYANOVA
Faculty of Professional Development and Retraining: SVIATLANA P. GURSKAYA

BREST STATE TECHNICAL UNIVERSITY

224017 Brest, vul. Moskovskaya 267
Telephone: (162) 42-33-93
E-mail: canc@bstu.by
Internet: www.bstu.by

Founded 1966

Faculties of civil engineering (civil engineering, production of building elements and structures, construction of roads and transport facilities, architecture), economics (accounting, analysis, audit; world economy and international economic relations; marketing), electronic and mechanical engineering (technology, equipment and automation of machine-building; automatic data processing systems; computers, systems and networks), extramural studies and preparatory training, water supply systems and soil conservation (water supply and sewage disposal systems, soil conservation and water resources management)

Rector: Prof. Dr P. S. POJTA

Library of 395,000 vols
Number of teachers: 499
Number of students: 6,438

BREST STATE UNIVERSITY 'A. S. PUSHKIN'

224016 Brest, bul. Kosmonavtov 21
Telephone: (162) 23-33-40
E-mail: box@brsu.brest.by
Internet: www.brsu.brest.by

Founded 1945

Rector: Prof. Dr MECHISLAV E. CHESNOVSKIY
First Pro-Rector: Prof. KONSTANTIN K. KRASOVSKIY
Pro-Rector for Academic Affairs: Prof. STANISLAV G. RACHEVSKIY
Pro-Rector for Admin. and Managerial Affairs: SERGEY V. KLIMUK
Pro-Rector for Educational Affairs: Prof. Dr ANNA N. SENDER
Pro-Rector for Educational and Social Affairs: Asst Prof. LIUDMILA A. GODUYKO
Pro-Rector for Scientific Affairs and Economics: Asst Prof. SERGEY A. MARZAN

DEANS

Faculty of Biology: NATALIA M. GOLUB
Faculty of Foreign Languages: SERGEY N. SIEVIERIN
Faculty of Geography: VLADIMIR I. BOYKO
Faculty of History: NATALYA P. GALIMOVA
Faculty of Law: YELENA N. GRIGOROVICH
Faculty of Mathematics: ALEXANDER Y. BUDKO
Faculty of Philology: OLGA A. FIELKINA
Faculty of Physical Education: NIKOLAY I. PRISTUPA
Faculty of Physics: IGOR I. MAKOYED
Faculty of Pre-School Education: LARISA D. GUSAROVA
Faculty of Pre-University Education: YELENA I. MIRSKAYA
Faculty of Psychology and Pedagogy: ALEKSANDER I. OSTAPUK
Faculty of Social Sciences and Pedagogics: ANATOLIY N. GIERASIEVICH

GOMEL STATE MEDICAL UNIVERSITY

246000 Gomel, Lange St 5
Telephone: (232) 74-41-21
E-mail: medinst@mail.gomel.by
Internet: www.medinstitut.gomel.by

Founded 1990
State control
Languages of instruction: Belarusian, English, Russian
Academic year: September to July

Rector: Prof. ANATOLY N. LYZIKOV
Vice-Rector for Academic Work: Assoc. Prof. ALEXANDR A. KOZLOVSKY
Vice-Rector for Admin. and Economic Work: SERGEY N. GLUSHKOV
Vice-Rector for Educational and Ideological Work: VICTOR M. UMANETS
Vice-Rector for Medical Work: Prof. VLADIMIR V. ANICHKIN
Head of Library: SVETLANA M. POLADIEVA

Library of 250,600 vols, 28,400 periodicals
Number of teachers: 500
Number of students: 3,500

Publication: *Problems of Health and Ecology*

DEANS

Faculty of General Medicine: Assoc. Prof. VYACHESLAV A. PODOLYAKO
Faculty of General Medicine for Overseas Students: Assoc. Prof. SVETLANA A. HODULEVA
Faculty of Medical Diagnostics: Assoc. Prof. ANDREY L. KALININ
Faculty of Pre-University Education: Assoc. Prof. MIKHAIL E. ABRAMENKO

GOMEL STATE UNIVERSITY 'F. SKORINA'

246699 Gomel, vul. Sovetskaya 104
Telephone: (232) 56-31-13
E-mail: mail@gsu.by
Internet: www.gsu.by

Founded 1969
State control
Languages of instruction: Belarusian, Russian
Academic year: September to July
Faculties of biology, economics, foreign languages, geology and geography, history, law, mathematics, philology, physical training, physics, psychology and preparatory training; France–Belarus Institute of Management, Institute of Qualification Improvement
Rector: Prof. Dr MIKHAIL V. SELKIN
First Pro-Rector: ALEKSANDR P. KARMAZIN
Library: 1m. vols
Number of teachers: 570
Number of students: 5,843
Publications: *Belarusian Language*, *Problems in Algebra*, *University News* (6 a year, in Belarusian, English and Russian)

GRODNO STATE AGRARIAN UNIVERSITY

230008 Grodno, vul. Tereshkovoy 28
Telephone: (152) 77-01-68
E-mail: ggay@uni-agro.grodno.by
Internet: www.uni.agro-grodno.com

Founded 1951
State control
Rector: VITOLD K. PESTIS
First Pro-Rector: ALEKSANDR A. DUDUK
Pro-Rector for Admin. Affairs: VALERIY N. TRIKUTS
Pro-Rector for Education: FEDOR N. LEONOV
Pro-Rector for Research: ALEKSANDR V. GLAZ
Librarian: NADEZHDA P. KHODOTCHUK
Library of 300,000 vols
Number of teachers: 209
Number of students: 3,842

DEANS

Faculty of Agronomy: FEDOR F. SEDLYAR
Faculty of Economics: IOSIF I. DEGTYAREVICH
Faculty of Plant Protection: GALINA A. ZEZYULINA
Faculty of Pre-University Training: REGINA K. YANKELEVICH
Faculty of Qualifications Improvement and Retraining of Agricultural Personnel: OLEG E. MOLYAVKO (Pro-Rector)
Faculty of Veterinary Medicine: MIKHAIL A. KAVRUS
Faculty of Zooengineering: EVGENIY A. DOBRUK

GRODNO STATE MEDICAL UNIVERSITY

230009 Grodno, ul. Gorkogo 80
Telephone: (152) 43-54-51
E-mail: mailbox@grsmu.by
Internet: www.grsmu.by

Founded 1958
State control
Languages of instruction: English, Russian
Academic year: September to June
Rector: Prof. VIKTOR A. SNEZHITSKY
Vice-Rector: VITALY V. VOROBYOV
Vice-Rector for Clinical Work: VLADIMIR L. ZVERKO
Vice-Rector for Research: VIKTOR V. ZINCHUK
Vice-Rector for Student Affairs: IGOR P. BOGDANOVICH
Pro-Rector for Medical Affairs: VLADIMIR L. ZVERKO

DEANS

Faculty of Foreign Students: ANDREY R. PLOTSKY
Faculty of General Medicine: GENNADIY G. MARMYSH
Faculty of Medical Diagnostics: EVGENY M. TISCHENKO
Faculty of Medical Psychology: TATYANA M. SHAMOVA
Faculty of Paediatrics: ANDREY L. GURIN

INTERNATIONAL SAKHAROV ENVIRONMENTAL UNIVERSITY

220070 Minsk, Dolgobrodskaya St 23
Telephone: (17) 230-69-98
E-mail: info@iseu.by
Internet: www.iseu.by

Founded 1992
State control
Academic year: September to June
Rector: Prof. SEMJON P. KUNDAS
Library of 150,000 vols
Number of teachers: 345
Number of students: 1,370

DEANS

Faculty of Advanced Training and Retraining: IVAN I. MATVEENKO
Faculty of Environmental Medicine: Asst Prof. MIKHAIL S. MAROZIK
Faculty of Environmental Monitoring: Prof. NIKOLAY V. PUSHKAREV
Faculty of Pre-University Training: Asst Prof. LYUDMILA M. SHEIKO

MINSK STATE LINGUISTIC UNIVERSITY

220034 Minsk, vul. Zakharova 21
Telephone: (17) 284-80-67
E-mail: info@mslu.by
Internet: www.mslu.by

Founded 1948
Schools of English, French, German, intercultural communication, retraining and teacher devt, Russian as a foreign language, Spanish, translation and interpreting
Rector: NATALYA P. BARANOVA
Library: 1m. vols and periodicals
Number of teachers: 737
Number of students: 7,659
Publications: *Foreign Languages in the Republic of Belarus* (4 a year), *Methodology of Teaching Foreign Languages* (1 a year), *Studies in Romanic and Germanic Languages* (1 a year), *Vestnik of MSLU: History, Philosophy and Economics* (1 a year), *Vestnik of MSLU: Phylology and Linguistics* (2 a year), *Vestnik of MSLU: Psychology, Didactics and Methods of Foreign Language Teaching* (1 a year)

MOGILEV STATE FOODSTUFFS UNIVERSITY

212027 Mogilev, pr. Shmidta 3
Telephone: (22) 244-03-63
E-mail: info@mgup.net
Internet: www.mgup.net

Founded 1973
State control
Rector: Prof. VYACHESLAV SHARSHUNOV
Library of 500,000 vols
Number of teachers: 250
Number of students: 5,530

DEANS

Faculty of Chemical Technology: T. I. PISKUN
Faculty of Economics: NADEZHDA V. ABRAMOVICH
Faculty of External Studies: A. V. OBOTUROV
Faculty of Mechanical Engineering: VALERIY P. CHIRKIN
Faculty of Pre-University Training: ELENA N. ANDREYCHIKOVA
Faculty of Technology: LIDIYA A. KASYANOVA

MOGILEV STATE UNIVERSITY 'A. A. KULESHOV'

220009 Minsk, vul. Dolgobrodskaya 23
Telephone: (17) 230-69-98
E-mail: rector@iseu.by
Internet: msu.mogilev.by

Founded 1913, present name and status 1997
Rector: Dr KONSTANTIN M. BONDARENKO
First Pro-Rector: Prof. Dr MIKHAIL I. VISHNEVSKIY
Pro-Rector for Academic Affairs: Dr VLADIMIR V. YASEV
Pro-Rector for Research: Dr NIKOLAY P. BUZUK
Library of 500,000 vols
Number of teachers: 450
Number of students: 7,600

P. O. SUKHOI STATE TECHNICAL UNIVERSITY OF GOMEL

246746 Gomel, pr. Oktyabrya 48
Telephone: (232) 40-20-36
E-mail: rector@gstu.by
Internet: www.gstu.by

Founded 1968
State control
Languages of instruction: Belarusian, Russian
Academic year: September to July
Rector: SERGEI I. TIMOSHIN
First Vice-Rector: OLEG D. ASENCHIK
Vice-Rector for Admin. and Maintenance Operation: SERGEI S. PRISCHEPOV
Vice-Rector for Education and Educative Work: VIKTOR V. KIRIENKO
Vice-Rector for Education and Instruction: ALEKSANDER V. SYCHEV
Vice-Rector for Research: ANDREI A. BOIKA
Library of 540,000 vols
Number of teachers: 400
Number of students: 8,000

DEANS

Faculty of Automation and Information Systems: GEORGIY I. SELIVERSTOV
Faculty of Correspondence: PETR V. LYCHEV
Faculty of Humanities and Economics: RAISA I. GROMYKO
Faculty of Mechanical Engineering: GRIGORY V. PETRISHIN
Faculty of Power Engineering: MIKHAIL N. NOVIKOV
Faculty of Pre-University Training: SERGEY A. YURIS
Faculty of Technology: IGOR B. ODARCHENKO
Upgrading and Retraining Institute: YURIY N. KOLESNIK

POLOTSK STATE UNIVERSITY

211440 Novopolotsk, vul. Blokhina 29
Telephone: (214) 53-20-12
E-mail: post@psu.by
Internet: www.psu.by

Founded 1968
State control
Rector: DMITRIY N. LAZOVSKIY
First Pro-Rector: NATALYA N. BELORUSOVA
Pro-Rector for Academic Affairs: VASILIY V. BULAKH
Pro-Rector for Admin. Affairs: VLADIMIR P. STRIZHAK
Pro-Rector for Education and Social Affairs: VIKENTIY G. TSYGANOK

Pro-Rector for Information Systems: DMITRIY O. GLUKHOV
Pro-Rector for Innovation: NIKOLAY N. POPOK
Pro-Rector for Int. Affairs: SERGEY V. PESHKUN
Pro-Rector for Maintenance and Construction: VILEN S. LEVIN
Pro-Rector for Research: FEDOR I. PANTALEENKO
Pro-Rector for the Environment: VLADIMIR K. LIPSKIY
Library of 427,000 vols
Number of teachers: 500
Number of students: 6,000

VITEBSK STATE ORDER OF PEOPLES' FRIENDSHIP MEDICAL UNIVERSITY

210023 Vitebsk, pr. Frunze 27
Telephone: (212) 21-04-33
E-mail: admin@vgmu.vitebsk.by
Internet: www.vgmu.vitebsk.by
Founded 1934
State control
Academic year: September to July
Languages of instruction: English, Russian
Attached clinic and stomatological polyclinic
Rector: Prof. VALERY PETROVICH DEIKALO
Vice-Rector for Admin. Affairs: SERGEI IVANOVICH ZHAGOLKIN
Vice-Rector for Clinical and Pharmaceutical Affairs: LEONID EGOROVICH KRISHTOPOV
Vice-Rector for Educational Work and Int. Affairs: Prof. Dr NATALLIA YURIEVNA KONEVALOVA
Vice-Rector for Pedagogical and Ideological Affairs: OLGA ARKADIEVNA SYRODOYEVA
Vice-Rector for Scientific Research Work: SERGEI ALBERTOVICH SUSHKOV
Library: 1.5m. vols
Number of teachers: 538
Number of students: 6,259
Publications: *Herald* (4 a year), *Immunopathology, Allergology, Infectology* (4 a year), *Maternity and Child Protection* (4 a year), *Pharmacy News* (4 a year), *Surgery News* (4 a year)

DEANS
Faculty for Mastering Skills of Specialists and Collective of Employees Re-training: Prof. RADETSKAYA LYUDMILA YEUGENIEVNA
Faculty of Overseas Students Training: Assoc. Prof. PRISTUPA VADIM VITALIEVICH
Faculty of Pedagogics and Psychology: Prof. KUNTSEVICH ZINAIDA STEPANOVNA
Faculty of Professional Orientation and Preparatory Training: Doc. PASHKOV ALEXANDER ALEXANDROVICH
Medical Faculty: Prof. Dr SEMENOV VALERIY MIHAILOVICH
Pharmaceutical Faculty: Assoc. Prof. KUGACH VALENTINA VASILIEVNA
Stomatological Faculty: Doc. KABANOVA SVETLANA ALEKSEYEVNA

VITEBSK STATE TECHNOLOGICAL UNIVERSITY

210035 Vitebsk, pr. Moskovskiy 72
Telephone: (212) 27-50-26
E-mail: vstu@vstu.vitebsk.by
Internet: www.vstu.vitebsk.by
Founded 1959
State control
Rector: Prof. VALERIY S. BASHMETOV
First Pro-Rector: IVAN A. MOSKALEV
Pro-Rector for Admin. Affairs: ALEKSEY N. SHUT
Pro-Rector for Education: ANATOLIY A. BELOV
Pro-Rector for Research: SERGEY M. BASHMETOV
Pro-Rector for Social and Economic Affairs and Construction: BORIS E. RYKLIN
Library of 300,000 vols
Number of teachers: 293
Number of students: 5,500 (incl. 2,500 external)

DEANS
Faculty of Arts and Technology: GALINA V. KAZARNOVSKAYA
Faculty of Civil Engineering and Technology: VITALIY K. SMELKOV
Faculty of Economics: VLADIMIR P. SHARSTNEV
Faculty of External Studies: ANATOLIY M. TIMOFEEV
Faculty of Mechanical Engineering and Technology: VALERIY I. OLSHANSKIY
Faculty of Pre-University Training and Vocational Guidance: ALEKSANDR P. SUVOROV
Faculty of Qualifications Improvement: IGOR M. KONTOROVICH

VITEBSK STATE UNIVERSITY 'P. M. MASHEROV'

210038 Vitebsk, pr. Moskovskiy 33
Telephone: (212) 21-58-66
E-mail: vsu@vsu.by
Internet: www.vsu.by
Founded 1910 as Teacher Training Institute; present name and status 1955
State control
Rector: Prof. ALEXANDER PETROVICH SOLODKOV
First Pro-Rector: Prof. ALEXANDER GLADKOV
Pro-Rector for Research: Prof. INNA MIHAILOVNA PRISHCHEPA
Pro-Rector for Studies: VASILIY MALINOVSKIY
Publications: *My i Chas*, *Vestnik VGU*

DEANS
Faculty of Belarusian Philology and Culture: VIKTOR I. NESTOROVICH
Faculty of Biology: VITALIY YA. KUZMENKO
Faculty of Graphic Arts: DMITRIY SENKO
Faculty of History: VALERIY SHOREC
Faculty of Law: ALEXANDER BOCHKOV
Faculty of Mathematics: LILIYA ALIZARCHIK
Faculty of Pedagogy: INNA SHARAPOVA
Faculty of Philology: LEONID M. VARDOMATSKIY
Faculty of Physics: URIY BOHAN
Faculty of Social Pedagogy and Psychology: SERGEY A. MOTOROV

YANKA KUPALA STATE UNIVERSITY OF GRODNO

230023 Grodno, vul. Ozheshko 22
Telephone: (152) 73-19-00
E-mail: mail@grsu.by
Internet: www.grsu.by
Founded 1940
State control
Academic year: September to June
Rector: Prof. Dr YAUHENI ROUBA
Sr Vice-Rector: Assoc. Prof. Dr SVIATLANA AHIIYAVETS
Vice-Rector for Academic Affairs: Dr ULADZIMIR BARSUKOU
Vice-Rector for Academic Affairs and Economy: Dr VASILI SIANKO
Vice-Rector for Academic Affairs and Quality Management: Dr YURY BIALYKH
Vice-Rector for Academic Affairs (IT and Int. Cooperation): Dr YURY VAITUKEVICH
Vice-Rector for Research and Innovations: Prof. Dr HENADZ KHATSKEVICH
Library of 718,300 vols
Number of teachers: 895
Number of students: 17,100
Publications: *Vestnik GrGU—Economics* (2 a year), *Vestnik GrGU—History, Philosophy, Political Science, Sociology* (3 a year), *Vestnik GrGU—Law* (4 a year), *Vestnik GrGU—Mathematics, Physics, Informatics, Computer Science and Management, Biology* (3 a year), *Vestnik GrGU—Philology, Pedagogics, Psychology* (3 a year)

DEANS
Faculty of Arts: Dr LIUDMILA CHARNILOUSKAYA
Faculty of Biology and Ecology: Prof. Dr VASILI BURDZ
Faculty of Economics and Management: Prof. Dr ULADZIMIR FATEEV
Faculty of Engineering and Construction: Dr ALLA VOLIK
Faculty of History and Sociology: Assoc. Prof. Dr EDMUND YARMUSIK
Faculty of Innovative Mechanic Engineering: Prof. Dr VASILI STRUK
Faculty of Law: Prof. Dr MIKALAI SILCHANKA
Faculty of Mathematics and Information Science: Dr ALENA LIVAK
Faculty of Pedagogy: Prof. Dr VIKTAR TARANTSEI
Faculty of Philology: Dr INA LISOUSKAYA
Faculty of Physical Training: Dr ANDREI NAVOICHYK
Faculty of Physics and Engineering: Dr HENADZ HACHKO
Faculty of Psychology: Dr. LILIYA DAUKSHA
Faculty of Tourism and Service: Dr SIARHEI DANSKIKH
Military Faculty: Assoc. Prof. ALIAKSANDR DZMITRUK

Other Institutes of Higher Education

Academy of Public Administration of the President of the Republic of Belarus: 220007 Minsk, vul. Moskovskaya 17; tel. (17) 222-82-05; e-mail rector@pacademy.edu.by; internet www.pacademy.edu.by; f. 1991, acquired presidential institution status 1995; 3 constituent institutes: Institute of Civil Service, Institute of Public Admin., Institute of Sr Management Personnel; library: 200,000 vols; Rector PETR KUKHARCHYK; publ. *Issues of Management*.

Academy of the Ministry of Internal Affairs: 220771 Minsk, pr. Pobeditelei 6; tel. (17) 284-31-15; e-mail info@amia.unibel.by; internet amia.nsys.by; f. 1958; faculties of distance education, forensic medicine, investigation, military studies, officer training and professional training; Rector VITALIY I. APARASEVICH.

Belarus State Academy of Arts: 220012 Minsk, pr. Nezavisimosti 81; tel. (17) 232-15-42; e-mail belam@user.unibel.by; internet belam.by.com; f. 1945; faculties of decorative-applied arts, fine arts and design and theatre; postgraduate courses in theatre art, television, cinema and visual arts, fine and decorative-applied arts and architecture, theory of arts, technical aesthetics and design; library: 83,538 vols; Rector Prof. RICHARD B. SMOLSKIY.

Belarus State Agricultural Academy: 213410 Mogilev raion, Gorki, vul. Michurina 5; tel. (2233) 5-14-20; internet www.belagro.org.by; f. 1840; faculties of accounting, agribusiness and law, agroecology, agronomy, animal husbandry, economics, mechanization, land management and hydromelioration; library: 1.0m. vols; 800 teachers; 11,000 students; Rector Prof. ALEKSANDR R. TSYGANOV; publ. collection of research works (1 a year).

Belarusian Medical Academy of Postgraduate Education: 220013 Minsk, vul. P.

Brovki 3; tel. (17) 232-25-83; e-mail rector@belmapo.edu.by; internet www.belmapo.edu.by; f. 1931; faculties of dentistry, paediatrics, public health and protection, surgery and therapy; attached Laboratory of Scientific Research; 16,000 students; Rector Prof. GENNADIY Y. KHULUP; Librarian ANNA A. KOLBASKO.

Belarusian State Academy of Music: 220030 Minsk, Internatsionalnaya vul. 30; tel. (17) 227-49-42; e-mail bgam@tut.by; internet www.bgam.edu.by; f. 1932; courses: piano, orchestral and folk instruments, singing, composition, pedagogics, musicology, ethnomusicology, choir and symphony conducting; library: 211,702 vols; 307 teachers; 979 students; Rector M. A. KOZINETS.

Minsk Institute of Management: 220102 Minsk, vul. Lazo 12; tel. (17) 242-97-97; e-mail mik@mikby.com; internet www.miu.by; f. 1991; faculties of accounting and finance, economics and law; Rector Dr NIKOLAY V. SUSHA.

Minsk State Higher Education College of Civil Aviation: 220096 Minsk, vul. Uborevitcha 17; tel. (17) 201-02-81; e-mail aviakollege@ivcavia.com; internet www.avia.by/mgvak_en.shtml; f. 1974; trains specialists in aircraft and engine technical exploitation, lifting and transportation, operation of building and road machinery, technical exploitation of aviation technology (electrical devices and light technical equipment), information technology systems and networks, air traffic control and operation; Head ALEXANDER I. NAUMENKO.

Vitebsk State Academy of Veterinary Medicine: 210026 Vitebsk, vul. 1-ya Dovatora 7/11; tel. (212) 37-20-44; e-mail vet@lib.belpak.vitebsk.by; f. 1924; faculties of correspondence studies, specialist upgrading, veterinary medicine and zooengineering; library: 340,000 vols; 348 teachers; 3,109 students; Rector A. I. YATUSEVICH.

BELGIUM

The Higher Education System

The higher education system in Belgium reflects divisions of language, with separate ministries of education for the Dutch (or Flemish), French (Walloon) and German-speaking communities. This division was enshrined in legislation passed in 1963, under which French was established as the medium of instruction in Wallonia, Flemish in Flanders and German in the East-Cantons (Ostkantone). Brussels, the capital, is officially bilingual (French and Flemish). Both public and private university-level institutions are funded through their respective communities, but Roman Catholic institutions are regarded as 'free' and account for about 60% of Belgium's students. A national study fund provides grants where necessary and around 20% of students receive scholarships. Within the French community, in 2004/05 there were 329 non-university higher education institutions and nine university-level institutions, and in 2007/08 a total of 152,624 students were enrolled in higher education (82,901 at non-university establishments and 69,723 at university-level establishments). In 2012 there were 10 universities, 21 Hautes Écoles, 16 Conservatoires and artistic institutes and the transnational University of Limburg, a collaboration between the University of Hasselt and the University of Maastricht (Netherlands) which provides Bachelor and Masters degrees in English and Dutch. Within the Flemish community, in 2009/10 there were 22 non-university higher education institutions (attended by 116,613 students) and seven university-level institutions (attended by 76,602 students). In 2012 there were five universities, 22 university colleges and five associations (formed by one university and one or several university colleges); the Higher Education Register also lists another 10 accredited institutes for higher education and five private institutes or academies of fine arts. German-speaking students typically enrol in institutions in the French community or in Germany itself.

The requirement for entrance into higher education is the Certificat d'Enseignement Secondaire or Diploma Secundair Onderwijs. Hogescholen (see below) are open to all applicants holding the required certificates or to those wishing to attend courses as a 'free' student. The latter category of students is only eligible for certificates, not diplomas, after completing part of these studies. Generally, there are no entrance examinations or selective admission systems in use. However, in specific areas like nautical sciences, civil engineering, dental and medical sciences, architecture and some art courses (audio-visual arts, music and dance), entrance examinations are compulsory.

Belgium began implementing the Bologna Process in higher education institutions in the 2004/05 academic year with reforms being carried out by all three communities. The traditional systems were gradually replaced and Bachelors and Masters degrees were fully implemented by 2008/09. Most universities and university-level institutions use the European Credit Transfer and Accumulation System (ECTS) and issue the Diploma Supplement for free. The Bachelors (which generally takes three years to complete) replaced a number of different degrees, notably one-cycle programmes of up to three years which resulted in either Gegradueerde (Flemish) or Graduat (Walloon), and two-cycle programmes of four or more years consisting of Candidat and Licencié (Walloon) or Kandidaat and Licentiaat (Flemish). The first part of the two-cycle programme (Candidat/Kandidaat) provided a general education, and lasted two years, whilst the second part (Licencié/Licentiaat) provided more specialized training over two or more years. A distinction should be made between the Professional Bachelors, which replaced the one-cycle/Graduate degree and which has a finality, and the Academic Bachelors, which replaced the Candidate degree and which gives access to Masters studies. The Masters (which takes one to two years) is broadly equivalent to the old degrees of complementary education, the Gediplomeerde in de Aanvullende Studiën (Flemish) and Diplômé d'Études Complémentaires (Walloon), and degrees of advanced studies, Diplômé d'Études Approfondies (Walloon) and Diploma van Grondige Studies (Flemish). The final, and highest, level of academic degree is the Doctorate, which has no time limit but is usually awarded three to four years after completion of a final university degree or some equivalent. Doctoral studies (which are defined in ECTS points in the French community, but not in the Flemish community) involve the presentation of a publicly defended thesis.

Non-university post-secondary education is provided by Hautes Écoles (in Wallonia), Hogescholen (in Flanders) and a number of specialist colleges of technology, agriculture, paramedical studies, economics, social studies and teacher training. In Walloon-controlled institutions, courses were previously divided into eight subject categories, leading either to a Graduat after a 'short' course of three years or a Licencié after a 'long' course of four years. In 2004/05 this system changed in line with the Bologna model. Hence, these Haute Écoles now offer Professional Bachelors degrees (180 ECTS) and Masters degrees (60 to 120 ECTS) in conjunction with universities. Furthermore, students can progress to a Diplôme de Spécialisation (DS) of 60 ECTS after the Professional Bachelors degree; this is particularly relevant for paramedical subjects. Programmes in the Hogescholen were also previously divided into 'long/short' courses of one or two cycles, but have now changed to the Bologna system. Hogescholen can offer Professional Bachelors degrees (180 ECTS) and Masters degree programmes in association with a university. Professional Bachelors degrees do not provide direct entry to a Masters degree programme; candidates have to complete a bridging programme of about 45 to 90 ECTS. In 2005 the Autonomous Hochschule of the German-speaking Community was founded in Eupen offering higher education courses specializing in teacher training and nursing.

Technical and vocational training is available either through an employer or an institution (secondary or higher level) and is divided into three categories: apprenticeship contract (usually lasting three years); industrial apprenticeships; and part-time work and/or training. Apprenticeships are rare in Belgium, with the majority of young people completing education in the regular upper secondary school system. Flanders in 2009 introduced the Higher Vocational Education Qualification Level 5 (Hoger Beroepsonderwijs—HBO5); in 2012 there were 47 HBO5 centres offering adult part-time and dual pathway qualifications.

The Joint Accreditation Body of the Netherlands and Flanders (Nederlands-Vlaamse Accreditatieorganisatie—NVAO) was established by Treaty in 2003 and formally ratified in 2005 as an independent body responsible for the accreditation of higher education programmes.

Regulatory and Representative Bodies

GOVERNMENT

Flemish Ministry of Education and Training: Hendrik Consciencegebouw, Koning Albert II-laan 15, 1210 Brussels; tel. (2) 553-50-70; internet www.ond.vlaanderen.be; Minister PASCAL SMET.

Ministry of the French-speaking Community, Office for Compulsory Education: pl. Surlet de Chokier 15/17, 1000 Brussels; tel. (2) 801-78-11; internet gouvernement.cfwb.be/competences-de-la-federation-wallonie-bruxelles/enseignement-obligatoire; Minister MARIE-MARTINE SCHYNS.

Ministry of the French-speaking Community, Office for Higher Education: Ave Louise, 65/9, 1050 Brussels; tel. (2) 801-74-11; internet gouvernement.cfwb.be/competences-de-la-federation-wallonie-bruxelles/enseignement-sup-rieur; Minister JEAN-CLAUDE MARCOURT.

Ministry of the German-speaking Community: Gospertstr. 1, 4700 Eupen; tel. (87) 78-96-13; attached to Department of Education, Vocational Training and Employment; Minister OLIVER PAASCH.

ACCREDITATION

Agence pour l'Evaluation de la Qualité de l'Enseignement Supérieur (Higher Education Quality Evaluation Agency): rue Adolphe Lavallée 1, 5ème étage, 1080 Brussels; e-mail presidence@aeqes.be; internet www.aeqes.be; f. 2002, present status 2008; Pres. MARIANNE COESSENS; Vice-Pres. VINCENT WERTZ.

ENIC-NARIC of the Federation Wallonia-Brussels (Belgium): NARIC of the Belgian French Community, Directorate Gen. for Non-Compulsory Education and Scientific Research, rue A. Lavallée 1, 1080 Brussels; tel. (2) 690-88-57; e-mail celine.nicodeme@cfwb.be; internet www.enseignement.be; f. 1984; Dir-Gen. CHANTAL KAUFMANN; Specialist CELINE NICODÈME.

NARIC Vlaanderen (Belgium): Agency for Quality Assurance in Education and Training, APL services division, Hendrik Consciencegebouw Toren C 2, Koning Albert II-laan 15, 1210 Brussels; tel. (2) 553-89-58; e-mail naric@vlaanderen.be; internet www.naric.be; f. 1984; attached to Flemish Min. of Education and Training, Agency for Quality Assurance in Education and Training; equivalences higher education, secondary education, adult education; application EC directive 2005/36 for regulated professions in the Flemish schools; attestations; information on equivalence matters; Coordinator DANIEL DE SCHRIJVER.

REGIONAL AND COMMUNITY BODIES

Conseil des Recteurs des Universités Francophones de Belgique (CReF) (Rectors' Conference of the French-speaking Community of Belgium): rue d'Egmont 5, 1000 Brussels; tel. (2) 504-93-00; e-mail vandevenne@cref.be; internet www.cref.be; f. 1990; Pres. PIERRE DE MARET; Vice-Pres. BERNARD RENTIER; Vice-Pres. BRUNO DELVAUX.

Conseil Général des Hautes Écoles (Regional Council of Hautes Écoles): rue Adolphe Lavallée 1, 1080 Brussels; tel. (2) 690-88-24; e-mail brigitte.twyffels@cfwb.be; internet www.enseignement.be; Dir BRIGITTE TWYFFELS (acting).

Conseil Interuniversitaire de la Communauté Française de Belgique (CIUF) (Interuniversity Council of the French-speaking Community in Belgium): rue d'Egmont 5, 1000 Brussels; tel. (2) 504-92-91; e-mail info@ciuf.be; internet www.ciuf.be; f. 2003; represents 9 univs. and univ.-level instns in the French-speaking community; advises on education policy; promotes cooperation between univs and univ.-level instns; Pres. BRUNO DELVAUX; Vice-Pres. BERNARD RENTIER; Sec. CLAUDE LALOUT.

Institut d'Encouragement de la Recherche Scientifique et de l'Innovation de Bruxelles/Instituut ter Bevordering van het Wetenschappelijk Onderzoek en de Innovatie van Brussel (Institute for the Encouragement of Scientific Research and Innovation of Brussels): Domaine Latour de Freins, rue Engeland 555, 1180 Brussels (Uccle); tel. (2) 600-50-34; e-mail info@irsib.irisnet.be; internet www.irsib.irisnet.be; f. 2003; promotes, supports and valorizes scientific research and technological innovation; provides financial support.

Vlaamse Hogescholenraad (VLHORA) (Flemish Council of University Colleges): Ravensteingalerij 27 bus 3, 1e verd, 1000 Brussels; tel. (2) 211-41-90; e-mail info@vlhora.be; internet www.vlhora.be; f. 1996, awarded statute of public utility institution by decree in 1998; gives advice to the Flemish authorities on all policy aspects regarding college education, scientific project research, social services and the practice of the arts; organizes and stimulates consultation between the institutions on all issues related to the univ. colleges (hogescholen); Chair. Prof. BERT HOOGEWIJS; Sec.-Gen. MARC VANDEWALLE.

Vlaamse Interuniversitaire Raad (VLIR) (Flemish Interuniversity Council): Ravensteingalerij 27, 1000 Brussels; tel. (2) 792-55-00; e-mail administratie@vlir.be; internet www.vlir.be; f. 1976; autonomous body financed by univs; advises on and presents proposals to min. with regard to univ. education; research activities; Chair. Prof. Dr PAUL VAN CAUWENBERGE; Sec.-Gen. Prof. Dr ROSETTE S' JEGERS.

Learned Societies

GENERAL

Académie Royale des Sciences, des Lettres et des Beaux-Arts de Belgique (Royal Academy of Science, Letters and Fine Arts of Belgium): Palais des Académies, rue Ducale 1, 1000 Brussels; tel. (2) 550-22-12; e-mail academieroyale@cfwb.be; internet www.academieroyale.be; f. 1772; colln of paintings, graphic works, sculptures, letters, memoirs and medals; video and audio cassette library and archive; 400 mems (200 ordinary, 200 assoc.); library of 600,000 vols; Pres. JEAN-LOUIS MIGEOT; Permanent Sec. HERVE HASQUIN; Librarian CLAIRE PASCAUD; publs *Bulletin de la Classe des Arts* (1 a year), *Bulletin de la Classe des Lettres et des Sciences Morales et Politiques*, *La Lettre des Académies* (4 a year), *Mémoires de l'Académie Royale de Belgique* (5–10 a year), *Nouvelle Biographie Nationale* (every 2 years).

Académie Royale des Sciences d'Outre-Mer/Koninklijke Academie voor Overzeese Wetenschappen (Royal Academy for Overseas Sciences): ave Louise 231, 1050 Brussels; tel. (2) 538-02-11; e-mail kaowarsom@skynet.be; internet www.kaowarsom.be; f. 1928, present name and status 1959; promotes scientific knowledge of overseas countries, esp. with particular devt problems; organizes colloquia, symposia, seminars and confs; 305 mems; Pres. JACQUES CHARLIER; Permanent Sec. DANIELLE SWINNE; publs *Actes Symposiums/Acta Symposia*, *Biographie belge d'Outre-Mer/Belgische Overzeese Biografie*, *Bulletin des Séances/Mededelingen der Zittingen* (4 a year), *Recueils d'études historiques/Historische bijdragen*.

Koninklijke Vlaamse Academie van België voor Wetenschappen en Kunsten (Royal Flemish Academy of Belgium for Science and the Arts): Paleis der Academiën, Hertogsstraat 1, 1000 Brussels; tel. (2) 550-23-23; e-mail info@kvab.be; internet www.kvab.be; f. 1938; promotes cooperation between different educational institutions; organizes scientific and cultural activities; 300 mems (incl. spec. foreign mems); library of 50,000 vols; Pres. Prof. Dr PIERRE JACOBS; Permanent Sec. Prof. Dr GÉRY VAN OUTRYVE D'YDEWALLE; publs *Academiae Analecta*, *Collectanea Biblica et Religiosa Antiqua*, *Collectanea Hellenistica*, *Collectanea Maritima*, *Fontes Historiae Artis Neerlandicae*, *Iuris Scripta Historica*, *Iusti Lipsi Epistolae*, *Memoirs*.

Attached Institute:

Commission Royale d'Histoire/Koninklijke Commissie voor Geschiedenis (Royal Historical Commission): Palais des Académies, rue Ducale 1, 1000 Brussels; tel. (2) 550-22-20; e-mail luc.moreau@cfwb.be; internet www.kcgeschiedenis.be; f. 1834; researches, analysis and publication of written sources concerning the history of Belgium; Pres. GUSTAAF JANSSENS; Vice-Pres. CLAUDE BRUNEEL; Sec. and Treas. GUY VANTHEMSCHE; publ. *Instruments de Travail* (irregular).

AGRICULTURE, FISHERIES AND VETERINARY SCIENCE

Fédération Wallonne de l'Agriculture: chaussée de Namur 47, 5030 Gembloux; tel. (81) 60-00-60; e-mail fwa@fwa.be; internet www.fwa.be; f. 2001; protects professional interests.

Attached Institute:

Committee of Agricultural Organizations in the EU (Copa): rue de Trèves 61 1040 Brussels; tel. (2) 287-27-11; e-mail mail@copa-cogeca.eu; internet www.copa-cogeca.eu; f. 1958; 60 mems, 36 partner orgs; Pres. PADRAIG WALSHE; Sec. Gen. PEKKA PESONEN.

ARCHITECTURE AND TOWN PLANNING

Association Royale des Demeures Historiques de Belgique (Royal Association for Historic Buildings): rue de Trèves 67, 1040 Brussels; tel. (2) 400-77-08; e-mail administration@demeures-historiques.be; internet www.demeures-historiques.be; f. 1934, present status 1958; Pres. HRH PRINCE LORENZ OF BELGIUM; Pres. Baron CARDON DE LICHTBUER; Sec. Gen. Baron JOSEPH DE DORLODOT; Treas. DIRK LEERMAKERS; publs *François-Emmanuel de Wasseige*, *La Maison d'Hier et d'Aujourd'hui* (4 a year).

Fédération Royale des Sociétés d'Architectes de Belgique: rue Ernest Allard 21, 1ère étage, 1000 Brussels; tel. (2) 512-34-52; e-mail info@fab-arch.be; internet www.fab-arch.be; f. 1905; Pres. LUC DELEUZE; Sec. GEORGES BRUTSAERT; Treas. PHILEMON WACHTELAER.

Société Centrale d'Architecture de Belgique: Maison des Architectes, rue Ernest Allard 21/4, 1000 Brussels; tel. (2) 511-34-92; e-mail info@scab.be; internet scab.archiscab.be; f. 1872; promotes architecture and town planning; 180 mems; library of 20,000 vols; Pres. SERGE ROOSE; Vice-Pres. RENAUD DARD-

ENNE; Sec. JEAN-PIERRE VIENNE; Treas. LAURENCE MERCIER.

BIBLIOGRAPHY, LIBRARY SCIENCE AND MUSEOLOGY

Archives et Bibliothèques de Belgique: blvd de l'Empereur 4, 1000 Brussels; tel. (2) 519-53-93; e-mail frankd@kbr.be; f. 1907; a sub-cttee of UNESCO, studies methods of standardization of bibliography; 350 mems; Pres. Dr FRANK DAELEMANS; publs *Archives et Bibliothèques de Belgique*, *Coll* (1 a year).

Association Professionnelle des Bibliothécaires et Documentalistes: Place de la Wallonie, 15, 6140 Fontaine-L'eveque; tel. (71) 52-31-93; e-mail info@apbd.be; internet www.apbd.be; f. 1975; promotes functions of library and information professionals; defends professional interests of librarians and archivists; 300 mems; Pres. LAURENCE BOULANGER; Vice-Pres. ALEXANDRE LEMAIRE; Vice-Pres. ANDRÉ MORUE; Sec. FABIENNE GÉRARD; Treas. GUY TONDREAU.

Service Belge des Echanges Internationaux/Belgische Dienst Internationale Ruil (Belgian International Exchange Service): Keizerslaan, 4 blvd de l'Empereur, 1000 Brussels; tel. (2) 519-53-94; e-mail nathael.istasse@kbr.be; f. 1889; information, documentation, exchange and transmission; Dir Dr NATHAËL ISTASSE; Librarian CHRISTOPHE JOUNIAUX; Librarian NATHALIE GEOFFROIT.

Vereniging van Antwerpse Bibliofielen (Antwerp Bibliophile Society): Museum Plantin-Moretus, Vrijdagmarkt 22, 2000 Antwerp; tel. (3) 221-14-67; e-mail pierre.meulepas@stad.antwerpen.be; internet www.boekgeschiedenis.be; f. 1877; fmrly Maatschappij der Antwerpsche Bibliophilen; conserves typographic heritage; promotes study of history of printed book; organizes excursions; 175 mems; Pres. MARCUS DE SCHEPPER; Vice-Pres. JEAN-PIERRE TRICOT; Sec. PIERRE MEULEPAS; Treas. NORBERT MOERMANS; publ. *De Gulden Passer* (2 a year).

Vlaamse Museumvereniging (Flemish Museums Association): Europawijk 30/205, 2400 Mol; tel. (14) 71-62-70; e-mail info@museumvereniging.be; internet www.museumvereniging.be; f. 1962, present name and status 1982; defends interests of museums and museum personnel; 650 mems; Pres. WIM DE VOS; Vice-Pres. SOFIER WILDE; Sec. PETER VAN DER PLAETSEN; Treas. ELKE MANSHOVEN; publs *Museumkatern* (4 a year), *VMV Nieuwsbrief*.

ECONOMICS, LAW AND POLITICS

Institut Belge de Science Politique/Belgisch Instituut voor Wetenschap der Politiek (Belgian Political Science Association): place Montesquieu 1/7, 1348 Louvain-la-Neuve; tel. (10) 47-40-48; e-mail absp-cf@uclouvain.be; f. 1951, present status 1996; Pres. BENOÎT RIHOUX; Vice-Pres. CORINNE GOBIN; Sec. RÉGIS DANDOY; Treas. NATHALIE PERRIN.

Société Royale d'Economie Politique de Belgique (Royal Belgian Society of Political Economy): c/o CIFOP, ave Général Michel 1B, 6000 Charleroi; tel. (71) 53-29-08; e-mail cattelain.marlene@cifop.be; internet www.cifop.be/groupe.php?id=24; f. 1855, present status 1997; promotes and contributes to progress of political economy; 400 mems; Pres. ETIENNE DE CALLATAY; Sec.-Gen. MARLÈNE CATTELAIN; Treas. JEAN-EDOUARD CARBONNELLE.

Union Royale Belge pour les Pays d'Outre-Mer (Royal Belgian Overseas Union): rue de Stassart 20, 1050 Brussels; tel. (2) 384-37-40; e-mail a.schoro@skynet.be; internet www.urome.be; f. 1912; gathers asscns of fmr colonies, cooperatives and Congolese living in Belgium; protects interests of veterans from Congo, Rwanda and Burundi and member asscns; organizes confs; 10,000 mems; Pres. ANDRÉ DE MAERE; Vice-Pres. GUIDO BOSTEELS; Vice-Pres. PAUL VANNÈS; Admin. and Treas. ELISABETH JANSSENS.

Vereniging voor Politieke Wetenschappen (Institute of Political Science): Van Evenstraat 2B, 3000 Leuven; tel. (16) 32-32-54; e-mail res.publica@soc.kuleuven.be; f. 1958; annual conf. jtly with Dutch Political Science Assn; PhD seminars; 700 mems; Pres. Prof. Dr MARC HOOGHE; publs *Belgian Political Yearbook* (Dutch, English and French), *Res Publica* (4 a year, in Dutch, English and French), *Res Publica Library*.

FINE AND PERFORMING ARTS

Association Belge de Photographie et de Cinématographie asbl (Belgian Association of Photography and Cinematography): rue de Sévigné, Anderlecht 1A, 1070 Brussels; tel. (47) 214-46-29; e-mail jacques.guilmin@hotmail.com; internet abpc066.hautetfort.com; f. 1874; provides training in photography and cinematography and exhibits works of members; 30 mems; Pres. JACQUES MAROQUIN; Sec. JACQUES GUILMIN; Treas. JEAN-LOUIS BECKMAN; publ. *Informations* (5 a year).

HISTORY, GEOGRAPHY AND ARCHAEOLOGY

Académie Royale d'Archéologie de Belgique/Koninklijke Academie voor Oudheidkunde van België (Royal Academy of Archaeology of Belgium): Palais des Académies, rue Ducale 1, 1000 Brussels; e-mail info@acad.be; internet www.acad.be; f. 1842; promotes study of archaeology and art history of Southern Low Countries, Liège and Belgium; grants Simone Bergmans Award to unpublished study on history of nat. art every 3 years; 100 mems (60 ordinary, 40 corresp.); Pres. Dr ALEXANDRA DE POORTER; Gen. Sec. Dr ISABELLE LECOCQ; publ. *Revue Belge d'Archéologie et d'Histoire de l'Art / Belgisch Tijdschrift voor Oudheidkunde en Kunstgeschiedenis* (1 a year).

Association Egyptologique Reine Elisabeth/Egyptologisch Genootschap Koningin Elisabeth (Queen Elizabeth Association of Egyptology): Parc du Cinquantenaire 10, 1000 Brussels; tel. (2) 741-73-64; e-mail aere.egke@kmkg-mrah.be; internet www.aere-egke.be; f. 1923; encourages Egyptological and papyrological research; promotes study of history and civilization of Pharaonic, Graeco-Roman and Christian Egypt; 650 mems; library of 30,000 vols; Chair. Comte ARNOUL D'ARSCHOT SCHOONHOVEN; Sec.-Gen. LUC DELVAUX; publs *Bibliographie Papyrologique* (4 a year), *Chronique d'Egypte* (2 a year).

Belgisch Genootschap voor Byzantijnse Studies/Société Belge d'Etudes Byzantines (Belgian Society for Byzantine Studies): Hertogstraat 1, 1000 Brussels; tel. (9) 264-40-28; e-mail erika.gielen@hiw.kuleuven.be; internet www.byzantium.be; f. 1956; 34 mems; Pres. Prof. KRISTOFFEL DEMOEN; Sec. Dr ERIKA GIELEN; publ. *Byzantion*.

Belgische Vereniging voor Aardrijkskundige Studies/Société Belge d'Etudes Géographiques (Belgian Society for Geographical Studies): W. de Croylaan 42, 3001 Heverlee; tel. (16) 32-24-27; f. 1931; centralizes and coordinates geographical research; 150 mems; Pres. J. CHARLIER; Sec. F. WITLOX; publ. *BELGEO* (2 a year).

Institut Archéologique du Luxembourg (Archaeological Institute of Luxembourg): rue des Martyrs 13–16, 6700 Arlon; tel. (63) 21-28-49; e-mail info@ial.be; internet www.ial.be; f. 1847; deployed between 2 museums; Archaeological Museum covers prehistoric period, Belgian-Roman period, Frankish period; Gaspar Museum displays works by Jean-Marie Gaspar and local art since 16th century; 500 mems; library of 25,000 vols; Pres. LOUIS LEJEUNE; publ. *Annales*.

Institut Archéologique Liégeois: Grand Curtius, quai de Maastricht 13, 4000 Liège; tel. (4) 232-98-60; e-mail info@ialg.be; internet www.ialg.be; f. 1850; promotes studies of history and archaeology and related sciences in the Dist. of Liège; 250 mems (200 ordinary, 50 corresp.); Pres. PIERRE GASON; Sec. MAURICE LORENZI.

Institut Géographique National/Nationaal Geografisch Instituut: Abbaye de la Cambre 13, 1000 Brussels; tel. (2) 629-82-82; e-mail sales@ngi.be; internet www.ign.be; f. 1831, present status 1976; land surveying and cartography; performs aerial photographic coverage of the territory; creates database; 267 mems; library of 15,000 maps; Dir-Gen. INGRID VANDEN BERGHE; publ. *Catalog* (1 a year).

Société Archéologique de Namur (Archaeological Society of Namur): Hôtel de Croix, rue Saintraint 3, 5000 Namur; tel. (81) 22-43-62; e-mail soc.arch.namur@scarlet.be; internet www.lasan.be; f. 1845; museum and library; discovery, conservation, implementation and publcation of cultural heritage of Namur; 450 mems; Pres. EMMANUEL BODART; Sec. JACQUES JEANMART; Treas. MICHEL GILBERT; publ. *Annales* (1 a year).

Société Royale Belge de Géographie (Royal Belgian Society of Geography): Campus ULB du Solbosch, CP 130/03, Ave F. D. Roosevelt, 50, 1050 Brussels; tel. (2) 650-68-02; e-mail srbg@ulb.ac.be; internet www.srbg.be; f. 1876; 100 mems; Pres. Prof. Dr CHRISTIAN VANDERMOTTEN; Sec.-Gen. Dr B. WAYENS; publ. *Belgeo* (4 a year).

Société Royale d'Archéologie de Bruxelles: c/o Université Libre de Bruxelles, CP 175, ave F. D. Roosevelt 50, 1050 Brussels; tel. (2) 650-24-86; e-mail secretariat@srab.be; internet www.srab.be; f. 1887; prevents destruction of monuments; sections for archaeology, and history of art; other collns in Musées Royaux d'Art et d'Histoire; organizes exhibitions, lectures, tours and excursions; 450 mems; library of 20,000 vols; Pres. A. DIERKENS; Vice-Pres. J. M. DUVOSQUEZ; Vice-Pres. C. L. DICKSTEIN; Sec.-Gen. A. VANRIE; publ. *Annales*.

Société Royale de Numismatique de Belgique/Koninklijk Belgisch Genootschap voor Numismatiek (Royal Numismatic Society of Belgium): c/o Cabinet des Médailles, Bibliothèque Royale de Belgique, blvd de l'Empereur 4, 1000 Brussels; tel. (2) 519-56-08; e-mail jm@bvdmc.com; internet www.numisbel.be; f. 1841; promotes numismatics and sigillography through publs and confs; 225 mems (12 hon. mems, 32 institutional mems, 42 foreign mems, 48 working mems, 91 corresp. mems); Pres. JOHAN VAN HEESCH; Vice-Pres. FRANÇOIS DE CALLATAŸ; Sec. CÉCILE ARNOULD; Treas. HUGUETTE TAYMANS; publ. *Revue Belge de Numismatique et de Sigillographie* (1 a year).

LANGUAGE AND LITERATURE

Académie Royale de Langue et de Littérature Françaises (Royal Academy of French Language and Literature): Palais des Académies, rue Ducale 1, 1000 Brussels; tel. (2) 550-22-72; e-mail alf@cfwb.be; internet www.arllfb.be; f. 1920; promotes

French language and literature; awards literary prizes; 40 mems (incl. 10 foreign mems); Dir YVES NAMUR; Vice-Dir RAYMOND TROUSSON; Permanent Sec. JACQUES DE DECKER; publs *Annuaire*, *Mémoires*.

Alliance Française de Bruxelles-Europe: rue de la Loi 26, 1040 Brussels; tel. (2) 788-21-60; e-mail info@alliancefr.be; internet www.alliancefr.be; f. 1945; offers courses and examinations in French language and culture; attached offices in Antwerp, Condroz-Meuse-Hesbaye, Hainaut, Kortrijk, Limburg, Verviers and Gand; 8 Belgian depts; library of 4,000 vols, 30 periodicals, 400 DVDs, 35 CD-ROMs, 300 brochures, 1,100 audio cassettes and CDs, 450 comics strips, 1,000 video cassettes, 50 exhibits; Dir THIERRY LAGNAU.

Association des Ecrivains Belges de Langue Française (Association of Belgian Writers in the French Language): Maison Camille Lemonnier-Maison des Ecrivains, chaussée de Wavre 150, 1050 Brussels; tel. (2) 512-29-68; e-mail a.e.b@skynet.be; internet www.ecrivainsbelges.be; f. 1902; 500 mems; library of 11,000 vols; awards prizes for essays, poetry and prose; Camille Lemonnier museum; Pres. JEAN-PIERRE DOPAGNE; Vice-Pres. MARIE NICOLAÏ; Vice-Pres. EMILE KESTEMAN; Sec. Gen. JEAN LACROIX; Treas. JEAN PIRLET; publ. *Nos Lettres* (10 a year).

British Council: Leopold Plaza, rue du Trône 108, 1050 Brussels; tel. (2) 227-08-40; e-mail enquiries@britishcouncil.be; internet www.britishcouncil.org/brussels; offers courses and exams in English language and British culture; promotes cultural exchange with the UK; also responsible for Luxembourg; Dir MARTIN HOPE.

Goethe-Institut: rue Belliard 58, 1040 Brussels; tel. (2) 230-39-70; e-mail info@bruessel.goethe.org; internet www.goethe.de/bruessel; f. 1959; offers courses and examinations in German language and culture; promotes cultural exchange with Germany; library of 20,000 vols, 90 periodicals; Dir SUSANNE HÖHN; Sec. CHANTAL BOERSEN.

Instituto Cervantes: ave de Tervurenlaan 64, 1040 Brussels; tel. (2) 737-01-90; e-mail cenbru@cervantes.es; internet bruselas.cervantes.es; offers courses and exams in Spanish language and culture; promotes cultural exchange with Spain and Spanish-speaking Latin and Central America; library of 25,000 documents, incl. books, periodicals, CDs, DVDs, video cassettes and CD-ROMs; Dir MARÍA DE LOS ÁNGELES GONZÁLEZ ENCINAR; Sec. NURIA BLANCO MARTÍNEZ.

International PEN Club, French-speaking Branch: c/o Huguette de Broqueville, ave des Cerfs 10, 1950 Kraainem (Bruxelles); tel. (2) 731-48-47; e-mail huguette.db@skynet.be; internet www.hdebroqueville.be; f. 1922; petitions for writers in prison; literary meeting with int. writers: French, Italy, Russian, German etc.; 540 mems; Pres. HUGUETTE DE BROQUEVILLE; Gen. Sec. ALISON JANE BELL.

International PEN Club, PEN-Centre Belgium: POB 12, King Albertpark, 2600 Antwerp-Berchem; e-mail info@penvlaanderen.be; internet www.penvlaanderen.be; Dutch-speaking br.; f. 1935; 195 mems; Pres. GEERT VAN ISTENDAEL; Vice-Pres. INGRID VANDER VEKEN; Sec. GUY POSSON; Treas. SUZANNE BINNEMANS; publ. *PEN-Tijdingen* (4 a year).

Koninklijke Academie voor Nederlandse Taal- en Letterkunde (Royal Academy of Dutch Language and Literature): Koningstraat 18, 9000 Ghent; tel. (9) 265-93-40; e-mail secretariaat@kantl.be; internet www.kantl.be; f. 1886; promotes literary and cultural life in Flanders; encourages research into Dutch language, culture and literature; 79 mems (30 ordinary, 5 extraordinary, 19 hon. mems, 25 foreign hon.); library of 50,000 vols; Pres. Prof. Dr MARCEL DE SMEDT; Permanent Sec. Prof. Dr WILLY VANDEWEGHE; publ. *Verslagen en Mededelingen* (3 a year).

Société Belge des Auteurs, Compositeurs et Editeurs (Belgian Society of Authors, Composers and Publishers): rue d'Arlon, 75–77, 1040 Brussels; tel. (2) 286-82-11; e-mail frontoffice@sabam.be; internet www.sabam.be; f. 1922; collection and distribution of copyrights; 25,000 mems; Chair. STIJN CONINX; Vice-Chair. TIMOTHY HAGELSTEIN; Vice-Chair. JAN VAN LANDEGHEM; Man. Dir CHRISTOPHE DEPRETER; publ. *Sabam Magazine* (4 a year).

Société de Langue et de Littérature Wallonnes (Society for Walloon Language and Literature): Université de Liège, place du XX Août 7, 4000 Liège; tel. (86) 34-44-32; e-mail sllw.be@skynet.be; internet users.skynet.be/sllw; f. 1856; promotes local literary productions in Walloon; 400 mems; library of 20,000 vols; Pres. GUY FONTAINE; Sec. MARC DUYSINX; Treas. JEAN BRUMIOUL; publs *Dialectes de Wallonie* (1 a year), *Littérature dialectale d'aujourd'hui* (1 a year), *Mémoire Wallonne* (1 a year), *Wallonnes* (4 a year).

Société d'Études Latines de Bruxelles (LATOMUS) absl (Brussels Society for Latin Studies): rue du Palais St Jacques 6, 7500 Tournai; e-mail latomus@belgacom.net; internet users.belgacom.net/latomus; f. 1936; promotes Latin studies, Roman history and archaeology in Belgium by publ. of books and journals; 750 mems; Dir-Gen. M. CARL DEROUX; publs *Collection Latomus*, *Review Latomus* (4 a year).

Société Littéraire de Liège: pl. de la République Française 5, 4000 Liège; tel. (4) 223-71-66; e-mail olivier.hamal@skynet.be; internet www.litteraire-liege.be; f. 1779; maintains archives and runs clubs and circles related to literature, art and history; 500 mems; Pres. OLIVIER HAMAL; Sec. JEAN-MARIE DE COUNE; Treas. BAUDOUIN RABAU.

MEDICINE

Académie Royale de Médecine de Belgique (Royal Academy of Medicine of Belgium): Palais des Académies, rue Ducale 1, 1000 Brussels; tel. (2) 550-22-55; e-mail contact@armb.be; internet www.armb.be; f. 1841, present status 2013; divs of biological sciences, human medicine, immunology, microbiology, parasitology, pharmacy, public health and forensic medicine, surgery and obstetrics, veterinary medicine; 300 mems; Pres. Prof. JACQUES BROTCHI; Permanent Sec. Prof. AUGUSTIN FERRANT; publs *Bulletin et Mémoires* (2 a year), *Proceedings of the Belgian Academies of Medicine* (1 a year, print and online, www.probram.be).

Association Belge de Santé Publique (Belgian Association of Public Health): c/o Scientific Institute of Public Health, rue Juliette Weytsman 14, 1050 Brussels; tel. (2) 642-57-09; e-mail jamila.buziarsist@wiv-isp.be; internet www.baph.be; f. 1938; promotes public health research in Belgium; 200 mems; Pres. Prof. Dr GUIDO VAN HAL; Vice-Pres. VÉRONIQUE TELLIER; Vice-Pres. WILLEM AELVOET; Sec. JAMILA BUZIARSIST; Treas. JOHAN VAN DER HEYDEN; publ. *Archives of Public Health*.

Association Royale des Sociétés Scientifiques Médicales Belges/Koninklijke Vereniging van de Belgische Medische Wetenschappelijke Genootschappen (Royal Association of Medical Scientific Societies of Belgium): ave Winston Churchill 11, bte 30, 1180 Brussels; tel. (2) 374-51-58; e-mail amb@skynet.be; internet www.arsmb-kvbmg.be; f. 1945; promotes Belgian medical socs; 4,000 mems; Pres. Dr D. VAN RAEMDONCK; Vice-Pres. Dr J. P. SQUIFFLET; Sec. Gen. Dr M. HOOGMARTENS; Treas. Dr PH. KOLH; publs *Acta Anaesthesiologica Belgica* (4 a year), *Acta Chirurgica Belgica* (6 a year), *Acta Neurologica Belgica* (4 a year), *Acta Orthopedica Belgica* (6 a year), *JBR-BTR* (Belgian Journal of Radiology, 6 a year).

Belgian Association for Cancer Research: Department of Medical Oncology, University Hospital Antwerpen, Wilrijkstraat 10, 2650 Antwerp; tel. (3) 821-33-75; e-mail jan.b.vermorken@uza.be; internet www.bacr.be; Pres. J. B. VERMORKEN; Vice-Pres. V. GREGOIRE; Sec. G. ANDRY; Treas. MARK DE RIDDER.

Koninklijke Academie voor Geneeskunde van België (Belgian Royal Academy of Medicine): Hertogsstraat 1, 1000 Brussels; tel. (2) 550-23-06; e-mail academiegeneeskunde@vlaanderen.be; internet www.academiegeneeskunde.be; f. 1938; promotes scientific research in fields of human medicine, pharmacy, veterinary medicine; awards scientific prizes; organizes meetings and confs.; 166 mems (80 ordinary, 55 foreign corresp., 22 hon., 9 foreign hon.); Pres. Prof. Dr BERNARD HIMPENS; Sec. Gen. Prof. Dr AART DE KRUIF; publ. *Dissertationes–Series Historica*.

Probio: ave de la Constitution 56/13, 1090 Brussels; tel. (2) 466-22-13; e-mail probio.service@swing.be; internet www.probio.be; f. 1977; promotes and defends profession of biology; determines conditions required to acquire and provide good training for both scientific and educational roles, esp. in biology; Pres. CATHERINE LAUMONIER; Vice-Pres. SYLVETTE DESCAMPS; Sec. MARIE DECUYPER; publs *PROBIO Revue* (2 a year), *PROBIO Service* (4 a year).

Société Belge de Médecine Tropicale/Belgische Vereniging voor Tropische Geneeskunde: Nationalestraat 155, Antwerp; tel. (3) 247-62-12; e-mail dvdr@itg.be; f. 1920; 569 mems (24 Belgian and foreign hon., 66 assoc., 85 titular, 394 corresp.); Sec. Prof. Dr B. GRYSEELS; publ. *Tropical Medicine and International Health* (12 a year).

Société Belge d'Ophtalmologie, section francophone (Belgian Society of Ophthalmology, French-speaking section): c/o Marlene Verlaeckt, Kapucijnenvoer 33, 3000 Louvain; tel. (16) 33-23-98; f. 1896; Sec. Prof. J. M. LEMAGNE; publ. *Bulletin* (4 a year).

NATURAL SCIENCES

General

Association pour la Promotion des Publications Scientifiques (APPS): 26 ave de l'Amarante, 1020 Brussels; tel. (2) 268-29-33; f. 1981; 80 mems and 20 assoc. mems; Pres. Dr JEAN BAUDET; publ. *Ingénieur et Industrie* (12 a year).

Société Royale des Sciences de Liège (Royal Society of Sciences of Liège): Institut de Mathématique de l'Université de Liège, B 37, Grande Traverse 12, 4000 Liège; tel. (4) 366-93-71; e-mail srsl@guest.ulg.ac.be; internet www.srsl-ulg.net; f. 1835; promotes biological, chemical, mathematical, mineral and physical sciences; 200 mems; Pres. GUY MAGHIN-ROGISTER; Sec.-Gen. Prof. JACQUES AGHION.

Société Scientifique de Bruxelles: 61 rue de Bruxelles, 5000 Namur; tel. (81) 72-41-36; e-mail anne-martine.baert@fundp.ac.be; f. 1875; 140 mems; Sec. Gen. GUY DEMORTIER; Admin. ANNE-MARTINE BAERT; publ. *Revue des Questions Scientifiques* (4 a year).

Biological Sciences

Belgian Society of Human Genetics: rue au Bois 22, 1950 Kraainem; e-mail helene.antoine-poirel@uclouvain.be; internet www.beshg.be; f. 2000; promotes research in human genetics; organizes scientific meetings; Pres. HÉLÈNE ANTOINE-POIREL; Sec. THOMY DE RAVEL DE L'ARGENTIÈRE; Treas. GUY VAN CAMP.

Belgische Vereniging voor Microbiologie (Belgian Society for Microbiology): Rega Institute, Minderbroedersstraat 10, 3000 Leuven; tel. 16337341; e-mail bsm.newsletter@gmail.com; internet www.belsocmicrobio.be; f. 1996; 240 mems; Chair. Prof. JOZEF ANNÉ; Sec. Prof. PAUL DE VOS.

Koninklijke Maatschappij voor Dierkunde van Antwerpen (Royal Zoological Society of Antwerp): Koningin Astridplein 26, 2018 Antwerp; tel. (3) 202-45-40; internet www.kmda.org; f. 1843; zoological and botanical gardens, aquarium, nature reserve, laboratories; educational and cultural services and scientific research; responsible for 3 instns: Antwerp Zoo, Planckendael and Queen Elisabeth Hall (concert hall); 32,000 mems; library of 34,000 vols; CEO DRIES HERPOELAERT; publ. *Zoo* (4 a year, in Dutch).

Société Belge de Biochimie et de Biologie Moléculaire (SBBBM)/Belgische Vereniging voor Biochemie en Moleculaire Biologie (BVBMB) (Belgian Society of Biochemistry and Molecular Biology): UCL-ICP 74.39, ave Hippocrate 74–75, 1200 Brussels; tel. (2) 764-74-39; e-mail info@biochemistry.be; internet www.biochemistry.be; f. 1951; promotes research in fields of sciences, medicine, pharmacy, agriculture, veterinary medicine; 700 mems; Pres. Dr ANNE-MARIE LAMBEIR; Sec. Prof. FRED R. OPPERDOES; Treas. Prof. YVES ENGELBORGHS.

Société Belge de Biologie Clinique/Belgische Vereniging voor Klinische Biologie (Belgian Society for Clinical Biology): Laboratoriumgeneeskunde, UZ Gasthuisberg, Herestraat 49, 3000 Leuven; tel. (16) 34-79-02; internet www.bvkb-sbbc.org; f. 1948, present name and status 1997; encourages research in clinical biology; promotes teaching of laboratory medicine; 350 mems; Pres. PIETER VERMEERSCH; Vice-Pres. ANNE DEMULDER; Vice-Pres. ALAIN VERSTRAETE; Sec. DELPHINE MARTINY; Treas. LUC VANDENVULCKE.

Société Royale Belge d'Entomologie/Koninklijke Belgische Vereniging voor Entomologie (Royal Belgian Entomological Society): rue Vautier 29, 1000 Brussels; tel. (2) 627-43-21; e-mail info@srbe-kbve.be; internet www.srbe-kbve.be; f. 1855; promotes study of insects; 250 mems; library of 23,000 vols; Pres. WOUTER DEKONINCK; Vice-Pres. MARC POLLET; Sec. KOEN SMETS; Treas. UGO DALL'ASTA; publs *Bulletin* (2 a year), *Catalogue des Coléoptères de Belgique* (irregular), *Mémoires* (irregular).

Société Royale de Botanique de Belgique/Koninklijke Belgische Botanische Vereniging (Royal Botanical Society of Belgium): c/o Pierre Meerts, chaussée de Wavre 1850, 1160 Brussles; tel. (2) 650-21-64; e-mail inparmen@ulb.ac.be; internet www.botany.be; f. 1862; promotes botany through scientific research, publs, confs and excursions; distributes awards for botanical research; 200 mems; Pres. Prof. LUDWIG TRIEST; Vice-Pres. ELMAR ROBBRECHT; Sec. PIERRE MEERTS; Treas. ANN BOGAERTS; publ. *Plant Ecology and Evolution* (2 a year).

Société Royale Zoologique de Belgique/Koninklijke Belgische Vereniging voor Dierkunde (Royal Belgian Zoological Society): Koninklijk Belgisch Instituut voor Natuurwetenschappen, Vautierstaat 29, 1000 Brussels; tel. (2) 650-40-38; e-mail bjz@ua.ac.be; internet www.naturalsciences.be/institute/associations/rbzs_website; f. 1863; promotes study of zoology; 400 mems; library of 1,500 periodicals; Pres. Dr P. MERGEN; Sec. Prof. Dr H. LEIRS; Treas. Dr E. VERHEYEN; publ. *Belgian Journal of Zoology* (2 a year).

Mathematical Sciences

Belgian Mathematical Society: Campus de la Plaine, CP 218/01, blvd du Triomphe, 1050 Brussels; tel. (3) 265-39-00; e-mail bms@ulb.ac.be; internet bms.ulb.ac.be; f. 1921; promotion of mathematical activities; defends interests of Belgian mathematicians; 190 mems; library of 170 vols; Pres. Prof. FRANÇOISE BASTIN; Sec. Prof. JAN VAN CASTEREN.

Conseil Supérieur de Statistique: WTCIII, blvd Simon Bolivar 30, 1000 Brussels; tel. (2) 277-71-69; e-mail philippe.mauroy@economie.fgov.be; internet statbel.fgov.be/fr/statistiques/organisation/css; f. 1841, present name 1946; supports devt of statistics; ensures quality and unity of statistical work of govt instns; develops regionalized statistics; 36 mems; Pres. MARTINE VAN WOUWE; Sec. PHILIPPE MAUROY; Sec. NADINE BUNTINX.

Physical Sciences

Geologica Belgica: rue Jenner 13, 1000 Brussels; tel. (2) 788-76-30; e-mail kris.piessens@naturalsciences.be; internet www.ulg.ac.be/geolsed/gb; f. 1887, present name 1999; promotes geological knowledge; organizes seminars, confs and field trips; awards prizes and distinctions; 250 mems; Pres. Prof. SARA VANDYCKE; Sec. Prof. RUDY SWENNEN; Treas. Dr KRIS PIESSENS; Librarian Dr XAVIER DEVLEESCHOUWER; publ. *Geologica Belgica* (2 or 3 a year).

Koninklijk Sterrenkundig Genootschap van Antwerpen/Société Royale d'Astronomie d'Anvers (Royal Astronomical Society of Antwerp): Antverpiagebouw, Sint-Antoniuslei 95, 2930 Brasschaat; tel. (3) 827-46-51; e-mail astroantverpia@hotmail.be; f. 1905; dissemination, teaching and aid for promotion of astronomy; 40 mems; Pres. FERDINAND DELATIN; Vice-Pres. WILLY DE KORT; Vice-Pres. ERIC VAN ACKER; publ. *Astronomische Gazet* (6 a year).

Société Astronomique de Liège (Liège Society of Astronomy): ave de Cointe 5, 4000 Liège; tel. (4) 253-35-90; e-mail sal@societeastronomiquedeliege.be; internet www.societeastronomiquedeliege.be; f. 1938; brings together amateurs of astronomy, and promotes public understanding; 700 mems; library of 1,600 vols; Pres. A. LAUSBERG; Sec. L. PAUQUAY; publ. *Le Ciel* (12 a year).

Société Géologique de Belgique (Geological Society of Belgium): Unité de documentation, B6 allée de la Chimie, 4000 Liège; tel. (4) 366-53-56; e-mail a.anceau@ulg.ac.be; f. 1874; br. in Brussels; 200 mems; Pres. Prof. JACQUELINE VANDER AUWERA; Sec. Gen. Dr ANNICK ANCEAU; publ. *Geologica Belgica* (4 a year).

Société Royale Belge d'Astronomie, de Météorologie et de Physique du Globe: ave Circulaire 3, 1180 Brussels; tel. (2) 373-02-53; internet www.srba.be; f. 1894; 800 mems; Pres. GUY SCHAYES; Treas. MARC VANDIEPENBEECK; publ. *Ciel et Terre* (6 a year).

Société Royale de Chimie (Royal Society of Chemistry): ULB, CP 160/07, ave F. D. Roosevelt 50, 1050 Brussels; tel. (2) 650-52-08; e-mail src@ulb.ac.be; internet www.src.be; f. 1887, current name adopted 1904; promotes study of chemistry and highlights contribution of chemistry to sciences; 600 mems; Pres. Prof. CLAUDINE BUESS-HERMAN; Sec.-Gen. Prof. JEAN-CLAUDE BRAEKMAN; Treas. PASCAL LAURENT; publ. *Chimie Nouvelle* (3 a year).

PHILOSOPHY AND PSYCHOLOGY

Société Philosophique de Louvain: c/o Institut Supérieur de Philosophie, place du Cardinal Mercier 14, 1348 Louvain-la-Neuve; tel. (10) 47-47-87; e-mail nathalie.frogneux@uclouvain.be; f. 1888; 71 mems; Pres. NATHALIE FROGNEUX; Sec. PIERRE DESTRÉE; Treas. HERVÉ POURTOIS.

RELIGION, SOCIOLOGY AND ANTHROPOLOGY

Institut Belge des Hautes Études Chinoises/Belgisch Instituut voor Hogere Chinese Studiën (Belgian Institute of Advanced Chinese Studies): c/o Musées Royaux d'Art et d'Histoire, parc du Cinquantenaire 10, 1000 Brussels; tel. (2) 741-73-55; e-mail inst.chin@kmkg-mrah.be; internet www.china-institute.be; f. 1929; promotes study of Chinese civilization; Sinology and Buddhism; lectures, courses on Chinese art, history, painting and calligraphy; offers scholarships to young Chinese pursuing graduate studies in Belgium; library of 60,000 vols; approx. 300 mems; Pres. ILSE TIMPERMAN; Dir JEAN-MARIE SIMONET; publ. *Mélanges Chinois et Bouddhiques* (every 2 years).

Ruusbroecgenootschap/Ruusbroec Institute: Grote Kauwenberg 34, 2000 Antwerp; tel. (3) 275-57-80; e-mail ingrid.deruyte@ua.ac.be; f. 1925, inc. as Centrum voor Spiritualiteit of Universiteit Antwerpen in 1973; soc. of Flemish Jesuits engaged in spiritual studies of Low Countries; library of 115,000 vols (incl. 30,000 old and rare books), 500 MSS, 35,000 devotional prints; Dir Prof. Dr THEO CLEMENS; Sec. INGRID DE RUYTE; Librarian ERNA VAN LOOVEREN; publ. *Ons Geestelijk Erf* (4 a year).

Société des Bollandistes (Society of Bollandistes): Blvd St Michel 24, 1040 Brussels; tel. (2) 740-24-21; e-mail info@bollandistes.be; internet www.bollandistes.be; f. 1630; research and publs in critical hagiography; library of 500,000 vols, 1,000 periodicals; Dir Dr ROBERT GODDING; publs *Analecta Bollandiana* (critical hagiography, 2 a year), *Subsidia Hagiographica* (irregular), *Tabularium Hagiographicum* (irregular).

Société Royale Belge d'Anthropologie et de Préhistoire/Koninklijke Belgische Vereniging voor Antropologie en Prehistorie (Royal Belgian Society of Anthropology and Prehistory): rue Vautier 29, 1000 Brussels; tel. (2) 627-41-45; e-mail srbap@naturalsciences.be; internet srbap.naturalsciences.be; f. 1882, current name adopted 1931; multidisciplinary study of man and cultures; promotes and disseminates scientific research in these areas; Pres. NATHALIE VANMUYLDER; Sec.-Gen. CAROLINE POLET; Treas. JEAN PIRET; 109 mems; publs *Anthropologie et Préhistoire* (1 a year), *Hominid Remains*.

TECHNOLOGY

Bureau de Normalisation (NBN) (Standards Bureau): rue de Birmingham 131, 1070 Brussels; tel. (2) 738-01-11; e-mail info@nbn.be; internet www.nbn.be; f. 1946; Belgian nat. mem. of the CEN (European Cttee for Standardization) and the ISO (Int. Org. for Standardization); establishes outline of standardization programmes; 962 mems; Pres. of Management Cttee MARC DE POORTER; publ. *NBN Revue* (10 a year).

Koninklijke Vlaamse Ingenieursvereniging (Royal Flemish Association of Engineers): Ingenieurshuis, Desguinlei 214, 2018 Antwerp; tel. (3) 260-08-40; e-mail info@kviv.be; internet www.kviv.be; f. 1928; protects professional interests of univ.-trained engineers; creates awareness of technical knowledge; promotes technology and engineering; 9,500 mems; Pres. PAUL VERSTRAETEN; Sec. Gen. Ir P. ERAUW; publs *Het Ingenieursblad* (12 a year), *Ingenieurs in Vlaanderen* (1 a year), *KVIV-Direkt* (12 a year).

Société Royale Belge des Electriciens/Koninklijke Belgische Vereniging der Elektrotechnici: c/o VUB-TW-ETEC, blvd de la Plaine 2, 1050 Brussels; tel. (2) 629-28-19; e-mail srbe-kbve@vub.ac.be; internet www.kbve-srbe.be; f. 1884, present status 1925; organizes seminars; promotes study and devt of electricity science; 1,600 mems; Sec. Gen. BRIGITTE SNEYERS; publ. *Revue E Tijdschrift* (4 a year).

Société Royale Belge des Ingénieurs et des Industriels: Hôtel Ravenstein, rue Ravenstein 3, 1000 Brussels; tel. (2) 511-58-56; f. 1885; 2,000 mems; Pres. PIERRE KLEES; publ. *SRBII info* (12 a year).

Research Institutes

GENERAL

Antwerp Management School: Sint-Jacobsmarkt 9–13, 2000 Antwerp; tel. (3) 265-49-89; e-mail info@antwerpmanagementschool.be; internet www.antwerpmanagementschool.be; attached to Univ. of Antwerp; academic and research support to management field; contributes to creation and dissemination of knowledge in collaboration with business world and public and social-profit orgs; Dean Prof. Dr PHILIP NAERT.

Centre d'Études Nord-Américaines de l'ULB: Université Libre de Bruxelles, ave F. D. Roosevelt 50, CP 175/01, 1050 Brussels; tel. (2) 650-38-07; e-mail mlebrun@admin.ulb.ac.be; internet www.ulb.ac.be/cena; f. 2008; attached to Univ. Libre de Bruxelles; promotes study of N America, esp. Canada, Mexico and United States; library of 6,000 vols; Dir SERGE JAUMAIN; Sec. MIREILLE LEBRUN.

Centre for European Studies: Rue du Commerce, 1000 Brussels; tel. (2) 300-80-04; e-mail info@thinkingeurope.eu; internet www.thinkingeurope.eu; f. 2007; advances centre-right thought; contributes to the formulation of EU and nat. policies; serves as a framework for nat. political foundations and academics; and stimulates public debate about the EU; Pres. WILFRIED MARTENS.

Centre for International Management and Development: Lange Sint Annastraat 7, 2000 Antwerp; tel. (3) 265-45-25; e-mail daniel.vandenbulcke@ua.ac.be; internet www.ua.ac.be/cimda; f. 1990; research related to investment, devt, multinationals and emerging economies; Chair. Prof. Dr DANIEL VAN DEN BULCKE; Vice-Chair. LUDO CUYVERS.

Centre for Research in Finance and Management: Rempart de la Vierge 8, 5000 Namur; tel. (81) 72-48-87; e-mail pierre.giot@fundp.ac.be; attached to Univ. of Namur; studying aspects of financial management of company and its interactions with financial markets, both empirical and theoretical; Head PIERRE GIOT.

Centrum voor Bedrijfsgeschiedenis: Prinsstraat 13, 2000 Antwerp; tel. (3) 265-42-52; e-mail helma.desmedt@ua.ac.be; attached to Univ. of Antwerp; research on history of port of Antwerp in 19th and 20th centuries; history of stock exchange and banking in Belgium; Dir Prof. Dr HELMA DE SMEDT.

Centrum voor Migratie en Interculturele Studies (Centre for Migration and Intercultural Studies): Prinsstraat 13, 2000 Antwerp; Lange Nieuwstraat 55, 2000 Antwerp; tel. (3) 265-59-69; e-mail ina.lodewyckx@ua.ac.be; internet www.ua.ac.be/cemis; f. 2005; attached to Univ. of Antwerp; multidisciplinary research in field of migration and intercultural society; Chair. DIRK VANHEULE; Dir CHRISTIANE TIMMERMAN.

Groupe de Recherche sur les Relations Ethniques, les Migrations et l'Egalité (GERME) (Group for Research on Ethnic Relations, Migration and Equality (GERME)): ave F. D. Roosevelt 50, CP 124, 1050 Brussels; tel. (2) 650-31-82; e-mail germe@ulb.ac.be; internet germe.ulb.ac.be; f. 1995; attached to Faculty of Social and Political Sciences, Univ. Libre de Bruxelles; promotes study on migration, racism; European dimensions of immigration policy and integration; Dir Prof. ANDREA REA; Dir Prof. DIRK JACOBS; Sec. ISABELLE RENNESON.

Instituut voor Ontwikkelingsbeleid en-beheer (Institute of Development Policy and Management): Prinsstraat 13, 2000 Antwerp; Lange Sint-Annastraat 7, 2000 Antwerp; tel. (3) 265-57-70; e-mail iob@uantwerp.be; internet www.uantwerp.be/iob; research on political economy of Great Lakes Region of Central Africa, devt evaluation and management, governance and devt, globalization and devt; library of 25,000 vols; Chair. TOM DE HERDT; Librarian HANS DE BACKER; publ. *L'Afrique des grands lacs: Annuaire* (1 a year).

Instituut voor Samenwerking tussen Universiteit en Arbeidersbeweging: Venusstraat 23, 2000 Antwerp; tel. (3) 265-58-86; e-mail els.peeters@ua.ac.be; internet www.ua.ac.be/isua; f. 1970; attached to Univ. of Antwerp; scientific research to guard interests of trade unions; Chair. Prof. MARC RIGAUX; Sec. DOMINIQUE KIEKENS.

Oostenrijk-Centrum Antwerpen (Austrian Centre Antwerp): Prinsstraat 13, 2000 Antwerp; tel. (3) 220-42-48; e-mail octant@ua.ac.be; internet www.ua.ac.be/octant; f. 1993, present status 1999; attached to Univ. of Antwerp; promotes cultural dialogue between central and northwestern Europe (BENELUX countries, France and Germany); plans research projects on topics of relevance to Austria; Man. Dir EVA STEINDORFER.

Steunpunt Gelijkekansenbeleid: Lange Nieuwstraat 55, 2000 Antwerp; tel. (3) 265-59-63; e-mail steunpuntgeka@ua.ac.be; internet www.ua.ac.be/sgk; f. 2002; br. in Hasselt; scientific and applied research to assess opportunities in society and to settle and support policies of Min. of Equal Opportunities; 4 research pillars linked to groups: women, elderly, homosexuals and immigrants; Dir Prof. Dr PETRA MEIER.

Universitair Wetenschappelijk Instituut voor Drugproblemen (University Scientific Institute for Drug Problems): Prinsstraat 13, 2000 Antwerp; tel. (3) 265-40-65; e-mail a.uwid@antwerpen.be; internet www.uwid.be; f. 2003; research, education and service provision in field of drug and substance abuse; Dir Prof. Dr BOB VERMERGHT.

AGRICULTURE, FISHERIES AND VETERINARY SCIENCE

Centre des Technologies Agronomiques: rue de la Charmille 16, 4577 Liège; tel. (85) 27-49-60; e-mail cta.stree@tiscali.be; internet www.ctastree.be; applied research-oriented teaching in agricultural field; Dir CHRISTIAN MARCHE.

Centre Wallon de Recherches Agronomiques (Walloon Agricultural Research Centre): rue de Liroux 9, 5030 Gembloux; tel. (81) 62-65-55; e-mail cra@cra.wallonie.be; internet www.cra.wallonie.be; f. 1872, present status 2002; attached to Regional Government of Wallonia; agricultural research at 8 research depts; has brs in Libramont and Mussy-la-Ville; encourages research in agriculture, horticulture, food processing industries and environmental sciences; Dir R. BISTON; publ. *Rapport d'activité*.

Centrum voor Onderzoek in Diergeneeskunde en Agrochemie/Centre d'Étude et de Recherches Vétérinaires et Agrochimiques (Veterinary and Agrochemical Research Centre): Groeselenberg 99, 1180 Brussels; tel. (2) 379-04-00; e-mail info@coda-cerva.be; internet www.coda-cerva.be; f. 1997 by merger between Nat. Veterinary Research Institute (INRV) and Chemical Research Institute (IRC); research sites in Brussels, Tervuren and Machelen; promotes scientific research in food production, animal health and public health; Gen. Man. Dr PIERRE KERKHOFS; publ. *Activiteitsverlag/Rapport d'activité* (1 a year).

ECONOMICS, LAW AND POLITICS

Centre for European Policy Studies: place du Congrès 1, 1000 Brussels; tel. (2) 229-39-11; e-mail info@ceps.eu; internet www.ceps.eu; f. 1983; serves as forum for debate on EU affairs; organizes task forces, conferences, meetings, briefings, training seminars; 130 institutional mems, 120 corporate mems; CEO KAREL LANNOO; Dir DANIEL GROS.

Centrum voor Beroepsvervolmaking Rechten: Venusstraat 23, 2000 Antwerp; tel. (3) 265-54-48; e-mail cbr@ua.ac.be; internet www.ua.ac.be/cbr; f. 1985; attached to Univ. of Antwerp; organizes training related to law; Dir PASCALE BUYCK; Sec. REINHILDE TULKENS; Sec. JUTTA LEDÈNE.

Europacentrum Jean Monnet: Prinsstraat 13, 2000 Antwerp; tel. (3) 265-40-88; e-mail evrard.claessens@ua.ac.be; attached to Univ. of Antwerp; study of European integration process and EU devts in Belgium; Dir Prof. Dr EVRARD CLAESSENS.

European Centre for Advanced Research in Economics and Statistics: ave F. D. Roosevelt 50, CP 114, 1050 Brussels; tel. (2) 650-30-75; e-mail ecares@ulb.ac.be; f. 1991, current name adopted 1999; promotes research in economics, econometrics and statistics; Head Prof. DAVY PAINDAVEINE.

Federal Planning Bureau: ave des Arts 47–49, 1000 Brussels; tel. (2) 507-73-11; e-mail contact@plan.be; internet www.plan.be; studies and projections on economic, social and environmental policy issues and on their integration within context of sustainable devt; Dir-Gen. MICHEL ENGLERT; Head of Admin. JAN VERSCHOOTEN.

Institut de Recherche Multidisciplinaire pour la Modélisation et l'Analyse Quantitative (Institute for Multidisciplinary Research in Quantitative Modelling and Analysis): voie du Roman Pays 34, 1348 Louvain-la-Neuve; tel. (10) 47-43-21; internet www.uclouvain.be/en-immaq; research in fields of economics, statistics, biostatistics, actuarial science, operations; Pres. Prof. RAINER VON SACHS.

Institut Royal des Relations Internationales (Royal Institute for International Relations): rue de Namur 69, 1000 Brussels;

tel. (2) 223-41-14; e-mail info@egmontinstitute.be; internet www.egmontinstitute.be; f. 1947; research in int. relations, int. economics, int. politics, int. law, European affairs; documentation centre covering EU integration, central Africa, European security and defence policy; archives; 1,000 mems; library of 500 vols; Chair. ETIENNE DAVIGNON; Vice-Chair. DIRK ACHTEN; Dir-Gen. MARC TRENTESEAU; publs *Egmont Papers* (irregular, online (www.egmontinstitute.be)), *Studia Diplomatica* (4 a year).

Studie Centrum voor Onderneming en Beurs: Prinsstr. 13, 2000 Antwerp; tel. (3) 265-35-38; e-mail frans.buelens@uantwerpen.be; internet www.scob.be; f. 1999; attached to Univ. of Antwerp; digitalizing stock exchange information; study of financial data and history of Belgian stock exchanges and companies listed on them; archives of Antwerp Stock Exchange (1858–2002), Liège Stock Exchange and Ghent Stock Exchange (1902–1992); Pres. Prof. Dr JAN ANNAERT.

EDUCATION

Centre for ASEAN Studies: Kipdorp 61, 2000 Antwerp; tel. (3) 275-50-34; e-mail ludo.cuyvers@ua.ac.be; internet webh01.ua.ac.be/cas; f. 1994; attached to Univ. of Antwerp; established jtly by Faculty of Applied Economics and Institute of Administrative Sciences of Univ. of Antwerp (RUCA); promotes inter-university cooperation projects with univs in SE Asia; Dir Prof. Dr LUDO CUYVERS; publs *ASEAN Business Case Studies*, *CAS Discussion Papers*.

Centre for European and International Business Education and Research: Prinsstraat 13, 2000 Antwerp; tel. (3) 265-50-28; e-mail liliane.vanhoof@ua.ac.be; attached to Univ. of Antwerp; Dir Prof. Dr LILIANE VAN HOOF.

Centrum Nascholing Onderwijs—University of Antwerp (Education Training Course Centre—University of Antwerp): Universiteitsplein 1, 2610 Antwerp (Wilrijk); tel. (3) 265-29-61; e-mail paul.reynders@ua.ac.be; internet www.ua.ac.be/cno; organizes in-service training for teachers, middle mans, dirs, secs, CLB staff and others involved in primary, secondary education (ASO, TSO, BSO and KSO) and colleges; Pres. Prof. Dr PETER VAN PETEGEM; Dir PAUL REYNDERS.

Centrum voor Begaafdheidsonderzoek: Grotesteenweg 40, 2000 Antwerp (Berchem); tel. (3) 297-30-88; e-mail info@cbo-antwerpen.be; internet www.cbo-antwerpen.be; f. 1998, present status 2007; guidance of gifted children and adolescents; organizes training for parents, teachers, dirs, CLB staff, physicians and all others involved in education; research into realization of opportunities for optimal devt of gifted children and adolescents and into difficulties children face at home and esp. at school; Dir TESSA KIEBOOM; publ. *Hoogbegaafd?!*.

Centrum voor Mexicaanse Studiën: Prinsstraat 9, 2000 Antwerp; tel. (3) 265-44-42; e-mail barbara.ortiz@ua.ac.be; internet www.ua.ac.be/cms; f. 1990; attached to Univ. of Antwerp; study and research on literature and history of Mexico; library of 15,000 vols; Chair. Prof. Dr JEAN VAN HOUTTE; Dir Prof. Dr ROBERT VERDONK.

Expertise Centrum Hoger Onderwijs: Venusstraat 35, 2000 Antwerp; tel. (3) 265-45-08; e-mail echo@ua.ac.be; internet www.ua.ac.be/echo; attached to Univ. of Antwerp; supports and develops activities aimed at improving and reforming education at Univ. of Antwerp and colleges in asscn (AUHA); organizes workshops and seminars; Dir Prof. Dr PETER VAN PETEGEM.

Instituut voor Joodse Studies (Institute of Jewish Studies): Prinsstraat 13, L.400, 2000 Antwerp; Lange Winkelstraat 40–42, 2000 Antwerp; tel. (3) 265-52-43; e-mail ijs@uantwerpen.be; internet www.uantwerpen.be/ijs; f. 2001; academic study of Judaism from historical, philological, cultural, literary, religious, philosophical and sociological perspectives; organizes lectures, language courses and confs; library of 6,000 vols; Dir Prof. Dr VIVIAN LISKA.

Instituut voor Onderwijs- en Informatiewetenschappen: Venusstraat 35, 2000 Antwerp; tel. (3) 265-45-08; e-mail ioiw@ua.ac.be; attached to Univ. of Antwerp; provides scientific research and training in education and library sciences; Pres. PAUL MAHIEU; Vice-Pres. JOZEF COLPAERT.

FINE AND PERFORMING ARTS

Aisthesis: Grote Kauwenberg 18, 2000 Antwerp; tel. (3) 220-43-04; e-mail luc.vandendries@ua.ac.be; f. 1972; attached to Univ. of Antwerp; promotes theatre field studies; Dir Prof. Dr LUK VAN DEN DRIES.

Centre d'Étude de la Peinture du XVe Siècle dans les Pays-Bas Méridionaux et la Principauté de Liège/Studiecentrum voor de 15de-Eeuwse Schilderkunst in de Zuidelijke Nederlanden en het Prinsbisdom Luik (Centre for the Study of 15th-Century Painting in the Southern Netherlands and the Principality of Liège): Royal Institute for Cultural Heritage, Jubelpark 1, 1000 Brussels; tel. (2) 739-68-66; e-mail helene.mund@kikirpa.be; internet xv.kikirpa.be; f. 1955; research into 15th-century Flemish painting; collects art; historical documentation; photographic archive; library of 6,000 vols; Chair. Dr CYRIEL STROO; Vice-Chair. LILIANE MASSCHELEIN-KLEINER; Sec. MYRIAM SERCK-DEWAIDE; Scientific Sec. H. MUND; publs *Contributions*, *Corpus*, *Répertoire*.

LANGUAGE AND LITERATURE

Centrum voor Grammatica, Cognitie en Typologie (Centre for Grammar, Cognition and Typology): Prinsstraat 13, 2000 Antwerp; tel. (3) 220-45-88; e-mail johan.vanderauwera@ua.ac.be; internet webhost.ua.ac.be/cgct; f. 1999; attached to Univ. of Antwerp; research on relationship between morphosyntactic and semantic structure, from functional-cognitive point-of-view; Dir Prof. Dr JOHAN VAN DER AUWERA; Vice-Dir NILSON GABAS, JR.

Centrum voor Tekstgenetica (Centre for Manuscript Genetics): Prinsstraat 13, 2000 Antwerp; tel. (3) 265-42-74; e-mail dirk.vanhulle@ua.ac.be; attached to Univ. of Antwerp; study of modern MSS and writing processes; genetic research on authors of second half of 19th and first half of 20th century; emphasis on work of Samuel Beckett and James Joyce; Dir Prof. Dr DIRK VAN HULLE; publ. *Genetic Joyce Studies (GJS)* (online).

Computational Linguistics and Psycholinguistics Research Centre: Lange Winkelstraat 40–42, 2000 Antwerp; tel. (3) 265-52-22; e-mail walter.daelemans@ua.ac.be; internet www.clips.ua.ac.be; attached to Univ. of Antwerp; research and resources in developmental psycholinguistics, corpus linguistics, and computational linguistics; investigates interdisciplinary combinations of these disciplines; Dir Prof. Dr WALTER DAELEMANS.

Instituut voor de Studie van de Letterkunde in de Nederlanden: Prinsstraat 13, 2000 Antwerp; tel. (3) 265-45-67; e-mail rosina.hoydonckx@ua.ac.be; attached to Univ. of Antwerp; researches and provides academic courses in field of Dutch and foreign-language literature in Netherlands; study of Dutch literature and foreign-language literature in low countries, esp. in French and Latin; Chair. PIET COUTTENIER; Sec. KEVIN ABSILLIS.

International Pragmatics Association: Prinsstraat 13, S. D. 222, 2000 Antwerp; tel. (3) 265-45-63; e-mail info@ipra.be; internet ipra.ua.ac.be; f. 1986 as IPrA Research Centre; attached to Univ. of Antwerp; study of language use; research on field of pragmatics as functional (i.e., cognitive, social and cultural) perspective on language and communication; Pres. JAN-OLA ÖSTMAN; Sec.-Gen. JEF VERSCHUEREN; Exec. Sec. ANN VERHAERT; publ. *Pragmatics* (4 a year).

Studie- en Documentatiecentrum Hugo Claus: Prinsstraat 13, 2000 Antwerp; tel. (3) 265-52-49; e-mail georges.wildemeersch@ua.ac.be; f. 1996; attached to Univ. of Antwerp; study of literature in Netherlands; study of work of Hugo Claus through publ. and organizes scientific and cultural meetings; Dir Prof. Dr GEORGES WILDEMEERSCH.

MEDICINE

Biomedisch Onderzoeksinstituut (Biomedical Research Institute): Agoralaan gebouw A, 3590 Diepenbeek; tel. (11) 26-93-03; e-mail biomed@uhasselt.be; internet www2.uhasselt.be/biomed; f. 1999; attached to Hasselt Univ.; research on pathogenic mechanisms of autoimmune diseases and physiopathological mechanisms of cell injury and cell death resulting from stress factors; devt of therapeutic approaches for autoimmune diseases; Dir Prof. Dr PIET STINISSEN; Vice-Dir Prof. Dr MARCEL AMELOOT.

Centrum voor Bekkenbodemkunde: Universiteitsplein 1, 2610 Antwerp (Wilrijk); tel. (3) 265-25-35; e-mail jeanjacques.wyndaele@ua.ac.be; attached to Univ. of Antwerp; Dir Prof. Dr JEAN-JACQUES WYNDAELE.

Centrum voor de Evaluatie van Vaccinaties (Centre for the Evaluation of Vaccination): Universiteitsplein 1, 2610 Antwerp (Wilrijk); tel. (3) 265-26-52; e-mail cev@ua.ac.be; internet www.ua.ac.be/cev; f. 1984, present status 2007; attached to Univ. of Antwerp; research on epidemiology of infectious diseases and economic evaluation of vaccination programmes; Dir Prof. Dr PIERRE VAN DAMME; Sec. EMMY ANGELS.

Centrum voor Huisartsgeneeskunde Antwerpen: Universiteitsplein 1, 2610 Antwerp (Wilrijk); tel. (3) 265-25-29; e-mail chris.monteyne@ua.ac.be; internet webh01.ua.ac.be/cha; f. 1972; research in primary health care; offers academic services and medical education; Dir Prof. Dr JOKE DENEKENS; Dir Prof. Dr PAUL VAN ROYEN.

Centrum voor Kankerpreventie: Universiteitsplein 1, 2610 Antwerp (Wilrijk); tel. (3) 265-26-53; e-mail rsc@ua.ac.be; attached to Univ. of Antwerp; Dir Prof. Dr JOOST WEYLER.

Centrum voor Thoracale Oncologie Groep Antwerpen: Universiteitsplein 1, 2610 Antwerpen (Wilrijk); tel. (3) 265-26-39; e-mail paul.germonpre@ua.ac.be; attached to Univ. of Antwerp; devt of uniform policy regarding control and treatment of disorders of thoracic oncology; Pres. PAUL GERMONPRÉ; Vice-Pres. ANNEKE LEFEBURE.

Collaborative Antwerp Psychiatric Research Institute: Universiteitsplein 1, 2610 Antwerp (Wilrijk); tel. (3) 265-24-09; e-mail bernard.sabbe@ua.ac.be; internet www.ua.ac.be/capri; f. 2002; attached to Univ. of Antwerp; scientific research in fields of psychiatry, epidemiology, genetics, cognitive neuroscience, experimental psychopathology and psychoneuropharmacology; Dir Prof. Dr BERNARD SABBE; Dir Prof. Dr D. DEBOUTTE.

Direction Opérationnelle Maladies Transmissibles et Infectieuses/Operationele Directie Overdraagbare en Besmettelijke Ziekten (Operational Direction Communicable & Infectious Diseases): rue Engeland 642, 1180 Brussels; tel. (2) 373-31-11; e-mail jmpirotte@wiv-isp.be; internet www.wiv-isp.be/odobz-domti; f. 1900, present name and status by merger between Institute of Hygiene and Epidemiology (IHE) and Pasteur Institute of Brabant (IPB); scientific biomedical research, analyses; has br. at Ixelles; Dir JEAN CONTENT.

Fondation Médicale Reine Elisabeth/ Geneeskundige Stichting Koningin Elisabeth (Queen Elisabeth Medical Foundation): ave J. J. Crocqlaan 3, 1020 Brussels; tel. (2) 478-35-56; e-mail fmre.gske@skynet.be; internet www.fmre-gske.be; f. 1926; supports medical research in field of neurobiology through several Belgian univ. laboratories; distributes grants and awards; Hon. Pres. HRH PRINCESS ASTRID; Pres. ALAIN SIAENS; Man. Dir VINCENT PARDOEN; Sec. ERIK DHONDT; Scientific Dir Prof. Dr BARON DE BARSY.

Institut Jules Bordet: blvd de Waterloo 121 1000 Brussels; tel. (2) 541-31-11; e-mail direction@bordet.be; internet www.bordet.be; f. 1939; research on oncology; attached to Univ. Libre de Bruxelles; Pres. Prof. R. TOLLET; Vice-Pres. R. GLINEUR; Gen. Dir O. VAN TIGGELEN.

Institut Neurologique Belge: rue de Linthout 150, 1040 Brussels; tel. (2) 737-85-60; f. 1925; Pres. Comte EDOUARD D'OULTREMONT; publs *Acta Neurologica, Psychiatrica Belgica*.

Institut Scientifique de Santé Publique/ Wetenschappelijk Instituut Volksgezondheid. (Scientific Institute of Public Health): rue Juliette Wytsman 14, 1050 Brussels; tel. (2) 642-51-11; internet www.wiv-isp.be; promotes scientific research in support of health policy; Belgian rep. at level of EU and World Health Organization, Organisation for Economic Cooperation and Development, and Council of Europe; Gen. Dir Dr JOHAN PEETERS.

Institute Born-Bunge: Universiteitsplein 1, Bldg T, 5th Fl., 2610 Antwerp (Wilrijk); tel. (3) 265-25-96; e-mail jjmneuro@uia.ac.be; internet www.bornbunge.be; f. 1933; attached to Univ. of Antwerp; research in neurological sciences and cardiology; Chair. Prof. Dr P. P. DE DEYN; Vice-Chair. and Man. Dir VAN DEN EYNDE.

Laboratoire d'Investigation et de Recherche Clinique: rue Héger-Bordet 1, CP 401/06, 1000 Brussels; tel. (2) 541-33-99; e-mail data.centre@bordet.be; attached to Université Libre de Bruxelles; diagnosis and treatment of tumours; Dir Prof. JEAN KLASTERSKY.

Rega-Instituut (Rega Institute for Medical Research): Minderbroedersstraat 10, 3000 Leuven; tel. (16) 33-73-41; e-mail wie-is-wie@kuleuven.be; internet www.kuleuven.be/rega; f. 1954; attached to Katholieke Universiteit van Leuven; consists of depts of medicine and pharmacology; Head GHISLAIN OPDENAKKER.

NATURAL SCIENCES

General

Centre for Research on the Epidemiology of Disasters: Clos Chapelle-aux-Champs, 30.94, 1200 Brussels; tel. (2) 764-33-27; e-mail contact@cred.be; internet www.cred.be; f. 1973; promotes research, training and technical expertise on humanitarian emergencies, with focus on public health and epidemiology; Dir Prof. DEBARATI GUHA-SAPIR.

Institut Royal des Sciences Naturelles de Belgique/Koninklijk Belgisch Instituut voor Natuurwetenschappen (Royal Belgian Institute of Natural Sciences): rue Vautier 29, 1000 Brussels; tel. (2) 627-42-11; e-mail info@naturalsciences.be; internet www.naturalsciences.be; f. 1846; biology, zoology, palaeontology, geology, anthropology; subdivided into 7 depts; library: see under Libraries and Archives; Gen. Dir CAMILLE PISANI; publs *Bulletin: Biology*, *Bulletin: Entomology*, *Bulletin: Palaeontology*, *Study Documents* (irregular).

Biological Sciences

Bio-Imaging Lab: Universiteitsplein 1, B 2610 Antwerp; tel. (3) 265-27-75; e-mail annemie.vanderlinden@uantwerpen.be; internet www.uantwerpen.be/en/rg/bio-imaging-lab; f. 1994; attached to Univ. of Antwerp; Dir Prof. Dr ANNEMIE VAN DER LINDEN.

Institut de Recherche Interdisciplinaire en Biologie Humaine et Moléculaire: route de Lennik 808, CP 602, 1070 Brussels; tel. (2) 555-41-33; e-mail iribhm@ulb.ac.be; internet www.ulb.ac.be/medecine/iribhm; research on molecular genetics, molecular oncology, enzymology and molecular pharmacology, cell biology, theoretical modelling, experimental biology, gene therapy; Dir Prof. GILBERT VASSART.

Jardin Botanique National de Belgique/ Nationale Plantentuin van België (National Botanic Garden of Belgium): Domein van Bouchout, Nieuwelaan 38, 1860 Meise; tel. (2) 260-09-20; e-mail office@br.fgov.be; internet www.br.fgov.be; f. 1870, current name adopted 1967; promotes research on tropical and European botany; gene bank of Phaseolinae; herbarium with over 2m. specimens; library of 200,000 vols, 300 journals; Dir-Gen. Dr STEVEN DESSEIN; publs *Distributiones plantarum africanarum* (irregular), *Dumortiera* (3 a year), *Flore d'Afrique Centrale* (irregular), *Flore illustrée des champignons d'Afrique Centrale* (1 a year), *Icones mycologicae* (irregular), *Opera Botanica Belgica* (irregular), *Scripta Botanica Belgica* (irregular), *Systematics and Geography of Plants* (2 a year).

Referentiecentrum voor Biologische Merkers van Geheugenstoornissen: Universiteitsplein 1, 2610 Antwerp; tel. (3) 265-26-17; e-mail peter.dedeyn@ua.ac.be; attached to Univ. of Antwerp; contributes to devt and characterization of biomarkers for dementia and Alzheimer's disease; develops biomarkers-based diagnostic models that can be used in clinical practice; Dir Prof. Dr PETER DE DEYN.

Vlaams Instituut voor Biotechnologie: Rijvisschestraat 120, 9052 Ghent; tel. (9) 244-66-11; e-mail info@vib.be; internet www.vib.be; f. 1996; research on translating scientific results into pharmaceutical, agricultural and industrial applications; Man. Dir JO BURY; Man. Dir RUDY DEKEYSER.

Mathematical Sciences

CFP-CeProMa (Center for Proteomics): Groenenborgerlaan 171, 2020 Antwerp; tel. (3) 265-33-88; e-mail frank.sobott@ua.ac.be; internet www.ceproma.ua.ac.be; f. 2003; attached to Univ. of Antwerp; metabolomics, proteomics and mass spectrometry; Dir Prof. Dr YVES GUISEZ; Sec. SUZANNE POOTERS.

VIB Departement Moleculaire Genetica (VIB Department of Molecular Genetics): Universiteitsplein 1, 2610 Antwerp (Wilrijk); tel. (3) 265-11-02; e-mail gisele.smeyers@molgen.vib-ua.be; internet www.molgen.ua.ac.be; attached to Univ. of Antwerp; research in field of human molecular genetics with focus on complex diseases of central and peripheral nervous system; Dir Prof. Dr CHRISTINE VAN BROECKHOVEN.

Direction Générale Statistique/General-direktion Statistik (Directorate General Statistics): Koning Albert II-laan 16, 1000 Brussels; tel. (2) 277-51-11; e-mail info.stat@economie.fgov.be; internet statbel.fgov.be; f. 1831; collects, processes and disseminates statistical data; Dir-Gen. A. VERSONNEN.

Physical Sciences

Centre d'Étude de l'Energie Nucléaire/ Studiecentrum voor Kernenergie (Belgian Nuclear Research Centre): Boeretang 200, 2400 Mol; tel. (14) 33-21-11; e-mail info@sckcen.be; internet www.sckcen.be; f. 1952, current name adopted 1957; promotes research on nuclear science and technology and ionizing radiation; reactor safety; fuel and materials irradiation; characterization and geological disposal of waste; decontamination and dismantling of facilities; radioprotection; nuclear services, incl. irradiation in BR2 and post-irradiation examination; Chair. FRANK DECONINCK; Dir-Gen. ERIC VAN WALLE; Sec.-Gen. CHRISTIAN LEGRAIN; publ. *Scientific Report* (1 a year).

Centrum voor Milieukunde (Centre for Environmental Sciences): Agoralaan gebouw D, 3590 Diepenbeek; tel. (11) 26-83-02; e-mail jaco.vangronsveld@uhasselt.be; internet www.uhasselt.be/cmk; f. 1997; attached to Hasselt Univ.; effects of abiotic stress factors at different biological org. levels: from molecular to ecosystem level; Dir Prof. Dr JACO VANGRONSVELD.

Institut d'Aéronomie Spatiale de Belgique/Belgisch Instituut voor Ruimte-Aëronomie (Belgian Institute for Space Aeronomy): ave Circulaire 3, 1180 Brussels; tel. (2) 373-04-04; e-mail info@aeronomie.be; internet www.aeronomie.be; f. 1964; promotes research in field of space aeronomy; disseminates knowledge resulting from application of space investigation methods; library of 3,000 vols and 150 periodicals; Dir Prof. PAUL C. SIMON; Head of Admin. MARC DELANCKER.

Institut d'Astronomie et d'Astrophysique (Institute of Astronomy and Astrophysics): blvd du Triomphe, CP 226, 1050 Brussels; tel. (2) 650-28-42; e-mail email@ulb.ac.be; internet www.astro.ulb.ac.be; attached to Univ. Libre de Bruxelles; research on nucleosynthesis, nuclear astrophysics, stellar evolution and chemical composition, binary stars, neutron stars; Dir ALAIN JORISSEN; Sec. NANCY TIGNÉE.

Institut Royal Météorologique de Belgique/Koninklijk Meteorologisch Instituut van België (Royal Meteorological Institute of Belgium): ave Circulaire 3, 1180 Brussels; tel. (2) 373-05-08; e-mail info@meteo.be; internet www.meteo.be; f. 1913; depts for aerology, aerometry, applied meteorology, climatology, geophysics and numerical calculus; Pres. Prof. Dr CH. BOUQUEGNEAU; Dir Dr D. GELLENS; publs *Bulletin Quotidien du temps* (1 a day), *Climatologie, Hydrologie* (1 a year), *Magnétisme terrestre, Marées terrestres à Dourbes, Observations climatologiques, Observations d'ozone* (4 a year), *Observations géophysiques*, *Observations ionosphériques* (12 a year), *Observations synoptiques*, *Rayonnement solaire*.

Instituut voor Milieu & Duurzame Ontwikkeling (Institute of Environment and Sustainable Development): Universiteitsplein 1, 2610 Antwerp (Wilrijk); Fort VI-str. 276, 2610 Antwerp (Wilrijk); tel. (3) 265-21-14; e-mail milieu@ua.ac.be; internet www.ua.ac.be/imdo; research in field of environmental education, environmental management, spatial planning, integrated water management, environmental policy; Pres. Prof. Dr PATRICK MEIRE.

Instituut voor Natuur- en Bosonderzoek (Research Institute for Nature and Forest): Kliniekstraat 25, 1070 Brussels; tel. (2) 525-02-00; e-mail info@inbo.be; internet www.inbo.be; research into sustainable management and use of natural resources; supports orgs for nature management, forestry, agriculture, hunting and fisheries; provides data to Flemish govt; has brs in Geraardsbergen, Groenendaal, Linkebeek; CEO Dr JURGEN TACK; Man. CHRISTEL FOSTIER.

Observatoire Royal de Belgique/Koninklijke Sterrenwacht van België (Royal Observatory of Belgium): ave Circulaire 3, 1180 Brussels; tel. (2) 373-02-11; e-mail rob_info@oma.be; internet www.astro.oma.be; f. 1826; astrometry, astrophysics, celestial mechanics, earth tides, fundamental astronomy, gravimetry, radioastronomy, satellite positioning, seismology, solar physics, time service; Dir RONALD VAN DER LINDEN; publs *Annuaire*, *Bulletin Astronomique*, *Communications*.

PHILOSOPHY AND PSYCHOLOGY

Centre for Metaphysics and Culture: Grote Kauwenberg 18, 2000 Antwerp; tel. (3) 265-43-41; e-mail guy.vanheeswijck@ua.ac.be; attached to Univ. of Antwerp; research into history of concept of metaphysics in ancient, medieval, modern and contemporary philosophy and into history of critique of metaphysics; Dir Prof. Dr GUIDO VANHEESWIJCK.

Centre National de Recherches de Logique/Nationaal Centrum voor Navorsingen in de Logica (Belgian National Centre for Research in Logic): Fondation Universitaire, rue d'Egmont 11, 1000 Brussels; e-mail cnrlncnl@logic-center.be; internet www.logic-center.be; f. 1955; promotes and coordinates research in logic; Pres. M. CRABBÉ; Sec. B. VAN KERKHOVE; Treas. A. PÉTRY; publs *Cahiers du Centre de Logique* (online, www.logic-center.be/cahiers), *Logique et Analyse* (4 a year).

Centrum voor Cultuurfilosofie (Center for Philosophy of Culture): Prinsstraat 13, 2000 Antwerp; tel. (3) 265-45-50; e-mail arthur.cools@uantwerpen.be; internet www.ua.ac.be/cultuurfilosofie; attached to Univ. of Antwerp; research on relation between reason and culture in modern and contemporary society from 3 perspectives: criticism of metaphysics and post-metaphysical thought, criticism of religion and secularization, modernism and criticism of representation.

Centrum voor Ethiek (Centre for Ethics): Prinsstraat 13, 2000 Antwerp; tel. (3) 265-43-12; e-mail willem.lemmens@uantwerpen.be; f. 2003; attached to Univ. of Antwerp; research on history of ethics and practical philosophy; contemporary meta-ethics and moral-psychology; business ethics; bioethics; Head Prof. Dr WILLEM LEMMENS.

Centrum voor Filosofische Psychologie (Centre for Philosophical Psychology): Prinsstraat 13, 2000 Antwerp; Office (S) D416, Grote Kauwenberg 18, 2000 Antwerp; tel. (3) 220-43-37; e-mail erik.myin@ua.ac.be; internet www.ua.ac.be/main.aspx?c=.philosophyofmind; f. 1999; attached to Univ. of Antwerp; research on philosophy of perception, linguistic communication, aesthetics and free will; Dir Prof. Dr ERIK MYIN.

RELIGION, SOCIOLOGY AND ANTHROPOLOGY

Centre d'Études et de Recherches Multimédia et Études Euro-Méditerranéennes et Orientales (CERM-EMO): c/o Mme Annie Delsaut, ave Maistriau, 8, 7000 Mons; Université de Mons, pl. du Parc 20, 7000 Mons; tel. (65) 39-45-16; e-mail cerm.umh@gmail.com; internet cermumons.be; f. 1978; incl. Euro–Mediterranean studies section, int. relations section and Arabic language, translation and interpreting (graduate studies); training and research (FTI and ISL) in translation and interpreting; Arabic, English, French (postgraduate studies and Phd); visio-interpreting (e-learning); audiovisual translation: respeaking, subtitling, audiodescription, dubbing and AT/CAT; library of 2,500 vols; Pres. Prof. H. SAFAR; Sec. NAJWA HAMAOUI.

Centre Interdisciplinaire d'Étude des Religions et de la Laïcité: ave F. D. Roosevelt 17, CP 108, 1050 Brussels; tel. (2) 650-38-49; e-mail bdecharn@ulb.ac.be; internet www.ulb.ac.be/philo/cierl; f. 1965, present name 2003; attached to Univ. Libre de Bruxelles; study of religious phenomena and spirituality in contemporary expressions from ancient polytheism, so-called primitive religions, great monotheistic religions and popular devotions, to beliefs of New Age; library of 226 vols; Dir Prof. BAUDOUIN DECHARNEUX; publs *Divin et Sacré*, *Le Figuier: Annales du Centre interdisciplinaire d'Etude des Religions et de la Laïcité de l'Université libre de Bruxelles*, *Problèmes d'Histoire des Religions*, *Spiritualités et Pensées libres*.

Centrum Pieter Gillis: Prinsstraat 13, 2000 Antwerp; tel. (3) 265-44-77; e-mail cpg@ua.ac.be; internet www.ua.ac.be/pietergillis; f. 2004; attached to Univ. of Antwerp; promotes respect for critical approach to and dialogue with other philosophies; promotes research on religious ideas and communities; Chair. Prof. WILLEM LEMMENS.

Centrum voor Longitudinaal en Levensloop Onderzoek (Research Centre for Longitudinal and Life Course Studies): Sint-Jacobstraat 2, 2000 Antwerp; tel. (3) 265-55-35; e-mail dimitri.mortelmans@uantwerpen.be; internet webh01.ua.ac.be/cello; f. 2003; attached to Univ. of Antwerp; colln of panel studies of Belgian households; research on family sociology and sociology of labour and Student Evaluations of Teaching (developer of the SET37-scale); Dir Prof. Dr DIMITRI MORTELMANS.

Centrum voor Rechtssociologie (Centre for Sociology of Law): Sint-Jacobstraat 2, 2000 Antwerp; tel. (3) 265-52-64; e-mail francis.vanloon@ua.ac.be; f. 1972; attached to Univ. of Antwerp; research on interface between law and society; Dir Prof. Dr FRANCIS VAN LOON.

Centrum voor Sociaal Beleid Herman Deleeck (Herman Deleeck Centre for Social Policy): Sint-Jacobstraat 2, 2000 Antwerp; tel. (3) 265-53-74; e-mail ingrid.vanzele@ua.ac.be; internet webhost.ua.ac.be/csb; f. 1972; attached to Univ. of Antwerp; empirical and multidisciplinary research on social inequality and wealth distribution in welfare state; Dir Prof. Dr BEA CANTILLON; Sec. INGRID VAN ZELE.

Centrum voor Stadsgeschiedenis: Prinsstraat 13, 2000 Antwerp; tel. (3) 265-49-54; e-mail stefanie.beghein@ua.ac.be; internet webh01.ua.ac.be/cstadg; attached to Univ. of Antwerp; research on aspects of urban culture, economics, religion, society, politics and instns of Middle Ages to present day to study mutual societies; studies on socio-economic and cultural history; Dir Prof. Dr BERT DE MUNCH; Sec. STEFANIE BEGHEIN; publ. *Stadsgeschiedenis* (2 a year).

Institut d'Études du Judaïsme (Institute for the study of Judaism): ave F. D. Roosevelt 17, 1050 Brussels; tel. (2) 650-33-48; e-mail iej@ulb.ac.be; internet www.ulb.ac.be/facs/philo/judaisme; f. 1959; attached to Univ. Libre de Bruxelles; studies, publs and documentation on contemporary Judaism; library of 10,000 vols; Pres. Prof. GUY HAARSCHER; Dir Prof. THOMAS GERGELY; publs *Mosaïque* (1 a year), *Nouvelles* (4 a year).

Institut de Sociologie (Institute of Sociology): ave Jeanne 44, CP 124, 1050 Brussels; tel. (2) 650-34-89; e-mail is@ulb.ac.be; internet is.ulb.ac.be/index.php?page=revues&hl=fr_fr; f. 1902; attached to Univ. Libre de Bruxelles; Dir NATHALIE ZACCAI-REYNERS; Sec. CATHERINE VANCLEVE; publs *Civilisations*, *L'Année sociale*, *Revue de l'Institut de Sociologie*, *Transitions*.

Ruusbroecgenootschap: Instituut voor de Geschiedenis van de Spiritualiteit in de Nederlanden tot ca. 1750 (Research Institute for the History of Christian Spirituality in the Low Countries until 1750): Prinsstraat 13, 2000 Antwerp; tel. (3) 265-57-89; e-mail thom.mertens@uantwerpen.be; internet www.uantwerpen.be/ruusbroec; f. 1925; attached to Faculty of Arts, Univ. of Antwerp; scientific research of history of Christian spirituality, ascetical and mystical, in low countries from conversion to 1750; interpretative and contextual study of religious literature in Netherlands; codicological and historical research on early days of Ruusbroecgenootschap in cultural and social perspectives; library of 120,000 vols, incl. 30,000 rare books, 500 MSS, 40,000 devotional prints (17th century–1850); Dir Prof. Dr THOM MERTENS; Sec. INGRID DE RUYTE; Librarian ERNA VAN LOOVEREN; publ. *Ons Geestelijk Erf: Journal for the History of Spirituality in the Low Countries* (4 a year).

TECHNOLOGY

Antwerp Institute for Enterprise Computing: Prinsstraat 13, 2000 Antwerp; e-mail carlos.debacher@ua.ac.be; attached to Univ. of Antwerp; education, research and services in terms of information technologies and methodologies applied within business context; Dir Prof. Dr CARLOS DE BACKER.

Centrum voor de Economische Studie van Innovatie en Technologie (Centre for Economic Study of Innovation and Technology): Prinsstraat 13, 2000 Antwerp; tel. (3) 220-40-54; e-mail wim.meeusen@ua.ac.be; internet webh01.ua.ac.be/cesit; attached to Univ. of Antwerp; research on technology and innovation; publishes papers and organizes seminars; Dir Prof. Dr WIM MEEUSEN; Dir Prof. Dr JEF PLASMANS.

Centrum voor Micro-en Sporenanalyse (Micro and Trace Analysis Centre): Universiteitsplein, 1, 2610 Antwerp (Wilrijk); tel. (3) 820-23-40; e-mail rene.vangrieken@ua.ac.be; f. 1980; attached to Univ. of Antwerp; research in analytical sciences: trace analysis and microscopic and surface elemental and molecular analysis; fundamental research for better understanding of processes and parameters governing those methods of analysis; devt of methods of analysis; Dir Prof. Dr RENÉ VAN GRIEKEN.

Centrum voor ZorgTechnologie: Universiteitsplein 1, 2610 Antwerp (Wilrijk); tel. (3) 265-23-12; e-mail czt@ua.ac.be; internet www.czt.be; f. 1991; attached to Univ. of Antwerp; devt of technological devices to help people with disabilities.

European Cooperation in Science and Technology (COST): ave Louise 149, 1050 Brussels; tel. (2) 533-38-00; e-mail office@cost.eu; internet www.cost.esf.org; provides platform for European scientists to cooperate on particular projects; nationally funded research on European level; key domains of research: biomedicine and molecular biosciences, food and agriculture, forests, materials, physics and nanosciences, chemistry, molecular sciences and technologies, earth system science and environmental management, information and communication technologies, transport and urban devt, individuals, societies, cultures and health; Pres. Dr ÁNGELES RODRÍGUEZ-PEÑA.

IMO-IMOMEC: Wetenschapspark 1, 3590 Diepenbeek; tel. (11) 26-88-26; e-mail imo-imomec@uhasselt.be; internet www.uhasselt.be/imo; f. 2001; attached to Hasselt Univ.; collaboration with IMOMEC (Institute for Materials Research in MicroElectronics), dept of IMEC (Interuniv. Micro Electronics Centre, Louvain); devt and characterization of new material systems with potential use in microelectronics, bioelectronics and nanotechnology; Dir Prof. Dr DIRK VANDERZANDE; Vice-Dir Prof. Dr MARC D'OLIESLAEGER.

Institut Meurice (IIF–IMC–ISI): ave Emile Gryzon 1, 1070 Brussels; tel. (2) 526-73-04; e-mail info@meurice.heldb.be; internet www.heldb.be/he/meurice; f. 1892, present status 1977; research and training centre for industrial engineers in chemistry and biochemistry; library of 80,000 vols, 110 periodicals, 1,000 CD-ROMs; Dir Dr Ir PATRICK DYSSELER.

Institut Scientifique de Service Public: rue du Chéra 200, 4000 Liège; tel. (4) 229-83-12; e-mail direction@issep.be; internet www.issep.be; f. 1990; attached to Walloon Government; applied research, devt and demonstration relating to natural resources, environment, technical and industrial security, solid fuels, radiocommunications; library of 11,000 vols; Gen. Man. M. LAMBERT.

Institute for Reference Materials and Measurements: Retieseweg 111, 2440 Geel; tel. (14) 57-12-11; e-mail jrc-irmm-info@ec.europa.eu; internet irmm.jrc.ec.europa.eu; f. 1957, current name adopted 1993; 1 of 7 institutes of Joint Research Centre (JRC); promotes common and reliable European measurement system; 6 areas of competence: reference materials, food analysis, bioanalysis, chemical reference measurements, radionuclide metrology, neutron physics; Dir KRZYSZTOF MARUSZEWSKI.

Institute for Transport and Maritime Management Antwerp: Kipdorp 59, 2000 Antwerp; tel. (3) 265-51-51; e-mail frank.vanlaeken@ua.ac.be; internet www.itmma.com; f. 1996; attached to Univ. of Antwerp; research on academic and practice-based maritime and logistics; Pres. Prof. THEO NOTTEBOOM; Dir FRANK VAN LAEKEN.

Instituut voor Mobiliteit: Universiteit Hasselt, Wetenschapspark 5, bus 6, 3590 Diepenbeek; tel. (11) 26-91-11; e-mail imob@uhasselt.be; internet www.uhasselt.be/imob; f. 2003; attached to Hasselt Univ.; research on solutions to problems within domains of mobility, safety and logistics; Dir Prof. Dr GEERT WETS.

Interdisciplinair Instituut voor Breedband Technologie (Interdisciplinary Institute for Broadband Technology): Gaston Crommenlaan 8, POB 102, 9050 Ghent; tel. (9) 331-48-00; e-mail info@ibbt.be; internet www.ibbt.be; promotes innovation in ICT, applications of broadband technology in particular; CEO WIM DE WAELE.

International Medical Equipment Collaborative: Kapeldreef 75, 3001 Leuven; tel. (16) 28-12-11; e-mail bezoek@imec.be; internet www2.imec.be; f. 1984; research in field of nanoelectronics; Pres. and CEO LUC VAN DEN HOVE.

Sustainable Energy Research: Prinsstraat 13, 2000 Antwerp; tel. (3) 265-49-85; e-mail aviel.verbruggen@uantwerpen.be; internet www.avielverbruggen.be; f. 2004; attached to Univ. of Antwerp; research on processes of scientific and technological innovation to contribute positively to sustainable devt, in its social, economic and ecological dimensions; Chair. Prof. Dr AVIEL VERBRUGGEN; Sec. LINDA TEUNKENS.

Von Karman Institute for Fluid Dynamics: chaussée de Waterloo 72, 1640 Rhode-St-Genese; tel. (2) 359-96-11; e-mail secretariat@vki.ac.be; internet www.vki.ac.be; f. 1956; multinational postgraduate teaching and research in aerodynamics; supported by countries of NATO; depts of aeronautics/aerospace, turbomachinery and propulsion, environmental fluid dynamics; library of 3,000 vols, 65,000 reports; Dir JEAN MUYLAERT.

Libraries and Archives

Antwerp

Erfgoedbibliotheek Hendrik Conscience: Hendrik Conscienceplein 4, 2000 Antwerp; tel. (3) 338-87-10; e-mail consciencebibliotheek@stad.antwerpen.be; internet www.consciencebibliotheek.be; f. 1481, reorganized 1834; Flemish and Dutch literature, history, humanities, local press, early printed books, history of printing, history of the book; 1m. vols; Dir AN RENARD; Curator for Antiquarian Books STEVEN VAN IMPE.

FelixArchief/Stadsarchief Antwerpen (Antwerp City Archives): Oudeleeuwenrui 29, 2000 Antwerp; tel. (3) 3389411; e-mail stadsarchief@stad.antwerpen.be; internet www.felixarchief.be; f. 1796; 26 km of documents concerning the admin. of Antwerp since the 13th century; history, genealogy, heraldry, cartography, sigillography; 11,000 specialized vols, 245 periodicals; Archivist INGE SCHOUPS.

Letterenhuis (House of Literature): Minderbroedersstr. 22, 2000 Antwerp; tel. (3) 222-93-20; e-mail letterenhuis@stad.antwerpen.be; internet www.letterenhuis.be; f. 1933, present name 2002, present status 2004; archives of Flemish literature, theatre, music, arts and culture; files and MSS can be seen on application; 55,000 files, 2m. letters and MSS, 50,000 posters, 130,000 photographs; Dir LEEN VAN DIJCK.

Rijksarchief te Antwerpen/Archives de l'État à Anvers (Antwerp State Archives): Kruibekesteenweg 39/1, 9120 Beveren; tel. (3) 236-73-00; e-mail rijksarchief.antwerpen@arch.be; internet arch.arch.be; f. 1896; history of province of Antwerp; documents from 12th century onwards; 17,000 microfilm colln; Head Dr MICHEL OOSTERBOSCH; Archivist Lic. ERIK HOUTMAN; Archivist Dr BART WILLEMS.

Rubenianum: Kolveniersstraat 20, 2000 Antwerp; tel. (3) 20-115-77; e-mail rubenianum@stad.antwerpen.be; internet www.rubenianum.be; f. 1962; library and documentation centre for study of 16th-and 17th-century Flemish art, esp. the works of Jordaens, Rubens and Van Dyck; 45,000 vols and exhibition catalogues, books on art, artists and art history, journals, sales catalogues, 150 periodicals; Curator VÉRONIQUE VAN DE KERCKHOF; Librarian UTE STAES; publs *Corpus Rubenianum Ludwig Burchard* (the complete edition of the works of Rubens), *The Rubenianum Quarterly*.

Universiteit Antwerpen—Bibliotheek Campus Drie Eiken (University of Antwerp—Campus Drie Eiken Library): Universiteitsplein 1, 2610 Antwerp; tel. (3) 265-21-45; e-mail helpdesk@library.uantwerpen.be; internet www.uantwerpen.be/library; f. 1972, fmrly known as Universitaire Insteling Antwerpen, current name adopted 2003; attached to Univ. of Antwerp; 1,380,000 vols; Chief Librarian TRUDI NOORDERMEER.

Universiteit Antwerpen—Bibliotheek Campus Middelheim/Groenenborger (University of Antwerp—Middelheimmuseum/Groenenborger Campus Library): Middelheimlaan 1, 2020 Antwerp; tel. (3) 265-37-94; e-mail helpdesk@library.uantwerpen.be; internet www.uantwerpen.be/library; f. 1965; mathematics and computer sciences: campus Middelheimlaan 1, 2020 Antwerp; natural sciences: Groenenborgerlaan 171, 2620 Antwerp; 75,000 vols; Head Librarian TRUDI NOORDERMEER.

Universiteit Antwerpen—Bibliotheek Stadscampus (University of Antwerp—Campus Library): Prinsstraat 13, 2000 Antwerp; tel. (3) 265-44-34; e-mail helpdesk@library.uantwerpen.be; internet www.uantwerpen.be/library; f. 1852; 1.43m. vols; Chief Librarian TRUDI NOORDERMEER; Librarian VERONIQUE REGA.

Arlon

Archives de l'État à Arlon: Parc des Expositions 9, 6700 Arlon; tel. (63) 22-06-13; e-mail archives.arlon@arch.be; f. 1849; documents concerning Province of Luxembourg since 12th century; 18 km of shelving; 100,000 vols; Archivist VINCENT PIRLOT.

Beveren

Archives de l'État à Beveren: Kruibekesteenweg 39/1, 9120 Beveren; tel. (3) 750-29-77; e-mail rijksarchief.beveren@arch.be; f. 1964; archives for judicial district of Dendermonde; 19th and 20th century archives of creators from provinces of West Flanders, East Flanders, Antwerp and Flemish Brabant; genealogical centre; Head JOHAN DAMBRUYNE.

Bruges

Archives de l'État à Bruges: Academiestraat 14–18, 8000 Bruges; tel. (50) 33-72-88; e-mail rijksarchief.brugge@arch.be; f. 1796; documents on Western Flanders since 12th century; Dept Head Dr MAURICE VANDERMAESEN.

Openbare Bibliotheek Brugge (Bruges Public Library): Kuipersstraat 3, 8000 Bruges; tel. (50) 47-24-00; e-mail bibliotheek@brugge.be; internet www.brugge.be/bibliotheek; f. 1798; colln of archives, CDs, CD-ROMs, DVDs, incunabula, medieval MSS, old prints; Dir SPEECKE LEEN; Librarian CALIS KOEN.

Brussels

Archives de l'État à Bruxelles (Anderlecht): Quai Demets 7, 1070 Brussels (Anderlecht); tel. (2) 524-61-15; e-mail archives.anderlecht@arch.be; f. 2002; repository auxiliary Street Hop; colln of microfilms of church records prior to 1795; public archives of Old Regime; contemporary public records; contemporary and ecclesiastical instns of Ancient Regime; contemporary and ancient notaries; Head LUC JANSSENS.

Archives de l'État dans les Provinces Wallonnes et la Communauté Germanophone: rue de Ruysbroeck 2, 1000 Brussels; tel. (2) 513-76-80; e-mail archives.wallonie@arch.be; Head of Dept CLAUDE DE MOREAU DE GERBEHAYE.

Archives de la Ville de Bruxelles: rue des Tanneurs 65, 1000 Brussels; tel. (2) 279-53-20; e-mail archives@brucity.be; internet archives.bruxelles.be; historical archive of city of Brussels; colln of newspapers and periodicals, maps and plans, posters and advertisements; iconographic colln; cartographic colln; cabinet of medals; 25,000 vols; Archivist ANNE VANDENBULCKE.

Archives du Palais Royal—Archief van het Koninklijk Paleis (Archives of the Royal Palace): rue Ducale 2/Hertogsstraat 2, 1000 Brussels; tel. (2) 551-20-20; e-mail cap@kppr.be; f. 1962; service of Cabinet of the King and Section of Belgian Gen. State Archives and State Archives in Provinces; records and archives produced by depts and services of palace since 1831 and private archives of some mems of the royal family; colln of maps, photographs and medals; library specialized on monarchy and political history of Belgium; music library of Queen Elisabeth; 8,721 vols; Head and Archivist GUSTAAF JANSSENS.

Archives et Musée du Centre Public d'Action Sociale de Bruxelles: rue Haute 298A, Brussels; tel. (2) 543-60-55; e-mail archives@cpasbru.irisnet.be; f. 1796; archives, books, objects and art works concerning hospitals, health care and welfare in Brussels since the 12th century; approx. 10 km archives; 15,000 vols; Archivist D. GUILARDIAN.

Archives Générales du Royaume/Algemeen Rijksarchief—Generalstaatsarchiv: rue de Ruysbroeck 2, 1000 Brussels; tel. (2) 513-76-80; e-mail archives.generales@arch.be; internet arch.arch.be; f. 1815; 50 km documents concerning Low Countries, Belgium and Brabant since 11th century; execution of legislation on Public Records; 400,000 vols; Gen. Archivist KAREL VELLE (acting).

Attached Centre:

Centre d'Études et de Documentation Guerre et Société Contemporaines (CEGES) (Centre for Historical Research and Documentation on War and Contemporary Society): Luchtscheepvaartsquare 29, 1070 Brussels; tel. (2) 556-92-11; e-mail cegesoma@cegesoma.be; internet www.cegesoma.be; f. 1967, present name 1997; colln incl. personal archives, archives of private orgs, of collaborators and collaborationist movements, of resistance fighters and resistance orgs, of official instns and services that existed only between 1939 and 1946; 62,000 vols, 4,000 periodicals; Dir RUDI VAN DOORSLAER; Head of Documentation Sector FABRICE MAERTEN; publ. *Belgisch Tijdschrift voor Nieuwste Geschiedenis/Revue belge d'Histoire contemporaine/Journal of Belgian History*.

Archives Générales du Royaume et Archives de l'État dans les Provinces: rue de Ruysbroeck 2, 1000 Brussels; tel. (2) 513-76-80; e-mail archives.generales@arch.be; central br. of state archives in Belgium; acquired govt and private archives; Head KAREL VELLE.

Bibliothèque Artistique de la Ville de Bruxelles: rue du Midi 144, 1000 Brussels; tel. (2) 506-10-35; e-mail bib.aca@brunette.brucity.be; internet www.bibliothequeartistique.be; f. 1886; colln about fine and applied arts and art history; 18,000 vols, 400 rare books from 17th and 18th centuries; more than 10,000 books on applied arts from 19th century, collns of photographs from 19th and early 20th centuries (architecture, applied arts, travel); Librarian AUDE CORBEAU.

Bibliothèque d'Art, École Nationale Supérieure des Arts Visuels de la Cambre: abbaye de la Cambre 21, 1000 Brussels; tel. (2) 626-17-86; e-mail bibliotheque@lacambre.be; internet www.lacambre.be; f. 1926; 60,000 vols; Librarian RÉGINE CARPENTIER.

Bibliothèque de l'Institut Royal des Sciences Naturelles de Belgique/Bibliotheek en Documentatiedienst van het Koninklijk Belgisch Instituut voor Natuurwetenschappen (Library and Documentation Service of the Royal Belgian Institute of Natural Sciences): rue Vautier 29, 1000 Brussels; tel. (2) 627-41-89; e-mail bib@naturalsciences.be; internet www.naturalsciences.be; f. 1846; 750,000 vols, Dautzenberg colln with rare vols, 7,000 periodicals, 35,000 geographical, hydrological and geological maps; Dir CAMILLE PISANI; Librarian LAURENT MEESE; publs *Bulletin de l'Institut Royal des Sciences Naturelles de Belgique, Série Biologie*, *Bulletin de l'Institut Royal des Sciences Naturelles de Belgique, Série Entomologie*, *Bulletin de l'Institut Royal des Sciences Naturelles de Belgique, Série Sciences de la Terre*.

Bibliothèque de l'Université Saint-Louis: blvd du Jardin Botanique 43, 1000 Brussels; tel. (2) 211-79-09; e-mail lib@usaintlouis.be; internet www.usaintlouis.be/sl/bib_bienvenue.html; f. 1858; specializes in law, economics, philosophy, political science and sociology; 260,000 vols; Librarian MARIE CLAUDE MINGUET; Librarian NICOLE PETIT.

Bibliothèque, Documentation, Publications du Ministère de l'Emploi et du Travail: Ernest Blerotstraat 1, 1070 Brussels; e-mail bibliotheek@werk.belgie.be; internet employment.belgium.be; f. 1896; primarily for staff; open by appointment to outside users; colln on labour and social security, management and org. of work, being at work, occupational safety, occupational health; 150,000 vols, 400 periodicals; Dir JEF CASSIMONS; Librarian ANKE COPPENS.

Bibliothèque du Parlement Fédéral Belge: rue de la presse 35, 1000 Brussels; tel. (2) 549-92-12; e-mail bibliotheque@lachambre.be; internet www.lachambre.be/accessible/lachambre_biblio_presentation.htm; f. 1831; colln of documents in law, politics, economics, social sciences, history and parliamentary politics; 550,000 vols, 2,900 periodicals, collns on microfilms, 290,000 monographs, 120 CD-ROM titles; Librarian MARC DETHIER.

Bibliothèque Espace 27 Septembre (Ministère de la Communauté Française): blvd Leopold II 44, 1080 Brussels; tel. (2) 413-31-48; e-mail bibli27sept@cfwb.be; internet www.bibli2709.cfwb.be; f. 1879; contains vols on admin. and law, all brs of science and pedagogy, educational books; open only to teachers and mems of French Dept; 600,000 vols, 900 periodicals; Dir J. M. ANDRIN.

Bibliothèque Fonds Quetelet (Fonds Quetelet Library): 50 Vooruitgangstraat, 1210 Brussels; tel. (2) 277-55-55; e-mail quetelet@economie.fgov.be; internet quetelet.economie.fgov.be; f. 1841; library of the Fed. Public Service Economy, SMEs, Self-Employed and Energy; reading room now closed to the public; 1.2m. vols on statistics, economic and social sciences, agriculture, 8,000 periodicals; Chief Librarian STEFAAN JACOBS; publ. *Aanwinsten=Accroissements* (online, www.economie.fgov.be/informations/quetelet/acquisitions_nl.htm).

Bibliothèque Royale de Belgique/Koninklijke Bibliotheek van België (Royal Library of Belgium): blvd de l'Empereur 4, 1000 Brussels; tel. (2) 519-53-11; e-mail info@kbr.be; internet www.kbr.be; f. 1837; nat. depository library; 6 sections of colln: valuable reserve, maps, music, prints, MSS, coins and medals; 5m. vols, 18,000 periodicals, 35,000 MSS, 35,000 rare printed books, 700,000 prints, 140,000 maps, 200,000 coins and medals, 10,000 records, 200,000 maps and plans units; Dir-Gen. PATRICK LEFÈVRE (acting).

Central Library of the European Commission: rue Van Maerlant 18, B-1049 Brussels; tel. (2) 295-29-76; e-mail central-library@ec.europa.eu; internet ec.europa.eu/libraries/doc/index_en.htm; f. 1958; a central library linking a system of specialized library/documentation units; forms part of EC's Directorate-Gen. for Education and Culture; sites in Brussels and Luxembourg; colln on subjects related to European integration and EU; 600,000 vols and periodicals; Head of Unit Dr JEAN HERDIES.

Hoofdstedelijke Openbare Bibliotheek (Capital City Public Library): Muntplein Prinsenstraat 8, 1000 Brussels; tel. (2) 229-18-40; e-mail info@hob.be; internet www.hob.be; books, CDs, CD-ROMs, video cassettes, DVDs, magazines, community information, newspapers and magazines.

Les Archives et Bibliothèques de l'Université Libre de Bruxelles: ave F. D. Roosevelt 50, CP 180, 1050 Brussels; tel. (2) 650-23-70; e-mail bibdir@ulb.ac.be; internet www.bib.ulb.ac.be; f. 1846; 8.5 km linear archives; 1,220,850 vols, 10,856 ejournals, 14,407 audiovisual items; Librarian Prof. JEAN-PIERRE DEVROEY.

NATO Multimedia Library, Public Diplomacy Division: Room Nb 123, 1110 Brussels; tel. (2) 707-44-14; e-mail multilib@hq.nato.int; internet www.nato.int/library; f. 1950; serves the int. staff, int. military staff, delegations and Partnership for Peace countries; subject areas: int. relations, defence and security, military questions and current world affairs; 14,000 vols, 200 periodicals; incl. NATO audiovisual material; Head Librarian ISABEL FERNANDEZ; publs *Acquisitions List* (12 a year), *Thematic Bibliographies* (10 a year).

SIST-DWTI (Scientific and Technical Information Service): Bâtiment Platinum, ave Louise 231, 1050 Brussels; tel. (2) 238-37-40; e-mail stis@stis.fgov.be; internet www.stis.fgov.be; f. 1964, current name and status 1997; provides information in fields of medicine, science and technology; focal point for library, documentation and information networks (nat. and int.); Dir Dr JEAN MOULIN; Sec. BRIGITTE BLANQUART.

Vrije Universiteit Brussel, Universiteitsbibliotheek: Pleinlaan 2, 1050 Brussels; tel. (2) 629-26-09; e-mail info@biblio.vub.ac.be; internet www.vub.ac.be/biblio; f. 1972; also has medical library; 565,000 vols, 380,000 monographs and 185,000 bound periodicals; Head Librarian Dr PATRICK VANOUPLINES.

Wetenschappelijke Bibliotheek van de Nationale Bank van België/Bibliothèque Scientifique de la Banque Nationale de Belgique (Scientific Library of the National Bank of Belgium): rue Montagne aux Herbes potagères-Warmoesberg 57, 1000 Brussels; tel. (2) 221-24-10; e-mail documentation@nbb

.be; internet www.nbb.be/library; colln of books and journals related to economics, finance and monetary policy; 100,000 vols, 1,300 periodicals.

Courtrai

Archives de l'État à Courtrai: G. Gezellestr. 1, 8500 Kortrijk; tel. (56) 21-32-68; e-mail rijksarchief.kortrijk@arch.be; internet www.arch.be; f. 1964; records of regional and local govt instns; colln of microfilms of parish registers and records of births of all municipalities in province of West Flanders; colln of journals, reference works and monographs in field of nat., regional and local history; Head MARC THERRY.

Archives de l'État dans les Provinces Flamandes: Guido Gezellestraat 1, 8500 Kortrijk; tel. (56) 22-10-23; e-mail rijksarchief.vlaanderen@arch.be; main dept archive of Flanders; Head of Dept MICHEL NUYTTENS.

Gembloux

Bibliothèque des Sciences Agronomiques: passage des Déportés 2, 5030 Gembloux; tel. (81) 62-21-03; e-mail bib.bsa@ulg.ac.be; internet www.bib.fsagx.ac.be; f. 1860; 100,000 vols, 1,000 journals, 120,000 monographs, 1,000 periodicals; Chief Librarian BERNARD POCHET; publ. *Biotechnologies, Agronomie, Société et Environnement* (4 a year).

Ghent

Liberaal Archief (Liberal Archives): Kramersplein 23, 9000 Ghent; tel. (9) 221-75-05; e-mail info@liberaalarchief.be; internet www.liberaalarchief.be; f. 1982, present status 2002; 10,000 m archives; archives of major liberal orgs; documents of Liberal Int. and Mont Pèlerin soc.; 48,000 vols, 2,500 periodicals; Pres. Prof. Dr JUUL HANNES; Sec. Prof. Dr GUY SCHRANS; Dir LUC PAREYN.

Rijksarchief te Gent/Archives de l'État à Gand: Geraard de Duivelstraat 1, 9000 Ghent; tel. (9) 225-13-38; e-mail rijksarchief.gent@arch.be; f. 1830; 7 km of documents (since 9th century): mainly County of Flanders (until 1795), Diocese of Ghent (until 1801), Province of Oost-Vlaanderen (until 1870), Dist. of Ghent; Head Dr THIJS LAMBRECHT.

Universiteitsbibliotheek Gent: Rozier 9, 9000 Ghent; tel. (9) 264-38-51; e-mail libservice@ugent.be; internet www.lib.ugent.be; f. 1797; open to public; 3m. vols, 5,060 MSS; Chief Librarian Dr SYLVIA VAN PETEGHEM.

Hasselt

Archives de l'État à Hasselt: Bampslaan 4, 3500 Hasselt; tel. (11) 22-17-66; e-mail rijksarchief.hasselt@arch.be; f. 1869; repository of Limburg State govts and individuals from 1040 to 2000; Head ROMBOUT NIJSSEN.

Bibliotheek van de XIOS Hogeschool: Vildersstraat 5, 3500 Hasselt; tel. (11) 37-06-03; e-mail danny.sneyers@xios.be; internet www.xios.be/bibliotheek; has br. at Diepenbeek; reference books and dictionaries, economics, business studies, social sciences, law, education, linguistics, mathematics, biology, physics, chemistry, engineering, technology, IT; 30,000 vols, 400 journals; Librarian DANNY SNEYERS.

Liège

Archives de l'État à Eupen: Kaperberg 2–4, 4700 Liège (Eupen); tel. (87) 55-43-77; e-mail staatsarchiv.eupen@arch.be; f. 1988; archives of public and private instns; stocks from 14th century; microfilm on church records and civil registers and civil communities in judicial district of Eupen; historical archives (mid-16th to 20th centuries) and newspaper colln (1827 to present); 30,000 vols; Dir ELS HERREBOUT; Archivist RENÉ ROHRKAMP.

Archives de l'État à Liège: rue du Chéra 79, 4000 Liège; tel. (4) 252-03-93; e-mail archives.liege@arch.be; internet arch.arch.be; f. 1794; state archives, Belgian fed. scientific and cultural institute; 26 km of public and private records relating to history of Liège district since 9th century; Dir Prof. Dr SÉBASTIEN DUBOIS; Archivist Dr LAURENCE DRUEZ; Archivist Dr BRUNO DUMONT; Archivist ANNE JACQUEMIN; publ. *Inventaires des Archives de l'Etat à Liège*.

Bibliothèque 'Chiroux-Croisiers': place des Carmes, 8, 4000 Liège; tel. (41) 232-86-86; e-mail chiroux@liege.be; f. 1907; general library; MSS, ancient works, maps; 1,300,000 vols, local history, architecture, Walloon dialectology, 1,000 periodicals; Dir J. P. ROUGE.

Bibliothèque de l'Institut Archéologique Liégeois: Grand Curtius, quai de Maastricht 13, 4000 Liège; tel. (4) 232-98-60; e-mail monique.merland@crmsf.be; internet www.ialg.be; f. 1850; archaeology, decorative arts; 27,000 vols (mostly periodicals); Librarian MONIQUE MERLAND; publ. *Bulletin de l'Institut Archéologique Liégeois* (1 a year).

Réseau des Bibliothèques de l'Université de Liège: Grande Traverse 12, bât. B37, 4000 Liège (Sart-Tilman); tel. (4) 366-52-90; e-mail bib.direction@ulg.ac.be; internet www.libnet.ulg.ac.be; f. 1817; institutional repository; spec. collns incl. Fonds Québecois (French Canadian literature and society); 5 depts: law, economics, management and social sciences Leon Graulich, philosophy and letters, agricultural sciences-Gembloux, science and technology, life sciences; 2,600,000 vols and pamphlets (incl. 12,000 current serials, 6,000 MSS and 500 early printed books); Chief Librarian Dr PAUL THIRION; publ. *Bibliotheca Universitatis Leodiensis*.

Louvain

K. U. Leuven Universiteitsbibliotheek: Mgr Ladeuzeplein 21, 3000 Leuven; tel. (16) 32-46-60; e-mail centrale.bibliotheek@bib.kuleuven.be; internet www.bib.kuleuven.be; f. 1636; 4,300,000 vols (of which 3m. in faculty and dept libraries), 1,000 MSS; Chief Librarian Prof. STEFAN GRADMANN; Sec. ELS SCHEERS.

Rijksarchief te Leuven/Archives de l'État à Louvain (State Archives in Leuven): Vaartstraat 24, 3000 Louvain; tel. (16) 31-49-54; e-mail rijksarchief.leuven@arch.be; internet www.arch.be; f. 2001; records creators based in province of Flemish Brabant; parish registers and civil registration of Flemish Brabant, Brussels and Walloon Brabant; Dir Prof. Dr EDDY PUT.

Louvain-la-Neuve

Archives de l'État à Louvain-la-Neuve: rue Paulin Ladeuze 16, 1348 Louvain-la-Neuve; tel. (10) 23-00-90; e-mail archives.louvain-la-neuve@arch.be; internet arch.arch.be; f. 2009; 7 km of archives; regional and local public records of old regime; ecclesiastical, business, notarial, govt and courts archives; scientific and admin. library; Head CATHERINE HENIN; Head FLORE PLISNIER; Head MARIE VAN EECKENRODE.

Bibliothèques de l'Université Catholique de Louvain: Grand Place 45, 1348 Louvain-la-Neuve; tel. (10) 47-81-87; e-mail contact-biul@uclouvain.be; internet www.uclouvain.be/biul.html; has 8 core libraries; 2m. vols, 8,000 current periodicals; Pres. of Central Library VINCENT YZERBYT; Chief Librarian CH.-H. NYNS.

Maredsous

Bibliothèque de l'Abbaye de Saint-Benoît: Abbaye de Maredsous, 5198 Denée; tel. (82) 69-91-55; e-mail biblioteque@maredsous.com; f. 1872; books of learning, esp. history and theology; 400,000 vols, 50,000 brochures; Chief Librarian IGNACE BAISE; publ. *Revue Bénédictine*.

Mechelen

Archdiocesan Archives, Mechelen: Varkensstraat 6, 2800 Mechelen; tel. (15) 29-84-22; e-mail archiv@diomb.be; archives of archdiocese of Mechelen-Brussels and its predecessors since 12th century; MSS and books; photographs, iconographs, souvenirs; Archivist Drs GERRIT VANDEN BOSCH.

Archief en Stadsbibliotheek: Goswin de Stassartstraat 145, 2800 Mechelen; tel. (15) 20-43-46; e-mail stadsarchief@mechelen.be; f. 1802; archives of city of Malines (Mechelen) since the 13th century and library of Great Ccl of the Netherlands; Archivist WILLY VAN DE VIJVER; publs *Catalogue méthodique de la Bibliothèque de Malines*, *Inventaire des Archives de la ville de Malines*.

Mons

Archives de l'État à Mons: ave des Bassins 66, 7000 Mons; tel. (65) 40-04-60; e-mail archives.mons@arch.be; internet arch.arch.be; f. 1834; 25,000 vols; archives since 10th century; archives from Abbeys and noble families of Hainaut; records of instns or orgs, families or individuals attached to territory; Head LAURENT HONNORÉ; Archivist JEAN-PIERRE NIEBER.

Bibliothèque de l'Université de Mons: rue Marguerite Bervoets 2, 7000 Mons; tel. (65) 37-30-55; e-mail bibliotheque.centrale@umons.ac.be; internet www.umons.ac.be; f. 1797, present status 1966; collns focus on humanities; heritage collns; 900,000 vols, 3,622 MSS and incunabula, maps, prints; Dir CATHERINE MASSELUS.

Université de Mons—Bibliothèques: Place du Parc 20, 7000 Mons; tel. (65) 37-30-57; e-mail martine.piens@umons.ac.be; internet www.umons.ac.be; f. 1837; has 9 br. libraries; 900,000 vols, 1,300 journals; Chief Librarian CATHERINE MASSELUS; Sec. MARTINE PIENS.

Namur

Archives de l'État à Namur: rue d'Arquet 45, 5000 Namur; tel. (81) 65-41-98; e-mail archives.namur@arch.be; internet arch.arch.be; f. 1848; documents concerning county and province of Namur since 8th century; Head EMMANUEL BODART.

Bibliothèque Centrale de la Province de Namur: chaussée de Charleroi 85, 5000 Namur; tel. (81) 77-67-16; e-mail bibliotheques@province.namur.be; central library in province of Namur; Librarian FRANÇOISE DURY.

Bibliothèque Universitaire Moretus Plantin: rue Grandgagnage 19, B-5000 Namur; tel. (81) 72-46-46; e-mail direction.bump@fundp.ac.be; internet www.bump.fundp.ac.be; f. 1921; attached to Univ. of Namur; history of W Europe, Classical, Roman and German philology, philosophy, law, economics, art, biomedical sciences, life sciences, earth sciences; 800,000 vols; spec. colln: rare books on natural sciences, 7,000 eperiodicals; Dir MARCEL REMON.

Sint Niklaas Waas

Bibliotheek voor Hedendaagse Dokumentatie (Library on Contemporary Documentation): Parklaan 2, 9100 Sint Niklaas Waas; tel. (3) 776-50-63; e-mail akses@skynet.be; f. 1964; private, political, social and economic library; spec. collns on governmental research, public admin.; US govt documents depository colln; 120,000 vols, 4,000 periodicals, 15,000 maps; Librarian JOHN HESS; publs *Bibliographical Series* (irregular), *Governmental Publications Survey* (1 a year).

Tournai

Archives de l'État à Tournai: rue des Augustins 20, 7500 Tournai; tel. (69) 22-53-76; e-mail archives.tournai@arch.be; f. 1834; records of external services of the Ministry of Finance; archives of families and enterprises; church archives; microfilms of registers and civil registers of district court; Head BERNARD DESMAELE.

Ypres

Stedelijke Openbare Bibliotheek (Urban Public Library): Weverijstraat 9, 8900 Ypres; tel. (57) 23-94-20; e-mail bibliotheek@ieper.be; internet bibliotheekieper.blogspot.com; f. 1839; gen. interest; colln of encyclopaedias, dictionaries, newspapers, magazines; 120,000 vols, 400 periodicals; Librarian EDDY BARBRY.

Museums and Art Galleries

Antwerp

Etnografisch Museum: Suikerrui 19, 2000 Antwerp; tel. (3) 220-86-00; e-mail etnografisch.museum@stad.antwerpen.be; f. 1988; arts and crafts of pre-literate and non-European people; library of 12,000 vols; Dir JAN VAN ALPHEN; publ. *Bulletin van de Vrienden van het Etnografisch Museum Antwerpen*.

FotoMuseum: Waalse Kaai 47, 2000 Antwerp; tel. (3) 242-93-00; e-mail info@fotografie.provant.be; internet www.fotomuseum.be; f. 1965, current name adopted 1980; colln of prints, cameras and photographic objects, and works by nat. and int. photographers; library of 35,000 vols; Dir ELVIERA VELGHE; Curator INGE HENNEMAN; Curator DOMINIQUE SOMERS; publ. *Extra*.

Koninklijk Museum voor Schone Kunsten (Royal Museum of Fine Arts Antwerp (KMSKA)): Lange Kievitstraat 111–113, POB 100, 2018 Antwerp; tel. (3) 224-95-50; e-mail info@kmska.be; internet www.kmska.be; f. 1890; collns of Flemish Primitives, early foreign schools, Rubens, 16th–17th-century Antwerp School, 17th-century Dutch School, works of Belgian artists since 19th century; important works of De Braekeleer, Ensor, Leys, Magritte, Permeke, Smits, Wouters; closed for renovation until 2018; colln highlights will be kept on display in other locations in the city; library of 70,000 vols; Admin-Gen. Dr PAUL HUVENNE; publs *Antwerp Royal Museum Annual* (2 a year), *Calendar* (4 a year), *Zaal Z* (4 a year).

Middelheimmuseum (Openluchtmuseum voor Beeldhouwkunst) (Open-air Museum of Sculpture): Middelheimlaan 61, 2020 Antwerp; tel. (3) 288-33-60; e-mail middelheimmuseum@stad.antwerpen.be; internet www.middelheimmuseum.be; f. 1950; colln of modern and contemporary sculpture, incl. Ai Weiwei, Arp, Bill, Bourdelle, Burden, Calder, Cragg, Duchamp-Villon, Gargallo, Graham, Kirkeby, Laurens, Maillol, Manzu, Marini, Moore, Muñoz, Nevelson, Rodin, Schütte, Soto, Weiner, West, Wotruba and Zadkine; colln of medals, sketches and prints; library of 60,000 vols; Curator SARA WEYNS; Librarian JOHAN VERMARIËN.

Museum Brouwershuis: Adriaan Brouwerstraat 20, 2000 Antwerp; tel. (3) 206-03-50; internet museum.antwerpen.be/brouwershuis; f. 1933; closed until further notice; 16th-century installations for water-supply to breweries, ccl chamber; Curator F. DE NAVE.

Museum Mayer van den Bergh: Lange Gasthuisstraat 19, 2000 Antwerp; tel. (3) 338-81-88; e-mail museum.mayervandenbergh@stad.antwerpen.be; internet www.museummayervandenbergh.be; f. 1904; paintings from 13th to 18th century, incl. Aertsen, Breughel, Bronzino, de Vos, Heda, Metsys, Mostaert; sculptures from 12th to 18th century; drawings from 16th to 19th century; applied art objects from Gothic age; Chief Curator Dr CLAIRE BAISIER.

Museum Plantin-Moretus/Prentenkabinet/Idem: Vrijdagmarkt 22–23, 2000 Antwerp; tel. (3) 221-14-50; e-mail museum.plantin.moretus@stad.antwerpen.be; internet www.museumplantinmoretus.be; f. 1876, print room f. 1938; UNESCO World Heritage site; 16th–18th-century patrician house with ancient printing office and foundry, engravings on copper and wood; typographical collns, drawings, prints and paintings by Rubens; illuminated MSS; rare books and atlases; library of 30,000 rare books (15th–18th century) and modern reference library on humanism and book history, family and business archives (16th–19th century); spec. collns: Max Horn Legacy, Ensemble Emile Verhaeren, 600 MSS; Dir IRIS KOCKELBERGH.

Museum Rockoxhuis (Rockox House Museum): Keizerstraat 10–12, 2000 Antwerp; tel. (3) 201-92-50; e-mail inforockoxhuis@kbc.be; internet www.rockoxhuis.be; f. 1977; colln of furniture, paintings, applied art.

Museum Smidt van Gelder: Lange Nieuwstraat 24, 2000 Antwerp; Belgiëlei 91, 2018 Antwerp; tel. (3) 239-06-52; e-mail museum.smidtvangelder@stad.antwerpen.be; internet museum.antwerpen.be/smidtvangelder; f. 1950; museum is closed temporarily to public; Chinese and European porcelains, 17th-century Dutch paintings, 18th-century French furniture; Curator CLARA VANDERHENST.

Museum van Hedendaagse Kunst Antwerpen: Leuvenstraat 32, 2000 Antwerp; tel. (3) 260-99-99; e-mail info@muhka.be; internet www.muhka.be; f. 1987; maintains archives; colln Vrielynck; colln of nat. and int. pre-cinema and film hardware; library of 18,000 vols; Dir BART DE BAERE; Exec. Dir ANN CEULEMANS; publs *Afterall*, *AS*.

Museum Vleeshuis | Klank van de Stad/ Vleeshuis Museum | Sounds of the City: Vleeshouwersstraat 38–40, 2000 Antwerp; tel. (3) 292-61-00; e-mail vleeshuis@stad.antwerpen.be; internet museum.antwerpen.be/vleeshuis; f. 1913, re-opened in 2006 as a music museum; presents the history of music and dance in Antwerp; instruments, prints, MSS, books, paintings and models portraying the story of minstrels, bell ringers, opera singers, church and domestic music; public concerts and dance events; library of 15,000 vols; Curator KAREL MOENS.

Nationaal Scheepvaartmuseum (Steen) (National Maritime Museum): Steenplein 1, 2000 Antwerp; tel. (3) 201-93-40; e-mail scheepmus@stad.antwerpen.be; f. 1952; maritime history, esp. concerning Belgium; colln exhibiting inland navigation, fishing, training ships, 'Belgica' expedition to North Pole, shipbuilding, pleasure craft; library of 43,000 vols; Asst Dir R. JALON.

Rubenshuis (Rubens House): Wapper 9–11, 2000 Antwerp; tel. (3) 201-15-55; e-mail rubenshuis@stad.antwerpen.be; internet www.rubenshuis.be; f. 1946; reconstruction of Rubens's house and studio; original 17th-century garden screen and garden pavilion; paintings by P. P. Rubens, his collaborators and pupils; 17th-century furnishings; Renaissance architecture and garden; Curator BEN VAN BENEDEN.

Van Mieghem Museum: Ernest Van Dijckkaai 9, 2000 Antwerp; tel. (3) 211-03-30; e-mail van.mieghem.museum@skynet.be; internet www.vanmieghemmuseum.com; colln of works of artist; sculpture and paintings; Curator ERWIN JOOS.

Volkskundemuseum: Gildekamersstraat 2–6, 2000 Antwerp; tel. (3) 220-86-66; f. 1907; folklore of Flemish provinces, esp. folk art and craft; library of 18,000 vols; Curator WERNER VAN HOOF.

Bouillon

Musée Ducal 'Les Amis de Vieux Bouillon': rue du Petit 1–3, 6830 Bouillon; tel. (61) 46-41-89; e-mail courrier@museeducal.be; f. 1947; archives, historical MSS and documents; archaeology, folklore; exhibition of history of Godefroy de Bouillon; small library; Curator Mme MICHEL GOURDIN.

Bruges

Musea Brugge: Dijver 12, 8000 Bruges; tel. (50) 44-87-11; e-mail musea@brugge.be; internet www.museabrugge.be; umbrella org. for 16 museums subdivided into 3 groups: Groeningemuseum (Artistic Works), Hospitaalmuseum and Bruggemuseum (historical museums); Dir Dr MANFRED SELLINK.

Attached Museums:

Bruggemuseum: Dijver 12, 8000 Bruges; tel. (50) 44-87-11; e-mail musea@brugge.be; internet www.brugge.be/internet/en/musea; f. 1997; 12 brs: Gruuthuse, Onthaalkerk Onze-Lieve-Vrouw, Archeologie, Gentpoort, Belfort, Lantaarntoren, Stadhuis, Brugse Vrije, Volkskunde, Sint-Janshuismolen, Koeleweimolen and Gezelle; library; Curator HUBERT DE WITTE.

Groeningemuseum (Municipal Art Gallery of Fine Arts): Dijver 12, 8000 Bruges; tel. (50) 44-87-11; e-mail musea@brugge.be; internet www.brugge.be/musea/fr/groeningefrans.htm; Belgian and Dutch paintings and etchings from late medieval times to present; artistic works from 15th to 21st century grouped in Groeninge Museum and Arentshuis; artworks from S Netherlands (Belgium) over a period of 6 centuries; Art Dir Dr MANFRED SELLINK.

Hospitaalmuseum: St John's Hospital, Mariastraat 38, 8000 Bruges; tel. (50) 44-87-11; e-mail musea@brugge.be; internet www.museabrugge.be; f. c. 1150; paintings by Hans Memling and Jan Provost, furniture and sculpture from 15th–19th century; medieval instruments and books; 17th-century pharmacy; colln of records, works of art, applied arts and medical instruments; colln related to healthcare, worship and monastery; has br. O.L.V.-ter-Potterie (Our Lady of the Potteries); Curator Dr MANFRED SELLINK.

Brussels

Bozar Palais des Beaux-Arts (Bozar Centre for Fine Arts): rue Ravensteinstraat 23, 1000 Brussels; tel. (2) 507-82-00; e-mail tickets@bozar.be; internet www.bozar.be; f. 1928; art exhibition; painting, sculpture, monumental art, applied arts, photography;

music concerts; archives; CEO PAUL DUJARDIN.

Horta Museum: rue Américain, 25, 1060 Brussels (Saint-Gilles); tel. (2) 543-04-90; e-mail info@hortamuseum.be; internet www.hortamuseum.be; f. 1969; furniture, utensils and art objects designed by Horta and his contemporaries; Horta's personal archives; photographic archives; Art Nouveau library; Pres. MARTINE WILLE.

Koninklijk Museum voor Midden-Afrika Musée Royal de l'Afrique Centrale/ Musée Royal de l'Afrique Centrale (Royal Museum for Central Africa): Leuvensesteenweg 13, 3080 Tervuren; tel. (2) 769-52-11; e-mail info@africamuseum.be; internet www.africamuseum.be; f. 1897, present name 1960; large collns in fields of prehistory, ethnography, native arts and crafts; geology, mineralogy, palaeontology; zoology (entomology, ornithology, mammals, reptiles); history, economics; archival documents about history of central Africa; library of 110,000 vols; Dir-Gen. GUIDO GRYSEELS; publs *Africana Linguistica*, *Annales* (5 publs dealing with botany, geology, zoology, humanities and economics), *Journal of Afrotropical Zoology (JAZ)*.

Musée & Jardins van Buuren (Museum & Gardens van Buuren): ave Léo Errera 41, 1180 Brussels; tel. (2) 343-48-51; e-mail info@museumvanbuuren.be; internet www.museumvanbuuren.com; f. 1975; rare furniture, carpets, stained-glass windows, sculptures and int. masterpieces; art decoration of garden; colln of Flemish and Italian paintings covering 5 centuries of art; open air exhibitions of contemporary sculptures.

Musée d'Ixelles/Museum van Elsene (Museum of Elsene): rue Jean Van Volsem 71, Ixelles, 1050 Brussels; tel. (322) 515-64-21; e-mail musee@ixelles.be; internet www.fading.museumofixelles.be; f. 1892; watercolours, drawings, engravings, sculptures, posters; works of Belgian and foreign schools; colln of works of realist, impressionist, luminist, neo-impressionist and symbolist, fauvism, expressionism, cubism, surrealism and abstraction; library of 3,000 vols (bibliographies); Dir CLAIRE LEBLANC.

Musée Juif de Belgique: rue des Minimes 21, 1000 Brussels; tel. (2) 512-19-63; e-mail z.seewald@mjb-jmb.org; internet www.new.mjb-jmb.org; f. 1946; 20,000 photographs relating to aspects of Jewish life in Belgium, Israel, Israeli-Palestine and Jewish Morocco; Jewish genealogy colln; worship and textile items; archives; music colln; art works; library of 25,000 vols; Pres. BARON SCHNEK; Curator ZAHAVA SEEWALD; Curator DANIEL DRATWA.

Musée René Magritte: rue Esseghem 135, 1090 Brussels; tel. (2) 428-26-26; e-mail info@magrittemuseum.be; internet www.magrittemuseum.be; documents over a biographical journey of artist; mascots, surrealist brochures, adverts, correspondence; paintings; drawings, sketches, studies, drawings in letters, illustrations in books and graphic works by artist; Curator ANDRÉ GARITTE.

Musée Royal de l'Armée et d'Histoire Militaire/Koninklijk Museum van het Leger en de Krijgsgeschiedenis (Royal Museum of the Armed Forces and of Military History): parc du Cinquantenaire 3, 1000 Brussels; tel. (2) 737-78-11; e-mail infocom@klm-mra.be; internet www.klm-mra.be; f. 1910; colln incl. int. military history from 10th century onwards; exhibits arms, uniforms, decorations, paintings, sculpture, maps; photographic and print colln; library of 450,000 vols and archives; Dir-Gen. DOMINIQUE HANSON; Curator PIET DE GRYSE; publs *Bulletin du MRA* (1 a year), *Bulletin van het KLM* (1 a year).

Musées Royaux d'Art et d'Histoire: 1040 Etterbeek, 1040 Brussels; tel. (2) 741-72-11; e-mail info@kmkg-mrah.be; internet www.kmkg-mrah.be; f. 1835; Dir-Gen. MICHEL DRAGUET (acting); Sec. DOMINIQUE COUPÉ; Sec. SYLVIE PAESEN; publ. *Musze* (3 a year).

Component Museums:

MIM—Musical Instruments Museum: Montagne de la Cour 2, 1000 Brussels; tel. (2) 545-01-30; e-mail info@mim.be; internet www.mim.be; f. 1877; exhibits musical instruments; library of 35,000 vols.

Musée d'Extrême-Orient: ave Van Praet 44, 1020 Brussels; tel. (2) 268-16-08; e-mail info@kmkg-mrah.be; internet www.kmkg-mrah.be; Chinese art, porcelain and furniture; Japanese architecture and decorative arts; Dir-Gen. MICHEL DRAGUET.

Musée du Cinquantenaire: parc du Cinquantenaire 10, 1000 Brussels; tel. (2) 741-72-11; e-mail info@kmkg-mrah.be; internet www.kmkg-mrah.be; f. 1835; archaeology of Belgium, the Americas, Asia, the Pacific and North-Islamic world, and of ancient Iran and Near East, Egypt, Greece and Rome; European decorative arts; library of 100,000 vols; Dir-Gen. MICHEL DRAGUET; publ. *Musze* (3 a year).

Pavillon Horta-Lambeaux: parc du Cinquantenaire, 1000 Brussels; tel. (2) 741-72-44; e-mail info@kmkg-mrah.be; internet www.kmkg-mrah.be; f. 1899; temporarily closed; marble relief of Human Passions; Dir-Gen. MICHEL DRAGUET.

Porte de Hal/Hallepoort: blvd du Midi, 1000 Brussels; tel. (2) 534-15-18; e-mail info@kmkg-mrah.be; internet www.kmkg-mrah.be; f. 1835; guild's armour parade of Archduke Albert and his horse naturalized; 'Charles Quint' cradle; painting of Anthonis Sallaert; temporary exhibitions; Dir-Gen. MICHEL DRAGUET.

Musées Royaux des Beaux-Arts de Belgique/Koninklijke Musea voor Schone Kunsten van België (Royal Museums of Fine Arts of Belgium): rue du Musée 9, 1000 Brussels; tel. (2) 508-32-11; e-mail info@fine-arts-museum.be; internet www.fine-arts-museum.be; f. 1801; temporarily closed; Brussels, medieval, Renaissance and modern pictures, drawings and sculpture; public and private collns of archives; library of 164,000 vols, 350,000 monographs and exhibition catalogues, 3,000 periodicals, 50 CD-ROMs; Chief Curator MICHEL DRAGUET; publ. *Bulletin*.

Attached Museums:

Musée Antoine Wiertz: rue Vautier 62, 1050 Brussels; tel. (2) 648-17-18; e-mail info@fine-arts-museum.be; internet www.fine-arts-museum.be; f. 1868; paintings by Antoine Wiertz; the artist's house and studio; Chief Curator MICHEL DRAGUET.

Musée Constantin Meunier: rue de l'Abbaye 59, 1050 Brussels; tel. (2) 648-44-49; e-mail info@fine-arts-museum.be; internet www.fine-arts-museum.be; f. 1939; paintings, drawings and sculptures by Constantin Meunier; the artist's house and studio; Dir MICHEL DRAGUET.

Musée d'Art Ancien (Museum of Ancient Art): rue de la Régence 3, 1000 Brussels; tel. (2) 508-32-11; e-mail info@fine-arts-museum.be; internet www.fine-arts-museum.be; f. 1801; 15th–18th-century paintings, drawings and sculpture; Chief Curator MICHEL DRAGUET.

Musée d'Art Moderne (Museum of Modern Art): rue de la Régence 3, 1000 Brussels; tel. (2) 508-32-11; e-mail info@fine-arts-museum.be; internet www.fine-arts-museum.be; f. 1984; paintings since 19th century, drawings and sculpture; Chief Curator MICHEL DRAGUET.

Musée Magritte Museum: rue de la Régence 3, 1000 Brussels; tel. (2) 508-32-11; e-mail info@fine-arts-museum.be; internet www.musee-magritte-museum.be; f. 1984; René Magritte colln; paintings, drawings, gouaches, posters, advertising work, letters, photographs, sculptures, films; Gen. Dir MICHEL DRAGUET.

Muséum des Sciences Naturelles (Museum of Natural Sciences): rue Vautier 29, 1000 Brussels; tel. (2) 627-42-11; e-mail info@naturalsciences.be; internet www.naturalsciences.be; f. 1846; colln of minerals, fossils, living animals; temporary exhibitions; dinosaur hall; library.

Museum Erasmus: rue du Chapitre 31, 1070 Brussels; tel. (2) 521-13-83; e-mail info@erasmushouse.museum; internet www.erasmushouse.museum; f. 1932; portraits, books, gothic sculpture, documents, paintings, early edns and MSS relating to Erasmus and other Humanists of 16th century; library of 12,000 vols; Curator Dr ALEXANDER VANAUTGAERDEN; publ. *Melissa 156* (6 a year).

Charleroi

Musée de la Photographie (Museum of Photography): ave Paul Pastur 11, 6032 Charleroi; tel. (71) 43-58-10; e-mail mpc.info@museephoto.be; internet www.museephoto.be; f. 1987; colln of 80,000 photographs and 3m. negatives; library of 13,000 vols; Dir XAVIER CANONNE; Curator MARC VAUSORT; Curator CHRISTELLE ROUSSEAU.

Musée des Beaux-Arts (Museum of Fine Arts): Place du Manège 1, 6000 Charleroi; tel. (71) 86-11-34; e-mail mba@charleroi.be; internet charleroi-museum.be/wps; works of Belgian artists, from 19th century to today, with links to region; sculptures, paintings, sketches, various drawings and archival materials; permanent collns of Museum of Fine Arts; Curator ALIBONI CORALY.

Courtrai

Musée Paul Delvaux (Paul Delvaux Museum): ave Paul Delvaux laan 42, 8670 Koksijde (St-Idesbald); tel. (58) 52-12-29; e-mail info@delvauxmuseum.com; internet www.delvauxmuseum.com; f. 1982; colln of paintings, drawings, prints by artist and his personal belongings.

Ghent

Design Museum Gent: Jan Breydelstraat 5, 9000 Ghent; tel. (9) 267-99-99; e-mail museum.design@gent.be; internet www.designmuseumgent.be; f. 1903; colln and exhibition of 20th-century art and contemporary design; 17th- and 18th-century furnishings; furniture, glass and ceramics by Alessandro Mendini, Ettore Sottsass, Michele de Lucchi, Massimo Iosa-Ghini, Michael Graves, Marco Zanini, Martine Bedin, Nathalie du Pasquier, Mateo Thun, Ron Arad, Maarten Van Severen, Richard Hutten, Hella Jongerius, Piet Stockmans, Nedda El-Asmar; digital photographic archive; Dir KATRIEN LAPORTE; Asst BERNADETTE DE LOOSE.

Het Huis Van Alijn (House Of Alijn): Kraanlei 65, 9000 Ghent; tel. (9) 269-23-50; e-mail info@huisvanalijn.be; internet www.huisvanalijn.be; digital photograph album; sound-recordings and film excerpts; temporary exhibitions; Dir SYLVIE DHAENE.

Museum voor Schone Kunsten (Ghent Museum of Fine Arts): Fernand Scribedreef

1, Citadelpark, 9000 Ghent; tel. (9) 240-07-00; e-mail museum.msk@gent.be; internet www.mskgent.be; f. 1798; ancient and modern paintings, sculpture, tapestries, prints and drawings; Flemish art from Middle Ages to first half of 20th century; library; Dir ROBERT HOOZEE.

Sint-Pietersabdij (St Peter's Abbey): Sint-Pietersplein 9, 9000 Ghent; tel. (9) 243-97-30; e-mail sintpietersabdij@gent.be; internet www.sintpietersabdijgent.be; f. 1958; exhibits works by nat. and int. artists; Dir DOREEN GAUBLOMME (acting).

STAM—Stadsmuseum Gent: Godshuizenlaan 2, 9000 Ghent; tel. (9) 267-14-00; e-mail stam@gent.be; internet www.stamgent.be; illustrates history of Ghent; temporary exhibitions; Dir CHRISTINE DE WEERDT.

Stedelijk Museum voor Actuele Kunst (Museum of Contemporary Art): Citadelpark, 9000 Ghent; tel. (9) 240-76-01; e-mail info@smak.be; internet www.smak.be; f. 1975; drawings, etchings, paintings, sculpture; featured movements incl. arte povera, cobra, conceptualism, minimalism, pop art; colln provides an overview of devts in international art from 1945 to present; library of 40,000 vols, 195 periodicals; Dir PHILIPPE VAN CAUTEREN; Man. Dir PHILIPPE VANDENWEGHE; Curator THIBAUT VERHOEVEN; Curator THOMAS CARON.

Liège

Collections Artistiques de l'Université de Liège: place du 20 août 7, 4000 Liège; tel. (4) 366-56-07; e-mail wittert@ulg.ac.be; internet www.ulg.ac.be/wittert; f. 1903; 30,000 prints and drawings, paintings of 15th and 16th century; modern Belgian paintings; 5,483 coins; colln of Zairian art and craft; works of African art, sculptures; photography colln; Dir Dr JEAN-PATRICK DUCHESNE; Sec. EMMANUELLE GROSJEAN.

Grand Curtius Museum: quai de Maastricht 13, 4000 Liège; tel. (4) 221-68-00; e-mail infograndcurtius@liege.be; internet www.grandcurtiusliege.be; f. 2009; 7,000 years of regional and int. artefacts; 5,200 items displayed in chronological or thematic order; Dir NICOLE DARDING; Curator CONSTANTIN CHARIOT.

Attached Museums:

Musée Curtius: quai de Maastricht 13, 4000 Liège; tel. (4) 221-83-83; f. 1909; chief sections: prehistory, Romano-Belgian and Frankish, Liège coins, decorative arts (from the Middle Ages to 19th century); annexe: lapidary colln in Palais de Justice; HQ of Archaeological Institute of Liège (*q.v.*).

Musée d'Ansembourg: Féronstrée 114, 4000 Liège; tel. (4) 221-94-02; e-mail webadmin@liege.be; internet www.liege.be/culture/musees/musee-d-ansembourg; f. 1905; collns of 18th-century decorative arts of Liège; reconstituted interiors.

Musée d'Armes: quai de Maastricht 13, 4000 Liège; tel. (4) 221-94-16; e-mail info@museedarms.be; internet www.museedarmes.be; f. 1883; books, specialized articles, archives, photographs; military weapons, hunting and sporting arms, ethnic weapons, ranging from prehistory to present; colln of decorations and insignia of knighthood; colln of 600 commemorative medals for Revolution, Consulate and First French Empire; Curator PHILIPPE JORIS; publ. *Amis du Musée d'Armes de Liège* (4 a year).

Musée d'Art Religieux et d'Art Mosan (Museum of Religious Art and Mosan Museum of Art): rue Mère-Dieu, 4000 Liège; tel. (4) 221-42-25; e-mail infograndcurtius@liege.be; sculptures from 11th century; plates, fabrics and paintings; works from Flemish school, French school, Brabant school and German school.

Musée du Verre: quai de Maastricht 13, 4000 Liège; tel. (4) 221-94-04; e-mail infograndcurtius@liege.be; f. 1959; all main centres of production, from earliest times to present, are represented.

Musées d'Archéologie et d'Arts Décoratifs de Liège: Institut Archéologique Liégeois, 13 quai de Maastricht, 4000 Liège; tel. (4) 221-94-04; e-mail infograndcurtius@liege.be; archaeological collns; Middle Palaeolithic stone tools discovered at Spy, in 1885–86.

Musée d'Art Moderne et d'Art Contemporain de la Ville de Liège: parc de la Boverie 3, 4020 Liège; tel. (4) 343-04-03; e-mail mamac@liege.be; internet www.mamac.be; f. 1981; modern paintings, sculptures and abstracts of Belgian School, French and foreign masters; collns of paintings and sculptures from 1850 to today; Curator FRANCINE DAWANS; Curator FRANÇOISE SAFIN.

Musée de la Vie Wallonne (Museum of Walloon Life): cour des Mineurs 1, 4000 Liège; tel. (4) 237-90-50; e-mail info@viewallonne.be; internet www.viewallonne.be; f. 1913; varied colln covering S Belgium in fields of ethnography, folklore, arts and crafts and history; 450,000 documents; private and public archives; library of 35,000 vols, video cassettes, CD-ROMs, 460 periodicals; Curator MARIE-CLAUDE THURION; publ. *Enquêtes* (1 a year).

Louvain

M-Museum Leuven: Vanderkelenstraat 28, 3000 Leuven; tel. (16) 27-29-29; e-mail m@leuven.be; internet www.mleuven.be; f. 1823; art works of Leuven and Brabant from Middle Ages to 19th century; Pres. DENISE VANDEVOORT; Vice-Pres. ELS BUELENS; Gen. Dir LUC DELRUE; Chief Curator VERONIQUE VANDEKERCHOVE.

Louvain-la-Neuve

Musée de Louvain-La-Neuve: Place Blaise Pascal 1, 1348 Louvain-la-Neuve; tel. (10) 47-48-41; e-mail accueil-musee@uclouvain.be; internet www.muse.ucl.ac.be; f. 1979; attached to Université Catholique de Louvain; permanent collns focus on 4 areas: ancient sculpture, African art, classical archaeology (primarily from Mainz) and colln of casts; Dir Prof. JOËL ROUCLOUX.

Mariemont

Musée Royal de Mariemont: chaussée de Mariemont 100, 7140 Mariemont (Morlanwelz); tel. (64) 21-21-93; e-mail info@musee-mariemont.be; internet www.musee-mariemont.be; f. 1975; antiquities from Egypt, Greece, Rome, China, Japan; nat. archaeology; Tournai porcelain; bookbindings; library of 130,000 vols, 400 periodicals; Dir MARIE-CÉCILE BRUWIER; Man. Dir DANIEL COURBE; publ. *Les Cahiers de Mariemont* (1 a year).

Mechelen

Stedelijke Musea Mechelen: Van Beethovenstraat 8–10, 2800 Mechelen; tel. (15) 29-40-30; e-mail stedelijkemusea@mechelen.be; internet www.stedelijkemusea.mechelen.be; f. 1844; Head Curator STROOBANTS BART.

Namur

Musée Archéologique de Namur: Halle al'Chair, Rue du Pont 21, 5000 Namur; tel. (81) 23-16-31; e-mail man.info@tvcablenet.be; f. 1855; archaeological collns: pre- and protohistoric, Roman and Merovingian; Head and Curator JEAN-LOUIS ANTOINE.

Musée de Groesbeeck-de Croix: rue Joseph Saintraint 3, 5000 Namur; tel. (81) 24-87-20; e-mail museedecroix@ville.namur.be; furniture and art works of 18th century; paintings, sculptures, ceramics, silverware, glassware and crystal; decorative arts; Head MARTINE GEORGE; Curator JOSINE DE FRAIPONT; Curator JACQUES TOUSSAINT.

Musée Félicien Rops: rue Fumal 12, 5000 Namur; tel. (81) 77-67-55; e-mail info@museerops.be; internet www.museerops.be; f. 1964; artist's etchings, drawings, paintings; temporary exhibitions.

Musée Provincial des Arts Anciens du Namurois: Hôtel de Gaiffier d'Hestroy, rue de Fer 24, 5000 Namur; tel. (81) 77-67-54; e-mail musee.arts.anciens@province.namur.be; internet www.museedesartsanciens.be; f. 1964; colln of paintings by Henri Bles; Oignies's Treasure; arts of Middle Ages and Renaissance of Namur; library of 50,000 vols; Dir and Chief Curator JACQUES TOUSSAINT; publ. *Journal des Musées*.

Sint-Martins-Latem

Museum Dhondt-Dhaenens: Museumlaan 14, 9831 Sint-Martens-Latem (Deurle); tel. (9) 282-51-23; e-mail info@museumdd.be; internet www.museumdd.be; f. 1968; works by James Ensor, Gust and Leon De Smet, Valerius De Saedeleer, Constant Permeke, Albert Servaes, Frits Van den Berghe, Gustave van de Woestyne and contemporary artists; Dir JOOST DECLERCQ; Curator TANGUY EECKHOUT.

Tournai

Musée d'Archéologie (Museum of Archaeology): rue des Carmes 8, 7500 Tournai; tel. (69) 22-16-72; e-mail musee.archeologie@tournai.be; internet www.tournai.be/musee-archeologie; divided into 3 sections: Quaternary, Gallo-Roman and Merovingian; Curator MARIANNE DELCOURT.

Musée d'Armes et d'Histoire Militaire (Museum of Weapons and Military History): rue Roc Saint Nicaise 59–61, 7500 Tournai; tel. (69) 21-19-66; e-mail musee.armes@tournai.be; internet www.tournai.be/musee-armes; f. 1930; weapons, military and civilian artefacts; Curator CHARLES DELIGNE.

Musée de Folklore (Folklore Museum): Réduit des Sions 32–36, 7500 Tournai; tel. (69) 22-40-69; e-mail musee.folklore@tournai.be; internet www.tournai.be/musee-folklore; f. 1930; colln exhibits porcelain, tin, printing, medicine, traditions and calendar customs, men's and women's civilian and military clothing evolution; reproduction of a relief ground plan of Tournai in the 17th century made out for King Louis XIV; Curator NICOLE DEMARET.

Musée des Beaux-Arts (Museum of Fine Arts): Enclos Saint-Martin, 7500 Tournai; tel. (11) 33-24-31; e-mail musee.beaux-arts@tournai.be; internet www.tournai.be/musee-beaux-arts; f. 1928; architecture, ancient paintings, works of nat. and int. artists; Curator JEAN-PIERRE DE RYCKE.

Musée d'Histoire et des Arts Décoratifs (Museum of History and Decorative Arts): rue Saint-Martin 50, 7500 Tournai; tel. (69) 33-23-53; e-mail tourisme@tournai.be; internet www.tournai.be/musee-arts-decoratifs; earthenware of 15th, 16th, 18th centuries; coins minted in Tournai between 12th and 17th centuries; silverware; Curator THOMAS BAYET.

Verviers

Musée d'Archéologie et de Folklore: rue des Raines 42, 4800 Verviers; tel. (87) 33-16-95; e-mail musees.verviers@skynet.be; internet www.lesmuseesenwallonie.be; f.

1959; history of art, archaeology, folklore, local history; Curator MARIE-PAULE DEBLANC.

Musée des Beaux-Arts et de la Céramique: rue Renier 17, 4800 Verviers; tel. (87) 33-16-95; e-mail musees.verviers@skynet.be; internet www.lesmuseesenwallonie.be; f. 1884; sculpture, Belgian paintings; European paintings from 14th to 19th century; ceramics of Europe and Asia; Chinese porcelain and Japanese, Saxony-Meissen, Delft pottery, sandstone Raeren; Dir MARIE-PAULE DEBLANC; publ. *Guide du Visiteur*.

Zulte

Roger Raveel Museum: Gildestraat 2–8, 9870 Zulte (Machelen); tel. (9) 381-60-00; e-mail rrm@rogerraveelmuseum.be; internet www.rogerraveelmuseum.be; exhibition of works by artist.

Universities

HASSELT UNIVERSITEIT

Campus Diepenbeek Agoralaan, Gebouw D, 3590 Diepenbeek
Telephone: (11) 26-81-11
E-mail: info@uhasselt.be
Internet: www.uhasselt.be
Founded 1971, present status 2001
State control
Languages of instruction: Dutch, English
Rector: Prof. Dr LUC DE SCHEPPER
Vice-Rector for Research: PAUL JANSSEN
Vice-Rector for Education: ERNA NAUWELAERTS
Permanent Sec.: MARK SMEYERS
Librarian: MARC GOOVAERTS
Library of 70,000 vols
Number of teachers: 530
Number of students: 2,700

DEANS

Faculty of Applied Economics: PIET PAUWELS
Faculty of Law: GUNTER MAES
Faculty of Medicine: PIET STINISSEN
Faculty of Sciences: JEAN MANCA

KATHOLIEKE UNIVERSITEIT LEUVEN
(Catholic University of Leuven)

Naamsestraat 22, 3000 Louvain (Leuven)
Telephone: (16) 32-40-10
E-mail: info@kuleuven.be
Internet: www.kuleuven.ac.be
Founded 1425, present status 1970
Private control
Languages of instruction: Dutch, English
Academic year: September to September
Rector: Prof. RIK TORFS
Vice-Rector for Biomedical Sciences: Prof. MINNE CASTEELS
Vice-Rector for Educational Policy: Prof. LUDO MELIS
Vice-Rector for Humanities and Social Sciences: Prof. FILIP ABRAHAM
Vice-Rector for Int. Policy: Prof. BART DE MOOR
Vice-Rector for Kortrijk Campus: Prof. JAN BEIRLANT
Vice-Rector for Research Policy: Prof. PETER MARYNEN
Vice-Rector for Science, Engineering and Technology: Prof. KAREN MAEX
Vice-Rector for Student Affairs: Prof. TINE BAELMANS
Gen. Man. for Univ. Admin.: Prof. KOENRAAD DEBACKERE
Librarian: MEL COLLIER
Library: see under Libraries and Archives
Number of teachers: 2,600
Number of students: 39,395
Publication: *Campuskrant* (10 a year)

DEANS

Faculty of Arts: Prof. LUK DRAYE
Faculty of Bioscience Engineering: Prof. Dr Ir POL COPPIN
Faculty of Business and Economics: Prof. Dr LUC SELS
Faculty of Canon Law: Prof. RIK TORFS
Faculty of Engineering: Prof. Ir LUDO FROYEN
Faculty of Kinesiology and Rehabilitation Science: Prof. CHRISTOPHE DELECLUSE
Faculty of Law: Prof. PAUL VAN ORSHOVEN
Faculty of Medicine: Prof. Dr BERNARD HIMPENS
Faculty of Pharmaceutical Sciences: Prof. A. VERBRUGGEN
Faculty of Psychology and Educational Sciences: Prof. Dr PATRICK ONGHENA
Faculty of Science: Prof. PETER LIEVENS
Faculty of Social Sciences: KATLIJN MALFLIET
Faculty of Theology: Prof. LIEVEN BOEVE
Institute of Philosophy: ANTOON VANDEVELDE

KU LEUVEN CAMPUS BRUSSELS

Warmoesberg 26, 1000 Brussels
Telephone: (2) 210-12-11
E-mail: feb.hubrussel@kuleuven.be
Internet: www.kuleuven.be/campus/athub/eng
Founded 1968 as Universitaire Faculteiten Sint-Aloysius, became Katholieke Universiteit Brussel 1991, merged with European Univ. College, VLEKHO and HONIM in 2007
Private control
Languages of instruction: Dutch, English
Academic year: September to June
Rector: Prof. Dr DIRK DE CEULAER
Library of 70,000 vols
Number of teachers: 1,000
Number of students: 9,000
Publications: *N9* (4 a year), *Tempo* (4 a year)

DEANS

Faculty of Arts: R. SLEIDERINK
Faculty of Economics and Business: T. VAN PUYENBROECK
Faculty of Law: B. DEMARSIN

PROFESSORS

ACX, R., Bank and Credit Sciences
BOUSSET, H., Dutch Literature
BRAEKMAN, W. L., English Literature
CARPENTIER, N.
DE BOECK, A.
DE CLERCQ, M., European Literature and Introduction to Modern Literature
DEFOORT, E., Modern French Texts
DEGADT, J., Economic Science and Social Statistics
DE LATHOUWER, L.
DELWAIDE, J.
DE MARTELAERE, P., Philosophic Anthropology
DEPREEUW, E.
DE SCHRYVER, J.
DESMET, J.
DE VIN, D., Dutch Literature
DEWINTER, L.
ELST, M.
FLEERACKERS, F.
FOBLETS, M.-C.
GEERAERTS, R.
GOOSSENS, W., Historic Introduction to Philosophy
GOTZEN, F., Introduction to Law
HEMMERECHTS, L.
HEYSSE, T.
JAKOBS, D.
JANSSENS, J., History of Medieval Dutch Literature
JANSSENS, P., Modern Times
LINDEMANS, J.-F., Traditional Logics
LOOSVELDT, G., Methods and Techniques of Social Sciences
MOONS, T., History of Antiquity
MUYLLE, J., Art and Cultural History
NELDE, P. H., Germanic Linguistics
OOSTERBOSCH, A., Physics
SCHOENMAECKERS, R.
SWYNGEDOUW, M.
TACQ, J., Sociology
VANDEN BROECKE, S.
VAN DEN WIJNGAERT, M., History of Modern Times
VANDEN WYNGAERD, G.
VAN DE WOESTYNE, I.
VANHEMELRYCK, F., History of Modern Times
VAN HOECKE, M., Introduction to Law
VERRETH, H.
VERSTRAELEN, L., Mathematics
VERTONGHEN, R., Accountancy
WINTGENS, L.

UNIVERSITÉ CATHOLIQUE DE LOUVAIN
(Catholic University of Louvain)

Place de l'Université 1, 1348 Louvain-la-Neuve
Telephone: (10) 47-21-11
E-mail: info-portail@uclouvain.be
Internet: www.uclouvain.be
Founded 1425, present status 1970
Private control
Language of instruction: French
Academic year: September to May
Rector: Prof. BRUNO DELVAUX
Vice-Rector for Health Sciences: Prof. PIERRE GIANELLO
Vice-Rector for Humanities: CAMILLE FOCANT
Vice-Rector for Human Resources Policy: Prof. JACQUES GRÉGOIRE
Vice-Rector for Student Affairs: DIDIER LAMBERT
Vice-Rector for Technology: Prof. PATRICK BERTRAND
Gen. Administrator: DOMINIQUE OPFERGELT
Librarian: CH.-H. NYNS
Library: see under Libraries and Archives
Number of teachers: 1,260
Number of students: 21,000
Publication: *Bulletin des Amis de Louvain*

DEANS

École Polytechnique de Louvain: Prof. F. DELANNAY
Faculty of Architecture, Architectural Engineering, Town Planning and Environmental Engineering: Prof. A. DE HERDE
Faculty of Arts and Letters: Prof. P.-A. DEPROOST
Faculty of Bio-engineering, Agronomy and Environment: Prof. J. MAHILLON
Faculty of Economic, Social and Political Sciences: Prof. CL. ROOSENS
Faculty of Law: Prof. B. DUBUISSON
Faculty of Medicine and Dentistry: Prof. A. GEUBEL
Faculty of Motor Sciences: Prof. T. ZINTZ
Faculty of Pharmacy and Biomedical Sciences: Prof. J. LECLERCQ
Faculty of Psychology and Educational Sciences: Prof. M. FRENAY
Faculty of Public Health: Prof. E. DARRAS
Faculty of Sciences (incl. veterinary medicine): Prof. J. GOVAERTS
Faculty of Theology: Prof. A. WÉNIN
Louvain School of Management: VÉRONIQUE SEMINERIO

UNIVERSITÉ DE LIÈGE
(University of Liège)

Place du 20-Août 7, 4000 Liège
Telephone: (4) 366-21-11
E-mail: international@ulg.ac.be
Internet: www.ulg.ac.be

Founded 1817, present status 1989
Language of instruction: French
Academic year: October to September

Rector: BERNARD RENTIER
Vice-Rector: ALBERT CORHAY
Vice-Rector for Evaluation and Quality: Prof. FREDDY COIGNOUL
Vice-Rector for Gembloux Agro-Bio-Tech: Prof. ERIC HAUBRUGE
Vice-Rector for Int. Relations: Prof. JEAN MARCHAL
Vice-Rector for Research: Prof. PIERRE WOLPER
Gen. Administrator: FRANÇOIS RONDAY
Gen. Dir for Education and Training: MONIQUE MARCOURT-DEFRENE

Library: see under Libraries and Archives
Number of teachers: 593
Number of students: 20,000

DEANS

Faculty of Applied Sciences: Prof. MICHEL HOGGE
Faculty of Law and Political Science—The Jean Constant Criminology School of Liège: Prof. OLIVIER CAPRASSE
Faculty of Medicine: Prof. GUSTAVE MOONEN
Faculty of Philosophy and Letters: Prof. JEAN-PIERRE BERTRAND
Faculty of Psychology and Education: Prof. SERGE BREDART
Faculty of Science: Prof. RUDI CLOOTS
Faculty of Veterinary Medicine: Prof. PIERRE LEKEUX
Gembloux Agro-Bio-Tech: PHILIPPE LEPOIVRE
HEC-Management School—ULg: THOMAS FROEHLICHER
Institute for Human and Social Sciences: DIDIER VRANCKEN

PROFESSORS WITH CHAIRS

Faculty of Applied Sciences (chemin des Chevreuils, 1, B52/3 Sart Tilman, 4000 Liège):

BOIGELOT, B., Computer Science
CESCOTTO, S., Mechanics of Materials
CHARLIER, R., Geomechanics and Engineering Geology
CRINE, M., Chemical Engineering
DASSARGUES, A., Hydrogeology and Environmental Geology
DE MARNEFFE, P.-A., Computer Science
DELHEZ, E., General Mathematics
DESTINE, J., Microelectronics
DUYSINX, P., Land Vehicle Engineering
ESSERS, J. A., Aerodynamics
FLEURY, CL., Aerospatial Structures
GERMAIN, A., Industrial Chemistry
GOLINVAL, J.-C., Vibration and Structure Identification
GRIBOMONT, P., Computer Science and Artificial Intelligence
HOGGE, M., Thermomechanics
JASPART, J.-P., Structural Adequacy of Techno-economic Performance and Operation Requirements
LEDUC, G., Computer Networks
MARCHAL, J., Transport Systems and Shipbuilding
PIRARD, E., Mineral Geo-Resources and Geological Imaging
PIRARD, J. P., Applied Physical Chemistry
PONTHOT, J.-P., Non Linear Digital LTAS-Mechanics
SEPULCHRE, R., Systems and Modelling
VERLY, J., Signal and Image Processing
WEHENKEL, L., Systems and Modelling
WOLPER, P., Computer Science

Faculty of Law and Political Science—The Jean Constant Criminology School of Liège (7 blvd du Rectorat, B 31, Sart Tilman, 4000 Liège):

BIQUET, C., Contract and Credit Law
CAPRASSE, O., Commercial Law
DE LEVAL, G., Civil Law
JACOBS, A., Criminal Law and Criminal Law Procedure
LECOCQ, P., Property and Evidentiary Law
LELEU, Y.-H., Family Law and Medical Law
PARENT, X., Tax Law
WAUTELET, P., Private International Law

Faculty of Medicine (ave de l'hôpital, 1, B 36 Sart Tilman, 4000 Liège):

ADELIN, A., Public Health Science
ANGENOT, L., Pharmacy
ANSSEAU, M., Psychiatry and Medical Psychology
BELAICHE, J., Hepato-gastroenterology
BONIVER, J., Anatomy and Pathological Cytology
BOURS, V., General and Human Genetics
CRIELAARD, J.-M., Physical Skills Evaluation and Conditioning
CROMMEN, J., Drug Analysis
DEFRAIGNE, J.-O., Cardiovascular and Thoracic Surgery
DEFRESNE, M.-P., Histology–Cytology
DE LEVAL, J., Urology
DE MOL, P., Medical Microbiology and Virology
D'ORIO, V., Emergency Medicine
FILLET, G., Haematology
FOIDART, J. M., Gynaecology–Obstetrics
GRISAR, T., Human and Pathological Biochemistry and Physiology
HEINEN, E., Human Histology
LIMME, M., Orthodontics and Paedodontics
MALAISE, M., Rheumatology
MEURISSE, M., Abdominal Surgery
MOONEN, G., Normal and Pathological Physiology
PIERARD, L., Cardiology
PIROTTE, B., Pharmaceutical Chemistry
REGINSTER, J.-Y., Epidemiology and Public Health
ROMPEN, E., Bucco-dental Surgery and Periodontics
SCHEEN, A., Diabetology, Nutrition and Metabolic Disorders
SCHOENEN, J., Neuro-anatomy

Faculty of Philosophy and Letters (place du 20-Août, 7, A1 (Centre Ville), 4000 Liège):

ALLART, D., Art History and Archaeology of Modern Times
BAJOMEE, D., Contemporary French Literature
BALACE, F., Contemporary History
BERTRAND, J.-P., 19th- and 20th-Century French Literature
CURRERI, L., Italian Language and Literature
DELVILLE, M., Modern English and American Literature
DOR, J., Medieval English Language and Literature
DUCHESNE, J.-P., Art History and Contemporary Archaeology
DUMORTIER, J.-L., Romance Language Teacher Training: French, Spanish, Italian
DURAND, P., Cultural Institutions and Information
GIOVANNANGELI, D., History of Modern and Contemporary Philosophy
GOB, A., Museology
KLINKENBERG, J.-M., Rhetoric and Semiology
KUPPER, J. L., History of the Middle Ages and Historical Geography
LAFFINEUR, R., Art History and Archaeology of Classical Antiquity
OTTE, M., Prehistoric Archaeology
RAXHON, P., Historical Criticism
TUNCA, O., Modern English Philology
VROMANS, J., Modern Dutch Language and Synchronic Linguistics
WINAND, J., Egyptology

Faculty of Psychology and Education (5 blvd du Rectorat, B 32 Sart Tilman, 4000 Liège):

BECKERS, J., Professional Teacher Training
BORN, M., Psychology of Criminality and Psycho-Social Development
BREDART, S., Cognitive Psychology
HANSENNE, M., Personality and Individual Differences Psychology
LECLERCQ, D., Economy and Rural Development
LEROY, J.-F., Social Psychology of Groups and Organizations
MEULEMANS, T., Neuropsychology
TIRELLI, E., Behavioural Neuroscience and Experimental Psychopharmacology

Faculty of Science (allée de la Chimie, 5, B6 Sart Tilman, 4000 Liège):

ADELIN, A.
BASTIN, F., Analysis, Functional Analysis, Wavelets
BECKERS, J., Physical Oceanography
BOULVAIN, F., Sedimentary Petrology
BOUQUEGNEAU, J.-M., Oceanology
CLOOTS, R., Structural Inorganic Chemistry
CUGNON, J., Theoretical Physics
DE PAUW, E., Physical Chemistry, Mass Spectrometry
DEMOULIN, V., Algology, Mycology and Experimental Systematics
DOMMES, J., Plant Molecular Biology and Biotechnology
DONNAY, J.-P., Geographic Information Systems and Mapping
FRANSOLET, A. M., Mineralogy
GHOSEZ, P., Theoretical Material Physics
LECOMTE, P., Geometry and Algorithm Theory
LUXEN, A., Synthetic Organic Chemistry
MARTIAL, J., Molecular Biology and Genetic Engineering
MOTTE, P., Functional Genomics and Plant Molecular Imaging
PETIT, F.-F., Geomorphology, Hydrography
RENTIER, B., Basic Virology
SCHOUMAKER-MERENNE, B., Economic Geography
SURDEJ, J., Extragalactic Astrophysics and Space Observation
THOME, J.-P., Animal Ecology and Ecotoxicology
THONART, PH., Microbiology
VANDEWALLE, N., Statistical Physics
VANDEWALLE, P., Functional and Developmental Morphology

Faculty of Veterinary Medicine (20 blvd du Colonster, B 42 Sart Tilman 4000 Liège):

BALLIGAND, M., Surgery and Surgical Clinical Practice in Small Animals
CLERCX, C., Small Animal Medical Pathology
COIGNOUL, F., Pathological Anatomy and Autopsies
DESMECHT, D., Special Pathology and Autopsies
GEORGES, M., Animal Genomics
GODEAU, J. M., Biochemistry
GUSTIN, P., Pharmacology, Pharmacotherapeutics and Toxicology
LEKEUX, P., Physiology
LEROY, P., Information Science Applied to Animal Husbandry
LOSSON, B., Parasitology and Pathology of Parasitic Diseases
MAINIL, J., Bacteriology and Pathology of Bacterial Diseases
SERTEYN, D., General Anaesthesiology and Surgical Pathology in Larger Animals

THIRY, E., Virology, Epidemiology, and Pathology of Viral Diseases
VANDERPLASSCHEN, A., Immunology and Vaccinology

Gembloux Agro-Bio-Tech (passage des Déportés, 2, 5030 Gembloux; tel. (81) 62-21-11; e-mail gembloux@ulg.ac.be; internet www.fsagx.ac.be):

BAUDOIN, J.-P., Agricultural Science
BOCK, L., Environmental Science and Technology
CLAUSTRIAUX, J.-J., Agricultural Science
DEBOUCHE, C., Environmental Science and Technology
DEROANNE, C., Chemistry and Bio-industries
DESTAIN, M.-F., Environmental Science and Technology
DU JARDIN, P., Agricultural Science
HAUBRUGE, E., Agricultural Science
LEBAILLY, P., Agricultural Science
LEPOIVRE, P., Agricultural Science
PAQUOT, M., Chemistry and Bio-Industries
PORTETELLE, D., Chemistry and Bio-industries
RONDEUX, J., Environmental Science and Technology
THEWIS, A., Agricultural Science
THONART, P., Chemistry and Bio-industries

HEC-Management School—ULg (rue Louvrex, 14, N1, 4000 Liège):

BAIR, J., International Relations
CHOFFRAY, J.-M., Computer Decision Support
CORHAY, A., Accounting and Finance
CORNET, A., Management of Human Resources and Organizations
CRAMA, Y., Operational Research and Production Management
DEFOURNY, J., Social Economy and Economic Systems
FELD, S., Development Economics
JURION, B., Political Economy
PAHUD DE MORTANGES, C., General Marketing
PICHAULT, F., Human Resource Management
SURLEMONT, B., International Management–Entrepreneurship

Institute for Human and Social Sciences (blvd du Rectorat, 7, B31, Sart Tilman, 4000 Liège):

PONCELET, M., Occupational Psychology
VRANCKEN, D., Sociological Practice

UNIVERSITÉ DE MONS
(University of Mons)

Place du Parc 20, 7000 Mons
Telephone: (65) 37-31-11
E-mail: martine.vanelslande@umh.ac.be
Internet: www.umh.ac.be

Founded 1965
Language of instruction: French
State control
Academic year: October to September

Rector: CALOGERO CONTI
Vice-Rector: BERNARD HARMEGNIES
Vice-Rector for Institutional and Regional Devt: GIUSEPPE PAGANO
Vice-Rector for Int. Relations: PIERRE DEHOMBREUX
Vice-Rector for Research: PHILIPPE DUBOIS
Administrator: DANY VINCE
Librarian: RENÉ PLISNIER

Library: see under Libraries and Archives
Number of teachers: 250
Number of students: 5,000

Publications: *Elément*, *Polytech.News*, *UMH Dedicace* (4 a year)

DEANS

Faculty of Architecture and Town Planning: NICOLAS PERCSY
Faculty of Engineering: Prof. PAUL LYBAERT
Faculty of Medicine and Pharmacy: Prof. ROBERT N. MULLER
Faculty of Psychology and Education: Prof. AGNÈS VAN DAELE
Faculty of Sciences: Prof. CHRISTIAN MICHAUX
Faculty of Translation and Interpretation: Prof. ALAIN PIETTE
Institute for Language Sciences: BERNARD HARMEGNIES
Warocqué Faculty of Economics and Business Management: Prof. KARIN COMBLE

PROFESSORS

ALEXANDRE, H., Biology and Embryology
BELAYEW, A., Molecular Biology
BIEMONT, E., Astrophysics and Spectroscopy
BREDAS, J.-L., Chemistry of New Materials
BRIHAYE, Y., Theoretical Physics and Mathematics
BRUYÈRE, V., Theoretical Computer Science
BRUYNINCKX, H., Linguistics and Data Processing
CHERON, G., Electrophysiology
COMBLÉ-DARJA, K., Accountancy and Finance
COUVREUR, P., Applied Statistics
DANG, N. N., Probability and Statistics
DE CONINCK, J., Molecular Modelling
DEFRAITEUR, R., Fiscal System
DEPOVER, C., Moulding Technology
DESMET, H., Social and Community Psychology
DONNAY-RICHELLE, J., Clinical Psychology
DOSIERE, M., Physics and Chemistry of Polymers
DUBOIS, P., Polymeric and Composite Materials
DUFOUR, P., Computer Sciences
DUPONT, P., Methodology and Formation
ESCARMELLE, J.-F., Public Economy
FALMAGNE, P., Biological Chemistry
FINET, C., Mathematical Analysis
FORGES, G., Language Teaching
GILLIS, P., Experimental and Biological Physics
GOCZOL, J., Microeconomics and Marketing
GODAUX, E., Neurosciences
HARMEGNIES, B., Metrology in Psychology and Education
HECQ, M., Analytical and Inorganic Chemistry
HERQUET, P., Physics
ISAAC-VANDEPUTTE, M.-T., Historical Bibliography
JANGOUX, M., Marine Biology
LAUDE, L., Solid State Physics
LEBRUN-CARTON, C., Mathematics
LOWENTHAL, F., Cognitive Sciences
LUX, B., Company Management and Economics
MAGEROTTE, G., Education of the Handicapped
MAHY, B., Economic Analysis
MICHAUX, CH., Logic Mathematics
PAGANO, G., Public Finance and Management
PLATTEN, J., General Chemistry
POURTOIS, J.-P., Psychosociology of Family and School Education
RADOUX, C., Mathematics and Number Theory
RASMONT, P., Zoology
SAUSSEZ, S., Anatomy
SPILLEBOUDT-DETERCK, M., Finance
SPINDEL, P., Mechanics and Gravitation
STANDAERT, S., International Economic Analysis
TEGHEM-LORIS, J., Mathematics and Actuarial Science
THIRY, P., Management Information Science
TOUBEAU, G., Histology
TROESTLER, C., Numerical Analysis
VAN DAELE, A., Psychology of Labour
VAN HAVERBEKE, Y., Organic Chemistry
VANSNICK, J.-C., Quantitative Methods
VERHEVE, D., Chemical Technology
WAUTELET, H., Experimental Photonics
WIJSEN, J., Information Systems Science

UNIVERSITÉ LIBRE DE BRUXELLES
(Free University of Brussels)

Ave F. D. Roosevelt 50, 1050 Brussels
Telephone: (2) 650-21-11
E-mail: infor-etudes@ulb.ac.be
Internet: www.ulb.ac.be

Founded 1834, present status 1970
Private control
Languages of instruction: English, French
Academic year: September to July

Rector: DIDIER VIVIERS
Pres.: ALAIN DELCHAMBRE
Vice-Pres.: MARTIN CASIER
Sec.: MONIQUE TAVERNIER
Librarian: Prof. JEAN-PIERRE DEVROEY

Library: see under Libraries and Archives
Number of teachers: 1,313
Number of students: 24,236

Publication: *Esprit Libre* (4 a year)

DEANS

Faculty of Applied Sciences/École polytechnique: JEAN-CLAUDE MAUN
Faculty of Architecture (la Cambre Horta): FRANCIS METZGER
Faculty of Law and Criminology: ANDRÉE PUTTEMANS
Faculty of Medicine: YVON ENGLERT
Faculty of Motor Sciences: NATHALIE GUISSARD
Faculty of Pharmacy: KARIM AMIGHI
Faculty of Philosophy and Letters: MANUEL COUVREUR
Faculty of Psychology and Education: ALAIN CONTENT
Faculty of Science: MARTINE LABBE
Faculty of Social and Political Sciences: JEAN-MICHEL DE WAELE
Institute of European Studies: MARIANNE DONY
School of Public Health: ALAIN LEVEQUE
Solvay Business School Faculty of Economics and Management: BRUNO VAN POTTELSBERGHE

UNIVERSITÉ SAINT-LOUIS-BRUXELLES
(Saint-Louis University, Brussels)

Blvd du Jardin Botanique 43, 1000 Brussels
Telephone: (2) 211-78-11
E-mail: info@usaintlouis.be
Internet: www.usaintlouis.be

Founded 1858, current name adopted 1948
Language of instruction: French
Academic year: September to June

Rector: JEAN-PAUL LAMBERT
Vice-Rector: FRANÇOIS OST

Library: see under Libraries and Archives
Number of students: 2,900

DEANS

Faculty of Economic, Social and Political Sciences: F. NILS
Faculty of Law: P. JADOUL
Faculty of Philosophy and Letters: L. VAN EYNDE

PROFESSORS

Faculty of Economic, Social and Political Sciences:

BERTRAND, P., Physics
CALLUT, J. P., English Language
CITTA-VANTHEMSCHE, M., Mathematics
D'ASPREMONT LYNDEN, C., Philosophy and Social Sciences

de Kerchove de Denterghem, A. M., Economics
Deprins, D., Statistics
de Ronge, Y., Accountancy
de Saint-Georges, P., Social Communication
de Stexhe, G., Philosophy and Ethics
Everaert-Desmedt, N., Semiology
Franck, C., Political Science
Gillardin, J., Introduction to Law
Guerra, F., Accountancy
Hardy, A., Mathematics
Hubert, M., Sociology
Lambert, J. P., Economics
Leclercq, N. C., Civil Law
Lepers, A., Accountancy
Loute, E., Mathematics and Computer Science
Marquet, J., Sociology
Mitchell, J., Economics
Rigaux, M.-F., Introduction to Law, Public Law
Servais, P., Economic and Social History
Simar, L., Statistics
Soete, J. L., Contemporary History
Sonveaux, E., Chemistry
Streydio, J. M., Physics
Strodiot, J. J., Mathematics
Tulkens, H., Political Economy
van Campenhoudt, L., Sociology
van Rillaer, J., Social and Industrial Psychology
Verhoeven, J., International Law
Wibaut, S., Political Economy
Witterwulghe, R., Political Economy

Faculty of Law:
Cartuyvels, Y., Introduction to Law
de Brouwer, J. L., Political Science
de Jemeppe, B., Dutch Language
de Theux, A., Introduction to Law
Deville, A., Sociology
Dillens, A. M., Philosophy
Dumont, H., Public Law
Gerard, P., Introduction to Law
Hanard, G., Roman Law
Jacob, R., Private Law
Loriaux, C., English
Mahieu, M., Introduction to Law
Nandrin, J. P., History
Ost, F., Introduction to Law
Segers, M. J., Psychology
Strowel, A., Introduction to Law
van de Kerchove, M., Introduction to Law
van Gehuchten, P. P., Law
Wanthy, X., Political Economy

Faculty of Philosophy and Letters:
Bousset, H., Dutch Authors and Literature
Braive, J., History
Brisart, R., Philosophy
Cauchies, J. M., History
Cheyns, A., Greek Philology and Authors
Cupers, J.-L., English Authors and Literature
Dauchy, S., History
de Ruyt, C., Ancient History and History of Art
Duchesne, J.-P., History of Art
Heiderscheidt, J., English Phonetics and Grammar
Jongen, R., German Phonetics and Grammar, Linguistics
Lenoble-Pinson, M., Modern French Grammar, Philology
Leonardy, E., German Literature
Loge, T., French Literature
Longree, D., Latin Philology and Authors
Maeschalck, M., Philosophy
Marrant, A., Latin Authors
Mattens, W., Dutch Grammar and Philology
Renard, M. C., French Authors, Modern Literatures, Italian and Spanish
Tock, B. M., History
Willems, M., Medieval French Literature
Xhardey, D., History of Greek and Latin Literature and Greek Philology

UNIVERSITEIT ANTWERPEN
(University of Antwerp)

Prinsstraat 13, 2000 Antwerp
Telephone: (3) 265-47-77
E-mail: internationalstudents@ua.ac.be
Internet: www.uantwerp.be

Founded 2003 by merger of Universitaire Centrum Antwerpen, Universitaire Faculteiten Sint-Ignatius Antwerpen and Universitaire Insteling Antwerpen
State control
Languages of instruction: Dutch, English
Academic year: September to July

Rector: Prof. Dr Alain Verschoren
Pres.: Prof. Dr Alex Vanneste
Chair of Education Council: Prof. Dr Joke Denekens
Chair of Research Council: Prof. Dr Jean-Pierre Timmermans
Chair of Services Council: Prof. Dr Johan Meeusen
Man.: Prof. Dr Bart Heijnen
Librarian: Trudi Noordermeer

Library: see under Libraries and Archives
Number of teachers: 997
Number of students: 18,800

Publications: *Bijdragen tot de Geschiedenis, CSB-Berichten, Economische Didaktiek, Gezelliana, Kroniek van de Gezellestudie, Het Teken van de Ram, In de Steigers, Miscellanea Neerlandica*

DEANS

Faculty of Applied Economics: Prof. Dr Rudy Martens
Faculty of Arts and Philosophy: Prof. Dr Bruno Tritsmans
Faculty of Law: Prof. Dr Gert Straetmans
Faculty of Medicine: Prof. Dr Paul Van De Heyning
Faculty of Pharmaceutical, Biomedical and Veterinary Sciences: Prof. Dr Frans Van Meir
Faculty of Political and Social Sciences: Prof. Dr Ria Janvier
Faculty of Science: Prof. Dr Herwig Leirs

UNIVERSITEIT GENT
(Ghent University)

Sint-Pietersnieuwstraat 25, 9000 Ghent
Telephone: (9) 264-31-11
E-mail: communicatie@ugent.be
Internet: www.ugent.be

Founded 1817
State control
Language of instruction: Dutch
Academic year: October to July

Rector: Prof. Paul Van Cauwenberge
Vice-Rector: Prof. Luc Moens
Govt Commr: Yannick De Clercq
Chief Academic Admin.: Prof. Koen Goethals
Chief Logistics Administrator: Dirk Mangeleer
Sec. of Board of Govs: Dirk Van Haelter

Library: see under Libraries and Archives
Number of teachers: 962
Number of students: 32,000

Publication: *Universiteit Gent* (8 a year)

DEANS

Faculty of Arts and Philosophy: Freddy Mortier
Faculty of Bioscience Engineering: Guido Van Huylenbroeck
Faculty of Economics and Business Administration: Marc De Clercq
Faculty of Engineering: Luc Taerwe
Faculty of Law: Piet Taelman
Faculty of Medicine and Health Sciences: Eric Mortier
Faculty of Pharmaceutical Sciences: Stefaan De Smedt
Faculty of Political and Social Sciences: Herwig Reynaert
Faculty of Psychology and Educational Sciences: Geert De Soete
Faculty of Sciences: Herwig Dejonghe
Faculty of Veterinary Sciences: Hubert De Brabander

PROFESSORS

Faculty of Arts and Philosophy (Blandijnberg 2, 9000 Ghent; tel. (9) 264-39-32):
Art, J., Modern History
Bourgeois, J., Archaeology and Ancient History of Europe
Commers, M., Philosophy and Moral Sciences
Decreus, F., Latin and Greek
Detrez, R., Slavonic and East-European Studies
Devos, I., Early Modern History
Devos, M., Dutch Linguistics
Kabuta, N., African Languages and Cultures
Laureys, G., Nordic Studies
Leman, M., Art, Music and Theatre Sciences
Moerloose, E., Languages and Cultures of South and East Asia
Pinxten, H., Comparative Sciences of Culture
Roegiest, E., Language and Communication
Slembrouck, S., English
Tanret, M., Languages and Cultures of the Near East and North Africa
Thoen, E., Medieval History
Verhulst, S., Romance Languages (Other than French)
Vervaeck, B., Dutch Literature
Willems, D., French
Willems, K., German

Faculty of Bioscience Engineering (Coupure Links 653, 9000 Ghent; tel. (9) 264-59-01):
Devlieghere, F., Food Safety and Food Quality
Janssen, C., Applied Ecology and Environmental Biology
Ottoy, J., Applied Mathematics, Biometrics and Process Control
Pieters, J., Biosystems Engineering
Reheul, D., Plant Production
Sorgeloos, P., Animal Production
Steurbaut, W., Crop Protection
Van Meirvenne, M., Soil Management
Van Oostveldt, P., Molecular Biotechnology
Verhé, R., Organic Chemistry
Verheyen, K., Forest and Water Management
Verloo, M., Applied Analytical and Physical Chemistry
Verstraete, W., Biochemical and Microbial Technology
Viaene, J., Agricultural Economics

Faculty of Economics and Business Administration (Hoveniersberg 24, 9000 Ghent; tel. (9) 264-34-61):
De Beelde, I., Accountancy and Corporate Finance
De Clercq, M., General Economics
Heene, A., Management, Innovation and Entrepreneurship
Omey, E., Social Economics
Vander Vennet, R., Financial Economics
Vanhoucke, M., Management Information Science and Operation Management
Van Kenhove, P., Marketing

Faculty of Engineering (Jozef Plateaustraat 22, 9000 Ghent; tel. (9) 264-79-50):

Bruneel, H., Telecommunications and Information Processing
De Baets, P., Mechanical Construction and Production
Degrieck, J., Materials Science and Engineering
De Rouck, J., Civil Engineering
De Zutter, D., Information Technology
Kiekens, P., Textiles
Leys, C., Applied Physics
Marin, G., Chemical Engineering and Technical Chemistry
Melkebeek, J., Electrical Energy, Systems and Automation
Sierens, R., Flow, Heat and Combustion Mechanics
Taerwe, L., Structural Engineering
Van Campenhout, J., Electronics and Information Systems
Van Keer, R., Mathematical Analysis
Van Landeghem, H., Industrial Management
Verschaffel, B., Architecture and Urban Planning

Faculty of Law (Universiteitstraat 4, 9000 Ghent; tel. (9) 264-67-62):

Bocken, H., Civil Law
Bouckaert, B., Legal Theory and Legal History
Erauw, J., Procedural Law, Arbitration and Private International Law
Humblet, P., Labour Law and Social Security Law
Maresceau, M., European Institute
Somers, E., International Public Law
Van Acker, C., Business Law
Van Crombrugge, S., Tax Law
Veny, L., Public Law
Vermeulen, G., Penal Law and Criminology

Faculty of Medicine and Health Sciences (Campus Heymans, De Pintelaan 185, 9000 Ghent; tel. (9) 332-41-90):

Cambier, D., Physical Therapy and Motor Rehabilitation
De Backer, G., Public Health
De Clercq, D., Movement and Sports Sciences
De Hemptinne, B., Surgery
De Maeseneer, J., General Practice and Primary Health Care
De Pauw, G., Dentistry
De Vos, M., Internal Medicine
De Wagter, C., Radiotherapy and Nuclear Medicine
Kestelyn, P., Opthalmology
Lambert, J., Dermatology
Lefebvre, R., Pharmacology
Matthys, D., Paediatrics and Medical Genetics
Mortier, E., Anaesthesiology
Piette, M., Forensic Medicine
Plum, J., Clinical Chemistry, Microbiology and Immunology
Temmerman, M., Uro-Gynaecology
Thierens, H., Basic Medical Sciences
Van Cauwenberge, P., Ornithol/Laryngology
Vandekerckhove, J., Biochemistry
Van Heeringen, C., Psychiatry and Medical Psychology
Verdonk, R., Physical Medicine and Orthopaedic Surgery
Verstraete, K., Radiology

Faculty of Pharmaceutical Sciences (Campus Heymans, Harelbekestraat 72, 9000 Ghent; tel. (9) 264-80-40):

Nelis, H., Pharmaceutical Analysis
Remon, J., Pharmaceutics
Van Peteghem, C., Bio-Analysis

Faculty of Political and Social Sciences (Universiteitstraat 8, 9000 Ghent; tel. (9) 264-67-80):

Biltereyst, D., Communication Studies
Bracke, P., Sociology
Coolsaet, H., Political Science
Walraet, A., Third World Studies

Faculty of Psychology and Educational Sciences (Henri Dunantlaan 2, 9000 Ghent; tel. (9) 264-63-41):

Broeckaert, E., Special Education
Claes, R., Personnel Management, Work and Organizational Psychology
Crombez, G., Experimental Clinical and Health Psychology
De Bie, M., Social Welfare Studies
De Corte, W., Data-Analysis
Hartsuiker, R., Experimental Psychology
Mervielde, I., Developmental, Personality and Social Psychology
Spoelders, M., Pedagogy
Valcke, M., Educational Studies
Verhaeghe, P., Psychoanalysis and Clinical Consulting

Faculty of Sciences (K. L. Ledeganckstraat 35, 9000 Ghent; tel. (9) 264-50-42):

Clauws, P., Solid State Sciences
De Clerck, F., Pure Mathematics and Computer Algebra
De Clercq, P., Organic Chemistry
De Maeyer, P., Geography
Depicker, A., Plant Biotechnology and Genetics
De Vos, P., Biochemistry and Microbiology
Hoste, S., Inorganic and Physical Chemistry
Huysseune, A., Biology
Jacobs, P., Geology and Soil Science
Ryckbosch, D., Subatomic and Radiation Physics
Sarlet, W., Mathematical Physics and Astronomy
Strijckmans, K., Analytical Chemistry
Vanden Berghe, G., Applied Mathematics and Computer Science
Van Der Straeten, D., Physiology
Van Roy, F., Biomedical Molecular Biology

Faculty of Veterinary Sciences (Salisburylaan 133, 9820 Merelbeke; tel. (9) 264-75-03):

De Backer, P., Pharmacology, Toxicology and Biochemistry
De Brabander, H., Veterinary Public Health and Food Safety
De Kruif, A., Obstetrics, Reproduction and Herd Health
Deprez, P., Internal Medicine and Clinical Biology of Large Animals
Duchateau, L., Physiology and Biometry
Gasthuys, F., Surgery and Anaesthesiology of Domestic Animals
Haesebrouck, F., Pathology, Bacteriology and Poultry Diseases
Simoens, P., Morphology
Van Bree, H., Veterinary Medical Imaging and Small Animal Orthopaedics
Van Ham, L., Medicine and Clinical Biology of Small Animals
Van Zeveren, A., Animal Nutrition, Genetics, Breeding and Ethology
Vercruysse, J., Virology, Parasitology and Immunology

VRIJE UNIVERSITEIT BRUSSEL
(Free University of Brussels)

Pleinlaan 2, 1050 Brussels
Telephone: (2) 629-21-11
E-mail: info@vub.ac.be
Internet: www.vub.ac.be

Founded 1834, present status 1970
Private control
Languages of instruction: Dutch, English
Academic year: October to July

Chair.: E. Van Gelder
Rector: Prof. Paul De Knop
Vice-Rector for Education: Prof. Y. Michotte
Vice-Rector for Research: Prof. L. Wyns
Vice-Rector for Student Policy: Prof. H. Casman
Gen. Dir: J. Van Leemput
Librarian: Patrick Vanouplines
Number of teachers: 1,883
Number of students: 10,198

Publications: *Akademos*, *Nieuw Tijdschrift van de VUB*, *VUB-Press*

DEANS

Department of Teacher Training: Nini Vrijens
Faculty of Arts and Philosophy: Prof. Dr. Piet Van de Craen
Faculty of Economic, Political and Social Sciences and Solvay Business School: Prof. Dr Joël Branson
Faculty of Engineering: Prof. Dr Jacques De Ruyck
Faculty of Law and Criminology: Prof. Dr G. Van Limberghen
Faculty of Medicine and Pharmacy: Prof. A. Dupont
Faculty of Physical Education and Physiotherapy: Prof. Dr Peter Van Roy
Faculty of Psychology and Educational Sciences: Prof. Dr Elias Willem
Faculty of Science and Bio-engineering Sciences: Patricia Provè

Institutions with University Status

FACULTÉ POLYTECHNIQUE DE MONS

Rue de Houdain 9, 7000 Mons
Telephone: (65) 37-40-30
E-mail: info.polytech@umons.ac.be
Internet: portail.umons.ac.be/fr/universite/facultes/fpms/pages/default.aspx

Founded 1837, current name adopted 1935
State control; attached to Univ. of Mons
Academic year: September to June

Rector: Prof. Calogero Conti
Dean: Paul Lybaert
Dept Dir: Christine Martens
Library: see under Libraries and Archives
Number of teachers: 70
Number of students: 1,000

Publications: *Bulletin de l'AIMS* (12 a year), *Mons Mines* (4 a year), *PolyTech News* (4 a year)

PROFESSORS

Ancia, Ph., Mining Engineering
Blondel, M., Electromagnetism and Telecommunications
Boucher, S., Theoretical Mechanics
Bouquegneau, C., General Physics
Broche, C., Electrotechnics
Conti, C., Theoretical Mechanics
Coussement, G., Fluid Mechanics, Applied Mechanics
Crappe, R., Microelectronics
De Haan, A., General Chemistry, Electrochemistry
De Meyer, M., Applied Chemistry and Biochemistry
Dehombreux, P., Mechanical Engineering
Delhaye, M., Electrotechnology
Delvosalle, C., Chemical and Biochemical Engineering
Dumortier, C., Metallurgy
Dupuis, C., Geology
Durand, Y., Mechanical Engineering
Dutoit, T., Signals Processing
Filippi, E., Mechanical Engineering
Fortemps, P., Mathematics, Operational Research
Frère, M., Thermodynamics

GUERLEMENT, G., Strength of Materials, Stability of Buildings
HANCQ, J., Signal Processing
HANTON, J., Fluid Mechanics, Applied Mechanics
LAMBLIN, D., Strength of Materials, Stability of Buildings
LAMQUIN, M., Electromagnetism and Telecommunications
LIBERT, G., Computer Science
LIÉNARD, PH., Metallurgy
LOBRY, J., Transport and Distribution of High-Voltage Electricity
LYBAERT, P., Heat Transfer
MACQ, D., Electronics
MANNEBACK, P., Computer Science
MEGRET, P., Electromagnetism and Telecommunications
MOINY, F., General Physics
PILATTE, A., Thermodynamics
PIRLOT, M., Mathematics, Operational Research
QUINIF, Y., Geology
REMY, M., Automation
RENGLET, M., Electronics
RENOTTE, CH., Automation
RIQUIER, Y., Metallurgy
SAUCEZ, PH., Mathematics, Operational Research
TEGHEM, J., Mathematics, Operational Research
TRÉCAT, J., Transport and Distribution of High-Voltage Electricity
TSHIBANGU, J. P., Mining Engineering
TUYTTENS, D., Mathematics, Operational Research
VANDER WOUWER, A., Automation
VANKERKEM, M., Business Administration
VERLINDEN, O., Theoretical Mechanics
WILQUIN, H., Architecture

FACULTÉ UNIVERSITAIRE DE THÉOLOGIE PROTESTANTE DE BRUXELLES/UNIVERSITAIRE FACULTEIT VOOR PROTESTANTSE GODGELEERDHEID TE BRUSSEL (Faculty of Protestant Theology)

Rue des Bollandistes 40, 1040 Brussels
Telephone: (2) 735-67-46
E-mail: info@protestafac.ac.be
Internet: www.protestafac.ac.be

Founded 1950
Private control (United Protestant Church)
Languages of instruction: French, Dutch

Head of Admin.: ANNE JOUÉ
Chair. of Admin. Board: PETER TOMSON
Dean of Dutch-speaking Section: Prof. PETER TOMSON
Dean of French-speaking Section: B. HORT
Sec.: DOMINIQUE DESCAMPS
Librarian: ELIANE EVRARD-GRCE

Library of 46,257 vols, 130 periodicals
Number of teachers: 20
Number of students: 110

Publications: *Analecta Bruxellensia* (1 a year), *Belgische Protestantse Biografieën / Biographies Protestantes Belges* (4 a year), *FACtualité / FACtualiteit* (4 a year), *Programme et Horaire des Cours / Studiegids* (1 a year)

PROFESSORS

Dutch-speaking Section:
DE LANGE, J., Practical Theology
REIJNEN, A. M., Ethics
SMELIK, K., Old Testament Studies, Hebrew
TOMSON, P., New Testament Studies, Greek
WIERSMA, J., Dogmatics, Philosophy
WILLEMS, W., Church History, History of Dogma and 16th-century History

French-speaking Section:
HORT, B., Dogmatics, History of Philosophy and Religious Philosophy
MUTOMBO, F., Old Testament Studies and Hebrew
REIJNEN, A. M., Church History, Ethics
ROUVIÈRE, C., Practical Theology
VAN MOERE, R., New Testament Studies
WILLEMS, W., Church History and Methodology

FACULTÉS UNIVERSITAIRES CATHOLIQUES DE MONS

Chaussée de Binche 151, 7000 Mons
Telephone: (65) 32-32-11
E-mail: international@fucam.ac.be
Internet: www.fucam.ac.be

Founded 1896 as Institut Supérieur Commercial et Consulaire, univ. status 1965
Private control
Language of instruction: French
Academic year: October to September

Rector: BART JOURQUIN
Vice-Rector: DOMINIQUE HELBOIS

Library of 28,000 vols, 9,700 periodicals
Number of teachers: 120
Number of students: 1,200

FACULTÉS UNIVERSITAIRES NOTRE-DAME DE LA PAIX

Rue de Bruxelles 61, 5000 Namur
Telephone: (81) 72-41-11
E-mail: info.etudes@fundp.ac.be
Internet: www.fundp.ac.be

Founded 1831
Language of instruction: French
Academic year: September to June

Rector: YVES POULLET
Vice-Rector: PHILIPPE LAMBIN
Gen. Man.: PAUL REDING
Chief Librarian: J. M. ANDRÉ

Library: see under Libraries and Archives
Number of teachers: 210
Number of students: 4,900

DEANS

Faculty of Arts: X. HERMAND
Faculty of Computer Science: J.-M. JACQUET
Faculty of Economics, Social Sciences and Management: A. DE CROMBRUGGHE
Faculty of Law: E. MONTERO
Faculty of Medicine: M. HERIN
Faculty of Sciences: R. SPORKEN

PROFESSORS

Faculty of Arts (rue J. Grafé 1, 5000 Namur; tel. (81) 72-42-07; e-mail dolores.bouchat@fundp.ac.be; internet www.fundp.ac.be/philo_lettres):
ALLARD, A., Classical Philology
BOSSE, A., German and Comparative Literature
BRACKELAIRE, J.-L., Psychology
BURNEZ, L., Prehistoric Art, Archaeology
DELABASTITA, D., English, General and Comparative Literature
DE RUYT, C., History of Ancient Art, Archaeology
DOYEN, A.-M., Greek Language and Literature
GANTY, E., Modern Philosophy
GIOT, J., French Linguistics
HANTSON, A., English Language, Linguistics
LEGROS, G., Romance Philology, Theory of Literature
LEIJNSE, E., Dutch, General and Comparative Literature
LENOIR, Y., History of Music
MARCHETTI, P., Classical Philology, Antiquity and Latin Authors
MORENO, P., Italian Language
NOËL, R., Medieval History
PETERS, M., German Language, Linguistics
PHILIPPART, G., Medieval History
RIZZERIO, L., Ancient Philosophy
SAUVAGE, P., History of the 19th and 20th Centuries
SELDESLACHTS, H., Latin Language, Greek and Latin Linguistics
VANDEN BEMDEN, Y., History of Post-Classical Art, Archaeology
VAN DEN BERGHE, K., Spanish Language
WEISSHAUPT, J., Dutch Language, Linguistics
WYNANTS, P., History of Belgian Institutions

Faculty of Computer Science (rue Grandgagnage 21, 5000 Namur; tel. (81) 72-49-66; e-mail doyen@info.fundp.ac.be; internet www.info.fundp.ac.be):
BERLEUR, J., Informatics and Sciences, Informatics and Rationality (Epistemological questions), Informatics and Society
BODART, F., Information Systems Design, Decision Support System, User/Machine Interface Engineering
BONAVENTURE, O., Computer Architecture, Computer Networks
FICHEFET, J., Graph Theory, Linear Programming, Numerical Analysis, Operations Research, Multicriteria Decision Aid, Management
HABRA, N., Software Engineering, Software Development
HAINAUT, J. L., Database Technology, Database Design, Database Engineering
JACQUET, J.-M., Programming Methodology, Programming Projects, Artificial Intelligence Techniques, Theory of Programming Languages
LE CHARLIER, B., Programming Methodology, Theory of Programming Languages, Abstract Interpretation
LECLERCQ, J.-P., Scientific Methods and Applications, Graph Theory
LESUISSE, R., Organization Design, Strategic Management and Information Systems, Organization Theory
LOBET-MARIS, C., Organization Theories, Psychological Aspects of Information Systems, Communication
NOIRHOMME-FRAITURE, M., Stochastic Processes, Simulation of Systems, Data Mining and Database Analysis, Performance Models and Evaluation
RAMAEKERS, J., Operating Systems, Performance and Measurement of Computer Systems, Computer System Reliability and Security
SCHOBBENS, P.-Y., Artificial Intelligence Techniques, Automatic Testing and Program Testing, Artificial Intelligence in DSSs, Language Theory

Faculty of Economics, Social Sciences and Management (rue de Bruxelles 61, 5000 Namur; tel. (81) 72-48-55; e-mail veronique.gilson@fundp.ac.be; internet www.fundp.ac.be/eco/eco.html):
BALAND, J.-M., Development Economics
BERTELS, K., Information Management
BODART, F., Management Information Systems
BRACKELAIRE, J. L., Psychology
CHEFFERT, J. M., Micro-economics
COLSON, B., Political Sociology and Comparative History of Institutions
DE COMBBRUGGHE DE PICQUENDAELE, A., International Trade Project Evaluation
DESCHAMPS, R., Macro-economics
GLEJSER, H., Econometrics, International and Interregional Economics

GREGOIRE, P., Corporate Finance and Portfolio Management
HOTTE, L., Industrial Economics, Development Economics
JACQUEMIN, J.-C., International Trade, Methods of Economic Investigation
JACQUES, J.-M., Business Policy, International Strategy
JAUMOTTE, CH., Political Economy, Regional and Sectoral Economic Analysis
LEGRAND, M., Epistemology, Philosophical Anthropology
LESUISSE, R., Computer Science
LOUVEAUX, F., Mathematical Statistics, Mathematical Programming, Operations Research
MANIQUET, F., Micro-economics
MIGNOLET, M., Fiscal Policy and Business Strategies, Macro-economics
NIZET, J., Sociology
PLATTEAU, J.-PH., Economic Development, Institutional Economics
PLATTEN, I., Finance and Financial Modelling
REDING, P., Money and Banking, Monetary Theory and Policy, International Monetary Economics
RIGAUX, N., Sociology
SCHEPENS, G., Operations Management, Management Information Systems
VALOGNES, F., Advanced Mathematics
VAN WYMEERSCH, C., Managerial Finance, Business Forecasting, Accounting
VAN YPERSELE, T., Public Economics, Regional Economics
WALLEMACQ, A., Human Resources Management
WUIDAR, J., Mathematics
WYNANTS, B., Introduction to Sociology
WYNANTS, P., History

Faculty of Law (Rempart de la Vierge 5, 5000 Namur; tel. (81) 72-47-94; e-mail secretariat.droit@fundp.ac.be):

COIPEL, M., Commercial Law
COIPEL, N., Methodology and Legal Sources
DIJON, X., Natural Law
DUPLAT, J.-L., Fiscal Law
FIERENS, J., Legal Methodology and Human Rights
KIGANAHÉ, Criminal Law
POULLET, Y., Roman Law
ROBAYE, R., History of Private Law
THIRY, PH., General Theory of Knowledge and Philosophy
THUNIS, X., Comparative Law and Law of Obligation
VUYE, H., Constitutional Law, Dutch Legal Terminology
WÉRY, P., General Principles of Private Law

Faculty of Medicine (rue de Bruxelles 61, 5000 Namur; tel. (81) 72-43-47; e-mail administration-medecine@fundp.ac.be; internet www.fundp.ac.be/medecine):

BOSLY, A., Immunology
DONCKIER, J., Endocrinology
DULIEU, J., Human Anatomy
FLAMION, B., Physiology, Pharmacology
GOFFINET, A., Special Physiology
HÉRIN, M., Histology, Embryology
JADOT, M., Human Biochemistry, General Biochemistry
LALOUX, P., Physiopathology
MARCHANOL, E., Human Physiology
MERCIER, M., Psychology and Medical Psychology
PIRONT, A., General Physiology
POUMAY, Y., General Histology
TRIGAUX, J. P., Radiological Anatomy
VANDERPAS, J., Epidemiology
ZECH, F., Microbiology

Faculty of Sciences (rue de Bruxelles 61, 5000 Namur; tel. (81) 72-54-35; e-mail decanat-sciences@fundp.ac.be; internet www.fundp.ac.be/sciences):

ANDRE, J.-M., Quantum Chemistry, Physical Chemistry
BLANQUET, GH., Molecular Infrared Spectroscopy and General Physics
B'NAGY, J., General Chemistry, Spectroscopy
BODART, F., Experimental Physics, Atomic and Nuclear Physics
CALLIER, F., Differential and Integral Calculus, Graph Theory
DE BOLLE, X., Statistics, Biostatistics, Bioinformatics
DELHALLE, J., General Chemistry
DEMORTIER, G., X-ray Physics, General Physics and Nuclear Physics
DEPIEREUX, E., Statistics, Biostatistics, Bioinformatics
DESCY, J.-P., Ecology
DEVOS, P., Endocrinology and Zoology
DUCHENE, J., Philosophy of Science
DURANT, F., Radiocrystallography and General Chemistry
EVRARD, G., Radiocrystallography
GIFFROY, J.-M., Anatomy, Embryology and Ethology of Animals
HALLET, V., Mineralogy, Geology
HARDY, A., Mathematics and Statistics
HENRARD, J., Mathematics, Celestial Mechanics, Astronomy
HEVESI, L., Organic Chemistry
HOUSSIAU, L., Experimental Physics, Thermodynamics
KESTEMONT, P., Ecology
KRIEF, A., Organic Chemistry
LAMBERT, D., Philosophy of Science
LAMBERTS, L., Analytical Chemistry
LAMBIN, P., Analytical Mechanics, Theoretical Physics
LETESSON, J. J., Microbiology, Immunology
LUCAS, A., Theoretical Solid State Physics and Quantum Physics
MAES, A., Mathematics, Differential and Integral Calculus
MASEREEL, B., Pharmaceutical Sciences, Biochemistry and Cytology
MEKHALIF, Z., General Chemistry, Physical Chemistry, Polymers
MESSIAEN, J., General Biology, Vegetal Physiology
MICHA, J.-CL., Ecology
NGUYEN, V. H., Differential and Integral Calculus, Optimization and Applied Mathematics
ORBAN-FERAUGE, F., Geography, Cartography
PAQUAY, R., Animal Physiology
PIREAUX, J.-J., Experimental Physics, Atomic and Molecular Physics
PIRSON, P., Methodology of Chemistry
RAES, M., Biochemistry
RASSON, J.-P., Probabilities
REMACLE, J., Biochemistry
REMON, M., Programming Statistics
ROUSSELET, D., Methodology of Biology
SCHNEIDER, M., Methodology of Mathematics
STOIKEN, R., Physics, Electronics
STRODIOT, J.-J., Optimization
SU, B. L., General Chemistry
THILL, G., Philosophy of Science
THIRAN, J.-P., Numerical Analysis
THIRY, P., Solid State Physics, General Physics
TOINT, PH., Algebra, Numerical Analysis
VAN CUTSEM, P., Biotechnology
VANDENHAUTE, J., Genetics
VERCAUTEREN, D., General Chemistry, Kinetics, Physical Chemistry
VIGNERON, J.-P., Solid State Physics

University-Level Institutions

ARCHITECTUURWETENSCHAPPEN VAN DE ARTESIS HOGESCHOOL ANTWERPEN

Mutsaardstraat 31, 2000 Antwerp
Telephone: (3) 205-61-70
E-mail: architectuurwetenschappen@artesis.be
Internet: www.artesis.be/architectuurwetenschappen
Founded 1663 by Teniers; ind. 1952
Dept Head: Prof. KOEN VAN DE VREKEN
Publication: *Antwerp Design Sciences Cahiers (ADSC)* (2 a year)

ARTESIS HOGESCHOOL ANTWERPEN

Keizerstraat 15, 2000 Antwerp
Telephone: (3) 213-93-00
E-mail: info@artesis.be
Internet: www.artesis.be
Chair.: CAMILLE PAULUS
Vice-Chair.: ROBERT VOORHAMME
Man. Dir: GUY AELTERMAN

ARTEVELDEHOGESCHOOL

Hoogpoort 15, 9000 Ghent
Telephone: (9) 234-00-00
E-mail: info@arteveldehs.be
Internet: www.arteveldehogeschool.be
Languages of instruction: Dutch, English
Academic year: September to June
Chair.: TONY VAN PARYS
Gen. Man.: Prof. Dr JOHAN VEECKMAN
Number of teachers: 1,100
Number of students: 12,000
Publication: *Arteveldemagazine*

COLLEGE OF EUROPE/COLLÈGE D'EUROPE

Dijver 11, 8000 Bruges
Telephone: (50) 47-71-11
E-mail: info@coleurope.eu
Internet: www.coleurope.eu
Founded 1949
Private control
Languages of instruction: English, French
Academic year: September to June
Postgraduate Institute of European Studies; br. in Natolin (Warsaw)
Pres. of Admin. Ccl: IÑIGO MENDEZ DE VIGO
Rector: Prof. PAUL DEMARET
Vice-Rector: EWA OŚNIECKA-TAMECKA
Library Dir: ERIC DE SOUZA
Library of 100,000 vols
Number of teachers: 200
Number of students: 330
Publication: *Collegium*

ÉCOLE DES HAUTES ÉTUDES COMMERCIALES

Rue Louvrex 14, 4000 Liège
Telephone: (4) 232-72-11
E-mail: info@hec.be
Internet: www.hec.be
Founded 1898
Language of instruction: French
Academic year: September to June
Pres.: YVES NOEL
Dir-Gen.: M. DUBRU
Academic Dir: LOUIS ESCH
Sec. Gen.: JACQUES DEFER
Librarian: M. A. THOMAS
Library of 12,000 vols

Number of teachers: 217
Number of students: 1,620

ÉCOLE PRACTIQUE DES HAUTES ÉTUDES COMMERCIALES

Ave K. Adenauer 3, 1200 Brussels
Telephone: (2) 772-65-75
E-mail: ephec@ephec.be
Internet: www.ephec.be
Founded 1969
Languages of instruction: English, French
Dir and Pres.: ALAIN GILBERT
Number of teachers: 240
Number of students: 3,000

ERASMUSHOGESCHOOL-BRUSSEL (Erasmus University College)

Nijverheidskaai 170, 1070 Brussels
Telephone: (2) 523-37-37
E-mail: info@ehb.be
Internet: www.erasmushogeschool.be
Founded 1995, merger of 10 colleges in and around Brussels
Private control
Language of instruction: Dutch
Man. Dir: LUC VAN DE VELDE
Admin. Dir: ERIKA EECKHOUT
Number of students: 4,500
Publications: *ehbmagazine*, *Medium—Tijdschrift voor Toegepaste Taalwetenschap* (3 a year), *Tijdschrift voor Bestuurswetenschappen en Publike Recht* (12 a year)

FACULTEIT VOOR VERGELIJKENDE GODSDIENSTWETENSCHAPPEN (Faculty for Comparative Study of Religions)

Bist 164, 2610 Antwerp (Wilrijk)
Telephone: (3) 830-51-58
E-mail: info@antwerpfvg.org
Founded 1980
Language of instruction: Dutch, English, French, German
Academic year: October to June
Chair. of Board: JEREMY ROSEN
Rector: CHRISTIAAN J. G VONCK
Deans: LYDIA BONTE, JAN VAN REETH, FRANK STAPPAERTS
Librarians: WU JEN, EDDY VAN LAERHOVEN, HUGO PEERLINCK, CHRISTIAN VANDEKERKHOVE
Library of 35,000 vols
Number of teachers: 44
Number of students: 120
Publication: *Acta Comparanda* (1 a year)

GROEP T—INTERNATIONALE HOGESCHOOL LEUVEN (Group T—International University College Leuven)

Andreas Vesaliusstraat 13, 3000 Leuven
Telephone: (16) 301030
E-mail: groupt@groupt.be
Internet: www.groupt.be
Founded 1888
State control
Languages of instruction: Dutch, English
Academic year: September to September
Pres.: Prof. Dr JOHAN DE GRAEVE
Dir-Gen.: PATRICK DE RYCK
Dean of Leuven Education College: STIJN DHERT
Dean of Leuven Engineering College: KOEN ENEMAN
Number of teachers: 168
Number of students: 2,507

HAUTE ÉCOLE ALBERT JACQUARD

Sq. Arthur Masson 1, 5000 Namur
Telephone: (81) 23-43-80
E-mail: presidence@heaj.be
Internet: www.heaj.be
Founded 1959, present name and status 1996
Private control
Academic year: September to June
Dir and Pres.: GUY BRIFFOZ

HAUTE ÉCOLE BLAISE PASCAL

Rue des Déportés 140, 6700 Arlon
Telephone: (63) 23-41-48
E-mail: info@hebp.be
Internet: www.hebp.be
Founded 1996
Dir and Pres.: RICHARD JUSSERET
Number of students: 1,300
Publication: *Le Pari*

HAUTE ÉCOLE CATHOLIQUE CHARLEROI-EUROPE

Pl. Brasseur 6, 6280 Loverval
Telephone: (71) 47-42-70
E-mail: peda.loverval@helha.be
Internet: www.hece.eu
Founded 1996
Rector: JEAN-LUC VREUX
Acad. Sec.: BERNARD RIGUELLE

HAUTE ÉCOLE CHARLEMAGNE

Rue des Rivageois 6, 4000 Liège
Telephone: (4) 254-76-00
E-mail: secr.rivageois@hech.be
Internet: www.lesrivageois.be
Founded 1874
Language of instruction: French
Dir and Pres.: CORINE MATILLARD
Number of teachers: 280
Number of students: 2,800

HAUTE ÉCOLE DE BRUXELLES

Chaussée de Waterloo 749, 1180 Brussels
Telephone: (2) 340-12-95
E-mail: heb@heb.be
Internet: www.heb.be
Academic year: September to June
Head: MARIANNE COESSENS
Librarian: J. P. GAHIDE
Librarian: O. GALMA
Library of 45,000 vols
Number of teachers: 189
Number of students: 2,200
Publication: *Équivalences* (2 a year)

HAUTE ÉCOLE DE LA COMMUNAUTÉ FRANÇAISE DU HAINAUT

Rue Pierre-Joseph Duménil 4, 7000 Mons
Telephone: (65) 34-79-83
E-mail: directeur-president@hecfh.be
Internet: www.hecfh.be
Founded 1996
State control
Language of instruction: French
Dir and Pres.: DENIS DUFRANE
Sec.: MICHEL POPIJN
Number of teachers: 333
Number of students: 3,000

HAUTE ÉCOLE DE LA COMMUNAUTÉ FRANÇAISE DU LUXEMBOURG SCHUMAN

Ave de Luxembourg 101, 6700 Arlon
Telephone: (63) 41-00-00
E-mail: cel.adm@hers.be
Internet: www.hers.be
State control
Dir and Pres.: MARC FOURNY
Number of teachers: 200
Number of students: 2,000

HAUTE ÉCOLE DE LA COMMUNAUTÉ FRANÇAISE PAUL-HENRI SPAAK

Rue Royale 150, 1000 Brussels
Telephone: (2) 227-35-01
E-mail: mejdoubi@he-spaak.be
Internet: www.he-spaak.be
Founded 1995
State control
Dir and Pres.: JACQUES LEBEGGE

HAUTE ÉCOLE DE LA PROVINCE DE LIÈGE

Ave Montesquieu 6, 4000 Liège
Telephone: (4) 237-96-05
E-mail: hepl@provincedeliege.be
Internet: haute-ecole.prov-liege.be
State control
Dir and Pres.: TONI BASTIANELLI
Number of students: 8,546

HAUTE ÉCOLE DE LA PROVINCE DE NAMUR

Rue Henri Blès 188–190, 5000 Namur
Telephone: (81) 77-67-56
E-mail: haute.ecole@province.namur.be
Internet: www.hepn.be
State control
Academic year: September to June
Dir and Pres.: FRANÇOISE GASPAR

HAUTE ÉCOLE DE LA VILLE DE LIÈGE

Rue Hazinelle 2, 4000 Liège
Telephone: (4) 223-28-08
E-mail: info@hel.be
Internet: www.hel.be
Founded 1996, by merger of l'Institut d'Enseignement Supérieur Pédagogique, l'École Communale Supérieure de Secrétariat, d'Administration et de Commerce, l'École Supérieure de Logopédie, l'Institut Supérieur d'Enseignement Technologique
Language of instruction: French
Academic year: September to July
Pres.: Dr ANDRÉ NOSSENT
Number of teachers: 250
Number of students: 2,200

HAUTE ÉCOLE DE NAMUR

Rue Saint-Donat 130, 5002 Namur
Telephone: (81) 46-85-00
E-mail: info@henam.be
Internet: www.henam.be
Founded 2007, by merger of Haute École Namuroise Catholique and Haute École d'Enseignement Supérieur de Namur
Private control
Language of instruction: French
Academic year: September to June
Dir and Pres.: DANIEL CHAVÉE
Number of students: 4,000

HAUTE ÉCOLE FRANCISCO FERRER DE LA VILLE DE BRUXELLES

Rue de la Fontaine 4, 1000 Brussels
Telephone: (2) 279-57-92
E-mail: sec.hefftech@brunette.brucity.be
Internet: www.brunette.brucity.be/heff
Publication: *Info-Ferrer*

HAUTE ÉCOLE GALILÉE

Rue Royale 336, 1030 Brussels
Telephone: (2) 613-19-20
E-mail: directeur.president@galilee.be
Internet: www.galilee.be
State control
Language of instruction: French
Academic year: September to July
Dir and Pres.: JOHN VAN TIGGELEN
Gen. Sec.: EVELYNE CROUSSE
Number of teachers: 520
Number of students: 3,800

HAUTE ÉCOLE LÉONARD DE VINCI

Pl. de l'Alma 2, 1200 Brussels
Telephone: (2) 761-06-80
E-mail: info@vinci.be
Internet: www.vinci.be
Founded 1995, by merger of 6 instns: ECAM, Institut Supérieur Industriel, École Normale Catholique du Brabant Wallon, Institut d'Enseignement Supérieur Parnasse-Deux Alice, Institut Libre Marie Haps, Institut Paul Lambin, Institut Supérieur d'Enseignement Infirmier
Academic year: September to June
Dir and Pres.: PAUL ANCIAUX
Sec.: HOURIA ZARKI
Number of teachers: 156
Number of students: 6,457

HAUTE ÉCOLE LIBRE DE BRUXELLES—ILYA PRIGOGINE

Ave Besme 97, 1190 Brussels
Telephone: (2) 349-68-11
E-mail: direction.presidence@helb-prigogine.be
Internet: www.helb-prigogine.be
Language of instruction: French
Academic year: September to June
Dir and Pres.: JEAN-MARIE MESKENS

HAUTE ÉCOLE LIBRE DU HAINAUT OCCIDENTAL

Quai des Salines 20, 7500 Tournai
Telephone: (69) 89-05-05
E-mail: secretariat@helho.be
Internet: www.helho.be
Language of instruction: French
Dir and Pres.: PHILIPPE DE CONINCK
Number of students: 1,500

HAUTE ÉCOLE LIBRE MOSANE

Mont Saint-Martin 41, 4000 Liège
Telephone: (4) 222-22-00
E-mail: info@helmo.be
Internet: www.helmo.be
Founded 2008
Language of instruction: French
Academic year: September to June
Dir and Pres.: ALEXANDRE LODEZ
Librarian: NICOLE GRAVIER
Library of 11,528 vols
Number of teachers: 720
Number of students: 6,500
Publication: *Nouvelles de l'Union Gramme* (4 a year)

HAUTE ÉCOLE LUCIA DE BROUCKÈRE

Ave Émile Gryzon 1, 1070 Brussels
Telephone: (2) 526-73-00
E-mail: info@heldb.be
Internet: www.heldb.be
State control
Language of instruction: French
Academic year: September to June
Dir and Pres.: PATRICK DYSSELER

HAUTE ÉCOLE PROVINCIALE DE HAINAUT CONDORCET

Chemin du Champ 17, 7000 Mons
Telephone: (65) 40-12-20
E-mail: communication@condorcet.be
Internet: www.condorcet.be
Founded 2009
Language of instruction: French
Academic year: September to June
Dir and Pres.: ALAIN SCANDOLO
Number of students: 8,000

HOGERE ZEEVAARTSCHOOL ANTWERPEN/ÉCOLE SUPÉRIEURE DE NAVIGATION D'ANVERS (Antwerp Maritime Academy)

Noordkasteel Oost 6, 2030 Antwerp
Telephone: (3) 205-64-30
E-mail: info@hzs.be
Internet: www.hzs.be
Founded 1834
Languages of instruction: Dutch, English, French
Gen. Man.: PATRICK BLONDÉ
Chair. of Board: PETER RAES
Librarian: HAN JACOBS
Number of students: 686

HOGESCHOOL GENT

Kortrijksesteenweg 14, 9000 Ghent
Telephone: (9) 243-33-33
E-mail: info@hogent.be
Internet: www.hogent.be
Founded 1995 by merger of 13 univ. colleges
State control
Languages of instruction: Dutch, English
Academic year: September to June
Rector: Dr ROBERT HOOGEWIJS
Chair.: Dr PAUL VAN CAUWENBERGE
Vice-Chair.: ELKE DECRUYNAERE
Library of 380,000 vols, 500 periodicals
Number of teachers: 1,134
Number of students: 13,887
Publication: *Volgende halte: HoGent* (8 a year)

DEANS

Business and Information Management: ANITA BERNARD
Education, Health and Social Work: MAURICE WALGRAEVE
School of Arts: Dr WIM DE TEMMERMAN
Science and Technology: PATRICK STEELANDT

HOGESCHOOL SINT-LUKAS BRUSSEL

Paleizenstraat 70, 1030 Brussels
Telephone: (2) 250-11-00
E-mail: info@sintlukas.be
Internet: www.sintlukas.be
Founded 1880
Private control
Pres.: JEAN-PIERRE RAMMANT
Vice-Pres.: HUGO CASAER
Number of students: 850

HOGESCHOOL VOOR WETENSCHAP & KUNST (University College for Sciences and Arts)

Koningsstraat 328, 1030 Brussels
Telephone: (2) 250-15-11
E-mail: info@wenk.be
Internet: www.wenk.be
Founded 1995
Languages of instruction: Dutch, English
Man. Dir: MARIA DE SMET

HOWEST: HOGESCHOOL WEST-VLAANDEREN

Marksesteenweg 58, 8500 Kortrijk
Telephone: (56) 24 12 90
E-mail: info@howest.be
Internet: www.howest.be
Founded 1995
Private control
Languages of instruction: Dutch, English
Chair.: JAN DURNEZ
Gen. Man.: LODE DE GEYTER
Number of students: 5,500

INSTITUT CATHOLIQUE DES HAUTES ÉTUDES COMMERCIALES

Blvd Brand Whitlock 2, 1150 Brussels
Telephone: (2) 739-37-11
E-mail: communication@ichec.be
Internet: www.ichec.be
Founded 1934
Languages of instruction: Dutch, English, French
Rector: BRIGITTE CHANOINE
Gen. Sec.: PIERRE FLAHAUT
Library of 16,000 vols
Number of teachers: 300
Number of students: 2,000
Publication: *Reflets et Perspectives de la Vie Economique*

INSTITUT COOREMANS

Place Anneessens 11, 1000 Brussels
Telephone: (2) 551-02-10
E-mail: heff.economique@he-ferrer.eu
Internet: www.brunette.brucity.be/ferrer/eco
Founded 1911
Academic year: September to June
Courses at Bachelors and Masters degree level in commerce and administration
Pres.: P. LAMBERT
Dir: LUC COOREMANS
Number of teachers: 80
Number of students: 400
Publication: *ECOO* (4 a year)

INSTITUT SUPÉRIEUR D'ARCHITECTURE INTERCOMMUNAL

Site Victor Horta, CP 248, blvd du Triomphe, 1050 Brussels
Telephone: (2) 650-50-52
E-mail: isahorta@ulb.ac.be
Internet: horta.ulb.ac.be
Founded 1711
Language of instruction: French
Associated with Free Univ. of Brussels and schools of architecture at Liège and Mons (ISAI); courses in architecture, restoration and heritage conservation, urban design
Academic Dean: FABRIZIO BUCELLA
Dir: JEAN-MARC STERNO
Library of 30,000 vols
Number of teachers: 60
Number of students: 650
Publication: *I.S.A.Br* (12 a year)

INSTITUUT VOOR TROPISCHE GENEESKUNDE/INSTITUT DE MÉDECINE TROPICALE (Institute of Tropical Medicine)

Nationalestraat 155, 2000 Antwerp
Telephone: (3) 247-66-66
E-mail: info@itg.be
Internet: www.itg.be
Founded 1906, Royal Decree 1931

Languages of instruction: French, English
Academic year: September to July

Chair.: CATHY BERX
Vice-Chair.: Prof. Dr ALAIN VERSCHOREN
Dir: Prof. Dr BRUNO GRYSEELS
Librarian: DIRK SCHOONBAERT

Library of 60,000 vols, 5,000 dissertations, 30,000 journals
Number of teachers: 120
Number of students: 800

Publications: *ITGPress* (irregular), *Studies in Health Services Organisation & Policy*, *Tropical Medicine and International Health* (12 a year)

KAREL DE GROTE-HOGESCHOOL

Brusselstraat 45, 2018 Antwerp
Telephone: (3) 613-13-13
E-mail: info@kdg.be
Internet: www.kdg.be

Founded 1995
Languages of instruction: Dutch, English
Gen. Man.: DIRK BROOS

Library of 130,000 vols, 23,000 audiovisual items
Number of teachers: 1,200
Number of students: 11,000

KATHOLIEKE HOGESCHOOL KEMPEN

Kleinhoefstraat 4, 2440 Geel
Telephone: (14) 56-23-10
E-mail: info@khk.be
Internet: www.khk.be

Founded 1995
Language of instruction: Dutch
Academic year: September to June

Pres.: KOEN GEENS
Vice-Pres.: LOUIS GENOE
Gen. Man.: MAURICE VAES
Number of students: 7,200

Publication: *Agora* (3 a year)

KATHOLIEKE HOGESCHOOL LEUVEN
(Leuven University College)

Abdij van Park 9, 3001 Heverlee
Telephone: (16) 37-57-00
E-mail: international@khleuven.be
Internet: www.leuvenuniversitycollege.be
State control
Languages of instruction: Dutch, English
Academic year: September to June

Pres.: WILLY INDEHERBERGHE
Gen. Dir: Dr TOON MARTENS

Number of teachers: 700
Number of students: 8,000

DEANS

Business Management: Dr LUC VANHILLE
Health and Technology: Dr TOON QUAGHEBEUR
Social Work: Dr IMRAN UDDIN
Teacher Education: WIM BERGEN

KATHOLIEKE HOGESCHOOL LIMBURG
(Limburg Catholic University College)

Agoralaan, Gebouw B, bus 1, 3590 Diepenbeek
Telephone: (11) 23-07-70
E-mail: informatie@khlim.be
Internet: www.khlim.be

Founded 1994, by merger of 9 schools

Gen. Dir: WILLY INDEHERBERGHE
Pres.: NORBERT VAN BROEKHOVEN
Vice-Pres.: KAREL PEETERS

Number of teachers: 700
Number of students: 6,000

KATHOLIEKE HOGESCHOOL SINT-LIEVEN

Gebroeders Desmetstraat 1, 9000 Ghent
Telephone: (9) 265-86-10
E-mail: info@kahosl.be
Internet: www.kahosl.be

Founded 1995, by merger of 8 instns
Languages of instruction: Dutch, English
Academic year: September to June

Man. Dir: Prof. Dr FRANK BAERT
Chair.: LUC SANTENS

Number of teachers: 700
Number of students: 6,400

KATHOLIEKE HOGESCHOOL VIVES—CAMPUS BRUGGE
(Catholic University College VIVES—Campus Bruges)

Xaverianenstraat 10, 8200 Bruges
Telephone: (50) 30-51-00
E-mail: info@vives.be
Internet: www.vives.be

Founded 2013 by merger of KATHO and KHBO
State control
Language of instruction: Dutch
Academic year: September to June

Pres.: WILLIAM DE GROOTE
Gen. Man.: PIET DE LEERSNYDER
Librarian: PATRICK VANDEGEHUCHTE

Library of 30,000 vols
Number of teachers: 4,200
Number of students: 12,000

DEANS

Biomedical and Paramedical Professions: Dr ISABEL VANSLEMBROUCK
Education and Teacher Training: JOHAN L. VANDERHOEVEN
Engineering Technology: Dr WIM HAEGEMAN
Management and Business Studies: JOHAN DE LANGHE
Nursing and Midwifery: NANCY BOUCQUEZ
Social Work: VEERLE DEKOCKERE

KATHOLIEKE HOGESCHOOL ZUID-WEST-VLAANDEREN

Doorniksesteenweg 145, 8500 Kortrijk
Telephone: (56) 26-41-60
E-mail: bachelor@katho.be
Internet: www.katho.be

Founded 1995
Private control

Pres.: ERIC HALSBERGHE

Number of teachers: 520
Number of students: 7,000

LESSIUS ANTWERPEN—MECHELEN

Jozef de Bomstraat 11, 2018 Antwerp
Telephone: (3) 206-04-80
E-mail: info@lessius.eu
Internet: www.lessius.eu

Founded 2000, following merger of Handelshogeschool (f. 1923) and Katholieke Vlaamse Hogeschool (f. 1919)
Languages of instruction: Dutch, English
Academic year: September to July

8 Campuses

Chair.: Prof. Dr KOEN GEENS
Man. Dir: JOHAN CLOET
Dir-Gen.: Prof. Dr FLORA CARRIJN
Dir of Finances: PHILIPPE MICHIELS

Number of teachers: 600
Number of students: 10,000

Publication: *Journal of Internationalisation and Localisation*

LESSIUS MECHELEN
(Lessius University College Mechelen)

Zandpoortvest 13, 2800 Mechelen
Telephone: (15) 36-91-02
E-mail: info@lessius.eu
Internet: www.lessius.eu
State control
Languages of instruction: Dutch, English

Man. Dir: JOHAN CLOET
Gen. Man.: PHILIPPE MICHIELS

Library of 40,000 vols
Number of students: 4,400

PLANTIJN HOGESCHOOL VAN DE PROVINCIE ANTWERPEN

Lange Nieuwstraat 101, 2000 Antwerp
Telephone: (3) 220-57-99
E-mail: info@plantijn.be
Internet: www.plantijn.be

Founded 1995
Language of instruction: Dutch
State control
Academic year: September to September

Gen. Man.: ERWIN SAMSON

Number of teachers: 442
Number of students: 3,648

PROVINCIALE HOGESCHOOL LIMBURG

Elfde-Liniestraat 24, 3500 Hasselt
Telephone: (11) 23-88-88
E-mail: phl@phl.be
Internet: www.phl.be

Founded 1995 by merger of 6 colleges of higher education
Languages of instruction: Dutch, English

Pres.: BEN LAMBRECHTS

Number of teachers: 620
Number of students: 5,000

DEANS

Department of Architecture: R. CUYVERS
Department of Arts: R. CUYVERS
Department of Bio: M. SCHEPERS
Department of Business: M. GAENS
Department of Education: M. HERMANS
Department of Healthcare: R. NELISSEN
Department of Music: L. LEURS

VLERICK LEUVEN GENT MANAGEMENT SCHOOL

Telephone: (9) 210-97-11
E-mail: info@vlerick.be
Internet: www.vlerick.com

Founded 1953
Academic year: September to July

Associated with Ghent Univ. and Katholieke Univ. Leuven

Dean: Prof. PHILIPPE HASPESLAGH
Librarian: ELKE PARREZ

Library of 11,000 vols, 30,000 online and printed journals
Number of teachers: 70
Number of students: 480 undergraduate students

Publication: *Vlerick reflect* (4 a year)

XIOS HOGESCHOOL LIMBURG

Agoralaan, Gebouw H, 3590 Diepenbeek
Telephone: (11) 26-00-46
E-mail: info@xios.be
Internet: www.xios.be
Private control
Languages of instruction: Dutch, English
Academic year: September to July

Vice-Chancellor: Prof. Dr DIRK FRANCO
Pres.: LUC HOUBRECHTS

Gen. Man.: Prof. Dr DIRK FRANCO
Library of 30,000 vols, 400 journals
Number of students: 3,000

Schools of Music, Art and Architecture

Académie des Beaux-Arts et des Arts Décoratifs de Tournai: rue de l'Hôpital Notre-Dame 14, 7500 Tournai; tel. (69) 84-12-63; internet www.actournai.be; f. 1756; courses in drawing, painting, textile design, interior design, advertising, digital arts, comics; Dir BERNARD BAY.

Académie Royale des Beaux-Arts de Bruxelles (Brussels Royal Academy of Fine Arts): rue du Midi 144, 1000 Brussels; tel. (2) 506-10-10; e-mail info@arba-esa.be; internet www.arba-esa.be; f. 1711; drawing, engraving, environmental art, illustration, interior design, painting, publicity and visual communication, sculpture, tapestry-textile creation; 80 teachers; 450 students; Dir MARC PARTOUCHE.

Conservatoire Royal d'Anvers/Koninklijk Conservatorium (Royal Conservatoire of Antwerp): Desguinlei 25, 2018 Antwerp; tel. (3) 244-18-00; e-mail conservatorium@artesis.be; internet www.artesis.be/conservatorium; f. 1898, present status 1995; language of instruction: Dutch, English, French, German; 4-year full-time academic education and professional training in theatre and related performing arts; 3 art colleges; 180 teachers; Pres. PASCALE DE GROOTE; Admin. Sec. ROGER QUADFLIEG; Librarian JAN DEWILDE.

Conservatoire Royal de Bruxelles: rue de la Régence 30, 1000 Brussels; tel. (2) 511-04-27; e-mail info@conservatoire.be; internet www.conservatoire.be; f. 1832; Bachelor and Masters courses in music, theatre and arts; library: 1m. vols, 13,000 MSS, 1,200 periodicals; 250 teachers; 500 students; Dir FRÉDÉRIC DE ROOS; Librarian PAUL PROSPÉ.

Conservatoire Royal de Mons: rue de Nimy 7, 7000 Mons; tel. (65) 34-73-77; e-mail crm.mons @ sup.cfwb.be; internet www.conservatoire-mons.be; f. 1820; courses in music and theatre; library: 30,000 vols; 420 students; Dir ANDRÉ FOULON.

Conservatoire Royal de Liège: rue Forgeur 14, 4000 Liège; tel. (4) 222-03-06; e-mail info@crlg.be; internet www.crlg.be; f. 1826; 80 professors; students taken from 15 years of age; all brs of music and theatre; Dir BERNARD DEKAISE; Sec. NANCY DEMET; Librarian PHILIPPE GILSON.

École Nationale Supérieure des Arts Visuels de la Cambre: Abbaye de la Cambre 21, 1000 Brussels; tel. (2) 626-17-80; e-mail lacambre@lacambre.be; internet www.lacambre.be; f. 1926; library: see under Libraries and Archives; 230 teachers; 631 students; Dir CAROLINE MIEROP.

École Supérieure des Arts Plastiques et Visuels: rue des Sœurs Noires 4A, 7000 Mons; tel. (65) 39-47-60; e-mail esapv.mons@esapv.be; internet www.esapv.be; courses in drawing, digital arts, painting, sculpture, interior architecture; Dir JEAN-PIERRE BENON; Librarian LINA VASAPOLLI.

École Supérieure des Arts Saint-Luc: rue d'Irlande 57, 1060 Brussels; tel. (2) 537-08-70; e-mail info@stluc-bruxelles.be; internet www.stluc-bruxelles.be; f. 1863; promotes debate on modern art; research and teaching; 130 teachers; 700 students; Dir FRANÇOISE KLEIN.

École Supérieure des Arts Saint-Luc: blvd de la Constitution 41, 4020 Liège; tel. (4) 341-80-00; e-mail info@saintluc.com; internet www.saintluc-liege.be; courses in practical arts and crafts, graphics, photography, painting, sculpture, interior architecture, industrial design, conservation and restoration of works of arts; 130 teachers; 1,300 students; Dir ERIC VAN DEN BERG; Librarian BRUNO VANDERMEULEN.

Etablissement Communal d'Enseignement Supérieur Artistique 'Le 75': ave Jean-François Debecker 10, 1200 Brussels; tel. (2) 761-01-22; e-mail le75@woluwe1200.be; internet www.leseptantecinq.be; f. 1969; courses in visual art, graphics, painting and photography; 230 students; Exec. Sec. PASCALE DE COSTER.

Institut des Arts de Diffusion: rue des Wallons 77, 1348 Louvain-La-Neuve; tel. (10) 47-80-20; e-mail iad@iad-arts.be; internet www.iad-arts.be; f. 1959; courses in audiovisual and performing arts; Dir SERGE FLAMÉ; Vice-Dir MICHEL WOUTERS.

Institut National Supérieur des Arts du Spectacle et Techniques de Diffusion: rue Thérésienne 8, 1000 Brussels; tel. (2) 511-92-86; e-mail info@insas.be; internet www.insas.be; f. 1962; advanced studies in dramatic art, cinema and broadcasting technique, incl. television; library: 6,000 vols, 300 periodicals; Dir LAURENT GROSS; Admin. Sec. MAGALI SONNET.

Institut Saint-Luc: chaussée de Tournai 7, 7520 Tournai (Ramegnies-Chin); tel. (69) 25-03-04; e-mail secretariat-secondaire@st-luc-tournai.be; internet www.islt.be; courses and technical training in photography, drawing, illustration, advertising; Dir D. MAURAGE; Asst Dir Dr WILMART.

Institut Supérieur d'Architecture de la Communauté Française—La Cambre: pl. Eugène Flagey 19, 1050 Brussels; tel. (2) 640-96-96; e-mail isacf@lacambre-archi.org; internet www.lacambre-archi.be; f. 1926; organizes confs, workshops and courses in architecture; library: 17,000 vols, 42 periodicals; Dir Prof. JEAN-LOUIS GENARD; Deputy Dir Dr GUY PILATE; Exec. Sec. SAMIRA BARFI; publ. *Pola* (1 a year).

Institut Supérieur de Musique et de Pédagogique: rue Juppin 28, 5000 Namur; tel. (81) 73-64-37; e-mail info@imep.be; internet www.imep.be; f. 1970; research, theoretical and practical training in music; organizes concerts, confs; Dir GUIDO JARDON; Librarian THIERRY BOUILLET.

Institut Supérieur Libre des Arts Plastiques/École de Recherche Graphique: rue du Page 87, 1050 Brussels; tel. (2) 538-98-29; e-mail secretariat@erg.be; internet www.erg.be; courses in photography, sculpture, videography, painting, drawing, comics, animation; Dir YVAN FLASSE.

Liège Académie Royale des Beaux-Arts de Liège: rue des Anglais 21, 4000 Liège; tel. (4) 221-70-77; e-mail administration@academieroyaledesbeauxartsliege.be; internet www.academieroyaledesbeauxartsliege.be; f. 1836; courses in tapestry, sculpture, photography, engraving, sketching; organizes workshops.

BELIZE

The Higher Education System

The provision of education in Belize is regulated by the Education Act of 1991 (most recently revised as the Education and Training Act in 2010) and is overseen by the Ministry of Education and Youth. The main institution of higher education is the University of Belize, which was established in 2000 as an amalgam of previously existing tertiary institutions, including the University College of Belize, the School of Nursing, the Teachers' College, the School of Agriculture and Belize Technical College. There is also an extramural branch (a School of Continuing Studies) of the University of the West Indies (UWI) in Belize and the University of Indianapolis, USA, awards degrees through the private sector Galen University in Cayo District, which was established in 2003. To ensure adequate provision of tertiary education, the number of junior colleges was increased in the 1990s; by 2014 there was a total of 10 junior colleges in Belize. Initially most of the junior colleges operated as extensions of high schools, but there has been a trend for them to become independent institutions. In 2009/10 the number of students enrolled in junior colleges totalled over 7,000 and the number enrolled in universities reached 4,000. Some 90% of these students were enrolled in the University of Belize (3,714) and Galen University (288), with the remaining following open and distance courses at UWI (some 495 students in 2011/12) or studying abroad. In 2011/12 there were 5,195 students enrolled in higher, technical or vocational colleges.

Admission to university or junior college is on the basis of attaining at least the minimum required scores in secondary school examinations (including GCE A-level or Caribbean Advanced Proficiency Examination). Holders of the Caribbean Examinations Council Secondary Education Certificate or GCE O-level take a preliminary year before entry to a degree. There are two degree levels, Associate and Bachelors, with the former lasting for two years and the latter for four. Junior colleges mainly offer two-year Associate degree programmes and certificate and diploma courses, while the University of Belize offers Associate and Bachelor degrees and a number of certificate and diploma programmes, and Galen University offers courses at both undergraduate and postgraduate level (including Masters degrees and PhD courses). Several undergraduate programmes at Galen University are offered in collaboration with the University of Indianapolis; graduates of these programmes receive a final certificate awarded by the University of Indianapolis. Graduates of junior colleges holding an Associate degree may transfer their credits and gain admission to the final two years of a Bachelors degree.

Other post-secondary non-university education and training is available either through the workplace or at colleges. Courses can be taken leading to qualifications from City and Guilds, London Chamber of Commerce and the Royal Society of Arts. There is also a network of Institutes for Technical and Vocational Education and Training (ITVETs—formerly known as Centres for Employment Training), which offer three levels of occupational industry-based courses leading directly to employment. The ITVETs enrol school leavers and those already in employment who wish to learn a trade or upgrade their occupational skills. The Education Sector Strategy 2011–16 made one of its priorities to increase enrolment in the six ITVETs, which each has a capacity of 200 students.

At present Belize does not have an appointed external agency responsible for quality assurance in the higher education sector, although since 2005 it has been a member of the Consejo Centroamericano de Acreditación de la Educación Superior (Central American Accreditation Council for Higher Education), a regional body whose purpose it is to harmonize and improve higher education in Central America. However, at a national level tertiary institutions obtain a licence to operate from the Ministry of Education and Youth, on the condition that they are able to demonstrate adequate financial and infrastructural resources. The National Accreditation Council Act, which was signed in 2004, presented plans for the establishment of a National Accreditation Council that would monitor quality assurance and educational standards at tertiary institutions; in early 2014, however, such a body had still not been set up. A Qualifications Framework for Member States of the Carribean Community was being finalised in 2014 for Belize to move from a five-tier to an eight-tier level regional qualifications framework in alignment with African, Asian, European and Pacific standards.

Regulatory Bodies

GOVERNMENT

Ministry of Education and Youth: West Block Bldg, 3rd Fl., Belmopan, Cayo Dist.; tel. 822-2380; e-mail moeducation.moes@gmail.com; internet moe.gov.bz; Minister PATRICK JASON FABER.

Ministry of Tourism and Culture: 106 South St, Belize City; tel. 227-2801; e-mail ceotourism@travelbelize.gov.bz; internet www.belize.gov.bz/index.php/ministry-of-tourism-and-culture; Minister JOSE MANUEL HEREDIA, JR.

Learned Society

NATURAL SCIENCES

Belize Audubon Society: 12 Fort St, POB 1001, Belize City; tel. 223-5004; e-mail base@btl.net; internet www.belizeaudubon.org; f. 1969; sustainable management of natural resources; manages 9 protected areas; 1,400 mems; Pres. EARL D. GREEN; Exec. Dir ANNA DOMINGUEZ HOARE.

Research Institute

NATURAL SCIENCES

Biological Sciences

Carrie Bow Marine Field Station—Caribbean Coral Reef Ecosystems (CCRE): c/o Smithsonian Marine Station, 5612 Old Dixie Highway, Fort Pierce, FL 34946-7303, USA; Carrie Bow Cay, Belize; e-mail paul@si.edu; internet ccre.si.edu; f. 1972; attached to the Smithsonian Instn's Nat. Museum of Natural History (USA); field laboratory; part of the Smithsonian Marine Science Network; Dir Dr VALERIE PAUL.

Environmental Research Institute: Price Center Rd, Univ. of Belize Pre-school Grounds, POB 340, Belmopan, Cayo Dist.; tel. 822-2701; e-mail info@eriub.org; internet eriub.org; f. 2010; attached to Univ. of Belize; also Calabash Caye Field Station (CCFS); Admin. and Science Dir Dr LEANDRA CHO-RICKETTS.

Libraries and Archives

Belize City

Leo Bradley Library: POB 287, Belize City; Princess Margaret Dr., Belize City; tel. 223-4248; e-mail nls@btl.net; internet www.bnlsis.org; f. 1935; nat. library service for Belize; incl. Nat. Colln; 45 brs in Belize; 100,000 vols; Chief Librarian JOY YSAGUIRRE.

Belmopan

Belize Archives Department: 26/28 Unity Blvd, Belmopan, Cayo Dist.; tel. 822-2247; e-mail archives@btl.net; internet www.belizearchives.gov.bz; f. 1965; 150,000 documents; Chief Archivist Dr HERMAN BYRD.

Universities

GALEN UNIVERSITY

62.5 W Highway, San Ignacio, Cayo Dist.
Telephone: 824-3226
E-mail: admissions@galen.edu.bz
Internet: galen.edu.bz
Founded 2003
Private control
Language of instruction: English
Faculties of arts and social sciences, business and entrepreneurship, education, science and technology
Pres.: Dr LOUIS ZABANEH
Provost: ALINE E. HARRISON
Registrar: RAUL AVILA
Number of students: 485

UNIVERSITY OF BELIZE

University Dr., POB 340, Belmopan, Cayo Dist.
Telephone: 822-3680
E-mail: admissions@ub.edu.bz
Internet: www.ub.edu.bz
Founded 2000
Pres.: Dr CARY FRASER
Provost: WILMA WRIGHT
Asst Provost: CYNTHIA THOMPSON
Chief Librarian: ERWIN WOODYE, JR.
Library of 45,000 vols

DEANS

Faculty of Education and Arts: Dr PRISCILLA BROWN-LOPEZ (acting)
Faculty of Management and Social Science: Dr VINCENT PALACIO
Faculty of Nursing, Allied Health and Social Work: Dr ABIGAIL MCKAY
Faculty of Science and Technology: Dr JOAQUIN URBINA

BENIN

The Higher Education System

The structure of the higher education system in Benin (known as Dahomey until 1975) is a legacy of its period as a French colony (1890–1960). It is dominated by the Université d'Abomey-Calavi (comprising six faculties and 19 institutions), which was founded in 1970 as Université du Dahomey. The university changed its name to Université Nationale du Bénin in 1975 and adopted its current name in 2001. In 2011/2012 it had approximately 69,700 students. A second university, in Parakou, with a student capacity of approximately 3,000, opened in 2001 and there is now a third university in Porto-Novo. In 2005/06 there was a total of 42,600 students enrolled in further and higher educational institutions. In recent years the private sector of tertiary education has expanded rapidly and the number of students has increased accordingly. By 2009 there were seven private universities and around 90 other private higher education institutions, many of which are affiliated to universities in France, Belgium and Canada.

The Ministry of Higher Education and Scientific Research is responsible for the higher education sector. The university rectors are government appointees, but deans of faculty are elected by their peers. State funding for higher education has been affected by economic problems and poor management, with the effect that more specialized private institutions have begun to emerge.

The Baccalauréat de l'Enseignement Secondaire is required for admission to first-cycle university courses. Qualifications are arranged in three cycles. The first cycle lasts for two years and leads to the Diplôme Universitaire d'Études Littéraires in humanities, the Diplôme Universitaire d'Études Scientifiques in science or the Diplôme d'Études Universitaires Générales in law and economics. The second cycle lasts for either one year after the Diplomas for the Licence, or two years for the Maîtrise. Finally, the third cycle (requiring the Maîtrise for entry) comprises either a programme of doctoral research (in law, economics or agronomy) for two or more years leading to the award of Doctorat de Troisième Cycle or a four-year postgraduate course leading to either a Diplôme d'Études Approfondies in arts and management or a Diplôme d'Études Supérieures Spécialisées in science.

Regulatory Bodies

GOVERNMENT

Ministry of Culture, Literacy, Crafts and Tourism: 01 BP 2037, Guincomey, Cotonou; tel. 21-30-70-10; e-mail sg@tourisme.gouv.bj; internet www.tourisme.gouv.bj; Minister BABALOLA JEAN-MICHEL HERVÉ ABIMBOLA.

Ministry of Higher Education and Scientific Research: 01 BP 348, Cotonou; tel. 21-30-06-81; e-mail sgm@recherche.gouv.bj; internet www.mesrs.bj/spip.php; Minister FRANÇOIS ABIOLA.

Ministry of Secondary Education, Technical and Professional Training, the Conversion and Integration of Youths: 10 BP 250, Cotonou; tel. 21-30-56-15; Minister ALASSANE SOUMANOU.

Research Institutes

GENERAL

Centre Régional de Recherche Sud-Bénin: Attogon; f. 1904; library of 2,000 vols and periodicals; Dir Dr J. DETONGNON.

Institut de Recherches Appliquées: BP 6, Porto Novo; f. 1942; library of 8,000 vols; Dir S. S. ADOTEVI; publ. *Etudes*.

AGRICULTURE, FISHERIES AND VETERINARY SCIENCE

Institut National des Recherches Agricoles du Bénin (INRAB): 01 BP 884, Cotonou; tel. 21-30-37-70; internet www.bj.refer.org/benin_ct/rec/inrab/inrab.htm; f. 1992 to replace the Direction de la Recherche Agronomique (DRA); Dir-Gen. DAVID YAO ARODOKOUN.

Station de Recherches sur le Cocotier de Semé-Podji: Semé-Podji; tel. 20-24-07-01; coconut research; f. 1949; attached to Institut des Recherches sur les Huiles et Oléagineux, France; Dir HONORÉ TCHIBOZO.

Station de Recherches sur le Palmier à Huile de Pobe: BP 1, Pobe; tel. 20-25-00-66; f. 1922; palm oil station; attached to Direction de la Recherche Agronomique/Ministère des Affaires Rurales, France; library of 70 vols, 54 reviews; Dir Dr MOÏSE HOUSSOU.

NATURAL SCIENCES

General

Institut de Recherche pour le Développement (IRD): BP 4414, Cotonou; see main entry in France chapter.

TECHNOLOGY

Office Béninois de Recherches Géologiques et Minières: BP 249, Cotonou; tel. 21-31-03-09; e-mail obrgm@intnet.bj; f. 1977; branch of Min. of Mining, Energy and Hydraulics; library of 8,000 vols, 10 current periodicals; Dir-Gen. NESTOR VEDOGBETON; publ. *OBRGM Actu* (4 a year).

Libraries and Archives

Porto Novo

Archives Nationales de la République du Bénin: BP 629, Porto Novo; tel. 20-24-66-09; f. 1914; Dir ELISE PARAISO; publs *Mémoire du Bénin* (irregular), *Répertoire d'archives* (irregular).

Bibliothèque Nationale du Bénin: BP 401, Porto Novo; tel. 20-21-25-85; e-mail bn.benin@bj.refer.org; internet www.bj.refer.org/benin_ct/tur/bnb; f. 1975; 35,000 vols; Dir NOËL H. AMOUSSOU.

Museums and Art Galleries

Abomey

Musée Historique d'Abomey: BP 25, Abomey; tel. 22-50-03-14; internet epa-prema.net/abomey/; f. 1943; colln incl. craftwork, drawings, jewellery and royal paraphernalia; Curator ZÉPHIRIN DAAVO.

Porto Novo

Musée National: c/o IRA, BP 6, Porto Novo; premises at Cotonou; Curator MARTIN AKABIAMU.

Universities

UNIVERSITÉ D'ABOMEY-CALAVI

Abomey-Calavi, BP 526, Cotonou

Telephone: 21-36-11-19
E-mail: vrcireip.uac@uac.bj
Internet: www.uac.bj

Founded 1970 as Université du Dahomey; became Université Nationale du Bénin 1975; present name 2001
State control
Language of instruction: French
Academic year: October to July

Rector: Prof. BRICE SINSIN
Vice-Rector and Dir for Academic Affairs: Prof. DA CRUZ MAXIME
Sec.-Gen.: Dr LÉON BANI BIO BIGOU
Librarian: PASCAL A. I. GANDAHO

Library of 50,000 vols
Number of teachers: 984
Number of students: 69,688

DEANS

Faculty of Agriculture: Prof. JOSEPH HOUNHOUIGAN
Faculty of Arts, Letters and Humanities: Prof. FLAVIEN GBETO
Faculty of Health Sciences: Prof. BENJAMIN FAYOMI
Faculty of Law: Prof. IGUE CHARLEMAGNE
Faculty of Science and Technology: CYPRIEN GNANVO

UNIVERSITÉ DE PARAKOU

BP 123, Parakou

Telephone: 23-61-07-12
E-mail: universite_parakou2001@yahoo.fr

Founded 2001
State control
Academic year: October to July

Rector: Prof. ALEXIS HOUNTONDJI
Vice-Rector: Dr AGNÈS THOMAS-ODJO
Registrar: Dr MOUHAMED PARAPE
Librarian: BIO TIKANDE

Library of 3,657 vols
Number of teachers: 28
Number of students: 3,020

DEANS

Faculty of Agricultural Sciences: Dr NESTOR SOKPON
Faculty of Economics: Prof. BARTHÉLÉMY BIAO
Faculty of Law and Policy: Dr OMAR FORTUNÉ ALAPINI
Institute of Technology and Management: Dr SIMÉON FAGNISSE
School of Medicine: Prof. SIMON A. AKPONA

BHUTAN

The Higher Education System

Traditionally, education in Bhutan was purely monastic; the establishment of the contemporary state education system was the result of the reforming zeal of the third King, Jigme Dorji Wangchuck (r. 1952–72). There are five main linguistic groups in Bhutan; Dzongkha, spoken in western Bhutan, is the official language but English is the medium of school instruction. Tertiary education includes various first degree courses offered by the 10 member colleges and institutes that comprise the Royal University of Bhutan (RUB), which was formally opened in 2003 (although most of its constituent institutions had been established in the late 1960s and early 1970s). The colleges and institutes are located across the country, and, like traditional university faculties, they each specialize in a specific area of study and research. Until 2010 the majority of students admitted to the constituent establishments of the RUB were wholly sponsored by the Government, although in 2010 the University did admit 177 self-financed students out of a total of 5,414 enrolments. In 2011, however, the University began a process to become independent of the state and a commission was formed to work on a new financing system based on student fees and funding. Adult literacy and non-formal education (NFE) programmes began in Bhutan in 1992, with the establishment of 10 pilot NFE centres targeting those who had left school before completing the curriculum and those without a formal education. The programme offered a one-year basic literacy programme together with a nine-month post-literacy course in Dzongkha covering practical issues such as agriculture, health and sanitation. In 2010 there were 714 NFEs with 12,901 adults enrolled.

Admission to higher education is made on the basis of completion of grade 12 and passing of examinations leading to award of either the Indian School Certificate or Bhutan Higher Secondary Education Certificate. Bachelors degrees which last for three to four years are offered at four of the colleges in the RUB. At postgraduate level, the University also offers a Postgraduate Certificate of Education (PGCE) and has recently introduced Postgraduate Diplomas in financial management, public administration and national law. The Masters degree is currently offered on a very limited basis. There are currently no doctoral programmes in Bhutan.

The Department of Human Resources (DHR) of the Ministry of Labour and Human Resources was founded in 1999 to supervise technical and vocational education and training. Within the Department, the Department of Occupational Standards (formerly Bhutan Vocational Qualifications Authority) has developed a three-tier Bhutan Vocational Qualifications Framework. The grades of occupational training offered by the six technical/vocational institutes currently operated by the DHR are Apprenticeship Training Programmes (lasting one year), Special Skills Development Programmes and Village Skills Development Programmes. These programmes, admission to which is mainly based on the completion of grade 10, train around 1,500 individuals every year. Constituent colleges/institutes of the RUB and a growing number of private institutions also offer technical and vocational programmes of education; the latter establishments focus particularly on IT training. The College of Natural Resources, which is under the administration of the Ministry of Agriculture and Forests, offers two- and three-year diploma courses in agriculture, forestry and animal husbandry. Courses in nursing and midwifery, pharmacy, medical laboratory technology, dental hygiene and ophthalmic assisting are available at the RUB's Royal Institute of Health Sciences; most of these programmes are of two years' duration and the entrance requirement is the completion of grade 10. The University also offers two courses in Bhutanese traditional medicine.

In 2011 the Government was pursuing ambitious plans to establish a Bhutan Education City on the outskirts of the capital city of Thimphu, as a public–private partnership with India. Although the Bhutan Education City Bill was passed in June 2012, it contained a large number of amendments; for example, limiting the land lease period to 30 rather than 99 years, potentially calling into question the financial viability of the project for the private sector.

The Tertiary Education Policy of the Kingdom of Bhutan 2010, approved by the Government in 2011, provides for an autonomous Bhutan Accreditation Council (BAC) to licence and provide quality assessment for tertiary programmes. Guidelines for BAC operation and a new Qualifications Framework were put into place in 2012.

Regulatory Bodies

GOVERNMENT

Department of Occupational Standards: Min. of Labour and Human Resources, POB 1036, Thongsel Lam, Lower Motithang, Thimphu; tel. (2) 333867; internet www.molhr.gov.bt/molhrsite/?page_id=363; attached to Min. of Labour and Human Resources; improves and monitors the quality of technical and vocational skills acquired by individuals through the Bhutan Vocational Qualifications Framework (BVQF); comprises 3 divs: standards and qualifications, assessment and certification, review and audit; Dir SANGAY DORJEE.

Ministry of Education: POB 112, Thimphu; tel. (2) 323825; e-mail minister@education.gov.bt; internet www.education.gov.bt; Minister LYONPO MINGBO DRUKPA.

Ministry of Home and Cultural Affairs: Tashichho Dzong, POB 133, Thimphu; tel. (2) 322301; e-mail lmd@mohca.gov.bt; internet www.mohca.gov.bt; Minister LYONPO DAMCHOE DORJI.

Learned Society

GENERAL

Royal Textile Academy of Bhutan: POB 1551, Chubachu, Thimpu; tel. (2) 335117; internet www.royaltextileacademy.org; f. 2005; promotes and preserves textiles of Bhutan; Exec. Dir RINZIN O. DORJI.

Research Institutes

ECONOMICS, LAW AND POLITICS

Centre for Bhutan Studies: POB 1111, Langjophakha, Thimphu; tel. (2) 321007; e-mail cbs@druknet.bt; internet www.bhutanstudies.org.bt; f. 1999; research on Bhutan's economy, history, religion, society, polity, culture; Pres. DASHO KARMA URA; publ. *Journal of Bhutan Studies* (2 a year).

NATURAL SCIENCES

Physical Sciences

Ugyen Wangchuck Institute for Conservation and Environment: Lamai Goempa, Bumthang; tel. (3) 631926; e-mail uwice@druknet.bt; internet www.uwice.gov.bt; attached to Min. of Agriculture and Forests; research areas incl. conservation biology, socio-economic and policy sciences, sustainable forestry, water resources; offers 1-year certificate course in environment, forestry and conservation; Dir NAWANG NORBU; Head of Research and Education SHERUB; Dean for Student and Training Affairs TIL BHADUR MONGAR.

Libraries and Archives

Thimphu

National Library & Archives of Bhutan: Kawangjangsa, Pedzoe Lam, GPO POB 185, Thimphu 11001; tel. (2) 324314; e-mail nlb@library.gov.bt; internet www.library.gov.bt; f.

1967; br in Kuenga Rabten, Trongsa; 12,700 Dzongkha/Chokey MSS and block-printed books, 90,000 Dzongkha/Chokey books in other forms; 15,000 foreign (mainly English) books; Dir DORJEE TSHERING; publ. *Rigter* (2 a year).

Thimphu Public Library: POB 295, Thimphu; tel. (2) 322814; f. 1980; incl. the Jigme Dorji Wangchuck Library (f. 1978); UN depository library; 20,000 vols; Librarian TSHEWANG ZAM; Asst Librarian TSHERING PHUNTSHO.

Museum

Paro

National Museum of Bhutan: POB 1227, Paro; Ta Dzong, Paro; tel. (8) 271511; e-mail nmb@druknet.net.bt; internet www.nationalmuseum.gov.bt; f. 1968; housed in 7-storey 17th-century fortress; gallery of paintings (Thankas), images, decorative art, arms, jewellery; copper, bronze, wood and bamboo objects, philately, photographs; natural history of Bhutan; reference library with books on Bhutan, Northern Buddhism, Tibetology, museology and conservation; Dir PHUNTSOK TASHI.

University

ROYAL UNIVERSITY OF BHUTAN (RUB)/DRUK GYYELZIN TSHULA LOPDHEY

POB 708, Semtokha, Thimphu
Telephone: (2) 336457
E-mail: vc_rub@rub.edu.bt
Internet: www.rub.edu.bt
Founded 2003
State control
Academic year: July to June, February to December (2 sessions)
Chancellor: HM JIGME KHESAR NAMGYEL WANGCHUCK
Chair.: Hon. Min. KHANDU WANGCHUK
Vice-Chancellor: Dr PEMA THINLEY
Dir for Academic Affairs: YANGKA
Dir for Research and External Relations: Dr DORJI THINLEY
Registrar: KEZANG DOMA
Number of teachers: 354
Number of students: 5,701 (4,998 full-time, 703 part-time)

Colleges

College of Natural Resources: Lobesa, P. O. Wangdue, Punakha Dzongkhag; tel. (2) 480509; e-mail webmaster@cnr.edu.bt; internet www.cnr.edu.bt; f. 1992, fmrly National Resources Training Institute; attached to Royal Univ. of Bhutan; faculties of agriculture, animal husbandry, extension and communication, forestry; library: 1,000 vols.

College of Science and Technology: POB 450, Rinchending, Phuentsholing, Chukha; tel. (5) 240056; e-mail director@cst.edu.bt; internet www.cst.edu.bt; f. 2001; attached to Royal Univ. of Bhutan; faculties of civil engineering, electrical engineering, electronics and communications engineering, information technology, science and humanities; Dir Dr CHEKI DORJI; Dean for Academic Affairs OM KAFLEY; Dean for Student Affairs NIMA DUKPA.

Gaeddu College of Business Studies: Gedu, Chukha; tel. (5) 282297; internet www.gcbs.edu.bt; f. 2008; attached to Royal Univ. of Bhutan; offers Bachelors degree in business administration, commerce; Dir LHATO JAMBA; Dean for Academic Affairs TANDIN CHHOPHEL; Dean for Student Affairs TSHEWANG NORBU.

Jigme Namgyel Polytechnic: Dewathang; tel. (7) 260286; internet www.jnp.edu.bt; f. 1972 as Royal Bhutan Polytechnic, present name and status 2006; attached to Royal Univ. of Bhutan; depts of admin. and support, civil engineering, electrical engineering, mechanical engineering, humanities, information technology; library: 2,000 vols; 41 teachers; 328 students; Prin. KEZANG CHADOR.

National Institute of Traditional Medicine: POB 297, Kawajangsa, Thimphu; tel. (2) 321473; e-mail pema.zangmo@gmail.com; internet www.nitm.edu.bt; f. 1971, present name 1992; attached to Royal Univ. of Bhutan; offers Bachelors degree in traditional medicine; Dir DORJI WANGCHUK; Dean for Student Affairs DOPHU.

Paro College of Education: Paro; tel. (8) 271487; e-mail pce@pce.edu.bt; internet www.pce.edu.bt; f. fmrly Nat. Institute of Education; attached to Royal Univ. of Bhutan; offers Bachelors in education; depts of arts and humanities, Dzongkha, English, health and physical education, information technology, mathematics, professional studies, science; 66 teachers; Dean for Academic Affairs DORJI THINLEY; Dean for Student Affairs PHUNTSHO DOLMA.

Royal Institute for Tourism and Hospitality: POB 1147, Upper Motithang, Thimphu; tel. (2) 331281; e-mail rith@rith.edu.bt; internet rith.edu.bt; f. 2003 as Hotel and Tourism Management Training Institute, present name 2010; offers diploma in tourism and hospitality.

Royal Institute of Health Sciences: Thimphu; internet www.rihs.edu.bt; f. 1974, present status 2003; attached to Royal Univ. of Bhutan; depts of basic science, community, midwifery, nursing; Dir Dr CHENCHO DORJEE; Dean for Academic Affairs DIKI WANGMO; Dean for Student Affairs KUNGZANG DORJI.

Royal Institute of Management: POB 416, Semtokha, Thimphu; tel. (2) 351013; internet www.rim.edu.bt; f. 1986, present status 1990; training courses for civil service and private sector at certificate, diploma and postgraduate diploma levels; depts of finance and business, information and communications technology, management devt, research and consultancy; library: 13,000 vols, 60 periodicals; 32 teachers; 292 students; Dir KARMA TSHERING; publ. *dZinchong Rigphel* (2 a year).

Royal Thimphu College: POB 1122, Ngabiphu, Thimphu; tel. (2) 351801; e-mail info@rtc.bt; internet www.rtc.bt; faculties of business studies, information technology, humanities, mathematics, social sciences; Dir TENZING YONTEN; Dean for Academic Affairs Dr SHIVARAJ BHATTARAI; Registrar NIM DEM.

Samtse College of Education: POB 329, Samtse; tel. (5) 365273; e-mail director@sce.edu.bt; internet www.sce.edu.bt; f. 1968, fmrly Nat. Institute of Education, present name and status 2003; attached to Royal Univ. of Bhutan; depts of Dzongkha, educational psychology, English, mathematics and information technology, professional studies, sciences, social sciences; library: 15,617 vols; 51 teachers; 662 students; Dir KALYZANG TSHERING; Dean for Academic Affairs DEKI C. GYAMTSO; Dean for Student Affairs NANDU GIRI; Chief Librarian YESHEY DORJI; publ. *Rig–Gter*.

Sherubtse College: Kanglung, Trashigang; tel. (4) 535100; e-mail director@sherubtse.edu.bt; internet www.sherubtse.edu.bt; f. 1983; attached to Royal Univ. of Bhutan; depts of botany, chemistry, computer science and mathematics, Dzongkha, economics, English, environmental studies, geography and planning, history, political science, physics, zoology; library: 35,000 vols; 46 teachers; 484 students; Dir Dr SINGYE NAMGYEL; Dean for Academic Affairs Dr SONAM WANGMO; Dean for Student Affairs TSHERING WANGDI; publ. *Sherub Doenme* (2 a year, in English).

BOLIVIA

The Higher Education System

Universities in Bolivia fall into five categories: public autonomous universities and members of the Sistema de la Universidad Boliviana (SUB, Bolivian University System—which is overseen by the Comité Ejecutivo de la Universidad Boliviana—CEUB, Executive Committee of the Bolivian University); public non-autonomous universities; public non-autonomous universities and members of the SUB; universities under special regime; and private universities. The first university to be established in Bolivia was the Universidad Mayor de San Francisco Xavier (UMSFX) founded in La Plata (now Sucre) in 1624. The Universidad Mayor de San Andrés (UMSS) and the Universidad Mayor de San Simón (UMSS) were founded in La Paz and Cochabamba, respectively, in the early 1830s. Several more university institutions were established in the late 1880s. There was a rapid expansion of the number of private universities in the 1990s.

There are 17 public universities, 11 of which undertake research according to the Act of the Constitution of the SUB and are classified as public autonomous universities as they are self-financing and free to develop their own programmes. There are also two public non-autonomous universities which follow the SUB and are members of the CEUB: the Escuela Militar de Ingeniería (Military School of Engineering) and the Universidad Católica Boliviana 'San Pablo' (Catholic University of Bolivia). These two institutions do not, however, have the authority to offer all types of degrees; the courses that they do offer are administered by the Bolivian Army and Catholic Church. There are four public universities that do not participate in the SUB, do not have autonomy and are administered directly by the Vice-Ministry of Higher Education within the Ministry of Education. This group of institutions consists of the Universidad Militar de las Fuerzas Armadas, the Universidad Pedagógica Nacional, the Universidad Públicade El Alto and the Universidad de la Policía Boliviana.

In 2010 there were 68 private universities, which have been offering degrees since the mid-1980s. Most private universities are members of the Asociación Nacional de Universidades Privadas, founded in 1992, but are under the supervision of the Vice-Ministry of Higher Education within the Ministry of Education. There were, in addition, 313 non-university, higher education institutes in 2010.

One university, the Universidad Andina Simón Bolívar (UASB) has special status in Bolivia as an international university with campuses in Ecuador, Peru, Venezuela, Colombia and Bolivia. It was established by the Parlamento Andina (Andean Parliament) in December 2005 and is considered an international centre of excellence in postgraduate training, research and providing services for the transfer of scientific and technological knowledge. The Bolivian campus in Sucre offers postgraduate programmes in subjects such as medicine, administration and management and law.

In 2008 the Government approved the establishment of three indigenous universities, known collectively as the Universidades Indígenas Bolivianas Comunitarias Interculturales Productivas (UNIBOL): these were an Aymara university, Tupac Katari University, in the town of Warisata near La Paz; a Quechua university, Casimiro Huanca University, in the central department of Cochabamba; and a Guarani university, Apiaguaiki Tupa University, in the southern department of Chuquisaca. Courses at Tupac Katari University were to focus on high plains agronomy, food and textile industry studies, veterinary medicine and animal husbandry. The Casimiro Huanca University was to specialize in the food industry, forestry and fishery cultivation. The Apiaguaiki Tupa University was to focus on hydrocarbons, fishery cultivation, veterinary medicine and animal husbandry. Students were expected to return to their communities upon completion of their studies, and to apply their newly acquired knowledge towards the improvement of their region. This was part of a strategy by the Government of Evo Morales to address the social and economic inequalities in Bolivia, particularly those that exist between the urban and rural populations.

The Servicio Plurinacional de Certificación de Competencias was created by the Government in 2008 with the aim of recognizing the skills needed for the modern labour market in Bolivia and of broadening the focus of the higher education system to include these skills, in addition to the traditional high-status subjects typically offered by universities. The Ley Avelino Siñani Elizardo Pérez (known as the Ley de Educación BolivianaLEB) promulgated in December 2010 established the educational priorities of the Government of Evo Morales, which focused on increasing enrolment and literacy rates, as well as ensuring greater access to education for all socio-economic groups. Within the Sistema Educativa Plurinacional established under the LEB, priorities for higher education were set out by the Educación Superior de Formación Profesional programme (ESFPProfessional Training in Higher Education) which aimed to provide Bolivia with the skills needed to improve its economy.

Undergraduate higher education in Bolivia is offered at four levels in the public sector: the Técnico Universitario Medio (two years), Técnico Universitario Superior (three years), Bachiller Universitario (four years) and the Licenciatura (five years). National standards establishing the general requirements for each of these levels were set following the Tenth National Congress of Universities in 2003, and have been applied to all undergraduate degrees at public autonomous universities since 2006. At undergraduate level private universities offer only the Técnico Universitario Superior and the Licenciatura. At postgraduate level there are four types of degrees: specialist degrees in medical disciplines, specialist degrees in non-medical disciplines, Masters and Doctoral studies. On completion of these courses, students receive an academic rather than a professional title. The Diploma de Bachiller Científico-Humanístico serves as the principle entry requirement for access to higher education. Unlike some other countries in Latin America, there is no national university entrance examination. Some universities have their own admissions policy which may include passing an entrance examination. In 2006/07, according to UNESCO figures, there were 352,554 students enrolled in tertiary education, of whom 283,708 were enrolled at public institutions.

Accreditation of higher education is carried out by the Consejo Nacional Evaluación y Acreditación de la Educación Superior (CONAES). CONAES was established in 2002 as an independent agency responsible for conducting external evaluation of degree programmes in public and private universities. The system of accreditation is mainly programmatic and not compulsory. As a member of the Mercado Común del Sur (MercosurSouthern Common Market), CONAES has already established an evaluation committee for first-level medical degrees so that these qualifications will be automatically recognized throughout all Mercosur member states. In 2008 the Comisión Nacional de Acreditación de Carreras Universitarias (CNACU) was established to coordinate, supervise and carry out external evaluations in line with Mercosur. Also under the new Constitution the 'Avelino Siñani-Elizardo Pérez' Education Law was passed in 2010 bringing into existence a new accreditation agency, the Agencia Plurinacional de Evaluación y Acreditación de la Educación Superior Universitaria (APEAESU) to oversee both public and private universities. Once the APEAESU is fully operational it will replace the CNACU.

In 2010 there were 313 non-university higher education institutions, including around 25 state Escuelas Normales

Superiores (teacher training institutes), two private Escuelas Normales Superiores and a large number of state technical education colleges. Although universities also offer teacher training courses, the majority of student teachers undertake their studies at the Escuelas Normales Superiores. The technical education colleges award successful students the Diploma de Técnico Superior after three years of study. The technical/vocational education sector is overseen by the Sistema Nacional de Educación Técnica y Tecnología, which was established in 1994 in accordance with the Education Reform Law.

Regulatory and Representative Bodies

GOVERNMENT

Ministry of Culture: Palacio Chico, Calle Ayacucho Esq. Potosí s/n, Casilla 7846, La Paz; tel. (2) 220-0910; e-mail despacho@minculturas.gob.bo; internet www.minculturas.gob.bo; Minister PABLO CESAR GROUX CANEDO.

Ministry of Education: Avda Arce 2147, Casilla 3116, La Paz; tel. (2) 244-2144; internet www.minedu.gob.bo; Minister Lic. ROBERTO AGUILAR GÓMEZ.

NATIONAL BODIES

Comité Ejecutivo de la Universidad Boliviana (Executive Committee of the Bolivian University): Avda Arce Esq. Pinilla 2606 y Hnos Manchego 2559, La Paz; tel. (2) 2435-302; e-mail secejec@ceub.edu.bo; internet www.ceub.edu.bo; Nat. Exec. Sec. EDUARDO CORTEZ BALDIVIESO.

Secretaría Nacional de Investigación, Ciencia y Tecnología (Secretariat for Research, Science and Technology): Avda Arce No 2606, La Paz; tel. (2) 2435-217; e-mail secejec@ceub.edu.bo; f. 1994; directs and coordinates activities related to research, science and technology in Bolivian univs; Nat. Sec. Ing. LEONARDO SUÁREZ; publ. *Revista Ciencia al Día*.

Learned Societies

GENERAL

Academia Boliviana de la Lengua (Bolivian Academy of Language): Calle Capitán Ravelo, pasaje Issac Eduardo 2643, La Paz; tel. (2) 2445-381; e-mail abodelalen@hotmail.com; internet www.abolen.org; f. 1927; corresp. Academy of the Real Academia Española in Madrid; 26 mems; Dir Dr RAÚL RIVADENEIRA PRADA; Vice-Dir Dr MARIO FRÍAS INFANTE; publ. *Revista*.

UNESCO Office La Paz: Casilla 5112, La Paz; Casilla de correos 5112, La Paz; tel. (2) 220-4009; e-mail la-paz@unesco.org; Dir YVES DE LA GOUBLAYE DE MENORVAL.

AGRICULTURE, FISHERIES AND VETERINARY SCIENCE

Sociedad Rural Boliviana (Bolivia Rural Society): Casilla 786, Edif. El Condor 10°, Of. 1005, La Paz; f. 1934; 30 assoc. mems; Pres. Ing. JOSÉ LUIS ARAMAYO V.; publs *Cotar, El Surco, IFAP News, Universitas*.

ARCHITECTURE AND TOWN PLANNING

Colegio de Arquitectos de Bolivia (College of Architects of Bolivia): Casilla 8779, La Paz; tel. (2) 2310-300; e-mail colegioarquitectoslp@gmail.com; internet www.bolivia-arquitectos.org; f. 1940; 3,000 mems; library of 5,000 vols; Pres. RIM SAFAR SAKKAL; Vice-Pres. LUIS FERNANDO ÁLVAREZ NÚÑEZ; Sec.-Gen. ISMAEL SUÁREZ SERRATE; publs *Arquitectura y Ciudad, CDALP Informa, Punku*.

HISTORY, GEOGRAPHY AND ARCHAEOLOGY

Sociedad de Estudios Geográficos e Históricos (Geographical and Historical Society): 21 de Mayo-Galeria Casco Viejo, Local 131, Santa Cruz de la Sierra; e-mail segh.scz@gmail.com; f. 1903; Pres. LUCIO AÑEZ; Sec. AVELINO PEREDO.

Sociedad Geográfica de La Paz (La Paz Geographical Society): Casilla 1487, Edif. Santa Mónica, 13 Plaza Abaroa, La Paz; f. 1889; depts of prehistory, history, folklore, geography; 580 mems; Pres. Dr GREGORIO LOZA BALSA; publ. *Boletín* (2 a year).

Sociedad Geográfica y de Historia 'Potosí' (Potosi Society of History and Geography): Casilla 39, Potosí; tel. (62) 22777; f. 1905; 20 mems; library of 4,000 vols; Pres. Prof. ALFREDO TAPIA VARGS; Sec. WALTER ZAVAL.

Sociedad Geográfica y de Historia 'Sucre' (Sucre Society of History and Geography): Plaza 25 de Mayo, Sucre; e-mail geo_historicasucre@hotmail.com; internet www.geograficasucre.8m.net; f. 1887; 8 mems; library of 3,000 vols; Pres. GASTÓN SOLARES ÁVILA.

LANGUAGE AND LITERATURE

Alliance Française: Calle F. Guachalla y 20 de Octubre, La Paz; tel. (2) 242-5004; e-mail infolapaz@alianzafrancesa.org.bo; internet www.alianzafrancesa.org.bo; offers courses and exams in French language and culture and promotes cultural exchange with France; attached teaching offices in Cochabamba, Santa Cruz, Tarija and Sucre; Dir MARIE GRANGEON-MAZAT.

Goethe-Institut: Avda Arce 2708, Casilla 2195, La Paz; tel. (2) 2431-916; e-mail info@lapaz.goethe.org; internet www.goethe.de/ins/bo/lap/esindex.htm; offers courses and exams in German language and culture and promotes cultural exchange with Germany; library of 10,000 vols; Dir MICHAEL FRIEDRICH.

PEN International—Bolivian Centre: CP 5920, Cochabamba; e-mail gabyvall@supernet.com.bo; internet www.pen-international.org/centres/bolivian-centre; f. 1931; 40 Bolivian mems; Pres. MELITA DEL CARPIO; Sec. GABY VALLEJO.

MEDICINE

Ateneo de Medicina de Sucre (Sucre Medicine Athenaeum): Sucre; Pres. Dr AGUSTÍN BENÁVIDES; Sec.-Gen. Dr ROMELIO A. SUBIETA.

Sociedad de Pediatría de Cochabamba (Paediatrics Society): Avda G. Villarroel No 1132, Edif. Confort 5to. oficina 5-E°, Cochabamba; tel. (4) 4488-416; f. 1945; 14 mems; Pres. Dra MARCELA MONTAÑO MORENO; Vice-Pres. Dra BLANCA TORRICO TERCEROS; Sec.-Gen. Dra JUDITH CHOQUE.

NATURAL SCIENCES

General

Academia Nacional de Ciencias de Bolivia (National Academy of Sciences of Bolivia): Avda 16 de Julio 1732, Paseo El Prado, Casilla de Correos 5829, La Paz; tel. (2) 2363-990; e-mail secretaria@aciencias.org.bo; internet www.aciencias.org.bo; f. 1960; 42 mems; library of 8,000 vols; Pres. Acad. GONZALO TABOADA LÓPEZ; Gen. Sec. Acad. JOSÉ ANTONIO BALDERRAMA GÓMEZ ORTEGA; Librarian TERESA OCHOA GONZÁLES; publs *Publicaciones* (irregular), *Revista* (2 a year).

Physical Sciences

Colegio de Géologos de Bolivia (College of Geologists of Bolivia): Edif. Sergeomin, Calle Federico Zuazo, Esq. Reyes Ortiz 1673, Casilla 8941, La Paz; e-mail cogebo@acelerate.com; internet cogebo.online.fr; f. 1961 as Sociedad Geológica Boliviana, current name adopted 1996; Pres. ENRIQUE ARTEAGA REQUENA; Vice-Pres. HUGO ALARCÓN BARRENECHEA; Sec.-Gen. ESTELA MINAYA.

TECHNOLOGY

Asociación de Ingenieros y Geólogos de Yacimientos Petrolíferos Fiscales Bolivianos (AIG—YPFB) (Association of Engineers and Geologists of Yacimientos Petrolíferos Fiscales Bolivianos): Casilla 401, La Paz; f. 1959; 4 brs: La Paz, Camiri, Cochabamba, Santa Cruz; 210 mems; Pres. Ing. JUAN CARRASCO; publ. *Revista Técnica de Yacimientos Petrolíferos Fiscales Bolivianos* (4 a year).

Research Institutes

GENERAL

Centro de Estudios Superiores Universitarios (University College Centre): Calle Calama E-02350 entre Nataniel Aguirre y Esteban Arce, Cochabamba; tel. (591-4) 4252-951; e-mail cesu@umss.edu.bo; internet www.cesu.umss.edu.bo; f. 1992; attached to Universidad Mayor de San Simón; offers Masters and Diploma courses; Dir MANUEL DE LA FUENTE PATIÑO.

Institut de Recherche pour le Dévelopement (IRD) (Research Institute for Development (IRD)): CP 9214, La Paz; Avda Hernando Siles No 5290 Esq. Calle 7-Obrajes, La Paz; tel. (2) 2782-969; e-mail bolivie@ird.fr; internet www.bolivie.ird.fr; geology, hydrobiology, medical entomology, agronomy, nutrition, hydrology, climatology, social sciences; see main entry under France; Representative JEAN-JACQUES GARDON.

AGRICULTURE, FISHERIES AND VETERINARY SCIENCE

Sistema Boliviano de Tecnología Agropecuaria (SIBTA) (The Bolivian System for Agricultural Technology (SIBTA)): Avda Héctor Ormachea 1000, Esq. Calle 12, 3°, Obrajes, La Paz; tel. (2) 2786-937; e-mail ucpsa@sibta.gov.bo; f. 1975; library of 47,000 vols, 260 periodicals; Dir Dr GONZALO ROMERO G.

ECONOMICS, LAW AND POLITICS

Centros de Planificación y Gestión (Centre of Planning and Management): Campus Universitario U.M.S.S. Edif. Decanato Facultadad de Ciencias Económicas-2°, Cochabamba; tel. (4) 4542-759; internet www.ceplag.edu.bo; f. 1999; attached to Universidad Mayor de San Simón; research in the areas of economics, accountancy, business administration, applied mathematics, social studies and space studies; Dir MAURICIO ROJAS RUIZ.

Instituto Nacional de Estadística (National Institute of Statistics): Casilla 6129, La Paz; Calle J. Carrasco 1391, Miraflores, La Paz; tel. (2) 2222-333; e-mail ceninf@ine.gob.bo; internet www.ine.gob.bo; f. 1937; nat., economic and social statistics and censuses; library of 10,500 vols, 370 periodicals; Exec. Dir Lic. RICARDO LARUTA RODRIGUEZ; publs *Actualidad Estadística* (52 a year), *Actualidad Estadística Departamental* (12 a year), *Anuario Estadística*, *Encuenta Integrada de Hogares* (1 a year).

HISTORY, GEOGRAPHY AND ARCHAEOLOGY

Instituto Geográfico Militar (Military Institute of Geography): Casilla 7641, La Paz; Avda Saavedra 2303, (Estado Mayor), La Paz; tel. (2) 2149-434; e-mail igm@ejercito.mil.bo; internet www.igmbolivia.gob.bo; f. 1936; geodesy, nat. topographical survey; Commandant Col HUGO MÉNDEZ SARAVIA.

LANGUAGE AND LITERATURE

Instituto Nacional de Estudios Lingüísticos (INEL) (National Institute of Linguistic Studies (INEL)): Junín 608, Casilla 7846, La Paz; f. 1965; attached to Instituto Nacional de Historia, Literatura y Antropología; linguistic, social and educational research and teaching; specializations: Quechua and Aymara; library of 1,200 vols; Dir VITALIANO HUANCA TORREZ; publs specialized papers, *Notas y Noticias Lingüísticas* (12 a year), *Yatiñataki*.

MEDICINE

Instituto de Cancerología 'Cupertino Arteaga' ('Cupertino Arteaga' Institute of Oncology): Hospital de Clínicas, Plaza de Libertad, Sucre; f. 1947; Dir Dr H. NUNEZ R.

Instituto Médico Sucre (Medical Institute): Calle San Alberto 32, Casilla 82, Sucre; e-mail inmedsuc@yahoo.com; f. 1895; research and production of vaccines and sera; library of 8,000 vols, incl. *Flora Peruviensis* and 16th-century edn of *Aforismos de Hipocrates*, 6,000 pamphlets; Pres. Dr EZEQUIEL L. OSORIO; Sec. Dr JOSÉ AGUIRRE; publ. *Revista* (4 a year).

Instituto Nacional de Medicina Nuclear (National Institute of Nuclear Medicine): CP 5795, La Paz; Calle Mayor Rafael Zubieta 1555, Miraflores, La Paz; tel. (2) 2226-116; e-mail inamen@caoba.entelnet.bo; f. 1962; Dir Prof. LUIS F. BARRAGÁN M.

NATURAL SCIENCES

Physical Sciences

Centro de Levantamientos Aeroespaciales y Aplicaciones de Sistemas de Información Geográfica para el Desarrollo Sostenible de los Recursos Naturales (Center for Aerospace survey and GIS Applications for Sustainable Development of Natural Resources): Edif. Multiacadémico 2do°. Universidad Mayor de San Simón, Cochabamba Cercado 5294; tel. (4) 4540-750; e-mail clas@clas.umss.edu.bo; internet www.clas.umss.edu.bo; f. 1996; attached to Universidad Mayor de San Simón; research based on Geographic Information Systems (GIS) and Remote Perception for the Sustainable Management of Natural Resources; offers postgraduate courses; Dir GUY GALINDO A.

Instituto de Ingeniería Sanitaria y Ambiental (Institute of Sanitary and Environmental Engineering): Avda Villazón No 1995 Pabellón 103, La Paz; tel. (2) 441519; e-mail iis@umsa.bo; internet iis.umsa.edu.bo; f. 1971; attached to Universidad Mayor de San Andrés; library of 800 vols; Dir JOSÉ DÍAZ BENAVENTE.

Instituto de Investigación y Desarrollo de Procesos Químicos (Institute for Research and Development of Chemical Processes): Av. Mariscal Santa Cruz Nº 1175 Ed. Facultad de Ingeniería 2º, La Paz; tel. (2) 2205-000; internet iideproq.umsa.edu.bo/ubicacion.html; f. 1994; attached to Universidad Mayor de San Andrés; Dir VIRGINIA ROJAS MERCADO.

Observatorio San Calixto (San Calixto Observatory): Casilla 12656, La Paz; Calle Indaburo 944, La Paz; tel. (2) 2406-222; e-mail osc@observatoriosancalixto.org; internet www.observatoriosancalixto.org; f. 1913; meteorology and seismology; library of 11,000 vols; Dir Dr ESTELA MINAYA; Sec. FABIOLA ZAVALA.

Servicio Nacional de Geología y Técnico de Minas (SERGEOTECMIN) (National Service of Geology and Mining Technicians (SERGEOTECMIN)): Casilla 2729, La Paz; Calle Federico Zuazo No 1673 esq. Reyes Ortíz Zona Central, La Paz; tel. (2) 231-1373; e-mail contactenos@sergeotecmin.gob.bo; internet www.sergeotecmin.gob.bo; f. 1956 as nat. dept, reorganized 1965, 1996 and 2004; 10 laboratories; library of 8,000 vols; Exec. Dir Eng. HUGO DELGADO; publ. *Boletín SERGEOTECMIN Informa* (3 a year).

RELIGION, SOCIOLOGY AND ANTHROPOLOGY

Centro de Estudios de Poblacion (Population Studies Center): Calle Calama E-235 (Edif. Ex-Banco Agrícola) 2°, Cochabamba; tel. (4) 4232-540; e-mail cep@umss.edu.bo; internet www.cep.umss.edu.bo; f. 1983; attached to Universidad Mayor de San Simón; Dir ROSE MARY SALAZAR.

Programa Integral de Rehabilitación de Áreas Históricas de Cochabamba (Comprehensive Rehabilitation Programme of Historic Areas of Cochabamba): Facultad de Arquitectura de la UMSS, Calle Jordán final este s/n Edif. Multifuncional, 3era planta, Cochabamba; tel. (4) 4540-084; e-mail gestionpatrimonio@msn.com; internet www.prahc.umss.edu.bo; f. 1998; attached to Universidad Mayor de San Simón; research and training institute for the protection and enhancement of heritage and cultural resources of Bolivia; Dir MARINA STURICH TAMAIN.

TECHNOLOGY

Instituto Boliviano de Ciencia y Tecnología Nuclear (Bolivian Institute of Nuclear Science and Technology): Casilla 4821, La Paz; Avda 6 de Agosto 2905, La Paz; tel. (2) 2433-481; e-mail ibten@datacom-bo.net; internet www.ibten.gob.bo; f. 1983; CEO LUIS ENRIQUE ROMERO BOLAÑOS (acting); Dir for Admin. OMAR MERCADO VELASCO; Dir for CIAN ISAAC LUNA LAURACIA.

Instituto de Investigaciones Industriales (Industrial Research Institute): Calle Ayacucho No 205 anexo Facultad de Ingeniería, La Paz; tel. 2110-923; e-mail maeindust@yahoo.es; internet www.iii.fi.umsa.bo; f. 1991; attached to Universidad Mayor de San Andrés; research in regards to modifying technology used in Bolivian industries; Dir GROVER PANDO VIAMONTT.

Libraries and Archives

Cochabamba

Biblioteca Central Universitaria 'José Antonio Arze' (Central University Library 'José Antonio Arze'): Casilla 992, Cochabamba; Avda Oquendo Esq. Sucre, Cochabamba; tel. (42) 31733; f. 1930; 30,000 vols; attached to Universidad Mayor de San Simón; Librarian RUTH VALENCIA; publ. *Boletín Bibliográfico*.

La Paz

Biblioteca Central de la Universidad Mayor de San Andrés (Central Library of Higher University of San Andrés): Avda Villazón 2170, La Paz; tel. (2) 2420-264; f. 1930; 70,000 vols; Dir TERESA ROCABADO.

Biblioteca del Instituto Boliviano de Estudio y Acción Social (Library of the Bolivian Institute for Study and Social Action): Avda Arce 2147, La Paz; spec. collns on social science, Boliviana, education and govt documents; 12,000 vols; Dir ELENA PEDDLE.

Biblioteca del Ministerio de Relaciones Exteriores (Library of the Ministry of Foreign Affairs): Plaza Murillo, Calle Ingavi Esq. Calle Junin, La Paz; tel. (2) 2408-900; f. 1930; 10,000 vols; private library; Dir Prof. PACÍFICO LUNA QUIJARRO.

Biblioteca Municipal 'Mariscal Andrés de Santa Cruz' (Municipal Library): Zona Central, Plaza del Estudiante, Calle Cañada Strongest Esq. México, La Paz; tel. (2) 2378-477; f. 1838; 35,000 vols; Dir YOLOTZIN SALDAÑA.

Biblioteca y Archivo Histórico de la Asamblea Legislativa Plurinacional (Library and Historical Archive of the Plurinational Legislative Assembly): Edif. de la Vicepresidencia, Calle Mercado, casi Esq. Ayacucho, No 308 7056, La Paz; tel. (2) 2142-671; f. 1911; literature on legislation, law, economics, political science and sociology; 6,000 modern monographs, 100 titles of old books; 100 journal titles, 10,000 copies of 16 titles of newspapers of nat. circulation, the political memory of the Legislature (Senate National Fund, the Chamber of Deputies); Documents 2006-2007 Constituent Assembly (Constituent Assembly Fund); audio recordings of legislative chambers and legislative sessions from 1947 to 2000 in various media, and publs produced or published by the Executive, Legislative, Judicial, Electoral and entities with legal bodies; publ. *Fuentes* (6 a year).

Biblioteca y Archivo Histórico del Honorable Congreso Nacional (Library and Historical Archives of the Honourable National Congress): Calle Mercado esq. Ayacucho No 308, La Paz; tel. (2) 214-2671; f. 1912; 22,000 vols; Dir VÍCTOR BERNAL SOLARES; Chief Librarian NELLY ARRAYA VASQUEZ; publ. *Reports of Congress*.

Cámara Nacional del Libro (National Book Chamber): Calle Capitan Ravelo 2116, La Paz; tel. (2) 2113-264; e-mail cabolib@entelnet.bo; internet www.cabolib.org.bo; f. 1945; Pres. CARLA MARÍA BERDEGUÉ.

Centro Nacional de Documentación Científica y Tecnológica (National Scientific and Technological Documentation Centre): Casilla 14538, La Paz; Avda Mariscal Santa Cruz 1175, Esq. Calle Ayacucho, La Paz; tel. (2) 359-583; e-mail iiicndct@huayna.umsa.edu.bo; internet www.bolivian.com/industrial/cndct; f. 1967; attached to Instituto de Investigaciones Industriales, Universidad Mayor de San Andrés; provides information for research and devt; depository library for FAO, WHO and ILO; 9,800 vols;

Dir Rubén Valle Vera; publ. *Actualidades* (4 a year).

Potosí

Biblioteca Central Universitaria (Central University Library): Universidad Autónoma 'Tomás Frías', Casilla 54, Avda del Maestro, Potosí; tel. (62) 27313; internet www.uatf.edu.bo/web_servicios/bibliotecas.php; f. 1942; 1 central library, 8 specialized libraries; 43,796 vols, 1,471 periodicals; Dir Julia B. de López; publs *Revista Científica, Revista de Ciencias, Revista Orientación Pedagógica*.

Sucre

Biblioteca Central de la Universidad Mayor de San Francisco Xavier (Central Library of the Higher University of St Francis Xavier): Plaza 25 de Mayo, Apdo 212, Sucre; internet www.usfx.info/edif/index.php?id=37; Incl. NetLibrary of 4,000 vols; Dir Agar Peñaranda.

Biblioteca y Archivo Nacionales de Bolivia (National Library and Archives of Bolivia): Casilla 793, Sucre; Calle Dalence 4, Sucre; tel. (4) 6451-481; e-mail abnb@entelnet.bo; internet www.archivoybibliotecanacionales.org.bo; f. 1836; 150,000 vols; Dir Gunnar Mendoza.

Museums and Art Galleries

La Paz

Museo 'Casa de Murillo' (House of Murillo Museum): Calle Apolinar Jaén 790, La Paz; tel. (2) 2280-758; f. 1950; former residential house of Don Pedro Domingo Murillo, folk and colonial art, paintings, furniture, national costume, herb medicine and magic from the 19th century.

Museo Costumbrista 'Juan de Vargas' (Juan de Vargas Customs Museum): Calle Sucre s/n, Esq. Jaén, La Paz; tel. (2) 2280-758; f. 1979; history and customs of La Paz.

Museo de Metales Preciosos Precolombinos (Columbian Museum of Precious Metals): Calle Jaén 777, Casilla 609, La Paz; tel. (2) 2280-329; f. 1983; pre-Hispanic archaeological pieces, anthropomorphic, zoomorphic and other priceless objects; Dir José de Mesa.

Museo Nacional de Arqueología (National Archaeological Museum): Calle Tihuanaco 93, Casilla Oficial, La Paz; tel. (2) 231-1621; f. 1846; archaeological and ethnographical collns; over 50,000 archaeological pieces; Lake Titicaca district exhibits; Dir Julio Cesar Velasquez Alquizaleth; publ. *Anales*.

Museo Nacional de Arte (National Art Museum): Casilla 11390, La Paz; Calle Socabaya Esq. Calle Comercio, La Paz; tel. (2) 2408-600; e-mail mna@mna.org.bo; internet www.mna.org.bo; f. 1964; housed in 18th-century baroque palace; colonial art, sculpture and furniture; Bolivian and Latin-American modern art; Dir Daniela Guzmán Vargas.

Potosí

Museo de la Casa Nacional de Moneda (Museum of the National Mint): Calle Ayacucho s/n, Potosí; tel. (2) 6223-986; e-mail moneda@cedro.pts.entelnet.bo; internet www.casanacionaldemoneda.org.bo; f. 1938; housed in the 'Casa de Moneda', the Royal Mint, f. 1572; colonial art, 18th-century wooden machinery, coins, historical archives, mineralogy, weapons, Indian ethnography, archaeology, modern art; Dir Luis Alfonso Fernández.

Sucre

Casa de la Libertad (Freedom House): CP 101, Sucre; Plaza 25 de Mayo 11, Sucre; tel. (4) 645-4200; e-mail cdl@casadelalibertad.org.bo; internet www.casadelalibertad.org.bo; f. 1886 as Casa de la Independencia; historical colln concerned with Independence, incl. Bolivian Declaration of Independence; library of 5,000 vols, 1,000 maps; publ. *Memorias*.

Museo Charcas (Charcas Museum): Simón Bolívar, 698 Esq. Pantaleón Dalence, Sucre; tel. (4) 645-6100; f. 1944; anthropological colln with pre-Inca archaeology; houses paintings by the half-indigenous Melchor Pérez Holguín, incl. his most famous work, San Juan de Dios; colln of mummified bodies; Dir Jaime Urioste Arana; publ. *Boletín Antropológico*.

Museo Nacional de Etnográfica y Folklore (National Museum of Ethnography and Folklore): CP 5817, Sucre; Calle Ingavi No 916, Esq. Jenaro Sanjinés, Sucre; tel. (2) 240-8640; e-mail musef@musef.org.bo; internet www.musef.org.bo; f. 1925, current name adopted 1962; attached to Cultural Foundation of the Central Bank of Bolivia; Dir Elvira Espejo Ayca; publ. *Revista del Museo Nacional de Etnografía y Folklore*.

Universities

UNIVERSIDAD AMAZÓNICA DE PANDO
(Amazonian University of Pando)

Avda 9 de Febrero, Esq. Teniente Coronel Cornejo, Pando

Telephone: (3) 842-2135

E-mail: recuap@hotmail.com

Internet: www.uap.edu.bo

Founded 1993

State control

Language of instruction: Spanish

Depts of biological and natural sciences, economics and finance, health sciences, legal, political and social sciences, science and technology

Rector: Ing. Ludwing Arcienega Baptista

Vice-Rector: Lic. Jose Luis Segovia

Sec.-Gen.: Lic. Ines Bautista Huallpara

UNIVERSIDAD ANDINA SIMÓN BOLÍVAR
(Andean University Simón Bolívar)

Calle Real Audiencia No 73, El Alto, Sucre

Telephone: (4) 646-0265

E-mail: info@uasb.edu.bo

Internet: www.uasb.edu.bo

Founded 1998

State control

Rector: Dr Jose Luis Gutiérrez Sardán

UNIVERSIDAD AUTÓNOMA DEL BENI 'JOSÉ BALLIVIÁN'
(Autonomous University of Beni 'José Ballivián')

Avda 6 de Agosto, Edif. Central 'Antonio Vaca Díez', 4°, Trinidad

Telephone: (46) 20744

E-mail: uabjb@uabjb.edu.bo

Internet: www.uabjb.edu.bo

Founded 1967

State control

Rector: Ing. Luis Carlos Zambrano Aguirre

Gen. Sec.: Dr Nelson Yañez Roca

Librarian: Lorgia S. de Tanaka

Library of 9,600 vols

Number of students: 15,000

Publication: *Revista Cientifica Agrociencias Amazonia*

DEANS

Faculty of Agricultural Sciences: Ing. Erwing Diederich del Aguila

Faculty of Economic Sciences: Lic. María René Guillen

Faculty of Forest Sciences: Ing. Luis Medina Alipa

Faculty of Health Sciences: Lic. Wilma Teresa Alarcón Balcázar

Faculty of Humanities and Educational Sciences: Julio Alberto Núñez Vela

Faculty of Legal, Political and Social Sciences: Dr Jesús Alfredo Ibáñez Vaca

Faculty of Livestock Sciences: Dra Francis Ferrier Abidar

UNIVERSIDAD AUTÓNOMA 'GABRIEL RENÉ MORENO'
(Gabriel René Moreno Autonomous University)

Plaza 24 de Septiembre, Santa Cruz de la Sierra

Telephone: (3) 336-5533

E-mail: uagrmrec@bibosi.scz.entelnet.bo

Internet: www.uagrm.edu.bo

Founded 1880

State control

Language of instruction: Spanish

Academic year: February to December

Rector: Saul Rosas Ferrufino

Vice-Rector: Abog. Oswaldo Ulloa Peña

Sec.-Gen.: Ing. Carlos Martinez Bonilla

Chief Financial Officer: Erwin Vaca Duran

Univ. Dir for Extension: Victor Alberto Ochoa Moya

Univ. Dir for Research: Julio Waldo Lopez Aparicio

Univ. Dir for Social Welfare: Hector Saldias Callejas

Librarian: Lic. José Melchor Mansilla

Library of 40,000 vols

Number of teachers: 1,400

Number of students: 78,000

Publication: *Universidad*

DEANS

Faculty of Agriculture: Ing. Juan Benigno Ortube Flores

Faculty of Economics and Finance: Lic. Vicente Remberto Cuellar Téllez

Faculty of Engineering, Computers and Telecommunications: Ing. Juan Carlos Alberto Contreras

Faculty of Exact Sciences and Technology: Ing. Juan Carlos Paz Castro

Faculty of Habitat, Integral Design and Art: Arq. Pedro Bazán Salvatierra

Faculty of Health Sciences: Dr Raúl Pedraza Leaños

Faculty of Humanities: Abog. Marcelo Javier Sossa Hoyos

Faculty of Juridical, Political and Social Sciences: Abog. Manfredo Menacho Aguilera

Faculty of Pharmaceutical and Biochemical Sciences: Lic. Blanca Elena Saldaña Gil

Faculty of Public Accounting: Lic. Ezequiel Paniagua Banegas

Faculty of Veterinary Medicine and Zootechnology: Dr Pablo Rosales Callejas

Polytechnic Faculty: Ing. Clover Herrera Domínguez

UNIVERSIDAD AUTÓNOMA 'JUAN MISAEL SARACHO'
(Juan Misael Saracho Autonomous University)

Avda Victor Paz E-0149, Casilla 51, Tarija
Telephone: (4) 664-5097
E-mail: rector@uajms.edu.bo
Internet: www.uajms.edu.bo

Founded 1946
State control
Language of instruction: Spanish
Academic year: March to December

Rector: Ing. MARCELO HOYOS MONTECINOS
Vice-Rector: Lic. ANCELMO RODRIGUEZ
Sec.-Gen.: Dra OLGA MARTINEZ

Publications: *Astro Información* (12 a year), *Visión Universitaria* (12 a year)

DEANS

Faculty of Agriculture and Forestry: Ing. ISMAEL ACOSTA GALARZA
Faculty of Dentistry: Dr CARLOS CONSTANTINO KUNCAR
Faculty of Economics and Finance: BERNARDO VARGAS MUÑOZ
Faculty of Health Sciences: Dr CARLOS FLORENCIO HOYOS DELFIN
Faculty of Humanities: Lic. EDWIN JIJENA
Faculty of Law and Political Sciences: Dr CARLOS PÉREZ RIVERO
Faculty of Sciences and Technology: Ing. LUIS ALBERTO YURQUINA FLORES
Grán Chaco Faculty: Lic. JAIME CONDORÍ ÁVILA
Integrated School of Bermejo: Lic. LUIS RICARDO COLPARI DÍAZ

UNIVERSIDAD AUTÓNOMA 'TOMÁS FRÍAS'
(Tomás Frías Autonomous University)

Casilla 36, Potosí
Avda del Maestro, Avda Civica s/n, Potosí
Telephone: (2) 2622-7300
E-mail: rector@rect.nrp.edu.bo
Internet: www.uatf.edu.bo

Founded 1892
State control
Language of instruction: Spanish
Academic year: April to November

Rector: Lic. VICTOR HUGO VILLEGAS
Vice-Rector: Ing. HUGO CAZON P.
Chief Librarian: Dr CARLOS LOAYZA MENDIZABAL

Number of teachers: 380
Number of students: 7,551

Publication: *Vida Universitaria*

DEANS

Faculty of Agriculture and Stockbreeding: Ing. AMILCAR MARISCAL CORTEZ
Faculty of Arts: Lic. LUIS TORRICO GAMARRA
Faculty of Economics, Finance and Administration: Lic. VALETÍN VIÑOLA QUINTANILLA
Faculty of Engineering: Ing. ALBERTO SCHMIDT QUEZADA
Faculty of Geological Engineering: Ing. DANIEL HOWARD BARRÓN
Faculty of Humanities and Social Sciences: Dr NESTOR GOITIA IRAHOLA
Faculty of Law: Dr JORGE QUILLAGUAMÁN SÁNCHEZ
Faculty of Mining: Ing. EDDY ROMAY MORALES
Faculty of Sciences: Lic. GONZALO POOL GARCÍA
Polytechnic: Téc. Sup. ENRIQUE ARROYO MAMANI

UNIVERSIDAD CATÓLICA BOLIVIANA 'SAN PABLO'
(San Pablo Catholic Bolivian University)

Avda 14 de Septiembre No 4807 Esq. Calle 2, Obrajes, La Paz
Telephone: (2) 278-2222
E-mail: rrppint@ucb.edu.bo
Internet: www.ucb.edu.bo

Founded 1966
Private control
Language of instruction: Spanish
Academic year: February to December

Grand Chancellor: Mgr JORGE HERBAS OBIPSO PRELADO DE AIQUILE
Rector: Mgr MARCO ANTONIO FERNÁNDEZ CALDERÓN
Vice-Rector for Academic Affairs: Dr JESÚS MUÑOZ DIEZ
Vice-Rector for Admin. and Finance: Dr CLAUDIO NACIF MUCKLED
Sec.-Gen.: Dr MARIO HOYOS

Publication: 5 Journals: Acta Nova, Ajayu, Ciencia y Cultura, Con-Sciencas Sociales, Punto Cero, Yachay

UNIVERSIDAD CRISTIANA DE BOLIVIA
(Christian University of Bolivia)

Km 5, Carretera al Norte, Santa Cruz de la Sierra
Telephone: (3) 342-6311
E-mail: info@ucebol.edu.bo
Internet: www.ucebol.edu.bo

Founded 1991
Private control
Language of instruction: Spanish

Rector: Dr EUN SHIL CHUNG

Publication: *Universidad Ciencia & Sociedad*

UNIVERSIDAD DE AQUINO BOLIVIA
(University of Aquino Bolivia)

Capitán Ravelo pasaje Isaac Eduardo, La Paz
Telephone: (2) 244-1044
E-mail: info@udabol.edu.bo
Internet: www.udabol.edu.bo

Founded 1995
Private control

Rector: Dr ANTONIO SAAVEDRA MUÑOZ

UNIVERSIDAD EMPRESARIAL MATEO KULJIS
(Mateo Kuljis Business University)

Calle 24 de Septiembre 444, 2321 Santa Cruz
Telephone: (3) 332-2211
E-mail: universidad@unikuljis.edu.bo
Internet: www.unikuljis.edu.bo

Founded 2000

Rector: Lic. IVO KULJIS FUTCHNER

UNIVERSIDAD EVANGÉLICA BOLIVIANA
(Bolivian Evangelical University)

Barrio Cruz del Sur U. V. 117 Avda Moscú, Santa Cruz de la Sierra
Telephone: (3) 356-0990
E-mail: uebmail@ueb.edu.bo
Internet: www.ueb.edu.bo

Founded 1980
Private control
Language of instruction: Spanish

Faculties of business sciences, communication and culture, health sciences, science and technology, social educational theology

Rector: Dr TIMOTEO SÁNCHEZ BEJARANO
Vice-Rector: Dra MARCELA VALENZUELA DE CAMACHO
Sec.-Gen.: Dra PURA AMPARO ZAPATA SAUCEDO

UNIVERSIDAD LOYOLA
(Loyola University)

Avda Busch 1191, Edif. 'El Sauce', La Paz
Telephone: (2) 222-4522
E-mail: uloyola@loyola.edu.bo
Internet: www.loyola.edu.bo

Founded 1995
Private control
Language of instruction: Spanish
Academic year: January to December

Faculties of economics and financial management, natural sciences, social sciences, technology

Pres.: Ing. HUMBERTO MENDIZÁBAL ORELLANA
Rector: Lic. JULIO ESTRADA VÁSQUEZ
Dir for Academic Affairs: Ing. RAMIRO AGUILAR CALDERÓN
Dir for Admin. and Financial Affairs: Arq. MARIA HILDA CABRERA MAYSER
Dir for Planning and Self-Evaluation: Ing. CHRISTIAN MENDIZÁBAL CABRERA
Sec.-Gen.: Dr OSCAR VARGAS DAROCA

UNIVERSIDAD MAYOR DE SAN ANDRÉS
(Higher University of San Andrés)

Avda Villazón 1995, Monoblock Central, La Paz
Telephone: (2) 244-1963
E-mail: webmaster@umsa.bo
Internet: www.umsa.bo

Founded 1830
State control
Language of instruction: Spanish
Academic year: January to December

Rector: FÁTIMA CONSUELO DOLZ DE MORENO
Vice-Rector: Dr LUIS FREDDY ROSSELL CASANOVA
Gen. Sec.: Lic. GERMÁN EMILIO MONTAÑO ARROYO
Academic Sec.: Lic. RAÚL ESPAÑA CUELLAR
Librarian: Lic. ELIANA MARTINEZ DE ASBUN

Library: see under Libraries and Archives

Publications: *Boletín Tesis*, *Gaceta Universitaria*, *Memorias Universitarias*

DEANS

Faculty of Agronomy: Ing. EDUARDO OVIEDO FARFAN
Faculty of Architecture, Arts, Design and Urbanism: Arq. WALTER ESPINOZA GARCIA
Faculty of Dentistry: Dr LUIS FREDDY ROSSELL CASANOVA
Faculty of Economics and Finance: Lic. CARLOS CLAVIJO VARGAS
Faculty of Engineering: Ing. ADHEMAR DAROCA MORALES
Faculty of Geology: Ing. GERMAN WILFREDO NUÑEZ ARAMAYO
Faculty of Humanities and Education: Lic. RAÚL GONZALO PAREDES ARANDA
Faculty of Law and Political Science: Dr JULIO ADELIO MALLEA RADA
Faculty of Medicine, Nursing, Nutrition and Medical Technology: Dr JULIO HERIBERTO CUEVAS LIZARRAGA
Faculty of Pharmacy and Biochemistry: Dr TITO ESTEVEZ MARTINI
Faculty of Pure and Natural Sciences: Dr MARIA EUGENIA GARCIA
Faculty of Social Sciences: Dr JOSÉ TEJEIRO VILLARROEL
Faculty of Technology: Lic. RAFAEL ONOFRE MONTES

UNIVERSIDAD MAYOR DE SAN SIMÓN
(Higher University of San Simón)

Avda Ballivián Esq. Reza 591, Cochabamba
Telephone: (4) 422-0717
E-mail: rector@umss.edu.bo
Internet: www.umss.edu.bo

Founded 1832
State control
Language of instruction: Spanish
Academic year: July to December

Rector: Dr LUCIO GONZALES CARTAGENA
Vice-Rector: Mgr. WALDO JIMENEZ VALDIVIA
Sec.-Gen.: Dr ROLANDO LÓPEZ HERBAS
Librarian: RUTH VALENCIA

Library: see under Libraries and Archives

DEANS

Faculty of Agriculture and Habitat Sciences: Arq. EDWIN MAGNE SOTOMAYOR
Faculty of Agriculture, Livestock, Forestry and Veterinary Sciences: Ing. JUAN VILLARROEL SOLIZ
Faculty of Biochemistry and Pharmaceutical Sciences: Dra JENNY KATYA PINTO DÁVALOS
Faculty of Dentistry: Dra DELIA AYALA ARAMBURO
Faculty of Economics: JULIO CÉSAR CAMACHO VALDIVIA
Faculty of Humanities and Education: Dr GREBY RIOJA MONTAÑO
Faculty of Legal and Political Sciences: Dra IRMA IVANOVIC CORRALES
Faculty of Medicine: Dr MANUEL ANTONIO MONROY DELGADILLO
Faculty of Science and Technology: Ing. HERNÁN FLORES GARCÍA
Faculty of Social Sciences: Dr JOSÉ ANTONIO ROCHA TORRICO
Polytechnical University Institute 'El Valle Alto': DAVID ABUJDER DAJUT

UNIVERSIDAD NACIONAL DE ORIENTE
(National University of the East)

Calle Libertad Esq. Andres Ibañez, Santa Cruz de la Sierra
Telephone: (3) 333-7577
E-mail: uno@uno.edu.bo
Internet: www2.uno.edu.bo

Founded 1999
State control

Rector: BORIS SANTOS GÓMEZ ÚZQUEDA
Vice-Rector for Academic Affairs: GIOVANNA MEDINA CAMARA
Vice-Rector for Admin. and Finance: Lic. NANCY LLANO
Sec.-Gen.: Abog. EDUARDO ENRIQUE ROCA DIAZ DE OROPEZA

DEANS

Faculty of Biochemistry and Pharmacy: Dra CAROLA VARGAS MENESES
Faculty of Dentistry: Dra PATRICIA MARTINEZ
Faculty of Law: Dr ANDRÉS SOSSA LINO
Faculty of Medicine: Dr HURTADO LORGIO
Faculty of Physiotherapy and Kinesiology: Lic. RENÉ WILSON PEREZ

UNIVERSIDAD NACIONAL 'SIGLO XX'
('Siglo XX' National University)

Calle Campero 36, Llallagua
Telephone: (2) 582-0222
E-mail: rectorado@unsxx.edu.bo
Internet: www.unsxx.edu.bo

Founded 1985
State control

Rector: Lic. PABLO RAMIRO MARTINEZ BUSTILLOS
Vice-Rector: JULIO OLIVAREZ ALANEZ
Chief Admin. Officer: VICTOR MAMANI ALVAREZ
Dir-Gen. for Extension: TERESA ALVARO CARRASCO
Dir-Gen. for Research: MARCIAL PLAZA SANTOS
Librarian: FLAVIO FERNÁNDEZ MARISCAL

UNIVERSIDAD NUR
(Nur University)

Av. Cristo Redentor No 100, Santa Cruz de la Sierra
Telephone: (3) 336-3939
E-mail: info@nur.edu
Internet: www.nur.edu

Founded 1985
Private control
Language of instruction: Spanish

Rector: Lic. WILLIAM SHOAIE

UNIVERSIDAD PRIVADA ABIERTA LATINOAMERICANA
(Latin American Private Open University)

Tupac Amaru 1800 Esq. Paso del Inca, Cochabamba
Telephone: (4) 445-4795
E-mail: upal@upal.edu
Internet: www.upal.edu

Founded 1990
Private control

Faculties of biochemistry and pharmacy, dentistry, marketing, medicine, psychology, social communication

Rector: Mgr. PATRICIA MIRANDA CHAVEZ
Vice-Rector: Mgr. RAMIRO FERNANDEZ GOMEZ
Vice-Rector for Admin.: Mgr. JIMMY CAMACHO VILLAZÓN

UNIVERSIDAD PRIVADA BOLIVIANA
(Bolivian Private University)

Avda Capitan Ustariz, km 6.5, Cochabamba
Telephone: (4) 437-7048
E-mail: upb@upb.edu
Internet: www.upb.edu

Private control

Rector: MANUEL OLAVE SARMIENTO
Vice-Rector for Academic Affairs: ALBERTO SANJINÉS UNZUETA
Vice-Rector for Admin. and Finance: Dr CARLOS AGUSTÍN ITURRICHA FERNÁNDEZ
Gen. Sec.: JUAN ANTONIO FERNÁNDEZ LEÓN

Publication: *Revistas Anteriores I & D*

DEANS

Faculty of Business and Law, Cochabamba: MARÍA ISABEL PUEYO ROY
Faculty of Business and Law, La Paz: OSCAR JORGE MOLINA TEJERINA
Faculty of Engineering, La Paz: OSCAR ALVARO VALDIVIESO TABORGA
Faculty of Engineering and Architecture, Cochabamba: Dr CÉSAR WILDE VILLAGOMEZ VILLARROEL

UNIVERSIDAD PRIVADA CUMBRE
(Cumbre Private University)

Avda Cantono No 580, entre Calle Mexico y Avda Centenario, Santa Cruz
Telephone: (3) 333-1319
E-mail: info@cumbre.edu.bo
Internet: www.cumbre.edu.bo

Private control
Language of instruction: Spanish

Faculties of business sciences, law, science and technology, social sciences

Rector: Dra SALOMÉ NASICA AZOGUE
Vice-Rector for Academic Affairs: Dr JOSÉ SAMIR MAKAREN CHÁVEZ
Sec.-Gen.: Lic. ANGELINO VASQUEZ ROCA

UNIVERSIDAD PRIVADA DE SANTA CRUZ DE LA SIERRA
(Private University of Santa Cruz de la Sierra)

Avda Paraguá y 4to. Anillo, Santa Cruz de la Sierra
Telephone: (3) 346-4000
E-mail: informaciones@upsa.edu.bo
Internet: www.upsa.edu.bo

Founded 1984
Private control
Language of instruction: Spanish

Rector: Lic. LAUREN MÜLLER DE PACHECO
Dir for Academic Affairs: Lic. VANYA ROCA URIOSTE
Dir for Research and Graduate Studies: Lic. JORGE ESTENSSORO MORENO
Sec.-Gen.: Lic. ROBERTO ANTELO SCOTT

DEANS

Faculty of Architecture, Design and Urbanism: Dr Arq. VICTOR HUGO LIMPIAS ORTIZ
Faculty of Business Sciences: Lic. MARY ESTHER PARADA DE SAUCEDO
Faculty of Engineering: Dr Ing. JAVIER ALANOCA GUTIÉRREZ
Faculty of Humanities and Communication: Lic. INGRID STEINBACH MÉNDEZ
Faculty of Law and Social Sciences: Dr FERNANDO NÚÑEZ JIMÉNEZ

UNIVERSIDAD PRIVADA DEL VALLE
(Private University of the Valley)

Calle Guillermina Martínez s/n, Tiquipaya, Cochabamba
Telephone: (4) 431-8800
Internet: www.univalle.edu

Founded 1988
Private control

Faculty of business and social sciences

Rector: Ing. GONZALO RUIZ MARTINEZ

Publications: *Compass Empresarial*, *Journal Boliviano de Ciencias* (online), *Revista de Investigacion e Informacion en Salud* (online)

DEANS

Faculty of Architecture and Tourism: ALBERTO ZEGARRA DORADO
Faculty of Health Sciences: CARLOS IRIARTE SAAVEDRA
Faculty of Informatics and Electronics: JUAN LUIS SILES HINOJOSA
Faculty of Technology: AUGUSTO CUADROS PRADO

UNIVERSIDAD PRIVADA DOMINGO SAVIO
(Dominic Savio Private University)

Avda Beni y 3er, Anillo Externo, Santa Cruz de la Sierra
Telephone: (3) 342-6600
Internet: www.upds.edu.bo

Founded 2001
Private control
Language of instruction: Spanish

Rector: CARLOS CUELLAR
Vice-Rector: WILSON ROSAS
Vice-Rector for Admin.: NORMA PACHECO
Sec.-Gen.: ISABEL ESTRADA
Librarian: JUAN CARLOS VIRUEZ A

DEANS

Faculty of Business Sciences: ROGER CHOQUE
Faculty of Humanities: JULVI MOLINA
Faculty of Law: JUAN PABLO SALDANA
Faculty of Technology: WILMER CAMPAS

UNIVERSIDAD PRIVADA FRANZ TAMAYO
(Franz Tamayo Private University)

Calle Héroes del Acre No 1855, Esq. Landaeta, La Paz

Telephone: (2) 248-4300
E-mail: informaciones@unifranz.edu.bo
Internet: www.unifranz.edu.bo

Founded 1993
Private control

Faculties of design and technology cross-media, economics and business, engineering, heath sciences, law and social sciences

Pres.: Arq. ABEL ÁGREDA MÉNDEZ
Vice-Pres.: Arq. VERÓNICA DE PAZOS
Rector: Dr PEDRO SÁENZ MUÑOZ

UNIVERSIDAD REAL
(Real University)

Calle Capitán Ravelo No 2329, La Paz

Telephone: (2) 244-4423
E-mail: ecapriles@ureal.edu.bo
Internet: www.ureal.edu.bo

Founded 1999
Private control

Rector: Ing. ESMERALDA CAPRILES ZAPATA
Academic Sec.: Lic. IVONNÉ N. RÍOS MADARIAGA

UNIVERSIDAD SAN FRANCISCO DE ASIS
(St Francis of Assisi University)

Avda 20 de Octubre Esq. Belisario Salinas, La Paz

Telephone: (2) 244-3773
Internet: www.usfa.edu.bo

Founded 2005
Private control
Language of instruction: Spanish

Rector: BORIS CRESPO

UNIVERSIDAD SAN FRANCISCO XAVIER DE CHUQUISACA
(St Francis Xavier of Chuquisaca University)

Regimiento Campos 180, Sucre

Telephone: (4) 645-3308
E-mail: dsa@usfx.info
Internet: www.usfx.info

Founded 1624
State control
Language of instruction: Spanish
Academic year: February to December (2 semesters)

Rector: Ing. WALTER ARÍZAGA CERVANTES
Vice-Rector: Ing. EDUARDO RIVERO ZURITA
Sec.-Gen.: EDGAR PEDRO SÉRNICH CÁCERES
Librarian: Dr RONALD GANTIER LEMOINE

Number of teachers: 1,000
Number of students: 37,000

Publications: *Archivos Bolivianos de Medicina, Revista del Instituto de Sociología Boliviana*

DEANS

Faculty of Agricultural Sciences: Ing. CARLOS PÉREZ POZOS
Faculty of Chemical, Pharmaceutical and Biochemical Sciences: Dr JUAN CARLOS PIZARRO CORTEZ
Faculty of Dentistry: Dr FERNANDO CAMARGO ARIZAGA
Faculty of Economics and Business: Lic. EDWIN VELASQUEZ SARAVIA
Faculty of Humanities: Lic. JUAN HINOJOSA GONZALEZ
Faculty of Law, Political and Social Sciences: Dra DORIS VIRGINIA KOLLE CASO
Faculty of Medicine: Dr PEDRO LEDEZMA MIRANDA
Faculty of Nursing and Midwifery: Lic. NANCY WILMA MANJÓN CALVIMONTES
Faculty of Public Accounting: Lic. EINER GONZALES GARCIA
Faculty of Technology: Ing. RICARDO CABALLERO CLAURE
Technical Faculty: Arq. HUMBERTO QUIROGA RIERA

UNIVERSIDAD SIMÓN I. PATIÑO
(Simón I. Patiño University)

Avda Villazón No 22, km 1A Sacaba, Cochabamba

Telephone: (4) 453-9930
E-mail: info@usip.edu.bo
Internet: www.usip.edu.bo

Founded 2007
Private control

Faculties of engineering, law, management and finance, natural resources management and environment, science and arts

Rector: SANTIAGO SOLOGUREN PAZ
Academic Dir: CIRO MIRANDA URIBE
Admin. Dir: AIDA MACILLA

UNIVERSIDAD TÉCNICA DE ORURO
(Technical University of Oruro)

Avda 6 de Octubre entre Ayacucho y Cochabamba, Oruro

Telephone: (252) 528-1745
E-mail: rectorado@uto.edu.bo
Internet: www.uto.edu.bo

Founded 1892
State control
Language of instruction: Spanish
Academic year: January to November

Rector: RUBEN MEDINACELI ORTIZ
Vice-Rector: Lic. AUGUSTO VELA CHACON
Gen. Sec.: Dr RAUL ARAOZ VELASCO
Admin. and Finance Dir: Lic. ALBERTO JAEN FUENTES
Librarian: SOFÍA A. ZUBIETA

Number of teachers: 487
Number of students: 10,403

Publications: *Revista de Cultura Boliviana, Revista de Derecho, Revista de Economía, Revista de Mecánica, Revista Metalúrgica, Revista Universitaria*

DEANS

Faculty of Agriculture, Animal and Veterinary Sciences: Ing. OSCAR IÑIGUEZ GUTIERRES
Faculty of Architecture and Town Planning: Arq. ANIBAL GUSTAVO VARGAS OROZA
Faculty of Economics and Finance: Lic. BENIGNO CABALLERO CLAURE
Faculty of Engineering: Ing. RAMIRO FRANZ ALIENDRE GARCIA
Faculty of Health Sciences: Dr OSCAR RODRIGO BALLADARES
Faculty of Legal, Political and Social Sciences: Dr MARCO ERNESTO JAIMES MOLINA
Technical College: Lic. FRANCISCO LAZARTE MARTINEZ

UNIVERSIDAD TÉCNICA PRIVADA COSMOS
(Cosmos Private Technical University)

Avda Blanco Galindo, km 7 1/2 Florida Norte, Bloque Central, Cochabamba

Telephone: (4) 437-4740
Internet: www.unitepc.edu.bo

Founded 1993
Private control

UNIVERSIDAD TECNOLÓGICA PRIVADA DE SANTA CRUZ
(Private Technological University of Santa Cruz)

Avda Noel Kempff Mercado, 3er, Anillo Interno No 715, Santa Cruz de la Sierra

Telephone: (3) 363-9000
E-mail: informaciones@utepsa.edu
Internet: www.utepsa.edu

Founded 1994
Private control
Language of instruction: Spanish

Faculties of business studies, law and social sciences, science and technology

Rector: Lic. L. ANTONIO CARVALHO SUÁREZ

Schools of Art and Music

Conservatorio Nacional de Música (National Conservatory of Music): Calle Reyes Ortiz Esq. Bravo, La Paz; tel. (2) 373-297; internet www.bolivia.com/empresas/cultura/conservatorio_musica/index.asp; f. 1907; library: 420 books, 3,900 scores; Dir ANTONIO ROBERTO BORDA.

Escuela Superior de Bellas Artes 'Hernando Siles' ('Hernando Siles' School of Fine Arts): Calle Rosendo Gutiérrez 323, La Paz; tel. (2) 244-2141; f. 1926; 210 students; Dir ALBERTO MEDINA MENDIETA.

BOSNIA AND HERZEGOVINA

The Higher Education System

Bosnia and Herzegovina emerged in its present form from the conflict that, from 1991, engulfed the republics hitherto constituting Yugoslavia. In accordance with the General Framework Agreement for Peace in Bosnia and Herzegovina, signed in 1995, Bosnia and Herzegovina is a single state, which consists of two political entities: the Federation of Bosnia and Herzegovina, principally comprising the Bosniak (Muslim)- and Croat-majority areas, and Republika Srpska, principally comprising the Serb-majority area. Although there is a central (state) Government of Bosnia and Herzegovina, based in Sarajevo, both constituent entities have their own governments. In the Federation of Bosnia and Herzegovina, higher education is the responsibility of the Ministry of Education and Science, based in Mostar, and in the Republika Srpska higher education is overseen by the Ministry of Education and Culture, based in Banja Luka. The state-level Ministry of Civil Affairs is responsible for coordinating the higher education activities of the country's two entities. At present, higher education is centrally funded. Although the cantons are responsible for financing higher education, only three of the 10 existing cantons coincide with university centres. There are no adequate resources at cantonal level for the financing of higher education and there is no provision for inter-cantonal cooperation in higher education. In 2012 talks were being held with European partners to reform higher education funding.

In 2008/09 in the country as a whole 105,488 students attended 39 higher education institutions, in both the public and private sectors, including eight state universities (with some 90 faculties, which were treated as higher education establishments), 14 private universities, specialist institutes and Visoke Skole (high schools/colleges). In August 2003 officials of the Federation, Republika Srpska, the cantonal Governments and the Interim District Government of Brčko signed an agreement to replace the country's three ethnically based education systems with a single unified system. (However, some local authorities remained resistant to the unification of the education system.) In the same year Bosnia and Herzegovina became a signatory to the Bologna Process. However, despite the immediate preparation of a new law pertaining to the implementation of a two-tier higher education system (as well as the European Credit Transfer System, ECTS, and the Diploma Supplement), the new Framework Law on Higher Education was not adopted until 2007. In accordance with this law the Centre for Information and Recognition of Qualifications in Higher Education and the Agency for Development of Higher Education and Quality Assurance were both established in 2008 as independent public organizations. In 2010 the Agency became an associate member of the European Association for Quality Assurance. In 2012, according to the Agency, there were 10 licensed public higher education institutions and 35 private ones.

Higher education admission is made on the basis of a Secondary School Leaving Certificate. Holders of a qualification from a professional school/apprenticeship may have to sit special entrance examinations. Higher education has been reorganized and credited according to the ECTS. Although a three-cycle structure already existed for most fields of study in all countries of former Yugoslavia, the new framework clearly corresponds with the Bologna scheme of three cycles of higher education: Bachelor, Masters and Doctoral programmes. According to the old, established system, there are four university degrees: two at undergraduate level (Diploma Višeg Obrazovanje and Diploma Visokog Obrazovanja) and two at postgraduate level (Magistar and Doktor Nauka). The Diploma Višeg Obrazovanje (Diploma of Higher Education) is a two- to three-year course, resulting in a professional title, but is not a full degree. The Diploma Visokog Obrazovanja (Advanced Diploma of Higher Education) is a full degree course of four to six years leading to a professional title. The Bologna undergraduate Bachelors degrees typically last for three to four years (earning 180 to 240 ECTS points). Upon completion students are awarded the title of Bachelor of Arts or Science. At postgraduate level, the Magistar (Masters) requires two years of research and defence of a thesis, and the Doktor Nauka (Doctor of Science) requires further research and defence of a thesis, but in a non-specified time frame. PhD courses can be taken after completing a postgraduate university course and typically last for three years. Higher education institutions also offer postgraduate specialist courses which last for one to two years (carrying 60 to 120 ECTS points) and through which students are awarded the title of a specialist in a profession or a certain specialist field (such as medicine).

In addition, Radnicki/Narodni Univerziteti (Workers'/People's Universities) offer a large variety of courses lasting from as little as two weeks to as much as two years. These institutions do not award degrees but offer specialized courses leading to a particular vocational qualification and are used mainly to rectify earlier deficiencies in an individual's education. Although these universities have proved popular since the Second World War, the number of students attending them is now decreasing. Two-year professional and technical courses are also offered by Vise Skole (post-secondary schools). These courses are also available at universities leading to the Diploma Višeg Obrazovanje.

Regulatory and Representative Bodies

GOVERNMENT

Federal Ministry of Culture and Sports: Obala Maka Dizdara 2, 71000 Sarajevo; tel. (33) 254-100; e-mail kabinet@fmksa.com; internet www.fmks.gov.ba; Minister SALMIR KAPLAN.

Federal Ministry of Education and Science: Ante Starčevića bb., 88000 Mostar; tel. (36) 355-700; e-mail info@fmon.gov.ba; internet www.fmon.gov.ba; Minister DAMIR MAŠIĆ.

ACCREDITATION

ENIC/NARIC Bosnia and Herzegovina: Min. of Civil Affairs, Sektor za obrazovanje/Education Sector (Unit for Collecting ENIC-NARIC Information), Vilsonovo šetalište 10, 71000 Sarajevo; tel. (33) 655-339; e-mail miljan.popic@mcp.gov.ba; internet www.mcp.gov.ba; Contact MILJAN POPIĆ.

Learned Societies

GENERAL

Akademija Nauka i Umjetnosti BiH (Academy of Sciences and Arts of Bosnia and Herzegovina): Bistrik 7, 71000 Sarajevo; tel. (33) 206-034; e-mail akademija@anubih.ba; internet www.anubih.ba; f. 1951 as the Scientific Soc., present name and status 1966; attached research institute: see Research Institutes; responsible for the overall devt of science and the arts by organizing scientific research and arts-related events, publishing papers written by its members and associates; 57 mems; library of 50,000 vols; Pres. Dr BOŽIDAR MATIĆ; Vice-Pres. Dr SLOBODAN LOGA; Sec.-Gen. Dr ZIJO PAŠIĆ; publs *Godišnjak* (Annals), *Herbologia*, *Ljetopis* (Yearbook), *Sarajevo Journal of Mathematics* (2 a year).

Hrvatsko Kulturno Društvo 'Napredak' (Napredak Croatian Cultural Society): Središnja uprava, Ulica Maršala Tita 56, 71000 Sarajevo; tel. (33) 222-876; e-mail ured@napredak.com.ba; internet www.napredak

.com.ba; f. 1902; 20,000 mems; Pres. FRANJO TOPIĆ; Sec.-Gen. VANJA RAVEN; publ. *Stecak* (cultural and social issues, 12 a year).

Srpsko Prosvjetno Kulturno Društvo 'Prosvjeta' Sarajevo (Prosvjeta Serbian Cultural and Educational Society, Sarajevo): Sime Milutinovića-Sarajlije 1, 71000 Sarajevo; tel. (33) 444-230; e-mail prosvjeta@bih.net.ba; internet www.prosvjeta.com.ba; f. 1902; science, art and literature; 220 mems; library of 3,000 vols; Pres. SAVO VLAŠKI; Gen. Sec. NENAD MARILOVIĆ; publ. *Bosanska Vila*.

Udruženje Gradjana Bošnjačka Zajednica Kulture 'Preporod' u BiH (Preporod Cultural Association of the Bosniak Community of Bosnia and Herzegovina): Branilaca Sarajeva 30, 71000 Sarajevo; tel. (33) 205-553.

UNESCO Office Sarajevo: Titova 48/4, 71000 Sarajevo; tel. (33) 222-792; e-mail sarajevo@unesco.org; Dir COLIN KAISER.

AGRICULTURE, FISHERIES AND VETERINARY SCIENCE

Bosnia and Herzegovina Small Animal Veterinary Association: Alipašina St 37, 71000 Sarajevo; tel. (33) 442-303; e-mail veterins@bih.net.ba; Pres. Dr JOSIP KRASNI.

ARCHITECTURE AND TOWN PLANNING

Društvo Urbanista Bosne i Hercegovine (Society of Town Planning of Bosnia and Herzegovina): Zavod za urbanizam, Aleja bosanskih vladara 6, 75000 Tuzla; tel. (35) 252-038; f. 1993; 500 mems; Pres. ZEHRA MORANKIĆ; publ. *URBO* (1 a year).

BIBLIOGRAPHY, LIBRARY SCIENCE AND MUSEOLOGY

Društvo Arhivskih Radnika Bosne i Hercegovine (Association of Archive Workers of Bosnia and Herzegovina): Franje Ledera 1, 75000 Tuzla; tel. (35) 252-620; Pres. Dr AZEM KOŽAR; publ. *Glasnik Arhiva i Društva Arhivski Radnika Bosne i Hercegovine* (1 a year).

Društvo Bibliotekara BiH (Librarians' Society of Bosnia and Herzegovina): Zmaja od Bosne 8B, 71000 Sarajevo; tel. (33) 275-325; f. 1949; 450 mems; Pres. NEVENKA HAJDAROVIĆ; publs *Bibliotekarstvo* (1 a year), *Bilten*.

ECONOMICS, LAW AND POLITICS

Advokatska Komora FBiH (Bar Association of Federation of Bosnia and Herzegovina): Obala Kulina Bana 6, 71000 Sarajevo; tel. (33) 261-090; internet www.advokomfbih.ba; Pres. BRANKO MARIĆ.

Advokatska-Odvjetnicka Komora Federacije Bosne i Hercegovine (Bar Association of the Federation of Bosnia and Herzegovina): Obala Kulina Bana 6, 71000 Sarajevo; tel. (33) 261-090; e-mail adkomfbh@bih.net.ba; internet www.advokomfbih.ba; 830 mems, incl. 670 attorneys and 160 law trainees; Pres. AMILA KUNOSIĆ-FERIZOVIĆ.

Udruženje Sudija i Sudaca u Federacije Bosne i Hercegovine (Association of Judges of the Federation of Bosnia and Herzegovina): Valtera Perića 15, Kancelarija udruženja br. 203, 71000 Sarajevo; tel. (33) 668-035; e-mail usfbih@bih.net.ba; internet www.usfbih.ba; f. 1996; advocacy and training; 320 mems; Pres. VILDANA HELIĆ; Vice-Pres. STJEPAN MIKULIĆ; Vice-Pres. GORAN SALIHOVIĆ; publ. *Mjesečni Casopis*.

Udruženje sudija Republike Srpske (Republic of Srpska Association of Judges): Aleja svetog Save bb., 78000 Banja Luka; tel. (51) 212-801; e-mail zlatko.kulenovic@pravosudje.ba; f. 2005; annual seminars on criminal and civil and administrative law; 300 mems; Pres. ZLATKO KULENOVIĆ; Sec. ŽIVANA BAJIĆ; publ. *Seminar Collected Texts* (3 a year).

EDUCATION

Pedagoško Društvo BiH (Pedagogical Society of Bosnia and Herzegovina): Djure Djakovića 4, 71000 Sarajevo.

FINE AND PERFORMING ARTS

Muzička Omladina Sarajeva BiH (Jeunesses Musicales of Sarajevo): Dalmatinska 2/1, 71000 Sarajevo; tel. (33) 665-713; e-mail muzomlsa@soros.org.ba; internet jm-sa.open.net.ba; f. 1958; organizes concerts and theatre events; 12,000 mems; library of 1,000 vols, record library of 1,000 items; Pres. REŠAD ARNAUTOVIĆ; Sec. SLAVICA ŠPOLJARIĆ.

Udruženje Muzičkih Umjetnika BiH (Association of Musicians of Bosnia and Herzegovina): Sv. Markovicá 1, 71000 Sarajevo.

HISTORY, GEOGRAPHY AND ARCHAEOLOGY

Društvo Istoričara BiH (Historical Society of Bosnia and Herzegovina): Račkog 1, Filozofski fakultet, 71000 Sarajevo.

Geografsko Društvo Republike Srpske (Geographical Society of Republic of Srpska): Mladena Stojanovica 2, 78000 Banja Luka; tel. (51) 235-625; e-mail info@gdrsbl.org; internet www.gdrsbl.org; publ. *Herald* (print and online, in Serbian and English).

Geografsko Društvo u Federaciji BiH (Geographical Society of Federation of Bosnia and Herzegovina): Zmaja od Bosne 35, 71000 Sarajevo; tel. (33) 645-328; e-mail info@geodrustvo.ba; internet www.geodrustvo.ba; f. 1947; 1,540 mems; Pres. Dr NUSRET DREŠKOVIĆ; Sec. EDIN HRELJA; publs *Geografski List* (5 a year), *Geografski Pregled, Nastava Geografije* (1 a year).

LANGUAGE AND LITERATURE

British Council: Ljubljianska 9, 71000 Sarajevo; tel. (33) 250-220; e-mail british.council@britishcouncil.ba; internet www.britishcouncil.ba; offers courses and examinations in English language and British culture; promotes cultural exchange with the UK; f. 1996; library of 6,500 vols; Dir MICHAEL MOORE; Deputy Dir GORJANA ŠEVELJ PEĆANAC.

Društvo Pisaca BiH (Association of Writers of Bosnia and Herzegovina): Kranjčevićeva 24, 71000 Sarajevo; tel. (33) 557-940; e-mail d_pisaca@bih.net.ba; f. 1993; organizes the Int. Festival of Poetry and Sarajevo Poetry days; 165 mems; library of 1,500 vols; Pres. GRADIMIR GOJER; Sec. MUHAMED CUROVAC; publs *Lica i Život* (4 a year), *Slovo* (12 a year).

Goethe-Institut: Bentbaša 1A, 71000 Sarajevo; tel. (33) 570-000; e-mail info@sarajevo.goethe.org; internet www.goethe.de/sarajevo; f. 2000, present bldg 2004; offers courses and examinations in German language and culture and promotes cultural exchange with Germany; Dir Dr PETRA RAYMOND; Deputy Dir Dr NINA WICHMANN.

PEN Centar u BiH (PEN Centre of Bosnia and Herzegovina): Vrazova 1, 71000 Sarajevo; tel. (33) 200-155; e-mail pencentear@bih.net.ba; internet www.penbih.ba; f. 1992; freedom of expression, dialogue culture, writing without borders, literary critics, and meetings connected to the above-mentioned issues; mem. of the PEN Int. org.; 92 mems; Pres. UGO VLAISAVLJEVIĆ; Exec. Dir. FERIDA DURAKOVIĆ; publ. *Novi Izraz, Literary and Art Critics Review* (4 a year).

MEDICINE

Društvo Ljekara BiH (Physicians' Society of Bosnia and Herzegovina): Zavod za zdravst-venu zaštitu BiH, Maršala Tita 7, 71000 Sarajevo.

Farmaceutsko društvo Republike Srpske (Pharmaceutical Society of Republika Srpske): Ranka Šipke 32, 78000 Banja Luka; tel. (51) 318-699; e-mail farmacia@teol.net; internet www.farmaceutskodrustvo.org; f. 1996; br. offices in Banja Luka, Doboj, Bijeljina, Foca, Sarajevo, Prijedor, Trebinje and Zvornik; training programmes, devt of health education; Pres. RADA AMIDŽIĆ.

Udruga/Udruženje Pedijatara u Bosni i Hercegovini (Paediatric Society in Bosnia and Herzegovina): Sveučilisna klinička bolnica Mostar Klinika za dječje bolest, 88000 Mostar; tel. (36) 343-348; e-mail tajnica@upubih.org; internet www.upubih.org; f. 2006 as legal successor of the Paediatric Asscn of Bosnia and Herzegovina in Sarajevo, registered with the Min. of Justice; disease prevention and health care; Pres. ZELJKO RONCEVIĆ; Vice-Pres. AMIRA SKAKA; Vice-Pres. ZDRAVKO KUZMAN.

Udruženje Farmakologa Federacije Bosne i Hercegovine (Association of Pharmacologists of the Federation of Bosnia and Herzegovina): Čekaluša 90/II, 71000 Sarajevo; tel. (33) 226-973; e-mail farma@bih.net.ba; f. 1980; organizes symposia, congresses; 68 mems; library of 5,000 vols; Pres. Prof. Dr NEDŽAD MULABEGOVIĆ; Sec. Asst Prof. SVJETLANA LOGA; publs *Bosnian Journal of Basic Medical Sciences* (6 a year), *Drug Plus* (1 a year).

Udruženje Stomatologa BiH (Dental Association of Bosnia and Herzegovina): School of Dentistry, Bolnicka 4A, 71000 Sarajevo; tel. (33) 214-259; e-mail medigan@bih.net.ba; internet www.usfbih.org.ba; f. 1997; 500 mems; Pres. Prof. MAIDA GANIBEGOVIĆ; Gen. Sec. DAJANA ČOLIĆ; publ. *Bilten Stomatologia BiH* (3 a year, in the nat. languages of Bosnia and Herzegovina and in English).

NATURAL SCIENCES

General

Društvo Fizičara u BiH (Physical Society in Bosnia and Herzegovina): Zmaja od Bosne 35, zgrada Prirodno-matematički fakultet, 71000 Sarajevo; tel. (33) 653-294; e-mail dfubih@gmail.com; internet www.drustvofizicara.com.ba; organizes competitions, seminars and lectures for the popularization of physics; Pres. RAJFA MUSEMIĆ; Vice-Pres. SLAVICA EREŠ-BRKIĆ; Vice-Pres REFIK FAZLIĆ; Vice-Pres. ZALKIDA HADŽIBEGOVIĆ.

Mathematical Sciences

Društvo Matematičara Republike Srpske (Society of Mathematicians of Republika Srpska): Bana Lazarevića 1, 78000 Banja Luka; tel. (51) 268-686.

PHILOSOPHY AND PSYCHOLOGY

Društvo Psihologa BiH (Association of Psychologists of Bosnia and Herzegovina): Aleja lipa 81, 71000 Sarajevo; tel. (33) 659-184; e-mail sekretar@dpfbih.ba; internet www.dpfbih.ba.

Društvo Psihologa Republike Srpske (Association of Psychologists of Republika Srpske): Bana Lazarevića 1, treći sprat, soba 47, 78000 Banja Luka; e-mail dprs@drustvo-psihologa.rs.ba; internet www.drustvo-psihologa.rs.ba; f. 2003; devt and application of theoretical and applied psychology; org. of professional education; Pres. Dr MILENA PASIĆ; Vice-Pres. SINISA LAKIĆ.

Research Institutes

GENERAL

Bošnjački Institut—Fondacija Adila Zulfikarpašića (Bosniak Institute—Adil Zulfikarpasic Foundation): Mula Mustafe Bašeskije 21, 71000 Sarajevo; tel. (33) 279-800; e-mail info@bosnjackiinstitut.ba; internet www.bosnjackiinstitut.ba; f. 1988 in Zurich, in Sarajevo 2001; researches into history, literature, art, language and religion of Bosniaks and other people of Bosnia and Herzegovina and promotion of their cultural and historical heritage; library of 150,000 vols; Dir AMINA RIZVANBEGOVIĆ DZUVIĆ; Archivist AMHET ZULFIKARPASIĆ; Head Librarian NARCISA PULJEK-BUBRIC.

Centre for Philosophical Research: Bistrik 7, 71000 Sarajevo; tel. (33) 560-700; e-mail akademija@anubih.ba; internet www.anubih.ba; attached to Acad. of Sciences and Arts of Bosnia and Herzegovina; Dir VLADIMIR PREMEC; publ. *Dialogue* (4 a year).

Kantonalni Zavod za Zaštitu Kulturno-Historisjkog i Prirodnog Naslijedja Sarajevo (Institute for the Protection of the Cultural, Historical and Natural Heritage of the Canton of Sarajevo): Josipa Štadlera 32, 71000 Sarajevo; tel. (33) 475-020; e-mail heritsa@bih.net.ba; internet www.spomenici-sa.ba; f. 1965; documentation of monuments; devt projects; surveys and studies; promotes awareness of culture, history and natural heritage; library of 15,000 vols; Dir MUNIB BULJINA; Exec. Dir VALIDA ČELIĆ-ČEMERLIĆ.

Orijentalni Institut u Sarajevu (Oriental Institute, Sarajevo): Zmaja od Bosne 8B, 71000 Sarajevo; tel. (33) 225-353; e-mail ois@bih.net.ba; internet www.ois.unsa.ba; f. 1950; history, philology and culture of the Ottoman Balkans and the Middle East; library of 10,900 vols, 1,640 periodicals; Scientific Advisor and Dir Dr BEHIJA ZLATAR; Archivist HADŽIJA HADŽIABDIĆ; publ. *Prilozi za orijentalnu filologiju/Revue de philologie orientale* (1 a year).

Zavod za Zaštitu Kulturnog, Historijskog i Prirodnog Naslijedja BiH (Institute for the Protection of the Cultural, Historical and Natural Heritage of Bosnia and Herzegovina): Alekse Šantića 8/III, 71000 Sarajevo; tel. (33) 663-299; e-mail h_c_bih@bih.net.ba; f. 1947; protection and preservation of monuments; conservation, registering of moveable and non-moveable heritage; colln of documents; raising awareness and evaluation of heritage, projects and studies; Dir DŽIHAD PAŠIĆ; publ. *Naše Starine*.

ARCHITECTURE AND TOWN PLANNING

Centar za Islamsku Arhitektura (Centre for Islamic Architecture): Blvr Mese Selimovića 85, 71000 Sarajevo; tel. (33) 459-780; e-mail centaria@bih.net.ba; internet www.rijaset.ba; f. 1995; attached to Rijaset Islamske Zajednice u Bosni i Hercegovini (Islamic Community in Bosnia and Herzegovina); restoration and reconstruction of damaged and destroyed religious sites; Dir KEMAL ZUKIĆ.

ECONOMICS, LAW AND POLITICS

Ekonomski Institut Sarajevo (Institute of Economics, Sarajevo): Branilaca Sarajevo 47, 71000 Sarajevo; tel. (33) 565-870; e-mail ekonomski.institut@efsa.unsa.ba; internet www.eis.ba; f. 1961; economic research for improvement of public policy and business consulting services, increasing competitiveness in the business sector; library of 12,400 vols; Dir Dr ANTO DOMAZET.

Ekonomski Institut Tuzla (Tuzla Institute of Economics): Zvonka Cerića 1, 75000 Tuzla; tel. (35) 214-657; Dir SEAD BABOVIĆ.

Human Rights Centre: Zmaja od Bosne 8, 71000 Sarajevo; tel. (33) 668-251; e-mail research@hrc.unsa.ba; internet www.hrc.unsa.ba; f. 1996; attached to Univ. of Sarajevo; contributes to the implementation of int. human rights through education and training, research and consulting, documentation and information services; library of 8,261 vols, 6,780 monographs, 828 serials, 658 theses; Dir SAŠA MADACKI; Librarian AIDA HAJRO; Librarian MAJA KALJANAC; Librarian NINA KARAĆ.

Institut za istraživanje zločina protiv čovječnosti i međunarodnog prava (Institute for Research of Crimes Against Humanity and International Law): ul. Halida Nazecica 4, 71000 Sarajevo; tel. (33) 561-350; e-mail info@institut-genocid.ba; internet www.institut-genocid.ba; f. 1992; attached to Univ. of Sarajevo; public scientific institution; provides analysis of crimes against int. law, human rights violations and genocide; Chair. for Board of Management Prof. Dr ISMET DIZDAREVIĆ; Chair. for Scientific Ccl Prof. Dr SMAIL ČEKIĆ.

HISTORY, GEOGRAPHY AND ARCHAEOLOGY

Institut za Istoriju (Institute of History): Alipašina 9, 71000 Sarajevo; tel. (33) 209-364; e-mail nauka@bih.net.ba; internet www.iis.unsa.ba; f. 1959; public research institute; deals with research work in field of history; library of 3,000 journals, 12,070 monographs, rare periodicals from the prewar and 1941–45 period; Dir Dr HUSNIJA KAMBEROVIĆ; Pres. Prof. Dr MUSTAFA IMAMOVIĆ; Sec. ASIDE ŠAHBEGOVIĆ; publ. *Prilozi* (Contributions, 1 a year).

LANGUAGE AND LITERATURE

Institut za Jezik (Institute of Language): Hasana Kikića 12, 71000 Sarajevo; tel. (33) 200-117; internet www.izj.unsa.ba; Dir ALEN KALAJDZIJA.

Language Institute: Hasana Kikića 12, 71000 Sarajevo; tel. (33) 200-117; e-mail insjezik@bih.net.ba; f. 1973; library of 3,200 vols; Dir Dr IBRAHIM ČEDIĆ; publs *Dijalektološki Zbornik* (Dialect Colln, irregular), *Književni jezik* (Literary Language, 4 a year), *Radovi* (Works, 1 a year).

Media Plan Institute: Antuna Branka Šimića 5/2, 71000 Sarajevo; tel. (33) 717-840; e-mail mediaplan@mediaplan.ba; internet www.mediaplan.ba; f. 1995; research into and analysis of the media; press clippings; educational projects, media campaigns, communication training; audiovisual productions; Pres. ZORAN UDOVIĆIĆ; Exec. Dir BOJANA ŠUTVIĆ.

NATURAL SCIENCES

Mathematical Sciences

Agencija za Statistiku Bosne i Hercegovine (Agency for Statistics of Bosnia and Herzegovina): Zelenih beretki 26, 71000 Sarajevo; tel. (33) 911-911; e-mail bhas@bhas.ba; internet www.bhas.ba; f. 1998; dir and 2 deputies consisting of 1 Serb, 1 Croat and 1 Muslim; documents statistical changes in economic, demographic and social fields, environment and natural resources; Dir ZDENKO MILINOVIĆ; Asst Dir MAIDA HASANBEGOVIC; publ. *First Release* (irregular).

Federalni Zavod za Statistiku (Institute of Statistics of the Federation of Bosnia and Herzegovina): Zeleni beretki 26, 71000 Sarajevo; tel. (33) 664-553; e-mail fedstat@fzs.ba; internet www.fzs.ba; f. 1997; organizes and conducts statistical research; library of 6,940 vols; Dir DERVIŠ ĐURĐEVIĆ; Sec. SUADA ĆUKOJEVIĆ; publs *Federacija BiH u Brojkama* (1 a year), *GDP* (1 a year), *Kanton u Brojkama* (1 a year), *Obrazovanje* (1 a year), *Poljoprivedra* (1 a year), *Pravosudje* (1 a year), *Socjalna Zaštita* (Statistical Bulletin, 1 a year), *Statistički Godisnjak* (1 a year), *Statistički Podaci o Privrednim i Drugim Kretanjima u Federacije BiH* (12 a year), *Statistički Podaci o Privrednim i Drugim Kretanjim o Kantonima* (12 a year), *Zaposlenost i Plaće* (1 a year).

Republički Zavod za Statistiku Republike Srpske (Republika Srpska Institute of Statistics): Veljka Mlađenovića 12D, 78000 Banja Luka; tel. (51) 332-700; e-mail stat@rzs.rs.ba; internet www.rzs.rs.ba; f. 1992; attached to Min. of Finance; performs statistical activity for the territory of Republika Srpska; Dir SLAVKO ŠOBOT; publs *Statistical Yearbook* (1 a year), *This is Republika Srpska* (1 a year, in Bosnian (Cyrillic) and English).

Physical Sciences

Federalni Meteorološki Zavod (Federal Hydrometeorological Institute): Bardakčije 12, 71000 Sarajevo; tel. (33) 276-701; e-mail kontakt@fhmzbih.gov.ba; internet www.fhmzbih.gov.ba; Dir ENES SARAČ.

Geodetski Zavod Bosne i Hercegovine (Geodetic Institute of Bosnia and Herzegovina): Blvr Meše Selimovića 95, 71000 Sarajevo; tel. (33) 469-357.

Institute of Meteorology: Hadži Loje 4, 71000 Sarajevo; f. 1891; Dir M. V. VEMIĆ.

Metalurški Institut 'Kemal Kapetanović' (Kemal Kapetanović Metallurgical Institute): Travnička cesta 7, 72000 Zenica; tel. (32) 247-999; e-mail miz@miz.ba; internet www.miz.ba; f. 1961, fmrly Hasan Brkić; attached to Univ. in Zenica; depts in physical metallurgy, chemistry, heat engineering, welding, metal casting, electrical engineering and automation; conducts research and devt in natural sciences, technological and architectural engineering, technical testing and analysis, education-related activities; Dir Dr MIRSADA ORUČ.

Zavod za Geologiju (Institute of Geology): Ustanička 11, Ilidža 71210 Sarajevo; tel. (33) 621-567; e-mail zgeolbih@bih.net.ba; internet www.fzzg.ba; f. 1946 as Geologic Research Institute of the Ministry of Industry and Mining; Asst Dir ALOJZ FILIPOVIĆ.

TECHNOLOGY

Institut za standardizaciju BiH (Institute for Standardization of Bosnia and Herzegovina): V. Radomira Putnika 34, 71123 Sarajevo; tel. (57) 310-560; e-mail stand@bas.gov.ba; internet www.bas.gov.ba; f. 1992 as Institut za standarde, mjeriteljstvo i intelektualno vlasništvo, current name adopted 2007; proposes the strategy of standardization in Bosnia and Herzegovina; participates in preparing technical regulations, develops and establishes the information system of standards; organizes and carries out specialist education of personnel in standardization area; adopted more than 12,000 int. and European standards by endorsement method; library of 950 vols; Dir GORAN TESANOVIĆ (acting); publ. *Glasnik Standardizacije* (4 a year).

Rudarski Institut: Rudarska 72, 75000 Tuzla; tel. (35) 282-406; e-mail rituzla@bih.net.ba; internet www.rudarski-institut.com

.ba; f. 1960; planning and consulting in mining, electrical, mechanical and civil engineering, geology, geo-engineering, occupational safety and environmental protection, testing materials and constructions; Dir Dr RASIM PIRIĆ.

Libraries and Archives

Banja Luka

Arhiv Republike Srpske (Archives of Republika Srpska): ul. Svetog Save 1, 78000 Banja Luka; tel. (51) 340-240; e-mail arhivrs@inecco.net; internet www.arhivrs.org; f. 1953; attached to Min. of Education and Culture; 12,000 vols, 15,000 photographs, 2,500 m of records from all periods; Dir Prof. LJILJANA RADOSEVIĆ.

Narodna i Univerzitetska Biblioteka Republike Srpske (National and University Library of Republika Srpska): Jevrejska 30, 78000 Banja Luka; tel. (51) 215-894; e-mail nubrs@urc.bl.ac.yu; internet www.nubrs.rs.ba; f. 1936; organizes continuous educational programmes for librarians; 500,000 vols; Dir RANKO RISOJEVIĆ; Library Sec. LJILJANA BABIĆ; publ. *National Bibliography of Republika Srpska*.

Bihać

Arhiv Unsko-sanskog Kantona Bihać (Una-Sana Canton Archives, Bihać): ul. Bosanskih banova 7, 77000 Bihać; tel. (37) 327-384; f. 1988; Dir Prof. OSMAN ALTIĆ.

Javna Biblioteka Unsko-sanskog Kantona (Una-Sana Canton Public Library): Trg Slobode 8, 77000 Bihać; tel. (37) 333-372; f. 1954; Dir REUF MUSTAFIĆ.

Fojnica

Franjevački Samostan Fojnica, Biblioteka (Library of the Franciscan Monastery, Fojnica): 71270 Fojnica; tel. (30) 832-081; e-mail samostan.fojnica@gmail.com; internet www.fojnica-samostan.com; f. 1463; 13,000 vols, 15 incunabula, archives incl. documents in Turkish and Bosnian; Guardian Fra NIKICA VUJICA.

Kraljeva Sutjeska

Franjevački Samostan Kraljeva Sutjeska, Biblioteka (Library of the Franciscan Monastery, Kraljeva Sutjeska): 72244 Kraljeva Sutjeska; tel. (32) 771-700; e-mail urednistvo@kraljeva-sutjeska.com; internet www.kraljeva-sutjeska.com; f. 1350; 11,000 vols, 31 incunabula, archives incl. parish registers and MSS in Bosnian Cyrillic and Turkish; Guardian ZORAN JAKOVIĆ.

Kreševo

Franjevački Samostan Kreševo, Biblioteka (Library of the Franciscan Monastery, Kreševo): 71260 Kreševo; tel. (30) 806-075; f. 1767; 25,000 vols, archive; Guardian Fra MATO CVIJETKOVIĆ.

Mostar

Arhiv Hercegovine Mostar (Archives of Herzegovina, Mostar): Trg 1 Maj 17, 88000 Mostar; tel. (36) 551-047; e-mail arhiv@cob.net.ba; f. 1954; records from the 13th century onwards; 9,000 vols; spec. Oriental colln of 800 MSS and 2,000 documents; Dir EDIN ČELEBIĆ; publ. *Hercegovina* (1 a year).

Narodna Biblioteka Mostar (Mostar Public Library): Marsala Tita bb., 88000 Mostar; tel. (36) 551-487; e-mail biblioteka@mostar.ba; Dir RASIM PRGUDA.

Mrkonjić Grad

Narodna Biblioteka, Mrkonjić Grad (National Library, Mrkonjić Grad): Svetog Save 1, 70260 Mrkonjić Grad; tel. (50) 220-271; e-mail kontakt@junbmg.info; internet www.junbmg.info; f. 1900 as Serbian Orthodox Church-Nikolajević Glee Club, present bldg 1973; activities incl. literary evenings, book promotions, professional and scientific lectures, exhibitions, round tables and workshops; 20,000 books; Dir BILJANA ĆELIĆ.

Sarajevo

Arhiv Bosne i Hercegovine (Archive of Bosnia and Herzegovina): Reisa Džemaludina Čauševića 6, 71000 Sarajevo; tel. (33) 206-492; e-mail info@arhivbih.gov.ba; internet www.arhivbih.gov.ba; f. 1947, current name adopted 1965; nat. archive; 11,000 m of documents from the 14th century to the present; 20,000 vols; Dir ŠABAN ZAHIROVIĆ; publ. *Glasnik*.

Arhiv Federacije Bosne i Hercegovine (Archive of the Federation of Bosnia and Herzegovina): Reisa Čauševića 6, 71000 Sarajevo; tel. (33) 214-481; e-mail info@arhivfbih.gov.ba; internet www.arhivfbih.gov.ba; f. 1994; entity archive; activities incl. archival processing and preservation, devt of archival service; Dir ADAMIRA JERKOVIĆA.

Biblioteka Grada Sarajeva (Sarajevo City Library): Mis Irbina 4, 71000 Sarajevo; tel. (33) 444-580; e-mail info@bgs.ba; internet www.bgs.ba; f. 1948; collects, restores, preserves and processes professional library materials, old and rare books; promotes information systems; 300,000 vols; Pres. RAMO KOLAR; Dir MESUD SMAJIĆ.

Gazi Husrev-begova biblioteka (Gazi Husrav-Bey Library): Gazi Husrev-begova 46, 71000 Sarajevo; tel. (33) 264960; e-mail ghbibl@bih.net.ba; internet www.ghb.ba; f. 1537; Oriental library; 90,000 vols of catalogue, incl. 11,000 Islamic MSS; Pres. AHMET ALIBAŠIĆ; Dir Dr MUSTAFA JAHIĆ; Sec. HAMIDA KARČIĆ; publs *Anali Gazi Husrevbegove biblioteke, Katalog arapskih, turskih i perzijskih rukopisa*.

Historijski Arhiv Sarajevo (Sarajevo Historical Archives): Alipašina 19, 71000 Sarajevo; tel. (33) 223-281; e-mail has@arhivsa.ba; internet www.arhivsa.ba; f. 1948; archive of the canton and city of Sarajevo; 3,000 m of documents; 20,000 vols; spec. colln of Ottoman MSS; Dir Prof. TONČI GRBELJA; publ. *Glas Arhiva Grada Sarajeva*.

Nacionalna i univerzitetska biblioteka Bosne i Hercegovine (National and University Library of Bosnia and Herzegovina): Zmaja od Bosne 8B, 71000 Sarajevo; tel. (33) 275-301; e-mail nubbih@nub.ba; internet www.nub.ba; f. 1945, destroyed 1992, reconstructed 1995; nat. deposit library; nat. agency for ISSN and ISMN; nat. bibliography centre; centre for permanent education of librarians; nat. centre for cooperative online bibliographic and information system and service; supports univ. research, educational and scientific work; 500,000 vols; Dir Dr ISMET OVČINA.

Zemaljski Muzej Bosne i Hercegovine, Biblioteka (National Museum of Bosnia and Herzegovina, Library): Zmaja od Bosne 3, 71000 Sarajevo; tel. (33) 586-321; e-mail z.muzej@zemaljskimuzej.ba; internet www.zemaljskimuzej.ba; f. 1888, present bldg 1913; archaeology, ethnology and natural sciences; 250,000 vols; Chief Librarian OLGA LALEVIĆ; publs *Glasnik Zemaljskog muzeja BiH—Arheologija* (scientific reports of the museum of Bosnia and Herzegovina; 3 series: Archaeology, Ethnology, Natural History, in Bosnian and English), *Glasnik Zemaljskog muzeja BiH—Etnologija* (scientific and professional reports of the National Museum of Bosnia and Herzegovina: Ethnology), *Glasnik Zemaljskog muzeja BiH—Natural History* (scientific and professional reports of the National Museum of Bosnia and Herzegovina: Natural History, in Bosnian and English).

Travnik

Kantonalni-Županijski Arhiv Travnik (Cantonal and County Archive, Travnik): ul. Školska bb., 72000 Travnik; tel. (30) 511-580; f. 1954; 8,900 m of documents; Dir Prof. JASMINA HOPIĆ.

Tuzla

Arhiv Tuzlanskog kantona (Archives of Tuzla Canton): ul. Franje Ledera 1, 75000 Tuzla; tel. (35) 252-620; e-mail arhiv.tk@bih.net.ba; internet www.arhivtk.com.ba; f. 1954 as Archive of Tuzla, current name adopted 1966; 1,380 m of documents from all periods; 20,000 vols; Dir Dr IZET ŠABOTIĆ; publ. *Archival Practice*.

Narodna i Univerzitetska Biblioteka 'Derviš Sušić' Tuzla (Public and University Library Derviš Sušić, Tuzla): Mihajla i Živka Crnogorčevića 7, 75000 Tuzla; tel. (35) 272-626; e-mail nubtz@nubtz.ba; internet www.nubtz.ba; f. 1946, present status 1986; gen. reference colln; works in science and arts, literature, history and philosophy, domestic and foreign rarities, doctoral and Masters papers, serial publs; 200,000 vols, 10,000 periodicals; Dir ENISA ŽUNIĆ.

Zenica

Opća Biblioteka Zenica (Zenica Public Library): Školska ul. 6, 72000 Zenica; tel. (32) 407-600; e-mail biblioze@biblioze.ba; internet www.biblioze.ba; f. 1954; 78,000 vols; Dir MIDHAT KASAP; Sec. RASMA SEHIC.

Museums and Art Galleries

Banja Luka

Muzej savremene umjetnosti Republike Srpske (Museum of Contemporary Art of Republika Srpska): Trg Srpskih Junaka 2, 78000 Banja Luka; tel. (51) 215-364; e-mail galrs@inecco.net; internet www.msurs.org; f. 1971; history, archaeology, ethnography, history of art, contemporary art, natural history of Republika Srpska; library of 5,500 vols, 500 journals; Dir LJILJANA LABOVIC-MARINKOVIĆ; Man. MILICA RADOJIČIĆ; Curator LANA PILIPOVIC; Curator ZANA VUKICEVIC.

Bihać

Muzej Unsko-sanskog Kantona (Una-Sana Canton Museum): ul. 5 Korpusa 2, 77000 Bihać; tel. (37) 229-743; f. 1953; archaeology, history, natural history, ethnography; attached museums: Kapetanova kula (The Captain's Tower), Museum of the first Session of AVNOJ; Dir DŽAFER MAHMUTOVIĆ.

Bijeljina

Muzej Semberija (Semberija Museum): Karadjordjeva 1, 76300 Bijeljina; tel. (65) 401-293; e-mail mbabic@rstel.net; f. 1970; archaeology, history, ethnography; 5,000 artefacts, 2,000 photographs; Resić collns of ceramics, tapestries by Milica Zorić-Colaković; library of 5,000 vols; Dir MIRKO BABIĆ.

Doboj

Regionalni Muzej Doboj (Doboj Regional Museum): ul. Vidovdanska br. 4, Doboj; tel. (32) 231-220; f. 1956; 16,000 items; archaeology, history, ethnography, photography; Dir DOBRILA BIJELIĆ.

Fojnica

Franjevački Samostan Duha Svetoga Fojnica (Franciscan Monastery Fojnica): ul. Fra Zvizdovića 4, 71270 Fojnica; tel. (30) 832-081; e-mail samostan.fojnica@gmail.com; internet www.fojnica-samostan.com; spec. colln of church clothes embroidered with gold, bishops' clothing and footwear, Roman and Greek coins; documents relating to the Franciscan order, Fojnica monastery and Fojnica, incl. inventories and parish registers, Ottoman land-related documents, 156 documents in Bosnian Cyrillic and 3,000 Turkish documents; Bosnian ecclesiastical and secular history, education, diaries and autograph letters; library of 37,000 vols, 5,500 vols. of old prints, incl. 15 incunabula, Fojnica Arms book, 19th-century periodicals; Guardian NIKICA VUJICA; publ. *Fojnička Škrinja*.

Kreševo

Franjevački Samostan Kreševo (Franciscan Monastery, Kreševo): 71260 Kreševo; tel. (87) 806-075; f. 1767; library of 17,000 vols, 92 periodicals; Guardian Fra MATO CVIJETKOVIĆ.

Mostar

Muzej Hercegovine (Museum of Herzegovina): Bajatova br. 4, 88000 Mostar; tel. (61) 707-307; e-mail muzej.herc@bih.net.ba; internet www.muzejhercegovine.com; f. 1950; archaeology, art, history, ethnography, numismatics; Dir ZDRAVKO ZVONIĆ; publ. *Kingdom Magazine*.

Prijedor

Muzej Kozara (Kozara Museum): Nikole Pašića, 79101 Prijedor; tel. (62) 221-334; f. 1953; regional museum; archaeology, history, ethnography, art; collns incl. 400 paintings of the Prijedor school, 900 archaeological exhibits, 5th century Celtic-Illyrian helmets, 400 artefacts from the Kozara region, 2,000 documents relating to the Second World War; Dir MILENKO RADIVOJEC.

Sarajevo

Ars Aevi—Museum of Contemporary Art Sarajevo: Centar Skenderija, Dom mladih, Terezija bb., 71000 Sarajevo; tel. (33) 216-919; e-mail arsaevi@arsaevi.ba; internet www.arsaevi.ba; f. 1992; contributed works of 161 int. artists form the Ars Aevi Colln; Gen. Dir ENVER HADŽIOMERSPAHIĆ; Exec. Dir AMILA ROMOVIĆ.

Historijski Muzej Bosne i Hercegovine (Historical Museum of Bosnia and Herzegovina): Zmaja od Bosne 5, 71000 Sarajevo; tel. (33) 656-629; e-mail histmuz@bih.net.ba; internet www.muzej.ba; f. 1945, current name adopted 1993, present bldg 1963; history since medieval times; archive material, objects, academic library, documentation centre (300,000 vols); colln of 2,600 paintings incl. work of artists from all regions of the fmr Yugoslavia; library of 20,000 vols; Dir MUHIBA KALJANAC.

Muzej Književnosti BiH (Literary Museum of Bosnia and Herzegovina): Sime Milutinovića Sarajlije 7, 71000 Sarajevo; tel. (33) 471-828; literature and theatre arts; collns incl. MSS, documents, photographs, paintings, books and newspaper clippings; Dir ALEKSANDAR LJILJAK; publ. *Baština*.

Muzej Sarajeva (Museum of Sarajevo): Josipa Štedlera 32, 71000 Sarajevo; tel. (33) 475-740; e-mail info@muzejsarajeva.ba; internet www.muzejsarajeva.ba; f. 1949; history, archaeology, fine and applied art; Dir MEVLIDA SERDAREVIĆ.

Branch Museums:

Despića Kuća (Despić House): Despićeva 2, 71000 Sarajevo; tel. (33) 215-531; Serbian merchant's house.

Muzej Jevreja BiH (Jewish Museum of Bosnia and Herzegovina): Velika Avlija bb., 71000 Sarajevo; tel. (33) 535-688; Dir ŽANKA DODIĆ-KARAMAN.

Muzej Sarajevska 1878–1918 (Museum of Sarajevo 1878–1918): Zelenih beretki 1, 71000 Sarajevo; tel. (33) 533-288; used as temporary exhibition space; Curator MIRSAD AVDIĆ.

Svrzina Kuća (Svrzo House): Glodjina 8, 71000 Sarajevo; tel. (33) 535-264; house of the Ottoman period; Curator AMRA MADIŽAREVIĆ.

Muzej Srpsko-pravoslavne Crkve (Museum of the Serbian Orthodox Church): Mula Mustafe Bašeskije 59, 71000 Sarajevo; tel. (33) 534-783; small colln of silver and gold church objects and robes; spec. colln of Cretan and locally painted icons from 17th century.

Umjetnička galerija Bosne i Hercegovine (Art Gallery of Bosnia and Herzegovina): Zelenih beretki br. 8, 71000 Sarajevo; tel. (33) 266-550; e-mail info@ugbih.ba; internet www.ugbih.ba; f. 1946; collns of modern art from Serbia, Montenegro and Bosnia and Herzegovina; spec. colln of works by Ferdinand Hodler; ancient icons and art; library of 3,000 vols; Dir Prof. MELIHA HUSEDŽINOVIĆ.

Zemaljski Muzej Bosne i Hercegovine (National Museum of Bosnia and Herzegovina): Zmaja od Bosne 3, 71000 Sarajevo; tel. (33) 668-027; e-mail z.muzej@zemaljskimuzej.ba; internet www.zemaljskimuzej.ba; f. 1888; prehistoric, Roman, Greek and medieval periods, ethnological, botanical, zoological, geological sections; botanical garden; library: see under Libraries and Archives; Dir Dr ADNAN BUSULADŽIĆ; publs *Glasnik Zemaljskog muzeja–Arheologija* (1 a year), *GZM–Etnologija* (1 a year), *GZM–Prirodne nauke* (1 a year), *Wissenschaftliche Mitteilungen A (Archäologie)* (irregular), *Wissenschaftliche Mitteilungen B (Volkskunde)* (irregular), *Wissenschaftliche Mitteilungen C (Naturwissenschaft)* (irregular).

Travnik

Zavičajni Muzej Travnik (Regional Museum, Travnik): Memed-paše Kukavice 1, 72270 Travnik; tel. (30) 814-140; e-mail muzej.travnik@bih.net.ba; f. 1950; Dir FATIMA MASLIĆ.

Trebinje

Muzej Hercegovine—Trebinje (Museum of Herzegovina, Trebinje): Stari Grad bb., 89101 Trebinje; tel. (59) 271-061; e-mail muzejhtr@teol.net; internet muzejhercegovine.org; f. 1952; archaeology, art, ethnography, history; library of 8,000 vols; Dir VESELJKO SALATIĆ; publ. *Tribunia* (history, archaeology, ethnology, art and culture).

Tuzla

Medjunarodna Galerija Portreta Tuzla (Tuzla International Portrait Gallery): ul. Slavka Mičića 13, 75000 Tuzla; tel. (35) 276-150; e-mail mgptuzla@inet.ba; internet www.mgp.ba; f. 1964; works by artists from Bosnia and Herzegovina and abroad, incl. int. artists like James Haim Pinto, Adela Bervukić; colln of 200 portraits; spec. colln of works by Izmet Mujezinović, whose studio forms a br. museum; Dir ĆAZIM SARAJLIĆ.

Muzej Istočne Bosne Tuzla (Museum of East Bosnia, Tuzla): Džindić mahala 21, 75000 Tuzla; tel. (35) 318321; e-mail muzej.ib@bih.net.ba; f. 1947; 15,000 archaeological artefacts incl. Celtic bronze jewellery, 12,000 historical artefacts from the Second World War; ethnography, natural history, art, numismatics; spec. colln of works by D. Mihajlović; library of 15,000 vols, 30,000 exhibits; Dir Prof. VESNA IŠABEGOVIĆ; Curator Prof. NATAŠA PERIĆ; publ. *Članci i gradja za kulturnu historiju istočne Bosne* (Articles and Study Materials for the Cultural History of East Bosnia, 1 a year).

Muzej Solane Tuzla (Tuzla Saltworks Museum): ul. Soli br. 3, 75000 Tuzla; tel. (35) 282 342; internet solana.ba/o-soli-2/muzej/; devoted to the Tuzla saltworks industry.

Zenica

Muzej Grada Zenice (Zenica Town Museum): Muhameda Seida Serdarevića bb., 72000 Zenica; tel. (32) 209-515; e-mail zemuzej@bih.net.ba; internet www.zemuzej.ba; f. 1966, present bldg 2007; archaeology, history, ethnography, geology, art; library of 2,000 titles (literature); Dir ADNADIN JAŠAREVIĆ; Sec. SANJA KAIKČIJA.

Universities

SVEUČILIŠTE U MOSTARU
(University of Mostar)

Trg hrvatskih velikana 1, 88000 Mostar
Telephone: (36) 310-778
E-mail: mail@sve-mo.ba
Internet: www.sve-mo.ba

Founded 1977, present name and status 1992
State control
Language of instruction: Croatian
Academic year: September to August

Rector: Prof. Dr VLADO MAJSTOROVIĆ
Pro-Rector: IVO ČOLAK
Pro-Rector: DRAŽENA TOMIĆ
Gen. Sec.: MARINKO JURILJ
Librarian: SLAVICA JUKA

Library of 15,200 vols
Number of teachers: 500
Number of students: 7,500

Publications: *Mostariensia* (2 a year), *Znanstveni glasnik* (2 a year)

DEANS

College of Nursing: LJUBO ŠIMIĆ
Faculty of Agriculture and Food Technology: Dr STANKO IVANKOVIĆ
Faculty of Civil Engineering: Prof. Dr IVO ČOLAK
Faculty of Economics: Prof. Dr IVAN PAVLOVIĆ
Faculty of Education: Prof. Dr ŠIMUN MUSA
Faculty of Law: Prof. Dr DRAGO RADIĆ
Faculty of Mechanical Engineering: Prof. Dr MILENKO OBAD
Faculty of Medicine: Prof. Dr LJERKA OSTOJIĆ

UNIVERZITET 'DŽEMAL BIJEDIĆ' U MOSTARU
(Džemal Bijedić University of Mostar)

USRC Midhat-Hujdur-Hujka, 88104 Mostar
Telephone: (36) 570-727
E-mail: info@unmo.ba
Internet: www.unmo.ba

Founded 1977
State control
Languages of instruction: Bosnian, Croatian, Serbian
Academic year: October to September

Rector: Dr SEAD PASIC
Vice-Rector for Education: Dr VAHIDA ZUJO
Vice-Rector for Int. Relations: Dr NINA BIJEDIC

Vice-Rector for Science and Research: Dr ELVIR ZLOMUSICA
Sec.-Gen.: ZORAN KAZAZIĆ
Chief Librarian: EDITA MULAOSMANOVIĆ

Library of 11,850 vols
Number of teachers: 250
Number of students: 5,000

Publication: *Revija za pravo i ekonomiju* (Law and Economics Review, 2 a year)

DEANS

Agromediterranean Faculty: Prof. Dr AHMED DZUBUR
Faculty of Civil Engineering: Dr SUAD SPAGO
Faculty of Economics: ADIL TRGO
Faculty of Education: Dr SALKO PEZO
Faculty of Humanities: Dr ADNAN VELAGIC
Faculty of Information Technology: Dr JASMIN AZEMOVIC
Faculty of Law: Dr ANITA DURAKOVIC
Faculty of Mechanical Engineering: Dr DAUT DENJO

UNIVERZITET U BANJOJ LUCI
(University of Banja Luka)

Blvd vojvode Petra Bojovića 1A, 78000 Banja Luka
Telephone: (51) 321-171
E-mail: info@unibl.rs
Internet: www.unibl.rs

Founded 1975
State control
Language of instruction: Serbian
Academic year: October to September

Rector: Prof. Dr STANKO STANIĆ
Vice-Rector for Human Resources and Other Issues: Prof. Dr DRASKO MARINKOVIĆ
Vice-Rector for Int. Relations: Prof. Dr VALERIJA SAULA
Vice-Rector for Scientific Research: Prof. Dr MILAN MATARUGA
Vice-Rector for Teaching and Students Issues: Prof. Dr SIMO JOKANOVIĆ
Sec.-Gen.: DJORDJE MARKEZ
Relations Officer: JELENA ROZIĆ
Librarian: LJILJA PETROVIĆ ZEĆIĆ

Library of 185,000 vols, 75 scientific magazines
Number of teachers: 1,100
Number of students: 17,000

DEANS

Academy of Arts: Prof. Dr. LUKA KECMAN
Faculty of Agriculture: Asst Prof. ALEKSANDAR OSTOJIĆ
Faculty of Architecture and Civil Engineering: Prof. Dr MILENKO STANKOVIĆ
Faculty of Economics: Prof. Dr NOVAK KONDIĆ
Faculty of Electrical Engineering: Prof. Dr BRANKO DOKIC
Faculty of Forestry: Prof. Dr ZORAN GOVEDAR
Faculty of Law: Prof. Dr VITOMIR POPOVIĆ
Faculty of Mechanical Engineering: Prof. Dr DARKO KNEZEVIC
Faculty of Medicine: Prof. Dr MILAN SKRBOBIC
Faculty of Mine Engineering: NADEZDA ĆALIĆ
Faculty of Natural Sciences and Mathematics: Prof. Dr RAJKO GNJATO
Faculty of Philology: Prof. Dr MLADENKO SADŽAK
Faculty of Philosophy: Prof. Dr DRAGO BRANKOVIĆ
Faculty of Physical Education and Sport: Prof. Dr SIMO VUKOVIC
Faculty of Political Sciences: Prof. Dr NENAD KECMANOVIĆ
Faculty of Technology: Prof. Dr MILOŠ SORAK

UNIVERZITET U BIHAĆU
(University of Bihać)

Pape Ivana Pavla II 2/II, 77000 Bihać
Telephone: (37) 222-022
E-mail: rektorat@unbi.ba
Internet: www.unbi.ba

Founded 1997
public control
Language of instruction: Bosnian

Rector: Prof. REFIK ŠAHINOVIĆ
Gen. Sec.: ASIJA CUCAK
Librarian: HALILAGIĆ DŽENITA

Number of teachers: 400
Number of students: 5,700

UNIVERZITET U ISTOČNOM SARAJEVU
(University of East Sarajevo)

Lukavica, Vuka Karadžića br. 30, 71123 Istočno Sarajevo
Telephone: (57) 340-464
E-mail: univerzitet@paleol.net
Internet: www.unssa.rs.ba

Founded 1992 as Univ. of Serb Sarajevo, current name adopted 2005
State control
Language of instruction: Serbian

Rector: Prof. Dr MITAR NOVAKOVIĆ
Vice-Rector for Education and Student Affairs: Prof. Dr ZORAN LJUBOJE
Vice-Rector for International Cooperation: Prof. Dr SLOBODAN MILOVANOVIĆ
Provost for Science and Research: Prof. Dr STEVAN TRBOJEVIĆ
Sec.-Gen.: VOJISLAV SUK

Number of teachers: 919
Number of students: 11,054

DEANS

Academy of Fine Arts: MIRKO TOLJIĆ
Academy of Music: Prof. Dr ZORAN RAKIĆ
Faculty of Agriculture: Prof. MIROSLAV BOGDANOVIĆ
Faculty of Economics (Brčko): Prof. Dr LJUBOMIR TRIFUNOVIĆ
Faculty of Economics (Pale): Prof. Dr NOVO PLAKALOVIĆ
Faculty of Electrotechnology: Prof. Dr BOŽIDAR KRSTAJIĆ
Faculty of Law: Prof. Dr RADOMIR LUKIĆ
Faculty of Mechanical Engineering: Prof. Dr DUSAN GOLUBOVIĆ
Faculty of Medicine: Prof. Dr VELJKO MARIĆ
Faculty of Pedagogy: Prof. Dr MOMČILO PELEMIŠ
Faculty of Philosophy: Prof. Dr MILENKO PIKULA
Faculty of Physical Sciences: Prof. Dr DANKO PRŽULJ
Faculty of Production and Management: Prof. Dr RADE IVANKOVIĆ
Faculty of Stomatology: Prof. Dr PETAR GRGIĆ
Faculty of Technology: Prof. Dr MILOVAN JOTANOVIĆ
Faculty of Theology: Prof. Dr PREDRAG PUZOVIĆ

UNIVERZITET U SARAJEVU
(University of Sarajevo)

Obala Kulina bana 7/II, 71000 Sarajevo
Telephone: (33) 565-118
E-mail: javnost@unsa.ba
Internet: www.unsa.ba

Founded 1949
State control
Academic year: September to September

Rector: Prof. Dr MUHAREM AVDISPAHIC
Vice-Rector: Prof. Dr ZEHRA KREHO
Vice-Rector: Prof. Dr FARUK MEKIC
Vice-Rector: Prof. Dr UGO VLAISAVLJEVIC
Vice-Rector: Prof. Dr DZENAN DJONLAGIC
Dir for National and Univ. Library: Dr ISMET OVCINA

Number of teachers: 1,335
Number of students: 34,000

Publications: *Pregled* (4 a year), *Pregled Predavanja* (1 a year)

DEANS

Academy of Fine Arts: Prof. AMELA HADZIMEJLIC-KECO
Academy of Music: Prof. Dr IVAN CAVLOVIC
Academy of Performing Arts: Prof. PJER ZALICA
Faculty of Agriculture and Food Science: Prof. Dr MIRSAD KURTOVIC
Faculty of Architecture: Prof. Dr RADA CAHTAREVIC
Faculty of Civil Engineering: Prof. Dr MUSTAFA HRASNICA
Faculty of Criminalistics, Criminology and Security Studies: Prof. Dr NEDZAD KORAJLIC
Faculty of Dental Medicine: Prof. Dr SEAD REDZEPAGIC
Faculty of Economics and Business: Prof. Dr ZELJKO SAIN
Faculty of Education: Prof. Dr UZEIR BAVCIC
Faculty of Electrical Engineering: Prof. Dr NARCIS BEHLILOVIC
Faculty of Forestry: Prof. Dr MIRZA DAUTBASIC
Faculty of Health Studies: Prof. Dr DIJANA AVDIC
Faculty of Law: Prof. Dr BORISLAV PETROVIC
Faculty of Mechanical Engineering: Prof. Dr EJUB DZAFEROVIC
Faculty of Medicine: Prof. Dr BAKIR MEHIC
Faculty of Natural Sciences and Mathematics: Prof. Dr RIFAT SKRIJELJ
Faculty of Pharmacy: Prof. Dr DAVORKA ZAVRSNIK
Faculty of Philosophy: Prof. Dr SALIH FOCO (acting)
Faculty of Political Sciences: Prof. Dr SACIR FILANDRA
Faculty of Sports Physical Education: Prof. Dr MUNIR TALOVIC
Faculty of Transport and Communications: Prof. Dr SAMIR CAUSEVIC
Faculty of Veterinary Sciences: Prof. Dr NIHAD FEJZIC

UNIVERZITET U TUZLI
(Tuzla University)

Dr Tihomila Markovića 1, 75000 Tuzla
Telephone: (35) 300-500
E-mail: rektorat@untz.ba
Internet: www.untz.ba

Founded 1976

Rector: Prof. Dr ENVER HALILOVIĆ
Vice-Rector for Academic and Student Affairs: Prof. Dr ADMEDINA SAVKOVIĆ
Vice-Rector for Finance and Devt: Prof. Dr SNJEŽANA MARIĆ (acting)
Vice-Rector for Int. Relations: Prof. Dr MIRSAD ĐONLAGIĆ
Vice-Rector for Science and Research: Dr NASER PRLJAČA (acting)
Sec.-Gen.: JASMINA BERBIĆ
Sec. of Senate: DELIĆ MIRSADA

Number of teachers: 737
Number of students: 16,500

DEANS

Academy of Drama: Prof. Dr VLADO KEROŠEVIĆ
Faculty of Economy: Prof. Dr SAFET KOZAREVI
Faculty of Education and Rehabilitation: Prof. Dr NEVZETA SALIHOVIĆ
Faculty of Electrical Engineering: Doc. Dr AMIR TOKIĆ
Faculty of Mathematics: FEHIM DEDAGIĆ

Faculty of Mechanical Engineering: Doc. Dr IZET ALIĆ
Faculty of Medicine: Prof. Dr FARID LJUCA
Faculty of Mining, Geology, Civil Engineering: Prof. Dr ABDULAH BAŠIĆ
Faculty of Pharmacy: Prof. Dr LEJLA BEGIĆ
Faculty of Philosophy: Prof. Dr ENVER HALILOVIĆ (acting)
Faculty of Science: Prof. Dr FEHIM DEDAGIĆ
Faculty of Sport and Physical Education: Prof. Dr BRANIMIR MIKIĆ
Faculty of Technology: Prof. Dr MIRJANA RADIĆ

UNIVERZITET U ZENICI
(University of Zenica)

Fakultetska 3, 72000 Zenica
Telephone: (32) 444-420
E-mail: rektorat@unze.ba
Internet: www.unze.ba
Founded 2000
Languages of instruction: Bosnian, Croatian, Serbian
Rector: Prof. Dr SABAHUDIN EKINOVIĆ
Vice-Rector for Education and Student Affairs: Dr SAFET BRDAREVIĆ
Vice-Rector for Scientific Research, Devt and Int. Cooperation: Dr DARKO PETKOVIĆ
Gen. Sec.: MEDIHA ARNAUT
Number of teachers: 210
Number of students: 3,200
Publications: *Didaktički putokazi* (education), *Mašinstvo* (mechanical engineering)

DEANS
Faculty of Economics: DŽEVAD ZEČIĆ
Faculty of Education: REFIK CATIĆ
Faculty of Health: SAHIB MUMINAGIĆ
Faculty of Law: SALIH JALIMAM
Faculty of Mechanical Engineering: Prof. Dr DUŠAN VUKOJEVIĆ
Faculty of Metallurgy and Materials Science: SULEJMAN MUHAMEDAGIĆ

BOTSWANA

The Higher Education System

Tertiary education is provided by the University of Botswana (which was attended by 17,678 students in 2011/12). The University of Botswana was founded in 1963 as the University of Basutoland (now Lesotho), Bechuanaland (now Botswana) and Swaziland at Roma, in Lesotho. It became the University of Botswana, Lesotho and Swaziland (UBLS) following the independence of Botswana and Lesotho in 1966, and has been known under its current name since 1982. The University of Botswana is funded mainly by the Government and receives some income from students' fees. The Department of Tertiary Education Financing is the country's main facilitator of tertiary education and training through its provision of a sustainable and transparent financial support system. A second state university, the Botswana International University of Science and Technology (BIUST), the main campus of which is currently under construction at Palapye, began offering undergraduate courses in August 2012; its administrative board was operating temporarily from Gaborone in the Botswana Examinations Council Complex. The new university was planned to have the capacity to accommodate 6,000 full-time equivalent students, and to offer research-intensive science, engineering and technology programmes at Bachelors, Masters and Doctoral (PhD) levels; however, there were reports that, owing to soaring costs, maladministration and various delays, the original proposals regarding the remit of the university might be downgraded. A campus of the private international Limkokwing University of Creative Technology, which has a total of nine campuses located in Africa, Europe and Asia, was opened in Gaborone in 2007. The university, comprising eight faculties, a lifestyle design academy and a sound and music design academy, offers a language course and a variety of Associate and Bachelors degrees in the arts; in 2008 the university had a total enrolment of around 6,000 students (the majority of whom were sponsored by the Government). In 2012 both BIUST and Limkokwing had only a letter of interim Authority from the Tertiary Education Council (TEC) and no programmes had been registered with the TEC. There are also more than 40 non-university tertiary establishments (in both the public and private sectors), including the Botswana College of Agriculture, the Botswana Institute of Administration and Commerce, the Botswana Polytechnic and the Institute of Development Management; these institutions offer a range of courses, including Certificates, Diplomas and Bachelors degrees, and are mainly focused on technical and vocational subjects. The Tertiary Education Council, which was established in 2003, promotes and coordinates the higher education sector in Botswana and is the principal regulatory body, maintaining a register of accredited programmes from Diploma to Doctoral level at public and private institutions. In 2008 the Botswana National Assembly approved a new tertiary education policy, entitled 'Towards a knowledge society', one of the aims of which was to more than double the ratio of young people entering tertiary education within two decades. The National Assembly also approved a new framework to help develop and integrate tertiary education. This involved the establishment of a Department of Tertiary Education Financing within the newly named Ministry of Education and Skills Development, a new National Qualifications Framework and a Human Resource Development Council.

The general entry requirement for undergraduate programmes (including Diplomas) is the Botswana General Certificate of Secondary Education, the local variant of the Cambridge Overseas School Certificate, either first or second division, with a credit in English language. At the University of Botswana, which is composed of seven faculties and a School of Graduate Studies, the standard undergraduate degree is the Bachelors, which comprises two two-year cycles; the main postgraduate degree is the Masters, taken after the Bachelors. Since 1997 the university has offered MPhil and PhD postgraduate degrees, both of which are carried out through supervised research. In 2008/09 the University of Botswana had some 1,028 postgraduate students.

Regulatory Bodies

GOVERNMENT

Ministry of Education and Skills Development: PMB 005, Gaborone; tel. 3655440; e-mail cde.registry@gov.bw; internet www.moe.gov.bw; Minister Dr PELONOMI VENSON-MOITOI.

Ministry of Youth, Sport and Culture: PMB 00514, Gaborone; Plot 50626, Samora Machel Dr., Gaborone; tel. 3682600; e-mail mysc_pro@gov.bw; internet www.mysc.gov.bw; Minister SHAW KGATHI.

NATIONAL BODY

Tertiary Education Council: Private Bag 108, Gaborone; Lot 60113, Extension 48, Block 7, Gaborone-West; tel. 3930741; e-mail info@tec.org.bw; internet www.tec.org.bw; f. 2003; promotes and coordinates tertiary education; maintains standards of teaching, examination, funding, research and cooperation among tertiary instns; accredits private tertiary instns; Chair. JACOB R. SWARTLAND; Deputy Chair. Dr K. J. GASENNELWE; Exec. Sec. Dr PATRICK MOLUTSI.

Learned Societies

GENERAL

Botswana Society: POB 71, Gaborone; tel. 3919745; e-mail botsoc@info.bw; internet www.botsoc.org.bw; f. 1968, in asscn with the Nat. Museum, Monuments and Art Gallery; encourages knowledge and research on Botswana in all fields; promotes cultural heritage tourism online and through publs; 100 mems; library of 48 vols; Chair. Dr JOSEPH TSONOPE; Vice-Chair. Prof. FRED MORTON; Exec. Sec. RAPELANG TSEBE; publ. *Botswana Notes and Records* (1 a year).

BIBLIOGRAPHY, LIBRARY SCIENCE AND MUSEOLOGY

Botswana Library Association: POB 1310, Gaborone; tel. 3552295; e-mail president@bla.org.bw; internet www.bla.org.bw; f. 1978; 60 mems; Pres. KGOMOTSO RADIJENG; Sec. STELLA NALEDI MADZIGIGWA; publs *Botswana Journal of Library and Information Science* (2 a year), *Journal*.

LANGUAGE AND LITERATURE

Alliance Française: POB 1817, Gaborone; Pudulogo Crescent, Plot 2939, Extension 10, Gaborone; tel. 3951650; e-mail af.gaborone@info.bw; internet www.alliance.org.za/branches/gaborone/home.aspx; offers courses and exams in French language and culture and promotes cultural exchange with France.

British Council: British High Commission Bldg, Queen's Rd, The Mall, POB 439, Gaborone; tel. 3953602; e-mail general.enquiries@britishcouncil.org.bw; internet www.britishcouncil.org/botswana; offers courses and exams in English language and British culture and promotes cultural exchange with the UK; Dir DAVID KNOX.

Research Institute

NATURAL SCIENCES

Physical Sciences

Geological Survey of Botswana: Private Bag 14, Lobatse; tel. 5330327; internet www.gov.bw/government/geology.htm; f. 1948; library of 2,000 vols, 151 periodicals; Dir TIYAPO NGWISANYI; publs *Bibliography of the Geology of Botswana* (every 5 years), *District Memoir*.

Libraries and Archives

Gaborone

Botswana National Archives and Records Services: Cnr State and Parliament Dr., Government Enclave, POB 239, Gaborone; tel. 3911820; e-mail archives@gov.bw; internet www.mysc.gov.bw/nars/index.php; f. 1967; central govt, district, tribal, business and private archives since c. 1885; audiovisual and machine-readable archives; records management for central govt, districts and parastatal orgs; oral tradition programmes; educational programmes and exhibitions; 17,000 vols, 45,000 archival documents; Dir LINDA MAGULA (acting); Sr Archivist MOSES T. MAFATLHE; Librarian M. S. MOROLONG; publ. *Archives Library Accessions List*.

Botswana National Library Service: Private Bag 0036, Gaborone; tel. 3952288; f. 1968; 23 br. libraries, 3 mobile libraries; 286 book box service points; 64 village reading rooms; 282,383 vols; Dir CONSTANCE B. MODISE; publs *National Bibliography of Botswana* (3 a year), *Quarterly Accessions List*, *Statistical Bulletin*.

Museums and Art Galleries

Gaborone

National Museum, Monuments and Art Gallery: Independence Ave, Private Bag 00114, Gaborone; tel. 3974616; e-mail national.museum@gov.bw; internet www.gov.bw/tourism/attractions/thenational.html; f. 1968; provides, through dioramas and graphic displays, a visual education in the devt of man in Botswana; preserves and promotes Botswana's cultural and natural heritage; operates mobile education service for rural primary schools; repository for scientific collns relating to Botswana; Nat. Herbarium contains 20,000 plant specimens; art gallery holds a colln of art of all races of Africa south of the Sahara, and exhibits works from the rest of the world; library of 7,000 vols and numerous journals; Dir SUSO R. MWEENDO; publs *The Zebra's Voice* (newsletter), *Zebra's Tales* (4 a year).

Mochudi

Phuthadikobo Museum: POB 367, Mochudi; tel. 5777238; e-mail phuthadikobo@botsnet.bw; internet www.kgabopreincts.org; f. 1975; archaeology, ethnography, photographic collns; conservation, community and environmental education; organizes arts and crafts, exhibitions, performing arts, festivals, silk screen printing workshop, heritage trails and tours; Dir VINCENT PHEMELO RAPOO.

Universities

LIMKOKWING UNIVERSITY OF CREATIVE TECHNOLOGY, BOTSWANA

Plot 59140, Block 7, Gaborone
Telephone: 3180135
E-mail: enquiry@limkokwing.edu.my
Internet: www.limkokwing.net/botswana
Founded 2007
Private control
Faculties of architecture and built environment, business management and globalization, communication, media and broadcasting, creativity in tourism and hospitality, design innovation, information and communication technology, multimedia creativity; HQs at Malaysia; other campuses in Bali, Borneo, Cambodia, Jakarta, Lesotho, Swaziland, UK
Library of 10,000 vols (incl. books, journals and electronic journals, video cassettes and CD-ROMs)

UNIVERSITY OF BOTSWANA

PMB 0022, Gaborone
Telephone: (35) 50000
Internet: www.ub.bw
Founded 1963 as Univ. of Basutoland (now Lesotho), Bechuanaland (now Botswana) and Swaziland at Roma (Lesotho), current name adopted 1982
State control
Language of instruction: English
Academic year: July to April
Vice-Chancellor: Prof. THABO T. FAKO
Deputy Vice-Chancellor for Academic Affairs: Prof. OTLOGETSWE TOTOLO
Deputy Vice-Chancellor for Finance and Admin.: DAVID BENJAMIN KATZKE
Deputy Vice-Chancellor for Student Affairs: Prof. LYDIA M. NYATI-SALESHANDO
Library of 576,534 vols
Number of teachers: 890
Number of students: 18,717
Publication: *Pula* (2 a year)

DEANS

Faculty of Education: Prof. R. TABULAWA
Faculty of Engineering and Technology: Dr O. KANYETO
Faculty of Health Sciences: Prof. Y. MASHALLA
Faculty of Humanities: Prof. K. H. MOAHI
Faculty of Science: Prof. M. P. MODISI
Faculty of Social Sciences: Prof. H. K. SIPHAMBE
School of Graduate Studies: Prof. G. O. ANDERSON

Colleges

Botswana College of Agriculture: Content Farm, Sebele, Gaborone; PMB 0027, Gaborone; tel. 3650100; internet www.bca.bw; f. 1967; associated instn of Univ. of Botswana; library: 29,810 vols, 118 periodicals; 79 teachers; 425 students; Prin. E. J. KEMSLEY.

Botswana Institute of Administration and Commerce: POB 10026, Gaborone; tel. 3956324; f. 1970; library: 7,000 vols; 73 teachers; Prin. L. L. SEBINA.

Institute of Development Management: POB 1357, Gaborone; tel. 3612100; e-mail directorb@idmbls.com; internet www.idmbls.com; f. 1974; management training in business management, education management, information management, administration of legal services; library: 8,000 vols (incl. spec. World Bank and SADCC collns); 30 teachers; 970 students; Regional Dir Dr M. KHAKHETLA.

BRAZIL

The Higher Education System

In 2011 there were an estimated 2,365 institutions of higher education in Brazil, of which some 90% were private. According to UNESCO figures, total enrolment in higher education was 6,929,324 in 2011, of whom 1,932,581 were students at public institutions. Universities (of which there were 190 in 2011) fall into five categories: federal, state, municipal, private and Catholic. Brazil's first institution of higher learning was the Escola Politécnica, the first engineering school in the Americas and the third in the world, founded in Rio de Janeiro in 1792. Several other institutes, specializing in civil and military engineering, medicine and sciences, were established in the early 1800s, and many of these subsequently developed into Brazil's modern-day universities.

Education at all public institutions of higher education is free. Federal universities are the most popular and competition to enter them is very fierce; they are administered by the federal Government. State universities are funded by the individual states, while municipal universities usually focus on one subject or provide professional training. Private universities are funded by private organizations and students' fees, and Catholic universities, while supported principally by the Catholic Church, are in fact open to students of all denominations. The Secretaria de Educação Superior (Secretariat of Higher Education) of the Ministry of Education has ultimate control of higher education, and the establishment of new institutions is authorized by the Conselho Nacional de Educação (CNE—National Education Council, which was established in 1995). In 2009 the development began of a new national system of evaluation, the Sistema Nacional da Avaliação da Educação Superior (SINAES). The Commisão Nacional de Avaliação da Educação Superior (CONAES—National Commission for the Evaluation of Higher Education) was established as the national body responsible for coordinating and supervising SINAES. CONAES accredits and assesses all federal and private universities at the undergraduate and postgraduate level (excluding stricto sensu programmes, see below), while state and municipal universities are accredited and assessed by the respective state council.

Aside from universities, higher education in Brazil is principally provided by Centros Universitários, the first of which was established in 1997, which offer degree programmes but do not undertake research, and by Faculdades. The latter are by far the most numerous higher education institutions in Brazil, and are divided into Faculdades Integradas, offering degree programmes in a limited number of disciplines, and Faculdades Isoladas, offering degree programmes in a single discipline. Faculdades are the least autonomous tertiary education institution in the country, while Centros Universitários enjoy considerable autonomy in the areas of curriculum, enrolment, finance and management. The establishment in 1995 of the CNE, together with legislative changes introduced in 1996 (Lei de Diretrizes e Bases de Educação Nacional: Lei 9.394, de 20 de dezembro de 1996) liberalizing the sector and enabling higher education institutions to function as profit-making entities, resulted in a rapid expansion of tertiary education. Private interests began to offer degrees and other higher education qualifications on a large scale. Between 2005 and 2009 the number of students engaged in higher education increased by 67%. Government expenditure on higher education during the same period, however, decreased by 2%. In 2009 government expenditure on the sector was equivalent to 0.8% of gross domestic product (GDP), significantly lower than the regional average.

Both public (federal, state, municipal) and private (including Catholic) universities base admissions on a combination of the secondary school diploma and entrance examinations (Vestibular) administered by individual institutions. However, since 1998 all universities, particularly those in the federal system, have been encouraged to adopt a standard examination administered by the Ministry of Education, the Exame Nacional do Ensino Médio (ENEM). There are three qualifications each at undergraduate and postgraduate level. Undergraduate degrees are between three and five years long, and consist of the Bacharel (excludes teacher training), Licenciado/Licenciado Plena (includes teacher training) and Título Profissional (professional title). Parallel to these degrees are cursos següênciais (sequential courses), which are non-degree courses in subjects such as business and management and which are mainly offered by private higher education institutions, the Extensão (extension courses) skills-based programmes and the Provão, an obligatory test designed to monitor teaching standards.

Postgraduate qualifications are divided into stricto sensu ('strict sense') and lato sensu ('wide sense'). Stricto sensu encompasses the classical postgraduate schema, consisting of the Mestrado/Mestrado Profissional (Masters/Professional Masters), which requires two to three years of study, and the Doutorado (Doctorate), which is awarded after three to four years of study and research following the Mestrado. Lato sensu programmes, which generally last only one year and do not hold graduate 'credit', are offered in vocational or professional fields and lead to the title of Especialização (Specialist) or, alternatively, a Certificado de Pós-Graduação Lato Sensu em Nível de Especialização in an applied discipline. The Coordenação de Aperfeiçoamento de Pessoal de Nível Superior (CAPES, Coordination for the Improvement of Personnel in Higher Education) is responsible for the development and consolidation of postgraduate courses, including research programmes at the Masters and Doctoral levels. The body also evaluates the national impact of peer reviewed publications and uses this to inform funding decisions. CAPES, which was established in 1951 and is attached to the Ministry of Education, is also responsible for the accreditation of postgraduate stricto sensu degrees (other postgraduate courses are accredited by CONAES).

Vocational and technical training, which has rapidly expanded in recent years in both the public and private sector, is separate from academic education, and is governed according to the Lei de Diretrizes e Bases da Educação Nacional (Educational Guidelines Law) of 1996, which established three levels of non-university, post-secondary education and training. The three levels are: nível básico, a first stage open to students of any educational attainment, and leading to a certificate of basic competency in a specific job or skill; nível técnico, which lasts one to two years, requires at least 11 years of basic education and is regulated by the Ministry of Education (and approved by state authorities); and nível tecnológica, the third and final level, providing vocational education of a higher education standard and lasting two to three years (courses at this level enable access to postgraduate study).

In 2009 the Secretaria de Educação Superior launched the Os Referenciais Curriculares Nacionais dos Cursos de Bacharelado e Licenciatura (Reference of National Curriculum of Bachelor and Degree Courses) with the aim of standardizing the content and quality of degree titles.

Regulatory and Representative Bodies

GOVERNMENT

Ministry of Culture: Esplanada dos Ministérios, Bloco B, Térreo, Brasília, DF 70068-900; tel. (61) 2024-2082; e-mail valecultura@cultura.gov.br; internet www.cultura.gov.br; Minister MARTA SUPLICY.

Ministry of Education: Esplanada dos Ministérios, Bloco L, 8° andar Gabinete, Brasília, DF 70047-900; tel. (61) 2022-7828; e-mail gabinetedoministro@mec.gov.br; internet www.mec.gov.br; Minister Prof. Dr ALOÍZIO MERCADANTE.

Ministry of Science, Technology and Innovation: Esplanada dos Ministérios, Bloco E, Brasília, DF 70067-900; tel. (61) 2033-7500; e-mail ministro@mct.gov.br; internet www.mct.gov.br; Minister CLÉLIO CAMPOLINA.

Instituto Nacional de Estudos e Pesquisas Educacionais Anísio Teixeira (INEP) (National Institute for Educational Studies and Research Anisio Teixeira): SRTVS Quadra 701, Bloco M, Edifício Sede do Inep, Brasília, DF 70340-909; tel. (61) 2104-8406; internet www.inep.gov.br; f. 1937; govt agency; promotes study and research of Brazilian education system; supports formation and implementation of education policy; Pres. REYNALDO FERNANDES; publ. *Prova Brasil* (irregular).

Secretaria de Educação Superior (SESu) (Secretariat of Higher Education): Ministério da Educação, Esplanada dos Ministérios, Bloco L, Brasília, DF 70047-903; tel. (61) 2104-8012; e-mail sesu@mec.gov.br; internet portal.mec.gov.br/sesu; attached to Min. of Education; Sec. AMARO LINS HENRIQUE PESSOA.

ACCREDITATION

Comissão Nacional de Avaliação da Educação Superior (CONAES) (National Commission for Evaluation of Higher Education): Edif. Sede do Conselho Nacional de Educação—CNESGAS, Av. L2 Sul, Quadra 607, Lote 50, Térreo, Sala 16, Brasília, DF 70200-670; tel. (61) 2022-7680; e-mail conaes@mec.gov.br; f. 2004; proposes and evaluates the processes of institutional evaluation and accreditation of courses and student performance; formulates proposals for the devt of HEIs; Pres. ROBERT EVAN VERHINE.

Conselho Nacional de Educação (CNE) (National Education Council): SGAS, Av. L/2, Quadra 607, Lote 50, Brasília, DF 70200-670; tel. (61) 2022-7700; e-mail edsonnunes@mec.gov.br; internet portal.mec.gov.br/cne; f. 1995; Pres. JOSÉ FERNANDES DE LIMA.

FUNDING

Coordenação de Aperfeiçoamento de Pessoal de Nível Superior (CAPES) (Coordination for the Improvement of Personnel in Higher Education): Setor Bancário Norte, Quadra 2, Bloco L, Lote 06, Brasília, DF 70040-020; tel. (61) 2104-8801; internet www.capes.gov.br; f. 1951; govt agency; funds stricto sensu postgraduate study of the sciences in Brazil and abroad; main objects are to deploy the human resources of graduate schools to help govt and public enterprises, to give student grants; evaluates and coordinates Masters and Doctors courses; funds over half of all eligible postgraduate students in Brazil; library of 126 vols; Pres. JORGE ALMEIDA GUIMARÃES; publ. *Revista Brasileira de Pós-Graduação* (3 a year).

NATIONAL BODIES

Associação de Educação Católica do Brasil (Association for Catholic Education in Brazil): Bloco 'C', Sala 102, Brasília, DF, 70722-530; tel. (61) 3533-5050; e-mail secretarioexecutivo@anec.org.br; internet www.anec.org.br; f. 1945; supervises 27 sections, with a total of 1,750 schools and seminaries; Pres. Fr JOSEPH MARINONI; publs *Cadernos AEC*, *Revista de Educação AEC* (4 a year).

Conselho de Reitores das Universidades Brasileiras (Council of Brazilian University Rectors): Prédio da Associação Médica de Brasília (AMBr), Setor de Clubes Esportivos Sul Trecho 3, Conj.06, 3° andar, Brasília, DF 70200-003; tel. (61) 3349-9010; e-mail crub@crub.org.br; internet www.crub.org.br; f. 1966; study of problems affecting higher education; 128 mems; library of 15,000 vols; Pres. WOLMIR THEREZIO AMADO; Exec. Sec. FERNANDA FIGUEIRÊDO TORRES PÓVOA; publ. *Revista Educação Brasileira* (2 a year).

Instituto Brasileiro de Educação, Ciência e Cultura (IBECC) (Brazilian Institute of Education, Science and Culture): Travessa Elodir Livramento de Freitas, 20 Centro, São João de Meriti, RJ; tel. (21) 2756-5504; e-mail contato@cursoibecc.com.br; internet www.cursoibecc.com.br; f. 1946; library of 1,500 vols; Exec. Sec. JOAQUIM CAETANO GENTIL NETO.

Learned Societies

GENERAL

Fundação Bunge (Bunge Foundation): Av. Maria Coelho Aguiar 215, Bloco D, 5° andar, São Paulo, SP 05804-900; tel. (11) 3741-2170; e-mail fundacao@bunge.com; internet www.fundacaobunge.org.br; f. 1955; promotes the advancement of science, language and literature, and arts in Brazil by granting every year the Bunge Foundation Award and the Bunge Foundation Youth Award; manages the Bunge Memory Center that contains over 200,000 images—printed photos, glass slides, chromes, engravings, paintings and maps, 1,300 boxes of assorted documents, 3,000 works of filmography; Chair. JACQUES MARCOVITCH; Exec. Dir CLÁUDIA CALAIS; publ. *Cidadania* (Citizenship, 6 a year, in Portuguese and English, print and online, www.fundacaobunge.org.br/jornal-cidadania).

Representação da UNESCO no Brasil (UNESCO Office in Brasília): CP 08563, Brasília, DF 70070-000; SAUS Quadra 5 Bloco H Lote 6, Edif. CNPq/IBICT/UNESCO, 9° andar, Brasília, DF 70070-912; tel. (61) 2106-3500; e-mail brasilia@unesco.org; internet www.unesco.org/brasilia; f. 1964 in Rio de Janeiro, present location 1972; Dir LUCIEN ANDRÉ MUÑOZ; publs *Debates* (education, natural sciences, social and human sciences, culture, communication and information, irregular, in Portuguese, English and Spanish), *Educação comparada: Panorama internacional e perspectivas* (International Handbook of Comparative Education, 1 a year, in Portuguese), *UNESCO News* (4 a year).

AGRICULTURE, FISHERIES AND VETERINARY SCIENCE

Associação Brasileira de Mecânica dos Solos e Engenharia Geotecnica (ABMS) (Brazilian Association for Soil Mechanics and Geotechnical Engineering): Av. Prof. Almeida Prado, 532, IPT, prédio 59, Cidade Universitaria, São Paulo, SP 05508-901; tel. (11) 3768-7325; e-mail abms@abms.com.br; internet www.abms.com.br; f. 1950; 1,100 mems; Pres. ANDRÉ PACHECO DE ASSIS; Sec.-Gen. ALESSANDER KORMANN; Treas. ARTUR QUARESMA; publ. *Soils and Rocks* (3 a year, in English, print and online, www.soilsandrocks.com.br).

Sociedade Nacional de Agricultura (SNA) (National Agricultural Society): Av. General Justo 171, 7° andar, Rio de Janeiro, RJ 20021-130; tel. (21) 3231-6350; e-mail sna@sna.agr.br; internet www.sna.agr.br; f. 1897; undergraduate course in animal science; extension courses in animal husbandry, organic production, gardening; veterinary medicine undergraduate course with Univ. Castelo Branco; campus in Rio de Janeiro acts as a networking org.; annual agribusiness congress; 10,000 mems; library of 45,000 vols; Pres. ANTONIO MELLO ALVARENGA; publs *A Lavoura* (6 a year), *Animal Business Brasil* (6 a year).

BIBLIOGRAPHY, LIBRARY SCIENCE AND MUSEOLOGY

Associação dos Arquivistas Brasileiros (Association of Brazilian Archivists): Av. Presidente Vargas 1733 sala 903, Rio de Janeiro, RJ 20210-030; tel. (21) 2507-2239; e-mail aab@aab.org.br; internet www.aab.org.br; f. 1971; cooperates with the govt, nat. and int. organizations on all matters relating to archives and documentation; organizes nat. congresses, study courses, confs; has achieved nat. legislation on archives; 300 mems; library of 1,000 vols; Pres. LUCIA MARIA VELLOSO DE OLIVEIRA; Sec.-Gen. LEILA ESTEPHANIO DE MOURA; Treas. RENATA SILVA BORGES; publ. *Arquivo & Administração* (2 a year, in Portuguese).

Federação Brasileira de Associações de Bibliotecários, Cientistas da Informação e Instituições (FEBAB) (Brazilian Federation of Library Associations, Information Scientists and Institutions): Rua Avanhandava, 40 -conj. 108/110, Bela Vista, São Paulo, SP 01306-000; tel. (11) 3257-9979; e-mail febab@febab.org.br; internet www.febab.org.br; f. 1959 to act for the regional library asscns at a nat. level; serves as a centre of documentation and bibliography for Brazil; organizes a biennial nat. congress; 16 mem. asscns; Pres. SIGRID KARIN WEISS DUTRA; Admin. and Financial Dir MÁRCIA ELISA GARCIA DE GRANDI; publ. *Revista Brasileira de Biblioteconomia e Documentação (RBBD)* (2 a year, in Portuguese with abstracts in English and Spanish, online, rbbd.febab.org.br).

ECONOMICS, LAW AND POLITICS

Instituto Brasileiro de Economia (Brazilian Institute of Economics): Fundação Getulio Vargas, Rua Barão de Itambi 60, Botafogo, Rio de Janeiro, RJ 22231-000; tel. (21) 3799-6799; e-mail ibre@fgv.br; internet portalibre.fgv.br; f. 1951; attached to Fundação Getulio Vargas; researches, analyses, publishes and disseminates macro-economic statistics and applied economic research; Dir LUIZ GUILHERME SCHYMURA DE OLIVEIRA; publs *Conjuntura Econômica* (The Brazilian Economy, 12 a year, in Portuguese and English), *Revista Agroanalysis* (12 a year).

Instituto dos Advogados Brasileiros (IAB) (Institute of Brazilian Lawyers): Av. Marechal Câmara 210, 5° andar, Centro, Rio de Janeiro, RJ 20020-080; tel. (21) 2240-3173; internet www.iabnacional.org.br; f. 1843; 1,141 mems; library: see under Libraries and Archives; Pres. FERNANDO FRAGOSO; Sec.-Gen. UBYRATAN GUIMARÃES CAVALCANTI; publs *Folha* (6 a year, online), *Revista* (1 a year), *Revista Digital* (4 a year, online).

EDUCATION

Fundação Carlos Chagas (Carlos Chagas Foundation): Av. Prof. Francisco Morato 1565, Jardim Guedala, São Paulo, SP 05513-900; tel. (11) 3723-3000; e-mail fcc@fcc.org.br; internet www.fcc.org.br; f. 1964; activities in the fields of human resources, educational research and educational evaluation; 184 mems; library: see under Libraries and Archives; Pres. Prof. Dr FERNANDO CALZA DE SALLES FREIRE; Admin. Dir Prof. Dr ANA MARIA OLIVAN; publs *Cadernos de Pesquisa* (3 a year), *Estudos em Avaliação Educacional* (2 a year).

Fundação Getúlio Vargas (Getúlio Vargas Foundation): Praia de Botafogo 190, Rio de Janeiro, RJ 22250-900; tel. (21) 3799-6000; e-mail faleconosco@fgv.br; internet portal.fgv.br; f. 1944; technical, scientific, educational and philanthropic activities; incl. 8 educational instns; 385 mems in Gen. Assembly; library: over 120,000 vols; Pres. Dr CARLOS IVAN SIMONSEN LEAL; publs *Agroanalysis* (12 a year), *Conjuntura Econômica* (12 a year), *Correio da UNESCO* (12 a year), *Estudos Históricos* (2 a year), *Revista Brasileira de Economia* (4 a year), *Revista de Administração de Empresas* (6 a year), *Revista de Administração Pública* (4 a year).

HISTORY, GEOGRAPHY AND ARCHAEOLOGY

Instituto Arqueológico, Histórico e Geográfico Pernambucano (Archaeological, Historical and Geographical Institute of Pernambuco): Rua do Hospício 130, Boa Vista, Recife, PE 50060-080; tel. (81) 3222-4952; e-mail contato@institutoarqueologico.com.br; internet www.institutoarqueologico.com.br; f. 1862; 185 mems (50 full-time, 130 corresp., 5 hon.); library of 25,000 vols; Pres. MARGARIDA DE OLIVEIRA CANTARELLI; First Sec. REINALDO CARNEIRO LEÃO; publ. *Revista do Instituto Arqueológico Pernambucano*.

Instituto do Ceará (Ceará Institute): Rua Barão do Rio Branco 1594, Fortaleza, CE 60025-061; tel. (85) 3231-6152; e-mail contato@institutodoceara.org.br; internet www.institutodoceara.org.br; f. 1887; incl. the following comms: History, MSS and Periodicals, Geography, Anthropology; 40 mems; library of 52,000 vols; Pres. JOSÉ AGUSTO BEZERRA; Gen. Sec. VALDELICE CARNEIRO GIRÃO; publ. *Revista* (1 a year).

Instituto Genealógico Brasileiro (Genealogical Institute): Rua Senador Egidio 34, 2º andar, sala 22, Centro, São Paulo, SP 01006-010; tel. (11) 3257-4840; f. 1930; library of 972 vols; Pres. SALVADOR DE MOYA; Sec. Dr JORGE BUENO DE MIRANDA; publs *Anuário Genealógico Brasileiro*, *Anuário Genealógico Latino*, *Biblioteca*, *Biblioteca Genealógica Brasileira*, *Genealógica Latina*, *Indices Genealógicos Brasileiros*, *Revista Genealógica Brasileira*, *Subsídios Genealógicos*.

Instituto Geológico (Geological Institute): Av. Miguel Stefano 3900, Água Funda, São Paulo, SP 04301-903; tel. (11) 5077-1155; e-mail igeologico@igeologico.sp.gov.br; internet www.igeologico.sp.gov.br; f. 1886; map colln, geological museum; 100 mems; library of 8,500 vols, 1,850 periodicals, 10,000 maps; Dir Dr RICARDO VEDOVELLO (acting); publ. *Revista*.

Instituto Histórico e Geográfico Brasileiro (Brazilian Historical and Geographical Institute): Av. Augusto Severo 8, 10° andar, Rio de Janeiro, RJ 20021-040; tel. (21) 2509-5107; e-mail gerencia@ihgb.org.br; internet www.ihgb.org.b; f. 1838; archive of 110,000 documents; museum of 1,100 items; regional socs in 22 states and the Fed. District; library of 560,000 vols; Pres. ARNO WEHLING; Sec. CYBELLE MOREIRA DE IPANEMA; Treas. FERNANDO TASSO FRAGOSO PIRES; publ. *Revista* (4 a year).

Sociedade Brasileira de Cartografia, Geodésia, Fotogrametria e Sensoriamento Remoto (Brazilian Society of Cartography, Geodesy, Photogrammetry and Remote Sensing): Av. Presidente Wilson 210, 7° andar, Rio de Janeiro, RJ 20030-021; tel. (21) 3203-5902; e-mail contato@cartografia.org.br; internet www.cartografia.org.br; f. 1958; 2,000 mems; Pres. PAULO CESAR TEIXEIRA TRINO; Sec.-Gen. Eng. JOSÉ HENRIQUE DA SILVA; publs *Proceedings of the Brazilian Congress of Cartography* (every 2 years), *Revista Brasileira de Cartografia* (4 a year, print and online, www.lsie.unb.br/rbc).

Sociedade Brasileira de Geografia (Brazilian Geographical Society): Rua Uruguaiana 39, Bloco B, 6º andar, Centro, Rio de Janeiro, RJ 20050-093; tel. (21) 2224-1223; e-mail sbgrj@socbrasileiradegeografia.com.br; internet www.socbrasileiradegeografia.com.br; f. 1883; 284 mems; library of 14,000 vols; Pres. Prof. Dr WILLIAM PAULO MACIEL; First Sec. Profa JORGE RUBEM FOLENA DE OLIVEIRA; publs *Estante Paranista*, *Revista*.

LANGUAGE AND LITERATURE

Academia Brasileira de Letras (Brazilian Academy of Letters): Av. Presidente Wilson 203, Castelo, Rio de Janeiro, RJ 20030-021; tel. (21) 3974-2500; e-mail academia@academia.org.br; internet www.academia.org.br; f. 1897; prepares Portuguese language dictionary; awards prizes for Brazilian works in prose, verse and drama; regional socs in Amazonas, Bahia, Ceará, Goiás, Minas Gerais, Paraíba, Pernambuco, Piauí, Rio Grande do Sul, São Paulo; 40 mems; library of 50,000 vols; Pres. ANA MARIA MACHADO; Gen. Sec. GERALDO HOLANDA CAVALCANTI; Librarian BARBOSA LIMA SOBRINHO; publ. *Revista Brasileira* (4 a year).

Alliance Française: Av. Presidente Antônio Carlos 58, 3º andar, Rio de Janeiro, RJ 20020-010; tel. (21) 2215-8522; e-mail centro@rioaliancafrancesa.com.br; internet www.aliancafrancesabrasil.com.br; f. 1885; offers courses and exams in French language and culture and promotes cultural exchange with France; 36 asscns and 9 corresp. centres in Brazil; Dir of Operations, Brazil LUCE RUDENT.

British Council: Embaixada Britânico, Setor de Embaixadas Sul, Quadra 801, Lote 8, Brasília, DF 70408-900; tel. (61) 2106-7500; e-mail centro.info@britishcouncil.org.br; internet www.britishcouncil.org/brasil.htm; f. 1945; offers courses and exams in English language and British culture and promotes cultural exchange with the UK; attached offices in Recife, Rio de Janeiro (teaching centre) and São Paulo (library); library of 6,500 vols of books in English; Dir JIM SCARTH.

Goethe-Institut: Rua Lisboa 974, São Paulo, SP 05413-001; tel. (11) 3296-7000; e-mail info@saopaulo.goethe.org; internet www.goethe.de/ins/br/lp/ptindex.htm; offers courses and exams in German language and culture and promotes cultural exchange with Germany; attached centres in Brasília, Curitiba, Porto Alegre, Rio de Janeiro and Salvador-Bahia; library of 15,000 vols, 60 periodicals; Dir and Regional Dir, South America Dr BRUNO FISCHLI.

Instituto Cervantes: Rua Visconde de Ouro Preto 62, Botafogo, Rio de Janeiro, RJ 22250-180; tel. (21) 3554 5910; e-mail adx3rio@cervantes.es; internet riodejaneiro.cervantes.es; offers courses and exams in Spanish language and culture and promotes cultural exchange with Spain and Spanish-speaking Latin and Central America; attached centre in São Paulo; Jose Garcia Nieto Library; Dir ANTONIO MARTÍNEZ LUCIANO.

PEN Clube do Brasil (International PEN Centre): Praia do Flamengo 172, 11° andar, Flamengo, Rio de Janeiro, RJ 22210-030; tel. (21) 2556-0461; e-mail pen@penclubedobrasil.org.br; internet www.penclubedobrasil.org.br; f. 1936; 106 mems; monthly free lectures; theatrical performances; Pres. CLÁUDIO AGUIAR; Exec. Sec. MARCIA AGRAU; Treas. ALCMENO BASTOS; publ. *Convivência* (irregular, online).

Sociedade Brasileira de Autores (Society of Authors): Av. Almirante Barroso 97, 3° andar, Rio de Janeiro, RJ 20031-005; tel. (21) 2240-7231; e-mail cadastro@sbat.com.br; internet www.sbat.com.br; f. 1917; non-profit-making org.; represents mem. authors and playwrights (by collecting and distributing royalties) whose work is performed abroad; collects and archives handwritten and typewritten MSS of plays; 6,000 mems; library of 6,000 vols, 33,538 plays; Pres. ADERBAL FREIRE-FILHO; publ. *Revista de Teatro* (irregular).

MEDICINE

Academia de Medicina de São Paulo (Medical Academy of São Paulo): Av. Brigadeiro Luís Antonio 278, 6º andar, Sala 3, São Paulo, SP 01318-901; tel. (11) 3105-4402; e-mail contato@academiamedicinasaopaulo.org.br; internet www.academiamedicinasaopaulo.org.br; f. 1895 as Sociedade de Medicina e Cirurgia; 130 mems; Pres. Prof. AFFONSO RENATO MEIRA; Gen. Sec. JOSÉ ROBERTO DE SOUZA BARATELLA.

Academia Nacional de Medicina (National Academy of Medicine): Av. General Justo 365, 7° andar, Rio de Janeiro, RJ 20021-130; tel. (21) 2524-1552; e-mail presidente@anm.org.br; internet www.anm.org.br; f. 1829; 683 mems; library of 11,000 vols, incl. 2,000 vols of rare and old books, 1,200 periodicals, 400 theses; library temporarily closed due to renovation work; Pres. PIETRO NOVELLINO; Sec.-Gen. JOSÉ ALVES GALVÃO; publ. *Anais* (2 a year).

Associação Bahiana de Medicina (ABM) (Bahia Medical Association): Rua Baependi, 162, Ondina, Salvador, BA 40170-070; tel. (71) 2107-9666; e-mail abm@abmnet.org.br; internet www.abmnet.org.br; f. 1894; Pres. Dr ANTONIO CARLOS VIEIRA LOPES; Sec.-Gen. Dr CÉSAR AUGUSTO DE ARAÚJO NETO; publs *Anais*, *Revista ABM* (3 a year, in Portuguese, print and online, www.abmnet.org.br/revista-abm).

Associação Brasileira de Farmacêuticos (Brazilian Pharmaceutical Association): Rua dos Andradas 96, 10° Andar, Centro, Rio de Janeiro, RJ 20051-001; tel. (21) 2233-3672; e-mail abf@abf.org.br; internet www.abf.org.br; f. 1916; comprises the following Comms: *Desenvolvimento Cultural* (Cultural Development); *Econômica e Etica Farmacêutica* (Pharmaceutical Economics and Ethics); *Legislação Comercial* (Commercial Legislation); *Legislação de Marcas e Patentes* (Trade Marks and Patents); *Legislação Sanitaria* (Sanitary Legislation); *Legislação Tributaria* (Tax Legislation); *Propaganda e Intercambio Associativo* (Propaganda and Exchange); attached museum; 950 mems (hon. and corresp.); library of 2,433 vols of books on pharmaceutical science and related areas, 450 titles of periodicals; Pres. Dr MARIA LETICE COUTO DE ALMEIDA; First Sec. Dr DENIR GOMES NOGUEIRA; Treas. DENISE HAMMES TORRES; publ. *Revista Brasileira de Farmácia* (3 a year, in Portuguese, English and Spanish, print and online, www.rbfarma.org.br).

Associação Médica Brasileira (AMB) (Brazilian Medical Association): Rua São Carlos do Pinhal 324, Bela Vista, São Paulo, SP 01333-903; tel. (11) 3178-6800; e-mail diretoria@amb.org.br; internet www.amb.org.br; f. 1951; 250,000 mems; Pres. FLORENTINO CARDOSO; Gen. Sec. ALDEMIR HUMBERTO SOARES; publs *Jornal AMB* (6 a year, online), *O Médico & Você* (4 a year), *Revista AMB* (6 a year, online).

Associação Paulista de Medicina (São Paulo Medical Association): Av. Brig. Luíz Antônio 278, Bela Vista, São Paulo, SP 01318-901; tel. (11) 3188-4200; e-mail comunica@apm.org.br; internet www.apm.org.br; f. 1930; 30,000 active mems, 432 corresp. mems; Pres. FLORISVAL MEINÃO; Sec.-Gen. PAULO CEZAR MARIANI; publs *Diagnóstico & Tratamento* (4 a year), *Revista da APM* (12 a year), *São Paulo Medical Journal* (6 a year, in English).

Sociedade Brasileira de Dermatologia (Brazilian Dermatological Society): Av. Rio Branco 39-18º andar, Rio de Janeiro, RJ 20090-003; tel. (21) 2253-6747; e-mail sbd@sbd.org.br; internet www.sbd.org.br; f. 1912; 3,872 mems, incl. 16 hon. and 56 corresp.; library of 4,000 vols, 200 periodicals; Pres. DENISE STEINER; Gen. Sec. Dr LEANDRA D'ORSI METSAVAHT; Treas. LENINHA VALÉRIO DO NASCIMENTO; publs *Anais Brasileiros de Dermatologia* (6 a year, in Portuguese and English, print and online, www.anaisdedermatologia.org.br), *Jornal* (6 a year, in Portuguese, print and online), *Revista Sensatez, Surgical & Cosmetic Dermatology* (4 a year, in Portuguese and English, print and online, www.surgicalcosmetic.org.br).

Sociedade Brasileira de Pediatria (Brazilian Society of Paediatrics): Rua Santa Clara, 292, Rio de Janeiro, RJ 22041-012; tel. (21) 2548-1999; internet www.sbp.com.br; f. 1910; 27 affiliated regional socs; Pres. EDUARDO DA SILVA VAZ; Sec.-Gen. MARILENE AUGUSTA R. CRISPINO SANTOS; publs *Jornal de Pediatria* (6 a year, print and online, www.jped.com.br), *Residência Pediátrica* (3 a year, online, www.residenciapediatrica.com.br).

NATURAL SCIENCES

General

Academia Brasileira de Ciências (Brazilian Academy of Sciences): Rua Anfilófio de Carvalho 29, 3° andar, Centro, Rio de Janeiro, RJ 20030-060; tel. (21) 3907-8100; e-mail abc@abc.org.br; internet www.abc.org.br; f. 1916; 602 mems; Pres. JACOB PALIS, JR; Vice-Pres. HERNAN CHAIMOVICH GURALNIK; publs *Anais da Academia Brasileira de Ciências* (4 a year), *Jovem Academia em Revista* (Young Academy in Review, 1 a year, in Portuguese and English).

Sociedade Brasileira para o Progresso da Ciência (Brazilian Society for the Advancement of Science): Rua Maria Antonia 294, 4° andar, Vila Buarque, São Paulo, SP 01222-010; tel. (11) 3259-2766; e-mail sbpc@sbpcnet.org.br; internet www.sbpcnet.org.br; f. 1948; 3,995 mems; Pres. Dr HELENA BONCIANI NADER; Sec.-Gen. Prof. Dr ALDO MALAVASI; publs *Anais* (1 a year, online), *Ciência e Cultura* (4 a year, print and online, cienciaecultura.bvs.br), *Ciência Hoje* (12 a year), *Jornal da Ciência* (26 a year, print and online, www.jornaldaciencia.org.br), *Revista Ciência Hoje das Crianças* (12 a year).

Biological Sciences

Sociedade Brasileira de Entomologia (Brazilian Entomological Society): CP 42672, São Paulo, SP 04299-970; tel. (11) 6161-3504; e-mail sbe@ib.usp.br; f. 1937; 400 mems; Pres. PEDRO GNASPINI NETTO; Sec. SÉRVIO TÚLIO PIRES AMARANTE; publ. *Revista Brasileira de Entomologia* (4 a year).

Physical Sciences

Associação Brasileira de Química (Brazilian Chemical Association): Av. Presidente Vargas 633 sala 2228, Centro, Rio de Janeiro, RJ 20071-004; tel. (21) 2224-4480; e-mail secretaria@abq.org.br; internet www.abq.org.br; f. 1922 as Sociedade Brasileira de Química, current name adopted 1951; affiliated to IUPAC; regional brs in Alagoas, Bahia, Ceará, Goiás, Maranhão, Mato Grosso, Minas Gerais, Pará, Pernambuco, Piauí, Rio de Janeiro, Rio Grande do Norte, Rio Grande do Sul and São Paulo; 3,000 mems; library of 3,000 vols; Pres. NEWTON MARIO BATTASTINI; Sec. ANTONIO CARLOS MAGALHÃES; Treas. ROBERIO FERNANDES ALVES DE OLIVEIRA; publs *Anais da Associação Brasileira de Química* (1 a year, print and online, www.abq.org.br/anais), *Revista de Química Industrial* (4 a year, print and online, www.abq.org.br/rqi).

PHILOSOPHY AND PSYCHOLOGY

Sociedade Brasileira de Filosofia (Brazilian Philosophy Society): Praça da República 54, Rio de Janeiro, RJ; f. 1927; 80 mems (8 hon., 5 Brazilian corresp., 12 foreign); Pres. Dr RICARDINA MARQUES DA SILVA; Sec.-Gen. Prof. ARNALDO CLARO DE SÃO THIAGO; publ. *Anais*.

RELIGION, SOCIOLOGY AND ANTHROPOLOGY

Comissão Nacional de Folclore (National Folklore Commission): CP 6565, Fortaleza, CE 60040-531; tel. (85) 9128-6058; e-mail comissaonacionaldefolclore@gmail.com; internet www.comissaonacionaldefolclore.org.br; f. 1947; dept of the Brazilian Institute of Education, Science and Culture (IBECC); Pres. LOURDES MACENA; Sec. SIMONE CASTRO.

TECHNOLOGY

Associação Brasileira de Metalurgia, Materiais e Mineração (Brazilian Metallurgy, Materials and Mining Association): Rua Antônio Comparato 218, Campo Belo, São Paulo, SP 04605-030; tel. (11) 5534-4333; e-mail abm@abmbrasil.com.br; internet www.abmbrasil.com.br; f. 1944; 5,500 mems; library of 5,000 vols, periodicals; Pres. ALFREDO HUALLEM; publs *Journal of Materials Research and Technology (jmr&t)* (4 a year, in English, online), *Metalurgia & Materiais* (12 a year, print and online, www.abmbrasil.com.br/revistamm), *Revista ABM* (6 a year), *Tecnologia em Metalurgia e Materiais* (4 a year, in Portuguese and English, print and online, www.tecnologiammm.com.br).

Associação de Engenharia Química (Association of Chemical Engineers): Av. Prof. Lineu Prestes 510, Bloco 19 Superior, Cidade Universitária, São Paulo, SP 05508-000; tel. (11) 3091-3746; e-mail aeq.usp@gmail.com; internet aeqpoli.wix.com/aeqpoli; f. 1944; 500 mems; Pres. PEDRO AUGUSTO SILVA BRACCO; Sec. BRUNO THEOZZO; Treas. LUCAS D'AVILA BRAGA.

Research Institutes

AGRICULTURE, FISHERIES AND VETERINARY SCIENCE

Centro de Energia Nuclear na Agricultura (Centre of Nuclear Energy in Agriculture): CP 96, Av. Centenário 303, Piracicaba, SP 13400-970; tel. (19) 3429-4600; e-mail diretoria@cena.usp.br; internet www.cena.usp.br; f. 1966; attached to Univ. de São Paulo; 68 researchers; 3 divs: tropical ecosystems, production of agro-industrial foods, devt of analytical and nuclear techniques; library of 9,000 vols and 366 periodicals; spec. colln: IAEA publs on life sciences; Dir Prof. Dr ANTONIO VARGAS DE OLIVEIRA FIGUEIRA; publ. *Scientia Agrícola* (print and online, www.esalq.usp.br/scientia).

Empresa Brasileira de Pesquisa Agropecuária (EMBRAPA) (Brazilian Agricultural Research Corporation): Parque Estacão Biológica s/n, Brasília, DF 70770-901; tel. (61) 3448-4433; e-mail presid@sede.embrapa.br; internet www.embrapa.br; f. 1973; attached to Min. of Agriculture; controls agricultural research in the country; 38 research centres, 3 service centres and 13 central divs; library of 120,000 vols; Pres. MAURÍCIO ANTÔNIO LOPES; publs *Cadernos de Ciência & Tecnologia* (4 a year, online, seer.sct.embrapa.br/index.php/cct), *Ciência para a Vida* (Science for Life, in Portuguese and English, print and online, revista.sct.embrapa.br), *Pesquisa Agropecuaria Brasileira* (12 a year, online, seer.sct.embrapa.br/index.php/pab), *Revista de Política Agrícola* (Journal of Agriculture Policy, in Portuguese and English), *Textos para Discussão* (irregular).

Research Centres:

Embrapa Acre: Rodovia BR 364, km 14, CP 321, Rio Branco, AC 69900-970; tel. (68) 3212-3200; e-mail cpafac.chgeral@embrapa.br; internet www.cpafac.embrapa.br; f. 1976; Gen. Chief EUFRAN FERREIRA DO AMARAL.

Embrapa Agrobiologia: Rodovia BR 465, km 47, Seropédica, RJ 23891-000; tel. (21) 3441-1500; internet www.cnpab.embrapa.br; f. 1993; Gen. Chief EDUARDO FRANCIA CARNEIRO CAMPELLO.

Embrapa Agroindústria de Alimentos: Av. das Americas 29501, Guaratiba, Rio de Janeiro, RJ 23020-470; tel. (21) 3622-9600; e-mail ctaa.sac@embrapa.br; internet www.ctaa.embrapa.br; f. 1971; food science and technology centre; library of 5,500 vols, 842 journal titles, 2,689 reprints. 715 theses, 555 proceedings, 150 technical standards, 172 pamphlets, 216 bibliographies; Gen. Chief LOURDES MARIA CORREA CABRAL.

Embrapa Agroindústria Tropical: Rua Dra Sara Mesquita 2270, Planalto do Pici, Fortaleza, CE 60511-110; tel. (85) 3391-7100; internet www.cnpat.embrapa.br; f. 1993; Gen. Chief Dr LUCAS ANTONIO DE SOUSA LEITE.

Embrapa Agropecuária do Oeste: BR 163, km 253.6, CP 449, Dourados, MS 79804-970; tel. (67) 3416-9700; internet www.cpao.embrapa.br; f. 1976; Gen. Chief GUILHERME LAFOURCADE ASMUS.

Embrapa Algodão: Rua Osvaldo Cruz 1143, Centenário, CP 174, Campina Grande, PB 58428-095; tel. (83) 3182-4300; e-mail sac@cnpa.embrapa.br; internet www.cnpa.embrapa.br; f. 1975; research on cotton; Gen. Chief MARIA AUXILIADORA LEMOS BARROS.

Embrapa Amapá: CP 10, Macapá, AP 68906-970; Rodovia Juscelino Kubitschek, km 5, n°2600, Macapá, AP 68903-419; tel. (96) 4009-9501; e-mail cpafap.sac@embrapa.br; internet www.cpafap.embrapa.br; f. 1980; Gen. Chief SILAS MOCHIUTTI.

Embrapa Amazônia Ocidental: Rodovia AM-010 km 29, Estrada Manaus/Itacoatiara, Manaus, AM 69011-970; tel. (92) 621-0300; internet www.cpaa.embrapa.br; f. 1975; rubber and oil-palm research;

library of 22,485 vols, 1,268 journals; Gen. Chief LUIZ MARCELO BRUM ROSSI.

Embrapa Amazônia Oriental: Travessa Dr Enéas Pinheiro s/n, CP 48, Belém, PA 66095-100; tel. (91) 3204-1000; internet www.cpatu.embrapa.br; f. 1975; Gen. Chief AUSTRELINO SILVEIRA FILHO.

Embrapa Arroz e Feijão: Rodovia GO-462, km 12, Zona Rural CP 179, Santo Antônio de Góias, GO 75375-000; tel. (62) 3533-2110; e-mail cnpaf.sac@embrapa.br.; internet www.cnpaf.embrapa.br; f. 1974; research on beans, cowpeas and rice; Gen. Chief PEDRO LUIZ OLIVEIRA DE ALMEIDA MACHADO.

Embrapa Caprinos e Ovinos: Estrada Sobral/Groaíras km 04, CP 145, Sobral, CE 62010-970; tel. (88) 3112-7400; e-mail adriana@cnpc.embrapa.br; internet www.cnpc.embrapa.br; f. 1975; research on goats; Gen. Chief Dr EVANDRO VASCONCELOS HOLANDA, JR.

Embrapa Cerrados: BR 020 km 18, Planaltina, DF 73310-970; tel. (61) 3388-9898; e-mail sac@cpac.embrapa.br; internet www.cpac.embrapa.br; f. 1975; Gen. Chief JOSÉ ROBERTO RODRIGUES PERES.

Embrapa Clima Temperado: Rodovia BR 392 km 78, CP 403, Pelotas, RS 96001-970; tel. (532) 3275-8100; e-mail cpact.chgeral@embrapa.br; internet www.cpact.embrapa.br; f. 1975; research on temperate fruit and vegetable crops and food technology; Gen. Chief CLENIO NAILTO PILLON.

Embrapa Florestas: Estrada da Ribeira km 111, CP 319, Colombo, PR 83411-000; tel. (41) 3675-5600; e-mail cnpf.sac@embrapa.br; internet www.cnpf.embrapa.br; f. 1978; forest research; Gen. Chief EDSON TADEU IEDE; publ. *Pesquisa Florestal Brasileira*.

Embrapa Gado de Corte: Av. Rádio Maia 830, Zona Rural, Campo Grande, MS 79106-550; tel. (67) 3368-2000; internet www.cnpgc.embrapa.br; f. 1976; research on beef cattle; Gen. Chief CLEBER OLIVEIRA SOARES.

Embrapa Gado de Leite: Rua Eugênio do Nascimento 610, Dom Bosco, Juiz de Fora, MG 36038-330; tel. (32) 3249-4700; internet www.cnpgl.embrapa.br; f. 1976; dairy research; Gen. Chief DUARTE VILELA.

Embrapa Hortaliças: Rodovia Brasília/Anápolis BR 060 km 09, Gama DF 70359-970; tel. (61) 3385-9000; e-mail cnph.sac@embrapa.br; internet www.cnph.embrapa.br; f. 1975; vegetable research.

Embrapa Informática Agropecuária: Av. André Tosello, 209, Barão Geraldo, CP 6041, Campinas, SP 13083-886; tel. (19) 3211-5700; internet www.cnptia.embrapa.br; Gen. Chief KLEBER XAVIER SAMPAIO DE SOUZA.

Embrapa Instrumentação: Rua XV de Novembro 1452, São Carlos, SP 13560-970; tel. (16) 2107-2800; e-mail cnpdia.sac@embrapa.br; internet www.cnpdia.embrapa.br; library of 5,850 vols, 322 theses, 246 periodical titles; Gen. Chief LUIZ HENRIQUE CAPPARELLI MATTOSO.

Embrapa Mandioca e Fruticultura: Rua Embrapa s/n, Cruz das Almas, BA 44380-000; tel. (75) 3312-8048; e-mail chgeral@cnpmf.embrapa.br; internet www.cnpmf.embrapa.br; f. 1973; research on cassava and tropical fruits; Gen. Chief Dr DOMINGO HAROLDO REINHARDT.

Embrapa Meio Ambiente: Rodovia SP 340, km 127.5, CP 69, Jaguariúna, SP 13820-000; tel. (19) 3311-2700; e-mail chgeral@cnpma.embrapa.br; internet www.cnpma.embrapa.br; f. 1982; library of 7,825 vols, 466 journals; Gen. Chief Dr CELSO VAINER MANZATO.

Embrapa Meio-Norte: Av. Duque de Caxias 5650, Bairro Buenos Aires, Teresina, PI 64006-220; tel. (86) 3089-9100; internet www.cpamn.embrapa.br; f. 1975; Gen. Chief CARGO LUIZ FERNANDO CARVALHO LEITE.

Embrapa Milho e Sorgo: Rodovia MG 424, km 65, 35701-970, Sete Lagoas, MG; tel. (31) 3027-1000; internet www.cnpms.embrapa.br; f. 1975; research on maize and sorghum; library of 5,500 vols, 65 periodicals; Gen. Chief Dr ANTÔNIO ÁLVARO CORSETTI PURCINO.

Embrapa Monitoramento por Satélite: Av. Soldado Passarinho 303, Fazenda Chapadão, Campinas, SP 13070-115; tel. (19) 3211-6200; internet www.cnpm.embrapa.br; f. 1989; Gen. Chief MATEUS BATISTELLA.

Embrapa Pantanal: Rua 21 de Setembro 1880, Bairro Nossa Senhora de Fátima, CP 109, Corumbá, MS 79320-900; tel. (67) 3234-5800; internet www.cpap.embrapa.br; f. 1975; research on beef cattle and pasture land; Gen. Chief EMIKO KAWAKAMI DE RESENDE.

Embrapa Pecuária Sudeste: Rodovia Washington Luiz km 234, São Carlos, SP 13560-970; tel. (16) 3411-5600; internet www.cppse.embrapa.br; f. 1975; library of 2,970 vols, 290 periodical titles, 7,008 leaflets, 3,900 reprints, 814 theses; Gen. Chief MAURÍCIO MELLO DE ALENCAR.

Embrapa Pecuária Sul: BR 153, km 603, CP 242, Bagé, RS 96401-970; tel. (32) 3240-4650; e-mail cppsul.sac@embrapa.br; internet www.cppsul.embrapa.br; f. 1975; Gen. Chief ALEXANDRE COSTA VARELLA.

Embrapa Recursos Genéticos e Biotecnologia: Parque Estacão Biológico, PqEB, Av. W5 Norte (final), CP 02372, Brasília, DF 70770-917; tel. (61) 3448-4700; e-mail sac@cenargen.embrapa.br; internet www.cenargen.embrapa.br; f. 1976; Gen. Chief MAURO CARNEIRO.

Embrapa Rondônia: Rodovia BR 364, km 5.5, Zona Rural, CP 127, Porto Velho, RO 76815-800; tel. (69) 3901-2510; e-mail sac@cpafro.embrapa.br; internet www.cpafro.embrapa.br; f. 1975; library of 15,000 vols; Gen. Chief CÉSAR AUGUSTO DOMINGUES TEIXEIRA.

Embrapa Roraima: Rodovia BR 174, km 8, Distrito Industrial, Boa Vista, RR 69301-970; tel. (95) 4009-7100; internet www.cpafrr.embrapa.br; f. 1981; library of 12,000 vols, 355 periodical titles; Gen. Chief FRANCISCO JOACI DE FREITAS LUZ.

Embrapa Semi-Árido: BR 428 km 152, Zona Rural, CP 23, Petrolina, PE 56302-970; tel. (87) 3866-3600; e-mail cpatsa.chgeral@embrapa.br; internet www.cpatsa.embrapa.br; f. 1975; library of 60,000 vols; Gen. Chief NATONIEL FRANKLIN DE MELO.

Embrapa Soja: Rodovia Carlos João Strass, Distrito de Warta, Londrina, PR 86001-970; tel. (43) 3371-6000; e-mail sac@embrapa.br; internet www.cnpso.embrapa.br; f. 1975; research on soya beans and sunflowers; Gen. Chief ALEXANDRE JOSÉ CATTELAN.

Embrapa Solos: Rua Jardim Botânico 1024, Jardim Botânico, Rio de Janeiro, RJ 22460-000; tel. (21) 2179-4500; internet www.cnps.embrapa.br; f. 1974; soil survey and conservation; Gen. Chief MARIA DE LOURDES BREFIN.

Embrapa Suínos e Aves: CP 21, Concórdia, SC 89700-000; tel. (49) 3441-0400; e-mail cnpsa.sac@embrapa.br; internet www.cnpsa.embrapa.br; f. 1975; research on pigs and poultry; library of 4,000 vols, 800 periodicals; Gen. Chief DIRCEU JOÃO DUARTE TALAMINI.

Embrapa Tabuleiros Costeiros: Av. Beira Mar 3250, CP 44, Aracajú, SE 49025-040; tel. (79) 4009-1300; e-mail cpatc.sac@embrapa.br; internet www.cpatc.embrapa.br; f. 1974; Gen. Chief EDSON DIOGO TAVARES.

Embrapa Trigo: Rodovia BR 285 km 174, CP 451, Passo Fundo, RS 99001-970; tel. (54) 3316-5800; e-mail cnpt.chgeral@embrapa.br; internet www.cnpt.embrapa.br; f. 1974; wheat research centre; Gen. Chief SÉRGIO ROBERTO DOTTO.

Embrapa Uva e Vinho: Rua Livramento 515, CP 130, Bento Gonçalves, RS 95700-000; tel. (54) 3455-8000; e-mail cnpuv.sac@embrapa.br; internet www.cnpuv.embrapa.br; f. 1975; research and devt in viticulture, temperate fruits and the wine industry; library of 10,000 vols, 545 journal titles; Gen. Chief Dr LUCAS DA RESSURREICAO GARRIDO.

Instituto Agronômico (Agronomic Institute): Av. Barão de Itapura 1481, CP 28, Campinas, SP 13012-970; tel. (19) 2137-0600; e-mail iacdir@iac.sp.gov.br; internet www.iac.sp.gov.br; f. 1887; basic and applied research on plants, soils, environment, farming methods and agricultural machinery; 11 centres: citriculture, coffee, ecophysiology and biophysics, engineering and automation, fruit, grains and fibres, horticulture, phytosanitary, soil and environmental resources, sugarcane, vegetable genetic resources; Technical Scientific Information Service; library of 200,000 vols; Dir-Gen. Dr SÉRGIO AUGUSTO MORAIS CARBONELL; publs *Bragantia* (2 a year), *Citrus Research & Technology* (print and online, revistalaranja.centrodecitricultura.br), *O Agronômico* (irregular).

Instituto Brasileiro do Meio Ambiente e dos Recursos Naturais Renováveis (IBAMA) (Brazilian Institute for the Environment and Renewable Natural Resources): SCEN trecho 2, Edif. Sede Ibama, CP 09566, Brasília, DF 70818-900; tel. (61) 3316-1212; e-mail presid.sede@ibama.gov.br; internet www.ibama.gov.br; f. 1989; attached to Min. of Environment; library of 65,000 vols; Pres. VOLNEY ZANARDI JR.

Instituto de Economia Agrícola (Agricultural Economics Institute): Av. Miguel Stefano 3900, Água Funda, CP 68029, São Paulo, SP 04301-903; tel. (11) 5067-0526; e-mail iea@iea.sp.gov.br; internet www.iea.sp.gov.br; f. 1942; affiliated to São Paulo Secretariat of Agriculture and Provision; provides information for state and federal govts and other interested bodies; library of 70,000 vols, 2,700 periodicals; Dir Dr VALQUÍRIA DA SILVA; publs *Agricultura em São Paulo* (irregular), *Informações Econômicas* (12 a year), *Informações Estatística da Agricultura* (1 a year).

Instituto de Pesquisas Veterinárias 'Desidério Finamor' (Institute of Veterinary Research): Estrada Municipal do Conde, 6000, Eldorado do Sul, RS 92990-000; tel. (51) 3481-3711; e-mail contato@ipvdf.rs.gov.br; internet www.ipvdf.rs.gov.br; f. 1949; attached to Fundação Estadual de Pesquisa Agropecuária; research and training in all aspects of animal health; 8 attached laboratories: bacteriology, bird-health, brucellosis, histopathology, leptospirosis, molecular biology, parasitology and virology; library of 1,400 vols; Dir ALEXANDER CENCI; publ. *Pesquisa Agropecuária Gaúcha*.

Instituto de Zootecnia (Institute of Animal Science and Pastures): Rua Heitor Penteado 56, Nova Odessa, SP 13460-000; tel. (19) 3466-9400; e-mail zootecnia@iz.sp.gov.br; internet www.iz.sp.gov.br; f. 1905; attached to Dept of Agriculture and Food Supply of the state of São Paulo; beef cattle, dairy cattle, goats, information science, pastures, pigs, reproduction and genetics, sheep, water buffaloes; library of 10,710 vols, 1,610 periodicals; Dir-Gen. SEBASTIÃO APARECIDO TEIXEIRA; publ. *Boletim de Indústria Animal* (2 a year).

Instituto Florestal (Estado de São Paulo) (São Paulo State Forestry Institute): Rua do Horto 931, CP 1322, São Paulo, SP 02377-000; tel. (11) 6231-8555; e-mail nuinfo@iflorest.sp.gov.br; internet www.iflorestsp.br; f. 1896; library of 7,500 vols, 2,000 periodicals; Dir MARIA CECÍLIA WEY DE BRITO; publs *Revista do Instituto Florestal* (2 a year), *Revista IF-Serie Registros* (irregular).

Organização Nacional de Proteção Fitossanitária (ONPF) (National Plant Protection Organization): Departamento de Sanidade Vegetal, Ministério da Agricultura, Pecuária e Abastecimento, Esplanada dos Ministérios, Bloco D, Anexo B, Sala 303-B, Brasília, DF; tel. (61) 3218-2675; e-mail dsv@agricultura.gov.br; internet www.agricultura.gov.br; f. 2005; Dir JOSÉ GERALDO BALDINI RIBEIRO.

EDUCATION

Instituto Nacional de Estudos e Pesquisas Educacionais 'Anísio Teixeira' (National Institute for Educational Studies and Research): Quadra 701, Bloco M, Edif. Sede do INEP, Brasília, DF 70340-909; tel. (61) 2022-3605; e-mail presidencia@inep.gov.br; internet www.inep.gov.br; f. 1938; attached to Min. of Education; library of 50,000 vols, 985 periodicals; Pres. Dr LUIZ CLÁUDIO COSTA; publs *Em Aberto*, *Revista Brasileira de Estudos Pedagógicos* (4 a year, in Portuguese with English abstracts).

HISTORY, GEOGRAPHY AND ARCHAEOLOGY

Instituto Brasileiro de Geografia e Estatística (Brazilian Institute of Geography and Statistics): Av. Franklin Roosevelt 166/10°andar, Castelo, Rio de Janeiro, RJ 20021-120; tel. (21) 2142-4501; e-mail ibge@ibge.gov.br; internet www.ibge.gov.br; f. 1936; produces and analyses statistical, geographical, cartographic, geodetic, demographic, socioeconomic, natural resources and environmental information; 27 state units, 27 documentation and dissemination centres, 581 data colln agencies; Pres. WASMÁLIA BIVAR; publs *Anuário Estatístico do Brasil*, *Revista Brasileira de Estatística*, *Revista Brasileira de Geografia*.

MEDICINE

Fundação 'Oswaldo Cruz' (Oswaldo Cruz Foundation): Av. Brasil 4365, Manguinhos, Rio de Janeiro, RJ 21045-900; tel. (21) 2598-4242; e-mail ferreirj@fiocruz.br; internet www.fiocruz.br; f. 1900; infectious and parasitic diseases, entomology, epidemiology, history of science, immunology, public health; tropical medicine, virology; library of 800,000 vols, 2,000 current periodicals; Pres. PAULO GADELHA; publs *Cadernos de Saúde Pública* (Reports in Public Health, 12 a year, print and online, www4.ensp.fiocruz.br/csp), *Ciência & Saúde Coletiva* (Science & Collective Health, print and online, www.cienciaesaudecoletiva.com.br), *História, Ciências, Saúde—Manguinhos* (4 a year, print and online, www.revistahcsmanguinhos.coc.fiocruz.br), *Memórias* (6 a year, print and online, memorias.ioc.fiocruz.br), *Revista Eletrônica de Comunicação Informação e Inovação em Saúde* (in Portuguese and English, online, www.reciis.cict.fiocruz.br), *Trabalho, Educação e Saúde* (Work, Education and Health, 3 a year).

Instituto 'Adolfo Lutz' (Adolfo Lutz Institute): Av. Dr Arnaldo 355, Cerqueira César, São Paulo, SP 01246-902; tel. (11) 3068-2802; internet www.ial.sp.gov.br; f. 1892; Central Laboratory of Public Health for the State of São Paulo; library of 50,000 vols, incl. periodicals; Dir-Gen. CRISTIANO CORRÊA DE AZEVEDO MARQUES; publ. *Revista*.

Instituto 'Benjamin Constant' (Benjamin Constant Institute): Av. Pasteur 350/368, Urca, Rio de Janeiro, RJ 22290-240; tel. (21) 3478-4442; e-mail ibc@ibc.gov.br; internet www.ibc.gov.br; f. 1854; attached to Min. of Education; educational institute for the blind; teaching and research; library of 15,000 vols; spec. Braille colln; Dir-Gen. MARIA ODETE SANTOS DUARTE; publs *Pontinhos* (4 a year), *Revista Benjamin Constant* (4 a year), *Revista Brasileira para Cegos* (4 a year).

Instituto Brasileiro de Estudos e Pesquisas de Gastroenterologia (IBEPEGE) (Brazilian Institute for Studies and Research in Gastroenterology): Rua Dr Seng 320, São Paulo, SP 01331-020; tel. (11) 3147-6227; f. 1963; study and research in gastroenterology, nutrition and psychosomatic medicine; postgraduate courses; library of 10,000 vols; Pres. Prof. JOSÉ FERNANDES PONTES; Vice-Pres. Dr JOSÉ VICENTE MARTINS CAMPOS; publ. *Arquivos de Gastroenterologia* (4 a year, print and online, www.scielo.br/ag.htm).

Instituto Butantan (Butantan Institute): Av. Vital Brasil 1500, São Paulo, SP 05503-900; tel. (11) 2627-9300; e-mail instituto@butantan.gov.br; internet www.butantan.gov.br; f. 1901; snake farm; Public Health Institute for research and the production of vaccines, sera; also research in genetics, virology, pathology; Hospital Vital Brasil (snake, spider and scorpion accidents); 16 laboratories; library of 96,000 vols on ophiology and biomedical sciences; Dir JORGE KALIL.

Instituto de Saúde (Institute of Health): Rua Santo Antonio 590, São Paulo, SP 01314-000; tel. (11) 3116-8504; e-mail isaude@isaude.sp.gov.br; internet www.isaude.sp.gov.br; f. 1969; organization and supervision of health service, research and activities in the field of mother and child care; evaluation of health technologies, health care, health services research, communication and public health, degenerative diseases, dermatology, hansenology, nutrition; library: see under Libraries and Archives; Dir-Gen. Dr LUIZA STERMAN HEIMANN; publ. *Boletim* (3 a year).

Instituto Evandro Chagas (Evandro Chagas Institute): Rodovia BR-316 km 7 s/n, Levilândia, Ananindeua, PA 67030-000; tel. (91) 3214-2213; e-mail contato@iec.pa.gov.br; internet www.iec.pa.gov.br; f. 1936; attached to Min. of Health; research in bacteriology, human ecology and environment, medical entomology, mycology, parasitology, pathology, virology; library of 50,000 vols, 134 current periodicals, 4,000 reprints; Dir ELISABETH CONCEIÇÃO DE OLIVEIRA SANTOS; publ. *Revista Pan-Amazônica de Saúde*.

Instituto Nacional de Cancer (Brazilian National Cancer Institute): Praça Cruz Vermelha 23, Centro, Rio de Janeiro, RJ 20230-130; tel. (21) 3207-1000; e-mail apoioadm@inca.gov.br; internet www.inca.gov.br; f. 1958; attached to Min. of Health; cell biology, experimental oncology, genetics, molecular biology, pharmacology; Dir-Gen. LUIZ ANTONIO SANTINI RODRIGUES DA SILVA.

Instituto Oscar Freire (Oscar Freire Institute): Rua Teodoro Sampaio 115, São Paulo, SP 05405-000; tel. (11) 3061-8408; e-mail mls@iof.fm.usp.br; internet www.fm.usp.br/iof; f. 1918; attached to Univ. of São Paulo; for instruction and research in forensic medicine; library of 4,200 vols; Chair. Prof. Dr CLÁUDIO COHEN; publ. *Saúde, Ética e Justiça* (2 a year).

Instituto Pasteur (Pasteur Institute): Av. Paulista 393, São Paulo, SP 01311-000; tel. (11) 3145-3157; e-mail ip_ouvidoria@pasteur.saude.sp.gov.br; internet www.saude.sp.gov.br/instituto-pasteur/; f. 1903; practical measures and theoretical studies aimed at preventing rabies and other viral encephalitis in humans; library of 5,000 vols and 1,083 periodicals; Dir LUCIANA HARDT.

Instituto 'Penido Burnier': Av. Andrade Neves 683, Botafogo, Campinas, SP 13013-161; tel. (19) 3232-5866; e-mail penido@penidoburnier.com.br; internet www.penidoburnier.com.br; f. 1920; anaesthesiology, ophthalmology, otolaryngology; library of 11,585 vols; Pres. Dr JOSÉ MARIA PENTEADO QUEIROZ ABREU FILHO; Exec. Dir Dr GUSTAVO BARBOSA ABREU; publ. *Arquivos IPB* (2 a year).

NATURAL SCIENCES

General

Centro de Ciências, Letras e Artes (Science, Letters and Arts Centre): Rua Bernardino de Campos 989, Centro, Campinas, SP 13010-151; tel. (19) 3231-2567; e-mail ccla@ccla.org.br; internet www.ccla.org.br; f. 1901; attached museum and art gallery; library of 120,000 vols, incl. 500 rare items; Pres. Eng MARINO ZIGGIATTI; Sec.-Gen. Dra MARIA LETICIA DE BARROS E GONCALVES; Librarian Dr LUIZ CARLOS RIBEIRO BORGES; publ. *Revista*.

Conselho Nacional de Desenvolvimento Científico e Tecnológico (CNPq) (National Council of Scientific and Technological Development): SHIS QI 1 Conjunto B, Blocos A, B, C e D, Lago Sul, Brasília, DF 71605-001; tel. (61) 2108-9000; e-mail coapg@cnpq.br; internet www.cnpq.br; f. 1951; attached to Min. of Science, Technology and Innovation; Pres. GLAUCIUS OLIVA.

Institut de Recherche pour le Développement (IRD) (Institute of Research for Development): CP 7091, Lago Sul, Brasília, DF 71635-971; SHIS, QL 16, Conj. 4, Casa 8, Lago Sul, Brasília, DF 71640-230; tel. (61) 3248-5323; e-mail bresil@ird.fr; internet www.brasil.ird.fr; f. 1979; HQ of the Brazilian delegation to Latin America; missions at various univs and research institutes; see main entry under France; Delegate to Brazil FRÉDÉRIC HUYNH.

Instituto Nacional de Pesquisas da Amazônia (National Research Institute for Amazonia): CP 2223, Manaus, AM 69080-971; Av. André Araújo 2936, Petrópolis, Manaus, AM 69067-375; tel. (92) 3643-3377; e-mail ascom@inpa.gov.br; internet www.inpa.gov.br; f. 1954; agronomics, biology, ecology, forestry, medicine, technology and spec. projects; wood colln; library of 48,000 items; Dir ADALBERTO LUIS VAL; publ. *Acta Amazônica* (4 a year, in Portuguese, English and Spanish, print and online, acta.inpa.gov.br).

Biological Sciences

Campo de Santana: Praça da República s/n, Centro, Rio de Janeiro, RJ 20211-360; tel. (21) 2323-3500; laid out 1870 by Auguste F. M. Glaziou, who collected 23,000 plants, including 700 trees; Herbário Glaziou forms the most noteworthy exhibit in the Botanical Div. of the Nat. Museum.

Centro de Pesquisa e Gestão de Recursos Pesqueiros Continentais (CEPTA) (Research and Management Centre for Continental Fish Resources): Rod. Pref. Euberto N. P. de Godoy s/n, CP 64, km 6.5, Pirassununga, SP 13630-970; tel. (19) 3565-1299; f. 1938; library of 26,024 vols; Dir LAERTE BATISTA DE OLIVEIRA ALVES; publ. *Boletim Técnico* (1 a year).

Fundação Ezequiel Dias (Ezequiel Dias Foundation): Rua Conde Pereira Carneiro 80, Gameleira, Belo Horizonte, MG 30510-010; tel. (31) 3314-4577; e-mail comunicacao@funed.mg.gov.br; internet www.funed.mg.gov.br; f. 1907; attached to the Minas Gerais state govt; health and welfare, biotechnology, immunology research; library; Pres. AUGUSTO MONTEIRO GUIMARÃES; Vice-Pres. EDUARDO JANOT PACHECO LOPES.

Herbário 'Barbosa Rodrigues' (Barbosa Rodrigues Herbarium): Av. Coronel Marcos Konder 800, Itajaí, SC 88301-302; tel. (47) 3348-8725; e-mail contato@hbr.org.br; internet hbriai.webnode.com.br; f. 1942; botany of southern Brazil, taxonomy, ecology; 186 mems; library of 19,200 vols; Pres. VITUS SCHLICKMANN ROETGER; Dir ADEMIR REIS; publs *Flora Ilustrada Catarinense* (1 a year), *Sellowia* (1 a year).

Instituto Biológico (Biological Institute): Av. Counselor Rodrigues Alves, 1252 Vila Mariana, São Paulo, SP 04014-002; tel. (11) 5571-9134; e-mail divulgacao@biologico.sp.gov.br; internet www.biologico.sp.gov.br; f. 1927; animal and plant protection; library of 13,000 vols, 105,000 periodicals; Dir-Gen. ANTONIO BATISTA FILHO; publs *Arquivos do Instituto Biológico* (4 a year), *O Biológico* (2 a year).

Instituto de Botânica (Botanical Institute): CP 68041, São Paulo, SP 04045-972; tel. (11) 5067-6000; e-mail biblioteca@ibot.sp.gov.br; internet www.ibot.sp.gov.br; f. 1938; herbarium of 400,000 plants; postgraduate course in plant diversity and the environment; library of 90,000 vols; Dir LUIZ MAURO BARBOSA; publ. *Hoehnea* (4 a year).

Instituto de Pesquisas do Jardim Botânico do Rio de Janeiro (Research Institute of the Botanical Gardens of Rio de Janeiro): Rua Jardim Botânico 1008, Jardim Botânico, Rio de Janeiro, RJ 22460-000; tel. (21) 2511-0511; e-mail jbrj@jbrj.gov.br; internet www.jbrj.gov.br; f. 1808; attached to Min. of the Environment, Water Resources and Amazonia; botanical research in systematics, wood anatomy (7,148 samples and 17,000 microscope plates), cytomorphology and ecology; botanical garden with 7,800 species and 11,000 specimens; herbarium with 350,000 samples; library of 15,000 vols, 50,000 periodicals, antiquarian colln of 3,000 vols; Pres. SAMYRA CRESPO; Dir RENATO CADER DA SILVA; publ. *Rodriguésia*.

Instituto Estadual do Ambiente (INEA) (State Environmental Institute): Assessoria de Comunicação, Av. Venezuela 110, Rio de Janeiro, RJ; f. 2009 to protect environment in Rio de Janeiro State and promote sustainable devt; Pres. LUIZ FIRMINO MARTINS PEREIRA; Vice-Pres. PAULO SCHIAVO.

Physical Sciences

Associação Internacional de Lunologia (International Association of Lunology): CP 322, Franca, São Paulo; f. 1969; publishes a review on lunar research carried out by all countries.

Centro Brasileiro de Pesquisas Físicas (Brazilian Centre for Physics Research): Rua Dr Xavier Sigaud 150, Urca, Rio de Janeiro, RJ 22290-180; tel. (21) 2141-7100; e-mail drica@cbpf.br; internet www.cbpf.br; f. 1949; library of 19,000 vols, 800 periodicals; Dir FERNANDO LÁZARO FREIRE, JR; Sec. IVANILDA GOMES FERREIRA; publ. *Ciência e Sociedade*.

Departamento Nacional da Produção Mineral (National Department of Mineral Production): SAN Quadra 01, Bloco B, Brasília, DF 70041-903; tel. (61) 3312-6666; e-mail dire@dnpm.gov.br; internet www.dnpm.gov.br; f. 1907; attached to Min. of Mines and Energy; Dir-Gen. SÉRGIO AUGUSTO DÂMASO DE SOUSA; publs *Anuário Mineral Brasileiro*, *Balanço Mineral Brasileiro*.

Instituto Nacional de Meteorologia (National Institute of Meteorology): Eixo Monumental Via S1 Sudoeste, Brasília, DF 70680-900; tel. (61) 2102-4602; e-mail acs.inmet@inmet.gov.br; internet www.inmet.gov.br; f. 1909; Dir ANTÔNIO DIVINO MOURA; publ. *Boletim Agroclimatológico*.

Laboratório de Análises (Analytical Laboratory): Av. Rodrigues Alves 81, Rio de Janeiro, RJ 20081-250; tel. (21) 223-7743; f. 1889; covers organic, inorganic and pharmaceutical chemistry, biochemistry and materials; library of 4,000 vols; Dir Prof. MARCELO DE M. MOURA.

Observatório Nacional (National Observatory): Rua General José Cristino 77, Bairro Imperial de São Cristovão, Rio de Janeiro, RJ 20921-400; tel. (21) 2580-2681; e-mail dir@on.br; internet www.on.br; f. 1827; library; astronomical, metrology of time and frequency and geophysical research programmes using 7 refractors, a Time Service at Rio de Janeiro and a Time Station at Brasília; operates 3 magnetic observatories; established seismograph network in Brazil; graduate programmes in astronomy and geophysics; Dir Dr JOÃO CARLOS COSTA DOS ANJOS; publs *Contribuições Científicas*, *Efemérides Astronômicas* (1 a year).

PHILOSOPHY AND PSYCHOLOGY

Instituto Neo-Pitagórico (Neo-Pythagorean Institute): CP 1047, Curitiba, PR 80001-970; Rua Prof. Dario Vellozo 460, Vila Izabel, Curitiba, PR 80320-260; tel. (41) 3242-1840; e-mail neo@pitagorico.org.br; internet www.pitagorico.org.br; f. 1909; courses in hierology, history of religion, occultism, parapsychology, philosophy, Pythagorean studies, theosophy; library of 21,000 vols; Pres. Dr ANAEL PINHEIRO DE ULHOA CINTRA; Sec. ELIZABETH GARZUZE DA SILVA ARAUJO; publs *A Lâmpada* (4 a year), *Biblioteca Neo-Pitagórica* (1 a year), *Circulares* (1 a year), *Templo da Paz* (3 a year).

RELIGION, SOCIOLOGY AND ANTHROPOLOGY

Fundação Joaquim Nabuco (Joaquim Nabuco Foundation): Av. 17 de Agosto 2187, Casa Forte, Recife, PE 52061-540; tel. (81) 3073-6363; e-mail presi@fundaj.gov.br; internet www.fundaj.gov.br; f. 1949; anthropological, economic, educational, geographical, historical, political, sociological, statistical and population studies about N and NE Brazil; attached museum; library of 60,238 vols; Pres. Dr FERNANDO JOSÉ FREIRE; publs *Cadernos de Estudos Sociais* (2 a year), *Ciência & Trópico* (2 a year).

TECHNOLOGY

Centro de Pesquisas e Desenvolvimento (CEPED) (Research and Development Centre): Km 0 Rodovia 512, Camaçari, BA 42810-440; tel. (71) 834-7300; internet www.ceped.ba.gov.br; f. 1969; research in agroindustrial and food technology, analysis, building materials, chemistry and petrochemistry, energy, environmental engineering, metallurgy, ores treatment, materials testing, mineralogy, quality control; library of 26,702 vols; Dir Dr SYLVIO DE QUEIROS MATTOSO; publ. *Tecbahia* (3 a year).

Comissão Nacional de Energia Nuclear (CNEN) (Commission for Nuclear Energy): Rua Gal Severiano n° 90, Botafogo, Rio de Janeiro, RJ 22290-901; tel. (21) 2173-2000; e-mail presidencia@cnen.gov.br; internet www.cnen.gov.br; f. 1956; supervisory nuclear agency, coordinates planning and financing of nuclear activities, promotes and executes research programmes, trains scientists and technicians; Pres. ANGELO FERNANDO PADILHA.

Attached Institutes:

Centro de Desenvolvimento da Tecnologia Nuclear (Nuclear Technology Development Centre): CP 941, Belo Horizonte, MG 30161-970; Av. Pres. Antônio Carlos, 6627, Campus UFMG, Belo Horizonte, MG 31270-901; tel. (31) 3069-3261; e-mail comunicacao@cdtn.br; internet www.cdtn.br; f. 1952; environmental and atomic energy research; applied research in medical radiology, radiotherapy and nuclear medicine; geological and metallogenic studies of uranium deposits; Dir JOÃO ROBERTO LOUREIRO DE MATTOS.

Centro Regional de Ciências Nucleares do Centro-Oeste (Regional Centre of Nuclear Sciences of the Midwest): BR 060, km 174,5, Abadia de Goiá, GO 75345-000; tel. (62) 3604-6001; e-mail crcnco@cnen.gov.br; internet www.crcn-co.cnen.gov.br; f. 1997; represents CNEN regionally in the Midwest of Brazil and the state of Goiás; conducts research in nuclear and environmental sciences; Coordinator ROSANGELA DA SILVEIRA CORREA.

Centro Regional de Ciências Nucleares do Nordeste (Regional Centre of Nuclear Sciences of the Northeast): Rua Prof. Luiz Freire n° 200, Cidade Universitária, Recife, PE 50740-540; tel. (81) 3797-8000; internet www.crcn.gov.br; f. 1995; represents CNEN regionally in the N and NE of Brazil; conducts nuclear research and devt; Dir FERNANDO ROBERTO DE ANDRADE LIMA.

Instituto de Engenharia Nuclear (Nuclear Engineering Institute): Rua Hélio de Almeida 75, Cidade Universitária, Ilha do Fundão, Rio de Janeiro, RJ 21941-906; tel. (21) 2173-3702; e-mail sampaio@ien.gov.br; internet www.ien.gov.br; f. 1962; pure and applied research and devt of uses of atomic energy, especially fast breeder reactors, instrumentation and control, cyclotron physics; library of 55,000 vols incl. books, journals, theses and technical reports; Dir PAULO AUGUSTO BERQUO DE SAMPAIO.

Instituto de Pesquisas Energéticas e Nucleares (Nuclear and Energy Research Institute): Av. Prof. Lineu Prestes 2242, Cidade Universitária, São Paulo, SP 05508-000; tel. (11) 3133-9000; e-mail pergunta@ipen.br; internet www.ipen.br; f. 1956; conducts pure and applied research in energy, mainly in nuclear sector; offers training courses; energy information centre; library of 21,214 books, 32,856 scientific reports, 18,066 scientific papers of the institute, 1,700 periodicals, 28,835 DVDs; Dir JOSÉ CARLOS BRESSIANI; Dir for Research, Devt and Education MARCELO LINARDI.

Instituto de Radioproteção e Dosimetria (Radiation Protection and Dosimetry Institute): Av. Salvador Allende s/n, Recreio dos Bandeirantes, Rio de Janeiro, RJ 22780-160; tel. (21) 2173-2701; e-mail ird@ird.gov.br; internet www.ird.gov.br; f. 1972; research and devt of radiation protection and dosimetry methods and standards; training courses on radiation protection for industries and health physics professionals; post-graduation course; Dir DEJANIRA DA COSTA LAURIA.

Instituto Brasileiro de Petróleo, Gás e Biocombustíveis (Brazilian Petroleum, Gas and Biofuels Institute): Av. Almirante Barroso 52, 26° andar, Centro, Rio de Janeiro, RJ 20031-000; tel. (21) 2112-9000; e-mail ibp@ibp.org.br; internet www.ibp.org.br; f. 1957; holds Brazilian standards for petroleum products and equipment; research in petroleum, gas, biofuels and petrochemical industries; mems: 200 companies; Pres. JOÃO CARLOS DE LUCA.

Instituto de Pesquisas Tecnológicas (Institute for Technological Research): Av. Prof. Almeida Prado 532 Cidade Universitária, Butantã, São Paulo, SP 05508-901; tel. (11) 3767-4000; e-mail imprensa@ipt.br; internet www.ipt.br; f. 1899; non-profit public corpn owned by the State of São Paulo; 8 technical divs: civil engineering, chemistry, economy and systems engineering, forest products, geology, mechanical and electrical engineering, metallurgy, transport technology; 4 technical centres: information technology and telecommunications, leather and footwear technology, technological improvement, technological information; library of 98,200 books, 4,315 periodicals, 1.1m. nat. and int. active and historical standards; Dir Pres. Dr FERNANDO JOSÉ GOMES LANDGRAF; publ. *Revista do IPT – Pesquisa & Tecnologia*.

Instituto de Tecnológia de Pernambuco (ITEP) (Technological Institute of the State of Pernambuco): Av. Prof. Luis Freire 700, Cidade Universitária, Recife, PE 50740-540; tel. (81) 3183-4399; e-mail itep@itep.br; internet www.itep.br; f. 1942; industrial research; library of 6,500 vols, 2,500 pamphlets, 1,503 periodical articles, 603 periodical titles, 63 dissertations, 4,673 technical standards and int. standards; Pres. FREFERICO CAVALCANTI MONTENEGRO; publ. *Revista Pernambucana de Tecnologia* (2 a year).

Instituto de Tecnológia do Paraná (Paraná Institute of Technology): Rua Prof. Algacyr Munhoz Mader 3775 Cidade Industrial de Curitiba, Curitiba, PR 81350-010; tel. (41) 3316-3000; e-mail tecpar@tecpar.br; internet www.tecpar.br; f. 1940; centres of energy, engineering of intelligent systems, industrial measurements, information and strategic studies, technological tests; research in all aspects of technology for the devt of the state; produces vaccines; nat. and int. exchange with orgs in the same field; library of 8,000 vols, 1,054 periodicals; Pres. JÚLIO C. FELIX; publs *Boletim Técnico* (6 a year), *Brazilian Archives of Biology and Technology* (6 a year, in English, print and online, www.babt.tecpar.br).

Instituto Nacional de Pesquisas Espaciais (INPE) (National Institute for Space Research): Av. dos Astronautas 1758, Jardim Granja, São José dos Campos, SP 12227-010; tel. (12) 3208-6000; e-mail diretor@dir.inpe.br; internet www.inpe.br; f. 1961, renamed in 1971; research areas: earth observation, satellite tracking and control, space and atmospheric sciences, space engineering and technology, weather forecast and climate studies; attached integration and testing laboratory; other laboratories in the field of combustion, computing and applied mathematics, plasma, propulsion, sensors and materials; library of 73,000 vols of books, theses, reports and maps, 160,000 journals; spec. map colln of 4,800 items; Dir Dr LEONEL FERNANDO PERONDI; publ. *Climanálise*.

Instituto Nacional de Tecnología (National Technological Institute): Av. Venezuela 82, Rio de Janeiro, RJ 20081-312; tel. (21) 2123-1018; e-mail domingos.naveiro@int.gov.br; internet www.int.gov.br; f. 1921; research in chemical industry, chemistry of natural products, computer-aided projects, corrosion, energy conservation, industrial design, metallurgy, pollution control, rubber and plastics; library of 49,000 vols of books, periodicals, theses, reports, technical standards; Dir DOMINGOS MANFREDI NAVEIRO; publ. *Informativo do INT*.

Libraries and Archives

Aracajú

Biblioteca Pública Epifânio Dória (Epifânio Dória Public Library): Prolongamento da Vila Cristina, s/n, Aracajú, SE 49015-000; tel. (79) 224-2127; f. 1851; 15,000 vols; Dir SÔNIA CARVALHO.

Belém

Arquivo Público do Estado do Pará (Pará Public Archives): Rua Campos Sales, 273, Comércio, Belém, PA 66019-050; tel. (91) 3219-1110; e-mail apep.secult@yahoo.com.br; internet www.apep.pa.gov.br; f. 1901; 742 vols; Dir GERALDO MÁRTIRES COELHO; publ. *Anais do Arquivo Público do Pará* (every 2 years).

Biblioteca Central Prof. Dr Clodoaldo Beckmann da Universidade Federal do Pará (Central Library of Prof Dr. Clodoaldo Beckmann Federal University of Pará): Rua Augusto Corrêa 1, Campus Universitário, Guamá, Belém, PA 66075-110; tel. (91) 3201-7110; e-mail bc@ufpa.br; internet bc.ufpa.br; f. 1962; 900,000 vols general colln, Amazon colln, theses and dissertations, rare books, DVD and CD-ROM works in Braille; Dir MARIA DAS GRAÇAS DA SILVA PENA.

Biblioteca do Grêmio Literário e Comercial Português (Library of the Portuguese Literary and Commercial Union): Rua Senador Manuel Barata 477/483, Belém, PA 66019-000; tel. (91) 3241-0918; internet www.gremioportugues.com.br/conteudo_fixo/detalhe/6/biblioteca; f. 1867; 29,568 vols; Chief Librarian ANTONIO PINHO.

Belo Horizonte

Biblioteca Pública Estadual Luiz de Bessa (Public Library): Praça da Liberdade 21, Funcionários, Belo Horizonte, MG 30140-010; tel. (31) 3269-1166; e-mail bibliotecapublica.sub@cultura.mg.gov.br; f. 1954; 280,000 vols, 5,124 vols of braille, 300 talking books; 600 brs; Dir MARIA DE FÁTIMA FALCI.

Sistema de Bibliotecas da UFMG (Library System UFMG): Av. Presidente Antônio Carlos 6627, Pampulha, Belo Horizonte, MG 31270-901; tel. (31) 3409-4609; e-mail sdir@bu.ufmg.br; internet www.bu.ufmg.br; f. 1927; colln of spec. documents; 650,000 vols, 6,000 maps, 14,763 rare works, 22,000 periodicals, 15,000 music scores; Dir MARIA ELIZABETH DE OLIVEIRA COSTA.

Brasília

Biblioteca Acadêmico Luiz Viana Filho (Library of the Federal Senate): Senado Federal, Praça dos Três Poderes, Palácio do Congresso (Anexo II—Térreo), Brasília, DF 70165-900; tel. (61) 3303-1267; e-mail biblioteca@senado.leg.br; internet www.senado.gov.br/sf/biblioteca; f. 1826; specializes in social sciences, law, politics, public admin., legislation; also works on literature, history and geography; 200,000 vols; 6,000 periodical titles, 8,000 rare books, 3m. newspaper clippings, the Senator Luiz Viana Filho colln with 12,000 vols, the Legal Deposit colln with works published by the Senate and the digital library with about 250,000 documents; Dir SIMONE BASTOS VIEIRA; publ. *Revista de Informação Legislativa* (4 a year, online).

Biblioteca Central, Universidade de Brasília (Central Library, University of Brasilia): Campus Universitário Darcy Ribeiro, Gleba A, Brasília, DF 70910-900; tel. (61) 3107-2676; e-mail emprestimos@bce.unb.br; internet www.bce.unb.br; f. 1962; 1,500,000 vols, 7,864 periodicals; maps colln, spec. colln of works by Cassiano Nunes and Carlos Lacerda; Dir EMIR JOSÉ SUAIDEN.

Biblioteca Demonstrativa Maria da Conceição Moreira Salles/Fundação Biblioteca Nacional (Demonstrative Library Maria da Conceição Moreira Salles/National Library Foundation): Av. W3 Sul, Entrequadras 506/507, Brasília, DF 70350-580; tel. (61) 3443-0852; e-mail bdb@bn.br; internet www.bdb.org.br; f. 1970; cultural activities, book club, music sessions, courses, workshops, authors' rights office; 110,617 vols; Dir and Pres. MAURO MANDELLI.

Biblioteca do Ministério da Justiça (Library of Ministry of Justice): Esplanada dos Ministérios, Ed. Sede Térreo, Brasília, DF 70064-900; tel. (61) 3429-3323; e-mail biblioteca@mj.br; f. 1940; colln covers agencies and units of the Min. of Justice; very rare colln of laws of Portuguese colonial period; 80,000 vols, 437 periodicals on law, economics, sociology, labour, and political science; 6,000 vols Goethe colln, Affonso Penna Jr colln, Brazilian legislation colln; Dir DOROTI TEREZITA HOF; publ. *Revista Arquivos do Ministério da Justiça*.

Biblioteca do Ministério do Trabalho e Emprego (Library of Ministry of Labour and Employment): Esplanada dos Ministérios, Bloco F, Ala B Ed, Anexo Térreo, Brasília, DF 70056-900; tel. (61) 2031-6186; f. 1871; 120 collns of newspapers; 19,000 vols; Librarian MARIA PAULA GARCIA CAMPOS DE ARAYO; publ. *Relação Anual de Informações Sociais*; publ. *Revista Carta Capital* (irregular).

Biblioteca Embaixador Antonio Francisco Azeredo da Silveira (Azeredo da Silveira Library): Palácio Itamaraty, Esplanada dos Ministérios, Bloco H, Anexo II, Térreo, Brasília, DF 70170-900; tel. (61) 3411-9103; e-mail biblio@itamaraty.gov.br; internet www.biblioteca.itamaraty.gov.br; f. 1906; attached to Dept of Communication and Documentation, Min. of Foreign Affairs; law, history, politics and economics; colln of UN documents; 100,000 vols, 590 periodical titles; Chief Librarian Bib. ELIZABETH MARIA DE MATTOS.

Biblioteca Nacional de Agricultura (BINAGRI) (National Library of Agriculture): Ministério da Agricultura, Pecuária e Abastecimento Esplanada dos Ministérios, Bloco D, Brasília, DF 70043-970; tel. (61) 3218-2828; f. 1904; central unit of National System of Agricultural Information and Documentation (SNIDA); responsible for establishing State libraries of agriculture in order to decentralize information sources; 400,000 vols, 7,032 serial titles, 216,000 microfiche documents; Coordinator and Librarian NEUZA ARANTES SILVA; publ. *Thesaurus para Indexação/Recuperação da Literatura Agrícola Brasileira*.

Centro de Documentação e Informação da Câmara dos Deputados do Brasil (Centre for Documentation and Information, Chamber of Deputies, Brazil): Palácio do Congresso Nacional, Praça dos Três Poderes,

Brasília, DF 70160-900; tel. (61) 3216-5777; e-mail informa.cedi@camara.gov.br; f. 1971; 200,000 vols, 4,700 vols of rare books; Dir ADOLFO FURTADO; Dir of Archives Unit FREDERICO DOS SANTOS.

Centro de Informação e Biblioteca em Educação (Centre for Library Information and Education): Esplanada dos Ministérios, Ministério da Educação, Bloco L, Ed. Sede, térreo, Zona Cívico-administrativa, Brasília, DF 70047-900; tel. (61) 2022-3960; e-mail cibec@inep.gov.br; internet portal.inep.gov.br/pesquisa-cibec-ocibec; f. 1981; specialized library on education; 21,000 vols, 844 periodicals; Coordinator-Gen. ALEX RICARDO MEDEIROS DA SILVEIRA.

Instituto Brasileiro de Informação em Ciência e Tecnologia (IBICT) (Brazilian Institute of Information in Science and Technology (IBICT)): Setor de Autarquias Sul (SAUS), Quadra 05 Lote 06 Bloco H, Brasília, DF 70070-912; tel. (61) 3217-6145; e-mail bib@ibict.br; internet www.ibict.br; f. 1954 as IBBD, current name adopted 1976; coordinates scientific and technical information services throughout the country; provides technical assistance, and training; 205,000 vols; Dir EMIR SUAIDEN; publ. *Ciência da Informação* (3 a year).

Curitiba

Biblioteca Central da Universidade Federal do Paraná (Central Library of the University of Paraná): CP 19051, Rua General Carneiro 370/380, Centro, Curitiba, PR 81531-990; tel. (41) 3360-5000; e-mail bc@ufpr.br; internet www.ufpr.br/portalufpr/servicos/bibliotecas; f. 1956; 13 specialized libraries; 350,000 vols; Dir GILBERTO DE CASTRO.

Biblioteca Pública do Paraná (Paraná Public Library): Rua Cândido Lopes 133, Curitiba, PR 80020-901; tel. (41) 3221-4900; e-mail bppgeral@pr.gov.br; internet www.bpp.pr.gov.br; f. 1954; 630,000 vols, incl. 1,026 periodicals, photographs and multimedia materials; Dir ROGÉRIO PEREIRA.

Florianópolis

Biblioteca Pública do Estado de Santa Catarina (Santa Catarina State Public Library): Rua Tenete Silveira 343, Centro, Florianópolis, SC 88010-301; tel. (48) 3028-8063; e-mail biblio@fcc.sc.gov.br; f. 1854; collns of rare books, braille and talking books; 115,000 vols; Dir ISABELA SALUM FETT.

Fortaleza

Biblioteca Pública Governador Menezes Pimentel (Governor Menezes Pimentel Public Library): Av. Presidente Castelo Branco 255, Centro, Fortaleza, CE 60010-000; tel. (85) 3101-2552; e-mail bpublica@secult.ce.gov.br; f. 1867 as Provincial Library of Caera; 115 m. vols, incl. books, periodicals, rare books, video cassettes, spoken books, braille books and CD-ROMs; Dir and Pres. MARIA DO SOCORRO SAMPAIO FLORES.

Biblioteca Universitária da Universidade Federal do Ceará (University Library of the Federal University of Ceará): Campus do Pici s/n, CP 6025, 60451-970 Fortaleza, CE 60451-970; tel. (85) 3366-9506; internet www.biblioteca.ufc.br; f. 1958; 164,429 vols; Dir FRANCISCO JONATAN SOARES.

João Pessoa

Biblioteca Pública do Estado da Paraíba (Paraíba Public Library): Rua General Osório 253, Centro, João Pessoa, PB 58000-000; tel. (83) 3218-4195; e-mail bibliotecafunesc@gmail.com; f. 1857; 130,000 vols; Dir CYBELLE NUNES.

Ouro Preto

Biblioteca Dr Amaro Lanari Júnior (Library of the Ouro Preto School of Mines): Campus da Universidade Federal de Ouro Preto, Morro do Cruzeiro Ouro Preto, MG 35400-000; tel. (31) 3559-1508; e-mail bibem@sisbin.ufop.br; internet www.sisbin.ufop.br; f. 1876; 50,000 vols, 1,900 periodicals; Exec. Coordinator CELINA BRASIL LUIZ; publ. *Revista*.

Pelotas

Biblioteca Pública Pelotense (Public Library Pelotense): Praça Coronel Pedro Osório 103, Pelotas, RS 96015-010; tel. (53) 3222-3856; f. 1875; museum, cultural exhibition; 150,000 vols; Pres. JOAQUIM SALVADOR COELHO PINHO.

Petrópolis

Biblioteca Central Municipal Gabriela Mistral (Central Municipal Library Gabriela Mistral): Praça Visconde de Mauá 305, Centro, Petrópolis, RJ 25685-380; tel. (24) 2233-1228; e-mail biblioteca@petropolis.rj.gov.br; internet www.petropolis.rj.gov.br; f. 1871; incorporates archive of 300,000 documents concerning admin. history of Petrópolis; 140,000 vols; Librarian MARIA HELENA DE AVELLAR PALMA.

Porto Alegre

Biblioteca Central da Universidade Federal do Rio Grande do Sul: Av. Paulo Gama 110, Térreo da Reitoria Prédio 12107, 90046-900 Porto Alegre, RS; tel. (51) 3308-3065; e-mail bcentral@bc.ufrgs.br; internet www.biblioteca.ufrgs.br; f. 1971; 32 br. libraries; 1,044,830 vols; Dir VIVIANE CARRION CASTANHO.

Biblioteca Pública do Estado do Rio Grande do Sul (Rio Grande do Sul State Public Library): Rua dos Andradas, 736, Centro, Porto Alegre, RS; tel. (51) 3224-5045; e-mail bpe.administracao@via-rs.net; internet www.bibliotecapublica.rs.gov.br; f. 1877; 250,000 vols incl. colln of works in Braille and audio books for visually impaired people; Dir MORGANA MARCON.

Recife

Biblioteca Central da Universidade Federal de Pernambuco (Central Library of the Federal University of Pernambuco): Av. Prof. Moraes Rego 1235, Cidade Universitária, Recife, PE 50670-901; tel. (81) 2126-8000; e-mail bcufpe@ufpe.br; internet www.ufpe.br; f. 1968; regional centre for the nat. bibliographic network organized by the Instituto Brasileiro de Informação em Ciência e Tecnologia (*q.v.*); 405,291 vols (incl. all deptl libraries), 8,603 periodicals; Dir ELILSON GÓIS; publs *BC-informa* (12 a year), *Sumários de Periódicos* (12 a year).

Biblioteca Pública do Estado de Pernambuco (Pernambuco State Public Library): Rua João Lira s/n, Santo Amaro, Recife, PE 50050-550; tel. (81) 3181-2642; e-mail sbm@educacao.pe.gov.br; internet www.biblioteca.pe.gov.br; f. 1852; 250,000 vols, incl. rare works, iconography, MSS, map colln, braille and journals; Coordinator MARIA LÚCIA BEZERRA FERREIRA.

Rio de Janeiro

Arquivo Nacional (National Archives): Praça da República, 173, Rio de Janeiro, RJ 20211-350; tel. (21) 2179-1228; e-mail pi@arquivonacional.gov.br; internet www.arquivonacional.gov.br; f. 1838; specializes in history of Brazil, technique of archives and legislation; 44,000 vols on geography, 8,000 rare books, 45 shelf-km of documents, 1.74 million photographs and negatives, 200 photo albums, 15,000 slides, 4,000 caricatures and cartoons, 3,000 posters, 300 drawings, 300 engravings and 20,000 illustrations; Dir-Gen. JAIME ANTUNES DA SILVA; publs *BIBA*, *Revista Acervo* (2 a year).

Biblioteca Bastos Tigre da Associação Brasileira de Imprensa (Bastos Tigre Library of Brazilian Press Association): Rua Araújo Porto Alegre 71, 12° andar, Rio de Janeiro, RJ 20030-010; tel. 2262-9822; e-mail biblioteca@abi.org.br; internet www.abi.org.br/biblioteca; f. 1908; 40,473 vols, 6,788 periodical titles; Pres. MAURÍCIO AZÊDO.

Biblioteca da Sociedade Brasileira de Cultura Inglesa: Rua São Clemente 258–3°, 4° e 5° andares, Botafogo, Rio de Janeiro, RJ 22260-000; tel. (21) 2528-8700; internet www.culturainglesa.net; f. 1934; 3 brs; 34,000 vols; Head Librarian MARIA DE FÁTIMA BORGES GONÇALVES; publ. *Library News*.

Biblioteca do Centro Cultural Banco do Brasil (Library of the Banco do Brasil Cultural Centre): Rua Primeiro de Março 66, 5° andar, Centro, Rio de Janeiro, RJ 20010-000; tel. (21) 3808-2020; e-mail ccbbrio@bb.com.br; f. 1931; spec. collns: rare books, Brazilian music and folklore; 125,000 vols; Dir KLEUBER DE PAIVA PEREIRA.

Biblioteca do Exército (Army Library): Palácio Duque de Caxias, Ala Marcílio Dias (3° andar), Centro, Rio de Janeiro, RJ 20221-260; tel. (21) 2519-5726; e-mail assinantes@bibliex.ensino.eb.br; internet www.bibliex.ensino.eb.br; f. 1881; general collns to supply cultural needs of the army; Dir Cel LUIZ EUGÊNIO DUARTE PEIXOTO; publs *Revista A Defesa Nacional* (3 a year), *Revista do Exército Brasileiro* (3 a year), *Revista Militar de Ciência e Tecnologia* (3 a year).

Biblioteca do Instituto dos Advogados Brasileiros (Library of Lawyers' Institute): Av. Marechal Câmara 210, 5° andar, Centro, Rio de Janeiro, RJ 20020-080; tel. (21) 2240-3921; internet www.iabnacional.org.br; f. 1897; archives the publs of Institute of Brazilian Lawyers and Order of Attorneys of Brazil; spec. collns incl. the works of Rui Barbosa; attached museum; 36,000 vols; Dir MAXIMUM FERNANDO DE ALMEIDA PIZARRO DRUMMOND.

Biblioteca do Ministério das Relações Exteriores no Rio de Janeiro (Library of the Ministry of Foreign Affairs in Rio de Janeiro): Palácio Itamaraty, Av. Marechal Floriano 196, Centro, Rio de Janeiro, RJ 20080-002; tel. (21) 2253-5730; f. 1906; history; rare books; see also under Brasília; 270,000 vols incl. periodicals; Dir SONIA DOYLE.

Biblioteca Nacional (National Library): Av. Rio Branco 219-39, Rio de Janeiro, RJ 20040-008; tel. (21) 3095-3879; e-mail infobn@bn.br; internet www.bn.br; f. 1810 with 60,000 vols from the Real Biblioteca brought to Brazil by the Royal Family of Portugal in 1808; spec. collns: Col. De Angelis (Brazilian and Paraguayan History), Col. Tereza Cristina Maria (donated by Emperor D. Pedro II, 1891), Col. Alexandre Rodrigues Ferreira (description with illustrations of travels in Amazônia by A. R. Ferreira, 1783–1792); 120,000 vols; Pres. PEDRO CORREA DO LAGO; publ. *Anais da Biblioteca Nacional*.

Biblioteca Popular do Leblon-Vinicius de Moraes: Av. Bartolomeu Mitre 1297, Gávea, Rio de Janeiro, RJ 22431-000; tel. (21) 2294-1598; f. 1946; 8,000 vols; Dir MARIA LEONICE DE ALMEIDA.

Biblioteca Pública de Copacabana: Av. N.S. de Copacabana 817, Copacabana, Rio de Janeiro, RJ 22050-002; tel. (21) 2255-0081; e-mail biblicopa@pcrj.rj.gov.br; f. 1954;

29,706 vols; Dir ANA MARIA COSTA DESLANDES.

Fundação Casa de Rui Barbosa (Rui Barbosa Foundation): Rua São Clemente 134, Rio de Janeiro, RJ 22260-000; tel. (21) 3289-4600; internet www.casaruibarbosa.gov.br; f. 1930, became Foundation 1966; incl. centre for research in law, philology and history, centre of Brazilian literature (over 50,000 documents), documentation centre with a library, Rui Barbosa archive, microfilm laboratory and paper restoration laboratory; museum and auditorium; 37,000 vols, 60,000 items that make up the file Rui Barbosa; Pres. MANOLO GARCIA FLORENTINO.

Fundação Instituto Brasileiro de Geografia e Estatística: Rua General Canabarro, nº 706, Maracanã, Rio de Janeiro, RJ 20271-200; tel. (21) 2142-4720; e-mail bibliotecacddi@ibge.gov.br; internet www.ibge.gov.br; f. 1977; attached to Centro de Documentação e Disseminação de Informações, Divisão de Biblioteca e Acervos Especiais; documentation and dissemination of research and studies in geoscience, environment, demography, social and economic indicators, nat. accounts, statistics; 48,000 vols, 2,105 periodicals, 20,000 maps, 115,000 photographs; Dir MARIA TERESA PASSOS BASTOS.

Serviço de Documentação da Marinha (Documentation Service of the Navy): Rua Dom Manuel, 15, Centro, Rio de Janeiro, RJ 20091-000; tel. (21) 3870-6721; e-mail admin@sdm.mar.mil.br; internet www.mar.mil.br/dphdm/sede.htm; f. 1943; maritime history of Brazil; incl. a naval museum and archives; naval library of 110,000 vols; Dir LUIS HENRIQUE DE AZEVEDO BRAGA; publ. *Revista Marítima Brasileira* (3 a year).

Sistema de Bibliotecas e Informação da Universidade Federal do Rio de Janeiro (Library and Information System of the Federal University of Rio de Janeiro): Av. Pasteur 250, Urca, Rm 106, Rio de Janeiro, RJ 22290-902; tel. (21) 2295-1595; e-mail sibi@sibi.ufrj.br; internet www.sibi.ufrj.br; f. 1983; coordinates 43 brs; maintains mem. of the Nat. Catalogue of Periodicals Online; 1,567,330 vols, 3.24m. periodicals; Coordinator PAULA MARIA ABRANTES COTTA DE MELLO.

Rio Grande

Biblioteca Rio-Grandense (Rio Grande Library): Rua General Osório 454, Bairro Centro, Rio Grande, RS 96200-400; tel. (53) 231-2842; e-mail contato@bibliotecariograndense.com.br; internet bibliotecariograndense.com.br; f. 1846; 400,000 vols, 7,600 maps; Pres. Dr JOÃO MARINONIO CARNEIRO LAGES; Dir Dr GILBERTO M. CENTENO CARDOSO.

Rio Negro

Biblioteca Pública Municipal Prof. Wenceslau Muniz (Prof. Wenceslau Muniz Municipal Public Library): Rua Getúlio Vargas 680, Centro, Rio Negro, PR 83880-000; tel. (47) 3645-1311; e-mail bibliotecapublicarn@yahoo.com.br.

Salvador

Biblioteca Pública do Estado da Bahia (Bahia State Public Library): Rua Gen. Labatut 27, Barris, Salvador, BA 40010-100; tel. (71) 3117-6000; e-mail bpeb.fpc@fpc.ba.gov.br; f. 1811 as Livraria Pública da Bahia, current name adopted 1984; 114,698 vols; Dir KILMA APARECIDA.

São José dos Campos

Biblioteca Pública 'Cassiano Ricardo' ('Cassiano Ricardo' Public Library): Rua XV de Novembro 99, Centro, São José dos Campos, SP 12210-070; tel. (12) 3921-6330; f. 1968; 70,000 vols and 8,500 periodicals; Dir ANA ELISABETE MARTINELLI GODINHO.

São Luís

Biblioteca Pública Benedito Leite (Benedito Leite Public Library): Praça Deodoro, s/n, Centro, São Luís, MA 65020-430; tel. (98) 3218-9910; e-mail bpbl@cultura.ma.gov.br; f. 1829; collns of more than 15,000 engravings, and newspapers since 1821; 45,000 vols; Dir JOSEANE MARIA DE SOUZA; Librarian ROBERTO TAMARA.

São Paulo

Arquivo do Estado de São Paulo (Public Archives of the State of São Paulo): Rua Voluntários da Pátria, 596, Santana, São Paulo, SP 02010-000; tel. (11) 2221-4785; e-mail faleconosco@arquivoestado.sp.gov.br; internet www.arquivoestado.sp.gov.br; f. 1892; 10 km of historical documents incl. MSS, photographs, illustrations, journals, magazines, maps, books and state records; preserves documents covering more than 400 years of history; 45,000 vols; Dir Dr FAUSTO COUTO SOBRINHO; publ. *Revista Histórica* (6 a year, online).

Biblioteca 'Ana Maria Poppovic': Av. Prof. Francisco Morato 1565, Jardim Guedala, São Paulo, SP 05513-900; tel. (11) 3723-3083; e-mail biblioteca@fcc.org.br; internet www.fcc.org.br/biblioteca; attached to Fundação Carlos Chagas; colln focused on education, childcare, women, statistics; contains publs of the Min. of Education and state depts of education; incl. Ariadne database that contains summaries of scholarly work on women, gender, sexuality and formal education; 23m. vols of books, periodicals, monographs, dissertations and theses, 432 audiovisual items; Head Librarian MARIA JOSÉ DE OLIVEIRA DE SOUZA; publs *Cadernos de Pesquisa* (3 a year), *Estudos em Avaliação Educacional* (2 a year).

Biblioteca do Instituto de Saúde (Health Institute Library): Av. Dr. Enéas Carvalho de Aguiar, 188, São Paulo, SP 05403-000; tel. (11) 3066-8000; internet www.isaude.sp.gov.br; f. 1969; 41,000 vols, valuable collection of works, reviews, maps on dermatology and Hansen's disease, and rare works since 1600; Dir CARMEN CAMPOS ARIAS PAULENAS.

Biblioteca 'George Alexander' (George Alexander Library): Rua da Consolação 896, Prédio 2, Consolação, São Paulo, SP 01302-907; tel. (11) 2114-8316; e-mail biblio.per@mackenzie.com.br; internet www.mackenzie.com.br; f. 1870 as Mackenzie Library, current name adopted 1926; 378,000 vols; 1,700 periodical titles; Librarian MARIA REGINA TRUGILHO.

Biblioteca Municipal Mário de Andrade (Municipal Library): Rua da Consolação 94, São Paulo, SP 01302-000; tel. (11) 3775-0002; f. 1925; incl. fmr Biblioteca Pública do Estado de São Paulo; 53,000 vols; 52,000 rare books, 8,774 vols of periodicals and 3,500 other documents; Dir LUIZ ARMANDO BAGOLIN; publ. *Revista da Biblioteca Mário de Andrade*.

BIREME—Centro Latino-Americano e do Caribe de Informação em Ciências da Saúde (Latin American and Caribbean Centre on Health Sciences Information): Rua Botucatu 862, São Paulo, SP 04023-901; tel. (11) 5576-9800; e-mail birdir@bireme.org; internet www.bireme.br; f. 1967; provides access to scientific and technical health information for devt and health research, education and care systems; 587,156 records of 27 countries, 851 journals, 475,503 articles, 77,165 monographs, 28,129 theses, 205,993 full texts; Dir ADALBERTO OTRANTO TARDELLI (acting); publ. *LILACS* (3 a year, online (lilacs.bvsalud.org)).

British Council Library and Information Centre: Rua Ferreira Araújo, 741 terreo Pinheiros, São Paolo SP 05428-002; tel. (11) 2126 7500; e-mail centro.info@britishcouncil.org.br; internet www.britishcouncil.org/brasil-quem-somos-biblioteca-e-centro-de-informacao.htm; 7,000 vols; Regional Dir Americas PETER ELLWOOD; Dir São Paulo ERIC KLUG.

Discoteca Oneyda Alvarenga: Centro Cultural São Paulo, Rua Vergueiro 1000, Paraíso, São Paulo, SP 01504-000; tel. (11) 3397-4071; e-mail ccsp@prefeitura.sp.gov.br; f. 1935; study and diffusion of Brazilian and int. classical, folk and popular music; colln of books, periodical titles on music; museum of folklore; 11,000 vols; 45,000 78 rpm discs, 26,000 33 rpm discs and 1,500 CDs, 62,000 scores; Librarian JÉSSICA BARRETO.

Sistema Integrado de Bibliotecas da Universidade de São Paulo (São Paulo University Integrated Library System): Rua da Praça do Relógio, 109, Bloco K, 4º andar, São Paulo, SP 05508-050; tel. (11) 3091-4195; e-mail atendimento@sibi.usp.br; internet www.usp.br/sibi; f. 1981; 43 libraries; 7,762,103 vols; Technical Dir Prof. Dr SUELI MARA SOARES PINTO FERREIRA.

Vitória

Arquivo Público Estadual do Espírito Santo (Public Archive of the State of Espírito Santo): Rua Sete de Setembro, 441, Centro, Vitória, ES 29001-970; tel. (27) 3223-7524; e-mail codeac@ape.es.gov.br; f. 1908.

Biblioteca Municipal Adelpho Poli Monjardim (Municipal Library Adelpho Poli Monjardim): Av. Jerônimo Monteiro 656, Centro, Vitória, ES; tel. (27) 3381-6925; f. 1941; 17,000 vols.

Museums and Art Galleries

Belém

Museu Paraense Emílio Goeldi (Goeldi Museum): Ave Magalhães Barata, 376, São Braz, Belém, PA 66040-170; tel. (91) 3219-3300; e-mail gabas@museu-goeldi.br; internet www.museu-goeldi.br; f. 1871 as the Museum of Pará; current name adopted 1900; attached to Min. of Science, Technology and Innovation; research instn; natural history, archaeology, anthropology and ethnography of the Amazon region; zoological and botanical collns and garden; colln of rare books; library of 200,000 vols; Dir Dr NILSON GABAS; Substitute Dir BENEDICTA BARROS; publ. *Destaque Amazônia* (4 a year).

Belo Horizonte

Museu Histórico Abílio Barreto (Abilio Barreto Historical Museum): Av. Prudente de Morais 202, Barrio Cidade Jardim, Belo Horizonte, MG 30380-002; tel. (31) 3277-8573; e-mail mhab.fmc@pbh.gov.br; f. 1943; local colln; spec. collns: original documentation of the Belo Horizonte Construction Commission, Minas Gerais provincial laws (1849–89); library; Dir THAÏS VELLOSO COUGO PIMENTEL.

Campinas

Museu de História Natural (Natural History Museum): Rua Cel Quirino 2, Bosque dos Jequitibás, Campinas, SP 13025-004; tel. (19) 3295-5850; e-mail museuaquario@terra.com.br; f. 1938; long term exhibitions presenting taxidermied specimens from biomes Mata Atlântica, Amazon Forest, Cerrado, and Pantanal; environmental education activities; Dir FLÁVIO JORGE ABRÃO.

Campo Grande

Museu das Culturas Dom Bosco (Dom Bosco Regional Museum): Av. Afonso Pena 7000, Parque das Nações Indígenas, Campo Grande, MS 79010-200; tel. (67) 3326-9788; e-mail info@mcdb.org.br; internet mcdb.org.br; f. 1951; archaeology, ethnographic, mineralogy, palaeontology and zoology; Dir ANTONIO TEIXEIRA.

Curitiba

Museu Oscar Niemeyer (Oscar Niemeyer Museum): Rua Marechal Hermes 999 Centro, Curitiba, PR 80530-230; tel. (41) 3350-4400; e-mail faleconosco@mon.org.br; internet www.museuoscarniemeyer.org.br; f. 2002; focuses on visual arts, architecture and design; 3,000 works of nat. and int. artists; Dir and Pres. CRISTIANO AUGUSTO SOLIS DE FIGUEIREDO MORRISSY.

Museu Paranaense (Paraná Museum): Rua Kellers, 289, Alto São Francisco, Curitiba, PR 80410-100; tel. (41) 3304-3300; e-mail museupr@seec.pr.gov.br; internet www.museuparanaense.pr.gov.br; f. 1876; historical, ethnographical and archaeological collns; 100 seat auditorium; library of 8,000 vols, 2,200 periodicals; colln of rare books on history of Paraná; Dir Dr RENATO AUGUSTO CARNEIRO, JR; publ. *Arquivos do Museu Paranaense*.

Fortaleza

Museu do Ceará (Ceará Museum): Rua São Paulo 51, Centro, Fortaleza, CE 60030-100; tel. (85) 3101-2610; e-mail musce@secult.ce.gov.br; f. 1932; history of Fortaleza and Ceará, ethnographical, archaeological and literary collns, abolition of slavery; Sec. FRANCISCO JOSÉ PINHEIRO.

Goiânia

Museu Goiano Zoroastro Artiaga (Zoroastro Artiaga State Museum): Praça Cívica 13, Setor Central, Goiânia, GO 74003-010; tel. (62) 3201-4676; e-mail hdefreitas@ig.com.br; f. 1946; history, geology, anthropology, local art, folklore; Dir HENRIQUE DE FREITAS.

Itu

Museu Republicano 'Convenção de Itu' (Itu Convention Republican Museum): Rua Barão de Itaim 67, Centro, SP 13300-160; tel. (11) 4023-0240; e-mail mrci@usp.br; internet www.mp.usp.br/mr; f. 1923; attached to Museu Paulista da Universidade de São Paulo (*q.v.*); colln incl. republican objects (for personal use, interior decoration, furniture, tools, weapons, coins and medals), iconographic documents (sculptures, paintings, prints, drawings, plans, maps and photographs) and textual documents (MSS and printed); training workshops for educators; library of 32,000 vols, 142 periodicals, 23 newspaper titles (1870—1930), photographs; spec. collns incl. Prudente de Morais colln, database 1870–1930 and bibliographical rarities; Dir Prof. Dra SHEILA WALBE ORNSTEIN; Supervisor Prof. Dra HELOISA MARIA SILVEIRA BARBUY; publ. *Boletim Informativo—SAMUR*.

Macapá

Museu Histórico do Amapá (Amapá Historical Museum): Av. Mário Cruz, 376, Centro, Macapá AP 68900-740; tel. (96) 3223-5441; e-mail museuhjcs@fundecap.ap.gov.br; f. 1948; zoology, archaeology, ethnography and numismatics; expeditions; Dir Prof. FERNANDO RODRIGUES.

Olinda

Museu Regional de Olinda (Regional Museum of Olinda): Rua do Amparo 128, Olinda, PE 53120-180; tel. (81) 3184-3159; e-mail ddcultural.fundarpe@gmail.com; f. 1934; historic and regional art; Dir ANA MARIA.

Ouro Preto

Museu da Inconfidência (History of Democratic Ideals and Culture): Praça Tiradentes 139, Centro, Ouro Preto, MG 35400-000; tel. (31) 3551-1121; e-mail inconfidencia@veloxmail.com.br; internet www.museudainconfidencia.gov.br; f. 1944; 18th- and 19th- century music MSS and works of art, documents related to Inconfidência Mineira, documents from the Notary Public's Office during the Colonial Period; library of 20,000 vols incl. titles in art, history of mining, literature, museology and religion; Dir RUI MOURÃO; publs *Isto é Inconfidência* (bulletin, 4 a year), *Oficiano do Inconfidência, Revista de Trabalho* (1 a year).

Museu de Ciência e Técnica da Escola de Minas (Science and Technology Museum of the School of Mines): Praça Tiradentes 20, Centro, Ouro Preto, MG 35400-000; tel. (31) 3559-3118; e-mail museu@ufop.br; internet www.museu.em.ufop.br; f. 1995; affiliated to the Universidade Federal de Ouro Preto; Dir Prof. Dr LEONARDO BARBOSA GODEFROID.

Petrópolis

Museu Imperial (Imperial Museum): Rua da Imperatriz 220, Petrópolis, RJ 25610-320; tel. (24) 2233-0300; e-mail mimp.faleconosco@museus.gov.br; internet www.museuimperial.gov.br; f. 1940; 11,024 period exhibits of Brazilian Empire (1808–89) and Petrópolis history, notably imperial regalia, jewels and apparel; historic archives of 200,000 MSS on Brazilian history in the 19th century; 20,000 photos, 1,000 maps and 2,000 iconographic items; library of 50,000 vols incl. 8,000 rare books; Dir MAURÍCIO VICENTE FERREIRA, JR; publ. *Anuário*.

Porto Alegre

Museu de Arte do Rio Grande do Sul Ado Malagoli (Art Museum of Rio Grande do Sul): Praça da Alfândega s/n°, Centro, Porto Alegre, RS 90010-150; tel. (51) 3227-2311; e-mail museu@margs.rs.gov.br; internet www.margs.rs.gov.br; f. 1954; paintings, sculptures, prints, drawings, installations, design; library: art library of 2,500 vols; Dir Dr GAUDÊNCIO FIDELIS; Chief Curator Dr JOSÉ FRANCISCO ALVES; publ. *Jornal do MARGS* (11 a year).

Museu 'Julio de Castilhos' (State Historical Museum): Rua Duque de Caxias 1205, Centro, Porto Alegre, RS 90010-283; tel. (51) 3221-3959; e-mail museu_juliodecastilhos@sedac.rs.gov.br; f. 1903; 10,100 exhibits of nat. history, incl. the 1835 Revolutionary period, the Paraguayan War, and colln of Indian pieces; armoury, antique furniture and slave pieces; library of 5,000 vols; Dir ROBERTO SCHMITT-PRYM.

Recife

Museu do Estado de Pernambuco (State Museum): Av. Rui Barbosa 960, Graças, Recife, PE 52011-040; tel. (81) 427-9322; f. 1929; local history, paintings; library of 4,000 vols, 110 periodicals, newspaper clippings, video cassettes; Superintendent SYLVIA SPOT.

Rio de Janeiro

Museu Aeroespacial (Aerospace Museum): Av. Marechal Fontenelle, 2000, Campo dos Afonsos, Rio de Janeiro, RJ 21740-000; tel. (21) 2108-8954; e-mail comsocial@musal.aer.mil.br; internet www.musal.aer.mil.br; f. 1976; houses colln of aircraft, aeronautical material and historical documents; Dir Brig. MÁRCIO BHERING CARDOSO.

Museu Carpológico do Jardim Botânico do Rio de Janeiro (Museum of Carpology of the Botanical Garden): Rua Pacheco Leão 915, Rio de Janeiro, RJ 22460-030; tel. (21) 2511-2749; e-mail jbrj@jbrj.gov.br; internet www.jbrj.gov.br; f. 1915; specializes in botany; colln of 6,200 fruits; Pres. SAMYRA CRESPO.

Museu da República (Museum of the Republic): Rua do Catete 153, Catete, Rio de Janeiro, RJ 22220-000; tel. (21) 3235-3693; e-mail museu@museudarepublica.org.br; internet www.museudarepublica.org.br; f. 1960; sited in Catete Palace, built 1858–67, fmr seat of Govt; exhibits of items belonging to former Presidents; spec. collns: history of Brazil, historical archive with 85,000 photographs and documents; library of 10,000 vols; Dir MAGALY DE OLIVEIRA CABRAL SANTOS.

Museu de Arte Moderna do Rio de Janeiro (Museum of Modern Art): Av. Infante Dom Henrique 85, Parque do Flamengo, Rio de Janeiro, RJ 20021-140; tel. (21) 3883-5600; e-mail atendimento@mamrio.org.br; internet www.mamrio.org.br; f. 1948; 12,000 art works; collns representing different countries; film archive; art exhibition; film screenings; research and document centre; library of 25,000 vols; Pres. CARLOS ALBERTO GOUVÊA CHATEAUBRIAND; Dir LUIZ SCHYMURA.

Museu de Ciências da Terra, Departamento Nacional de Produção Mineral (Earth Sciences Museum, National Department of Mineral Production): Av. Pasteur 404, 2° andar, Urca, Rio de Janeiro, RJ 22290-240; tel. (21) 2295-7596; e-mail mcter.dnpm@dnpm.gov.br; internet www.dnpm.gov.br; f. 1907; colln of fossils, minerals, rocks, gems, ore minerals and meteorites from Brazil and other countries; Dir DIOGENES DE ALMEIDA CAMPOS.

Museu do Índio (Museum of the Indian): Rua das Palmeiras 55, Botafogo, Rio de Janeiro, RJ 22270-070; tel. (21) 3214-8700; e-mail comunicacao@museudoindio.gov.br; internet www.museudoindio.gov.br; f. 1953; ethnology, ethnohistory, museology, linguistics, documentation; conducts research into Indian societies and cultures; scientific archives (documents, photographs, films and music); library of 28,000 vols; Dir. JOSÉ CARLOS LEVINHO; publ. *Museo ao Vivo*.

Museu do Instituto Histórico e Geográfico Brasileiro (Museum of the Brazilian Historical and Geographical Institute): Av. Augusto Severo 8, 12 andar, Glória, Rio de Janeiro, RJ 20021-040; tel. (21) 2252-4430; e-mail info@ihgb.org.br; internet www.ihgb.org.br; f. 1838; history, geography and ethnography colln; Pres. ARNO WEHLING.

Museu e Arquivo Histórico do Centro Cultural Banco do Brasil (Museum and Historical Archives of the Banco do Brasil Cultural Centre): Rua Primeiro de Março 66, Centro, Rio de Janeiro, RJ 20010-000; tel. (21) 3808-2020; e-mail ccbbrio@bb.com.br; f. 1989; colln of banknotes and coins from Brazil and other countries, documents relating to the economic history of Brazil and to the Banco do Brasil; library: see under Libraries and Archives; Dir MARCELO MENDONÇA.

Museu Histórico da Cidade do Rio de Janeiro (Historical Museum of Rio de Janeiro): Estrada Santa Marinha s/n, Gávea, Rio de Janeiro, RJ 22451-240; tel. (21) 2512-2353; e-mail mcrj@pcrj.rj.gov.br; f. 1934; library of 4,000 vols; Dir BEATRIZ DE VICQ CARVALHO.

Museu Histórico Nacional (National Historical Museum): Praça Marechal Âncora, Rio de Janeiro, RJ 20021-200; tel. (21) 2550-9221; e-mail mhn.comunicacao@museus.gov.br; internet www.museuhistoriconacional.com.br; f. 1922; colIns of ceramics, coins, furniture, ivory, medals, paintings, prints, vehicles, weapons, besides historical exhibits; organizes courses in museology, national history, arts; library of 50,000 vols, incl. works of the 16th century, pamphlets, periodicals and spec. materials in art, food, genealogy, heraldry, history of Brazil and Portugal, museology and numismatics; Dir VERA LÚCIA BOTTREL TOSTES; Sec. ROZIMAR VIANNA DOS SANTOS.

Museu Nacional (National Museum): Quinta da Boa Vista, São Cristóvão, Rio de Janeiro, RJ 20940-040; tel. (21) 2562-6900; e-mail museu@mn.ufrj.br; internet www.museunacional.ufrj.br; f. 1818 as the Royal Museum; attached to Federal Univ. of Rio de Janeiro; sections: anthropology, botany, entomology, geology and palaeontology, invertebrates and vertebrates, archaeology, ethnolinguistics; 4m. specimens; library of 482,037 vols incl. periodicals, thesis and dissertations, multimedia, brochures, folios, rare books, CD-ROMs, DVDs, maps, microfiches, microfilms and monographs; Dir Prof. SÉRGIO ALEX KUGLAND DE AZEVEDO; publs *Arquivos* (irregular), *Boletim: Antropologia* (irregular), *Boletim: Botânica* (irregular), *Boletim: Geologia* (irregular), *Boletim: Zoologia* (irregular), *Estudos de Antropologia Social* (2 a year).

Museu Nacional de Belas Artes (National Museum of Fine Arts): Av. Rio Branco 199, Centro, Rio de Janeiro, RJ 20.040-008; tel. (21) 3299-0600; e-mail mnba@museus.gov.br; internet www.mnba.gov.br; f. 1937; collns of Brazilian and European paintings and sculpture; graphic arts and furniture; primitive art, numismatics, posters, photographs; exhibitions and educational services; library of 12,000 vols incl. rare works, journals, monograms and catalogues; Dir MONICA FIGUEIREDO BRAUNSCHWEIGER XEXÉO; publ. *Boletim*.

Museus 'Raymundo Ottoni de Castro Maya': Rua Murtinho Nobre 93, Santa Teresa, RJ 20241-050; tel. (21) 3970-1126; e-mail chacara@museuscastromaya.com.br; internet www.museuscastromaya.com.br; f. 1962; attached to Min. of Culture; 2 museums: Museu da Chácara do Céu (modern Brazilian and European art, works by Jean Baptiste Debret and 19th-century European traveller artists, Luso-Brazilian furniture) and Museu do Açude (Chinese pottery and sculpture, 17th- to 19th-century Portuguese tiles and sculpture, Luso-Brazilian furniture, contemporary installations in 19th-century manor house); library of 8,000 vols of Brazilian and European literature, publs of early 19th-century travellers; Dir VERA MARIA ABREU DE ALENCAR; Admin. Advisor ROBERTO DE ALMEIDA BISHOP.

Rio Grande

Museu Oceanográfico 'Prof. Eliézer de Carvalho Rios' (Oceanographic Museum): CP 379, Rua Heitor Perdigão 10, Rio Grande, RS 96200-970; tel. (53) 3230-5364; e-mail museu@furg.br; f. 1953; attached to Fundação Universidade Federal do Rio Grande; oceanography, ichthyology, malacology, mammalogy; large shell colln, cetaceans colln; library; Dir Oc. Ms. LAURO BARCELLOS.

Sabará

Museu do Ouro (Gold Museum): Rua da Intendência s/n°, Centro, Sabará, MG; tel. (31) 3671-1848; e-mail mdo@museus.gov.br; internet www.museudoouro.com; f. 1945; 3 sections: technical, historical, artistic; antique methods of gold-mining and smelting; gold ingots; 749 objects incl. furniture, armour, porcelain, religious imagery and mining objects; library of 4,972 vols on historical and cultural aspects of Minas Gerais, Brazil's colonization, slavery, cultural heritage, historic preservation, mining, architecture, handicrafts and numismatics; 35,000 documents; Dir RICARDO ALFREDO DE CARVALHO ROSA.

Salvador

Museu Henriqueta Catharino (Henriqueta Catharino Museum): Rua Monsenhor Flaviano, N°02, Politeama, Salvador, BA 40080-136; tel. (71) 3329-5522; e-mail contato@institutofeminino.com.br; f. 1933; attached to Fundação Instituto Feminino da Bahia; collns of religious art, Brazilian art and feminine apparel; gold, silver, jewellery, clothing, weapons, furniture, porcelain, textiles; Museu de Arte Popular; library; Dir SONIA MARIA MOREIRA DE SOUZA BASTOS.

São Paulo

Museu da Língua Portuguesa (Portuguese Language Museum): Praça da Luz, s/n °, Centro, São Paulo, SP; tel. (11) 3322-0080; e-mail museu@museulp.org.br; internet www.museulinguaportuguesa.org.br; f. 2006; films in Portuguese on everyday life, totems dedicated to people who shaped Brazilian Portuguese; offers free courses, lectures and seminars; Dir ISA GRINSPUN FERRAZ.

Museu de Arqueologia e Etnologia da Universidade de São Paulo e Serviço de Biblioteca e Documentação: Av. Prof. Almeida Prado 1466, Cidade Universitária, São Paulo, SP 05508-070; tel. (11) 3091-4905; internet www.mae.usp.br; f. 1964; comprises 1.5m. items; library of 75,000 vols, incl. 19,000 books and 32,000 vols of print periodicals; Museum Dir Dr MARIA BEATRIZ BORBA FLORENZANO; Library Dir ELIANA ROTOLO; publs *Revista do Museu de Arqueologia e Etnologia* (1 a year), *Sumários de Periódicos* (6 a year).

Museu de Arte Contemporânea da Universidade de São Paulo (Contemporary Art Museum of São Paulo University): Av. Pedro Álvares Cabral, 1301, São Paulo, SP 04094-050; tel. (11) 5573-9932; e-mail informac@edu.usp.br; internet www.mac.usp.br; f. 1963; permanent exhibition of int. and Brazilian plastic arts; library of 9,000 vols, 18 titles of current periodicals, 32,000 catalogues, 27,000 slides and 1,400 newspaper clippings; Dir TADEU CHIARELLI.

Museu de Arte de São Paulo (São Paulo Museum of Arts): Av. Paulista 1578, Cerqueira César São Paulo, SP 01310-200; tel. (11) 3251-5644; e-mail atendimento@masp.art.br; internet www.masp.art.br; f. 1947; classical and modern paintings, Italian, Spanish, Dutch, Flemish and French schools; also representative works by Portinari and Lasar Segall; depts of theatre, music, cinema, art history, exhibitions, printing, photography and education; library of 60,000 vols about culture and art; Dir Pres. BEATRIZ MENDES GONÇALVES PIMENTA CAMARGO.

Museu de Arte Sacra (Sacred Art Museum of São Paulo): Av. Tiradentes 676, Luz, São Paulo, SP 01102-000; tel. (11) 3326-5393; e-mail mas@museuartesacra.org.br; internet www.museuartesacra.org.br; f. 1970, fmrly Museu da Curia Metropolitana; sacred art, furniture, numismatics, paintings, silverware, jewellery, textiles, etc.; library of 4,500 vols, incl. rare liturgical books; Dir Exec. JOSÉ CARLOS MARÇAL DE BARROS.

Museu de Zoologia, Universidade de São Paulo (Museum of Zoology, University of São Paulo): Av. Nazaré 481, Ipiranga, São Paulo, SP 04263-000; tel. (11) 2065-8100; e-mail mz@edu.usp.br; internet www.mz.usp.br; f. 1939; 7m. specimens of neotropical and world fauna; library of 248,000 vols; Dir Prof. Dr HUSSAM EL DINE ZAHER; publs *Arquivos de Zoologia, Papeis Avulsos de Zoologia*.

Museu Florestal 'Octávio Vecchi' (Forestry Museum): Rua do Horto 931, Bairro Horto Florestal, São Paulo, SP 02377-000; tel. (11) 2231-8555; internet www.iflorestal.sp.gov.br/museu/index.asp; f. 1931; a dependency of the Forestry Institute of the Sec. of State for Environment; forestry and forest technology, collns of local timber; Dir DALMO DIPPOLD VILAR.

Museu Paulista da Universidade de São Paulo (São Paulo University Museum): Parque da Independência s/n°, Ipiranga, São Paulo, SP 04263-000; tel. (11) 2065-8000; e-mail mp@usp.br; internet www.mp.usp.br; f. 1895; 125,000 units; history, material culture, historical and numismatic specimens; collns of furniture and stamps; library of 26,466 vols, 2,300 periodical titles, 2,892 reprints; Dir Prof. Dr SHEILA WALBE ORNSTEIN; publs *Anais do Museu Paulista, Cadernos de São Paulo*.

Pinacoteca do Estado de São Paulo (State Art Gallery of São Paulo): Praça da Luz 02, Luz, São Paulo, SP 01120-010; tel. (11) 3324-1000; internet www.pinacoteca.org.br; f. 1905; Brazilian art from 19th century to the present; temporary and permanent exhibitions, workshops, lectures, int. meetings; library of 10,000 vols, 3,440 exhibition catalogues; Exec. Dir MARCELO MATTOS ARAUJO.

Teresina

Museu do Piauí 'Odilon Nunes' (Piauí Museum): Praça Marechal Deodoro da Fonseca s/n, Centro, Teresina, PI 64000-160; tel. (86) 3221-6027; e-mail museudopiaui@ig.com.br; f. 1934; historical, cultural and artistic exhibitions; Dir DORA MEDEIROS.

Vitória

Museu Solar Monjardim (Solar Museum Monjardim): Av. Paulino Müller s/n°, Jucutuquara, Vitória, ES 29040-470; tel. (27) 3223-6609; f. 1939 as State Museum; inc. 1967 to Universidade Federal do Espírito Santo; history, sacred art, furniture, porcelain, paintings, arms, books, silverware and photographs.

Universities and University Centres

Higher education institutions in Brazil fall into one of six categories: universities, university centres, single-faculty non-university tertiary institutions (hereafter simply referred to as faculties), integrated non-university tertiary education institutions (hereafter integrated HEIs), centres for technological education, and higher schools or institutes. All told there are over 2,400 institutions. Owing to space limitations we cannot list them all, and so have restricted our listings to universities and university centres. The numbers of other types of higher education institutions will be given for each state.

Acre

In Acre, there are eight faculties and one higher school.

UNIVERSITY

UNIVERSIDADE FEDERAL DO ACRE
(Federal University of Acre)

CP 500, Rio Branco, AC 69915-900
Campus Universitario, Rodovia BR 364, km 04, nº 6637, Distrito Industrial, Rio Branco, AC 69920-900
Telephone: (68) 3901-2500
E-mail: reitoria@ufac.br
Internet: www.ufac.br
Founded 1971
federal control
Language of instruction: Portuguese
Academic year: January to December
Rector: Prof. Dr MINORU MARTINS KINPARA
Vice-Rector for Student Affairs: Prof. ANTONIO CARLOS FONSECA PONTES, JR
Pro-Rector for Admin.: THIAGO ROCHA DOS SANTOS
Pro-Rector for Devt and Human Resources: FILOMENA MARIA OLIVEIRA DA CRUZ
Pro-Rector for Extension and Culture: Prof. Dr ENOCK DA SILVA PESSOA
Pro-Rector for Planning: Prof. ALEXANDRE RICARDO HID
Pro-Rector for Research and Postgraduate Affairs: Prof. Dr JOSIMAR BATISTA FERREIRA
Pro-Rector for Undergraduate Affairs: Profa Dra MARIA SOCORRO NERI MEDEIROS DE SOUZA
Library Dir: MARCELINO GERALDO MENEZES MONTEIRO
Library of 46,000 vols
Number of teachers: 274
Number of students: 2,013
Publication: *Revista Elementos*

Alagoas

In Alagoas, there are 17 faculties, one integrated HEI, one centre for technological education and six higher schools or institutes.

UNIVERSITIES

UNIVERSIDADE ESTADUAL DE CIÊNCIAS DA SAÚDE DE ALAGOAS
(State University of Health Sciences of Alagoas)

Rua Doutor Jorge de Lima 113, Trapiche da Barra, Maceió, AL 57010-300
Telephone: (82) 3315-6701
E-mail: reitoria@uncisal.edu.br
Internet: www.uncisal.edu.br
Founded 2005
State control
Language of instruction: Portuguese
Academic year: January to December
Centres of distance education, health sciences, integrative sciences, technology
Rector: Profa Dra ROZANGELA MARIA DE ALMEIDA FERNANDES WYSZOMIRSKA
Vice-Rector: Profa Dra ALMIRA ALVES DOS SANTOS
Pro-Rector for Admin.: Dr JOSÉ NOBRE PIRES
Pro-Rector for Extension: GERALDO MAGELLA TEIXEIRA
Pro-Rector for Personnel Management: MARTHA BARBOSA DUARTE
Pro-Rector for Research and Postgraduate Affairs: MARIA DO CARMO BORGES TEIXEIRA
Pro-Rector for Student Affairs: ROSIMEIRE RODRIGUES CAVALCANTI
Pro-Rector for Undergraduate Affairs: PAULO JOSÉ MEDEIROS DE SOUZA COSTA
Library Man.: MONALISA ALVES BARROS
Library of 15,196 vols, 913 periodicals, 423 cassettes, 585 CD-ROMS, 25 DVDs

UNIVERSIDADE FEDERAL DE ALAGOAS
(Federal University of Alagoas)

Campus A. C. Simões, Av. Lourival Melo Mota s/n, Cidade Universitária, Maceió, AL 57072-900
Telephone: (82) 3214-1051
E-mail: atendimento@nti.ufal.br
Internet: www.ufal.br
Founded 1961
federal control
Language of instruction: Portuguese
Academic year: March to December (2 semesters)
Rector: Dr EURICO DE BARROS LÔBO FILHO
Vice-Rector: Dra RACHEL ROCHA DE ALMEIDA BARROS
Pro-Rector for Extension: EDUARDO SARMENTO DE LYRA
Pro-Rector for Institutional Management: Dr VALMIR DE ALBUQUERQUE PEDROSA
Pro-Rector for Personnel and Work Management: SÍLVIA REGINA CARDEAL
Pro-Rector for Research and Postgraduate Affairs: Dra SIMONI MARGARETI PLENTZ MENEGHETTI
Pro-Rector for Student Affairs: PEDRO NELSON BONFIM GOMES RIBEIRO
Pro-Rector for Undergraduate Affairs: Dr AMAURI DA SILVA BARROS
Number of teachers: 907
Number of students: 6,128

Amapá

In Amapá, there are eight faculties and four integrated HEIs.

UNIVERSITY

UNIVERSIDADE FEDERAL DO AMAPÁ
(Federal University of Amapá)

Rod. Juscelino Kubitschek, Macapá, AP 68903-419
Telephone: (96) 3312-1700
E-mail: unifap@unifap.br
Internet: www.unifap.br
federal control
Language of instruction: Portuguese
Academic year: January to December
Rector: JOSÉ CARLOS TAVARES CARVALHO
Vice-Rector: ANTONIO SERGIO MONTEIRO FILOCREAO
Pro-Rector for Admin.: SELONIEL BARROSO DOS REIS
Pro-Rector for Extension and Community Affairs: STEVE WANDERSON CALHEIROS DE ARAUJO
Pro-Rector for Inter-Institutional Cooperation: GUTEMBERG DE VILHENA SILVA
Pro-Rector for Personnel Management: SILVIA SAMPAIO CHAGAS GOMES
Pro-Rector for Planning: ROSILENE SEABRA DE AGUIAR
Pro-Rector for Research and Postgraduate Affairs: ALAAN UBAIARA BRITO
Pro-Rector for Undergraduate Affairs: ADELMA DAS NEVES NUNES BARROS

Amazonas

In Amazonas, there are nine faculties, one centre for technological education and three higher schools or institutes.

UNIVERSITIES

UNIVERSIDADE DO ESTADO DO AMAZONAS
(State University of Amazonas)

Av. Djalma Batista 3578, Flores, Manaus, AM 69050-010
Telephone: (92) 3646-7508
E-mail: reitoria@uea.edu.br
Internet: www.uea.edu.br
Founded 2001
State control
Language of instruction: Portuguese
Academic year: January to December
Rector: Dr CLEINALDO DE ALMEIDA COSTA
Vice-Rector: Dr RAIMUNDO DE JESUS TEIXEIRA BARRADAS
Pro-Rector for Admin.: MARCOS ANDRÉ FERREIRA ESTÁCIO
Pro-Rector for Extension and Community Affairs: Dr CARLOSSANDRO CARVALHO DE ALBUQUERQUE
Pro-Rector for Planning: Dr FABIANA LUCENA OLIVEIRA
Pro-Rector for Research and Postgraduate Affairs: Dr MARIA PAULA GOMES MOURÃO
Pro-Rector for Undergraduate Affairs: LUCIANO BALBINO DOS SANTOS
Library Dir: JEANE MACELINO GALVES
Number of teachers: 1,931
Number of students: 23,465 (22,654 undergraduate, 811 postgraduate)
Publications: *Aboré* (online, www.revistas.uea.edu.br/old/abore), *Areté* (2 a year, online, www.revistas.uea.edu.br/arete), *Hiléia* (2 a year, online, www.pos.uea.edu.br/direitoambiental/?dest=revista)

UNIVERSIDADE FEDERAL DO AMAZONAS
(Federal University of Amazonas)

Av. Gen. Rodrigo Otávio 6200, Coroado I, Manaus, AM 69077-000
Telephone: (92) 3305-1489
E-mail: ascom@ufam.edu.br
Internet: www.ufam.edu.br
Founded 1962
federal control
Language of instruction: Portuguese
Academic year: March to December
Rector: Profa Dra MÁRCIA PERALES MENDES SILVA
Vice-Rector: Prof. Dr HEDINALDO NARCISO LIMA
Pro-Rector for Admin.: RICARDO JOSE BAPTISTA CAVALCANTE
Pro-Rector for Extension: Prof. LUIZ FREDERICO MENDES DOS REIS ARRUDA
Pro-Rector for Planning and Institutional Devt: Prof. MARIOMAR DE SALES LIMA
Pro-Rector for Research and Postgraduate Affairs: Prof. Dr GILSON VIEIRA MONTEIRO
Pro-Rector for Technological Innovation: Profa Dra MARIA DO PERPÉTUO SOCORRO RODRIGUES CHAVES
Pro-Rector for Undergraduate Teaching: Prof. LUCÍDIO ROCHA SANTOS
Library Dir: CÉLIA SIMONETTI BARBALHO
Library of 320,808 vols, 18,005 periodicals
Number of teachers: 777
Number of students: 22,000 (20,000 undergraduate, 2,000 postgraduate)
Publications: *Boletim Estatístico*, *Caderno de Humanidades e Ciências Sociais*, *Maloca Digital* (online, www.malocadigital.ufam.edu.br/maloca), *Mutações* (online,

www.relem.info), *Scientia Amazonia* (3 a year, in Portuguese, English and Spanish, online, www.scientia.ufam.edu.br)

UNIVERSITY CENTRES

CENTRO UNIVERSITÁRIO DE ENSINO SUPERIOR DO AMAZONAS
(University Centre for Higher Education in Amazonas)

Rua Pedro Dias Leme 203, Flores, Manaus, AM 69058-818
Telephone: (92) 3643-4200
E-mail: secretaria@ciesa.br
Internet: www.ciesa.br
Language of instruction: Portuguese
Academic year: January to December
Courses in accounting, business administration, computer science, economics, education, executive secretary, law, social communication, tourism
Academic Sec.: SORANDA TABOSA DE CARVALHO

CENTRO UNIVERSITÁRIO DO NORTE
(Northern University Centre)

Av. Joaquim Nabuco 1232, Centro, Manaus, AM 69020-031
Telephone: (92) 3212-5000
E-mail: contato@uninorte.com.br
Internet: www.uninorte.com.br
Founded 1994, present status 2004
Private control
Language of instruction: Portuguese
Academic year: January to December
Schools of health sciences, humanities and social sciences, science and technology; graduate school
Pres.: MILTON CAMARGO
Rector: VICENTE DE PAULO QUEIROZ NOGUEIRA
Dir for Finance: MARCELO JOSÉ FRUTUOSO MEDEIROS
Dir for Operations: RAIMUNDO EXPEDITO DE OLIVEIRA
Dir for Planning and Academic Support: MARIA IZOLDA DE OLIVEIRA BARRETO
Academic Sec.: GISELLE PINTO

CENTRO UNIVERSITÁRIO LUTERANO DE MANAUS
(Lutheran University Centre of Manaus)

Av. Carlos Drummond de Andrade 1460, Conjunto Atílio Andreazza, Bairro Japiim II, Manaus, AM 69077-730
Telephone: (92) 3616-9800
E-mail: acsmao@ulbra.br
Internet: www.ulbra.br/manaus
Private control; attached to Universidade Luterana do Brasil
Language of instruction: Portuguese
Academic year: January to December
Courses in architecture and urbanism, business administration, chemical, civil, electrical, environmental and mechanical engineering, law, nursing, psychology, technology in logistics
Gen. Dir: VALDEMAR SJLENDER
Coordinator for Admin.: CÉLIA REGINA PESSOA
Coordinator for Extension, Research and Postgraduate Affairs: FERNANDA LÚCIA PEREIRA COSTA
Coordinator for Teaching: SÔNIA LEMOS
Sec.-Gen.: MADSON DENES

Bahia

In Bahia, there are 104 faculties, three integrated HEIs, one centre for technological education and 16 higher schools or institutes.

UNIVERSITIES

UNIVERSIDADE CATÓLICA DO SALVADOR
(Catholic University of Salvador)

Largo do Campo Grande 07, Campo Grande, Salvador, BA 40080-121
Telephone: (71) 3329-8601
E-mail: ascom@ucsal.br
Internet: www.ucsal.br
Founded 1961
Private control
Languages of instruction: Portuguese, French, English
Chancellor: Dom MURILO SEBASTIÃO RAMOS KRIEGER
Rector: Prof. JOSÉ CARLOS ALMEIDA DA SILVA
Vice-Rector: Profa LILIANA MERCURI DE ALMEIDA
Librarian: SONIA RODRIGUES
Number of teachers: 690
Number of students: 12,000

UNIVERSIDADE ESTADUAL DE FEIRA DE SANTANA
(State University of Santana Feira)

Av. Transnordestina s/n, Novo Horizonte, Feira de Santana, BA 44036-900
Telephone: (75) 3161-8000
E-mail: reitor@uefs.br
Internet: www.uefs.br
Founded 1976
State control
Language of instruction: Portuguese
Academic year: March to December
Rector: JOSÉ CARLOS BARRETO DE SANTANA
Vice-Rector: GENIVAL CORREIA DE SOUZA
Pro-Rector for Admin. and Finance: ROSSINE CERQUEIRA DA CRUZ
Pro-Rector for Extension: MARIA HELENA DA ROCHA BESNOSIK
Pro-Rector for Research and Graduate Studies: LAILA MARIA ASSIS ARAÚJO
Pro-Rector for Undergraduate Teaching: RUBENS EDSON ALVES PEREIRA
Librarian: ISABEL CRISTINA NASCIMENTO SANTANA
Library of 72,700 vols
Number of teachers: 500
Number of students: 4,200
Publications: *Intercampus*, *Sitientibus* (2 a year)

UNIVERSIDADE FEDERAL DA BAHIA
(Federal University of Bahia)

Palácio da Reitoria, Rua Augusto Viana s/n, Canela, Salvador, BA 40110-909
Telephone: (71) 3283-7072
Internet: www.ufba.br
Founded 1946
State control
Academic year: February to December
Rector: Prof. DORA LEAL ROSA
Vice-Rector: Prof. LUIZ ROGÉRIO BASTOS LEAL
Pro-Rector for Admin.: DIRCEU MARTINS
Pro-Rector for Extension: BLANDINA FELIPE VIANA
Pro-Rector for Graduate Affairs: ROBERT EVAN VERHINE
Pro-Rector for People Devt: ANTÔNIO EDUARDO MOTA PORTELA
Pro-Rector for Planning and Budget: MARIA ISABEL PEREIRA VIANNA
Pro-Rector for Undergraduate Affairs: Prof. RICARDO CARNEIRO DE MIRANDA FILHO
Pro-Rector for Research, Devt and Innovation: MARCELO EMBIRUÇU
Pro-Rector for Student Affairs: DULCE TAMARA DA ROCHA LAMEGO DA SILVA
Librarian: JUCÉLIA DE OLIVEIRA SANTOS
Library: central library and 35 departmental libraries, with 531,000 vols
Number of teachers: 1,812
Number of students: 16,836
Publication: *Universitas*

UNIVERSIDADE SALVADOR
(University of Salvador)

Campus Costa Azul, Ed. Civil Empresarial, Rua Doutor José Peroba 251, STIEP, Salvador, BA 41770-235
Telephone: (71) 3021-2800
E-mail: webmarketing@unifacs.br
Internet: www.unifacs.br
Founded 1972
Private control
Dir and Pres.: MARCELO HENRIK
Chancellor: Prof. MANOEL BARROS SOBRINHO
Rector: MARCIA BARROS
Library of 61,000 vols, 485 periodicals
Number of teachers: 151
Number of students: 3,693

UNIVERSITY CENTRES

CENTRO UNIVERSITÁRIO ESTÁCIO DA BAHIA
(Bahia University Centre)

Rua Barão de Cotegipe, nº 147, Calçada, Salvador, BA
Telephone: (71) 3316-8200
2 Campuses in Fratelli Vita and Gilberto Gil

CENTRO UNIVERSITÁRIO JORGE AMADO
(Jorge Amado University Centre)

Av. Luis Viana, n. 6775, Paralela, Salvador, BA 41745-130
Telephone: (71) 3206-8000
Internet: www.fja.edu.br
Founded 1999
Attached to the Whitney International University System
Pres.: MARCOS ALMEIDA
Vice-Pres. for Institutional Relations: MÁRIO CALMON
Rector: GUILHERME MARBACK
Publications: *Órbita - Revista de Comunicação* (2 a year), *Praxis - Revista de historia e cultura* (1 a year), *Seara Jurídica - Revista de Direito*

Ceará

In Ceará, there are 36 faculties, eight integrated HEIs and one centre for technological education.

UNIVERSITIES

UNIVERSIDADE DE FORTALEZA
(University of Fortaleza)

Av. Washington Soares 1321, Edson Queiroz, Fortaleza, CE 60811-905
Telephone: (85) 3477-3000
E-mail: reitoria@unifor.br
Internet: www.unifor.br
Founded 1973
Private control
Language of instruction: Portuguese
Academic year: January to December

Chancellor: AIRTON JOSÉ VIDAL QUEIROZ
Rector: FATIMA MARIA FERNANDES VERAS
Vice-Rector for Admin.: JOSÉ MARIA GONDIM FELISMINO, JR
Vice-Rector for Extension and Univ. Community: RANDAL MARTINS POMPEU
Vice-Rector for Research and Postgraduate Affairs: LILIA MAIA DE MORAIS SALES
Vice-Rector for Undergraduate Affairs: HENRIQUE LUIS DO CARMO E SÁ
Dir for Communication and Marketing: EROTILDE HONÓRIO SILVA
Dir for Planning: JOSÉ RENATO FERREIRA BARRETO
Librarian: LEONILHA MARIA BRASILEIRO LESSA

Library of 330,000 vols, incl. books, periodicals, theses, proceedings, pamphlets, video cassettes, CD-ROMs, DVDs
Number of teachers: 1,200
Number of students: 25,000

Publications: *Pensar—Revista de Ciências Jurídicas* (4 a year), *Revista Brasileira em Promoção da Saúde* (4 a year), *Revista Ciência e Pesquisa UNIFOR, Revista Ciências Administrativas* (2 a year), *Revista de Humanidades* (2 a year), *Revista Mal-estar e Subjetividade* (Malaise and Subjectivity, 2 a year, in Portuguese, English, French and Spanish), *Revista Tecnologia* (2 a year)

UNIVERSIDADE ESTADUAL DO CEARÁ
(State University of Ceará)

Av. Paranjana 1700, Campus do Itaperi, Fortaleza, CE 60714-903
Telephone: (85) 3101-9600
E-mail: reitor@uece.br
Internet: www.uece.br

Founded 1975
State control
Language of instruction: Portuguese
Academic year: March to December

Academic centres of applied social studies, education, health sciences, humanities, science and technology; faculty of veterinary sciences

Rector: Prof. Dr JOSÉ JACKSON COELHO SAMPAIO
Vice-Rector and Pro-Rector for Planning: Prof. HIDELBRANDO DOS SANTOS SOARES
Pro-Rector for Admin.: ESAÚ TORRES FRADIQUE ACCIOLY
Pro-Rector for Extension: Profa LÚCIA HELENA FONSÊCA GRANGEIRO
Pro-Rector for Postgraduate Affairs and Research: Prof. JERFFESON TEIXEIRA DE SOUZA
Pro-Rector for Student Affairs: Prof. ANTÔNIO DE PÁDUA SANTIAGO DE FREITAS
Pro-Rector for Undergraduate Affairs: Profa MARCÍLIA CHAGAS BARRETO
Library Dir: ANA NERI BARRETO DE AMORIN

Library of 91,697 vols
Number of teachers: 1,071
Number of students: 17,837

Publications: *Kalagatos* (2 a year), *Revista Lumen Ad Viam*

UNIVERSIDADE ESTADUAL DO VALE DO ACARAÚ
(Acaraú Valley State University)

Av. da Universidade 850, Campus de Betânia, Sobral, CE 62040-370
Telephone: (88) 3677-4271
E-mail: reitoria@uvanet.br
Internet: www.uvanet.br

Founded 1968
State control
Language of instruction: Portuguese
Academic year: January to December

Rector: MARIA PALMIRA SOARES DE MESQUITA
Pro-Rector for Admin.: MANOEL DE CASTRO CARNEIRO NETO
Pro-Rector for Continuing Education: (vacant)
Pro-Rector for Extension: JOSÉ FALCÃO SOBRINHO
Pro-Rector for Planning: FÁTIMA LÚCIA FÁTIMA LÚCIA
Pro-Rector for Research and Postgraduate Affairs: ISRAEL ROCHA BRANDÃO
Pro-Rector for Student Affairs: JOSÉ CÂNDIDO FERNANDES
Pro-Rector for Undergraduate Affairs: MÁRCIA MORAIS DE MELO
Library Dir: MARIA CLAUDINEIDE TELES CARNEIRO

Library of 71,454 vols, incl. 69,495 books, 714 periodical titles, 1,003 dissertations and theses
Number of teachers: 257
Number of students: 9,717

Publications: *Essentia* (2 a year), *Revista da Casa da Geografia de Sobral* (2 a year, in Portuguese with English abstracts, print and online, www.uvanet.br/rcgs), *Revista Helius* (online, www.uvanet.br/helius), *Revista Historiar* (2 a year, online, www.uvanet.br/historiar), *Revista Homem, Espaço e Tempo* (Man, Space and Time, 2 a year, online)

UNIVERSIDADE FEDERAL DO CEARÁ
(Federal University of Ceará)

Av. da Universidade 2853, Benfica, Fortaleza, CE 60020-181
Telephone: (85) 3366-7300
E-mail: reitor@ufc.br
Internet: www.ufc.br

Founded 1955
federal control
Language of instruction: Portuguese
Academic year: January to December

Centres for agricultural sciences, humanities, sciences, technology; faculties of economics, business administration and accounting, education, law, pharmacy, dentistry and nursing; institutes of culture and arts, medicine, physical education and sports

Rector: Prof. JESUALDO PEREIRA FARIAS
Vice-Rector: Prof. HENRY DE HOLANDA CAMPOS
Pro-Rector for Admin.: Profa DENISE MARIA MOREIRA CHAGAS CORREA
Pro-Rector for Extension: Profa MÁRCIA MARIA TAVARES MACHADO
Pro-Rector for Personnel Management: Prof. SERAFIM FIRMO DE SOUZA FERRAZ
Pro-Rector for Planning: Prof. ERNESTO DA SILVA PITOMBEIRA
Pro-Rector for Research and Postgraduate Affairs: Prof. GIL DE AQUINO FARIAS
Pro-Rector for Student Affairs: Prof. CIRO NOGUEIRA FILHO
Pro-Rector for Undergraduate Affairs: Prof. CUSTÓDIO LUÍS SILVA DE ALMEIDA
Sec. for Institutional Devt: Prof. WAGNER BANDEIRA ANDRIOLA
Library Dir: FRANCISCO JONATAN SOARES

Library of 468,016 vols, 7,826 ebooks
Number of teachers: 3,935
Number of students: 34,597 (26,956 undergraduate, 7,641 postgraduate)

Publication: *Revista Universidade Pública* (6 a year)

UNIVERSIDADE REGIONAL DO CARIRI
(Regional University of Cariri)

Rua Cel. Antônio Luis, 1161, Pimenta, Crato, CE 63100-000
Telephone: (88) 3102-1212
E-mail: urca@urca.br
Internet: www.urca.br

Founded 1986
State control
Language of instruction: Portuguese
Academic year: February to December

Centres of applied social sciences, arts, biological and health sciences, education, humanities, science and technology

Rector: ANTONIA OTONITE DE OLIVEIRA CORTEZ
Vice-Rector: JOSÉ PATRÍCIO PEREIRA MELO
Pro-Rector for Planning: JOÃO LUÍS DO NASCIMENTO MOTA
Pro-Rector for Postgraduate Affairs and Research: MARIA ARLENE PESSOA DA SILVA
Pro-Rector for Student Affairs: BERILO BARROSO MENDES, JR

Number of students: 9,000

Publications: *Cadernos de Cultura e Ciência* (2 a year), *Macabéa—Revista Eletrônica Do Netlli* (2 a year, online), *Miguilim—Revista Eletrônica do Netlli* (3 a year, online), *Revista Direito & Dialogicidade* (1 a year, online)

Distrito Federal

In Distrito Federal, there are 49 faculties, five integrated HEIs and 15 centres for technological education.

UNIVERSITIES

UNIVERSIDADE CATÓLICA DE BRASÍLIA
(Catholic University of Brasília)

QS 07, Lote, 01, EPCT, Águas Claras, Taguatinga Sul, DF 71966-700
Telephone: (61) 3356-9000
E-mail: ucb@ucb.br
Internet: www.ucb.br

Founded 1974

Centres for applied social sciences, education and humanities, life sciences, science and technology

Rector: Prof. Dr AFONSO CELSO TANUS GALVÃO
Pro-Rector for Academics: Prof. Dr JORGE HAMILTON SAMPAIO
Pro-Rector for Admin.: Prof. VANJIVALDO DA SILVA
Sec.-Gen.: JOSÉ TEIXEIRA DA COSTA NAZARETH

Library of 263,679 vols, incl. 219,946 books, 40,976 periodicals, 672 ejournals, 1,665 video cassettes, 9 databases; 1,092 vols of spec. collns
Number of teachers: 831
Number of students: 20,000

Publications: *Direito em Ação* (2 a year), *Revista Brasileira de Ciência e Movimento* (4 a year), *Revista Brasileira de Economia de Empresa* (3 a year), *Revista de Análise Econômica do Direito* (Economic Analysis of Law Review, 2 a year, in Portuguese, English and Spanish, online), *Revista do Mestrado em Direito* (online), *Revista Technologia da Informação* (2 a year)

UNIVERSIDADE DE BRASÍLIA
(University of Brasília)

Campus Universitário Darcy Ribeiro, Brasília, DF 70910-900
Telephone: (61) 3107-3300
E-mail: unb@unb.br
Internet: www.unb.br

Founded 1962
Private control
Language of instruction: Portuguese
Academic year: March to December

Faculties of agronomy and veterinary medicine, architecture and urbanism, communication, economics, business administration and accounting, education, health sciences, information science, information and documentation science, law, medicine, physical education, technology

Rector: IVAN MARQUES DE TOLEDO CAMARGO
Vice-Rector: SONIA BÁO
Dean for Admin.: LUÍS AFONSO BERMÚDEZ
Dean for Community Affairs: Profa DENISE BOMTEMPO
Dean for Extension: THÉRÈSE HOFMANN GATTI RODRIGUES DA COSTA
Dean for Personnel Management: Profa Dra GARDENIA ABBAD
Dean for Planning and Budgeting: CARLOS ALBERTO MÜLLER LIMA TORRES
Dean for Research and Postgraduate Affairs: Prof. Dr JAIME MARTINS DE SANTANA
Dean for Undergraduate Studies: MAURO LUIZ RABELO
Central Library Dir: EMIR JOSÉ SUAIDEN

Library: see under Libraries and Archives
Number of teachers: 2,308
Number of students: 39,640 (30,727 undergraduate, 8,913 graduate)

Publications: *Revista Humanidades* (4 a year), *UnB Revista* (4 a year)

UNIVERSITY CENTRES

CENTRO UNIVERSITÁRIO DE BRASÍLIA
(University Centre of Brasília)

SEPN 707/907, Campus do UniCEUB, Asa Norte, Brasília, DF 70790-075

Telephone: (61) 3966-1200
E-mail: central.atendimento@uniceub.br
Internet: www.uniceub.br

Founded 1968
Private control
Language of instruction: Portuguese
Academic year: January to December

Rector: GETÚLIO AMÉRICO MOREIRA LOPES
Vice-Rector: EDEVALDO ALVES DA SILVA
Pro-Rector for Academic Affairs: ELIZABETH REGINA LOPES MANZUR
Pro-Rector for Admin. and Finance: EDSON ELIAS ALVES DA SILVA
Sec.-Gen.: MAURÍCIO DE SOUSA NEVES FILHO

Library of 240,000 vols, 1,800 nat. and 8,195 int. periodicals, 3,200 items of spec. colln

CENTRO UNIVERSITÁRIO DO DISTRITO FEDERAL
(University Centre of the Federal District)

SEP/SUL EQ704/904 Conj.A, Brasília, DF 70390-045

Telephone: (61) 3704-8888
E-mail: udf@udf.edu.br
Internet: udf.edu.br

Founded 1967
Language of instruction: Portuguese
Academic year: January to December

Rector: Prof. Dr RENATO PADOVESE
Pro-Rector for Academic Affairs: Profa Dra BEATRIZ MARIA ECKERT-HOFF

Library of 42,000 vols
Number of teachers: 950
Number of students: 33,000

CENTRO UNIVERSITÁRIO PLANALTO DO DISTRITO FEDERAL
(University Centre of the Federal District Plateau)

Av. Pau Brasil lote 02 s/n, Águas Claras, Brasília, DF

Telephone: (61) 3435-2200
Internet: www.uniplandf.edu.br

Founded 2007
Private control
Language of instruction: Portuguese
Academic year: January to December

Rector: Prof. Dr YUGO OKIDA
Dir: Prof. GERALDO MAGELA
Coordinator for Assessment: Prof. JÚLIO CELSO NOGUCHI
Coordinator for Education: Prof. Dr RUBENS FIDALGO CUNHA
Coordinator for Research and Postgraduate Affairs: Profa Dra ELOÍSA CANGIANI
Coordinator for Student Assistance: Profa TELMA ARANTES

Publication: *Cesubra Scientia*

Espírito Santo

In Espírito Santo, there are 79 faculties, six integrated HEIs, one centre for technological education and 13 higher schools or institutes.

UNIVERSITIES

UNIVERSIDADE FEDERAL DO ESPÍRITO SANTO
(Federal University of Espírito Santo)

Av. Fernando Ferrar 514, Goiabeiras, Vitória, ES 29075-910

Telephone: (27) 4009-2200
E-mail: reitoria@npd.ufes.br
Internet: www.ufes.br

Founded 1954 as state univ., present status 1961
federal control
Language of instruction: Portuguese
Academic year: March to December

Rector: REINALDO CENTODUCATTE
Vice-Rector: MARIA APARECIDA SANTOS CORRÊA BARRETO
Pro-Rector for Admin.: Prof. Dr AMARÍLIO FERREIRA NETO
Pro-Rector for Extension: Prof. Dr APARECIDO JOSÉ CIRILLO
Pro-Rector for Personnel Management and Student Affairs: MARIA LUCIA CASATE
Pro-Rector for Planning and Institutional Devt: Prof. MAXIMILIAN SERGUEI MESQUITA
Pro-Rector for Research and Postgraduate Affairs: NEYVAL COSTA REIS, JR
Pro-Rector for Undergraduate Affairs: Profa Dra MARIA AUXILIADORA DE CARVALHO CORASSA
Central Library Dir: ARLETE FRANCO

Number of teachers: 1,000
Number of students: 10,200

Publications: *Argumentum* (2 a year, print and online, periodicos.ufes.br/argumentum), *Caderno de Pesquisa da UFES* (2 a year, print and online, periodicos.ufes.br/educacao), *(Con)textos Linguísticos* (2 a year, print and online, periodicos.ufes.br/contextoslinguisticos), *Dimensões: Revista de História da UFES* (2 a year, print and online, periodicos.ufes.br/dimensoes), *Geografares* (in Portuguese, English, French and Spanish, print and online, periodicos.ufes.br/geografares), *Jornal Laboratório, Journal UFES, Litteræ* (2 a year, online, periodicos.ufes.br/litterae), *Primeira Mão, RCP—Revista Universo Pedagógico, Revista de Cultura da UFES, Revista Sofia do Departamento de Filosofia, Revista Você da Secretaria de Cultura da UFES*

UNIVERSIDADE VILA VELHA
(Vila Velha University)

Av. Comissário José Dantas de Melo n° 21, Boa Vista, Vila Velha, ES 29102-920

Telephone: (27) 3421-2001
E-mail: reitor@uvv.br
Internet: www.uvv.br

Founded 1976, present name and status 2011
Private control
Language of instruction: Portuguese
Academic year: February to December

Rector: MANOEL CECILIANO SALLES DE ALMEIDA
Vice-Rector: LUCIANA DANTAS DA SILVA PINHEIRO
Pro-Rector for Academic Affairs: HERÁCLITO AMANCIO PEREIRA, JR
Pro-Rector for Admin.: EDSON FRANCO IMMAGINÁRIO
Pro-Rector for Extension and Culture: MARLY IMPERIAL GARABELI
Pro-Rector for Innovation and Devt: PAULO RÉGIS VESCOVI
Pro-Rector for Research and Postgraduate Affairs: MARCO ANTONIO OLIVA CANO
Dir for Library: MARLENE ELIAS POZZATTO

Library of 127,190 vols

Publication: *Scientia*

UNIVERSITY CENTRES

CENTRO UNIVERSITÁRIO DO ESPÍRITO SANTO
(University Centre of Espírito Santo)

Av. Fioravante Rossi 2930, Bairro Martinelli, Colatina, ES 29703-900

Telephone: (27) 3723-3000
Internet: www.unesc.br

Founded 2004
Private control
Language of instruction: Portuguese
Academic year: January to December

Rector: PERGENTINO VASCONCELOS, JR

Library of 57,620 vols

Publication: *UNESC em Revista* (2 a year)

CENTRO UNIVERSITÁRIO SÃO CAMILO
(São Camilo University Centre)

Rua São Camilo de Léllis 01, Bairro Paraíso, Cachoeiro de Itapemirim, ES 29304-910

Telephone: (28) 3526-5911
E-mail: bibli@saocamilo-es.br
Internet: www.saocamilo-es.br/centrouniversitario

Founded 1989
Private control
Language of instruction: Portuguese
Academic year: January to December

Rector: JOÃO BATISTA GOMES DE LIMA
Vice-Rector: AMÉRICO PINHO DE CRISTO
Pro-Rector for Academic Affairs: MARCOS OLIVEIRA ATHAYDE
Pro-Rector for Admin.: JOSÉ BESSA BARROS
Librarian: IRONETE FIRMO VIEIRA

Goiás

In Goiás, there are 57 faculties, 2 integrated HEIs, 3 centres for technological education and 9 higher schools or institutes.

UNIVERSITIES

PONTIFÍCIA UNIVERSIDADE CATÓLICA DE GOIÁS
(Pontifical Catholic University of Goiás)

Av. Universitária 1440, Setor Universitário, Goiânia, GO 74605-010

Telephone: (62) 3946-1000
E-mail: reitoria@pucgoias.edu.br
Internet: www.pucgoias.edu.br

Founded 1959
Private control

Language of instruction: Portuguese
Academic year: January to December

51 Bachelors, 14 Masters and 3 doctoral degrees

Chancellor: Rev. ARCHBISHOP OF GOIÂNIA
Rector: Prof. WOLMIR THEREZIO AMADO
Vice-Rector: Profa OLGA IZILDA RONCHI
Pro-Rector for Admin.: Prof. DANIEL RODRIGUES BARBOSA
Pro-Rector for Communications: Prof. EDUARDO RODRIGUES DA SILVA
Pro-Rector for Extension and Student Support: Profa MÁRCIA DE ALENCAR SANTANA
Pro-Rector for Health: Prof. SÉRGIO ANTÔNIO MACHADO
Pro-Rector for Institutional Devt: Profa HELENISA MARIA GOMES DE OLIVEIRA NETO
Pro-Rector for Postgraduate Affairs and Research: Profa SANDRA DE FARIA
Pro-Rector for Undergraduate Affairs: Profa SÔNIA MARGARIDA GOMES SOUSA
Chief of Staff: Prof. LORENZO LAGO
Librarian: IRENE TOSCANO PASCOAL

Number of teachers: 1,317
Number of students: 25,000

Publications: *Caminhos* (2 a year), *Educativa* (2 a year), *Estudos* (4 a year), *Flash* (52 a year), *Fragmentos de Cultura* (4 a year), *Guará* (1 a year), *Habitus* (2 a year), *Momento* (52 a year), *Mosaico* (2 a year), *Panorama* (2 a year), *Ser* (2 a year)

UNIVERSIDADE DE RIO VERDE
(University of Rio Verde)

Fazenda Fontes do Saber, CP 104, Rio Verde, GO 75901-970
Telephone: (64) 3620-2200
Internet: www.fesurv.br

Founded 1973, present name and status 2003
Private control
Language of instruction: Portuguese
Academic year: January to December

Campuses in Caiapônia, Cristalina, Nerópolis

Rector: Prof. Dr SEBASTIÃO LÁZARO PEREIRA
Vice-Rector: Profa MARIA FLAVINA DAS GRAÇAS COSTA
Pro-Rector for Admin. and Planning: Prof. CARMO DOS REIS DE SOUSA
Pro-Rector for Extension, Culture and Student Affairs: Prof. FERDINANDO AGOSTINHO
Pro-Rector for Postgraduate Affairs and Research: Prof. NAGIB YASSIN
Pro-Rector for Undergraduate Affairs: Profa HELEMI OLIVEIRA GUIMARÃES DE FREITAS

UNIVERSIDADE ESTADUAL DE GOIÁS
(State University of Goiás)

BR 153 Quadra Área, km 99, Anápolis, GO 75132-903
Telephone: (62) 3328-1403
E-mail: reitor@ueg.br
Internet: www.ueg.br

Founded 1999
State control
Language of instruction: Portuguese
Academic year: January to December

Academic units of distance education, exact sciences and technology, socio-economic sciences and humanities; 39 attached univ. units in the state of Goiás

Rector: HAROLDO REIMER
Vice-Rector: VALCEMIA GONÇALVES DE SOUSA NOVAES
Pro-Rector for Extension, Culture and Student Affairs: Profa DANÚSIA ARANTES FERREIRA BATISTA DE OLIVEIRA
Pro-Rector for Planning, Management and Finance: Profa Dra SUELI MARTINS DE FREITAS ALVES
Pro-Rector for Research and Postgraduate Affairs: Prof. Dr IVANO ALESSANDRO DEVILLA
Pro-Rector for Undergraduate Affairs: Profa MARIA OLINDA BARRETO

Number of students: 18,800

Publications: *Revista de História*, *Revista Temporis*

UNIVERSIDADE FEDERAL DE GOIÁS
(Federal University of Goiás)

CP 131, Campus Samambaia, Goiânia, GO 74001-970
Telephone: (62) 3521-1000
E-mail: cai@cai.ufg.br
Internet: www.ufg.br

Founded 1960
federal control
Language of instruction: Portuguese
Academic year: January to December

Faculties of business administration, accounting and economics, communication and library sciences, dentistry, education, humanities and philosophy, law, letters, mathematics, medicine, nursing, nutrition, pharmacy, physical education, visual arts; schools of civil, computer, electrical and mechanical engineering, veterinary sciences

Rector: Prof. Dr EDWARD MADUREIRA BRASIL
Vice-Rector: Prof. Dr ERIBERTO FRANCISCO BEVILAQUA MARIN
Pro-Rector for Admin. and Finance: Prof. Dr ORLANDO AFONSO VALLE DO AMARAL
Pro-Rector for Community Affairs: JÚLIO CÉSAR PRATES
Pro-Rector for Extension and Culture: Prof. Dr ANSELMO PESSOA NETO
Pro-Rector for Institutional Devt and Human Resources: Prof. JEBLIN ANTONIO ABRAO
Pro-Rector for Research and Postgraduate Affairs: Profa Dra DIVINA DAS DORES DE PAULA CARDOSO
Pro-Rector for Undergraduate Affairs: Profa Dra SANDRAMARA MATIAS CHAVES
Librarian: VALRIA MARIA SOLEDADE DE ALMEIDA

Library of 215,950 vols
Number of teachers: 1,800
Number of students: 18,324 (16,233 undergraduate, 1,521 graduate, 570 doctoral)

Publications: *Ateli Geogrfico* (4 a year), *Boletim Goiano de Geografia* (2 a year), *Cincia Animal Brasileira* (4 a year), *Comunicação & Informação* (2 a year), *Histria Revista* (2 a year), *Inter-Ao* (2 a year), *Msica Hodie* (2 a year), *Pensar a Prtica* (4 a year), *Pesquisa Agropecuria Tropical* (2 a year), *Philsophos—Revista de Filosofia* (2 a year), *Revista de Biologia Neotropical* (2 a year), *Revista de Patologia Tropical* (4 a year), *Revista Eletrônica de Enfermagem* (4 a year), *Revista Eletrônica de Farmcia* (4 a year), *Signtica* (2 a year), *Sociedade e Cultura* (2 a year)

Maranhão

In Maranhão, there are 19 faculties, one centre for technological education and eight higher schools or institutes.

UNIVERSITIES

UNIVERSIDADE ESTADUAL DO MARANHÃO
(State University of Maranhão)

Cidade Universitária Paulo VI, CP 9, São Luís, MA
Telephone: (98) 3245-5461
E-mail: pra@uema.br
Internet: www.uema.br

Founded 1981
State control
Language of instruction: Portuguese
Academic year: January to December

Centres of agricultural sciences, applied social sciences, education, exact and natural sciences, science and technology; 20 attached campuses

Rector: Prof. JOSÉ AUGUSTO SILVA OLIVEIRA
Pro-Rector for Admin.: Prof. WALTER CANALES SANT'ANA
Pro-Rector for Extension and Student Affairs: Profa VÂNIA LOURDES MARTINS FERREIRA
Pro-Rector for Planning: ANTÔNIO PEREIRA E SILVA
Pro-Rector for Research and Postgraduate Affairs: Prof. Dr PORFIRIO CANDANEDO GUERRA
Pro-Rector for Undergraduate Affairs: MARIA AUXILIADORA GONCALVES CUNHA

Library of 31,180 vols, incl. 26,432 books, 1,200 periodicals, 1,756 theses and dissertations, 1,565 CD-ROMs and DVDs, 122 musical scores

UNIVERSIDADE FEDERAL DO MARANHÃO
(Federal University of Maranhão)

Av. dos Portugueses 1966, Bacanga, São Luís, MA 65085-580
Telephone: (98) 3272-8000
E-mail: atendimento@ufma.br
Internet: www.ufma.br

Founded 1966
federal control
Academic year: January to December

Rector: Prof. Dr NATALINO SALGADO FILHO
Vice-Rector: ANTÔNIO JOSÉ SILVA OLIVEIRA
Pro-Rector for Extension: MARIZE BARROS ROCHA ARANHA
Pro-Rector for Human Resources: MARIA ELISA CANTANHEDE LAGO BRAGA BORGES
Pro-Rector for Management and Finance: JOSÉ AMÉRICO DA COSTA BARROQUEIRO
Pro-Rector for Research and Postgraduate Affairs: FERNANDO CARVALHO SILVA
Pro-Rector for Teaching: SONIA MARIA CORREA PEREIRA MUGSCHL
Librarian: MARIA DA GRAÇA MONTEIRO FONTOURA

Number of teachers: 867
Number of students: 8,895

Mato Grosso

In Mato Grosso, there are 46 faculties, seven integrated HEIs, two centres for technological education and four higher schools or institutes.

UNIVERSITIES

UNIVERSIDADE DE CUIABÁ
(Cuiabá University)

Av. Beira Rio 3100, Cuiabá, MT 78015-480
Telephone: (65) 3363-1000
E-mail: unic@zaz.com.br
Internet: www.unic.br

Founded 1988
Private control
Language of instruction: Portuguese
Academic year: January to December

Rector: ALTAMIRO BELO GALINDO

Library of 58,000 vols, 261 periodicals
Number of teachers: 408
Number of students: 9,053

UNIVERSIDADE DO ESTADO DE MATO GROSSO
(State University of Mato Grosso)

Av. Tancredo Neves 1095, Cavalhada II, Cáceres, MT 78200-000
Telephone: (65) 3221-0000
E-mail: reitoriaunemat@unemat.br
Internet: www.unemat.br

Founded 1993
State control
Language of instruction: Portuguese
Academic year: January to December

12 Attached campuses

Rector: ADRIANO APARECIDO SILVA
Vice-Rector: DIONEI JOSÉ DA SILVA
Pro-Rector for Admin.: VALTER GUSTAVO DANZER
Pro-Rector for Extension and Culture: VERA LÚCIA DA ROCHA MAQUEA
Pro-Rector for Financial Management: ARIEL LOPES TORRES
Pro-Rector for Planning and IT: WEILY TORO MACHADO
Pro-Rector for Research and Postgraduate Affairs: ÁUREA REGINA ALVES IGNÁCIO
Pro-Rector for Student Affairs: CELSO FANAIA TEIXEIRA
Pro-Rector for Undergraduate Affairs: ANA MARIA DI RENZO

Publications: *Caderno Fênix Ciência* (2 a year), *Caderno Fênix Ciência do Estudante* (2 a year), *Educação, Cultura, e Sociedade* (2 a year, online), *História e Diversidade* (online), *Revista Alere*, *Revista Ave Palavra* (2 a year), *Revista da Faculdade de Educação* (2 a year), *Revista de Ciências Agro-Ambientais* (2 a year), *Revista Ecos* (2 a year), *Revista Eventos Pedagógicos* (2 a year, online), *Revista Fronteira Digital* (2 a year, online), *Revista Moinhos* (2 a year, online)

UNIVERSIDADE FEDERAL DE MATO GROSSO
(Federal University of Mato Grosso)

Av. Fernando Corrêa da Costa nº 2367, Bairro Boa Esperança, Cuiabá, MT 78060-900
Telephone: (65) 3615-8000
E-mail: reitora@ufmt.br
Internet: www.ufmt.br

Founded 1970
federal control
Language of instruction: Portuguese
Academic year: April to May

Schools of administration and accounting, agronomy and veterinary sciences, architecture, engineering and technology, economics, nutrition, law, nursing, physical education; institutes of agricultural and technology sciences, biological and health sciences, exact and natural sciences, human and social sciences

Rector: Profa MARIA LÚCIA CAVALLI NEDER
Vice-Rector: Prof. JOÃO CARLOS DE SOUZA MAIA
Pro-Rector for Admin.: VALÉRIA CALMON CERISARA
Pro-Rector for Culture and Extension: LUIS FABRÍCIO CIRILLO DE CARVALHO
Pro-Rector for Planning: Profa ELISABETH APARECIDA FURTADO DE MENDONÇA
Pro-Rector for Postgraduate Teaching: Profa LENY CASELLI ANZAI
Pro-Rector for Research: Prof. JOANIS TILEMAHOS ZERVOUDAKIS
Pro-Rector for Student Assistance: Profa MYRIAN THEREZA DE MOURA SERRA
Pro-Rector for Undergraduate Teaching: Profa IRENE CRISTINA DE MELLO
Pro-Rector for Araguaia Campus: Prof. JOSÉ MARQUES PESSOA
Pro-Rector for Rondonópolis Campus: Prof. JAVERT MELO VIEIRA
Pro-Rector for Sinop Campus: Prof. MARCO ANTÔNIO ARAÚJO PINTO
Sec. for Communication and Media: Prof. BENEDITO DIELCIO MOREIRA
Sec. for Information Technology and Communication: Prof. ALEXANDRE MARTINS DOS ANJOS
Sec. for Institutional Relations: Prof. SERGIO HENRIQUE ALLEMAND MOTTA
Sec. for Int. Relations: Prof. PAULO TEIXEIRA DE SOUSA, JR
Sec. for Personnel Management: DOMINGOS SÁLVIO SANT'ANA

Library of 300,000 vols
Number of teachers: 1,300
Number of students: 18,000

Publications: *Advances in Forestry Science*, *Biodiversidade* (1 a year), *Boletim do Grupo de Pesquisa da Flora, Vegetação e Etnobotânica (FLOVET)*, *Coletâneas do Nosso Tempo*, *Máthema* (2 a year), *Mídias Interativas Digitais (MID)*, *Polifonia* (2 a year), *Revista de Ciências Contábeis* (2 a year), *Revista de Educação Pública* (4 a year), *Revista de Estudos Sociais* (2 a year), *Revista Mato-Grossense de Geografia*

Mato Grosso do Sul

In Mato Grosso do Sul, there are 24 faculties, eight integrated HEIs and five centres for technological education.

UNIVERSITIES

UNIVERSIDADE ANHANGUERA-UNIDERP
(Anhanguera University)

CP 2153, Campo Grande, MS 79003-010
Rua Ceará 333, Bairro Miguel Couto, Campo Grande, MS 79003-010
Telephone: (67) 3348-8000
E-mail: reitoria.uniderp@aesapar.com
Internet: www.uniderp.br

Founded 1996 as Universidade para o Desenvolvimento do Estado e da Região do Pantanal, present name 2008
Private control
Language of instruction: Portuguese
Academic year: January to December

Rector: Profa LEOCÁDIA AGLAÉ PETRY LEME
Pro-Rector for Extension: Prof. IVO ARCÂNGELO VENDRUSCULO BUSATO
Pro-Rector for Research and Postgraduate Affairs: Profa Dra LUCIANA PAES DE ANDRADE
Pro-Rector for Undergraduate Affairs: Prof. Dr EDUARDO DE OLIVEIRA ELIAS
Central Library Coordinator: KELLY CRISTINA DE SOUZA

Library of 140,448 vols, incl. 137,448 books, 3,000 periodicals
Number of teachers: 240
Number of students: 5,100

UNIVERSIDADE CATÓLICA DOM BOSCO
(Don Bosco Catholic University)

Av. Tamandaré 6000, Jardim Seminário, Campo Grande, MS 79117-900
Telephone: (67) 3312-3300
E-mail: reitoria@unibosco.br
Internet: site.ucdb.br

Founded 1993, fmrly Faculdades Unidas Católicas de Mato Grosso
Private control
Language of instruction: Portuguese
Academic year: January to December

Rector: JOSÉ MARINONI
Pro-Rector for Academics and Devt: CONCEIÇÃO APARECIDA GALVES BUTERA
Pro-Rector for Admin.: Ir ALTAIR M. GONÇALO DA SILVA
Pro-Rector for Extension and Community Affairs: LUCIANE PINHO DE ALMEIDA
Pro-Rector for Pastoral Affairs: Ir GILLIANNO JOSE MAZZETTO DE CASTRO
Pro-Rector for Research and Postgraduate Affairs: HEMERSON PISTORI

Library of 120,000 vols
Number of teachers: 200

Publications: *Interações—Revista Internacional de Desenvolvimento Local* (Interactions—International Journal of Local Development, 2 a year), *Jornal UCDB* (12 a year), *Multitemas* (2 a year), *Revista do Direito* (6 a year), *Revista Koembá Pytã* (2 a year), *Tellus* (2 a year)

UNIVERSIDADE ESTADUAL DE MATO GROSSO DO SUL
(State University of Mato Grosso do Sul)

Cidade Universitária de Dourados, CP 351, Dourados, MS 79804-970
Telephone: (67) 3902-2360
E-mail: reitoria@uems.br
Internet: www.uems.br

Founded 1993
State control
Language of instruction: Portuguese
Academic year: January to December

Rector: Prof. Dr FÁBIO EDIR DOS SANTOS COSTA
Vice-Rector: Profa Dra ELEUZA FERREIRA LIMA
Pro-Rector for Admin. and Planning: Prof. Dr JELLY MAKOTO NAKAGAKI
Pro-Rector for Extension, Culture and Community Affairs: Prof. Dr EDMILSON DE SOUZA
Pro-Rector for Human Resources: ADRIANA ROCHAS DE CARVALHO FRUGULI MOREIRA
Pro-Rector for Research and Postgraduate Affairs: Profa Dra CARLA VILLAMAINA CENTENO
Pro-Rector for Teaching: SILVANE APARECIDA DE FREITAS
Chief Librarian: DEOCLECIO VIEIRA MACHADO

Publications: *Revell*, *Web Revista Linguagem, Educação e Memória*

UNIVERSIDADE FEDERAL DA GRANDE DOURADOS
(Federal University of Dourados Region)

Rua João Rosa Góes 1761, Vila Progresso, CP 322, Dourados, MS 79825-070
Telephone: (67) 3410-2002
E-mail: reitoria@ufgd.edu.br
Internet: www.ufgd.edu.br

Founded 1969, present name and status 1979
federal control
Language of instruction: Portuguese
Academic year: January to December

Faculties of agricultural sciences, biological and environmental sciences, business administration, accounting and economics, communication, arts and letters, education, engineering, exact sciences and technology, health sciences, human sciences, indigenous inter-cultural studies, law and international relations

Rector: Prof. Dr DAMIÃO DUQUE DE FARIAS
Vice-Rector: Prof. Dr WEDSON DESIDÉRIO FERNANDES
Pro-Rector for Admin.: Prof. SIDNEI AZEVEDO DE SOUZA

Pro-Rector for Community and Student Affairs: Profa Dra CERES MORAES
Pro-Rector for Extension and Culture: Profa Dra CELIA REGINA DELÁCIO FERNANDES
Pro-Rector for Institutional Assessment and Planning: Profa Dra SILVANA DE ABREU
Pro-Rector for Personnel Management: Prof. AMILTON LUIZ NOVAES
Pro-Rector for Postgraduate Teaching and Research: Prof. Dr CLÁUDIO ALVES VASCONCELOS

Publications: *Agrarian* (4 a year), *ArReDia* (2 a year), *EaD & Tecnologias Digitais na Educação* (2 a year), *Educação e Fronteiras* (3 a year, online), *Entre-Lugar* (2 a year), *Fronteiras: Revista de História* (2 a year), *Horizontes: Revista de Educação* (2 a year), *Monções: Revista de Relações Internacionais da UFGD* (2 a year, in Portuguese, English, French and Spanish), *Ñanduty*, *Premissas*, *Raído* (2 a year), *Revista Eletrônica História em Reflexão* (2 a year, online), *Revista Videre* (2 a year)

UNIVERSIDADE FEDERAL DE MATO GROSSO DO SUL
(Federal University of Mato Grosso do Sul)

Cidade Universitária s/n, CP 549, Campo Grande, MS 79070-900
Telephone: (67) 3345-7010
E-mail: reitoria@ufms.br
Internet: www.ufms.br

Founded 1970
federal control
Language of instruction: Portuguese
Academic year: March to December

Centres of biological and health sciences, humanities and social sciences, science and technology; faculties of computing, dentistry, medicine, veterinary medicine and animal science; campuses in Aquidaúana, Corumbá, Três Lagoas

Rector: Dr MARIA TEREZA FERREIRA DUENHAS MONREAL
Vice-Rector: Dr JOÃO RICARDO FILGUEIRAS TOGNINI
Pro-Rector for Admin.: CLAODINARDO FRAGOSO DA SILVA
Pro-Rector for Extension, Culture and Student Affairs: VALDIR SOUZA FERREIRA
Pro-Rector for Infrastructure: JULIO CESAR GONÇALVES
Pro-Rector for Personnel Management: ROBERT SCHIAVETO DE SOUZA
Pro-Rector for Planning, Budget and Finance: MARIZE TEREZINHA LOPES PEREIRA PERES
Pro-Rector for Research and Postgraduate Affairs: DERCIR PEDRO DE OLIVEIRA
Pro-Rector for Undergraduate Teaching: HENRIQUE MONGELLI
Central Library Coordinator: LUCIA REGINA VIANNA OLIVEIRA

Minas Gerais

In Minas Gerais, there are 222 faculties, 15 integrated HEIs, six centres for technological education and 60 higher schools or institutes.

UNIVERSITIES

PONTIFÍCIA UNIVERSIDADE CATÓLICA DE MINAS GERAIS
(Pontifical Catholic University of Minas Gerais)

Av. Dom José Gaspar 500, bairro Coração Eucarístico, Belo Horizonte, MG 30535-901
Telephone: (31) 3319-4444
E-mail: central@pucminas.br
Internet: www.pucminas.br

Founded 1958
Academic year: February to December

Chancellor: WALMOR OLIVEIRA DE AZEVEDO
Rector: Prof. JOAQUIM GIOVANI MOL GUIMARÃES
Vice-Rector: Prof. PATRÍCIA BERNARDES
Head of Office of the Rector: Prof. PAULO ROBERTO DE SOUSA
Pro-Rector for Extension: Prof. WANDERLEY CHIEPPE FELIPPE
Pro-Rector for Financial Management: Prof. PAULO SÉRGIO GONTIJO CARMO
Pro-Rector for Graduate Affairs: Prof. MARIA INÊS MARTINS
Pro-Rector for Logistics and Infrastructure: Prof. RÔMULO ALBERTINI RIGUEIRA
Chief Librarian: CÁSSIO JOSÉ DE PAULA

Library of 200,000 vols
Number of teachers: 2,032
Number of students: 44,043

Publications: *Journal PUC Minas* (12 a year), *No Pique da PUC* (52 a year), *PUC Informa* (52 a year), *Revista Scripta* (2 a year).

AFFILIATED FOUNDATION

Fundação Dom Cabral: Rua Bernardo Guimarães 3071, Sto. Agostinho, Belo Horizonte, MG 30140-083; tel. (31) 275-3466; f. 1976

UNIVERSIDADE DE ITAÚNA
(University of Itaúna)

Rodovia MG 431 km 45, CP 100, Itaúna, MG 35680-142
Telephone: (37) 3249-3000
E-mail: uit@uit.br
Internet: www.uit.edu.br

Founded 1965
Private control
Academic year: March to December

Rector: Prof. FAIÇAL DAVID FREIRE CHEQUER
Vice-Rector: Prof. IRINEU CARVALHO DE MACEDO
Chancellor: Dr RALPH BATISTA DE MAULAZ
Pro-Rector for Admin. and Finance: Dr MATOZINHO FERREIRA BARBOSA
Pro-Rector for Teaching and Academic Affairs: Dra TERESINHA ALVES DE ALMEIDA
Librarian: ANICÉIA AP. DE RESENDE FERREIRA
Librarian: JOSÉ MARIA PEREIRA NUNES

Library of 150,000 vols
Number of teachers: 200
Number of students: 2,200

Publications: *Cadernos de Extensão*, *Odonto-Itaúna*

UNIVERSIDADE DE UBERABA
(University of Uberaba)

Av.Guilherme Ferreira, 217, Bairro Centro, Uberaba, MG 38010-200
Telephone: (34) 3319-6600
E-mail: divulgacao@uniube.br
Internet: www.uniube.br

Founded 1947 as Faculdade de Odontologia do Triângulo Mineiro; current name adopted 1988

Rector: MARCELO PALMÉRIO
Pro-Rector for Higher Education: Profa INARA BARBOSA PENA ELIAS
Pro-Rector for Research, Postgraduates and Extension: Prof. Dr JOSÉ BENTO ALVES
Admin. Man. for Library: DORA SIVIERI

Publication: *Revista Jurídica UNIJUS* (2 a year)

UNIVERSIDADE ESTADUAL DE MONTES CLAROS
(State University of Montes Claros)

CP 126, Montes Claros, MG 39401-089
Campus Universitário Prof. Darcy Ribeiro, Vila Mauricéia, Montes Claros, MG 39401-089
Telephone: (38) 3229-8000
E-mail: reitoria@unimontes.br
Internet: www.unimontes.br

Founded 1962
State control

Rector: Prof. JOÃO DOS REIS CANELA
Vice-Rector: Prof. MARIA IVETE SOARES DE ALMEIDA
Pro-Rector for Education: Prof. JOÃO FELÍCIO RODRIGUES NETO
Pro-Rector for Extension: Prof. MARINA RIBEIRO QUEIRÓZ
Pro-Rector for Planning, Management and Finance: Prof. JUVENTINO RUAS DE ABREU JR
Pro-Rector for Postgraduate Affairs: Prof. HERCÍLIO MARTELLI JÚNIOR
Pro-Rector for Research: Prof. VICENTE RIBEIRO ROCHA JÚNIOR

Library of 100,000 vols, 2,609 periodicals
Number of teachers: 368
Number of students: 4,667

Publication: *Revista Unimontes Científica* (2 a year, online, www.ruc.unimontes.br)

UNIVERSIDADE FEDERAL DE ITAJUBÁ
(Federal University of Itajubá)

Av. BPS 103, bairro Pinheirinho, Itajubá, MG 37500-903
Telephone: (35) 3629-1101
E-mail: maua@unifei.edu.br
Internet: www.unifei.edu.br

Founded 1913 as Instituto Eletrotécnico e Mecânico de Itajubá, became Instituto Eletrotécnico de Itajubá 1936 and Escola Federal de Engenharia de Itajubá 1968, current name adopted 2002

Rector: Prof. Dr DAGOBERTO ALVES DE ALMEIDA
Vice-Rector: Prof. Dr PAULO SIZUO WAKI
Chief of Staff: Prof. Dra ELIANE GUIMARÃES PEREIRA MELLONI
Pro-Rector for Extension: Prof. JOSÉ WANDERLEY MARANGON LIMA
Pro-Rector for Research and Postgraduate Affairs: Prof. CARLOS EDUARDO DA SILVA SANCHES
Pro-Rector for Undergraduate Affairs: Prof. EGON LUIZ MÜLLER JR
Librarian: CRISTIANE CARPINTEIRO

Library of 37,000
Number of teachers: 183
Number of students: 2,581

Publication: *Pesquisa e Desenvolvimento Tecnológico* (4 a year)

UNIVERSIDADE FEDERAL DE JUIZ DE FORA
(Federal University of Juiz de Fora)

Rua José Lourenço Kelmer s/n, Campus Univ., Bairro São Pedro, Juiz de Fora, MG 36036-900
Telephone: (32) 2102-3911
E-mail: faleconosco@ufjf.edu.br
Internet: www.ufjf.br

Founded 1960
federal control
Language of instruction: Portuguese
Academic year: March to December

Rector: HENRIQUE DUQUE DE MIRANDA CHAVES FILHO
Vice-Rector: JOSÉ LUIZ REZENDE PEREIRA

Pro-Rector for Academic Affairs: Flávio Iassuo Takakura
Pro-Rector for Extension: Prof. Marcelo Soares Dulci
Pro-Rector for Planning and Management: Alexandre Zanini
Pro-Rector for Postgraduate Affairs: Fernando Salgueiro Perobelli
Pro-Rector for Research: Marta Tavares D'Agosto
Pro-Rector for Student Affairs: Maria Elizabete de Oliveira
Pro-Rector for Undergraduate Affairs: Eduardo Magrone
Librarian: Adriana Aparecida de Oliveira
Number of teachers: 988
Number of students: 18,868
Publications: *Boletim do Centro de Biologia da Reprodução* (1 a year), *Boletim do Instituto de Ciências Biológicas* (1 a year), *Educacão em Foco* (2 a year), *Ética e Filosofia Política* (2 a year), *Locus* (1 a year), *Revista do Hospital Universitário* (4 a year), *Revista do Instituto de Ciências Exatas* (1 a year), *Revista Eletrônica de História do Brasil* (2 a year)

UNIVERSIDADE FEDERAL DE LAVRAS
(Federal University of Lavras)

Campus Universitário Ufla, s/n, Inácio Valetim, CP 3037 Lavras, MG 37200-000
Telephone: (35) 3829-1122
E-mail: reitoria@reitoria.ufla.br
Internet: www.ufla.br
Founded 1908 as Agricultural School of Lavras, univ. status 1994
State control
Chancellor: José Roberto Soares Scolforo
Vice-Chancellor: Édila Vilela de Resende Von Pinho
Publications: *Ciência e Agrotecnologia*, *Revista Linearidades*

UNIVERSIDADE FEDERAL DE MINAS GERAIS
(Federal University of Minas Gerais)

Av. Antônio Carlos 6627, Pampulha, CP 1621, Belo Horizonte, MG 31270-901
Telephone: (31) 3409-5000
E-mail: info@cointer.ufmg.br
Internet: www.ufmg.br
Founded 1927
State control
Language of instruction: Portuguese
Academic year: February to December
Rector: Clélio Campolina Diniz
Vice-Rector: Rocksane de Carvalho Norton
Pro-Rector for Human Resources: Roberto do Nascimento Rodrigues
Pro-Rector for Planning and Devt: João Antônio de Paula
Dir of Libraries: Maria Elizabeth de Oliveira Costa
Library of 22,305 vols., 783,549 periodicals and 100,000 other items
Number of teachers: 2,743
Number of students: 49,254
Publications: *Arquivos da Escola de Veterinária da UFMG*, *Barroco*, *Diversa* (1 a year), *Estudos Germânicos*, *Kriterion*, *Manuelzão* (12 a year), *Revista Brasileira de Estudos Políticos*

UNIVERSIDADE FEDERAL DE OURO PRETO
(Federal University of Ouro Preto)

Rua Diogo de Vasconcelos 122, Pilar, Ouro Preto, MG 35400-000
Telephone: (31) 3559-1189
E-mail: reitoria@ufop.br
Internet: www.ufop.br
Founded 1969
federal state control
Academic year: February to December
Rector: Dr Marcone Jamilson Freitas Souza
Vice-Rector: Dr Célia Maria Fernandes Nunes
Chief of Staff: Prof. José Armando Ansaloni
Pro-Rector for Admin.: Sílvia Maria de Paula Alves Rodrigues
Pro-Rector for Extension: Prof. Dr Rogério Santos Oliveira
Pro-Rector for Graduate Affairs: Prof. Dr Marsilius Sousa Freitas da Rocha
Pro-Rector for Planning and Devt: Prof. Dr João Luiz Martins
Pro-Rector for Research and Postgraduate Studies: Prof. Dr Valdei Lopes de Araujo
Pro-Rector for Student and Community Affairs: Rafael Magdalena
Exec. Coordinator for Library: Celina Brazil Luiz
Number of teachers: 390
Number of students: 5,200 (4,800 undergraduate, 400 postgraduate)
Publications: *Jornal da UFOP* (12 a year), *Jornal Revirarte*, *Revista da Escola de Minas* (4 a year), *Revista de Historia* (3 a year), *Revista de Pesquisa da UFOP* (4 a year), *Revista Juridica* (1 a year).

CONSTITUENT INSTITUTES

Institute of Arts and Culture: Rua Coronel Alves 55, Ouro Preto, MG 35400-000; f. 1981; Dean Guiomar Gramont.

Institute of Exact and Biological Sciences: Campus Universitario, Morro do Cruzeiro, Ouro Preto, MG 35400-000; e-mail iceb@iceb.ufop.br; f. 1982; Dean João Martins.

Institute of Human and Social Sciences: Rua do Seminário, Mariana, MG 35420-000; f. 1979; Dean Ivan A. Almeida.

School of Mines: Praça Tiradentes 20, Ouro Preto, MG 35400-000; e-mail diretor@em.ufop.br; f. 1876; Dean Antonio Gomes.

School of Pharmacy: Rua Costa Sena 171, Ouro Preto, MG 35400-000; f. 1839; Dean Lisiane da Silveira Eu

UNIVERSIDADE FEDERAL DE SÃO JOÃO DEL REI
(Federal University of São João del Rei)

Praça Frei Orlando, 170, Centro, São João del-Rei, MG 36307-352
Telephone: (32) 3379-2300
E-mail: reitoria@ufsj.edu.br
Internet: www.ufsj.edu.br
Founded 1980
State control
Rector: Valéria Heloísa Kemp
Vice-Rector: Sérgio Augusto Araújo da Gama Cerqueira
Pro-Rector for Extension and Community Action: Prof. Paulo Henrique Caetano
Pro-Rector for Management and People Devt: Prof. Adriana Amorim da Silva
Pro-Rector for Planning and Devt: Prof. Cláudio Sérgio Teixeira de Souza
Pro-Rector for Postgraduate Affairs and Research: Prof. Paulo Henrique Caetano
Pro-Rector for Student Affairs: Prof. Dimas José de Resende
Library of 110,000 vols
Publication: *A Vertentes*

UNIVERSIDADE FEDERAL DE UBERLÂNDIA
(Federal University of Uberlândia)

Av. João Naves de Ávila, n° 2121, Bairro Santa Mônica, Uberlândia, MG 38408-100
Telephone: (34) 3239-4411
Internet: www.ufu.br
Founded 1969
Academic year: March to December
Rector: Prof. Elmiro Santos Resende
Vice-Chancellor: Prof. Eduardo Nunes Guimaraes
Chief of Staff: Prof. José Antônio Galo
Pro-Rector for Culture and Student Affairs: Dalva Maria Silva de Oliveira
Pro-Rector for Planning and Management: José Francisco Ribeiro
Pro-Rector for Research and Postgraduate Affairs: Marcello Emílio Beletti
Pro-Rector for Undergraduate Affairs: Marisa Lomônaco de Paula Naves
Dir of Library: Kelma Patrícia de Souza
Library of 163,631 vols, 5,636 periodicals
Number of teachers: 1,320
Number of students: 12,500
Publications: *Ciência e Engenharia*, *Economia e Ensaios*, *Educação e Filosofia*, *Ensino em Revista*, *Letras & Letras*, *Revista do CEBIM*, *Revista do CETEC*, *Revista do Direito, Sociedade e Natureza*, *Veterinária e Notícias*

UNIVERSIDADE FEDERAL DE VIÇOSA
(Federal University of Viçosa)

Av. P. H. Rolfs s/n, Campus Universitário, CP 384, Viçosa, MG 36571-000
Telephone: (31) 3899-2796
E-mail: reitoria@mail.ufv.br
Internet: www.ufv.br
Founded 1926, frmly Univ. Rural do Estado de Minas Gerais
State control
Language of instruction: Portuguese
Academic year: March to November
Rector: Nilda de Fátima Ferreira Soares
Vice-Rector: Demetrius David da Silva
Pro-Rector for Admin.: Leiza Maria Granzinolli
Pro-Rector for Community Affairs: Sylvia do Carmo Castro Franceschini
Pro-Rector for Education: Vicente de Paula Lélis
Pro-Rector for Extension and Culture: Gumercindo Souza Lima
Pro-Rector for Personnel Management: Luiz Antônio Abrantes
Pro-Rector for Planning and Budget: Sebastião Tavares de Rezende
Pro-Rector for Research and Postgraduate Affairs: Eduardo Seiti Gomide Mizubuti
Dir of Library: Doris Magna de Avelar Oliveira
Library of 177,467 vols, 7,604 periodical titles, 43,970 serials, 29,053 theses, 1,298 rare works, 2,641 works in braille
Number of teachers: 786
Number of students: 9,584 (incl. 815 at high school level)
Publications: *Administração Pública e Gestão Social – APGS* (4 a year, online, www.apgs.ufv.br), *Engenharia na Agricultura*, *Revista Ação Ambiental* (6 a year, online, www.acaoambiental.ufv.br), *Revista Arvore* (The Tree Magazine, 6 a year, online, www.revistas.cpd.ufv.br), *Revista Brasileira de Agropecuária Sustentável – PEC/UFV* (2 a year, online, www.rbas.com.br), *Revista Brasileira de Armazenamento* (2 a year), *Revista CERES* (6 a year, online, www.ceres.ufv.br), *Revista de Ciências Humanas* (2 a year,

online, www.cch.ufv.br), *Revista de Economia e Agronegócio* (1 a year), *Revista de Educação em Perspectiva* (1 a year), *Revista ELO – Diálogo em Extensão – PEC/UFV* (online, www.elo.ufv.br), *Revista Mineira de Educação Física* (online, www.revistamineiraefi.ufv.br), *Revista Oikos* (2 a year), *Revista Ponto de Vista* (1 a year, online, www.coluni.ufv.br)

UNIVERSIDADE FEDERAL DO TRIÂNGULO MINEIRO
(Federal University of Triângulo Mineiro)

Av. Frei Paulino, 30, Abadia, Uberaba, MG 38025-180
Telephone: (34) 3318-5000
E-mail: reitoria@reitoria.uftm.edu.br
Internet: www.uftm.edu.br
Founded 1953
State control
Rector: VIRMONDES RODRIGUES, JR
Vice-Rector: ANA LÚCIA DE ASSIS SIMÕES
Pro-Rector for Admin.: JOÃO ULISSES RIBEIRO
Pro-Rector for Extension: VIRGINIA RESENDE SILVA WEFFORT
Pro-Rector for Human Resources: ANA PALMIRA SOARES SANTOS
Pro-Rector for Planning and Devt: CARLA COSTA FIGUEIREDO
Pro-Rector for Research and Post Graduate Affairs: DALMO CORREIA FILHO
Pro-Rector for Student Affairs and Community Action: ROSIMÁR ALVES QUERINO
Pro-Rector for Teaching: ACIR MÁRIO KARWOSKI
Publication: *Revista Triângulo*

UNIVERSIDADE FEDERAL DOS VALES DO JEQUITINHONHA E MUCURI
(Federal University of the Valleys of Jequitinhonha and Mucuri)

Rua da Glória, nº 187, Centro, Diamantina, MG 39100-000
Telephone: (38) 3532-1200
Internet: www.ufvjm.edu.br
Founded 1953
State control
Rector: Prof. Dr PEDRO ANGELO ALMEIDA ABREU
Publication: *Revista Vozes dos Vales*

UNIVERSIDADE JOSÉ DO ROSARIO VELLANO
(José do Rosario Vellano University)

Rodovia MG 179, km 0, Campus Universitário, CP23, Alfenas, MG 37130-000
Telephone: (35) 3299-3000
E-mail: unifenas@unifenas.br
Internet: www.unifenas.br
Founded 1988 as Univ. de Alfenas, current name adopted 2002
Private control
Academic year: February to December
Rector: Dr MARIA DO ROSÁRIO ARAÚJO VELANO
Vice-Rector: Dra VIVIANE ARAÚJO VELANO CASSIS
Pro-Rector for Academics: Prof. JOÃO BATISTA MAGALHÃES
Pro-Rector for Admin. and Finance: Dra LARISSA ARAÚJO VELANO DOZZA
Pro-Rector for Planning and Devt: Dra VIVIANE ARAÚJO VELANO CASSIS
Library of 86,373 vols, 3,593 periodicals
Number of teachers: 896
Number of students: 10,544
Publications: *Jornal da UNIFENAS* (12 a year), *Revista da Universidade de Alfenas* (2 a year, in Portuguese and English)

UNIVERSITY CENTRES

CENTRO UNIVERSITÁRIO DA FUNDAÇÃO EDUCACIONAL GUAXUPÉ

Av. Dona Floriana, 463, Centro, Guaxupé, MG 37800-000
Telephone: (35) 3551-5267
Internet: www.unifeg.edu.br
Rector: Prof. JOSÉ LÁZARO DE SOUZA

CENTRO UNIVERSITÁRIO DE BELO HORIZONTE

Av. Prof. Mário Werneck, 1685 - Estoril, Belo Horizonte, MG 30455-610
Telephone: (31) 3319-9500
E-mail: falecomoreitor@unibh.br
Internet: www.unibh.br
Rector: Prof. RIVADÁVIA C. DRUMMOND DE ALVARENGA NETO

CENTRO UNIVERSITÁRIO DE CARATINGA

Av. Moacir de Matos, 49, Caratinga, MG 35300-047
Telephone: (33) 3322-7900
E-mail: reitoria@funec.br
Internet: www.unec.edu.br
Founded 1963
Rector: ANTONIO FONSECA DA SILVA
Pro-Rector for Admin.: EUGÊNIO MARIA GOMES
Pro-Rector for Postgraduate Affairs, Research and Extension: JOAQUIM FELÍCIO JÚNIOR
Pro-Rector for Teaching: ROBERTO SANTOS BARBIÉRI
Library Dir: PAULO CÉSAR DOS SANTOS

CENTRO UNIVERSITÁRIO DE FORMIGA

Av. Dr. Arnaldo Sena, 328, Água Vermelha, Formiga, MG 35570-000
Telephone: (37) 3329-1400
Internet: www.uniformg.edu.br
Founded 1963
Rector: Prof. MARCO ANTONIO DE SOUSA LEÃO
Vice-Rector: Prof. SEBASTIÃO ALVES DA SILVEIRA
Library of 60,818 vols
Publication: *Conexão Ciência*

CENTRO UNIVERSITÁRIO DE ITAJUBÁ

Av. Dr. Antônio Braga Filho 687, Varginha, Itajubá, MG, 37501-002
Telephone: (35) 3629-8400
E-mail: reitoria@fepi.br
Internet: www.fepi.br
Founded 1965
Rector: Profa CIDÉLIA MARIA BARBOSA LIMA
Vice-Rector and Pro-Rector for Admin.: Prof. ERWIN ROLF MÁDISSON, JR
Pro-Rector for Academics: Profa MAGDA CRISTINA NASCIMENTO ROCHAEL
Library of 17,582 vols
Publication: *Revista Científic*

CENTRO UNIVERSITÁRIO DE LAVRAS

Rua Padre José Poggel, 506, Centenário, Lavras, MG 37200-000
Telephone: (35) 3694-8170
E-mail: reitoria@unilavras.edu.br
Internet: www.unilavras.edu.br
Founded 2001
Rector: CHRISTIANE AMARAL LUNKES ARGENTA

CENTRO UNIVERSITÁRIO DE PATOS DE MINAS

Rua Major Gote, nº 808, Caiçaras, Patos de Minas, MG 38702-054
Telephone: (34) 3823-0300
E-mail: unipam@unipam.edu.br
Internet: www.unipam.edu.br
Founded 1968
Rector: Prof. MILTON ROBERTO DE CASTRO TEIXEIRA
Library of 83,938 vols
Publication: *Revista Jurisvox* (print and online, jurisvox.unipam.edu.br)

CENTRO UNIVERSITÁRIO DE SETE LAGOAS

Av. Marechal Castelo Branco, 2765 Santo Antônio, Sete Lagoas, MG 35701-242
Telephone: (31) 2106-2106
Internet: www.unifemm.edu.br
Founded 1966
Rector: ANTÔNIO FERNANDINO DE CASTRO BAHIA FILHO
Pro-Rector for Academics: JOSÉ HAMILTON RAMALHO
Pro-Rector for Admin. and Finance: ERASMO BRUNO GONÇALVES
Library of 1,700
Publication: *Maestria*

CENTRO UNIVERSITÁRIO DO CERRADO-PATROCÍNIO

Av. Liria Terezinha Lassi Capuano; 466, Patrocínio, MG 38740-000
Telephone: (34) 3839-3737
Internet: www.unicerp.edu.br
Founded 2005
Rector: IÊDA PEREIRA DE MAGALHÃES MARTINS
Sec.-Gen.: NEIDE DE FÁTIMA SILVA BERNARDES
Librarian: LEATRICE ARAÚJO PICCIN
Publications: *Revista Athos & Ethos*, *Revista Rumos*, *Revista Saúde e Meio Ambiente*, *UNIJURIS - Revista Juridica do Cerrado*

CENTRO UNIVERSITÁRIO DO LESTE DE MINAS GERAIS

Rua Bárbara Heliodora, 725, Bom Retiro, MG 35160-215
Telephone: (31) 3846-5500
Internet: www.unilestemg.br
Founded 1969
Rector: GENÉSIO ZEFERINO DA SILVA FILHO
Library of 100,000
Publications: *Biologium*, *Funcional*, *Revista Enfermagem Integrada*, *Revista Movimentum* (2 a year)

CENTRO UNIVERSITÁRIO DO PLANALTO DE ARAXÁ (UNIARAXÁ)

Av. Ministro Olavo Drumond, 05, São Geraldo, Araxá, MG 38180-129
Telephone: (34) 3669-2000
Internet: www.uniaraxa.edu.br
Rector: Prof. VÁLTER GOMES

CENTRO UNIVERSITÁRIO DO SUL DE MINAS (UNIS-MG)

Av. Cel. José Alves, 256 Vila Pinto, Varginha, MG 37010-540
Telephone: (35) 3219-5000
Internet: www.unis.edu.br
Founded 2001

Rector: Prof. STEFANO BARRA GAZZOLA

CENTRO UNIVERSITÁRIO DO TRIÂNGULO

Av. Nicomedes Alves dos Santos, 4545, Gávea, Uberlândia, MG 38411-106
Telephone: 344009-9000
Internet: unitri.edu.br
Founded 1924
Rector: Prof. MARLENE SALGADO DE OLIVEIRA
Vice-Rector: Prof. JOSÉ MARIA MINA
Pro-Rector for Research, Graduate Studies and Extension: Prof. CLOTILDE MARIA KORNDÖRFER
Librarian: DORIZA VAZ

CENTRO UNIVERSITÁRIO METODISTA 'IZABELA HENDRIX'

Av. Dr. Àlvaro Camargos, 205, São Jão Batista, Belo Horizonte, MG 31515-200
Telephone: (31) 3582-2472
Internet: www.metodistademinas.edu.br
Founded 1904
Rector: MÁRCIA NOGUEIRA AMORIM

CENTRO UNIVERSITÁRIO NEWTON PAIVA

R. José Cláudio Rezende, 420, Estoril Belo Horizonte, MG 30455-590
Telephone: (31) 3516-2300
Internet: www.newtonpaiva.br
Founded 1998
Rector: LUIZ CARLOS DE SOUZA VIEIRA

CENTRO UNIVERSITÁRIO UNA (UNA)

Rua José Cláudio Rezende, 80, Estoril, Belo Horizonte, MG 30455-590
Telephone: (31) 3235-7300
E-mail: reitoria@una.br
Internet: www.una.br
Rector: ÁTILA SIMÕES

Pará

In Pará, there are 19 faculties, one integrated HEI, one centre for technological education and seven higher schools or institutes.

UNIVERSITIES

UNIVERSIDADE DA AMAZÔNIA (University of Amazônia)

Av. Alcindo Cacela 287, Belém, PA 66060-902
Telephone: (91) 4009-3000
E-mail: reitor@unama.br
Internet: www.unama.br
Founded 1974
Private control
Language of instruction: Portuguese
Academic year: January to December
Centres of applied social studies, biological and health sciences, humanities and education, science and technology; institute of legal sciences; 3 campuses in Belém and 1 campus in Ananindeua
Rector: Profa ANA CÉLIA BAHIA SILVA
Vice-Rector: Prof. ANTÔNIO DE CARVALHO VAZ PEREIRA
Pro-Rector for Research, Postgraduate Affairs and Extension: Profa NÚBIA MARIA MACIEL
Pro-Rector for Teaching: EVARISTO REZENDE
Library Dir: MARIA CÉLIA SANTANA DA SILVA
Library of 121,000 vols, 3,219 periodicals
Number of teachers: 400
Number of students: 10,300

UNIVERSIDADE DO ESTADO DO PARÁ (State University of Pará)

Rua do Una nº 156, Belém, PA 66050-540
Telephone: (91) 3299-2200
E-mail: ascom@uepa.br
Internet: www.uepa.br
Founded
State control
Language of instruction: Portuguese
Academic year: February to December
Centres of biological sciences and health, natural sciences and technology, nursing, physical education, social sciences and education
Rector: JUAREZ ANTÔNIO SIMÕES QUARESMA
Vice-Rector: RUBENS CARDOSO DA SILVA
Pro-Rector for Extension: MARIA MARIZE DUARTE
Pro-Rector for Management and Planning: LÉONY NEGRÃO
Pro-Rector for Research and Postgraduate Affairs: JOFRE JACOB FREITAS
Pro-Rector for Undergraduate Affairs: ANA DA CONCEIÇÃO OLIVEIRA
Number of teachers: 803
Number of students: 14,943 (14,721 undergraduate, 222 postgraduate)
Publications: *Revista Cocar* (2 a year), *Revista Cognição e Educação Matemática, Revista Comunicação Universitária* (2 a year), *Revista Educação em Foco, Revista Observatório da Religião*

UNIVERSIDADE FEDERAL DO PARÁ (Federal University of Pará)

CP 479, Belém, PA 66075-110
Av. Augusto Corrêa 1, Guamá, Belém, PA 66075-110
Telephone: (91) 3201-7000
E-mail: reitor@ufpa.br
Internet: www.ufpa.br
Founded 1957
federal control
Language of instruction: Portuguese
Academic year: March to December
Institutes of applied social sciences, arts, biological sciences, coastal studies, education, exact and natural sciences, geosciences, health sciences, legal sciences, letters and communication, philosophy and humanities, science and mathematics, technology, veterinary medicine; campuses in Abaetetuba, Altamira, Belém, Bragança, Breves, Cametá, Capanema, Castanhal, Marabá, Soure, Tucuruí
Rector: Prof. Dr CARLOS EDILSON DE ALMEIDA MANESCHY
Vice-Rector: Prof. Dr HORACIO SCHNEIDER
Pro-Rector for Admin.: Prof. EDSON ORTIZ DE MATOS
Pro-Rector for Devt and Personnel Management: JOÃO CAUBY DE ALMEIDA, JR
Pro-Rector for Extension: Prof. Dr FERNANDO ARTHUR DE F. NEVES
Pro-Rector for Int. Relations: Prof. FLÁVIO AUGUSTO SIDRIM NASSAR
Pro-Rector for Planning and Institutional Devt: RAQUEL TRINDADE BORGES
Pro-Rector for Research and Postgraduate Affairs: Prof. Dr EMMANUEL ZAGURY TOURINHO
Pro-Rector for Undergraduate Studies: Profa Dra MARLENE RODRIGUES MEDEIROS FREITAS
Library Dir: MARIA DAS GRAÇAS DA SILVA PENA
Library of 1,088,650 vols
Number of teachers: 2,310
Number of students: 39,236
Publications: *Cadernos de Pós-Graduação em Direito da UFPA, Cadernos do Centro de Filosofia e Ciências Humanas, Humanitas, MOARA, Revista do Centro do Ciências Jurídicas, Revista do Centro Sócio-Econômico, Revista do Tecnológico, Ver a Educação*

UNIVERSIDADE FEDERAL RURAL DA AMAZÔNIA (Federal Rural University of the Amazon)

Av. Presidente Tancredo Neves nº 2501, Bairro Montese, Belém, PA 66077-901
Telephone: (91) 3210-5184
E-mail: ascom.ufra@gmail.com
Internet: www.ufra.edu.br
federal control
Language of instruction: Portuguese
Academic year: January to December
Rector: Prof. SUEO NUMASAWA
Vice-Rector: Prof. PAULO DE JESUS SANTOS
Pro-Rector for Admin. and Finance: Prof. KEDSON RAUL DE SOUZA LIMA
Pro-Rector for Extension: Prof. DJACY BARBOSA RIBEIRO
Pro-Rector for Personnel Management: RANYELLE FORO DE SOUSA
Pro-Rector for Planning and Institutional Devt: Prof. ANTÔNIO CORDEIRO DE SANTANA
Pro-Rector for Research and Technological Devt: Prof. IZILDINHA DE SOUZA MIRANDA
Pro-Rector for Student Affairs: Prof. MANOEL SEBASTIÃO PEREIRA DE CARVALHO
Pro-Rector for Teaching: Prof. MARCEL DO NASCIMENTO BOTELHO
Publications: *Boletim Técnico Científico do Cepnor* (Tropical Journal of Fisheries and Aquatic Sciences, 2 a year), *Revista de Ciências Agrárias* (Amazonian Journal of Agricultural and Environmental Sciences, 4 a year, in Portuguese and English)

Paraíba

In Paraíba, there are 24 faculties, one integrated HEI, one centre for technological education, and five higher schools or institutes.

UNIVERSITIES

UNIVERSIDADE ESTADUAL DA PARAÍBA (State University of Paraíba)

Av. das Baraúnas 351, Campus Universitário, Campina Grande, PB 58429-500
Telephone: (83) 3315-3300
E-mail: reitoria@uepb.edu.br
Internet: www.uepb.edu.br
Founded 1966
State control
Language of instruction: Portuguese
Academic year: March to December
Centres of agricultural and environmental sciences, applied social sciences, biological and health sciences, education, exact and applied sciences, humanities, legal sciences, science and technology; campuses in Araruna, Campina Grande, Catolé do Rocha, Guarabira, João Pessoa, Lagoa Seca, Monteiro, Patos
Rector: Prof. Dr ANTONIO GUEDES RANGEL, JR
Vice-Rector: Prof. Dr JOSÉ ETHAN DE LUCENA BARBOSA
Pro-Rector for Admin.: CÉLIA REGINA DINIZ
Pro-Rector for Arts and Culture: FRANCISCO PEREIRA DA SILVA, JR
Pro-Rector for Extension: Prof. JOSÉ PEREIRA DA SILVA

Pro-Rector for Financial Management: GIOVANA CARNEIRO PIRES FERREIRA
Pro-Rector for Infrastructure: Prof. Dr ALVARO LUIS DE FARIAS
Pro-Rector for Personnel Management: SANDY GONZAGA DE MELO
Pro-Rector for Planning and Budgeting: Prof. MISAEL ELIAS DE MORAIS
Pro-Rector for Postgraduate Affairs and Research: Profa Dra MARIA JOSÉ LIMA DA SILVA
Pro-Rector for Student Affairs: NÚBIA DO NASCIMENTO MARTINS
Pro-Rector for Technical and Distance Education: Profa ELIANE DA MOURA SILVA
Pro-Rector for Undergraduate Affairs: Prof. ELI BRANDÃO
Head Librarian: MANUELA MAIA
Library of 65,000 vols
Number of teachers: 650
Number of students: 10,000
Publications: *A Barriguda* (online, www.abarriguda.org.br), *Alpharrabios* (2 a year, online, eduep.uepb.edu.br/alpharrabios), *Catálogo Geral* (1 a year), *Dataveni@* (2 a year), *Informativo UEPB*, *Pesquisa Brasileira em Odontopediatria e Clínica Integrada* (4 a year), *Qualit@s* (2 a year, online), *Revista de Biologia e Farmácia (BioFar)* (4 a year, print and online, sites.uepb.edu.br/biofar), *Revista de Estudos Internacionais* (2 a year, online, www.revistadeestudosinternacionais.com), *Revista Sociopoética* (online, eduep.uepb.edu.br/sociopoetica), *Roteiro*, *Tarairiú* (2 a year, online)

UNIVERSIDADE FEDERAL DA PARAÍBA
(Federal University of Paraíba)

Cidade Universitária, João Pessoa, PB 58051-900
Telephone: (83) 3216-7200
E-mail: gabinete@reitoria.ufpb.br
Internet: www.ufpb.br
Founded 1955
federal control
Language of instruction: Portuguese
Academic year: March to December
Centres of agricultural sciences, applied sciences, applied social sciences, education, exact and natural sciences, health sciences, humanities, arts and letters, legal sciences, medicine, technology
Rector: MARGARETH DE FÁTIMA FORMIGA MELO DINIZ
Vice-Rector: EDUARDO RAMALHO RABENHORST
Pro-Rector for Admin.: CLIVALDO SILVA DE ARAÚJO
Pro-Rector for Community Affairs: ORLANDO DE CAVALCANTI VILLAR
Pro-Rector for Personnel Management: FRANCISCO RAMALHO DE ALBUQUERQUE
Pro-Rector for Planning: MARCELO SOBRAL DA SILVA
Pro-Rector for Postgraduate Affairs and Research: ISAAC ALMEIDA DE MEDEIROS
Pro-Rector for Student Assistance: THOMPSON LOPES DE OLIVEIRA
Pro-Rector for Undergraduate Affairs: ARIANE NORMA MENEZES DE SÁ
Dir for Central Library: SÔNIA SUELY ARAÚJO PESSOA ROSAS
Number of teachers: 1,423
Number of students: 19,203
Publications: *Acta Semiotica et Linguistica* (2 a year), *Arquivo & Sociedade: Estudos, Culturas Midiáticas* (2 a year), *Cultura & Tradução* (every 2 years), *Diversidade Religiosa* (2 a year), *Espaço do Currículo* (2 a year), *Gaia Scientia* (2 a year), *Informação e Sociedade: Estudos* (3 a year), *Journal of Urban and Environmental Engineering (JUEE)* (2 a year, print and online, journal-uee.org), *MORINGA—Artes do Espetáculo* (2 a year), *Perspectivas em Gestão & Conhecimento* (2 a year), *Pesquisa Brasileira em Ciência da Informação e Biblioteconomia (PBCIB)* (2 a year), *Prima Facie—Direito, História e Política* (2 a year, online), *Problemata—Revista Internacional de Filosofia* (2 a year), *Revista de Arqueologia*, *Revista Artemis* (2 a year), *Revista Brasileira de Ciência da Saúde* (4 a year), *Revista Brasileira de Engenharia Agrícola e Ambiental* (4 a year), *Revista de Ciências Sociais—Política & Trabalho* (2 a year), *Revista de Iniciação Científica em Relações Internacionais* (2 a year), *Revista do Mestrado Profissional Gestão em Organizações Aprendentes* (2 a year), *Revista Economia e Desenvolvimento* (2 a year), *Revista Estudos Geoambientais*, *Revista Evidenciação Contábil & Finanças* (4 a year), *Revista Gênero & Direito* (irregular), *Revista Graphos* (2 a year), *Revista Nordestina de Biologia* (1 a year), *Revista Palavrar*, *Revista Religare* (2 a year), *Revista Temas em Educação* (2 a year, online), *Revista Sebastiana* (2 a year, online), *Sæculum—Revista de História* (2 a year)

UNIVERSIDADE FEDERAL DE CAMPINA GRANDE
(Federal University of Campina Grande)

Rua Aprígio Veloso 882, Bairro Universitário, Campina Grande, PB 58429-900
Telephone: (83) 2101-1000
Internet: www.ufcg.edu.br
Founded 2002, from 4 existing campuses of the Univ. Fed. da Paraíba
federal control
Language of instruction: Portuguese
Academic year: January to December
Centres of agrifood technology, biological and health sciences, education and health, electrical and computer engineering, humanities, legal and social sciences, rural health and technology, science and technology, sustainable devt of semi-arid areas, teacher training, technology and natural resources
Rector: JOSÉ EDÍLSON DE AMORIM
Vice-Rector: VICEMÁRIO SIMÕES
Pro-Rector for Admin. and Finance: ALEXANDRE JOSÉ DE ALMEIDA GAMA
Pro-Rector for Community Affairs: EDMILSON LÚCIO DE SOUSA, JR
Pro-Rector for Postgraduate Affairs: BENEMAR ALENCAR DE SOUSA
Pro-Rector for Research and Extension: ROSILENE DIAS MONTENEGRO
Pro-Rector for Teaching: LUCIANO BAROSI DE LEMOS
Sec.: VÂNIA SUELI GUIMARÃES ROCHA
Sec. for Human Resources: HOMERO GUSTAVO CORREIA RODRIGUES
Sec. for Planning and Institutional Assessment: VICEMÁRIO SIMÕES
Chief of Staff: VÂNIA SUELI GUIMARÃES ROCHA
Publications: *Ariús* (1 a year), *Raizes* (2 a year), *Revista Brasileira de Engenharia Agrícola e Ambiental (AGRIAMBI)* (4 a year), *Sheculum* (1 a year)

UNIVERSITY CENTRE

CENTRO UNIVERSITÁRIO DE JOÃO PESSOA
(University Centre of João Pessoa)

BR 230, km 22, Água Fria, João Pessoa, PB 58053-000
Telephone: (83) 2106-9200
E-mail: aai@unipe.br
Internet: www.unipe.br
Founded 1971
Private control
Language of instruction: Portuguese
Academic year: January to December
Courses in accounting, architecture and urbanism, business administration, civil engineering, computer networks, computer science, dentistry, fashion design, internet systems, law, nursing, physical education, physiotherapy, psychology, speech
Rector: Profa ANA FLÁVIA PEREIRA DA FONSECA
Pro-Rector for Postgraduate Affairs, Research and Extension: Profa IANY CAVALCANTI DA SILVA BARROS
Pro-Rector for Undergraduate Teaching: Profa Dra MARIA IZABEL CAVALCANTI CABRAL
Librarian: Profa ANA MARIA HENRIQUES E SILVA
Library of 145,000 vols
Publications: *Direito e Desenvolvimento* (2 a year), *InterScientia* (3 a year)

Paraná

In Paraná, there are 120 faculties, seven integrated HEIs and 19 centres for technological education.

UNIVERSITIES

PONTIFÍCIA UNIVERSIDADE CATÓLICA DO PARANÁ
(Pontifical Catholic University of Paraná)

Rua Imaculada Conceição 1155, Bairro Prado Velho, Curitiba, PR 80215-901
Telephone: (41) 3271-1515
E-mail: imprensa@pucpr.br
Internet: www.pucpr.br
Founded 1959
Private control
Language of instruction: Portuguese
Academic year: February to December (2 semesters)
Grand Chancellor: DOM MOACYR JOSÉ VITTI (Archbishop of Curitiba)
Rector: Ir CLEMENTE IVO JULIATTO
Vice-Rector: PAULO OTÁVIO MUSSI AUGUSTO
Pro-Rector for Academic Affairs: EDUARDO DAMIÃO DA SILVA
Pro-Rector for Admin. and Devt: JOSÉ LUIZ CASELA
Pro-Rector for Community Affairs: MÁSIMO DELLA JUSTINA
Pro-Rector for Research and Postgraduate Affairs: WALDEMIRO GREMSKI
Chief of Staff: SARA REGINA HOKAI
Sec.-Gen.: KÁTIA MARIA BIESEK
Central Library Coordinator: HELOISA HELENA ANZOLIN
Number of teachers: 1,200
Number of students: 20,400
Publications: *Archives of Oral Research* (3 a year, in English), *Círculo de Estudos Bandeirantes* (1 a year), *Estudos de Biologia* (2 a year, in Portuguese and English), *Estudos de Medicina* (4 a year), *Estudos Nietzsche* (2 a year), *Fisioterapia em Movimento* (4 a year), *Locus* (1 a year), *Psicologia Argumento* (4 a year), *PUC-PR em Dados* (1 a year), *Revista Acadêmica Ciências Agrárias e Ambientais* (4 a year), *Revista Brasileira de Estratégia (REBRAE)* (4 a year), *Revista Brasileira de Gestão Urbana* (2 a year, in Portuguese, English, French and Spanish), *Revista de Direito Econômico e Socioambiental* (2 a year), *Revista de Estudos da Comunicação* (4 a year), *Revista de Filosofia* (2 a year),

Revista Diálogo Educacional (4 a year), *Revista Pistis & Praxis—Teologia e Pastoral* (2 a year), *Verba Iuris* (1 a year), *Vida Universitária* (12 a year)

DEANS

School of Agricultural Sciences and Veterinary Medicine: HUMBERTO MACIEL FRANÇA MADEIRA
School of Architecture and Design: CARLOS DOMINGOS NIGRO
School of Business: CARLOS AUGUSTO CANDÊO FONTANINI
School of Communication and Arts: ELIANE CRISTINE FRANCISCO MAFFEZZOLLI
School of Education and Humanities: MARIA LOURDES GISI
School of Health and Biosciences: SÉRGIO SURUGI DE SIQUEIRA
School of Law: ALVACIR ALFREDO NICZ
School of Medicine: ALBERTO ACCIOLY VEIGA
University Polytechnic: VIDAL MARTINS

UNIVERSIDADE ESTADUAL DE LONDRINA
(State University of Londrina)

CP 10011, Londrina, PR 86055-900
Campus Universitário, Rodovia Celso Garcia Cid, PR 445, km 380, Londrina, PR 86055-900
Telephone: (43) 3371-4000
E-mail: proaf@uel.br
Internet: www.uel.br

Founded 1971
State control
Language of instruction: Portuguese
Academic year: February to December

Centres of agrarian sciences, applied social studies, biological sciences, education, communication and arts, exact sciences, health sciences, letters and human sciences, physical education, technology and urbanism

Rector: Profa Dra NÁDINA APARECIDA MORENO
Vice-Rector: BERENICE QUINZANI JORDÃO
Pro-Rector for Admin. and Finance: HIDEAKI WILSON TAKAHASHI
Pro-Rector for Extension: CRISTIANNE CORDEIRO NASCIMENTO
Pro-Rector for Human Resources: ITAMAR ANDRE RODRIGUES DO NASCIMENTO
Pro-Rector for Planning: LUIS FERNANDO PINTO DIAS
Pro-Rector for Research and Postgraduate Affairs: Prof. Dr MÁRIO SÉRGIO MANTOVANI
Pro-Rector for Undergraduate Affairs: Prof. Dr LUDOVIKO CARNASCIALI DOS SANTOS
Chief of Staff: Profa Dra MARIA JÚLIA GIANNASI KAIMEN
Sec.-Gen.: DEISE MARY GARBELINI BERGAMIN
Central Library Dir: Profa Dra MARIA ELISABETE CATARINO

Library of 153,360 vols, incl. 135,740 books, 9,380 theses and 8,240 pamphlets; 6,444 periodical titles; 5,169 units of spec. collns
Number of teachers: 1,600
Number of students: 16,000

Publications: *Antíteses* (2 a year), *ASSOBRAFIR Ciência* (2 a year), *Discursos Fotográficos* (2 a year), *Entretextos* (2 a year), *Estudos Interdisciplinares em psicologia* (2 a year), *Geografia (Londina)* (2 a year), *Germinal: Marxismo e Educação em Debate* (1 a year), *História e Ensino* (1 a year), *Informação e Informação* (2 a year), *Mediações—Revista de Ciências Sociais* (2 a year), *Portal de Cartografia* (1 a year), *Projética* (2 a year), *Revista de Estudos Contábeis* (2 a year), *Revista do Direito Público* (3 a year), *Revista Espaço para Saúde* (2 a year), *Scientia Iuris* (2 a year), *Semina: Ciências Agrárias* (4 a year), *Semina: Ciências Biológicas e da Saúde* (2 a year), *Semina: Ciências Exatas e Tecnológicas* (2 a year), *Semina: Ciências Sociais e Humanas* (2 a year), *Signun: Estudo da Linguagem* (2 a year)

UNIVERSIDADE ESTADUAL DE MARINGÁ
(State University of Maringá)

Av. Colombo 5790, Jardim Universitário, Maringá, PR 87020-900
Telephone: (44) 3011-4040
E-mail: fadec@wnet.com.br
Internet: www.uem.br

Founded 1970
State control
Language of instruction: Portuguese
Academic year: March to December

Rector: Prof. Dr JÚLIO SANTIAGO PRATES FILHO
Vice-Rector: Profa Dra NEUSA ALTOÉ
Pro-Rector for Admin.: Prof. MARCELO SONCINI RODRIGUES
Pro-Rector for Extension and Culture: Prof. Dr JOSÉ GILBERTO CATUNDA SALES
Pro-Rector for Human Resources and Community Affairs: Profa Dra SONIA LUCY MOLINARI
Pro-Rector for Research and Postgraduate Affairs: Prof. Dr MAURO ANTONIO DA SILVA SÁ RAVAGNANI
Pro-Rector for Teaching: Profa Dra EDNÉIA REGINA ROSSI
Chief of Staff: Prof. Dr MAURICIO ANTONIO CUSTÓDIO DE MELO
Central Library Dir: MARINALVA APARECIDA SPOLON DE ALMEIDA

Library of 161,680 vols, 257,160 periodicals, 4,347 pamphlets, 3,554 monographs, 5,743 theses, 3,515 microfiches, 944 CD-ROMs and DVDs
Number of teachers: 1,300
Number of students: 9,800

Publications: *A Economia em Revista*, *Caderno da Semana de Geografia*, *Caderno de METEP*, *Cadernos de Administração*, *Jornal Alfabetizando*, *Revista Apontamentos*, *Revista de Educação Física*, *Revista de Psicologia*, *Revista Diálogos*, *Revista Enfoque-Reflexão Contábil*, *Revista Tecnológica*, *Unimar*, *Unimar Jurídica*, *Universidade e Sociedade*

UNIVERSIDADE ESTADUAL DE PONTA GROSSA
(State University of Ponta Grossa)

Av. Gen. Carlos Cavalcanti 4748, Campus de Uvaranas, Ponta Grossa, PR 84030-900
Telephone: (42) 3220-3000
E-mail: uepg@uepg.br
Internet: www.uepg.br

Founded 1970
State control
Language of instruction: Portuguese
Academic year: February to November

Rector: CARLOS LUCIANO SANTANA VARGAS
Vice-Rector: (vacant)
Pro-Rector for Admin. Affairs: Prof. Dr ARIANGELO HAUER DIAS
Pro-Rector for Extension and Cultural Affairs: Profa Dra GISELE ALVES DE SÁ QUIMELLI
Pro-Rector for Human Resources: ANA MARIA SALLES ROSA SOLAK
Pro-Rector for Planning: ALTAIR JUSTINO
Pro-Rector for Research and Postgraduate Affairs: Prof. Dr BENJAMIM DE MELO CARVALHO
Pro-Rector for Undergraduate Affairs: GRACIETE TOZETTO GÓES
Chief of Staff: CARLOS ROBERTO FERREIRA
Librarian: MARIA LUIZA FERNANDES BERTHOLINO

Library of 98,000 vols, 2,772 periodical titles
Number of teachers: 700
Number of students: 11,400

Publications: *Emancipação* (2 a year), *General Catalogue* (1 a year), *Lumiar: Revista de Ciências Jurídicas* (2 a year), *Muitas Vozes* (2 a year), *Olhar de Professor* (2 a year), *Práxis Educativa* (2 a year), *Publicatio UEPG* (published in 4 parts: *Applied Social Sciences, Biological Sciences and Health, Exact and Earth Sciences, Agriculture and Engineering Sciences, Human Sciences, Linguistics, Letters and Art*; each 2 a year), *Revista de História Regional* (2 a year), *Revista Internacional de Folkcomunicação* (2 a year), *Revista Latino-Americana de Geografia e Gênero* (2 a year), *Teacher Eyes Review* (1 a year), *Terr@ Plural* (2 a year), *UniLetras* (2 a year), *UPEG em Números* (2 a year)

UNIVERSIDADE ESTADUAL DO CENTRO-OESTE
(State University of Central West)

Rua Padre Salvador 875, Santa Cruz, CP 730, Guarapuava, PR 85015-430
Telephone: (42) 3621-1000
E-mail: secretaria_deadm@yahoo.com.br
Internet: www2.unicentro.br

Founded 1997
State control
Language of instruction: Portuguese
Academic year: January to December

Academic units of agricultural and environmental sciences, applied social sciences, exact sciences and technology, health sciences, humanities, letters and arts

Rector: Prof. ALDO NELSON BONA
Vice-Rector: Prof. OSMAR AMBRÓSIO DE SOUZA
Pro-Rector for Admin.: AMARILDO HERSEN
Pro-Rector for Extension and Culture: Prof. MARQUIANA DE FREITAS VILAS BOAS GOMES
Pro-Rector for Human Resources: ROSELI DE OLIVEIRA MACHADO
Pro-Rector for Planning: Prof. SILVANO SIMÕES ROCHA
Pro-Rector for Research and Postgraduate Affairs: Prof. MARCOS VENTURA FARIA
Pro-Rector for Teaching: Profa MÁRCIA TEREZINHA TEMBIL

Publications: *Ambiência* (3 a year), *Analecta* (2 a year), *Revista Brasileira de Tecnologia Aplicada nas Ciências Agrárias* (4 a year), *Revista Capital Científico* (3 a year, online), *Revista Ciências Exatas e Naturais* (2 a year), *Revista Guairacá* (1 a year), *Revista Interfaces*, *Revista Salus* (2 a year)

UNIVERSIDADE ESTADUAL DO OESTE DO PARANÁ
(State University of West Parana)

Rua Universitária 1619, CP 701, Jardim Universitário, Cascavel, PR 85819-110
Telephone: (45) 3220-3000
E-mail: gabinete@unioeste.br
Internet: www.unioeste.br

Founded 1991
State control
Language of instruction: Portuguese
Academic year: January to December

Rector: PAULO SERGIO WOLFF
Vice-Rector: CARLOS ALBERTO PIACENT
Pro-Rector for Admin. and Finance: ROSICLEI FÁTIMA LUFT
Pro-Rector for Extension: Prof. Dr GILMAR BAUMGARTNER
Pro-Rector for Human Resources: AMARILDO JORGE DA SILVA
Pro-Rector for Planning: JANDIR FERRERA DE LIMA
Pro-Rector for Research and Postgraduate Affairs: SILVIO CÉSAR SAMPAIO

Pro-Rector for Undergraduate Affairs: LILIAM FARIA PORTO BORGES
Central Library Coordinator: NEUSA FAGUNDES
Library of 53,000 vols, 23,000 periodicals
Number of teachers: 400
Number of students: 6,000
Publication: *Revista Línguas & Letras*

UNIVERSIDADE FEDERAL DO PARANÁ
(Federal University of Paraná)

Rua 15 de Novembro 1299, Centro, Curitiba, PR 80060-000
Telephone: (41) 3360-5001
E-mail: gabinetereitor@ufpr.br
Internet: www.internacional.ufpr.br
Founded 1912
federal control
Language of instruction: Portuguese
Academic year: March to December
Rector: Prof. Dr ZAKI AKEL SOBRINHO
Vice-Rector: ROGÉRIO ANDRADE MULINARI
Pro-Rector for Admin.: PAULO ROBERTO ROCHA KRÜGER
Pro-Rector for Extension and Culture: Profa Dra DEISE CRISTINA DE LIMA PICANÇO
Pro-Rector for Personnel Management: ADRIANO DO ROSÁRIO RIBEIRO
Pro-Rector for Research and Postgraduate Affairs: Prof. Dr EDILSON SERGIO SILVEIRA
Pro-Rector for Student Affairs: RITA DE CÁSSIA LOPES
Pro-Rector for Undergraduate and Professional Education: Profa Dra MARIA AMÉLIA SABBAG ZAINKO
Librarian: LÍGIA ELIANA SETENARESKI
Library: see under Libraries and Archives
Number of teachers: 1,800
Number of students: 30,000
Publications: *Boletim Paranaense de Geociências* (2 a year), *Dens* (2 a year), *Desenvolvimento e Meio Ambiente* (2 a year), *História: Questões & Debates* (2 a year), *Nerítica* (1 a year), *RAEGA* (1 a year), *Revista de Economia* (2 a year), *Revista de Faculdade de Direito* (2 a year), *Revista Letras* (2 a year), *Scientia Agraria* (2 a year)

UNIVERSIDADE NORTE DO PARANÁ
(University of North Paraná)

Av. Paris 675, Jardim Piza, Londrina, PR 86041-120
Telephone: (43) 3371-7700
E-mail: reitoria@unopar.br
Internet: www.unopar.br
Founded 1972
Private control
Language of instruction: Portuguese
Academic year: January to December
Centres of applied business and social sciences, biological and health sciences, exact sciences and technology, humanities, education, communication and arts
Rector: Prof. CLEBER FAGUNDES RAMOS
Vice-Rector and Pro-Rector for Teaching: Prof. HÉLIO RODOLFO NAVARRO
Pro-Rector for Distance Learning: Profa ELISA MARIA DE ASSIS
Pro-Rector for Extension: Profa WILMA JANDRE MELO
Pro-Rector for Postgraduate Affairs and Research: Prof. HÉLIO HIROSHI SUGUIMOTO
Librarian: EDUARDO MARCOS FAHL
Publications: *Revista Unopar Científica Ciências Biológicas e da Saúde* (4 a year), *Revista Unopar Científica Ciências Exatas eTecnológicas* (1 a year), *Revista Unopar Científica Ciências Humanas e Educação* (2 a year), *Revista Unopar Científica Ciências Jurídicas e Empresariais* (2 a year)

Pernambuco

In Pernambuco, there are 74 faculties, three integrated HEIs, two centres for technological education and 14 higher schools or institutes.

UNIVERSITIES

UNIVERSIDADE CATÓLICA DE PERNAMBUCO
(Catholic University of Pernambuco)

Rua do Príncipe 526, Boa Vista, Recife, PE 50050-900
Telephone: (81) 2119-4016
E-mail: assecom@unicap.br
Internet: www.unicap.br
Founded 1951
Private control
Language of instruction: Portuguese
Academic year: February to December (2 semesters)
Centres of biological and health sciences, legal sciences, social sciences, theology and humanities
Rector: Fr PEDRO RUBENS FERREIRA OLIVEIRA
Pro-Rector for Academic Affairs: Profa Dra ALINE MARIA GREGO
Pro-Rector for Admin.: LUCIANO JOSÉ PINHEIRO BARROS
Pro-Rector for Community Affairs: Fr LÚCIO FLÁVIO RIBEIRO CIRNE
Librarian: JAÍSE DA C. LEÃO
Library of 314,700 vols, 153,060 periodicals
Number of teachers: 575
Number of students: 13,353
Publication: *Symposium* (2 a year)

UNIVERSIDADE DE PERNAMBUCO
(University of Pernambuco)

Av. Agamenon Magalhães s/n, Bairro Santo Amaro, Recife, PE 50100-010
Telephone: (81) 3183-3674
E-mail: reitor@upe.br
Internet: www.upe.br
Founded 1965
Private control
Language of instruction: Portuguese
Academic year: January to December
Rector: Prof. CARLOS FERNANDO DE ARAÚJO CALADO
Vice-Rector: Prof. RIVALDO MENDES DE ALBUQUERQUE
Pro-Rector for Admin. Affairs: Prof. Dr PEDRO HENRIQUE DE BARROS FALCÃO
Pro-Rector for Extension and Culture: Prof. GILBERTO DIAS ALVES
Pro-Rector for Planning: Prof. Dr BÉDA BARKOKÉBAS, JR
Pro-Rector for Postgraduate Affairs and Research: Profa Dra VIVIANE COLARES SOARES DE ANDRADE AMORIM
Pro-Rector for Undergraduate Affairs: Profa IZABEL CHRISTINA DE AVELAR SILVA
Librarian: LÍDIA PONTUAL
Library of 8,000 vols, 8,302 periodicals (390 titles)
Number of teachers: 879
Number of students: 11,928 (10,968 undergraduate, 350 postgraduate, 610 extension)
Publications: *Revista de Pesquisa em Saúde*, *Revista Eletrônica Formação*, *Revista Eletrônica Historien*

UNIVERSIDADE FEDERAL DE PERNAMBUCO
(Federal University of Pernambuco)

Av. Prof. Moraes Rego 1235, Cidade Universitária, Recife, PE 50670-901
Telephone: (81) 2126-8000
E-mail: gabinete@ufpe.br
Internet: www.ufpe.br
Founded 1946
federal control
Language of instruction: Portuguese
Academic year: March to December
Centres of applied social sciences, arts and communication, biological sciences, education, exact and natural sciences, health sciences, law, philosophy and humanities, technology and geosciences; 3 campuses in Recife, Caruaru and Vitória de Santo Antão
Rector: Prof. ANÍSIO BRASILEIRO DE FREITAS DOURADO
Vice-Rector: Prof. SILVIO ROMERO DE BARROS MARQUES
Pro-Rector for Academic Affairs: ANA MARIA SANTOS CABRAL
Pro-Rector for Extension: EDILSON FERNANDES DE SOUZA
Pro-Rector for Personnel Admin. and Quality of Life: LENITA ALMEIDA AMARAL
Pro-Rector for Planning, Budgeting and Finance: Prof. HERMANO PERRELLI DE MOURA
Pro-Rector for Research and Postgraduate Affairs: Prof. FRANCISCO DE SOUSA RAMOS
Pro-Rector for Student Affairs: CLAUDIO HELIOMAR VICENTE DA SILVA
Library: see under Libraries and Archives
Number of teachers: 2,140
Number of students: 34,607 (27,753 undergraduate, 4,348 postgraduate, 2,506 doctoral)
Publications: *Revista Anthropológicas* (2 a year), *Revista Brasileira de Geografia Física* (2 a year), *Revista de Estudos Universitários*, *Revista de Geografia* (3 a year)

UNIVERSIDADE FEDERAL DO VALE DO SÃO FRANCISCO
(Federal University of São Francisco Valley)

Av. José de Sá Maniçoba s/n, Centro, Petrolina, PE 56304-205
Telephone: (87) 2101-6831
E-mail: reitoria@univasf.edu.br
Internet: www.univasf.edu.br
Founded 2002
federal control
Language of instruction: Portuguese
Academic year: January to December
Rector: Prof. Dr JULIANELI TOLENTINO DE LIMA
Vice-Rector: Prof. Dr TÉLIO NOBRE LEITE
Pro-Rector for Extension: Profa Dra LÚCIA MARISY SOUZA RIBEIRO DE OLIVEIRA
Rector for Planning and Institutional Devt: Prof. Dr JOSÉ RAIMUNDO CORDEIRO NETO
Pro-Rector for Research, Postgraduate Affairs and Innovation: Prof. Dr HELINANDO PEQUENO DE OLIVEIRA
Pro-Rector for Student Affairs: ISABEL CRISTINA SAMPAIO ANGELIM
Pro-Rector for Teaching: LEONARDO RODRIGUES SAMPAIO
Dir for Libraries: LUCÍDIO LOPES DE ALENCAR
Library of 40,000 vols
Publication: *Guarany*

UNIVERSIDADE FEDERAL RURAL DE PERNAMBUCO
(Federal University of Rural Pernambuco)

Rua Dom Manoel de Medeiros s/n, Dois Irmãos, Recife, PE 52171-900
Telephone: (81) 3320-6000
E-mail: reitoria@reitoria.ufrpe.br
Internet: www.ufrpe.br

Founded 1912
federal control
Language of instruction: Portuguese
Academic year: January to December

Academic units in Garanhuns and Serra Talhada; depts of agronomy, animal science, biology, business administration, chemistry, education, fisheries and aquaculture, forestry science, history, letters and human sciences, mathematics, molecular sciences, morphology and physiology, physical education, physics, rural technology, social sciences, statistics and computing, veterinary medicine

Rector: Profa MARIA JOSÉ DE SENA
Vice-Rector: Prof. MARCELO BRITO CARNEIRO LEÃO
Pro-Rector for Admin.: Prof. MOACYR CUNHA FILHO
Pro-Rector for Extension: Prof. DELSON LARANJEIRA
Pro-Rector for Planning: Prof. LUIZ FLÁVIO ARREGUY MAIA FILHO
Pro-Rector for Research and Postgraduate Affairs: Profa MARIA MADALENA PESSOA GUERRA
Pro-Rector for Student Affairs.: Prof. SEVERINO MENDES DE AZEVEDO, JR
Pro-Rector for Undergraduate Teaching: Profa MÔNICA MARIA LINS SANTIAGO
Librarian: MÁRIO HENRIQUE VAREJÃO

Library of 135,175 vols, 1,153 nat. and 737 int. periodicals, 1,983 multimedia items
Number of teachers: 700
Number of students: 8,000

Publications: *Anais* (1 a year), *Caderno Ômega* (irregular), *Medicina Veterinária* (online), *Revista Brasileira de Ciências Agrárias* (online), *Revista Custos e Agronegócio* (online)

Piauí

In Piauí, there are 25 faculties, one centre for technological education and nine higher schools or institutes.

UNIVERSITIES

UNIVERSIDADE ESTADUAL DO PIAUÍ
(State University of Piauí)

Rua João Cabral 2231, Bairro Pirajá, Teresina, PI 64002-150
Telephone: (86) 3213-7398
E-mail: ascom.uespi@gmail.com
Internet: www.uespi.br

Founded 1985
State control
Language of instruction: Portuguese
Academic year: January to December

Centres of applied social sciences, education, communications and arts, health sciences, humanities and letters, natural sciences, technology and urbanism

Rector: Prof. CARLOS ALBERTO PEREIRA DA SILVA
Vice-Rector: Prof. NOUGA CARDOSO BATISTA

Library of 59,000 vols, 5,050 periodicals
Number of teachers: 359
Number of students: 7,001

UNIVERSIDADE FEDERAL DO PIAUÍ
(Federal University of Piauí)

Campus Universitário Ministro Petrônio Portella, Bairro Ininga, Teresina, PI 64049-550
Telephone: (86) 3215-5525
E-mail: comunicacao@ufpi.edu.br
Internet: www.ufpi.br

Founded 1968
federal control
Language of instruction: Portuguese
Academic year: March to November

Centres of agricultural sciences, education, health sciences, humanities and letters, natural sciences, technology

Rector: Prof. Dr JOSÉ ARIMATÉIA DANTAS LOPES
Vice-Rector: Profa Dra NADIR DO NASCIMENTO NOGUEIRA
Pro-Rector for Admin.: JOVITA MARIA TERTO MADEIRA NUNES
Pro-Rector for Extension: Prof. Dr MIGUEL FERREIRA CAVALCANTE FILHO
Pro-Rector for Planning: Prof. Dr JOSÉ ARIMATÉIA DANTAS LOPES
Pro-Rector for Research and Postgraduate Affairs: Prof. Dr SAULO CUNHA DE SERPA BRANDÃO
Pro-Rector for Student and Community Affairs: Profa Dra NADIR DO NASCIMENTO NOGUEIRA
Pro-Rector for Undergraduate Teaching: Profa Dra MARIA DO SOCORRO LEAL LOPES
Dir for Libraries: GERALDO BATISTA DE MOURA FILHO

Library of 205,200 vols
Number of teachers: 1,104
Number of students: 11,612

Publications: *Arquivo Jurídico* (2 a year, online), *Cadernos de Pesquisa em Ciência Política* (2 a year), *Fundamentos* (2 a year, online), *Revista Científica de Produção Animal* (2 a year)

Rio de Janeiro

In Rio de Janeiro, there are 73 faculties, nine integrated HEIs, three centres for technological education and 23 higher schools or institutes.

UNIVERSITIES

PONTIFÍCIA UNIVERSIDADE CATÓLICA DO RIO DE JANEIRO
(Pontifical Catholic University of Rio de Janeiro)

Rua Marquês de São Vicente 225, Edif. Pe. Leonel Franca, 8 andar, Gávea, CP 38097, Rio de Janeiro, RJ 22451-900
Telephone: (21) 3527-1001
E-mail: incoming-ccci@puc-rio.br
Internet: www.puc-rio.br

Founded 1941
Private control
Academic year: March to December

Chancellor: ORANI JOÃO TEMPESTA
Rector: Prof. Fr JOSAFÁ CARLOS DE SIQUEIRA
Vice-Pres.: Fr FRANCISCO IVERN SIMÓ
Vice-Rector for Academic Affairs: Prof. JOSÉ RICARDO BERGMANN
Vice-Rector for Admin. Affairs: Prof. LUIZ CARLOS SCAVARDA DO CARMO
Vice-Rector for Community Affairs: Prof. AUGUSTO LUIZ DUARTE LOPES SAMPAIO
Vice-Rector for Devt Affairs: Prof. SERGIO BRUNI
Librarian: Dra DOLORES RODRIGUEZ PERES

Library of 600,000 vols
Number of teachers: 1,162
Number of students: 20,000

Publication: *Anuário*

DEANS

Medical Centre: Prof. Dr HILTON AUGUSTO KOCH
Social Sciences Centre: Profa LUIZ ROBERTO AZEVEDO CUNHA
Technical and Scientific Centre: Prof. JOSÉ ALBERTO DOS REIS PARISE
Theology and Human Sciences Centre: Profa MARIA CLARA BINGEMER

UNIVERSIDADE CASTELO BRANCO
(University Castelo Branco)

Av. Santa Cruz 1631, Realengo, Rio de Janeiro, RJ 21710-250
Telephone: (21) 3216-7700
E-mail: prouni@castelobranco.br
Internet: www.castelobranco.br

Founded 1994
Private control

Rector: VERA COSTA GISSONI

Library of 142,091 vols
Number of teachers: 167
Number of students: 5,914

UNIVERSIDADE CATÓLICA DE PETRÓPOLIS
(Catholic University of Petrópolis)

Av. Benjamin Constant 213, Centro, Petrópolis, RJ 25610-130
Telephone: (24) 2244-4000
E-mail: faleconosco@ucp.br
Internet: www.ucp.br

Founded 1953
Private control
Academic year: February to December

Rector: PEDRO PAULO DE CARVALHO ROSA
Vice-Rector: MARCELO VIZANI
Pro-Rector for Academic Affairs: REGINA MÁXIMO
Pro-Rector for Admin. Affairs: PADRE LUÍS
Librarian: MARIA DAS NEVES FRANCA LEITE KRÜGER

Library of 100,000 vols
Number of teachers: 220
Number of students: 4,300

Publications: *O Communitário* (12 a year), *Revista UCP* (3 a year)

UNIVERSIDADE DE NOVA IGUAÇU
(University of Nova Iguaçu)

Av. Augusto Távora 2134, Jardim Redenção, Nova Iguaçu, RJ 26275-580
Telephone: (21) 2765-4000
E-mail: unig@unig.br
Internet: www.unig.br

Founded 1993
Private control

Rector: Prof. ANDRÉ NASCIMENTO MONTEIRO
Pro-Rector for Admin.: JOSÉ CARLOS DE MELO
Pro-Rector for Postgraduate Studies, Research and External Relations: TARCILA FONSECA HUGUENIN
Pro-Rector for Undergraduate Studies: CARLOS HENRIQUE MELO REIS

Library of 85,748 vols, 1,355 periodicals
Number of teachers: 900
Number of students: 12,300

Publications: *In Solidum*, *InterFace*, *Revista de Ciência & Tecnologia*, *Revista de Ciências Biológicas e da Saúde*

UNIVERSIDADE DO ESTADO DO RIO DE JANEIRO
(State University of Rio de Janeiro)

Rua São Francisco Xavier 524, Maracanã, Rio de Janeiro, RJ 20550-900
Telephone: (21) 2334-0797
E-mail: dci@sr2.uerj.br
Internet: www.uerj.br

Founded 1950
State control
Language of instruction: Portuguese
Academic year: March to December (2 semesters)

Rector: RICARDO VIEIRALVES DE CASTRO
Vice-Rector: PAULO ROBERTO VOLPATO DIAS
Pro-Rector for Extension and Culture: REGINA LÚCIA MONTEIRO HENRIQUES
Pro-Rector for Postgraduate Affairs and Research: MONICA DA COSTA PEREIRA LAVALLE HEILBRON
Pro-Rector for Undergraduate Affairs: LENÁ MEDEIROS DE MENEZES
Librarian: SILVIA MARIA GAGO DA COSTA

Number of teachers: 2,350
Number of students: 31,000

Publications: *Cadernos de Antropologia da Imagem*, *Em Pauta*, *Espaço e Cultura*, *Geo UERJ*, *Logos*, *Matraga*, *Qfwfq*, *Revista de Enfermagem da UERJ*, *Revista do Centro de Estudos da Faculdade de Odontologia da UERJ* (2 a year), *UERJ em Questão*, *Informe UERJ*, *UERJ emdia*

DEANS

Biomedical Centre:
- Faculty of Dentistry: MARIA ISABEL DE CASTRO DE SOUZA
- Faculty of Medicine: Profa ALBANITA VIANA DE OLIVEIRA
- Faculty of Nursing: Profa Dra HELENA MARIA SCHERLOWSKI LEAL DAVID
- Institute of Biology: JOSÉ JORGE DE CARVALHO
- Institute of Nutrition: INÊS RUGANI RIBEIRO DE CASTRO
- Institute of Social Medicine: Prof. RICARDO TAVARES

Education and Humanities Centre:
- Faculty of Education: Profa ROSANA GLAT
- Institute of Letters: MARIA ALICE GONÇALVES ANTUNES
- Institute of Physical Education and Sport: JOÃO GONZAGA DE OLIVEIRA
- Institute of Psychology: ELEONÔRA TORRES PRESTRELO

Social Science Centre:
- Faculty of Administration and Finance: Prof. LUIZ DA COSTA LAURENCEL
- Faculty of Economics: Prof. RALPH MIGUEL ZERKOUVISKY
- Faculty of Law: Prof. ANTONIO CELSO ALVES PEREIRA
- Faculty of Social Service: CLEIER MARCONSIN
- Institute of Philosophy and Human Sciences: DIRCE ELEONORA NIGRO SOLIS

Technology and Science Centre:
- Faculty of Engineering: Profa MARIA EUGÊNIA GOUVÊA
- Faculty of Geology: LELIA MARIA DE ARAUJO KALIL THIAGO
- Faculty of Physics: LUCIA DE ASSIS ALVES
- Institute of Chemistry: Prof. MARCO ANTONIO DA COSTA
- Institute of Geosciences: Profa ANA LÚCIA TRAVASSOS ROMANO
- Institute of Mathematics and Statistics: Profa GERALDO MAGELA DA SILVA

UNIVERSIDADE DO GRANDE RIO
(University of Rio Grande)

Rua Prof. José de Souza Herdy 1160, Bairro 25 de Agosto Duque de Caxias, Duque de Caxias, RJ 25071-202
Telephone: (21) 2672-7777
Internet: www.unigranrio.br

Founded 1994
Private control
Academic year: January to December

Rector: ARODY CORDEIRO HERDY
Pro-Rector for Academic Admin.: Prof. CARLOS DE OLIVEIRA VARELLA
Pro-Rector for Community and Extension: Profa Dra SÔNIA REGINA MENDES DOS SANTOS
Pro-Rector for Devt: Prof. JOSÉ LUIZ ROSA LORDELLO
Pro-Rector for Postgraduate Affairs and Research: Prof. EMILIO ANTONIO FRANCISCHETTI

Library of 110,535 vols
Number of teachers: 550
Number of students: 10,457

Publications: *Revista ComUnigranrio*, *Revista de Administração e Ciências Contábeis da Unigranrio* (online), *Revista de Direito da Unigranrio* (2 a year), *Revista de Educação, Ciências e Matemática* (4 a year), *Revista Eletrônica do Instituto de Humanidades*, *Revista Magistro* (2 a year), *Revista Rede de Cuidados em Saúde*, *Saúde & Ambiente em Revista* (2 a year)

UNIVERSIDADE ESTÁCIO DE SÁ
(University of Estacio de Sá)

Rua do Bispo 83, Rio Comprido, Rio de Janeiro, RJ 20261-060
Telephone: (21) 2503-7000
Internet: www.estacio.br

Founded 1988
Private control

Rector: PAULA CALEFFI
Vice-Rector for Admin. and Finance: ABÍLIO GOMES DE CARVALHO, JR
Vice-Rector for Extension, Continuing Education and Culture: CIPRIANA NICOLITT CORDEIRO PARANHOS
Vice-Rector for Graduate Affairs: VINÍCIUS DA SILVA SCARPI
Vice-Rector for Institutional Relations: JOÃO LUIS TENREIRO BARROSO
Vice-Rector for Post Graduation and Research: LUCIANO VICENTE DE MEDEIROS

Library of 36,063 vols, 9,474 titles, 421 journal titles
Number of teachers: 634
Number of students: 100,000
Publications: *ADM.MADE*, *JurisPoiesis*

UNIVERSIDADE FEDERAL DO ESTADO DO RIO DE JANEIRO
(Federal University of the State of Rio de Janeiro)

Av. Pasteur 296, Urca, Rio de Janeiro, RJ 22290-240
Telephone: (21) 2542-7350
E-mail: reitoria@unirio.br
Internet: www.unirio.br

Founded 1979
federal control

Rector: LUIZ PEDRO SAN GIL JUTUCA
Vice-Rector: JOSÉ DA COSTA FILHO
Pro-Rector for Admin.: NÚRIA MENDES SANCHES
Pro-Rector for Extension and Culture: DIÓGENES PINHEIRO
Pro-Rector for Graduate Affairs: LOREINE HERMIDA DA SILVA E SILVA
Pro-Rector for Planning: JANAINA SPECHT DA SILVA MENEZES
Pro-Rector for Research: RICARDO SILVA CARDOSO
Dir of Central Library: EROTILDES DE LIMA MATTOS

Library of 200,000 vols in the areas of biomedical and exact sciences, humanities and arts
Number of teachers: 575
Number of students: 5,620

DEANS

- Center for Arts and Letters: Profa CAROLE GUBERNIKOFF
- Centre for Biological Sciences and Health: Prof. ANA MARIA MENDES MONTEIRO WANDELLI
- Centre for Engineering and Technology: Prof. LUIZ AMÂNCIO MACHADO DE SOUSA JR
- Center for Humanities and Social Sciences: Prof. IVAN COELHO DE SÁ
- Center for Law and Political Science: Profa ROSÂNGELA MARIA DE AZEVEDO GOMES

UNIVERSIDADE FEDERAL DO RIO DE JANEIRO
(Federal University of Rio de Janeiro)

Ave Pedro Calmon, 550–2º. Andar Prédio da Reitoria–Gabinete do Reitor Cidade Universitária, Rio de Janeiro, RJ 21941-901
Telephone: (21) 2598-1618
E-mail: reitoria@reitoria.ufrj.br
Internet: www.ufrj.br

Founded 1920 as Univ. do Rio de Janeiro, became Univ. do Brasil 1937, current name adopted 1967
State control

Rector: LEVI CARLOS ANTONIO DA CONCEICAO
Vice-Rector: Prof. ANTÔNIO JOSÉ LEDO ALVES DA CUNHA
Pro-Rector for Extension: PABLO CESAR BENETTI
Pro-Rector for Graduate Affairs: Profa ANGELA ROCHA DOS SANTOS
Pro-Rector for Management and Governance: ARACELI CRISTINA DE SOUSA FERREIRA
Pro-Rector for Planning, Devt and Finance: CARLOS RANGEL RODRIGUES
Pro-Rector for Research: DEBORA FOGUEL
Pro-Rector for Staff: ROBERTO ANTONIO GAMBINE MOREIRA

Library: 43 libraries
Number of teachers: 3,844
Number of students: 54,480
Publication: *Jornal da UFRJ*

DEANS

- Centre of Health Sciences: Profa. MARIA FERNANDA SANTOS QUINTELA DA COSTA NUNES
- Centre of Juridical and Economic Sciences: Profa. MARIA LÚCIA TEIXEIRA WERNECK VIANNA
- Centre of Letters and Arts: Profa. FLORA DE PAOLI FARIA
- Centre of Mathematics and Natural Sciences: Prof. JOÃO GRACIANO MENDONÇA FILHO
- Centre of Philosophy and Human Sciences: Profa. MARCELO MACEDO CORREA E CASTRO
- Centre of Technology: Prof. WALTER ISSAMU SUEMITSU

UNIVERSIDADE FEDERAL FLUMINENSE
(Fluminense Federal University)

Rua Miguel de Frias 9, Icaraí, Niterói, RJ 24220-900
Telephone: (21) 2629-5000
E-mail: gabinete@gar.uff.br
Internet: www.uff.br

Founded 1960 as Fed. Univ. of the State of Rio de Janeiro, current name adopted 1965
Academic year: March to December
Rector: ROBERTO DE SOUZA SALLES
Vice-Rector: SIDNEY LUIZ DE MATOS MELLO
Pro-Rector for Extension: Prof. WAINER DA SILVEIRA E SILVA
Pro-Rector for Research, Postgraduate Studies and Innovation: ANTONIO CLAUDIO LUCAS DA NÓBREGA
Pro-Rector for Student Affairs: Prof. SÉRGIO JOSÉ XAVIER DE MENDONÇA
Pro-Rector for Undergraduate Affairs: RENATO CRESPO PEREIRA
Chief Admin. Officer: ALDERICO MENDONÇA FILHO
Librarian: JOÃO CARLOS GOMES RIBEIRO
Library: 26 libraries with 420,000 vols
Number of teachers: 2,637
Number of students: 26,050 (23,982 undergraduate, 2,068 postgraduate)
Publications: *Antropolítica* (2 a year, online, www.uff.br/antropolitica), *Contracampo* (4 a year, online, www.uff.br/contracampo/index.php/revista), *Revista da Faculdade de Educação*, *Revista de Ciências Médicas*, *Revista Puerubim* (4 a year, online, www.uff.br/feuffrevistaquerubim)

UNIVERSIDADE FEDERAL RURAL DO RIO DE JANEIRO
(Federal Rural University of Rio de Janeiro)

BR 465 km 7, Seropédica, RJ 23890-000
Telephone: (21) 2681-4600
E-mail: gabinete@ufrrj.br
Internet: www.ufrrj.br
Founded 1910 as Escola Superior de Agronomia e Medicina Veterinária
federal control
Language of instruction: Portuguese
Academic year: March to December (2 semesters)
Rector: Profa ANA MARIA DANTAS SOARES
Vice-Rector: Prof. EDUARDO MENDES CALLADO
Pro-Rector for Admin. Affairs: Prof. PEDRO PAULO DE OLIVEIRA SILVA
Pro-Rector for Extension: Profa KATHERINA COUMENDOUROS
Pro-Rector for Financial Affairs: Profa NIDIA MAJEROWICZ
Pro-Rector for Graduate Affairs: Profa LÍGIA MACHADO
Pro-Rector for Research: Prof. ROBERTO CARLOS COSTA LELIS
Pro-Rector for Student Affairs: Prof. CESAR AUGUSTO DA ROS
Dir of Library: MIRIAN ELISABETE DA PENHA NEVES
Library of 44,233 vols
Number of teachers: 612
Number of students: 6,303
Publications: *Ciências da Vida* (2 a year), *Ciências Exatas e da Terra* (2 a year), *Ciências Humanas e Sociais* (2 a year)

DIRECTORS

Institute of Agronomy: Prof. ANTONIO CARLOS DE SOUZA ABBOUD
Institute of Biology: Prof. Dr ILDEMAR FERREIRA
Institute of Forestry: Prof. Dr JOÃO VICENTE DE F. LATORRACA
Institute of Mathematical Sciences: JOÃO BATISTA NEVES DA COSTA
Institute of Technology: Prof. HÉLIO FERNANDES MACHADO, JR
Institute of Veterinary Science: Prof. ZELSON GIACOMO LÓSS
Multidisciplinary Institute: ALEXANDRE FORTES

UNIVERSIDADE GAMA FILHO
(University Gama Filho)

Rua Manuel Vitorino 553, Piedade, Rio de Janeiro, RJ 20740-900
Telephone: (21) 2599-7100
E-mail: faleconosco@eadugf.com.br
Internet: www.ugf.br
Founded 1972
Private control
Language of instruction: Portuguese
Academic year: February to December
Chancellor: Prof. Dr PAULO GAMA FILHO
Vice-Chancellors: Prof. LUIZ ALFREDO GAMA FILHO, Prof. PAULO CESAR GAMA FILHO
Rector: Prof. SÉRGIO DE MORAES DIAS
Vice-Rector for Academic Affairs: Dr MANOEL JOSÉ GOMES TUBINO
Vice-Rector for Admin.: Prof. PREDUÊNCIO FERREIRA
Vice-Rector for Community: Prof. PERALVA DE MIRANDA DELGADO
Vice-Rector for Devt: Prof. AYRTON LUIZ GONÇALVES
Vice-Rector for Planning and Coordination: Prof. SÉRGIO DE MORAES DIAS
Sec.-Gen.: Dra MARIA CECÍLIA NUNES AMARANTE
Librarian: Profa LÚCIA BEATRIZ R. T. PARANHOS DE OLIVEIRA
Library of 400,000 vols, 130,000 periodicals
Number of teachers: 1,080
Number of students: 15,500
Publications: *Artus* (2 a year), *Ciência* (2 a year), *Ciência Humana* (2 a year), *Ciência Social* (2 a year)

DEANS

Biological and Health Sciences Centre: Prof. JOAQUIM JOSÉ DO AMARAL CASTELLÕES
Human Sciences Centre: Profa PAULINA CELI GAMA DE CARVALHO
Sciences and Technology Centre: Prof. SÉRGIO FLORES DA SILVA
Social Sciences Centre: Prof. HENRIQUE LUÍS ARIENTE

UNIVERSIDADE SALGADO DE OLIVEIRA
(Salgado de Oliveira University)

Rua Lambari 10, Trindade, São Gonçalo, RJ 24456-570
Telephone: (21) 2138-3432
E-mail: universo@universo.edu.br
Internet: www.universo.edu.br
Founded 1976, recognized in 1993
Private control
Rector: Profa MARLENE SALGADO DE OLIVEIRA
Library of 59,000 vols, 32,859 periodicals
Number of teachers: 426
Number of students: 20,995

UNIVERSIDADE SANTA ÚRSULA
(Santa Ursula University)

Rua Fernando Ferrari 75, Botafago, Rio de Janeiro, RJ 22231-040
Telephone: (21) 2552-4750
E-mail: usu@usu.br
Internet: www.usu.br
Founded 1938
Rector: MARIA DO CARMO BITTENCOURT
Library of 10,000 vols, periodicals, maps and charts
Number of teachers: 425
Number of students: 7,639

UNIVERSIDADE SEVERINO SOMBRA
(University Severino Sombra)

Av. Expedicionário Oswaldo Ramos de Almeida Ramos, nº 280, Centro, Vassouras, RJ 27700-000
Telephone: (24) 2471-8200
E-mail: reitoria@uss.br
Internet: www.uss.br
Founded 1969
Private control
Rector: Dr MARCO ANTONIO SOARES DE SOUZA
Pro-Rector for Health Sciences: Prof. Dr GUSTAVO MENDES GOMES
Pro-Rector for Humanities: Prof. ALYNE FRANÇA RIVELLO
Pro-Rector for Medical Sciences: Prof. Dr JOÃO CARLOS DE SOUZA CÔRTES, JR
Pro-Rector for Research and Graduate Affairs: Prof. Dr. JULIO CÉSAR DA SILVA
Pro-Rector for Science and Technology: Prof. JOSÉ THOMAZ DE CARVALHO
Pro-Rector for Univ. Extension: Profa. CONSUELO MENDES
Library of 46,000 vols, 708 periodicals
Number of teachers: 207
Number of students: 2,034
Publication: *Revista Eletrônica*

UNIVERSIDADE VEIGA DE ALMEIDA
(Veiga de Almeida University)

Rua Ibituruna 108, Bloco B, 3° andar, Tijuca, Rio de Janeiro, RJ 20271-020
Telephone: (21) 2574-8888
Internet: www.uva.br
Founded 1992
Private control
Dir and Pres.: LUIS VIDAL
Rector: ARLINDO VIANNA
Pro-Rector for Graduate Affairs: KÁTIA PASSOS
Pro-Rector for Graduate Studies and Research: BEATRIZ BALENA
Pro-Rector for Student Affairs: DIANA MAGALDI
Library of 66,000 vols, 1,007 periodicals
Number of teachers: 333
Number of students: 6,864
Publications: *Revista Aquila*, *Trivium*

UNIVERSITY CENTRES

CENTRO UNIVERSITÁRIO CELSO LISBOA

Rua 24 de Maio, 797 Engenho Novo, Rio de Janeiro, RJ 20950-092
Telephone: (21) 3289-4747
Internet: www.celsolisboa.edu.br
Founded 1971
Rector: ANA CAROLINA LISBOA
Library of 50,000 vols

CENTRO UNIVERSITÁRIO DE BARRA MANSA—UBM

Rua Vereador Pinho de Carvalho, n° 267 Centro, Barra Mansa, RJ 27330-550
Telephone: (24) 3325-0222
E-mail: pro.com@ubm.br
Internet: www.ubm.br
Founded 1961 as Sociedade Barramansense de Ensino Superior, univ. status and present name 1997
Private control
Rector: GUILHERME DE CARVALHO CRUZ
Pro-Rector for Admin.: FÉRES OSRRAIA NADER
Pro-Rector for Communications: LEANDRO ÁLVARO CHAVES
Library Coordinator: MARGARETH MÁRCIA FARIA MAGALHÃES
Library of 56,490 vols, 500 periodicals

Publications: *Caderno de Cultura Referencia* (4 a year), *Revista Cientifica* (2 a year), *Revista Eletrônica do Curso de Direito*, *Revista Eletrônica do Curso de Medicina Veterinária*

CENTRO UNIVERSITÁRIO DE VOLTA REDONDA

Av. Paulo Erlei Alves Abrantes, nº 1325, Três Poços, Volta Redonda, RJ 27240-560

Telephone: (24) 3340-8400
Internet: www.foa.org.br

Founded 1993

Rector: Profa Dra CLAUDIA YAMADA UTAGAWA
Pro-Rector for Academics: DIMITRI RAMOS ALVES
Pro-Rector for Postgraduate Affairs, Research and Extension: KÁTIA MIKA NISHIMURA
Librarian: GABRIELA LEITE FERREIRA

Publication: *Revista Praxis Online* (2 a year, www.foa.org.br/praxis)

CENTRO UNIVERSITÁRIO FLUMINENSE

Rua Tenente Coronel Cardoso, 349 - Centro Campos dos Goytacazes, Rio de Janeiro, RJ 28013-460

Telephone: (22) 2101-3350
Internet: www.uniflu.edu.br

Founded 2004

Rector: Profa REGINA COELI SARDINHA SILVA
Pro-Rector for Admin: Profa ANA LÚCIA SANGUEDO BOYNARD MENDONÇA
Pro-Rector for Teaching, Research and Extension: Profa DIRCÉA BRANCO DE MENEZES GOMES

CENTRO UNIVERSITÁRIO GERALDO DI BIASE

Rodovia Benjamin Ielpo, km 11 (Estrada Barra do Piraí - Valença), Barra do Piraí, RJ 27101-090

Telephone: (24) 2447-4700
Internet: www.ferp.br

Founded 1968

Rector: GERALDO DI BIASE FILHO

Library of 55,000 vols

Publication: *Revista Episteme Transversalis*

CENTRO UNIVERSITÁRIO METODISTA BENNETT
(Bennett Methodist University Centre)

Rua Marquês de Abrantes 55, Flamengo, Rio de Janeiro, RJ 22230-060

Telephone: (21) 3509-1000
E-mail: imb@bennett.br
Internet: www.bennett.br

Founded 1887

Academic year: February to December

Dir Gen.: Prof. WILSON ROBERTO ZUCCHERATO
Dir of College: Profa GILKA SILVIA DE REZENDE FIGUEIREDO

Library of 38,746 vols, 60,461 rare books, catalogues, monographs, brochures, references, theses, architectural and maps; 1,453 periodical titles, 1,238 multimedia records and 1,478 copies on DVD's, CD-ROM and video cassette
Number of teachers: 258
Number of students: 3,548

CENTRO UNIVERSITÁRIO MOACYR SREDER BASTOS

Rua Engenheiro Trindade, nº 229, Campo Grande, Rio de Janeiro, RJ 23050-290

Telephone: (21) 2413-5727
E-mail: coordenacao@msb.br
Internet: www.msb.br

Founded 1969

Rector: (vacant)
Vice-Rector: Prof. BRUNO BASTOS

Publication: *Revista Prociência*

Rio Grande do Norte

In Rio Grande do Norte, there are 15 faculties, one centre for technological education and four higher schools or institutes.

UNIVERSITIES

UNIVERSIDADE DO ESTADO DO RIO GRANDE DO NORTE
(State University of Rio Grande do Norte)

Rua Almino Afonso 478, Centro, Mossoró, RN 59610-210

Telephone: (84) 3315-2145
E-mail: reitoria@uern.br
Internet: www.uern.br

Founded 1968
State control
Language of instruction: Portuguese
Academic year: May to March (2 semesters)

Faculties of arts and letters, economics, education, exact and natural sciences, health sciences, law, nursing, philosophy and social sciences, physical education

Rector: Prof. Dr PEDRO FERNANDES RIBEIRO NETO
Vice-Rector: Prof. ALDO GONDIM FERNANDES
Pro-Rector for Admin.: Prof. LAURO GURGEL DE BRITO
Pro-Rector for Extension: Prof. FRANCISCO VANDERLEI DE LIMA
Pro-Rector for Human Resources and Student Affairs: LÚCIA MUSMEE FERNANDES PEDROSA
Pro-Rector for Planning: FÁBIO LÚCIO RODRIGUES
Pro-Rector for Research and Postgraduate Affairs: JOÃO MARIA SOARES
Pro-Rector for Undergraduate Affairs: Profa Dra MOÊMIA GOMES DE OLIVEIRA MIRANDA
Gen. Coordinator for Libraries: LAURO AUGUSTO RIBEIRO, JR

Number of teachers: 797
Number of students: 11,000

Publications: *Contexto* (2 a year), *Diálogo das Letras* (2 a year, online), *Revista Colineares* (2 a year), *Revista Colóquio—Administração & Ciência*, *Revista Expressão—Trabalhos em Educação e Linguagem* (2 a year), *Revista Extendere* (2 a year, online), *Revista Geotemas* (2 a year), *Revista Química: Ciência, Tecnologia e Sociedade* (2 a year), *Revista Sertões* (2 a year, online), *Revista Turismo: Estudos e Práticas* (2 a year), *Terra e Sal* (2 a year)

UNIVERSIDADE FEDERAL DO RIO GRANDE DO NORTE
(Federal University of Rio Grande do Norte)

CP 1524, Campus Universitário Lagoa Nova, Natal, RN 59078-970

Telephone: (84) 3215-3883
E-mail: gabinete@reitoria.ufrn.br
Internet: www.ufrn.br

Founded 1958
federal control
Language of instruction: Portuguese
Academic year: February to December (2 semesters)

Centres of applied social sciences, biosciences, health sciences, education, exact and natural sciences, humanities, arts and letters, technology; schools of agriculture, music, science and technology

Rector: ANGELA MARIA PAIVA CRUZ
Pro-Rector for Admin.: JOÃO BATISTA BEZERRA
Pro-Rector for Extension: EDMILSON LOPES, JR
Pro-Rector for Personnel Management: MIRIAN DANTAS DOS SANTOS
Pro-Rector for Planning and Gen. Coordination: JOÃO EMANUEL EVANGELISTA DE OLIVEIRA
Pro-Rector for Postgraduate Affairs: EDNA MARIA DA SILVA
Pro-Rector for Research: VALTER JOSÉ FERNANDES, JR
Pro-Rector for Undergraduate Affairs: ALEXANDRE MENEZES
Central Library Dir: ANA CRISTINA CAVALCANTI TINÔCO

Number of teachers: 1,679
Number of students: 27,605

Publications: *Bagoas—Estudos Gays: Gêneros e Sexualidades* (2 a year, print and online, periodicos.ufrn.br/bagoas), *Biblio-Canto* (2 a year, print and online, periodicos.ufrn.br/bibliocanto), *Cronos* (2 a year, print and online, periodicos.ufrn.br/cronos), *Imburana: Revista do Núcleo Câmara Cascudo de Estudos Norte-Rio-Grandenses* (2 a year, online, periodicos.ufrn.br/imburana), *Journal of Respiratory and Cardio-Vascular Physical Therapy* (2 a year, in English, print and online, periodicos.ufrn.br/revistadefisioterapia), *Journal of Surgical and Clinical Research* (2 a year, in English, print and online, periodicos.ufrn.br/jscr), *Mneme—Revista de Humanidades* (2 a year, online, periodicos.ufrn.br/mneme), *Revista Ambiente Contábil* (2 a year), *Revista Direito E-nergia* (irregular, print and online, periodicos.ufrn.br/direitoenergia), *Revista Educação em Questão* (4 a year, print and online, periodicos.ufrn.br/educacaoemquestao), *Revista Inter-Legere* (2 a year, print and online, periodicos.ufrn.br/interlegere), *Revista Odisseia* (2 a year, online, periodicos.ufrn.br/odisseia), *Revista Porto* (2 a year, print and online, periodicos.ufrn.br/porto), *Revista PublICa* (2 a year, print and online, periodicos.ufrn.br/publica), *Saberes: Revista Interdisciplinar de Filosofia e Educação* (1 a year, print and online, periodicos.ufrn.br/saberes), *Sociedade e Território* (2 a year. print and online, periodicos.ufrn.br/sociedadeeterritorio), *Vivência: Revista de Antropologia* (2 a year, online, periodicos.ufrn.br/vivencia)

UNIVERSIDADE FEDERAL RURAL DO SEMI-ÁRIDO
(Federal Rural University of Semi-Árido)

Av. Francisco Mota 572, Bairro Costa e Silva, Mossoró, RN 59625-900

Telephone: (84) 3317-8300
E-mail: reitor@ufersa.edu.br
Internet: www.ufersa.edu.br

Founded 2005
federal control
Language of instruction: Portuguese
Academic year: January to December

Courses in accounting, agronomy, animal science, biotechnology, business administration, computer science, ecology, engineering, forestry, mathematics, science and technology, veterinary medicine

Rector: Prof. JOSÉ DE ARIMATEA DE MATOS
Vice-Rector: Prof. FRANCISCO ODOLBERTO DE ARAÚJO

Pro-Rector for Admin.: ANAKLÉA MELO SILVEIRA DA CRUZ COSTA
Pro-Rector for Community Affairs: RODRIGO SÉRGIO
Pro-Rector for Extension and Culture: Prof. Dr LUIZ AUGUSTO VIEIRA CORDEIRO
Pro-Rector for Personnel Management: KELIANE DE OLIVEIRA CAVALCANTE
Pro-Rector for Planning: GEORGE BEZERRA RIBEIRO
Pro-Rector for Research and Postgraduate Affairs: Prof. RUI SALES, JR
Pro-Rector for Undergraduate Affairs: Prof. Dr AUGUSTO CARLOS PAVÃO
Dir for Libraries: KEINA CRISTINA SANTOS SOUSA E SILVA
Library of 32,640 vols
Publications: *Acta Veterinaria Brasilica* (4 a year), *Journal of Animal Behaviour and Biometeorology* (4 a year, in Portuguese and English), *Revista Caatinga* (4 a year), *Revista de Informação do Semiárido* (2 a year)

UNIVERSIDADE POTIGUAR
(Potiguar University)

Av. Floriano Peixoto, 295, Petrópolis, Natal, RN 59012-500
Telephone: (84) 3215-1234
E-mail: vicereitoria@unp.br
Internet: www.unp.br
Founded 1981, present name and status 1996
Private control
Language of instruction: Portuguese
Academic year: March to November
Schools of business and management, communications and arts, education, engineering and exact sciences, health, hospitality, law
Rector: Profa SÂMELA SORAYA GOMES DE OLIVEIRA
Pro-Rector for Academics: Profa SANDRA AMARAL DE ARAÚJO
Librarian: FERNANDA ANDRÉA S. DE SOUZA
Library of 249,547 vols, 33,207 periodicals, 7,315 multimedia items
Number of teachers: 249
Number of students: 5,813
Publications: *Catussaba: Revista Cientifica da Escola da Saúde* (2 a year, online), *Connexio: Revista Cientifica da Escola de Gestão e Negócio* (2 a year, online), *Quipus* (2 a year, online), *Revista Eletrônica do Mestrado em Administração* (2 a year, online), *Revista Juris Rationis* (2 a year, online), *RUnPetro* (2 a year, online)

Rio Grande do Sul

In Rio Grande do Sul, there are 69 faculties, one integrated HEI, three centres for technological education and 10 higher schools or institutes.

UNIVERSITIES

PONTIFÍCIA UNIVERSIDADE CATÓLICA DO RIO GRANDE DO SUL
(Pontifical Catholic University of Rio Grande do Sul)

Av. Ipiranga 6681, Partenon, Porto Alegre, RS 90619-900
Telephone: (51) 3320-3500
E-mail: aaii@pucrs.br
Internet: www.pucrs.br
Founded 1948
Private control
Language of instruction: Portuguese
Academic year: March to December
Faculties of aeronautical sciences, architecture and urbanism, biosciences, business administration, accounting and economics, chemistry, dentistry, education, engineering, informatics, law, letters, mathematics, medicine, nursing, nutrition and physiotherapy, pharmacy, philosophy and human sciences, physical education and sport science, physics, psychology, social communication, social service, theology
Chancellor: Dom DADEUS GRINGS
Rector: Prof. Dr JOAQUIM CLOTET
Vice-Rector: Prof. Dr EVILÁZIO TEIXEIRA
Pro-Rector for Academic Affairs: Profa Dra SOLANGE MEDINA KETZER
Pro-Rector for Admin. and Finance: Prof. Dr RICARDO MELO BASTOS
Pro-Rector for Extension and Community Affairs: Prof. Dr SÉRGIO LUIZ LESSA DE GUSMÃO
Pro-Rector for Research, Innovation and Devt: Prof. Dr JORGE LUIS NICOLAS AUDY
Dir for Uruguaiana Campus: Prof. CLEITON TAMBELLINI BORGES
Librarian: Prof. CÉSAR AUGUSTO MAZZILLO
Number of teachers: 1,896
Number of students: 33,000
Publications: *Análise—Revista de Administração* (2 a year, print and online), *Aviation in Focus—Journal of Aeronautical Sciences* (2 a year, in Portuguese and English, online), *BELT—Brazilian English Language Teaching Journal* (2 a year, in English, online), *Biociências* (2 a year), *Brasil* (2 a year), *Ciência & Saúde* (4 a year, online), *Civitas—Revista de Ciências Sociais* (3 a year), *Conversas & Controvérsias* (2 a year, online), *Direito e Justiça* (2 a year), *Educação* (3 a year), *Educação Por Escrito* (2 a year), *Estudos Ibero-Americanos* (2 a year), *Hifen* (2 a year), *Intuitio* (2 a year, online), *Letrônica* (2 a year), *Mundo Jovem* (12 a year), *Navegações* (2 a year), *Odontociência* (2 a year), *Oficina do Historiador* (online), *Psico* (4 a year, in Portuguese, English and Spanish), *Revista de Medicina da PUCRS* (4 a year), *Revista FAMECOS* (3 a year), *Revista Odonto Ciência* (4 a year, in Portuguese and English), *Scientia Medica* (4 a year, in Portuguese, English and Spanish), *Sessões do Imaginário* (2 a year), *Sistema Penal & Violência* (2 a year), *Teocomunicação* (2 a year), *Textos & Contextos* (2 a year, online), *Veritas* (3 a year)

UNIVERSIDADE CATÓLICA DE PELOTAS
(Catholic University of Pelotas)

Rua Félix da Cunha 412, Centro, Pelotas, RS 96010-000
Telephone: (53) 2128-8220
E-mail: ucpel@ucpel.tche.br
Internet: www.ucpel.tche.br
Founded 1960
Private control
Language of instruction: Portuguese
Academic year: February to December
Centres of education and communication, life and health sciences, law, economic and social sciences; institutes of philosophy, religious culture, theology; attached polytechnic
Chancellor: JAYME HENRIQUE CHEMELLO
Rector: Dr JOSÉ CARLOS PEREIRA BACHETTINI, JR
Pro-Rector for Academic Affairs: Profa PATRÍCIA HAERTEL GIUSTI
Pro-Rector for Admin.: Prof. EDUARDO LUIS INSAURRIAGA DOS SANTOS
Coordinator for Continuing Education: JOSÉ LUIS SILVEIRA DA COSTA
Coordinator for Extension: RENATO DA SILVA DELLA VECHIA
Coordinator for Research and Postgraduate Affairs: RICARDO TAVARES PINHEIRO
Coordinator for Teaching: IEDA LOURDES GOMES DE ASSUMPÇÃO
Coordinator for Undergraduate Affairs: JOSÉ ANTÔNIO WEYKAMP DA CRUZ
Head of Central Library: CRISTIANE DE FREITAS CHIM
Library of 140,570 vols, 57,045 periodicals, 7,401 monographs, 1,009 theses and dissertations, 104 technical standards, 615 cassettes, 543 CD-ROMs, 563 DVDs
Number of teachers: 443
Number of students: 6,189
Publications: *Ecos Revista* (2 a year), *Razão e Fé* (2 a year), *Revista Linguagem & Ensino* (2 a year), *Sociedade em Debate* (2 a year, online)

UNIVERSIDADE DA REGIÃO DE CAMPANHA
(University of the Region of Campanha)

Av. Tupy Silveira 2099, Bagé, RS 96400-110
Telephone: (53) 3242-8244
E-mail: ascom@urcamp.tche.br
Internet: www.urcamp.tche.br
Founded 1989
municipal control
Language of instruction: Portuguese
Academic year: January to December
Depts of accounting, advertising and marketing, agronomy, architecture and urbanism, biological sciences, business administration, civil engineering, environmental management, education, information systems, journalism, law, nursing, nutrition, pharmacy, physical education, physiotherapy, psychology, veterinary medicine; campuses in Alegrete, Caçapava do Sul, Dom Pedrito, Itaqui, Santana do Livramento, São Borja, São Gabriel
Rector: Profa LIA MARIA HERZER QUINTANA
Pro-Rector for Academic Affairs: Profa MARILENE SILVEIRA
Pro-Rector for Admin.: Prof. RICARDO RIBEIRO
Pro-Rector for Postgraduate Affairs, Research and Extension: Prof. PAULO RICARDO EBERT SIQUEIRA
Library of 230,000 vols
Number of teachers: 578
Number of students: 6,985
Publication: *Revista do Centro de Ciências da Economia e Informática* (2 a year)

UNIVERSIDADE DE CAXIAS DO SUL
(University of Caxias do Sul)

CP 1352, Rua Francisco Getúlio Vargas 1130, Caxias do Sul, RS 95070-560
Telephone: (54) 3218-2100
E-mail: reitoria@ucs.br
Internet: www.ucs.br
Founded 1967
Private control
Language of instruction: Portuguese
Academic year: January to October
Rector: Prof. ISIDORO ZORZI
Vice-Rector and Pro-Rector for Research, Innovation and Institutional Devt: Prof. JOSÉ CARLOS KÖCHE
Pro-Rector for Academic Affairs: EVALDO ANTONIO KUIAVA
Sub-Rector for Vinhedos Campus: MIGUEL ÂNGELO SANTIN
Dir for Admin. and Finance: GILBERTO HENRIQUE CHISSINI
Dir for Região das Hortênsias Campus: ANA LÍDIA WEBER BISOL
Dir for Vacaria Campus: MARINA BRITO BOSCHI
Dir for Vale do Caí Campus: CARMEN CECILIA SCHMITZ
Chief Librarian: MARCOS HÜBNER

Library of 578,650 vols, 8,911 nat. and 2,191 foreign periodicals, 25,744 multimedia items
Number of teachers: 1,098
Number of students: 27,599
Publications: *ANTARES (Letras e Humanidades)* (2 a year, online), *Caderno da Editora da Universidade de Caxias do Sul*, *Cadernos de Pequisa* (irregular), *Coletânea, Cultura e Saber* (2 a year), *Comunicado* (irregular), *Conexão: Comunicação e Cultura* (2 a year), *Conjectura: Filosofia e Educação* (3 a year), *Direito Ambiental e Sociedade* (2 a year), *Do Corpo: Ciências e Artes*, *Jornal Multicampi e Cadernos de Pesquisa*, *Métis: História & Cultura* (2 a year), *Revista Chronos*, *Revista de Ciências Médicas* (2 a year), *Revista do CCET* (2 a year), *Revista Faculdade de Direito* (2 a year), *Revista Jovens Pesquisadores* (1 a year), *Rosa dos Ventos* (2 a year), *Sensu* (2 a year)

UNIVERSIDADE DE CRUZ ALTA
(University of Cruz Alta)

Campus Universitário Dr Ulysses Guimarães, Rodovia Municipal Jacob Della Méa, km 5.6, Parada Benito, Cruz Alta, RS 98020-290
Telephone: (55) 3321-1500
E-mail: reitoria@unicruz.edu.br
Internet: www.unicruz.edu.br
Founded 1988
Private control
Language of instruction: Portuguese
Academic year: January to December
Rector: Elizabeth Fontoura Dorneles
Vice-Rector for Admin.: Fábio Dal-Soto
Vice-Rector for Postgraduate Affairs, Research and Extension: Cléia Rosani Baiotto
Vice-Rector for Undergraduate Affairs: Sirlei de Lourdes Lauxen
Library of 82,000 vols
Number of teachers: 165
Number of students: 2,600
Publications: *Ciência & Tecnologia* (2 a year, online), *Di@logus* (2 a year, online), *Revista Biomotriz* (2 a year), *Revista Gestão e Desenvolvimento em Contexto* (2 a year, online)

UNIVERSIDADE DE PASSO FUNDO
(University of Passo Fundo)

BR 285, Passo Fundo, RS 99052-900
Telephone: (54) 3316-8100
E-mail: informacoes@upf.br
Internet: www.upf.br
Founded 1968
Private control
Language of instruction: Portuguese
Academic year: March to November (2 semesters)
Faculties of agronomy and veterinary medicine, arts and communication, business administration and accounting, dentistry, economics, education, engineering and architecture, law, medicine, physical education and physiotherapy; institutes of biological sciences, geosciences and exact sciences, philosophy and human sciences
Rector: José Carlos Carles de Souza
Vice-Rector for Admin.: Agenor Dias de Meira, Jr
Vice-Rector for Extension and Community Affairs: Bernadete Maria Dalmolin
Vice-Rector for Research and Postgraduate Affairs: Leonardo José Gil Barcellos
Vice-Rector for Undergraduate Affairs: Neusa Maria Henriques Rocha
Librarian: Laíde Cristina Mühl
Library of 280,000 vols
Number of teachers: 1,100
Number of students: 22,000
Publications: *Desenredo* (2 a year), *Espaço Pedagógico* (2 a year), *Revista Brasileira de Ciências do Envelhecimento Humano* (3 a year), *Revista Brasileira de Computação Aplicada* (2 a year), *Revista da Faculdade de Odontologia* (3 a year), *Revista de Ciências Exatas Aplicadas e Tecnológicas* (2 a year), *Revista História: Debates e Tendências* (2 a year), *Revista Justiça do Direito* (2 a year), *Revista Sul-americana de Engenharia Estrutural* (3 a year), *Secretariado Executivo em Revist@* (1 a year)

UNIVERSIDADE DE SANTA CRUZ DO SUL
(Santa Cruz do Sul University)

Av. Independência 2293, Bairro Universitário, Santa Cruz do Sul, RS 96815-900
Telephone: (51) 3717-7300
E-mail: info@unisc.br
Internet: www.unisc.br
Founded 1993
Private control
Language of instruction: Portuguese
Academic year: January to December
Rector: Vilmar Thomé
Vice-Rector: Eltor Breunig
Pro-Rector for Admin.: Prof. Jaime Laufer
Pro-Rector for Extension and Community Relations: Profa Ana Luisa Teixeira de Menezes
Pro-Rector for Planning and Institutional Devt: Prof. João Pedro Schmidt
Pro-Rector for Research and Postgraduate Affairs: Profa Rosângela Gabriel
Pro-Rector for Undergraduate Affairs: Profa Carmen Lúcia de Lima Helfer
Library of 26,000 vols
Number of teachers: 650
Number of students: 12,587 (11,106 undergraduate, 1,481 postgraduate)
Publications: *Barbarói* (2 a year), *Caderno de Pesquisa* (2 a year), *Cinergis* (2 a year), *Estudos do CEPE* (2 a year), *Reflexão & Ação* (2 a year), *Revista de Epidemiologia e Controle de Infecção* (4 a year), *Revista do Desenvolvimento Regional (REDES)* (3 a year), *Revista do Direito* (3 a year), *Revista Jovens Pesquisadores* (1 a year), *Rizoma* (2 a year), *Signo* (2 a year), *Tecno-Lógica* (2 a year)

UNIVERSIDADE DO VALE DO RIO DOS SINOS
(University of Vale do Rio dos Sinos)

Av. Unisinos 950, São Leopoldo, RS 93022-000
Telephone: (51) 3591-1122
E-mail: atendimento@unisinos.br
Internet: www.unisinos.br
Founded 1969
Private control
Language of instruction: Portuguese
Academic year: February to December
Rector: Prof. Dr Marcelo Fernandes de Aquino
Vice-Rector: Prof. Dr Jose Ivo Follmann
Pro-Rector for Academic Affairs: Pedro Gilberto Gomes
Pro-Rector for Admin.: Prof. João Zani
Library Dir: Dr Lodomilo Augusto Mallmann
Library of 700,000 vols
Number of teachers: 1,108
Number of students: 30,320
Publications: *Arquitetura Revista* (2 a year), *BASE: Revista de Administração e Contabilidade da Unisinos* (3 a year, in Portuguese, English and Spanish), *Calidoscópio* (3 a year), *Ciências Sociais Unisinos* (3 a year), *Contextos Clínicos* (2 a year), *Controvérsia* (2 a year), *Educação Unisinos* (3 a year), *Filosofia Unisinos* (3 a year), *Fronteiras* (3 a year), *Gaea—Journal of Geoscience* (2 a year), *História Unisinos* (3 a year), *Jornal Unisinos* (4 a year), *Journal of Applied Computing Research* (2 a year, in English), *Neotropical Biology and Conservation* (3 a year, in English), *Otra Economía* (2 a year), *Perspectiva Econômica* (2 a year, online), *Questões Transversais—Revista de Epistemologias da Comunicação* (2 a year), *Revista de Estudos Constitucionais, Hermenêutica e Teoria do Direito* (2 a year), *Strategic Design Research Journal* (3 a year), *Verso & Reverso* (3 a year)

DEANS
Polytechnic School: Carlos Moraes
School of Business Management: Yeda Swirski de Souza
School of Creative Industries: Ana Maria Guimarães
School of Health Sciences: Vera Regina Röhnelt Ramires
School of Humanities: Adriano Naves de Brito
School of Law: Vicente de Paulo Barretto

UNIVERSIDADE ESTADUAL DO RIO GRANDE DO SUL
(State University of Rio Grande do Sul)

Rua 7 de Setembro 1156, Centro, Porto Alegre, RS 90010-191
Telephone: (51) 3288-9000
E-mail: reitor@uergs.edu.br
Internet: www.uergs.edu.br
Founded 2004
Private control
Language of instruction: Portuguese
Academic year: January to December
Rector: Prof. Dr Fernando Guaragna Martins
Vice-Rector: Profa Dra Sita Mara Lopes Sant'anna
Pro-Rector for Extension: Profa Dra Sílvia Santin Bordin
Pro-Rector for Research and Postgraduate Affairs: Marc François Richter
Pro-Rector for Teaching: Leonardo Alvim Beroldt da Silva

UNIVERSIDADE FEDERAL DE CIÊNCIAS DA SAÚDE DE PORTO ALEGRE
(Federal University of Health Sciences of Porto Alegre)

Rua Sarmento Leite 245, Porto Alegre, RS 90050-170
Telephone: (51) 3303-9000
E-mail: reitoria@ufcspa.edu.br
Internet: www.ufcspa.edu.br
Founded 1953 as Fundação Faculdade Federal de Ciências Médicas de Porto Alegre; present name and status 2008
federal control
Language of instruction: Portuguese
Academic year: January to December
Rector: Miriam da Costa Oliveira
Vice-Rector: Luis Henrique Telles da Rosa
Pro-Rector for Admin.: Roseane Alfama Inhaquites
Pro-Rector for Extension and Community Affairs: Deisi Cristina Gollo Marques Vidor
Pro-Rector for Planning: Liane Nanci Rotta
Pro-Rector for Research and Postgraduate Affairs: Rodrigo Della Méa Plentz

Pro-Rector for Undergraduate Affairs: MARIA TEREZINHA ANTUNES
Librarian and Archivist: RUTH BORGES FORTES DE OLIVEIRA
Number of students: 1,500

UNIVERSIDADE FEDERAL DE PELOTAS
(Federal University of Pelotas)

Rua Gomes Carneiro 1, Centro, Pelotas, RS 96010-610
Telephone: (53) 3921-1401
E-mail: reitor@ufpel.edu.br
Internet: www.ufpel.edu.br
Founded 1883 as Imperial Escola de Medicina Veterinária e de Agricultura Prática; current name adopted 1969
State control
Academic year: March to December
Rector: MAURO AUGUSTO BURKERT DEL PINO
Vice-Rector: CARLOS ROGÉRIO MAUCH
Pro-Rector for Admin.: ANTÔNIO CARLOS DE FREITAS CLEFF
Pro-Rector for Extension Services and Culture: ANTÔNIO CARLOS MARTINS DA CRUZ
Pro-Rector for Human Resources: SÉRGIO BATISTA CHRISTINO
Pro-Rector for Planning and Devt: LUIZ OSÓRIO ROCHA DOS SANTOS
Pro-Rector for Research and Postgraduate Affairs: DENISE PETRUCCI GIGANTE
Pro-Rector for Student Affairs: ROSANE MARIA DOS SANTOS BRANDÃO
Pro-Rector for Undergraduate Affairs: FABIANE TEJADA DA SILVEIRA
Number of teachers: 948
Number of students: 9,989
Publications: *Cadernos de Educação* (1 a year), *Dissertatio* (1 a year), *Expresso Extensão* (1 a year), *História da Educação* (1 a year), *Jornal da UFPel* (12 a year), *Revista Acadêmica de Medicina* (1 a year), *Revista Brasileira de Agrociência* (2 a year)

UNIVERSIDADE FEDERAL DE SANTA MARIA
(Federal University of Santa Maria)

Campus Universitário–Camobi, Santa Maria, RS 97105-900
Telephone: (55) 3220-8000
E-mail: gabinetereitor@ufsm.br
Internet: www.ufsm.br
Founded 1960
federal control
Academic year: March to December (2 semesters)
Centres of arts and letters, education, health sciences, natural and exact sciences, physical education and sports, rural sciences, social and human sciences, technology; attached agricultural college, polytechnic, technical college
Rector: Prof. FELIPE MARTINS MÜLLER
Vice-Rector: Prof. DALVAN JOSÉ REINERT
Pro-Rector for Admin.: ANDRÉ LUIS KIELING RIES
Pro-Rector for Extension: Prof. JOÃO RODOLPHO AMARAL FLÔRES
Pro-Rector for Infrastructure: Prof. VALMIR BRONDANI RAMAL
Pro-Rector for Personnel Management: VANIAD E FÁTIMA BARROS ESTIVALETE
Pro-Rector for Planning: CHARLES JACQUES PRADE
Pro-Rector for Postgraduate Affairs and Research: Prof. HELIO LEÃES HEY
Pro-Rector for Student Affairs: Prof. UBIRATAN TUPINAMBÁ DA COSTA
Pro-Rector for Undergraduate Affairs: Prof. Dr ORLANDO FONSECA
Librarian: MARIA INEZ FIGUEIREDO FIGAS MACHADO
Library of 339,620 vols, incl. 101,013 books, 205,081 periodicals, 20,790 theses and dissertations, 7,249 pamphlets, 5,488 other material
Number of teachers: 4,642
Number of students: 25,665 (20,292 undergraduate, 5,373 postgraduate)
Publications: *Animus: Revista Interamericana de Comunicação Mediática* (2 a year, online), *Cadernos de Comunicação* (2 a year), *Ciência e Natura* (2 a year), *Ciência Florestal* (4 a year), *Ciência Rural, Economia e Desenvolvimento* (2 a year), *Educação* (3 a year), *Extensão Rural* (2 a year), *Fragmentum* (4 a year), *Geografia Ensino & Pesquisa* (3 a year), *Kinesis* (2 a year), *Literatura e Autoritarismo* (2 a year), *Revista Brasilerira de Agroameteorologia*, *Revista de Administração da UFSM* (3 a year, in Portuguese with English abstracts), *Revista de Enfermagem da UFSM* (3 a year, online), *Revista de Gestão e Avaliação Educacional* (2 a year, online), *Revista Direitos Emergentes na Sociedade Global* (2 a year), *Revista Educação Especial* (3 a year), *Revista Saúde (Santa Maria)* (2 a year), *Revista Sociais e Humanas* (3 a year), *Século XXI—Revista de Ciências Sociais* (2 a year)

UNIVERSIDADE FEDERAL DO PAMPA
(Federal University of Pampa)

Av. General Osório, 900, Bagé, RS 96400-100
Telephone: (53) 3240-5400
E-mail: reitora@unipampa.edu.br
Internet: www.unipampa.edu.br
Founded 2008
federal control
Language of instruction: Portuguese
Academic year: January to December
10 Attached campuses
Rector: ULRIKA ARNS
Vice-Rector: ALMIR BARROS DA SILVA SANTOS NETO
Pro-Rector for Admin.: EVERTON BONOW
Pro-Rector for Extension: Profa VERA LÚCIA CARDOSO MEDEIROS
Pro-Rector for Personnel Management: CLAUDIA DENISE DA SILVEIRA TÔNDOLO
Pro-Rector for Planning, Devt and Evaluation: VANESSA RABELO DUTRA
Pro-Rector for Postgraduate Affairs: Prof. Dr RICARDO JOSÉ GUNSKI
Pro-Rector for Research: EDUARDO CERETTA MOREIRA
Pro-Rector for Student and Community Affairs: Profa Dra SIMONE BARROS DE OLIVEIRA
Pro-Rector for Undergraduate Affairs: ELENA MARIA BILLIG MELLO
Coordinator for Library Systems: VANESSA ABREU DIAS

UNIVERSIDADE FEDERAL DO RIO GRANDE
(Federal University of Rio Grande)

Rua Alfredo Huch 475, Centro, Rio Grande, RS 96201-900
Telephone: (53) 3233-8600
E-mail: reitor03@super.furg.br
Internet: www.furg.br
Founded 1969
federal control
Language of instruction: Portuguese
Academic year: March to November
Rector: Prof. Dr JOÃO CARLOS BRAHM COUSIN
Vice-Rector: Prof. ERNESTO LUIZ CASARES PINTO
Pro-Rector for Extension and Culture: RITA PATTA RACHE
Pro-Rector for Infrastructure: GUILHERME LERCH LUNARDI
Pro-Rector for Personnel Management and Devt: CLAUDIO PAZ DE LIMA
Pro-Rector for Planning and Admin.: MOZART TAVARES MARTINS FILHO
Pro-Rector for Research and Postgraduate Affairs: DANILO GIROLDO
Pro-Rector for Student Affairs: DARLENE TORRADA PEREIRA
Pro-Rector for Undergraduate Affairs: CLEUZA MARIA SOBRAL DIAS
Dir for Libraries: ROSELI PRESTES
Library of 127,890 vols, 14,230 periodicals, 4,470 theses, 3,894 pamphlets, 287 maps, 1,883 CD-ROMs
Number of teachers: 700
Number of students: 4,700
Publications: *Ambiente & Educação—Revista de Educação Ambiental* (2 a year, print and online, www.seer.furg.br/ambeduc), *Atlântica* (2 a year, print and online, www.seer.furg.br/atlantica), *BIBLOS* (2 a year, print and online, www.seer.furg.br/biblos), *Historiæ* (3 a year, print and online, www.seer.furg.br/hist), *JURIS* (1 a year, print and online, www.seer.furg.br/juris), *MOMENTO—Diálogos em Educação* (2 a year, print and online, www.seer.furg.br/momento), *Revista Brasileira de Educação Ambiental* (1 a year, print and online, www.seer.furg.br/revbea), *Revista Didática Sistêmica* (2 a year, print and online, www.seer.furg.br/redsis), *Revista Eletrônica do Mestrado de Educação Ambiental* (2 a year, online, www.seer.furg.br/remea), *SINERGIA* (2 a year, in Portuguese with English abstracts, print and online, www.seer.furg.br/sinergia), *VETOR—Revista de Ciências Exatas e Engenharias* (2 a year, print and online, www.seer.furg.br/vetor), *VITTALLE—Revista de Ciências da Saúde* (2 a year, in Portuguese with English abstracts, print and online, www.seer.furg.br/vittalle)

UNIVERSIDADE FEDERAL DO RIO GRANDE DO SUL
(Federal University of Rio Grande do Sul)

Av. Paulo Gama 110, Bairro Farroupilha, Porto Alegre, RS 90040-060
Telephone: (51) 3308-6000
E-mail: reitor@gabinete.ufrgs.br
Internet: www.ufrgs.br
Founded 1934
federal control
Language of instruction: Portuguese
Academic year: March to November
Rector: Prof. CARLOS ALEXANDRE NETTO
Vice-Rector and Pro-Rector for Academic Coordination: Prof. RUI VICENTE OPPERMANN
Pro-Rector for Extension: SANDRA DE DEUS
Pro-Rector for Human Resources: Prof. MAURÍCIO VIEGAS DA SILVA
Pro-Rector for Planning and Admin.: ÁRIO ZIMMERMANN
Pro-Rector for Postgraduate Affairs: Profa VLADIMIR PINHEIRO DO NASCIMENTO
Pro-Rector for Research: JOSÉ CARLOS FRANTZ
Pro-Rector for Student Affairs: Prof. ANGELO RONALDO PEREIRA DA SILVA (acting)
Pro-Rector for Undergraduate Affairs: SÉRGIO ROBERTO KIELING FRANCO
Dir for Libraries: VIVIANE CARRION CASTANHO
Library of 825,000 vols
Number of teachers: 2,730
Number of students: 43,620 (26,468 undergraduate, 8,927 graduate, 8,225 specialization)
Publications: *Acta Scientiae Veterinariae*, *Análise Econômica* (2 a year), *Anos 90* (2 a year), *Art e Educação em Revista* (2 a

year), *Caderno de Farmácia* (2 a year), *Cadernos de Sociologia* (2 a year), *Educação e Realidade* (2 a year), *Educação, Subjetividade e Poder* (2 a year), *Egatea* (2 a year), *Em Pauta* (2 a year), *Epistéme* (2 a year), *Forjamento* (2 a year), *Horizontes Antropológicos* (2 a year), *Humanas* (2 a year), *Intexto* (2 a year), *Jornal do SAJU* (2 a year), *Napaea* (2 a year), *Notas Técnicas* (2 a year), *Organon* (2 a year), *Pesquisas* (2 a year), *Porto Artes* (2 a year), *Psicologia: Reflexão e Crítica* (2 a year), *Revista da Faculdade de Direito* (2 a year), *Revista da Faculdade de Odontologia* (2 a year), *Revista de Biblioteconomia e Comunicação* (2 a year), *Revista de Informática Teórica e Aplicada* (2 a year), *Revista Gaúcha de Enfermagem* (a year), *Revista HCPA* (2 a year), *Revista Movimento* (2 a year), *Revista Perfil* (2 a year)

UNIVERSIDADE LUTERANA DO BRASIL
(Lutheran University of Brazil)

Av. Farroupilha 8001, Bairro São José, Canoas, RS 92425-900

Telephone: (51) 3477-4000
E-mail: ulbra@ulbra.br
Internet: www.ulbra.br

Founded 1988
Private control
Language of instruction: Portuguese
Academic year: January to December

Rector: MARCOS FERNANDO ZIEMER
Pro-Rector for Academic Affairs: RICARDO WILLY RIETH
Pro-Rector for Planning and Admin.: ROMEU FORNECK
Deputy Pro-Rector for Classroom Teaching: PEDRO ANTONIO GONZÁLEZ HERNÁNDEZ
Deputy Pro-Rector for Distance Education: PEDRO LUIZ PINTO DA CUNHA
Deputy Pro-Rector for Extension and Community Affairs: VALTER KUCHENBECKER
Deputy Pro-Rector for Postgraduate Affairs, Research and Innovation: ERWIN FRANCISCO TOCHTROP, JR

Library of 346,000 vols, 1,285 periodicals
Number of teachers: 1,762
Number of students: 17,557

Publications: *Revista Acta Scientiae*, *Stomatos*

UNIVERSIDADE REGIONAL DO NOROESTE DO ESTADO DO RIO GRANDE DO SUL
(Regional University of the Northwest of the State of Rio Grande do Sul)

Rua do Comércio, 3000, Bairro Universitário, Ijuí, RS 98700-000

Telephone: (55) 3332-0200
E-mail: reitoria@unijui.edu.br
Internet: www.unijui.edu.br

Founded 1985
Private control
Language of instruction: Portuguese
Academic year: March to December

Rector: MARTINHO LUIS KELM
Vice-Rector for Admin.: LAERDE SADY GEHRKE
Vice-Rector for Postgraduate Affairs, Research and Extension: EVELISE MORAES BERLEZI
Vice-Rector for Undergraduate Affairs: CÁTIA MARIA NEHRING
Librarian: ELEDA PASSINATO SAUSEN

Library of 359,578 vols, incl. 224,983 books, 98,075 periodicals, 16,308 pamphlets, 8,873 monographs, 2,806 theses and dissertations, 1,366 reports, 2,320 CD-ROMs, 261 maps, 535 catalogues, 657 technical standards, 1,180 multimedia items
Number of teachers: 569
Number of students: 9,500

Publications: *Coleção Situação de Estudos* (2 a year), *Contexto & Educação* (4 a year), *Contexto e Saúde* (2 a year), *Desenvolvimento em Questão* (2 a year), *Direito em Debate* (2 a year), *Educação nas Ciências* (2 a year), *Espaços da Escola* (4 a year), *Formas & Linguagens* (2 a year), *Leitura e Revista* (2 a year), *Revista AD Homimen Tomo I* (2 a year), *Revista de Estudos de Administracão* (2 a year)

UNIVERSIDADE REGIONAL INTEGRADA DO ALTO URUGUAI E DAS MISSÕES
(Integrated Regional University)

Av. Sete de Setembro 1621, CP 743, Erechim, RS 99700-000

Telephone: (54) 2107-1255
E-mail: urireitoria@st.com.br
Internet: www.uricer.edu.br

Founded 1992
Private control
Language of instruction: Portuguese
Academic year: January to December

Depts of agricultural sciences, applied social sciences, biological sciences, engineering and computing, exact and natural sciences, health sciences, humanities, linguistics, letters and arts

Rector: Prof. LUIZ MARIO SILVEIRA SPINELLI
Pro-Rector for Admin.: CLÓVIS QUADROS HEMPEL
Pro-Rector for Research, Extension and Postgraduate Affairs: GIOVANI PALMA BASTOS
Pro-Rector for Teaching: ROSANE VONTOBEL RODRIGUES

Library of 204,000 vols, 5,130 periodicals
Number of teachers: 425
Number of students: 8,337

Rondônia

In Rondônia, there are 24 faculties, three integrated HEIs and two centres for technological education.

UNIVERSITY

FUNDAÇÃO UNIVERSIDADE FEDERAL DE RONDÔNIA
(Foundation Federal University of Rondônia)

Campus Universitário, BR 364 km 9.5, Porto Velho, RO 76801-059

Telephone: (69) 2182-2100
E-mail: reitoria@unir.br
Internet: www.unir.br

Founded 1982
federal control
Academic year: March to December

Faculties of education, exact sciences, health sciences, and social sciences

Rector: Profa Dra MARIA BERENICE ALHO DA COSTA TOURINHO
Vice-Rector: Profa Dra MARIA CRISTINA VICTORINO DE FRANÇA
Pro-Rector for Admin.: IVANDA SOARES DA SILVA
Pro-Rector for Culture, Extension and Student Affairs: Prof. RUBENS VAZ CAVALCANTE
Pro-Rector for Postgraduate Affairs and Research: ARI MIGUEL TEIXEIRA OTT
Pro-Rector for Planning: OSMAR SILVA
Pro-Rector for Undergraduate Affairs: JORGE LUIZ COIMBRA DE OLIVEIRA
Librarian: LUZIMAR BARBOSA CHAVES

Number of teachers: 300
Number of students: 4,800

Publications: *Anais da Semana Educa* (1 a year), *Gaia* (1 a year), *Presença: Cadernos de Criação* (4 a year), *Primeira Versão*, *Revista de Administração e Negócios da Amazônia* (4 a year), *Revista de Desenvolvimento e Ambiente Amazônico* (2 a year, online), *Revista Eletrônica Língua Viva* (2 a year, online), *Revista Igarapé* (2 a year), *Revista Pesquisa & Criação* (2 a year)

Roraima

In Roraima, there are five faculties.

UNIVERSITIES

UNIVERSIDADE ESTADUAL DE RORAIMA
(State University of Roraima)

Rua Sete de Setembro 231, Canarinho, Boa Vista, RR

Telephone: (95) 2121-0933
E-mail: ascomuerr@gmail.com
Internet: www.uerr.edu.br

Founded 2005
State control
Language of instruction: Portuguese
Academic year: January to December

Rector: JOSÉ HAMILTON GONDIM SILVA
Vice-Rector: ILMA DE ARAÚJO XAUD

Number of teachers: 246
Number of students: 5,324 (5,158 undergraduate, 166 postgraduate)

Publication: *Ambiente: Gestão e Desenvolvimento* (2 a year)

UNIVERSIDADE FEDERAL DE RORAIMA
(Federal University of Roraima)

Av. Cap. Ene Garcez, n° 2413, Bairro Aeroporto, Boa Vista, RR 69304-000

Telephone: (95) 3621-3100
E-mail: reitoria@ufrr.br
Internet: www.ufrr.br

Founded 1989
federal control
Language of instruction: Portuguese
Academic year: January to December

Centres for administrative science and economics, agricultural sciences, communication, letters and visual arts, education, human sciences, health sciences, science and technology, studies in biodiversity

Rector: Profa Dra GIOCONDA SANTOS E SOUZA MARTINEZ
Vice-Rector: Prof. REGINALDO GOMES DE OLIVEIRA
Pro-Rector for Admin.: RAILMA SALES DE SOUSA
Pro-Rector for Infrastructure: JOEL CARLOS MOIZINHO
Pro-Rector for Personnel Management: Profa Dra MARIA EDITH ROMANO SIEMS-MARCONDES
Pro-Rector for Planning: MANOEL ALVES BEZERRA, JR
Pro-Rector for Research and Postgraduate Affairs: ROSÂNGELA DUARTE
Pro-Rector for Student Affairs and Extension: MARIA DAS GRAÇAS SANTOS DIAS
Pro-Rector for Teaching and Undergraduate Affairs: FÁBIO LUIZ WANKLER

Library of 102,260 vols, 2,023 periodicals
Number of teachers: 456
Number of students: 4,200

Publications: *Acta Geográfica* (4 a year), *Examãpaku: Revista Eletrônica de Ciências Sociais, História e Relações Internacionais* (2 a year), *Revista Agro@mbiente* (3 a year, online), *Revista de Administração de Roraima* (2 a year)

Santa Catarina

In Santa Catarina, there are 71 faculties, three integrated HEIs, one centre for technological education and 13 higher schools or institutes.

UNIVERSITIES

UNIVERSIDADE COMUNITÁRIA REGIONAL DE CHAPECÓ
(Community University of the Region of Chapecó)

Av. Senador Attílio Fontana 591E, CP 1141, Efapi, Chapecó, SC 89809-000

Telephone: (49) 3321-8000
E-mail: reitoria@unochapeco.edu.br
Internet: www.unochapeco.edu.br
Private control
Language of instruction: Portuguese
Academic year: January to December

Rector: Prof. ODILON LUIZ POLI
Vice-Rector for Admin.: Prof. ANTONIO ZANIN
Vice-Rector for Planning and Devt: Prof. CLAUDIO ALCIDES JACOSKI
Vice-Rector for Teaching, Research and Extension: Profa MARIA APARECIDA LUCCA CAOVILLA

Publications: *Revista Cadernos do CEOM*, *Revista FisiSenectus*, *Revista Grifos*

UNIVERSIDADE DA REGIÃO DE JOINVILLE
(University of the Region of Joinville)

Rua Paulo Malschitzki 10, Zona Industrial Norte, Joinville, SC 89201-972

Telephone: (47) 3461-9000
E-mail: univille@univille.br
Internet: www.univille.edu.br

Founded 1992
Private control
Language of instruction: Portuguese
Academic year: February to December

Rector: Profa Dra SANDRA APARECIDA FURLAN
Vice-Rector: Prof. Dr ALEXANDRE CIDRAL
Pro-Rector for Admin. Affairs: Prof. Dr RAUL LANDMANN
Pro-Rector for Educational Affairs: Profa SIRLEI DE SOUZA
Pro-Rector for Extension and Community Affairs: Prof. Dr CLEITON VAZ
Pro-Rector for Research and Postgraduate Affairs: Profa Dra DENISE ABATTI KASPER SILVA
Univ. Library Coordinator: MARLENE FEUSER WESTRUPP

Library of 154,831 vols, 2,962 periodicals
Number of teachers: 626
Number of students: 8,604

Publications: *Acta Biológica Catarinense* (1 a year), *Revista Confluências Culturais* (2 a year), *Revista Saúde e Meio Ambiente* (2 a year), *Revista Sul-Brasileira de Odontologia*, *Universo UNIVILLE* (3 a year)

PROFESSORS

ADAMOVSKI, M.
AGUIAR, A.
AGUIAR, D.
AGUIAR, J.
AGUSTINI, M.
ALCANTARA, V.
ALMEIDA, S.
ALVES, C.
ALVES, M.
ALVES, M.
ALVES, R.
ALVES, W.
AMARAL, C.
AMARAL, C.
AMARAL, J.
AMARO, J.
AMORIM, C.
AMORIM, V.
ANDRADES, K.
ANDRIOLI, D.
ANELLO, J.
ANTONELLO, C.
APATI, G.
AQUINO, L.
ARAUJO, J.
ARCHER, M.
AREAS, P.
ARRUDA, C.
AUGUSTIN, E.
AVELAR, M.
AVILA, L.
AZEVEDO, J.
BAGGENSTOSS, R.
BAHIENSE, A.
BAHIENSE, F.
BALDIN, N.
BANDEIRA, D.
BARG, J.
BARP, J.
BARROS, S.
BARROS, V.
BASSOLI, K.
BASTOS, I.
BATALHA, W.
BATISTA, J.
BATTI, H.
BAUMER, J.
BAZZO, G.
BECKER, R.
BEDIN, A.
BELTRAO, J.
BEPPLER, A.
BERNARDES, J.
BERTOLOTTO, F.
BIAZI, G.
BITTENCOURT, E.
BOARETTO, K.
BOEHM, L.
BOHN, L.
BORBA, M.
BOUSFIELD, P.
BRAMMER, R.
BRANCO, B.
BRASILINO, F.
BRAVO, R.
BREHM, T.
BRENNEISEN, I.
BROTERO, M.
BUBLITZ, G.
BUFFON, I.
BURG, M.
CABRAL, N.
CAMPOS, E.
CAMPOS, R.
CAPUTO, R.
CARDOSO, C.
CARDOSO, H.
CARDOZO, V.
CARELLI, E.
CARELLI, M.
CARVALHO, H.
CARVALHO, M.
CASTELLANI, S.
CASTRO, A.
CAVALCANTI, A.
CAVASSIN, R.
CECATO, M.
CICOGNA, P.
CIDRAL, A.
CIPRIANI, T.
CLEMENTE, A.
COAN, W.
COELHO, A.
COELHO, C.
COELHO, I.
COELHO, L.
COLELLA, V.
COLLERE, V.
COLUSSO, S.
COLVERO, J.
CONCEICAO, F.
CONDE, I.
CORAZZA, E.
CORDEIRO, A.
CORDEIRO, I.
CORDEIRO, M.
CORDEIRO, M.
CORREA, C.
CORREA, F.
COSTA, C.
COSTA, E.
COSTA, F.
COSTA, I.
COSTA, L.
CREMER, M.
CREMONINI, R.
CRESTANI, J.
CRISTOFOLINI, R.
CROCOMO, T.
CRUZ, A.
CRUZ, C.
CRUZ, G.
CUNHA, A.
CYRINO, L.
CYRINO, L.
DALONSO, Y.
DAUDT, C.
DEMARCH, S.
DEMARCHI, G.
DEMETRIO, A.
DENK, A.
DIAS, J.
DICKIE, I.
DOBNER, V.
DONOFRIO, M.
DORNEL, R.
DORNELLES, S.
DUARTE, C.
DUPRAT, M.
DUTRA, J.
DUTRA, M.
ERHARDT, B.
ERZINGER, G.
EVERLING, M.
EXTERKOETTER, M.
EXTERKOETTER, S.
FATIMA, I.
FEDALTO, C.
FEIJO, R.
FERNANDES, E.
FERREIRA, A.
FERREIRA, C.
FERREIRA, D.
FERREIRA, E.
FERREIRA, J.
FERREIRA, L.
FERREIRA, R.
FERREIRA, S.
FIGARI, M.
FIGUEIREDO, N.
FILHO, C.
FILHO, C.
FILHO, F.
FILHO, J.
FILHO, M.
FINARDI, A.
FINDLAY, E.
FLEISCHMANN, E.
FLORIANI, S.
FLORIANO, J.
FLORIANO, J.
FONSECA, R.
FONTANA, K.
FONTANA, V.
FONTOURA, A.
FRANCA, J.
FRANCA, P.
FRANCA, R.
FRANCALACCI, C.
FRANCISCO, M.
FRANCO, S.
FRANZONI, D.
FRANZONI, J.

FRIEDRICH, C.
FRONZA, M.
FUCKNER, C.
FURLAN, S.
FURTADO, W.
GABARDO, C.
GAMA, G.
GANSKE, C.
GARCIA, B.
GARCIA, C.
GARCIA, M.
GARCIA, R.
GERENT, M.
GERN, R.
GIRALDI, A.
GOMES, N.
GOMES, T.
GONCALVES, A.
GONCALVES, M.
GONCALVES, S.
GRANDO, M.
GRAZZIOTTIN, G.
GREGORI, F.
GROSSL, C.
GROSSL, L.
GRUBER, V.
GRUNBERG, P.
GSCHWENDTNER, L.
GUALBERTO, P.
GUBERT, L.
GUEDES, S.
GUIMARAES, G.
GUIMARAES, L.
GUSSO, L.
HAGEMANN, B.
HARGER, L.
HARITSCH, F.
HEINZELMANN, M.
HESS, C.
HEYDER, C.
HOEPFNER, C.
HOFFMANN, G.
HOMRICH, A.
HUBER, G.
HUBNER, J.
HUGO, V.
IETKA, M.
IGNARRA, R.
IMHOF, A.
INIGO, R.
IWAYA, J.
JACOVICZ, E.
JAHN, A.
JORGE, F.
JOSE, A.
JUNQUEIRA, R.
KALB, C.
KASSULKE, A.
KASTEN, H.
KEMPNER, J.
KEMPNER, N.
KERBER, G.
KLEINUBING, H.
KLEMANN, M.
KLUG, J.
KNEUBUEHLER, P.
KOBS, C.
KOENIG, A.
KOERBEL, A.
KOERNER, R.
KOHARA, S.
KOHLS, W.
KONESKI, J.
KORQUIEVICZ, F.
KOSLOWSKI, L.
KRICHELDORF, F.
KROHL, D.
KRUGER, S.
KUSSUMOTO, C.
LAMAS, N.
LANDMANN, R.
LAPA, F.
LEITE, M.
LEITE, S.
LEITZKE, T.
LEME, S.
LEMOS, R.
LENZI, A.
LEONHARDT, J.
LESSA, C.
LIEDKE, M.
LIMA, C.
LIMA, D.
LIMA, F.
LIMA, G.
LIMA, G.
LIMA, H.
LIMA, J.
LIMA, L.
LIPRERI, J.
LOBO, M.
LOMBARDI, M.
LONGO, A.
LOPES, C.
LOPES, M.
LORENZI, L.
LORENZI, R.
LUCA, R.
LUFIEGO, R.
LUZ, E.
LUZ, J.
MACANEIRO, C.
MACHADO, K.
MACHADO, L.
MACHADO, L.
MACHADO, O.
MADEIRA, L.
MAGRI, P.
MALBURG, T.
MALLON, F.
MARANGONI, C.
MARCELINO, R.
MARQUES, A.
MARQUES, D.
MARQUES, S.
MARTINS, A.
MARTINS, E.
MARTINS, R.
MARTINS, S.
MASTROENI, M.
MASTROENI, S.
MATOS, F.
MATOS, S.
MATOS, S.
MATTOS, R.
MAZZETTI, G.
MEDEIROS, C.
MEDEIROS, G.
MEDEIROS, I.
MEDEIROS, L.
MEDEIROS, M.
MEDEIROS, R.
MEDEIROS, R.
MEDEIROS, S.
MEDEIROS, V.
MELLO, R.
MELO, A.
MELO, J.
MELO, L.
MELO, M.
MENDES, A.
MENDES, C.
MENDES, D.
MENDONCA, W.
MENESTRINA, E.
MERKLE, M.
MEURER, B.
MEYER, J.
MIERS, J.
MIGUEL, L.
MILESKI, C.
MINIKOVSKY, A.
MIRANDA, A.
MIRANDA, O.
MIYAMOTO, R.
MIZUNO, J.
MODRO, N.
MONTAGNOLI, M.
MORAES, L.
MORAES, T.
MOREIRA, K.
MOREIRA, V.
MORENO, W.
MORGENSTERN, E.
MORO, C.
MOTA, S.
MOTTA, S.
MOUGA, D.
MUELLER, M.
MULLER, A.
MULLER, I.
MUNHOZ, E.
NASCIMENTO, D.
NASCIMENTO, L.
NASCIMENTO, M.
NAU, L.
NENEVE, M.
NENEVE, M.
NENEVE, M.
NETO, A.
NETO, P.
NETO, W.
NETTO, S.
NEVES, V.
NIEMEYER, C.
NOBREGA, M.
NOLLI, D.
NOVAIS, T.
NUNES, A.
NUNES, M.
ODEBRECHT, C.
OLIVEIRA, A.
OLIVEIRA, C.
OLIVEIRA, D.
OLIVEIRA, E.
OLIVEIRA, M.
OLIVEIRA, M.
OLIVEIRA, R.
OLIVEIRA, R.
OLIVEIRA, S.
OLIVEIRA, T.
ORICOLLI, A.
OTERO, D.
OTERO, D.
PABIS, F.
PACHECO, M.
PAIANO, H.
PAIVA, E.
PAIVA, M.
PAN, M.
PANDOLFO, P.
PASINI, E.
PAULO, L.
PAYAO, J.
PAZA, A.
PEDACK, J.
PEDROSO, G.
PEDROSO, M.
PEREIRA, C.
PEREIRA, E.
PEREIRA, I.
PEREIRA, J.
PEREIRA, M.
PEREIRA, S.
PERES, D.
PERIN, V.
PERINI, C.
PESCE, M.
PETRY, R.
PEYERL, D.
PEZZIN, A.
PEZZINI, B.
PEZZINI, M.
PFEIFER, A.
PILZ, C.
PINHEIRO, P.
PINHO, M.
PINTO, A.
PINTO, A.
PINTO, L.
PIVA, A.
PIVA, W.
PIZZATTO, J.
POERNER, A.
POPE, L.
PORCHER, L.
POSSAMAI, F.
POSSAMAI, T.

PRASS, G.
PRESTINI, S.
PRETTO, F.
PROVEZI, J.
QUADROS, K.
QUEIROZ, P.
RAFAEL, M.
RAFFAELI, I.
RAMIN, E.
RAMOS, M.
RAMOS, M.
RAMOS, S.
RAMPINELLI, J.
RANK, S.
REBERTI, A.
REBERTI, H.
REINERT, M.
REIS, L.
REIS, M.
RENNER, G.
RIANI, J.
RIBEIRO, C.
RIBEIRO, S.
RICHTER, E.
RINNERT, C.
ROBERT, I.
ROBERTO, A.
ROCHA, F.
ROCHA, I.
RODRIGUES, G.
RODRIGUES, J.
RODRIGUES, L.
RODRIGUES, L.
ROJAS, C.
ROMAO, L.
RONSONI, R.
ROSA, A.
ROSA, A.
ROSA, I.
ROSA, L.
ROSENDO, D.
ROSINI, N.
ROTHBARTH, R.
RUCKL, N.
RUDNICK, S.
S.THIAGO, D.
SA, C.
SALIN, M.
SALLES, D.
SANCHEZ, M.
SANTANA, N.
SANTOS, A.
SANTOS, A.
SANTOS, G.
SANTOS, G.
SANTOS, S.
SAUER, K.
SCAINI, F.
SCALABRINI, E.
SCHAPITZ, O.
SCHEIDEMANTEL, M.
SCHEJELINSKI, A.
SCHELBAUER, M.
SCHEMMER, A.
SCHIESSL, F.
SCHLINDWEIN, I.
SCHMIDT, C.
SCHMOECKEL, P.
SCHNEIDER, A.
SCHNEIDER, C.
SCHNEIDER, R.
SCHOLZ, F.
SCHOLZE, E.
SCHOSSLAND, S.
SCHRAMM, C.
SCHROEDER, A.
SCHROEDER, H.
SCHROEDER, M.
SCHUBERT, E.
SCHUBERT, R.
SCHUBERT, S.
SCHUEDA, M.
SCHULENBURG, H.
SCHULENBURG, R.
SCHULTER, N.
SCHULZE, G.
SCHULZE, M.
SCHWARZ, G.
SCHWINGEL, F.
SELL, C.
SERAPIAO, C.
SERPA, S.
SILVA, D.
SILVA, D.
SILVA, E.
SILVA, E.
SILVA, E.
SILVA, G.
SILVA, J.
SILVA, J.
SILVA, L.
SILVA, L.
SILVA, L.
SILVA, L.
SILVA, M.
SILVA, M.
SILVA, P.
SILVA, R.
SILVA, R.
SILVA, V.
SILVEIRA, L.
SILVEIRA, M.
SILVEIRA, P.
SIMAO, V.
SIQUEIRA, M.
SOARES, E.
SOARES, L.
SOBRAL, J.
SOCOOWSKI, J.
SOETHE, V.
SOSSAI, F.
SOUSA, M.
SOUTO, V.
SOUZA, E.
SOUZA, I.
SOUZA, N.
SOUZA, O.
SOUZA, S.
SPITZNER, G.
STAHN, S.
STAMM, E.
STEFFEN, A.
STEGLICH, E.
STEGLICH, V.
STIEGLER, N.
SZABUNIA, S.
TAMANINE, A.
TAMANINI, E.
TAMBOSI, S.
TAVARES, R.
THIAGO, E.
TIRECK, E.
TIRONI, F.
TODESCAT, E.
TONTINI, M.
TORRENS, B.
TORRENS, E.
TRAPP, V.
TREML, C.
TREML, E.
TREML, G.
TRIGO, N.
TURECK, C.
UNGER, G.
UNGER, P.
VALENTIM, C.
VALENTIM, L.
VALOR, N.
VARGAS, H.
VAZ, C.
VENERA, J.
VENERA, R.
VERAS, T.
VETORAZZI, V.
VEXANI, J.
VICENZI, T.
VIEIRA, C.
VIEIRA, J.
VIESI, C.
VIZZOTTO, D.
VOIGT, J.
VOOS, J.
WAGNER, T.
WANZUITA, R.
WEINGRILL, P.
WEINZIERL, W.
WENDHAUSEN, A.
WESTPHAL, E.
WESTPHAL, G.
WESTRUPP, D.
WESTRUPP, M.
WIESE, J.
WIESE, M.
WIESE, V.
WISBECK, E.
WITT, M.
WITT, M.
WOLF, S.
WYREBSKI, J.
XAVIER, J.
ZAFFARI, G.
ZANGARI, B.
ZANGHELINI, A.
ZANINI, K.
ZESKA, M.
ZETOLA, M.
ZIMATH, M.
ZIMMERMANN, C.
ZUCCO, C.
ZUGE, G.
ZULAUF, J.

UNIVERSIDADE DE BLUMENAU
(University of Blumenau)

Rua Antônio da Veiga 140, Sala A 201, Blumenau, SC 89012-900

Telephone: (47) 3321-0214
E-mail: cri@furb.br
Internet: www.furb.br

Founded 1968
Private control
Language of instruction: Portuguese
Academic year: January to December

Rector: Prof. JOÃO NATEL POLLONIO MACHADO
Vice-Rector: Profa GRISELDES FREDEL BOOS
Pro-Rector and Dean of Education: Prof. ANTÓNIO ANDRÉ CHIVANGA BARROS
Pro-Rector for Admin.: Prof. UDO SCHROEDER
Pro-Rector for Research, Postgraduate Affairs, Extension and Culture: Prof. Dr MARCOS RIVAIL DA SILVA
Library Dir: DARLAN JEVAER SCHMITT

Library of 481,900 vols
Number of teachers: 850
Number of students: 11,000

Publications: *Dynamis–Revista Tecno-Científica*, *Revista de Divulgação Cultural*, *Revista de Estudos Ambientais*, *Revista de Negócios*, *Revista Jurídica*

UNIVERSIDADE DO CONTESTADO
(University of Contestado)

Av. Presidente Nereu Ramos 1071, Mafra, SC 89300-000

Telephone: (47) 3641-5500
E-mail: reitoria@unc.br
Internet: www.unc.br

Founded 1997
State control
Language of instruction: Portuguese
Academic year: January to December

Rector: JOSÉ ALCEU VALÉRIO
Vice-Rector for Academic Affairs: Prof. VILSON POHLENZ
Vice-Rector for Admin. and Planning: Prof. Dr CARLOS EDUARDO CARVALHO
Librarian: JOSIANE LIEBL MIRANDA

Library of 170,860 vols, 1,041 nat. and 128 foreign periodical titles, 6,392 CD-ROMs
Number of teachers: 300
Number of students: 5,500

Publications: *Ágora: Revista de Divulgação Científica* (2 a year), *DRd—Desenvolvi-*

mento Regional em debate (2 a year), *Saúde e meio ambiente: Revista Interdisciplinar* (2 a year)

UNIVERSIDADE DO ESTADO DE SANTA CATARINA
(State University of Santa Catarina)

Av. Madre Benvenuta 2007, Itacorubi, Florianópolis, SC 88035-001
Telephone: (48) 3321-8000
E-mail: reitor@udesc.br
Internet: www.udesc.br
Founded 1965
State control
Language of instruction: Portuguese
Academic year: March to December
Rector: ANTÔNIO HERONALDO DE SOUSA
Vice-Rector: MARCUS TOMASI
Pro-Rector for Academics: LUCIANO EMILIO HACK
Pro-Rector for Admin.: VINÍCIUS ALEXANDRE PERUCCI
Pro-Rector for Extension, Culture and Community: MAYCO MORAIS NUNES
Pro-Rector for Planning: GERSON VOLNEY LAGEMANN
Pro-Rector for Research and Postgraduate Studies: ALEXANDRE AMORIM DOS REIS
Librarian: LÚCIA MARENGO
Library of 186,960 vols, 82,984 titles
Number of teachers: 765
Number of students: 13,325
Publications: *Human Factors in Design* (2 a year), *PerCursos* (2 a year), *REAVI—Revista Eletrônica do Alto Vale do Itajaí* (2 a year, online), *Revista Ciclos* (2 a year), *Revista da UDESC*, *Revista Educação, Artes e Inclusão* (1 a year), *Revista Gestão Organizacional*, *Revista Linhas* (2 a year, online), *Revista Palíndromo* (2 a year), *Tempo e Argumento* (2 a year), *UDESC em Ação* (1 a year), *Urdimento—Revista de Estudos em Artes Cênicas* (2 a year)

UNIVERSIDADE DO EXTREMO SUL CATARINENSE
(University of Extreme South Catarinense)

Av. Universitária 1105, Bairro Universitário, Criciúma, SC 88806-000
Telephone: (48) 3431-2500
E-mail: iro@unesc.net
Internet: www.unesc.net
Founded 1997
Private control
Language of instruction: Portuguese
Academic year: January to December
Rector: GILDO VOLPATO
Vice-Rector: MÁRCIO ANTÔNIO FIORI
Number of teachers: 585
Number of students: 10,901 (9,893 undergraduate, 952 postgraduate and 56 doctoral)
Publication: *Revista Científica*

UNIVERSIDADE DO OESTE DE SANTA CATARINA
(University of the West of Santa Catarina)

Rua Getúlio Vargas 2125, Bairro Flor de Serra, Joaçaba, SC 89600-000
Telephone: (49) 3551-2000
E-mail: reitor@unoesc.edu.br
Internet: www.unoesc.edu.br
Founded 1968
State control
Language of instruction: Portuguese
Academic year: February to December
Rector: ARISTIDES CIMADON
Vice-Rector for Academics: NELSON SANTOS MACHADO
Vice-Rector for Videira Campus: ANTONIO CARLOS DE SOUZA
Vice-Rector for West São Miguel Campus: VITOR CARLOS D'AGOSTINI
Vice-Rector for Xanxerê Campus: GENESIO TÉO
Library of 302,850 vols, 5,525 nat. and 431 foreign periodicals, 2,968 CD-ROMs
Number of teachers: 800
Number of students: 13,700
Publications: *Espaço Jurídico* (2 a year), *Roteiro* (2 a year, online)

UNIVERSIDADE DO SUL DE SANTA CATARINA
(University of Southern Santa Catarina)

Av. José Acácio Moreira 787, Bairro Dehon, CP 370, Tubarão, SC 88704-900
Telephone: (48) 3279-1000
E-mail: unisul@unisul.br
Internet: www.unisul.br
Founded 1967
municipal control
Language of instruction: Portuguese
Academic year: March to November
Rector: SEBASTIÃO SALÉSIO HERDT
Vice-Rector and Pro-Rector for Teaching, Research and Extension: MAURI LUIZ HEERDT
Sec.-Gen.: MIRIAN MARIA DE MEDEIROS
Pro-Rector for Institutional Devt: LUCIANO RODRIGUES MARCELINO
Pro-Rector for Operations and Academic Services: VALTER ALVES SCHMITZ NETO
Dir for Grande Florianópolis Campus: HÉRCULES NUNES DE ARAÚJO
Dir for Tubarão Campus: HEITOR WENSING, JR
Univ. Librarian: ELIA DA SILVA
Library of 159,960 vols, incl. 119,474 books, 32,941 periodicals, 708 theses and dissertations, 323 technical standards, 1,523 monographs, 3,137 reference titles, 775 annals, 342 maps, 141 CD-ROMs
Number of teachers: 1,641
Number of students: 25,000
Publication: *Jornal* (10 a year)

UNIVERSIDADE DO VALE DO ITAJAÍ
(University of Vale do Itajaí)

Rua Uruguai 458, Centro, CP 360, Itajaí, SC 88302-202
Telephone: (47) 3341-7500
E-mail: reitoria@univali.rsc-sc.br
Internet: www.univali.br
Founded 1970, present name and status 1989
municipal control
Language of instruction: Portuguese
Academic year: January to December
Rector: MÁRIO CESAR DOS SANTOS
Vice-Rector: AMÂNDIA MARIA DE BORBA
Pro-Rector for Research, Postgraduate Affairs, Extension and Culture: VALDIR CECHINEL FILHO
Pro-Rector for Teaching: CÁSSIA FERRI
Int. Affairs Office Coordinator: Prof. Dr J. M. LUNA
Librarian: CRISTIANI REGINA ANDRETTI
Library of 103,000 vols, 18,000 periodicals
Number of teachers: 1,200
Number of students: 26,100
Publications: *Alcance* (4 a year), *Novos Estudos Jurídicos* (2 a year), *Revista de Arte e Cultura, Turismo e Ação* (2 a year)

UNIVERSIDADE FEDERAL DE SANTA CATARINA
(Federal University of Santa Catarina)

Campus Reitor João David Ferreira Lima, Bairro Trindade, CP 476, Florianópolis, SC 88040-900
Telephone: (48) 3721-9000
E-mail: gabinete@reitoria.ufsc.br
Internet: www.ufsc.br
Founded 1960
federal control
Language of instruction: Portuguese
Academic year: March to December
Centres of agrarian sciences, biological sciences, biomedical sciences, communication, education, engineering and technology, health sciences, legal sciences, philosophy and social sciences, physical education, physics and mathematics, social and economic sciences
Rector: ROSELANE NECKEL
Vice-Rector: LÚCIA HELENA PACHECO
Pro-Rector for Admin.: ANTÔNIO CARLOS MONTEZUMA BRITO
Pro-Rector for Extension: EDISON DA ROSA
Pro-Rector for Planning and Budgeting: BEATRIZ AUGUSTO DE PAIVA
Pro-Rector for Postgraduate Affairs: JOANA MARIA PEDRO
Pro-Rector for Research: JAMIL ASSEREUY FILHO
Pro-Rector for Undergraduate Affairs: ROSELANE FÁTIMA CAMPOS
Number of teachers: 1,610
Number of students: 34,500
Publications: *Biotemas* (2 a year), *Ciências da Saúde* (2 a year), *Ciências Humanas* (2 a year), *Fragmentos* (2 a year), *Geosul* (2 a year), *Graf & Tec* (2 a year), *Ilha do Desterro* (2 a year), *Katalysis* (2 a year), *Motrivivência—Políticas Públicas* (2 a year), *Perspectiva* (2 a year), *Principia* (2 a year), *Seqüência* (2 a year), *Travessia* (2 a year)

São Paulo

In São Paulo, there are 415 faculties, 50 integrated HEIs, one centre for technological education and 53 higher schools or institutes.

UNIVERSITIES

PONTIFÍCIA UNIVERSIDADE CATÓLICA DE CAMPINAS
(Pontifical Catholic University of Campinas)

Rua Mal. Deodoro, 1099, Centro Campinas, Campinas, SP 13010-920
Telephone: (19) 3343-7000
E-mail: reitoria@puc-campinas.edu.br
Internet: www.puc-campinas.edu.br
Founded 1941
Private control
Language of instruction: Portuguese
Academic year: February to December
Chancellor: Dom BRUNO GAMBERINI
Rector: Profa Dra ANGELA DE MENDONÇA ENGELBRECHT
Vice-Rector: Prof. Dr EDUARD PRANCIC
Pro-Rector for Admin.: Prof. Dr RICARDO PANNAIN
Pro-Rector for Extension and Communitarian Subjects: Profa Dra VERA ENGLER CURY
Pro-Rector for Research and Graduate and Postgraduate Courses: Profa Dra VERA ENGLER CURY
Pro-Rector for Undergraduate Courses: Prof. Dr GERMANO RIGACCI JÚNIOR
Sec.-Gen.: Prof. JOSÉ BENEDITO DE ALMEIDA DAVID

Librarian: MARIA MAKIKO M.

Library of 162,208 vols, 4,169 journal titles
Number of teachers: 1,000
Number of students: 20,000

Publications: *Cadernos da FACECA*, *Cadernos de Extensão*, *Cadernos de Serviço Social*, *Cadernos do CCH*, *Revista Bióikos*, *Revista Comunicarte*, *Revista de Ciências Médicas*, *Revista de Educação*, *Revista de Nutrição*, *Revista Estudos de Psicologia*, *Revista Humanitas*, *Revista Jornalismo*, *Revista Jurídica*, *Revista Letras*, *Revista Notícia Bibliográfica e Histórica*, *Revista Oculum Ensaios*, *Revista Phrónesis*, *Revista Reflexão*, *Revista TransInformação*

DIRECTORS OF CENTRES

Centre for Communication Sciences: Prof. WAGNER JOSÉ GERIBELLO
Centre for Economics and Administration: Prof. EDUARD PRANCIC
Centre for Humanities and Applied Social Sciences (CCHSA): Prof. PAULO SÉRGIO LOPES GONÇALVES
Centre for Life Sciences: Profa MIRALVA APARECIDA DE JESUS SILVA
Centre for Mathematical, Environmental and Technological Sciences: Prof. ORANDI MINA FALSARELLA

DIRECTORS OF FACULTIES

Centre for Communication Sciences (tel. (19) 3343-7192; e-mail clc@puc-campinas.edu.br; internet www.puc-campinas.edu.br/clc):

Faculty of Advertising and Publicity: Profa FLAILDA BRITO GARBOGGINI
Faculty of Journalism: Profa ROGÉRIO EDUARDO RODRIGUES BAZI
Faculty of Letters: Prof. CARLOS DE AQUINO PEREIRA
Faculty of Public Relations: Profa CLÁUDIA MARIA DE C. CAFVALHO
Faculty of Tourism: Profa LAURA UMBELINA SANTI
Faculty of Visual Arts: Profa FLÁVIO SHIMODA

Centre for Economics and Administration (tel. (19) 3343-7099; e-mail cea@puc-campinas.edu.br; internet www.puc-campinas.edu.br/cea):

Faculty of Accounting: Prof. MARCOS FRANCISCO RODRIGUES SOUZA
Faculty of Admin.: Prof. PAULO ANTÔNIO G. L. ZUCCOLOTTO
Faculty of Economics: Prof. LINEU CARLOS MAFFEZOLI

Centre for Humanities and Applied Social Sciences (tel. (19) 3343-7299; e-mail cch@puc-campinas.edu.br; internet www.puc-campinas.edu.br):

Faculty of Education: Profa LUZIA SIQUEIRA VASCONCELOS
Faculty of History: Prof. JOÃO MIGUEL TEIXEIRA DE GODOY
Faculty of Law: Prof. LÚIS ARLINDO FERIANI
Faculty of Library Science: Profa MARIANGELA PISONI ZANAGA
Faculty of Philosophy: Prof. JOSÉ ANTONIO TRASFERETTI
Faculty of Physical Education and Sports: Prof. WAGNER ROBERTO BERGAMO
Faculty of Social Sciences: Prof. PEDRO ROCHA LEMOS
Faculty of Social Services: Profa VÂNIA MARIA CAIO
Faculty of Theology and Religious Studies: Prof. ELISIÁRIO CÉSAR CABRAL

Centre for Life Sciences (Av. John Boyd Dunlop s/n, Jardim Ipaussurama, Campinas, SP 13060-904; tel. (19) 3343-6800; e-mail ccv@puc-campinas.edu.br; internet www.puc-campinas.edu.br/ccv):

Faculty of Biological Sciences: Profa MARIÂNGELA CAGNONI RIBEIRO
Faculty of Dentistry: Prof. JOSÉ IGNÁCIO TOLEDO JÚNIOR
Faculty of Medicine: Prof. JOSÉ ESPIN NETO
Faculty of Nursing: Profa MARIA APARECIDA GAMPER NUNES
Faculty of Nutrition: Profa ANGELA DE CAMPOS TRENTIN
Faculty of Occupational Therapy: Profa LIANA MAURA NAKED TANNUS
Faculty of Pharmacy: GUSTAVO HENRIQUE DA SILVA
Faculty of Physical Therapy: Profa ROSANGELA MARIA FRANCO GUERRA DA COSTA
Faculty of Psychology: Profa HELENA BAZANELLI PREBIANCHI
Faculty of Speech Therapy and Audiology: Profa MARIENE TERUMI UMEOKA HIDAKA

Centre for Mathematical, Environmental and Technological Sciences (tel. (19) 3343-7314; e-mail ceatec@puc-campinas.edu.br; internet www.puc-campinas.edu.br/ceatec):

Faculty of Architecture and Urban Planning: Prof. RICARDO DA SOUZA CAMPS BADARÓ
Faculty of Chemistry: Prof. DALMO MENDELLI
Faculty of Civil Engineering: Prof. JOÃO CARLOS ROCHA BRAZ
Faculty of Computer Engineering: Prof. RICARDO LUÍS DE FREITAS
Faculty of Electrical Engineering: Profa NORMA REGGIANI
Faculty of Environmental Engineering: Profa SUELI DO CARMO BETTINE
Faculty of Geography: Prof. DAMARIS PUGA DE MORÃES
Faculty of Mathematics: Prof. ELIANA DAS NEVES AREAS
Faculty of Systems Analysis: Prof. JOSÉ ESTEVÃO PICARELLI

PONTIFÍCIA UNIVERSIDADE CATÓLICA DE SÃO PAULO
(Pontifical Catholic University of São Paulo)

Rua Monte Alegre 984, Perdizes, São Paulo, SP 05014-901

Telephone: (11) 3670-8000
E-mail: reitoria@pucsp.br
Internet: www.pucsp.br

Founded 1946
Private control
Academic year: February to December (2 semesters)

Grand Chancellor: Dom ODILO PEDRO SCHERER (Archbishop of São Paulo)
Rector: Profa Dra ANNA MARIA MARQUES CINTRA
Vice-Rector: Prof. Dr JOSÉ EDUARDO MARTINEZ
Pro-Rector for Continuing Education: Profa Dra ALEXANDRA FOGLI SERPA GERALDINI
Pro-Rector for Culture and Community Relations: Profa Dra ROSANA NUNES DOS SANTOS
Pro-Rector for Graduate Affairs: Profa Dra MARIA MARGARIDA CAVALCANTI LIMENA
Pro-Rector for Planning, Devt and Management: Prof. Dr. LAWRENCE CHUNG KOO
Pro-Rector for Postgraduate Affairs and Research: Profa Dra MARIA AMALIA PIE ABIB ANDERY
Chief of Staff: Prof. Dr LAFAYETTE POZZOLI
Librarian: ANA MARIA RAPASSI

Library of 250,000 vols
Number of teachers: 1,700
Number of students: 35,000

Publications: *Cadernos Metrópole* (2 a year), *Cognitio* (1 a year), *Delta—Documentação de Estudos em Linguística Teórica Aplicada* (2 a year), *Distúrbios da Comunicação* (4 a year), *Educação Matemática Pesquisa* (2 a year), *Galáxia* (2 a year), *Hypnos* (2 a year), *Kairós* (2 a year), *Pesquisa & Debate* (2 a year), *Projeto História* (2 a year), *The ESPecialist* (2 a year)

DEANS

Faculty of Biological Sciences: Prof. WALTER BARRELLA
Faculty of Economics and Business: JUAREZ TORINO BELLI
Faculty of Education: NEIDE NOFFS
Faculty of Human Sciences and Health: MARIA AMÁLIA ANDERY
Faculty of Law: MARCELO FIGUEIREDO
Faculty of Mathematical and Physical Sciences: Prof. FERNANDO ANTONIO DE CASTRO GIORNO
Faculty of Medical Sciences and Health: JOSÉ EDUCARDO MARTINEZ
Faculty of Philosophy, Communication, Languages and Arts: SANDRA MRAZ
Faculty of Psychology: Profa MARIA DA GRAÇA MARCHINA GONÇALVES
Faculty of Sciences and Technology: LUIZ CARLOS CAMPOS
Faculty of Social Sciences: MARGARIDA LIMENA
Faculty of Social Work: Profa MARIA ROSÂNGELA BATISTONI
Faculty of Theology: VALERIANO DOS SANTOS

UNIVERSIDADE BANDEIRANTE DE SÃO PAULO
(Bandeirante University of São Paulo)

Av. Dr. Rudge Ramos, 1501, São Bernardo do Campo, SP 09639-000

Telephone: (11) 4362-9000
E-mail: uniban@ns.uniban.br
Internet: www.uniban.br

Founded 1994
Private control
Academic year: February to December

Chancellor: Prof. ANTONIO CARBONARI NETTO
Rector: Prof. GILBERTO LUIZ MORAES SELBER
Pro-Rector for Academics: Profa ANA MARIA FERREIRA DE MATTOS RETTL
Pro-Rector for Admin. and Finance: ANTONIO FONSECA DE CARVALHO
Pro-Rector for Operations: ANTONIO AUGUSTO DE OLIVEIRA COSTA

Library of 557,125 vols, 900 periodicals
Number of teachers: 1,200
Number of students: 30,000

UNIVERSIDADE BRAZ CUBAS
(Braz Cubas University)

Av. Francisco Rodrigues Filho 1233, Vila Mogilar Mogi das Cruzes, Mogi das Cruzes, SP 08773-380

Telephone: (11) 4791-8000
E-mail: candidato@brazcubas.br
Internet: www.brazcubas.br

Founded 1940, univ. status 1986
Private control
Language of instruction: Portuguese
Academic year: February to December

Chancellor: Prof. NAIR GRINBERG
Rector: Prof. MAURÍCIO CHERMANN
Pro-Rector for Admin.: Prof. SAUL GRINBERG
Pro-Rector for Community Affairs: Prof. IRAM ALVES DOS SANTOS
Pro-Rector for Finance: Prof. ISRAEL ALVES DOS SANTOS
Pro-Rector for Planning: Prof. DAVI CHERMANN
Sec.-Gen.: PÉRCIO CHAMMA JR
Librarian: JANDIRA MARIA COUTINHO

Library of 97,000 vols
Number of teachers: 512
Number of students: 10,494

UNIVERSIDADE CATÓLICA DE SANTOS
(Catholic University of Santos)

Av. Conselheiro Nébias, 300, Vila Matias Santos, Santos, SP 11015-002
Telephone: (13) 3205-5555
E-mail: secgeral@unisantos.com.br
Internet: www.unisantos.com.br

Founded 1951, recognized 1986

Rector: Prof. MARCOS MEDINA LEITE
Librarian: MARIA RITA DE CÁSSIA REBELLO NASTASI

Library of 58,000 vols, 945 periodicals
Number of teachers: 537
Number of students: 7,015

Publications: *Revista Leopoldianum* (3 a year), *Revista Pesquiseduca*

UNIVERSIDADE CIDADE DE SÃO PAULO
(City University of São Paulo)

Rua Cesário Galeno 448/475, Tatuapé, São Paulo, SP 03071-000
Telephone: (11) 2178-1212
E-mail: gabreit@unicid.br
Internet: www.eadunicid.com.br

Founded 1992
Private control

Rector: RUBENS LOPES DA CRUZ
Chancellor: PAULO EDUARDO SOARES DE OLIVEIRA NADDEO

Library of 103,000 vols, 1,200 periodicals
Number of teachers: 550
Number of students: 12,000

UNIVERSIDADE CRUZEIRO DO SUL
(South Cross University)

Av. Dr Ussiel Cirilo 225, São Paulo, SP 08060-070
Telephone: (11) 2037-5700
Internet: www.unicsul.br

Founded 1993
Private control

Rector: Profa Dra SUELI CRISTINA MARQUESI
Pro-Rector for Distance Education: Prof. Dr CARLOS FERNANDO DE ARAUJO, JR
Pro-Rector for Extension and Community Affairs: Profa Dra JANICE VALIA DE LOS SANTOS
Pro-Rector for Postgraduate Affairs and Research: Prof. Dr DANILO ANTONIO DUARTE
Pro-Rector for Undergraduate Affairs: Prof. Dr LUIZ HENRIQUE AMARAL

Library of 500,000 vols, 194 periodicals
Number of teachers: 250
Number of students: 10,000

UNIVERSIDADE DE FRANCA
(University of Franca)

Av. Dr Armando Salles Oliveira 201, Parque Universitário, Franca, SP 14404-600
Telephone: (16) 3711-8888
E-mail: reitoria@unifran.br
Internet: www.unifran.br

Founded 1970
Private control

Chancellor: Dr CLOVIS EDUARDO PINTO LUDOVICE
Rector: Profa ESTER REGINA VITALE

Library of 58,000 vols, 1,300 periodicals
Number of teachers: 200
Number of students: 6,300

UNIVERSIDADE DE MARÍLIA
(University of Marilia)

Av. Higyno Muzzy Filho, 1001 Campus Universitário, Marília, SP 17525–902
Telephone: (14) 2105-4000
E-mail: falecom@unimar.br
Internet: www.unimar.com.br

Founded 1956
Private control
Academic year: February to December (2 semesters)

Rector: MÁRCIO MESQUITA SERVA
Vice-Rector: REGINA LÚCIA OTTAIANO LOSASSO SERVA
Pro-Rector: MARIA BEATRIZ DE BARROS MORAES TRAZZI
Pro-Rector: JOSÉ ROBERTO MARQUES DE CASTRO
Pro-Rector: MARCO ANTONIO TEIXEIRA E SUELY FADUL VILLIBOR FLORY
Sec.-Gen.: GENI DE ALMEIDA COLLA
Head of Library: MARIA CÉLIA ARANHA RAMOS

Library of 65,438 vols, 128,455 copies
Number of teachers: 350
Number of students: 7,000

Publications: *Argumentum* (1 a year), *Asuntamentos Humanos* (1 a year), *Ciências Humanas* (1 a year), *Ciências Odontológicas* (1 a year), *Comunicação Veredas* (1 a year), *Unimar Ciências* (2 a year), *Unimídia* (6 a year), *Uninformativo* (1 a year)

UNIVERSIDADE DE MOGI DAS CRUZES
(University of Mogi Das Cruzes)

Av. Dr Cândido Xavier de Almeida Souza 200, Mogi das Cruzes, SP 08780-911
Telephone: (11) 4798-7000
E-mail: reitoria@umc.br
Internet: www.umc.br

Founded 1973
Private control
Language of instruction: Portuguese
Academic year: February to December

Chancellor: Prof. MANOEL BEZERRA DE MELO
Vice-Chancellor: Profa MARIA COELI BEZERRA DE MELO
Rector: Profa REGINA COELI BEZERRA DE MELO
Vice-Rector: Dra ROSELI DOS SANTOS FERRAZ VERAS
Pro-Rector for Graduate Affairs of Campus HQ: Prof. Dr CLAUDIO JOSÉ ALVES DE BRITO
Pro-Rector for Graduate Affairs of Other Campuses: Prof. ANTONIO DE OLIVAL FERNANDES
Pro-Rector for Postgraduate Affairs, Research and Extension: Prof. Dr MIGUEL LUIZ BATISTA JÚNIOR
Librarian: DECLEIA MARIA FAGANELLO

Library of 148,087 vols
Number of teachers: 836
Number of students: 21,000

Publication: *Entre Nós* (12 a year)

UNIVERSIDADE DE RIBEIRÃO PRETO
(University of Ribeirão Preto)

Av. Costábile Romano 2201, Ribeirânia, Ribeirão Preto, SP 14096-900
Telephone: (16) 3603-7000
Internet: www.unaerp.br

Founded 1985
Private control

Rector: Profa ELMARA LUCIA DE OLIVEIRA BONINI CORAUCI

Library of 134,555 vols, incl. books, monographs, dissertations, theses, periodicals, sheet music, rare books and multimedia materials
Number of teachers: 400
Number of students: 7,500

UNIVERSIDADE DE SANTO AMARO
(University of Santo Amaro)

Rua Prof. Enéas de Siqueira Neto 340, Cidade Dutra, São Paulo, SP 04829-300
Telephone: (11) 2141-8500
E-mail: pesquisaunisa@unisa.br
Internet: www.unisa.br

Founded 1968 as Instituição de Ensino Superior; current name adopted 1994
Private control

Rector: MARGARETH ROSE PRIEL
Vice-Rector: JOSÉ DOUGLAS DALLORA
Pro-Rector for Distance Education: ANGELITA MARÇAL FLORES
Pro-Rector for Postgraduate Affairs, Research and Extension: ELOI FRANCISCO ROSA
Pro-Rector for Undergraduate Affairs: SONIA REGINA LEITE DE ALMEIDA PRADO

Library of 57,000 vols, 700 periodicals
Number of teachers: 500
Number of students: 7,800

Publications: *Revista de Enfermagem*, *Revista Maranhão*

UNIVERSIDADE DE SÃO FRANCISCO
(University of São Francisco)

Rua Antonieta Leitão, 129 Freguesia do Ó, São Paulo, SP
Telephone: (11) 4034-8170
E-mail: imprensa@usf.edu.br
Internet: www.usf.com.br

Founded 1976, university status 1985
Private control
Language of instruction: Portuguese
Academic year: February to December

Chancellor: FIDÊNCIO VANBOEMMEL
Rector: HÉCTOR EDMUNDO HUANAY ESCOBAR
Vice-Rector: JOEL ALVES DE SOUSA JR
Pro-Rector for Admin. and Planning: EROS PACHECO NETO
Pro-Rector for Education, Research and Postgraduate Affairs: IARA ANDREA ALVARES FERNANDES
Gen. Sec.: PAULO POZEBON
Librarian: IVANI BENASSI

Library of 232,427 vols, 1,299 print journals
Number of teachers: 821
Number of students: 17,561

Publications: *Cadernos do IFAN* (4 a year), *InformIPPEX* (12 a year), *Horizontes*, *Psico-USF*, *Semeando* (12 a year)

UNIVERSIDADE DE SÃO PAULO

Cidade Universitária, Rua da Reitoria 109, São Paulo, SP 05508-900
Telephone: (11) 3091-1000
E-mail: gr@usp.br
Internet: www.usp.br

Founded 1934
State control
Academic year: March to November

Campuses in São Paulo, Bauru, San Carlos, Lorena, Piracicaba, Pirassununga, Ribeirão Preto, San Sebastian

Rector: JOÃO GRANDINO RODAS
Vice-Rector: HÉLIO NOGUEIRA DA CRUZ
Vice-Rector for Admin: ANTONIO ROQUE DECHEN
Vice-Rector for International Relations: ALUISIO AUGUSTO COTRIM SEGURADO
Chief of Staff: ALBERTO CARLOS AMADIO
Pro-Rector for Culture and Univ. Extension: MARIA ARMINDA DO NASCIMENTO ARRUDA
Pro-Rector for Postgraduate Studies: VAHAN AGOPYAN

Pro-Rector for Research: MARCO ANTONIO ZAGO
Pro-Rector for Undergraduate Studies: TELMA MARIA TENÓRIO ZORN
Sec.-Gen.: Dr RUBENS BEÇAK
Library: see under Libraries and Archives
Number of teachers: 5,500
Number of students: 82,000
Publications: *Anagrama*, *Boletim de Botânica* (2 a year), *Boletim IG/USP—Série Científica* (1 a year), *Brazilian Journal of Veterinary Research and Animal Science* (6 a year), *Educação e Pesquisa—FE* (2 a year), *Espaço Aberto*, *Estilos da Clínica* (2 a year), *Pesquisa Odontológica Brasileira* (4 a year), *Revista Alterjor* (2 a year), *Revista Angelus Novus*, *Revista Brasileira de Ciências Farmacêuticas—IQ/FCF* (3 a year), *Revista Brasileira de Educação Física e Esporte*, *Revista Brasileira de Oceanografia* (2 a year), *Revista da Escola de Enfermagem* (4 a year), *Revista da Faculdade de Direito* (1 a year), *Revista de Administração* (4 a year), *Revista de Fisioterapia* (2 a year), *Revista de Psicologia USP* (2 a year), *Revista de Saúde Pública* (6 a year), *Revista de Terapia Ocupacional* (4 a year), *Revista do Instituto de Medicina Tropical de SP* (6 a year), *Revista do Museu de Arqueologia e Etnologia* (1 a year), *Revista Música* (2 a year), *Revista Paulista de Educação Física* (2 a year), *Revista USP* (4 a year), *Scientia Agrícola—ESALQ* (4 a year), *Sinopses—FAU* (irregular)

DEANS

Faculty of Animal Husbandry and Food Engineering (Pirassununga): Prof. Dr HOLMER SAVASTANO, Jr
Faculty of Architecture and Town Planning: Prof. Dr SYLVIO BARROS SAWAYA
Faculty of Dentistry: Prof. Dr CARLOS DE PAULA EDUARDO
Faculty of Dentistry (Bauru): Prof. Dr LUIZ FERNANDO PEGORARO
Faculty of Dentistry (Ribeirão Preto): Prof. Dr OSWALDO LUIZ BEZZON
Faculty of Economics, Administration and Accounting: Prof. Dr CARLOS ROBERTO AZZONI
Faculty of Economics, Administration and Accounting (Ribeirão Preto): Prof. Dr RUDINEI TONETO
Faculty of Education: Profa Dra SONIA TERESINHA DE SOUSA PENIN
Faculty of Law: Prof. Dr JOÃO GRANDINO RODAS
Faculty of Law (Ribeirão Preto): Prof. Dr IGNÁCIO MARIA POVEDA VELASCO
Faculty of Medicine: Prof. Dr MARCOS BOULOS
Faculty of Medicine (Ribeirão Preto): Prof. Dr BENEDITO CARLOS MACIEL
Faculty of Pharmaceutical Sciences: Prof. Dr JORGE MANCINI FILHO
Faculty of Pharmaceutical Sciences (Ribeirão Preto): Prof. Dr AUGUSTO CÉSAR CROPANESE SPADARO
Faculty of Philosophy, Literature and Human Sciences: Profa Dra SANDRA MARGARIDA NITRINI
Faculty of Philosophy, Sciences and Literature (Ribeirão Preto): Prof. Dr SEBASTIÃO DE SOUSA ALMEIDA
Faculty of Public Health: Prof. Dr CHESTER LUIZ GALVÃO CÉSAR
Faculty of Veterinary Medicine and Zootechnics: Prof. Dr JOSÉ ANTONIO VISINTIN
Institute of Biomedical Sciences: Prof. Dr LUIZ ROBERTO GIORGETTI DE BRITTO
Institute of Biosciences: Profa Dra WELLINGTON BRAZ CARVALHO DELITTI
Institute of Chemistry: Prof. Dr HANS VIERTLER
Institute of Chemistry (São Carlos): Prof. Dr EDSON ANTONIO TICIANELLI
Institute of Geophysics, Astronomy and Atmospheric Sciences: Profa Dra MÁRCIA ERNESTO
Institute of Geosciences: Prof. Dr COLOMBO CELSO GAETA TASSINARI
Institute of Mathematical Sciences and Computing Systems (São Carlos): Prof. Dr JOSÉ ALBERTO CUMINATO
Institute of Mathematics and Statistics: Prof. Dr PAULO DOMINGOS CORDARO
Institute of Oceanography: Prof. Dr ANA MARIA S. PIRES VANIN
Institute of Physics: Prof. Dr ALEJANDRO SZANTO DE TOLEDO
Institute of Physics (São Carlos): Prof. Dr GLAUCIUS OLIVA
Institute of Psychology: Profa Dra EMMA OTTA
'Luiz de Queiroz' Higher School of Agriculture: Prof. Dr ANTONIO ROQUE DECHEN
Polytechnic School: Prof. Dr IVAN GILBERTO SANDOVAL FALLEIROS
School of Communication and Arts: Prof. Dr MAURO WILTON DE SOUSA
School of Engineering (Lorena): Prof. Dr NEI FERNANDES DE OLIVEIRA, Jr
School of Engineering (São Carlos): Profa Dra MARIA DO CARMO CALIJURI
School of Nursing: Profa Dra ISILIA APARECIDA SILVA
School of Nursing (Ribeirão Preto): Profa Dra MARIA DAS GRAÇAS BOMFIM DE CARVALHO
School of Physical Education and Sport: Prof. Dr GO TANI
School of Physical Education and Sport (Ribeirão Preto): Prof. Dr VALDIR JOSÉ BARBANTI

UNIVERSIDADE DE SOROCABA
(University of Sorocaba)

Km 92.5, Rod Raposo Tavares, Sorocaba, SP 18023-000
Telephone: (15) 2101-7000
E-mail: uniso@uniso.br
Internet: www.uniso.br
Founded 1994
Academic year: February to December
Rector: Prof. Dr FERNANDO DE SÁ DEL FIOL
Pro-Rector for Academics: Prof. Dr JOSÉ MARTINS DE OLIVEIRA, JR
Pro-Rector for Admin.: Prof. Dr ROGÉRIO AUGUSTO PROFETA
Library of 225,000,000 vols, 995 periodicals
Number of teachers: 300
Number of students: 7,300
Publications: *Quaestio—Revista de Estudos de Educação* (2 a year), *Revista de Estudos Universitários* (2 a year)

UNIVERSIDADE DE TAUBATÉ
(University of Taubaté)

Rua Quatro de Março 432, Centro, Taubaté, SP 12020-270
Telephone: (12) 3625-4295
E-mail: reitoria@unitau.br
Internet: www.unitau.br
Founded 1976
municipal control
Academic year: March to November
Rector: Dr JOSÉ RUI CAMARGO
Vice-Rector: Dr MARCOS ROBERTO FURLAN
Pro-Rector for Admin.: Prof. Dr FRANCISCO JOSÉ GRANDINETTI
Pro-Rector for Economy and Finance: Prof. Dr LUCIANO RICARDO MARCONDES DA SILVA
Pro-Rector for Extension and Community Relations: Prof. Dr ANA JOSÉ FELÍCIO GOUSSAIN MURADE
Pro-Rector for Research and Postgraduate Affairs: Prof. Dr EDSON APARECIDA DE ARAÚJO QUERIDO OLIVEIRA
Pro-Rector for Students: Profa Dra NARA LÚCIA PERONDI FORTES
Pro-Rector for Undergraduates: Profa Dra ANA JULIA URIAS DOS SANTOS ARAUJO
Chief Librarian: MÁRCIA MARIA DE MOURA RIBEIRO
Library of 214,000 vols
Number of teachers: 700
Number of students: 15,000
Publications: *Ambiente and Água—An Interdisciplinary Journal of Applied Science*, *Caminhos em Lingüística Aplicada*, *Clínica e Pesquisa em Odontologia—UNITAU*, *Revista Biociências*, *Revista Ciências Exatas*, *Revista Ciências Humanas*, *Revista de Extensão da Universidade de Taubaté*, *Revista G&DR*, *Revista Periodontia*, *Revista UNITAU*

DEANS

Agricultural Sciences: LUCIANO RICARDO MARCONDES DA SILVA
Architecture: MOACYR PAULISTA CORDEIRO
Civil Engineering: ALEX THAUMATURGO DIAS
Dentistry: SANDRA MÁRCIA HABITANTE
Economics, Accounting and Management: Profa MARLENE FERREIRA SANTIAGO
Electrical Engineering: WILTON NEY DO AMARAL PEREIRA
Law: FERNANDO ANTONIO BARBOSA ROMEIRO
Mechanical Engineering: CARLOS ANTONIO VIEIRA
Medicine: ANTONIO CARLOS BARTOLOMUCCI
Nursing: SILVIA MAIRA PEREIRA CINTRA
Physical Education: APARECIDA DE FÁTIMA FERRAZ QUERIDO
Physiotherapy: ULYSSES FERNANDES ERVILHA
Psychology: MARILZA TEREZINHA SOARES DE SOUZA
Social Communications: MARCELO TADEU DOS REIS PIMENTEL
Social Sciences and Languages: SOLANGE TERESINHA RICARDO DE CASTRO
Social Work: MARIA AUXILIADORA ÁVILA DOS SANTOS SÁ

PROFESSORS

ABRAHAM, R.
ABRAO SAAD, W.
ABRUCEZE, S.
ABUD MARCELINO, M.
ABUD MARTINS, A.
AKIYAMA, M.
ALBERNAZ CRESPO, A.
ALEGRE SALLES, V.
ALGADO, A.
ALVES CARRINHO, M.
ALVES CORRÊA, V.
ALVES MARTINS, I.
ALVES SOARES, D.
AMBROSETTI, N.
ANBINDER, A.
ANDRADE BRISOLA, E.
ANTONIO BOVO, L.
APARECIDA RIBEIRO, M.
ARRUDA FILHO, E.
ASSINI BALBUENO, E.
AUXILIADORA PINTO, C.
BARBAGALLO, L.
BARBANERA, M.
BARBERIO, A.
BARBOSA ROMEIRO, F.
BARONE Jr, T.
BARROS DINIZ, N.
BARTOLOMUCCI, A.
BASSO SCHMITT, A.
BATISTA TUFFI, V.
BAUAB PUZZO, M.
BOAL TEIXEIRA, M.
BOLL, A.
BORGES GLAUS LEÃO, M.
BRANCO ROMEIRO, R.

Brás Roque, R.
Brenol Lages, R.
Britto, M.
Buchler Zorrón, A.
Bueno Costa, J.
Burini, D.
Bussolotti, J.
Cabral Jr, J.
Camargo, J.
Camargo Antoniazzi, M.
Camargo Ortiz Monteiro, P.
Cantanhede Guarnieri, O.
Cappellanes, C.
Cardoso, M.
Cardoso, N.
Cardoso Jorge, A.
Carelli Barreto, L.
Carlos Pinto, E.
Carniello, M.
Cavaglieri, A.
Cavalca Cortelli, S.
Cavalcante, K.
Celso Pellogia, M.
Cembraneli Jr, L.
Cervantes, J.
César Jr, C.
Cesar Pires, O.
Cesar Reis, R.
César Vieira, M.
Chaves, C.
Cinelli Moreira, P.
Cirelli, G.
Claro Neves, A.
Cobo, V.
Coimbra Mazzini, R.
Constantino, E.
Cordeiro, M.
Corrêa, J.
Cortelli, J.
Costa, V.
Costa Ferraz, U.
Costa Nascimento, L.
Costa Sodré, P.
Cruz Loures Merkx, A.
Cusma Pelogia, N.
Cusmanich, K.
Custodio, T.
Da Conceição Rivoli Costa, M.
Da Costa, J.
Da Costa, L.
Da Costa E Silva, L.
Da Costa Reis, M.
Da Costa Zöllner, M.
Da Cruz Galvão Júnior, L.
Da Cunha Filho, S.
Da Cunha Oliveira, M.
Da Mota, A.
Da Rosa, L.
Da Silva, A.
Da Silva, A.
Da Silva, C.
Da Silva, D.
Da Silva, E.
Da Silva, E.
Da Silva, J.
Da Silva, L.
Da Silva, M.
Da Silva, M.
Da Silva, R.
Da Silva, R.
Da Silva, R.
Da Silva, T.
Da Silva Almeida, A.
Da Silva Jr, J.
Da Silva Richetto, K.
Da Silva Santos, T.
Da Silva Souza, J.
Da Silveira Luz, M.
Da Trindade Siqueira, M.
Da Veiga, S.
Dalla Vecchia Grassi, A.
Dalombardi, J.
Damilano, J.
Daortiz Abrahão, J.
Das Neves Cavalcanti, B.
Dasimões Florençano, J.
Davoli Arizono, A.
De Albuquerque Camara Neto, I.
De Almeida, A.
De Almeida, J.
De Almeida, L.
De Almeida Candelária, L.
De Almeida Macedo, E.
De Almeida Nascimento, E.
De Alvarenga, M.
De Andrade, L.
De Aquino Freitas, R.
De Arantes Gomes Eller, R.
De Araújo, C.
De Araújo, D.
De Araújo, R.
De Araujo Querido Oliveira, E.
De Assis Claro, C.
De Assis Coelho, F.
De Ávila Moreira, M.
De Azeredo Freitas, L.
De Azevedo, A.
De Azevedo, D.
De Barros, D.
De Barros, J.
De Barros Rezende Filho, C.
De Brito, L.
De Brito Marques, E.
De Campos, J.
De Campos Almeida Vieira, C.
De Carli Bueri Mattos, R.
De Carvalho, A.
De Carvalho, M.
De Carvalho, P.
De Carvalho Almeida, E.
De Carvalho Galizia, P.
De Cássia Rigotti Vilela Monteiro, R.
De Castro, A.
De Castro, M.
De Castro, P.
De Castro, R.
De Castro, S.
De Castro Folgueras, L.
De Castro Moura, J.
De Cerqueira, A.
De Faria, A.
De Faria E Silva, L.
De Fátima Camargo Dias Ferreira, M.
De Fátima Da Silva, M.
De Fatima Ferraz Querido, A.
De Freitas, D.
De Freitas Carpegeani, C.
De Jesus Filho, J.
De Lemos, M.
De Lima, J.
De Lima E Silva, M.
De Mattos, A.
De Mattos Moraes Dos Santos, T.
De Medeiros, A.
De Medeiros, J.
De Mello, B.
De Mello Rode, S.
De Melo, F.
De Melo, J.
De Miranda, G.
De Moraes, M.
De Moraes, V.
De Moraes Rocha Medeiros Freitas Lourenco, R.
De Morais, V.
De Moura, J.
De Moura, L.
De Moura Marques, M.
De Moura Ribeiro, M.
De Moura Santos, A.
De Oliveira, A.
De Oliveira, A.
De Oliveira, C.
De Oliveira, C.
De Oliveira, E.
De Oliveira, F.
De Oliveira, J.
De Oliveira, L.
De Oliveira, M.
De Oliveira, P.
De Oliveira, T.
De Oliveira Brazil, J.
De Oliveira Carvalho, M.
De Oliveira Chamon, E.
De Oliveira Filho, J.
De Oliveira Mukai, A.
De Oliveira Rabay, F.
De Oliveira Sanches, F.
De Oliveira Silva, O.
De Paula, C.
De Paula, M.
De Paula, P.
De Paula Posso, I.
De Paula Posso, R.
De Paula Prisco Cunha, V.
De Rezende, A.
De Sa Rodrigues, C.
De Sá Rodrigues Tadeucci, M.
De Santis Teixeira, C.
De Santos, R.
De Silva, C.
De Siqueira, O.
De Siqueira Renda, V.
De Sousa Almeida, R.
De Souza, L.
De Souza, L.
De Souza, M.
De Souza, M.
De Souza, P.
De Souza E Silva, R.
De Souza Quirino, M.
De Souza Romero, T.
De Souza Soares, A.
De Toledo, J.
De Toledo, M.
De Toledo Netto, A.
De Toledo Piza Filho, P.
De Toledo Souza, R.
De Vasconcellos, R.
Del'arco jr, A.
Dellu, M.
Destro, M.
Di Angelis Coelho, B.
Dias, A.
Dias Colombo, C.
Dias Raposo Filho, P.
Do Amaral Pereira, W.
Do Nascimento, A.
Do Nascimento, J.
Do Patrocínio, M.
Do Patrocínio Nunes, L.
Do Prado, P.
Do Prado Láua, M.
Do Rego, M.
Dolores Alves Cocco, M.
Donizete Guinalz, R.
Dos Reis, L.
Dos Reis Ervilha, F.
Dos Reis Pimentel, M.
Dos Santos, A.
Dos Santos, A.
Dos Santos, A.
Dos Santos, C.
Dos Santos, I.
Dos Santos, J.
Dos Santos, M.
Dos Santos, M.
Dos Santos, R.
Dos Santos, S.
Dos Santos, S.
Dos Santos, S.
Dos Santos, T.
Dos Santos Araujo, A.
Dos Santos Filho, A.
Dos Santos Sá, M.
Dos Santos Targa, M.
Duarte Abdala, R.
Echeverria, S.
Effrin Pupio, C.
Elias jr, M.
Ervilha, U.
Esper Berthoud, C.
Esteves, J.
Esteves Veiga, J.
Faria Neto, A.
Fazenda, A.
Fernandes Barbosa, W.
Fernandes Ferreira, J.

FERNANDES RUIVO, G.
FERNANDEZ, J.
FERNANDO FISCH, G.
FERREIRA, F.
FERREIRA, L.
FERREIRA NASCIMENTO, G.
FERREIRA SANTIAGO, M.
FERREIRA SANTOS, A.
FERREIRA VIAGI, A.
FERRI-DE-BARROS, J.
FIGUEIREDO NEJAR, E.
FILHO, N.
FILHO, J.
FIORE Jr, M.
FORTES NETO, P.
FORTES SOARES D'AZEVEDO, M.
FORTES VIEGAS, T.
FRANCA, H.
FREIRE, E.
FROIO TOLEDO, M.
GALVÃO VILLELA SANTOS, F.
GALVEIAS LOPES, P.
GARCIA LOPES ROSSI, M.
GERASI CABRAL, R.
GERMANO BASSI, D.
GONÇALVES, A.
GONÇALVES, J.
GONÇALVES, J.
GONÇALVES, M.
GONÇALVES, T.
GONÇALVES CARDOSO, M.
GONÇALVES CONTREIRA, A.
GONÇALVES FILHO, J.
GONÇALVES FRANCO, D.
GOULART, B.
GOULART, V.
GOULART GOUVEA, L.
GOUSAIN MURADE, J.
GRANDINETTI, F.
GUIDI DAMASCENO, A.
GUIMARÃES AZEVEDO, A.
GUIMARÃES FELICIANO, G.
GUIMARÃES FILHO, R.
GUIOTO ABREU, W.
HABITANTE, S.
HAMZAGIC, M.
HENRIQUES LUIS, P.
HIDENORI ENARI, E.
HIROSHI MURAGAKI, W.
INOCENTE, N.
ISRAEL, E.
JOAO BERTOLI, C.
JUNQUEIRA BARBOSA, M.
KAJITA, T.
KALIL KOBBAZ, A.
KASSAB, B.
KATHER NETO, J.
KNUPP RODRIGUES, J.
KOMATSU, M.
LABINAS, A.
LEONEL GALDINO, M.
LETÍCIA ALVES, G.
LIMA, A.
LIMA SALGADO, F.
LIPORONI, P.
LOPES BONATO, L.
LOPES SILVA, J.
LORENZO ACÁCIO, G.
LOURIVAL FERRAZZA, J.
LUCAREVSCHI, B.
LUCCHESI, M.
LUIS NOHARA, E.
LUIZ LOUSADA, S.
LUIZ MARIOTO, J.
LUIZ MONTEIRO, R.
MANDELBAUN, S.
MANFREDINI, C.
MARCELO, J.
MARCHI, A.
MARCHINI, L.
MARCITELLI, R.
MARCOS VALADÃO, M.
MARQUES, R.
MARTIN, I.
MARTINS, N.
MARTINS PRIANTE, A.
MASCARENHAS TORRES, M.
MAURICIO, L.
MAZZEO MACHADO, L.
MEDRANO BALBOA, R.
MELO, G.
MELO VIÉGAS, R.
MENDES FARIA, G.
MERLI LAMOSA, D.
MISAILIDIS LERENA, M.
MONEGATTI MATTEI, S.
MONTEIRO, R.
MONTEIRO ARREZZE, B.
MONTEIRO ILKIU, A.
MOREIRA, M.
MOREIRA, M.
MOREIRA PINTO, J.
MOREIRA ROSA, L.
MORELLI, A.
MOURA LINDEGGER, L.
MOURÃO, F.
MOURE CÍCERO, C.
MUNIZ Jr, J.
NATALINO PEREIRA, E.
NAVES SILVA, T.
NERY CONDE MALTA, F.
NETO, J.
NOGUEIRA ASSAD, M.
NOGUEIRA REZENDE, P.
NORDI, J.
OKAMOTO, T.
OSVALDO CIMASCHI NETO, E.
PAIVA VIANNA, L.
PALLOS, D.
PANZA, E.
PARANHOS GOMES DOS SANTOS, E.
PARQUET BIZARRIA, F.
PARQUET BIZARRIA, J.
PASKEWICKS, V.
PASTOUKHOV, V.
PEDRO PERES, M.
PELEGRINE GUIMARÃES, D.
PENA MATOS, A.
PEREIRA, S.
PEREIRA, T.
PEREIRA CINTRA, S.
PEREIRA IEMINI, M.
PEREIRA LEÃO, M.
PEREIRA LEITE, M.
PERONDI FORTES, N.
PESCATORE ALVES, C.
PIMENTEL, E.
PINHEIRO WERNECK, M.
PINTO, C.
PINTO, R.
PIRES CLEMENTE, R.
PIRTOUSCHEG, N.
PRADO SCHERMA, A.
PRATA ROCHA, R.
PRATI, A.
PROLUNGATTI CESAR, M.
PÚPIO MARCONDES, M.
QUERIDO, A.
QUERIDO GUISARD, R.
RAMOS ANALIO, R.
RAMOS MOTA, J.
REGINA NAMURA, M.
REMBRANDT GUTLICH, G.
RESCHILIAN, P.
REZENDE, M.
RIBEIRO LARA, L.
RIBEIRO PEÃO, G.
RIBEIRO QUINTAIROS, P.
RIZZARDI MAZZINI, X.
ROBERTO FURLAN, M.
ROBERTO MARTINS, M.
ROCHA, R.
ROCHA Jr, A.
RODRIGUES, A.
RODRIGUES, D.
RODRIGUES, E.
RODRIGUES FERNANDES, T.
RODRIGUES PELOGIA, A.
RODRIGUES TEIXEIRA, F.
ROSSI, R.
RUGGERI, C.
RUV LEMES, M.
SABA, E.
SALIM MINHOTO, E.
SALLES CAUDURO, R.
SALVIO CARRIJO, D.
SARTORI, A.
SASHAKI, S.
SEBE TONZAR, E.
SERAFIM, A.
SERAFINI, F.
SILVA ARTUSI, M.
SILVA LAGE MARQUES, J.
SILVA MEDEIROS, H.
SIMÕES ARAUJO, E.
SOARES, R.
SOUZA LOPES E SILVA, A.
SREE VANI, G.
STEINLE CAMARGO, L.
STELLATI, C.
STEVANATO, E.
TADEU IAOCHITE, R.
TÁPIAS OLIVEIRA, E.
TEIXEIRA, M.
TEIXEIRA BATISTA, G.
TEIXEIRA BRANCO COSTA, M.
TEIXEIRA BRAZÃO, C.
TEIXEIRA SOARES, M.
TONINI, A.
TUBALDINI SOUZA, M.
TUFFI, G.
UENO, M.
URRUCHI, W.
VASCONCELOS, M.
VELLOSO, V.
VENEZIANI PASIN, L.
VIANNA BRITO, E.
VIEIRA, C.
VIEIRA BASILI, M.
VIEIRA FISCH, S.
VILLELA CHAGAS, R.
VOLTOLINI, J.
WANDERLEY TERNI, A.
WELLAUSEN DIAS, N.
YOKO UYENO, E.
ZERAIK ARMANI, M.
ZÖLLNER, N.

ATTACHED RESEARCH INSTITUTES

Basic Institute of Biosciences: tel. (12) 3629-7909; Dir Profa Dra ANA JÚLIA URIAS DOS SANTOS ARAÚJO.

Basic Institute of Exact Sciences: tel. (12) 3629-3804; Dir EURICO ARRUDA FILHO.

Basic Institute of Human Sciences: tel. (12) 3622-2474; Dir MAURÍLIO JOSÉ DE OLIVEIRA CAMELLO

UNIVERSIDADE DO OESTE PAULISTA—UNOESTE (University of West São Paulo—UNOESTE)

Rua José Bongiovani 700, Presidente Prudente, SP 19050-920

Telephone: (18) 3229-2000
E-mail: contact@unoeste.br
Internet: www.unoeste.br

Founded 1972
Private control
Language of instruction: Portuguese
Academic year: February to December

Rector: ANA CARDOSO MAIA DE OLIVEIRA LIMA
Vice-Rector: ANA CRISTINA DE OLIVEIRA LIMA
Dean for Academic Affairs: Dr JOSÉ EDUARDO CRESTE
Dean for Admin. Affairs: MARIA REGINA DE OLIVEIRA LIMA
Dean for Extension and Community Action: ANGELITA IBANHES DE ALMEIDA OLIVEIRA LIMA
Dean for Research and Graduate Studies: Dr ADILSON EDUARDO GUELFI
Library of 49,053 vols, 155,813 copies, 95,664 periodicals
Number of teachers: 828
Number of students: 12,300

Publications: *Colloquium Agrariae* (2 a year, online, revistas.unoeste.br/revistas/ojs/index.php/ca), *Colloquium Exactarum* (2 a year, online, revistas.unoeste.br/revistas/ojs/index.php/ce), *Colloquium Humanarum* (2 a year, online, revistas.unoeste.br/revistas/ojs/index.php/ch), *Colloquium Vitae* (2 a year, online, revistas.unoeste.br/revistas/ojs/index.php/cv), *Identidade Científica* (2 a year, online, revistas.unoeste.br/revistas/ojs/index.php/ic)>

UNIVERSIDADE DO SAGRADO CORAÇÃO
(Sacred Heart University)

Rua Irmã Arminda 10–50, Bauru, SP 17011-160
Telephone: (14) 2107-7000
E-mail: reitoria@usc.br
Internet: www.usc.br
Founded 1953
Academic year: February to November
Private control
Rector: Dra Sis. SUSANA DE JESUS FADEL
Vice-Rector and Pro-Rector for Academic Affairs: Dra Sis. ILDA BASSO
Pro-Rector for Admin.: Profa Sis MARIA INÊS PÉRICO
Pro-Rector for Extension and Community Action: Profa Sis JUCÉLIA MELO
Pro-Rector for Research and Postgraduate Affairs: Profa Dra SANDRA DE OLIVREIRA SAES
Librarian: ALESSANDRA CARRIEL VIEIRA
Library of 243,883 vols
Number of teachers: 300
Number of students: 6,000
Publications: *Boletim Cultural* (1 a year), *Cadernos de Divulgação Cultural* (1 a year), *Revista Camoniana*, *Revista Mimesis* (2 a year), *Revista Salusvita* (in Portuguese and English)

DEANS

College of Business Administration: Ir MARIA INÊS PÉRICO
College of Liberal Arts: Ir MARIA APARECIDA LIMA
College of Sciences: Ir LEILA MARIA VIEIRA
College of Social Sciences: DANIELA LUCHESSI
Committee on Ethics: Dr RODRIGO RICCI VIVAN
Lato Sensu Courses: EDSON CARLOS VIEIRA DE MELO
Research: Dr RODRIGO RICCI VIVAN
Scientific Initiation Projects: Dr ALBERTO DE VITTA

UNIVERSIDADE DO VALE DO PARAÍBA
(University of Vale do Paraíba)

Av. Shishima Hifumi 2911, Urbanova, São José dos Campos, SP 12244-000
Telephone: (12) 3947-1000
Internet: www.univap.br
Founded 1992
Private control
Rector: Prof. Dr JAIR CÂNDIDO DE MELO
Vice-Rector: Profa Dra SANDRA MARIA FONSECA DA COSTA
Pro-Rector for Graduation, Continuing Education and Evaluation: Prof. SAMUEL ROBERTO XIMENES COSTA
Pro-Rector for Research and Postgraduate Affairs: Profa Dra SANDRA MARIA FONSECA DA COSTA
Pro-Rector for Univ.-Society Integration: Profa Dra MARIA REGINA DE AQUINO SILVA
Library of 59,000 vols, 539 periodicals
Number of teachers: 269
Number of students: 6,255
Publication: *Revista UniVap*

UNIVERSIDADE ESTADUAL DE CAMPINAS
(State University of Campinas)

Cidade Universitária 'Zeferino Vaz', Campinas, SP 13083-970
Telephone: (19) 3521-7000
E-mail: gabinete@rei.unicamp.br
Internet: www.unicamp.br
Founded 1966
State control
Academic year: March to December
Rector: Prof. Dr JOSÉ TADEU JORGE
Pro-Rector for Extension and Community Action: Prof. Dr JOÃO FREDERICO DA COSTA AZEVEDO MEYER
Pro-Rector for Postgraduate Affairs: Profa Dra ITALA MARIA LOFFREDO D'OTTAVIANO
Pro-Rector for Research: Profa Dra GLÁUCIA MARIA PASTORE
Pro-Rector for Undergraduate Affairs: Prof. LUÍS ALBERTO MAGNA
Pro-Rector for Univ. Devt: Profa Dra TERESA DIB ZAMBON ATVARS
Number of teachers: 1,800
Number of students: 28,000
Publications: *Jornal da Unicamp* (12 a year), *Revista Aulas*

UNIVERSIDADE ESTADUAL PAULISTA 'JULIO DE MESQUITA FILHO'
(São Paulo State University)

Av. Eng. Luiz Edmundo Carrijo Coube, 1000, Bauru, São Paulo, SP 17033-360
Telephone: (11) 3252-0521
E-mail: arex@reitoria.unesp.br
Internet: www.unesp.br
Founded 1976, incorporating previous existing faculties in São Paulo State
State control
Academic year: February to December
Affiliated faculties: faculty of technology, Zona Leste and faculty of technology, Guaratinguetá
Rector: JULIO CEZAR DURIGAN
Vice-Rector: MARILZA VIEIRA CUNHA RUDGE
Pro-Rector for Admin.: Prof. Dr CARLOS ANTONIO GAMERO
Pro-Rector for Extension: Profa MARIÂNGELA SPOTTI LOPES FUJITA
Pro-Rector for Postgraduate Affairs: EDUARDO KOKUBUN
Pro-Rector for Research: Profa Dra MARIA JOSÉ SOARES MENDES GIANNINI
Pro-Rector for Undergraduate Affairs: Prof. Dr LAURENCE DUARTE COLVARA
Librarian: MARGARET ALVES ANTUNES
Library: 30 libraries
Number of teachers: 3,300
Number of students: 44,000
Publications: *Alfa* (linguistics, 1 a year), *Alimentos e Nutrição* (1 a year), *ARBS* (biomedical sciences, 1 a year), *ARTunesp* (1 a year), *Científica* (agronomy, 1 a year), *Didática* (education, 1 a year), *Eclética Química* (chemistry, 1 a year), *Geociências* (2 a year), *História* (1 a year), *Naturália* (1 a year), *Perspectivas* (1 a year), *Revista de Ciêcias Farmacêuticas* (2 a year), *Revista de Engenharia e Ciências Aplicadas* (1 a year), *Revista de Geografia* (geography, 1 a year), *Revista de Matemática e Nutrição* (1 a year), *Revista de Odontologia da UNESP* (2 a year), *Transformação* (philosophy, 1 a year), *Veterinária e Zootecnia* (1 a year)

DIRECTORS

Araçatuba Campus:

Faculty of Dentistry (Rua José Bonifácio 1193, Araçatuba, SP 16015-050; tel. (18) 3636-3200; e-mail diretor@foa.unesp.br; internet www.foa.unesp.br):

Prof. ANA MARIA PIRES SOUBHIA

Araraquara Campus:

Faculty of Dentistry (R. Humaitá 1680, Araraquara, SP 14801-903; tel. (16) 3301-6300; e-mail diretor@foar.unesp.br; internet www.foar.unesp.br):

Profa Dra ANDREIA AFFONSO BARRETTO MONTANDON

Faculty of Pharmaceutical Sciences (Rodovia Araraquara–Jaú km 1, Araraquara, SP 14801-902; tel. (16) 3301-6880; e-mail diretor@fcfar.unesp.br; internet www.fcfar.unesp.br):

Profa Dra CLEOPATRA DA SILVA PLANETA

Faculty of Sciences and Humanities (Rodovia Araraquara–Jaú km 1, Araraquara, SP 14800-901; tel. (16) 3301-6200; e-mail diretor@fclar.unesp.br; internet www.fclar.unesp.br):

Prof. Dr ARNALDO CORTINA

Institute of Chemistry (R. Prof. Francisco Degni s/n, Bairro Quitandinha, Araraquara, SP 14801-970; tel. (16) 3301-6600; e-mail diretor@foar.unesp.br; internet www.iq.unesp.br):

Prof. Dr LEONARDO PEZZA

Assis Campus:

Faculty of Sciences and Humanities (Av. Dom Antonio 2100, Assis, SP 19806-900; tel. (18) 3302-5800; e-mail diretor@assis.unesp.br; internet www.assis.unesp.br):

Dr IVAN ESPERANÇA ROCHA

Bauru Campus:

Faculty of Architecture, Arts and Communication (Avda Eng. Luiz Edmundo Carrijo Coube s/n, Bauru, SP 17033-360; tel. (14) 3103-6000; e-mail diretor@faac.unesp.brr; internet www.faac.unesp.br):

Prof. Dr NILSON GHIRARDELLO

Faculty of Engineering (Eng. Luiz Edmundo Carrijo Coube s/n, Bauru, SP 17033-360; tel. (14) 3103-6000; e-mail diretor@feb.unesp.br; internet www.feb.unesp.br):

Prof. Dr EDSON ANTONIO CAPELLO SOUSA

Faculty of Sciences (Eng. Luiz Edmundo Carrijo Coube s/n, Bauru, SP 17033-360; tel. (14) 3103-6000; e-mail diretor@fc.unesp.br; internet www.fc.unesp.br):

Prof. DAGMAR AP. CYNTHIA FRANÇA HUNGER

Botucatu Campus:

Faculty of Agronomical Sciences (R. José de Barros Barbosa, 1780, Botucatu, SP 18610-307; tel. (14) 3811-7100; e-mail diretor@fca.unesp.br; internet www.fca.unesp.br):

Dr JOÃO CARLOS CURY SAAD

Faculty of Medicine (Distrito de Rubião Júnior s/n, Botucatu, SP 18618-970; tel. (14) 3811-6000; e-mail diretor@fmb.unesp.br; internet www.fmb.unesp.br):

Prof. Dr PASCOAL

Faculty of Veterinary Medicine and Animal Husbandry (Distrito de Rubião Júnior s/n, Botucatu, SP 18618-000; tel. (14) 3811-6002; e-mail diretor@fmvz.unesp.br; internet www.fmvz.unesp.br):

Prof. Dr JOSÉ PAES DE ALMEIDA NOGUEIRA PINTO

Institute of Biosciences (Distrito de Rubião Júnior s/n, Botucatu, SP 18618-000; tel. (14) 3811-6000; e-mail diretor@ibb.unesp.br; internet www.ibb.unesp.br):

Profa Dra MARIA DALVA CESARIO

Dracena Campus:

Dracena Campus (Rod. Comte. João Ribeiro de Barros, km 651, Métropole, SP 17900-000; tel. (18) 3821-8200; internet www.dracena.unesp.br):

Prof. Dr JOSÉ ANTONIO MARQUES

Franca Campus:

Faculty of History, Law and Social Services (R. Major Claudiano 1.488, Franca, SP 14400-690; tel. (16) 3711-1804; e-mail diretor@franca.unesp.br; internet www.franca.unesp.br):

Prof. Dr HELIO BORGHI

Guaratinguetá Campus:

Faculty of Engineering (Av. Dr Ariberto Pereira da Cunha 333, Guaratinguetá, SP 12500-000; tel. (12) 3123-2800; e-mail direcao@feg.unesp.br; internet www.feg.unesp.br):

Prof. Dr TÂNIA C. A. M. DE AZEVEDO

Ilha Solteira Campus:

Faculty of Engineering (Av. Brasil Centro 56, Ilha Solteira, SP 15385-000; tel. (18) 3743-1000; e-mail gd@feis.unesp.br; internet www.feis.unesp.br):

Prof. Dr VICENTE LOPES JUNIOR

Itapeva Campus:

Itapeva Campus (R. Geraldo Alckmin 519, Itapeva, SP 18049-010; tel. (15) 3524-9100; internet www.itapeva.unesp.br):

Prof. Dr MARCUS TADEU TIBÚRCO GONÇALVES

Jaboticabal Campus:

Faculty of Agricultural and Veterinary Sciences (Prof. Paulo Donato Castellane s/n, Jaboticabal, SP 14884-900; tel. (16) 322-4250; e-mail diretor@fcav.unesp.br; internet www.fcav.unesp.br):

Prof. Dr ROBERVAL VIEIRA

Marília Campus:

Faculty of Philosophy and Sciences (Av. Hygino Muzzi Filho 737, Marília, SP 17525-900; tel. (14) 3402-1300; e-mail diretor@marilia.unesp.br; internet www.marilia.unesp.br):

Prof. Dr MARIA CANDIDA SOARES DEL MASSO

Ourinhos Campus:

Ourinhos Campus (R. Dom José Marello 749, Vila Perino, SP 19911-760; tel. (14) 3302-5800; e-mail joaolima@ourinhos.unesp.br; internet www.ourinhos.unesp.br):

Prof. Dr JOÃO LIMA SANT'ANNA NETTO

Presidente Prudente Campus:

Faculty of Science and Technology, Presidente Prudente (R. Roberto Simonsen 305, Presidente Prudente, SP 19060-900; tel. (18) 229-5300; e-mail dirfct@prudente.unesp.br; internet www.prudente.unesp.br):

Prof. Dr NERI ALVES

Registro Campus:

Registro Campus (R. Tamekeshi Takano 05, Centro, SP 11900-000; tel. (13) 3822-2230; e-mail benez@registro.unesp.br; internet www.registro.unesp.br):

Prof. SÉRGIO HUGO BENEZ

Rio Claro Campus:

Institute of Biosciences (Av. 24-A 1515, Bela Vista, Rio Claro, SP 13500-900; tel. (19) 3526-1400; e-mail dirib@rc.unesp.br; internet www.rc.unesp.br):

Prof. Dr AMILTON FERREIRA

Institute of Geosciences and Exact Sciences (Rua Dez 2527, Rio Claro, SP 13500-230; tel. (19) 534-0326; e-mail diretor@caviar.igce.unesp.br):

Profa Dra MARIA RITA CAETANO CHANG

Rosana Campus:

Rosana Campus (Av. dos Barrageiros s/n, Primavera, SP 19274-000; tel. (18) 3284-9201; e-mail coordenadoria@rosana.unesp.br; internet www.rosana.unesp.br):

Prof. Dr MESSIAS MENGHETTI JÚNIOR

São José do Rio Preto Campus:

Institute of Biosciences, Humanities and Exact Sciences (Ruo Cristóvão Colombo 2265, São José do Rio Preto, SP 15054-000; tel. (17) 221-2200; e-mail diretor@ibilce.unesp.br; internet www.ibilce.unesp.br):

Profa Dr JOHNNY RIZZIERI OLIVEIRA

São José dos Campos Campus:

Faculty of Dentistry (Av. Engenheiro Francisco José Longo 777, São José dos Campos, SP 12245-000; tel. (12) 3947-9000; e-mail diretor@fosjc.unesp.br; internet www.fosjc.unesp.br):

Profa Dra MARIA AMÉLIA MÁXIMO DE ARAÚJO

São Paulo Campus:

Institute of Arts (Rua Dom Luiz Lasagna 400, Ipiranga, São Paulo, SP 04266-030; tel. (11) 274-4733; e-mail diretor@ia.unesp.br; internet www.ia.unesp.br):

Profa Dra MARISA TRENCH O. FONTERRADA

Institute of Theoretical Physics (Rua Pamplona 145, São Paulo, SP 01405-900; tel. (11) 3177-9090; e-mail gkrein@iff.unesp.br; internet www.iff.unesp.br):

Profa Dr GASTÃO I. KREIN

São Vicente Campus:

São Vicente Campus (Praça Infante Don Henrique s/n, São Vicente, SP 011330-205; tel. (13) 3569-9403; e-mail coordenadoria@csv.unesp.br; internet www.csv.unesp.br):

Prof. Dr MARCELO ANTONIO AMARO PINHEIRO

Sorocaba Campus:

Sorocaba Campus (Av. Três de Marco 511, Alto da Boa Vista, SP 18087-180; tel. (15) 3238-3401; e-mail direcao@sorocaba.unesp.br; internet www.sorocaba.unesp.br):

Prof. Dr GALDENORO BOTURA JÚNIOR

Tupã Campus:

Tupã Campus (Av. Domingas da Costa Lopes 780, Tupã, SP 17602-660; tel. (14) 3404-4200; e-mail ejsimon@tupa.unesp.br; internet www.tupa.unesp.br):

Prof. Dr ELIAS JOSÉ MARELLO

COMPLEMENTARY UNITS

Aquaculture Centre: Rodovia Carlos Tonanni km 5, Jaboticabal, SP 14870-000; tel. (16) 3203-2500; e-mail fatima@caunesp.unesp.br; Dir Profa Dra ELISABETH CRISCUOLO URBINATI.

Centre for Education and Cultural Radio and Television: Av. Eng. Luiz Edmundo Carrijo Coube s/n°, Bauru, SP 17033-360; tel. (14) 230-5486; e-mail dir-rad@faac.unesp.br; Dir Prof. Dr MURILO CÉSAR SOARES.

Centre for Environmental Studies (CEA): Av. 24-A 1.515, Rio Claro, SP 13506-900; tel. (19) 534-7298; e-mail cea@life.ibrc.unesp.br; Dir Prof. Dr NIVAR GOBBI.

Centre for the Study of Venom and Venomous Animals (CEVAP): Distrito de Rubião Junior s/n°, Botucatu, SP 18610-000; tel. (14) 6821-2121; e-mail cevap@botunet.com.br; Dir Prof. Dr CARLOS ALBERTO DE MAGALHÃES LOPES.

Centre for Tropical Root Crops (CERAT): Fazenda Experimental Lageado, CP 237, Botucatu, SP 18603-970; tel. (14) 6802-7158; e-mail seccerat@fca.unesp.br; internet www.cerat.unesp.br; Dir Profa Dra ELISABETH CRISCUOLO URBINATI.

Centre of Excellence in Dental Care (CAOE): Rod. Marechal Rondon km 527, Araçatuba, SP 16015-050; tel. (18) 622-4125; e-mail saguiar@foa.unesp.br; Dir Profa Dra SANDRA MARIA H. C. AVILA DE AGUIAR.

Institute of Meteorological Research (IPMet): Av. Eng Luiz Edmundo Carrijo Coube s/n, Bauru, SP 17033-360; tel. (14)3103-6028; e-mail diretoria@ipmet.ipmet.unesp.br; internet www.ipmet.unesp.br; Dir Prof. Dr LUIS VICENTE DE ANDRADE SCALVI; Dean Prof. ROVERTO VICENTE CALHEIROS.

Isotopes Centre: Distrito de Rubião Júnior s/n, Botucatu, SP 18618-000; tel. (14) 6821-1171; e-mail ducatti@ibb.unesp.br; Dir Prof. Dr CARLOS DUCATTI

UNIVERSIDADE FEDERAL DE SÃO CARLOS
(Federal University of São Carlos)

Rodovia Washington Luiz, km 235, Monjolinho, SP 310, São Carlos, SP 13565-905

Telephone: (16) 3351-8111
E-mail: reitoria@ufscar.br
Internet: www.ufscar.br

Founded 1970
federal control
Language of instruction: Portuguese
Academic year: March to December

Campuses in São Carlos, Sorocaba and Araras

Chancellor: ALOIZIO MERCADANTE
Rector: Prof. Dr TARGINO DE ARAÚJO FILHO
Vice-Rector: Prof. Dr ADILSON JESUS APARECIDO DE OLIVEIRA
Pro-Rector for Extension: Profa Dra CLÁUDIA MARIA SIMÕES MARTINEZ
Provost for Extension: Profa Dra MARINA SILVEIRA PALHARES
Provost for Postgraduate Studies: Prof. Dr BERNARDO ARANTES DO NASCIMENTO TEIXEIRA
Provost for Research: Prof. Dr CLAUDIO SHYINTI KIMINAMI
Provost for Undergraduate Studies: Profa Dra EMILIA FREITAS DE LIMA
Librarian: LIGIA MARIA SILVA E SOUZA

Library of 191,500 vols
Number of teachers: 981
Number of students: 12,094

Publications: *Cadernos de Terapia Ocupacional, Click Ciência, Revista Brasileira de Fisioterapia, Revista Eletrônica de Educação, Revista Gestão e Produção, Revista Olhar, Revista Universitária do Audiovisual*

UNIVERSIDADE FEDERAL DE SÃO PAULO
(Federal University of São Paulo)

Rua Sena Madureira, 1500, 5° andar, São Paulo, SP 04021-001

Telephone: (11) 5576-4000
E-mail: reitoria@unifesp.br
Internet: www.unifesp.br

Founded 1933 fmrly Escola Paulista de Medicina

Rector: SORAYA SOUBHI SMAILI
Vice-Rector: VALERIA PETRI
Pro-Rector for Admin.: JANINE SCHIRMER
Pro-Rector for Extension: FLORIANITA COELHO BRAGA CAMPOS
Pro-Rector for Planning: ESPER ABRAO CAVALHEIRO
Pro-Rector for Postgraduates and Research: MARIA LUCIA OLIVEIRA DE SOUZA FORMIGONI
Pro-Rector for Student Affairs: ANDREA RABINOVICI
Pro-Rector for Undergraduates: MARIA ANGÉLICA PEDRA MINHOTO

Library of 9,000 vols, 8,079 journals, 10,600 theses
Number of teachers: 650
Number of students: 4,000

Publications: *Pensata, Revista Internacional de Humanidades Médicas* (in Portuguese and Spanish), *Revista Neurociências*

UNIVERSIDADE GUARULHOS
(Guarulhos University)

Praça Cap. Alberto Mendes Júnior, 88 Centro, Guarulhos, SP 07023-070
Telephone: (11) 2475-8300
E-mail: reitor@ung.br
Internet: www.ung.br

Founded 1970
Private control
Language of instruction: Portuguese
Academic year: February to December

Chancellor: Prof. ANTONIO VERONEZI
Rector: Profa Dra LUCIANE LÚCIO PEREIRA
Pro-Rector for Graduate Affairs: MARIO ALBERTO MARCONDES PERITO

Library of 179,424 vols, 840 periodicals
Number of teachers: 1,000
Number of students: 18,000

Publications: *Education Magazine* (2 a year), *Geosciences Magazine* (2 a year), *Health Magazine* (2 a year), *Third Sector Magazine* (2 a year)

UNIVERSIDADE IBIRAPUERA
(Ibirapuera University)

Av. Interlagos, 1329 Chácara Flora, São Paulo, SP 04661-100
Telephone: (11) 5694-7900
E-mail: unib@unib.br
Internet: www.unib.br

Founded 1969
Private control

Rector: JORGE BASTOS
Librarian: PAOLA CARVALHO

Library of 69,000 vols, 1,936 periodicals
Number of teachers: 317
Number of students: 10,829

UNIVERSIDADE METODISTA DE PIRACICABA
(Methodist University of Piracicaba)

Rua Rangel Pestana 762, CP 68, Piracicaba, SP 13400-901
Telephone: (19) 3124-1515
E-mail: falecomreitor@unimep.br
Internet: www.unimep.br

Founded 1881 as Colégio Piracicabano, recognized 1975
Private control
Languages of instruction: Portuguese, Spanish
Academic year: March to December

Rector: Prof. Dr GUSTAVO JACQUES DIAS ALVIM
Pro-Rector for Extension and Community Affairs: Prof. Dr JOSUÉ ADAM LAZIER
Pro-Rector for General Postgraduate Lato Sensu: Prof. CARLOS ALBERTO ZEM
Pro-Rector for Postgraduation and Research: Profa Dra ROSANA MACHER TEODORI
Pro-Rector for Undergraduate Affairs: Profa Dra THERESA BEATRIZ FIGUEIREDO SANTOS
Librarian: REGINA FRACETO

Library of 360,000 vols
Number of teachers: 680
Number of students: 15,000

Publications: *Cadernos de Direito* (law), *Impulso* (humanities and social sciences), *Revista Brasileira de Educação Especial*, *Revista de Ciência e Tecnologia*, *Revista de Odontologia*, *Saúde em Revista*

UNIVERSIDADE METODISTA DE SÃO PAULO
(Methodist University of São Paulo)

R. Alfeu Tavares, 149, Rudge Ramos, CP 5002, São Bernardo do Campo, SP 09641-000
Telephone: (11) 4366-5000
E-mail: reitoria@metodista.br
Internet: www.metodista.br

Founded 1997

Rector: Prof. Dr MARCIO DE MORAES
Vice-Rector: CLOVIS PINTO DE CASTRO
Pro-Rector for Distance Education: LUCIANO SATHLER ROSA GUIMARÃES
Pro-Rector for Extension and Community Affairs: PAULO BESSA DA SILVA
Pro-Rector for Personnel Management and Infrastructure: ELAINE LIMA DE OLIVEIRA
Pro-Rector for Postgraduate Affairs and Research: FÁBIO BOTELHO JOSGRILBERG
Pro-Rector for Undergraduate Affairs: VERA LÚCIA GOUVÊA STIVALETTI

Library of 97,000 vols, 4,900 periodicals
Number of teachers: 537
Number of students: 27,500

Publications: *Revista da Faculdade de Administração e Economia*, *Revista do Curso de Direito*, *Revista Organizações em Contexto*

UNIVERSIDADE METROPOLITANA DE SANTOS
(Metropolitan University of Santos)

Rua da Constituição n° 374, Vila Nova, Santos, SP 11015-470
Telephone: (13) 3226-3400
E-mail: infounimes@unimes.com.br
Internet: www.unimes.com.br

Founded 1968 as Centro de Estudos Unificados Bandeirante; current name adopted 1985
Private control

Rector: Profa RENATA GARCIA DE SIQUEIRA VIEGAS
Pro-Rector for Academic Affairs: Prof. DANIEL CARREIRA

Library of 59,000 vols, 233 periodicals
Number of teachers: 405
Number of students: 5,034

UNIVERSIDADE PAULISTA
(Paulista University)

Rua Dr Bacelar 1212, Vila Clementino, São Paulo, SP 04026-002
Telephone: (11) 5586-4000
Internet: www2.unip.br

Founded 1988
Private control

Rector: Prof. Dr JOÃO CARLOS DI GENIO
Vice-Rector for Extension: Prof. Dr PASCHOAL LAERCIO ARMONIA
Vice-Rector for Planning, Admin. and Finance: Prof. FÁBIO ROMEU DE CARVALHO
Vice-Rector for Postgraduate Affairs and Research: Prof. Dr YUGO OKIDA
Vice-Rector for Undergraduate Affairs: Profa. Dra MARÍLIA ANCONA-LOPEZ
Vice-Rector for Univ. Units: Profa MELÂNIA DALLA TORRE

Library of 1,170,943 vols, 3,300 periodicals
Number of teachers: 2,519
Number of students: 57,064

UNIVERSIDADE PRESBITERIANA MACKENZIE
(Mackenzie Presbyterian University)

Rua da Consolação 930, Consolação, São Paulo, SP 01302-907
Telephone: (11) 2114-8000
E-mail: reitoria@mackenzie.br
Internet: www.mackenzie.br

Founded 1870
Private control
Academic year: March to December

Pres.: Dr MAURICIO MELO DE MENEZES
Vice-Pres.: Dr PEDRO RONZELLI, JR
Rector: Prof. Dr BENEDITO GUIMARÃES AGUIAR NETO
Vice-Rector: Dr MARCEL MENDES
Sec.-Gen.: Prof. NELSON CALLEGARI
Dean for Academic Affairs: Dra ESMERALDA RIZZO
Dean for Extension: Prof. Dr CLEVERSON PEREIRA DE ALMEIDA
Dean for Graduate Courses and Research: Prof. Dr MOISES ARI ZILBER
Librarian: ROSELY BIANCONCINI MULIN

Library of 342,784 vols, 262 periodicals
Number of teachers: 1,488
Number of students: 40,000

Publications: *Horacinho*, *Jornal Análise*, *O Picareta*, *Oráculo*, *Perfil Mackenzie*, *Revista de Engenharia e Computação*, *Revista Mackenzie*, *Revista Psicologia: Teoria e Prática*, *Revista Todas as Letras*

UNIVERSIDADE SANTA CECÍLIA
(St Cecilia University)

Rua Oswaldo Cruz 277, Boqueirão, Santos, SP 11045-907
Telephone: (13) 3202-7101
E-mail: assecom@unisanta.br
Internet: www.unisanta.br

Founded 1961
Private control
Academic year: February to December

Chancellor: Dr MILTON TEIXEIRA
Pres.: Dra LÚCIA M. TEIXEIRA FURLANI
Vice-Pres.: Profa MARIA CECÍLIA P. TEIXEIRA
Rector: Dra SÍLVIA ÂNGELA TEIXEIRA PENTEADO
Pro-Rector for Academics: Profa ZULEIKA DE A. SENGER GONÇALVES
Pro-Rector for Admin.: Dr MARCELO PIRILO TEIXEIRA
Pro-Rector for Community: Prof. EMÍLIA MARIA PIRILO
Chief Librarian: ANA MARIA RACCIOPI SILVEIRA

Library of 107,000 vols
Number of teachers: 640
Number of students: 13,000

Publications: *Ceciliana*, *Revista de Estudo*

UNIVERSIDADE SÃO JUDAS TADEU
(University of São Judas Tadeu)

Rua Taquari 546, Mooca, São Paulo, SP 03166-000
Telephone: (11) 2799-1677
Internet: www.usjt.br

Founded 1985
Private control

Chancellor: Prof. ALZIRA ALTENFELDER SILVA MESQUITA
Rector: Prof. JOSÉ REINALDO ALTENFELDER SILVA MESQUITA
Pro-Rector for Extension: Prof. LILIAN BRANDO GARCIA MESQUITA
Pro-Rector for Research and Postgraduate Affairs: Prof. ALBERTO MESQUITA FILHO
Pro-Rector for Undergraduate Affairs: Prof. LUÍS ANTÔNIO BAFFILE LEONI

Library of 70,000 vols, 2,066 periodicals
Number of teachers: 733
Number of students: 18,410

Publications: *Integração* (4 a year), *Revista Plural Digitalizada*

UNIVERSITY CENTRES

CENTRO REGIONAL UNIVERSITÁRIO DE ESPÍRITO SANTO DO PINHAL

Av. Helio Vergueiro Leite, S/N, Jardim Universitário, Espìrito Santo do Pinhal, SP
Telephone: (19) 3651-9600
E-mail: atendimento@unipinhal.edu.br
Internet: www.unipinhal.edu.br

Rector: Dr ELISEU MARTINS

Library of 90,000 vols

CENTRO UNIVERSITÁRIO ADVENTISTA DE SÃO PAULO

Estrada de Itapecerica, 5859, Capão Redondo, São Paulo, SP 05858-001
Telephone: (11) 2128-6000
E-mail: faleconosco-sp@unasp.edu.br
Internet: www.unasp.edu.br
Founded 1923
Rector: EULER PEREIRA BAHIA
Pro-Rector for Admin.: ÉLNIO ÁLVARES DE FREITAS
Pro-Rector for Graduate Affairs: SILVIA CRISTINA DE OLIVEIRA QUADROS
Pro-Rector for Research, Postgraduate Affairs and Extension: TÂNIA DENISE KUNTZE
Sec.-Gen.: MARCELO FRANCA ALVES

CENTRO UNIVERSITÁRIO ANHANGÜERA DE SÃO PAULO

Estr. do Campo Limpo, 288 - Jardim São Luís, São Paulo, SP 05777-000
Telephone: (11) 2268-0010
E-mail: assessoria@anhanguera.com
Founded 2005
Dir: LINEIA VEZZO
Library of 8,153 vols

CENTRO UNIVERSITÁRIO BELAS ARTES DE SÃO PAULO

Rua Dr. Álvaro Alvim, 90, Vila Mariana, São Paulo, SP 04018-010
Telephone: (11) 5576-7300
E-mail: relacionamento@belasartes.br
Internet: www.belasartes.br
Founded 1925
CEO and Rector: Prof. Dr PAUL ANTONIO GOMES CARDIM
Publication: *Revista Belas Artes*

CENTRO UNIVERSITÁRIO CAPITAL

Av. Paes de Barros, 2761, São Paulo, SP, 03149-100
Telephone: (11) 2065-1000
Internet: www.unicapital.edu.br
Founded 1969 as Faculdade Pais de Barros, present status 1999
Rector: Dr ADRIANO AUGUSTO FERNANDES

CENTRO UNIVERSITÁRIO CATÓLICO SALESIANO AUXILIUM
(Catholic Auxilium Salesian University Centre)

Rodoviária Teotônio Vilela, 3821, Jardim Alvorada, Araçatuba, SP, 16400-505
Telephone: (18) 3636-5252
E-mail: unisalesiano@salesiano-ata.br
Internet: www.unisalesiano.edu.br
Founded 2006
Rector: Fr PAUL FERNANDO VENDRAME
Pro-Rector for Teaching, Research and Extension: Prof. HELOISA HELENA DA SILVA ROVERY

CENTRO UNIVERSITÁRIO CENTRAL PAULISTA

Rua Pedro Bianchi, 111, Vila Alps, São Carlos, SP 13570-300
Telephone: (16) 3363-2111
Internet: www.unicep.edu.br
Founded 1972
Rector: Prof. APARECIDO NERES SANTANA
Publications: *Revista Multiciência*, *Revista UniPaulistana* (2 a year)

CENTRO UNIVERSITÁRIO DA FUNDAÇÃO EDUCACIONAL DE BARRETOS

Av. Prof. Roberto Frade Monte, 389 - Aeroporto Barretos, São Paulo, SP 14783-226
Telephone: (17) 3321-6411
E-mail: reitoria@feb.br
Internet: www.feb.br
Rector: Prof. Dr REGINALDO DA SILVA
Pro-Rector for Extension and Culture: Profa MARIA PAULA BARCELLOS DE CARVALHO
Pro-Rector for Graduate Affairs: Profa Dra SISSI KAWAI MARCOS
Pro-Rector for Postgraduate Affairs and Research: Prof. Dr FERNANDA SCARMATO DE ROSA
Publications: *Ciência e Cultura*, *Revista Eletrônica de Direito Febre*

CENTRO UNIVERSITÁRIO DA FUNDAÇÃO EDUCACIONAL INACIANA PE SABÓIA DE MEDEIROS

Rua Tamandaré, 688, São Paulo, MG 01525-000
Telephone: (11) 3274-5200
Internet: www.fei.edu.br
Founded 1945
Rector: Prof. Dr FÁBIO DO PRADO
Vice-Rector for Extension and Community Activities: Profa Dra RIVANA BASSO FABBRI MARINO
Vice-Rector for Teaching and Research: Prof. Dr MARCELO ANTONIO PAVANELLO
Publication: *Revista Domínio FEI*

CENTRO UNIVERSITÁRIO DAS FACULDADES ASSOCIADAS DE ENSINO FAE

Largo Engenheiro Paulo de Almeida Sandeville, 15, Jardim Santo André, São João da Boa Vista, SP 13870-377
Telephone: (19) 3623-3022
E-mail: secretaria@fae.br
Internet: www.fae.br
Founded 1961 as Faculdade de Ciências Econômicas de São João da Boa Vista, current status 2001
Rector: Prof. Dr. FRANCISCO DE ASSIS CARVALHO ARTEN
Vice-Rector: Profa Dra MARIA HELENA CIRNE DE TOLEDO

CENTRO UNIVERSITÁRIO DE ARARAS 'DR. EDMUNDO ULSON'

Av. Ernani Lacerda de Oliveira, 100, Parque Santa Cândida, Araras, São Paulo, SP 13603-112
Telephone: (19) 3321-8000
Internet: www.unar.edu.br
Founded 1971
Rector: Profa MARIA TEREZINHA PIRES BARBOSA ULSON
Vice-Rector: Prof. Dr JOSÉ MARTA FILHO

CENTRO UNIVERSITÁRIO DE FRANCA

Av. Major Nicácio, 2433 Bairro São José, São Paulo, SP 14401-135
Telephone: (16) 3713-4688
E-mail: facef@facef.br
Internet: site.unifacef.com.br
Founded 1951
Rector: Prof. Dr ALFREDO JOSÉ MACHADO NETO
Vice-Rector: Prof. Dr PAULO DE TARSO OLIVEIRA
Pro-Rector for Academics: Prof. Dr SHEILA FERNANDES PIMENTA E OLIVEIRA
Pro-Rector for Community Affairs and Extension: Prof. Dr MELISSA FRANCHINI CAVALCANTI BANDOS

CENTRO UNIVERSITÁRIO DE JALES

Av. Francisco Jales, 1851, Jales, SP 15700-000
Telephone: (17) 3622-1620
Internet: www.unijales.edu.br
Founded 1967
Rector: MARIA CHRISTINA F. S. BERNARDO
Library of 34,000 vols

CENTRO UNIVERSITÁRIO DE LINS

Av. Nicolau Zarvos, 1925, Lins, SP 16401-905
Telephone: (14) 3533-3200
E-mail: unilins@unilins.edu.br
Internet: www.unilins.edu.br
Founded 2001
Rector: Prof. MILTON LÉO

Sergipe

In Sergipe, there are nine faculties, one centre for technological education and two higher schools or institutes.

UNIVERSITIES

UNIVERSIDADE FEDERAL DE SERGIPE
(Federal University of Sergipe)

Cidade Universitária, Av. Marechal Rondon s/n, Jardim Rosa Elze, São Cristóvão, SE 49100-000
Telephone: (79) 2105-6600
E-mail: internationalcommunication@ufs.br
Internet: www.ufs.br
Founded 1967
federal control
Language of instruction: Portuguese
Academic year: May to February
Centres of applied social sciences, biological and health sciences, education and human sciences, exact sciences and technology; also centre for distance higher education
Rector: Prof. ANGELO ROBERTO ANTONIOLLI
Vice-Rector: Prof. ANDRÉ MAURÍCIO CONCEIÇÃO DE SOUZA
Pro-Rector for Admin.: ABEL SMITH MENEZES
Pro-Rector for Extension and Community Affairs: Profa Dra MARIA DA CONCEIÇÃO ALMEIDA VASCONCELOS
Pro-Rector for Postgraduate Affairs and Research: MARCUS EUGÊNIO OLIVEIRA LIMA
Pro-Rector for Student Affairs: Profa Dra MARIA LÚCIA MACHADO ARANHA
Pro-Rector for Undergraduate Affairs: Prof. Dr JONATAS SILVA MENESES
Central Library Dir: ZERLAIDE PIMENTEL
Library of 195,260 vols, 5,314 periodical titles
Number of teachers: 400
Number of students: 5,900
Publications: *Jornal* (26 a year), *Revista* (irregular), *Revista EDaPECI* (2 a year)

UNIVERSIDADE TIRADENTES
(Tiradentes University)

Rua Lagarto, 264, Aracajú, SE 49010-390
Telephone: (79) 3218-2100
E-mail: asscom@unit.br
Internet: www.unit.br
Founded 1972
Private control
Language of instruction: Portuguese
Academic year: January to December

Rector: JOUBERTO UCHÔA DE MENDONÇA
Vice-Rector: AMÉLIA MARIA CERQUEIRA UCHOA
Superintendent-Gen.: JOUBERTO UCHÔA DE MENDONÇA, JR
Superintendent for Academics: EDUARDO PEIXOTO ROCHA
Superintendent for Admin. and Finance: ANDRÉ TAVARES ANDRADE
Superintendent for Institutional Relations and Market: IHANMARCK DAMASCENO DOS SANTOS
Dir for Libraries: MARIA EVELI DE BARROS FREIRE
Library of 35,650 vols, 15,325 periodicals
Number of teachers: 400
Number of students: 11,700
Publications: *Caderno de Graduação* (2 a year), *Ideias e Inovação* (2 a year), *Interfaces Científica* (4 a year), *Revista Fragmenta* (3 a year)

Tocantins

In Tocantins, there are 26 faculties, one integrated HEI and three centres for technological education.

UNIVERSITIES

UNIVERSIDADE DO TOCANTINS (University of Tocantins)

108 Sul Alameda 11 Lote 03, CP 173, Palmas, TO 77020-122
Telephone: (63) 3218-2947
E-mail: comunicacao@unitins.br
Internet: www.unitins.br
Founded 1990
Private control
Language of instruction: Portuguese
Academic year: January to December
Courses in accounting, business administration, education, engineering, information systems, law, letters, mathematics, public administration, social work
Rector: JOABER DIVINO MACEDO
Coordinator for Libraries: LAYSSE NOLETO BALBINO

UNIVERSIDADE FEDERAL DO TOCANTINS (Federal University of Tocantins)

Av. NS 15, 109 Norte, Plano Diretor Norte, Palmas, TO 77001-090
Telephone: (63) 3232-8035
E-mail: reitor@uft.edu.br
Internet: www.uft.edu.br
Founded 2003
federal control
Language of instruction: Portuguese
Academic year: January to December
Rector: MÁRCIO ANTÔNIO DA SILVEIRA
Vice-Rector: ISABEL CRISTINA AULER PEREIRA
Pro-Rector for Admin. and Finance: JOSÉ PEREIRA GUIMARÃES NETO
Pro-Rector for Assessment and Planning: ANA LÚCIA DE MEDEIROS
Pro-Rector for Extension and Culture: GEORGE FRANÇA
Pro-Rector for Research and Postgraduate Affairs: WALDECY RODRIGUES
Pro-Rector for Student and Community Affairs: Prof. Dr GEORGE LAURO RIBEIRO DE BRITO
Pro-Rector for Undergraduate Affairs: BERENICE FEITOSA DA COSTA AIRES
Coordinator for System of Libraries: EDSON DE SOUSA OLIVEIRA
Library of 242,345 vols
Publications: *EntreLetras*, *Revista Questão de Opinião*

BRUNEI

The Higher Education System

The Universiti Brunei Darussalam (UBD, founded in 1985) is the principal institution of higher education. In 1988 the Sultan Hassanal Bolkiah Institute of Education was merged into the university, and in 2008 it was announced that the Princess Rashidah College of Nursing (established in 1986) was to merge with the UBD's Institute of Medicine (which was renamed as the PAPRSB Institute of Health Sciences in 2010). A second university, the Universiti Islam Sultan Sharif Ali, was founded in 2007 to offer Islamic education. In the same year the status of the Seri Begawan Training College for Teachers of Islamic Religion was upgraded when it became the Seri Begawan University College for Teachers of Islamic Religion. Malay is the official language of instruction at higher education institutions, but courses are also taught in English and Arabic (especially Islamic education). The Ministry of Education is responsible for higher education.

Students with a minimum of two 'A' Level passes are eligible for entry to the Universiti Brunei Darussalam or other tertiary institutions or to be awarded scholarships to study abroad. The Institut Teknologi Brunei (ITB), which was established in 1986, provides courses leading to a Higher National Certificate (part-time) or a Higher National Diploma (full-time) and Bachelors degree courses at the Faculty of Engineering and the Faculty of Business and Computing. The ITB was officially upgraded to university status in 2008, but retained its original name. Bachelors degrees at the Universiti Brunei Darussalam last for four to six years and programmes operate on a US-style 'credit' system, with a minimum number required for graduation. In 2010 there were 5,903 students enrolled in higher education institutions.

In 2010 there were 13 nursing/technical/vocational colleges in Brunei, attended by a total of 3,398 students. The Sistem Pendidikan Negara Abad Ke-21 (SPN 21, National Education System for the 21st Century), which was approved by the Ministry of Education in 2008, aimed to achieve a participation rate of at least 50% in post-secondary education, including students pursuing vocational and technical training. New technical/vocational courses and qualifications were to be introduced as part of the SPN 21, namely a three-year National Skill Certificate, a three-year Diploma and a four-year sandwich Degree, which includes a one-year placement in industry.

Regulatory and Representative Bodies

GOVERNMENT

Ministry of Culture, Youth and Sports: Simpang 336-17, Jalan Kebangsaan, Bandar Seri Begawan BA 1210; tel. 2382911; e-mail info@kkbs.gov.bn; internet www.kkbs.gov.bn; Minister Pehin Dato' Haji HAZAIR BIN HAJI ABDULLAH.

Ministry of Education: Old Airport Rd, Bandar Seri Begawan, Berakas BB 3510; tel. 2381133; e-mail feedback@moe.gov.bn; internet moe.gov.bn; Minister Pehin Dato' Haji AWANG ABU BAKAR BIN HAJI APONG.

ACCREDITATION

Brunei Darussalam National Accreditation Council: B211, 2nd Fl., Block B, Min. of Education, Old Airport Rd, Berakas BB 3510; tel. (2) 381133; e-mail mkpk@moe.edu.bn; internet www.moe.edu.bn/web/moe/dept/highedu/sbnac; f. 1990; ensures and maintains the quality and standard of educational credentials; considers and evaluates the status and quality of qualifications awarded by local and overseas instns; Exec. Sec. ADININ MD SALLEH (acting).

Learned Societies

LANGUAGE AND LITERATURE

Alliance Française: No 1A, Simpang 46, Kg Kiarong, Jalan Dato Ratna, Negara; tel. (2) 654245; e-mail education@afbrunei.com; internet www.afbrunei.com; offers courses and exams in French language and culture and promotes cultural exchange with France.

Research Institutes

AGRICULTURE, FISHERIES AND VETERINARY SCIENCE

Brunei Agricultural Research Centre, Department of Agriculture: Dept of Agriculture, Min. of Industry and Primary Resources, Jalan Tutong, Kilanas BF 2520; tel. (2) 661894; e-mail barc001@brunet.bn; internet www.brunet.bn/gov/doa/barc.htm; f. 1984, present name since 1995; 100 mems; Head of Div. Pengiran Hajah ROSIDAH BINTI PENGIRAN HAJI METUSSIN.

HISTORY, GEOGRAPHY AND ARCHAEOLOGY

Brunei History Centre: Ministry of Culture, Youth and Sports, BS 8610 Bandar Seri Begawan; tel. (2) 240166; e-mail sejarah@brunet.bn; internet www.history-centre.gov.bn; f. 1982; attached to Min. of Culture, Youth and Sports; research on Brunei's history and genealogies, and history of Brunei's Sultan, royal families, and state dignitaries; Dir Haji MOHAMED JAMIL AL-SUFRI; publs *Darussalam* (The Abode of the Peace, 1 a year), *Pusaka* (Heritage, 2 a year).

Library

Bandar Seri Begawan

Language and Literature Bureau Library: Jalan Elizabeth II, Bandar Seri Begawan BS8711; tel. (2) 235501; e-mail kb_perpustakaan@brunet.bn; internet www.dbplibrary.gov.bn; f. 1961; 1 central and 4 full-time brs; 5 mobile units; reference and lending facilities open to the public; 600,000 vols in Malay and English; Chief Librarian Haji ABU BAKAR BIN HAJI ZAINAL; publs *Accessions List*, indexes.

Museums and Art Galleries

Bandar Seri Begawan

Brunei Museum: Jalan Kota Batu, Bandar Seri Begawan BD 1510; tel. (2) 244545; e-mail bmdir@brunet.bn; internet www.museums.gov.bn; f. 1965; ethnographical, historical, archaeological displays; natural history, oriental arts and cultural heritage collns; legal depository; library of 77,813 vols, Borneo colln of 2,492 vols, 63,927 local publs; Dir Haji MATASSIM BIN HAJI JIBAH; publs *Berita Muzium* (4 a year), *Brunei Darussalam National Bibliography* (1 a year), *Brunei Museum Journal* (1 a year).

Constitutional History Gallery: Jalan Sultan, Bandar Seri Begawan BD 1510; tel. (2) 238360; f. 1984; Dir Pengiran Haji HASHIM BIN PENGIRAN HAJI MOHAMED JADID.

Malay Technology Museum: Brunei Museums Dept, Jalan Kota Batu, Bandar Seri Begawan, BD 1510; tel. (2) 244545; e-mail bmethno@brunet.bn; internet www.museums.gov.bn; f. 1988; exhibitions of traditional industries and handicrafts, Malay traditional technologies, research on Brunei indigenous ethnic groups; 26 mems; Curator of Ethnography PUDARNO BINCHIN; Museum Officer JAHRANI HAJI ABAS; Museum Officer SHARIANA HAJI NAIM; publ. *The Brunei Museum Journal*.

Royal Regalia Building: Jalan Sultan, Bandar Seri Begawan BS 8610; tel. (2) 238360; internet www.museums.gov.bn/bangunan2.htm; f. 1992; Dir Haji MATASSIM BIN HAJI JIBAH.

Universities

INSTITUT TEKNOLOGI BRUNEI

Tungku Link, Gadong, Bandar Seri Begawan 1410

Telephone: (2) 461020

Internet: www.itb.edu.bn

Founded 1986

B/TEC HND and BEng courses

Dir: Haji MOHAMED YUSRA BIN HAJI ABDUL HALIM

Registrar: Haji MOHAMMAD BIN HAJI HIDUP

Librarian: Hajah PUSPARAINI BINTI HAJI THANI
Library of 35,000 vols
Number of teachers: 83
Number of students: 483

UNIVERSITI BRUNEI DARUSSALAM

Jalan Tungku Link, Gadong BE 1410
Telephone: (2) 463001
E-mail: office.ipro@ubd.edu.bn
Internet: www.ubd.edu.bn

Founded 1985, the Sultan Hassanal Bolkiah Institute of Education was integrated into the Univ. in 1988, the Institute of Islamic Studies was integrated into the Univ. in 1999, Princess Rashida College of Nursing was integrated into the Univ. in 2008
State control
Languages of instruction: Malay, English
Academic year: August to May (2 semesters)
Chancellor: HM Sultan Haji HASSANAL BOLKIAH MU'IZZADDIN WADDAULAH
Pro-Chancellor: Dr MUDA HAJI AL-MUHTADEE BILLAH
Vice-Chancellor: Dr HAJI ZULKARNAIN HANAFI
Registrar and Sec.: RUBIAH YACUB (acting)
Chief Librarian: Dr HAJI AWG SUHAIMI BIN HAJI ABDUL KARIM
Library of 345,160 vols
Number of teachers: 403
Number of students: 4,728
Publications: *al-Islam: jurnal ilmiah Fakulti Pengajian Islam*, *Brunei Darussalam Journal of Health*, *Brunei International Journal of Science and Mathematics Education* (1 a year), *International Journal of Special Education*, *Janang*, *Journal of Applied Research in Education (JAIRE)* (1 a year), *Jurnal undang-undang syariah Brunei Darussalam*, *Purih*, *Science and Mathematics Technical Education*, *Scientia Bruneiana*, *South East Asia: A Multidisciplinary Journal*, *Studies in Education*, *Tinjauan: policy and management review*

DEANS
Academy of Brunei Studies: Assoc. Prof. AMPUAN DR HAJI BRAHIM BIN AMPUAN HAJI TENGAH
Educational Technology Centre: HASNAN SAWAL
Faculty of Arts and Social Science: Dr YABIT ALAS
Faculty of Business, Economics and Policy Studies: Dr TEO SIEW YEAN
Faculty of Science: Prof. DATO HAJI MOHAMED ABDUL MAJID
Graduate Studies and Research: Assoc. Prof. Dr DAVID YOUNG
Information, Communication and Technology Centre: LIM SEI GUAN
Language Centre: Dr HAJI NOOR AZAM BIN OKMB HAJI OTHMAN
PAPRSB Institute of Health Sciences: Dr HAJAH MASLINA BINTI HAJI MOHSIN
Sultan Haji Omar Ali Saifuddien Institute of Islamic Studies: Dr NUROL HUDA
Sultan Hassanal Bolkiah Institute of Education: Dr JAINATUL HALIDA BINTI HAJI JAIDIN

UNIVERSITI ISLAM SULTAN SHARIF ALI (UNISAA)

Jalan Tungku, Gadong BE 1410
Telephone: (2) 463001
E-mail: info@unissa.edu.bn
Internet: www.unissa.edu.bn
Founded 2007
State control
Rector: Pengiran Dato' Seri Setia Dr Haji MOHAMMAD BIN PENGIRAN HAJI ABD RAHMAN
Permanent Academic Advisor: Prof. Dato' Dr MUNIR YAACOB
Registrar: Haji TARIP BIN HAJI MAT YASSIN
Bursar: Haji SULAIMAN BIN LATIP
Dean for Student Affairs: Pengiran Haji SAIFUL BAHRIN BIN PENGIRAN HAJI KULA

DEANS
Faculty of Arabic Language and Islamic Civilization: Prof. Madya Dr ARIF KARKHI ABUKHUDAIRI
Faculty of Business and Management Science: (vacant)
Faculty of Shariah and Law: Dr AYMAN ABDEL RAOUF SALEH
Faculty of Usuluddin: Dr SABER AHMAD TAHA

Colleges

There are Adult Education Centres attached to colleges and schools.

Jefri Bolkiah College of Engineering: POB 63, Kuala Belait 6000; internet www.brunet.bn/php/chongrms/jbcehome.htm; f. 1970; craft, technical, mathematics and English courses; 78 teachers; 350 students; Prin. MICHAEL LIM (acting).

Sultan Saiful Rijal Technical College: POB 914, Simpang 125, Jalan Muara; tel. (2) 331077; e-mail mtssr@brunet.bn; internet www.mtssr.edu.bn; f. 1985; engineering and business courses; 195 teachers; 1,000 students; Dir Pengiran SUHAIMI BIN PENGIRAN HAJI BAKAR (acting).

BULGARIA

The Higher Education System

Higher education is supported by the State through the aegis of the Ministry of Education and Science. During the mid-1990s the higher education system was extensively reorganized, with a degree system introduced and many foundations renamed. Higher education is governed by the Higher Education Act (amended 1999, 2001, 2004 and 2010); according to the 2010 amendments, part of which replaced the existing Academic Degrees and Titles Act, Bulgarian universities were to be permitted to bestow academic titles (previously granted by an independent, external body, the Higher Attestation Commission, which was to be disbanded). In 2010/11 there were 25,511 students enrolled in colleges and 255,659 enrolled in 44 universities and equivalent institutions (including Spetzializirano Visshe Uchilishte—specialized higher education schools). In mid-1999 tuition fees for students at public universities were introduced.

Admission to higher education is on the basis of the Diploma of Completed Secondary Education and successful entrance examinations (including the State Maturity Examination). The autonomy of higher education institutions allows them to set their own criteria for admission. Under the 2001 and 2004 amendments to the Higher Education Act, Bulgaria has implemented changes in line with the Bologna Process (although a three-cycle system was already in place). The obligatory national credit transfer system, which was introduced in 2004, is comparable to the European Credit Transfer and Accumulation System (ECTS). Since 2005 all graduates of higher education institutions have automatically received the Diploma Supplement. The principal undergraduate degree is the Bachelors, which requires four years of study culminating in defence of a thesis; according to the 2010 amendments to the Higher Education Act, three-year Bachelor degrees were to be introduced over the following five years. There is also a range of Diploma and Diploma Specialist programmes. The Masters degree requires five years of study (or one more year after the Bachelors) ending with either state examinations or defence of a thesis. Finally, there are three types of Doctorate, each requiring at least three years of study following the Masters: Doctors, Doctor of Sciences, and Doctor Honoris Causa.

Post-secondary non-tertiary vocational and technical training is mostly obtained within the framework of the secondary education system. Educational programmes lasting two years are offered by both state and private schools. In addition, there are currently some 38 colleges (29 incorporated into the structures of the universities and nine independent establishments), which offer relatively short-term, vocationally orientated training. The National Agency for Vocational Education and Training, established in 2000, oversees the quality and development of courses.

The National Evaluation and Accreditation Agency is responsible for evaluating and accrediting institutions of higher education. In 2010 the Government indicated that, as part of the amendments to the Higher Education Act, there were plans to change the existing system of university accreditation.

Regulatory and Representative Bodies

GOVERNMENT

Ministry of Culture: 'Al. Stamboliiski' Blvd 17, 1040 Sofia; tel. (2) 9400900; e-mail press@mc.government.bg; internet www.mc.government.bg; Minister PETER STOYANOVICH.

Ministry of Education and Science: St Prince Dondukov 2A, 1000 Sofia; tel. (2) 9217799; e-mail press_mon@mon.bg; internet www.minedu.government.bg; Minister ANELIYA KLISAROVA.

ACCREDITATION

ENIC/NARIC Bulgaria: Nat. Centre for Information and Documentation (NACID), G. M. Dimitrov Blvd 52A, 1125 Sofia; tel. (2) 8173824; e-mail naric@nacid.bg; internet www.enic-naric.net/index.aspx?c=bulgaria; Exec. Dir for NACID VANYA GRASHKINA.

National Evaluation and Accreditation Agency: Tsarigradsko Shose Blvd 125, Bldg 5, 4th Fl., North Wing, 1113 Sofia; tel. (2) 8077811; e-mail info@neaa.government.bg; internet www.neaa.government.bg; statutory body for evaluation, accreditation and monitoring of quality in HEIs and scientific orgs; 11 mems: 1 chair., 6 reps from HEIs, 1 from the Bulgarian Acad. of Sciences, 1 from the Nat. Centre of Agricultural Science, 2 reps from the Min. of Education and Science; Chair. Prof. Dr BOYAN BIOLCHEV; Deputy Chair. Prof. DANAIL LAZAROV DANAILOV; Sec.-Gen. MILA NENCHEVA PENELOVA.

NATIONAL BODY

Bulgarian Rectors' Conference: c/o Agricultural Univ., Mendeleev Blvd 12, 4000 Plovdiv; tel. (32) 633232; e-mail info@rectorsbg.com; internet rectorsbg.zavas.org; Rector Prof. DIMITAR GREKOV; Pres. Prof. YORDANKA KUZMANOVA.

Learned Societies

GENERAL

Bulgarian Academy of Sciences: Noemvri St 15, 1040 Sofia; tel. (2) 9795333; e-mail presidentbas@cu.bas.bg; internet www.bas.bg; f. 1869 as Bulgarian Learned Soc., present name 1911; attached research institutes: see under Research Institutes; 224 mems (57 academicians, 84 corresp., 2 hon., 81 foreign); library: see under Libraries and Archives; Vice-Pres. and Acting Pres. Prof. EUGENE NICKOLOV; publs *Balgaristika/Bulgarica* (2 a year), *Comptes rendus de l'Académie Bulgare des Sciences* (12 a year), *Spisanie na Balgarskata Akademija na Naukite* (Journal of the Bulgarian Academy of Sciences), various spec. publs on science and the arts.

Bulgarian Comparative Education Society: Blvd Shipchenski prohod 69A, 1574 Sofia; tel. (2) 8311198; e-mail bces.conference@bgcell.net; internet bces.home.tripod.com; f. 1991; promotes historical, methodological and practical aspects of comparative education; organizes, coordinates and supports research; cooperates with scholars, research orgs, instns, societies in Bulgaria and abroad; Chair. Dr Hab. NIKOLAY POPOV.

National Centre of Public Health and Analyses: Acad. Iv. Geshov Blvd 15, 1431 Sofia; tel. (2) 8056444; e-mail ncpha@ncpha.government.bg; internet ncphp.government.bg; attached to Min. of Health; Dir Assoc. Prof. Dr CHRISTIAN GRIVA; publs *Bulgarian Journal of Public Health* (4 a year), *Public Health Statistics* (1 a year).

Union of Publishers in Bulgaria: Alabin St 58, 1000 Sofia; tel. (2) 9864251; e-mail office@sib.bg; internet www.sib.bg; f. 2000; non-governmental asscn that defends the freedom of the press, the independence of journalists and encourages their work so that soc. is objectively informed; 22 mems; Chair. LYUBOMIR PAVLOV; Exec. Dir RADOMIR TCHOLAKOV.

Union of Scientists in Bulgaria: Madrid Blvd 39, 2nd Fl., 1505 Sofia; tel. (2) 9441157; e-mail science@usb-bg.org; internet www.usb-bg.org; f. 1944; works in the area of science and research, education, innovations, environment, health care, information, informatics and information technologies, int. cooperation, social assistance, tourism and recreation; organizes more than 150 scientific events annually—int. and nat. scientific congresses, nat. and regional confs with foreign participation, scientific sessions, seminars, round table discussions; 4,000 mems; Pres. Prof. Dr DAMYAN DAMYANOV; publs *Nauka* (6 a year), *Science* (6 a year).

AGRICULTURE, FISHERIES AND VETERINARY SCIENCE

Scientific and Technical Union of Specialists in Agriculture: G.S. Rakovski St 108, 1000 Sofia; tel. (2) 9876513; f. 1965; Pres. Prof. Dr VALIO VALEV; Sec. DIMITAR RADULOV; publ. *Buletin Vnedreni Novosti*.

Soil Resources Agency: Shose Bankia St 7, 1331 Sofia; tel. (2) 8248798; e-mail soilsurv@mail.netplus.bg; f. 1959; analytical research of soil; verifies the quality of agricultural land, and applies finding in legal cases; assesses deterioration risks posed by erosion, contamination, salinity, acidity/alkalinity and bogginess; cartographic information and reports; creation and maintenance of the State Digital Map of Soil and Agricultural Land Grades and Soil Resource Geographical Information System, both overseen by the Min. of Agriculture and Food; Exec. Dir DAMJAN MIHALEV; Gen. Sec. TSENKA CHERNOGOROVA.

ARCHITECTURE AND TOWN PLANNING

Union of Architects in Bulgaria: Krakra St 11, 1504 Sofia; tel. (2) 9438321; e-mail sab@bularch.org; internet www.bularch.eu; f. 1965; develops and extends its professional cooperation with the Chamber of the Architects in Bulgaria and other related Bulgarian, foreign and int. orgs in the area of architecture; documentation and conservation of monuments; 2,200 mems; library of 6,000 vols; Chair. GEORGI BAKALOV; Sec. Gen. VANIA FURNADJIEVA; publ. *Architecture* (6 a year).

ECONOMICS, LAW AND POLITICS

Bulgarian Association of Criminology: Vitosha 2, 1000 Sofia; tel. (2) 9874751; f. 1986; Pres. Assoc. Prof. Y. BOYADZHIEVA.

Bulgarian Association of International Law: H. C. Belite Brezi, Bldg 6, ap. 31, 1680 Sofia; f. 1962; attached to Int. Law Asscn; 60 mems; Pres. Prof. ALEXANDER YANKOV; Sec. Gen. Prof. MARGARIT GANEV; Treas. Dr EVGUENIY JICHEV; publ. *Trudove po Mezhdunarodno Pravo* (every 3 years).

Union of Economists: G. S. Rakovski St 108, 1000 Sofia; tel. (2) 9871847; f. 1968; Pres. Prof. S. ALEXANDROV; Sec. I. POPOV.

FINE AND PERFORMING ARTS

Union of Bulgarian Actors: Narodno Sabranie Sq. 12, 1000 Sofia; tel. (2) 9870725; e-mail office@uba.bg; internet www.uba.bg; f. 1921 as Union of Bulgarian Artists; 600 mems; library of 6,000 vols; Chair. HRISTO MUTAFCHIEV; publ. *Teatar*.

Union of Bulgarian Artists: Shipka St 6, 1504 Sofia; tel. (2) 9444141; e-mail info@sbhart.com; internet www.sbhart.com; f. 1893 as Asscn of the Artists in Bulgaria, present name 1959; protects the interests of its mems and promotes Bulgarian visual culture nationally and internationally; 3,000 mems; library of 9,000 vols; Pres. LYUBEN GENOV; publs *Dekorativno Izkustvo*, *Promishlena Estetika* (Information Bulletin, in Bulgarian only).

Union of Bulgarian Composers: ul. Ivan Vazov, 1000 Sofia; tel. (2) 9881560; e-mail mail@ubc-bg.com; internet www.ubc-bg.com; f. 1933 as Contemporary Music Soc., present name 1954; 230 mems; library of 25,280 books, scores and recordings; Pres. PETAR LIONDEV; Vice-Pres. VELISLAV ZAIMOV.

Union of Bulgarian Film Makers: Dondukov Blvd 67, 1504 Sofia; tel. (2) 9461069; e-mail sbfd@sbfd-bg.com; internet www.filmmakersbg.org; f. 1934; 1,000 mems; Pres. IVAN PAVLOV; Admin. Sec. RENI ZLATANOVA; publ. *KINO* (6 a year).

HISTORY, GEOGRAPHY AND ARCHAEOLOGY

Bulgarian Geographical Society: Tsar Osvoboditel 15, 1000 Sofia; tel. (2) 9858261; f. 1918; Pres. Prof. P. V. PETROV; Sec. L. TSANKOVA; publs *Geoecologija*, *Geografija*, *Geografijata Dnes*.

LANGUAGE AND LITERATURE

Alliance Française: Dragan Tsankov St 34A, POB 1015, 4000 Plovdiv; tel. (32) 631342; e-mail afbg@afbg.org; internet www.afbg.org; f. 1904; offers courses and exams in French language and culture and promotes cultural exchange with France; attached offices in Blagoevgrad, Burgas, Kazanlak, Pleven, Stara Zagora, Varna and Veliko Tărnovo; library of 17,000 vols, 950 video cassettes, 600 audio cassettes, 350 CDs, 105 CD-ROMs; Dir TÉOPHANA BRADINSKA-ANGELOVA; publ. *Alliances* (2 a year).

Balkanmedia Association: Luibotran 96, 1407 Sofia; tel. (2) 8622497; e-mail balkanmedia90@gmail.com; f. 1990; ind. non-profit org. for mass media and communication culture in the Balkan countries; 36 assoc. mems (from all Balkan countries); Pres. ROSSEN MILEV; publs *Balkanmedia*, *Scriptura Mundi* (Writings of the World).

British Council: Krakra St 7, 1504 Sofia; tel. (2) 9424344; e-mail bc.sofia@britishcouncil.bg; internet www.britishcouncil.org/bulgaria; f. 1991; offers courses and exams in English language and British culture; promotes cultural exchange with the UK; teaching centre; Dir IAN STEWART.

Bulgarian Philologists' Society: c/o Ezik i literatura, Moskovska St 13, 1000 Sofia; tel. (2) 9862561; e-mail ezik_i_literatura@abv.bg; f. 1977; Pres. Prof. S. HADZHIKOSEV; publ. *Ezik i literatura* (4 a year).

Goethe-Institut: Budapesta St 1, POB 1384, 1000 Sofia; tel. (2) 9390100; e-mail info@sofia.goethe.org; internet www.goethe.de/sofia; f. 1989; offers courses and exams in German language and culture; promotes cultural exchange with Germany; library of 11,000 vols; Dir Dr RUDOLF BARTSCH; Sec. OLJA MATEEVA.

Union of Bulgarian Journalists: Graf Ignatiev St 4, 1000 Sofia; tel. (2) 9872808; e-mail sbj_bg@mail.bg; internet sbj-bg.eu; f. 1944; 5,500 mems; Pres. MILEN VALKOV; Gen. Sec. SNEZHANA TODOROVA.

Union of Bulgarian Writers: Pl. Slavejkova 2A, 1000 Sofia; tel. (2) 880031; f. 1913; 495 mems; Pres. N. HAITOV; publs *Bulgarian Writer*, *Plamak*, *Slavejche*.

Union of Translators in Bulgaria: Slavic 29, 1000 Sofia; tel. (2) 9864500; e-mail office@bgtranslators.org; internet www.bgtranslators.org; f. 1974, present status 2001; non-profit org.; represents and defends the professional and creative rights of its mems; raises the quality of translation; Bureau translation translates about 46 languages; Chair. Prof. Dr EMILIA STAYCHEVA; publ. *Panorama*.

MEDICINE

Bulgarian Society for Parasitology: Tsar Osvoboditel Blvd 1, 1000 Sofia; tel. (2) 9792313; e-mail ieppcom@bas.bg; internet www.bsparasitology.org; f. 1965 as Soc. of Parasitologists in Bulgaria, present name 1999; conducts research on parasitological aspects of biology, human and veterinary medicine, agriculture and forestry; organizes annual meetings, lectures; 187 mems; Pres. Prof. Dr BOYKO B. GEORGIEV; Sec. Dr DENITSA TEOFANOVA; Treas. Dr ANETA YONEVA.

Bulgarian Society of Neurology: Ljuben Russev St 1, 113 Sofia; tel. (2) 9702300; e-mail neurologybg@gmail.com; internet www.nevrologiabg.com; f. 1987; Exec. Dir and Pres. Prof. Dr IVAN MILANOV; publ. *Bulgarian Neurology Journal*.

Bulgarian Society of Sports Medicine and Kinesitherapy: Nat. Sports Acad. 'Vasil Levski', Dept of Sports Medicine, Studentski grad, 1700 Sofia; tel. (2) 4012345; e-mail bsssmk@abv.bg; f. 1953; 65 mems; Chair. Assoc. Prof. DIANA DIMITROVA; Vice-Chair. Assoc. Prof. EVGENIA DIMITROVA; Sec. Gen Dr MARIELA SIRAKOVA; publs *Medicina i Sport*, *Sports & Science* (12 a year).

Union of the Bulgarian Medical Societies: Nat. Centre of Public Health Protection, 12th Fl., Room 19, Ivan Geshov Blvd 15, 1431 Sofia; tel. (2) 9541156; e-mail info@medunion-bg.org; internet www.medunion-bg.org; f. 1968; promotes research and contributes to maintaining high professional qualities among medical professionals by developing a modern system for continuous medical training; 10,000 mems, 71 mem socs; Chair. Prof. TODOR POPOV; publ. *Modern Medicine* (6 a year).

NATURAL SCIENCES

Biological Sciences

Bulgarian Botanical Society: c/o Institute of Botany, Bulgarian Acad. of Sciences, Acad. Georgi Bonchev St., Blvd 23, 1113 Sofia; tel. (2) 9792153; e-mail bgbotsoc@gmail.com; internet www.bio.bas.bg; f. 1923; researches, preserves and promotes the flora and fauna of Bulgaria; Sec. M. ANCHEV.

Bulgarian Society of Natural History: D. Zankov 8, 1164 Sofia; tel. (2) 666594; f. 1896; 1,000 mems; Pres. Prof. D. VODENICHAROV; Sec. S. DIMITROVA; publ. *Priroda i Znanie* (10 a year).

Mathematical Sciences

Union of Bulgarian Mathematicians: Acad. Georgi Bonchev Blvd 8, 1113 Sofia; tel. (2) 8738076; e-mail smb.sofia@gmail.com; internet www.math.bas.bg/smb; f. 1898; 2,000 mems; Pres. PETER KENDEROV; Sec. Dr SAVA GROZDEV; publ. *Mathematics and Education in Mathematics* (1 a year).

Physical Sciences

Bulgarian Geological Society: Akad. Georgi Bonchev St, Bldg 24, 1113 Sofia; tel. (2) 9792250; internet www.bgd.bg; f. 1925; 340 mems; library of 21,000 vols (incl. books, journals, maps and unique archive documents); Pres. Prof. DIMITAR SINNYOVSKI; Sec. Prof. Dr LYUBOMIR METODIEV; Treas. Prof. Dr EUGENIA TARASSOVA; publs *Proceedings of Bulgarian Geological Society* (1 a year), *Review of the Bulgarian Geological Society* (3 a year).

Union of Physicists in Bulgaria: 5 James Bourchier Blvd, 1164 Sofia; tel. (2) 627660; e-mail upb@phys.uni-sofia.bg; internet www.phys.uni-sofia.bg/~upb/index.html; f. 1971 as Bulgarian Physical Soc., present name and status 1989; Pres. Prof. Dr ALEXANDER PETROV; Exec. Sec. PENKA GANCHEVA LAZAROVA; publs *Bulgarian Journal of Physics* (in English), *The World of Physics* (in Bulgarian).

PHILOSOPHY AND PSYCHOLOGY

Bulgarian Pedagogical Society: Shipchenski prohod 69A, 1547 Sofia; tel. (2) 720893; f. 1975; Pres. Prof. G. BIZHKOV.

Bulgarian Philosophical Association: 15 Tsar Osvoboditel Blvd, Sofia Univ., 1504 Sofia; tel. (88) 8383073; f. 1968; 320 mems; Pres. Prof. IVAN KALCHEV; Sec. R. KRIKORIAN; publs *Filosofia* (Philosophy, 12 a year), *Filosofski Alternativi* (Philosophical Alternatives, 12 a year), *Filosofski Forum* (Philosophical Forum, 4 a year), *Filosofski Vestnik* (Philosophical News, 4 a year).

Bulgarian Psychological Society: 52 Cherkovna St, 1505 Sofia; tel. (2) 8435854; e-mail office@psychology-bg.org; internet www.psychology-bg.org; f. 1969; Pres. and CEO Dr Plamen Dimitrov; Sec. Zh. Balev; publ. *Balgarsko Spisanie po Psikhologija*.

RELIGION, SOCIOLOGY AND ANTHROPOLOGY

Bulgarian Sociological Association: c/o Dr. Svetla Koleva, Institute of Sociology, Bulgarian Academy of Sciences, 13A Moskovska St., 1000 Sofia; tel. (2) 9809522; e-mail bsa@sociology.bas.bg; internet www.bsa-bg.org; f. 1959 as Sociological Assn, present name 1969; professional non-profit org.; carries out theoretical and empirical research, teaching and publishing activities in the field of sociology in Bulgaria; conducts congresses, confs. and seminars; Pres. Svetla Koleva; Sec. Diana Nenkova; publ. *Sociological Problems* (4 a year).

TECHNOLOGY

Bulgarian Astronautical Society: Acad. G. Bonchev Str., bl. 1, SRTI, 1113 Sofia; tel. (2) 9793451; e-mail pangelov@space.bas.bg; f. 1957; 300 mems; library of 3,000 vols; Pres. Prof. Petar Getsov; Vice-Pres. Prof. Plamen Angelov; Scientific Sec. Prof. Elisaveta Alexandrova.

Federation of the Scientific-Technical Unions in Bulgaria: 108 G. S. Rakovski St, POB 431, 1000 Sofia; tel. (2) 9877230; e-mail info@fnts-bg.org; internet www.fnts.bg; f. 1893 as Bulgarian Engineering-Architectural Asscn, current name adopted 1992; non-profit asscn; organizes congresses, confs, symposia, seminars and workshops; participates in the drafting of laws and other normative documents related to science and technology; carries out qualification activity through its Centre for Professional Education and Qualification; 15,000 mems; Pres. Prof. Ivan Yatchev; publ. *Technosfera*.

Scientific and Technical Union of Civil Engineering: G. S. Rakovski St 108, 1000 Sofia; tel. (2) 9884678; f. 1965; Pres. Dr E. Milchev; Sec. M. Ruseva; publs *Stroitel 2000*, *Stroitelstvo*.

Scientific and Technical Union of Forestry: G. S. Rakovski St 108, 1000 Sofia; tel. (2) 9883683; e-mail ntsl@mail.bg; f. 1965; Pres. V. Brezin; Sec. S. Savov; publs *Celuloza i Hartija*, *Darvoobrabotvashta i mebelna Promislenost*.

Scientific and Technical Union of Mining, Geology and Metallurgy: G. S. Rakovski St 108, 1000 Sofia; tel. (2) 9875727; e-mail nts-mdgm@speedbg.net; f. 1965; Pres. Prof. V. Stoyanov; Sec. V. Genevski; publs *Metalurgija*, *Rudodobiv*.

Scientific and Technical Union of Power Engineers: G. S. Rakovski St 108, 5th Fl., Office 505, 1000 Sofia; tel. (2) 9884158; e-mail energy@fnts-bg.org; internet www.ntse-bg.org; f. 1965; carries out vocational training activities and supports the devt of creative ideas and initiatives of its mems; participates in the devt and discussion of laws, regulations, rules, instructions and other regulations on energy, environment, protecting people from harmful effects and the protection of tangible property against damage and destruction resulting from the use of energy; conducts scientific and technical events; Pres. Prof. Simeon Batov; Sec. Eng. D. Tomov; publ. *Energetika*.

Scientific and Technical Union of Textiles, Clothing and Leather: G. S. Rakovski St 108, 1000 Sofia; tel. (2) 9881641; f. 1965; Pres. Prof. E. Kantchev; Sec. I. Mechev; publs *Kozhi i Obuvki*, *Tektil i obleklo*.

Scientific and Technical Union of the Food Industry: G. S. Rakovski St 108, 1000 Sofia; tel. (2) 9874744; e-mail hvp_magazine@go.com; f. 1965; Pres. A. Petrov; publ. *Hranitelna promishlenost*.

Scientific and Technical Union of Transport: G. S. Rakovski St 108, 1000 Sofia; tel. (2) 9325680; f. 1965; participates in policy making in the field of transport research and technological devt; Pres. K. Ermenkov; Sec. St. Gaidarov; publs *Patishta*, *Zelezopaten Transport*.

Scientific and Technical Union of Water Affairs in Bulgaria: Nat. Science and Technology, 4th Fl., Office 419, G. S. Rakovski St 108, 1000 Sofia; tel. (2) 9885303; e-mail stuwa@stuwa.org; internet www.stuwa.org; f. 1966; Chair. Eng. Plamen Slavchev Nikiforov; Sec. Gen. Eng. Margarita Pavlova Siarova; publ. *Vodno delo* (Water Affairs).

Scientific-Technical Union of Mechanical Engineering: Rakovski St 108, 1000 Sofia; tel. (2) 9877290; e-mail nts-bg@mech-ing.com; internet www.mech-ing.com; f. 1965; supports the industrial devt of Bulgaria; protects and represents the professional, intellectual and social interests of its mems; organizes congress and confs at Motuato and Foundry; 900 mems; Pres. Prof. Georgi Popov; Sec. Dr Raicho Georgiev; publ. *Machinery, Technology, Materials* (12 a year).

Union of Chemists in Bulgaria: G. S. Rakovski St 108, 1000 Sofia; tel. (2) 9875812; e-mail chem@fnts-bg.org; internet www.unionchem.org; f. 1901; non-profit org.; scientific and technical work; nat. and int. scientific confs. and symposia; Pres. Prof. Venko Nikolaev Beshkov; Sec. Nayden Naydenov Christ; publ. *Chemistry and Industry* (2 a year).

Union of Electronics, Electrical Engineering and Telecommunications: G. S. Rakovski St 108, 1000 Sofia; tel. (2) 9879767; e-mail ceec@mail.bg; internet www.ceec.fnts.bg; f. 1965; non-profit org.; scientific and technical events; confs, symposia, seminars, roundtables, discussions; devt of draft laws, regulations, programmes; training activities; int. cooperation; 1,300 mems; Chair. Prof. Prof. Ivan Stoyanov Yatchev; Deputy-Pres. Prof. Todorov Seferin Mirchev; Exec. Dir Prof. Dr Ivan Vasilev Nikolov; publ. *Elektrotechnica i Elektronica* (12 a year).

Union of Surveyors and Land Managers in Bulgaria: G. S. Rakovski St 108, POB 431, 1000 Sofia; tel. (2) 9875852; e-mail office@geodesy-union.org; internet www.geodesy-union.org; f. 1922; 200 mems; Pres. Prof. Dr Ing. G. Milev; Sec. St. Bogdanov; publ. *Geodesija, Kartografija, Zemeustrojstvo* (6 a year).

Research Institutes

AGRICULTURE, FISHERIES AND VETERINARY SCIENCE

Agricultural Institute: Simeon Veliki Blvd 3, 9700 Shumen; tel. (54) 830448; e-mail agr_inst@abv.bg; internet www.agricinst.eu; f. 2000 by merger of Institute of Buffalo, Institute of Pig Breeding and the Institute of Sugar Beet; research activity in stockbreeding; library of 10,900 vols; Dir Dr Apostol Apostolov; Scientific Sec. Dr Kalin Dimov; publs *Bulgarian Journal of Agricultural Science*, *Genetica i selectija* (4 a year), *Zhivotnovadni Nauki* (8 a year).

Central Medical Veterinary Research Institute: P. Slaveykov 15, 1606 Sofia; tel. (2) 9521277; e-mail director@iterra.net; f. 1901; Dir Prof. Dr S. P. Martinov.

Dairy Research Institute: 3700 Vidin; tel. (94) 23204; f. 1959; library of 8,000 vols; Dir A. Kozhev; publ. *Advanced Experience* (2 a year).

Dobrudzha Agricultural Institute: General Toshevo, 9521 Dobrich Dist.; tel. (58) 603125; e-mail dai_gt@dobrich.net; internet www.dai-gt.org; f. 1940; nat. research centre for breeding and farming practices of field crops; produces pre-basic and basic seed of guaranteed origin and quality; develops new biotechnological methods in selection of field crops; library of 32,000 vols; Dir Dr Ivan Kiryakov; Scientific Sec. Dr Nina Nenova; publ. *Field Crops Studies*.

Field Crops Institute: G. Dimitrov St 2, 6200 Chirpan; tel. (416) 93133; e-mail iptp@abv.bg; internet www.iptp-chirpan.org; f. 1925, part of the Agricultural Acad. at the Min. of Agriculture and Food, Sofia; breeding of high-yielding and high-quality cotton and durum wheat cultivars; devt of cotton and durum wheat cultivation technologies and elements of technologies for main field crops cultivation under irrigation and in dry conditions; laboratory and field experiments with various crops, machinery, fertilizers, pesticides, growth regulators and defoliants; study of technological parameters of cotton fibre and durum wheat grain; information provision; laboratory analysis of soil and plant samples; seed-production of cotton and durum wheat; library of 16,000 vols; Dir Assoc. Prof. Dr Neli Valkova; Scientific Sec. Assoc. Prof. Dr Ana Stoilova.

Fisheries Industry Institute: Industrialna 3, 8000 Burgas; tel. (56) 840522; f. 1965; Dir Dr Zh. Nechev.

Food Research and Development Institute—Plovdiv: Vasil Aprilov St 154, 4003 Plovdiv; tel. (32) 952109; e-mail office@canri.org; internet www.canri.org; f. 1962, current name adopted 2010; develops and transfers new technologies and products in food industry; library of 19,000 vols; Dir Prof. Dr Nanyo Nanev.

Forest Research Institute: St Kliment Ohridski Blvd 132, 1756 Sofia; tel. (2) 9620442; e-mail forestin@bas.bg; internet www.fribas.org; f. 1928; attached to Bulgarian Acad. of Sciences; library of 39,000 vols; Dir Prof. Alexander Haralanov Alexandrov; publs *Nauka za gorata* (Forest Science, 4 a year), *Silva Balcanica* (2 a year).

Freshwater Fisheries Research Institute: V. Levski St 248, 4003 Plovdiv; tel. (32) 956033; f. 1978; Dir G. Grozev.

Fruit Growing Institute—Plovdiv: Ostromila 12, 4004 Plovdiv; tel. (32) 692349; e-mail instov@infotel.bg; internet www.fruitgrowinginstitute.com; f. 1950, fmrly Fruit Growing Experimental Station, current name adopted 1952; attached to Agricultural Acad., Min. of Agriculture and Food; research, incl. breeding, genetic resources and biotechnology, fruit growing technologies; extension activities; service in the field of fruit growing; Dir Dr Argir Zhivondov; Scientific Sec. Dr Petya Gercheva.

Institute for Plant Genetic Resources 'K. Malkov': Druzhba Blvd 2, 4122 Sadovo (Plovdiv Dist.); tel. (32) 629026; e-mail ipgr_sadovo@abv.bg; internet www.ipgrbg.com; f. 1902 as an agricultural experimental station, current name adopted 2001; attached to Agricultural Acad., Min. of Agriculture and Food; plant genetic resources programme; offers free germplasm exchange, registration and free storage of plant accessions; library of 30,000 vols; Dir Prof. TENCHO CHOLAKOV; Scientific Sec. Prof. Dr RUSKA RUSEVA.

Institute for Roses, Essential and Medical Cultures: Osvobozhdenie Blvd 49, 6100 Kazanlak; tel. (431) 62039; e-mail iremk@iremk.net; internet www.iremk.net; f. 1907; introduction, selection and reproduction of essential oil and medical plants; technology devt for essential oil and medical plants; licensed testing laboratory for analyses and certificate issuing for oils, drugs, plant extracts, sowing seeds, cosmetics and pharmaceuticals; natural cosmetic production; library of 3,600 vols; Dir Prof. Dr KIRILOV NEDKO NEDKOV.

Institute for the Control of Foot and Mouth Disease and Dangerous Infections: Trakia 75, 8800 Sliven; tel. (44) 22039; f. 1974; Dir R. KASABOV.

Institute of Agricultural Economics: Tsarigradsko Shose 125, Blvd 1, 1113 Sofia; tel. (2) 9710014; e-mail office@iae-bg.com; internet www.iae-bg.com; f. 1935; research and devt in economics, sociology, ecology and management of agriculture and food–beverage industry; library of 10,850 vols, 5,560 periodicals; Dir Assoc. Prof. RUMEN POPOV GROZDANOV; Scientific Sec. Prof. Dr TSVETANA KOSEVA KOVACHEVA.

Institute of Agriculture—Karnobat: 1 Industrialna St., 8400 Karnobat; tel. (559) 22702; e-mail iz_karnobat@mail.bg; internet www.iz-karnobat.org; f. 1925, fmrly Barley Research Institute, present name 2001; barley, oat and coriander breeding; investigations on cultivation technologies and crop protection; library of 17,000 vols; Dir Assoc. Prof. I. MIHOV; Scientific Sec. Dr B. DYULGEROVA.

Institute of Agriculture—Kyustendil: Sofjisko Shose St, 2500 Kyustendil; tel. (78) 522612; e-mail iz_kn@abv.bg; internet www.iz-kyustendil.org; f. 1929; attached to Agricultural Acad., Min. of Agriculture and Food; research instn for investigation of theoretical and practical problems in agriculture; introduction of Bulgarian and foreign innovations in the area; assistance to the growers; library of 9,000 vols; Dir Prof. Dr DIMITAR DOMOZETOV; Scientific Sec. Assoc. Prof. Dr VENERA TASEVA.

Institute of Agriculture 'Obraztsov Chiflik': Prof. Ivan Ivanov St 1, 7007 Ruse; tel. (82) 820801; e-mail izs.rousse@gmail.com; internet www.izs-ruse.org; f. 1905; attached to Agricultural Acad.; develops scientific, applied and service activities in the field of breeding of field crops and vine, seed science and agrotechnics; Dir Assoc. Prof. Dr GALINA PANAYOTOVA; Scientific Sec. Assoc. Prof. EVGENIYA DOBREVA ZHEKOVA-NEDELCHEVA.

Institute of Animal Science: Pochivka 1, 2232 Kostinbrod; tel. (721) 68940; e-mail inst_anim_sci@abv.bg; internet www.ias.bg; f. 1950; attached to Bulgarian Agricultural Acad., Min. of Agriculture and Food; research in biochemistry, physiology, reproduction, nutrition, genetics of farm animal, sheepbreeding, cattlebreeding, horsebreeding, poultry, apiculture, rabbits; 9 scientific depts; library of 26,200 vols; Dir Assoc. Prof. Dr MAYA IGNATOVA; Scientific Sec. Prof. PENKA MARINOVA.

Institute of Fisheries and Aquaculture: Primorski 4, Blvd 4, POB 72 9000 Varna; tel. (52) 231852; e-mail aquaculture@migton.net; f. 1932; attached to Nat. Center of Agricultural Sciences, Min. of Agriculture and Food; library of 24,000 vols; Dir Dr LILIANA HADJINIKOLOVA; publ. *Proceedings* (1 a year).

Institute of Forage Crops—Pleven: Gen. Vladimir Vazov St 89, 5800 Pleven; tel. (64) 805882; e-mail ifc@el-soft.com; internet www.ifc-pleven.org; f. 1954; attached to Agricultural Acad.; nat. centre for complex scientific and applied researches and devt activities, advises and trains in the field of breeding of forage production, crop technology and animal nutrition; Dir Prof. Dr ATANAS PETROV KIRILOV; Scientific Sec. Assoc. Prof. Dr ANELIA ILIEVA KATOVA.

Institute of Grains and Feed Industry: Kostinbrod 2, 2232 Sofia 2; tel. (721) 2084; f. 1965; library of 9,050 vols, 16 periodicals; Dir M. MACHEV.

Institute of Soil Science 'Nikola Poushkarov': Shousse Bankya St 7, 1080 Sofia; tel. (2) 8246141; e-mail soil@mail.bg; internet www.iss-poushkarov.org; f. 1947, present name 1960; attached to Agricultural Acad.; research, conservation and restoration of soil resources; management of agriculture and ecosystems; Dir Dr NIKOLAI DINEV; Scientific Sec. Prof. Dr DIMITRANKA STOYCHEVA; publs *Journal of Balkan Ecology* (4 a year, in English), *Soil Science, Agrochemistry and Ecology* (6 a year, in Bulgarian with English abstract).

Institute of Soya Bean Growing: POB 8, 5200 Pavlikeni; tel. (610) 2275; f. 1925; Dir Dr G. GEORGIEV.

Institute of Tobacco and Tobacco Products: 4108 Plovdiv; tel. (32) 672364; e-mail itti@pl.bia-bg.com; internet www.ttpi-bg.com; f. 1944; conducts comprehensive studies of fundamental and applied nature to help solve problems arising in the selection, maintenance, production of tobacco and tobacco seeds, crop protection from pests, drying, handling and processing of tobacco, chemistry of tobacco and tobacco smoke; library of 40,000 vols; Dir Assoc. Prof. Dr HRISTO BOZUKOV; Scientific Sec. Prof. Dr PENKA ZAPRYANOVA; publ. *Bulgarian Tobacco* (6 a year).

Institute of Viticulture and Oenology: Kala tepe 1, POB 62, 5800 Pleven; tel. (64) 822161; f. 1902 as State Control Station in Viticulture and Oenology, present name 1944; Dir Prof. P. ABRASHEVA.

Institute of Water Problems: Acad. G. Bonchev St, Bl.1 1113 Sofia; tel. (2) 722572; e-mail water_management@meteo.bg; internet www.iwp.bas.bg; f. 1963; attached to Bulgarian Acad. of Sciences; carries out theoretical and applied investigations and develops methods, models, software, technologies and installations concerning water resource use and protection; Dir Prof. Eng. OHANES SANTOURDJIAN; Scientific Sec. Assoc. Prof. Dr Eng. IGOR NIAGOLOV; publ. *Vodni Problemi* (Water Problems, 1 a year).

Maize Research Institute: 3230 Knezha; tel. (91) 322211; f. 1924; Dir Prof. K. ANGELOV.

Maritsa Vegetable Crops Research Institute: Brezovsko Shose St 32, 4000 Plovdiv; tel. (32) 951227; e-mail balkanvegetables@gmail.com; internet www.balkanvegetables.eu; f. 1930; attached to Bulgarian Agricultural Acad.; research emphasizes vegetable quality by improving biological value and sensory characteristics, pest and disease resistance, high temperature and drought tolerance; library of 20,500 vols; Dir Prof. Dr MASHEVA STOYKA PETKOVA.

National Wine and Spirituous Beverages Research Institute Ltd: Tsar Boris 3rd Blvd 134, 1618 Sofia; tel. (2) 8184950; e-mail office@wineinbg.org; internet www.wineinbg.org; f. 1952; research incl. chemistry and microbiology of wine and spirits production; Exec. Dir CHRISTO BOEVSKY.

Plant Protection Institute: Panayot Volov St 35, 2230 Kostinbrod; tel. (721) 66061; e-mail protection@infotel.bg; internet www.ppi-bg.org; f. 1936, present location 1961; depts of biological and integrated pest control, entomology and radiobiology, prognosis, toxicology, phytopathology and plant immunity, herbology; library of 15,343 vols (incl. 6,744 books, 2,573 periodicals, 6,026 magazines); Dir Assoc. Prof. Dr OLIA EVTIMOVA KARADJOVA; Scientific Sec. Assoc. Prof. Dr HRISTINA TODOROVA KRUSTEVA.

Regional Veterinary Institute: Nezavisimost Blvd 111, 4000 Plovdiv; tel. (32) 260868; f. 1936; library of 10,000 vols; Dir D. ARNAUDOV.

Regional Veterinary Institute: Slavjanska St 5, 5000 Veliko Tărnovo; tel. (62) 621669; f. 1932; library of 11,840 vols; Dir Prof. V. RADOSLAVOV.

Regional Veterinary Research Institute and Centre: Slavyanska St 58, 6000 Stara Zagora; tel. (42) 26732; f. 1931; Dir Assoc. Prof. N. NIKOLOV.

Research Institute for Irrigation, Drainage and Hydraulic Engineering: Tsar Boris III Blvd 136, 1618 Sofia; tel. (2) 563001; e-mail riidhe@sf.cit.bg; f. 1953; library of 18,000 vols; Dir Asst Prof. Dr PLAMEN PETKOV; publ. *Proceedings* (every 3 years).

Research Institute for Land Reclamation and Agricultural Mechanization: Bansko shosse St 3, IMM, 1331 Sofia; tel. (2) 8257170; e-mail imm_2001@mail.bg; internet www.e-imm2001-ncan-bg.com; f. 1949; nat. centre for strategic and applied research, extension and training in the fields of irrigated agriculture and mechanization of crop husbandry and animal breeding; library of 22,000 vols; Dir Prof. Dr MIHO YANKOV MIHOV; Scientific Sec. Assoc. Prof. Dr GEORGI DIMITROV KOSTADINOV; publ. *Agricultural Engineering* (6 a year, scientific journal).

Research Institute of Mountain Stockbreeding and Agriculture: V. Levski St 281, 5600 Trojan; tel. (670) 62802; e-mail rimsa@mail.bg; internet www.rimsa.eu; f. 1978, fmrly State Fruit Nursery (f. 1910); solves complex issues concerning agriculture in mountainous and foothill regions; Dir Prof. Dr MARIN METODIEV TODOROV.

Scientific and Production Enterprise with Sugar Beet Research Institute 'Prof. Ivan Ivanov': Carev Brod, 9747 Shumen Dist.; tel. (54) 55102; f. 1926; Dir Assoc. Prof. S. KRASTEV.

Scientific and Production Institute for Veterinary Preparations 'Vetbiopharm': 3000 Vratsa; tel. (92) 649485; f. 1942; library of 5,000 vols; Dir Dr T. NIKOLOV.

Veterinary Institute of Immunology Ltd: Bakareno Shose 1, 1360 Sofia; tel. (2) 263170; f. 1942; Pres. Prof. Dr STEFANOV.

ARCHITECTURE AND TOWN PLANNING

Centre for Architectural Studies: Akad. G. Bonchev St 1, 1113 Sofia; tel. (2) 8724620; e-mail danizen@iwt.bas.bg; internet www.bas.bg/arch; f. 1949 as Institute for Urbanism and Architecture, present name 1995; attached to Bulgarian Acad. of Sciences; history of architecture and urban planning from ancient period to modern times, architectural stylistic influences, and comparative studies in the larger context of Balkan and European architecture, continuity in architectural traditions through the ages; new ideas in Europe and their impact on world architecture; preservation of architectural heritage and devt of cultural tourism; Dir Prof. Dr KONSTANTIN BOJADJIEV; Research Sec. Dr ANTON GOUGOV.

National Centre for Regional Development: Alabin 16–20, 1000 Sofia; tel. (2)

9800312; e-mail office@ncrdhp.bg; internet www.ncrdhp.bg; f. 1960; library of 9,000 vols; Exec. Dir Prof. Dr VESSELINA TROEVA; publ. *Series for the Municipalities* (6 a year).

ECONOMICS, LAW AND POLITICS

Economic Research Institute: Aksakov St 3, POB 788, 1040 Sofia; tel. (2) 8104010; e-mail ineco@iki.bas.bg; internet www.iki.bas.bg; f. 1949 as Institute of Economics; attached to Bulgarian Acad. of Sciences; library of 40,000 vols; Dir Prof. Dr MITKO ATANASOV DIMITROV; Scientific Sec. ISKRA BOGDANOVA CHRISTOVA-BALKANSKA; publs *Ikonomicheska Misal* (Economic Thought, 6 a year), *Ikonomicheski Izsledvania* (Economic Studies, 4 a year).

Institute for Legal Studies: Serdica St 4, 1000 Sofia; tel. (2) 9874902; e-mail ipn_ban@bas.bg; internet www.ipn-bg.org; f. 1947; attached to Bulgarian Acad. of Sciences; library of 36,356 vols, 21,156 books and 15,200 periodicals; Dir Prof. TSVETANA KAMENOVA (acting); Scientific Sec. Dr PETAR BONCHOVSKI (acting); publ. *Pravna Misal* (Legal Thought, 4 a year).

Research Institute of Forensic Sciences and Criminology: POB 934, 1000 Sofia; tel. (2) 9829006; e-mail int.27@mvr.bg; internet www.nikk.mvr.bg; f. 1968; Dir KOSTADIN BOBEV; publ. *Scientific Proceedings* (1 a year).

EDUCATION

National Institute for Education—Centre for Higher Education Research: Tsarigradsko Shose 125, Blvd 5, 1113 Sofia; tel. (2) 9717224; f. 1996; non-profit org.; supports educational policy, strategy and priorities for change and enhancement of Bulgarian education in the perspective of the wider European integration; library of 100,000 vols; Head Dr ROSITZA PENKOVA; publ. *Strategies for Policy in Science and Education*.

FINE AND PERFORMING ARTS

Institute of Art Studies: Krakra St 21, 1000 Sofia; tel. (2) 9442414; e-mail office@artstudies.bg; internet www.artstudies.bg; f. 1947; attached to Bulgarian Acad. of Sciences; carries out studies on ancient, medieval and contemporary art and culture; focuses on collecting and preserving art documentation and analysis of art phenomena, both professional and vernacular, associated with the Bulgarian legacy and its role in the construction of European culture; library of 45,000 vols; Dir Prof. Dr ALEXANDER YANAKIEV; publs *Bulgarsko muzikoznanie* (4 a year), *Problemi na izkustvoto* (Art Studies Quarterly, 4 a year).

HISTORY, GEOGRAPHY AND ARCHAEOLOGY

Centre for Population Studies: Acad. G. Bonchev St, Bldg 6, 6th Fl., 1113 Sofia; tel. (2) 9793030; e-mail cps@cc.bas.bg; internet cps.bas.bg; f. 2002, fmrly Institute of Demography (f. 1990); attached to Bulgarian Acad. of Sciences; nat. unit for theoretical and applied demographic studies; research on the population of Bulgaria; aim of identifying the laws and determinants of its evolution as well as population strategy and policy concerns within the context of European integration and the global devt trend; Dir Assoc. Prof. Dr GENOVEVA MIHOVA (acting); Scientific Sec. Dr KREMENA BORISSOVA-MARINOVA; publ. *Naselenie*.

Institute for Balkan Studies & Center of Thracology 'Prof. Alexander Fol': 13 Moskovska St, 1000 Sofia; tel. (2) 981-58-53; e-mail thracologia@live.com; internet www.thracologia.org; f. 1972 as Institute of Thracology, merger with Institute for Balkan Studies 2010, present name 2010; attached to Bulgarian Acad. of Sciences; Thracian history, culture and language; library of 6,000 vols; Dir Prof. SVETLANA YANAKIEVA; Scientific Sec. Prof. Dr IRINA SHOPOVA; publ. *Orpheus* (Journal of Indo-European and Thracian studies, 1 a year).

Institute of Historical Studies: Shipchenski Prohod Blvd 52, Block 17, 1113 Sofia; tel. (2) 870-8513; e-mail ihistory@ihist.bas.bg; internet www.ihist.bas.bg; f. 1947; attached to Bulgarian Acad. of Sciences; works in the field of theoretical and specialized problems of Bulgarian nat., political, social, religious and cultural history from the establishment of the Bulgarian state to the present day, as well as on problems of world history and int. relations; library of 60,000 vols; Dir Prof. Dr ILIYA TODEV; Scientific Sec. Prof. Dr DANIEL VATCHKOV; publs *Bulgarian Historical Review* (2 a year), *Istoritcheski Pregled* (3 a year).

National Institute of Archaeology with Museum: Saborna St 2, 1000 Sofia; tel. (2) 9882406; e-mail naim@naim.bg; internet www.naim.bg; f. 1892; attached to Bulgarian Acad. of Sciences; exercises scholarly and methodological control on field research into prehistory, classical antiquity and the Middle Ages; colln and exhibition on cultural heritage of present day Bulgaria; library of 18,478 vols incl. 7,644 books, 10,834 periodicals; Dir Assoc. Prof. Dr LYUDMIL VAGALINSKI; Scientific Sec. Assoc. Prof. Dr MARIA GUROVA; publ. *Archaeology* (4 a year).

National Institute of Geophysics, Geodesy and Geography: Acad. G. Bonchev St, Blvd 3, 1113 Sofia; tel. (2) 9793322; e-mail office@geophys.bas.bg; internet www.niggg.bas.bg; f. 2010 by merger of Geophysical Institute (f. 1960), Geographical Institute (f. 1950), Central Laboratory of Geodesy (f. in 1948) and Central Laboratory for Seismic Mechanics and Earthquake Engineering (f. 1982); attached to Bulgarian Acad. of Sciences; conducts basic and applied research in the fields of geophysics, seismology, earthquake engineering, geodesy and geography in order to support the sustainable devt of Bulgaria; library of 17,000 vols; Head of Dept Assoc. Prof. STOYAN NEDKOV; Head of Section Prof. BORIS KOLEV; Head of Section Assoc. Prof. GEORGI ZHELEZOV; publs *Bulgarian Geophysical Journal* (1 a year), *Problems of Geography* (4 a year).

LANGUAGE AND LITERATURE

Cyrillo-Methodian Research Centre: Moskovska St 13, POB 432, 1000 Sofia; tel. (2) 9870261; e-mail kmnc@bas.bg; internet www.kmnc.bg; f. 1914 as Clement Commission, present name 1980; attached to Bulgarian Acad. of Sciences; comprehensive study and publishing of the translated and original works of Cyril and Methodius, the Slavonic, Greek and Latin sources on the Cyrillo-Methodian activities; support of bibliographic database and scientific archive of rare publs and MSS copies; Dir Prof. Dr SLAVIA BARLIEVA; Scientific Sec. Dr TATIANA MOSTROV; publs *Kirilo-Metodievski studii* (Cyrillo-Methodian Studies, 1 a year), *Palaeobulgarica / Starobalgaristica* (4 a year).

Institute for the Bulgarian Language: Shipchenski Prohod Blvd 52, Block 17, 1113 Sofia; tel. (2) 722302; e-mail ibl@ibl.bas.bg; internet www.ibl.bas.bg; f. 1942, present name 2004; attached to Bulgarian Acad. of Sciences; Dir Prof. Dr SVETLA KOEVA; Scientific Sec. Assoc. Prof. Dr IVONA KARACHOROVA; publs *Bulgarian Language*, *Linguistique Balkanique*.

Institute of Literature: Shipchenski Prohod Blvd 52, Bldg 17, 7th and 8th Fls, 1113 Sofia; tel. (2) 9792990; e-mail director@ilit.bas.bg; internet www.ilit.bas.bg; f. 1948; attached to Bulgarian Acad. of Sciences; researches on Bulgarian literature from the Middle Ages to the present day, in its theoretical, historical, cultural and comparative aspects; library of 114,795 vols; Dir Assoc. Prof. Dr EDEN TRAYKOVA; Scientific Sec. Assoc. Prof. Dr KAMEN MIKHAILOV; publs *Literaturna misal* (Literary Thought, 2 a year, print and online), *Scripta & e-Scripta* (1 a year, journal of interdisciplinary medieval studies), *Starobulgarska literatura* (Old Bulgarian Literature).

MEDICINE

Centre of Physiotherapy and Rehabilitation: Ovcha Kupel 2B, 1618 Sofia; tel. (2) 562824; f. 1949; Dir Assoc. Prof. P. NIKOLOVA.

Institute of Obstetrics and Gynaecology: Zdrave 2, 1431 Sofia; tel. (2) 5172200; f. 1976; library of 2,000 vols; Exec. Dir Assoc. Prof. V. ZLATKOV; publs *Akusherstvo i Ginekologia* (Obstetrics and Gynaecology, 12 a year), *Problems of Obstetrics and Gynaecology* (1 a year).

MHATEM 'N.I. Pirogov': Totleben Blvd 21, 1606 Sofia; tel. (2) 9154411; internet www.pirogov.bg; f. 1951, fmrly Institute 'N.I. Pirogov'; Chair. MATEY MATEEV; Exec. Dir Prof. DIMITAR RADENKOVSKI; publ. *Emergency Medicine* (magazine).

National Center of Infectious and Parasitic Diseases: Yanko Sakazov Blvd 26, 1504 Sofia; tel. (2) 9446999; e-mail ncipd@ncipd.org; internet www.ncipd.org; f. 1972; courses in epidemiology, microbiology, virology, parasitology and immunology and allergology; training; Dir Prof. Dr TODOR KANTARDZHIEV; publs *Infektologiya*, *Problems of Infectious and Parasitic Diseases*.

National Centre of Haematology and Transfusiology: Plovdivsko Pole St 6, 1756 Sofia; tel. (2) 9701235; f. 1948; Dir Prof. Dr T. LISSITCHKOV; publ. *Clinical and Transfusional Haematology*.

National Centre of Radiobiology and Radiation Protection: Sv. G. Sofijski, Blvd 3, Bldg 7, 1606 Sofia; tel. (2) 9549875; e-mail ncrrp@ncrrp.org; internet www.ncrrp.org; f. 1963; attached to Min. of Health; research, education and training, monitoring and control on occupationally exposed persons and radiological equipment, methodology, diagnostics and prophylaxis of radiation injury, emergency at nuclear accident sites; Dir Prof. Dr RADOSTINA TENEVA GEORGIEVA.

National Drug Institute: Blvd Yanko Sakazov 26, 1504 Sofia; tel. (2) 9434046; e-mail ndi@bg400.bg; f. 1949; Dir Dr BORISLAV BORISOV.

National Heart Hospital: Konoviza St 65, 1309 Sofia; tel. (2) 9217180; e-mail nkb@hearthospital.bg; internet www.hearthospital.bg; f. 1962; Chair. YANI NINKOVA.

Specialized Hospital for Active Treatment in Oncology (SHATO): Plovdivsko Pole 6, 1756 Sofia; tel. (2) 8076299; e-mail info@sbaloncology.bg; internet www.sbaloncology.bg; f. 1952 as Nat. Oncological Centre; library of 22,000 vols; Exec. Dir Assoc. Prof. Dr ZDRAVKA VASSILEVA-VALERIANOVA; publ. *Oncology* (4 a year).

State Institute of Endocrinology and Gerontology: Dame Gruev 6, 1303 Sofia; tel. (2) 9877201; f. 1972; Dir Prof. B. LOZANOV.

University Clinical Centre of Gastroenterology—Sofia: UMBAL 'Tsaritsa Giovanna—ISUL', 8 St Bialo More, 1527 Sofia; tel. (2) 9432277; e-mail hirurgi@isul.eu; f. 1959; Dir Prof. Dr DAMIAN DAMIANOV.

University Clinical Dialysis Centre—Sofia: 1st 'St Georgi Sofiiski' Blvd, 1431 Sofia; tel. (2) 9230463; e-mail firstkhd_org@yahoo.com; internet www.kcd.medfac-sofia.eu; f. 1967; attached to Clinic of Urology at the Chair of Surgery in the Medical Univ.—Sofia; researches on haemodialysis, peritoneal dialysis and related complications; Head Assoc. Prof. Dr DIANA HRISTOVA YONOVA-IVANCHEVA.

NATURAL SCIENCES

Biological Sciences

Acad. M. Popov Institute of Plant Physiology: Acad. Georgi Bonchev St, Bldg 21, 1113 Sofia; tel. (2) 9792606; e-mail karanov@obzor.bio21.bas.bg; internet www.bio21.bas.bg/ipp; f. 1948 as Institute of Biology, present name 1964; attached to Bulgarian Acad. of Sciences; depts of experimental algology, mineral nutrition and water relations, photosynthesis, plant stress molecular biology, regulation of plant growth and devt; Dir Prof. Dr SNEZHANA DONCHEVA; publ. *Genetics and Plant Physiology*.

Institute of Biodiversity and Ecosystem Research: Yurii Gagarin St 2, 1113 Sofia; tel. (2) 8717195; e-mail iber@iber.bas.bg; internet www.iber.bas.bg; f. 2010 by merger of Institute of Zoology, Institute of Botany and the Central Laboratory of Gen. Ecology; attached to Bulgarian Acad. of Sciences; research in theoretical and applied aspects of ecology, biodiversity, environmental conservation and sustainable use of biological resources; training and education in botany, mycology, zoology, ecology, hydrobiology, conservation biology, environmental genetics, parasitology, evolutionary biology and other closely related scientific areas; provides reliable and sound scientific basis and methodological approaches within areas of its research competence; library of 25,500 vols; Dir Assoc. Prof. Dr VALKO BISERKOV; Scientific Sec. Dr SNEZHANA GROZEVA.

Institute of Biology and Immunology of Reproduction Academy 'Kiril Bratanov': Tsarigradsko Shose Blvd 73, 1113 Sofia; tel. (2) 9711395; e-mail ibir@abv.bg; internet www.ibir.bas.bg; f. 1938 as Institute for Artificial Insemination and Breeding Diseases, present name 1994; attached to Bulgarian Acad. of Sciences; library of 11,680 vols; Dir Prof. Dr DIMITRINA STEFANOVA KACHEVA; Scientific Sec. Prof. Dr MARIA GEORGIEVA IVANOVA.

Institute of Biophysics and Biomedical Engineering: Acad. Georgi Bonchev St, Bldg 105, 1113 Sofia; tel. (2) 9793607; e-mail office@biomed.bas.bg; internet www.biomed.bas.bg; f. 2010 by merger of Institute of Biophysics (f. 1967) with Centre of Biomedical Engineering 'Prof. Ivan Daskalov' (f. 1994); attached to Bulgarian Acad. of Sciences; depts of excitable structures, lipid–protein interactions in biological membranes, photoexcitable membranes, electroinduced and adhesive properties, biomacromolecules and biomolecular interactions, processing and analysis of biomedical data and signals, QSAR and molecular modelling, biomechanics and control of movements, bioinformatics and mathematical modelling; Dir Prof. Dr ANDON KOSSEV; Scientific Sec. Assoc. Prof. Dr TANIA PENCHEVA; publs *International Journal Bioautomation* (4 a year), *Journal of Geometry and Symmetry in Physics* (4 a year), *Notes on Intuitionistic Fuzzy Sets*, *Notes on Number Theory and Discrete Mathematics*.

Institute of Experimental Morphology, Pathology and Anthropology with Museum: Acad. G. Bonchev St, Bldg 25, 1113 Sofia; tel. (2) 9792311; e-mail iempam@bas.bg; internet www.iempam.bas.bg; f. 2010 by merger of the Institute of Experimental Morphology and Anthropology with Museum and the Institute of Experimental Pathology and Parasitology; attached to Bulgarian Acad. of Sciences; conducts fundamental and applied research in the field of human and veterinary medicine; focuses on morphology, cell biology, pathology and anthropology; Dir Prof. Dr NINA ATANASSOVA; Scientific Sec. Assoc. Prof. MASHENKA DIMITROVA; publs *Acta Morphologica et Anthropologica* (1 a year), *Journal of Anthropology* (1 a year).

Institute of Genetics 'Acad. Doncho Kostoff': Tsarigradsko Shose, 13 Km, 1113 Sofia; tel. (2) 9746228; e-mail genetika@bas.bg; internet ig.bas.bg; f. 1910, present name 1987; attached to Bulgarian Acad. of Sciences; library of 27,069 vols (incl. 10,625 books, 15,995 periodicals, 401 microfilms and microcards); Dir Prof. Dr KOSTADIN GECHEFF; Scientific Sec. Assoc. Prof. Dr GANKA GANEVA; publ. *Genetics and Breeding* (2 a year).

Institute of Molecular Biology 'Roumen Tsanev': Acad. Georgi Bonchev St, Bldg 21, 1113 Sofia; tel. (2) 8728050; e-mail info@bio21.bas.bg; internet www.bio21.bas.bg/imb; f. 1960; attached to Bulgarian Acad. of Sciences; library of 5,000 vols; Dir Prof. ANDREY KARSHIKOFF; Scientific Sec. Assoc. Prof. ROUMIANA MIRONOVA.

Institute of Neurobiology: Acad. Georgi Bonchev 23, 1113 Sofia; tel. (2) 9792151; e-mail neurobiology@bio.bas.bg; internet www.bio.bas.bg/neurobiology; f. 1947, fmrly Institute of Physiology; attached to Bulgarian Acad. of Sciences; basic and applied research in the field of neurophysiology, neuropharmacology, neuroanatomy, psychopharmacology, psychophysiology, psychophysics and neurotoxicology; Dir Prof. Dr R. RADOMIROV; Scientific Sec. Dr CATHERINE ILIONOVA STAMBOLIEVA.

Institute of Zoology: 1 Tsar Osvoboditel Blvd, 1000 Sofia; tel. (2) 9885115; e-mail zoology@zoology.bas.bg; f. 1947 by merger of Zoology and Entomology depts of fmr Royal Institutes of Natural Sciences; attached to Bulgarian Acad. of Sciences; depts of biology and ecology of terrestrial animals, experimental zoology, faunology and zoogeography, hydrobiology, protozoology, taxonomy; library of 15,000 vols, 27,000 periodicals and journals; Dir Prof. Dr PARASKEVA MICHAILOVA; Scientific Sec. Assoc. Prof. Dr SNEJANA GROZEVA; publs *Acta Zoologica Bulgarica* (3 a year), *Catalogus Faunae Bulgaricae* (1 a year), *Fauna bulgarica* (1 a year).

Stephan Angeloff Institute of Microbiology: Georgi Bonchev St 26, 1113 Sofia; tel. (2) 9793157; e-mail micb@microbio.bas.bg; internet www.microbio.bas.bg; f. 1947 as Institute of Microbiology; attached to Bulgarian Acad. of Sciences; depts of general microbiology, applied microbiology, infectious microbiology, virology, immunology; Dir Prof. Dr HRISTO NAJDENSKI; Scientific Sec. Assoc. Prof. Dr LYUBKA DOUMANOVA.

Mathematical Sciences

Institute of Mathematics and Informatics: Acad. Georgi Bonchev St, Block 8, 1113 Sofia; tel. (2) 9793828; e-mail office@math.bas.bg; internet www.math.bas.bg; f. 1947; attached to Bulgarian Acad. of Sciences; researches and trains specialists and exercises long-range, consistent policy related to the fundamental trends in the devt of mathematics, computer science and information technologies; Dir Prof. STEFAN DODUNEKOV; Scientific Sec. Prof. NELI DIMITROVA; publs *Fractional Calculus and Applied Analysis*, *Mathematica Balkanica* (4 a year), *Mathematica Plus*, *Physico-Mathematical Journal* (4 a year), *PLISKA*, *Serdica Journal of Computing*, *Serdica Mathematical Journal* (4 a year).

Physical Sciences

'Acad. Evgeni Budevski' Institute of Electrochemistry and Energy Systems: Acad. Georgi Bonchev St, Bldg 10, 1113 Sofia; tel. (2) 8722545; internet www.bas.bg/cleps; f. 1967 as Central Laboratory of Electrochemical Power Sources; attached to Bulgarian Acad. of Sciences; electrochemical studies; research and devt of electrochemical energy sources and information systems; electrochemical materials science; electrochemical methods, techniques and instrumentation; devt and application of electronic science tools; Dir Prof. Dr DARIA VLADIKOVA; Deputy Dir Prof. Dr TAMARA PETKOVA; Scientific Sec. Assoc. Prof. Dr ANTONIA STOYANOVA; publs *Bulgarian Chemical Communications* (4 a year), *ICIS* (online).

Central Laboratory of Geodesy: Acad. Georgi Bonchev St, Bldg 1, 1113 Sofia; tel. (2) 8720841; e-mail clgdimi@argo.bas.bg; internet clg.cc.bas.bg; f. 1948; attached to Bulgarian Acad. of Sciences; research in estimation theory and statistics, geodetic astronomy, global, regional and local geodynamics, space geodesy, physical and mathematical geodesy; library of 10,000 vols; Dir Assoc. Prof. Dr DIMITAR DIMITROV; Deputy Dir and Scientific Sec. Assoc. Prof. Dr IVAN GEORGIEV; publ. *Geodesy* (2 a year).

Central Laboratory of Solar Energy & New Energy Sources: Tsarigradsko Shose Blvd 72, 1784 Sofia; tel. (2) 8778448; e-mail solar@phys.bas.bg; internet www.senes.bas.bg; f. 1977; attached to Bulgarian Acad. of Sciences; specializes in the field of photovoltaics research; Dir Prof. Dr PETKO VITANOV; Scientific Sec. Assoc. Prof. Dr MARUSHKA SENDOVA-VASSILEVA.

Geological Institute 'Strashimir Dimitrov': Acad. Georgi Bonchev St, Bldg 24, 1113 Sofia; tel. (2) 8723563; e-mail geolinst@geology.bas.bg; internet www.geology.bas.bg; f. 1947; attached to Bulgarian Acad. of Sciences; basic and applied research studies of the geoenvironment of the Bulgarian territory aiming to support the sustainable devt of contemporary society and harmonic safe control of the issues associated with geohazards; library of 80,000 vols; Dir Assoc. Prof. Dr DONCHO KARASTANEV; Scientific Sec. Prof. Dr KRISTALINA STOYKOVA; publs *Engineering Geology and Hydrogeology* (2 a year), *Geochemistry, Mineralogy and Petrology* (1 a year), *Geologica Balcanica* (4 a year), *Review of the Bulgarian Geological Society* (3 a year).

Georgi Nadjakov Institute of Solid State Physics: Tsarigradsko Shose Blvd 72, 1784 Sofia; tel. (2) 8758061; e-mail director@issp.bas.bg; internet www.issp.bas.bg; f. 1972, current name adopted 1982; attached to Bulgarian Acad. of Sciences; fundamental and applied research in fields of laser physics, condensed matter physics, microelectronics, spectroscopy and optics; Dir Prof. Dr ALEXANDER G. PETROV; First Deputy Dir Prof. Dr KIRIL BLAGOEV; Second Deputy Dir Prof. Dr ISAK BIVAS; Scientific Sec. Assoc. Prof. Dr MARINA PRIMATAROWA.

Institute of Catalysis: Acad. Georgi Bonchev St, Bldg 11, 1113 Sofia; tel. (2) 9793563; e-mail icatalys@ic.bas.bg; internet www.ic.bas.bg; f. 1983; attached to Bulgarian Acad. of Sciences; theory and practice of catalysis; elaboration of new catalysts; devt of new catalytic processes; investigation of the kinetics and mechanism of catalytic processes; creation of models of catalytic processes and elementary acts; research and devt of technologies for catalyst manufactures; coordination of the research activities in the field of catalysis in Bulgaria; Dir Prof. Dr SLAVCHO RAKOVSKY; Scientific Sec. Asst Prof. Dr SILVIA TODOROVA; publs *Proceedings of the International Symposium on Electron Paramagnetic Resonance, Proceedings of the International Symposium on Heterogeneous Catalysis*.

Institute of General and Inorganic Chemistry: Acad. Georgi Bonchev St, Bldg 11, 1113 Sofia; tel. (2) 8724801; e-mail info@svr.igic.bas.bg; internet www.igic.bas.bg; f. 1960; attached to Bulgarian Acad. of Sciences; Dir Prof. Dr PLAMEN STEFANOV; Scientific Sec. Prof. Dr EKATERINA ZHECHEVA.

Institute of Mechanics: Acad. Georgi Bonchev St, Bldg 4, 1113 Sofia; tel. (2) 9796420; e-mail office@imbm.bas.bg; internet www.imbm.bas.bg; f. 1977, present name 1993; attached to Bulgarian Acad. of Sciences; theoretical and experimental research, consultation and experts' reports, metrology measurements, construction of scientific devices and education of highly qualified specialists in theoretical and applied mechanics, biomechanics and mechatronics; main fields of research incl. mechanics of multibody systems, solid mechanics, fluid mechanics, biomechanics and physicochemical mechanics; library of 8,000 vols; Dir Prof. VASIL KAVARDJIKOV; Scientific Sec. Prof. Dr VASSIL MITEV VASSILEV; publs *Journal of Theoretical and Applied Mechanics* (4 a year), *Series in Applied Mathematics and Mechanics, Series on Biomechanics*.

Institute of Nuclear Research and Nuclear Energy: Tsarigradsko Shose Blvd 72, 1784 Sofia; tel. (2) 9743761; e-mail inrne@inrne.bas.bg; internet www.inrne.bas.bg; f. 1972; attached to Bulgarian Acad. of Sciences; Dir Assoc. Prof. Dr DIMITAR VASILEV TONEV; Scientific Sec. Assoc. Prof. Dr ANNA ANDREEVA DAMIANOVA; publ. *Proceedings of the International School on Nuclear Physics*.

Institute of Oceanology 'Fridtjof Nansen': First May St 40, POB 152, 9000 Varna; tel. (52) 370486; e-mail office@io-bas.bg; internet www.io-bas.bg; f. 1973 as Institute for Marine Research and Oceanology, current name adopted 1985; attached to Bulgarian Acad. of Sciences; research in the field of biology, chemistry, coastal dynamics and ocean technology, geology, ecology, marine physics; consulting and expert services; training; library of 10,000 vols; Dir Prof. Dr ATANAS PALAZOV; Scientific Sec. Prof. Dr GALINA SHTEREVA; publ. *Oceanologia*.

Institute of Optical Materials and Technologies 'Academician Jordan Malinovski': Acad. Georgi Bonchev St 109, POB 95, 1113 Sofia; tel. (2) 8720073; e-mail iomt@iomt.bas.bg; internet www.iomt.bas.bg; f. 2012 by merger of Central Laboratory of Photo-Processes with Central Laboratory of Optical Recording and Processing of Information; attached to Bulgarian Acad. of Sciences; examination of interaction of hard materials with different types of radiation as microwave and x-ray radiation, electron and ion-beam radiation, light and laser radiation in the ultraviolet and the visible; Dir Prof. Dr NIKOLA MALINOVSKI; Scientific Sec. Assoc. Prof. Dr ELENA STOYKOVA.

Institute of Organic Chemistry with Centre of Phytochemistry: Acad. Georgi Bonchev St, Bldg 9, 1113 Sofia; tel. (2) 9606112; e-mail iochem@orgchm.bas.bg; internet www.orgchm.bas.bg; f. 1960; attached to Bulgarian Acad. of Sciences; focuses on clarifying the relationship between synthesis, structure and reactivity of organic compounds; isolation, determination of structure and practical application of natural compounds; determination of structure and the function of proteins, enzymes and peptides; study of the thermal and catalytic transformations of hydrocarbons; Dir Prof. Dr PETKO IVANOV; Scientific Sec. Assoc. Prof. Dr MARGARITA POPOVA.

Institute of Polymers: Acad. Georgi Bonchev St, Block 103-A, 1113 Sofia; tel. (2) 8700309; e-mail instpoly@polymer.bas.bg; internet www.polymer.bas.bg; f. 1960; attached to Bulgarian Acad. of Sciences; research and education in macromolecular sciences relevant to devt and application of polymers and polymeric materials; Dir Assoc. Prof. Dr NELI KOSEVA; Scientific Sec. Assoc. Prof. Dr DILYANA PANEVA.

National Institute of Meteorology and Hydrology: Tsarigradsko Shose Blvd 66, 1784 Sofia; tel. (2) 4624710; e-mail office@meteo.bg; internet www.meteo.bg; f. 1890 as the principal meteorological station for Bulgaria, present name 1991; attached to Bulgarian Acad. of Sciences; main provider of the scientific research and operational activities in meteorology, climatology, agrometeorology and hydrology; library of 25,572 vols (incl. 9,677 books, 15,895 periodicals); Dir Prof. Dr GEORGI KORTCHEV; Scientific Sec. Prof. Dr TANIA MARINOVA; publ. *Bulgarian Journal of Meteorology and Hydrology*.

Rostislaw Kaischew Institute of Physical Chemistry: Acad. Georgi Bonchev St, Bldg 11, 1113 Sofia; tel. (2) 8727550; e-mail physchem@ipc.bas.bg; internet www.ipc.bas.bg; f. 1958; attached to Bulgarian Acad. of Sciences; crystal growth, interface colloid science phase formation, electrochemical deposition and metal dissolution; electrochemically obtained materials and corrosion processes; amorphous materials; Dir Prof. Dr VESSELA TSAKOVA; Scientific Sec. Assoc. Prof. Dr TSVETINA DOBROVOLSKA.

Rozhen National Astronomical Observatory: POB 136, 4700 Smolyan; tel. (30) 958356; e-mail office@astro.bas.bg; internet www.nao-rozhen.org; f. 1981; attached to Institute of Astronomy, Bulgarian Acad. of Sciences; fundamental studies in the field of astronomy and astrophysics; library of 5,000 vols; Dir Dr TANYU BONEV.

Solar-Terrestrial Influences Laboratory: Acad. Georgi Bonchev St, Block 3, 1113 Sofia; tel. (2) 8700229; internet www.stil.bas.bg; f. 1990; attached to Bulgarian Acad. of Sciences; fundamental space research and its application in solar-terrestrial physics; in situ and remote investigation of the geospace, planets and interplanetary space; study of global change and ecosystems and heliobiology and telemedicine and eHealth; Dir Dr TSVETAN PANTALEEV DACHEV; Scientific Sec. IRINA MITKOVA STOILOVA; publs *Advances in Space Research, Comptes Rendus de l'Académie Bulgare des Sciences, Journal of Atmospheric and Solar-Terrestrial Physics*.

Space Research and Technology Institute: Acad. Georgi Bonchev St, Block 1, 1113 Sofia; tel. (2) 9883503; e-mail office@space.bas.bg; internet www.space.bas.bg; f. 1975, present name and status 2010; attached to Bulgarian Acad. of Sciences; fundamental and applied investigations in space physics, astrophysics, image processing, remote sensing, life sciences, scientific equipment; preparation and realization of experiments in the region of space investigation and usage from the board of automatic and navigated spacecraft; investigation on control systems, air- and spacecraft and equipment for them; activity for creation of cosmic materials and technologies and their transfer in the nat. economy; Dir Prof. Dr PETAR GETSOV; Scientific Sec. Prof. Dr GARO MARDIROSSIAN; publ. *Aerospace Research in Bulgaria* (1 a year).

PHILOSOPHY AND PSYCHOLOGY

Institute for the Study of Societies and Knowledge: Moskovska St 13A, 1000 Sofia; tel. (2) 9809086; e-mail institutesk@gmail.com; internet www.issk-bas.org; f. 2010 by merger of Institute for Philosophical Research, Institute of Sociology and Centre for Science Studies and History of Science; attached to Bulgarian Acad. of Sciences; depts of ethics, aesthetics and cultural studies, anthropology and religious studies, history of philosophy, logic, ontology and epistemology, social theories, sociology of science and education, public politics, social control, identities, empirical social research, history of science; library of 53,817 vols, incl. books and periodicals; Dir Prof. Dr RUMIANA STOILOVA; Scientific Sec. Assoc. Prof. Dr ANNA MANTAROVA; publs *Balkan Journal of Philosophy* (2 a year), *Philosophical Alternatives* (6 a year), *Sociological Problems* (6 a year).

Institute of Psychology: Acad. Georgi Boncchev St, Bldg 6, Fl. 5, 1113 Sofia; tel. (2) 8703217; e-mail psycho@ipsyh.bas.bg; f. 1973 as Laboratory of Psychology, present name 1990; attached to Bulgarian Acad. of Sciences; Dir Prof. Dr BOZHIDAR DIMITROV; Scientific Sec. Assoc. Prof. Dr ELIANA PENCHEVA; publ. *Psychological Research*.

RELIGION, SOCIOLOGY AND ANTHROPOLOGY

Institute of Ethnology and Folklore Studies with Ethnographic Museum: Acad. Georgi Bonchev St., Bldg 6, 1113 Sofia; tel. (2) 8052611; e-mail folklor@bas.bg; internet www.folklor.bas.bg; f. 2010 by merger of Ethnographic Institute and Museum and the Institute of Folklore; attached to Bulgarian Acad. of Sciences; carries out research on various aspects of Bulgarian traditional and contemporary culture; Balkan ethnology; Balkan and Slavic folklore; anthropology of oral traditions, music and dance, folk arts and visual forms; intangible cultural heritage; library of 4,200 vols, 73 periodicals; Dir Prof. Dr LOZANKA PEYCHEVA; Scientific Sec. Dr EKATERINA ATANASOVA; publ. *Bulgarian Folklore* (4 a year).

Institute of Sociology: Moskovska St 13A, 1000 Sofia; tel. (2) 9809086; e-mail info@sociology-bg.org; internet www.old-sociology.issk-bas.org; f. 1968; attached to Bulgarian Acad. of Sciences; conducts theoretical and applied research in the fields of social communities, social stratification and social mobility, social pathology, sociology of labour, orgs. and politics, sociology of education, science and technologies, ethno-sociology, sociology of religions and everyday life, regional and global devt; Dir Prof. Dr DIMITAR VELKOV DIMITROV; Scientific Sec. Assoc. Prof. Dr ANNA IVANOVA MANTAROVA; publ. *Sociological Problems* (4 a year).

TECHNOLOGY

'Academician Emil Djakov' Institute of Electronics: Tsarigradsko chaussee Blvd 72, 1784 Sofia; tel. (2) 8750077; e-mail die@ie.bas.bg; internet www.ie-bas.dir.bg; f. 1963; attached to Bulgarian Acad. of Sciences; conducts research on applied physics and engineering such as high-tech material fabrication, treatment and analysis, nanosciences and nanotechnologies, nanoelectronics, photonics, optoelectronics, quantum optics, environmental monitoring, biomedical photonics; has 12 laboratories; Dir Dr SANKA GATEVA; Scientific Sec. Dr EKATERINA BORISOVA.

Central Laboratory of Applied Physics: St Petersburg Blvd 61, 4000 Plovdiv; tel. (32) 635019; e-mail clap@mbox.digsys.bg; internet www.bas.bg/plovdiv; f. 1979 as Laboratory of Applied Physics, present status and name 1995; attached to Bulgarian Acad. of Sciences; scientific investigation, research and devt work and production in the field of electronics, micro- and optoelectronics, semiconductor sensors and sensor devices and production technologies; Dir Prof. Dr LILYANA KOLAKLIEVA; Scientific Sec. Assoc. Prof. Dr LYDIA BEDIKIAN.

Central Laboratory of Mechatronics and Instrumentation: Acad. Georgi Bonchev, Bldg 1, 1113 Sofia; tel. (2) 8723571; internet www.clmi.bas.bg; f. 1994; attached to Bulgarian Acad. of Sciences; Dir Assoc. Prof. Dr TANIO TANEV; Academic Sec. Assoc. Prof. Dr VASIL TRENEV.

Central Laboratory of Physico-Chemical Mechanics: Acad. Georgi Bonchev St, Bldg 1, 1113 Sofia; tel. (2) 8718182; e-mail clphchm@clphchm.bas.bg; f. 1972; attached to Bulgarian Acad. of Sciences; nat. coordinator of research in the field of mechanics and technology of non-metallic composite materials for constructions; Dir Assoc. Prof. Dr NIKOLAY BAROVSKY; Scientific Sec. Prof. Dr RUMIANA KOTSILKOVA; publs *Non-Metallic Composite Materials* (2 a year), *Physico-Chemical Mechanics* (2 a year).

Central Laboratory of Seismic Mechanics and Earthquake Engineering: Acad. Georgi Bonchev St, Bldg 3, 1113 Sofia; tel. (2) 9712407; e-mail clsmseeof@geophys.bas.bg; f. 1982; attached to Bulgarian Acad. of Sciences; seismic risk assessment of urban areas, bldgs and structures; monitors strong ground motion; reduces the effects of earthquakes; elaborates standard documents for design and construction in seismic regions; trains scientific and engineering specialists and improves public earthquake knowledge; Dir Dr Eng. SVETOSLAV SIMEONOV; Vice-Dir Dr Eng. DIMITAR STEFANOV; Scientific Sec. Dr Eng. KIRIL HDJIYSKI.

Institute of Chemical Engineering: Acad. Georgi Bonchev Str., Bldg 103, 1113 Sofia; tel. (2) 8702088; e-mail ichemeng@bas.bg; internet www.bas.bg/iceng; f. 1961 as Dept for Mass Transfer Processes, present name and status 1986; attached to Bulgarian Acad. of Sciences; nat. research centre for chemical engineering and bioengineering science; fundamental and applied research in the fields of hydrodynamics, heat and mass transfer processes in multiphase systems, methods for optimal use and storage of energy, chemical engineering problems in catalysis, practical aspects of biochemical processes, computer simulation and control of chemical systems; comprises 6 research laboratories; Dir Prof. Dr VENKO BESCHKOV; Scientific Sec. Dr TSVETAN SAPUNDZHIEV.

Institute of Information and Communication Technologies: Acad. G. Bonchev St, Block 25A, 1113 Sofia; tel. (2) 8708494; e-mail iict@bas.bg; internet www.iict.bas.bg; f. 2010 by merger of Institute for Parallel Processing, Institute of Information Technologies and Institute of Computer and Communication Systems; attached to Bulgarian Acad. of Sciences; conducts research in the fields of computer networks and architecture, parallel algorithms, scientific computations, mathematical methods for sensor data processing, linguistic modelling, information technologies for security, grid technologies and applications, technologies for knowledge management and processing, optimization and decision making, signal processing and pattern recognition, information processes and systems, intelligent systems, embedded intelligent technologies, communication systems and services, hierarchical systems; Dir Prof. Dr SVETOZAR DIMITROV MARGENOV (acting); Scientific Sec. Dr GENNADY PAVLOVICH AGRE; publs *Cybernetics and Information Technologies* (in English, online, www.cit.iit.bas.bg/index.html), *Mathematica Balkanica* (in English and French, online, www.math-balkanica.info), *Problems of Engineering Cybernetics and Robotics* (in English and Russian, online, www.iit.bas.bg/pecr/index.html).

Institute of Laser Technology: Galichitsa 33A, 1326 Sofia; tel. (2) 688913; f. 1980; Dir Prof. I. KHRISTOV.

Institute of Metal Science, Equipment and Technologies 'Acad. A. Balevski' with Hydroaerodynamics Centre: Shipchenski prohod Str. 67, 1574 Sofia; tel. (2) 4626200; internet www.ims.bas.bg; f. 1967 as Institute of Metal Science and Technology of Metals, present name 2010; attached to Bulgarian Acad. of Sciences; conducts fundamental and applied research in the field of metal science and heat treatment, casting, crystallization, structure and properties of metals, alloys and composites on metal base, plasticity and fracture of materials, destruction of materials, functionality and reliability of construction, ship hydrodynamics, aerodynamics, water transport, ocean and coastal engineering, marine and river disasters and crises, national security and defence; Dir STEFAN VODENICHAROV; Scientific Sec. Dr NIKOLAY LICHKOV; publs *Engineering Sciences* (4 a year, in Bulgarian and English), *Journal of Materials Science and Technology* (4 a year, in English).

Institute of Mineralogy and Crystallography 'Acad. Ivan Kostov': Acad. Georgi Bonchev St, Bldg 107, 1113 Sofia; tel. (2) 9797055; e-mail mincryst@interbgc.com; internet www.clmc.bas.bg; f. 1995, fmrly Central Laboratory of Mineralogy and Crystallography, present name 2010; attached to Bulgarian Acad. of Sciences; basic studies and applied research; consulting; expertise service and analytic activities; practical applications of scientific results and training of highly qualified specialists in the field of mineralogy and crystallography; investigation and modelling of natural and technogenic mineral systems; Dir Dr ZHELYAZKO DAMYANOV; Scientific Sec. Dr VILMA PETKOVA.

Institute of Systems Engineering and Robotics 'Saint Apostle and Gospeller Matthew': Acad. G. Bonchev Str., Bldg 2, POB 79, 1113 Sofia; tel. (2) 8732614; internet www.iser.bas.bg; f. 2010 by merger of Institute for Control and System Research and Central Laboratory for Mechatronics and Instrumentation; depts of sensors, actuators and measurement technologies, bioengineering, integrated systems, hybrid systems, robotized executive mechanisms and intelligent systems, unique instruments, components and structures, mechatronic technological systems, modelling and fractal analysis of information systems, complexes and networks; Dir Prof. Dr CHAVDAR ROUMENIN; Scientific Sec. Prof. Dr SIYA LOZANOVA.

Technological Institute of Agricultural Engineering: Lipnitsa Blvd 106, 7005 Ruse; tel. (82) 441921; f. 1962; Dir T. KAYRIAKOV.

Libraries and Archives

Burgas

Library PK Yavorov: Aleko Bogoridi Blvd 21, 8000 Burgas; tel. (56) 842753; e-mail director@burglib.org; internet www2.burglib.org; f. 1888; literary and cultural centre; performs organizational and methodological features of the territory of Burgas region; 560,000 vols; Dir NATALIA KOTSEVA.

Plovdiv

'Ivan Vazov' Public Library: Avksentii Veleshki Str. 17, 4000 Plovdiv; tel. (32) 654901; e-mail nbiv@libplovdiv.com; internet www.libplovdiv.com; f. 1879; 140,000 vols (incl. scientific materials, fiction, incunabula, rare and valuable edns, reference books, Bulgarian and foreign periodicals, audiovisual materials, electronic publications); Dir DIMITAR MINEV; publ. *Yearbook* (1 a year).

Ruse

'Lyuben Karavelov' Regional Library: Dondukov Korsakov 1, 7000 Ruse; tel. (82) 820130; e-mail libruse@libruse.bg; internet www.libruse.bg; f. 1888; 700,000 vols; Dir THEODORA EVTIMOVA.

Shumen

Public Library 'Stilian Chilingirov': Slavianski Blvd 19, 9700 Shumen; tel. (54) 877093; e-mail libshumen@abv.bg; internet www.libshumen.org; f. 1922; 750,000 vols; Dir KRASIMIRA ALEKSANDROVA.

Sofia

Archives State Agency: 5 Moskovska Str., 1000 Sofia; tel. (2) 9400101; e-mail daa@archives.government.bg; internet www.archives.government.bg; f. 1951; implements nat. policy on collecting, preserving, arranging and use of historically valuable archival records; administers 2 central and 6 regional archives; 34,900 vols, 140 periodicals; Chair. IVAN KOMITSKI; Vice-Chair. Assoc. Prof. Dr VARBAN TODOROV; Chief Sec. GEORGI CHERNEV; publs *Arhiven Pregled* (Archival Review, 4 a year), *Izvestiya na Darzhavnite Arhivi* (2 a year).

Central Agricultural Library: Tsarigradsko Shose Blvd125, Block 1, 1113 Sofia; tel. (2) 8706081; e-mail csb@abv.bg; internet www.agrobiblioteki.eu; f. 1962; attached to Institute of Agricultural Information; documentation centre of nat. and int. literature of the agriculture, food science and forestry industry; 510,000 vols; Dir Dr SIMONA RALCHEVA; Head of Library MARGARITA STAMATOVA; publs *Agricultural Economics and Management*, *Agricultural Engineering*, *Agricultural Science*, *Animal Science*, *Bulgarian Journal of Agricultural Science*, *Plant Science*, *Soil Science Agrochemistry and Ecology*.

Central Library of the Bulgarian Academy of Sciences: 1, Noemvri Str. 15, 1040 Sofia; tel. (2) 9878966; e-mail library@cl.bas.bg; internet www.cl.bas.bg; f. 1869; maintains 33 spec. libraries of the acad.; provides information services for the scientific potential of Bulgarian Acad. of Sciences and the country; 2,100,000 vols; Dir Dr DINCHO KRASTEV; Deputy Dir DANIELA ATANASOVA; publs *Bulgaristika/Bulgarica*, *Bulgarian Chemical Communications* (4 a year), *Philosophical Alternatives*, *Problemi na spetsialnite biblioteki–tematichen sbornik*, *Psychological Investigations*.

Central Medical Library—MU Sofia: Sv. G. Sofiyski St 1, 1431 Sofia; tel. (2) 9523171; e-mail cml.mu.sofia@gmail.com; internet www.medun.acad.bg; f. 1918; research for medical, dental, pharmacy and public health information; scientific research and education; exchange of information resources with local and int. scientific instn and orgs; publishing and editorial activities; 338,591 vols, 250,090 books and 88,318 periodicals; Dir Dr LYDIA TACHEVA; Head of Library and Information Activities PENKA KOTSILKOVA; publs *Acta Medica Bulgarica* (2 a year, in English), *Actual Dentistry* (3 a year, in Bulgarian and English), *Acupuncture* (3 a year, in Bulgarian and English), *Allergology, Clinical Immunology & Clinical Laboratory* (2 a year), *Bulgarian Medical Journal* (4 a year, in Bulgarian and English), *Cardiovascular Diseases* (4 a year, in Bulgarian and English), *Endocrine diseases* (2 a year, in Bulgarian and English), *Gastroenterology* (2 a year), *General Medicine* (4 a year, in Bulgarian and English), *Health Management and Health Policy* (3 a year, in Bulgarian and English), *Information for Nursing Staff* (4 a year, in Bulgarian and English), *Medical Review* (4 a year, in Bulgarian and English), *Neurology and Psychiatry* (2 a year, in Bulgarian and English), *Pediatrics & Infectious diseases* (4 a year, in Bulgarian and English), *Scripta Periodica* (4 a year, in English), *Surgery* (3 a year, in Bulgarian and English).

Central Research and Technical Library at the National Centre for Information and Documentation: NACID, MD. GM Dimitrov Blvd 50, 1125 Sofia; tel. (2) 8173841; e-mail ctb@nacid-bg.net; f. 1962; collects, stores and makes available various types of Bulgarian and foreign publs, incl. monographs, reference books, encyclopaedias, dictionaries, magazines and periodicals, bibliographic and referral issues, reports from scientific confs held nationally and internationally, dissertations; 396,900 vols, 13,000 journals, periodicals, bibliographic publs, 77,000 reports of scientific confs, 19,000 UN reports, 14,000 dissertations, 103,000 co literatures, 900 CD-ROMs, DVDs; Dir for SLIS VALENTINA SLAVCHEVA; publs *Advances in Bulgarian Science* (1 a year), *Infosviat* (4 a year).

Central State Archives: Moskovska Str. 5, 1000 Sofia; tel. (2) 9400179; e-mail cda@archives.government.bg; internet www.archives.government.bg/6-central_state_archives; f. 1952; attached to Archives State Agency; has 1,739,277 archival units; documents activities of state instns, political parties, state and private companies and enterprises, from the mid-19th century to recent times; personal papers of eminent Bulgarians; Dir STEFKA PETROVA.

Centre for European Studies: G. M. Dimitrov 52A, 1125 Sofia; tel. (2) 9712411; e-mail ces@mail.cesbg.org; f. 1990; European Documentation Centre receiving all official publs of EC; Dir I. SHIKOVA; publ. *Europa* (12 a year).

Institute of Agricultural Information (with Central Agricultural Library): Tsarigradsko Shose 125, Bldg 1, 1113 Sofia; tel. (2) 8705558; e-mail csb@abv.bg; f. 1961; library and information services in agriculture; Dir MARGARITA STAMATOVA; Librarian ROUMYANA VASSILEVA; publ. *Bulgarian Journal of Agricultural Science*.

Library and Information Services of University of Architecture, Civil Engineering and Geodesy: 1 Hristo Smirnenski Blvd, 1046 Sofia; tel. (2) 9635245; e-mail lib@uacg.bg; internet www.uacg.bg; f. 1942; holds MSS, theses, grey literature, microfilms, spec. colln of art and graphics albums, reference books and encyclopaedias in Bulgarian, English, French, German, Italian, Polish, Russian, Spanish and other Slavonic languages covering areas of architecture, art, agricultural sciences, economics, environmental sciences, geodesy, mathematics, physics, philosophy, political and social sciences, technics; 90,000 vols; Dir PERSIDA TOMOVA RAFAILOVA.

Library of the Union of Bulgarian Actors: 6 Slavyanska Str., Sofia; tel. (2) 9873872; e-mail library@uba.bg; internet www.uba.bg; plays and drama materials from the end of the 19th and beginning of the 20th centuries; open to mems of soc.; 6,000 vols; Librarian IVANKA SHINDAROVA; Librarian VESELA PAVLOVA; publ. *Homo Ludens*.

National Centre for Information and Documentation: G. M. Dimitrov Blvd 52A, 1125 Sofia; tel. (2) 8173824; e-mail nacid@nacid-bg.net; internet mail.nacid.bg; f. 1993; attached to Min. of Education and Science; management models, structure, control and resources ensuring popular education, higher education, youth and science systems; information products and services in the field of education and science; 2,552,070 vols; Exec. Dir VANYA GRASHKINA; publs *Advances in Bulgarian Science* (1 a year, in English), *Scientific and Technical Publications in Bulgaria* (4 a year, in English).

St Cyril and Methodius National Library: Vasil Levski Blvd 88, 1037 Sofia; tel. (2) 9882811; e-mail nl@nationallibrary.bg; internet www.nationallibrary.bg; f. 1878, present bldg 1953; holds Slavonic and foreign language MSS, incunabula, rare and valuable edns, Bulgarian historical archives, maps and graphics, official publs, music publs and recordings, foreign books and periodicals, reference books, specialized collns, dept of Oriental collns; 7,753,188 vols incl. 1,714,211 vols of books, 1,367,487 serials, 209,490 graphic documents, 12,991 cartographic documents, 5,547 MSS, 3,124,974 archives, 5,889 electronic records and 17 electronic databases; Dir Prof. Dr BORYANA HRISTOVA; Sec. VIOLETA BOZHKOVA; publs *Journal Biblioteka* (6 a year), *Proceedings* (1 a year).

Scientific Archives of the Bulgarian Academy of Sciences: 15 Noemvri 1, 1040 Sofia; tel. (2) 9884046; e-mail office_sa@cl.bas.bg; internet archiv.cl.bas.bg; f. 1947; MSS and 110,000 scientific dossiers; historical archives containing documents on the history of the Bulgarian state, science and orthodox church; Head Prof. Dr RUZHA SIMEONOVA; publ. *Proceedings of the scientific archive*.

Sofia City Library: 4 Slaveikov Sq., 1000 Sofia; tel. (2) 9862169; e-mail libsofdir@libsofia.bg; internet www.libsofia.bg; f. 1898, present status 2000; Sofia local history colln; also a municipal culture institute; 872,228 vols of books, 35,283 periodicals, 8,682 black and white drawings, 1,862 maps, 9,242 scores, 12,669 sound records, 292 official editions, 2,241 slides and films and 322 pictures; Dir MIHAIL BELCHEV.

University Library 'St Kliment Ohridski': Tsar Osvoboditel Blvd 15, 1043 Sofia; tel. (2) 8467584; e-mail lsu@libsu.uni-sofia.bg; internet www.libsu.uni-sofia.bg; f. 1888; provides interlibrary and int. interlibrary loans; comprises 24 br. libraries; 2,001,000 vols; Dir Dr ANNA ANGELOVA; Deputy Dir BILIANA YAVRUKOVA; Sec. BISTRA DRAGOLOVA.

Stara Zagora

Regional Library 'Zaharii Ukyazhesky': Ruski Blvd 46, 6000 Stara Zagora; tel. (42) 648131; e-mail snmlib@abv.bg; f. 1954; 419,000 vols; Dir SNEZHANA MARINOVA.

Rodina Library: Ruski Blvd 17, 6000 Stara Zagora; tel. (42) 630113; e-mail lib@rodina-bg.org; internet www.rodina-bg.org; f. 1860; 300,000 vols of books, periodicals, graphic and cartographic issues, books of notes, records, cassettes, film strips, CDs.

Varna

'Pencho Slaveykov' Public Library—Varna: Slivnitsa Blvd 34, 9000 Varna; tel. (52) 659136; e-mail office@libvar.bg; internet www.libvar.bg; f. 1883; depository of Bulgarian nat. literature since 1945; 773,000 vols; Man. Dir EMILIYA STANEVA-MILKOVA.

Veliko Tărnovo

Public Library P. R. Slaveykov—Veliko Turnovo: Ivanka Boteva St 2, 5000 Veliko Tărnovo; tel. (62) 620208; e-mail prs@libraryvt.com; internet www.libraryvt.com; f. 1889; third nat. depository library; 586,873 vols; Dir IVAN ALEXANDROV; Deputy Dir KALINA IVANOVA.

Vidin

Regional Library 'Mihalacky Gergiev': Bdintsi Pl. 1, 3700 Vidin; tel. (94) 601704; e-mail libvidin@vidin.net; internet www.libvidin.net; f. 1863; 299,322 vols incl. 286,083 books, 3,696 periodicals, 2,186 graphic edns, 2,025 printed music, 11 MSS, 499 CDs, 122 DVDs; Dir DESISLAVA IVANOVA VENCHOVA.

Museums and Art Galleries

Blagoevgrad

Blagoevgrad Regional History Museum: Rila St 1, Varosha Block, 2700 Blagoevgrad; tel. (73) 885370; e-mail im_bld@yahoo.com; f. 1951; archaeology, ethnography, fine arts, history, natural history; library of 17,000 vols; Dir K. GRANCHAROVA.

Burgas

Regional Museum, Burgas: Slavianska St 69, 8000 Burgas; tel. (56) 820344; e-mail main@burgasmuseums.bg; internet www.burgasmuseums.bg; f. 1912, present status 2000; organizes research and study of cultural heritage; archaeological, ethnographic, historical and natural history expositions; Dir TSONYA DRAZHEVA; publ. *Bulletin of Museums of Southeast Bulgaria* (1 a year).

Dobrich

Regional Museum of History—Dobrich: 18 Konstantin Stoilov St, p. k. 131, 9300 Dobrich; tel. (58) 603256; e-mail rim_dobrich@abv.bg; internet www.dobrichmuseum.bg; f. 1953; holds 150,000 items; depts of archaeology, ethnography, literature and art, modern history, nat. revival period, nature; library of 20,000 vols; Dir KOSTADIN KOSTADINOV; publ. *Dobrudzha* (1 a year).

Haskovo

Regional Museum of History—Haskovo: Svoboda Sq. 19, 6300 Haskovo; tel. (38) 624237; internet www.haskovomuseum.com; f. 1952; Dir VALENTIN DIMITROV.

Kalofer

Hristo Botev National Museum: 5 Hristo Botev St, 4370 Kalofer; tel. (3133) 5271; e-mail musei_botev@abv.bg; f. 1944; birthplace of Hristo Botev, poet, revolutionary and rebel against Ottoman rule; objects and clothes showing Bulgarian life in the past; exhibit of rose oil and lace production; Dir A. NIKOLOVA.

Karlovo

'Vasil Levski' Museum—Karlovo: General Kartsov St 57, 4300 Karlovo; tel. (335) 93489; e-mail v_levski_museum@mail.orbitel.bg; internet www.vlevskimuseum-bg.org; f. 1937; named after Vasil Levski (1837-73), founder of Bulgarian Revolutionary Central Committee, which liberated Bulgaria from Ottoman rule; consists of Levski's birth house, an exhibition hall with personal items, photographs, documents and works of art; memorial chapel preserving hair of Vasil Levski; Dir DORA CHAUSHEVA.

Kazanlak

National Park-Museum 'Shipka-Buzluzha': Kazanlak Directorate, P. R. Slaveykov St 8, 6100 Kazanlak; tel. (431) 62495; e-mail shipkamuseum@mail.bg; internet www.shipkamuseum.org; f. 1956; monuments connected with the liberation of Bulgaria from Ottoman rule; Dir DANCHO DANCHEV.

Lovech

Regional Museum of History: Todor Kirkov Str. 1, 5500 Lovech; tel. (68) 601382; e-mail imlovech@yahoo.com; f. 1895; holds 70,000 exhibits; restoration and conservation activities; photography services; exhibition area for temporary exhibits; Dir IVAN LALEV.

Montana

Regional Museum of History: Tsar Boris III 2, 3400 Montana; tel. (96) 28481; f. 1953; Dir U. DERAKCHIISKA.

Pazardzhik

Art Gallery 'Stanislav Dospevsky': Pl. K. Velichkov 15, 4400 Pazardzhik; tel. (34) 444152; e-mail citygallerypz@abv.bg; f. 1963; Dir BABACHEV.

Regional Historical Museum of Pazardzhik: Pl. K. Velichkov 15, 4400 Pazardzhik; tel. (34) 443113; e-mail museumpz@abv.bg; internet historymuseumpazardzhik.jimdo .com; f. 1911; house museum of Constantine Velichkov; permanent exhibition of Lapidarium findings, archaeology, history of Pazardzhik before and after liberation, ethnography; library of 11,000 vols; Dir DIMITAR ZLATKOV MITREV; publ. *Homeland* (every 2 years).

Pernik

Regional Museum of History: Fizkulturna St 2, 2300 Pernik; tel. (76) 603118; e-mail muzeum@rotop.com; f. 1953 as a city museum, present status 1959, present name 1969; sections of archaeology, ethnography, labour movement, socialistic devt, mine and coal devt, nat. history; Dir EMILIYA VELINOVA.

Pleven

Regional Historical Museum—Pleven: Stoyan Zaimov Str. 3, 5800 Pleven; tel. (64) 822623; e-mail plevenmuseum@dir.bg; internet www.plevenmuseum.dir.bg; f. 1903 as Archaeological Soc., present location 1984, present name and status 2000; gen. history with a natural science section; units: archaeology, history of Bulgaria from 15th to 19th century, modern history, ethnography, nature, stocks and scientific records, public relations, studio for restoration and conservation, photo-laboratory, library; basic museum colln over 180,000 items and 25,000 coins; library of 10,000 vols of scientific literature and periodicals; Dir STEFKA GRIGOROVA (acting); publ. *Museum Studies in North-Western Bulgaria* (1 a year).

Plovdiv

Archaeological Museum—Plovdiv: Saedinenie sq. 1, 4000 Plovdiv; tel. (32) 633106; e-mail ram.plovdiv@gmail.com; internet www.archaeologicalmuseumplovdiv.org; f. 1882, present status 1920; colln of 100,000 museum artefacts related to history of Plovdiv, prehistoric, Thracian, ancient Greek, Roman, medieval, Bulgarian revival art; numismatic colln of 1,500 coins; ethnographic and historical documents; library of 13,000 vols; Dir Prof. Dr KOSTADIN KISIOV; publs *Pulpudeva*, *Yearbook of the Regional Archaeological Museum-Plovdiv* (in Bulgarian with annotations in English).

City Gallery of Fine Arts: 'Saborna' St 14A, 4000 Plovdiv; tel. (32) 635322; e-mail ghgpl@abv.bg; f. 1952; collects, treasures and popularizes Bulgarian fine arts, painting, graphic art, sculpture, applied arts, photography, icon colln, and Mexican art; holds colln of 6,900 items; Dir KRASIMIR LINKOV.

Regional Ethnographic Museum—Plovdiv: Dr Chomakov Str. 2, 4000 Plovdiv; tel. (32) 625257; e-mail ethnograph@abv.bg; internet www.ethnograph.info; f. 1917; 40,000 artefacts exhibiting traditional material and spiritual culture of the population of Plovdiv and Rodopi; permanent exhibition of agricultural tools and utensils, craftsman's articles and tools, textiles and clothing, furniture and interior, musical instruments and ritual properties, paintings, icons, statuettes, woodcarvings and metal figures; Dir Dr ANGEL YANKOV.

Regional History Museum—Plovdiv: Saedinenie Sq. 1, 4000 Plovdiv; tel. (32) 629409; e-mail hm_plovdiv@mail.bg; internet www.historymuseumplovdiv.org; f. 1951; collects, preserves and popularizes historical evidence from the past of Plovdiv and Plovdiv region from 15th to 20th century; colln of 60,000 artefacts incl. cold steel and firearms, orders and medals, armament, personal belongings, printed publs, apparel and items from town's everyday life, photos and documents; Dir STEFAN SHIVACHEV; Chief Curator MARIA KARADECHEVA.

Regional Natural History Museum of Plovdiv: Hrysto G. Danov str. 34, 4000 Plovdiv; tel. (32) 626683; e-mail pnm_plovdiv@abv.bg; internet rnhm.org; f. 1955, present name 2006; collns in minerals, botany, invertebrates, freshwater aquarium, 'Sea bottom' exhibiting colln from the Caribbean Sea, the Atlantic Ocean and the Mediterranean, fishes, amphibians and reptiles, birds, mammals; library of 7,740 vols; Dir Dr OGNIAN TODOROV; Chief Curator MIROSLAV ANTOV.

Rila

Rila Monastery National Museum: Rilski Monastir, 2643 Rila (Sofia Dist.); tel. (70) 542208; e-mail rila_monastery@abv.bg; internet www.rilamonastery.pmg-blg.com; f. 1961, present status 1976; Bulgarian art and architecture during the Ottoman period, Bulgarian history and history of the monastery; Dir P. MITEV.

Ruse

Regional Museum of History: Al. Batenberg Sq. 3, POB 60, 7000 Ruse; tel. (82) 825002; e-mail pr@museumruse.com; internet www.museumruse.com; f. 1904, present name and status 2000; archaeology, ethnography, history of Bulgaria, modern and contemporary history, nature; colln of 130,000 items; library of 15,340 vols; Dir Prof. Dr NIKOLAY IVANOV NENOV; publ. *Izvestija*.

Shumen

Regional Museum of History—Shumen: Slavianski Blvd 17, 9700 Shumen; tel. (54) 875487; e-mail museum_shumen@abv.bg; internet www.museum-shumen.eu; f. 1904; incl. 3 nat. archaeological reserves, 4 house museums, preserved sites; maintains main exhibition in Shumen city museum and 7 smaller museums, specializing in history and archaeology of the region; collns of armoury, jewellery, numismatic and sphragistic colln, old printed books, film posters; 150,000 artefacts; library of 25,000 vols, incl. scientific literature and periodicals; Dir GEORGI MAYSTORSKI.

Sofia

Boyana Church National History Museum: 1–3 Boyansko Ezero St, 1616 Sofia; tel. (2) 9592966; e-mail nmbc@nmbc .orbitel.bg; internet www.boyanachurch.org; f. 1947; medieval orthodox painting; Dir MARIANA HRISTOVA-TRIFONOVA.

Dimitar Blagoev Museum: ul. Lajos Koshut 34, 1606 Sofia; tel. (2) 523145; f. 1948; house of the founder of the Bulgarian Social-Democratic Party, containing documents and personal items; Dir R. RUSSEV.

Georgi Dimitrov National Museum: Opalchenska 66, 1303 Sofia; tel. (2) 320149; f. 1951; Dir VERA DICHEVA.

Ivan Vazov Memorial House: Ivan Vazov St 10, 1000 Sofia; tel. (2) 881270; f. 1926; house of the Bulgarian poet; colln of personal belongings such as clothes, books, presents and awards; his workroom is preserved in its original state; Curator I. BACHEVA.

National Ethnographical Museum: Moskovska St 6A, 1000 Sofia; tel. (2) 9884191; e-mail eim_bas@mail.bg; internet mdl.cc.bas .bg/ethnography; f. 1978; contains elements of Renaissance, Baroque Vienna, reminiscent of French palaces of the 18th century; 50,000 artefacts; library of 22,221 vols; Dir Prof. Dr RACHKO POPOV; Deputy Dir Prof. Dr HOPE TENEVA; Scientific Sec. Prof. Dr ELYA TSANEVA; publs *Bulgarian Ethnology*, *Ethnologia Balcanica* (1 a year).

National Gallery of Decorative Arts: Cerni vrah Blvd 2, 1421 Sofia; tel. (2) 9630758; f. 1976; works from the 1950s to the present; library of 2,000 vols; Dir ZDRAVKO MAVRODIEV.

National Institute of Archaeology with Museum Bulgarian Academy of Sciences: Saborna Str. 2, 1000 Sofia; tel. (2) 9882406; e-mail naim@naim.bg; internet naim.bg; f. 1892; permanent exhibitions on prehistory, classical antiquity and the Middle Ages; numismatic and ethnographic colln; temporary exhibitions; facilitates archaeological research; Dir Dr LYUDMIL VAGALINSKI; Scientific Sec. Dr MARIA GUROVA; publ. *Arheologia* (4 a year).

National Museum of Bulgarian Literature: ul. Rakovski 138, 1000 Sofia; tel. (2) 9882493; f. 1976; Dir DZH. KAMENOV.

National Museum of Ecclesiastical History and Archaeology: Sv. Nedelya Sq. 19, 1000 Sofia; tel. (2) 890115; Dir N. KHADZHIEV.

National Museum of History: 16 Vitoshko lale Str., 1618 Sofia; tel. (2) 9554280; e-mail nim1973@abv.bg; internet www .historymuseum.org; f. 1973, present location 2000; more than 680,000 exhibits, incl. colln from Palaeolithic, Neolithic, Chalcolithic, Bronze, Iron, Roman, Middle-Late Middle ages; numismatics, adornments, jewellery, embroideries, weapons, uniforms and civil clothes and accessories, traditional clothes, applied and fine arts, documents from the nat. revival, modern history of Bulgaria, also maps, printed materials, manufacture samples; 4 brs; Dir Dr BOZHIDAR DIMITROV.

National Museum of Military History: Cherkovna Str. 92, 1505 Sofia; tel. (2) 9461805; e-mail m.museum@bol.bg; internet www.militarymuseum.bg; f. 1916; attached to Min. of Defence; more than 1m. artefacts; collects, registers and popularizes Bulgarian and European military artefacts (arms, uniforms, flags, photographs); organizes educational programmes for students and school children; 2 brs in Varna and 1 in Krumovo; library of 15,000 vols; Dir Dr SONIA PENKOVA; publ. *Proceedings of the National Museum of Military History*.

National Museum of Natural History: Tsar Osvoboditel Blvd 1, 1000 Sofia; tel. (2) 9882894; e-mail contact@nmnhs.com; internet www.nmnhs.com; f. 1889 as Royal Prince's Natural History Museum; attached to Bulgarian Acad. of Sciences; 1m. specimens and samples, incl. 460 mammal species, 1,990 bird species, reptile and amphibian colln, 480,000 specimens of insects and 300,000 specimens of other invertebrates; colln also incl. mineral species from around the world and more than 30,000 samples of fossil invertebrates; br. at Asenovgrad; library of 7,887 vols of periodicals, 2,427 books; Dir Prof. Dr NIKOLAI SPASSOV; Scientific Sec. Dr ZDRAVKO HUBENOV; Public Relations Officer SILVIA TOSHEVA; publ. *Historia naturalis bulgarica* (1 a year).

National Polytechnic Museum: Opulchenska 66, 1303 Sofia; tel. (2) 9318018; e-mail polytechnic@abv.bg; internet www.polytechnicmuseum.org; f. 1968; 22,000 exhibits incl. collns of instruments of time-measurement, transport, photo and cinema technique, optics, sound tracking and sound reproduction, radio and TV, calculation technique, musical mechanisms, geodesic instruments, measurement technique, household technique, sewing machines, typewriters, physical appliances, communication technique; 3 brs; scientific archive incl. 2,000 archive units; library of 12,000 vols; Dir Dr EKATERINA TSEKOVA; Deputy Dir. EMIL DAVCHEV; publs *Annual of the National Polytechnical Museum, Technitartché*.

Sofia Art Gallery: Gen. Gurko Str. 1, 1000 Sofia; tel. (2) 9872181; e-mail sghg@sghg.bg; internet www.sghg.bg; f. 1928, present name and status 1952, present location 1973; conserves, maintains and studies art heritage; modern Bulgarian art; collns of paintings, graphics, sculpture, contemporary art and photography; Dir ADELINA FILEVA; Chief Curator Dr MARIA VASSILEVA.

Sofia Museum of History: Exarh Yossif 27, 1000 Sofia; tel. (2) 9833755; e-mail p_mitanov@yahoo.com; f. 1952; library of 16,000 vols.

Sopot

Ivan Vazov House Museum—Sopot: Vasil Levski 1, 4330 Sopot; tel. (3134) 8650; e-mail vazovmuseum_sopot@abv.bg; internet www.vazovmuseum.com; f. 1935; birthplace of the writer (1850–1921); Head STEFAN FILCHEV.

Stara Zagora

Regional Museum of History: 42 Ruski Blvd, 6000 Stara Zagora; tel. (42) 919206; e-mail rim@museum.starazagora.net; internet www.museum.starazagora.net; f. 1907, present name and status 1953; sections of pre-history, antique archaeology, medieval archaeology, Bulgarian history, ethnology, numismatics; library of 7,600 vols (incl. books and periodicals); Dir Dr SVETLA DIMITROVA.

Trojan

Museum of Folk Craft and Applied Arts: Pl. Vazrashdane, POB 46, 5600 Trojan; tel. (670) 22062; f. 1962; library of 2,700 vols; Dir T. TOTEVSKI; publ. *Cultural and Historical Inheritance of Trojan Region* (1 a year).

Tryavna

Museum of Wood Carving and Icon Painting: Captain Dyado Nikola Sq. 7, 5350 Tryavna; tel. (677) 62278; e-mail tryavna_museum@mail.bg; internet www.tryavna-museum.com; f. 1963; woodcarving and icon-painting; incl. 8 museum bldgs: Angel Kunchev House Museum, Asian and African Art Museum, Daskalov House Museum, Icon Painting Museum, Old School Museum, Raykov House Museum, Slaveykov House Museum; library of 4,535 vols; Dir JULIA NINOVA (acting).

Varna

Varna Museum of Archaeology: Maria Louisa Blvd 41, 9000 Varna; tel. (52) 681011; e-mail archaeological@museumvarna.com; internet www.archaeo.museumvarna.com; f. 1906; br. open-air museums: Roman Baths, Aladzha Monastery, 'Stone Forest' Nat. Park; 100,000 colln of artefacts showing prehistory, Thracian, antiquity, middle ages, ottoman periods; library of 24,000 vols of periodicals, 7,000 monographs; Dir Prof. Dr VALENTIN PLETNYOV; publs *Acta Musei Varnaensis, Izvestija na narodniya muzei Varna* (1 a year).

Veliko Tărnovo

Ethnographic Museum of Veliko Tărnovo: Ivan Vazov St 35, POB 281, 5000 Veliko Tărnovo; tel. (62) 604010; e-mail studio@studiohotel-vt.com; f. 2012; library of 4,600 vols; Man. Dir D. MARINOV.

Regional Museum of History—Veliko Tărnovo: Nikola Pikolo Str. 6, 5000 Veliko Tărnovo; tel. (62) 682511; e-mail rimvt@abv.bg; internet www.museumvt.com; f. 1871; comprises Archaeological Museum, Museum of the Bulgarian Revival and Constituent Assembly, Museum of Contemporary History, Museum of Prison, Sarafkina's House, Slaveikov House, Architectural reserve 'Arbanasi', Konstantsalieva's House, Museum of History in the town of Kilifarev, Philip Totyo House, Archaeological reserve 'Nicopolis ad Istrum', Ethnographic complex 'Osenarska reka'; organizes annual conf.; library of 12,000 vols; Dir IVAN TSAROV; Admin. Sec MARGARITA KUNEVA; Chief Curator VIOLETA PAVLOVA; publ. *Proceedings* (1 a year).

Vidin

Historical Museum Vidin: Tsar Simeon Veliki Str. 13, 3700 Vidin; tel. (94) 601710; e-mail museumvd@mail.bg; internet www.museum-vidin.domino.bg; f. 1910; units of archaeology, numismatics, ethnography, modern history, recent history, Bulgarian history (15th to 19th century); library of 4,600 vols; Dir FIONERA FILIPOVA.

Vratsa

Regional Historical Museum Vratsa: Hristo Boteva Sq. 2, 3000 Vratsa; tel. (92) 620373; e-mail vratsamuseum@mail.bg; internet www.vratsamuseum.com; f. 1952; depts of archaeology, Bulgarian history of 15th to 19th century, ethnography, modern history, contemporary history, art gallery; library of 4,500 vols; Dir ILIYA DIMITROV STOYANOV.

Universities

AGRAREN UNIVERSITET PLOVDIV
(Agricultural University Plovdiv)

Mendeleev Blvd 12, 4000 Plovdiv
Telephone: (32) 654200
E-mail: rector@au-plovdiv.bg
Internet: www.au-plovdiv.bg

Founded 1945, present name and status 2001
State control
Academic year: September to June

Rector: Prof. Dr DIMITAR GREKOV
Vice-Rector: Prof. Dr HRISTINA YANCHEVA
Vice-Rector: Prof. Dr KRASIMIR IVANOV

Library of 215,000 vols of books, reference materials, textbooks, scientific periodicals and CDs
Number of teachers: 350
Number of students: 2,700

Publications: *Agricultural Sciences* (2 a year), *Scientific Works of the Agricultural University Plovdiv* (4 a year)

DEANS

Dept of Languages and Sports: GALINA SESTRIMSKA (Dir)
Faculty of Agronomy: Dr BOJIN BOJINOV
Faculty of Economics: Dr GEORGI BOGOEV
Faculty of Plant Protection and Agroecology: Dr YANKO DIMITROV
Faculty of Viticulture and Horticulture: Dr KRASSIMIR MIHOV

PROFESSORS

ALADJADJIYAN, A., Mathematics, Computer Science and Physics
ATANASOV, H., Botany and Agrometeorology
CHRIST, K., Economics
CHOLAKOV, D., Horticulture
DZHELEPOV, G., Mathematics, Computer Science and Physics
DZHUGALOV, H., Arboriculture
FERDINANDOV, D., Animal Science
GESHEV, Z., Tourism
HARIZANOVA, B., Entomology
IVANOV, K., General Chemistry
KAMBUROVA, M., General Chemistry
LECHEVA, I., Entomology
MANDRADJHIEV, S., Agricultural Mechanization
MERANZOVA, A., Land Reclamation and Surveying
PANDELIEV, S., Viticulture
ROYTCHEV, V., Viticulture
SAMALIEV, H., Entomology
STANCHO, D., Ecology and Environment
STOIMENOV, V., Animal Science
STOYKOV, A., Animal Science
SVETLEVA, D., Plant Genetics
TONEV, S., Agriculture and Herbology
VASSILEVA, M., General Chemistry
YANCHEVA, H., Crop
YANKOV, D., Accounting and Finance
ZOROVSKI, P., Agroecology and Agroecosystems and Protection of Population

AMERIKANSKI UNIVERSITET V BULGARIA
(American University in Bulgaria)

1 Georgi Izmirliev Sq., 2700 Blagoevgrad
Telephone: (73) 888306
E-mail: admissions@aubg.bg
Internet: www.aubg.bg

Founded 1991
Private control
Language of instruction: English
Academic year: August to May

Academic depts of arts, languages and literature, business management, computer science, economics, history and civilizations, journalism and mass communication; mathematics and science, politics and European studies

Pres.: Dr W. MICHAEL EASTON
Provost: STEVEN SULLIVAN
Vice-Pres. for Finance and Admin.: ALEXANDER ALEXANDROV
Vice-Pres. for Institutional Advancement: SANI SILVENNOINEN
Dean for Faculty: LUCIA MIREE

Dean for Students: LYDIA KRISE
Registrar: EVELINA TERZIEVA
Library Dir: SOPHIA KATSARSKA

Library of 105,000 vols, 72,000 ebooks, 10,000 print vols, 36,000 ejournal titles, magazines and newspapers, audiovisual materials and many electronic databases
Number of teachers: 78 (51 full-time and 27 part-time)
Number of students: 1,044
Publication: *AUBG Today* (2 a year)

PROFESSORS

CHRISTOZOV, D., Computer Science
CRIPPS, J., Business
FORTNER, R., Journalism and Mass Communication
GALLETLY, J., Computer Science
IVANOVA, T., Mathematics
KARAGIOZOV, V., Computer Science
KELBECHEVA, E., History and Civilizations
MATEEV, M., Business
MIREE, L., Business
MUTAFCHIEV, L., Mathematics and Science
POLICH, J., Journalism and Mass Communications
POPOV, A., Mathematics and Science
STEFANOVICH, M., History and Civilizations
STOYTCHEV, O., Mathematics and Science

BURGASKI SVOBODEN UNIVERSITET (Burgas Free University)

San Stefano St 62, 8000 Burgas
Telephone: (56) 900400
Internet: www.bfu.bg

Founded 1991
Private control
Academic year: October to June

Pres.: Prof. Dr PETKO CHOBANOV
Rector: Prof. Dr VASIL YANKOV
Vice-Rector for Academic Affairs: Dr MILEN BALTOV
Vice-Rector for Research and Int. Cooperation: Prof. Dr GALYA HRISTOZOVA
Dir for Library: DIANA ADAMOVA

Library of 120,000 vols
Number of teachers: 615
Number of students: 7,000
Publications: *Business Directions*, *Modern Humanities*

DEANS

Faculty of Business Studies: Prof Dr PETKO CHOBANOV
Faculty of Computer Science and Engineering: Prof. DIMITAR JUDAH
Faculty of Humanities: Dr EVELINA DINEVA
Faculty of Legal Studies: Prof. Dr MOMYANA GUNEVA

PROFESSORS

(some professors teach in more than 1 faculty)

Faculty of Business Studies:
GROZDANOV, B.
STANKOV, P. C.
YANKOV, V. N.

Faculty of Computer Science and Engineering:
JUDAH, D. D.
LAZAROV, A. D.
STAMOVA, I. M.

Faculty of Humanities:
HRISTOZOV, G. M.
LUKOVA, K. G.

Faculty of Legal Studies:
DRAGIEV, A. D.
ENCHEV, T. T.
IVANOV, I. V.
KYNDEVA-SPIRIDO, E. V.
ZLATAREV, E. N.

BURGAS PROF. ASSEN ZLATAROV UNIVERSITY

Prof. Yakimov Blvd 1, 8010 Burgas
Telephone: (56) 860041
E-mail: rector@btu.bg
Internet: www.btu.bg

Founded 1963 as Higher Institute of Chemical Technology, present name 1995
State control
Language of instruction: English
Academic year: September to July

Rector: Prof. PETKO PETKOV
Vice-Rector for Int. Cooperation Studies: Dr MAGDALENA SABEVA MITKOVA
Vice-Rector for Quality Training, Accreditation and Staff: Dr GEORGIEV BRATOVAN KOPRINAROV
Vice-Rector for Research: Prof. VALENTIN ANDREEV NENOV
Vice-Rector for Student Affairs: Dr PETRANKA PIPEVA TODOROVA DIMITROVA
Dir for Academic Affairs: C. MAEVSKA
Dir for Library: Dr IRENA MARKOVSKA

Library of 256,000 vols incl. 184,000 books, 33,000 periodicals, 37,000 patents and standards, 2,000 other library materials
Number of teachers: 320
Number of students: 3,918
Publication: *Godishnik*

DEANS

College of Tourism: Dr MARY NIKOVA (Dir)
Faculty of Natural Science: Prof. RADOSTIN KUTSAROV
Faculty of Social Science: Prof. DIMITAR TODOROV GOGOV
Faculty of Technical Science: Dr STOIKO PETROV
Medical College: Dr MIMI GEORGIEVA STOYCHEVA (Dir)
Technical College: Prof. B. MECHKOV (Dir)

HIMIKO TEHNOLOGIČEN I METALURGIČEN UNIVERSITET (University of Chemical Technology and Metallurgy)

St Kliment Ohridski Blvd 8, 1756 Sofia
Telephone: (2) 8163120
E-mail: rector@uctm.edu
Internet: www.uctm.edu

Founded 1953 as Dept of the State Polytechnic, present name and status 1995
State control
Languages of instruction: Bulgarian, English, French, German
Academic year: September to July

Rector: Prof. Dr MITKO GEORGIEV
Vice-Rector for Accreditation and Quality: Dr SENIA TERZIEVA
Vice-Rector for Education: Prof. NIKOLAI DISHOVSKI
Vice-Rector for Scientific Activities: Dr EDUARD KLIEN
Dir for Library: Prof. MAYA PENCHEVA

Library of 70,000 vols
Number of teachers: 297
Number of students: 4,000
Publication: *Journal of the University of Chemical Technology and Metallurgy* (4 a year, in English)

DEANS

Faculty of Chemical and System Engineering: Dr PESHKO JAMBOV
Faculty of Chemical Technology: Prof. Dr VLADIMIR BOJINOV
Faculty of Metallurgy and Material Science: Dr EMIL MIHAILOV

PROFESSORS

ANGELOVA, D.
BECHEV, R.
BOJINOV, V.
DISHOVSKI, N.
DOMBALOV, I.
GERGINOV, A.
HADJOV, K.
ILIEVA, M.
IVANOVA, J.
KUMANOVA, B.
NENKOVA, S.
PANEV, S.
PELOVSKI, J.
PENCHEV, I.
TZVETKOV, T.
VEZENKOV, L.

LESOTEHNICHESKI UNIVERSITET (University of Forestry)

10 Kliment Ohridski Blvd, 1756 Sofia
Telephone: (2) 9625997
E-mail: rektor@ltu.bg
Internet: www.ltu.bg

Founded 1953, present name and status 1995
State control
Languages of instruction: Bulgarian, English
Academic year: September to June (2 terms)

Rector: Prof. Dr VESSELIN STAMENOV BREZIN
Vice-Rector for Accreditation, Int. Integration and Public Relations: Dr PETAR ZHELEV STOYANOV
Vice-Rector for Educational Activities: Prof. Dr IVAN PETROV PALIGOROV
Vice-Rector for Scientific and Devt Activities: Prof. Dr RUMEN IGNATOV TOMOV
Library Dir: YULIYANA IVANOVA YOSIFOVA

Library of 10,900 vols of books, dissertations, periodicals
Number of teachers: 350
Number of students: 3,500
Publications: *Forest Ideas*, *Management and Sustainable Development*, *Propagation of Ornamental Plants*, *Woodworking and Furniture Production*

DEANS

Faculty of Agronomy: Dr ZHIVKO VASILEV ZHIVKOV
Faculty of Business Management: Dr VLADISLAV IVANOV TODOROV
Faculty of Ecology and Landscape Architecture: Prof. Dr ATANAS DIMITROV KOVACHEV
Faculty of Forest Industry: Dr NENO TRICHKOV
Faculty of Forestry: Dr MILKO HRISTOV MILEV
Faculty of Veterinary Medicine: Prof. Dr BOGDAN YANEV AMINKOV

PROFESSORS

ASPARUCHOV, K., Harvesting Machinery and Technology
DIMITROV, E., Basis of Forestry
DINKOV, B., Wood Technology
GENCHEVA, S., Ecology and Conservation, Soil Science
GERASIMOV, SV., Zoology
GRIGOROV, P., Sawing of Timber
KAVALOV, A., Furniture Technology
KOLAROV, D., Plant Physiology
KOVACHEV, G., Veterinary Medicine
KULELIEV, J., Planting Trees and Flowers
KYUCHUKOV, G., Furniture Construction
MICHOV, I., Forest Mensuration
PAVLOV, D., Phytocenology
PAVLOVA, EK., Ecology
PUCHALEV, G., Organization and Planting in Landscape Architecture
RAICHEV, A., Thermodynamics, Heat and Mass Transfer
SHECHTOV, CH., Automation of Technological Processes
SHKTILYANOVA, EL., Floriculture
TASEV, G., Machinery and Technology in Agronomy
VAKAZELOV, I., Dendrology

VIDELOV, H., Hydrothermal Treatment of Wood
YOROVA, K., Soil Science
YOSIFOV, N., Particle-Board Technology

MEDICINSKI UNIVERSITET PLEVEN (Medical University Pleven)

Sv. Kliment Ohridski Str. 1, 5800 Pleven
Telephone: (64) 884101
E-mail: rector@mu-pleven.bg
Internet: www.mu-pleven.bg

Founded 1974
State control
Languages of instruction: Bulgarian, English
Academic year: September to June (2 semesters)

Rector: Prof. Dr GRIGOR GORTCHEV
Vice-Rector for Education: PETYO BOCHEV
Vice-Rector for European Integration and Int. Cooperation: Dr ANGELIKA VELKOVA
Vice-Rector for Quality of Education and Accreditation: Dr VENETA LYUBENOVA SHOPOVA
Vice-Rector for Science: Dr MARIYA SREDKOVA
Chief Librarian: GABRIEL GEORGIEV

Library of 82,287 vols, 120 periodicals
Number of teachers: 360
Number of students: 2,044

Publication: *Journal of Biomedical and Clinical Research* (2 a year)

DEANS

College of Medical Science: Dr PAVLINA YORDANOVA (Dir)
Dept of Language and Specialized Training: MARGARITA ALEXANDROVA (Dir)
Faculty of Health Care: Dr TOMOV SLAVCHOV
Faculty of Medicine: Dr DIMITAR KONSTANTINOV GOSPODINOV
Faculty of Public Health: Dr GENA GRANCHAROVA

MEDICINSKI UNIVERSITET PLOVDIV (Medical University of Plovdiv)

15A Vassil Aprilov Blvd, 4002 Plovdiv
Telephone: (32) 602207
E-mail: rector@meduniversity-plovdiv.bg
Internet: www.meduniversity-plovdiv.bg

Founded 1945 as Higher Medical Institute, present name and status 2002
State control
Languages of instruction: Bulgarian, English
Academic year: September to June (2 terms)

Rector: Prof. Dr STEFAN STOILOV KOSTIANEV
Vice-Rector for Education and Postgraduate Study: Prof. Dr MARIA KUKLEVA-TODOROVA
Vice-Rector for Hospital Coordination: Assoc. Prof. Dr BORISLAV KITOV
Vice-Rector for Int. Relations and Project Activity: Prof. Dr MARIANA ATANASOVA MURDJEVA
Vice-Rector for Quality and Accreditation: Prof. Dr STEFAN TODOROV SIVKOV

Library of 190,000 vols
Number of teachers: 806
Number of students: 4,500

Publication: *Folia Medica* (4 a year)

DEANS

Dept of Languages and Specialized Training: Assoc. Prof. Dr SVETLA PACHEVA-KARABOVA (Dir)
Faculty of Dental Medicine: Assoc. Prof. Dr GEORGI TODOROV
Faculty of Medicine: Assoc. Prof. Dr NIKOLAY BOYADZHIEV
Faculty of Pharmacy: Assoc. Prof. Dr LYUDMIL LUKANOV
Faculty of Public Health: Prof. Dr RUMEN STEFANOV
Medical College: Assoc. Prof. Dr NIKOLETA TRAYKOVA-DZHAMBAZOVA (Dir)

MEDICINSKI UNIVERSITET 'PROF. DR PARASKEV STOYANOV'—VARNA (Medical University 'Prof. Dr Paraskev Stoyanov'—Varna)

'Marin Drinov' St 55, 9002 Varna
Telephone: (52) 677050
E-mail: uni@asclep.muvar.acad.bg
Internet: www.mu-varna.bg

Founded 1961 as Higher Medical Institute Varna, present name 2002
Academic year: September to June

Rector: Prof. Dr KRASIMIR IVANOV
Vice-Rector for Career Devt Research and Postgraduate Education: Dr RINALDO SHISHKOV
Vice-Rector for Teaching: Prof. Dr ALBENA KEREKOVSKA
Vice-Rector for Int. Cooperation, Accreditation and Quality: Prof. TODORKA KOSTADINOVA
Dir for Library: PETRANA MILEVA

Library of 150,000 vols incl. 109,000 books, 40,000 periodicals and 1,000 CD-ROMs
Number of teachers: 382 (172 full profs and assoc. profs, 210 asst profs and lecturers)
Number of students: 2,182

Publications: *Biomedical Reviews* (1 a year), *Health Economics and Management*, *Infoacademica*, *Intern. Bulletin of Otorhinolaryngology*

DEANS

Dept of Foreign Languages: Prof. Dr VIOLETA KASPARIAN TACHEVA (Dir)
Faculty of Dental Medicine: Prof. Dr TSVETAN TONCHEV LYUBENOV
Faculty of Medicine: Dr RADOSLAV RADEV
Faculty of Pharmacy: Prof. Dr DIMITAR ATANASOV DIMITROV
Faculty of Public Health: Dr IVANOVA RAYCHEVA EMANUELA DI-MUTAFOVA
Medical College: Prof. Dr NESTEROV NEGREV NEGRIN (Dir)

MEDICINSKI UNIVERSITET SOFIA (Medical University of Sofia)

Acad. Ivan Geshov Blvd 15, 1431 Sofia
Telephone: (2) 9523791
E-mail: rector@mu-sofia.bg
Internet: www.mu-sofia.bg

Founded 1917 as medical faculty of Sofia Univ., present name and status 1995
State control
Academic year: September to June

Rector: Prof. Dr VANYO MITEV
Vice-Rector for Academic Affairs: Prof. RUMENOVA SASHKA POPOVA
Vice-Rector for Education: Prof. SASHKA RUMENOVA POPOVA
Vice-Rector for Int. Integration and Project Financing: Prof. RADOMIR LYUBOMIROV UGRINOV
Vice-Rector for Postgraduate Studies: VASIL DIMITROV
Vice-Rector for Research: Prof. GENKA IVANOVA PETROVA-TASHKOVA
Sec.: Prof. ALEXEI ALEXEYEV YORDANOV

Library of 500,422 vols
Number of teachers: 1,408
Number of students: 6,155

Publications: *Acta Medica Bulgarica* (2 a year), *Problems of Dental Medicine*

DEANS

Faculty of Dental Medicine: Prof. Dr ANTON FILCHEV
Faculty of Medicine: Prof. Dr MARIN MARINOV
Faculty of Pharmacy: Prof. NICHOLAS LAMBOV
Faculty of Public Health: Prof. Dr TZEKOMIR VODENICHAROV
Medical College: Prof. Dr VIHREN PETKOV

MINNO-GEOLOŽKI UNIVERSITET 'SV. IVAN RILSKI' (University of Mining and Geology 'St Ivan Rilski')

Studentski grad 'Prof. Boyan Kamenov' St, 1700 Sofia
Telephone: (2) 8060300
E-mail: maillist-mgu@mgu.bg
Internet: www.mgu.bg

Founded 1953
Academic year: October to June (2 terms)

Rector: Prof. Dr LYUBEN IVANOV TOTEV
Vice-Rector for Devt of Academic Staff: Prof. Dr DIMITAR STOYANOV ANASTASOV
Vice-Rector for Education and Student Affairs: Dr VYARA GEORGIEVA POZHIDAEVA
Vice-Rector for Int. Cooperation and Projects: Dr STEFKA DIMITROVA PRISTAVOVA
Vice-Rector for Research Activities: Dr PAVEL EVSTATIEV PAVLOV
Librarian: K. DRAGANOVA

Library of 90,000 vols, 61,000 books, 29,000 periodicals
Number of teachers: 230
Number of students: 2,500

Publication: *Godishnik* (1 a year)

DEANS

Faculty of Geoexploration: Dr EFROSIMA PETROVA ZANEVA-DOBRANOVA
Faculty of Mining Electromechanics: Dr DIANA DECHEVA TASHEVA
Faculty of Mining Technology: Prof. Dr IVAN MIHAYLOV NISHKOV

PROFESSORS

Department of Humanities (tel. (2) 8060324; e-mail department@mgu.bg):
STAMATOV, A., Philosophy

Faculty of Geoexploration (tel. (2) 8060221; e-mail dekangpf@mgu.bg):
LILKOV, V., Physics
KORTENSKI, J., Geology and Exploration of Mineral Deposits
RADICHEV, R., Applied Geophysics

Faculty of Mining Electromechanics (tel. (2) 8060509):
AVGELOV, V., Mathematics
FETVADJIEV, G., Mechanization of Mines
KARTZELIN, E., Electrification of Mining Production
TRICHKOV, K., Electrical Engineering

Faculty of Mining Technology (tel. (2) 8060206; e-mail inishkov@gmail.com):
ANASTASOV, D., Underground Mining of Mineral Deposits
MICHAYLOV, M., Mine Ventilation
NISHKOV, I., Processing and Recycling of Mineral Resources
PANAYOTOV, V., Processing and Recycling of Mineral Resources
PANAYATOVA, M., Chemistry
TOTEV, L., Underground Construction
VELEV, V., Economy and Management
YOVKOV, K., Mine Surveying and Geodesy
ZLATANOV, P., Opencast Mining of Mineral Deposits and Blasting Activities

NOV BULGARKI UNIVERSITET (New Bulgarian University)

Ovcha Kupel 21, Montevideo St, 1618 Sofia
Telephone: (2) 8110247
E-mail: top.info@nbu.bg
Internet: www.nbu.bg

Founded 1991
Private control

Languages of instruction: Bulgarian, English, French

Rector: Dr PLAMEN BOCHKOV
Vice-Rector: Dr MARIN MARINOV
Vice-Rector for Int. Affairs and Public Relations: Prof. Dr KRISTIAN BANKOV
Vice-Rector for Research Activities: Dr LJUDMIL GEORGIEV

Library of 162,300 vols, 1,800 reference works, 480 periodicals
Number of teachers: 500
Number of students: 12,000

Publications: *Entelegentno* (Intelligent), *Kant*, *Praven Pregled* (Legal Matters), *Sledva* (To be continued)

DEANS

Graduate School: ROSSEN STOIANOV
School of Basic Education: Dr NIKOLAI ARABADZHIISKI
Undergraduate School: TOMA TOMOV

PLOVDIVSKI UNIVERSITET 'PAISII HILENDARSKI'
(Paisii Hilendarski University of Plovdiv)

24 Tsar Asen St, 4000 Plovdiv
Telephone: (32) 261363
E-mail: iro@uni-plovdiv.bg
Internet: www.uni-plovdiv.bg

Founded 1961, fmrly 'Paisii Hilendarski' Higher Pedagogical Institute, Plovdiv, present name and status 1972
State control
Academic year: October to June

Rector: Dr ZAPRYAN KOZLUDZHOV
Asst Rector: RUMEN KIROV
Vice-Rector for Int. Relations and Scientific Research: Prof. Dr NEVENA MILEVA
Dir for Library: MILKA YANKOVA

Library of 348,045 vols, incl. books, periodicals, textbooks, reference guides
Number of teachers: 603 (85 full profs, 196 assoc. profs and 322 asst profs)
Number of students: 15,236 (11,694 full-time and 3,542 part-time)

Publications: *Journal Plovdiv University*, *Nauchni Trudove*

DEANS

Faculty of Biology: Prof. AT. DONEV
Faculty of Chemistry: Prof. AT VENKOV
Faculty of Economics: Assoc. Prof. M. MIHAILOVA
Faculty of Education: Dr R. TANK
Faculty of Languages and Literature: Dr ZIVKO IVANOV
Faculty of Law: Prof. G. PETROVA
Faculty of Mathematics and Computer Science: Prof. D. MEKEROV
Faculty of Pedagogics: Assoc. Prof. P. RADEV
Faculty of Philology: Prof. Iv. KUTSAROV
Faculty of Philosophy and History: Assoc. Prof. KRASIMIRA KRASTANOVA
Faculty of Physics: Prof. G. MEKISHEV

PROFESSORS

ALEKSANDROV, A.
ANDREEV, G.
ANGELOV, A.
ANGELOV, P., Zoology
ATANASOV, A., Theoretical Physics
BACHVAROV, G.
BALABANOV, N., Nuclear Physics
DIMITROV, R., Technology of Inorganic Chemistry
DONEV, A., Zoology
DRUMEVA, E.
FUTEKOV, L., Analytical Chemistry
GOLEMINOV, C.
GOLEVA, P.
GRUEV, B.
IVANOV, A., Microbiology
IVANOV, S., Technology of Organic Chemistry
JENKINS, D.
KARTALOV, A.
KATSARKOVA, V.
KIRYAKOV, I.
KOLAROV, N.
KUTSAROV, I., Morphology of Modern Bulgarian Language
KUZMANOVA, A.
LAZAROV, K.
MIHAYLOVA, M.
MIHOVSKI, S.
MINKOV, I., Plant Physiology
MITEV, D., Zoology
MOLLOV, T., Algebra
MRACHKOV, V.
NIKOLOVA, M., Anatomy and Physiology
PAPANOV, G.
PETROV, P.
POPCHEV, I.
POPOV, P.
SAPAREV, O.
SAPKOVA, I.
SAVOV, E.
TSEKOV, G.
VELCHEV, N., Physics of Dielectrics
VENKOV, A.
YORDANOV, Y

RUSENSKI UNIVERSITET 'ANGEL KANCHEV'
('Angel Kanchev' University of Ruse)

Studentska St 8, 7017 Ruse
Telephone: (82) 888465
E-mail: secretary@uni-ruse.bg
Internet: www.uni-ruse.bg

Founded 1945 as a higher technical school, present name and status 1995
State control
Academic year: September to July
Brs in Razgrad and Silistra

Rector: Prof. Dr HRISTO BELOEV
Vice-Rector for Admissions and Education: Prof. Dr MIHAIL ILIEV
Vice-Rector for European Integration and Int. Cooperation: Dr YULIANA POPOVA
Vice-Rector for Staff and Research Devt: Prof. Dr ANGEL SMRIKAROV
Sec. Gen.: Dr TANYA GROZEVA
Dir for Library: Mag. Prof. EMILIA KIRILOVA LEHOVA

Library of 411,134 vols, incl. 334,427 books, 43,870 periodicals
Number of teachers: 480
Number of students: 10,000

Publication: *Nauchni Trudove*

DEANS

Agrarian and Industrial Faculty: Dr PLAMEN KANGALOV
Faculty of Business and Management: Dr EMIL GEORGIEV TRIFONOV
Faculty of Electrical Engineering, Electronics and Automation: Dr VALENTIN STOYANOV
Faculty of Law: Prof. Dr LACHEZAR IVANOV DACHEV
Faculty of Mechanical and Manufacturing Engineering: Dr BRANKO SOTIROV
Faculty of Natural Sciences and Education: Prof. Dr MARGARITA TEODOSIEVA
Faculty of Public Health and Healthcare: Dr TODORKA STEFANOVA
Faculty of Science and Education: Prof. MARGARITA TEODOSIEVA
Faculty of Transport: Dr ROSSEN IVANOV

PROFESSORS

Agrarian and Industrial Faculty:

ENCHEV, K.
GUZHGULOV, G.
MITKOV, A.
ORLOEV, N.
PARASHKEVOV, I.

Faculty of Business and Management:

PAPAZOV, KR.

Faculty of Electrical Engineering, Electronics and Automation:

ANDONOV, K.

Faculty of Law:

MICHEV, N.

Faculty of Mechanical and Manufacturing Engineering:

IVANOV, V.
KANEV, M.
POPOV, G.
TOMOV, B.
VELCHEV, S.
VITLIEMOV, VL.

Faculty of Transport:

ANDREEV, D.
ILIEV, L.
LIUBENOV, SL.
NENOV, P.
SIMEONOV, D.

SHUMENSKI UNIVERSITET 'EPISKOP KONSTANTIN PRESLAVSKI'
(Konstantin Preslavski University of Shumen)

Universitetska St 115, 9700 Shumen
Telephone: (54) 830495
E-mail: rector@shu-bg.net
Internet: www.shu.bg

Founded 1971
State control
Academic year: September to June

Rector: Prof. Dr hab. MARGARITA GEORGIEVA
Vice-Rector for Accreditation, Evaluation and Quality Assurance of Education and Academic Staff: Dr BOGDANA GEORGIEVA
Vice-Rector for Economic Affairs and Academic Staff: Prof. Dr hab. GEORGI KOLEV
Vice-Rector for Educational Affairs: Dr ZHIVKO ZHEKO
Vice-Rector for Science, Research and Int. Relations: Dr RUMYANA TODOROVA
Dir for Library: MARIANA PETEVA

Library of 362,568 vols, 170 periodicals
Number of teachers: 445
Number of students: 7,000

Publication: *Godishnik* (1 a year)

DEANS

Faculty of Education: Dr hab. MARGARITA BONEVA
Faculty of Humanities: Prof. Dr Hab. IVELINA SAVOVA
Faculty of Mathematics and Computer Science: Dr RUSANKA G. PETROVA
Faculty of Natural Sciences: Prof. Dr DOBROMIR ENCHEV
Faculty of Technical Sciences: Dr IVAN KRASTEV TSONEV

SOFIISKI UNIVERSITET 'SVETI KLIMENT OHRIDSKI'
(Sofia University 'St Kliment Ohridski')

Tsar Osvoboditel Blvd 15, 1504 Sofia
Telephone: (2) 9308200
E-mail: rector@uni-sofia.bg
Internet: www.uni-sofia.bg

Founded 1888 as School of Higher Education, present status 1904, present name 1905
State control
Academic year: September to June (2 terms)

Rector: Prof. Dr hab. IVAN ILCHEV
Vice-Rector for Education-Bachelors and Masters Degree Programmes: Dr MILENA STEFANOVA

Vice-Rector for Education-PhD Students and Continuing Education: Prof. Dr hab. ANASTAS GERDJIKOV
Vice-Rector for Information Activities, Academic Staff and Admin.: Prof. Dr hab. ALBENA CHAVDAROVA
Vice-Rector for Management Control and Public Procurement: Dr YURIY KUCHEV
Vice-Rector for Research and Project Affairs: Prof. Dr hab. RUMEN PANKOV
Sec. Gen.: DETELINA ILIEVA
Dir for Library: Prof. ANNA ANGELOVA

Library: see under Libraries and Archives
Number of teachers: 1,608
Number of students: 25,454
Publication: *Godishnik*

DEANS

Faculty of Biology: Dr MARIELA ODJAKOVA
Faculty of Chemistry and Pharmacy: Prof. Dr hab. TONY GEORGIEV SPASOV
Faculty of Classical and Modern Philology: Prof. Dr hab. TSVETAN TEOFANOV
Faculty of Economics and Business Administration: Dr TODOR POPOV
Faculty of Education: Dr BONCHO GOSPODINOV
Faculty of Geology and Geography: Dr MARIN IVANOV
Faculty of History: Dr PLAMEN DIMITROV MITEV
Faculty of Journalism and Mass Communication: Dr TEODORA PETROVA
Faculty of Law: Prof. Dr SASHO GEORGIEV PENOV
Faculty of Mathematics and Informatics: Prof. Dr hab. IVAN SOSKOV
Faculty of Medicine: Prof. Dr LYUBOMIR SPASOV
Faculty of Philosophy: Prof. Dr DIMITAR ANGELOV DENKOV
Faculty of Physics: Prof. Dr hab. ALEXANDER DREISCHUH
Faculty of Preschool and Primary School Education: Prof. Dr DIMITAR GYUROV
Faculty of Slavic Studies: Prof. Dr hab. PANAYOT KARAGYOZOV
Faculty of Theology: Dr ALEXANDER OMARCHEVSKI

PROFESSORS

Faculty of Biology:
BOZHILOVA, E., Botany
IVANOVA, I., Plant Physiology
KIMENOV, G., Plant Physiology
KOLEV, D., Biochemistry
MARGARITOV, N., Hydrobiology and Ichthyology
MINKOV, I., Human and Animal Physiology
TEMNISKOVA, D., Botany
VLAHOV, S., General and Industrial Microbiology

Faculty of Chemistry and Pharmacy:
ALEKSANDROV, S., Analytical Chemistry
BONCHEV, P., Analytical Chemistry
DOBREV, A., Organic Chemical Technology
FAKIROV, S., Organic Chemical Technology
GALABOV, B., Organic Chemical Technology
IVANOV, I., Physical Chemistry
KALCHEVA, B., Organic Chemical Technology
KOSTADINOV, K., Inorganic Chemical Technology
LAZAROV, D., Inorganic Chemical Technology
MARKOV, P., Organic Chemistry
PANAYOTOV, I., Physical Chemistry
PETROV, B., Organic Chemical Technology
PETSEV, N., Organic Chemistry
PLATIKANOV, D., Physical Chemistry
RADOEV, B., Physical Chemistry
TOSHEV, B., Physical Chemistry

Faculty of Classical and Modern Philology:
ALEKSIEVA, B., English Philology
BOEV, E., Eastern Languages
BOGDANOV, B., Classical Philology
BOYADZHIEV, D., Classical Philology
DAKOVA, N., German Philology
DELIIVANOVA, B., German Philology
GALABOV, P., Romance Philology
KANCHEV, I., Ibero-Romance Philology
PARASHKEVOV, B., German Philology
PETKOV, P., German Philology
SHURBANOV, A., English Philology

Faculty of Economics and Business Administration:
BEHAR, H., History of Economics
SERGIENKO, R., General Economic Theory

Faculty of Geology and Geography:
BACHVAROV, M., Geography of Tourism
ESKENAZI, G., Mineralogy, Petrology and Economic Geology
KANCHEV, D., Economic Geography
MANDOV, G., Geology and Palaeontology
PETROV, P., Geography

Faculty of History:
ANGELOV, P., Bulgarian History
BAEVA, I., Modern History
DASKALOV, G., Byzantine History
DRAGANOV, D., Modern History
GAGOVA, K., Ancient History and Thracian Studies
GAVRILOV, B., Modern History
ILCHEV, I., Byzantine History
KAIMAKAMOVA, M., Bulgarian History
KALINOVA, E., Bulgarian History
KOLEVA, I., Ethnography
MATANOV, H., Byzantine History
POPOV, D., Ancient History and Thracian Studies

Faculty of Journalism and Mass Communication:
DIMITROV, V., Radio Journalism
KARAIVANOVA, P., Journalism
PANAYOTOV, F., History of Journalism
SEMOV, M., Theory of Journalism

Faculty of Law:
BOYCHEV, G., Theory of State Law
GERDZHIKOV, O., Civil Law
MIHAYLOV, D., Criminal Law
PAVLOVA, M., Civil Law
PETKANOV, G., Finance Law
POPOV, P., Civil Law
SREDKOVA, K., Civil Law
STOYCHEV, S., Constitutional and Administrative Law
TSANKOVA, Ts., Civil Law
ZAHAROV, V., Theory of State Law
ZIDAROVA, I., International Law

Faculty of Mathematics and Informatics:
BOYANOV, B., Numerical Analysis and Algorithms
DENCHEV, R., Complex Analysis and Topology
GENCHEV, T., Differential Equations
HADZHIIVANOV, N., Education in Mathematics and Computer Sciences
HOROSOV, E., Differential Equations
HRISTOV, E., Complex Analysis and Topology
LILOV, L., Analytical Mechanics
MARKOV, K., Continuous Media Mechanics
POPIVANOV, N., Differential Equations
SKORDEV, D., Mathematical Logic and Applications
STANILOV, G., Education in Mathematics and Computer Sciences
TROYANSKI, S., Mathematical Analysis
ZAPRYANOV, Z., Continuous Media Mechanics

Faculty of Philosophy:
ALEKSANDROV, P., History of Psychology
ANDONOV, A., Philosophy
BOYADZHIEV, T., History of Philosophy
DESEV, L., Social Psychology
DINEV, V., Philosophical Anthropology
FOL, A., History of Culture
GENCHEV, N., History of Culture
GERGOVA, A., Book Science
GINEV, V., Theory of Culture
GRADEV, D., Social Psychology
KARASIMEONOV, G., Political Science
KRUMOV, K., Social Psychology
MIHAILOVSKA, E., Sociology
MITEV, P. E., Political Science
NESHEV, K., Ethics
PETKOV, K., Sociology
RADEV, R., History of Philosophy
SIVILOV, L., Epistemology
STEFANOV, I. I., Sociology
VASILEV, N., Philosophy
VENEDIKOV, Y., Sociology
ZNEPOLOSKY, I., Theory of Culture

Faculty of Physics:
APOSTOLOV, A., Solid State Physics
DENCHOV, G., Geophysics
DINEV, S., Quantum Electronics
GEORGIEV, G., Quantum Electronics
ILIEV, M., Condensed Matter Physics
IVANOV, G., Astronomy
KAMENOV, P., Nuclear Physics and Energetics
KUTSAROV, S., Electronics
LALOV, I., Condensed Matter Physics
LUKYANOV, A., Nuclear Physics and Energetics
MARTINOV, N., Condensed Matter Physics
MATEEV, M., Theoretical Physics
NIKOLOV, N., Plasma Physics
PANCHEV, S., Meteorology and Geophysics
POPOV, A., Semiconductor Physics
SALTIEV, S., Quantum Electronics
SLAVOV, B., Quantum and Nuclear Physics
ZAHARIEV, Z., Theoretical Physics
ZHELYASKOV, I., Plasma Physics

Faculty of Preschool and Primary School Education:
BALTADZHIEVA, A., Special Education
BIZHKOV, G., Primary Education
DOBREV, Z., Special Education
KOLEV, J., Primary Education
PETROV, P., Primary Education
RADEVA, B., Anatomy
TSVETKOV, D., Primary Education
ZDRAVKOVA, S., Primary Education

Faculty of Slavic Studies:
BIOLCHEV, B., Slavonic Literature
BOEVA, L., Russian Literature
BOYADZHIEV, T., Bulgarian Language
BOYADZHIEV, Z., Linguistics
BRESINSKI, S., Bulgarian Language
BUNDZHALOVA, B., Russian Language
BUYUKLIEV, I., Slavonic Linguistics
CHERVENKOVA, I., Russian Language
CHOLAKOV, Z., Bulgarian Literature
DIMCHEV, K., Teaching Methods of Bulgarian Language and Literature
DOBREV, I., Studies on Cyril and Methodius
GEORGIEV, N., Theory of Literature
HADZHIKOSEV, S., Theory of Literature
MINCHEVA, A., Studies on Cyril and Methodius
NITSOLOVA, R., Bulgarian Language
PASHOV, P., Bulgarian Language
PAVLOV, I., Slavonic Literature
PAVLOVA, R., Russian Language
POPIVANOV, L., Theory of Literature
POPOVA, V., Bulgarian Language
RADEVA, V., Bulgarian Language
TROEV, P., Russian Literature
VASILEV, M., Bulgarian Literature
VIDENOV, M., Bulgarian Language
YANEV, S., Bulgarian Literature
YOTOV, T., Russian Language

Faculty of Theology:
DENEV, I., Practical Theology
HUBANCHEV, A., Christian Philosophy
KIROV, T., Moral Theology
KOEV, T., Dogmatics
MADZHUROV, N., Christian Philosophy

POPTODOROV, R., Canon Law
SHIVAROV, N., Old Testament Studies
SLAVOV, S., Old Testament Studies
STOYANOV, H., Church History

TEHNIČESKI UNIVERSITET GABROVO (Technical University of Gabrovo)

4 H. Dimitar, 5300 Gabrovo
Telephone: (66) 827777
E-mail: info@tugab.bg
Internet: www.tugab.bg

Founded 1964 as Higher Technical Institute for Part-Time Studies, present name and status 1995
Academic year: September to June

Rector: Prof. Dr RAYCHO TODOROV ILARIONOV
Vice-Rector for Academic Affairs: Dr PETAR KOLEV PETROV
Vice-Rector for Int. Cooperation and Public Relations: Dr TSVETELINA ALEXANDROVA GANKOVA
Vice-Rector for Research and Devt: Dr ILIYA SLAVOV ZHELEZAROV
Sec. Gen.: Dr IRINA STEFANOVA ALEXANDROVA
Dir for Library: JOLIEN DIMITROVA CHRIST

Library of 170,000 vols
Number of teachers: 240
Number of students: 7,219

Publication: *Journal of the Technical University of Gabrovo* (2 a year)

DEANS

Faculty of Economics: Dr ANGELINA PENCHEVA PENCHEVA
Faculty of Electrical Engineering and Electronics: Dr MINCHO VANEV SIMEONOV
Faculty of Mechanical and Precision Engineering: Dr PENKA MILCHEVA NEDELCHEVA

TEHNIČESKI UNIVERSITET SOFIA (Technical University of Sofia)

Kliment Ohridski Blvd 8, 1000 Sofia
Telephone: (2) 9652111
E-mail: office_tu@tu-sofia.bg
Internet: www.tu-sofia.bg

Founded 1945, present name 1995
Academic year: September to June

Rector: Prof. MARIN HRISTOV
Vice-Rector for Academic Staff and Coordination: Prof. Eng. VESKO KRUMOV PANOV
Vice-Rector for Education, Quality and Accreditation: Prof. GEORGI SLAVCHEV MIHOV
Vice-Rector for Int. Integration and Public Relations: Prof. Eng. VALERI MARKOV MLADENOV
Vice-Rector for Research and Devt: Eng. IVAN MLADENOV KRALOV
Admin. Dir: VALENTIN IVANOV DIMITROV
Librarian: A. DIMITROVA

Library of 153,517 vols
Number of teachers: 1,309
Number of students: 18,000

Publication: *Nov Tehničeski Avangard* (12 a year)

DEANS

English Language Dept of Engineering: Eng. TASHO ANGELOV TASHEV
Dept of Applied Physics: Prof. IVAN MITEV UZUNOV
Dept of Foreign Languages and Applied Linguistics: VESELA D. FRENGOVA
Faculty of Applied Mathematics and Informatics: Prof. KETI GEORGIEVA PEEVA
Faculty of Automatics: Prof. Dr Eng. EMIL KOSTOV NIKOLOV
Faculty of Computer Systems and Control: Prof. Dr Eng. OGNYAN NAKOV NAKOV
Faculty of Electrical Engineering: Prof. Dr Eng. IVAN STOYAN YATCHEV
Faculty of Electronic Engineering and Technology: Dr Eng. EMIL DIMITROV MANOLOV
Faculty of German Engineering Education and Industrial Management: Eng. STEFAN ANGELOV STEFANOV
Faculty of Machine Technology: Prof. Dr Eng. GEORGI DIMITROV TODOROV
Faculty of Management: Prof. Dr Eng. MLADEN STEFANOV VELEV
Faculty of Mechanical Engineering: Prof. Dr Eng. LUBOMIR VANKOV DIMITROV
Faculty of Power Engineering and Power Machines: Prof. Dr Eng. BONCHO IVANOV BONEV
Faculty of Telecommunications: Prof. Dr Eng. VLADIMIR KOSTADINOV POULKOV
Faculty of Transport: Dr Eng. TEODOSI PETROV EVTIMOV
French-Language Faculty of Electrical Engineering: Prof. Eng. IVAN MOMCHILOV MOMCHEV

TEHNIČESKI UNIVERSITET VARNA (Technical University of Varna)

Studenska St 1, 9010 Varna
Telephone: (52) 302444
E-mail: rectorat@tu-varna.bg
Internet: www.tu-varna.bg

Founded 1962 as Higher Mechanical and Electrical Engineering Institute, present name 1990
State control
Languages of instruction: Bulgarian, English
Academic year: September to July

Rector: Prof. Dr OBED AZARIA FARHI
Deputy Rector for Academic Affairs: Prof. Dr MARIA IVANOVA MARINOVA
Vice-Rector for Accreditation and Devt: Dr. ROSSEN NIKOLOV VASILEV
Vice-Rector for Int. Cooperation and European Integration: Dr. VENTZISLAV TSEKOV VALCHEV
Vice-Rector for Scholar and Applied Scientific Research: Prof. Dr HRISTO KOSTOV SKULEV
Dir for Library: Prof. MARIANA TODOROVA

Library of 200,000 vols
Number of teachers: 359
Number of students: 6,600

Publications: *Acta Universitatis Pontica Euxinus* (2 a year), *Annual Proceedings*, *Computer Science and Technologies* (3 a year), *Heat Engineering* (2 a year), *Machinery Mechanics* (3 a year), *Mechanical Engineering* (3 a year)

DEANS

Electrical Engineering Faculty: Dr Eng. MARINELA YORDANOVA
Electronic Engineering Faculty: Dr Eng. ROZALINA DIMOVA
Faculty of Automation and Computing: Prof. Dr PETAR ANTONOV
Faculty of Marine Sciences and Ecology: Dr Eng. NIKOLAY NIKOLAEV MINCHEV
Manufacturing Engineering Faculty: Prof. Dr Eng. ANGEL DIMITROV
Shipbuilding Faculty: Dr Eng. PLAMEN DICHEV

PROFESSORS

DIMITROV, A., Internal Combustion Engines
DJAGAROV, N., Electrical Engineering
FARHI, O., Automation
GEORGIEV, D., Mechanical Engineering
GERASIMOV, K. K., Electrical Engineering
IVANOV, V., Science of Art
MILKOV, V., Engineering Mechanics
MINCHEV, N., Engineering Mechanics
MIRCHEV, A., Economics
NIKOV, N., Welding
RUSEV, R., Materials Science
STAVREV, D., Physical Metallurgy and Metals Engineering

TODOR KABLESHKOV UNIVERSITY OF TRANSPORT

Geo Milev Str. 158, 1574 Sofia
Telephone: (2) 9709240
E-mail: office@vtu.bg
Internet: www.vtu.bg

Founded 1922 as State Railway School, present name and status 2000
State control
Language of instruction: Bulgarian
Academic year: September to August

Rector: Prof. Dr PETAR KOLEV KOLEV
Vice-Rector for Academic Affairs: Dr RUMEN KOSTADINOV ULUCHEV
Vice-Rector for Research and Int. Activities: Assoc. Prof. Dr DANIELA TODOROVA

Library of 50,000 vols
Number of teachers: 140
Number of students: 2,500

Publication: *Mechanics, Transport, Communications* (online (www.mtc-aj.com))

DEANS

Faculty of Machinery and Construction Technologies in Transport: Prof. Dr VALENTIN ALEKSANDROV NIKOLOV
Faculty of Telecommunications and Electrical Equipment in Transport: Prof. Dr IVAN KOSTADINOV MILENOV
Faculty of Transport Management: Prof. Dr. TOSHO TRIFONOV KACHAUNOV

TRAKIYSKI UNIVERSITET (Trakia University)

Students' Campus, 6000 Stara Zagora
Telephone: (42) 670204
E-mail: info@uni-sz.bg
Internet: www.uni-sz.bg

Founded 1995 by merger of Higher Institute of Animal Sciences and Veterinary Medicine and Higher Institute of Medicine
State control
Languages of instruction: Bulgarian, English
Academic year: September to July

Rector: Prof. Dr IVAN KOSTADINOV STANKOV
Asst Rector: Dr DOBRI YARKOV
Vice-Rector for Admin., Economical and Information Activities: Dr IVANKA ZHELEVA ZHELYAZKOVA
Vice-Rector for Scientific Research and Int. Activities: Dr ANNA NAYDENOVA TOLEKOVA
Vice-Rector for Student Affairs: Prof. Dr IVAN TODOROV VASHIN
Sec. Gen: Dr TANYA GOCHEVA TANEVA
Dir for Library: G. DAKOVSKA

Library of 360,000 vols (incl. monographs, reference books, books and scientific periodicals)
Number of teachers: 543
Number of students: 7,686

Publications: *Agricultural Science and Technology* (4 a year, online, tru.uni-sz.bg/ascitech), *Bulgarian Journal of Veterinary Medicine* (4 a year, online, tru.uni-sz.bg/bjvm), *Trakia Journal of Sciences* (biomedical sciences and social sciences series, 4 a year, online, tru.uni-sz.bg/tsj)

DEANS

Faculty of Agriculture: Prof. Dr RADOSLAV SLAVOV
Faculty of Economics: Dr IVAN GEORGIEV
Faculty of Education: Prof. Dr KRASSIMIR MUSTAFCHIEVA
Faculty of Medicine: Dr MAYA GULUBOVA
Faculty of Technics and Technology-Yambol: Dr KRASIMIRA GEORGIEVA

Faculty of Veterinary Medicine: Dr MIHNI LYUTSKANOV STOYANOV

UNIVERSITET PO ARHITEKTURA, STROITELSTVO I GEODEZIA
(University of Architecture, Civil Engineering and Geodesy)

Hristo Smirnenski Blvd 1, 1046 Sofia
Telephone: (2) 9635245
E-mail: aceint@uacg.bg
Internet: www.uacg.bg
Founded 1942 as Higher Technical School, present name and status 1995
State control
Languages of instruction: Bulgarian, English, German
Academic year: September to June
Rector: Prof. Dr Eng. KRASIMIR VELKOV PETROV
Vice-Rector for Academic Affairs: Dr NEDYALKO IVANOV BONCHEV
Vice-Rector for Int. Relations and Postgraduate Qualification: Prof. Dr Eng. PLAMEN BOGDANOV MALDJANSKI (acting)
Vice-Rector for Research and Design Affairs: Dr Eng. BOGOMIL VESELINOV PETROV
Vice-Rector for Social and Living Affairs: Prof. Dr Eng. MILCHO GEORGIEV LEPEOV
Asst Rector: Eng. DIMITAR NIKOLAEV VITANOV
Dir for Library: PERSIDA TOMOVA RAFAILOVA
Library: see under Libraries and Archives
Number of teachers: 576 (364 full-time, 212 part-time)
Number of students: 5,000
Publication: *Annals* (1 a year)

DEANS

Dept of Applied Linguistics and Physical Culture: BORISLAV NIKOLOV KOLEV
Faculty of Architecture: Dr ASEN METODIEV PISARSKI
Faculty of Geodesy: Prof. Dr Eng. BORISLAV DIMITROV MARINOV
Faculty of Hydraulic Engineering: Dr Eng. IRINA STOYKOVA KOSTOVA
Faculty of Structural Engineering: Dr Eng. IVAN DIMITROV MARKOV
Faculty of Transportation Engineering: Prof. Dr Eng. STOYO PETKOV TODOROV

PROFESSORS

Faculty of Architecture (tel. (2) 9635245; e-mail dean_far@uacg.bg):
- DIMITROV, S., Urban Planning
- HARALAMPIEV, H., Drawing and Modelling
- KRASTEV, T., History of Architecture
- TROEVA, D., Urban Planning

Faculty of Geodesy (tel. (2) 9662201; e-mail dean_fgs@uacg.bg):
- VALEV, G., Geodesy

Faculty of Hydraulic Engineering (tel. (2) 8656648; e-mail dean_fhe@uacg.bg):
- ARSOV, R., Water Supply and Sewerage
- DIMITROV, G., Water Supply and Sewerage
- KALINKOV, P., Water Supply and Sewerage
- MARADJIEVA, M., Hydraulics and Hydrology
- MLADENOV, K., Theoretical Mechanics

Faculty of Structural Engineering (tel. (2) 9635245; e-mail dean_fce@uacg.bg):
- BARAKOV, T., Reinforced Concrete Structures
- BAYCHEV, I., Building Mechanics
- DAKOV, D., Steel, Timber and Plastic Structures
- DRAGANOV, N., Steel, Timber and Plastic Structures
- GOSPODINOV, G., Building Mechanics
- JANCHULEV, A., Organization and Economics of Construction
- KIROV, N., Building Technology and Mechanization
- NAZARSKI, D., Building Materials and Insulation
- STAJKOV, P., Steel, Timber and Plastic Structures

Faculty of Transportation Engineering (tel. (2) 9662201; e-mail dean_fte@uacg.bg):
- DOULEVSKI, E., Bridges, Tunnels, Harbours
- GICHEV, T., Mathematics
- KONSTANTINOV, M., Mathematics
- TRIFONOV, I., Road Engineering

UNIVERSITET PO HRANITELNI TECHNOLOGII
(University of Food Technology)

Maritsa Blvd 26, 4000 Plovdiv
Telephone: (32) 643005
E-mail: rector_uft@uft-plovdiv.bg
Internet: uft-plovdiv.bg
Founded 1953 as Higher Institute of Food and Flavour Industries, current name adopted 2003
State control
Academic year: September to July
Rector: Prof. Dr NIKOLO TENEV DINKOV
Vice-Rector for Int. and Informative Activity: Prof. Dr NIKOLAY DIMITROV MENKOV
Vice-Rector for Scientific Activity: Dr PANTELEI PETROV DENEV
Vice-Rector for Students Affairs: Prof. Dr ALBENA STOYANOVA STOYANOVA
Dean for Faculty: Prof. Dr YORDANKA NIKOLOVA ALEXIEVA
Dean for Learning and Student Social Work: Dr TODOROVA VENELIN POPOVA
Head of Univ. Library: IVANKA N. KUNEVA
Library of 150,000 vols
Number of teachers: 210 full-time
Number of students: 3,174
Publications: *Scientific Journals in Food Technology* (irregular), *Scientific Works of UFT* (1 a year)

DEANS

Economic Faculty: Prof. Dr YORDANKA NIKOLOVA ALEXIEVA
Faculty of Technology: DIMITROV STEFCHO KEMILEV
Technical Faculty: Dr BORISOV VENTZISLAV NENOV

PROFESSORS

Economic Faculty:
- ALEXIEVA, Y., Tourism, Catering, Hotel and Restaurant Operations and Management
- BAEVA, M., Food, Nutrition and Dietetics
- HADJIEV, B., Industrial Business and Entrepreneurship, Industrial Management
- HADZHIKINOVA, M., Environmental Engineering in the Food Industry, Environmental Safety
- JORDANOV, J., Food Industry Economics, Tourist Industry Economics

Faculty of Technology:
- DENEV, P., Organic Chemistry, Chemistry of Food
- DENKOVA, Z., Microbiology of Food
- HADZHIKINOV, D., Technology of Sugar, Sugar Products, Starch and Starch Hydrolysates
- KRASTANOV, A., Biotechnology
- MARINOV, M., Technology of Wine and Beer
- MOLLOV, P., Canning and Refrigeration Technology; Analysis and Control of Food Products
- PERIFANOVA, M., Technology of Plant Oils
- SIMOV, Z., Technology of Milk
- STOYANOVA, A., Technology of Essential Oils, Perfumery and Cosmetics
- VASILEV, K., Technology of Meat and Fish

Technical Faculty:
- DAMYANOV, Automation, Information and Control Engineering
- RASHEVA, V., Heat Engineering
- STEFANOV, S., Food Industry Machine Building, Packaging of Foods
- VASILEV, S., Mechanics and Machinery

UNIVERSITET ZA NACIONALNO I SVETOVNO STOPANSTVO
(University of National and World Economy)

Studentski grad 'Hristo Botev', 1700 Sofia
Telephone: (2) 8195211
E-mail: rectorss@unwe.acad.bg
Internet: www.unwe.acad.bg
Founded 1920 as Free Univ. of Political and Economic Sciences, present name and status 1995
Academic year: October to July
Rector: Prof. Dr. STATTY VASILEV STATTEV
Vice-Rector for Education in Bachelor Degree: Prof. Dr OGNIAN GEORGIEV SIMEONOV
Vice-Rector for Education in Masters Degree Programmes and Distance Learning: Prof. Dr VESELKA HRISTOVA PAVLOVA
Vice-Rector for Electronic Organization: Prof. Dr VALENTIN STEPHANOV KISIMOV
Vice-Rector for Scientific Research Activity and Int. Projects: Prof. Dr VALENTIN DIMITROV GOEV
Sec.-Gen.: Dr MARCHO IANAKIEV MARKOV
Dir for Library: STANKA TZENOVA
Library of 500,000 vols
Number of teachers: 531
Number of students: 19,556
Publications: *Godishnik na UNSS*, *Ikonomicheski Alternativi* (12 a year), *Nauchni Trudove* (2 a year)

DEANS

Business Faculty: Prof. Dr JORDANKA HRISTOVA JOVKOVA
Faculty of Applied Informatics and Statistics: Prof. Dr KAMELIA GEORGIEVA STEFANOVA
Faculty of Economics of Infrastructure: Prof. Dr HRISTO PARVANOV PURVANOV
Faculty of Finance and Accounting: Prof. Dr SNEZHANKA ALEKSANDROVA BASHEVA
Faculty of General Economics: Dr LILIA JOTOVA BORISOVA
Faculty of International Economy and Politics: Prof. Dr ANTOANETA GEORGIEVA VASILEVA
Faculty of Law: Prof. Dr HRISTINA TODOROVA BALABANOVA
Faculty of Management and Administration: Prof. Dr MARGARITA CVETANOVA HARIZANOVA-CHOLAKOVA

VARNA FREE UNIVERSITY 'CHERNORIZETS HRABAR'

Chaika Resort, 9007 Varna
Telephone: (52) 365088
E-mail: rector@vfu.bg
Internet: www.vfu.bg
Founded 1991, present status 1995
Academic year: October to June (2 semesters)
Rector: Prof. Dr ANNA NEDYALKOVA
Vice-Rector for Educational Affairs: Prof. GALYA GERCHEVA
Vice-Rector for Scientific Research: Prof. Dr PAVEL PAVLOV
Asst Rector: Dr KRASIMIR NEDYALKOV
Dir for Library: MARIA MINKOVA
Number of teachers: 500
Number of students: 10,000

DEANS

Faculty of Architecture: Prof. Dr STEFAN TERZIEV
Faculty of Law: Prof. Dr PETAR HRISTOV
International Economics and Administration Faculty: Dr EMIL PANUSHEV

VARNENSKI SVOBODEN UNIVERSITET (University of Economics—Varna)

77 Kniaz Boris I Blvd, 9002 Varna
Telephone: (52) 660212
E-mail: rector@ue-varna.bg
Internet: www.ue-varna.bg
Founded 1920 as Higher School of Commerce
State control
Academic year: September to June
Rector: Prof. Dr PLAMEN BLAGOV ILIEV
Vice-Rector for Academic Affairs: Dr EVGENI PETROV STANIMIROV
Vice-Rector for Int. Cooperation and Public Relations: Dr VIOLETA JANEVA DIMITROVA
Vice-Rector for PSC and Finance: Dr STOYAN ANDREEV STOYANOV
Vice-Rector for Research: Dr VESELIN IVANOV HADZHIEV
Dir for Library: ROSSITZA ZARKOVA
Library of 270,000 vols
Number of teachers: 270
Number of students: 12,000
Publications: *Economic Research* (3 a year), *Godishnik*, *Izvestya*, *News* (magazine of Univ. of Economics-Varna), *University news* (bulletin), *Yearbook of the University of Economics-Varna*

DEANS

Faculty of Economics: Prof. Dr DANCHO JANKOV DANCHEV
Faculty of Finance and Accounting: Dr SLAVI DIMITROV GENOV
Faculty of Informatics: Dr TODORKA BORISOVA ATANASOVA
Faculty of Management: Prof. Dr MARIN NAJDENOV NESHKOV

PROFESSORS

ATANASOV, B. I., Mathematical Sciences
DANCHEV, D. J., Economics and Management of Commerce
DOCHEV, D. T., Mathematical Sciences
DONEV, K. I., Accountancy
FILIPOVA, F. A., Accountancy
GENOV, G. D., Accountancy
ILIEV, P. B., Economics and Management of Construction
ILIEV, P. S., Informatics
JAKIMOVA, I. G., General Economic Theory
KALINKOV, K. S., Economics and Management of Construction
KKARAKASHEVA, L. V., International Economic Relations
KOEV, J. D., Management
KOVACHEV, Z. S., General Economic Theory
LICHEV, I. K., Management
MARCHEV, F. G., Philosophical Sciences
MIHAJLOV, P. I., General Economic Theory
MINCHEV, S., Organic Chemistry
MLADENOVA, Z. K., General Economic Theory
NESHKOV, M. N., Economics and Organization of Tourism
RADILOV, D. S., Statistics
RAKADZHIJSKA, S. G., Economics and Organization of Tourism
STANCHEVA, A. R., Management
SULOVA, N. P., Economics and Management of Commerce
TODOROV, T. N., Economics and Management of Industry
TOMOVA, S. T., Physical Education and Sport
UZUNOVA, J. D., Marketing
VACHKOV, S. M., Finance and Credit
VLADIMIROV, V. K., General Economic Theory

'VASIL LEVSKI' NATIONAL MILITARY UNIVERSITY

Bulgaria Blvd 76, 5006 Veliko Tărnovo
Telephone: (62) 618822
E-mail: nvu@nvu.bg
Internet: www.nvu.bg
Founded 1878, present name and status 2002
State control
Faculties of artillery, air defence and CIS, aviation, land forces; depts of foreign languages, language and physical training; institute for research and innovation
Rector: TSVETAN GEORGIEV HARIZANOV
Vice-Rector: Col COSTA BAYCHEV BAEV
Vice-Rector for Academic and Scientific Activities: Col Prof. Dr GEORGI VASILEV KAMARASHEV
Library of 149,111 vols

VELIKO TĂRNOVSKI UNIVERSITET 'SV. KIRIL I METODII' (St Cyril and St Methodius University of Veliko Turnovo)

Teodosii Tarnovski St 2, 5003 Veliko Tărnovo
Telephone: (62) 620189
E-mail: mbox@uni-vt.bg
Internet: www.uni-vt.bg
Founded 1963 as Brothers Cyril and Methodius Higher Institute of Education, present name and status 1971
State control
Academic year: October to June
Rector: Prof. Dr hab. PLAMEN ANATOLIEV LEGKOSTUP
Vice-Rector for Academic Affairs and Accreditation: Dr PETKO STEFANOV PETKOV
Vice-Rector for European Integration and Int. Cooperation: Dr BAGRELIYA SABCHEVA BORISOVA
Vice-Rector for Financial and Economic Policy: Dr MARIYA MINKOVA PAVLOVA
Asst Rector: Dr MILEN VASILEV MIHOV
Sec. Gen.: OLEG YANKOV BOZHANOV
Dir for Library: Prof. Dr hab. SAVA YORDANOV VASSILEV
Library of 380,000 vols, 42,000 periodicals, rare and valuable books, electronic and other materials
Number of teachers: 853
Number of students: 14,000
Publications: *Archives of Historical and Geographical Research* (4 a year), *Epochi* (4 a year), *Pir* (1 a year), *Proglas* (4 a year), *Slovo I Obraz* (Word and Image), *Works of the University* (1 a year)

DEANS

Br. Vratsa College of Education: Prof. MARINELA VELIKOVA MIHOVA (Dir)
Faculty of Economics: Prof. Dr Hab. BAYKO PETKOV BAYKOV
Faculty of Education: Dr ROZALIA YORDANOVA KOUZMANOVA-KARTALOVA
Faculty of Fine Arts: BORIS ZHELEV GEORGIEV
Faculty of History: Dr ANDREY DIMOV ANDREEV
Faculty of Law: Dr TSVETAN GEORGIEV SIVKOV
Faculty of Mathematics and Informatics: Prof. Dr GEORGI STOYANOV TODOROV
Faculty of Modern Languages: Prof. Dr HRISTO ILIEV BONDZHOLOV
Faculty of Orthodox Theology: Prof. Dr DIMITAR MARINOV KIROV
Faculty of Philosophy: Dr ILIYA DOCHEV STOYKOV
Pleven College of Education: Dr ROSITSA DIMITROVA DIMKOVA (Dir)

VISSHE UCHILISHTE PO ZASTRAKHOVANE I FINANSI (VUZF University)

Gusla St 1, 1618 Sofia
Telephone: (2) 4015812
E-mail: office@vuzf.bg
Internet: www.vuzf.bg
Founded 2002
Private control
Courses in finance, insurance and social insurance, management, marketing
Pres.: Prof. Dr GRIGORII VAZOV
Vice-Pres.: DETELINA SMILKOVA
Exec. Dir: RADOSTIN VAZOV
Deputy Rector for Educational Activities and Quality Management: Prof. Dr YORDAN HRISTOSKOV
Deputy Rector for Research and Devt and Institutional Relations: Prof. Dr NIKOLAY IVANOV

YUGOZAPADEN UNIVERSITET 'NEOFIT RILSKI' (South-West University 'Neofit Rilski')

Ivan Michailov St 66, 2700 Blagoevgrad
Telephone: (73) 885505
E-mail: info@swu.bg
Internet: www.swu.bg
Founded 1975 as a br. of Sofia Univ. 'St. Kliment Ohridski'
State control
Academic year: September to July
Rector: Prof. Dr IVAN MIRCHEV
Vice-Rector for Accreditation, Master Programmes and Continuing Education: Dr RAYA MADGEROVA
Vice-Rector for Educational Activities–Bachelor Programmes: Dr TRAYAN POPKOCHEV
Vice-Rector for Research: Dr BORISLAV YURUKOV
Asst Rector: NIKOLAY TAHOV
Library Dir: HEAVEN NAYDENOVA
Library of 155,000 vols
Number of teachers: 1,000
Number of students: 10,000

DEANS

Faculty of Arts: Prof. Dr JORDAN GOSHEV
Faculty of Economics: Prof. Dr GANCHO GANCHEV
Faculty of Law and History: Dr GABRIELA BELOVA
Faculty of Mathematics and Natural Sciences: Dr STEFAN STEFANOV
Faculty of Pedagogy: Dr MARGARITA KOLEVA
Faculty of Philology: Dr ANTHONY STOILOV
Faculty of Philosophy: GEORGI APOSTOLOV
Faculty of Public Health and Sports: Prof. STOYAN IVANOV
Technical College: IVANKA GEORGIEVA (Dir)

Academies and Institutes

Academy of Music, Dance and Fine Arts: Todor Samodumov St 2, POB 783, 4000 Plovdiv; tel. (32) 601441; e-mail office@artacademyplovdiv.com; internet www.artacademyplovdiv.com; f. 1964 as Bulgarian State Conservatory in Sofia, present name 1995; 105 teachers; 972 students; Rector Prof. MILCHO VASILEV; Vice-Rector for Artistic Activities Prof. DANIELA DZHENEVA; Vice-Rector for Research and Postgraduate Studies Prof. DORA SLAVCHEVA; Vice-Rector for Student Affairs Dr JULIAN KUYUMDZHIEVA; publ. *Art Spectrum* (4 a year).

Bulgarian–Romanian Interuniversity Europe Center: Studentska St 8, 7017 Ruse; tel. (82) 825667; e-mail brie@uni-ruse

.bg; internet www.brie.uni-ruse.bg; f. 2001; attached to Rusenski Universitet 'Angel Kanchev'; offers postgraduate degrees in European studies and public administration, European studies and regional cooperation; operates through collaboration between the Rusenski Universitet 'Angel Kanchev' and the Academia de Studii Economice *q.v.*; Dir MIMI KORNAZHEVA.

College of Economics and Administration—Plovdiv: 13 Kuklensko Shose, Plovdiv; tel. (32) 266935; e-mail info@cea.bg; internet www.cea.bg; f. 2003; programmes in accounting, business administration, finance, marketing, public order management, tourism management; library: 3,100 vols; 2,500 students; Pres. Prof. GEORGI MANOLOV; Rector Prof. DIMITAR DIMITROV.

European College of Economics and Management: Zadruga Str. 18, 4004 Plovdiv; tel. (32) 672362; e-mail info@ecem.org; internet www.ecem.org; f. 2001; offers courses in accountancy and control, business administration, corporate economics, management of tourism and public administration; library: 7,800 vols of documents, 4,700 full-text magazines; 2,000 students; Pres. Prof. Dr MARIANA MIHAILOVA; Rector Prof. TSVETAN KOTSEV; Vice-Rector for Academic Affairs Prof. Dr MARIA KAPITANOVA.

G. S. Rakovski National Defence Academy: Evlogi and Hristo Georgiev No. 82, 1504 Sofia; tel. (2) 9226510; e-mail rectorrdsc@md.government.bg; internet rdsc.md.government.bg; f. 1912; higher education and scientific research on issues of nat. security and defence; faculties of national security and defence, command and staff; incl. defence advanced research institute and language training dept; library: 420,000 vols in Academic Library and 250,000 books in Military History Library; 1,000 students; Commandant DIMITAR ANGELOV; Deputy-Commandant for Academic Affairs and Research Col Dr PETAR NIKOLOV MOLLOV; Deputy-Commandant for Admin. and Logistics Col Dr LYUBOMIR TSVETKOV SIMEONOV; publ. *Military Journal* (10 a year).

Higher School 'Agricultural College' Plovdiv: Dunav Blvd 78, 4003 Plovdiv; tel. (32) 960360; e-mail agri_college@mail.bg; f. 1992, present name 1997, present status 2003; courses in agrarian economics, alternative tourism, agrotechnologies, business administration, economics of tourism, technologies in horticulture and wine production; Rector Prof. Dr Eng. DIMITAR KIRILOV DIMITROV; Vice-Rector for Education and Int. Cooperation Prof. Dr MARIANA IVANOVA; Vice-Rector for Research Dr VASKO VASSILEV.

Higher School 'College of Telecommunications and Post': Student City, St 'Academician Stefan Mladenov' 1, 1700 Sofia; tel. (2) 8622893; e-mail rector@hctp.acad.bg; internet www.hctp.acad.bg; f. 1922, present name and status 1997; depts of communications management, fundamental training, telecommunication technologies, wireless communications and broadcasting; Rector Prof. Dr IVAN KURTEV; Deputy Rector for Research Activity Dr STEFAN POPOV; Asst Rector JULIAN BAT.

Higher School—College Telematics: Parchevich St 26, 6000 Stara Zagora; tel. (42) 630206; e-mail coppk@abv.bg; f. 1989; offers professional courses and specialized language courses, incl. English, French, German, Italian, Russian, Spanish; Rector Prof. Dr CHRISTO SANTULOV.

International University College: Bulgaria St 3, 9300 Dobrich; tel. (58) 655620; e-mail admission@vumk.eu; internet www.vumk.eu; f. 1992; depts of economics and management, foreign languages, hospitality; campuses in Sofia and Varna; library: 12,500 vols; 1,400 students; Rector Dr TODOR RADEV; Vice-Rector Dr VESELIN BLAGOEV; Vice-Rector for Academic Affairs and Academic Dir Dr STANISLAV IVANOV; Dir for Library ELENA KOEVA-YURCHENKO; publ. *The European Journal of Tourism Research* (2 a year).

Ministry of the Interior Academy: c/o Min. of Interior, Shesti Septemvri Str. 29, 1000; tel. (2) 9825000; internet www.mvr.bg/en/aboutus/structuralunits/educational/academi.htm; f. 2002; attached to Min. of Interior; training state officials, incl. faculties of security, police, fire and emergency safety; organizes nat. and int. confs, seminars and research.

Nacionalna Akademija za Teatralno i Filmovo Izkustvo (National Academy of Theatre and Film Arts): G. S. Rakovski St 108A, POB 100, 1000 Sofia; tel. (2) 9231351; e-mail rector.office@natfiz.bg; internet natfiz.bg; f. 1948, present name and status 1995; academic year October to July; offers drama theatre acting, puppet theatre acting, physical theatre, drama theatre directing, puppet theatre directing, stage and screen design; screen arts and stage arts management; library: 63,000 vols; 87 teachers; 560 students; Rector Prof. Dr LUBOMIR HALACHEV; Asst Rector VLADIMIR KUZMANOV; Head of Academic Affairs ANELIA TSVETKOVA; Sec. PAULINE DASKALOVA; publ. *108A Magazine*.

Nacionalna Hudojestvena Akademija (National Academy of Art Sofia): Shipka St 1, 1000 Sofia; tel. (2) 9881701; e-mail art_academy@yahoo.com; internet www.nha-bg.org; f. 1896 as State Drawing School, reorganized as an acad. 1921; 131 teachers; 800 students; Rector Prof. SVETOSLAV KOKALOV; Vice-Rector for Educational Activity and Devt of Academic Staff Prof. VIKTOR PAUNOV; Vice-Rector for Scientific and Artistic Activity Prof. Dr SVILEN STEFANOV; Librarian DARINKA DIUKMEDJIEVA; publ. *The Art of Drawing* (1 a year).

National Music Academy 'Prof. Pancho Vladigerov': Evlogi i Hristo Georgiev Blvd 94, 1505 Sofia; tel. (2) 4409740; e-mail info@nma.bg; internet www.nma.bg; f. 1921, fmrly State Academy of Music, present name 2006; 220 teachers; 995 students; Rector Prof. Dr DIMITAR MOMTCHILOV; Vice-Rector for Academic Opera Theatre and Art Activities of the Vocal Faculty Prof. ILKA BORISOVA POPOVA; Vice-Rector for Art Activities and Academic Orchestra Work Prof ANATOLI DOBREV KRASTEV; Vice-Rector for Academic and Methodological Research Prof. Dr PRAVDA ATANASOVA GORANOV; publ. *Godishnik*.

National Sports Academy 'Vassil Levski': Studentski grad, 1700 Sofia; tel. (2) 4012345; internet www.nsa.bg; f. 1942 as Higher School for Physical Education, present name 1999; Rector Dr PENCHO GESHEV; Vice-Rector for Education Dr NIKOLAY IZOV; Vice-Rector for Quality of Education and Accreditation Prof. Dr DIMITAR MIHAILOV; Vice-Rector for Research, Project and Int. Affairs Prof. Dr DANIELA DASHEVA.

N. Y. Vaptsarov Naval Academy: 73 Vasil Drumev St, 9026 Varna; tel. (52) 552228; e-mail info@naval.acad.bg; internet www.naval-acad.bg; f. 1881 as Machine School for the Navy, present name 1949; trains specialists for the Navy and for the merchant marine in all areas of maritime life; research and devt; Commandant BOYAN MEDNIKAROV.

Stopanska Akademija 'D. A. Tsenov' (D. A. Tsenov Academy of Economics): Em. Chakarov Str. 2, 5250 Svishtov; tel. (631) 66201; e-mail rectorat@uni-svishtov.bg; internet www.uni-svishtov.bg; f. 1936 as D. A. Tsenov Higher School of Commerce, present name 1995; library: 192,748 vols of periodicals, 200,000 vols of books, 15 int. databases; 320 teachers; 10,000 students; Rector Prof. Dr VELICHKO ADAMOV; Vice-Rector for Scientific Research and Devt of Academic Staff Prof. Dr IVAN VARBANOV; Vice-Rector for Student, Information and Social Policy Dr TEODORA DIMITROVA; Vice-Rector for Undergraduate and Graduate Training Prof. Dr LYUBEN KIREV; publs *Biznes—Upravlenie* (4 a year), *Dialogue* (4 a year, online), *Economic World Library* (6 a year), *Narodnostopanski Arhiv* (4 a year).

Technical College of Lovech: S. Saev St 31, 5500 Lovech; tel. (68) 603929; e-mail tklovech@mail.bg; internet www.tklovech.org; f. 1990; attached to Tehničeski Universitet Gabrovo; depts of computer systems and technologies, electrical engineering, mechanical engineering; Dir Dr VASIL KOCHEVSKI.

Theatre College 'Luben Groys': Bulgaria Sq. 1, NDK, Admin. Bldg, 12th Fl., Suite 7A, 1000 Sofia; tel. (2) 9862025; e-mail lgroys_college@yahoo.com; internet www.lgrois.50megs.com/en; f. 1991, present status 2002.

BURKINA FASO

The Higher Education System

Higher education in Burkina Faso dates from the establishment of a teacher-training institute in 1965, which, after several name changes, became known as the Université de Ouagadougou (UO) in 1972. In addition to the UO there is a polytechnic university at Bobo-Dioulasso, which was founded in 1997, and in 2005 the Université de Koudougou was established (incorporating the town's existing institute of teacher training); there are also five private officially recognized universities and some 38 private officially recognized higher education institutions. French is the language of instruction in the majority of institutions. The number of students enrolled at tertiary-level institutions in 2008/09 was 47,500. The three state-run universities are government-funded, with additional financial resources provided by bilateral or multilateral agreements and the universities' own revenue streams. Higher education is the responsibility of the Ministry of Secondary and Higher Education; however, there do not currently appear to be any coherent criteria in place for assessment and accreditation in the higher education sector.

The UO, Université Polytechnique de Bobo-Dioulasso and Université de Koudougou have similar, five-tier administrative structures consisting of a Board of Directors, a University Assembly, a University Council, institutions and departments. The Board of Directors consists of representatives from the government ministries, the institution's administrative staff, trade unions' representatives, academic staff and students. The University Assembly decides university policy and is summoned by the President at least twice a year. Its members are drawn from the Directors, teaching, administrative and technical staff, students and representatives from government ministries. The President runs the university with the aid of the Vice-Presidents and a Secretary-General. Finally, institutions are administered by Directors, who report directly to the President.

Admission to higher education is based on the award of the Baccalauréat or Bachelier du Second Degré. Higher education awards are arranged in three cycles. The first cycle lasts two years and leads to award of the Diplôme d'Études Universitaires Générales (DEUG), Premier Cycle d'Études Médicales (PCEM), Diplôme Universitaire d'Études Littéraires (DUEL), Diplôme Universitaire d'Études Scientifiques (DUES) or Diplôme Universitaire de Technologie (DUT). The second cycle lasts one year after the first cycle for the Licence degree, two years for the Maîtrise, three years for Diplôme d'Ingénieur or four years for a degree in medicine. Finally, the third cycle comprises doctoral-level studies undertaken following the second cycle. The Diplôme d'Études Supérieures Spécialisées (DESS) or the Diplôme d'Études Approfondies (DEA) are awarded after one-year courses in subjects such as mathematics, biology, chemistry, law, economics and linguistics, and the Doctorat de troisième cycle or Doctorat de spécialité are awarded following two to three further years of study after the DEA. In medicine, the Doctorat d'État en Médecine is awarded following a further one year of studying on completion of the four-year second-cycle course. Since 2005, in an attempt to enable greater mobility for Burkinabè students, steps have been taken (with varying degrees of success) to adopt the licence-maîtrise-doctorat system (LMD, in line with the European Bologna Process). The LMD system was adopted officially in UO from 2011 onwards and in the Université Polytechnique de Bobo-Dioulasso from 2012 onwards. In addition to higher education awards, the main vocational award is the Diplôme, which requires two years of study.

Students undertaking technical or vocational courses attend a lycée technique, where they can study for two years and obtain the Brevet d'Études Professionnelles (the more vocational option), or study for three years and obtain the more academic and technical Baccalauréat Technique.

Regulatory Bodies

GOVERNMENT

Ministry of Culture, Tourism and Communication: 11 BP 852, Ouagadougou 11; tel. 50-33-09-63; e-mail mctc@cenatrin.bf; internet www.culture.gov.bf; Minister BABA HAMA.

Ministry of National Education and Literacy: 03 BP 7032, Ouagadougou 03; tel. 50-30-66-00; internet www.meba.gov.bf; Minister KOUMBA BOLY BARRY.

Ministry of Scientific Research and Innovation: Ouagadougou; Minister GNISSA ISAÏE KONATÉ.

Ministry of Secondary and Higher Education: 03 BP 7047, Ouagadougou 03; tel. 50-33-73-34; e-mail messrsxxsg@yahoo.ca; internet www.messrs.gov.bf; Minister Prof. MOUSSA OUATTARA.

Research Institutes

GENERAL

Centre National de la Recherche Scientifique et Technologique: BP 7047, Ouagadougou 03; tel. 50-32-46-48; e-mail dg.cnrst@fasonet.bf; internet www.cnrst.bf; f. 1950, 1968 incorporated into Ministère de l'Education Nationale, 1978 into Ministère de l'Enseignement Supérieur et de la Recherche Scientifique; basic and applied research in humanities, social sciences, natural sciences, agriculture, energy, medicine; library of 20,000 vols; Dir-Gen. BASILE L. GUISSOU; publs *CNRST-Information* (6 a year), *Eurêka* (4 a year), *Sciences et Technique* (2 a year).

Institut de Recherche pour le Développement (IRD): BP 182, Ouagadougou 01; tel. 50-30-67-37; e-mail ird-bobo@ird.fr; internet www.burkina-faso.ird.fr; f. 1968; hydrology, geography, agronomy, botany, medical entomology, economics, demography, anthropology, pedology, ethnology, geology, sociology; see main entry under France; Dir JEAN-PIERRE GUENGANT.

AGRICULTURE, FISHERIES AND VETERINARY SCIENCE

Centre de Coopération Internationale en Recherche Agronomique pour le Développement (CIRAD): ave du Président Kennedy, BP 596, Ouagadougou 01; tel. 50-30-70-70; e-mail jacques.pages@cirad.fr; f. 1963; natural resource management and environmental protection; improved crop and livestock production; agroeconomics; remote sensing and geographical information systems; agrifoods; Regional Dir for Continental West Africa JACQUES PAGÈS; publ. *Rapport Scientifique* (1 a year).

Institut de l'Environnement et de Recherches Agricoles: BP 8645, Ouagadougou 04; tel. 50-34-71-12; e-mail inera.direction@fasonet.bf; f. 1978; research in arable and livestock farming, forestry, agricultural machinery, natural resources, management and farming systems; library of 2,500 vols, 2,500 documents; Dir Dr FRANÇOIS LOMPO; publ. *Science et Technique* (2 a year).

EDUCATION

Institut Pédagogique du Burkina: BP 7043, Ouagadougou; tel. 50-33-63-63; f. 1976 by the Min. of Nat. Education and Literacy, for the devt of methods and courses in primary education; library of 16,000 vols (Min. of Nat. Education and Literacy Library); Dir-Gen. JUSTINE TAPSOBA; publ. *Action, Réflexion et Culture* (8 a year).

TECHNOLOGY

Bureau de Recherches Géologiques et Minières (BRGM): BP 86, Ouagadougou; tel. 50-33-50-42; see main entry under France.

Libraries and Archives

Ouagadougou

Bibliothèque Nationale du Burkina: 03 LP 7007, Ouagadougou 03; tel. 50-32-63-63; internet www.culture.gov.bf/site_ministere/m.c.a.t/ministere/ministere_sr_bn.htm; f. 1988; attached to Min. of Culture, Tourism and Communication; Dir-Gen. ABEL NADIE.

Centre National des Archives: Présidence du Faso, BP 7030, Ouagadougou; tel. 50-33-61-96; f. 1970; Dir DIDIER E. OUEDRAOGO.

Museum

Ouagadougou

Musée National: 08 BP 11186, Ouagadougou; located at: Ave Oubritenga, Ouagadougou; tel. 50-30-73-89; internet www.culture.gov.bf/site_ministere/textes/etablissements/etablissements_museenational.htm; f. 2003; 4,000 artefacts; Dir Prof. ALIMATA SAWADOGO.

Universities

UNIVERSITÉ DE OUAGADOUGOU

03 BP 7021, Ouagadougou 03
Telephone: 50-30-70-64
E-mail: info@univ-ouaga.bf
Internet: www.univ-ouaga.bf

Founded 1969, present status 1974
State control
Language of instruction: French
Academic year: October to June

Pres.: Prof. GUSTAVE KABRE
Vice-Pres.: Prof. HAMIDOU TOURE
Vice-Pres.: Prof. DIARRA YE OUATTARA
Vice-Pres.: Prof. TANGA PIERRE ZOUNGRANA
Sec. Gen.: MAMIDOU KONE
Librarian: CLÉMENT NIKIEMA

Library of 70,000 vols
Number of teachers: 395
Number of students: 21,309

Publications: *Annales* (2 a year), *Cahiers du Centre d'Études, Centre d'études et de recherches en lettres, sciences humaines et sociales, de Documentation et de Recherches Economiques et Sociales* (4 a year), *Revue burkinabè de Droit* (2 a year)

DEANS

Burkinabè Institute of Arts and Crafts: STANISLAS OUARO
Faculty of Exact and Applied Sciences: KARFA TRAORÉ
Faculty of Health Sciences: AROUNA OUÉDRAOGO
Faculty of Humanities and Social Sciences: WILLY MOUSSA BATENGA
Faculty of Letters, Arts and Communication: AMADOU BISSIRI
Faculty of Life and Earth Sciences: GÉRARD ZOMBRÉ
Institute of Population Sciences: BAYA BANZA
Pan-African Institute of Research Studies on Media, Information and Communication: SERGE THÉOPHILE BALIMA

UNIVERSITÉ POLYTECHNIQUE DE BOBO-DIOULASSO

01 BP 1091, Bobo-Dioulasso 01
Telephone: 20-98-06-35
E-mail: oga@fasonet.bf
Internet: www.univ-bobo.bf

Founded 1997
State control
Language of instruction: French
Academic year: October to July

Pres.: Prof. ANICET GEORGES OUÉDRAOGO
Vice-Pres. for Teaching and Pedagogic Innovation: Prof. MARIE YVES THÉODORE TAPSOBA
Vice-Pres. for Research, Prospective and Int. Cooperation: Prof. ABOUBACAR TOGUYÉNI
Dir for Int. Cooperation: Dr MIPRO HIEN

Number of teachers: 130
Number of students: 4,500

Colleges

Centre d'Études Economiques et Sociales d'Afrique Occidentale (CESAO): BP 305, Bobo-Dioulasso; tel. 20-97-10-17; e-mail cesao.bobo@fasonet.bf; f. 1960; areas of study incl. the enhancement of rural orgs on an institutional level, the promotion of women, faith and humanity, community health, admin. of the devt of rural communities, environment and land admin., savings and investments in rural areas, devt projects; library: 14,000 vols and 77 periodicals; Dir ROSALIE OUOBA; publ. *Construire Ensemble* (6 a year).

École Inter-États d'Ingénieurs de l'Equipement Rural (EIER): BP 7023, Ouagadougou 03; tel. 50-30-20-53; f. 1968 by governments of 14 francophone African states; 3-year postgraduate diploma course; hydraulics, civil engineering, refrigeration technology, sanitary engineering; Dir MICHEL GUINAUDEAU.

BURUNDI

The Higher Education System

In the early 1960s higher education in Burundi consisted of three institutions: the Institute of Agriculture of Ruanda-Urundi, the Institut Facultaire of Usumbura, and the Faculty of Science of Usumbura. In 1964 these three institutions merged to form the Université Officielle de Bujumbura (UOB). At present, the main institution of higher education is the Université du Burundi (UB), which was founded in 1973 following a merger of the UOB, the École Normale Supérieure and the École Nationale d'Administration. In 1989, in order to optimize the use of the resources allocated to higher education, the School of Journalism, the School of Commerce, the Institute of Town Planning and Development, and the Institute of Agriculture were integrated into the UB. The university currently has eight faculties and five institutes. The UB's funding is derived from an annual grant from the State included in the budget of the Ministry of Higher Education and Scientific Research; financial and other contributions from bilateral and multilateral cooperation; officially approved gifts and bequests; remuneration or income from work, studies and research carried out by the university at the request of and on behalf of public or private persons; and fees paid by students as registration fees, etc. The UB's senior management consists of a Board of Directors, a Rector and a Vice-Rector. The administration of the university comprises three Directorates: the Academic Services Directorate, the Directorate of Research, and the Administration and Finance Directorate. The Rectorial Council, composed of the Rector (Chairman), Vice-Rector, Director for Academic Services, Director for Research and Innovation, Deans of Faculties and Institutes, and two student representatives, meets at least once every two months.

In 2008/09 24,290 students were enrolled in higher education. The main language of instruction is French. The Minister of Higher Education and Scientific Research is responsible for higher education, although the Université du Burundi enjoys a relative degree of autonomy. There is also a growing private higher education sector and there are currently some seven private universities. The Hope Africa University, which is affiliated to the Free Methodist Church and which was established in Bujumbura in 2004 (having relocated from Nairobi, Kenya), is currently the largest and fastest growing university in Burundi, with some 4,000 students enrolled in February 2011 (the UB has around 3,100 students). At present, no accreditation body for higher education appears to exist in Burundi (the accreditation process, such as it is, is carried out by the Government).

The Diplôme des Humanités Complètes is the standard secondary education qualification required for admission to higher education. In a number of subjects, including mathematics, physics and civil engineering, students also have to pass an entrance examination. Undergraduate education consists of three stages: the Candidature is a programme of general studies lasting two years; the Diplôme de Licence requires a further two years of study; and in medicine the professional title Docteur en Médecin is awarded after four years of study following the Candidature. In the fields of civil and agronomic engineering, courses last five years and lead to the award of the Diplôme d'Ingénieur. The main postgraduate qualification is the Diplôme d'Études Approfondies. There are two stages of postgraduate study in the field of medicine: six years of study leads to the award of a professional doctorate in medicine, and the completion of a further five years of study and presentation of a thesis in a specialized area such as surgery, internal medicine, clinical biology, paediatrics or gynaecology leads to the award of a special doctorate. In 2011 the Université du Burundi was preparing to adopt a system of courses and qualifications in line with the European Bologna Process.

Five technical institutes/faculties within the Université du Burundi also offer higher vocational education, usually courses of three to four years leading to the award of the Diplôme d'Ingénieur Technicien.

Regulatory Bodies

GOVERNMENT

Ministry of Higher Education and Scientific Research: Bujumbura; Minister Dr JOSEPH BUTORE.

Ministry of Primary and Secondary Education, Professional and Vocational Training and Literacy: Bujumbura; Minister ROSE GAHIRU.

Ministry of Youth, Sports and Culture: Bujumbura; tel. 22226822; Minister ADOLPHE RUKENKANYA.

Research Institutes

AGRICULTURE, FISHERIES AND VETERINARY SCIENCE

Institut des Sciences Agronomiques du Burundi: BP 795, Bujumbura; tel. 22223390; e-mail isabu@usan-bu.net; internet www.asareca.org/naris/isabu; f. 1962; agronomical research and farm management; library of 11,500 vols, 120 periodicals; Dir-Gen. Dr JEAN NDIKURANA.

TECHNOLOGY

Direction Générale de la Géologie et des Mines (General Directorate of Geology and Mines): Ministère de l'Energie et des Mines, BP 745, Bujumbura; tel. 22222278; Dir-Gen. Dr AUDACE NTUNGICIMPAYE.

Libraries and Archives

Bujumbura

Archives Nationales du Burundi (National Archives of Burundi): Min. of Youth, Sports and Culture, BP 1095 Rohero II, Bujumbura; Ave Kunkiko, Bujumbura; tel. 22225051; 26,000 vols; Dir NICODÈME NYANDWI.

Bibliothèque de l'Université du Burundi: BP 1320, Bujumbura; tel. 22222857; f. 1961; 192,000 vols, 554 periodicals; Chief Librarian THARLISSE NSABIMANA.

Museums and Art Galleries

Bujumbura

Musée Vivant de Bujumbura: Min. of Youth, Sports and Culture, BP 1095 Rohero II, Bujumbura; Ave Kunkiko, Bujumbura; tel. 22226852; f. 1977; attached to Min. of Youth, Sports and Culture; part of Centre de Civilisation Burundaise; reflects the life of the Burundi people in all its aspects; incl. a reptile house, aquarium, aviary, traditional Rugo dwelling, open-air theatre, fishing museum, botanical garden, herpetology centre, musical pavilion, and crafts village; Dir EMMANUEL NIRAGIRA.

Gitega

Musée National de Gitega: 223 Magarama (Pl. de la Révolution), BP 110, Gitega; tel. 22402359; e-mail mapfarakoraj@yahoo.com; f. 1955; history, archaeology, ethnography, arts, folk traditions, arms; Curator JACQUES MAPFARAKORA.

National Universities

UNIVERSITÉ DE MWARO

Ave des Etats-Unis, 18, BP 553 Bujumbura
Siège du Campus à Kibumbu, BP 26 Mwaro
Telephone: 22243953
E-mail: info@universitemwaro.org
Internet: www.universitemwaro.org
State control

Faculties of administration and business management and law; 1 institute

Number of teachers: 157 (incl. full-time and part-time)
Number of students: 182

UNIVERSITÉ DU BURUNDI

BP 1550, Bujumbura
Telephone: 2242353
E-mail: rectorat@ub.edu.bi
Internet: www.ub.edu.bi

Founded 1960, renamed as Université Officielle de Bujumbura 1964, current name adopted 1974
State control
Academic year: October to September
Language of instruction: French
Pres. of Admin. Ccl: MARC RWABAHUNGU
Rector: Prof. ALEXANDRE HATUNGIMANA
Vice-Rector: Prof. JACQUES BUKURU
Dir for Academic Services: Prof. SYLVIE HATUNGIMANA
Dir for Admin. and Finance: VÉNÉRAND NIZIGIYIMANA
Dir for Research and Innovation: Prof. VESTINE NTAKARUTIMANA
Chief Librarian: APOLLINAIRE YENGAYENGE

Number of teachers: 239
Number of students: 3,100

Publications: *Actes de la Conférence des Universités des Etats Membres de la CEPGL* (1 a year), *Actes de la Semaine de l'Université* (1 a year), *Le Flambeau* (1 a year), *Le Héraut* (6 a year), *Revue de l'Université* (4 a year)

DEANS
Faculty of Agriculture: BONAVENTURE NIYOYANKANA
Faculty of Applied Sciences: JOSEPH NZEYIMANA
Faculty of Economic and Administrative Sciences: PASCAL RUTAKE
Faculty of Law: Prof. STANISLAS MAKOROKA
Faculty of Letters and Humanities: Prof. MELCHIOR NTAHONKIRIKYE
Faculty of Medicine: Prof. THEODORE NIYONGABO
Faculty of Psychology and Education: Prof. PAUL NKUNZIMANA
Faculty of Sciences: Prof. DÉO DOUGLAS NIYONZIMA

Private Universities

INSTITUT SUPÉRIEUR DE GESTION ET D'INFORMATIQUE (ISGE)
(Higher Institute of Business Management)

BP 6624, Bujumbura
Ave de la Révolution No. 38, Bujumbura
Telephone: 22219861
Founded 1987
Private control

UNIVERSITÉ DE NGOZI

BP 137, Ngozi
Telephone: 22302259
E-mail: info@univ-ngozi.org
Internet: www.univ-ngozi.org

Founded 1999
Private control

Faculties of agronomy; arts and sciences; law, economics and administrative sciences; maths and computer; medicine

Rector: ABBÉ APPOLINAIRE BANGAYIMBAGA
Vice-Rector: BONAVENTURE BANGURAMBONA

Number of teachers: 160 (incl. 38 full-time, 122 part-time)
Number of students: 1,180

UNIVERSITÉ DU LAC TANGANYIKA
(University of Lake Tanganyika)

BP 5403, Mutanga, Bujumbura
Ave des Palmiers 6, Bujumbura
Telephone: 243645
E-mail: webmaster@ult.bi

Founded 2000
Private control

Faculties of law; management science and applied economics; social sciences, policy and administration
Number of students: 2,662

UNIVERSITÉ ESPOIR D'AFRIQUE
(Hope Africa University)

BP 238, Bujumbura
Telephone: 22237973
Internet: hopeafricauniversity.org

Founded 2000 in Nairobi, present location 2003
Private control
Languages of instruction: English, French

Faculties of arts and sciences, business and professional studies, educational sciences, engineering, health sciences

Dir: Dr ELIE BUCONYORI
Number of students: 4,000

UNIVERSITÉ LUMIÈRE DE BUJUMBURA

BP 1368, Bujumbura
Telephone: 22248733
E-mail: ntukapaul@yahoo.com
Internet: www.ulbu.bi

Founded 2000
Private control

Pres.: Rev. CHANOINE PAU NTUKAMAZINA
Rector: Dr GRÉGOIRE NJEJIMANA
Sec.-Gen.: RUTOMERA PIERRE CLAVER
Number of students: 1,826

DEANS
Faculty of Theology: Rev. DONALD WERNER

UNIVERSITÉ MARTIN LUTHER KING
(Martin Luther King University)

BP 2393, Bujumbura
Telephone: 243944
E-mail: umlku@yahoo.fr
Private control

Colleges

Ecole Normale Supérieure (ENS) (Higher Teachers' Training School): 28th November Blvd, BP 6983, Bujumbura; tel. 22258945; e-mail info@ens.bi; internet www.ens.bi; f. 1965, present status 1999; depts of applied sciences, languages and social sciences, natural sciences; 79 teachers; 2,000 students.

Institut Supérieur d'Agriculture (Higher Institute of Agriculture): BP 35, Gitega; tel. 402605; e-mail rectorat@bibilio.ub.edu.bi; f. 1983; attached to Min. of Higher Education and Scientific Research; courses in tropical agriculture, stockbreeding, agricultural engineering, food technology; 213 students; publ. *Revue des Techniques Agricoles Tropicales* (2 a year).

Institut Supérieur de Techniciens de l'Aménagement et de l'Urbanisme: BP 2720, Bujumbura; tel. 22223694; f. 1983; attached to Min. of Public Works and Urban Devt; 100 students; library: 863 vols; Dir SALVATOR NAHIMANA.

Lycée Technique: POB 4618, Bujumbura; tel. 22259480; f. 1949; training apprentices, craftsmen and professional workers; 4 workshops: mechanics, masonry, carpentry, electrical assembling; 450 students.

CAMBODIA

The Higher Education System

The oldest institution of higher education is the Royal University of Phnom-Penh, founded in 1960. The higher education system was severely affected by the coup of 1975 and the Khmer Rouge regime (1975–79), but has enjoyed a renaissance in recent years with the restoration of pre-Khmer Rouge institutions and the foundation of numerous private establishments. The first private higher education institution, Norton University, commenced operations in 1997, and by 2010 there was a total of more than 50 private higher education institutions in Cambodia. Public institutions of higher education now include universities of agriculture, fine arts and health sciences (administered by the appropriate government ministry). Higher education is regulated by the Department of Higher Education, within the Ministry of Education, Youth and Sport (MoEYS). The key roles of the Department are: to develop overall policy and strategy, license institutions to operate, assist in developing the requisite academic programmes and management tools to enable institutions to meet accreditation standards, and improve quality and efficiency nationwide. The Accreditation Committee of Cambodia was established in 2003 to develop quality standards within higher education. Foundation year standards are already in operation and a set of institutional standards has been drawn up. The Foundation Year Course Assessment is a prerequisite for enrolment in a Bachelors degree. Although there is currently no fully accredited internationally recognized university degree available in Cambodia, a number of universities offer such degrees in conjunction with other countries.

To gain admission to higher education students must (in most cases) possess the Diploma of Upper Secondary Education and pass the competitive national entrance examination. Higher education, which is based on a system of credit allocation, lasts for up to nine years, including undergraduate and postgraduate study. Until 1993 the most common undergraduate qualification was the Diploma of Higher Education, but since then several other degrees have been introduced, including two-year Associate degrees and Bachelors degrees lasting four to six years. Postgraduate degrees include Masters degrees, which are undertaken on completion of a Bachelors degree and take two or three years, and Doctorate degrees, which entail the defence of a thesis and generally last for at least three years. In 2009 there were 76 higher education institutions, the majority of which were located in Phnom-Penh; 33 of them were public and 43 were private. Total higher education enrolment increased from 25,080 in 2000/01 to 161,516 in 2009/10, and was expected to expand considerably during the next few years, with plans to open two new universities in 2013/14. In 2009 the MoEYS sent 415 students to study overseas and 51 graduates in Cambodia were from overseas. MoEYS admitted 56 foreign students to study in Cambodian universities in that year.

Technical and vocational educational and training courses (entrance into which requires the Diploma of Lower Secondary Education) are one to three years in length, and the Department of Technical Vocational Education and Training (DTVET) has established criteria for certificate- and Diploma-level studies.

In May 2009 the Government announced that the World Bank was to donate US $15m. between 2010 and 2015 to support tertiary education in private and public universities and institutes in Cambodia. The aim of the five-year programme was to boost standards, provide scholarships for needy students and improve academic research and financial management.

Regulatory and Representative Bodies

GOVERNMENT

Ministry of Culture and Fine Arts: 227 Blvd Norodom, Phnom-Penh; tel. (23) 218148; e-mail info@mcfa.gov.kh; internet www.mcfa.gov.kh; Minister PHOEUNG SAKONA.

Ministry of Education, Youth and Sport: 80 Blvd, Preah Norodom, Phnom-Penh; tel. (23) 210134; e-mail info@moeys.gov.kh; internet www.moeys.gov.kh; Minister HANG CHUON NARON.

ACCREDITATION

Accreditation Committee of Cambodia: 3/F, Bldg No. 134, cnr of Monivong and Kampuchea Krom Blvd, Phnom-Penh; tel. (23) 224620; internet www.acc.gov.kh; f. 2003; assures and works to improve the quality of higher education instns in Cambodia; meets int. standards through accreditation; Chair. SOK AN.

Learned Societies

GENERAL

UNESCO Office Phnom-Penh: POB 29, Phnom-Penh; House 38, Samdech Sothearos Blvd, Phnom-Penh; tel. (23) 426726; e-mail phnompenh@unesco.org; internet www.un.org.kh/unesco; Head ANNE LEMAISTRE.

AGRICULTURE, FISHERIES AND VETERINARY SCIENCE

Cambodian Society of Agriculture: POB 01, 14 Monireth St, Phnom-Penh; tel. (23) 219692; e-mail cardi@bigpond.com.kh; f. 1998; attached to Cambodia-IRRI-Australia Project; 144 mems; Pres. MAK SOLIENG; Sec. TOUCH SAVY; publ. *Cambodian Journal of Agriculture* (irregular).

HISTORY, GEOGRAPHY AND ARCHAEOLOGY

Authority for the Protection and Management of Angkor and the Region of Siem Reap (APSARA): 187 Pasteur St, Chaktomuk, Daun Penh, Phnom-Penh; tel. (23) 720315 Angkor Preservation Compound, Siem Reap; tel. (63) 760080; internet www.autoriteapsara.org; f. 1995; depts of admin., monuments and archaeology 1, monuments and archaeology 2, urbanism and urban planning, Angkor tourist devt, water and forest, demography, public order and cooperation; publs *Journal* (12 a year), *Udaya—Journal of Khmer Studies* (irregular).

Royal Angkor Foundation: Budapest Hegedű u. 9, 1061 Budapest, Hungary; tel. (1) 3224270; e-mail info@angkor.org.hu; internet www.angkor.org.hu; f. 1992; safeguards the monuments and relics of the ancient Khmer civilization, establishing projects and gathering data; Hon. Co-Pres. HM NORODOM SIHANOUK (King of Cambodia); Hon. Co-Pres. ÁRPÁD GÖNCZ (fmr Pres. of Hungary); Chair. of Supervisory Board GÁBOR BARTA.

NATURAL SCIENCES

Biological Sciences

Parks Society of Cambodia: POB 2680, Phnom-Penh; 280B, St 146, Group 32, Sangkat Toek Laaok II, Khan Toul Kork, Phnom-Penh; tel. (16) 813700; e-mail vibolparkssociety@hotmail.com; internet parkssociety-cambodia.netfirms.com; NGO responsible for community devt, environmental education and the preservation of 10 wildlife reserves, 7 nat. parks, 3 protected landscapes and 3 multiple-use areas.

RELIGION, SOCIOLOGY AND ANTHROPOLOGY

Buddhist Association Khmer Republic: c/o Buddhist Institute Library, POB 1047, Phnom-Penh; tel. (23) 212046.

Research Institutes

ECONOMICS, LAW AND POLITICS

Cambodia Development Resource Institute: POB 622, Phnom-Penh; 56 St 315, Tuol Kork, Phnom-Penh; tel. (23) 881701; internet www.cdri.org.kh; f. 1990; research in macroeconomic policy, rural livelihoods, governance and decentralization, natural resources and the environment, poverty analysis and monitoring; library of 15,250 vols, 100 periodicals; Dir LARRY STRANGE; Coordinator of the Centre for Peace and Devt ROMDUOL HUY; publs *Annual Development Review* (1 a year), *Cambodia Development Review* (4 a year), *Flash Report on the Cambodian Economy* (12 a year).

Cambodian Institute for Cooperation and Peace: POB 1007, Phnom-Penh; Phum Paung Peay, Sangkat Phnom-Penh Thmey, Khan Sen Sok, Phnom-Penh; tel. (12) 819953; e-mail cicp@everyday.com.kh; internet www.cicp.org.kh; f. 1994; library of 4,000 vols in Khmer, English and French; Admin. SOTHEARA CHHORN.

Cambodian Institute of Human Rights: POB 550, 30, St 57, Sangk at Boeung Keng Kong 1, Khan Chamcar Morn, Phnom-Penh; tel. (23) 210596; e-mail chir@camnet.com.kh; f. 1993 by UN Transitional Authority in Cambodia; Dir KASSIE NEOU.

Centre for Social Development: POB 1346, Phnom-Penh; House 19, St 57, Sangkat Boeung Trabek, Keng Kang I Khan Chamkar Mon, Phnom-Penh; tel. (23) 364735; internet www.bigpond.com.kh/users/csd; f. 1995; promotes democratic values through research, training, advocacy and debate; Pres. CHEA VANNATH; publ. *Bulletin* (12 a year).

MEDICINE

National Institute of Public Health: POB 1300, Phnom-Penh; No 2, St 289, Toul Kork, Phnom-Penh; tel. (23) 880345; e-mail info@niph.org.kh; internet www.niph.org.kh; f. 1997; attached to Min. of Health; advises on govt policy and trains senior staff; school of public health; Dir Prof. UNG SAM AN; Deputy Dir CHHEA CHHORVANN.

RELIGION, SOCIOLOGY AND ANTHROPOLOGY

World Buddhism Association for Development, Cambodia Regional Center: No 11C, Rd 1986, Sangkat Phnom-Penh, Termei, Khan Kussey Keo, Phnom-Penh; tel. (23) 368506.

Libraries and Archives

Phnom-Penh

Documentation Centre of Cambodia: POB 110, Phnom-Penh; 70E, King Norodom Sihanouk Blvd, Phnom-Penh; tel. (23) 211875; e-mail dccam@online.com.kh; internet www.dccam.org; f. 1995, as field office of the Cambodian Genocide Program at Yale University, USA; became fully autonomous instn in 1997; information resource centre on the Khmer Rouge regime; Dir YOUK CHHANG.

National Archives of Cambodia: POB 1109, Phnom-Penh; St 61, Oknha Hing Pen, near Wat Phnom, Phnom-Penh; tel. (23) 430582; e-mail archives.cambodia@camnet.com.kh; internet www.nac.gov.kh; f. 1863; records of Résidence Supérieure du Cambodge (French colonial admin.), 1863–1954; post-colonial govt collns; records of Khmer Rouge regime and 1979 genocide tribunal; periodicals and newspapers in French, Khmer, Vietnamese and Chinese; photographic colln, poster colln; film archive; Dir KY LIM.

National Library of Cambodia: St 92, Daun Penh Dist., Phnom-Penh; tel. (23) 430609; e-mail khlot.vibolla@biblionationallibrarycamb.org; f. 1924; 103,635 vols; spec. colln of original palm-leaf MSS, 700 manuscript titles on microfilm; French Indo-China colln; Dir KHLOT VIBOLLA; publ. *Books-in-Print Cambodia*.

Museums and Art Galleries

Phnom-Penh

National Museum of Cambodia: POB 2341, Phnom-Penh; 13th St, Sangkat Chey Chumneas, Khan Daun Penh, Phnom-Penh; tel. (23) 211753; e-mail museum_cam@camnet.com.kh; internet www.cambodiamuseum.info; f. 1920; Dir KONG VIREAK.

Tuol Sleng Genocide Museum: St 113, Phnom-Penh; tel. (23) 300698; f. 1975.

National Universities

BUDDHIST INSTITUTE

POB 1047, Phnom Penh
Sangkat Tonle Basak, Khan Chamkamon, Phnom-Penh
Telephone: (23) 212046
E-mail: info@budinst.gov.kh
Internet: www.budinst.gov.kh
Founded 1930; attached to Min. of Religion and Cults
State control
Dir: NGUON VAN CHANTHY
Publication: *Kambuja Soriya* (4 a year)

CHEA SIM UNIVERSITY OF KAMCHAYMEAR

GPOB 865, Phnom-Penh
Smong Choeung Commun, Kamchay Mear Dist., Prey Veng
Telephone: (17) 888166
E-mail: mvu-camb@forum.org.kh
Internet: www.csuk.edu.kh
Founded 1993 as Maharishi Vedic Univ., current name adopted 2008; attached to Min. of Education, Youth and Sport
State control
Offers Bachelors and Masters courses in agriculture and management; smaller campuses in Kampong Cham and Prey Veng
Pres.: UK THAUN
Dir for Int. Relations: SETH KHAN
Number of students: 3,000

ECONOMICS AND FINANCE INSTITUTE

c/o Min. of Economy and Finance, St 90, Sangkat Wat Phnom, Khan Daun Penh, Phnom-Penh
Telephone: (23) 430556
E-mail: sengsrengefi@yahoo.co.uk
Internet: efi.mef.gov.kh
Founded 1997; attached to Min. of Economy and Finance
State control
Dir: SENG SRENG
Deputy Sec. Gen.: Dr HEAN SAHIB

INSTITUTE OF HEALTH SCIENCE OF ROYAL CAMBODIAN ARMED FORCES

Russian Fed. Blvd, Tek Thla Commun, Russey Keo Dist., Phnom-Penh
Telephone: (16) 932876
E-mail: iahs2005@yahoo.com; attached to Min. of Education, Youth and Sport
State control
Dir: Dr SOKHON LON

INSTITUTE OF TECHNOLOGY OF CAMBODIA

Russian Fed. Blvd., Sangkat Toek leak 1, Khan Tuolkok, Phnom-Penh
Telephone: (23) 880370
E-mail: direction@itc.edu.kh
Internet: www.itc.edu.kh; attached to Min. of Education, Youth and Sport
State control
Dir: P. HOEURNG SACKONA

KAMPONG CHAM NATIONAL SCHOOL OF AGRICULTURE

Nat. Rd 7, Veal Vong Commune, Kampong Cham Dist., Kampong Cham
Telephone: (42) 340187; attached to Min. of Agriculture, Forestry and Fisheries
State control

NATIONAL INSTITUTE OF BUSINESS

St 217, Phum Trea, Sangkat Steung Mean Chey, Khan Mean Chey, Phnom-Penh
Telephone: (23) 424591
E-mail: nib@nib.edu.kh
Internet: www.nib.edu.kh
Founded 1979 as School of Central Commercial Technique, present status 1994, current name adopted 2001; attached to Min. of Education, Youth and Sport
State control
Offers diplomas and Bachelors degrees

NATIONAL INSTITUTE OF EDUCATION

123, Norodom Blvd, Sangkat Chaktomok, Khan Doun Penh, Phnom-Penh
Telephone: (23) 332342
E-mail: nieimkoch@yahoo.com
State control; attached to Min. of Education, Youth and Sport
Dir: IM KOCH
Number of students: 500

NATIONAL POLYTECHNIC INSTITUTE OF CAMBODIA

Phum Sre Reachas, Samrong Krom, Khan Dangkor, Phnom-Penh
Telephone: (12) 964401
E-mail: info@npic.edu.kh
Internet: www.npic.edu.kh
Founded 2005; attached to Min. of Social Affairs, Veterans and Youth Rehabilitation
State control
Offers courses in automobile engineering, CAD/CAM, civil engineering, culinary art (bakery and cookery), electronic engineering, electrical engineering, information technology, mechanical engineering, tourism and hospitality
Dir: HE SOPHOAN PICH
Pres.: HE PHEARIN BUN
Co-Pres.: Prof. Dr SUNG CHUL KIM
Vice-Pres.: Dr YONG WOO LEE

NATIONAL TECHNICAL TRAINING INSTITUTE

Russian Blvd, Sangkat Teukthla Khan Sensok, Phnom-Penh
Telephone: (23) 883039
E-mail: info@ntti.edu.kh
Internet: www.ntti.edu.kh
Founded 1999 as Preach Kossomak Technical and Vocational Training Centre, pre-

sent name and status 2001; attached to Min. of Labour and Vocational Training

State control

Offer Bachelors and Masters degrees in civil engineering and electrical engineering; diploma courses in business information technology, civil engineering and technology in electricity

Dir: YOK SOTHY

NATIONAL UNIVERSITY OF MANAGEMENT (NUM)

Cnr of Monivong Blvd. and St 96 (Christopher Howes), Phnom-Penh

Telephone: (23) 428120

E-mail: horpeng@num.edu.kh

Internet: www.num.edu.kh; attached to Min. of Education, Youth and Sport

State control

Academic year: September to July

Rector: HE Dr LOR SOCHEAT

Vice-Rector for Academics, Research and Library: HE Dr PIC PHIRUM

Vice-Rector for Accounting: CHHUM CHHONLY

Vice-Rector for Admin. and Personnel: NOU SETHA

Vice-Rector for Int. Relations and Career Placement: SENG BUNTHOEUN

Number of teachers: 650

Number of students: 20,000

Publication: *NUM Research Series*

DEANS

Faculty of Economics: SIM SOVICHA

Faculty of Information Technology: CHHAY PHANG

Faculty of Law: NEAU SARETH

Faculty of Management: SOU PHALLA

PREAH KOSSOMAK POLYTECHNIC INSTITUTE

Russian Blvd, Sangkat Toek Tla, Khan Reusey Keo, Phnom-Penh

Telephone: (11) 909148

E-mail: ppi@camnet.com.kh

Internet: www.rumdoul.com/ppi

Founded 1965 as Centre de formation Professionnelles des Cadres Technique, present name and status 2001; attached to Min. of Labour and Vocational Training

State control

Languages of instruction: English, French, Khmer

Offers degrees in business admin., civil engineering, electrical engineering, electronic engineering, information technology; diplomas in civil construction, electricity, electronic, information technology

Dir: HEM CHANTHA

Number of teachers: 81

PREK LEAP NATIONAL SCHOOL OF AGRICULTURE

Russey Keo, POB 1319, Phnom-Penh

Rd 6A, Prek Leap, Russey Keo, Phnom-Penh

Telephone: (23) 219746

E-mail: info@pnsa.edu.kh

Internet: www.pnsa.edu.kh

Founded 1950, present status 1984; attached to Min. of Agriculture, Forestry and Fisheries

State control

Languages of instruction: English, Khmer

Academic year: September to June

Dir: PHAT MUNY

Vice-Dir: Assoc. Prof. KHANNARITH LAM

Number of teachers: 450

Number of students: 2,300

DEANS

Faculty of Agricultural Economics: VENGHENG VA

Faculty of Cadastral and Land Management: TRY EAM

Faculty of Information Technology: TOUCH LONG

ROYAL ACADEMY OF CAMBODIA

Campus 2, Fed. of Russia Blvd, Sangkat Tuk Laak 1, Khan Tuol Kok, Phnom-Penh 12156

POB 2070, Phnom-Penh

Telephone: (23) 890180

E-mail: hacademy@camnet.com.kh

Internet: www.rac.edu.kh

Founded 1965, disbanded 1975 due to civil war, re-established 1997; attached to Office of the Ccl of Mins

Languages of instruction: English, Khmer

State control

Academic year: October to June

Offers a range of masters and doctoral programmes; promotes research in all major academic areas and organizes scientific forums

Library of 10,000 vols

Pres.: LOK CHUUTEAR KLOT THIDA

Under-General Sec. for Admin. and Finance: CHHUN SUM BUN

Under-General Sec. for Training and Research: CHEA NENG.

SUB-INSTITUTES

Institute of Biology, Medicine and Agriculture: tel. (12) 835306; Dir Dr SAM SOPHEAN.

Institute of Culture and Fine Arts: tel. (12) 733336; Dir Dr CHHAY YIHEANG.

Institute of Humanities and Social Sciences: tel. (11) 919044; Dir Dr ROS CHANTRABOT.

Institute of National Language: tel. (12) 836040; Dir (vacant).

Institute of Science and Technology: tel. (11) 951849; Dir Dr CHAN PORN

ROYAL UNIVERSITY OF AGRICULTURE

POB 2696, Khan Dangkor, Phnom-Penh

Telephone: (23) 219753

E-mail: info@rua.edu.kh

Internet: www.rua.edu.kh

Founded 1964, present status 1999; attached to Min. of Agriculture, Forestry and Fisheries

Rector: Dr NGO BUNTHAN

Number of teachers: 220

Number of students: 1,100

DEANS

Faculty of Agricultural Economics and Rural Development: BORA KATHY

Faculty of Agricultural Technology and Management: KANG KROESNA

Faculty of Agro-Industry: KONG THONG

Faculty of Agronomy: SOPHAL CHOUNG

Faculty of Animal Science and Veterinary Medicine: PHITH LOAN CHHUM

Faculty of Fisheries: CHHOUK BORIN

Faculty of Forestry: MONIN VON

Faculty of Land Management and Land Administration: VUNG SETHA

Graduate School: Dr THAVRAK HOUN (acting)

ROYAL UNIVERSITY OF FINE ARTS

St 184, Chey Chumneas Commune, Daun Penh, Phnom-Penh

Telephone: (23) 986417

E-mail: rufa@camnet.com.kh

Internet: www.rufa.edu.kh

Founded 1918 as École des Arts Cambodgiens, merged with Nat. Theatre School 1965, closed 1975, re-opened as School of Fine Arts 1980, original name and status restored 1993; attached to Min. of Culture and Fine Arts

Faculties of archaeology, architecture and urban studies, choreographic arts, music, plastic arts

Rector: KEOUN TUK

Vice-Rector and Dean of Choreographic Arts: CHHIENG PROEUNG

ROYAL UNIVERSITY OF LAW AND ECONOMICS

Preah Monivong, Phnom-Penh 12305

Telephone: (23) 211565

E-mail: fle@khmerson.com

Internet: www.rule.edu.kh

Founded 1948 as Nat. Institute of Law, Politics and Economics, incorporated into the Univ. of Phnom-Penh as Faculty of Law and Economics 1957, independent univ. status 2003; attached to Min. of Education, Youth and Sport

State control

Language of instruction: Khmer

Academic year: October to July

Faculties of economics and management, law, public admin.; graduate schools of law and economics and management

Rector: YUOK NGOY (acting)

Number of teachers: 266 (84 full-time, 112 visiting Cambodian lecturers and 70 foreign visiting lecturers)

Number of students: 4,802

ROYAL UNIVERSITY OF PHNOM-PENH

Russian Fed. Blvd, Toul Kork, Phnom-Penh

Telephone: (23) 883-640

E-mail: secretary@rupp.edu.kh

Internet: www.rupp.edu.kh

Founded 1960 as Royal Khmer Univ., renamed Phnom-Penh Univ. 1970, closed 1975–79, re-opened 1980, current name adopted 1996; attached to Min. of Education, Youth and Sport

State control

Languages of instruction: English, French, Khmer

Academic year: September to June

Rector: Prof. LAV CHHIV EAV

Vice-Rector for Acad. and Admin. Affairs: PONN CHHAY

Vice-Rector for Curriculum and QA: HE SOK VANNY

Vice-Rector for Gen. Management of CJCC, Youth and Cultural Exchange Programme: OUM RAVY

Vice-Rector for Gen. Management of IFL: SUOS MAN

Vice-Rector for Research, Postgraduate Programme and Int. Relations: HANG CHANTHON

Librarian: SEN SENG

Library of 39,000 vols

Number of teachers: 420

Number of students: 9,000

DEANS

Faculty of Science: ING HENG

Faculty of Social Science and Humanities: KIM SOVANNKIRY

Institute of Foreign Languages: Dr MEAS VANNA

SVAY RIENG UNIVERSITY

Nat. Rd 1, Chambak Village, Sangkat Chek, Svay Rieng
Telephone: (44) 715776
E-mail: info@sru.edu.kh
Internet: www.sru.edu.kh
Founded 2006; attached to Min. of Education, Youth and Sport
State control
Faculties of agriculture; art, humanity and foreign language; business admin.; science and technology; social science
Rector: TUM SARAVUTH

UNIVERSITE DES SCIENCES DE LA SANTE
(University of Health Sciences)

73, Preah Monivong Blvd, Phnom-Penh
Telephone: (23) 430732
E-mail: uhsc@univ-sante.edu.kh
Internet: uhs.edu.kh
Founded 1946 as School for Medical Officers, current name adopted 1997, current status 2001; attached to Min. of Health
Faculties of medicine, pharmacy, odontostomatology
Rector: VONTHANAK SAPHONN

UNIVERSITY OF BATTAMBANG

Nat. Rd 5, Prek Preah Sdech Commune, Battambang
Telephone: (53) 952905
E-mail: info@ubb.edu.kh
Internet: www.ubb.edu.kh
Founded 2007; attached to Min. of Education, Youth and Sport
State control
Academic year: August to September (2 semesters)
Faculties of agriculture and food processing; arts education and humanities; business administration and tourism; science and technology; sociology and community development
Rector: Dr VISALSOK TOUCH

Private Universities

ANGKOR CITY INSTITUTE

Main Campus, Seam Reap
Telephone: (23) 990424
E-mail: aci@camintel.com; attached to Min. of Education, Youth and Sport
Private control
Dir: SEOUN HOK

ANGKOR UNIVERSITY

Borey Seang Nam, Phum Khna, Khum Chreav, Srok Siem Reap, Khet Siem Reap, Angkor
Telephone: (92) 256086
E-mail: info@angkor.edu.kh
Internet: www.angkor.edu.kh
Founded 2004; attached to Min. of Education, Youth and Sport
Private control
Rector: HE NEAK OKNHA SEANG NAM
Vice-Rector: SHIN HO CHUL
Vice-Rector: YUN LINNE

ASIA EURO UNIVERSITY

832 ABCD, Kampuchea Krom Blvd, Sangkat Teuk Laak I, Khan Toul Kork, Phnom-Penh 12156
Telephone: (11) 757485
E-mail: info@aeu.edu.kh
Internet: www.aeu.edu.kh
Founded 2005; attached to Min. of Education, Youth and Sport
Private control
Rector: DUONG LEANG
Dir for Admin: SEANG SOVANN

DEANS

Faculty of Arts, Humanities and Languages: LY BUNSAN

ASIA PACIFIC INSTITUTE

189, Mao Tse Toung Blvd, Khan Chamkarmorn, Phnom-Penh
Telephone: (23) 985823
E-mail: steveloun@gmx.net; attached to Min. of Education, Youth and Sport
Private control
Dir: CHHENG LY

BELTEI INTERNATIONAL INSTITUTE

25A, St 105, Boeng Prolit, Khan 7 Makara, Phnom-Penh
Telephone: (12) 823666
E-mail: info@beltei.edu.kh
Internet: www.beltei.edu.kh
Founded 2002; attached to Min. of Education, Youth and Sport
Private control
10 Campuses
Dir: HE CHHENG LY

BUILD BRIGHT UNIVERSITY

Tonle Basac Bldg, Grey Bldg, Samdech Sothearos Blvd, Phnom-Penh
Telephone: (23) 987700
E-mail: info@bbu.edu.kh
Internet: www.bbu.edu.kh
Founded 2000 as Faculty of Management and Law, present name and status 2002; attached to Min. of Education, Youth and Sport
Private control
Rector: VIRAKCHEAT IN
Pres.: Assoc. Prof. DIEP SEIHA
Vice-Pres. for Acad. and Student Affairs: Assoc. Prof. MEAS REN RITH
Vice-Pres. for Admin. Affairs: Asst Prof. IN VIRACHEY
Vice-Pres. for Finance and Property: PROK VEASNA
Vice-Pres. for Legal Affairs and Coordination: Assoc. Prof. LAM CHEA
Vice-Pres. for Postgraduate Studies: Prof. Dr TAPAS RANJAN DASH
Number of students: 12,000

DEANS

Faculty of Business Management: SAMRITH CHANHENG
Faculty of Education and Languages: KE CHHUM PANHA
Faculty of Engineering and Architecture: SOK KHOM
Faculty of Law and Social Sciences: OEURN SOKHA
Faculty of Science and Technology: CHI KIM Y
Faculty of Tourism and Hospitality: EM KHEDY

CAMBODIAN MEKONG UNIVERSITY

9B, St 271, Sangkat Tek Thla, Khan Sen Sok, Phnom-Penh 12102
Telephone: (23) 882211
E-mail: info@mekong.edu.kh
Internet: www.mekong.edu.kh; attached to Min. of Education, Youth and Sport
Private control
Chancellor: ICH SENG
Vice-Chancellor: BAN THERO
Library of 10,000 vols

DEANS

Faculty of Arts, Humanities and Foreign Language: CHENG KIMSAN
Faculty of Economics: LONG SOPHAT
Faculty of Law: PEN PICHSALY
Faculty of Management and Tourism: KON SKAISHANN
Faculty of Science: CHEA CHHOUN HONG
Faculty of Social Science: SUGITA SHIN

CAMBODIAN UNIVERSITY FOR SPECIALTIES

Bldg F, Toul Kork Village, Sangkat Toul Sangke, Khan Russey Keo, Phnom-Penh
Telephone: (23) 350828
E-mail: info@cus.edu.kh
Internet: www.cus.edu.kh; attached to Min. of Education, Youth and Sport
Private control
Campuses in Banteaymeanchey, Battambang, Kamport, Kampong Cham, Kampong Thom
Rector: HE SDOEUNG SOKHOM
Vice-Rector for Admin. Affairs: CHHUN NOCH
Vice-Rector for Foundation and Academic Affairs: SOEUR YAN
Vice-Rector for Research and Devt Affairs: Dr MEAS BORA

CHAMROEUN UNIVERSITY OF POLYTECHNOLOGY

88, St 350, Khan Chamkarmorn, Phnom-Penh
Telephone: (11) 987795
E-mail: cup@camintel.com.kh
Internet: www.cup.edu.kh
Founded 2002; attached to Min. of Education, Youth and Sport
Private control
Rector: HE Dr CHEA CHAMROEUN

HUMAN RESOURCES UNIVERSITY

Bldg 2, St 163, Sangkat Olympic, Khan Chamkamorn, Phnom-Penh
Telephone: (23) 987826
E-mail: info@hru.edu.kh
Internet: www.hru.edu.kh
Founded 1998, current name adopted 2005, present status 2007; attached to Min. of Education, Youth and Sport
Private control
Faculties of arts, humanity and languages; business administration and tourism; law and political science; science and technology; social science and economics
Rector: SENG PHALLY
Vice-Rector: EK MONOSEN
Vice-Rector: OK SOPHEA

ICS UNIVERSITY

14, St 214, Sangkat Beoung Raing, Khan Daun Penh, Phnom-Penh
Telephone: (23) 724062
E-mail: info_bss@ics.edu.kh
Internet: www.ics.edu.kh; attached to Min. of Education, Youth and Sport

Private control
Rector: KHUON SUDARY

IIC UNIVERSITY OF TECHNOLOGY

Bldg 650, Nat. Rd 2, Sankat Chak, Angre Krom, Khan Mean Chey, Phnom-Penh
Telephone: (23) 425 148
E-mail: info@iic.edu.kh
Internet: www.iic.edu.kh
Founded 1999 as Int. Institute of Cambodia, present name and status 2008; attached to Min. of Education, Youth and Sport
Private control
Rector: CHHUON CHAN THAN
Number of teachers: 29
Number of students: 500

INSTITUTE FOR BUSINESS EDUCATION

315, St Charles De Gaulle Blvd, Sangkat Orussey II, Khan 7 Makara, Phnom-Penh
Telephone: (23) 990980
E-mail: info@ibe.edu.kh
Internet: www.ibe.edu.kh
Founded 2006; attached to Min. of Education, Youth and Sport
Private control
Faculties of business and English
Deputy Dir: YOK SETTHA

INSTITUTE OF CAMBODIA

314, Nat. Rd 5, O Ambel Dist., Bantey Meanchay
Telephone: (12) 737578
E-mail: ic.edu.bmc@yahoo.com; attached to Min. of Education, Youth and Sport
Private control
Rector: VIN SOCHEAT

INSTITUTE OF MANAGEMENT AND DEVELOPMENT

Peal Nhek I, Phtes Prey, Sampov Meas, Pursat
Telephone: (52) 951519
E-mail: mensethy@camintel.com
Internet: www.imd.edu.kh
Founded 2006; attached to Min. of Education, Youth and Sports
Private control
Dir: MEN SETHY

INSTITUTE OF MANAGEMENT SCIENCE

Monivong St, Khom Kompong Cham, Kompong Cham Dist., Kompong Cham
Telephone: (12) 873539; attached to Min. of Education, Youth and Sport
Private control
Rector: SENG LYMENG

INSTITUTE OF TECHNOLOGY AND MANAGEMENT

St 180, Khan Daun Pen, Phnom-Penh
Telephone: (23) 982229
E-mail: itm@online.com.kh
Founded 1999; attached to Min. of Education, Youth and Sport
Private control
Dir: SOK BUN LIM

INTERED INSTITUTE

Level 5 of Phnom Penh Center, Sothearos Blvd, Khan Chamkarmorn, Phnom-Penh
Telephone: (23) 993866
E-mail: info@intered.edu.kh; attached to Min. of Education, Youth and Sport
Private control
Rector: UNG DIPOLA

INTERNATIONAL UNIVERSITY

Cnr of Sts 1984 & 1011, Sangkat Phnom-Penh Thmey, Khan Russey Keo, Phnom-Penh 12100
Telephone: (17) 926969
E-mail: iusabo@yahoo.com
Internet: www.iu.edu.kh
Founded 2002; attached to Min. of Education, Youth and Sport
Private control
Languages of instruction: Khmer, French, English
7 Faculties and 1 postgraduate institute; offers 40 degree programmes ranging from assoc. to doctoral degrees
Hon. Chair.: HE Dr OUK RABUN
Pres.: HE Prof. UON SABO
Vice-Pres.: Dr SEUN SAMBATH
Vice-Pres.: HE Prof. SABO OJANO
Dir for Int. Relations: Dr ANBIN EZHILAN
Number of students: 1,250

KHEMARAK UNIVERSITY

Sothearos Blvd and Preah Sihanouk Blvd cnr, Phnom-Penh Center, Block D, Phnom-Penh
Telephone: (23) 6336296
E-mail: khemarak_university@yahoo.com
Internet: www.khemarak.com; attached to Min. of Education, Youth and Sport
Private control
Faculties of agricultural science and rural devt, art and linguistics, business admin. and tourism, educational science, humanities, law and economic science, political science and int. relations, professional training centre and research, science technology and information
Rector: Dr SOK TOUCH

KHMER UNIVERSITY OF TECHNOLOGY AND MANAGEMENT

Sangkat 4, Khan Mittapheap, Sihanoukville
Telephone: (34) 933718
E-mail: info@kutm-shv.com
Internet: www.kutm-shv.com
Private control
Rector: Dr HONG CHAN SOKHA
Librarian: CHHAY CHANDARET
Librarian: SAM ROTHA

LIMKOKWING UNIVERSITY OF CREATIVE TECHNOLOGY

120–126, St 1986, Sangkat Phnom Penh Thmei, Khan Sen Sok, Phnom-Penh
Telephone: (23) 995733
E-mail: enquiry@limkokwing.edu.kh
Internet: www.limkokwing.edu.kh
Founded 1991 in Malaysia
Private control
Campuses in Botswana, People's Republic of China, Indonesia, Lesotho, Malaysia, Swaziland, UK
Pres.: Dr LIM KOK WING

NEWTON THILAY UNIVERSITY

100, St Pasteur, Psar Tmey 3, Khan Daun Penh, Phnom-Penh
Telephone: (23) 224807
E-mail: info.ntu@ntu.edu.kh; attached to Min. of Education, Youth and Sport
Private control
8 Faculties and 1 training centre
Rector: CHEA THILAY

NORTON UNIVERSITY

Cnr St 118 & 19 & 130, Sangkat Phsar Chas, Khan Daun Penh, Phnom-Penh
Telephone: (23) 982166
E-mail: info@norton-u.com
Internet: www.norton-u.com; attached to Min. of Education, Youth and Sport
Private control
Rector: CHAN SOK KHIENG
Dir for Admin. and Personnel: KAO SAM OL
Dir for Information Technology Dept: OUR PHIRUN
Dir for Int. Relations: RODRIGO C. PASCO
Registrar: NGOV SIMRONG
Library of 4,000 vols

DEANS
College of Sciences: HAS BUNTON
College of Social Sciences: TRY SOTHEARITH

PAÑÑĀSĀSTRA UNIVERSITY OF CAMBODIA

92–94, Maha Vithei Samdech Sothearos, Phnom-Penh
Telephone: (23) 990153
E-mail: info@puc.edu.kh
Internet: www.puc.edu.kh
Founded 1997; attached to Min. of Education, Youth and Sport
Private control
Faculties of arts, letters and humanities; business and economics; communication and media art; education; law and public affairs; mathematics, science and engineering; medicine and health sciences; social sciences and int. art
Pres.: Dr CHEA SAN CHANTHAN
Dir for Library System: MAO KOLAP

PHNOM PENH INTERNATIONAL UNIVERSITY

Bldg 36, St 169, Sangkat Veal Vong, Khan 7 Makara, Phnom-Penh
Telephone: (23) 999908
E-mail: info@ppiu.edu.kh
Internet: www.ppiu.edu.kh
Founded 2006 by merger of Int. Institute of Cambodia and Asean Univ.
Private control
Rector: TEP KOLAP
Sr Vice-Rector: HIN SAM ATH
Vice-Rector for Acad. Affairs: KHOV MEAS
Vice-Rector for Admin. and Finance: KEO KUYLY
Head of Academic Ccls: SREY BUN DOEUN
Number of teachers: 30

DEANS
Faculty of Business and Tourism: SREY CHANTHY
Faculty of Education: KEA LEAPH
Faculty of Law and Economics: LY KONGSOCHAN
Faculty of Science and Information Technology: (vacant)

SACHAK ASIA DEVELOPMENT INSTITUTE

47Eo, St 348, Sangkat Toul Svay Prey I, Kanh Chamkarmon, Phnom-Penh
Telephone: (12) 603148
E-mail: info@sadi.edu.kh
Internet: www.sadi.edu.kh
Founded 2004; attached to Min. of Education, Youth and Sport
Private control

Faculties of business management, computer science, economics, English and hotel tourism

Dir: NHEM SACHAK

SETEC INSTITUTE

92, St 110, Russian Fed. Blvd, Sangkat Teuk Laak I, Khan Toul Kork, Phnom-Penh
Telephone: (23) 880612
E-mail: info@setecu.com
Internet: www.setecu.com; attached to Min. of Education, Youth and Sport
Private control

Offers Bachelors degrees in business admin. skills and English, computer and local area networking, software engineering, software programming and database management system, website and multimedia devt; also offers Masters degrees in business management, database admin., application devt, networking technology

Dir: NGOUN SOKVENG

Library of 2,000 books and magazines

SITC UNIVERSITY

315, St Saldegol, Sangkat Oreushi 2, Khan 7 Makara, Phnom-Penh
Telephone: (12) 914321
E-mail: sii@online.com.kh; attached to Min. of Education, Youth and Sport
Private control

Vice-Dir: Dr MICHEL YU

UNIVERSITY OF CAMBODIA

POB 116, Phnom-Penh 12000
145, Preah Norodom Blvd, Phnom-Penh
Telephone: (23) 993274
E-mail: info@uc.edu.kh
Internet: www.uc.edu.kh

Founded 2003; attached to Min. of Education, Youth and Sport
Private control

Chair.: HE Dr AUN PORN MONIROTH
Chancellor: Dr HARUHISA HANDA
Pres.: Dr KAO KIM HOURN
Vice-Pres. for Academic Affairs: Dr ANGUS D. MUNRO
Dir. for Admin.: POR MALIS

Library of 50,000 books, periodicals, magazines

Publication: *Journal of Cambodian Studies*

UNIVERSITY OF MANAGEMENT AND ECONOMICS

POB 303, Battambang
5 St, Prakpreah sdech Commune, Battambang
Telephone: (17) 868386
E-mail: umecambodia@gmail.com
Internet: www.ume.edu.kh

Founded 1998 as Battambang High Education Center, renamed as Institute of Management and Economics 2000, current name adopted 2005; attached to Min. of Education, Youth and Sport
Private control

Hon. Chair.: Dr BUTH KIMSEAN
Chair.: Prof. Dr TEP KHUNNAL
Pres.: Prof. TUN PHEAKDEY
Vice-Pres.: Prof. Dr CHUM LAY
Vice-Pres.: Prof. Dr NORING THA
Vice-Pres.: Prof. Dr PRIEN HIEP
Vice-Pres.: Prof. Dr TUN NARITH

Library of 12,000 vols
Number of teachers: 92
Number of students: 3,879

UNIVERSITY OF PUTHISASTRA

55, St 180, Sangkat Boeung Raing, Khan Daun Penh, Phnom-Penh
Telephone: (23) 220476
E-mail: info@puthisastra.edu.kh
Internet: www.puthisastra.edu.kh

Founded 2007
Private control
Academic year: October to August

Chair.: Dr HENG VONG BUNCHHAT
Pres.: HE SOK PUTHVYUTH
Vice-Rector for Int. Affairs: STEPHEN PATERSON
Vice-Rector for Student Affairs: KY RAVIKUN
Chief of Admin.: IM PIDO TEVY

Library of 6,000 books, magazines

DEANS

Faculty of Computer Science and Microsoft IT Academy Dept: ONG WITHYARD
Language Department: HENG RATTANA

UNIVERSITY OF SOUTH EAST ASIA

Seam Reap
Telephone: (63) 6901696
E-mail: info@usea.edu.kh
Internet: www.usea.edu.kh

Founded 2006; attached to Min. of Education, Youth and Sport
Private control

Rector: SEIN SOVANNA

VANDA INSTITUTE OF ACCOUNTING

216–218, Mao Tse Toung Blvd, Sangkat Tomnop Toek, Khan Chamkarmon, Phnom-Penh
Telephone: (23) 213563
E-mail: vanda@camnet.com.kh
Internet: www.vanda.edu.kh

Founded 1997 as Vanda Centre, current name adopted 2002; attached to Min. of Education, Youth and Sport
Private control

Offers Bachelors and Masters degrees in accounting, auditing and political science

Dir: HENG VANDA

Library of 5,000 vols
Number of students: 2,749

WESTERN UNIVERSITY

15, St 528, Sangkat Boeung kak I, Khan ToulKork, Phnom-Penh
Telephone: (23) 998233
E-mail: info_wu@western.edu.kh
Internet: www.western.edu.kh/wu

Founded 2003; attached to Min. of Education, Youth and Sport
Private control

Rector: HE TE LAURENT
Vice-Rector for Acad. Affairs and Research: HE RONG CHHORNG
Vice-Rector for Admin and Finance: AO VENG
Registrar: TOM BANDOS

Library of 5,000 vols, 100 journals and periodicals

DEANS

Faculty of Arts, Humanities and Language: PRUDENT INJEELI
Faculty of Social Science, Management and Hotel-Tourism: PEH BUNTONG
Graduate School: HE RONG CHHORNG

ZAMAN UNIVERSITY

St 315, No. 8, Boeng Kok 1, Toul Kork, Phnom-Penh
Telephone: (23) 996111
E-mail: info@zamanuniversity.com
Internet: www.zamanuniversity.com

Founded 2010
Private control
Academic year: October to September

Faculties of arts, humanities and languages; economics and administrative sciences; engineering; information and computer technologies

Rector: Dr ERKAN POLATDEMIR

CAMEROON

The Higher Education System

As a result of Cameroon's mixed colonial heritage, there are separate education systems in the former British- and French-administered regions. East Cameroon was a French colony from 1916 to 1960, when it became independent and was known as the Republic of Cameroon. A merger with the smaller, British-run provinces of Southern Cameroon in 1961 led to the creation of the Federal Republic of Cameroon. The current name of the country, the Republic of Cameroon, was adopted in 1984. British- and French-based educational systems now operate in the respective former provinces, and English and French are the respective official languages of instruction. The Université de Yaoundé I (formerly Federal University of Cameroon) was established in 1962 and operates on a decentralized principle, with five regional campuses, each devoted to a different field of study. Five new state universities were created by presidential decree in 1993: Buéa, Douala, Dschang, Ngaoundéré and Yaoundé II. As part of a process of decentralizing Cameroon's public higher education sector, a seventh state university was inaugurated in the far north of the country in 2008, the Université de Maroua. The University of Buéa teaches solely in English, while the six other state-managed universities are run on the francophone model (although in principle, they are considered to be bilingual institutions). In 2010 the eighth state university was signed into existence; the Université de Bamenda held its first competitive intake of students in the 2012/13 academic year. There are also a number of private universities in Cameroon, including the Bamenda University of Science and Technology, the International University (Bamenda), the Victor Fotso University Institute of Technology and the Université Catholique de l'Afrique Centrale. There was a total of 174,100 students enrolled at universities in 2008/09. The Ministry of Higher Education is responsible for maintaining standards and for accreditation in both the public and private higher education sectors. In 2003 seven private institutions signed 'creation agreements' with the Ministry of Higher Education; such agreements initiate the process by which educational institutions seek authorization for their establishment.

Chancellors are government appointees and are the executive heads of universities. The Chancellor oversees the appointments of Deans of faculty, Heads of department and Directors of professional schools in consultation with the Vice-Chancellor. The Governing Council is presided over by the Vice-Chancellor, and includes the Deans, Directors, members of the academic staff and representatives from government and labour organizations.

Admission to university requires the Baccalauréat or two GCE Advanced level examinations and four GCE Ordinary level examinations. In 2006 the Cameroonian Government introduced a Bologna-style (Licence-Maîtrise-Doctorat or Bachelors-Masters-Doctorate) system of higher education which aimed to bring the Cameroonian education system more in line with the European university structure. As part of the new degree structure, which was implemented from the 2007/08 academic year, new curricula and a system of transferable credits (similar to the European Credit Transfer and Accumulation System—ECTS—within the Bologna system) were introduced. University education is divided into three cycles, the first at undergraduate level and the second and third at postgraduate level. The first cycle generally comprises a three- to four-year programme leading to the award of the Licence/Bachelors or various diploma programmes (Diplômes) lasting up to six years. The second cycle, at postgraduate level, consists of a two-year programme undertaken following the Licence/Bachelors and leading to the award of a Maîtrise/Masters degree; in addition, there is the Diplôme d'Etudes Professionnelles Approfondies (DEPA), which is a three-semester postgraduate qualification offered mainly in the field of management. The third cycle consists of doctoral studies: three to five years of study after the Maîtrise for the Doctorat du Troisième Cycle or Doctor of Philosophy (PhD). The latter degree requires the public defence of a thesis before an appointed panel.

An increasing number of specialist institutions (both public and private) offer vocational education and technical training in a broad range of subjects; the most common awards at these institutions are diplomas and courses lasting for two to three years.

Regulatory Bodies

GOVERNMENT

Ministry of Art and Culture: Quartier Hippodrome, Yaoundé; tel. 2222-6579; Minister AMA TUTU MUNA.

Ministry of Employment and Professional Training: Yaoundé; tel. 2222-0186; Minister ZACHARIE PÉRÉVET.

Ministry of Higher Education: 2 ave du 20 Mai, BP 1457, Yaoundé; tel. 2222-1770; e-mail aowono@uycdc.uninet.cm; internet www.minesup.gov.cm; Minister Prof. JACQUES FAME NDONGO.

Ministry of Scientific Research and Innovation: BP 1457, Yaoundé; tel. 2223-2412; e-mail info@minresi.net; internet www.minresi.net; Minister Dr MADELEINE TCHUINTÉ.

Learned Societies

GENERAL

UNESCO Office Yaoundé: POB 12909, Yaoundé; Immeuble Stamatiades, 2e étage, Yaoundé; tel. 2222-5763; internet www.unesco.org/fr/yaounde; f. 1991; designated Cluster Office for Cameroon, Chad and CAR; 19 mems; Dir BERNARD HADJADJ.

LANGUAGE AND LITERATURE

Alliance Française: BP 441, Ngaoundéré; tel. (237) 251826; e-mail alliance.ngaoundere@free.fr; internet alliance.ngaoundere.free.fr; offers courses and exams in French language and culture and promotes cultural exchange with France; attached teaching offices in Bamenda, Buea, Dschang, Garoua and L'Adamaoua; Pres. LUC DJAOUKIDO.

British Council: Immeuble Christo, ave Charles de Gaulle, BP 818, Yaoundé; tel. 2221-1696; e-mail bc-yaounde@britishcouncil.cm; internet www.britishcouncil.org/cameroon; offers courses and exams in English language and British culture and promotes cultural exchange with the UK; attached teaching centre in Douala; Dir JENNY SCOTT; Teaching Centre Man. TOM HINTON.

Goethe-Institut: Quartier Bastos, BP 1067, Yaoundé; tel. (237) 22214409; e-mail info@yaounde.goethe.org; internet www.goethe.de/ins/cm/fr/yao.html?wt_sc=cameroun; offers courses and exams in German language and culture and promotes cultural exchange with Germany; library of 6,000 vols; Dir IRENE BARK.

Research Institutes

GENERAL

Institut de Recherche pour le Développement (IRD): Représentation ORSTOM, BP 1857, Yaoundé; tel. 2220-1508; e-mail orstyde@ird.uninet.cm; internet www.ird.fr; f. 1944; see main entry under France; Representative FRANÇOIS RIVIÈRE.

AGRICULTURE, FISHERIES AND VETERINARY SCIENCE

Humid Forest Ecoregional Centre: BP 2008, Yaoundé; tel. (237) 22227449; f. 1980; Dir A. M. MAINO.

Institut de la Recherche Agricole pour le Développement: BP 2123, Yaoundé; tel. (273) 22223362; e-mail contact@

irad-cameroun.org; internet www.iradcameroun.org; f. 1979; agriculture, agronomy, botany, entomology, phytopathology, pedology; 6 research centres, 16 stations; library of 2,600 vols, 2,500 brochures, 450 periodicals; Dir Dr J. A. AYUK-TAKEM; publs *Mémoires et Travaux de l'IRA*, *Science et Technique (Series Sciences Agronomiques et Zootechniques* (4 a year).

ECONOMICS, LAW AND POLITICS

Institut de Formation et de Recherche Démographiques: BP 1556, Yaoundé; tel. 2222-2471; e-mail iford@iford-cm.org; f. 1972 with the cooperation of the UN; training and research on demographic phenomena and their links with economic and social factors; library of 17,000 vols; Dir AKOTO ELIWO; publ. *Annales* (3 a year).

Institut des Relations Internationales du Cameroun (IRIC): BP 1637, Yaoundé; tel. 2231-0305; e-mail iric@uycdc.uninet.cm; f. 1971 by the Federal Government, the Carnegie Endowment for International Peace, the Swiss Division for Technical Cooperation and others; library of 65,000 vols; Dir Dr JEAN-EMMANUEL PONDI; Sec. Gen. SAMUEL ENOH BESONG; publ. *Cameroon Review of International Studies* (1 a year).

EDUCATION

Centre National d'Education: POB 1457 Yaoundé; tel. (237) 22234012; f. 1979; attached to Min. of Scientific Research and Innovation; Dir ELISABETH TAMAJONG.

HISTORY, GEOGRAPHY AND ARCHAEOLOGY

Institut de Recherches Géologiques et Minières: POB 4110, Yaoundé; tel. 22210316; e-mail contact@irgm-cameroon.org; internet www.irgm-cameroun.org; f. 1979; research on natural hazards like volcanic eruptions, earthquakes and gas emissions; Dir GEORGES E. EKODECK.

Institut National de Cartographie: BP 157, Ave Mgr.-Vogt, Yaoundé; tel. 2222-2921; e-mail inc@incsdncmr.undp.org; f. 1945; cartography, geography, GIS and remote sensing; Dirs PAUL MOBY ETIA; Dir MICHEL SIMEU KAMDEM.

LANGUAGE AND LITERATURE

Centre International de Recherche et de Documentation sur les Traditions et les Langues Africaines (CERDOTOLA): BP 479, Yaoundé; tel. 2230-3144; e-mail cerdotola@yahoo.com; internet www.cerdotola.com; f. 1978; 20 mem. countries; library in process of formation; Exec. Sec. Prof. CHARLES BINAM BIKOI.

MEDICINE

Institut de Recherches Médicales et d'Etudes des Plantes Médicinales: BP 8013, Yaoundé; tel. (237) 2233221; f. 1979; attached to Min. of Scientific Research and Innovation; library of 1,000 vols, 50 periodicals; Dir ESSAME OYONO; publs *Cahiers*, *Science et Technique*.

NATURAL SCIENCES

Physical Sciences

Direction de la Météorologie Nationale du Cameroun: BP 186, Douala; tel. 33421635; e-mail bangawa2001@yahoo.fr; internet www.meteo-cameroon.net; f. 1934; Dir PHILIPPE RICHARD; publs *Annales Climatologiques* (irregular), *RCM: Résumé Climatologique Mensuel* (12 a year), *Résumé Mensuel du Temps* (12 a year).

TECHNOLOGY

Compagnie Française pour le Développement des Fibres Textiles (CFDT): BP 1699, Douala; brs at Garoua, Maroua, Mora, Touboro and Kaele; textile research.

Libraries and Archives

Bamenda

British Council Learning and Information Centre: Bamenda Urban Council Library, Commercial Ave, POB 622, Bamenda; tel. 3336-2011; e-mail anyeoscar@yahoo.co.uk; f. 1995; 15,000 vols; Information Officer EMMANUEL NGANG.

Yaoundé

Archives Nationales: BP 1053, Yaoundé; tel. 2223-0078; f. 1952; conserves and classifies all documents relating to the Republic; 15,000 vols; Dir AMADOU POKEKO.

Bibliothèque Nationale du Cameroun: Ministère de la Culture, Yaoundé; tel. 2223-7002; 64,000 vols; Dir NGOTOBO NGOTOBO.

Museums and Art Galleries

Bamenda

International Museum and Library—Akum: POB 389, Bamenda; f. 1948; local and foreign artefacts of interest to researchers and students of sociology, anthropology and archaeology; brasswork, paintings, beaded work, clay figures, animal skins, masks, postage stamps, iron work, sculpture, stools, traditional costumes, films and books; Curator PETER S. ATANGA.

Kumbo-Nso

Musa Heritage Gallery (Mus'Art): POB 21, Kumbo; Bamfem Quarter, Kumbo; tel. 7937-2652; e-mail administration@musartgallery.org; internet www.musartgallery.org; f. 1996; cultural democratization and heritage preservation of arts, music, arts and crafts of the Western Grassfields region of Cameroon; 400 artefacts; preservation, education and promotion of cultural legacy of the Grass fields of Cameroon; Dir PETER M. MUSA.

Universities

UNIVERSITÉ DE BUÉA

POB 63, Buea
Telephone: 3332-2134
E-mail: registrar@ubuea.net
Internet: www.ubuea.net
Founded 1977 (opened 1986) as Buea Univ. Centre, present name and status 1992
State control
Languages of instruction: English, French, Spanish
Academic year: September to June
Chancellor: Dr PETER AGBOR TABI
Pro-Chancellor: Prof. VICTOR ANOMAH NGU
Vice-Chancellor: Dr DOROTHY L. NJEUMA
Deputy Vice-Chancellor for Control: Prof. SAMMY BEBAN CHUMBOW
Deputy Vice-Chancellor for Research and Cooperation: Prof. SAMSON ABANGMA
Deputy Vice-Chancellor for Teaching: Prof. VINCENT P. K. TITANJI
Registrar: Dr HERBERT NGANJO ENDELEY
Librarian: ROSEMARY SHAFACK
Library of 35,000 vols
Number of teachers: 208 (93 full-time, 115 part-time)
Number of students: 3,300
Publication: *Epasa Moto* (1 a year)

DEANS

Faculty of Arts: Prof. EMMANUEL GWAN ACHU
Faculty of Education: Dr GRACE EWENE
Faculty of Health Sciences: Dr THEODOSA MCMOLI
Faculty of Science: Dr NZUMBE MESAPE NTOKO
Faculty of Social and Management Sciences: Prof. CORNELIUS LAMBI

CONSTITUENT INSTITUTE

Advanced School of Translators and Interpreters (ASTI): Dir Dr ETIENNE ZÉ AMVELA

UNIVERSITÉ CATHOLIQUE DE L'AFRIQUE CENTRALE

BP 11628, Yaoundé
Telephone: 2223-7400
E-mail: ucac.icy-nk@camnet.cm
Internet: www.cm.refer.org/edu/ram3/univers/ucac/ucac.htm
Founded 1989
Private control (Catholic Church)
Languages of instruction: English, French
Academic year: October to July
Rector: Abbé OSCAR EONE EONE
Vice-Rector: Abbé OLIVIER MASSAMBA LOUBELO
Sec. Gen.: JOSEPH KONO OWONA
Dir for Devt and Cooperation: GILLES NOUDJAG
Head Librarian: Dr PATRICK ADESO (acting)
Library of 39,341 vols
Number of teachers: 90
Number of students: 1,692
Publication: *Cahiers de l'U.C.A.C.* (1 a year)

DEANS

Faculty of Social Sciences and Management: Prof. Dr JACQUES FDRY
Faculty of Theology: Père Dr ANTOINE BABÉ
School of Nursing: Soeur RENÉE GEOFFRAY

UNIVERSITÉ DE DOUALA

BP 2701, Douala
Telephone: (237) 33401128
E-mail: infos.udla@univ-douala.com
Internet: www.univ-douala.com
Founded 1993
State control
Languages of instruction: English, French
Academic year: October to July
Rector: Prof. DIEUDONNÉ OYONO
Vice-Rector for Research, Cooperation and Relations with World Business: HELENE NTONE KOUO
Sec. Gen.: Prof. ALICE DELPHINE TANG
Head of Library: CHANTALE MOUKOKO
Number of teachers: 140
Number of students: 6,500
Publications: *Arts Review* (1 a year), *Revue de Sciences Economiques et de Management* (4 a year), *Technologie et Développement* (every 2 years).

CONSTITUENT INSTITUTES

Ecole Normale Supérieure de l'Enseignement Technique: BP 1872, Douala; Dir Dr CLAUDE BEKOLO.

Ecole Supérieure des Sciences Economiques et Commerciales: BP 1931,

Douala; e-mail infos.essec@univ-douala.com; Dir Dr EMMANUEL KAMDEM.

Faculté des Lettres et des Sciences Humaines: BP 3132, Douala; Dean Prof. SAMUEL EFOUA MBOZO'O.

Faculté des Sciences: BP 24157, Douala; Dean Prof. ADOLPHE MUKENGUE IMANO.

Faculté des Sciences Economiques et de Gestion Appliquée: BP 4032, Douala; Dean Prof. MARIE THÈRÈSE UM NGOUEM.

Faculté des Sciences Juridiques et Politiques: BP 4982, Douala; Dean Dr ANDRÉ AKAME AKAME.

Institut Universitaire de Technologie: BP 8698, Douala; Dir Dr LOUIS MAX AYINA OHANDJA

UNIVERSITÉ DE DSCHANG

POB 96, Dschang
Telephone: 3345-1092
Founded 1993
State control
Languages of instruction: English, French
Academic year: October to July

Rector: Prof. ANACLET FOMETHE
Vice-Rector for Inspection: Prof. LAURE PAULINE FOTSO
Vice-Rector for Research and Cooperation: Prof. JOHN MUCHO NGUNDAM
Vice-Rector for Teaching: Prof. ONGLA JEAN
Sec. Gen.: Prof. MARTHE ISABELLE ATANGANA ABOLO
Librarian: DJIDERE VALÈRE

Library of 26,780 books
Number of teachers: 330
Number of students: 14,000

Publications: *Les Echos* (Law and Politics, 4 a year), *NKA* (Arts and Humanities, 2 a year), *Sciences et Développement* (Agriculture, 2 a year)

DEANS

Faculty of Agronomy and Agricultural Sciences: Dr MANGELI YACOUBA
Faculty of Economics and Management Sciences: Prof. TAFAH EDOKAT OKI EDWARD
Faculty of Law and Political Science: Prof. FRANÇOIS ANOUKAHA
Faculty of Letters and Social Sciences: Prof. CHARLES ROBERT DIMI
Faculty of Sciences: Prof. PIERRE TANE
Fotso Victor Institute of Technology: MÉDARD FOGUE

UNIVERSITÉ DE NGAOUNDÉRÉ

BP 454, Ngaoundéré
Telephone: 22254001
E-mail: rectorat_ngaoundere@yahoo.fr
Founded 1977, opened 1982, present name since 1993
State control
Languages of instruction: English, French
Academic year: October to July

Rector: Prof. PAUL-HENRI AMVAM ZOLLO
Vice-Rector for Control and Internal Evaluation: Prof. DAVID BEKOLLÉ
Vice-Rector for Research and Cooperation and Relations with the Business World: Prof. IBRAHIMA ADAMOU
Vice-Rector for Teaching, Professionalization and Devt of Information Technology: Prof. BEDA TIBI
Sec. Gen.: Prof. RÉMY SYLVESTRE BOUELET

Library of 60,000 vols
Number of teachers: 365
Number of students: 16,000

Publications: *Annales de la Faculté des Arts, Lettres et Sciences Humaines* (1 a year), *Cahiers juridiques et politiques*, *Ngaoundéré-Anthropos* (social science review, 1 a year), *Revue de la Faculté des Sciences juridiques et politiques* (juridical and political science review, 1 a year)

DEANS

Faculty of Arts, Humanities and Social Sciences: Dr IYA MOUSSA
Faculty of Economics and Management Science: Prof. VICTOR TSAPI
Faculty of Laws and Political Science: Prof. ATANGANA AMOUGOU JEAN LOUIS
Faculty of Science: Prof. LUCIEN DIEUDONNÉ BITOM
Institute of Technology: Dr ALI AHMED
School of Agro-Industrial Sciences: Prof. NSO JONG EMMANUEL (Dir)
Prof. ISMAIL NGOUNOUNO
School of Veterinary Medicine and Animal ScienceProf. ANDRÉ ZOLI PAGNAH

PROFESSORS

Faculty of Economics and Management Science:
FEUDJO, J. R.
TSAPI, V.

Faculty of Law and Political Science:
AKAM AKAM, A.
TIENTCHEU NJIAKO, A.

Faculty of Science:
AMVAM ZOLLO, P.-H.
BEKOLLÉ, D.
LOURA BENGUELLA, B.
MAPONGMETSEM, P. M.
NGO BUM, E.
NGOUNOUNO, I.
OUMAROU, B.
TCHUENGUEM FOHOUO, F. N.

School of Agro-Industrial Sciences:
DZUDIE, T.
KAMGA, R.
KAPSEU, C.
KAYEM, J.
MBOFUNG, C. M. F.
NGASSOUM, M. B.
TCHIEGANG, C.

UNIVERSITÉ DE YAOUNDÉ I

BP 337, Centre Province, Yaoundé
Telephone: 2222-0744
E-mail: cdc@uycdc.uninet.cm
Founded 1962
State control
Languages of instruction: English, French
Academic year: October to July

Rector: JEAN TABI-MANGA
Vice-Rector for Inspection: MAURICE AURÉLIEN SOSSO
Vice-Rector for Research and Cooperation: (vacant)
Vice-Rector for Teaching: MAURICE AURÉLIEN SOSSO
Sec. Gen.: ELIE-CLAUDE NDJITOYAP NDAM
Librarian: ALEXIS EYANGO MOUEN

Library of 90,000 vols
Number of teachers: 929
Number of students: 20,343

Publications: *Annales de la Faculté des Lettres*, *Annales de la Faculté des Sciences*, *Sosongo* (Cameroon review of the arts, 1 a year), *Syllabus* (review of the Ecole Normale Supérieure)

DEANS

Faculty of Arts: Prof. EMMANUEL GWAN ACHU
Faculty of Medicine and Biomedical Science: Prof. AMOUGOU AKOA
Faculty of Sciences: Prof. MAURICE A. SOSSO

UNIVERSITÉ DE YAOUNDÉ II

POB 18, Soa
Telephone: 7220-1154
E-mail: info@univ-yde2.org
Internet: www.univ-yde2.org
Founded 1993
State control
Academic year: October to July

Rector: Prof. JEAN TABI MANGA
Vice-Rector for Academic Affairs: Prof. PAUL GÉRARD POUGOUÉ
Vice-Rector for Inspection: Prof. PIERRE OWONA ATEBA
Vice-Rector for Research and Cooperation: Prof. ADOLPHE MINKOA SHE
Sec. Gen.: Dr LISETTE ELOMO NTONGA (acting)

Number of teachers: 271
Number of students: 13,768

Publications: *African Review of Political Strategy* (1 a year), *Cameroon Review of International Relations* (2 a year), *Fréquence Sud* (2 a year), *Les Cahiers de l'IFORD* (52 a year), *Revue Africaine des Sciences Economiques et de Gestion* (2 a year), *Revue Africaine des Sciences Juridiques* (2 a year)

DEANS

Faculty of Economics and Management: Prof. GEORGES KOBOU
Faculty of Law and Political Science: Prof. VICTOR-EMMANUEL BOKALLI

PROFESSORS

Faculty of Economics and Management:
BEKOLO, E. B.
GANKOU, J. M.
NDJIEUNDE, G.
TOUNA, M.

Faculty of Law and Political Science:
ALETUM, M. T.
ANOUKAHA, F.
KONTCHOU, K. A.
MINKOA, S. A.
NGWAFOR, E. N.
NTAMARK, P. Y.
OWONA, J.
POUGOUE, P. G.

Advanced School of Mass Communication:
BOYOMO, A. L. C.
CHINJI, K. F.
FAME, N.

International Relations Institute of Cameroon:
OYONO, D.

ATTACHED INSTITUTES

Centre for Study and Research in Economics and Management: tel. 2223-7389; Coordinator Assoc. Prof. SÉRAPHIN FOUDA.

Centre for Study and Research in International Community Law: tel. 2221-4234; Coordinator Assoc. Prof. MAURICE KAMTO

Colleges

Ecole Nationale d'Administration et de Magistrature: BP 7171, Yaoundé; tel. 2223-1308; f. 1959; library: 11,000 vols; 85 teachers (10 full-time, 75 part-time); 1,063 students; Dir. V. MOUTTAPA.

Institut d'Administration des Entreprises: BP 337, Yaoundé; 150 students; Dir G. NDJIEUNDE.

CANADA

The Higher Education System

Under legislation passed in 1982, the 10 provinces and three territories individually enjoy autonomy over their respective higher education sectors; however, the Council of Ministers of Education, Canada was created by the provincial and territorial ministers of education in 1967 to take collective decisions in the national interest. The provincial and territorial governments provide the majority of funding to their public post-secondary institutions, with the remainder of funding coming from tuition fees, the federal Government, and research grants. The Association of Universities and Colleges of Canada (AUCC) is the national organization of university executive heads. In 2011/12 there were 95 public and private institutes authorized to offer degrees in the 10 Canadian provinces. Most are conferred by universities/university colleges and their affiliated and federated institutions, as well as by colleges of applied science, applied arts and technology. Conservatories and some community colleges are also authorized to offer degrees. The only federal institution with degree-granting powers is the Royal Military College of Canada; there are no universities in Canada's three territories. In 2008/09 an estimated 1,112,370 students were enrolled in post-secondary education (not including the Northwest Territories, Nunavut Territory and Yukon Territory); in 2011 there were 941,857 full-time and 294,596 part-time students (incl. undergraduates and postgraduates). The official languages of Canada are French and English, but English is the language of instruction in most universities except in the province of Québec, where French is used.

The standard administrative structure for a university consists of two governing bodies, a Board of Governors or Regents and a Senate or Academic Council. In addition, a Vice-Chancellor, President, Principal or Rector is responsible for administrative and academic management. Higher education funding varies according to the province or territory in question. The only consistent admissions criteria for undergraduate studies include successful completion of grade 12 of secondary school or, in Québec, candidates are required to take the Diplôme d'Etudes Collégiales (study for which lasts two years) at a Collège d'enseignement général et professionnel (CEGEP) since schooling at primary and secondary level in this province lasts only 11 years; otherwise, higher education institutes are free to set their own entrance criteria. Subjects such as law and medicine require the passing of an entrance examination.

Though there may be provincial or territorial peculiarities, the university degree system conforms to the Bachelors/Masters/Doctorate schema. The Bachelors (Baccalaureat in Québecois) is a three- to four-year programme the format of which varies from institution to institution, with some following the US-style credits system. Some Bachelors programmes include an element of research and are known as Honours (these courses, however, are not offered within the Francophone system of higher education). Following Bachelors are Masters (Maîtrise) programmes of two years, which fall into two classifications: Taught and Research. Finally, the qualification Doctor of Philosophy (PhD, or Philosophiae Doctor) requires three to five years of study following the Masters.

Post-secondary technical and vocational education is provided by a wide range of institutions, including community and professional colleges, conservatories and technical institutes; the most common qualifications attained at these establishments are the Certificate and Diploma, the latter generally requiring two to three years of study. However, in recent years, some of these institutions have started to offer Bachelors and Applied Bachelors degrees in response to the changing requirements of business, industry and the public service sectors.

Unlike in the USA, there is no central system of accreditation for post-secondary institutions in Canada, although a number of regulatory authorities perform this function for certain professional programmes (such as law, medicine, engineering and architecture) within these institutions. However, procedures and regulations are in place in each province and territory that provide ongoing assessment of the overall quality equivalent to 'accreditation' as it is commonly understood. In addition, it is generally held that membership of the AUCC implies that an institution is offering university-level programmes of nationally acceptable standards. The Canadian Education and Training Accreditation Commission (CETAC, founded in 1984) provides a voluntary system of non-governmental self-regulation of Canada's private post-secondary institutions. There is also the Association of Accrediting Agencies of Canada, which was established in 1994 and provides a national network of professional education accrediting bodies.

In March 2011 in an historic pact believed to be the first of its kind in Canada, the Atlantic Policy Congress of First Nations Chiefs and the Association of Atlantic Universities signed a memorandum of understanding to improve access to post-secondary education for aboriginal people.

Regulatory and Representative Bodies

GOVERNMENT

Council of Ministers of Education, Canada (CMEC)/Conseil des Ministres de l'Education (Canada): Suite 1106, 95 St Clair Ave W, Toronto, ON M4V 1N6; tel. (416) 962-8100; e-mail info@cmec.ca; internet www.cmec.ca; Chair. Hon. RAMONA JENNEX; Dir-Gen. ANDREW PARKIN.

ACCREDITATION

Association of Accrediting Agencies of Canada/Association des Agences d'Agrément du Canada: POB 370, 1-247 Barr St, Renfrew, ON K7V 1J6; tel. (613) 432-9491; e-mail info@aaac.ca; internet www.aaac.ca; f. 1994; pursues excellence in standards and processes of accreditation to foster the highest quality of professional education; Chair. MARLENE WYATT.

Canadian Education and Training Accreditation Commission (CETAC): 590 Queen St, Suite 310, Fredericton, NB E3B 7H9; tel. (506) 459-4546; e-mail info@cetac.ca; internet www.cetac.ca; f. 1984; responsible for institutional accreditation of private post-secondary institutions in Canada; provides nat. accrediting service with established nat. standards; Nat. Commr BILL RICHES; Nat. Commr CAROL LOWTHERS; Nat. Commr CHRISTOPHER HOPE.

Canadian Information Centre for International Credentials (CICIC): 95 St Clair Ave W, Suite 1106, Toronto ON M4V 1N6; tel. (416) 962-9725; e-mail info@cicic.ca; internet cicic.ca; f. 1990; collects, organizes and distributes information; acts as a nat. clearing house and referral service; supports the recognition of Canadian and int. educational and occupational qualifications; promotes int. mobility by advocating wider recognition of higher education and professional qualifications; Coordinator NATASHA SAWH; Information Officer MICHAEL RINGUETTE; Admin. Officer NOELLINE IP YAM.

NATIONAL BODIES

Association of Atlantic Universities/Association des Universités de l'Atlantique: Suite 403, 5657 Spring Garden Rd, Halifax, NS B3J 3R4; tel. (902) 425-4230; e-mail info@atlanticuniversities.ca; internet www.atlanticuniversities.ca; f. 1964; 16 univs in the Atlantic region of Canada and in the W Indies, which offer programmes leading to a degree or have degree-granting status; Exec. Dir PETER HALPIN; Dir for Operations CORINA KENT.

Association of Canadian Community Colleges/Association des Collèges Communautaires du Canada (ACCC): Suite 200, 1223 Michael St N, Ottawa, ON K1J

7T2; tel. (613) 746-2222; e-mail info@accc.ca; internet www.accc.ca; f. 1972; nat. voluntary membership org. to represent colleges and institutes to govt, business and industry, both in Canada and worldwide; interacts with fed. depts and agencies on the mems' behalf; links college capabilities to nat. industries; organizes confs and workshops for college staff, students and board mems to facilitate networking and participation in nat. and int. activities such as sector studies, awards programmes and linkages; Pres. and CEO JAMES KNIGHT.

Association of Registrars of the Universities and Colleges of Canada (ARUCC)/ Association des Registraires des Universités et Collèges du Canada: c/o France Myette, Sec. Treas., ARUCC, Univ. de Sherbrooke, 2500 blvd de l'Université, Sherbrooke QC J1K 2R1; tel. (819) 821-7685; e-mail france.myette@usherbrooke.ca; internet www.arucc.unb.ca; f. 1964; Pres. DAVID HINTON.

Association of Universities and Colleges of Canada (AUCC): 350 Albert St (Suite 600), Ottawa, ON K1R 1B1; tel. (613) 563-1236; e-mail info@aucc.ca; internet www.aucc.ca; f. 1911; Pres. and CEO PAUL DAVIDSON; Chair. DAVID BARNARD.

Canadian Bureau for International Education/Bureau Canadien de l'Education Internationale: 220 Laurier Ave W, Suite 1550, Ottawa, ON K1P 5Z9; tel. (613) 237-4820; e-mail info@cbie.ca; internet www.cbie.ca; f. 1966; promotes int. devt and intercultural understanding through a broad range of educational activities in Canada and abroad; 3 divs: research, devt and membership, scholarships and awards, centre for central and Eastern Europe; library of 300 vols and journals; Chair. Dr ROBERT MCCULLOCH; publ. *E-Internationalist* (irregular).

Canadian Network for Innovation in Education (CNIE)/Réseau Canadien pour l'Innovation en Education (RCIE): Suite 204, 260 Dalhousie St, Ottawa, ON K1N 7E4; tel. (613) 241-0018; e-mail cnie-rcie@cnie-rcie.ca; internet www.cnie-rcie.ca; f. 2007; Pres. DIANE JANES; Dir for Admin. TIM HOWARD; publs *Canadian Journal of Learning and Technology* (3 a year), *Journal of Distance Education* (3 a year).

National Research Council Canada: Bldg M-58, 1200 Montréal Rd, Ottawa, ON K1A 0R6; tel. (613) 993-9101; e-mail info@nrc-cnrc.gc.ca; internet www.nrc.ca; f. 1916; carries out research and devt in engineering, information technology, life sciences, physical sciences, technology and industry support; Pres. JOHN R. MCDOUGALL; Exec. Vice-Pres. and Sec. Gen. PATRICIA MORTIMER.

Learned Societies

GENERAL

Académie des Lettres du Québec: CP 8888, Succursale Centre-ville, Montréal, QC H3C 3P8; tel. (514) 987-3000; e-mail secretariat@academiedeslettresduquebec.ca; internet academiedeslettresduquebec.ca; f. 1944; 38 mems; Pres. JACQUES ALLARD; publ. *Les Ecrits* (3 a year).

Canadian Council for International Co-operation/Conseil Canadien pour la Coopération Internationale: 1 Nicholas St, Suite 300, Ottawa, ON K1N 7B7; tel. (613) 247-7007; e-mail info@ccic.ca; internet www.ccic.ca; f. 1968 (fmrly Overseas Institute of Canada, f. 1961); coordination centre for voluntary agencies working in int. devt; 115 mems; Chair. JEAN-PIERRE MASSÉ; publ. *Directory of Canadian NGOs*.

Royal Canadian Academy of Arts: 401 Richmond St West (Suite 375), Toronto, ON M5V 3A8; tel. (416) 408-2718; e-mail rcaarts@interlog.com; internet www.rca-arc.ca; f. 1880; Pres. ALISON HYMAS.

Royal Canadian Institute for the Advancement of Science: 700 University Ave, H7-D, Toronto, ON M5G 1X6; tel. (416) 977-2983; e-mail royalcanadianinstitute@sympatico.ca; internet www.royalcanadianinstitute.org; f. 1849; promotes knowledge of science; 600 mems; Pres. BRUCE GITELMAN; Sec. DUNCAN JONES; Treas. JOHN GRANT.

Royal Society of Canada: 170 Waller St, Ottawa, ON K1N 9B9; tel. (613) 991-6990; e-mail info@rsc.ca; internet www.rsc.ca; f. 1882; 1,800 fellows; Pres. YVAN GUINDON; Hon. Sec. ROBERT MAJOR; publs *RSC News* (3 a year), *Présentations* (1 a year), *Proceedings* (1 a year).

AGRICULTURE, FISHERIES AND VETERINARY SCIENCE

Agricultural Institute of Canada: Suite 900, 280 Albert St, Ottawa, ON K1P 5G8; tel. (613) 232-9459; e-mail office@aic.ca; internet www.aic.ca; f. 1920; organizes and unites all workers in scientific and technical agriculture; serves as a medium where progressive ideas for improvements in agricultural education, investigation, publicity and extension work can be discussed and recommended for adoption; represents 6,500 scientists and agrologists; publs *Canadian Journal of Animal Science* (4 a year), *Canadian Journal of Plant Science* (4 a year), *Canadian Journal of Soil Science* (4 a year).

Canadian Forestry Association: 1027 Pembroke St E, Pembroke, ON K8A 3M4; tel. (613) 732-7068; e-mail dlemkay@bell.net; internet www.canadianforestry.com; f. 1900; conservation org. providing educational materials and programmes to raise awareness of the wise use of forest, wildlife and water resources; 354 mems; Chair. BARRY WAITO; Gen. Man. DAVE LEMKAY.

Canadian Society of Animal Science: 9 Corvus Court, Suite 900, Ottawa, ON K2E 7Z4; tel. (613) 232-9459; e-mail info@aic.ca; internet www.csas.net; f. 1925; attached to Agricultural Institute of Canada (*q.v.*); provides opportunities for discussion of problems, improvement and coordination of research, extension and teaching; encourages publication of scientific and educational material relating to animal and poultry industries; holds annual meetings, produces occasional papers and presents awards to members; 550 mems; Pres. DUANE MCCARTNEY; Sec. and Treas. CHRISTIANE GIRARD; publ. *Canadian Journal of Animal Science* (4 a year).

Canadian Veterinary Medical Association/Association Canadienne des Médecins Vétérinaires: 339 Booth St, Ottawa, ON K1R 7K1; tel. (613) 236-1162; e-mail kallen@cvma-acmv.org; internet www.cvma-acmv.org; f. 1948; 4,000 mems; publs *Canadian Journal of Veterinary Research* (4 a year), *Canadian Veterinary Journal* (12 a year).

ARCHITECTURE AND TOWN PLANNING

Canadian Society of Landscape Architects/Association des Architectes Paysagistes du Canada: POB 13594, Ottawa, ON K2K 1X6; tel. (613) 622-5520; e-mail info@csla.ca; internet www.csla.ca; f. 1934; 1,100 mems; Exec. Dir FRAN PAUZÉ; publs *Bulletin* (6 a year), *Landscapes/Paysages* (4 a year).

Royal Architectural Institute of Canada: 55 Murray St, Suite 330, Ottawa, ON K1N 5M3; tel. (613) 241-3600; e-mail info@raic.org; internet www.raic.org; f. 1908; 3,500 mems; Pres. CHRIS FILLINGHAM; Exec. Dir JON F. HOBBS; publ. *Update/En Bref* (4 a year).

BIBLIOGRAPHY, LIBRARY SCIENCE AND MUSEOLOGY

ASTED (Association pour l'Avancement des Sciences et des Techniques de la Documentation) Inc. (Association for the advancement of documentation sciences and techniques): 2065 rue Parthenais, Bureau 387, Montréal, QC H2X 3T1; tel. (514) 281-5012; e-mail info@asted.org; internet www.asted.org; f. 1973; 500 mems; Pres. SYLVIE THIBAULT (acting); Exec. Dir FRANCIS FARLEY-CHEVRIER (acting); publs *Documentation et bibliothèques* (4 a year), *Nouvelles de l'ASTED* (online only).

Bibliographical Society of Canada/La Société Bibliographique du Canada: POB 19035, 360 Bloor St W, Walmer, Toronto, ON M5S 3C9; e-mail secretary@bsc-sbc.ca; internet www.bsc-sbc.ca/en/bschome.html; f. 1946; 260 mems; Pres. LINDA QUIRK; Sec. GRETA GOLICK; publ. *Papers/Cahiers* (2 a year).

Canadian Association of Law Libraries: POB 1570, Kingston, ON K7L 5C8; tel. (613) 531-9338; e-mail office@callacbd.ca; internet www.callacbd.ca; f. 1961; promotes law librarianship, develops and increases the usefulness of Canadian law libraries, and fosters a spirit of cooperation among them, provides a forum for meetings and cooperates with other similar orgs; 500 mems; Pres. JANINE MILLER; Admin. Officer ELIZABETH HOOPER; publs *CALL Newsletter* (5 a year), *Canadian Law Library* (5 a year).

Canadian Library Association: 1150 Morrison Dr. Suite 400, Ottawa, ON K2H 8S9; tel. (613) 232-9625; e-mail info@cla.ca; internet www.cla.ca; f. 1946; 3,000 mems; Pres. MARIE DEYOUNG; Exec. Dir VALOREE MCKAY.

Canadian Museums Association/Association des Musées Canadiens: 280 Metcalfe, Suite 400, Ottawa, ON K2P 1R7; tel. (613) 567-0099; e-mail info@museums.ca; internet www.museums.ca; f. 1947; advancement of public museums and art galleries services in Canada; 2,000 mems; Exec. Dir JOHN G. MCAVITY; publ. *Muse* (6 a year).

ECONOMICS, LAW AND POLITICS

Canadian Bar Association: 500–865 Carling Ave, Ottawa, ON K1S 5S8; tel. (613) 237-1988; e-mail info@cba.org; internet www.cba.org; f. 1914; promotes admin. of justice and uniformity of legislation; also promotes a high standard of legal education, training and ethics; 38,000 mems; Pres. ROBERT BRUN; CEO JOHN HOYLES; Treas. ANNETTE HORST; publs *CCCA Magazine*, *National*, *The Canadian Bar Review*.

Canadian Economics Association: Dept of Economics, Brock Univ., 500 Glenridge Ave, St Catharines, ON L2S 3A1; tel. (905) 688-5550; e-mail office@economics.ca; internet www.economics.ca; f. 1967; non-partisan asscn promoting the advancement of economic knowledge through the encouragement of study and research, the issuing of publs and the furtherance of free and informed discussion of economic questions; 1,400 mems; Pres. GERARD GAUDET; Exec. Dir ANNE MOTTE; Sec. and Treas. FRANCES WOOLLEY; publs *Canadian Journal of Economics/Revue Canadienne d'Economique*, *Canadian Public Policy/Analyse de Politique*.

Canadian Institute of Chartered Accountants: 277 Wellington St W, Toronto, ON M5V 3H2; tel. (416) 977-3222; internet www.cica.ca; f. 1902; 70,000 mems; Chair. ALAIN BENEDETT; Pres. and CEO KEVIN J. DANCEY; publ. *CA Magazine* (12 a year).

Canadian Institute of International Affairs: Suite 302, 205 Richmond St W, Toronto, ON M5V 1V3; tel. (416) 977-9000; e-mail mailbox@ciia.org; internet www.ciia.org; f. 1928; 1,400 mems in 15 brs; library of 8,000 vols; Chair. The Hon. ROY MACLAREN; Pres. and CEO DOUGLAS GOOLD; publs *Behind the Headlines, International Journal* (4 a year), *Canadian Foreign Relations Index* (1 a year, CD-ROM; 12 a year, online).

Canadian Political Science Association/Association Canadienne de Science Politique: 260 Dalhousie St, Suite 204, Ottawa, ON K1N 7E4; tel. (613) 562-1202; e-mail cpsa-acsp@cpsa-acsp.ca; internet www.cpsa-acsp.ca; f. 1912; organizes annual conf.; awards prizes; runs the Parliamentary Internship Programme and Ontario Legislative Internship Programme; 1,500 mems; Administrator MICHELLE HOPKINS; publ. *Canadian Journal of Political Science/Revue canadienne de science politique* (4 a year).

EDUCATION

Canadian Education Association/Association Canadienne d'education: 119 Spadina Ave, Suite 705, Toronto, ON M5V 2L1; tel. (416) 591-6300; e-mail info@cea-ace.ca; internet www.cea-ace.ca; f. 1891; 300 mems; Chair. ROGER PAUL; Vice-Chair. MICHELE JACOBSEN; Pres. and CEO RON CANUEL; publs *CEA Handbook/Ki-es-Ki* (1 a year), *Education Canada* (5 a year).

Canadian Society for the Study of Education: Suite 204, 260 Dalhousie St, Ottawa, ON K1N 7E4; tel. (613) 241-0018; e-mail csse-scee@csse.ca; internet www.csse-scee.ca; f. 1972; holds annual conf.; promotes educational research; 1,000 mems; Dir for Admin. TIM G. HOWARD; publ. *Canadian Journal of Education* (4 a year).

FINE AND PERFORMING ARTS

Canada Council for the Arts/Conseil des Arts du Canada: POB 1047, 350 Albert St, Ottawa, ON K1P 5V8; tel. (613) 566-4365; internet www.canadacouncil.ca; f. 1957; provides grants and services to professional Canadian artists and arts orgs; maintains secretariat for Canadian Commission for UNESCO; administers Public Lending Right Comm. and Canada Council Art Bank; administers Killam Program of prizes and fellowships to Canadian research scholars, and recognizes achievement through a number of prizes, incl. Governor General's Literary Awards, Molson Prizes and Glenn Gould Prize; 11 mems; Chair. JOSEPH L. ROTMAN; Vice-Chair. SIMON BRAULT; Dir ROBERT SIRMAN.

Canadian Film Institute: 2 Daly Ave, Suite 120, Ottawa, ON K1N 6E2; tel. (613) 232-6727; e-mail info@cfi-icf.ca; internet www.cfi-icf.ca; f. 1935; encourages and promotes the study, appreciation and use of motion pictures and television in Canada; hosts annual film festivals: the EU Film Festival, the Latin American Film Festival, and Ottawa Int. Animation Festival; presents ongoing Canadian film programming; curates Canadian film programmes internationally; publishes texts on Canadian cinema; undertakes educational activities in local schools, colleges and univs; Exec. Dir TOM MCSORLEY.

Canadian Music Centre (Centre de Musique Canadienne): 20 St Joseph St, Toronto, ON M4Y 1J9; tel. (416) 961-6601; e-mail info@musiccentre.ca; internet www.musiccentre.ca; f. 1959; 700 mems; library of 20,000 vols, 15,000 scores; Exec. Dir ELISABETH BIHL.

Sculptors' Society of Canada/Canadian Sculpture Centre: 500 Church St, Toronto, ON M4Y 2C8; tel. (647) 435-5858; e-mail gallery@cansculpt.org; internet www.cansculpt.org; f. 1928; Pres. JUDI MICHELLE YOUNG; Vice-Pres. RICHARD MCNEILL; Sec. MARLENE KAWALEZ.

Society of Composers, Authors and Music Publishers of Canada (SOCAN): 41 Valleybrook Drive, Toronto, ON M3B 2S6; tel. (416) 445-8700; e-mail socan@socan.ca; internet www.socan.ca; f. 1990; copyright collective for the communication and performance of musical works; licenses music in Canada; distributes royalties to its members for the use of their music overseas; offices in Dartmouth, Edmonton, Toronto, Montréal, Vancouver, Toronto; 80,000 mems; Pres. PIERRE-DANIEL RHEAULT; publs *Music Means Business/Le Rhytme de vos Affaires* (2 a year), *Words & Music/Paroles & Musique* (4 a year).

Visual Arts Ontario: Suite 225, 215 Spadina Ave, Toronto, ON M5T 2C7; tel. (416) 591-8883; e-mail info@vao.org; internet www.vao.org; f. 1973; 3,600 mems; Exec. Dir HENNIE L. WOLFF; publs *Agenda* (4 a year), *Hidden Agenda* (8 a year).

HISTORY, GEOGRAPHY AND ARCHAEOLOGY

Canadian Association of Geographers: Dept of Geography, McGill Univ., 425-805 Sherbrooke St W, Montréal, QC H3A 2K6; tel. (514) 398-4946; e-mail cag@geog.mcgill.ca; internet www.cag-acg.ca; f. 1951; 800 mems; Pres. CHRIS SHARPE; Sec.-Treas. ALAN NASH; publs *The CAG Newsletter* (6 a year), *The Canadian Geographer* (4 a year), *The Directory* (1 a year).

Canadian Historical Association/Société Historique du Canada: 501–130 Albert St, Ottawa, ON K1P 5G4; tel. (613) 233-7885; e-mail cha-shc@cha-shc.ca; internet www.cha-shc.ca; f. 1922; 1,200 mems; promotes historical research and public interest in history; annual meeting awards; prizes affiliated committees advocacy; Exec. Dir Dr MICHEL DUQUET; publs *Bulletin* (3 a year), *Canada's Ethnic Groups* (2 a year), *Journal of the CHA/Revue de la SHC* (2 a year), *Register of Dissertations/Répertoire des thèses* (online), *Short Book Series* (2 a year).

Château Ramezay Museum/Musée du Château Ramezay: 280 Notre Dame E, Montréal, QC H2Y 1C5; tel. (514) 861-3708; e-mail info@chateauramezay.qc.ca; internet www.chateauramezay.qc.ca; f. 1895; 250 mems; library of 8,000 books; Dir ANDRÉ J. DELISLE; Sec. SUZANNE LALUMIÈRE; publ. *La Lettre de Ramezay* (Ramezay Letter, 3 a year).

Genealogical Association of Nova Scotia: 3045 Robie St, Suite 222, Halifax, NS B3K 4P6; tel. (902) 454-0322; e-mail gans@chebucto.ns.ca; internet www.chebucto.ns.ca/recreation/gans; f. 1982; 1,000 mems; Pres. JANICE FRALIC-BROWN; publ. *The Nova Scotia Genealogist* (3 a year).

Genealogical Institute of the Maritimes/Institut Généalogique des Provinces Maritimes: POB 36022, Canada Post Postal Office, 5675 Spring Garden Rd, Halifax, NS B3J 1G0; internet nsgna.ednet.ns.ca/gim; f. 1983; education and research in genealogy; offers certification and registration of individuals undertaking genealogical research for the public; 44 mems.

Institut d'Histoire de l'Amérique Française: 261 Bloomfield Ave, Montréal, QC H2V 3R6; tel. (514) 278-2232; e-mail ihaf@ihaf.qc.ca; internet www.ihaf.qc.ca; f. 1946; 1,000 mems; Pres. Prof. ALAIN BEAULIEU; Sec. Prof. BRIGITTE CAULIER; publ. *Revue d'histoire de l'Amérique Française* (4 a year).

Ontario Historical Society: 34 Parkview Ave, Willowdale, ON M2N 3Y2; tel. (416) 226-9011; e-mail ohs@ontariohistoricalsociety.ca; internet www.ontariohistoricalsociety.ca; f. 1888; 3,000 mems; Exec. Dir PATRICIA K. NEAL; publs *OHS Bulletin* (5 a year), *Ontario History* (2 a year).

Royal Canadian Geographical Society: 1155 Lola St, Suite 200, Ottawa, ON K1K 4C1; tel. (613) 745-4629; e-mail rcgs@rcgs.org; internet www.rcgs.org; f. 1929; 204,000 mems; Pres. PAUL RUEST; CEO JOHN GEIGER; publ. *Canadian Geographic* (10 a year).

Royal Nova Scotia Historical Society: POB 2622, Halifax, NS B3J 3P7; internet www.rnshs.ca; f. 1878; history, biography, social studies of provincial past; 350 mems; Pres. Dr BERTRUM MACDONALD; Sec. JOHN MACLEOD; publ. *Journal* (1 a year).

Société Généalogique Canadienne Française: 3440 rue Davidson, Montréal, QC H1W 2Z5; tel. (514) 527-1010; e-mail info@sgcf.com; internet www.sgcf.com; f. 1943; studies and publs on the origins and history of French Canadian families since 1615; 3,400 mems; library of 21,300 vols, 3m. cards on marriages, 4,500 microfilms; Pres. GISÈLE MONARQUE; Dir-Gen. MICHELINE PERREAULT; publ. *Mémoires* (4 a year).

Waterloo Historical Society: c/o Kitchener Public Library, 85 Queen St N, Kitchener, ON N2H 2H1; tel. (519) 743-0271; e-mail whs@whs.ca; internet www.whs.ca; f. 1912; local history; colln at Kitchener Public Library; Grace Schmidt Room of Local History; 275 mems; Sec. JOHN ARNDT; publ. *Waterloo Historical Society Annual Volume.*

LANGUAGE AND LITERATURE

Alliance Française: 352 MacLaren St, Ottawa, ON K2P 0M6; tel. (613) 234-9470; e-mail com@af.ca; internet www.af.ca; f. 1905; offers courses and examinations in French language and culture and promotes cultural exchange with France; attached offices in Calgary, Edmonton, Halifax, Mississauga, Moncton, North York, Regina, Saskatoon, Toronto, Vancouver, Victoria and Winnipeg; Dir HERVÉ DEVOULON.

British Council: British High Commission, 80 Elgin St, Ottawa, ON K1P 5K7; tel. (514) 886-5863; e-mail education.enquiries@ca.britishcouncil.org; internet www.britishcouncil.org/canada; promotes education in and cultural exchange with the UK; Dir LILIANA BIGLOU.

Canadian Authors Association: 6 West Street N, Suite 203, Orillia, ON L3V 5B8; tel. (705) 325-3926; e-mail admin@canadianauthors.org; internet www.canadianauthors.org; f. 1921; 500 mems; administers awards; annual conf.; workshops and seminars; Exec. Dir ANITA PURCELL; Assoc. Dir COURTNEY THOMPSON; Program Dir NOELLE BICKLE; publs *Canadian Author eZine* (4 a year), *The Canadian Writer's Guide* (irregular).

Canadian Linguistic Association/Association Canadienne de Linguistique: Département d'Études Françaises, University of Western Ontario, London, N6A 3K7; e-mail aclcla@mun.ca; internet homes.chass.utoronto.ca/~cla-acl; f. 1954; advances study of linguistics and languages in Canada; 220 mems; Pres. FRANCE MARTINEAU; Sec. ILEANA

PAUL; Treas. CARRIE DYCK; publ. *The Canadian Journal of Linguistics / La Revue Canadienne de Linguistique* (3 a year).

Goethe-Institut: 1626 Blvd St-Laurent, Suite 100, Montréal, QC H2X 2T1; tel. (514) 499-0159; e-mail info@montreal.goethe.org; internet www.goethe.de/montreal; f. 1962; offers courses and examinations in German language and culture and promotes cultural exchange with Germany; attached centres in Ottawa; library of 7,500 vols, 20 periodicals, incl. German newspapers, magazines, CDs and DVDs; Dir MANFRED STOFFL.

PEN Canada: 24 Ryerson Ave, Suite 301, Toronto, ON M5T 2P3; tel. (416) 703-8448; e-mail queries@pencanada.ca; f. 1983; 300 mems; Pres. CHARLIE FORAN; Vice-Pres. RANDY BOYAGODA.

MEDICINE

Academy of Medicine: c/o Library and Information Services, Univ. Health Network, Toronto General Hospital, 200 Elizabeth St, EN1-418, Toronto, ON M5G 2C4; tel. (416) 340-3259; f. 1907; Librarian MARGARET ALIHARAN.

Canadian Association for Anatomy, Neurobiology and Cell Biology/Association Canadienne d'Anatomie, de Neurobiologie et de Biologie Cellulaire: c/o Dr MICHAEL KAWAJA, Dept of Anatomy and Cell Biology, Queen's University, Kingston, ON K7L 3N6; tel. (613) 533-2864; e-mail kawajam@post.queensu.ca; f. 1956; 147 mems; Pres. Dr RIC DEVON; Sec. Dr MICHAEL KAWAJA; publ. *The Bulletin* (1 a year).

Canadian Association of Optometrists: 234 Argyle Ave, Ottawa, ON K2P 1B9; tel. (613) 235-7924; e-mail info@opto.ca; internet www.opto.ca; f. 1948; Pres. Dr PAUL GENEAU; Dir-Gen. LAURIE CLEMENT; Sec. and Treas. Dr BARRY THIENES; publ. *The Canadian Journal of Optometry / La Revue Canadienne d'Optométrie* (4 a year).

Canadian Dental Association: 1815 Alta Vista Drive, Ottawa, ON K1G 3Y6; tel. (613) 523-1770; e-mail reception@cda-adc.ca; internet www.cda-adc.ca; f. 1902; Pres. Dr LOUIS DUBÉ; publs *Communiqué* (6 a year), *Journal* (11 a year).

Canadian Lung Association: 1750 Courtwood Crescent, Suite 300, Ottawa, ON K2C 2B5; tel. (613) 569-6411; e-mail info@lung.ca; internet www.lung.ca; f. 1900; 10 provincial member associations (Alberta, British Columbia, Québec, Nova Scotia, Saskatchewan, Manitoba, New Brunswick, Newfoundland and Labrador, Ontario, Prince Edward Island), 1 territorial association (NW Territories); associated professional societies: Canadian Thoracic Society, Canadian Physiotherapy Cardio-Respiratory Society, Canadian Nurses' Respiratory Society, Respiratory Therapy Society; publ. *Canadian Respiratory Journal* (8 a year).

Canadian Medical Association: 1867 Alta Vista Drive, Ottawa, ON K1G 3Y6; e-mail pubs@cma.ca; internet www.cma.ca; f. 1867; 60,000 mems; Pres. Dr COLIN MACMILLAN; Sec.-Gen. WILLIAM THOLL; Hon. Treas. Dr JOHN RAPIN; publs *Canadian Association of Radiologists Journal* (6 a year), *Canadian Journal of Emergency Medicine* (4 a year), *Canadian Journal of Rural Medicine* (4 a year), *Canadian Journal of Surgery* (6 a year), *Canadian Medical Association Bulletin* (26 a year), *Canadian Medical Association Journal—CMAJ* (25 a year), *Health Care News* (12 a year), *Journal of Psychiatry and Neuroscience* (5 a year), *Strategy Magazine*.

Canadian Paediatric Society/Société Canadienne de Pédiatrie: 2305 St Laurent Blvd, Ottawa, ON K1G 4J8; tel. (613) 526-9397; e-mail info@cps.ca; internet www.cps.ca; f. 1923; 2,000 mems; Pres. C. ROBIN WALKER; publ. *Paediatrics and Child Health* (6 a year).

Canadian Pharmacists Association: 1785 Alta Vista Dr., Ottawa, ON K1G 3Y6; tel. (613) 523-7877; e-mail cpha@pharmacists.ca; internet www.pharmacists.ca; f. 1907; 9,000 mems; Pres. GARTH MCCUTCHEON; publs *Compendium of Non Prescription Products* (English only), *Compendium of Pharmaceuticals and Specialties* (English and French edns, 1 a year), *Patient Self-Care* (English only), *Therapeutic Choices* (English only).

Canadian Physiological Society: c/o Canadian Federation of Biological Societies, 305-1750 Courtwood Crescent, Ottawa, ON K2C 2B5; tel. (613) 225-8889; internet www.cps.cfbs.org; f. 1936; 300 mems; Pres. Dr CHRIS CHEESEMAN; Sec. Dr C. ELAINE CHAPMAN; Treas. Dr DOUG JONES; publ. *The Canadian Journal of Physiology and Pharmacology* (12 a year).

Canadian Psychiatric Association/Association des Psychiatres du Canada: 141 Laurien Ave West, Suite 701, Ottawa, ON K1P 5J3; tel. (613) 234-2815; e-mail cpa@cpa-apc.org; internet www.cpa-apc.org; f. 1951; promotes research into psychiatric disorders; foster high standards of professional practice in clinical care, education and research; 2,950 mems; Chair. Dr DONALD ADDINGTON; CEO ALEX SAUNDERS; publ. *The Canadian Journal of Psychiatry* (12 a year).

Canadian Public Health Association: 404–1525 Carling Ave, Ottawa, ON K1Z 8R9; tel. (613) 725-3769; e-mail info@cpha.ca; internet www.cpha.ca; f. 1910; represents public health in Canada with links to int. public health community; 1,170 mems; Chair. Dr LYNN MCINTYRE; Exec. Dir IAN CULBERT; publ. *Canadian Journal of Public Health* (6 a year, print and online (cjph.cpha.ca)).

Canadian Society for Nutritional Sciences: c/o Dr SUSAN WHITING, Div. Nutrition and Dietetics, College of Pharmacy and Nutrition, 110 Science Place, Univ. of Saskatchewan, Saskatoon, SK S7N 5C9; internet www.nutritionalsciences.ca; f. 1957; extends knowledge of nutrition by research, discussion of research reports, and exchange of information; 340 mems; Pres. SUSAN WHITING; Sec. GUYLAINE FERLAND; publ. *Nutrition / Forum de Nutrition* (2 a year).

Pharmacological Society of Canada: c/o Dept of Physiology and Pharmacology, M216 Medical Sciences Bldg, Univ. of Western Ontario, London, ON N6A 5C1; e-mail robert.mcneill@usask.ca; internet www.physpharm.med.uwo.ca; f. 1956; 320 mems; Pres. Dr J. ROBERT MCNEILL; Sec. Dr FIONA PARKINSON; publ. *Canadian Journal of Physiology and Pharmacology*.

Royal College of Physicians and Surgeons of Canada: 774 Echo Dr., Ottawa, ON K1S 5N8; tel. (613) 730-8177; e-mail info@rcpsc.edu; internet rcpsc.medical.org; f. 1929; sets standards for postgraduate medical education of specialists in Canada; accredits postgraduate specialist education programmes; acts as nat. examining body to certify medical, surgical and laboratory specialists; offers a professional devt programme; 39,270 mems; CEO Dr ANDREW PADMOS; publ. *Royal College Outlook* (4 a year).

NATURAL SCIENCES

General

Association Francophone pour le Savoir (Acfas): 425 rue de la Gauchetière Est, Montréal, QC H2L 2M7; tel. (514) 849-0045; e-mail acfas@acfas.ca; internet www.acfas.ca; f. 1923; popularizes science by means of lectures, meetings, awards, publications; 6,000 mems; Pres. CLAIRE V. DE LA DURANTAYE; publs *Découvrir* (6 a year), *Les Cahiers de l'Acfas* (2–3 a year).

Nova Scotian Institute of Science: c/o Reference and Research Services, Killam Memorial Library, 6225 University Ave, POB 15000, Halifax, NS B3H 4R2; e-mail nsis@chebucto.ns.ca; internet www.chebucto.ns.ca; f. 1862; 120 mems; Pres. Dr MICHELLE PAON; Vice-Pres. TOM RAND; Sec. LINDA MARKS; publ. *Proceedings* (irregular).

Biological Sciences

Canadian Phytopathological Society: c/o Joanne McWilliams, KW Neatby Bldg, Agriculture and Agri-Food Canada, 960 Carling Ave, Ottawa, ON K1A 0C6; internet www.cps-scp.ca; f. 1929; 500 mems; Pres. RICHARD MARTIN; Sec. DEENA ERRAMPALLI; publs *Canadian Journal of Plant Pathology* (4 a year), *News* (4 a year).

Canadian Society for Cellular and Molecular Biology: Centre de recherche, Hôtel-Dieu de Québec, 11 Côte du Palais, Quebec, QC G1R 2J6; e-mail contact@csbmcb.ca; internet www.csbmcb.ca; f. 1966; 400 mems; Pres. Dr DAVID ANDREWS; Sec. C. CASS; publ. *Bulletin* (3 a year).

Canadian Society for Immunology: c/o Immunology Research Group, University of Calgary, 2500 University Dr. NW, Calgary, AB T2N 1N4; tel. (403) 492-0712; e-mail membership@csi-sci.ca; f. 1966; 400 mems; Pres. Dr JOHN SCHRADER; Sec. and Treas. Dr DONNA CHOW.

Canadian Society of Microbiologists/Société Canadienne des Microbiologistes: c/o Canadian Fed. of Biological Societies, 305-1750 Courtwood Crescent, Ottawa, ON K2C 2B5; tel. (613) 225-8889; e-mail info@csm-scm.org; internet www.csm-scm.org; f. 1951; 500 mems; Man. WAFAA ANTONIOUS; publs *CSM Newsletter* (3 a year), *Programme and Abstracts* (1 a year).

Cercles des Jeunes Naturalistes: 4101 Sherbrooke est, Suite 262, Montréal, QC H1X 2B2; tel. (514) 252-3023; e-mail cjn@cam.org; internet www.cjn.cam.org; f. 1931; 1,500 mems; Pres.-Gen. YVES BREAULT; Dir LAURE BOUCHARD; publs *Les Naturalistes* (4 a year), *Nouvelles CJN* (12 a year).

Entomological Society of Canada: 393 Winston Ave, Ottawa, ON K2A 1Y8; tel. (613) 725-2619; e-mail entsoc.can@bellnet.ca; internet esc-sec.org; f. 1863; 500 mems; Pres. Dr MAYA EVENDEN; Sec. Dr ANNABELLE FIRLEJ; publ. *The Canadian Entomologist* (6 a year).

Genetics Society of Canada/Société de Génétique du Canada: c/o E. K. Consulting, 53 Slalom Gate Rd, Collingwood, ON L9Y 5B1; tel. (613) 232-9459; internet www.life.biology.mcmaster.ca/gsc; f. 1956; 425 mems; Pres. VIRGINIA WALKER; Treas. JOHN BELL; Sec. CAROLYN J. BROWN; publs *Bulletin* (4 a year), *Genome* (6 a year).

Manitoba Naturalists Society: 401–63 Albert St, Winnipeg, MB R3B 1G4; tel. (204) 943-9029; e-mail mns@escape.ca; internet www.manitobanature.ca; f. 1920; 1,500 mems; Pres. LARRY DE MARCH; Exec. Dir GORDON FARDOE.

Société de Protection des Plantes du Québec: c/o Secretary, 1643 chemin des Lacs, Vincent Phillion, Station de recherches agricoles, CP 480, Saint-Faustin-Lac carré, QC J0T 1J2; e-mail ltartier@sympatico.ca; internet www.sppq.qc.ca; f. 1908; 225 mems; Pres. DANNY RIOUX; Sec. LÉON TARTIER; Treas. GAÉTAN BOURGEOIS; publs *Echos phytosanitaires* (4 a year), *Phytoprotection* (3 a year).

Société Linnéenne du Québec: 1040 Belvédère, Sillery, QC G1S 3G3; tel. (418) 683-2432; internet ecoroute.uqcn.qc.ca/group/slq; f. 1929; 800 mems; Pres. JEAN-PAUL L'ALLIER; Dir AGATHE SAVARD; publ. *Le Linnéen* (4 a year).

Vancouver Natural History Society: POB 3021, Vancouver, BC V6B 3X5; tel. (604) 876-7694; e-mail jpmccall@telus.net; internet www.naturevancouver.ca; f. 1918; promotes interest in nature, conserves natural resources, protects endangered species and ecosystems; 700 mems; Pres. DAPHNE NAGORSEN; Dir and Treas. JEREMY MCCALL; publ. *Discovery* (1 a year).

Mathematical Sciences

Canadian Mathematical Society/Société Mathématique du Canada: 209–1725 St Laurent blvd, Ottawa, ON K1G 3V4; tel. (613) 733-2662; e-mail office@cms.math.ca; internet www.cms.math.ca; f. 1945, inc. 1979; promotes the discovery, learning and application of mathematics; 960 mems; Pres. KEITH TAYLOR; Exec. Dir and Sec. JOHAN RUDNICK; Treas. DAVID RODGERS; publs *Canadian Journal of Mathematics* (6 a year), *Canadian Mathematical Bulletin* (4 a year), *CMS Notes* (6 a year), *CRUX with Mayhem* (8 a year).

Physical Sciences

Canadian Association of Physicists/Association Canadienne des Physiciens et Physiciennes: MacDonald Bldg (Suite 112), 150 Louis Pasteur, Ottawa, ON K1N 6N5; tel. (613) 562-5614; e-mail capmgr@uottawa.ca; internet www.cap.ca; f. 1945; 2,000 mems; Pres. Dr HENRY VAN DRIEL; Exec. Dir FRANCINE M. FORD; Sec. and Treas. Dr DAVID LOCKWOOD; publ. *Physics in Canada* (4 a year).

Canadian Meteorological and Oceanographic Society/Société Canadienne de Météorologie et d'Océanographie: Station 'D', POB 3211, Ottawa, ON K1P 6H7; tel. (613) 990-0300; e-mail exec-dir@cmos.ca; internet www.cmos.ca; f. 1939 as Canadian Br. of the Royal Meteorological Soc., current name adopted 1984; promotes meteorology and oceanography; organizes meetings, lectures, publs, prizes and awards, scholarships, education, public outreach; information cooperation with science asscns; 800 mems; Pres. Dr HARINDER AHLUWALIA; Exec. Dir Dr ANDREW BELL; publs *Atmosphere-Ocean* (4 a year), *Congress Program and Abstracts* (1 a year).

Canadian Society for Analytical Sciences and Spectroscopy/Société de Spectroscopie du Canada: POB 46122, 2339 Ogilvie Rd, Ottawa, ON K1J 9M7; internet www.csass.org; f. 1957; 350 mems; Pres. DIANE BEAUCHEMIN; Sec. TERESA SWITZER; publ. *Canadian Journal of Analytical Sciences and Spectroscopy*.

Canadian Society for Molecular Biosciences/Société Canadienne de Biochimie et de Biologie Moléculaire et Cellulaire: c/o Wafaaa Antonium, Rofail Conference and Management Service, 17 Dossette Way, Ottawa, ON K1G 4S3; tel. (613) 421-7229; e-mail contact@csmb-scbm.ca; f. 1958; 1,000 mems; Pres. Dr ANDREW J. SIMMONDS.

Canadian Society of Petroleum Geologists: 540 Fifth Ave SW (Suite 160), Calgary, AB T2P 0M2; tel. (403) 264-5610; e-mail cspg@cspg.org; internet www.cspg.org; f. 1927; 3,400 mems; Pres. CRAIG LAMB; Business Man. TIM HOWARD; publs *Bulletin of Canadian Petroleum Geology* (4 a year), *Reservoir* (11 a year).

Chemical Institute of Canada: 130 Slater St, Suite 550, Ottawa, ON K1P 6E2; tel. (613) 232-6252; e-mail info@cheminst.ca; internet www.cheminst.ca; f. 1945; 27 local sections, 16 subject divisions, 116 student chapters and 3 constituent societies—Canadian Society for Chemical Engineering, the Canadian Society for Chemical Technology and the Canadian Society for Chemistry; Exec. Dir ROLAND ANDERSSON; publs *Canadian Chemical News* (10 a year), *Canadian Journal of Chemical Engineering* (6 a year).

Geological Association of Canada: c/o Dept of Earth Sciences, Rm ER4063, Memorial University of Newfoundland, St John's, NL A1B 3X5; tel. (709) 737-7660; e-mail gac@mun.ca; internet www.gac.ca; f. 1947; advances the science of geology and related fields of study and promotes a better understanding thereof throughout Canada; 2,500 mems; Pres. Dr STEPHEN JOHNSTON; Sec. and Treas. Dr TOBY RIVERS; publs *Geolog* (4 a year), *Geoscience Canada* (4 a year).

Royal Astronomical Society of Canada: 203-4920 Dundas St W, Toronto, ON M9A 1B7; tel. (416) 924-7973; e-mail nationaloffice@rasc.ca; internet www.rasc.ca; f. 1890; 4,400 mems; Exec. Sec. JO TAYLOR; publs *Journal* (6 a year), *Observers' Handbook* (1 a year).

Society of Chemical Industry (Canadian Section): 247 Ridgewood Rd, Toronto, ON M1C 2XC; tel. (416) 708-8924; internet www.soci.org; f. 1902; fosters contact between chemical industry, univs and Govt; rewards achievement in industry and universities; promotes int. contact; 150 mems; Administrator BETH GALLOWAY.

PHILOSOPHY AND PSYCHOLOGY

Canadian Philosophical Association/Association Canadienne de Philosophie: Saint Paul Univ., 223 Main St, Ottawa, ON K1S IC4; tel. (613) 236-1393; e-mail acpa@ustpaul.ca; internet www.acpcpa.ca; f. 1958; promotes philosophical scholarship in Canada and represents Canadian philosophers; 800 mems; Exec. Dir LOUISE MOREL; publ. *Dialogue: Canadian Philosophical Review/Revue canadienne de philosophie* (4 a year, in French and English).

Canadian Psychological Association/Société Canadienne de Psychologie: 141 Laurier Ave W, Suite 702, Ottawa, ON K1P 5J3; tel. (613) 237-2144; e-mail cpa@cpa.ca; internet www.cpa.ca; f. 1939; 4,500 mems; Exec. Dir Dr JOHN C. SERVICE; publs *Canadian Journal of Behavioural Science* (4 a year), *Canadian Journal of Experimental Psychology* (4 a year), *Canadian Psychology* (4 a year), *Psynopsis* (4 a year).

RELIGION, SOCIOLOGY AND ANTHROPOLOGY

Association for the Advancement of Scandinavian Studies in Canada (AASSC): 643 University College, Winnipeg, MB R3T 2M8; tel. (204) 474-6628; f. 1982; 120 mems; Pres. JOHN TUCKER; Sec. KATHY HANSON; publs *Newsbulletin* (2 a year), *Scandinavian-Canadian Studies* (1 a year).

Canadian Association of African Studies/Association Canadienne des Etudes Africaines: CAAS/ACEA Administrator, 4-17E Old Arts Bldg University of Alberta, Edmonton, AB T6G 2E6; e-mail caas@ualberta.ca; internet www.arts.ualberta.ca/~caas; f. 1970; aims to improve the Canadian public's knowledge and awareness of Africa; provides a link between Canadian and African scholarly and scientific communities; 310 mems; Admin. LOUISE ROLINGHER; publ. *Canadian Journal of African Studies/Revue Canadienne des Etudes Africaines* (3 a year).

Canadian Association for Latin American and Caribbean Studies/Association Canadienne des Etudes Latino-Américaines et des Caraïbes: 8–17 Kaneff Tower, York Univ., 4700 Keele St, Toronto, ON M3J 1P3; e-mail calacs@yorku.ca; internet www.can-latam.org; f. 1969; 350 mems; Pres. NATHALIE GRAVEL; Treas. JESSICA STITES MOR; publ. *Canadian Journal of Latin American and Caribbean Studies* (2 a year).

Canadian Society of Biblical Studies: c/o Michele Murray, Dept of Religion, Bishop's University, Lennoxville, QC J1M 1Z7; tel. (819) 822-9600; e-mail mmurray@ubishops.ca; internet www.ccsr.ca/csbs; f. 1933; 287 mems; Pres. DAVID HAWKIN; Exec. Sec. M. MURRAY; publ. *Bulletin* (1 a year).

TECHNOLOGY

Canadian Academy of Engineering/Académie Canadienne du Génie: 180 Elgin St, Suite 1402, Ottawa, ON K2P 2K3; tel. (613) 235-9056; e-mail info@acad-eng-gen.ca; internet www.acad-eng-gen.ca; f. 1987; provides ind. and expert advice on matters of nat. importance concerning engineering; highlights exceptional engineering achievements; works by cooperation with nat. and int. academies; 260 mems; Pres. RON NOLAN; Sec. and Treas. Dr JOHN MCLAUGHLIN; Exec. Dir PHILIP COCKSHUTT.

Canadian Aeronautics and Space Institute: 350 Terry Fox Dr., Suite 104, Kanata, ON K2K 2W5; tel. (613) 591-8787; e-mail casi@casi.ca; internet www.casi.ca; f. 1954; 2,000 mems; Pres. DAVID MUIR; Exec. Dir GEOFFREY LANGUEDOC; publs *Canadian Aeronautics and Space Journal* (4 a year), *Canadian Journal of Remote Sensing* (4 a year).

Canadian Council of Professional Engineers: 180 Elgin St, Suite 1100, Ottawa, ON K2P 2K3; tel. (613) 232-2474; e-mail info@engineerscanada.ca; internet www.engineerscanada.ca; f. 1936; 152,000 constituent asscns; CEO CHANTAL GUAY.

Canadian Electricity Association: 1155 rue Metcalfe, Bureau 1120, Montréal, QC H3B 2V6; tel. (514) 866-6121; e-mail info@canelect.ca; internet www.canelect.ca; f. 1891; 2,500 individual mems; Pres. H. R. KONOW; publs *Connections* (10 a year), *Electricity* (1 a year).

Canadian Institute of Mining, Metallurgy and Petroleum: Xerox Tower, Suite 1210, 3400 de Maisonneuve Blvd W, Montréal, QC H3Z 3B8; tel. (514) 939-2710; e-mail cim@cim.org; internet www.cim.org; f. 1898; 10,500 mems; Pres. WARREN HOLMES; Exec. Dir JEAN VAVREK; publ. *Journal of Canadian Petroleum Technology* (10 a year).

Engineering Institute of Canada: 1295 Hwy 2E, Kingston, ON K7L 4V1; tel. (613) 547-5989; e-mail info@eic-ici.ca; internet www.eic-ici.ca; f. 1887; 16,000 mems and 13 mem. socs; Pres. Prof. Dr KERRY ROWE; Exec. Dir B. JOHN PLANT.

Research Institutes

GENERAL

Alberta Innovates—Technology Futures: 250 Karl Clark Rd, Edmonton,

AB T6N 1E4; tel. (780) 450-5111; e-mail referral@albertainnovates.ca; internet www.albertatechfutures.ca; f. 2010 by merger of Alberta Ingenuity, Alberta Research Ccl, iCORE and nanoAlberta; library of 20,000 vols, 3,500 reports, 100 current periodicals; CEO GARY ABACH.

InNOVAcorp: 101 Research Dr., Woodside Industrial Park, Dartmouth, NS B2Y 4T6; tel. (902) 424-8670; e-mail corpcomm@innovacorp.ns.ca; f. 1995; assists firms based in Nova Scotia to develop and market products, particularly in the fields of advanced engineering, information technology and oceans technology; library of 20,000 vols; CEO Dr ROSS MCCURDY; publ. *Progress Report* (4 a year).

National Research Council of Canada/Conseil National de Recherches Canada: 1200 Montréal Rd, Bldg M-58, Ottawa, ON K1A 0R6; tel. (613) 993-9101; e-mail info@nrc-cnrc.gc.ca; internet www.nrc-cnrc.gc.ca; f. 1916; integrated science and technology agency of the federal Govt; provides scientific and technological information through Canada Institute for Scientific and Technical Information and industrial support through Industrial Research Assistance Programme; research carried out by 16 research institutes linked to 3 technology groups: biotechnology, information and telecommunications technologies, and manufacturing technologies; Pres. MICHAEL RAYMONT (acting); Sec. Gen. PAT MORTIMER; publs *Biochemistry and Cell Biology* (6 a year), *Canadian Geotechnical Journal* (6 a year), *Canadian Journal of Botany* (12 a year), *Canadian Journal of Chemistry* (12 a year), *Canadian Journal of Civil Engineering* (6 a year), *Canadian Journal of Earth Sciences* (12 a year), *Canadian Journal of Fisheries and Aquatic Sciences* (12 a year), *Canadian Journal of Forest Research* (12 a year), *Canadian Journal of Microbiology* (12 a year), *Canadian Journal of Physics* (12 a year), *Canadian Journal of Physiology and Pharmacology* (12 a year), *Canadian Journal of Zoology* (12 a year), *Environmental Reviews* (4 a year), *Genome* (6 a year).

North-South Institute: 55 Murray St, Suite 500, Ottawa, ON K1N 5M3; tel. (613) 241-3535; e-mail nsi@nsi-ins.ca; internet www.nsi-ins.ca; f. 1976; policy-relevant research on issues of relations between industrialized and developing countries; research related to int. cooperation, democratic governance and conflict prevention; library of 10,000 vols, 300 periodicals; Pres. and CEO JOSEPH K. INGRAM; publ. *Canadian Development Report* (1 a year).

Nunavut Research Institute: POB 1720, Iqaluit, NU X0A 0H0; tel. (867) 979-7279; e-mail slcnri@nunanet.com; internet pooka.nunanet.com/~research; f. 1978; current name adopted 1995; publ. *Research Compendium* (1 a year).

Process Research ORTECH Corporation: 2350 Sheridan Park Dr., Mississauga, ON L5K 2T4; tel. (905) 822-4941; e-mail info@processortech.com; internet www.processortech.com; f. 1928 as Ontario Research Foundation, privatized 1999; library of 10,000 vols; Pres. Dr R. SRIDHAR.

RPC (Research and Productivity Council): 921 College Hill Rd, Fredericton, NB E3B 6Z9; tel. (506) 452-1212; e-mail info@rpc.ca; internet www.rpc.ca; f. 1962; professional and technical services to help industry develop new products and innovative solutions to operating problems; depts incl. chemical and biotechnical services, engineering materials and diagnostics, food, fisheries and aquaculture, inorganic analytical services, product innovation, and process and environmental technology; library: information centre with 21,000 vols, 250 periodicals, inter-library loan services, access to on-line databases; Exec. Dir Dr P. LEWELL.

Saskatchewan Research Council: 125-15 Innovation Blvd, Saskatoon, SK S7N 2X8; tel. (306) 933-5400; e-mail info@src.sk.ca; internet www.src.sk.ca; f. 1947; assists the population of Saskatchewan in strengthening the economy and securing the environment by means of research, devt and the transfer of innovative scientific and technological solutions, applications and services; provides research, devt and technology commercialization; library of 25,000 vols, 5,500 in-house publs and 300 periodicals; Pres. and CEO LAURIER SCHRAMM.

Vizon SciTech Inc.: BC Research Complex, 3650 Wesbrook Mall, Vancouver, BC V6S 2L2; tel. (604) 224-4331; internet www.vizonscitech.com; f. 1944 as British Columbia Research Inc. (BCRI), current name adopted 2004; conducts technological research in fields of applied biology, applied chemistry, engineering-physics.

AGRICULTURE, FISHERIES AND VETERINARY SCIENCE

Canadian Forest Service: Ottawa, ON K1A 0E4; f. 1899; forest production, tree improvement, forest statistics and the environmental aspects of forestry, pests, fire, carbon monitoring, industrial competitiveness; supports FPInnovations (see Research Institutes, Technology) and research at Canadian forestry schools; Asst Deputy Minister JIM FARRELL; publs *Annual State of Canada's Forests*, *CFS Research Notes*, *Forestry Technical Reports*, *Information Reports Digest*.

Research Establishments:

Great Lakes Forestry Centre: Box 490, 1219 Queen St East, Sault Ste Marie, ON P6A 5M7; Dir-Gen. E. KONDO.

Laurentian Forestry Centre: 1055 rue du PEPS, BP 10380, Ste-Foy, QC G1V 4C7; tel. (418) 648-5847; Dir-Gen. N. LAFRENIÈRE.

Maritimes Forestry Service: Box 4000, Fredericton, NB E3B 5P7; Dir-Gen. H. OLDHAM.

Northern Forestry Centre: 5320 122nd St, Edmonton, AB T6H 3S5; Dir-Gen. G. MILLER.

Pacific Forestry Centre: 506 West Burnside Rd, Victoria, BC V8Z 1M5; Dir-Gen. C. WINGET.

Dominion Arboretum: Bldg 72, Central Experimental Farm, Ottawa, ON K1A 0C6; tel. (613) 995-3700; f. 1886; evaluation of woody plants for cold hardiness and adaptability; display area of 35 ha; special living collections; Dir Dr H. DAVIDSON.

MEDICINE

Canadian Cancer Society Research Institute: 55 St Clair Ave W, Suite 300, Toronto, ON M4V 2Y7; tel. (416) 961-7223; e-mail ccsri@cancer.ca; internet www.cancer.ca/research; f. 1947; research grant-awarding agency; Pres. and CEO Dr PAMELA FRALICK; Vice-Pres. for Research CHRISTINE WILLIAMS.

Canadian Institutes of Health Research: Ninth Fl., 160 Elgin St, Ottawa, ON K1A 0W9; tel. (613) 941-2672; e-mail info@cihr-irsc.gc.ca; internet www.cihr-irsc.gc.ca; f. 2000; creates new scientific knowledge and enables its translation to make Canadian health services and products more effective and to strengthen the health care system; composed of 13 institutes; provides leadership and support to health researchers and trainees; Pres. Dr ALAIN BEAUDET; publs *Communiqué* (4 a year, in English and French), *Report of the President* (1 a year).

Cancer Care Ontario: 620 University Ave, Suite 1500, Toronto, ON M5G 2L7; tel. (416) 971-9800; e-mail publicaffairs@cancercare.on.ca; internet www.cancercare.on.ca; f. 1943; prevention, diagnosis, treatment, supportive care, education and research in cancer; Pres. and CEO Dr TERRENCE SULLIVAN; publ. *Cancer Care*.

Dentistry Canada Fund: 427 Gilmour St, Ottawa, ON K2P 0R5; tel. (613) 236-4763; e-mail information@dcf-fdc.ca; f. 1902; Pres. and Chair. Dr BERNARD DOLANSKY; Exec. Dir RICHARD MUNRO.

NATURAL SCIENCES

General

Arctic Institute of North America: Univ. of Calgary, 2500 University Dr., NW, ES-1040, Calgary, AB T2N 1N4; tel. (403) 220-7515; e-mail arctic@ucalgary.ca; internet www.arctic.ucalgary.ca; f. 1945; multidisciplinary research on physical, biological and social sciences; library of 40,000 vols; Exec. Dir Dr MARIBETH MURRAY; publ. *Arctic* (4 a year).

International Development Research Centre: POB 8500, 150 Kent St, Ottawa, ON K1G 3H9; tel. (613) 236-6163; e-mail info@idrc.ca; internet www.idrc.ca; f. 1970 by act of the Canadian Parliament; library of 60,000 vols, 5,000 serials, 1,000 pamphlets and annual reports; Pres. Dr DAVID M. MALONE; publ. *IDRC in_focus Collection*.

Natural Sciences and Engineering Research Council of Canada (NSERC): 350 Albert St, Ottawa, ON K1A 1H5; tel. (613) 995-5992; e-mail comm@nserc.ca; internet www.nserc.ca; f. 1978; supports both basic university research through research grants and project research through partnerships of universities with industry, as well as the advanced training of highly qualified people in both areas; Pres. TOM BRZUSTOWSKI; publ. *NSERC Contact* (newsletter).

Biological Sciences

Huntsman Marine Science Centre: 1 Lower Campus Rd, St Andrews, NB E5B 2L7; tel. (506) 529-1200; e-mail huntsman@huntsmanmarine.ca; internet www.huntsmanmarine.ca; f. 1969 with the cooperation of universities and the federal Government; Dir W. D. ROBERTSON; publ. *Newsletter (In Depth)* (4 a year).

Jardin Botanique de Montréal: 4101 Sherbrooke St E, Montréal, QC H1X 2B2; tel. (514) 872-1400; e-mail jardin_botanique@ville.montreal.qc.ca; internet espacepourlavie.ca; f. 1931; 22,000 plant species and cultivars, 30 thematic gardens; educational, conservation and research activities; affiliated botanical and horticultural socs; library of 30,000 vols on botany, horticulture, landscaping and natural sciences, 60,000 vols of periodicals (500 titles); Botanist-Librarian CELINE ARSENEAULT; publs *Index Seminum* (every 2 years), *Quatre-temps* (Amis du Jardin Botanique, 4 a year).

Physical Sciences

Algonquin Radio Observatory: c/o Natural Resources Canada, Geodetic Survey Div., 615 Booth St, Room 440, Ottawa, ON K1A 0E9; tel. (613) 996-4410; e-mail aro@thoth.ca; f. 1959.

David Dunlap Observatory: 123 Hillsview Dr., Richmond Hill, ON L4C 1T3; tel. (905) 883-0174; internet www.theddo.ca; f. 1935;

attached to Univ. of Toronto; library of 30,000 vols; Chair. PAUL MORTFIELD.

Dominion Astrophysical Observatory: 5071 West Saanich Rd, Victoria, BC V9E 2E7; tel. (250) 363-0001; f. 1918; library of 20,000 vols; Dir Dr JAMES E. HESSER.

Geological Survey of Canada: 601 Booth St, Ottawa, ON K1A 0E8; tel. (613) 996-3919; e-mail ess-esic@nrcan-rncan.gc.ca; internet gsc.nrcan.gc.ca; f. 1842; regional centres in Dartmouth, NS, Ste-Foy, QC, Calgary, AB, Vancouver and Sidney, BC, and associated with Iqaluit, NU, Nunavut Geoscience Centre, NU; Asst Deputy Min. MARK COREY; publ. *GSC Information Circular*.

Toronto Biomedical NMR Centre: Dept of Medical Genetics and Microbiology, Univ. of Toronto Medical Sciences Building, Rm 1233, Toronto, ON M5S 1A8; f. 1970; Dir Dr A. A. GREY.

RELIGION, SOCIOLOGY AND ANTHROPOLOGY

Canadian Federation for the Humanities and Social Sciences: Suite 300, 275 Bank St, Ottawa, ON K2P 2L6; tel. (613) 238-6112; e-mail info@ideas-idees.ca; internet www.ideas-idees.ca; f. 1941; Exec. Dir PAUL LEDWELL.

International Center for Research on Language Planning/Centre International de Recherche en Aménagement Linguistique: Pavillon De Koninck, Cité Universitaire, Sainte-Foy, QC G1K 7P4; tel. (418) 656-3232; f. 1967; research on language planning, description of oral and written Quèbec French, new information technologies, learning of a second language; library of 6,000 vols, 50 periodicals; Exec. Dir D. DESHAIES.

Social Sciences and Humanities Research Council of Canada/Conseil de Recherches en Sciences Humaines du Canada: 350 Albert St, POB 1610, Ottawa, ON K1P 6G4; tel. (613) 992-0691; e-mail info@sshrc-crsh.gc.ca; internet www.sshrc-crsh.gc.ca; f. 1977; Pres. Dr CHAD GAFFIELD.

TECHNOLOGY

Atomic Energy of Canada, Ltd (AECL): 2251 Speakman Dr., Mississauga, ON L5K 1B2; tel. (905) 823-9040; internet www.aecl.ca; f. 1952; devt of economic nuclear power, scientific research and development in the nuclear energy field, and marketing of nuclear reactors; Chair. J. RAYMOND FRENETTE; Pres. and CEO ROBERT VAN ADEL.

Attached Laboratories:

AECL Research, Chalk River Laboratories: Chalk River, ON K0J 1J0; f. 1944; nuclear reactors (NRU, NRX, Pool Test Reactor and ZED-2), Tandem Accelerating Super Conducting Cyclotron, equipment for nuclear research and engineering development.

AECL Research, Whiteshell Laboratories: Pinawa, MB R0E 1L0; f. 1960; I-10/1 Accelerator, Underground Research Laboratory, equipment for nuclear research and engineering development.

BC Advanced Systems Institute: 1048, 4720 Kingsway, Burnaby, BC V5H 4N2; tel. (604) 438-2752; e-mail asi@asi.bc.ca; internet www.asi.bc.ca; f. 1986; promotes research and devt in high-technology areas such as microelectronics and artificial intelligence; Pres. and CEO VICTOR JONES.

Canada Centre for Inland Waters/ Centre Canadien des Eaux Intérieures: 867 Lakeshore Rd, POB 5050, Burlington, ON L7R 4A6; tel. (905) 336-4981; f. 1967; freshwater research complex of the depts of environment and fisheries and oceans; freshwater environmental and fisheries research and monitoring; cooperative management by cttee of institutional dirs.

Attached Research Institutes:

Bayfield Institute: 867 Lakeshore Rd, POB 5050, Burlington, ON L7R 4A6; attached to Dept of Fisheries and Oceans; comprises of Great Lakes Laboratory for Fisheries and Aquatic Sciences; Fisheries and Habitat Management; Canadian Hydrographic Service; Small Craft Harbours br.; and support for shipping. Together with the Freshwater Research Institute in Winnipeg, it provides the federal Fisheries and Oceans programme for the Central and Arctic Region.

National Water Research Institute: 867 Lakeshore Rd, POB 5050, Burlington, ON L7P 3M1; tel. (905) 336-4675; e-mail nwriscience.liaison@ec.gc.ca; internet www.ec.gc.ca/inre-nwri; attached to Environment Canada's Science and Technology br.; freshwater research facility; operates 2 main centres: Canada Centre for Inland Waters and National Hydrology Research Centre; brs focus on aquatic ecosystem impacts, protection and management research, science liaison, monitoring and research support; comprises the Nat. Laboratory for Environmental Testing (NLET) and programme office for the UN's Global Environment Monitoring System (GEMS/Water); library of 58,000 vols, 105 print journals, 105 online journals; Dir-Gen. Dr JOHN H. CAREY; publ. *NWRI Contributions*.

FPInnovations—Forintek Division: Head Office and Western Laboratory, 2665 E Mall, Vancouver, BC V6T 1W5; tel. (604) 224-3221; e-mail info@fpinnovations.ca; internet www.fpinnovations.ca; f. 1979, fmrly Forintek Canada Corp.; pulp and paper, forestry and forest products research, contract research and technical services, solid wood products research; Pres. and CEO PIERRE LAPOINTE; Chief Financial Officer Y. NADON.

Institute for Aerospace Studies: 4925 Dufferin St, Toronto, ON M3H 5T6; tel. (416) 667-7700; e-mail info@utias.utoronto.ca; internet www.utias.utoronto.ca; f. 1949; attached to Univ. of Toronto; undergraduate and graduate studies; research in aerospace science and engineering, and associated fields; serves industrial research and development needs in government and industry; facilities for experimental and computational research; library of 80,000 vols; Dir Prof. D. W. ZINGG; publ. *Progress Report* (1 a year).

Libraries and Archives

Alberta

Calgary Public Library: 616 Macleod Trail SE, Calgary, AB T2G 2M2; tel. (403) 260-2600; e-mail dearlibrary@calgarypubliclibrary.com; internet www.calgarypubliclibrary.com; f. 1912; 2.4m. items; 16 brs; spec. sections on petroleum; Dir GERRY MEEK.

City of Edmonton Archives: 10440 108th Ave, Edmonton, AB T5H 3Z9; tel. (780) 496-8711; e-mail cms.archives@edmonton.ca; internet www.edmonton.ca/archives; f. 1971; 10,000 vols, also MSS, newspapers, slides, city records, photographs and maps of the city; Man. (vacant).

Edmonton Public Library: 7 Sir Winston Churchill Sq., Edmonton, AB T5J 2V4; tel. (780) 496-7000; internet www.epl.ca; f. 1913; 1,766,809 print items, 242,934 audiovisual items; Dir for Libraries LINDA C. COOK.

Glenbow Library and Archives: 130 Ninth Ave SE, Calgary, AB T2G 0P3; tel. (403) 268-4204; e-mail library@glenbow.org; internet www.glenbow.org; f. 1955; 80,000 vols, 700,000 photographs and a large colln of MSS materials, chiefly on western and northern Canada.

Legislature Library: 216 Legislature Bldg, 10800–97 Ave, Edmonton, AB T5K 2B6; tel. (780) 427-2473; e-mail library@assembly.ab.ca; internet www.assembly.ab.ca/lao/library; f. 1906; 425,000 vols; Legislature Librarian VALERIE FOOTZ.

Parkland Regional Library: 5404 56th Ave, Lacombe, AB T4L 1G1; tel. (403) 782-3850; e-mail rsheppard@prl.ab.ca; internet www.prl.ab.ca; f. 1959; Dir RONALD SHEPPARD.

Provincial Archives of Alberta: 8555 Roper Rd, Edmonton, AB T6E 5W1; tel. (780) 427-1750; e-mail paa@gov.ab.ca; internet culture.alberta.ca/archives/default.aspx; f. 1963; holdings incl. non-current Alberta govt records, private papers, church records, municipal records, photographs, taped oral history interviews, films, video cassettes and maps pertaining to the history of Alberta; regular exhibitions; reference library colln with focus on W Canadiana, local/community histories and archival literature (12,000 vols); Exec. Dir and Provincial Archivist LESLIE LATTA-GUTHRIE.

University of Alberta Library: 5-07 Cameron Library, Edmonton, AB T6G 2J8; tel. (403) 492-3790; f. 1909; 4,809,303 vols, 3,690,989 microforms; Chief Librarian ERNIE INGLES; Dir KAREN ADAMS; publ. *Library Editions* (2 a year).

University of Calgary Library: 2500 University Dr. NW, Calgary, AB T2N 1N4; tel. (403) 220-5953; e-mail libinfo@ucalgary.ca; internet library.ucalgary.ca; f. 1966; 7,678,394 vols,; Univ. Librarian H. THOMAS HICKERSON.

British Columbia

British Columbia Archives: 655 Belleville St, Victoria, BC V8W 9W2; tel. (250) 387-1952; e-mail access@bcarchives.gov.bc.ca; internet www.bcarchives.gov.bc.ca; f. 1893; 71,000 items of printed material, 7,000 linear metres of MSS and govt records, 5m. photographs, 9,000 paintings, 35,000 maps, charts and architectural plans, 25,000 hours of sound recordings, 4,000 cans of moving images; Provincial Archivist GARY A. MITCHELL.

Fraser Valley Regional Library: Admin. Centre, 34589 Delair Rd, Abbotsford, BC V2S 5Y1; tel. (604) 859-7141; internet www.fvrl.ca; f. 1930; 900,000 vols, 10,000 talking books, also incl. electronic resources DVDs, CDs, ebooks; CEO ROB O'BRENNAN.

Greater Victoria Public Library: 735 Broughton St, Victoria, BC V8W 3H2; tel. (250) 382-7241; internet www.gvpl.ca; f. 1864; 940,749 vols; CEO MAUREEN SAWA.

Legislative Library: Parliament Bldgs, Victoria, BC V8V 1X4; tel. (250) 387-6510; e-mail llbc.ref@leg.bc.ca; internet www.llbc.leg.bc.ca; f. 1863; 200,000 vols; Dir PETER GOURLAY.

Public Library InterLINK: 7252 Kingsway, Lower Level, Burnaby, BC V5E 1G3; tel. (604) 517-8441; e-mail info@interlinklibraries.ca; internet www.interlinklibraries.ca; f. 1994; federation of 18 autonomous public libraries sharing resources and services and providing open access to all mem. libraries; spec. services: audiobooks for the visually impaired (46,056 vols), multilingual books, staff training video cassettes, children's educational video cassettes; Man. of Operations RITA AVIGDOR; Exec. Dir MICHAEL BURRIS.

Simon Fraser University, W. A. C. Bennett Library: 8888 University Blvd, Burnaby, BC V5A 1S6; tel. (778) 782-4658; e-mail libhelp@sfu.ca; internet www.lib.sfu.ca; f. 1965; 1,214,111 vols, 937,181 microforms; Univ. Librarian Dr CHARLES ECKMAN.

University of British Columbia Library: 1961 East Mall, Vancouver, BC V6T 1Z1; tel. (604) 822-6375; internet www.library.ubc.ca; f. 1915; 5.5m. vols, 65,000 print and electronic serial subscriptions, 261,000 ebooks, 5.2m. microforms; Univ. Librarian Dr W. PETER WARD.

Vancouver Island Regional Library: Box 3333, Nanaimo, BC V9R 5N3; tel. (250) 758-4697; e-mail info@virl.bc.ca; internet virl.bc.ca; f. 1936; 1,172,571 vols; Exec. Dir ROSEMARY BONNANO.

Vancouver Public Library: 350 West Georgia St, Vancouver, BC V6B 6B1; tel. (604) 331-3603; e-mail info@vpl.ca; internet www.vpl.ca; f. 1887; 2,641,444 vols; Chief Librarian SANDRA SINGH.

Vancouver School of Theology Library: 6050 Chancellor Blvd, Vancouver, BC V6T 1X3; tel. (604) 822-9430; e-mail gmcleod@vst.edu; internet www.vst.edu; f. 1971; 85,000 vols; Library Dir GILLIAN MCLEOD.

Manitoba

Archives of Manitoba: 200 Vaughan St, Winnipeg, MB R3C 1T5; tel. (204) 945-3971; e-mail archives@gov.mb.ca; internet www.gov.mb.ca/archives/index.html; f. 1884; 5,500 linear ft private MSS, 65,000 linear ft Manitoba govt and court records, 8,000 linear ft Hudson's Bay Co Archives records, 130,000 architectural drawings, 1.2m. photographs, 32,000 maps, 300 paintings, 5,500 prints and drawings, 7,000 sound records; spec. collns: Red River Settlement and Red River Disturbance, Lt-Governors' papers, Winnipeg General Strike, Canadian Airways Ltd, archives of the Ecclesiastical Province of Rupert's Land, records of local govts and school divs, Archives of Manitoba legal and judicial history; Archivist of Manitoba GORDON DODDS.

Legislative Library of Manitoba: Rm 100, 200 Vaughan St, Winnipeg, MB R3C 1T5; tel. (204) 945-4330; e-mail legislative_library@gov.mb.ca; internet www.manitoba.ca/leglib; f. 1870; Legislative Librarian (vacant); publs *Monthly Checklist of Manitoba Government Publications* (online), *Selected New Titles* (8 a year, online).

Manitoba Culture, Heritage and Tourism—Public Library Services Branch: 300-1011 Rosser Ave, Brandon, MB R7A 0L5; tel. (204) 726-6590; e-mail pls@gov.mb.ca; f. 1972; 45,000 vols, 10,000 ebooks; Dir (vacant); publ. *Manitoba Public Library Statistics* (1 a year).

Manitoba Law Library Inc., Great Library: 331–408 York Ave, Winnipeg, MB R3C 0P9; tel. (204) 945-1958; internet www.cbsc.org; f. 1877; attached to Law Society of Manitoba; 50,000 vols; Librarian R. GARTH NIVEN.

University of Manitoba Libraries: Winnipeg, MB R3T 2N2; tel. (204) 474-9881; e-mail marina_webster@umanitoba.ca; internet www.umanitoba.ca/libraries; f. 1877; 2m. vols, 520,000 govt publs, 157,500 other print items (maps, performance music, textbook collection, etc.), 2.7m. microforms, 31,000 audiovisual items, 9,000 serial titles; Dir CAROLYNNE PRESSER.

New Brunswick

Bibliothèque Champlain (Université de Moncton): 18 ave Antonine-Maillet, Moncton, NB E1A 3E9; tel. (506) 858-4012; internet www.umoncton.ca/umcm-bibliotheque-champlain; f. 1965; 661,008 vols, 24,274 periodicals; Head Librarian MARTHE BRIDEAU.

Harriet Irving Library: Univ. of New Brunswick, POB 7500, Fredericton, NB E3B 5H5; tel. (506) 453-4740; e-mail library@unb.ca; internet www.lib.unb.ca; f. 1790; 1,141,807 vols and 3,103,813 (equivalent vols) microforms; Dir for Libraries JOHN D. TESKEY.

Legislative Library: Box 6000, Fredericton, NB E3B 5H1; tel. (506) 453-2338; e-mail library.biblio-info@gnb.ca; f. 1841; 35,000 vols; Librarian MARGARET PACEY.

Mount Allison University Libraries and Archives: Mount Allison Univ., 49 York St, Sackville, NB E4L 1C6; tel. (506) 364-2562; e-mail bgnassi@mta.ca; internet www.mta.ca/library; f. 1840; 454,000 vols, 515,000 microforms, 282,000 documents; Univ. Librarian BRUNO GNASSI.

Provincial Archives of New Brunswick: POB 6000, Fredericton, NB E3B 5H1; tel. (506) 453-2122; e-mail provincial.archives@gnb.ca; internet archives.gnb.ca; f. 1968; collects and preserves documents bearing on all aspects of the history of New Brunswick; holds textual records from the legislature, govt offices, courts and private sources; 19,000 linear m of textual records, 339,000 photographs, 374,000 maps, plans and architectural items, 25,000 microfilm; Provincial Archivist FRED FARRELL.

Newfoundland and Labrador

Newfoundland and Labrador Public Libraries: 48 St George's Ave, Stephenville, NL A2N 1K9; tel. (709) 643-0900; internet www.nlpl.ca; f. 1934; provides public library services, incl. books, magazines, newspapers, large-print and spoken-word books, DVDs, computers with free internet access, digital cameras; 1,300,000 vols at 96 libraries; Exec. Dir SHAWN TETFORD.

The Rooms Corporation of Newfoundland and Labrador—The Rooms Provincial Archives Division: POB 1800, St John's, NL A1C 5P9; 9 Bonaventure Ave, St John's, NL A1C 5P9; tel. (709) 757-8030; e-mail archives@therooms.ca; internet www.therooms.ca; f. 1960, refounded 2005; Provincial Archivist, Newfoundland and Labrador and Dir, The Rooms Provincial Archives Division GREG WALSH.

Provincial Resource Library: Arts and Culture Centre, St John's, NL A1B 3A3; tel. (709) 737-3946; f. 1934; 181,604 vols (incl. Newfoundland Collection); Man. MICHELLE WALTERS.

Queen Elizabeth II Library: Memorial Univ. of Newfoundland, St John's, NL A1B 3Y1; tel. (709) 737-7428; e-mail lbusby@mun.ca; internet www.library.mun.ca; f. 1925; 1,724,807 vols, 1,977,982 microform units; Librarian LORRAINE BUSBY.

Nova Scotia

Angus L. Macdonald Library: St Francis Xavier Univ., POB 5000, Antigonish, NS B2G 2W5; tel. (902) 867-2267; e-mail circdesk@stfx.ca; internet library.stfx.ca; f. 1853; 762,000 vols; spec. colln: Celtic history, literature and language; Librarian LYNNE MURPHY; publ. *The Antigonish Review* (4 a year).

Dalhousie University Libraries: Halifax, NS B3H 4H8; tel. (902) 494-3601; internet libraries.dal.ca; 1,877,524 vols, 1,036,747 print monograph titles, 198,993 e-monograph titles, 453,284 microform units, 423,549 govt documents, 5,063 MSS and archives, 11,985 printed music scores, 94,886 cartographic materials, 47,000 graphic materials, 13,213 audio materials, 1,595 film and video materials; Univ. Librarian DONNA BOURNE-TYSON.

Halifax Regional Library: 60 Alderney Dr., Dartmouth, NS B2Y 4P8; tel. (902) 490-5744; internet www.halifaxpubliclibraries.ca; f. 1996; 898,532 books (fiction, non-fiction, reference, rapid read, multilingual), 51,202 periodicals, 41,099 CDs, 55,471 DVDs, 30,816 video cassettes, 8,440 audio cassettes, 5,613 talking books; CEO JUDITH HARE.

Nova Scotia Archives: 6016 University Ave, Halifax, NS B3H 1W4; tel. (902) 424-6060; e-mail nsarm@gov.ns.ca; internet www.gov.ns.ca/nsarm; f. 1929; provincial govt records; family, political, personal and business papers; maps, plans, charts; photographs, paintings; microfilmed files of leading newspapers; film, television and sound archives; genealogical records; research library of 50,000 vols; Provincial Archivist LOIS YORKE.

Nova Scotia Legislative Library: Province House, 1726 Hollis St, Halifax, NS B3J 2P8; tel. (902) 424-5932; e-mail murphymf@gov.ns.ca; internet www.gov.ns.ca/legislature/library; f. 1862; 170,000 vols; Librarian MARGARET MURPHY; publ. *Publications of the Province of Nova Scotia* (12 a year and 1 a year).

Vaughan Memorial Library, Acadia University: POB 4, 50 Acadia St, Wolfville, NS B4P 2P6; tel. (902) 585-1249; e-mail libweb@acadiau.ca; internet library.acadiau.ca; f. 1843; 1,000,000 vols and govt documents, ejournals; Univ. Librarian SARA LOCHHEAD.

Nunavut Territory

Nunavut Public Library Services: POB 189A, Iqaluit, NU X0A 0H0; tel. (867) 979-5400; e-mail nuic@gov.nu.ca; br. libraries in Arctic Bay, Arviat, Baker Lake, Cambridge Bay, Clyde River, Igloolik, Kugluktuk, Pangnirtung, Pond Inlet and Rankin Inlet.

Branch Library:

Iqaluit Centennial Library: POB 189A, Iqaluit, NU X0A 0H0; tel. (867) 979-5400; e-mail nuic@gov.nu.ca; Librarian TORI-LYNNE EVANS.

Ontario

Canada Institute for Scientific and Technical Information: 1200 Montréal Rd, M-55, Ottawa, ON K1A 0R6; tel. (613) 998-8544; e-mail info.cisti@nrc-cnrc.gc.ca; internet cisti-icist.nrc-cnrc.gc.ca; f. 1974, fmrly National Science Library; attached to Nat. Research Ccl Canada; Dir-Gen. BERNARD DUMOUCHEL.

Canadian Agriculture Library: Sir John Carling Bldg, Agriculture and Agri-Food Canada, Ottawa, ON K1A 0C5; tel. (613) 759-7068; internet www.agr.gc.ca/cal; f. 1910; specializes in agriculture, biology, biochemistry, economics, entomology, food sciences, plant science, veterinary medicine; serves 24 field libraries; 1m. vols, 22,200 serials; Dir DANIELLE JACQUES.

Carleton University Library: 1125 Colonel By Dr., Ottawa, ON K1S 5B6; tel. (613) 520-2735; e-mail university.librarian@carleton.ca; internet www.library.carleton.ca; f. 1942; 1,782,483 vols, 10,486 serial subscriptions, 1,513,714 items (microforms, maps, audiovisual items), 12,025 electronic journals; Univ. Librarian and Copyright Officer MARGARET HAINES.

Earth Sciences Information Centre: 601 Booth St, Ottawa, ON K1A 0E8; tel. (613) 996-3919; e-mail esic@nrcan.ac.ca; internet www.nrcan.gc.ca/ess/esic; f. 1842; component of Natural Resources Canada; interlibrary loans, online retrospective searching; 400,000 vols, 260,000 geological maps; Head of ESIC Services PAULINE MCDONALD (acting).

Hamilton Public Library: 55 York Blvd, POB 2700, Station A, Hamilton, ON L8N 4E4; tel. (905) 546-3200; e-mail kroberts@hpl.ca; internet www.hpl.hamilton.on.ca; f. 1889; 1,492,467 vols and 1,876 periodicals; spec. collns of local history, Canadiana to 1950, govt documents; Chief Librarian KEN ROBERTS.

John W. Graham Library, University of Trinity College: 6 Hoskin Ave, Toronto, ON M5S 1H8; tel. (416) 978-2653; e-mail ask.grahamlibrary@utoronto.ca; internet www.trinity.utoronto.ca; f. 1851; 215,000 vols; spec. collns: Anglican Church of Canada Colln, Churchill Colln, G8/G20 Colln, SPCK Colln, Strachan Colln, W. Speed Hill Colln (works of Richard Hooker), Upjohn-Waldie Colln (works of Eric Gill and other fine printing); Nicholls Librarian and Dir for Graham Library LINDA WILSON CORMAN.

Library and Archives Canada: 395 Wellington St, Ottawa, ON K1A 0N4; tel. (613) 996-5115; e-mail reference@lac-bac.gc.ca; internet www.collectionscanada.gc.ca; f. 2004, following merger of National Library of Canada (f. 1953) and National Archives of Canada (f. 1872), incl. Canadian Postal Archives; depository of all Canadian publs, public records and historical material; 71,000 films and documentaries, 2.5m. architectural drawings, plans and maps, 21.3m. photographic images, 270,000 hours of audio and visual recordings, 343,000 works of art, Canadian sheet music and 200,000 recordings related to music in Canada, Canadian postal archive, medals, seals, posters and coats of arms, nat., provincial and territorial newspapers, periodicals, MSS, microforms and theses, more than 1m. portraits of Canadians; Librarian and Archivist Dr DANIEL CARON; publ. *Annual Review*.

Library of Parliament: Ottawa, ON K1A 0A9; tel. (613) 995-1166; e-mail info@parl.gc.ca; internet www.parl.gc.ca; f. 1867; 407,500 vols in integrated systems, 510,000 microforms; Parliamentary Librarian WILLIAM YOUNG; publs *Quorum* (1 a day, during session), *Radar* (1 a day, during session), *Current Issue Reviews* (12 a year), *Research Publications* (12 a year).

Library of the Pontifical Institute of Medieval Studies: 4th Floor, 113 St Joseph St, Toronto, ON M5S 1J4; tel. (416) 926-7146; e-mail pims.library@utoronto.ca; internet www.pims.ca; f. 1929; principal research resource for the Institute's Mellon Fellows, postdoctoral candidates for the Licence in Medieval Studies, and for the faculty and doctoral students of the Univ. of Toronto's Centre for Medieval Studies; 120,000 vols, 210 periodicals, 15 MSS codices, 300 MSS charters, 10,000 folios of MSS on photostats, 250,000 folios of MSS on microfilm; Pres. RICHARD ALWAY; Dir JONATHAN BENGTSON.

London Public Library: 251 Dundas St, London, ON N6A 6H9; tel. (519) 661-4600; e-mail info@lpl.london.on.ca; internet www.lpl.london.on.ca; f. 1894; 934,001 vols, 172,975 non-book materials; CEO and Chief Librarian SUSANNA HUBBARD KRIMMER.

McMaster University Libraries: 1280 Main St West, Hamilton, ON L8S 4L6; tel. (905) 525-9140; e-mail libinfo@mcmaster.ca; internet www.mcmaster.ca/library; f. 1887; 1,717,799 vols, 1,488,305 microform items, 175,000 non-print items, 10,976 linear metres archival material, 6,292 serial subscriptions; Librarian GRAHAM R. HILL.

National Defence Headquarters Library: 101 Colonel By Dr., Ottawa, ON K1A 0K2; tel. (613) 995-2213; e-mail libraryndhq@forces.gc.ca; internet www.collectionscanada.gc.ca; f. 1903; 30,000 vols incl. military Canadiana; Librarian J. BRIAN GRIER.

Natural Resources Canada, Headquarters Library: 580 Booth St, Ottawa, ON K1A 0E4; tel. (613) 996-8282; internet www.nrcan-rncan.gc.ca; f. 1958; 65,000 vols and bound periodicals, 3,000 reports; Dir S. E. HENRY.

Ontario Legislative Library: Legislative Bldg, Queen's Park, Toronto, ON M7A 1A9; tel. (416) 325-3900; f. 1867; 58,440 monograph titles; Exec. Dir (vacant).

Ottawa City Archives: 1st Fl., Bytown Pavilion, 111 Sussex Dr., Ottawa, ON K1N 1J1; tel. (613) 580-2424; e-mail archives@ottawa.ca; f. 1976; repository of public records of civic administration and other historical material; spec. collns: genealogy, heraldry, local railroad history; City Archivist DAVE BULLOCK.

Ottawa Public Library/Bibliothèque Publique d'Ottawa: 120 Metcalfe St, Ottawa, ON; tel. (613) 580-2940; e-mail feedback@biblioottawalibrary.ca; internet www.biblioottawalibrary.ca; f. 1906; 2.5m. vols; City Librarian BARBARA CLUBB.

Queen's University Library: Stauffer Library, 101 Union St, Kingston, ON K7L 5C4; tel. (613) 533-2519; internet library.queensu.ca; f. 1842; 2,380,675 vols, 3,792,624 other items; Univ. Librarian MARTHA WHITEHEAD.

Supreme Court of Canada Library: 301 Wellington St, Ottawa, ON K1A 0J1; tel. (613) 996-8120; e-mail library@scc-csc.ca; internet www.scc-csc.gc.ca; 200,000 vols; Dir ROSALIE FOX.

Toronto Public Library: 789 Yonge St, Toronto, ON M4W 2G8; tel. (416) 393-7131; internet www.tpl.toronto.ca; City Librarian JOSEPHINE BRYANT; publ. *What's On* (4 a year).

University of Ottawa Library Network: 65 University Private, Ottawa, ON K1N 6N5; tel. (613) 562-5883; e-mail reference@uottawa.ca; internet www.biblio.uottawa.ca; f. 1848; library contains more than 4.5m. items, incl. more than 1,250,000 monographs, 19,000 current periodicals, 1.9m. microforms; tens of thousands of music scores, sound recordings and audiovisual items; hundreds of thousands of slides, aerial photographs, maps and govt publications; electronic resources; Univ. Chief Librarian LESLIE WEIR.

University of Toronto Libraries: Toronto, ON M5S 1A5; tel. (416) 978-8580; e-mail utweb@library.utoronto.ca; internet www.library.utoronto.ca; f. 1891; 10,342,574 vols, 32,485 serials, 5,372,000 microforms, 1,695,060 other non-book items (maps, sound recordings, audiovisual, MSS titles, aerial photographs, etc.), 32,912 online journals; Chief Librarian CAROLE MOORE.

University of Waterloo Library: 200 University Ave, Waterloo, ON N2L 3G1; tel. (519) 888-4567; e-mail gsoffice@uwaterloo.ca; internet www.lib.uwaterloo.ca; f. 1957; 2,046,934 vol, 1,715,194 microform pieces, 3,998 print titles, 31,585 electronic serials titles; University Librarian K. MARK HASLETT; publ. *Bibliography* (irregular).

University of Western Ontario Libraries: London, ON N6A 3K7; tel. (519) 661-2111; internet www.lib.uwo.ca; f. 1878; 3,546,496 vols, 9,756 print serials subscriptions; 480,985 ebooks, 54,790 ejournals; 4,062,350 microforms; 1,823,011 audio, video graphic and other spec. materials; Univ. Librarian JOYCE C. GARNETT.

Victoria University Library (E. J. Pratt Library): 71 Queen's Park Crescent East, Toronto, ON M5S 1K7; tel. (416) 585-4470; e-mail victoria.library@utoronto.ca; internet library.vicu.utoronto.ca; f. 1836; 300,000 vols; spec. collns: humanities (gen.), religions and theology; Northrop Frye, S. T. Coleridge, William Blake and his contemporaries, Hogarth Press, Tennyson, V. Woolf, Bloomsbury Group, Wesleyana, Norman Jewison Archive, E. J. Pratt; George Baxter (books and prints); 19th-century Canadian poetry, French and French-Canadian literature (Rièse colln); folklore; Senator Keith Davey; posters (Paris riots of 1968); contemporary poets; univ. archives; Chief Librarian LISA J. SHERLOCK.

Prince Edward Island

Confederation Centre Public Library: Box 7000, Charlottetown, PE C1A 8G8; tel. (902) 368-4642; e-mail ccpl@gov.pe.ca; internet www.library.pe.ca; f. 1773; 72,000 vols; Chief Librarian TRINA O'BRIEN LEGGOTT.

Prince Edward Island Public Library Service: POB 7500, 89 Red Head Rd, Morell, PE C0A 1S0; tel. (902) 961-7320; e-mail plshq@gov.pe.ca; internet www.library.pe.ca; f. 1933; 340,000 vols in regional system of 26 public libraries; Dir for Libraries and Archives KATHLEEN EATON.

Public Archives and Records Office of Prince Edward Island: POB 1000, Charlottetown, PE C1A 7M4; tel. (902) 368-4290; e-mail archives@gov.pe.ca; internet www.gov.pe.ca/archives; f. 1964; Provincial Archivist JILL MACMICKEN-WILSON.

Québec

Bibliothèque de l'Assemblée Nationale du Québec: Edifice Pamphile-Lemay, Québec, QC G1A 1A3; tel. (418) 643-4408; e-mail bibliotheque@assnat.qc.ca; internet www.assnat.qc.ca; f. 1802; law and legislation, political science, parliamentary procedure, history, official publs of Québec, newspapers; 955,000 vols; Dir HÉLÈNE GALARNEAU; Librarian VALÉRIE BOURDEAU; publs *Bulletin* (4 a year), *Débats de l'Assemblée législative 1867–1962* (irregular), *Journal des débats: index* (irregular).

Bibliothèque de la Compagnie de Jésus (BCJ): Collège Jean-de-Brébeuf, L. B4–25, 3200 chemin Côte-Ste-Catherine, Montréal, QC H3T 1C1; tel. (514) 342-9342; e-mail bcj@brebeuf.qc.ca; f. 1882; 197,000 vols; Dir MARC UMBA.

Bibliothèque de l'Université Laval: Cité Universitaire, Québec, QC G1K 7P4; tel. (418) 656-3344; internet www.bibl.ulaval.ca; f. 1852; 5,000,000 vols, 24,422 periodicals, 19,500 films, 140,000 maps; Dir Dr SYLVIE DELORME; publ. *Répertoire des vedettes-matière* (2 a year, CD-ROM).

Bibliothèques de l'Université de Montréal: CP 6128, Succursale Centre-ville, Montréal, QC H3C 3J7; tel. (514) 343-6905; e-mail biblios@bib.umontreal.ca; internet www.bib.umontreal.ca; f. 1928; 3,106,971 vols, 21,087 current periodicals, 1,650,557 microforms, 189,164 audiovisual documents; Dir for Libraries RICHARD DUMONT.

Bibliothèque de Montréal: Édifice Gaston-Miron, 1210 rue Sherbrooke Est, Bureau 002, Montréal, QC H2L 1L9; tel. (514) 872-4055; internet bibliomontreal.com; f. 1902; 2,102,600 vols, of which 51,700 books, 20,757 pamphlets, 43,900 pictures and photographs, 1,547 maps, 3,035 slides and 99,200 microforms related to Canada and its history; Dir JACQUES PANNETON.

Bibliothèque et Archives Nationales du Québec: 2275 rue Holt, Montréal, QC H2G 3H1; tel. (514) 873-1100; e-mail info@banq.qc.ca; internet www.banq.qc.ca; f. 1967; merged with Archives Nationales du Québec (f. 1920) 2006; 4m. vols; Conservation Centre and Grande Bibliothèque in Montréal; 9 archive centres (Chicoutimi, Gatineau, Montréal, Québec, Rimouski, Rouyn-Noranda, Sept-Iles, Sherbrooke,Trois-Rivières); Chair and CEO LISE BISSONNETTE; publ. *À rayons ouverts* (4 a year).

CAIJ—Montréal: Palais de Justice, 17e étage, 1 rue Notre-Dame est, local 17.50, Montréal, QC H2Y 1B6; tel. (514) 866-2057; e-mail mlaforce@caij.qc.ca; f. 1828; 100,000 vols; Librarian MIREILLE LAFORCE.

Concordia University Libraries: 1455 de Maisonneuve Blvd W, Montréal, QC H3G 1M8; tel. (514) 848-2424; e-mail libadmin@alcor.concordia.ca; internet library.concordia.ca; f. 1974; 2,730,000 vols; Univ. Librarian GERALD BEASLEY.

Departmental Library, Aboriginal Affairs and Northern Development Canada: Room 1400, 10 Wellington St, Gatineau, QC K1A 0H4; tel. (819) 997-0811; e-mail reference@ainc-inac.gc.ca; internet www.aadnc-aandc.gc.ca; f. 1966; 100,600 vols, 20,000 bound periodicals, 2,000 rare books, 3,500 govt documents, 3,000 microfilm reels, incl. records relating to Indian affairs; Chief Librarian JULIA FINN.

Fraser-Hickson Institute Library: 16 Westminster N, Suite 100, Montréal-Ouest, QC H4X 1Z1; tel. (514) 489-5301; e-mail frances@fraserhickson.ca; internet www.fraserhickson.ca; f. 1870; colln of archives of the Mercantile Library Asscn (Montréal); partnership with the YMCA; 150,000 vols; Dir FRANCES W. ACKERMAN; Reader Services Man. ISABEL RANDALL.

McGill University Libraries: 3459 McTavish St, Montréal, QC H3A 1Y1; tel. (514) 398-4734; e-mail doadmin.library@mcgill.ca; internet www.mcgill.ca/library; f. 1829; 4.4m. vols (incl. govt documents), 3,805 print and 77,041 electronic current periodicals, 1,792,136 microtexts; Dean C. COLLEEN COOK; Assoc. Dir, Planning and Resources DIANE KOEN.

Osler Library of the History of Medicine: McGill Univ., McIntyre Medical Sciences Bldg, 3655 Promenade Sir William Osler, 3rd Fl., Montréal, QC H3G 1Y6; tel. (514) 398-4475; e-mail osler.library@mcgill.ca; internet www.mcgill.ca/library/branches/osler; f. 1929; history of medicine and allied sciences; 104,521 vols; Head Librarian CHRISTOPHER LYONS.

Philatelic Collections, Library and Archives Canada: 550 blvd de la Cité, Gatineau, QC K1A 0N4; tel. (613) 996-5115; internet www.collectionscanada.gc.ca/philately-postal; f. 1988, fmrly Canadian Postal Archives; acquisition, preservation, description of philatelic records and related material; Manager PASCAL LEBLOND.

Saskatchewan

Regina Public Library: 2311 12th Ave, Regina, SK S4P 3Z5; tel. (306) 777-6000; e-mail askalibrarian@reginalibrary.ca; internet www.reginalibrary.ca; f. 1908; 665,928 vols; Library Dir JEFF BARBER; publs *@ the Library* (6 a year), *Community Information Catalogue*, *Regina Public Library Film Catalogue*, *RPL Theatre Calendar* (6 a year).

Saskatchewan Legislative Library: 234-2405 Legislative Dr., Regina, SK S4S 0B3; tel. (306) 787-2276; e-mail reference@legassembly.sk.ca; internet www.legassembly.sk.ca/library; f. 1878, current name adopted 1905; social sciences, law and history; colln of govt documents and W Canadiana; 152,500 vols, 522,000 sheets of microfiche, 6,300 reels of microfilm, 3,200 CD-ROMs, 760 audio, video and film recordings; Legislative Librarian MELISSA BENNETT; publ. *Checklist of Saskatchewan Government Publications* (12 a year).

Saskatchewan Provincial Library and Literacy Office: 409A Park St, Regina, SK S4N 5B2; tel. (306) 787-2972; internet www.learning.gov.sk.ca/provinciallibrary; f. 1953; coordinates library services in the province; 97,000 vols, specializing in library science, multilingual books and last copy fiction; Provincial Librarian and Exec. Dir BRETT WAYTUCK.

Saskatoon Public Library: 311 23rd St E, Saskatoon, SK S7K 0J6; tel. (306) 975-7558; internet www.saskatoonlibrary.ca; f. 1913; 824,258 vols, 75,348 DVDs, 63,322 CDs, 2,198 VGs, 46,985 magazines, 604,559 books; Dir for Libraries ZENON ZUZAK; Deputy Library Dir ANN-MARIE MATHIEU.

University of Saskatchewan Libraries: 3 Campus Dr., Saskatoon, SK S7N 5A4; tel. (306) 966-5927; internet www.library.usask.ca; f. 1909; main library and 6 brs with 1,871,000 vols, 15,423 current journals, 3,054,000 items on microform, 427,902 govt documents and pamphlets, Adam Shortt colln of Canadiana, Conrad Aiken colln of published works; Russell Green music MSS; Dir for Libraries F. WINTER.

Wapiti Regional Library: 145 12th St East, Prince Albert, SK S6V 1B7; tel. (306) 764-0712; e-mail wapiti@panet.pa.sk.ca; f. 1950; 5,263,600 vols; Regional Dir JOHN MURRAY.

Museums and Art Galleries

Alberta

Art Gallery of Alberta: 2 Sir Winston Churchill Sq., Edmonton, AB T5J 2C1; tel. (780) 422-6223; e-mail info@youraga.ca; internet www.youraga.ca; f. 1924; Canadian and int. drawing, painting, printmaking, sculpture and photography; devt and presentation of original exhibitions of contemporary and historical art from Alberta, Canada and around the world; art education and public programmes; colln of more than 6,000 objects; exhibits, preservation of art and visual culture; Exec. Dir GILLES HEBERT; Deputy Dir CATHERINE CROWSTON.

Banff Park Museum: Box 900, Banff, AB T1L 1K2; tel. (403) 762-1558; e-mail banff.vrc@pc.gc.ca; internet www.parkscanada.gc.ca/lnh-nhs/ab/banff/index-e.asp; f. 1895; Historic Sites Supervisor STEVE MALINS.

Buffalo Nations Museum: 1 Birch Ave (Box 850), Banff, AB T1L 1A8; tel. (403) 762-2388; e-mail buffalonations@telus.net; f. 1951 as Luxton Museum; promotes education and awareness of the Northern Plains and Canadian Rockies Indians; natural history exhibits; Pres. HAROLD HEALY.

Department of Earth and Atmospheric Sciences Museum, University of Alberta: Edmonton, AB T6G 2E3; tel. (780) 492-2518; e-mail eas.inquiries@ualberta.ca; internet easweb.eas.ualberta.ca; f. 1912; geology, meteorites, mineralogy, invertebrate and vertebrate palaeontology, stratigraphy; Collns and Museums Administrator A. J. LOCOCK.

Glenbow Museum: 130 Ninth Ave SE, Calgary, AB T2G 0P3; tel. (403) 268-4100; e-mail glenbow@glenbow.org; internet www.glenbow.org; f. 1966; library of 100,000 vols, archives of 1,250,000 photos and negatives; Pres. Dr ROBERT R. JANES; Chair., Board of Governors ROBERT G. PETERS; publ. *Experience* (3 a year).

Medicine Hat Museum and Art Gallery: 1302 Bomford Crescent, Medicine Hat, AB T1A 5E6; tel. (403) 502-8580; e-mail esplanade@medicinehat.ca; internet www.esplanade.ca; f. 1967; cultural and natural history, palaeontology, and primitive peoples representative of SE Alberta; art gallery; monthly exhibits by Canadian and international artists.

Royal Alberta Museum: 12845 102nd Ave, NW, Edmonton, AB T5N 0M6; tel. (780) 453-9100; internet www.royalalbertamuseum.ca; f. 1967; exhibitions and educational programmes in cultural history of Alberta and archaeology, geology, life sciences and biodiversity, palaeontology and environments, quaternary palaeontology and environments of Alberta; numismatics.; Exec. Dir CHRIS ROBINSON.

Royal Tyrrell Museum of Palaeontology: POB 7500, Highway 838 Midland Provincial Park, Drumheller, AB T0J 0Y0; tel. (403) 823-7707; e-mail tyrrell.info@gov.ab.ca; internet www.tyrrellmuseum.com; f. 1985; library of 50,000 vols, special biographical collection on Joseph Burr Tyrrell; Dir ANDREW NEUMAN.

British Columbia

H. R. MacMillan Space Centre: 1100 Chestnut St, Vancouver, BC V6J 3J9; tel. (604) 738-7827; e-mail tcromwell@spacecentre.ca; internet www.spacecentre.ca; f. 1988; administers the H. R. MacMillan Space Centre, H. R. MacMillan Planetarium and Gordon Southam Observatory; multimedia astronomy shows, laser shows, exhibitions, Observatory activities, lectures; 1,000 mems; Exec. Dir ROB APPLETON; publ. *Starry Messenger* (4 a year).

Helmcken House Museum: c/o Royal BC Museum, 675 Belleville St, Victoria, BC V8W 9W2; tel. (250) 356-7226; internet www.royalbcmuseum.bc.ca; Curator of Human History, Royal BC Museum LORNE HAMMOND.

Museum of Northern British Columbia: 100 First Ave W, Prince Rupert, BC V8J 1A8; tel. (250) 624-3207; e-mail mnbc@citytel.net; internet www.museumofnorthernbc.com; f. 1924; exhibits cover 10,000 years of human habitation, incl. First Nations culture, local pioneer history and natural history; art gallery; library of 800 vols (50 rare); Dir ROBIN WEBER; Curator SUSAN MARSDEN.

Royal British Columbia Museum: 675 Belleville St, Victoria, BC V8W 9W2; tel. (250) 356-7226; e-mail reception@royalbcmuseum.bc.ca; internet www.royalbcmuseum.bc.ca; f. 1886; contains reference collections and exhibits pertaining to natural history and human history of BC; CEO Prof. JACK LOHMAN.

Vancouver Art Gallery: 750 Hornby St, Vancouver, BC V6Z 2H7; tel. (604) 662-4700; e-mail info@vanartgallery.bc.ca; internet www.vanartgallery.bc.ca; f. 1931; Canadian and foreign art by contemporary artists and major historical figures; library of 25,000 vols; Dir KATHLEEN BARTELS; publ. *Members' Newsletter* (3 a year).

Vancouver Maritime Museum: 1905 Ogden Ave, Vancouver, BC V6J 1A3; tel. (604) 257-8300; e-mail director@vancouvermaritimemuseum.com; internet www.vancouvermaritimemuseum.com; f. 1958; maritime history, local and int. heritage vessels, RCMP *St Roch* Arctic patrol vessel, school programmes, lectures and summer festivals; library of 10,000 vols; Exec. Dir SIMON ROBINSON; publ. *Signals* (4 a year).

Manitoba

Manitoba Museum of Man and Nature: 190 Rupert Ave, Winnipeg, MB R3B 0N2; tel. (204) 956-2830; e-mail info@manitobamuseum.ca; f. 1965; human and natural history of Manitoba; planetarium; 'Touch the Universe' interactive science centre; library of 26,000 vols; Exec. Dir CLAUDETTE LECLERC; publ. *Happenings* (6 a year).

Winnipeg Art Gallery: 300 Memorial Blvd, Winnipeg, MB R3C 1V1; tel. (204) 786-6641; e-mail inquiries@wag.ca; internet www.wag.ca; f. 1912; library of 24,000 vols; Dir Dr STEPHEN BORYS.

New Brunswick

Beaverbrook Art Gallery: POB 605, Fredericton, NB E3B 5A6; tel. (506) 458-8545; e-mail emailbag@beaverbrookartgallery.org; internet www.beaverbrookartgallery.org; f. 1959; Man. for Public Programming ADDA MIHAILESCU; publ. *Tableau* (2 a year).

Fort Beauséjour (Fort Cumberland National Historic Site of Canada): 111 Fort Beauséjour Rd, Aulac, NB E4L 2W5; tel. (506) 364-5080; e-mail fort.beausejour@pc.gc.ca; internet www.pc.gc.ca/lhn-nhs/nb/beausejour/default.asp; f. 1926 fort was built by French in 1751, renamed Fort Cumberland by the British; declared nat. historic site 1926; Interpretation Officer and Coordinator JULIETTE BULMER.

Miramichi Natural History Museum: 149 Wellington St, Miramichi NB E1N 1L7; e-mail mirnathist@nb.aibn.com; f. 1880; 5,000 specimens of decorative arts, fine arts, human history and natural sciences; Curator KEN WEATHERBY.

New Brunswick Museum: 277 Douglas Ave, Saint John, NB E2K 1E5; tel. (506) 643-2300; e-mail nbmuseum@nbm-mnb.ca; internet www.nbm-mnb.ca; f. 1842; archives, library, fine art, decorative art, natural science and history; CEO JANE FULLERTON.

York-Sunbury Historical Society Museum: POB 1312, Fredericton, NB E3B 5C8; tel. (506) 455-6041; e-mail yorksun@nbnet.nb.ca; f. 1932; domestic and military exhibits of Fredericton and area; housed in British Officers' Quarters of 1840; Exec. Dir KATE MOSSMAN.

Newfoundland and Labrador

The Rooms Corporation of Newfoundland and Labrador—Provincial Museum and Art Gallery: POB 1800, St John's, NL A1C 5P9; 9 Bonaventure Ave, St John's, NL A1C 5P9; tel. (709) 757-8020; e-mail information@therooms.ca; internet www.therooms.ca; f. 2005; colln of over 8,000 works from historical, contemporary, international, crafts and folk art; Canadian works, including a Jean-Paul Riopelle; more than 1m. archeological items and natural history specimens; native artefacts; the world's largest Beothuk colln; Dir for Provincial Museum ANNE CHAFE; Dir for Provincial Art Gallery SHIELA PERRY.

Subsidiary Museums:

Mary March Regional Museum and Loggers' Exhibit: Grand Falls–Windsor, NL; tel. (709) 292-4522; e-mail pwells@nf.aibn.com; internet www.nfmuseum.com; Curator PENNY WELLS.

Southern Newfoundland Seamen's Museum: Grand Bank, NL; tel. (709) 832-1484; e-mail gwcrews@nf.aibn.com; internet www.nfmuseum.com; Curator GERALD CREWS.

Nova Scotia

Art Gallery of Nova Scotia: 1723 Hollis St, POB 2262, Halifax, NS B3J 3C8; tel. (902) 424-5280; e-mail infodesk@gov.ns.ca; internet www.artgalleryofnovascotia.ca; f. 1975; Dir and Chief Curator JEFFREY SPALDING; Dir for Devt BERNARD DOUCET; publ. *The Journal*.

Fort Anne National Historic Site and Museum: POB 9, Annapolis Royal, NS B0S 1A0; tel. (902) 532-2321; e-mail information@pc.gc.ca; internet www.pc.gc.ca; f. 1917; Superintendent Operations THERESA BUNBURY.

Fortress of Louisbourg National Historic Site: 259 Park Service Rd, Louisbourg, NS B1C 2L2; tel. (902) 733-2280; e-mail louisbourg.info@pc.gc.ca; internet fortress.uccb.ns.ca; f. 1963; District Dir CAROL WHITFIELD.

Maritime Museum of the Atlantic: 1675 Lower Water St, Halifax, NS B3J 1S3; tel. (902) 424-7890; e-mail mmalibry@gov.ns.ca; internet museum.gov.ns.ca/mma/; f. 1982; naval and merchant shipping history; *Titanic* and Halifax explosion exhibitions; small boat collection; collection of 20,000 photographs and 5,000 books; Dir MICHAEL MURRAY.

Museum of Natural History: 1747 Summer St, Halifax, NS B3H 3A6; tel. (902) 424-7353; e-mail museum-info@gov.ns.ca; internet naturalhistory.novascotia.ca; f. 1868 as the Provincial Museum; current name adopted 1947; attached to Nova Scotia Museum; Dir CALUM EWING.

Ontario

Art Gallery of Hamilton: 123 King St West, Hamilton, ON L8P 4S8; tel. (905) 527-6610; e-mail info@artgalleryofhamilton.com; internet www.artgalleryofhamilton.com; f. 1914; 9,000 works, mainly Canadian paintings, sculpture and graphics; also art from the USA, UK and other European countries; library of 2,000 vols; Pres. and CEO LOUISE DOMPIERRE; publ. *Insights* (members' magazine, 3 a year).

Art Gallery of Ontario: 317 Dundas St W, Toronto, ON M5T 1G4; tel. (416) 979-6648; internet www.ago.net; f. 1900; European and N American art since 15th century; Inuit art in all forms; Henry Moore; research; library of 250,000 vols; Dir and CEO MATTHEW TEITELBAUM; Dir, Collns and Research DENNIS REID; publ. *Art Matters Magazine* (4 a year).

Canada Science and Technology Museum Corporation: POB 9724, Station T, Ottawa, ON K1G 5A3; tel. (613) 991-6090; e-mail info@technomuses.ca; internet technomuses.ca; f. 1967; Pres. and CEO DENISE AMYOT; publs *Collection Profile* (11 a year, also in electronic edn), *Curator's Choice* (irregular, also in electronic edn), *Material History Review* (2 a year).

Canadian Museum of Nature: POB 3443 Station D, Ottawa, ON K1P 6P4; tel. (613) 566-4700; e-mail questions@mus-nature.ca; internet www.nature.ca; f. 1912; research and collns in the areas of botany, evolution, mineralogy, palaeobiology and zoology; houses the Centre for Traditional Knowledge, National Herbarium, the Biological Survey of Canada and the Canadian Centre for Biodiversity; library of 36,000 vols, 2,000 periodical titles (200 active subscriptions); Pres. and CEO JOANNE DICOSIMO.

Collingwood Museum: POB 556, 45 St Paul St, Collingwood, ON L9Y 4B2; tel. (705) 445-4811; e-mail museum@collingwood.ca; internet www.collingwood.ca/museum; f. 1904; exhibits, children's programming, adult lectures, display, programming, research, spec. events; Supervisor SUSAN WARNER.

Dundurn Castle: 610 York Blvd, Hamilton, ON L8R 3H1; tel. (905) 546-2872; Curator WILLIAM NESBITT.

Jordan Historical Museum of the Twenty: 3802 Main St, Jordan, ON L0R 1S0; tel. (905) 562-5242; f. 1953; Curator HELEN BOOTH.

Leacock Museum: Old Brewery Bay, 50 Museum Dr., Orillia, ON L3V 6K5; tel. (705) 326-5578; e-mail leacock@mail.transdata.ca; internet leacockmuseum.com; f. 1957; summer home, correspondence, MSS, personal effects of Stephen Butler Leacock; Curator DAPHNE MAINPRIZE.

Marine Museum of Upper Canada: Exhibition Place, Toronto, ON M5T 1R5; tel. (416) 392-1765; e-mail can-thb@immedia.ca; f. 1959; preserves and interprets the marine history of Toronto, Toronto Harbour and Lake Ontario; collns include 1932 steam tug *Ned Hanlan* in dry dock; Curator JOHN SUMMERS.

Museum London: 421 Ridout St N, London, ON N6H 5H4; tel. (519) 661-0333; e-mail ramurray@museumlondon.ca; internet www.museumlondon.ca; f. 1940; 25,000 historical artefacts, incl. paintings, prints, drawings and sculptures; undertakes collection and conservation of fine art and artefacts; exhibitions, lectures, films, workshops, tours and live performances; 900 mems; Exec. Dir BRIAN MEEHAN; publ. *At the Museum* (4 a year).

National Arts Centre: 53 Elgin St, Box 1534, Station B, Ottawa, ON K1P 5W1; tel. (613) 947-7000; e-mail info@nac-cna.ca; internet www.nac-cna.ca; f. 1969; consists of Southam Hall (2,300 seats), theatre (950 seats), studio (300 seats), 4th stage (140 seats); resident 60-mem. NAC orchestra, English and French theatre, dance, opera, workshops, artist devt; 700 performances a year; Chair. JULIA FOSTER; Pres. and CEO PETER HERNNDORF.

National Gallery of Canada: 380 Sussex Dr., POB 427 Station A, Ottawa, ON K1N 9N4; tel. (613) 990-1985; e-mail info@gallery.ca; internet national.gallery.ca; f. 1880; largest colln of Canadian art in the world; collns incl. large and important prints and drawings colln; historical and contemporary Canadian and international photography colln; Canadian art colln; Inuit colln; European colln; large contemporary colln; site incl. Canadian Museum of Contemporary Photography; operates largest travelling exhibition programme in N America; library of 275,000 vols; Dir PIERRE THÉBERGE; publs *National Gallery of Canada Review* (1 a year), *Vernissage* (4 a year).

Ontario Science Centre: 770 Don Mills Rd, Toronto, ON M3C 1T3; tel. (416) 696-1000; e-mail contact.centre@ontariosciencecentre.ca; internet www.ontariosciencecentre.ca; f. 1969; more than 600 exhibits in all fields of science and technology; library of 11,000 vols; CEO LESLEY LEWIS; Chief Operating Officer GRANT TROOP; Librarian VALERIE HATTEN.

Queen's University Museums: Miller Hall, Union St, Kingston, ON K7L 3N6.

Royal Ontario Museum: 100 Queen's Park, Toronto, ON M5S 2C6; tel. (416) 586-8000; e-mail info@rom.on.ca; internet www.rom.on.ca; f. 1912, opened in March 1914; natural history and world cultures; conservation and preservation; education and public programmes; library and archives; library of 175,000 vols; spec. collns 5,000 vols; Dir

JANET CARDING; Deputy Dir for Colls and Research Dr MARK ENGSTROM; Head of Library and Archives ARTHUR SMITH; publ. *ROM: The Magazine of the Royal Ontario Museum* (3 a year).

Attached Institution:

George R. Gardiner Museum of Ceramic Art: 111 Queen's Park, Toronto, ON M5S 2C7; tel. (416) 586-8080; e-mail mail@gardinermuseum.com; internet gardinermuseum.com; f. 1984.

Tom Thomson Memorial Art Gallery: 840 First Ave West, Owen Sound, ON N4K 4K4; tel. (519) 376-1932; e-mail ttag@tomthomson.org; internet www.tomthomson.org; f. 1967; Tom Thomson paintings, memorabilia; changing exhibitions of historic and contemporary art; Dir and Curator STUART REID.

Upper Canada Village: RR1, Morrisburg, ON K0C 1X0; tel. (613) 543-3704; internet www.uppercanadavillage.com; f. 1961; 45 restored bldgs portraying a rural community c. 1866; spec. colln of 19th-century archival materials, incl. family and business records, photographs and social history documents from eastern Ontario; library of 5,000 vols; Man. GEOFF WAYCIK.

Prince Edward Island

Confederation Centre Art Gallery and Museum: 145 Richmond St, Charlottetown, PE C1A 1J1; tel. (902) 628-6111; e-mail artgallery@confederationcentre.com; internet www.confederationcentre.com; f. 1964; nat. colln of 15,000 works of Canadian art since 19th century: paintings, drawings, prints, sculpture and photography; Harris Colln (paintings, drawings, MSS and records of Robert Harris, 1849–1919); temporary exhibitions on historical research and the contemporary artist; Dir JON TUPPER; Registrar and Curatorial Man. KEVIN RICE.

Québec

Canadian Museum of History: 100 Laurier St, Gatineau, QC K1A 0M8; tel. (819) 776-7173; e-mail library@historymuseum.ca; internet www.historymuseum.ca; f. 1856 as Geological Museum, current name adopted 2013; archaeology, ethnology, folk culture studies, history of Canada, linguistics, physical anthropology; study collns open to qualified researchers and gen. public; incl. Archaeological Survey of Canada, Canadian Children's Museum, Canadian Centre for Folk Culture Studies, Canadian Ethnology Service, Canadian Postal Museum, Canadian War Museum and other elements; library of 200,000 vols, of which 70,000 accessible to public; Pres. and CEO Dr MARK O'NEILL.

Centre Canadien d'Architecture/Canadian Centre for Architecture: 1920 rue Baile, Montréal, QC H3H 2S6; tel. (514) 939-7000; e-mail ref@cca.qc.ca; internet www.cca.qc.ca; f. 1979, present status 1989; research centre and museum; study programmes, exhibitions, publications, seminars, lectures and internships; library of 235,500 printed monographs (incl. rare books); 5,000 runs of periodicals, a number of spec. collns; architecture-related artefacts (such as toys and souvenir models); ephemera; Founding Dir and Pres. of the Board PHYLLIS LAMBERT.

Insectarium de Montréal: 4581 rue Sherbrooke Est, Montréal, QC H1X 2B2; tel. (514) 872-1400; e-mail insectarium@ville.montreal.qc.ca; internet www.ville.montreal.qc.ca/insectarium; f. 1990; colln of 160,000 insects; Dir ANNE CHARPENTIER.

McCord Museum of Canadian History: 690 Sherbrooke St West, Montréal, QC H3A 1E9; tel. (514) 398-7100; e-mail info@mccord.mcgill.ca; internet www.musee-mccord.qc.ca; f. 1921; Exec. Dir Dr VICTORIA DICKENSON.

Montréal Biodôme: 4777 ave Pierre-de-Coubertin, Montréal, QC H1V 1B3; tel. (514) 868-3000; e-mail biodome@ville.montreal.qc.ca; internet www.biodome.qc.ca; f. 1992; museum of the environment; live collns, containing more than 4,800 animals of 230 species, and 750 plants species in four recreated ecosystems found in the Americas; housed in the velodrome used for the 1976 Olympic Games; Dir RACHEL LÉGER.

Montréal Museum of Fine Arts: 1380 Sherbrooke St West, Montréal, QC H3G 2T9; tel. (514) 285-2000; e-mail webmaster@mbamtl.org; internet www.mmfa.qc.ca; f. 1860; permanent colln of paintings (European and Canadian), sculptures, decorative arts and drawings; art from Asia, Africa and Oceania; library of 90,000 vols, 930 serial publs, and slides; Pres. BRIAN M. LEVITT; Dir NATHALIE BONDIL; publ. *M* (3 a year).

Musée d'art Contemporain de Montréal: 185 St Catherine St W, Montréal, QC H2X 3X5; tel. (514) 847-6226; e-mail info@macm.org; internet www.macm.org; f. 1964; exhibits contemporary Québecois, Canadian and int. art; organizes multimedia events, art workshops, lectures; library of 38,000 vols and exhibition catalogues, 713 periodicals, 8,000 visual archives, 1,000 video cassettes and audio items, 12,000 artists' files and bibliographic database; Dir and Chief Curator JOHN ZEPPETELLI (acting); publ. *Le Magazine*.

Musée de l'Amérique Française (Museum of French North America): 9 rue de la Vieille-Université, CP 460, succ., Haute-Ville, QC G1R 4R7; tel. (418) 528-0157; e-mail archives@mcq.org; internet www.mcq.org; f. 1806, as Musée du Séminaire de Québec, current name adopted 1983; attached to Musée de la Civilisation complex; library of 180,000 vols; Museum Dir DANIELLE POIRÉ; Archives Dir PIERRE BAIL.

Musée du Québec/Musée National des Beaux-Arts du Québec: Parc des Champs de Bataille, Québec, QC G1R 5H3; tel. (418) 643-2150; e-mail info@mnba.qc.ca; internet www.mnba.qc.ca; f. 1933; paintings, sculptures, drawings, prints, photographs, decorative art objects, interior design pieces; colln of 24,000 items relating to Québecois art and artists; Exec. Dir Dr JOHN R. PORTER.

Planétarium de Montréal: 1000 rue Saint-Jacques Ouest, Montréal, QC H3C 1G7; tel. (514) 872-4530; e-mail info@planetarium.montreal.qc.ca; internet www.planetarium.montreal.qc.ca; f. 1966; Dir PIERRE LACOMBE.

Redpath Museum: 859 Sherbrooke St W, Montréal, QC H3A 2K6; tel. (514) 398-4086; e-mail redpath.museum@mcgill.ca; internet www.mcgill.ca/redpath; f. 1882; promotes biological, geological, and cultural heritage through scientific research, collns-based study and education; Dir DAVID GREEN.

Saskatchewan

MacKenzie Art Gallery: 3475 Albert St, Regina, SK S4S 6X6; tel. (306) 522-4250; e-mail mackenzie@uregina.ca; internet www.mackenzieartgallery.ca; f. 1954; permanent colln of Canadian historical and contemporary art, int. art since the 19th century, permanent colln displays and travelling exhibitions; public programmes; library: Resource Centre of 3,500 vols; Exec. Dir STUART REID; Curator TIMOTHY LONG; publs *At the MacKenzie* (3 a year), *@ the MacKenzie* (12 a year, online).

Mendel Art Gallery and Civic Conservatory (Saskatoon Gallery and Conservatory Corporation): 950 Spadina Crescent East, POB 569, Saskatoon, SK S7K 3L6; tel. (306) 975-7610; e-mail mendel@mendel.ca; internet www.mendel.ca; f. 1964; library of 10,000 vols; Exec. Dir and CEO RICHARD MOLDENHAUER (acting); publ. *Folio* (4 a year).

Musée Ukraina Museum: POB 26072, Saskatoon, SK S7K 8C1; tel. (306) 244-4212; e-mail ukrainamuseum@sasktel.net; internet www.mumsaskatoon.com; f. 1953; ethnographic collns representing the spiritual, material and folkloric culture of Ukraine; Pres. PATRICIA MIALKOWSKY.

Prince Albert Historical Museum: 10 River St E, Prince Albert, SK S6V 8A9; tel. (306) 764-2992; e-mail historypa@citypa.com; internet www.historypa.com; f. 1923 as Prince Albert Historical Soc.; library: 300,000 images, 15,000 documents and over 400 maps all relating to Prince Albert housed in the Bill Smiley Archive; Pres. DENNIS OGRODNICK; Man. and Curator MICHELLE TAYLOR.

Royal Saskatchewan Museum: College Ave and Albert St, Regina, SK S4P 3V7; tel. (306) 787-2815; e-mail rsminfo@gov.sk.ca; internet www.gov.sk.ca/rsm; f. 1906; Earth Sciences Gallery depicts 2.5 billion years of Saskatchewan's geological history; First Nations Gallery traces 12,000 years of aboriginal history and culture; Paleo Pit interactive gallery; Megamunch, a roaring robotic Tyrannosaurus rex; Life Sciences Gallery features the flora, fauna and landscapes of Saskatchewan's diverse eco-regions; Dir DAVID BARON.

Saskatchewan Western Development Museum: 2935 Lorne Ave, Saskatoon, SK S7J 0S5; tel. (306) 934-1400; e-mail info@wdm.ca; internet www.wdm.ca; f. 1949; library of 15,000 historical vols, maps, photographs; Exec. Dir JOAN CHAMP; publ. *Sparks off the Anvil* (6 a year).

Universities and Colleges

ACADIA UNIVERSITY

15 University Ave, Wolfville, NS B4P 2R6
Telephone: (902) 542-2201
E-mail: ask.acadia@acadiau.ca
Internet: www2.acadiau.ca

Founded 1838
State control
Language of instruction: English
Academic year: September to April

Chancellor: LIBBY BURNHAM
Pres. and Vice-Chancellor: RAY IVANY
Academic Vice-Pres.: Dr TOM HERMAN
Assoc. Vice-Pres. for Finance and Treas.: MARY MACVICAR
Vice-Pres. for Finance and Admin. and Chief Financial Officer: DARRELL YOUDEN
Sr Dir for Communications and Public Affairs: SCOTT ROBERTS
Registrar: ROSEMARY JOTCHAM
Vice-Pres. for Enrolment and Student Services and Univ. Librarian: SARA LOCHHEAD

Library: see under Libraries and Archives
Number of teachers: 248 (211 full-time, 37 part-time)
Number of students: 3,480 (3,100 full-time, 380 part-time)

DEANS

Faculty of Arts: Dr BARRY MOODY (acting)
Faculty of Professional Studies: Dr HEATHER HEMMING
Faculty of Pure and Applied Sciences: Dr PETER WILLIAMS
Faculty of Theology: Dr HARRY GARDNER
Research and Graduate Studies: Dr DAVID MACKINNON

PROFESSORS

ARCHIBALD, T., Mathematics
ASH, S., Business Administration
ASHLEY, T. R.
BAILET, D., French
BALDWIN, D., History
BARR, S. M., Geology
BAWTREE, M., English
BEDINGFIELD, E. W., Recreation and Kinesiology
BEST, J., French
BISSIX, G., Recreation and Kinesiology
BOOTH, P., Classics
BOWEN, K., Sociology
CABILIO, P., Mathematics
CAMERON, B. W., Geology
CONRAD, M. R., History
DABORN, G. R., Biology
DADSWELL, M., Biology
DAVIES, J. E., Economics
DAVIES, R. A., English
FISHER, S. F., Music
GRIFFITH, B., Education
HERMAN, T. B., Biology
HOBSON, P., Economics
HORVATH, P., Psychology
JOHNSTON, E. M., Nutrition
LATTA, B., Physics
LEITER, M. P., Psychology
LOOKER, E. D., Sociology
MACLATCHY, C. S., Physics
MCLEOD, W., Kinesiology
MATTHEWS, B., History
MOODY, B. M., History
MOUSSA, H., Economics
MULDNER, T., Computer Science
NESS, G., Recreation and Kinesiology
OGILVIE, K. K., Chemistry
OLIVER, L., Computer Science
O'NEILL, P. T. H., Psychology
PARATTE, H. D., French
PIPER, D., Education
PYRCZ, G. E., Political Science
RAESIDE, R. P., Geology
RIDDLE, P. H., Music
ROSCOE, J. M., Chemistry
ROSCOE, S., Chemistry
SACOUMAN, R. J., Sociology
SPARKMAN, R., Business
STEWART, I., Political Science
STEWART, R., English
STILES, D. A., Chemistry
SUMARAH, J., Education
SYMON, S., Psychology
TOEWS, D. P., Biology
TOMEK, I., Computer Science
TOWNLEY, P., Economics
TRITES, A. A., Theology
TRUDEL, A., Computer Science
TUGWELL, M., Economics
VAN WAGONER, N. A., Geology
VERSTRAETE, B. C., Classics
WILSON, R. S., Theology

AFFILIATED COLLEGE

Acadia Divinity College: Wolfville; e-mail agi@acadiau.ca; f. 1968; Prin. L. MCDONALD

ALGOMA UNIVERSITY

1520 Queen St East, Sault Ste Marie, ON P6A 2G4
Telephone: (705) 949-2301
E-mail: info@algomau.ca
Internet: www.algomau.ca
Founded 1965 as an affiliate of Laurentian Univ. in Sudbury, present name and status 2008
State control
Language of instruction: English
Academic year: September to April
Pres.: Dr RICHARD MYERS
Academic Dean: Dr ARTHUR H. PERLINI
Registrar: DAVID MARASCO
Library of 124,849 vols, 436,900 ebooks, 129,434 ejournals
Number of teachers: 57
Number of students: 1,253

ATHABASCA UNIVERSITY

1 University Dr., Athabasca, AB T9S 3A3
Telephone: (780) 675-6100
Internet: www.athabascau.ca
Founded 1970
provincial control
Language of instruction: English
Open univ. providing undergraduate and Masters-level courses for adult, non-residential students, with emphasis on distance and online education
Chair., Governing Ccl: JOY ROMERO
Pres.: Dr FRITS PANNEKOEK (acting)
Vice-Pres. for Academic Affairs: Dr MARGARET HAUGHE
Vice-Pres. for Advancement: Dr LORI VAN-ROOIZEN
Registrar: JIM DARCY
Librarian: S. SCHAFER
Library of 143,261
Number of teachers: 258
Number of students: 31,250
Publications: *Aurora* (interviews with leading thinkers and writers), *Electronic Journal of Sociology*, *Globalization*, *IRRODDL* (research for Open and Distance Learning), *Radical Pedagogy*, *Sport and the Human Animal*, *Theory and Science*, *Trumpeter*

BISHOP'S UNIVERSITY

Sherbrooke, QC J1M 1Z7
Telephone: (819) 822-9600
E-mail: recruitment@ubishops.ca
Internet: www.ubishops.ca
Founded 1843, constituted a univ. by Royal Charter 1853
Academic year: September to May
Language of instruction: English
Chancellor: SCOTT GRIFFIN
Prin.: MICHAEL GOLDBLOOM
Vice-Prin.: Dr MICHAEL CHILDS
Vice-Prin. for Admin. and Finance: HÉLÈNE ST-AMAND
Registrar and Sec. Gen.: RUTH SHEERAN
Librarian: WENDY DURRANT
Dean of Student Affairs: BRUCE STEVENSON
Number of teachers: 109 (full-time)
Number of students: 2,850
Publication: *Journal of Eastern Township Studies* (2 a year)

DEANS

School of Arts and Sciences: Dr JAMIE CROOKS
School of Education: Dr CATHERINE BEAUCHAMP
Williams School of Business: Dr STEVE HARVEY

BRANDON UNIVERSITY

270 18th St, Brandon, MB R7A 6A9
Telephone: (204) 728-9520
E-mail: president@brandonu.ca
Internet: www.brandonu.ca
Founded 1899, gained full autonomy July 1967
public control
Language of instruction: English
Academic year: September to April
Chancellor: MICHAEL DECTER
Pres.: Dr DEBORAH POFF
Vice-Pres. for Academic and Research: Dr DEAN CARE (acting)
Vice-Pres. for Admin. and Finance: SCOTT J. B. LAMONT
Dean for Students: DAVID ROWLAND
Univ. Registrar: GREG COATES (acting)
Univ. Librarian: CHRIS HURST (acting)
Number of teachers: 208 (full- and part-time)
Number of students: 3,000 (full- and part-time)
Publications: *Canadian Journal of Native Studies*, *Journal of Rural and Community Development*

DEANS

Faculty of Arts: Dr BRUCE STRANG
Faculty of Education: Dr GLENN COCKERLINE (acting)
Faculty of Health Studies: Dr NOREEN EK (acting)
Faculty of Music: Dr MICHAEL KIM
Faculty of Science: Dr PHILLIP GOERNERT (acting)

BROCK UNIVERSITY

500 Glenridge Ave, St Catharines, ON L2S 3A1
Telephone: (905) 688-5550
E-mail: regist@brocku.ca
Internet: www.brocku.ca
Founded 1964
provincial control
Academic year: September to April
Language of instruction: English
Chancellor: NED GOODMAN
Pres. and Vice-Chancellor: JACK LIGHTSTONE
Provost and Vice-Pres. for Academics: MURRAY KNUTTILA
Vice-Pres. for Admin.: STEVEN PILLAR
Registrar: BARB DAVIS
Librarian: BARBARA MCDONALD
Library of 2,194,400 vols
Number of teachers: 583
Number of students: 17,877
Publications: *View Book* (1 a year), *Surgite* (2 a year)

DEANS

Faculty of Applied Health Sciences: JOANNE MACLEAN
Faculty of Business: PHILIP KITCHEN
Faculty of Education: FOINA BLAIKIE
Faculty of Graduate Studies: MARILYN ROSE
Faculty of Mathematics and Science: RICK CHEEL
Faculty of Social Sciences: THOMAS DUNK

CAPE BRETON UNIVERSITY

POB 5300, 1250 Grand Lake Rd, Sydney, NS B1P 6L2
Telephone: (902) 539-5300
E-mail: welcome@capebretonu.ca
Internet: www.cbu.ca
Founded 1974
State control
Language of instruction: English
Academic year: September to April
Depts of anthropology/sociology, biology, chemistry, communication, community studies, education, engineering, finance and information management, health sciences and emergency management, history and culture, indigenous studies, languages and letters, mathematics, nursing, organizational management, philosophy and religious studies, physics and geology, political science, psychology
Chancellor: ANNETTE VERSCHUREN
Pres. and Vice-Chancellor: Dr DAVID WHEELER
Vice-Pres. for Academic and Professional Studies and Provost: Dr ROBERT BAILEY

Vice-Pres. for Int. and Aboriginal Affairs: GORDON MACINNIS
Vice-Pres. for External Affairs: Dr KEITH BROWN
Vice-Pres. for Student Services and Registrar: ALEXIS MANLEY
Dean of Research and Graduate Studies: Dr DALE KEEFE
Library of 532,290 vols, 800 periodicals
Number of teachers: 153
Number of students: 3,600

DEANS

School of Arts and Social Sciences: Dr ARJA VAINIO-MATTILA
School of Professional Studies: Dr ROBERT BAILEY
School of Science and Technology: Dr DAVID MCCORQUODALE
Shannon School of Business Studies: Dr DAVID RAE

PROFESSORS

School of Arts and Social Sciences:
- BROADHEAD, L. A., Political Science
- JOHNSON, D., Political Science
- MACKINNON, R., Community Studies
- MOLLOY, A., Political Science
- MULLAN, D., History
- REYNOLDS, A., History
- ROLLS, J., Communication
- STEWART, R. S., Philosophy

School of Science and Technology:
- BRITTEN, A., Chemistry
- MACINTYRE, P., Psychology
- MACLELLAN, E., Engineering
- MCCANN, S., Psychology
- MCCORQUODALE, D., Biology
- MIADONYE, A., Chemistry
- TANCHAK, M., Biology

Shannon School of Business:
- JOHNSTONE, H., Accounting
- SCOTT, J., Organization Management

ATTACHED RESEARCH INSTITUTES

The mailing address is that of the University

Beaton Institute: e-mail beaton@cbu.ca; repository of Cape Breton social, economic, political and cultural history; Dir WENDY ROBICHEAU.

Children's Rights Centre: e-mail childrens_rights@cbu.ca; f. 1996; conducts research and provides public education on children's rights; monitors implementation of UN Children's Rights Convention in Nova Scotia and Canada; Co-Dir Prof. KATHERINE COVELL; Co-Dir Prof. BRIAN HOWE.

Institute for Integrative Science and Health: f. 1996; provides support, training, policy advice and research in community economic devt; Dir Dr GERTRUDE MACINTYRE

CARLETON UNIVERSITY

1125 Colonel By Dr., Ottawa, ON K1S 5B6
Telephone: (613) 520-2600
E-mail: infocarleton@carleton.ca
Internet: www.carleton.ca
Founded 1942
provincial control
Language of instruction: English
Academic year: September to May
Chancellor: MARC GARNEAU
Pres. and Vice-Chancellor: Dr RICHARD VAN LOON
Vice-Pres. for Academic Affairs and Provost: ALAN HARRISON
Vice-Pres. for Advancement: LUCINDA BOUCHER
Vice-Pres. for Finance and Admin.: DUNCAN WATT
Vice-Pres. for Research: FERIDUN HAMDULLAHPUR
Asst Vice-Pres. for Devt and Alumni: SERGE ARPIN
Asst Vice-Pres. for Enrolment Management: SUSAN GOTTHEIL
Librarian: MARTIN FOSS
Library: see under Libraries and Archives
Number of teachers: 786
Number of students: 22,535
Publications: *Research and Works* (4 a year), *The President's Report* (1 a year)

DEANS

Faculty of Arts and Social Science: MICHAEL SMITH
Faculty of Engineering: SAMI MAHMOUD
Faculty of Public Affairs and Management: KATHERINE GRAHAM
Faculty of Science: JEAN-GUY GODIN
Faculty of Graduate Studies and Research: ROGER BLOCKLEY

CHAIRS AND DIRECTORS

Faculty of Arts and Social Science (330 Paterson Hall, 1125 Colonel By Drive, Ottawa, ON K1S 5B6; tel. (613) 520-2355; internet www.carleton.ca/fass):
- Canadian Studies: F. ROCHER
- English Language and Literature: R. HOLTON
- Environmental Studies: N. DOUBLEDAY
- French: C. DOUTRELEPONT
- Geography: S. DALBY
- History: E. P. FITZGERALD
- Humanities: S. WILSON
- Interdisciplinary Studies: K. ARNUP
- Philosophy: J. DRYDYK
- Psychology: J. LOGAN (acting)
- Sociology and Anthropology: C. GORDON
- Studies in Art and Culture: B. GILLIINGHAM (acting)
- Women's Studies: P. RANKIN
- Centre for Applied Language Studies: I. PRINGLE

Faculty of Engineering (3010 Minto Centre, 1125 Colonel By Drive, Ottawa, ON K1S 5B6; tel. (613) 520-5790; internet www.carleton.ca/engineeringdesign):
- Architecture: G. HAIDER
- Civil and Environmental Engineering: G. HARTLEY (acting)
- Electronics: L. ROY
- Industrial Design: L. FRANKEL
- Mechanical and Aerospace Engineering: R. BELL
- Systems and Computer Engineering: R. GOUBRAN

Faculty of Public Affairs and Management (D391 Loeb Building, 1125 Colonel By Drive, Ottawa, ON K1S 5B6; tel. (613) 520-3741; e-mail melanie_thompson@carleton.ca; internet www.carleton.ca/pam):
- Business: V. KUMAR
- Criminology and Criminal Justice: B. WRIGHT
- Economics: A. RITTER
- European and Russian Studies: P. DUTKIEWICZ
- International Affairs: F. HAMPSON
- Journalism and Communication: C. DORNAN
- Law: C. SWAN
- Political Economy: R. MAHON
- Political Science: C. BROWN
- Public Administration: L. PAL
- Social Work: C. LUNDY

Faculty of Science (3239 Herzberg Laboratories, 1125 Colonel By Drive, Ottawa, ON K1S 5B6; tel. (613) 520-4388; e-mail odscience@ccs.carleton.ca; internet www.carleton.ca/science):
- Biochemistry: M. SMITH
- Biology: J. CHEETHAM
- Chemistry: G. BUCHANAN
- Computational Sciences: L. COPLEY
- Computer Science: D. HOWE
- Earth Sciences: C. SCHROEDER-ADAMS
- Environmental Science: D. WIGFIELD
- Geography: S. DALBY
- Integrated Science Studies: I. MUNRO
- Mathematics and Statistics: C. GARNER
- Physics: P. KALYNDAK
- Psychology: J. LOGAN

CONCORDIA UNIVERSITY

Sir George Williams Campus, 1455 de Maisonneuve blvd West, Montréal, QC H3G 1M8
Loyola Campus, 7141 Sherbrooke St West, Montréal, QC H4B 1R6
Telephone: (514) 848-2424
Internet: www.concordia.ca
Founded 1974 by merger of Sir George Williams Univ. (f. 1948) and Loyola College (inc. 1899)
provincial control
Language of instruction: English
Academic year: May to April
Chancellor and Univ. Secretariat: ERIC MOLSON
Pres. and Vice-Chancellor: Prof. FREDERICK H. LOWY
Provost: DAVID GRAHAM
Vice-Provost for Academic Affairs: ROBERT M. ROY
Vice-Provost for Academic Relations: RAMA BHAT
Vice-Provost for Teaching and Learning: OLLIVIER DYENS
Exec. Dir for Office of the Pres.: GARY MILTON
Registrar: LINDA HEALEY
Dir for Libraries: GERALD BEASLEY
Library: see under Libraries and Archives
Number of teachers: 1,837 (884 full-time, 953 part-time)
Number of students: 31,175
Publications: *Canadian Jewish Studies* (1 a year), *Canadian Journal of Irish Studies* (2 a year), *Canadian Journal of Research in Early Childhood Education* (2 a year), *Journal of Canadian Art History / Annales d'Histoire de L'art Canadien* (2 a year), *Journal of Religion and Culture* (1 a year), *Revue de l'Institut Simone de Beauvoir Institute Review* (1 a year)

DEANS

Faculty of Arts and Science: BRIAN LEWIS
Faculty of Engineering and Computer Science: ROBIN DREW
Faculty of Fine Arts: CATHERINE WILD
John Molson School of Business: SANJAY SHARMA

DALHOUSIE UNIVERSITY

Halifax, NS B3H 4R2
Telephone: (902) 494-2450
E-mail: registrar@dal.ca
Internet: www.dal.ca
Founded 1818, merged with Technical Univ. of Nova Scotia 1997
Private control
Language of instruction: English
Academic year: September to August
Chancellor: Dr FRED FOUNTAIN
Pres. and Vice-Chancellor: Dr THOMAS D. TRAVES
Vice-Pres. for Academic and Provost: Dr CAROLYN WATTERS
Vice-Pres. for External: FLOYD DYKEMAN
Vice-Pres. for Finance and Admin: KEN BURT
Vice-Pres. for Research: Dr MARTHA CRAGO
Vice-Pres. for Student Services: BONNIE NEUMAN
Registrar: ASA KACHAN
Librarian: DONNA BOURNE-TYSON

Library: see under Libraries and Archives
Number of teachers: 1,131 (full-time and part-time)
Number of students: 18,268

DEANS

Faculty of Agriculture: Dr HAROLD COOK
Faculty of Architecture: CHRISTINE MACY
Faculty of Arts and Social Sciences: ROBERT SUMMERBY-MURRAY
Faculty of Computer Science: MICHAEL SHEPHERD
Faculty of Dentistry: THOMAS BORAN
Faculty of Engineering: JOSHUA LEON
Faculty of Graduate Studies: BERNARD BOUDREAU
Faculty of Health Professions: WILLIAM WEBSTER
Faculty of Law: KIMBERLEY BROOKS
Faculty of Management: PEGGY CUNNINGHAM
Faculty of Medicine: TOM MARRIE
Faculty of Science: CHRIS MOORE

PROFESSORS

Faculty of Architecture (tel. (902) 494-3971; e-mail arch.office@dal.ca; internet archplan.dal.ca):

CAVANAGH, E., Architecture
GRANT, J., Planning
KROEKER, R., Architecture
MACKAY-LYONS, B., Architecture
MACY, C., Architecture
PALERMO, F., Planning
POULTON, M., Planning
PROCOS, D., Architecture
WANZEL, J., Architecture

Faculty of Arts and Social Sciences (tel. (902) 494-1440; e-mail fass@dal.ca):

APOSTLE, R., Sociology and Social Anthropology
AUCOIN, P. C., Political Science
BAKVIS, H., Political Science
BARKER, W., English
BARKOW, J. H., Sociology and Social Anthropology
BAXTER, J., English
BAYLIS, F., Philosophy
BEDNARSKI, H. E., French
BINKLEY, M. E., Sociology and Social Anthropology
BOARDMAN, R., Political Science
BURNS, S., Philosophy
CAMPBELL, R. M., Philosophy
CROWLEY, J. E., History
CURRAN, J. V., German (Chair.)
DAVIS, J., Political Science
DE MEO, P., French
DIEPEVEEN, L. P., English
FURROW, M. M., English
HANKEY, W., Classics (King's)
HANLON, G., History
HARVEY, F., Political Science
HUEBERT, R., English
KIRK, J. M., Spanish
LI, T. J., Sociology and Social Anthropology
LUCKYJ, C., English
MARTIN, R., Philosophy
MIDDLEMISS, D., Political Science
NEVILLE, C., History (Chair.)
OORE, I., French
OVERTON, D. R., Theatre
PARPART, J., International Development Studies
PEREIRA, N. G. O., History and Russian
PERINA, P., Theatre
RUNTE, H. R., French
SCHOTCH, P., Philosophy
SCHROEDER, D., Music
SCHWARZ, H. G., German
SCULLY, S., Classics
SERVANT, G. W., Music
SHAW, T. W., Political Science
SHERWIN, S., Philosophy
SMITH, J., Political Science (Chair.)
STARNES, C. J., Classics (King's)
STONE, M. I., English
TETREAULT, R., English
THIESSEN, V., Sociology and Social Anthropology
TRAVES, T., History
VINCI, T., Philosophy
WAINWRIGHT, J. A., English and Canadian Studies
WATERSON, K., French

Faculty of Computer Science (tel. (902) 494-2093):

BODORIK, P.
BORWEIN, J.
BROWN, J. I.
COX, P.
FARRAG, A.
GENTLEMAN, M.
GRUNDKE, E.
HITCHCOCK, P.
JOST, A.
KEAST, P.
MACDONALD, N.
MILOS, E.
RAU-CHAPLIN, A.
RIORDAN, D.
SAMPALLI, S.
SCRIMGER, J. N.
SHEPHERD, M.
SLONIM, J.
WACH, G.
WATTERS, C. R.

Faculty of Dentistry (tel. (902) 494-2824):

LEE, J. M., Applied Oral Sciences
LONEY, R., Dental Clinical Sciences
PRECIOUS, D. S., Oral and Maxillofacial Science
PRICE, R. B. T., Dental Clinical Science
RYDING, H. A., Applied Oral Sciences (Acting Chair.)
SUTOW, E. J., Applied Oral Sciences

Faculty of Engineering (tel. (902) 494-3267; e-mail dean.engineering@dal.ca):

ALI, N. A., Civil Engineering
ALLEN, P., Mechanical Engineering
AL-TAWEEL, A., Chemical Engineering
AMYOTTE, P., Chemical Engineering
BASU, P., Mechanical Engineering
BEN-ABDALLAH, N., Biological Engineering (Head)
CADA, M., Electrical and Computer Engineering
CALEY, W. F., Mining and Metallurgical Engineering
CHEN, Z., Electrical and Computer Engineering
CHUANG, J. M., Mechanical Engineering
EL-HAWARY, M., Electrical and Computer Engineering
EL-MASRY, E., Electrical and Computer Engineering (Head)
FELS, M., Chemical Engineering
FENTON, G., Engineering Mathematics
GHALY, A., Biological Engineering
GILL, T., Food Science and Technology
GREGSON, P., Electrical and Computer Engineering
GUNN, E., Industrial Engineering
GUPTA, Y., Chemical Engineering (Head)
HUGHES, F. L., Electrical and Computer Engineering
ISLAM, M., Civil Engineering
KALAMKAROV, A., Mechanical Engineering
KEMBER, G., Engineering Mathematics
KIPOUROS, G., Mining and Metallurgical Engineering
KUJATH, M., Mechanical Engineering
MILITZER, J., Mechanical Engineering
PAULSON, A. T., Food Science and Technology
PEGG, M., Chemical Engineering
PHILLIPS, W., Engineering Mathematics (Head)
RAHMAN, M., Engineering Mathematics
ROBERTSON, W., Engineering Mathematics
ROCKWELL, M., Mining and Metallurgical Engineering
SANDBLOM, C., Industrial Engineering
SATISH, M., Civil Engineering
SPEERS, R. A., Food Science and Technology (Head)
TROTTIER, J.-F., Civil Engineering
UGURSAL, M., Mechanical Engineering
WATTS, K., Biological and Mechanical Engineering
YEMENIDJIAN, N., Mining and Metallurgical Engineering (Head)
ZOU, D. H., Mining and Metallurgical Engineering

Faculty of Health Professions (tel. (902) 494-3327; internet healthprofessions.dal.ca):

School of Health and Human Performance:

HOLT, L. E.
LYONS, R. F.
MALONEY, T.
SINGLETON, J.
UNRUH, A.

School of Health Services Administration:

MCINTYRE, L.
NESTMAN, L.
RATHWELL, T. (Dir)

School of Nursing:

BUTLER, L. (Dir)
DOWNE-WAMBOLDT, B. (Dir)
KEDDY, B. A.

School of Occupational Therapy:

TOWNSEND, E. (Dir)

College of Pharmacy:

SKETRIS, I.
YEUNG, P. K. F.

School of Physiotherapy:

KOZEY, C. L.
MAKRIDES, L. (Dir)
TURNBULL, G. I.

Maritime School of Social Work:

DIVINE, D.
WIEN, F. C.

Faculty of Law (tel. (902) 494-3495; e-mail lawinfo@dal.ca):

ARCHIBALD, B.
BLACK, V.
DEVLIN, R.
KAISER, H. A.
KINDRED, H. M.
MCCONNELL, M. L.
MACKAY, A. W.
POTHIER, D. L.
THOMAS, P.
THOMPSON, D. A. R.
THORNHILL, E. M. A.
VANDERZWAGG, D.
WOODMAN, F. L.
YOGIS, J. A.

Faculty of Management (tel. (902) 494-2582; internet www.management.dal.ca):

School of Business Administration:

BROOKS, M. R.
CONRAD, J.
DUFFY, J.
FOOLADI, I.
MACLEAN, L. C.
MCNIVEN, J. D.
MEALIEA, L. W.
OPPONG, A.
ROSSON, P.
SANKAR, Y.
SCHELLINCK, D. A.

School of Public Administration:

AUCOIN, P. C.
BAKVIS, H.
BROWN, M. P.
MCNIVEN, J. D.
SIDDIQ, F.
SULLIVAN, K.
TRAVES, T.

School of Resource and Environmental Studies:

COHEN, F. G.
CÔTÉ, R.
DUINKER, P. (Dir)
WILLISON, J. H.

Faculty of Medicine (tel. (902) 494-6592; e-mail dean.medicine@dal.ca; internet www .medicine.dal.ca):

ALDA, H., Psychiatry
ALEXANDER, D., Surgery
ALLEN, A. C., Paediatrics, Obstetrics and Gynaecology
ANDERSON, D. R., Medicine, Community Health and Epidemiology
ANDERSON, P. A., Urology
ANDERSON, R., Microbiology and Immunology
ARMSON, A., Obstetrics and Gynaecology
ATTIA, E., Surgery
BARNES, S., Physiology and Biophysics, Ophthalmology
BASKETT, T., Obstetrics and Gynaecology
BAYLIS, F., Bioethics
BENSTED, T., Medicine
BITTER-SUERMANN, H., Surgery
BLAY, J., Pharmacology
BONJER, H. J., Surgery
BORTOLUSSI, R., Paediatrics
BRECKENRIDGE, W. C., Biochemistry
BROWN, M. G., Community Health and Epidemiology
BRYSON, S., Paediatrics
BYERS, D., Paediatrics
CAMERON, I., Family Medicine
CAMFIELD, C., Paediatrics
CAMFIELD, P. R., Paediatrics
CASSON, A., Surgery and Pathology
CHAUHAN, B., Ophthalmology, Physiology and Biophysics
CLEMENTS, J. C., Biomedical Engineering
COHEN, M. M., Paediatrics
CONNOLLY, J., Medicine
COOK, H. W., Paediatrics
COONAN, T., Anaesthesia (Head)
COWDEN, E., Medicine (Head)
COX, J., Medicine
CROCKER, J. F. S., Paediatrics
CROLL, R. P., Physiology and Biophysics
CRUESS, A. F., Ophthalmology (Chair.)
CURRIE, R. W., Anatomy and Neurobiology
DANIELS, C., Diagnostic Radiology
DEVITT, H., Anaesthesia
DOANE, B. K., Psychiatry
DOOLEY, J., Paediatrics
DOOLITTLE, W. F., Biochemistry
DOWNIE, J. W., Pharmacology
DUCHARME, J., Emergency Medicine
DUNCAN, R., Microbiology and Immunology
DUNPHY, B., Obstetrics and Gynaecology
FARRELL, S., Obstetrics and Gynaecology
FERNANDEZ, L. A. V., Medicine
FERRIER, G. R., Pharmacology
FINE, A., Physiology and Biophysics
FINLEY, G. A., Anaesthesia
FINLEY, J. P., Paediatrics
FORWARD, K., Pathology, Medicine, Microbiology and Immunology
FOX, R. A., Medicine
FRANK, B. W., Division of Medical Education
FRENCH, A., Biomedical Engineering, Physiology and Biophysics
GAJEWSKI, J., Urology
GARDNER, M. J., Medicine
GASS, D. A., Family Medicine
GOLDBLOOM, R., Paediatrics
GRAVES, G., Obstetrics and Gynaecology (Head)
GRAY, M. W., Biochemistry (Head)
GREER, W., Pathology
GREGSON, P., Biomedical Engineering
GROSS, M., Surgery
GRUNFIELD, E., Medicine, Community Health and Epidemiology
GUERNSEY, D. L., Pathology, Physiology, Biophysics and Ophthalmology
HAASE, D. A., Medicine
HALL, R., Anaesthesia and Pharmacology
HALPERIN, S., Paediatrics
HANDA, S. P., Medicine
HANLY, J. G., Medicine
HAYES, V., Family Medicine
HEATHCOTE, J. G., Ophthalmology and Pathology (Head)
HIRSCH, D., Medicine and Psychiatry
HOLNESS, R. O., Surgery
HOPKINS, D. A., Anatomy and Neurobiology
HORACEK, B. M., Physiology, Biophysics and Biomedical Engineering
HORACKOVA, M., Physiology and Biophysics
HOSKIN, D. W., Microbiology, Immunology, and Pathology
HOWLETT, S., Pharmacology
HUGENHOLZ, H., Surgery
HUNG, O. R., Anaesthesia and Pharmacology
HYNDMAN, J. C., Surgery
IMRIE, D., Anaesthesia
ISA, N. N., Obstetrics and Gynaecology
ISSEKUTZ, A., Paediatrics and Pathology
ISSEKUTZ, T. B., Paediatrics, Microbiology, Immunology and Pathology
JAMIESON, C. G., Surgery
JOHNSTON, B. L., Medicine, Community Health and Epidemiology
JOHNSTON, G. C., Microbiology and Immunology (Head)
JOHNSTONE, D. E., Medicine
KAZIMIRSKI, J., Division of Medical Education
KELLS, C., Medicine
KELLY, M., Pharmacology
KELLY, M. E., Ophthalmology
KENNY, N. P., Paediatrics and Bioethics and Division of Medical Education
KHANNA, V. N., Medicine
KIBERD, B. A., Medicine
KIRBY, R. L., Medicine and Biomedical Engineering
KISELY, S. R., Community Health and Epidemiology, Psychiatry
KRONICK, J., Paediatrics (Head)
KUTCHER, S., Psychiatry
LAIDLAW, T., Division of Medical Education
LANGILLE, D. B., Community Health and Epidemiology
LANGLEY, G. R., Medicine
LAROCHE, G. R., Ophthalmology
LAWEN, J. G., Urology
LAZIER, C. B., Biochemistry
LEBLANC, R. P., Ophthalmology
LEBRON, G., Diagnostic Radiology
LEE, M., Applied Oral Sciences and Biomedical Engineering
LEE, P. W. K., Microbiology, Immunology and Pathology
LEE, T., Microbiology, Immunology and Pathology
LEIGHTON, A. H., Psychiatry
LESLIE, R. A., Anatomy, Neurobiology and Psychiatry (Head)
LO, C. D., Diagnostic Radiology
LUDMAN, H., Paediatrics
MACAULAY, R., Pathology
MACDONALD, A. S., Surgery
MACDONALD, N., Paediatrics
MCDONALD, T. F., Physiology and Biophysics
MCGRATH, P. J., Paediatrics, Psychiatry and Psychology
MACLACHLAN, R., Family Medicine (Head)
MACLEAN, L. D., Community Health and Epidemiology
MCMILLAN, D., Paediatrics
MAHONY, D. E., Microbiology and Immunology
MALATJALIAN, D. A., Pathology and Medicine
MANN, K. V., Division of Medical Education
MANN, O. E., Medicine
MARSHALL, J., Pathology, Microbiology and Immunology
MASSOUD, E., Surgery
MAXNER, C. E., Medicine and Opthalmology
MEINERTZHAGEN, I., Psychology, Physiology and Biophysics
MENDEZ, I., Surgery
MILLER, R. A., Medicine
MILLER, R. M., Diagnostic Radiology
MORRIS, I. R., Anaesthesia
MORRIS, S. F., Surgery
MOSHER, D., Medicine
MOSS, M. A., Pathology (Head)
MURPHY, P., Physiology and Biophysics (Head)
MURRAY, T. J., Medicine
NACHTIGAL, M., Pharmacology
NASHON, B. J., Surgery and Urology
NASSAR, B. A., Pathology, Medicine and Urology
NEUMANN, P. E., Anatomy and Neurobiology
NORMAN, R., Urology (Head)
O'NEILL, B., Medicine, Community Health and Epidemiology
PADMOS, M., Medicine
PALMER, F. B. ST. C., Biochemistry (Head)
PARKHILL, W. S., Surgery
PELZER, D., Physiology and Biophysics and Division of Medical Education
PETERSON, T., Medicine and Pharmacology
PHILLIPS, S., Medicine
POLLAK, T., Medicine
POULIN, C., Community Health and Epidemiology
POWELL, C., Medicine
PURDY, R. A., Medicine
RAMSEY, M., Ophthalmology
RASMUSSON, D., Physiology and Biophysics
RENTON, K. W., Pharmacology
RO, H., Biochemistry
ROBERTSON, G. S., Pharmacology and Psychiatry
ROBERTSON, H. A., Pharmacology and Medicine (Head)
ROBINSON, K. S., Medicine
ROCKER, G., Medicine
ROCKWOOD, K., Medicine
ROWDEN, G., Pathology and Medicine
ROWE, R. C., Medicine
RUSAK, B., Psychiatry, Psychology and Pharmacology
RUTHERFORD, J., Anatomy and Neurobiology
SADLER, R. M., Medicine
SAWYNOK, J., Pharmacology
SCHLECH, W., Medicine
SEMBA, K., Anatomy and Neurobiology
SHUKLA, R. C., Anaesthesia
SIMPSON, D., Medicine
SINCLAIR, D., Emergency Medicine
SINGER, R. A., Biochemistry
STANISH, W. D., Surgery
STEWART, R. D., Anaesthesia, Emergency Medicine and Division of Medical Education
STEWART, S., Psychology
STOKES, A., Psychiatry (Acting Head)
STOLTZ, D. B., Microbiology and Immunology
STONE, R. M., Surgery (Head)
STROINK, G., Biomedical Engineering
STUTTARD, C., Microbiology and Immunology
SULLIVAN, J., Surgery
TURNBULL, G. K., Medicine
VAN DEN HOF, M., Obstetrics and Gynaecology
VANZANTEN, S., Medicine, Community Health and Epidemiology
VAUGHN, P., Division of Medical Education
WALLACE, C. J. A., Biochemistry
WALSH, N., Pathology
WARD, T., Paediatrics

WASSERSUG, R. J., Anatomy and Neurobiology
WEAVER, D., Medicine and Biomedical Engineering
WEST, M. L., Medicine
WILKINSON, M., Physiology, Biophysics, Obstetrics and Gynaecology
WOLF, H. K., Physiology and Biophysics
WRIGHT, J. R., Pathology, Surgery and Biomedical Engineering
YABSLEY, R. H., Surgery

Faculty of Science (tel. (902) 494-2373; e-mail science@dal.ca; internet www.science.dal.ca):

BARRESI, J., Psychology
BEAUMONT, C., Oceanography
BENTZEN, P., Biology and Oceanography
BOUDREAU, B. P., Oceanography (Chair.)
BOWEN, A. J., Oceanography
BOYD, R. J., Chemistry (Chair.)
BRADFIELD, F. M., Economics
BROWN, J., Mathematics and Statistics
BROWN, R. E., Psychology
BRYSON, S. E., Psychology
BURFORD, N., Chemistry
BURNELL, D. J., Chemistry
BURTON, P., Economics
CAMERON, T. S., Chemistry
CAMFIELD, C., Psychology
CHATT, A., Chemistry
CLARKE, D. B., Earth Sciences
CLEMENTS, J., Mathematics and Statistics
COLEY, A., Mathematics and Statistics, Physics
CONNOLLY, J. F., Psychology
COXON, J. A., Chemistry
CROLL, R. P., Biology
CULLEN, J., Oceanography
DAHN, J. R., Chemistry and Physics
DARVESH, S., Chemistry
DASGUPTA, S., Economics
DILCHER, K., Mathematics and Statistics
DUNHAM, P. J., Psychology
DUNLAP, R., Physics
FENTRESS, J. C., Biology
FIELD, C. A., Mathematics and Statistics
FINLEY, G. A., Psychology
FOURNIER, R. O., Oceanography
FREEDMAN, W., Biology (Chair.)
GABOR, G., Mathematics and Statistics
GELDART, D. J., Physics
GIBLING, M. R., Earth Sciences (Chair.)
GRANT, J., Oceanography
GREATBATCH, R., Oceanography and Physics
GRINDLEY, B., Chemistry
GUPTA, R. P., Mathematics and Statistics
HALL, B. K., Biology
HAMILTON, D. C., Mathematics and Statistics
HAY, A., Oceanography
HILL, P. S., Oceanography
HILLS, E. L., Biology
HUTCHINGS, J. A., Biology
ISCAN, T., Economics
IVERSON, S. J., Biology
JAMIESON, R. A., Earth Sciences
JERICHO, M. H., Physics
JOHNSTON, M. O., Biology
KAY-RAINING BIRD, E., Psychology
KEAST, P., Mathematics and Statistics (Chair.)
KLEIN, R. M., Psychology
KREUZER, H. J., Physics
KUSALIK, P. G., Chemistry
KWAK, J. C., Chemistry
LANE, P. A., Biology
LEE, R., Biology
LEONARD, M. L., Biology
LESSER, B., Economics (Chair.)
LEWIS, M., Oceanography
LOLORDO, V. M., Psychology
LOUDEN, K. E., Oceanography
LYONS, R., Psychology
MCGRATH, P. J., Psychology
MCMULLEN, P., Psychology
MACRAE, T., Biology
MEINERTZHAGEN, I. A., Psychology
MITCHELL, D. E., Psychology
MOORE, C. L., Psychology
MOORE, R. M., Oceanography
MORIARTY, K., Mathematics and Statistics, and Physics
MYERS, R. A., Biology
NOWAKOWSKI, R., Mathematics and Statistics
O'DOR, R. K., Biology
OSBERG, L. S., Economics
PACEY, P. D., Chemistry
PARÉ, R., Mathematics and Statistics
PATON, B. E., Physics
PATRIQUIN, D. G., Biology
PHILLIPS, D., Psychology
PHIPPS, S. A., Economics
PINCOCK, J. A., Chemistry
POHAJDAK, B., Biology
RAJORA, O. P., Biology
REYNOLDS, P. H., Earth Sciences and Physics
ROBERTSON, H., Psychology
RUDDICK, B., Oceanography
RUSAK, B., Psychology and Psychiatry
SCHEIBLING, R., Biology
SCOTT, D., Earth Sciences
SEMBA, K., Psychology
SHAW, S., Psychology
STEWART, S., Psychology
STROINK, G., Physics (Chair.)
SUTHERLAND, W. R., Mathematics and Statistics
TAN, K. K., Mathematics and Statistics
TAYLOR, K., Mathematics and Statistics
THOMPSON, K., Mathematics and Statistics, and Oceanography
WACH, G. D., Earth Sciences
WALDE, S., Biology
WEAVER, D. F., Chemistry and Division of Neurology
WENTZELL, P. D., Chemistry
WHITE, M. A., Chemistry and Physics
WHITEHEAD, H., Biology
WILLISON, J. H. M., Biology and Resource, Environmental Studies
WOOD, R. J., Mathematics and Statistics
WRIGHT, J. M., Biology
XU, K., Economics
ZWANZIGER, J. W., Chemistry and Physics

Henson College of Continuing Education (tel. (902) 494-2526; e-mail henson-info@dal.ca):

BENOIT, J.
FRASER, L.
NOVACK, J.

DOMINICAN COLLEGE OF PHILOSOPHY AND THEOLOGY

96 Empress Ave, Ottawa, ON K1R 7G3
Telephone: (613) 233-5696
E-mail: info@collegedominicain.ca
Internet: www.collegedominicain.ca

Founded 1909 as 'Studium Generale' of Order of Friars Preachers in Canada, current name adopted 1967
Private control
Languages of instruction: English, French
Academic year: September to April

Chancellor: ANDRÉ DESCÔTEAUX
Pres. and Regent of Studies: MAXIME ALLARD
Vice-Pres.: FRANCIS PEDDLE
Vice-Pres.: JEAN-FRANÇOIS MÉTHOT
Registrar: HERVÉ TREMBLAY
Librarian: PHILIP FRASER

Library of 120,000 vols, 500 periodicals
Number of teachers: 25
Number of students: 635 (127 full-time, 508 part-time)

DEANS

Faculty of Philosophy: EDUARDO ANDÚJAR
Faculty of Theology: MICHEL GOURGUES
Institute of Pastoral Theology: DANIEL CADRIN (Dir)

LAKEHEAD UNIVERSITY

955 Oliver Rd, Thunder Bay, ON P7B 5E1
Telephone: (807) 343-8110
E-mail: commun@lakeheadu.ca
Internet: www.lakeheadu.ca

Founded 1965, fmrly Lakehead College of Arts, Science and Technology, 1956, and Lakehead Technical Institute, 1946
Academic year: September to April

Chancellor: ARTHUR MAURO
Pres.: Dr BRIAN J.R. STEVENSON
Provost and Vice-Pres. for Academic Affairs: Dr MOIRA MCPHERSON
Vice-Pres. for Admin. and Finance: MICHAEL PAWLOWSKI
Vice-Pres. for Student Affairs: MARIAN RYKS-SZELEKOVSZKY
Vice-Pres. for Research: Dr RUI WANG
Registrar: BRENDA WINTER
Librarian: ANNE DEIGHTON

Number of teachers: 240
Number of students: 8,000

DEANS

Faculty of Business Administration: Dr BAHRAM DADGOSTAR
Faculty of Education: Dr JOHN O'MEARA
Faculty of Engineering: Dr HENRI T. SALIBA
Faculty of Graduate Studies: Dr PHILIP HICKS (acting)
Faculty of Health and Behavioural Sciences: Dr LORI LIVINGSTON
Faculty of Medicine: Dr ROGER STRASSER
Faculty of Natural Resource Management: Dr ULF RUNESSON
Faculty of Science and Environmental Studies: Dr ANDREW P. DEAN
Faculty of Social Sciences and Humanities: Dr GILLIAN SIDDALL

LAURENTIAN UNIVERSITY OF SUDBURY

935 Ramsey Lake Rd, Sudbury, ON P3E 2C6
Telephone: (705) 675-1151
E-mail: admission@laurentian.ca
Internet: www.laurentian.ca

Founded 1960
provincially assisted, non-denominational
Languages of instruction: French, English(-certain depts offer parallel courses in both languages)
Academic year: September to April

Depts of anthropology, behavioural neuroscience, biology, classical studies, commerce and administration, earth science, education (English), education (French), English, environmental earth science, ethics studies, film studies, folklore, geography, history, liberal science, mathematics and computer science, midwifery, modern languages and literatures, music, native human services, native studies, nursing, philosophy, physics and astronomy, political science, psychology, radiation therapy, religious studies, social work, sociology, sport psychology, sports administration

Pres.: JUDITH WOODSWORTH
Vice-Pres. for Admin.: ROBERT F. BOURGEOIS
Academic Vice-Pres. for Anglophone Affairs: SUSAN SILVERTON
Academic Vice-Pres. for Francophone Affairs: HARLEY D'ENTREMONT
Registrar: RON SMITH
Dir of Library: LIONEL BONIN
Dir for Centre for Continuing Education: DENIS MAYER
Dir for Div. of Physical Education: ROGER COUTURE

Dir for Graduate Studies and Research: PAUL COLILLI
Number of teachers: 377 (full-time)
Number of students: 9,100

DEANS

Humanities and Social Sciences: JOHN ISBISTER
Management: HUGUETTE BLANCO
Professional Schools: ANNE-MARIE MAWHINEY
Sciences and Engineering: PATRICE SAWYER

CONSTITUENT INSTITUTIONS

Collège Universitaire de Hearst: Hearst, ON P0L 1N0; internet www.univhearst.edu; f. 1952; Rector R. TREMBLAY; Registrar J. DOUCET.

FEDERATED UNIVERSITIES

Huntington University: Ramsey Lake Rd, Sudbury, ON P3E 2C6; f. 1960; related to United Church of Canada; Pres.-Principal KEVIN MCCORMICK; Registrar A. HOOD.

Thorneloe University: 935 Ramsey Lake Rd, Sudbury, ON P3E 2C6; tel. (705) 673-1730; e-mail info@thorneloe.ca; internet www.thorneloe.ca; Pres. R. DERRENBACKER; Registrar I. MACLENNAN.

University of Sudbury: Ramsey Lake Rd, Sudbury, ON P3E 2C6; e-mail usudburyalumni@usudbury.ca; f. 1957; conducted by the Jesuit Fathers; Pres. ANDRII KRAWCHUK; Registrar L. BEAUPRÉ

McGILL UNIVERSITY

845 Sherbrooke St W, Montréal, QC H3A 2T5
Telephone: (514) 398-4455
Internet: www.mcgill.ca
Founded 1821 by legacy of Hon. James McGill
provincial control
Language of instruction: English
Academic year: September to May (2 terms)
Chancellor: H. ARNOLD STEINBERG
Prin. and Vice-Chancellor: HEATHER MUNROE-BLUM
Provost: Prof. ANTHONY C. MASI
Deputy Provost for Student Life and Learning: Prof. MORTON J. MENDELSON
Vice-Prin. for Admin. and Finance: MICHAEL L. RICHARDS
Vice-Prin. for Devt and Alumni Relations: MARC WEINSTEIN
Vice-Prin. for Health Affairs: Dr RICHARD I. LEVIN
Vice-Prin. for Research and Int. Relations: Prof. RIMA ROZEN
Exec. Head of Public Affairs: VAUGHAN DOWIE
Sec. Gen.: STEPHEN STROPLE
Registrar and Exec. Dir for Enrolment Services: KATHLEEN MASSEY
Dir for Libraries: DIANE KOEN
Library: see under Libraries and Archives
Number of teachers: 1,627
Number of students: 35,300
Publications: *McGill Journal of Education* (3 a year), *McGill Journal of Medicine* (2 a year), *McGill Journal of Middle East Studies* (1 a year), *McGill Reporter* (6 a year), *McGill University Health Centre, The McGill Journal of Political Economy* (1 a year), *The McGill Journal of Political Studies* (1 a year), *The McGill Law Journal* (4 a year), *MUHC Ensemble*

DEANS

Centre for Continuing Education: Dr JUDITH POTTER
Desautels Faculty of Management: Prof. PETER TODD
Faculty of Agricultural and Environmental Sciences: Prof. CHANDRA A. MADRAMOOTOO
Faculty of Arts: Prof. CHRISTOPHER P. MANFREDI
Faculty of Dentistry: Dr PAUL ALLISON
Faculty of Education: Dr HÉLÈNE PERRAULT
Faculty of Engineering: CHRISTOPHE PIERRE
Faculty of Law: Prof. DANIEL JUTRAS
Faculty of Medicine: Dr RICHARD I. LEVIN
Faculty of Religious Studies: Dr ELLEN AITKEN
Faculty of Science: MARTIN GRANT
Graduate and Postdoctoral Studies: MARTIN KREISWIRTH
Schulich School of Music: DON MCLEAN

INCORPORATED COLLEGES AND CAMPUSES

Macdonald Campus: 21111 Lakeshore Rd, Ste Anne de Bellevue, QC H9X 3V9; e-mail info.macdonald@mcgill.ca.

Royal Victoria College: Montréal; Warden F. TRACY.

AFFILIATED BODIES

Montreal Diocesan Theological College: 3473 University St, Montréal, QC H3A 2A8; e-mail info@dio-mdtc.ca; Prin. J. M. SIMONS.

Presbyterian College: 3495 University St, Montréal, QC H3A 2A8; Prin. J. VISSERS.

United Theological College: 3521 University St, Montréal, QC H3A 2A9; e-mail admin@utc.ca; Prin. P. JOUDREY

McMASTER UNIVERSITY

Hamilton, ON L8S 4L8
Telephone: (905) 525-9140
E-mail: agrob@mcmaster.ca
Internet: www.mcmaster.ca
Founded 1887 in Toronto, present location 1930
Private control
Language of instruction: English
Academic year: September to April
Chancellor: Dr L. R. WILSON
Pres. and Vice-Chancellor: Dr PATRICK DEANE
Provost and Vice-Pres. for Academic Affairs: Dr ILENE BUSCH-VISHNIAC
Vice-Pres. for Admin.: ROGER COULDREY
Vice-Pres. for Health Sciences: Dr JOHN KELTON
Vice-Pres. for Research and Int. Affairs: Dr MO ELBESTAWI
Vice-Pres. for Univ. Advancement: MARY WILLIAMS
Registrar: MELISSA POOL (acting)
Librarian: JEFF TRZECIAK
Library: see under Libraries and Archives
Number of teachers: 4,287
Number of students: 26,170
Publications: *Journal of the Bertrand Russell Archives* (4 a year), *McMaster University Library Research News, The Research Bulletin* (12 a year)

DEANS

Faculty of Business: Dr ROBERT MCNUTT (acting)
Faculty of Engineering: Dr DAVID WILKINSON
Faculty of Health Sciences: Dr JOHN KELTON
Faculty of Humanities: Dr SUZANNE CROSTA
Faculty of Science: Dr JOHN CAPONE
Faculty of Social Sciences: Dr CHARLOTTE YATES
Graduate Studies: Dr ALLISON SEKULER
Principal of the Divinity College: Dr STANLEY PORTER

PROFESSORS

Faculty of Engineering:

BAETZ, B. W., Civil Engineering
BEREZIN, A. A., Engineering Physics
CAPSON, D. W., Electrical and Computer Engineering
CASSIDY, D. T., Engineering Physics
CHANG, J. S., Engineering Physics
DEEN, M. J., Electrical and Computer Engineering
DICKSON, J. M., Chemical Engineering
DRYSDALE, R. G., Civil Engineering
ELBESTAWI, M. A., Mechanical Engineering
FRANEK, F., Computing and Software
GARLAND, W. J., Engineering Physics
GERSHMAN, A. B., Electrical and Computer Engineering
GHOBARAH, A., Civil Engineering
HAUGEN, H., Engineering Physics
HRYMAK, A. N., Chemical Engineering
IRONS, G. A., Materials Science and Engineering
JANICKI, R., Computing and Software
JESSOP, P. E., Engineering Physics
JOHARI, G. P., Materials Science and Engineering
KITAI, A. H., Engineering Physics
KLEIMAN, R. N., Engineering Physics
KREYMAN, K., Computing and Software
LOUTFY, R., Chemical Engineering
LUO, Z.-Q., Electrical and Computing Engineering
LUXAT, J. C., Engineering Physics
MACGREGOR, J. F., Chemical Engineering
MAIBAUM, T., Computing and Software
MARLIN, T. E., Chemical Engineering
MASCHER, P., Engineering Physics
PARNAS, D. L., Computing and Software
PELTON, R. H., Chemical Engineering
PETRIC, A., Materials Science and Engineering
PIETRUSZCZAK, S., Civil Engineering
PRESTON, J. S., Engineering Physics
QIAO, S., Computing and Software
REILLY, J. P., Electrical and Computer Engineering
SIVAKUMARAN, K. S., Civil Engineering
SMITH, P. M., Electrical and Computer Engineering
STOLLE, D. F. E., Civil Engineering
SZABADOS, B., Electrical and Computer Engineering
SZYMANSKI, T. H., Electrical and Computer Engineering
TAYLOR, P. A., Computing and Software
TERLAKY, T., Computing and Software
THOMPSON, D. A., Engineering Physics
TODD, T. D., Electrical and Computer Engineering
TSANIS, I. K., Civil Engineering
VLACHOPOULOS, J. A., Chemical Engineering
WEAVER, D. S., Mechanical Engineering
WILKINSON, D. S., Materials Science and Engineering
WONG, K. M., Electrical and Computer Engineering
WOOD, P. E., Chemical Engineering
WU, X., Electrical and Computer Engineering
XU, G., Materials Science and Engineering
ZHU, S., Chemical Engineering
ZIADA, S., Mechanical Engineering
ZUCKER, J. I., Computing and Software

Faculty of Health Sciences:

ADACHI, R., Medicine
ANDREWS, D. W., Biochemistry
ANTONY, M., Psychiatry
ANVARI, M., Surgery
ARNOLD, A., Medicine
ARSENAULT, L., Pathology
ARTHUR, H. M., School of Nursing
ATKINSON, S. A., Paediatrics
BALL, A. K., Pathology
BARR, R. D., Paediatrics
BAUMANN, M. A., School of Nursing
BELBECK, L. W., Pathology
BIRCH, S., Clinical Epidemiology and Biostatistics
BLAJCHMAN, M, Pathology
BOYLE, M. H., Psychiatry
BROWNE, R. M., School of Nursing

BUCHANAN, M. R., Pathology
BUTLER, R. G., Pathology
CAPONE, J. P., Biochemistry
CHAMBERS, L. W., Clinical Epidemiology and Biostatistics
CHEN, V., Pathology
CHERNESKY, M., Paediatrics
CHIRAKAL, R., Radiology
CHURCHILL, D. N., Medicine
CILISKA, D. K., School of Nursing
COATES, G., Radiology
COBLENTZ, C., Radiology
COLLINS, S. M., Medicine
CONNOLLY, S. J., Medicine
COOK, D. J., Medicine
CRANKSHAW, D. J., Obstetrics and Gynaecology
CROITORU, K., Medicine
CUNNINGHAM, C., Psychiatry
DAYA, S., Obstetrics and Gynaecology
DENBURG, J. A., Medicine
DENBURG, S. D., Psychiatry
DICENSO, A., School of Nursing
FAHNESTOCK, M., Psychiatry
FARGAS-BABJAK, A., Anaesthesia
FERNANDES, C., Medicine
FIRNAU, G., Radiology
GAFNI, A. J., Clinical Epidemiology and Biostatistics
GAULDIE, J., Pathology
GERBER, G. E., Biochemistry
GERSTEIN, H. C., Medicine
GINSBERG, J. S., Medicine
GOLDSMITH, C. H., Clinical Epidemiology and Biostatistics
GROVER, A. K., Medicine
GROVES, D., Pathology
GUPTA, R. S., Biochemistry
GUYATT, G. H., Clinical Epidemiology and Biostatistics
HARNISH, D. G., Pathology
HARVEY, J. T., Surgery
HASSELL, J. A., Biochemistry
HATTON, M. W. C., Pathology
HAYNES, R. B., Clinical Epidemiology and Biostatistics
HEIGENHAUSER, G. J. F., Medicine
HENRY, J., Psychiatry
HOLDER, D. A., Medicine
HOLLAND, F. J., Paediatrics
HUCKER, S. J., Psychiatry
HUGHES, D., Obstetrics
HUIZINGA, J. D., Medicine
HUNT, R. H., Medicine
HUTCHISON, B. G., Family Medicine
ISSENMAN, R. M., Paediatrics
JORDANA, M., Pathology
KARMALI, M. A., Pathology
KATES, N., Psychiatry
KAUFMAN, K. J., Family Medicine
KEARON, C., Medicine
KELTON, J. G., Pathology
KILLIAN, K. J., Medicine
KIRBY, T. Medicine
KIRPALANI, H., Paediatrics
KWAN, C. Y., Medicine
LATIMER, E. J., Family Medicine
LAW, M. C., Rehabilitation Science
LEE, R. M. K. W., Anaesthesia
LEVINE, M., Clinical Epidemiology and Biostatistics
LEVITT, C. A., Family Medicine
LONN, E., Medicine
LUDWIN, D., Medicine
LUKKA, H., Medicine
MCDERMOTT, M. R., Pathology
MACMILLAN, H., Psychiatry
MACPHERSON, A., Medicine
MAHONY, J., Pathology
MAJUMDAR, B., School of Nursing
MCKELVIE, R., Medicine
MANDELL, L., Medicine
MAZUREK, M., Medicine
MCQUEEN, M., Pathology
MEYER, R., Medicine
MISHRA, R. K., Psychiatry
MOAYYEDI, P., Medicine
MOHIDE, P. T., Obstetrics and Gynaecology
MOLLOY, D. W., Medicine
MORILLO, C., Medicine
MUGGAH, H. F., Obstetrics and Gynaecology
NAHMIUS, C., Radiology
NEAME, P., Pathology
NEVILLE, A., Medicine
NIEBOER, E., Biochemistry
NILES, L. P., Psychiatry
NORMAN, G. R., Clinical Epidemiology and Biostatistics
O'BYRNE, P., Medicine
OFOSU, F., Pathology
OROVAN, W. L., Surgery
PAES, B. A., Paediatrics
PANJU, A., Medicine
PATTERSON, C. J. S., Medicine
PATTERSON, M., Radiology
PERDUE, M. H., Pathology
PINELLI, J. M., School of Nursing
RADHI, J., Pathology
RATHBONE, M. P., Medicine
RICHARDS, C. D., Pathology
RIDDELL, R., Radiology
RONEN, G. M., Paediatrics
ROSENBAUM, P. L., Paediatrics
ROSENFELD, J. M., Pathology
ROSENTHAL, K. L., Pathology
ROTSTEIN, C. M. F., Medicine
RUSTHOVEN, J., Medicine
RYAN, E., Psychiatry
SALAMAS, S., Pathology
SCHMIDT, B. K., Paediatrics
SCHULMAN, S., Medicine
SEARS, M. R., Medicine
SEGGIE, J., Psychiatry
SHANNON, H. S., Clinical Epidemiology and Biostatistics
SHARMA, A., Medicine
SMAILL, F., Pathology
SNIDER, D., Pathology
SOLOMON, P., School of Rehabilitation Science
SOMERS, S., Radiology
STEER, P., Paediatrics
STEINER, M., Psychiatry
STODDART, G. L., Clinical Epidemiology and Biostatistics
STRATFORD, P., School of Rehabilitation Science
SUR, R., Medicine
SWINSON, R. P., Psychiatry
SZATMARI, P., Psychiatry
SZECHTMAN, H., Psychiatry
TEO, K., Medicine
TOUGAS, G., Medicine
TURNBULL, J. D., Medicine
TURPIE, I. D., Medicine
UPTON, A. R. M., Medicine
VAN DER SPUY, R., Medicine
VERMA, D. K., Family Medicine
VICKERS, J. D., School of Nursing
WALKER, I. R., Medicine
WALTER, S. D., Clinical Epidemiology and Biostatistics
WARKENTIN, T., Pathology
WATTS, J. L., Paediatrics
WAYE, J., Pathology
WEBBER, C., Radiology
WEITZ, J., Medicine
WESSEL, J., Rehabilitation Science
WHELAN, D., Paediatrics
WHITTON, A., Medicine
WITELSON, S. F., Psychiatry
WRIGHT, G. D., Biochemistry
YANG, D. S. C., Biochemistry
YOUNG, E., Pathology
YOUNGLAI, E. V., Obstetrics and Gynaecology
YUSUF, S., Medicine
ZHOROV, B., Biochemistry

Faculty of Humanities:

ADAMSON, J., English
AHMED, A., French
ALLEN, B. G., Philosophy
ALSOP, J. D., History
ARTHUR, R. T. W., Philosophy
BAYARD, C. A., French
BOWERBANK, S., English
CLARK, D. L., English
CROSTA, S., French
DUNBABIN, K. M. D., Classics
FERNS, H. J., English
GAUVREAU, J. M., History
GIROUX, H., English and Communications Studies
GOELLNICHT, D. C., English
GRIFFIN, N. J., Philosophy
HITCHCOCK, D. L., Philosophy
JEAY, M. M., French
JONES, H., Classics
KACZYNSKI, B. M., History
KING, J., English
KOLESNIKOFF, N., Modern Languages and Linguistics
MAGINNIS, H. B. J., School of the Arts
MURGATROYD, P., Classics
NELLES, H. V., History
O'CONNOR, M. E., English
OSTOVICH, H. M., English
RAHIMIEH, N., English and Comparative Literature
RAPOPORT, P., School of the Arts
RENWICK, W., School of the Arts
SILCOX, M., English
STROINSKA, M., Modern Languages and Linguistics
WALMSLEY, P., English
WALUCHOW, W. J., Philosophy
WEAVER, J. C., History
YORK, L. M., English

Faculty of Science:

ALAMA, S., Mathematics and Statistics
ALLAN, L. G., Psychology
BAIN, A. D., Chemistry
BALAKRISHNAN, N., Mathematics and Statistics
BARBIER, J. R. H., Chemistry
BECKER, S., Psychology
BENNETT, P., Psychology
BERLINSKY, A. J., Physics and Astronomy
BRONSARD, L., Mathematics and Statistics
BROOK, M. A., Chemistry
CHETTLE, D. R., Physics and Astronomy
CHOUINARD, V. A., School of Geography and Geology
COUCHMAN, H. M., Physics and Astronomy
CRAIG, W., Mathematics and Statistics
DALY, M., Psychology
DE CATANZARO, D. A., Psychology
DICKIN, A. P., School of Geography and Geology
DRAKE, J. J., School of Geography and Geology
ELLIOTT, S. J., School of Geography and Geology
EYLES, C. H., School of Geography and Geology
EYLES, J. D., School of Geography and Geology
FENG, S., Mathematics
FINAN, T. M., Biology
GAULIN, B. D., Physics and Astronomy
GOLDING, B., Biology
GREEDAN, J. E., Chemistry
GUAN, P., Mathematics and Statistics
HALL, F. L., School of Geography and Geology
HAMBLETON, I., Mathematics and Statistics
HARRIS, R. S., School of Geography and Geology
HARRIS, W. E., Physics and Astronomy
HART, B. T., Mathematics and Statistics
HIGGS, P. G., Physics and Astronomy
HITCHCOCK, A. P., Chemistry
HOPPE, F. M., Mathematics and Statistics
HURD, T. R., Mathematics and Statistics
JACOBS, J. R., Biology

KALLIN, C., Physics and Astronomy
KANAROGLOU, P. S., School of Geography and Geology
KOLASA, J., Biology
KOLSTER, M., Mathematics and Statistics
LEIGH, W. J., Chemistry
LEVY, B. A., Psychology
LEWIS, T. L., Psychology
LIAW, K. L., School of Geography and Geology
LUKE, G. M., Physics and Astronomy
MCCARRY, B. E., Chemistry
MACDONALD, P. D. M., Mathematics and Statistics
MAURER, D. M., Psychology
MIN-OO, M., Mathematics and Statistics
MOORE, G. H., Mathematics and Statistics
MORRIS, W. A., School of Geography and Geology
MOTHERSILL, C. E., Medical Physics and Applied Radiological Science
MURPHY, K. M., Psychology
NICAS, A. J., Mathematics and Statistics
NURSE, C. A., Biology
O'DONNELL, M. J., Biology
PUDRITZ, R. E., Physics and Astronomy
RACINE, R. J., Psychology
RAINBOW, A. J., Biology
ROLLO, C. D., Biology
SAWYER, E. T., Mathematics and Statistics
SCHELLHORN, H., Biology
SCHROBILGEN, G. J., Chemistry
SEKULER, A., Psychology
SHI, A., Physics and Astronomy
SIEGEL, S., Psychology
SINGH, R. S., Biology
STOVER, H., Chemistry
SUTHERLAND, P., Physics and Astronomy
TERLOUW, J. K., Chemistry
TRAINOR, L. J., Psychology
VALERIOTE, M. A., Mathematics and Statistics
VENUS, D., Physics and Astronomy
VIVEROS-AGUILER, R., Mathematics and Statistics
WANG, M. Y. K., Mathematics and Statistics
WELCH, D. L., Physics and Astronomy
WERETILNYK, E. A., Biology
WERSTIUK, N. H., Chemistry
WILSON, C. D., Physics and Astronomy
WILSON, M. I., Psychology
WOLKOWICZ, G. S. K., Mathematics and Statistics
WOO, M. K., School of Geography and Geology
WOOD, C. M., Biology
YIP, P. C. Y., Mathematics and Statistics

Faculty of Social Sciences:
ARCHIBALD, W. P., Sociology
ARONSON, J. H., School of Social Work
BLIMKIE, C. J. R., Kinesiology
BROWN, R. A., Social Work
CAIN, R., Social Work
CANNON, A., Anthropology
CARROLL, B. A., Political Science
CHAN, K. S. Y., Economics
COLARUSSO, J. J., Anthropology
COLEMAN, W. D., Political Science
COOPER, M. O., Anthropology
CUNEO, C. J., Sociology
DENTON, M. A., Gerontology
DOOLEY, M. D., Economics
ELLIOTT, D., Kinesiology
FEIT, H. A., Anthropology
FINSTEN, L., Anthropology
FOX, J. D., Sociology
HERRING, D. A., Anthropology
HICKS, A. L., Kinesiology
HURLEY, J. E., Economics
JACEK, H. J., Political Science
JONES, S. R. G., Economics
KROEKER, P. T., Religious Studies
KUBURSI, A. A., Economics
LEACH, J. E., Economics
LEE, T. D., Kinesiology
LEVITT, C. H., Sociology
LEWCHUK, W., Economics
LEWIS, T. J., Political Science
MCCARTNEY, N., Kinesiology
MAGEE, L. J., Economics
MENDELSON, A., Religious Studies
MESTELMAN, S., Economics
MIALL, C., Sociology
MULLER, R. A., Economics
PORTER, T., Political Science
RACINE, J., Economics
RICE, J. J., School of Social Work
RODMAN, W. L., Anthropology
SALE, D. G., Kinesiology
SATZEWICH, V., Sociology
SAUNDERS, S. R., Anthropology
SCARTH, W. M., Economics
SCHULLER, E. M., Religious Studies
SHAFFIR, W. B., Sociology
SPENCER, B. G., Economics
SPROULE-JONES, M. H., Political Science
STARKES, J., Kinesiology
STEIN, M. B., Political Science
STUBBS, R. W., Political Science
VEALL, M. R., Economics
WATT, M. S., School of Social Work
WHITE, P. G., Kinesiology
YATES, C. A. B., Political Science

School of Business:
ABAD, P. L., Management Science and Information Systems
AGARWAL, N. C., Human Resources and Management
BABA, V., Business
BART, C. K., Marketing
CHAMBERLAIN, T. W., Finance and Business Economics
CHEUNG, C. S., Finance and Business Economics
COOPER, R. G., Marketing
DEAVES, R., Finance and Business Economics
HACKETT, R. D., Human Resources and Management
KLEINSCHMIDT, E. J., Marketing
KWAN, C. C. Y., Finance and Business Economics
MEDCOF, J. W., Human Resources and Management
MILTENBURG, J. G., Management Science and Information Systems
MOUNTAIN, D. C., Finance and Business Economics
PARLAR, M., Management Science and Information Systems
ROSE, J. B., Human Resources and Management
SHEHATA, M. M., Accounting
STEINER, G., Management Science and Information Systems
WESOLOWSKY, G. O., Management Science and Information Systems
YUAN, Y., Management Science and Information Systems
ZEYTINOGLU, F. I., Human Resources and Management

Divinity College (1280 Main St, W, Hamilton, ON L8S 4R1; tel. (905) 525-9140; internet www.macdiv.ca):
HORNSELL, M. J. A., Old Testament and Hebrew
LONGENECKER, R. N., New Testament
PORTER, S. E., New Testament

MEMORIAL UNIVERSITY OF NEWFOUNDLAND

POB 4200, Elizabeth Ave, St John's, NL A1C 5S7
Telephone: (709) 864-8000
Internet: www.mun.ca

Founded 1925 by Provincial Government as Memorial University College, present status 1949
Academic year: September to August (3 semesters)
Language of instruction: English
Chancellor: Gen. RICK HILLIER
Pres. and Vice-Chancellor: Dr GARY KACHANOSKI
Vice-Pres. for Academic and Pro Vice-Chancellor: Dr DAVID WARDLAW
Vice-Pres. for Admin.: KENT DECKER
Vice-Pres. for Research: Dr CHRISTOPHER LOOMIS
Vice-Pres. for Grenfell Campus: Dr MARY BLUECHARDT
Registrar: GLENN COLLINS
Librarian: LORRAINE BUSBY
Number of teachers: 2,143
Number of students: 18,746
Publications: *Canadian Folklore Canadien* (2 a year), *Communicator* (4 a year), *Culture and Tradition* (1 a year), *Echos du Monde Classique/Classical Views* (3 a year), *Gazette* (26 a year), *Labour/Le Travail* (2 a year), *Luminus* (3 a year), *Newfoundland Quarterly* (4 a year), *Regional Language Studies* (1 a year), *Research Matters* (3 a year), *The Muse* (52 a year)

DEANS AND DIRECTORS

Faculty of Arts: Dr NOEL ROY (acting)
Faculty of Business Administration: Dr WILFRED ZERBE
Faculty of Education: Dr ALICE COLLINS (acting)
Faculty of Engineering and Applied Science: Dr JOHN QUAICOE
Faculty of Human Kinetics: Dr ANTHONY CARD
Faculty of Medicine: Dr JAMES ROURKE
Faculty of Science: Dr MARK ABRAHAMS
School of Graduate Studies: Dr NOREEN GOLFMAN
School of Lifelong Learning: KAREN KENNEDY
School of Music: ELLEN WATERMAN
School of Nursing: Dr JUDITH MCFERTRIDGE-DURDLE
School of Pharmacy: Dr CARLO MARRA
School of Social Work: E. DOW

PROFESSORS

Faculty of Arts:
ALLEN, T. J.
BATH, A. J., Geography
BELL, D. N., Religious Studies
BELL, T. J., Physical Geography
BISHOP, N. B., French and Spanish
BORNSTEIN, C., Philosophy
BRADLEY, J., Linguistics
BRANIGAN, P., Linguistics
BROWN, S. C., Anthropology
BUBENIK, V., Linguistics
BUTLER, K., Physical Geography
BUTRICA, J., Classics
BYRNE, P., English
CATTO, N. R., Physical Geography
CHADWICK, A., French and Spanish
CHERWINSKI, W. J., History
CLARKE, S., Linguistics
CLOSE, D., Philosophy
CROCKER, S., Religious Studies
CULLUM, L., Religious Studies
DEAL, M., Anthropology
DEN OTTER, A. A., History
DEROCHE, M., Religious Studies
DYCK, C., Linguistics
EDINGER, E., Physical Geography
FEEHAN, J. P., Economics
FELT, L. F., Sociology
FISCHER, L., History
GRAHAM, D. E., French and Spanish
HARGER-GRINLING, V. A., French and Spanish
HARRIS, P. F., Linguistics

HART, P., History
HAWKIN, D. J., Religious Studies
HILL, R., Sociology
HILLER, J. K., History
HOUSE, J. D., Sociology
JACOBS, J. D., Geography
JOHNSTONE, F., Sociology
JONES, G. P., English
KENNEDY, J. C., Anthropology
LAI, T. T. L., Philosophy
LATUS, A., Philosophy
LEYTON, E. H., Anthropology
LYNDE, D., English
MCKENZIE, M., Linguistics
MANNION, J. J., Geography
MAXWELL, D. V., Philosophy
MAY, J. D., Economics
NARVAËZ, P., Folklore
NICHOL, D. W., English
NICHOL, K., Geography
NURSE, D., Linguistics
O'DEA, S., English
O'DWYER, B., English
PANJABI, R. K., History
PARKER, K. I., Religious Studies
PARKER, M., Classics
PETERS, H., English
POCIUS, G., Folklore
PORTER, J., Religious Studies
RAINEY, L., Religious Studies
RENOUF, P., Anthropology
ROLLMAN, H., Religious Studies
ROSENBERG, N., Folklore
ROY, N., Economics
RYAN, S., History
SCHRANK, B., English
SCHRANK, W. E., Economics
SHARPE, C., Geography
SHAWYER, A. J., Geography
SHORROKS, G., English Language and Literature
SHUTE, M., Religious Studies
SIMMS, A., Geography
SIMMS, E., Geography
SIMPSON, E., Philosophy
SMITH, P., Folklore
STAFFORD, A., Philosophy
STAVELEY, M., Geography
STOREY, C., Economic Geography
TANNER, A., Anthropology
THOMSPON, D., Philosophy
TSOA, E., Economics
TUCK, J. A., Anthropology
WHITE, R. W., Geography
WOOD, C., Geography

Faculty of Business Administration:

BARNES, J. G., Marketing
FASERUK, A. J., Business Administration
KUBIAK, W., Quantitative Methods
PARSONS, J., Information Systems
SAHA, S., Organizational Behaviour
SEXTY, R. W., Management and Policy
SKIPTON, M. D., Management and Policy
SOOKLAL, L. R., Human Resource Management and Organizational Theory
STEWART, D. B., Business Administration
WITHEY, M. J., Organizational Behaviour

Faculty of Education:

BARRELL, B., Education
BROWN, J., Education
BURNABY, B. J., Education
CAHILL, M., Education
CANNING, P., Education
CROCKER, R. K., Education
DOYLE, C. P., Education
GARLIE, N. W., Education
GLASSMAN, M. S., Education
HADLEY, N. H., Education
JEFFREY, G. H., Education
KELLEHER, R. R., Education
KELLY, U., Education
KENNEDY, W., Education
KIM, K. S., Education
MANN, B. L., Education
NESBIT, W. C., Education
OLDFORD-MATCHIM, J., Education
ROBERTS, B. A., Education
SHARPE, D. B., Education
SINGH, A., Education
STEVENS, K., Education
TRESLAN, D., Education

Faculty of Engineering and Applied Sciences:

ABDI, M., Mechanical Engineering
ADLURI, S., Civil Engineering
AHMED, M. H., Electrical and Computer Engineering
BASS, D. W., Mathematics and Statistics and Engineering
BOOTON, M., Mechanical Engineering
BOSE, N., Engineering
BRUCE-LOCKHART, M., Engineering
CLAUDE, D., Engineering
COLES, C., Civil Engineering
GEORGE, G., Electrical and Computer Engineering
GILL, E., Electrical and Computer Engineering
GOSINE, R., Electrical and Computer Engineering
HADDARA, M. M. R., Engineering
HAWBOLDT, K., Civil Engineering
HEYS, H., Electrical and Computer Engineering
HINCHEY, M., Mechanical Engineering
HUSAIN, T., Engineering
IQBAL, T., Electrical and Computer Engineering
JEYASURYA, B., Electrical and Computer Engineering
JORDAAN, I. J., Ocean Engineering
KHAN, F., Mechanical Engineering
KREIN, L., Mechanical Engineering
LI, C., Electrical and Computer Engineering
LYE, L., Engineering
MALONEY, C., Electrical and Computer Engineering
MASEK, V., Electrical and Computer Engineering
NIEFER, R., Engineering
NORVELL, T., Electrical and Computer Engineering
O'YOUNG, S., Electrical and Computer Engineering
PETERS, D., Electrical and Computer Engineering
POPESCU, R., Engineering
QUAICOE, J., Electrical and Computer Engineering
RAHMAN, M., Electrical and Computer Engineering
SABIN, G., Mechanical Engineering
SESHADRI, R., Mechanical Engineering
SHARAN, A., Mechanical Engineering
SHARP, J. J., Engineering
SHIROKOFF, J., Mechanical Engineering
SWAMIDAS, A. S. J., Engineering
VEITCH, B., Engineering
WILLIAMS, F., Engineering

Faculty of Medicine:

BEAR, J. C., Medicine (Genetics)
BROSNAN, J. T., Biochemistry and Medicine
BROSNAN, M. E., Biochemistry and Medicine
CARAYANNIOTIS, G., Medicine and Endocrinology
CORBETT, D. R., Medicine
GADAG, V., Biostatistics
GILLESPIE, L. L., Oncology
HANSEN, P. A., Medicine
HERZBERG, G. R., Biochemistry and Medicine
HOEKMAN, T., Biophysics
HOOVER, R., Biochemistry
HULAN, H., Biochemistry
KEOUGH, K., Biochemistry
LIEPINS, A., Medicine (Cell Sciences)
MARTIN, A. M., Biochemistry
MICHALAK, T. I., Medicine
MICHALSKI, C. J., Medicine (Molecular Biology)
MOODY-CORBETT, F., Physiology
NEUMAN, R. S., Medicine (Pharmacology)
PATER, A., Medicine (Molecular Biology)
PATERNO, G., Medicine (Oncology)
RAHIMTULA, A. D., Biochemistry and Medicine
SCOTT, T. M., Medicine (Anatomy)
VASDEV, S. C., Medicine (Biochemistry)
WEST, R., Pharmacy and Medicine

Faculty of Science:

ADAMEC, R. E., Psychology
ADAMS, R. J., Psychology
AFANASSIEV, I., Physics
AKSU, A. E., Earth Sciences
ANDERSON, R., Psychology
ANDREWS, E., Psychology
ANDREWS, T., Physics
ARLETT, C., Psychology
BARTHA, M., Computer Science
BARTLETT, R., Statistics
BODWELL, G. J., Chemistry
BOURGAULT, D., Physics
BRIDSON, J., Chemistry
BROWN, J. A., Psychology
BRUNNER, H., Mathematics and Statistics
BURDEN, E., Earth Sciences
BURRY, J. H., Mathematics
BURTON, D., Biology
BURTON, M., Biology
BUTTON, C., Psychology
CALON, T. J., Earth Sciences
CARR, S. M., Biology
CHO, C. W., Physics
CLOUTER, M. J., Physics
COLBO, M. H., Biology
COLLINS, M., Biology
COURAGE, M., Psychology
CURNOE, S., Physics
DABINETT, P., Biology
DAVIDSON, W. S., Biochemistry, Molecular Biology
DEBRUYN, J. R., Physics
DEYOUNG, B., Physics
DRIEDZIC, W., Biochemistry, Molecular Biology
DUNBRACK, R. L., Biochemistry, Molecular Biology
DUNNING, G., Earth Sciences
EDDY, R. H., Mathematics and Statistics
EDINGER, E., Biology
EVANS, J., Psychology
FAHRAEUS-VAN RAE, G., Biology
FINNEY-CRAWLEY, J., Biology
FLETCHER, G. L., Ocean Sciences Centre (Biology)
GALE, J. E., Earth Sciences
GAMPERL, K., Biology
GARDNER, G., Biology
GASKILL, H. S., Mathematics
GEORGHIOU, P., Chemistry
GIEN, T. T., Physics
GILLARD, P., Computer Science
GOODAIRE, E. G., Mathematics and Statistics
GOSSE, V., Psychology
GOW, J., Biology
GRANT, M. J., Psychology
GREEN, J. M., Biology
GREEN, J. M., Psychology
HADDEN, K., Psychology
HAEDRICH, R. L., Ocean Sciences Centre (Biology)
HALL, J., Earth Sciences
HANNAH, E., Psychology
HANNAH, T. E., Psychology
HARLEY, C. A., Psychology
HEATH, P. R., Mathematics and Statistics
HERMANUTZ, L., Biology
HISCOTT, R. N., Earth Sciences
HODYCH, J. P., Earth Sciences
HOOPER, R., Biology
HURICH, C. A., Earth Sciences
INDARES, A.-D., Earth Sciences

INNES, D., Biology
JABLONSKI, C. R., Chemistry
JENNER, G., Earth Sciences
JONES, I., Biology
JONES, I., Psychology
KNOECHEL, R., Biology
LAGOWSKI, J., Physics
LARSON, D. J., Biology
LEE, D., Biology
LEITCH, A. M., Earth Sciences
LEWIS, J. C., Physics
LIEN, J., Psychology
LOADER, C. E., Chemistry
LUCAS, C. R., Chemistry
MCKIM, W., Psychology
MADDIGAN, R., Psychology
MALSBURY, C., Psychology
MARTIN, G., Psychology
MASON, R. A., Earth Sciences
MEYER, R., Earth Sciences
MILLER, E., Psychology
MILLER, H. G., Earth Sciences
MILLER, T., Biology
MINIMIS, G., Computer Science
MOESER, S., Psychology
MONTEVECCHI, W. A., Psychology
MORROW, M. R., Physics
MURRIN, F., Biology
MYERS, J. S., Earth Sciences
NARAYANASWAMI, P. P., Mathematics and Statistics
PARMENTER, M. M., Mathematics and Statistics
PARSONS, J., Biology
PARSONS, J., Computer Science
PATEL, T. R., Biochemistry and Biology
PENNEY, C. G., Psychology
PETERSEN, C., Psychology
PICKUP, P. G., Chemistry
PODUSKA, K., Physics
POIRIER, R., Chemistry
QUINLAN, G. M., Earth Sciences
QUIRION, G., Physics
RABINOWITZ, F. M., Psychology
REVUSKY, B., Psychology
RICH, N. H., Physics
RIVERS, C. J. S., Earth Sciences
ROSE, B., Psychology
ROSE, G., Marine Institute
SCHNEIDER, D. C., Ocean Sciences Centre
SCOTT, P., Biology
SHAWYER, B. L. R., Mathematics and Statistics
SHERRICK, M., Psychology
SIWEI, L., Computer Science
SKINNER, D., Psychology
SLAWINSKI, M., Earth Sciences
SMITH, F., Physics
SNELGROVE, P., Biology
STAVELY, B. E., Biology
STEIN, A. R., Chemistry
STENSON, G. B., Psychology
STOREY, A. E., Psychology
SUMMERS, D., Mathematics and Statistics
SUTRADHAR, B. C., Mathematics and Statistics
SYLVESTER, P. J., Earth Sciences
TANG, J., Computer Science
THOMPSON, R. J., Ocean Sciences Centre
VOLKOFF, H., Biology
VIDYASANKAR, K., Computer Science
WADLEIGH, M., Earth Sciences
WALSH, D., Physics
WANG, C. A., Computer Science
WARKENTIN, I., Psychology
WHITEHEAD, J. P., Physics
WHITMORE, M. D., Physics
WHITTICK, A., Biology
WILSON, M., Earth Sciences
WILTON, D. H. C., Earth Sciences
WRIGHT, J. A., Earth Sciences
WROBLEWSKI, J. S., Ocean Sciences Centre (Physics)
ZEDEL, L., Physics
ZUBEREK, W. M., Computer Science

School of Nursing:
LARYEA, M., Nursing
School of Pharmacy:
WEST, R., Pharmacy

MOUNT ALLISON UNIVERSITY

Sackville, NB E4L 1E4
Telephone: (506) 364-2600
E-mail: ldillman@mta.ca
Internet: www.mta.ca

Founded 1839
Private control
Language of instruction: English
Academic year: September to May

Chancellor: JOHN BRAGG
Pres. and Vice-Chancellor: Dr ROBERT CAMPBELL
Provost and Vice-Pres. for Academics and Research: Dr STEPHEN MCCLATCHIE
Vice-Pres. for Admin. and Finance: D. J. STEWART
Registrar: CHRIS PARKER
Librarian: BRUNO GNASSI

Library of 1,200,000 vols
Number of teachers: 130
Number of students: 2,250

DEANS

Faculty of Arts: Dr HANS VANDERLEEST
Faculty of Science: Dr JEFF OLLERHEAD
Faculty of Social Sciences: Dr ROB SUMMERBY-MURRAY

PROFESSORS

AIKEN, R., Biology
BAERLOCHER, F. J., Biology
BAKER, C., Mathematics and Computer Science
BEATTIE, M., Mathematics and Computer Science
BEATTIE, R., Mathematics and Computer Science
BELKE, T., Psychology
BLAGRAVE, M., English
BOGAARD, P., Philosophy
BURKE, R., Fine Arts
COHEN, I., Classics
CRAIG, T., English
FLEMING, B., Sociology
FOX, M., Geography and Environment
HAWKES, B., Physics
HOLOWNIA, T., Fine Arts
HUDSON, R., Commerce
HUNT, W., Political Science
IRELAND, R., Biology
KACZMARSKA, I., Biology
MACMILLAN, C., English
POLEGATO, R., Commerce
ROSEBRUGH, B., Mathematics and Computer Science
STEWART, J. M., Biochemistry
STRAIN, F., Economics
TUCKER, M., Political Science
VARMA, P., Physics
VERDUYN, C., English
VOGAN, N., Music
WESTCOTT, S., Chemistry

MOUNT SAINT VINCENT UNIVERSITY

Halifax, NS B3M 2J6
Telephone: (902) 457-6117
E-mail: admissions@msvu.ca
Internet: www.msvu.ca

Founded 1925
Language of instruction: English
Academic year: September to April, 2 summer sessions

Chancellor: MARY LOUISE BRINK
Pres. and Vice-Chancellor: Dr SHEILA A. BROWN
Vice-Pres. for Academics: Dr DONNA WOOLCOTT
Vice-Pres. for Admin.: AMANDA WHITEWOOD
Registrar: J. LYNNE THERIAULT
Univ. Librarian: LILLIAN BELTAOS

Number of teachers: 232 (151 full-time, 81 part-time)
Number of students: 4,500

Publications: *Atlantis* (4 a year), *Folia Montana*, *The Connection* (12 a year)

DEANS

Arts and Sciences: Dr SHEVA MEDJUCK
Professional Studies: Dr MARY LYON
Student Affairs: Dr CAROL HILL

NIPISSING UNIVERSITY

100 College Dr., Box 5002, North Bay, ON P1B 8L7
Telephone: (705) 474-3450
E-mail: liaison@nipissingu.ca
Internet: www.nipissingu.ca

Founded 1967 as Nipissing College, affiliated to Laurentian Univ. of Sudbury; merged with North Bay Teachers' College 1973, present status and name 1992
Academic year: September to August

Chancellor: DAVID B. LIDDLE
Pres.: Dr DENNIS R. MOCK
Vice-Pres. of Academic Affairs and Research: Dr. PETER RICKETTS
Vice-Pres. of Admin. and Finance: VICKY PAINE-MANTHA
Dean of Applied and Professional Studies: Dr. RICK VANDERLEE
Dean of Arts and Science: Dr CRAIG COOPER
Dean of Education: Dr RON WIDERMAN
Registrar: ANDREA ROBINSON
Exec. Dir. for Library Services: BRIAN NETTLEFOLD

Number of teachers: 170
Number of students: 7,170

NOVA SCOTIA AGRICULTURAL COLLEGE

Truro, NS B2N 5E3
Telephone: (902) 893-6722
E-mail: reg@nsac.ns.ca
Internet: www.nsac.ns.ca

Founded 1905

Pres.: Dr PHILIP HICKS
Vice-Pres. for Academics: Dr BRUCE GRAY
Vice-Pres. for Admin.: Dr BERNIE MACDONALD
Registrar: T. DOLHANTY
Librarian: B. R. WADDELL

Library of 19,000 vols
Number of teachers: 69
Number of students: 900

Publication: *NSAC College Calendar*

NOVA SCOTIA COLLEGE OF ART AND DESIGN (NSCAD)

5163 Duke St, Halifax, NS B3J 3J6
Telephone: (902) 422-7381
E-mail: admissions@nscad.ns.ca
Internet: www.nscad.ca

Founded 1887
Academic year: September to April

Depts of craft, design, fine art, foundation, graduate studies, historical and critical studies, media art

Pres.: DAVID B. SMITH
Sr Vice-Pres. for Academic Affairs and Research: KENN HONEYCHURCH
Vice-Pres. for Finance and Admin.: PETER FLEMMING
Registrar: LAURELLE LEVERT
Library Dir: ILGA LEJA

Library of 50,000 vols, 220 art periodicals, 140,000 colour slides, large holding of films and video cassettes (incl. Canada Council Art Bank colln)
Number of teachers: 53
Number of students: 1,100 (800 full-time, 300 part-time)

QUEEN'S UNIVERSITY AT KINGSTON

99 University Ave, Kingston, ON K7L 3N6
Telephone: (613) 533-2000
E-mail: liaison@post.queensu.ca
Internet: www.queensu.ca
Founded 1841
Language of instruction: English
Academic year: September to May (2 terms)
Chancellor: Dr DAVID A. DODGE
Vice-Chancellor and Prin.: Dr DANIEL WOOLF
Rector: NICK DAY
Provost and Vice-Prin. for Academics: Dr B. SILVERMAN
Vice-Prin. for Advancement: Dr T. HARRIS
Vice-Prin. for Human Resources: R. MORRISON
Vice-Prin. for Finance and Admin.: C. DAVIS
Vice-Prin. for Research: Dr K. ROWE
Registrar: J. BRADY
Librarian: PAUL WIENS
Number of teachers: 2,567
Number of students: 22,477
Publication: *Queen's Quarterly* (4 a year)

DEANS

Faculty of Arts and Science: Dr A. MACLEAN
Faculty of Education: Dr S. ELLIOTT
Faculty of Engineering and Applied Science: Dr K. WOODHOUSE
Faculty of Health Sciences: Dr R. REZNICK
Faculty of Law: W. FLANAGAN
School of Business: Dr D. SAUNDERS
School of Graduate Studies: Dr B. BROUWER
Student Affairs: Dr J. LAKER

PROFESSORS

Some staff teach in more than one faculty.

Faculty of Applied Science (Ellis Hall, Kingston, ON K7L 3N6; tel. (613) 533-2055; e-mail appsci@post.queensu.ca; internet appsci.queensu.ca):

AITKEN, G. J. M., Electrical and Computer Engineering
ANDERSON, R. J., Mechanical Engineering
ARCHIBALD, J. F., Mining Engineering
BEAULIEU, N. C., Electrical and Computer Engineering
BIRK, A. M., Mechanical Engineering
BOYD, J. D., Materials and Metallurgical Engineering
BRYANT, J. T., Mechanical Engineering
CAMERON, J., Materials and Metallurgical Engineering
CAMPBELL, T. I., Civil Engineering
CARTLEDGE, J. C., Electrical and Computer Engineering
DANESHMEND, L. K., Mining Engineering
DAUGULIS, A. J., Chemical Engineering
GRANDMAISON, E. W., Chemical Engineering
HALL, K., Civil Engineering
HAMACHER, V. C., Electrical and Computer Engineering
HARRIS, T. J., Chemical Engineering
JESWIET, J., Mechanical Engineering
JORDAN, M. P., Mechanical Engineering
KAMPHUIS, J. W., Civil Engineering
KORENBERG, M., Electrical and Computer Engineering
KRSTIC, V. D., Materials and Metallurgical Engineering
KUEPER, B., Civil Engineering
MCKINNON, S. D., Mining Engineering
MCLANE, P. J., Electrical and Computer Engineering
MITCHELL, R. J., Civil Engineering
MOUFTAH, H. T., Electrical and Computer Engineering
MULVENNA, C. A., Mechanical Engineering
NEUFELD, R. J., Chemical Engineering
OOSTHUIZEN, P. H., Mechanical Engineering
PICKLES, C. A., Materials and Metallurgical Engineering
POLLARD, A., Mechanical Engineering
ROSE, K., Civil Engineering
SAIMOTO, S., Materials and Metallurgical Engineering
SEN, P. C., Electrical and Computer Engineering
SMALL, C. F., Mechanical Engineering
SURGENOR, B. W., Mechanical Engineering
TAVARES, S. E., Electrical and Computer Engineering
TURCKE, D. J., Civil Engineering
VAN DALEN, K., Civil Engineering
WATT, W. E., Civil Engineering
WYSS, U. P., Mechanical Engineering
YEN, W.-T., Mining Engineering

Faculty of Arts and Science (Mackintosh-Corry Hall, Room F300, Kingston, ON K7L 3N6; tel. (613) 533-2470; internet www.queensu.ca/artsci):

AARSSEN, L. W., Biology
AKENSON, D. H., History
AKL, S. G., Computing and Information Science
ATHERTON, D. L., Physics
BAIRD, M. C., Chemistry
BAKAN, A. B., Political Studies
BAKHURST, D., Philosophy
BANTING, K. G., Politics
BEACH, C. M., Economics
BECKE, A. D., Chemistry
BENINGER, R. J., Psychology
BERG, M., English
BERGIN, J., Economics
BERMAN, B. J., Politics
BERNHARDT, D., Economics
BICKENBACH, J. E., Philosophy
BLY, P. A., Spanish and Italian
BOADWAY, R. W., Economics
BOAG, P. T., Biology
BOGOYAVLENSKIJ, O. I., Mathematics and Statistics
BROWN, R. S., Chemistry
BURKE, F., Film
CALLE-GRUBER, M., French
CAMPBELL, H. E. A., Mathematics and Statistics
CARMICHAEL, D. M., Geological Sciences
CARMICHAEL, H. L., Economics
CASTEL, B., Physics
CHRISTIANSON, P., History
CLARK, A. H., Geology
CONAGHAN, C. M., Politics
CORDY, J. R., Computing and Information Science
CRAWFORD, R. G., Computing and Information Science
CRUSH, J., Geography
CUDDY, L. L., Psychology
DALRYMPLE, R. W., Geology
DAVIDSON, R., Economics
DE CAEN, D. J. P., Mathematics and Statistics
DIXON, J. M., Geology
DONALD, M. W., Psychology
DUNCAN, M. J., Physics
DU PREY, P. D., Art
ELTIS, D., History
ERDAHL, R. M., Mathematics and Statistics
ERRINGTON, E. J., History
FINLAYSON, J., English
FISHER, A., Music
FLATTERS, F. R., Economics
FLETCHER, R., Physics
FORTIER, S., Chemistry
FOX, M. A., Philosophy
FROST, B. J., Psychology
GEKOSKI, W. L., Psychology
GERAMITA, A. V., Mathematics and Statistics
GILBERT, R. E., Geography
GLASGOW, J., Computing and Information Science
GOHEEN, P. G., Geography
GREGORY, A. W., Economics
GREGORY, D. A., Mathematics and Statistics
GUNN, J. A. W., Politics
HAGEL, D. K., Classics
HAGLUND, D. G., Politics
HAMILTON, R., Sociology
HAMM, J.-J. N., French
HANES, D. A., Physics
HARRISON, J. P., Physics
HARTWICK, J. M., Economics
HELLAND, J., Art
HELMSTAEDT, H., Geology
HENRIKSEN, R. N., Physics
HERZBERG, A. M., Mathematics and Statistics
HEYWOOD, J. C., Art
HIRSCHORN, R. M., Mathematics and Statistics
HODSON, P. V., Biology
HOLDEN, R. R., Psychology
HOLMES, J., Geography
HUGHES, I., Mathematics and Statistics
HUNTER, B. K., Chemistry
JAMES, N. P., Geology
JEEVES, A. H., History
JIRAT-WASIVTYNSKI, V., Art
JOHNSTONE, I. P., Physics
JONKER, L. B., Mathematics and Statistics
KALIN, R., Psychology
KANI, E., Mathematics and Statistics
KILPATRICK, R. S., Classics
KNAPPER, C., Psychology
KNOX, V. J., Psychology
KOBAYASHI, A., Women's Studies
KYMLICKA, W., Philosophy
KYSTER, T. K., Geology
LAKE, K. W., Physics
LAYZELL, D. B., Biology
LEDERMAN, S., Psychology
LEGGETT, W. C., Biology
LEIGHTON, S. R., Philosophy
LELE, J. K., Politics
LESLIE, J. R., Physics
LESLIE, P. M., Politics
LEVISON, M., Computing and Information Science
LEWIS, F. D., Economics
LINDSAY, R. C. L., Psychology
LOBB, R. E., English
LOCK, F. P., English
LOGAN, G. M., English
LOVELL, W. G., Geography
LYON, D., Sociology
MACARTNEY, D. H., Chemistry
MCCAUGHEY, J. H., Geography
MCCOWAN, J. D., Chemistry
MCCREADY, W. D., History
MCDONALD, A. B., Physics
MCINNIS, R. M., Economics
MCKAY, I. G., History
MACKINNON, J. G., Economics
MCLATCHIE, W., Physics
MACLEAN, A. W., Psychology
MACLEOD, A. M., Philosophy
MCTAVISH, J. D., Art
MALCOLMSON, R. W., History
MANUTH, V., Art
MARSHALL, W. L., Psychology
MEWHORT, D., Psychology
MILNE, F., Economics
MINGO, J. A., Mathematics and Statistics
MONKMAN, L. G., English
MONTGOMERIE, R. D., Biology
MOORE, E. G., Geography
MORRIS, G. P., Biology
MUIR, D. W., Psychology
MURTY, M. R. P., Mathematics and Statistics

NARBONNE, G. M., Geology
NATANSOHN, A. L., Chemistry
O'NEILL, P. J., German
ORZECH, M., Mathematics and Statistics
OSBORNE, B. S., Geography
OVERALL, C. D., Philosophy
PAGE, S. C., Politics
PALMER, B. D., History
PEARCE, G. R. F., Sociology
PEARCE, T. H., Geology
PENTLAND, C. C., Politics
PERLIN, G. C., Politics
PETERS, R. D., Psychology
PIKE, R. M., Sociology
PLANT, R. L., Drama
PLAXTON, W. C., Biology
PRACHOWNY, M. F. J., Economics
PRADO, C. G., Philosophy
PRITCHARD, J., History
QUINSEY, V. L., Psychology
RASULA, J., English
RAY, A., Economics
REEVE, W. C., German
RIDDELL, J. B., Geography
ROBERTS, L. G., Mathematics and Statistics
ROBERTSON, B. C., Physics
ROBERTSON, R. J., Biology
ROBERTSON, R. M., Biology
ROSENBERG, M. W., Geography
SACCO, V. F., Sociology
SAYER, M., Physics
SCHROEDER, F. M., Classics
SHENTON, R. W., History
SILVERMAN, R. A., Sociology
SKILLICORN, D. B., Computing and Information Science
SMITH, G. S., History
SMITH, G. W., Economics
SMOL, J., Biology
SNIDER, D. L., Sociology
SNIECKUS, U. A., Chemistry
SPARKS, G. R., Economics
STAYER, J. M., History
STEVENSON, J. M., Physical and Health Education
STONE, J. A., Chemistry
STOTT, M. J., Physics
SYPNOWICH, C., Philosophy
SZAREK, W. A., Chemistry
TAYLOR, D. R., Physics
TAYLOR, P. D., Mathematics and Statistics
TENNENT, R. D., Computing and Information Science
THOMSON, C. J., Geology
TINLINE, R. R., Geography
VANLOON, G. W., Chemistry
VERNER, J. H., Mathematics and Statistics
WALKER, V. K., Biology
WANG, S., Chemistry
WARDLAW, D. M., Chemistry
WARE, R., Economics
WEISMAN, R. G., Psychology
WIEBE, M. G., English
WOLFE, L. A., Physical and Health Education
YOUNG, P. G., Biology
YUI, N., Mathematics and Statistics
ZAMBLE, E., Psychology
ZAREMBA, E., Physics
ZUK, I. B., Education
ZUREIK, E. T., Sociology

Faculty of Education (tel. (613) 533-6205; e-mail regoff@educ.queensu.ca; internet educ.queensu.ca):

HUTCHINSON, N. L.
KIRBY, J. R.
MUNBY, A. H.
O'FARRELL, L.
RUSSELL, T.
UPITIS, R. B.
WILSON, R. J.

Faculty of Health Sciences (tel. (613) 533-2544; e-mail jeb8@post.queensu.ca; internet meds.queensu.ca):

ADAMS, M. A., Pharmacology and Toxicology
ANASTASSIADES, T. P., Medicine
ANDREW, R. D., Anatomy and Cell Biology
ARBOLEDA-FLOREZ, J. E., Psychiatry
ASTON, W. P., Microbiology and Immunology
BENNETT, B. M., Pharmacology and Toxicology
BIRTWHISTLE, R. V., Family Medicine
BOEGMAN, R. J., Pharmacology and Toxicology
BRIEN, J. F., Pharmacology and Toxicology
BRUNET, D. G., Medicine
BURGGRAF, G. W., Medicine
BURKE, S. O., School of Nursing
CARSTENS, E. B., Microbiology and Immunology
CHAPLER, C. K., Physiology
CLARK, A. F., Biochemistry
COLE, S. P. C., Pathology
COTE, G. P., Biochemistry
CRUESS, A. F., Ophthalmology
DA COSTA, L. R., Medicine
DAGNONE, L. E., Emergency Medicine
DAVIES, P. L., Biochemistry
DEELEY, R. G., Pathology
DELISLE, G. J., Microbiology and Immunology
DEPEW, W. T., Medicine
DOW, K. E., Paediatrics
DUFFIN, J. M., Health Sciences
DWOSH, I. L., Medicine
EISENHAUER, E. A., Radoncology
ELCE, J. S., Biochemistry
ELLIOTT, B. E., Pathology
FERGUSON, A. V., Physiology
FISHER, J. T., Physiology
FLYNN, T. G., Biochemistry
FORD, P. M., Medicine
FORKERT, P. G., Anatomy and Cell Biology
FROESE, A. B., Anaesthesia
GORWILL, R. H., Obstetrics and Gynaecology
HALL, S. F., Otolaryngology
HEATON, J. P. W., Urology
HOLDEN, J. J. A., Psychiatry
HUDSON, R. W., Medicine
JACKSON, A. C., Medicine
JARRELL, K. F. J., Microbiology and Immunology
JHAMANDAS, K., Pharmacology and Toxicology
JONEJA, M. G., Anatomy and Cell Biology
JONES, G., Biochemistry
KAN, F. W. K., Anatomy and Cell Biology
KISILEVSKY, R., Pathology
KROPINSKI, A. M., Microbiology and Immunology
LAMB, M. W., School of Nursing
LAWSON, J. S., Psychiatry
LILLICRAP, D. P., Pathology
LUDWIN, S. K., Pathology
MCCREARY, B., Psychiatry
MAK, A. S., Biochemistry
MANLEY, P. N., Pathology
MASSEY, T. E., Pharmacology and Toxicology
MERCER, C. D., Surgery
MILNE, B., Anaesthesia
MORALES, A., Urology
MUNT, P. W., Medicine
NAKATSU, K., Pharmacology and Toxicology
NESHEIM, M. E., Biochemistry
NICKEL, J. C., Urology
NOLAN, R. L., Diagnostic Radiology
O'CONNOR, H. M., Emergency Medicine
O'DONNELL, D. E., Medicine
OLNEY, S. J., Rehabilitation Therapy
PANG, S. C., Anatomy and Cell Biology
PATER, J. L., Community Health and Epidemiology
PATERSON, W. G., Medicine
PICHORA, D. R., Surgery
POOLE, R. K., Microbiology and Immunology
PROSS, H. F., Microbiology and Immunology
RACZ, W. J., Pharmacology and Toxicology
RAPTIS, L. H., Microbiology and Immunology
REID, R. L., Obstetrics and Gynaecology
REIFEL, C., Anatomy and Cell Biology
RICHMOND, F. J., Physiology
RIOPELLE, R. J., Medicine
ROSE, P. K., Physiology
SHANKS, G. L., Rehabilitation Medicine
SHIN, S. H., Physiology
SHORTT, S. E. D., Community Health and Epidemiology
SIMON, J. B., Medicine
SINGER, M. A., Medicine
SMITH, B. T., Paediatrics
SZEWCZUK, M. R., Microbiology and Immunology
WALKER, D. M. C., Emergency Medicine
WEAVER, D. F., Medicine
WHERRETT, B. A., Paediatrics
WIGLE, R. D., Medicine
WILSON, C. R., Family Medicine

Faculty of Law (Macdonald Hall, Kingston, ON K7L 3N6; tel. (613) 533-2220; e-mail llb@gsilver.queensu.ca; internet gsilver.queensu.ca/law):

ADELL, B. L.
ALEXANDROWICZ, G. W.
BAER, M. G.
BALA, N. C.
CARTER, D. D.
DELISLE, R. J.
EASSON, A. J.
HARVISON YOUNG, A.
LAHEY, K. A.
MAGNUSSON, D. N.
MANSON, A. S.
MULLAN, D. J.
SADINSKY, S.
STUART, D. R.
WEISBERG, M. A.

School of Business (Dunning Hall, Kingston, ON K7L 3N6; tel. (613) 533-2330; e-mail info@business.queensu.ca; internet business.queensu.ca):

ANDERSON, D. L.
ARNOLD, S. J.
BARLING, J. I.
COOPER, W. H.
DAUB, M. A. C.
GALLUPE, R. B.
GORDON, J. R. M.
JOHNSON, L. D.
MCKEEN, J. D.
MORGAN, I. G.
NEAVE, E. H.
NIGHTINGALE, D. V.
NORTHEY, M. E.
PETERSEN, E. R.
RICHARDSON, A. J.
RICHARDSON, P. R.
RUTENBERG, D. P.
TAYLOR, A. J.
THORNTON, D. B.

School of Policy Studies (tel. (613) 533-6555; e-mail policy@policy.queensu.ca; internet gsilver.queensu.ca/sps):

LEISS, W.
WILLIAMS, T. R.

School of Urban and Regional Planning (tel. (613) 533-2188; e-mail williamj@post.queensu.ca; internet info.queensu.ca/surp):

LEUNG, H. L.
QADEER, M. A.
SKABURSKIS, A.

AFFILIATED COLLEGE

Queen's Theological College: Kingston, ON K7L 3N6; f. 1841; Prin. Rev. H. E. Llewellyn

REDEEMER UNIVERSITY COLLEGE

777 Garner Rd East, Ancaster, ON L9K 1J4
Telephone: (905) 648-2131
E-mail: adm@redeemer.on.ca
Internet: www.redeemer.on.ca

Founded 1976, present status 1982, current name adopted 2000
Language of instruction: English
Private control
Academic year: September to May

Pres.: Dr Hubert Krygsman
Vice-Pres. for Academics: Dr Jacob Ellens
Vice-Pres. for Admin. and Finance: Fred Verwoerd
Registrar: Richard Wikkerink
Librarian: Janny Eikelboom

Library of 100,000 vols
Number of teachers: 48
Number of students: 915

DEANS

Arts and Foundations: Dr David Zietsma
Natural Sciences and Social Sciences: Dr Doug Needham

ROYAL MILITARY COLLEGE OF CANADA

POB 17000 Stn Forces, Kingston, ON K7K 7B4
Telephone: (613) 541-6000
E-mail: liaison@rmc.ca
Internet: www.rmc.ca

Founded 1876
Languages of instruction: English, French
Academic year: September to May

Chancellor and Pres.: The Min. of Nat. Defence
Commandant: Brig. Gen. J. M. J. Leclerc
Prin. and Dir of Studies: Dr J. S. Cowan
Registrar: Cdr Deborah A. Wilson
Dir for Cadets: Col W. N. Peters
Chief Librarian: B. Cameron

Library of 380,000 vols
Number of teachers: 174
Number of students: 865 (760 undergraduate, 105 graduate)

DEANS

Arts: Dr J. J. Sokolsky
Continuing Studies: Dr M. F. Bardon
Engineering: Dr J. A. Stewart
Graduate Studies and Research: Dr B. J. Fugère
Science: Dr R. F. Marsden

PROFESSORS

Akhras, G., Civil Engineering
Al-Khalili, D., Electrical Engineering
Allard, P. E., Electrical Engineering
Amami, M., Business Administration
Amphlett, J. C., Chemistry
Antar, Y., Electrical Engineering
Bardon, M. F., Mechanical Engineering
Barrett, A. J., Mathematics
Batalla, E., Physics
Bathurst, R. J., Civil Engineering
Beaty, A., Civil Engineering
Benabdallah, H., Mechanical Engineering
Benesch, R., Mathematics
Bennett, L., Chemistry and Chemical Engineering
Benson, M., French Studies
Boness, R. J., Mechanical Engineering
Bonin, H. W., Chemical Engineering
Bonnycastle, S., English
Bradley, P., Military Psychology and Leadership
Buckley, J., Physics
Bui, T., Chemistry and Chemical Engineering
Bussieres, P., Mechanical Engineering
Chaudhry, M. L., Mathematics
Chikhani, A. Y., Electrical Engineering
Constantineau, P., Politics and Economics
Creber, K., Chemistry and Chemical Engineering
Davies Bouchard, S., Continuing Studies
Deplanche, D., Electrical and Computer Engineering
Dreiziger, N. A. F., History
Dunnett, P., Political and Economic Science
DuQuesnay, D., Mechanical Engineering
Eder, W. E., Mechanical Engineering
Erki, M., Civil Engineering
Errington, J., History
Farooq, M., Electrical Engineering
Finan, J., Politics and Economics
Fjarlie, E. J., Mechanical Engineering
Fugere, J., Mathematics and Computer Science
Gagnon, Y., Politics and Economics
Gauthier, N., Physics
Gervais, R., Mathematics
Godard, R., Mathematics and Computer Science
Gravel, P., Mathematics and Computer Science
Haddad, L., Mathematics and Computer Science
Hassan-Yari, H., Politics and Economics
Haycock, R. G., History
Hefnawi, M., Electrical and Computer Engineering
Hurley, W., Business Administration
Ion, A., History
Isac, G., Mathematics and Computer Science
Jenkins, A. L., Engineering Management
Klepak, H., History
Labbe, M., Mathematics and Computer Science
Labonte, G., Mathematics
Lachaine, A. R., Physics
Lagueux, P.-A., French Studies
Laplante, J. P., Chemistry
Lewis, B., Chemistry and Chemical Engineering
Luciuk, L., Politics and Economics
McDonough, L., Politics and Economics
McKercher, B., History
Maloney, S., War Studies
Mann, R. F., Chemical Engineering
Moffatt, W. C., Mechanical Engineering
Mongeau, B., Electrical Engineering
Mukherjee, B. K., Physics
Neilson, K. E., History
Noel, J.-M., Physics
Pottier, R. H., Chemistry
Quillard, G., French Studies
Racey, T. J., Physics
Ranganathan, S., Mathematics
Reimer, K., Chemistry and Chemical Engineering
Roberge, P. R., Chemistry
Rochon, P., Physics
St Pierre, A., Business Administration
Schurer, C., Physics
Seguin, G., Electrical Engineering
Shepard, T., Electrical Engineering
Shoucri, R. M., Mathematics
Simms, B. W., Engineering Management
Sokolsky, J. J., Political Science
Sri, P. S., English
Stacey, M., Physics
Stewart, A., Civil Engineering
Tarbouchi, M., Electrical and Computer Engineering
Thompson, W. T., Chemical Engineering
Torrie, G. M., Mathematics
Treddenick, J. M., Economics
Vincent, T. B., English
Weir, R. D., Chemical Engineering
Whelau, D., Mathematics and Computer Science
Whitehorn, A. J., Political Science
Wilson, J. D., Electrical Engineering

ROYAL ROADS UNIVERSITY

2005 Sooke Rd, Victoria, BC V9B 5Y2
Telephone: (250) 391-2511
E-mail: learn.more@royalroads.ca
Internet: www.royalroads.ca

Founded 1995

Pres. and Vice-Chancellor: Dr Allan Cahoon
Vice-Pres. for Academic Affairs and Provost: Dr Peter Meekison (acting)
Vice-Pres. and Chief Information Officer: Dan Tulip
Vice-Pres. for RRU Foundation and Chief Devt Officer: Dan Spinner
Vice-Pres. for Univ. Relations: Roberta Mason (acting)
Univ. Librarian: (vacant)
Number of students: 3,000

DEANS

Faculty of Management: Dr Pedro Marquez
Faculty of Social and Applied Science: Dr Jim Bayer
Faculty of Tourism and Hotel Management: Dr Nancy Arsenault

RYERSON UNIVERSITY

350 Victoria St, Toronto, ON M5B 2K3
Telephone: (416) 979-5000
E-mail: international@ryerson.ca
Internet: www.ryerson.ca

Founded 1948 as Ryerson Institute of Technology; became Ryerson Polytechnical Institute 1964 and Ryerson Polytechnic University 1993; current name adopted 2001
provincial control
Language of instruction: English
Academic year: September to April

Chancellor: G. Raymond Chang
Pres. and Vice-Chancellor: Sheldon Levy
Provost and Vice-Pres. for Academic Affairs: Dr Alan Shepard
Vice-Provost for Academics: Dr Mehmet Zeytinoglu (acting)
Vice-Provost for Faculty Affairs: Dr Michael Dewson
Vice-Provost for Students: Dr Heather Lane Vetere
Vice-Provost for Univ. Planning Office: Dr Paul Stenton
Vice-Pres. for Admin. and Finance: Linda Grayson
Vice-Pres. for Research and Innovation: Dr Tas Venetsanopoulos
Vice-Pres. for Univ. Advancement: Adam Kahan
Registrar: Keith Alnwick
Chief Librarian: Madeleine Lefebvre

Number of teachers: 771
Number of students: 24,475 (full-time)

DEANS

Faculty of Arts: Dr Carla Cassidy
Faculty of Business: Tom Knowlton
Faculty of Communication and Design: Dr Daniel Doz (acting)
Faculty of Community Services: Dr Usha George
Faculty of Engineering, Architecture and Science: Dr Mohamed Lachemi
School of Graduate Studies: Dr Maurice Yeates
Ted Rogers School of Management: Dr Ken Jones
The G. Raymond Chang School of Continuing Education: Dr Gervan Fearon

ST FRANCIS XAVIER UNIVERSITY

POB 5000, Antigonish, NS B2G 2W5
Telephone: (902) 867-3931
E-mail: pr@stfx.ca
Internet: www.stfx.ca

Founded 1853
Language of instruction: English
Academic year: September to May

Chancellor: Most Rev. RAYMOND LAHEY
Pres.: Dr SEAN E. RILEY
Vice-Pres. for Academic Affairs: Dr RON JOHNSON
Vice-Pres. for Admin.: RAMSAY DUFF
Vice-Pres. for Student Services: JANA LUKER
Vice-Pres. for Univ. Advancement: PETER FARDY
Vice-Pres. and Dir of Coady International Institute: M. COYLE
Dir for University Extension: R. WEHRELL
Registrar: J. STARK
Librarian: LYNNE MURPHY

Library: see under Libraries and Archives
Number of teachers: 200
Number of students: 5,200 (4,200 full-time, 1,000 part-time)

Publications: *Antigonish Review* (literary), *Xavieran Annual*, *Xavieran Weekly*

DEANS

Faculty of Arts: M. MCGILLIVRAY
Faculty of Science: E. MCALDUFF

PROFESSORS

ANDERSON, A., Earth Sciences
AQUINO, M., Chemistry
ASPIN, M., Modern Languages
BALDNER, S., Philosophy
BECK, J., Chemistry
BELTRAMI, H., Earth Sciences
BERNARD, I., Education
BICKERTON, J., Political Science
BIGELOW, A., Psychology
BILEK, L., Human Kinetics
BROOKS, G. P., Psychology
BUCKLAND-NICKS, J., Biology
CALLAGHAN, T., Psychology
CLANCY, P., Political Science
DEMONT, E., Biology
DEN HEYER, K., Psychology
DOSSA, S. A., Political Science
DUNCAN, C. M., Business Administration
EDWARDS, J., Psychology
EL-SHEIKH, S., Economics
GALLANT, C. D., Mathematics, Statistics and Computer Science
GALLANT, L., Business Administration
GALLANT, M., Human Kinetics
GARBARY, D., Biology
GERGE, A., Music
GERRIETS, M., Economics
GILLIS, A., Nursing
GRANT, J., Education
GRENIER, Y., Political Science
HARRISON, J. F., Political Science
HENKE, P., Psychology
HOGAN, M. P., History
HOLLOWAY, S., Political Science
HUNTER, D., Physics
JACKSON, W., Sociology and Anthropology
JACONO, J., Nursing
JAN, N., Physics
JOHNSON, R. W., Psychology
KLAPSTEIN, D., Chemistry
KOCAY, V., Modern Languages
LANGILLE, E., Modern Languages
LIENGME, B., Chemistry
MCALDUFF, E., Chemistry
MACCAULL, W., Mathematics, Statistics and Computer Science
MACDONALD, B., Religious Studies
MACDONALD, M. Y., Religious Studies
MACEACHERN, A., Mathematics, Statistics and Computer Science
MACFARLANE, E., Nursing
MCGILLIVRAY, M., English
MACINNES, D., Sociology and Anthropology
MADDEN, R. F., Business Administration
MARAGONI, G., Chemistry
MARQUIS, P., English
MARSHALL, W. S., Biology
MELCHIN, M., Earth Sciences
MENSCH, J., Philosophy
MILNER, P., English
MURPHY, J. B., Earth Sciences
NACZK, M., Human Nutrition
NASH, R., Sociology and Anthropology
NEWSOME, G. E., Biology
NILSEN, K., Celtic Studies
NORRIS, J., Education
ORR, J., Education
PALEPU, R., Chemistry
PHILLIPS, P., History
PHYNE, J., Anthropology and Sociology
QUIGLEY, A., Adult Education
QUINN, J., Mathematics, Statistics and Computer Science
QUINN, W. R., Engineering
RASMUSSEN, R., Human Kinetics
SCHUEGRAF, E. J., Mathematics, Statistics and Computer Science
SEYMOUR, N., Biology
SMITH, D., English
SMITH, G., Music
SMITH-PALMER, T., Chemistry
STANLEY-BLACKWELL, L., History
STEINITZ, M. O., Physics
SWEET, W., Philosophy
TAYLOR, J., English
TRITES, G., Information Systems
WALLBANK, B., Physics
WANG, P., Mathematics, Statistics and Computer Science
WEHRELL, R., Extension
WILPUTTE, E., English
WOOD, D., English
WRIGHT, E., Psychology

ATTACHED INSTITUTE

Coady International Institute: POB 5000, Antigonish, NS B2G 2W5; tel. (902) 867-3960; e-mail coadycom@stfx.ca; internet www.coady.stfx.ca; f. 1959; runs leadership and organization devt programmes with peoples of Third World countries; diploma and certificate courses in Canada, also training courses and projects overseas; library of 13,000 vols, 90 periodicals; Dir Dr JOHN GAVENTA

SAINT MARY'S UNIVERSITY

923 Robie St, Halifax, NS B3H 3C3
Telephone: (902) 420-5400
E-mail: public.affairs@smu.ca
Internet: www.smu.ca

Founded 1802
public control
Academic year: September to May

Chancellor: Dr ROBERT KELLY
Pres. and Vice-Chancellor: Dr J. COLIN DODDS
Vice-Pres. for Academics and Research: Dr DAVID GAUTHIER
Vice-Pres. for Admin.: GABRIELLE MORRISON
Vice-Pres. for Finance: LARRY CORRIGAN
Assoc. Vice-Pres. and Registrar: Dr PAUL DIXON
Librarian: MARIE DE YOUNG

Library of 291,000 vols and 27,000 electronic data
Number of teachers: 246
Number of students: 8,539 (6,309 full-time, 2,230 part-time)

DEANS

Faculty of Arts: Dr ESTHER E. ENNS
Faculty of Graduate Studies and Research: Dr KEVIN VESSEY
Faculty of Science: Dr STEVEN SMITH
Sobey School of Business: Dr DAVID WICKS

PROFESSORS

AMIRKHALKHAI, S., Economics
ARYA, P. L., Economics
BARRETT, G., Sociology
BOWLBY, P., Religious Studies
BOYLE, W. P., Engineering
CATANO, V. M., Psychology
CHAMARD, J. C., Management
CHARLES, A., Finance and Management Science
CHENG, T., Accounting
CHESLEY, G. R., Accounting
CHRISTIANSEN-RUFFMAN, L., Sociology and Women's Studies
CLARKE, D., Astronomy and Physics
CONE, D., Biology
DAR, A., Economics
DARLEY, J., Psychology
DAS, H., Management
DAVIS, S., Anthropology
DEUPREE, R., Astronomy and Physics
DIXON, P., Finance and Management Science
DOAK, E. J., Economics
DODDS, J. C., Finance and Management Science
DOSTAL, J., Geology
ELSON, C., Chemistry
EMMS, R., Modern Languages and Classics
ERICKSON, P. A., Anthropology
FARRELL, A., Modern Languages and Classics
FITZGERALD, P., Management
GORMAN, B., Accounting
GUENTHER, D., Astronomy and Physics
HAIGH, E., History
HARTNELL, B., Mathematics and Computing Science
HARVEY, A., Economics
HILL, K., Psychology
HOWELL, C. D., History and Atlantic Canada Studies
KATZ, W., English
KELLOWAY, K., Management and Psychology
KIANG, M.-J., Mathematics and Computing Science
KIM, C., Marketing
KONAPASKY, R., Psychology
LANDES, R., Political Science
LARSEN, M. J., English
LEE, E., Finance and Management Science
LINGRAR, P., Mathematics and Computing Science
MCCALLA, R., Geography
MACDONALD, M., Economics and Women's Studies
MACDONALD, R. A., English
MCGEE, H., Anthropology
MCMULLEN, J., Sociology
MICIAK, A., Marketing
MILLAR, H., Finance and Management Science
MILLS, A., Management
MILLWARD, H., Geography
MITCHELL, G., Astronomy and Physics
MORRISON, J. H., History and Asian Studies
MUIR, P., Mathematics
MUKHOPADHYAY, A. K., Economics
MURPHY, J., Religious Studies
OWEN, V., Geology
PARKER, R., English
PENDSE, S., Management
PE-PIPER, G., Geology
RAND, J., Biology
REID, J. G., History and Atlantic Canada Studies
RICHARDSON, D. H. S., Biology
SASTRY, V., Engineering
SEAMEN, A., English
SIDDIQUI, Q., Geology
STRONGMAN, D., Biology and Forensic Science
SWINGLER, D., Engineering
TARNAWSKI, V., Engineering
THOMAS, G., English
TURNER, D. G., Astronomy and Physics
TWOMEY, R. J., History

VAUGHAN, K., Chemistry
VELTMEYER, H., Sociology, International Development Studies
VESSEY, K., Biology
WAGAR, T., Management
WEIN, S., Philosophy
YOUNG, N., Accounting

SIMON FRASER UNIVERSITY

8888 University Dr., Burnaby, BC V5A 1S6
Telephone: (778) 782-3111
E-mail: sfumpr@sfu.ca
Internet: www.sfu.ca
SFU Vancouver: 515 West Hastings St, Vancouver, BC V6B 5K3
Telephone: (778) 782-5000
Internet: www.sfu.ca
SFU Surrey: 250–13450 102nd Ave, Surrey, BC V3T 0A3
Telephone: (778) 782-7400
Internet: www.sfu.ca
Founded 1963
provincial control
Language of instruction: English
Academic year: September to August (3 terms of 4 months each)
Chancellor: Dr ANNE GIARDINI
Pres. and Vice-Chancellor: Dr MICHAEL STEVENSON
Vice-Pres. for Academic Affairs: Dr JON DRIVER
Vice-Pres. for Research: Dr MARIO PINTO
Registrar and Sec. of Senate: KATE ROSS
Librarian: LYNN COPELAND
Library of 1,000,000 vols
Number of teachers: 942
Number of students: 30,313
Publications: *Canadian Journal of Communication* (4 a year), *International History Review* (4 a year), *West Coast Line* (3 a year)

DEANS

Faculty of Applied Sciences: NIMAL RAJAPAKSE
Faculty of Arts and Social Sciences: JOHN CRAIG
Faculty of Business Administration: DANIEL SHAPIRO
Faculty of Communication, Art and Technology: CHERYL GEISLER
Faculty of Education: KRIS MAGNUSSON
Faculty of Environment: JOHN PIERCE
Faculty of Health Sciences: JOHN O'NEIL
Faculty of Science: Dr MICHAEL PLISCHKE (acting)
Graduate Studies: WADE PARKHOUSE

PROFESSORS

Faculty of Applied Sciences (9861 Applied Sciences Bldg, Burnaby; tel. (604) 291-4724; internet fas.sfu.ca):

School of Communication:

ANDERSON, R. S.
GRUNEAU, R.
HACKETT, R. A.
HARASIM, L. M.
KLINE, S.
LABA, M.
LEWIS, B. S.
LORIMER, R. M.
RICHARDS, W. D.
TRUAX, B. D.

School of Computing Science:

ATKINS, M. S.
BHATTACHARYA, B. K.
BURTON, F. W.
CAMERON, R. D.
DAHL, V.
DELGRANDE, J. P.
FUNT, B. V.
HADLEY, R. F.
HAN, J. W.
HELL, P.
HOBSON, R. F.
KAMEDA, T.
LI, Z. N.
LIESTMAN, A. L.
LUK, W. S.
PETERS, J. G.
POPOWICH, F.
SHERMER, T. C.
YANG, Q.

School of Engineering Science:

BIRD, J. S.
BOLOGNESI, C. R.
CAVERS, J. K.
CHAPMAN, G. H.
DILL, J. C.
GRUVER, W. A.
GUPTA, K. K.
HARDY, R. H. S.
HO, P. K. M.
HOBSON, R. F.
JONES, J. D.
LEUNG, A. M.
PARAMESWARAN, M.
PAYANDEH, S.
RAWICZ, A. H.
SAIF, M.
STAPLETON, S. P.
SYRZYCKI, M.

School of Kinesiology:

BAWA, P. N. S.
DICKINSON, J.
FINEGOOD, D. T.
GOODMAN, D.
HOFFER, J. A.
MACKENZIE, C. L.
MACLEAN, D. R.
MARTENIUK, R. G.
MORRISON, J. B.
PARKHOUSE, W. S.
ROSIN, M.
TIBBITS, G.

School of Resource and Environmental Management Programme:

DE LA MERE, W. K.
GILL, A. M.
GOBAS, F.
PETERMAN, R. M.
WILLIAMS, P. W.

Faculty of Arts (6168 Academic Quadrangle, Burnaby; tel. (604) 291-4414; internet www.sfu.ca/arts):

Archaeology:

BURLEY, D. V.
DRIVER, J. C.
FLADMARK, K. R.
GALDIKAS, B. M. F.
HAYDEN, B. D.
NANCE, J. D.
NELSON, D. E.
SKINNER, M. F.

School for the Contemporary Arts:

ALOI, S. A.
DIAMOND, M.
GOTFRIT, M. S.
MACINTYRE, D. K.
SNIDER, G.
TRUAX, B. D.
UNDERHILL, O.

School of Criminology:

BOYD, N. T.
BRANTINGHAM, P. J.
BRANTINGHAM, P. L.
BROCKMAN, J.
BURTCH, B.
CHUNN, D. E.
CORRADO, R. R.
FAITH, K.
GORDON, R. M.
GRIFFITHS, C. T.
JACKSON, M. A.
LOWMAN, J.
MENZIES, R. J.
VERDUN-JONES, S. N.

Economics:

ALLEN, D. W.
BOLAND, L. A.
CHANT, J. F.
DEVORETZ, D. J.
DEAN, J. W.
DOW, G.
EASTON, S. T.
HARRIS, R. G.
JONES, R. A.
KENNEDY, P. E.
MAKI, D. R.
MUNRO, J. M.
OLEWILER, N. D.
SCHMITT, N.
SPINDLER, Z. A.

English:

COE, R. M.
DELANY, P.
DELANY, S.
DJWA, S.
GERSON, C.
MEZEI, K.
MIKI, R. A.
STOUCK, D.
STURROCK, J.

French:

DAVISON, R.
FAUQUENOY, M. C.
VISWANATHAN, J.

Geography:

BAILEY, W. G.
GILL, A. M.
HAYTER, R.
HICKIN, E. J.
PIERCE, J. T.
ROBERTS, A. C. B.
ROBERTS, M. C.

Gerontology Program:

GUTMAN, G.
WISTER, A. V.

History:

BOYER, R. E.
CLEVELAND, W. L.
DEBO, R. K.
DUTTON, P. E.
FELLMAN, M. D.
GAGAN, D. P.
HUTCHINSON, J. F.
JOHNSTON, H. J. M.
LITTLE, J. I.
PARR, J.
STEWART, M. L.
STUBBS, J. O.

Humanities:

ANGUS, I.
DUGUID, S.
DUTTON, P. E.
MEZEI, K.
WALLS, J. W.

Latin American Studies:

BROHMAN, J. A C.

Linguistics:

GERDTS, D. B.
MCFETRIDGE, P.
ROBERTS, E. W.
SAUNDERS, R.

Philosophy:

HANSON, P. P.
JENNINGS, R. E.
ZIMMERMAN, D.

Political Science:

COHEN, L. J.
COHN, T. H.
COVELL, M. A.
ERICKSON, L. J.

GRIFFIN COHEN, M. G.
HOWLETT, M.
MCBRIDE, S.
MEYER, P.
ROSS, D. A.
SMITH, P. J.
STEVENSON, H. M.
WARWICK, P. V.

Psychology:

ALEXANDER, B. K.
BOWMAN, M. L.
HART, S. D.
KIMBALL, M.
KREBS, D. L.
MCFARLAND, C. G.
MISTLBERGER, R.
MORETTI, M. M.
ROESCH, R. M.
WHITTLESEA, B. W. A.

Sociology and Anthropology:

DYCK, N.
GEE, E.
HOWARD, M.
KENNY, M.
MACLEAN, D. R.

Women's Studies:

GRIFFIN COHEN, M. G.
KIMBALL, M. M.
STEWART, M. L.
WENDELL, S.

Faculty of Business Administration (3302 Lohn Building, Burnaby; tel. (604) 291-3708; internet www.bus.sfu.ca):

CHOO, E. U.
CLARKSON, P. M.
FINLEY, D. R.
GRAUER, R. R.
LOVE, C. E.
MAUSER, G. A.
MEREDITH, L. N.
PINFIELD, L. T.
POITRAS, G.
RICHARDS, J. G.
SHAPIRO, D. M.
TUNG, R. L.
VINING, A. R.
WATERHOUSE, J. H.
WEDLEY, W. C.
WEXLER, M. N.
WYCKHAM, R. G.
ZAICHKOWSKY, J. L.

Faculty of Education (8622 Education Building, Burnaby; tel. (604) 291-3395; internet www.educ.sfu.ca):

BAILIN, S.
BARROW, R.
CASE, R.
DE CASTELL, S. C.
EGAN, K.
GEVA-MAY, I.
GRIMMETT, P. P.
MAMCHUR, C. M.
MARTIN, J.
OBADIA, A. A.
RICHMOND, S.
TOOHEY, K.
WINNE, P. H.
WONG, B. Y. L.
ZAZKIS, R.

Faculty of Science (P9451 Shrum Science Centre, Burnaby; tel. (604) 291-4590; internet www.sfu.ca/~science):

Biological Sciences:

ALBRIGHT, L. J.
BECKENBACH, A. T.
BORDEN, J. H.
BRANDHORST, B. P.
CRESPI, B. J.
DILL, L. M.
FARRELL, A. P.
GRIES, G. J.
HAUNERLAND, N. H.
LAW, F. C. P.
MATHEWES, R. W.
PUNJA, Z. K.
RAHE, J. E.
ROITBERG, B. D.
WINSTON, M. L.
YDENBERG, R. C.

Chemistry:

BENNET, A. J.
CORNELL, R. B.
D'AURIA, J. D.
GAY, I. D.
HILL, R. H.
HOLDCROFT, S.
JONES, C. H. W.
MALLI, G. L.
PERCIVAL, P. W.
PINTO, B. M.
POMEROY, R. K.
RICHARDS, W. R.
SEN, D.
SLESSOR, K. N.

Earth Sciences:

HICKIN, E. J.
ROBERTS, M. C.

Mathematics:

BERGGREN, J. L.
BORWEIN, J. M.
BORWEIN, P. B.
BROWN, T. C.
GRAHAM, G. A. C.
HELL, P.
LACHLAN, A. H.
LEWIS, A. S.
REILLY, N. R.
RUSSELL, R. D.
SHEN, C. Y.

Molecular Biology and Biochemistry:

BAILLIE, D. L.
BRANDHORST, B. P.
CORNELL, R. B.
DAVIDSON, W. S.
HONDA, B. M.
RICHARDS, W. R.
SEN, D.
SMITH, M. J.

Physics:

BALLENTINE, L. E.
BECHHOEFER, J. L.
BOAL, D. H.
BOLOGNESI, C. R.
CLAYMAN, B. P.
CROZIER, E. D.
ENNS, R. H.
FRINDT, R. F.
HEINRICH, B.
KAVANAGH, K. L.
KIRCZENOW, G.
PLISCHKE, M.
SCHEINFEIN, M. R.
THEWALT, M. L. W.
TROTTIER, H. D.
VETTERLI, M.
WATKINS, S.

Statistics and Actuarial Science:

LOCKHART, R. A.
MACLEAN, D. R.
ROUTLEDGE, R. D.
SCHWARZ, C. J.
SITTER, R. R.
SWARTZ, T. B.

ATTACHED INSTITUTES

Behavioural Ecology Research Group: tel. (604) 291-3664; f. 1989; Dir Dr LAWRENCE M. DILL.

Canadian Centre for Studies in Publishing: tel. (604) 291-5240; f. 1987; Dir Dr R. M. LORIMER.

Centre for Coastal Science and Management: tel. (778) 772-4653; e-mail lauriew@sfu.ca; Dir Dr P. GALLAGHER.

Centre for Education, Law and Society: tel. (604) 291-4484; e-mail cels@sfu.ca; f. 1984; Dir Dr W. CASSIDY.

Centre d'Études Francophones Québec-Pacifique: tel. (604) 291-3544; Dir Dr G. POIRIER.

Centre for Experimental and Constructive Mathematics: tel. (604) 291-5617; f. 1993; Dir Dr J. BORWEIN.

Centre for Innovation in Management: tel. (604) 291-4183; Dir Dr E. LOVE.

Centre for Labour Studies: tel. (604) 291-5827; Dir Dr M. LEIER.

Centre for Policy Research on Science and Technology: Vancouver, BC V6B 5K3; tel. (778) 782-5114; internet www.sfu.ca/cprost; f. 1989; Dir Prof. D-Y JIN.

Centre for Restorative Justice: f. 2001; Dir Dr R. M. GORDON; Dir Dr E. ELLIOTT.

Centre for Scientific Computing: tel. (604) 291-4819; Dir Dr R. RUSSELL.

Centre for Scottish Studies: tel. (604) 291-5515; Dir Dr S. DUGUID.

Centre for the Study of Government and Business: e-mail csgb@csgb.ubc.ca; internet www.csgb.ubc.ca; Co-Dirs Dr T. ROSS; Co-Dir Dr A. R. VINING.

Centre for Systems Science: tel. (604) 291-4588; Dir Dr S. ATKINS.

Centre for Tourism Policy and Research: tel. (604) 291-3103; f. 1989; Dir Dr P. WILLIAMS.

Chemical Ecology Research Group: tel. (604) 291-3646; f. 1981; Dir Dr J. H. BORDEN.

Community Economic Development Centre: tel. (604) 291-5849; e-mail cedc@sfu.ca; internet www.sfu.ca/cedc; f. 1989; Dir Dr M. ROSELAND.

Cooperative Resource Management Institute: tel. (604) 291-4683; f. 1998; Dir R. PETERMAN.

Criminology Research Centre: tel. (604) 291-4040; f. 1978; Dir Dr W. GLACKMAN.

David Lam Centre for International Communication: tel. (604) 291-5021; e-mail dlam-info@sfu.ca; f. 1989; Dir Dr J. W. WALLS.

Feminist Institute for Studies on Law and Society: f. 1990; Co-Dirs Dr D. CHUNN; Co-Dir Dr W. CHAN.

Gerontology Research Centre: tel. (604) 291-5062; e-mail gero@sfu.ca; f. 1982; Dir Dr G. GUTMAN.

Institute for Canadian Urban Research Studies: tel. (604) 291-3515; Dir Dr PATRICIA L. BRANTINGHAM.

Institute of Governance Studies: tel. (604) 291-4994; e-mail igs@sfu.ca; Dir P. J. SMITH.

Institute for the Humanities: tel. (604) 291-5516; e-mail sgz@sfu.ca; Dir Dr D. GRAYSTON.

Institute of Micromachine and Microfabrication Research: tel. (604) 291-4971; e-mail paramesw@sfu.ca; Dir Dr A. M. PARAMESWARAN.

Institute for Studies in Criminal Justice Policy: tel. (604) 291-4040; f. 1980; Dir Dr M. A. JACKSON.

Institute for Studies in Teacher Education: tel. (604) 291-4937; Co-Dirs P. GRIMMETT; Co-Dir Dr M. F. WIDEEN.

International Centre for Criminal Law Reform and Criminal Justice Policy: tel. (604) 822-9875; e-mail icclr@law.ubc.ca; f. 1991; Exec. Dir F. M. GORDON.

Logic and Functional Programming Group: tel. (604) 291-3426; f. 1990; Dir Dr V. DAHL.

Mental Health, Law and Policy Institute: 207-1502 Island Park Walk, Vancouver; tel. (778) 782-3370; e-mail roesch@sfu.ca; internet members.psyc.sfu.ca/labs/mhlpi; f. 1991; Dir Prof. RON ROESCH.

Pacific Institute for the Mathematical Sciences: tel. (604) 291-4376; f. 1996; Dir Dr P. BORWEIN.

Research Institute on South-Eastern Europe: tel. (604) 291-5597; Dir Dr A. GEROLYMATOS.

TRIUMF: 4004 Wesbrook Mall, Vancouver BC; tel. (604) 222-1047; e-mail communications@triumf.ca; internet www.triumf.ca.

Western Canadian Universities Marine Biological Station (Bamfield): tel. (250) 728-3301; e-mail info@bms.bc.ca; f. 1969; Dir Dr A. N. SPENCER.

W. J. VanDusen BC Business Studies Institute: tel. (604) 291-4183; f. 1982; Dir Dr E. LOVE

TRENT UNIVERSITY

1600 West Bank Drive, Peterborough, ON K9J 7B8

Telephone: (705) 748-1332
E-mail: liaison@trentu.ca
Internet: www.trentu.ca

Founded 1963
Language of instruction: English
Academic year: September to April (2 semesters with reading periods intervening; summer sessions also available)

Chancellor: Dr ROBERTA BONDAR
Pres. and Vice-Chancellor: BONNIE M. PATTERSON
Vice-Pres. for Academic Affairs and Provost: SUSAN APOSTLE-CLARK
Vice-Pres. for Administration: DON O'LEARY
Vice-Pres. for External Relations and Advancement: DIANNE LISTER
Registrar: SUSAN SALUSBURY
Senior Director of Public Affairs: DON CUMMING
Univ. Librarian: ROBERT F. CLARKE

Number of teachers: 467 (325 full-time, 142 part-time)
Number of students: 8,050 undergraduates (6,688 full-time, 1,362 part-time), 277 postgraduates

DEANS

Faculty of Arts and Science: CHRISTINE MCKINNON
Faculty of Graduate Studies: DOUGLAS EVANS

PROFESSORS

ARVIN, M. C., Economics
BANDYOPADHYAY, P., Comparative Development Studies
BERRILL, D., School of Education
BERRILL, M., Biology
BISHOP, J., Business Administration
BRUNGER, A. G., Geography
BUTTLE, J., Geography
CHOUDRY, S., Economics
COGLEY, J. G., Geography
CONOLLY, L. W., English Literature
CURTIS, D. C. A., Economics
DAWSON, P. C., Physics
DELLAMORA, R. J., English Literature and Cultural Studies
DILLON, P., Environmental Studies, Chemistry
EVANS, D., Environmental Studies
EVANS, W., Environmental Studies, Physics
FEKETE, J. A., English Literature, Cultural Studies
FOX, M., Environmental Studies, Biology
HAGMAN, R. S., Anthropology
HEALY, P. F., Anthropology
HEITLINGER, A., Sociology
HURLEY, R., Computer Studies, Science
HUXLEY, C. V., Sociology and Comparative Development Studies
JAMIESON, S., Anthropology
JOHNSTON, G. A., English Literature
JONES, E. H., History
JURY, J. W., Physics and Computer Studies
KANE, S., English Literature, Cultural Studies
KATZ, S., Sociology
KEEFER, S., English Literature
KENNETT, D. J., Psychology
KINZL, K. H., Ancient History and Classics
KITCHEN, H. M., Economics
LAFLEUR, P., Geography
LASENBY, D. C., Biology
LEM, W., International Development Studies and Women's Studies
LEWARS, E. G., Chemistry
MCCASKILL, D. N., Native Studies
MCKENNA-NEWMAN, C., Geography
MCKINNON, C., Philosophy
MAXWELL, E. A., Mathematics
METCALFE, C., Environmental Studies
MILLOY, J., Native Studies and History
MITCHELL, O. S., English Literature
MORRISON, D. R., International Development Studies
NADER, G. A., Geography
NEUFELD, J. E., English Literature
NEUMANN, M., Philosophy
NOL, E., Biology
NORIEGA, T. A., Hispanic Studies
PAEHLKE, R. C., Political Studies, Environmental Studies
PALMER, B., Canadian Studies
PARNIS, M., Chemistry
PATTERSON, B., Business Administration
PETERMAN, M., English Literature
PICKEL, A., Political Studies
POLLOCK, Z., English Literature
POOLE, D. G., Mathematics
REKER, G. T., Psychology
SANGSTER, J., History and Women's Studies
SHEININ, D., History
SLAVIN, A. J., Physics
SMITH, C. T., Psychology
SO, J. K.-F., Anthropology
STANDEN, S. D., History
STOREY, I. C., Ancient History and Classics
STRUTHERS, J. E., Canadian Studies, History
SUTCLIFFE, J., Biology
SVISHCHEV, I., Chemistry
TAMPLIN, M., Anthropology
TAYLOR, C., Geography
TAYLOR, G., History
TINDALE, C., Philosophy
TOPIC, J. R., Anthropology
TORGERSON, D., Environmental and Resource Studies
TROMLY, F. B., English Literature
WADLAND, J. H., Canadian Studies
WALDEN, K., History
WERNICK, A. L., Cultural Studies
WHITE, B., Biology
WINOCUR, G., Psychology
ZHOU, B., Mathematics

TRINITY WESTERN UNIVERSITY

7600 Glover Rd, Langley, BC V2Y 1Y1

Telephone: (604) 888-7511
E-mail: suderman@twu.ca
Internet: www.twu.ca

Founded 1962, university status 1985
Private control
Language of instruction: English
Academic year: September to April

Pres.: Dr JONATHAN RAYMOND
Provost: Dr DENNIS JAMESON
Vice-Pres. for Academic Affairs: Dr DENNIS JAMESON
Vice-Pres. for Advancement: DAVID COONS
Vice-Pres. for Finance: DALE CLARK
Assoc. Provost for Student Life: SHELDON LOEPPKY
Registrar: GRANT MCMILLAN
Librarian: TED GOSHULAK

Library of 430,000 items
Number of teachers: 305 (165 full-time, 140 part-time)
Number of students: 3,500

DEANS

Faculty of Humanities and Social Sciences: Dr ROBERT BURKINSHAW
Faculty of Natural and Applied Sciences: Dr KEN RADANT, Dr KA YIN LEUNG
School of Arts, Media and Culture: Dr DAVID SQUIRES
School of Business and Economics: ANDREA SOBERG
School of Graduate Studies: Dr WILLIAM ACTON
School of Human Kinetics: Dr BLAIR WHITMARSH

UNIVERSITÉ DE MONCTON

Moncton, NB E1A 3E9

Telephone: (506) 858-4000
E-mail: info@umoncton.ca
Internet: www.umoncton.ca

Founded 1864 as St Joseph's Univ., current name adopted 1963
Language of instruction: French
public control
Academic year: September to April

Chancellor: LOUIS R. COMEAU
Rector: YVON FONTAINE
Vice-Rector for Academic Research: NEIL BOUCHER
Vice-Rector for Edmundston Campus: PAUL ALBERT
Vice-Rector for Human Resources and Admin.: NASSIR EL-JABI
Vice-Rector for Shippagan Campus: JOCELYNE ROY VIENNEAU
Sec. Gen.: LYNNE CASTONGUAY (acting)
Librarian: ALAIN ROBERGE

Number of teachers: 389 full-time
Number of students: 5,881 (5,063 full-time, 818 part-time)

Publication: *La Revue*

DEANS

Moncton Campus:

Faculty of Administration: GASTON LEBLANC
Faculty of Arts and Social Sciences: ISABELLE MCKEE-ALLAIN
Faculty of Education: JEAN-FRANÇOIS RICHARD
Faculty of Engineering: PAUL A. CHIASSON
Faculty of Forestry: JEAN-MARIE BINOT
Faculty of Health Sciences and Community Services: PAUL-EMILE BOURQUE
Faculty of Higher Studies and Research: LISA DUBOIS
Faculty of Law: ODETTE SNOW
Faculty of Sciences: FRANCIS LEBLANC

DIRECTORS

Edmundston Campus:

Academic Services: JACQUES PAUL COUTURIER
Arts and Letters: BLANCA NAVARRO-PARDIÑAS
Business Administration: FRANCOIS BOUDREAU
Education: PIERRETTE FORTIN
Human Sciences: LUC VIGNEAULT
School of Nursing: FRANCE L. MARQUIS
Sciences: LUC FRENETTE

Moncton Campus:

School of Kinesiology and Recreology: JEAN-GUY VIENNEAU
School of Nursing: SYLVIE ROUBICHAUD-EKSTRAND

School of Nutrition and Home Economics: SLIMANE BELBRAOUET
School of Psychology: DOUGLAS FRENCH
School of Social Work: HÉLÈNE ALBERT

Shippagan Campus:

Arts and Human Sciences: BENOIT FERRON
Management: ZINE KHELIL
Nursing: SUZANNE OUELLET
Sciences: ELISE MAYRAND

UNIVERSITÉ DE MONTRÉAL

CP 6128, Station Centre-ville, Montréal, QC H3C 3J7
Telephone: (514) 343-6111
E-mail: international@umontreal.ca
Internet: www.umontreal.ca

Founded 1878
public control
Language of instruction: French
Academic year: September to August

Chancellor: LOUISE ROY
Rector: GUY BRETON
Vice-Rector for Academic Affairs and Deputy Rector: HÉLÈNE DAVID
Vice-Rector for Devt and Graduate Relations: DONAT TADDEO
Vice-Rector for Finance and Infrastructure: ÉRIC FILTEAU
Vice-Rector for Human Resources and Planning: ANNE-MARIE BOISVERT
Vice-Rector for Research and Int. Relations: JOSEPH HUBERT
Vice-Rector for Student Affairs and Continuing Education: LOUISE BÉLIVEAU
Gen. Sec.: ALEXANDRE CHABOT
Registrar: PIERRE CHENARD
Librarian: RICHARD DUMONT

Library: see under Libraries and Archives
Number of teachers: 6,856
Number of students: 56,927

Publications: *Cahiers d'Histoire*, *Cahiers du Centre d'études de l'Asie de l'Est*, *Cinémas*, *CIRCUIT* (North American modern music), *Collection Tiré à part* (School of Industrial Relations), *Criminologie*, *Études françaises*, *Géographie physique et Quaternaire*, *Gestion*, *L'Actualité Economique*, *La Gazette des Sciences mathématiques du Québec*, *Le Médecin vétérinaire du Québec*, *META*, *Journal des traducteurs*, *Paragraphes*, *Revue des Sciences de l'Education*, *Revue Juridique Thémis*, *Sociologie et sociétés*, *Surfaces*, *Théologiques*

DEANS

Faculty of Arts and Sciences: GÉRARD BOISMENU
Faculty of Continuing Education: RAYMOND LALANDE (Administrator)
Faculty of Dental Medicine: GILLES LAVIGNE
Faculty of Education Sciences: LOUISE POIRIER
Faculty of Environment Design: GIOVANNI DE PAOLI
Faculty of Graduate Studies: LOUISE BÉLIVEAU
Faculty of Law: GILLES TRUDEAU
Faculty of Medicine: JEAN-LUCIEN ROULEAU
Faculty of Music: SYLVAIN CARON
Faculty of Nursing: FRANCINE GIRARD
Faculty of Pharmacy: PIERRE MOREAU
Faculty of Theology: JEAN-CLAUDE BRETON
Faculty of Veterinary Medicine: RAYMOND S. ROY

PROFESSORS

Faculty of Arts and Sciences

Department of Anthropology:

BEAUCAGE, P.
BERNIER, B.
BIBEAU, G.
CHAPAIS, B.
CHAPDELAINE, C.
CLERMONT, N.
LEAVITT, J.
MEINTEL, D.
MULLER, J.-C.
PANDOLFI, M.
PARADIS, L. I.
SMITH, P.
THIBAULT, P.
TOLSTOY, P.
VERDON, M.

Department of Biology:

ANCTIL, M.
BOISCLAIR, D.
BOUCHARD, A.
BROUILLET, L.
CABANA, T.
CAPPADOCIA, M.
CARIGNAN, R.
HARPER, P.-P.
LEGENDRE, P.
MOLOTCHNIKOFF, S.
MORSE, D.
PINEL-ALLOUL, B.
SAINI, H. S.
SIMON, J.-P.

Department of Chemistry:

BEAUCHAMP, A. L.
BERTRAND, M.
BRISSE, F.
CARRINGTON, T.
CHARETTE, A.
D'AMBOISE, M.
DUGAS, H.
DUROCHER, G.
ELLIS, T. H.
HANESSIAN, S.
HUBERT, J.
LAFLEUR, M.
REBER, C.
ST-JACQUES, M.
WINNIK, F. M.
WUEST, J. D.
ZHU, J.

Department of Classical and Medieval Studies:

FASCIANO, D.

Department of Communication:

CARON, A. H.
GIROUX, L.
LAFRANCE, A. A.
RABOY, M.

Department of Comparative Literature:

CHANADY, A.
GUÉDON, J.-C.
KRYSINSKI, W.
MOSER, W.

Department of Computing Sciences and Operational Research:

ABOULHAMID, E. M.
BRASSARD, G.
CERNY, E.
DSSOULI, R.
FERLAND, J. A.
FLORIAN, M.
FRASSON, C.
GENDREAU, M.
JAUMARD, B.
LAPALME, G.
L'ÉCUYER, P.
MCKENZIE, P.
MARCOTTE, P.
MEUNIER, J.
NGUYEN, S.
POTVIN, J.-Y.
STEWART, N.
VAUCHER, J.

School of Criminology:

BROCHU, S.
BRODEUR, J.-P.
CUSSON, M.
LANDREVILLE, P.
OUIMET, M.
TREMBLAY, P.
TRÉPANIER, J.

Department of Demography:

LAPIERRE-ADAMCYK, E.
PICHÉ, V.

Department of Economics:

BOSSERT, W.
BOYER, M.
BRONSARD, C.
DUDLEY, L.
DUFOUR, J.-M.
GAUDET, G.
GAUDRY, M. J. I.
HOLLANDER, A.
LACROIX, R.
MARTENS, A.
MARTIN, F.
MONTMARQUETTE, C.
POITEVIN, M.
RENAULT, É.
VAILLANCOURT, F.

School of Educational Psychology:

CHARLEBOIS, P.
GAGNON, C.
LARIVÉE, S.
LEBLANC, M.
NORMANDEAU, S.
VAN GIJSEGHEM, H.
VITARO, F.

Department of English Studies:

MARTIN, R. K.

Department of French Studies:

BEAULIEU, J.-P.
CAMBRON, M.
GAUVIN, L.
HÉBERT, F.
LAFLÈCHE, G.
LAROSE, J.
MELANÇON, R.
MICHAUD, G.
NEPVEU, P.
PIERSSENS, M.
SOARE, A.
VACHON, S.

Department of Geography:

BRYANT, C. R.
CAVAYAS, F.
COFFEY, W.
COMTOIS, C.
COMTOIS, P.
COURCHESNE, F.
DE KONINCK, R.
FOGGIN, P. M.
GANGLOFF, P.
GRAY, J. T.
MANZAGOL, C.
MAROIS, C.
RICHARD, P. J. H.
ROY, A. G.
SINGH, B.
THOUEZ, J.-P.

Department of Geology:

BOUCHARD, M. A.
MARTIGNOLE, J.
TRZCIENSKI, W. E.

Department of History:

ANGERS, D.
BOGLIONI, P.
DICKINSON, J. A.
HUBERMAN, M.
KEEL, O.
LÉTOURNEAU, P.
LUSIGNAN, S.
MORIN, C.
PERREAULT, J. Y.
RABKIN, Y.
RAMIREZ, B.
ROUILLARD, J.
SUTTO, C.

Department of History of Art:
DE MOURA SOBRAL, L.
DUBREUIL, N.
GAUDREAULT, A.
KRAUSZ, P.
LAFRAMBOISE, A.
LAMOUREUX, J.
LAROUCHE, M.
LHOTE, J.-F.
MARSOLAIS, G.
NAUBERT-RISER, C.
TOUSIGNANT, S.
TRUDEL, J.

School of Industrial Relations:
BOURQUE, R.
BROSSARD, M.
CHICHA, M.-T.
COUSINEAU, J.-M.
DOLAN, S.
DURAND, P.
GUÉRIN, G.
MURRAY, G.
SIMARD, M.
TRUDEAU, G.

School of Library and Information Sciences:
BERTRAND-GASTALDY, S.
COUTURE, C.
DESCHATELETS, G.
LAJEUNESSE, M.
SAVARD, R.

Department of Linguistics and Translation:
CONNORS, K.
CORMIER, M. C.
FORD, A.
HOSINGTON, B.
JAREMA-ARVANITAKIS, G.
KITTREDGE, R.
MEL'ČUK, I. A.
MÉNARD, N.
MORIN, J.-Y.
MORIN, Y.-C.
NUSELOVICI NOUSS, A.
PATRY, R.
ST-PIERRE, P.
SCHULZE-BUSACKER, E.
SINGH, R.

Department of Literature and Modern Languages:
BOUCHARD, J.
PECK, J.
RÄKEL, H.-H.

Department of Mathematics and Statistics:
ARMINJON, P.
BÉLAIR, J.
BENABDALLAH, K.
BILODEAU, M.
BRUNET, R.
CLÉROUX, R.
DELFOUR, M.
DUFRESNE, D.
FRIGON, M.
GAUTHIER, P.
GIRI, N. C.
GIROUX, A.
HUSSIN, V.
JOFFE, A.
LALONDE, F.
LÉGER, C.
LEPAGE, Y.
LESSARD, S.
PATERA, J.
PERRON, F.
RAHMAN, Q. I.
REYES, G.
ROSENBERG, I.
ROUSSEAU, C.
ROY, R.
SABIDUSSI, G.
SAINT-AUBIN, Y.
SANKOFF, D.
SCHLOMIUK, D.
TURGEON, J.
WINTERNITZ, P.
ZAIDMAN, S.

Department of Philosophy:
BAKKER, E. J.
BODEÜS, R.
DUCHESNEAU, F.
GAUTHIER, Y.
GRONDIN, J.
LAGUEUX, M.
LAURIER, D.
LEPAGE, F.
LÉVESQUE, C.
PICHÉ, C.
ROY, J.
SEYMOUR, M.

Department of Physics:
BASTIEN, P.
CAILLÉ, A.
CARIGNAN, C.
COCHRANE, R. W.
DEMERS, S.
FONTAINE, G.
GOULARD, B.
LAPOINTE, J.-Y.
LAPRADE, R.
LEONELLI, R.
LÉPINE, Y.
LEROY, C.
LESSARD, L.
LEWIS, L. J.
LONDON, D.
MICHAUD, G.
MOFFAT, A.
MOISAN, M.
ROORDA, S.
TARAS, P.
TEICHMANN, J.
VINCENT, A.
WESEMAEL, F.
ZACEK, V.

Department of Politics:
BÉLANGER, A.-J.
BERNIER, G.
BLAIS, A.
BOISMENU, G.
CLOUTIER, É.
DION, S.
DUQUETTE, M.
ÉTHIER, D.
FAUCHER, P.
FORTMANN, M.
JENSON, J.
MONIÈRE, D.
NADEAU, R.
NOËL, A.
SOLDATOS, P.
THÉRIEN, J.-P.

Department of Psychology:
BERGERON, J.
BOUCHARD, M.-A.
BRUNET, L.
CLAES, M.
COMEAU, J.
COSSETTE-RICARD, M.
CYR, M.
DAVID, H.
DOYON, J.
DUBÉ, L.
FAVREAU, O.
FORTIN, A.
GRANGER, L.
HACCOUN, R.
HODGINS, S.
LASRY, J.-C.
LASSONDE, M.
LECOMTE, C.
LEPORE, F.
MATHIEU, M.
NADEAU, L.
PAGÉ, M.
PERETZ, I.
PERRON, J.
ROBERT, M.
SABOURIN, M.
SAVOIE, A.
STRAVYNSKI, A.
TREMBLAY, R. E.
WRIGHT, J.
ZAVALLONI, M.

School of Social Work:
BERNIER, D.
CHAMBERLAND, C.
GROULX, L. H.
LEGAULT, G.
MAYER, R.
PANET-RAYMOND, J.
RINFRET-RAYNOR, M.
RONDEAU, G.

Department of Sociology:
BERNARD, P.
FOURNIER, M.
HAMEL, J.
HAMEL, P.
HOULE, G.
JUTEAU, D.
LAURIN, N.
MCALL, C.
MAHEU, L.
RACINE, L.
RENAUD, J.
RENAUD, M.
ROCHER, G.
SALES, A.
VAILLANCOURT, J.-G.

Faculty of Dental Medicine

Department of Dental Prosthesis:
BALTAJIAN, H.
BOUDRIAS, P.
LAMARCHE, C.
PRÉVOST, A.
TACHÉ, R.

Department of Oral Health:
CHARLAND, R.
JULIEN, M.
KANDELMAN, D.
LAVIGNE, G.
MASSEREDJIAN, V.
REMISE, C.
TURGEON, J.
WECHSLER, M.

Department of Stomatology:
DONOHUE, W. B.
DUNCAN, G.
DUPUIS, R.
DUQUETTE, P.
FOREST, D.
LEMAY, H.
MICHAUD, M.
NANCI, A.

Faculty of Education Sciences

Department of Curriculum and Instruction:
BEER-TOKER, M.
CHARLAND, J.-P.
GAGNÉ, G.
LEMOYNE, G.
PAINCHAUD, G.
PARET, M.-C.
PIERRE, R.
RETALLACK-LAMBERT, N.
SAINT-JACQUES, D.
THÉRIEN, M.
VAN GRUNDERBEECK, N.

Department of Education and Educational Administration Studies:
AJAR, D.
BOURGEAULT, G.
BRASSARD, A.
CHENÉ, A.
CRESPO, M.
DUPUIS, P.
JOFFE-NICODÈME, A.
LESSARD, C.
PELLETIER, G.
PROULX, J.-P.
TARDIF, M.
TRAHAN, M.
VAN DER MAREN, J.-M.

Department of Psychopedagogy and Andragogy:

COMEAU, M.
DUFRESNE-TASSÉ, C.
GAUDREAU, J.
LANGEVIN, J.
LÉVESQUE, M.
MARCHAND, L.
TREMBLAY, N.

Faculty of Environmental Design

School of Architecture:

ADAMCZYK, G.
DALIBARD, J.
DAVIDSON, C. H.
MARSAN, J.-C.

School of Industrial Design:

CAMOUS, R. F.
FINDELI, A.
LECLERC, A.

Department of Kinesiology:

ALAIN, C.
ALLARD, P.
GAGNON, M.
GARDINER, P. F.
LABERGE, S.
LAVOIE, J.-M.
LÉGER, L.
PÉRONNET, F.
PROTEAU, L.

School of Landscape Architecture:

CINQ-MARS, I.
JACOBS, P.
LAFARGUE, B.
POULLAOUEC-GONIDEC, P.

Institute of Urbanism:

BARCELO, A.-M.
BLANC, B.
BOISVERT, M. A.
CARDINAL, A.
GARIÉPY, M.
LESSARD, M.
MCNEIL, J.
PARENTEAU, R.
SOKOLOFF, B.
TRÉPANIER, M.-O.

Faculty of Law:

BENYEKHLEF, K.
BICH, M.-F.
BOISVERT, A.-M.
BRISSON, J.-M.
CHEVRETTE, F.
CIOTOLA, P.
CÔTÉ, P.-A.
CÔTÉ, P. P.
CRÉPEAU, F.
DESLAURIERS, P.
DUMONT, H.
FABIEN, C.
FRÉMONT, J.
GAGNON, J. D.
GOLDSTEIN, G.
GRUNING, D.
HÉTU, J.
KNOPPERS, B. M.
LABRÈCHE, D.
LAJOIE, A.
LAMONTAGNE, D.-C.
LEFEBVRE, G.
LEROUX, T.
LLUELLES, D.
MACKAAY, E.
MOLINARI, P.
NEUWAHI, N.
PINARD, D.
POPOVICI, A.
ROCHER, G.
TALPIS, J.
TREMBLAY, A.
TREMBLAY, L.
TRUDEL, P.
TURP, D.
VIAU, L.

WOEHRLING, J.

Faculty of Medicine

Department of Anaesthesiology:

BLAISE, G.
DONATI, F.
HARDY, J.-F.

Department of Biochemistry:

BOILEAU, G.
BOUVIER, M.
BRAKIER-GINGRAS, L.
BRISSON, N.
CRINE, P.
DAIGNEAULT, R.
DESGROSEILLERS, L.
LANG, F. B.
ROKEACH, L. A.
SKUP, D.
SYGUSCH, J.

Department of Family Medicine:

BEAULIEU, M.-D.
MILLETTE, B.

Department of Health Administration:

BÉLAND, F.
BLAIS, R.
CHAMPAGNE, F.
CONTANDRIOPOULOS, A.-P.
DENIS, J.-L.
DUSSAULT, G.
LAMARCHE, P.
SICOTTE, C.
TILQUIN, C.

Department of Medicine:

AYOUB, J.
BICHET, D.
BRADLEY, E.
BRAZEAU, P.
BUTTERWORTH, R. F.
CARDINAL, J.
CHIASSON, J.-L.
D'AMOUR, P.
DELESPESSE, G. J. T.
DUQUETTE, P.
GOUGOUX, A.
GRASSINO, A.
HALLÉ, J.-P.
HAMET, P.
HUET, M.
LACROIX, A.
LAPLANTE, L.
LECOURS, A. R.
LE LORIER, J.
MALO, J.-L.
MARLEAU, D.
MARTEL-PELLETIER, J.
MATTE, R.
MES-MASSON, A.-M.
NADEAU, R.
NATTEL, S.
PELLETIER, J.-P.
PERREAULT, C.
POITRAS, P.
POMIER-LAYRARGUES, G.
RASIO, E.
SARFATI, M.
SÉNÉCAL, J.-L.
TREMBLAY, J.
VINAY, P.

Department of Microbiology and Immunology:

AUGER, P.
COHEN, É.
DE REPENTIGNY, L.
HALLENBECK, P.
LEMAY, G.
MENEZES, J. P. C. A.
MONTPLAISIR, S.
MORISSET, R.
SEKALY, R.-P.

Department of Nutrition:

DELISLE, H.
DES ROSIERS, C.
GARREL, D.

GAVINO, V.
HOUDE-NADEAU, M.
LÉVY, E.
POEHLMAN, É.
PRENTKI, M.
SERRI, O.
SIMARD-MAVRIKAKIS, S.
VAN DE WERVE, G.

Department of Obstetrics and Gynaecology:

BÉLISLE, S.
DROUIN, P.

Department of Occupational and Environmental Health:

CARRIER, G.
CHAKRABARTI, S. K.
GÉRIN, M.
KRISHNAN, K.
VIAU, C.
ZAYED, J.

Department of Ophthalmology:

BOISJOLY, H.
LABELLE, P.

Department of Paediatrics:

ALVAREZ, F.
BARD, H.
CHEMTOB, S.
FOURON, J.-C.
FRAPPIER, J.-Y.
GAGNAN-BRUNETTE, M.
GAUTHIER-CHOUINARD, M.
LABUDA, D.
LACROIX, J.
LAMBERT, M.
LAPOINTE, N.
RASQUIN-WEBER, A.-M.
ROBITAILLE, P.
ROUSSEAU, É.
SEIDMAN, E.
TEASDALE, F.
VANASSE, M.
VAN VLIET, G.
WEBER, M.
WILKINS, J.

Department of Pathology and Cellular Biology:

BENDAYAN, M.
CHARTRAND, P.
DESCARRIES, L.
GIROUX, L.
KESSOUS, A.
LATOUR, J.-G.
SCHÜRCH, W.

Department of Pharmacology:

CARDINAL, R.
DE LÉAN, A.
DUMONT, L.
DU SOUICH, P.
ÉLIE, R.
GASCON-BARRÉ, M.
LAMBERT, C.
LAROCHELLE, P.
LAVOIE, P.-A.
MOMPARLER, R.
YOUSEF, I.

Department of Physiology:

ANAND-SRIVASTAVA, M.
BERGERON, M.
BERTELOOT, A.
BILLETTE, J.
CASTELLUCCI, V.
COUTURE, R.
DE CHAMPLAIN, J.
DREW, T. B.
FELDMAN, A. G.
GULRAJANI, R.
KALASKA, J. F.
LACAILLE, J.-C.
LAMARRE, Y.
LAVALLÉE, M.
LEBLANC, A.-R.
MAESTRACCI, D.
MALO, C.

READER, T. A.
ROBERGE, F.
ROSSIGNOL, S.
SAUVÉ, R.
SMITH, A.

Department of Preventive and Social Medicine:

BRODEUR, J.-M.
DASSA, C.
FOURNIER, P.
LABERGE-NADEAU, C.
LAMBERT, J.
MAHEUX, B.
PHILIPPE, P.
PINEAULT, R.
POTVIN, L.
SÉGUIN, L.
SIEMIATYCKI, J.

Department of Psychiatry:

AMYOT, A.
CHOUINARD, G.
LALONDE, P.
LEMAY, M.-L.
MONDAY, J.
MONTPLAISIR, J. Y.
SAUCIER, J.-F.
WEISSTUB, D. N.

Department of Radiology, Radio-Oncology and Nuclear Medicine:

BRETON, G.
LAFORTUNE, M.
SAMSON, L.

School of Rehabilitation:

ARSENAULT, B.
BOURBONNAIS, D.
CHAPMAN, C. E.
DUTIL, E.
FERLAND, F.
FORGET, R.
GAUTHIER-GAGNON, C.
GRAVEL, D.
WEISS-LAMBROU, R.

School of Speech Pathology and Audiology:

GAGNÉ, J.-P.
GETTY, L.
JOANETTE, Y.
LE DORZE, G.
SKA, B.

Department of Surgery:

BEAUCHAMP, G.
BERNARD, D.
CAOUETTE-LABERGE, L.
CARRIER, M.
CHARLIN, B.
DALOZE, P.
DUBÉ, S.
DURANCEAU, A.
LABELLE, H.
PAGÉ, P.
PAQUIN, J.-M.
RIVARD, C.-H.
ROBIDOUX, A.
SMEESTERS, C.
VALIQUETTE, L.
WASSEF, R.

Faculty of Music:

BELKIN, A.
DESROCHES, M.
DURAND, M.
EVANGELISTA, J.
GUERTIN, M.
LEFEBVRE, M.-T.
LEROUX, R.
LONGTIN, M.
NATTIEZ, J.-J.
PANNETON, I.
PICHÉ, J.
POIRIER, R.
RIVEST, J.-F.
SMOJE, D.
VAILLANCOURT, L.

Faculty of Nursing:

DUCHARME, F.
DUQUETTE, A.
GAGNON, L.
GOULET, C.
GRENIER, R.
KÉROUAC, S.
REIDY, M.
RICARD, N.

School of Optometry:

BEAULNE, C.
CASANOVA, C.
FAUBERT, J.
KERGOAT, H.
LOVASIK, J. V.
PTITO, M.
SIMONET, P.

Faculty of Pharmacy:

ADAM, A.
BESNER, J.-G.
BISAILLON, S.
BRAZIER, J.-L.
CARTILIER, L.
GAGNÉ, J.
LAURIER, C.
MCMULLEN, J.-N.
MAILHOT, C.
ONG, H.
TURGEON, J.
VARIN, F.
WINNIK, F.
YAMAGUCHI, N.

Faculty of Theology:

DUHAIME, J.
NADEAU, J.-G.
PETIT, J.-C.

Faculty of Veterinary Medicine

Department of Clinical Sciences:

BLAIS, D.
BONNEAU, N, H.
BOUCHARD, E.
BRETON, L.
CARRIER, M.
CÉCYRE, A. J.
CHALIFOUX, A.
COUTURE, Y.
CUVELLIEZ, S.
D'ALLAIRE, S.
DI FRUSCIA, R.
DUBREUIL, P.
LAMOTHE, P. J.
LAROUCHE, Y.
LAVERTY, S.
LAVOIE, J.-P.
MARCOUX, M.
PARADIS, M.
VAILLANCOURT, D.
VRINS, A.

Department of Pathology and Microbiology:

BIGRAS-POULIN, M.
DROLET, R.
DUBREUIL, D.
EL AZHARY, Y.
FAIRBROTHER, J. M.
FONTAINE, M.
GIRARD, C.
GOTTSCHALK, M.
HAREL, J.
HIGGINS, R.
JACQUES, M.
LALLIER, R.
LARIVIÈRE, S.
MITTAL, K. R.
MORIN, M.
ROY, R. S.
SCHOLL, D. T.
SILIM, A. N.

Department of Veterinary Biomedicine:

BARRETTE, D.
BISAILLON, A.
DALLAIRE, A.
DEROTH, L.
GOFF, A. K.
LARIVIÈRE, N.
LUSSIER, J. G.
MURPHY, B. D.
SILVERSIDES, D. W.
SIROIS, J.
SMITH, L. C.
TREMBLAY, A. V.

AFFILIATED INSTITUTIONS

Ecole des Hautes Etudes Commerciales: 3000 ch. de la Côte-Sainte-Catherine, Montréal, QC H3T 2A7; tel. (514) 340-6000; f. 1907; Dir JEAN-MARIE TOULOUSE.

Ecole Polytechnique: 2500 ch. de Polytechnique, Montréal, QC H3T 1J4; tel. (514) 340-4711; f. 1873; Dir RÉJEAN PLAMONDON

UNIVERSITÉ DE SHERBROOKE

2500 blvd de l'Université, Sherbrooke, QC J1K 2R1
Telephone: (819) 821-7000
E-mail: admission@usherbrooke.ca
Internet: www.usherbrooke.ca

Founded 1954
Private control
Language of instruction: French
Academic year: SeptemberAugust

Chancellor: H. E. Mgr LUC CYR (Catholic Archbishop of Sherbrooke)
Rector: LUCE SAMOISETTE
Vice-Rector for Admin.: JOANNE ROCH
Vice-Rector for Personnel and Students Life: MARTIN BUTEAU
Vice-Rector for Research: JACQUES BEAUVAIS
Vice-Rector for Studies: LUCIE LAFLAMME
Sec. Gen. and Vice-Rector for Int. Relations: JOCELYNE FAUCHER
Registrar: FRANCE MYETTE
Librarian: SYLVIE BELZILE

Library of 1,676,000 vols
Number of teachers: 3,400
Number of students: 37,000

UNIVERSITÉ DU QUÉBEC

475 rue de Parvis, Québec, QC G1K 9H7
Telephone: (418) 657-3551
E-mail: infoormation@uquebec.ca
Internet: www.uquebec.ca

Founded 1968
State control
Language of instruction: French

Pres.: SYLVIE BEAUCHAMP
Vice-Pres. for Admin. and Finance: ISABELLE BOUCHER
Vice-Pres. for Teaching and Research: LYNE SAUVAGEAU
Sec. Gen.: ANDRÉ G. ROY
Dir for Communication: VALÉRIE REUILLARD (acting)
Librarian: (vacant)

Library of 2,340,000 vols
Number of teachers: 2,619
Number of students: 92,000

Publications: *Étudier dans le réseau de' l Université du Québec* (1 a year), *Luniversité en quelques chiffres* (1 a year).

CONSTITUENT INSTITUTIONS

Université du Québec en Abitibi-Témiscamingue

445 blvd de l'Université, Rouyn-Noranda, QC J9X 5E4
Telephone: (819) 762-2922
E-mail: registraire@uqat.ca
Internet: www.uqat.uquebec.ca

Founded 1981 as Centre d'études universitaires, current name adopted 1984

Rector: JULES ARSENAULT

Vice-Rector for Resources: L. BERGERON
Vice-Rector for Teaching and Research: ROGER CLAUX
Registrar: N. MURPHY
Dir for Services: N. MURPHY
Sec. Gen.: J. TURGEON
Librarian: A. BÉLAND

Library of 201,000 vols
Number of teachers: 75
Number of students: 2,843 (911 full-time and 1,932 part-time)

Université du Québec à Chicoutimi

555 blvd de l'Université, Chicoutimi, QC G7H 2B1
Telephone: (418) 545-5011
E-mail: regist@uqac.ca
Internet: www.uqac.ca

Founded 1969
State control
Language of instruction: French
Academic year: September to April

Rector: MICHEL BELLEY
Sec. Gen.: MARTIN CÔTÉ
Registrar: CLAUDIO ZOCCASTELLO
Librarian: GILLES CARON

Library of 250,000 vols
Number of teachers: 225
Number of students: 6,500 (3,200 full-time, 3,300 part-time)

Publication: *UQACtualité* (4 a year)

Université du Québec en Outaouais

CP 1250, Succursale Hull, Gatineau, QC J8X 3X7
Telephone: (819) 595-3900
E-mail: registraire@uqo.ca
Internet: www.uqo.ca

Founded 1970
Language of instruction: French
Academic year: September to June

Rector: JEAN VAILLANCOURT
Sec. Gen.: LUC MAURICE
Registrar: ROBERT BONDAZ
Librarian: HÉLÈNE LAROUCHE

Library of 210,000 vols
Number of teachers: 184
Number of students: 5,492 (2,884 full-time, 2,608 part-time)

Publication: *Savoir Outaouais* (3 a year)

Université du Québec à Montréal

CP 8888, Succ. Centre-ville, Montréal, QC H3C 3P8
Telephone: (514) 987-3000
E-mail: registrariat@uqam.ca
Internet: www.regis.uqam.ca

Founded 1969

Rector (vacant)
Vice-Rector for Academic Services and Technological Devt: MICHEL ROBILLARD
Vice-Rector for Academics and Research: LYNN DRAPEAU
Vice-Rector for Human Resources and Admin. Affairs: ALAIN DUFOUR
Vice-Rector for Partnership and External Affairs: PAULE LEDUC (acting)
Vice-Rector for Strategic and Financial Planning and Gen. Sec.: LOUISE DANDURAND
Registrar: CLAUDETTE JODOIN
Librarian: JEAN-PIERRE CÔTÉ

Library of 2,388,000 vols
Number of teachers: 903
Number of students: 37,395 (18,406 full-time, 18,989 part-time)

Université du Québec à Rimouski

300 allée des Ursulines, Rimouski, QC G5L 3A1
Telephone: (418) 723-1986
E-mail: uqar@uqar.uquebec.ca
Internet: www.uqar.ca

Founded 1969
State control
Language of instruction: French
Academic year: September to April (2 semesters)

Rector: JEAN-PIERRE OUELLET
Vice-Rector for Admin. and Human Resources: MARJOLAINE VIEL
Vice-Rector for Teaching and Research: FRANÇOIS DESCHÊNES
Sec. Gen.: ALAIN CARON
Librarian: DENIS BOISVERT

Library of 226,384 vols
Number of teachers: 215
Number of students: 6,684 (3,441 full-time, 3,243 part-time)

Publications: *Ľuniversitaire: Magazine de lUQAR* (4 a year), *UQAR-Info* (8 a year).

ATTACHED CENTRE

Oceanography Centre: Dir V. KOUTITONSKY

Université du Québec à Trois-Rivières

3351 blvd des Forges, CP 500, Trois-Rivières, QC G9A 5H7
Telephone: (819) 376-5045
E-mail: crmultiservice@uqtr.ca
Internet: www.uqtr.ca

Founded 1969
provincial control
Academic year: September to April

Rector: GHISLAIN BOURQUE
Vice-Rector for Admin. and Finance: RENÉ GARNEAU
Sec. Gen.: ANDRÉ GABIAS
Registrar: NORMAND SHAFFER

Library of 500,000 vols
Number of teachers: 352
Number of students: 11,427 (6,650 full-time, 4,777 part-time)

Publication: *En Tête*

Ecole Nationale d'Administration Publique

555 blvd Charest Est, Québec, QC G1K 9E5
Telephone: (418) 641-3000

Founded 1969

Dir-Gen.: PIERRE DE CELLES

Library of 90,000 vols
Number of teachers: 59
Number of students: 1,143

Ecole de Technologie Supérieure

1100 rue Notre-Dame Ouest, Montréal, QC H3C 1K3
Telephone: (514) 396-8800
E-mail: admission@etsmtl.ca
Internet: www.etsmtl.ca

Founded 1974

Dir-Gen.: YVES BEAUCHAMP

Library of 65,000 vols
Number of teachers: 126

INRS-Institut Armand-Frappier

531 blvd des Prairies, Laval, QC H7V 1B7
Telephone: (450) 687-5010

Founded 1938

Human, animal, environmental health (immunity, infectious diseases, cancer, epidemiology, biotechnologies, toxicology, pharmacodiomistry sciences)

Dir-Gen.: CHARLES DOZOIS

Library of 10,000 vols
Number of teachers: 45
Number of students: 170

Institut National de la Recherche Scientifique

490 de la Couronne, Québec, QC G1K 9A9
Telephone: (418) 654-4677
E-mail: communications@adm.inrs.ca
Internet: www.inrs.ca

Founded 1969
Language of instruction: French

Dir-Gen.: DANIEL CODERRE

Library of 58,000 vols
Number of teachers: 155
Number of students: 642

Télé-université

Tour de la Cité, 2600 blvd Laurier, 7e étage, Québec, QC G1V 4V9
Telephone: (418) 657-2262
E-mail: info@teluq.ca

Founded 1972
Distance-learning programmes

Dir-Gen.: A. MARREC

Library of 12,000 vols
Number of teachers: 35
Number of students: 5,716 (258 full-time, 5,458 part-time)

UNIVERSITÉ LAVAL

Québec, QC G1V 0A6
Telephone: (418) 656-2131
E-mail: accueil@sg.ulaval.ca
Internet: www.ulaval.ca

Founded 1852, Royal Charter signed December 1852, Pontifical Charter 1876, Provincial Charter 1970
Language of instruction: French
Academic year: September to August

Rector: DENIS BRIÈRE
Vice-Rector for Academic Int. Activities: BERNARD GARNIER
Vice-Rector for Admin. and Finances: JOSÉE GERMAIN
Vice-Rector for Human Resources: MICHEL BEAUCHAMP
Vice-Rector for Research and Creation: EDWIN BOURGET
Deputy Vice-Rector for Research and Creation: CHRISTIANE PICHÉ
Dir for Continuing Education: PIERRE DIONNE
Dir for Undergraduate Studies: SERGE TALBOT
Dean for Graduate Studies: MARIE AUDETTE
Sec. Gen.: MONIQUE RICHER
Registrar: DANIELLE FLEURY
Librarian: SILVIE DELORME

Library: see under Libraries and Archives
Number of teachers: 1,587
Number of students: 37,295 (24,415 full-time, 12,880 part-time)

Publications: *Anthropologie et Sociétés* (anthropology), *Cahiers de Droit* (law), *Cahiers de Géographie du Québec* (geography), *Cahiers de Recherche* (1 a year, economics), *CRIRES* (education), *Communication* (mass communication), *Didaskalia* (2 a year, education), *Ecoscience* (biology), *Ethnologies* (1 a year, journal of Canadian folklore studies), *Études Internationales* (4 a year, international studies), *Études Inuits* (2 a year, Inuit studies), *Études Littérataires* (3 a year, literature), *Langues et Linguistique* (linguistics), *L'Année Francophone Internationale (L'AFI)* (literary), *Laval Théologique et Philosophique* (theology and philosophy), *Les Cahiers du Journalisme* (journalism), *Recherches Féministes* (feminism), *Recherches Sociographiques* (1 a year, Quebec studies), *Rédiger* (1 a year, technical writing), *Relations Industrielles* (industrial relations), *Revue d'Histoire Intellectuelle de l'Amérique Française* (12 a year), *Revue Scientifique* (education), *Service Social* (online, social work), *Visio* (history)

DEANS AND DIRECTORS

Faculty of Administrative Sciences: ROBERT W. MANTHA
Faculty of Agriculture and Food Sciences: JEAN-PAUL LAFOREST
Faculty of Dentistry: ANDRÉ FOURNIER
Faculty of Education: MARCEL MONETTE
Faculty of Forestry and Geomatics: ROBERT BEAUREGARD
Faculty of Law: PIERRE LEMIEUX
Faculty of Letters: THIERRY BELLEGUIC
Faculty of Medicine: PIERRE JACOB DURAND
Faculty of Music: PAUL CADRIN
Faculty of Nursing Sciences: DIANE MORIN
Faculty of Pharmacy: JEAN-PIERRE GRÉGOIRE
Faculty of Philosophy: LUC LANGLOIS
Faculty of Sciences and Engineering: GUY GENDRON
Faculty of Social Sciences: FRANÇOIS BLAIS
Faculty of Theology and Religious Sciences: MARC PELCHAT
Faculty of Urban Planning, Architecture and Visual Arts: RICHARD PLEAU
Québec Institute of Higher International Studies: PAUL GAUTHIER

PROFESSORS

Faculty of Administrative Sciences (Pavillon Palasis-Prince, Bureau 1322, Québec, QC G1K 7P4; tel. (418) 656-2180; e-mail fsa@fsa.ulaval.ca; internet www.fsa.ulaval.ca):

AUDET, M., Management
BANVILLE, C., Management Information Systems
BEAULIEU, M.-C., Finance and Insurance
BÉDARD, J., Accounting (Sciences)
BÉLIVEAU, D., Marketing
BELLEMARE, G., Finance and Insurance
BERGERON, F., Management Information Systems
BERNIER, G., Finance and Insurance
BHERER, H., Management
BLAIS, R., Management
BOCTOR, F. F., Operations and Decision Systems
BOIRAL, O., Management
BOULAIRE, C., Marketing
BOURDEAU, L., Management
BRUN, J.-P., Management
CARPENTIER, C., Accounting (School)
CAYER, M., Management
CORMIER, E., Accounting (School)
COULOMBE, D., Accounting (Sciences)
D'AVIGNON, G. R., Operations and Decision Systems
DES ROSIERS, F., Management
DIONNE, P., Management
FISCHER, P. K., Finance and Insurance
GARAND, D. J., Management
GARNIER, B., Management
GASCON, A., Operations and Decision Systems
GASSE, Y., Management
GAUTHIER, A., Operations and Decision Systems
GAUVIN, S., Marketing
GENDRON, M., Finance and Insurance
GOSSELIN, M., Accounting (School)
GRISÉ, J., Management
HASKELL, N., Marketing
KETTANI, O., Operations and Decision Systems
KISS, L. N., Operations and Decision Systems
LACASSE, N., Management
LAI, V. S., Finance and Insurance
LAMOND, B., Operations and Decision Systems
LANDRY, R., Management
LANG, P., Operations and Decision Systems
LEE-GOSSELIN, H., Management
LESCEUX, D., Marketing
LETARTE, P.-A., Management
MANTHA, R. W., Management Information Systems
MARTEL, A., Operations and Decision Systems
MOFFET, D., Finance and Insurance
MONTREUIL, B., Operations and Decision Systems
NADEAU, L., Accounting (School)
NADEAU, R., Operations and Decision Systems
PAQUETTE, S., Accounting (Sciences)
PARÉ, P.-V., Accounting (School)
PASCOT, D., Management Information Systems
POULIN, D., Management
PRÉMONT, P. E., Management Information Systems
RENAUD, J., Operations and Decision Systems
RIDJANOVIC, D., Management Information Systems
RIGAUX-BRICMONT, B., Marketing
ROY, M.-C., Management Information Systems
ROY, M.-J., Management
SAINT PIERRE, J., Finance and Insurance
SEROR, ANN C., Management
SU, Z., Management
SURET, J.-M., Accounting (School)
VERNA, G., Management
VÉZINA, R., Marketing
ZINS, M., Marketing

Faculty of Agriculture and Food Sciences (Pavillon Paul-Comtois, Bureau 1122, Québec, QC G1K 7P4; tel. (418) 656-3145; e-mail fsaa@fsaa.ulaval.ca; internet www.fsaa.ulaval.ca):

ALLARD, G., Plant Science
AMIOT, J., Food Science and Nutrition
ANGERS, P., Food Science and Nutrition
ANTOUN, H., Soils and Agricultural Engineering
ARUL, J., Food Science and Nutrition
ASSELIN, A., Plant Science
BAILEY, J. L., Animal Sciences
BEAUCHAMP, C. J., Plant Science
BEAUDOIN, P., Agricultural Economics and Consumer Sciences
BEAUDRY, M., Food Science and Nutrition
BÉLANGER, R., Plant Science
BELZILE, F., Plant Science
BENHAMOU, N., Plant Science
BERGERON, R., Animal Sciences
BERNIER, J.-F., Animal Sciences
BLACKBURN, M., Soils and Agricultural Engineering
BRODEUR, J., Plant Science
CAILLIER, M., Soils and Agricultural Engineering
CALKINS, P., Agricultural Economics and Consumer Sciences
CAREL, M., Agricultural Economics and Consumer Sciences
CARON, J., Soils and Agricultural Engineering
CASTAIGNE, F., Food Science and Nutrition
CESCAS, M. P., Soils and Agricultural Engineering
CHALIFOUR, F. P., Plant Science
CHAREST, P.-M., Plant Science
CHOUINARD, Y., Animal Sciences
COLLIN, J., Plant Science
DANSEREAU, B., Plant Science
DEBAILLEUL, G., Agricultural Economics and Consumer Sciences
DESJARDINS, Y., Plant Science
DESPRES, J.-P., Food Science and Nutrition
DESROSIERS, T., Food Science and Nutrition
DION, P., Plant Science
DOSTALER, D., Plant Science
DOYEN, M., Agricultural Economics and Consumer Sciences
DUFOUR, J. C., Agricultural Economics and Consumer Sciences
EMOND, J.-P., Soils and Agricultural Engineering
FLISS, I., Food Science and Nutrition
FORTIN, J., Soils and Agricultural Engineering
GALIBOIS, I., Food Science and Nutrition
GALLICHAND, J., Soils and Agricultural Engineering
GAUTHIER, S., Food Science and Nutrition
GERVAIS, J.-P., Agricultural Economics and Consumer Services
GOSSELIN, A., Plant Science
GOUIN, D., Agricultural Economics and Consumer Sciences
GOULET, J., Food Science and Nutrition
JACQUES, H., Food Science and Nutrition
KARAM, A., Soils and Agricultural Engineering
LACHANCE, M. J., Agricultural Economics and Consumer Sciences
LAFOREST, J.-P., Animal Sciences
LAGACÉ, R., Soils and Agricultural Engineering
LAMARCHE, B., Food Science and Nutrition
LAMBERT, R., Agricultural Economics and Consumer Sciences
LAPOINTE, G., Food Science and Nutrition
LARUE, B., Agricultural Economics and Consumer Sciences
LAVERDIÈRE, M.-R., Soils and Agricultural Engineering
LEFRANÇOIS, M., Animal Sciences
LEMIEUX, S., Food Science and Nutrition
LEROUX, G., Plant Science
LEVALLOIS, R., Agricultural Economics and Consumer Sciences
LOCONG, A., Food Science and Nutrition
MAKHLOUF, J., Food Science and Nutrition
MARQUIS, A., Soils and Agricultural Engineering
MARTEL, R., Food Science and Nutrition
MARTIN, F., Agricultural Economics and Consumer Sciences
MICHAUD, D., Plant Science
MORISSET, M., Agricultural Economics and Consumer Sciences
OLIVIER, A., Plant Science
OUELLET, D., Food Science and Nutrition
PAQUIN, P., Food Science and Nutrition
PARENT, D., Animal Science
PARENT, L. E., Soils and Agricultural Engineering
PELLERIN, D., Animal Sciences
PERRIER, J.-P., Agricultural Economics and Consumer Sciences
PICARD, G., Food Science and Nutrition
POTHIER, F., Animal Science
POULIOT, Y., Food Science and Nutrition
RATTI, C., Soils and Agricultural Engineering
RIOUX, J.-A., Plant Science
ROBITAILLE, J., Agricultural Economics and Consumer Sciences
ROCHEFORT, L., Plant Science
ROMAIN, R., Agricultural Economics and Consumer Sciences
ROY, D., Food Science and Nutrition
ST-LOUIS, R., Agricultural Economics and Consumer Sciences
SIRARD, M.-A., Animal Science
SUBIRADE, M., Food Science and Nutrition
THÉRIAULT, R., Soils and Agricultural Engineering
TURGEON, S., Food Science and Nutrition
TURGEON-O'BRIEN, H., Food Science and Nutrition
VOHL, J.-C., Food Science and Nutrition
VUILLEMARD, J.-C., Food Science and Nutrition
WEST, E. G., Agricultural Economics and Consumer Sciences
ZEE, J., Food Science and Nutrition

Faculty of Architecture, Planning and Visual Arts (Édifice du Vieux-Séminaire de Québec, 1 Côte de la Fabrique, Bureau 2230, Québec, QC G1R 3V6; tel. (418) 656-2546; e-mail faaav@faaav.ulaval.ca; internet www.faaav.ulaval.ca):

BLAIS, M., Architecture
CARRIER, M., Planning
CASAULT, A., Architecture
CHAINE, F., Visual Arts
CLOUTIER, L., Visual Arts
COSSETTE, M. A., Visual Arts
CÔTÉ, P., Architecture
DEMERS, C., Architecture
DESPRÉS, C., Architecture
DUBÉ, C., Planning
GIRARD, G., Visual Arts
JEAN, M., Visual Arts
LAVOIE, C., Planning
LEE-GOSSELIN, M., Planning
LEMIEUX, R., Visual Arts
MALENFANT, N., Visual Arts
MILL, R., Visual Arts
NAYLOR, D., Visual Arts
PICHÉ, D., Architecture
PLEAU, R., Architecture
POTVIN, A., Architecture
POULIOT, S., Visual Arts
ROCHON, A., Visual Arts
RODRIGUEZ-PINZON, M., Planning
TEYSSOT, G., Architecture
THÉRIAULT, M., Planning
TREMBLAY, G.-H., Architecture
VACHON, E., Architecture
VACHON, G., Architecture
VILLENEUVE, P., Planning
ZWIEJSKI, J., Architecture

Faculty of Dentistry (Pavillon de Médecine Dentaire, Bureau 1615, Québec, QC G1K 7P4; tel. (418) 656-2247; e-mail fmd@fmd.ulaval.ca; internet www.ulaval.ca/fmd):

BASTIEN, R.
BERNARD, C.
CARON, C.
CHMIELEWSKI, W.
FOURNIER, A.
GAGNON, G.
GAGNON, P.
GAUCHEN, H.
GIASSON, L.
GOULET, J.-P.
GRENIER, D.
LACHAPELLE, D.
MORAND, M.-A.
MORIN, S.
NICHOLSON, L.
PAYANT, L.
PERUSSE, R.
PROULX, M.
ROBERT, D.
ROUABHIA, M.
ROY, S.
VALOIS, M.

Faculty of Education (Pavillon des Sciences de l'Éducation, Québec, QC G1K 7P4; tel. (418) 656-3062; e-mail fse@fse.ulaval.ca; internet www.fse.ulaval.ca):

ARRIOLA-SOCOL, M., Foundations and Interventions in Education
BÉLANGER, J.-D., Teaching and Learning Studies
BOISCLAIR, A., Teaching and Learning Studies
BOIVIN, M.-D., Foundations and Interventions in Education
BOUCHARD, P., Foundations and Interventions in Education
BOURASSA, B., Foundations and Interventions in Education
CARDIN, J.-F., Teaching and Learning Studies
CARDU, H., Foundations and Interventions in Education
CLOUTIER, R., Foundations and Interventions in Education
DEBLOIS, L., Teaching and Learning Studies
DENIGER, M.-A., Foundations and Interventions in Education
DÉSAUTELS, J., Teaching and Learning Studies
DESGAGNÉ, S., Teaching and Learning Studies
DIAMBOMBA, M., Foundations and Interventions in Education
DIONNE, J., Teaching and Learning Studies
DRAPEAU, S., Foundations and Interventions in Education
DROLET, J.-L., Foundations and Interventions in Education
FOUNTAIN, R. M. B., Teaching and Learning Studies
FOURNIER, G., Foundations and Interventions in Education
FOURNIER, J.-P., Teaching and Learning Studies
GAGNON, J., Physical Education
GAGNON, R., Teaching and Learning Studies
GAULIN, C., Teaching and Learning Studies
GAUTHIER, C., Teaching and Learning Studies
GERVAIS, F., Teaching and Learning Studies
GIASSON, J., Teaching and Learning Studies
GUAY, F., Foundations and Interventions in Education
GUERETTE, C., Teaching and Learning Studies
GUILBERT, L., Teaching and Learning Studies
HAMEL, T., Foundations and Interventions in Education
JACQUES, M., Teaching and Learning Studies
JEANRIE, C., Foundations and Interventions in Educations
JEFFREY, D., Teaching and Learning Studies
KASZAP, M., Teaching and Learning Studies
LACHANCE, L., Foundations and Interventions in Education
LAFERRIÈRE, T., Teaching and Learning Studies
LANDRY, C., Foundations and Interventions in Education
LAPOINTE, C., Foundations and Interventions in Education
LAROCHELLE, M., Teaching and Learning Studies
LAROSE, S., Teaching and Learning Studies
LE BOSSE, Y., Foundations and Interventions in Education
LECLERC, C., Foundations and Interventions in Education
LEGAULT, M., Teaching and Learning Studies
MARANDA, M.-F., Foundations and Interventions in Education
MARCOUX, Y., Foundations and Interventions in Education
MARTEL, D., Physical Education
MASSOT, A., Foundations and Interventions in Education
MOISSET, J.-J., Foundations and Interventions in Education
MONETTE, M., Foundations and Interventions in Education
MURA, R., Teaching and Learning Studies
NADEAU, G.-A., Physical Education
PAGÉ, P., Teaching and Learning Skills
PELLETIER, P., Teaching and Learning Skills
PLANTE, J., Foundations and Interventions in Education
RATTE, J., Foundations and Interventions in Education
ROY-BUREAU, L., Teaching and Learning Skills
ROYER, E., Teaching and Learning Studies
ST-LAURENT, L., Teaching and Learning Studies
SAMSON, J., Physical Education
SAVARD, C., Physical Education
SIMARD, C., Teaching and Learning Studies
SIMARD, D., Teaching and Learning Skills
SPAIN, A., Foundations and Interventions in Education
TALBOT, S., Physical Education
THERIAULT, G., Physical Education
TROTTIER, C., Foundations and Interventions in Education
VALOIS, P., Foundations and Interventions in Education
VINCENT, S., Teaching and Learning Skills
ZIARKO, H., Teaching and Learning Skills

Faculty of Forestry and Geomatics (Pavillon Abitibi-Price, Bureau 1151, Québec, QC G1K 7P4; tel. (418) 656-3880; e-mail ffg@ffg.ulaval.ca; internet www.ffg.ulaval.ca):

ALLARD, M., Geography
BAUCE, É., Wood and Forest Sciences
BEAUDOIN, M., Wood and Forest Sciences
BEAULIEU, B., Geomatics
BEAUREGARD, R., Wood and Forest Sciences
BÉDARD, Y., Geomatics
BÉGIN, J., Wood and Forest Sciences
BÉGIN, Y., Geography
BÉLANGER, L., Wood and Forest Sciences
BELLEFLEUR, P., Wood and Forest Sciences
BERNIER, L., Wood and Forest Sciences
BHIRY, N., Geography
BOULIANNE, M., Geomatics
BOUSQUET, J., Wood and Forest Sciences
BOUTHILLER, L., Wood and Forest Sciences
BRIÈRE, D., Wood and Forest Sciences
CAMIRÉ, C., Wood and Forest Sciences
CHEVALLIER, J.-J., Geomatics
CLOUTIER, A., Wood and Forest Sciences
CONDAL, A., Geomatics
DESROCHERS, A., Wood and Forest Sciences
DESSUREAULT, M., Wood and Forest Sciences
EDWARDS, G., Geomatics
FILION, L., Geography
FORTIN, Y., Wood and Forest Sciences
GODBOUT, C., Wood and Forest Sciences
HERNANDEZ PENA, R., Wood and Forest Sciences
LALONDE, M., Wood and Forest Sciences
LEBEL, L., Wood and Forest Sciences
LOWELL, K., Wood and Forest Sciences
MARGOLLIS, H., Wood and Forest Sciences
MERCIER, G., Geography
MUNSON, A., Wood and Forest Sciences
PICHÉ, Y., Wood and Forest Sciences
PIENITZ, R., Geography
PLAMONDON, A. P., Wood and Forest Sciences
PLANTE, F., Geomatics
POTHIER, D., Wood and Forest Sciences
RIEDL, B., Wood and Forest Sciences
RUEL, J.-C., Wood and Forest Sciences
ST-HILAIRE, M., Geography
SANTERRE, R., Geomatics
STEVANOVIC, J. T., Wood and Forest Sciences
THIBEAULT, J.-R., Wood and Forest Sciences
TREMBLAY, F., Wood and Forest Sciences
VIAU, A., Geomatics

Faculty of Law (Pavillon Charles-DeKoninck, Bureau 2407, Québec, QC G1K 7P4; tel. (418) 656-2131, ext. 6134; e-mail fd@fd.ulaval.ca; internet www.ulaval.ca/fd):

ARBOUR, M.
BELLEAU, M.-C.
BOUCHARD, C.
BRETON, R.
BROCHU, F.
COTE-HARPER, G.
CRÊTE, R.

DELEURY, E.
DESLAURIERS, J.
DUPLE, N.
FERLAND, D.
GARDNER, D.
GIROUX, L.
GOUBAU, D.
HALLEY, P.
ISSALYS, P.
LANGEVIN, L.
LAQUERRE, P.
LAREAU, A.
LAUZIÈRE, L.
LEMIEUX, D.
LEMIEUX, P.
MANGANAS, A.
MELKEVILL, B.
NORMAND, S.
OTIS, G.
PRUJINER, A.
RAINVILLE, P.
ROUSSEAU, G.
TREMBLAY, G.
TURGEON, J.

Faculty of Letters (Pavillon Charles-De Koninck, Bureau 3254, Québec, QC G1K 7P4; tel. (418) 656-3460; e-mail fl@fl.ulaval.ca; internet www.fl.ulaval.ca):

AUGER, P., Languages and Linguistics
AUGER, R., History
BACZ, B., Languages and Linguistics
BAKER, P., History
BAUDOU, A., Literature
BEAUCHAMP, M., Information and Communication
BEAUDET, M.-A., Literature
BEAUSOLEIL, P., Information and Communication
BELANGER, R., History
BELLEGUIC, T., Literature
BERNIER, J., History
BISAILLON, J., Languages and Linguistics
BOISVERT, L., Languages and Linguistics
BOIVIN, A., Literature
BORGONOVO, C., Languages and Linguistics
BOULANGER, J.-C., Languages and Linguistics
CARANI, M., History
CARDIN, M., History
CAULIER, B., History
CHARRON, J., Information and Communication
CLERC, I., Information and Communication
COSSETTE, J. C., Information and Communication
CUMMINS, S., Languages and Linguistics
DAGENAIS, B., Information and Communication
DAIGLE, J., History
DAVIAULT, A., Literature
DE BONVILLE, J., Information and Communication
DE KONINCK, Z., Languages and Linguistics
DE LA GARDE, R., Information and Communication
DEMERS, F., Information and Communication
DEMERS, G., Languages and Linguistics
DESDOUITS, A.-M., History
DESHAIES, D., Languages and Linguistics
DOLAN, C., History
DUBÉ, P., History
DUFFLEY, P., Languages and Linguistics
DUMONT, F., Literature
ESPANOL, E. M., Languages and Linguistics
FAITELSON-WEISER, S., Languages and Linguistics
FINETTE, L., Literature
FORTIER, A.-M., Literature
FORTIN, M., History
FYSON, D., History
GAGNÉ, M., Literature
GARON, L., Information and Communication
GAUTHIER, G., Information and Communication
GRENIER, D., History
GRIGNON, M., History
GUEVEL, Z., Languages and Linguistics
GUILBERT, L., History
HÉBERT, C., Literature
HERMON, E., History
HUMMEL, K., Languages and Linguistics
HUOT, D., Languages and Linguistics
HUOT-LEMONNIER, F., Languages and Linguistics
JOLICOEUR, L., Languages and Linguistics
JUNEAU, M., Languages and Linguistics
KAREL, D., History
KEGLE, C., Literature
KOSS, B. J., History
KUGLER, M., Information and Communication
LABERGE, A., History
LACHARITÉ, D. P., Languages and Linguistics
LADOUCEUR, J., Languages and Linguistics
LAPOINTE, M., History
LAVIGNE, A., Information and Communication
LEBEL, E., Information and Communication
LEMELIN, B., History
LEMIEUX, J., Information and Communication
LÉTOURNEAU, J., History
LOWE, R., Languages and Linguistics
LUKIC, R., History
MANNING, A., Languages and Linguistics
MARCHAND, J., Information and Communication
MARTIN, P., Languages and Linguistics
MATHIEU, J., History
MERCIER, A., Literature
MOORE, E., History
MOSER VERREY, M., Literature
MOUSSETTE, M., History
NAKOS, D., Languages and Linguistics
NGUYEN-DUY, V., Information and Communication
NIQUETTE, M., Information and Communication
OUELLET, J., Languages and Linguistics
PAQUETTE, G., Information and Communication
PAQUOT, A., Languages and Linguistics
PARADIS, C., Languages and Linguistics
PARKS, S. E., Languages and Linguistics
PELLETIER, E., Literature
PERELLI-CONTOS, I., Literature
PERESTRELO, F., Languages and Linguistics
PICARD, J.-C., Information and Communication
PIETTE, C., History
POIRIER, C., Languages and Linguistics
PONTBRIAND, J.-N., Literature
PRÉVOST, P., Languages and Linguistics
RIVET, J., Information and Communication
ROY, L., Literature
SADETSKY, A., Languages and Linguistics
ST-GELAIS, R., Literature
SAINT JACQUES, D., Literature
SAUVAGEAU, F., Information and Communication
THENON, L., Literature
THÉRY, C., Literature
THOMAS, N. H., Literature
TREMBLAY, G., Geography
TURGEON, L., History
VALLIÈRES, M., History
VAN DER SCHWEREN, E., Literature
VERREAULT, C., Languages and Linguistics
VINCENT, D., Languages and Linguistics
WATINE, T., Information and Communication

Faculty of Medicine (Pavillon Ferdinand-Vandry, Bureau 1214, Québec, QC G1K 7P4; tel. (418) 656-5245; e-mail fmed@fmed.ulaval.ca; internet www.fmed.ulaval.ca):

ABDOUS, B., Social and Preventive Medicine
AKOUM, A., Obstetrics and Gynaecology
ALARY, M., Social and Preventive Medicine
ALLEN, T., Family Medicine
AMZICA, F., Anatomy and Physiology
AUBIN, M., Family Medicine
AUDETTE, M., Medical Biology
AUGER, F., Surgery
AYOTTE, P., Social and Preventive Medicine
BACHELARD, H., Medicine
BACHVAROV, D., Medicine
BAIRAM, A., Paediatrics
BAIRATI, I., Surgery
BARDEN, N., Anatomy and Physiology
BASTIDE, A., Obstetrics and Gynaecology
BEAUCHAMP, D., Medical Biology
BEAUCHEMIN, J.-P., Family Medicine
BEAULIEU, A., Medicine
BEDARD, P., Medicine
BÉLANGER, A., Anatomy and Physiology
BÉLANGER, A. Y., Rehabilitation
BÉLANGER, L., Medical Biology
BERGERON, J., Obstetrics and Gynaecology
BERGERON, M. G., Medical Biology
BERGERON, R., Family Medicine
BERNARD, P.-M., Social and Preventive Medicine
BERNATCHEZ, J.-P., Psychiatry
BERNIER, V., Medical Biology
BILODEAU, A., Family Medicine
BISSONNETTE, E., Medicine
BLANCHET, J., Obstetrics and Gynaecology
BLONDEAU, F., Family Medicine
BLONDEAU, L., Medicine
BOGATY, P., Medicine
BOIVIN, G., Medical Biology
BORGEAT, P., Anatomy and Physiology
BOUCHARD, J.-P., Medicine
BOUCHER, F., Paediatrics
BOULAY, M. R., Social and Preventive Medicine
BOULET, L.-P., Medicine
BOURBONNAIS, R., Rehabilitation
BOURGOIN, S.-G., Anatomy and Physiology
BRAILOVSKY, C. A., Family Medicine
BRASSARD, N., Obstetrics and Gynaecology
BRISSON, C., Social and Preventive Medicine
BRISSON, J., Social and Preventive Medicine
CABANAC, M., Anatomy and Physiology
CANDAS, B., Anatomy and Physiology
CAPADAY, C., Anatomy and Physiology
CARRIÈRE, M., Rehabilitation
CARUSO, M., Medical Biology
CHAHINE, M., Medicine
CHAKIR, J., Medicine
CHARRON, J., Medical Biology
CLOUTIER, A., Paediatrics
CORBEIL, J., Anatomy and Physiology
CORMIER, Y., Medicine
CÔTÉ, C., Rehabilitation
CÔTÉ, J., Anaesthesiology
CÔTÉ, L., Medicine
COUET, J., Medicine
CUSAN, L., Anatomy and Physiology
DE KONINCK, M., Social and Preventive Medicine
DE KONINCK, Y., Psychiatry
DE SERRES, G., Medical Biology
DE WALS, P., Social and Preventive Medicine
DELAGE, R., Medicine
DERY, P., Paediatrics
DESCHÊNES, M., Anatomy and Physiology
DESHAIES, Y., Anatomy and Physiology
DESLAURIERS, J., Surgery
DESMEULES, M., Medicine
DEWAILLY, F., Social and Preventive Medicine
DIONNE, C., Rehabilitation
DIONNE, F. T., Social and Preventive Medicine
DODIN, S. D., Obstetrics and Gynaecology
DOILLON, C., Surgery

DORÉ, F. M., Medicine
DORVAL, J., Paediatrics
DOUVILLE, Y., Surgery
DROLET, G., Medicine
DUMESNIL, J.-G., Medicine
DURAND, P.-J., Social and Preventive Medicine
FAURE, R., Paediatrics
FLAMAND, L., Anatomy and Physiology
FOREST, J.-C., Medical Biology
FORTIER, M.-A., Obstetrics and Gynaecology
FORTIN, J.-P., Social and Preventive Medicine
FRADET, Y., Surgery
FRÉMONT, P., Rehabilitation
FRENETTE, J., Family Medicine and Rehabilitation
GAGNON, F., Psychiatry
GAILIS, L., Medicine
GERMAIN, L., Surgery
GERVAIS, M., Rehabilitation
GIRARD, J. E., Social and Preventive Medicine
GLENN, J., Medical Biology
GOSSELIN, J., Anatomy and Physiology
GOVINDAN, M. J., Anatomy and Physiology
GRAVEL, C., Psychiatry
GUAY, G., Medicine
GUÉRIN, S., Anatomy and Physiology
GUIDOIN, R., Surgery
HANCOCK, R., Medical Biology
HUDON, C., Paediatrics
HUOT, J., Medicine
JEANNOTTE, L., Medical Biology
JOBIN, J., Medicine
JULIEN, J.-P., Anatomy and Physiology
JULIEN, P., Medicine
KHANDJIAN, E. W., Medical Biology
KINKEAD, R., Paediatrics
KINGMA, J. G., Medicine
L'ARRIÈRE, M., Rehabilitation
LABBÉ, J., Paediatrics
LABBÉ, R., Medical Biology
LABELLE, Y., Medical Biology
LABERGE, C., Medicine
LABRECQUE, M., Family Medicine
LABRIE, C., Anatomy and Physiology
LABRIE, F., Anatomy and Physiology
LACASSE, Y., Medicine
LAFRAMBOISE, R., Paediatrics
LAGACÉ, R., Medical Biology
LAGASSE, P.-P., Social and Preventive Medicine
LAJOIE, P., Social and Preventive Medicine
LALANNE, M., Medical Biology
LAMBERT, R. D., Obstetrics and Gynaecology
LAMONTAGNE, R., Family Medicine
LANDRY, J., Medicine
LANGELIER, M., Medicine
LANGLOIS, S., Medicine
LANIVIÈLE, R., Medicine
LAROCHELLE, L., Anatomy and Physiology
LATULIPPE, L., Medicine
LAVIOLETTE, M., Medicine
LAVOIE, J., Medical Biology
LEBEL, M., Medicine
LEBLANC, R., Social and Preventive Medicine
LEBLOND, P., Medicine
LECLERC, P., Medical Biology
LEDUC, Y., Family Medicine
LELIÈVRE, M., Paediatrics
LEMAY, A., Obstetrics and Gynaecology
LETARTE, R., Medical Biology
LEVALLOIS, P., Social and Preventive Medicine
LEVESQUE, D., Medicine
LÉVESQUE, R., Medical Biology
LIN, S.-X., Anatomy and Physiology
LUU, T. V., Anatomy and Physiology
MCFADYEN, B. J., Rehabilitation
MAHEUX, R., Obstetrics and Gynaecology
MALOUIN, F., Rehabilitation
MALTAIS, F., Medicine
MARCEAU, F., Medicine
MARCEAU, N., Medicine
MARCHAND, R., Anatomy and Physiology
MARCOUX, H., Family Medicine
MARCOUX, S., Social and Preventive Medicine
MARETTE, A., Anatomy and Physiology
MARTINEAU, R., Medical Biology
MAUNSELL, E., Social and Preventive Medicine
MAURIEGE, P., Social and Preventive Medicine
MAZIADE, M., Psychiatry
MERETTE, C., Psychiatry
MEYER, F., Social and Preventive Medicine
MIRAULT, M.-E., Medicine
MOFFET, H., Rehabilitation
MONTGRAIN, N., Psychiatry
MORISSETTE, J., Anatomy and Physiology
MOSS, T., Medical Biology
MOURAD, M. W., Medicine
MURTHY, M.-R.-V., Medical Biology
NACCACHE, P.-H., Medicine
NADEAU, A., Medicine
NADEAU, L., Medical Biology
NOREAU, L., Rehabilitation
OUELLETTE, M., Medical Biology
PAINCHAUD, G., Psychiatry
PAPADOPOULO, B., Medical Biology
PARENT, A., Anatomy and Physiology
PELLETIER, G.-H., Anatomy and Physiology
PERUSSE, L., Social and Preventive Medicine
PHILIPPE, E., Anatomy and Physiology
PIBAROT, P., Medicine
PIEDBOEUF, B., Paediatrics
POIRIER, D., Anatomy and Physiology
POIRIER, G., Medical Biology
POMERLEAU, G., Psychiatry
POUBELLE, P., Medicine
POULIN, R., Anatomy and Physiology
PUYMIRAT, J., Medicine
RATTÉ, C., Psychiatry
RAYMOND, V., Anatomy and Physiology
RICHARD, D., Anatomy and Physiology
RICHARDS, C. L., Rehabilitation
RIOUX, F., Medicine
RIVEST, S., Anatomy and Physiology
ROBERGE, C., Medical Biology
ROBICHAUD, L., Rehabilitation
ROUILLARD, C., Medicine
ROULEAU, J., Medicine
ROUSSEAU, F., Medical Biology
ROY, M., Obstetrics and Gynaecology
SALESSE, C., Otorhinolaryngology and Ophthalmology
SATO, M., Anatomy and Physiology
SATO, S., Medical Biology
SAUCIER, D., Family Medicine
SAVARD, P., Medicine
SEGUIN, C., Anatomy and Physiology
SERIES, F., Medicine
SHAH, G., Medical Biology
SIMARD, J., Anatomy and Physiology
STERIADE, M., Anatomy and Physiology
SULLIVAN, R., Obstetrics and Gynaecology
TALBOT, J., Medical Biology
TANGUAY, R., Medicine
TEASDALE, N., Social and Preventive Medicine
TESSIER, P., Medical Biology
TETREAULT, S., Rehabilitation
TETU, B., Medical Biology
THIVIERGE, J., Psychiatry
TREMBLAY, A., Social and Preventive Medicine
TREMBLAY, J.-P., Anatomy and Physiology
TREMBLAY, M. J., Medical Biology
TREMBLAY, Y., Obstetrics and Gynaecology
TRUDEL, L., Rehabilitation
VENRREAULT, R., Social and Preventive Medicine
VERRET, S., Paediatrics
VEZINA, M., Social and Preventive Medicine
VILLENEUVE, E., Psychiatry
VINCENT, C., Rehabilitation
VINCENT, M., Medicine

Faculty of Music (Pavillon Louis-Jacques-Casault, Bureau 3312, Québec, QC G1K 7P4; tel. (418) 656-7061; e-mail mus@mus.ulaval.ca; internet www.ulaval.ca/mus):

BOULET, M.-M.
CADRIN, P.
DUCHARME, M.
LAFLAMME, S.
MASSON-BOURQUE, C.
MATHIEU, L.
PAPILLON, A.
PARENT, N.
PINSON, J.-P.
RINGUETTE, R.
ROBERGE, M.-A.
STUBER, U.
TEREBESI, G.

Faculty of Nursing Sciences (Pavillon Paul-Comtois, Bureau 4106, Québec, QC G1K 7P4; tel. (418) 656-3356; e-mail fsi@fsi.ulaval.ca; internet www.ulaval.ca/fsi):

BLONDEAU, D.
CÔTÉ, E.
DALLAIRE, C.
EBACHER, M.-F.
FILLION, L.
GODIN, G.
HAGAN, L.
LEPAGE, L.
MORIN, D.
O'NEILL, M.
PATENAUDE, L.
PELLETIER, L.
PROVENCHER, H.
VIENS, C.

Faculty of Pharmacy (Pavillon Ferdinand-Vandry, Bureau 2241, Québec, QC G1K 7P4; tel. (418) 656-3211; e-mail pha@pha.ulaval.ca; internet www.pha.ulaval.ca):

BEAULAC-BAILLARGEON, L.
BELANGER, P. M.
CASTONGUAY, A.
DALEAU, P.
DESGAGNÉ, M.
DI PAOLO-CHENEVERT, T.
DIONNE, A.
DORVAL, M.
GRÉGOIRE, J.-P.
GUILLEMETTE, C.
JUHASZ, J.
MOISAN, J.
RICHER, M.
TREMBLAY, M.
VÉZINA, C.

Faculty of Philosophy (Pavillon Félix-Antoine-Savard, Bureau 644, Québec, QC G1K 7P4; tel. (418) 656-2244; e-mail fp@fp.ulaval.ca; internet www.fp.ulaval.ca):

BÉGIN, L.
BILODEAU, R.
BOSS, G.
CUNNINGHAM, H.-P.
DE KONINCK, T.
KNEE, P.
LAFLEUR, C.
LANGLOIS, L.
NARBONNE, J.-M.
PARIZEAU, M.-H.
PELLETIER, Y.
RICARD, M.-A.
SASSEVILLE, M.
THIBAUDEAU, V.
TOURNIER, F.

Faculty of Sciences and Engineering (Pavillon Alexandre-Vachon, Bureau 1033, Québec, QC G1K 7P4; tel. (418) 656-2163; e-mail fsg@fsg.ulaval.ca; internet www.fsg.ulaval.ca):

ADAM, L., Actuarial Science
AIT-KADI, D., Mechanical Engineering
AMIOT, P. L., Physical Engineering and Optics

ANCTIL, F., Civil Engineering
ANDERSON, A., Biology
AUGER, M., Chemistry
BARBEAU, C., Chemistry
BARIBEAU, L., Mathematics and Statistics
BARRETTE, C., Biology
BASTIEN, J., Civil Engineering
BAZIN, C., Mining, Metallurgical and Materials Engineering
BEAUDOIN, G., Geology and Geological Engineering
BEAULIEU, D., Civil Engineering
BEAULIEU, J.-M., Computer Science
BEAUPRÉ, D., Civil Engineering
BÉDARD, D., Actuarial Science
BÉDARD, G., Physical Engineering and Optics
BELISLE, C., Mathematics and Statistics
BELKHITER, N., Computer Science
BERGEVIN, R., Electrical and Computer Engineering
BERNATCHEZ, L., Biology
BORRA, E. F., Physical Engineering and Optics
BOUCHARD, C., Civil Engineering
BOUDREAU, D., Chemistry
BOUKOUVALAS, J., Chemistry
BOURBONNAIS, Y., Biochemistry and Microbiology
BOUSMINA, M. M., Chemical Engineering
BRISSON, J., Chemistry
BUI, M. D., Computer Science
CARDOU, A., Mechanical Engineering
CARMICHAEL, J.-P., Mathematics and Statistics
CASSIDY, C., Mathematics and Statistics
CASSIDY, D. P., Geology and Geological Engineering
CHAIB-DRAA, B., Computer Science
CHARLET, G., Chemistry
CHÊNEVERT, R., Chemistry
CHIN, S. L., Physical Engineering and Optics
CHOUINARD, J.-Y., Electrical and Computer Engineering
CLOUTIER, C., Biology
COSSETTE, H., Actuarial Science
CROS, J., Electrical and Computer Engineering
CURODEAU, A., Mechanical Engineering
D'AMOURS, S., Mechanical Engineering
DARVEAU, A., Biochemistry and Microbiology
DE CHAMPLAIN, A., Mechanical Engineering
DE KONINCK, J.-M., Mathematics and Statistics
DEL VILLAR, R., Mining, Metallurgical and Materials Engineering
DESBIENS, A., Electrical and Computer Engineering
DESCHÊNES, C., Mechanical Engineering
DESHARNAIS, J., Computer Science
DESLAURIERS, N., Biochemistry and Microbiology
DODSON, J., Biology
DORÉ, G., Civil Engineering
DUBE, L. J., Physical Engineering and Optics
DUBÉ, D., Mining, Metallurgical and Materials Engineering
DUCHESNE, J., Geology and Geological Engineering
DUGUAY, M.-A., Electrical and Computer Engineering
DUMAS, G., Mechanical Engineering
DUPUIS, C., Computer Science
DUSSAULT, P., Biochemistry and Microbiology
FAFARD, M., Civil Engineering
FORIERO, A., Civil Engineering
FORTIER, L., Biology
FORTIER, P., Electrical and Computer Engineering
FORTIER, R., Geology and Geological Engineering
FORTIN, A., Mathematics and Statistics
FRENETTE, M., Biochemistry and Microbiology
FYTAS, K., Mining, Metallurgical and Materials Engineering
GAKWAYA, A., Mechanical Engineering
GALSTIAN, T., Physics, Physical Engineering and Optics
GALVEZ-CLOUTIER, R., Civil Engineering
GANGULY, U. S., Electrical and Computer Engineering
GARNIER, A., Chemical Engineering
GAUTHIER, G., Biology
GELINAS, P. J., Geology and Geological Engineering
GENDRON, G., Mechanical Engineering
GENEST, C., Mathematics and Statistics
GERVAIS, J.-J., Mathematics and Statistics
GHALI, E., Mining, Metallurgical and Materials Engineering
GHAZZALI, N., Mathematics and Statistics
GIGUÈRE, M., Actuarial Science
GLOVER, P., Geology and Geological Engineering
GOSSELIN, C., Mechanical Engineering
GOUDREAU, S., Mechanical Engineering
GOULET, V., Actuarial Science
GOURDEAU, F., Mathematics and Statistics
GRANDJEAN, B., Chemical Engineering
GRENIER, D., Electrical and Computer Engineering
GUDERLEY, H., Biology
GUENETTE, R., Mathematics and Statistics
GUERTIN, M., Biochemistry and Microbiology
GUILLOT, M., Mechanical Engineering
HADJIGEORGIOU, J., Mining, Metallurgical and Materials Engineering
HEBERT, R., Geology and Geological Engineering
HIMMELMAN, J., Biology
HODGSON, B. R., Mathematics and Statistics
HODOUIN, D., Mining, Metallurgical and Materials Engineering
HOULE, G., Biology
HUOT, J., Biology
JACQUES, M., Actuarial Science
JOHNSON, L. E., Biology
JONCAS, G., Physics, Physical Engineering and Optics
KALIAGUINE, S., Chemical Engineering
KIRKWOOD, D., Geology and Geological Engineering
KNYSTAUTAS, E., Physics, Physical Engineering and Optics
KONRAD, J.-M., Civil Engineering
KRETSCHMER, D., Mechanical Engineering
KROEGER, H., Physics, Physical Engineering and Optics
LACROIX, R., Chemical Engineering
LAPOINTE, L., Biology
LARACHI, F., Chemical Engineering
LAROCHE, G., Mining, Metallurgical and Materials Engineering
LAROCHELLE, J., Biology
LAROCHELLE, S., Electrical and Computer Engineering
LAURENDEAU, D., Electrical and Computer Engineering
LAVOIE, M. C., Biochemistry and Microbiology
LEBOEUF, D., Civil Engineering
LECLERC, M., Chemistry
LEDUY, A., Chemical Engineering
LE HUY, H., Electrical and Computer Engineering
LEMAY, J., Mechanical Engineering
LEMIEUX, C., Biochemistry and Microbiology
LEMIEUX, G., Biochemistry and Microbiology
LEROUEIL, S., Civil Engineering
LESSARD, P., Civil Engineering
LESSARD, R. A., Physics, Physical Engineering and Optics
LEVASSEUR, M., Biology
LÉVEILLÉ, G., Actuarial Science
LÉVESQUE, B., Mechanical Engineering
LÉVESQUE, C., Mathematics and Statistics
LOCAT, J., Geology and Geological Engineering
LUONG, A., Actuarial Science
MCBREEN, P. H., Chemistry
MCCARTHY, N., Physics, Physical Engineering and Optics
MACIEL, Y., Mechanical Engineering
MALDAGUE, X., Electrical and Computer Engineering
MANOUZI, H., Mathematics and Statistics
MARCEAU, E., Actuarial Science
MARCHAND, J., Civil Engineering
MARCHAND, M., Computer Science
MARCHAND, P., Computer Science
MARLEAU, L., Physics, Physical Engineering and Optics
MARTEL, H., Physics, Physical Engineering and Optics
MASSE, J.-C., Mathematics and Statistics
MATHIEU, P., Physics, Physical Engineering and Optics
MINEAU, G., Computer Science
MOINEAU, S., Biochemistry and Microbiology
MORSE, B., Civil Engineering
MOULIN, B., Computer Sciences
NGUYEN-DANG, T.-T., Chemistry
PALLOTTA, D., Biology
PAQUETTE, N., Biology
PARASZCZAK, J., Mining, Metallurgical and Materials Engineering
PARIZEAU, M., Electrical and Computer Engineering
PAYETTE, S., Biology
PEZOLET, M., Chemistry
PHILIPPIN, G., Mathematics and Statistics
PICARD, A., Civil Engineering
PICHÉ, M., Physics, Physical Engineering and Optics
PIERRE, R., Mathematics and Statistics
PIGEON, M., Civil Engineering
PINEAULT, S., Physics, Physical Engineering and Optics
PLANETA, S., Mining, Metallurgical and Materials Engineering
POMERLEAU, A., Electrical and Computer Engineering
POULIN, R., Mining, Metallurgical and Materials Engineering
RANCOURT, D., Mechanical Engineering
RANSFORD, T.-J., Mathematics and Statistics
RICHARD, M. J., Mechanical Engineering
RITCEY, A.-M., Chemistry
RIVEST, L.-P., Mathematics and Statistics
ROBERT, C., Physics, Physical Engineering and Optics
ROBERT, J.-L., Civil Engineering
ROCHELEAU, M., Geology and Geological Engineering
RODRIGUE, D., Chemical Engineering
ROY, C., Chemical Engineering
ROY, D., Physics, Physical Engineering and Optics
ROY, P.-H., Biochemistry and Microbiology
ROY, R., Physics, Physical Engineering and Optics
RUSCH, L. A., Electrical and Computer Engineering
SEGUIN, M. K., Geology and Geological Engineering
SERODES, J.-B., Civil Engineering
SHENG, Y., Physics, Physical Engineering and Optics
TARASIEWICZ, R., Mechanical Engineering
TAWBI, N., Computer Science
TÊTU, M., Electrical and Computer Engineering
THERRIEN, R., Geology and Geological Engineering
TOURIGNY, N., Computer Science

TREMBLAY, P., Electrical and Computer Engineering
TREMBLAY, R., Physics, Physical Engineering and Optics
TURCOTTE, J., Chemistry
TURMEL, M., Biochemistry and Microbiology
VADEBONCOEUR, C., Biochemistry and Microbiology
VALLÉE, R., Physics, Physical Engineering and Optics
VIAROUGE, P., Electrical and Computer Engineering
VINCENT, W. F., Biology
VO VAN, T., Mining, Metallurgical and Materials Engineering
VOYER, N., Chemistry
WITZEL, B., Physics, Physical Engineering and Optics
ZACCARIN, A., Electrical and Computer Engineering

Faculty of Social Sciences (Pavillon Charles-DeKoninck, Bureau 3456, Québec, QC G1K 7P4; tel. (418) 656-2615; e-mail fss@fss.ulaval.ca; internet www.fss.ulaval.ca):

ARCAND, B., Anthropology
AUDET, M., Industrial Relations
BACCIGALUPO, A., Political Science
BAKARY, T., Political Science
BARIBEAU, J., Psychology
BARITEAU, C., Anthropology
BARLA, P., Economics
BARRE, A., Industrial Relations
BEAUCHAMP, C., Sociology
BEAUDREAU, B. C., Economics
BEAUDRY, M., Social Work
BÉLANGER, G., Economics
BÉLANGER, J., Industrial Relations
BÉLANGER, L., Political Science
BERNARD, J.-T., Economics
BERNIER, C., Industrial Relations
BERNIER, J., Industrial Relations
BLAIS, F., Political Science
BLOUIN, R., Industrial Relations
BOISVERT, J.-M., Psychology
BOIVIN, J., Industrial Relations
BOIVIN, M., Psychology
BOLDUC, D., Economics
BOUCHER, N., Social Work
BOUSQUET, N., Sociology
BRETON, G., Political Science
CARMICHAEL, B., Economics
CHALIFOUX, J.-J., Anthropology
CLAIN, O., Sociology
CLOUTIER, R., Psychology
COMEAU, Y., Social Work
CONSTANTANOS, C., Economics
CÔTÉ, P., Political Science
COUILLARD, M.-A., Anthropology
CRÊTE, J., Political Science
DAGENAIS, H., Anthropology
DAMANT, D., Social Work
DARVEAU-FOURNIER, L., Social Work
DECALUWE, B., Economics
DELAGE, D., Sociology
DEOM, E., Industrial Relations
DERRIENNIC, J.-P., Political Science
DESÈVE, M., Sociology
DESROCHERS, S., Psychology
DESSY, S. E., Economics
DIGUER, L., Psychology
DOMPIERRE, J., Industrial Relations
DORAIS, L.-J., Anthropology
DORAIS, M., Social Work
DORÉ, F.-Y., Psychology
DRAINVILLE, A., Political Science
DUCLOS, J.-Y., Economics
DUFORT, F., Psychology
DUHAIME, G., Sociology
DUMAIS, A., Sociology
DUMONT, S., Social Work
ELBAZ, M., Anthropology
EVERETT, J., Psychology
FOREST, P. G., Political Science
FORTIN, A., Sociology
FORTIN, B., Economics
FORTIN, C., Psychology
FORTIN, D., Social Work
GAGNÉ, G., Sociology
GAUTHIER, J., Psychology
GENEST, S., Anthropology
GILES, A. J., Industrial Relations
GINGRAS, A.-M., Political Science
GISLAIN, J.-J., Industrial Relations
GONZALEZ, P., Economics
GORDON, S. F., Economics
GOSSELIN, G., Political Science
GOULET, S., Psychology
GRONDIN, S., Psychology
GUAY, L., Sociology
HERVOUET, G., Political Science
HUDON, R., Political Science
HUNG, N. M., Economics
HURTUBISE, Y., Social Work
IMBEAU, L., Political Science
KHALAF, L. A., Economics
KIROUAC, G., Psychology
LABRECQUE, M.-F., Anthropology
LACOMBE, S., Sociology
LACOUTURE, Y., Psychology
LACROIX, G., Economics
LADOUCEUR, R., Psychology
LAFLAMME, G., Industrial Relations
LAFLAMME, R., Industrial Relations
LAFLEUR, G.-A., Political Science
LAFOREST, G., Political Science
LAMONDE, F., Industrial Relations
LAMOUREUX, D., Political Science
LANDREVILLE, P., Psychology
LANGLOIS, L., Industrial Relations
LANGLOIS, S., Sociology
LAPOINTE, P.-A., Industrial Relations
LAUGRAND, F. B., Anthropology
LAVALLÉE, M., Psychology
LAVOIE, F., Psychology
LEBLANC, G., Economics
LINDSAY, J., Social Work
LORANGER, M., Psychology
MACE, G., Political Science
MARCOUX, R., Sociology
MASSÉ, R., Anthropology
MERCIER, J., Industrial Relations
MERCIER, J., Political Science
MERCURE, D., Sociology
MONTREUIL, S., Industrial Relations
MOREL, S., Industrial Relations
MORIN, C.-M., Psychology
NORMANDIN, L., Psychology
PAQUIN, L., Economics
PELLETIER, R., Political Science
PEPIN, M., Psychology
PETRY, F., Political Science
PICHÉ, C., Psychology
POCREAU, J.-B., Psychology
POIRIER, S., Anthropology
ROLAND, M., Economics
SABOURIN, S., Psychology
SAILLANT, F., Anthropology
SAINT-ARNAUD, P., Sociology
SAINT-YVES, A., Psychology
SAMSON, L., Economics
SAVARD, J., Psychology
SENECAL, C., Psychology
SEXTON, J., Industrial Relations
SHEARER, B., Economics
SIMARD, J.-J., Sociology
SIMARD, M., Social Work
TESSIER, L., Social Work
TESSIER, R., Psychology
THWAITES, J., Industrial Relations
TRUCHON, M., Economics
TRUDEL, F., Anthropology
TURCOTTE, D., Social Work
TURMEL, A., Sociology
VAN AUDENRODE, M., Economics
VEILLETTE, D., Sociology
VEZINA, A., Social Work
VÉZINA, J., Psychology
VINET, A., Industrial Relations
ZYLBERBERG, J., Political Science

Faculty of Theology and Religious Studies (Pavillon Félix-Antoine-Savard, Bureau 832, Québec, QC G1K 7P4; tel. (418) 656-3576; e-mail ftsr@ftsr.ulaval.ca; internet www.ftsr.ulaval.ca):

AUBERT, M.
BRODEUR, R.
CÔTÉ, L.
CÔTÉ, P.-R.
COUTURE, A.
FARRELL, S. E.
FAUCHER, A.
FORTIN, A.
HURLEY, R.
KEATING, B.
LEMIEUX, R.
MAGER, R.
PAINCHAUD, L.
PASQUIER, A.
PELCHAT, M.
POIRIER, P.-H.
RACINE, J.
ROBERGE, R. M.
ROUTHIER, G.
VIAU, M.

UNIVERSITÉ SAINTE-ANNE

Church Point, NS B0W 1M0
Telephone: (902) 769-2114
E-mail: admission@usainteanne.ca
Internet: www.usainteanne.ca
Founded 1890
Language of instruction: French
Academic year: September to April

Chancellor: LOUIS DEVEAU
Pres.: Dr ANDRÉ ROBERGE
Vice-Pres. for Academics: Dr NEIL BOUCHER
Registrar: MURIELLE COMEAU PÉLOQUIN
Librarian: CÉCILE POTHIER-COMEAU

Library of 84,000 vols
Number of teachers: 51
Number of students: 481
Publication: *Port Acadie* (1 a year)

UNIVERSITY OF ALBERTA

Edmonton, AB T6G 2M7
Telephone: (780) 492-3113
E-mail: info@ualberta.ca
Internet: www.ualberta.ca
Founded 1908
provincial control
Language of instruction: English, French
Academic year: September to August

Chancellor: LINDA HUGHES
Pres.: Dr INDIRA V. SAMARASEKERA
Provost and Vice-Pres. for Academic Affairs: Dr CARL G. AMRHEIN
Vice-Pres. for External Relations: DEBRA POZEGA OSBURN
Vice-Pres. for Facilities and Operations: DON HICKEY
Vice-Pres. for Finance and Admin.: PHYLLIS CLARK
Vice-Pres. for Research: Dr LORNE BABIUK
Registrar: GERRY KENDAL
Vice-Provost and Chief Librarian: ERNIE INGLES
Library: see under Libraries and Archives
Number of teachers: 3,520
Number of students: 37,588
Publications: *Calendar* (1 a year), *Folio* (23 a year), *The New Trail* (3 a year)

DEANS

Alberta School of Business: Prof. MIKE PERCY
Augustana Campus: Dr ALLEN BERGER
Campus St-Jean: Dr MARC ARNAL
Faculty of Agricultural, Life and Environmental Sciences: JOHN KENNELLY
Faculty of Arts: LESLEY CORMACK (acting)
Faculty of Education: Dr FERN SNART (acting)

Faculty of Engineering: DAVID LYNCH
Faculty of Extension: Dr KATY CAMPBELL
Faculty of Graduate Studies and Research: Dr MAZI SHIRVANI
Faculty of Law: PHILIP BRYDEN
Faculty of Medicine and Dentistry: PHILIP BAKER
Faculty of Native Studies: Dr ELLEN BIELAWSKI
Faculty of Nursing: Dr ANITA MOLZAHN
Faculty of Pharmacy and Pharmaceutical Sciences: Dr JAMES KEHRER
Faculty of Physical Education and Recreation: Dr KERRY MUMMERY
Faculty of Rehabilitation Medicine: Dr MARTIN FERGUSON-PELL
Faculty of Science: GREGORY TAYLOR
School of Library and Information Studies: Dr LISA M. GIVEN (acting)
School of Public Health: Dr SYLVIE STACHENKO (acting)

AFFILIATED COLLEGES

North American Baptist College: 11525 23rd Ave, Edmonton, AB T6J 4T3; Pres. Dr M. DEWEY.

St Joseph's College: Edmonton, AB T6G 2J5; tel. (780) 492-7681; internet www.stjosephscollege.ca; library of 25,000 vols; Pres. Dr T. SCOTT.

St Stephen's College: Edmonton, AB T6G 2J6; e-mail st.stephens@ualberta.ca; f. 1909; Prin. and Dean Dr EARLE SHARAM

UNIVERSITY OF BRITISH COLUMBIA

2329 West Mall, Vancouver, BC V6T 1Z4
Telephone: (604) 822-2211
E-mail: presubc@interchange.ubc.ca
Internet: www.ubc.ca
Founded 1908
Academic year: September to August
Chancellor: SARAH MORGAN-SILVESTER
Pres. and Vice-Chancellor: Prof. STEPHEN J. TOOPE
Vice-Pres. for Academics and Provost: DAVID H. FARRAR
Vice-Pres. for Devt and Alumni Engagement: BARBARA MILES
Vice-Pres. for External, Legal and Community Relations: STEPHEN OWEN
Vice-Pres. for Finance, Resources and Operations: PIERRE OUILLET
Vice-Pres. for Research and Int.: JOHN HEPBURN
Vice-Pres. for Students: BRIAN SULLIVAN
Registrar: R. A. SPENCER
Librarian: INGRID PARENT
Number of teachers: 4,669
Number of students: 50,332
Publications: *BC Asian Review* (1 a year), *BC Studies* (4 a year), *BC Studies: The British Columbian Quarterly* (4 a year), *Canadian Journal of Botany* (4 a year), *Canadian Journal of Civil Engineering* (6 a year), *Canadian Journal of Women and the Law* (1 a year), *Canadian Literature* (4 a year), *PRISM International* (4 a year), *University Calendar* (winter and summer), *Yearbook of International Law*

DEANS

College for Interdisciplinary Studies: MIKE BURGESS (Principal)
College of Health Disciplines: LOUISE NASMITH (Principal)
Faculty of Applied Science: TYSEER ABOUL-NASR
Faculty of Arts: GAGE AVERILL
Faculty of Dentistry: CHARLES SHULER
Faculty of Education: JON SHAPIRO
Faculty of Forestry: JOHN INNES
Faculty of Graduate Studies: BARBARA EVANS
Faculty of Land and Food Systems: MURRAY B. ISMAN
Faculty of Law: MARY ANNE BOBINSKI
Faculty of Medicine: GAVIN STUART
Faculty of Pharmaceutical Sciences: ROBERT D. SINDELAR
Faculty of Science: SIMON PEACOCK
Sauder School of Business: DANIEL F. MUZYKA

PROFESSORS

Faculty of Agricultural Sciences

Department of Agroecology:

BLACK, A.
CHANWAY, C.
CHENG, K.
CHIENG, S.-T.
COPEMAN, R.
CRONK, Q.
ELLIS, B.
ISMAN, M.
JOLLIFFE, P.
LAVKULICH, L.
MCKINLEY, S.
MYERS, J.
RAJAMAHENDRAN, R.
SCHREIER, H.
SHACKLETON, D.
TAYLOR, I.
UPADHYAYA, M.
WEARY, O.

Department of Community and the Environment:

CONDON, P.
PATERSON, D.
QUAYLE, M.

Department of Food, Nutrition and Health:

BARR, S.
CHENG, K.
DURANCE, T.
KITTS, D.
LI-CHAN, E.
THOMPSON, J.
VAN VUUREN, H.
VERCAMMEN, J.

Faculty of Applied Science

Department of Chemical and Biological Engineering:

BERT, J.
BOWEN, B.
CHIENG, S.
DUFF, S.
ENGLEZOS, P.
GRACE, J.
HATZIKIRIAKOS, S.
JIM JIM, C.
KEREKES, R.
LO, K.
OLOMAN, C.
PIRET, J.
SMITH, K.
WATKINSON, P.

Department of Civil Engineering:

ADEBAR, P.
BANTHIA, N.
FANNIN, R.
FOSCHI, R.
HALL, E.
HALL, K. J.
ISSACSON, M.
LAWRENCE, G.
MAVINIC, D.
MINDESS, S.
NAVIN, F.
RUSSELL, A.
SEXSMITH, R.
STEIMER, S.

Department of Electrical and Computer Engineering:

DAVIES, M.
DUMONT, G.
IVANOV, A.
JAEGER, N.
KRISHNAMURTHY, V.
LAWRENCE, P.
LEUNG, C.
LEUNG, V.
PULFREY, D.
SALEH, R.
WARD, R.

Department of Mechanical Engineering:

ALTINTAS, Y.
CALISAL, S.
CHERCHAS, D.
DE SILVA, C.
EVANS, R.
GADALA, M.
GREEN, S.
HILL, P.
HODGSON, M.
HUTTON, S.
RAJAPAKSE, N.
SALCUDEAN, M.
SASSANI, F.
SCHAJER, G.
YELLOWLEY, I.

Department of Metals and Materials Engineering:

DREISINGER, D.
POURSARTIP, A.
REED, R.
TROCZYNSKI, T.
TROMANS, D.

Department of Mining Engineering:

MEECH, J.
SCOBLE, M.
WILSON, W.

Faculty of Arts

Department of Anthropology:

MATSON, R.
MILLER, B.

Department of Art History, Visual Art and Theory:

COHODAS, M.
EDER, R.
GUILBAUT, S.
LUM, K.
O'BRIAN, J.
WATSON, S.
WINDSOR-LISCOMBE, R.

Department of Asian Studies:

DUKE, M.
NOSCO, P.
OBEROI, H.
SCHMIDT, J.
TAKASHIMA, K.-I.

Department of Classical, Near Eastern and Religious Studies:

BARRETT, A. A.
HARDING, P.
SULLIVAN, S.
TODD, R.
WILLIAMS, E.

Department of Economics:

COPELAND, B.
DIEWERT, E.
ESWARAN, M.
EVANS, R.
GREEN, D.
KOTWAL, A.
LEMIEUX, T.
PATERSON, D.
REDISH, A.
RIDDELL, C.

Department of French, Hispanic and Italian Studies:

BOCCASSINI, D.
HODGSON, R.
MCEACHERN, J.
RAOUL, V.
SARKONAK, R.
TESTA, C.
URRELLO, A.

Department of Geography:

BARNES, T.
CHURCH, M.
GREGORY, D.
HIEBERT, D.
LEY, D.
McCLUNG, D.
McKENDRY, I.
OKE, T.
PRATT, G.
ROBINSON, J.
SLAYMAKER, O.
STEYN, D.
STULL, R.
WYNN, G.

Department of Germanic Studies:

MORNIN, E.
PETERSEN, K.
PETRO, P.
STENBERG, P.

Department of History:

FRIEDRICHS, C.
KRAUSE, P.
LARY, D.
NEWELL, D.
RAY, A.
UNGER, R.
WARD, P.

Department of Linguistics:

PULLEYBLANK, D.
STEMBERGER, J.
VATIKIOTIS-BATESON, E.

School of Music:

BENJAMIN, W.
BERINAUM, M.
BUTLER, G.
CHATMAN, S.
COOP, J.
DAWES, A.
HAMEL, K.
READ, J.
SHARON, R.
TENZER, M.

Department of Philosophy:

BEATTY, J.
IRVINE, A.
RUSSELL, P.
SAVITT, S.
SCHABAS, M.
WILSON, C.

Department of Political Science:

JOB, B.
JOHNSTON, R.
LASELVA, S.
MARANTZ, P.
MAUZY, D.
RESNICK, P.
TENNANT, P.
TUPPER, A.
WALLACE, M.

Department of Psychology:

ALDEN, L.
CHANDLER, M.
COREN, S.
DUTTON, D.
ENNS, J.
GORZALKA, B.
GRAF, P.
HAKSTIAN, R.
LEHMAN, D.
LINDEN, W.
PINEL, J.
TEES, R.
WALKER, L.
WARD, L.
WERKER, J.

Department of Sociology:

CREESE, G.
CURRIE, D.
ELLIOTT, B.
ERICSON, R.
GUPPY, N.
JOHNSON, G.
JOPPKE, C.
MATTHEWS, D.

Department of Theatre, Film and Creative Writing:

ALDERSON, S.
DURBACH, E.
GARDINER, R.
McWHIRTER, G.
MAILLARD, K.
WASSERMAN, J.

Faculty of Dentistry

Department of Oral Biological and Medical Sciences:

BRUNETTE, D.
CLARK, C.
DIEWERT, V.
DONALDSON, D.
HANNAM, A.
LARJAVA, H.
LOWE, A.
OVERALL, C.
UITTO, V.-J.
YEN, E.

Department of Oral Health Sciences:

CLARK, C.
DIEWERT, V.
HANNAM, A.
LOWE, A.
McENTEE, M.

Faculty of Education

Faculty of Curriculum Studies:

CHALMERS, F. G.
ERICKSON, G.
GASKELL, P.
IRWIN, R.
KINDLER, A.
PETERAT, L.
PIRIE, S.

Department of Educational and Counselling Psychology, and Special Education:

AMUNDSON, N.
ARLIN, M.
BORGEN, W.
BUTLER, D.
DANILUK, J.
KAHN, S.
LONG, B.
PORATH, M.
SIEGEL, L.
WESTWOOD, M.
YOUNG, R.
ZUMBO, B.

Department of Educational Studies:

ADAM-MOODLEY, K.
BARMAN, J.
BOSHIER, R.
BROWN, D.
FISHER, D.
KELLY, D.
PRATT, D. D.
ROMAN, L.
RUBENSON, K.
SCHUETZE, H.
SHIELDS, C.
SORK, T.
STRONG-BOAG, V.
UNGERLEIDER, C. S.

Faculty of Forestry:

AVRAMIDIS, S.
BARKER, J.
BARRETT, D.
BUNNELL, F.
CHAFWAY, C.
EL-KASSABY, Y.
EVANS, P.
FANNIN, J.
GUY, R.
HALEY, D.
HOBERG, G.
INNES, J.
KIMMINS, J.
KLINKA, K.
McLEAN, J.
MARTIN, K.
MURTHA, P.
RITLAND, K.
RUDDICK, J.
VAN DER KAMP, B.

Faculty of Law:

BAKAN, J.
BLACK, W.
BLOM, J.
BOYD, S.
BOYLE, C.
BURNS, P.
ELLIOT, R.
FARQUHAR, K.
GRANT, I.
JACKSON, M.
LEBARON, L. M.
McDOUGALL, B.
PATERSON, R.
PAVLICH, D.
PUE, W.
SHEPPARD, A.
WEILER, J.
YOUNG, C.

Faculty of Medicine

Department of Anatomy:

BRESSLER, B.
CHURCH, J.
CRAWFORD, B.
EMERMAN, J.
NAUS, C.
OVALLE, W.
SLONECKER, C.
VOGL, A.
WEINBERG, J.

School of Audiology and Speech Sciences:

JOHNSTON, J.
STAPELLS, D.

Department of Biochemistry and Molecular Biology:

BRAYER, G.
BROWNSEY, R.
CULLIS, P.
DEDHAR, S.
FINLAY, B.
MACGILLIVRAY, R.
McINTOSH, L.
MACKIE, G.
MAUK, A.
MOLDAY, R.
ROBERGE, M.
SADOWSKI, I.

Department of Family Practice:

BASSETT, K.
BATES, J.
CALAM, B.
DONNELLY, M.
GRAMS, G.
GRZYBOWSKI, S.
KHAN, K.
KLEIN, M.
KUHL, D.
LIVINGSTONE, V.
McKENZIE, D.
SCOTT, I.
TAUNTON, J.
WHITESIDE, C.
WIEBE, C.
WOOLLARD, R.

Department of Healthcare and Epidemiology:

BARER, M.
BLACK, C.
HERTZMAN, C.
KAZANJIAN, A.
KENNEDY, S.
MATHIAS, R.
SCHECHTER, M.
SHEPS, S.

SINGER, J.
TESCHKE, K.

Faculty of Medical Genetics:

BURGESS, M.
EAVES, C.
FIELD, L.
FRIEDMAN, J.
HALL, J.
HIETER, P.
JEFFERIES, W.
JURILOFF, D.
KAY, R.
MCGILLIVRAY, B.
MCMASTER, W.
MAGER, D.
ROSE, A.
SADOVNICK, A.

Department of Medicine:

ABBOUD, R.
BAI, T.
BEATTIE, B.
BIRMINGHAM, C.
BOWIE, W.
BRUNHAM, R.
CAIRNS, J.
CALNE, D.
CHOW, A.
EAVES, A.
EISEN, A.
ESDAILE, J.
FLEETHAM, J.
FREEMAN, H.
HO, V.
HUMPHRIES, R.
KEOWN, P.
KERR, C.
LAM, S.
LUI, H.
MCLEAN, D.
MANCINI, G.
MONTANER, J.
OGER, J.
OSTROW, D.
PAGE, G.
PARÉ, P.
PATY, D.
PELECH, S.
PRIOR, J.
QUAMME, G.
RABKIN, S.
REINER, N.
RIVERS, J.
ROAD, J.
RUSSELL, J.
SCHELLENBERG, R.
SCHRADER, J.
SCHULZER, M.
STEIN, H.
STEINBRECHER, U.
STIVER, H.
STOESSL, J.
SUTTON, R.
TSUI, J.
WALLEY, K.
WANG, Y.
WONG, N.
WRIGHT, J.
YEUNG, M.

Department of Physiology:

BAIMBRIDGE, K.
BUCHAN, A.
FEDIDA, D.
MCINTOSH, C.
NAUS, C. C.
PEARSON, J

Department of Radiology:

COOPERBERG, P.
CULHAM, G.
LI, D.
LYSTER, D.
MACKAY, A.
MÜLLER, N.
MUNK, P.

Department of Surgery:

WARNOCK, G.

Faculty of Science

Department of Botany:

DEWREEDE, R.
DOUGLAS, C.
GANDERS, F.
GLASS, A.
GREEN, B.
GRIFFITHS, A.
MADDISON, W.
TAYLOR, F.
TAYLOR, I.
TOWERS, G.
TURKINGTON, R.

Department of Chemistry:

ANDERSEN, R.
BLADES, M.
BROOKS, D.
BURNELL, E.
COMISAROW, M.
DOLPHIN, D.
DOUGLAS, D.
FLEMING, D.
FRYZUK, M.
FYFE, C.
GERRY, M.
HEPBURN, J.
HERRING, G.
LEGZDINS, P.
MCINTOSH, L.
MITCHELL, K.
ORVIG, C.
PATEY, G.
PIERS, E.
SAWATZKY, G.
SCHEFFER, J.
SHAPIRO, M.
SHERMAN, J.
SHIZGAL, B.
STORR, A.
TANNER, M.
WITHERS, S.

Department of Computer Science:

ASCHER, U.
BOOTH, K.
CONDON, A.
FRIEDMAN, J.
KICZALES, G.
KIRKPATRICK, D.
KLAWE, M.
LAKSHMANAN, L.
LITTLE, J.
LOWE, D.
MACKWORTH, A.
NG, R.
PAI, D.
PIPPENGER, N.
POOLE, D.
ROSENBERG, R.
WOODHAM, R.

Department of Earth and Ocean Sciences:

ANDERSEN, R.
BOSTOCK, M.
BUSTIN, M.
CLARKE, G.
CLOWES, R.
FLETCHER, K.
GROAT, L.
HARRISON, P.
HEALEY, M.
HSIEH, W.
HUNGR, O.
INGRAM, G.
OLDENBURG, D.
RUSSELL, K.
SMITH, L.
SMITH, P.
STEYN, D.
STULL, R.
TAYLOR, M.
ULRYCH, T.
WEIS, D.

Department of Mathematics:

ANSTEE, R.
BLUMAN, G.
BOYD, D.
CARRELL, J.
FOURNIER, J.
GHOUSSOUB, N.
LAM, K.
LOEWEN, P.
MACDONALD, J.
MARCUS, B.
PEIRCE, A.
PERKINS, E.
SEYMOUR, B.
SJERVE, D.
SLADE, G.
WARD, M.

Department of Microbiology and Immunology:

HANCOCK, R. E. W.
JEFFERIES, W. A.
KRONSTAD, J. W.
SMIT, J.
SPIEGELMAN, G.
TEH, H.-S.
WEEKS, G.

Department of Statistics:

HARRY, J.
HECKMAN, N.
PETKAU, J.
VAN EEDEN, C.
ZAMAR, R.
ZIDEK, J.

Department of Zoology:

ADAMSON, M.
BERGER, J.
BLAKE, R.
BROCK, H.
GASS, C.
GOSLINE, J.
GRIGLIATTI, T.
JONES, D.
MILSOM, W.
MOERMAN, D.
MYERS, J.
PAULY, D.
PITCHER, T.
RANDALL, D.
SCHLUTER, D.
SINCLAIR, T.
SMITH, J.
SNUTCH, T.
STEEVES, J.
TETZLAFF, W.
WALTERS, C.

Sauder School of Business

Division of Accounting:

FELTHAM, G.
SIMUNIC, D.

Division of Finance:

GIAMMARINO, R.
HAMILTON, S.
HEINKEL, R.
KRAUS, A.
LEVI, M.

Division of Law:

WAND, Y.

Division of Marketing:

GRIFFIN, D.
WEINBERG, C.

Division of Operations and Logistics:

ATKINS, D.
GRANOT, D.
GRANOT, F.
MCCORMICK, T.
OUM, T.
PUTERMAN, M.
QUEYRANNE, M.
ZHANG, A.
ZIEMBA, W.

Division of Strategy and Business Economics:

ANTWEILER, W.
BOARDMAN, A.
BRANDER, J.
FRANK, M.
HELSLEY, R.
NAKAMURA, M.
NEMETZ, P.
ROSS, T.
SPENCER, B.
VERTINSKY, I.
WINTER, R.

School of Architecture:

BROCK, L.
COLE, R.
CONDON, P.
MACDONALD, C.
PATKAU, P.
WAGNER, G.
WALKEY, R.
WOJTOWICZ, J.

School of Human Kinetics:

CROCKER, P.
FRANKS, I.
MCKENZIE, D.
RHODES, E.
TAUNTON, J.

School of Journalism:

LOGAN, D.

School of Library, Archival and Information Studies:

DURANTI, L.
HAYCOCK, K.
RASMUSSEN, E.

School of Nursing:

ACORN, S.
ANDERSON, J.
BOTTORFF, D.
CARTY, E.
HILTON, A.
JOHNSON, J.
PATERSON, B.
THORNE, S.

School of Social Work and Family Studies:

CHRISTENSEN, C.
MARTIN-MATHEWS, A.
PERLMAN, D.
RUSSELL, M.
WHITE, J.

THEOLOGICAL COLLEGES

Carey Hall and Carey Theological College: 5920 Iona Drive, Vancouver, BC V6T 1J6; tel. 224-4308; e-mail info@carey-edu.ca; internet www.careytheologicalcollege.ca; Prin. Dr B. F. STELCK.

Regent College: 5800 University Blvd, Vancouver, BC V6T 2E4; tel. 224-3245; e-mail reception@regent-college.edu; internet www.regent-college.edu; Private control; language of instruction: English; academic year September to April; Pres. ROD WILSON; Academic Dean PAUL WILLIAMS; publ. *CRUX*.

St Andrew's Hall: 6040 Iona Drive, Vancouver, BC V6T 2E8; tel. (604) 822-9720; Dean Rev. B. J. FRASER.

St Mark's College: 5935 Iona Drive, Vancouver, BC V6T 1J7; tel. 224-3311; internet www.stmarkscollege.ca; Prin. Dr JOHN D. DENNISON.

Vancouver School of Theology: 6000 Iona Drive, Vancouver, BC V6T 1L4; tel. (604) 228-9031; internet www.vst.edu; an ecumenical school of theology, inc. 1971; continues work of the Anglican Theological College of BC and Union College of BC; provides theological education for laymen, for future clergy and for graduates in theology; Prin. Dr KENNETH MACQUEEN

UNIVERSITY OF CALGARY

2500 University Dr. NW, Calgary, AB T2N 1N4
Telephone: (403) 220-5110
E-mail: reginfo@ucalgary.ca
Internet: www.ucalgary.ca

Founded 1945 as a br. of the University of Alberta; gained full autonomy 1966
Language of instruction: English
Academic year: July to June

Chancellor: JIM DINNING
Pres.: Dr ELIZABETH CANNON
Provost and Vice-Pres. for Academic Affairs: ALAN HARRISON
Vice-Pres. for Devt.: GARY DURBENIUK
Assoc. Vice-Pres. for External Relations: CATHERINE BAGNELL STYLES
Vice-Pres. for Facilities Management and Devt.: BOB ELLARD
Vice-Pres. for Finance and Services: JONATHAN GEBERT
Vice-Pres. for Research: Dr ROSE GOLDSTEIN
Registrar: D. B. JOHNSTON
Chief Information Officer for Information Technologies: H. A. ESCHE

Number of teachers: 2,761
Number of students: 29,000

Publications: *Abstracts of English Studies*, *Arctic Journal* (Arctic Institute of North America), *Ariel: Review of International English Literature*, *Calgary Alumni*, *Canadian Energy Research Institute publs* (irregular), *Canadian Ethnic Studies*, *Canadian and International Education* (2 a year), *Canadian Journal of Law and Society* (1 a year), *Canadian Journal of Philosophy* (4 a year), *Classical Views—Echos du monde classique*, *International Journal of Man-Machine Studies* (12 a year), *Journal of Child and Youth Care*, *Journal of Comparative Family Studies*, *Journal of Educational Thought* (3 a year), *University Gazette* (26 a year)

DEANS

Faculty of Arts: KEVIN MCQUILLAN
Faculty of Education: DENNIS SUMARA
Faculty of Environmental Design: Dr NANCY POLLOCK-ELLWAND
Faculty of Graduate Studies: Dr FRED HALL
Faculty of Kinesiology: Dr WAYNE GILES
Faculty of Law: ALASTAIR R. LUCAS
Faculty of Medicine: Dr TOM FEASBY
Faculty of Nursing (Calgary): DIANNE TAP
Faculty of Nursing (Qatar): SHEILA EVANS
Faculty of Science: Dr KEN BARKER
Faculty of Social Work: Dr GAYLA ROGERS
Schulich School of Engineering: Dr ANIL MEHROTRA
Haskayne School of Business: Dr LEONARD WAVERMAN
Continuing Education: Dr SCOTT MCLEAN (Dir)

PROFESSORS

ADDICOTT, J. F., Biological Sciences
ADDINGTON, D. E. N., Psychiatry
AGOPIAN, E. E., Music
ANDREWS, J. W., Division of Applied Psychology
ARCHER, C. I., History
ARCHER, D. P., Anaesthesia and Clinical Neurosciences
ARCHER, K. A., Political Science
ARCHIBALD, J. A., Linguistics
ARMSTRONG, G. D., Microbiology and Infectious Diseases
ARTHUR, N. M., Division of Applied Psychology
ASTLE, W. F., Surgery
ATKINSON, M. H., Medicine
AUER, R. N., Clinical Neurosciences and Pathology and Laboratory Medicine
AUSTIN, C. D., Social Work
BACK, T. G., Chemistry
BANKES, N. D., Law
BARCLAY, R. M. R., Biological Sciences
BARKER, K. E., Computer Science
BARRY, D., Political Science
BAUWENS, L., Mechanical Engineering
BECH-HANSEN, N. T., Medical Genetics and Surgery
BECKER, W. J., Clinical Neurosciences and Medicine
BEHIE, L. A., Chemical and Petroleum Engineering
BELENKIE, I., Medicine
BELL, A. G., Music
BELL, D. M., Music
BELYEA, B., English
BENEDIKTSON, H., Pathology and Laboratory Medicine
BENNETT, S., English
BENTLEY, L. R., Geology and Geophysics
BERCUSON, D. J., History
BERSHAD, D. L., Art
BEZDEK, K., Mathematics and Statistics
BIDDLE, F. G., Paediatrics and Biochemistry and Molecular Biology and Medical Genetics
BINDING, P. A., Mathematics and Statistics
BIRSS, V. I., Chemistry
BISZTRICZKY, T., Mathematics and Statistics
BLAND, B. H., Psychology
BOND, R. B., English
BOS, L. P., Mathematics and Statistics
BOSETTI, B. L., Education
BOWAL, P. C., Haskayne School of Business
BOYCE, J. R., Economics
BRADLEY, J., Computer Science
BRANNIGAN, A., Sociology
BRANT, R. F., Community Health Sciences
BRAY, R. C., Surgery
BRENKEN, B. A., Mathematics and Statistics
BRENT, D. A., Communication and Culture
BROWDER, L. W., Biochemistry and Molecular Biology and Oncology
BROWN, C. A., Law
BROWN, C. B., Medicine, Oncology, Biochemistry and Molecular Biology
BROWN, J. L. S., Environmental Design
BROWN, J. S., Music
BROWN, K., French, Italian and Spanish
BROWN, R. J., Geology and Geophysics
BROWN, T. G., Civil Engineering
BROWNELL, A. K. W., Clinical Neurosciences and Medicine
BRUCE, C. J., Economics
BRUEN, A. A., Mathematics and Statistics
BRUTON, L. T., Electrical and Computer Engineering
BULLOCH, A. G. M., Physiology and Biophysics
BURET, A. G., Biological Sciences
BURGESS, E. D., Medicine
BURKE, M. D., Mathematics and Statistics
BUTZNER, J. D., Paediatrics
CAIRNCROSS, J. G., Clinical Neurosciences
CAIRNS, K. V., Division of Applied Psychology
CAMERON, E., Art
CAMPBELL, G. W., French, Italian and Spanish
CAMPBELL, N. R. C., Medicine
CANNON, M. E., Geomatics Engineering
CARTER, S. A., History
CAVEY, M. J., Biological Sciences
CERI, H., Biological Sciences
CHACONAS, G., Biochemistry, Molecular Biology, Microbiology and Infectious Diseases
CHADEE, K., Microbiology and Infectious Diseases
CHANG, K.-W., Mathematics and Statistics
CHEN, S. R. W., Physiology, Biophysics, Biochemistry and Molecular Biology
CHINNAPPA, C. C., Biological Sciences
CHIVERS, T., Chemistry
CHUA, J. H., Haskayne School of Business
CHURCH, D. L., Pathology and Laboratory Medicine and Medicine
CHURCH, J. R., Economics

CLARK, A. W., Pathology and Laboratory Medicine and Clinical Neurosciences
CLARK, P. D., Chemistry
CLARKE, M. E., Paediatrics and Psychiatry
CLEVE, R. E., Computer Science
COCKETT, J. R. B., Computer Science
COELHO, V. A., Music
COLE, W. C., Pharmacology and Therapeutics
COLEMAN, H. D. J., Social Work
COLIJN, A. W., Computer Science
COLLINS, D. G., Social Work
COLLINS, J. R., Mathematics and Statistics
CONLY, J. M., Pathology and Laboratory Medicine
COOK, F. A., Geology and Geophysics
COOPER, F. B., Political Science
COPPES, M. J., Oncology and Paediatrics
CORENBLUM, B., Medicine
COUCH, W. E., Mathematics and Statistics
COWIE, R. L., Medicine and Community Health Sciences
CROSS, J. C., Biochemistry, Molecular Biology, Obstetrics and Gynaecology
CURRY, B., Pathology and Laboratory Medicine and Clinical Neurosciences
DAIS, E. E., Law
DANSEREAU, E. D. M., French, Italian and Spanish
DAVIES, J. M., Anaesthesia
DAVIES, W. K. D., Geography
DAVIS, R. C., English
DAVISON, J. S., Physiology and Biophysics
DAY, R. L., Civil Engineering
DEACON, P. G., Art
DELONG, K. G., Music
DEWEY, D. M., Paediatrics
DICKIN, J. P., Faculty of Communication and Culture
DICKINSON, J. A., Family Medicine and Community Health Sciences
DOBSON, K. S., Psychology
DORT, J. C., Surgery
DOWTY, A., Political Science
DRAPER, D. L., Geography
DUCKWORTH, K., Geology and Geophysics
DUGAN, J. S., Drama
DUGGAN, M. A., Pathology, Laboratory Medicine, Obstetrics and Gynaecology
DUNN, J. F., Radiology, Physiology and Biophysics
DUNSCOMBE, P. B., Oncology
DYCK, R. H., Psychology
EAGLE, C. J., Anaesthesia
EATON, B. C., Economics
EBERLY, W. M., Computer Science
EDWARDS, M. V., Music
EGGERMONT, J. J., Physiology and Biophysics and Psychology
EINSIEDEL, E. F., Communications and Culture
EL-BADRY, M. M., Civil Engineering
EL-GUEBALY, M. A., Psychiatry
EL-SHEIMY, N. M., Geomatics Engineering
ELHAJJ, R. S., Computer Science
ELLIOTT, R. J., Haskayne School of Business
ELOFSON, W. M., History
EMES, C. G., Kinesiology
ENGLE, J. M., Music
ENNS, E. G., Mathematics and Statistics
EPSTEIN, M., Mechanical and Manufacturing Engineering
ERESHEFSKY, M. F., Philosophy
ESLINGER, L. M., Religious Studies
FACCHINI, P. J., Biological Sciences
FARFAN, P. C. M., Drama and English
FATTOUCHE, M. T., Electrical and Computer Engineering
FAUVEL, O. R., Mechanical and Manufacturing Engineering
FEDIGAN, L. M., Anthropology
FERRIS, J. R., History
FEWELL, J. E., Obstetrics and Gynaecology, Paediatrics and Physiology and Biophysics
FICK, G. H., Community Health Sciences
FLANAGAN, T. E., Political Science
FLETCHER, W. A., Clinical Neurosciences and Surgery
FONG, T. C., Radiology
FORD, G. T., Medicine
FOREMAN, C. L., Music
FOREMAN, K. J., Drama
FOUTS, G. T., Psychology
FRANCIS, R. D., History
FRANK, A. W., Sociology
FRANK, C. B., Surgery
FRENCH, R. J., Physiology and Biophysics
FRIDERES, J. S., Sociology
FRIESEN, J. W., Faculty of Education
FRITZLER, M. J., Medicine, Biochemistry and Molecular Biology
FUJITA, D. J., Biochemistry and Molecular Biology
GABOR, P. A., Social Work
GAISFORD, J. D., Economics
GEDAMU, L., Biological Sciences
GETZ, D. P., Haskayne School of Business
GHALI, W. A., Medicine and Community Health Sciences
GHANNOUCHI, F., Electrical and Computer Engineering
GHENT, E. D., Geology and Geophysics
GILES, W. R., Physiology and Biophysics and Medicine
GILL, B., French, Italian and Spanish
GILL, M. J., Medicine
GILLIS, A. M., Medicine
GORDON, D. V., Economics
GORDON, T. M., Geology and Geophysics
GOREN, H. J., Biochemistry and Molecular Biology
GORESKY, G. V., Anaesthesia and Paediatrics
GRAHAM, J. R., Social Work
GRAVEL, R. A., Cell Biology and Anatomy
GREEN, F. H. Y., Pathology and Laboratory Medicine
GREENBERG, S., Computer Science
GU, P., Mechanical and Manufacturing Engineering
GUPTA, A., Management
HABIBI, H. R., Biological Science
HAGEN, N. A., Oncology and Medicine
HAJI, I. H., Philosophy
HALL, B. L., Social Work
HANLEY, D. A., Medicine
HANLEY, P. J., Medicine
HARASYM, P. H., Office of Medical Education and Community Health Sciences
HARDER, L. D., Biological Sciences
HARDING, T. G., Chemical and Petroleum Engineering
HARPER, T. L., Environmental Design
HART, D. A., Microbiology and Infectious Diseases, Medicine
HARTMAN, F. T., Civil Engineering
HASLETT, J. W., Electrical and Computer Engineering
HAWE, H. P., Community Health Sciences
HAWKES, R. B., Cell Biology and Anatomy
HAWKINS, R. W., Communication and Culture
HEBERT, Y. M., Faculty of Education
HECKEL, W., Greek and Roman Studies
HELMER, J. W., Archaeology
HENDERSON, C. M., Geology and Geophysics
HERMAN, R. J., Medicine
HERWIG, H. H., History
HERZOG, W., Kinesiology
HETTIARATCHI, J. P. A., Civil Engineering
HEXHAM, I. R., Religious Studies
HEYMAN, R. D., Faculty of Education
HIEBERT, B. A., Division of Applied Psychology
HILLER, H. H., Sociology
HO, M., Microbiology, Infectious Diseases and Medicine
HODGINS, D. C., Psychology
HOGAN, D. B., Medicine and Clinical Neurosciences and Community Health Sciences
HOLLENBERG, M. D., Pharmacology and Therapeutics
HU, B., Clinical Neurosciences, Cell Biology and Anatomy
HUBER, R. E., Biological Sciences
HUGHES, M. E., Law
HULL, R. D., Medicine
HULLIGER, M., Clinical Neurosciences and Physiology and Biophysics
HUNT, J. D., Civil Engineering
HUSHLAK, G. M., Art
HYNES, M. F., Biological Sciences
IRVINE-HALLIDAY, D., Electrical and Computer Engineering
ISMAEL, J. S., Social Work
ISMAEL, T. Y., Political Science
JACOB, J. C., Faculty of Education
JADAVJI, T., Microbiology and Infectious Diseases and Paediatrics
JAMESON, E., History
JARDINE, D. W., Faculty of Education
JARRELL, J. F., Obstetrics and Gynaecology
JEJE, A. A., Chemical and Petroleum Engineering
JENNETT, P. A., Office of Medical Education and Community Health Sciences
JIRIK, F. R., Biochemistry and Molecular Biology
JOHNSON, E. A., Biological Sciences
JOHNSON, J. M., Obstetrics and Gynaecology
JOHNSTON, R. H., Electrical and Computer Engineering
JOHNSTON, R. N., Biochemistry and Molecular Biology
JOLDERSMA, H., Germanic, Slavic and East Asian Studies
JONES, A. R., Medicine and Oncology
JONES, D. C., Faculty of Education
JONES, V. J., Haskayne School of Business
JORDAN, W. S., Music
JOY, M. M., Religious Studies
JULLIEN, G. A., Electrical and Computer Engineering
KALBACH, M. H., Sociology
KALER, K. V. I., Electrical and Computer Engineering
KANTZAS, A., Chemical and Petroleum Engineering
KAPLAN, B. J., Paediatrics
KARGACIN, G. J., Physiology and Biophysics
KARIM, G. A., Mechanical and Manufacturing Engineering
KATZENBERG, M. A., Archaeology
KAUFFMAN, S. A., Biological Sciences, Physics and Astronomy
KAWAMURA, L. S., Religious Studies
KEAY, B. A., Chemistry
KEENAN, T. P., Environmental Design
KEITH, D. W., Chemical and Petroleum Engineering and Economics
KEITH, R. C., Political Science
KELLNER, J. D., Paediatrics, Microbiology and Infectious Diseases
KEREN, M., Communication and Culture and Political Science
KERTZER, A. E., English
KERTZER, J. M., English
KLASSEN, J., Pathology and Laboratory Medicine and Medicine
KLINE, D. W., Psychology
KLINE, T. J., Psychology
KNEEBONE, R. D., Economics
KNOLL, P. J., Law
KNOPFF, R., Political Science
KNUDTSON, M. L., Cardiac Sciences and Medicine
KOOPMANS, H. S., Physiology and Biophysics and Psychology
KOOYMAN, B. P., Archaeology
KOSTYNIUK, R. P., Art
KRAUSE, F. F., Geology and Geophysics
KREBES, E. S., Geology and Geophysics
KUBES, P., Physiology and Biophysics and Medicine
KURTZ, S. M., Education
LACHAPELLE, G. J., Geomatics Engineering
LAFLAMME, C., Mathematics and Statistics
LAFRENIÈRE, R., Surgery
LAI, D. W. L., Social Work
LAING, W. J. H., Art

LAMOUREUX, M. P., Mathematics and Statistics
LANGE, I. R., Obstetrics and Gynaecology
LARTER, S. R., Geology and Geophysics
LAU, D. C. W., Medicine
LAWTON, D. C., Geology and Geophysics
LEAHY, D. A., Physics and Astronomy
LEE, S. S., Medicine
LEE, T. G., Environmental Design
LEES-MILLER, S. P., Biochemistry and Molecular Biology
LEON, L. J., Electrical and Computer Engineering
LEUNG, H. K. Y., Electrical and Computer Engineering
LEVIN, G. J., Music
LEVY, J. C., Law
LEVY, R. M., Environmental Design
LEWKONIA, R. M., Medicine and Paediatrics and Medical Genetics
LINES, L. R., Geology and Geophysics
LOUIE, T. J., Medicine, Microbiology and Infectious Diseases
LOUTZENHISER, R. D., Pharmacology and Therapeutics
LOVE, J. A., Environmental Design
LUCAS, A. R., Law
LUKASIEWICZ, S. A., Mechanical and Manufacturing Engineering
LUKOWIAK, K., Physiology and Biophysics
LYTTON, J., Biochemistry, Molecular Biology, Physiology and Biophysics
MCCALLUM, P. M., English
MCCAULEY, F. E. R., Biological Sciences
MCCLELLAND, R. W., Social Work
MCCONNELL, C. S., Art
MCCREADY, W. O., Religious Studies
MCCULLOUGH, D. T., Drama
MACDONALD, D. L., English
MCGHEE, J. D., Biochemistry and Molecular Biology
MCGILLIS, R. F., English
MCGILLIVRAY, M. D., English
MACINTOSH, B. R., Kinesiology
MACINTOSH, J. J., Philosophy
MCKENZIE, K. J., Economics
MCKEOUGH, A. M., Division of Applied Psychology
MCKINNON, J. G., Surgery and Oncology
MCMORDIE, M. J., Environmental Design, Communication and Culture
MCMULLAN, W. E., Haskayne School of Business
MACNAUGHTON, W. K., Physiology and Biophysics
MCRAE, R. N., Economics
MCWHIR, A. R., English
MAES, M. A., Civil Engineering
MAHER, P. M., Haskayne School of Business
MAHONEY, K. E., Law
MAINI, B. B., Chemical and Petroleum Engineering
MAINS, P. E., Biochemistry and Molecular Biology
MANDIN, H., Medicine
MARTIN, R. H., Paediatrics and Medical Genetics
MARTIN, S. L., Law
MARTINUZZI, R., Mechanical and Manufacturing Engineering
MASH, E. J., Psychology
MATO, D., Art
MAURER, F. O., Computer Science
MEDDINGS, J. B., Medicine
MEEUWISSE, W. H., Kinesiology
MEHROTRA, A. K., Chemical and Petroleum Engineering
MEHTA, S. A., Chemical and Petroleum Engineering
MIDHA, R., Clinical Neurosciences
MILONE, E. F., Physics and Astronomy
MINTCHEV, M. P., Electrical and Computer Engineering
MITCHELL, D. B., Communication and Culture
MITCHELL, I., Paediatrics
MITCHELL, L. B., Cardiac Science and Medicine
MITCHELL, S. H., Education
MOAZZEN-AHMADI, N., Physics and Astronomy
MOCQUAIS, P. Y. A., French, Italian and Spanish
MODY, C. H., Medicine, Microbiology and Infectious Diseases
MOHAMAD, A. A., Mechanical and Maufacturing Engineering
MOLLIN, R. A., Mathematics and Statistics
MOORE, R. G., Chemical and Petroleum Engineering
MORCK, D. W., Biological Sciences
MORTON, F. L., Political Science
MUELLER, J. H., Division of Applied Psychology
MUNRO, M. C., Haskayne School of Business
MURPHREE, J. S., Physics and Astronomy
MURRAY, R. W., Linguistics
MURRAY, S. C., Kinesiology
MUZIK, I., Civil Engineering
MYLES, S. T., Surgery and Clinical Neurosciences
NATION, J. G., Obstetrics and Gynaecology and Oncology
NAULT, B. R., Haskayne School of Business
NEU, D. E., Haskayne School of Business
NEUFELDT, A. H., Faculty of Education
NEUFELDT, R. W., Religious Studies
NICHOLSON, W. K., Mathematics and Statistics
NIELSON, N., Haskayne School of Business
NIGG, B. M., Kinesiology
NKEMDIRIM, L. C., Geography
NORTON, P. G., Family Medicine
NOSAL, M., Mathematics and Statistics
NOSEWORTHY, T. W., Community Health Sciences
OETELAAR, G. A., Archaeology
OKONIEWSKI, M., Electrical and Computer Engineering
OSBORN, G. D., Geology and Geophysics
OSLER, M. J., History
PARKER, J. R., Computer Science
PATTISON, D. R. M., Geology and Geophysics
PAUL, R., Chemistry
PEREIRA ALMAO, P. R., Chemical and Petroleum Engineering
PERL, A. D., Political Science
PERREAULT, J. M., English
PIERS, W. E., Chemistry
PINEO, G. F., Medicine and Oncology
PITTMAN, Q. J., Physiology and Biophysics
POLLAK, P. T., Medicine, Cardiac Sciences, Pharmacology and Therapeutics
PONAK, A. M., Haskayne School of Business
PONTING, J. R., Sociology
POON, M.-C., Medicine and Paediatrics
POST, J. R., Biological Sciences
POWELL, D. G., Family Medicine
PRICE, G. D., Music
PROUD, D., Physiology and Biophysics
PRUSINKIEWICZ, P., Computer Science
PYRCH, T., Social Work
RABIN, H. R., Microbiology, Infectious Diseases and Medicine
RADTKE, H. L., Psychology
RAFFERTY, N. S., Law
RAMRAJ, V. J., English
RANGACHARI, P. K., Pharmacology and Therapeutics
RANGAYYAN, R. M., Electrical and Computer Engineering
RASPORICH, B. J., Communication and Culture
RATTNER, J. B., Cell Biology and Anatomy and Biochemistry and Molecular Biology and Oncology
RAY, D. I., Political Science
RAYMOND, S., Archaeology
REID, D. M., Biological Sciences
REMMERS, J. E., Medicine, Physiology and Biophysics
REVEL, R. D., Environmental Design
REYNOLDS, J. D., Physiology, Biophysics and Medicine
RIABOWOL, K. T., Biochemistry and Molecular Biology
RIEDIGER, C. L., Geology and Geophysics
RITCHIE, J. R. B., Haskayne School of Business
ROBERTSON, S. E., Division of Applied Psychology
ROHLEDER, T. R., Haskayne School of Business
ROKNE, J. G., Computer Science
RONSKY, J. L., Mechanical and Manufacturing Engineering
RORSTAD, O. P., Medicine
ROSS, W. A., Environmental Design
ROTH, S. H., Pharmacology and Therapeutics, and Anaesthesia
ROTHERY, M. A., Social Work
ROUNTHWAITE, H. I., Law
ROWNEY, J. I. A., Haskayne School of Business
ROWSE, J. G., Economics
RUDY, S. A., English
RUHE, G., Computer Science and Electrical and Computer Engineering
RUSSELL, A. P., Biological Sciences
SAINSBURY, R. S., Psychology
SAMUELS, M. T., Division of Applied Psychology
SANDERS, B. C., Physics and Astronomy
SANDS, G. W., Mathematics and Statistics
SANTAMARIA, P., Microbiology and Infectious Diseases
SARNAT, H. B., Paediatrics, Clinical Neurosciences Pathology and Laboratory Medicine
SAUER, N. W., Mathematics and Statistics
SAUNDERS, I. B., Law
SAUVE, R. S., Paediatrics and Community Health Sciences
SCHACHAR, N. S., Surgery
SCHNETKAMP, P. P. M., Biochemistry and Molecular Biology, and Physiology and Biophysics
SCHRYVERS, A. B., Microbiology and Infectious Diseases
SCHULZ, R. A., Haskayne School of Business
SCHWARZ, K.-P., Geomatics Engineering
SCIALFA, C. T., Psychology
SCOLLNIK, D. P. M., Mathematics and Statistics
SCOTT, R. B., Paediatrics
SEGAL, E. L., Religious Studies
SENSEN, C. W., Biochemistry and Molecular Biology
SERLETIS, A., Economics
SESAY, A. B., Electrical and Computer Engineering
SETTARI, A., Chemical and Petroleum Engineering
SEVERSON, D. L., Pharmacology and Therapeutics
SHAFFER, E. A., Medicine
SHANTZ, D. H., Religious Studies
SHAPIRO, B. L., Education
SHARKEY, K. A., Physiology and Biophysics
SHAW, W. J. D., Mechanical and Manufacturing Engineering
SHELDON, R. S., Medicine
SHIELL, A. M., Community Health Sciences
SHRIVE, N. G., Civil Engineering
SICK, G. A., Haskayne School of Business
SIDERIS, M. G., Geomatics Engineering
SIMMINS, G., Art
SINGHAL, N., Paediatrics
SMART, A., Anthropology
SMART, P. J., Anthropology
SMITH, D. D. B., History
SMITH, D. G., Geography
SMITH, D. J., Kinesiology
SMITH, F. R., Physiology and Biophysics
SMITH, G. B., Drama
SMITH, M. R., Electrical and Computer Engineering
SNIATYCKI, J. Z., Mathematics and Statistics

SNYDER, F. F., Paediatrics, Medical Biochemistry and Medical Biology
SOKOL, P. A., Microbiology and Infectious Diseases
SPENCER, R. J., Geology and Geophysics
SPRATT, D. A., Geology and Geophysics
STALKER, M. A., Law
STAM, H. J., Psychology
STAMP, R. M., Education
STAUM, M. S., History
STELL, W. K., Cell Biology and Anatomy and Surgery
STEWART, R. R., Geology and Geophysics
STOCKING, J. R., Art
STOREY, D. G., Biological Sciences
STOUGHTON, N. M., Haskayne School of Business
SUCHOWERSKY, O., Clinical Neurosciences
SUTHERLAND, C. T., Communication and Culture
SUTHERLAND, F. R., Surgery and Oncology
SUTHERLAND, G. R., Clinical Neurosciences
SUTHERLAND, L. R., Medicine and Community Health Sciences
SVRCEK, W. Y., Chemical and Petroleum Engineering
SWAIN, M. G., Medicine
SYED, N. I. S., Cell Biology, Anatomy, Physiology and Biophysics
TARAS, D., Communication and Culture
TARAS, D. G., Haskayne School of Business
TAY, R. S. T., Civil Engineering
TAYLOR, A. R., Physics and Astronomy
TAYLOR, M. S., Economics
TEMPLE, W. J., Surgery and Oncology
TER KEURS, H. E. D., Cardiac Sciences, Medicine, Physiology and Biophysics
TESKEY, G. C., Psychology
TESKEY, W. F., Geomatics Engineering
THOMAS, R. E., Family Medicine
THOMPSON, D. A. R., Environmental Design
THURSTON, W. E., Community Health Sciences
TIELEMAN, D. P., Biological Sciences
TOEWS, J. A., Psychiatry
TOMM, K. M., Psychiatry
TOOHEY, P. G., Greek and Roman Studies
TREBBLE, M. A., Chemical and Petroleum Engineering
TRIGGLE, C. R., Pharmacology and Therapeutics
TRUTE, B., Social Work and Nursing
TSENKOVA, S., Environmental Design
TURNER, L. E., Electrical and Computer Engineering
TURNER, R. W., Cell Biology, Anatomy, Physiology and Biophysics
TUTTY, L. M., Social Work
TYBERG, J. V., Cardiac Sciences, Medicine, Physiology and Biophysics
UNGER, B. W., Computer Science
URBANSKI, S. J., Pathology and Laboratory Medicine
VANBALKOM, W. D., Education
VAN DER HOORN, F. A., Biochemistry and Molecular Biology
VANDERSPOEL, J., Greek and Roman Studies
VAN DE SANDE, J. H., Biochemistry and Molecular Biology
VAN HERK, A., English
VAN ROSENDAAL, G. M. A., Medicine
VEALE, W. L., Physiology and Biophysics
VERBEKE, A. C. M., Haskayne School of Business
VERHOEF, M. J., Community Health Sciences and Medicine
VICKERS, J. N., Kinesiology
VINOGRADOV, O., Mechanical and Manufacturing Engineering
VIOLATO, C., Community Health Sciences
VIZE, P. D., Biological Sciences
VOGEL, H. J., Biological Sciences
VOORDOUW, G., Biological Sciences
VREDENBURG, H., Haskayne School of Business
WAISMAN, D. M., Biochemistry and Molecular Biology
WALKER, D. C., French, Italian and Spanish
WALKER, S., Environmental Design
WALL, A. J., French, Latin and Spanish
WALLACE, J. L., Physiology and Biophysics, and Pharmacology and Therapeutics and Medicine
WALLS, W. D., Economics
WALSH, M. P., Biochemistry and Molecular Biology
WAN, R. G., Civil Engineering
WANG, Y., Electrical and Computer Engineering
WANNER, R. A., Sociology
WARNICA, J. W., Cardiac Sciences and Medicine
WATERS, N. M., Geography
WEBBER, C. F., Education
WEISS, S., Cell Biology and Anatomy and Pharmacology and Therapeutics
WESTRA, H. J., Greek and Roman Studies
WHITE, T. H., Haskayne School of Business
WHITELAW, W. A., Medicine
WIEBE, S., Clinical Neurosciences, Paediatrics and Community Health Sciences
WIERZBA, I., Mechanical and Manufacturing Engineering
WILLIAMS, H. C., Mathematics and Statistics
WILLIAMSON, C. L., Computer Science
WILMAN, E. A., Economics
WILSON, M. G., Social Work
WINCHESTER, W. I. S., Education
WONG, N. C. W., Medicine
WONG, R. C. K., Civil Engineering
WONG, S. L., Biological Sciences
WOODROW, P., Art
WOODROW, R. E., Mathematics and Statistics
WOODS, D. E., Microbiology and Infectious Diseases
WRIGHT, L. M., Nursing
WU, P. P. C., Geology and Geophysics
WYVILL, B. L. M., Computer Science
YACOWAR, M., Art
YANG, X. J., Germanic, Slavic and East Asian Studies
YAU, A. W., Physics and Astronomy
YEUNG, E. C. J., Biological Sciences
YONG, V. W., Oncology and Clinical Neurosciences
YOON, J. W., Microbiology and Infectious Diseases and Paediatrics
YOUNG, D. B., Biochemistry, Molecular Biology and Oncology
ZAMPONI, G. W., Physiology, Biophysics, Pharmacology and Therapeutics
ZANZOTTO, L., Civil Engineering
ZAPF, M. K., Social Work
ZEKULIN, N. G. A., Germanic, Slavic and East Asian Studies
ZIEGLER, T., Chemistry
ZOCHODNE, D. W., Clinical Neurosciences
ZVENGROWSKI, P. D., Mathematics and Statistics

UNIVERSITY OF GUELPH

Guelph, ON N1G 2W1
Telephone: (519) 824-4120
Internet: www.uoguelph.ca

Founded 1964 from Ontario Agricultural College, Ontario Veterinary College and Macdonald Institute, formerly affiliated to the Univ. of Toronto
private/provincial control
Language of instruction: English
Chancellor: L. M. ALEXANDER
Pres. and Vice-Chancellor: ALASTAIR SUMMERLEE
Provost and Vice-Pres. for Academic Affairs: MAUREEN MANCUSO (acting)
Vice-Pres. for Alumni Affairs and Devt: PAMELLA HEALEY (acting)
Vice-Pres. for Finance and Admin.: NANCY SULLIVAN
Vice-Pres. for Research: ALAN WILDEMAN
Vice-Provost and Chief Academic Officer: MICHAEL NIGHTINGALE
Librarian: M. RIDLEY
Library: 2.5m. vols
Number of teachers: 750
Number of students: 14,000
Publications: *Graduate Calendar*, *President's Report*, *Undergraduate Calendar*

DEANS

College of Arts: JACQUELINE MURRAY
College of Biological Science: MICHAEL EMES
College of Physical and Engineering Science: PETER TREMAINE
College of Social and Applied Human Sciences: ALUN JOSEPH
Faculty of Environmental Sciences: M. R. MOSS
Faculty of Graduate Studies: ISOBEL HEATHCOTE
Ontario Agricultural College: CRAIG PEARSON
Ontario Veterinary College: A. H. MEEK

UNIVERSITY OF KING'S COLLEGE

Halifax, NS B3H 2A1
Telephone: (902) 422-1271
E-mail: admissions@ukings.ns.ca
Internet: www.ukings.ca

Founded 1789 by United Empire Loyalists; granted Royal Charter 1802, entered into asscn with Dalhousie Univ. 1923
Language of instruction: English
Academic year: September to May
Chancellor: MICHAEL MEIGHEN
Pres. and Vice-Chancellor: WILLIAM BARKER
Vice-Pres.: KIM KIERANS
Registrar: E. YEO
Bursar: G. G. SMITH
Librarian: H. DRAKE PETERSEN
Number of teachers: 51
Number of students: 1,158
Publication: *The Hinge* (1 a year)

PROFESSORS

BARKER, W., English
BISHOP, M., French
BURNS, S. A. M., Philosophy
CROWLEY, J., History
HANKEY, W. J., Classics
HUEBERT, R., English
KIMBER, S., Journalism
STARNES, C. J., Classics
VINCI, T., Philosophy

UNIVERSITY OF LETHBRIDGE

4401 University Dr., Lethbridge, AB T1K 3M4
Telephone: (403) 320-5700
E-mail: inquiries@uleth.ca
Internet: www.uleth.ca

Founded 1967
provincial control
Language of instruction: English
Academic year: September to April (2 semesters), also summer sessions
Chancellor: ROBERT HIRONAKA
Pres. and Vice-Chancellor: WILLIAM HENRY CADE
Provost and Vice-Pres. for Academic Affairs: SEAMUS O'SHEA
Vice-Pres. for Finance and Admin.: NANCY WALKER
Registrar: LESLIE LAVERS
Chief Librarian: JUDY HEAD
Number of teachers: 248 full-time
Number of students: 8,230
Library of 498,000 vols
Publication: *Annual Calendar*

DEANS

Faculty of Arts and Science: CHRISTOPHER NICOL
Faculty of Education: Dr JANE O'DEA
Faculty of Management: Dr JOHN USHER
School of Fine Arts: C. SKINNER
School of Health Sciences: LYNN BASFORD
School of Graduate Studies: ALAM SHAMSUL

UNIVERSITY OF MANITOBA

Winnipeg, MB R3T 2N2
Telephone: (204) 474-8880
E-mail: registrar@umanitoba.ca
Internet: www.umanitoba.ca

Founded 1877
Language of instruction: English
Academic year: September to April (2 terms)

Chancellor: Dr WILLIAM NORRIE
Pres. and Vice-Chancellor: Dr DAVID T. BARNARD
Vice-Pres. for Academic and Provost: JOANNE C. KESELMAN
Vice-Pres. for Admin.: DEBORAH MCCALLUM
Vice-Pres. for External: ELAINE GOLDIE
Vice-Pres. for Research: DIGVIR JAYAS (acting)
Dir for Libraries: C. PRESSER

Library of 2,000,000 vols
Number of teachers: 1,142
Number of students: 26,800

DEANS

Faculty of Agricultural and Food Sciences: Dr MICHAEL TREVAN
Faculty of Architecture: Dr DAVID R. WITTY
Faculty of Arts: RICHARD SIGURDSON
Faculty of Dentistry: ANTHONY IACOPINO
Faculty of Education: JOHN WIENS
Faculty of Engineering: DOUGLAS RUTH
Faculty of Environment: LESLIE KING
Faculty of Graduate Studies: Dr TONY SECCO
Faculty of Human Ecology: R. BIRD
Faculty of Law: HARVEY SECTER
Faculty of Management: J. L. GRAY
Faculty of Medicine: B. K. E. HENNEN
Faculty of Nursing: D. M. GREGORY
Faculty of Pharmacy: D. COLLINS
Faculty of Physical Education and Recreation Studies: D. W. HRYCAIKO
Faculty of Science: Dr MARK WHITMORE
Faculty of Social Work: BOB MULLALY

PROFESSORS

Faculty of Agricultural and Food Sciences:

BALLANCE, G. M., Plant Science
BJARNASON, H., Agribusiness and Agricultural Economics
BLANK, G., Food Science
BOYD, M. S., Agribusiness and Agricultural Economics
BRITTON, M. G., Biosystems Engineering
BRÛLÉ-BABEL, A. L., Plant Science
CAMPBELL, L. D., Animal Science
CENKOWSKI, S., Biosystems Engineering
CONNOR, M. L., Animal Science
DRONZEK, B. L., Plant Science
ENTZ, M., Plant Science
GALLOWAY, T. D., Entomology
GOH, T. B., Soil Science
GUENTER, W., Animal Science
HILL, R. D., Plant Science
HOLLEY, R. A., Food Science
HOLLIDAY, N. J., Entomology
JAYAS, D. S., Biosystems Engineering
KRAFT, D. F., Agribusiness and Agricultural Economics
MACKAY, P. A., Entomology
MACMILLAN, J. A., Agribusiness and Agricultural Economics
MCVETTY, P. B. E., Plant Science
MUIR, W. E., Biosystems Engineering
PRITCHARD, M. K., Plant Science
RACZ, G. J., Soil Science
REMPHREY, W. R., Plant Science
ROUGHLEY, R. E., Entomology
SCANLON, M. G., Food Science
SCARTH, R., Plant Science
VESSEY, J. K., Plant Science
WITTENBERG, K. M., Animal Science
ZHANG, Q., Biosystems Engineering

Faculty of Architecture:

COX, M. G., Interior Design
MACDONALD, R. I., Environmental Design
NELSON, C., Landscape Architecture
RATTRAY, A. E., Landscape Architecture
THOMSEN, C. H., Landscape Architecture

Faculty of Arts:

ALBAS, D. C., Sociology
ANNA, T. E., History
ARNASON, D. E., English
BAILEY, P. C., History
BARBER, D. G., Geograpy
BRIERLEY, J. S., Geography
BUMSTED, J. M., History
BUTEUX, P. E., Political Studies
CAMERON, N. E., Economics
CHERNOMAS, R., Economics
COMACK, A. E., Sociology
COOLEY, D. O., English
COSMOPOULOS, M. B., Classics
DEAN, J. M., Economics
DEBICKI, M., Political Studies
DELUCA, R., Psychology
EATON, W. O., Psychology
FERGUSON, B. G., History
FINLAY, J. L., History
FINNEGAN, R. E., English
FORTIER, P., French, Spanish and Italian
FRIESEN, G. A., History
GERUS, O. W., History
GONICK, C. W., Economics
GORDON, D. K., French, Spanish and Italian
GREENFIELD, H. J., Anthropology
GRISLIS, E., Religion
HALLI, S. S., Sociology
HELLER, H., History
HINZ, E. J., English
HUM, D., Economics
JOHNSON, C. G., English
JUDD, E. R., Anthropology
KENDLE, J. E., History
KESELMAN, H. J., Psychology
KESELMAN, J. C., Psychology
KINNEAR, E. M., History
KINNEAR, M. S. R., History
KULCHYSKI, P., Native Studies
KWONG, J., Sociology
LEBOW, M. D., Psychology
LEVENTHAL, L. Y., Psychology
LINDEN, E. W., Sociology
LOBDELL, R. A., Economics
LOXLEY, J., Economics
MCCANCE, D., Religion
MCCARTHY, D. J., Philosophy
MARTIN, D. G., Psychology
MARTIN, G. L., Psychology
MATHESON, C., Philosophy
NAHIR, M., Linguistics
NICHOLS, J. D., Linguistics
NICKELS, J. B., Psychology
NORTON, W., Geography
OAKES, J. E., Native Studies
O'KELL, R. P., English
PEAR, J. J., Psychology
PERRY, R. P., Psychology
PHILLIPS, P. A., Economics
RAMU, G. N., Sociology
REA, J. E., History
REMPEL, H., Economics
ROBERTS, L., Sociology
RUBENSTEIN, H., Anthropology
SCHAFER, A. M., Philosophy
SCHLUDERMANN, E. H., Psychology
SCHLUDERMANN, S., Psychology
SEGALL, A., Sociology
SHAVER, R. W., Philosophy
SHKANDRIJ, M., German and Slavic Studies
SIMPSON, W., Economics
SINGER, M., Psychology
SMIL, V., Geography
SMITH, G. C., Geography
SPRAGUE, D. N., History
STAMBROOK, F. G., History
STEIMAN, L. B., History
SZATHMÁRY, J. E., Anthropology
TAIT, R. W., Psychology
THOMAS, P. G., Political Studies
TODD, D., Geography
TOLES, G. E., English
WALZ, E. P., English
WATERMAN, A. M. C., Economics
WEIL, H. S., English
WIEST, R. E., Anthropology
WILLIAMS, D. L., English
WILSON, L. M., Psychology
WOLF, K., Icelandic
WOLFART, H. C., Linguistics
WORTLEY, J. T., History

Faculty of Dentistry:

BHULLAR, R. P.
BOWDEN, G. H. W.
DAWES, C.
DE VRIES, J.
FLEMING, N.
HAMILTON, I. R.
KARIM, A. C.
LAVELLE, C. L. B.
LOVE, W. B.
SCOTT, J. E.
SINGER, D. L.
SUZUKI, M.
WILTSHIRE, W.

Faculty of Education:

BARTELL, R., Educational Administration, Foundations and Psychology
CAP, O., Curriculum, Teaching and Learning
CHINIEN, C., Curriculum, Teaching and Learning
CLIFTON, R. A., Postsecondary Studies, Educational Administration, Foundations and Psychology
FREEZE, D. R., Educational Administration, Foundations and Psychology
GREGOR, A. D., Postsecondary Studies, Educational Administration, Foundations and Psychology
HARVEY, D. A., Curriculum, Teaching and Learning
HLYNKA, L. D., Curriculum, Teaching and Learning
JENKINSON, D. H., Curriculum, Teaching and Learning
KESELMAN, J. C., Educational Administration, Foundations and Psychology
KIRBY, D. M., Postsecondary Studies
LEVIN, B., Educational Administration, Foundations and Psychology
LONG, J. C., Educational Administration, Foundations and Psychology
MAGSINO, R., Educational Administration, Foundations and Psychology
MORPHY, D. R., Postsecondary Studies
PERRY, R. P., Postsecondary Studies
POROZNY, G. H. J., Curriculum, Teaching and Learning
ROBERTS, L. W., Postsecondary Studies
SCHULZ, W. E., Educational Administration, Foundations and Psychology
SEIFERT, K. L., Educational Administration, Foundations and Psychology
STAPLETON, J. J., Educational Administration, Foundations and Psychology
STINNER, A. O., Curriculum, Teaching and Learning
STRAW, S. B., Curriculum, Teaching and Learning
YOUNG, J. C., Educational Administration, Foundations and Psychology
ZAKALUK, B. L., Curriculum, Teaching and Learning

Faculty of Engineering:
- BALAKRISHNAN, S., Mechanical and Industrial
- BASSIM, M. N., Mechanical and Industrial
- BRIDGES, G. E. J., Electrical and Computer
- BURN, D. H., Civil and Geological
- CAHOON, J. R., Mechanical and Industrial
- CARD, H. C., Electrical and Computer
- CHATURVEDI, M. C., Mechanical and Industrial
- CIRIC, I. M. R., Electrical and Computer
- CLAYTON, A., Civil and Geological
- GOLE, A. M., Electrical and Computer
- GRAHAM, J., Civil and Geological
- KINSNER, W., Electrical and Computer
- LAJTAI, E. Z., Civil and Geological
- LEHN, W., Electrical and Computer
- MCLAREN, P. G., Electrical and Computer
- MCLEOD, R. D., Electrical and Computer
- MARTENS, G. O., Electrical and Computer
- MENZIES, R. W., Electrical and Computer
- MUFTI, A. A., Civil and Geological
- OLESZKIEWICZ, J. A., Civil and Geological
- ONYSHKO, S., Electrical and Computer
- PAWLAK, M., Electrical and Computer
- POLYZOIS, D., Civil and Geological
- POPPLEWELL, N., Mechanical and Industrial
- RAGHUVEER, M. R., Electrical and Computer
- RUTH, D. W., Mechanical and Industrial
- SEBAK, A., Electrical and Computer
- SEPEHRI, N., Mechanical and Industrial
- SHAFAI, L., Electrical and Computer
- SHAH, A. H., Civil and Geological
- SHWEDYK, E., Electrical and Computer
- SOLIMAN, H. M., Mechanical and Industrial
- STIMPSON, B., Civil and Geological
- STRONG, D., Mechanical and Industrial
- THOMSON, D. J., Electrical and Computer
- THORNTON-TRUMP, A. B., Mechanical and Industrial
- WOODBURY, A. D., Civil

Faculty of Human Ecology:
- BERRY, R. E., Family Studies
- BIRD, R. P., Foods and Nutrition
- BOND, J. B., Family Studies
- ESKIN, N. A. M., Foods and Nutrition
- HARVEY, C. D. H., Family Studies

Faculty of Law:
- ANDERSON, D. T.
- BUSBY, K.
- DEUTSCHER, D.
- ESAU, A.
- GUTH, D. J.
- HARVEY, D. A. C.
- IRVINE, J. C.
- MCGILLIVRAY, A.
- NEMIROFF, G.
- OSBORNE, P. H.
- PENNER, R.
- SECTER, H. L.
- SNEIDERMAN, B.
- STUESSER, L.
- VINCENT, L.

Faculty of Management:
- BARTELL, M., Business Administration
- BECTOR, C. R., Business Administration
- BHATT, S. K., Business Administration
- BRUNING, E. R., Marketing
- BRUNING, N. S., Business Administration
- ELIAS, N. S., Accounting and Finance
- FROHLICH, N., Business Administration
- GODARD, J. H., Business Administration
- GOOD, W. S., Marketing
- GOULD, L. I., Accounting and Finance
- GRAY, J. L., Business Administration
- HILTON, M. W., Accounting and Finance
- HOGAN, T. P., Business Administration
- MCCALLUM, J. S., Accounting and Finance
- NOTZ, W. W., Business Administration
- OWEN, B. E., Business Administration
- ROSENBLOOM, E. S.
- STARKE, F. A., Business Administration

Faculty of Medicine:
- ADAMSON, I. Y. R., Pathology
- ANDERSON, J., Human Anatomy and Cell Science
- ANGEL, A., Medicine and Physiology
- AOKI, F. Y., Continuing Medical Education, Medical Microbiology, Medicine, Pharmacology and Therapeutics
- ARNETT, J. L., Clinical Health Psychology and Continuing Medical Education
- ARTHUR, G., Biochemistry and Medical Genetics
- BAKER, S., Medicine
- BARAGAR, F., Medicine
- BARAKAT, S., Psychiatry
- BARAL, E., Medicine, Radiology
- BARWINSKY, J., Cardiothoracic Surgery
- BEBCHUK, W., Psychiatry
- BECKER, A., Paediatrics and Child Health
- BEGLEITER, A., Medicine, Pharmacology and Therapeutics
- BERCZI, I., Immunology
- BLACK, G., Surgery
- BLAKLEY, B., Otolaryngology
- BOOTH, F., Paediatrics and Child Health
- BORODITSY, R., Obstetrics, Gynaecology and Reproductive Sciences
- BOSE, D., Anaesthesia, Medicine, Pharmacology and Therapeutics
- BOSE, R., Pharmacology and Therapeutics
- BOW, E., Medical Microbiology
- BOWDEN, G. H., Medical Microbiology
- BOWMAN, D. M., Medicine
- BOWMAN, W. D., Paediatrics and Child Health
- BRANDES, L. J., Medicine, Pharmacology and Therapeutics
- BRISTOW, G. K., Anaesthesia
- BRUNHAM, R. C., Medical Microbiology, Medicine, Obstetrics, Gynaecology and Reproductive Sciences
- BRUNI, J. E., Human Anatomy and Cell Science
- CARR, I., Pathology
- CARTER, S. A., Medicine and Physiology
- CASIRO, O., Paediatrics and Child Health
- CATTINI, P., Physiology, Pharmacology and Therapeutics
- CHERNICK, V., Paediatrics and Child Health
- CHOY, P. C., Biochemistry and Molecular Biology
- CHUDLEY, A. E., Continuing Medical Education, Human Genetics, Paediatrics and Child Health
- COOMBS, C., Medical Microbiology
- COOPER, J., Community Health Sciences
- CRAIG, D. B., Anaesthesia
- CRISTANTE, L., Surgery
- CUMMING, G. R., Paediatrics and Child Health
- DANZINGER, R. G., General Surgery
- DAVIE, J. R., Biochemistry and Molecular Biology
- DEAN, H., Paediatrics and Child Health
- DUBO, H. I. C., Medicine
- DUKE, P. C., Anaesthesia
- EL-GABALAWY, H., Medicine
- EVANS, J. A., Community Health Sciences, Human Genetics, Paediatrics and Child Health
- FERGUSON, C. A., Paediatrics and Child Health
- FINE, A., Medicine
- FORESTER, J., Medicine
- FORGET, E., Community Health Sciences
- GARTNER, J., Immunology, Pathology
- GEIGER, J., Pharmacology and Therapeutics
- GERRARD, J. M., Paediatrics and Child Health
- GLAVIN, G., Pharmacology and Therapeutics
- GORDON, R., Radiology
- GREENBERG, C. R., Human Genetics, Paediatrics and Child Health
- GREWAR, D. A. I., Family Medicine, Paediatrics and Child Health
- GUIJON, F., Obstetrics, Gynaecology and Reproductive Sciences
- HALL, P. F., Obstetrics, Gynaecology and Reproductive Sciences
- HAMERTON, J. L., Paediatrics and Child Health
- HAMMOND, G. W., Medical Microbiology, Medicine
- HARDING, G. M., Medical Microbiology, Medicine
- HARVEY, D. A., Community Health Sciences
- HASSARD, T. H., Community Health Sciences
- HAVENS, B., Community Health Sciences
- HAYGLASS, K. T., Immunology
- HELEWA, M., Obstetrics, Gynaecology and Reproductive Sciences
- HERSHFIELD, E. A., Community Health Sciences
- HERSHFIELD, E. S., Medicine
- HOESCHEN, R., Medicine
- HOGAN, T. P., Community Health Sciences
- HORNE, J. M., Community Health Sciences
- HOSKING, D., Surgery
- HUDSON, R., Anaesthesia
- HUGHES, K. R., Physiology
- IRELAND, D. J., Otolaryngology
- JAY, F. T., Medical Microbiology
- JEFFERY, J., Medicine
- JOHNSTON, J. B., Medicine
- JORDAN, L. M., Physiology
- KARDAMI, E., Human Anatomy and Cell Science
- KATZ, P., Psychiatry
- KAUFERT, J. M., Community Health Sciences
- KAUFERT, P. A., Community Health Services
- KAUFMAN, B. J., Medicine
- KEPRON, M. W., Medicine
- KIRK, P. J., Family Medicine
- KIRKPATRICK, J. R., Continuing Medical Education, General Surgery
- KREPART, G. V., Obstetrics, Gynaecology and Reproductive Sciences
- KROEGER, E. A., Physiology
- KRYGER, M., Medicine
- LABELLA, F. S., Pharmacology and Therapeutics
- LATTER, J., Medicine
- LAUTT, W. W., Pharmacology and Therapeutics
- LEJOHN, H. B., Human Genetics
- LERTZMAN, M., Continuing Medical Education, Medicine
- LEVI, C. S., Radiology
- LEVITT, M., Medicine
- LIGHT, B., Medicine
- LIGHT, R. B., Medical Microbiology
- LONGSTAFFE, S., Paediatrics and Child Health
- LYONS, E. A., Radiology, Obstetrics, Gynaecology and Reproductive Sciences
- MCCARTHY, D. S., Medicine
- MCCLARTY, B., Radiology
- MCCLARTY, G. A., Medical Microbiology
- MCCOSHEN, J. A., Obstetrics, Gynaecology and Reproductive Sciences
- MCCREA, D. A., Physiology
- MCCULLOUGH, D. W., Continuing Medical Education, Otolaryngology
- MACDOUGALL, B., Medicine
- MCILWRAITH, R., Clinical Health Psychology
- MCKENZIE, J. K., Community Health Sciences
- MAKSYMIUK, A., Medicine
- MINK, G., Medicine
- MINUK, G. Y., Medicine, Pharmacology and Therapeutics

MOFFATT, M. E., Community Health Services, Paediatrics and Child Health
MOWAT, M., Biochemistry and Medical Genetics
MURPHY, L. C., Biochemistry and Molecular Biology, Medicine
MURPHY, L. J., Medicine and Physiology
MURRAY, R., Community Health Sciences
MUTCH, A., Anaesthesia
NAGY, J. I., Physiology
NAIMARK, A., Physiology
NANCE, D. M., Pathology
NICOLLE, L., Medicine, Medical Microbiology
OEN, K., Paediatrics and Child Health
OLWENY, C., Medicine
O'NEIL, J. D., Community Health Sciences
ONG, B. Y., Anaesthesia
OPPENHEIMER, L., General Surgery
ORR, F. W., Pathology
PANAGIA, V., Human Anatomy and Cell Science, Physiology
PARKINSON, D., Neurosurgery
PASTERKAMP, H., Paediatrics and Child Health
PATERSON, J. A., Human Anatomy and Cell Science
PEELING, J., Pharmacology and Therapeutics
PEELING, W. J., Radiology
PENNER, B., Medicine
PENNER, S. B., Pharmacology and Therapeutics
PETTIGREW, N., Pathology
PIERCE, G. N., Physiology
PLUMMER, F. A., Medical Microbiology, Medicine
POSTL, B., Community Health Sciences, Paediatrics and Child Health
POSTUMA, R., General Surgery
RAMSEY, E., Surgery
REED, M. H., Continuing Medical Education, Paediatrics and Child Health, Radiology
RENNIE, W., Orthopaedic Surgery
RHODES, R., Pathology
RIESE, K. T., General Surgery and Otolaryngology
RIGATTO, H., Paediatrics and Child Health, Obstetrics, Gynaecology and Reproductive Sciences
ROBERTS, D., Medicine
RONALD, A. R., Community Health Sciences, Medical Microbiology, Medicine
ROOS, L. L., Community Health Sciences
ROOS, N. P., Community Health Sciences
ROY, R., Clinical Health Psychology
RUSH, D., Medicine
SCHACTER, B., Medicine
SCHROEDER, M., Paediatrics and Child Health
SESHIA, M. M. K., Obstetrics, Gynaecology and Reproductive Sciences, Paediatrics and Child Health
SHEFCHY, S., Physiology
SHIU, R. P. C., Physiology
SHOJANIA, A. M., Medicine, Paediatrics and Child Health, Pathology
SIMONS, F. E. R., Immunology, Paediatrics and Child Health
SIMONS, K., Paediatrics and Child Health
SINGAL, P. K., Physiology
SITAR, D., Medicine, Pharmacology and Therapeutics
SMYTH, D. D., Continuing Medical Education, Pharmacology and Therapeutics
SMYTHE, D., Medicine
SNEIDERMAN, B. M., Community Health Sciences
STANWICK, R. S., Community Health Sciences
STEPHENS, N. L., Physiology
STRANC, M. F., Plastic Surgery
SZATHMÁRY, E. J. E., Human Genetics
TENENBEIN, M., Community Health Sciences, Medicine, Pharmacology and Therapeutics, Paediatrics and Child Health
THLIVERIS, J. A., Human Anatomy and Cell Science
THOMSON, I., Anaesthesia
UNRUH, H. W., Surgery
VRIEND, J., Human Anatomy and Cell Science
WALKER, J., Clinical Health Psychology
WARREN, C. P. W., Continuing Medical Education, Medicine
WARRINGTON, R. J., Immunology and Medicine
WEST, M., Surgery
WILKINS, J. A., Immunology, Medicine, Medical Microbiology
WILLIAMS, T., Medical Microbiology, Paediatrics and Child Health
WOODS, R. A., Human Genetics
WRIGHT, J. A., Biochemistry and Molecular Biology
WROGEMANN, K., Biochemistry and Molecular Biology, Human Genetics
YASSI, A., Community Health Sciences
YOUNES, M., Medicine
YOUNG, T. K., Community Health Sciences
ZELINSKI, T., Biochemistry and Medical Genetics

Faculty of Nursing:

BEATON, J. I.
DEGNER, L. F.
GREGORY, D. M.

Faculty of Pharmacy:

BRIGGS, C. J.
COLLINS, D.
GRYMONPRE, R.
HASINOFF, B.
SIMONS, K. J.
TEMPLETON, J. F.
ZHANEL, G.

Faculty of Physical Education and Recreation Studies:

ALEXANDER, M. J. L.
DAHLGREN, W. J.
GIESBRECHT, G.
HARPER, J.
HRYCAIKO, D. W.
JANZEN, H. F.
READY, A. E.

Faculty of Science:

ABRAHAMS, M., Zoology
AITCHISON, P. W., Mathematics
ARNASON, A. N., Computer Science
AYRES, L. D., Geological Sciences
BALDWIN, W. G., Chemistry
BARBER, R. C., Physics and Astronomy
BELL, M. G., Mathematics
BERRY, T. G., Mathematics
BIRCHALL, J., Physics and Astronomy
BLUNDEN, P., Physics and Astronomy
BOOTH, J. T., Botany
BREWSTER, J. F., Statistics
BUTLER, M., Microbiology
CHARLTON, J. L., Chemistry
CHENG, S. W., Statistics
CHOW, A., Chemistry
CLARK, G. S., Geological Sciences
COLLENS, R. J., Computer Science
DAVISON, N. E., Physics and Astronomy
DICK, T. A., Zoology
DOOB, M., Mathematics
DUCKWORTH, H. W., Chemistry
EALES, J. G., Zoology
ELIAS, R. J., Geological Sciences
ENS, W., Physics and Astronomy
FALK, W., Physics and Astronomy
FU, J. C., Statistics
GERHARD, J. A., Mathematics
GHAHRAMANI, F., Mathematics
GRATZER, G., Mathematics
GUO, B., Mathematics
GUPTA, C. K., Mathematics
GUPTA, N. D., Mathematics
HALDEN, N. M., Geological Sciences
HAWTHORNE, F. C., Geological Sciences
HOSKINS, J. A., Computer Science
HOSKINS, W. D., Mathematics
HRUSKA, F. E., Chemistry
HUEBNER, E., Zoology
HUNTER, N. R., Chemistry
JAMIESON, J. C., Chemistry
JANZEN, A. F., Chemistry
KELLY, D., Mathematics
KENKEL, N. C., Botany
KING, P. R., Computer Science
KLASSEN, G. R., Microbiology
KOCAY, W. L., Computer Science
KRAUSE, G., Mathematics
LAKSER, H., Mathematics
LAST, W. M., Geological Sciences
LOEWEN, P. C., Microbiology
LOLY, P. D., Physics and Astronomy
MACARTHUR, R. A., Zoology
MCKINNON, D. M., Chemistry
MACPHERSON, B. D., Statistics
MAEBA, P. Y., Microbiology
MEEK, D. S., Computer Science
MENDELSOHN, N. S., Mathematics
MOON, W., Geological Sciences
MORRISH, A. H., Physics and Astronomy
O'NEIL, J. D. J., Chemistry
OSBORN, T. A., Physics and Astronomy
PADMANABHAN, R., Mathematics
PAGE, J. H., Physics and Astronomy
PAGE, S. A., Physics and Astronomy
PARAMESWARAN, M. R., Mathematics
PLATT, C., Mathematics
PUNTER, D., Botany
RIEWE, R. R., Zoology
ROBINSON, G. G. C., Botany, Environmental Science Program
ROSHKO, R. M., Physics and Astronomy
SAMANTA, M., Statistics
SCHAEFER, T., Chemistry
SCUSE, D. H., Computer Science
SEALY, S. G., Zoology
SECCO, A. S., Chemistry
SHARMA, K. S., Physics and Astronomy
SHERRIFF, B. L., Geological Sciences
SHIVAKUMAR, P. N., Mathematics
SICHLER, J., Mathematics
SOUTHERN, B. W., Physics and Astronomy
STANTON, R. G., Computer Science
STEWART, J. M., Botany
SUZUKI, I., Microbiology
SVENNE, J. P., Physics and Astronomy
TABISZ, G. C., Physics and Astronomy
TELLER, J. C., Geological Sciences
THOMAS, R. S. D., Mathematics
TRIM, D. W., Mathematics
VAN OERS, W. T. H., Physics and Astronomy
VAN REES, G. H. J., Computer Science
WALLACE, R., Chemistry
WALTON, D. J., Computer Science
WESTMORE, J. B., Chemistry
WIENS, T. J., Zoology
WILLIAMS, G., Physics and Astronomy
WILLIAMS, H. C., Computer Science
WILLIAMS, J. J., Mathematics
WOODS, R. G., Mathematics
WRIGHT, J. A., Microbiology
ZETNER, P. W., Physics and Astronomy

Faculty of Social Work:

FUCHS, D. M.
ROY, R.
TRUTE, B.

School of Art:

AMUNDSON, D. O.
BAKER, M. C.
FLYNN, R. K.
HIGGINS, S. B.
MCMILLAN, D. S.
PURA, W. P.
SAKOWSKI, R. C.
SCOTT, C. W.

School of Dental Hygiene:

BOWDEN, G. H. W.

DAWES, C.
FLEMING, N.
HAMILTON, I. R.
JAY, F.
KARIM, A. C.
LAVELLE, C. L. B.
SCOTT, J. E.
SINGER, D. L.

School of Medical Rehabilitation:

ANDERSON, J., Occupational Therapy
COOPER, J. E., Occupational Therapy
LOVERIDGE, B., Physical Therapy

School of Music:

ENGBRECHT, H.
JENSEN, K.
LONIS, D.
WEDGEWOOD, R.

Continuing Education Division:

PERCIVAL, A.

ATTACHED INSTITUTE

Natural Resources Institute: e-mail nriinfo@umanitoba.ca; Dir Dr C. EMDAD HAQUE.

AFFILIATED COLLEGES

St Andrew's College: 29 Dysart Rd, Winnipeg, MB R3T 2M7; tel. (204) 474-8995; e-mail st_andrews@umanitoba.ca; f. 1964 (Ukrainian Orthodox Church); library of 45,000 vols; Rector and Dean of Theology Rev. Fr. ROMAN BOZYK; publ. *Faith & Culture*.

St Boniface College: 200 Cathedral Ave, St Boniface, MB R2H 0H7; tel. (204) 233-0210; f. 1818 (Roman Catholic); Rector P. RUEST.

St John's College: 400 Dysart Rd, Winnipeg, MB R3T 2M5; tel. (204) 474-8531; f. 1849 (Anglican); Warden and Vice-Chancellor Dr J. HOSKINS.

St Paul's College: 430 Dysart Rd, Winnipeg, MB R3T 2M6; tel. (204) 474-8575; e-mail stpauls@umanitoba.ca; f. 1926 (Roman Catholic); Rector J. J. STAPLETON.

University College: 500 Dysart Rd, Winnipeg, MB R3T 2M8; tel. (204) 474-9522; Provost G. WALZ

UNIVERSITY OF NEW BRUNSWICK

UNB Fredericton POB 4400, Fredericton, NB E3B 5A3
Telephone: (506) 453-4666
UNB Saint John 100 Tucker Park Rd, POB 5050 Saint John NB E2L 4L5
Telephone: (506) 648-5500
Internet: www.unb.ca
Founded 1785
provincial control
Language of instruction: English
Academic year: September to May
Chancellor: RICHARD CURRIE
Pres.: JOHN MCLAUGHLIN
Vice-Pres. for Academic Affairs and Fredericton Campus: Dr ANTHONY SECCO (acting)
Vice-Pres. for Finance and Corporate Services: DANIEL V. MURRAY
Vice-Pres. for Research: Dr GREGORY S. KEALEY
Vice-Pres. (Saint John Campus): Dr ROBERT MACKINNON
Comptroller: LARRY GUITARD
Sec.: STEPHEN STROPLE
Registrar: TOM BUCKLEY
Dir. for Devt and Donor Relations: SUSAN MONTAGUE
Librarian: JOHN TESKEY
Number of teachers: 679
Number of students: 10,880 (9,430 full-time, 1,450 part-time)
Publications: *Acadiensis*, a historical journal of the Atlantic provinces (2 a year), *Experience UNB* (1 a year), *Fiddlehead* (short stories and poetry, 4 a year), *Graduate Studies Calendar*, *International Fiction Review*, *Research Inventory* (1 a year), *Studies in Canadian Literature* (3 a year), *Summer School Calendar*, *Undergraduate Calendar*

DEANS

Fredericton Campus:

Faculty of Administration: DANIEL COLEMAN
Faculty of Arts: Dr JAMES S. MURRAY (acting)
Faculty of Computer Science: ALI GHORBANI
Faculty of Education: SHARON RICH (acting)
Faculty of Engineering: DAVID COLEMAN
Faculty of Forestry and Environmental Management: IAN METHVEN (acting)
Faculty of Kinesiology: TERRY R. HAGGERTY
Faculty of Law: PHILIP BRYDEN
Faculty of Nursing: CHERYL GIBSON
Faculty of Science: ALLAN SHARP
School of Graduate Studies: GWEN DAVIES (acting)

Saint John Campus:

Faculty of Arts: Dr JOANNA EVERITT
Faculty of Business: REGENA FARNSWORTH (acting)
Faculty of Science, Applied Science and Engineering: Dr RUTH SHAW

PROFESSORS

Fredericton Campus:

Faculty of Administration:

ABEKAH, J.
ANGELES, R.
ARCELUS, F. J.
ASKANAS, W.
BETTS, N.
BOOTHMAN, B.
COLEMAN, D.
DU, D.
DUNNETT, J.
DUPLESSIS, D.
EISELT, H. A.
FLINT, D.
GAUDES, A.
GRANT, S.
HINTON, J.
KABADI, S.
LAUGHLAND, A. R.
LIM, W.
MAHER, E.
MAHER, R.
MITRA, D.
NAIR, K. P. K.
NASIEROWSKI, W.
NEVERS, R.
OTCHERE, I.
OTUTEYE, E.
OUYANG, M.
POST, P.
RAHIM, M. A.
RASHID, M.
RITCHIE, P.
ROY, J. A.
SHARMA, B.
SHEPPARD, R. G.
SIMYAR, F.
SRINIVASAN, G.
THOMAS, M. E.
TOLLIVER, J.
TRENHOLM, B.
WHALEN, H.
WIELMAKER, M.
ZULUAGA, L.

Faculty of Arts:

AHERN, D., Philosophy
ALLEN, J. G., Political Science
ALMEH, R., Sociology
ANDREWS, J., English
AUSTIN, D., English
BALL, J., International Development Studies
BALL, J. C., English
BEDFORD, A., International Development Studies
BEDFORD, D., Law and Society
BEDFORD, D., Women's Studies
BEDFORD, D. W., Political Science
BLACK, D., Anthropology
BONNETT, J., History
BOWDEN, G., Sociology
BRANDER, J. R. G., Economics
BROWN, A., French
BROWN, A., Women's Studies
BROWN, J. S., History
BYERS, E. S., Psychology
CAMPBELL, G., History
CANITZ, A. E., English
CARRIERE, M., French
CHARRON, D., French
CHARTERS, D., History
CICHOCKI, W., French
CLARK, D. A., Psychology
CONRAD, M., History
COOK, B. A., Economics
CULVER, K., Law in Society
CULVER, K., Philosophy
CUPPLES, B. W., Philosophy
DAVIES, G., English
D'ENTREMONT, B., Psychology
DICKSON, V., Economics
DOERKSEN, D., English
DONALDSON, A. W., Psychology
DUECK, C., Culture and Language Studies
DUPLESSIS, D., Law in Society
FALKENSTEIN, L., English
FARNWORTH, M., Economics
FERGUSON, B., Economics
FIELDS, D. L., Psychology
FRANK, D., History
GANTS, D. L., English
GEYSSEN, J. W., Classics and Ancient History
HAMLING, A., Women's Studies
HARRISON, D., Sociology
HIEW, C. C., Psychology
HORNE, C., Linguistics
HORNOSTY, J., Women's Studies
HORNOSTY, J. M., Sociology
HOWE, J. M., Sociology
JARMAN, M., English
KEALEY, G. S., History
KEALEY, L., History
KENNEDY, S., History
KERR, W., Classics and Ancient History
KERR, W., Law in Society
KLINCK, A., English
KUFELDT, K., Sociology
LACHAPELLE, D., Psychology
LANTZ, V., Economics
LARMER, R., Philosophy
LAUTARD, E. H., Sociology
LAW, S., Economics
LEBLANC, D., French
LECKIE, R., English
LEMIRE, B., History
LEMIRE, B. J., History
LEVINE, L., Economics
LINTON, M., Culture and Language Studies
LOREY, C., Culture and Language Studies
LOVELL, P. R., Anthropology
LOW, J., Sociology
MCDONALD, T., Economics
MCFARLAND, J., International Development Studies
MCGAW, R. L., Economics
MCTAVISH, L., Women's Studies
MARTIN, R., English
MIEDEMA, B., Sociology
MILLS, M. J., Classics and Ancient History
MILNER, M., History
MITRA, K., International Development Studies
MULLALY, E. J., English
MURRAY, J., Classics and Ancient History
MURRAY, J. S., Classics and Ancient History
MURRAY, K., Political Science
MURRELL, D., Economics

MYATT, A. E., Economics
NASON-CLARK, N., Sociology and Women's Studies
NEILL, W., Philosophy
NEILSON, L., Law in Society
PAPPONET-CANTAT, C., Anthropology and International Development Studies
PARENTEAU, W. M., History
PASSARIS, C. E., Economics
PIERCEY, D., Psychology
PLAICE, E., Anthropology
PLOUDE, R. J., English
POOL, G., International Development Studies
POOL, G. R., Anthropology
POULIN, C., Law in Society
POULIN, C., Psychology
POULIN, C., Women's Studies
RAHMANIAN, A., Philosophy
REHORICK, D. A., Sociology
REID, A., Culture and Language Studies
REZUN, M., Economics, International Development Studies and Political Science
RIDEOUT, V., Sociology
RIMMER, M. P., English
ROBBINS, W., Women's Studies
ROBBINS, W. J., English
ROBINSON, G. B., Psychology
ROWCROFT, J. E., Economics
SCHERF, K., English
SHANNON, C., Women's Studies
SIGURDSON, R., Political Science
SPINNER, B., Psychology
STOPPARD, J. M., Psychology
TASIC, V., Linguistics
THOMPSON, D. G., History
TRYPHONOPOULOS, D., English
TURNER, R. S., History
VAN DEN HOONAARD, W. C., Sociology
VIAU, R., French
VILLIARD, P., Linguistics
WAITE, G. K., History
WHITEFORD, G., International Development Studies
WIBER, M., Anthropology
WISNIEWSKI, L. J., Sociology
WORKMAN, T., Anthropology

Faculty of Computer Science:
BHAVSAR, V. C.
COOPER, R. H.
DEDOUREK, J. M.
DESLONGCHAMPS, G.
DU, W.
EVANS, P.
FRITZ, J.
GHORBANI, A. A.
HORTON, J. D.
KENT, K.
KURZ, B. J.
MACNEIL, D. G.
NICKERSON, B. G.
WASSON, W. D.
ZHANG, H.

Faculty of Education:
ALLEN, P., Adult and Vocational Education
BERRY, K., Educational Foundations
BEZEAU, L., Educational Foundations
BURGE, E., Adult and Vocational Education
CASHION, M., Educational Foundations
CLARKE, G. M., Curriculum and Instruction
COOPER, T. G., Curriculum and Instruction
EYRE, L., Health Education
GILL, B., Educational Administration
HUGHES, A. S., Curriculum and Instruction
LEAVITT, R., Curriculum and Instruction
MYERS, S., Health Education
NASON, P. N., Curriculum and Instruction
OTT, H. W., Educational Foundations
PAUL, L., Curriculum and Instruction
PAZIENZA, J., Curriculum and Instruction
RADFORD, K., Curriculum and Instruction
REHORICK, S., Curriculum and Instruction
SEARS, A., Curriculum and Instruction
SMALL, M. S., Curriculum and Instruction
SOUCY, D. A., Curriculum and Instruction
STEVENSON, M., Electrical and Computer Engineering
STEWART, J. (acting), Educational Foundations
SULLENGER, K., Science Education
WHITEFORD, G., Curriculum and Instruction
WILLMS, J. D., Educational Foundations

Faculty of Engineering:
BENDRICH, G., Chemical Engineering
BIDEN, E., Mechanical Engineering
BISCHOFF, P. H., Civil Engineering
BONHAM, D. J. (acting), Mechanical Engineering
CHANG, L., Electrical and Computer Engineering
CHAPLIN, R. (acting), Chemical Engineering
CHAPLIN, R. A. (acting), Chemical Engineering
COLEMAN, D. J., Geodesy and Geomatics
COLPITTS, B. (acting), Electrical and Computer Engineering
COUTURIER, M. (acting), Chemical Engineering
DARE, P., Geodesy and Geomatics (Chair)
DAWE, J. L. (acting), Civil Engineering
DIDUCH, C. (acting), Electrical Engineering
DORAISWAMI, R., Electrical Engineering
EIC, M., Chemical Engineering
HILL, E. F. (acting), Electrical Engineering
HUDGINS, B., Electrical and Computer Engineering
HUSSEIN, E. (acting), Mechanical Engineering
INNES, J. D., Civil Engineering
IRCHA, M. C., Civil Engineering
LANGLEY, R. B. (acting), Geodesy and Geomatics Engineering
LEE, Y. C., Geodesy and Geomatics
LEWIS, J. E., Electrical Engineering
LISTER, D., Chemical Engineering
LOVELY, D., Electical and Computer Engineering
LOWRY, B. (acting), Chemical Engineering
LUKE, D. M. (acting), Electrical Engineering
LYON, D., Mechanical Engineering
MCLAUGHLIN, J. D. (acting), Geodesy and Geomatics Engineering
MAYER, L., Geodesy and Geomatics Engineering
NI, Y., Chemical Engineering
NICHOLS, S. E. (acting), Geodesy and Geomatics
PARKER, P. A. (acting), Electrical Engineering
ROGERS, R. J., Mechanical Engineering
SHARAF, A. M. M., Electrical Engineering
SOUSA, A. C. M., Mechanical Engineering
SULLIVAN, P., Mechanical Engineering
TAYLOR, J. H. (acting), Electrical Engineering
TERVO, R., Electrical and Computer Engineering
THOMAS, M. D. A. (acting), Civil Engineering
VALSANGKAR, A. J. (acting), Civil Engineering
VANICEK, P., Geodesy and Geomatics Engineering
WAUGH, L. M., Civil Engineering

Faculty of Forestry and Environmental Management:
AFZAL, M. (acting)
ARP, P. A.
BECKLEY, T.
BOURQUE, C.
CHUI, Y.
CUNJAK, R.
CURRY, A.
DAUGHERTY, D.
DIAMOND, T.
ERDLE, T.
FORBES, G.
JAEGER, D.
JORDAN, G.
KEPPIE, D. M.
KERSHAW, J.
KRASOWSKI, M.
LANTZ, V.
LEBLON, B.
MACLEAN, D.
MENG, C.-H.
QUIRING, D. T. W.
ROBAK, E. W.
ROBERTS, M. R.
SAVIDGE, R.
SCHNEIDER, M. H.
SERGEANT, B.
SMITH, I.
ZUNDEL, P.

Faculty of Kinesiology:
BURKARD, J.
HAGGERTY, T. R.
PATON, G. A.
SEXSMITH, J.
STEVENSON, C. L.
WRIGHT, P. H.

Faculty of Law:
BELL, D. G.
BIRD, R. W.
BLADON, G. L.
CHATERJEE, A.
DORE, K. J.
FLEMING, D. J.
GOCHNAUER, M. L.
KUTTNER, T. S.
LAFOREST, A.
MCCALLUM, M. E.
MCEVOY, J. P.
MATHEN, C.
PEARLSTON, K.
PENNEY, S.
SIEBRASSE, N.
TOWNSEND, D.
VEITCH, E.
WILLIAMSON, J. R.

Faculty of Nursing:
ERICSON, P.
GETTY, G.
GIBSON, C.
GILBEY, V. J. U.
LEWIS, K.
OUELLET, L.
RUSH, K. L.
STORR, G.
WIGGINS, N.
WUEST, J.

Faculty of Science:
ADAM, A. G., Chemistry
BALCOLM, B., Chemistry
BANERJEE, P. K., Mathematics and Statistics
BARCLAY, D. W., Mathematics and Statistics
BROSTER, B., Geology
CASHION, P. J., Biology
CHERNOFF, W. W., Mathematics and Statistics
COOMBS, D. H., Biology
COOPER, R., Chemistry
CWYNAR, L., Biology
CULP, J., Biology
CUNJAK, R., Biology
DESLONGCHAMPS, G., Chemistry
DIAMOND, A., Biology
DILWORTH, T. G., Biology
FORBES, G., Biology
GEGENBERG, J., Mathematics and Statistics
HAMZA, A., Mathematics and Statistics
HUSAIN, V., Mathematics and Statistics
INGALLS, C., Mathematics and Statistics
JONES, C., Mathematics and Statistics
KEPPIE, D. M., Biology (also under Faculty of Forestry and Environmental Management)
LENTZ, D., Geology

LINTON, C., Physics
LYNCH, W. H., Biology
MCKELLAR, R., Mathematics and Statistics
MAGEE, D., Chemistry
MARCHAND, E., Mathematics and Statistics
MASON, G. R., Mathematics and Statistics
MATTAR, S., Chemistry
MONSON, B. R., Mathematics and Statistics
MUREIKA, R. A., Mathematics and Statistics
NEVILLE, J., Chemistry
NI, Y., Chemistry
PASSMORE, J., Chemistry
PICKERILL, R. K., Geology
RIDING, R. T., Biology
ROSS, W. R., Physics
SAUNDERS, G., Biology
SEABROOK, W. D., Biology
SHARP, A. R., Physics
SIVASUBRAMANIAN, P., Biology
SPRAY, J., Geology
THAKKAR, A., Chemistry
TIMOTHY, J. G., Physics
TINGLEY, D., Mathematics and Statistics
TUPPER, B. O. J., Mathematics and Statistics
TURNER, T. R., Mathematics and Statistics
VILLEMURE, G., Chemistry
WHITE, J. C., Geology
WHITTAKER, J. R., Biology
WILLIAMS, P. F., Geology
YOO, B. Y., Biology

Saint John Campus:

Faculty of Arts:

BELANGER, L., French
BEST, L., Psychology
BOTH, L., Psychology
BRADLEY, M. T., Psychology
CAMPBELL, M. A., Psychology
CAVALIERE, P. A., History
CHILDS, J., Economics
DARTNELL, M., Political Science
DESSERUD, D., Political Science
DI TOMMASO, E., Psychology
DONNELLY, F., History and Politics
EVERITT, J., Political Science
GENDREAU, P., Psychology
GODDARD, M. J., Psychology
HILL, R., Economics
HILL, V., French
HYSON, S., Political Sciences
JEFFREY, L., Political Sciences
KABIR, M., Social Science
LINDSAY, D., History
MARQUIS, G., History
MOIR, R., Economics
MOSHIRI, S., Economics
NKUNZIMANA, O., French
PONS-RIDLER, S., Humanities and Languages
RIDLER, N. B., Social Science
SELIM, M., Economics
SNOOK, B., Psychology
TAUKULIS, H., Psychology
TONER, P., History and Politics
WHITNEY, R., History
WILSON, A., Psychology

Faculty of Business:

CHALYKOFF, J.
DAVIS, C. H.
DAVIS, G.
GILBERT, E.
MINER, F. C.
PIKE, E.
ROUMI, E.
STERNICZUK, H.
WANG, S.
WONG, J.

Faculty of Science, Applied Science and Engineering:

ALDERSON, H., Mathematical Sciences
ALDERSON, T., Mathematical Sciences
BECKETT, B. A., Physical Sciences
BOONE, C., Engineering
BUCHANAN, J., Nursing (non-professorial Head, acting)
CHOPIN, T., Biology
CHRISTIE, J., Engineering
COTTER, G. T., Engineering (Head)
DE'BELL, K., Mathematical Sciences
FEICHT, A., Chemistry (Chair.)
GAREY, L. E., Mathematics, Statistics and Computer Science
GUPTA, R. D., Mathematics, Statistics and Computer Science
HALCROW, K., Biology
HAMDAN, M., Mathematics, Statistics and Computer Science
HUMPHRIES, R., Physical Sciences
KAMEL, M. T., Mathematics, Statistics and Computer Science
KAYSER, M., Physical Sciences
LEUNG, C.-H., Physical Sciences
LITVAK, M. K., Biology
LOGAN, A., Physical Sciences
MCCULLUM, D., Engineering
MACDONALD, B., Biology
MACLATCHY, D., Biology
MAHANTI, P., Computer Science and Applied Statistics
NUGENT, L., Nursing
PRASAD, R. C., Engineering
PUNNEN, A., Mathematical Sciences
RILEY, E., Engineering
ROCHETTE, R., Biology
SHAW, R., Computer Science and Applied Statistics
SOLLOWS, K., Engineering
STOICA, G., Mathematical Sciences
TERHUNE, J. M., Biology
THOMPSON, C., Computer Science and Applied Statistics (Chair.)
WAGSTAFF, J., Physical Sciences
WALTON, B., Engineering
WILSON, L., Physical Sciences
XU, L.-H., Physical Sciences

ATTACHED COLLEGES

Renaissance College: Dean Dr PIERRE ZUNDEL.

Saint John College: e-mail sjcol@unbsj.ca.

FEDERATED UNIVERSITY

St Thomas University: Fredericton, NB; e-mail admissions@stu.ca; f. 1910; Pres. DANIEL O'BRIEN

UNIVERSITY OF NORTHERN BRITISH COLUMBIA

3333 University Way, Prince George, BC V2N 4Z9
Telephone: (250) 960-5555
E-mail: registrar-info@unbc.ca
Internet: www.unbc.ca

Founded 1990; full opening 1994
Language of instruction: English
Academic year: September to May (2 semesters)

Chancellor: Dr JOHN MACDONALD
Pres.: Dr GEORGE IWAMA
Provost: Dr MARK DALE
Vice-Pres. for Admin. and Finance: EILEEN BRAY
Vice-Pres. for External Relations: ROB VAN ADRICHEM
Vice-Pres. for Research: Dr GAIL FONDAHL
Registrar: JOHN DEGRACE
Univ. Librarian: NANCY BLACK
Number of teachers: 178 (full-time); 204 (part-time)
Number of students: 4,177

DEANS

College of Arts, Social and Health Sciences: Dr JOHN YOUNG
College of Science and Management: Dr WILLIAM MCGILL
Graduate Programs: Dr IAN HARTLEY
Student Success and Enrolment Management: Dr PAUL MADAK

UNIVERSITY OF OTTAWA

550 Cumberland St, Ottawa, ON K1N 6N5
Telephone: (613) 562-5700
Internet: www.uottawa.ca

Founded 1848
independent, provincially assisted
Languages of instruction: English, French
Academic year: September to August (undergraduate 2 semesters, graduate 3 terms)

Chancellor: HUGUETTE LABELLE
Pres. and Vice-Chancellor: ALLAN ROCK (acting)
Vice-Pres. for Academic Affairs: ROBERT MAJOR
Vice-Pres. for Research: MONA NEMER
Vice-Pres. for Resources: VICTOR SIMON
Vice-Pres. for Univ. Relations: (vacant)
Asst Vice-Pres. for Strategic Enrolment Management and Registrar: FRANÇOIS CHAPLEAU
Sec. Gen.: PIERRE-YVES BOUCHER
Librarian: LESLIE WEIR
Library: see under Libraries and Archives
Number of teachers: 1,737 (936 full-time, 801 part-time)
Number of students: 36,460 (29,800 full-time, 6,660 part-time)

DEANS

Faculty of Arts: GEORGE LANG
Faculty of Education: MARIE JOSÉE BERGER
Faculty of Engineering: CLAUDE LAGUE
Faculty of Graduate and Post-doctoral Studies: GARY SLATER
Faculty of Health Sciences: DENIS PRUD'HOMME
Faculty of Law: SEBASTIAN GRAMMOND (Acting Dean, Civil Law: BRUCE FELDTHUSEN (Common Law)
Faculty of Medicine: JACQUES E. BRADWEJN
Faculty of Science: ANDRÉ DABROWSKI
Faculty of Social Sciences: FRANCOIS HOULE
Telfer School of Management: MICHEÁL J. KELLY

PROFESSORS

Faculty of Arts (internet www.uottawa.ca/academic/arts):

BARBIER, J. A., History
BEHIELS, M. D., History
BERTHIAUME, P., French Literature
BRISSET, A., Translation and Interpretation
BURGESS, R., Classics
CARLSON, D., English
CASTILLO DURANTE, D., French Literature
CHILDS, D., English Literature
CHOQUETTE, R., Religious Studies
CLAYTON, J. D., Russian
CRAM, R., Music
DAIGLE, J.-G., History
DAVIS, D. F., History
DE BRUYN, F., English
DELISLE, J., Translation and Interpretation
DONSKOV, A., Russian
EGERVARI, T., Visual Arts
FERGUSON, S., Communication
FERRIS, I., English
FLOYD, C., Music
FORGET, D., French Literature
FRENCH, H. M., Geography
FROEHLICH, A. J. P., Theatre
GAFFIELD, C. M., History
GAJEWSKI, K., Geography
GELLMAN, S., Music
GEURTS, M.-A., Geography
GILBERT, A., Geography
GIROU-SWIDERSKI, M., French Literature
GOLDENBERG, N., Religious Studies

GOODLUCK, H., Linguistics
GRISE, Y., French Literature
HIRSCHBUHLER, P., Linguistics
HUNTER, D. G., Philosophy
IMBERT, P. L., French Literature
JARRAWAY, D., English Literature
JOHNSON, P. G., Geography
KILMER, M. F., Classics and Religious Studies
KUNSTMANN, P. M. F., French Literature
LABELLE, N., Music
LA BOSSIÈRE, C. R., English Literature
LACHANCE, P. F., History
LAFON, D., French Literature
LANGLOIS, A., Geography
LAPIERRE, A., Linguistics
LAURIOL, B., Geography
LEMELIN, S., Music
LEPAGE, Y. G., French Literature
LEVY, P., Communication
LEWKOWICZ, A. G., Geography
LONDON, A., English Literature
LUGG, A. M., Philosophy
LYNCH, G., English
MAKARYK, I. R., English
MANGANIELLO, D., English
MAYNE, S., English
MERKLEY, P., Music
MOSER, W., Modern Languages and Literature
MOSS, J., English
MUNOZ-LICERAS, J., Modern Languages and Literature
PIVA, M., History
POPLACK, S., Linguistics
PUMMER, R. E., Religious Studies
RADLOFF, B., English
RAMPTON, D. P., English
REID, L., Visual Arts
RIVERO, M. L., Linguistics
ROBERTS, R. P., Translation and Interpretation
RUANO DE LA HAZA, J., Modern Languages and Literature
SEGUIN, H., Second Language Institute
STAINES, D., Arts
STICH, K. P., English
STOLARIK, M. M., History
STROCCHI, L. G., Modern Languages and Literature
VAILLANCOURT, P.-L., French Literature
VANDENDORPE, C., French Literature
VILLA, B. L., History
VON MALTZAHN, N., English
WELLAR, B. S., Geography
WESCHE, M. B., Centre for Second Language Learning
WILSON, K. G., English
YARDLEY, J. C., Classics

Faculty of Education (internet www.uottawa.ca/academic/education):

BÉLAIR, L.
BERGER, M.-J.
BOURDAGES, J. J.
COOK, S.
COUSINS, B.
FORGETTE-GIROUX, R.
FORTIN, J.-C.
GAGNE, E.
GIROUX, A.
HERRY, Y.
JEFFERSON, A. L.
LAVEAULT, D.
LEBLANC, R. N.
MACDONALD, C.
MASNY, D.
MICHAUD, J. P.
ST-GERMAIN, M.
TAYLOR, M.

Faculty of Engineering (internet www.eng.uottawa.ca):

ABOULNASR, T. T., Engineering
ADAMOWSKI, K., Civil Engineering
CHENG, S.-C., Mechanical Engineering
DHILLON, B. S., Engineering Management
DROSTE, R. L., Civil Engineering
EVGIN, E., Civil Engineering
FAHIM, A. E., Mechanical Engineering
GARDNER, N. J., Civil Engineering
GARGA, V. K., Civil Engineering
HADDAD, Y. M., Mechanical Engineering
HALLETT, W. L. H., Mechanical Engineering
KENNEDY, K. J., Civil Engineering
LIANG, M., Mechanical Engineering
MCLEAN, D. D., Chemical Engineering
MUNRO, M. B., Mechanical Engineering
NARBAITZ, R. M., Civil Engineering
NEALE, G. H., Chemical Engineering
NECSULESCU, D.-S., Engineering Management
REDEKOP, D., Mechanical Engineering
SAATCIOGLU, M., Civil Engineering
TANAKA, H., Engineering
TAVOULARIS, S., Mechanical Engineering
THIBAULT, J., Chemical Engineering
TOWNSEND, D. R., Civil Engineering

School of Information Technology and Engineering:

BOCHMANN, G. V.
CADA, M.
CHOUINARD, J.-Y.
DELISLE, G. Y.
DUBOIS, E.
GEORGANAS, N. D.
GIBBONS, D.-T.
HALL, T.
IONESCU, D.
KARMOUCH, A.
MCNAMARA, D. A.
MATWIN, S. J.
MOUFTAH, H. T.
OROZCO, B.-L.
PETRIU, E.
PROBERT, R. L.
RAYMOND, J.
SKUCE, D. R.
STOJMENOVIC, I.
SZPAKOWICZ, S.
URAL, H.
YANG, O. W.
YONGACOGLU, A. M.

Faculty of Health Sciences

School of Human Kinetics:

HARVEY, J.
LAMONTAGNE, M.
ORLICK, T. D.
RAIL, G.
ROBERTSON, G. E.
TRUDEL, P.

School of Nursing:

CRAGG, E. C.
EDWARDS, N.
FOTHERGILL-BOURBONNAIS, F.
O'CONNOR, A.

School of Rehabilitation Sciences:

DURIEUX-SMITH, A., Audiology and Speech-language Pathology

Faculty of Law (internet www.uottawa.ca/academic/droit-law):

Civil Law Section:

ARCHAMBAULT, J.-D.
BEAULNE, J.
BELLEAU, C.
BISSON, A.-F.
BOIVIN, M.
BOUDREAULT, M.
BRAEN, A.
DUPLESSIS, Y.
EMANUELLI, C.
GRONDIN, R.
JODOUIN, A.
LACASSE, J.-P.
MORIN, M.
PELLETIER, B.
PROULX, D.
VINCELETTE, D.

Common Law Section:

DES ROSIERS, N.
JACKMAN, M.
KRISHNA, V.
MCRAE, D. M.
MAGNET, J. E.
MANWARING, J. A.
MENDES, E. P.
MORSE, B. W.
PACIOCCO, D. M.
PERRET, L.
RATUSHNY, E. J.
RODGERS, S.
SHEEHY, E.
SULLIVAN, R.
ZWEIBEL, E.

Faculty of Management:

ADJAOUD, F.
CALVET, A. L.
CARO, D. H. J.
DE LA MOTHE, J.
DOUTRIAUX, J.
GANDHI, D. K.
GOH, S.
HENAULT, G. M.
HENIN, C. G.
JABES, J.
KELLY, M. J.
KERSTEN, G.
KINDRA, G. S.
LANE, D.
MANGA, P.
MICHALOWSKI, W.
NASH, J. C.
SIDNEY, J. B.
WRIGHT, D. J.
ZEGHAL, D.
ZUSSMAN, D.

Faculty of Medicine (internet www.uottawa.ca/academic/med):

ALTOSAAR, I., Biochemistry, Microbiology and Immunology
ANDERSON, P. J., Biochemistry, Microbiology and Immunology
BAENZIGER, J., Biochemistry, Microbiology and Immunology
BERNATCHEZ-LEMAIRE, I., Cellular and Molecular Medicine (Pharmacology)
BROWN, E., Biochemistry, Microbiology and Immunology
CHAN, A. C., Biochemistry, Microbiology and Immunology
CHEN, Y., Epidemiology and Community Medicine
CHEUNG, D. W., Cellular and Molecular Medicine (Pharmacology)
DE BOLD, A. J., Pathology and Laboratory Medicine
DILLON, J. R., Biochemistry, Microbiology and Immunology
DIMOCK, K. D., Biochemistry, Microbiology and Immunology
FRANKS, D., Pathology and Laboratory Medicine
FRYER, J. N., Cellular and Molecular Medicine (Anatomy)
GELFAND, T., History of Medicine
GIBB, W., Obstetrics and Gynaecology
HACHE, R. J. G., Medicine
HAKIM, A. M., Medicine
HÉBERT, R., Medicine
HINCKE, M., Cellular and Molecular Medicine (Anatomy)
JASMIN, B. J., Cellular and Molecular Medicine (Physiology)
KACEW, S., Cellular and Molecular Medicine (Pharmacology)
KRANTIS, A., Cellular and Molecular Medicine (Physiology)
KREWSKI, D., Medicine
LABOW, R., Surgery
LEMAIRE, S., Cellular and Molecular Medicine (Pharmacology)
MCBURNEY, M. W., Medicine

McDowell, I. W., Epidemiology and Community Medicine
Maler, Leonard, Cellular and Molecular Medicine (Anatomy)
Marcel, Y. L., Pathology and Laboratory Medicine
Marshall, K. C., Cellular and Molecular Medicine (Physiology)
Milne, R. W., Pathology and Laboratory Medicine
Mussivand, T. F., Surgery
Nair, R. C., Epidemiology and Community Medicine
Parry, D. J., Cellular and Molecular Medicine (Physiology)
Peterson, L. M., Cellular and Molecular Medicine (Physiology)
Rousseaux, C., Cellular and Molecular Medicine
St John, R. K., Medicine
Sattar, S. A., Biochemistry, Microbiology and Immunology
Spasoff, R. A., Epidemiology and Community Medicine
Staines, W., Cellular and Molecular Medicine (Anatomy)
Tanphaichitr, N., Obstetrics and Gynaecology
Tsang, B. K., Obstetrics and Gynaecology
Tuana, B. S., Cellular and Molecular Medicine (Pharmacology)
Walker, P., Medicine
Wells, G., Medicine
Yao, Z., Biochemistry, Microbiology and Immunology

Faculty of Science (internet www.science.uottawa.ca):
Alvo, M., Mathematics and Statistics
Arnason, J. T., Biology
Bao, X., Physics
Brabec, T., Physics
Bonen, L., Biology
Burgess, W. D., Mathematics and Statistics
Castonguay, C., Mathematics and Statistics
Chapleau, F., Biology
Clark, I. B., Earth Sciences
Currie, D. J., Biology
Dabrowski, A. R., Mathematics and Statistics
Detellier, C. G., Chemistry
Durst, T., Chemistry
Fallis, A. G., Chemistry
Fenwick, J. C., Biology
Fowler, A., Earth Sciences
Gambarotta, S., Chemistry
Giordano, T., Mathematics and Statistics
Handelman, D. E., Mathematics and Statistics
Hattori, K., Earth Sciences
Hickey, D. A., Biology
Hodgson, R. J. W., Physics
Ivanoff, G. B., Mathematics and Statistics
Joos, B., Physics
Kaplan, H., Chemistry
LaLonde, A. E., Earth Sciences
Lean, D. R., Biology
Longtin, A., Physics
McDonald, D. R., Mathematics and Statistics
Moon, T. W., Biology
Morin, A., Biology
Neher, E., Mathematics and Statistics
Perry, S. F., Biology
Pestov, V., Mathematics and Statistics
Philogène, B. J. R., Biology
Racine, M. L., Mathematics and Statistics
Rancourt, D., Physics
Richeson, D., Chemistry
Rossman, W., Mathematics and Statistics
Roy, D., Mathematics and Statistics
Sankoff, D., Mathematics and Statistics
Sayari, A. H., Chemistry
Scaiano, J. C., Chemistry
Scott, P. J., Mathematics and Statistics
Stadnik, Z., Physics
Teitelbaum, H., Chemistry
Veizer, J., Earth Sciences

Faculty of Social Sciences (internet www.uottawa.ca/academic/socsci):
Andrew, C. P., Political Science
Beauchesne, L., Criminology
Cardinal, L., Political Science
Cellard, A., Criminology
Chossudovsky, M., Economics
Coulombe, S., Economics
Crelinsten, R., Criminology
da Rosa, V. M. P., Sociology
Denis, A. B., Sociology
Denis, S., Political Science
Gabor, T., Criminology
Grenier, G., Economics
Hastings, J. R., Criminology
Havet, J. L., Sociology
Laczko, L., Sociology
Laux, J. K., Political Science
Lavoie, M., Economics
Los, M. J., Criminology
Mellos, K., Political Science
Moggach, D., Political Science
Murphy, R. J., Sociology
Pires, A., Criminology
Poulin, R., Sociology
Roberts, J., Criminology
Seccareccia, M., Economics
Tahon, M.-B., Sociology
Thériault, J. Y., Sociology
Tremblay, M., Political Science
Waller, I., Criminology

School of Psychology:
Bielajew, C.
Campbell, K. B.
Cappeliez, P.
Clement, R.
Firestone, P.
Flynn, R.
Fouriezos, G.
Girodo, M.
Hunsley, J.
Johnson, S.
Ledingham, J.
Lee, C.
LeMyre, L.
Merali, Z.
Messier, C.
Mook, B.
Pelletier, L.
Ritchie, P.
Sarrazin, G.
Schneider, B.
Tougas, F.
Whiffen, V.
Younger, A.

School of Social Work:
Coderre, C.
Home, A. M.
St-Amand, N.
Tougas, F.

FEDERATED UNIVERSITY

Saint Paul University: 223 Main St, Ottawa, ON K1S 1C4; e-mail info@ustpaul.ca; internet www.ustpaul.ca; Rector Rev. Prof. Dale Schlitt

DEANS

Faculty of Canon Law: Rev. Roch Pagé
Faculty of Human Sciences: Jean-Guy Goulet
Faculty of Theology: Rev. David Perrin

PROFESSORS

Faculty of Canon Law:
Huels, J.
Mendonça, Rev. A.
Morrisey, Rev. F. G.
Page, R.

Faculty of Human Sciences:
Bégin, B.
Daviau, P.
Goulet, J.-G.
Meier, A.
Mooren, T.
Rigby, P.

Faculty of Theology:
Coyle, J. K.
Dumais, Rev. M.
Martínez de Pisón, R.
Melchin, K.
Pambrun, J.
Peelman, Rev. A.
Provencher, Rev. M. N.
Schlitt, Rev. D. M.
Van den Hengel, Rev. J.
Walters, G.

UNIVERSITY OF PRINCE EDWARD ISLAND

550 University Ave, Charlottetown, PE C1A 4P3
Telephone: (902) 566-0439
E-mail: registrar@upei.ca
Internet: upei.ca

Founded 1969 by merger of St Dunstan's University (f. 1855) and Prince of Wales College (f. 1834)
Academic year: September to May

Chancellor: Don McDougall
Pres. and Vice-Chancellor: Alaa Abd-El-Aziz
Vice-Pres. for Acad.: Jim Randall
Vice-Pres. for Admin. and Finance: Phil Hooper
Registrar: Kathy Kielly
Univ. Librarian: Dawn Hooper

Library: see under Libraries and Archives
Number of teachers: 192 (full-time)
Number of students: 4,600

DEANS

Faculty of Arts: Don Desserud
Faculty of Business Administration: Dr Alan Duncan
Faculty of Education: Dr Miles Turnbull
Faculty of Nursing: Dr Kim Critchley
Faculty of Science: Dr Christian Lacroix
Faculty of Veterinary Medicine: Dr Don Reynolds

UNIVERSITY OF REGINA

3737 Wascana Parkway, Regina, SK S4S 0A2
Telephone: (306) 585-4111
E-mail: admissions@uregina.ca
Internet: www.uregina.ca

Founded 1911 as Regina College, current name adopted 1974
State control
Language of instruction: English
Academic year: May to April (3 semesters)

Chancellor: Dr William F. Ready
Vice-Chancellor and Pres.: Dr Vianne Timmons
Provost and Vice-Pres. for Academic Affairs: Dr Thomas Chase
Vice-Pres. for Admin.: David Button
Vice-Pres. for External Relations: Barbara Pollock
Vice-Pres. for Research: Dr Dennis Fitzpatrick
Exec. Dir: Annette Revet
Registrar: Dr John Metcalfe
Librarian: William Sgrazzutti

Library: 2.1m. items and 3,700 periodicals
Number of teachers: 498
Number of students: 12,878 (9,917 full-time, 2,961 part-time)

Publications: *@Archer* (12 a year), *Degrees* (2 a year), *Degrees Magazine*, *Wascana Review* (2 a year)

DEANS

Faculty of Arts: Dr RICHARD KLEER (Dir)
Faculty of Business Administration: Dr MORINA RENNIE
Faculty of Education: Dr JAMES MCNINCH
Faculty of Engineering and Applied Science: Dr PAITOON TONTIWACHWUTHIKUL
Faculty of Fine Arts: Dr SHEILA PETTY
Faculty of Kinesiology and Health Studies: Dr CRAIG CHAMBERLIN
Faculty of Nursing: Dr DAVID GREGORY
Faculty of Science: Dr DANIEL GAGNON
Faculty of Social Work: Dr CRAIG CHAMBERLIN
Graduate Studies and Research: Dr ROD KELLN

PROFESSORS

ALFANO, DENNIS P., Psychology
ANDERSON, LEONA, Religious Studies
ANDERSON, ROBERT, Business Admin.
ASHTON, NEIL W., Biology
ASMUNDSON, GORDON, Kinesiology and Health Studies
AUSTIN, BRYAN J., Business Admin.
BERGMAN, KATHERINE, Geology
BLACKSTONE, MARY, Theatre
BLAKE, RAYMOND, History
BRENNAN, WILLIAM, History
BRIGHAM, R. MARK, Biology
BROAD, DAVID, Social Work
CHAN, CHRISTINE, Engineering
CHANNING, LYNN, Music
CHAPCO, WILLIAM, Biology
CHERLAND, MEREDITH, Education
CHOW, SUI, Psychology
CONWAY, JOHN, Sociology and Social Studies
CRUIKSHANK, JANE, Social Work
DAI, LIMING, Engineering
DIAZ, HARRY, Sociology and Social Studies
DOLMAGE, ROD, Education
DONG, MINGZHE, Engineering
DRURY, SHADIA, Philosophy, Political Science
DURST, DOUG, Social Work
EVANS, DENNIS, Visual Arts
FARENICK, DOUGLAS, Mathematics and Statistics
FISHER, J. C., Mathematics
GAUTHIER, DAVID, Geography
GILLIGAN, BRUCE, Mathematics
GINGRICH, PAUL, Sociology and Social Studies
GRIFFITHS, JOHN, Music
GU, YONGAN, Engineering
HADJISTAVROPOULOS, HEATHER, Psychology
HADJISTAVROPOULOUS, THOMAS, Psychology
HAMILTON, HOWARD, Computer Science
HANDEREK, KELLY, Theatre
HANSEN, PHILLIP, Philosophy
HART, PAUL, Education
HAYFORD, ALISON, Sociology
HEINRICH, KATHERINE, Mathematics and Statistics
HOWARD, WILLIAM, English
HUANG, GUO, Engineering
HUBER, GARTH, Physics
IDEM, RAPHAEL, Engineering
ITO, JACK, Business Admin.
JEFFREY, BONNIE, Social Work
JIN, YEE-CHUNG, Engineering
JOHNSON, SHANTHI, English
KELLN, RODNEY, Chemistry and Biochemistry
KESTEN, CYRIL, Education
KIPLING BROWN, ANN, Education
KIRKLAND, STEPHEN, Mathematics and Statistics
KNUTTILA, K. MURRAY, Sociology and Social Studies
KORTÉ, HERBERT, Philosophy
LAVACK, ANNE, Business Admin.
LEAVITT, PETER, Biology
LEDREW, JUNE, Kinesiology and Health Studies
LEESON, HOWARD, Political Science
LENTON-YOUNG, GERALD, Theatre
LOLOS, GEORGE, Physics
LOUIS, CAMERON, English
MCINTOSH, RICHARD, Mathematics and Statistics
MACLENNAN, RICHARD, Justice Studies
MAEERS, MHAIRI (VI), Education
MAGUIRE, BRIEN, Computer Science
MALLOY, DAVID, Kinesiology and Health Studies
MARCHILDON, GREGORY, Johnson-Shoyama Graduate School of Public Policy
MASLANY, GEORGE, Social Work
MATHIE, EDWARD, Physics
MISSKEY, WILLIAM, Systems Engineering
PALMER, RONALD, Electronic Systems Engineering
PAPANDREOU, ZISIS, Physics
PARANJAPE, RAMAN, Electronic Systems Engineering
PAUL, ALEXANDER, Geography
PETTY, SHEILA, Media Studies
PFEIFER, JEFFREY, Justice, Psychology
PICKARD, GARTH, Education
PITSULA, JAMES, History
QING, HAIRUO, Geology
RAUM, J. RICHARD, Music
RENNIE, MORINA, Business Admin.
ROBINSON, ANNABEL, Classics
RUDDICK, NICHOLAS, English
SAUCHYN, DAVID, Geography
SAXTON, LAWRENCE, Computer Science
SHAMI, JEANNE, English
SHARMA, SATISH, Systems Engineering
SMYTHE, WILLIAM, Psychology
SOIFER, ELDON, Philosophy
STARK, CANNIE, Psychology
STREIFLER, LEESA, Visual Arts
SZABADOS, BELA, Philosophy
TOMKINS, JAMES, Mathematics
TONTIWACHWUTHIKUL, PAITOON, Engineering
TYMCHAK, MICHAEL, Education
WALL, KATHLEEN, English
WATKINSON, AILSA, Social Work
WEE, ANDREW, Chemistry and Biochemistry
WIDDIS, RANDY, Geography
YAKEL, NORM, Education
YANG, XUE-DONG, Computer Science
YAO, YIYU, Computer Science
ZHANG, CHANG, Computer Science
ZIARKO, WOJCIECH, Computer Science

FEDERATED COLLEGES

Campion College: 3737 Wascana Parkway, Regina, SK S4S 0A2; tel. (306) 586-4242; e-mail campion.college@uregina.ca; internet www.campioncollege.ca; f. 1917; library of 50,000 vols; Pres. Dr JOHN MEEHAN; Academic Dean Prof. FRANK OBRIGEWITSCH.

First Nations University of Canada: 1 First Nations Way, Regina, SK S4S 7K2; tel. (306) 790-5950; e-mail info@firstnationsuniversity.ca; internet www.firstnationsuniversity.ca; f. 1975; library of 55,200 vols, incl. the Eeniwuk Colln of 5,000 titles, supporting research in native studies; Pres. CHARLES PRATT (acting); Vice-Pres. for Academic Affairs Dr BERNIE SELINGER.

Luther College: Regina, SK S4S 0A2; tel. (306) 585-5444; e-mail lutherreg@uregina.ca; internet www.luthercollege.edu; f. 1913; Pres. Dr BRUCE PERLSON; Academic Dean Dr MARY VETTER.

ATTACHED INSTITUTES

Canadian Institute for Peace, Justice and Security: tel. (306) 585-4779; internet www.uregina.ca/arts/cipjs; Dir Dr JEFFREY PFEIFER.

Centre for Academic Technologies: tel. (306) 337-2400; e-mail cat@uregina.ca; internet www.uregina.ca/cat/home.html; Dir Dr VI MAEERS.

Institut Français: Regina; tel. (306) 585-4828; e-mail institut@uregina.ca; internet institutfrancais.uregina.ca/home.htm; Dir DOMINIQUE SARNY.

Organizational and Social Psychology Research Unit: tel. (306) 585-5268; e-mail cannie.stark@uregina.ca; internet uregina.ca/~starkc; Dir CANNIE STARK.

Saskatchewan Institute of Public Policy: Univ. of Regina, College Ave Campus, Regina, SK S4S 0A2; tel. (306) 585-5777; e-mail sipp@uregina.ca; internet www.uregina.ca/sipp; Dir IAN PEACH.

Saskatchewan Instructional Development and Research Unit of the Faculty of Education: tel. (306) 585-4537; e-mail contactus@education.uregina.ca; internet education.uregina.ca/index.php?id=38; f. 1985; Dir Dr MICHAEL TYMCHAK.

Saskatchewan Population Health and Evaluation Research Unit (SPHERU): tel. (306) 585-5674; e-mail spheru@uregina.ca; internet www.spheru.ca; Dir Dr GEORGE MASLANY (acting).

Social Policy Research Unit: Faculty of Social Work, Univ. of Regina, Regina, SK S4S 0A2; tel. (306) 585-5643; e-mail social.policy@uregina.ca; Dir Dr GARSON HUNTER.

Teaching Development Centre: Dir J. MCNINCH.

University of Regina Press: tel. (306) 585-4758; e-mail uofrpress@uregina.ca; internet www.uofrpress.caRegina; Dir Dr BRUCE WALSH

UNIVERSITY OF SASKATCHEWAN

105 Administration Pl., Saskatoon, SK S7N 5A2
Telephone: (306) 966-1212
E-mail: askus@usask.ca
Internet: www.usask.ca

Founded 1907
State control
Language of instruction: English
Academic year: September to August

Pres. and Chancellor: R. P. MACKINNON
Provost and Vice-Pres. for Academic Affairs: BRETT FAIRBAIRN
Vice-Pres. for Finance and Resources: RICHARD FLORIZONE
Vice-Pres. for Research: KAREN CHAD
Univ. Sec.: LEA PENNOCK
Registrar: R. ISINGER
Librarian: F. WINTER

Library: 2.046m. vols, 3.087m. microforms, 449,171 govt documents and pamphlets
Number of teachers: 1,090
Number of students: 21,367 (17,863 undergraduate, 3,504 graduate)

DEANS

College of Agriculture and Bioresources: M. BUHR
College of Arts and Science: PETER STOICHEFF
College of Dentistry: G. S. USWAK
College of Education: C. REYNOLDS
College of Engineering: E. BARBER
College of Graduate Studies and Research: L. MARTZ
College of Kinesiology: C. D. RODGERS
College of Law: B. BILSON
College of Medicine: W. ALBRITTON
College of Nursing: L. BUTLER (acting)
College of Pharmacy and Nutrition: DAVID HILL
College of Veterinary Medicine: Dr DOUGLAS FREEMAN
Edwards School of Business: D. TARAS

PROFESSORS

ADAMS, G. P., Veterinary Biomedical Sciences
AKKERMAN, A., Geography
ALBRITTON, W. L., Paediatrics
ALLEN, A. L., Veterinary Pathology
ALTMAN, M., Economics
ANDERSON, D. W., Soil Science

ANGEL, J. F., Biochemistry
ANSDELL, K. M., Geological Sciences
ARCHIBOLD, O. W., Geography
ATKINSON, M., Political Studies
AXWORTHY, C. S., Law
BAILEY, J. V., Large Animal Clinical Sciences
BAKER, C. G., Dentistry
BARANSKI, A. S., Chemistry
BARBER, E. M., Agricultural and Bioresource Engineering
BARBER, S. M., Large Animal Clinical Sciences
BARBOUR, S. L., Civil Engineering
BARTH, A. D., Large Animal Clinical Sciences
BASINGER, J. F., Geological Sciences
BATTISTE, M., Educational Foundations
BAXTER-JONES, A. D. G., Kinesiology
BELL, K. T. M., Art and Art History
BELL, L. S., Art and Art History
BERENBAUM, S. L., Nutrition and Dietetics
BERGSTROM, D. J., Mechanical Engineering
BETTANY, J. R., Soil Science
BIDWELL, P. M., Languages and Linguistics
BILSON, R. E., Law
BINGHAM, W., Paediatrics
BLACKSHAW, S. L., Psychiatry
BLAKLEY, B. R., Veterinary Biomedical Sciences
BOLTON, R. J., Electrical and Computer Engineering
BONHAM-SMITH, P. C., Biology
BORSA, J., Women's and Gender Studies
BORTOLOTTI, G. R., Biology
BOWDEN, M. A., Law
BOWEN, R. C., Psychiatry
BOYD, C. W., Management and Marketing
BRAWLEY, L., Kinesiology
BREMNER, M., Mathematics and Statistics
BRENNA, D. S., Drama
BRETSCHER, P. A., Microbiology and Immunology
BROOKE, J. A., Mathematics and Statistics
BROWN, W. J., Agricultural Economics
BROWN, Y. M. R., Nursing
BUCHANAN, F. C., Animal and Poultry Science
BUGG, J. D., Mechanical Engineering
BUNT, R. B., Computer Science
BURBRIDGE, B., Medical Imaging
BURNELL, P., History
BURTON, R. T., Mechanical Engineering
BUTLER, L., Nursing
CALDER, R. L., English
CAMPBELL, D. C., Anaesthesia
CAMPBELL, J., Psychology
CAMPBELL, J. R., Veterinary Large Animal Science
CARD, C. E., Veterinary Large Animal Science
CARD, R. T., Medicine
CARR-STEWART, S., Educational Admin.
CARTER, JR, J. A., Computer Science
CASSON, A., Psychiatry
CHAD, K., Kinesiology
CHAPMAN, D., Anatomy and Cell Biology
CHARTRAND, P., Law
CHEDRESE, P. J., Obstetrics, Gynaecology and Reproductive Sciences
CHIBBAR, R. N., Plant Sciences
CHILIBECK, P., Kinesiology
CHILTON, N., Biology
CHIRINO-TREJO, J. M., Veterinary Microbiology
CHIVERS, D. P., Biology
CLARKE, P. L., Industrial Relations and Organizational Behaviour
CLASSEN, H. L., Animal and Poultry Science
COCKCROFT, D. W., Medicine
COOLEY, R. W., English
COOPER-STEPHENSON, K. D., Law
CORCORAN, M., Anatomy and Cell Biology
COTTER, W. B., Law
COTTON, D. J., Medicine
COULMAN, B. E., Plant Science
CROSSLEY, D. J., Philosophy
CROWE, T. G., Agricultural and Bioresource Engineering
CSAPO, G., Music
CUMING, R. C. C., Law
CUSHMAN, D. O., Economics
DABNI, C. B., Management and Marketing
DAKU, B. L. F., Electrical and Computer Engineering
DALAI, A. K., Chemical Engineering
D'ARCY, C., Psychiatry
DAVIS, A. R., Biology
DAVIS, G. R., Physics and Engineering Physics
DAYTON, E. B., Philosophy
DE BOER, D. H., Geography
DELBAERE, L. T. J., Biochemistry
DENHAM, W. P., English
DENIS, W. B., Sociology
DESAUTELS, M., Physiology
DEUTSCHER, T. B., History
DEVON, R. M., Anatomy and Cell Biology
DICK, R., Physics and Engineering Physics
DICKINSON, H. D., Sociology
DICKSON, G., Nursing
DILLON, J. R., Biology
DODDS, D. E., Electrical and Computer Engineering
DOUCETTE, J. R., Anatomy and Cell Biology
DOWLING, P. M., Veterinary Biomedical Sciences
DUGGLEBY, W. D., Nursing
DUKE, T., Small Animal Clinical Sciences
DUST, W., Surgery
DYCK, L. E., Psychiatry
DYCK, R. F., Medicine
EAGER, D. L., Computer Science
ECHEVARRIA, E. C., Economics
ELLIS, J. A., Veterinary Microbiology
ENGLAND, G. J., Industrial Relations and Organization Behaviour
ENTWISTLE, G., Accounting
ERVIN, A. M., Religious Studies and Anthropology
FAIRBAIRN, B. T., History
FARIED, S. O., Electrical and Computer Engineering
FAULKNER, R. A., Kinesiology
FERGUSON, L. M., Nursing
FINDLAY, L. M., English
FLANNIGAN, R. D., Law
FLYNN, M., Educational Psychology and Special Education
FORSYTH, G. W., Veterinary Biomedical Sciences
FOWLER, D. B., Plant Sciences
FOWLER-KERRY, S. E., Nursing
FRANKLIN, S., Geography
FULTON, M. E., Agricultural Economics
FURTAN, W. H., Agricultural Economics
GANDER, R. E., Electrical and Computer Engineering
GEORGE, G. N., Geological Sciences
GERMIDA, J. J., Soil Science
GIESY, J. P., Veterinary Biomedical Sciences
GINGELL, S. A., English
GOLDIE, H. A., Microbiology and Immunology
GOPALAKRISHNAN, V., Pharmacology
GORDON, J. R., Veterinary Microbiology
GORECKI, D. K. J., Pharmacy
GRAHAM, B. L., Medicine
GRAHN, B. H., Small Animal Clinical Sciences
GRANT, P. R., Psychology
GRAY, R. S., Agricultural Economics
GREER, J. E., Computer Science
GRIEBEL, R. W., Surgery
GUSTA, L. V., Plant Sciences
GUSTHART, J. L., Kinesiology
GUTWIN, C., Computer Science
HAIGH, J. C., Veterinary Large Animal Sciences
HAINES, D. M., Veterinary Microbiology
HAINES, L. P., Educational Psychology and Special Education
HAMILTON, D. L., Veterinary Biomedical Sciences
HANDY, J. R., History
HARDING, A. J., English
HARRIS, D. I., Music
HARRIS, R. L., English
HARRISON, E. L., Physical Therapy
HARVEY, B. L., Plant Sciences
HAUG, M. D., Civil and Geological Engineering
HAYES, S. J., Microbiology and Immunology
HEMMINGS, S. J., Medicine
HENDERSON, J. R., English
HENDRY, M. J., Geological Sciences
HERTZ, P. B., Mechanical Engineering
HIEBERT, L. M., Veterinary Biomedical Sciences
HILL, G. A., Chemical Engineering
HIROSE, A., Physics and Engineering Physics
HOBBS, J. E., Agricultural Economics
HOEPPNER, V. H., Medicine
HOLM, F. A., Plant Sciences
HOOVER, J. N., Dentistry
HOWARD, S. P., Microbiology and Immunology
HOWE, E. C., Economics
HUBBARD, J. W., Pharmacy
HUCL, P. J., Plant Sciences
HULL, P. R., Medicine
HURST, T. S., Medicine
IRVINE, D., Family Medicine
ISAAC, G., Management and Marketing
ISH, D., Law
JACKSON, M. L., Veterinary Pathology
JELINSKI, M. D., Large Animal Clinical Sciences
JOHNSTON, G. H. F., Surgery
JUURLINK, B. H. J., Anatomy and Cell Biology
KALRA, J., Pathology
KASAP, S. O., Electrical and Computer Engineering
KASIAN, G. F., Paediatrics
KEIL, J. M., Computer Science
KEITH, R. G., Surgery
KELLY, I. W., Educational Psychology and Special Education
KENT, C. A., History (Acting Head)
KERR, W. A., Agricultural Economics
KERRICH, R. W., Geological Sciences
KHACHATOURIANS, G. G., Applied Microbiology and Food Science
KHANDELWAL, R. L., Medical Biochemistry
KIRK, A., Medicine
KOLB, N. R., Physics and Engineering Physics
KOLBINSON, D. A., Diagnostic and Surgical Sciences
KONCHAK, P. A., Dentistry
KORDAN, B., Political Studies
KORINEK, V. J., History
KOUSTOV, A. V., Physics and Engineering Physics
KOZINSKI, J. A., Chemical Engineering
KRAHN, J., Pathology
KREYSZIG, W. K., Music
KRONE, P. H., Anatomy and Cell Biology
KUHLMANN, F.-V., Mathematics and Statistics
KUHLMANN, S., Mathematics and Statistics
KULSHRESHTHA, S. N., Agricultural Economics
KULYK, W. M., Anatomy and Cell Biology
KUSALIK, A. J., Computer Science
LAARVELD, B., Animal and Poultry Science
LAFERTÉ, S., Biochemistry
LEE, J. S., Biochemistry
LEHMKUHL, D. M., Biology
LEIGHTON, F. A., Veterinary Pathology
LEPNURM, R., Management and Marketing
LI, P. S., Sociology
LI, X. M., Psychiatry
LLEWELLYN, E. J., Physics and Engineering Physics
LOH, L. C., Medical Biochemistry
LONG, R. J., Industrial Relations and Organization Behaviour
LOW, N. H., Applied Microbiology and Food Science
LOWRY, N., Paediatrics
LUCAS, R. F., Economics
MAAKA, R., Native Studies

McCalla, G. I., Computer Science
McCrosky, C., Electrical and Computer Engineering
MacDonald, M. B., Nursing
MacDougall, B., Native Studies
McKay, G., Pharmacy
MacKinnon, J. C., History
McKinnon, J. J., Animal and Poultry Science
MacKinnon, R. P., Law
McLennan, B. D., Biochemistry
MacLennan, J., Professional Communication in Engineering
McMullen, L. M., Psychology
McNeill, D., Music
Majewski, M., Chemistry
Manson, A. H., Physics and Engineering Physics
Mapletoft, R. J., Large Animal and Clinical Sciences
Marciniuk, D. D., Medicine
Martin, J. R., Mathematics and Statistics
Martz, L. W., Geography
Matheson, T. J., English
Maulé, C. P., Agricultural and Bioresource Engineering
Mehta, M. D., Sociology
Merriam, J. B., Geological Sciences
Messier, F., Biology
Meyer, D. A., Archaeology
Michelmann, H. J., Political Studies
Middleton, D., Veterinary Pathology
Miket, M. J., Mathematics and Statistics
Miller, J. R., History
Misra, V., Veterinary Microbiology
Moewes, A., Physics and Engineering Physics
Monture, P. A., Sociology
Moulding, M. B., Restorative and Prosthetic Dentistry
Muhajarine, N., Community Health and Epidemiology
Muir, G. D., Veterinary Biomedical Sciences
Nazarali, A. J., Pharmacy
Neufeld, E. M., Computer Science
Norman, K. E., Law
Ogle, K. D., Family Medicine
Olatunbosun, O. A., Obstetrics, Gynaecology and Reproductive Sciences
Olfert, M. R., Agricultural Economics
Ovsenek, N. C., Anatomy and Cell Biology
Packota, G. V., Dentistry
Painter, M., Management and Marketing
Pan, Y., Geological Sciences
Parkinson, D. J., English
Paterson, P. G., Nutrition and Dietetics
Patterson, W., Geology
Pato, M. D., Medical Biochemistry
Patrick, G. W., Mathematics and Statistics
Pedras, M. S. C., Chemistry
Peng, D.-Y., Chemical Engineering
Pennock, D. J., Soil Science
Peternelj-Taylor, C. A., Nursing
Petrie, L., Veterinary Large Animal Sciences
Pfeifer, K., Philosophy
Pharr, J. W., Veterinary Anaesthesiology, Small Animal Clinical Sciences
Phillips, B., Management and Marketing
Phillips, F., Accounting
Phillips, P. W. B., Political Studies
Pierson, R. A., Obstetrics, Gynaecology and Reproductive Sciences
Polley, L. R., Veterinary Microbiology
Pomeroy, J., Geography
Pooler, J. A., Geography
Popkin, D. R., Obstetrics, Gynaecology and Reproductive Sciences
Post, K., Small Animal Clinical Sciences
Pratt, B. R., Geological Sciences
Proctor, L. F., Curriculum Studies
Pugsley, T. S., Chemical Engineering
Pywell, R. E., Physics and Engineering Physics
Qualtiere, L. F., Pathology
Quigley, T. L., Law
Ralph, E. G., Curriculum Studies
Rangacharyulu, C., Physics and Engineering Physics
Rank, G. H., Biology
Rawlings, N. C., Veterinary Biomedical Sciences
Reed, M. G., Geography
Reeder, B. A., Community Health and Epidemiology
Reeves, M. J., Civil and Geological Engineering
Regnier, R. H., Educational Foundations
Relke, D., Women's and Gender Studies
Remillard, A. J., Pharmacy
Renaut, R. W., Geological Sciences
Renihan, P. J., Educational Administration
Reynolds, C., Educational Administration
Rhodes, C. S., Large Animal Clinical Sciences
Richardson, J. S., Pharmacology
Roesler, W. J., Biochemistry
Romo, J. T., Plant Sciences
Rosaasen, K. A., Agricultural Economics
Rosenberg, A. M., Paediatrics
Rosser, B. W. C., Anatomy and Cell Biology
Rossnagel, B. G., Crop Development Centre
Rowland, G. G., Plant Sciences
Rudachyk, L., Physical Medicine and Rehabilitation (Acting Head)
Rutledge Harding, S., Pathology
St Louis, L. V., Economics
Salt, J. E., Electrical and Computer Engineering
Sankaran, K., Paediatrics
Sawatzky, J. E., Nursing
Sawhney, V. K., Biology
Saxena, A., Pathology
Schissel, B., Sociology
Schmutz, S. M., Animal and Poultry Science
Schoenau, G. J., Mechanical Engineering
Schoney, R. A., Agricultural Economics
Schreyer, D., Anatomy and Cell Biology
Schwier, R. A., Curriculum Studies
Scoles, G. J., Plant Sciences
Semchuk, K. M., Nursing
Shand, P. J., Applied Microbiology and Food Science
Shantz, S., Art and Art History
Sharma, R. K., Pathology
Sheridan, D. P., Medicine
Shevchuk, Y. M., Pharmacy
Shmon, C. L., Small Animal Clinical Sciences
Shoker, A., Medicine
Simko, E., Veterinary Pathology
Singh, B., Veterinary Biomedical Sciences
Singh, J., Veterinary Biomedical Sciences
Sinha, B. M., Religious Studies
Smart, M. E., Small Animal Clinical Sciences
Smith, B. L., Nursing
Smolyakov, A., Physics and Engineering Physics
Sofko, G. J., Physics and Engineering Physics
Soteros, C. E., Mathematics and Statistics
Sparks, G. A., Civil and Geological Engineering
Spink, K. S., Kinesiology
Srinivason, R., Mathematics and Statistics
Stamler, L. R. L., Nursing
Steele, T. G., Physics and Engineering Physics
Steer, R. P., Chemistry
Steeves, J. S., Political Studies
Stephanson, R. A., English
Stewart, L., History
Stewart, N. J., Nursing
Stoicheff, R. P., English
Stookey, J. M., Veterinary Large Animal Sciences
Story, D. C., Political Studies
Sulakhe, P. V., Physiology
Sutherland, J. K., Restorative and Prosthetic Dentistry
Suveges, L. G., Pharmacy
Szmigielski, J., Mathematics and Statistics
Szyszkowski, W., Mechanical Engineering
Takaya, K., Electrical and Computer Engineering
Tannous, G. F., Finance and Management Science
Taylor, S. M., Small Animal Clinical Sciences
Tempier, R., Psychiatry
Teplitsky, P. E., Restorative and Prosthetic Dentistry
Thacker, P. A., Animal and Poultry Science
Thomlinson, W., Physics and Engineering Physics
Thompson, V. A., Psychology
Thornhill, J. A., Physiology
Thorpe, D. J., English
Townsend, H. G. G., Veterinary Internal Medicine
Tremblay, M., Kinesiology
Tyler, R. T., Applied Microbiology and Food Science
Tymchatyn, E. D., Mathematics and Statistics
Vaidyanathan, G., Accounting
Van Rees, K. C. J., Soil Science
Vandenberg, A., Plant Sciences
Vandervort, L. A., Law
Verge, V. M. K., Anatomy and Cell Biology
von Baeyer, C. L., Psychology
Waiser, W. A., History
Waldner, C. L., Large Animal Clinical Sciences
Waldram, J. B., Psychology
Walker, E. G., Anthropology and Archaeology
Walker, K. D., Educational Administration
Walley, F. L., Soil Science
Waltz, W. L., Chemistry
Ward, A., Curriculum Studies
Ward, D. E., Chemistry
Warrington, R. C., Biochemistry
Wason-Ellam, L., Curriculum Studies
Watson, L. G., Mechanical Engineering
Waygood, E. B., Biochemistry
West, N. H., Physiology
Wetzel, K. W., Industrial Relations and Organizational Behaviour
White, G. N., Family Medicine
Whiting, S. J., Nutrition and Dietetics
Wickett, R. E. Y., Educational Foundations
Wilson, D. G., Veterinary Large Animal Sciences
Wilson, T. W., Medicine
Wishart, T. B., Psychology
Wobeser, G. A., Veterinary Pathology
Woodhouse, H., Educational Foundations
Wormith, J. S., Psychology
Worobetz, L. J., Medicine
Wotherspoon, T. L., Sociology
Xiao, C., Physics and Engineering Physics
Xiao, W., Microbiology and Immunology
Yong-Hing, K., Surgery
Yu, P. H., Psychiatry
Zello, G. A., Nutrition and Dietetics
Zhang, C., Mechanical Engineering
Zichy, F. A., English
Ziola, B., Pathology

FEDERATED COLLEGE

St Thomas More College: 1437 College Dr., Saskatoon, SK. S7N 0W6; Pres. Rev. G. Smith.

AFFILIATED COLLEGES

Briercrest College: 510 College Dr., Caronport, SK S0H 0S0; e-mail info@briercrest.ca; Pres. Rev. D. Uglem.

Central Pentecostal College: 1303 Jackson Ave, Saskatoon, SK S7H 2M9; Pres. Rev. D. Stiller.

College of Emmanuel and St Chad: 1337 College Dr., Saskatoon, SK S7N 0W6; e-mail emmanuel.stchad@usask.ca; Prin. Rev. W. D. Deller.

Gabriel Dumont College: Exec. Dir C. Racette.

Lutheran Theological Seminary: 114 Seminary Crescent, Saskatoon, SK S7N 0X3; e-mail lutheran.seminary@usask.ca; Pres. D. E. Buck.

St Andrew's College: 1121 College Dr., Saskatoon, SK S7N 0W3; tel. (306) 966-8970; e-mail standrews.college@usask.ca; internet www.standrews.ca; language of instruction: English; Prin. L. Calvert.

St Peter's College: POB 10, Muenster, SK S0K 2Y0; e-mail spc@stpeters.sk.ca; Pres. G. Kobussen

UNIVERSITY OF TORONTO

27 King's College Circle, Toronto, ON M5S 1A1
Telephone: (416) 978-2011
Internet: www.utoronto.ca
Founded 1827
Private control
Language of instruction: English
Academic year: September to May (May to August, summer session)
Chancellor: Hon. David R. Peterson
Pres.: David Naylor
Vice-Pres. and Provost: Cheryl Misak
Vice-Pres. and Chief Advancement Officer: David Palmer
Vice-Pres. for Business Affairs: Catherine Riggall
Vice-Pres. for Human Resources and Equity: Angela Hildyard
Vice-Pres. for Research: Paul Young
Vice-Pres. for Univ. Relations: Judith Wolfson
Vice-Pres. and Prin. for Univ. of Toronto at Mississauga: Ian Orchard
Vice-Pres. and Prin. for Univ. of Toronto at Scarborough: Franco Vaccarino
Chief Librarian: Carole Moore
Library: see under Libraries and Archives
Number of teachers: 3,771
Number of students: 73,685
Publications: *Bulletin*, *Calendars*, *President's Report*, *The Graduate*, *Undergraduate Admission Handbook*

DEANS

Faculty of Applied Science and Engineering: Cristina Amon
Faculty of Architecture, Landscape and Design: Richard M. Sommer
Faculty of Arts and Science: Meric Gertler
Faculty of Dentistry: David Mock
Faculty of Forestry: C. T. Smith
Faculty of Information: Seamus Ross
Faculty of Law: Mayo Moran
Faculty of Medicine: Catharine Whiteside
Faculty of Music: Russell Hartenberger
Lawrence S. Bloomberg Faculty of Nursing: Sioban Nelson
Leslie Dan Faculty of Pharmacy: Henry J. Mann
Faculty of Physical Education and Health: Bruce Kidd
Factor-Inwentash Faculty of Social Work: Faye Mishna
Ontario Institute of Studies in Education: Jane Gaskell
School of Continuing Studies: Marilynn Booth
School of Graduate Studies: Brian Corman
Rotman School of Management: Roger Martin
Dalla Lana School of Public Health: Jack Mandel
School of Public Policy and Governance: Mark Stabile

PROFESSORS

Faculty of Applied Science and Engineering:
Aarabi, P., Electrical and Computer Engineering
Abdelrahman, T., Electrical and Computer Engineering
Adams, B. J., Civil Engineering
Aitchison, J., Electrical and Computer Engineering
Allen, D., Chemical Engineering
Balke, S. T., Chemical Engineering
Bawden, W., Civil Engineering
Bidleman, T., Chemical Engineering
Birkemoe, P. C., Civil Engineering
Bonert, R., Electrical and Computer Engineering
Boocock, D. G. B., Chemical Engineering
Boulton, P. I. P., Electrical Engineering
Byer, P. H., Civil Engineering
Chaffey, C. E., Chemical Engineering
Charles, M. E., Chemical Engineering
Cheng, Y., Chemical Engineering
Chow, P., Electrical and Computer Engineering
Cluett, W., Chemical Engineering
Cobbold, R. S. C., Institute of Biomedical Engineering
Collins, M. P., Civil Engineering
Cormack, D. E., Chemical Engineering
Coyle, T., Chemical Engineering
Curran, J. H., Civil Engineering
Davies, S., Electrical and Computer Engineering
Davison, E. J. A., Electrical Engineering
Dawson, F., Electrical and Computer Engineering
Dewan, S. B., Electrical Engineering
Diamond, M., Chemical Engineering
Diosady, L. L., Chemical Engineering
Edwards, E., Chemical Engineering
Eizenman, M., Electrical and Computer Engineering
Erb, U., Materials Science
Evans, G., Chemical Engineering
Farnood, R., Chemical Engineering
Foulkes, F. R., Chemical Engineering
Fox, M. S., Industrial Engineering
Francis, B. A., Electrical Engineering
Frecker, R., Electrical and Computer Engineering
Fulthorpe, R., Chemical Engineering
Goldenberg, A. A., Mechanical Engineering
Gulack, P., Electrical and Computer Engineering
Hatzinakos, D., Electrical and Computer Engineering
Herman, P., Electrical and Computer Engineering
Hooton, R., Civil Engineering
Iravani, M. R., Electrical and Computer Engineering
Jacobsen, H.-A., Electrical and Computer Engineering
James, D. F., Mechanical Engineering
Jardine, A. K. S., Industrial Engineering
Jia, C., Chemical Engineering
Joy, M., Electrical and Computer Engineering
Karney, B., Civil Engineering
Kawaji, M., Chemical Engineering
Kirk, D. W., Chemical Engineering
Konrad, A., Electrical and Computer Engineering
Kortschot, M., Chemical Engineering
Kschischang, F., Electrical and Computer Engineering
Kuhn, D., Chemical Engineering
Kunov, H., Biomedical Engineering
Kwong, R. H., Electrical Engineering
Lavers, J. D., Electrical Engineering
Lee, E. S., Electrical Engineering
Lehn, P., Electrical and Computer Engineering
Leon-Garcia, A., Electrical Engineering
Li, D., Mechanical Engineering
Lo, H.-K., Electrical and Computer Engineering
Luus, R., Chemical Engineering
McKague, A., Chemical Engineering
Mandelis, A., Mechanical Engineering
Mann, S., Electrical and Computer Engineering
Martin, K., Electrical Engineering
Measures, R. M., Aerospace Studies
Meguid, S. A., Mechanical Engineering
Miller, E. J., Civil Engineering
Mims, C. A., Chemical Engineering
Mohanty, B., Civil Engineering
Ojha, M., Chemical Engineering
Packer, J. A., Civil Engineering
Paradi, J., Chemical Engineering
Park, C., Mechanical Engineering
Pasupathy, S. P., Electrical Engineering
Perovic, D., Materials Science
Reeve, D. W., Chemical Engineering
Rose, J., Electrical and Computer Engineering
Sain, M., Chemical Engineering
Salama, C. A. T., Electrical Engineering
Santerre, J., Chemical Engineering
Sargent, E., Electrical and Computer Engineering
Saville, B., Chemical Engineering
Sefton, M. V., Chemical Engineering
Semlyen, A., Electrical and Computer Engineering
Sevcik, K., Electrical and Computer Engineering
Sheikh, S. A., Civil Engineering
Shoichet, M., Chemical Engineering
Sleep, B., Civil Engineering
Smith, K. C., Electrical Engineering
Smith, P. W., Electrical Engineering
Sodhi, R., Engineering
Sousa, E., Electrical and Computer Engineering
Terzopoulos, D., Electrical and Computer Engineering
Tran, H. N., Chemical Engineering
Trass, O., Chemical Engineering
Turksen, I. B., Industrial Engineering
Vecchio, F. J., Civil Engineering
Venetsanopoulos, A. N., Electrical Engineering
Venter, R. D., Mechanical Engineering
Vranesic, Z. G., Electrical Engineering
Wallace, J. S., Mechanical Engineering
Wang, Z., Materials Science
Wania, F., Chemical Engineering
Ward, C. A., Mechanical Engineering
Wonham, W. M., Electrical Engineering
Woodhouse, K., Chemical Engineering
Wright, P. M., Civil Engineering
Yan, N., Chemical Engineering
Yip, C., Chemical Engineering
Young, R., Civil Engineering
Zaky, S. G., Electrical Engineering
Zandstra, P., Chemical Engineering
Zukotynski, S., Electrical Engineering

Faculty of Architecture, Landscape and Design:
Corneil, C. S.
Eardley, A.

Faculty of Arts and Science:
Abbatt, J., Chemistry
Abouhaidar, M. G., Botany
Abraham, R. G., Astronomy and Astrophysics
Accinelli, R. D., History
Adler, E., Political Science
Aivazian, V. A., Economics
Alloway, T. M., Psychology
Anderson, G. M., Geology
Anderson, J. B., Botany
Arnheim, C., Geography
Arthur, J. G., Mathematics
Aster, S., History
Astington, J., English
Bacchus, F., Computer Science
Bailey, D. C., Physics
Bailey, R. C., Physics
Baird, J., English
Baker, M., Economics

BAKICH, O., Slavic Languages and Literature
BALDUS, B., Sociology
BARNES, C. J., Slavic Languages and Literature
BARRETT, F. M., Zoology
BARRETT, S. C. H., Botany
BARZDA, V., Physics
BASHKEVIN, S., Political Science
BEINER, R. S., Political Science
BENJAMIN, D., Economics
BERGER, C. C., History
BERKOWITZ, M. K., Economics
BEWELL, A., English
BIERSTONE, E., Mathematics
BINNICK, R. I., Linguistics
BIRGENEAU, R. J., Physics
BISZTRAY, G., Slavic Languages and Literature
BLAKE, T., Botany
BLANCHARD, P. H., History
BLAND, J. S., Mathematics
BLISS, J. M., History
BLOOM, T., Mathematics
BODDY, J., Anthropology
BODEMANN, M., Sociology
BOLTON, C. T., Astronomy
BOND, J., Astronomy and Astrophysics
BOONSTRA, R., Life Sciences
BORODIN, A. B., Computer Science
BOTHWELL, R., History
BOURNE, L. S., Geography
BOYD, M., Sociology
BRAUN, A., Political Science
BRITTON, J., Geography
BROOK, T. J., History, East Asian Studies
BROOKS, D. R., Zoology
BROWN, I. R., Zoology
BROWN, J. R., Philosophy
BROWN, R. M., Humanities
BROWNLEE, J. S., East Asian Studies
BRUDNER, A., Political Science
BRUMER, P. W., Chemistry
BRYAN, R. B., Geography
BRYANT, J., Sociology
BRYM, R. J., Sociology
BUCHWEITZ, R., Mathematics
BUNCE, M., Geography
BURKE, J. F., Spanish and Portuguese
BURTON, F. D., Anthropology
CAMERON, D. R., Political Science
CANFIELD, J. V., Philosophy
CAPOZZI, R., Italian Studies
CARLBERG, R. G., Physical Sciences
CARR, J. L., Economics
CASAS, F. R., Economics
CHAMBERLIN, J. E., English
CHEETHAM, M., Fine Art
CHEN, J., Geography
CHIN, J., Chemistry
CHING, J. C., Religious Studies
CLARKE, W. H., Astronomy
CLIVIO, G. P., Italian Studies
CODE, R. F., Physics
COOK, S. A., Computer Science
CORMAN, B., English Literature
CORNEIL, D. G., Mathematics, Computer Science
CRAWFORD, G., Anthropology
CRUDEN, S., Geology
CUMMINS, W. R., Botany
CUNNINGHAM, F. A., Philosophy, Political Science
DANESI, M., Italian Studies
DAY, R. B., Political Economy
DE KERCKHOVE, D., French
DE QUEHEN, A. H., English
DE SOUSA, R., Philosophy
DEL JUNCO, A., Mathematics
DENGLER, N. G., Botany
DENNY, M. G. S., Economics
DENT, J., History
DESAI, R. C., Physics
DEWAR, M., Classics
DEWEES, D. N., Political Economy
DIAMOND, M., Geography
DION, P.-E., Near Eastern Studies
DONALDSON, D., Chemistry
DONNELLY, M. W., Political Science, East Asian Studies
DRUMMOND, J. R., Physics
DUNLOP, D. J., Physics
EDWARDS, E., Botany
EDWARDS, R. N., Physics
EISENBICHLER, K., Italian
ELLIOTT, G. A., Mathematics
ENRIGHT, W. H., Mathematics, Computer Science
ERICKSON, B. H., Sociology
ESPIE, G., Botany
EVANS, M. J., Statistics
EYLES, N., Physical Sciences
FAIG, M., Economics
FALKENHEIM, V. C., Political Science, East Asian Studies
FARRAR, D., Chemistry
FENNER, A., German
FIUME, E., Computer Science
FOOT, D. K., Economics
FORBES, H. D., Political Science
FORGUSON, L. W.
FRANCESCHETTI, A., Italian Studies
FRIEDLANDER, J. B., Mathematics
FRIEDMANN, H. B., Sociology
FUSS, M. A., Economics
GAD, G. H. K., Geography
GALLOWAY, J. H., Geography
GARTNER, R. I., Sociology
GEORGES, M., Chemistry
GERTLER, M. S., Geography
GERVERS, M., History
GILLIS, A. R., Sociology
GITTINS, J., Geology
GOERING, J., History
GOLDSTEIN, M., Mathematics
GOLDSTICK, D., Philosophy
GOTLIEB, C., Computer Science
GOURIEROUX, C., Economics
GRAHAM, I. R., Mathematics
GREENWOOD, B., Geography
GREENWOOD, B., Geology
GREER, A. R., History
GREINER, P. C., Mathematics
GRIFFEN, P. A., Physics
GROSS, M. R., Zoology
GUNDERSON, M. K., Economics
GWYNNE, D. T., Biology
HAGAN, J. L., Sociology
HALLS, H. C., Geological Sciences
HANNIGAN, J., Sociology
HANSELL, R. I. C., Zoology
HARVEY, D., Geography
HARVEY, E., Sociology
HARVEY, E. R., English
HAYHOE, R., East Asian Studies
HEALEY, A., English
HEATH, M. C., Botany
HEHNER, E. C. R., Computer Science
HELMSTADTER, R. J., History
HIGGINS, V. J., Botany
HIGGS, D. C., History
HINTON, G. E., Computer Science
HIRST, G., Computer Science
HOLDOM, B., Physics
HORGEN, P. A., Botany
HORI, K., Physics
HORTON, S., Economics
HOWARD, K., Geology
HOWARD, P. J., English
HOWELL, N., Sociology
HOWSON, S. K., Social Sciences
HUTCHEON, L. A., English
INGHAM, J. N., History
INWOOD, B. C., Classics, Philosophy
ISRAEL, M., History
IVRII, V., Mathematics
JAAKSON, R., Geography
JACKSON, H., English
JACKSON, K. R., Computer Science
JACOBS, A. E., Physics
JEFFREY, L., Mathematics
JELLINEK, M., Physics
JEPSON, A. D., Computer Science
JOHN, S., Physics
JOHNSON, W. M. L. A., Fine Art
JOHNSTON, A., English
JONES, A., Classics
JONES, C. L., Sociology
JUMP, G. V., Economics
JURDJEVIC, V., Mathematics
KAPRAL, R. E., Chemistry
KAPRANOV, M., Mathematics
KAY, L., Chemistry
KEE, H.-K., Physics
KEITH, W. J., English
KERVIN, J. B., Sociology
KEY, A. W., Physics
KHESIN, B., Mathematics
KHOVANSKII, A., Mathematics
KIM, H., Mathematics
KIM, Y.-B., Physics
KLAUSNER, D. N., English
KLEIN, M. A., History
KLUGER, R. H., Chemistry
KOFMAN, L., Astronomy
KRAMER, C. E., Slavic Languages and Literature
KRIEGER, P., Physics
KRULL, U., Chemistry
KUKLA, A., Psychology, Philosophy
LAMBEK, M. J., Anthropology
LANCASHIRE, A. C., English
LANCASHIRE, D. I., English
LANTZ, K. A., Slavic Languages and Literature
LAUTENS, M., Chemistry
LEDUC, L., Political Science
LEE, M. J., Physics
LEE, R. B., Anthropology
LEGGATT, A. M., English
LEHMAN, A. B., Computer Science
LEVESQUE, H. J., Computer Science
LO, H.-K., Physics
LOGAN, R., Physics
LORIMER, J. W., Mathematics
LUKE, M., Physics
LUONG, H. V., Anthropology, East Asian Studies
LUSTE, G. J., Physics
LYNN, R., East Asian Studies
LYUBICH, M., Mathematics
MCCLELLAND, R. A., Chemistry
MCDONALD, P., Chemistry
MCILWRAITH, T., Geography
MAGEE, J., Classics
MAGILL, D. W., Sociology
MAGNUSSON, L., English
MAGOCSI, P. R., Political Science
MALLOCH, D. W., Botany
MANNERS, I., Chemistry
MARGORIBANKS, R., Physics
MARTIN, J. F., Physics
MARTIN, P. G., Astronomy
MATHEWSON, G. F., Political Economy
MATHON, R. A., Mathematics, Computer Science
MATUS, J., English
MELINO, A., Economics
MENDELSOHN, E., Mathematics, Computer Science
MENDELZON, A. O., Computer Science
MENZINGER, M., Chemistry
MERRILEES, B., French
MIALL, A. D., Geology
MICHELSON, W., Sociology
MIKHALKIN, G., Mathematics
MILKEREIT, B., Physics
MILLER, R., Chemistry
MILLER, R., Physics
MILMAN, P., Mathematics
MIMS, C., Chemistry
MINTZ, J., Economics
MIRON, J. R., Geography
MITROVICHA, J. X., Physics
MOCHNACKI, S., Astronomy
MOGGRIDGE, D. E., Economics
MOORE, G., Physics
MORGAN, K. P., Philosophy

MORRIS, G. K., Zoology
MORRIS, R., Chemistry
MORRIS, S. W., Physics
MORRISON, J. C., Philosophy
MUNK, L., English
MUNRO, D. S., Geography
MURNAGHAN, F., Mathematics
MURRAY, H., English
MURRAY, N., Astronomy
MURTY, V., Mathematics
MYLES, J., Sociology
MYLOPOULOS, J., Computer Science
NACHMAN, A., Mathematics
NEDELSKI, J., Political Science
NETTERFIELD, B., Physics
NEUMAN, S., English
NOYES, J. K., German
O'DAY, D., Zoology
O'DONNELL, P. J., Physics
OLIVER, W. A., French
ORCHARD, A., English
ORCHARD, I., Zoology
ORR, R. S., Physics
ORWIN, C. L., Political Science
OSBORNE, M., Economics
O'TOOLE, R., Sociology
OZIN, G. A., Chemistry
PANGLE, T. L., Political Science
PATERSON, J. M., French
PAULY, P., Political Science, Economics
PEET, A., Physics
PELTIER, W. R., Physics
PERCY, J. R., Astronomy
PERRON, P., French
PIETROPAOLO, D., Italian
PITASSI, T., Computer Science
POLANYI, J. C., Chemistry
POPPITZ, E., Physics
POWELL, J., Chemistry
PRIESTLEY, L. C., East Asian Studies
PRUESSEN, R. W., History
PUGLIESE, G., Italian
RACKOFF, C. W., Computer Science
RAYSIDE, D. M., Political Science
REDEKOP, M., English
REIBETANZ, J. H., English
REID, D., Fine Art
REID, F. J., Economics
REISZ, R. R., Zoology
REITZ, J. G., Sociology
RELPH, T., Geography
REPKA, J. S., Mathematics
RICE, K. D., Linguistics
RICHARDSON, D. S., Fine Art
RISING, J. D., Zoology
ROBIN, P. Y., Geological Science
ROSENTHAL, J., Mathematics
ROSENTHAL, P., Mathematics
ROSSOS, A., History
RUBINOFF, A., Political Science
RUTHERFORD, P., History
SALAFF, J. W., Sociology
SANDBROOK, K. R. J., Political Science
SANDERS, G., East Asian Studies
SAVARD, P., Physics
SCHWARTZ, D. V., Political Science
SCOTT, S. D., Geology
SEAGER, W. E., Philosophy
SEAQUIST, E. R., Astronomy
SEARY, P. D., English
SECO, L., Mathematics
SELICK, P., Mathematics
SELIGER, F., German
SEVCIK, K. C., Computer Science
SHAW, W. D., English
SHEN, V., East Asian Studies
SHEPHERD, T., Physics
SHERK, A., Mathematics
SHERWOOD LOLLAR, B., Geology
SHI, S., Economics
SHUB, M., Mathematics
SIGMON, B. A., Anthropology
SILCOX, P., Political Science
SIMEON, R., Political Science, Law
SIOW, A., Economics
SIPE, J. E., Physics
SKOGSTAD, G. D., Political Science
SMITH, J. J. B., Zoology
SMYTH, D., History
SOECKI, S., English
SOHM, P. L., Fine Art
SOLOMON, P. H., Political Science
SOLOMON, S., Political Science
SPOONER, E. T., Geology
SPRULES, W. G., Zoology
STATT, B., Physics
STEIN, J., Political Science
STEINBERG, A., Physics
STERNBERG, R., Spanish and Portuguese
STEVENS, P., English
STREN, R. E., Political Science
STRONG, K., Physics
SULEM, C., Mathematics
SULLIVAN, R., English
SUMNER, L. W., Philosophy
TAILLEFER, L., Physics
TALL, F. D., Mathematics
TANNER, J., Sociology
TANNY, S., Mathematics
TEICHMAN, J., Political Science
TEPPERMAN, L. J., Sociology
TERZOPOULOS, D., Computer Science
THOMPSON, J. C., Chemistry
THOMPSON, M., Chemistry
THOMPSON, R. P., Philosophy
THOMSON, L., English
THYWISSEN, J., Physics
TOBE, S. S., Zoology
TOWNSEND, D., English
TREBILOCK, M., Economics
TREFLER, D., Economics
TRISCHUK, W., Physics
TROTT, D., French
TUOHY, C., Political Science
TURNER, D. H., Anthropology
URQUHART, A. I. F., Philosophy
VAN DRIEL, H. M., Physics
VIPOND, R., Political Science
VIRAG, B., Mathematics
WAGLE, N. K., History
WALKER, M. B., Physics
WATERHOUSE, D. B., East Asian Studies
WEI, J., Physics
WEINRIB, L., Political Science
WEISS, W. A., Mathematics
WELLMAN, B. S., Sociology
WESTGATE, J. A., Geology
WHEATON, B., Sociology
WHITE, G., Political Science
WHITE, R. R., Geography
WHITTINGTON, S. G., Chemistry
WILLIAMS, D. D., Life Sciences
WILSON, F. F., Philosophy
WOLFE, D., Political Science
WOOLDRIDGE, T. R., French
WORTMAN, D. B., Computer Science
YOUNG, R. P., Geology
YOUSON, J. H., Zoology
YU, E., Computer Science
ZIMMERMAN, A. M., Zoology

Faculty of Dentistry:
BENNICK, A.
DAVIES, J.
DEPORTER, D. A.
ELLEN, R. P.
FERRIER, J. M.
FREEMAN, E.
HEERSCHE, J. N. M.
LEAKE, J. L.
LEVINE, N.
LEWIS, D. W., Community Dentistry
LOCKER, D.
MCCOMB, D.
MCCULLOCH, C. A.
MAIN, J. H. P., Oral Pathology
MAYHALL, J. T.
MELCHER, A. H.
MOCK, D.
PILLIAR, R. M.
SANDHAM, H. J.
SESSLE, B. J.
SODEK, J.
SYMINGTON, J. M.
TEN CATE, A. R.
TENENBAUM, H. C.
WATSON, P. A.
ZARB, G. A., Prosthodontics

Faculty of Law:
BEATTY, D. M.
BENSON, P.
BRUDNER, A.
BRUNÉE, J.
CHAPMAN, B.
COOK, R.
COSSMAN, B.
DANIELS, R.
DEWEES, D.
DICKENS, B.
DYZENHAUS, D.
FLOOD, C.
FRIEDLAND, M.
GREEN, A.
HAGAN, J.
JANISCH, H.
LANGILLE, B.
LEE, I.
MACKLEM, P.
NEDELSKY, J.
PHILLIPS, J.
RÉAUME, D.
RIPSTEIN, A.
ROACH, K.
ROGERSON, C.
SIMEON, R.
SOSSIN, R.
TREBILOCK, M.
WADDAMS, S.
WEINRIB, E.
WEINRIB, L.

Faculty of Medicine:
ABEL, S., Otolaryngology
ACKERMANN, U., Physiology
ADAMSON, S., Obstetrics and Gynaecology, Paediatrics
ADELI, K., Pathobiology
ANDERSON, G. H., Nutrition and Food Sciences
ANDREWS, B. J., Medical Genetics and Microbiology
ANDRULIS, I., Pathobiology, Microbiology
ARCHER, M. C., Nutritional Studies
ARROWSMITH, C., Immunology
ASA, S., Pathobiology
ATWOOD, H. L., Physiology
AUBIN, J., Medical Biophysics
AXELRAD, A. A., Medical Biophysics
BAINES, A. D., Clinical Biochemistry
BAKER, R. R., Medicine
BARKER, G., Anaesthesia
BAUMAL, R., Pathology
BAZETT-JONES, D., Biochemistry
BELIK, J., Paediatrics
BENCHIMOL, S., Medical Biophysics
BENSON, L., Paediatrics
BERGERON, C., Pathobiology
BEVAN, D., Anaesthesia
BHAVNANI, B., Obstetrics and Gynaecology
BIGGAR, W. D., Paediatrics
BISSONETEE, B., Anaesthesia
BLAKE, J., Obstetrics and Gynaecology
BLANCHETTE, V., Paediatrics
BLENCOWE, B., Medical Research, Microbiology
BLUMENTHAL, A., Pathobiology
BOCKING, A., Obstetrics and Gynaecology, Physiology
BOGGS, J., Pathobiology
BOGNAR, A., Microbiology
BOHN, D., Anaesthesia
BOONE, C., Medical Research
BOONSTRA, R., Zoology, Physiology
BOUFFET, E., Paediatrics
BOYD, N., Medical Biophysics
BRESLIN, C., Ophthalmology
BRET, P.
BRONSKILL, M., Immunology

BROWN, D., Otolaryngology
BRUBAKER, P., Physiology
BRUNTON, J., Pathobiology
BUNCIC, R., Ophthalmology
BURNHAM, W. M., Pharmacology
BURNS, P., Medical Biophysics
BUSTO, U., Pharmacology
BUTANY, J., Pathobiology
BUTLER, D., Physiology
BYRICK, R., Anaesthesia
CAMERMAN, N., Biochemistry
CAMPBELL, J. B., Microbiology
CARLEN, P. L., Medicine
CASPER, R. F., Obstetrics and Gynaecology
CHALLIS, J., Physiology and Obstetrics
CHAMBERLAIN, D., Pathobiology
CHAN, H. S., Biochemistry
CHAN, S. L., Paediatrics
CHAN, V. L., Microbiology
CHARLTON, M. P., Physiology
CHETTY, R., Pathobiology
CHIANG, L., Pathobiology
CHITAYAT, D., Paediatrics
CHUNG, F. F., Anaesthesia
CLARKE, D., Biochemistry
CLARKE, J. T. R., Paediatrics
COATES, A., Paediatrics, Physiology
COLE, D., Pathobiology
COLE, P., Otolaryngology
COLGAN, T., Pathobiology
COVENS, A., Obstetrics and Gynaecology
CRUZ, T., Pathobiology
CRYSDALE, W. S., Otolaryngology
CUNNANE, S., Nutritional Sciences
CUNNINGHAM, A., Medical Biophysics
DANEMAN, A., Medical Imaging
DANEMAN, D., Paediatrics
DANSKA, J., Medical Biophysics
DEBER, C. M., Medical Biophysics
DEBONI, U., Physiology
DENNIS, J., Pathobiology
DE PETRILLO, A. D., Obstetrics and Gynaecology
DIAMANDIS, E., Pathobiology
DIAMANT, N. E., Physiology
DICK, J. E., Microbiology
DIRKS, F., Medicine
DIRKS, P., Medicine
DIXON, W., Ophthalmology
DORIAN, P., Pharmacology
DOSCH, H., Paediatrics
DOSTROVSKY, J. O., Physiology
DRUCKER, D. J., Pathobiology
DRUTZ, H., Obstetrics and Gynaecology
DUBE, I., Pathobiology
DUFFIN, J., Anaesthesia
DULLIN, J., Medical Biophysics
DURIE, P., Paediatrics
EASTERBROOK, M., Ophthalmology
EDWARDS, A., Medical Research, Microbiology
ELLEN, R., Pathobiology
ELLIS, D., Otolaryngology
EMILI, A., Medical Research, Microbiology
FARINE, D., Obstetrics and Gynaecology
FELDMAN, B. M., Paediatrics
FELDMAN, F., Ophthalmology
FERNIE, G. R., Surgery
FIEDBERG, J., Otolaryngology
FISH, E., Medical Biophysics
FISHER, R. H. G., Family and Community Medicine
FONG, I., Pathobiology
FORNASIER, V., Pathobiology
FORSTNER, G. G., Paediatrics
FORSTNER, J., Biochemistry
FOSTER, F. S., Medical Biophysics
FOX, A., Medical Imaging
FOX, G., Anaesthesia
FRECKER, R., Biomedical Engineering
FREEDMAN, J., Pathobiology
FREEDMAN, M., Paediatrics
FREEDOM, R., Paediatrics
FREEDOM, R., Pathobiology
FREEMAN, J., Otolaryngology
FRIESEN, J., Medical Research
FROM, L., Medicine
GALLIE, B., Ophthalmology
GALLINGER, S., Pathobiology
GANOZA, M. C., Medical Research
GARE, D., Obstetrics and Gynaecology
GARIÉPY, J., Medical Biochemistry
GARVEY, M. B., Medicine
GEARY, D., Paediatrics
GEORGE, S., Pharmacology
GILDAY, D., Medical Imaging
GOLDMAN, B. S., Surgery
GOLDSTEIN, M. B., Medicine
GOTLIEB, A. I., Pathology
GRANT, D., Pharmacology
GREENBERG, G. R., Medicine
GREENBERG, M. L., Paediatrics
GREENBLATT, J. F., Medical Research
GREENWALD, M., Paediatrics
GREENWOOD, C., Nutritional Sciences
GRINSTEIN, S., Biochemistry
GRYNPAS, M., Pathobiology
GUHA, A., Medical Biochemistry
GULLANE, P. J., Otolaryngology
GURD, J., Biochemistry
HALLIDAY, W., Pathobiology
HAMPSON, D., Pharmacology
HANLEY, W., Paediatrics
HANNA, W., Pathobiology
HANNAH, M., Obstetrics and Gynaecology
HARRISON, R., Otolaryngology
HASLAM, R., Paediatrics
HAWKE, M., Pathobiology, Otolaryngology
HAY, J. B., Immunology
HEDLEY, D., Medical Biophysics
HEERSCH, J., Pharmacology
HELM, T., Paediatrics
HENKELMAN, R. M., Medical Biophysics
HERSCHORN, S., Urology
HILL, R., Medical Biophysics
HILLIARD, R., Paediatrics
HINEK, A., Pathobiology
HO PING KONG, Medicine
HOWELL, P., Biochemistry
HUGHES, T., Medical Research
HUNT, J. W., Medical Biophysics
HYDE, M., Otolaryngology
IKURA, M., Medical Biophysics
INABA, T., Pharmacology
INGLES, C. J., Medical Research
ISCOVE, N., Medical Biochemistry
ISENMAN, D. E., Biochemistry
JEEJEEBHOY, K. N., Medicine
JOHNSSTON, K. W., Vascular Surgery
JOHNSTON, M., Pathobiology
JORGENSEN, A. O., Anatomy and Cell Biology
JOTHY, S., Pathobiology
JULIUS, M., Medical Biophysics
KAHN, H. (acting), Pathobiology
KAIN, K., Pathobiology
KALNINS, V. I., Histology
KANDEL, R., Pathobiology
KAPLAN, D., Medical Genetics
KARMALI, M., Pathobiology
KAY, L., Biochemistry
KEELEY, F., Biochemistry, Pathobiology
KERBEL, R., Medical Biophysics, Pathobiology
KHANNA, J. M., Pharmacology
KHOKHA, R., Medical Biophysics, Pathobiology
KISH, S., Pharmacology
KLIP, A., Biochemistry, Paediatrics
KOREN, G., Paediatrics, Pharmacology
KOVACS, K., Pathobiology
KRAFT, S., Ophthalmology
KRAFTCHIK, B., Paediatrics
KRAICER, J., Physiology
KRAUSE, H., Medical Research
KUCHARCZYK, W., Radiology
KUKSIS, A., Medical Research
KUNOV, H., Otolaryngology
LANGER, B., Surgery
LANGILLE, B. L., Pathology
LAWEE, D. H., Family and Community Medicine
LEPOCK, J., Medical Biophysics
LETARTE, M., Medical Biophysics
LEVY, G. A., Medicine
LEWIS, P. N., Biochemistry
LI, R.-K., Pathobiology
LICKLEY, L., Physiology
LICKRISH, G., Obstetrics and Gynaecology
LIEBGOTT, B., Anatomy
LIEW, C. C., Clinical Biochemistry
LINGWOOD, C., Biochemistry
LIU, F.-F., Medical Biophysics, Physiology
LIVINGSTONE, R. A., Obstetrics and Gynaecology
LOGAN, W. J., Paediatrics
LOW, D., Pathobiology
LYE, S., Obstetrics and Gynaecology
MACDONALD, J. F., Physiology
MCGEER, A., Pathobiology
MCGRAIL, S., Otolaryngology
MCINNES, R. R., Paediatrics
MACKAY, M., Biomedical Communications
MCKEE, N., Plastic Surgery
MACLENNAN, D. H., Medical Research
MAHURAN, D., Pathobiology
MAK, T.-W., Medical Biophysics
MARKS, A., Neurobiology
MARSDEN, P., Medical Biophysics, Pathobiology
MARSHALL, V. W., Behavioural Science
MAZER, C. D., Anaesthesia
MESSNER, H., Medical Biophysics
MICKLE, D., Pathobiology
MICKLEBOROUGH, L., Cardiac Surgery
MILGRAM, N., Pharmacology
MILLER, F., Physiology
MINDEN, M., Medical Biophysics
MOCK, D., Pathobiology
MOSCARELLO, M., Pathobiology
MORAN, L., Biochemistry
MORAN, M. F., Medical Research
MORGAN, J. E., Obstetrics and Gynaecology
MORTIMER, C. B., Ophthalmology
MROSOVSKY, N., Physiology
NAG, S., Pathobiology
NAGY, A., Medical Genetics
NARANJO, C. A., Pharmacology
NEDZELSKI, J. M., Otolaryngology
NOBLE, W. H., Anaesthesia
NOYEK, A. M., Otolaryngology
O'BRIEN, P., Pharmacology
O'BRODOVICH, H., Paediatrics, Physiology
O'DOWD, B., Pharmacology
OHASHI, P., Medical Biophysics
OHLSSON, A., Paediatrics
OKEY, A. B., Pharmacology
OLIVIERI, N., Paediatrics
OPAS, M., Pathobiology
ORSER, B., Anaesthesia, Physiology
OSMOND, D. H., Physiology
OTTENSMEYER, F. P., Medical Biophysics
PACE-ASCIAK, C., Pharmacology
PAI, E., Biochemistry
PAIGE, C., Medical Biophysics
PANG, C., Physiology
PANG, K., Pharmacology
PANTALONY, D., Pathobiology
PAPPO, A., Paediatrics
PAPSIN, F. R., Obstetrics and Gynaecology
PARKER, J., Ophthalmology
PARKER, J. D., Pharmacology
PAVLIN, C., Ophthalmology
PENCHARZ, P., Paediatrics
PENN, L., Medical Biophysics
PENNINGER, J., Medical Biophysics
PERLMAN, M., Paediatrics
PETERS, W. J., Plastic Surgery
PINKERTON, P. H., Pathology
PLEWES, D., Medical Biophysics
POST, M., Pathobiology, Physiology
PRITZKER, K., Pathobiology
PRUD'HOMME, G., Pathobiology
PULLEYBLANK, D. E., Biochemistry
RABINOVITCH, M., Paediatrics
RACHLIS, A., Pathobiology
RAJALAKSHMI, S., Pathobiology
RAUTH, A., Medical Biophysics

READ, S. E., Paediatrics, Pathobiology
REGAN, M., Ophthalmology
REITHMEIER, R., Biochemistry
RENLUND, R., Physiology
REZNICK, R., General Surgery
RICHARDSON, C., Medical Biophysics
RIDDELL, R., Pathobiology
RITCHIE, J. W. K., Obstetrics and Gynaecology
ROBERTS, E., Paediatrics
ROBINSON, G., Psychiatry
ROIFMAN, C., Paediatrics
ROSE, D., Medical Biophysics
ROTSTEIN, O. D., Surgery
ROWLANDS, J. A., Medical Biophysics
RUTKA, J., Pathobiology
SADOWSKI, P. D., Medical Genetics, Pathobiology
SARMA, D., Pathobiology
SAUDER, D. N., Medicine
SCHATZKER, J., Surgery
SCHIMMER, B. P., Medical Research
SCHLICHTER, L., Physiology
SCHMITT-ULMS, G., Pathobiology
SCULLY, H., Cardiac Surgery
SEGALL, J., Biochemistry, Medical Genetics
SEIDELMAN, W. E., Family and Community Medicine
SELLERS, E. M., Pharmacology
SERMER, M., Obstetrics and Gynaecology
SESSLE, B., Dentistry
SETH, A., Pathobiology
SHAH, C. P., Preventive Medicine and Biostatistics
SHARPE, J. A., Otolaryngology
SHEAR, N., Pharmcology
SHEK, P., Pathobiology
SHERMAN, P., Paediatrics, Pathobiology
SHIER, R. M., Obstetrics and Gynaecology
SHIME, J., Obstetrics and Gynaecology
SHULMAN, H. S., Radiology
SHULMAN, M. J., Immunology, Medical Genetics
SILVERMAN, M., Medicine
SIMOR, A., Pathobiology
SIU, C. H., Medical Research
SLINGER, P., Anaesthesia
SNEAD, III, O. C., Paediatrics
SODEK, J., Biochemistry
SOLE, M. J., Medicine
SONNENBERG, H., Physiology
SPEAKMAN, J., Ophthalmology
SQUARE, P., Speech-Language Pathology
SQUIRE, J., Pathobiology
STEIN, H., Ophthalmology
STEINER, G., Medicine
STEWART, D. J., Pathobiology
STEWART, P. A., Anatomy and Cell Biology
SUN, A., Physiology
TALLETT, S., Paediatrics
TANNOCK, I., Medical Biophysics
TANSWELL, A., Paediatrics
TATOR, C. H., Surgery
TAYLOR, G., Pathobiology
TAYLOR, I. M., Anatomy
TEMPLETON, D. M., Pathobiology
TENENBAUM, H., Pathobiology
TERBRUGGE, K., Medical Imaging
THOMPSON, L., Nutrition
THORNER, P., Pathobiology
TIMMER, V., Botany
TOMLINSON, D., Otolaryngology
TRIMBLE, W. S., Biochemistry
TRITCHLER, D., Medical Biophysics
TROPE, G., Ophthalmology
TSAO, M., Medical Biophysics, Pathobiology
TWEED, D., Physiology
UETECHT, J., Pharmacology
VAN DER KOOY, D. J., Anatomy and Cell Biology
VAN NOSTRAND, P., Otolaryngology
VAN TOL, H., Pharmacology
VAS, S., Pathobiology
VELLEND, H., Medicine
VRANIC, M., Physiology
WADDELL, J. P., Surgery
WALFISH, P. G., Otolaryngology
WANG, Y.-T., Pathobiology
WANLESS, I., Pathobiology
WARSH, J., Pharmacology
WEISBROD, G., Medical Imaging
WEISER, W., Medical Imaging
WEITZMAN, S., Paediatrics
WEKSBERG, R., Paediatrics
WELLS, J., Pharmacology
WELLS, P., Pharmacology
WILLIAMS, D., Biochemistry
WILLINSKY, R., Medical Imaging
WILSON, B., Medical Biophysics
WILSON, G., Pathobiology
WILSON, S., Medical Imaging
WILSON-PAUWELS, L., Biomedical Communications
WITTNICH, C., Cardiac Surgery
WOJTOWICZ, J., Physiology
WOLEVER, T., Nutritional Sciences
WONG, J. T. F., Biochemistry
WONG, P.-Y., Pathobiology
WONG, S., Medical Biophysics
WOOD, L., Medical Biophysics
WOOD, M., Medical Imaging
WOODGETT, J., Medical Biophysics
WOOLRIDGE, N., Biomedical Communications
WU, T. W., Clinical Biochemistry
YAFFE, M., Medical Biophysics
YIP, C. C., Medical Research
YOO, S.-J., Medical Imaging
ZAMEL, N., Otolaryngology
ZHOU, M., Physiology

Faculty of Music:

ARMENIAN, R., Director of Orchestral Activities
HARTENBERGER, R., Percussion, Graduate Coordinator
HATZIS, C., Composition
HAWKINS, J., Theory and Composition
LAUFER, E. C., Music Theory
MACDONALD, L., Voice Studies
SHAND, P. M., Music Education

Faculty of Nursing:

GALLOP, R.
HILLAN, E.
HODNETT, E.
MCKEEVER, P.
O'BRIEN-PALLAS, L.
PRINGLE, D.
STEVENS, B.

Faculty of Pharmacy:

O'BRIEN, P. J.
PANG, K. S.
PERRIER, D. G.
ROBINSON, J. B.
SEGAL, H.
STIEB, E. W., History of Pharmacy
THIESSEN, J. J.
UETRECHT, J. P.

Faculty of Social Work:

BARBER, J.
BOGO, M.
HULCHANSKI, D.
LIGHTMAN, E.
MCDONALD, L.
NEYSMITH, S.
SHERA, W.

Joseph L. Rothman School of Management:

AIVAZIAN, V., Finance
AMBURGEY, T. (acting), Strategic Management
AMERNIC, J. (acting), Accounting
BAUM, J. (acting), Strategic Management
BEATTY, D. (acting), Strategic Management
BERKOWITZ, M. (acting), Finance
BERMAN, O. (acting), Operations Management
BIRD, R. (acting), Economics
BOOTH, L. (acting), Finance
BORINS, S. (acting), Public Management
BREAN, D. (acting), Business Economics
BROOKS, L. (acting), Business Ethics and Accounting
CALLEN, J. (acting), Accounting
D'CRUZ, J. (acting), Strategic Management
DOBSON, W. (acting), International Business
DUAN, J.-C. (acting), Finance
EVANS, M. (acting), Organizational Behaviour
FELDMAN, M. (acting), Business Economics
FLECK, J. (acting), Business Government Relations
GOLDEN, B. (acting), Strategic Management
GUNZ, H. (acting), Organizational Behaviour
HALPERN, P. (acting), Finance
HORSTMANN, I. (acting), Business Economics
HUGHES, P. (acting), Strategic Management, Space Systems
HULL, J. (acting), Finance
HYATT, D. (acting), Business Economics
KIRZNER, E. (acting), Finance
KOLODNY, H. (acting), Organizational Behaviour
LATHAM, G. (acting), Organizational Effectiveness
MCCURDY, T. (acting), Finance
MARTIN, R. (acting), Strategic Management
MENZEFRICKE, U. (acting), Operations Management
MINTZ, J. (acting), Taxation
MITCHELL, A. (acting), Marketing
MOORTHY, S. (acting), Marketing
ONDRACK, D. (acting), Organizational Behaviour
PAULY, P. (acting), Economics
SMIELIAUSKAS, W. (acting), Accounting
SOMAN, D. (acting), Marketing
STARK, A. (acting), Strategic Management
STRANGE, W. (acting), Urban Economics
TOMBAK, M. (acting), Technology Management
TREFLER, D. (acting), Business Economics
WHITE, A. (acting), Finance
WHYTE, G. (acting), Organizational Behaviour
WILSON, T. (acting), Economics

Ontario Institute for Studies in Education:

ACKER, S. (acting), Sociology and Equity Studies in Education, Theory and Policy Studies in Education
ASTINGTON, J., Human Development
BECK, C., Curriculum, Teaching and Learning
BIEMILLER, A. J.
BOGDAN, D., Theory and Policy and Studies in Education
BOYD, D., Theory and Policy Studies in Education
COLE, A., Adult Education
CONNELLY, M., Curriculum, Teaching and Learning
CORTER, C. M.
CUMMING, A., Curriculum, Teaching and Learning
CUMMINS, J., Curriculum, Teaching and Learning
DARROCH-LOZOWSKI, V., Curriculum, Teaching and Learning
DAVIE, L., Curriculum, Teaching and Learning
DEI, G., Sociology and Equity Studies in Education
DIAMOND, P.
EICHLER, M., Sociology and Equity Studies in Education
FARRELL, J., Curriculum, Teaching and Learning, Theory and Policy Studies in Education
GASKELL, J., Sociology and Equity Studies in Education

GEVA, E., Curriculum, Teaching and Learning
GUTTMAN, M. A., Counselling Psychology
HANNAY, L., Curriculum, Teaching and Learning
HARVEY, E., Sociology and Equity Studies in Education
HAYHOE, R., Theory and Policy Studies in Education
HELLER, M., Sociology and Equity Studies in Education
HODSON, D., Curriculum, Teaching and Learning
JENKINS, J., Human Development
JORDAN, A., Curriculum, Teaching and Learning
KEATING, D., Human Development
KNOWLES, J. G., Adult Education
LABRIE, N., Curriculum, Teaching and Learning
LANG, D., Theory and Policy Studies in Education
LAPKIN, S., Curriculum, Teaching and Learning
LEITHWOOD, K., Theory and Policy Studies in Education
LENSKYJ, H., Sociology and Equity Studies in Education
LEVINE, D., Theory and Policy Studies in Education
LEWIS, M., Human Development
LIVINGSTONE, D., Sociology and Equity Studies in Education
MCLEAN, R., Curriculum, Teaching and Learning
MIEZITIS, S., Teacher Education
MILLER, J., Curriculum, Teaching and Learning
MISGELD, D., Theory and Policy Studies in Education
MOORE, C., Human Development
NG, R., Adult Education, Sociology and Equity Studies in Education
O'SULLIVAN, E., Adult Education
OATLEY, K., Human Development
OLSON, D., Human Development
PASCAL, C., Theory and Policy Studies in Education
PIERSON, R. R., Sociology and Equity Studies in Education
PIRAN, N., Counselling Psychology
PORTELLI, J., Theory and Policy Studies in Education
QUARTER, J., Adult Education
ROSS, J., Curriculum, Teaching and Learning
RYAN, J., Theory and Policy Studies in Education
SCARDAMALIA, J., Curriculum, Teaching and Learning
SIMON, R., Curriculum, Teaching and Learning
SKOLNIK, M., Theory and Policy Studies in Education
SPADA, N., Curriculum, Teaching and Learning
STANOVICH, K., Curriculum, Teaching and Learning
STERMAC, L., Counselling Psychology
SWAIN, M., Curriculum, Teaching and Learning
THIESSEN, D., Curriculum, Teaching and Learning
TROPER, H., Theory and Policy Studies in Education
VOLPE, R., Human Development
WIENER, J., Human Development
WILLOWS, D., Curriculum, Teaching and Learning
WILSON, D., Curriculum, Teaching and Learning, Theory and Policy Studies in Education

School of Graduate Studies:
ANGENOT, M., Comparative Literature
BEATTIE, J. M., Criminology
BOND, R. J., Theoretical Astronomy
BRYDEN, R., Drama
COHEN, J. S., Graduate Studies
DOOB, A. N., Criminology
HACKING, I. M., History and Philosophy of Science and Technology
HARIANTO, F., International Studies
HEALEY, A. D., Medieval Studies
HERNANDEZ, C., International Studies
KAISER, N., Theoretical Astronomy
LEVERE, T. H., History and Philosophy of Science and Technology
MARKER, L. L., Drama
MARTIN, P. G., Theoretical Astronomy
NESSELROTH, P. W., Comparative Literature
PESANDO, J. E., Policy Analysis
RIGG, A. G., Medieval Studies
SHEARING, C. D., Criminology
STENNING, P. C., Criminology
STOCK, B. C., Comparative Literature
TREMAINE, S. D., Theoretical Astronomy
VALVERDE, M. V., Criminology
WINSOR, M. P., History and Philosophy of Science and Technology

School of Physical Education and Health:
COREY, P.
DONNELLY, P.
FERNIE, G.
GOODE, R.
JACOBS, I.
LEITH, L.
LENSKYJ, H.
MCCLELLAND, J.
MCKEE, N.
PLYLEY, M.
VOLPE, R.

UNIVERSITY COLLEGES

Erindale College/University of Toronto at Mississauga: 3359 Mississauga Rd N, Mississauga, ON L5L 1C6; tel. 828-5211; f. 1964; Prin. IAN ORCHARD.

Innis College: 2 Sussex Ave, Toronto, ON M5S 1J5; tel. 978-7023; e-mail registrar .innis@utoronto.ca; internet www.utoronto .ca/innis; f. 1964; Prin. F. CUNNINGHAM.

New College: 300 Huron St, Toronto, ON M5S 3JO; tel. 978-2461; e-mail newcollege .registrar@utoronto.ca; internet utt2.library .utoronto.ca/www/new_college/index.htm; f. 1962; Pres. DAVID KLANDFIELD.

Scarborough College: 1265 Military Trail, Scarborough, ON M1C 1A4; tel. 287-8872; e-mail helpdesk@utsc.utoronto.ca; f. 1964; Prin. R. P. THOMPSON.

University College: 15 King's College Circle, Toronto, ON M5S 3H7; tel. 978-3170; e-mail uc.principal@utoronto.ca; f. 1853; Prin. PAUL J. PERRON.

Woodsworth College: 117–119 St George St, Toronto, ON M5S 1A9; tel. 978-2411; e-mail info@wdw.utoronto.ca; f. 1974; Prin. N. M. MELTZ.

FEDERATED UNIVERSITIES

University of St Michael's College: 81 St Mary St, Toronto, ON M5S 1J4; tel. (416) 926-1300; f. 1958; conducted by the Basilian Fathers; Pres. Dr ANNE ANDERSON.

University of Trinity College: 6 Hoskin Ave, Toronto, ON M5S 1H8; tel. (416) 978-2522; f. 1851; Vice-Chancellor and Provost R. PAINTER.

Victoria University, Toronto: 73 Queen's Park Cres., Toronto, ON M5S 1K7; tel. (416) 585-4524; f. 1836; Pres. E. KUSHNER.

FEDERATED COLLEGES

Emmanuel College: 75 Queen's Park Cres., Toronto, ON M5S 1K7; tel. (416) 585-4539; f. 1928; theological college associated with The United Church of Canada; Prin. MARK G. TOULOUSE.

Knox College: 59 St George St, Toronto, ON M5S 2E5; tel. (416) 978-4500; e-mail knox .college@utoronto.ca; Presbyterian theological college; Prin. Rev. Dr RAYMOND HUMPHRYES (acting).

Regis College: 15 St Mary St, Toronto, ON M4Y 2R5; tel. (416) 922-5474; e-mail inquiries@regiscollege.ca; f. 1930; Roman Catholic theological college (Society of Jesus); Pres. Rev. JOHN E. COSTELLO.

Wycliffe College: 5 Hoskin Ave, Toronto, ON M5S 1H7; tel. (416) 979-2870; Anglican theological college; Prin. Rev. H. S. HILCHEY (acting).

AFFILIATED INSTITUTES

Massey College: University of Toronto, Toronto, ON M5S 2E1; tel. (416) 978-2895; e-mail porter@masseycollege.ca; f. 1963; residential college for graduates and senior scholars engaged in research; Master J. S. DUPRE.

Pontifical Institute of Medieval Studies: 59 Queen's Park Cres. East, Toronto, ON M5S 2C4; tel. (416) 926-7142; internet www .pims.ca; affiliated to Univ. of St Michael's College; grants degrees in its own right, offering pontifical Licentiate in Medieval Studies (MSL) and Doctorate in Medieval Studies (MSD); Pres. Dr RICHARD M. ALWAY

UNIVERSITY OF VICTORIA

3800 Finnerty Rd, Victoria, BC V8P 5C2
Telephone: (250) 721-7211
E-mail: ucom@uvic.ca
Internet: www.uvic.ca
Founded 1963
provincial control
Language of instruction: English
Academic year: September to April
Chancellor: MURRAY FARMER
Pres. and Vice-Chancellor: Dr DAVID H. TURPIN
Vice-Pres. for Academic Affairs and Provost: Dr REETA TREMBLAY
Vice-Pres. for External Relations: CARMEN CHARETTE
Vice-Pres. for Finance and Operations: GAYLE GORRILL
Vice-Pres. for Research: Dr HOWARD BRUNT
Univ. Sec.: Dr JULIA EASTMAN
Registrar: LAUREN CHARLTON
Univ. Librarian: JONATHAN BENGTSON
Number of teachers: 790
Number of students: 19,646
Publications: *Calendar* (1 a year), *Malahat Review*, *The Ring*

DEANS

Faculty of Business: Dr SAUL KLEIN
Faculty of Education: Dr TED RIECKEN
Faculty of Engineering: Dr THOMAS TIEDJE
Faculty of Fine Arts: Dr SARAH BLACKSTONE
Faculty of Graduate Studies: Dr DAVID W. CAPSON
Faculty of Human and Social Development: Dr MARY ELLEN PURKIS (acting)
Faculty of Humanities: Dr JOHN ARCHIBALD
Faculty of Law: Prof. DONNA GRESCHNER (acting)
Faculty of Science: Dr ROBERT LIPSON
Faculty of Social Sciences: Dr PETER KELLER

PROFESSORS

AGATHOKLIS, P., Electrical and Computer Engineering
ANDERSON, J., Educational Psychology and Leadership Studies
ANDRACHUK, G. P., Hispanic and Italian Studies

ANTONIOU, A., Electrical and Computer Engineering
ARMITAGE, A., Social Work
AUSIO, J., Biochemistry and Microbiology
AVIO, K. L., Economics
BACHOR, D. G., Psychological Foundations
BALFOUR, W. J., Chemistry
BARCLAY, J. A., Mechanical Engineering
BARNES, C., Earth and Ocean Sciences
BARNES, G. E., Child and Youth Care
BASKERVILLE, P. A., History
BAVELAS, J. B., Psychology
BEDESKI, R. E., Political Science
BENNETT, C., Political Science
BENOIT, C., Sociology
BERRY, E. I., English
BEST, M. R., English
BHARGAVA, V. K., Electrical and Computer Engineering
BHAT, A. K. S., Electrical and Computer Engineering
BLANK, K., English
BOAG, D. A., Faculty of Business
BOHNE, C., Chemistry
BORNEMANN, J., Electrical and Computer Engineering
BORROWS, J., Law
BRADLEY, K. R., Classics
BRENER, R., Visual Arts
BROWNING-MOORE, A., Music
BRUNT, H., Nursing
BRYANT, D., Pacific and Asian Studies
BUB, D., Psychology
BUCKLEY, J. T., Biochemistry and Microbiology
BURKE, R. D., Biology
CAMPBELL, M., Human and Social Development
CARROLL, W. K., Sociology
CASSELS, J. L., Law
CASSWELL, D. G., Law
CELONA, J., Music
CHAPMAN, R., Earth and Ocean Sciences
CHAPPELL, N. L., Sociology
COBLEY, E., English
COCKAYNE, E. J., Mathematics and Statistics
COOPERSTOCK, F. I., Physics and Astronomy
COWARD, H. G., History
CROIZIER, L., Writing
CROIZIER, R. C., History
CUNNINGHAM, J. B., Public Administration
CUTT, J., Public Administration
DEARDEN, P., Geography
DEVOR, H., Sociology
DIACU, F., Mathematics and Statistics
DIMOPOULOS, N., Electrical and Computer Engineering
DIPPIE, B. W., History
DIXON, R. A., Psychology
DJILALI, N., Mechanical Engineering
DOBELL, A. R., Public Administration
DOCHERTY, D., Physical Education
DONALD, L. H., Anthropology
DONG, Z., Mechanical Engineering
DOST, S., Mechanical Engineering
DYSON, L., Psychological Foundations
EDWARDS, A. S., English
EL GUIBALY, F. H., Electrical and Computer Engineering
ENGINEER, M., Economics
ESLING, J., Linguistics
FELLOWS, M., Computer Science
FERGUSON, G. A., Law
FLEMING, T., Education
FOSS, J., Philosophy
FOSTER, H., Law
FOSTER, H. D., Geography
FOWLER, R., Social and Natural Sciences
FRANCE, H., Psychological Foundations
FYLES, T. M., Chemistry
GALAMBOS, N., Psychology
GALLAGHER, Nursing
GALLOWAY, J., Law
GARRETT, C., Physics, Earth and Ocean Sciences
GARTRELL, D., Sociology
GIBSON-WOOD, C., History in Art
GIFFORD, R. D., Psychology
GILES, D. E., Economics
GILLIN, M., Law
GLICKMAN, B., Biology
GOOCH, B. N. S., English
GOUGH, T. E., Chemistry
GRANT, P. J., English
GREGORY, P. T., Biology
GULLIVER, A., Electrical and Computer Engineering
HALL, B., Curriculum and Instruction
HANLEY, B., Curriculum and Instruction
HARKER, W. J., Education
HARRINGTON, D., Chemistry
HARRIS, C., Communication and Social Foundations
HARTWICK, F. D. A., Physics and Astronomy
HARVEY, B., Psychological Foundations
HAWRYSHYN, C., Biology
HEDLEY, R. A., Sociology
HILLS, M., Nursing
HOCKING, M., Chemistry
HODGINS, J., Creative Writing
HOEFER, W. J. R., Electrical and Computer Engineering
HOGYA, G., Theatre
HORITA, R. E., Physics and Astronomy
HORSPOOL, R. N., Computer Science
HOWE, B. L., Physical Education
HOWELL, R. G., Law
HUENEMANN, R. W., Faculty of Business
HULTSCH, D. F., Psychology
ILLNER, R., Mathematics and Statistics
ISHIGURO, E. E., Biochemistry and Microbiology
JOHNSON, T. D., Education
JONES, J. C. H., Economics
KAMBOURELI, S., English
KAY, W. W., Biochemistry and Microbiology
KEELER, R., Physics and Astronomy
KELLER, A., English
KELLER, P., Geography
KERBY-FULTON, K., English
KESS, J. F., Linguistics
KINDERMAN, W., Music
KIRLIN, R. L., Electrical and Computer Engineering
KLUGE, E.-H., Philosophy
KOENIG, D., Sociology
KOOP, B., Biology
KREBS, H., Music
KUEHNE, V., Child and Youth Care
KWOK, H. H. L., Electrical and Computer Engineering
LAI, D. C.-Y., Geography
LANGFORD, J. W., Public Administration
LAPPRAND, M., French Language and Literature
LAZAREVICH, G., Music
LEADBEATER, B., Psychology
LEEMING, D. J., Mathematics and Statistics
LIDDELL, P., Germanic Studies
LIEDTKE, W. W., Education
LINDSAY, D., Psychology
LISCOMB, K., History in Art
LIVINGSTON, N., Biology
LONERGAN, S. C., Geography
LU, W.-S., Electrical and Computer Engineering
MCCANN, L., Geography
MCDAVID, J. C., Public Administration
MCDORMAN, T., Law
MCDOUGALL, I., Music
MCLAREN, A. G., History
MCLAREN, J. P. S., Law
MACGREGOR, J. N., Public Administration
MACPHERSON, G. R. I., History
MAGNUSSON, W., Political Science
MALONEY, M. A., Law
MANNING, E. G., Computer Science, Electrical and Computer Engineering
MARTIN-NEWCOMBE, Y., Communication and Social Foundations
MASSON, M. E. J., Psychology
MATEER, C., Psychology
MAYFIELD, M., Education
MAZUMDER, A., Biology
M'GONIGLE, R., Environmental Studies
MIERS, C. R., Mathematics and Statistics
MILLER, D., Computer Science
MISRA, S., Biochemistry and Microbiology
MITCHELL, D. H., Anthropology
MITCHELL, R. H., Chemistry
MOEHR, J. R., Health Information Service
MOLZAHN, A., Nursing
MORE, B. E., Music
MORGAN, C. G., Philosophy
MOSK, C. A., Economic Relations with Japan
MULLER, H., Computer Science
MURPHY, P., Communication and Social Foundations
MUZIO, J. C., Computer Science
MYRVOLD, W., Computer Science
NANO, F., Biochemistry and Microbiology
NEILSON, W. A. W., Law
NG, I., Business
NICHOLS, D., Physical Education
NIEMANN, O., Geography
OGMUNDSON, R., Sociology
OLAFSON, R. W., Biochemistry and Microbiology
OLESKY, D., Computer Science
OLESON, J. P., Classics
OSBORNE, J., History in Art
PAETKAU, V., Biochemistry
PEARSON, T. W., Biochemistry and Microbiology
PENCE, A. R., Child and Youth Care
PFAFFENBERGER, W. E., Mathematics and Statistics
PHILLIPS, J., Mathematics and Statistics
PICCIOTTO, C. E., Physics and Astronomy
PINDER, W. C., Business
PORTEOUS, J. D., Geography
PRINCE, M. J., Social Policy
PRITCHET, C. J., Physics
PROTTI, D. J., Health Information Science
PROVAN, J. W., Mechanical Engineering
PUTNAM, I., Mathematics and Statistics
RANGER, L., Music
REED, W. J., Mathematics and Statistics
REID, R. G. B., Biology
REITSMA-STREET, M., Child and Youth Care
RICKS, F. A. S., Child and Youth Care
RIEDEL, W. E., Germanic Studies
RING, R. A., Biology
ROMANIUK, P., Biochemistry and Microbiology
ROTH, E., Anthropology
ROTH, W.-M., Social and Natural Sciences
ROY, P., History
RUSKEY, F., Computer Science
RUTHERFORD, M., Economics
SAGER, E. W., History
ST PETER, C., Women's Studies
SCARFE, C. D., Physics and Astronomy
SCHAAFSMA, J., Economics
SCHAARSCHMIDT, G. H., Slavonic Studies
SCHOFIELD, J. A., Economics
SCHULER, R., English
SCHWANDT, E., Music
SCOBIE, S. A. C., English
SERRA, M., Computer Science
SHERWOOD, N., Biology
SHRIMPTON, G., Greek and Roman Studies
SMITH, D., Geography
SOUROUR, A. R., Mathematics and Statistics
SRIVASTAVA, H. M., Mathematics and Statistics
STEPANENKO, Y., Mechanical Engineering
STEPHENSON, P. H., Anthropology
STOBART, S. R., Chemistry
STORCH, J., Nursing
STOREY, V., Communication and Social Foundations
STRAUSS, E., Psychology
STRONG, D. F., Earth and Ocean Sciences
STUCHLY, M., Electrical and Computer Engineering
SYMINGTON, R. T. K., Germanic Studies
THALER, D., French Language and Literature

THATCHER, D. S., English
TUCKER, J., English
TULLER, S., Geography
TULLY, J., Political Science
TUNNICLIFFE, V. J., Earth and Ocean Sciences, Biology
TURNER, N., Environmental Studies
UHLEMANN, M. R., Education
VALGARDSON, W. D., Creative Writing
VAN DEN DRIESSCHE, R., Biology
VAN EMDEN, M., Computer Science
VAN GYN, G., Physical Education
VANCE, J. H., Education
VANDENBERG, D. A., Physics
VICKERS, G. W., Mechanical Engineering
VOGT, B., Music
VON ADERKAS, P., Biology
WADGE, W. W., Computer Science
WALDRON, M. A., Law
WALKER, R. B. J., Political Science
WALTER, G. R., Economics
WAN, P. C., Chemistry
WARBURTON, R., Sociology
WATTON, A., Physics and Astronomy
WEAVER, A., Earth and Ocean Sciences
WELCH, S. A., History in Art
WENGER, H. A., Physical Education
WHITICAR, M., Earth and Ocean Sciences
WILL, H. J., Public Administration
WILLIAMS, T., English
WILSON, J., Political Science
WOLFF, R., Business
WOON, YUEN-FONG, Pacific Asian Studies
WU, Z., Sociology
WYNAND, D., Creative Writing
YORE, L. D., Education
YOUDS, R., Visual Arts
YOUNG, J., Philosophy
ZIELINSKI, A., Electrical and Computer Engineering
ZIMMERMAN, D., History
ZUK, W., Arts in Education

UNIVERSITY OF WATERLOO

Waterloo, ON N2L 3G1
Telephone: (519) 888-4567
E-mail: registrar@uwaterloo.ca
Internet: www.uwaterloo.ca
Founded 1957
provincially supported
Language of instruction: English
Chancellor: PREM WATSA
Pres. and Vice-Chancellor: FERIDUN HAMDULLAHPUR
Vice-Pres. for Academic Affairs and Provost: GEOFFREY MCBOYLE
Vice-Pres. for Admin. and Finance: DENNIS E. HUBER
Vice-Pres. for Univ. Relations: TIM JACKSON
Vice-Pres. for Univ. Research: GEORGE DIXON
Assoc. Provost for Academic and Student Affairs: CHRIS READ
Assoc. Provost for Graduate Studies: SUE HORTON
Assoc. Provost for Human Resources and Student Services: MARILYN THOMPSON
Assoc. Provost for Information Systems and Technology: DAVID WALLACE
Registrar: RAY DARLING
Univ. Librarian: MARK HASLETT
Library: 2m. vols
Number of teachers: 1,062
Number of students: 30,861
Publications: *Alternatives* (6 a year), *Environments Journal* (3 a year), *New Quarterly*

DEANS

Faculty of Applied Health Sciences: SUSAN ELLIOT
Faculty of Arts: DOUGLAS PEERS
Faculty of Engineering: PEARL SULLIVAN
Faculty of Environmental Studies: ANDRE ROY
Faculty of Mathematics: IAN GOULDEN
Faculty of Science: TERRY MCMAHON

FEDERATED UNIVERSITY

St Jerome's University: Waterloo, ON N2L 3G3; f. 1864; federated 1960; Roman Catholic, conducted by the Congregation of the Resurrection; Pres. D. PERRIN.

AFFILIATED COLLEGES

Conrad Grebel University College: Waterloo, ON N2L 3G6; e-mail congreb@uwaterloo.ca; f. 1961; Pres. H. PAETKAU.

Renison University College: Waterloo, ON N2L 3G4; e-mail more@renison.uwaterloo.ca; f. 1959, affiliated 1960; Prin. G. CARTWRIGHT.

St Paul's University College: Waterloo, ON N2L 3G5; e-mail stpauls@uwaterloo.ca; f. 1962; Prin. G. BROWN

UNIVERSITY OF WINDSOR

Windsor, ON N9B 3P4
Telephone: (519) 253-3000
E-mail: registr@uwindsor.ca
Internet: www.uwindsor.ca
Founded 1857
provincially assisted
Language of instruction: English
Academic year: September to May (2 semesters)
Chancellor: Dr EDWARD LUMLEY
Vice-Chancellor and Pres.: Dr ALAN WILDEMAN
Vice-Pres. for Admin. and Finance: STEPHEN WILLETTS
Vice-Pres. for Univ. Advancement: MICHAEL SALTER (acting)
Provost and Vice-Pres. for Academics: Prof. NEIL GOLD
Vice-Provost for Students and Registrar: Prof. BRIAN MAZER (acting)
Librarian: GWENDOLYN EBBETT
Number of teachers: 428 (full-time)
Number of students: 16,180 (full-time and part-time)
Publications: *Review*, *The Lance* (52 a year), *Windsor University Magazine* (4 a year)

DEANS

Faculty of Arts and Social Science: Dr CECIL HOUSTON
Faculty of Education: Dr PAT ROGERS
Faculty of Engineering: Dr GRAHAM T. READER
Faculty of Graduate Studies and Research: Dr JIM FRANK
Faculty of Human Kinetics: Dr ROBERT BOUCHER
Faculty of Law: Prof. BRUCE ELMAN
Faculty of Nursing: Dr ELAINE DUFFY
Faculty of Science: Dr MARLYS KOSCHINSKY
Odette School of Business: Dr ALLAN CONWAY

PROFESSORS

Faculty of Arts and Social Science:
AMORE, R. C., Political Sciences
ATKINSON, C. B., English
BABE, R. E., Communication Studies
BALANCE, W. D., Psychology
BAXTER, I., Visual Arts
BÉLANGER, S., Visual Arts
BERTMAN, S., Classical Studies
BIRD, H. W., Classical Studies
BLAIR, J. A., Philosophy
BROOKS, S., Political Science
BROWN-JOHN, C. L., Political Science
BUTLER, E. G., Music
CASSANO, P., French
COHEN, J. S., Psychology
DEANGELIS, J. R., Visual Arts
DEVILLERS, J. P., French
DILWORTH, T. R., English
DITSKY, J. M., English
GOLD SMITH, S. B., Visual Arts
HANSON, J., Music
HAWKINS, F. R., Social Work
HOLOSKO, M. J., Social Work
HOUSEHOLDER, R., Music
KING, J. N., Religious Studies
KINGSTONE, B. D., French
KLINCK, D. M., History
LAKHAN, V. C., Geography
LINTON, J. M., Communication Studies
MCCRONE, K. E., History
MACKENDRICK, L. K., English
MADY KELLY, D., Dramatic Art
MURRAY, J., History
PAGE, J. S., Psychology
PALMER, D., Music
PHIPPS, A. G., Geography
PINNELL, W. H., Dramatic Art
REYNOLDS, D. V., Psychology
ROMSA, G. H., Geography
ROURKE, B. P., Psychology
SCHNEIDER, F. W., Psychology
SODERLUND, W. C., Political Science
STARETS, M., French
STEBELSKY, I., Geography
TRENHAILE, A. S., Geography
VAN DEN HOVEN, A., French
WARREN, B., Dramatic Art
WHITNEY, B., Religious Studies
WINTER, J. P., Communication Studies

Faculty of Education:
CRAWFORD, W. J. I.
KUENDIGER, E.
LAING, D. A.
MORTON, L.
WILLIAMS, N. H.

Faculty of Engineering:
AHMADI, M., Electrical Engineering
ALFA, A. S., Industrial Engineering and Manufacturing Systems Engineering
ALPAS, A. T., Mechanical, Automotive and Materials Engineering
ASFOUR, A. A., Civil and Environmental Engineering
BEWTRA, J. K., Civil and Environmental Engineering
BISWAS, N., Civil and Environmental Engineering
BUDKOWSKA, B. B., Cultural and Environmental Engineering
DUTTA, S. P., Industrial Engineering and Manufacturing Systems Engineering
EL MARAGHY, H., Industrial Engineering and Manufacturing Systems Engineering
EL MARAGHY, W., Industrial Engineering and Manufacturing Systems Engineering
FRISE, P. R., Mechanical, Automotive and Materials Engineering
HEARN, N., Civil and Environmental Engineering
KWAN, H. K., Electrical Engineering
LASHKARI, R. S., Industrial Engineering and Manufacturing Systems Engineering
MADUGULA, M. K. S., Civil and Environmental Engineering
MILLER, W. C., Electrical Engineering
NORTH, W., Mechanical, Automotive and Materials Engineering
RAJU, G. R. G., Electrical Engineering
RANKIN, G. W., Mechanical, Automotive and Materials Engineering
READER, G. T., Mechanical, Automotive and Materials Engineering
SID-AHMED, M., Electrical Engineering
SOLTIS, J., Electrical Engineering
TABOUN, S., Industrial Engineering and Manufacturing Systems Engineering
WANG, H., Industrial Engineering and Manufacturing Systems Engineering
WATT, D. F., Mechanical, Automotive and Materials Engineering

WILSON, N. W., Mechanical, Automotive and Materials Engineering

Faculty of Human Kinetics:

BOUCHER, R. L., Athletics and Recreational Studies
MARINO, W., Kinesiology
OLAFSON, G. A., Kinesiology
SALTER, M. A., Kinesiology
WEESE, W. J., Kinesiology

Faculty of Law:

BERRYMAN, J.
BOGART, W. A.
BUSHNELL, I. S.
CARASCO, E. F.
CONKLIN, W.
ELMAN, B.
GOLD, N.
IRISH, M.
MAZER, B. M.
MENEZES, J. R.
MOON, R. J.
MURPHY, P. T.
STEWART, G. R.
WEST, J. L.
WILSON, L. C.
WYDRZYNSKI, C. J.

Faculty of Science

(Some professors are also attached to the Faculty of Engineering)

AL-AASM, I. S., Earth Sciences
ANGLIN, P., Economics
AROCA, R., Chemistry and Biochemistry
ATKINSON, J. B., Physics
BANDYOPADHYAY, S., Computer Science
BARRON, R. M., Mathematics and Statistics
BAYLIS, W. E., Physics
BRITTEN, D. J., Mathematics and Statistics
CAMERON, W. S., Nursing
CARON, R. J., Mathematics and Statistics
CARTY, L., Nursing
CHANDNA, O. P., Mathematics and Statistics
CIBOROWSKI, J. J. H., Biological Sciences
COTTER, D. A., Biological Sciences
DRAKE, G. W., Physics
DRAKE, J. E., Chemistry and Biochemistry
FACKRELL, H. B., Biological Sciences
FAN, Y., Economics
FORTUNE, J. N., Economics
FROST, R. A., Computer Science
FUNG, K. Y., Mathematics and Statistics
GENCAY, R., Economics
GILLEN, W. J., Economics
GLASS, E. N., Physics
HAFFNER, G. D., Biological Sciences
HUDEC, P. P., Earth Sciences
KALONI, P. N., Mathematics and Statistics
KENT, R. D., Computer Science
LEMIRE, F. W., Mathematics and Statistics
LOEB, S. J., Chemistry and Biochemistry
LOVETT DOUST, J. N., Biological Sciences
LOVETT DOUST, L., Biological Sciences
MCCONKEY, J. W., Physics
MCDONALD, J. F., Mathematics and Statistics
MCINTOSH, J. M., Chemistry and Biochemistry
MACISAAC, H. J., Biological Sciences
MAEV, R. G., Physics
MUTUS, B., Chemistry and Biochemistry
PAUL, S. R., Mathematics and Statistics
SALE, P. F., Biological Sciences
SIMPSON, F., Earth Sciences
SMITH, T. E., Earth Sciences
STEPHAN, D. W., Chemistry and Biochemistry
STRICK, J. C., Economics
SUH, S. C., Economics
TAYLOR, N. F., Chemistry and Biochemistry
THOMAS, B. C., Nursing
THOMAS, D., Biological Sciences
TRACY, D. S., Mathematics and Statistics
TUREK, A., Earth Sciences
WARNER, A., Biological Sciences
WONG, C. S., Mathematics and Statistics
ZAMANI, N. G., Mathematics and Statistics

Odette School of Business Administration:

ANDIAPPAN, P.
ANEJA, Y. P.
ARMSTRONG-STASSEN, M.
BRILL, P. H.
CHANDRA, R.
DICKINSON, J. R.
FARIA, A. J.
FIELDS, M.
HUSSEY, R.
KANTOR, J.
LAM, W. P.
MORGAN, A.
OKECHUKU, C.
PUNNETT, B. J.
SINGH, J.
TEMPLER, A.
THACKER, J. W.
WITHANE, S.

FEDERATED UNIVERSITY

Assumption University: 400 Huron Church Rd, Windsor, ON; e-mail cbertrand@assumptionu.ca; Pres. Rev. U. E. PARÉ.

AFFILIATED COLLEGES

Canterbury College: 172 Patricia Rd, Windsor, ON; e-mail canter@uwindsor.ca; Prin. D. T. A. SYMONS.

Iona College: Sunset Ave, Windsor, ON; e-mail office@ionacollege.edu; Prin. Rev. D. G. GALSTON

UNIVERSITY OF WINNIPEG

515 Portage Ave, Winnipeg, MB R3B 2E9
Telephone: (204) 786-7811
Internet: www.uwinnipeg.ca

Founded 1871, univ. status 1967
controlled jtly by the Govt of Manitoba and the United Church of Canada
Language of instruction: English
Academic year: September to April

Chancellor: H. SANDFORD RILEY
Vice-Chancellor and Pres.: LLOYD AXWORTHY
Vice-Pres. for Academic Affairs: BRIAN STEVENSON
Vice-Pres. for Finance and Admin.: BILL BALAN
Vice-Pres. for Human Resources, Audit and Sustainability: LAUREL REPSKI
Vice-Pres. for Research and Int.: NEIL BESNER
Corporate Sec. and Gen. Counsel: VALERIE GILROY

Number of teachers: 330
Number of students: 9,394

DEANS

Faculty of Arts: DAVID FITZPATRICK
Faculty of Business and Economics: MICHAEL BENARROCH
Faculty of Continuing Education: ERIN STEWART
Faculty of Education: KEN MCCLUSKEY
Faculty of Science: RODNEY HANLEY
Faculty of Theology: JAMES CHRISTIE
The Collegiate: ROBERT BEND

PROFESSORS

ABD-EL-AZIZ, Chemistry
ABIZADEH, S., Economics
BAILEY, D. A., History
BASILEVSKY, A., Statistics
BECKER, G., Psychology
BOTTERILL, C., Sport Psychology
BRADBURY, H., Psychology
BROWN, J., History
BROWN, W., Economics
BURLEY, D., History
CARLYLE, W. J., Geography
CARTER, T., Geography
CHAN, F. Y., Business Computing
CHEAL, D. J., Sociology
CLARK, J., Psychology
CLOUTIS, E., Geography
DANNEFAER, S., Physics
DAY, P., Religious Studies
DONG, X.-Y., Economics
EVANS, M., English
FEHR, B., Psychology
FORBES, S., Biology
FRIESEN, K., Chemistry
GINSBERG, J., Mathematics
GOLDEN, M., Classics
GRANT, H., Economics
GRANZBERG, G., Anthropology
GREENHILL, P., Women's Studies
HARVEY, C. J., French Studies
HATHOUT, S., Geography
HOWLADER, H., Statistics
HUEBNER, J., Biology
IZYDORCZYK, Z., English
KERR, D. P., Physics
KHAN, R. A., Political Science
KOBES, R., Physics
KUNSTATTER, G., Physics
KYDON, D. W., Physics
LEHR, J., Geography
LEO, C., Political Science
MCCORMACK, A. R., History
MCCORMACK, R., History
MCDOUGALL, I., Classics
MCINTYRE, M., Psychology
MAYS, A., Education
MEADWELL, K., French Studies
MEIKLEJOHN, C., Anthropology
MILLS, A., Political Science, Anthropology
MOODIE, G. E. E., Biology
NNADI, J., French Studies
NODELMAN, P. M., English
NORTON, R., Psychology
NOVEK, J., Sociology
PARAMESWARAN, U., English
PEELING, J., Chemistry
PIP, E., Biology
POLYZOI, E., Education
RANNIE, W., Geography
ROCKMAN, G., Psychology
RODRIGUEZ, L., French
SCHAEFER, E., Psychology
SCOTT, G., Geography
SELWOOD, J., Geography
SPIGELMAN, M., Psychology
STANIFORTH, R., Biology
STONE, D. Z., History
STRUB, H., Psychology
TOMCHUK, E., Physics
TOMLINSON, G., Chemistry
VISELLI, S., French Studies
WIEGAND, M., Biology
WRIGHT, C., Political Science
YOUNG, R. J., History

ATTACHED INSTITUTES

Institute of Urban Studies: 515 Portage Ave, Winnipeg; e-mail ius@uwinnipeg.ca; internet www.uwinnipeg.ca/ius; Dir JINO DISTASIO; publ. *Canadian Journal of Urban Research*.

Menno Simons College: 515 Portage Ave, Winnipeg; e-mail msc@uwinnipeg.ca; Pres. EARL DAVEY

WESTERN UNIVERSITY OF CANADA

1151 Richmond St, London, ON N6A 3K7
Telephone: (519) 661-2111
E-mail: reg-admissions@uwo.ca
Internet: www.westernu.ca

Founded 1878
Language of instruction: English
Academic year: September to April

Chancellor: JOSEPH L. ROTMAN
Pres. and Vice-Chancellor: AMIT CHAKMA
Provost and Vice-Pres. for Academic Affairs: JANICE DEAKIN
Vice-Pres. for External Affairs: Dr KEVIN GOLDTHORP
Vice-Pres. for Research: JOHN CAPONE
Vice-Pres. for Resources and Operations: GITTA KULCZYCKI
Vice-Provost for Academic Programs and Students and Registrar: JOHN DOERKSEN
Vice-Provost for the School of Graduate and Postdoctoral Studies: LINDA MILLER
Univ. Librarian: JOYCE GARNETT

Library of 4,676,586 vols, 4,175,097 microforms, 83,507 ejournals, 6,862 print serials, 155 print subscriptions
Number of teachers: 1,408 full-time
Number of students: 31,243

Publications: *Alumni Gazette* (magazine, 3 a year), *Ivey Business Journal*, *Mediations*, *Medical Journal*, *Reflections*, *The Gazette*, *The President's Report*, *The Science Terrapin*, *Western News*, *Western Research Undergrad Journal*

DEANS

Don Wright Faculty of Music: BETTY ANNE YOUNKER
Faculty of Arts and Humanities: MICHAEL MILDE
Faculty of Education: VICKI SCHWEAN
Faculty of Engineering: ANDY HRYMAK
Faculty of Health Sciences: JIM WEESE
Faculty of Information and Media Studies: TOM CARMICHAEL
Faculty of Law: W. IAIN SCOTT
Faculty of Science: CHARMAINE DEAN
Faculty of Social Science: BRIAN TIMNEY
Richard Ivey School of Business: ROBERT KENNEDY
Schulich School of Medicine and Dentistry: MICHAEL STRONG

PROFESSORS

Faculty of Arts and Humanities (tel. (519) 661-3043; internet www.uwo.ca/arts):

ADAMS, S. J., English
BELL, J. L., Philosophy
BENTLEY, D. M. R., English
BRENNAN, S., Philosophy (Head)
BROWN, C. G., Classical Studies (Head)
BROWN, H., Philosophy
BRUSH, K., Visual Arts
CROWTHER, N. B., Classical Studies
DAVEY, F. W., English
DEMOPOULOS, W. G., Philosophy
ELLIOTT, B., Visual Arts
ESTERHAMMER, A., English, Modern Languages and Literatures
FALKENSTEIN, L., Philosophy
GEDALOF, A., Film Studies
GITTINGS, C., Film Studies (Head)
GOLDSCHLAGER, A. J., French
GRODEN, M. L., English
HARPER, W. L., Philosophy
HOFFMASTER, C. B., Philosophy
KNEALE, J. D., English (Head)
KREISWIRTH, M., English
LEE, A. M., Women's Studies (Head)
LENNON, T. M., Philosophy
LEONARD, J., English
LITTLEWOOD, A. R., Classical Studies
MAHON, P., Visual Arts (Head)
MARRAS, A., Philosophy
MAYNARD, P. L., Philosophy, Visual Arts
MURISON, L., Classical Studies
POOLE, R., English
PURDY, A., French
RAJAN, T., English
RANDALL, M., French
SOMERSET, J. A. B., English
TENNANT, J., French (Head)
THOMSON, C., French

Faculty of Education (tel. (519) 661-3182; internet www.uwo.ca/edu):

CUMMINGS, A.
DICKINSON, G. M.
LESCHIED, A.
MAJHANOVICH, S. E. W.
PEARSON, A. T.

Faculty of Engineering (tel. (519) 661-2128; internet www.eng.uwo.ca):

ADAMIAK, K., Electrical and Computer
BADDOUR, R. E., Civil and Environmental
BARTLETT, F. M. P., Civil and Environmental
BASSI, A., Chemical and Biochemical
BERRUTI, F., Dean's Office, Chemical and Biochemical
BRIENS, C. L., Chemical and Biochemical
DE LASA, H., Chemical and Biochemical
EL NAGGAR, H., Civil and Environmental
FLORYAN, J. M., Mechanical and Materials
GREASON, W. D., Electrical and Computer
HONG, H. P., Civil and Environmental
JIANG, J., Electrical and Computer
JOHNSON, J. A., Mechanical and Materials
JUTAN, A., Chemical and Biochemical
KARAMANEV, D., Chemical and Biochemical
KHAYAT, R. E., Mechanical and Materials
KNOPF, G. K., Mechanical and Materials
PATEL, R. V., Electrical and Computer
ROHANI, S., Chemical and Biochemical
SHANG, J. Q., Civil and Environmental
SHINOZAKI, D. M., Mechanical and Materials
SIDHU, T. S., Electrical and Computer
SIMONOVIĆ, S., Civil and Environmental
SINGH, A. V., Mechanical and Materials
VANFUL, E., Civil and Environmental
ZHU, J., Chemical and Biochemical

Faculty of Health Sciences (tel. (519) 661-4249; internet www.uwo.ca/fhs):

BAKA, R., Kinesiology
BELCASTRO, A. N., Kinesiology
BUCKOLZ, E., Kinesiology
CARRON, A. V., Kinesiology
DOYLE, P., Communication Sciences and Disorders
FORCHUK, C., Nursing
GARLAND, J., Physical Therapy
GOLDENBERG, D., Nursing
HALL, C. R., Kinesiology
IWASIW, C., Nursing
JAMIESON, D., Communication Sciences and Disorders
JOHNSON, C. S., Kinesiology
LASCHINGER, H., Nursing
LEMON, P., Kinesiology
MCWILLIAM, C., Nursing
MEIER, K. V., Kinesiology
MORROW, L. D., Kinesiology
MYERS, A. M., Kinesiology
NOBLE, E., Kinesiology
ORCHARD, C., Nursing (Head)
OVEREND, T., Physical Therapy (Head)
PATERSON, D. H., Kinesiology
PICHÉ, L. A., Kinesiology
SALMONI, A., Kinesiology (Head)
SEEWALD, R. C., Communication Sciences and Disorders
SEMOTIUK, D., Kinesiology
SUMSION, T., Occupational Therapy (Head)
TREVITHICK, J. R., Kinesiology
TRUJILLO, S., Health Sciences (Head)
VANDERVOORT, A. A., Physical Therapy
WATSON, R., Communication Sciences and Disorders (Head)
WEESE, W. J., Kinesiology

Faculty of Information and Media Studies (tel. (519) 661-3542; internet www.fims.uwo.ca):

BABE, R. E.
CRAVEN, T. C.
HARRIS, R. M.
PARR, J.
ROSS, C. L.
SPENCER, D.
VAUGHAN, L. Q.
WILKINSON, M. A.

Faculty of Law (tel. (519) 661-3346; internet www.law.uwo.ca):

BARTON, P. G.
BROWN, C.
EDGAR, T.
HOLLAND, W. H.
HOLLOWAY, I.
HOVIUS, B.
MCLAREN, R. H.
MERCER, P.
SOLOMON, R.
USPRICH, S. J.
WELLING, B.

Don Wright Faculty of Music (tel. (519) 661-2043; e-mail music@uwo.ca; internet www.music.uwo.ca):

BRACEY, J. P., Music Performance Studies
FISKE, H., Music Education
GRIER, J., Music History
HEARD, A., Theory and Composition
KOPROWSKI, P. P., Theory and Composition
MCKAY, J., Music Performance Studies (Head)
NOLAN, C., Theory and Composition (Head)
PARKS, R. S., Theory and Composition
TOFT, R. E., Music History (Head)
WOODFORD, P., Music Education (Head)

Faculty of Science (tel. (519) 661-3040; e-mail science@uwo.ca; internet www.uwo.ca/sci):

BAILEY, R., Biology
BAINES, K. M., Chemistry (Head)
BAIRD, N. C., Chemistry
BARRON, J. L., Computer Science
BATTISTA, J., Medical Biophysics (Head)
BAUER, M. A., Computer Science (Head)
BELLHOUSE, D. R., Statistical and Actuarial Sciences
BOIVIN, A., Mathematics
BRANDL, C., Biochemistry (Head)
CAMPBELL, K., Epidemiology and Biostatistics (Head)
CASS, F. P. A., Mathematics
CAVENEY, S., Biology
CORLESS, R. M., Applied Mathematics; Computer Science; Philosophy (Head, Applied Mathematics)
COTTAM, M. G., Physics and Astronomy
DAY, A. W., Biology
DEAN, P. A. W., Chemistry
DEBRUYN, J. R., Physics and Astronomy (Joint Head)
EATON, D. W. S., Earth Sciences
ELIAS, V. W., Applied Mathematics
ESSEX, G. C., Applied Mathematics
FENTON, M. B., Biology (Head)
FLORYAN, J. M., Applied Mathematics
GUTHRIE, J. P., Chemistry and Biochemistry
HEINICKE, A. G., Mathematics
HICOCK, S. R., Earth Sciences
HOCKING, W. K., Physics and Astronomy
HOLT, R. A., Physics and Astronomy
HUANG, Y., Chemistry
HUNER, N. P. A., Biology
JARDINE, J. F., Mathematics
JEFFREY, D. J., Applied Mathematics
JIN, J., Earth Sciences
JONES, B. L., Physics and Astronomy (Joint Head)
JÜRGENSEN, H., Computer Science
JUTAN, A., Applied Mathematics
KANE, R. M., Mathematics (Head)
KANG, C. Y., Biology
KERR, M. A., Chemistry
KHALKHALI, M., Mathematics
KOVAL, S. F., Earth Sciences, Microbiology and Immunology
KRISHNA, P., Biology
KULPERGER, R. J., Statistical and Actuarial Sciences

LACHANCE, M. A., Biology, Microbiology and Immunology
LAU, L. W. M., Physics and Astronomy
LEAIST, D. G., Chemistry
LEHMAN, M., Anatomy and Cell Biology (Head)
LENNARD, W. N., Physics and Astronomy
LIPSON, R. H., Chemistry
LONGSTAFFE, F. J., Earth Sciences
LUTFIYYA, H., Earth Sciences
MCKEON, D. G. C., Applied Mathematics
MCLEOD, A. I., Statistical and Actuarial Sciences
MCNEIL, J. N., Biology
MADHAVJI, J. W., Computer Science
MARTIN, R. R., Chemistry
MERCER, R. E., Computer Science
MILLAR, J. S., Biology
MILNES, P., Mathematics
MINÀC, J., Mathematics
MIRANSKY, V. A., Applied Mathematics
MITTLER, S., Physics and Astronomy
NESBITT, H. W., Earth Sciences (Head)
NORTON, P. R., Chemistry
PAYNE, N. C., Chemistry
PLINT, A. G., Earth Sciences
PODESTA, R. B., Biology
POTTER, P., History of Medicine (Head)
PROVOST, S., Statistical and Actuarial Sciences
PUDDEPHATT, R. J., Chemistry
RAY, A. K., Applied Mathematics
RENNER, L. E., Mathematics
RILEY, D. M., Mathematics
ROHANI, S., Applied Mathematics
ROSNER, S. D., Physics and Astronomy
RYLETT, R. J., Physiology and Pharmacology (Head)
SECCO, R. A., Earth Sciences
SHAM, T. K., Chemistry
SHAW, G. S., Biochemistry and Chemistry
SHOESMITH, D. W., Chemistry
SICA, R. J., Physics and Astronomy
SINGH, M. R., Physics and Astronomy
SINGH, S. M., Biology
STANFORD, D. A., Statistical and Actuarial Sciences
STILLMAN, M. J., Chemistry
TRICK, C. G., Biology
USSELMAN, M. C., Chemistry
VALVANO, M., Microbiology and Immunology (Head)
WATT, S., Computer Science
WEEDON, A. C., Chemistry
WORKENTIN, M. S., Chemistry
WREN, J. C., Chemistry
YU, P., Applied Mathematics
YU, S., Computer Science
ZHANG, K., Computer Science
ZINKE-ALLMANG, M., Physics and Astronomy

Faculty of Social Science (tel. (519) 661-2053; internet www.ssc.uwo.ca):

ABELSON, D., American Studies (Joint Head)
ABELSON, D., Political Science (Head)
ALLAHAR, A., Sociology
ALLEN, N., Psychology
ASHMORE, P. E., Geography
AVERY, D. H., History
AVISON, W. R., Sociology
BEAUJOT, R. P., Sociology
BHATIA, K. B., Economics
BOYER, R. S., Economics
BURGESS, D. F., Economics
CAIN, D. P., Psychology
CARROLL, M., Sociology
CHEN, X., Psychology
CHHEM, R. K., Anthropology
CLARK, S., Sociology
CODE, W. R., Geography
CONNIDIS, I. A., Sociology
CÔTE, J. E., Sociology
CREIDER, C., Linguistics (Joint Head)
CREIDER, C. A., Anthropology (Head)
CYBULSKI, J. S., Anthropology
DARNELL, R., First Nations Studies (Joint Head)
DAVENPORT, P., Economics
DAVIES, J. B., Economics
ELLIS, C., Anthropology
EMERY, G., History
ESSAS, V., Psychology
FISHER, W. A., Psychology
FLEMING, K., Management and Organizational Studies (Head)
FLEMING, M., Political Science
FORSTER, B., History (Head)
GARDINER, M., Sociology
GOODALE, M., Psychology
GRABB, E. G., Sociology
GREEN, M. B., Geography
HAMPSON, E., Psychology
HARSHMAN, R., Psychology
HEAP, D., Linguistics (Joint Head)
HELE, K., First Nations Studies (Joint Head)
HERNANDEZ-SAENZ, L. M., Latin American Studies (Head)
HEWITT, W. E., Sociology
JOHNSTON, A., American Studies (Joint Head)
KATZ, A. N., Psychology
KAVALIERS, M., Psychology
KELLOW, M., International Relations (Head)
KING, R. H., Geography
KNIGHT, J., Economics
KUIPER, N. A., Psychology
LUCKMAN, B. H., Geography
LUPKER, S. J., Psychology
MCBEAN, G., Geography, Political Science
MCDOUGALL, J. N., Political Science
MCQUILLAN, K., Sociology
MCRAE, K., Psychology
MARTIN, R. A., Psychology
MAXIM, P. S., Sociology
MEYER, J. P., Psychology
MOLTO, J. E., Anthropology
MORAN, G., Psychology
NEUFELD, R. W. J., Psychology
OLSON, J. M., Psychology
OSSENKOPP, K.-P., Psychology (Head)
PAUNONEN, S. V., Psychology
PEREZ, A., Political Science
RIDDELL-DIXON, E., Political Science
ROBINSON, C. M. G. F., Economics
ROLLMAN, G. B., Psychology
RUSHTON, J. P., Psychology
SANCTON, A. B., Political Science
SELIGMAN, C., Psychology
SHATZMILLER, M., History
SHERRY, D., Psychology
SHRUBSOLE, D., Geography (Head)
SLIVINSKI, A., Economics (Head)
SMART, C. C., Geography
SORRENTINO, R. M., Psychology
SPENCE, M. W., Anthropology
TIMNEY, B. N., Psychology
VERNON, P. A., Psychology
VERNON, R. A., Political Science
WANG, J., Geography
WHALLEY, J., Economics
WHITE, C., Anthropology
WHITE, J., Sociology (Head)
WHITEHEAD, P. C., Sociology
WINTROBE, R. S., Economics
YOUNG, R. A., Political Science

Richard Ivey School of Business (tel. (519) 661-3485; e-mail info@ivey.uwo.ca; internet www.ivey.uwo.ca):

ATHANASSAKOS, G.
BEAMISH, P. W.
BELL, P. C.
CONKLIN, D. W.
DAWAR, N.
DEUTSCHER, T. H.
FISHER, R. J.
FOERSTER, S. R.
GANDZ, J.
HARDY, K. G.
HATCH, J. E.
HENDRICKS, K. B.
HIGGINS, C. A.
HOWELL, J. M.
KALYMON, B.
KONRAD, A. M.
ROTHSTEIN, M. G.
SCHAAN, J. L.
SHACKEL, D. S. J.
VAN DEN BOSCH, M. B.
WHITE, R. W.
WILSON, J. G.
WYNANT, L.

Schulich School of Medicine and Dentistry (tel. (519) 661-3459; internet www.med.uwo.ca):

ADAMS, P. C., Medicine
ALBORES, A., Physiology and Pharmacology
ANG, L. C., Pathology
ARNOLD, J. M. O., Medicine
AVISON, W. R., Paediatrics; Epidemiology and Biostatistics
BAILEY, S. I., Surgery
BALL, E. H., Biochemistry
BANTING, D. W., Dentistry
BARR, R. M., Medicine
BATTISTA, J. J., Oncology
BAUMAN, G., Oncology (Head)
BELL, D. A., Medicine
BEND, J. R., Pathology
BERTRAND, M. A., Obstetrics and Gynaecology
BLAKE, P. G., Medicine
BOLLI, P., Medicine
BORRIE, M. J., Medicine
BOUGHNER, D. R., Medicine
BOURNE, R. B., Surgery
BRANDL, C. J., Biochemistry
BRIDGER, W. A., Biochemistry
BROWN, J. B., Family Medicine
BROWN, J. D., Clinical Neurological Sciences
BROWN, J. E., Medicine
CANHAM, P. B., Medical Biophysics
CECHETTO, D. F., Anatomy and Cell Biology
CERNOVSKY, Z. Z., Psychiatry
CHACONAS, G., Biochemistry
CHAMBERS, A. F., Oncology
CHAN, F. P., Anatomy and Cell Biology
CHANG, D. C. H., Anaesthesia and Perioperative Medicine (Head)
CHERIAN, G. M., Pathology
CHHEM, R. K., Diagnostic Radiology and Nuclear Medicine
CIRIELLO, J., Physiology and Pharmacology
CLARK, W. F., Medicine
COLCLEUGH, R. G., Surgery
COOK, M. A., Physiology and Pharmacology
COOK, R. A., Biochemistry
COOKE, J. D., Physiology and Pharmacology
CORDY, P. E., Medicine
CUNNINGHAM, I. A., Diagnostic Radiology and Nuclear Medicine
DALEY, T. D., Pathology
DEKABAN, G. A., Microbiology and Immunology
DELOVITCH, T. L., Microbiology and Immunology
DENSTEDT, J. D., Surgery (Head)
DIXON, S. J., Physiology and Pharmacology
DONNER, A. P., Epidemiology and Biostatistics
DREYER, J. F., Medicine
DRIEDGER, A. A., Medicine
DROST, D. J., Diagnostic Radiology and Nuclear Medicine
DUNN, S. D., Biochemistry
EDMONDS, M. W., Medicine
ELLIS, C. G., Medical Biophysics
FEIGHTNER, J. W., Family Medicine
FELDMAN, R. D., Medicine
FENSTER, A., Diagnostic Radiology and Nuclear Medicine

FERGUSON, G. G., Clinical Neurological Sciences
FINNIE, K. J. C., Medicine
FISHER, W. A., Medicine
FISMAN, S. N., Psychiatry (Head)
FLINTOFF, W., Microbiology and Immunology
FLUMERFELT, B. A., Anatomy and Cell Biology
FOWLER, P. J., Surgery
FRAHER, L. J., Medicine
FREEMAN, T., Family Medicine (Head)
FREWEN, T. C., Paediatrics (Head)
GAGNON, R., Obstetrics and Gynaecology
GARCIA, B. M., Pathology (Head)
GEORGE, C. F. P., Medicine
GERACE, R. V., Medicine
GILBERT, J. J., Pathology
GIROTTI, M. J., Surgery
GIRVAN, D. P., Surgery
GLOOR, G. B., Biochemistry
GOODALE, M. A., Physiology and Pharmacology
GRANT, C. W., Biochemistry
GUENTHER, L. C., Medicine
GUPTA, M. A., Psychiatry
HAASE, P., Anatomy and Cell Biology
HACHINSKI, V., Clinical Neurological Sciences
HAHN, A. F. G., Clinical Neurological Sciences
HAMMOND, J. R., Physiology and Pharmacology
HAMPSON, E., Psychiatry
HAN, V. K. M., Paediatrics
HANIFORD, D. B., Biochemistry
HARRIS, K. A., Surgery
HAYES, K. C., Physical Medicine and Rehabilitation
HEGELE, R. A., Medicine
HENNING, J. L., Physiology and Pharmacology
HERBERT, C. P., Family Medicine
HILL, D. J., Medicine
HOBBS, B. B., Diagnostic Radiology and Nuclear Medicine
HODSMAN, A. B., Medicine
HOFFMASTER, C. B., Family Medicine
HOLLIDAY, R. L., Surgery
HOLLOMBY, D. J., Medicine (Head)
HOOPER, P., Ophthalmology (Head)
HORE, J., Physiology and Pharmacology
HOWARD, J. M., Paediatrics
HRAMIAK, I. M., Medicine
HRYCYSHYN, A. W., Anatomy and Cell Biology
HUANG, G., Physiology and Pharmacology
HUFF, M. W., Medicine
HUMEN, D. P., Medicine
HUNTER, G. K., Dentistry
HURST, L. N., Surgery
JAFFE, P. G., Psychiatry
JAIN, S. C., Psychiatry
JAMIESON, D. G., Medicine
JEVNIKAR, A. M., Medicine
JOHNSON, C., Medicine
JOHNSON, K. C., Epidemiology and Biostatistics
JONES, D. L., Physiology and Pharmacology
JUNG, J. H., Paediatrics
KANG, C. Y., Microbiology and Immunology
KARLIK, S. J., Diagnostic Radiology and Nuclear Medicine
KARMAZYN, M., Physiology and Pharmacology
KENNEDY, T. G., Physiology and Pharmacology
KIDDER, G. M., Physiology and Pharmacology
KIERNAN, J. A., Anatomy and Cell Biology
KING, G. J., Surgery
KIRK, M. E., Pathology
KLEIN, G. J., Medicine
KOGON, S. L., Dentistry
KOREN, G., Paediatrics; Medicine
KOROPATNICK, D. J., Oncology
KOSTUK, W. J., Medicine
KRONICK, J. B., Medicine
KVIETYS, P. R., Physiology
LAIRD, D. W., Anatomy and Cell Biology
LAJOIE, G., Biochemistry
LAMPE, H. B., Otolaryngology
LANNIGAN, R., Microbiology and Immunology
LEASA, D. J., Medicine
LEE, D. H., Diagnostic Radiology and Nuclear Medicine
LEE, T. Y., Diagnostic Radiology and Nuclear Medicine
LEFCOE, M. S., Diagnostic Radiology and Nuclear Medicine
LELLA, J. W., History of Medicine
LEUNG, L. W. S., Clinical Neurological Sciences
LEWIS, J. F., Medicine
LINDSAY, R. M., Medicine
LO, T. C., Biochemistry
LOWNIE, S., Clinical Neurological Sciences (Joint Head)
MCCARTHY, G. M., Dentistry
MCCORMACK, D. G., Medicine
MCDONALD, J. W., Medicine
MCFADDEN, D. G., Microbiology and Immunology
MCFADDEN, R. G., Medicine
MCGRATH, P. A., Paediatrics
MCKENZIE, F. N., Surgery
MCLACHLAN, R. S., Clinical Neurological Sciences
MACRAE, D. L., Otolaryngology (Joint Head)
MAO, Y., Epidemiology and Biostatics
MAROTTA, J. T., Clinical Neurological Sciences
MENDONCA, J., Psychiatry
MENKIS, A. H., Surgery
MILLWARD, S. F., Diagnostic Radiology and Nuclear Medicine
MORRIS, V. L., Microbiology
MUIRHEAD, J. M., Medicine
MURKIN, J. M., Anaesthesia and Perioperative Medicine
NARAYANAN, N., Physiology and Pharmacology
NATALE, R., Obstetrics and Gynaecology
NEUFELD, R. W. J., Psychiatry
NICHOLSON, R. L., Diagnostic Radiology and Nuclear Medicine
NICOLLE, D. A., Opthalmology
NISKER, J. A., Obstetrics and Gynaecology
NORMAN, R. M. G., Psychiatry
NORRIS, J. W., Clinical Neurological Sciences
NOVICK, R. J., Surgery
PARNES, L. S., Otolaryngology
PATERSON, N. A. M., Medicine
PAYTON, K. B., Medicine
PERSAD, E., Psychiatry
PETERS, T. M., Diagnostic Radiology and Nuclear Medicine
PETERSEN, N. O., Biochemistry
POTTER, P. M. J., History of Medicine and Science
POZNANSKY, M. J., Biochemistry
PRABHAKARAN, V. M., Biochemistry
PRATO, F. S., Diagnostic Radiology and Nuclear Medicine
RALLEY, F. E., Anaesthesia and Perioperative Medicine
RALPH, E. D., Medicine
RANKIN, R. N., Diagnostic Radiology and Nuclear Medicine (Head)
REID, G., Microbiology and Immunology
REYNOLDS, R. P., Medicine
RICE, G. P. A., Clinical Neurological Sciences
RICHARDSON, B. S., Obstetrics and Gynaecology (Head)
RIEDER, M J., Paediatrics
RODGER, N. W., Medicine
RORABECK, C. H., Surgery
ROTH, J. H., Surgery
RUTLEDGE, F. S., Medicine
RUTT, B. K., Diagnostic Radiology and Nuclear Medicine
RYLETT, R. J., Physiology and Pharmacology
SANDHU, H. S., Dentistry (Head)
SANGSTER, J. F., Family Medicine
SHAW, G. S., Biochemistry
SHERAR, M. D., Oncology
SHKRUM, M. J., Pathology
SHOUKRI, M. M., Epidemiology and Biostatics
SHUM, D. T. W., Pathology
SILCOX, J. A., Obstetrics and Gynaecology
SIMS, S. M., Physiology and Pharmacology
SINGH, B., Microbiology and Immunology
SINGHAL, S. K., Microbiology and Immunology
SOLIMAN, G. L., Medicine
SPENCE, J. D., Clinical Neurological Sciences
STEWART, M. A., Family Medicine
STILLER, C. R., Medicine
STRONG, M. J., Clinical Neurological Sciences (Joint Head)
TAVES, D. H., Diagnostic Radiology and Nuclear Medicine
TEASELL, R. W., Physical Medicine and Rehabilitation (Head)
TEPPERMAN, B. L., Physiology and Pharmacology
THOMPSON, R. T., Diagnostic Radiology and Nuclear Medicine
TRICK, C. G., Microbiology and Immunology
TYML, K., Medical Biophysics
URBAIN, J. L. C. P., Diagnostic Radiology and Nuclear Medicine
VALVANO, M. A., Microbiology and Immunology
VAN DYK, J., Oncology
VILIS, T., Physiology and Pharmacology
VILOS, G., Obstetrics and Gynaecology
VINGILIS, E. R., Family Medicine
WALL, W. J., Surgery
WEAVER, L. C., Physiology and Pharmacology
WESTON, W., Family Medicine
WEXLER, D., Medicine
WHITE, D. J., Surgery
WILLIAMSON, P. C., Psychiatry
WILLIS, N. R., Ophthalmology
WILSON, J. X., Physiology and Pharmacology
WISENBERG, G., Medicine
WRIGHT, E., Otolaryngology (Joint Head)
WRIGHT, J. G., Epidemiology and Biostatistics
WYSOCKI, G. P., Pathology
YANG, K., Obstetrics and Gynaecology
YEE, R., Medicine
YOUNG, G. B., Clinical Neurological Sciences
ZAMIR, M., Medical Biophysics
ZHONG, Z., Surgery

AFFILIATED INSTITUTIONS

Brescia University College: 1285 Western Rd, London, ON N6G 1H2; e-mail brescia@uwo.ca; internet www.uwo.ca/brescia; f. 1919; Prin. T. TOPIĆ

PROFESSORS

SNYDER, J., Philosophy
TOPIC, T., Anthropology

Huron University College: 1349 Western Rd, London, ON N6G 1H3; e-mail huron@uwo.ca; internet www.huronuc.on.ca; f. 1863; Prin. Dr R. LUMPKIN

PROFESSORS

BLOCKER, J. S., History
CRIMMINS, J. E., Political Science
HAMILTON, G., Theology
HYLAND, P., English

McCarthy, D. R., English
Read, C., History
Schachter, J. P., Philosophy
Xu, D., Economics

King University College: 266 Epworth Ave, London, ON N6A 2M3; e-mail kings@uwo.ca; internet www.uwo.ca/kings; f. 1912 (Seminary), 1955 (College); Prin. Dr Gerald Killan

PROFESSORS

Bahcheli, T., Political Science
Baruss, I., Psychology
Brown, H., Philosophy and Religious Studies
Brown, J., Social Work
Compton-Brouwer, R., History
Gorassini, D. R., Psychology
Harman, L., Sociology
Irving, A., Social Work
Killan, G., History
Kopinak, K., Sociology
Lella, J. W., Sociology
MacGregor, D., Sociology
O'Connor, T., Religious Studies
Paterson, G. H., English
Prieur, M. R., Religious Studies
Skinner, N. F., Psychology
Werstine, P., English

WILFRID LAURIER UNIVERSITY

75 University Ave, Waterloo, ON N2L 3C5
Telephone: (519) 884-1970
Internet: www.wlu.ca
Founded 1911, fmrly Waterloo Lutheran University, current name adopted 1973
State control
Language of instruction: English
Academic year: September to April (2 terms)
Chancellor: Bob Rae
Pres. and Vice-Chancellor: Dr Max Blouw
Vice-Pres. for Academic Affairs: Dr Deborah MacLatchy
Vice-Pres. for Finance and Admin.: Jim Butler
Registrar: Dr John Metcalfe
Librarian and Archivist: Sharon Brown
Number of teachers: 838 (410 full-time, 428 part-time)
Number of students: 14,750 (12,700 full-time, 2,050 part-time)
Publications: *Anthropologica* (2 a year), *Canadian Bulletin of Medical History/Bulletin Canadien D'histoire de la Médecine* (2 a year), *Canadian Social Work Review/Revue Canadienne de Service Social* (2 a year), *Dialogue: Canadian Philosophical Review/Revue Canadienne de Philosophie* (4 a year), *Leisure/Loisive* (4 a year), *Studies in Religion/Sciences Religieuses* (4 a year), *Toronto Journal of Theology* (4 a year), *Topia: A Canadian Journal of Cultural Studies* (2 a year)

DEANS

Faculty of Arts and Science: Dr Robert Campbell
Faculty of Graduate Studies: Dr Adele Reinhartz
Faculty of Music: Dr Charles Morrison
Faculty of Science: Dr Arthur Szabo
Faculty of Social Work: Prof. Luke Fusco
School of Business and Economics: Dr Scott Carson
Waterloo Lutheran Seminary: Dr Richard Crossman

YORK UNIVERSITY

4700 Keele St, Toronto, ON M3J 1P3
Telephone: (416) 736-2100
Internet: www.yorku.ca
Founded 1959, ind. 1965
public control
Academic year: September to April
Chancellor: Roy McMurtry
Pres. and Vice-Chancellor: Mamdouh Shoukri
Pres. and CEO York Univ. Foundation and Vice-Pres. (Dev): Paul Marcus
Vice-Pres. for Academics: Sheila Embleton
Vice-Pres. for Finance and Admin.: Gary Brewer
Vice-Pres. for Research and Innovation: Stan Shapson
Vice-Pres. for Students and Alumni: Robert J. Tiffin
Univ. Sec. and Gen. Counsel: Harriet Lewis
Number of teachers: 1,415 (full-time)
Number of students: 52,290
Publications: *Profiles* (4 a year), *York Gazette* (37 a year)

DEANS

Faculty of Education: Alice Pitt
Faculty of Environmental Studies: Barbara Rahder (acting)
Faculty of Fine Arts: Barbra Sellers-Young
Faculty of Graduate Studies: Douglas Peers
Faculty of Liberal Arts and Professional Studies: Martin Singer
Faculty of Pure and Applied Science: Gillian E. Wu
Glendon College: Kenneth McRoberts (Principal)
Osgoode Hall Law School: Patrick J. Monahan
Schulich School of Business: Dezso Horvath

PROFESSORS

Faculty of Education:

Britzman, D. P.
Bunch, G.
Ewoldt, C.
Heshusius, L.
Piper, T. C.
Rogers, P. K.
Shapson, S.

Faculty of Environmental Studies:

Bell, D. V. J.
Daly, G. P.
Found, W. C.
Greer-Wootten, B.
Homenuck, H. P. M.
Spence, E. S.
Victor, P. A.
Wekerle, G. R.
Wilkinson, P. F.

Faculty of Fine Arts:

Bieler, T., Visual Arts
Métraux, G. P. R., Visual Arts
Morris, P., Film and Video
Rubin, D., Theatre
Sankaran, T., Music
Tenney, J., Music
Thurlby, M., Visual Arts
Tomcik, A., Visual Arts
Whiten, T., Visual Arts

Faculty of Liberal Arts and Professional Studies:

Abramson, M., Mathematics and Statistics
Adelman, H., Philosophy
Anisef, P., Sociology
Appelbaum, E., Economics
Armstrong, C., History
Armstrong, P., Sociology
Arthur, R. G., Humanities
Axelrod, P., Social Science
Bartel, H., Administrative Studies
Bayefsky, A. F., Political Science
Beer, F. F., English
Bialystok, E., Psychology
Birbalsingh, F. M., English
Blum, A. F., Sociology
Bordessa, R., Geography
Brown, M. G., Humanities
Burns, R. G., Mathematics and Statistics
Butler, G. R., Humanities
Callaghan, B., English
Carley, J., English
Chambers, D., Physical Education
Code, L. B., Philosophy
Cohen, D., English
Cotnam, J., French Studies
Cowles, M. P., Psychology
Cuff, R. D., History
Cummings, M. J., English
Danziger, L., Economics
Darroch, A. G. L., Sociology
Davies, D. I., Social Science and Sociology
Davis, C. A., Physical Education
Dewitt, D. B., Political Science
Donnenfeld, S., Economics
Dosman, E. J., Political Science
Dow, A. S., Mathematics and Statistics
Drache, D., Political Science
Drost, H., Economics
Egnal, M. M., History
Ehrlich, S. L., Languages, Literatures and Linguistics
Ellenwood, W. R., English
Embleton, S. M., Languages, Literatures and Linguistics
Endler, N. S., Psychology
Faas, E., Humanities
Fancher, R. E., Psychology
Fichman, M., Humanities
Fleming, S. J., Psychology
Fletcher, F. J., Political Science
Flett, G. L., Psychology
Fowler, B. H., Physical Education
Freeman, D. B., Geography
Frolic, M. B., Political Science
Gill, S., Political Science
Gledhill, N., Physical Education
Gray, P. T., Humanities
Grayson, J. P., Sociology
Green, B. S., Sociology
Green, L. J. M., Philosophy
Greenberg, L., Psychology
Greenglass, E. R., Psychology
Greer-Wootten, B., Geography
Guiasu, S., Mathematics and Statistics
Guy, G. R., Languages, Literatures and Linguistics
Haberman, A., Humanities
Harries-Jones, P., Anthropology
Harris, L. R., Psychology
Hattiangadi, J. N., Philosophy
Heidenreich, C., Geography
Hellman, J., Political Science and Social Science
Hellman, S., Political Science
Herren, M., Classics and Humanities
Hill, A. R., Geography
Hobson, D. B., Humanities
Hoffman, R. C., History
Hruska, K. C., Mathematics and Statistics
Innes, C., English
Irvine, W. D., History
Jarvie, I. C., Philosophy
Kanya-Forstner, A. S., History
Kaplan, H., Political Science and Social Science
Kater, M. H., History
Katz, E., Economics
King, R. E., Languages, Literatures and Linguistics
Kleiner, I., Mathematics and Statistics
Kochman, S. O., Mathematics and Statistics
Kohn, P. M., Psychology
Landa, J. T., Economics
Lanphier, C. M., Sociology
Lennox, J. W., English
Levy, J., Nursing
Leyton-Brown, D., Political Science
Lightman, B. V., Humanities
Lipsig-Mummé, C., Social Science
Lovejoy, P. E., History
Luxton, M., Social Science
McRoberts, K. H., Political Science

MADRAS, N. N., Mathematics and Statistics
MAHANEY, W. C., Geography
MAIDMAN, M. P., History
MALLIN, S. B., Philosophy
MANN, S. N., History
MASON, S. N., Humanities
MASSAM, B. H., Geography
MASSAM, H., Mathematics and Statistics
MENDELSOHN, D. J., Languages, Literatures and Linguistics
MOUGEON, R., French Studies
MULDOON, M. E., Mathematics and Statistics
MURDIE, R. A., Geography
NAGATA, J., Anthropology
NELLES, H. V., History
NOBLE, D., Social Science
NORCLIFFE, G. B., Geography
NORTH, L., Political Science
O'BRIEN, G. L., Mathematics and Statistics
OKADA, R., Psychology
OLIN, P., Mathematics and Statistics
OLIVER, P. N., History
ONO, H., Psychology
PANITCH, L., Political Science
PELLETIER, J. M., Mathematics and Statistics
PEPLER, D. J., Psychology
PLOURDE, C., Economics
POLKA, B., Humanities
POPE, R. W. F., Languages, Literatures and Linguistics
PROMISLOW, S. D., Mathematics and Statistics
PYKE, S., Psychology
RADFORD, J. P., Geography
REGAN, D. M., Psychology
RENNIE, D. L., Psychology
ROBBINS, S. G., Physical Education
RODMAN, M. C., Anthropology
ROGERS, N. C. T., History
SALISBURY, T., Mathematics and Statistics
SAUL, J. S., Social Science
SHANKER, S. G., Philosophy
SHTEIR, A. B., Humanities
SHUBERT, A., History
SILVERMAN, M., Anthropology
SIMMONS, H., Political Science
SIMPSON-HOUSLEY, P., Geography
SMITHIN, J. N., Economics
SOLITAR, D., Mathematics and Statistics
STAGER, P., Psychology
STEINBACH, M. J., Psychology
STEPRANS, J., Mathematics and Statistics
SUBTELNY, O., History and Political Science
THOLEN, W., Mathematics and Statistics
UNRAU, J. P., English
VAN ESTERIK, P., Anthropology
WAKABAYASHI, B. T., History
WATSON, W. S., Mathematics and Statistics
WEISS, A. I., Computer Science and Mathematics
WHITAKER, R., Political Science
WHITELEY, W. J., Mathematics and Statistics
WILSON, B. A., Humanities
WONG, M., Mathematics and Statistics
WOOD, J. D., Geography
WU, J., Mathematics and Statistics

Faculty of Pure and Applied Science:
ALDRIDGE, K. D., Earth and Atmospheric Science
ARJOMANDI, E., Computer Science
BARTEL, N. H., Physics and Astronomy
BOHME, D. K., Chemistry
CAFARELLI, E. D., Physical Education
CALDWELL, J. J., Natural Science, Physics and Astronomy
CANNON, W. H., Physics and Astronomy
COLMAN, B., Biology
COUKELL, M. B., Biology
DAREWYCH, J. W., Physics and Astronomy
DAVEY, K. G., Biology
DE ROBERTIS, M. M., Physics and Astronomy
DYMOND, P. W., Computer Science
FENTON, M. B., Biology and Environmental Science
FILSETH, S. V., Chemistry
FORER, A., Biology
FREEDHOFF, H. S., Physics and Astronomy
GLEDHILL, N., Physical Education
GOODINGS, J. M., Chemistry
HARRIS, G. W., Chemistry
HASTIE, D. R., Chemistry
HEATH, I. B., Biology
HEDDLE, J. A. M., Biology
HILLIKER, A. J., Biology
HOLLOWAY, C. E., Chemistry
HOOD, D. A., Physical Education
HOPKINSON, A. C., Chemistry
HORBATSCH, M., Physics and Astronomy
INNANEN, K. A., Physics and Astronomy
JARRELL, R. A., Natural Science
JARVIS, G. T., Earth and Atmospheric Science
KONIUK, R., Physics and Astronomy
LAFRAMBOISE, J. G., Physics and Astronomy
LEE-RUFF, E., Chemistry
LEVER, A. B. P., Chemistry
LEZNOFF, C. C., Chemistry
LICHT, L. E., Biology and Environmental Science
LIU, J. W. H., Computer Science
LOGAN, D. M., Biology and Natural Science
LOUGHTON, B. G., Biology
MCCALL, M., Physics and Astronomy
MCCONNELL, J. C., Earth and Atmospheric Science
MCQUEEN, D. J., Biology and Environmental Science
MALTMAN, K. R., Mathematics and Statistics
MILLER, J. R., Physics and Astronomy
PACKER, L. D. M., Biology
PEARLMAN, R. E., Biology
PRINCE, R. H., Physics and Astronomy
RUDOLPH, J., Chemistry
SALEUDDIN, A. S. M., Biology
SAPP, J. A., Biology
SHEPHERD, G. G., Earth and Atmospheric Science
SIU, K. W. M., Chemistry
SMYLIE, D. E., Earth and Atmospheric Science
STAUFFER, A. D., Mathematics and Statistics, Physics and Astronomy
STEEL, C. G., Biology
TAYLOR, P. A., Earth and Atmospheric Science
TOURLAKIS, G., Computer Science
TSOTSOS, J. K., Computer Science
WEBB, R. A., Biology

Osgoode Hall Law School:
ARTHURS, H. W.
BROOKS, W. N.
GEVA, B.
GRAY, R. J. S.
HASSON, R. A.
HATHAWAY, J. C.
HOGG, P. W.
HUTCHINSON, A. C.
MCCAMUS, J. D.
MANDEL, M. G.
MONAHAN, P. J.
MOSSMAN, M. J.
RAMSAY, I. D.
SALTER, R. L.
SLATTERY, B.
VAVER, D.
WATSON, G. D.
WILLIAMS, S. A.
ZEMANS, F. H.

Schulich School of Business:
BURKE, R. J., Organizational Behaviour, Industrial Relations
BUZACOTT, J., Management Science
COOK, W. D., Management Science
CRAGG, A. W., Business Ethics
DERMER, J. D., Policy
FENWICK, I. D., Marketing
HEELER, R. M., Marketing
HORVATH, D., Policy
LITVAK, I. A., Policy
MCKELLAR, J., Real Property Development
MCMILLAN, C. J., Policy
MORGAN, G. H., Organizational Behaviour, Industrial Relations
OLIVER, C. E., Organizational Behaviour, Industrial Relations
PAN, Y., International Business
PETERSON, R., Policy
PRISMAN, E., Finance
ROBERTS, G. S., Finance
ROSEN, L. S., Accounting
THOMPSON, D. N., Marketing
TRYFOS, P., Management Science
WHEELER, D. C., Business and Sustainability
WILSON, H. T., Policy
WOLF, B. M., Economics

Glendon College:
ABELLA, I. M., History
ALCOCK, J., Psychology
BAUDOT, A., French Studies
DOOB, P. B., English
GENTLES, I. J., History
HORN, M. S. D., History
KIRSCHBAUM, S. J., Political Science
KLEIN-LATAUD, C., Translation
MAHANT, E., Political Science
MORRIS, R. N., Sociology
MOYAL, G. J. D., Philosophy
OLSHEN, B. N., English and Multidisciplinary Studies
ONDAATJE, P. M., English
SHAND, G. B., English
TATILON, C., French Studies
TWEYMAN, S., Philosophy
WALLACE, R. S., English
WHITFIELD, A., Translation

ATTACHED INSTITUTES

Canadian Centre for German and European Studies: Kaneff Tower, 7th Fl., York Univ., 4700 Keele St, Toronto, ON M3J 1P3; e-mail ccges@yorku.ca; internet ccges.apps01.yorku.ca/wp.

Centre for Atmospheric Chemistry: 006 Steacie Science, York Univ., 4700 Keele St, Toronto, ON M3J 1P3; tel. (416) 736-5410; e-mail cac@yorku.ca; internet cac.yorku.ca; Dir Assoc. Prof. ROBERT MCLAREN.

Centre for Feminist Research: 6th Floor, York Research Tower, York Univ., 4700 Keele St, Toronto, ON M3J 1P3; e-mail cfr@yorku.ca; Dir E. DUA.

Centre for Health Studies: 214 York Lanes, York Univ., Toronto, ON M3J 1P3; Dir G. D. FELDBERG.

Centre for International and Security Studies: 375 York Lanes, York Univ., 4700 Keele St, Toronto, ON M3J 1P3; e-mail dmutimer@yorku.ca; Dir D. B. DEWITT.

Centre for Jewish Studies: 260 Vanier College, York Univ., 4700 Keele St, Toronto, ON M3J 1P3; Dir M. G. BROWN.

Centre for Practical Ethics: 102 McLaughlin, York Univ., 4700 Keele St, Toronto, ON M3J 1P3; Dir D. SHUGARMAN.

Centre for Public Law and Public Policy: 435 Osgoode, York Univ., 4700 Keele St, Toronto, ON M3J 1P3; e-mail ycppl@yorku.ca; Dir P. J. MONAHAN.

Centre for Refugee Studies: 322 York Lanes, York Univ., 4700 Keele St, Toronto, ON M3J 1P3; e-mail crs@yorku.ca; Dir P. PENZ.

Centre for Research in Earth and Space Science: 249 Petrie Science Bldg, York Univ., 4700 Keele St, Toronto, ON M3J 1P3; Dir G. SHEPHERD.

Centre for Research on Latin America and the Caribbean: 240 York Lanes, York Univ., Toronto, ON M3J 1P3; e-mail cerlac@yorku.ca; Dir V. PATRONI.

Centre for Research on Work and Society: 6th Floor, York Research Tower, York Univ., Toronto, ON M3J 1P3; e-mail crws@yorku.ca; internet www.crws.yorku.ca; Co-Dir LEAH VOSKO; Co-Dir MARK THOMAS; Co-Dir STEPHANIE ANN ROSS.

Centre for the Study of Computers in Education: S869 Ross, York Univ., 4700 Keele St, Toronto, ON M3J 1P3; Dir R. D. OWSTON.

Centre for Vision Research: Lassonde Building, York Univ., 4700 Keele St, Toronto, ON M3J 1P3; internet cvr.yorku.ca; Dir Dr. LAURENCE HARRIS; Admin. TERESA MANINI.

Institute for Social Research: 5075 TEL Bldg, York Univ., 4700 Keele St, Toronto, ON M3J 1P3; tel. (416) 736-5061; e-mail isrnews@yorku.ca; internet www.isr.yorku.ca.

Jack and Mae Nathanson Centre on Transnational Human Rights, Crime and Security: 3067 Ignat Kaneff Bldg, Osgoode Hall Law School, York Univ., 4700 Keele St, Toronto, ON M3J 1P3; tel. (416) 736-5586; e-mail nathansoncentre@osgoode.yorku.ca; internet nathanson.osgoode.yorku.ca; Dir F. TANGUAY-RENAUD.

Joint Centre for Asia Pacific Studies: 270 York Lanes, York Univ., 4700 Keele St, Toronto, ON M3J 1P3; Dir B. FROLIC.

LaMarsh Centre for Research on Violence and Conflict Resolution: 217 York Lanes, York Univ., 4700 Keele St, Toronto, ON M3J 1P3; e-mail lamarsh@yorku.ca; Dir D. J. PEPLER.

Robarts Centre for Canadian Studies: 7th Fl., Kaneff Tower, York Univ., 4700 Keele St, Toronto, ON M3J 1P3; e-mail robarts@yorku.ca; Dir C. COATES.

York Centre for Applied Sustainability: 355 Lumbers, York Univ., 4700 Keele St, Toronto, ON M3J 1P3; Dir D. BELL

Schools of Art and Music

Alberta College of Art and Design: 1407 14th Ave NW, Calgary, AB T2N 4R3; tel. (403) 284-7600; e-mail admissions@acad.ca; internet www.acad.ab.ca; f. 1926; library: 28,578 vols and colln of 124,845 slides, 75 periodical titles; 100 teachers; 1,000 students; Pres. LANCE CARLSON.

Banff Centre: POB 1020, Banff, AB T1L 1H5; tel. (403) 762-6100; internet www.banffcentre.ca; f. 1933; offers programmes in arts (aboriginal arts, audio, press, new media, creative electronic environment, dance, media and visual arts, music, opera, theatre, writing, curatorial practice), leadership development, aboriginal leadership and management, mountain culture, environmental issues; Pres. and CEO MARY E. HOFSTETTER; Sr Vice-Pres. for Programming JOANNE MORROW; Vice-Pres. and CFO J. A. NUTT.

Conservatoire de Musique de Montréal: 4750 ave Henri-Julien, Montréal, QC H2T 2C8; tel. (514) 873-4031; e-mail cmm@mcc.gouv.qc.ca; internet www.mcc.gouv.ca/conservatoire/montreal.htm; f. 1942; 76 teachers; 340 students; library: 58,000 books and scores, 125 rare books, 20 MSS, 10,000 recordings and 80 periodicals; Dir ISOLDE LAGACÉ.

Conservatoire de Musique de Québec: 270 rue St-Amable, Québec, QC G1R 5G1; tel. (418) 643-2190; e-mail cmq@mcc.gouv.qc.ca; internet www.mcc.gouv.gc.ca/conservatoire/quebec.htm; f. 1944; library: 68,000 vols, recordings, scores and periodicals; 50 teachers; 250 students; Dir GUY CARMICHAEL.

Maritime Conservatory of Performing Arts: 6199 Chebucto Rd, Halifax, NS B3L 1K7; tel. (902) 423-6995; e-mail admin@maritimeconservatory.com; internet www.maritimeconservatory.com; f. 1887; 80 teachers; 1,200 students; Chair. WILLIAM WEBSTER.

Ontario College of Art and Design: 100 McCaul St, Toronto, ON M5T 1W1; tel. (416) 977-6000; internet www.ocad.on.ca; f. 1876; library: 24,000 vols, 225 periodical subscriptions, 44,000 pictures, 70,000 slides, etc.; 200 teachers; 2,329 students; Pres. RON SHUEBROOK; Exec. Vice-Pres. PETER CALDWELL; Financial Aids and Awards Officer KELLY DICKINSON; Dir for Library JILL PATRICK.

Royal Canadian College of Organists: 204 St George St, Suite 204, Toronto, ON M5R 2N5; tel. (416) 929-6400; e-mail rcco@the-wire.com; internet www.rcco.ca; f. 1909; Pres. F. ALAN REESOR; Vice-Pres. PATRICIA WRIGHT; Treas. DON TIMMINS; publs *Organ Canada* (4 a year), *The American Organist* (12 a year, in asscn with American Guild of Organists).

Royal Conservatory of Music: 273 Bloor St West, Toronto ON M5S 1W2; tel. (416) 408-2824; e-mail communityschool@rcmusic.ca; internet www.rcmusic.ca; f. 1886; 350 teachers; 10,000 students; Pres. PETER C. SIMON; Deans JEFF MELANSON; Dean RENNIE REGEHR.

CABO VERDE

The Higher Education System

Cabo Verde has little history of higher education. During five centuries of colonial rule in the archipelago Portugal did not draft any known plans for the establishment of a university for Cabo Verde. After the granting of independence in 1975, the number of students enrolled in secondary education increased markedly, and the demand for higher education began to be addressed with the creation of several institutes of higher studies to train teachers and health workers. Most Cabo Verdeans studied abroad; in 2002/03 there were 1,743 Cabo Verdean students studying at overseas universities. However, the cost of foreign study was high. Thus, as domestic demand increased throughout the 1990s, more concrete plans were made for establishing a university. The Universidade Jean Piaget de Cabo Verde was founded in 2001 in the capital city of Praia (with a smaller second location in Mindelo on São Vicente); the privately operated university offers both undergraduate and graduate degrees, as well as continuing education courses. The administrative staff of the university includes a Rector and a Vice-Rector. According to the 2004 statutes of the university, the Administrador Geral presides over the Advisory Council, represents the university in legal matters and proposes the budget (in addition to other duties). A second university, the state-run Universidade de Cabo Verde, was established in 2006 by the merger of two institutes operating in two different locations: the Instituto Superior de Educação in Praia and the Instituto Superior de Engenharia e Ciências do Mar (Higher Institute of Engineering and Marine Science) in Mindelo; in 2007 a third institute—the Instituto Nacional de Investigação e Desenvolvimento Agrário in São Jorge dos Órgãos (the National Institute of Agricultural Research and Development)—was incorporated into the university. In 2008/09 there were 8,465 students in higher education. By 2009/10 there were nine institutes of higher education—five universities, three Institutos Superiors, and Mindeo Escola Internacional de Arte—with a total enrolment of 10,144 students; this figure rose again in 2010/11 to 11,769. Also, in 2007, the first professional training centre for mechanics, metalworkers, plumbers and electricians was opened.

Regulatory Bodies

GOVERNMENT

Ministry of Culture: Praia, Santiago; tel. 261-05-67; Minister MÁRIO LÚCIO MATIAS DE SOUSA MENDES.

Ministry of Education and Sport: Palácio do Governo, Várzea, CP 111, Praia, Santiago; tel. 261-05-10; e-mail cci.mees@palgov.gov.cv; internet www.minedu.gov.cv; Minister Dra FERNANDA MARIA DE BRITO MARQUES.

Ministry of Higher Education, Science and Innovation: Palácio do Governo, Várzea, CP 111, Praia, Santiago; tel. 261-02-32; e-mail mesci.govcv@gmail.com; internet www.mesci.gov.cv; Minister Dr ANTÓNIO LEÃO DE AGUIAR CORREIA E SILVA.

Learned Society

LANGUAGE AND LITERATURE

Alliance Française: Rua de Santo Antonio, CP 37, Mindelo; tel. 232-11-49; e-mail afmsvcapvert@cvtelecom.cv; offers courses and exams in French language and culture and promotes cultural exchange with France.

Research Institute

ECONOMICS, LAW AND POLITICS

Instituto Nacional de Estatística de Cabo Verde (Cabo Verde National Statistical Institute): Ave Cidade de Lisboa, CP 116, Praia; tel. 261-38-27; e-mail inecv@ine.gov.cv; internet www.ine.cv; Pres. ANTÓNIO DOS REIS DUARTE.

Library

Praia

Biblioteca de Assembleia Nacional (National Assembly Library): Achada de Santo António, CP 20-A, Praia, Santiago; tel. 262-32-90; internet www.parlamento.cv/biblioteca; f. 1985; 5,000 vols, 100 periodicals; Dir ALBERTINA GRAÇA.

University

UNIVERSIDADE JEAN PIAGET DE CABO VERDE

Campus Universitário da Cidade da Praia, CP 775, Cidade de Praia, Santiago

Telephone: 262-90-85

E-mail: info@caboverde.ipiaget.cv

Internet: www.unipiaget.cv

Founded 2001; attached to Instituto Piaget, Portugal

Academic year: October to July

Courses in architecture, business information, chemistry and physics teaching, civil construction engineering, communications science, hotel and tourism management, education science, economics and management, English language and literature teaching, information systems and engineering, mathematics teaching, nursing, pharmaceutical sciences, physiotherapy, professional education, Portuguese language and literature teaching, psychology, sociology

Rector: Prof. Dr ESTELA PINTO RIBEIRA LAMAS

Vice-Rector: Prof. Dr JORGE SOUSA BRITO

Gen. Administrator: Prof. Dr DAVID RIBEIRO LAMAS

Number of teachers: 50

Number of students: 650

College

Instituto Superior de Engenharia e Ciências do Mar (ISECMAR) (Higher Institute of Engineering and Marine Science): CP 163, Ribeira de Julião, São Vicente; tel. 232-65-61; e-mail info@isecmar.cv; internet www.isecmar.cv; f. 1984; depts of electrical and mechanical engineering, electronic and computer engineering, marine biology and aquatic research, natural and human sciences, nautical sciences; Pres. ELISA FERREIRA SILVA.

CENTRAL AFRICAN REPUBLIC

The Higher Education System

Until the late 1960s higher education was closely linked to the former colonial power, France, from which the Central African Republic (CAR) had gained its independence in 1960. Students either travelled to France to study or attended the Foundation for Higher Education in Central Africa, established by the French to serve the CAR, Gabon, Chad and the Republic of Congo. The state-run Université de Bangui was founded in 1969 and remains the CAR's only university. The university has five faculties: law and economics, literature and humanities, science, health sciences, and juridical and political science. It also has four institutes and one teacher-training school: the Higher Institute of Rural Development, the Higher Institute of Technology, the Institute of Business Management, the Institute of Applied Linguistics and the École Normale Supérieure. In addition, the visiting campus and official academic headquarters of the international intergovernmental university framework EUCLID (Pôle Universitaire Euclide/Euclid University) are located at the Université de Bangui. The provision of state-funded higher education was severely disrupted during the 1990s and early 2000s, owing to the inadequacy of financial resources. The Ministry of National Education, Higher Education and Research oversees public higher education institutions. The medium of instruction at higher education level is French. In 2008/09 there were 10,427 students in further and higher education. Construction began in February 2012 on Université Newtech Institut, a project financed in part by the African Development Bank.

The University Council is the administrative and executive body of the Université de Bangui, and the Rector is the institutional head. All appointments and promotions are based on recommendations made to the Minister of National Education, Higher Education and Research by the University Council.

The secondary school Baccalauréat or Diplôme de Bachelier de l'Enseignement du Second Degré are the main criteria for admission to university. A special entrance exam is organized for students who do not have the Baccalauréat. University education is divided into two cycles. The first cycle results in the award of a Diplôme for which two years of study in an area of specialization (general studies, literature, science, economics, law or teaching) are required. The second cycle lasts for a year following this and leads to the award of the Licence degree, after which an additional year of study results in the award of a Maîtrise degree. The only doctoral qualification awarded by the Université de Bangui is the Doctorat en Médecine, which requires six years of study. The Université de Bangui also offers vocational education in agricultural, technical and engineering fields. Courses last for two to three years and lead to the award of Brevet de Technicien Supérieur, Diplôme Universitaire de Technologie or Diplôme d'Ingénieur de Technologie. Postgraduate education is currently unavailable in the CAR.

The higher education system in the CAR is beset by numerous and complex challenges. For decades, various governments have failed to provide adequate funding for the education system or regular and decent pay for its employees. Strikes by students and professors have led to the curtailment of academic years. The system suffers severe deficiencies in quality and does not satisfy real labour-market demand.

Regulatory Bodies

GOVERNMENT

Ministry of Basic, Secondary and Technical Education: Bangui; Minister MARCEL LOUDÉGUÉ.

Ministry of National Education, Higher Education and Research: BP 791, Bangui; tel. 61-08-38; Minister RAINALDY SIOKE.

Ministry of the Promotion of Arts and Culture: Bangui; tel. 61-39-69; Minister BRUNO YAPANDE.

Learned Society

LANGUAGE AND LITERATURE

Alliance Française: cnr rue de l'Industrie/rue du Poitou, BP 971, Bangui; tel. 61-49-41; e-mail afbangui@yahoo.fr; offers courses and exams in French language and culture and promotes cultural exchange with France.

Research Institutes

AGRICULTURE, FISHERIES AND VETERINARY SCIENCE

Institut de Recherches Agronomiques de Boukoko (Agricultural Research Institute): BP 44, M'Baiki, Boukoko; f. 1948; research into tropical agriculture and plant diseases, fertilization and entomology; library of 2,740 vols; Dir M. GONDJIA.

ECONOMICS, LAW AND POLITICS

Département des Études de Population à l'Union Douanière et Économique de l'Afrique Centrale: BP 1418, Bangui; tel. 61-45-77; f. 1964; Dir JEAN NKOUNKOU.

MEDICINE

Institut Pasteur: BP 983, Bangui; tel. 61-45-76; e-mail ipb@pasteur.cf; f. 1961; research on viral haemorrhagic fevers, polio virus, tuberculosis, HIV/AIDS and simian retroviruses; WHO Regional Centre for poliomyelitis in Africa; 110 researchers; Dir Dr ALAIN LE FAOU.

RELIGION, SOCIOLOGY AND ANTHROPOLOGY

Mission Sociologique du Haut-Oubangui: BP 68, Bangassou; f. 1954; sociological and archaeological study of socs and cultures from the CAR, espec. from the Gbaya, Nzakara and Zandé countries; historical maps and sociological documents; Head Prof. E. DE DAMPIERRE; publ. *Recherches Oubanguiennes*.

Library

Bangui

Bibliothèque Universitaire de Bangui: BP 1450, Bangui; tel. 61-20-00; f. 1980; 26,000 vols, 600 periodicals (Central Library); 9,144 vols École Normale Supérieure; 5,240 vols, 168 periodicals Faculty of Health Sciences; Dir JOSEPH GOMA-BOUANGA.

University

UNIVERSITÉ DE BANGUI
(University of Bangui)

Ave des Martyrs, BP 1450, Bangui
Telephone: 61-20-00
Internet: ww.univ-bangui.net
Founded 1969
public control
Language of instruction: French
Academic year: October to June

Rector: GUSTAVE BOBOSSI SERENGBE
Vice-Rector: Dr JOACHIM ROUAULD
Sec. Gen.: Dr NOËL NGOULO
Librarian: EMMANUEL FEIKELE

Library: see under Libraries and Archives
Number of teachers: 243
Number of students: 15,000

Publications: *Annales de l'Université de Bangui Wambesso*, *Espace Francophone*, *Revue d'Histoire et d'Archéologie Centrafricaine*

DEANS

Faculty of Economics and Management: Dr EMMANUEL MBETID BESSAN

Faculty of Health Sciences: Prof. GERARD GRESENGUET
Faculty of Law: Dr ISMAILA SY
Faculty of Letters and Humanities: Dr CLEMENT-ANICET GUIYAMA-MASSOGO
Faculty of Sciences: Prof. JEAN-LAURENT SISSA MAGALE

Colleges

École Nationale d'Administration et de la Magistrature (ENAM) (National School of Administration and Judiciary): BP 1450, Bangui; tel. 61-04-88; State control; f. as school for future civil students and magistrates; curriculum now oriented to workshops for benefit of public-sector workers; Dir-Gen. ISAAC EDGAR BENAM.

École Nationale des Arts (National School of Arts): BP 349, Bangui; f. 1966; dance, dramatic art, music and plastic arts.

CHAD

The Higher Education System

The main institution of higher education is the Université de N'Djamena, which was founded as the Université de Tchad in 1971 and adopted its current name in 1994. In addition, there are five other universities—the Université Adam Barka d'Abéché (founded 2003) and the Université de Moundou (which opened in 2008 and is financed entirely by oil revenue), Université d'Ati (2008), and the universities at Doha (not yet functional) and Sahr (which regroups the Institut Universitaire des Sciences Agronomiques et de l'Environnement and the Ecole Normale Supérieur de l'Enseignement Technique); there are also some 80 other private institutes of higher education. Students at the Université de N'Djamena, who currently number some 6,000, are each entitled to receive a monthly bursary allowance from the Government. In 2011 a new campus was being built at the Université de N'Djamena which was reported to have the capacity to accommodate another 50,000 students. The languages of instruction are French and Arabic. Some 20,394 students were enrolled at tertiary education institutions in 2008/09 and 22,130 in 2009/10.

Higher education in Chad is influenced by the French model, in which universities are under direct government supervision. The Ministry of Higher Education and Scientific Research Training oversees research activities through the National Committee of Scientific and Technical Research. The ministry has power over most education institutions in which teaching and research activities are performed. Some specialized institutions are supervised by other ministries. There is currently no external accreditation agency for higher education programmes, although the Ministry of Higher Education and Scientific Research maintains a register of recognized higher education institutions in the country. In 1990 the Government adopted a development strategy entitled Education-Formation-Emploi (EFE—Education-Training-Employment). The strategy, made up of five programmes corresponding to five sectors of the education system, sought to improve the education system's efficiency and increase access to education. It focused on teacher training, curriculum design and the rationalization of management. The Government was committed to improving the management of public resources in an attempt to meet structural adjustment programmes, and directed its attention to investment and basic education. As a result, inadequate resources were allocated to higher education. EFE strategists decided to increase student enrolment, particularly to scientific and technological disciplines. The resulting growth served only to exacerbate existing imbalances. The implementation of EFE strategy has since stalled owing to a lack of resources, and the reforms have yet to yield satisfactory results.

The Baccalauréat de l'Enseignement du Second Degré is required for admission to university. University-level education consists of three cycles. The first cycle involves two years of study and leads to one of four diplomas, depending on the student's area of specialization: Diplôme Universitaire de Lettres Modernes (humanities), Diplôme d'Etudes Universitaires Général (general studies), Diplôme Universitaire de Sciences (sciences) and Diplôme Universitaire de Sciences Juridiques, Economiques et de Gestion (social sciences). The second cycle leads to the award of the Licence after one year of study following the award of the Diplôme, and the Maîtrise after a further one or two years of study and the defence of a thesis. The third cycle consists of a one- to two-year postgraduate course following the Maîtrise and leads to the award of the Diplôme d'Etudes Approfondies or the Diplôme d'Etudes Supérieures Spécialisées; holders of these two qualifications are eligible to register on a doctoral programme. In the academic year 2006/07 a number of higher education institutions commenced the transition to the European-style (Licence-Maîtrise-Doctorat) system.

The Baccalauréat de l'Enseignement du Second Degré is also required for admission to non-university higher education and professional training courses. Higher technical and vocational programmes are offered by several public and private institutes in various fields, such as agriculture, technology, computer science, accountancy and management. These courses last for two to three years and lead to the award of the Brevet de Technicien Supérieur or the Diplôme Universitaire de Technologie.

Regulatory Bodies

GOVERNMENT

Ministry of Culture, Youth and Sport: BP 519, N'Djamena; tel. 52-26-58; Minister ABDOULAYE NGARDIGUINA.

Ministry of Higher Education and Scientific Research: BP 743, N'Djamena; tel. 51-61-58; Minister Prof. MACKAYE HASSANE TAISSO.

Research Institutes

AGRICULTURE, FISHERIES AND VETERINARY SCIENCE

Institut de Recherches du Coton et des Textiles Exotiques (IRCT): BP 764, N'Djamena; f. 1939; cotton research (agronomy, entomology and genetics); Head of station at Bebedja M. RENOU; Regional Dir M. YEHOUESSI.

Laboratoire de Recherches Vétérinaires et Zootechniques de Farcha: BP 433, N'Djamena; tel. 52-74-75; f. 1952; veterinary and stock-breeding research and production of vaccines; training; library of 3,500 vols; Dir Dr HASSANE MAHAMAT HASSANE.

EDUCATION

Centre de Recherche, des Archives et de Documentation, Commission Nationale pour l'UNESCO: BP 731, N'Djamena; Sec. Gen. Dr KHALIL ALIO; publ. *COMNAT: Bulletin d' Information*.

RELIGION, SOCIOLOGY AND ANTHROPOLOGY

Institut National des Sciences Humaines: BP 1117, N'Djamena; tel. 51-62-68; f. 1961; anthropology, ethno-sociology, geography, history, linguistics, oral traditions, palaeontology, prehistory, proto-history, social sciences, sociolinguistics, sociology; 6 researchers; library of 1,000 vols and 400 archive documents; Dir MOUKTHAR DJIBRINE MAHAMAT; Gen. Sec. DJONG-YANG OÜANLARBO; publ. *Revue de Tchad*.

Museum

N'Djamena

Musée National: BP 638, N'Djamena; tel. 51-33-75; f. 1963; attached to Institut National des Sciences Humaines (see above); 100 collns; in process of re-formation; depts of ethnography, palaeontology, prehistory and archaeology, scientific archives; Dir DJAMIL MOUSSA NENE.

University

UNIVERSITÉ DE N'DJAMENA (UNDJ)

BP 1117, Ave Mobutu, N'Djamena
Telephone: 51-44-44
E-mail: rectorat@intnet.td
Internet: www.undt.info

Founded 1971 as Université de Tchad; present title 1994
State control
Languages of instruction: French, Arabic
Academic year: October to June

Rector: Prof. RODOUMTA KOINA
Vice-Rector: ZAKARIA KHIDIR FADOUL

Sec. Gen.: MAHAMAT ADOUM DOUTOUM
Int. Relations Officer: GILBERT LAWANE
Librarian: MAHAMAT SALEH

Library of 30,000 vols
Number of teachers: 203
Number of students: 5,183

Publication: *Annuaire*

DEANS

Faculty of Arts and Human Sciences: AHMED N'GARE

Faculty of Exact and Applied Sciences: AHMAT CHARFADINE

Faculty of Health Sciences: DJADA DJIBRINE ATIM

Faculty of Law and Economics: BENJAMEN DJIKOLOUM BENAN (acting)

Colleges

Ecole Nationale d'Administration et de Magistrature: BP 768, N'Djamena; f. 1963; set up by the Govt and controlled by an Admin. Ccl to train students as public servants; Dir N. GUELINA.

Institut Supérieur des Sciences de l'Education: BP 473 N'Djamena; tel. 51-44-87; f. 1992; depts of teacher training for primary education, teacher training for secondary education and teacher training for technical and professional education; Dir MAYORE KARYO.

CHILE

The Higher Education System

The Real Universidad de San Felipe de Santiago, founded in 1738, was the first higher learning establishment in Chile. The replacement of this institution by the Universidad de Chile in 1842 marked the beginning of the country's formal higher education system. There are currently three main types of higher education institution in Chile: public and private universities (universidades públicas and universidades privadas), professional institutes (institutos profesionales) and professional training centres (centros de formación profesional). The 25 publicly funded, so-called 'traditional' universities (of which 16 are public and nine are private) are members of the Consejo de Rectores, while 'non-traditional' private universities come under the jurisdiction of the Consejo Nacional de Educación. In 2012, according to government figures, there were 1,127,181 students enrolled in tertiary education, of whom around 60% were studying at universities, 27% at professional institutes and 13% at professional training centres. More than 80% of these students were enrolled at private institutions. In 2011 there were 229 higher education institutions in Chile, comprising 25 traditional universities, 39 non-traditional universities, 48 professional institutes and 117 professional training centres. The number of private universities has expanded considerably in recent years as part of the general decentralization and privatization of the Chilean education system ushered in on the final day of the military regime of Gen. Augusto Pinochet by the 1990 Ley Orgánica Constitucional de Enseñanza (LOCE, Organic Constitutional Law on Education). This legislation allowed the creation of universities and other higher learning institutions by private interests as profit-making entities, and resulted in a proliferation of such establishments. Consequently, Chile has one of the highest levels of university fees in the world and state funding covers only around 10%–15% of the total cost for each student in the public sector. Despite a system of government loans and scholarships for disadvantaged students, Chile is still regarded as one of the most expensive countries in the world in which to be a higher education student. According to figures from the Organisation for Economic Co-operation and Development (OECD), the Chilean Government allocated just 0.8% of total public expenditure to tertiary education in 2009, the lowest figure of any OECD country.

Students require the Licencia de Educación Media to be admitted to university. Admittance into one of the 25 'traditional' universities requires the student to sit an entrance examination called the Prueba de Selección Universitaria (PSU), which was introduced in 2003 and is managed by the Ministry of Education. There are three levels of university qualifications in Chile, one undergraduate and two postgraduate. Undergraduates study for three years for the Bachiller or for four or more years for the Licenciado. Postgraduates study for two to four years following the Licenciado to receive the Magister, and then for a further two to three years for the Doctorado (requiring the submission of a thesis).

Technical and vocational training is co-ordinated by the Instituto Nacional de Capitación Profesional, which administers and accredits qualifications and institutions. Entrance requirements are the same as those for university-level education. At sub-degree level, the Técnico de Nivel Superior or Técnico Universitario is awarded by the professional training centres after two to three years of classroom-based study and practical assessments, while the professional institutes offer degree courses of four to five years leading to a professional title (rather than a Licenciado). At postgraduate level, the professional institutes offer the postítulo programme (lasting one to three years, of which the Diplomado is the most common) in place of the Magister, but do not offer doctoral degrees.

As an associate member state of the Mercado Común del Sur (Mercosur), Chile is a participant of El Mecanismo Experimental de Acreditación de Carreras del Mercosur, which has accredited Chilean degrees in disciplines including agronomy, medicine and engineering. The Comisión Nacional de Acreditación de Pregrado (CNAP) was established in 1999 to ensure national standards are met at undergraduate level. The accreditation process, which is voluntary, consists of both the accreditation of degrees and institutions. Technical committees of university academics assess the standard of degrees. The Comisión Nacional de Acreditación de Posgrado (CONAP) was established in 1999 to monitor standards of postgraduate degrees. In 2006 the Agency for National Quality Assurance in Higher Education came into law and the Comisión Nacional de Acreditación (CNA) was given power to accredit all autonomous institutions (including technical training centres) for undergraduate and graduate programmes; however, accreditation still seems to be on a voluntary basis.

Discontent among the student population regarding the role of the private sector in Chile's higher education system has increased in recent years, with large demonstrations taking place in 2011, 2012 and 2013. The impeachment of the Minister of Education, Harald Beyer, in April 2013, and the arrest of two university rectors and a former president of the CNA, following the discovery of serious financial irregularities linked to a corruption scandal at the CNA, resulted in increased criticism of the system. When Michelle Bachelet was elected president in late 2013 she promised to reform the sector and introduce free higher education for all, despite having failed to introduce such changes during her first presidential term. The proposals included the establishment of a Higher Education Secretariat that would oversee spending and enforce the prohibition of government subsidies to for-profit institutions. The proposed agency would also introduce mandatory, universal accreditation for the sector.

Regulatory and Representative Bodies

GOVERNMENT

Ministry of Education: Ave Libertador Bernardo O'Higgins 1371, 7°, Santiago; tel. (2) 24066000; e-mail consultas@mineduc.cl; internet www.mineduc.cl; Minister Carolina Schmidt Zaldívar.

National Commission for Culture and the Arts: Paseo Ahumada 11, 9°, 10° y 11°, Santiago; tel. (2) 26189000; e-mail oirs@cultura.gob.cl; internet www.cultura.gob.cl; Minister Roberto Ampuero.

ACCREDITATION

Comisión Nacional de Acreditación (National Accreditation Commission): Santa Lucía 360, 6°, Santiago; tel. (2) 26201100; e-mail contacto@cnachile.cl; internet www.cnachile.cl; f. 2006; ind. body set up to verify and promote the quality of univs, professional institutes and self-governing technical training centres, and of the courses and programmes they offer; 13 mems; Pres. Matko Koljatic; Exec. Sec. Paula Beale.

Consejo Nacional de Educación (National Council of Education): Marchant Pereira 844, Providencia, Santiago; tel. (2) 23413412; e-mail consultas@cned.cl; internet www.cned.cl; f. 1990, fmrly Consejo Superior de Educación, reorganized and current name adopted 2009; accredits new univs, professional institutes and technical training centres; promotes devt of research on higher education and school education; Pres. Ignacio Irarrázaval Llona; publs *Revista Calidad en la Educación* (2 a year), *Serie Seminarios Internacionales* (1 a year).

NATIONAL BODY

Consejo de Rectores de las Universidades Chilenas (Council of Rectors of Chilean Universities): Alameda 1371, 4°, Casilla 14798, Santiago; tel. (2) 24268620; e-mail cruch@consejoderectores.cl; internet www.consejoderectores.cl; f. 1954; coordinates the academic activities of its mem. instns, develops policies aimed at enhancing higher-education activities, promotes changes in laws regulating univ. studies and student financial aid; 25 mem. univs; Pres. CAROLINA SCHMIDT ZALDÍVAR; Gen. Sec. CLAUDIA REYES GUTIÉRREZ.

Learned Societies

GENERAL

Instituto de Chile (Institute of Chile): Almirante Montt 453, 6500445 Santiago; tel. (2) 26854400; internet www.institutodechile.cl; f. 1964; promotes cultural, humanistic and scientific studies; Pres. Dr RODOLFO ARMAS MERINO; Gen. Sec. Dr ABRAHAM SANTIBÁÑEZ MARTÍNEZ; publ. *Anales*.

Constituent Academies:

Academia Chilena de Bellas Artes (Chilean Academy of Fine Arts): Almirante Montt 453, 6500445 Santiago; tel. (2) 26854400; e-mail acchbear@ctcinternet.cl; internet www.institutodechile.cl/bellasartes; f. 1964; 40 mems; Pres. SANTIAGO VERA RIVERA; Sec. RAMÓN NÚÑEZ VILLARROEL.

Academia Chilena de Ciencias (Chilean Academy of Sciences): Almirante Montt 454, Santiago; tel. (2) 24812841; internet www.academia-ciencias.cl; f. 1964; 62 mems; Pres. JUAN ASENJO; Sec. FRANCISCO HERVE ALLAMAND; publ. *Figuras señeras de la Ciencia en Chile* (irregular).

Academia Chilena de Ciencias Sociales, Políticas y Morales (Chilean Academy of Social, Political and Moral Sciences): Almirante Montt 454, 8320105 Santiago; tel. (2) 26854416; e-mail acchcsso@ctcinternet.cl; internet www.institutodechile.cl/cienciassociales; f. 1964; 36 mems; library of 7,000 vols; Pres. JOSÉ LUIS CEA EGAÑA; Sec. JAIME ANTÚNEZ ALDUNATE; publ. *Anales* (1 a year).

Academia Chilena de la Historia (Chilean Academy of History): Almirante Montt 454, 6500445 Santiago; tel. (2) 26854414; e-mail acchhist@tie.cl; internet www.institutodechile.cl/historia; f. 1933; 36 mems; library of 2,500 vols; Pres. RICARDO COUYOUMDJIAN BERGAMALI; Sec. ISIDORO VÁZQUEZ DE ACUÑA; publs *Archivo de D. Bernardo O'Higgins* (irregular), *Boletín de la Academia* (2 a year).

Academia Chilena de la Lengua (Chilean Academy of Language): Almirante Montt 453, 6500445 Santiago; tel. (2) 26854413; e-mail acadchileng@terra.cl; internet www.institutodechile.cl/lengua; f. 1885; fmrly Academia Chilena; corresp. mem. of the Real Academia Española, Madrid; 36 mems; Dir ALFREDO MATUS OLIVIER; Sec. JOSÉ LUIS SAMANIEGO ALDAZÁBAL; publ. *Boletín de la Academia Chilena*.

Academia Chilena de Medicina (Chilean Academy of Medicine): Almirante Montt 453, 6500445 Santiago; tel. (2) 26854417; e-mail cblamey@tie.cl; internet www.institutodechile.cl/medicina; f. 1964; 120 mems; library of 900 vols; Pres. RODOLFO ARMAS MERINO; Sec. JOSÉ ADOLFO RODRÍGUEZ PORTALES; publ. *Proceedings on the Chilean History of Medicine*.

Regional Bureau for Education in Latin America and the Caribbean/Oficina Regional de Educación para América Latina y el Caribe (OREALC/UNESCO Santiago): Casilla 127, Correo 29, CP 665692, Santiago; Enrique Delpiano 2058 Plaza Pedro de Valdivia Providencia, Santiago; tel. (2) 24724600; e-mail comunicaciones.santiago@unesco.org; internet www.unesco.org/santiago; f. 1963; assists mem. states in defining strategies for further devt of their education policies, dissemination of knowledge, formulation of public policy guidelines, provision of advisory services and technical support to countries of the region, promotion of dialogue, exchange and cooperation; 37 mem. states; Dir JORGE SEQUEIRA.

AGRICULTURE, FISHERIES AND VETERINARY SCIENCE

Colegio de Ingenieros Forestales de Chile (College of Forestry Engineers of Chile): San Isidro 22, Of. 503, Santiago; tel. (2) 23610047; e-mail jsalas@surnet.cl; internet www.cifag.cl; f. 1982; 350 mems; Pres. JORGE GOFFARD SILVA; publs *Actas de las Jornadas Forestales* (2 a year), *Renarres* (6 a year), *Revista Mundo Forestal* (4 a year), *Revista Nuestra Tierra* (6 a year).

Sociedad Agronómica de Chile (Agronomical Society of Chile): Calle MacIver 120, Of. 36, Casilla 4109, Santiago; tel. (2) 26384881; e-mail sociedad.agronomica.chile@gmail.com; internet www.sach.cl; f. 1910; 1,900 mems; library of 1,600 vols; Pres. HORST BERGER; Sec. CARMEN GLORIA DE VAL I.; publ. *Simiente* (3 a year).

Sociedad Chilena de Producción Animal A.G. (Chilean Society of Animal Production A.G.): c/o Señora Carmen Gallo S., Facultad de Ciencias Veterinarias, Universidad Austral de Chile, Casilla 567, Valdivia; tel. (45) 2215706; internet www.sochipa.cl; f. 1979; 115 mems; Pres. CLAUDIA BARCHIESI F.; Sec./Treas. ADRIÁN CATRILEO S.

Sociedad Nacional de Agricultura (National Society of Agriculture): Tenderini 187, 8320232 Santiago; tel. (2) 25853377; e-mail comunicaciones@sna.cl; internet www.sna.cl; f. 1838; library of 3,500 vols; research in agricultural, social and economic problems; controls a plant genetics experimental station and a broadcasting chain with stations in several cities; register of pedigree cattle kept; technical assistance to farmers; annual int. and agricultural show since 1869, and home show since 1980; Pres. PATRICIO CRESPO URETA; Vice-Pres. MARÍA GRACIA CARIOLA CUBILLOS; Vice-Pres. RECAREDO OSSA BALMACEDA; publs *El Vocero*, *Informe Semanal*, *Revista El Campesino* (4 a year).

ARCHITECTURE AND TOWN PLANNING

Colegio de Arquitectos de Chile (Chilean College of Architects): Avda Libertador B. O'Higgins 115, Santiago; tel. (2) 23532300; e-mail contacto@colegioarquitectos.com; internet www.colegioarquitectos.com; f. 1942; Chilean and foreign architects working in Chile; 5,500 mems; library of 2,000 vols, 2,500 journals; Pres. SEBASTIAN GRAY AVINS; Sec. Gen. JOSE ROSAS VERA; publs *Bienal de Arquitectura* (every 2 years), *Congreso Nacional de Arquitectos* (every 2 years), *Revista CA* (4 a year).

BIBLIOGRAPHY, LIBRARY SCIENCE AND MUSEOLOGY

Colegio de Bibliotecarios de Chile, A.G. (Librarians Association of Chile, A.G.): Diagonal Paraguay 383, Depto 122, Torre 11, Santiago; tel. (2) 22225652; e-mail cbc@uplink.cl; internet www.bibliotecarios.cl; f. 1969; 1,891 mems; Pres. GABRIELA PRADENAS BOBADILLA; Sec. Gen. VÍCTOR CANDIA ARANCIBIA; publ. *Eidisis* (4 a year).

ECONOMICS, LAW AND POLITICS

Servicio Médico Legal (Forensic Medicine Service): Avda La Paz 1012, Independencia, Santiago; tel. (2) 27823500; internet www.sml.cl; f. 1915; attached to Min. of Justice; 305 mems; library of 800 vols; Dir Dr PATRICIO BUSTOS STREETER; publ. *Revista de Medicina Legal* (3 a year).

FINE AND PERFORMING ARTS

Asociación Plástica Latina Internacional de Chile (APLICH) (Chilean International Plastic Arts Association): c/o Museo Nacional Bellas Artes, Parque Forestal, Casilla 3209, Santiago; tel. (2) 24991600; internet www.mnba.cl; f. 1880; library of 100,000 vols; Dir ROBERTO FARRIOL; Sec. VERÓNICA MUÑOZ; publ. *APLICH al Día*.

HISTORY, GEOGRAPHY AND ARCHAEOLOGY

Instituto Geográfico Militar (Military Geographical Institute): Nueva Santa Isabel 1640, Santiago; tel. (2) 24109300; e-mail igm@igm.cl; internet www.igm.cl; f. 1922; 400 mems; library of 4,000 vols, 25,000 maps; Dir Col LEONARDO IVÁN PÉREZ ÁLVAREZ; publ. *Revista Terra Australis* (1 a year).

Sociedad Chilena de Historia y Geografía (Chilean Society of History and Geography): Casilla 1386, Santiago; Calle Londres 65, Santiago; tel. (2) 6382489; f. 1911; 304 mems; library of 12,600 vols; Pres. SERGIO MARTÍNEZ BOEZA; Sec. Gen. ROBERTO COBO DE LA MOZA; publs *Revista Chilena de Historia y Geografía*, related works.

LANGUAGE AND LITERATURE

British Council: Avda Ricardo Lyon 222, Of. 2001, 7510125 Providencia, Santiago; tel. (2) 24106900; e-mail info@britishcouncil.cl; internet www.britishcouncil.cl; offers courses and exams in English language and British culture and promotes cultural exchange with the UK; Dir ANDREW CHADWICK.

Goethe-Institut: Avda Holanda 100, 7510021 Providencia, Santiago; tel. (2) 29528000; e-mail info@santiago.goethe.org; internet www.goethe.de/ins/cl/sao/esindex.htm; f. 1961; offers courses and exams in German language and culture and promotes cultural exchange with Germany; library of 8,500 vols; Dir JUDITH MAIWORM; Dir REINHARD MAIWORM.

Sociedad Chilena de Lingüística (Chilean Linguistics Society): Casilla 394, 11 Santiago; tel. (41) 2203001; internet www.sochil.cl; f. 1971; over 100 mems; Pres. Dr BERNARDO RIFFO; Dir Dr PILAR ALVAREZ-SANTULLANO; publ. *Actas*.

MEDICINE

Colegio de Químico-Farmacéuticos y Bioquímicos de Chile (College of Pharmacists and Biochemists of Chile): Casilla 1136, Santiago; Merced 50, Santiago; tel. (2) 26392505; e-mail comunicaciones@colegiofarmaceutico.cl; internet www.colegiofarmaceutico.cl; f. 1942; 2,500 regional councils in 13 towns; Pres. MAURICIO HUBERMAN; Sec. Dra PAMELA MILLA N.

Sociedad Chilena de Cancerología y Hematología (Chilean Society of Hematology and Cancerology): Calle Pérez Valenzuela 1520, Of. 502, Providencia, Santiago; tel. (2) 2358357; internet www.cancerologia

.cl; f. 1954; 142 mems; Pres. Dr CESAR DEL CASTILLO SANTA MARIA; Gen. Sec. Dr HERNAN PULGAR; publ. *Revista Chilena de Cancerología* (4 a year).

Sociedad Chilena de Cardiología y Cirugía Cardiovascular (Chilean Society of Cardiovascular Surgery and Cardiology): Alfredo Barros Errázuriz 1954, Of. 1601, Providencia, Santiago; tel. (2) 22690076; e-mail sochicar@entelchile.net; internet www.sochicar.cl; f. 1949; Pres. Dra IVONNE ARAMBURÚ MUÑOZ; Vice-Pres. Dr ALEJANDRO MARTINEZ SEPÚLVEDA; publ. *Revista Chilena de Cardiología* (3 a year).

Sociedad Chilena de Dermatología y Venereología (Chilean Society of Dermatology and Venereology): Avda Vitacura 5250, Of. 202, Vitacura, Santiago; tel. (2) 26519160; e-mail secretaria@sochiderm.cl; internet www.sochiderm.cl; f. 1938; Pres. Dr JOSE HONO; Gen. Sec. Dr ELIANA FAÚNDEZ; publ. *Revista Sochiderm* (4 a year).

Sociedad Chilena de Endocrinología y Diabetes (Chilean Society of Diabetes and Endocrinology): Bernarda Morín 488, 2°, Providencia, Santiago; tel. (2) 27535555; internet www.soched.cl; f. 1961; Pres. Dr GILBERTO GONZÁLEZ V.; Sec. Gen. Dr FRANCISCO CORDERO A.

Sociedad Chilena de Enfermedades Respiratorias (Chilean Society of Respiratory Diseases): Santa Magdalena 75, Of. 701, Providencia, Santiago; tel. (2) 22316292; e-mail ser@serchile.cl; internet www.serchile.cl; f. 1930; 410 mems; Pres. Dr LUIS ASTORGA FUENTES; Sec. Dra CLAUDIA ASTUDILLO MAGGIO; publ. *Revista Chilena de Enfermedades Respiratorias* (4 a year).

Sociedad Chilena de Gastroenterología (Chilean Society of Gastroenterology): El Trovador 4280, Of. 909, Las Condes, Santiago; tel. (2) 23425004; e-mail schgastro@schge.cl; internet sociedadgastro.cl; f. 1938; Pres. Dr RODRIGO ZAPATA LARRAÍN; Sec. Dra SOLANGE AGAR FARNÉ; publs *Gastroenterología Latinoamericana* (1 a year), *Normas de Diagnóstico en Enfermedades Digestivas*.

Sociedad Chilena de Inmunología (Chilean Society of Immunology): Avda Independencia 1027, Santiago; tel. (2) 29786347; e-mail info@sochin.cl; internet www.sochin.cl; f. 1972; 55 active mems; Pres. Dr ÁNGEL OÑATE CONTRERAS; Sec. DARWIN SÁEZ POBLETE.

Sociedad Chilena de Obstetricia y Ginecología (Chilean Society of Obstetrics and Gynaecology): Román Díaz 205, Of. 205, Providencia, Santiago; tel. (2) 22350133; e-mail sochog@entelchile.net; internet www.sochog.cl; f. 1935; 409 mems; Pres. Dr HERNAN MUÑOZ; Sec. Dr OMAR NAZZAL; publ. *Revista Chilena de Obstetricia y Ginecología* (6 a year, online).

Sociedad Chilena de Oftalmología (Chilean Society of Ophthalmology): Avda Luís Pasteur 5280, Of. 104 Vitacura, Santiago; tel. (2) 2185950; e-mail contacto@sochiof.cl; internet www.sochiof.cl; f. 1931; 600 mems; library of 650 vols, spec. colln of video cassettes; Pres. Dr PEDRO BRAVO C.; Pres. GONZALO MATUS M.; Sec. Dr JAVIER CORVALÁN R.; publs *Archivos Chilenos de Oftalmología* (2 a year), *Revista Informativa* (10 a year).

Sociedad Chilena de Ortopedia y Traumatología (Chilean Society of Orthopaedics and Traumatology): Evaristo Lillo 78, Of. 81, Las Condes, Santiago; tel. (2) 22072151; e-mail schot@schot.cl; internet www.schot.cl; f. 1949; 508 mems; library of 500 vols; Pres. Dr EDUARDO AHUMADA; Sec. Dr ALDO GIOLITO; publ. *Revista Chilena de Ortopedia y Traumatología* (4 a year).

Sociedad Chilena de Pediatría (Chilean Society of Pediatrics): CP 6841638, Casilla 593, Correo 11, Santiago; Alcalde Eduardo Castillo Velasco 1838, Ñuñoa, Santiago; tel. (2) 22371598; e-mail contacto@sochipe.cl; internet www.sochipe.cl; f. 1922; 1,230 mems; Pres. Dr HERNÁN SEPÚLVEDA R.; Sec. Gen. Dr MARIO VILDOSO F.

Sociedad Chilena de Reumatología (Chilean Society of Rheumatology): Avda 11 de Septiembre 2214, 12°, Of. 126, Providencia, Santiago; tel. (2) 28644113; e-mail sochire@entelchile.net; internet www.sochire.cl; f. 1950; Pres. Dr LUIS LIRA WELLDT; Sec. Gen. Dra ANNELISE GOECKE SARIETO.

Sociedad de Cirujanos de Chile (Chilean Society of Surgeons): Casilla 2843, Santiago; Román Díaz 205, Of. 401, Santiago; tel. (2) 22362831; e-mail info@cirujanosdechile.cl; internet www.cirujanosdechile.cl; f. 1949; 640 mems; Pres. Dr MARIO URIBE M.; Sec. Gen. Dr CRISTIAN OVALLE L.; publ. *Revista Chilena de Cirugía* (6 a year).

Sociedad de Endodoncia de Concepción (Concepción Society of Endodontics): San Martín 1384 Edif. Plaza del Arco, Concepción; tel. (41) 2225897; e-mail socendoconcepcion@gmail.com; internet www.socendoconcepcion.cl; Pres. RODRIGO GONZALEZ COFRE; Sec. Dra MARIA EUGENIA CARRASCO.

Sociedad de Farmacología de Chile (Society of Pharmacology of Chile): Avda Independencia 1027, Independencia, Santiago; tel. (2) 29786050; e-mail secretaria@sofarchi.cl; internet www.sofarchi.cl; f. 1979; 88 mems; Pres. Dr RAFAEL BURGOS A.; Sec. ANGÉLICA MARÍA G. HIDALGO; publ. *Revista de Farmacología de Chile* (irregular).

Sociedad de Neurocirugía de Chile (Chilean Society of Neurosurgery): Esmeralda 678 (2° interior), Santiago; tel. (2) 26334149; e-mail sociedad@neurocirugia.cl; internet www.neurocirugia.cl; f. 1957; 100 mems; Sec. Dr RENÉ CORVALÁN LATAPIA; publ. *Revista Chilena de Neurocirugía* (2 a year).

Sociedad de Neurología, Psiquiatría y Neurocirugía de Chile (Chilean Society of Neurology, Psychiatry and Neurosurgery): Carlos Silva Vildósola 1300 Departmento 22, Providencia, Santiago; tel. (2) 22329347; e-mail presidencia@sonepsyn.cl; internet www.sonepsyn.cl; f. 1932; Pres. Dr FERNANDO IVANOVIC-ZUVIC; publ. *Revista Chilena de Neuro-Psiquiatría* (4 a year).

Sociedad de Ortodoncia de Chile (Society of Dentistry of Chile): Del Inca 4446, Of. 205, Esq. Américo Vespucio Sur, Las Condes, Santiago; tel. (2) 22062036; e-mail info@sortchile.cl; internet www.sortchile.cl; f. 1942; 200 mems; Pres. Dr ANDRÉS GOYCOOLEA; Sec. Dr VERÓNICA ARRIAGADA; publ. *Revista Chilena de Ortodoncia* (2 a year).

Sociedad Médica de Santiago (Santiago Medical Society): Bernarda Morín 488, Providencia, Santiago; tel. (2) 27535500; e-mail smschile@smschile.cl; internet www.smschile.cl; f. 1869; 1,600 mems; library: 50 periodical titles; Pres. Dr GUILLERMO ACUÑA LEIVA; Sec. Dr HECTOR UGALDE PRIETO; publ. *Revista Médica de Chile* (12 a year).

NATURAL SCIENCES

Biological Sciences

Sociedad de Microbiología de Chile (Society of Microbiology of Chile): Canadá 253, 3°, Of. F, Santiago; tel. (2) 22093503; e-mail socbiol@manquehue.net; internet www.somich.cl; f. 1964; 194 mems; Pres. Dr NICOLAS GUILIANI; Sec. Dr CLAUDIA SAAVEDRA; publ. *Acta Microbiológica* (2 a year).

Sociedad Chilena de Entomología (Chilean Society of Entomology): Casilla 21132, Santiago; tel. (2) 6804635; internet www.insectachile.cl; f. 1922; 170 mems; library of 4,000 periodicals; Pres. Prof. ALEJANDRO VERA S.; Sec. Ing. Agr. SERGIO ROTHMANN T.; publ. *Revista Chilena de Entomología* (1 a year).

Sociedad de Biología de Chile (Biology Society of Chile): Canadá 253, Depto F, Providencia, Santiago; tel. (2) 22093503; e-mail socbiol@biologiachile.cl; internet www.biologiachile.cl; f. 1928; 565 mems; Pres. Dra ROSALBO LAGOS; Sec. GINO CORSINI; publs *Biological Research* (2 a year), *Noticiario* (12 a year), *Revista Chilena de Historia Natural* (4 a year).

Sociedad de Genética de Chile (Genetics Society of Chile): Diagonal Cervantes 683, Of. 213, Santiago; tel. (2) 26387046; e-mail sochigen@adsl.tie.cl; internet www.sochigen.cl; f. 1964; 100 mems; Pres. MAURICIO MORAGA; Sec. SERGIO FLORES; publs *Biological Research*, *Revista Chilena de Historia Natural*.

Sociedad de Vida Silvestre de Chile (Wildlife Society of Chile): Rocío Sanhueza Caba, Casilla 164, Valdivia; tel. (63) 215846; e-mail enlace.svsch@surnet.cl; internet svsch.ceachile.cl; f. 1975; 300 mems; Pres. CLAUDIA GIL; Exec. Sec. ROCIO SANHUEZA; publs *Enlace* (1 a year), *Gestión Ambiental* (1 a year).

Mathematical Sciences

Sociedad de Matemática de Chile (Mathematical Society of Chile): Canadá 253, Departamento F, Providencia, Santiago; tel. (2) 22489260; e-mail somachi@manquehue.net; internet www.somachi.cl; f. 1976; 250 mems; Pres. SAMUEL NAVARRO; Sec. ANA DE LA MAZA.

Physical Sciences

Asociación Chilena de Astronomía y Astronáutica (Chilean Association of Astronomy and Astronautics): Casilla 3904, Santiago; tel. (2) 6327556; internet www.achaya.cl; f. 1957; union of amateur astronomers; arranges courses and lectures; astronomy, astrophotography, radioastronomy, telescope-making; owns the observatory of Mt Pochoco, near Santiago; 350 mems; library of 1,000 vols; Pres. PEDRO AILLAPÁN FERRADA; Sec. JUAN ROA PARDO; publ. *Boletín ACHAYA* (6 a year).

Asociación Chilena de Sismología e Ingeniería Antisísmica (Chilean Association of Seismology and Earthquake Engineering): Blanco Encalada 2002, 4°, Santiago; tel. (2) 978-4372; e-mail mmualin@ing.uchile.cl; internet www.achisina.cl; f. 1963; Pres. PATRICIO BONELLI CANABES.

Comisión Chilena de Energía Nuclear (Chilean Commission of Nuclear Energy): Amunátegui 95, Casilla 188-D, Santiago; tel. (2) 24702511; e-mail oirs@cchen.cl; internet www.cchen.gov.cl; f. 1964; research, devt and applications of the pacific uses of nuclear energy; library of 9,000 vols; Pres. RENATO AGURTO-COLIMA; Exec. Dir Dr JAIME SALAS-KURTE; publ. *Nucleotécnica* (1 a year).

Comité Oceanográfico Nacional (CONA) (National Oceanographic Committee (CONA)): Casilla 324, Valparaíso; Errázuriz 254, Playa Ancha, Valparaíso; tel. (32) 2266521; e-mail cona@shoa.cl; internet www.cona.cl; f. 1971; 28 mem. instns; coordinates oceanographic activities among univs and govt research instns; Pres. Capt. PATRICIO J. C. CARRASCO; Exec. Sec. Capt. FERNANDO J. MINGRAM; publ. *Ciencia y Tecnología del Mar* (2 a year).

Liga Marítima de Chile (Maritime League of Chile): Casilla 1345, Valparaíso; Avda Errázuriz 471, 2°, Valparaíso; tel. (32) 2255179; e-mail ligamar@tie.cl; internet www.ligamar.cl; f. 1914; runs course in nautical education; brs in Iquique, Tocopilla, Santiago, Concepción, Tomé, Valdivia, Puerto Montt and Punta Arenas; 1,350 mems; Pres. Rear Admiral ERI SOLIS OYARZÚN; Dir Sec. Atty JUAN CARLOS GALDAMEZ NARANJO; publ. *Mar* (1 a year).

Sociedad Chilena de Física (Chilean Society of Physics): c/o Dr Juan Carlos Retamal, Casilla 307, Correo 2, Santiago; c/o Dr Juan Carlos Retamal, Depto de Física, Universidad de Santiago de Chile, Avda Ecuador 3493 Estación Central, Santiago; tel. (2) 27181200; e-mail jretamal@lauca.usach.cl; internet fisica.usach.cl; f. 1965; attached to Universidad de Santiago de Chile; 250 mems; Pres. Dr JUAN CARLOS RETAMAL; Sec. Dr LUIS ROA.

Sociedad Chilena de Fotogrametría y Percepción Remota (Chilean Society of Photogrammetry and Remote Sensing): Instituto Geográfico Militar de Chile, Nueva Santa Isabel 1640, Santiago; tel. (2) 4109314; e-mail igm@igm.cl; internet www.igm.cl; library of 5,000 vols, 25,000 maps; Pres. Col RODRIGO MATURANA NADAL; publ. *Revista Geografica de Chile: Terra Australis* (1 a year).

Sociedad Chilena de Química (Chilean Society of Chemistry): Paicaví 170 Departmento 19, Concepción; tel. (41) 2227815; e-mail sociedadchilenadequimica@gmail.com; internet www.schq.cl; f. 1945; 1,000 mems; library of 1,500 vols and 400 periodicals; Pres. Dr ADELIO MATAMALA VÁSQUEZ; Sec. Dr CLAUDIO JIMÉNEZ AGUILA.

Sociedad de Bioquímica y Biología Molecular de Chile (Society for Biochemistry and Molecular Biology of Chile): c/o Dr Marcelo López Lastra, Laboratorio de Virología Molecular, Facultad de Medicina, Pontificia Universidad Católica, Marcoleta 391, Santiago; tel. (2) 3548182; e-mail secretariasbbm@gmail.com; internet www.sbbmch.cl; f. 1974; 130 mems; Pres. Dr SERGIO LAVANDERO GONZÁLEZ; Sec. Dr ANDREW QUEST.

Sociedad Geológica de Chile (Geological Society of Chile): Valentin Letelier 20, Of. 401, Santiago; tel. (2) 26712415; e-mail info@sociedadgeologica.cl; internet www.sociedadgeologica.cl; f. 1962; 434 mems; Pres. REYNALDO CHARRIER GONZÁLEZ; Sec. MARCELO FARÍAS THIERS; publs *Comunicaciones* (1 a year), *Revista Geológica de Chile* (2 a year).

TECHNOLOGY

Asociación Interamericana de Ingeniería Sanitaria y Ambiental (Inter-American Association of Sanitary and Environmental Engineering): Barros Errázuriz 1954, 10°, Of. 1007, Providencia, Santiago; tel. (2) 22690085; e-mail aidischi@aidis.cl; internet www.aidis.cl; f. 1979; Pres. Ing. ALEXANDER CHECHILNITZKY ZWICKY; Dir Sec. JORGE CASTILLO GONZÁLEZ; publ. *Revista* (4 a year).

Colegio de Ingenieros de Chile, AG (Chilean College of Engineers): Avda Santa María 0508, Casilla 7520378, Providencia, Santiago; tel. (2) 25701900; e-mail colegio@ingenieros.cl; internet www.ingenieros.cl; f. 1958; professional engineering assen; 23,000 mems; Pres. FERNANDO AGÜERO GARCÉS; Sec. Gen. CRISTIAN HERMANSEN REBOLLEDO; publs *C. I. Informa* (12 a year), *Ingenieros* (4 a year).

Instituto de Ingenieros de Chile (Institute of Engineers of Chile): San Martín N° 352, Santiago; tel. (2) 26726997; e-mail iing@iing.cl; internet www.iing.cl; f. 1888; 800 mems; library of 2,100 vols; Pres. TOMÁS GUENDELMAN BEDRACK; Sec. IVÁN ALVAREZ VALDÉS; publs *Anales*, *Revista Chilena de Ingeniería*.

Instituto de Ingenieros de Minas de Chile (Institute of Mining Engineers of Chile): Encomenderos 260, Of. 31, Casilla 14668, Correo 21, Santiago; tel. (2) 25862545; e-mail instituto@iimch.cl; internet www.iimch.cl; f. 1930; 1,200 mems; Pres. LEOPOLDO CONTRERAS C.; publ. *Minerales* (6 a year).

Sociedad Chilena de Tecnología en Alimentos (Chilean Society of Food Technology): Echaurren 149, Santiago; tel. (2) 6966236; e-mail sochital@lauca.usch.cl; f. 1963; Pres. Dr JOSÉ MIGUEL BASTÍAS MONTES; Sec. Dra GRACIELA BUGUEÑO BUGUEÑO; publ. *Alimentos* (4 a year).

Sociedad Nacional de Minería (National Society of Mining): Avda Apoquindo 3000 (5°), Las Condes, Santiago; tel. (2) 28207000; e-mail sonami@sonami.cl; internet www.sonami.cl; f. 1883; library of 20,000 digital reports, 20,000 plans, 5,000 spec. documents; Pres. ALBERTO SALAS MUÑOZ; Sec. Gen JORGE RIESCO VALDIVIESO; publ. *Revista Boletín Minero*.

Research Institutes

AGRICULTURE, FISHERIES AND VETERINARY SCIENCE

Instituto de Fomento Pesquero (Fisheries Research Institute): Blanco 839, Valparaíso; tel. (32) 2151500; e-mail info@ifop.cl; internet www.ifop.cl; f. 1964; 400 mems; library of 9,000 vols; Dir LUIS PAROT DONOSO.

Instituto de Investigaciones Agropecuarias (Research Institute for Agriculture): Fidel Oteíza 1956, 11°,12° y 15°, Providencia, Santiago; tel. (2) 25771000; f. 1964; conducts research on plant and livestock production, horticulture, viticulture, oenology, field crops; library: see under Libraries and Archives; Nat. Dir PEDRO BUSTOS VALDIVIA; publs *Agricultura Técnica* (4 a year), *Bibliografía Agrícola Chilena* (1 a year), *Memoria Anual*, *Tierra Adentro* (6 a year).

Instituto Forestal (Forestry Institute): Casilla 109C, Concepción; Camino a Coronel km 7.5, Concepción; tel. (41) 2853260; e-mail oirs@infor.cl; internet www.infor.cl; f. 1961; library of 9,000 vols; Pres. LUIS MAYOL BOUCHON; Librarian PILAR LEIVA; publs *Boletín de Precios Forestales*, *Ciencia e Investigación Forestal*.

ECONOMICS, LAW AND POLITICS

Centre of Economic and Administrative Research: San Ignacio 414, Santiago; tel. (2) 6954010; Dir CARLOS RETAMAL UMPIERREZ.

Centre of Housing Research: José Joaquin Prieto 10001, Casilla 6D San Bernardo; tel. (2) 5585311; Dir ALFONSO RAPOSO MOYANO.

Centre of Juridical Research: Lord Cochrane 417, Santiago; tel. (2) 6957533; Dir RUBEN CELIS RODRIGUEZ.

Instituto Latinoamericano y del Caribe de Planificación Económica y Social (ILPES) (Latin American and Caribbean Institute for Economic and Social Planning): Avda Dag Hammarskjöld 3477, Vitacura, Casilla 179-D, Santiago; tel. (2) 22102507; e-mail ilpes@cepal.org; internet www.ilpes.cl; f. 1962; permanent body within the Economic Comm. for Latin America and the Caribbean (ECLAC), which is a part of the UN; supports mem. countries in strategic planning and management of public affairs, by providing training, advisory and research services; library of 60,000 vols, documents and periodicals; Dir JORGE MATTAR; Sec. DANIELA GEBHARD; publs *Panorama de la Gestión Pública*, *Series Gestión Pública*, *Series Manuales*.

Instituto Nacional de Estadísticas (National Statistical Institute): Casilla 498, Correo 3, Santiago; Paseo Bulnes 418, Santiago; tel. (2) 28924000; e-mail ine@ine.cl; internet www.ine.cl; f. 1843; library of 16,104 vols; Dir Nat. JUAN EDUARDO COEYMANS AVARIA; publs *Compendio Estadístico* (1 a year), *Indicadores Mensuales* (12 a year), *Metodologías*, *Revista Estadística y Economía* (2 a year).

EDUCATION

Centro de Investigación y Desarrollo de la Educación (CIDE) (Centre for Research and Development in Education (CIDE)): Erasmo Escala 1825, Santiago; tel. (2) 28897100; e-mail cide@reuna.cl; internet www.cide.cl; f. 1965; attached to Universidad Alberto Hurtado; research into education and the family, education and work, education and social values; library of 50,000 vols, 7,000 documents; Dir DASLAV OSTOIC MUÑOZ.

Latin American Information and Documentation Network for Education (Latin American Information and Documentation Network for Education): Casilla 13608, Santiago; tel. (2) 26987153; e-mail reduc@cide.cl; internet www.reduc.cl; f. 1977; network of different educational research instns; aims to disseminate information on education for research and policy making; documentation centre of 20,000 research summaries; 27 mem. instns; Dir GONZALO GUTIÉRREZ.

HISTORY, GEOGRAPHY AND ARCHAEOLOGY

Instituto de Investigaciones Arqueológicas y Museo 'R. P. Gustavo Le Paige' (Archeological Research Institute and Museum 'R.P. Gustavo Le Paige'): San Pedro de Atacama; tel. (55) 851002; e-mail museospa@ucn.cl; internet www3.ucn.cl/museo/detalle.asp; f. 1985; affiliated to the Universidad Católica del Norte, Antofagasta; research in archaeology and anthropology; postgraduate courses (MA and PhD); library of books, 5,000 periodicals; Dir Dr AGUSTÍN LLAGOSTERA M.; publ. *Estudios Atacameños* (irregular).

MEDICINE

Instituto de Medicina Experimental del Servicio Nacional de Salud (Institute of Experimental Medicine of the National Health Service): Avda Irarrázaval 849, Casilla 3401, Santiago; tel. (2) 22497930; f. 1937; affiliated to WHO; physiology, neuroendocrinology and cancer research; maintains tumour bank, available for use by other research centres; library of 6,800 vols; Dir Dr SERGIO YRARRÁZAVAL; Chief Sec. Mrs BERTA IRIBIRRA.

Instituto de Salud Pública de Chile (Public Health Institute of Chile): Avda Marathon 1000, Ñuñoa, Santiago; tel. (2) 25755201; internet www.ispch.cl; f. 1980; centre for vaccine production, nat. control of pharmaceutical, food and cosmetic products, and for coordination of nat. network of health laboratories; 600 mems; library of 9,142 vols (Central Scientific Library 3,600 vols; Centre of Occupational Health and Air Pollution Library 5,542 vols); Dir JORGE SÁNCHEZ VEGA; publs *Laboratorio al Día*, *Manual de Bioseguridad*, *Manuales de Procedimiento de Laboratorio Clínico*.

NATURAL SCIENCES

General

Centro de Información de Recursos Naturales (CIREN) (Centre for Information on Natural Resources): Avda Manuel Montt 1164, Providencia, 7501556 Santiago; tel. (2) 22008900; e-mail ciren@reuna.cl; internet www.ciren.cl; f. 1964; gathers data and provides a central information service in the areas of climate, soil, water, fruit production, afforestation, mining, agricultural resources; holds a landowners register; library of 11,000 vols, 150 journals; Pres. ÁLVARO CRUZAT OCHAGAVÍA.

Physical Sciences

Comité Nacional de Geografía, Geodesía y Geofísica (National Geographical, Geodetic and Geophysical Committee): Nueva Santa Isabel 1640, Santiago; tel. (2) 4109314; e-mail igm@igm.cl; f. 1979; encourages and coordinates research in fields of geography, geodetics and geophysics; represents Chile in the Int. Union for Geodesy and Geophysics-IUGG; Dir JUAN GUTTIÉREZ PALACIOS; Dir Col RODRIGO MATURANA NADAL.

Dirección Meteorológica de Chile (Meteorological Bureau): Casilla 140, Sucursal Matucana, Estación Central, Santiago; Avda Portales 3450, Estación Central, Santiago; tel. (2) 24364538; e-mail dimetche@meteochile.cl; internet www.meteochile.cl; f. 1884; library of 3,000 vols; Dir GUILLERMO NAVARRO SCHLOTTERBECK; publ. monthly bulletins on agrometeorology, climate and ultraviolet radiation.

European Southern Observatory (ESO): Casilla 19001, Avda Alonso de Córdova 3107, Vitacura, Santiago; tel. (2) 24633000; e-mail contacto@eso.org; internet www.eso.org; f. 1962; operates 3 observational sites in the Chilean Atacama Desert; ESO Representative in Chile VALENTINA RODRIGUEZ.

Instituto Antártico Chileno (Chilean Antarctic Institute): 1055 Plaza Muñoz Gamero, Punta Arenas; tel. (61) 2298100; e-mail inach@inach.cl; internet www.inach.gob.cl; f. 1964; promotes devt of scientific research, technology and innovation in Antarctica following int. standards; participates in the Antarctic Treaty System and related int. forums; strengthening of Punta Arenas as gateway; organizes activities and evaluation of knowledge regarding Antarctica in the nat. community; advises the Min. of Foreign Affairs on Antarctica matters; 43 mems; library of 4,100 vols, 11,600 periodicals, 3,000 monographs; Dir Dr JOSÉ RETAMALES ESPINOZA; publs *Boletín Antártico Chileno* (2 a year), *Programa Nacional de Ciencia Antártica* (1 a year, in English and Spanish).

Instituto de Ciencias Naturales Alexander von Humboldt (Alexander von Humboldt Institute of Natural Sciences): Avda. Universidad de Chile 02800, Antofagasta; tel. (55) 2637401; e-mail info@iio.cl; internet www.iio.cl; attached to Faculty of Marine Science and Bioresources, Univ. de Antofagasta; research in marine life of N coast of Chile, coastal marine systems; Dir JOSE M. RIASCOS; Sec. MARÍA RAQUEL PÉREZ.

Instituto Isaac Newton (Isaac Newton Institute): Casilla 8–9, Correo 9, Santiago; tel. (2) 22172013; e-mail inewton@terra.cl; internet www.ini.cl; f. 1978; promotes astronomy in 9 Eastern European and Eurasian countries; Dir GONZALO ALCAINO; publs *Astronomical Journal* (10 a year), *Astronomy and Astrophysics* (70 a year), *Astrophysical Journal* (10 a year).

Observatorio Astronómico Nacional (National Astronomical Observatory): Camino El Observatorio 1515, Las Condes, Santiago; tel. (2) 29771091; e-mail secretaria@das.uchile.cl; internet www.das.uchile.cl; f. 1852; attached to Universidad de Chile; Repsold Meridian circle, Transit instrument, Gauthier refractor astrograph, Heyde visual refractor, Danjon astrolabe and Zeiss transit instruments; astronomical station at Cerro El Roble; library of 7,247 vols; Dir Prof. GUIDO GARAY.

Observatorio Interamericano de Cerro Tololo (Cerro Tololo Inter-American Observatory): Colina El Pino s/n, Casilla 603, La Serena; tel. (51) 2205200; e-mail ctio@noao.edu; internet www.ctio.noao.edu; f. 1963; astronomical observation of stars only observable in the S hemisphere; library of 21,405 vols; Dir Dr NICOLE S. VAN DER BLIEK.

Servicio Hidrográfico y Oceanográfico de la Armada de Chile (Hydrographic and Oceanographic Service of the Chilean Navy): Errazuriz 254, Playa Ancha, Valparaíso; tel. (32) 2266666; e-mail shoa@shoa.cl; internet www.shoa.cl; f. 1874; hydrographic surveys, nautical charts and publs, oceanography, maritime safety, nat. oceanographic data centre; library of 12,700 vols; Dir Capt. PATRICIO J. C. CARRASCO H.; publs *Anuario Hidrográfico* (1 a year), *Derroteros de la Costa de Chile*, *Tablas de Marea de la Costa de Chile* (1 a year).

Servicio Nacional de Geología y Minería (National Geology and Mining Service): Casilla 10465, Santiago; Avda Santa María 0104, Providencia, Santiago; tel. (2) 24825500; e-mail msuarez@sernageomin.cl; internet www.sernageomin.cl; f. 1981; library of 30,000 vols, 15,000 aerial photographs, 200 satellite photographs, 600 periodical titles, 6,000 maps; Nat. Dir JULY POBLETE; publ. *Revista Geológica de Chile* (2 a year).

RELIGION, SOCIOLOGY AND ANTHROPOLOGY

Instituto de Investigaciones Antropológicas (Institute for Anthropological Research): Avda Angamos 601 Antofagasta; tel. (55) 2637201; internet www.uantof.cl/pages/unidades_acad/instituto_inves_antropologica.html; attached to Universidad de Antofagasta; research in archaeology, anthropology, linguistics and literature of N Chile; Dir ROBERT LEHNERT SANTANDER.

Instituto de la Patagonia (Patagonia Institute): Avda Bulnes 01890, Casilla 113-D, Punta Arenas; tel. (61) 207051; internet www.umag.cl/facultades/instituto; f. 1969; scientific, cultural and social devt of the S American region; library of 5,901 vols, 20,234 journals; Dir Dr CARLOS RÍOS CARDOZA; Librarian XIMENA SILVA.

TECHNOLOGY

Comisión Nacional de Investigación Científica y Tecnológica (CONICYT) (National Commission for Scientific and Technological Research): Canadá 308, Providencia, Santiago; tel. (2) 23654400; internet www.conicyt.cl; f. 1969; govt agency in charge of studying, planning and proposing nat. scientific and technological policy to the govt and developing, promoting and improving science and technology; mem. of ICSU and FID; library of 4,500 vols; Pres. MATEO BUDINICH DIEZ; Exec. Dir MARÍA ELENA BOISIER PONS; publs *C & T* (12 a year, online), *Panorama Científico* (12 a year).

Instituto de Investigaciones y Ensayes de Materiales (IDIEM) (Institute for Materials Research and Testing): Plaza Ercilla 883, Santiago; tel. (2) 29784151; e-mail idiem@idiem.uchile.cl; internet www.idiem.uchile.cl; f. 1898; attached to Universidad de Chile; library of 8,000 vols; Dir FERNANDO YAÑEZ URIBE.

Instituto Nacional de Normalización (National Institute of Standardization): Matías Cousiño 64, 6°, Santiago; tel. (2) 24458800; e-mail info@inn.cl; internet www.inn.cl; f. 1973; library: 160,000 technical standards; Pres. TOMÁS FLORES JAÑA.

Libraries and Archives

Concepción

Dirección de Bibliotecas Universidad de Concepción (Directorate of Libraries University of Concepción): Barrio Universitario, Casilla 1807, 160-C, Correo 3, Concepción; tel. (41) 2204403; e-mail infobib@udec.cl; internet www.bib.udec.cl; f. 1926; incl. Central library, Library of the Faculty of Law and Social Sciences, Humanities Faculty Library, School of Medicine Library Dr. Maria Antonieta Muñoz U., Faculty of Dentistry Library, Library of the Faculty of Architecture, Planning and Geography, Library of the Faculty of Physical and Mathematical Sciences, Library of the Faculty of Biological Sciences, Chillan Campus Library, Academic Unit Los Angeles Library and Colln 'Eula'; 425,250 vols, 6,315 periodicals; Dir OLGA MORA MARDONES.

Santiago

Archivo Nacional (National Archive): Miraflores 50, Santiago; tel. (2) 24135500; e-mail archivo.nacional@archivonacional.cl; internet www.archivonacional.cl; f. 1927; incl. historic and public admin. collns; Dir OSVALDO VILLASECA; publ. *Revista Archivo Nacional* (1 a year).

Biblioteca Central, Instituto de Investigaciones Agropecuarias (Central Library, Institute of Agricultural Research): Fidel Oteíza 1956, 11°, 12° y 15°, Providencia, 7083150, Santiago; tel. (2) 25771000; internet www.inia.cl; f. 1964; 18,000 vols, 31,800 documents and papers, incl. Chilean colln, 675 current periodicals, 9,764 Chilean univ. theses; Head Librarian SONIA ELSO; publs *Agricultura Técnica* (4 a year, online), *Bibliografía Agrícola Chilena* (online), *Collection Libros INIA* (irregular), *Serie Actas* (irregular), *Tierra Adentro* (6 a year).

Biblioteca del Congreso Nacional (Library of the National Congress): Huérfanos 1117, 2°, Clasificador Postal 1199, Santiago; tel. (2) 22701700; internet www.bcn.cl; f. 1883; 1m. vols and 5,600 periodicals on law, social sciences, politics and economics, human sciences and literature; 13,500 leaflets, 12,000 rare books, 1,353 maps and topographical charts, 4m. Chilean press cuttings, official depository for int. orgs, legal depository for nat. publs; Dir ALFONSO PÉREZ GUÍÑEZ; Asst Dir FELIPE VICENCIO EYZAGUIRRE; publs *Alerta Informativa*, *Serie Estudios*, *Temas de Actualidad*, *Visión Semanal*.

Biblioteca Nacional de Chile (National Library): Avda Libertador Bernardo O'Higgins 651, Santiago; tel. (2) 23605232; e-mail biblioteca.nacional@bndechile.cl; internet www.bibliotecanacional.cl; f. 1813; 3.5m. vols, 75,000 MSS, 83 incunabula; Dir ANA TIRONI; publs *Bibliografía Chilena* (1 a year), *Mapocho* (2 a year), *Referencias Críticas*.

Dirección del Sistema de Bibliotecas de la Universidad de Santiago de Chile (Library System of the University of Santiago de Chile): Dr. Enrique Kirberg No 4, Ex-Schatchtebeck, Estación Central, Santiago; tel. (2) 27182600; e-mail ximena.sobarzo@usach.cl; internet www.biblioteca

.usach.cl; f. 1979; 292,175 vols; Dir XIMENA SOBARZO SÁNCHEZ.

Sistema de Bibliotecas UC (Library System UC): Vicuña Mackenna 4860, Casilla 306, Correo 22, Santiago; tel. (2) 23542678; internet bibliotecas.uc.cl; f. 1901; attached to Pontificia Universidad Católica de Chile; 10 university libraries; 1,779,508 vols, incl. 625,538 books, 69,609 thesis, 1,061,015 periodicals, 43,346 brochures and other materials; Dir EVELYN MIREYA DIDIER CARRASCO.

Servicios de Información y Bibliotecas (Library and Information Services): Avda Diagonal Paraguay 265, Of. 703, Santiago; tel. (2) 29782583; e-mail sisib@uchile.cl; internet www.uchile.cl/bibliotecas; f. 1843, reorganized 1936; attached to Universidad de Chile; 48 mem. libraries; 3m. vols, private collns of Pedro Montt and Pablo Neruda; Dir GABRIELA ORTÚZAR.

Valdivia

Sistema de Bibliotecas, Universidad Austral de Chile (Library System, University Austral of Chile): Avda Eduardo Morales s/n, Campus Isla Teja, Valdivia; tel. (63) 2221290; e-mail biblio@uach.cl; internet www.biblioteca.uach.cl; f. 1962; specializes in science; 167,321 vols, 39,000 journal titles; Dir LUIS VERA CARTES.

Valparaíso

Biblioteca Central de la Universidad Técnica 'Federico Santa María' (Central Library of the Technical University 'Federico Santa Maria'): Avda España 1680, Edif. U, Valparaíso; tel. (32) 2654147; e-mail casa .central@bib.utfsm.cl; internet www.bib .utfsm.cl; f. 1926; audiovisual material: cassettes, video cassettes, maps, microfilms, slides; specializes in science and technology; 167,000 vols, 2,400 periodicals; Dir HUMBERTO RAVEST BECERRA; publs *Gestión Tecnológica* (4 a year), *Scientia: Serie A Mathematical Sciences*.

Biblioteca de la Pontificia Universidad Católica de Valparaíso (Library of the Pontifical Catholic University of Valparaíso): Avda Brasil 2950, Valparaíso; tel. (32) 2273260; e-mail mfernand@ucv.cl; internet biblioteca.ucv.cl; f. 1928; 335,000 vols; Dir MARISOL FERNANDEZ; publ. *Electronic Journal of Biotechnology*.

Biblioteca Publica No 1 'Santiago Severin' de Valparaíso (Public Library No 1 'Santiago Severin' of Valparaiso): Plaza Simón Bolívar, Valparaíso; tel. (32) 2213375; e-mail b001bc1@abretumundo.cl; f. 1873; 94,149 vols, incl. a colln of historical books on Chile and America and a colln of 17th to 19th-century books; 166,814 periodicals; Dir YOLANDA SOTO VERGARA.

Museums and Art Galleries

Angol

Museo Dillman S. Bullock (Dillman S. Bullock Museum): Casilla 8-D, Angol; Km 5 Camino Angol–Collipulli, Angol; tel. (45) 712395; e-mail museodbullock@yahoo.es; f. 1946; gen. local flora and fauna; local archaeological colln; also undertakes research, scientific expeditions; library of 5,000 vols; Dir ALBERTO E. MONTERO.

Antofagasta

Antofagasta Museum: José Manuel Balmaceda 2786, Antofagasta; tel. (55) 2227016; e-mail museo.antofagasta@museosdibam.cl; internet www.museodeantofagasta.cl; f. 1984; archaeology, history, ethnography, geology, bibliographic colln; scenes from coastal zone of the Antofagasta region with the pre-historic littoral and the environment occupations; library of 3,000 vols; Dir IVO DAVOR KUZMANIC PIEROTIC.

Arica

Museo Arqueológico San Miguel de Azapa (Archaeological Museum of San Miguel de Azapa): Camino Azapa km 12, Arica; tel. (58) 205555; e-mail masma@uta.cl; internet www.uta.cl/masma; f. 1967; attached to Dept of Anthropology, Univ. of Tarapacá; exhibits communicate univ. research on pre-Columbian, colonial and modern native people; library of 8,000 vols; Dir JULIA CÓRDOVA G. (acting); publs *Chungara* (2 a year), *Cuadernos de Trabajo* (irregular).

Concepción

Museo de Historia Natural de Concepción (Concepción Natural History Museum): Maipú 2359, Plaza Acevedo, Concepción; tel. (41) 2310932; e-mail museo.concepcion@ museosdibam.cl; internet www .museodehistorianaturaldeconcepcion.cl; f. 1902; library of 6,732 vols; Dir MARCO SÁNCHEZ AGUILERA; publ. *Comunicaciones del Museo de Concepción*.

Museo de Hualpén (Hualpén Museum): Camino Desembocadura s/n, Hualpén; tel. (41) 2426399; f. 1882; collns of Greek, Roman and Egyptian archaeology; Chilean arms and numismatic collns; Oriental art; Chilean and American folk art; Chilean archaeology; 18th- and 19th-century furniture; Dir MARTÍN DOMÍNGUEZ.

Copiapó

Museo Regional de Atacama (Regional Museum of Atacama): Casilla 134, Copiapó; Atacama 98, Copiapó; tel. (52) 2212313; e-mail museo.atacama@museosdibam.cl; internet www.museodeatacama.cl; f. 1973; archaeology, mineralogy, ecology and history; library of 15,000 vols; Dir MIGUEL CERVELLINO.

Iquique

Museo Antropológico de Iquique (Anthropological Museum of Iquique): c/o Rector, Universidad Arturo Prat, Avda Arturo Prat 2120, Iquique; internet www .unap.cl; f. 1987; attached to the Centro de Estudios del Desierto of the Univ.; permanent exhibition showing the cultural devt of the people of the region from 10,000 BC to AD 1900; research in archaeology, rural devt of farming communities, history and ethnography; specialized library; Dir Arq. ÁLVARO CAREVIĆ RIVERA; publ. research findings.

Museo Regional de Iquique (Iquique Regional Museum): Calle Paseo Baquedano 951, Iquique; tel. (57) 544719; e-mail contacto@museoregionaliquique.cl; internet museoregionaliquique.cl; f. 1960; attached to the Dept of Social Devt of the Municipality of Iquique; permanent exhibition of regional archaeology, ethnography and history; Dir FRANCISCO TÉLLEZ CANCINO.

La Serena

Museo Arqueológico de La Serena (La Serena Archaeological Museum): Cordovez Esq. Cienfuegos s/n, La Serena; tel. (51) 672210; e-mail mals@museosdibam.cl; internet www.museoarqueologicolaserena.cl; f. 1943; sections on archaeology, prehistory, physical anthropology, colonial history, ethnology and palaeontology; library of 23,000 vols, 18,000 slides, 28,200 photographs; Dir GABRIEL COBO CONTRERAS.

Linares

Museo de Arte y Artesanía de Linares (Museum of Arts and Crafts of Linares): Casilla Postal 280, Linares; Avda Valentín Letelier 572, Linares; tel. (73) 2210662; e-mail museo.linares@museosdibam.cl; internet www.museodelinares.cl; f. 1966; arts and crafts from the Inca period to the present; clay miniatures; colln of Huaso implements; ceramics; exhibition of history and people of Linares; confs, lectures, films; library of 2,500 vols; Dir and Curator PATRICIO ACEVEDO LAGOS.

Ovalle

Museo del Limari (Limari Museum): Covarrubias Esq. Antofagasta, Casilla 59, Ovalle; tel. (53) 2433680; e-mail museo .limari@museosdibam.cl; internet www .museolimari.cl; f. 1963; archaeology (esp. local); Dir DANIELA SERANI ELLIOTT.

Puerto Williams

Museo Antropológico 'Martín Gusinde' (Anthropological Museum 'Martin Gusinde'): Aragay-Gusinde, Puerto Williams; tel. (61) 2621043; e-mail museo.martingusinde@ museosdibam.cl; internet www .museoantropologicomartingusinde.cl; f. 1975; history and geography of the southern most archipelagos of the Americas; aboriginal culture, flora, fauna and minerals of the area; library of 500 vols; Dir ALBERTO SERRANO FILLOL.

Punta Arenas

Museo Regional de Magallanes (Magallanes Regional Museum): Centro Cultural Braun-Menéndez, Hernando de Magallanes 949, Punta Arenas; tel. (61) 2242049; internet www.museodemagallanes.cl; f. 1967 as Museo de la Patagonia, current name adopted 1983; Patagonian history; library of 3,500 vols; Dir PAOLA ANDREA GRENDI ILHARREBORDE.

Museo Salesiano 'Maggiorino Borgatello' (Salesian Museum 'Maggiorino Borgatello'): Avda Bulnes 336, Casilla 347, Punta Arenas; tel. (61) 2221001; e-mail musborga@ hotmail.com; internet www .museomaggiorinoborgatello.cl; f. 1893; scientific and ethnographical (notable relics of extreme S American and Tierra del Fuegan tribes), Patagonic history, Antarctic continent vision, petroleum industry; library of 2,000 vols on history, geography, ethnography, the Salesian presence in the region; Scientific Dir Prof. SALVATORE CIRILLO DAMA.

Santiago

Museo Chileno de Arte Precolombino (Chilean Museum of Pre-Columbian Art): Casilla 3687, Bandera 361, Santiago; tel. (2) 29281500; e-mail leyzaguirre@ museoprecolombino.cl; internet www .precolombino.cl; f. 1981; 5,000 items of pre-Columbian art and 1,000 items in ethnographic collns from Mapuche and Aymara cultures; textiles, ceramics, metalwork, stone sculptures; colln of photographs, slides, video and audio cassettes; laboratory for textile and pottery conservation; archaeological research; research on pre-Columbian music, rock art, Tiahuanaco, Aymara, Atacama and Araucanian cultures, prehistoric architecture, Andean textiles and symbolism; educational programmes; music archive; library of 7,500 vols, 500 periodicals, spec. colln of pre-Columbian art, conservation and archaeology, 1,900 reprints and audiovisual archive; Dir CARLOS ALDUNATE DEL SOLAR; publ. *Boletín del Museo Chileno de Arte Precolombino* (2 a year).

Museo de Arte Colonial de San Francisco (Colonial Art Museum of San Francisco): Avda Libertador Bernardo O'Higgins 834, Santiago; tel. (2) 26398737; e-mail museocolonial.sanfrancisco@gmail.com; internet www.museosanfrancisco.com; f. 1968; 16th- to 19th-century art (esp. 17th-century paintings); the life of St Francis and San Diego de Alcalá depicted in pictures; also other religious works of art, furniture, icons, embroidery, sculpture, carving, woodwork and metalwork; Dir FRANCISCO GARCÍA SÁNCHEZ.

Museo de Arte Contemporáneo (Contemporary Art Museum): Parque Forestal frente a Calle Mosqueto, Santiago; tel. (2) 29771741; e-mail dirmac@uchile.cl; internet www.mac.uchile.cl; f. 1947; contemporary and fine arts; Dir FRANCISCO BRUGNOLI BAILONI.

Museo de Arte Popular Americano (Museum of American Folk Art): Avda Libertador Bernardo O'Higgins 227, Santiago; tel. (2) 26396139; e-mail mapa@uchile.cl; internet www.mapa.uchile.cl; f. 1943; objects of American folk art, incl. pottery, basketware, wood and metal objects, Araucanian silverware; Dir NURY GONZALEZ.

Museo de la Educación Gabriela Mistral (Gabriela Mistral Museum of Education): Chacabuco 365, Santiago; tel. (2) 6818169; e-mail desarrollo.megm@museosdibam.cl; internet www.museodelaeducacion.cl; f. 1941; permanent exhibition on Chilean educational history; central themes of heritage and memory; organizes seminars, workshops and training in education, culture and soc.; works in the fields of gender and women studies, science, childhood, diversity in schools; library of 40,000 vols, photographic archive of 6,000 images; Dir Dr MARÍA ISABEL ORELLANA RIVERA.

Museo Histórico Nacional (National Historical Museum): Plaza de Armas 951, Santiago; tel. (2) 24117010; e-mail extension@mhn.cl; internet www.museohistoriconacional.cl; f. 1911; pre-Hispanic period to the present; costume, iconographic, arms, arts and crafts, and numismatic collns; dept of education; research in textile, paper and photographic restoration; library of 12,000 vols; Dir DIEGO MATTE PALACIOS.

Museo Nacional de Bellas Artes (National Museum of Fine Arts): Casilla 3209, Santiago; Parque Forestal s/n, Correo Central, Santiago; tel. (2) 24991600; e-mail milan.ivelic@mnba.cl; internet www.mnba.cl; f. 1880; paintings, engravings, etchings and sculpture, Chilean and European paintings; library of 15,000 vols; Dir ROBERTO FARRIOL.

Museo Nacional de Historia Natural (National Museum of Natural History): Casilla 787, Santiago; Parque Quinta Normal, Santiago; tel. (2) 26804603; e-mail comunicaciones@mnhn.cl; internet www.mnhn.cl; f. 1830; depts of zoology, entomology, hydrobiology, botany, mineralogy, palaeontology, anthropology, museology, education; library of 25,000 vols; Curator CLAUDIO GOMEZ; Chief Librarian PAOLA GONZALEZ; publ. *Publicación Ocasional*.

Talca

Museo O'Higginiano y de Bellas Artes de Talca (O'Higginiano Museum and the Fine Arts of Talca): 1 Norte No 875, Talca; tel. (71) 2615883; e-mail museodetalca@gmail.com; internet www.museodetalca.cl; f. 1964; paintings, sculpture, Chilean history, archaeology, religious artefacts, antique furniture, arms; library of 430 vols; Dir ALEJANDRO MORALES YAMAL; publ. *La Casona Durante la Colonia*.

Temuco

Museo Regional de la Araucania (Araucania Regional Museum): Avda Alemania 084, Casilla 481, Temuco; tel. (45) 2747948; f. 1940; archaeological, artistic and ethnographic exhibits of Araucanian and Mapuche Indians of S Chile; exhibits on colonization of Araucania and history of Temuco city; research section; library of 886 vols about Mapuche culture and regional history; 1,400 reprints and maps; Dir MIGUEL CHAPANOFF CERDA.

Valdivia

Museo Histórico y Antropológico 'Mauricio Van de Maele' (Historical and Anthropological Museum 'Mauricio Van de Maele'): Los Laureles s/n, Isla Teja, Valdivia; tel. (63) 212872; e-mail secmuseologica@uach.cl; internet www.museosaustral.cl; f. 1967; attached to Universidad Austral de Chile; centre for conservation of historical monuments, archaeology, museums and historical archives; undertakes teaching, research, training of museum staff, conservation, museology; library of 3,000 vols, 4,000 photographs; Dir LEONOR ADÁN A.

Valparaíso

Museo de Historia Natural de Valparaíso (Natural History Museum of Valparaíso): Calle Condell 1546, Valparaíso; tel. (32) 2544840; e-mail andrea.vivar@museosdibam.cl; internet www.mhnv.cl; f. 1876; natural sciences and anthropology; library of 3,000 vols; Dir LOREDANA ROSSO ELORRIAGA; publ. *Anales*.

Vicuña

Museo Gabriela Mistral de Vicuña (Gabriela Mistral Museum of Vicuña): Casilla 50, Vicuña; Calle Gabriela Mistral 759, Vicuña; tel. (51) 2411223; e-mail museo.vicuna@museosdibam.cl; f. 1971; documents, photographs and personal effects of poet Gabriela Mistral; replica of birthplace of poet, talks, films, music; library of 6,000 vols; Dir RODRIGO IRIBARREN AVILÉS.

Viña del Mar

Museo Comparativo de Biología Marina: Facultad de Ciencias del Mar y de Recursos Naturales, Universidad de Valparaíso, Casilla 5080, Reñaca, Viña del Mar; tel. (32) 2507824; e-mail ricardo.bravo@uv.cl; f. 1955; echinoderms, molluscs and other invertebrates; fishes from the coastal regions of the SE Pacific; marine biology library; Curator Dr RICARDO BRAVO; publ. *Revista de Biología Marina y Oceanografía*.

Traditional Universities

PONTIFICIA UNIVERSIDAD CATÓLICA DE CHILE (Pontifical Catholic University of Chile)

Avda Libertador Bernardo O'Higgins 340, Santiago
Telephone: (2) 23542000
E-mail: soporte@puc.cl
Internet: www.puc.cl
Founded 1888
Private control
Academic year: March to December

Grand Chancellor: Mgr RICARDO EZZATTI ANDRELLO
Vice-Grand Chancellor: CRISTIÁN RONCAGLIOLO PACHECO
Rector: Dr IGNACIO SÁNCHEZ
Pro-Rector: GUILLERMO MARSHALL
Vice-Pres. for Academics: ROBERTO GONZÁLEZ
Vice-Pres. for Communications and Continuing Education: LUZ MÁRQUEZ DE LA PLATA
Vice-Pres. for Finance and Management Affairs: PATRICIO DONOSO
Vice-Pres. for Research: JUAN LARRAÍN
Sec. Gen.: MARIO CORREA
Librarian: MARÍA LUISA ARENAS

Library: see under Libraries and Archives
Number of teachers: 1,586
Number of students: 18,000

Publications: *Revista Humanitas* (every 2 years), *Revista Universitaria* (4 a year)

DEANS

Faculty of Agronomy: JUAN IGNACIO DOMÍNGUEZ COVARRUBIAS
Faculty of Architecture and Fine Arts: MARIO UBILLA SANZ
Faculty of Arts: RAMÓN LÓPEZ CAULY
Faculty of Biological Sciences: JUAN CORREA MALDONADO
Faculty of Chemistry: BÁRBARA LOEB LUSCHOW
Faculty of Communication: SILVIA PELLEGRINI RIPAMONTI
Faculty of Economics and Management Sciences: FRANCISCO ROSENDE RAMÍREZ
Faculty of Education: CRISTIÁN COX DONOSO
Faculty of Engineering: JUAN CARLOS DE LA LLERA MARTÍN
Faculty of History, Geography and Political Sciences: PATRICIO BERNEDO PINTO
Faculty of Law: ROBERTO GUERRERO VALENZUELA
Faculty of Mathematics: MARTIN CHUAQUI FARRÚ
Faculty of Medicine: LUIS IBÁÑEZ ANRÍQUE
Faculty of Philosophy: LUIS MARIANO DE LA MAZA SAMHABER
Faculty of Physics: MARÍA CRISTINA DEPASSIER TERÁN
Faculty of Social Sciences: PEDRO MORANDÉ COURT
Faculty of Theology: FREDY PARRA CARRASCO

BRANCH CAMPUS

Sede Regional de Villarrica: Casilla 111; Dir Mgr PAUL WEVERING WEIDEMANN

PONTIFICIA UNIVERSIDAD CATÓLICA DE VALPARAÍSO (Pontifical Catholic University of Valparaíso)

Avda Brasil 2950, Casilla 4059, Valparaíso
Telephone: (32) 2273000
E-mail: rector@ucv.cl
Internet: www.ucv.cl
Founded 1928
Private control
Languages of instruction: Spanish, English
Academic year: March to December

Grand-Chancellor: Mgr GONZALO DUARTE GARCÍA DE CORTÁZAR
Vice-Grand Chancellor: DIETRICH LORENZ DAIBER
Rector: CLAUDIO ELÓRTEGUI RAFFO
Vice-Rector for Academics: NELSON VÁSQUEZ LARA
Vice-Rector for Devt Affairs: ARTURO CHICANO JIMÉNEZ
Vice-Rector for Research and Advanced Studies: JOEL SAAVEDRA ALVEAR
Sec. Gen.: ARTURO MENA LORCA
Registrar: PAULA DROGUETT MEGE
Librarian: ATILIO BUSTOS GONZÁLEZ

Library: see under Libraries and Archives
Number of teachers: 500
Number of students: 13,000

Publications: *Electronic Journal of Biotechnology* (online), *Revista de Derecho* (online), *Revista de Estudios Histórico-Jurídicos* (online), *Revista Geográfica de Valparaíso* (online), *Revista Investiga-*

ciones Marinas (online), *Revista Perspectiva Educacional*, *Revista Philosophica*, *Revista Signos* (online)

DEANS

Faculty of Agronomy: JOSÉ A. OLAETA COSCORROZA
Faculty of Architecture: DAVID LUZA CORNEJO
Faculty of Economics and Administration: BERNARDO DONOSO RIVEROS
Faculty of Engineering: EDMUNDO LÓPEZ ESTAY
Faculty of Law: ALAN BRONFMAN VARGAS
Faculty of Natural Resources: GABRIEL YANY GONZÁLEZ
Faculty of Philosophy and Education: JOSÉ MARÍN RIVEROS
Faculty of Science: ROSA VERA ARAVENA
Institute of Theology: KAMEL HARIRE SEDA

UNIVERSIDAD ARTURO PRAT
(Arturo Prat University)

Avda Arturo Prat 2120, Iquique
Telephone: (57) 2526000
E-mail: admision@unap.cl
Internet: www.unap.cl
Founded 1984
State control
Language of instruction: Spanish
Academic year: March to December
Pres.: NÉSTOR ARAYA BLAZINA
Rector: GUSTAVO SOTO BRINGAS
Sec.: SERGIO ETCHEVERRY GUTIÉRREZ
Librarian: ROBERTO JIMÉNEZ RAMÍREZ
Number of teachers: 500
Number of students: 5,300
Publication: *Revista Corpus Iuris Regionis*

UNIVERSIDAD AUSTRAL DE CHILE
(Austral University of Chile)

Independencia 641, Valdivia
Telephone: (63) 2221277
Internet: www.uach.cl
Founded 1954
Private control
Language of instruction: Spanish
Academic year: March to December
Rector: Dr VÍCTOR CUBILLOS GODOY
Pro-Rector: JUAN OMAR COFRÉ
Vice-Rector for Academic Affairs: Dr HERNÁN POBLETE WILSON
Vice-Rector for Economic and Admin. Affairs: Mag. AGUSTÍN QUEVEDO GODOY
Sec. Gen.: Dr JAVIER MILLAR SILVA
Registrar: MARIA BARRIGA RAMÍREZ
Dean for Campus Puerto Montt: RENATO WESTERMEIER HITSCHFELD
Dir for Library: Mag. LUIS VERA CARTES
Library: see under Libraries and Archives
Number of teachers: 1,237
Number of students: 12,500
Publications: *Agro Sur*, *Archivos de Medicina Veterinaria*, *AUS*, *Bosque*, *Cuadernos de Cirugía*, *Estudios Filológicos*, *Estudios Pedagógicos*, *Gestión Turística*, *Revista Austral de Ciencias Sociales*

DEANS

Faculty of Agriculture: RICARDO FUENTES PÉREZ
Faculty of Economic and Administration Sciences: JORGE DÍAZ CASTRO
Faculty of Engineering Sciences: FREDY RÍOS MARTÍNEZ
Faculty of Forestry Sciences: VICTOR SANDOVAL VÁSQUEZ
Faculty of Juridical and Social Sciences: ANDRÉS BORDALÍ SALAMANCA
Faculty of Medicine: CLAUDIO FLORES WÜRTH
Faculty of Philosophy and Humanities: YANKO GONZÁLEZ CANGAS
Faculty of Sciences: Dr MARIO PINO QUIVIRA
Faculty of Veterinary Science: RAFAEL BURGOS AGUILERA

UNIVERSIDAD CATÓLICA DE LA SANTÍSIMA CONCEPCIÓN
(Catholic University of the Most Holy Conception)

Caupolicán 491, Concepción
Telephone: (41) 2345000
E-mail: ucsc@ucsc.cl
Internet: www.ucsc.cl
Founded 1991
Private control; financially supported by the State
Chancellor: FERNANDO CHOMALI GARIB
Rector: JUAN MIGUEL CANCINO CANCINO
Sec. Gen.: TERESA DEL CARMEN LOBOS DEL FIERRO
Vice-Rector for Academic Affairs: JORGE FERNANDO PLAZA DE LOS REYES ZAPATA
Vice-Rector for Financial and Admin. Affairs: JORGE GALLEGUILLOS PIZARRO
Vice-Rector for Communications: GONZALO SANHUEZA PALMA
Library of 73,000 vols, 2,311 periodicals
Number of teachers: 300
Number of students: 6,000

DEANS

Faculty of Communication, History and Social Sciences: MARIO URZÚA ARACENA
Faculty of Economics and Administration: IVÁN VALENZUELA DÍAZ
Faculty of Education: JAIME CONSTENLA NÚÑEZ
Faculty of Engineering: HUBERT MENNICKENT MENA
Faculty of Law: FERNANDO ARTURO MONSALVE BASAÚL
Faculty of Medicine: Dr CLAUDIO LERMANDA SOTO
Faculty of Science: Dr JUAN CANCINO CANCINO

ATTACHED INSTITUTE

Instituto Tecnológico (Institute of Technology): Caupolicán 491, Concepción; tel. (41) 2345000; internet it.ucsc.cl; Dir GABRIEL HIDALGO AEDO

UNIVERSIDAD CATÓLICA DE TEMUCO
(Catholic University of Temuco)

Manuel Montt 056, Casilla 15-D, 4780000 Temuco
Telephone: (45) 205205
E-mail: dara@uct.cl
Internet: www.uct.cl
Founded 1991
Private control; financially supported by the State
Academic year: March to December
Chancellor: HÉCTOR EDUARDO VARGAS BASTIDAS
Rector: Dr ALIRO BÓRQUEZ SALINAS
Pro-Rector: ARTURO HERNÁNDEZ SALLÉS
Vice-Rector for Academic Affairs: Dr FERNANDO PEÑA CORTÉS
Vice-Rector for Finance and Admin.: Dr MARCELO TONEATTI BASTIDAS
Vice-Rector for Int. Affairs: Dr DAVID FIGUEROA HERNÁNDEZ
Library of 90,053 vols, 4,100 periodicals
Number of teachers: 213
Number of students: 6,854

DEANS

Faculty of Arts and Humanities: Dr GINETTE CASTRO YANEZ
Faculty of Education: Dr PAULA RIQUELME BRAVO
Faculty of Engineering: Dr XIMENA PETIT BREUILH SEPULVEDA
Faculty of Law: EDUARDO CASTILLO VIGOUROUX
Faculty of Natural Resources: Dr CELSO NAVARRO C.
Faculty of Social Sciences: Dr JOSÉ MANUEL ZAVALA CEPEDA
Institute of Theological Studies: Dr TIBALDO ZOLEZZI CID (Dir)
School of Health: MARCELA ANDAUR RADEMACHER

ATTACHED RESEARCH INSTITUTES

Centre of Sociocultural Studies: tel. (45) 205626; e-mail tduran@uct.cl; Dir Dra TERESA DURÁN PÉREZ.

Centre of Sustainable Development: tel. (45) 205629; e-mail cds@uct.cl; Dir Dr ANDRÉS YURJEVIC MARSCHAL.

Institute of Regional Studies: tel. (45) 205685; e-mail artufilu@uct.cl; Dir ARTURO HERNANDEZ SALLÁS

UNIVERSIDAD CATÓLICA DEL MAULE
(Catholic University of Maule)

Avda San Miguel 3605, Talca
Telephone: (71) 2203100
E-mail: ucm_comunica@ucm.cl
Internet: www.ucm.cl
Founded 1991
Private control; financially supported by the State
Grand-Chancellor: HORACIO VALENZUELA ABARCA
Rector: Dr DIEGO DURÁN JARA
Vice-Rector for Academic Affairs: Dra PILAR ZAMORA
Vice-Rector for Finance and Admin.: JUAN ANTONIO GUTIÉRREZ
Vice-Rector for Research and Graduate Affairs: VÍCTOR HUGO MONZÓN GODOY
Sec. Gen.: PATRICIO GATICA MANDIOLA
Library of 50,000 vols, 227 periodicals
Number of teachers: 200
Number of students: 6,000

DEANS

Faculty of Agrarian and Forestry Sciences: NELSON LOYOLA LÓPEZ
Faculty of Basic Sciences: RAÚL BECERRA HUENCHO
Faculty of Education: OSVALDO JIRÓN
Faculty of Engineering: JUAN FRANCISCO FIGUEROA
Faculty of Health Sciences: SARA HERRERA LEYTON
Faculty of Medicine: RAUL SILVA PRADO
Faculty of Social and Economic Sciences: RODRIGO SALCEDO HANSEN
Faculty of Religion and Philosophy: MARCELO CORREA

UNIVERSIDAD CATÓLICA DEL NORTE
(Catholic University of the North)

Avda Angamos 0610, Antofagasta
Telephone: (55) 355002
E-mail: mcamus@ucn.cl
Internet: www.ucn.cl
Founded 1956
Language of instruction: Spanish
Private control
Academic year: March to December
Chancellor: PABLO LIZAMA RIQUELME
Rector: JORGE TABILO ÁLVAREZ
Vice-Rector for Academic Affairs: RODRIGO FERNANDO ALDA VARAS
Vice-Rector for HQ: JAIME MERUANE ZUMELZU
Vice-Rector for Economic Affairs: MARÍA JACQUELINE FUENTES HERNÁNDEZ

Vice-Rector for Research and Technological Devt: MARÍA CECILIA HERNÁNDEZ VERA
Gen. Sec.: VICTORIA GONZÁLEZ STUARDO
Librarian: SERGIO ARCE MOLINA
Library of 114,000 vols
Number of teachers: 400
Number of students: 11,000
Publications: *Cuadernos de Arquitectura, Estudios Atacameños, Norte: Revista Divulgacíon de Ciencias, Tecnologia y Cultura, Revista de Derecho, Revista Proyecciones, Revista Reflejos, Revista Vertiente, Tercer Milenio*

DEANS
Antofagasta Campus (tel. (55) 2355000):
Faculty of Economics and Management: FERNANDO AURELIO ALVAREZ CASTILLO
Faculty of Engineering and Construction Science: ALEX MILTON COVARRUBIAS ARANDA
Faculty of Engineering and Geological Sciences: TEODORO POLITIS JARAMIS
Faculty of Humanities: MARIANA BARGSTED ARAVENA
Faculty of Sciences: RAMON LUIS CORREA SOTO
Coquimbo Campus (Larrondo 1281, Coquimbo; tel. (51) 2209701):
Faculty of Marine Sciences: ALFONSO EDUARDO SILVA ARANCIBIA
Faculty of Medicine: SERGIO ANDRES HABERLE TAPIA

UNIVERSIDAD DE ANTOFAGASTA
(University of Antofagasta)

Avda Angamos 601, Antofagasta
Telephone: (55) 637325
E-mail: rectoria@uantof.cl
Internet: www.uantof.cl
Founded 1981
State control
Language of instruction: Spanish
Academic year: March to January
Rector: LUIS ALBERTO LOYOLA MORALES
Vice-Rector for Academic Affairs: HERNÁN SAGUA FRANCO
Vice-Rector for Finance: YÉSSICA AGUILERA COVARRUBIA
Vice-Rector for Research, Innovation and Postgraduate Affairs: CARLOS RIQUELME SALAMANCA
Gen. Sec.: MACARENA SILVA BOGGIANO
Librarian: KATHERINE JARA ALARCÓN
Number of teachers: 300
Number of students: 6,000
Publications: *Estudios Oceanológicos, Hombre y Desierto, Innovación*

DEANS
Faculty of Basic Sciences: GUILLERMO MONDACA
Faculty of Education and Human Sciences: JUAN PANADES VARGAS
Faculty of Engineering: PEDRO CÓRDOVA
Faculty of Health Sciences: MARCOS CIKUTOVIĆ
Faculty of Law: DOMINGO CLAPS
Faculty of Marine Science and Bioresources: HERNAN BAEZA

UNIVERSIDAD DE ATACAMA
(University of Atacama)

Copayapu 485, Copiapó
Telephone: (52) 206500
Internet: www.uda.cl
Founded 1981
State control
Language of instruction: Spanish
Academic year: March to December
Rector: CELSO ARIAS MORA
Vice-Rector: JORGE NAVEA C.
Gen. Sec.: RODRIGO PÉREZ L.
Librarian: MARIANELA VIVANCO CORTÉS
Number of teachers: 100
Number of students: 3,000
Publications: *Revista de Derecho de Aguas* (1 a year), *Revista de Derecho de Minas* (1 a year), *Revista de Ingeniería* (1 a year)

DEANS
Faculty of Engineering: CELSO ARIAS M.
Faculty of Humanities and Education: OSCAR PAINÉAN BUSTAMANTE
Faculty of Law: RODRIGO PÉREZ LISICIC
Faculty of Natural Sciences: RENÉ MAURELIA GÓMEZ

ATTACHED INSTITUTES
Instituto Asistencia a la Minería: Casilla 240, Copiapó; tel. (52) 212006; Dir JUAN NAVEA DANTAGNAN.
Instituto de Investigaciones Científicas y Tecnológicas: Casilla 240, Copiapó; tel. (52) 218770; Dir GERMÁN CÁCERES ARENAS.
Instituto Derecho de Minas y Aguas: Moneda 673, 8° piso, Santiago; tel. (2) 6328290; Dir ALEJANDRO VERGARA BLANCO.
Instituto Tecnológico: Casilla 240, Copiapó; tel. (52) 206750; e-mail timur.padilla@uda.cl; internet www.tecnologico.uda.cl; Dir TIMUR PADILLA BOCIĆ

UNIVERSIDAD DE CHILE
(University of Chile)

Avda Libertador Bernardo O'Higgins 1058, Casilla 10-D, Santiago
Telephone: (2) 29782000
Internet: www.uchile.cl
Founded 1738 as Universidad Real de San Felipe, inaugurated 1843 as Universidad de Chile
State control
Academic year: March to December
Campuses at Andrés Bello, Beauchef, Juan Gómez Millas, Norte, Sur
Rector: Prof. VÍCTOR PÉREZ VERA
Pro-Rector: Prof. ROSA DEVÉS ALESSANDRI
Vice-Rector for Academics: Prof. PATRICIO ACEITUNO GUTIÉRREZ
Vice-Rector for Finance and Institutional Management: Prof. FRANCISCO MARTÍNEZ CONCHA
Vice-Rector for Communications: SONIA MONTECINO AGUIRRE
Vice-Rector for Research and Devt: SERGIO LAVANDERO GONZÁLEZ
Chief of Staff: CECILIA CODDOU SCHILLING
Library: see under Libraries and Archives
Number of teachers: 3,000 (incl. all br. instns)
Number of students: 25,000
Publications: *Actualidad Universitaria* (12 a year), *Anales de la Universidad de Chile* (1 a year), *Anuario Astronómico* (1 a year), *Bizantion Nea Hellas, Boletín Chileno de Parasitología* (4 a year), *Boletín de Filología* (2 a year), *Boletín Interamericano de Educación Musical* (1 a year), *Comentarios Sobre la Situación Económica, Cuadernos de Ciencia Política* (4 a year), *Cuadernos de Historia* (1 a year), *Desarrollo Rural* (2 a year), *Estudios Internacionales* (4 a year), *Ocupación y Desocupación Encuesta Nacional* (2 a year), *Política* (2 a year), *Revista Chilena de Antropología* (1 a year), *Revista Chilena de Historia del Derecho, Revista Chilena de Humanidades* (1 a year), *Revista Comunicaciones en Geología* (1 a year), *Revista de Derecho Económico, Revista de Derecho Público, Revista de Filosofía* (1 a year), *Revista Económica y Administración* (4 a year), *Revista Musical Chilena* (2 a year), *Revista Psiquiátrica Clínica* (1 a year), *Terra Aridae* (2 a year), *U Noticias* (12 a year)

DEANS
Faculty of Agriculture: Prof. ANTONIO LIZANA MALINCONI
Faculty of Architecture and Town Planning: Prof. LEOPOLDO PRAT VARGAS
Faculty of Business and Economics: Prof. MANUEL AGOSIN TRUMPER
Faculty of Chemical and Pharmaceutical Sciences: LUIS NÚÑEZ VERGARA
Faculty of Dentistry: Prof. JORGE GAMONAL ARAVENA
Faculty of Fine Arts: Prof. CLARA CÁRDENAS SQUELLA
Faculty of Forestry and Nature Conservation: Prof. JAVIER GONZÁLEZ MOLINA
Faculty of Law: Prof. ROBERTO NAHUM ANUCH
Faculty of Medicine: Prof. CECILIA SEPÚLVEDA CARVAJAL
Faculty of Philosophy and Humanities: MARÍA EUGENIA GÓNGORA DÍAZ
Faculty of Mathematics and Physical Sciences: Prof. FRANCISCO BRIEVA RODRÍGUEZ
Faculty of Sciences: Prof. VÍCTOR CIFUENTES GUZMÁN
Faculty of Social Sciences: Prof. MARCELO ARNOLD CATHALIFAUD
Faculty of Animal and Veterinary Sciences: Prof. SANTIAGO URCELAY VICENTE

ATTACHED INSTITUTES
Clinical Hospital of the University of Chile: Diego Portales 449, Cerro Barón, Valparaiso; Dir Dr ITALO BRAGHETTO.
Instituto de Estudios Internacionales (Institute of International Studies): Condell 249, Santiago; tel. (2) 24961200; e-mail inesint@uchile.cl; internet www.iei.uchile.cl; library of 13,000 vols, 245 journals; 24 teachers; 74 students; Dir JOSÉ MORANDÉ; publ. *Estudios Internacionales* (3 a year), *Visiones Internacionales* (online).
Institute of Nutrition and Food Technology: Avda José Pedro Alessandri 5540, Santiago; Dir FERNANDO VIO.
Institute of Public Affairs: Santa Lucia 240, Santiago; Dir OSVALDO SUNKEL

UNIVERSIDAD DE CONCEPCIÓN
(University of Concepción)

Casilla 160-C, Correo 3, Concepción
Víctor Lamas 1290, Concepción
Telephone: (41) 2204000
E-mail: foro@udec.cl
Internet: www.udec.cl
Founded 1919
Private control
Language of instruction: Spanish
Academic year: March to January
Rector: SERGIO LAVANCHY MERINO
Vice-Rector for Academic Affairs: ERNESTO FIGUEROA HUIDOBRO
Vice-Rector for Admin. and Finance: ALBERTO LARRAÍN PRAT
Gen. Sec.: RODOLFO WALTER DÍAZ
Library Dir: OLGA MORA MARDONES
Number of teachers: 1,400
Number of students: 16,800
Publications: *Acta Literaria, Agro-Ciencia* (2 a year), *Atenea* (12 a year), *Gayana, Informativo de Rectoría—PANORAMA, Revista de Derecho* (4 a year), *RLA—Revista de Lingüística Aplicada*

DEANS
Faculty of Agricultural Engineering: JOSÉ LUIS ARUMÍ R.
Faculty of Agriculture: RAÚL CERDA GONZÁLEZ

Faculty of Architecture, Planning and Geography: BERNARDO SUAZO PEÑA
Faculty of Biological Sciences: NELSON CARVAJAL BAEZA
Faculty of Chemical Sciences: ADELIO RICARDO MATAMALA VÁSQUEZ
Faculty of Dentistry: ALEX BUSTOS LEAL
Faculty of Economic and Administrative Sciences: JUAN SAAVEDRA GONZÁLEZ
Faculty of Education: ABELARDO CASTRO HIDALGO
Faculty of Engineering: JOEL ZAMBRANO VALENCIA
Faculty of Forestry Sciences: MANUEL SÁNCHEZ OLATE
Faculty of Humanities and Art: PATRICIO OYANEDER JARA
Faculty of Law and Social Sciences: JOSÉ LUIS DIEZ SCHWERTER
Faculty of Medicine: RAÚL GONZÁLEZ RAMOS
Faculty of Natural Sciences and Oceanography: MARCUS SOBARZO B.
Faculty of Pharmacy: CARLOS CALVO MONFIL
Faculty of Physics and Mathematics: RODOLFO ARAYA DURÁN
Faculty of Social Sciences: JORGE MIGUEL ROJAS HERNÁNDEZ
Faculty of Veterinary Medicine: ALEJANDRO SANTA MARÍA SANZANA

UNIVERSIDAD DE LA FRONTERA
(University of the Frontier)

Avda Francisco Salazar, Casilla 54-D, 01145 Temuco
Telephone: (56) 2325000
E-mail: comunicaciones@ufrontera.cl
Internet: www.ufro.cl

Founded 1981
State control
Academic year: March to December (2 semesters)

Rector: Prof. SERGIO BRAVO ESCOBAR
Vice-Rector for Academic Affairs: Dr JUAN MANUEL FIERRO BUSTOS
Vice-Rector for Admin. and Finance: HERNÁN FUENTES SALGADO
Vice-Rector for Research and Postgraduate Affairs: Dr
Sec. Gen.: Dr PLINIO DURÁN GARCÍA
Library Dir: ROBERTO ARAYA NAVARRO

Number of teachers: 700
Number of students: 9,000

Publications: *Cubo* (1 a year), *Chilean Review of Biological Medical Sciences* (2 a year), *International Journal of Morphology* (4 a year), *Lengua y Literatura Mapuche* (2 a year), *Memoria Institucional* (1 a year), *Revista Educación y Humanidades* (1 a year), *Revista Investigaciones en Educación* (1 a year), *Revista Médica del Sur* (2 a year), *Revista Nuestra Muestra* (2 a year), *Vertientes UFRO* (4 a year)

DEANS

Faculty of Agricultural and Forestry Sciences: RODOLFO PIHÁN SORIANO
Faculty of Dentistry: Dr RAMÓN FUENTES FERNÁNDEZ
Faculty of Education and Humanities: Dr CARLOS DEL VALLE ROJAS
Faculty of Engineering and Administration: Dr CRISTIAN BORNHARDT BRACHMANN
Faculty of Medicine: Dr EDUARDO HEBEL WEISS

PROFESSORS

Faculty of Agricultural and Forestry Sciences (Francisco Salazar 01145; tel. (45) 325630; e-mail aliroc@ufro.cl; internet www .agrofor.ufro.cl):

MARÍN, P., Forestry Sciences
SORIANO, R., Agricultural Production
VENEGAS, J., Agricultural Sciences and Natural Resources

Faculty of Education and Humanities (Francisco Salazar 01145; tel. (45) 325370; e-mail hcarrasc@ufro.cl; internet educacionyhumanidades.ufro.cl):

CHÁVEZ, J., Social Sciences
FELMER, L., Psychology
MÉNDEZ, I., Education
RIBERA, E., Language, Literature and Communication
SALAZAR, C., Physical Education, Sports and Recreation
TRABOL, H., Social Work

Faculty of Engineering and Administration (Arturo Prat 321; tel. (45) 325800; e-mail decing@ufro.cl; internet fica.ufro.cl/web):

BARRA, M., Chemical Sciences
BARRERA, A., Mathematics Engineering
BRACHMANN, C., Chemical Engineering
BRICEÑO, I., Electrical Engineering
JARA, F., Administration and Economy
SALAZAR, G., Systems Engineering
SANHUEZA, M., Physical Sciences
VEGA, H., Mathematics and Statistics
VILLASEÑOR, M., Mechanical Engineering
VON-BISCHOFFSHAUSEN, G., Civil Engineering

Faculty of Medicine (Manuel Montt 112; tel. (45) 325700; e-mail decanmed@ufro.cl; internet www.med.ufro.cl):

ARAYA ORÓSTICA, J., Pathology
CONCHA, S., Medicine (specialized)
CORTES, H., Public Health
ESPINOZA, B., Basic Sciences
FERNÁNDEZ, L., Paediatrics and Infant Surgery
FERNÁNDEZ, R., Integral Odontology
FREDES, E., Surgery and Traumatology
FRENE, E., Internal Medicine
FUENTES, L., Mental Health and Psychiatry
GONZÁLEZ, M., Pre-clinical Sciences
VALLEJOS, C., Obstetrics and Gynaecology

UNIVERSIDAD DE LA SERENA
(University of La Serena)

Benavente 980, La Serena
Telephone: (51) 2204000
E-mail: uls@userena.cl
Internet: www.userena.cl

Founded 1981
State control
Academic year: March to December

Campuses at Andrés Bello, Coquimbo, Ignacio Domeyko, Isabel Bongard, Limarí, Molina Garmendia

Rector: Dr NIBALDO AVILÉS PIZARRO
Vice-Rector for Academic Affairs: Dr JORGE CATALÁN AHUMADAS
Vice-Rector for Finance and Admin.: Dra MARÍA MARCELA AGUIRRE SALGADO
Gen. Dir of Student Affairs: MIGUEL ZULETA CERECEDA
Sec. Gen.: SERGIO ZEPEDA MALUENDA
Librarian: Lic. MARÍA A. CALABACERO JIMÉNEZ

Number of teachers: 600
Number of students: 8,000

Publications: *Revista Actas de Logos* (1 a year), *Revista Crisalida* (1 a year), *Revista de Investigación y Desarrollo* (1 a year), *Revista Humus* (1 a year), *Revista Logos* (1 a year), *Revista Omnibus* (1 a year), *Revista Temas de Educación* (1 a year)

DEANS

Faculty of Engineering: Dr Ing. ALBERTO CORTÉS ÁLVAREZ
Faculty of Humanities: Dra MARÍA ZÚÑIGA CARRASCO
Faculty of Sciences: Dr GUSTAVO LABBÉ MORALES
Faculty of Social Sciences and Economics: JORGE FERNÁNDEZ LABRA

UNIVERSIDAD DE LOS LAGOS
(University of Los Lagos)

Casilla 933, Osorno
Avda Alcalde Fuchslocher 1305, Osorno
Telephone: (64) 2333000
E-mail: rectoria@ulagos.cl
Internet: www.ulagos.cl

Founded 1993, fmrly Instituto Profesional de Osorno
State control
Language of instruction: Spanish
Academic year: March to December

Campuses at Puerto Montt, Santiago, Chiloe, Osorno

Rector: OSCAR GARRIDO ALVAREZ
Vice-Rector for Academic Affairs: JUAN LUIS CARTER BELTRAN
Vice-Rector for Admin. and Finance: PAULA BEDECARRATZ
Vice-Rector for Planning and Devt: OSCAR DIAZ
Vice-Rector for Research and Graduate Studies: EGON MONTECINOS
Gen. Sec.: DIANA KISS DE ALEJANDRO
Librarian: ARTURO RUBIO

Library of 40,200 vols
Number of teachers: 220
Number of students: 12,000

Publications: *Alpha*, *Biota*, *Leader*

UNIVERSIDAD DE MAGALLANES
(University of Magallanes)

Avenida Bulnes 01855, Punta Arenas
Telephone: (61) 2207000
Internet: www.umag.cl

Founded 1964, previously br. of Universidad Técnica del Estado
State control
Language of instruction: Spanish

Rector: Dr VÍCTOR FAJARDO MORALES
Vice-Rector for Academic Affairs: JUAN OYARZO PÉREZ
Sec. Gen.: RUTH ORTIZ SUAZO
Librarian: ILUMINANDA ROJAS PALACIOS

Library of 58,902 vols, 17,153 journals
Number of teachers: 188
Number of students: 3,800

Publications: *Anales del Instituto de la Patagonia*, *Austroumag*, *Magallania*

DEANS

Faculty of Economics and Law: LUIS POBLETE DAVANZO
Faculty of Engineering: Dr HUMBERTO OYARZO PÉREZ
Faculty of Humanities, Social Sciences and Health Sciences: Dr JUAN YUDIKIS PRELLER
Faculty of Sciences: VÍCTOR DÍAZ HUENTELICÁN

UNIVERSIDAD DE PLAYA ANCHA
(University of Playa Ancha)

Edif. Puntángeles, 6°, Avda Playa Ancha 850, Playa Ancha, Valparaíso
Telephone: (32) 2500100
E-mail: mbaxman@upla.cl
Internet: www.upla.cl

Founded 1948
State control
Languages of instruction: Spanish, English, French, German
Academic year: March to December

Rector: PATRICIO SANHUEZA VIVANCO
Pro-Rector: CARMEN IBAÑEZ CASTILLO
Vice-Rector for Academic Affairs: TITO LARRONDO GONZÁLEZ

Vice-Rector for Admin. and Financial Affairs: EDUARDO FAIVOVICH BORTNIK
Vice-Rector for Postgraduate Affairs and Research: DANIEL LÓPEZ STEFONI
Gen. Sec.: GINETTE BOBILLIER
Librarian: MARIA EUGENIA OLGUIN STEENBECKER
Number of teachers: 400
Number of students: 7,000
Publications: *Diálogos Educacionales*, *Diccionario Ejemplificado de Chilenismos*, *Nueva Revista del Pacífico*, *Notas Históricas y Geográficas*, *Proyección Universitaria*, *Revista de Orientación*, *Visiones Científicas*

DEANS
Faculty of Art: ALBERTO TEICHELMANN SHUTTLETON
Faculty of Education: LUIS ALBERTO DÍAZ ARANCIBIA
Faculty of Health Sciences: MIRTA CROVETTO MATTASSI
Faculty of Humanities: JUAN SAAVEDRA ÁVILA
Faculty of Natural and Exact Sciences: JOSÉ RUBIO VALENZUELA
Faculty of Physical Education: ELÍAS MARÍN VALENZUELA

UNIVERSIDAD DE SANTIAGO DE CHILE
(University of Santiago de Chile)

Avda Libertador Bernardo O'Higgins No 3363, Santiago
Telephone: (2) 27180000
E-mail: dae@usach.cl
Internet: www.usach.cl
Founded 1849 as Escuela de Artes y Oficios, renamed Universidad Técnica del Estado 1947, current name adopted 1981
State control
Language of instruction: Spanish
Academic year: March to December
Rector: Dr JUAN MANUEL ZOLEZZI CID
Pro-Rector: PEDRO PALOMINOS BELMAR
Vice-Rector for Academic Affairs: FERNANDA KRI AMAR
Vice-Rector for Finances and Management: JUAN PABLO AGUIRRE
Vice-Rector for Research and Devt: Dr ÓSCAR BUSTOS CASTILLO
Vice-Rector for Student Support: MANUEL ARRIETA SANHUEZA
Sec. Gen.: GUSTAVO ROBLES
Librarian: MARÍA ISABEL PARRA
Library of 250,000 vols
Number of teachers: 1,200
Number of students: 20,000
Publications: *Avances en Investigación y Desarrollo*, *Educación en Ingeniería*, *Mantención e Industria* (4 a year), *Comunicación Universitaria*, *Contribuciones Científicas y Tecnológicas*, *Cuadernos de Humanidades*

DEANS
Faculty of Administration and Economics: SILVIA FERRADA VERGARA
Faculty of Chemistry and Biology: GUSTAVO ZÚÑIGA NAVARRO
Faculty of Engineering: RAMÓN BLASCO SÁNCHEZ
Faculty of Humanities: AUGUSTO SAMANIEGO MESSIAH
Faculty of Medicine: HUMBERTO GUAJARDO SAINZ
Faculty of Sciences: RAFAEL LABARCA BRIONES
Faculty of Technology: GUMERCINDO VILCA CÁCERES
School of Architecture: ALDO HIDALGO HERMOSILLA
School of Journalism: MARGARITA PASTENE VALLADARES
School of Psychology: EMILIO MOYANO DÍAZ
Undergraduate Programme: MARCELA ORELLANA MUERMANN

UNIVERSIDAD DE TALCA
(University of Talca)

2 Norte 685, Talca
Telephone: (71) 2200200
Internet: www.utalca.cl
Founded 1981
State control
Language of instruction: Spanish
Academic year: March to December
Rector: ÁLVARO ROJAS MARÍN
Vice-Rector for Academic Affairs: GILDA CARRASCO SILVA
Vice-Rector for Finance and Admin.: MARITZA FAILLA LEÓN
Vice-Rector for Innovation, Devt and Technology Transfer: GONZALO HERRERA JIMÉNEZ
Vice-Rector for Student Affairs: SERGIO MATUS FUENZALIDA
Vice-Rector for Undergraduate Affairs: MARÍA INÉS ICAZA PÉREZ
Sec. Gen.: JOHANN ALLESCH PEÑAILILLO
Librarian: RAÚL RAVANAL
Number of teachers: 500
Number of students: 8,000
Publications: *Acontecer* (12 a year), *Ius et Praxis* (2 a year), *Panorama Socio Económico* (1 a year), *Revista de Estudios Constitucionales*, *Revista de Estudios Seriados en Gestión de Salud*, *Revista Neuma*, *Revista Interamericana de Ambiente y Turismo (Riat)*, *Universum* (1 a year)

DEANS
Faculty of Agronomy: HERNÁN PAILLÁN LEGUE
Faculty of Business Administration: ARCADIO CERDA URRUTIA
Faculty of Engineering: CLAUDIO TENREIRO LEIVA
Faculty of Forestry Sciences: IVÁN CHACÓN CONTRERAS
Faculty of Health Sciences: CARLOS PADILLA ESPINOZA
Faculty of Juridical and Social Sciences: JORGE DEL PICÓ RUBIO
Faculty of Psychology: EDGAR VOGEL GONZÁLEZ

UNIVERSIDAD DE TARAPACÁ
(University of Tarapaca)

Gral Velásquez 1775, Casilla 7-D, Arica
Telephone: (58) 205100
E-mail: mesacentral@uta.cl
Internet: www.uta.cl
Founded 1981
State control
Language of instruction: Spanish
Academic year: March to December
Library of 80,242 vols, 499 periodicals
Rector: EMILIO RODRÍGUEZ PONCE
Vice-Rector for Academic Affairs: VICTORIA ESPINOSA SANTOS
Vice-Rector for Finance and Admin.: LUIS TAPIA ITURRIETA
Librarian: PATRICIA CASTILLO OCHOA
Library of 80,000 vols, 622 periodicals
Number of teachers: 250
Number of students: 8,000
Publications: *Chungará* (2 a year), *Diálogo Andino* (2 a year), *Idesia* (2 a year), *Limite* (1 a year), *Revista Facultad de Ingeniería* (1 a year), *Revista de Fisica* (1 a year)

DEANS
College of Business Administration: LUIS MELLA SALINAS
Faculty of Agronomy: VITELLIUS GOYKOVIC CORTÉS
Faculty of Health Sciences: LUÍS ALVAREZ INOSTROZA
Faculty of Education and Humanities: ALFONSO DÍAZ AGUAD
Faculty of Electrical Engineering: RICARDO OVALLE CUBILLOS
Faculty of Sciences: CARLOS LEIVA SAJURIA
Faculty of Social Sciences and Law: IVÁN BARRIENTOS BORDOLI
School of Industrial Engineering, Computer Science and Systems: HERNÁNDO BUSTOS ANDREU
School of Mechanical Engineering: JAIME VILLANUEVA ÁGUILA

PROFESSORS
Faculty of Engineering:
ARACENA PIZARRO, D.
BARRAZA SOTOMAYOR, B.
BECK FERNÁNDEZ, H.
BENAVIDES SILVA, J.
BORJAS MONTERO, R.
BUSTOS ANDREU, H.
CAMPOS TRONCOSO, J.
COHEN HORNICKEL, W.
CORREA ARANEDA, E.
DÍAZ ROJAS, H.
DURÁN ARRIAGADA, R.
ESPINOZA VALLEDOR, J.
ESTUPIÑAN PULIDO, E.
FERNÁNDEZ MAGGI, M.
FIGUEROA PÉREZ, H.
FLORES CONDORI, C.
FUENTES HEINRICH, E.
FUENTES ROMERO, R.
GALLEGOS ARAYA, A.
GÁLVEZ SOTO, E.
GODOY RAMSAY, J.
GONZÁLEZ ARAYA, A.
GUÍRRIMAN CARRASCO, R.
HARNISCH VELOSO, I.
JERALDO CASTRO, A.
MARCHIONI CHOQUE, I.
MENDIZABAL JIMÉNEZ, H.
MUÑOZ ESPINOSA, J.
OSSANDON DÍAZ, H.
OSSANDON NUÑEZ, Y.
OVALLE CUBILLOS, R.
PAZ SEGURA, G.
PEDRAJA REJAS, L.
PONCE LÓPEZ, E.
RAMÍREZ VARAS, I.
RODRÍGUEZ ESTAY, A.
SANHUEZA HORMAZABAL, R.
SANZ CANTILLANA, T.
SAPIAÍN ARAYA, R.
TARQUE COSSIO, S.
TORRES ORTÍZ, E.
TORRES SILVA, H.
VALDÉS GONZÁLEZ, H.
VALDIVIA PINTO, R.
VERGARA DÍAZ, J.
VILLALOBOS ABARCA, J.
VILLANUEVA AGUILA, J.
VILLARROEL GONZÁLEZ, C.
ZAMORANO LUCERO, M.

Faculty of Sciences:
ALVAREZ INOSTROZA, L.
BARRIENTOS NUÑOZ, V.
BELTRAN BARRIOS, R.
BOGGIONI CASANOVA, S.
BÓRGUEZ BENITT, CELIA
BRAVO AZLÁN, H.
CABALLERO PETTERSEN, H.
CABELLO FERNÁNDEZ, G.
CALISTO PÉREZ, H.
CAMPOS ORTEGA, H.
CANDIA ANDRADE, M.
CARO ARAYA, M.
CASTRO SANTANDER, F.
CISTERNAS RIVEROS, M.
CORNEJO PONCE, L.
CORRALES MUÑOZ, J.

Cortés Gajardo, W.
Cruz Marino, A.
Espinoza Navarro, O.
Fernández Carvajal, I.
Flores Araya, J.
Flores Franculic, A.
Galaz Leiva, S.
Glass Sadia, B.
González Flores, M.
Hernández Villaseca, L.
Laime Condori, D.
Lavín Becerra, L.
Lazo Núñez, E.
Lea Rodríguez, L.
Leiva Sajuria, C.
Lobato Acosta, I.
López Peric, H.
Lorca Pizarro, S.
Martín García, E.
Medina Díaz, M.
Meneses Vera, C.
Montalvo Villalba, M.
Moscoso Zárate, D.
Naranjo Gárate, A. M.
Olivares Toledo, V.
O'Nell Sequeira, M.
Ortega Araya, A.
Ortega Rojas, A.
Pachá Bustamente, A.
Palleros Santos, H.
Pedreros Avendaño, M.
Pérez Moretti, N.
Quelopana del Valle, A.
Quioza Palominos, S.
Reyes Rubilar, T.
Rey Mas, V.
Rivas Avila, M.
Rojas Espinoza, E.
Rojas Troncoso, M.
Román Flores, H.
Sanhueza Collinao, M.
Ubeda de la Cerda, C.
Valenzuela Estrada, M.
Vasquez Rojas, M. I.
Vilaxa Olcay, A.
Villanueva Díaz, H.
Villegas Bravo, J.
Zúñiga Aguirre, J.
Zúniga Salas, P.

Faculty of Social Sciences, Business Studies and Administration:

Alburquenque Eliash, M.
Alfonso Vargas, J.
Alfred Alfaro, F.
Alvarez Rosales, N.
Barrientos Bordoli, I.
Belmonte Schwarzbaum, E.
Bernal Peralta, J.
Briones Morales, L.
Bussenius Risco, J. C.
Cabrales Gómez, F.
Cayo Rios, G.
Chacama Rodríguez, J.
Chaigneau Orfanoz, S.
Cisternas Arapio, B.
Contreras Cordano, M.
Córdova González, J.
Cuadra Peralta, A.
Donoso Muñoz, M.
Espinoza Verdejo, A.
Ferreira Reyes, R.
Figueroa Guachalla, M.
Flores Tapia, E.
González Cortés, H.
Gutiérrez Samohod, A.
Henriquez Aguilera, A.
Jiménez Quñones, P.
Karmelic Pavlov, V.
Leal Soto, F.
LeBlanc Valenzuela, L.
Muñiz Ovalle, I.
Muñoz Abella, G.
Navarrete Alvarez, M.
Ochoa de la Maza, O.
Palma Quiroz, A.
Parra Suazo, O.
Peralta Montecinos, J.
Pulido Roccatagliata, S.
Ramírez Huanca, D.
Rodríguez Ponce, E.
Romero Romero, J.
Ruíz Larral, C.
Salas Palacios, R.
Santoro Vargas, C.
Standen Ramírez, V.
Storey Meza, R.
Ulloa Torres, H.
Viera Castillo, D.

UNIVERSIDAD DE VALPARAÍSO
(Valparaiso University)

Blanco 951, Valparaíso

Telephone: (32) 2507000
E-mail: vinculos@uv.cl
Internet: www.uv.cl

Founded 1981; previously br. of Univ. of Chile
State control
Academic year: 2 terms, beginning March and August

Rector: Aldo Valle Acevedo
Pro-Rector: Christian Corvalán Rivera
Sec. Gen.: Osvaldo Corrales Jorquera

Number of teachers: 2,000
Number of students: 18,000

Publications: *Revista de Biología Marina*, *Revista de Ciencias Sociales*

DEANS

Faculty of Architecture: Juan Luis Moraga Lacoste
Faculty of Dentistry: Gastón Zamora Alvarez
Faculty of Economics and Administration: Ricardo Barril Villalobos
Faculty of Humanities: Carlos Martel Llano
Faculty of Law and Social Sciences: Alberto Balbontín Retamales
Faculty of Marine Sciences and Natural Resources: Ricardo Bravo Méndez
Faculty of Medicine: Antonio Orellana Tobar, Faculty of Pharmacy: María Soledad Lobos Salvo
Faculty of Sciences: Quintín Molina Vega

UNIVERSIDAD DEL BÍO-BÍO
(Bío-bío University)

Avda Collao 1202, Casilla 5-C, Concepción

Telephone: (41) 3111200
E-mail: rector@ubiobio.cl
Internet: www.ubiobio.cl

Founded 1988
State control
Language of instruction: Spanish
Academic year: March to December

Campus also at Avda Andrés Bello s/n, Chillán

Pres.: Fernando Toledo Montiel
Rector: Dr Héctor Guillermo Gaete Feres
Pro-Rector: Gloria Gómez Vera
Vice-Rector for Academic Affairs: Aldo Ballerini Arroyo
Vice-Rector for Financial Affairs: Luis Améstica Rivas
Sec. Gen.: Ricardo Ponce Soto

Number of teachers: 600
Number of students: 9,000

Publications: *Arquitecturas del Sur* (3 a year), *Cuadernos de Edificación en Madera* (3 a year), *Maderas: Ciencia y Tecnología* (2 a year), *Memoria Anual Institucional* (1 a year), *Mercado de Suelo de Concepción* (3 a year), *Proyección UBB*, *Theoría* (1 a year), *Tiempo y Espacio* (1 a year)

DEANS

Faculty of Architecture, Construction and Design: Cecilia Poblete Arredondo
Faculty of Business Management: Hermosilla Umana Benito
Faculty of Education and Humanities (Chillán): Marco Aurelio Reyes Coca
Faculty of Engineering: Peter Backhouse Erazo
Faculty of Health and Food Sciences: Patricia Letelier Sanz
Faculty of Sciences: Mauricio Cataldo Monsalves

UNIVERSIDAD METROPOLITANA DE CIENCIAS DE LA EDUCACIÓN
(Metropolitan University of Educational Sciences)

Avda Jose Pedro Alessandri 774, Ñuñoa, Santiago

Telephone: (2) 22412400
E-mail: contacto@umce.cl
Internet: www.umce.cl

Founded 1889

Rector: Jaime Espinosa Araya
Vice-Rector: Tatiana Díaz Arce
Sec. Gen.: Ramiro Aguilar Baldomar
Librarian: María Isabel Bruce

Number of teachers: 450
Number of students: 5,000

Publications: *Academia*, *Acta Entomológica Chilena*, *Dimensión Histórica de Chile*, *Educación Física*

DEANS

Faculty of Arts and Physical Education: Patricia Vásquez Prieto
Faculty of Basic Sciences: Juan Vargas Marín
Faculty of Education: Ana María Figueroa Espinola
Faculty of History, Geography and Literature: María Isabel Sáenz-Villarroel Sánchez

UNIVERSIDAD TÉCNICA 'FEDERICO SANTA MARÍA'
(Technical University of Federico Santa Maria)

Avda España 1680, Valparaíso

Telephone: (32) 2654000
E-mail: dgc@usm.cl
Internet: www.usm.cl

Founded 1926
Private control
Language of instruction: Spanish
Academic year: March to December

Rector: Dr Ing. José Rodríguez Péres
Vice-Rector for Academic Affairs: Dr Marcello Visconti
Vice-Rector for Economic and Admin. Affairs: Dr Pedro Gajardo
Sec. Gen.: Jerome Mac Auliffe
Library Dir: Humberto Ravets

Library: see under Libraries and Archives
Number of teachers: 1,100
Number of students: 19,000

Publications: *Gestión Tecnológica* (2 a year), *Revista Industrias* (4 a year), *Scientia* (1 a year).

BRANCH CAMPUSES

Campus Rancagua: Gamero 212, Rancagua; e-mail info.rancagua@usm.cl; Dir Claudio Waghorn.

Campus Santiago: Avda Santa María 6400, Vitacura, Santiago; e-mail comunicaciones-cs-v@usm.cl; Dir Carlos Castro.

Sede José Miguel Carrera: Avda Federico Santa María 6090, Viña del Mar; Dir ROSENDO ESTAY MARTÍNEZ.

Sede Rey Balduino de Bélgica: Avda Alemparte 943, Talcahuano; Dir ALEX ERIZ SOTO

UNIVERSIDAD TECNOLÓGICA METROPOLITANA
(Metropolitan University of Technology)

Calle Dieciocho 161, Casilla 9845, Santiago
Telephone: (2) 27877500
E-mail: rectoria@utem.cl
Internet: www.utem.cl
Founded 1981 as Instituto Profesional de Santiago; current name adopted 1993
Rector: LUIS PINTO FAVERIO
Vice-Rector for Academic Affairs: MARISOL DURÁN SANTIS
Vice-Rector for Admin. and Financial Affairs: ALBERTO RODRÍGUEZ ARRIAGADA
Vice-Rector for Technology Transfer and Extension: MARIO TORRES ALCAYAGA
Gen. Sec.: PATRICIO BASTÍAS ROMÁN
Librarian: XIMENA SÁNCHEZ STAFORELLI
Number of teachers: 500
Number of students: 5,600
Publication: *Trilogía*

DEANS

Faculty of Administration and Economics: ENRIQUE MATURANA LIZARDI
Faculty of Construction and Town and Country Planning: VÍCTOR HUGO POBLETE PULGAR
Faculty of Engineering: CRESCENTE URRUTIA ORTEGA
Faculty of Humanities and Social Communication Technology: ANA GAVILANES BRAVO
Faculty of Natural Sciences, Mathematics and the Environment: MANUEL JERIA ORELL

Private Autonomous Universities

UNIVERSIDAD ACADEMIA DE HUMANISMO CRISTIANO
(Academy of Christian Humanism University)

Condell 343, Providencia, Santiago
Telephone: (2) 27878000
E-mail: admision@academia.cl
Internet: www.academia.cl
Founded 1975
Private control
Pres.: JOSÉ FERNANDO GARCÍA SOTO
Rector: JOSÉ BENGOA CABELLO
Vice-Rector of Academics: LORETO HOECKER PIZARRO
Sec. Gen.: LUIS RIVERA

DEANS

Faculty of Arts: CARLOS ZAMORA PÉREZ
Faculty of Education: LUIS OSANDÓN
Faculty of Social Science: CECILIA LEBLANC

UNIVERSIDAD ADOLFO IBÁÑEZ
(Adolfo Ibáñez University)

Avda Padre Hurtado 750, Viña del Mar
Telephone: (32) 2503500
E-mail: paula.fernandez@uai.cl
Internet: www.uai.cl
Founded 1953
Private control
Language of instruction: Spanish
Academic year: March to December
Rector: ANDRÉS BENÍTEZ
Vice-Rector for Academic Affairs: RAFAEL MACHERONE
Vice-Rector for Economic and Admin. Affairs: CATALINA BOBENRIETH
Gen. Sec.: AGUSTÍN ANTOLA
Dean of Undergraduates: FRANCISCO JOSÉ COVARRUBIAS
Librarian: MARÍA ZINA JIMÉNEZ
Number of teachers: 50 full-time
Number of students: 2,000
Publications: *Cuadernos Jurídicos* (3 a year), *Informe Económico* (4 a year), *INTUS LEGERE: Anuario de Filosofía, Historia y Letras* (1 a year)

DEANS

School of Business: MANOLA SÁNCHEZ
Faculty of Engineering and Science: ALEJANDRO JADRESIĆ
Faculty of Law: RODRIGO CORREA
Faculty of Liberal Arts: LUCÍA SANTA CRUZ
School of Government: LEONIDAS MONTES
School of Journalism: ASCANIO CAVALLO
School of Psychology: JORGE SANHUEZA

UNIVERSIDAD ADVENTISTA DE CHILE
(Chile Adventist University)

Calle Camino las Mariposas, km 12, Chillán Bio-bío
Telephone: (42) 2433500
E-mail: contacto@unach.cl
Internet: www.unach.cl
Founded 1906
Private control
Rector: RICARDO A. GONZÁLEZ
Vice-Rector for Academics: RAMÓN PÉREZ S.
Vice-Rector for Finance: ADRIÁN SEGUI
Vice-Rector for Student Devt: ANTONIO PARRA
Sec. Gen.: LILIAN SCHMIED
Dir for Library: VALENTINA WEVAR J.
Library of 106,045 vols

DEANS

Faculty of Education and Social Sciences: Dr PATRICIO MATAMALA
Faculty of Engineering and Business: HANS ALBÁN P.
Faculty of Health Sciences: Dra GISELA MALDONADO L.
Faculty of Theology: Dr WALTER ALAÑA HUAPALLA

UNIVERSIDAD ALBERTO HURTADO
(Alberto Hurtado University)

Almirante Barroso 10, Santiago
Telephone: (2) 26920200
E-mail: admision@uahurtado.cl
Internet: www.uahurtado.cl
Founded 1997
Private control
Rector: FERNANDO MONTES MATTE
Pro-Rector: JORGE LARRAÍN IBÁÑEZ
Vice-Rector for Academics: PEDRO MILOS HURTADO
Vice-Rector for Integration and Univ. Relations: FERNANDO VERDUGO RAMÍREZ DE ARELLANO
Sec. Gen.: MATÍAS PROVOSTE
Dir for Libraries: PATRICIA ORTIZ
Library of 246,631 vols
Publications: *La Revista Latinoamericana de Psicología Social Ignacio Martín Baró* (2 a year, online, www.rimb.cl), *Revista Diké*, *Revista Persona y Sociedad* (4 a year, print and online, www.personaysociedad.cl)

DEANS

Faculty of Business and Economics: JORGE RODRÍGUEZ GROSSI
Faculty of Education: DASLAV OSTOIC MUÑOZ
Faculty of Law: PEDRO IRURETA URIARTE
Faculty of Philosophy and Humanities: EDUARDO SILVA ARÉVALO
Faculty of Psychology: MAURICIO ARTEAGA MANIEU
Faculty of Social Sciences: FRANCISCA MÁRQUEZ

UNIVERSIDAD BOLIVARIANA
(Bolivarian University)

Calle Huerfanos 1805, Santiago
Telephone: (02) 25776536
E-mail: informaciones@ubolivariana.cl
Internet: www.ubolivariana.cl
Founded 1987
Private control
Rector: RICARDO MEDINA MUÑOZ
Library of 16,000
Publications: *Revista Austerra*, *Revista Babel*, *Revista Polis*

UNIVERSIDAD CATÓLICA CARDENAL RAÙL SILVA HENRIQUEZ
(Catholic University Cardinal Raùl Silva Henriquez)

General Jofré 462, Santiago
Telephone: (2) 24601100
Internet: ww3.ucsh.cl
Founded 1982
Private control
Pres. and Grand Chancellor: ALBERTO LORENZELLI
Rector: JORGE BAEZA CORREA
Vice-Rector for Academics: MANUEL PÉREZ PASTÉN
Vice-Rector for Student Devt: FERNANDO VERGARA HENRÍQUEZ
Vice-Rector for Admin. and Finance: GUILLERMO ESCOBAR ALANIZ
Sec. Gen.: PATRICIO ROSENDE LYNCH
Library of 118,966 vols

DEANS

Faculty of Education: JAIME BRITO FARÍAS
Faculty of Religion and Philosophy: CARLOS ÁBRIGO OTEY
Faculty of Social Sciences, Law and Economics: ALVARO ACUÑA VERCELLI

UNIVERSIDAD CENTRAL
(Central University)

Toesca 1783, Santiago
Telephone: (2) 25826000
E-mail: guia@ucentral.cl
Internet: www.ucentral.cl
Founded 1982
Private control
Language of instruction: Spanish
Academic year: March to January
Rector: RAFAEL ROSELL AIQUELRAFAEL
Vice-Rector for Academic Affairs: SILVANA COMINETTI COTTI-COMETTI
Vice-Rector for Admin. and Finance: RICARDO MARTÍNEZ PASSEK
Vice-Rector for Institutional Devt: GERMÁN CORREA DÍAZ
Gen. Sec.: OMAR AHUMADA MORA
Librarian: NELLY CORNEJO MENESES
Number of teachers: 700
Number of students: 6,200
Publications: *Parthenon* (2 a year), *Perspectiva*, *Revista de Arquitectura*, *Revista de Derecho*, *Revista de Psicología*, *Universidad y Sociedad*

DEANS

Faculty of Architecture and Town and Country Planning: RODRIGO DE LA CRUZ BENAPRES
Faculty of Communications: JUANITA ROJAS CISTERNAS
Faculty of Economics and Administration: ROBERTO CASTRO TAPIA
Faculty of Education: JOSÉ LUIS REYES FUENTES
Faculty of Engineering: NÉSTOR GONZÁLEZ VALENZUELA
Faculty of Health Sciences: BERNANDO JAVIER MORALES CATALÁN
Faculty of Law and Social Sciences: ANDRÉS NAUDÓN FIGUEROA
Faculty of Physical Sciences and Mathematics: SERGIO QUEZADA GONZÁLEZ
Faculty of Politics and Public Administration: MARCO MORENO PÉREZ
Faculty of Social Sciences: OSVALDO TORRES GUTIÉRREZ

UNIVERSIDAD DE ACONCAGUA
(Aconcagua University)

Pedro Herrera Balharry s/n, San Felipe
Telephone: (34) 2511414
E-mail: sede.sanfelipe@uac.cl
Internet: www.uac.cl

Founded 1990
Private control

Rector: JOSÉ FRANCISCO AGUIRRE OSSA
Vice-Rector for Academics: PÍO VALDÉS NAGEL
Vice Rector for Admin. and Finance: GASTÓN ZEGARD LATRACH
Sec. Gen.: SERGIO ANABALÓN MUÑOZ

UNIVERSIDAD DIEGO PORTALES
(Diego Portales University)

Avda Manuel Rodríguez Sur 415, Santiago 8370179
Telephone: (2) 26762000
E-mail: admision@udp.cl
Internet: www.udp.cl

Founded 1982

Rector: CARLOS PEÑA GONZÁLEZ
Vice-Rector for Academic Affairs and Research: CRISTÓBAL MARÍN CORREA
Sec. Gen: JOSÉ JULIO LEÓN REYES
Librarian: PAULINA GODOY

Number of teachers: 1,200
Number of students: 11,000

Publication: *El Portaliano*

DEANS

Faculty of Architecture, Design and Art: MATHÍAS KLOTZ
Faculty of Business: FERNANDO LEFORT GORCH
Faculty of Communication: CECILIA GARCÍA HUIDOBRO MAC AULIFFE
Faculty of Education: HORACIO WALKER LARRAÍN
Faculty of Engineering: RODRIGO GARRIDO HIDALGO
Faculty of Law: JUAN ENRIQUE VARGAS VIANCOS
Faculty of Medicine: PATRICIA MUÑOZ CASAS DEL VALLE
Faculty of Psychology: ADRIANA KAULINO
Faculty of Social Sciences and History: MANUEL VICUÑA URRUTIA

UNIVERSIDAD FINIS TERRAE
(Finis Terrae University)

Avda Pedro de Valdivia 1509, Providencia, Santiago
Telephone: (2) 24207100
Internet: www.finisterrae.cl

Founded 1988
Private control

Rector: CRISTIAN NAZER A.
Vice-Rector for Academics: ROBERTO VEGA
Vice-Rector for Communications: CONSTANZA LÓPEZ
Vice-Rector for Devt: BRUNO KRUMENAKER
Vice-Rector for Finance: PABLO BARROS
Sec. Gen.: ROBERTO SALIM-HANNA
Dir for Library: NOLLY HERRERA ACUÑA

DEANS

Faculty of Architecture and Design: FELIPE ASSADI
Faculty of Arts: ENRIQUE ZAMUDIO
Faculty of Business and Economics: MIGUEL LEÓN
Faculty of Civil Engineering: MIGUEL LEÓN
Faculty of Dentistry: SERGIO SÁNCHEZ
Faculty of Education and Family Sciences: LUZ MARÍA BUDGE
Faculty of Law: MIGUEL SCHWEITZER
Faculty of Medicine: ALBERTO DOUGNAC

UNIVERSIDAD GABRIELA MISTRAL
(Gabriela Mistral University)

Avda Ricardo Lyon 1177, Providencia, Santiago
Telephone: (2) 24144545
E-mail: admision@ugm.cl
Internet: www.ugm.cl

Founded 1981
Academic year: March to January

Communication, digital arts, economics, education, engineering, humanities, law and social sciences, management, psychology

Rector: ALDO GIACCHETTI PASTOR
Pro-Rector: LISANDRO SERRANO SPOERER
Vice-Rector for Academic Affairs: KIYOSHI FUKUSHI MANDIOLA
Vice-Rector for Admin. and Finance: ISABEL MARGARITA MANDIOLA SERRANO
Librarian: CARMEN BUSQUETS

Number of teachers: 450
Number of students: 3,500

UNIVERSIDAD LOS LEONES
(Los Leones University)

Zenteno 234, Metro La Moneda, Santiago
Telephone: (2) 26521200
E-mail: admision@ipleones.cl
Internet: www.uleones.com

Founded 1981
Private control

Rector: FERNANDO VICENCIO
Vice-Rector for Academics: EMILIO GAUTIER

Library of 22,000 vols

UNIVERSIDAD MAYOR
(Mayor University)

Manuel Montt 367, Santiago
Telephone: (2) 23281190
E-mail: registro.estudiantes@umayor.cl
Internet: www.umayor.cl

Founded 1988

Faculty of engineering, institute for art and media technology and institute of communication and new technologies
Private control

Rector: RUBÉN COVARRUBIAS GIORDANO
Vice-Rector for Academics and Quality Assurance: RENÉ SALAMÉ MARTÍN
Vice-Rector for Devt: ERICH VILLASEÑOR MALDONADO
Vice-Rector for Admin. and Finance: PATRICIO SOTO CARAMORI
Vice-Rector for Regions: HUGO CUMSILLE NEIRA

DEANS

Faculty of Medicine: Dr JUAN GIACONI G.
Faculty of Agriculture and Forestry: EDUARDO VENEZIAN LEIGH
Faculty of Education: CORNELIO WESTENENK
Faculty of Dentistry: Dr GUSTAVO MONCADA
Faculty of Business and Entrepreneurship: FELIPE MORANDÉ LAVÍN
Faculty of Architecture, Design and Construction: FERNANDO MARÍN CRUCHAGA
Faculty of Law: CLARA SZCZARANSKI CERDA
Faculty of Arts: HÉCTOR NOGUERA
Faculty of Science: Dr PATRICIO A. MANQUE

UNIVERSIDAD MIGUEL DE CERVANTES
(Miguel de Cervantes University)

Calle Merced 385, Santiago
Telephone: (2) 23809610
E-mail: admision@umcervantes.cl
Internet: www.umcervantes.cl

Founded 1996
Private control

Accounting, audit, commercial engineering, education, political science and public administration, psychology, right, risk prevention and environment, social work

Rector: GUTENBERG MARTÍNEZ OCAMICA
Vice-Rector for Academics: FRANCISCA ORTEGA FREI
Vice-Rector for Admin. and Finance: MAURICIO ESPINOSA SANHUEZA
Vice-Rector for Communications and Extension: JORGE MALDONADO ROLDÁN
Sec. Gen.: MERCEDES AUBÁ ASVICIO
Dir for Libraries: GASTÓN GONZALEZ CARREÑO

Library of 10,500 vols, 180 periodicals

UNIVERSIDAD PEDRO DE VALDIVIA
(Pedro de Valdivia University)

Huérfanos 1546, Santiago
Telephone: (2) 28285890
Internet: www.upv.cl

Founded 2006
Private control

Rector: ALDO BIAGINI ALARCÓN
Vice-Rector for Academics: PAULINA MARAMBIO DÍAZ
Vice-Rector for Admin. and Finance: MARCO CONTRERAS ARAVENA
Vice-Rector for Campus Antofagasta: JUAN FUENTES VILLEGAS
Vice-Rector for Campus La Serena: FERNANDO DÍAZ MOLINA
Vice-Rector for Campus Sur: RICARDO BOCAZ SEPÚLVEDA
Sec. Gen: LUIS SOLÍS VÁSQUEZ

DEANS

Faculty of Agricultural Sciences: SERGIO BOASSI ROCUANT
Faculty of Architecture, Design and Communication: RICARDO CASTILLO VON BENNEWITZ
Faculty of Education: ANDREA FARÍAS DELANO
Faculty of Engineering: LUIS MARTÍNEZ CERNA
Faculty of Health Sciences: DANIELA ESPINOZA ALVARADO
Faculty of Legal and Social Sciences: MACARENA FERNÁNDEZ UNDURRAGA
Faculty of Medical Sciences: HERNÁN MONASTERIO IRAZOQUE
Faculty of Nursing: PÍA BAEZA VICUÑA

UNIVERSIDAD SAN SEBASTIÁN
(San Sebastián University)

Campus Las Tres Pascualas, Lientur 1457, Concepción
Telephone: (41) 22400001
E-mail: concepcion@uss.cl

Internet: www.uss.cl
Founded 1989
Private control
Academic year: March to December
Campuses at Santiago, Concepción, Valdivia, Osorno, Puerto Montt
Rector: RICARDO RIESCO JARAMILLO
Pro-Rector: LUIS CORDERO BARRERA
Vice-Rector for Academic Affairs: OSCAR CRISTI MARFIL
Vice-Rector for Campus Clinics: GHISLAINE ARCIL GREVE
Vice-Rector for Communications: WILLIAM DÍAZ ROMÁN
Vice-Rector for Concepción Campus: JAVIER VERA JÜNEMANN
Vice-Rector for Economic and Admin. Affairs: SERGIO MENA JARA
Vice-Rector for Osorno Campus: SERGIO HERMOSILLA PÉREZ
Vice-Rector for Planning and Devt: ANDRÉS FLORES MELLADO
Vice-Rector for Puerto Montt Campus: JOSÉ GUILLERMO LEAY RUIZ
Vice-Rector for Quality Assurance: GONZALO PUENTES SOTO
Vice-Rector for Research and Postgraduate Affairs: ALEJANDRO ALBORNOZ SATELER
Vice-Rector for Santiago Campus: PATRICIO GAETE MAUREIRA
Vice-Rector for Social Responsibility and Extension: ANA VICTORIA DURRUTY CORRAL
Vice-Rector for Valdivia Campus: ANGELO ROMANO VIRAGO
Gen. Sec.: SANDRA GUZMÁN MARTÍNEZ
Librarian: MARGARITA VALDERRAMA CÁCERES
Library of 6,000 vols
Number of teachers: 180
Number of students: 1,800

DEANS
Faculty of Architecture, Art and Design: ALBERT TIDY
Faculty of Dentistry: SERGIO CASTRO ALFARO
Faculty of Economics and Business: HUGO LAVADOS MONTES
Faculty of Education: RODRIGO FERNÁNDEZ DONOSO
Faculty of Engineering and Technology: PEDRO RAMÍREZ GLADE
Faculty of Health: FERNANDO QUIROGA DUBORNAIS
Faculty of Law: XAVIER ARMENDARIZ SALAMERO
Faculty of Medicine: MARIO FERNÁNDEZ GUTIÉRREZ
Faculty of Nursing: ASTRID OURCILLEÓN ANTOGNONI
Faculty of Psychology: CLAUDIO ORELLANA FERNÁNDEZ
Faculty of Sciences of Physical Activity: PATRICIA ACUÑA FUENTES
Faculty of Veterinary Medicine: ÁLVARO BERRÍOS SALAS

UNIVERSIDAD SANTO TOMÁS
(Saint Thomas University)

Avda Ejército 146, Barrio Universitario, Santiago
Telephone: (600) 4444444
E-mail: redsocial@santotomas.cl
Internet: www.santotomas.cl
Founded 1988
Private control
Rector: JAIME VATTER GUTIÉRREZ
Vice-Rector for Academics: ÁNGELA VIVANCO MARTÍNEZ
Vice-Rector for Professional Institute and Technical Training Center: JUAN CARLOS ERDOZÁIN ACEDO
Vice-Rector for Quality Assurance: FERNANDO DE LA JARA GOYENECHE
Vice-Rector for Admissions and Student Affairs: ANA MARÍA PELEGRÍ KRISTIC
Vice-Rector for Corporate Affairs: HERNÁN SWART FIGUEROA
Vice-Rector for Admin. and Human Resources: ENRIQUE GÓMEZ BRADFORD
Vice-Rector for Finance and Management Control: JUAN PABLO GUZMÁN ALDUNATE
Vice-Rector for Process and Information Technology: LEOPOLDO CÁRDENAS PÉREZ
Sec. Gen.: PATRICIO CEPEDA SILVA
Number of teachers: 3,880
Number of students: 28,000
Publications: *Berit Internacional*, *IUS Publicum*, *Revista Ciencias Sociales*

DEANS
Faculty of Education: PAULINA DITTBORN CORDUA
Faculty of Engineering: ÓSCAR MIMICA ROKI
Faculty of Health: ANDREA SOLÍS AGUIRRE
Faculty of Law: ANÍBAL RODRÍGUEZ LETELIER
Faculty of Management: PATRICIO ARRAU PONS
Faculty Natural Resources and Veterinary Medicine: JORGE CROSSLEY CABEZÓN
Faculty of Science: CARMEN ESPOZ LARRAÍN
Faculty of Social Sciences: MACARENA LUCAR ARCE

Professional Institutes

Instituto Profesional de Chile (Professional Institute of Chile): República 285, Santiago; tel. (2) 27224800; e-mail contacto@ipchile.cl; internet www.ipchile.cl; f. 1981; campuses also in La Serena, Rancagua, San Joaquín, Temuco; Rector JORGE NARBONA LEMUS; Vice-Rector for Academics FELIPE EDUARDO VIDAL ROJAS; Vice-Rector for Admin. ALEJANDRA RUTTIMANN CURTZE; Vice-Rector for Admissions and Communications CRISTÓBAL RAMÍREZ RODRÍGUEZ; Vice-Rector for Quality Assurance SERGIO SCHMIDT YURASZECK.

Instituto Profesional de ENAC/Centro de Formación Téchnica (Professional Institute of ENAC): Alameda 2182, metro República, Santiago; tel. (2) 24738828; internet www.enac.cl; f. 1982; Rector CAROLINA DUCCI BUDGE; Vice-Rector for Academics MARIA OLGA CAMUS POBLETE; Vice-Rector for Admin. and Finance LUIS ALBERTO GUAJARDO MONRROY; Vice-Rector for Research, Devt and Student Affairs DEBORAH SINGER CERDA; Sec. Gen. JAVIERA DIAZ SCHMIDT.

Instituto Profesional de la Universidad Andrés Bello (AIEP) (Professional Institute of Andres Bello University (AIEP)): Avda Providencia 727, Santiago; tel. (2) 24027901; e-mail admision@aiep.cl; internet www.aiep.cl; f. 1960; campuses at Calama, Antofagasta, La Serena, San Felipe, Viña del Mar, Valparaíso, Barrio Universitario, Providencia, Bellavista, San Joaquín, Rancagua, San Fernando, Curicó, Talca, Concepción, Los Ángeles, Temuco, Osorno, Puerto Montt; faculties of art and communication, business, comprehensive aesthetics, construction and civil works, costume design, design, engineering, food hospitality and tourism health, social development, sound television and speech, sport; Rector FERNANDO MARTÍNEZ SANTANA; Pro-Rector PATRICIA CABELLO PEDRASA; Vice-Rector for Academics ALEJANDRO ZAMORANO JONES; Vice-Rector for Admissions and Communications JAVIER NAVARRO CUBILLOS; Vice-Rector for Finance NILS LILLIEGREN NOBOA; Vice-Rector for Operations RODRIGO GUZMÁN POSAVAC.

Instituto Profesional del Valle Central (Professional Institute of Valle Central): Barros Arana 160, Concepción; tel. (41) 2669250; e-mail admin@vallecentral.cl; internet www.vallecentral.cl; f. 1996; Rector LUIS HORACIO ROJAS M.; Vice-Rector for Academics ALEJANDRO SALINAS LÒPEZ; Vice-Rector for Admin. and Finance ALBERTO VILLA CONTRERAS.

Instituto Profesional La Araucana (Araucana Professional Institute): Ejército 171, Metro los Héroes, Santiago; tel. (02) 24271057; internet www.iplaaraucana.cl; f. 1980; campuses in Concepción, Curaco de Vélez, Curicó, La Serena, Melipilla, Osorno, Quilicura, San Antonio, San Bernardo, Temuco, Viña del Mar; Rector MARCOS BURICH MAESTRI.

Instituto Profesional Los Leones (Los Leones Professional Institute): Arturo Prat No 274, metro University of Chile, Santiago; tel. (2) 26521200; e-mail dae@ipleones.cl; internet www.ipleones.cl/ip; f. 1981; campus also in Viña del Mar; Rector FERNANDO VICENCIO.

Instituto Profesional Santo Tomas (Saint Thomas Professional Institute): Avda Ejército 146, Barrio Universitario, Santiago; tel. (600) 4444444; internet www.santotomas.cl/ipcft; campuses also in Antofagasta, Copiapó, Iquique, La Serena, Ovalle, San Joaquín, Viña del Mar; Pres. JUAN HURTADO VICUNA; Rector ANSONIA LILLO TOR; publ. *N-Portada*.

PEOPLE'S REPUBLIC OF CHINA

The Higher Education System

Some of the oldest institutions of higher education in the world are to be found in the People's Republic of China (for example, Hunan University dates back to the establishment of Yuelu Academy in 976). Tertiary education has expanded dramatically over the last decade or so, making China's higher education system the world's largest in absolute numbers. Higher education is dominated by state institutions, although some private establishments have been established in recent years, and administration reflects the centralized nature of the State. During the 1950s a number of higher education establishments were designated 'key' institutions and received better staff, facilities and funding. The term 'key institution' is now officially defunct but is still used to denote the most prestigious institutions (which currently number around 70 and which, not surprisingly, attract the best students). The Cultural Revolution (1966–76) led to radical changes in the higher education system, as entrance examinations and continuous assessment were abolished; however, many of the changes were later reversed (the National University Entrance Examination—Gaokao—was re-introduced in 1977). Following university unrest in 1989, including the Tiananmen Square protests in Beijing, students were required to undergo a year of political 'training' prior to university entrance. Further reforms were launched in 1992, under which institutions were given greater autonomy in decision-making (although central government retained responsibility for overall planning and management). There was also a trend towards mergers, which led to a decrease in the number of higher education institutions, from 1,984 in 1998 to 1,731 in 2004; however, by 2009 the number of establishments had risen substantially again to reach a total of 2,305. In that year a total of 21.45m. students were enrolled in higher education; this figure rose in 2011 to 23.08m. Also in 2011 there were 2,101 state higher education institutions (incl. junior colleges), 386 non-state institutions and 309 state approved independent colleges. A new higher education reform programme was launched in early 2000, with the aim of modernizing courses and teaching materials and improving pedagogy.

Laws regulating the higher education system include the 1996 Law on Vocational Education, the 1998 Law on Higher Education and the 2004 Regulations on Academic Degrees. In 1986 the stipend system for university and college students was replaced with a new scholarship and loan system. From 1997 all higher education institutions officially started charging tuition fees; the level of fees has been rising steadily since then. Tuition fees and miscellaneous charges are now the major sources of income for colleges and universities, while state appropriations are used to cover the salaries for university employees.

Performance in the National University Entrance Examination represents the main criterion for admission to higher education. Additionally, students may be required to undergo political education and perform some form of industrial or agricultural labour. The examination is conducted on a national basis and students are tested on three compulsory subjects (Chinese, mathematics and a foreign language—usually English) and on one to three additional subjects in their specialized field of either science or the humanities. Competition to gain places at the most reputable institutions is particularly fierce. Since 2003 the entrance examination system has been undergoing reform, with a rising number of the 'key'/'prestigious' universities using independent examinations (in addition to the national examination). The university-level degree system, which is offered at universities, colleges and academies with degree-awarding powers, consists of Xueshi (Bachelors), Shuoshi (Masters) and Boshi (Doctorate). Bachelors degree courses last four years (five years for medical courses) and conform to one of the 249 programmes defined by the Ministry of Education. Entry to Masters degree programmes is based on a two-cycle, very competitive entrance examination. In 1989 it was announced that selection of postgraduate students would also be on the basis of 'moral' and physical fitness. A Masters degree requires two to three years of further study after the Bachelors, including research and the submission and defence of a thesis. The Doctorate (PhD) is awarded after a minimum of three years of study following the Masters and concludes with the submission and defence of a thesis.

Diplomas from technical and vocational education at tertiary level are available from a number of different types of institution, and usually require two to three years of study. Institutions offering technical and vocational education include vocational technology colleges, vocational universities, radio and television universities (Dianda, which currently number around 1,300) and spare-time universities (Yeda). The programmes, which are open to senior school graduates in both the academic and vocational streams, involve a large amount of course work. Students are generally required to complete some form of field study as part of their studies. In 2011 there were 356 state and non-state approved adult higher education institutions in operation. Vocational education is supervised by the Ministry of Education and Ministry of Human Resources and Social Security.

The early 21st century has seen considerable growth in online higher education, which is of particular benefit to students living in remote and underdeveloped regions and to students who failed university entrance examinations.

Regulatory and Representative Bodies

GOVERNMENT

Ministry of Culture: 10 Chao Yang Men Bei Dajie, Chao Yang Qu, 100020 Beijing; tel. (10) 59881114; e-mail chinaculture@chinadaily.com.cn; internet www.ccnt.gov.cn; Minister CAI WU.

Ministry of Education: 37 Damucang Hutong, Xidan, 100816 Beijing; tel. (10) 66096114; e-mail english@moe.edu.cn; internet www.moe.edu.cn; Minister YUAN GUIREN.

Ministry of Science and Technology: 15 B, Fuxing Rd, Beijing, 100862; e-mail officemail@mail.most.gov.cn; internet www.most.gov.cn; Minister Dr WAN GANG.

FUNDING

China Scholarship Council: Level 13, Bldg A3 No. 9, Chegongzhuang Ave, 100044 Beijing; tel. (10) 66093900; e-mail webmaster@csc.edu.cn; internet www.csc.edu.cn; f. 1994; attached to Min. of Education; provides financial assistance to Chinese citizens wishing to study abroad and to foreign citizens wishing to study in China; Chair. ZHANG XINSHENG; Sec.-Gen. ZHANG XIUQIN.

NATIONAL BODY

China Education Association for International Exchange: 37 Damucang Hutong, Xicheng Dist., Beijing 100816; 160 Fuxingmen Nei Dajie, 100031 Beijing; tel. (10) 66416080; e-mail info@ceaie.edu.cn; internet chn.ceaie.edu.cn; f. 1981; not-for-profit org. conducting int. educational exchanges; 159 mem. instns; Pres. ZHANG XINSHENG; Sec.-Gen. Prof. JIANG BO.

Learned Societies

GENERAL

Chinese Academy of Sciences: 52 San Li He Rd, 100864 Beijing; tel. (10) 68597289; e-mail cas_en@stimes.cn; internet www.cas.ac.cn; f. 1949; academic divs of chemistry, earth sciences, information technical sciences, life sciences and medicine, mathematics and physics, technological sciences; attached research institutes: see under Research Institutes; 633 mems, 13 foreign mems; library: see under Libraries and Archives; Pres. Prof. BAI CHUNLI; Vice-Pres. ZHAN WENLONG; Vice-Pres. DING ZHONGLI; Vice-Pres. YIN HEJUN; Sec.-Gen. Prof. ZHU XUAN.

Chinese Academy of Social Sciences: 5 Jianguomen Nei Da Jie, 100732 Beijing; tel. (10) 65137744; e-mail cssnenglish@yahoo.com.cn; internet www.cass.net.cn; f. 1977; attached research institutes: see under Research Institutes; Pres. WANG WEIGUANG; Sec.-Gen. ZHU JINCHANG.

UNESCO Office Beijing: Waijiaogongyu 5-13-3, Jianguomenwai Compound, Beijing 100600; tel. (10) 65322828; e-mail beijing@unesco.org; internet www.unescobeijing.org; designated Cluster Office for People's Republic of China, Democratic People's Republic of Korea, Japan, Mongolia and Republic of Korea; Dir YASUYUKI AOSHIMA.

AGRICULTURE, FISHERIES AND VETERINARY SCIENCE

China Society of Fisheries: East Third Ring Rd, 100122 Beijing; tel. (10) 59199605; e-mail csfish@csfish.org.cn; internet www.csfish.org.cn; f. 1963; 19,589 mems; library of 12,000 vols; Pres. ZHANG YANXI; publs *Deep-sea Fisheries, Freshwater Fisheries, Journal of Fisheries of China, Marine Fisheries, Scientific Fish Farming*.

Chinese Academy of Agricultural Mechanization Sciences: 1 Beishatan, Deshengmen Wai, 100083 Beijing; tel. (10) 64882223; e-mail info@caams.org.cn; internet www.caams.org.cn; f. 1956; Pres. LI SHU JUN; publs *China Agricultural Mechanization* (6 a year), *Farm Machinery* (12 a year), *Rural Mechanization* (6 a year), *Tractor and Automobile Drivers* (6 a year), *Transactions of the Chinese Society of Agricultural Machinery* (4 a year).

Chinese Academy of Agricultural Sciences: 12 Zhongguancun South St, Beijing; tel. (10) 82109475; e-mail diccaas@caas.cn; internet www.caas.net.cn; f. 1957; 40 attached research institutes; library of 650,000 vols, 7,000 periodicals; Pres. LI JIAYANG; publs *Acta Agronomica Sinica, Acta Horticulturae Sinica, Acta Phyliphulacica Sinica*.

Chinese Academy of Forestry: Wan Shou Shan, 100091 Beijing; tel. (10) 62582211; internet www.caf.ac.cn; f. 1958; 4,700 mems; attached research institutes: see Research Institutes; library of 400,000 vols; Pres. ZHANG SHOUGONG; publs *Chemistry and Industry of Forest Products, China Forestry Abstracts, Foreign Forest Product Industry Abstracts, Foreign Forestry Abstracts, Forestry Research, Forestry Science and Technology, Scientia Silvae Sinicae, Wood Industry, World Forestry Research*.

Chinese Association of Agricultural Science Societies: Min. of Agriculture, 11 Nongzhanguan Nanli, 100026 Beijing; f. 1917; Pres. HONG FUZENG; Sec.-Gen. LI HUAIZHI.

Chinese Sericulture Society: Sibaidu, Zhenjiang, 212018 Jiangsu Province; tel. (511) 5616661; f. 1963; 10,000 mems; library of 50,000 vols; Pres. XIANG ZHONGHUAI; Sec.-Gen. ZHUANG DAHUAN; publ. *Sericultural Science* (4 a year).

Chinese Society for Horticultural Science: 12 Zhongguancun Nandajie, Beijing 100081; tel. (10) 68919528; e-mail ivfcaas@public3.bta.net.cn; f. 1930; 3,000 mems; Pres. ZHU DEWEI; publ. *Acta Horticulturae Sinica* (6 a year).

Chinese Society of Forestry: Wanshoushan, 100091 Beijing; tel. (10) 62889815; e-mail csfoffice@forestry.ac.cn; internet www.csf.org.cn; f. 1917, current name adopted 1951; 87,225 mems; Pres. JIANG ZEHUI; Sec. Gen. GUAN SONGLIN; publ. *Scientia Silvae Sinicae* (6 a year).

Chinese Society of Tropical Crops: Baodao Xincun, Danzhou, Hainan Province; tel. (898) 23300157; e-mail scutafao@yahoo.com; f. 1978; 4,474 mems; library of 250,000 vols; Chair. ZENG YUZHUANG; Chair. YU RANGSHUI; Sec.-Gen. ZHENG WENRONG; publ. *Chinese Journal of Tropical Crops* (4 a year).

Crop Science Society of China: 12 Zhongguancun South St, 100081 Beijing; tel. (10) 82108616; e-mail zwxh@caas.cn; internet www.chinacrops.org; f. 1961; attached to Institute of Crop Sciences, Chinese Academy of Agricultural Sciences; 20,000 mems; Dir ZHAI HUQU; publs *Acta Agronomica Sinica* (6 a year), *Crop Journal* (6 a year).

Soil Science Society of China: POB 821, 210008 Nanjing; tel. (25) 86881532; e-mail sssc@issas.ac.cn; f. 1945; academic exchange; scientific popularization; education and training; consultation for decision-making; technical service; int. cooperation; talents recommendation, reward and recognition; 17,600 mems; Pres. Prof. ZHOU JIANMIN; Vice Sec.-Gen. WEIDONG YAN; publs *Acta Pedologica Sinica* (6 a year), *Arid Zone Research* (6 a year), *Journal of Soil and Water Conservation* (6 a year), *Soil Bulletin* (6 a year), *Pedosphere* (6 a year).

ARCHITECTURE AND TOWN PLANNING

Architectural Society of China: 9 Sanlihe Rd, 100835 Beijing; tel. (10) 88082238; e-mail asc@mail.cin.gov.cn; f. 1953; 30,000 mems; library of 25,000 vols; Pres. SONG CHUNHUA; publs *Architectural Journal* (12 a year), *Architectural Knowledge* (12 a year), *Journal of Building Structure* (6 a year).

Chinese Society for Urban Studies: Bai Wanzhuang, 100835 Beijing; tel. (10) 68393424; e-mail zhaibh@mail.cin.gov.cn; internet www.urbanstudies.org.cn; f. 1984; part of Min. of Housing and Urban-Rural Construction; 30,000 mems; Pres. ZHOU GANSHI; Sec.-Gen. GU WENXUAN; publ. *Urban Studies* (6 a year).

BIBLIOGRAPHY, LIBRARY SCIENCE AND MUSEOLOGY

Chinese Archives Society: 21 Fengshen Hutong, Beijing; tel. (10) 66175130; f. 1981; 7,412 mems; Chair. SHEN ZHENGLE; publ. *Archive Science Study* (4 a year).

Chinese Association of Natural Science Museums: 126 Tian Chiao St, 100050 Beijing; tel. (10) 67053997; e-mail cansm@vip.sina.com; internet www.cansm.org; f. 1980; 1,520 mems (1200 individual mems and 320 group mems); Sec. Gen. XIE YENGHUAN; publ. *China Nature* (6 a year).

Chinese Society of Library Science: 39 Bai Shi Qiao Rd, 100081 Beijing; tel. (10) 68415566; f. 1979; 10,150 mems; Pres. LIU DEYOU; publ. *Journal of Library Science in China* (6 a year, in Chinese).

ECONOMICS, LAW AND POLITICS

China Law Society: 63 Bing Ma Si Hutong, 100034 Beijing; tel. (10) 66150114; f. 1949; ind. academic instn for study of the Chinese socialist legal system; 110,000 mems; library of 40,000 vols, incl. China Catalogue of Law Books; Pres. REN JIANXIN; Sec. Gen. SONG SHUTAO; publs *China Law Yearbook, Democracy and Law Journal, Law of China*.

Chinese Legal History Society: Law Dept, Beijing Univ., Haidian Dist., Beijing 100871; tel. (10) 62561166; f. 1979; studies history of Chinese and foreign legal systems; 300 mems; Pres. Prof. ZHANG GUOHUA; Chief Sec. RAO XINXIAN; publs *Communications of Legal History, Review of Legal History*.

Chinese Research Society for the Modernization of Management: c/o China Association for Science and Technology, Sanlihe, Xijiao, Beijing; tel. (10) 68318877 ext. 524; f. 1978; Pres. XIE SHAOMING; publ. *Modernization of Management*.

HISTORY, GEOGRAPHY AND ARCHAEOLOGY

Chinese Society for Future Studies: 32 Baishiqiao Rd, Haidian Dist., 100081 Beijing; f. 1979; 1,000 mems; CEO DU DAGONG; publ. *Future and Development* (4 a year).

Chinese Society of Geodesy, Photogrammetry and Cartography: Baiwanzhuang, Beijing; tel. (10) 68992229; f. 1959; 3,000 mems; Pres. Prof. WANG ZHIZHUO; Sec.-Gen. Prof. YANG KAI; publ. *Acta Geodetica et Cartographica Sinica*.

Chinese Society of Oceanography: 1 Fuxingmenwai Ave, 100860 Beijing; tel. (10) 68047602; e-mail xuehuimishuchu@hotmail.com; Pres. PENG DEQING.

Geographical Society of China: No. A11, Datun Rd, Beijing 100101; tel. (10) 64870663; e-mail gsc@igsnrr.ac.cn; internet www.gsc.org.cn; f. 1909; 31 provincial divs; special comms: cartography, climatology, economic geography, environmental geography and chemical geography, geographical information systems, geomorphology and quaternary studies, historical geography, human geography, hydrography, marine geography, medical geography, physical geography, quantitative geography, sustained agriculture and rural development, tourist geography, urban geography, world geography; working comms: academic affairs, edition and publication, geographical education, int. scientific and technical cooperation (China Nat. Cttee for Int. Geographical Union—IGU), popularization of geographical knowledge, young geographers; br. socs: coastal open region, Changjang river research, desert research, environmental remote sensing, glaciology and geocryology, mountain research; geographical construction in the arid and semi-arid region; 18,900 mems; Pres. LU DADAO; Sec.-Gen. ZHANG GUOYOU; publs *Acta Geographica Sinica* (6 a year), *China National Geography* (12 a year), *Economic Geography* (6 a year), *Historical Geography* (4 a year), *Human Geography* (6 a year), *Journal of Geographical Sciences* (4 a year, English edn), *Journal of Glaciology and Geocryology* (6 a year), *Journal of Mountain Science* (6 a year), *Journal of Remote Sensing* (6 a year), *World Regional Studies* (4 a year).

LANGUAGE AND LITERATURE

Alliance Française: 18 Gongtixilu, Guangcai Guojigongyu, Chaoyang Dist., Beijing 100020; tel. (10) 65532678; e-mail info.beijing@afchine.org; internet www.alliancefrancaise.org.cn; offers courses and exams in French language and culture and promotes cultural exchange with France; attached teaching centres in Chengdu, Guangzhou, Nanjing, Shanghai and Wuhan.

British Council: Cultural and Education Section, British Embassy, 4th Fl., Landmark Bldg Tower 1, 8 N Dongsanhuan Rd, Chaoyang Dist., Beijing 100004; tel. (10) 6590-6903; e-mail enquiry@britishcouncil.org.cn; internet www.britishcouncil.org/china; offers courses and exams in English language and British culture and promotes cultural exchange with the UK; attached offices in Shanghai, Guangzou and Chongqing; Dir and Cultural Counsellor MICHAEL O'SULLIVAN.

Chinese Writers' Association: 2 Shatanbeijie, 100720 Beijing; f. 1949; 20,000 mems; Chair. TIE NING; publs *Chinese Writers* (6 a year), *Minority Literature* (12 a year), *People's Literature* (12 a year), *Poetry* (12 a year).

Goethe-Institut: Cyber Tower, Bldg B, 17th Fl., No 2, Zhong Guan Cun S Ave, 100086 Beijing; tel. (10) 82512909; e-mail info@peking.goethe.org; internet www.goethe.de/ins/cn/pek/deindex.htm; offers courses and exams in German language and culture and promotes cultural exchange with Germany; attached centres in Shanghai; library of 10,000 vols; Head PETER ANDERS.

MEDICINE

China Association of Acupuncture–Moxibustion: 16 Dongzhimen Nanxiaojie, 100700 Beijing; tel. (10) 64014411; e-mail d12@cast.org.cn; internet www.caam.cn; f. 1979; 19,000 mems; Pres. LIU BAOYAN; publ. *Chinese Acupuncture and Moxibustion*.

China Association of Traditional Chinese Medicine: East St, 9 Bldg B, 100061 Beijing; tel. (10) 64060498; internet www.catcm.org.cn; f. 1979; 80,000 mems; Hon. Pres. ZHANGHONG KUI; publ. *China Journal of Traditional Chinese Medicine* (6 a year).

Chinese Academy of Medical Sciences and Peking Union Medical College: 9 Dongdan Santiao, 100730 Beijing; tel. 553447; f. 1917 (College), 1956 (Academy); attached research institutes: see Research Institutes; Pres. Dr BA DENIAN; publ. *Chinese Medical Sciences Journal*.

Chinese Anti-Cancer Association: 52 Fucheng, Haidian Dist., Beijing 100036; tel. (10) 88148749; e-mail yuhui@caca.org.cn; internet www.caca.org.cn; f. 1985; 40,000 mems; Pres. Dr XU GUANGWEI; publs *Cancer Rehabilitation* (6 a year), *Chinese Journal of Cancer Biotherapy* (4 a year), *Chinese Journal of Cancer Research* (4 a year), *Chinese Journal of Clinical Oncology* (12 a year), *Journal of Practical Oncology* (6 a year), *Research on Prevention and Treatment of Cancer* (6 a year).

Chinese Anti-Tuberculosis Association: 42 Dung-si-xi-da St, Beijing; tel. 553685; Pres. HUANG DINGCHEN.

Chinese Association for Mental Health: 5 An Kang Hutong, De Wai, Beijing 100088; tel. (10) 82085385; e-mail camh@camh.org.cn; internet www.camh.org.cn; f. 1985; 30,000 mems; Pres. CAI ZHUOJI; Sec.-Gen. LI ZHANJIANG; publs *Chinese Journal of Clinical Psychology* (4 a year), *Chinese Journal of Health Psychology* (6 a year), *Chinese Mental Health Journal* (12 a year).

Chinese Association of Integrated Medicine: 16 Beixincang, Dongzhimennei, Beijing; tel. (10) 64010688; f. 1981; 66,492 mems; Pres. CHEN KAIXIAN; Sec.-Gen. MU DAWEI; publ. *Chinese Journal of Integrative Medicine* (12 a year in Chinese, 4 a year in English).

Chinese Medical Association: 42 Dongsi Xidajie, 100710 Beijing; tel. (10) 85158136; e-mail intl@cma.org.cn; internet www.cma.org.cn; f. 1915; 500,000 mems; library of 80,000 vols; Pres. CHEN ZHU; publs *Chinese Journal of Internal Medicine* (12 a year), *Chinese Journal of Surgery* (12 a year), *Chinese Medical Journal* (12 a year, in English), *National Medical Journal of China* (12 a year).

Chinese Nursing Association: 42 Dongsi Xidajie, 100710 Beijing; tel. (10) 65265331; internet www.cna-cast.org.cn; f. 1909; Pres. LI XIUHUA; publs *Journal of Nursing* (12 a year), *Journal of Nursing Eduction*.

Chinese Nutrition Society: Guang'an Men, Xuanwu Dist., Beijing 100053; tel. (10) 83554781; e-mail mm@cnsoc.org; internet www.cnsoc.org; f. 1981; 7,026 mems; Pres. GE KEYOU; publ. *Acta Nutrimenta* (4 a year, in Chinese and English).

Chinese Pharmaceutical Association: A38 Lishi Rd N, Beijing 100810; tel. (10) 68316576; internet www.cpa.org.cn; f. 1907; Pres. DING LIXIA.

Chinese Pharmacological Society: 1 Xian Nong Tan St, 100050 Beijing; tel. (10) 63165211; e-mail muxin@imm.ac.cn; internet www.cnphars.org; f. 1979; Pres. Prof. DU GUANHUA; Sec.-Gen. Prof. ZHANG YONGXIANG; publs *Acta Pharmacologica Sinica*, *Chinese Journal of Pharmacology and Toxicology*, *Chinese Pharmacological Bulletin*, *Pharmacology and Clinics of Chinese Materia Medica*.

NATURAL SCIENCES

General

China Association for Science and Technology (CAST): 3 Fuxing Rd, 100863 Beijing; tel. (10) 68571898; e-mail english@cast.org.cn; internet www.cast.org.cn; f. 1958; organizes academic exchanges, int. confs and in-service training for scientists, engineers and technicians; library of 50,000 vols; Pres. HAN QIDE.

Chinese Society for Oceanology and Limnology: 7 Nanhai Rd, 266071 Qingdao; tel. (532) 82898611; f. 1950; attached to Institute of Oceanology, Chinese Academy of Sciences; 8,000 mems; Pres. QIN YUNSHAN; Sec. Gen. ZHOU MINGJIANG; publs *Chinese Journal of Oceanology and Limnology* (4 a year, in English), *Oceanologia et Limnologia Sinica* (6 a year, in Chinese).

Chinese Society of the History of Science and Technology: 137 Chao Nei St, Beijing 100010; tel. (10) 64043989; f. 1980; 1,500 mems; Pres. X. ZEZONG; Pres. LU YONGXIANG; publs *China Historical Materials of Science and Technology* (4 a year), *Studies in the History of Natural Sciences* (4 a year).

National Natural Science Foundation of China (NSFC): Beijing; tel. (10) 62327001; e-mail bic@nsfc.gov.cn; internet www.nsfc.gov.cn; depts of chemical sciences, earth sciences, eng. and materials science, information sciences, life sciences, management sciences, mathematical and physical sciences; does not have any research entities; directs, coordinates and financially supports basic research and applied basic research, identifies and fosters scientific talents, promotes science and technology; receives research proposals from univs and other institutions, prepares peer reviews and sessions of evaluation panels; provides advisory services on major issues related to the nat. strategic devt of basic and applied basic research in China; supports activities of nat. professional science foundations; develops cooperative relations with scientific orgs in other countries; Pres. CHEN YIYU; Vice-Pres. WANG JIE; Vice-Pres. SHEN WENQING; Vice-Pres. SUN JIAGUANG; Vice-Pres. SHEN YAN; Vice-Pres. YAO JIANNIAN; publ. *Guide to Programs* (1 a year).

Biological Sciences

Biophysical Society of China: 15 Datun Rd, Chaoyang Dist., Beijing 100101; tel. (10) 64889869; e-mail bscott@sun5.ibp.ac.cn; internet bsc.org.cn; f. 1980; 2,300 mems; Pres. Prof. ZHAO NANMING; Sec.-Gen. Prof. SHEN XUN; publs *Acta Biophysica Sinica* (4 a year), *Progress in Biochemistry and Biophysics* (6 a year).

Botanical Society of China: 20 Naxincun, Xiangshan, Beijing 100093; tel. (10) 62591431; e-mail bsco@public.bta.net.cn; 15,000 mems; Pres. KUANG TINGYUN; publs *Acta Botanica Sinica* (12 a year), *Acta Phytoecologica et Geobotanica Sinica* (4 a year), *Acta Phytotaxonomica* (6 a year), *Bulletin of Biology* (12 a year), *Chinese Bulletin of Botany* (4 a year), *Plants* (6 a year).

China Zoological Society: 19 Zhongguancun Rd, Beijing; tel. (10) 62552368; e-mail czs@panda.ioz.ac.cn; f. 1934; 11,600 mems; Pres. CHEN DAYUAN; publs *Acta Arachnologica Sinica* (2 a year), *Acta Parasitologica et Medica Entomologica Sinica* (4 a year), *Acta Theriologica Sinica* (4 a year), *Acta Zoologica Sinica* (6 a year), *Acta Zootaxonomica Sinica* (4 a year), *Chinese Journal of Zoology* (6 a year).

Chinese Association for Physiological Sciences: 42 Dongsixidajie, 100710 Beijing; tel. (10) 65278802; e-mail xiaoling3535@126.com; internet www.caps-china.org; Pres. WANG XIAOMIN.

Chinese Association of Animal Science and Veterinary Medicine: 33 Nongfengli, Dongdaqiao, Chao Yang Dist., 100020 Beijing; tel. (10) 65005934; e-mail caavxshb@public.bta.net.cn; f. 1936; 50,000 mems; Pres. WU CHANGXIN; Sec.-Gen. YAN HANPING; publs *Chinese Journal of Animal and Veterinary Sciences*, *Chinese Journal of Animal Science*, *Chinese Journal of Veterinary Medicine*.

Chinese Society for Anatomical Sciences: 42 Dongsi Xidajie, 100710 Beijing; tel. (10) 65296459; e-mail d07@cast.org.cn; internet www.csas.org.cn; f. 1920; 3,000 mems; Pres. Prof. LI YUNQING; publs *Acta Anatomica Sinica* (4 a year), *Chinese Journal of Anatomy* (4 a year), *Chinese Journal of Clinical Anatomy* (4 a year), *Chinese Journal of Histochemistry and Cytochemistry* (4 a year), *Journal of Neuroanatomy* (4 a year), *Progress of Anatomical Sciences* (4 a year).

Chinese Society for Microbiology: 1 Beichen West Rd, 100101 Beijing; tel. (10) 64807200; e-mail csm@sun.im.ac.cn; internet csm.im.ac.cn; f. 1952; 16,000 mems; Pres. Prof. ZIXIN DENG; publs *Acta Microbiologica Sinica*, *Acta Mycologica Sinica*, *Chinese Journal of Biotechnology*, *Chinese Journal of Virology*, *Chinese Journal of Zoonoses*, *Microbiology China*.

Chinese Society of Biochemistry and Molecular Biology: Room 210, 31A Fl., 319 Yueyang Rd, 200031 Shanghai; tel. (21) 54921088; e-mail csbmb@sibs.ac.cn; internet www.csbmb.org.cn; f. 1979; 5,100 mems; Pres. WANG ZHIXIN; Sec. Gen. KING NAIHE; publs *Chemistry of Life* (6 a year), *Chinese Journal of Biochemistry and Molecular Biology* (6 a year).

Chinese Society of Environmental Sciences: 54 Honglian Nancun, 100082 Beijing; tel. (10) 82211021; e-mail cses@chinacses.org; internet www.chinacses.org; f. 1978; 42,000 mems; Pres. JIANG ZHENGHUA.

Chinese Society of Plant Biology: Room 101, Bldg 3B, 319 Yueyang Rd, 200031 Shanghai; tel. (21) 54922859; e-mail cspb@sibs.ac.cn; internet www.cspp.cn; f. 1963; 5,000 mems; Dir Prof. ZHIHONG XU; Sec. Gen. ZHUHUA HE; publs *Acta Phytophysiologica Sinica* (4 a year), *Plant Physiology Communications* (6 a year).

Ecological Society of China: Shuangqing Rd, 100085 Beijing; tel. (10) 62849101; e-mail esc@rcees.ac.cn; internet www.esc.org.cn; f. 1979; 7,800 mems; Pres. Prof. DONG MING; Sec. Gen. Prof. TAO JIANPING; publs *Acta Ecologica Sinica* (6 a year), *Journal of*

Applied Ecology (4 a year), *Journal of Ecology* (6 a year).

Entomological Society of China: 19 Zhongguancun Rd, Haidian, 100080 Beijing; tel. (10) 62565687; e-mail wangmm@panda.ioz.ac.cn; f. 1944; 11,000 mems; Pres. ZHANG GUANGXUE; Gen. Sec. LI DIANMO; publs *Acta Entomologica Sinica* (in Chinese), *Acta Parasitologica et Medica* (in Chinese), *Acta Zootaxonomia Sinica* (in Chinese), *Entomological Knowledge* (in Chinese), *Entomologia Sinica* (in Chinese).

Genetics Society of China: 1 W Beichen Rd, Chaoyang Dist., Beijing 100101; tel. (10) 64806635; f. 1978; 400 nat. mems, 6,600 mems of local socs; Pres. JIAYANG LI; Sec.-Gen. YONGBIAO XUE; publs *Acta Genetica Sinica*, *Hereditas* (6 a year).

Palaeontological Society of China: 39 East Beijing Rd, 210008 Nanjing; tel. (25) 83282138; e-mail psc@nigpas.ac.cn; internet www.china-psc.org.cn; f. 1929; 1,230 mems; Pres. YANG QUN; Sec. Gen. WANG YONGDONG; publ. *Acta Palaeontologica Sinica* (4 a year).

Mathematical Sciences

Chinese Mathematical Society: 55 Zhong Guan Cun East Rd, 100080 Beijing; tel. (10) 62551022; e-mail cms@math.ac.cn; internet www.cms.org.cn; f. 1935; 50,000 mems; Pres. M. A. ZHIMING; Sec. Gen. WANG CHANGPING; publ. *Acta Mathematica Sinica* (in Chinese and English).

Physical Sciences

Acoustical Society of China: 21 Beisihuan Xilu, 100080 Beijing; tel. (10) 62554285; e-mail asc@mail.ioa.ac.cn; f. 1985; 3,685 mems; Pres. TIAN JING; publs *Applied Acoustics* (4 a year), *Chinese Journal of Acoustics* (4 a year, English version of *Acta Acustica*), *Noise and Vibration Control*.

Chinese Academy of Meteorological Sciences: 46 South Zhongguancun St, 100081 Beijing; tel. (10) 68406206; e-mail wlb@cams.cma.gov.cn; internet www.cams.cma.gov.cn; f. 1956, current name adopted 1991; attached research institutes: see under Research Institutes; Pres. DUAN YIHONG; Vice-Pres. WANG HUAIGANG.

Chinese Aerodynamics Research Society: POB 2425, Beijing; Pres. ZHUANG GENGGAN.

Chinese Astronomical Society: Purple Mountain Observatory 2 West Beijing Rd, 210008 Nanjing; tel. (25) 83332036; e-mail cas.nj@pmo.ac.cn; internet astronomy.pmo.cas.cn; f. 1922; 401 mems; Pres. CUI XIANGQUN; Sec.-Gen. YANG JI; publs *Acta Astronomica Sinica* (24 a year), *Acta Astrophysica Sinica* (4 a year).

Chinese Chemical Society: POB 2709, Beijing 100190; tel. (10) 62568157; e-mail zcc@iccas.ac.cn; internet www.ccs.ac.cn; f. 1932; promotes popularization and devt of science and application of chemistry by uniting and organizing chemists; improves social mem.'s scientific accomplishment; promotes growth of people and sustainable devt of nat. economy; practices high technology innovation in China; organizes nat. symposia, seminars and int. academic meetings; 50,000 mems; Pres. Prof. JIANNIAN YAO; Sec.-Gen Prof. ZHENZHONG YANG; publs *Acta Chimica Sinica* (12 a year), *Chinese Journal of Chemistry* (6 a year).

Chinese Geological Survey: 45 Fu Wai St, 100037 Beijing; tel. (10) 58584680; e-mail metadata@mail.cgs.gov.cn; internet www.cgs.gov.cn; f. 1959; attached to Min. of Land and Resources; responsible for the centralized deployment and implementation of China's basic, public and strategic geological investigation and mineral exploration; provides basic geological information and data for the nat. economy; attached institutes: see Research Institutes; Dir-Gen. MENG XIANLAI; publs *Acta Geologica Sinica*, *Geological Review*.

Chinese Geophysical Society: China Univ. for Nationalities, Beijing Rd, 100081 Beijing; tel. (10) 68729347; e-mail zgdqwl@163.com; internet www.cgs.org.cn; f. 1947; 14,414 mems; Dir GUO JIAN; publs *China Geophysics*, *Chinese Journal of Geophysics*.

Chinese High-Energy Physics Society: POB 918, Beijing 100039; tel. (10) 68235910; e-mail zhouxb@alpha02.ihep.ac.cn; internet www.ihep.ac.cn; f. 1981; 962 mems; Chair. DAI YUANBEN; Sec.-Gen. HUANG TAO; publs *High Energy Physics and Nuclear Physics* (12 a year), *Modern Physics* (6 a year).

Chinese Meteorological Society: 46 Zhongguancun South Ave, 100081 Beijing; tel. (10) 68407634; e-mail cmsams@cms1924.org; internet www.cms1924.org; f. 1924; 21,000 mems; Pres. Prof. Dr QIN DAHE (acting); Sec.-Gen. WANG CHUNYI; publs *Acta Meteorologica Sinica* (6 a year, in English), *Meteorological Knowledge* (12 a year, in Chinese).

Chinese Nuclear Physics Society: POB 275-50, Beijing 102413; tel. (10) 69358003; e-mail zhusy@ciae.ac.cn; internet www.cnps.ac.cn; f. 1979; 600 mems; Pres. Prof. HUANQIAO ZHANG; Sec.-Gen. Prof. SHENGYUN ZHU; publ. *Nuclear Physics Review* (4 a year).

Chinese Nuclear Society: POB 2125, Beijing 100822; tel. (10) 68531473; e-mail cns@cnnc.com.cn; internet www.ns.org.cn; f. 1980; 8,894 mems; Pres. WANG NAIYAN; publ. *Chinese Journal of Nuclear Science and Technology*.

Chinese Physical Society: POB 603, Beijing 100080; tel. (10) 82649019; e-mail cps@aphy.iphy.ac.cn; internet www.cps-net.org; f. 1932; attached to Chinese Association for Science and Technology; 42,000 mems; Pres. YANG GUO-ZHEN; Sec.-Gen. WANG EN-GE; publs *Acta Physica Sinica* (12 a year, in Chinese), *Chinese Journal of Chemical Physics* (6 a year, in Chinese), *Chinese Physics* (12 a year, in English), *Chinese Physics Letters* (12 a year, in English), *College Physics* (12 a year, in Chinese), *Communications in Theoretical Physics* (12 a year, in English), *Physics Teaching* (12 a year, in Chinese), *Progress in Physics* (4 a year, in Chinese), *Wuli* (Physics, 12 a year, in Chinese).

Chinese Society for Mineralogy, Petrology and Geochemistry: 46 Guanshui Rd, Guiyang 550002, Guizhou Province; tel. (851) 5895823; e-mail csmpg@vip.skleg.cn; internet www.gyig.ac.cn/society; f. 1978; 6,500 mems; library of 10,000 vols and periodicals; Pres. Prof. HU RUIZHONG; publs *Acta Mineralogica Sinica* (4 a year), *Acta Petrologica Sinica* (12 a year), *Geochemica* (6 a year), *Journal of Paleography* (6 a year), *The Chinese Journal of Geochemistry* (4 a year, in English).

Chinese Society for Rock Mechanics and Engineering: POB 9825, 100029 Beijing; tel. (10) 82998163; e-mail csrme@163.com; internet www.csrme.com; f. 1985; 14 corporate mems, 554 individual mems; Pres. Prof. QIAN QIHU (acting); Sec.-Gen. Prof. WU FAQUAN; publs *Chinese Journal of Rock Mechanics and Engineering* (in Chinese), *Chinese Journal of Underground Space and Engineering* (in Chinese), *Journal of Rock Mechanics and Geotechnical Engineering* (in English), *News of Rock Mechanics and Engineering* (4 a year, in Chinese).

Chinese Society of Space Research: 1 Zhonguancun Nan'ertiao, 100080 Beijing; tel. (10) 62559882; e-mail cssr@cssar.ac.cn; f. 1980; 3,073 mems; Pres. Prof. GU YIDONG; publ. *Journal of Space Science* (4 a year).

Geological Society of China: 26 Baiwanzhuang Dajie, 100037 Beijing; tel. (10) 68311539; e-mail cgdzxh@163bj.com; internet www.geosociety.org.cn; f. 1922; 71,000 mems; Pres. ZHANG HONGREN; publs *Acta Geologica Sinica* (4 a year), *Geology Review* (24 a year).

Seismological Society of China: 5 Minzu Daxue Nanlu, 100081 Beijing; tel. (10) 68417858; f. 1979; 1,250 mems; Pres. Prof. ZHANG GUOMIN; publ. *Acta Seismologica Sinica* (4 a year, Chinese and English edns).

PHILOSOPHY AND PSYCHOLOGY

Chinese Psychological Society: Institute of Psychology, Chinese Academy of Sciences, Datun Rd, Jia 10 Hao, Chaoyang Dist., Beijing 100101; tel. (10) 64855830; e-mail xuehui@psych.ac.cn; internet www.cpsbeijing.org; f. 1921; organizes annual conference on various topics by br. committees; Nat. Congress of Psychology every two years; open lectures to public; promotion of psychological science through the internet; seminars organized for professionals in other fields; 2,000 mems; Pres. Prof. KAN ZHANG; Sec.-Gen. Prof. YUFANG YANG; publs *Acta Psychologica Sinica* (6 a year), *Psychological Science* (6 a year).

TECHNOLOGY

Chemical Industry and Engineering Society of China: 53 Xiaoguan Jie, 100029 Beijing; tel. (10) 64441885; e-mail ciesc@ciesc.cn; internet www.ciesc.cn; f. 1922; 60,000 mems; Pres. CAO XIANGHONG; Sec. Gen. HONG DINGYI; publs *Chinese Journal of Chemical Engineering* (6 a year), *Journal of Chemical Industry and Engineering* (12 a year).

China Association of Lighting Industry: Room 230, 6 Dongchang'an St, 100740 Beijing; tel. (10) 65135872; e-mail wenqidong@chineselighting.org; internet www.chineselighting.org; f. 1989; Pres. LIU SHENGPING.

China Civil Engineering Society: 9 Sanlihe Rd, 100835 Beijing; tel. (10) 58934710; e-mail master@cces.net.cn; internet www.cces.net.cn; f. 1912; Pres. MAO YISHENG; Sec. Gen. ZHANG YAN; publ. *Civil Engineering Journal* (12 a year).

China Computer Federation: POB 2704, Beijing 100080; tel. (10) 62562503; e-mail ccf@ns.ict.ac.cn; internet www.ccf.org.cn; f. 1962, fmrly Chinese Information Processing Soc.; 40,000 mems; Chair. ZHANG XIAOXIANG; Sec. Gen. CHEN SHUKAI; publs *Chinese Journal of Advanced Software Research*, *Chinese Journal of Computers*, *Journal of Computer-aided Design and Computer Graphics*, *Journal of Computer Science and Technology* (in English), *Journal of Software*.

China Electrotechnical Society: 46 Sanlihe Rd, POB 2133, Beijing 100823; tel. (10) 68595358; e-mail cesintl@public.bta.net.cn; internet www.ces.org.cn; f. 1981; 50,000 mems; Pres. WU XIAOHUA; Sec.-Gen. DUAN RUICHUN; publs *Electrical Engineering* (12 a year), *Transactions of China Electrotechnical Society* (12 a year).

China Energy Research Society: 54 Sanlihe Rd, 100045 Beijing; tel. (10) 68511816; e-mail cers@mx.cei.gov.cn; internet www.cers.org.cn; f. 1981; 18,000 mems; Chair. CHAI SONGYUE.

China Engineering Graphics Society: POB 85, Beijing 100083; tel. (10) 82317091; Pres. TANG RONGXI; publ. *Computer Aided Drafting, Design and Manufacturing* (2 a year).

China Fire Protection Association: 5th Fl., Fire Station, 19A Huawei XiLi, Chaoyang Dist., Beijing 100021; China Fire, 48, Banbuqiao Rd, Xuanwu, Beijing 100054; tel. (10) 51232677; e-mail english@china-fire.org; internet www.china-fire.com; f. 1984; 30,000 mems; Pres. SUN LUN; publs *Fire Protection in China*, *Fire Science and Technology*, *Fire Technique and Products Information*.

China Society for Scientific and Technical Information: 15 Fuxing Rd, Beijing; tel. (10) 68014024; internet www.cssti.org.cn; f. 1964; organizes academic activities about information science and technology; 13,000 mems; Pres. WU HENG; publ. *Journal of the China Society for Scientific and Technical Information* (6 a year).

Chinese Academy of Engineering (CAE): POB 3847, 100038 Beijing; 3 Fuxing Rd, Beijing; tel. (10) 68530187; e-mail info@cae.cn; internet www.cae.ac.cn; f. 1994; 616 academicians; Pres. XU KUANGDI; Sec. HE ZHONGWEI.

Chinese Academy of Space Technology: 31 Zhongguancun Nandajie, 100081 Beijing; tel. (10) 68197125; e-mail market@cast.cn; internet www.cast.cn; f. 1968; attached research institutes: see under Research Institutes; 4 mems; Pres. YANG BAOHUA.

Chinese Association of Automation: POB 2728, Beijing 100080; tel. (10) 62544415; e-mail wangh@iamail.ia.ac.cn; internet www.gongkong.com; f. 1961; 40,000 mems; Pres. Prof. CHEN HANFU; Pres. Prof. YANG JIACHI; Pres. Prof. DAI RUWAI; publs *Acta Automatica Sinica* (6 a year), *Automation Panorama* (6 a year), *Information and Control* (6 a year), *Pattern Recognition and Artificial Intelligence* (4 a year), *Robot* (6 a year).

Chinese Ceramic Society: 11 Sanlihe Rd, 100831 Beijing; tel. (10) 57811248; e-mail zggsyxh@sina.com; internet www.chinaexhibition.com/official_site/21-603-the_chinese_ceramic_society_(ccs).html; f. 1945; 30,000 mems; Pres. XU YONGMO; Sec.-Gen. JIN ZHANPING; publ. *Journal of the Chinese Ceramic Society* (6 a year).

Chinese Hydraulic Engineering Society: 2-2 Baiguang Rd, 100053 Beijing; tel. (10) 63202163; e-mail ches@mwr.gov.cn; internet www.ches.org.cn; f. 1931; promotes devt of water resources, science and technology; 93,309 mems; Pres. ZHU ERMING; Sec. Gen. CAO ZHENG QI; publs *Journal of Geotechnical Engineering* (6 a year), *Journal of Hydraulic Engineering* (12 a year), *Journal of Sediment Research* (6 a year).

Chinese Mechanical Engineering Society: 11th Fl., Bldg 4, Zhuyu Int., 9 Shouti S Rd, Haidian Dist., Beijing 100048; tel. (10) 68799038; e-mail headquarters@cmes.org; internet www.cmes.org; f. 1936; 180,000 mems; Pres. Dr ZHOU JI; Gen. Sec. ZHANG YAN-MIN; publs *Chinese Journal of Mechanical Engineering* (6 a year, in English), *China Mechanical Engineering* (6 a year, in Chinese), *Journal of Mechanical Engineering* (6 a year, in Chinese).

Chinese Petroleum Society: POB 766, Liu Pu Kang, Beijing 100724; tel. (10) 62095615; f. 1979; 60,000 mems; library: 20,000 books, 560 periodicals; Pres. JIN ZHONGCHAO; Sec.-Gen. LU JIMENG; publ. *Acta Petrolei Sinica* (Exploration and Development, and Refining and the Petrochemical Industry, each edn 4 a year).

China Railway Society: 10 Fuxing Rd, POB 2499, Beijing; e-mail yangzm25@yahoo.com.cn; internet www.crs.org.cn; f. 1978; railway transport, construction and rolling stock manufacture; academic exchanges, technological consultation, technical research and devt; 78,000 mems; Chair. SUN YONGFU; Sec.-Gen. LU CHANGQING; publs *Railway Journal*, *Railway Knowledge*.

Chinese Society for Metals: 46 Dongsi Xidajie, Beijing 100711; tel. (10) 65133322; e-mail csmoffice@csm.org.cn; internet www.csm.org.cn; f. 1956; 100,000 mems; library of 50,000 vols, 20,000 serials, 1,270 periodicals; Pres. WENG YUQING; Sec.-Gen. LI WENXIU; publs *Acta Metallurgica Sinica* (12 a year, in Chinese; 6 a year, in English), *China Metallurgy* (6 a year), *Iron and Steel* (12 a year), *Journal of Materials Science and Technology* (6 a year).

Chinese Society of Aeronautics and Astronautics: 5 Liangguochang Rd, Dongcheng Dist., 100010 Beijing; tel. (10) 84923943; e-mail office@csaa.org.cn; internet www.csaa.org.cn; f. 1964; 21,800 mems; Pres. LIU GAOZHUO; Sec.-Gen. ZHANG JUEN; publs *Acta Aeronautica et Astronautica Sinica* (6 a year), *Aerospace Knowledge* (12 a year), *Chinese Journal of Aeronautics* (4 a year), *Journal of Aeronautical Materials* (6 a year), *Journal of Aerospace Power* (6 a year), *Model Airplane* (6 a year).

Chinese Society of Astronautics (CSA): POB 838, 100830 Beijing; 2 Yue Tan Beixiao Tie, Beijing; tel. (10) 68768622; e-mail csa_heinlein@yahoo.com.cn; internet www.csaspace.org.cn/heinlein/hlindex-en.htm; f. 1979; 10,000 mems; Pres. LIU JIYUAN; Sec.-Gen. Prof. YANG, JUNHUA; publs *Space Exploration*, *Journal*.

Chinese Society for Electrical Engineering: 1 Lane 2, Baiguang Rd, 10076 Beijing; tel. (10) 63415928; e-mail csee@csee.org.cn; internet www.csee.org.cn; f. 1934 as Chinese Society for Electrical Engineers, current name adopted 1958; 100,000 mems; Chair. CHEN FENG; publ. *Electricity* (4 a year).

Chinese Society of Engineering Thermophysics: POB 2706, Zhongguancun, Beijing; f. 1978; 5,000 mems; Sec.-Gen. Prof. XU JIANZHONG; publ. *Journal of Engineering Thermophysics* (4 a year).

Chinese Society of Naval Architects and Marine Engineers: 5 Yuetanbeijie, 100861 Beijing; tel. (10) 59517926; e-mail csname@csname.org.cn; internet www.csname.org.cn; f. 1943; Dir JIN XIANGJUN; Sec. Gen. LUO JIYAN; publs *Naval and Merchant Ships* (12 a year), *Shipbuilding of China* (4 a year), *Ship Engineering* (6 a year).

Chinese Society of Theoretical and Applied Mechanics (CSTAM): 15 Bei Si Huan Xi Rd, 100190 Beijing; tel. (10) 62559209; e-mail office@cstam.org.cn; internet www.cstam.org.cn; f. 1957; 21,000 mems; Chair. Prof. HU HAIYAN; publs *Acta Mechanica Sinica* (6 a year, in English 4 a year), *Acta Mechanica Solida Sinica* (6 a year, in English 4 a year), *Engineering Mechanics* (4 a year), *Explosion and Shock Waves* (4 a year), *Journal of Computational Mechanics* (4 a year), *Journal of Experimental Mechanics* (4 a year), *Mechanics and Practice* (6 a year).

Chinese Textile Engineering Society: 3 Yanjing Li, 100025 Beijing; tel. (10) 65016537; f. 1930; 60,000 mems; Pres. SUN RUIZHE.

Nonferrous Metals Society of China: B12, Fuxing Rd, Beijing 100814; tel. (10) 63971451; e-mail nfsoc@public.bta.net.cn; internet www.nfsoc.org.cn; f. 1984; 39,000 mems; Pres. KANG YI; Sec.-Gen. NIU YINJIAN; publs *Journal of Nonferrous Metals* (4 a year, with English Abstracts), *Journal of Rare Metals* (4 a year, with English version), *Transactions of Nonferrous Metals Society of China* (4 a year, with English version).

Society of Automotive Engineers of China: 46 Fucheng Rd, 100036 Beijing; tel. (10) 68121894; e-mail sae@sae-china.org; internet www.sae-china.com; f. 1963; 1,520 mems; Exec. Vice-Pres. and Sec.-Gen. ZHANG JINHUA; publs *Auto Fan* (12 a year), *Automotive Engineering* (6 a year).

Systems Engineering Society of China: Institute of Systems Science, Zhongguancun, Beijing 100080; tel. (10) 62541827; internet www.amss.iss.ac.cn.sesc; f. 1980; 3,000 individual mems, 150 collective mems; Pres. CHEN, GUANGYA; Sec.-Gen. WANG, SHOUYANG; publs *Journal of Systems Science and Systems Engineering* (4 a year, in English), *Journal of Transportations Systems Engineering and Information Technology* (4 a year, in English), *Systems Engineering* (4 a year), *Systems Engineering—Theory and Practice* (12 a year).

Research Institutes

AGRICULTURE, FISHERIES AND VETERINARY SCIENCE

Chinese Research Institute of the Wood Industry: Wan Shou Shan, 100091 Beijing; attached to Chinese Acad. of Forestry.

Forestry Research Institute: Wan Shou Shan, Beijing 100091; tel. (10) 62888862; e-mail lumz@www.caf.ac.cn; internet nic6.forestry.ac.cn; f. 1953; attached to Chinese Acad. of Forestry; research into silviculture, tree cultivation, soil science, agroforestry, prevention of desertification, ornamental plants, biotechnology; 148 mems; Dir Prof. Dr LU MENG ZHU; publ. *Forest Research* (6 a year).

Institute of Soil Science: 71 East Beijing Rd, 210008 Nanjing; tel. (25) 86881114; e-mail iss@issas.ac.cn; internet www.issas.cas.cn; f. 1953; attached to Chinese Acad. of Sciences; research areas incl. soil resources and their management, soil fertility and its regulation, soil environment and health, and soil biota and safety; library of 250,000 vols; Dir-Gen. Prof. SHEN RENFANG; Deputy Dir Dr JIANG XIN; publs *Acta Pedologica Sinica*, *Pedosphere* (6 a year, in English), *Soils*.

Research Institute of Resources Insects: Bailongsi, 650224 Kunming; tel. (871) 3860027; e-mail xu@sohu.net; internet www.riricaf.org; f. 1995; attached to Chinese Acad. of Forestry; Dir CHEN XIAOMING; Deputy Dir SHI LEI.

Sub-Tropical Forestry Research Institute: Fuyang 311400, Zhejiang Province; attached to Chinese Acad. of Forestry; Dir YANG PEISHOU.

Tropical Forestry Research Institute: Longdong, 510520 Guangzhou, Guandong Province; attached to Chinese Acad. of Forestry.

BIBLIOGRAPHY, LIBRARY SCIENCE AND MUSEOLOGY

State Archives Bureau of China: 21 Feng Sheng Hutong, Beijing; tel. (10) 665797; f. 1954; Dir FENG ZIZHI; publ. *Archival Work* (12 a year).

ECONOMICS, LAW AND POLITICS

Academy of Marxism of the Chinese Academy of Social Sciences: Rd Jianguomennei Da Jie, No 5, Beijing; e-mail wangzb@cass.org.cn; internet myy.cass.cn; f. 1980; attached to Chinese Acad. of Social Sciences; Dir ENFU CHENG; publs *International Critical Thought* (in English), *Marxism Digest* (in Chinese), *Study of Marxism* (in Chinese).

Institute of American Studies: 3 Zhangzhizhong Rd, 100007 Beijing; tel. (10) 64039046; internet ias.cass.cn; f. 1981; attached to Chinese Acad. of Social Sciences; Dir HUANG PING; publ. *American Studies Quarterly*.

Institute of East European, Russian and Central Asian Studies: POB 1103, 100007 Beijing; tel. (10) 4014006; f. 1976; attached to Chinese Acad. of Social Sciences; library of 60,000 vols, 280 periodicals; Dir Prof. ZHANG WENWU.

Institute of Economics: 2 Yuetanxiaojie North, Fuchengmenurai, 100836 Beijing; tel. (10) 68030264; e-mail kyc-jjs@cass.org.cn; internet ie.cass.cn; f. 1929, current name adopted 1977; attached to Chinese Acad. of Social Sciences; library of 700,000 vols; Dir PEI CHANGHONG; publs *China's Economic History Research Journal* (4 a year), *Economic Perspectives* (12 a year), *Economic Research Journal* (12 a year).

Institute of European Studies: 5 Jianguomennei Ave, 100732 Beijing; tel. (10) 65138428; e-mail ies@cass.net.cn; internet europeanstudies.org; f. 1980; attached to Chinese Acad. of Social Sciences; Dir Prof. ZHOU HONG; publ. *Chinese Journal for European Studies* (6 a year).

Institute of Industrial Economics: 2 Yuetanbeixiao St, Fuchengmenwai, 100836 Beijing; internet www.gjs.cass.cn; f. 1978; attached to Chinese Acad. of Social Sciences; Dir HUANG QUN HUI.

Institute of Latin American Studies: POB 1113, Beijing; tel. (10) 64014009; e-mail ilas@cass.org.cn; internet www.ilas.cass.cn; f. 1961; attached to Chinese Acad. of Social Sciences; Dir ZHENG BINGWEN.

Institute of Law: 15 Shatan Beijie, 100720 Beijing; tel. (10) 64035493; e-mail ky_law@cass.org.cn; internet www.iolaw.org.cn; f. 1958; attached to Chinese Acad. of Social Sciences; Dir LI LIN.

Institute of Political Science: 28 MCC Bldg, 7th Fl., Shuguang Xili, 100028 Beijing; tel. (10) 59868153; internet www.chinaps.cass.cn; f. 1985; attached to Chinese Acad. of Social Sciences; Dir YAN JIAQI.

Institute of West Asian and African Studies: 3 Zhangzhizhong Rd, 100007 Beijing; f. 1961; attached to Chinese Acad. of Social Sciences; Dir-Gen. Prof. YANG GUANG; publ. *West Asia and Africa* (6 a year).

Institute of World Economics and Politics: 5 Jianguomennei Ave, 100732 Beijing; tel. (10) 85196063; internet www.iwep.org.cn; f. 1980; attached to Chinese Acad. of Social Sciences; Dir ZHANG YUYAN.

Japanese Studies Institute: Dong Yuan, 3 Zhangzhizhong Rd, 100007 Beijing; f. 1980; attached to Chinese Acad. of Social Sciences; Dir HE FANG.

Quantitative and Technical Economics Institute: 5 Jianguomennei Ave, Beijing 100732; tel. (10) 65137561; e-mail tswang@mx.cei.gov.cn; internet www.iqte-cass.org; f. 1982; attached to Chinese Acad. of Social Sciences; Dir WANG TONGSAN; publ. *Quantitative and Technical Economics* (12 a year).

Rural Development Institute: Ritan Rd, Beijing; tel. (10) 65275067; internet www.cass.net.en/chinese/s04-nfs/s04-nfs.htm; f. 1978; attached to Chinese Acad. of Social Sciences; Dir Prof. ZHANG XIAOSHAN; publs *Chinese Rural Economy* (12 a year), *Chinese Rural Survey* (6 a year).

Taiwan Studies Institute: 15 Poshangcun, Haidian Dist., Beijing 100091; tel. (10) 62883311; f. 1984; attached to Chinese Acad. of Social Sciences; Dir XU SHIQUAN; publ. *Taiwan Studies* (4 a year).

HISTORY, GEOGRAPHY AND ARCHAEOLOGY

Chinese Academy of Surveying and Mapping: 28 Lianhuachi West Road, 100830 Beijing; tel. (10) 63880803; e-mail office@casm.ac.cn; internet www.casm.ac.cn; f. 1959; library of 50,000 vols; Pres. ZHANG JIXIAN; publs *Remote Sensing Information*, *Trends in Science and Technology of Surveying and Mapping*.

Institute of Archaeology: 27 Wangfujing Dajie, 100710 Beijing; tel. (10) 85115250; e-mail archaeology@cass.org.cn; f. 1950; attached to Chinese Acad. of Social Sciences; Dir WANG WEI.

Institute of World History: 1 Dongcheng HuTong, Wangfujing St, 100006 Beijing; tel. (10) 65248571; e-mail szhyjb-sjlss@cass.org.cn; internet www.worldhistory.cass.cn; f. 1964; attached to Chinese Acad. of Social Sciences; library of 100,000 vols; Dir YU PEI.

Northeast Institute of Geography and Agroecology: 4888 Shengbei St, 130102 Changchun; tel. (431) 85542266; e-mail neigae@neigae.ac.cn; internet www.neigae.ac.cn; f. 1958, current name adopted 2002; attached to Chinese Acad. of Sciences; research areas incl. agroecology, wetland ecology, remote sensing and GIS, environment science and regional devt; Dir Prof. HE XINGYUAN.

LANGUAGE AND LITERATURE

Foreign Literature Institute: 5 Jianguomennei Ave, Beijing 100732; attached to Chinese Acad. of Social Sciences; Dir ZHANG YU.

Institute of Ethnic Literature: 5 Jianguomennei Ave, Beijing 100732; tel. (10) 65138025; e-mail iel-scholarship@cass.org.cn; internet www.ilnm.cass.net.cn; f. 1981; attached to Chinese Acad. of Social Sciences; Dir TANG XIAOGING; Dir CHAO GEJIN; publ. *Studies of Ethnic Literature* (4 a year).

Institute of Linguistics: 5 Jianguomennei Dajie, Beijing 100732; tel. (10) 65737403; f. 1950; attached to Chinese Acad. of Social Sciences; Dir SHEN JIAXUAN; publs *Contemporary Linguistics*, *Dialects*, *The Chinese Language and Writing*.

Journalism Institute: 2 Jintai Rd W., Chaoyang District, 100026 Beijing; e-mail globaljournalism@mail.tsinghua.edu.cn; attached to Chinese Acad. of Social Sciences; Dir SUN XUPEI.

MEDICINE

Cancer Institute and Hospital: 17 Panjiayuan, POB 2258, 100021 Beijing; tel. (10) 67781331; internet www.cicams.ac.cn; f. 1958 as Ritan Hospital, current name adopted 1983; attached to Chinese Acad. of Medical Sciences; Dean HE JEI.

Fuwai Hospital: A167 Beilishi Rd, 100037 Beijing; tel. (10) 88398700; e-mail fuwaih@public.bta.net.cn; f. 1956; attached to Chinese Acad. of Medical Sciences and Peking Union Medical College.

Institute of Basic Medical Sciences: 5 Dongdan Santiao, Beijing 100005; tel. (10) 65134466; e-mail zheng@public3.bta.net.cn; attached to Chinese Acad. of Medical Sciences; Dir ZHENG DEXIAN.

Institute of Blood Transfusion: 76 Huacai Rd, 610052 Chengdu; tel. (28) 83340579; e-mail sxs268@hotmail.com; internet www.camsibt.cn; f. 1958; attached to Chinese Acad. of Medical Sciences and Peking Union Medical College; Dir YANG CHENGMIN; publ. *Chinese Journal of Blood Transfusion*.

Institute of Haematology and Blood Diseases Hospital: 228 Nanjing Rd, 300020 Tianjin; tel. (22) 707939; f. 1957; attached to Chinese Acad. of Medical Sciences and Peking Union Medical College; Dir HAO YUSHU.

Institute of Laboratory Animal Sciences: 5 Pan Jia Yuan Nan Li, Chao Yang Dist., 100021 Beijing; e-mail suoban@cnilas.org; internet www.cnilas.org; f. 1980; attached to Chinese Acad. of Medical Sciences; Dir Prof. QIN CHUAN.

Institute of Materia Medica: 1 Xiannongtan St, 100050 Beijing; tel. (10) 63036794; e-mail info@imm.ac.cn; internet www.imm.ac.cn; f. 1958; attached to Chinese Acad. of Medical Sciences and Peking Union Medical College; research and discovery of innovative drugs for treating or preventing human diseases; Dir Prof. JIANG JIANDONG.

Institute of Microcirculation: 5 Dongdan Santiao, 100005 Beijing; tel. (10) 65126407; f. 1984; attached to Chinese Acad. of Medical Sciences and Peking Union Medical College; Dir Prof. XIU RUIJUAN.

Institute of Radiation Medicine: 238 Baidi Rd, 300192 Tianjin; tel. (22) 85682291; e-mail office@irm-cams.ac.cn; internet www.irm-cams.ac.cn; f. 1959; attached to Chinese Acad. of Medical Sciences and Peking Union Medical College; Dir FAN FEIYUE.

Medicinal Plant Development Institute: 151 Ma Lian Wa North Rd, Haidian Dist., Beijing 100094; tel. (10) 62896288; e-mail implad@implad.ac.cn; internet www.implad.ac.cn; f. 1983; attached to Chinese Acad. of Medical Sciences; library of 30,000 vols; Dir Prof. CHEN SHILIN.

Shanghai Institute of Materia Medica: 555 Zu Chong Zhi Rd, Zhang Jiang Hi-Tech Park, Pudong, 201203 Shanghai; tel. (21) 50806600; e-mail suoban@simm.ac.cn; internet www.simm.ac.cn; f. 1932; attached to Chinese Acad. of Sciences; devt of new drugs; library of 80,000 vols, 600 current periodicals; Dir Prof. JIANG HUA-LIANG; publ. *Acta Pharmocologica Sinica*.

NATURAL SCIENCES

General

Fujian Institute of Research on the Structure of Matter: 155 Yangqiao Rd West, 350002 Fuzhou; tel. (591) 83714517; e-mail fjirsm@fjirsm.ac.cn; internet www.fjirsm.ac.cn; f. 1960; attached to Chinese Acad. of Sciences; focuses on structural chemistry, energy catalysis, nanomaterials, crystal engineering, photoelectric materials, laser technology integration and applications, electronic information, advanced manufacturing and power engineering; library of 75,000 vols; Dir Prof. HONG MAOCHUN; publ. *Chinese Journal of Structural Chemistry* (6 a year).

Institute of Oceanology: 7 Nanhai Rd, Qingdao 266071; tel. (532) 2879062; e-mail iocas@ms.qdio.ac.cn; f. 1950; attached to Chinese Acad. of Sciences; library of 180,000 vols; Dir XIANG JIANHAI; publs *Chinese Journal of Oceanology and Limnology* (4 a year, in English), *Marine Sciences* (6 a year, in Chinese), *Oceanologia et Limnologia Sinica* (6 a year, in Chinese), *Studia Marina Sinica* (1 a year, in Chinese with English abstracts).

Institute of the History of Natural Sciences: 137 Chao Nei St, Beijing 100010; tel. (10) 64043989; e-mail zhouping@ihns.ac.cn; internet www.ihns.ac.cn; f. 1957; attached to Chinese Acad. of Sciences; library of 150,000 vols; Dir Prof. DUN LIU; publs *China Historical Materials of Science and Technology* (4 a year), *Studies in the History of Natural Sciences* (4 a year).

Qinghai Institute of Salt Lakes: 18 Xinning Rd, 810008 Xinning; tel. (971) 6304306; e-mail szxx@isl.ac.cn; internet www.isl.cas.cn; f. 1965; attached to Chinese Acad. of Sciences; research on geoscience, chemistry and chemical engineering of salt lakes and related fields; library of 100,000 vols; Dir DONGPING DUAN; publ. *Journal of Salt Lake Research*.

South China Sea Institute of Oceanology: 164 West Xingang Rd, Guangzhou 510301; tel. (20) 84452227; internet www.scsio.ac.an; f. 1959; attached to Chinese Acad. of Sciences; library of 95,546 vols; Dir Dr SHI PING; publs *Journal of Tropical Oceanology* (6 a year), *Nanhai Studia Marina Sinica* (irregular, Chinese with English abstracts).

Biological Sciences

Institute of Applied Ecology: 72 Wenhua Rd, 110016 Shenyang; tel. (24) 83970304; e-mail syiae@iae.ac.cn; internet www.iae.cas.cn; f. 1954; attached to Chinese Acad. of Sciences; focuses on forest science, soil science, botany, microbiology and environmental sciences; library of 95,000 vols; Dir Prof. HAN XINGGUO; publs *Chinese Journal of Applied Ecology* (12 a year), *Chinese Journal of Ecology* (12 a year).

Institute of Biophysics: 15 Datun Rd, Chaoyang Dist., 100101 Beijing; tel. (10) 64889872; e-mail office@ibp.ac.cn; internet www.ibp.cas.cn; f. 1958; attached to Chinese Acad. of Sciences; Dir-Gen. TAO XU; publ. *Acta Biophysica Sinica*.

Institute of Botany: 20 Nanxincun, 100093 Beijing; tel. (10) 62836215; e-mail fangjingyun@ibcas.ac.cn; internet www.ibcas.ac.cn; f. 1928; attached to Chinese Acad. of Sciences; research areas incl. systematic and evolutionary botany, vegetation and environmental change, plant molecular physiology and devt, photosynthesis, and the sustainable use of plant resources; Dir JINGYUN FANG; publs *Journal of Integrative Plant Biology* (12 a year), *Journal of Plant Ecology* (4 a year, in Chinese and English), *Journal of Systematics and Evolution*.

Institute of Developmental Biology: POB 2707, Beijing; f. 1980; attached to Chinese Acad. of Sciences; specializes in biotechnology of fish and mammals; Dir YAN SHAOYI.

Institute of Genetics and Developmental Biology: Datun Rd, Andingmenwai, Beijing 100101; tel. (10) 64889331; e-mail genetics@genetics.ac.cn; internet www.genetics.ac.cn; attached to Chinese Acad. of Sciences; Dir Prof. JIAYANG LI.

Institute of Hydrobiology: Luojiashan, Wuhan 430072, Hubei Province; tel. (27) 68780789; e-mail zhh@ihb.ac.cn; internet www.ihb.ac.cn; f. 1930; attached to Chinese Acad. of Sciences; freshwater ecology, fisheries, biotechnology and molecular biology, aquatic environment protection; library of 70,000 vols; fish museum; Dir Dr. GUI JIANFANG; publ. *Acta Hydrobiologica Sinica* (6 a year).

Institute of Microbiology: 13 Beiyitiao, Zhongguancun, Haidian Dist., Beijing 100080; tel. (10) 62552178; e-mail gaof@im.ac.cn; internet www.im.ac.cn; f. 1958; attached to Chinese Acad. of Sciences; 380 mems; Dir Prof. GEORGE F. GAO; publs *Acta Microbiologica Sinica* (6 a year), *Chinese Journal of Biotechnology* (6 a year), *Microbiology* (6 a year), *Mycosystema* (4 a year).

Institute of Vertebrate Palaeontology and Palaeoanthropology: 142 Xizhimenwai St, 100044 Beijing; tel. (10) 68354669; e-mail kjc@ivpp.ac.cn; internet www.ivpp.cas.cn; f. 1929, current name adopted 1960; attached to Chinese Acad. of Sciences; research focuses on the morphology, taxonomy, phylogeny, paleoecology, and spatial and temporal distribution of the various vertebrate groups, as well as other relevant biogeographical, paleoclimatological, developmental and molecular biological problems; library of 100,000 vols; Dir Dr ZHONGHE ZHOU; publ. *Vertebrata PalAsiatica* (4 a year).

Institute of Zoology: 1 Beichen West Rd, 100101 Beijing; tel. (10) 64807098; e-mail ioz@ioz.ac.cn; internet www.ioz.cas.cn; f. 1928, current name adopted 1962; attached to Chinese Acad. of Sciences; Dir Prof. KANG LE; publs *Acta Entomologica Sinica* (4 a year), *Acta Zoologica Sinica* (6 a year), *Acta Zootaxonomica Sinica* (4 a year), *Chinese Bulletin of Entomology* (6 a year), *Chinese Journal of Zoology* (6 a year, in English), *Insect Science* (4 a year, in English), *Integrative Zoology* (in English).

Kunming Institute of Zoology: Kunming 650223, Yunnan Province; tel. (871) 5190390; internet english.kiz.cas.cn; f. 1959; attached to Chinese Acad. of Sciences; library of 180,000 vols; Dir Prof. ZHANG YAPING; publ. *Zoological Research* (4 a year).

Nanjing Institute of Geology and Palaeontology: 39 East Beijing Rd, 210008 Nanjing; tel. (25) 83282105; e-mail chxzh@nigpas.ac.cn; internet www.nigpas.cas.cn; f. 1951; attached to Chinese Acad. of Sciences; library of 280,000 vols; Dir Dr YANG QUN; publs *Acta Micropalaeontologica Sinica* (4 a year), *Acta Palaeontologica Sinica* (4 a year), *Journal of Stratigraphy* (4 a year), *Palaeoworld* (4 a year).

Research Centre for Environmental Sciences: POB 2871, 18 Shuangqing Rd, Haidian, Beijing 100085; tel. (10) 62923549; e-mail zhb@rcees.ac.cn; internet www.rcees.ac.cn; f. 1975; attached to Chinese Acad. of Sciences; library of 20,000 vols; Dir Dr JIANG GUIBIN; publs *Acta Ecologica Sinica* (6 a year), *Acta Scientiae Circumstantiae* (12 a year, with English abstracts), *Asian Journal of Ecotoxicology* (6 a year), *Chinese Journal of Environmental Engineering* (12 a year), *Huanjing Huaxue* (Environmental Chemistry, 12 a year), *Huanjing Kexue* (Environmental Sciences, 12 a year), *Journal of Environmental Sciences* (12 a year).

Shanghai Institute of Biochemistry and Cell Biology: 320 Yue-Yang Rd, 200031 Shanghai; tel. (21) 54920000; e-mail sibcb@sibs.ac.cn; internet www.sibcb.ac.cn; f. 2000 by merger of Shanghai Institute of Biochemistry and Shanghai Institute of Cell Biology; attached to Chinese Acad. of Sciences; research on protein science; gene, RNA and epigenetic regulation; signal transduction; cell and stem cell biology; cancer and other diseases; Dir Prof. LIN ANNING.

Shanghai Institutes for Biological Sciences: 319 Yueyang Rd, 200031 Shanghai; tel. (21) 64317102; e-mail yangzh@shb.ac.cn; internet www.sibs.cas.cn; f. 1999 by merger of Shanghai Institute of Biochemistry, Shanghai Institute of Cell Biology, Shanghai Institute of Physiology, Shanghai Brain Research Institute, Shanghai Institute of Materia Medica, Shanghai Institute of Plant Physiology, Shanghai Institute of Entomology and Shanghai Research Center of Biotechnology; attached to Chinese Acad. of Sciences; Pres Dr MIANHENG JIANG.

South China Botanical Garden: 723 Xingke Rd, Tianhe Dist., Guangzhou, 510650, Guangdong Province; tel. (20) 37252531; e-mail scbg@scbg.ac.cn; internet english.scib.cas.cn; f. 1929; attached to Chinese Acad. of Sciences; global change, ecosystem service, environmental degradation, ecological restoration, plant systematic and evolutionary biology, biodiversity, conservation and sustainable utilization, agriculture, food quality and safety, phytochemical resources, sustainable use of plant gene engineering; library of 35,000 vols, 54,000 journals; Dir Dr HONGWEN HUNAG; publ. *Journal of Tropical and Sub-tropical Botany* (12 a year).

Xishuangbanna Tropical Botanical Garden: 666303 Menglun, Mengla County; tel. (691) 8715071; e-mail office@xtbg.org.cn; internet www.xtbg.cas.cn; f. 1959; attached to Chinese Acad. of Sciences; scientific research, species preservation, public education; library of 50,000 vols; Dir Prof. Dr CHEN JIN.

Mathematical Sciences

Institute of Applied Mathematics: 55 Zhongguancun East Rd, 100080 Beijing; tel. (10) 62651344; e-mail iam@amt.ac.cn; internet www.amt.ac.cn; f. 1979; attached to Chinese Acad. of Sciences; Dir GU FUZHOU.

Institute of Mathematics: 55 Zhongguancun East Rd, 100190 Beijing; tel. (10) 62651275; e-mail mathlab@math.ac.cn; internet www.math.ac.cn; f. 1952; attached to Chinese Acad. of Sciences; Dir ZHOU XIANGYU; publ. *Acta Mathematica Sinica* (in Chinese and English).

Physical Sciences

Changchun Institute of Applied Chemistry: 5625 Ren Min St, 130022 Changchun; tel. (431) 85687300; e-mail ciac@ciac.jl.cn; internet www.ciac.cas.cn; f. 1948 as Northeast Industrial Institute, current name adopted 1978; attached to Chinese Acad. of Sciences; library of 120,000 vols; Dir Prof. AN LIJIA; publs *Chinese Journal of Analytical Chemistry* (12 a year), *Chinese Journal of Applied Chemistry* (6 a year).

Changchun Institute of Optics, Fine Mechanics and Physics: 3888 Dong Nanhu Rd, 130033 Changchun; tel. (431) 86176813; e-mail ciomp@ciomp.ac.cn; internet www.ciomp.cas.cn; f. 1952 as Institute of Instrumentation, merged with Changchun Institute of Physics and current name adopted 1999; attached to Chinese Acad. of Sciences; luminescence and its application, integrated optics; library of 200,000 vols; Dir XUAN MING; publs *Chinese Journal of Liquid Crystal and Displays* (4 a year), *Chinese Journal of Luminescence* (4 a year).

Chengdu Institute of Geology and Mineral Resources: 2 Renmin N Rd, 610081 Chengdu; tel. (28) 83231057; e-mail cdcgs2011@163.com; internet www.chengdu.cgs.gov.cn; f. 1962; attached to Chinese Acad. of Geological Sciences; Dir DING JUN.

China Institute of Atomic Energy: POB 275, 102413 Beijing; tel. (10) 69357493; e-mail fancm@iris.ciae.ac.cn; internet www.ciae.ac.cn; f. 1950 as Institute of Modern Physics, current name adopted 1958; attached to Chinese Acad. of Sciences; depts of nuclear physics, reactor engineering, radiochemistry, isotope, nuclear technology application, and radiation safety; Pres. WAN GANG; publs *Atomic Energy Science and Technology* (6 a year), *Journal of Chinese Mass Spectrometry Society*, *Journal of Isotopes* (4 a year), *Journal of Nuclear and Radiochemistry* (4 a year).

Cold and Arid Regions Environmental and Engineering Research Institute: 320 Donggang West Rd, 730000 Lanzhou; tel. (931) 4967606; e-mail caorui@lzb.ac.cn; internet www.careeri.cas.cn; f. 1999; attached to Chinese Acad. of Sciences; library of 546,246 vols, 23,968 periodicals; Dir Prof. MA WEI; publs *Journal of Desert Research* (4 a year, in Chinese), *Journal of Glaciology and Geocryology* (4 a year, in Chinese),

Plateau Meteorology (4 a year, in Chinese), *Sciences of Cold and Arid Regions* (in English).

Dalian Institute of Chemical Physics: 457 Zhongshan Rd, 116023 Dalian; tel. (411) 84379163; internet www.dicp.ac.cn; f. 1949; attached to Chinese Acad. of Sciences; library of 70,000 vols; Dir Prof. Dr Tao Zhang; publs *Chinese Journal of Catalysis* (12 a year), *Chinese Journal of Chromatography* (6 a year), *Journal of Natural Gas Chemistry* (4 a year).

Guangzhou Institute of Chemistry: Academia Sinica, Guangzhou 510650; tel. (20) 85231815; e-mail cyha@gic.ac.cn; internet www.gic.ac.cn; f. 1958; attached to Chinese Acad. of Sciences; library of 80,000 vols; Dir Chengyong Ha; publs *Guangzhou Chemistry* (4 a year), *Journal of Cellulose Science and Technology* (4 a year).

Institute of Acoustics: 17 Zhongguancun St, Beijing 100080; tel. (10) 62553765; e-mail lig@mail.ioa.ac.cn; internet www.ioa.ac.cn; f. 1964; attached to Chinese Acad. of Sciences; Dir Li Qihu.

Institute of Atmospheric Sounding: 7 Block 11, Hepingli, Beijing; attached to Chinese Acad. of Meteorological Sciences.

Institute of Chemistry: No 2 Zhongguancun North St, 100190 Beijing; tel. (10) 62554001; e-mail jwzhang@iccas.ac.cn; internet www.ic.cas.cn; f. 1956; attached to Chinese Acad. of Sciences; library of 100,000 vols; Dir Zhang Deqing; publ. *Chinese Journal of Polymer Science* (12 a year).

Institute of Climatology: 7 Block 11, Hepingli, Beijing; attached to Chinese Acad. of Meteorological Sciences.

Institute of Geochemistry: Chinese Academy of Sciences, 73 Guanshui Rd, Guiyang 550002, Guizhou; tel. (851) 5895095; e-mail zengyiqiang@vip.gyig.ac.cn; f. 1966; attached to Chinese Acad. of Sciences; library of 150,000 vols; Dir Liu Congqiang; publs *Acta Mineralogica Sinica* (4 a year), *Bulletin of Mineralogy, Petrology and Geochemistry* (4 a year), *Chinese Journal of Geochemistry* (4 a year, in English), *Geology-Geochemistry* (4 a year).

Institute of Geology: 26 Baiwanzhuang Rd, Beijing 100037; tel. (10) 68999664; e-mail geoinst@cags.net.cn; internet igeo.cags.ac.cn; f. 1956; attached to Chinese Acad. of Geological Sciences; researches on geological sciences; main areas of research: regional geology, tectonic geology, palaeontology; library of 30,000 vols; publ. *Acta Petrologica Et Minerologica* (6 a year).

Institute of Geology and Geophysics: 19 Beitucheng West Rd, 100029 Beijing; tel. (10) 82998001; e-mail suoban@mail.iggcas.ac.cn; internet www.igg.cas.cn; f. 1999 by merger of Institute of Geology (f. 1951) and Institute of Geophysics (f. 1950); attached to Chinese Acad. of Sciences; Dir Prof. Zhu Rixiang; publ. *Acta Petrological Sinica* (12 a year).

Institute of Geomechanics: 11 S Minzudaxue Rd, 100081 Beijing; tel. (10) 68412303; internet www.geomech.ac.cn; f. 1956; attached to Chinese Acad. of Geological Sciences; conducts new tectonic movement research, energy and mineral resources survey, crustal stability evaluation, research on geological disasters and quaternary geoenvironment; Pres. Prof. Long Changxing; publ. *Journal of Geomechanics* (4 a year).

Guangzhou Institute of Geochemistry: 511 Kehua St, Wushan, 510640 Guangzhou; tel. (20) 85290281; e-mail wumanqing@gig.ac.cn; internet www.gig.cas.cn; f. 1993, merger of Changsha Institute of Geotectonics 2002; attached to Chinese Acad. of Sciences; library of 120,000 vols; Pres. Prof. Yigang Xu.

Institute of High Energy Physics: 19B YuquanLu, 100049 Beijing; tel. (10) 88233093; e-mail ihep@ihep.ac.cn; internet www.ihep.cas.cn; f. 1973; attached to Chinese Acad. of Sciences; Dir Prof. Wang Yifang; publs *High Energy Physics and Nuclear Physics* (12 a year), *Modern Physics* (6 a year).

Institute of Karst Geology: 50 Qixing Rd, 541004, Guangxi Autonomous Region; internet www.karst.ac.cn; attached to Chinese Acad. of Geological Sciences; Dir Jiang Yuchi.

Institute of Metal Research: 72 Wenhua Rd, 110016 Shenyang; tel. (24) 23971500; e-mail syli@imr.ac.cn; internet www.imr.cas.cn; f. 1953, merged with Institute of the Corrosion and Protection of Metals 1999; attached to Chinese Acad. of Sciences; focuses on high performance metallic materials, new types of inorganic nonmetallic materials and advanced composite materials; library of 120,000 vols, 2,500 periodicals; Dir Prof. Yang Rui; publs *Acta Metallurgica Sinica* (12 a year, in Chinese and English), *Chinese Journal of Materials Research* (in Chinese), *Corrosion Science and Protection Technology* (in Chinese), *Journal of Chinese Society for Corrosion and Protection* (in Chinese), *Journal of Materials Science and Technology* (6 a year, in English).

Institute of Mineral Resources: 26 Baiwanzhuang Rd, 100037 Beijing; tel. (10) 68999026; e-mail sunwh@263.net; f. 1956; attached to Chinese Acad. of Geological Sciences.

Institute of Physics: Third S St 8, Zhongguancun, 100090 Beijing; tel. (10) 82649361; internet www.iop.cas.cn; f. 1950, current name adopted 1958; attached to Chinese Acad. of Sciences; research on condensed matter physics, optical physics, atomic and molecular physics, plasma physics, soft matter physics, condensed matter theory and computation physics; Dir Yupeng Wang.

Institute of Process Engineering: 1 Beiertiao, Zhongguancun, Beijing; e-mail office@home.ipe.ac.cn; internet www.ipe.ac.cn; f. 1958; attached to Chinese Acad. of Sciences; library of 171,500 vols; Dir Prof. Jinghai Li; publs *Chinese Journal of Process Engineering* (6 a year), *Chinese Journal of Spectroscopy Laboratory* (6 a year), *Computer and Applied Chemistry* (6 a year).

Institute of Theoretical Physics: Academia Sinica, POB 2735, Beijing 100080; tel. (10) 62555058; f. 1978; attached to Chinese Acad. of Sciences; library of 10,000 vols; Dir Ou-Yang Zhong Can; publ. *Communications in Theoretical Physics* (12 a year, in English).

Institute of Weather Modification: 7 Block 11, Hepingli, Beijing; attached to Chinese Acad. of Meteorological Sciences.

Lanzhou Institute of Physics: POB 94, 730000 Lanzhou; tel. (931) 8264461; e-mail market@spacechina.com; internet www.lipcast.cn; f. 1962; attached to Chinese Acad. of Space Technology.

Nanjing Center, China Geological Survey: 534 Zhongshan E. Rd, Nanjing 210016, Jiangsu Province; tel. (25) 84600446; internet www.nanjing.cgs.gov.cn; f. 1962; attached to Chinese Geological Survey; publ. *Resources Survey and Environment*.

National Research Center for Geoanalysis: 26 Baiwanzhuang Rd, 100037 Beijing; tel. (10) 68327982; e-mail nrcga@cags.ac.cn; f. 1978; attached to Chinese Acad. of Geological Sciences.

National Time Service Center: POB 18, Lintong, Xian; tel. (29) 83890326; e-mail kyc@ntsc.ac.cn; internet www.ntsc.cas.cn; f. 1966 as Shaanxi Astronomical Observatory, current name adopted 2001; attached to Chinese Acad. of Sciences; library of 3,500 vols; Dir Prof. Guo Ji; publ. *Journal of Time and Frequency* (2 a year).

Purple Mountain Observatory: 2 West Beijing Rd, 210008 Nanjing; tel. (25) 83332000; internet www.pmo.cas.cn; f. 1934; attached to Chinese Acad. of Sciences; research on high-energy astrophysics, solar physics and space astronomy exploration technology; star formation through the universe and corresponding terahertz technology; artificial satellite orbital dynamics and probe methods; planetary science, ephemeral astronomy and deep space exploration; observational cosmology and galaxy formation; library of 36,000 vols; Dir Ji Yang; publs *Acta Astronomica Sinica* (4 a year), *Chinese Astronomy and Astrophysics*.

Shanghai Astronomical Observatory: 80 Nandan Rd, Shanghai 200030; tel. (21) 64384522; e-mail shao@shao.ac.cn; internet www.center.shao.ac.cn; f. 1872; attached to Chinese Acad. of Sciences; library of 80,000 vols; Dir Prof. Zhao Junliang; publs *Annals of Shanghai Observatory*, *Progress in Astronomy* (4 a year).

Shanghai Institute of Applied Physics: POB 800-204, 201800 Shanghai; tel. (21) 59553998; e-mail sinap@sinap.ac.cn; internet www.sinap.ac.cn; f. 1959 as Shanghai Institute of Nuclear Research, current name adopted 2003; attached to Chinese Acad. of Sciences; Dir Prof. Zhao Zhentang; publs *Journal of Radiation Research and Radiation Processing* (4 a year), *Nuclear Science and Techniques* (4 a year), *Nuclear Technology* (12 a year, in Chinese).

Shanghai Institute of Microsystem and Information Technology: 865 Changning Rd, 200050 Shanghai; tel. (21) 62511070; e-mail director@mail.sim.ac.cn; internet www.sim.cas.cn; f. 1928 as Shanghai Institute of Metallurgy, current name adopted 2001; attached to Chinese Acad. of Sciences; Dir Xi Wang; publ. *Journal of Functional Materials and Devices*.

Shanghai Institute of Organic Chemistry: 345 Fenglin Lu, Shanghai 200032; tel. (21) 64163300; e-mail sioc@mail.sioc.ac.cn; internet www.sioc.ac.cn; f. 1950; attached to Chinese Acad. of Sciences; library of 300,000 vols; Dir Prof. Jiang Biao; publs *Acta Chimica Sinica* (12 a year, in Chinese), *Chinese Journal of Chemistry* (12 a year, in English), *Organic Chemistry* (12 a year, in Chinese).

Shenyang Institute of Geology and Mineral Resources: 25 Beilingdajie, 110032 Shenyang; tel. (24) 86843110; attached to Chinese Acad. of Geological Sciences.

Southwestern Institute of Physics: POB 15, Leshan, 614007 Sichuan; POB 432, Chengdu 610041, Sichuan Province; tel. (28) 2932304; e-mail wb@swip.ac.cn; f. 1965; attached to China Nat. Nuclear Corpn; controlled nuclear fusion and application of intermediate technology; library of 150,000 vols, 630 periodicals; Dir Prof. Pan Chuanhong; publ. *Nuclear Fusion and Plasma Physics* (4 a year).

Tianjin Institute of Geology and Mineral Resources: 4 8th Rd, Dazhigu, 300170 Tianjin; tel. (22) 24314292; e-mail tjigmr@public.tpt.tj.cn; internet www.coi.gov.cn/english/eoverview/edzkc; f. 1962; attached to Chinese Acad. of Geological Sciences; Dir Prof. Lu Songnian; publ. *Progress in Precambrian Research* (4 a year).

Xi'an Center of Geological Survey: 438 Eastern to Youyi Rd, 710054 Xian; e-mail bella_xacgs@hotmail.com; internet www.xian.cgs.gov.cn; f. 1962 as Xi'an Institute of

Geology and Mineral Resources, current name adopted 2006; attached to Chinese Acad. of Geological Sciences; Dir-Gen. LI WENYUAN.

Yichang Institute of Geology and Mineral Resources: 37 Gangyaolu, 443003 Yichang; tel. (717) 6346941; attached to Chinese Acad. of Geological Sciences.

Yunnan Astronomical Observatory: Phoenix Hill, 650011 Kunming; e-mail ynaobgs@ynao.ac.cn; internet www1.ynao.ac.cn; f. 1972; attached to Chinese Acad. of Sciences; library of 35,000 vols; Dir HAN ZHANWEN; publ. *Publications of Yunnan Observatory* (4 a year).

PHILOSOPHY AND PSYCHOLOGY

Institute of Psychology: 16 Lincui Rd, 100101 Beijing; tel. (10) 64872070; e-mail suozhang@psych.ac.cn; internet www.psych.cas.cn; f. 1951; attached to Chinese Acad. of Sciences; library of 145,000 vols, 1,500 periodicals; Dir Dr XIAOLAN FU; publs *Acta Psychologica Sinica* (4 a year), *Advances in Psychological Science*, *PsyCh Journal*.

Philosophy Institute: 5 Jianguomennei Ave, Beijing 100732; f. 1977; attached to Chinese Acad. of Social Sciences; Dir XING FONSI.

RELIGION, SOCIOLOGY AND ANTHROPOLOGY

Institute of Population and Labour Economics: 5 Jianguomennei Ave, Beijing 100732; tel. (10) 85195417; e-mail iple@cass.org.cn; internet iple.cass.cn; f. 1980; attached to Chinese Acad. of Social Sciences; library of 10,000 vols; Dir Prof. FANG CAI; publs *China Labour Economics* (4 a year), *Population Science of China* (6 a year).

Institute of Sociology: 5 Jianguomennei Ave, 100732 Beijing; e-mail ios@cass.org.cn; internet www.cs-en.cass.cn; f. 1980; attached to Chinese Acad. of Social Sciences; Dir Prof. LI PEILIN; publs *Sociological Studies* (6 a year), *Youth Studies* (6 a year).

Institute of World Religions: 5 Jianguomennei St, 100732 Beijing; tel. (10) 65138521; e-mail kyc-zjs@cass.org.cn; internet iwr.cass.cn; f. 1964; attached to Chinese Acad. of Social Sciences; Dir Prof. ZHUO XINPING; publs *Studies on World Religions* (4 a year), *World Religious Culture* (4 a year).

Nationalities Studies Institute: Baishiqiao, Beijing; attached to Chinese Acad. of Social Sciences; Dir ZHAONA SITU.

TECHNOLOGY

Beijing Institute of Control Engineering: POB 729, 100080 Beijing; f. 1968; attached to Chinese Acad. of Space Technology.

Beijing Institute of Spacecraft Systems Engineering: POB 9628, Beijing 100086; attached to Chinese Acad. of Space Technology.

Chemical Processing and Forest Products Utilization Research Institute: Longpan Rd, Nanjing, Jiangsu Province; attached to Chinese Acad. of Forestry.

China Coal Research Institute: 5 Qingniangou Rd, Hepingli, Beijing 100013; tel. (10) 84262809; e-mail info@coalpreparation.org; internet www.ccri.ac.cn; f. 1957; Dir Prof. Dr ZHANG YUZHUO; publs *Coal Science and Technology* (12 a year, in Chinese), *Journal of China Coal Society* (12 a year, in Chinese; 2 a year, in English).

China National Space Administration: POB 2940, Beijing; 8 Fucheng Rd, Haidian District, 100037 Beijing; tel. (10) 68516733; e-mail webmaster@cnsa.gov.cn; internet www.cnsa.gov.cn; coordinates and implements nat. space policy and devt of space science, technology and industry, and arranges bilateral technical and scientific programmes, incl. launch of space probes; Sec. SUN YAN.

China State Bureau of Technical Supervision (CSBTS): POB 8010, Beijing; tel. (10) 62025835; f. 1988; research and devt for nat. standards and quality control; colln of nat. standards from 56 countries; Dir-Gen. ZHU YULI; publs *Standards Journal*, *Technical Supervision Journal*.

Institute of Automation: 95 Zhongguancun East Rd, 100190 Beijing; tel. (10) 62551575; e-mail info@ia.ac.cn; internet www.ia.cas.cn; f. 1956; attached to Chinese Acad. of Sciences; focuses on intelligent processing of information, intelligent control of complex systems and integrated intelligent systems; Dir DONGLIN WANG; publs *Acta Automatica Sinica* (6 a year, in Chinese), *International Journal of Automation and Computing*.

Institute of Coal Chemistry: 27 S Taoyuan Rd, 030001 Taiyuan; tel. (351) 4041267; e-mail dzb@sxicc.ac.cn; internet www.sxicc.cas.cn; f. 1954, current name adopted 1961; attached to Chinese Acad. of Sciences; research on energy and the environment, advanced materials and green chemistry; Dir Dr JIANGUO WANG; publs *Journal of Fuel Chemistry and Technology* (24 a year), *New Carbon Materials* (6 a year).

Institute of Computing Technology: 6 Kexueyuan S Rd, Zhongguancun, 100190 Beijing; tel. (10) 62601166; e-mail office@ict.ac.cn; internet www.ict.ac.cn; f. 1956; attached to Chinese Acad. of Sciences; Dir Dr NINGHUI SUN; publs *Chinese Journal of Computers* (12 a year), *Journal of Computer Research and Development*, *Journal of Computer-Aided Design and Graphics*, *Journal of Computer Science and Technology* (in English).

Institute of Electronics: 17 Zhongguancun Rd, POB 2702, Beijing 100080; tel. (10) 62554424; internet www.ie.ac.cn; f. 1956; attached to Chinese Acad. of Sciences; library of 35,000 vols; Dir Prof. YIN HEJUN; publs *Journal of Electronics and Information Technology* (12 a year, in Chinese), *Journal of Electronics (China)* (6 a year, in English).

Institute of Engineering Mechanics, China Earthquake Administration: 29 Xuefu Rd, 150086 Harbin; tel. (451) 86652500; e-mail iem@iem.net.cn; internet www.iem.net.cn; f. 1954, current name adopted 1998; attached to China Seismological Bureau; library of 110,000 vols; Dir WANG ZIFA; publs *Earthquake Engineering and Engineering Vibration* (4 a year), *Journal of Natural Disasters* (4 a year), *World Information on Earthquake Engineering* (4 a year).

Institute of Engineering Thermophysics: 11 Beisihuanxi Rd, 100190 Beijing; tel. (10) 62554126; e-mail iet@iet.cn; internet www.iet.cas.cn; f. 1956; attached to Chinese Acad. of Sciences; research in energy, power and the environment; Dir QIN WEI; publs *Journal of Engineering Thermodynamics* (4 a year), *Journal of Thermal Science*.

Institute of Hydrogeology and Environmental Geology: 92 Zhongshan Donglu, 050803 Hebei; tel. (311) 88021122; internet www.iheg.org.cn; f. 1956; attached to Chinese Acad. of Geological Sciences.

Institute of Mechanics: 15 Beisihuanxi Rd, 100190 Beijing; tel. (10) 62560914; e-mail imech@imech.ac.cn; internet www.imech.cas.cn; f. 1956; attached to Chinese Acad. of Sciences; Dir FAN JING.

Institute of Optics and Electronics: POB 350, Shuangliu, Chengdu, Sichuan Province; tel. (28) 85100341; e-mail dangban@ioe.ac.cn; internet www.ioe.cas.cn; f. 1970; attached to Chinese Acad. of Sciences; library of 90,000 vols; Dir Prof. ZHANG YUDONG; publ. *Opto-Electronics Engineering* (12 a year).

Institute of Semiconductors: 35A QingHua East Rd, POB 912, 100083 Beijing; tel. (10) 82304210; e-mail semi@red.semi.ac.cn; internet www.semi.ac.cn; f. 1960; attached to Chinese Acad. of Sciences; Dir LI SHU-SHEN.

Institute of Systems Science: 1A Nansi St, Zhongguancun, Beijing 100080; tel. (10) 62541830; e-mail contact@amss.ac.cn; internet www.iss.ac.cn; f. 1979; attached to Chinese Acad. of Sciences; Dir Prof. XIAO-SHAN GAO; publs *Journal of Systems Science and Complexity*, *Journal of Systems Science and Mathematics* (4 a year), *Journal of Systems Science and Systems Engineering* (6 a year).

Institute of the Multipurpose Utilization of Mineral Resources: Third Ave South 5, Chengdu; tel. (371) 85592163; e-mail bgs@imumr.cn; internet www.imumr.cn; f. 1953; attached to Chinese Acad. of Geological Sciences; library of 200,000 vols; Dir Prof. Dr ZHANG KEREN; publ. *Conservation and Utilization of Mineral Resources* (6 a year).

Shanghai Institute of Ceramics: 1295 Ding Xi Rd, 200050 Shanghai; tel. (21) 52412990; e-mail siccas@sunm.shcnc.ac.cn; internet www.sic.ac.cn; f. 1959 as Shanghai Institute of Ceramic Chemistry and Engineering, current name adopted 1984; attached to Chinese Acad. of Sciences; library of 80,000 vols; Dir LIXIN SONG; publ. *Journal of Inorganic Materials* (6 a year).

Shanghai Institute of Optics and Fine Mechanics: POB 800-211, Shanghai, 201800; tel. (21) 69918000; e-mail hxlin@siom.ac.cn; internet www.siom.ac.cn; attached to Chinese Acad. of Sciences; laser science and technology; Dir Prof. ZHU JIANQING; publs *Acta Optica Sinica* (12 a year, in Chinese), *Chinese Journal of Lasers* (12 a year, in Chinese), *Chinese Optics Letters* (12 a year, in English).

Shanghai Institute of Technical Physics: 500 Yutian Rd, Shanghai 200083; tel. (21) 65420850; e-mail sitp@mail.sitp.ac.cn; internet www.sitp.ac.cn; f. 1958; attached to Chinese Acad. of Sciences; infrared technology and physics, optoelectronics and remote sensing; library of 40,000 vols; Dir WANG JIANYU; publ. *Chinese Journal of Infrared and Millimetre Waves* (6 a year).

Xian Institute of Optics and Precision Mechanics: 17 Xinxi Rd, New Industrial Park, Xian Hi-Tech Industrial Devt Zone, Xian; tel. (29) 88887565; e-mail info@opt.ac.cn; internet www.opt.cas.cn; f. 1962; attached to Chinese Acad. of Sciences; research on optoelectronic engineering and basic optics; library of 120,000 vols; Dir Prof. ZHAO WEI; publ. *Acta Photinica Sinica* (6 a year).

Xian Institute of Space Radio Technology: POB 165, 710000 Xian; tel. (29) 5290500; f. 1965; attached to Chinese Acad. of Space Technology; Pres. and CEO SHI PINGYAN.

Libraries and Archives

Baoding

Hebei University Library: 2 Hezuo Rd, Baoding, Hebei Province; tel. (312) 5022922 ext. 417; f. 1921; 1,960,000 vols, 3,923 current periodicals, 3,000 back copies; spec. colln: 4,397 vols of Chinese ancient books, incl. local chronicles and family trees; Dir LOU CHENGZHAO; publ. *Journal of Hebei University*.

Beijing

Beijing Normal University Library: Xinjiekouwai Dajie, 100875 Beijing; tel. (10) 62208163; internet www.lib.bnu.edu.cn; f. 1902; 435.3m. vols; Dir ZHANG QIWEI.

Capital Library: 15 Guozijian St, Dongcheng Dist., Beijing; tel. (10) 67358114; internet www.clcn.net.cn; f. 1913; municipal library; 2,574,000 vols, 142,000 current periodicals; spec. collns incl. traditional opera, folk customs; Dir JIN PEILIN.

Central Archives of China: Wenquan, Haidian Dist., Beijing; tel. (10) 62556611; f. 1959; revolutionary historical archives from the 4th May movement of 1919 to the founding of the People's Republic in 1949, and archives of CPC and central govt offices; 8,000,000 files; Curator WANG GANG; publs *CPC Documents*, *Central Archives of China Series*, *Collection of PCC Documents*, etc.

Centre for Documentation and Information, Chinese Academy of Social Sciences: 5 Jianguomennei Ave, Beijing 100732; tel. (10) 65126393; e-mail kyc-tsg@cass.org.cn; internet www.lib.cass.org.cn; f. 1985; attached to Chinese Acad. of Social Sciences; administrates Chinese Soc. of Social Sciences Information; 2,400,000 vols; Dir YANG PEICHAO; publs *Diogenes* (2 a year, in Chinese), *Social Sciences Abroad* (6 a year).

First Historical Archives of China: Palace Museum inside Xihuamen, 100031 Beijing; tel. (10) 63096487; f. 1925; 10,000,000 files; historical archives of Ming and Qing Dynasties; Curator XING YONGFU; publ. *Historical Archives* (4 a year).

Institute of Medical Information: 3 Yabaolu, Chaoyang Dist., Beijing 100020; tel. (10) 65122340; e-mail qianq@imicams.ac.cn; internet www.library.imicams.ac.cn; f. 1958; attached to Chinese Acad. of Medical Sciences and Peking Union Medical College; Dir Prof. DAI TAO.

Institute of Scientific and Technical Information of China (ISTIC): 15 Fuxing Rd, 100038 Beijing; tel. (10) 58882589; internet www.istic.ac.cn; f. 1956; 18,000,000 items from China and abroad, incl. research reports, conference proceedings, periodicals, patents, standards, catalogues and samples and audiovisual material; Dir-Gen. ZHU WEI; publs *Journal of Scientific and Technical Information*, *Review of World Inventions*, *Scientific and Technical Trends Abroad*.

Library of the Chinese Academy of Sciences: 33 Beisihuanxilu, Zhongguancun, 100080 Beijing; tel. (10) 82626684; e-mail office@mail.las.ac.cn; internet www.las.ac.cn; f. 1950; spec. collns incl. local chronicles, collected works of the Ming and Qing Dynasties, 40,000 rubbings from stone tablets, 600,000 rare books, 28 web-based databases, 38 CD-ROM databases; 5,200,000 vols, 8,636 current periodicals, 51,000 reports of conference proceedings; Chief Deputy Dir ZHANG XIAOLIN; publs *Chinese Biotechnology* (12 a year), *Chinese Mathematical Abstracts* (6 a year), *Chinese Physical Abstracts* (6 a year), *High Technology and Industrialization* (12 a year), *Library and Information Service* (12 a year), *New Technology of Library and Information Service* (12 a year), *Progress in Chemistry* (6 a year), *R&D Information* (12 a year), *Science and Technology International* (12 a year).

National Library of China: 33 Zhongguancun Nandajie, Haidian Dist., Beijing 100081; tel. (10) 88545023; e-mail interco@publicf.nlc.gov.cn; internet www.nlc.gov.cn; f. 1909; 22,000,000 vols, 21,000 current periodicals, 1,100,000 microforms and audiovisual items; spec. collns incl. 291,696 vols of rare books of imperial libraries in the Southern Song, Ming and Qing Dynasties; all kinds of Chinese publs, incl. those in minority languages; foreign books, periodicals and newspapers, UN publs and govt publs of certain countries; blockprinted editions, books of rubbings, and other antique items; Dir Prof. REN JIYU; publs *Documents* (4 a year), *Journal of the National Library of China* (4 a year), *National Bibliography*.

Peking University Library: Haidian Dist., Beijing 100871; tel. (10) 62751051; e-mail office@lib.pku.edu.cn; internet www.lib.pku.edu.cn; f. 1902; 5,736,401 books, 708,424 vols of bound periodicals, spec. colln: 1,600,000 vols of thread-bound Chinese ancient books, incl. 200,000 vols of rare books, 70,000 rubbings, copy of *Complete Works of Shakespeare* (publ. 1623), Dante's *Divine Comedy* (publ. 1896), and plays by Schiller, 529,446 vols of ebooks, 47,010 ejournals, 466 databases; Dir Prof. QIANG ZHU; publ. *Journal of Academic Libraries* (6 a year).

Renmin University of China Library: 175 Haidian Rd, Beijing; tel. (10) 62511371; internet www.lib.ruc.edu.cn; f. 1937; rich colln of philosophy of Marxism, law, economics, modern and contemporary history of China; 3.5m. vols; spec. colln: Chinese revolutionary documents in liberated and base areas, ancient rare books of Song, Yuan, Ming and Qing Dynasties (2,400 titles); Dir Prof. SUN QUAN.

Tsinghua University Library: Qinghuayuan, West Suburb, 100084 Beijing; tel. (10) 62782137; e-mail bgs@lib.tsinghua.edu.cn; internet www.lib.tsinghua.edu.cn; f. 1912; 3.5m. vols incl. 300,000 thread-bound ancient books, 3,000 monographs or textbooks; Dir XUE FANGYU.

Changchun

Jilin Provincial Library: 1162 Xinmin St, Changchun; tel. (431) 85632100; internet www.jlplib.com.cn; f. 1909; 3m. vols; Dir BAO SHENGHUA; publ. *Research in Library Science* (6 a year).

Jilin University Library: Qianjin St, 130012 Changchun; tel. (431) 8923189; internet www.lib.jlu.edu.cn; f. 1946; 585m. vols; spec. colln: local chronicles, clan trees, Asian Series, documents of Manchurian railways; Dir Prof. WANG JIAN.

Northeast Normal University Library: 138 Renmin St, 130024 Changchun; tel. (431) 84536093; internet www.library.nenu.edu.cn; f. 1946; publs from time of the War of Resistance against Japan; rare Chinese ancient books; 2,300,000 vols, 4,000 current periodicals, 11,600 back copies; Dir SUN ZHONGTIAN; publ. *Jilin Libraries of Colleges and Universities* (4 a year).

Changsha

Hunan Provincial Library: 169 North Shaoshan Rd, 410011 Changsha; tel. (731) 84129413; internet www.library.hn.cn; f. 1904; 3,400,000 vols.

Chengdu

Sichuan Provincial Library: 6 Lu Zongfu, 610016 Chengdu; tel. (28) 6659219; e-mail sctsg@qq.com; f. 1940; 3,760,000 vols, 13,485 periodicals, historical material; Dir WANG ENLAI (acting); publ. *Librarian* (6 a year).

Chongqing

Chongqing Library: 106 Phoenix Day Rd, 400037 Chongqing; tel. (23) 65210822; internet www.cqlib.cn; f. 1947; 460m. vols; Dir REN JING.

Dalian

Dalian Library: 7 Changbai, Xigang District, Dalian; tel. (411) 39662300; internet www.dl-library.net.cn; f. 1907; 4.51m. vols; Curator ZHANG BENYI.

Fuzhou

Fujian Provincial Library: 227 Hudong Lu, Fuzhou; tel. (591) 87507075; f. 1911; 3.3m. vols, 4,350 current periodicals, historical material; spec. collns incl. data on Taiwan and Southeast Asia.

Guangzhou

Zhongshan Library of Guangdong Province: 211 Wenming Rd, Guangzhou, Guangdong Province; tel. (20) 330676; f. 1912; spec. collns incl. research materials on Dr Sun Yatsen; 3,300,000 vols, 6,000 current periodicals, historical documents; Dir HUANG JUNGUI; publs *Journal of Guangdong Libraries* (4 a year), *Library Tribune* (4 a year).

Guilin

Guilin Library of Guangxi Zhuang Autonomous Region: 15 North Ronghu Rd, Guilin, Guangxi Zhuang Autonomous Region; tel. (773) 223494; f. 1909; 1,380,000 vols, 15,275 current periodicals, historical material; Deputy Dir YANG JIANHONG; publs *Catalogue of Guangxi Local Documents*, *Catalogue of Materials on Guangxi Minority Study* (vols 1–2).

Guiyang

Guizhou Provincial Library: 31 Beijing Rd, Guiyang, Guizhou Province; tel. (851) 25562; f. 1937; 1,270,000 vols, 5,000 periodicals, historical material; publs *Chronological Table of the Historical Calamities of Guizhou Province*, *Collected Papers on the Mineral Products of Guizhou Province*, *Journal* (4 a year).

Hangzhou

Zhejiang Provincial Library: 38 Shuguang Rd, Hangzhou 310007, Zhejiang Province; tel. (571) 87999812; e-mail bgs@zjlib.net.cn; internet www.zjlib.net.cn; f. 1900; 4,210,000 vols, 7,526 current periodicals; Chief Officer CHENG XIAOLIAN; publ. *Library Science Research and Work* (4 a year).

Harbin

Heilongjiang Provincial Library: No 218 Changjiang Rd, Nangang Dist., 150090 Harbin, Heilongjiang Province; tel. (451) 85990586; e-mail hljstsg@sina.com; f. 1958; spec. collns incl. Russian publs, 1920s–1940s Japanese publs; 2,928,193 vols, 2,371,484 books; 133,693 ancient books; 6,602 rare books; 438,675 newspapers and periodicals; 35,866 audiovisual documents and microcopies; 82,168 other documents; Dir GAO WENHUA; publ. *Library Development* (12 a year).

Hefei

Anhui Provincial Library: 38 Wuhu Rd, Hefei, Anhui Province; tel. (551) 257602; f. 1913; 2,108,608 vols, 5,400 current periodicals, 30,000 antique books, historical documents; Dir WANG BAO SHENG; publ. *Library Work* (4 a year).

Jinan

Shandong Provincial Library: 275 Daminhu Rd, Jinan; tel. (531) 612338; internet www.sdlib.com; f. 1909; 6.12m. vols.

Shandong University Library: Jinan; tel. (531) 88364902; internet www.lib.sdu.edu.cn; f. 1901; 77% of holdings are on liberal arts; spec. colln: rare books, rubbings from stone inscriptions, calligraphy and paintings, revolutionary documents; 4,434,296 vols; Dir Prof. XU WEN-TIAN.

Kunming

Yunnan Provincial Library: 2 South Cuihu Rd, Kunming; tel. (871) 532851; internet www.ynlib.cn; f. 1909; 2,150,000 vols, 7,172 periodicals, historical material.

Lanzhou

Gansu Provincial Library: 488 South Riverside Rd, 730000 Lanzhou; tel. (931) 28982; internet www.gslib.com.cn; f. 1916; 2,400,000 vols, historical material; spec. collns incl. Imperial Library of Qianlong; Dir PAN YINSHENG; publ. *Library and Information* (4 a year).

Nanchang

Jiangxi Provincial Library: 160 N Hongdu Rd, 330046 Nanchang; tel. (791) 8513364; f. 1920; 2,200,000 vols, 6,600 periodicals, historical material; publ. *Journal of the Jiangxi Society of Library Science* (4 a year).

Nanjing

Nanjing Library: 66 Chengxian St, Nanjing, Jiangsu Province; tel. (25) 57717619; e-mail ntbgs@sina.com; internet www.jslib.com.cn; f. 1907; 7,790,000 vols, 8,000 current periodicals, 1,700,000 ancient books; Exec. Dir MA NING; publ. *New Century Library* (6 a year).

Nanjing University Library: 22 Hankou Rd, 210093 Nanjing; tel. (25) 3592943; e-mail tsgzxb@library.nju.edu.cn; internet lib.nju.edu.cn; f. 1902; systematic colln of literature, history, philosophy, economics, law, mathematics, physics, chemistry, astronomy, geology, geography, meteorology, environmental science, computer science, biology and medicine, in Chinese and foreign languages; 3,560,000 vols, 5,000 current periodicals, 566,400 bound vols of periodicals; spec. colln: 1,452 titles of rare books (Song, Yuan, Ming and Qing Dynasties), 10,000 sheets of rubbings from stone inscriptions, many paintings, MSS and handcopies, 4,600 titles (40,000 vols) of local chronicles, mainly of Jiangsu and Sichuan Provinces, also books on orientalism, bibliography and archaeology; Dir Prof. ZHANG YIBING; publ. *Journal of Serials Management and Research* (2 a year).

Second Historical Archives of China: 309 East Zhongshan Rd, 210016 Nanjing; tel. (25) 84800747; internet www.shac.net.cn; f. 1951; 1,800,000 files, 200,000 periodicals; Curator ZHAI YUXIA.

Shanghai

East China Normal University Library: 3663 N Zhongshan Rd, 200062 Shanghai; tel. (21) 62232317; internet www.lib.ecnu.edu.cn; f. 1951; collns on pedagogy, psychology, geography, classical philosophy, local histories and bibliography; earliest edns of thread-bound Chinese ancient books of the Song Dynasty and of foreign books (publ. 1630); rubbings from stone inscriptions; 424.6m. vols; Dir WANG XIJING; publ. *Library Information* (12 a year).

Fudan University Library: 220 Handan Rd, 200433 Shanghai; tel. (21) 65643592; e-mail liboffice@fudan.edu.cn; internet www.library.fudan.edu.cn; f. 1922; 5m. vols, 400,000 rare ancient Chinese books; Dir Prof. GE JIANXIONG.

Shanghai Library: Huaihai Rd, Shanghai; tel. (21) 3273176; e-mail service@libnet.sh.cn; internet www.library.sh.cn; f. 1952; 53m. vols; Dir ZHU QING ZHO; publs *Catalog of Chinese Series, Contents of Modern Chinese Journals, Catalog of Shanghai Library Collections of Local Histories, Catalog of Works and Translations by Guo Moruo.*

Shenyang

Liaoning Provincial Library: 111 Wanliutanglu, 110015 Shenyang; tel. (24) 24822449; e-mail wzgl@lnlib.com; internet www.lnlib.com; f. 1948 current name adopted 1955; 1,923,366 vols, 13,307 periodicals; Dir WANG XIAOWEN.

Tianjin

Nankai University Library: 94 Weijin Rd, Tianjin 300071; tel. (22) 23502410; e-mail tsg@nankai.edu.cn; internet www.lib.nankai.edu.cn; f. 1919; 3,145,805 vols, 3,349 current periodicals, 511,159 bound copies of periodicals; spec. collns: 2,000 titles of rare books, 4,000 titles of local chronicles, 10,000 reference books, complete set of 100 periodicals with back issues of more than 50 years, 5,946 audiovisual items, 1,689 multimedia CD-ROMs, 51 databases; Dir Prof. YAN SHIPING; publs *Catalog of Rare Books Held by Nankai University Library, Catalog of Thread-Bound Ancient Books Held by Nankai University Library.*

Tianjin Library: 12 Chengdedao Rd, Heping Dist., Tianjin; tel. (22) 27406249; e-mail lib@tju.edu.cn; internet www.lib.tju.edu.cn; f. 1895; 2.4m. vols, 8,251 current periodicals; Dir DONG CHANGXU; publ. *Library Work and Research* (4 a year).

Wuhan

Hubei Provincial Library: 45 Wuluo Rd, 430060 Wuhan; tel. (27) 88846080; f. 1904; 4.96m. vols; Dir XIONG JINSHAN; publ. *Library & Information Science Tribune* (4 a year).

Wuhan University Library: Mt Luojiashan, Wuhan; tel. (27) 7872290; e-mail jwshen@lib.whu.edu.cn; internet www.lib.whu.edu.cn; f. 1913; 13,360,000 vols incl. 200,000 ancient Chinese books; colln of works on basic theories, and newspapers and periodicals published before 1949; Dir SHEN JIWU.

Xiamen

Xiamen University Libraries: 422 Siming Nan Rd, Xiamen, Fujian Province; tel. (592) 2186127; e-mail dehong@xmu.edu.cn; internet library.xmu.edu.cn; f. 1921; publs on natural and social sciences, esp. economics, biology, chemistry and data on Southeast Asia and Taiwan; 4,270,000 vols, 3,000,000 vols of ebooks and ejournals; Dean XIAO DEHONG.

Xian

Shaanxi Provincial Library: 146 Xi Ave, Xian, Shaanxi Province; f. 1909; 2,300,000 vols.

Xian Jiaotong University Library: Xianning Rd, 710049 Xian; tel. (29) 82668103; e-mail ref@mail.lib.xjtu.edu.cn; internet www.lib.xjtu.edu.cn; f. 1896; colln of scientific and technical publs, complete sets of 15 sci-tech periodicals with a history of over 100 years; 3,910,000 vols, 5,214 current periodicals; Dir Prof. LI RENHOU.

Xining

Qinghai Provincial Library: 66 Xiguan Dajie, Xining; tel. (971) 6134733; f. 1935; 1.4m. vols; publ. *Libraries in Qinghai* (4 a year).

Yinchuan

Ningxia Library: Tongxin Rd N, Yinchuan; tel. (951) 2021986; internet www.nxlib.cn; f. 1958; 1,300,000 vols.

Zhengzhou

Henan Provincial Library: 150 Song Shan Nan Rd, Zhengzhou; tel. (371) 67181499; internet www.henanlib.gov.cn; f. 1909; 2,360,000 vols, 4,419 current periodicals, 700,000 antique books, historical material; Dir TONG JIYONG; publ. *Journal of Henan Libraries* (4 a year).

Museums and Art Galleries

Beijing

Arthur M. Sackler Museum of Art and Archaeology: Peking University, School of Archaeology and Museology, Beijing 100871; tel. (10) 62751667; f. 1993; attached to Peking Univ.; Dir Prof. ZHAO HUI.

Beijing Lu Xun Museum: 19, Gongmenkou Ertiao, Fuchengmennei St, Beijing, 100034; tel. (10) 66164080; e-mail huangsheng2@263.net; internet www.luxunmuseum.com; f. 1956; confs; exhibitions; library of 30,000 vols; Curator HUANG QIAOSHENG; publ. *Lu Xun Research* (12 a year).

Beijing Museum of Natural History: 126 Tianqiao South St, Dongcheng Dist., Beijing; tel. (10) 67020641; e-mail office@bmnh.org.cn; internet www.bmnh.org.cn; f. 1951; specimen collns, scientific researches and scientific popularization in areas as paleontology, biology and anthropology; exhibitions about ancient life, animals, plants and human beings; temporary exhibitions; library of 50,000 vols; Dir MENG QINGJIN; publs *China Nature* (with English contents, jtly with the China Wildlife Conservation Asscn, the Chinese Asscn of Natural Science Museums and Beijing Natural History Museum), *Memoirs* (with English abstract).

Geological Museum of China: 15 Yangrouhutong, Xisi, Beijing 100034; tel. (10) 66557402; e-mail ngmc@public2.bta.net.cn; f. 1916; Dir CHENG LIWEI.

Military Museum of the Chinese People's Revolution: 9 Fuxing Rd, 100038 Beijing; tel. (10) 66866244; f. 1958; Curator SHI ZHIHONG; publ. *Military History* (6 a year).

National Museum of China: 16 East Chang'an Ave, Beijing 100006; tel. (10) 65118983; e-mail info@chnmuseum.cn; internet www.chnmuseum.cn; f. 2003 by merger of Nat. Museum of Chinese History (f. 1912) and Nat. Museum of Chinese Revolution (f. 1950); ancient Chinese historical artefacts and documents since prehistoric times; modern Chinese art and history since 1840; archaeology, history and art; Dir LU ZHANGSHEN; publs *Journal of National Museum of China, Modern China and Cultural Relics.*

Palace Museum: 4 Jingshan Qian Jie, 100009 Beijing; tel. (10) 65132255; internet www.dpm.org.cn; f. 1925; paintings, ceramics, bronzes, jades, applied arts, calligraphy, carvings, coins, furniture, arms, decorative arts, musical instruments, clocks, seals, toys; library of 700,000 vols; Dir ZHENG XINMIAO; publs *Forbidden City* (6 a year), *Palace Museum Journal* (6 a year).

Quanzhou

Quanzhou Museum for Overseas Communications History: Quanzhou City, Fujian Province; tel. (595) 226655; f. 1959; Chinese foreign trade and China's int. relations in the fields of culture, science and religion; Curator WANG LIANMAO; publ. *Research into Overseas Communications History* (published jointly with the China Society of Research on Overseas Communications History, 2 a year).

Shanghai

Shanghai Museum: 201 Ren Min Da Dao, Shanghai 200003; tel. (21) 63723500; e-mail webmaster@shanghaimuseum.net; internet www.shanghaimuseum.net; f. 1952; library of 200,000 vols; Dir CHEN XIEJUN.

Universities and Colleges

ANHUI UNIVERSITY

3 Feixi Rd, Hefei 230039, Anhui Province
Telephone: (551) 5106114
Internet: www.ahu.edu.cn

Founded 1928
Academic year: September to July

Pres.: HUAN DEKUAN
Vice-Pres.: LAN XI JIE
Vice-Pres.: WEI SUI
Vice-Pres.: WU LIANG
Vice-Pres.: YI YOU MIN
Head of Graduate Dept: WANG XING HAI
Head of Graduate Dept: ZHU SHI QUN
Librarian: XU JUN DA

Number of teachers: 1,100
Number of students: 26,787

Publications: *Anhui University Law Review* (2 a year), *Hui Study* (1 a year), *Journal of Anhui University* (natural sciences, 6 a year), *Journal of Anhui University* (philosophy and social science, 6 a year)

DEANS

Business Administration: ZHOU YA NA
Chinese: TAO XIN MIN
Economics: RONG ZHAO ZI
Electrical Science and Technology: CHEN JUN NING
Foreign Studies: HUANG QING LONG
History: WU CHUN MEI
Law: LI MING FA
Life Science: LI JIN HUA
Management: XIE YANG QUN
Mathematics and Computing Science: JIANG WEI
Philosophy: LI XIA
Physics and Material Science: SHI SHOU HUA

PROFESSORS

BA, ZHAO LIN, Chinese
CAO, ZHUO LIANG, Physics and Material Science
CHEN, DAO GUI, Chinese
CHEN, GUI JING, Mathematics and Computing Science
CHEN, HUA YOU, Mathematics and Computing Science
CHEN, JUN NING, Electrical Science and Technology
CHEN, QIN, Life Science
CHEN, SHENG QING, Law
CHEN, ZHANG JIN, Physics and Material Science
CHENG, JING RONG, Physics and Material Science
DOU, REN SHENG, Physics and Material Science
DU, PENG CHENG, Business Administration
DU, XIAN NENG, Mathematics and Computing Science
FAN, YI ZHENG, Mathematics and Computing Science
FANG, BIN, Electrical Science and Technology
FANG, QING QING, Physics and Material Science
FANG, XIANG ZHENG, Physics and Material Science
FENG, YI MING, Economics
GAO, QING WEI, Electrical Science and Technology
GE, CHUANG LI, Electrical Science and Technology
GE, LI FENG, Electrical Science and Technology
GU, RONG BAO, Mathematics and Computing Science
GU, ZU DAO, Chinese
GUAN, XIN LIN, Business Administration
GUO, JIAN YOU, Physics and Material Science
HAN, JIA HUA, Physics and Material Science
HE, JIA QING, Life Science
HU, GUO GUANG, Physics and Material Science
HU, MAO LIN, Mathematics and Computing Science
HU, SHU HE, Mathematics and Computing Science
HU, YAN JUN, Electrical Science and Technology
HUANG, PEI, Life Science
JIA, HAI JI, Economics
JIANG, WEI, Mathematics and Computing Science
KE, DAO MING, Electrical Science and Technology
KONG, FAN CHAO, Mathematics and Computing Science
LI, CAI FU, Management
LI, JIN HUA, Life Science
LI, MING FA, Law
LI, SHOU SHEN, Economics
LI, XIA, Philosophy
LI, XIAO HUI, Electrical Science and Technology
LI, XIU SONG, History
LI, YU CHENG, Life Science
LIU, XIN FANG, History
LOU, PING, Physics and Material Science
LU, QIN YI, History
LU, RONG SHAN, Economics
LU, YING BIN, Economics
MA, REN JIE, Management
MA, XIU SHUI, Electrical Science and Technology
MING, JUN, Electrical Science and Technology
REN, KAI, Philosophy
RONG, ZHAO ZI, Economics
SHENG, YE SHOU, Life Science
SHENG, ZHAO XUAN, Mathematics and Computing Science
SHI, FU YUAN, Electrical Science and Technology
SHI, SHOU HUA, Physics and Material Science
SHI, XIANG QIAN, Philosophy
SUN, YI KAI, Philosophy
SUN, YU FA, Electrical Science and Technology
SUN, ZHAO QI, Physics and Material Science
TANG, HUA QUAN, Chinese
TANG, QI XUE, History
TAO, XIN MIN, Chinese
WANG, DA MING, Chinese
WANG, DAO MING, Economics
WANG, DAO QING, Chinese
WANG, HUI, Management
WANG, LIANG LONG, Mathematics and Computing Science
WANG, RONG, Law
WANG, XIN YI, History
WANG, YI PING, Life Science
WANG, YIN HAI, Physics and Material Science
WANG, YONG DE, Chinese
WANG, YU, Life Science
WEI, WEI, Economics
WEN, CHUN RU, Philosophy
WU, CHUN MEI, History
WU, JIA RONG, Chinese
XIAO, JIAN, Mathematics and Computing Science
XIAO, YA ZHONG, Life Science
XIE, YANG QUN, Management
XIONG, XIAO QI, Economics
XU, CHANG QING, Mathematics and Computing Science
XU, CHENG ZHI, Chinese
XU, JIAN HUA, Mathematics and Computing Science
XU, JUN DA, Philosophy
XU, ZAI GUO, Chinese
XU, ZHANG CHENG, Physics and Material Science
YAN, PENG FEI, Mathematics and Computing Science
YANG, FANG ZHI, Economics
YANG, SHANG JUN, Mathematics and Computing Science
YANG, XIAO LI, Chinese
YAO, XUE BIAO, Physics and Material Science
YE, LIU, Physics and Material Science
YI, YOU MIN, Physics and Material Science
YONG, XI QI, Mathematics and Computing Science
YU, BEN LI, Physics and Material Science
YUE, FANG SUI, Chinese
YUE, JIE XIAN, Philosophy
ZENG, FAN YIN, Economics
ZHA, XIANG DONG, Life Science
ZHANG, BU CHANG, Life Science
ZHANG, JIAN FENG, Economics
ZHANG, JIN XI, History
ZHANG, LU GAO, Chinese
ZHANG, NENG WEI, Philosophy
ZHANG, QI YOU, Chinese
ZHANG, ZI XIA, History
ZHENG, MING ZHEN, Philosophy
ZHOU, HUAI YU, History
ZHOU, LI ZHI, Life Science
ZHOU, NAN, Law
ZHOU, SHENG MING, Physics and Material Science
ZHOU, YA NA, Business Administration
ZHOU, ZHI YUAN, History
ZHOU, ZHONG ZE, Life Science
ZHU, SHI QUN, Philosophy
ZHU, XUE SHAN, Law
ZHU, ZONG YAN, Economics

BEIHANG UNIVERSITY

37 Xue Yuan Rd, 100191 Beijing
Telephone: (10) 82317114
E-mail: xiaoban@buaa.edu.cn
Internet: www.buaa.edu.cn

Founded 1952, current name adopted 2002
State control
Languages of instruction: Chinese, English
Academic year: September to August

Pres.: HUAI JINPENG
Vice-Chancellor: WEI ZHIMIN
Vice-Chancellor: ZHANG GUANGJUN
Vice-Chancellor: WANG JIANZHONG
Vice-Chancellor: TAO CHI
Deputy Sec.: LI JUNFENG

Library of 1,100,000 vols, 98,000 periodicals
Number of teachers: 3,359
Number of students: 27,811 (14,428 graduates, 12,715 undergraduates, 668 other)

Publications: *Acta Aeronautica et Astronautica Sinica* (12 a year), *Acta Materiae Compositae Sinica* (4 a year), *Aerospace Knowledge* (12 a year), *China Aeronautical Education* (4 a year), *College English* (6 a year), *DADDM* (2 a year), *Journal* (4 a year), *Journal of Aerospace Power* (4 a year), *Journal of Engineering Graphics* (2 a year), *Model World* (4 a year)

DEPARTMENTAL DEANS

Automatic Control: Prof. LI XINGSHAN

Computer Sciences and Engineering: Prof. JIN MAOZHONG
Electronic Engineering: Prof. ZHANG XIAOLIN
Flying Vehicle Design and Applied Mechanics: Prof. WANG JINJUN
Foreign Languages: Prof. LI BAOKUN
Manufacturing Engineering: Prof. TANG XIAOQING
Materials Science and Engineering: Prof. XU HUIBIN
Mechanical and Electrical Engineering: Prof. YANG ZONGXU
Propulsion: Prof. LI QIHAN
Systems Engineering: Prof. YANG WEIMIN

BEIJING BROADCASTING UNIVERSITY

Ding Fu Zhuang St, Chao Yang District, Beijing 10024
Telephone: (10) 65779319
Internet: www.cuc.edu.cn

Founded 1954
Min. of Education control
Academic year: August to July

Pres.: LIU JI NAN

Number of teachers: 772
Number of students: 28,000

Publications: *Asia Media and Communication Studies* (1 a year), *Journal of Beijing Broadcasting University* (modern communication, 4 a year), *Journal of Beijing Broadcasting University* (natural science, 4 a year), *Media Studies* (irregular)

DEANS

Advertising Studies: HUANG SHENG MIN
Animation: LU SHENG ZHAN
Film and Television Arts: LI XING GUO
Information Engineering and Science: LI JIAN ZENG
International Communication: XU QIN YUAN
Journalism and Communication: DING JUN JIE
Literature: MIAO DI
Media Management: ZAN YAN QUAN
Presentation Art: LI XIAO HUA
Social Sciences: GAO HUI RAN
Television: GAO XIAO HONG

PROFESSORS

BI, GEN HUI, Film and Television Arts
CAI, CHAO SHI, Information Engineering
CAI, GUO FEN, International Communication
CAI, WEN MEI, Journalism and Communication
CAO, LU, Journalism and Communication
CAO, QING RUI, Film and Television Arts
CHEN, BIAN ZHI, International Communication
CHEN, JING SHENG, Broadcasting
CHEN, WEI XING, International Communication
CHEN, YUAN MENG, International Communication
DING, JUN JIE, Journalism and Communication
DONG, HUA MIAO, Film and Television Arts
DU, HAN FENG, Literature
FENG, SONG CHE, Social Sciences
FU, JUN QING, Journalism and Communication
GAO, FU AN, Film and Television Arts
GAO, FU AN, Media Management
GAO, XIAO HONG, Television
GUAN, LING, Film and Television Arts
GUO, ZHEN ZHI, Television
HA, YAN QIU, Journalism and Communication
HE, LAN, International Communication
HE, SU LIU, Television
HE, XIAO BING, Film and Television Arts
HOU, MIN, Broadcasting
HUANG, JING HUA, Advertising Studies
HUANG, ZHI XUN, Information Engineering
HUO, WEN LI, Television
JIA, FOU, Animation
JIANG, XIU HUA, Information Engineering
JIN, GUI RONG, Film and Television Arts
KE, HUI XIN, Journalism and Communication
LEI, YUE JIE, Journalism and Communication
LI, DONG, Information Engineering
LI, JIAN ZENG, Information Engineering
LI, JIAN ZENG, Science
LI, SHENG LI, Film and Television Arts
LI, XING GUO, Film and Television Arts
LI, ZENG RUI, Information Engineering
LI, ZENG RUI, Science
LI, ZUO FENG, Literature
LIANG, MING, Film and Television Arts
LIANG, YI GAO, Journalism and Communication
LIANG, ZHENG LI, Media Management
LIN, ZHENG BAO, Information Engineering
LIU, JIAN BO, Information Engineering
LIU, JING LIN, Journalism and Communication
LIU, LI WEN, Literature
LIU, LI WEN, Film and Television Arts
LIU, SHU LIANG, Film and Television Arts
LIU, TING, Film and Television Arts
LIU, YE YUAN, Film and Television Arts
LU, GUI ZHEN, Information Engineering
LU, JIAN, Film and Television Arts
LU, SHENG ZHAN, Animation
LU, YING KUN, Film and Television Arts
LUO, LI, Broadcasting
MAO, ZHI JI, Information Engineering
MIAO, DI, Literature
NI, XUE LI, Film and Television Arts
PAN, YE, Film and Television Arts
PENG, HUI GUO, Animation
PU, ZHEN YUAN, Literature
QIN, YU MING, Television
REN, SU QIN, Social Sciences
REN, YUAN, Television
SHENG, QIN, Information Engineering
SHI, MIN YONG, Animation
SHI, XU SHENG, Film and Television Arts
SONG, PEI YI, Film and Television Arts
SONG, PEI YI, Media Management
WANG, CHUN ZHI, Information Engineering
WANG, HONG, Television
WANG, MING YA, Film and Television Arts
WANG, WEI, International Communication
WANG, WU LU, Journalism and Communication
WANG, XIAO HONG, Television
WANG, YA PING, Animation
WEI, YONG ZHENG, Social Sciences
WU, YIN, Television
WU, YU, Broadcasting
XING, XIN, Broadcasting
YANG, FENG JIAO, Television
YANG, LEI, Information Engineering
YANG, LU PING, Television
YANG, XIAO LU, Film and Television Arts
YAO, XIAO OU, Literature
YE, FENG YING, Television
YOU, FEI, Film and Television Arts
YUAN, QING FENG, Film and Television Arts
ZAN, YAN QUAN, Media Management
ZENG, XIANG MIN, Television
ZENG, ZHI HUA, Broadcasting
ZHANG, FEN ZHU, Film and Television Arts
ZHANG, GE DONG, Film and Television Arts
ZHANG, GUI ZHEN, International Communication
ZHANG, JING, Literature
ZHANG, JUN, Animation
ZHANG, QI, Information Engineering
ZHANG, SHU, Journalism and Communication
ZHANG, XIAO FENG, Social Sciences
ZHANG, YAN, Film and Television Arts
ZHANG, YAN, Journalism and Communication
ZHANG, YONG HUI, Information Engineering
ZHANG, YU HUA, Film and Television Arts
ZHAO, SHU PING, Television
ZHAO, XIAO GUANG, Literature
ZHAO, YU MING, Journalism and Communication
ZHONG, TAO, Literature
ZHONG, YI QIAN, Advertising Studies
ZHOU, HONG GUO, Media Management
ZHOU, HUA BIN, Film and Television Arts
ZHOU, JING BO, Film and Television Arts
ZHOU, YONG, Film and Television Arts
ZHOU, YUE LIANG, Film and Television Arts

BEIJING FILM ACADEMY

4 Xi Tu Cheng Rd, 100088 Beijing
Telephone: (10) 82045433
E-mail: admit@bfa.edu.cn
Internet: www.bfa.edu.cn

Founded 1950, current name adopted 1956

Depts of basic education, cinematography, directing, film and TV technology, film studies, fine arts, management, screenwriting, sound recording; schools of animation, continuing education, performing arts, photography

Pres.: ZHANG HUIJUN
Vice-Pres.: WANG LIGUANG
Vice-Pres.: XIE XIAOJING
Vice-Pres.: SUN LIJUN
Vice-Pres.: WANG HONGHAI
Vice-Pres.: NI YUEHONG
Vice-Pres.: WANG HONGMIN

Library of 300,000 vols
Number of teachers: 263
Number of students: 2,364

Publication: *Journal*

BEIJING FOREIGN STUDIES UNIVERSITY

3 West Ring Rd, 100089 Beijing
Telephone: (10) 88816215
E-mail: bwxzb@bfsu.edu.cn
Internet: www.bfsu.edu.cn

Founded 1941
State control
Academic year: September to July

Schools of Chinese language and literature, English and int. studies, English for specific purposes, int. business, Russian

Pres.: PENG LONG
Vice-Pres.: JIA DEZHONG
Vice-Pres.: JIA WENJIAN
Vice-Pres.: YAN GUOHUA

Library: 1.01m. vols
Number of teachers: 600
Number of students: 7,000

Publications: *Foreign Language Teaching and Research*, *Foreign Literatures*, *International Forum*, *Soviet Art and Literature*

BEIJING FORESTRY UNIVERSITY

Xiaozhuang, Haidian Dist., 100083 Beijing
Telephone: (10) 62338279
E-mail: service@bjfu.edu.cn
Internet: www.bjfu.edu.cn

Founded 1952

Colleges of environmental science and engineering, forestry, information science and technology, material science and technology, nature conservation, science; schools of economics and management, foreign languages, humanities and social sciences, landscape architecture, soil and water conservation, technology

Pres.: SONG WEIMING
Vice-Pres.: JIANG ENLAI
Vice-Pres.: ZHANG QIXIANG
Librarian: Prof. GAO RONGFU

Library of 560,000 vols
Number of teachers: 1,806
Number of students: 31,000

BEIJING INSTITUTE OF TECHNOLOGY

7 Bai Shi Giao, Hai Ding Dist., Beijing 100081
Telephone: (10) 68914246
Internet: www.bit.edu.cn
Founded 1940
State control
Academic year: September to July
Pres: KUANG JINGMING
Vice-Pres.: HOU GUANGMING
Vice-Pres.: LI ZHIXIANG
Vice-Pres.: YANG BIN
Vice-Pres.: ZHAO CHANGLU
Head of Graduate Dept: KUANG JINGMING
Librarian: CAO SHU REN
Number of teachers: 3,000
Number of students: 31,000
Publications: *Journal of Beijing Institute of Technology* (natural sciences, 6 a year), *Journal of Beijing Institute of Technology* (social sciences, 6 a year)

DEANS

School of Chemical Engineering and Materials: ZHOU, TONG LAI
School of Computers and Control: HOU, CHAO ZHEN
School of Design Art: ZHANG, NAI REN
School of Humanities and Social Sciences: XI, QIAO JUAN
School of Information Engineering: WANG, YUE
School of Management and Economics: WANG, XIU CUN
School of Mechatronic Engineering: LIU, LI
School of Science and Technology: XU, WEN GUO
School of Software: WANG, SHU WU
School of Vehicle and Transport Engineering: XU, CHUN GUANG

PROFESSORS

AN, JIAN PING, Information and Communication Engineering
BA, YAN ZHU, Optics Engineering
BAI, CHUN HUA, Mechatronic Engineering
BI, SHI HUA, Mechatronic Engineering
CAI, HONG YAN, Material Science and Engineering
CAO, GEN RUI, Apparatus Science and Technology
CAO, YUAN DA, Computer Science and Technology
CHAI, RUI JIAO, Mechatronic Engineering
CHEN, DONG SHENG, Vehicle and Transport Engineering
CHEN, HUI YAN, Vehicle and Transport Engineering
CHEN, JIA BIN, Control Science and Engineering
CHEN, JIE, Control Science and Engineering
CHEN, SHU FENG, Electronic Science and Technology
CHEN, SI ZHONG, Vehicle and Transport Engineering
CHEN, XIANG GUANG, Control Science and Engineering
CUI, ZHAN ZHONG, Mechatronic Engineering
DA, YA PING, Control Science and Engineering
DING, HONG SHENG, Vehicle and Transport Engineering
DONG, YU PING, Material Science and Engineering
DOU, LI HUA, Control Science and Engineering
DU, ZHI MING, Mechatronic Engineering
FAN, NING JUN, Mechatronic Engineering
FAN, TIAN YOU, Applied Mathematics
FAN, XIAO ZHONG, Computer Science and Technology
FEI, YUAN CHUN, Electronic Science and Technology
FENG, CHANG GEN, Mechatronic Engineering
FENG, SHUN SHAN, Mechatronic Engineering
FU, MENG YING, Control Science and Engineering
GAN, REN CHU, Management Science and Engineering
GAO, BEN QING, Electronic Science and Technology
GAO, CHUN QING, Electronic Science and Technology
GAO, MEI GUO, Information and Communication Engineering
GAO, SHI QIAO, Engineering Mechanics
GAO, ZHI YUN, Optics Engineering
GE, WEI GAO, Applied Mathematics
GE, YUN SHAN, Vehicle and Transport Engineering
GOU, BING CONG, Electronic Science and Technology
GU, LIANG, Vehicle and Transport Engineering
GU, ZHI MIN, Computer Science and Technology
GUO, QIAO, Control Science and Engineering
HAN, BAO LING, Vehicle and Transport Engineering
HAN, BO TANG, Management Science and Engineering
HAN, FENG, Mechatronic Engineering
HAN, YUE QIU, Information and Communication Engineering
HE, PEI KUN, Information and Communication Engineering
HOU, CHAO ZHEN, Control Science and Engineering
HOU, GUANG MING, Management Science and Engineering
HU, CHANG WEN, Chemistry
HU, GENG KAI, Solid Mechanics
HUANG, FENG LEI, Mechatronic Engineering
HUANG, RUO, Vehicle and Transport Engineering
JIA, YUN DE, Computer Science and Technology
JIAO, QING JIE, Mechatronic Engineering
JIAO, YONG HE, Vehicle and Transport Engineering
KANG, JING LI, Mechatronic Engineering
KONG, LING JIA, Vehicle and Transport Engineering
KONG, ZHAO JUN, Management Science and Engineering
KUANG, JING MING, Information and Communication Engineering
LI, JIA ZE, Electronic Science and Technology
LI, JIAN, Management Science and Engineering
LI, JIN LIN, Management Science and Engineering
LI, KE JIE, Mechatronic Engineering
LI, LIN, Apparatus Science and Technology
LI, PING, Mechatronic Engineering
LI, SHI YI, Apparatus Science and Technology
LI, SHI YI, Mechatronic Engineering
LI, XIAO LEI, Vehicle and Transport Engineering
LI, ZHI XIANG, Management Science and Engineering
LIAO, NING FANG, Optics Engineering
LIN, YI, Vehicle and Transport Engineering
LIU, LI, Mechatronic Engineering
LIU, YU SHU, Computer Science and Technology
LIU, ZAO ZHEN, Control Science and Engineering
LIU, ZAO ZHEN, Mechatronic Engineering
LIU, ZHAO DU, Vehicle and Transport Engineering
LIU, ZHI WEN, Information and Communication Engineering
LONG, TENG, Information and Communication Engineering
LONG, XIN PING, Mechatronic Engineering
LU, GUANG SHU, Material Science and Engineering
LU, XIN, Electronic Science and Technology
LUO, WEI XIONG, Information and Communication Engineering
LUO, YUN JUN, Material Science and Engineering
MA, BAO HUA, Mechatronic Engineering
MA, BIAO, Vehicle and Transport Engineering
MA, CHAO CHEN, Vehicle and Transport Engineering
MA, SHU YUAN, Apparatus Science and Technology
MAI, XIAO QING, Mechatronic Engineering
MAO, ER KE, Information and Communication Engineering
MEI, FENG XIANG, Applied Mathematics
NING, GUO QIANG, Optics Engineering
NING, JIAN GUO, Mechatronic Engineering
NING, JIAN GUO, Solid Mechanics
OU, YU XIANG, Material Science and Engineering
PENG, ZHENG GUANG, Control Science and Engineering
QI, ZAI KANG, Mechatronic Engineering
QUAN, WEI QI, Optics Engineering
REN, XUE MEI, Control Science and Engineering
SHA, DING GUO, Apparatus Science and Technology
SHAO, BIN, Chemistry
SHENG, TING ZHI, Information and Communication Engineering
SHI, FENG, Computer Science and Technology
SHI, FU GUI, Applied Mathematics
SONG, HAN TAO, Computer Science and Technology
SONG, ZHEN GUO, Mechatronic Engineering
SUI, SHU YUAN, Mechatronic Engineering
SUN, FENG CHUN, Vehicle and Transport Engineering
SUN, GUANG CHUAN, Information and Communication Engineering
SUN, LIANG, Applied Mathematics
SUN, YE BAO, Vehicle and Transport Engineering
SUN, YU NAN, Electronic Science and Technology
TAN, HUI MIN, Material Science and Engineering
TAN, HUI MIN, Mechatronic Engineering
TAO, RAN, Information and Communication Engineering
WANG, BO, Control Science and Engineering
WANG, FU CHI, Material Science and Engineering
WANG, GUO YU, Vehicle and Transport Engineering
WANG, JIAN ZHONG, Mechatronic Engineering
WANG, PEI LAN, Mechatronic Engineering
WANG, QING LIN, Control Science and Engineering
WANG, SHUN TING, Control Science and Engineering
WANG, XIAO LI, Vehicle and Transport Engineering
WANG, XIAO MO, Information and Communication Engineering
WANG, XING WEN, Mechatronic Engineering
WANG, YONG TIAN, Optics Engineering
WANG, YU, Control Science and Engineering
WANG, YUE, Information and Communication Engineering
WU, QI ZONG, Management Science and Engineering
WU, QING HE, Control Science and Engineering
WU, SI LIANG, Information and Communication Engineering
WU, WEN HUI, Material Science and Engineering
XIA, EN JUN, Management Science and Engineering
XIANG, CHANG LE, Vehicle and Transport Engineering
XIE, JING HUI, Optics Engineering
XING, JIAN GUO, Electronic Science and Technology

XU, GENG GUANG, Mechatronic Engineering
XU, XIAO WEN, Electronic Science and Technology
XU, XING ZHONG, Applied Mathematics
XUE, WEI, Optics Engineering
YAN, JI XIANG, Electronic Science and Technology
YANG, JUN, Engineering Mechanics
YANG, RONG JIE, Material Science and Engineering
YANG, SHU YIN, Mechatronic Engineering
YAO, XIAO XIAN, Mechatronic Engineering
YI, JIANG, Mechatronic Engineering
YU, XIN, Electronic Science and Technology
YUAN, SHI HUA, Vehicle and Transport Engineering
ZENG, FENG ZHANG, Management Science and Engineering
ZENG, QING XUAN, Mechatronic Engineering
ZHAN, SHOU YI, Computer Science and Technology
ZHANG, CHENG NING, Vehicle and Transport Engineering
ZHANG, CHUN LIN, Vehicle and Transport Engineering
ZHANG, FU JUN, Vehicle and Transport Engineering
ZHANG, JING LIN, Mechatronic Engineering
ZHANG, PING, Mechatronic Engineering
ZHANG, QI, Mechatronic Engineering
ZHANG, QIANG, Management Science and Engineering
ZHANG, QING MING, Engineering Mechanics
ZHANG, TONG ZHUANG, Vehicle and Transport Engineering
ZHANG, WEI ZHENG, Vehicle and Transport Engineering
ZHANG, YONG FA, Solid Mechanics
ZHANG, YOU TONG, Vehicle and Transport Engineering
ZHANG, YU HE, Control Science and Engineering
ZHANG, YUN HONG, Chemistry
ZHAO, CHANG LU, Vehicle and Transport Engineering
ZHAO, CHANG MING, Electronic Science and Technology
ZHAO, DA ZUN, Optics Engineering
ZHAO, HONG KANG, Electronic Science and Technology
ZHAO, XING QI, Material Science and Engineering
ZHAO, YUE JIN, Apparatus Science and Technology
ZHEN, LIAN, Mechatronic Engineering
ZHENG, HONG FEI, Vehicle and Transport Engineering
ZHENG, LIAN, Control Science and Engineering
ZHONG, QIU HAI, Control Science and Engineering
ZHOU, JIAN, Applied Mathematics
ZHOU, LI WEI, Optics Engineering
ZHOU, TONG LAI, Chemistry
ZHU, DONG HUA, Management Science and Engineering
ZUO, ZHEN XING, Vehicle and Transport Engineering

BEIJING JIAOTONG UNIVERSITY

Shang Yuan Cun, Xi Zhi Men Wai, Hai Ding Dist., Beijing 100044
Telephone: (10) 51688421
Internet: www.njtu.edu.cn

Founded 1921
Academic year: September to July

Pres.: TAN ZHEN HUI
Vice-Pres.: CHEN FENG
Vice-Pres.: LI XUE WEI
Vice-Pres.: NING BIN
Vice-Pres.: WANG JIA QIONG
Head of Graduate Department: WANG YONG SHENG
Librarian: SHA SHU LI

Number of teachers: 2,500
Number of students: 15,000
Publication: *Journal* (6 a year)

DEANS

School of Civil Engineering and Architecture: XU ZHAO YI
School of Computer and Information Technology: RUAN QIU QI
School of Economy and Management: WANG JIA QIONG
School of Electrical Engineering: ZHENG QIONG LIN
School of Electronics and Information Engineering: ZHANG SI DONG
School of Humanities and Social Science: GUO HAI YUN
School of Mechanical, Electronic and Control Engineering: SUN SHOU GUANG
School of Science: ZHANG PING ZHI
School of Traffic and Transportation: SUN QUAN XIN

PROFESSORS

BI, YING, Humanities and Social Science
CHANG, YAN XUN, Science
CHEN, CHANG JIA, Electronics and Information Engineering
CHEN, HOU JIN, Electronics and Information Engineering
CHEN, JING YAN, Economy and Management
CHEN, SHI RONG, Humanities and Social Science
CHEN, SHU MIN, Humanities and Social Science
CHEN, XI SHENG, Economy and Management
CHEN, YIN HANG, Electronics and Information Engineering
CHENG, ZHEN WEI, Science
DENG, ZHEN BO, Science
DING, HUI PING, Economy and Management
DONG, BAO TIAN, Traffic and Transportation
DU, YAN LIANG, Mechanical Engineering
FAN, YU, Electrical Engineering
FANG, YUE FA, Mechanical Engineering
FENG, QI BO, Science
FENG, YAN QUAN, Science
FENG, YU MIN, Electronics and Information Engineering
GAO, WEN, Humanities and Social Science
GAO, YU CHEN, Civil Engineering and Architecture
GAO, ZI YOU, Traffic and Transportation
GUAN, KE YING, Science
GUAN, ZHONG LIANG, Economy and Management
HAN, BAO MING, Traffic and Transportation
HAO, RONG TAI, Electrical Engineering
HE, QING FU, Mechanical Engineering
HE, SHI WEI, Traffic and Transportation
HOU, YAN BIN, Science
HOU, ZHONG SHENG, Electronics and Information Engineering
HU, SI JI, Traffic and Transportation
HUANG, LEI, Economy and Management
HUANG, MEI, Electrical Engineering
HUANG, SHI HUA, Science
JI, JIA LUN, Traffic and Transportation
JIA, LI, Mechanical Engineering
JIA, LI MIN, Traffic and Transportation
JIA, YUAN HUA, Traffic and Transportation
JIANG, JIU CHUN, Electrical Engineering
JIANG, ZHONG HAO, Science
JIN, XIN MIN, Electrical Engineering
JIN, ZONG ZE, Mechanical Engineering
JU, SONG DONG, Economy and Management
LI, CHENG SHU, Electronics and Information Engineering
LI, DE CAI, Mechanical Engineering
LI, PEI XUAN, Economy and Management
LI, QIANG, Mechanical Engineering
LI, SI ZE, Science
LI, WEN XING, Economy and Management
LI, XUE WEI, Economy and Management
LIN, BO LIANG, Traffic and Transportation
LIN, DAI DAI, Economy and Management
LIU, CHANG BIN, Economy and Management
LIU, JIAN KUN, Civil Engineering and Architecture
LIU, JUN, Traffic and Transportation
LIU, KAI, Traffic and Transportation
LIU, KUN HUI, Science
LIU, MING GUANG, Electrical Engineering
LIU, WEI NING, Civil Engineering and Architecture
LIU, YAN PEI, Science
LIU, YAN PING, Economy and Management
LIU, YI SHENG, Economy and Management
LIU, ZUO YI, Traffic and Transportation
LV, YONG BO, Traffic and Transportation
MA, JIAN JUN, Traffic and Transportation
MAO, BAO HUA, Traffic and Transportation
NIE, YU XIN, Science
NING, TI GANG, Electronics and Information Engineering
NU, YI HONG, Economy and Management
OU, GUO LI, Economy and Management
QIAO, CHUN SHENG, Civil Engineering and Architecture
QU, HONG XIANG, Mechanical
RONG, CHAO HE, Economy and Management
SHA, FEI, Electronics and Information Engineering
SHANG, PENG JIAN, Science
SHAO, CHUN FU, Traffic and Transportation
SHEN, JIN SHENG, Traffic and Transportation
SHENG, XIN ZHI, Science
SHI, DING HUAN, Traffic and Transportation
SHI, MEI XIA, Economy and Management
SHI, ZHI FEI, Civil Engineering and Architecture
SHI, ZHONG HENG, Civil Engineering and Architecture
SONG, SHOU XIN, Economy and Management
SUN, QUAN XIN, Traffic and Transportation
SUN, SHOU GUANG, Mechanical Engineering
TAN, ZHEN HUI, Electronics and Information Engineering
TANG, TAO, Electronics and Information Engineering
TANG, TAO, Electronics and Information Engineering
TANG, ZHEN MIN, Electronics and Information Engineering
WANG, JIA QIONG, Economy and Management
WANG, JUN HONG, Electronics and Information Engineering
WANG, LI DE, Electrical Engineering
WANG, LIAN JUN, Civil Engineering and Architecture
WANG, MENG SHU, Civil Engineering and Architecture
WANG, WEI, Electrical Engineering
WANG, XI SHI, Electronics and Information Engineering
WANG, YAN YONG, Traffic and Transportation
WANG, YAO QIU, Economy and Management
WANG, YI, Electrical Engineering
WANG, YONG SHENG, Science
WANG, YUAN FENG, Civil Engineering and Architecture
WANG, YUE SHENG, Civil Engineering and Architecture
WEI, QING CHAO, Civil Engineering and Architecture
WEI, XUE YE, Electronics and Information Engineering
WU, CHONG QING, Science
WU, LIU, Science
XIA, HE, Civil Engineering and Architecture
XIAO, GUI PING, Traffic and Transportation
XIE, JI LONG, Mechanical Engineering
XIN, SHU MING, Mechanical Engineering
XIU, NAI HUA, Science
XU, TAO BO, Economy and Management
XU, YU GONG, Mechanical Engineering
XU, ZHAO YI, Civil Engineering and Architecture
YAN, FENG PING, Electronics and Information Engineering

YAN, GUI PING, Civil Engineering and Architecture
YAN, HONG SEN, Mechanical Engineering
YANG, HAO, Traffic and Transportation
YANG, QIN SHAN, Civil Engineering and Architecture
YANG, QING XIN, Mechanical Engineering
YANG, SHAO PU, Mechanical Engineering
YANG, ZHAO XIA, Traffic and Transportation
YAO, BIN, Economy and Management
YAO, PEI JI, Economy and Management
YAO, QIAN FENG, Civil Engineering and Architecture
YE, SHU JUN, Economy and Management
YI, XIANG YONG, Traffic and Transportation
YU, LEI, Traffic and Transportation
YU, QING, Traffic and Transportation
YUAN, LU QU, Economy and Management
YUAN, ZHEN ZHOU, Traffic and Transportation
ZHA, JIAN ZHONG, Mechanical, Electronic and Control Engineering
ZHAN, HE SHENG, Economy and Management
ZHANG, CHAO, Traffic and Transportation
ZHANG, GUO WU, Traffic and Transportation
ZHANG, HONG KE, Electronics and Information Engineering
ZHANG, HONG RU, Civil Engineering and Architecture
ZHANG, LEI, Economy and Management
ZHANG, LI, Electrical Engineering
ZHANG, LIN CHANG, Electronics and Information Engineering
ZHANG, LU XIN, Civil Engineering and Architecture
ZHANG, MING YU, Economy and Management
ZHANG, QIU SHENG, Economy and Management
ZHANG, SI DONG, Electronics and Information Engineering
ZHANG, WEN JIE, Economy and Management
ZHANG, XI, Traffic and Transportation
ZHANG, XI QING, Science
ZHANG, XIAO DONG, Electrical Engineering
ZHANG, XIAO QING, Electrical Engineering
ZHANG, XING CHEN, Traffic and Transportation
ZHANG, YI HUANG, Electrical Engineering
ZHANG, YU XIN, Traffic and Transportation
ZHANG, YUN TONG, Economy and Management
ZHANG, ZHI WEN, Traffic and Transportation
ZHANG, ZHONG YI, Traffic and Transportation
ZHANG, ZI MAO, Civil Engineering and Architecture
ZHAO, CHENG GAN, Civil Engineering and Architecture
ZHAO, JIAN, Economy and Management
ZHENG, QIONG LIN, Electrical Engineering
ZHONG, YAN, Traffic and Transportation
ZHOU, LEI SHAN, Traffic and Transportation
ZHOU, XI DE, Electrical Engineering
ZHOU, YU HUI, Electrical Engineering
ZHU, HENG JUN, Mechanical Engineering
ZHU, HONG, Science
ZHU, JIA SHAN, Traffic and Transportation
ZHU, XI, Civil Engineering and Architecture
ZHU, XIAO NING, Traffic and Transportation

BEIJING LANGUAGE AND CULTURE UNIVERSITY

15 Xue Yuan Rd, Haidian Dist., Beijing 100083
Telephone: (10) 82303086
E-mail: zhaosh3@blcu.edu.cn
Internet: www.blcu.edu.cn
Founded 1962
State control
Languages of instruction: Arabic, Chinese, English, French, German, Italian, Japanese, Korean, Portuguese, Russian, Spanish
Academic year: September to July
Pres.: CUI XILIANG
Vice-Pres.: QI DEXIANG
Vice-Pres.: CAO ZHIYUN
Dir for Int. Students Dept: WU ZHIYONG
Head of Graduate School: HUA ZHANG
Head of Library: KAI ZHANG
Library of 1,000,000 vols
Number of teachers: 1,100
Number of students: 12,000
Publications: *Chinese Culture Research* (4 a year), *Chinese Teaching in the World* (4 a year), *Language Teaching and Linguistic Studies* (6 a year)

DEANS

College of Advanced Chinese Training: QIU JUN
College of Chinese Language Studies: GUO PENG
College of Foreign Languages: NING YIZHONG
College of Humanities and Social Sciences: HUA XUECHENG
College of Information Sciences: LIU GUILONG
College of Intensive Chinese Studies: CHI LANYING
Continuing (Network) Education College: LI WEI
International Business School: LIU KE

PROFESSORS

CHEN, JUAN, Humanities and Social Sciences
CUI, XI LIANG, Humanities and Social Sciences
DU, DAO MING, Humanities and Social Sciences
FAN, LI, Foreign Languages
FANG, MING, Humanities and Social Sciences
HAN, DE MIN, Humanities and Social Sciences
HAN, JING TAI, Humanities and Social Sciences
HU, YU LONG, Foreign Languages
HUANG, ZHUO YUE, Humanities and Social Sciences
JIAO, FENG, Information Sciences
LI, LI CHENG, Chinese Language
LI, TIE CHENG, Humanities and Social Sciences
LI, WEI, Finance
LI, YANG, Chinese Language
LI, YAN SHU, Foreign Languages
LIANG, XIAO SHENG, Humanities and Social Sciences
LIU, XUN, Humanities and Social Sciences
LIU, GUI LONG, Information Sciences
LIU, KE, Finance
LV, WEN HUA, Humanities and Social Sciences
MA, SHU DE, Chinese Language
MA, ZHEN SHENG, Humanities and Social Sciences
NING, YI ZHONG, Foreign Languages
QIU, MING, Foreign Languages
SHEN, ZHI JUN, Chinese Language
SHI, DING GUO, Humanities and Social Sciences
SONG, ROU, Information Sciences
WANG, YE XIN, Chinese Language
WANG, ZHEN YA, Foreign Languages
XU, SHU AN, Humanities and Social Sciences
YAN, CHUN DE, Humanities and Social Sciences
ZHENG, GUI YOU, Humanities and Social Sciences
ZHENG, WANG PENG, Humanities and Social Sciences
ZHU, WEN JUN, Foreign Languages

BEIJING NORMAL UNIVERSITY

19 Xinjiekouwai St, 100875 Beijing
Telephone: (10) 58806183
E-mail: ipo@bnu.edu.cn
Internet: www.bnu.edu.cn
Founded 1902
State control
Academic year: September to July
Pres.: DONG QI
Vice-Pres.: CHEN GUANGJU
Vice-Pres.: HAO FANGHUA
Vice-Pres.: CAO WEIDONG
Vice-Pres.: GE JIANPING
Vice-Pres.: YANG GENG
Librarian: Prof. JIANG LU
Library: see under Libraries and Archives
Number of teachers: 3,100
Number of students: 22,000
Publications: *Comparative Education Review* (12 a year), *Foreign Language Teaching in Schools* (12 a year), *Journal* (Natural Science edn: 4 a year; Social Science edition: 6 a year), *Journal of Historiography* (12 a year)

BEIJING SPORT UNIVERSITY

Zhongguancun, Hai Ding District, Beijing 100084
Telephone: (10) 62989047
Internet: www.bupe.edu.cn
Founded 1953
State control
Academic year: September to July
Pres.: YANG HUA
Vice-Pres.: ZHONG BIN SHU
Vice-Pres.: HE ZHEN WEN
Vice-Pres.: CHI JIAN
Head of Graduate Dept: CHI JIAN
Librarian: LIU CAI XIA
Number of teachers: 5,000
Number of students: 540
Publications: *China Method of Body Mechanics* (2 a year), *China School Sport* (6 a year), *Journal* (4 a year)

DEANS

School of Gym Education: ZHOU DIAN MIN
School of Gym Management: QIN CHUN LIN
School of Human Sport: XIE MIN HAO
School of Sports Coaching: YUAN ZUO SHENG
School of Wu Shu: LIU BAO CAI

PROFESSORS

GUI, XIANG, Wu Shu
JIN, JI CHUN, Human Sport Science
JIN, YING HUA, Gym Management
LIU, DA QING, Sports Coaching
MEN, HUI FENG, Wu Shu
MENG, WEN DI, Gym Management
QI, GUO YING, Gym Education
QIN, CHUN LIN, Gym Management
SU, PI REN, Gym Education
SUN, BAO LI, Gym Management
WANG, MIN XIANG, Gym Education
WANG, QIAN, Gym Education
WANG, RUI YUAN, Human Sport Science
WANG, WEI, Sports Coaching
XIA, HUAN ZHEN, Gym Education
XIE, MIN HAO, Human Sport Science
XIONG, XIAO ZHENG, Gym Management
XU, SHENG HONG, Sports Coaching
YAO, XIA WEN, Gym Education
YUAN, DAN, Gym Management
YUAN, ZUO SHENG, Sports Coaching
ZHANG, GUANG DE, Wu Shu
ZHAO, LIAN JIA, Gym Education
ZHOU, DENG SONG, Gym Education
ZHU, RUI QI, Wu Shu

BEIJING UNIVERSITY OF BUSINESS AND TECHNOLOGY

11/33 Fucheng Rd, 100048 Beijing
Telephone: (10) 68904774
E-mail: webmaster@btbu.edu.cn
Internet: www.btbu.edu.cn
Founded 1950
Academic year: September to July

Schools of art and communication, business, computer and information engineering, economics, food science and chemical engineering, foreign languages, law, material science and mechanical engineering, Marxism, science

Pres.: Prof. TAN XIANGYONG
Vice-Pres.: SUN BAOGUO
Vice-Pres.: XIE ZHIHUA
Vice-Pres.: LI CHAOXIAN
Vice-Pres.: ZHANG YUN
Vice-Pres.: FANG DEYING
Librarian: GAO YUNZHI

Library: 2.03m. vols, 2,600 magazines and periodicals
Number of teachers: 800
Number of students: 14,000

Publications: *Commercial Economy Research* (12 a year), *Correspondence Department Report* (4 a year), *Journal* (6 a year)

BEIJING UNIVERSITY OF CHEMICAL TECHNOLOGY

15 Bei San Huan East Rd, Chao Yang Dist., Beijing 100029
Telephone: (10) 64434820
E-mail: office@buct.edu.cn
Internet: www.buct.edu.cn

Founded 1958
Academic year: September to July

Pres.: WANG ZI GAO
Vice-Pres.: DING JU YUAN
Vice-Pres.: WANG GUI
Vice-Pres.: ZHAO SU ZHEN
Vice-Pres.: ZUO YU
Head of Graduate Dept: FU ZHI FENG CO
Librarian: ZHANG YU CHUAN

Number of teachers: 1,800
Number of students: 16,900

Publications: *Journal of Beijing University of Chemical Technology* (natural sciences, 6 a year), *Journal of Beijing University of Chemical Technology* (social sciences, 4 a year)

DEANS

College of Chemical Engineering: ZHANG ZE YAN
College of Economics and Management: YAO FEI
College of Information Science and Technology: ZHAO HENG YONG
College of Life Sciences and Technology: TAN TIAN WEI
College of Literature and Law: FU YU LONG
College of Machine Electricity Engineering: WANG KUI SHENG
College of Materials Science and Engineering: YU DING SHENG
College of Science: JIANG GUANG FENG
Professional Technology Institute: XU XI TANG

PROFESSORS

CAO, LIU LIN, Information Science and Technology
CAO, ZHI QING, Machine Electricity Engineering
CHEN, BIAO HUA, Chemical Engineering
CHEN, CHANG SHU, Literature and Law
CHEN, JIAN FENG, Chemical Engineering
CHEN, XIAO CHUN, Chemical Engineering
CHEN, YAO QI, Literature and Law
CHEN, ZHONG LI, Literature and Law
CUI, WEI QI, Literature and Law
DANG, ZHI MIN, Materials Science and Engineering
DUAN, XUE, Science
FENG, LIAN XUN, Machine Electricity Engineering
GAO, ZHENG MING, Chemical Engineering
GENG, XIAO ZHEN, Machine Electricity Engineering
GUO, FEN, Chemical Engineering
GUO, KAI, Chemical Engineering
HAI, RE TI, Chemical Engineering
HE, JING, Science
HUA, YOU QING, Materials Science and Engineering
HUANG, LI, Materials Science and Engineering
HUANG, MIN LI, Materials Science and Engineering
HUANG, MING ZHI, Materials Science and Engineering
HUANG, XIONG BIN, Chemical Engineering
JI, SHENG FU, Chemical Engineering
JIANG, BO, Machine Electricity Engineering
JIN, RI GUANG, Materials Science and Engineering
LI, CHANG JIANG, Science
LI, CHUN XI, Chemical Engineering
LI, DIAN QING, Science
LI, HANG QUAN, Materials Science and Engineering
LI, HONG GUANG, Information Science and Technology
LI, QI FANG, Materials Science and Engineering
LI, QUN SHENG, Chemical Engineering
LI, WU SI, Economics and Management
LI, XIAO YU, Materials Science and Engineering
LI, XIU JIN, Chemical Engineering
LI, YUE CHENG, Chemical Engineering
LI, ZHI LIN, Materials Science and Engineering
LIU, FENG XIN, Information Science and Technology
LIU, HUI, Chemical Engineering
LIU, JIE, Materials Science and Engineering
LIU, KUN YUAN, Chemical Engineering
LIU, WEI, Chemical Engineering
MA, YUN YU, Life Sciences and Technology
MAO, BING QUAN, Science
MO, DE JU, Information Science and Technology
PAN, LI DENG, Information Science and Technology
PANG, YAN BIN, Information Science and Technology
QIAN, CAI FU, Machine Electricity Engineering
QIAO, JIN LIANG, Materials Science and Engineering
QU, YI XIN, Chemical Engineering
SHENG, WEI YONG, Literature and Law
SONG, HUAI HE, Materials Science and Engineering
SU, HAI JIA, Life Sciences and Technology
SUN, JUN, Economics and Management
TAN, TIAN WEI, Life Sciences and Technology
WANG, FANG, Life Sciences and Technology
WANG, JIAN HONG, Chemical Engineering
WANG, JIAN LIN, Information Science and Technology
WANG, KUI SHENG, Machine Electricity Engineering
WANG, MING MING, Economics and Management
WANG, WEN CHUAN, Chemical Engineering
WANG, XUE WEI, Information Science and Technology
WANG, ZI GAO, Chemical Engineering
WEI, GANG, Materials Science and Engineering
WEI, JIE, Materials Science and Engineering
WU, CHONG GUANG, Information Science and Technology
WU, DE ZHEN, Materials Science and Engineering
WU, GANG, Materials Science and Engineering
WU, XIANG ZHI, Chemical Engineering
WU, YI XIAN, Materials Science and Engineering
XIONG, RONG CHUN, Materials Science and Engineering
XU, CHUN CHUN, Materials Science and Engineering
XU, GUANG JUN, Economics and Management
XU, HONG, Machine Electricity Engineering
XU, PENG HUA, Machine Electricity Engineering
YANG, QI, Science
YANG, RU, Materials Science and Engineering
YANG, WANG TAI, Materials Science and Engineering
YANG, WEN SHENG, Science
YANG, YUAN YI, Science
YANG, ZU RONG, Chemical Engineering
YAO, FEI, Economics and Management
YIN, DENG XIANG, Literature and Law
YU, DING SHENG, Materials Science and Engineering
YUAN, DE YU, Literature and Law
YUAN, QI PENG, Life Sciences and Technology
ZHANG, JING CHANG, Science
ZHANG, LI QUN, Materials Science and Engineering
ZHANG, MEI LING, Machine Electricity Engineering
ZHANG, MING GUO, Literature and Law
ZHANG, PENG, Life Sciences and Technology
ZHANG, WEI DONG, Chemical Engineering
ZHANG, XING YING, Materials Science and Engineering
ZHANG, YING KUI, Economics and Management
ZHANG, YU CHUAN, Materials Science and Engineering
ZHANG, ZE YAN, Chemical Engineering
ZHAO, BAO YUAN, Economics and Management
ZHAO, HENG YONG, Information Science and Technology
ZHAO, SHU QING, Information Science and Technology
ZHAO, SU HE, Materials Science and Engineering
ZHEN, DAN XING, Chemical Engineering
ZHONG, CHONG LI, Chemical Engineering
ZHOU, HENG JIN, Materials Science and Engineering
ZHU, QUN XIONG, Information Science and Technology

BEIJING UNIVERSITY OF CHINESE MEDICINE

11 East Rd, Bei San Huan, Chao Yang Dist., Beijing 100029
Telephone: (10) 64213841
Internet: www.bjucmp.edu.cn

Founded 1956
Min. of Education control
Academic year: September to July

Pres.: ZHENG SHOU ZE
Vice-Pres.: QIAO WANG ZHONG
Vice-Pres.: WANG QING GUO
Vice-Pres.: WEI TIAO MAO
Vice-Pres.: XU XIAO
Heads of Graduate Dept: TU YA
Librarian: ZHANG QI CHENG

Number of teachers: 2,705
Number of students: 9,925

Publications: *Chinese Medicine Education* (6 a year), *Journal of Beijing University of Chinese Medicine* (6 a year), *Journal of Beijing University of Chinese Medicine* (clinical studies, 4 a year)

DEANS

College of Acupuncture: GU SHI ZE
College of Basic Medicine: GUO XIA ZHEN
College of Chinese Traditional Medicine: LI JIA SHI
College of Nursing: ZHANG MEI
Network Education College: YU YONG JIE

PROFESSORS

BAI, LING MIN, Chinese and Western Medicine
CHEN, JIA XU, Chinese Medicine (Diagnostics)
CHEN, LI XIN, Chinese and Western Medicine
CHEN, MING, Basic Medicine
CHEN, SHU CHANG, Chinese Medicine (Surgery)
CHEN, XIN YI, Chinese and Western Medicine
FENG, QIAN JIN, Chinese and Western Medicine
FU, YAN LING, Basic Medicine
GAO, XUE MIN, Chinese Medicine (Clinical)
GAO, YAN BING, Chinese Medicine
GAO, YING, Chinese Medicine
GU, LI GANG, Chinese and Western Medicine
GU, SHI ZE, Acupuncture
GUO, WEI QIN, Chinese Medicine
GUO, XIA ZHEN, Basic Medicine
GUO, YA JIAN, Chinese Medicine (Traditional)
HAO, RUI FU, Chinese Medicine
HAO, WANG SHAN, Basic Medicine
HOU, JIA YU, Chinese Medicine (Traditional)
HU, LI SHENG, Chinese and Western Medicine
HUANG, QI FU, Chinese and Western Medicine
JI, SHAO LIANG, Chinese Medicine (Diagnostics)
JIANG, LI SHENG, Basic Medicine
JIANG, LIANG GUO, Chinese Medicine
JIN, GUANG LIANG, Basic Medicine
JIN, ZHE, Chinese and Western Medicine
LI, FENG, Chinese Medicine (Diagnostics)
LI, GUO ZHANG, Chinese and Western Medicine
LI, JIA SHI, Chinese Medicine (Traditional)
LI, JIN XIANG, Chinese Medicine
LI, NAI QING, Chinese and Western Medicine
LI, PENG TAO, Chinese and Western Medicine
LI, RI QING, Chinese Medicine (Surgery)
LI, SHI FAN, Basic Medicine
LI, XUE WU, Acupuncture
LI, YU HANG, Basic Medicine
LI, YUN GU, Chinese Medicine (Traditional)
LIANG, RONG, Chinese Medicine (Diagnostics)
LIN, QIAN, Chinese and Western Medicine
LIU, JIN MING, Chinese Medicine
LIU, TIAN JUN, Acupuncture
LIU, TONG HUA, Chinese Medicine
LIU, YAN CHI, Basic Medicine
LU, WEI XING, Chinese and Western Medicine
LU, YUN RU, Chinese Medicine (Traditional)
LU, ZHAO LIN, Basic Medicine
LV, REN HE, Chinese Medicine
MENG, QING GANG, Basic Medicine
NIU, JIAN ZHAO, Chinese and Western Medicine
NIU, XIN, Chinese and Western Medicine
QIAO, YAN JIANG, Chinese Medicine (Traditional)
QIU, QUAN YING, Chinese and Western Medicine
QU, SHUANG QING, Basic Medicine
REN, TIAN CHI, Chinese Medicine (Traditional)
SHI, REN BIN, Chinese Medicine (Traditional)
SONG, NAI GUANG, Basic Medicine
SU, JING, Basic Medicine
SUN, JIAN NING, Chinese Medicine (Traditional)
SUN, YING LI, Chinese and Western Medicine
TANG, QI SHENG, Chinese Medicine
TANG, YI PENG, Chinese and Western Medicine
TIAN, DE LU, Chinese Medicine
TIAN, JING ZHOU, Chinese Medicine
TU, YA, Acupuncture
WANG, HONG TU, Basic Medicine
WANG, JI FENG, Chinese and Western Medicine
WANG, QI, Basic Medicine
WANG, QING GUO, Basic Medicine
WANG, SHUO REN, Chinese and Western Medicine
WANG, TIAN FANG, Chinese Medicine (Diagnostics)
WANG, WEI, Chinese and Western Medicine
WANG, WEN QUAN, Chinese Medicine (Traditional)
WANG, XIN YUE, Chinese Medicine
WANG, YU LAI, Chinese Medicine
WEI, LU XUE, Chinese Medicine (Traditional)
WU, WEI PING, Chinese Medicine
XIAO, PEI GEN, Chinese Medicine (Traditional)
XU, LIN, Chinese and Western Medicine
XU, QIU PING, Chinese Medicine (Traditional)
YAN, JI LAN, Basic Medicine
YAN, JIAN HUA, Basic Medicine
YAN, YU NING, Chinese Medicine (Traditional)
YAN, ZHENG HUA, Chinese Medicine (Clinical)
YANG, JING XIANG, Chinese Medicine
YANG, SHU PENG, Chinese Medicine (Traditional)
YE, YONG AN, Chinese Medicine
ZHANG, BING, Chinese Medicine (Clinical)
ZHANG, QI CHENG, Basic Medicine
ZHANG, YAN SHENG, Chinese Medicine (Surgery)
ZHANG, YUN LING, Chinese Medicine
ZHAO, JI PING, Acupuncture
ZHAO, JIN XIN, Chinese Medicine
ZHOU, PING AN, Chinese Medicine
ZHOU, YI HUAI, Chinese Medicine

BEIJING UNIVERSITY OF POSTS AND TELECOMMUNICATIONS

10 Xi Tu Cheng Rd, 100876 Beijing
Telephone: (10) 62281949
E-mail: admissions@bupt.edu.cn
Internet: www.bupt.edu.cn

Founded 1955; attached to Min. of Industry and Information Technology
Academic year: September to July

Pres.: WANG YAJIE
Vice-Pres.: REN XIAOMIN
Vice-Pres.: YANG FANG-CHUN
Vice-Pres.: WEN XIANG-MING

Library: 1.1m. vols
Number of teachers: 2,000
Number of students: 22,000

Publications: *Academic Journal of BUPT* (4 a year), *Journal of China University of Posts and Telecommunications*

DEANS

School of Computer Science: YANG FANGCHUN
School of Digital Media and Design Arts: LI XUEMING
School of Economics and Management: ZHOU HONGREN
School of Information and Communication Engineering: GUO JUN

BEIJING UNIVERSITY OF TECHNOLOGY

100 Ping Le Yuan, Chao Yang Dist., Beijing 100226
Telephone: (10) 67392239
Internet: www.bjpu.edu.cn

Founded 1960
Academic year: September to July

Pres.: FAN, BO YUAN
Vice-Pres.: HOU, YI BIN
Head of Graduate Dept: JIANG, YI JIAN
Librarian: FEI, REN YUAN

Number of teachers: 1,100
Number of students: 26,000

Publication: *Journal* (4 a year)

DEANS

College of Applied Science: ZHANG, ZHONG ZHAN
College of Architecture Engineering: HUO, DA
College of Computer Science: ZHANG, SHU JIE
College of Economics and Management: LI, JING WEN
College of Electronic Information and Control Engineering: WANG, PU
College of Energy and Environmental Engineering: MA, CHONG FANG
College of Foreign Languages: WANG, FU XIANG
College of Humanities and Social Sciences: LU, XUE YI
College of Life Science and Bio-Engineering: ZENG, YI
College of Material Science and Engineering: NIE, ZHA REN
College of Mechanical Engineering and Applied Electronics Technology: YANG, JIAN WU
College of Software Engineering: HOU, YI BIN

PROFESSORS

BAO, CHANG CHUN, Electronic Information and Control Engineering
CAO, WANG LIN, Architecture Engineering
CHEN, GUANG HUA, Material Science and Engineering
CHEN, JIAN XIN, Electronic Information and Control Engineering
CHEN, YANG ZHOU, Electronic Information and Control Engineering
CHENG, CAO ZONG, Applied Science and Physics
CHENG, SHUI YUAN, Energy and Environmental Engineering
CUI, PING YUAN, Electronic Information and Control Engineering
DAI, HONG XING, Energy and Environmental Engineering
DI, RUI HUA, Computer Science
DU, XIU LI, Architecture Engineering
DUAN, JIAN MIN, Electronic Information and Control Engineering
FEI, REN YUAN, Mechanical Engineering and Applied Electronics Technology
GUO, BAI NING, Computer Science
HAN, FU RONG, Economics and Management
HE, CUN FU, Mechanical Engineering and Applied Electronics Technology
HE, HONG, Energy and Environmental Engineering
HE, RUO QUAN, Architecture Engineering
HE, ZI NIAN, Energy and Environmental Engineering
HOU, BI HUI, Applied Science and Physics
HOU, YI BIN, Computer Science
HUANG, LU CHENG, Economics and Management
HUANG, TI YUN, Economics and Management
HUO, DA, Architecture Engineering
JIANG, YI JIE, Applied Science and Physics
KANG, BAO WEI, Electronic Information and Control Engineering
KANG, TIAN FANG, Energy and Environmental Engineering
LEI, YONG PING, Material Science and Engineering
LI, DE SHENG, Mechanical Engineering and Applied Electronics Technology
LI, GANG, Laser Engineering
LI, HUI MING, Economics and Management
LI, JING WEN, Economics and Management
LI, SHOU MEI, Applied Science and Physics
LI, XIAO YAN, Material Science and Engineering
LI, ZHEN BAO, Architecture Engineering
LI, ZHI GUO, Electronic Information and Control Engineering
LIAO, HU SHENG, Computer Science
LIU, CHUN NIAN, Computer Science
LIU, XIAO MING, Architecture Engineering

LIU, YOU MING, Applied Science and Physics
LIU, ZHONG LIANG, Energy and Environmental Engineering
LU, XUE YI, Economics and Management
MA, CHONG FANG, Energy and Environmental Engineering
MA, GUO YUAN, Energy and Environmental Engineering
NIE, ZHA REN, Material Science and Engineering
PENG, YONG ZHEN, Energy and Environmental Engineering
REN, FU TIAN, Architecture Engineering
REN, ZHEN HAI, Energy and Environmental Engineering
RUAN, XIAO GANG, Electronic Information and Control Engineering
SHANG, DE GUANG, Mechanical Engineering and Applied Electronics Technology
SHE, YUAN BIN, Energy and Environmental Engineering
SHENG, GUANG DI, Electronic Information and Control Engineering
SHENG, LAN SUN, Electronic Information and Control Engineering
SHI, YAO WU, Material Science and Engineering
SONG, ROU, Computer Science
SUI, YUN KANG, Mechanical Engineering and Applied Electronics Technology
TAO, LIAN JIN, Architecture Engineering
TAO, SHI QUAN, Applied Science and Physics
WAN, SU CHUN, Architecture Engineering
WANG, DA YONG, Applied Science and Physics
WANG, DAO, Energy and Environmental Engineering
WANG, GUANG TAO, Architecture Engineering
WANG, LI, Applied Science and Physics
WANG, PU, Electronic Information and Control Engineering
WANG, SONG GUI, Applied Science and Physics
WU, BIN, Mechanical Engineering and Applied Electronics Technology
WU, GUO WEI, Economics and Management
WU, WU CHEN, Electronic Information and Control Engineering
WU, YONG LUN, Mechanical Engineering and Applied Electronics Technology
XIA, DING GUO, Energy and Environmental Engineering
XUE, LIU GEN, Applied Science and Physics
XUE, SU GUO, Architecture Engineering
YAN, HUI, Material Science and Engineering
YAN, WEI MING, Architecture Engineering
YANG, HONG RU, Applied Science and Physics
YAO, HAI LOU, Applied Science and Physics
YI, BAO CAI, Computer Science
YIN, SHU YAN, Mechanical Engineering and Applied Electronics Technology
YIN, SHU YAN, Material Science and Engineering
YU, JIAN, Energy and Environmental Engineering
YU, KUAN XIN, Applied Science and Physics
YU, YUE QING, Mechanical Engineering and Applied Electronics Technology
ZENG, YI, Energy and Environmental Engineering
ZHANG, AI LIN, Architecture Engineering
ZHANG, HONG BIN, Computer Science
ZHANG, HONG BIN, Electronic Information and Control Engineering
ZHANG, HUI HUI, Mechanical Engineering and Applied Electronics Technology
ZHANG, JIE, Energy and Environmental Engineering
ZHANG, JIU JIE, Material Science and Engineering
ZHANG, WANG RONG, Electronic Information and Control Engineering
ZHANG, WEI, Mechanical Engineering and Applied Electronics Technology
ZHANG, WEN XIONG, Material Science and Engineering
ZHANG, YI GANG, Architecture Engineering
ZHANG, ZE, Applied Science and Physics
ZHANG, ZHEN HAI, Applied Science and Physics
ZHANG, ZHI GANG, Applied Science and Physics
ZHANG, ZHONG ZHAN, Applied Science and Physics
ZHONG, NING, Computer Science
ZHONG, RU GANG, Energy and Environmental Engineering
ZHOU, DA SEN, Energy and Environmental Engineering
ZHOU, MEI LING, Material Science and Engineering
ZHOU, WEI, Architecture Engineering
ZHOU, XI YUAN, Architecture Engineering
ZHOU, YU WEN, Energy and Environmental Engineering
ZONG, GANG, Economics and Management
ZUO, TIE XUN, Applied Science and Physics
ZUO, TIE YONG, Material Science and Engineering

CAPITAL MEDICAL UNIVERSITY

10 Xitoutiao, You Anmen, Fengtai Dist., Beijing 100069
Telephone: (10) 83911199
E-mail: guohechu@ccmu.edu.cn
Internet: www.ccmu.edu.cn

Founded 1960
Academic year: September to July

Pres.: LU ZHAOFENG
Vice-Pres.: FAN QI
Vice-Pres.: WANG SONGLING
Vice-Pres.: WANG XIAOMIN
Vice-Pres.: WANG YUHUI
Vice-Pres.: XIAN FUHUA
Head of Graduate Dept: LU ZHAOFENG
Librarian: WANG JIEZHEN

Number of teachers: 2,500

Publications: *Journal* (4 a year), *School of Public Health* (4 a year)

DEANS

Biomedical Engineering Institute: LIU ZHICHENG
Eighth Faculty of Clinical Medicine: XI XIUMING
Faculty of Mental Health: CAI ZHUOJI
Faculty of Nursing: LI SHUJIA
Faculty of Obstetrics and Gynaecology: CHEN BAOYING
Faculty of Paediatrics: LI ZHONGZHI
Faculty of Rehabilitation: YOU HONG
Faculty of Stomatology: ZHENG SUN
Fifth Faculty of Clinical Medicine: DAI JIANPING
First Faculty of Clinical Medicine: ZHANG JIAN
Fourth Faculty of Clinical Medicine: LIU HONGBO
Ninth Faculty of Clinical Medicine: ZHAO CHUNHUI
School of Basic Medical Sciences: CHEN TIEJUN
School of Chemical Biology and Pharmaceutical Sciences: PENG SHIQI
School of Chinese Traditional Medicine: QI FANG
School of Health Administration and Education: LIANG WANNIAN
School of Public Health and Family Medical Science: WANG WEI
Second Faculty of Clinical Medicine: GAO DONGCHEN
Sixth Faculty of Clinical Medicine: ZHANG GUANGZHAO
Third Faculty of Clinical Medicine: GAO JUZHONG

PROFESSORS

AN, WEI, School of Basic Medical Sciences
AN, YUNQING, School of Basic Medical Sciences
BAI, YUXING, Faculty of Stomatology
CAI, ZHUOJI, Faculty of Mental Health
CHANG, XHIWEN, Fourth Faculty of Clinical Medicine
CHE, NIANCONG, School of Chinese Traditional Medicine
CHEN, BAOTIAN, Sixth Faculty of Clinical Medicine
CHEN, BAOYING, Faculty of Obstetrics and Gynaecology
CHEN, BIAO, First Faculty of Clinical Medicine
CHEN, HAIYING, School of Chinese Traditional Medicine
CHEN, HUIDE, Third Faculty of Clinical Medicine
CHEN, HUIRU, Fourth Faculty of Clinical Medicine
CHEN, JUN, School of Basic Medical Sciences
CHEN, SHAN, Fourth Faculty of Clinical Medicine
CHEN, TIEJUN, School of Basic Medical Sciences
CHEN, XUESHI, Faculty of Mental Health
CHEN, YILIN, First Faculty of Clinical Medicine
CHEN, YINGCHUN, Sixth Faculty of Clinical Medicine
CHEN, YUPING, Sixth Faculty of Clinical Medicine
CHEN, ZHAN, Sixth Faculty of Clinical Medicine
CUI, GUOHUI, School of Chemical Biology and Pharmaceutical Sciences
CUI, SHUQI, School of Public Health and Family Medical Science
DAI, JIANPING, Fifth Faculty of Clinical Medicine
DAI, XINGHUA, Faculty of Obstetrics and Gynaecology
DAO, HONG, School of Public Health and Family Medical Science
DING, BOTAN, Faculty of Rehabilitation
DING, ZONGYI, Faculty of Paediatrics
DONG, PEIQING, Sixth Faculty of Clinical Medicine
DONG, ZONGJUN, First Faculty of Clinical Medicine
DU, FENGHE, Fifth Faculty of Clinical Medicine
DU, LINDONG, Second Faculty of Clinical Medicine
DUAN, YANPING, School of Chinese Traditional Medicine
DUAN, ZHONGPING, Ninth Faculty of Clinical Medicine
FAN, DONGPO, Fifth Faculty of Clinical Medicine
FAN, MING, School of Basic Medical Sciences
FAN, XUNMEI, Faculty of Paediatrics
FANG, DEYUN, First Faculty of Clinical Medicine
GAO, BAOQIN, Fifth Faculty of Clinical Medicine
GAO, CHUNJIN, Third Faculty of Clinical Medicine
GAO, DONGCHEN, Second Faculty of Clinical Medicine
GAO, FENG, Faculty of Obstetrics and Gynaecology
GAO, JUZHONG, Third Faculty of Clinical Medicine
GAO, MINGZHE, Sixth Faculty of Clinical Medicine
GAO, PEIYI, Fifth Faculty of Clinical Medicine
GAO, WENZHU, Faculty of Rehabilitation
GAO, XIULAI, School of Basic Medical Sciences
GAO, YIMIN, School of Chinese Traditional Medicine
GUAN, DELIN, Third Faculty of Clinical Medicine
GUO, AIMIN, School of Public Health and Family Medical Science
GUO, SONG, Faculty of Mental Health

GUO, XIUHUA, School of Public Health and Family Medical Science
HAN, DEMIN, Fourth Faculty of Clinical Medicine
HAN, LING, Sixth Faculty of Clinical Medicine
HE, YAN, Fifth Faculty of Clinical Medicine
HU, DAYI, Third Faculty of Clinical Medicine
HU, YAMEI, Faculty of Paediatrics
HU, YINYUAN, Faculty of Rehabilitation
HUA, QI, First Faculty of Clinical Medicine
HUANG, JIEYING, Second Faculty of Clinical Medicine
HUANG, SHUZHEN, Faculty of Mental Health
JI, SHURONG, Faculty of Rehabilitation
JIA, HONGTI, School of Basic Medical Sciences
JIA, JIANPING, First Faculty of Clinical Medicine
JIA, JIDONG, Second Faculty of Clinical Medicine
JIANG, BING, School of Health Administration and Education
JIANG, TAO, Fifth Faculty of Clinical Medicine
JIANG, WENHUA, First Faculty of Clinical Medicine
JIANG, ZAIFANG, Faculty of Paediatrics
JIANG, ZUONING, Faculty of Mental Health
JIN, RUI, Ninth Faculty of Clinical Medicine
JU, LIRONG, School of Public Health and Family Medical Science
LI, BIN, Fourth Faculty of Clinical Medicine
LI, CUIYING, Faculty of Stomatology
LI, FEI, First Faculty of Clinical Medicine
LI, HONGPEI, Fifth Faculty of Clinical Medicine
LI, JIANPING, School of Health Administration and Education
LI, KUNCHENG, First Faculty of Clinical Medicine
LI, LIN, First Faculty of Clinical Medicine
LI, LIN, School of Health Administration and Education
LI, PING, Sixth Faculty of Clinical Medicine
LI, REN, Third Faculty of Clinical Medicine
LI, SHUJIA, Faculty of Nursing
LI, SHUREN, Second Faculty of Clinical Medicine
LI, XIA, Biomedical Engineering Institute
LI, YONGJIE, First Faculty of Clinical Medicine
LI, YUJING, Faculty of Stomatology
LI, ZHI'AN, Sixth Faculty of Clinical Medicine
LI, ZHIZIA, Fourth Faculty of Clinical Medicine
LI, ZHONGZHI, Faculty of Paediatrics
LIAN, SHI, First Faculty of Clinical Medicine
LIANG, WANNIAN, School of Health Administration and Education
LING, FENG, First Faculty of Clinical Medicine
LIU, BIN, Fourth Faculty of Clinical Medicine
LIU, CHANGGUI, Second Faculty of Clinical Medicine
LIU, HONGBO, Fourth Faculty of Clinical Medicine
LIU, HONGGANG, Fourth Faculty of Clinical Medicine
LIU, JINGZHONG, Third Faculty of Clinical Medicine
LIU, LEI, Fourth Faculty of Clinical Medicine
LIU, NONG, School of Basic Medical Sciences
LIU, WEIZHEN, School of Basic Medical Sciences
LIU, XICHENG, Faculty of Paediatrics
LIU, YONGBIN, Faculty of Rehabilitation
LIU, ZHICHENG, Biomedical Engineering Institute
LONG, JIE, Fifth Faculty of Clinical Medicine
LU, HUIZHANG, First Faculty of Clinical Medicine
LU, SHIQI, School of Basic Medical Sciences
LUAN, GUOMING, Fifth Faculty of Clinical Medicine
LUO, SHIQI, Fifth Faculty of Clinical Medicine
LUO, SHUQIAN, Biomedical Engineering Institute
MA, BINRONG, Biomedical Engineering Institute
MA, CHANGSHENG, Sixth Faculty of Clinical Medicine
MA, DAQING, Second Faculty of Clinical Medicine
MA, DONGLI, Fourth Faculty of Clinical Medicine
MENG, XU, Sixth Faculty of Clinical Medicine
NI, JIAYI, First Faculty of Clinical Medicine
PAN, JULI, Faculty of Stomatology
PENG, SHIQI, School of Chemical Biology and Pharmaceutical Sciences
QI, FANG, School of Chinese Traditional Medicine
QI, YING, Fourth Faculty of Clinical Medicine
QIAN, YING, School of Chinese Traditional Medicine
QIAO, ZHIHENG, Faculty of Rehabilitation
QU, RENYOU, Third Faculty of Clinical Medicine
SHE, KUNLING, Faculty of Paediatrics
SHEN, LUHUA, Second Faculty of Clinical Medicine
SHEN, YIN, Faculty of Paediatrics
SHI, SHENGGEN, Faculty of Stomatology
SHI, XIAOLIN, School of Basic Medical Sciences
SHI, XIANG'EN, Fifth Faculty of Clinical Medicine
SHI, YUYING, Fourth Faculty of Clinical Medicine
SONG, MAOMIN, Fifth Faculty of Clinical Medicine
SONG, WEIXIAN, Fourth Faculty of Clinical Medicine
SUN, BAOZHEN, Fourth Faculty of Clinical Medicine
SUN, BO, Fifth Faculty of Clinical Medicine
SUN, JIANBANG, First Faculty of Clinical Medicine
SUN, YANQING, Sixth Faculty of Clinical Medicine
SUN, ZHENG, Faculty of Stomatology
TANG, XHAOQU, School of Basic Medical Sciences
TIAN, XHU'EN, Faculty of Mental Health
WANG, BANGKANG, Faculty of Stomatology
WANG, BAOGUO, Fifth Faculty of Clinical Medicine
WANG, CHEN, Third Faculty of Clinical Medicine
WANG, DEXIN, Second Faculty of Clinical Medicine
WANG, ENXHEN, Fifth Faculty of Clinical Medicine
WANG, HUILING, Sixth Faculty of Clinical Medicine
WANG, JIE, Fifth Faculty of Clinical Medicine
WANG, PEIYAN, Third Faculty of Clinical Medicine
WANG, SONGLING, Faculty of Stomatology
WANG, SUQIU, Fifth Faculty of Clinical Medicine
WANG, TIANYOU, Second Faculty of Clinical Medicine
WANG, WEI, School of Public Health and Family Medical Science
WANG, WENWEI, Fourth Faculty of Clinical Medicine
WANG, XHENFU, Fourth Faculty of Clinical Medicine
WANG, XHIGANG, Second Faculty of Clinical Medicine
WANG, XHONGCHENG, Fifth Faculty of Clinical Medicine
WANG, XIAOLIANG, School of Chemical Biology and Pharmaceutical Sciences
WANG, XIAOMIN, School of Basic Medical Sciences
WANG, XIAOYAN, School of Health Administration and Education
WANG, YADONG, School of Health Administration and Education
WANG, YIZHEN, Fifth Faculty of Clinical Medicine
WANG, YONGJUN, Fifth Faculty of Clinical Medicine
WANG, YU, Second Faculty of Clinical Medicine
WANG, ZHONGGAO, First Faculty of Clinical Medicine
WENG, XINAHI, Third Faculty of Clinical Medicine
WENG, YONGZHEN, Faculty of Mental Health
WU, AINGHUA, Sixth Faculty of Clinical Medicine
WU, FENGYI, Third Faculty of Clinical Medicine
WU, HAO, Ninth Faculty of Clinical Medicine
WU, MINYUAN, Faculty of Paediatrics
WU, SHUZENG, Sixth Faculty of Clinical Medicine
WU, XUESHI, Sixth Faculty of Clinical Medicine
WU, ZHAOSU, Sixth Faculty of Clinical Medicine
XI, XIUMING, Eighth Faculty of Clinical Medicine
XIANG, XIUKUN, Fourth Faculty of Clinical Medicine
XIAO, RONG, School of Public Health and Family Medical Science
XU, QUNYAN, School of Basic Medical Sciences
XUE, MING, School of Health Administration and Education
YANG, BAOQIN, School of Chinese Traditional Medicine
YANG, HUI, School of Basic Medical Sciences
YANG, JINKUI, Fourth Faculty of Clinical Medicine
YANG, SHAOXU, Fifth Faculty of Clinical Medicine
YANG, SHENGHUI, Faculty of Stomatology
YANG, YUNPING, Faculty of Mental Health
YAO, CHONGHUA, Sixth Faculty of Clinical Medicine
YAO, TIANQIAO, Sixth Faculty of Clinical Medicine
YOU, HONG, Faculty of Rehabilitation
YOU, KAITAO, Third Faculty of Clinical Medicine
YU, CHUNJIANG, First Faculty of Clinical Medicine
YU, ZELI, Fourth Faculty of Clinical Medicine
YUAN, ZHENGGUO, School of Chinese Traditional Medicine
YUE, YUN, Third Faculty of Clinical Medicine
ZHAN, ZHENTING, Faculty of Stomatology
ZHANG, BINXI, Fourth Faculty of Clinical Medicine
ZHANG, CHANGHUAI, Second Faculty of Clinical Medicine
ZHANG, FENGXIAN, Third Faculty of Clinical Medicine
ZHANG, GUANGZHAO, Sixth Faculty of Clinical Medicine
ZHANG, HONGYU, Third Faculty of Clinical Medicine
ZHANG, JIAN, First Faculty of Clinical Medicine
ZHANG, JIGU, Faculty of Mental Health
ZHANG, JINCAI, Faculty of Stomatology
ZHANG, JINRONG, Sixth Faculty of Clinical Medicine
ZHANG, JINZHE, Faculty of Paediatrics
ZHANG, JIZHI, Faculty of Mental Health
ZHANG, PENGTIAN, Second Faculty of Clinical Medicine
ZHANG, QIUHAN, First Faculty of Clinical Medicine
ZHANG, SHIJI, Faculty of Mental Health
ZHANG, SHUMIN, School of Chinese Traditional Medicine
ZHANG, SHUWEN, Second Faculty of Clinical Medicine
ZHANG, YU, First Faculty of Clinical Medicine
ZHANG, YUHAI, Second Faculty of Clinical Medicine
ZHANG, ZHAOGUANG, Sixth Faculty of Clinical Medicine

ZHANG, ZHAOQI, Sixth Faculty of Clinical Medicine
ZHANG, ZHITAI, Sixth Faculty of Clinical Medicine
ZHAO, CHUNHUI, Ninth Faculty of Clinical Medicine
ZHAO, DONG, Sixth Faculty of Clinical Medicine
ZHAO, JIZONG, Fifth Faculty of Clinical Medicine
ZHAO, MING, School of Chemical Biology and Pharmaceutical Sciences
ZHAO, YADU, Fifth Faculty of Clinical Medicine
ZHAO, YI, Second Faculty of Clinical Medicine
ZHAO, YUANLI, Fifth Faculty of Clinical Medicine
ZHENG, BANGHE, Fourth Faculty of Clinical Medicine
ZHENG, JIE, School of Basic Medical Sciences
ZHENG, YI, Faculty of Mental Health
ZHOU, BING, Fourth Faculty of Clinical Medicine
ZHOU, QIWEN, Sixth Faculty of Clinical Medicine
ZHOU, YAOTING, School of Chinese Traditional Medicine
ZHOU, YUJIE, Sixth Faculty of Clinical Medicine
ZHU, XINPING, School of Basic Medical Sciences

CAPITAL NORMAL UNIVERSITY

105 Xi San Huan, Beijing 100037
Telephone: (10) 68900974
Internet: www.cnu.edu.cn

Founded 1954
Bureau of Education of Beijing
Academic year: September to July

Pres.: XIANG YUAN XU
Vice-Pres.: HUI LI GONG
Vice-Pres.: JIAN CHENG LIU
Vice-Pres.: JIAN SHE ZHOU
Vice-Pres.: WAN LIANG WANG
Head of Graduate Dept: JING HE LIANG
Librarian: YUE HU

Number of teachers: 1,147
Number of students: 24,905 (12,786 full-time, 12,119 part-time)

Publications: *Education Art* (12 a year), *Journal of Capital Normal University (Natural Sciences Edition)* (4 a year), *Journal of Capital Normal University (Social Sciences Edition)* (6 a year), *Language Teaching in Middle School* (12 a year), *Middle School Math* (12 a year)

DEANS

College of Biology: HE YIKUN
College of Education: MEN FANHUA
College of Environmental Resources and Tourism: GONG HUILI
College of Fine Arts: SUN ZHIJUN
College of Foreign Languages: YANG YANG
College of Information Technology: WANG WANSEN
College of International Culture: LIU XIAOTIAN
College of Music: YANG QING
College of Political Sciences and Law: WANG SHUMENG
Department of Chemistry: ZHANG ZHUOYONG
Department of Educational Technology: AI LUN
Department of History: SONG JIE
Department of Mathematics: ZHENG CHONGYOU
Department of Physics: ZHANG CUNLIN
Elementary Education College: WANG ZHIQIU
Physical Teaching and Research Section: SUN JIANHUI
School of Literature: WU SHIJING
Teaching and Research Division of Marxism: LI SONGLIN
University English Teaching and Research Division: XIE FUZHI

PROFESSORS

AN, YUFENG, Political Sciences and Law
BI, LUO, Environmental Resources and Tourism
CAI, TUANYAO, Biology
CHANG, RUILUN, Fine Arts
CHEN, XINXIA, Political Sciences and Law
CHI, YUNFEI, History
DAI, LIN, Fine Arts
DIAO, YONGZHA, Marxism
DONG, ZHONGXUN, Fine Arts
DU, XIAOSHI, Music
DU, XIXIAN, Fine Arts
FAN, YANNING, Political Sciences and Law
FANG, PING, Education
FANG, YAN, Physics
FU, HUA, Environmental Resources and Tourism
GONG, HUILI, Environmental Resources and Tourism
GU, XUEXIN, Chemistry
HAO, CHUNWEN, History
HE, YIKUN, Biology
HUANG, MEIYING, Music
HUO, LONGGUANG, Mathematics
JIN, QIONGHUA, Chemistry
LAN, WEI, Political Sciences and Law
LEI, DA, Music
LI, AIGUO, Fine Arts
LI, FULI, Physics
LI, JIAYANG, Biology
LI, SHUPEI, Mathematics
LI, SONGLIN, Marxism
LI, XIA, Chemistry
LI, YARU, Marxism
LIAN, SHAOMING, History
LIANG, JINGHE, History
LIN, LI, Foreign Languages
LIU, DACHUN, Mathematics
LIU, LIMIN, Foreign Languages
LU, XIAOMING, Chemistry
MENG, FANHUA, Education
NIE, YUEYAN, Political Sciences and Law
NING, HONG, Education
NING, KE, History
QI, SHIRONG, History
QIU, YUNHUA, Literature
REN, DONG, Biology
SHAO, HUIBO, Chemistry
SHEN, JINGLING, Physics
SHI, SHENGMING, Mathematics
SHUI, SHUFENG, Political Sciences and Law
SONG, JIE, History
SUN, ZHIJUN, Fine Arts
TAN, FENGTAI, Education
TANG, CHONGQIN, Music
TAO, DONGFENG, Literature
TIAN, BAO, Education
WANG, ANGUO, Music
WANG, CHANGCHUN, Education
WANG, DESHENG, Literature
WANG, GUANGMING, Literature
WANG, JIANPING, Education
WANG, LU, Educational Technology
WANG, SHIPING, Physics
WANG, SHUMENG, Political Sciences and Law
WANG, SHUQIN, Political Sciences and Law
WANG, ZHIQIU, Elementary Education
WEI, GUANGQI, History
WEN, LISHU, Political Sciences and Law
WU, JIANGPING, Mathematics
WU, SHIJING, Literature
XIA, JIGUO, History
XIA, LIMIN, Political Sciences and Law
XIE, CHENGREN, History
XING, HONGJUN, Physics
XING, YONGFU, Education
XU, PEIJUN, Physics
XU, YUZHEN, Education
YANG, QING, Music
YANG, SHENGPING, Political Sciences and Law
YANG, YANG, Foreign Languages
YANG, YUE, Biology
YE, XIAOBING, History
YIN, LIPING, Biology
YIN, TIELIANG, Music
YIN, WEIPING, Mathematics
ZHAN, LIJUAN, Music
ZHANG, CUNLIN, Physics
ZHANG, GUOLI, Music
ZHANG, JUNDA, Education
ZHANG, YONGHUA, Chemistry
ZHANG, ZHUOYONG, Chemistry
ZHAO, XUEZHI, Mathematics

CENTRAL ACADEMY OF FINE ARTS

8 Hua Jia Di Nan Jie, Chaoyang Dist., Beijing 100102
Telephone: (10) 64771018
E-mail: xujia@cafa.edu.cn
Internet: www.cafa.edu.cn

Founded 1950
Min. of Education control
Academic year: September to July

Pres.: PAN GONGKAI
Vice-Pres.: FAN DIAN
Head of Graduate Department: CHU DI
Librarian: SHEN JIANDONG

Number of teachers: 141
Number of students: 1,000

Publications: *Art Research* (4 a year), *World Art* (4 a year)

DEANS

Art History Department: YIN JINAN
Art Education Department: JIN JIAZHEN
Chinese Painting Department: TIAN LIMING
First-year Foundation Programme: WEN GUOZHANG
Mural Painting Department: SUN JINGBO
Oil Painting Department: DAI SHIHE
Printmaking Department: SU XINPING
School of Architecture: LU PINJING
School of Design: WANG MIN
School of Humanities: YIN JINAN
Sculpture Department: SUI JIANGUO

PROFESSORS

CAO, LI, Mural Painting
CHAO, GE, Oil Painting
CHEN, WENYI, Mural Painting
DAI, SHIHE, Oil Painting
DING, YILIN, Oil Painting
FAN, DI'AN, Humanities
GAO, RONGSHENG, Printmaking
HONG, PENGSHENG, Humanities
HU, JIANCHENG, Oil Painting
HU, WEI, Chinese Painting
HU, YUE, Architecture
HUANG, WEI, Architecture
LI, LINZUO, Mural Painting
LU, SHENGZHONG, Oil Painting
LU, PINJING, Architecture
LUO, SHIPING, Humanities
MA, LU, Oil Painting
QIU, ZHENZHONG, Chinese Painting
SU, XINPING, Printmaking
SUI, JIANGUO, Sculpture
SUN, JIABO, Sculpture
SUN, JINGBO, Mural Painting
TAN, PING, Design
TANG, YONGLI, Chinese Painting
TIAN, LIMING, Chinese Painting
WANG, MIN, Design
WANG, YONG, Chinese Painting
WEN, GUOZHANG, First-year Foundation Program
WU, CHANGJIANG, Printmaking
YIN, JINAN, Art History
ZHOU, ZHIYU, Design

CENTRAL CHINA NORMAL UNIVERSITY (HUAZHONG NORMAL UNIVERSITY)

152 Luoyu Rd, Wuhan 430079, Hubei Province

Telephone: (27) 67868133
E-mail: www@ccnu.edu.cn
Internet: www.ccnu.edu.cn

Founded 1903
Min. of Education control
Academic year: September to July

Pres.: MA MING
Vice-Pres.: HUANG YONGLING
Vice-Pres.: LE GUANGZHOU
Vice-Pres.: LI ZONGKAI
Vice-Pres.: PANG XIANGNONG
Vice-Pres.: YANG ZHENGNONG
Librarian: ZUO BIN

Number of teachers: 1,200
Number of students: 20,000

Publications: *Foreign Literature Studies* (6 a year), *Journal of Central China Normal University* (humanities and social science, 6 a year), *Journal of Central China Normal University* (natural sciences, 6 a year)

DEANS

College of Networking Academy: ZHANG YOULIANG
Department of Computer Science: TAN LIANSHENG
Department of Information Management: WANG XUEDONG
Department of Information Technology: ZHANG GUOPING
Department of Sociology: JIANG LIHUA
School of Chemistry: YANG GUANGFU
School of City and Environmental Science: ZENG JUXIN
School of Economics: CAO YANG
School of Foreign Language and Literature: ZHANG WEIYOU
School of History and Culture: WANG YUDE
School of Life Science: CHEN QICAI
School of Literature: LI XIANGNONG
School of Management: WU JINSHENG
School of Mathematics and Statistics: DENG YINBIN
School of Music: TIAN XIAOBAO
School of Physics and Technology: WANG ENKE
School of Political Science and Law: LIN JIAN

PROFESSORS

BAI, GUOZHONG, Information Management
CAI, JINQUAN, History and Culture
CAI, XU, Physics and Technology
CAO, YANG, Economics
CHEN, CHUANLI, Mathematics and Statistics
CHEN, GUOSHENG, Life Science
CHEN, HONGWEI, Foreign Language and Literature
CHEN, JIANXIAN, Literature
CHEN, JISHENG, Physics and Technology
CHEN, QICAI, Life Science
CHEN, QUN, Mathematics and Statistics
CHEN, YIN'E, Sociology
CHEN, YOULIN, Foreign Language and Literature
CHU, ZEXIANG, Literature
DAI, JIANYE, Literature
DENG, HONGGUANG, History and Culture
DENG, XIANRUI, City and Environmental Science
DENG, YINBIN, Mathematics and Statistics
DING, MINGWU, Chemistry
DING, YIHUA, History and Culture
FENG, GANG, Computer Science
FU, HUIHUA, Life Science
GAO, HUAPING, Literature
GONG, SHENGSHENG, City and Environmental Science
GU, YONGXING, History and Culture
GU, ZHIHUA, History and Culture
GUO, JUN, Foreign Language and Literature
GUO, TUOYING, Mathematics and Statistics
HAN, KEFANG, Physics and Technology
HAN, XUNGUO, Music
HE, BAIGEN, City and Environmental Science
HE, HONGWU, Chemistry
HE, JIANMING, History and Culture
HE, SUI, Mathematics and Statistics
HE, TINGTING, Computer Science
HE, XUEFENG, Sociology
HONG, HUAZHU, Life Science
HOU, FUDE, Physics and Technology
HU, JINZHU, Computer Science
HU, XIANGMING, Physics and Technology
HU, YAMIN, Literature
HU, ZONGQIU, Chemistry
HUA, XIANFA, Foreign Language and Literature
HUANG, HUAWEN, History and Culture
HUANG, QINGYANG, Life Science
HUANG, WANHUI, Computer Science
HUANG, XIAOQUN, Foreign Language and Literature
HUANG, XINTANG, Physics and Technology
HUANG, YONGLIN, Literature
HUANG, ZHENGBO, History and Culture
HUANG, ZHONGLIAN, Foreign Language and Literature
JIA, YA, Physics and Technology
JIA, ZHIJIE, Physics and Technology
JIN, BOXIN, City and Environmental Science
JIN, CONG, Computer Science
JING, CAIRUI, City and Environmental Science
LI, BANGJI, Computer Science
LI, GAOXIANG, Physics and Technology
LI, JIALIN, Physics and Technology
LI, JIAQING, City and Environmental Science
LI, JIARONG, Physics and Technology
LI, QIRONG, History and Culture
LI, TAOSHENG, Mathematics and Statistics
LI, WENXIN, Life Science
LI, XIANGNONG, Literature
LI, XIAOYAN, Computer Science
LI, XINGRUN, Life Science
LI, XUEBAO, Life Science
LI, YADAN, Foreign Language and Literature
LI, ZHIYANG, Physics and Technology
LI, ZHONGHUA, Chemistry
LIANG, MIAOYUAN, Computer Science
LIAO, MEIZHEN, Foreign Language and Literature
LIAO, ZHANRU, Chemistry
LIN, DELI, Life Science
LIU, ANHAI, Literature
LIU, FENG, Physics and Technology
LIU, GUSHENG, History and Culture
LIU, LIANSHOU, Physics and Technology
LIU, SHAOJUN, History and Culture
LIU, SHENGHUA, Chemistry
LIU, SHENGJIA, City and Environmental Science
LIU, SHENGXIANG, Life Science
LIU, SHOUHUA, Literature
LIU, WEI, History and Culture
LIU, WU, Physics and Technology
LIU, XIANLONG, Mathematics and Statistics
LIU, YONGHONG, Foreign Language and Literature
LIU, ZHAOJIE, Chemistry
LOU, CEQUN, Information Management
LU, GUANGHAN, Chemistry
LU, WUQIANG, City and Environmental Science
LUO, BANGCHENG, Mathematics and Statistics
LUO, DEHUI, History and Culture
MA, CHENGWU, Literature
MA, MIN, History and Culture
MENG, DAZHONG, Physics and Technology
MOU, JIMEI, Physics and Technology
NIE, ZHENDAO, Foreign Language and Literature
PENG, CHANGZHENG, History and Culture
PENG, JIANXIN, Life Science
PENG, NANSHENG, History and Culture
QIU, BAOSHENG, Life Science
QIU, ZIHUA, Literature
SHAO, QINGYU, City and Environmental Science
SHEN, JIE, Sociology
SHEN, ZHENGYU, Literature
SU, BAIMEI, Foreign Language and Literature
SUN, WENXIAN, Literature
TAN, BANGHE, Literature
TAN, CHUANFENG, City and Environmental Science
TAN, HONG, Mathematics and Statistics
TAN, LIANSHENG, Computer Science
TANG, CHENGCHUN, Physics and Technology
TAO, JIAYUAN, City and Environmental Science
TIAN, SONGQING, City and Environmental Science
WAN, JIAN, Chemistry
WANG, ENKE, Physics and Technology
WANG, GUOSHENG, Literature
WANG, GUOXIU, Life Science
WANG, LIHUA, Sociology
WANG, MANJUN, Literature
WANG, QINGSHENG, Literature
WANG, QIZHOU, Literature
WANG, WEIJUN, Information Management
WANG, XIANPEI, Literature
WANG, XUEDONG, Information Management
WANG, YANGANG, Chemistry
WANG, YOUNIAN, Literature
WANG, YUDE, History and Culture
WANG, YUFENG, Life Science
WANG, ZELONG, Literature
WEI, CHANGHUA, Computer Science
WU, GANG, Life Science
WU, QI, History and Culture
WU, YI, Sociology
WU, YUANFANG, Physics and Technology
XIA, MINGYUAN, Mathematics and Statistics
XIA, XIAOBIN, Life Science
XIANG, JIQUAN, Sociology
XIAO, DEBAO, Computer Science
XIE, MINYU, Mathematics and Statistics
XIN, FUYI, Literature
XIN, LAISHUN, History and Culture
XIONG, TIEJI, History and Culture
XIU, DIAO, Literature
XU, QIAOLI, City and Environmental Science
XU, SENLIN, Mathematics and Statistics
XU, ZUHUA, Literature
YAN, CHANGHONG, History and Culture
YAN, GUOZHENG, Mathematics and Statistics
YAN, SHAOXIANG, History and Culture
YANG, BAOLIANG, City and Environmental Science
YANG, CHANG, History and Culture
YANG, CHUNBIN, Physics and Technology
YANG, GUANGFU, Chemistry
YANG, SHAO, Life Science
YANG, SHUANGHUA, Computer Science
YANG, XU, Life Science
YAO, WEIJUN, History and Culture
YI, HONGGEN, Foreign Language and Literature
YOU, LIRONG, Sociology
YU, GUANGMING, City and Environmental Science
YU, ZEHUA, Life Science
ZENG, JUXIN, City and Environmental Science
ZENG, LIANMAO, City and Environmental Science
ZENG, QINGQIANG, Foreign Language and Literature
ZHAN, CHANGGUO, Chemistry
ZHAN, ZHENGKUN, Chemistry
ZHANG, AIDONG, Chemistry
ZHANG, CHANGNIAN, Music
ZHANG, FAN, Information Management
ZHANG, GUOPING, Physics and Technology
ZHANG, KAIQUAN, History and Culture
ZHANG, LIDE, Physics and Technology
ZHANG, LONGSHENG, Foreign Language and Literature
ZHANG, QUANMING, History and Culture
ZHANG, SANXI, Literature

ZHANG, SHAOYAN, Economics
ZHANG, WEIYOU, Foreign Language and Literature
ZHANG, YINGLIN, Foreign Language and Literature
ZHANG, YONGJIAN, Literature
ZHANG, YUNENG, Literature
ZHANG, ZHENGMING, History and Culture
ZHAO, YIJUN, Life Science
ZHENG, QUAN, Mathematics and Statistics
ZHENG, XIAOPING, Physics and Technology
ZHOU, DAICUI, Physics and Technology
ZHOU, GUOLIN, History and Culture
ZHOU, JIYUAN, Life Science
ZHOU, XIAOMING, Literature
ZHOU, ZHENGRONG, Mathematics and Statistics
ZHOU, ZONGKUI, Sociology
ZHU, CHANGJIANG, Mathematics and Statistics
ZHU, CHUANFANG, Chemistry
ZHU, XINDE, Chemistry
ZHU, YING, History and Culture
ZOU, SHANGHUI, City and Environmental Science
ZUO, BIN, Sociology

CENTRAL CONSERVATORY OF MUSIC

43 Bao Jia St, Beijing 100031
Telephone: (10) 66425598
E-mail: ccom@ccom.edu.cn
Internet: www.ccom.edu.cn

Founded 1950
Min. of Culture control
Academic year: September to July

Pres.: WANG CIZHAO
Vice-Pres.: LI XU
Vice-Pres.: LIU KANGHUA
Vice-Pres.: XU CHANGJUN
Vice-Pres.: ZHOU HAIHONG
Head of Graduate Dept: WANG CIZHAO
Librarian: ZHOU HAIHONG

Number of teachers: 278
Number of students: 1,665

Publication: *Haihong Journal of the Central Conservatory of Music* (4 a year)

DEANS

Composition Department: TANG JIANPING
Conducting Department: YU FENG
General Education Department: LIANG JING
Music Education Department: GAO JIANJIN
Musicology Department: ZHANG BOYU
Orchestral Instruments Department: LIU PEIYAN
Piano Department: YANG MING
Traditional Instruments Department: ZHAO HANYANG
Voice and Opera Department: LIU DONG

PROFESSORS

BIAN, MENG, Piano
CAI, ZHOANGDE, Musicology
CHEN, BIGANG, Piano
CHEN, DANBU, Composition
CHEN, ZIMIN, Musicology
CHENG, DA, Voice and Opera
DU, MINGXIN, Composition
DU, TAIHANG, Piano
DUAN, PINGTAI, Composition
GAO, JIANJIN, Music Education
GUI, XILI, Traditional Instruments
GUO, SHUZHEN, Voice and Opera
GUO, WENJING, Composition
HAN, XIAOMING, Orchestral Instruments
HAN, ZHIHONG, Piano
HAN, ZHONGJIE, Conducting
HE, RONG, Orchestral Instruments
HEI, HAITAO, Voice and Opera
HU, SHIXI, Voice and Opera
HU, ZHIHOU, Traditional Instruments
HUANG, HE, Traditional Instruments
HUANG, PEIYING, Piano
HUANG, XIAOHE, Musicology
LI, GUANGHUA, Traditional Instruments
LI, HENG, Traditional Instruments
LI, JITI, Composition
LI, MENG, Traditional Instruments
LI, QIFENG, Piano
LI, XIANGTING, Traditional Instruments
LI, XINCHANG, Voice and Opera
LI, YINGHUA, Musicology
LI, ZHENGUI, Traditional Instruments
LIANG, DANA, Orchestral Instruments
LIANG, NING, Voice and Opera
LIN, SHICHENG, Traditional Instruments
LIN, YAXIONG, Musicology
LIU, CHANGFU, Traditional Instruments
LIU, DONG, Voice and Opera
LIU, LIN, Composition
LIU, PEIYAN, Orchestral Instruments
LIU, YUAN, Composition
LUO, ZHONGRONG, Composition
MA, HONGHAI, Voice and Opera
PAN, BIXIN, Musicology
PAN, CHUN, Piano
PENG, KANGLIANG, Voice and Opera
PINI, YAXUO, Voice and Opera
SHENG, LIHONG, Composition
SONG, JIN, Musicology
TAI, ER, Piano
TANG, JIANPING, Composition
TIAN, LIANTAO, Musicology
WANG, CIZHAO, Musicology
WANG, SHUHE, Musicology
WANG, XIANLIN, Voice and Opera
WANG, XIUFENG, Voice and Opera
WANG, YAOLING, Orchestral Instruments
WU, SHIKAI, Composition
WU, ZHUQIANG, Composition
XIE, HUAZHEN, Piano
XU, CHANGJUN, Composition
XU, XIN, Conducting
YANG, HONGNIAN, Conducting
YANG, JUN, Piano
YANG, MING, Piano
YAO, HENGLU, Composition
YE, XIAOGANG, Composition
YU, FENG, Conducting
YU, RUNYANG, Musicology
YU, SUXIAN, Composition
YU, ZHIGANG, Musicology
YUAN, JINGFANG, Musicology
ZHANG, BOYU, Musicology
ZHANG, JIANYI, Voice and Opera
ZHANG, LIPING, Voice and Opera
ZHANG, QIAN, Musicology
ZHANG, SHAO, Traditional Instruments
ZHAO, BIXUAN, Voice and Opera
ZHAO, DENGYING, Voice and Opera
ZHAO, HANYANG, Traditional Instruments
ZHAO, RUILIN, Orchestral Instruments
ZHENG, XIAOYING, Conducting
ZHENG, ZHUXIANG, Musicology
ZHONG, ZILIN, Musicology
ZHOU, GUANGREN, Piano
ZHOU, HAIHONG, Musicology
ZHOU, QINGQING, Musicology
ZHU, DUN, Orchestral Instruments
ZHU, YIBING, Orchestral Instruments

CENTRAL SOUTH UNIVERSITY

Changsha 410083, Hunan Province
Telephone: (731) 8879225
E-mail: homepage@csu.edu.cn
Internet: www.csu.edu.cn

Founded 1952
Academic year: September to July

Pres.: HUANG BOYUN
Vice-Pres.: CHEN QIYUAN
Vice-Pres.: CHEN ZHIYA
Vice-Pres.: HU TIEHUI
Vice-Pres.: LI GUIYUAN
Vice-Pres.: QIU GUANZHOU
Head of Graduate Dept: LIU YILUN
Librarian: FANG ZHENG

Publications: *International Chinese Nursing Journal* (4 a year), *Journal of Central South University* (6 a year), *Journal of Central South University* (medical sciences, 6 a year), *Journal of Central South University* (social sciences, 6 a year), *Transactions of Nonferrous Metals Society of China* (6 a year)

DEANS

School of Basic Medical Sciences: WEN JIFANG
School of Business: CHEN XIAOHONG
School of Chemistry and Chemical Engineering: HUANG KELONG
School of Civil Engineering and Architecture: YU ZHIWU
School of Energy and Power Engineering: ZHOU DIAOMIN
School of Fine Arts: DAI DUAN
School of Foreign Languages: TU GUOYUAN
School of Geoscience and Environmental Engineering: DAI TAGEN
School of Info-Physics and Geomatics Engineering: TANG JINGTIAN
School of Information Science and Engineering: GUI WEIHUA
School of Law: QI DUOJUN
School of Literature: OU YANG YOUQUAN
School of Materials Science and Engineering: YI DANQING
School of Mathematical Sciences and Computing Technology: ZOU JIEZHONG
School of Mechanical and Electrical Engineering: WU YUNXIN
School of Medical Technology and Information: GUO QULIAN
School of Metallurgic Science and Engineering: LI JIE
School of Nursing: HE GUOPING
School of Pharmaceutical Sciences: LI YUANJIAN
School of Physics, Sciences and Technology: YANG BINGCHU
School of Politics and Public Administration: LI JIANHUA
School of Public Health: XIAO SHUIYUAN
School of Resources Processing and Bioengineering: HU YUEHUA
School of Resources and Safety Engineering: LI XIBING
School of Stomatology: JIAN XINCHUN
School of Traffic and Transportation Engineering: SHI FENG

PROFESSORS

CAI, HONGWEI, Medical Technology and Information
CAI, ZIXING, Information Science and Engineering
CAO, JIAN, Physics, Sciences and Technology
CAO, XING, Business
CHANG, YETIAN, Medical Technology and Information
CHEN, FANGPING, Medical Technology and Information
CHEN, FENG, Materials Science and Engineering
CHEN, HAIBO, Mathematical Sciences and Computing Technology
CHEN, HUANXIN, Civil Engineering and Architecture
CHEN, HUANXIN, Energy and Power Engineering
CHEN, JIAN'ER, Information Science and Engineering
CHEN, KANGHUA, Powder Metallurgy
CHEN, LIQUAN, Chemistry and Chemical Engineering
CHEN, QIYUAN, Chemistry and Chemical Engineering
CHEN, SHIZHU, Materials Science and Engineering
CHEN, SONGQIAO, Information Science and Engineering
CHEN, XIAOHONG, Business

CHEN, XIAOQING, Chemistry and Chemical Engineering
CHEN, XIAOSONG, Mathematical Sciences and Computing Technology
CHEN, XIUFANG, Civil Engineering and Architecture
CHEN, YIZHUANG, Politics and Public Administration
CHEN, YUEWU, Foreign Languages
CHEN, YUXIANG, Bioscience and Technology
CHEN, ZHENXING, Chemistry and Chemical Engineering
CHEN, ZHIGANG, Information Science and Engineering
CHEN, ZHONGWEN, Foreign Languages
DAI, BINXIANG, Mathematical Sciences and Computing Technology
DAI, DUAN, Fine Arts
DAI, GONGLIAN, Civil Engineering and Architecture
DENG, CHAO, Business
DENG, DEHUA, Civil Engineering and Architecture
DENG, FEIYAOI, Chemistry and Chemical Engineering
DENG, HANWU, Pharmaceutical Sciences
DENG, RUIJIAO, Nursing
DENG, TIANSHENG, Business
DU, YONG, Powder Metallurgy
FAN, XIANGRU, Business
FAN, XIANLONG, Foreign Languages
FAN, XIAOHUI, Resources Processing and Bioengineering
FAN, XIAOPING, Information Science and Engineering
FANG, LIGANG, Civil Engineering and Architecture
FANG, PING, Medical Technology and Information
FANG, YUNXIANG, Pharmaceutical Sciences
FANG, ZHENG, Chemistry and Chemical Engineering
FENG, QIMING, Resources Processing and Bioengineering
FU, HELIN, Civil Engineering and Architecture
GAN, SIQING, Mathematical Sciences and Computing Technology
GAN, WEIPING, Materials Science and Engineering
GAO, YANG, Business
GONG, FAN, Chemistry and Chemical Engineering
GONG, YANPING, Business
GU, JINGHUA, Resources Processing and Bioengineering
GU, YINGYING, Chemistry and Chemical Engineering
GUAN, LUXIONG, Chemistry and Chemical Engineering
GUI, WEIHUA, Information Science and Engineering
GUO, GUANGHUA, Physics, Sciences and Technology
GUO, QULIAN, Medical Technology and Information
GUO, SHAOHUA, Civil Engineering and Architecture
GUO, XIANGRONG, Civil Engineering and Architecture
HAN, JINGQUAN, Foreign Languages
HAN, QINGLAN, Business
HAN, XULI, Information Science and Engineering
HAN, XULI, Mathematical Sciences and Computing Technology
HE, BOQUAN, Resources Processing and Bioengineering
HE, GUOPING, Nursing
HE, HONGBO, Physics, Sciences and Technology
HE, HONGQU, Business
HE, JISHAN, Business
HE, XUEWEI, Literature
HE, YUNBO, Foreign Languages
HOU, MANLING, Chemistry and Chemical Engineering
HOU, ZHENTING, Mathematical Sciences and Computing Technology
HU, HUIPING, Chemistry and Chemical Engineering
HU, HUOSHENG, Information Science and Engineering
HU, KAI, Politics and Public Administration
HU, WEIXIN, Bioscience and Technology
HU, YUEHUA, Resources Processing and Bioengineering
HU, ZHENHUA, Business
HUANG, BOYUN, Materials Science and Engineering
HUANG, FANGLIN, Civil Engineering and Architecture
HUANG, JIAN, Chemistry and Chemical Engineering
HUANG, JIANBO, Business
HUANG, JIANREN, Foreign Languages
HUANG, KELONG, Chemistry and Chemical Engineering
HUANG, LANFANG, Chemistry and Chemical Engineering
HUANG, PEIYUN, Materials Science and Engineering
HUANG, PEIYUN, Powder Metallurgy
HUANG, QIZHONG, Powder Metallurgy
HUANG, SHENGSHENG, Resources Processing and Bioengineering
HUANG, YANPING, Politics and Public Administration
HUANG, YONG'AN, Foreign Languages
HUANG, ZHUCHENG, Resources Processing and Bioengineering
HUO, GUOJING, Civil Engineering and Architecture
HUO, YAOHUI, Powder Metallurgy
JIA, WEIJIA, Information Science and Engineering
JIAN, XINCHUN, Stomatology
JIANG, DONGJIU, Nursing
JIANG, DONGMEI, Nursing
JIANG, JINZHI, Chemistry and Chemical Engineering
JIANG, SHAOJIAN, Energy and Power Engineering
JIANG, TAO, Resources Processing and Bioengineering
JIANG, XINHUA, Information Science and Engineering
JIANG, YIMIN, Physics, Sciences and Technology
JIANG, YUREN, Chemistry and Chemical Engineering
JIN, ZHANPENG, Materials Science and Engineering
LAN, XIAOJUN, Medical Technology and Information
LENG, WUMING, Civil Engineering and Architecture
LI, BAIQING, Foreign Languages
LI, DENGQING, Medical Technology and Information
LI, HE, Energy and Power Engineering
LI, HONGJIAN, Physics, Sciences and Technology
LI, HUANDE, Pharmaceutical Sciences
LI, JIANHUA, Politics and Public Administration
LI, JIE, Chemistry and Chemical Engineering
LI, JUNPING, Mathematical Sciences and Computing Technology
LI, LIANG, Civil Engineering and Architecture
LI, LIPING, Business
LI, MINGSHENG, Business
LI, SONGREN, Resources Processing and Bioengineering
LI, XIAOBIN, Energy and Power Engineering
LI, XIAORU, Chemistry and Chemical Engineering
LI, XIBIN, Powder Metallurgy
LI, XUE, Mathematical Sciences and Computing Technology
LI, YANGCHENG, Mathematical Sciences and Computing Technology
LI, YANGSHENG, Fine Arts
LI, YANLIN, Foreign Languages
LI, YIBING, Information Science and Engineering
LI, YIBING, Physics, Sciences and Technology
LI, YIMIN, Powder Metallurgy
LI, YIZHI, Business
LI, YUANGAO, Chemistry and Chemical Engineering
LI, YUANJIAN, Pharmaceutical Sciences
LI, ZIRU, Business
LIANG, HONG, Chemistry and Chemical Engineering
LIANG, LAIYIN, Business
LIANG, XIMING, Information Science and Engineering
LIANG, YIZENG, Chemistry and Chemical Engineering
LIAO, SHENGMING, Civil Engineering and Architecture
LIAO, SHENGMING, Energy and Power Engineering
LIU, AIDONG, Business
LIU, BAOCHEN, Civil Engineering and Architecture
LIU, CHANGQING, Chemistry and Chemical Engineering
LIU, DONGRONG, Business
LIU, GUOPING, Information Science and Engineering
LIU, JIAJIA, Chemistry and Chemical Engineering
LIU, JIANSHE, Resources Processing and Bioengineering
LIU, KAIYU, Chemistry and Chemical Engineering
LIU, LIHANG, Politics and Public Administration
LIU, LIYING, Pharmaceutical Sciences
LIU, MINGJING, Foreign Languages
LIU, QINGTAN, Civil Engineering and Architecture
LIU, SHIJUN, Chemistry and Chemical Engineering
LIU, SUQIN, Chemistry and Chemical Engineering
LIU, WEIJUN, Mathematical Sciences and Computing Technology
LIU, XIAOCHUN, Medical Technology and Information
LIU, XINXING, Resources Processing and Bioengineering
LIU, XIONGFEI, Physics, Sciences and Technology
LIU, YANPING, Bioscience and Technology
LIU, YAZHENG, Business
LIU, YEXIANG, Energy and Power Engineering
LIU, YIRONG, Mathematical Sciences and Computing Technology
LIU, YONGHE, Medical Technology and Information
LIU, YONGMEI, Business
LIU, YOUNIAN, Chemistry and Chemical Engineering
LIU, ZAIMING, Mathematical Sciences and Computing Technology
LIU, ZEMIN, Literature
LIU, ZHIYI, Materials Science and Engineering
LIU, ZHUMING, Materials Science and Engineering
LUO, AIJING, Medical Technology and Information
LUO, AN, Information Science and Engineering
LUO, DAYONG, Information Science and Engineering
LUO, JIAOWAN, Mathematical Sciences and Computing Technology
LUO, WENDONG, Physics, Sciences and Technology
LUO, XIAOLING, Business
LUO, XINXING, Business

LUO, XUEGANG, Basic Medical Sciences
LUO, YIMING, Chemistry and Chemical Engineering
LUO, ZIQIANG, Basic Medical Sciences
LU, HAIBO, Powder Metallurgy
LU, XICHEN, Politics and Public Administration
LU, YAOHUAI, Politics and Public Administration
MA, CHENGYIN, Chemistry and Chemical Engineering
MAN, RUILIN, Chemistry and Chemical Engineering
MAO, XUANGUO, Literature
MEI, MEIZHI, Energy and Power Engineering
MENG, ZE, Foreign Languages
NIU, YINJIAN, Resources Processing and Bioengineering
OU YANG, YOUQUAN, Literature
PAN, QINGLIN, Materials Science and Engineering
PANG, CHUNYAO, Chemistry and Chemical Engineering
PEN, JINDING, Foreign Languages
PENG, JIEYING, Stomatology
PENG, LIMIN, Civil Engineering and Architecture
PENG, PINGYI, Politics and Public Administration
PENG, XIAOQI, Energy and Power Engineering
PENG, XIAOQI, Physics, Sciences and Technology
PENG, YUELIN, Mathematical Sciences and Computing Technology
QIAN, DONG, Chemistry and Chemical Engineering
QIN, XIAOQUN, Basic Medical Sciences
QIU, KEQIANG, Chemistry and Chemical Engineering
QIU, YUNREN, Chemistry and Chemical Engineering
QU, LONG, Chemistry and Chemical Engineering
QU, XUANHUI, Powder Metallurgy
RAO, QIUHUA, Civil Engineering and Architecture
RAO, YUELEI, Business
REN, FENGLIAN, Chemistry and Chemical Engineering
REN, JIFAN, Literature
RUAN, JIANMING, Powder Metallurgy
SHE, XIEBIN, Foreign Languages
SHEN, CHAOHONG, Business
SHEN, MEILAN, Mathematical Sciences and Computing Technology
SHEN, QUNTAI, Information Science and Engineering
SHI, RONGHUA, Information Science and Engineering
SHI, ZHANGMING, Energy and Power Engineering
SHU, WANGEN, Chemistry and Chemical Engineering
SI, SHIHUI, Chemistry and Chemical Engineering
SONG, HUIPING, Bioscience and Technology
SU, YUCHANG, Materials Science and Engineering
SUN, XIANGMING, Fine Arts
SUN, ZHENQIU, Mathematical Sciences and Computing Technology
TAN, DAREN, Medical Technology and Information
TAN, GUANZXHENG, Information Science and Engineering
TAN, MENGQUN, Basic Medical Sciences
TAN, XIPEI, Politics and Public Administration
TAN, YUNJIE, Foreign Languages
TANG, HONG'E, Civil Engineering and Architecture
TANG, RUIREN, Chemistry and Chemical Engineering
TANG, XIANHUA, Mathematical Sciences and Computing Technology
TANG, YOUGEN, Chemistry and Chemical Engineering
TANG, ZHANGUI, Stomatology
TAO, XINLU, Nursing
TU, GUOYUAN, Foreign Languages
TU, LING, Stomatology
WAN, ZHONG, Mathematical Sciences and Computing Technology
WANG, DIANZUO, Resources Processing and Bioengineering
WANG, GUOSHUN, Business
WANG, HANQING, Energy and Power Engineering
WANG, HUI, Chemistry and Chemical Engineering
WANG, JIABAO, Mathematical Sciences and Computing Technology
WANG, JIANQIANG, Business
WANG, JIANXIU, Chemistry and Chemical Engineering
WANG, JIGUI, Medical Technology and Information
WANG, LINGSEN, Powder Metallurgy
WANG, MENGJUN, Civil Engineering and Architecture
WANG, MING'AN, Medical Technology and Information
WANG, MINGMING, Nursing
WANG, MINGPU, Materials Science and Engineering
WANG, SHIPING, Basic Medical Sciences
WANG, SHUHUA, Resources Processing and Bioengineering
WANG, XIAOCHUN, Medical Technology and Information
WANG, XINGHUA, Civil Engineering and Architecture
WANG, YAN, Chemistry and Chemical Engineering
WANG, YIJUN, Information Science and Engineering
WANG, YONGHE, Civil Engineering and Architecture
WANG, YUECHUAN, Literature
WANG, ZHANGHUA, Literature
WANG, ZHIFA, Materials Science and Engineering
WANG, ZHIZHONG, Mathematical Sciences and Computing Technology
WEI, RENYONG, Information Science and Engineering
WEN, JIFANG, Basic Medical Sciences
WEN, YUSONG, Civil Engineering and Architecture
WU, JINMING, Business
WU, KUN, Mathematical Sciences and Computing Technology
WU, LIANGGANG, Business
WU, LIXIANG, Basic Medical Sciences
WU, XIANCHENG, Politics and Public Administration
XIA, CHANGQING, Materials Science and Engineering
XIA, JIAHUI, Bioscience and Technology
XIA, JINLAN, Resources Processing and Bioengineering
XIANG, SHU, Mathematical Sciences and Computing Technology
XIAO, LIMING, Foreign Languages
XIAO, TIEJIAN, Politics and Public Administration
XIAO, XIANZHONG, Basic Medical Sciences
XIAO, XIAODAN, Medical Technology and Information
XIAO, XU, Business
XIAO, ZEQIANG, Energy and Power Engineering
XIE, RUHE, Energy and Power Engineering
XIE, XIAOLI, Stomatology
XIE, YOUJUN, Civil Engineering and Architecture
XIONG, LUMAO, Politics and Public Administration
XIONG, XIANG, Powder Metallurgy
XIONG, YAN, Pharmaceutical Sciences
XU, HUI, Physics, Sciences and Technology
XU, JICHENG, Materials Science and Engineering
XU, QINGSONG, Mathematical Sciences and Computing Technology
XU, ZHISHENG, Civil Engineering and Architecture
YAN, AIMIN, Business
YAN, ZHEN, Literature
YANG, BINGCHU, Physics, Sciences and Technology
YANG, CHANGXIN, Information Science and Engineering
YANG, CHANGYING, Foreign Languages
YANG, DONGLIANG, Chemistry and Chemical Engineering
YANG, GUOLIN, Civil Engineering and Architecture
YANG, HUAMING, Resources Processing and Bioengineering
YANG, JUNSHENG, Civil Engineering and Architecture
YANG, SHOUKANG, Foreign Languages
YANG, WEIWEN, Business
YANG, XINRONG, Information Science and Engineering
YANG, ZHANHONG, Chemistry and Chemical Engineering
YE, BOLONG, Civil Engineering and Architecture
YE, HONGQI, Chemistry and Chemical Engineering
YE, MEIXIN, Civil Engineering and Architecture
YI, DANQING, Energy and Power Engineering
YI, JIANHONG, Powder Metallurgy
YI, MAOZHONG, Powder Metallurgy
YIN, ZHIMIN, Materials Science and Engineering
YIN, ZHOULAN, Chemistry and Chemical Engineering
YU, DEQUAN, Literature
YU, PING, Basic Medical Sciences
YU, SHENGHUA, Mathematical Sciences and Computing Technology
YU, SHOUYI, Information Science and Engineering
YU, ZHIWU, Civil Engineering and Architecture
YUAN, DONGYUAN, Physics, Sciences and Technology
YUAN, JINGEN, Civil Engineering and Architecture
YUAN, LEPING, Business
YUAN, MINGLIANG, Resources Processing and Bioengineering
YUAN, XIUGUI, Mathematical Sciences and Computing Technology
YUE, YIDING, Business
ZENG, CHANGQIU, Politics and Public Administration
ZENG, DONGMING, Chemistry and Chemical Engineering
ZENG, QINGFU, Basic Medical Sciences
ZENG, QINGREN, Basic Medical Sciences
ZENG, QINGYUAN, Civil Engineering and Architecture
ZENG, SUMIN, Materials Science and Engineering
ZENG, YUHUA, Nursing
ZENG, ZHICHENG, Basic Medical Sciences
ZHANG, CHENGPING, Foreign Languages
ZHANG, CONGYI, Foreign Languages
ZHANG, HANJUN, Mathematical Sciences and Computing Technology
ZHANG, HONGYAN, Mathematical Sciences and Computing Technology
ZHANG, HUAILIANG, Fine Arts
ZHANG, JIANXIANG, Basic Medical Sciences
ZHANG, JIASHENG, Civil Engineering and Architecture
ZHANG, JINGSHENG, Resources Processing and Bioengineering
ZHANG, JINRU, Chemistry and Chemical Engineering
ZHANG, LONGKUAN, Foreign Languages

ZHANG, NAN, Civil Engineering and Architecture
ZHANG, PINGMIN, Chemistry and Chemical Engineering
ZHANG, QINGJIN, Resources Processing and Bioengineering
ZHANG, QISEN, Civil Engineering and Architecture
ZHANG, QUAN, Energy and Power Engineering
ZHANG, SENKUAN, Foreign Languages
ZHANG, SHIMIN, Chemistry and Chemical Engineering
ZHANG, SIQI, Materials Science and Engineering
ZHANG, TAIMING, Chemistry and Chemical Engineering
ZHANG, TAISHAN, Information Science and Engineering
ZHANG, XINGXIAN, Foreign Languages
ZHANG, XINMIN, Materials Science and Engineering
ZHANG, XU, Foreign Languages
ZHANG, YAOJUN, Foreign Languages
ZHAO, WANGDA, Civil Engineering and Architecture
ZHAO, YAOLONG, Information Science and Engineering
ZHENG, ZHIQIAO, Materials Science and Engineering
ZHENG, ZHOUSHUN, Mathematical Sciences and Computing Technology
ZHON, HONG, Chemistry and Chemical Engineering
ZHONG, MEIZUO, Medical Technology and Information
ZHONG, SHI'AN, Chemistry and Chemical Engineering
ZHONG, YOUXUN, Literature
ZHOU, CHAOYANG, Civil Engineering and Architecture
ZHOU, CHUNSHAN, Chemistry and Chemical Engineering
ZHOU, DEBI, Chemistry and Chemical Engineering
ZHOU, DIAOMIN, Energy and Power Engineering
ZHOU, FEIMENG, Chemistry and Chemical Engineering
ZHOU, JICHENG, Physics, Sciences and Technology
ZHOU, KECHAO, Powder Metallurgy
ZHOU, KESHENG, Physics, Sciences and Technology
ZHOU, LIUXI, Foreign Languages
ZHOU, MINGDA, Chemistry and Chemical Engineering
ZHOU, NAIJUN, Energy and Power Engineering
ZHOU, PIN, Energy and Power Engineering
ZHOU, QIAN, Energy and Power Engineering
ZHOU, SHIQIONG, Civil Engineering and Architecture
ZHOU, TAO, Chemistry and Chemical Engineering
ZHU, DEQING, Resources Processing and Bioengineering
ZHU, KAICHENG, Physics, Sciences and Technology
ZHU, NIANQIONG, Nursing
ZHUANG, JIANMING, Resources Processing and Bioengineering
ZOU, BEIJI, Information Science and Engineering
ZOU, JIEZHONG, Mathematical Sciences and Computing Technology
ZUO, TIEYONG, Materials Science and Engineering

CENTRAL UNIVERSITY FOR NATIONALITIES

27 Nan Da Rd, Zhongguancun, Haidian Dist., Beijing 100081
Telephone: (10) 68932544
E-mail: cunofficexz@sina.com
Internet: www.cun.edu.cn

Founded 1951
State Ethnic Affairs Commission control
Academic year: September to July

Pres.: RONG SHIXIANG
Vice-Pres.: AI'BI BULA
Vice-Pres.: CHEN LI
Vice-Pres.: GUO WEIPING
Vice-Pres.: HUANG FENGXIAN
Vice-Pres.: JIN YASHENG
Vice-Pres.: REN ZHONGXIA
Vice-Pres.: YAN YUMING
Head of Graduate Dept: CHEN LI
Librarian: LI DELONG

Number of teachers: 700
Number of students: 13,000

Publications: *Journal of the Central University for Nationalities* (natural sciences, 4 a year), *Journal of the Central University for Nationalities* (philosophy and social sciences, 6 a year)

DEANS

School of Arts: YIN HUILI
School of Education: WANG JUN
School of Ethnology and Sociology: YANG SHENGMIN
School of Foreign Language: HE KEYONG
School of Law: ZHU JING'AN
School of Literature, Journalism and Communication: BAI WEI
School of Management: LI JUNQING
School of Music: MENG XINYANG
College of Dance: SU ZIHONG
College of Economics: LIU YONGJI
College of Life and Environment Science: FENG JINZHAO
College of National Minorities: LI JINFANG
College of Science and Engineering: FENG JINZHAO
Department of History: LI HONGBIN
Department of Philosophy and Religion: GONG YUKUAN
Department of Physics: WEI XIAOKANG
Preparatory Department: SONG TAICHENG
Research Institute of Tibet: BANBAN DUOJIE

PROFESSORS

BAI, RUNSHENG, Literature, Journalism and Communication
BAI, WEI, Literature, Journalism and Communication
BAI, YINTAI, National Minority Study
BANBAN, DUOJIE, Tibetan Studies
BI, MUXUN, Literature, Journalism and Communication
BU, ZHONGJIAN, Philosophy and Religion
CHEN, CHANGPING, Ethnology and Sociology
CHEN, FANGYING, Science and Engineering
CHEN, JIANJIAN, Tibetan Studies
CHEN, NAN, History
CUI, GUANZHI, Science and Engineering
DALI, ZHABU, History
DING, HONG, Ethnology and Sociology
DING, SHIQING, National Minority Study
FENG, JINZHAO, Life and Environment Science
FENG, JINZHAO, Science and Engineering
FU, CHENGZHOU, Literature, Journalism and Communication
FU, YIXIN, Education
GEN, SHIMIN, National Minority Study
GENG, YUFANG, Tibetan Studies
GESANG, DUNZHU, Tibetan Studies
GESANG, JUMIAN, Tibetan Studies
GONG, YUKUAN, Philosophy and Religion
HA, JINGXIONG, Education
HAMITI, TIEMUER, National Minority Study
HASHI, E'ERDUN, National Minority Study
HE, JINRUI, Philosophy and Religion
HE, KEYONG, Foreign Languages
HE, QIMIN, Philosophy and Religion
HE, WEI, Science and Engineering
HU, SHAOHUA, History
HU, ZHENHUA, National Minority Study
HUANG, KAI, Science and Engineering
HUOXIGE, TAOKETAO, National Minority Study
JI, YONGHAI, National Minority Study
JIAO, YUGUO, Life and Environment Science
JIN, RIGUANG, Music
LI, BINQUAN, Tibetan Studies
LI, GUIZHI, History
LI, HONGBIN, History
LI, JINFANG, National Minority Study
LI, JUNQING, Management
LI, KUI, Arts
LI, XINCHANG, Music
LI, YAN, National Minority Study
LI, YAN, Law
LIN, JING, Music
LIU, BINGJIANG, Arts
LIU, JIANMING, Literature, Journalism and Communication
LIU, JINZHEN, Science and Engineering
LIU, YONGJI, Economics
LIU, YONGZHOU, Literature, Journalism and Communication
LU, SHAO'EN, Music
MEN, DUHU, National Minority Study
MENG, XINYANG, Music
PIAO, CHANGTIAN, Music
SHANG, YANBIN, History
SHAO, XIANSHU, Ethnology and Sociology
SHEN, JIA, Music
SONG, RUBU, National Minority Study
SU, ZIHONG, Dance
TAO, LIPAN, Literature, Journalism and Communication
TENG, XING, Education
WANG, JUN, Education
WANG, RAO, Tibetan Studies
WANG, TIANJIN, Economics
WANG, YUANXIN, National Minority Study
WANG, ZHONGHAN, History
WANGMEN, TIEGA, National Minority Study
WEI, FENGRONG, Science and Engineering
WU, LIJI, National Minority Study
XIAO, XIURONG, Management
XING, FUCHON, Science and Engineering
XING, LI, Literature, Journalism and Communication
XU, LUYA, Foreign Languages
XU, SHOUCHUN, Science and Engineering
XU, WANBANG, Ethnology and Sociology
XU, YONGZHI, History
XU, YONGZHI, Management
YANG, CONG, Economics
YANG, ROOMING, Life and Environment Science
YANG, SHENGMIN, Ethnology and Sociology
YAO, NIANCI, History
YIN, HUILI, Arts
YU, KESEN, Literature, Journalism and Communication
YU, QIMING, Philosophy and Religion
ZENG, SHIQI, National Minority Study
ZHANG, GONGJIN, National Minority Study
ZHANG, GUANGHUA, Science and Engineering
ZHAO, KANG, Tibetan Studies
ZHAO, SHILIN, Philosophy and Religion
ZHOU, LI, Management
ZHOU, RUNNIAN, Tibetan Studies
ZHU, JING'AN, Law
ZHU, ZHENGYUAN, Science and Engineering

CENTRAL UNIVERSITY OF FINANCE AND ECONOMICS

39 Xue Yuan Nan Rd, Beijing 100081
Telephone: (10) 62289132
E-mail: wlb@cufe.edu.cn
Internet: www.cufe.edu.cn

Founded 1949
Min. of Education control
Academic year: September to July

Pres.: WANG GUANGQIAN
Vice-Pres.: CHEN MING
Vice-Pres.: LI JUNSHENG

Vice-Pres.: WANG GUOHUA
Vice-Pres.: YUAN DONG
Head of Graduate Dept: QI LAN
Librarian: HAN ZHIPING

Number of teachers: 500
Number of students: 14,000 (6,800 full-time, 7,200 part-time)

Publication: *Journal of the Central University of Finance and Economics* (12 a year)

DEANS

Business School: SUN GUOHUI
College of Culture and Communication: WANG QIANG
Department of Athletics Economy and Management: GAO HAN
Department of Economic Mathematics: CHEN WENDENG
Department of Foreign Languages: WANG XIAOHONG
Department of Insurance: HAO YANSU
Department of Investment Economics: WANG YAOQI
Department of Sociology: LI ZHIJUN
School of Accountancy: MENG YAN
School of Economics: JIN ZHESONG
School of Finance: SHI JIANPING
School of Information: WANG LUBIN
School of Law: GAN GONGEN
School of Public Finance and Administration: MA HAITAO

PROFESSORS

BAO, XIAOGUANG, Culture and Communication
CHEN, WENDENG, Economic Mathematics
CUI, XINJIAN, Business
DONG, CHENGZHANG, Information
GAN, GONGEN, Law
HAN, FULING, Finance
HAO, YANSU, Insurance
HOU, RONGHUA, Economics
HUO, PEI, Finance
HUO, QIANG, Finance
JIANG, WEIZHUANG, Public Finance and Administration
JIANG, XIAN, Economics
JIN, ZHESONG, Economics
LAN, CUIPAI, Law
LI, BAOREN, Public Finance and Administration
LI, JIAN, Finance
LI, JIXIONG, Insurance
LI, JUNSHENG, Public Finance and Administration
LI, SHUANG, Accountancy
LI, XIAOLIN, Insurance
LI, YAN, Public Finance and Administration
LI, ZHIJUN, Sociology
LIAO, SIPING, Culture and Communication
LIU, HENG, Public Finance and Administration
LIU, HONGXIA, Accountancy
LIU, YANG, Economics
MA, HAITAO, Public Finance and Administration
MENG, YAN, Accountancy
MIAO, RUNSHENG, Accountancy
PAN, JINSHENG, Finance
PAN, SHENGCHU, Information
QI, HUAIJIN, Accountancy
QI, LAN, Economics
SHI, JIANPING, Finance
SHI, SHULIN, Law
SUN, BAOWEN, Information
SUN, GUOHUI, Business
WANG, GUOHUA, Public Finance and Administration
WANG, JINYING, Business
WANG, JUNCAI, Accountancy
WANG, KEJING, Economics
WANG, LUBIN, Information
WANG, PEIZHEN, Finance
WANG, QIANG, Culture and Communication
WANG, RUIHUA, Accountancy
WANG, YONGJUN, Public Finance and Administration
WANG, YONGPING, Accountancy
WEI, ZHENXIONG, Accountancy
WEN, QIAN, Economics
WU, ZHENZHI, Finance
XI, SHUQIN, Accountancy
XU, SHANHUI, Finance
XU, XIANGYU, Investment Economics
YANG, JINGUANG, Accountancy
YANG, ZHIQING, Public Finance and Administration
YAO, SUI, Finance
ZHANG, BIQIONG, Finance
ZHANG, LIQIN, Finance
ZHANG, SHUJUN, Business
ZHANG, TIEGANG, Economics
ZHAO, LIFENG, Economics
ZHAO, XUEHENG, Public Finance and Administration

CHANG'AN UNIVERSITY

Nan Er Huan Rd, Xian 710064, Shaanxi Province

Telephone: (29) 82334104
E-mail: xbmsk@chd.du.cn
Internet: www.xahu.edu.cn

Founded 2000
Min. of Education control
Academic year: September to July

Pres.: ZHOU XU HONG
Vice-Pres.: LI YUN JI
Vice-Pres.: LIU BO QUAN
Vice-Pres.: LIU JIAN CHAO
Vice-Pres.: MA JIAN
Head of Graduate Dept: LU PENG MIN
Librarian: SHA AI MIN

Number of teachers: 3,438
Number of students: 36,383

Publications: *Automobile Racing Driver* (12 a year), *China Journal of Highway and Transport* (4 a year), *Journal of Chang'an University* (architecture and environmental sciences, 6 a year), *Journal of Chang'an University* (natural sciences, 6 a year), *Journal of Chang'an University* (philosophy and social sciences, 6 a year), *Journal of Earth Sciences and Environment* (4 a year), *Journal of Traffic and Transportation Engineering* (4 a year), *Road Machinery and Construction Machanization* (12 a year)

DEANS

College of Applied Technology: HU XUE MEI
College of Construction Engineering: WANG YI HONG
College of Earth Science and Land Resources Management: LI YONG
College of Environmental Science and Engineering: WANG WEN KE
College of Foreign Languages: LI MIN QUAN
College of Geology Engineering and Geomatics: PENG JIAN MIN
College of Highway Engineering: XU YUE
College of Information Engineering: HE YI QU
School of Construction Machinery: FENG ZHONG XU
School of Economics and Management: ZHOU GUO GUANG
School of Humanities and Social Science: LIU JI FA
School of Science: FENG JIAN HU

PROFESSORS

CHEN, DE CHUAN, Highway Management
CHEN, HONG, Traffic Engineering
CHEN, KUAN MIN, Traffic Engineering
CHEN, ZHI XIN, Geology Engineering and Geomatics
CHEN, ZHONG DA, Highways
DAI, JING LIANG, Highways
DONG, QIAN LI, Economics and Management
DOU, MING JIAN, Highway Disaster Prevention and Cure
DU, DONG JU, Geology Engineering and Geomatics
FAN, WEN, Geology Engineering and Geomatics
FENG, JIAN HU, Science
FENG, ZHEN YU, Science
FENG, ZHONG XU, Construction Machinery
GUAN, WEI XING, Environmental Science and Engineering
GUO, YUAN SHU, Information Engineering
HAN, SEN, Highways
HAO, PEI WEN, Highways
HAO, XIAN WU, Bridges
HE, AN MING, Science
HE, SHUANG HAI, Bridges
HE, YI QU, Information Engineering
HU, DA LIN, Bridges
HU, YONG BIAO, Construction Machinery
HU, YUE, Bridges
HU, ZHAO TONG, Bridges
HUANG, PING MIN, Bridges
JIANG, CHANG YI, Earth Science and Land Resources Management
JIAO, SHENG JIE, Construction Machinery
JU, YONG FENG, Information Engineering
LEI, SHENG YOU, Geognosy and Tube Engineering
LI, PEI CHENG, Environmental Science and Engineering
LI, QING CHUN, Geology Engineering and Geomatics
LI, XIU, Geology Engineering and Geomatics
LI, YONG, Earth Science and Land Resources Management
LI, YUN FENG, Environmental Science and Engineering
LI, ZI QING, Bridges
LIU, BAO JIAN, Geognosy and Tube Engineering
LIU, JI FA, Humanities and Social Science
LIU, JIAN XIN, Bridges
LIU, LAI JUN, Bridges
LIU, YONG JIAN, Bridges
LONG, SHUI GEN, Construction Machinery
LU, KANG CHENG, Geognosy and Tube Engineering
LU, PENG MIN, Construction Machinery
MA, JIANG MING, Science
MA, RONG GUO, Traffic Engineering
MA, TIAN SHAN, Economics and Management
MAO, YAN LONG, Geology Engineering and Geomatics
MEN, YU MING, Geology Engineering and Geomatics
NI, WANG KUI, Geology Engineering and Geomatics
PEI, XIAN ZHI, Earth Science and Land Resources Management
PENG, JIAN MIN, Geology Engineering and Geomatics
QIAN, ZHUANG ZHI, Earth Science and Land Resources Management
SHA, AI MIN, Highways
SHEN, AI QIN, Highways
SHI, YONG MIN, Highway Management
SONG, YI FAN, Bridges
SU, SHENG RUI, Geology Engineering and Geomatics
TAN, CHENG QIAN, Geology Engineering and Geomatics
TIAN, WEI PING, Highway Disaster Prevention and Cure
WANG, BIN GANG, Highways
WANG, HU, Science
WANG, WEN KE, Environmental Science and Engineering
WANG, XIAO MOU, Geognosy and Tube Engineering
WANG, XUAN CANG, Highway Management
WEI, GUANG SHENG, Science
WU, XIAO GUANG, Highway Management
XIA, YONG XU, Geognosy and Tube Engineering

Xie, Yong Li, Geognosy and Tube Engineering
Xu, Hai Cheng, Economics and Management
Xu, Jing Liang, Road Reconnaissance
Xue, Chun Ji, Earth Science and Land Resources Management
Yan, Bao Jie, Traffic Engineering
Yang, Bin Cheng, Bridges
Yang, Shao Wei, Road Reconnaissance
Yang, Xiao Hua, Geognosy and Tube Engineering
Yang, Xing Ke, Earth Science and Land Resources Management
Yi, Guan Sheng, Science
Zhang, Chao, Highways
Zhang, Deng Liang, Highways
Zhang, Jun, Geology Engineering and Geomatics
Zhang, Qin, Geology Engineering and Geomatics
Zhang, Zhi Qiang, Geology Engineering and Geomatics
Zhao, Fa Shuo, Geology Engineering and Geomatics
Zhe, Xue Sen, Geognosy and Tube Engineering
Zheng, Chuan Chao, Highways
Zheng, Nan Xiang, Highways
Zhou, Guo Guang, Economics and Management
Zhou, Wei, Traffic Engineering
Zhou, Xu Hong, Bridges
Zhu, Guang Ming, Geology Engineering and Geomatics

CHENGDU UNIVERSITY OF TECHNOLOGY

1st East Third Rd, Chenghua, Erxianqiao, Chengdu 610059, Sichuan Province
Telephone: (28) 84078898
Internet: www.cdut.edu.cn

Founded 1956
provincial control
Academic year: September to July

Pres.: Liu Jiaduo
Vice-Pres.: Huang Runqiu
Vice-Pres.: Ni Shijun
Vice-Pres.: Tan Shumin
Vice-Pres.: Wang Yingchuan
Librarian: Li Yong

Library of 1,170,000 vols
Number of teachers: 2,021
Number of students: 25,000

Publications: *Computing Techniques for Geophysical Exploration* (4 a year), *Journal* (6 a year), *Journal of Geological Hazards and Environment Preservation* (4 a year), *Journal of Mineralogy and Petrology* (4 a year), *Scientific and Technological Management of Land and Resources* (6 a year)

DEANS

Australian Institute of Tourism and Hospitality: Li Yusheng
College of Applied Techniques and Automation Engineering: Ge Liangquan
College of Energy Resources: Zhang Shaonan
College of Environment and Civil Engineering: Xu Qiang
College of Foreign Languages and Cultures: Luo Yijun
College of Geosciences: Sun Chuanmin
College of Humanities and Law: Li Quanhui
College of Information Engineering: Wang Xuben
College of Information Management: Guo Ke
College of Materials and Bioengineering: Wang Ling
Commercial College: Li Yusheng

PROFESSORS

Cao, Jinwen, College of Information Management
Cao, Junxing, College of Information Engineering
Chen, Buke, College of Energy Resources
Chen, Changquan, College of Information Management
Chen, Hongde, Geosciences College
Chen, Junming, Australian Institute of Tourism and Hospitality
Chen, Wanjiang, Commercial College
Cheng, Xia, Commercial College
Deng, Lin, College of Information Engineering
Deng, Tianlong, College of Materials and Bioengineering
Ding, Zhaoyu, Network Education College
Fan, Biwei, College of Materials and Bioengineering
Fang, Fang, College of Applied Techniques and Automation Engineering:
Feng, Wenguang, College of Energy Resources
Fu, Guanghai, Commercial College
Fu, Ronghua, College of Environment and Civil Engineering
Fu, Rulin, College of Information Engineering
Ge, Liangquan, College of Applied Techniques and Automation Engineering:
Gu, Xuexiang, Geosciences College
Guo, Jiang, College of Information Engineering
Guo, Ke, College of Information Management
He, Mingsheng, College of Applied Techniques and Automation Engineering:
He, Zhengwei, Geosciences College
He, Zhenhua, College of Information Engineering
Hong, Zhiquan, College of Information Engineering
Hu, Guangmang, College of Information Engineering
Hu, Yuanlai, College of Information Management
Huang, Dilong, College of Information Engineering
Huang, Jijun, Geosciences College
Huang, Runqiu, College of Environment and Civil Engineering
Huang, Sijing, Geosciences College
Jia, Suyuan, College of Environment and Civil Engineering
Kong, Fanjing, College of Foreign Languages and Cultures
Kuang, Jianchao, College of Information Management
Li, Hongmu, College of Applied Techniques and Automation Engineering:
Li, Juchu, College of Applied Techniques and Automation Engineering:
Li, Liangming, Commercial College
Li, Luming, College of Information Engineering
Li, Quanhui, College of Humanities and Law
Li, Rui, College of Information Engineering
Li, Shusheng, College of Environment and Civil Engineering
Li, Tianbin, College of Environment and Civil Engineering
Li, Wuquan, College of Foreign Languages and Cultures
Li, Yusheng, Commercial College
Li, Zhengwen, College of Information Engineering
Li, Zheqin, College of Environment and Civil Engineering
Li, Zhiquan, College of Information Engineering
Lie, Dexin, College of Environment and Civil Engineering
Lin, Li, Geosciences College
Liu, Dengzhong, Geosciences College
Liu, Hanchao, College of Environment and Civil Engineering
Liu, Hongjun, College of Information Management
Liu, Jiaduo, Geosciences College
Liu, Maocai, College of Information Management
Liu, Shugen, College of Energy Resources
Liu, Xianfan, Geosciences College
Lu, Kun, College of Applied Techniques and Automation Engineering:
Lu, Zhengyuan, College of Energy Resources
Luo, Mei, College of Applied Techniques and Automation Engineering:
Luo, Runtian, College of Foreign Languages and Cultures
Luo, Shengxian, College of Information Engineering
Luo, Yijun, College of Foreign Languages and Cultures
Ma, Runze, Geosciences College
Ma, Yuxiao, College of Applied Techniques and Automation Engineering:
Miao, Fang, College of Information Engineering
Ni, Shijun, College of Applied Techniques and Automation Engineering:
Peng, Dajun, College of Energy Resources
Qie, Jinling, College of Information Engineering
Qiu, Kehui, College of Materials and Bioengineering
Ren, Guangming, College of Environment and Civil Engineering
Sha, Jichang, College of Information Management
Sheng, Zhongming, College of Energy Resources
Shi, He, Geosciences College
Shi, Zhejin, College of Energy Resources
Sun, Chuanmin, Geosciences College
Sun, Shuxia, Network Education College
Tan, Jianxiong, Geosciences College
Tang, Juxing, Geosciences College
Tian, Jingchun, Geosciences College
Tong, Chunhan, College of Applied Techniques and Automation Engineering:
Tuo, Xianguo, College of Information Engineering
Wan, Xinnan, College of Environment and Civil Engineering
Wang, Chengshan, Geosciences College
Wang, Hongfeng, Geosciences College
Wang, Honghui, College of Energy Resources
Wang, Huizhou, College of Foreign Languages and Cultures
Wang, Lansheng, College of Environment and Civil Engineering
Wang, Ling, College of Materials and Bioengineering
Wang, Mohui, College of Materials and Bioengineering
Wang, Shitian, College of Environment and Civil Engineering
Wang, Xiaochun, College of Environment and Civil Engineering
Wang, Xinzhuang, College of Information Management
Wang, Xuben, College of Information Engineering
Wang, Yuncheng, College of Energy Resources
Wang, Yunsheng, College of Environment and Civil Engineering
Wang, Zaiqi, College of Foreign Languages and Cultures
Wei, Guiming, College of Information Management
Wen, Chunqi, Geosciences College
Wu, Shan, Geosciences College
Xi, Dashun, College of Information Engineering
Xian, Yuanfu, Geosciences College
Xiang, Yang, College of Energy Resources
Xiao, Cixun, College of Information Engineering
Xing, Wenxiang, College of Information Management
Xu, Guosheng, College of Energy Resources

XU, MO, College of Environment and Civil Engineering
XU, QIANG, College of Environment and Civil Engineering
YAN, HELIN, Geosciences College
YANG, SHAOGUO, College of Information Engineering
YANG, WUNIAN, Geosciences College
YANG, ZHENGXI, Geosciences College
YI, GUAN, College of Applied Techniques and Automation Engineering:
YI, HAISHENG, Geosciences College
YIN, HUIAN, College of Materials and Bioengineering
ZHANG, CHENGJIANG, College of Applied Techniques and Automation Engineering:
ZHANG, QICHUN, College of Materials and Bioengineering
ZHANG, SHAONAN, College of Energy Resources
ZHANG, ZUOYUAN, College of Environment and Civil Engineering
ZHAO, BING, Geosciences College
ZHAO, QIHUA, College of Environment and Civil Engineering
ZHAO, XIAFEI, College of Energy Resources
ZHAO, XIGUI, College of Energy Resources
ZHAO, ZESONG, Commercial College
ZHEN, HUAN, College of Foreign Languages and Cultures
ZHEN, MINGHUA, Geosciences College
ZHEN, RONGCAI, Geosciences College
ZHONG, BENSHAN, College of Information Engineering
ZHONG, YONGJIAN, Commercial College
ZHOU, JIAJI, College of Information Engineering
ZHOU, RONGSHENG, College of Applied Techniques and Automation Engineering:
ZHOU, SICHUN, College of Applied Techniques and Automation Engineering:
ZHOU, XIXIANG, College of Information Engineering
ZHU, CHUANGYE, Geosciences College
ZHU, JIESHOU, College of Information Engineering

CHENGDU UNIVERSITY OF TRADITIONAL CHINESE MEDICINE

37 Shierqiao Rd, Chengdu 610075
Telephone: (28) 87784542
E-mail: wsc@cdutcm.edu.cn
Internet: www.cdutcm.edu.cn

Founded 1956
State control
Languages of instruction: Chinese, English
Academic year: September to August

Pres.: Prof. ZHU BIDE
Vice-Pres.: FU CHUNHUA
Vice-Pres.: LIANG FANRONG
Vice-Pres.: LUO CAIGUI
Vice-Pres.: XIE KEQING
Chief Admin. Officer: XU, LIAN
Librarian: JIANG YONGGUANG

Library of 602,000 vols
Number of teachers: 1,678
Number of students: 10,095

Publications: *Academic Journal* (4 a year), *Higher Education Research into Traditional Chinese Medicine* (4 a year)

CHINA AGRICULTURAL UNIVERSITY

2 West of Yuanmingyuan Rd, Haidian Dist., Beijing 100094
Telephone: (10) 62732394
Internet: www.cau.edu.cn

Founded 1905
Academic year: September to July

Pres.: CHEN ZHANGLIANG
Vice-Pres.: FU ZETIAN
Vice-Pres.: JIANG SHUREN
Vice-Pres.: MA JIANSHENG
Vice-Pres.: SUN QIXIN
Vice-Pres.: TAN XIANGYONG
Vice-Pres.: ZHANG DONGJUN
Head of Graduate Department: CHEN ZHANGLIANG
Librarian: ZHANG QUAN

Number of teachers: 1,170
Number of students: 18,425

Publications: *Chinese Journal of Veterinary Medicine*, *Journal* (natural sciences, 6 a year)

DEANS

College of Agronomy and Biotechnology: DAI JINGRUI
College of Animal Science and Technology: LI DEFA
College of Biology Science: WU WEIHUA
College of Economic Management: WANG XIUQING
College of Food Science and Nutritional Engineering: LUO YUNBO
College of Humanities and Development: LI XIAOYUN
College of Information and Electrical Engineering: YANG RENGANG
College of International Studies: MENG FANXI
College of Resources and Environment: ZHANG FUSUO
College of Science: JIAO QUNYING
College of Veterinary Medicine: WANG MING
College of Water Conservation and Civil Engineering: WANG FUJUN

PROFESSORS

AO, GUANGMING, Biological Sciences
CAI, WANZHI, Agronomy and Biotechnology
CAO, YIPING, Resources and the Environment
CAO, ZHIPING, Resources and the Environment
CHANG, JINSHI, Water Conservation and Civil Engineering
CHEN, BAOFENG, Economic Management
CHEN, BU, Agronomy and Biotechnology
CHEN, HUANWEI, Resources and the Environment
CHEN, JIA, Biological Sciences
CHEN, JIANPING, Resources and the Environment
CHEN, MIN, Food Science and Nutritional Engineering
CHEN, QINGYUN, Agronomy and Biotechnology
CHEN, SANFENG, Biological Sciences
CHEN, SHAOJIANG, Agronomy and Biotechnology
CHEN, WENXIN, Biological Sciences
CHEN, YONGFU, Biological Sciences
CHEN, ZHANGLIANG, Agronomy and Biotechnology
CHENG, XU, Agronomy and Biotechnology
CUI, JIANYUN, Food Science and Nutritional Engineering
CUI, SHENG, Biological Sciences
CUI, ZONGJUN, Agronomy and Biotechnology
DAI, JINGRUI, Agronomy and Biotechnology
DENG, NAIYANG, Science
DENG, XIMIN, Agronomy and Biotechnology
DUAN, CHANGQING, Food Science and Nutritional Engineering
FENG, GONG, Humanities and Development
FENG, GU, Resources and the Environment
FENG, KAIWEN, Economic Management
FENG, SHAOYUAN, Water Conservation and Civil Engineering
FU, ZHIYI, Science
GAO, JUNPING, Agronomy and Biotechnology
GAO, QIJIE, Humanities and Development
GAO, WANGSHENG, Agronomy and Biotechnology
GAO, XIWU, Agronomy and Biotechnology
GAO, YANXIANG, Food Science and Nutritional Engineering
GONG, LIMIN, Animal Science and Technology
GONG, YUANSHI, Resources and the Environment
GONG, ZHIZHONG, Biological Sciences
GUO, SHUNTANG, Food Science and Nutritional Engineering
GUO, XIQING, Information and Electrical Engineering
GUO, YANGDONG, Agronomy and Biotechnology
GUO, YUHAI, Agronomy and Biotechnology
GUO, YUYUAN, Agronomy and Biotechnology
GUO, ZEJIAN, Agronomy and Biotechnology
HAN, BEIZHONG, Food Science and Nutritional Engineering
HAN, CHENGGUI, Agronomy and Biotechnology
HAN, JIANGUO, Animal Science and Technology
HAN, YUZHEN, Biological Sciences
HAN, ZHENHAI, Agronomy and Biotechnology
HAO, JINMIN, Resources and the Environment
HE, GUANGWEN, Economic Management
HE, XIURONG, Economic Management
HOU, CAIYUN, Food Science and Nutritional Engineering
HU, XIAOSONG, Food Science and Nutritional Engineering
HU, YUEGAO, Agronomy and Biotechnology
HUANG, GUANHUA, Water Conservation and Civil Engineering
HUANG, WEIDONG, Food Science and Nutritional Engineering
HUANG, WENBIN, Science
HUANG, YUANFANG, Resources and the Environment
HUANG, ZHIYONG, Agronomy and Biotechnology
JI, BAOPING, Food Science and Nutritional Engineering
JI, CHENG, Animal Science and Technology
JI, HAIYAN, Information and Electrical Engineering
JIA, WENSUO, Agronomy and Biotechnology
JIA, ZHIHAI, Animal Science and Technology
JIAN, HENG, Agronomy and Biotechnology
JIANG, RONGFENG, Resources and the Environment
JIANG, SHUREN, Science
JIANG, WEIBO, Food Science and Nutritional Engineering
JIAO, QUNYING, Science
JIAO, SHIYAN, Animal Science and Technology
KANG, DINGMING, Agronomy and Biotechnology
KANG, SHAOZHONG, Water Conservation and Civil Engineering
KE, BINGSHENG, Economic Management
LEI, TINGWU, Water Conservation and Civil Engineering
LENG, PING, Agronomy and Biotechnology
LI, BAOGUO, Resources and the Environment
LI, BAOMING, Water Conservation and Civil Engineering
LI, CHONGJIU, Science
LI, CHUNJIAN, Resources and the Environment
LI, DAWEI, Biological Sciences
LI, DEFA, Animal Science and Technology
LI, GENGLONG, Economic Management
LI, GUANGYONG, Water Conservation and Civil Engineering
LI, GUOHUI, Science
LI, GUOXUE, Resources and the Environment
LI, HUAIFANG, Agronomy and Biotechnology
LI, JI, Resources and the Environment
LI, JIANMIN, Agronomy and Biotechnology
LI, JIANQIANG, Agronomy and Biotechnology
LI, JIANSHENG, Agronomy and Biotechnology
LI, JILUN, Biological Sciences
LI, LITE, Food Science and Nutritional Engineering
LI, LONG, Resources and the Environment
LI, MINZAN, Information and Electrical Engineering
LI, NAN, Science
LI, NING, Biological Sciences

LI, OU, Humanities and Development
LI, PING, Economic Management
LI, SHAOKUN, Agronomy and Biotechnology
LI, SHENGLI, Animal Science and Technology
LI, SHUHUA, Agronomy and Biotechnology
LI, WEIJIONG, Resources and the Environment
LI, XIAOLIN, Resources and the Environment
LI, XIAOYUN, Humanities and Development
LI, XUEFENG, Science
LI, YAN, Biological Sciences
LI, YING, Biological Sciences
LI, ZANDONG, Biological Sciences
LI, ZHAOHU, Agronomy and Biotechnology
LI, ZICHAO, Agronomy and Biotechnology
LIAN, LINSHENG, Animal Science and Technology
LIAN, ZHENGXING, Animal Science and Technology
LIN, CONG, Water Conservation and Civil Engineering
LIN, DEGUI, Veterinary Medicine
LIN, QIMEI, Resources and the Environment
LIN, SHAN, Resources and the Environment
LIU, GUOJIE, Agronomy and Biotechnology
LIU, GUOQIN, Biological Sciences
LIU, LIMING, Resources and the Environment
LIU, QINGCHANG, Agronomy and Biotechnology
LIU, YONGGONG, Humanities and Development
LIU, ZHIYONG, Agronomy and Biotechnology
LOU, CHENGHOU, Biological Sciences
LU, FENGJU, Economic Management
LU, JUAN, Economic Management
LU, YAHAI, Resources and the Environment
LU, ZHIGUANG, Resources and the Environment
LUO, YUNBO, Food Science and Nutritional Engineering
MA, CHANGWEI, Food Science and Nutritional Engineering
MA, CHENGWEI, Water Conservation and Civil Engineering
MAO, DARU, Resources and the Environment
MENG, FANXI, International College
MENG, QINGXIANG, Animal Science and Technology
MI, GUOHUA, Resources and the Environment
MIN, SHUNGENG, Science
NIU, TIANGUI, Food Science and Nutritional Engineering
PAN, SHENQUAN, Agronomy and Biotechnology
PAN, XUEBIAO, Resources and the Environment
PENG, YOULIANG, Agronomy and Biotechnology
QIAO, JUAN, Economic Management
QIAO, ZHONG, Economic Management
QIN, FU, Economic Management
QIN, YAODONG, Resources and the Environment
REN, DONGTAO, Biological Sciences
REN, FAZHENG, Food Science and Nutritional Engineering
REN, LI, Resources and the Environment
REN, SHUMEI, Water Conservation and Civil Engineering
SHEN, DEZHONG, Resources and the Environment
SHEN, JIANZHONG, Veterinary Medicine
SHEN, ZUORUI, Agronomy and Biotechnology
SHI, DAZHAO, Agronomy and Biotechnology
SHI, JIEPING, Food Science and Nutritional Engineering
SHI, YUANCHUN, Resources and the Environment
SONG, YUAN, Biological Sciences
SU, DECHUN, Resources and the Environment
SU, ZHEN, Biological Sciences
SUN, BAOQI, Agronomy and Biotechnology
SUN, CHUANQING, Agronomy and Biotechnology
SUN, JUNSHE, Food Science and Nutritional Engineering
SUN, QIXIN, Agronomy and Biotechnology
SUN, YURUI, Information and Electrical Engineering
SUN, ZHEN, Resources and the Environment
TAN, XIANGYONG, Economic Management
TENG, GUANGHUI, Water Conservation and Civil Engineering
TIAN, WEIMING, Economic Management
WANG, AIGUO, Animal Science and Technology
WANG, BIN, Biological Sciences
WANG, CHUDUAN, Animal Science and Technology
WANG, DEHAI, Humanities and Development
WANG, FANG, Animal Science and Technology
WANG, FUJUN, Water Conservation and Civil Engineering
WANG, GUOYING, Biological Sciences
WANG, HEXIANG, Biological Sciences
WANG, HONGGUANG, Agronomy and Biotechnology
WANG, HUANHUA, Information and Electrical Engineering
WANG, HUAQI, Agronomy and Biotechnology
WANG, HUIMIN, Agronomy and Biotechnology
WANG, JIANHUA, Agronomy and Biotechnology
WANG, JINGGUO, Resources and the Environment
WANG, KU, Information and Electrical Engineering
WANG, MAO, Biological Sciences
WANG, MING, Veterinary Medicine
WANG, PU, Agronomy and Biotechnology
WANG, SHIPING, Food Science and Nutritional Engineering
WANG, SHOUCAI, Agronomy and Biotechnology
WANG, TAO, Biological Sciences
WANG, XIUQING, Economic Management
WANG, XUECHEN, Biological Sciences
WANG, YIMING, Information and Electrical Engineering
WEN, BOYING, Information and Electrical Engineering
WO, YUMING, Animal Science and Technology
WU, PING, Information and Electrical Engineering
WU, WEIHUA, Biological Sciences
WU, WENLIANG, Resources and the Environment
XIA, GUOLIANG, Biological Sciences
XIAO, HAIFENG, Economic Management
XIAO, XINGGUO, Biological Sciences
XIE, GUANGHUI, Agronomy and Biotechnology
XIN, XIAN, Economic Management
XU, HUIYUAN, Economic Management
XU, MINGLIANG, Agronomy and Biotechnology
XU, XUEFENG, Agronomy and Biotechnology
XUE, WENTONG, Food Science and Nutritional Engineering
YAN, TAILAI, Information and Electrical Engineering
YANG, DING, Agronomy and Biotechnology
YANG, HANCHUN, Veterinary Medicine
YANG, JIANCHANG, Agronomy and Biotechnology
YANG, MINGHAO, Information and Electrical Engineering
YANG, NING, Animal Science and Technology
YANG, PEILING, Water Conservation and Civil Engineering
YANG, QIULIN, Economic Management
YANG, RENGANG, Information and Electrical Engineering
YANG, XIAOBING, Agronomy and Biotechnology
YANG, ZHIFU, Resources and the Environment
YE, JINGZHONG, Humanities and Development
YE, ZHIHUA, Agronomy and Biotechnology
YI, MINGFANG, Agronomy and Biotechnology
YU, HUAIJIANG, Humanities and Development
YU, JIALIN, Biological Sciences
YU, RUIPING, Veterinary Medicine
YU, ZHENRONG, Resources and the Environment
YUAN, MING, Biological Sciences
ZANG, RIHONG, Economic Management
ZENG, SHENMING, Animal Science and Technology
ZENG, SHIMAI, Agronomy and Biotechnology
ZHAI, ZHIXI, Agronomy and Biotechnology
ZHANG, BAOGUI, Resources and the Environment
ZHANG, CONG, Resources and the Environment
ZHANG, DAPENG, Biological Sciences
ZHANG, FENGRONG, Resources and the Environment
ZHANG, FUSUO, Resources and the Environment
ZHANG, KEJIA, Veterinary Medicine
ZHANG, LONG, Agronomy and Biotechnology
ZHANG, QIN, Animal Science and Technology
ZHANG, QINGWEN, Agronomy and Biotechnology
ZHANG, RUAN, Animal Science and Technology
ZHANG, SHAOYING, Food Science and Nutritional Engineering
ZHANG, SHUQIU, Biological Sciences
ZHANG, WEI, Information and Electrical Engineering
ZHANG, XIAOMING, Animal Science and Technology
ZHANG, ZHENGHE, Economic Management
ZHANG, ZHENXIAN, Agronomy and Biotechnology
ZHANG, ZHONGJUN, Agronomy and Biotechnology
ZHANG, ZHONGZHI, Veterinary Medicine
ZHAO, DEMING, Veterinary Medicine
ZHAO, GUANGYONG, Animal Science and Technology
ZHAO, LIANGJUN, Agronomy and Biotechnology
ZHAO, MING, Agronomy and Biotechnology
ZHENG, DAWEI, Resources and the Environment
ZHENG, HANG, Biological Sciences
ZHOU, HE, Animal Science and Technology
ZHU, DAOLIN, Resources and the Environment
ZHU, DEHAI, Information and Electrical Engineering
ZHU, DEJU, Resources and the Environment
ZHU, QIZHEN, Humanities and Development
ZHU, SHIEN, Animal Science and Technology
ZUO, QIANG, Resources and the Environment
ZUO, TING, Humanities and Development

CHINA CENTRAL RADIO AND TELEVISION UNIVERSITY

160 Fuxingmen Nei St, Beijing 100031
Telephone: (10) 66412407
E-mail: fao@crtvu.edu.cn
Internet: www.crtvu.edu.cn
Founded 1979 on the 'open univ.' principle
State control
Academic year: September to July
44 Provincial campuses, 961 br. schools
Pres.: ZHANG YAOXUE
Vice-Pres.: RUAN ZHIYONG
Vice-Pres.: SUN LUYI
Vice-Pres.: YAN BING
Vice-Pres.: YU YUNXIU
Library Dir: SUN LUYI
Library of 100,000 vols (CRTVU), 32,869,000 vols (provinces)
Number of teachers: 188 full-time, 565 part-time (CRTVU)
Number of teachers: 42,500 full-time, 31,500 part-time (provinces)
Number of students: 2,300,000
Publication: *Distance Education in China* (6 a year)

CHINA FOREIGN AFFAIRS UNIVERSITY

24 Zhanlan Rd, Xicheng, Beijing 100037
Internet: www.cfau.edu.cn

Founded 1955

Academic year: September to July

Pres.: WU JIANMING
Vice-Pres.: QIN YAQING
Vice-Pres.: QU XING
Head of Graduate Dept: ZHENG QIRONG
Vice-Librarian: JIAN LEYI

Library of 23,500
Number of teachers: 170
Number of students: 1,600

Publication: *Journal* (4 a year)

DEANS

English: FAN SHOUYI
Foreign Affairs: ZHANG LILI
International Economics: JIANG RUIPING
International Law: JIN KESHENG

PROFESSORS

CHU, GUANGYOU, English
FAN, SHOUYI, English
HUANG, JINQI, English
JIANG, RUIPING, International Economics
QIN, YAQING, English
QU, XING, Foreign Affairs
REN, XIAOPING, English
SU, HAO, Foreign Affairs
WANG, SHAOREN, English
XIONG, ZHIYONG, Foreign Affairs
YANG, XUEYAN, English
YUAN, SHIBING, English
ZHANG, LILI, Foreign Affairs
ZHANG, YITING, English
ZHENG, QIRONG, Foreign Affairs

CHINA MEDICAL UNIVERSITY

Bei Er Rd, He Ping Dist., Shenyang 110001, Liaoning Province
Telephone: (24) 23265491
Internet: www.cmu.edu.cn

Founded 1931

Provincial Dept of Education control

Academic year: September to July

Pres.: ZHAO QUN
Vice-Pres.: HAN MINTAN
Vice-Pres.: HE QINCHENG
Vice-Pres.: SUN BAOZHI
Vice-Pres.: ZHAO LIKUI
Head of Graduate Dept: ZHAO QUN
Librarian: NENG DIZHI

Number of teachers: 6,126
Number of students: 19,602 (11,094 full-time, 8,508 part-time)

Publications: *Chinese Journal of Health Statistics* (6 a year), *Chinese Journal of Practical Ophthalmology* (12 a year), *Journal* (6 a year), *Journal of China Clinical Medical Imaging* (4 a year), *Liaoning Journal of Pharmacy and Clinical Remedies* (4 a year), *Liaoning Journal of Practical Diabetology* (4 a year), *Paediatric Emergency Medicine* (4 a year), *Practical Journal for Rural Doctors* (6 a year), *Progress of Anatomical Sciences* (4 a year), *Progress in Japanese Medicine* (12 a year)

DEANS

College of Basic Medical Sciences: BAI SHULING
College of Nursing: LI XIAOHAN
College of Public Health: SUN GUIFAN
Department of Information Management and Information Systems: ZHAO YUHONG
Department of Social Science: GUO SHUYING
Faculty of Forensic Medicine: WANG BAOJIE
First Clinical College and First Affiliated Hospital: LI JIGUANG
Fourth Clinical College and Fourth Affiliated Hospital: HAN JIANPING
School of Pharmacy: JIN XIN
School of Stomatology and Affiliated Stomatological Hospital: AI HONGJUN
Second Clinical College and Second Affiliated Hospital: GUO QIYONG
Third Clinical College and Third Affiliated Hospital: XU JIANJUN

PROFESSORS

AI, HONGJUN, Stomatology
AN, XHUNLI, Basic Medical Sciences
BAI, SHULING, Basic Medical Sciences
BAO, ZHONGXIAO, Basic Medical Sciences
CAI, JINGYUAN, First Clinical College
CAI, JIQUN, Basic Medical Sciences
CAI, YUAN, Public Health
CAI, ZHIDAO, First Clinical College
CAO, YAMING, Basic Medical Sciences
CHANG, TIANHUI, Basic Medical Sciences
CHEN, HONGDUO, First Clinical College
CHEN, JUNQING, First Clinical College
CHEN, LIANG, First Clinical College
CHEN, SHUZHENG, Second Clinical College
CHEN, YUHUA, Basic Medical Sciences
CHU, HANG, First Clinical College
CUI, JIANJUN, Second Clinical College
CUI, LEI, Information Management and Information Systems
DAI, XIANWEI, Second Clinical College
DENG, XIANGDONG, First Clinical College
DENG, YAN, Stomatology
DING, LUOLAN, First Clinical College
DING, MEI, Forensic Medicine
DONG, XIAOJIE, Basic Medical Sciences
DONG, YULAN, Basic Medical Sciences
DU, XUEBIN, Social Science
DUAN, ZHIQUAN, First Clinical College
FAN, GUANGYU, First Clinical College
FAN, SHUDUO, Basic Medical Sciences
FANG, JINWU, First Clinical College
FANG, XIUBIN, Basic Medical Sciences
FU, BAOYU, First Clinical College
GAO, DIANWEN, Second Clinical College
GU, CHUNJIU, First Clinical College
GUAN, DAWEI, Forensic Medicine
GUO, DUISHAN, Second Clinical College
GUO, SHUYING, Social Science
HAN, JIANPING, Fourth Clinical College
HAN, YUKUN, Second Clinical College
HE, AN'GUANG, First Clinical College
HE, QINCHENG, Information Management and Information Systems
HE, SANGUANG, First Clinical College
HE, XIUQIN, First Clinical College
HONG, JIAKANG, Basic Medical Sciences
HONG, YANG, Basic Medical Sciences
HOU, XIANGMING, First Clinical College
HUANG, JIANQUN, First Clinical College
JI, SHIJUN, Second Clinical College
JIA, XINSHAN, Basic Medical Sciences
JIANG, RUOLAN, First Clinical College
JIN, CHUNLIAN, Basic Medical Sciences
JIN, WANBAO, Basic Medical Sciences
JIN, XIN, Pharmacy
LI, FUCAO, Basic Medical Sciences
LI, HOUWEN, First Clinical College
LI, JIGUANG, First Clinical College
LI, JINMING, Basic Medical Sciences
LI, LIYUN, First Clinical College
LI, SHAOYING, First Clinical College
LI, SHUQIN, Second Clinical College
LI, XIAOHAN, Nursing
LI, XINGYUAN, Second Clinical College
LI, XIULLING, First Clinical College
LI, YAN, Second Clinical College
LI, YUQUAN, Second Clinical College
LI, ZHENCHUN, Stomatology
LI, ZHENG, Second Clinical College
LI, ZHI, Basic Medical Sciences
LI, ZHUQIN, First Clinical College
LIU, CHUNRONG, First Clinical College
LIU, ENJIE, Basic Medical Sciences
LIU, ENQING, Second Clinical College
LIU, GUOLIANG, First Clinical College
LIU, HONGQIN, Second Clinical College
LIU, JUHUI, Forensic Medicine
LIU, JUNTING, Forensic Medicine
LIU, JUNTING, Pharmacy
LIU, LANQING, Second Clinical College
LIU, LIMIN, Forensic Medicine
LIU, SHUJIE, Stomatology
LIU, XIUMEI, First Clinical College
LIU, YANG, Public Health
LIU, YINGMIN, Second Clinical College
LIU, ZHENLIN, Public Health
LU, CHANGLONG, Basic Medical Sciences
LU, JINGMING, Second Clinical College
LU, SHENGMIN, Second Clinical College
MENG, FANHAO, Pharmacy
MU, HUACHUN, Basic Medical Sciences
PAN, YAPING, Stomatology
PAN, ZHIMIN, First Clinical College
PANG, XINING, Basic Medical Sciences
PEI, ZHUGUO, Second Clinical College
PIAO, AIYING, Second Clinical College
QIU, XUESHAN, Basic Medical Sciences
QU, MING, First Clinical College
REN, CHONG, First Clinical College
SHEN, KUI, First Clinical College
SHI, LIDE, Basic Medical Sciences
SHI, YUXIU, Basic Medical Sciences
SONG, FANGJI, First Clinical College
SONG, JIJIE, Basic Medical Sciences
SONG, JINDAN, Basic Medical Sciences
SONG, MIN, Basic Medical Sciences
SUN, GUIFAN, Public Health
SUN, GUIYUAN, Basic Medical Sciences
SUN, JIANCHUN, Second Clinical College
SUN, KAILAI, Basic Medical Sciences
SUN, LIGUANG, Basic Medical Sciences
TANG, HAO, Basic Medical Sciences
TIAN, XUSHENG, Basic Medical Sciences
WANG, BAOJIE, Forensic Medicine
WANG, CHUN, Fourth Clinical College
WANG, DEWEN, Forensic Medicine
WANG, DEZHI, Second Clinical College
WANG, ENHUA, Basic Medical Sciences
WANG, GUIZHEN, Basic Medical Sciences
WANG, HAIPENG, Basic Medical Sciences
WANG, HAIYI, Second Clinical College
WANG, HE, Basic Medical Sciences
WANG, HONGDA, First Clinical College
WANG, HUAILIANG, Basic Medical Sciences
WANG, HUIZHEN, Second Clinical College
WANG, LIANYING, Second Clinical College
WANG, LIJUN, Second Clinical College
WANG, LIYU, Social Science
WANG, MINGQIAN, Second Clinical College
WANG, SHUBAO, First Clinical College
WANG, SHULAN, First Clinical College
WANG, TIE, Second Clinical College
WANG, WEILIN, Second Clinical College
WANG, XINGDUO, First Clinical College
WANG, XUEYING, Second Clinical College
WANG, YANFENG, Second Clinical College
WANG, YUXIN, Stomatology
WANG, ZHAOGUAN, Second Clinical College
WANG, ZHAOYUAN, Stomatology
WEI, KELUN, Second Clinical College
WU, BAOMIN, Second Clinical College
WU, HUAZHANG, Social Science
WU, JINGTIAN, First Clinical College
WU, KEGUANG, Second Clinical College
WU, YIJIANG, Fourth Clinical College
WU, YINGYU, Second Clinical College
WU, ZHENHUA, Second Clinical College
XIE, HUIFANG, Second Clinical College
XU, ZHAOFA, Public Health
XU, ZHENXING, First Clinical College
XUE, XINDONG, Second Clinical College
XUE, YIXUE, Basic Medical Sciences
YANG, GUORUI, First Clinical College
YANG, JUN, Public Health
YANG, SHILIN, Second Clinical College
YANG, XIANGHONG, Basic Medical Sciences
YANG, XIAODONG, Stomatology
YANG, YUXIU, First Clinical College
YAO, XINGJIA, Public Health
YIN, HONGNIAN, First Clinical College
YIN, SHUGUO, Second Clinical College

YU, BINGXHI, Basic Medical Sciences
YU, RUNJIANG, First Clinical College
YUAN, ZHUANG, Second Clinical College
ZENG, DINGYIN, First Clinical College
ZHA, HONGYAN, Basic Medical Sciences
ZHANG, DAORONG, Basic Medical Sciences
ZHANG, GANZHONG, First Clinical College
ZHANG, HAIPENG, Basic Medical Sciences
ZHANG, HONG, Basic Medical Sciences
ZHANG, JIAXING, Second Clinical College
ZHANG, JINGRONG, First Clinical College
ZHANG, LIFENG, Basic Medical Sciences
ZHANG, SHULAN, Second Clinical College
ZHANG, XUE, Basic Medical Sciences
ZHAO, CHONGZHI, Second Clinical College
ZHAO, GUIZHEN, Second Clinical College
ZHAO, GUOGUI, Second Clinical College
ZHAO, LIJUAN, First Clinical College
ZHAO, SHUFENG, Basic Medical Sciences
ZHAO, SHUXIA, Second Clinical College
ZHAO, YKUN, Basic Medical Sciences
ZHAO, YUHONG, Information Management and Information Systems
ZHONG, MING, Stomatology
ZHOU, BAOSEN, Public Health
ZHOU, WEI, Social Science
ZHOU, XIJING, First Clinical College
ZHOU, YONGDE, Second Clinical College
ZHU, LIPING, Basic Medical Sciences

CHINA PHARMACEUTICAL UNIVERSITY

Xuan Wu Men, Yan Zi Ji, Nanjing 210009, Jiangsu Province
Telephone: (25) 3271319
Internet: www.cpu.edu.cn

Founded 1936
Min. of Education Control
Academic year: September to July

Pres.: WU XIAOMING
Vice-Pres.: LI FENGWEN
Vice-Pres.: PAN YUJIAN
Vice-Pres.: WANG GUANGJI
Vice-Pres.: ZHANG XIAOLIAN
Head of Graduate Dept: CHU MINZUO
Librarian: MA SHIPING

Library of 700,000 vols
Number of teachers: 610
Number of students: 8,880

Publications: *Journal of China Pharmaceutical University* (6 a year), *Medical Evolution* (6 a year), *Medicine Annual of China*, *Medicine Education* (4 a year)

DEANS

Basic Institute: TAO LU
Department of Foreign Languages: DU HUI
Institute of Physical Education: WANG YONGTAO
School of Biological Pharmacy: WANG WEN
School of Economics and Economic School of International Medicine: GU HAI
Schools of Medicine and Chinese Traditional Medicine: KONG LINGYI

PROFESSORS

DAI, DEZAI, Medicine
GAO, SHANLIN, Chinese Traditional Medicine
GAO, XIANGDONG, Biological Pharmacy
GU, HAI, Economic School of International Medicine
HU, YUZHU
HUA, WEIYI, Medicine
HUANG, WENLONG, Medicine
JI, HUI, Medicine
JI, MIN, Medicine
KONG, LINGYI, Chinese Traditional Medicine
LIANG, JINGYU, Chinese Traditional Medicine
LIU, JINGJING, Biological Pharmacy
LIU, WENYING, Medicine
LIU, XIAODONG, Chinese Traditional Medicine
LIU, XIAODONG, Medicine
MA, SHIPING, Chinese Traditional Medicine
NI, KUNYI
PENG, SIXUN, Medicine
PING, QINENG, Medicine
QIAN, ZHIYU, Medicine
SHAO, RONG, Economic School of International Medicine
SHEN, ZILONG, Biological Pharmacy
TU, SHUCI, Medicine
WANG, GUANGJI, Medicine
WANG, QIUJUAN, Medicine
WANG, WEN, Biological Pharmacy
WU, WUTONG, Biological Pharmacy
WU, XIAOMING, Medicine
XI, TAO, Biological Pharmacy
XIANG, BINGREN
YANG, ZHONGLIN, Chinese Traditional Medicine
YE, WENCAI, Chinese Traditional Medicine
YOU, QIDONG, Medicine
YU, BOYANG, Chinese Traditional Medicine
ZHANG, LUYONG, Medicine
ZHANG, YIHUA, Medicine
ZHANG, ZHENGHANG, Medicine
ZHOU, JIANPING, Medicine
ZHU, DANNI, Chinese Traditional Medicine
ZHU, JIABI, Medicine

CHINA UNIVERSITY OF GEOSCIENCES (WUHAN)

Yujiashan, 388 Lumo Rd, Wuhan 430074, Hubei Province
Telephone: (27) 87481030
E-mail: xb@dns.cug.edu.cn
Internet: www.cug.edu.cn

Founded 1952
Academic year: September to July

21 Colleges which offer 49 Bachelors degree courses, 65 Masters degree courses and 30 doctoral courses

Pres.: ZHANG, JINGAO
Vice-Pres.: OUYANG JIANPING
Vice-Pres.: WANG YANXIN
Vice-Pres.: XING XIANGQIN
Vice-Pres.: YAO SHUZHEN

Library of 1,167,000 vols, 3,852 periodicals
Number of teachers: 2,800
Number of students: 23,600

Publications: *Chinese Journal of Engineering Geophysics*, *Earth Science*, *Geological Science and Technology Information*, *Journal of China University of Geosciences* (in English and Chinese), *Journal of Geoscience Translations*

CHINA UNIVERSITY OF MINING AND TECHNOLOGY

Xuzhou 221008, Jiangsu Province
Telephone: (516) 3885745
Internet: www.cumt.edu.cn

Founded 1909
State control
Academic year: September to July

Pres.: Prof. XIE HEPING
Vice-Pres.: Prof. GE SHIRONG
Vice-Pres.: Prof. KE WENJIN
Vice-Pres.: Prof. LUO CHENG XUAN
Vice-Pres.: Prof. SUNG XUEFENG
Vice-Pres.: Prof. WANG JIANPING
Vice-Pres.: Prof. WANG YUEHAN
Registrar: Prof. XING YONGCHANG
Dir for Int. Div.: ZHENG ZHENKANG
Librarian: Prof. TANG YI

Library of 330,000 vols
Number of teachers: 3,817
Number of students: 30,942

Publication: *Journal* (4 a year in Chinese, 2 a year in English)

HEADS OF ACADEMIC DIVISIONS

College of Adult Education: ZHANG FUSHENG
College of Applied Science and Technology: FAN ZHONGQI
Department of Physical Education: CHI ZHONGJUN
School of Architecture and Civil Engineering: ZHOU GUOQING
School of Chemical Engineering: LIU JIONGTIAN
School of Computer Science and Technology: XIA SHIXIONG
School of Environment and Spatial Informatics: HAN BAOPING
School of Foreign Studies: YANG SHU
School of Information and Electrical Engineering: JIANG JIANGUO
School of Mechatronic and Materials Engineering: DUAN XIONG
School of Mineral and Energy Resources Engineering: CAI QINGXIANG
School of Resources and Geoscience: LIN JIAN
School of Management: NIE RUI
School of Politics, Literature and Law: WANG YAN
School of Science: MIAO XIEXIN

CHINA UNIVERSITY OF PETROLEUM

2 North Rd, Dongying 257061, Shandong Province
Telephone: (546) 8392241
Internet: www.hdpu.edu.cn

Founded 1953
State control
Academic year: September to July

Pres.: TONG ZHAOQI
Vice-Pres: SHAN HONGHONG
Vice-Pres: SUN HAIFENG
Vice-Pres: TONG XINHUA
Vice-Pres: WANG RUIHE
Vice-Pres: ZHA MING
Head of Graduate Dep: WANG RUIHE
Librarian: ZHANG ZHONGXUE

Number of teachers: 1,000
Number of students: 23,500

Publication: *Journal of China University of Petroleum* (6 a year)

DEANS

College of Architecture, Transport and Storage Engineering: ZHANG GUOZHONG
College of Chemistry and Chemical Engineering: JIN YOUHAI
College of Computer and Communication Engineering: DUAN YOUXIANG
College of Economic Administration: ZHANG ZAIXU
College of Foreign Languages: LUAN SHUWEN
College of Geo-Resources and Information: YIN XINGYAO
College of Humanities and Social Science: XIA CHONGYA
College of Information and Control Engineering: TIAN XUEMING
College of Mathematics and Computer Science: LI WEIGUO
College of Mechanical and Electronic Engineering: QI MINGXIA
College of Petroleum Engineering: YAO JUN
College of Physical Education: WEI RULI
College of Physics, Science and Technology: GUAN JITENG

PROFESSORS

BAI, LIANPING, Information and Control Engineering
CHAO, KE, Humanities and Social Science
CHEN, GANGHUA, Geo-Resources and Information
CHEN, JIANMIN, Petroleum Engineering
CHEN, SHIYUE, Geo-Resources and Information
CHEN, YUEMING, Petroleum Engineering
CHENG, YUANFANG, Petroleum Engineering

DAI, JUNSHENG, Geo-Resources and Information
DU, JINLIANG, Humanities and Social Science
FAN, YIREN, Geo-Resources and Information
FANG, JIANHUI, Physics, Science and Technology
GAO, YIFA, Petroleum Engineering
GUAN, ZHICHUAN, Petroleum Engineering
GUANG, JITENG, Physics, Science and Technology
HAN, ZHIYONG, Petroleum Engineering
HE, LIMIN, Architecture, Transport and Storage Engineering
JIA, RUIGAO, Physics, Science and Technology
JIANG, HUA, Humanities and Social Science
JIANG, YOULU, Geo-Resources and Information
JIANG, ZAIXING, Geo-Resources and Information
JIN, QIANG, Geo-Resources and Information
LI, GUOHUA, Physical Education
LI, HANLIN, Geo-Resources and Information
LI, MINGZHONG, Petroleum Engineering
LI, SHURONG, Information and Control Engineering
LI, WEIGUO, Mathematics and Computational Science
LI, YUANCHENG, Physics, Science and Technology
LI, YUXING, Architecture, Transport and Storage Engineering
LI, ZHAOMIN, Petroleum Engineering
LI, ZILI, Architecture, Transport and Storage Engineering
LIANG, JINGUO, Architecture, Transport and Storage Engineering
LIN, CHENGYAN, Geo-Resources and Information
LIU, HUIQING, Petroleum Engineering
LIU, RUNHUA, Information and Control Engineering
LIU, ZHAN, Geo-Resources and Information
LUAN, SHUWEN, Foreign Languages
MA, XIGENG, Information and Control Engineering
MEN, FUDIAN, Physics, Science and Technology
QIU, SHIWEI, Architecture, Transport and Storage Engineering
QIU, ZHENGSONG, Petroleum Engineering
SHAN, YIXIAN, Information and Control Engineering
SHEN, ZHONGHOU, Petroleum Engineering
SHU, HENGMU, Architecture, Transport and Storage Engineering
SONG, DESHENG, Foreign Languages
SUN, BAOJIANG, Petroleum Engineering
SUN, JIANMENG, Geo-Resources and Information
SUN, XIULI, Foreign Languages
TIAN, XUEMIN, Information and Control Engineering
WAN, JIANHUA, Geo-Resources and Information
WANG, HUAQIN, Foreign Languages
WANG, JIANJUN, Humanities and Social Science
WANG, QINGTING, Foreign Languages
WANG, RUIHE, Petroleum Engineering
WANG, SHUTING, Foreign Languages
WANG, WEIFENG, Geo-Resources and Information
WANG, YANJIANG, Information and Control Engineering
WANG, YONGGANG, Geo-Resources and Information
XIA, CHONGYA, Humanities and Social Science
XING, LIANJUN, Physical Education
XU, MINGHAI, Architecture, Transport and Storage Engineering
XU, YIJI, Petroleum Engineering
XUE, SHIFENG, Architecture, Transport and Storage Engineering
YAN, XIANGZHEN, Architecture, Transport and Storage Engineering
YANG, DEWEI, Architecture, Transport and Storage Engineering
YANG, SHAOCHUN, Geo-Resources and Information
YANG, WEI, Physics, Science and Technology
YAO, JUN, Petroleum Engineering
YIN, XINGYAO, Geo-Resources and Information
YU, RANGANG, Architecture, Transport and Storage Engineering
YU, ZHAOXIAN, Physics, Science and Technology
YUAN, HONGCHAN, Foreign Languages
ZHAN, YONGLIANG, Architecture, Transport and Storage Engineering
ZHANG, GUOZHONG, Architecture, Transport and Storage Engineering
ZHANG, JIASHENG, Information and Control Engineering
ZHANG, QI, Petroleum Engineering
ZHANG, RONGHUA, Humanities and Social Science
ZHANG, ZHAOHUI, Information and Control Engineering
ZHAO, FULIN, Petroleum Engineering
ZHAO, XIUTAI, Petroleum Engineering
ZHAO, XIYU, Humanities and Social Science
ZHAO, YONGJUN, Geo-Resources and Information
ZHENG, JINWU, Information and Control Engineering
ZHONG, JIANHUA, Geo-Resources and Information
ZHOU, DETIAN, Humanities and Social Science
ZHOU, XIAOJUN, Petroleum Engineering
ZHOU, YAOQI, Geo-Resources and Information

CHINA UNIVERSITY OF POLITICAL SCIENCE AND LAW

Yuanyuan Rd, Chang Ping, Beijing 102249
Telephone: (10) 69745577
Internet: www.cupl.edu.cn

Founded 1952
State control
Academic year: September to July

Pres.: XU XIANMING
Vice-Pres.: JIE ZHANYUAN
Vice-Pres.: MA KANGMEI
Vice-Pres.: ZHANG BAOSHENG
Vice-Pres.: ZHANG GUILIN
Vice-Pres.: ZHANG LIUHUA
Head of Graduate Dept: ZHU YONG
Librarian: ZENG ERSHU

Number of teachers: 1,400
Number of students: 21,325

Publications: *Journal of China University of Political Science and Law (Tribune of Political Science and Law)* (6 a year), *Journal of Comparative Law* (6 a year)

DEANS

Business School: SUN XUANZHONG
Criminal and Judicial School: WANG MU
International Law School: WANG CHUANLI
Law School: MA HUAIDE
School of American and Comparative Law: XU CHUANXI
School of Foreign Languages: LI LI
School of German and Comparative Law: MI JIAN
School of Political and Public Management: ZHU WEIJIU

PROFESSORS

CAI, DINGJIAN, Law
CAI, TUO, Political and Public Management
CHE, HU, American and Comparative Law
CHEN, GUANGZHONG, Procedural Law
CHEN, HONGTAI, Political and Public Management
CHEN, LIJUN, Law
CHENG, XIAOXIANG, International Law
CONG, RIYUN, Political and Public Management
CUI, YONGDONG, Law
DING, MEI, German and Comparative Law
DONG, SHUJUN, Criminal and Judicial Law
DU, XINLI, International Law
DUAN, DONGHUI, International Law
FAN, CHONGYI, Procedural Law
FENG, XIA, International Law
GAO, JIAWEI, German and Comparative Law
GU, YONGZHONG, Procedural Law
HAO, WEIHUA, American and Comparative Law
HE, JIAHONG, Procedural Law
HONG, DAODE, Criminal and Judicial Law
HOU, TINGZHI, Business School
HU, WENZHENG, Business School
HUANG, DAOXIU, Foreign Languages
HUANG, YISI, Foreign Languages
JIANG, RUJIAO, International Law
JIAO, HONGCHANG, Law
JIAO, MEIZHEN, Foreign Languages
LANG, PEIJUAN, Law
LE, GUOAN, Criminal and Judicial Law
LI, JUQIAN, International Law
LI, LI, Foreign Languages
LI, MING, Research of Legal Historiography
LI, WEI, International Law
LI, XIAO, Business School
LIN, QIAN, Research of Legal Historiography
LIU, BANGHUI, Criminal and Judicial Law
LIU, CHANGMIN, Political and Public Management
LIU, GENJU, Criminal and Judicial Law
LIU, GUANGAN, Research of Legal Historiography
LIU, HONGYING, Law
LIU, JINGUO, Law
LIU, JUNSHENG, Political and Public Management
LIU, LI, International Law
LIU, MU, Criminal and Judicial Law
LIU, SHANCHUN, Law
LIU, SHEN, Law
LONG, MENGHUI, Foreign Languages
MA, CHENGYUAN, International Law
MA, HUAIDE, Law
MA, ZHIBING, Research of Legal Historiography
MI, JIAN, German and Comparative Law
MO, SHIJIAN, International Law
PAN, QIN, Criminal and Judicial Law
PENG, YANAN, American and Comparative Law
QI, DONGXIANG, American and Comparative Law
QI, XIANGQUAN, International Law
QU, CHAOLI, Political and Public Management
QU, XINJIU, Criminal and Judicial Law
RUAN, QILIN, Criminal and Judicial Law
SHI, XIAOLI, International Law
SHI, YAJUN, Political and Public Management
SHU, GUOYING, German and Comparative Law
SONG, YINGHUI, Procedural Law
SUN, XUANZHONG, Business School
WANG, CHUANLI, International Law
WANG, JIANCHENG, Procedural Law
WANG, JIANXIN, Political and Public Management
WANG, JIE, Law
WANG, MU, Criminal and Judicial Law
WANG, RENBO, Law
WANG, SHUNAN, Criminal and Judicial Law
WU, MINGYANG, Business School
XIAO, JIANHUA, Procedural Law
XIN, CHONGYANG, International Law
XU, CHUANXI, American and Comparative Law
XU, HAIMING, International Law
XU, HAOMING, German and Comparative Law
XU, SHIHONG, Institute of Legal Ancient Books Arrangement
XUAN, ZENGYI, International Law
XUE, GANGLING, Law

YANG, FAN, Business School
YANG, FAN, International Law
YANG, RONGXIN, Procedural Law
YANG, YANG, Political and Public Management
YANG, YUGUAN, Procedural Law, German and Comparative Law
YUE, LILING, German and Comparative Law
ZHANG, GUILIN, Political and Public Management
ZHANG, GUOJUN, Business School
ZHANG, JINFAN, Research of Legal Historiography
ZHANG, LI, International Law
ZHANG, LIYING, International Law
ZHANG, SHENG, Law
ZHANG, SHUYI, Law
ZHANG, XIAOMU, International Law
ZHANG, ZHONGQIU, Research of Legal Historiography
ZHAO, BAOCHENG, Criminal and Judicial Law
ZHAO, WEI, International Law
ZHAO, XIANGLIN, International Law
ZHAO, YIMIN, International Law
ZHENG, XIANWEN, Institute of Legal Ancient Books Arrangement
ZHENG, YONGLIU, German and Comparative Law
ZHOU, JIANHAI, International Law
ZHOU, ZHONGHAI, International Law
ZHU, JIANGENG, International Law
ZHU, WEIJIU, Political and Public Management
ZHU, YONG, Research of Legal Historiography
ZHU, ZIQIN, International Law

CHINESE TRADITIONAL OPERA COLLEGE

3 Li Ren St, 100054 Beijing
Telephone: (10) 63535156
Founded 1978
Pres.: YU LIN
Vice-Pres.: GE SHILIANG
Vice-Pres.: ZHU WENXIANG
Librarian: LIU SHIYUAN
Library of 150,000 vols
Number of teachers: 246
Number of students: 329
Publication: *Traditional Opera Art* (4 a year)

CHONGQING UNIVERSITY

Chongqing, 400044
Telephone: (23) 65102391
E-mail: fao@cqu.edu.cn
Internet: www.cqu.edu.cn
Founded 1929
State control
Languages of instruction: Chinese, English
Academic year: February to January
Pres.: Prof. LIN JIANHUA
Vice-Pres.: Prof. LIU QING
Librarian: TANG YIKE
Library: 3.6m. vols
Number of teachers: 5,800
Number of students: 48,000
Publication: *Journal* (8 a year)

DEANS

Faculty of Architecture: Prof. ZHANG SIPING
Faculty of Arts and Science: Acad. WU YUNDONG
Faculty of Communication: Prof. HUANG ZONGMING
Faculty of Engineering: Prof. LIU QING
Law School: Prof. CHEN ZHONGLIN
School of Economics and Business Administration: Prof. LIU XING

CHONGQING UNIVERSITY OF MEDICAL SCIENCES

1 Medicine Rd, Yu Zhong, Chongqing 400046
Telephone: (23) 68804034
Internet: www.cqums.edu.cn
Founded 1956
Academic year: September to July
Pres.: LEI HAN
Vice-Pres.: DENG SHIXIONG
Vice-Pres.: DONG ZHI
Vice-Pres.: HUANG AILONG
Vice-Pres.: WANG LIHUA
Vice-Pres.: XIE PENG
Librarian: LU CHANGHONG
Library of 570,000 vols
Number of teachers: 4,374
Number of students: 8,923
Publications: *Chinese Journal of Hepatology* (6 a year), *Journal of Chongqing Medical University* (6 a year), *Journal of Paediatric Pharmacy* (6 a year), *Journal of Ultrasound in Clinical Medicine* (6 a year), *Research in Medical Education* (6 a year)

DEANS

College of Basic Medicine: WANG YAPING
Department of Biomedical Engineering: WANG ZHIBIAO
Department of Medical Examining: TU ZHIGUANG
Department of Medical Imaging: REN HONG
Department of Reproductive Medical Science: WANG YINGXIONG
Institute of Humanity and Social Science: FENG ZHEYONG

PROFESSORS

CHEN, SHOUTIAN, Medical Imaging
CONG, YULONG, Medical Examining
DAI, YONG, Medical Examining
DONG, ZHI, Pharmacy
FENG, ZHEYONG, Humanities and Social Science
HU, GUOHU, Basic Medicine
JIANG, JIKAI, Medical Examining
KANG, GEFEI, Medical Examining
LEI, PEIYING, Medical Imaging
LEI, XIAOKUN, Humanities and Social Science
LI, HUIZHI, Pharmacy
LI, QINGEN, Pharmacy
LI, SHAOLIN, Basic Medicine
LIU, DAWEI, Preventive Medicine
LU, CHANGHONG, Basic Medicine
LUO, JIA, Medical Imaging
LUO, YUNPENG, Basic Medicine
MI, CAN, Basic Medicine
NING, BAODONG, Basic Medicine
PENG, HUIMING, Basic Medicine
QIU, ZONGYING, Pharmacy
QUAN, XUEMO, Medical Imaging
REN, HONG, Medical Imaging
SONG, FANGZHOU, Basic Medicine
SUN, SHANQUAN, Basic Medicine
TANG, SIJIE, Basic Medicine
TANG, WEIXUE, Basic Medicine
TU, ZHIGUANG, Medical Examining
WANG, RUIHUA, Preventive Medicine
WANG, WEIWEI, Basic Medicine
WANG, YANG, Preventive Medicine
WANG, YAPING, Basic Medicine
WANG, YINGXIONG, Reproductive Medical Science
WANG, ZHIBIAO, Biomedical Engineering
WANG, ZHIGANG, Medical Imaging
WU, FENG, Biomedical Engineering
XIANG, LIKE, Basic Medicine
XIE, ZHENGXIANG, Basic Medicine
YANG, ZHENGWEI, Basic Medicine
YANG, ZHIBANG, Basic Medicine
YI, YONGFENG, Basic Medicine
YU, YU, Basic Medicine
ZHANG, NENG, Basic Medicine
ZHAO, JIANNONG, Medical Imaging
ZHENG, ZHAOCHUN, Basic Medicine
ZHOU, CHENGHE, Pharmacy
ZHOU, JIANZHONG, Medical Imaging
ZHOU, QIXIN, Basic Medicine
ZHU, DAOYIN, Basic Medicine

DALIAN MARITIME UNIVERSITY

1 Linghai Rd, Dalian 116026, Liaoning Province
Telephone: (411) 84727149
E-mail: iceodmu@gmail.com
Internet: www.dlmu.edu.cn
Founded 1909
State control
Academic year: September to July
Pres.: Prof. WU ZHAOLIN
Vice-Pres.: Dr SUN LICHENG
Vice-Pres.: Dr SUN PEITING
Vice-Pres.: WEN XIAOQIN
Registrar: WANG YUEHUI
Librarian: PANG FUWEN
Number of teachers: 728
Number of students: 12,722
Publications: *Higher Education Research in Areas of Communications* (2 a year), *Journal* (6 a year), *Liaoning Navigation* (4 a year), *World Shipping* (6 a year)

DEANS

Adult Education College: DING YONG
Automation and Electrical Engineering College: WANG XINGCHEN
Business College: FAN HOUMING
Computer Science and Technology College: ZHANG WEISHI
Electronic Information College: ZHANG SHUFANG
Environmental Science and Engineering College: DING YONGSHENG
Humanities and Social Sciences College: FENG WENHUA
International Cooperation College: ZHANG SHIPPING
Law College: QU GUANGQING
Marine Engineering College: REN GUANG
Navigation College: DONG FANG
Shipping Management College: YANG ZHAN

DALIAN UNIVERSITY OF TECHNOLOGY (DUT)

2 Linggong Rd, Ganjingzi Dist., Dalian 116023, Liaoning Province
Telephone: (411) 4678300
E-mail: dut@dlut.edu.cn
Internet: www.dlut.edu.cn
Founded 1949 as Dalian Institute of Technology
State control
Academic year: September to July
Units incl. 14 schools, 50 research institutes and 4 Nat. Key Laboratories
Pres.: Prof. CHENG GENGDONG
Vice-Pres.: Prof. JIANG DEXUE
Vice-Pres.: Prof. KONG XIANJING
Vice-Pres.: Prof. SHEN HONGSHU
Vice-Pres.: Prof. WANG LIANSHENG
Vice-Pres.: Prof. XUE GUANG
Librarian: XIE MAOZHAO
Library of 1,840,000 vols, 8,000 periodicals
Number of teachers: 1,297
Number of students: 22,344 (incl. 5,883 postgraduate)
Publications: *Journal* (6 a year), *Journal of Computational Mechanics* (4 a year), *Journal of Mathematical Research and Exposition* (4 a year), *Journal of Social Sciences* (4 a year)

DAQING PETROLEUM INSTITUTE

Daqing 151400, Heilongjiang Province
Telephone: (459) 4653232

Internet: www.dqpi.net
Founded 1960
State control
Academic year: September to July
Pres.: LIU YANG
Vice-Pres.: LIU YONG JIAN
Vice-Pres.: LU YAN FANG
Vice-Pres.: SONG ZHI CHEN
Vice-Pres.: YANG XIAO LONG
Number of teachers: 1,762
Number of students: 10,000
Publications: *Journal* (4 a year), *Petroleum Industry Technology* (4 a year)

DEANS

College of Building Construction Engineering: SUN JIAN GANG
College of Computing and Information Technology: MA RUI MIN
College of Continuing Education: ZHAO JIN LIN
College of Earth Sciences: SHI SHANG MING
College of Economics and Management: SHAO QIANG
College of Electricity and Information Engineering: DUAN YU BO
College of Electronic Engineering: WANG MING JI
College of Foreign Languages: QIU XUE HE
College of Humanities: KUAN JIN LIN
College of Mathematics: WANG SHOU TIAN
College of Mechanical Science and Engineering: WANG ZUN CE
College of Oil Engineering Institute: CUI HAI QING

PROFESSORS

AI, CHI, Oil Engineering
BAI, XING HUA, Earth Sciences
CAO, YU QUAN, Electricity and Information Engineering
CHANG, YU LIAN, Mechanical Science and Engineering
CHEN, TAO PING, Oil Engineering
CHEN, XUE MEI, Mechanical Science and Engineering
CUI, HAI QING, Oil Engineering
CUI, ZHEN HUA, Mechanical Science and Engineering
DAI, GUANG, Mechanical Science and Engineering
DU, HONG LIE, Earth Sciences
DUAN, YU BO, Electricity and Information Engineering
FAN, HONG FU, Oil Engineering
FU, GUANG, Earth Sciences
FU, GUANG JIE, Electricity and Information Engineering
GAO, BING KUN, Electricity and Information Engineering
GUO, YU FENG, Electronic Engineering
HAN, GUO YOU, Mechanical Science and Engineering
HAN, HONG SHENG, Oil Engineering
HAO, WEN SEN, Mechanical Science and Engineering
JIA, WEN JU, Computing and Information Technology
JIA, ZHEN QI, Oil Engineering
JIANG, MING HU, Mechanical Science and Engineering
JIN, SHAO XIAN, Electronic Engineering
KANG, WANG LI, Oil Engineering
KONG, LING BIN, Mathematics
LI, BAO YAN, Mechanical Science and Engineering
LI, CHUN SHENG, Computing and Information Technology
LI, CONG XIN, Computing and Information Technology
LI, JIE, Earth Sciences
LI, XIAO PING, Mathematics
LI, YAN JIE, Mathematics
LING, JING LONG, Earth Sciences
LIU, JU BAO, Mechanical Science and Engineering
LIU, SU LIN, Mechanical Science and Engineering
LIU, TIE NAN, Electricity and Information Engineering
LIU, XIAO YAN, Earth Sciences
LIU, YANG, Oil Engineering
LIU, YI KUN, Oil Engineering
LIU, YONG JIAN, Oil Engineering
LU, LING JIE, Computing and Information Technology
LU, SHUANG FANG, Earth Sciences
LU, YAN FANG, Earth Sciences
MA, RUI MIN, Computing and Information Technology
MA, SHI ZHONG, Earth Sciences
NUAN, QING DE, Mechanical Science and Engineering
REN, FU SHAN, Mechanical Science and Engineering
REN, WEI JIAN, Electricity and Information Engineering
SHAO, QIANG, Economics and Management
SHI, SHANG MING, Earth Sciences
SONG, KAO PING, Oil Engineering
SONG, YU LING, Humanities
SUN, BO TAO, Foreign Languages
SUN, JIAN GANG, Building Construction Engineering
SUN, YAN BIN, Economics and Management
SUN, YU XUE, Oil Engineering
TANG, GUO WEI, Computing and Information Technology
WANG, DE MING, Oil Engineering
WANG, HENG JIU, Economics and Management
WANG, JING QI, Earth Sciences
WANG, MING JI, Electronic Engineering
WANG, SHOU TIAN, Mathematics
WANG, WEN GUANG, Earth Sciences
WANG, XIU MING, Earth Sciences
WANG, ZUN CE, Mechanical Science and Engineering
WU, WEN XIANG, Oil Engineering
XIA, HUI FENG, Oil Engineering
XU, BU YUN, Mechanical Science and Engineering
XU, SHAO HUA, Computing and Information Technology
YAN, TIE, Oil Engineering
YI, ZHI AN, Computing and Information Technology
ZENG, ZHAO YING, Mathematics
ZHANG, CHANG HAI, Mathematics
ZHANG, DA WEI, Oil Engineering
ZHANG, JI HUA, Foreign Languages
ZHANG, JING, Earth Sciences
ZHANG, YONG HONG, Mechanical Science and Engineering
ZHANG, YU BIN, Mechanical Science and Engineering
ZHAO, WEI MIN, Mechanical Science and Engineering
ZHAO, ZI GANG, Oil Engineering
ZHOU, QING LONG, Mechanical Science and Engineering
ZHU, JUN, Mechanical Science and Engineering

DONGBEI UNIVERSITY OF FINANCE AND ECONOMICS

217 Jianshan St, 116025 Dalian
Telephone: (411) 4691503
E-mail: dufe1952@pub.dl.inpta.net.cn
Internet: www.dufe.edu.cn
Founded 1952
State control
Languages of instruction: Chinese, English
Academic year: September to July
Pres.: Prof. XIA CHUNYU
Vice-Pres.: Prof. MA GUOQIANG
Vice-Pres.: LI DONGYANG
Vice-Pres.: Prof. XIA CHUNYU
Vice-Pres.: WU XIANHUA
Vice-Pres.: QUE CHENGYU
Vice-Pres.: LV WEI
Librarian: ZHANG LI
Library of 900,000 vols
Number of teachers: 560
Number of students: 11,820 (incl. 5,680 correspondence)
Publication: *Research on Finance and Economics Issues*

DONGHUA UNIVERSITY

1882 West Yan-An Rd, 200051 Shanghai
Telephone: (21) 62378595
E-mail: ico@dhu.edu.cn
Internet: www.dhu.edu.cn
Founded 1951 as East China Textile Institute of Science and Technology, re-named China Textile Univ. 1985, current name adopted 1999
Academic year: September to July
Colleges of chemistry, chemical engineering and biotechnology, foreign language, humanities, material science and engineering, mechanical engineering, textile; schools of computer science and technology, environmental science and engineering, information science and technology, science
Pres.: XU MINGZHI
Vice-Pres.: SONG LIQUN
Vice-Pres.: YU JIANYONG
Vice-Pres.: CHEN ZHAOYING
Vice-Pres.: LIU CHUNHONG
Vice-Pres.: QIU GAO
Librarian: Prof. YU MING
Library of 810,000 vols and periodicals
Number of teachers: 2,800
Number of students: 30,000
Publications: *Journal* (6 a year, English edn 2 a year), *Textile Technology Overseas* (6 a year)

EAST CHINA NORMAL UNIVERSITY

3663 North Zhongshan Rd, 200241 Shanghai
Telephone: (21) 62233333
E-mail: webmaster@ecnu.edu.cn
Internet: www.ecnu.edu.cn
Founded 1951
Academic year: September to July (2 semesters)
Schools of art, business, communication, design, education science, finance and statistics, foreign languages, humanities and social science, life sciences, preschool and special education, psychology and cognitive science, public admin., science and engineering, social devt, software engineering
Pres.: CHEN QUN
Vice-Pres.: LIN ZAIYONG
Vice-Pres.: REN YOUQUN
Vice-Pres.: FAN JUN
Vice-Pres.: ZHU ZIQIANG
Vice-Pres.: GUO WEILU
Vice-Pres.: SUN ZHENRONG
Librarian: HUANG XIUWEN
Library of 3,535,000 vols
Number of teachers: 4,000
Number of students: 26,000
Publications: *Applied Probability and Statistics* (4 a year), *East Europe and Central Asia Today* (6 a year), *Journal of Educational Science* (4 a year), *Journal of Natural Sciences* (4 a year), *Journal of Philosophy and Social Sciences* (6 a year), *Psychological Science* (6 a year), *Research into the Theory of Ancient Literature* (irregular), *Theoretical Studies in Literature and Art* (6 a year), *World Geography Research* (2 a year)

EAST CHINA UNIVERSITY OF SCIENCE AND TECHNOLOGY

130 Meilong Rd, 200237 Shanghai
Telephone: (21) 4775678
Internet: www.ecust.edu.cn

Founded 1952 as East China Univ. of Chemical Technology, current name adopted 1993

Schools of art, design and media; bioengineering; business; chemical engineering; chemistry and molecular engineering; foreign languages; humanities; information science and engineering; law; materials science and engineering; mechanical and power engineering; pharmacy; resource and environmental engineering; science; social and public admin.

Pres.: QIAN XUHONG
Vice-Pres.: CHEN YINGNAN
Vice-Pres.: YU JIANGUO
Vice-Pres.: MA YULU
Vice-Pres.: TU SHANDONG
Vice-Pres.: YANG CUNZHONG
Vice-Pres.: QIAN FENG

Library of 2,450,000 vols
Number of teachers: 3,700
Number of students: 16,300

Publication: *Journal* (6 a year)

FORMER SHANGHAI MEDICAL UNIVERSITY

138 Yixueyuan Lu, Shanghai 200032
Telephone: (21) 64041900
Internet: www.shmu.edu.cn

Founded 1927 as Fourth Zhongshan Univ. Medical College, current name adopted 1985
State control

Pres.: WEIPING WANG
Vice-Pres.: CAO SHILONG
Vice-Pres.: CHEN JIE
Vice-Pres.: PENG YUWEN
Vice-Pres.: WANG WEIPING
Vice-Pres.: XIE RONGGUO
Chief Admin. Officer: HU TIANNE
Librarian: CHEN GUIZHANG

Library of 490,000 vols
Number of teachers: 8,778
Number of students: 5,074

Publication: *Acta* (6 a year)

FUDAN UNIVERSITY

220 Handan Rd, Shanghai 200433
Telephone: (21) 65642222
Internet: www.fudan.edu.cn

Founded 1905, present status 2000, following merger with Shanghai Medical Univ.
State control
Languages of instruction: Chinese, English
Academic year: September to July (2 semesters)

Pres.: Prof. YANG, YULIANG
Exec. Vice-Pres.: Prof. WANG, WEIPING
Exec. Vice-Pres.: ZHANG, YIHUA
Vice-Pres.: Prof. CAI, DAFENG
Vice-Pres.: Prof. CHEN, XIAOMAN
Vice-Pres.: Prof. GUI, YONGHAO
Vice-Pres.: LIN, JI
Vice-Pres.: XU, ZHENG
Librarian: Prof. QIN ZENGFU

Library of 4,330,000 vols
Number of teachers: 2,481
Number of students: 26,792 (full-time) and 20,670 studying at the schools of Continuing Education and Online Education

Publications: *Fudan Natural Sciences Journal*, *Fudan Social Sciences Journal*, *Mathematics Annals Acta* (6 a year)

DEANS

School of Economics: Prof. HONG YUANPENG
School of Information Science and Engineering: LI-RONG ZHENG
School of International Cultural Communication: Prof. ZHU YONGSHENG
School of International Relations and Public Affairs: Prof. YONG LONGTU
School of Journalism: Prof. DING GANLIN
School of Law: (vacant)
School of Life Sciences: Prof. LI YUYANG
School of Management: LU XIONGWEN
School of Mathematical Sciences: WANG YONGZHEN (Vice-Dean)
School of Social Development and Public Policy: Prof. PENG XIZHE

FUJIAN AGRICULTURAL AND FORESTRY UNIVERSITY

350002 Jinshan
Telephone: (591) 83778235
E-mail: ruibi123@126.com
Internet: www.fafu.edu.cn

Founded 1936
State control
Language of instruction: Chinese

Colleges of adult education, animal science, crop science, economics and trade

Pres.: Prof. LAN SIREN
Librarian: HU FANPING

Library of 560,000 vols
Number of teachers: 1,600
Number of students: 24,000

Publications: *Current Communications on Overseas Agricultural Science and Technology*, *Journal of Entomology in Eastern China*, *Journal of Fujian Agricultural University*, *Overseas Agricultural Science: Sugarcane*, *Wuyi Science*

FUJIAN MEDICAL UNIVERSITY

88 Jiaotong Rd, Fuzhou 350004, Fujian Province
Telephone: (591) 3568821
E-mail: infor@mail.fjmu.edu.cn
Internet: www.fjmu.edu.cn

Founded 1937

Pres.: Prof. WU ZHONGFU
Vice-Pres.: LIN KEHUA
Vice-Pres.: LUO GUEILIN
Head of Postgraduate Dept: KANG YUANYUAN
Librarian: HUANG HUISHANG

Library of 258,448 vols
Number of teachers: 398
Number of students: 2,306

Publications: *Journal*, *Medical Education Study*

FUJIAN NORMAL UNIVERSITY

8 Shang San Rd, Cang Shan Section, Fuzhou 350007, Fujian Province
Telephone: (591) 83456156
Internet: www.fjtu.edu.cn

Founded 1907
Dept of Education of Fujian control
Academic year: September to July

Pres.: LI JIANPING
Vice-Pres.: HUANG HANSHENG
Vice-Pres.: LI MIN
Vice-Pres.: WANG ZHENGLU
Vice-Pres.: WANG WENDING
Vice-Pres.: ZHENG YISHU
Head of Graduate Dept: LI JIANPING
Librarian: WAN BAOCHUAN

Number of teachers: 2,500
Number of students: 30,000

Publications: *Journal* (natural sciences, 6 a year), *Journal* (philosophy and social sciences, 6 a year), *Mathematics of Fujian Middle School* (6 a year)

DEANS

College of Physical Education and Sports Science: MEI XUEXIONG
School of Bioengineering: LI MIN
School of Chemistry and Material Science: HU BINGHUAN
School of Economy: LI JIANJIAN
School of Educational Sciences and Technology: YU WENSEN
School of Foreign Languages: LIN DAJIN
School of Geographical Sciences: YANG YUSHENG
School of Humanities: CHEN QINGYUAN
School of Law: GUO TIEMIN
School of Mathematics and Computer Science: LI YONGQING
School of Media: YAN CHUNJUN
School of Music: ZHENG JINYANG
School of Physics and Optoelectronic Technology: XIE SHUSEN
School of Public Administration: HE YILUN
School of Society and History: LIN JINSHUI
School of Software: WENG ZUMAO
School of Tourism: ZHENG YAOXIN

PROFESSORS

CAI, XIULING, Economics
CHAI, YUPING, Public Administration
CHEN, GUIRONG, Public Administration
CHEN, GUORUI, Physical Education and Sports Science
CHEN, HUOPING, Educational Sciences and Technology
CHEN, JUNQIN, Physical Education and Sports Science
CHEN, KAI, Foreign Languages
CHEN, LIANGYUAN, Humanities
CHEN, QINGYUAN, Humanities
CHEN, RONG, Physical Education and Sports Science
CHEN, SHAOHUI, Economics
CHEN, SHAOPING, Chemistry and Material Science
CHEN, TIECHENG, Physical Education and Sports Science
CHEN, WEIZHEN, Foreign Languages
CHEN, YIPING, Bioengineering
CHEN, YONGCHUN, Public Administration
CHEN, YOUQIANG, Bioengineering
CHEN, ZEPING, Humanities
CHEN, ZHENG, Economics
CHENG, LIGUO, Educational Sciences and Technology
DAI, CONGTENG, Foreign Languages
DAI, XIANQUN, Society and History
DU, CHANGZHONG, Foreign Languages
GANG, SONG, Bioengineering
GAO, JIANMIN, Bioengineering
GU, YEPING, Humanities
GUO, TIEMIN, Economics
HE, YILUN, Public Administration
HONG, MING, Educational Sciences and Technology
HONG, YANGUO, Bioengineering
HU, BINGHUAN, Chemistry and Material Science
HU, CANGZE, Society and History
HU, ZHIGANG, Chemistry and Material Science
HUANG, AILING, Educational Sciences and Technology
HUANG, GUANGYANG, Educational Sciences and Technology
HUANG, GUOSHENG, Society and History
HUANG, GUOXIONG, Public Administration
HUANG, HANSHENG, Physical Education and Sports Science
HUANG, JIANZHONG, Bioengineering
HUANG, JIAYE, Economics
HUANG, RENXIAN, Educational Sciences and Technology
HUANG, ZHIGAO, Physics and Optoelectronic Technology

LAN, XUEFEI, Music
LI, HONGCAI, Physics and Optoelectronic Technology
LI, JIANJIAN, Economics
LI, JIANPING, Economics
LI, MIN, Bioengineering
LI, RONGBAO, Foreign Languages
LI, SHUZHEN, Public Administration
LI, XIANGMIN, Public Administration
LIAN, CHENGYE, Society and History
LIAN, RONG, Educational Sciences and Technology
LIN, BENCHUN, Foreign Languages
LIN, DAJIN, Foreign Languages
LIN, GUOPING, Society and History
LIN, JING, Educational Sciences and Technology
LIN, JINHUO, Chemistry and Material Science
LIN, JINSHUI, Society and History
LIN, LIN, Bioengineering
LIN, QING, Economics
LIN, SHANLANG, Economics
LIN, XIUGUO, Public Administration
LIN, ZHANG, Foreign Languages
LIN, ZIHUA, Economics
LIU, HUIYU, Society and History
LIU, JIANQIU, Bioengineering
LIU, RONGFANG, Chemistry and Material Science
LIU, YAMENG, Foreign Languages
LIU, YONGGENG, Humanities
MAO, NING, Bioengineering
MEI, XUEXIONG, Physical Education and Sports Science
PAN, XINHE, Humanities
PAN, YUTENG, Public Administration
QIAO, JIANZHONG, Music
QIU, LING, Foreign Languages
QIU, YISHEN, Physics and Optoelectronic Technology
QIU, YONGQU, Educational Sciences and Technology
SHI, QIAOQIN, Bioengineering
SU, XIAOQING, Physical Education and Sports Science
SU, ZHENFANG, Public Administration
SUN, SHAOZHEN, Humanities
TAN, XUEXHUN, Humanities
TANG, WENJI, Society and History
WANG, GUOHONG, Bioengineering
WANG, HANMIN, Humanities
WANG, JIANDE, Society and History
WANG, KE, Humanities
WANG, YAOHUA, Music
WANG, ZHENGLU, Society and History
WANG, ZHIBO, Public Administration
WEN, RI, Society and History
WENG, JIABAO, Chemistry and Material Science
WENG, YINTAO, Humanities
WENG, ZUMAO, Computer Software
WU, YOUGEN, Economics
WU, ZONGHUA, Chemistry and Material Science
XI, YANG, Humanities
XIAO, HUASHAN, Bioengineering
XIE, BIZHEN, Society and History
XIE, SHUSEN, Physics and Optoelectronic Technology
XU, HONGFENG, Physical Education and Sports Science
XU, MING, Educational Sciences and Technology
XU, YONG, Physics and Optoelectronic Technology
YAN, CHUNJUN, Humanities
YAN, YOUWEI, Educational Sciences and Technology
YANG, KONGCHI, Educational Sciences and Technology
YANG, MINGRU, Bioengineering
YANG, XINHUA, Public Administration
YANG, YUSHENG, Geographical Sciences
YANG, ZHAOFENG, Bioengineering
YE, YIDUO, Educational Sciences and Technology
YOU, YONGLONG, Bioengineering
YU, GECHUN, Public Administration
YU, WENSEN, Educational Sciences and Technology
YUAN, SHUQI, Geographical Sciences
ZENG, CONGSHENG, Geographical Sciences
ZHAN, GUANQUN, Society and History
ZHANG, DINGHUA, Bioengineering
ZHANG, HANJIN, Physical Education and Sports Science
ZHANG, HUARONG, Economics
ZHANG, WENGONG, Chemistry and Material Science
ZHANG, YANDING, Bioengineering
ZHEN, XIAOHUA, Society and History
ZHENG, DAXIAN, Geographical Sciences
ZHENG, JINYANG, Music
ZHENG, YI, Bioengineering
ZHENG, YOUXIAN, Public Administration
ZHU, HEJIAN, Geographical Sciences
ZHU, JIAN, Economics
ZHU, JINZI, Bioengineering
ZHU, LING, Humanities
ZHUANG, HUIRU, Bioengineering
ZHUANG, TAO, Foreign Languages
ZUAN, ZHENGFANG, Public Administration

FUZHOU UNIVERSITY

523 Industry Rd, Fuzhou 350002, Fujian Province
Telephone: (591) 3739513
Internet: www.fzu.edu.cn

Founded 1958

Academic year: September to July

Pres.: WU MIN SHENG
Vice-Pres.: CHEN GUO NAN
Vice-Pres.: FAN GENG HUA
Vice-Pres.: FANG ZHEN ZHENG
Vice-Pres.: FU XIAN ZHI
Head of Graduate Dept: LIN SHU WEN
Head of Graduate Dept: LIU SONG QING
Librarian: ZHANG WEN DE

Number of teachers: 1,200
Number of students: 20,000

Publications: *Journal* (natural sciences, 6 a year), *Journal* (philosophy, 4 a year)

DEANS

Napier College: XIE LIU HUI
School of Biological Science and Technology: RAO PING FAN
School of Civil Engineering and Architecture: CHEN BAO CHUN
School of Electric Engineering and Automation: CHEN BAO CHUN
School of Environment and Resources: XU HAN QIU
School of Foreign Languages: WU SONG JIANG
School of Humanities and Social Sciences: LIN YI
School of Law: CHEN QUAN SHENG
School of Management: CHEN GUO HONG
School of Materials Sciences and Engineering: CHEN XIAN SHENG
School of Mathematics and Computer Science: WANG XIAO DONG
School of Mechanical Engineering: GAO CHENG HUI
School of Physics and Information Engineering: YU LUN
School of Public Management: WANG JIAN
School of Software: FAN GENG HUA
School of Zhi Cheng: TANG YI ZHU
Sunshine College: CHEN GONG LIN

PROFESSORS

CAI, JIN DING, Electrical Engineering and Automation
CHEN, BAO CHUN, Civil Engineering and Architecture
CHEN, CHONG, Electrical Engineering and Automation
CHEN, FU JI, Public Management
CHEN, GUO HONG, Management
CHEN, LE SHAN, Mechanical Engineering
CHEN, LI, Mechanical Engineering
CHEN, RONG SI, Management
CHEN, SEN, Civil Engineering and Architecture
CHEN, SHU MEI, Mechanical Engineering
CHEN, XIAN SHENG, Materials Science and Engineering
CHEN, XIAO WEI, Foreign Languages
CHEN, XIN, Physics and Information Engineering
CHEN, XIN SHU, Civil Engineering and Architecture
DU, MING, Electrical Engineering and Automation
FANG, ZHEN ZHENG, Civil Engineering and Architecture
GAO, CHENG HUI, Mechanical Engineering
GUO, ZONG REN, Electrical Engineering and Automation
HU, JI RONG, Management
HU, XIAO RONG, Civil Engineering and Architecture
HUANG, KE AN, Management
HUANG, SHU ZHANG, Management
HUANG, WEN XIN, Management
HUANG, YAO ZHI, Mechanical Engineering
HUANG, ZHI GANG, Management
JIAN, WEN BIN, Environment and Resources
LAN, ZHAO HUI, Mechanical Engineering
LEI, DE SEN, Public Management
LIN, GUO RONG, Mechanical Engineering
LIN, QIANG, Physics and Information Engineering
LIN, SHU WEN, Mechanical Engineering
LIN, TONG, Mechanical Engineering
LIN, YI, Humanities and Social Sciences
LIN, YING XING, Management
LIN, YOU WEN, Management
LIN, YUAN QING, Management
LIU, MING HUA, Environment and Resources
LIU, YAN BIN, Mechanical Engineering
PAN, YAN, Management
PENG, DA WEN, Civil Engineering and Architecture
QI, KAI, Civil Engineering and Architecture
QIAN, KUANG WU, Materials Science and Engineering
QIU, GONG WEI, Electrical Engineering and Automation
RAO, PING FAN, Biological Science and Technology
RUAN, YU ZHONG, Materials Science and Engineering
SHENG, FEI MIN, Environment and Resources
SU, KAI XIONG, Physics and Information Engineering
SUN, QIU BI, Management
TANG, DE PING, Materials Science and Engineering
TANG, DIAN, Materials Science and Engineering
TANG, LI HONG, Public Management
TANG, NING PING, Electrical Engineering and Automation
WANG, JIAN, Public Management
WANG, QIN MIN, Physics and Information Engineering
WANG, WEI YI, Management
WANG, YING MING, Public Management
WANG, ZHONG LAI, Biological Science and Technology
WU, HAN GUANG, Electrical Engineering and Automation
WU, SONG JIANG, Foreign Languages
WU, XING NAN, Humanities and Social Sciences
XI, YONG QIN, Public Management
XIE, ZHI XIN, Civil Engineering and Architecture
XU, DOU DOU, Humanities and Social Sciences
XU, HAN QIU, Environment and Resources
YANG, FU WEN, Electrical Engineering and Automation

YANG, XIAO XIANG, Mechanical Engineering
YE, ZHONG HE, Mechanical Engineering
YEA, ZHONG, Management
YU, LUN, Physics and Information Engineering
YUAN, BING LING, Humanities and Social Sciences
ZHANG, BAI, Management
ZHANG, BEI MIN, Electrical Engineering and Automation
ZHANG, QI SHAN, Management
ZHANG, MAO XUN, Mechanical Engineering
ZHANG, QI SHAN, Mechanical Engineering
ZHANG, QIONG, Materials Science and Engineering
ZHANG, YE, Management
ZHENG, JIAN LAN, Civil Engineering and Architecture
ZHENG, SHI BIAO, Physics and Information Engineering
ZHENG, ZHEN, Civil Engineering and Architecture
ZHENG, ZHEN FEI, Civil Engineering and Architecture
ZHOU, RUI ZHONG, Civil Engineering and Architecture
ZHOU, XIAO LIANG, Management
ZHU, YONG CHUN, Civil Engineering and Architecture
ZHU, ZU PING, Mechanical Engineering

GANSU AGRICULTURAL UNIVERSITY

1 Yingmencun, 730070 Lanzhou
Telephone: (931) 7632459
E-mail: hzqiu@gsau.edu.cn
Internet: www.gsau.edu.cn

Founded 1958
Academic year: September to July

Colleges of animal science and technology, agronomy, economy management, extended education, food science and engineering, foreign languages, forestry science, grassland sciences, humanities, information sciences and technology, life science and technology, resources and environmental sciences, science, technology, veterinary medicine

Pres.: Prof. WU JIANMIN
Vice-Pres.: BI YANG
Vice-Pres.: YU JIHUA
Librarian: LIU XI

Library: 1.5m. vols
Number of teachers: 1,668
Number of students: 18,030

Publications: *Journal of Grassland and Turf* (4 a year), *University Journal* (12 a year)

GUANGDONG PHARMACEUTICAL UNIVERSITY

40 Guang Han Zhi, Guangzhou, 510224 Guangdong
Telephone: 4429040
Internet: www.gdpu.edu.cn

Founded 1958, current name adopted 2005

Pres.: Prof. ZHU JIAYONG (acting)
Vice-Pres.: ZHANG JIANHUA
Vice-Pres.: ZHANGYOU DUO
Vice-Pres.: CHEN YANZHONG
Librarian: LIAO MING QING

Library of 160,000 vols
Number of teachers: 1,243
Number of students: 30,000

Publication: *Journal*

PROFESSORS

FENGHE, H., Pharmacology
FENGMING, Z., Epidemiology
JINCHENG, H., Pharmaceutical Chemistry
JINGXIAN, J., Internal Medicine
JINGZHI, H., Human Parasitology
JIPENG, L., Pharmacognosy
MUXIAN, L., Biochemistry
PUSHENG, W., Traditional Chinese Medicine
QIHUA, W., Human Anatomy
QIYUN, Y., Phytochemistry
QIZHANG, D., Pharmacology
SHIDE, S., Statistics
YIYUAN, Z., Dermatology
ZHICHENG, C., Hygiene
ZHUHUA, L., Microbiology

GUANGXI NORMAL UNIVERSITY

Yan Shan, Gui Lin 541004, Guangxi Province
Telephone: (773) 5812081
E-mail: info@mailbox.gxnu.edu.cn
Internet: www.gxnu.edu.cn

Founded 1932
Min. of Education control
Academic year: September to July

Pres.: LIANG HONG
Vice-Pres.: LAN CHANGZHOU
Vice-Pres.: LIU JIANBING
Vice-Pres.: LIU MUREN
Vice-Pres.: WANG JIE
Vice-Pres.: YI ZHONG
Vice-Pres.: ZHONG RUITIAN
Librarian: YAO QIAN

Library of 2,060,000 vols
Number of teachers: 1,043
Number of students: 40,000

Publication: *Journal of Guangxi Normal University* (4 a year)

DEANS

College of Foreign Studies: LIU ZHAOZHONG
College of Life Science: QIN XINMING
College of Politics and Public Management: TAN PEIWEN
College of Physics and Information Technology: WANG QIANG
Department of Resources and Environmental Science: HE XINGCUN
Educational Science College: GAO JINLING
School of Chemistry and Chemical Engineering: LIANG FUPEI
School of Culture and Tourism: ZHOU ZUOMING
School of Law and Business: LUO ZHISONG
School of Sports: LIANG ZHUPING

PROFESSORS

CAI, CHANGZHUO, International Culture and Education
CHEN, HONGJIANG, Politics and Public Management
CHEN, JITANG, Foreign Studies
CHEN, QIN, Politics and Public Management
CHEN, XIONGZHANG, Culture and Tourism
CHEN, ZHAOBIN, Physical Education
CHEN, ZHENFENG, Chemistry and Chemical Engineering
CUI, TIANSHUN, Resources and Environmental Science
CUI, YAODONG, Mathematics and Computer Science
DENG, BIYANG, Chemistry and Chemical Engineering
DENG, PEIMING, Mathematics and Computer Science
DING, CHANGMING, Mathematics and Computer Science
FENG, CUNHUA, Mathematics and Computer Science
GUO, LILIANG, Physical Education
HE, LINXIA, Culture and Tourism
HE, XIANGLIN, Foreign Studies
HE, XINGCUN, Resources and Environmental Science
HU, DALEI, Chinese Studies
HUANG, BINLIAN, Physics and Information Technology
HUANG, CHENGMING, Life Science
HUANG, JIESHAN, Social Sciences
HUANG, RUIXIONG, Social Sciences
HUANG, SHEN, Physical Education
HUANG, WEILIN, Chinese Studies
HUANG, ZHUSHENG, Law and Business
JIANG, GUOCHENG, Life Science
JIANG, SHIHUI, Educational Science
JIANG, YIMING, Chemistry and Chemical Engineering
LEI, REI, Chinese Studies
LI, DUNXIANG, Law and Business
LI, FUBO, Chinese Studies
LI, HONGHAN, Educational Science
LI, JIANG, Chinese Studies
LI, LAILONG, Chinese Studies
LI, LU, Educational Science
LI, XIAO, Foreign Studies
LI, YI, Resources and Environmental Science
LI, ZHIQING, Physical Education
LIANG, FUPEI, Chemistry and Chemical Engineering
LIANG, HONG, Chemistry and Chemical Engineering
LIANG, ZHUPING, Physical Education
LIAO, GUOWEI, Chinese Studies
LIN, FENGMIN, Social Sciences
LIN, SHIMIN, Mathematics and Computer Science
LIU, MUREN, Physics and Information Technology
LIU, XIAOLIN, Culture and Tourism
LIU, XINGJUN, Chinese Studies
LIU, YING, International Culture and Education
LIU, ZHAOZHONG, Foreign Studies
LU, XIAO, Physics and Information Technology
LU, YUTAI, Foreign Studies
LUO, GUILIE, Mathematics and Computer Science
LUO, XIAOSHU, Physics and Information Technology
LUO, XINGKAI, Physics and Information Technology
LUO, ZHISONG, Law and Business
MAI, YONGXIONG, Chinese Studies
MO, DAOCAI, Chinese Studies
MO, QIXUN, Chinese Studies
PO, JINZE, Foreign Studies
QI, PEIFANG, Politics and Public Management
QIN, YONGSONG, Mathematics and Computer Science
QIN, ZIXIONG, Physics and Information Technology
QUE, ZHEN, Chinese Studies
REN, GUANWEN, Culture and Tourism
SHEN, JIAZHUANG, Chinese Studies
SHI, GUIYU, Life Science
SU, GUIFA, Chemistry and Chemical Engineering
SUN, JIANYUAN, Chinese Studies
TAN, DEQING, Chinese Studies
TAN, PEIWEN, Politics and Public Management
TAN, ZHAOYI, Culture and Tourism
TANG, DEHAI, Educational Science
TANG, FUCHENG, Mathematics and Computer Science
TANG, GAOYUAN, Foreign Studies
TANG, LING, Culture and Tourism
TANG, ZHAOQING, Life Science
TENG, DINGMING, Chinese Studies
TONG, GUANGZHENG, Law and Business
WANG, CHAOYUAN, Chinese Studies
WANG, CHENGMING, Mathematics and Computer Science
WANG, DEFU, Social Sciences
WANG, DEMING, Chinese Studies
WANG, JIE, Chinese Studies
WANG, QIANG, Physics and Information Technology
WANG, XIANGJUN, Politics and Public Management
WANG, ZHIYING, Chinese Studies
WEI, HAN, Foreign Studies
WENG, JIAQIANG, Physics and Information Technology

WU, DIANHUA, Mathematics and Computer Science
XIE, XIANG, Physical Education
XU, JIWANG, Foreign Studies
XU, XUEFU, Educational Science
XU, XUEYING, Educational Science
XUE, YUEGUI, Life Science
YAN, XIAOWEI, Mathematics and Computer Science
YANG, LIYAN, Law and Business
YANG, QIGUI, Mathematics and Computer Science
YANG, SHANCHAO, Mathematics and Computer Science
YANG, SHUJIE, Chinese Studies
YANG, YONGBING, Physics and Information Technology
YANG, YONGLIANG, Physical Education
YAO, DAILIANG, Chinese Studies
YE, YONGJI, Arts Department
YI, XING, Politics and Public Management
YI, ZHONG, Mathematics and Computer Science
YIN, LINGLING, Physical Education
YU, PING, Mathematics and Computer Science
YUAN, BINYE, Foreign Studies
ZHANG, LIQUN, Chinese Studies
ZHANG, MINGFEI, Chinese Studies
ZHANG, SHICHAO, Mathematics and Computer Science
ZHAO, SHULIN, Chemistry and Chemical Engineering
ZHONG, RUITIAN, Politics and Public Management
ZHOU, LIANGREN, Foreign Studies
ZHOU, QUANLIN, Foreign Studies
ZHOU, SHANYI, Life Science
ZHOU, SHIZHONG, Law and Business
ZHU, CONGBIN, Culture and Tourism
ZHU, JUNQIANG, Law and Business
ZHU, SHOUXING, Chinese Studies

GUANGXI TRADITIONAL CHINESE MEDICAL UNIVERSITY

179 Mingxiudong Rd, Nanning, Guangxi Zhuang Autonomous Region
Telephone: (771) 3137577
E-mail: tangnong@gxtcmu.edu.cn
Internet: www.gxtcmu.edu.cn

Founded 1956

Pres.: Prof. WEI GUIKANG
Vice-Pres: Prof. LI WEITAI
Vice-Pres: Assoc. Prof. ZHU HUA
Vice-Pres: Assoc. Prof. DEN JIAGANG
Librarian: LI JIANGUANG

Library of 300,000 vols
Number of teachers: 296
Number of students: 1,849

Publications: *Guangxi Journal of Traditional Chinese Medicine*, *Study in Higher Education of Traditional Chinese Medicine*

GUANGXI UNIVERSITY

100 Daxue Rd, Nanning, 530005 Guangxi
Telephone: (771) 3235229
E-mail: gjc@gxu.edu.cn
Internet: www.gxu.edu.cn

Founded 1928
State control
Academic year: September to June

Pres.: ZHAO YANLIN
Librarian: Prof. CHEN DAGUANG

Library: 2.5m. vols
Number of teachers: 3,722
Number of students: 24,205

Publication: *Guangxi University Journal*

DEANS

College of Adult Education: Prof. HE BAOCHONG
College of Agronomy: Prof. MO TIANYAN
College of Animal Science and Technology: Prof. YANG NIANSHENG
College of Biological Technology and Sugar Industrial Engineering: Prof. LU JIAJIONG
College of Business: Prof. LIU CHAOMING
College of Culture and Mass Communication: Prof. LIANG YANG
College of Chemistry and Chemical Engineering: Prof. TONG ZHANGFA
College of Civil Engineering: Prof. YAN LIUBIN
College of Computer Science and Information Technology: Prof. LI TAOSHEN
College of Electrical Engineering: Prof. LU ZUPEI
College of Foreign Languages: Prof. ZHOU YI
College of Forestry: Prof. JIN DAGANG (Exec. Vice-Dean)
College of Law: Prof. MENG QINGUO
College of Mechanical Engineering: Prof. LI SHANGPING
College of Natural Resources and the Environment: Prof. MA SHAOJIAN
College of Sciences: Prof. XI HONGJIAN
College of Social Sciences and Management: Prof. XIE SHUN
Department of Physical Education: Prof. XU MINGRONG
Department of Teacher Training: Prof. WANG HAIYIN (Vice-Dean)

GUANGZHOU UNIVERSITY

230 Wai Huan Xi Rd, Guangzhou Higher Education Mega Centre, Guangzhou 510006
Telephone: (20) 86394493
E-mail: faogzu@21cn.com
Internet: www.gzhu.edu.cn

Founded 1983, merged with 8 other institutions of higher education 2000
Academic year: September to July

Pres.: Prof. LIN WEIMING
Vice-Pres.: Prof. CHEN WANPENG
Vice-Pres.: Prof. LI XUNGUI
Vice-Pres.: Prof. LONG SHAOFENG
Vice-Pres.: Prof. SHU YANG
Vice-Pres.: Prof. XU CIRONG
Vice-Pres.: Prof. YU GUOYANG
Dir for Academic Affairs: Prof. YU QICAI
Dir for Academic Research: Prof. XIAN QIAOLING
Dir for the Institute for Higher Education Research: Prof. HUANG JIAQUAN
Dir for the International Office: Prof. LI YI
Dir for Postgraduate Affairs: Prof. YAO PO
Library Dir: Prof. ZHANG BAIYING

Library of 182,000 vols
Number of teachers: 2,372
Number of students: 31,333

Publication: *Journal* (12 a year)

GUANGZHOU UNIVERSITY OF TRADITIONAL CHINESE MEDICINE

12 Airport Rd, Guangzhou 510405, Guangdong Province
Telephone: (20) 36588233
Internet: www.gzhtcm.edu.cn

Founded 1956
Dept of Education of Guangdong control
Academic year: September to July

Pres.: FENG XINSONG
Vice-Pres.: CHEN YINGHUA
Vice-Pres.: LI JIANJUN
Vice-Pres.: LIN PEICHENG
Vice-Pres.: WANG NINGSHENG
Vice-Pres.: XU ZHIWEI
Head of Graduate Dept: QIU SHIJUN
Librarian: LI JIAN

Number of teachers: 1,025
Number of students: 3,000

Publications: *Journal* (6 a year), *New Journal of Traditional Chinese Medicine* (12 a year), *Traditional Chinese Drug Research and Clinical Pharmacology* (6 a year)

DEANS

First School of Medicine: DENG TIETAO
School of Acupuncture and Massage: CAI TIEQU
School of Basic Medical Sciences: CHEN QUN
School of Chinese Traditional Medicine: CHEN WEIWEN
School of Economy and Administration: QIU HONGZHONG
School of Information Technology: CHEN SU
School of Nursing: HE YANPING
Second School of Medicine: LU YUBO
Third School of Medicine: ZHUANG HONG

PROFESSORS

CAI, TIEQU, Acupuncture and Massage
CHEN, DACAN, Medicine
CHEN, JINGHE, Medicine
CHEN, JIPAN, Medicine
CHEN, QUN, Basic Medical Sciences
CHEN, SU, Information Technology
CHEN, WEIWEN, Chinese Traditional Medicine
CHEN, XHAOFENG, Basic Medical Sciences
CHEN, ZHIQIANG, Medicine
CHENG, YI, Chinese Traditional Medicine
DENG, TIETAO, Medicine
GAO, YOUHENG, Chinese Traditional Medicine
HUANG, SHAOYING, Medicine
I, JIEFEN, Basic Medical Sciences
JIN, RUI, Medicine
LAI, WEN, Basic Medical Sciences
LAI, XINSHENG, Acupuncture and Massage
LI, HANJIN, Basic Medical Sciences
LI, JINGBO, Basic Medical Sciences
LI, RENXIAN, Medicine
LI, RI, Chinese Traditional Medicine
LI, WANYAO, Acupuncture and Massage
LI, WEI, Chinese Traditional Medicine
LI, WEIMIN, Chinese Traditional Medicine
LI, YIWEI, Nursing
LIANG, SONGMIN, Chinese Traditional Medicine
LIN, LI, Chinese Traditional Medicine
LIU, HUANLAN, Basic Medical Sciences
LIU, JUN, Medicine
LIU, SHICHANG, Medicine
LIU, XIAOBIN, Basic Medical Sciences
LUO, RONGJING, Basic Medical Sciences
LUO, YUNJIAN, Medicine
LU, YUBO, Medicine
OU, YONGXIN, Basic Medical Sciences
OUYANG, HUIQING, Medicine
PAN, YI, Basic Medical Sciences
PENG, SHENGQUAN, Medicine
QIU, HEMING, Medicine
QIU, HONGZHONG, Economy and Administration
WANG, HONGQI, Basic Medical Sciences
WU, MIMAN, Basic Medical Sciences
WU, QINGHE, Chinese Traditional Medicine
XIONG, MANQI, Medicine
XU, HONGHUA, Chinese Traditional Medicine
XU, NENGGUI, Acupuncture and Massage
XU, ZHIWEI, Basic Medical Sciences
YANG, SHUNYI, Acupuncture and Massage
YANG, ZHIMIN, Medicine
YUAN, HAO, Medicine
ZHANG, HONG, Acupuncture and Massage
ZHANG, JIAWEI, Acupuncture and Massage
ZHOU, DAIHAN, Medicine
ZHOU, LILING, Chinese Traditional Medicine
ZHUANG, LIXING, Acupuncture and Massage

GUIZHOU UNIVERSITY

Guiyang
Telephone: (851) 3851187
E-mail: fa@gzu.edu.cn

Internet: www.gzu.edu.cn

Founded 1902 as Guizhou Institute of Higher Learning, current name adopted 1950, merged with Guizhou Univ. of Technology 2004

Colleges of agriculture, art, chemical engineering, civil engineering and building construction, computer science and information, continuing education, economics, electrical engineering, forestry, humanities, international studies, law, life science, management, materials and metallurgical, mechanical engineering, mining, resource and environment engineering, science, science and technology, vocational education, zoology

Pres.: ZHENG QIANG
Vice-Pres.: KIM TAO

Library: 3.7m. vols
Number of teachers: 2,530
Number of students: 44,588

Publications: *Journal of Guizhou University, Journal of Guizhou University of Technology, Journal of Mountain Agriculture and Biology*

HARBIN ENGINEERING UNIVERSITY

145 Nantong St, Harbin 150001, Heilongjiang Province
Telephone: (451) 2519212
E-mail: heu@public.hr.hl.cn
Internet: www.hrbeu.edu.cn

Founded 1953
Academic year: September to July

Pres.: Prof. QIU CHANGHUA
Sec. of the Univ. Party Cttee: LIU ZHIGANG

Library of 900,000 vols
Number of teachers: 2,200
Number of students: 23,000

Publications: *Applied Science and Technology, Journal of HEU, Overseas Science and Technology*

HARBIN INSTITUTE OF TECHNOLOGY

92 West Dazhi St, 150001 Harbin
Telephone: (451) 86412114
E-mail: president@hit.edu.cn
Internet: www.hit.edu.cn

Founded 1920
State control

Pres.: Prof. WANG SHUGUO
Vice-Pres.: DENG ZONGQUAN
Vice-Pres.: HAN JIECAI
Vice-Pres.: DING XUEMEI
Vice-Pres.: GUO BIN
Librarian: SHI HUILAI

Library of 1,000,000 vols
Number of teachers: 2,944
Number of students: 42,695

Publications: *Higher Engineering Education, Journal, Metal Science and Technology, Studying Computers, Technology of Energy Conservation*

DEANS

School of Astronautics: Prof. JIA SHILOU
School of Computer and Electrical Engineering: Prof. HONG WENXUE
School of Electric Mechanical Engineering: Prof. WANG SHUGUO
School of Energy Science and Engineering: Prof. WANG ZUWEN
School of Humanities and Social Sciences: Prof. JIANG ZHENHUA
School of Management: LI YIJUN
School of Materials Science and Engineering: Prof. ZHAO LIANCHENG
School of Science: Prof. GENG WANZHEN

HARBIN MEDICAL UNIVERSITY

194 Xuehu Rd, Nan Gang, Harbin 150086, Heilongjiang Province
Telephone: (451) 86671349
Internet: www.hrbmu.edu.cn

Founded 1926
Dept of Education of Heilongjiang Province control
Academic year: September to July

Pres.: YANG BAOFENG
Vice-Pres.: CAO DEPIN
Vice-Pres.: LI YUKUI
Vice-Pres.: LIU WENCHUAN
Vice-Pres.: WO ZHENZHONG
Head of Graduate Dept: ZHANG BAOXING
Librarian: YUE WEIPING

Number of teachers: 1,151
Number of students: 9,228 (6,414 full-time, 2,814 part-time)

Publications: *Chinese Journal of Endemiology* (6 a year), *Journal* (6 a year)

DEANS

Branch of Harbin Medical University: ZHANG SHIXUE
Department of Bioinformatics: LI XIA
First School of Medicine: ZHOU JIN
School of Basic Medical Sciences: FU SONGBIN
School of Mouth Cavity Medical Science: ZHANG BIN
School of Nursing: LI JIANFENG
School of Pharmacy: ZHU DALING
School of Public Health: SUN CHANGHAO
Second School of Medicine: ZHANG QIFAN

PROFESSORS

AI, MINGLI, Medicine
BAI, XINZHI, Medicine
BAO, XIUZENG, Pharmacy
BAO, YONGPING, Public Health
BI, WENSHU, Medicine
BI, ZHENGGANG, Medicine
CHEN, BINGQING, Public Health
CHEN, GENGXIN, Medicine
CHEN, LI, Public Health
CHEN, SHUXIANG, Medicine
CHEN, XIUJIE, Pharmacy
CHENG, DEQING, University Branch
CHENG, LIHA, Medicine
CHENG, ZHI, Basic Medical Sciences
CHI, ZIANG, Medicine
CUI, HAO, Medicine
CUI, HONGBIN, Public Health
CUI, LIANBIN, Medicine
CUI, SHI, Medicine
CUI, YUNPU, Medicine
DAI, HAIBIN, Medicine
DAI, QINSHUN, Medicine
DAI, ZE, University Branch
DU, XIUXHEN, Medicine
DU, ZHIMIN, Pharmacy
FAN, LIHUA, Public Health
FU, LU, Medicine
FU, SHIYING, Medicine
FU, SONGBIN, Basic Medical Sciences
GAO, GUANGMING, Dentistry
GAO, GUANGXIN, University Branch
GAO, RUIJU, Medicine
GAO, SHANLING, Medicine
GONG, LINGTAO, University Branch
GU, SUYI, Medicine
GUAN, JINGMING, Medicine
GUAN, YONGMEI, Medicine
GUAN, ZHENZHONG, Medicine
GUO, LUNSHU, University Branch
GUO, ZHENG, Bioinformatics
HAN, DE'EN, Medicine
HAN, DEWEN, University Branch
HAN, FENGPING, Medicine
HAN, MINGZI, Medicine
HAN, XIANGYANG, Medicine
HAO, LI, University Branch
HONG, FENGYANG, Medicine
HONG, WANQING, Medicine
HU, SHUANGJIU, Medicine
HU, XIAOCHEN, Medicine
HUANG, YONGLIN, Medicine
HUANG, ZHENGSONG, Medicine
JI, YUBIN, Pharmacy
JI, ZHUANZHEN, University Branch
JIA, GUODONG, Medicine
JIANG, GUIQIN, Medicine
JIANG, HONGCHI, Medicine
JIANG, LIJING, Medicine
JIANG, XUEHAI, Medicine
LI, BAIXIANG, Public Health
LI, BANQUAN, Medicine
LI, BAOJIE, Medicine
LI, BAOXIN, Pharmacy
LI, BIN, Medicine
LI, BO, Basic Medical Sciences
LI, CHANGXHUN, Medicine
LI, CHUNMING, Medicine
LI, HEYU, Medicine
LI, JIANFENG, Nursing
LI, JIXUE, Medicine
LI, KANG, Public Health
LI, PEILING, Medicine
LI, QIUJIE, Nursing
LI, SHULIN, Medicine
LI, WEIMIN, Medicine
LI, XIA, Bioinformatics
LI, XIA, Pharmacy
LI, XIAOYUN, Medicine
LI, XIULAN, Medicine
LI, YURONG, Basic Medical Sciences
LI, ZHIXU, Medicine
LI, ZUNYI, Medicine
LIN, XUESONG, University Branch
LIN, YIJIA, Medicine
LIU, BAOLIN, Public Health
LIU, BOSONG, Medicine
LIU, DEXIANG, University Branch
LIU, ENZHONG, Medicine
LIU, FENGJI, Medicine
LIU, FENGZHI, Pharmacy
LIU, HAITANG, Medicine
LIU, HONG, Dentistry
LIU, HONGYUAN, Public Health
LIU, JINJIE, University Branch
LIU, RUIHAI, Public Health
LIU, SHUDE, Medicine
LIU, TIEFU, Medicine
LIU, WENZHU, Medicine
LIU, XIANJUN, Medicine
LIU, YUFENG, Medicine
LIU, ZHICHENG, Public Health
LOU, GUIRONG, Medicine
LU, DAGUANG, Medicine
LU, LEI, Medicine
LU, MINGJUN, Public Health
MA, YINGJI, Medicine
MENG, FANCHAO, Medicine
MENG, HUANBIN, Medicine
QI, YOUCHENG, Medicine
QIAO, GUOFENG, Pharmacy
QIN, HUADONG, Medicine
QIU, FENGQIN, Medicine
QIU, ZHONGYI, Medicine
QU, RENHAI, Medicine
QU, XIUFEN, Medicine
QUAN, HUDE, Public Health
SANG, YIMIN, Medicine
SHENG, YUCHEN, Medicine
SHI, YUZHI, Medicine
SI, ZHUANG, Medicine
SONG, CHUNFANG, Medicine
SONG, CUIPING, Medicine
SONG, ZHIMIN, University Branch
SUN, AHIBO, Medicine
SUN, CHANGHAO, Public Health
SUN, GANG, University Branch
SUN, JIANPING, Pharmacy
SUN, KAOXIANG, Pharmacy
SUN, KEMIN, Medicine
SUN, XIANCHAO, Medicine
SUN, YUNQIAO, Medicine
TAN, TIEZHENG, Medicine
TAN, WENHUA, Medicine
TIAN, SULI, Medicine

WANG, BINYOU, Public Health
WANG, BOWEN, Medicine
WANG, CAIXIA, University Branch
WANG, CHUNXIANG, Medicine
WANG, FUJING, Medicine
WANG, GUIZHAO, Medicine
WANG, GUOQING, Medicine
WANG, HUIMIN, Medicine
WANG, JINGHUA, Medicine
WANG, JINGHUA, University Branch
WANG, JUNCHENG, Medicine
WANG, LI, University Branch
WANG, LING, Pharmacy
WANG, LINGSHAN, Medicine
WANG, MENGXUE, Medicine
WANG, MINGJUN, Medicine
WANG, NAIQIAN, Medicine
WANG, SHENGFA, Medicine
WANG, SHOUREN, Medicine
WANG, TAIHE, Medicine
WANG, XIAOFENG, Medicine
WANG, XIUFAN, Medicine
WANG, ZHIBANG, Medicine
WANG, ZHIGUO, Pharmacy
WEI, LINYU, Medicine
WU, DEQUAN, Medicine
WU, KUN, Public Health
WU, LIJIE, Public Health
WU, LINHUA, Pharmacy
WU, QUNHONG, Public Health
WU, YONGWEN, Medicine
XI, ZHENSHAN, Medicine
XING, JIE, University Branch
XU, JUNRU, Medicine
XU, LINSHENG, Medicine
XU, XUGUANG, Medicine
YANG, BAOFENG, Pharmacy
YANG, FUMING, Medicine
YANG, SHIXHUN, Medicine
YANG, WEILIANG, Medicine
YANG, XUEWEI, Medicine
YAO, LI, Medicine
YE, YUANZHU, Medicine
YIN, HUIQING, Medicine
YIN, KESEN, University Branch
YIN, XIAOQIAN, Medicine
YU, BO, Medicine
YU, DANPING, Medicine
YU, JINGHAI, Pharmacy
YU, JINGYUAN, Medicine
YU, WEIGANG, Medicine
YU, WEIPING, Public Health
YU, XIUXIAN, University Branch
YU, ZHONGSHU, Medicine
YUAN, XIZHEN, University Branch
YUAN, FENG, Medicine
YUE, WU, Medicine
ZHANG, BAOKU, Medicine
ZHANG, BIN, Dentistry
ZHANG, FENGMING, Basic Medical Sciences
ZHANG, JUN, University Branch
ZHANG, MINGWEN, Medicine
ZHANG, PENG, Medicine
ZHANG, QIFAN, Medicine
ZHANG, SHUQI, Basic Medical Sciences
ZHANG, SHUTAO, Medicine
ZHANG, TINGDONG, Medicine
ZHANG, XIANGLI, University Branch
ZHANG, XIAOXIAN, Medicine
ZHANG, XICHEN, University Branch
ZHANG, XINYING, Medicine
ZHANG, XIUQI, Medicine
ZHANG, XIYU, Medicine
ZHANG, YAN, Medicine
ZHANG, YINA, Medicine
ZHANG, YUCHENG, Medicine
ZHANG, YUCHUN, Medicine
ZHANG, ZHONGYI, Public Health
ZHAO, CHANGJI, Medicine
ZHAO, SHUZHEN, Medicine
ZHAO, YASHUANG, Public Health
ZHAO, ZHIHAI, Medicine
ZHONG, ZHENYU, Medicine
ZHOU, JIN, Medicine
ZHOU, WENXUE, Medicine
ZHOU, XIAOMING, Medicine
ZHOU, YUQOI, University Branch
ZHOU, ZHONGFANG, Medicine
ZHU, DALING, Pharmacy
ZHU, GUICHUN, Medicine
ZHU, QUAN, Medicine
ZHU, SHUYING, Medicine
ZHU, SIHE, Medicine
ZHU, XIUYING, Medicine
ZHU, YAN, Medicine

HARBIN NORMAL UNIVERSITY

1 Danan Rd, Liming Dist., Harbin 150080, Heilongjiang Province
Telephone: (451) 86376222
E-mail: chinahsdwsc@126.com
Internet: www.hrbnu.edu.cn

Founded 1951
Academic year: September to July

Pres.: CHEN SHUTAO
Vice-Pres.: FU DAOBIN
Vice-Pres.: FU JUNLONG
Vice-Pres.: LU YUSUN
Vice-Pres.: SUN FUGUANG
Vice-Pres.: WANG XUANZHANG
Vice-Pres.: WANG ZHONGQIAO
Librarian: GUO SHIMING

Library of 3,340,000 vols
Number of teachers: 3,695
Number of students: 31,835

Publications: *Continuing Education Research* (6 a year), *Heilongjiang Researches on Higher Education* (6 a year), *Natural Science Journal of Harbin Normal University* (6 a year), *Northern Forum* (6 a year)

DEANS

College of Arts: LU XUSUN
College of Computer Science and Mathematics: WANG YUWEN
College of Education Science and Technology: ZHAO HENIN
College of Life and Environment: ZHAO WENGE
College of Literature: GUO CONGLIN
College of Physics and Chemistry: LU SHUCHENG
College of Politics, Law and Economics Management: XU XIAOFENG
College of Sports Sciences: LIU ZHONGWU
Foreign Language Institute: JIANG TAO

PROFESSORS

CHEN, SHUTAO, Computer Science and Mathematics
DAI, BOQING, Physics and Chemistry
FENG, SUYUN, Literature
FU, DAOBIN, Literature
GAO, HUIMING, Arts
GE, YUNCHENG, Physics and Chemistry
GE, ZHIYI, Literature
GUO, CONGLIN, Literature
HUA, DEZUN, Life and Environment
LI, CHANGYU, Literature
LI, JILIN, Life and Environment
LU, SHUCHENG, Physics and Chemistry
LU, YUSUN, Arts
LUO, ZHENYA, Literature
SONG, WEN, Computer Science and Mathematics
SUN, MUTIAN, Literature
TAO, YABIN, Arts
TIAN, GUOWEI, Life and Environment
WANG, LISAN, Arts
WANG, TONGCHANG, Education Science and Technology
WANG, XUANZHANG, Physics and Chemistry
WANG, YUWEN, Computer Science and Mathematics
WANG, ZHONGQIAO, Literature
XU, GUOLIN, Physics and Chemistry
XU, HENGYONG, Physics and Chemistry
XU, XIANGLING, Life and Environment
XU, XIAOFENG, Literature
YU, LIJIE, Life and Environment
ZHANG, JINGCHI, Literature
ZHANG, JUNMING, Politics, Law and Economics Management
ZHANG, YONGZHENG, Computer Science and Mathematics
ZHAO, HENIN, Education Science and Technology
ZHAO, YUNLONG, Arts
ZHOU, JINXIAN, Literature

HARBIN UNIVERSITY OF SCIENCE AND TECHNOLOGY

57 Xuefu Rd, Nan Gang, Harbin 150080, Heilongjiang Province
Telephone: (451) 86390114
E-mail: wzgl@hrbust.edu.cn
Internet: www.hrbust.edu.cn

Founded 1953
Academic year: September to July

Pres.: ZHAO QI
Vice-Pres.: DU GUANGCUN
Vice-Pres.: LI DAYONG
Vice-Pres.: TENG CUNXIAN
Vice-Pres.: WU JUNFENG
Vice-Pres.: ZHAO HONG
Head of Graduate Dept: ZHEN MINLI
Librarian: CHEN JIE

Library of 173,800 vols
Number of teachers: 2,379
Number of students: 19,907

Publications: *Electric Machines and Control* (4 a year), *Journal* (6 a year), *Science, Technology and Management* (6 a year)

DEANS

College of Applied Science: CUI YUNAN
College of Chemistry and Environmental Engineering: LIU BO
College of Computer and Control Science: QIAO PEILI
College of Electrical and Electronic Engineering: WEI XINLAO
College of International Culture Education: ZHAO DAWEI
College of Material Science and Engineering: GUO ERJUN
College of Observation Technology and Communications Engineering: YU XIAOYANG
Foreign Language Institute: LUI LIQUN
School of Economics and Management: XIU GUOYI
School of Law: ZHANG YING
School of Mechanical Engineering: SHAO JUNPENG
Software College: LIU SHENGHUI

PROFESSORS

CHEN, DEYUN, Computer and Control Science
CHEN, DONGYAN, Applied Science
CHEN, GUANGHAI, Applied Science
CHEN, RONGDUO, Economics and Management
CHEN, YUQUAN, Mechanical Engineering
CUI, YUNAN, Applied Science
DENG, CAIXIA, Applied Science
DU, DESHENG, Computer and Control Science
DU, KUNMEI, Electrical and Electronic Engineering
DUAN, TIEQUN, Mechanical Engineering
FAN, JINGYUN, Material Science and Engineering
FAN, YONG, Material Science and Engineering
GAO, ANBANG, Mechanical Engineering
GAO, CHANGYUAN, Economics and Management
GAO, ZHONGWEN, Computer and Control Science
GE, BAOJUN, Electrical and Electronic Engineering
GE, JIANGHUA, Mechanical Engineering

GUO, ERJUN, Material Science and Engineering
GUO, JIANYING, Observation Technology and Communications Engineering
HE, ZHONGXIAO, Computer and Control Science
HU, BAOXIA, Computer and Control Science
JI, DONGHAI, Applied Science
JI, ZHESHENG, Material Science and Engineering
JING, XU, Computer and Control Science
KONG, FANLIANG, Applied Science
LEI, QINGQUAN, Electrical and Electronic Engineering
LI, DAYONG, Material Science and Engineering
LI, DONGMEI, Applied Science
LI, FENGZHEN, Material Science and Engineering
LI, GECHENG, Computer and Control Science
LI, HONGXIA, Economics and Management
LI, LEI, Economics and Management
LI, QUANLI, Computer and Control Science
LI, WEILI, Electrical and Electronic Engineering
LI, YUMING, Chemistry and Environmental Engineering
LI, ZHENJIA, Mechanical Engineering
LI, ZHONGHUA, Electrical and Electronic Engineering
LIANG, JINGXI, Economics and Management
LIANG, YANPING, Electrical and Electronic Engineering
LIN, JIAQI, Applied Science
LIU, BO, Chemistry and Environmental Engineering
LIU, RUNTAO, Applied Science
LIU, SHENGHUI, Computer and Control Science
LIU, WEIJUN, Mechanical Engineering
LIU, WENLI, Electrical and Electronic Engineering
LIU, XIANLI, Mechanical Engineering
LIU, XINGJIA, Mechanical Engineering
LUO, XIAOGUANG, Economics and Management
MA, HONGFEI, Economics and Management
MA, HUAIJIAN, Observation Technology and Communications Engineering
MENG, DAWEI, Electrical and Electronic Engineering
PAN, ZHUANGYUAN, Applied Science
QI, LIANGQUN, Economics and Management
QIAO, PEILI, Computer and Control Science
REN, FUJUN, Mechanical Engineering
SHAO, JUNPENG, Mechanical Engineering
SHAO, TIEZHU, Economics and Management
SHI, LIANSHENG, Material Science and Engineering
SONG, JIASHENG, Economics and Management
SONG, RUNBIN, Material Science and Engineering
SUI, XIULING, Mechanical Engineering
SUN, FENGLIAN, Material Science and Engineering
SUN, LIJIONG, Computer and Control Science
SUN, MINGSONG, Computer and Control Science
SUN, QUANYING, Mechanical Engineering
SUN, XIAOJUN, Chemistry and Envirnomental Engineering
TAN, GUANGYU, Mechanical Engineering
TENG, CUNXIAN, Economics and Management
WAN, GUOQIN, Material Science and Engineering
WANG, HONGQI, Economics and Management
WANG, LIPING, Material Science and Engineering
WANG, MUKUN, Observation Technology and Communications Engineering
WANG, PEIDONG, Computer and Control Science
WANG, TONG, Mechanical Engineering
WANG, XUAN, Applied Science
WANG, XUDONG, Electrical and Electronic Engineering
WANG, YIJIE, Applied Science
WANG, YUDONG, Economics and Management
WEI, XINLAO, Electrical and Electronic Engineering
WEN, JIABIN, Electrical and Electronic Engineering
WU, HONGBO, Economics and Management
WU, JUNFENG, Computer and Control Science
WU, YUBIN, Material Science and Engineering
WU, ZHONGYANG, Computer and Control Science
XIAOXU, Material Science and Engineering
XIU, GUOYI, Economics and Management
XU, LI, Mechanical Engineering
XU, XIAOCUN, Mechanical Engineering
YANG, JIAXIANG, Electrical and Electronic Engineering
YANG, MINGGUI, Mechanical Engineering
YIN, JINGHUA, Applied Science
YOU, BO, Mechanical Engineering
YU, HUILI, Mechanical Engineering
YU, LI, Economics and Management
YU, XIAOYANG, Observation Technology and Communications Engineering
YU, YANDONG, Material Science and Engineering
YUAN, JIANXIONG, Mechanical Engineering
ZHAI, LILI, Economics and Management
ZHANG, CUNXI, Electrical and Electronic Engineering
ZHANG, CUNYI, Mechanical Engineering
ZHANG, DECHENG, Economics and Management
ZHANG, GUOJIE, Economics and Management
ZHANG, JIAZHEN, Mechanical Engineering
ZHANG, LIYONG, Observation Technology and Communications Engineering
ZHANG, XIANYOU, Material Science and Engineering
ZHANG, XIAOHONG, Electrical and Electronic Engineering
ZHANG, YONGDE, Mechanical Engineering
ZHANG, YONGJUN, Mechanical Engineering
ZHANG, ZHONGMING, Mechanical Engineering
ZHAO, DAWEI, Economics and Management
ZHAO, HONG, Electrical and Electronic Engineering
ZHAO, XINLUO, Economics and Management
ZHEN, DIANCUN, Electrical and Electronic Engineering
ZHEN, MINLI, Mechanical Engineering

HEBEI MEDICAL UNIVERSITY

361 Zhongshan East Rd, Shijiazhuang City 050017, Hebei Province
Telephone: (311) 6048177
E-mail: fad@hebmu.edu.cn
Internet: www.hebmu.edu.cn

Founded 1915
Academic year: September to July

Pres.: WEN JINKUN
Vice-Pres: DUAN HUIJUN
Vice-Pres: JI HAIJIN
Vice-Pres: WANG RUNTIAN
Vice-Pres: WANG GENGXIN
Vice-Pres: WANG YANTIAN
Vice-Pres: ZHANG ZHANKUI
Head of Graduate School: CONG BIN
Librarian: MO ZHENYUN

Library of 541,000 vols
Number of teachers: 887
Number of students: 12,753

Publications: *Chinese Journal of Ultrasonography* (12 a year), *Clinical Focus* (6 a year), *Journal* (6 a year)

HEBEI NORMAL UNIVERSITY

Number 20, E Rd, Second Ring S, Yuhua Dist., Shijiazhuang 050024, Hebei Province
Telephone: (311) 80789793
E-mail: hnuio@sina.com
Internet: www.hebtu.edu.cn

Founded 1902
State control
Language of instruction: Chinese
Academic year: September to July

Pres.: Prof. Dr JIANG CHUNLAN
Vice-Pres: Prof. Dr DAI JIANBING
Vice-Pres.: Prof. Dr DENG MINGLI
Vice-Pres.: Prof. Dr GAO FULU
Vice-Pres.: Prof. LU JUNHENG
Vice-Pres.: Prof. Dr WANG CHANGHUA
Vice-Pres.: Prof. WANG CHUNLI
Vice-Pres.: Prof. Dr YANG HUANJIN
Librarian: Prof. Dr HOU DENGLU

Library of 3,270,000 vols
Number of teachers: 2,863
Number of students: 56,769 (30,985 undergraduate, 3,519 graduate, 22,265 part-time)

Publications: *Journal of Hebei Normal University (Education Science Edition)* (4 a year), *Journal of Hebei Normal University (Nature Science Edition)* (4 a year), *Journal of Hebei Normal University (Social Science Edition)* (4 a year)

DEANS

College of Business: Prof. FENG MEI
College of Chemistry and Material Science: Prof. MENG LINGPENG
College of Education Science: Prof. XUE YANHUA
College of Fine Arts and Design: Prof. JIANG SHIGUO
College of Foreign Languages: Prof. Dr LI ZHENGSHUAN
College of History and Culture: Prof. WU JIQING
College of Information Technology: Prof. ZHAO DONGMEI
College of Journalism and Communication: Prof. TONG WENYAO
College of Law and Political Science: Prof. ZHANG JILIANG
College of Life Science: Prof. GUO YI
College of Literature: Prof. YAN FULING
College of Mathematics and Information Science: Prof. MI JUSHENG
College of Music: Prof. ZHANG YUEJIN
College of Physical Education: Prof. HE YUXIU
College of Physics and Information Engineering: Prof. LIU YING
College of Public Administration: Prof. ZHAO XIAOLAN
College of Resources and the Environment: Prof. GE JINGFENG
College of Software: Prof. ZHANG ZILONG
College of Tourism: Prof. LU ZI
College of Vocational and Technology: Prof. DIAO ZHENJUN
Huihua College: Prof. CAI XINHUA

PROFESSORS

BAI, ZIMING, Foreign Languages
CHANG, CONGQIAN, Foreign Languages
CHEN, CHAO, Literature
CHEN, HUI, Literature
CHENG, RUZHEN, Mathematics and Information
CUI, JIYIN, Literature
CUI, ZHIYUAN, Literature
DENG, MINGLI, Mathematics and Information
DI, ZHAOYING, Mathematics and Information
DING, REN, Mathematics and Information
DONG, JUNMIN, Foreign Languages
DU, JIANZHENG, Education Science
DUAN, XIAOYING, Foreign Languages

DUAN, ZHEREN, Foreign Languages
FAN, SHUCHENG, Law and Political Science
GAO, SHUNSHENG, Mathematics and Information
GAO, SUOGANG, Mathematics and Information
GAO, TING, Mathematics and Information
GAO, XINFA, Resources and Environment Science
GAO, YUANXIANG, Resources and Environment Science
GAO, ZHIHUAI, Foreign Languages
GE, JINGFENG, Resources and Environment Science
GU, ZHONGQUAN, Foreign Languages
GUI, DINGKANG, Foreign Languages
GUO, BAOLIANG, Literature
GUO, QUNYING, Foreign Languages
HE, ANBAO, Foreign Languages
HE, LIANFA, Mathematics and Information
HU, WENLIANG, Resources and Environment Science
HU, YINGTONG, Foreign Languages
HUANG, HONGQUAN, Foreign Languages
HUANG, HONGXU, Foreign Languages
HUANG, HUAFANG, Resources and Environment Science
JIANG, CHUNLAN, Mathematics and Information
KANG, QINDE, Mathematics and Information
LEI, JIANGUO, Mathematics and Information
LI, SHIJU, Law and Political Science
LI, SUO, Literature
LI, TIANGUI, Law and Political Science
LI, XILONG, Literature
LI, YANNIAN, Literature
LI, ZHENGSHUAN, Foreign Languages
LIANG, YI, Foreign Languages
LIANG, ZHIHE, Mathematics and Information
LIE, WUJUN, Mathematics and Information
LIU, HONG, Education Science
LIU, HUANQUN, Foreign Languages
LIU, MING, Education Science
LIU, SHITIAN, Law and Political Science
LIU, YAN, Resources and Environment Science
LIU, ZHONGMING, Law and Political Science
LU, ZHONGYI, Education Science
LU, ZI, Resources and Environment Science
MA, HENGJUN, Literature
MA, RENHUI, Resources and Environment Science
MA, YUN, Literature
MENG, GUOHUA, Foreign Languages
MI, JUSHENG, Mathematics and Information
NAN, YUESHENG, Resources and Environment Science
PAN, BINXIN, Foreign Languages
QIAN, JINPING, Resources and Environment Science
QIAO, YUYING, Mathematics and Information
SHI, GUOXING, Education Science
SHI, JINGXIU, Literature
SU, BAORONG, Literature
TANG, GUOZENG, Law and Political Science
TIAN, XIUYUN, Law and Political Science
WANG, CHANGHUA, Literature
WANG, DELIN, Education Science
WANG, FENGMIN, Law and Political Science
WANG, FUISHENG, Foreign Languages
WANG, JIANXUN, Foreign Languages
WANG, WEI, Resources and Environment Science
WANG, XIN, Education Science
WANG, YANYING, Mathematics and Information
WANG, ZHENCHANG, Foreign Languages
WU, WEIREN, Foreign Languages
WU, XIUHUA, Literature
WU, ZHENGDE, Mathematics and Information
XIAO, GUIQING, Law and Political Science
XING, JIANCHANG, Literature
XU, JIANPING, Literature
XU, QINGHAI, Resources and Environment Science
YAN, KELE, Education Science
YANG, CHUNHONG, Mathematics and Information
YANG, DONG, Literature
YANG, TONGYONG, Literature
YI, SHENGLEI, Foreign Languages
YI, WEI, Foreign Languages
ZHAI, HONGCHANG, Education Science
ZHAN, YUANJIE, Resources and Environment Science
ZHANG, CHENGZONG, Resources and Environment Science
ZHANG, GUOYING, Foreign Languages
ZHANG, JI, Law and Political Science
ZHANG, JILIANG, Law and Political Science
ZHANG, JUNCAI, Literature
ZHANG, JUNHAI, Resources and Environment Science
ZHANG, WENXIANG, Law and Political Science
ZHANG, YIWEN, Resources and Environment Science
ZHANG, YOUHUI, Mathematics and Information
ZHANG, ZHENGGUO, Mathematics and Information
ZHANG, ZILONG, Mathematics and Information
ZHENG, ZHENFENG, Literature
ZHUANG, BIAO, Literature

HEBEI UNIVERSITY

1 Hezuo Rd, Baoding 071002, Hebei Province
Telephone: (312) 5079709
E-mail: hbu@mail.hbu.edu.cn
Internet: www.hbu.edu.cn

Founded 1921
Hebei Province control
Academic year: September to July

Pres.: WANG HONGRUI
Vice-Pres.: HA MINGHU
Vice-Pres.: LI SHUANGYIN
Vice-Pres.: SUN HANWEN
Vice-Pres.: SUN JINGYUAN
Vice-Pres.: WEI SUI
Head of Graduate College: HA MINGHU
Librarian: LI ZHENGANG

Library of 3,170,000 vols
Number of teachers: 2,500
Number of students: 47,500

Publications: *Journal* (natural sciences, 6 a year), *Journal* (philosophy and social sciences, 6 a year)

DEANS

College of Arts: YANG WENHUI
College of Chemistry and Environment Science: MA FENGRU
College of Economics: GU LIUBAO
College of Education: HE GUOQIN
College of Electronic and Information Engineering: WANG PEIGUANG
College of Foreign Languages: LI ZUOWEN
College of Industry and Commerce: WANG HONGRUI
College of Life Science: REN GUODONG
College of Literature: LI JINSHAN
College of Machinery and Civil Engineering: ZHANG JIANHUI
College of Management: SUN JIANFU
College of Mathematics and Computer Studies: WANG XIZHAO
College of Medicine: YANG GENGLIANG
College of Physics and Technology: HAN LI
College of Political Science and Law: LIU ZHIGANG
College of Quality and Technical Supervision: LI XIAOTING
Faculty of Journalism and Communication: BAI GUI

PROFESSORS

BA, XINWU, Chemistry and Environment Science
BAI, GUI, Journalism and Communication
BAI, SHUQIN, Political Science and Law
BI, WUQIN, Political Science and Law
BIAN, ZHAOLING, Management
CAI, HAIBO, Arts
CAO, MINGLUN, Foreign Languages
CAO, RU, Journalism and Communication
CAO, YUPING, Life Science
CHEN, JUNYING, Education
CHEN, SHUANGXIN, Arts
CHEN, ZHIGUO, Economics
CHENG, CHANGYU, Economics
CHENG, XINXUAN, Management
DING, JIHUI, Machinery and Civil Engineering
DING, XIAOZHENG, Journalism and Communication
DONG, LIFANG, Physics and Technology
DONG, ZHENGXIN, Economics
DU, HAO, Journalism and Communication
DU, YOUJUN, Journalism and Communication
FANG, BAOAN, Management
FANG, YOULIANG, Machinery and Civil Engineering
FENG, XIUQI, Education
FENG, YULONG, Life Science
FU, SONGTAO, Education
GAO, JUNGANG, Chemistry and Environment Science
GAO, SHUJUN, Management
GU, LIUBAO, Economics
GU, XIAOHUA, Management
GU, ZHONGLIANG, Arts
GUO, BAOZENG, Electronic and Information Engineering
GUO, FULIANG, Literature
GUO, JIAN, Arts
GUO, JIAN, Industry and Commerce
GUO, SHIXIN, Economics
GUO, XUYUAN, Literature
HAN, CHENGWU, Literature
HAN, LI, Physics and Technology
HAN, PANGSHAN, Arts
HAN, PANSHAN, Literature
HAN, XIUJING, Economics
HE, GUOQIN, Education
HE, XUELI, Life Science
HE, ZHIPU, Arts
HOU, GUANYING, Journalism and Communication
HOU, YUHUA, Management
HU, NING, Arts
HU, YAN, Management
HUA, ZHUXIN, Industry and Commerce
HUANG, GENGZHUO, Arts
HUANG, PENGZHANG, Management
JIAN, MIN, Arts
JIANG, JIANYUN, Literature
JIANG, JIZHI, Life Science
JIANG, LIHUA, Economics
JIAO, GUOZHANG, Journalism and Communication
JIAO, MAOLIN, Literature
JIE, YONGJUN, Arts
KAN, ZHENRONG, Life Science
KANG, SHUSHENG, Economics
KANG, XIANJIANG, Life Science
KONG, LINGHONG, Political Science and Law
LI, FANGHUA, Electronic and Information Engineering
LI, GANSHUN, Economics
LI, GUOHUA, Literature
LI, HEPING, Political Science and Law
LI, HUARUI, Literature
LI, JINSHAN, Literature
LI, JINZHENG, Literature
LI, JITAI, Chemistry and Environment Science
LI, LINJIE, Economics
LI, RENKAI, Literature
LI, SHU, Economics
LI, SHUANGJIE, Economics
LI, SHUQI, Machinery and Civil Engineering
LI, SUMIN, Education
LI, TONGSHUANG, Chemistry and Environment Science
LI, WENCAI, Literature

LI, WENXIU, Machinery and Civil Engineering
LI, XIAOTING, Quality and Technical Supervision
LI, XIAOWEI, Physics and Technology
LI, YAHONG, Journalism and Communication
LI, YANAN, Journalism and Communication
LI, YANBIN, Arts
LI, ZUOWEN, Foreign Languages
LIANG, SUZHEN, Political Science and Law
LIAO, XIANGRU, Life Science
LIU, CUIYING, Management
LIU, HUIWEN, Journalism and Communication
LIU, JINZHONG, Literature
LIU, JINZHU, Arts
LIU, SIJIN, Literature
LIU, YONGRUI, Education
LIU, YUKAI, Literature
LIU, ZHIGANG, Political Science and Law
LIU, ZHIQIANG, Physics and Technology
LIU, ZHIQIANG, Electronic and Information Engineering
LU, HONGPING, Economics
LU, MINGFANG, Physics and Technology
LU, ZIZHENG, Journalism and Communication
MA, CHENGLIAN, Journalism and Communication
MA, YANLING, Management
MAO, ZHUOLIANG, Foreign Languages
MEI, BAOSHU, Arts
MENG, SHIEN, Management
PEI, GUIFEN, Economics
PENG, YINGCAI, Physics and Technology
PENG, YINGCAI, Electronic and Information Engineering
QI, YI, Arts
QIAO, YUNXIA, Journalism and Communication
REN, GUODONG, Life Science
RONG, XINFANG, Foreign Languages
SONG, DENGYUAN, Electronic and Information Engineering
SONG, RUITIAN, Physics and Technology
SONG, YAOWU, Education
SUN, HANWEN, Chemistry and Environmental Science
SUN, SHENGCUN, Journalism and Communication
SUN, ZHIZHONG, Economics
TAO, DAN, Journalism and Communication
TIAN, JIANMING, Literature
TIAN, JUNFENG, Mathematics and Computer Science
WANG, BAOXING, Education
WANG, HONGRUI, Electronic and Information Engineering
WANG, HONGRUI, Industry and Commerce
WANG, JINYING, Economics
WANG, JUNJIE, Journalism and Communication
WANG, JUNLI, Life Science
WANG, PEIGUANG, Electronic and Information Engineering
WANG, QIN, Economics
WANG, SHUHUI, Management
WANG, WENLI, Electronic and Information Engineering
WANG, XIZHAO, Mathematics and Computer Science
WANG, YANLING, Journalism and Communication
WANG, YINSHUN, Physics and Technology
WANG, ZHENCHAO, Electronic and Information Engineering
WU, GENGZHEN, Journalism and Communication
WU, HONGCHENG, Education
WU, YAQING, Economics
WU, YONGZHEN, Management
XIE, CHANGFA, Education
XIONG, RENWANG, Arts
XU, JINGZHI, Physics and Technology
XU, MING, Journalism and Communication
XUE, KEMIU, Literature
YANG, BAOZHONG, Literature
YANG, GENGLIANG, Chemistry and Environment Science
YANG, GENGLIANG, Medicine
YANG, WENHUI, Arts
YANG, XIUGUO, Journalism and Communication
YANG, XUEXIN, Industry and Commerce
YAO, ZIHUA, Chemistry and Environment Science
ZHANG, DAOCHUAN, Life Science
ZHANG, DEQIANG, Chemistry and Environment Science
ZHANG, JIANHUI, Machinery and Civil Engineering
ZHANG, LIPING, Life Science
ZHANG, LIXIN, Education
ZHANG, RISHENG, Education
ZHANG, SHUANGCAI, Management
ZHANG, WEI, Journalism and Communication
ZHANG, WENCHUAN, Arts
ZHANG, YANJING, Political Science and Law
ZHANG, YUKE, Economics
ZHAO, YANYAN, Medicine
ZHEN, SHUQING, Political Science and Law
ZHENG, YUNLONG, Physics and Technology
ZHENG, ZHITING, Literature
ZHU, BAOCHENG, Life Science
ZHU, MINGSHENG, Life Science

HEBEI UNIVERSITY OF ECONOMICS AND BUSINESS

47 Xue Fu Rd, 050061 Shijiazhuang
Telephone: (311) 87655607
E-mail: ies@heuet.edu.cn
Internet: www.heuet.edu.cn

Founded 1995 by merger of Hebei Institute of Finance and Economics, Hebei Univ. of Economics and Trade and Hebei Business College

Pres.: JI LIANGGANG
Vice-Pres.: GENG YANJUN
Vice-Pres.: SHEN FUPING
Vice-Pres.: LIU JIANPING
Vice-Pres.: WU JIANQI
Vice-Pres.: CHAI ZHENGUO
Vice-Pres.: WU YIQING

Library of 250,000 vols
Number of teachers: 1,950
Number of students: 31,000

Publication: *Economics and Management*

HEFEI UNIVERSITY OF TECHNOLOGY

193 Tunxi Rd, 230009, Hefei
Telephone: (551) 4655210
Internet: www.hfut.edu.cn

Founded 1945

Schools of architecture and arts, biotechnology and food engineering, chemical engineering, civil engineering, computer and information, electric engineering and automation, humanities, instrument science and opto-electronic engineering, machinery and automobile engineering, management, material science and engineering, resources and environment, sciences

Pres.: XU WEI FIR
Vice-Pres.: ZHAO HAN
Vice-Pres.: WU CHENG
Vice-Pres.: LIU ZHIFENG
Registrar: ZHOU XU
Librarian: SUN XUANYIN

Number of teachers: 4,513
Number of students: 18,216

Publications: *Engineering Mathematics, Forecasting, Journal, Teaching and Study of Industrial Automation, Techniques Abroad, Tribology Abroad*

HEILONGJIANG UNIVERSITY OF CHINESE MEDICINE

24 Dongli Section He Ping Rd, Harbin 150040, Heilongjiang Province
Telephone: (451) 82118254
Internet: www.hljucm.net

Founded 1959

Academic year: September to July

Pres.: KUANG HAIXUE
Vice-Pres.: CHENG WEI
Vice-Pres.: LI BINGZHI
Vice-Pres.: LI JINGXIAO
Vice-Pres.: WANG XIJUN
Head of Graduate Dept: NING XIE
Librarian: YOU YANJUN

Number of teachers: 370
Number of students: 5,002 (4,817 full-time, 185 part-time)

Publications: *Acts of Chinese Medicine and Pharmacology* (6 a year), *Information on Traditional Chinese Medicine* (6 a year), *Journal of Clinical Acupuncture and Moxibustion* (12 a year)

DEANS

First School of Medicine: TIAN ZHENKUN
School of Basic Medical Sciences: LI YI
School of Human Sciences: TONG ZILIN
School of Pharmacy: LI YONGJI
Second School of Medicine: SUN ZHONGREN

PROFESSORS

AN, LIWEN, Medicine
CHEN, HONGBIN, Basic Medical Sciences
CHENG, WEIPING, Medicine
DAI, TIECHENG, Medicine
DONG, QINGPING, Medicine
DU, XIAOWEI, Pharmacy
DUAN, FUJIN, Basic Medical Sciences
GAO, QUANGUO, Basic Medical Sciences
GONG, ZHANYUE, Medicine
GU, JIALE, Medicine
HAN, BO, Medicine
HOU, LIHUI, Medicine
HUI, XIULI, Medicine
JIA, GUIZHI, Pharmacy
JIANG, DEYOU, Basic Medical Sciences
JIN, SHUYING, Basic Medical Sciences
KANG, GUANGSHENG, Basic Medical Sciences
KUANG, HAIXUE, Pharmacy
LI, JINGXIA, Medicine
LI, LINGGEN, Medicine
LI, QIUHONG, Pharmacy
LI, TINGLI, Pharmacy
LI, YADONG, Basic Medical Sciences
LI, YAN, Medicine
LI, YANBING, Pharmacy
LI, YI, Basic Medical Sciences
LI, YONGJI, Pharmacy
LIU, HANDE, Human Sciences
LIU, HUASHENG, Basic Medical Sciences
LIU, JIANQIU, Medicine
LIU, JILI, Human Sciences
LIU, YUANZHANG, Medicine
LU, BINGWEN, Basic Medical Sciences
LUO, HONGSHI, Medicine
MA, YINGLI, Pharmacy
MENG, RI, Pharmacy
NIE, YUNAHENG, Medicine
QU, JIE, Human Sciences
QUAN, HONG, Pharmacy
SONG, LIQUN, Medicine
SU, LIANJIE, Pharmacy
SU, YUNMING, Basic Medical Sciences
SUN, HUI, Pharmacy
SUN, WEIZHENG, Medicine
SUN, ZHONGREN, Medicine
TIAN, ZHENKUN, Medicine
TIAN, ZHENKUN, Pharmacy
TONG, ZILIN, Human Sciences
WANG, DEMIN, Medicine
WANG, DONG, Pharmacy
WANG, FEI, Basic Medical Sciences
WANG, GANG, Medicine

WANG, HEPING, Pharmacy
WANG, JIANMING, Pharmacy
WANG, LI, Basic Medical Sciences
WANG, TIECE, Basic Medical Sciences
WANG, XIAXIAN, Basic Medical Sciences
WANG, XIJUN, Pharmacy
WANG, XING, Medicine
WANG, XUEHUA, Basic Medical Sciences
WANG, YUMEI, Medicine
WANG, YUXI, Medicine
WU, BOYAN, Basic Medical Sciences
XIE, JINGRI, Medicine
YAN, JING, Pharmacy
YU, JIABIN, Pharmacy
YU, XIAOHONG, Basic Medical Sciences
ZHANG, FULI, Basic Medical Sciences
ZHANG, YOUTANG, Basic Medical Sciences
ZHANG, ZHIMIN, Basic Medical Sciences
ZHAO, WENJING, Basic Medical Sciences
ZHOU, DECHEN, Basic Medical Sciences
ZHOU, LING, Medicine
ZHOU, MIN, Basic Medical Sciences
ZHOU, WI, Medicine
ZHOU, YABIN, Medicine
ZHU, YONGZHI, Medicine
ZHU, ZHIZHEN, Basic Medical Sciences

HENAN UNIVERSITY

Ming Lun Rd, Kaifeng 475001, Henan Province
Internet: www.henu.edu.cn

Founded 1912
Academic year: September to July

Pres.: GUAN AIHE
Vice-Pres.: GUO TIANBANG
Vice-Pres.: HUANG YABIN
Vice-Pres.: LU KEPING
Vice-Pres.: SHI QUANSHENG
Vice-Pres.: WANG FAZENG
Vice-Pres.: ZHAO GUOXIANG
Librarian: LI JINGWEN

Number of teachers: 3,600
Number of students: 240,000

Publications: *Chinese Quarterly Journal of Mathematics*, *Journal* (6 a year), *Journal of Henan University Chemical Research* (4 a year), *Quarterly Journal of Pure and Applied Mathematics*

DEANS

Faculty of History and Culture: ZHANG QIANHONG
College of Arts: ZHAO WEIMING
College of Civil Engineering: BAO PENG
College of Communication and Journalism: LI JIANWEI
College of Economics: DI MINGZAI
College of Environmental Planning: QIN YAOCHEN
College of Foreign Languages: ZHANG KEDING
College of Life Science: SONG CHUNPENG
College of Medicine: MA YUANFANG
School of Business Administration: WEI CHENGLONG
School of Chemistry Engineering: CUI YUANCHENG
School of Computer and Information Engineering: LIU XIANSHENG
School of Mathematics and Information Science: LI QISHENG
School of Physics and Information Optoelectronics: ZHANG WEIFENG

PROFESSORS

CHEN, CHANGYUAN, History and Culture
CHEN, JIAHAI, Arts
CHEN, SHOUXIN, Mathematics and Information Science
CHENG, MINGSHENG, History and Culture
DI, MINGZHAI, Economics
DING, SHENGYAN, Environmental Planning
DING, SHENGYAN, Life Science
DONG, FACAI, Life Science
GAO, HAILIN, History and Culture
GAO, JIANGUO, Economics
GAO, JIANHUA, Environmental Planning
GONG, LIUZHU, History and Culture
GU, YUZONG, Physics and Information Optoelectronics
HOU, XUN, Physics and Information Optoelectronics
HU, CHANGLIU, Mathematics and Information Science
HU, CONGE, Mathematics and Information Science
HU, YUXIN, Life Science
HUANG, YABIN, Physics and Information Optoelectronics
JIA, XINGQIN, Mathematics and Information Science
JIA, YUYING, History and Culture
JU, QINGLIN, Arts
LI, CHENGDE, History and Culture
LI, GUANGYI, History and Culture
LI, GUOQIANG, Mathematics and Information Science
LI, JIANWEI, Communication and Journalism
LI, JIE, Business Administration
LI, MING, History and Culture
LI, QISHENG, Mathematics and Information Science
LI, RUI, Mathematics and Information Science
LI, SUOPING, Life Science
LI, YONGWEN, Environmental Planning
LI, YUJIE, History and Culture
LI, ZHENHONG, History and Culture
LIN, JIAKUN, History and Culture
LIU, BINSHAN, Foreign Languages
LIU, HONG, Arts
LIU, JIANZHONG, Business Administration
LIU, KUNTAI, History and Culture
LU, ZHENGUANG, Communication and Journalism
MA, JIANHUA, Environmental Planning
MA, LING, Arts
MA, XIAOQUAN, History and Culture
MAO, HAITAO, Physics and Information Optoelectronics
MIAO, CHANGHONG, Environmental Planning
MIAO, CHENG, Life Science
MIAO, SHUMEI, History and Culture
MO, YUJUN, Physics and Information Optoelectronics
NIU, JIANQIANG, History and Culture
OU, ZHENGWEN, History and Culture
QI, LING, Economics
QIAN, HUAISUI, Environmental Planning
QIN, MINGZHOU, Environmental Planning
QIN, YAOZHEN, Environmental Planning
SANG, FUDE, Life Science
SHAN, LUN, Life Science
SONG, CHUNPENG, Life Science
SONG, YINGLI, Communication and Journalism
SU, KEWU, Economics
SUN, QIULIN, Environmental Planning
TAN, CHENGLIN, Environmental Planning
TANG, GUIQIN, Arts
WAN, SONGYU, History and Culture
WANG, CHANGSHUN, Physics and Information Optoelectronics
WANG, CHUMING, Economics
WANG, FAZHENG, Environmental Planning
WANG, JILIN, History and Culture
WANG, JINGYE, Communication and Journalism
WANG, JINXIAN, Business Administration
WANG, XINGYU, Business Administration
WANG, YANFA, Arts
WANG, ZHANGUO, Physics and Information Optoelectronics
WANG, ZHENDUO, Communication and Journalism
WEI, CHENGLONG, Economics
WEI, QIANZHI, History and Culture
WENG, YOUWEI, History and Culture
WU, TAO, History and Culture
WU, XUELI, Foreign Languages
XU, XINGYA, Economics
YAN, ZHAOXIANG, History and Culture
YANG, HAIJUN, Communication and Journalism
YANG, XUEZHI, Mathematics and Information Science
YAO, BOHUA, Mathematics and Information Science
YAO, YINGTING, History and Culture
YI, GUOSHENG, Physics and Information Optoelectronics
YI, QIXIANG, History and Culture
YU, BAOLONG, Physics and Information Optoelectronics
YU, JINFU, Economics
ZHANG, DEZONG, History and Culture
ZHANG, JIATAI, History and Culture
ZHANG, JIN, Foreign Languages
ZHANG, KUN, Economics
ZHANG, MINGLIANG, Mathematics and Information Science
ZHANG, QIANHONG, History and Culture
ZHANG, QIUZHOU, History and Culture
ZHANG, RUFA, Communication and Journalism
ZHANG, TAIHAI, Business Administration
ZHANG, TIANDING, Communication and Journalism
ZHANG, WEIFENG, Physics and Information Optoelectronics
ZHANG, XINGMAO, Economics
ZHANG, XIUYING, Business Administration
ZHANG, ZHONGLIANG, Communication and Journalism
ZHANG, ZHONGSUO, Physics and Information Optoelectronics
ZHAO, BINDONG, Environmental Planning
ZHAO, BUYUN, History and Culture
ZHAO, JIANGUO, Communication and Journalism
ZHAO, WEIMING, Arts
ZHAO, ZHENQIAN, Arts
ZHAO, ZHIFA, Economics
ZHENG, HUISHENG, History and Culture
ZHOU, BAOZHU, History and Culture
ZHU, SHAOHOU, History and Culture

HENAN UNIVERSITY OF TRADITIONAL CHINESE MEDICINE

1 Jinshui Rd, Zhengzhou 450008, Henan Province
Telephone: (371) 65962930
E-mail: henantcm@gmail.com
Internet: www.henantcm.net

Founded 1958
State control
Language of instruction: Chinese, English
Academic year: September to July

Pres.: Prof. YULING ZHENG
Vice-Pres.: Prof. LI JIANSHENG
Librarian: LAI QIANKAI

Library of 959,000 vols
Number of teachers: 2,842
Number of students: 17,701

Publications: *Henan Traditional Chinese Medicine* (12 a year), *Journal* (6 a year)

PROFESSORS

CHEN, R. F., Internal Medicine
DING, Y., Paediatrics
FENG, M. Q., Traditional Chinese Medicine
GAO, T. S., Traditional Chinese Medicine
HOU, S. L., Traditional Materia Medica
JI, C. R., Traditional Materia Medica
LI, X. W., Traditional Chinese Medicine
LI, Z. H., Traditional Chinese Medicine
LI, Z. S., Internal Medicine
LOU, D. F., Traditional Chinese Medicine for Traumatology
LU, S. C., Qigong
MA, Z. H., Traditional Chinese Medicine
SHANG, C. C., Traditional Chinese Medicine
SHAO, J. M., Acupuncture
SHI, G. Q., Traditional Chinese Medicine

SHUN, L. H., Acupuncture
SUN, C. Q., Physiology
SUN, H. B., Parasitology
SUN, J. Z., Internal Medicine
TANG, S., Traditional Chinese Medicine
WANG, A. B., History of Traditional Chinese Medicine
WANG, R. K., Diagnostics
WANG, Y. M., Pharmaco-Chemistry
YANG, L. Y., Anatomy
YANG, Y. S., Traditional Materia Medica
ZHANG, G. Q., Traditional Materia Medica
ZHENG, J. M., Traditional Chinese Medicine for Paediatrics

HOHAI UNIVERSITY

1 Xikang Rd, 210098 Nanjing
Telephone: (25) 3323777
E-mail: intloffice@hhu.edu.cn
Internet: www.hhu.edu.cn

Founded 1915, fmrly East China Technical Univ. of Water Resources, current name adopted 1985
State control
Languages of instruction: Chinese, English
Academic year: September to July

Pres.: Prof. XU HUI
Vice-Pres.: JU PING
Vice-Pres.: ZHUYUE LONG
Vice-Pres.: TANG HONGWU
Vice-Pres.: WANG CHAO
Librarian: DONG TINGSONG

Library of 1,858,000 vols
Number of teachers: 3,383
Number of students: 40,000

Publications: *Advances in Science and Technology of Water Resources* (6 a year), *Journal of Economics of Water Resources* (6 a year), *Journal of Hohai University (Natural Sciences)* (6 a year), *Water Resources Protection* (6 a year), *Water Science and Engineering* (4 a year)

DEANS

College of Civil Engineering: Prof. ZHUO JIASHOU
College of Computer and Information Engineering: Assoc. Prof. ZHU YAOLONG
College of Electrical Engineering: Prof. YANG JINTANG
College of Harbour, Waterway and Coastal Engineering: Prof. ZHANG CHANGKUAN
College of Mechanical and Electrical Engineering: Prof. JIN YAHE
College of International Industry and Commerce: Assoc. Prof. ZHANG YANG
College of Technical Economics: Prof. ZHENG CHUIYONG
College of Water Conservancy and Hydropower Engineering: Prof. SUO LISHENG
College of Water Resources and Environment: Prof. WANG HUIMIN

HUAQIAO UNIVERSITY

Quanzhou 362011, Fujian
Telephone: (595) 2693630
E-mail: zsc@hqu.edu.cn
Internet: www.hqu.edu.cn

Founded 1960
State control

Pres.: Prof. WU CHENGYE
Vice-Pres: Prof. GUO HENGQUN
Vice-Pres: Assoc. Prof. LI JIMIN
Vice-Pres: Assoc. Prof. LI JIMIN
Registrar: Prof. HONG SHANGREN
Librarian: Prof. ZHANG WEIBIN

Library of 775,449 vols, 16,235 periodicals
Number of teachers: 542 (full-time)
Number of students: 12,000

Publications: *Journal of Huaqiao University* (Natural science and social science editions, 4 a year, in Chinese), *Research in Higher Education by Overseas Chinese* (2 a year, in Chinese)

DEANS

College of Economic Management: Prof. YE MINGQIANG
College of Electromechanical Engineering and Automation: Prof. XU XIPENG
College of Foreign Languages: Assoc. Prof. WANG HUAIHUI
College of Information Science and Engineering: Prof. GUO HENGQUN
College of Materials Science and Engineering: Prof. WU JIHUAI
College of Teaching Chinese as a Foreign Language: Assoc. Prof. LI HONG
Fujian Conservatory of Music: Prof. CAI JIKUN

HUAZHONG AGRICULTURAL UNIVERSITY

Shizhishan, Wuhan 430070, Hubei Province
Telephone: (27) 87282026
E-mail: studyinhau@gmail.com
Internet: www.hzau.edu.cn

Founded 1898, current name adopted 1985
State control
Languages of instruction: Chinese, English
Academic year: September to July

Pres.: ZHANG DUANPIN
Vice-Pres.: CHEN HUANCHUN
Vice-Pres.: GAO CHI
Vice-Pres.: LI GUIFANG
Vice-Pres.: LI MINGJIA
Vice-Pres.: LIU GUIYOU
Vice-Pres.: WANG CHUANXIN
Vice-Pres.: XIE CONGHUA
Librarian: WAN JIQIN

Library of 620,000 vols
Number of teachers: 2,215
Number of students: 15,000

Publication: *Journal* (4 a year)

DEANS

College of Adult Education: ZHANG DUANPIN
College of Animal Husbandry and Veterinary Science: BI DINGREN
College of Arts and Humanities and Social Science: LI CHONGGUANG
College of Basic Sciences: CHEN CHANGSHUI
College of Economics and Trade: WANG YAPENG
College of Engineering and Technology: ZHANG YANLIN
College of the Fishing Industry: XIE CONGXIN
College of Food Science and Technology: PAN SIYI
College of Horticulture and Forestry Science: BAO MANZHU
College of Land Management: WANG YAPENG
College of Life Sciences and Technology: ZHANG QIFA
College of Plant Science and Technology: ZHANG XIANLONG
College of Resources and Environment: CAI CHONGFA

HUAZHONG UNIVERSITY OF SCIENCE AND TECHNOLOGY

1037 Luoyu Rd, Wuhan 430074, Hubei Province
Telephone: (27) 87542157
E-mail: chengrw@126.com
Internet: www.hust.edu.cn

Founded 1953
Academic year: September to July

Pres.: Prof. FAN MINGWU
Vice-Pres.: Prof. CAO SHUQIN
Vice-Pres.: Prof. DING HANCHU
Vice-Pres.: Prof. DING LIEYUN
Vice-Pres.: Prof. FENG XIANGDONG
Vice-Pres.: Prof. FENG YOUMEI
Vice-Pres.: Prof. HUANG GUANGYING
Vice-Pres.: Prof. LI PEIGEN
Vice-Pres.: Prof. LIU XIANJUN
Vice-Pres.: Prof. WANG CHENG
Vice-Pres.: Prof. XIANG JIZHOU
Librarian: Assoc. Prof. WU JINWEI

Library of 2,070,000 vols, 550,000 vols of periodicals in Chinese and foreign languages
Number of teachers: 4,000
Number of students: 50,000

Publications: *Applied Mathematics*, *China's Organic Chemistry and Cellular Chemistry*, *Chinese Medicine Digest* (detection and clinical), *Clinical Cardiology*, *Clinical Gastroenterology*, *Clinical Haematology*, *Clinical Otolaryngology*, *Clinical Urology*, *Clinic Emergency*, *Foreign Medicine and Molecular Biology*, *Foreign Medicine* (social medicine), *Gastroenterology in Combined Traditional Chinese Medicine and Western Medicine*, *HUST Journal* (in separate natural sciences, social sciences and medical sciences editions), *Hydroelectric Energy*, *Internal Emergency*, *Journal of Higher Education*, *Journal of Solid State Mechanics*, *Linguistics Study*, *Medicine and Society*, *New Architecture*, *Nursing*, *Practice of Radiology*, *Radiant Diagnosis* (Chinese medical digest), *Research in Higher Education of Engineering*, *Sino-German Tumour Clinic*

DEANS

School of Architecture and Urban Planning: Prof. YUAN PEIHUANG
School of Civil Engineering and Mechanics: Prof. CHEN CHUANYAO
School of Computer Science and Technology: Prof. LU ZHENGDIAN
School of Economics: Prof. XU CHANGSHENG
School of Education: Prof. ZHANG YINGQIANG
School of Electrical and Electronics Engineering: Prof. GU CHENGLIN
School of Energy and Power Engineering: Prof. LIU WEI
School of Environmental Science and Engineering: Prof. SHEN YUNFENG
School of Humanities: Prof. ZHANG SHUGUANG
School of Hydropower and Information Engineering: Prof. WU ZHONGRU
School of Information Technology and Engineering: Prof. HUANG DEXIU
School of Journalism and Information Communication: Prof. WU TINGJUN
School of Law: Prof. LUO YUZHONG
School of Life Science and Technology: Prof. LUO QINGMING
School of Management: Prof. ZHANG JINLONG
School of Materials Science and Engineering: Prof. LI DEQUN
School of Mechanical Science and Engineering: Prof. SHAO XINYU
School of Public Administration: Prof. XIA SHUZHANG
School of Science: Prof. YE ZHAOHUI
School of Software Engineering: Prof. CHEN CHUANBO
School of Traffic Science and Engineering: Prof. ZHAO YAO
Tongji Medical School: Prof. XIANG JIZHOU

HUBEI UNIVERSITY

11 Xueyuan Rd, Wuchang, Wuhan 430062, Hubei Province
Telephone: (27) 88663896
E-mail: xiaoban@hubu.edu.cn
Internet: www.hubu.edu.cn

Founded 1931
Hubei Province control
Academic year: September to July

Pres.: WU CHUANXI

Vice-Pres.: GU HAOSHUANG
Vice-Pres.: LI JINHE
Vice-Pres.: YAN MINGMING
Vice-Pres.: ZHOU JIMING
Librarian: ZHANG WEIHUA

Library of 1,520,000 vols
Number of teachers: 1,000
Number of students: 12,700

Publications: *Acta Arachnologica Sinica* (2 a year), *Chinese Journal of Colloids and Polymers* (4 a year), *Journal* (4 a year), *Journal of the Adult Education College of Hubei University* (6 a year)

DEANS

Faculty of Arts: LUN ZUNMING
Faculty of Chemistry and Materials Science: WANG SHIMIN
Faculty of Education: JIN GUOPING
Faculty of Foreign Studies: XU QIUMEI
Faculty of History and Culture: GUO YING
Faculty of Philosophy: DAI MAOTANG
Institute of Physics and Electronic Technology: WANG HAO
School of Business: LIU JIANPING
School of Life Science: CHEN JIAN
School of Resources and the Environment: LI ZHAOHUA

PROFESSORS

BIAN, XIANGYI, Arts
CAO, WANQIANG, Physics and Electronic Technology
CHAN, SHAOHUA, Physics and Electronic Technology
CHANG, SHIYUAN, Chemistry and Materials Science
CHEN, PEIZHI, Chemistry and Materials Science
CHEN, QIUHUI, Mathematics and Computer Science
CHEN, TIANYOU, Business
CHEN, YIHAN, Physics and Electronic Technology
CHEN, YOUQING, Education
CHEN, ZHIHUI, Physics and Electronic Technology
CHEN, ZHUXING, Chemistry and Materials Science
CHENG, CHONGZHEN, Business
CHENG, SIHUI, Education
CHENG, YUANFA, Physics and Electronic Technology
DAI, MAOTANG, Philosophy
FENG, CHUANQI, Chemistry and Materials Science
FENG, HAO, Business
GAO, LU, History and Culture
GONG, GUIFANG, Foreign Studies
GONG, QUN, Philosophy
GU, HAOSHUANG, Physics and Electronic Technology
GU, PEI, History and Culture
GUAN, RONG, Chemistry and Materials Science
GUO, KANGSONG, Arts
GUO, YING, History and Culture
HAN, HUA, Education
HE, PEIXIN, Chemistry and Materials Science
HU, SHUGUANG, Chemistry and Materials Science
HUANG, SHIQIANG, Chemistry and Materials Science
HUANG, YUEHUI, Arts
JIANG, CHANG, Philosophy
JIANG, TAO, Chemistry and Materials Science
JIN, CONG, Mathematics and Computer Science
JIN, KEZHONG, Arts
LEI, TINAN, Education
LI, JUANWEN, Business
LI, JUANWEN, Resources and the Environment
LI, LUOQING, Mathematics and Computer Science
LI, YAN, Chemistry and Materials Science
LI, ZHAOHUA, Resources and the Environment
LI, ZONGRONG, Mathematics and Computer Science
LIU, CHUANE, Arts
LIU, HEGUO, Mathematics and Computer Science
LIU, JIANPING, Business
LIU, SHENGWU, Arts
LIU, ZHUNMING, Arts
LOU, ZHAOWEN, Chemistry and Materials Science
LU, DEPING, Chemistry and Materials Science
LU, ZHILU, Foreign Studies
QIN, ZHAOGUI, History and Culture
SHAO, CHANGGUI, Physics and Electronic Technology
SHI, JINPING, Business
SHU, HUAI, Arts
SONG, KEFU, Arts
TAN, SHUKUI, Business
TIAN, FANJI, Mathematics and Computer Science
TU, HUAIZHANG, Arts
WAN, CHANGGAO, Mathematics and Computer Science
WANG, HAO, Physics and Electronic Technology
WANG, HONGLING, Business
WANG, JIAZHI, Foreign Studies
WANG, SHENGFU, Chemistry and Materials Science
WANG, SHIMIN, Chemistry and Materials Science
WANG, YANG, History and Culture
WANG, ZHENGXIANG, Resources and the Environment
WU, CHUANXI, Mathematics and Computer Science
WU, MIN, Mathematics and Computer Science
XIA, QINGHUA, Chemistry and Materials Science
XIAN, KEN, Mathematics and Computer Science
XIANG, SONG, Foreign Studies
XIAO, DE, Business
XIAO, WEIDONG, Chemistry and Materials Science
XIE, FEIHOU, Education
XIE, JUFANG, Physics and Electronic Technology
XU, QIUMEI, Foreign Studies
XU, XUEJUN, Education
XU, ZHUSHUN, Chemistry and Materials Science
YAN, CUIE, Chemistry and Materials Science
YAN, MEIFU, Education
YAN, MINGMING, Education
YAN, XUEJUN, Business
YANG, JIANBO, Arts
YANG, YAOKUN, Philosophy
YE, YONG, Chemistry and Materials Science
YI, HONGCHUAN, Arts
YOU, WULI, Foreign Studies
ZHANG, BICHENG, Chemistry and Materials Science
ZHANG, HESHENG, Chemistry and Materials Science
ZHANG, JIANMING, Business
ZHANG, QINGZONG, Foreign Studies
ZHANG, TIANJIN, Physics and Electronic Technology
ZHAO, SHAOYI, Mathematics and Computer Science
ZHENG, YUMEI, Mathematics and Computer Science
ZHOU, DEJUN, History and Culture
ZHOU, HAO, Foreign Studies
ZHOU, TAOSHENG, Physics and Electronic Technology
ZHU, JIANZHEN, History and Culture
ZHU, WEIMING, Arts

HUNAN AGRICULTURAL UNIVERSITY

Fu Rong District, Changsha 410128, Hunan Province
Telephone: (731) 4618001
Internet: www.hunau.net

Founded 1951
Academic year: September to July

Pres.: ZHOU QINGMING
Vice-Pres.: BO LIANYANG
Vice-Pres.: FU SHAOHUI
Vice-Pres.: LU XIANGYANG
Vice-Pres.: PENG KEQIN
Vice-Pres.: ZHU YINGSHENG
Librarian: XIAO QIMING

Library of 909,600 vols
Number of teachers: 978
Number of students: 34,259

Publications: *Crop Research* (4 a year), *Journal* (4 a year)

DEANS

College of Bio-Safety Science and Technology: GAO BIDA
College of Economics Management: ZENG WEI
College of Engineering Technology: SUN SONGLIN
College of Resources and the Environment: DUAN JIANNAN
College of Science: RAO LIQUN
Faculty of Food Science and Technology: XIA YANBIN
Institute of Computing and Information Engineering: SHEN YUE
School of Agriculture: WANG GUOHUAI
School of Literature: QU LINYAN

PROFESSORS

BO, LIANYANG, Bio-Safety Science and Technology
CHEN, JINXIANG, Agriculture
CUI, GUOXIAN, Agriculture
DAI, LIANGYING, Bio-Safety Science and Technology
DENG, FANGMING, Food Science and Technology
DUAN, JIANNAN, Resources and the Environment
FANG, ZHI, Resources and the Environment
GAO, BIDA, Bio-Safety Science and Technology
GAO, YINGWU, Engineering Technology
GUAN, CHUNYUN, Agriculture
GUO, QINGQUAN, Agriculture
HUANG, HUANG, Agriculture
HUANG, YIHUAN, Food Science and Technology
HUANG, ZHENGQUAN, Literature
LAO, LIQUN, Science College
LI, FINGJUN, Bio-Safety Science and Technology
LI, XINGHUI, Food Science and Technology
LI, XUN, Agriculture
LIAO, BOHAN, Resources and the Environment
LIAO, XIAOLAN, Bio-Safety Science and Technology
LIU, DEHUA, Food Science and Technology
LIU, GUOHUA, Agriculture
LIU, QIANG, Resources and the Environment
LIU, ZHONGHUA, Food Science and Technology
LIU, ZHONGSONG, Agriculture
LUO, JUNWU, Food Science and Technology
LUO, KUAN, Bio-Safety Science and Technology
MA, MEIHU, Food Science and Technology
OU YANG, XIRONG, Agriculture
PENG, XILIN, Literature
QU, LINYAN, Literature
RONG, XIANGMING, Resources and the Environment
SHENG, XIAOBANG, Agriculture
SHI, ZHAOPENG, Food Science and Technology

SHUN, HUANLIANG, Agriculture
TAN, JICAI, Food Science and Technology
TAN, JICAI, Bio-Safety Science and Technology
TAN, XINGHE, Food Science and Technology
TANG, CHUYU, Engineering Technology
TANG, QIYUAN, Agriculture
TU, LIAOMEI, Agriculture
WANG, GUOHUAI, Agriculture
WANG, GUOLIANG, Agriculture
WANG, GUOPING, Bio-Safety Science and Technology
WEN, LIZHANG, Bio-Safety Science and Technology
WU, LIYOU, Bio-Safety Science and Technology
XI, YANBIN, Food Science and Technology
XIA, YANBIN, Food Science and Technology
XIAO, QIMING, Bio-Safety Science and Technology
XIAO, TIEGUANG, Bio-Safety Science and Technology
YAN, HEHONG, Agriculture
YANG, RENBIN, Resources and the Environment
YANG, WEILI, Food Science and Technology
YANG, ZHIJIAN, Agriculture
ZENG, FUSHENG, Economics Management
ZENG, QINGRU, Resources and the Environment
ZHANG, FUQUAN, Agriculture
ZHANG, XIWEI, Economics Management
ZHANG, YANGZHU, Resources and the Environment
ZHOU, DONGSHENG, Agriculture
ZHOU, JIHENG, Agriculture
ZHOU, MEILAN, Agriculture
ZHOU, QINGMING, Agriculture
ZHU, QI, Food Science and Technology

HUNAN NORMAL UNIVERSITY

36 Lu Shan Rd, He Xi, Changsha 410081, Hunan Province
Telephone: (731) 8883131
E-mail: study@hunnu.edu.cn
Internet: www.hunnu.edu.cn
Founded 1938
Min. of Education control
Academic year: September to July
Pres.: LIU XIANG RONG
Vice-Pres.: GONG WEI ZHONG
Vice-Pres.: JIANG JI CHENG
Vice-Pres.: LIANG SONG PING
Vice-Pres.: ZHOU JING MING
Head of Graduate Dept: CHEN JIAN CHU
Head of Graduate Dept: SHI OU
Librarian: YAN ZHAO HUI
Number of teachers: 1,000
Number of students: 22,000
Publications: *Ancient Chinese Research* (4 a year), *Chinese Literature Research* (4 a year), *Consumer Economy* (4 a year), *Journal* (education science, 6 a year), *Journal* (medicine, irregular), *Journal* (social science, 6 a year), *Life Science Research* (4 a year), *Modern Law* (4 a year)

DEANS

College of Commerce: LIU MAO SONG
Department of Computer Education: WANG LU YA
School of Chemistry and Chemical Engineering: XIE QING JI
School of Education Science: ZHANG CHUAN SUI
School of Foreign Languages: HUANG ZHEN DING
School of International Chinese Culture: JI XUE FENG
School of Law: JIANG XIN MIAO
School of Life Science: WU XIU SHAN
School of Literature: TAN GUI LIN
School of Mathematics and Computer Science: DONG XIN HAN
School of Medicine: FU XIAO HUA
School of Physical Education: LI YAN LING
School of Tourism: XIE JUN GUI

PROFESSORS

CAI, XUE BING, Law
CHEN, BO, Chemistry and Chemical Engineering
CHEN, CHUAN MIAO, Mathematics and Computer Science
CHEN, HUAN GEN, Mathematics and Computer Science
CHEN, JIA QIN, Life Science
CHEN, LIANG BI, Life Science
CHEN, YUN LIANG, Law
CHEN, ZE, Life Science
CHEN, ZUO HONG, Life Science
CUI, ZHEN HUA, International Chinese Culture
DENG, HONG WEN, Life Science
DENG, LE, Life Science
DENG, LE, Chemistry and Chemical Engineering
DENG, XUE JIAN, Life Science
DONG, XIN HAN, Mathematics and Computer Science
DU, XUE TANG, Mathematics and Computer Science
FANG, KUI, Mathematics and Computer Science
FU, PENG, Life Science
FU, ZAI HUI, Chemistry and Chemical Engineering
GU, YONG GENG, Mathematics and Computer Science
GUO, JING YUN, Mathematics and Computer Science
HAO, SAN RU, Computer Education
HE, DING SHENG, Chemistry and Chemical Engineering
HOU, YAO PING, Mathematics and Computer Science
HUANG, JIAN PING, Computer Education
HUANG, YI NONG, Tourism
HUANG, YUAN QIU, Mathematics and Computer Science
JI, XUE FENG, International Chinese Culture
JIANG, XIAN FU, Law
JIANG, XIAO CHENG, Life Science
JIANG, XIN MIAO, Law
JIN, GUANG HUI, Physical Education
JIN, ZU JUN, Mathematics and Computer Science
LENG, GANG SONG, Mathematics and Computer Science
LI, AI NIAN, Law
LI, FANG CHENG, Life Science
LI, HAI TAO, Chemistry and Chemical Engineering
LI, JIAN ZONG, Life Science
LI, SHUANG YUAN, Law
LI, XIAN BO, Law
LI, YAN LING, Physical Education
LI, ZE LIN, Chemistry and Chemical Engineering
LIANG, SONG PING, Life Science
LIU, HONG, Mathematics and Computer Science
LIU, KE MING, Life Science
LIU, MING YAO, Life Science
LIU, SHAO JUN, Life Science
LIU, YING DI, Life Science
LIU, YUN, Life Science
LIU, ZHEN XIU, Mathematics and Computer Science
LUO, CHEN, Life Science
MA, MING, Chemistry and Chemical Engineering
MA, WEI PING, Physical Education
NUAN, SHENG, Life Science
PENG, XIAN JING, Life Science
QIAN, GUANG MING, Mathematics and Computer Science
QIN, ZHENG DI, Computer Education
QIU, MENG SHENG, Life Science
QIU, XI MIN, Chemistry and Chemical Engineering
QU, FU DONG, Tourism
QUAN, HUI YUN, Mathematics and Computer Science
REN, JI CUN, Chemistry and Chemical Engineering
SHEN, JIAN HUA, Mathematics and Computer Science
SHEN, WEN XUAN, Mathematics and Computer Science
SHI, SHAO RONG, Physical Education
SHI, XIAN LIANG, Mathematics and Computer Science
SHI, YING GUANG, Mathematics and Computer Science
SUN, HONG TAO, Physical Education
TAN, PING PING, Physical Education
WANG, BAO HE, Life Science
WANG, GUI GUO, Law
WANG, GUO QIU, Mathematics and Computer Science
WANG, HONG QUAN, Life Science
WANG, LU YA, Computer Education
WANG, XIAN CHUN, Life Science
WANG, XIAN TAO, Mathematics and Computer Science
WU, XIU SHAN, Life Science
XIA, LI QIU, Life Science
XIANG, KAI NAN, Mathematics and Computer Science
XIAO, BEI GENG, Law
XIAO, XIAO MING, Chemistry and Chemical Engineering
XIE, JING YUN, Life Science
XIE, JUN GUI, Tourism
XIE, QING JI, Chemistry and Chemical Engineering
XU, CHUN XIAO, Tourism
XU, DA, Mathematics and Computer Science
XU, FEI XIONG, Tourism
XU, MAN CAI, Chemistry and Chemical Engineering
XU, MENG LIANG, Life Science
YAN, HENG MEI, Life Science
YANG, XIANG QUN, Mathematics and Computer Science
YANG, XIN JIAN, Mathematics and Computer Science
YAO, SHOU ZHUO, Chemistry and Chemical Engineering
YI, CHANG MIN, Life Science
YIN, DA ZHONG, Life Science
YIN, DONG HONG, Chemistry and Chemical Engineering
YUAN, WU ZHOU, Life Science
ZENG, YUE, Chemistry and Chemical Engineering
ZHANG, BAI ZHEN, Physical Education
ZHANG, JIAN, Life Science
ZHANG, TIAN XIAO, Life Science
ZHANG, XUAN JIE, Life Science
ZHANG, YAO, Mathematics and Computer Science
ZHANG, ZHI GUANG, Life Science
ZHENG, YAN, Tourism
ZHENG, YUAN MIN, Law
ZHOU, GONG JIAN, Life Science
ZHOU, JIAN SHE, Physical Education
ZHOU, TIE JUN, Physical Education
ZHOU, XIN YI, Computer Education
ZHU, QI DING, Mathematics and Computer Science

HUNAN UNIVERSITY

Yule, 410082 Changsha
Telephone: (731) 8822745
E-mail: xiaoban@hnu.edu.cn
Internet: www.hnu.edu.cn
Founded 976 as Yuelu Acad., became Hunan Institute of Higher Education 1903, Hunan Univ. 1926, Hunan Nat. Univ. 1937, South-Central Institute of Civil Engineer-

ing 1953, Hunan Institute of Technology between 1953 and 1959, and Hunan Univ. 1959, merged with Hunan College of Finance and Economics 2000

State control

Colleges of architecture, Chinese language and literature, civil engineering, electrical and information engineering, environmental science and engineering, finance and statistics, foreign languages and int. studies, information science and engineering, journalism and communication and film and television arts, marxism studies, materials and engineering, mathematics and econometrics, mechanical vehicle engineering; schools of biology, business admin., chemistry and chemical engineering, design, economy and trade, law, physics and microelectronics science

Pres.: ZHAO YUEYU

Library of 2,380,000 vols
Number of teachers: 1,950
Number of students: 34,800

INNER MONGOLIA AGRICULTURAL UNIVERSITY

Xinjian East Rd, Beyong Nanmen, Huhehaote 010018, Inner Mongolia Autonomous Region
Telephone: (471) 4301576
Internet: www.imau.edu.cn

Founded 1952
provincial control
Academic year: September to July

Pres.: LI CHANGYOU
Vice-Pres.: HOU XIANZHI
Vice-Pres.: LI JINQUAN
Vice-Pres.: REN QIANG
Vice-Pres.: WANG LINHE
Vice-Pres.: ZHENG JUNBAO

Library of 750,000 vols
Number of teachers: 1,010
Number of students: 18,800

Publication: *Journal* (4 a year)

DEANS

College of Agriculture: YU ZHUO
College of Animal Science and Animal Medicine: LI JINQUAN
College of Biology Engineering: ZHOU HUANMIN
College of Computing and Information Engineering: PEI XICHUN
College of Ecology and the Environment: WANG MINQIU
College of Economics Management: XIU CHANGBO
College of Forestry: ZHANG QIULIANG
College of Forestry Engineering: WANG XIAOLIANG
College of Humanities and Social Sciences: GAO CHAO
College of Mechanical and Electrical Engineering: WANG CHUNGUANG
College of Water Conservancy and Civil Engineering: JI BAOLIN

PROFESSORS

AN, SHOUQIN, Forestry
AO, CHANGJIN, Animal Science and Medicine
AO, RIGELE, Animal Science and Medicine
BAI, SHULAN, Forestry
CAO, GUIFANG, Animal Science and Medicine
CHANG, JINBAO, Forestry
CHAO, LUNBAGEN, Water Conservancy and Civil Engineering
CHEN, YAXIN, Water Conservancy and Civil Engineering
CUI, ZHIGUO, Animal Science and Medicine
DAO, ERJI, Animal Science and Medicine
DE, LIGEERSANG, Food Science and Engineering
DOU, WEIGUO, Mechanical and Electrical Engineering
DU, WENLIANG, Mechanical and Electrical Engineering
FAN, MINGSHOU, Agriculture
FENG, LIN, Forestry
GA, ERDI, Animal Science and Medicine
GAO, CHAO, Humanities and Social Sciences
GE, RILE, Forestry
GUANG, PINGYUAN, Animal Science and Medicine
GUO, LIANSHENG, Ecology and the Environment
GUO, LIANSHENG, Forestry
HE, YINFENG, Food Science and Engineering
HOU, XIANZHI, Animal Science and Medicine
HU, HEBATEER, Animal Science and Medicine
JIN, SHUGUANG, Animal Science and Medicine
LI, CHANGYOU, Water Conservancy and Civil Engineering
LI, JINQUAN, Animal Science and Medicine
LI, LIANGUO, Agriculture
LI, PEIFENG, Animal Science and Medicine
LI, QINGFENG, Ecology and the Environment
LI, YUNZHANG, Animal Science and Medicine
LIU, DEFU, Ecology and the Environment
LIU, KELI, Agriculture
LIU, YONG, Economics Management
LIU, ZHENGYI, Animal Science and Medicine
MA, SHUOSHI, Mechanical and Electrical Engineering
MA, XUEEN, Animal Science and Medicine
MANG, LAI, Animal Science and Medicine
MO, LIGEN, Biology Engineering
PANG, BAOPING, Agriculture
PEI, XICHUN, Computer and Information Engineering
QI, TONGCHUN, Mechanical and Electrical Engineering
QIAO, CHEN, Agriculture
QIAO, GUANGHUA, Economics Management
QIAO, LING, Animal Science and Medicine
QIN, HUA, Food Science and Engineering
SAI, YINCHAOKETU, Biology Engineering
SHANG, SHIYOU, Mechanical and Electrical Engineering
SHENG, XIANGDONG, Water Conservancy and Civil Engineering
SHENG, ZHIYI, Animal Science and Medicine
SHI, HAIBIN, Water Conservancy and Civil Engineering
SI, YA, Humanities and Social Sciences
TAN, PENZHEN, Humanities and Social Sciences
TIAN, DE, Mechanical and Electrical Engineering
TIAN, ZIHUA, Agriculture
TONG, SHUMIN, Mechanical and Electrical Engineering
WAN, TAO, Biology Engineering
WANG, BINXIU, Economics Management
WANG, CHUNGUANG, Mechanical and Electrical Engineering
WANG, CHUNJIE, Animal Science and Medicine
WANG, HAOFU, Humanities and Social Sciences
WANG, LAI, Biology Engineering
WANG, LIMING, Forestry
WANG, LINHE, Ecology and the Environment
WEN, HENG, Water Conservancy and Civil Engineering
WU, NI, Animal Science and Medicine
WU, SHUQING, Animal Science and Medicine
XIU, CHANGBO, Economics Management
XU, ZHIXIN, Ecology and the Environment
XUE, HERU, Computer and Information Engineering
YAN, SUMEI, Animal Science and Medicine
YAN, WEI, Ecology and the Environment
YAN, WEI, Forestry
YANG, BAOSHOU, Animal Science and Medicine
YANG, MINGSHAO, Mechanical and Electrical Engineering
YANG, XIAOYE, Animal Science and Medicine
YAO, FENGTONG, Economics Management
YAO, YUNFENG, Ecology and the Environment
YU, ZHUO, Agriculture
YUAN, XIUYING, Forestry
YUN, JINGFENG, Ecology and the Environment
YUN, XINGFU, Agriculture
YUN, YUEHUA, Humanities and Social Sciences
ZHANG, DEMIAN, Mechanical and Electrical Engineering
ZHANG, HEPING, Food Science and Engineering
ZHANG, LILING, Animal Science and Medicine
ZHANG, QIULIANG, Forestry
ZHANG, SHAOYING, Agriculture
ZHANG, XINLING, Economics Management
ZHANG, ZHIYI, Mechanical and Electrical Engineering
ZHAO, GENBAO, Computing and Information Engineering
ZHAO, SHIJIE, Mechanical and Electrical Engineering
ZHAO, YUANFENG, Economics Management
ZHAO, ZHENHUA, Animal Science and Medicine
ZHAO, ZHIGONG, Animal Science and Medicine
ZHOU, HUANMIN, Animal Science and Medicine
ZHOU, HUANMIN, Biology Engineering

INNER MONGOLIA UNIVERSITY

235 Daxue West Rd, Huhehaote 010021, Inner Mongolia Autonomous Region
Telephone: (471) 4992241
Internet: www.imu.edu.cn

Founded 1957
Academic year: September to July

Pres.: XU RIGAN
Vice-Pres.: CHEN GUOQING
Vice-Pres.: HU GEJILETU
Vice-Pres.: LI YANJUN
Vice-Pres.: LIANG XIXIA
Vice-Pres.: TONG GUOQING
Head of Graduate Dept: LIANG XIXIA
Librarian: A LATANCANG

Number of teachers: 1,447
Number of students: 20,000

Publications: *Journal* (humanities and social sciences, 6 a year), *Journal* (natural sciences, 6 a year), *Journal* (philosophy and social sciences, 6 a year)

DEANS

Academy of Mongolian Studies: BAI YINMENDE
College of Art: LI YULIN
College of Chemistry and Chemical Engineering: SU HAIQUAN
College of Computer Science: GAO GUANGLAI
College of Continuing Education: FU WENJUN
College of Economics and Management: GUO XIAOCHUAN
College of Foreign Languages: LI KANING
College of Humanities: QIAN JIANMEI
College of Life Science: YANG JIE
College of Physical Education: YU ZHIHAI
College of Public Administration: JIN HAIHE
College of Science and Technology: BAN SHILIANG
College of Vocational Technology: CHAI JINYI
School of Law: DING WENYING

PROFESSORS

A, LATANCANG, Science and Technology
BAI, XUELIANG, Life Science
BAN, SHILIANG, Science and Technology
BAO, QINGDE, Humanities
BAO, WENHAN, Humanities
BO, YINHUI, Humanities
BU, LINBEILE, Mongolian Studies
BU, RENBATU, Mongolian Studies
CHEN, GUOQING, Science and Technology

CHEN, YOUZUN, Law
CONG, ZHIJIE, Public Administration
DU, LIKE, Humanities
EN, HE, Mongolian Studies
GE, RILETU, Mongolian Studies
GUO, XIAOCHUAN, Economics and Management
HAO, WEIMIN, Mongolian Studies
HE, JIANG, Life Science
HU, TINGMAO, Life Science
JIA, GUISHENG, Public Administration
JIN, HAIHE, Public Administration
LANG, BAORU, Humanities
LI, HONG, Science and Technology
LI, QIANZHONG, Science and Technology
LI, SHUXIN, Humanities
LI, XIAOCHUN, Humanities
LIAN, ZIXIN, Public Administration
LIANG, XIXIA, Science and Technology
LIU, AIHUA, Public Administration
LIU, CHENG, Mongolian Studies
LIU, LIHUA, Public Administration
LIU, XIN, Public Administration
LUO, LIAOFU, Science and Technology
MA, JI, Humanities
MA, ZHANXIN, Economics and Management
MENG, BIN, Economics and Management
MENG, HUIJUN, Economics and Management
MING, YUE, Public Administration
NIU, JIANMING, Life Science
NIU, JINGZHONG, Humanities
QING, GEERTAI, Mongolian Studies
QUAN, FU, Mongolian Studies
REN, WEIDE, Public Administration
REN, YUFENG, Humanities
SHI, ZHENGJI, Humanities
SUN, JIONG, Science and Technology
SUN, KAIMIN, Public Administration
TONG, CHUAN, Life Science
WANG, HONGYAN, Law
WANG, MEICUI, Economics and Management
WANG, YAN, Economics and Management
WANG, YINGCHUN, Life Science
WU, QILATU, Mongolian Studies
WU, YINGJI, Life Science
WU, YUNNA, Public Administration
XU, RIGAN, Life Science
YANG, CHI, Life Science
YANG, JIE, Life Science
YANG, XINMIN, Science and Technology
YU, ZHIHAI, Public Administration
YUN, GUOHONG, Science and Technology
ZHANG, CUIZHEN, Public Administration
ZHANG, FENGMING, Law
ZHANG, ZHIZHONG, Public Administration
ZHAO, MIN, Public Administration
ZHEN, XIUYU, Humanities
ZHOU, QINGSHU, Mongolian Studies

INNER MONGOLIA UNIVERSITY FOR NATIONALITIES

22 Huolinhe Rd, Tongliao 028043, Inner Mongolia Autonomous Region
Telephone: (475) 8313292
Internet: www.imun.edu.cn

Founded 1960
Academic year: September to July

Pres.: WANG DINGZHU
Vice-Pres.: LIU ZONGRUI
Vice-Pres.: MA GUOWEN
Vice-Pres.: PAN XIANG
Vice-Pres.: XIAO JIANPING
Head of Graduate Dept: XING PENGNIN
Librarian: DONG SHALI

Library of 700,000 vols
Number of teachers: 2,262
Number of students: 31,271

Publications: *Journal* (natural sciences; 6 a year in Chinese, 2 a year in Mongolian), *Journal* (social sciences, 6 a year)

DEANS

College of Arts: (vacant)
College of Education Science: (vacant)
College of Law and History: PU FANDA
College of Literature: XU WENHAI
College of Mathematics and Computer Science: (vacant)
College of Mongolian Medicine: BA GENNA
College of Mongolian Studies: (vacant)
College of Sports: (vacant)

PROFESSORS

A, GULA, Mongolian Medicine
AN, GUANBU, Mongolian Medicine
BA, GENNA, Mongolian Medicine
BA, RIGEQI, Mongolian Medicine
BAI, YANMANDULA, Mongolian Medicine
PU, FANDA, Law and History
XUN, WENHAI, Literature
YANG, AMING, Mongolian Medicine

JIANGNAN UNIVERSITY

1800 Lihu Rd, Wuxi 214122, Jiangsu Province
Telephone: (510) 85913623
Internet: www.jiangnan.edu.cn

Founded 1902
State control
Academic year: September to July

Pres.: CHEN JIAN
Vice-Pres.: FENG BIAO
Vice-Pres.: JIANG ZHONGPING
Vice-Pres.: LOU GUODONG
Vice-Pres.: WANG WU
Vice-Pres.: ZHU TUO
Head of Graduate Dept: ZHANG HAO
Librarian: ZHANG YIXIN

Number of teachers: 1,504
Number of students: 19,600

Publication: *Journal of Southern Yangtze University* (edns: food and biotechnology, natural sciences, humanities and social science, 6 a year; beverage and frozen food industry, 4 a year)

DEANS

Department of Art: WANG JIANYAN
Department of Civil Engineering: HUA YUAN
Department of International Studies: GUO XIHUA
Department of Physical Education: YANG RONGLIN
School of Biotechnology: XU YAN
School of Business: FU XIANZHI
School of Chemical and Materials Engineering: FANG YUN
School of Communication and Control Engineering: JI ZHICHENG
School of Continuing Education: HUANG ZHENGMING
School of Design: GUO WEIMIN
School of Education: CHEN MINGXUAN
School of Food Science and Technology: ZHANG HAO
School of Foreign Studies: DONG JIANQIAO
School of Information Technology: WANG SHITONG
School of Law and Politics: ZHU TONGDAN
School of Literature: XU XINGHAI
School of Mechanical Engineering: ZHANG QIUJU
School of Medicine: LI HUAZHONG
School of Science: (vacant)
School of Textiles and Clothing: FANG KUANJUN

PROFESSORS

CAO, GUANGQUN, Chemical and Materials Engineering
CHEN, ANJUN, Mechanical Engineering
CHEN, JIAN, Biotechnology
CHEN, JIONG, Literature
CHEN, ZHENGXING, Food Science and Technology
DENG, ZIMEI, Law and Politics
DING, WEIGUO, Commerce
DING, XIAOLIN, Food Science and Technology
DONG, YUZI, Information Technology
DU, GUOCHENG, Biotechnology
FANG, HANWEN, Literature
FANG, KUANJUN, Textiles
FENG, BIAO, Food Science and Technology
GAO, WEIDONG, Textiles
GE, MINGQIAO, Textiles
GU, GUOXIAN, Biotechnology
GU, WENYING, Food Science and Technology
GU, YAOLIN, Information Technology
GU, YIFAN, Literature
GUO, SHIDONG, Food Science and Technology
HUANG, HUANCHU, Law and Politics
HUANG, WEINING, Food Science and Technology
HUANG, ZHIHAO, Literature
HUANG, ZHONGJING, Law and Politics
JIANG, BO, Food Science and Technology
JIANG, CHENGYONG, Literature
JIN, JIAN, Biotechnology
JIN, QIRONG, Biotechnology
JIN, ZHENGYU, Food Science and Technology
LE, GUOWEI, Food Science and Technology
LI, HUAZHONG, Biotechnology
LI, SHIGUO, Mechanical Engineering
LI, WEIJIANG, Biotechnology
LIU, HUANMING, Law and Politics
LUN, SHIYI, Biotechnology
MA, JIANGUO, Food Science and Technology
MA, QIFAN, Commerce
MAO, ZHONGGUI, Biotechnology
MENG, QING-EN, Law and Politics
PAN, BEILEI, Food Science and Technology
QIU, AIYONG, Food Science and Technology
QUAN, WENHAI, Biotechnology
SHAO, JIYONG, Commerce
SHI, YONGHUI, Food Science and Technology
SIMA, NAN, Literature
SUN, HONG, Literature
SUN, YANTANG, Information Technology
SUN, ZHIHAO, Biotechnology
SUN, ZHOUNIAN, Literature
TANG, JIAN, Food Science and Technology
TAO, BOHUA, Literature
TAO, WENYI, Biotechnology
WANG, SHITONG, Information Technology
WANG, WU, Biotechnology
WANG, YONGFENG, Literature
WANG, ZHANG, Food Science and Technology
WANG, ZHENGXIANG, Biotechnology
WANG, ZHIWEI, Mechanical Engineering
WU, GE, Commerce
WU, GEMING, Literature
WU, PEIZONG, Biotechnology
WU, XIANZHANG, Biotechnology
XIA, WENSHUI, Food Science and Technology
XIE, ZHENRONG, Law and Politics
XU, WENBO, Information Technology
XU, XINGHAI, Literature
XU, YAN, Biotechnology
XU, ZHENGYUAN, Information Technology
YAO, HUIYUAN, Food Science and Technology
YAO, JINMING, Literature
YU, SHIYING, Food Science and Technology
YUAN, HUIXIN, Mechanical Engineering
YUAN, ZHENHUI, Law and Politics
ZENG, YOUXIN, Commerce
ZHANG, GENYI, Food Science and Technology
ZHANG, HEGUAN, Commerce
ZHANG, JIWEN, Information Technology
ZHANG, KECHANG, Biotechnology
ZHANG, MIN, Food Science and Technology
ZHANG, QIUJU, Mechanical Engineering
ZHANG, XINCHANG, Mechanical Engineering
ZHANG, XINGYUAN, Biotechnology
ZHANG, XIQING, Mechanical Engineering
ZHANG, YIXIN, Information Technology
ZHANG, YONGXIN, Literature
ZHANG, YUZHONG, Mechanical Engineering
ZHAO, GUANGAO, Biotechnology
ZHAO, JIANGUO, Biotechnology
ZHAO, YONGWU, Mechanical Engineering
ZHOU, HUIMING, Food Science and Technology
ZHOU, QING, Biotechnology

ZHOU, WUCHUN, Literature
ZHU, TONGDAN, Law and Politics
ZHU, ZHIFENG, Textiles
ZHUGE, HONGYUN, Literature
ZHUGE, JIAN, Biotechnology

JIANGSU UNIVERSITY

301 Xuefu Rd, Zhenjiang 212013, Jiangsu Province
Telephone: (511) 8780048
Internet: www.ujs.edu.cn
Founded 2001
Academic year: September to July
Pres.: YANG JICHANG
Vice-Pres.: CAO YOUQING
Vice-Pres.: SONG JINGZHANG
Vice-Pres.: SONG YUQING
Vice-Pres.: SUN YUKUN
Vice-Pres.: XU HUAXI
Vice-Pres.: YUAN SHOUQI
Vice-Pres.: YUAN YINNAN
Vice-Pres.: ZHAO JIEWEN
Head of Graduate Dept: MAO HANPING
Librarian: SONG SHUNLIN
Number of teachers: 900
Number of students: 26,320
Publication: *Journal* (6 a year, edns: higher education, medicine, natural sciences, social sciences)

DEANS
College of Adult Education: XIN JUNKANG
Faculty of Science: TIAN LIXIN
School of Art Education: ZHU ZHENGLUN
School of Automotive and Traffic Engineering: CAI YIXI
School of Biological and Environmental Engineering: WU CHUNDU
School of Chemistry and Chemical Engineering: XIE JIMIN
School of Computer Science and Telecommunications: JU SHIGUANG
School of Electrical and Information Engineering: LIU GUOHAI
School of Energy Resources and Power Engineering: YANG MINGUAN
School of Foreign Languages: LUO XINMIN
School of Humanities and Social Sciences: DA YUANYI
School of Industrial and Business Administration: MEI QIANG
School of Materials Engineering: (vacant)
School of Mechanical Engineering: LI PINGPING
School of Medical Technology: XU WENRONG
School of Medicine: XU HUAXI
School of Normal Education: CHEN LIN
School of Pharmacy: XU XIMING

PROFESSORS
BAO, BINGHAO, Mechanical Engineering
CAI, LAN, Mechanical Engineering
CHEN, CUIYING, Mechanical Engineering
CHEN, GUOXIANG, Humanities and Social Sciences
CHEN, JIN, Mechanical Engineering
CHEN, LIZHEN, Business Administration
CHEN, ZHAOZHANG, Electrical and Information Engineering
CHEN, ZHIGANG, Materials Engineering
CHENG, LI, Electrical and Information Engineering
CHENG, XIANYI, Computer Science and Telecommunications
CHENG, XIAONONG, Materials Engineering
CHONG, KAI, Mechanical Engineering
DAI, QIXUN, Materials Engineering
DING, GUILIN, Mechanical Engineering
DING, JIANNING, Mechanical Engineering
DONG, DEFU, Humanities and Social Sciences
FAN, MING, Business Administration
GE, XIAOLAN, Mechanical Engineering
GU, JINAN, Mechanical Engineering
HE, YOUSHI, Business Administration
HE, ZHIGUO, Art
HUANG, GENLIANG, Materials Engineering
HUANG, XIQUAN, Medical Technology
JIN, LIFU, Humanities and Social Sciences
JU, SHIGUANG, Computer Science and Telecommunications
KONG, YUSHENG, Business Administration
LEI, YUCHENG, Materials Engineering
LI, BOQUAN, Mechanical Engineering
LI, CHANGSHENG, Mechanical Engineering
LI, DETAO, Energy Resources and Power Engineering
LI, PINGPING, Mechanical Engineering
LI, XINCHENG, Mechanical Engineering
LI, YAOMING, Mechanical Engineering
LI, ZHENGMING, Electrical and Information Engineering
LIN, HONGYI, Energy Resources and Power Engineering
LIU, AIZHEN, Foreign Languages
LIU, FENGYING, Computer Science and Telecommunications
LIU, GUOHAI, Electrical and Information Engineering
LIU, JIANYI, Business Administration
LIU, QIUSHENG, Business Administration
LU, ZHANGPING, Mechanical Engineering
LU, ZHENGNAN, Business Administration
LUO, DEFU, Materials Science and Engineering
LUO, TIGAN, Energy Resources and Power Engineering
LUO, XINMIN, Materials Engineering
LUO, ZHIGAO, Mechanical Engineering
MA, LVZHONG, Mechanical Engineering
MAO, HANPING, Mechanical Engineering
MEI, QIANG, Business Administration
QI, HONG, Energy Resources and Power Engineering
QIAO, ZHAOHUA, Humanities and Social Science
QIU, BAIJING, Mechanical Engineering
REN, NAIFEI, Mechanical Engineering
SHAO, HONGHONG, Materials Engineering
SHAO, SHIHE, Medical Technology
SHEN, XIANGQIAN, Materials Engineering
SHI, GUOHONG, Business Administration
SI, NAICHAO, Materials Engineering
SONG, SHUNLIN, Computer Science and Telecommunications
SONG, XINNAN, Energy Resources and Power Engineering
SONG, YUQING, Computer Science and Telecommunications
SUN, JIAGUANG, Computer Science and Telecommunications
SUN, YUKUN, Electrical and Information Engineering
WANG, CUNTANG, Mechanical Engineering
WANG, GANG, Computer Science and Telecommunications
WANG, GUICHENG, Mechanical Engineering
WANG, QIAN, Energy Resources and Power Engineering
WANG, SHULIN, Mechanical Engineering
WANG, SHUQI, Materials Engineering
WANG, ZE, Energy Resources and Power Engineering
WEI, QI, Energy Resources and Power Engineering
WEN, JIANLONG, Energy Resources and Power Engineering
WU, YANYOU, Mechanical Engineering
XIAO, TIEJUN, Computer Science and Telecommunications
XIE, GANG, Humanities and Social Sciences
XU, HUAXI, Medical Technology
XU, WENRONG, Medical Technology
XU, XIMING, Pharmacy
YANG, JICHANG, Mechanical Engineering
YANG, MINGUAN, Energy Resources and Power Engineering
YANG, PING, Mechanical Engineering
YAO, GUANXIN, Business Administration
ZHAN, YONGZHAO, Computer Science and Telecommunications
ZHANG, BINGSHENG, Humanities and Social Sciences
ZHANG, JIAN, Business Administration
ZHANG, RONGBIAO, Electrical and Information Engineering
ZHANG, YONGKANG, Mechanical Engineering
ZHANG, ZHUMEI, Humanities and Social Sciences
ZHAO, BUHUI, Electrical and Information Engineering
ZHAO, DEAN, Electrical and Information Engineering
ZHAO, JIN, Business Administration
ZHAO, XICANG, Business Administration
ZHAO, YANPING, Business Administration
ZHAO, YUTAO, Materials Engineering
ZHOU, HONG, Medical Technology
ZHOU, JIANZHONG, Mechanical Engineering
ZHOU, JUN, Mechanical Engineering
ZHOU, TIANJIAN, Medical Technology
ZHOU, ZHICHU, Humanities and Social Sciences
ZHU, HUANGQIU, Electrical and Information Engineering
ZHU, WEIXING, Electrical and Information Engineering
ZUO, RAN, Energy Resources and Power Engineering

JIANGXI AGRICULTURAL UNIVERSITY

Meiling, Nanchang 330045, Jianxi Province
E-mail: ieojau@yahoo.com.cn
Internet: www.jxau.edu.cn
Founded 1940
public control
Language of instruction: Chinese
Academic year: September to June
Pres.: Prof. HUANG LUSHENG
Library: over 1,000,000 vols
Number of teachers: 1,500
Number of students: 26,000
Publication: *Journal*

JILIN UNIVERSITY

10 Qianwei Rd, Changchun 130012
Telephone: (431) 5166885
E-mail: fsc@jlu.edu.cn
Internet: www.jlu.edu.cn
Founded 1946, merged in 2001 with Jilin Univ. of Technology (f. 1955), Norman Bethune Univ. of Medical Sciences (f. 1939), Changchun Univ. of Science and Technology (f. 1951) and Changchun Institute of Posts and Telecommunications (f. 1947), to form new Jilin Univ.
Academic year: September to July (2 semesters).
Colleges of administration studies, art, biology and agricultural engineering, chemistry, clinical medicine, communications engineering, computer science and technology, construction engineering, economics, economics and information, electronics and engineering, environment and resources, foreign languages, geological exploration and information technology, geological sciences, law, life sciences, literature and arts, machinery and engineering, management studies, materials science and engineering, mathematics, motor car engineering, nursing, pharmacy, philosophy and sociology, physical education, physics, public health sciences, stomatology, transport
Pres.: LIU ZHONGSHU
Head of Graduate School: QIU SHILUN
Librarian: BAO CHENGGUAN
Library of 2,510,000 vols

Publications: *Chemical Research in Chinese Universities* (Chinese and English edns), *Higher Education Research and Practice*, *Journal of Demography*, *Journal of Historical Studies*, *Journal of Natural Science*, *Legal Systems and Social Development*, *Mathematics of Northeastern China*, *Modern Japanese Economy*, *Northeast Asian Forum*

JINAN UNIVERSITY

601 Huangpu West Rd, Guangzhou 510632, Guangdong Province
Telephone: (20) 85220010
E-mail: officex@jnu.edu.cn
Internet: www.jnu.edu.cn

Founded 1906
Academic year: September to July

Pres.: LIU RENHUAI
Vice-Pres.: HU JUN
Vice-Pres.: JI ZONGAN
Vice-Pres.: JIA YIMIN
Vice-Pres.: JIANG SHUZHUO
Vice-Pres.: LU DAXIANG
Vice-Pres.: WANG HUA
Vice-Pres.: YE QIN
Head of Graduate Dept: GU WEIFANG
Librarian: ZHU LINA

Number of teachers: 1,477
Number of students: 22,000

Publications: *Chinese Journal of Pathophysiology* (6 a year), *Ecological Science* (4 a year), *Economic Front* (12 a year), *Jinan Higher Education Research* (6 a year), *Journal* (6 a year), *Journal of the College of Chinese Language and Culture of Jinan University* (4 a year), *South-East Asian Studies* (6 a year)

DEANS

College of Chinese Language and Culture: BAO CHAO
College of Continuing Education: HAO ZHAOZHOU
College of Economics: LIU SHAOBO
College of Foreign Studies: LIANG DONGHUA
College of Information Science and Technology: BO YUANHUAI
College of Journalism and Communication: CAI MINGZE
College of Liberal Arts: SUN WEIMING
College of Life Science and Technology: ZHOU TIANHONG
College of Pharmacy: ZHANG RONGHUA
College of Science and Engineering: ZHANG YONGLIN
International School: SUN BOHUA
Management School: SUI GUANGJUN
Medical School: SU BAOGUI
School of Law: ZHOU XIANZHI
Shenzhen College of Tourism: LIU ZEPENG
Zhuhai Special Economic Zone College: HU JUN

PROFESSORS

AO, NINGJIAN, Life Science and Technology
CAI, JIYE, Life Science and Technology
CAI, MINGZE, Journalism and Communication
CAO, BAOLIN, Liberal Arts
CAO, YUNHUA, Law
CHEN, CHUSHENG, Liberal Arts
CHEN, EN, Economics
CHEN, QIAOZHI, Law
CHEN, WEIMING, Liberal Arts
CHEN, XIAOJIN, Liberal Arts
CHEN, XINGDAN, Science and Engineering
CHEN, XUEMEI, Economics
CHEN, YINYUAN, Life Science and Technology
CHEN, YONGLIANG, Economics
CHENG, GUOBIN, Liberal Arts
DENG, QIAOBIN, Chinese
DONG, JIANXIN, Management
DONG, TIANCE, Journalism and Communication
DU, JINMIN, Finance
DUAN, SHUNSHAN, Life Science and Technology
FEI, YONG, Liberal Arts
FENG, BANGYAN, Economics
FENG, XIAOYUN, Economics
GAO, WEINONG, Liberal Arts
GAO, YINGJUN, Science and Engineering
GONG, WEIPING, Economics
GU, GUOYAO, Finance
GUO, SHUHAO, Life Science and Technology
HAN, BOPING, Life Science and Technology
HAN, ZHAOZHOU, Statistics
HE, WENTAO, Finance
HONG, AN, Life Science and Technology
HU, JUN, Management
HU, JUN, Zhuhai SEZ College
HU, SHIZHEN, Economics
HUANG, DEHONG, Management
HUANG, YAOXIONG, Life Science and Technology
JI, MANHONG, Liberal Arts
JI, ZONG-AN, Liberal Arts
JIA, YIMIN, Liberal Arts
JIANG, DUXIAO, Life Science and Technology
JIANG, SHUZHUO, Chinese
JIN, LAHUA, Science and Engineering
LI, BOQIAO, Law
LI, GUISHENG, Life Science and Technology
LI, WEI, Life Science and Technology
LI, YIJUN, Life Science and Technology
LI, YUFANG, Economics
LIN, FUYONG, Zhuhai SEZ College
LIN, LIQIONG, Economics
LIN, RUPENG, Journalism and Communication
LING, WENQUAN, Management
LIU, DEXUE, International Economics and Trade
LIU, JIALIN, Journalism and Communication
LIU, JIANPING, Statistics
LIU, JIESHENG, Life Science and Technology
LIU, RENHUAI, Science and Engineering
LIU, SHAOBO, Finance
LIU, SHAOJIN, Chinese
LIU, YIN, Law
LIU, YINGLIANG, Life Science and Technology
LIU, ZHENGGANG, Liberal Arts
LIU, ZHENGWEN, Life Science and Technology
LU, JUNHUA, Pharmacy
MA, MINGDA, Liberal Arts
MA, QIUFENG, Journalism and Communication
MA, ZHIRONG, Zhuhai SEZ College
MEI, LINHAI, Economics
NIU, DESHENG, Economics
OUYANG, JIANMING, Life Science and Technology
PAN, SHANPEI, Life Science and Technology
PANG, QICHANG, Science and Engineering
QIU, SHUSEN, Liberal Arts
RAO, PENGZI, Chinese
SHAO, JINGMIN, Chinese
SU, BAOHE, Zhuhai SEZ College
SU, DONGWEI, Finance
SUI, GUANGJUN, Management
SUN, BOHUA, International School
SUN, DONGCHUAN, Zhuhai SEZ College
SUN, HANXIAO, Pharmacy
TAN, TIAN, Journalism and Communication
TAN, YUE, Finance
TANG, KAIJIAN, Liberal Arts
TANG, SHUNQING, Life Science and Technology
TANG, SHUZE, Science and Engineering
WANG, CONG, Finance
WANG, FUCHU, Economics
WANG, HUA, Management
WANG, LIEYAO, Liberal Arts
WANG, XIANGPING, Zhuhai SEZ College
WANG, XINMIN, Liberal Arts
WANG, YANKUN, Chinese
WANG, YIFEI, Pharmacy
WANG, YING, Life Science and Technology
WEI, ZHONGLIN, Liberal Arts
WEN, BEIYAN, Law
WU, CHAOBIAO, Statistics
WU, JIANG, Economics
WU, LIGUANG, International Economics and Trade
WU, XIANZHONG, Management
XIA, HONGSHENG, Management
XIANG, JUNJIAN, Life Science and Technology
XIE, QINAN, Statistics
XU, SHIHAI, Life Science and Technology
YANG, QIGUANG, Liberal Arts
YANG, XING, Finance
YANG, YING, Economics
YANG, YUFENG, Life Science and Technology
YAO, XINSHENG, Pharmacy
YE, CHUNLING, Pharmacy
YE, WENCAI, Pharmacy
YIN, HUA, Science and Engineering
YIN, PINGHE, Life Science and Technology
YU, DINGCHENG, Economics
YU, RONGMIN, Pharmacy
YU, YOULONG, Science and Engineering
ZENG, JIANXIONG, Journalism and Communication
ZENG, YAOYING, Life Science and Technology
ZHAN, BOHUI, Chinese
ZHANG, JIE, International Economics and Trade
ZHANG, QIFAN, Liberal Arts
ZHANG, QIZHONG, Life Science and Technology
ZHANG, RONGHUA, Pharmacy
ZHANG, SENWEN, Science and Engineering
ZHANG, SHIJUN, Liberal Arts
ZHANG, XIAOHUI, Liberal Arts
ZHANG, YAOHUI, Zhuhai SEZ College
ZHANG, YONGLIN, Science and Engineering
ZHANG, YUANMING, Life Science and Technology
ZHANG, YUCHUN, Liberal Arts
ZHANG, ZIYONG, Life Science and Technology
ZHAO, JIAMIN, Finance
ZHENG, WENJIE, Life Science and Technology
ZHONG, JINGANG, Science and Engineering
ZHOU, CHANGREN, Life Science and Technology
ZHOU, LIXIN, Life Science and Technology
ZHOU, TIANHONG, Life Science and Technology
ZHOU, XIANZH, Law
ZHU, CHENGPING, Liberal Arts
ZHU, WEIJIE, Life Science and Technology

JINAN UNIVERSITY

601 West Guangzhou, 510632, Guangdong
Telephone: (20) 5516511
Internet: www.jnu.edu.cn

Founded 1906, univ. status 1927
State control
Language of instruction: Chinese
Academic year: September to July

Pres.: Prof. HU JUN
Vice-Pres.: Prof. JIANG SHUZHUO
Vice-Pres.: Prof. LU DAXIANG
Vice-Pres.: Prof. YE KIN
Vice-Pres.: Prof. ZHOU TIANHONG
Vice-Pres.: Prof. LIU JIESHENG
Vice-Pres.: Prof. LIN RUPENG
Vice-Pres.: Prof. SONG XIANZHONG
Vice-Pres.: Prof. RAO MIN
Dir for Library: HE RENJIN

Library of 1,347,000 vols
Number of teachers: 1,819
Number of students: 46,949

Publications: *Journal I — Literature, History, Economics*, *Journal II — Science, Technology, Medicine*, *Jinan Education*, *World Literature and Arts*

KUNMING MEDICAL UNIVERSITY

191 West Renmin Rd, 650031 Kunming
Telephone: (871) 5354878
E-mail: sskmu@hotmail.com
Internet: www.kmmc.cn

Founded 1956 as Kunming Medical College
Academic year: September to August (2 semesters)

Pres.: Prof. RUNSHENG JIANG

Library: 1m. vols
Number of teachers: 1,450
Number of students: 15,000

KUNMING UNIVERSITY OF SCIENCE AND TECHNOLOGY

727 South Jingming Rd, 650500 Kunming
Telephone: (871) 65915166
E-mail: intex@kmust.edu.cn
Internet: www.kmust.edu.cn

Founded 1954
State control
Academic year: September to July

Pres.: Prof. ZHANG YINGJIE
Vice-Pres.: LUO LIHUI
Vice-Pres.: TIAN JUN
Vice-Pres.: YANG BAO JIAN
Vice-Pres.: WANG HUA
Librarian: Prof. LIU ZHONGHUA

Library: 2.72m. vols
Number of teachers: 2,200
Number of students: 36,300

Publications: *Journal*, *Research in Higher Education in KUST*, *Science and Technology in KUST*

LANZHOU UNIVERSITY

222 Tianshui Nanlu, Lanzhou 730000, Gansu Province
Telephone: (931) 8912126
E-mail: news@lzu.edu.cn
Internet: www.lzu.edu.cn

Founded 1909
Academic year: September to July (2 semesters)

Pres.: ZHOU XUHONG
Vice-Pres.: AN LIZHE
Vice-Pres.: CHEN FAHU
Vice-Pres.: GAN HUI
Vice-Pres.: JING TAO
Vice-Pres.: XU SHENGCHENG
Dir for Pres. Office: ZHANG ZHENGGUO
Librarian: SHA YONGZHONG

Number of teachers: 1,779
Number of students: 28,358

Publications: *Collections of Articles on Dunhuang Studies*, *Historical and Geographical Review of Northwest China*

LIAONING NORMAL UNIVERSITY

Da Lian 116029, Liaoning Province
Telephone: (411) 2158235
Internet: www.lnnu.edu.cn

Founded 1951
provincial control
Academic year: September to July

Pres.: QU QINGBIAO
Vice-Pres.: HAN ZHENGLIN
Vice-Pres.: QU WEI
Librarian: ZHAO YUNSHENG

Library of 1,330,000 vols
Number of teachers: 1,897
Number of students: 25,200

Publication: *Journal* (6 a year)

DEANS

College of the City and Environment: LIN XIANSENG
College of Education: FU WEILI
College of Film and Television Art: GAO GUANGFU
College of Foreign Languages: MA YANGGANG
College of History and Tourism: XIE JINGFANG
College of Law: YU PEILIN
College of Life Science: HOU HESHENG
College of Literature: WANG WEIPING
College of Management: ZHAO ZHONGWEN
College of Physics and Electronic Technology: PAN FENG
College of Politics: SHI YIJUN
College of Sports: HE MINXUE
Faculty of Chemistry and Chemical Engineering: JIAO QIANGZHU
School of Mathematics: HAN YOUFA

PROFESSORS

BI, ZHIGUO, Politics
CAI, MIN, Education
CHANG, JINCHANG, History and Tourism
CHANG, RUOSONG, Education
CHEN, DACHAO, Education
CHEN, LIU, Literature
CHEN, TUYUN, Mathematics
CHENG, XIAOGUANG, Foreign Languages
DIAO, YANBIN, Literature
DONG, GUANGCAI, Foreign Languages
DONG, XUEDONG, Mathematics
DU, LIN, Literature
DU, RUIZHI, Mathematics
DU, XINGZHI, History and Tourism
FAN, YINGHENG, Chemistry and Chemical Engineering
FANG, HONGXIAO, Life Science
FENG, CHUNLIANG, Chemistry and Chemical Engineering
FU, WEILI, Education
GAO, BO, Management
HAN, YOUFA, Mathematics
HAN, YUCHANG, Education
HE, MINXUE, Sports
HOU, HESHENG, Life Science
HOU, LIN, Life Science
HU, ZHENKAI, Education
HUANG, BIN, Sports
JIANG, HUA, Life Science
JIN, CHENGJI, Sports
JIN, HONGYUAN, Education
JIN, RENSHU, Management
LI, CHUNLIN, Literature
LI, JINXIANG, Chemistry and Chemical Engineering
LI, LAIZHI, Management
LI, RENXI, Life Science
LI, TIANJIAN, Mathematics
LI, XUGUANG, Foreign Languages
LI, YAOZHENG, City and Environment Studies
LI, YINGJUN, Chemistry and Chemical Engineering
LIANG, GUIZHI, Literature
LIANG, SHUSHENG, Physics and Electronic Technology
LIN, HUA, Sports
LIN, XIANSHENG, City and Environment Studies
LIU, FANFU, Foreign Languages
LIU, FUGENG, Foreign Languages
LIU, PEIHAN, Politics
LIU, WANQI, Law
LIU, WEN, Education
LIU, XIUCHUN, Politics
LIU, ZHEQING, Mathematics
LUAN, WEIXIN, City and Environment Studies
LU, FENGYING, Law
LU, GUOFENG, Sports
MA, DONGYU, History and Tourism
MA, JIANSHENG, Education
MA, JUNSHAN, Literature
MA, YOUHUI, Life Science
MENG, DEXIU, Foreign Languages
MENG, ZHAOYUAN, Politics
NIU, SHUYUN, Chemistry and Chemical Engineering
PAN, FENG, Physics and Electronic Technology
QI, GUOYING, Physics and Electronic Technology
QU, GUANG, Literature
QU, JIANWU, Politics
QU, QINGBIAO, Politics
QU, WEI, Foreign Languages
SANG, DEJING, Life Science
SHI, LEI, Chemistry and Chemical Engineering
SHI, YIJUN, Politics
SHUN, RENAN, Chemistry and Chemical Engineering
SHUN, YUANGANG, Education
SONG, HUA, History and Tourism
TAO, YANG, Foreign Languages
TIAN, GUANGLIN, History and Tourism
WANG, BING, Foreign Languages
WANG, CHANGSHENG, Chemistry and Chemical Engineering
WANG, GUANLIN, Life Science
WANG, HONG, Sports
WANG, JIPENG, Literature
WANG, LI, Literature
WANG, QIHUA, Life Science
WANG, QINGJIAN, Mathematics
WANG, WEIPING, Literature
WANG, XIUWU, Life Science
WANG, XIUXIANG, Sports
WANG, YAOGUANG, Sports
WANG, YI, Literature
WANG, ZHIWEN, Physics and Electronic Technology
WEI, HUAZHONG, Education
WU, DESHENG, Literature
WU, ZHIHUA, Life Science
XIE, JINGFANG, History and Tourism
XIE, LIN, Mathematics
XIE, MINGJIE, Life Science
XU, YINGJUN, Foreign Languages
YAN, BANGYI, Literature
YAN, ZHILI, Sports
YANG, HONG, Life Science
YANG, LIZHU, Education
YANG, MING, Education
YANG, XIAO, Education
YANG, XIUXIANG, Politics
YANG, YINGJIE, History and Tourism
YANG, ZHONGZHI, Chemistry and Chemical Engineering
YI, HUAINING, City and Environment Studies
YOU, WANSHENG, Chemistry and Chemical Engineering
YU, BING, Literature
YU, DAHUA, History and Tourism
YU, PEILING, Law
YU, WENQIAN, Sports
YUAN, XUEHAI, Mathematics
YUE, ZHONGXING, Physics and Electronic Technology
ZHANG, AIJUN, Politics
ZHANG, GUICHUN, Education
ZHANG, GUIREN, Politics
ZHANG, LIHUA, Education
ZHANG, NINGSHENG, Education
ZHANG, QI, Education
ZHANG, SHUMIN, Chemistry and Chemical Engineering
ZHANG, WEIDONG, Life Science
ZHANG, XIAONING, Foreign Languages
ZHANG, YAOGUANG, City and Environment Studies
ZHAO, YI, History and Tourism
ZHAO, YUBAO, History and Tourism
ZHAO, ZHENYING, History and Tourism
ZHAO, ZHONGWEN, Management
ZHONG, GUIQING, City and Environment Studies
ZHOU, DANHONG, Chemistry and Chemical Engineering
ZHOU, WEI, Life Science
ZHOU, XIAOYAN, Education
ZHOU, ZHIQIANG, Politics
ZHU, NINGBO, Education
ZHU, ZHIJUN, Politics

LIAONING TECHNICAL UNIVERSITY

Fu Xin 3350461, Liaoning
E-mail: webmaster@lntu.edu.cn
Internet: www.lntu.edu.cn

Founded 1958
State control
Academic year: September to July

Constituent colleges and depts in the following areas: architecture and civil engineering; business management; electrical and information engineering; electrical engineering; foreign languages; geomatics engineering; journalism and communication; materials science and engineering; mechanical engineering; mechanics and engineering sciences; politics and law resources and environmental engineering; software; technology and economics

Pres.: SHI JINFENG
Vice-Pres.: MA ZHUANG
Vice-Pres.: PAN YISHAN
Vice-Pres.: SHAO LIANGBIN
Vice-Pres.: WANG JIREN
Vice-Pres.: ZHANG SHUSEN
Vice-Pres.: ZHANG ZUOGANG
Head of Graduate Dept: LIANG BING
Librarian: LIE JIE

Number of teachers: 1,349
Number of students: 25,000

Publications: *Journal* (natural sciences, 6 a year), *Journal* (social sciences, 4 a year)

PROFESSORS

FU, XINGWU, Electrical Engineering
GUO, FENGYI, Electrical Engineering
HUI, XIAOWEI, Electrical and Information Engineering
LI, WEIDONG, Electrical Engineering
LI, XIAOZHU, Electrical Engineering
LI, YIJIE, Electrical and Information Engineering
LI, ZHENGZHONG, Geomatics Engineering
LIU, JIANHUI, Electrical and Information Engineering
LU, SHIKUI, Electrical Engineering
MENG, QINGCHUN, Electrical Engineering
QIAO, YANGWEN, Geomatics Engineering
SONG, WEIDONG, Geomatics Engineering
SUN, JINGUANG, Electrical and Information Engineering
SUN, PENGYONG, Electrical and Information Engineering
WANG, JIAGUI, Geomatics Engineering
WANG, YUFENG, Electrical Engineering
XING, BAOJUN, Electrical Engineering
YE, JINGLOU, Electrical and Information Engineering
YE, JINGLOU, Electrical Engineering
ZHAO, GUOCAI, Electrical Engineering
ZHAO, GUOQIANG, Electrical Engineering
ZHU, HUA, Electrical Engineering

LIAONING UNIVERSITY

66 Chongshan Middle Rd, Shenyang 110036, Liaoning Province
Telephone: (24) 86842756
E-mail: office@lnu.edu.cn
Internet: www.lnu.edu.cn

Founded 1948
Min. of Education control
Academic year: September to July

Pres.: CHENG WEI
Vice-Pres.: LIU ZHICHAO
Vice-Pres.: MU HUAIZHONG
Vice-Pres.: ZANG SHULIANG
Vice-Pres.: ZHANG WEI
Head of Graduate Dept: XU PING
Librarian: YANG XIAOJUN

Number of teachers: 1,200
Number of students: 23,000

Publications: *Journal* (natural sciences, 4 a year), *Journal* (philosophy and social sciences, 6 a year), *Research of Japan* (4 a year)

DEANS

Asia-Australia College of Business: ZHOU JIE
College of Adult Education: MA YONGJUN
College of Business Management: GAO CHUANG
College of Chemistry and Engineering: SONG XIMING
College of Cultural Communication: GAO KAIZHENG
College of Economics: LIN MUXI
College of Foreign Languages: CHEN FENG
College of Higher Professional Techniques: YU ZHONGCHENG
College of Information Science and Technology: SHI XIANGBIN
College of Law: YANG SONG
College of Philosophy and Public Administration: SHAO XIAOGUANG
College of Radio, Film and Television: HU GUANGHUI
Faculty of Environmental Science: LI FAYUN
Faculty of History: DING HAIBIN
Faculty of Life Sciences: ZHOU RENQING
Faculty of Mathematics: DAI TIANMIN
Faculty of Physics: GUO YONGXIN
Sun Wah International Business School: CHENG WEI

PROFESSORS

BI, XIAOHUI, Philosophy and Public Administration
CHE, WEIYI, Mathematics
CHEN, CHUNGUANG, Information Science and Technology
CHEN, FENG, Foreign Languages
CHEN, XIN, Chemistry and Engineering
DAI, BOXUN, Business Management
DAI, TIANMIN, Mathematics
DING, HAIBIN, History
DING, NING, Information Science and Technology
DONG, SHOUYI, History
DONG, WENCHENG, Cultural Communication
FANG, BAOLIN, Business Management
GAO, CHUANG, Business Management
GAO, KAIZHENG, Cultural Communication
GAO, YANGKUI, Foreign Languages
GU, KUIXIANG, History
GUO, HUOXUN, Philosophy and Public Administration
GUO, JIE, Law
GUO, WENSHENG, Chemistry and Engineering
GUO, YONGXIN, Physics
HAO, JIANSHE, Law
HU, YUHAI, History
JIA, SHUFENG, Foreign Languages
JIAO, RUNMING, History
JIN, LISHUN, Business Management
LI, CHUNGUANG, History
LI, JUEXIAN, Mathematics
LI, LIPING, Information Science and Technology
LI, TIEMIN, Life Sciences
LI, YONGCHANG, History
LIN, MUXI, Economics
LIU, DUCAI, Law
LIU, FULIN, Mathematics
LIU, LIGANG, Business Management
LIU, WEIZHI, Cultural Communication
LIU, XINGZHI, Chemistry and Engineering
LU, JIERONG, Philosophy and Public Administration
LU, DIANZHEN, Chemistry and Engineering
LU, FANG, Mathematics
LU, GUOCHEN, Philosophy and Public Administration
LUO, JUNBO, Mathematics
MA, LIJUAN, Foreign Languages
NIU, BIN, Information Science and Technology
PENG, HAORONG, Business Management
QI, LIQUAN, Chemistry and Engineering
QI, ZHENGHUI, History
QIN, YONGLU, Information Science and Technology
QU, DELAI, Cultural Communication
REN, JI, Law
SHAO, XIAOGUANG, Philosophy and Public Administration
SHEN, GUIFENG, Physics
SHEN, HONGDA, Business Management
SHI, XIANGBIN, Information Science and Technology
SHI, YING, Law
SONG, XIMING, Chemistry and Engineering
SUN, HONGLIE, Mathematics
SUN, LI, Law
TANG, XIAOHUA, Business Management
TIAN, YUFENG, Information Science and Technology
TU, GUANGSHE, Cultural Communication
WANG, CHUNFEI, Cultural Communication
WANG, CHUNRONG, Cultural Communication
WANG, JUN, Chemistry and Engineering
WANG, QIUYU, Life Sciences
WANG, WEI, Cultural Communication
WANG, WEIFAN, Mathematics
WANG, WENCI, Foreign Languages
WANG, XIANGFENG, Cultural Communication
WU, CHUNYU, Physics
WU, WENZHONG, Foreign Languages
WU, XINJIE, Physics
XIAO, SHENG, Business Management
XING, ZHIREN, Law
XU, HAOGUANG, Cultural Communication
XU, ZHIGANG, Cultural Communication
XUE, JIANSHENG, Information Science and Technology
YANG, JIAZHEN, Chemistry and Engineering
YANG, LINRUI, Law
YANG, MING, Law
YANG, SONG, Law
YU, ZHONGZHUO, Business Management
ZANG, SHULIANG, Chemistry and Engineering
ZENG, XIAOFEI, Life Sciences
ZHANG, CHENGHUA, Physics
ZHANG, FENG, Chemistry and Engineering
ZHANG, JIE, History
ZHANG, LIZHEN, History
ZHANG, XIANGDONG, Chemistry and Engineering
ZHANG, YOUHUI, Information Science and Technology
ZHAO, BINGGUI, Law
ZHAO, DEZHI, Philosophy and Public Administration
ZHAO, GUOXING, Information Science and Technology
ZHAO, LINGHE, Cultural Communication
ZHENG, YONGFAN, Mathematics
ZHOU, FEI, Philosophy and Public Administration
ZHOU, RENQING, Life Sciences
ZHU, MINGLUN, Cultural Communication
ZUO, ZHICHENG, Foreign Languages

NANCHANG UNIVERSITY

235 Nanjing East Rd, Nanchang 330047, Jiangxi Province
Telephone: (791) 8305499
Internet: www.ncu.edu.cn

Founded 1940
State control
Academic year: September to July

Pres.: ZHOU WENBIN
Vice-Pres.: CHENG YANGGUO
Vice-Pres.: FU MINGFU
Vice-Pres.: GAN XIAOQING
Vice-Pres.: LI JIANMIN
Vice-Pres.: LIU SANQIU
Vice-Pres.: SHAO HONG
Vice-Pres.: XIE MINGYONG
Head of Graduate Dept: LI MING
Librarian: HE XIAOPING

Number of teachers: 1,253
Number of students: 45,000

Publications: *Journal* (engineering and technology, 4 a year), *Journal* (humanities and social sciences, 6 a year), *Journal* (natural sciences, 4 a year)

DEANS

Centre for Public Administration Programmes: TAO XUERONG
College of Architectural Engineering: GUI GUOQING
College of Art and Design: XIONG MANLING
College of Information Engineering: CHEN KEN
College of Life Sciences: ZHU YOULIN
College of Mechanics and Engineering: LIU HESHENG
College of Natural Science: LIU NIANHUA
College of Science and Technology: HE JIESHAN
College of Software: LU XIAOYONG
School of Chemistry and Materials Science: ZHOU LANG
School of Economics and Management: YIN JIDONG
School of Environmental Science and Engineering: HU ZHAOJI
School of Foreign Languages: FANG KEPING
School of Humanities and Social Sciences: LI DONGNI

PROFESSORS

BAO, ZHONGXU, Mechanics and Engineering
CAO, DEHE, Humanities and Social Sciences
CAO, YUSHENG, Life Sciences
CHEN, DONGYOU, Humanities and Social Sciences
CHEN, XINLING, Humanities and Social Sciences
DENG, SHUILAN, Economics and Management
DENG, ZEYUAN, Life Sciences
FU, XIAOLONG, Art and Design
GAO, GUOZHEN, Mechanics and Engineering
GAO, YINYU, Life Sciences
GONG, LIANSHOU, Humanities and Social Sciences
GU, XINGBIN, Humanities and Social Sciences
GU, ZHENGSHI, Mechanics and Engineering
HE, CHENGHONG, Mechanics and Engineering
HE, YUN, Economics and Management
HU, PING, Humanities and Social Sciences
HU, QING, Humanities and Social Sciences
HU, ZHAOJI, Environmental Science and Engineering
HUANG, JIHUA, Mechanics and Engineering
HUANG, XIJIA, Economics and Management
HUANG, XINJIAN, Economics and Management
JIANG, BOQUAN, Environmental Science and Engineering
JIANG, SHUISHENG, Mechanics and Engineering
JIN, LAHUA, Environmental Science and Engineering
LI, CHENGGUI, Humanities and Social Sciences
LI, DONGNI, Humanities and Social Sciences
LI, SHENGMEI, Humanities and Social Sciences
LI, XIANTAN, Economics and Management
LIN, BO, Environmental Science and Engineering
LIU, HESHENG, Mechanics and Engineering
LIU, LUNXIN, Humanities and Social Sciences
LIU, NIANHUA, Natural Science
LIU, QIJING, Environmental Science and Engineering
LIU, RENSHENG, Humanities and Social Sciences
LIU, WEIDONG, Mechanics and Engineering
LIU, XIAOHONG, Environmental Science and Engineering
LIU, XIAOQIN, Art and Design
LIU, YING, Mechanics and Engineering
LU, BINGFU, Humanities and Social Sciences
LU, SHENGPING, Art and Design
LU, XIANFENG, Mechanics and Engineering
LU, XIAOYONG, Economics and Management
LU, XIXING, Humanities and Social Sciences
MA, WEI, Economics and Management
NI, YONGNIAN, Life Sciences
PENG, DIYUN, Economics and Management
QIU, ZUMIN, Environmental Science and Engineering
RUAN, RONGSHENG, Life Sciences
SUN, RISHENG, Environmental Science and Engineering
SUN, YONG, Art and Design
WAN, FANGZHEN, Humanities and Social Sciences
WAN, JINBAO, Environmental Science and Engineering
WANG, DEBAO, Humanities and Social Sciences
WANG, LIANGSHENG, Art and Design
WANG, XIANGYANG, Art and Design
WANG, ZHEPING, Humanities and Social Sciences
WEI, LI, Economics and Management
WEN, SHIHUA, Humanities and Social Sciences
WU, LUSHEN, Mechanics and Engineering
WU, XIAOWEI, Humanities and Social Sciences
XIAO, ANKUN, Mechanics and Engineering
XIE, MINGYONG, Life Sciences
XIE, YONG, Economics and Management
XIN, YONG, Mechanics and Engineering
XIONG, JIANXIN, Art and Design
XIONG, MANLING, Art and Design
XIONG, RUIWEN, Mechanics and Engineering
XIONG, XIANGHUI, Mechanics and Engineering
XU, YANG, Life Sciences
YANG, GUOTAI, Mechanics and Engineering
YANG, MINGLANG, Art and Design
YANG, XUECHUN, Mechanics and Engineering
YANG, XUEPIN, Humanities and Social Sciences
YAO, YAPING, Humanities and Social Sciences
YI, PING, Humanities and Social Sciences
YIN, JIDONG, Economics and Management
YIN, XINGFAN, Humanities and Social Sciences
YING, YULONG, Life Sciences
YU, RANGYAO, Humanities and Social Sciences
YUAN, LIHUA, Humanities and Social Sciences
ZHAN, ZHIYOU, Humanities and Social Sciences
ZHANG, HUA, Mechanics and Engineering
ZHANG, NING, Natural Science
ZHANG, RENMU, Humanities and Social Sciences
ZHANG, SHENGYANG, Humanities and Social Sciences
ZHANG, YUMING, Economics and Management
ZHANG, YUSHENG, Humanities and Social Sciences
ZHANG, ZHIYONG, Humanities and Social Sciences
ZHAO, LIQIU, Economics and Management
ZHENG, DIANMO, Environmental Science and Engineering
ZHENG, WEIXIAN, Life Sciences
ZHENG, XIANGQING, Economics and Management
ZHENG, XIAOJIANG, Humanities and Social Sciences
ZHOU, GUOFA, Environmental Science and Engineering
ZHOU, PINGYUAN, Humanities and Social Sciences
ZHOU, SHU, Art and Design
ZHOU, TIANRUI, Mechanics and Engineering
ZHOU, WENBIN, Environmental Science and Engineering
ZHOU, YAOWANG, Humanities and Social Sciences
ZHU, CHUANXI, Natural Science

NANJING AGRICULTURAL UNIVERSITY

1 Weigang Rd, Nanjing 210095, Jiangsu Province
Telephone: (8625) 84395366
Internet: www.njau.edu.cn
Founded 1952
Min. of Education control
Academic year: September to July

Pres.: ZHENG XIAOBO
Vice-Pres.: CAO WEIXING
Vice-Pres.: QU FUTIAN
Vice-Pres.: SUN JIAN
Vice-Pres.: WANG YAONAN
Vice-Pres.: XU XIANG
Vice-Pres.: ZHOU GUANGHONG
Librarian: GAO RONGHUA

Number of teachers: 2,400
Number of students: 24,000

Publications: *Agricultural Education of China* (6 a year), *Agricultural History of China* (4 a year), *Animal Husbandry and Veterinary Science* (6 a year), *Chinese Animal Products and Food* (6 a year), *Journal* (natural sciences, 4 a year), *Journal* (social sciences, 4 a year)

DEANS

College of Adult Education: XU XIANG
College of Agronomy: WAN JIANMIN
College of Animal Science and Technology: WANG TIAN
College of Economics and Management: ZHONG FUNING
College of Engineering: DING WEIMIN
College of Food Science and Technology: LU ZHAOXIN
College of Foreign Studies: XU XIANG
College of Horticulture: XILIN HOU
College of Humanities and Social Sciences: WANG SIMING
College of Information Science and Technology: GAO RONGHUA
College of International Education: YAN ZHIMING
College of Life Sciences: XU LANGLAI
College of Plant Protection: HAN ZHAOJUN
College of Public Management (incorporating College of Land Management): (vacant)
College of Resources and Environmental Sciences: SHEN QIRONG
College of Science: YANG CHUNLONG
College of Veterinary Medicine: ZOU SIXIANG
Graduate School: ZHENG XIAOBO

PROFESSORS

BAO, ENDONG, Veterinary Medicine
BIAN, XINMIN, Agronomy
CAI, QINGSHENG, Agronomy
CAI, QINGSHENG, Life Sciences
CAO, WEIXING, Agronomy
CHEN, FUYAN, Veterinary Medicine
CHEN, JIE, Veterinary Medicine
CHEN, JINFENG, Horticulture
CHEN, MAO, Humanities and Social Sciences
CHEN, QIUSHENG, Veterinary Medicine
CHEN, WANMING, Economics and Management
CHEN, WEIHUA, Veterinary Medicine
CHEN, WENLIN, Humanities and Social Sciences
CHEN, XIAOMIN, Resources and Environmental Sciences
CHENG, CHUNYOU, Foreign Languages
CHU, BAOJIN, Economics and Management
DAI, HAOGUO, Plant Protection
DENG, ZHAOCHUN, Foreign Languages
DING, WEIMIN, Engineering
DONG, MINGSHENG, Food Science and Technology
DONG, SHUANGLIN, Plant Protection
GAI, JUNYI, Agronomy
GAO, GUANG, Land Science
GE, JIQI, Land Management

GONG, YIQIN, Horticulture
GU, HUANZHANG, Economics and Management
GU, ZHENXIN, Food Science and Technology
GUAN, HENGLU, Humanities and Social Sciences
GUO, JIANHUA, Plant Protection
GUO, QIAOSHENG, Horticulture
GUO, SHIRONG, Horticulture
GUO, WEIMING, Horticulture
HAN, ZHAOJUN, Plant Protection
HONG, XIAOYUE, Plant Protection
HOU, GUANGXU, Foreign Languages
HOU, HANQING, Information Science and Technology
HOU, JIAFA, Veterinary Medicine
HOU, XILIN, Horticulture
HU, FENG, Resources and Environmental Sciences
HU, JINBO, Humanities and Social Sciences
HU, QIUHUI, Food Science and Technology
HU, YUANLIANG, Veterinary Medicine
HUANG, KEHE, Veterinary Medicine
HUANG, SHUIQING, Information Science and Technology
HUANG, WEIYI, Resources and Environmental Sciences
HUANG, YAO, Resources and Environmental Sciences
HUI, FUPING, Humanities and Social Sciences
JI, CHANGYING, Engineering
JIANG, HANHU, Food Science and Technology
JIANG, MINGYI, Life Sciences
JIANG, PING, Veterinary Medicine
LAN, YEQING, Land Science
LEI, ZHIHAI, Veterinary Medicine
LI, BAOPING, Plant Protection
LI, SHUNPENG, Resources and Environmental Sciences
LI, XIANGRUI, Veterinary Medicine
LI, YANGHAN, Agronomy
LI, YUEYUN, Economics and Management
LIANG, YONGCHAO, Resources and Environmental Sciences
LIN, MAOSONG, Plant Protection
LIU, BAOJIN, Economics and Management
LIU, DAJUN, Agronomy
LIU, DEHUI, Resources and Environmental Sciences
LIU, HONGLIN, Animal Science and Technology
LIU, LEI, Information Science and Technology
LIU, YOULIANG, Agronomy
LIU, YOUZHAO, Land Management
LIU, ZHAOPU, Resources and Environmental Sciences
LU, CHENGPING, Veterinary Medicine
LU, DAXIN, Engineering
LU, ZHAOXIN, Food Science and Technology
LU, ZUOMEI, Agronomy
LUO, WEIHONG, Agronomy
MA, KAI, Horticulture
MENG, LING, Plant Protection
MENG, LINGJIE, Economics and Management
NIU, YOUQI, Information Science and Technology
OU, MINGHAO, Land Management
PAN, GENXIN, Resources and Environmental Sciences
PAN, JIANJUN, Resources and Environmental Sciences
PENG, JISHENG, Humanities and Social Sciences
PENG, ZENGQI, Food Science and Technology
QIANG, SHENG, Agronomy
QIANG, SHENG, Life Sciences
QIN, LIJUN, Foreign Languages
QU, FUTIAN, Land Management
SHEN, JINLIANG, Plant Protection
SHEN, QIRONG, Resources and Environmental Sciences
SHEN, YIXIN, Animal Science and Technology
SHEN, YONGLIN, Veterinary Medicine
SHEN, ZHENGUO, Agronomy
SHEN, ZHENGUO, Life Sciences
SHENG, BANGYUE, Humanities and Social Sciences
SUN, HANGSHENG, Economics and Management
SUN, JIN, Resources and Environmental Sciences
TANG, YIZU, Agronomy
TU, KANG, Food Science and Technology
WANG, GENLIN, Animal Science and Technology
WANG, GUOJIE, Veterinary Medicine
WANG, HUAIMING, Economics and Management
WANG, JIANMIN, Agronomy
WANG, JINSHENG, Plant Protection
WANG, KAI, Economics and Management
WANG, KERONG, Plant Protection
WANG, LINYUN, Animal Science and Technology
WANG, RONG, Economics and Management
WANG, SIMING, Humanities and Social Sciences
WANG, TIAN, Animal Science and Technology
WANG, WANMAO, Land Management
WANG, XIAOHUA, Engineering
WANG, XIAOLONG, Veterinary Medicine
WANG, YINQUAN, Foreign Languages
WANG, YUQUAN, Land Science
WHONG, ZHIWEI, Resources and Environmental Sciences
WU, QINSHENG, Horticulture
WU, YIDONG, Plant Protection
WU, YULIN, Economics and Management
XIE, ZHUANG, Animal Science and Technology
XU, JIANHUA, Plant Protection
XU, LIANGLAI, Life Sciences
XU, LIREN, Veterinary Medicine
XU, XIANG, Economics and Management
XU, YIWEN, Humanities and Social Sciences
YAN, HUOQI, Humanities and Social Sciences
YAN, PEISHI, Animal Science and Technology
YANG, HONG, Land Science
YANG, LIANFANG, Plant Protection
YANG, LIGUO, Animal Science and Technology
YANG, MINGMIN, Land Science
YANG, QIANG, Veterinary Medicine
YANG, QING, Life Sciences
YANG, SHIHU, Agronomy
YANG, ZHIMIN, Life Sciences
YE, YIGUANG, Economics and Management
YIN, WENQING, Engineering
YING, RUIYAO, Economics and Management
YU, DEYUE, Agronomy
ZHAI, BAOPING, Plant Protection
ZHANG, BING, Economics and Management
ZHANG, CHUNLAN, Resources and Environmental Sciences
ZHANG, FANG, Humanities and Social Sciences
ZHANG, GUOTAI, Agronomy
ZHANG, HAIBIN, Veterinary Medicine
ZHANG, HONGSHENG, Agronomy
ZHANG, JINGSHUN, Economics and Management
ZHANG, RONGXIAN, Agronomy
ZHANG, SHAOLING, Horticulture
ZHANG, SHUXIA, Veterinary Medicine
ZHANG, TIANZHEN, Agronomy
ZHANG, WEIQIANG, Engineering
ZHANG, ZHEN, Horticulture
ZHAO, RUQIAN, Veterinary Medicine
ZHENG, XIAOBO, Plant Protection
ZHENG, YONGHUA, Food Science and Technology
ZHONG, FUNING, Economics and Management
ZHOU, GUANGHONG, Food Science and Technology
ZHOU, LIXIANG, Resources and Environmental Sciences
ZHOU, MINGGUO, Plant Protection
ZHOU, SHUDONG, Economics and Management
ZHOU, YINGHENG, Economics and Management
ZHU, JUN, Life Sciences
ZHU, SIHONG, Engineering
ZHU, WEIYUN, Animal Science and Technology
ZHU, YUELIN, Horticulture
ZONG, LIANGGANG, Resources and Environmental Sciences
ZOU, SIXIANG, Veterinary Medicine

NANJING FORESTRY UNIVERSITY

159 Longpan Rd, Nanjing 210037, Jiangsu Province
Telephone: (25) 85427131
E-mail: interpro@njfu.edu.cn
Internet: www.njfu.edu.cn

Founded 1952
State control
Language of instruction: Chinese
Academic year: September to June

Pres.: Prof. CAO FULIANG
Vice-Pres.: Prof. LI PINGPING
Vice-Pres.: Prof. WANG HAO
Vice-Pres.: Prof. ZHAO MAOCHENG
Librarian: Prof. CHAO CHEN

Library of 1,500,000 vols
Number of teachers: 1,100
Number of students: 30,000 (incl. 4000 postgraduate)

Publications: *Bamboo Research*, *China Forestry Science and Technology*, *Forestry Energy Conservation*, *Interior Design and Construction*, *Journal of Nanjing Forestry University (Humanities)*, *Journal of Nanjing Forestry University (Social Sciences)*

DEANS

College of Automobile and Traffic Engineering: Prof. JIANGXIAO MA
College of Chemical Engineering: Prof. FEI WANG
College of Civil Engineering: Prof. PING YANG
College of Economics and Management: Prof. ZUOMING WEN
College of Forest Resources and Environment: Prof. JIANREN YE
College of Furniture and Industrial Design: Prof. ZHIHUI WU
College of Information Science and Technology: Prof. YUNFEI LIU
College of Landscape Architecture: Prof. LIANGGUI WANG
College of Light Industry Science and Engineering: Prof. HUI ZHANG
College of Mechanical and Electronic Engineering: Prof. HONGPING ZHOU
College of Wood Science and Technology: Prof. HANDONG ZHOU

PROFESSORS

CHEN GUOLIANG, Forest Economics
CHEN ZHI, Chemical Processing of Forest Products
HUA YUKUN, Wood Processing
LI ZHONGZHENG, Chemical Processing of Forest Products
SHEN GUANFU, Forest Mechanics
SU JINYUN, Forest Engineering
XIONG WENYUE, Forest Ecology
ZHU ZHENGDE, Forest Botany

NANJING INSTITUTE OF METEOROLOGY

114 Pancheng New St, Nanjing 210044, Jiangsu Province
Telephone: (25) 8731102
E-mail: nimemail@nim02.njim.edu.cn
Internet: www.njim.edu.cn

Founded 1960
State control
Languages of instruction: Chinese, English
Academic year: September to July

Pres.: SUN ZHAOBO
Vice-Pres.: LU WEISONG
Dean: ZHAO XUEYU

Chief Admin. Officer: Xu Kai
Librarian: Pang Xinguo

Library of 500,000 vols
Number of teachers: 450
Number of students: 8,000

Publications: *Journal* (4 a year), *Meteorological Education and Science and Technology* (4 a year)

NANJING MEDICAL UNIVERSITY

140 Hanzhong Rd, 210029 Nanjing
Telephone: (25) 6612696
E-mail: gjchen18@njmu.edu.cn
Internet: www.njmu.edu.cn

Founded 1934 as Jiangsu Provincial College of Health Policy and Management, current name adopted 1993

Schools of basic medical sciences, continuing education, foreign languages, health policy and management, int. education, nursing, pharmacy, public health, stomatology

Pres.: Chen Qi
Vice-Pres.: Hu Gang
Vice-Pres.: Zhang Zhu Fan
Vice-Pres.: Wang Hong
Vice-Pres.: Xiayou Bing
Vice-Pres.: Shen Hongbing
Librarian: Zhang Zhenghui

Library of 910,000 vols
Number of teachers: 1,570
Number of students: 13,000

Publications: *Journal of Biomedical Research* (6 a year), *Journal of Nanjing Medical University (Basic Sciences)* (12 a year), *Journal of Nanjing Medical University (Social Sciences)*

NANJING NORMAL UNIVERSITY

122 Ninghai Rd, 210097 Nanjing
Telephone: (25) 3720999
Internet: www.nnu.cn

Founded 1902
State control
Academic year: September to August

Pres.: Prof. Song Yongzhong
Vice-Pres.: Lingfu Chen
Vice-Pres.: Jian Wang
Vice-Pres.: Kangning Wu
Vice-Pres.: Jinwen Xia
Vice-Pres.: Baiqi Pan
Vice-Pres.: Guoxiang Chen

Library of 3,207,600 vols
Number of teachers: 1,740
Number of students: 32,426

Publications: *Fine Arts Education in China*, *Periodicals of Nanjing Normal University*, *References for Educational Research*

NANJING UNIVERSITY

22 Hankou Rd, Nanjing 210093, Jiangsu
Telephone: (25) 3593186
Internet: www.nju.edu.cn

Founded 1902
State control
Language of instruction: Chinese
Academic year: September to June

Pres.: Jiang Shusheng
Vice-Pres: Chen Jun
Vice-Pres: Hon Yinxing
Vice-Pres: Min Tiejun
Vice-Pres: Shin Jianjun
Vice-Pres: Zhang Daliang
Vice-Pres: Zhang Yibin
Librarian: Qian Chengdan

Number of teachers: 2,400
Number of students: 27,000

Publications: *Approximation Theory and its Application*, *Contemporary Foreign Literature*, *Geology in Higher Education*, *Journal* (humanities and social sciences), *Journal* (natural sciences), *Journal of Computer Science*, *Journal of Inorganic Chemistry*, *Mathematics in Higher Education*, *Mathematics Review* (2 a year), *Progress in Physics*, *Research in Higher Education*

DEANS

Adult Education School: Wang Jianqiang
Graduate School: Chen Chongqing
International Business School: Zhao Shuming
Medical School: Han Xiaodong
School of Chemistry and Chemical Engineering: Pam Yi
School of Foreign Studies: Wang Shouren
School of Geoscience: Wang Ying
School of Humanities: Dong Jian
School of Intensive Instruction in Sciences and Liberal Arts: Lu Dexin
School of Law: Shao Jiandong (acting)
School of Life Science: Zhang Hongzu
School of Natural Sciences: Gong Changde
School of Technology: Sun Zhongxiu

NANJING UNIVERSITY OF AERONAUTICS AND ASTRONAUTICS

29 Yudao Rd, Nanjing 210016, Jiangsu Province
Telephone: (25) 4892424
E-mail: office@nuaa.edu.cn
Internet: www.njmu.edu.cn

Founded 1952
Academic year: September to July

Pres.: Hu Haiyan
Vice-Pres.: Chen Xiachu
Vice-Pres.: Liang Dewang
Vice-Pres.: Nie Hong
Vice-Pres.: Wang Guinong
Vice-Pres.: Wang Yongliang
Vice-Pres.: Wu Qingxian
Vice-Pres.: Wu Yizhao
Head of Graduate Dept: Hu Haiyan
Librarian: Huang Yinhui

Number of teachers: 1,300
Number of students: 22,725

Publication: *Journal* (6 a year)

DEANS

College of Advanced Vocational Education: Jiang Wei
College of Aerospace Engineering: Xu Xiwu
College of Art: Liu Canming
College of Automation Engineering: Liu Jianye
College of Civil Aviation: Shen Yuankang
College of Economics and Management: Liu Sifeng
College of Energy and Power Engineering: Zhang Jingzhou
College of Humanities and Social Sciences: Wang Yan
College of Information Science and Technology: Ben De
College of Material Science and Engineering: Tao Jie
College of Mechanical Engineering: Zhu Di
College of Natural Sciences: Yan Xiaohong

PROFESSORS

Ai, Jun, Aerospace Engineering
An, Yukun, Natural Sciences
Ang, Haisong, Aerospace Engineering
Bao, Ming, Aerospace Engineering
Bao, Mingbao, Humanities and Social Sciences
Cai, Qiming, Economics and Management
Cao, Yunfeng, Automation Engineering
Chang, Haiping, Energy and Power Engineering
Che, Guangji, Art
Chen, Da, Material Science and Engineering
Chen, Daolian, Automation Engineering
Chen, Guoping, Aerospace Engineering
Chen, Hongquan, Aerospace Engineering
Chen, Huaihai, Aerospace Engineering
Chen, Qi, Economics and Management
Chen, Qian, Aerospace Engineering
Chen, Renliang, Aerospace Engineering
Chen, Songcan, Information Science and Technology
Chen, Wei, Energy and Power Engineering
Chen, Xin, Automation Engineering
Chen, Zhiliang, Aerospace Engineering
Dang, Yaoguo, Economics and Management
Deng, Zhiquan, Automation Engineering
Ding, Qiulin, Information Science and Technology
Ding, Yunliang, Aerospace Engineering
Du, Jida, Aerospace Engineering
Fan, Yinhe, Energy and Power Engineering
Fang, Xiande, Aerospace Engineering
Gan, Minliang, Civil Aviation
Gao, Deping, Energy and Power Engineering
Gao, Deping, Civil Aviation
Gao, Zheng, Aerospace Engineering
Ge, Ning, Energy and Power Engineering
Gong, Chunying, Automation Engineering
Gu, Hongbin, Civil Aviation
Gu, Zhiming, Natural Sciences
Gu, Zhongquan, Aerospace Engineering
Guan, De, Aerospace Engineering
Guo, Rongwei, Energy and Power Engineering
Guo, Wanlin, Aerospace Engineering
Han, Jinglong, Aerospace Engineering
He, Jiangsheng, Humanities and Social Sciences
He, Jianping, Material Science and Engineering
Hu, Haiyan, Aerospace Engineering
Hu, Jun, Energy and Power Engineering
Hu, Minghua, Civil Aviation
Hu, Mingmin, Aerospace Engineering
Huang, Hulin, Energy and Power Engineering
Huang, Jinquan, Energy and Power Engineering
Huang, Mingge, Aerospace Engineering
Huang, Shengguo, Civil Aviation
Huang, Shula, Art
Huang, Zaixing, Aerospace Engineering
Huang, Zhengxin, Humanities and Social Sciences
Ji, Honghu, Energy and Power Engineering
Jiang, Bin, Automation Engineering
Jiang, Keshen, Economics and Management
Li, Bangyi, Economics and Management
Li, Dong, Humanities and Social Sciences
Li, Nan, Economics and Management
Li, Pengtong, Natural Sciences
Li, Shunming, Energy and Power Engineering
Li, Ziquan, Material Science and Engineering
Li, Zongzhi, Humanities and Social Sciences
Lian, Qiangui, Humanities and Social Sciences
Liang, Dakai, Aerospace Engineering
Liang, Dewang, Energy and Power Engineering
Liu, Canming, Art
Liu, Renpei, Material Science and Engineering
Liu, Sifeng, Economics and Management
Liu, Weihua, Aerospace Engineering
Liu, Xianbin, Aerospace Engineering
Liu, Yiping, Economics and Management
Liu, Yu, Information Science and Technology
Lu, Lizhi, Humanities and Social Sciences
Ma, Jie, Humanities and Social Sciences
Meng, Fanchao, Humanities and Social Sciences
Miao, Jianjun, Humanities and Social Sciences
Ming, Xiao, Aerospace Engineering
Nie, Hong, Aerospace Engineering

NING, XUANXI, Economics and Management
PENG, CAN, Economics and Management
QIAN, XIAOLIN, Information Science and Technology
RUAN, XINBO, Automation Engineering
SHENG, SONGBO, Natural Sciences
SHI, YUNLONG, Humanities and Social Sciences
SONG, BAOYIN, Aerospace Engineering
SONG, YINGDONG, Energy and Power Engineering
SUN, JIANGUO, Energy and Power Engineering
SUN, JIUHOU, Aerospace Engineering
SUN, LIANGXIN, Aerospace Engineering
TAN, QINGMEI, Humanities and Social Sciences
TANG, DENGBIN, Aerospace Engineering
TAO, JIE, Material Science and Engineering
TONG, MINGBO, Aerospace Engineering
WANG, CAIYONG, Art
WANG, HUAMING, Aerospace Engineering
WANG, JIANDONG, Information Science and Technology
WANG, KAIFU, Aerospace Engineering
WANG, LUJIE, Humanities and Social Sciences
WANG, XINWEI, Aerospace Engineering
WANG, YAN, Humanities and Social Sciences
WANG, YONGLIANG, Aerospace Engineering
WEI, MINXIANG, Energy and Power Engineering
WEN, WEIDONG, Energy and Power Engineering
WU, DAIZHAO, Aerospace Engineering
WU, DINGMIN, Humanities and Social Sciences
WU, WENLONG, Aerospace Engineering
XIA, HONGSHAN, Civil Aviation
XIA, PINQI, Aerospace Engineering
XIAO, JUN, Material Science and Engineering
XIAO, PING, Humanities and Social Sciences
XIE, SHAOJUN, Automation Engineering
XING, YAN, Automation Engineering
XIONG, KE, Aerospace Engineering
XU, DAZHUAN, Information Science and Technology
XU, GUOHUA, Aerospace Engineering
XU, JINFA, Aerospace Engineering
XU, QIANG, Humanities and Social Sciences
XU, ZONGZE, Information Science and Technology
YANG, LILI, Art
YAO, WEIXING, Aerospace Engineering
YE, ZHIFENG, Energy and Power Engineering
YIN, HONGYOU, Natural Sciences
YU, XIONGQING, Aerospace Engineering
YU, XIWU, Aerospace Engineering
YUAN, SHENFANG, Aerospace Engineering
YUE, QIN, Natural Sciences
ZHANG, BUREN, Humanities and Social Sciences
ZHANG, CHENGLIN, Aerospace Engineering
ZHANG, GUODAI, Natural Sciences
ZHANG, JINGZHOU, Energy and Power Engineering
ZHANG, KUNYUAN, Energy and Power Engineering
ZHANG, LINGMI, Aerospace Engineering
ZHANG, LUMING, Natural Sciences
ZHANG, ZENGCHANG, Aerospace Engineering
ZHAO, CHUNSHENG, Aerospace Engineering
ZHAO, JIANXING, Energy and Power Engineering
ZHAO, MIN, Automation Engineering
ZHAO, NING, Aerospace Engineering
ZHAO, YOUQUN, Energy and Power Engineering
ZHENG, QI, Art
ZHENG, SHIJIE, Aerospace Engineering
ZHOU, CHUANRONG, Aerospace Engineering
ZHOU, DEQUN, Economics and Management
ZHOU, JIANJIANG, Information Science and Technology
ZHOU, LI, Aerospace Engineering
ZHU, JIANYING, Civil Aviation
ZHU, JINDONG, Humanities and Social Sciences
ZHU, JINFU, Civil Aviation
ZHU, WUJIA, Information Science and Technology
ZHU, ZHAODA, Information Science and Technology
ZUO, HONGFU, Civil Aviation

NANJING UNIVERSITY OF FINANCE AND ECONOMICS

3 Wenyuan Rd, Xianlin College Town, 210023 Nanjing
Telephone: (25) 84028504
Internet: www.njue.edu.cn

Founded 1956, present status 1981
State control
Academic year: September to July

Schools of accounting, business administration, economics, finance, international economics and business, public finance and taxation

Pres.: Dr XU CONGCAI
Vice-Pres.: WANG JIANMING
Vice-Pres.: WANG KAITIAN
Vice-Pres.: XU CHENGMING
Vice-Pres.: YUAN PING
Vice-Pres.: JIAO FUMIN
Librarian: CHENG YONGBO

Library of 2,030,000 vols
Number of teachers: 1,680
Number of students: 20,000

Publication: *Journal of Nanjing University of Economics*

NANJING UNIVERSITY OF POSTS AND TELECOMMUNICATIONS

66 Xin Mofan Ma Lu, 210003 Nanjing
Telephone: (25) 85866888
E-mail: nupt@njupt.edu.cn
Internet: www.njupt.edu.cn

Founded 1942
Academic year: September to July

Pres.: YANG ZHEN
Vice-Pres.: WANG CHENGKUAN
Vice-Pres.: LI JIANYU
Vice-Pres.: ZHU HONGBO
Vice-Pres.: WANG GUOPING
Vice-Pres.: WANG ZONGRONG
Vice-Pres.: JIANG GUOPING
Vice-Pres.: YAN XIAOHONG
Librarian: YANG ZHUYING

Library of 1,405,300 vols
Number of teachers: 1,622
Number of students: 16,771

Publications: *Journal of Social Science*, *NUPT Periodical*

PROFESSORS

BI HOUJIE, Image Communications
CAO WEI, Microwave Communications
CHEN TINGBIAO, Information Engineering
CHEN XI SHENG, Telecommunications Engineering
FENG GUANGZENG, Satellite Communications
HU JIANZHANG, Information Engineering
JU TI, Computer Engineering Science
KAN JIAHAI, Mathematics
LI BIAOQING, Telecommunications Engineering
LUO CHANGLONG, Computer Science
MEI ZHUOCHUN, Communication and Electronic Systems
MI ZHENGKUN, Communications Engineering
QI YUSHENG, Mobile Communication
QIN TINGKAI, Electrical Engineering
SHEN JINLONG, Computer Communication
SHEN YUANLONG, Electrical Engineering
SUN JINLUN, Communications Engineering
TANG JIAYI, Computer Science
WANG SHAOLI, Computer Communication
WANG SHUOPING, Electrical Engineering
WU XINYU, Electrical Engineering
WU ZHIZHONG, Electrical Engineering
XU CHENGQI, Telecommunications Engineering
YANG ZHUYING, Electrical Engineering
YIE ZHANGZHAO, Mathematics
YU ZHAOMIN, Information Engineering
ZHANG LIJUN, Telecommunications Engineering
ZHANG SHUNYI, Computer Communications
ZHANG XIAOQIANG, Communication Systems
ZHANG ZHIYONG, Electrical Engineering
ZHANG ZONGCHENG, Information Engineering
ZHENG BAOYU, Telecommunications Engineering
ZHU XIUCHANG, Information Engineering

NANJING UNIVERSITY OF SCIENCE AND TECHNOLOGY

200 Xiao Lingwei, Nanjing 210094, Jiangsu Province
Telephone: (25) 84315567
Internet: www.njust.edu.cn

Founded 1953
Min. of Industry and Information Technology control
Academic year: September to July

Chair.and Univ. Council: GENFU CHEN
Pres.: XIAOFENG WANG
Vice-Pres.: DAQING MA
Vice-Pres.: GANG LIU
Vice-Pres.: SHANZHI YANG
Vice-Pres.: WENYU SONG
Vice-Pres.: XIN WANG
Vice-Pres.: YIMIN XUAN
Vice-Pres.: YINKANG XIANG
Head of Graduate Dept: XIN WANG
Librarian: MIN ZHAO

Number of teachers: 1,466
Number of students: 20,283

Publications: *Higher Education Digest* (12 a year), *Journal* (natural sciences, 6 a year), *Journal* (social sciences, 6 a year), *Journal of Ballistics* (4 a year), *Journal of Explosive Materials* (6 a year), *Journal of Optoelectronic Information* (6 a year)

DEANS

Department of Foreign Languages: QUAN ZHANG
Department of Materials Science and Engineering: JINCHUN MEI
School of Adult Education: YUNLEI ZHANG
School of Automation: YUMING BO
School of Chemical Engineering: LIANJUN WANG
School of Computer Science: ZHENMIN TANG
School of Economics and Management: GUANGPING HUI
School of Electronic Engineering and Optoelectronic Technology: QIAN CHEN
School of Humanities and Social Sciences: JIANPING QIAN
School of International Education: WANG QINYOU
School of Joint Education: YUZHEN KE
School of Mechanical Engineering: YONG HE
School of Natural Science: XIAOPING YANG
School of Power Engineering: HAO WANG
Vocational and Technical College: ZHANG YUEXIN

PROFESSORS

AN, LICHAO, Chemical Engineering
BO, LIANFA, Electronic Engineering and Optoelectronic Technology
BO, YUMING, Automation Engineering
CAI, CHUN, Chemical Engineering
CAO, CONGYONG, Mechanical Engineering
CHANG, BENKANG, Electronic Engineering and Optoelectronic Technology

CHEN, GUANG, Materials Science and Engineering
CHEN, GUOLIANG, Materials Science and Engineering
CHEN, HEJUAN, Mechanical Engineering
CHEN, LEI, Electronic Engineering and Optoelectronic Technology
CHEN, QIAN, Electronic Engineering and Optoelectronic Technology
CHEN, QINGWEI, Automation Engineering
CHEN, RUSHAN, Electronic Engineering and Optoelectronic Technology
CHEN, YANRU, Electronic Engineering and Optoelectronic Technology
CHENG, YI, Chemical Engineering
CUI, CHONG, Materials Science and Engineering
DAI, YUEWEI, Automation Engineering
DENG, KAIMING, Natural Science
DU, YULAN, Economics and Management
DUAN, QIJUN, Mechanical Engineering
FAN, BAOCHUN, Power Engineering
FAN, XINMIN, Materials Science and Engineering
FANG, DAGANG, Electronic Engineering and Optoelectronic Technology
FANG, ZHIJIE, Chemical Engineering
FANG, ZILIANG, Mechanical Engineering
FENG, JUNWEN, Economics and Management
GAN, LIREN, Economics and Management
GEN, JIHUI, Power Engineering
GONG, GUANGRONG, Mechanical Engineering
GU, KEQIU, Mechanical Engineering
GU, XIAOHUI, Mechanical Engineering
GUO, ZHI, Automation Engineering
HAN, YUQI, Economics and Management
HAN, ZHIJUN, Economics and Management
HAN, ZIPENG, Power Engineering
HAO, JIANCHU, Chemical Engineering
HE, ANZHI, Natural Science
HE, QIHUAN, Chemical Engineering
HE, YONG, Mechanical Engineering
HE, ZHAOJI, Humanities and Social Sciences
HOU, XIAOXIA, Automation Engineering
HOU, YUANLONG, Mechanical Engineering
HU, KAIJIE, Humanities and Social Sciences
HU, WEILI, Automation Engineering
HUANG, JIN-AN, Automation Engineering
HUANG, YINSHENG, Chemical Engineering
HUANG, ZHENGYA, Chemical Engineering
HUI, JUNMING, Chemical Engineering
HUI, XIAOHUA, Electronic Engineering and Optoelectronic Technology
JIANG, JIANFANG, Automation Engineering
JIANG, LIPING, Electronic Engineering and Optoelectronic Technology
JIANG, RENYUAN, Mechanical Engineering
JIN, ZHONG, Computer Science
KANG, XIAODONG, Economics and Management
LAN, SHAOHUA, Computer Science
LI, BAOMING, Power Engineering
LI, CHENGJUN, Chemical Engineering
LI, DONGBO, Mechanical Engineering
LI, FENGSHENG, Chemical Engineering
LI, HONGCHANG, Chemical Engineering
LI, HUIZHONG, Materials Science and Engineering
LI, XIANGYIN, Natural Science
LI, XIAONING, Mechanical Engineering
LI, XINGGUO, Electronic Engineering and Optoelectronic Technology
LI, YAJUN, Mechanical Engineering
LI, YING, Mechanical Engineering
LI, ZHENHUA, Natural Science
LIANG, RENJIE, Mechanical Engineering
LIU, DABIN, Chemical Engineering
LIU, FENGYU, Computer Science
LIU, HONGYING, Chemical Engineering
LIU, JIACONG, Chemical Engineering
LIU, KUI, Humanities and Social Sciences
LIU, ZHONG, Electronic Engineering and Optoelectronic Technology
LIU, ZULIANG, Chemical Engineering
LOU, LANGHONG, Materials Science and Engineering
LU, CHUNXU, Chemical Engineering
LU, JIAN, Natural Science
LU, JINHUI, Electronic Engineering and Optoelectronic Technology
LU, LUDE, Chemical Engineering
LU, MING, Chemical Engineering
LUO, GUOWEI, Electronic Engineering and Optoelectronic Technology
MA, DAWEI, Mechanical Engineering
MA, YIZHONG, Economics and Management
MENG, YINGJUN, Electronic Engineering and Optoelectronic Technology
MOU, SHANXIANG, Electronic Engineering and Optoelectronic Technology
NI, OUQI, Chemical Engineering
NI, XIAOWU, Natural Science
PAN, GONGPEI, Chemical Engineering
PAN, RENMING, Chemical Engineering
PAN, ZHENGWEI, Mechanical Engineering
PENG, JINHUA, Chemical Engineering
PENG, XINHUA, Chemical Engineering
PU, XIONGZHU, Mechanical Engineering
QIAN, JIANPING, Automation Engineering
QIAN, LINFANG, Mechanical Engineering
SHEN, PEIHUI, Mechanical Engineering
SHEN, RUIQI, Chemical Engineering
SHENG, ANDONG, Automation Engineering
SHI, LIANJIE, Materials Science and Engineering
SHI, TIANHUA, Economics and Management
SHI, XIANGQUAN, Electronic Engineering and Optoelectronic Technology
SONG, YAOLIANG, Electronic Engineering and Optoelectronic Technology
SUN, GUIXIANG, Humanities and Social Sciences
SUN, HUAIJIANG, Computer Science
SUN, JIANPING, Economics and Management
SUN, JINSHENG, Automation Engineering
SUN, JINTAO, Electronic Engineering and Optoelectronic Technology
SUN, YAMIN, Computer Science
SUN, YU, Mechanical Engineering
TAN, LEBIN, Mechanical Engineering
TANG, ZHENMIN, Computer Science
TAO, CHUNKAN, Electronic Engineering and Optoelectronic Technology
WANG, DAYONG, Humanities and Social Sciences
WANG, FENGYUN, Chemical Engineering
WANG, HUAKUN, Mechanical Engineering
WANG, JIANXIN, Electronic Engineering and Optoelectronic Technology
WANG, JIANYU, Automation Engineering
WANG, JINGTAO, Materials Science and Engineering
WANG, JUNDE, Chemical Engineering
WANG, KEHONG, Materials Science and Engineering
WANG, LIANGGUO, Natural Science
WANG, LIANGMING, Power Engineering
WANG, LIANGMO, Mechanical Engineering
WANG, LIANJUN, Chemical Engineering
WANG, NAIYAN, Chemical Engineering
WANG, SHUMEI, Computer Science
WANG, XIAOMING, Mechanical Engineering
WANG, XIN, Chemical Engineering
WANG, YUSHI, Mechanical Engineering
WANG, ZESHAN, Chemical Engineering
WANG, ZHIQUAN, Automation Engineering
WEI, YUNYANG, Chemical Engineering
WEI, ZHIHUI, Natural Science
WEN, CHUNSHENG, Power Engineering
WU, HUIZHONG, Computer Science
WU, JIANG, Materials Science and Engineering
WU, JUNJI, Power Engineering
WU, XIAOBEI, Automation Engineering
XIA, DESHEN, Computer Science
XIAO, HEMING, Chemical Engineering
XIONG, DANGSHENG, Materials Science and Engineering
XU, FUMING, Chemical Engineering
XU, HOUQIAN, Power Engineering
XU, JIANCHENG, Mechanical Engineering
XU, JIANZHONG, Electronic Engineering and Optoelectronic Technology
XU, MING, Chemical Engineering
XU, MINGYOU, Power Engineering
XU, SHENGYUAN, Automation Engineering
XU, WANHE, Mechanical Engineering
XU, ZHENXIANG, Chemical Engineering
XU, ZHILIANG, Automation Engineering
XUAN, YIMIN, Power Engineering
XUE, HENGXIN, Economics and Management
XUE, XIAOZHONG, Power Engineering
YAN, LIANHE, Chemical Engineering
YANG, CHENGWU, Power Engineering
YANG, DETONG, Materials Science and Engineering
YANG, SHUIYANG, Humanities and Social Sciences
YANG, SHULIN, Chemical Engineering
YANG, XIAOPING, Natural Science
YANG, XUJIE, Chemical Engineering
YANG, ZHENYU, Computer Science
YAO, JUN, Humanities and Social Sciences
YE, YOUPEI, Computer Science
YIN, XIAOCHUN, Natural Science
YIN, ZHENGZHOU, Mechanical Engineering
YU, ANPING, Economics and Management
YU, YONGGANG, Power Engineering
YUAN, JUNTANG, Mechanical Engineering
YUAN, YAXIONG, Power Engineering
ZHANG, BAOMIN, Electronic Engineering and Optoelectronic Technology
ZHANG, CHI, Chemical Engineering
ZHANG, FENG, Power Engineering
ZHANG, FUXIANG, Mechanical Engineering
ZHANG, GONGXUAN, Computer Science
ZHANG, HONG, Computer Science
ZHANG, MINGYAN, Economics and Management
ZHANG, SHAOFAN, Power Engineering
ZHANG, TIE, Mechanical Engineering
ZHANG, XI, Mechanical Engineering
ZHANG, XIAOBING, Power Engineering
ZHANG, YOULIANG, Mechanical Engineering
ZHANG, YUE, Mechanical Engineering
ZHANG, YUEJUN, Chemical Engineering
ZHANG, ZHONGLIN, Economics and Management
ZHANG, ZHONGXIONG, Electronic Engineering and Optoelectronic Technology
ZHAO, BAOCHANG, Chemical Engineering
ZHAO, CHUNXIA, Computer Science
ZHAO, HUICHANG, Electronic Engineering and Optoelectronic Technology
ZHENG, JIANGUO, Mechanical Engineering
ZHONG, QIN, Chemical Engineering
ZHOU, BOSEN, Materials Science and Engineering
ZHOU, KEDONG, Mechanical Engineering
ZHOU, SHUGE, Electronic Engineering and Optoelectronic Technology
ZHOU, WEILIANG, Chemical Engineering
ZHOU, XIANZHONG, Automation Engineering
ZHU, JINAN, Mechanical Engineering
ZHU, RIHONG, Electronic Engineering and Optoelectronic Technology
ZHU, XIANCHEN, Economics and Management
ZHU, XIAOHUA, Electronic Engineering and Optoelectronic Technology
ZOU, YUN, Automation Engineering

NANJING UNIVERSITY OF TECHNOLOGY

Gu Lou Section, 5 New Model Rd, Nanjing 210009, Jiangsu Province
Telephone: (25) 83587018
E-mail: xiaoban@njut.edu.cn
Internet: www.njut.edu.cn
Founded 1902
Dept of Education of Jiangsu Province control
Academic year: September to July
Pres.: OUYANG PINGKAI
Vice-Pres.: SHU FANG
Vice-Pres.: SUN CHUANSONG

Vice-Pres.: SUN WEIMIN SUN
Vice-Pres.: WANG JINMING
Vice-Pres.: XU NANPING
Vice-Pres.: ZAI JINMIN
Vice-Pres.: ZHU YAO
Head of Graduate Dept: HAN PINGFANG
Librarian: ZHANG ZHENGHUI

Number of teachers: 1,000
Number of students: 23,000

Publications: *Journal* (natural sciences, 6 a year), *Journal* (social sciences, 4 a year)

DEANS

College of Architecture and Urban Planning: WU JILIANG
College of Artistic Design: LIU WEIQING
College of Automation: LIN JINGUO
College of Chemistry and Chemical Engineering: XU NANPING
College of Civil Engineering: CHEN GUOXING
College of Economics and Management: HE HONGJIN
College of Foreign Languages and International Exchange: YIN FULIN
College of Information Science and Engineering: YANG XIAOJIAN
College of Law and Politics: LI BIN
College of Life Sciences and Pharmaceutical Engineering: ZHOU HUA
College of Management Science and Engineering: NIE QIBO
College of Materials Science and Engineering: XU ZHONGZI
College of Mechanical and Power Engineering: TU SHANDONG
College of Sciences: YU BIN
College of Urban Construction, Safety and Environmental Engineering: JIANG JUNCHENG

PROFESSORS

CAI, RUIYING, Information Science and Engineering
CAI, ZHIFU, Mechanical and Power Engineering
CEI, CHENGJIAN, Information Science and Engineering
CHEN, BIAO, Mechanical and Power Engineering
CHEN, CHANGLIN, Chemistry and Chemical Engineering
CHEN, GUOXING, Civil Engineering
CHEN, HONGLING, Chemistry and Chemical Engineering
CHEN, SU, Chemistry and Chemical Engineering
CHEN, XIANYI, Materials Science and Engineering
CUI, KEQING, Mechanical and Power Engineering
CUI, QUN, Chemistry and Chemical Engineering
DAI, SHUHE, Mechanical and Power Engineering
DENG, MIN, Materials Science and Engineering
FAN, YIQUAN, Chemistry and Chemical Engineering
GONG, JIANMING, Mechanical and Power Engineering
GONG, YANFENG, Urban Construction, Safety and Environmental Engineering
GU, BOQIN, Mechanical and Power Engineering
GU, HEPING, Chemistry and Chemical Engineering
GUAN, GUOFENG, Chemistry and Chemical Engineering
GUO, LUCUN, Materials Science and Engineering
HE, HONGJIN, Economics and Management
HE, JIAPENG, Urban Construction, Safety and Environmental Engineering
HUANG, PEI, Chemistry and Chemical Engineering
HUANG, YOUDIAO, Mechanical and Power Engineering
HUANG, ZHENREN, Mechanical and Power Engineering
JIAN, MIAOFU, Materials Science and Engineering
JIANG, JUNCHENG, Urban Construction, Safety and Environmental Engineering
JIANG, JUNCHENG, Mechanical and Power Engineering
JIN, SUMIN, Mechanical and Power Engineering
JIN, WANQIN, Chemistry and Chemical Engineering
LI, BIN, Law and Politics
LI, DONGXU, Materials Science and Engineering
LI, LIQUAN, Materials Science and Engineering
LI, XIANGYING, Foreign Languages and International Exchange
LI, YONGSHENG, Mechanical and Power Engineering
LIN, JINGUO, Automation
LIN, XIAO, Chemistry and Chemical Engineering
LING, XIANG, Mechanical and Power Engineering
LIU, WEIQING, Artistic Design
LIU, XIAOQIN, Chemistry and Chemical Engineering
LIU, ZHONGWEN, Chemistry and Chemical Engineering
LU, JINGUI, Information Science and Engineering
LU, LEI, Materials Science and Engineering
LU, WEILIAN, Automation
LU, XIAOHUA, Chemistry and Chemical Engineering
LU, XIAOPING, Chemistry and Chemical Engineering
LU, YINONG, Materials Science and Engineering
MA, GONGXUN, Mechanical and Power Engineering
MA, ZHENGFEI, Chemistry and Chemical Engineering
PAN, YU, Management Science and Engineering
PAN, ZHIHUA, Materials Science and Engineering
QIAO, XU, Chemistry and Chemical Engineering
QIU, TAI, Materials Science and Engineering
SHEN, LINJIANG, Sciences
SHEN, SHIMING, Mechanical and Power Engineering
SHEN, XIAODONG, Materials Science and Engineering
SHI, JUN, Chemistry and Chemical Engineering
SHI, MEIREN, Chemistry and Chemical Engineering
SUN, WEIMIN, Civil Engineering
TANG, MINGSHU, Materials Science and Engineering
TU, SHANDONG, Mechanical and Power Engineering
WANG, HUI, Information Science and Engineering
WANG, JUN, Chemistry and Chemical Engineering
WANG, TINGWEI, Materials Science and Engineering
WANG, YANRU, Chemistry and Chemical Engineering
WANG, YONGPING, Architecture and Urban Planning
WANG, ZHUOJUN, Law and Politics
WEI, PING, Life Sciences and Pharmaceutical Engineering
WEI, WUJI, Materials Science and Engineering
WU, CHENGZHEN, Materials Science and Engineering
WU, JILIANG, Architecture and Urban Planning
XIAO, WANRU, Sciences
XU, NANPING, Chemistry and Chemical Engineering
XU, YANHUA, Urban Construction, Safety and Environmental Engineering
XU, ZHONGZI, Materials Science and Engineering
YAN, SHENG, Materials Science and Engineering
YANG, XIANNING, Chemistry and Chemical Engineering
YANG, XIAOJIAN, Information Science and Engineering
YAO, CHENG, Sciences
YAO, HUQING, Chemistry and Chemical Engineering
YAO, XIAO, Materials Science and Engineering
YEI, XUCHU, Materials Science and Engineering
YIN, CHENBO, Mechanical and Power Engineering
YIN, FULIN, Foreign Languages and International Exchange
YIN, XIA, Mechanical and Power Engineering
YU, BIN, Sciences
YUN, ZHI, Chemistry and Chemical Engineering
ZENG, CHONGYU, Chemistry and Chemical Engineering
ZENG, YANWEI, Materials Science and Engineering
ZHANG, GANDAO, Life Sciences and Pharmaceutical Engineering
ZHANG, HONG, Mechanical and Power Engineering
ZHANG, JUN, Materials Science and Engineering
ZHANG, LIJING, Urban Construction, Safety and Environmental Engineering
ZHANG, LIXIONG, Chemistry and Chemical Engineering
ZHANG, QITU, Materials Science and Engineering
ZHANG, SHAOMING, Materials Science and Engineering
ZHANG, WEI, Materials Science and Engineering
ZHANG, YAMING, Chemistry and Chemical Engineering
ZHAO, HESHENG, Architecture and Urban Planning
ZHAO, SHILIN, Materials Science and Engineering
ZHAO, YINGKAN, Automation
ZHENG, FENGQIN, Mechanical and Power Engineering
ZHOU, CHANGYU, Mechanical and Power Engineering
ZHOU, HUA, Life Sciences and Pharmaceutical Engineering
ZHU, DUNRU, Chemistry and Chemical Engineering
ZHU, HONG, Materials Science and Engineering
ZHU, XURONG, Chemistry and Chemical Engineering
ZHUANG, JUN, Mechanical and Power Engineering

NANJING UNIVERSITY OF TRADITIONAL CHINESE MEDICINE

282 Hanzhong Rd, Nanjing 210029, Jiangsu Province
Telephone: (25) 86798005
Internet: www.njutcm.edu.cn

Founded 1954
Academic year: September to July

Pres.: XIANG PING
Vice-Pres.: CHEN DIPING
Vice-Pres.: LIU SHENLIN
Vice-Pres.: WU MIANHUA

Librarian: JI WENHUI

Library of 4,320,000 vols
Number of teachers: 1,308
Number of students: 6,000

Publication: *Journal* (6 a year)

DEANS

College of Basic Medicine: ZHANG MINGQIN
College of Pharmacy: DING ANWEI
First Clinical Medical College: (vacant)
School of Commercial Management and Trade: (vacant)
School of Foreign Languages: (vacant)
Second Clinical Medical College: LI ZHONGREN

PROFESSORS

BIAN, HUIMIN, Pharmacy
CAI, BAOCHANG, Pharmacy
CHEN, JIANWEI, Pharmacy
DING, ANWEI, Pharmacy
DING, SHUHUA, Clinical Medicine
FANG, TAIHUI, Pharmacy
GUO, LIWEI, Pharmacy
HUANG, YAOZHOU, Pharmacy
LI, XIANG, Pharmacy
LIU, HANQING, Pharmacy
PENG, GUOPING, Pharmacy
QIN, MINGZHU, Pharmacy
WANG, SHOUCHUAN, Clinical Medicine
WU, DEKANG, Pharmacy
WU, HAO, Pharmacy
YAN, DAONAN, Clinical Medicine
YU, XIAOWEI, Clinical Medicine
ZHOU, FUYI, Clinical Medicine
ZHU, QUAN, Pharmacy

ATTACHED RESEARCH INSTITUTES

Botanical Refinement Engineering Research Centre: Dir GUO LIWEI.

Jiangsu Province Research and Development Centre for Marine Pharmaceuticals: Dir WU HAO

NANKAI UNIVERSITY

94 Weijin Rd, Tianjin 300071
Telephone: (22) 23508208
E-mail: xb@office.nankai.edu.cn
Internet: www.nankai.edu.cn

Founded 1919

Academic year: September to July

Pres.: Prof. HOU ZIXIN
Vice-Pres: CHEN HONG
Vice-Pres: CHEN XUEQI
Vice-Pres: CHEN YONGCHUAN
Vice-Pres: GENG YUNQI
Vice-Pres: PANG JINJU
Vice-Pres: ZHANG JING
Librarian: Prof. YAN SHIPING

Library of 2,900,000 vols
Number of teachers: 1,465
Number of students: 23,000

Publications: *Journal* (4 a year), *Nankai Economics Studies* (6 a year), *Nankai Journal* (6 a year), *Nankai Management Review* (6 a year)

DEANS

College of Adult Education: Prof. JING HONGGANG
College of Chemistry: Prof. GUAN NAIJIA
College of Chinese Language and Culture: Prof. SHI FENG
College of Economics: Prof. ZHOU LIQUN
College of Economics and Societal Development: Prof. HOU ZIXIN
College of Environmental Science and Engineering: Prof. ZHU TAN
College of Foreign Languages and Literature: Prof. WANG JIANYI
College of History: Prof. LI ZHIAN
College of Ideological and Cultural Education: Prof. LI YI
College of Information Science and Technology: Prof. WU GONGYI
College of International Business: Prof. LI WEIAN
College of Law and Political Science: Prof. ZHU GUANGLEI
College of Life Sciences: Prof. GENG YUNQI
College of Literature: Prof. CHEN HONG
College of Mathematics: Prof. LONG YIMING
College of Medicine: Prof. ZHU TIANHUI
College of Modern Distance Education: Prof. LEI ZONGBAO
College of Occupational Technology: Prof. SU LICHUN
College of Physics: Prof. XU JINGJUN
Software College: Prof. HUANG YALOU
Teda College: Prof. XIAN GUOMING

PROFESSORS

College of Chemistry (tel. (22) 23508470; e-mail hxx@office.nankai.edu.cn):

Department of Chemistry:

BU XIANHE, Inorganic Chemistry
CAI ZUNSHENG, Physical Chemistry
CAO YURONG, Organic Chemistry
CHENG JINPEI, Inorganic Chemistry
CHENG PENG, Inorganic Chemistry
DENG GUOCAI, Inorganic Chemistry
GUAN NAIJIA, Physical Chemistry
HE JIAQI, Inorganic Chemistry
HE XIWEN, Analytical Chemistry
HU QINGMEI, Organic Chemistry
HUANG JIAXIAN, Polymer Chemistry
HUANG WEIPING, Inorganic Chemistry
HUANG ZHIRONG, Analytical Chemistry
JIANG ZONGHUI, Inorganic Chemistry
LI FANGXING, Polymer Chemistry
LIAO DAIZHENG, Inorganic Chemistry
LIN HUAKUAN, Physical Chemistry
LIU YU, Physical Chemistry
MENG JIBEN, Organic Chemistry
SHEN HANXI, Inorganic Chemistry
SHEN PANWEN, Analytical Chemistry
SONG LICHENG, Organic Chemistry
WANG BAIQUAN, Organic Chemistry
WANG XINSHENG, Organic Chemistry
WANG YONGMEI, Organic Chemistry
WU SHIHUA, Inorganic Chemistry
XU SHANSHENG, Organic Chemistry
YAN SHIPING, Inorganic Chemistry
YAN XIUPING, Analytical Chemistry
YANG GUANGMING, Inorganic Chemistry
YANG XIULIN, Physical Chemistry
YIN LIHUA, Inorganic Chemistry
YOU YINGCAI, Polymer Chemistry
YUAN MANXUE, Physical Chemistry
ZHANG BAOLONG, Organic Chemistry
ZHANG BAOSHEN, Polymer Chemistry
ZHANG GUIZHU, Analytical Chemistry
ZHANG ZHIHUI, Physical Chemistry
ZHAO HONGXI, Physical Chemistry
ZHAO ZUEZHANG, Physical Chemistry
ZHU CHANGYING, Polymer Chemistry
ZHU SHOURONG, Physical Chemistry
ZHU XIAOQING, Organic Chemistry
ZHU ZHIANG, Physical Chemistry
ZUO JU, Polymer Chemistry
ZUO YUMIN, Organic Chemistry

Department of Materials Chemistry:

CHE YUNXIA, Inorganic Chemistry
CHEN JUN, Materials Chemistry
CHEN TIEHONG, Physical Chemistry
GAO XUEPING, Materials Chemistry
LIU SHUANGXI, Physical Chemistry
SONG DEYING, Materials Chemistry
SUN BO, Inorganic Chemistry
TAO KEYI, Physical Chemistry
XIANG SHOUHE, Physical Chemistry
YAN JIE, Materials Chemistry
YUAN HUATUNG, Materials Chemistry
ZHENG WENJUN, Physical Chemistry

College of Chinese Language and Culture (tel. (22) 23501687; e-mail hy@office.nankai.edu.cn):

CUI JIANXIN, Modern Chinese
GUO JIMAO, Modern Chinese
SHI FENG, Chinese Linguistics
SHI XIANGDONG, Ancient Chinese

College of Economics (tel. (22) 23508981; e-mail jjxy@office.nankai.edu.cn):

Department of Economics:

HE ZILI, Comparative Economics
JIA GENLIANG, Development Economics
JING WEIMIN, Transitional Economics
LIU CHUNBIN, Agro-economics
LIU JUNMIN, Macroeconomics and Virtual Economics
WANG SHUYING, Industrial Economics
WEN HAICHI, Labour Economics
ZHANG RENDE, Comparative Economics
ZHANG SHIQING, Macroeconomics and Microeconomics
ZHANG TONGYU (acting), Political Economy
ZHAO JIN, History of Economics
ZHU GUANGHUA, Political Economy

Department of Finance:

LI ZHIHUI, International Finance
LIU YUCAO, International Finance
MA JUNLU, International Finance

Department of International Economics and Trade:

GAO LEYONG, International Economic Theories, International Investment
LI KUNWANG, Theory and Policy of International Trade
LIU ZHONGLI, International Trade Management
TONG JIADONG, International Trade, Economics of International Integration
XUE JINGXIAO, International Economics, Japanese Economy
YANG CANYING, Open Economy
ZHANG ZHICHAO, Public Finance, Economics of Development

Department of Risk Management and Insurance:

JIANG SHENGZHONG, Research, Insurance Management
LIU MAOSHAN, Research, Insurance Economics
XIAO YUNRU, Research, Actuarial Mathematics

College of Environmental Science and Engineering (tel. (22) 23508807; e-mail hjxy@office.nankai.edu.cn):

Department of Environmental Engineering and Management:

BAI ZHIPENG, Air Pollution Chemistry, Environmental Risk Assessment
LIU MAO, Environmental Safety Assessment
WAN QISHAN, Water Pollution Control
ZHU TAN, Environmental Planning and Management
ZHUANG YUANYI, Environmental Engineering

Department of Environmental Science:

CHEN FUHUA, Environmental Chemistry
DAI SHUGUI, Environmental Chemistry
FU XUEQI, Environmental Chemistry
HU GUOCHEN, Environmental Biology
HUANG GUOLAN, Environmental Chemistry
JIN ZHAOHUI, Environmental Chemistry
SUN HONGWEN, Environmental Chemistry, Environmental Pollution Control
ZHANG BAOGUI, Environmental Chemistry, Analytic Chemistry
ZHU LIN, Environmental Biology

College of Foreign Languages and Literature (tel. (22) 23509292; e-mail wyxy@office.nankai.edu.cn):

Department of English Language and Literature:

CHANG YAOXIN, English Literature
CUI YONGLU, English Translation
GU QI'NAN, English Literature
JIANG HUASHANG, English Literature
LIU SHICONG, English Translation
SU LICHANG, English Linguistics
MA QIUWU, English Linguistics
WANG HONGYIN, English Translation
WANG WENHAN, English Literature
WEI RONGCHENG, English Literature
YAN QIGANG, English Literature
ZHANG MAIZENG, English Linguistics

Department of General Literature:

LI JINGYU, English Language
SUO JUNMEI, English Language
WANG SHIBIN, English Language
XUE CHEN, English Language
ZHANG JUNZHI, English Language
ZHANG WENQI, English Language
ZHOU SHUJIE, English Language

Department of Japanese Language and Literature:

LIU GUIMIN, Japanese Literature and Linguistics
WANG JIANYI, Japanese Literature and Linguistics

Department of Western Languages and Literature:

CHEN XI, Comparative Linguistics
YAN GUODONG, Sino-Russian Cultural Relations, Comparative Culture
ZHANG ZHITING, French Literature

College of History (tel. (22) 23508422; e-mail lizhian@nankai.edu.cn):

Department of History:

CHANG JIANHUA, Ancient Chinese History
CHEN ZHENJIANG, Modern and Contemporary Chinese History
CHEN ZHIQIANG, Ancient and Medieval World History
FENG ERKANG, Ancient Chinese History
HA QUAN'AN, Ancient and Medieval World History
HOU JIE, Modern and Contemporary Chinese History
JIANG PEI, Modern and Contemporary Chinese History
JIANG SHENGLI, Historiography
LI ZHI'AN, Ancient Chinese History
LI XISUO, Modern and Contemporary Chinese History
LIN HEKUN, Modern and Contemporary World History
LIU MIN, Ancient Chinese History
LIU ZEHUA, Ancient Chinese History
MA SHILI, Modern and Contemporary World History
SUN LIQUN, Ancient Chinese History
WANG DUNSHU, Ancient and Medieval World History
WANG XIANMING, Modern and Contemporary Chinese History
XU TAN, Ancient Chinese History
ZHANG FENTIAN, Ancient Chinese History
ZHANG GUOGANG, Ancient Chinese History

Department of Philosophy:

CHANG JIAN, Western Philosophy
CHEN YANQING, Marxist Philosophy
CUI QINGTIAN, Logical Philosophy
HAN QIANG, Chinese Philosophy
LI NA, Logical Philosophy
LI JIANSHANG, Scientific and Technological Philosophy
LI XIANGHAI, Chinese Philosophy
LIU WENYING, Chinese Philosophy
LU YANG, Aesthetics
REN XIAOMING, Logical Philosophy
WANG NANSHI, Marxist Philosophy
XUE FUXING, Aesthetics
YAN MENGWEI, Marxist Philosophy

Department of Relics and Museum Studies:

LIU YI, Museology
ZHU FENGHAN, Ancient Chinese History

College of Ideological and Cultural Education (tel. (22) 23507985; e-mail jyxy@office.nankai.edu):

CAO JIE, Marxist Theories and Ideological and Political Education
DING JUN, Political Economics
DOU AIZHI, History of the Chinese Communist Party
LI JIANSONG, Political Economics
LI YI, Marxist Philosophy
LIU JINGQUAN, History of the Chinese Communist Party
SHAO YUNRUI, History of the Chinese Communist Party
WANG YUANMING, Marxist Philosophy
WU DONGSHENG, Marxist Theories and Ideological and Political Education
YANG YONGZHI, Theoretical Thoughts of Deng Xiaopin
ZHANG HONGGUANG, Scientific and Technological Philosophy
ZHAO TIESUO, History of the Chinese Communist Party

College of Information Science and Technology (tel. (22) 23505705; e-mail nkit@nankai.edu.cn):

CHANG SHENGJIANG, Optical Information Processing
CHEN WENJU, Nonlinear Optical Physics and Materials Optoelectronics for Optical Information
DONG YUANYI, Photonics Technology and Modern Optical Communication
FANG ZHILIANG, Optical Information Processing
FU RULIAN, Laser and Biomedical Optics
GENG XINHUA, Photo-electronic Technology and Applications
HAN WEIHENG, Computer Software
LIN MEIRONG, Nonlinear Optical Physics and Materials, Optoelectronics for Optical Information
LIU FULAI, Optical Information Processing
MU GUOGUANG, Optical Information Processing
SHEN JINYUAN, Optical Information Processing
SUN YUN, Photo-electronic Materials and Technology
SUN ZHONGLI, Photo-electronic Technology, Semiconductor Materials and Devices
TANG GUOQING, Molecular Electronic Spectroscopy and Biomedical Photomaps
WANG QINGREN, Pattern Recognition and Intelligent Systems
WANG ZHAOQI, Optical Information Processing
WANG ZONGPAN, Photo-electronic Technology and Applications
XIONG SHAOZHEN, Optoelectronic Devices and Technology, Display Electronics
YUAN SHUZHONG, Fibre Communication and Fibre Sensors
ZHAI HONGCHEN, Institute of Modern Optics
ZHANG GUILAN, Nonlinear Optical Physics and Materials
ZHANG YANXIN, Optical Information Processing, Neural Networks and Pattern Recognition
ZHAO QIDA, Fibre Communication and Fibre Sensors
ZHU XIAONONG, Applications of Femtosecond Laser Science and Technology

Department of Automation:

CHEN QIUSHUANG, Job Shop Schedule Systems, DEDS System
CHEN ZENGQIANG, Adaptive, Predictive and Intelligent Control
SUN YONGHUA, Adaptive Control Systems
TU FENGSHENG, Integrated Computer Manufacturing Systems
WANG XIUFENG, Modelling and Identification, Financial Decision Support Systems
WANG ZHIBAO, Financial Decision Support Systems
YUAN ZHUZHI, Adaptive and Predictive Control, Intelligent Communication

Department of Communications Engineering:

LI WENCHEN, Radio Communications
WU YUE, Radio Communications

Department of Computer Science and Technology:

BAI GANG, Pattern Recognition
LI QINGCHENG, Embedded Operating Systems
LIU JING, Computer Architecture
LU ZHICAI, Intelligent Control and Communication Networks
SUN GUIRU, Software Engineering
WU GONGYI, Computer Networks
YANG YULU, Computer Architecture
YUAN XIAOJIE, Database Technology, Data Warehousing, Data Mining
ZHU YAOTING, Multimedia Technology and Network Teaching

Department of Electronic Information Science and Technology:

LI WEIXIANG, Systems and System Design
YAN SHAOLIN, Superconductor Electronics, Communications Science and Technology
YANG WENXIA, Net Communication

Department of Electronic Science and Technology:

FANG LAN, Superconductivity, Electronics
SHAO SHUMIN, Vacuum Science and Technology, Functional Materials and Devices

Department of Microelectronics:

JIA XIANGLUAN, VLSI and System Design
NIU WENCHENG, Transducer Technology and Systems
NIU XIUQING, VLSI and System Design
QIN SHICAI, VLSI and System Design

College of International Business (tel. (22) 23500603; e-mail alison41@eyou.com):

Department of Accounting:

FENG YANQI, International Accounting
LIU ZHIYUAN, Managerial Accounting
ZHOU XIAOSU, Financial Accounting

Department of Financial Management:

QI YINFENG, Corporate Finance
WANG QUANXI, Corporate Finance

Department of Human Resource Management:

LI WINJIAN, Human Resource Management
WU GUOCUN, Human Resource Management, Human Resource Development
XIE JINYU, Human Resource Management, Strategic Human Resource Management

Department of Information Systems and Management:

YAN JIANYUAN, Management Information Systems, Logistics Management

Department of International Business:

HAN JINGLUN, Management
JIA LANXIANG, Management
LI FEI, Management
LI GUOJING, Management
QI ANBANG, Management
WANG YINGJUN, Management
ZHANG YULI, Management

Department of Library Science:

LIU YUZHAO, Library Management

WANG ZHIJIN, Library Management

Department of Marketing:

FAN XIUCHENG, Service Marketing Management
HAN DECHANG, Marketing
WU XIAOYUN, Global Marketing Management

Department of Tourism Management:

LI TIANYUAN, Tourism Marketing
QI SHANHONG, Tourism Business Management
WANG JIAN, Tourism Development

College of Law and Political Science (tel. (22) 23501400; e-mail fzxy@nankai.edu.cn; internet nkfzxy.my163.com):

Department of Law:

BAI HUA, Theory of Law
FU SCHICHENG, Administrative Law
HOU XINYI, Theory of Law
HU SHIKAI, Theory of Law
LI YUNWU, Forensic Medicine
QI DAOMENG, Environmental Law
ZHAO ZHENGQUN, Administrative Law
ZHU JINGAN, International Private Law

Department of Political Science:

CAI TUO, International Relations
GE QUAN, Political Science
SHEN YAPING, Public Administration
WANG ZHENGYI, International Relations
YANG LONG, Political Science
YIN YANJUN, International Relations
ZHANG RUIZHUANG, International Relations
ZHU GUANGLEI, Political Science

Department of Sociology:

GUAN XINPING, Social Policy
HOU JUNSHENG, Applied Sociology
LIU JUNJUN, Applied Sociology
PENG HUAMIN, Social Work
WANG CHUHUI, Applied Sociology
WANG XINJIAN, Social Psychology
YUE GUOAN, Social Psychology

College of Life Sciences (tel. (22) 23501846; e-mail sky@office.nankai.edu.cn):

Department of Biochemistry:

CAO YOUJIA, Biochemistry and Molecular Biology, Signals Transduction and Apoptosis
CHEN QIMIN, Microbiology and Molecular Genetics, Molecular Virology
DU RONGQIAN, Molecular Biology
GENG YUNQI, Molecular Virology
HUANG XITAI, Biochemistry and Molecular Biology, Structure of Nucleic Acids and Gene Chips
WANG NINGNING, Plant Molecular Biology
WANG SHUFANG, Plant Physiology
WANG YONG, Plant Molecular Biology
YE LIHONG, Protein Biochemistry
YU ZIRAN, Purification and Characterization of Human Growth Hormones Expressed in Insect Cells
YU XINDA, Gene Engineering in Eukaryotic Cells

Department of Biology:

BU WENJUN, Zoological Systematics
CHEN QIANG, Biosensors, Biophysical Chemistry
CHEN RUIYANG, Cytogenetics
GAO YUBAO, Botany and Plant Ecology
LI HOUHUN, Insect Taxonomy, Zoogeography
LIU ANXI, Animal Physiology and Biochemistry
QIU ZHAOZHI, Zootaxy and Parasitology
SONG WENQIN, Molecular Cytogenetics
WANG XINHUA, Systematic Zoology
ZHENG LEYI, Zoological Systematics

Department of Microbiology:

BAI GANG, Molecular Immunology
DIAO HUXIN, Study of Petroleum Microorganisms
LIU FANG, Microbiological Sources and Molecular Biology
LIU RULIN, Microbiology
REN GAIXIN, Insect Microbiology
WANG LEI, Bacterial Genetics and Evolution
XING LAIJUN, Modern Mycology
YANG WENBO, Resource Bacteriology and Engineering

College of Literature (tel. (22) 23508247; e-mail chinese@wxy.nankai.edu.cn; internet www.nankai.chinese.edu.cn):

Department of Art Design:

XUE YI, Art Design

Department of Basic Cultural Education:

NING JIAYU, Ancient Chinese Literature

Department of Chinese Language and Literature:

CHEN HONG, Ancient Chinese Literature
HONG BO, Ancient Chinese
LI JIANGUO, Ancient Chinese Literature
LIU LILI, Literature and Art Science
LU SHENGJIANG, Ancient Chinese Literature
LUO ZONGQIANG, Ancient Chinese Literature
MA QINGZHU, Modern Chinese
MENG ZHAOLIAN, Ancient Chinese Literature
NING JIAYU, Ancient Chinese Literature
PENG XIUYIN, Literature and Art Science
QIAO YIGANG, Modern and Contemporary Chinese Literature
SHI FENG, Experimental Phonetics
SUN CHANGWU, Ancient Chinese Literature
TAO MUNING, Ancient Chinese Literature
WANG LIXIN, Comparative and World Literature
WANG ZHIGENG, Comparative and World Literature
XING KAI, Languages and Literature of Ethnic Minorities in China
XU XIANGLIN, Ancient Chinese Literature
ZENG XIAOYU, Languages and Literature of Ethnic Minorities in China
ZHANG YI, Ancient Chinese Literature
ZHOU JIAN, Modern Chinese

Department of Eastern Art:

CHEN YUPU, Chinese Painting
FAN ZENG, Chinese Painting
HAN CHANGLI, Chinese Painting
SHEN QUAN, Chinese Painting

Department of Mass Communication:

LUO DERONG, Editorial and Publishing Science
ZHAO HANG, Editorial and Publishing Science

College of Mathematics (tel. (22) 23501233; e-mail longym@nankai.edu.cn; internet www.math.nankai.edu.cn):

Department of Financial Information and Technology:

CHEN WANYI, Control Theory, Financial Mathematics
WANG GONGSHU, Applied Statistics
WANG HONG, Control Theory

Department of Information and Probability:

FU FANGWEI, Coding Theory, Bioinformation
GUO JUNYI, Stochastic Process, Risk Theory
LIANG PU, Coding Theory, Bioinformation
SHEN SHIYI, Coding Theory, Bioinformation
WANG YONGJIN, Probability, Stochastic Process
WU RONG, Probability, Stochastic Process
ZHOU XINGWEI, Harmonic Analysis, Wavelet Analysis

Department of Mathematics:

DENG SHAOQIANG, Lie Groups and Lie Algebras
DING GUANGGUI, Functional Analysis
GU PEI, Algebra, Group Metahomomorphisms
GUO JINGMEI, Differential Topology
HOU ZIXIN, Lie Groups and Lie Algebras
HUANG YUMIN, Partial Differential Equations
LIANG KE, Lie Groups and Lie Algebras
LIN JINKUN, Algebraic Topology
LIU CHUNGEN, Nonlinear Analysis
MENG DAOJI, Basic Mathematics, Algebra, Lie Therapy

Department of Scientific Computing and Applied Software:

HU JIANGWEI, Numerical Mathematics
TIAN CHUNSONG, Numerical Mathematics

Department of Statistics:

WANG ZHAOJUN, Experimental Design, Statistical Process Control
ZHANG RUNCHU, Experimental Design, Multivariate Analysis, Applied Statistics

College of Medicine (tel. (22) 23509842; e-mail zhuth@nankai.edu.cn):

LIU WEN, Anatomy
ZHU TIANHUI, Medical Genetics

College of Physics (tel. (22) 23501490; e-mail physics@nankai.edu.cn; internet www.physics.nankai.edu.cn):

Department of Physics:

CAI CHONGHAI, Evaluation of Nuclear Data
CHEN TIANLUN, Nonlinear Dynamics, Partial Physics Theory
DING DATONG, Nuclear Magnetic Resonance, Computational Materials, Mesoscopic Physics
GAO CHENGQUN, Nuclear Physics
HU BEILAI, Statistical Physics, Plasma Physics
HUANG WUQUN, Nonlinear Dynamics
LI BAOHUI, Nuclear Magnetic Resonance, Computational Physics
LI XUEQIAN, Phenomenology of High Energy Physics
LU ZHENQIU, Inverse Scattering Physics and Imaging Techniques
LUO MA, Perturbative Chromodynamic Power Electronics
MENG XINHE, Particle Physics and the Universe, Mesoscopic Physics
NING PINGZHI, Nuclear Physics
SHEN HONG, Nuclear Physics
WEN JINGSONG, Micro-atmospheric Science Suspension Mechanics
ZHOU WENZHUANG, Crystallology
ZHU YAPING, X-Ray Crystallology

Department of Optical and Electrical Science:

LÜ FUYUN, Photoelectron Laser and Modern Optical Communication
LÜ KECHENG, Photoelectron Laser and Modern Optical Communication
SHENG QIUQIN, Opto-electronics and Optical Fibre Communication, Optical Sensors

Department of Biophysical Science:

YANG WENXIU, Cellular and Molecular Informatics, Cellular and Membrane Biophysics

Software College (tel. (22) 23500526; e-mail cs@nankai.edu.cn; internet www.cs.nankai.edu.cn):

HUANG YALOU, Intelligent Robot Systems, Intelligent Information Processes

Department of Physical Education (tel. (22) 23502801; e-mail tyb@office.nankai.edu.cn):

WANG YUZHU, Track and Field
XING CHUNGUI, Volleyball
YANG XIANGDONG, Basketball (Dir)
ZHAO SHIJIE, Track and Field

Institute of Ancient Chinese Culture Studies (tel. (22) 23509662; e-mail chinese@wxy.nankai.edu.cn; internet www.nankai.chinese.edu.cn):

YE JIAYING, Ancient Chinese Literature and Culture

Institute of Economics (tel. (22) 23503997; e-mail zhoulq@public.tpt.tj.cn):

CAO ZHENLIANG, Regional Economic Theory
CHEN ZHONGSHENG, Socialist Economic Theory
LIU XIN, Capitalist Economic Theory
PANG JINJU, Socialist Economic Theory
WANG YURU, History of Modern Economic Development
ZHOU BING, Socialist Economic Theory
ZHOU LIQUN, Socialist Economic Theory

Institute of Elemento-Organic Chemistry (tel. (22) 23508629; e-mail yss@office.nankai.edu.cn):

CHEN RUYU, Organic Chemistry
CHENG JUNRAN, Organic Chemistry
FANG JIANXIN, Organic Chemistry
GAO RUYU, Organic Chemistry
HAN JIAXIANG, Organic Chemistry
HUANG RUNQIU, Organic Chemistry
LI JING, Organic Chemistry
LI JINSHAN, Organic Chemistry
LI SHUZHENG, Organic Chemistry
LI ZHENGMING, Organic Chemistry
LIAO RENAN, Organic Chemistry
LIU HUAYIN, Organic Chemistry
LIU LUNZU, Organic Chemistry
TANG CHUCHI, Organic Chemistry
WANG GUANGYUAN, Organic Chemistry
XIE QINGLAN, Organic Chemistry
YANG HUAZENG, Organic Chemistry
ZHANG ZHENGZHI, Organic Chemistry
ZHANG ZUXIN, Organic Chemistry
ZHENG JIANU, Organic Chemistry
ZHOU QILIN, Organic Chemistry

Institute of History (tel. (22) 23508903; e-mail lg433@eyou.com):

BAI XINLIANG, Ancient Chinese History
DU JIAJI, Ancient Chinese History
LIN YANQING, Ancient Chinese History
NAN BINGWEN, Ancient Chinese History
WANG MAOHE, Ancient Chinese History

Institute of International Economic Law (tel. (22) 23500694; e-mail shixuey@fm365.com; internet www.nkfzxy.my163.com):

CHENG BAOKU, International Economic Law
SHI XUEYING, International Economic Law

Institute of International Economics (tel. (22) 23508291; e-mail iitnk@office.nankai.edu.cn):

CHEN LIGAO, Open Economy
DAI JINPING, International Finance
LI RONGLIN, International Trade
QIU LICHENG, International Investment and Business
TENG WEIZAO, International Investment and Business
XIANG GUOMING, International Investment and Business
ZHANG CHENG, International Investment and Business
ZHANG XIAOTONG, Econometrics
ZHANG YANGUI, International Investment and Business

Institute of Modern Research Management (tel. (22) 23508439; e-mail nkimm@public.tpt.tj.cn):

LE WEIAN, Corporate Governance
ZHANG JINCHENG, Service Management and Strategic Management

Institute of Mathematics (tel. (22) 23501029; e-mail nim@nankai.edu.cn):

CHEN YONGCHUAN, Combinatorics
FANG FUQUAN, Geometric Topology
FU LEI, Algebraic Geometry
GE MOLIN, Theoretical Physics
LI XUELIANG, Theory of Graphs and Combinatorial Optimizations
LONG YIMING, Nonlinear Analysis
ZHANG WEIPING, Differential Geometry
ZHOU XINGWEI, Harmonic Analysis, Wavelet Analysis

Institute of Molecular Biology (tel. (22) 23501846; e-mail sky@office.nankai.edu.cn):

CAI BAOLI, Biodegradation and Biotechnology
GAO CAICHANG, Biochemistry and Molecular Biology
LI MINGGANG, Plant Molecular Biology
QIAO MINGQIANG, Molecular Microbiology and Microbial Technology
YU YAOTING, Biomaterials and Enzyme Engineering
ZHANG JINHONG, Enzyme Engineering and Biomedical Materials
ZHANG JU, Medical Genetics
ZHENG JIANYU, Molecular Biology
ZHANG XIAODONG, Tumour Molecular Biology

Institute of Modern Optics (tel. (22) 23502275; e-mail xxxy@office.nankai.edu.cn):

CHANG SHENGJIANG, Optical Information Processing
CHEN WENJU, Nonlinear Optical Physics and Materials
DONG XIAOYI, Photonics Technology and Modern Optical Communication
FANG ZHILIANG, Optical Engineering
FU RULIAN, Laser and Biomedical Optics
KAI GUIYUN, Fibre Communications and Fibre Sensors
LIN MEIRONG, Nonlinear Optical Physics and Materials
LIU FULAI, Optical Engineering
MU GUOGUANG, Optical Information Processing
SHEN JINYUAN, Optical Information Processing
TANG GUOQING, Molecular Electronic Spectroscopy and Biomedicine Photomaps
WANG ZHAOQI, Optical Information Processing
YUAN ZHUZHONG, Fibre Communications and Fibre Sensors
ZHAI HONGCHEN, Optical Information Processing, Optics Engineering
ZHANG GUILAN, Nonlinear Optical Physics and Materials
ZHANG YANXIN, Optical Information Processing Neural Networks and Pattern Recognition
ZHAO QIDA, Fibre Communications and Fibre Sensors
ZHU XIAONONG, Applications of Femtosecond Laser Science and Technology

Institute of Photoelectronics (tel. (22) 23502778; e-mail xxxy@office.nankai.edu.cn):

GENG XINHUA, Photoelectronic Technology and Applications
SUN YAN, Photoelectronic Materials and Technology
SUN ZHONGLIN, Photoelectronic Technology, Semiconductor Materials and Devices
WANG ZONGPAN, Photoelectronic Technology and Applications
XIONG SHAOZHEN, Optoelectronic Devices and Technology, Display Electronics

Institute of Polymer Chemistry (tel. (22) 23501386; e-mail gfzs@office.nankai.edu.cn):

HE BINGLIN, Polymer Chemistry
HUANG WENQIANG, Polymer Chemistry
LI CHAOXING, Polymer Chemistry
LI CHENXI, Polymer Chemistry
LI HONG, Polymer Chemistry
MA JIANBIAO, Polymer Chemistry
MI HUAIFENG, Biochemistry
SHI LINQI, Polymer Chemistry
SHI ZUOQING, Polymer Chemistry
WANG GUOCHANG, Polymer Chemistry
WU QIANG, Polymer Chemistry
YAN HUSHENG, Polymer Chemistry
YUAN ZHI, Polymer Chemistry
ZHANG BANGHUA, Polymer Chemistry
ZHANG ZHENGPU, Polymer Chemistry

Institute of Population and Development (tel. (22) 23508012; e-mail rks@office.nankai.edu.cn):

LI JIANMIN, Economics of Population and Labour
TAN LIN, Economics of Population and Labour
YUAN XIN, Economics of Population and Labour

APEC Study Centre (tel. (22) 23501573; e-mail apecnk@office.nankai.edu.cn):

GONG ZHANKUI, Regional Economic Cooperation, International Trade and Investment

Chinese Philology Research Centre (tel. (22) 23507855; e-mail chinese@wxy.nankai.edu.cn; internet www.nankai.chinese.edu.cn):

HE LEYUE, Chinese Philology
XIANG GUANGZHONG, Chinese Philology
ZHAO XIANCUO, Chinese Philology

Photonics Research Centre (tel. (22) 23503697; e-mail zhangcp@nankai.edu.cn; internet www.physics.nankai.edu.cn):

LIU SIMIN, Nonlinear Optics, Solid Spectrum
TIAN JIANGUO, Photonics
XU JINGJUN, Condensed Matter Physics and Photonic Devices
ZHANG CHUNPING, Photonics and Biomedical Photonics
ZHANG GUANGYIN, Solid Spectrum, Photonics and Laser Physics

Transnational Studies Centre (tel. (22) 23505235; e-mail ctsnk@office.nankai.edu.cn):

CHEN LIGAO, Open Economy
DAI JINPING, International Finance
QIU LICHENG, International Investment and Business
XIAN GUOMING, International Investment and Business
ZHANG CHENG, International Investment and Business
ZHANG XIAOTONG, Econometrics
ZHANG YANGUI, International Investment and Business

NINGXIA MEDICAL COLLEGE

Sheng Li South Rd, Yinchuan 750004, Ningxia Province
Telephone: (951) 4095934
Internet: www.nxmc.edu.cn
Founded 1958
Academic year: September to July
Pres.: SHUN TAO
Vice-Pres.: CHEN SHENGCHUN
Vice-Pres.: DAI XIUYING
Vice-Pres.: LI ZHENGZHI
Vice-Pres.: SHI WEIZHONG
Vice-Pres.: ZHANG JIANZHONG
Head of Graduate Dept: LI ZHENGZHI
Librarian: WANG HUIFANG
Library of 200,000 vols
Number of teachers: 811
Number of students: 7,500
Publication: *Journal* (6 a year)

DEANS

Department of Basic Medicine: WANG YANRONG
Department of Chinese Medicine: NIU YANG
Department of Clinical Medicine: WANG HUIXING

Department of Dentistry: MA MING
Department of Public Health: SONG QIRU
School of Nursing: ZHANG LIN
School of Pharmacy: ZHANG DONGNIN

PROFESSORS

GAO, WENHUA, Public Health
HOU, LINGLING, Chinese Medicine
HU, SANGPING, Basic Medicine
JIANG, HOUWEN, Chinese Medicine
JIN, ZHIJUN, Public Health
LI, YUCHUN, Chinese Medicine
LI, ZHENGZHI, Public Health
LIU, XIUFANG, Public Health
QIAN, LIQUN, Public Health
SONG, QIRU, Public Health
WANG, YANRONG, Basic Medicine
WANG, ZHONGJIU, Chinese Medicine
WEN, RUNLING, Public Health
ZHANG, YUJIE, Chinese Medicine
ZHANG, ZHENXIANG, Public Health
ZHU, YUDONG, Chinese Medicine

NORTH CHINA ELECTRIC POWER UNIVERSITY

204 Qingnian Rd, Baoding 071003, Hebei Province
Telephone: (312) 5024952
Internet: www.ncepu.edu.cn

Founded 1958
State control

Pres.: LIU JI ZHEN
Vice-Pres.: AN LIAN SUO
Vice-Pres.: LEI YING QI
Vice-Pres.: LI HE MING
Vice-Pres.: PENG ZHEN ZHONG
Head of Graduate Dept: AN LIAN SUO
Head of Graduate Dept: DING CHANG FU
Librarian: KONG ZHENGHUI

Number of teachers: 2,348
Number of students: 20,000

Publications: *Electric Power Higher Education* (4 a year), *Electric Power Information* (4 a year), *Electric Power Record* (4 a year), *Journal* (4 a year), *Modern Electric Power* (6 a year)

DEANS

Department of English: DAI ZHONG XIN
School of Adult Education: AN LIAN SUO
School of Applied Mathematics: LU ZHAN HUI
School of Applied Physics: ZHANG XIAO HONG
School of Automation: (vacant)
School of Computer Science and Technology: ZHU YONG LI
School of Dynamical Engineering: YANG YONG PING
School of Economic Management: QI JIAN XUN
School of Electrical and Communications Engineering: (vacant)
School of Electrical Engineering: CUI XIANG
School of Environmental Engineering: ZHAO YI
School of Humanity and Social Sciences: LI JU YING
School of Mechanical Engineering: (vacant)
School of Physical Education: YAN GUO QIANG

PROFESSORS

AI, XIN, Electrical Engineering
BAO, HAI, Electrical Engineering
CAO, CHUN MEI, Applied Physics
CHEN, SHENG JIAN, Computer Science and Technology
CHEN, WU, Computer Science and Technology
CHEN, YING MIN, Environmental Engineering
CUI, XIANG, Electrical Engineering
DAI, ZHONG XIN, English Department
DONG, XING HUI, Computer Science and Technology
DU, JIAN GUO, Computer Science and Technology
FANG, LU GUANG, Physical Education
FENG, HUI, Environmental Engineering
GUAN, RONG HUA, Applied Physics
GUO, LEI, English Department
HE, YONG GUI, Economics and Management
HU, MAN YIN, Environmental Engineering
HU, ZHI GUANG, Environmental Engineering
HUANG, YUAN SHENG, Economics and Management
JIA, ZHENG YUAN, Economics and Management
JIANG, GEN SHAN, Applied Physics
LI, JU YING, Humanities and Social Sciences
LI, QI, Applied Physics
LI, QUAN HUA, Physical Education
LI, SHOU XIN, Environmental Engineering
LIN, BI YING, Computer Science and Technology
LIU, ZHI YUAN, Humanities and Social Sciences
LU, FANG CHENG, Electrical Engineering
LU, ZHAN HUI, Applied Mathematics
MA, XIN SHUN, Applied Mathematics
NIU, DONG XIAO, Economics and Management
QI, JIAN XUN, Economics and Management
SUN, JIAN GUO, Computer Science and Technology
SUN, WEI, Economics and Management
WAN, SHI WEI, Applied Physics
WANG, BAO YI, Computer Science and Technology
WANG, CUI RU, Computer Science and Technology
WANG, JING MIN, Economics and Management
WANG, MIN, Humanities and Social Sciences
WU, KE HE, Computer Science and Technology
XIAO, XIANG NING, Electrical Engineering
XING, MIAN, Applied Mathematics
YAN, GUO QIANG, Physical Education
YANG, QI XUN, Electrical Engineering
YI, LIAN QING, Environmental Engineering
YI, ZENG QIAN, Applied Physics
YUAN, YONG TAO, Environmental Engineering
ZHANG, SHENG HAN, Environmental Engineering
ZHANG, TIAN XIN, Humanities and Social Sciences
ZHANG, XIAO HONG, Applied Physics
ZHANG, XU ZHEN, Humanities and Social Sciences
ZHANG, ZHEN SHENG, Environmental Engineering
ZHAO, WEN XIA, Applied Mathematics
ZHAO, YI, Environmental Engineering
ZHENG, GU PING, Computer Science and Technology
ZHU, LING, Electrical Engineering
ZHU, YONG LI, Computer Science and Technology

NORTHEAST FORESTRY UNIVERSITY

26 Hexing Rd, Harbin 150040, Heilongjiang Province
Telephone: (451) 821990015
E-mail: faob@public.hr.hl.cn
Internet: www.nefu.edu.cn

Founded 1952
Academic year: September to July (2 semesters)

Pres.: Prof. YANG CHUANPING
Vice-Pres.: CAO JUN
Vice-Pres.: SUN ZHENGLIN
Dean for Graduate School: HU HAIQING
Librarian: WANG KEQI

Library of 570,000 vols
Number of teachers: 2,781
Number of students: 21,000

Publications: *Bulletin of Botany Research* (4 a year), *Chinese Wildlife* (4 a year), *Forest Fire Protection* (4 a year), *Forestry Finance and Accounting* (12 a year), *Forestry Research in Northern China* (4 a year, in English), *Journal of Northeast Forestry University* (4 a year, in English), *Science of Logging Engineering* (6 a year)

HEADS OF COLLEGES AND DEPARTMENTS

College of Civil Engineering: Prof. HE DONGPO
College of Electromechanical Engineering: Prof. SONG WENLONG
College of Foreign Languages: Prof. WANG DAN
College of Forest Products: Prof. DI XUEYING
College of Forest Resources and Environment: Prof. WANG FENGYOU
College of Humanities: Prof. WANG YAOXIAN
College of Information and Computer Engineering: WANG NIHONG
College of Landscape Architecture: Prof. XU DAWEI
College of Science: Prof. LI BING
College of Transportation: Prof. CHU JIANGWEI
College of Wildlife Resources: Prof. JIA JINGBO
Correspondence College: Prof. KANG JIANYING
Department of Physical Education: Prof. MO SHONGSHAN
Normal College: Prof. SONG YE

PROFESSORS

DING, B., Silviculture
GE, M., Wood Science, Wood Chemistry
HU, Y., Forest Entomology
HUANG, Q., Plan Statistics
JIANG, M., Forestry Economics
LI, G., Forest Resources
LI JIAN, Wood Science and Technology, Wood Surface Chemistry
LI JINGWEN, Ecosystems, Community Ecology
LIU, G., Financial Accounting
LU, R., Wood and Composites Technology and Manufacturing
MA, J., Wildlife Management, Natural Reserves
MA, L., Forest Machinery
NIE, S., Phytocommunity Ecology, Phytotaxonomy
SHAO, L., Forest Disease Epidemiology, Taxonomy of Pathogenic Fungi
SHI, J., Forest Engineering
WANG, F., Ecosystems, Community Ecology
WANG, Y., Ecosystems, Physical and Chemical Ecology
WANG, Z., High Yield Forests
XIAN, K., Forest Protection, Water and Soil Conservation
XIANG, C., Taxonomy of Pathogenic Fungi, Management of Forest Diseases
YUE, S., Pest Control
ZHOU, X., Ecosystems, Economic Ecology
ZHOU, Y., Phytocommunity Ecology, Phytotaxonomy
ZHU, G., Forestry Vehicles, Sawing Equipment
ZU, Y., Unlinear Phytoecology

NORTHWEST UNIVERSITY

Tai Bai Bei Lu, 710069 Xian
Telephone: (29) 88302244
E-mail: lxsbgs@nwu.edu.cn
Internet: www.nwu.edu.cn

Founded 1902
State control
Academic year: September to August

Pres.: Prof. FANG GUANGHUA
Vice-Pres.: CHEN CHAO
Vice-Pres.: GAO LING
Vice-Pres.: LI HAO
Vice-Pres.: WANG YAO-YU

Vice-Pres.: YANGCHUN DE
Vice-Pres.: ZHANG YUNXIANG
Librarian: Prof. ZHANG WENPENG

Library: 1.6m. vols
Number of teachers: 2,400
Number of students: 26,000

Publications: *Journal* (4 a year), *Literature of the Tang Dynasty*, *Middle East*, *Studies in Higher Education*, *Studies in the History of North Western China*

NORTHWESTERN POLYTECHNICAL UNIVERSITY

Xian 710072, Shaanxi Province
Telephone: (29) 8493119
E-mail: office@nwpu.edu.cn
Internet: www.nwpu.edu.cn
Founded 1938
State control
Languages of instruction: Chinese, English
Academic year: September to July (2 semesters)

Hon. Pres.: Prof. JI WENMEI
Pres.: Prof. JIANG CHENGYU
Vice-Pres: Prof. GAO DEYUAN
Vice-Pres: Prof. WANG RUNXIAN
Vice-Pres: Prof. WANG WEI
Vice-Pres: Prof. YUAN JIANPING
Dean for Studies: Prof. WAN XIANPENG
Dir for Foreign Affairs: Prof. TANG HONG
Librarian: Prof. GOU WENXUAN

Number of teachers: 1,400
Number of students: 28,000

Publications: *Journal of Theoretical and Applied Mechanics* (4 a year), *Mechanical Science and Engineering* (4 a year), *University Journal* (4 a year)

DEANS

College of Astronautics: Prof. ZHOU JUN
College of Civil Aviation Engineering: Prof. SUN QIN
College of Continuing Education: Prof. WEI SHENGMIN
College of Management: Prof. YE ZHENGYIN
College of Marine Engineering: SONG BAOWEI
College of Materials Science: Prof. LI HEJUN
Graduate School: Prof. JIANG CHENGYU
School of Mechatronic Engineering: Prof. ZHANG DINGHUA

PROFESSORS

AI, J. L., Aircraft Design
AN, J. W., Aircraft Automatic Control
BAI, C. R., Aerodynamics
CAI, W. D., Computer Application
CAI, Y. H., Aero-engines
CAO, C. N., Physics
CHEN, C. L., Physics
CHEN, G. D., Mechanics
CHEN, K. A., Noise Control
CHEN, M., Gyroscope and Inertial Navigation
CHEN, S. L., Flight Mechanics
CHEN, Z., Metallic Materials and Heat Treatment
CHENG, G., Signal Measuring and Instruments
CHENG, L. F., Physical Metallurgy
CHU, W. L., Aero-engines
CUI, Y. Z., China Revolutionary History
DAI, G. Z., Theory and Application of Automatic Control
DANG, J. B., Solid Mechanics
DENG, Z. C., Mechanics
DING, X. Q., Applied Mathematics
DUAN, Z. M., Signal Circuit and Systems Engineering
FAN, D., Aero-engines
FAN, M. F., China Revolutionary History
FAN, X. D., High Polymer Material
FAN, X. Y., Computer Application
FANG, Q., Flight Mechanics
FANG, Z. D., Mechanical Engineering
FENG, D., Traditional Chinese Painting
FENG, J. L., Linguistics (Japanese)
FU, H. Z., Physical Metallurgy
FU, L. Z., Mathematics
GAN, X. Y., Linguistics (English)
GAO, D. Y., Computer Science and Engineering
GAO, M. T., Drafting
GAO, X. G., Command Systems Engineering
GAO, Z. H., Aerodynamics
GE, W. J., Machinery Design and Manufacturing
GOU, D. B., Track and Field Sports
GOU, W. X., Solid Mechanics
GU, L. X., Guided Missile Design
GUO, H. Z., Metal Forming
GUO, L., Intelligent Signal Processing
GUO, X. P., Physical Metallurgy
HAO, C. Y., Space Vehicle Design
HE, C. A., Theory and Application of Automatic Control
HE, E. M., Aircraft Control
HE, G. Q., Rocket Engine
HE, H. C., Computer and Artificial Intelligence
HE, M. Y., Signal Circuit and Systems Engineering
HE, W. P., Space Flight Manufacturing Engineering
HE, X. S., General Mechanics
HE, Y. Y., Automatic Control
HU, X. L., Physical Chemistry
HU, Z. G., Computer Software
HUANG, J. G., Applied Electronic Technology
HUANG, Q. Q., Structure Intensity
HUANG, W. D., Physical Metallurgy
JIANG, C. Y., Space Flight Manufacturing Engineering
JIANG, D. W., Applied Mathematics
JIANG, J. S., Structural Mechanics
JIANG, Z. J., Computer Software
JIAO, G. Q., Solid Mechanics
JIE, W. Q., Physical Metallurgy
JIN, B. S., Mechanics of Materials
JING, Z. R., Electronic Engineering
KANG, F. J., Automatic Control
KANG, R. K., Machinery Manufacturing
LAI, X. X., Dialectics of Nature
LEI, Y., Signal Processing
LI, B. X., Rocket Engines
LI, E. P., Physics
LI, F. G., Metal Plasticity Processing
LI, F. W., Aerodynamics
LI, H. J., Metallic Materials and Heat Treatment
LI, H. L., Physical Metallurgy
LI, H. X., Aerodynamics
LI, J. L., Mathematics
LI, J. Z., Political Economy
LI, K. Z., Metallic Materials and Heat Treatment
LI, M. Q., Metal Forming
LI, S. J., Magnetos
LI, S. P., Plasticity Processing
LI, T. H., Materials Processing
LI, W. H., Computer Applications
LI, W. J., Aircraft Design
LI, X. Q., Drafting
LI, Y., Space Flight Manufacturing Engineering
LI, Y. J., Guided Missile Automatic Control
LI, Y. L., Fracture Mechanics
LI, Y. Z., Applied Polymer Science
LI, Z. H., Computer Software
LI, Z. S., Underwater Technology
LIAN, B. W., Radio Communication
LIAN, X. C., Aero-engines
LIANG, G. Q., Space Flight Manufacturing Engineering
LIANG, G. Z., Physical and Chemistry Experiment
LIANG, S. X., Equipment Management
LIAO, M. F., Aero-engines Intensity
LIN, H., Electric Technology
LIU, B., Aero-engines
LIU, B. M., Metal Plasticity Processing
LIU, D., Solid Mechanics
LIU, G., Mechanical Design
LIU, J. H., Welding
LIU, L., Physical Metallurgy
LIU, W. G., Electrical Machinery and Control
LIU, X. L., Aircraft Automatic Control
LIU, Z. T., Metallic Materials and Heat Treatment
LU, B. T., Metallic Materials and Heat Treatment
LU, C. D., Machinery Manufacturing
LU, G. Z., Aircraft Structure Intensity
LU, J. C., Automatic Control
LU, S., Engine Structure Intensity
LU, Z. Z., Solid Mechanics
LUO, C. R., Physics
LUO, X. B., Mathematics
MA, R. Q., Electric Engineering
MA, X. Q., Space Flight Manufacturing Engineering
MA, Y. L., Underwater Acoustics Engineering
MAO, G. W., Rocket Engines
MENG, B. A., Track and Field Sports
MENG, J. M., Linguistics (English)
MO, R., Computer Design
MU, D. J., Theory and Application of Automatic Control
NING, R. C., High Polymer Material
NIU, P. C., Mathematics
OU, Y. J., Applied Mathematics
PAN, J. Y., Management Engineering
PAN, Q., Automatic Control
PEI, C. M., Signal Processing
QI, L. H., Metal Art
QI, S. H., High Polymer Material
QIAN, Z. B., Hot Motive Equipment of the Torpedo
QIAO, S. R., Metallic Materials and Heat Treatment
QIAO, Z. D., Computational Aerodynamics
QIN, X. S., Machinery Manufacturing
QIN, Y. Y., Gyroscope and Inertial Navigation
QING, H. Y., Chemistry
QU, S. R., Drafting
REN, X. M., Aero-engines
SHEN, J., Physical Metallurgy
SHI, H. S., Radio Communication
SHI, K. M., Linguistics (German)
SHI, X. F., Administration
SHI, X. H., Mechanical Engineering
SHI, X. Q., Linguistics (French)
SHI, Y. K., Electrical Equipment
SHI, Y. M., Applied Mathematics
SHI, Y. Y., Ergonomics
SHI, Z. K., Theory and Application of Automatic Control
SONG, B. F., Aircraft Design
SONG, B. W., Machinery Manufacturing
SONG, Z. M., Applied Physics
SU, C. W., Applied Mathematics
SU, K. H., Chemistry
SUN, C., Signal Processing
SUN, G. Z., Drafting
SUN, J. C., Applied Acoustics and Noise Control Engineering
SUN, Q., Aircraft Design
SUN, S. D., Machinery Manufacturing
TANG, G. P., Mathematics
TANG, H., Personnel Management
TANG, S., Flight Mechanics
TANG, Y. Z., Aircraft Automatic Control
TAO, H., Space Flight Manufacturing Engineering
TIAN, C. S., Metallic Materials and Heat Treatment
TIAN, Z., Mathematics
TONG, S. R., Equipment Management
TONG, X. Y., Aircraft Design
TU, Q. P., Signal Processing
WAN, X. P., Aircraft Design
WANG, B., Physics
WANG, J., Linguistics (English)
WANG, J. B., Aircraft Manufacture Engineering
WANG, J. F., Financial Accounting

WANG, L., Rocket Engines
WANG, L. D., Physics
WANG, R. M., Compound Materials
WANG, R. X., Numerically Controlled Machine Tools
WANG, S. M., Basic Electrical Training
WANG, S. M., Mechanics
WANG, W., Aircraft Automatic Control
WANG, X. M., Automatic Control and Computer Application
WANG, Y. C., Hot Motive Equipment of the Torpedo
WANG, Y. M., Underwater Acoustics Engineering
WANG, Y. S., Radio Technology
WANG, Z. S., Motive Equipment Control Engineering
WEI, B. B., Physical Metallurgy
WEI, F., Mechanics of Materials
WEI, S. M., Ergonomics
WENG, Z. Q., Navigation Systems
WU, D. Y., Heat Energy Engineering
WU, H., Aero-engines
WU, J., Computer Software
WU, J. J., Space Flight Manufacturing Engineering
WU, X. G., Torpedo Control
WU, Z. Y., Armoured Concrete Systems
XI, D. K., Aerodynamics
XI, S. M., Metallic Materials and Heat Transfer
XIAO, Y. L., Mathematics
XIE, F. Q., Metal Surface Corrosion
XIN, K., Linguistics (English)
XU, D. M., Torpedo Automatic Control
XU, J. D., Microwave and Antenna Technology
XU, M., Aerodynamics
XU, W., Applied Mathematics
XU, Y. D., Physical Metallurgy
XU, Z., Applied Mathematics
YAN, J., Aircraft Navigation Control
YAN, J. G., Automatic Control
YANG, G. C., Physical Metallurgy
YANG, H., Space Flight Technology
YANG, H. C., Computer Design
YANG, J., Aircraft Automatic Control
YANG, N. D., Systems Engineering
YANG, S. Q., Welding
YANG, Y. F., Linguistics (English)
YANG, Y. N., Aerodynamics
YANG, Y. Q., Metallic Materials and Heat Transfer
YANG, Y. S., Electrical Technology
YANG, Z. C., Solid Mechanics
YANG, Z. Y., Computer Applications
YAO, Z. K., Metal Forming
YE, Z. L., Applied Mathematics
YE, Z. Y., Aerodynamics
YU, H. X., Radio Communication
YUAN, J. P., Flight Mechanics
YUAN, W. Z., Machinery Manufacturing
YUAN, Z. K., Dialectics of Nature
YUE, Z. F., Aircraft Design
ZHANG, A., Command Systems Engineering
ZHANG, B. Q., Aerodynamics
ZHANG, D., Guided Missile Design
ZHANG, D. H., Ergonomics
ZHANG, D. S., Structural Mechanics
ZHANG, H. C., Theory and Application of Automatic Control
ZHANG, H. F., Thermal and Solar Energy Engineering
ZHANG, H. G., Linguistics (German)
ZHANG, H. S., Signal Circuit and Systems Engineering
ZHANG, K. S., Solid Mechanics
ZHANG, K. Y., Applied Mathematics
ZHANG, L. T., Physical Metallurgy
ZHANG, Q. X., Physical Metallurgy
ZHANG, Q. Y., High Polymer Material
ZHANG, S. S., Equipment Engineering
ZHANG, W. G., Aircraft Navigation Control
ZHANG, W. H., Space Flight Manufacturing Engineering
ZHANG, X. A., Building Structure
ZHANG, X. K., Space Flight Manufacturing Engineering
ZHANG, X. M., Detonator Technology
ZHANG, Y. M., Torpedo Design
ZHANG, Y. Y., Computer Software
ZHANG, Y. Z., Automatic Control
ZHAO, J. L., Modern Optics Application
ZHAO, J. W., Sound Electronic Engineering of Water
ZHAO, R. C., Signal and Graph Processing
ZHAO, S. Z., Machinery Manufacturing
ZHAO, X. A., Linguistics (English)
ZHAO, X. M., Mathematics
ZHAO, X. P., Solid Mechanics
ZHAO, Y. S., General Mechanics
ZHAO, Z. W., Computer Software
ZHI, B. S., Automatic Control
ZHI, X. Z., General Mechanics
ZHOU, D. Y., Command Systems Engineering
ZHOU, J., Aircraft Navigation Control
ZHOU, J. H., Analysis and Design of Control Systems
ZHOU, Q., Automatic Control
ZHOU, W. C., Physical Metallurgy
ZHOU, X. S., Computer Applications
ZHOU, Y. H., Physical Metallurgy
ZHOU, Z., Flight Mechanics
ZHU, H. R., Heat Energy Engineering
ZHU, J. Q., Aero-engines
ZHU, M. Q., Measurement Control in Mechanical Engineering
ZHU, X. P., Automatic Control
ZHU, Y. A., Computer Applications
ZOU, G. R., Materials Processing Engineering

PEKING UNION MEDICAL COLLEGE

9 Dong Dan San Tiao, Dongcheng Dist., Beijing 100730
Telephone: (10) 65295912
E-mail: liudp@pumc.edu.cn
Internet: www.pumc.edu.cn

Founded 1917
Academic year: September to July

Pres.: LIU DEPEI
Vice-Pres.: HE WEI
Vice-Pres.: LIU QIAN
Vice-Pres.: LU CHONGMEI
Vice-Pres.: QI KEMING
Vice-Pres.: SONG XUEMIN
Head of Graduate Dept: LIU DEPEI
Librarian: WANG ZHAOLING

Number of teachers: 3,328

Publications: *Acta Academiae Medicinae Sinicae* (6 a year), *Bilingual Journal of Medicine International* (6 a year), *Chinese Chemical Letters* (12 a year), *Journal of Asian Natural Products Research* (4 a year)

DEANS

Cancer Hospital: ZHAO PING
Fu Wai Hospital: HU SHENGSHOU
Institute of Materia Medica: WANG XIAOLIANG
Institute of Medical Biology Technology: JIANG JIANDONG
Orthopaedic Surgery Hospital: QI KEMING
Peking Union Medical College Hospital: LIU QIAN
School of Basic Medical Sciences: ZHENG DEXIAN
School of Nursing: SHEN NING

PROFESSORS

BAO, XIULAN, Peking Union Medical College Hospital
CAI, BOQIANG, Peking Union Medical College Hospital
CAI, LIXING, Peking Union Medical College Hospital
CAI, WEIMING, Cancer Hospital
CAO, JIMIN, School of Basic Medical Sciences
CHEN, CUANXIA, Peking Union Medical College Hospital
CHEN, DECHANG, Peking Union Medical College Hospital
CHEN, GUOZHANG, Orthopaedic Surgery Hospital
CHEN, HONGSHAN, Institute of Medical Biology Technology
CHEN, JIE, Peking Union Medical College Hospital
CHEN, TINGYUAN, Peking Union Medical College Hospital
CHEN, XI, Fu Wai Hospital
CHU, DATONG, Cancer Hospital
DAI, JINGLEI, Cancer Hospital
DAI, YUHUA, Peking Union Medical College Hospital
DONG, JINGWU, Peking Union Medical College Hospital
DONG, YI, Peking Union Medical College Hospital
FAN, JINCAI, Orthopaedic Surgery Hospital
FANG, DEFU, School of Basic Medical Sciences
FANG, QI, Peking Union Medical College Hospital
GAO, JUZHEN, Cancer Hospital
GAO, RUNLIN, Fu Wai Hospital
GU, DAZHONG, Cancer Hospital
GU, DONGFENG, Fu Wai Hospital
GUAN, YAN, Peking Union Medical College Hospital
GUANG, YAO, Peking Union Medical College Hospital
GUI, LAI, Orthopaedic Surgery Hospital
GUO, HUIYUAN, Institute of Medical Biology Technology
GUO, YUZHEN, Peking Union Medical College Hospital
HA, XIANGWEN, Cancer Hospital
HAO, YUZHI, Cancer Hospital
HE, ZHAMA, Fu Wai Hospital
HE, ZHUGEN, Cancer Hospital
HONG, FENGYI, Cancer Hospital
HONG, WANJUN, Cancer Hospital
HU, JINGQUN, Cancer Hospital
HU, SHENGSHOU, Fu Wai Hospital
HUANG, GUOJUN, Cancer Hospital
HUANG, HANYUAN, Peking Union Medical College Hospital
HUANG, LIANG, Institute of Materia Medica
HUANG, XIZHEN, Peking Union Medical College Hospital
HUANG, YIRONG, Cancer Hospital
HUI, RUTAI, Fu Wai Hospital
JI, BAOHUA, Peking Union Medical College Hospital
JI, XIAOCHENG, Peking Union Medical College Hospital
JIANG, JIANDONG, Institute of Medical Biology Technology
JIANG, MING, Peking Union Medical College Hospital
JIANG, XIUFANG, Peking Union Medical College Hospital
JIANG, ZHUMING, Peking Union Medical College Hospital
JIAO, HAIYAN, Peking Union Medical College Hospital
JIN, LAN, Peking Union Medical College Hospital
LI, CHANGLING, Cancer Hospital
LI, DIANDONG, Institute of Medical Biology Technology
LI, HANHONG, Peking Union Medical College Hospital
LI, JIAXIU, Cancer Hospital
LI, KUI, Cancer Hospital
LI, LIHUAN, Fu Wai Hospital
LI, LING, Cancer Hospital
LI, LONGYU, Peking Union Medical College Hospital
LI, QINGHONG, Cancer Hospital
LI, SENKAI, Orthopaedic Surgery Hospital
LI, TAISHENG, Cancer Hospital
LI, ZEJIAN, Peking Union Medical College Hospital
LIANG, XIAOTIAN, Institute of Materia Medica

LIANG, ZHIQUAN, School of Basic Medical Sciences
LIU, DAWEI, Peking Union Medical College Hospital
LIU, DEPEI, School of Basic Medical Sciences
LIU, FUSHENG, Cancer Hospital
LIU, GENTAO, Institute of Materia Medica
LIU, JINGSHENG, School of Basic Medical Sciences
LIU, LIYING, Cancer Hospital
LIU, QIAN, Peking Union Medical College Hospital
LIU, RUIXUE, Peking Union Medical College Hospital
LIU, SHUFAN, Cancer Hospital
LIU, TONGHUA, Peking Union Medical College Hospital
LIU, XINFAN, Cancer Hospital
LIU, YULING, Institute of Materia Medica
LIU, YUQING, Fu Wai Hospital
LIU, ZHONGXUN, Institute of Medical Biology Technology
LOU, ZHIXIAN, Institute of Medical Biology Technology
LU, CHONGMEI, School of Nursing
LU, NING, Cancer Hospital
LU, WEIXUAN, Peking Union Medical College Hospital
LUO, HUIYUAN, Peking Union Medical College Hospital
LUO, WEICI, Peking Union Medical College Hospital
MIAO, YANJUN, Cancer Hospital
OU YANG, HAN, Cancer Hospital
PAN, QINJING, Cancer Hospital
PAN, YANRUO, Peking Union Medical College Hospital
PU, JIELIN, Fu Wai Hospital
QI, KEMING, Orthopaedic Surgery Hospital
QI, MEIFU, Peking Union Medical College Hospital
QI, YONGFA, Cancer Hospital
QIANG, TUNAN, Cancer Hospital
QIAO, SHUBIN, Fu Wai Hospital
QIN, DEXING, Cancer Hospital
QIU, GUIXING, Peking Union Medical College Hospital
QIU, HUIZHONG, Peking Union Medical College Hospital
REN, YUZHU, Peking Union Medical College Hospital
SHAO, YONGFU, Cancer Hospital
SHEN, NING, School of Nursing
SHI, MULAN, Cancer Hospital
SHI, YUANKAI, Cancer Hospital
SONG, ZONGLU, Peking Union Medical College Hospital
SU, XUEZENG, Cancer Hospital
SUN, GENGTIAN, Cancer Hospital
SUN, JIANHENG, Cancer Hospital
SUN, LI, Cancer Hospital
SUN, LIXHONG, Fu Wai Hospital
SUN, NIANGU, Peking Union Medical College Hospital
SUN, YAN, Cancer Hospital
SUN, YINGLONG, Fu Wai Hospital
TANG, BANGCI, Peking Union Medical College Hospital
TANG, PINGZHANG, Cancer Hospital
TANG, WEISONG, Peking Union Medical College Hospital
TU, GIYI, Cancer Hospital
WANG, DANHUA, Peking Union Medical College Hospital
WANG, JIAQI, Orthopaedic Surgery Hospital
WANG, JINWAN, Cancer Hospital
WANG, LIANGJUN, Cancer Hospital
WANG, LUHUA, Cancer Hospital
WANG, MEI, Cancer Hospital
WANG, QILU, Cancer Hospital
WANG, SHIZHEN, Peking Union Medical College Hospital
WANG, XHISHI, Peking Union Medical College Hospital
WANG, XIAOMING, School of Basic Medical Sciences
WANG, YIPENG, Peking Union Medical College Hospital
WEI, MIN, Peking Union Medical College Hospital
WU, AIRU, Cancer Hospital
WU, NING, Cancer Hospital
WU, NING, Peking Union Medical College Hospital
WU, YANGFENG, Fu Wai Hospital
XI, ZHI, Cancer Hospital
XU, BINGHE, Cancer Hospital
XU, BINGZE, Cancer Hospital
XU, CHENGSU, School of Basic Medical Sciences
XU, GUOZHEN, Cancer Hospital
XU, JINGQIN, Peking Union Medical College Hospital
XU, LETIAN, Peking Union Medical College Hospital
XU, ZHENGANG, Cancer Hospital
YANG, GONGHUAN, School of Basic Medical Sciences
YANG, LIN, Cancer Hospital
YANG, YAOJIN, Fu Wai Hospital
YANG, ZIBIN, School of Basic Medical Sciences
YE, QIBIN, Peking Union Medical College Hospital
YIN, WEIBO, Cancer Hospital
YOU, KAI, Peking Union Medical College Hospital
YU, DEQUAN, Institute of Materia Medica
YU, GAOZHI, Cancer Hospital
YU, GUORUI, Cancer Hospital
YU, HONGZHAO, Cancer Hospital
YU, MENGXUE, Peking Union Medical College Hospital
YU, XHIHAO, Cancer Hospital
YUE, JILIANG, Orthopaedic Surgery Hospital
ZENG, XIAOFENG, Peking Union Medical College Hospital
ZENG, XUAN, School of Basic Medical Sciences
ZHAN, RUGANG, Cancer Hospital
ZHANG, BAONING, Cancer Hospital
ZHANG, DAWEI, Cancer Hospital
ZHANG, DECHANG, School of Basic Medical Sciences
ZHANG, DECHAO, Cancer Hospital
ZHANG, DELI, Peking Union Medical College Hospital
ZHANG, FENCHUN, Peking Union Medical College Hospital
ZHANG, HONGXING, Cancer Hospital
ZHANG, HUILAN, Fu Wai Hospital
ZHANG, JIANXI, Peking Union Medical College Hospital
ZHANG, SHIYUAN, Peking Union Medical College Hospital
ZHANG, WENHUA, Cancer Hospital
ZHANG, XHIXIAN, Cancer Hospital
ZHANG, XIANGRU, Cancer Hospital
ZHANG, XUE, School of Basic Medical Sciences
ZHANG, YOUJU, Peking Union Medical College Hospital
ZHANG, ZHENHAN, Peking Union Medical College Hospital
ZHANG, ZHIPING, Institute of Medical Biology Technology
ZHAO, MIN, Orthopaedic Surgery Hospital
ZHAO, PING, Cancer Hospital
ZHAO, SHIHUA, Fu Wai Hospital
ZHAO, SHIMIN, Peking Union Medical College Hospital
ZHAO, YAN, Peking Union Medical College Hospital
ZHAO, YUPEI, Peking Union Medical College Hospital
ZHEN, YONGSU, Institute of Medical Biology Technology
ZHENG, DEXIAN, School of Basic Medical Sciences
ZHONG, SHOUGUANG, Peking Union Medical College Hospital
ZHOU, JICHANG, Cancer Hospital
ZHOU, QIAN, Peking Union Medical College Hospital
ZHOU, XHUNWU, Cancer Hospital
ZHOU, YANMIN, Peking Union Medical College Hospital
ZHU, CHUANQIU, Peking Union Medical College Hospital
ZHU, DAHIA, School of Basic Medical Sciences
ZHU, GUANGJI, School of Basic Medical Sciences
ZHU, JUN, Fu Wai Hospital
ZHU, LI, Peking Union Medical College Hospital
ZHU, WENLING, Peking Union Medical College Hospital
ZHU, XIAODONG, Fu Wai Hospital
ZHUANG, HONGXING, Orthopaedic Surgery Hospital
ZHUI, YUANYU, Peking Union Medical College Hospital

PEKING UNIVERSITY

5 Yiheyuan Rd, Haidian, Beijing 100871
Telephone: (10) 62752114
Internet: www.pku.edu.cn

Founded 1898
Languages of instruction: Chinese, English
Academic year: September to June

Pres.: ZHOU QIFENG
Vice-Pres.: CHEN ZHANGLIANG
Vice-Pres.: CHI HUISHENG
Vice-Pres.: HAN QIDE
Vice-Pres.: HAO PING
Vice-Pres.: HE FANGCHUAN
Vice-Pres.: LII ZHAOFENG
Vice-Pres.: LIN JIUXIANG
Vice-Pres.: LIN JUNJING
Vice-Pres.: MIN WEIFANG
Registrar: LI KE'AN
Librarian: DAI LONGJI

Library of 4,610,000 vols
Number of teachers: 4,537
Number of students: 55,000

Publication: *Peking University Academic Journal*

QINGHAI NATIONALITIES COLLEGE

25 Ba Yi Rd, Xining 810007, Qinghai Province
Telephone: (971) 76803
Internet: www.qhmu.edu.cn

Founded 1949

Pres.: DUO JIE JIAN ZAN
Vice-Pres: SHAO DESHAN
Vice-Pres: Assoc. Prof. YU DEYUAN
Vice-Pres: ZHUO MA CAI DAN
Librarian: YAO KERANG

Library of 550,000 vols
Number of teachers: 330
Number of students: 1,572

Publications: *Journal of Qinghai Nationalities Institute*, *Qinghai Nationalities Research*

PROFESSORS

FENG, Y., Theory of Arts
HU, A., Ancient Chinese
MI, Y., History of Chinese
ZHU, K., Modern Literature

QUFU NORMAL UNIVERSITY

57 Jingxuanxi Rd, Qufu 273165, Shandong Province
Telephone: (537) 4458831
Internet: www.qfnu.edu.cn

Founded 1955
Academic year: September to July

Pres.: TIAN DEQUAN
Librarian: DU YU

Library of 1,880,000 vols
Number of teachers: 2,200
Number of students: 42,000

Publications: *Journal* (4 a year), *Qilu Journal* (6 a year)

DEANS

College of Literature: XUE YONGWU
College of Mathematics Science: (vacant)

PROFESSORS

CHEN, KESHOU, Literature
CHEN, QINGPING, Literature
DAN, CHENGBIN, Literature
GAO, SHANGQU, Literature
LIU, FENGGUANG, Literature
LIU, XINSHENG, Literature
LIU, YAOJIN, Literature
PU, ZHAOLIN, Literature
QIAN, JIAQING, Literature
TANG, XUENING, Literature
XU, ZHENGUI, Literature
XUE, YONGWU, Literature
ZHANG, LIANRANG, Literature
ZHANG, QUANZHI, Literature
ZHAO, DONGSHUAN, Literature
ZHAO, LIMING, Literature
ZHENG, JIEWEN, Literature

ATTACHED RESEARCH INSTITUTE

Adult Education College: Dir DU YIDE

RENMIN UNIVERSITY OF CHINA

59 Zhongguancun St, 100872 Beijing
Telephone: (10) 62511081
E-mail: rmdxxb@ruc.edu.cn
Internet: www.ruc.edu.cn

Founded 1937, current name adopted 1950
State control

Pres.: Prof. CHEN YULU
Vice-Pres.: YANG HUILIN
Vice-Pres.: LI KANGTAI
Vice-Pres.: LI SHAOGONG
Vice-Pres.: LUO GUOJIE
Vice-Pres.: MA SHAOMENG
Vice-Pres.: YANG DEFU
Vice-Pres.: ZHENG HANGSHENG
Librarian: DAI YI

Number of teachers: 1,850
Number of students: 24,565

Publications: *Archival News* (6 a year), *Economic Theory and Business Management*, *International Journalism World* (4 a year), *Learned Journal of the People's University of China* (6 a year), *Population Research*, *Teaching and Research*

SHAANXI NORMAL UNIVERSITY

199 Chang'an South Rd, Xian 710062, Shaanxi Province
Telephone: (29) 85308992
Internet: www.snnu.edu.cn

Founded 1944
Min. of Education control
Academic year: September to July

Pres.: FANG YU
Vice-Pres.: XIAO ZHENGHONG
Vice-Pres.: ZHANG JIANXIANG
Vice-Pres.: ZHAO BIN
Vice-Pres.: ZHOU DEMING
Head of Graduate Dept: LI JIKAI
Librarian: YANG ENCHENG

Number of teachers: 2,600
Number of students: 40,000

Publications: *Journal* (natural sciences, 4 a year), *Journal* (philosophy and social sciences, 6 a year)

DEANS

College of Arts: HU YUKANG
College of Chemistry and Materials Science: ZHANG CHENGXIAO
College of Chinese Language and Literature: LI XIJIAN
College of Computer Science: FENG DEMIN
College of Educational Science: YOU XUJUN
College of Food Engineering: CHEN JINPING
College of Foreign Languages: MA ZHENYI
College of Further Education: JIA WENXING
College of History and Civilization: JIA ERQIANG
College of International Business: LI ZHONGMIN
College of Life Sciences: WANG ZHEZHI
College of Mathematics and Information Science: WU JIANHUA
College of News and Media: LIU LU
College of Physical Education: LI ZHENBIN
College of Physics and Information Technology: ZHAO WEI
College of Political Economy: WANG ZHENYA
College of Teachers and Administrators: GONG JIANGUO
College of Tourism and the Environment: HUANG CHUNCHANG
e-College: LU JIURU

PROFESSORS

CAO, HAN, Computer Science
CAO, HUAIXIN, Mathematics and Information Science
CAO, WEIAN, History and Civilization
CHANG, JINCANG, History and Civilization
CHEN, FENG, History and Civilization
CHEN, JINPING, Life Science
CHEN, JINPING, Food Engineering
CHEN, XIAORUI, Educational Science
CHEN, YASHAO, Chemistry and Materials Science
DANG, HUAIXING, Chinese Language and Literature
DU, HONGKE, Mathematics and Information Science
DU, JIULIN, Physics and Information Technology
DU, WENYU, History and Civilization
DUAN, YUFENG, Food Engineering
FANG, YU, Chemistry and Materials Science
FENG, DEMING, Computer Science
FENG, WENLOU, Chinese Language and Literature
FU, SHAOLIANG, Chinese Language and Literature
GUO, MIN, Computer Science
GUO, QINNA, Chinese Language and Literature
HAO, WENWU, Educational Science
HE, JUHOU, Computer Science
HU, ANSHUN, Chinese Language and Literature
HU, DAODAO, Chemistry and Materials Science
HU, JI, History and Civilization
HU, MANCHENG, Chemistry and Materials Science
HUANG, QIN-AN, Mathematics and Information Science
HUANG, YUAN, Life Science
HUO, SONGLIN, Chinese Language and Literature
HUO, YOUMING, Chinese Language and Literature
JI, GUOXING, Mathematics and Information Science
JIA, ERQIANG, History and Civilization
LI, BAOLIN, Chemistry and Materials Science
LI, BAOXIN, Chemistry and Materials Science
LI, GUOQING, Educational Science
LI, HONGWU, Educational Science
LI, HUISHI, Mathematics and Information Science
LI, JIANFENG, Food Engineering
LI, JIKAI, Chinese Language and Literature
LI, QUANLU, Physics and Information Technology
LI, SHENGGANG, Mathematics and Information Science
LI, WANSHE, Mathematics and Information Science
LI, XIJIAN, Chinese Language and Literature
LI, YONGFANG, Physics and Information Technology
LI, YONGMING, Mathematics and Information Science
LI, YUMIN, History and Civilization
LI, ZHEN, Chinese Language and Literature
LIAN, ZHENMIN, Life Science
LIANG, DAOLI, Chinese Language and Literature
LIN, SHUYU, Physics and Information Technology
LIU, FENGDAO, Chinese Language and Literature
LIU, JING, Chinese Language and Literature
LIU, LU, News and Media
LIU, PENG, Physics and Information Technology
LIU, XINKE, Educational Science
LIU, XINPING, Mathematics and Information Science
LIU, ZHAOTIE, Chemistry and Materials Science
LIU, ZONGHUAI, Chemistry and Materials Science
LU, JIURU, Chemistry and Materials Science
LUO, ZENGRU, Mathematics and Information Science
MA, GEDONG, Chinese Language and Literature
MA, ZHENDUO, Foreign Languages
MIAO, RUNCAI, Physics and Information Technology
NIU, YONG, Physics and Information Technology
QIU, GUOYONG, Computer Science
QIU, NONGXUE, Food Engineering
QIU, XUENONG, Life Science
QU, YAJUN, Chinese Language and Literature
REN, YI, Life Science
RUN, QINGSHENG, Chinese Language and Literature
SHANG, ZHIYUAN, Physics and Information Technology
SHE, XIAOPING, Life Science
SUN, RUNGUANG, Physics and Information Technology
TANG, YIGONG, History and Civilization
TIAN, CHENRUI, Life Science
TIAN, JIANRONG, Educational Science
WANG, BO, Chemistry and Materials Science
WANG, CHENRUI, Food Engineering
WANG, GUOJUN, Mathematics and Information Science
WANG, HUI, History and Civilization
WANG, SHUANGHUAI, History and Civilization
WANG, WENLIANG, Chemistry and Materials Science
WANG, XIAOAN, Life Science
WANG, XIAOMING, Computer Science
WANG, XILI, Computer Science
WANG, XIN, Physics and Information Technology
WANG, YINGZONG, Physics and Information Technology
WANG, YINHUI, Computer Science
WANG, ZHEZHI, Life Science
WANG, ZHIWU, Chinese Language and Literature
WEI, GENGYUAN, Chinese Language and Literature
WEI, JIANGUO, Chinese Language and Literature
WEI, JUNFA, Chemistry and Materials Science
WU, BAOWEI, Mathematics and Information Science
WU, HONGBO, Mathematics and Information Science
WU, JIANHUA, Mathematics and Information Science
WU, YANSHENG, Chinese Language and Literature
WU, ZHENQIANG, Computer Science
XI, GENGSI, Life Science
XIAO, ZHENGHONG, History and Civilization

XING, XIANGDONG, Chinese Language and Literature
XUE, PINGSHUAN, History and Civilization
YANG, CUNTANG, History and Civilization
YANG, ENCHENG, Chinese Language and Literature
YANG, HEQING, Chemistry and Materials Science
YANG, HONGKE, Chinese Language and Literature
YANG, WANMIN, Physics and Information Technology
YANG, ZUPEI, Chemistry and Materials Science
YIN, SHENGPING, History and Civilization
YOU, XILIN, Chinese Language and Literature
YOU, XUQUN, Educational Science
YUAN, LIN, History and Civilization
ZANG, ZHEN, History and Civilization
ZHANG, CHENGXIAO, Chemistry and Materials Science
ZHANG, GUOJUN, Chinese Language and Literature
ZHANG, JIANHUA, Mathematics and Information Science
ZHANG, JIANMIN, Physics and Information Technology
ZHANG, JIANZHONG, Mathematics and Information Science
ZHANG, MAORONG, History and Civilization
ZHANG, XIAOLING, Chemistry and Materials Science
ZHANG, XINKE, Chinese Language and Literature
ZHANG, XUEZHONG, Chinese Language and Literature
ZHANG, YUHU, Chemistry and Materials Science
ZHANG, ZHIQI, Chemistry and Materials Science
ZHANG, ZHUJUN, Chemistry and Materials Science
ZHAO, BIN, Mathematics and Information Science
ZHAO, SHICHAO, History and Civilization
ZHAO, WANGQIN, Chinese Language and Literature
ZHENG, XINGWANG, Chemistry and Materials Science
ZHENG, ZHEMIN, Life Science
ZHOU, TIANYOU, History and Civilization

SHAANXI UNIVERSITY OF SCIENCE AND TECHNOLOGY

49 Renmin West Rd, Xianyang 712081, Shaanxi Province
Telephone: (910) 3579500
Internet: www.sust.edu.cn

Founded 1958
Academic year: September to July

Pres.: LUO HONGJIE
Vice-Pres.: CAO JUJIANG
Vice-Pres.: CUI JIHUA
Vice-Pres.: SHEN YIDING
Vice-Pres.: ZHANG MEIYUN
Head of Graduate Dept: ZHANG XIAOLEI
Librarian: GAO DONGQIANG

Number of teachers: 900
Number of students: 18,000

Publications: *Journal* (6 a year), *The Future* (6 a year)

DEANS

College of Chemistry and Chemical Engineering: ZHANG GUANGHUA
College of Computer and Information Engineering: CHEN HUA
College of Design: YANG JUNSHUN
College of Electrical and Electronic Engineering: MENG YANJING
College of Electromechanical Engineering: DANG XINAN
College of Life Sciences and Engineering: CHEN HE
College of Management: YAN YUJIE
College of Materials Science and Engineering: WANG XIUFENG
College of Paper Manufacture Engineering: ZHANG MEIYUN
College of Resources and the Environment: MA JIANZHONG
College of Science: LIN XIAOLIN
College of Vocational Technology (Xian): LI WENHAN
College of Vocational Technology (Xianyan): ZHANG WEIPING
Department of Foreign Languages: LI XIAOHONG

PROFESSORS

CHEN, HE, Life Sciences and Engineering
CHEN, HUA, Computer and Information Engineering
CHEN, JUNZHI, Chemistry and Chemical Engineering
CHEN, MANRU, Design
CHEN, TAILUN, Science
CHENG, FENGXIA, Resources and the Environment
DANG, HONGSHE, Electrical and Electronic Engineering
DANG, SISHAN, Science
DANG, XIN-AN, Electromechanical Engineering
DONG, WENBIN, Life Sciences and Engineering
DU, RUIQING, Foreign Languages
GAN, JIANZHI, Design
GONG, TAISHENG, Resources and the Environment
HOU, ZAIEN, Science
LI, GUOXING, Science
LI, LINSHENG, Chemistry and Chemical Engineering
LI, XI, Electrical and Electronic Engineering
LI, XIAORUI, Chemistry and Chemical Engineering
LI, ZHONGJIN, Chemistry and Chemical Engineering
LIN, XIAOLIN, Computer and Information Engineering
LIU, SHUXING, Life Sciences and Engineering
LU, JIALI, Life Sciences and Engineering
LU, XINGFANG, Resources and the Environment
LUO, CANGXUE, Life Sciences and Engineering
LUO, HONGJIE, Materials Science and Engineering
MA, JIANZHONG, Resources and the Environment
MENG, YANJING, Electrical and Electronic Engineering
MIAO, HONGYAN, Materials Science and Engineering
NING, DUO, Electrical and Electronic Engineering
QI, XIANGJUN, Life Sciences and Engineering
QIANG, XIHUAI, Resources and the Environment
SHAN, JINGMIN, Design
SHEN, YIDING, Chemistry and Chemical Engineering
SONG, HONGXIN, Life Sciences and Engineering
SUN, YU, Electrical and Electronic Engineering
TIAN, SANDE, Life Sciences and Engineering
WANG, DEZHONG, Design
WANG, FENG, Materials Science and Engineering
WANG, HONGRU, Resources and the Environment
WANG, JIANGEN, Resources and the Environment
WANG, LIANJIE, Life Sciences and Engineering
WANG, MENGXIAO, Electrical and Electronic Engineering
WANG, QUANJIE, Resources and the Environment
WANG, XIUFENG, Materials Science and Engineering
WANG, XUECHUAN, Resources and the Environment
XU, JIANZHONG, Foreign Languages
XU, MUDAN, Life Sciences and Engineering
YANG, JIANZHOU, Chemistry and Chemical Engineering
YANG, JUNSHUN, Design
YU, CONGZHEN, Resources and the Environment
YU, DAYUAN, Electrical and Electronic Engineering
ZHANG, CHUANBO, Resources and the Environment
ZHANG, GUANGHUA, Chemistry and Chemical Engineering
ZHANG, XIAOLEI, Resources and the Environment
ZHANG, ZHENGXI, Computer and Information Engineering
ZHENG, ENRANG, Electrical and Electronic Engineering
ZHOU, LIAN, Materials Science and Engineering
ZHU, ZHENFENG, Materials Science and Engineering

SHANDONG AGRICULTURAL UNIVERSITY

61 Dai Zong St, Taian 271018, Shandong Province
Telephone: (538) 8242291
E-mail: xb@sdau.cdu.cn
Internet: www.sdau.edu.cn

Founded 1906
Dept of Education of Shandong control
Academic year: September to July

Pres.: WEN FUJIANG
Vice-Pres.: DONG SHUTING
Vice-Pres.: YAO LAICHANG
Vice-Pres.: ZHANG JINGHE
Vice-Pres.: ZHANG XIANSHENG
Head of Graduate Dept: WANG ZHENLIN
Librarian: ZHANG XIANIQI

Number of teachers: 1,151
Number of students: 20,000

Publications: *Journal* (natural sciences, 4 a year), *Journal* (social sciences, 4 a year), *Shandong Journal of Animal Husbandry and Veterinary Science* (6 a year)

DEANS

College of Agricultural Resources and Environment: SHI YANXI
College of Agronomy: WANG HONGGANG
College of Animal Technology: TAN JINGHE
College of Chemistry and Materials Science: ZHOU JIE
College of Economy and Management: HU JILIAN
College of Food Science and Engineering: DONG HAIZHOU
College of Foreign Languages: LI ZHILING
College of Forestry: MU ZHIMEI
College of Horticulture: WANG XIUFENG
College of Humanities and Law: SUN YANQUAN
College of Hydrology and Civil Engineering: LIU FUSHENG
College of Information Science and Technology: WANG YUNCHENG
College of Life Sciences: ZHENG CHENGCHAO
College of Mechanical and Electronic Engineering: ZHENG WEI
College of Plant Protection: LI DUOCHUAN
College of Science: ZHOU JIE

PROFESSORS

AI, SHIYUN, Chemistry and Materials Science
CAI, TONGJIE, Animal Technology
CHANG, WEISHAN, Animal Technology
CHEN, XUESEN, Horticulture
CHENG, SHUHAN, Information Science and Technology
CUI, DECAI, Life Sciences
CUI, WEI, Humanities and Law
CUI, WEIZHENG, Forestry
CUI, YANSHUN, Animal Technology
CUI, ZHIZHONG, Animal Technology
DIAO, YOUXIANG, Animal Technology
DING, AIYUN, Plant Protection
DING, SHIFEI, Information Science and Technology
DONG, HAIZHOU, Food Science and Engineering
DONG, JINLING, Economy and Management
DONG, SHUTING, Agronomy
DU, SHOUJUN, Humanities and Law
FAN, WEIXING, Animal Technology
FAN, ZHICHENG, Horticulture
FENG, CHENGMING, Electromechanical Engineering
FENG, YONGJUN, Agricultural Resources and Environment
GAO, HUA, Information Science and Technology
GAO, HUA, Science
GAO, HUIYUAN, Life Sciences
GAO, QINGRONG, Agronomy
GAO, RONGQI, Agronomy
GUANGLIANG, DONGYE, Agricultural Resources and Environment
GUO, HUABEI, Information Science and Technology
GUO, HUABEI, Science
GUO, XINMIN, Electromechanical Engineering
HA, YIMING, Science
HE, MINGRONG, Agronomy
HU, CHANGHAO, Agronomy
HU, JILIAN, Economy and Management
HU, YANJI, Agronomy
JIANG, LIN, Chemistry and Materials Science
JIANG, YONGBIN, Economy and Management
JIN, XIANG, Chemistry and Materials Science
KANG, JINGFENG, Electromechanical Engineering
KONG, LINGRANG, Agronomy
LI, ANFEI, Agronomy
LI, DEQUAN, Life Sciences
LI, DUOCHUAN, Plant Protection
LI, FUCHANG, Animal Technology
LI, JIRONG, Horticulture
LI, JIYE, Hydrology and Civil Engineering
LI, QIANG, Plant Protection
LI, QINGQI, Agronomy
LI, RUXIN, Electromechanical Engineering
LI, TONGSHU, Animal Technology
LI, XIANGDONG, Agronomy
LI, XIANGDONG, Plant Protection
LI, XIANLI, Horticulture
LI, ZENGJIA, Agronomy
LI, ZHAOHUI, Plant Protection
LI, ZHENSHENG, Plant Protection
LIANG, XUETIAN, Hydrology and Civil Engineering
LIN, HAI, Animal Technology
LIN, HONGXIAO, Hydrology and Civil Engineering
LIN, QUANYE, Forestry
LING, CHENGHOU, Electromechanical Engineering
LIU, CHUANBAO, Hydrology and Civil Engineering
LIU, CHUNSHENG, Agricultural Resources and Environment
LIU, FUSHENG, Hydrology and Civil Engineering
LIU, KAIQI, Plant Protection
LIU, LIANWE, Science
LIU, LIANWEI, Chemistry and Materials Science
LIU, SHIDANG, Animal Technology
LIU, XIAOGUANG, Plant Protection
LIU, YAN, Foreign Languages
LIU, ZHONGXIANG, Animal Technology
LU, FUSUI, Chemistry and Materials Science
LU, FUSUI, Science
LUO, WANCHUN, Plant Protection
MA, SHUSHENG, Hydrology and Civil Engineering
MENG, QINGWEI, Life Sciences
MENG, XIANGDONG, Horticulture
MIAO, LIANG, Information Science and Technology
MU, LIYI, Plant Protection
MU, ZHIMEI, Forestry
NIE, JUNHUA, Agricultural Resources and Environment
PANG, QINGJIANG, Hydrology and Civil Engineering
PEIZHENG, ZHANG, Food Science and Engineering
QI, SHUJUN, Foreign Languages
QU, XIANGJIN, Science
SHAN, LUN, Agronomy
SHEN, XIANG, Horticulture
SHI, JIANMIN, Economy and Management
SHI, PEI, Agronomy
SHI, YANXI, Agricultural Resources and Environment
SHU, HUAIRUI, Horticulture
SHUHAN, CHENG, Science
SONG, JIANCHENG, Agronomy
SU, LANZHEN, Agronomy
SUN, MINGGAO, Forestry
SUN, XUGEN, Forestry
SUN, YANQUAN, Humanities and Law
SUN, ZHONGXU, Horticulture
TAN, JINGHE, Animal Technology
TIAN, BO, Plant Protection
TIAN, JICHUN, Agronomy
TIAN, QIZHUO, Agronomy
WAN, JIACHUAN, Economy and Management
WAN, YONGSHAN, Agronomy
WANG, DECHUN, Economy and Management
WANG, HANZHONG, Life Sciences
WANG, HONGGANG, Agronomy
WANG, HONGMO, Economy and Management
WANG, HUIMING, Electromechanical Engineering
WANG, KAIYUN, Plant Protection
WANG, LIQIN, Horticulture
WANG, SHUYING, Animal Technology
WANG, XIANZE, Life Sciences
WANG, XIUFENG, Horticulture
WANG, YUNCHENG, Information Science and Technology
WANG, YUNCHENG, Science
WANG, ZELI, Life Sciences
WANG, ZHENLIN, Agronomy
WANG, ZHONGHUA, Animal Technology
WEI, JIANGCHUN, Plant Protection
WEN, FUJIANG, Life Sciences
XING, SHIYAN, Forestry
XU, HONGFU, Plant Protection
XU, KUN, Horticulture
XU, WEIAN, Plant Protection
XUE, XINGLI, Economy and Management
XUESONG, HUANG, Food Science and Engineering
YAN, YANCHUN, Life Sciences
YAN, ZHENYUAN, Hydrology and Civil Engineering
YANG, DI, Humanities and Law
YANG, HONGQIANG, Horticulture
YANG, JIHUA, Forestry
YANG, QUANMING, Animal Technology
YANG, XUECHENG, Economy and Management
YANG, ZAIBIN, Animal Technology
YIN, XIANGCHU, Plant Protection
YIN, XUNHE, Animal Technology
YIN, YANPING, Agronomy
YU, SONGLIE, Agronomy
YU, XIANCHANG, Horticulture
YU, YIMIN, Hydrology and Civil Engineering
YU, YUANJIE, Agronomy
YU, ZHENWEN, Agronomy
YUE, YONGSHENG, Animal Technology
ZENG, YONGQING, Animal Technology
ZHAI, HENG, Horticulture
ZHANG, CHUNQING, Agronomy
ZHANG, GUANGMIN, Plant Protection
ZHANG, LIANGCHENG, Hydrology and Civil Engineering
ZHANG, MIN, Agricultural Resources and Environment
ZHANG, TIANYU, Plant Protection
ZHANG, XIANSHENG, Life Sciences
ZHANG, XIAOHUI, Electromechanical Engineering
ZHANG, ZHIGUO, Agricultural Resources and Environment
ZHAO, GENGXING, Agricultural Resources and Environment
ZHAO, HONGKUN, Animal Technology
ZHAO, LANYONG, Forestry
ZHAO, TANFANG, Agronomy
ZHENG, CHENGCHAO, Life Sciences
ZHENG, GUOSHENG, Life Sciences
ZHOU, JIE, Chemistry and Materials Science
ZHOU, JIE, Science
ZHOU, YANPING, Economy and Management
ZHU, FENGGANG, Chemistry and Materials Science
ZHU, FENGGANG, Science
ZHU, LUSHENG, Agricultural Resources and Environment
ZHU, RUILIANG, Animal Technology
ZOU, QI, Life Sciences

SHANDONG INSTITUTE OF ECONOMICS

4 East Yanzishan Rd, Jinan 250014, Shandong

Telephone: (531) 8934161

Internet: www.china-sd.com/business/sdjjxy/home2e.htm

Founded 1958

Pres.: Prof. HU JIJIAN
Vice-Pres: LI RENQUAN
Vice-Pres: Prof. LIU SHIFAN
Vice-Pres: Prof. REN HUI
Librarian: LI ZIRUI

Number of teachers: 322
Number of students: 2,118

Publications: *Accountant*, *Shandong Economy*, *Statistics and Management*

SHANDONG UNIVERSITY

Shanda Nanlu, Jinan 250100, Shandong Province

Telephone: (531) 8364701

Internet: www.sdu.edu.cn

Founded 1901

Min. of Education control

Academic year: September to July

Pres.: ZHAN TAO
Vice-Pres.: FAN HONGJIAN
Vice-Pres.: FANG HONGJIAN
Vice-Pres.: HU JIACHEN
Vice-Pres.: LI CHENGJUN
Vice-Pres.: WANG QILONG
Vice-Pres.: YU XIUPING
Vice-Pres.: ZHANG YONGBING
Head of Graduate Dept: WANG QILONG
Librarian: SU WEIZHI

Number of teachers: 3,154
Number of students: 50,000

Publications: *Folk Custom Research* (4 a year), *Journal of Literature, History and Philosophy* (6 a year), *Journal of Shandong University* (edns of engineering science, health science, natural sciences, philosophy and social sciences, 6 a year), *Studies of Zhouyi* (6 a year), *Young Thinker* (6 a year)

DEANS

School of Business Administration: XU XIANGYI
School of Chemistry and Chemical Engineering: JIANG JIANZHUANG
School of Civil Engineering: CAO SHENGLE
School of Computer Science and Technology: MENG XIANGXU
School of Continuing Education: ZHUANG PING
School of Control Science and Engineering: JIA LEI
School of Dentistry: YANG PISHAN
School of Economics: ZANG XUHENG
School of Electrical Engineering: ZHAO JIANGUO
School of Energy and Power Engineering: PAN JIHONG
School of Environmental Science and Engineering: GAO BAOYU
School of Fine Arts: LI XIAOFENG
School of Foreign Languages and Literature: WANG SHOUYUAN
School of History and Culture: WANG YUJI
School of Information Science and Engineering: YUAN DONGFENG
School of Law: CHEN JINZHAO
School of Life Sciences: QU YINBO
School of Literature and Journalism: CHEN YAN
School of Marxist Theory of Education: ZHOU XIANGJUN
School of Materials Science and Engineering: JIANG MINHUA
School of Mathematics: LIU JIANYA
School of Mechanical Engineering: LI JIANFENG
School of Medicine: ZHANG YUN
School of Nursing: LOU FENGLAN
School of Pharmacy: LOU HONGXIANG
School of Philosophy and Social Development: FU YOUDE
School of Physics and Microelectronics: XIE SHIJIE
School of Political Science and Public Administration: LIU YUAN
School of Public Health: ZHAOS ZHONGTANG

PROFESSORS

BAI, ZENGLIANG, Life Sciences
BAO, SITAO, Literature and Journalism
BAO, XIAOMING, Life Sciences
BAO, YIFEI, Civil Engineering
BIAN, XIUFANG, Materials Science and Engineering
BU, YUXIANG, Chemistry and Chemical Engineering
CAI, LUZHONG, Information Science and Engineering
CAI, ZHENGTING, Chemistry and Chemical Engineering
CAO, CHENGBO, Chemistry and Chemical Engineering
CAO, QINGJIE, Mathematics
CAO, SHENGLE, Civil Engineering
CHAO, ZHONGCHEN, History and Culture
CHEN, CHUANZHONG, Materials Science and Engineering
CHEN, DAIRONG, Chemistry and Chemical Engineering
CHEN, GUANJUN, Life Sciences
CHEN, HONG, Foreign Languages and Literature
CHEN, JIGUANG, Civil Engineering
CHEN, KAOSHAN, Life Sciences
CHEN, LIANBI, Medicine
CHEN, QINGLAI, Civil Engineering
CHEN, SHANGSHENG, History and Culture
CHEN, SHAOZHU, Mathematics
CHEN, SHENHAO, Chemistry and Chemical Engineering
CHEN, XIAO, Chemistry and Chemical Engineering
CHEN, XISHEN, Materials Science and Engineering
CHEN, YAN, Literature and Journalism
CHEN, ZENGJING, Mathematics
CHEN, ZHIJUN, Business Administration
CHEN, ZIAN, History and Culture
CHENG, XINGKUI, Physics and Microelectronics
CHENG, ZHAOLIN, Mathematics
CHI, ZHENMING, Life Sciences
CONG, YAPING, Foreign Languages and Literature
CUI, DAYONG, History and Culture
CUI, XI, Public Health
CUI, XING, Medicine
CUI, ZHAOJIE, Environmental Science and Engineering
DING, RONGGUI, Business Administration
DING, SHILIANG, Physics and Microelectronics
DING, SHILIANG, Chemistry and Chemical Engineering
DING, YUANMING, Philosophy and Social Development
DUAN, QI, Mathematics
EHRLICH, M. A., Philosophy and Social Development
FAN, JINXUE, Law
FAN, XIULING, Business Administration
FANG, HUI, History and Culture
FANG, LEI, Political Science and Public Administration
FENG, DACHENG, Chemistry and Chemical Engineering
FENG, DIANMEI, Law
FENG, MEILI, Nursing
FENG, SHENGYU, Chemistry and Chemical Engineering
FU, YONGJUN, Philosophy and Social Development
FU, YOUDE, Philosophy and Social Development
GAN, YING, Business Administration
GAO, BAOYU, Chemistry and Chemical Engineering
GAO, BAOYU, Environmental Science and Engineering
GAO, JIANGUO, Philosophy and Social Development
GAO, PEIJI, Life Sciences
GAO, RUWEI, Physics and Microelectronics
GAO, YINGMAO, Medicine
GAO, ZHENMING, Information Science and Engineering
GE, BENYI, Literature and Journalism
GENG, HAORAN, Materials Science and Engineering
GENG, JIANHUA, Literature and Journalism
GENG, ZUNJING, Civil Engineering
GONG, YAOQIN, Medicine
GU, LUANZHAI, History and Culture
GU, QINGMIN, Medicine
GU, YUEZHU, Chemistry and Chemical Engineering
GUAN, SHAOJI, History and Culture
GUAN, XIAOJUN, Materials Science and Engineering
GUO, DAJUN, Mathematics
GUO, JIDE, Foreign Languages and Literature
GUO, YANLI, Literature and Journalism
HAN, SHENGHAO, Physics and Microelectronics
HAO, AIYOU, Chemistry and Chemical Engineering
HAO, JINGCHENG, Chemistry and Chemical Engineering
HE, MAO, Physics and Microelectronics
HE, ZHONGHUA, Philosophy and Social Development
HONG, XIAOGUANG, Computer Science and Technology
HOU, WANGUO, Chemistry and Chemical Engineering
HOU, XUEYUAN, Information Science and Engineering
HU, JIFAN, Physics and Microelectronics
HU, PEICHU, Mathematics
HU, WEICHENG, Medicine
HU, WEIQING, History and Culture
HU, WENRONG, Environmental Science and Engineering
HU, XINSHENG, History and Culture
HU, ZHENGMING, Business Administration
HUANG, FAYOU, Literature and Journalism
HUANG, FENG, Life Sciences
HUANG, QINGZHI, Political Science and Public Administration
HUANG, SHENG, Civil Engineering
HUANG, WANHUA, Literature and Journalism
HUANG, XIRONG, Chemistry and Chemical Engineering
JI, AIGUO, Pharmacy
JI, FAHAN, Literature and Journalism
JI, PEIRONG, Political Science and Public Administration
JI, YUNXIA, Foreign Languages and Literature
JIA, LEI, Control Science and Engineering
JIA, ZHIPING, Computer Science and Technology
JIANG, BAOFA, Public Health
JIANG, JIANZHUANG, Chemistry and Chemical Engineering
JIANG, MINHUA, Materials Science and Engineering
JIANG, QINGLI, Environmental Science and Engineering
JIANG, SHENG, History and Culture
JIANG, SHOULI, Mathematics
JIANG, YONG, Philosophy and Social Development
JIN, WENRUI, Chemistry and Chemical Engineering
KONG, FANJIN, Literature and Journalism
KONG, JIAN, Life Sciences
KONG, LINGREN, History and Culture
LI, CHUANLIN, Computer Science and Technology
LI, DAIBIN, Control Science and Engineering
LI, DAXING, Mathematics
LI, FENGXIAN, Environmental Science and Engineering
LI, GANZUO, Chemistry and Chemical Engineering
LI, GUOJUN, Mathematics
LI, HONGWEI, Life Sciences
LI, HUA, Physics and Microelectronics
LI, JIANFENG, Literature and Journalism
LI, JIE, Public Health
LI, JINGZHOU, Computer Science and Technology
LI, JINYU, Physics and Microelectronics
LI, JUN, Business Administration
LI, MUSEN, Materials Science and Engineering
LI, QIN, Philosophy and Social Development
LI, QINGZHONG, Computer Science and Technology
LI, QIQIANG, Control Science and Engineering
LI, SHAOMING, Foreign Languages and Literature
LI, SHUCAI, Civil Engineering
LI, WEI, History and Culture
LI, XIAO, History and Culture
LI, XIAOYAN, Chemistry and Chemical Engineering
LI, XUEQING, Computer Science and Technology
LI, XUEZHEN, Foreign Languages and Literature
LI, YAJIANG, Materials Science and Engineering
LI, YUCHEN, Computer Science and Technology
LI, YUEZHONG, Life Sciences
LI, ZHENZHONG, Medicine
LI, ZHONGYOU, Materials Science and Engineering
LIANG, HUIXING, Law
LIANG, ZUOTANG, Physics and Microelectronics
LIAO, QUN, Literature and Journalism
LIE, JIE, Philosophy and Social Development
LIE, JIE, Computer Science and Technology

LIN, JIANQIANG, Life Sciences
LIN, JUREN, Philosophy and Social Development
LIN, LU, Mathematics
LIN, MING, Law
LIN, XINYING, Public Health
LIU, BAOYU, Law
LIU, CHENGBO, Chemistry and Chemical Engineering
LIU, FENGJUN, History and Culture
LIU, GANG, Business Administration
LIU, GUIZHEN, Mathematics
LIU, HONGWEI, Business Administration
LIU, JIANYA, Mathematics
LIU, JIAZHUANG, Mathematics
LIU, JU, Information Science and Engineering
LIU, KAI, Medicine
LIU, LUPENG, Philosophy and Social Development
LIU, PING, History and Culture
LIU, RONGXING, Computer Science and Technology
LIU, SHIGUO, Law
LIU, SHUMEI, Foreign Languages and Literature
LIU, SHUTANG, Control Science and Engineering
LIU, SHUWEI, Medicine
LIU, TIANLU, History and Culture
LIU, XIANXI, Medicine
LIU, XINLI, Philosophy and Social Development
LIU, YIHUA, Physics and Microelectronics
LIU, YU-AN, Political Science and Public Administration
LIU, YUFENG, History and Culture
LIU, YUNGANG, Control Science and Engineering
LIU, YUTIAN, Electrical Engineering
LIU, ZHAOLI, Mathematics
LIU, ZHAOXU, Nursing
LIU, ZHENQIAN, Foreign Languages and Literature
LIU, ZHIYU, Medicine
LIU, ZONGLIN, Chemistry and Chemical Engineering
LOU, FENGLAN, Nursing
LOU, HONGXIANG, Pharmacy
LU, JUNWEI, History and Culture
LU, WEIZHONG, Foreign Languages and Literature
LU, YAO, History and Culture
LUAN, FENGSHI, History and Culture
LUO, FUTENG, Literature and Journalism
MA, FENGSHU, Political Science and Public Administration
MA, GUANGHAI, Philosophy and Social Development
MA, HONGLEI, Physics and Microelectronics
MA, JUN, Computer Science and Technology
MA, LIXIAN, Medicine
MA, LONGQIAN, Literature and Journalism
MA, RUIFANG, Literature and Journalism
MA, SHAOHAN, Mathematics
MEI, LIANGMO, Physics and Microelectronics
MENG, LIRONG, Computer Science and Technology
MENG, XIANGCAI, History and Culture
MENG, XIANGXU, Computer Science and Technology
MIAO, JUNYING, Life Sciences
MIAO, QINGHAI, Physics and Microelectronics
MIAO, RUNTIAN, Philosophy and Social Development
MIAO, XINGWEI, Foreign Languages and Literature
MIN, GUANGHUI, Materials Science and Engineering
MO, WENCHUAN, Business Administration
NING, FEI, Computer Science and Technology
NIU, YUNQING, Literature and Journalism
PAN, AILING, Business Administration
PANG, SHOUYING, Literature and Journalism
PENG, SHIGE, Mathematics
PENG, YUHUA, Information Science and Engineering
PENG, ZHIZHONG, Business Administration
QI, GUIJIE, Business Administration
QI, YANPING, Law
QIAN, ZENGYI, Literature and Journalism
QIAO, YIZHENG, Control Science and Engineering
QIAO, YOUMEI, History and Culture
QU, YINBO, Life Sciences
REN, DENGYI, Materials Science and Engineering
REN, QUAN, Information Science and Engineering
REN, XIANGHONG, History and Culture
RUI, HONGXING, Mathematics
SHANG, QINGSEN, Civil Engineering
SHANG, YU, Philosophy and Social Development
SHAO, LIHUA, Public Health
SHENG, YUQI, Literature and Journalism
SHI, BING, Computer Science and Technology
SHI, KAIQUAN, Mathematics
SHI, LIANYUN, Business Administration
SHI, YUMING, Mathematics
SONG, GANG, Medicine
SUI, QINGMEI, Control Science and Engineering
SUN, DEJUN, Chemistry and Chemical Engineering
SUN, HONGJIAN, Chemistry and Chemical Engineering
SUN, JILIN, Literature and Journalism
SUN, KANGNING, Materials Science and Engineering
SUN, NAZHENG, Mathematics
SUN, SIXIU, Chemistry and Chemical Engineering
SUN, TONGJING, Control Science and Engineering
SUN, WENSHENG, Medicine
SUN, XINQIANG, Law
SUN, YINGCHUN, Foreign Languages and Literature
SUN, ZIMEI, Literature and Journalism
TAN, HAOZHE, Literature and Journalism
TAN, SHIBAO, History and Culture
TAN, YEBANG, Chemistry and Chemical Engineering
TANG, ZIHENG, Literature and Journalism
TIAN, GUOHUI, Control Science and Engineering
TIAN, XUELEI, Materials Science and Engineering
WAN, JIANCHENG, Computer Science and Technology
WANG, CHENGRUI, Physics and Microelectronics
WANG, CHUNLEI, Physics and Microelectronics
WANG, DEGANG, Business Administration
WANG, FENGSHAN, Pharmacy
WANG, FUTAI, Business Administration
WANG, HAIYANG, Computer Science and Technology
WANG, HUAIJING, Medicine
WANG, JIANMIN, Political Science and Public Administration
WANG, JIANWU, Chemistry and Chemical Engineering
WANG, JIAYE, Mathematics
WANG, JIEZHEN, Public Health
WANG, JINFENG, Physics and Microelectronics
WANG, JINXING, Life Sciences
WANG, JIYANG, Materials Science and Engineering
WANG, JUNJU, Foreign Languages and Literature
WANG, KEMING, Physics and Microelectronics
WANG, KEMING, Materials Science and Engineering
WANG, LILI, Foreign Languages and Literature
WANG, LIPING, Law
WANG, PEIYUAN, Literature and Journalism
WANG, PENG, Life Sciences
WANG, PING, Literature and Journalism
WANG, QILONG, Chemistry and Chemical Engineering
WANG, QING, Civil Engineering
WANG, QINGYOU, Information Science and Engineering
WANG, QUANJUAN, Civil Engineering
WANG, RENQING, Life Sciences
WANG, RUBIN, Pharmacy
WANG, SHANBO, Philosophy and Social Development
WANG, SHAOXING, Political Science and Public Administration
WANG, SUMEI, Public Health
WANG, TIANHONG, Life Sciences
WANG, WEI, Mathematics
WANG, WENCHENG, Literature and Journalism
WANG, WENQIAO, Mathematics
WANG, XIAOSHU, Literature and Journalism
WANG, XIAOYI, History and Culture
WANG, XIAOYUN, Mathematics
WANG, XINCHUN, Philosophy and Social Development
WANG, XINGYUAN, Business Administration
WANG, XINNIAN, Physics and Microelectronics
WANG, XUEDIAN, History and Culture
WANG, YIMING, Business Administration
WANG, YOUZHI, Civil Engineering
WANG, YUJI, History and Culture
WANG, YUZHEN, Control Science and Engineering
WANG, ZHIFU, Materials Science and Engineering
WANG, ZHIYU, Public Health
WANG, ZHOUMING, Literature and Journalism
WANG, ZUNONG, Life Sciences
WANG, ZUOCHENG, Materials Science and Engineering
WEI, ZHONGLI, Mathematics
WEN, SHULIN, Materials Science and Engineering
WU, AIHUA, Business Administration
WU, JIAN, Chemistry and Chemical Engineering
WU, RUNTING, Literature and Journalism
WU, XIAOJUAN, Information Science and Engineering
WU, YAOHUA, Control Science and Engineering
WU, YOUSHI, Materials Science and Engineering
WU, ZHEN, Mathematics
XIA, GUANGMIN, Life Sciences
XIA, HAIRUI, Physics and Microelectronics
XIA, YUEYUAN, Physics and Microelectronics
XIANG, FENGNING, Life Sciences
XIAO, JINMING, Law
XIAO, MIN, Life Sciences
XIAO, XIA, Foreign Languages and Literature
XIE, HONGXIANG, Literature and Journalism
XIE, HUI, Law
XIE, KEQIN, Public Health
XIE, QUBING, Physics and Microelectronics
XIE, SHIJIE, Physics and Microelectronics
XIONG, ZHIPING, Civil Engineering
XU, BIN, Materials Science and Engineering
XU, CHAO, Literature and Journalism
XU, DONG, Materials Science and Engineering
XU, GUIFA, Public Health
XU, GUIYING, Chemistry and Chemical Engineering
XU, MINGYU, Mathematics
XU, PING, Life Sciences
XU, QIULIANG, Computer Science and Technology
XU, WENFANG, Pharmacy
XU, XIANGYI, Business Administration
XU, YANSHENG, Civil Engineering
YAN, BINGGANG, Philosophy and Social Development
YANG, DANPING, Mathematics
YANG, HUIXIN, Business Administration
YANG, JINGHE, Chemistry and Chemical Engineering

YANG, LIANZHONG, Mathematics
YANG, LUHUI, Political Science and Public Administration
YANG, RUIZHI, Literature and Journalism
YANG, XUEJIN, Business Administration
YANG, YANZHAO, Chemistry and Chemical Engineering
YI, HONGXUN, Mathematics
YIN, YANSHENG, Materials Science and Engineering
YU, GUANG, Business Administration
YU, GUANGHAI, History and Culture
YU, HONGXIA, Public Health
YU, XIUPING, Medicine
YUAN, DONGFENG, Information Science and Engineering
YUAN, SHISHUO, Literature and Journalism
YUAN, YIRANG, Mathematics
YUE, QINGYAN, Environmental Science and Engineering
ZENG, GUANGZHOU, Computer Science and Technology
ZENG, ZHENYU, History and Culture
ZHAN, TAO, Mathematics
ZHANG, CAIMING, Computer Science and Technology
ZHANG, CHANGKAI, Life Sciences
ZHANG, CHENGHUI, Control Science and Engineering
ZHANG, CHUNGUANG, Chemistry and Chemical Engineering
ZHANG, CHUNLING, Public Health
ZHANG, HENG, Medicine
ZHANG, HUAZHONG, Computer Science and Technology
ZHANG, JIANYE, Medicine
ZHANG, JINLONG, History and Culture
ZHANG, JUREN, Life Sciences
ZHANG, KELI, Literature and Journalism
ZHANG, LIHENG, History and Culture
ZHANG, LINING, Medicine
ZHANG, NAIJIAN, Physics and Microelectronics
ZHANG, PEILIN, Physics and Microelectronics
ZHANG, PEIZHONG, Civil Engineering
ZHANG, QINGFAN, Control Science and Engineering
ZHANG, QINGZHU, Pharmacy
ZHANG, RUILIN, Physical Education
ZHANG, SHUNHUA, Mathematics
ZHANG, SHUXUE, History and Culture
ZHANG, SHUZHENG, Literature and Journalism
ZHANG, TAO, History and Culture
ZHANG, TIQIN, Business Administration
ZHANG, XIEN, Political Science and Public Administration
ZHANG, XINGYU, Information Science and Engineering
ZHANG, XIUMEI, Medicine
ZHANG, XIWEI, History and Culture
ZHANG, XUEJUN, Literature and Journalism
ZHANG, XUEYAO, Physics and Microelectronics
ZHANG, YULIN, Control Science and Engineering
ZHANG, YUZHEN, Life Sciences
ZHANG, YUZHONG, Life Sciences
ZHAO, AIGUO, History and Culture
ZHAO, BINGXIN, Business Administration
ZHAO, GUOQUN, Materials Science and Engineering
ZHAO, JIANGUO, Electrical Engineering
ZHAO, JINGHUA, Business Administration
ZHAO, SHENGZI, Information Science and Engineering
ZHAO, WEIMIN, Medicine
ZHAO, XIAOFAN, Life Sciences
ZHAO, ZHONGTANG, Public Health
ZHENG, CHUN, Literature and Journalism
ZHENG, FENGLAN, Literature and Journalism
ZHENG, LIQIANG, Chemistry and Chemical Engineering
ZHENG, PEIXIN, History and Culture
ZHENG, XUNZUO, Literature and Journalism
ZHONG, MAIYING, Control Science and Engineering
ZHONG, WEILIE, Physics and Microelectronics
ZHOU, GENYAN, Medicine
ZHOU, GUANGYUAN, History and Culture
ZHOU, HONGXING, Mathematics
ZHOU, LAIXIANG, Literature and Journalism
ZHOU, XIAOYU, History and Culture
ZHU, DAMING, Computer Science and Technology
ZHU, RUIFU, Materials Science and Engineering
ZHU, WEISHEN, Civil Engineering

SHANGHAI INTERNATIONAL STUDIES UNIVERSITY

550 Dalian Rd (W), 200083 Shanghai
Telephone: (21) 35373612
E-mail: fao@shisu.edu.cn
Internet: www.shisu.edu.cn

Founded 1949 as Foreign Language College, current name adopted 1994

Schools of humanities, international business, international finance and trade, international journalism, law, media and communication, social sciences

Pres.: CAO DEMING
Vice-Pres.: FENG QINGHUA
Vice-Pres.: ZHANG FENG
Vice-Pres.: YANG LI
Vice-Pres.: ZHOU CHENG

Library of 920,000 vols
Number of teachers: 1,305
Number of students: 10,343

Publications: *Arabian World* (4 a year), *Comparative Literature* (2 a year), *English Self-study* (12 a year), *Foreign Languages* (6 a year), *Foreign Language World* (4 a year), *International Survey* (4 a year), *Media in Foreign Language Instructions* (4 a year)

SHANGHAI JIAOTONG UNIVERSITY

1954 Hua Shan Rd, Shanghai 200030
Telephone: (21) 62812444
E-mail: wangxuanban@yahoo.com.cn
Internet: www.sjtu.edu.cn

Founded 1896
Academic year: September to July

Pres.: ZHANG JIE
Vice-Pres.: CHEN GANG
Vice-Pres.: LIN ZHONGQIN
Vice-Pres.: YE QUYUAN
Vice-Pres.: YIN JIE
Vice-Pres.: ZHANG SHIMIN
Vice-Pres.: ZHANG WENJUN
Vice-Pres.: ZHU ZHENGGANG
Librarian: CHEN ZHAONEN

Library of 1,826,000 vols
Number of teachers: 2,889
Number of students: 36,100 (incl. 18,100 postgraduates)

Publication: *Journal* (6 a year, also in English)

HEADS OF SCHOOLS

Department of Physical Education: SUN QILING
Department of Plasticity Technology: RUAN XUEYU
School of Chemistry and Chemical Engineering: TANG XIAOZHENG
School of Civil Engineering and Mechanics: LIU ZHENGXING
School of Electric Power Engineering: HOU ZHIJIAN
School of Electronics and Information Technology: XI YUGENG
School of Foreign Languages: ZHENG SHUTANG
School of Humanities and Social Sciences: YE DUNPING
School of Life Sciences and Technology: TANG ZHANGCHENG
School of Machinery Engineering: YAN JUNQI
School of Management: ZHANG XIANG
School of Materials Science and Engineering: WU JIANSHENG
School of Naval Architecture and Ocean Engineering: LI RUNPEI
School of Power and Energy Resources Engineering: XU JIJUN
School of Science: SHI ZHONGCI

SHANGHAI NORMAL UNIVERSITY

100 Guilin Rd, Nanjing 200234, Jiangsu Province
Telephone: (21) 64322881
Internet: www.shtu.edu.cn

Founded 1954
Academic year: September to July

Pres.: YU LIZHONG
Vice-Pres.: JIANG WEIYI
Vice-Pres.: LIU ZHIGANG
Vice-Pres.: LU JIANPING
Vice-Pres.: XIANG JIAXIANG
Librarian: CAO XU

Library of 2,600,000 vols
Number of teachers: 1,181
Number of students: 40,000

Publications: *Chinese University Academic Abstracts* (6 a year), *Journal* (6 a year)

DEANS

Architecture Engineering College: LIU JIANXIN
Engineering College of Machinery and Electronics Information: LIN XIAOYUN
Fine Arts College: XU WANGYAO
Life and Environmental Sciences College: LI HEXING
Mathematics and Science College: ZHANG JIZHOU
School of Arts: XIE JING
School of Commerce: FU HONGCHUN
School of Education: LU JIAMEI
School of European Culture and Trade: MAO XUNCHENG
School of Foreign Languages: GU DAXIN
School of Law and Politics: SHANG HONGRI
School of Literature: SUN XUN
School of Music: DAI DINGCHENG
Sports College: LU CHANGYA

PROFESSORS

CAI, LONGQUAN, Foreign Languages
CAO, TONG, Life and Environmental Sciences
CAO, XU, Literature
CEN, GUOZHEN, Education
CHEN, KEJIAN, Law and Politics
CHEN, MINGZHENG, Arts
CHEN, WEI, Literature
CHEN, WEIPING, Law and Politics
CHENG, XINGHUA, Foreign Languages
CHENG, ZHEHUAN, Law and Politics
DAI, DINGCHENG, Music
DENG, MINGDE, Foreign Languages
FAN, KAITAI, Literature
FAN, WUYUN, Literature
FANG, GUANGCHANG, Law and Politics
FEI, HELIANG, Mathematics and Science
FU, HONGCHUN, Commerce
GAN, FENG, Law and Politics
GAO, HUIZHU, Law and Politics
GAO, JIANHUA, Mathematics and Science
GU, DAXI, Foreign Languages
GU, HAIGEN, Education
HE, YUNFENG, Law and Politics
HONG, XIAOXIA, Law and Politics
HUANG, BAOHUA, Literature
JIA, HUANZHEN, Arts
JIANG, CHUANGUANG, Law and Politics
KANG, AISHI, Arts
LI, HEXING, Life and Environmental Sciences
LI, JIAHOU, Arts
LI, SHENG, Law and Politics
LI, SHI, Literature

LI, WEIHUI, Commerce
LI, WEIMING, Sports
LI, XIAOYUN, Machinery and Electronics Information Engineering
LI, YIZHEN, Life and Environmental Sciences
LI, ZHIGUO, Commerce
LIU, DANQING, Literature
LIU, JIANXIN, Architecture
LIU, YANYAN, Law and Politics
LU, CHANGYA, Sports
LU, JIAMEI, Education
LU, RUOPING, Arts
LU, RUZHAN, Literature
MA, DELING, Law and Politics
MEI, ZIHAN, Literature
MI, ZHENG, Arts
QI, LUYANG, Literature
REN, ZHONGLUN, Literature
SHANG, HONGRI, Law and Politics
SHAO, YONG, Literature
SHEN, HEBO, Life and Environmental Sciences
SHI, YONGBING, Mathematics and Science
SHUN, XUN, Literature
SUN, JINGRAO, Literature
SUN, XUSHENG, Sports
SUN, YUWEI, Law and Politics
TAN, WEIGUO, Foreign Languages
TANG, LIXING, Literature
TAO, BENYI, Literature
WANG, CUIYING, Sports
WANG, GUORONG, Mathematics and Science
WANG, JIREN, Literature
WANG, TIANQU, Literature
WANG, XIAODUN, Literature
WANG, XINQIU, Foreign Languages
WANG, YANMING, Mathematics and Science
WEI, SHIXIAN, Arts
WENG, MINHUA, Literature
WU, HONGLIN, Arts
WU, JINGDONG, Law and Politics
WU, JUNMING, Life and Environmental Sciences
WU, QUANXI, Life and Environmental Sciences
WU, XIAQIN, Life and Environmental Sciences
XIA, HUIXIAN, Education
XIE, LIMIN, Education
XU, SHIYI, Literature
XU, WEIHONG, Arts
XUE, HESHENG, Commerce
XUE, SIJIA, Life and Environmental Sciences
YAN, GWENHU, Literature
YANG, DONG, Sports
YANG, JIANLONG, Literature
YANG, ZHONGHUA, Mathematics and Science
YANG, ZHONGNAN, Life and Environmental Sciences
YE, HUANIAN, Foreign Languages
YE, HUANIAN, Literature
YU, XIBING, Life and Environmental Sciences
YUAN, BING, Literature
YUAN, FENG, Law and Politics
YUE, RONGXIAN, Mathematics and Science
ZHANG, JIZHOU, Mathematics and Science
ZHANG, ZIQIANG, Machinery and Electronics Information Engineering
ZHAO, XIAONAN, Arts
ZHENG, KELU, Literature
ZHOU, GENYU, Life and Environmental Sciences
ZHOU, ZHONGZHI, Law and Politics
ZHU, SHUNQUAN, Mathematics and Science
ZHU, XIANSHENG, Literature

SHANGHAI SECOND MEDICAL UNIVERSITY

280 S Chongqing Rd, Shanghai 200025
Telephone: (21) 63846590
E-mail: wxb@shsmu.edu.cn
Internet: www.shsmu.edu.cn

Founded 1952

Languages of instruction: Chinese, English, French
Academic year: September to July

Chancellor: FAN GUANRONG
Vice-Chancellor: Prof. CHEN ZHIXING
Vice-Chancellor: Prof. QIAN GUANXIANG
Vice-Chancellor: Prof. ZHUANG MENGHU
Vice-Chancellor: Assoc. Prof. ZHU ZHENGGANG
Registrar: Prof. CAI WEI
Librarian: Assoc. Prof. ZHANG WENHAO

Library of 420,000 vols
Number of teachers: 3,379
Number of students: 5,000

Publications: *Chinese Journal of Endocrinology and Metabolism* (in Chinese), *Journal of Clinical Paediatrics* (in Chinese), *Journal of Shanghai Second Medical University* (in Chinese and English), *Shanghai Journal of Immunology* (in Chinese)

DEANS

College of Basic Medical Sciences: Prof. LU YANG
Department of Social Sciences: XIANG YANG
Faculty of Clinical Medicine in Ren Ji Hospital: Prof. FAN GUANRONG
Faculty of Clinical Medicine in Rui Jin Hospital: Prof. LI HONGWEI
Faculty of Clinical Medicine in No. 6 People's Hospital: Prof. LIN FAXIONG
Faculty of Paediatrics and Clinical Medicine in Xin Hua Hospital: Prof. SHEN XIAOMIN
Health School: Assoc. Prof. WU XIANGQIAN
Junior Medical College in Bao Gang Hospital: JUN SHENGJI
School of Stomatology: Prof. ZHANG ZHIYUAN

SHANGHAI UNIVERSITY

99 Shangda Rd, 200444 Shanghai
Telephone: (21) 56331820
E-mail: cie@mail.shu.edu.cn
Internet: www.shu.edu.cn

Founded 1922

Colleges of continuing education, fine arts, int. exchange, science; schools of communications and information engineering, computer engineering and science, digital arts, economics, environmental and chemical engineering, film and TV arts and technology, foreign languages, law, liberal arts, life sciences, management, materials science and engineering, mechatronic engineering and automation, physical education, Sino-European school of social sciences, sociology and political science

Pres.: LUO HONGJIE
Vice-Pres.: LI YOUMEI
Vice-Pres.: YE ZHIMING
Vice-Pres.: WANG MIN
Vice-Pres.: TANG HAO
Vice-Pres.: WU MINGHONG

Library: 4m. vols
Number of teachers: 2,890
Number of students: 37,800

Publications: *Advances in Manufacturing* (4 a year), *Applied Mathematics and Mechanics* (12 a year, in English), *Journal of the Operations Research Society of China* (4 a year)

SHANGHAI UNIVERSITY OF FINANCE AND ECONOMICS

777 Guoding Rd, Shanghai 200433
Telephone: (21) 65903505
E-mail: wxb@mail.shufe.edu.cn
Internet: www.shufe.edu.cn

Founded 1917
Ministry of Education control
Academic year: September to July

Pres.: TAN MIN
Vice-Pres.: CONG SHUHAI
Vice-Pres.: HUANG LINFANG
Vice-Pres.: SUN ZHENG
Vice-Pres.: WANG HONGWEI
Vice-Pres.: ZHOU ZHONGFEI
Head of Graduate Dept: FENG ZHENGQUAN
Librarian: LI XIAOYE

Number of students: 20,000

Publications: *Economics and Management of Foreign Countries* (12 a year), *Higher Education of Finance and Economics* (4 a year), *Journal* (6 a year), *Journal of Finance and Economics* (12 a year)

DEANS

Department of Foreign Languages: WANG XIAOQUN
Department of Information Management: LIU LANJUAN
Department of Physical Education: CHEN XIAO
Department of Statistics: HAN XIAOLIANG
School of Accountancy: CHEN XINYUAN
School of Applied Mathematics: CHEN QIHONG
School of Economics: TIAN GUOQIANG
School of Finance: DAI GUOQIANG
School of Humanities: ZHANG XIONG
School of International Business Management: SUN HAIMING
School of Law: ZHOU ZHONGFEI
School of MBA Programmes: LUO ZUWANG
School of Public Economy Administration: JIANG HONG

PROFESSORS

BIAN, ZUWU, Statistics
CHANG, NING, Statistics
CHAO, GANGLING, Marketing
CHE, WEIHAN, International Economics
CHEN, HUIQIN, Statistics
CHEN, QIHONG, Applied Mathematics
CHEN, QIJIE, Marketing
CHEN, WENHAO, Accountancy
CHEN, XIAO, Physical Education
CHEN, XINKANG, Marketing
CHEN, XINYUAN, Accountancy
CHEN, YUN, Public Economy Administration
CHENG, ENFU, Economics
CHU, MINWEI, Public Economy Administration
CHU, YIYUN, Accountancy
CONG, SHUHAI, Public Economy Administration
DAI, GUOQIANG, Banking
DING, BANGKAI, Law
DONG, FENGGU, Statistics
DOU, JIANMING, Statistics
DU, XUNCHENG, Economics
FEI, FANGYU, International Finance
GAN, CHUNHUI, Industry Economics
GU, GUIDING, Applied Mathematics
GU, GUOZHU, Humanities
GUO, SHIZHENG, Public Economy Administration
GUO, YUDAN, International Trade
HAN, QING, Economics
HAN, XIAOLIANG, Statistics
HE, JIANMIN, Tourism Management
HE, YUCHANG, Economics
HU, JINGBEI, Economics
HU, YIJIAN, Public Economy Administration
HU, YIMING, Accountancy
HU, YONGGANG, Economics
HUO, WENWEN, Finance
JIANG, HONG, Public Economy Administration
JIANG, YIHONG, Accountancy
JIN, DEHUAN, Finance
LAN, YISHENG, International Trade
LI, XIAOYE, Humanities
LI, XIAOYU, Statistics
LI, XIN, Economics
LIANG, ZHIAN, Applied Mathematics
LIAO, YINLIN, Statistics
LIN, JUE, International Economics

LIU, HANLIANG, Statistics
LIU, LIJUAN, Resource Management
LIU, YONGMING, Banking
LU, PINYUE, Humanities
LU, SHIMIN, Banking
LU, WANZHONG, Statistics
LUO, ZUWANG, Humanities
MA, GUOXIAN, Public Economy Administration
MI, WENZHAN, Humanities
PAN, FEI, Accountancy
PEI, YIRAN, Humanities
PENG, JIAQIANG, Humanities
QI, ZHIXIANG, Humanities
QU, WEIDONG, International Finance
SHAO, JIANLI, Statistics
SHENG, BANGHE, Humanities
SHI, BINGCHAO, Banking
SHI, XIQUAN, International Finance
SU, JUNHE, Statistics
SUN, HAIMING, Industry Economics
SUN, YUNWU, Statistics
SUN, ZHENG, Accountancy
TAN, MIN, Economics
TAN, ZHENG, Information Management
TAO, TINGFANG, Tourism Management
WANG, DEFA, Statistics
WANG, HONGWEI, Public Economy Administration
WANG, HUILING, Statistics
WANG, LIMING, Statistics
WANG, LIYA, Foreign Languages
WANG, SONGNIAN, Accountancy
WANG, XIAOMING, Statistics
WANG, XIAOQUN, Foreign Languages
WANG, XINXIN, Marketing
WANG, XUEMIN, Statistics
WANG, YU, Business Management
WU, LONGSHENG, Resource Management
XI, JUNYANG, International Finance
XIA, JIANMING, Business Management
XIE, ZHIGANG, Finance
XU, DAJIAN, Humanities
XU, GUOXIANG, Statistics
XU, JIANPING, Humanities
XU, JINLIANG, Finance
XU, ZHENDAN, Accountancy
XUE, HUACHENG, Information Management
YAN, GUANGHUA, Business Management
YANG, DAKAI, Public Economy Administration
YANG, GONGPU, Industry Economics
YANG, JUNCHANG, Public Economy Administration
YANG, NAN, Statistics
YIN, CHENGYUAN, Applied Mathematics
YING, SHICHANG, Finance
YOU, JIARONG, Accountancy
YU, DINGWEI, Statistics
YU, ZHIYOU, Finance
YUAN, HONGQI, Accountancy
YUE, YAOXING, International Trade
ZAN, TINGQUAN, Information Management
ZHANG, CHUN, Accountancy
ZHANG, JUE, Humanities
ZHANG, MIAO, Statistics
ZHANG, MING, Accountancy
ZHANG, MINGFANG, Statistics
ZHANG, XIONG, Humanities
ZHANG, YAN, Humanities
ZHANG, YAOTING, Economics
ZHANG, YINJIE, Economics
ZHAO, JIANYONG, Accountancy
ZHAO, XIAOJU, Banking
ZHAO, XIAOLEI, Economics
ZHAO, XIAOSHENG, Foreign Languages
ZHOU, ZHONGFEI, Law
ZHU, BAOHUA, Economics
ZHU, GUOHUA, Industry Economics
ZHU, JIANZHONG, Statistics
ZHU, MINGXIONG, Statistics
ZHU, PINGFANG, Economics
ZHU, RONGEN, Accountancy
ZHU, YINGPING, Humanities
ZHU, ZHONGDI, International Economics

SHANTOU UNIVERSITY

243 University Rd, Shantou 515063, Guangdong Province
Telephone: (754) 2902350
Internet: www.stu.edu.cn

Founded 1981
provincial control
Academic year: September to July

Pres.: XU XIAOHU
Vice-Pres.: LI YUGUANG
Vice-Pres.: WU GUANGGUO
Vice-Pres.: XIANG BING
Vice-Pres.: XIAO ZELI
Vice-Pres.: ZHENG YI
Head of Graduate Dept: WANG ZHAN
Librarian: HUANG TING

Number of teachers: 630
Number of students: 12,868 (8,254 full-time, 4,614 part-time)

Publications: *Chinese Literature* (6 a year), *Journal* (4 a year), *Journal* (humanities and social sciences edition, 6 a year), *Journal* (natural science edition, 4 a year)

DEANS

College of Business: XUE YUNKUI
College of Engineering: GONG LEIGUANG
College of Law: ZHOU WEI
College of Literature: FENG SHANG
College of Medicine: LI YUGUANG
College of Science: LI DAN
Department of Physical Education: XU BIN
Department of Social Science: CHENG JIAMING
School of Art and Design: JIN DAIQIANG
School of Journalism and Communication: CHEN WANYING

PROFESSORS

CAO, BINGYUAN, Science
CHEN, FANGJING, Literature
CHEN, GUOQIANG, Science
CHEN, HANWEN, Business
CHEN, HONGLIN, Science
CHEN, MAOHUAI, Medicine
CHEN, WANYING, Journalism and Communication
CHEN, YAN, Art and Design
CHENG, JIAMING, Social Science
DING, XIAOJUN, Medicine
DING, ZHAOKUN, Science
DU, DANMING, Business
DU, GANGJIAN, Law
DU, LUNLUN, Literature
DUAN, MINGKE, Medicine
FANG, JIE, Science
GAO, KUNSHAN, Science
GONG, LEIGUANG, Engineering
GUO, XIANGUO, Medicine
GUO, XISHEN, Science
HAN, YALI, Science
HANG, JIAN, Art and Design
HE, SHAOHENG, Medicine
HERFORD, P. M., Journalism and Communication
HU, XINGRONG, Journalism and Communication
HUANG, CHANGJIANG, Science
HUANG, DONGYANG, Medicine
HUANG, XUELAN, Law
HUANG, YAN, Business
HUANG, YUANMING, Science
HUO, XIA, Medicine
JIANG, XUEWU, Medicine
JIN, DAIQIANG, Art and Design
KONG, KANGMEI, Medicine
LAN, SHENG, Science
LI, DAN, Science
LI, ENMIN, Medicine
LI, GUICANG, Literature
LI, KANGSHENG, Medicine
LI, PING, Law
LI, QING, Art and Design
LI, SHENGPING, Engineering
LI, YUGUANG, Medicine
LIN, FURONG, Science
LIN, SHUNCHAO, Medicine
LIU, JIANBIN, Engineering
LIU, XIAOHUA, Science
LOU, ZENGJIAN, Science
LUO, WENHONG, Medicine
MA, WENHUI, Science
MAI, JIEHUA, Science
MO, YAN, Literature
NI, ZHENHUA, Engineering
QI, DAQING, Business
QI, WEILI, Medicine
QIAN, SHUANRU, Medicine
QIAN, ZHIQIANG, Art and Design
QIN, DANIAN, Medicine
QIU, HANYING, Medicine
QIU, QINGCHUN, Science
SHEN, MINFEN, Engineering
SHI, GANGGANG, Medicine
SU, MIN, Medicine
TIAN, DONGPING, Medicine
WANG, CHEN, Medicine
WANG, FUREN, Literature
WANG, HUIGE, Medicine
WANG, JUNMING, Science
WANG, SHOUZHI, Art and Design
WANG, YINHE, Science
WANG, ZIYUAN, Science
WU, GUANGFUO, Science
WU, JIANXHONG, Medicine
WU, RENHUA, Medicine
WULAN, HASHI, Science
XIANG, BING, Business
XIAO, TAN, Science
XIE, HUICAI, Engineering
XIE, ZHUANGNING, Engineering
XU, JIANHENG, Medicine
XU, LUHANG, Law
XU, XIAOHU, Medicine
XU, ZONGLING, Business
XUE, YUNKUI, Business
YANG, SHOUZHI, Science
YANG, ZHONGQIANG, Science
YE, RUISONG, Science
YIN, YEGAO, Science
YUAN, ZHOU, Journalism and Communication
ZHAO, XIAOHUA, Engineering
ZHENG, XHIPEI, Medicine
ZHENG, YI, Engineering
ZHOU, WEI, Law

SHANXI AGRICULTURAL UNIVERSITY

Taigu 030801, Shaanxi Province
Telephone: (354) 6288211
E-mail: sxauxb@sxau.edu.cn
Internet: www.sxau.edu.cn

Founded 1950
provincial control
Academic year: September to July

Pres.: DONG CHANGSHENG
Vice-Pres.: CUI KEYONG
Vice-Pres.: WANG JUNDONG
Vice-Pres.: YUE WENBIN
Librarian: KANG CHENGYE

Number of teachers: 602
Number of students: 7,300

Publications: *Journal* (natural sciences, 4 a year), *Journal* (social sciences, 4 a year), *Study of Agriculture in Higher Education* (6 a year)

DEANS

College of Adult Education: REN JIAYAN
College of Agriculture: LI SHENGCAI
College of Animal Technology: LI HONGQUAN
College of Economics and Trade: (vacant)
College of Engineering Technology: (vacant)
College of Food Science and Engineering: HAO LIPING
College of Forestry: (vacant)
College of Horticulture: REN JIAYAN
College of Life Sciences: (vacant)

College of Resources and Environmental Science: SUN TAISEN
College of Social Science: (vacant)
Department of Modern Education and Technology: (vacant)

PROFESSORS

BAI, ZHONGKE, Resources and Environmental Science
CHANG, MINGCHANG, Food Science and Engineering
DONG, CHANGSHENG, Animal Technology
FAN, WENHUA, Resources and Environmental Science
HAN, JUCAI, Agriculture
HAO, JIANPING, Agriculture
HAO, LIN, Food Science and Engineering
HAO, LIPING, Food Science and Engineering
HE, YUNCHUN, Agriculture
HONG, JIANPING, Resources and Environmental Science
LI, BINGLIN, Agriculture
LI, HONGQUAN, Animal Technology
LI, SHENGCAI, Agriculture
LIN, DAYI, Resources and Environmental Science
LIU, HUIPING, Agriculture
LU, XIN, Resources and Environmental Science
MA, LIZHEN, Food Science and Engineering
PANG, QUANHAI, Animal Technology
SUN, TAISEN, Resources and Environmental Science
TANG, CHAOZHONG, Animal Technology
WANG, HONGFU, Agriculture
WANG, JUNDONG, Animal Technology
WANG, RUFU, Food Science and Engineering
WANG, SHENGUI, Resources and Environmental Science
WANG, YUGUO, Agriculture
WANG, ZHIRUI, Animal Technology
WANG, ZHIYA, Resources and Environmental Science
WEN, WEIYE, Animal Technology
WU, CAI-E, Food Science and Engineering
XIE, YINGHE, Resources and Environmental Science
YANG, JINZHONG, Agriculture
YANG, WUDE, Agriculture
ZHANG, HENG, Resources and Environmental Science
ZHAO, LIZHI, Agriculture

SHANXI UNIVERSITY

36 Wu Cheng Rd, Taiyuan 030006, Shaanxi Province
Telephone: (351) 7010944
E-mail: xiaoban@sxu.edu.cn
Internet: www.sxu.edu.cn

Founded 1902
provincial control
Academic year: September to July

Pres.: GUICHUN GUI
Vice-Pres.: JIA SUOTANG
Vice-Pres.: LIU WEIQI
Vice-Pres.: LIU ZHENSHENG
Vice-Pres.: QI FENG
Vice-Pres.: XING LONG
Head of Graduate Dept: GAO CE
Librarian: LI JIALIN

Number of teachers: 1,105
Number of students: 18,817 (11,905 full-time, 6,912 part-time)

Publications: *Acta Sinica Quantum Optica* (philosophy and social sciences, 4 a year), *Journal* (natural sciences, 4 a year), *Journal* (philosophy and social sciences, 4 a year), *Journal of Teachers' College of Shanxi University* (4 a year), *Shanxi Library Journal* (6 a year)

DEANS

College of Fine Arts: WANG ERXI
College of Music: WANG LIANG
College of Physical Education: LI JIANYING
College of Physics and Electronics Engineering: LIANG JIUQING
Department of History: LI SHUJI
Department of Mathematics: LI SHENGJIA
School of Chemistry and Engineering: ZHAO YONGXIANG
School of Chinese Language and Literature: QIAO QUANSHENG
School of Computer Science and Information Technology: LIANG JIYE
School of Economics: LIU JIANSHENG
School of Education Science: HOU HUAIYIN
School of Environmental Science and Resources: GUO DONGSHENG
School of Foreign Languages: NIE JIANZHONG
School of Law: WANG JIJUN
School of Life Science and Technology: MA ENBO
School of Management: CAO LIJUN
School of Philosophy and Sociology: QIAO RUIJIN
School of Political Science and Public Administration: LI LUQU

PROFESSORS

AN, XIMENG, Philosophy and Sociology
BI, FUSHENG, Philosophy and Sociology
CAO, LIJUN, Management
CHEN, JINSHENG, Law
CHEN, SHIBIN, Music
CHEN, ZHAOBIN, Chemistry and Engineering
CHENG, RENGAN, History
DENG, BING, Chemistry and Engineering
DONG, CHUAN, Chemistry and Engineering
DONG, YUMING, Law
FAN, WENBIAO, Environmental Science and Resources
FAN, YINGFANG, Chemistry and Engineering
GAO, XING, Music
GONG, RONGDE, Fine Arts
GUO, DONGSHENG, Environmental Science and Resources
GUO, GUICHUN, Philosophy and Sociology
GUO, YUXIANG, Fine Arts
HAN, JIANRONG, Life Science and Technology
HAN, XIANGMING, Education Science
HAN, ZHIMO, Fine Arts
HAO, JIANGRUI, Physics and Electronics Engineering
HONG, LIANGZHEN, Chinese Language and Literature
HOU, HUAIYIN, Education Science
HU, JIANHUA, Physical Education
HU, MINGLIANG, Foreign Languages
HUANG, FENGCHUN, Chemistry and Engineering
HUANG, SHUPING, Chemistry and Engineering
JIA, LIANFENG, Physics and Electronics Engineering
JIA, SHUOTANG, Physics and Electronics Engineering
JIA, XINCHUN, Mathematics
JIA, XIUYING, Foreign Languages
JIN, WEIJUN, Chemistry and Engineering
KANG, JINSHENG, Chinese Language and Literature
LAI, YUNZHONG, Physics and Electronics Engineering
LAN, HUANG, Chinese Language and Literature
LI, DEREN, Fine Arts
LI, FUYI, Mathematics
LI, JIANYING, Physical Education
LI, JINLONG, Physical Education
LI, LUQU, Political Science and Public Administration
LI, RUINING, Physics and Electronics Engineering
LI, SHENGJIA, Mathematics
LI, SHUJI, History
LI, WENDE, Chemistry and Engineering
LI, YUE'E, Foreign Languages
LI, ZHENGMIN, Chinese Language and Literature
LI, ZHIQIANG, Economics
LI, ZHONGHAO, Physics and Electronics Engineering
LIANG, JIAHUA, Management
LIANG, JIUQING, Physics and Electronics Engineering
LIANG, JIYE, Computer Science and Information Technology
LIANG, LIPING, Political Science and Public Administration
LIANG, ZHANDONG, Mathematics
LIU, BO, Chemistry and Engineering
LIU, CHAO, Music
LIU, GUIHU, Chinese Language and Literature
LIU, HAILIANG, Foreign Languages
LIU, HONGBING, Music
LIU, JIANSHENG, Economics
LIU, SHUQING, Chinese Language and Literature
LIU, WENSEN, Physics and Electronics Engineering
LIU, XHENSHENG, Chemistry and Engineering
LIU, XIAOHUI, Life Science and Technology
LIU, XIAOLI, Physical Education
LIU, YEPING, Fine Arts
LIU, ZHENSHENG, Chemistry and Engineering
MA, AIPING, Law
MA, ENBO, Life Science and Technology
MA, GUIBIN, Chemistry and Engineering
MA, HAILIANG, Foreign Languages
MA, WEIHUA, Law
MA, YONGMING, Chemistry and Engineering
MA, YUSHAN, History
MENG, ZIQIANG, Life Science and Technology
MIAO, DUOQIAN, Mathematics
NIE, HONGYIN, Chinese Language and Literature
NIE, YIXIN, Physics and Electronics Engineering
PAN, JINGHAO, Chemistry and Engineering
PAN, QING, Physics and Electronics Engineering
PANG, RENJI, Foreign Languages
PEI, CHENGFA, Economics
PEI, CHENGFA, Management
PENG, KUIXI, Physics and Electronics Engineering
PENG, YUNYE, Law
QIAO, DECAI, Physical Education
QIAO, QUANSHENG, Chinese Language and Literature
QIAO, RUIJIN, Philosophy and Sociology
QIN, XUEMEI, Chemistry and Engineering
REN, JIANGUO, Chemistry and Engineering
SHI, YAN, Physical Education
SHUANG, SHAOMIN, Chemistry and Engineering
SONG, BINGYAN, Philosophy and Sociology
SU, CHUNSHENG, Chinese Language and Literature
TIAN, YANNI, Chemistry and Engineering
WANG, HAI, Physics and Electronics Engineering
WANG, JIJUN, Law
WANG, JUNMIN, Physics and Electronics Engineering
WANG, LAN, Life Science and Technology
WANG, LIANG, Music
WANG, RONGSHENG, History
WANG, SHIYING, Mathematics
WANG, XIANMING, History
WANG, YI, Law
WANG, YINTIAN, History
WANG, YUANZHI, Law
WANG, ZHENGREN, Foreign Languages
WEI, GUANHLAI, History
WU, GAOSHOU, Philosophy and Sociology
WU, MIN, Political Science and Public Administration
WU, MINZHONG, Political Science and Public Administration
XIA, XHIXHONG, Chemistry and Engineering
XIANG, LILING, Management

XIE, CHANGDE, Physics and Electronics Engineering
XIE, JIAOLIANG, Life Science and Technology
XIE, SHULIAN, Life Science and Technology
XIE, YINGPING, Life Science and Technology
XING, LONG, History
XU, BINGSHENG, Chinese Language and Literature
XU, GENQI, Mathematics
XU, YONGMIN, Philosophy and Sociology
YAN, FENGWU, Chinese Language and Literature
YAN, JURANG, Mathematics
YANG, BINSHENG, Chemistry and Engineering
YANG, JUPING, History
YANG, LIAN, Chinese Language and Literature
YANG, PIN, Chemistry and Engineering
YANG, SUPING, Life Science and Technology
YI, HUILAN, Life Science and Technology
YU, GUODONG, Foreign Languages
YUE, QIANHOU, History
ZHANG, CUIYING, Management
ZHANG, FENG, Life Science and Technology
ZHANG, HENG, Chinese Language and Literature
ZHANG, JINGSHI, Education Science
ZHANG, JINTUN, Environmental Science and Resources
ZHANG, KUANSHOU, Physics and Electronics Engineering
ZHANG, MIN, Chinese Language and Literature
ZHANG, MINGYUAN, Fine Arts
ZHANG, RU, Chinese Language and Literature
ZHANG, RUIRONG, Music
ZHANG, SHENGWAN, Chemistry and Engineering
ZHANG, TIANCAI, Physics and Electronics Engineering
ZHANG, XIAOGE, Music
ZHANG, XINWEI, Management
ZHANG, YIXIAN, Life Science and Technology
ZHANG, ZHAO, Chemistry and Engineering
ZHANG, ZHUANGHUA, Life Science and Technology
ZHAO, AIMIN, Mathematics
ZHAO, JIANGUO, Chinese Language and Literature
ZHAO, RUIMIN, History
ZHAO, XIAOJUN, Law
ZHAO, YONGXIANG, Chemistry and Engineering
ZHAO, YUXIA, Philosophy and Sociology
ZHAO, ZHAOMING, Life Science and Technology
ZHOU, GUOSHENG, Physics and Electronics Engineering

SHENYANG AGRICULTURAL UNIVERSITY

120 Dongling Rd, Shenyang 110161, Liaoning Province
Telephone: (24) 88421121
Internet: www.syau.edu.cn

Founded 1952
Academic year: September to July

Pres.: ZHANG YULONG
Vice-Pres.: LI TIANLAI
Vice-Pres.: LIU GUANGLIN
Vice-Pres.: MENG QINGCHENG
Head of Graduate Dept: JIN BAOLIAN
Librarian: DUAN YUXI

Number of teachers: 859
Number of students: 20,105

Publications: *Chinese Journal of Soil Science* (6 a year), *Higher Agricultural Education* (12 a year), *Journal* (natural sciences, 6 a year), *Journal* (social sciences, 4 a year), *Journal of Pig Rearing* (6 a year), *New Agriculture* (12 a year)

DEANS

College of Agronomy: CAO MINJIAN
College of Biological Science and Technology: ZHANG LIJUN
College of Economics and Trade: FANG TIANKUN
College of Engineering: LI CHENGHUA
College of Food Science: LIU CHANGJIAN
College of Forestry: LIU MINGGUO
College of Horticulture: LI ZUOXUAN
College of Information and Electrical Engineering: PU ZAILIN
College of Land and the Environment: WANG QIUBING
College of Plant Protection: FU JUNFAN
College of Practical Technology: YANG YINSHAN
College of Science and Technology: (vacant)
College of Veterinary Science: HU JIANMING
College of Water Resources: WANG TIELIANG

PROFESSORS

BEI, NAXIN, Plant Protection
BIAN, QUANLIAN, Veterinary Science
CAO, MINJIAN, Agronomy
CAO, YUANYIN, Plant Protection
CAO, ZHIQIANG, Agronomy
CHEN, ENFENG, Land and the Environment
CHEN, JIE, Plant Protection
CHEN, WENFU, Agronomy
CHEN, XIAOFEI, Water Resources
CHEN, XISHI, Land and the Environment
CHEN, ZHENWU, Agronomy
CHENG, GUOHUA, Biological Science and Technology
CHENG, YULAI, Food Science
CHI, DAOCAI, Water Resources
CONG, BIN, Plant Protection
DAI, PENGJUN, Economics and Trade
DONG, WENXUAN, Horticulture
DU, GUANGMING, Horticulture
DU, SHAOFAN, Veterinary Science
DUAN, YUXI, Plant Protection
FANG, TIANKUN, Economics and Trade
FENG, HUI, Horticulture
FU, JUNFAN, Plant Protection
GAO, DESAN, Biological Science and Technology
GAO, GUOPING, Forestry
GAO, XINGLIAN, Engineering
GUAN, LIANZHU, Land and the Environment
GUO, XIUWU, Horticulture
GUO, YUHUA, Agronomy
HAN, XIAORI, Land and the Environment
HE, JUNSHI, Water Resources
HE, LILI, Horticulture
HOU, LIBAI, Agronomy
HU, JIANMIN, Veterinary Science
HUANG, RUIDONG, Agronomy
HUI, SHURONG, Basic Education
JI, JIANWEI, Information and Electrical Engineering
JI, MINGSHAN, Plant Protection
JI, MINGXI, Water Resources
JI, SHUJUAN, Food Science
JIANG, QILIANG, Plant Protection
LAN, QINGGAO, Economics and Trade
LI, BAOFA, Engineering
LI, BAOHUA, Basic Education
LI, BAOJIANG, Horticulture
LI, BINGCHAO, Basic Education
LI, CHENGHUA, Engineering
LI, GUOJIE, Insititute of Higher Education
LI, JIANNAN, Biological Science and Technology
LI, TIANLAI, Horticulture
LI, XINHUA, Food Science
LI, YONGKUI, Engineering
LI, YUXIA, Basic Education
LI, ZUOXUAN, Horticulture
LIANG, CHENGHUA, Land and the Environment
LIANG, JINGYI, Plant Protection
LIN, GUOLIN, Land and the Environment
LIU, CHANGJIANG, Food Science
LIU, MINGGUO, Forestry
LIU, RONGHOU, Engineering
LIU, ZHIHENG, Plant Protection
LIU, ZHONGQIN, Economics and Trade
LU, GUOZHONG, Plant Protection
LU, JIE, Economics and Trade
LU, SHUXIA, Biological Science and Technology
LUO, GUANGBIN, Veterinary Science
MAO, TAO, Food Science
MENG, XIANJUN, Food Science
MI, YONGNING, Water Resources
NIU, SHEN, Centre for Analysis and Testing
PU, ZAILIN, Information and Electrical Engineering
QIN, LI, Biological Science and Technology
QIU, LICHUN, Engineering
REN, WENTAO, Engineering
SHEN, XIANGQUN, Horticulture
SHI, ZHENSHENG, Agronomy
SI, LONGTING, Horticulture
SUN, JUNDE, Land and the Environment
TANG, YONG, Biological Science and Technology
WANG, BOLUN, Agronomy
WANG, CHUNPING, Economics and Trade
WANG, HONGPING, Plant Protection
WANG, HUICHENG, Engineering
WANG, JINGKUAN, Land and the Environment
WANG, JINMIN, Agronomy
WANG, LIXUE, Water Resources
WANG, QINGXIANG, Agronomy
WANG, QIUBING, Land and the Environment
WANG, SHAOBIN, Agronomy
WANG, XIAOQI, Plant Protection
WANG, XUEYING, Biological Science and Technology
WEI, YUTANG, Horticulture
WU, LUPING, Horticulture
WU, YUANHUA, Plant Protection
XIAO, SHENGAN, Social Science
XIE, FUTI, Agronomy
XU, XIAOMING, Physical Education
XU, ZHENGJIN, Agronomy
YAN, HONGWEI, Forestry
YANG, GUIQIN, Veterinary Science
YANG, SHOUREN, Agronomy
YANG, YONG, Information and Electrical Engineering
YI, YANLI, Land and the Environment
YIN, MINGFANG, Forestry
YU, ZHONGTAO, Social Science
ZHAI, YINLI, Economics and Trade
ZHANG, BAOSHI, Agronomy
ZHANG, KAIBIN, Horticulture
ZHANG, LIJUN, Biological Science and Technology
ZHANG, LONGBU, Agronomy
ZHANG, SHUSHEN, Plant Protection
ZHANG, XIURAN, Information and Electrical Engineering
ZHANG, YONGMING, Social Science
ZHANG, YULIN, Social Science
ZHANG, YULONG, Land and the Environment
ZHANG, ZHIHONG, Horticulture
ZHANG, ZULI, Engineering
ZHAO, YUJUN, Veterinary Science
ZHOU, BAOLI, Horticulture
ZHOU, HONGFEI, Agronomy
ZHOU, QILONG, Information and Electrical Engineering
ZHOU, YANMING, Centre for Analysis and Testing

SHENZHEN UNIVERSITY

Nanhai Rd 3688, Shenzhen 518060, Guangdong Province
Telephone: (755) 26534940
E-mail: szufao@szu.edu.cn
Internet: www.szu.edu.cn

Founded 1983
State control
Languages of instruction: English, Mandarin
Academic year: September to July

Pres.: Prof. LI QINGQUAN
Vice-Pres.: Prof. DU HONGBIAO
Vice-Pres.: Prof. LI FENGLIANG
Vice-Pres.: Prof. LI JUN
Vice-Pres.: Prof. RUAN SHUANGCHEN
Vice-Pres.: Prof. XU CHEN
Vice-Pres.: Prof. XING MIAO
Registrar: Prof. XU CHEN
Librarian: Prof. ZHANG DAOYI

Library: 3.28m. vols, 2.12m. ebooks
Number of teachers: 2,580
Number of students: 34,000

Publications: *Shenzhen University Journal* (social sciences and humanities), *Shenzhen University Journal* (natural sciences), *World Architecture Review*

DEANS

College of Architecture and Civil Engineering: Prof. AI ZHIGANG
College of Art and Design: Prof. WU HONG
College of Chemistry and Chemical Engineering: Prof. LIU JIANHONG
College of Chinese: Prof. JING HAIFENG
College of Civil Engineering and Urban Planning: Prof. WANG JIAYUAN
College of Computer and Software Engineering: Prof. CHEN GUOLIANG
College of Continuing Education: Prof. CHEN YANPING
College of Economics: Prof. CHEN YONG
College of Electronics and Electrical Engineering: Prof. XU PING
College of Foreign Languages: Prof. JIANG DAOCHAO
College of Golf Sport and Management: Prof. ZHANG XIAO CHUN
College of Information Engineering: Prof. LI XIA
College of International Exchange: Prof. WANG QING'GUO
College of Law: Prof. HUANG YAYING
College of Life Sciences: Prof. NI JIAZAN
College of Management: Prof. CHEN ZHIMIN
College of Mass Communication: Prof. WU YUMIN
College of Materials Sciences: Prof. ZENG XIERONG
College of Mathematics and Computational Science: Prof. CHEN ZHIBING
College of Mechtronics and Automation Engineering: Prof. XU GANG
School of Medicine: Prof. JIANG WENQI
College of Optical Engineering: Prof. NIU HANBEN
College of Physics and Physical Engineering: Prof. FAN PING
Normal College: Prof. ZHANG BIGONG

SICHUAN AGRICULTURAL UNIVERSITY

12 Xinkang Rd, Yaan 625014, Sichuan Province
Telephone: (835) 2882233
Internet: www.sicau.edu.cn

Founded 1906 as Sichuan Tong Sheng Agricultural School, subordinated to Nat. Sichuan Univ. in 1935, current name adopted 1985
Academic year: September to July

Schools and faculties: agronomy, animal science, economical management in agriculture and forestry, environmental engineering, forestry and grass science, humanities and social sciences, information and engineering technology, land resource management, life science, plant protection, veterinary science, vocational technology; Further Education College

Pres.: WEN XINTIAN
Vice-Pres.: REN ZHENGLONG
Vice-Pres.: YANG WENYU
Vice-Pres.: ZHANG QIANG
Vice-Pres.: ZHENG YOULIANG
Vice-Pres.: ZHU QING
Librarian: XIA JIMING

Library of 2,000,000 vols
Number of teachers: 1,500
Number of students: 28,000

Publication: *Journal* (4 a year)

SICHUAN UNIVERSITY

24 S Section 1, Yihuan Rd, Chengdu 610065, Sichuan Province
Telephone: (28) 85402443
Internet: www.scu.edu.cn

Founded 1896
State control
Academic year: September to July

Pres.: ZHAO YANXIU
Vice-Pres.: LI ZHIQIANG
Vice-Pres.: LIU YINGMING
Vice-Pres.: TANG DENGXUE
Vice-Pres.: XIE HEPING
Vice-Pres.: YANG JIRUI
Vice-Pres.: ZHANG WEIGUO
Vice-Pres.: ZHAO ZHAODA
Head of Graduate Dept: LIU YINGMING
Librarian: LI BINGYAN

Library of 4,847,300 vols
Number of teachers: 1,035
Number of students: 44,003

Publication: *Journal* (edns: natural sciences, 6 a year; engineering, 12 a year; medicine, 4 a year; philosophy and social sciences, 4 a year)

DEANS

College of Art: (vacant)
College of Chemistry: HU CHANG WEI
College of Economics and Management: ZHOU GUANG YAN
College of Foreign Languages and Cultures: SHI JIAN
College of Literature and Journalism: CAO SHUNQING
College of Mathematics: LI AN MIN
College of Physical Science and Technology: GONG MIN
College of Politics: WANG GUO MIN
College of Polymer Science and Engineering: YANG MING BO
College of Software Engineering: ZHOU JI LIU
College of Water Resources and Hydropower: LIANG CHUAN
School of Architecture and the Environment: FAN YU BO
School of Chemistry and Engineering: ZHU JIA HUA
School of Community and Sanitation: MA XIAO
School of Computer Science and Engineering: (vacant)
School of Electricity and Electronic Information: ZHAO ZHUO YAO
School of History and Culture: WANG TING ZHI
School of Law: (vacant)
School of Life Sciences: CHEN FANG
School of Manufacturing Science and Engineering: YIN GUO FU
School of Materials Science and Engineering: (vacant)
School of Physical Education: TANG CHENG
School of Pre-Clinical and Forensic Medicine: HOU YI PING
School of Tourism: (vacant)
West China College of Stomatology: ZHOU XUE DONG
West China School of Pharmacy: ZHANG ZHI RONG

PROFESSORS

AI, NAN SHAN, Architecture and the Environment
AO, FAN, Foreign Languages and Cultures
CAO, GUANG FU, Mathematics
CAO, YI PING, Electronics and Information Engineering
CAO, YI, Life Sciences
CAO, YU RONG, Politics
CENG, ZONG YONG, Life Sciences
CHEN, DAO BANG, Pre-Clinical and Forensic Medicine
CHEN, DE BEN, Chemistry
CHEN, GAO LIN, Economics and Management
CHEN, GUO DI, Pre-Clinical and Forensic Medicine
CHEN, HONG CHAO, Chemistry
CHEN, JIAN KANG, Water Resources and Hydropower
CHEN, JUN KAI, Architecture and the Environment
CHEN, KANG YANG, Law
CHEN, QIAN DE, Architecture and the Environment
CHEN, QIAO, Pre-Clinical and Forensic Medicine
CHEN, TIAN LANG, Chemistry
CHEN, WEN JUN, Chemistry
CHEN, YONG GE, Law
CHEN, ZE FANG, Chemistry
CHEN, ZHONG RONG, Foreign Languages and Cultures
CHENG, LI, Tourism
CHENG, XI LIN, Foreign Languages and Cultures
DAI, ZONG KUN, Electronics and Information Engineering
DAN, DE ZHONG, Architecture and the Environment
DENG, XIAO KANG, Pre-Clinical and Forensic Medicine
DENG, ZHEN HUA, Pre-Clinical and Forensic Medicine
DOU, HOU SONG, Chemistry
FAN, HONG, Architecture and the Environment
FAN, YU BO, Architecture and the Environment
FANG, GUO ZHEN, Chemistry
FANG, SHU XIN, History and Culture
FENG, YI JUN, Chemistry
FENG, ZE HUI, Foreign Languages and Cultures
FU, HE JIAN, Chemistry
FU, HUA LONG, Life Sciences
GAO, CHUN HUA, Manufacturing Science and Engineering
GAO, RONG, Life Sciences
GU, BIN, Life Sciences
GU, ZHONG BI, Electronics and Information Engineering
GUAN, PENG, Pre-Clinical and Forensic Medicine
HE, CHANG RONG, Water Resources and Hydropower
HE, JIANG DA, Water Resources and Hydropower
HE, JING XU, Law
HE, PEI YU, Electronics and Information Engineering
HE, PING, Foreign Languages and Cultures
HE, QING, History and Culture
HE, XING JIN, Life Sciences
HE, YA PING, Pre-Clinical and Forensic Medicine
HE, YU EN, Chemistry
HOU, XIAN DENG, Chemistry
HU, HUO ZHEN, Life Sciences
HU, JIA YUAN, Chemistry
HU, JUN MEI, Pre-Clinical and Forensic Medicine
HUANG, DE CHANG, Economics and Management
HUANG, FA LUN, Mathematics
HUANG, GUANG LIN, Chemistry
HUANG, NAN JING, Mathematics
HUANG, NIAN CI, Electricity and Electronic Information
HUANG, NING, Pre-Clinical and Forensic Medicine

HUANG, SHAN, Electricity and Electronic Information
HUANG, YING, Pre-Clinical and Forensic Medicine
JIANG, BO, Chemistry
JIANG, CHENG FA, Chemistry and Engineering
JIANG, WEN JU, Architecture and the Environment
JIN, MING, Law
JING, DONG, Electricity and Electronic Information
JU, XIAO MING, Water Resources and Hydropower
KANG, ZHEN HUANG, Architecture and the Environment
KE, JI GUI, Foreign Languages and Cultures
LEI, YONG XUE, Politics
LI, AN MIN, Mathematics
LI, BO HUAI, Tourism
LI, DE YU, Architecture and the Environment
LI, FANG, Chemistry
LI, FU HAI, Economics and Management
LI, GUO CHENG, Electricity and Electronic Information
LI, HONG, Pre-Clinical and Forensic Medicine
LI, HUI, Chemistry and Engineering
LI, JIAN MING, Chemistry and Engineering
LI, JIAO, Foreign Languages and Cultures
LI, JIE, Politics
LI, JU CAI, Chemistry
LI, KE FENG, Water Resources and Hydropower
LI, LIANG, Pre-Clinical and Forensic Medicine
LI, MENG LONG, Chemistry
LI, PING, Law
LI, RUI XIANG, Chemistry
LI, SHI YAN, Economics and Management
LI, TAO, History and Culture
LI, XIAO SONG, Infrastructure and Sanitation
LI, YAO ZHONG, Chemistry
LI, YING BI, Pre-Clinical and Forensic Medicine
LI, YING, Chemistry
LI, ZAN, Law
LI, ZHANG ZHENG, Architecture and the Environment
LI, ZHI SHU, Computer Science and Engineering
LI, ZHONG FU, Mathematics
LI, ZHONG MING, Polymer Science and Engineering
LIANG, BING, Chemistry and Engineering
LIANG, JI HUA, Mathematics
LIANG, YUAN DI, Economics and Management
LIAO, LIN CHUAN, Pre-Clinical and Forensic Medicine
LIN, BI GUO, Foreign Languages and Cultures
LIN, DA QUAN, Manufacturing Science and Engineering
LIU, CHANG JUN, Electronics and Information Engineering
LIU, DONG QUAN, Software Engineering
LIU, FEI PENG, Electricity and Electronic Information
LIU, GUANG ZHONG, Economics and Management
LIU, JIA YONG, Electronics and Information Engineering
LIU, LI MIN, Foreign Languages and Cultures
LIU, MIN, Pre-Clinical and Forensic Medicine
LIU, NIAN, Electricity and Electronic Information
LIU, QI CHAO, Software Engineering
LIU, RONG ZHONG, Manufacturing Science and Engineering
LIU, SHAN JUN, Water Resources and Hydropower
LIU, SHENG QING, Manufacturing Science and Engineering
LIU, TIAN QI, Electricity and Electronic Information
LIU, TING HUA, Polymer Science and Engineering
LIU, YI FEI, History and Culture
LIU, YU SHENG, Electricity and Electronic Information
LONG, JIAN ZHONG, Electronics and Information Engineering
LONG, KUI, Foreign Languages and Cultures
LONG, WEI, Manufacturing Science and Engineering
LONG, YUN FANG, Infrastructure and Sanitation
LONG, ZONG ZHI, Law
LUO, DI LUN, Foreign Languages and Cultures
LUO, LIN, Water Resources and Hydropower
LUO, LIN, Architecture and the Environment
LUO, MAO KANG, Mathematics
LUO, MEI MING, Chemistry
LUO, SU QIONG, Infrastructure and Sanitation
LUO, TE JUN, Architecture and the Environment
LUO, WAN BO, Computer Science and Engineering
LUO, XIANG LIN, Polymer Science and Engineering
LV, GUANG HONG, Computer Science and Engineering
LV, TAO, Mathematics
MA, HONG, Mathematics
MA, LI TAI, Foreign Languages and Cultures
MENG, YAN FA, Life Sciences
MU, CHUN LAI, Mathematics
NIE, GANG, Politics
NING, YUAN ZHONG, Electricity and Electronic Information
PEI, JUE MIN, Architecture and the Environment
PENG, BANG BEN, History and Culture
PENG, LIAN GANG, Mathematics
QI, JIAN GUO, Pre-Clinical and Forensic Medicine
QIN, SHI LUN, Architecture and the Environment
QIU, WANG SHENG, Foreign Languages and Cultures
QU, ZHAO YANG, Pre-Clinical and Forensic Medicine
SHI, JIAN, Foreign Languages and Cultures
SHI, YING PING, Tourism
SHU, QIN, Electricity and Electronic Information
SONG, HANG, Chemistry and Engineering
SONG, WEI, Economics and Management
SUN, CHENG JUN, Infrastructure and Sanitation
SUN, JIN QUAN, History and Culture
SUN, QI, Mathematics
TAN, DA LU, Architecture and the Environment
TAN, XIAO PING, Architecture and the Environment
TAN, YANG, Pre-Clinical and Forensic Medicine
TANG, JIA LING, Polymer Science and Engineering
TANG, LEI, Law
TANG, NING JIU, Computer Science and Engineering
TANG, YA, Architecture and the Environment
TAO, LI, Economics and Management
TU, SHANG YIN, Foreign Languages and Cultures
TU, YUAN ZHAO, Electricity and Electronic Information
WAN, JIA YI, Chemistry
WANG, DAO HUI, Electricity and Electronic Information
WANG, FAN, Pre-Clinical and Forensic Medicine
WANG, GUO MIN, Politics
WANG, JIAN PING, Law
WANG, LEI, Pre-Clinical and Forensic Medicine
WANG, LI, Water Resources and Hydropower
WANG, LI, Life Sciences
WANG, QI ZHI, Architecture and the Environment
WANG, QING YUAN, Architecture and the Environment
WANG, SHU YU, Foreign Languages and Cultures
WANG, XIAO LU, Foreign Languages and Cultures
WANG, YA JING, Pre-Clinical and Forensic Medicine
WANG, YING HAN, Polymer Science and Engineering
WANG, ZHEN XUE, Electronics and Information Engineering
WEI, XIN PING, Water Resources and Hydropower
WEI, ZHONG HAI, Politics
WEN, CHU AN, Foreign Languages and Cultures
WU, JIANG, Chemistry
WU, JIN, Pre-Clinical and Forensic Medicine
WU, QING, Pre-Clinical and Forensic Medicine
WU, XIAN HONG, Foreign Languages and Cultures
WU, ZHI HUA, Polymer Science and Engineering
XIA, SU LAN, Chemistry and Engineering
XIANG, TAO, Pre-Clinical and Forensic Medicine
XIANG, ZHAO YANG, Law
XIAO, AN FU, Foreign Languages and Cultures
XIAO, SHEN XIU, Chemistry
XIAO, XU, Politics
XIE, BANG HU, Polymer Science and Engineering
XIONG, FENG, Architecture and the Environment
XU, DAO YI, Mathematics
XU, HENG, Life Sciences
XU, LAN, Electronics and Information Engineering
XUE, YING, Chemistry
YANG, FANG JU, Pre-Clinical and Forensic Medicine
YANG, GANG, Polymer Science and Engineering
YANG, HONG GENG, Electricity and Electronic Information
YANG, HONG YU, Computer Science and Engineering
YANG, JIANG, Economics and Management
YANG, JIE, Chemistry
YANG, JUN LIU, Architecture and the Environment
YANG, SHI WEN, History and Culture
YANG, SUI QUAN, Law
YANG, WAN QUAN, Electronics and Information Engineering
YANG, WU NENG, Foreign Languages and Cultures
YANG, YI, Manufacturing Science and Engineering
YANG, YI, Life Sciences
YANG, ZHEN ZHI, Tourism
YANG, ZHENG GUANG, Politics
YE, GUANG DOU, Polymer Science and Engineering
YI, DAN, Foreign Languages and Cultures
YI, XU FU, Pre-Clinical and Forensic Medicine
YIN, HUA QIANG, Architecture and the Environment
YIN, YONG XIANG, Chemistry and Engineering
YOU, XIAN GUI, Chemistry and Engineering
YU, JIAN HUA, Architecture and the Environment
YU, ZHONG DE, Software Engineering
YUAN, DAO HUA, Computer Science and Engineering
YUAN, DE CHENG, Foreign Languages and Cultures
YUAN, DE QI, Chemistry
YUAN, LI HUA, Chemistry

YUAN, PENG, Water Resources and Hydropower
YUAN, YONG MING, Chemistry
YUAN, ZHI RUN, Architecture and the Environment
YUE, LI MIN, Pre-Clinical and Forensic Medicine
ZENG, CHENG MING, Life Sciences
ZENG, LING FU, Infrastructure and Sanitation
ZHANG, CHAO, Electricity and Electronic Information
ZHANG, DAI RUN, Electricity and Electronic Information
ZHANG, DE XUE, Mathematics
ZHANG, GUANG KE, Water Resources and Hydropower
ZHANG, HONG WEI, Computer Science and Engineering
ZHANG, HUA, Electricity and Electronic Information
ZHANG, JIAN ZHOU, Computer Science and Engineering
ZHANG, KE RONG, Infrastructure and Sanitation
ZHANG, LIN, Water Resources and Hydropower
ZHANG, PIN, Pre-Clinical and Forensic Medicine
ZHANG, WEI NIAN, Mathematics
ZHANG, WEI, Pre-Clinical and Forensic Medicine
ZHANG, XIN PEI, Architecture and the Environment
ZHANG, XU, Mathematics
ZHANG, YI ZHONG, Electricity and Electronic Information
ZHANG, YONG KUI, Chemistry and Engineering
ZHAO, CHANG SHEN, Polymer Science and Engineering
ZHAO, CHENG YU, Life Sciences
ZHAO, SHI PING, Manufacturing Science and Engineering
ZHAO, YUN, Life Sciences
ZHENG, CHANG YI, Chemistry
ZHENG, HUA, Politics
ZHONG, SHU LIN, Chemistry
ZHONG, YIN PING, Polymer Science and Engineering
ZHOU, AN MIN, Electronics and Information Engineering
ZHOU, BO, Architecture and the Environment
ZHOU, BU XIANG, Electricity and Electronic Information
ZHOU, GUANG YA, Foreign Languages and Cultures
ZHOU, JI LIU, Software Engineering
ZHOU, JIAN LUE, Chemistry
ZHOU, LI MING, Pre-Clinical and Forensic Medicine
ZHOU, WEI, Law
ZHOU, XUE, Pre-Clinical and Forensic Medicine
ZHOU, YI, Tourism
ZHU, HUI, Foreign Languages and Cultures
ZHU, XIN MIN, Economics and Management
ZHU, YUN MIN, Mathematics
ZHUANG, CHENG SAN, Computer Science and Engineering
ZUO, WEI MIN, Law

SOOCHOW UNIVERSITY

1 Shi Xin St, Suzhou 215006, Jiangsu Province
E-mail: mail@suda.edu.cn
Internet: www.suda.edu.cn

Founded 1900
Academic year: September to July

Pres.: QIAN PEIDE
Vice-Pres.: BAI LUN
Vice-Pres.: GE JIANYI
Vice-Pres.: ZHANG XUEGUANG
Vice-Pres.: ZHU XIULIN
Head of Graduate Dept: ZHU SHIQUN
Librarian: WANG GUOPING

Library of 3,320,000 vols
Number of teachers: 1,200
Number of students: 32,300

Publication: *Journal of Suzhou University* (edns: engineering sciences, medical science, 6 a year; natural sciences, philosophy and social science, 4 a year)

DEANS

College of Politics and Public Management: ZHOU KEZHEN
Institute of Pollution and Public Health: TONG JIAN
Material Engineering Institute: CHEN GUOQIANG
School of Agricultural Science and Technology: SHEN WEIDE
School of Chemistry and Chemical Engineering: JI SHUNJUN
School of Computer Science and Technology: ZHU QIAOMING
School of Electronic Information: ZHAO HEMING
School of Foreign Languages: WANG LABAO
School of Life Sciences: ZHANG XUEGUANG
School of Literature Department: LUO SHIJIN
School of Mathematical Sciences: WANG LABAO
School of Mechanical and Electronic Engineering: RUI YANNIAN
School of Medicine: WU AIQIN
School of Physical Education and Sports: WANG JIAHONG
School of Social Science: WANG LABAO

PROFESSORS

BAO, SHIQIAO, Medicine
CAO, YONGLUO, Mathematical Sciences
CAO, YONGLUO, Mechanical and Electronic Engineering
CHEN, LINSEN, Computer Science and Technology
CHEN, QINGGUAN, Mechanical and Electronic Engineering
CHEN, ZIXING, Medicine
CUI, ZHIMING, Mechanical and Electronic Engineering
FENG, ZHIHUA, Mechanical and Electronic Engineering
FU, GEYAN, Mechanical and Electronic Engineering
GAO, FANGYING, Social Science
GAO, QI, Medicine
GU, ZHENLUN, Medicine
GU, ZONGJIANG, Medicine
GUI, SHIHE, Mechanical and Electronic Engineering
HONG, FASHUI, Life Sciences
HU, HUACHENG, Medicine
HUA, RENDE, Art
HUANG, QIANG, Medicine
JIANG, WENKAI, Physical Education and Sports
JIANG, XINGHONG, Medicine
JIN, WEIXING, Social Science
LAN, QING, Medicine
LI, DECHUN, Medicine
LIANG, JUN, Art
LIAO, LIANGYUN, Art
LIU, CHUNFENG, Medicine
LIU, ZHIHUA, Medicine
LU, HUIMIN, Medicine
LU, JIAN, Social Science
MA, WEIZHONG, Literature
QIAN, HAIXIN, Medicine
QIN, ZHENGHONG, Medicine
RUI, YANNIAN, Mechanical and Electronic Engineering
SHEN, YULIANG, Mathematical Sciences
SHEN, ZHENYA, Medicine
SHI, GUANGYU, Mechanical and Electronic Engineering
SHI, SHIHONG, Mechanical and Electronic Engineering
SONG, HUICHUN, Life Sciences
SUN, JUNYING, Medicine
SUN, MINZHI, Physical Education and Sports
TANG, TIANSI, Medicine
TANG, ZHENGPEI, Social Science
TANG, ZHINGMING, Mathematical Sciences
TIAN, JIUMAI, Physical Education and Sports
TU, YIFENG, Chemistry and Chemical Engineering
WAN, JIEQIU, Commerce
WANG, GUANGWEI, Commerce
WANG, GUOPING, Social Science
WANG, JIAHONG, Physical Education and Sports
WANG, ZHAOYUE, Medicine
WEI, XIANGDONG, Social Science
WEN, DUANGAI, Medicine
WU, DEPEI, Medicine
WU, HAORONG, Medicine
WU, JINCHANG, Medicine
XIA, CHAOMING, Medicine
XIA, CHUNLIN, Medicine
XU, HAOWEN, Physical Education and Sports
XUE, YONGQUAN, Medicine
YAN, CHUNYIN, Medicine
YANG, JICHENG, Medicine
YANG, XIANGJUN, Medicine
YIN, YUNXING, Mechanical and Electronic Engineering
YU, HONGBING, Mathematical Sciences
YU, TONGYUAN, Social Science
YU, ZHENG, Social Science
ZANG, ZHIFEI, Social Science
ZHANG, LIN, Physical Education and Sports
ZHANG, MING, Social Science
ZHANG, PENGCHUAN, Art
ZHANG, RI, Medicine
ZHANG, SHIMING, Medicine
ZHANG, XIQING, Medicine
ZHANG, XUEGANG, Life Sciences
ZHANG, XUEGUANG, Medicine
ZHANG, ZHAOYU, Social Science
ZHAO, ZENGYAO, Commerce
ZHONG, KANGMIN, Mechanical and Electronic Engineering
ZHOU, DAI, Medicine
ZHOU, JIANPENG, Chemistry and Chemical Engineering
ZHU, CONGBING, Social Science
ZHU, JIANG, Life Sciences
ZHUGE, HONGXIANG, Medicine
ZHUGE, KAI, Art

SOUTH CHINA AGRICULTURAL UNIVERSITY

Wushan, Guangzhou 510642, Guangdong Province
Telephone: (20) 85280007
E-mail: office@scau.edu.cn
Internet: www.scau.edu.cn

Founded 1909
state (provincial) control
Academic year: September to July

Pres.: Prof. LUO SHIMING
Vice-Pres.: Prof. CHEN BEIGUANG
Vice-Pres.: Assoc. Prof. CHEN CHANGSHENG
Vice-Pres.: Prof. LUO XIWEN
Librarian: YE JINGHUA

Library of 700,000 vols
Number of teachers: 753
Number of students: 12,501

Publications: *Guangdong Agricultural Sciences* (jtly published with Guangdong Acad. of Agricultural Science, 12 a year), *Journal* (4 a year), *Poultry Husbandry and Disease Control* (12 a year)

DEANS

College of Adult Education: Prof. NIU BAOJUN
College of Biotechnology: Prof. PENG XINXIANG
College of Economics and Trade: Prof. LI DASHENG

College of Forestry: Prof. CHEN XIMU
College of Liberal Arts: Prof. ZHANG WENFANG
College of Resources and Environment: Prof. LI HUAXING
College of Science: Prof. ZHANG GUOQUAN
Department of Agronomy: Prof. ZHANG GUIQUAN
Department of Animal Medicine: Prof. ZENG ZHENLING
Department of Animal Science: Prof. FENG DINGYUAN
Department of Food Science: Assoc. Prof. LI BIN
Department of Horticulture: Assoc. Prof. CHEN RIYUAN
Department of Physical Education: Assoc. Prof. WANG CHANGQING
Department of Sericulture: Assoc. Prof. XU XINGYAO
Polytechnic College: Prof. OU YINGGANG

PROFESSORS

BI, Y. Z., Animal Nutrition and Immunology
CAO, Y., Silkworm Biotechnology
CHEN, B.G., Forest Ecology
CHEN, D. C., Pomology
CHEN, W. K., Insect Toxicology
CHEN, W. X., Post-harvest Physiology of Fruit and Vegetables
CHEN, X. M., Plant Systematics and Evolution
CHEN, Y. S., Animal Genetics and Breeding
CHEN, Y. Q., Food Biochemistry
CHEN, Z. L., Veterinary Medicine
CHEN, Z. Q., Crop Genetics and Breeding
FAN, H. Z., Plant Pathology
FAN, X. L., Soil Chemistry
FENG, D. Y., Animal Nutrition and Feed Science
FENG, Q. H., Veterinary Medicine
FU, C., Economic Policy and Development
FU, W. L., Animal Physiology
GAO, X. B., Plant Pathology
GU, D. J., Insect Ecology
GUO, Z. F., Plant Physiology and Molecular Biology
HONG, T. S., Agricultural Mechanization
HUANG, B. Q., Insecticide
HUANG, H. B., Fruit Tree Physiology
HUANG, Q. Y., Veterinary Microbiology
HUANG, X. Y., Food Nutrition
HUANG, Z. L., Biochemistry
JI, Z. L., Agricultural Product Storage and Processing
JIAN, Y. Y., Plant Biotechnology
JIANG, H., Agricultural Economics and Management
JIANG, Z. D., Plant Pathology
KONG, X. M., Veterinary Pathology
LAN, S. F., Ecological Energy and Value of Energy
LI, B. T., Plant Taxonomy
LI, D. S., Economics of Agricultural Engineering
LI, G. Q., Veterinary Parasitology
LI, H. X., Soil Science
LI, J. P., Soil Chemistry
LI, K. F., Wood Science
LI, M. Q., Plant Physiology
LI, Z. L., Crop Cultivation
LIANG, G. W., Insect Ecology
LIANG, J. N., Crop Cultivation
LIAO, Z. W., Soil Science and the Environment
LIN, J. R., Silkworm Genetics and Breeding
LIN, S. Q., Pomology
LIN, Y. G., Genetic Engineering
LU, Y. G., Plant Genetics
LUO, B. L., Agricultural Economics and Management
LUO, F. H., Forest Management
LUO, S. M., Agroecology
LUO, X. W., Agricultural Mechanization
MEI, M. T., Plant Biotechnology
OU, Y. G., Agricultural Engineering
PAN, Q. H., Plant Pathology
PANG, X. F., Insect Ecology and Taxonomy
PENG, X. X., Plant Physiology and Molecular Biology
REN, S. X., Insect Ecology
SUN, Y. M., Food Chemistry
TAN, Z. W., Plant Genetics and Breeding
TIE, L. Y., Fashion Design
WAN, B. H., Plant Genetics and Breeding
WANG, D. L., Tea Science
WANG, J., Forest Pathology
WANG, S. Z., Landscape Gardening
WANG, Z. S., Animal Ecology
WANG, Z. Z., Plant Pathology
WEN, S. M., Agricultural Economics and Management
WU, H., Botany
WU, Q. T., Agricultural Environment Protection
XIAO, H. G., Plant Pathology
XIN, C. A., Poultry Disease
XU, F. C., Plant Physiology
XU, H. H., Insect Toxicology
XU, X. Y., Silkworm Pathology
YAN, X. L., Plant Nutrition
YANG, G. F., Animal Genetics and Breeding
YANG, Y. S., Genetic Engineering
ZENG, L., Insect Ecology
ZENG, Z. L., Veterinary Pharmacology
ZHANG, G. Q., Crop Genetics and Breeding
ZHANG, T. L., Agricultural Mechanization
ZHANG, W. F., Agricultural Economics and Management
ZHANG, X. Q., Animal Genetics and Breeding
ZHANG, Y. H., Agricultural Economics and Management

SOUTH CHINA NORMAL UNIVERSITY

Shipai, Guangzhou 510631, Guangdong Province
Telephone: (20) 85210169
Internet: www.scnu.edu.cn
Founded 1933
Academic year: September to July

Pres.: WANG GUOJIAN
Vice-Pres.: HU SHEJUN
Vice-Pres.: HUANG LIYA
Vice-Pres.: LI YONGJIE
Vice-Pres.: LIU MING
Vice-Pres.: MO LEI
Vice-Pres.: QIAN XIANBIN
Vice-Pres.: WU YINGMIN
Head of Graduate Dept: XIAO HUA
Librarian: ZHU JIANLIANG

Number of teachers: 2,400
Number of students: 60,600

Publications: *High School Physics Education* (12 a year), *Journal* (6 a year), *Journal of Physical Education* (6 a year), *Oriental Culture* (6 a year)

DEANS

College of Economics and Management: LI YONGJIE
College of Educational Information Technology: XU FUYING
College of Foreign Languages: (vacant)
College of Humanities: KE HANLING
College of International Culture: LI SHENGBING
College of Life Sciences: MA GUANGZHI
College of Optoelectronics Technology: LIU SONGHAO
College of Physics and Telecommunications Engineering: LIU QIONGFA
College of Politics and Law: HU ZEHONG
College of Sports Science: ZHOU AIGUANG
Department of Art: HUANG LIYA
Department of Chemistry: ZENG HEPING
Department of Computer Science: BAO SUSU
Department of Geography: XU XIANGJUN
Department of Mathematics: HUANG ZHIDA
Department of Music: CHENG JIANPING
Department of Tourism Management: GAN QIAOLIN
School of Continuing Education: HUANG ZHIYING
School of Education Science: MO LEI

PROFESSORS

BAO, ZONGTI, Physics and Telecommunications Engineering
BIN, JINHUA, Life Sciences
CHANG, HONGSEN, Physics and Telecommunications Engineering
CHEN, HAO, Physics and Telecommunications Engineering
CHEN, HUOWANG, Computer Science
CHEN, JUNFANG, Physics and Telecommunications Engineering
CHEN, QI, Sports Science
CHEN, XIANGLIN, Life Sciences
CHEN, XINMIN, Economics and Management
CHEN, YAOSHENG, Economics and Management
CHEN, YONGSHAO, Mathematics
CHEN, YUQUN, Mathematics
CHEN, ZHANGHE, Life Sciences
DENG, SHUXUN, Sports Science
DING, SHIJIN, Mathematics
DING, XIN, Educational Information Technology
DONG, WULUN, Economics and Management
FANG, XINGQI, Economics and Management
FENG, YOUHE, Mathematics
GAN, QIAOLIN, Tourism Management
GAO, SHIAN, Mathematics
HAO, XUANMING, Sports Science
HE, ZHENGJIANG, Physics and Telecommunications Engineering
HU, LIAN, Physics and Telecommunications Engineering
HU, XIAOMING, Sports Science
HUANG, KUANROU, Sports Science
HUANG, LIREN, Mathematics
HUANG, WENFANG, Life Sciences
HUANG, YUSHAN, Sports Science
LI, DONGFENG, Life Sciences
LI, HONGQING, Life Sciences
LI, JIANYING, Economics and Management
LI, JIDONG, Economics and Management
LI, KEDONG, Educational Information Technology
LI, LING, Life Sciences
LI, SHAOSHAN, Life Sciences
LI, SHIJIE, Mathematics
LI, WEISHAN, Chemistry
LI, WEN, Mathematics
LI, YIJUN, Sports Science
LI, YONGJIE, Economics and Management
LI, YUNLIN, Educational Information Technology
LIN, CHANGHAO, Mathematics
LIN, YONG, Economics and Management
LING, JIANGHUAI, Economics and Management
LIU, BOLIAN, Mathematics
LIU, CHENGYI, Sports Science
LIU, QIONGFA, Physics and Telecommunications Engineering
LIU, SONGHAO, Optoelectronics
LIU, YUQIANG, Mathematics
LU, YUANZHEN, Sports Science
MO, LEI, Education Science
PAN, RUICHI, Life Sciences
PENG, BIYU, Economics and Management
SANG, XINMIN, Educational Information Technology
SHEN, WENHUAI, Mathematics
SUN, DAOCHUN, Mathematics
SUN, RUYONG, Life Sciences
TAN, HUA, Sports Science
TANG, SHANGYONG, Mathematics
TANG, ZAIXIN, Economics and Management
TANG, ZHILIE, Physics and Telecommunications Engineering
TONG, QINGXI, Geography
WANG, ANLI, Life Sciences
WANG, LINQUAN, Mathematics

WANG, QIAN, Sports Science
WANG, WEINA, Life Sciences
WANG, XIAOJING, Life Sciences
WENG, PEIXUAN, Mathematics
WU, CHAOLIN, Economics and Management
XIA, HUA, Physics and Telecommunications Engineering
XIAO, GUOQIANG, Sports Science
XIAO, PENG, Life Sciences
XIONG, JIANWEN, Physics and Telecommunications Engineering
XIONG, JINCHENG, Mathematics
XU, FUYING, Educational Information Technology
XU, JIE, Life Sciences
XU, XIAOYANG, Sports Science
XU, XUAN, Chemistry
YANG, WENXUAN, Sports Science
YANG, YONGHUA, Economics and Management
YE, QINGSHENG, Life Sciences
YI, FAHUAI, Mathematics
YU, YING, Chemistry
YUANG, GUANLING, Physics and Telecommunications Engineering
ZENG, HEPING, Chemistry
ZHANG, JIANWU, Economics and Management
ZHANG, JUNPENG, Physics and Telecommunications Engineering
ZHANG, MOUCHENG, Mathematics
ZHANG, ZHIYONG, Sports Science
ZHENG, ZHI, Chemistry
ZHAO, XUEZENG, Economics and Management
ZHOU, AIGUANG, Sports Science
ZHU, JIANJUN, Life Sciences
ZUO, ZAISHI, Mathematics

SOUTH CHINA UNIVERSITY OF TECHNOLOGY

381 Wushan Rd, 510641 Guangzhou
Telephone: (20) 87114470
E-mail: scuta04@scut.edu.cn
Internet: www.scut.edu.cn

Founded 1952
State control
Academic year: September to July

Pres.: WANG YINGJUN
Vice-Pres.: PENG SHUOLONG
Vice-Pres.: QIU XUEQING
Vice-Pres.: ZHU MIN
Vice-Pres.: ZHANG XICHUN
Vice-Pres.: DANG ZHI

Library of 5,160,000 vols
Number of teachers: 2,330
Number of students: 101,999

Publications: *Control Theory and Applications*, *Journal*

DEANS

School of Architecture: HE JINGTANG
School of Arts: HE PING
School of Automation Science and Engineering: Prof. LI YUANQING
School of Bioscience and Bioengineering: TAN WEN
School of Business Administration: ZHU GUILONG
School of Chemistry and Chemical Engineering: Prof. Dr ZHENGGUO ZHANG
School of Civil Engineering and Transportation: Prof. Dr SU CHENG
School of Computer Science and Engineering: HAN GUOQIANG
School of Economics and Commerce: SONG HAI
School of Electric Power: LI LICHENG
School of Electronic and Information Engineering: XU XIANGMIN
School of Foreign Languages: ZHONG SHUNENG
School of Ideology and Politics: LIU SHEXIN
School of International Education: Prof. AN RAN

SOUTH WESTERN UNIVERSITY OF FINANCE AND ECONOMICS

55 Guanghua St, Chengdu 610074, Sichuan Province
Telephone: (28) 7352937
Internet: www.swufe.edu.cn

Founded 1950
State control
Academic year: September to July

Pres.: WANG YUGUO
Vice-Pres.: FENG XIDE
Vice-Pres.: LIU CAN
Vice-Pres.: ZHAO DEWU
Head of Graduate Dept: ZHAO ZHENXIAN
Librarian: LIU FANGJIAN

Library of 1,000,000 vols
Number of teachers: 1,300
Number of students: 14,000

Publications: *Finance and Economics* (6 a year), *The Economist*

DEANS

Department of Economical Mathematics: XIANG KAILI
School of Accounting: PENG SHAOBING
School of e-Commerce: PU GUOQUAN
School of Economics: LI PING
School of Economic Information Engineering: SHAOBING SONG
School of Finance: YIN MENGBO
School of Insurance: AI SUNLIN
School of International Business: CHENG MINXUAN
School of Law: GAO JINKANG
School of Public Administration: YIN QINGSHUANG
School of Public Finance and Taxation: WANG GUOQING
School of Statistics: SHI DAIMIN

PROFESSORS

AI, SUNLIN, Insurance
CAI, CHUN, Accounting
CAO, TINGGUI, Finance
CHEN, MINGLI, Law
CHEN, SUYU, Law
CHEN, YONGSHENG, Finance
CHEN, YUANHONG, Accounting
CHENG, MINXUAN, International Business
CHENG, QIAN, Public Finance and Taxation
DENG, GUANJUN, e-Commerce
DING, RENZHONG, Economics
DU, ZHIHAN, Economic Mathematics
FAN, XINGJIAN, Accounting
FENG, JIAN, Accounting
FENG, XIDE, Economics
FENG, YADONG, Law
FU, DAIGUO, Accounting
FU, HONGCHUN, Economics
GAO, JINKANG, Law
GUO, FUCHU, Accounting
HE, ZERONG, Finance
JIANG, LING, Economics
JIANG, YUMEI, Law
KUANG, SONG, Economic Information Engineering
LI, NANCHENG, Statistics
LI, PING, Economics
LI, SHI, Statistics
LIN, WANXIANG, Accounting
LIN, YI, Insurance
LIU, CAN, Economics
LIU, RONG, Public Finance and Taxation
LIU, SHIBAI, Economics
MA, XIAO, Public Finance and Taxation
MU, LIANGPING, Economics
NI, KEQIN, Finance
PAN, XUEMO, Accounting
PANG, HAO, Statistics
PENG, SHAOBING, Accounting
REN, ZHIJUN, Economics
SHEN, XIAOMEI, Public Administration
SHI, DAIMIN, Statistics
SUN, RONG, Insurance
TU, KAIYI, International Business
WANG, GUOQING, Public Finance and Taxation
WANG, XIANGXI, e-Commerce
WANG, YONGXI, Economics
WANG, YUGUO, Economics
WANG, ZHIAN, Accounting
XIANG, KAILI, Economic Mathematics
XIANG, RONGMEI, Statistics
XIE, JIANMIN, e-Commerce
XIE, SHENGZHI, Economic Information Engineering
XIE, ZHILONG, e-Commerce
XING, QIANGGUO, Public Administration
XU, LANG, Statistics
YIN, MENGBO, Finance
YIN, QINGSHUANG, Public Administration
YIN, YINPIN, Public Finance and Taxation
YIN, ZHONGMING, International Business
YUAN, WENPING, Economics
YUE, CAISHEN, Law
ZENG, KANGLIN, Finance
ZENG, XIAOLING, Accounting
ZHANG, HEJIN, Finance
ZHANG, KUANHAI, Economic Information Engineering
ZHANG, QIAOYUN, Finance
ZHANG, WEI, Economics
ZHANG, XINCAI, e-Commerce
ZHAO, DEWU, Accounting
ZHENG, JINGJI, Economics
ZHONG, CHENG, e-Commerce
ZHOU, GUANGDA, Statistics
ZHOU, HONGYUAN, Finance
ZHOU, QIHAI, Economic Information Engineering
ZHOU, XIAOLIN, Public Finance and Taxation
ZHU, MINGXI, Public Finance and Taxation
ZHUO, ZHI, Insurance

SOUTHEAST UNIVERSITY

Si Pai Lou 2, Nanjing 210096
Telephone: (25) 83792412
E-mail: oic@seu.edu.cn
Internet: www.seu.edu.cn

Founded 1902
State control

Pres.: Prof. YI HONG
Vice-Pres.: Prof. LIU BO
Vice-Pres.: Prof. PU YUEPU
Vice-Pres.: Prof. ZHAO QIMAN
Vice-Pres.: Prof. HU MINQIANG
Vice-Pres.: Prof. ZHENG JIAMAO
Vice-Pres.: Prof. SHEN JIONG
Vice-Pres.: Prof. WANG BAOPING

Library: 3.3m. vols
Number of teachers: 2,269
Number of students: 41,090

Publication: *Journal*

DIRECTORS

Chien-shiung Wu College: Prof. LI AIQUN
College of Continuing Education: ZHUANG BAOJIE
College of Integrated Circuits: Prof. SHI LONGXING
College of International Students: Prof. HUANG KAI
Department of Mathematics: Prof. LIU JIJUN
Department of Physics: Prof. YANG YONGHONG
Department of Physical Education: Prof. CAI XIAOBO
Research Institute of SEU in Changzhou: Prof. LIU JINGNAN
Research Institute of SEU in Suzhou: HU MINQIANG
School of Architecture: Prof. WANG JIANGUO
School of Arts: Prof. WANG TINGXIN
School of Automation: Prof. FEI SHUMIN
School of Biological Science and Medical Engineering: Prof. GU NING

School of Computer Science and Engineering: Prof. LUO JUNZHOU
School of Chemistry and Chemical Engineering: Prof. LIN BAOPING
School of Civil Engineering: Prof. WU GANG
School of Economics and Management: Prof. XU KANGNING
School of Electrical Engineering: Prof. HUANG XUELIANG
School of Electronic Science and Engineering: Prof. SHI LONGXING
School of Energy and Environment: Prof. JIN BAOSHENG
School of Foreign Languages: Prof. LI XIAOXIANG
School of Humanities: Prof. FAN HEPING
School of Information Science and Engineering: Prof. YOU XIAOHU
School of Instrument Science and Engineering: Prof. SONG AIGUO
School of Material Science and Engineering: Prof. PAN YE
School of Mechanical Engineering: Prof. TANG WENCHENG
School of Medicine: Prof. TENG GAOJUN
School of Public Health: Prof. LIU PEI
School of Transportation: Prof. WANG WEI

SOUTHWEST JIAOTONG UNIVERSITY

111 N 1, Er Huan Rd, Chengdu 610031, Sichuan Province
Telephone: (28) 87600114
Internet: www.swjtu.edu.cn

Founded 1896
State control
Academic year: September to July

Pres.: ZHOU BENKUAN
Vice-Pres: CHEN ZHIJIAN
Vice-Pres: HUANG QING
Vice-Pres: JIANG GEFU
Vice-Pres: LIN ANLIN
Vice-Pres: PU DEZHANG
Vice-Pres: YANG LIZHONG
Head of Graduate Dept: HUANG QING
Librarian: DONG DEZHEN

Number of teachers: 1,961
Number of students: 20,000

Publication: *Journal* (natural sciences, 6 a year, in Chinese and English)

DEANS

College of Foreign Languages: XIA WEIRONG
College of Traffic and Transportation: ZHANG DIANYE
Faculty of Software: WU GUANG
School of Art and Communication: WANG SHUNHONG
School of Architecture: QIU JIAN
School of Civil Engineering: LI QIAO
School of Computer Science and Communications Engineering: FAN PINGZHI
School of Economics and Management: JIA JIANMIN
School of Electrical Engineering: LI QUNZHEN
School of Environmental Science and Engineering: LIU BAOJUN
School of Material Science and Engineering: HUANG NAN
School of Mechanical Engineering: XU MINGHENG

PROFESSORS

CAI, HUAI, Computer Science and Communications Engineering
CAI, YING, Civil Engineering
CEN, MINYI, Civil Engineering
CHE, HUIMIN, Civil Engineering
CHEN, JUNYING, Material Science and Engineering
CHEN, XIANGDONG, Computer Science and Communications Engineering
CHEN, XIAOCHUAN, Electrical Engineering
CHENG, QIANGONG, Civil Engineering
DAI, GUANGZE, Material Science and Engineering
DENG, RONGGUI, Civil Engineering
DENG, YOUQIANG, Economics and Management
DENG, YUCAI, Civil Engineering
DIAO, MINGBI, Economics and Management
FAN, HONG, Computer Software
FAN, LILI, Economics and Management
FAN, PINGZHI, Computer Science and Communications Engineering
FANG, XUMING, Computer Science and Communications Engineering
FENG, BO, Material Science and Engineering
FENG, QUANYUAN, Computer Science and Communications Engineering
FENG, XIAOYUN, Electrical Engineering
FU, YONGSHENG, Environmental Science and Engineering
GAO, BO, Civil Engineering
GAO, LONGCHANG, Economics and Management
GAO, SHIBIN, Electrical Engineering
GUAN, BAOSHU, Civil Engineering
GUO, JIN, Computer Science and Communications Engineering
GUO, YAOHUANG, Economics and Management
HE, CHUAN, Civil Engineering
HE, DAKE, Computer Science and Communications Engineering
HE, GUANGHAN, Civil Engineering
HU, HOUTIAN, Civil Engineering
HU, PEI, Economics and Management
HU, XIEWEN, Civil Engineering
HUANG, DENGSHI, Economics and Management
HUANG, DINGFU, Civil Engineering
HUANG, NAN, Material Science and Engineering
HUANG, ZEWEN, Material Science and Engineering
JIA, JIANMIN, Economics and Management
JIA, ZHIYONG, Economics and Management
JIANG, GUANLU, Civil Engineering
JIANG, QI, Material Science and Engineering
JIANG, SHIZHONG, Civil Engineering
JIN, WEIDONG, Electrical Engineering
LAO, YUANCHANG, Civil Engineering
LENG, YONGXIANG, Material Science and Engineering
LI, CHENGHUI, Civil Engineering
LI, CHENGZHONG, Computer Science and Communications Engineering
LI, JUN, Economics and Management
LI, QIAO, Civil Engineering
LI, QUNZHEN, Electrical Engineering
LI, XIAOHONG, Material Science and Engineering
LI, YADONG, Civil Engineering
LI, YONGSHU, Civil Engineering
LI, YUANFU, Civil Engineering
LI, ZHI, Electrical Engineering
LIAO, HAILI, Civil Engineering
LIU, DAN, Environmental Science and Engineering
LIU, HANWEI, Material Science and Engineering
LIU, XUEYI, Civil Engineering
LIU, ZHENGPING, Civil Engineering
LU, CHANGJIANG
LU, HELIN, Civil Engineering
LU, YANG, Civil Engineering
LU, ZHENQIN, Civil Engineering
LUO, BIN, Computer Science and Communications Engineering
LUO, YUANLIANG, Economics and Management
MA, YONGQIANG, Computer Science and Communications Engineering
MOU, RUIFANG, Environmental Science and Engineering
PAN, WEI, Computer Science and Communications Engineering
PENG, DAIYUAN, Computer Science and Communications Engineering
PENG, QIYUAN, Traffic and Transportation
PU, JINHUI, Civil Engineering
QI, TAIYUE, Civil Engineering
QIAN, DONGSHENG, Civil Engineering
QIANG, YONGJIU, Civil Engineering
QIU, WENGE, Civil Engineering
QUE, YANJUN, Civil Engineering
SHI, BENSHAN, Economics and Management
SU, BIN, Computer Software
SUN, LINFU, Civil Engineering
TANG, XIAOHU, Computer Science and Communications Engineering
WAN, FUGUANG, Civil Engineering
WANG, BEN, Electrical Engineering
WANG, CHENGZHANG, Economics and Management
WANG, JIN, Material Science and Engineering
WANG, JUNSHI, Material Science and Engineering
WANG, MINGNIAN, Civil Engineering
WANG, PING, Civil Engineering
WANG, QIAN, Economics and Management
WANG, YONG, Material Science and Engineering
WONG, JIE, Material Science and Engineering
WU, GUANG, Civil Engineering
WU, GUANG, Environmental Science and Engineering
WU, GUANG, Computer Software
WU, GUANGNING, Electrical Engineering
WU, ZHENYE, Economics and Management
XIA, WEIRONG, Foreign Languages
XIAO, JIAN, Electrical Engineering
XIE, QIANG, Civil Engineering
XU, JIANPING, Electrical Engineering
YAN, CHUANPENG, Material Science and Engineering
YANG, BANGCHENG, Material Science and Engineering
YANG, CHUAN, Material Science and Engineering
YANG, JIMEI, Economics and Management
YANG, LIZHONG, Civil Engineering
YANG, LIZHONG, Environmental Science and Engineering
YANG, PING, Material Science and Engineering
YANG, SHUNSHENG, Environmental Science and Engineering
YANG, YONGGAO, Computer Software
YAO, LINGKAN, Civil Engineering
YE, ZIRONG, Economics and Management
YI, SIRONG, Civil Engineering
YIN, ZHIBEN, Computer Science and Communications Engineering
YIN, ZHIBEN, Computer Software
ZENG, HUASANG, Computer Science and Communications Engineering
ZHANG, CUIFANG, Computer Science and Communications Engineering
ZHANG, DIANYE, Traffic and Transportation
ZHANG, JIANQIANG, Environmental Science and Engineering
ZHANG, JIASHU, Computer Science and Communications Engineering
ZHANG, JICHUN, Civil Engineering
ZHANG, KUNLUN, Electrical Engineering
ZHANG, WEI, Economics and Management
ZHANG, XIYAN, Material Science and Engineering
ZHAO, LEI, Civil Engineering
ZHAO, RENDA, Civil Engineering
ZHAO, SHANRUI, Civil Engineering
ZHAO, YUGUANG, Civil Engineering
ZHENG, KAIFENG, Civil Engineering
ZHOU, DEPEI, Civil Engineering
ZHOU, GUOHUA, Economics and Management
ZHOU, RONGHUI, Computer Science and Communications Engineering
ZHOU, SHAOBING, Material Science and Engineering
ZHOU, ZHONGRONG, Material Science and Engineering
ZHOU, ZUOWAN, Material Science and Engineering

ZHU, BING, Civil Engineering
ZHU, CHANGJIN, Computer Science and Communications Engineering
ZHU, DEGUI, Material Science and Engineering
ZHU, FENG, Electrical Engineering
ZHU, WENHAO, Material Science and Engineering
ZHUANG, SHENGXIAN, Electrical Engineering

SOUTHWEST PETROLEUM UNIVERSITY

Chengdu, Nanchong 637001, Sichuan Province
Telephone: (817) 2642301
Internet: aa.swpu.edu.cn/en
Founded 1958
provincial control
Academic year: September to July
Pres.: DU ZHIMIN
Vice-Pres: CHEN CICHANG
Vice-Pres: SUN YIPING
Vice-Pres: ZHAO JINZHOU
Vice-Pres: ZHOU MAO
Librarian: REN HAO
Library of 1,473,000 vols
Number of teachers: 888
Number of students: 15,951
Publications: *Higher Petroleum Education* (4 a year), *Journal* (4 a year)

PROFESSORS

BENG, JUN, Resources and the Environment
CHEN, JINGSHAN, Petroleum Exploration
CHEN, PING, Petroleum Engineering
CHENG, SHIQI, Resources and the Environment
DENG, JIANMING, Petroleum Engineering
DU, ZHIMIN, Petroleum Engineering
DUAN, DARONG, Electronic Information
GUO, XIAOYANG, Petroleum Engineering
HONG, QINYU, Depositation
HU, XINGQI, Electronic Information
HUANG, BINGGUANG, Petroleum Engineering
HUANG, LINJI, Petroleum Engineering
HUANG, ZHIYU, Electronic Information
JIANG, PING, Resource Science and Engineering
KANG, YILI, Petroleum Engineering
LI, BINGYUAN, Petroleum Engineering
LI, CHANGJUN, Petroleum Engineering
LI, CHUANLIANG, Petroleum Engineering
LI, CHUNFU, Resource Science and Engineering
LI, QIAN, Petroleum Engineering
LI, SHILUN, Petroleum Engineering
LI, YINGCHUAN, Petroleum Engineering
LI, YUN, Petroleum Engineering
LI, ZHIPING, Petroleum Engineering
LIAN, ZHANGHUA, Petroleum Engineering
LIANG, ZHENG, Resource Science and Engineering
LIAO, XIMING, Resources and the Environment
LIEHUI, Petroleum Engineering
LIU, CHONGJIAN, Petroleum Engineering
LUO, MINGGAO, Resources and the Environment
LUO, PINGYA, Petroleum Engineering
MA, DEKUN, Resource Science and Engineering
PU, XIAOLIN, Petroleum Engineering
QIN, QIRONG, Resources and the Environment
SHEN, ZHAOGUO, Survey and Exploration of Mineral Products
SHI, TAIHE, Petroleum Engineering
SUN, LIANGTIAN, Petroleum Engineering
WANG, TINDONG, Resources and the Environment
WANG, XINZHI, Resources and the Environment
WANG, YUAN, Petroleum Engineering
YAN, QIBIN, Survey and Exploration of Mineral Products
YANG, SHIGUANG, Electronic Information
YAO, ANLIN, Building Engineering
YUAN, ZONGMING, Petroleum Engineering
ZHANG, BAILIN, Resources and the Environment
ZHANG, FAN, Resources and the Environment
ZHANG, MINGHONG, Resource Science and Engineering
ZHANG, PENG, Resource Science and Engineering
ZHANG, TINSHAN, Resources and the Environment
ZHAO, JINZHOU, Petroleum Engineering
ZHAO, LIQIANG, Petroleum Engineering
ZHAO, LIZHI, Electronic Information
ZHOU, KAIJI, Petroleum Engineering

SOUTHWEST UNIVERSITY OF POLITICAL SCIENCE AND LAW

2 Zhuangzhi Rd, Shapingba, Chongqing 400031
Telephone: (23) 65382114
Internet: www.swupl.edu.cn
Founded 1953
Academic year: September to July
Pres.: LONG ZONGZHI
Vice-Pres.: FU ZITANG
Vice-Pres.: LI CHUNRU
Vice-Pres.: LIU JUN
Vice-Pres.: WANG JIANHUA
Head of Graduate Dept: YANG SHUMING
Librarian: ZOU YULI
Library of 800,000 vols
Number of teachers: 1,000
Number of students: 20,000
Publications: *Contemporaneity Law School* (6 a year), *Journal* (6 a year)

DEANS

School of Administration: CAO DAYOU
School of Administrative Law: (vacant)
School of Applied Law: LI WEI
School of Civil and Business Law: ZHAO WANYI
School of Criminology: GUAN GUANGCHENG
School of Economic and Trade Law: TANG QINGYANG
School of Economics: LIU LUJI
School of Foreign Languages: SONG LEI
School of Law: CHEN ZHONGLIN
School of Media: ZHAO ZHONGJI
School of Politics and Public Affairs: RAN ZHI

PROFESSORS

BAI, SHENG, Administration
CAO, DAYOU, Administration
CHANG, YI, Law
CHEN, JINQUAN, Administrative Law
CHEN, WEI, Civil and Business Law
CHEN, ZHONGLIN, Law
DENG, RUIPING, Economic and Trade Law
FU, ZITANG, Economic and Trade Law
FU, ZITANG, Law
GAO, SHAOXIAN, Law
GUAN, GUANGCHENG, Criminology
HAN, TIANSEN, Economic and Trade Law
HU, GUANGZHI, Economic and Trade Law
HU, RUKUI, Politics and Public Affairs
HU, SHICHENG, Criminology
HUI, YIN, Environment and International Law
LAI, DAQING, Economic and Trade Law
LI, CHANGQI, Economic and Trade Law
LI, JINRONG, Economic and Trade Law
LI, KAIGUO, Civil and Business Law
LI, PEIZE, Law
LI, SHENGYU, Administrative Law
LI, WEI, Law Application
LI, YONGSHENG, Law
LI, ZUJUN, Law
LIAO, ZHONGHONG, Law
LIN, RUIYING, Politics and Public Affairs
LIU, LUJI, Economics
LIU, XIANGSHU, Economic and Trade Law
LONG, ZONGZHI, Law
LU, DAIFU, Economic and Trade Law
RAN, ZHI, Politics and Public Affairs
REN, ZUYAO, Economics
SHI, HUIRONG, Civil and Business Law
SONG, LEI, Foreign Languages
SONG, YUBO, Administration
SUN, CHANGYONG, Law
TIAN, PINGAN, Law
WAN, YINGZHONG, Economics
WANG, LIRONG, Law
WANG, SHIHU, Civil and Business Law
WANG, XUEHUI, Administrative Law
WEN, ZHENGBANG, Administrative Law
WU, YUE, Economic and Trade Law
XIAO, YUNSHU, Foreign Languages
XU, JINGCUN, Law
XU, MINGYUE, Economic and Trade Law
YANG, SHUMING, Economic and Trade Law
YU, RONGGEN, Law
ZENG, DAIWEI, Administrative Law
ZENG, FANYUE, Politics and Public Affairs
ZHANG, GENG, Civil and Business Law
ZHANG, QIAN, Administrative Law
ZHANG, SHIDI, Media
ZHANG, YUMIN, Civil and Business Law
ZHAO, MING, Administrative Law
ZHAO, WANYI, Civil and Business Law
ZHAO, XUEQING, Economic and Trade Law
ZHAO, ZHONGJI, Media
ZHENG, CHUANKUN, Administrative Law
ZHONG, MINGZHAO, Economic and Trade Law
ZHU, JIANHUA, Law
ZUO, KAIDA, Politics and Public Affairs

SUN YAT-SEN UNIVERSITY

135 Xingang Rd, Guangzhou 510275, Guangdong Province
Telephone: (20) 84111583
E-mail: adpo@sysu.edu.cn
Internet: www.sysu.edu.cn
Founded 1924
State control
Academic year: September to July
Pres.: HUANG DAREN
Vice-Pres.: CHEN RUZHU
Vice-Pres.: CHEN WEILING
Vice-Pres.: CHEN YUCHUAN
Vice-Pres.: LIANG QINGYIN
Vice-Pres.: LI PING
Vice-Pres.: WANG JIANPING
Vice-Pres.: XU JIARUI
Vice-Pres.: XU NINGSHENG
Vice-Pres.: XU YUANTONG
Vice-Pres.: YAN GUANGMEI
Vice-Pres.: YU SHIYOU
Librarian: CHENG HUANWEN
Library of 4,170,000 vols
Number of teachers: 7,700
Number of students: 41,000
Publications: *Journal* (natural sciences and social sciences edns, each 4 a year), *Journal of the Graduates*, *Pearl River Delta Economy*, *South China Population*

HEADS OF SCHOOLS

College of Continuing Education: Prof. ZHAO GUODU
Graduate School: Prof. HUANG DAREN
Guang Hua School of Stomatology: Prof. LING JUNQI
Lingnan (University) College: Prof. SHU YUAN
School of Business: Prof. WEI MINGHAI
School of Chemistry and Chemical Engineering: Prof. CHEN XIAOMING
School of Environmental Science and Engineering: Prof. SUN XIAOMING
School of Foreign Languages: Prof. HUANG GUOWEN

School of Geographical Science and Planning: Prof. BAO JIGANG
School of Humanities: Prof. CHEN CHUNSHENG
School of Information Science and Technology: Prof. HUANG JIWU
School of Law and Political Science: Prof. REN JIANTAO
School of Life Sciences: Prof. XU ANLONG
School of Mathematics and Computational Science: Prof. ZHU XIPING
School of Physics and Engineering: Prof. XU NINGSHENG
School of Nursing: Prof. YOU LIMING
School of Overseas Educational Exchange: Prof. XU NINGSHENG
School of Pre-Clinical Medicine: Prof. XIE FUKANG
School of Public Health: LING WENHUA

TAIYUAN UNIVERSITY OF TECHNOLOGY

West Fen River Park, Taiyuan, Shanxi Province
Telephone: (351) 6010140
E-mail: xiaoban@tyut.edu.cn
Internet: www.tyut.edu.cn

Founded 1902
Academic year: September to July

Pres.: XIE KECHANG
Vice-Pres: GUO MINTAI
Vice-Pres: HAO JIANGGONG
Vice-Pres: HU BOYAN
Vice-Pres: LU MING
Vice-Pres: LU ZHENGUANG
Vice-Pres: MA FUCHANG
Vice-Pres: XU BINGSHE
Head of Graduate Dept: LING KAICHENG
Librarian: WANG SHENGKUN

Library of 1,830,000 vols
Number of teachers: 1,506
Number of students: 15,659

Publications: *Coal Transformation* (4 a year), *Journal* (natural sciences, 6 a year; social sciences, 4 a year), *Journal of Social Science of Shanxi High Schools* (12 a year), *Journal of Systemic Dialectics* (4 a year)

DEANS

College of Architecture and Environmental Engineering: (vacant)
College of Chemical Engineering and Technology: (vacant)
College of Economics Management: NIU CHONGHUAI
College of Electrical and Power Engineering: BU QINGHUA
College of Humanities: (vacant)
College of Information Engineering: XIE KEMING
College of Materials Science and Engineering: XU BINGSHE
College of Mechanical Engineering: (vacant)
College of Mining Engineering: KANG LIXUN
College of Science: (vacant)
College of Textile Engineering and Arts: (vacant)

PROFESSORS

BU, QINGHUA, Electrical and Power Engineering
CHEN, JUNJIE, Information Engineering
DUAN, FU, Information Engineering
DUAN, KANGLIAN, Mining Engineering
FANG, JINGHUA, Electrical and Power Engineering
GUO, YONGYI, Mining Engineering
HAN, FUCHUN, Electrical and Power Engineering
JIA, XIAOCHUAN, Electrical and Power Engineering
KANG, LIXUN, Mining Engineering
LI, XUEZHONG, Mining Engineering
NIU, CHONGHUAI, Economics Management
REN, PINGZHAO, Electrical and Power Engineering
SONG, JIANCHENG, Electrical and Power Engineering
TIAN, QUZHEN, Mining Engineering
WANG, HANBIN, Economics Management
ZHANG, JIANPING, Economics Management
ZHAO, YIFANG, Mining Engineering
ZHAO, YUHUAI, Electrical and Power Engineering

TIANJIN CONSERVATORY OF MUSIC

57 11th Meridian Rd, 300171 Tianjin
Telephone: (22) 24160049
E-mail: yuanzhang@tjcm.edu.cn
Internet: www.tjcm.edu.cn

Founded 1958

Pres.: XU CHANGJUN (acting)
Vice-Pres: FANG JIAN JUN
Vice-Pres: JIN XUEDONG
Vice-Pres: TANGYUE QI
Librarian: Assoc. Prof. WANG ZHIJIAN

Library of 200,000 vols
Number of teachers: 406
Number of students: 3,000

Publication: *Music Study and Research* (4 a year)

DEANS

Chinese Traditional Music: Assoc. Prof. SONG GUOSHENG
Composition: Prof. CHEN ENGUANG
Education: Assoc. Prof. YANG LIZHONG
Orchestra: Prof. YAN ZHENGPING
Vocal: Assoc. Prof. XIA ZHONGHENG

TIANJIN MEDICAL UNIVERSITY

22 Qi Xiang Tai Rd, Heping Dist., 300070 Tianjin
Telephone: (22) 341234
Internet: www.tijmu.edu.cn

Founded 1951 as Tianjin Medical College, current name adopted 1993

Pres.: Prof. YONGFENG SHANG
Vice-Pres.: CUI YITAI
Vice-Pres.: FANG PEIHUA
Vice-Pres.: LI JINGFU
Vice-Pres.: XING KEHAO
Chief Librarian: BAI JINGWEN

Library of 1,226,600 vols
Number of teachers: 1,550
Number of students: 9,697

Publications: *Foreign Medicine* (4 a year), *Journal of Tianjin Medical College* (4 a year), *Medical Education Research* (2 a year), *Medical Inquiry* (6 a year), *Medical Translation* (4 a year)

PROFESSORS

Dermatology:
FU ZHIYI
SHEN JIANMING

Endocrinology:
LI LIANGE
MA LIYUN
PANG ZHILING

Internal Medicine:
CHENG YUQIAN
DU WENBIN
HUANG NAIXIA
HUANG TIGANG
HUANG XIANGQIAN
SHI YUSHU
WANG PEIXIAN
YIN WEI
ZHOU JINTAI

Isotope:
FANG PEIHUA
LU TIZHANG
ZHENG MIAORONG

Neurology:
CHEN SHIJUN
JIANG DEHUA
PU PEIYU
XUE QINGCHENG
YANG LUCHUN

Obstetrics and Gynaecology:
JIAO SHUZHU
ZHAI ZHANCAN

Ophthalmology:
SONG GUOXIANG
WANG YANHUA
YING SHIHAO
YUAN JIAQING
ZHANG LIANJING

Otorhinolaryngology:
GUO QIXIN
WANG YANYOU
YAN CHENGXIAN

Paediatrics:
HUANG HONGHAI
LIU YUJI

Radiology:
HE NENGSHU
LIAN ZHONGCHENG
LI JINGXUE
WU ENHUI
YANG TIANEN
ZHAO CHANGJIANG

Stomatology:
HOU ZHIYAN
SUN XUEMIN

Surgery:
DAI ZHIHUA
DONG KEQUAN
GUO SHIFU
LI QINGRUI
LIU ZIKUAN
SHENG XIKUN
WANG PENGZHI
WU XIANZHONG
YU SONGTING

TIANJIN NORMAL UNIVERSITY

241 Weijing Rd, Tianjin 300074
Telephone: (22) 23540025
E-mail: msk@mail.tjnu.edu.cn
Internet: www.tjnu.edu.cn

Founded 1958
Academic year: September to July

Pres.: GAO YUBAO
Vice-Pres.: WANG GUILIN
Vice-Pres.: WANG YAOJIN
Vice-Pres.: XU JIANDONG

Library of 2,140,000 vols
Number of teachers: 2,113
Number of students: 30,000

Publication: *Journal* (4 a year)

DEANS

College of Basic Education: WANG GONGLIANG
College of Biology and Chemistry: GU BINHONG
College of Chemistry and Environment Science: (vacant)
College of Computer and Information Engineering: (vacant)
College of Economics: (vacant)
College of Education Science: GAO HENGLI
College of Foreign Languages: GU GANG
College of History and Culture: HOU JIANXIN
College of Literature: MENG ZHAOYI
College of Management: (vacant)
College of Mathematics: (vacant)
College of News and Communication: LIU WEIDONG

College of Physical Culture and Science: ZHANG JINNIAN
College of Physics and Electronic Information: CHANG XIANGRONG
College of Politics and Public Administration: GAO JIAN
Institute of Arts: SHUN GUANGJUN

PROFESSORS

BA, XINSHENG, History and Culture
BAO, YUANKAI, Arts
BI, GUANGJI, Physics and Electronic Information
CHANG, SHIYAN, Politics and Public Administration
CHEN, SHANGWEI, Politics and Public Administration
CHEN, XU, Biology and Chemistry
CHEN, YAN, Literature
CHEN, YUANLONG, Arts
CUI, FENGFU, Mathematics
DING, WEIMING, Economics
DONG, SIDAI, Politics and Public Administration
DUO, LIAN, Biology and Chemistry
FENG, JINCHENG, Biology and Chemistry
GAO, HENGWEN, Literature
GAO, JIAN, Politics and Public Administration
GAO, JIE, Management
GE, LUNHONG, Foreign Languages
GONG, ZUOMING, Chemistry and Environment Science
GU, BINHONG, Biology and Chemistry
GU, GANG, Foreign Languages
GU, WEIQING, Management
GUO, JIAN, Mathematics
GUO, QINGZHU, Foreign Languages
HAO, GUISHENG, Politics and Public Administration
HAO, JINKU, Biology and Chemistry
HE, CHENGQUAN, Chemistry and Environment Science
HONG, SONGLING, Economics
HOU, JIANXIN, History and Culture
HOU, RUNSHENG, Physical Culture and Science
LI, BAOYI, Mathematics
LI, DAPENG, Literature
LI, HUA, Literature
LI, JIECHUAN, History and Culture
LI, LONGZHU, Management
LI, PEIWU, Chemistry and Environment Science
LI, XUEZHI, History and Culture
LI, YI, Physics and Electronic Information
LI, YIJIN, Literature
LI, YUNXING, Foreign Languages
LI, ZHENGANG, Physics and Electronic Information
LIAO, QIBING, Physical Culture and Science
LIU, CHUNMAO, Management
LIU, DONGHUA, Biology and Chemistry
LIU, HONG, Economics
LIU, LILI, Biology and Chemistry
LIU, QIANG, Biology and Chemistry
LIU, SHIMING, Politics and Public Administration
LIU, WEIDONG, News and Communication
LIU, XIANGJUN, Biology and Chemistry
LIU, XIAOLAN, Biology and Chemistry
LIU, YUZHEN, Foreign Languages
LONG, XIUQING, History and Culture
LU, GUANGYUAN, Physics and Electronic Information
MA, DEPU, Politics and Public Administration
MA, JUNMING, History and Culture
MA, RUIJIANG, History and Culture
MA, YI, News and Communication
MAO, JIANYAO, Mathematics
MENG, ZHAOYI, Literature
MIU, FANGMING, Biology and Chemistry
PAN, RONG, History and Culture
PANG, ZHUOHENG, History and Culture
PENG, JINRONG, Economics
PENG, YONGKANG, Biology and Chemistry
PING, HUIYUAN, Literature
RONG, CHANGHAI, Politics and Public Administration
SHEN, LAIFAN, Arts
SHUN, HUIMIN, Economics
SHUN, QIFENG, Arts
SONG, CHANGLI, Literature
SONG, YI, Arts
TIAN, QINGJUN, Physics and Electronic Information
WAN, QUAN, Economics
WAN, TANGMING, Literature
WANG, FU, Arts
WANG, GUANGMING, Mathematics
WANG, GUOSHOU, Literature
WANG, JIANING, Foreign Languages
WANG, JINGAN, Biology and Chemistry
WANG, JINLING, Biology and Chemistry
WANG, TONGQI, Politics and Public Administration
WANG, XINHUA, Economics
WANG, XIUGE, Politics and Public Administration
WANG, YAN, Basic Education College
WANG, YAPING, History and Culture
WANG, YONGCHENG, Physics and Electronic Information
WANG, YUBEN, Mathematics
WANG, ZHENYING, Biology and Chemistry
WEI, WENYUAN, Mathematics
WEI, ZIGUANG, Biology and Chemistry
WU, CHUNHUA, Politics and Public Administration
XIA, XIAOYANG, Physics and Electronic Information
XIAO, LIJUN, History and Culture
XU, DATONG, Politics and Public Administration
XU, DELING, Economics
XU, LIMIAO, Chemistry and Environment Science
XU, RONGKUN, Arts
XU, YONGLONG, Management
XU, ZHELIN, Mathematics
YAN, YONGXIN, Management
YANG, JIALING, Biology and Chemistry
YANG, XIYUN, History and Culture
YOU, ZHEQING, Physics and Electronic Information
YU, JINCHENG, Politics and Public Administration
ZENG, YUEXIN, Physics and Electronic Information
ZHAI, CHANGMING, Politics and Public Administration
ZHANG, FUYE, Arts
ZHANG, JIER, Mathematics
ZHANG, JINGNIAN, Physical Culture and Science
ZHANG, LINJIE, Literature
ZHANG, QIYING, Economics
ZHANG, WENHUI, Biology and Chemistry
ZHANG, XIN, Biology and Chemistry
ZHANG, ZHIYONG, Physics and Electronic Information
ZHAO, DENGYING, Arts
ZHAO, JIE, Physics and Electronic Information
ZHAO, LIMING, Literature
ZHAO, LIZHU, Foreign Languages
ZHENG, LIANBING, Biology and Chemistry
ZHONG, YUXIU, Foreign Languages
ZHU, SHAOHONG, Mathematics

TIANJIN POLYTECHNIC UNIVERSITY

63 Chenglinzhuang Rd, Hedong District, Tianjin 300160
Telephone: (22) 24528000
E-mail: zxb@tjpu.edu.cn
Internet: www.tjpu.edu.cn
Founded 1958
Academic year: September to July
Pres.: Prof. ZHANG, HONGWEI
Vice-Pres.: Prof. JIANG XIUMING
Vice-Pres.: Prof. XIAO CHANGFA
Vice-Pres.: Assoc. Prof. YANG HONG
Vice-Pres.: YANG JIDI
Dir of Int. Office: Prof. LI YUXIANG
Dir of Int. Office: Prof. LI YUXIANG
Librarian: HANG GUANGFENG
Library of 700,000 vols, 2,100 periodicals
Number of teachers: 1,086
Number of students: 23,600
Publication: *Journal* (6 a year)

HEADS OF SCHOOLS AND COLLEGES

College of Adult Education: Prof. YANG XIULAN
College of Vocational Technology: Prof. YANG, XIULAN
School of Accounting: Prof. WEI, YAPING
School of Art Design: Prof. XU, DONG
School of Computer Technology and Automation: Prof. HANG, QUIRI
School of Economics: Prof. ZHAO, HONG
School of Foreign Languages: Assoc. Prof. YU, XIAODAN
School of Humanities and Law: Prof. ZHANG, CHUNHONG
School of Information and Communications Engineering: Prof. MIAO, CHANYUN
School of International Culture: Prof. LI YUXIANG
School of Management: Assoc. Prof. WU, ZHONGYUAN
School of Material Science and Chemical Engineering: Prof. CHENG, LI
School of Mechanical and Electronic Engineering: Prof. WU BAOLIN
School of Science: Prof. SUN MINGZHU
School of Textiles and Clothing: Prof. WANG, RUI
Institute of Function Fibre: Prof. MA, YAJING
Institute of Laser Processing: Prof. YANG, XICHEN
Institute of Membrane Technology: Prof. LI, XINMIN
Institute of Textile Composite Material: Prof. LI, JIALU

There are 38 research institutes and laboratories.

TIANJIN UNIVERSITY

92 Weijin Rd, 300072 Tianjin
Telephone: (22) 27406146
E-mail: ies@tju.edu.cn
Internet: www.tju.edu.cn
Founded 1895 as Peiyang Univ., current name adopted 1951
State control
Academic year: August to September (2 semesters)
Pres.: Prof. LI JIAJUN
Vice-Pres.: Prof. YU JIANXING
Vice-Pres.: Prof. FENG YAQING
Vice-Pres.: Prof. SHU GEQUN
Vice-Pres.: Prof. LIU DONGZHI
Vice-Pres.: Prof. YUAN YINGJIN
Librarian: Prof. YANG JIACHENG
Library: 2.4m. vols
Number of teachers: 4,407
Number of students: 29,907
Publications: *Collection of Research Achievements*, *Journal* (4 a year), various departmental publs

DEANS

School of Architecture: Prof. ZHANG QI
School of Civil Engineering: LIAN JIJIAN
School of Computer Science and Technology: DANG JIAN-WU
School of Computer Software: MENG ZHAOPENG
School of Electrical Engineering and Automation: Prof. SUNG YUGENG
School of Electronic Information Engineering: MA JIANGUO

School of Environmental Science and Engineering: CHEN GUANYI
School of Liberal Art and Law: LI XU
School of Management and Economics: Prof. WEI ZHANG
School of Materials Science and Engineering: Prof. ZHEN DUO CUI
School of Mechanical Engineering: Prof. WANG SHUXIN
School of Pharmaceutical Science and Technology: Dr JAY SIEGEL
School of Precision Instruments and Opto-Electronics Engineering: Prof. ZENG ZHOUMO
School of Sciences: ZHANG CHUNTING

TIANJIN UNIVERSITY OF COMMERCE

East Entrance of Jinba Rd, Beichen Dist., Tianjin 300134
Telephone: (22) 26667666
Internet: www.tjuc.edu

Founded 1980

Pres.: Prof. LIU SHUHAN

Library of 400,000 vols, 1,817 periodicals
Number of teachers: 839
Number of students: 15,000

Publication: *University Journal*

DEANS

College of Administration: ZHANG GUOWANG
College of Biological Technology and Food Science: PANG GUANGCHANG
College of Economy and Trade: BAI LING
College of Information Engineering: LIU DUO
College of International Exchange: KOU XIAOXUAN
College of Law and Politics: SHI RUIJIE
College of Mechanical Engineering: (vacant)
College of Science: YU YILIANG
College of Tourism Administration: WANG WENJUN
School of Foreign Languages: PAUL CHILTON

TIANJIN UNIVERSITY OF SCIENCE & TECHNOLOGY

1038 Dagu Nanlu, 300222 Tianjin
Telephone: (22) 8340538
E-mail: tjili@tju.edu.cn
Internet: www.tust.edu.cn

Founded 1958
State control
Languages of instruction: Chinese, English

Pres.: CAO XIAOHONG
Vice-Pres.: ZHANG JIANGUO
Vice-Pres: WANG XUEKUI
Vice-Pres: YAN XUEYUAN
Vice-Pres: WANG SHUO

Library: 1.6m. vols
Number of teachers: 1,750
Number of students: 17,000

Publication: *Journal*

TIBET UNIVERSITY

36 Jiangsu Rd, Chengguan, Lhasa, Tibet Autonomous Region
Telephone: (891) 6324482
E-mail: master@utibet.edu.cn
Internet: www.utibet.edu.cn

Founded 1951 as Tibet Cadres School, current name and status 1985
State control
Main degree areas: biology and geography, chemistry, Chinese and English, economics and management, mathematics and physics, politics and history, Tibetan art and music, Tibetan language

Pres.: PUB TSERING

Library of 800,000 vols
Number of teachers: 1,124
Number of students: 9,924

TONGJI MEDICAL COLLEGE

13 Hang Kong Lu, 430030 Wuhan
Telephone: (27) 83692777
Internet: www.tjmu.edu.cn

Founded 1907
State control
Languages of instruction: Chinese, English, German
Academic year: September to July

Chancellor: Prof. LIU SHUMAO
Pres.: Prof. XUE DELIN
Vice-Pres.: Prof. LIU JIHONG
Vice-Pres.: Prof. AN RUI
Vice-Pres.: Prof. CHEN JIANGUO
Deputy Librarian: Prof. XU FENGYING

Library of 500,000 vols
Number of teachers: 2,692
Number of students: 7,962

Publications: *Acta Universitatis Medicinae Tongji* (6 a year, in Chinese and English), *China Higher Medical Education* (6 a year, in Chinese), *Journal* (4 a year, in Chinese), various departmental publs

DIRECTORS

College of Basic Medicine: Prof. SHI YOU'EN
College for Continuing Medical Education: Prof. XIANG CHUNTING
College of Pharmacy: Prof. TIAN SHIXIONG
College of Public Health: Prof. CHEN XUEMIN
Faculty of Foreign Languages: Prof. ZHANG HONGQING
Faculty of Forensic Medicine: Prof. QIN QISHENG
Faculty of Maternal and Child Health: Prof. LIU XIAOXIAN
Faculty of Medical Library and Information Sciences: Prof. LI DAOPING (Deputy Dir)
Faculty of Paediatrics: Prof. HONG GUANGXIANG
Faculty of Social Sciences: Prof. HU JICHUN
First College of Clinical Medicine: (vacant)
Second College of Clinical Medicine: Prof. HONG GUANG XIANG

TONGJI UNIVERSITY

1239 Siping Rd, Shanghai 200092
Telephone: (21) 65982200
E-mail: webmaster@tongji.edu.cn
Internet: www.tongji.edu.cn

Founded 1907

Pres.: PEI GANG
Vice-Pres.: CHEN YIYI
Vice-Pres.: CHEN XIAOLONG
Vice-Pres.: DONG QI
Vice-Pres.: JIANG CHANGJUN
Vice-Pres.: LI YONGSHENG
Vice-Pres.: WU JIANG
Vice-Pres.: ZHENG HUIQIANG
Librarian: SHEN JINHUA

Number of teachers: 6,350 (incl. 645 profs)
Number of students: 77,516 (incl. 14,312 postgraduates)

Publications: *Tongji Journal*, several technical publications

DEANS

College of Architecture and Urban Planning: CHEN BINZHAO
College of Computer Science: XUAN GUORONG
College of Economics and Management: HUANG YUXIANG
College of Environmental Engineering: LIU SUIQING
College of Humanities and Law: DENG WEIZHI
College of Mechanical Engineering: MAO QINGXI
College of Structural Engineering: FAN LICHU
Graduate School: WU QIDI
Professional Education and Correspondence School: WU QIDI
Sino-German School: WU QIDI

TSINGHUA UNIVERSITY

1 Qing Hua Yuan, Haidian Dist., Beijing 100084
Telephone: (10) 62782015
E-mail: lbzhz@tsinghua.edu.cn
Internet: www.tsinghua.edu.cn

Founded 1911 as Tsinghua Xuetang; renamed Tsinghua School 1912; univ. section added 1925; became Nat. Tsinghua Univ. 1928; re-structured 1952
State control
Languages of instruction: Chinese, English
Academic year: September to January, February to June (2 semesters)

Pres.: Prof. GU BINGLIN
Vice-Pres.: Prof. CHEN JINING
Vice-Pres.: Prof. CHENG JIANPING
Vice-Pres.: Prof. KANG KEJUN
Vice-Pres.: Prof. QIU YONG
Vice-Pres.: Prof. XIE WEIHE
Vice-Pres.: Prof. YUAN SI
Vice-Pres.: Prof. ZHANG FENGCHANG
Provost: Prof. YUAN SI
Librarian: Prof. DENG JINGKANG

Library: 3.76m. vols
Number of teachers: 7,186
Number of students: 31,643

Publications: *China MediaTech* (in Chinese), *Computer Education* (in Chinese), *Decorative Arts* (in Chinese), *Experimental Technology and Management* (in Chinese), *Frontiers of Environmental Science & Engineering in China* (in English), *Journal of Tsinghua University (Philosophy and Social Science)* (in Chinese), *Journal of Tsinghua University (Science and Technology)* (in Chinese), *Modern Education Technology* (in Chinese), *Physics and Engineering* (in Chinese), *Tsinghua Journal of Education* (in Chinese), *Tsinghua Law Review* (in Chinese), *Tsinghua Science and Technology* (6 a year, in English), *World Architecture* (in Chinese)

DEANS

Academy of Art and Design: Prof. FENG YUAN, Prof. ZHENG SHUYANG
Graduate School: Prof. GU BINGLIN
Institute of Nuclear and New Energy Technology: Prof. ZHANG ZUOYIN
School of Aerospace: WANG YONGZHI, Prof. LIANG XINGANG
School of Architecture: Prof. ZHU WENYI
School of Civil Engineering: Prof. CHEN YONGCAN
School of Economics and Management: Prof. QIAN YINGYI
School of Humanities and Social Sciences: Prof. LI QIANG
School of Information Science and Technology: Prof. SUN JIAGUANG
School of Journalism and Communication: Prof. FAN JINGYI, Prof. YIN HONG
School of Law: Prof. WANG ZHENMIN
School of Life Sciences: Prof. SHI YIGONG
School of Marxism: Prof. XING BENSI, Prof. AI SILIN
School of Mechanical Engineering: Prof. YOU ZHENG
School of Medicine: Prof. WU JIEPING, Prof. SHI YIGONG
School of Public Policy and Management: Prof. XUE LAN
School of Sciences: Prof. ZHU BANGFEN
Teaching and Research Division of Physical Education: Prof. CHEN WEIQIANG

UNIVERSITY OF ELECTRONIC SCIENCE AND TECHNOLOGY OF CHINA

4 N Jian She Rd, 610054 Chengdu
Telephone: (28) 83202316
E-mail: dag@uestc.edu.cn
Internet: www.uestc.edu.cn

Founded 1956 as Chengdu Institute of Radio Engineering, current name adopted 1988
Academic year: September to July
Schools of automation engineering; computer science and engineering; electronic engineering; energy science and engineering; foreign languages; information and software engineering; life science and technology; management and economics; marxism education; mathematical sciences; mechatronics engineering; microelectronics and solid-state electronics; optoelectronic information; physical electronics; political science and public administration
Pres.: Prof. LI YAN RONG
Vice-Pres.: YUMIN MING
Vice-Pres.: MA ZHENG
Librarian: Prof. WU WEIGONG
Library of 2,570,000 vols
Number of teachers: 2,100
Number of students: 30,000
Publication: *University Journal* (6 a year)

UNIVERSITY OF INTERNATIONAL BUSINESS AND ECONOMICS

10 Hui Xin Dong Jie, 100029 Beijing
Telephone: (10) 64492327
E-mail: sie@uibe.edu.cn
Internet: www.uibe.edu.cn

Founded 1951
Academic year: September to July
Pres.: Prof. JIANJUN SHI
Vice-Pres: Prof. YANG FENGHUA
Librarian: SHI SHIYU
Number of teachers: 813
Number of students: 17,000
Publications: *University Journal* (6 a year), *International Business* (12 a year), *Japanese Language Studies* (12 a year)

DEANS

Department of Graduate Studies: Assoc. Prof. LIU YUAN
Faculty of Customs Administration: Assoc. Prof. ZHENG JUNTIAN
Faculty of Economic Information Management: Assoc. Prof. DANG JIAN
Faculty of Humanities: Assoc. Prof. ZHENG BAOYIN
School of Continuing Education: Prof. YANG FENGHUA
School of International Business Management: Prof. MA CHUNGUANG
School of International Studies: Prof. WANG XUEWEN
School of International Trade and Economics: Prof. LIN GUIJUN
School of Law: Prof. SHEN SIBAO

PROFESSORS

School of International Trade and Economics:
YE CAIWEN
WANG SHAOXI, International Trade
WANG SHOUCHUN, International Trade
XUE RONGJIU, International Business
CHEN TONGCHOU, International Trade
LI XIAOXIAN, International Trade
QIU NIANZHU, International Trade
SHI YUCHUAN
QIAO RONGZHEN, International Trade
LI KANG
XIA SHEN
WANG YUQING, Technology Trade
YU JUNNIAN
ZHAO XIUCHEN
LIU SHUNIAN
XIA XIURUI, History of China's Foreign Trade
FEI XIUMEI, International Finance
SHI YUXING, International Finance
LEI RONGDI, International Insurance
YAN QIMING, International Transport
WANG LINSHENG
LI KANGHUA
ZHANG XIGU
MENG JICHENG
LI SHI
CHU XIANGYIN
XIA YOUFU
LIN GUIJUN

School of International Business Management:
PENG YUSHU, Accountancy
HU HENIAN, Financial Management
GAO GUOPEI, International Marketing
MA CHUNGUANG, International Management
LIU YAOWEI
JIA HUAIQIN, Statistics
XU ZIJIAN
YU SHULIAN

School of International Studies:
SUN WEIYAN
HUANG ZHENHUA
FANG MAOTIAN
WANG XUEWEI, Business English
HE ZENGMEI, English
WU SHUNCHANG, English
WU FENG, Linguistics (English)
ZHANG BINGZI, Business English
YANG CHAOGUANG, Linguistics
SHI TIANLU, Business English
LU YONG, Business Russian
YANG NAIJUN, Linguistics (Russian)
DAI MINGPEI, Business French
XIAO TIANYOU, Linguistics (Italian)
ZIANG XINDAO, Linguistics (Korean)
ZHAO RUN, German Economics
YANG YANHONG
WANG ZHENGFU, Business German
ZHANG SUWO
SUN JIANQIU
YAN SHANMING
CHEN ZHUNMIN
LI WEIZHONG
LI WENTIAN
WANG TIANQING
ZHENG YUMIAO
HUANG MEIBO
CHENG HAIBO
DING HENGQI
ZHANG CAILIANG, Linguistics (German)
LIAO YAZHANG
CHEN JIANPING
LI BOJIE
CHANG LI
LI ZHENGZHONG
ZHU KAI

School of Law:
SHEN DAMING
SHEN SIBAO
GAO XIQING
WANG JUN

School of Continuing Education:
YANG FENGHUA

Faculty of Humanities:
GE GUANGQIAN, Political Economy
CHEN YUJIE, Political Economy
JIANG YONGHE
GUAN XIGUO
ZHANG YINGJU
LI ZUOSHU
ZHANG FANJIA
CHEN YANLIN
WANG XUEMIN
HUANG WEIZHI
LUO HANXIN

Faculty of Economic Information Management:
CAO ZELAN
YU JINKANG
LI XIAO

UNIVERSITY OF INTERNATIONAL RELATIONS

12 Po Shang Cun, Hai Ding Dist., Beijing 250014
Telephone: (10) 62861310
E-mail: yzxx@uir.cn
Internet: www.uir.edu.cn

Founded 1949
Academic year: September to July
Schools: continuing education, culture and communication, English language, Japanese and French language, law, Marxism and Leninism, national economy, national politics, science and technology information
Number of teachers: 1,000

UNIVERSITY OF SCIENCE AND TECHNOLOGY BEIJING

30 Xue Yuan Rd, 100083 Beijing
Telephone: (10) 62332541
E-mail: dfa@ustb.edu.cn
Internet: www.ustb.edu.cn

Founded 1952 as Beijing Institute of Iron and Steel Technology, current name adopted 1988
State control
Schools of applied science; automation; chemical and biological engineering; civil and environmental engineering; computer and communication engineering; Dongling school of economics and management; foreign studies; humanities and social science; materials science and engineering; mathematics; mechanical engineering; metallurgical and ecological engineering
Pres.: Prof. LUO WEIDONG
Vice-Chancellor: CHEN XI
Vice-Chancellor: XIE HUI
Vice-Chancellor: ZHANG WENMING
Library of 837,000 vols
Number of teachers: 2,902
Number of students: 22,399
Publications: *Higher Education Research*, *Journal of UST Beijing*

UNIVERSITY OF SCIENCE AND TECHNOLOGY OF CHINA

96 Jinzhai Rd, Hefei 230026, Anhui Province
Telephone: (551) 3601000
E-mail: iao@ustc.ac.cn
Internet: www.ustc.edu.cn

Founded 1958 by Chinese Acad. of Sciences
Academic year: September to July (2 semesters)
Schools of: chemistry and materials science, computer science and technology, continuing education, earth and space sciences, engineering science, the gifted young, humanities and social science, information science and technology, life sciences, management, nuclear science and technology, physical sciences, software engineering
Pres.: ZHU QINGSHI
Vice-Pres.: CHENG YI
Vice-Pres.: HOU JIANGUO
Vice-Pres.: LI DING
Vice-Pres.: LI GUODONG
Vice-Pres.: XU WU
Sec.-Gen.: WANG KEQIANG
Dir for Foreign Affairs: ZHANG MENGPING
Library of 1,620,000 vols, 230,000 periodicals
Number of teachers: 1,162 (full-time)

Number of students: 15,500 (incl. 8,100 postgraduates)
Publications: *Chinese Journal of Low Temperature Physics, Education and Modernization, Experimental Mechanics, Journal, Journal of Chemical Physics*

WEST CHINA CENTRE OF MEDICAL SCIENCES

17 Renminnanlu 3 Duan, Chengdu 610044, Sichuan Province
Telephone: (28) 85501047
E-mail: dff@wcums.ecu.cn
Internet: www.wcums.edu.cn
Founded 1910
State control; attached to Sichuan Union Univ.
Languages of instruction: Chinese, English
Academic year: September to July (2 semesters)
Pres.: XIE HEPING
Vice-Pres.: BAO LANG
Vice-Pres.: LI HONG
Vice-Pres.: ZHANG ZHAODA
Chief Admin. Officer: BU HONG
Librarian: LI BINYAN
Library of 650,000 vols
Number of teachers: 1,057
Number of students: 4,998
Publications: *Chinese Journal of Medical Genetics, Chinese Journal of Ocular Fundus Diseases, Chinese Journal of Reparative and Reconstructive Surgery, Journal of West China University of Medical Sciences, Modern Preventive Medicine, West China Journal of Pharmaceutical Sciences, West China Journal of Stomatology, West China Medical Journal*

DEANS

School of Basic Medical Sciences: Dr HOU YIPING
School of Continued Education: Dr HUO TINGFU
School of Medicine: Dr SHI YINGKANG
School of Pharmacy: WANG FENGPENG
School of Public Health: Dr MA XIAO
School of Stomatology: Dr ZHOU XUEDONG

DISTINGUISHED PROFESSORS

Faculty of Forensic Medicine:
WU MEIYUN, Forensic Medicine

School of Basic Medical Sciences:
BAO LANG, Pathophysiology
CAI MEIYING, Immunology
CHEN HUAIQING, Biomedical Engineering
CHEN JUNJIE, Biochemistry
CHEN MANLING, Biochemistry
DAI BAOMIN, Pathophysiology
FU MINGDE, Biochemistry
HU XIAOSHU, Parasitology
LI RUIXIANG, Anatomy
LIU BINGWEN, Biochemistry
LU ZHENSHAN, Histology and Embryology
OU KEQUN, Histology and Embryology
WANG BOYAO, Pathophysiology
WU LIANGFANG, Histology and Embryology
ZHU BIDE, Histology and Embryology

School of Pharmacy:
LI TUN, Pharmaceutics
LIAO GONGTIE, Pharmaceutics
LU BIN, Pharmaceutics
WANG FENGPENG, Chemistry of Natural Medicinal Products
WANG XIANKAI, Pharmaceutical Chemistry
WENG LINGLING, Pharmaceutical Chemistry
XU MINGXIA, Pharmaceutical Chemistry
ZHENG HU, Pharmaceutical Chemistry
ZHONG YUGONG, Pharmaceutical Chemistry

School of Public Health:
LI CHANGJI
LI XIAOSONG, Health Statistics
NI ZONGZAN
PENG SHUSHENG, Nutrition and Food Hygiene
SUN MIANLING, Environmental Health
WANG RUISHU, Nutrition and Hygiene
WANG ZHIMING, Occupational Health and Occupational Diseases
WU DESHENG, Environmental Health
YANG SHUQIN, Health Statistics
ZHANG CHAOWU
ZHANG CHENLIE, Occupational Health and Occupational Diseases

School of Stomatology:
CAO YONGLIE, Orthodontics
DU CHUANSHI, Prosthodontics
LI BINGQU, Oral Medicine
LI SHENWEI, Maxillofacial Surgery
LIU TIANJIA, Oral Medicine
LUO SONGJIAO, Orthodontics
MAO ZHUYI, Maxillofacial Surgery
WANG DAZHANG, Maxillofacial Surgery
WANG HANZHANG, Maxillofacial Surgery
WEI ZHITONG, Orthodontics
WEN YUMING, Maxillofacial Surgery
YUE SONGLING, Oral Medicine
ZHANG YUNHUI, Oral Medicine
ZHAO YUNFENG, Orthodontics
ZHOU XIUKUN, Orthodontics

West China School of Medicine:
CAO ZEYI, Obstetrics and Gynaecology
CAO ZHONGLIANG, Infectious Diseases
CHEN WENBIN, Internal Medicine
DENG XIANZHAO, Genito-Urinary Surgery
FANG QIANXUN, Ophthalmology
GAO LIDA, Neural Surgery
HU TINGZE, Paediatric Surgery
HUANG DEJIA, Diagnostic Imaging
HUANG MINGSHENG, Psychiatry and Mental Health
LEI BINGJUN, Infectious Diseases
LI GANDI, Pathology
LI XIUJUN, Internal Medicine
LIAO QINGKUI, Paediatrics
LIN DAICHENG, Otolaryngology
LIU XIEHE, Psychiatry and Mental Health
LUO CHENGREN, Ophthalmology
LUO CHUNHUA, Paediatrics
MIN PENGQIU, Diagnostic Imaging
OUYANG QIN, Gastroenterology
PENG ZHILAN, Obstetrics and Gynaecology
SHEN WENLU, General Surgery
SHI YINGKANG, Cardiological Surgery
TANG TIANZHI, Nuclear Medicine
TANG ZEYUAN, Paediatrics
WANG SHILANG, Obstetrics and Gynaecology
WANG ZENGLI, Internal Medicine
WEI FUKANG, Paediatric Surgery
XIAO LUJIA, General Surgery
YAN LUNAN, General Surgery
YAN MI, Ophthalmology
YANG GUANGHUA, Pathology
YANG YURU, Genito-Urinary Surgery
YANG ZHIMING, Orthopaedics
ZHANG ZIZHONG, Medical Genetics
ZHANG ZHAODA, General Surgery
ZHAO LIANSAN, Infectious Diseases

WUHAN UNIVERSITY

Wuhan 430072, Hubei Province
Telephone: (27) 87882547
E-mail: wupo@whu.edu.cn
Internet: www.whu.edu.cn
Founded 1893
Academic year: September to July
Pres.: Prof. LIU JINGNAN
Vice-Pres.: Prof. CHEN ZHAOFANG
Vice-Pres.: Prof. HUANG CONGXIN
Vice-Pres.: Prof. HU DEKUN
Vice-Pres.: Prof. LI QINGQUAN
Vice-Pres.: Prof. LIU JINGNAN
Vice-Pres.: Prof. LI WENXIN
Vice-Pres.: Prof. LONG XIAOLE
Vice-Pres.: Prof. WU JUNPEI
Sec.-Gen.: Prof. REN XINNIAN
Dir of Foreign Affairs Office: Assoc. Prof. PENG YUANJIE
Librarian: Prof. YAN JINWEI
Number of teachers: 5,000
Number of students: 40,000
Publications: *Economic Review* (6 a year), *French Studies* (every 2 years), *Journal* (humanities edn, in Chinese; social sciences edn, in Chinese; natural sciences edn, in English; engineering edn, in Chinese; information sciences edn, in English and Chinese; medical science edn, in Chinese), *Journal of Analytical Science* (6 a year), *Journal of Audiology and Speech Pathology* (4 a year), *Journal of Mathematical Medicine* (6 a year), *Journal of Mathematics* (4 a year), *Knowledge of Library Information* (4 a year), *Law Review* (6 a year), *Stroke and Nervous Diseases* (4 a year), *Writing* (12 a year)

DEANS

Business: Prof. ZHOU MAORONG
Chemistry and Molecular Science: Prof. PANG DAIWEN
Civil Engineering: Prof. ZHU YIWEN
Computer Science: Prof. HE YANXIANG
Dynamics and Mechanics: Prof. WU QINGMING
Electrical Engineering: Prof. CHEN YUNPING
Foreign Languages: Prof. WANG XIUZHEN
Geomatics: Prof. LI JIANCHENG
Humanities: Prof. GUO QIYONG
Information Management (Library and Information Science): Prof. MA FEICHENG
International Relations: (vacant)
Journalism and Communications: Prof. LUO YICHENG
Law: Prof. ZENG LINGLIANG
Life Science: Prof. HE GUANGCUN
Materials Science and Engineering: (vacant)
Mathematics and Probability: Prof. CHEN HUA
Medicine: Prof. FAN MINGWEN
Pharmacy: (vacant)
Photoelectronics and Information Service: Prof. KE HENGYU
Physics: Prof. SHI JING
Political Science and Management: Prof. TAN JUNJIU
Public Health: (vacant)
Public Management: Prof. DENG DASONG
Remote Sensing and Information Engineering: Prof. WANG YOUCHUAN
Resources and Environmental Science: Prof. LIU YAOLIN
Stomatology: Prof. FAN MINGWEN
Urban Studies: Prof. ZHAO BING
Water Resources and Hydropower Engineering: Prof. TAN GUANGMING

WUHAN UNIVERSITY OF TECHNOLOGY

122 Luoshi Rd, Wuhan 430070, Hubei Province
Telephone: (27) 87658253
Internet: www.whut.edu.cn
Founded 1945
State control
Academic year: September to July
Schools: economics, material science and engineering, literature and law, international studies, arts and design, natural sciences, resources and environmental engineering, mechatronic engineering, automotive engineering, automation, computer science and technology, information engineering, civil engineering and architecture, transpor-

tation, navigation, energy and power engineering, management sciences; depts of logistics engineering, humanities, chemical engineering, physical education, Institutes: continuing education, network education

Pres.: ZHOU ZUDE
Vice-Pres: CHEN DONGSHENG
Vice-Pres: LI HAIYING
Vice-Pres: TAO DEXIN
Vice-Pres: YAN XINGPING
Vice-Pres: ZHANG LIANMENG
Vice-Pres: ZHANG QINGJIE
Librarian: XIAO JINSHENG

Library of 2,720,000 vols
Number of teachers: 2,400
Number of students: 37,000

Publication: *Journal* (editions: management and information engineering; material sciences (in English); social sciences; transportation science and engineering)

PROFESSORS

CAI, CHANGXIU, Mechanical Design and Theory
CHANG, ZHIHUA, Automotive Engineering
CHEN, BINKANG, Ship-Building and Marine Structure Design
CHEN, DINGFANG, Manufacturing Engineering and Automation
CHEN, GONGYU, Management Science and Engineering
CHEN, GUOHONG, Management Science and Engineering
CHEN, MINGZHAO, Marine Engineering
CHEN, TIEQUN, Automotive Engineering
CHEN, WEN, Material Physics and Chemistry
CUI, KERUN, Marine Engineering
DENG, CHUNAN, Automotive Engineering
DENG, MINGRAN, Management Science and Engineering
FENG, ENDE, Ship-Building and Marine Structure Design
FU, ZHENGYI, Material Processing Engineering
GAO, XIAOHONG, Marine Engineering
GONG, WENQI, Mineralogy
GU, BICHONG, Mechanical Design and Theory
HU, RONGQIANG, Mechanical Design and Theory
HU, SHUGUANG, Material Science and Engineering
HU, SHUHUA, Management Science and Engineering
JIANG, CANGRU, Structural Engineering
JIANG, DESHENG, Material Science and Engineering
JIANG, ZHENGFENG, Mechanical Design and Theory
LI, BIQING, Management Science and Engineering
LI, GANGYAN, Mechanical Design and Theory
LI, HAIYING, Management Science and Engineering
LI, LAYUAN, Transportation Information Engineering and Control
LI, QIANG, Material Physics and Chemistry
LI, SHIPU, Material Science and Engineering
LI, ZHIMING, Mechanical Design and Theory
LI, ZHUOQIU, Structural Engineering
LIN, QITAI, Mineralogy
LIN, ZONGSHOU, Material Science and Engineering
LIU, GUOXIN, Management Science and Engineering
LIU, HANXING, Material Physics and Chemistry
LIU, ZUOMING, Mechanical Design and Theory
LIU, ZUYUAN, Fluid Mechanics
LU, KAISHENG, Marine Engineering
LU, LING, Transportation Information Engineering and Control
MEI, BINGCHU, Material Processing Engineering
MO, YIMIN, Mechanical Design and Theory
NAN, CEWEN, Material Physics and Chemistry
OU YANG, SHIXI, Material Science and Engineering
PAN, CHUNXU, Material Processing Engineering
PENG, SHAOMIN, Structural Engineering
QU, WEILIAN, Structural Engineering
SHEN, CHENWU, Ship-Building and Marine Structure Design
SUN, GUOZHENG, Mechanical Design and Theory
TAO, DEXIN, Manufacturing Engineering and Automation
WAN, JUNKANG, Management Science and Engineering
WANG, CENGFANG, Ship-Building and Marine Structure Design
WANG, DEXUN, Fluid Mechanics
WANG, JIEDE, Ship-Building and Marine Structure Design
WANG, LUNKANG, Fluid Mechanics
WANG, SHAOMEI, Mechanical Design and Theory
WANG, ZHONGFAN, Automotive Engineering
WU, BOLIN, Material Physics and Chemistry
WU, DAIHUA, Structural Engineering
XIA, YUANYOU, Structural Engineering
XIAO, HANLIANG, Application Engineering for Load-Carrying Equipment
XIAO, JINSHENG, Marine Engineering
XIE, KEFAN, Management Science and Engineering
XIONG, QIANXING, Transportation Information Engineering and Control
XUE, YIYU, Automotive Engineering
YAN, SHILIN, Structural Engineering
YAN, XINGPING, Application Engineering for Load-Carrying Equipment
YAN, YUHUA, Material Physics and Chemistry
YANG, MINGZHONG, Mechanical Design and Theory
YUAN, CHUXIONG, Mineralogy
YUAN, RUNZHANG, Material Science and Engineering
ZHANG, LEWEN, Fluid Mechanics
ZHANG, LIANMENG, Material Processing Engineering
ZHANG, QINGJIE, Material Science and Engineering
ZHANG, SHIXIONG, Mineralogy
ZHANG, YOULING, Automotive Engineering
ZHANG, ZHONGPU, Mechanical Design and Theory
ZHAO, XIUJIAN, Material Physics and Chemistry
ZHONG, LUO, Structural Engineering
ZHOU, YICHEN, Marine Engineering
ZHOU, ZAOJIAN, Ship-Building and Marine Structure Design
ZHOU, ZUDE, Manufacturing Engineering and Automation
ZHU, MEIQI, Ship-Building and Marine Structure Design
ZHU, RUIGENG, Mineralogy
ZHU, XICHAN, Automotive Engineering

XI'AN SHIYOU UNIVERSITY

E Rd, 710065 Xian
Telephone: (29) 88382261
E-mail: waiban@xsyu.edu.cn
Internet: www.xsyu.edu.cn

Founded 1958 as Xian Petroleum Institute, current name adopted 2003
Language of instruction: English

Pres.: QU ZHAN
Vice-Pres.: BAI LI
Vice-Pres.: FANG MING
Vice-Pres.: ZENG PING

Library of 280,000 vols, 2,000 periodicals
Number of teachers: 1,600
Number of students: 21,100

PROFESSORS

CHEN XIAOZHENG, Petroleum Economics
FU XINGSHENG, Earth Strata Slope Angles, Well-Logging Methods and Instruments
GAO CHENGTAI, Well-Testing
GAO JINIAN, Applied Electric-Hydraulic Control Technology
HU QI, Petroleum Instruments
LI DANG, Mechanism of High-Energy Gas Fracturing
LU JIAO, Petroleum Instruments
PANG JUFENG, Physics and Nuclear Well Logging
SHENG DICHENG, Walking Beam Pumping Units
WANG JIAHUA, Computers
WANG SHIQING, Mechanical Engineering
WANG YIGONG, Management Systems of Petroleum Machinery
WU KUN
WU YIJIONG, Pumping Wells
ZHANG SHAOHUAI, Drilling
ZHANG ZONGMING, Petroleum Tectonics of China
ZHAO GUANGCHANG, Economics and Management

XIAMEN UNIVERSITY

422 Siming Rd S, 361005 Xiamen
Telephone: (592) 2180000
E-mail: xmupo@xmu.edu.cn
Internet: www.xmu.edu.cn

Founded 1921
State control
Academic year: September to July

Schools of chemistry and chemical engineering, economics, foreign languages and cultures, humanities, information science and technology, journalism and communication, law, life sciences, public affairs, management, mathematical sciences, physics and mechanical and electrical engineering

Pres.: Prof. ZHU CHONGSHI
Vice-Pres.: Prof. YANG BIN
Vice-Pres.: Prof. WU TAI KWONG
Vice-Pres.: JIN NENGMING
Vice-Pres.: ZHAN ZINLI
Librarian: CHEN MINGGUANG

Library of 3,100,000 vols
Number of teachers: 4,900
Number of students: 38,000

Publication: *Journal of Xiamen University (Natural Science Edition)* (6 a year)

XIAN INTERNATIONAL STUDIES UNIVERSITY

437 S Changan Rd, Xian 710061, Shaanxi Province
Telephone: (29) 85309274
Internet: www.xisu.edu.cn

Founded 1952
provincial control
Academic year: September to July

Pres.: DU RUIQING
Vice-Pres.: CHU CHU
Vice-Pres.: HU XISHE
Vice-Pres.: LIU YUELIAN
Head of Graduate Dept: YANG XIWEN
Librarian: YANG YONGCAI

Library of 901,000 vols

Publications: *Foreign Language Education* (6 a year), *Human Geography* (6 a year), *Journal of Xian Foreign Languages Institute* (4 a year)

DEANS

Department of French: ZHANG PING
Department of German: WEN RENBAI
School of Audiovisual Communication: QIN YAMING

School of Culture and Communication: HU RUIHUA
School of Eastern Languages and Culture: ZHANG SEHNGYU
School of Economics: PAN HUIXIA
School of Tourism: DANG JINXUE

PROFESSORS

DANG, JINXUE, Tourism
FENG, GUANG, Audiovisual Communication
GAO, YAOTING, German Studies
HU, RUIHUA, Culture and Communication
LI, QIUQUAN, Tourism
LIN, KAI, Audiovisual Communication
LIU, JIANQIANG, Eastern Languages and Culture
MA, YONGPING, Eastern Languages and Culture
WANG, XINGZHONG, Tourism
WANG, XINRONG, Eastern Languages and Culture
WEI, GENYUAN, Audiovisual Communication
WEN, RENBAI, German Studies
YAO, BAORONG, Tourism
YUAN, JIANPING, Russian Studies
ZHANG, BAONING, Culture and Communication
ZHANG, CONG, Culture and Communication
ZHANG, SHENGYU, Eastern Languages and Culture
ZHENG, MINGJIANG, Culture and Communication

XIAN JIAOTONG UNIVERSITY

28 West Xianning Rd, Xian 710049
Telephone: (29) 2668234
E-mail: mailxjtu@xjtu.edu.cn
Internet: www.xjtu.edu.cn
Founded 1896
State control
Academic year: September to July (2 semesters)
Pres.: ZHENG NANNING
Registrar: LI NENGGUI
Admin. Officer: LIU BIN
Librarian: ZHOU JINGEN
Number of teachers: 3,241
Number of students: 26,410 (incl. 5,504 postgraduate)
Publications: *Applied Mechanics* (4 a year), *Engineering Mathematics* (4 a year), *Journal* (4 a year), *Journal of Economic Sciences* (4 a year), *Journal of Medical Sciences* (4 a year), *Journal of Social Sciences* (4 a year)

DEANS

Graduate School: XU TONGMO
School of Accountancy: XHANG TIANXI
School of Architectural Engineering and Mechanics: CHEN YIHENG
School of Continuing Education: SUN BI
School of Economics and Finance: XUE MOUHONG
School of Electrical and Communications Engineering: ZHU SHIHUA
School of Electrical Engineering: WANG ZHAOAN
School of Energy and Power Engineering: HUI SHEN
School of Environmental and Chemical Engineering: CHENG GUANGXU
School of Foreign Languages: BAI YONGQUAN
School of Humanities and Social Science: LIU YONGFU
School of Life Sciences and Technology: WAN MINGXI
School of Management: XI YOUMIN
School of Materials Science and Engineering: XU KEWEI
School of Mechanical Engineering: XING JIANDONG
School of Medical Science: YAN JIANQUN
School of Network Education: YU DEHONG
School of Science: XU ZONGBEN
School of Stomatology: (vacant)

There are 64 research institutes and 126 research laboratories.

XIAN UNIVERSITY OF ARCHITECTURE AND TECHNOLOGY

13 Yanta Rd, Xian 710055, Shaanxi
Telephone: (29) 2202121
E-mail: jianda@webmail.xauat.edu.cn
Internet: www.xauat.edu.cn
Founded 1956
Academic year: September to July
Pres.: Prof. XU DELONG
Vice-Pres.: Prof. DUAN ZHISHAN
Vice-Pres.: Prof. GAN ANSHENG
Vice-Pres.: Prof. WANG XIAOCHANG
Vice-Pres.: Assoc. Prof. MA JIANHUA
Head of the Graduate School: Assoc. Prof. YUAN SHOUQIAN
Librarian: Prof. LIU JIAPING
Library of 1,000,800 vols
Number of teachers: 2,100
Number of students: 22,518
Publications: *Journal* (4 a year), *Science and Technology of Xian University of Architecture and Technology* (4 a year), *Study of Higher Education*

XIAN UNIVERSITY OF SCIENCE AND TECHNOLOGY

58 Yanta Rd, Mid Sector, Xian 710054, Shaanxi Province
Telephone: (29) 5583033
E-mail: iecc@xust.sn.cn
Internet: www.xust.sn.cn
Founded 1958
Academic year: September to July
Pres.: Prof. CHANG XINTAN
Vice-Pres.: Prof. HAN JIANGSHUI
Vice-Pres.: Prof. LU JIANJUN
Vice-Pres.: Prof. MA HONGWEI
Vice-Pres.: Prof. YANG GENGSHE
Librarian: Prof. WANG TINGMAN
Library of 580,000 vols
Number of teachers: 750
Number of students: 14,200
Publications: *Higher Education Research* (6 a year), *Journal* (12 a year), *Scientech Talent Market* (6 a year)

XIAN UNIVERSITY OF TECHNOLOGY

5 Jinhua Rd (South), Xian 710048, Shaanxi Province
Telephone: (29) 82312541
E-mail: xzb@mail.xaut.edu.cn
Internet: www.xaut.edu.cn
Founded 1949, until 1993, Shaanxi Institute of Mechanical Engineering
Jt Min. of Education and Provincial control
Academic year: September to July
Pres.: Prof. CHEN ZHIMING
Vice-Pres.: Prof. CUI DUWU
Vice-Pres.: Prof. FU YOUMING
Vice-Pres.: Prof. LIU DING
Vice-Pres.: Prof. ZHANG MIAOFENG
Librarian: Prof. SHI JUNPING
Library of 800,000 vols
Number of teachers: 1,050
Number of students: 26,200
Publications: *Foundry Technology* (6 a year), *Journal of Shaanxi Water Power* (4 a year), *Journal of Xian University of Technology* (4 a year)

DEANS

Faculty of Automation Engineering and Information Science: Prof. GAO YONG
Faculty of Computer Science and Engineering: Prof. ZHANG YIKUN
Faculty of Humanities and Social Sciences: Prof. LI QINGMING
Faculty of Management: Prof. DANG XINHUA
Faculty of Materials Science and Engineering: Prof. FAN ZHIKANG
Faculty of Mechanical Engineering: Prof. LI YAN
Faculty of Printing and Packaging Engineering: Prof. WANG JIAMIN
Faculty of Science: Prof. HE QINXIANG
Faculty of Water Conservancy and Hydroelectric Power: Prof. LUO XINGQI
Polytechnic College: Prof. WANG HUI

XIANGTAN UNIVERSITY

Yanggutang, Xiangtan 411105, Hunan Province
Telephone: (732) 8292130
E-mail: ecc@xtu.edu.cn
Internet: www.xtu.edu.cn
Founded 1975
State control
Language of instruction: Chinese
Pres.: Prof. LUO HE'AN
Number of teachers: 1,309
Number of students: 31,600
Publications: *Journal* (social science and natural science editions), *Journal* (philosophy and social sciences series, 6 a year), *Journal* (natural science series, 4 a year), *Transaction of Chinese Verse* (4 a year)

XIDIAN UNIVERSITY

2 S Tai Bai Rd, Xian 710071, Shaanxi Province
Telephone: (29) 8202221
E-mail: master@xidian.edu.cn
Internet: www.xidian.edu.cn
Founded 1937
State control
Academic year: September to July
Pres.: DUAN BAOYAN
Vice-Pres: CAO TIANSHUN
Vice-Pres: CHEN YONG
Vice-Pres: HAO YUE
Vice-Pres: LI RUFENG
Vice-Pres: YU NANNAN
Librarian: FAN LAIYAO
Library of 860,000 vols
Number of teachers: 1,900
Number of students: 15,000
Publication: *Journal* (editions: physical and social sciences)

DEANS

School of Computer Science and Engineering: WU BO
School of Economics and Management: ZHAO PENGWEI
School of Electronic Engineering: JIAO LICHENG
School of Humanities: ZHAO BOFEI
School of Mechatronics: JIA JIANYUAN
School of Science: WU ZHENSEN
School of Technical Physics: AN YUYING
School of Telecommunications Engineering: LI JIANDONG

PROFESSORS

BAI, BAOMING, Telecommunications Engineering
CAI, XIQIAO, Software Engineering
CHEN, BOXIAO, Electronic Engineering
CHEN, JIANJUN, Mechatronic Engineering
CHEN, PING, Computer Science and Engineering
DUAN, ZHENHUA, Computer Science and Engineering
FENG, DAZHENG, Electronic Engineering

FU, FENGLIN, Telecommunications Engineering
GAO, XINBO, Electronic Engineering
GAO, YOUXING, Computer Science and Engineering
GONG, JIEMIN, Software Engineering
GONG, SHUXI, Electronic Engineering
GUO, BAOLONG, Mechatronic Engineering
HU, QIYING, Economics and Management
HUANG, LIYU, Electronic Engineering
JI, HONGBING, Electronic Engineering
JIA, JIANYUAN, Mechatronic Engineering
JIANG, ZHEXIN, Economics and Management
JIAO, LICHENG, Electronic Engineering
JIAO, YONGCHANG, Electronic Engineering
LI, BINGBING, Telecommunications Engineering
LI, HUA, Economics and Management
LI, WEIYING, Telecommunications Engineering
LI, YUSHAN, Electronic Engineering
LI, ZHIWU, Mechatronic Engineering
LIANG, CHANGHONG, Electronic Engineering
LIU, FANG, Computer Science and Engineering
LIU, HONGWEI, Electronic Engineering
LIU, HONGWEI, Science
LIU, JIAN, Software Engineering
LIU, MING, Mechatronic Engineering
LIU, QIZHONG, Electronic Engineering
LIU, ZHIJING, Computer Science and Engineering
MA, JIANFENG, Computer Science and Engineering
MA, JINPING, Electronic Engineering
NIU, ZHONGQI, Electronic Engineering
QIU, YANG, Mechatronic Engineering
QIU, YUANYING, Mechatronic Engineering
REN, ZHICHUN, Economics and Management
SHI, GUANGMING, Electronic Engineering
SUN, XIAOZI, Electronic Engineering
WANG, ANMIN, Economics and Management
WANG, BAOSHU, Computer Science and Engineering
WANG, JIALI, Mechatronic Engineering
WANG, LI, Software Engineering
WEN, XIAONI, Economics and Management
WEN, YOUKUI, Economics and Management
WEN, ZHENGZHONG, Mechatronic Engineering
WU, SHUNJUN, Electronic Engineering
XIE, YONGJUN, Electronic Engineering
XING, MENGDAO, Electronic Engineering
XU, CHUNXIANG, Economics and Management
XU, GUOHUA, Economics and Management
XU, LUPING, Electronic Engineering
YANG, WANHAI, Electronic Engineering
ZENG, PING, Computer Science and Engineering
ZENG, XINGWEN, Telecommunications Engineering
ZHANG, FUSHUN, Electronic Engineering
ZHANG, HUI, Telecommunications Engineering
ZHANG, JUNYING, Computer Science and Engineering
ZHANG, PING, Mechatronic Engineering
ZHANG, SHIXUAN, Electronic Engineering
ZHANG, SHOUHONG, Electronic Engineering
ZHANG, YONGRUI, Mechatronic Engineering
ZHAO, GUOQING, Electronic Engineering
ZHAO, KE, Mechatronic Engineering
ZHAO, PENGWEI, Economics and Management
ZHAO, WEI, Economics and Management
ZHAO, WENPING, Economics and Management
ZHAO, YIGONG, Electronic Engineering
ZHI, BOQING, Mechatronic Engineering
ZHOU, WEI, Mechatronic Engineering

XINJIANG UNIVERSITY

14 Sheng Li Rd, Urumqi 830046, Xinjiang Uygur Autonomous Region
Telephone: (991) 8582221
E-mail: icec12@xju.edu.cn
Internet: www.xju.edu.cn

Founded 1924; merged with Xinjiang Engineering Institute 2000
Academic year: September to July

Teaching units: colleges of adult education; chemistry and chemical engineering; construction engineering; electrical engineering; foreign languages; information science and engineering; liberal arts; mechanical engineering; science and technology; economics and management; law; depts of physics; textile engineering; institute of life sciences and technology; institute of mathematics and systematic science; institute of resources and environmental science; higher vocational and technical college; Research Institutes: Institute of Altaic Study; Institute of Applied Chemistry; Institute of Architectural Design; Institute of Arid Ecology; Institute of Central Asian Culture; Institute of Demography; Institute of Economics; Institute of Mathematical Theory

Rector: ANIWER AMUT
Vice-Rector: AZHAT SULITAN
Vice-Rector: TASHPLAT TYIP
Vice-Rector: ZHANG XIAOFAN
Librarian: WANG KAIYUAN

Library of 1,330,000 vols
Number of teachers: 1,830
Number of students: 39,000 (incl. 784 postgraduate)

Publication: *Xinjiang University Journal* (natural sciences and social sciences versions)

YANBIAN UNIVERSITY

977 Gongyuan Rd, Yanji 133002, Jilin Province
Telephone: (433) 2713167
Internet: www.ybu.edu.cn

Founded 1949
provincial control
Academic year: September to July

Pres.: JIN BINMIN
Vice-Pres: GAI TONGXIANG
Vice-Pres: LI SHUIJIN
Vice-Pres: PIAO YONGHAO
Vice-Pres: YU YONGHE
Head of Graduate Dept: CUI XIONGHAN
Librarian: HAN ZHE

Library of 1,400,000 vols
Number of teachers: 1,345
Number of students: 16,447

Publications: *Chinese Studies*, *Collection of Papers on Korean Issues*, *Collection of Papers on Korean Nationality*, *Collection of Papers on North and South Korean Studies*, *Dongjiang* ('Eastern Border'), *Journal* (editions: agricultural, medical, sciences and engineering and social science), *Oriental Philosophy Research*

DEANS

College of Agriculture: ZHANG SHOUFA
College of Art: JIANG GUANGXUN
College of Chinese Language and Culture: (vacant)
College of Economics and Management: XUAN DONGRI
College of Foreign Languages: (vacant)
College of Medicine: CUI JIONGMO
College of Nursing: JIN DONGXU
College of Pharmacy: CUI JIONGMO
College of Physical Education: LIU QIXIAO
College of Science and Engineering: WU XUE
College of Science and Technology: WU XUE
Normal College: CUI CHENGRI
School of Law: CHEN ZHENMING

PROFESSORS

AN, GUOFENG, Chinese Language and Culture
BAI, HONGAI, Foreign Languages
CAI, MEIHUA, Normal College
CAO, XIULING, Chinese Language and Culture
CHEN, YANQIU, Agriculture
CUI, CHENGXUE, Normal College
CUI, RONGYI, Science and Technology
CUI, SHENGYUN, Science and Technology
CUI, TAIJI, Chinese Language and Culture
CUI, YONGCHUN, Art
FANG, HAOFAN, Normal College
FANG, MEISHAN, Art
FANG, NANZHU, Agriculture
FEI, HONGGEN, Normal College
FU, WEIJIE, Agriculture
GU, GUANGRUI, Science and Technology
GUO, ZHENPING, Science and Technology
HE, YUNPENG, Law
HUANG, ZHENJI, Chinese Language and Culture
JIANG, HAISHUN, Law
JIANG, JIJIAN, Agriculture
JIANG, LONGFAN, Normal College
JIANG, RISHAN, Science, Technology and Engineering
JIANG, YONGZHE, Physical Education
JIANG, YUN, Normal College
JIN, BINGHUO, Normal College
JIN, BINGMIN, Normal College
JIN, CHENGGAO, Normal College
JIN, CHUNZHI, Physical Education
JIN, DONGRI, Science and Technology
JIN, HAIGUO, Agriculture
JIN, HELU, Law
JIN, HEWAN, Pharmacy and Nursing
JIN, HEYAN, Normal College
JIN, HUALIN, Economics and Management
JIN, HUXIONG, Normal College
JIN, JIANGLONG, Agriculture
JIN, JISHI, Normal College
JIN, JUNCHENG, Art
JIN, KUANXIONG, Normal College
JIN, LONGZHE, Physical Education
JIN, QIANGYI, Normal College
JIN, XIANGHUA, Chinese Language and Culture
JIN, XINGGUANG, Agriculture
JIN, XINGSAN, Art
JIN, XUECHUN, Law
JIN, YINGXIONG, Physical Education
JIN, YONGCHUN, Law
JIN, YONGHAO, Science and Technology
JIN, YONGSHOU, Foreign Languages
JIN, YUANZHE, Medicine
JIN, ZHEHUA, Normal College
JIN, ZHEHUI, Foreign Languages
JIN, ZHENGYI, Normal College
JIN, ZHEZHU, Normal College
LI, AISHUN, Art
LI, BAOQI, Law
LI, CHUNYU, Pharmacy and Nursing
LI, GUANFU, Normal College
LI, MINDE, Foreign Languages
LI, MINZI, Art
LI, SHANJI, Science and Technology
LI, SHENGLONG, Art
LI, WUJI, Foreign Languages
LI, YUNJUN, Science and Technology
LI, ZONGXUN, Normal College
LIAN, ZHEMAN, Science and Technology
LIN, CHENGHU, Foreign Languages
LIN, JINSHU, Economics and Management
LIU, XIANHU, Agriculture
LU, CHENG, Agriculture
LU, LONGSHI, Agriculture
MA, JINKE, Normal College
MENG, FANPING, Medicine
NAN, CHENGYU, Foreign Languages
PAN, CHANGHE, Normal College
PIAO, CHENGXIAN, Economics and Management
PIAO, XIUHAO, Economics and Management
PU, SHIZHEN, Law
PU, TAIZHU, Normal College
PU, XIANGFAN, Science and Technology
PU, YUMING, Normal College
PU, ZHE, Medicine

PU, ZHENGYANG, Normal College
QU, BOHONG, Agriculture
QUAN, LONGHUA, Foreign Languages
QUAN, XUEXI, Normal College
QUAN, YU, Foreign Languages
QUAN, ZONGXUE, Science and Technology
SHAO, JINGBO, Science and Technology
SUN, DEBIAO, Normal College
SUN, DONGZHI, Medicine
SUN, SHU, Medicine
TIAN, GUANRONG, Science, Technology and Engineering
WANG, GUIFEN, Science and Technology
WANG, KEPING, Chinese Language and Culture
WANG, XIAOBO, Normal College
WEI, ZHIFANG, Normal College
WEN, ZHAOHAI, Normal College
WU, MINGGEN, Agriculture
WU, XUE, Science, Technology and Engineering
XIANG, KIAMING, Art
XU, JI, Normal College
XU, MINGZHE, Normal College
XU, WENYI, Medicine
XU, YUANXIAN, Law
XUAN, DONGRI, Economics and Management
YAN, CHANGGUO, Agriculture
YIN, BINGZHU, Science, Technology and Engineering
YIN, TAISHUN, Law
YU, CHUNHAI, Normal College
YU, CHUNXI, Foreign Languages
YU, YANCUN, Normal College
ZHANG, JINGZHONG, Normal College
ZHANG, MIN, Agriculture
ZHANG, SHOU, Science and Technology
ZHANG, SHOUFA, Agriculture
ZHANG, ZHENAI, Foreign Languages
ZHAO, ENHUA, Physical Education
ZHAO, JINGCHUN, Foreign Languages
ZHAO, LIANHUA, Science and Technology
ZHENG, DAHAO, Agriculture
ZHENG, RINAN, Normal College
ZHENG, XIANRI, Foreign Languages
ZHENG, YONGZHEN, Normal College
ZHOU, ZHIYUAN, Normal College

YANGZHOU UNIVERSITY

88 Daxue Rd South, Yangzhou 225009, Jiangsu Province
Telephone: (514) 7971850
Internet: www.yzu.edu.cn

Founded 1902
provincial control
Academic year: September to July

Pres.: GUO RONG
Vice-Pres: FANG HONGJIN
Vice-Pres: FENG CHAONIAN
Vice-Pres: HU JIAXING
Vice-Pres: LIU CHAO
Vice-Pres: YANG JIADONG
Vice-Pres: ZHOU XINGUO
Head of Graduate Dept: YUAN JIANLI
Librarian: ZHANG ZHENGHUI

Number of teachers: 2,000
Number of students: 46,000 (30,000 full-time, 16,000 part-time)

Publications: *Journal* (editions: higher education study, humanities and social sciences, 6 a year; agricultural and life sciences, natural sciences, 4 a year), *Journal of Taxation College of Yangzhou University* (4 a year)

DEANS

Guangling College: LIU YANQING
School of Agriculture: WANG YULONG
School of Animal Science and Technology: CHEN GUOHONG
School of Architectural Science and Engineering: LIU PING
School of Arts: ZHANG MEILIN
School of Biological Sciences and Biotechnology: JIAO XIN'AN
School of Chemistry and Chemical Engineering: HU XIAOYA
School of Chinese Language and Literature: YAO WENFANG
School of Economics: JIANG NAIHUA
School of Educational Science and Technology: CHEN JIALILN
School of Environmental Science and Engineering: FENG KE
School of Foreign Languages: YU HONGLIANG
School of Information Engineering: CHEN LING
School of Law: JIAO FUMIN
School of Management: CHEN YAO
School of Mathematical Sciences: WANG HONGYU
School of Mechanical Engineering: ZHOU YIPING
School of Medicine: TANG YAO
School of Physical Education: TONG ZHAOGANG
School of Physical Science and Technology: CHEN XIAOBING
School of Social Development: ZHOU JIANCHAO
School of Tourism and Food Science: LU XINGUO
School of Veterinary Science: QIN AIJIAN
School of Water Conservation and Hydraulic Engineering: CHEN JIANKANG

PROFESSORS

BAN, JIQING, Chinese Language and Literature
BAO, ZHENQIANG, Information Engineering
BI, QIAO, Physical Science and Technology
CAI, CHUANREN, Mathematical Science
CAO, JINHUA, Social Development
CHANG, HONG, Animal Science and Technology
CHEN, GUOHONG, Animal Science and Technology
CHEN, JIALILN, Educational Science and Technology
CHEN, JIANKANG, Water Conservancy and Hydraulic Engineering
CHEN, JIANMIN, Biological Sciences and Biotechnology
CHEN, LING, Information Engineering
CHEN, RONGFA, Mechanical Engineering
CHEN, XIAOBING, Physical Science and Technology
CHEN, XIAOMING, Management
CHEN, YAO, Management
CHENG, JILIN, Water Conservancy and Hydraulic Engineering
CHENG, YONG, Veterinary Science
CHOU, BAOYUN, Water Conservancy and Hydraulic Engineering
CHOU, ZHIGANG, Physical Education
CHU, XUN, Water Conservancy and Hydraulic Engineering
DAI, XHIYI, Agriculture
DIAO, SHUREN, Social Development
DING, JIATONG, Animal Science and Technology
DING, LI, Medicine
DONG, GUOYAN, Chinese Language and Literature
ER, RONGBEN, Chinese Language and Literature
FAN, MING, Management
FANG, HONGYUAN, Water Conservancy and Hydraulic Engineering
FANG, WENLI, Foreign Languages
FEI, XUN, Social Development
FENG, KE, Environmental Science and Engineering
FENG, YONGSHAN, Medicine
GAO, HUIMING, Medicine
GAO, SONG, Veterinary Science
GE, XIAOQUN, Medicine
GU, FENG, Chinese Language and Literature
GU, NONG, Chinese Language and Literature
GU, RUIXIA, Tourism and Food Science
GU, SHILIANG, Agriculture
GUO, XIA, Chemistry and Chemical Engineering
HE, DAREN, Physical Science and Technology
HU, JINGGUO, Physical Science and Technology
HU, RONG, Medicine
HU, XIAOYA, Chemistry and Chemical Engineering
HU, XUENONG, Information Engineering
HU, XUEQIN, Economics
HUA, CHANGYOU, Social Development
HUANG, CHENG, Economics
HUANG, QIAN, Medicine
HUANG, QIANG, Chinese Language and Literature
HUANG, SHUCHENG, Economics
HUANG, SHUCHENG, Tourism and Food Science
HUO, WANLI, Arts
JI, MINGCHUN, Medicine
JI, SUYUE, Mathematical Science
JIANG, NAIHUA, Economics
JIAO, FUMIN, Law
JIAO, WENFENG, Social Development
JIAO, XIN'AN, Biological Sciences and Biotechnology
JIN, YINGEN, Biological Sciences and Biotechnology
JIN, YU, Physical Education
LI, BICHUN, Animal Science and Technology
LI, CHANGJI, Chinese Language and Literature
LI, CUNHUA, Information Engineering
LI, GUOLI, Medicine
LI, HOUDA, Veterinary Science
LI, JIANJI, Veterinary Science
LI, JINYU, Animal Science and Technology
LI, SHIHAO, Agriculture
LIANG, JIANSHENG, Biological Sciences and Biotechnology
LIN, ZHIGUI, Mathematical Science
LIU, CHAO, Water Conservancy and Hydraulic Engineering
LIU, CHENG, Social Development
LIU, GANG, Management
LIU, HONG, Chinese Language and Literature
LIU, MOXIANG, Medicine
LIU, PING, Architectural Science and Engineering
LIU, XIUFAN, Veterinary Science
LIU, YAN, Architectural Science and Engineering
LIU, YANQING, Medicine
LIU, YONGJUN, Physical Science and Technology
LIU, ZHUHAN, Mathematical Science
LIU, ZONGPING, Veterinary Science
LU, JIANFEI, Agriculture
LU, LINGUANG, Water Conservancy and Hydraulic Engineering
LU, XINGUO, Tourism and Food Science
MAO, YUYANG, Tourism and Food Science
MO, YUEPING, Information Engineering
PAN, XHAOWEI, Physical Education
PIAO, PING, Medicine
QIANG, JIANYA, Tourism and Food Science
QIANG, JING, Medicine
QIANG, ZHONGHAO, Economics
QIN, AIJIAN, Veterinary Science
QIN, XINGFANG, Economics
SHAO, YAOCHUN, Physical Science and Technology
SHEN, JIE, Information Engineering
SHI, MINGYI, Medicine
SHI, YONGFAN, Physical Education
SU, PEIQING, Medicine
SUN, GUORONG, Biological Sciences and Biotechnology
SUN, HUAICHANG, Veterinary Science
TIAN, HANYUN, Chinese Language and Literature
TONG, ZHAOGANG, Physical Education
WANG, BAO'AN, Veterinary Science
WANG, HANDONG, Veterinary Science

WANG, HONGRONG, Animal Science and Technology
WANG, HONGYU, Mathematical Science
WANG, JIANJUN, Medicine
WANG, JUN, Chinese Language and Literature
WANG, LINSUO, Water Conservancy and Hydraulic Engineering
WANG, LONGTAI, Mechanical Engineering
WANG, QINGREN, Social Development
WANG, XINGCHI, Management
WANG, XINGLONG, Animal Science and Technology
WANG, YEMING, Architectural Science and Engineering
WANG, YONGPING, Chinese Language and Literature
WANG, YONGPING, Social Development
WANG, YOUPING, Biological Sciences and Biotechnology
WANG, YULONG, Agriculture
WANG, ZHAOLONG, Biological Sciences and Biotechnology
WANG, ZONGYUAN, Veterinary Science
WEI, JUN, Physical Education
WEI, SHANHAO, Chinese Language and Literature
WEI, WANHONG, Biological Sciences and Biotechnology
WU, JIAN, Management
WU, SHANZHONG, Social Development
WU, YANTAO, Veterinary Science
WU, ZHOUWEN, Chinese Language and Literature
XIAO, SHUFENG, Chinese Language and Literature
XIONG, DEPING, Economics
XU, DEMING, Chinese Language and Literature
XU, JIANZHONG, Chinese Language and Literature
XU, LICHUN, Medicine
XU, MINGLIANG, Biological Sciences and Biotechnology
XU, WEIPING, Social Development
XU, YIMIN, Veterinary Science
YAN, JUN, Physical Education
YANG, BENHONG, Social Development
YANG, JIADONG, Economics
YANG, QIANPU, Social Development
YANG, SHUHE, Mechanical Engineering
YAO, WENFANG, Chinese Language and Literature
YIN, SHIXUE, Environmental Science and Engineering
YIN, XINCHUN, Information Engineering
YU, HAIPENG, Economics
YUAN, JIANLI, Architectural Science and Engineering
YUAN, XINMING, Water Conservancy and Hydraulic Engineering
ZENG, LI, Mechanical Engineering
ZHANG, HONGCHENG, Agriculture
ZHANG, HONGLIANG, Chinese Language and Literature
ZHANG, HONGQUAN, Medicine
ZHANG, JUN, Physical Education
ZHANG, MIANG, Chemistry and Chemical Engineering
ZHANG, MINLI, Architectural Science and Engineering
ZHANG, PEIJIAN, Medicine
ZHANG, QIJUN, Chinese Language and Literature
ZHANG, QING, Law
ZHANG, RUIHONG, Mechanical Engineering
ZHANG, TIANPING, Information Engineering
ZHANG, ZHENGANG, Medicine
ZHAO, GUOQI, Animal Science and Technology
ZHAO, ZONGFANG, Agriculture
ZHOU, JIANCHAO, Social Development
ZHOU, MINGYAO, Water Conservancy and Hydraulic Engineering
ZHOU, XIAOXIA, Medicine
ZHOU, XINTIAN, Social Development
ZHOU, YIPING, Mechanical Engineering
ZHOU, YIPING, Social Development
ZHU, XIASHI, Chemistry and Chemical Engineering
ZHU, YONGZE, Medicine
ZHUANG, LIN, Social Development

YANSHAN UNIVERSITY

438 Hebei Ave, Qinhuangdao 066004, Hebei Province
Telephone: (335) 8057100
E-mail: headmaster@ysu.edu.cn
Internet: www.ysu.edu.cn

Founded 1960
provincial control
Academic year: September to July

Pres.: LIU HONGMIN
Vice-Pres.: KONG XIANGDONG
Vice-Pres.: LI QIANG
Vice-Pres.: LIU BIN
Vice-Pres.: WANG YONGCHANG
Vice-Pres.: XING GUANGZHONG
Vice-Pres.: YANG YULIN
Head of Graduate Dept: ZHAO YONGSHENG
Librarian: ZHANG FUCHENG

Library of 600,000 vols
Number of teachers: 1,321
Number of students: 28,000

Publication: *Journal* (editions: natural science, philosophy and social sciences, 4 a year)

DEANS

College of Civil Engineering and Mechanics: (vacant)
College of Economic Administration: YUAN YE
College of Electrical Engineering: GUAN XINPING
College of Environmental and Chemical Engineering: BAI MINGHUA
College of Fine Art: ZHANG JIAXIN
College of Foreign Languages: (vacant)
College of Humanities and Law: WU YONG
College of Information Science and Engineering: KONG LINGFU
College of Material Science and Engineering: TIAN YONGJUN
College of Mechanical Engineering: ZHANG QING
College of Science: JIN XILI

PROFESSORS

AN, ZIJUN, Mechanical Engineering
BAI, MINGHUA, Environmental and Chemical Engineering
BI, WEIHONG, Information Science and Engineering
CHANG, DANHUA, Information Science and Engineering
CUI, YUNQI, Mechanical Engineering
DONG, HONGXUE, Foreign Languages
DONG, SHIMIN, Mechanical Engineering
DU, FENGSHAN, Mechanical Engineering
FANG, BAOGUO, Humanities and Law
GAO, DIANKUI, Mechanical Engineering
GAO, DIANRONG, Mechanical Engineering
GAO, FENG, Mechanical Engineering
GAO, SHIYOU, Mechanical Engineering
GAO, YINGJIE, Mechanical Engineering
GONG, JING'AN, Mechanical Engineering
GUO, BAOFENG, Mechanical Engineering
GUO, JINGFENG, Information Science and Engineering
GUO, XIJUAN, Information Science and Engineering
HAN, DECAI, Mechanical Engineering
HAN, PEIFU, Information Science and Engineering
HAN, XIAOJUAN, Mechanical Engineering
HOU, LANTIAN, Information Science and Engineering
HU, GUODONG, Mechanical Engineering
HU, ZHANQI, Mechanical Engineering
HUANG, ZHEN, Mechanical Engineering
HUI, JIXING, Humanities and Law
JIANG, SHIPING, Mechanical Engineering
JIANG, WANLU, Mechanical Engineering
JIN, ZHENLIN, Mechanical Engineering
JING, TIANFU, Material Science and Engineering
KONG, LINGFU, Information Science and Engineering
KONG, XIANGDONG, Mechanical Engineering
LI, BAODONG, Humanities and Law
LI, FULIANG, Humanities and Law
LI, JINLIANG, Mechanical Engineering
LI, JIUTONG, Mechanical Engineering
LI, KUIYING, Material Science and Engineering
LI, QIANG, Mechanical Engineering
LI, WEIMIN, Mechanical Engineering
LI, XIANKUI, Mechanical Engineering
LI, YUPENG, Mechanical Engineering
LIAN, JIACHUANG, Mechanical Engineering
LIU, GUOHUA, Information Science and Engineering
LIU, HONGMIN, Mechanical Engineering
LIU, RIPING, Material Science and Engineering
LIU, XIPING, Mechanical Engineering
LIU, YONGSHAN, Information Science and Engineering
LIU, ZEQUAN, Foreign Languages
LIU, ZHUBO, Mechanical Engineering
LU, XIUCHUN, Mechanical Engineering
LU, YI, Mechanical Engineering
NIE, SHAOMIN, Mechanical Engineering
PAN, MINGHAN, Information Science and Engineering
PENG, YAN, Mechanical Engineering
QIAO, CHANGSUO, Mechanical Engineering
QIN, SIJI, Mechanical Engineering
REN, YUNLAI, Mechanical Engineering
SHEN, GUANGXIAN, Mechanical Engineering
SHEN, LIMIN, Information Science and Engineering
SHEN, XIAOMEI, Humanities and Law
SHENG, YIPING, Environmental and Chemical Engineering
SHI, RONG, Mechanical Engineering
SONG, GUOSEN, Information Science and Engineering
SUN, HUIXUE, Mechanical Engineering
SUN, XUGUANG, Mechanical Engineering
TANG, JINGLIN, Mechanical Engineering
WANG, CHENGRU, Information Science and Engineering
WANG, FUSHENG, Foreign Languages
WANG, HAIRU, Mechanical Engineering
WANG, JUN, Mechanical Engineering
WANG, QINGXUE, Humanities and Law
WANG, XINSHENG, Information Science and Engineering
WANG, YIQUN, Mechanical Engineering
WANG, YONGCHANG, Mechanical Engineering
WEI, LIBO, Humanities and Law
WEN, DESHENG, Mechanical Engineering
WU, XIAOMING, Mechanical Engineering
WU, YONG, Humanities and Law
WU, YUEMING, Mechanical Engineering
XIAO, HONG, Mechanical Engineering
XU, CHENGQIAN, Information Science and Engineering
XU, HONGXIANG, Mechanical Engineering
XU, LIZHONG, Mechanical Engineering
XU, RUI, Material Science and Engineering
YANG, YULIN, Mechanical Engineering
YE, DEQIAN, Information Science and Engineering
YU, DESHENG, Information Science and Engineering
YU, DONGLI, Material Science and Engineering
YU, ENLIN, Mechanical Engineering
YU, JIANPING, Foreign Languages
YU, RONGJIN, Information Science and Engineering
YU, YUFENG, Information Science and Engineering

ZHANG, HAI, Mechanical Engineering
ZHANG, LIYING, Mechanical Engineering
ZHANG, QING, Mechanical Engineering
ZHANG, QISHENG, Mechanical Engineering
ZHANG, TAO, Mechanical Engineering
ZHANG, TONGYI, Mechanical Engineering
ZHANG, WEIDONG, Foreign Languages
ZHANG, WENZHI, Mechanical Engineering
ZHANG, ZHONGYI, Humanities and Law
ZHAO, JINGYI, Mechanical Engineering
ZHAO, JUN, Mechanical Engineering
ZHAO, TIESHI, Mechanical Engineering
ZHAO, YONGHE, Mechanical Engineering
ZHAO, YONGSHENG, Mechanical Engineering
ZHENG, SHENGXUAN, Information Science and Engineering
ZHOU, CHAO, Mechanical Engineering
ZHOU, QINGTIAN, Mechanical Engineering
ZHU, GUANGRONG, Humanities and Law
ZOU, MUCHANG, Information Science and Engineering

YANTAI UNIVERSITY

32 Qingquan Rd, 264005 Yantai
Telephone: (535) 6902143
E-mail: iaoyu5@ytu.edu.cn
Internet: www.ytu.edu.cn

Founded 1984
State control
Languages of instruction: Chinese, English

Depts of civil and commercial law, history of Chinese minorities, physical chemistry, theoretical physics, mechanical manufacturing and automation

Pres.: Dr FANG SHAOKUN
Vice-Pres.: JIANGLIN CHANG

Library: 2.4m. vols
Number of teachers: 1,966
Number of students: 3,839

Publication: *Journal*

YUNNAN UNIVERSITY

2 N Cuihu Rd, Kunming 650091, Yunnan Province
Telephone: (871) 5148533
Internet: www.ynu.edu.cn

Founded 1923
State control
Academic year: September to July

Pres.: Prof. WU SONG
Vice-Pres.: Prof. WANG RONG
Vice-Pres.: Prof. HONG PINJIE
Vice-Pres.: Prof. LIN CHAOMIN
Vice-Pres.: Prof. NI HUIFANG
Vice-Pres.: Prof. ZHANG KEQIN
Vice-Pres.: Prof. CHEN SHIBO
Registrar: Prof. YANG JIAHE
Librarian: Prof. WANG WENGGUAN

Library of 1,170,000 vols
Number of teachers: 888
Number of students: 7,160

Publication: *The Ideological Front* (6 a year)

PROFESSORS

Dianchi School (tel. (871) 5172513):
WU JIANGUO, Chemistry

School of Adult Education (tel. (871) 5147702):
DU CHAO, Analytical Chemistry
SHI PENGFEI, Ancient Chinese Literature
WANG JIALIN, Analytical Chemistry
WANG SHIDONG, Fluxional Dynamic Systems

School of Computer Science (tel. (871) 5031597):
LI TAILING, Electronic Circuits and Communication
LI TIANMU, Electronics and Information Systems
LIU WEIYI, Fuzzy Database Theory
TIAN ZHILIANG, Management Operating Systems
ZHENG WENXING, Correspondence

School of Development Research (tel. (871) 5031453):
CHEN LIN, Systems Engineering
LIAO HONGZHI, Systems Engineering
MAO YUGONG, Management Science
XIAO XIAN, History of International Relations
YANG MANSU, History of International Relations
YANG SHOUCHUANG, Ethnic History

School of Economics (tel. (871) 5033613):
CHEN JIANBO, Economic Statistics
GUO SHUHUA, Finance
HONG HUAXI, Economics
HU QIHUI, Economics
JIN RONG, Economics
LI DEPU, Economics
LU ZHAOHE, Demology
MA JUN, Accountancy
PAN JIANXING, Mathematical Statistics
SHI BENZHI, Investment
SHI LEI, Economic Statistics
SUN WENSHUANG, Mathematical Statistics
WANG XUEREN, Economics
XU GUANGYUAN, Economics
YENG XIANMING, Finance
ZHANG JIANHUA, Foreign Trade
ZHANG JIN, Economic Statistics
ZHU YINGGENG, Ideological History of Western Economics

School of Foreign Languages (tel. (871) 5033629):
GONG NINGZHU, Lao, Vietnamese
LI JIGANG, English
XU FENG
ZHANG XINHE, English

School of Humanities (tel. (871) 5033607):
JIN DANYUAN, Aesthetics
LI CONGZONG, Modern Literature
LI JIABIN, Ancient World History
LI YAN, History of the Chinese Feudal Economy
LIN CHAOMIN, Ethnic History
QIAO CHUANZAO, Writing
SUN QINHUA, Literary Language
TANG MIN, Modern World History
WANG KAILIAN, Classical Chinese Language
XU KANGMING, Modern World History
YANG ZHENKUN, Modern Literature
YOU ZHONG, History of Chinese Minorities
ZHANG FUSAN, Ethnic and Folk Literature
ZHANG GUOQING, Classical Chinese Writings
ZHANG XINCHANG, History and Archives of Chinese Minorities
ZHU HUIRONG, Historical Geography

School of Law (tel. (871) 5184816):
CHEN ZIGUO, Civil Law
XU ZHISHAN, Constitution

School of Life Sciences and Chemistry (tel. (871) 5031412):
DAI SHUSHAN, Physics and Chemistry
HE SENQUAN, Organic Chemistry
HONG PINJIE, Microwave Plasma
HU ZHIHAO, Botany
HUANG SUHUA, Botany
LI LIANG, Organic Chemistry
LI QIREN, Plant Cell Engineering
LIU FUCHU, Organic Chemistry
LIU SONGYU, Analytical Chemistry
LIU XINHUA, Soil Ecology
TAO YUANQI, Quantum Organic Chemistry
WANG CHANGYI, Organic Chemistry
XU QIHENG, Analytical Chemistry
YANG CHUNJIN, Inorganic Chemistry
YANG PIPENG, Organic Chemistry
YIN JIANGUO, Inorganic Chemistry
ZAN RUIGUANG, Cell Biology
ZHENG ZHUO, Microbiology
ZUO YANGXIAN, Invertebrates

School of Public Administration (tel. (871) 5033609):
CHEN GUOXING, Socialism
CUI YUNWU, Public Administration
GAO LI, Ethics
HOU YIHONG, Management Psychology
JIANG ZIHUA, Politics
JIN ZIQIANG, Current Chinese Politics
KUANG ZHIMING, Politics
LI BIN, Philosophy
LIU JIAZHI, Philosophy
LIU YUNHANG, Aesthetics
WANG YANBING, Sociology
XIONG SIYUAN, Economics
YANG JIQIONG, Current Chinese Politics
ZENG JIAN, Dialectics
ZHOU PING, Politics

School of Sciences (tel. (871) 5032012):
CAO KEFEI, Physics
CHEN ZHONGZHANG, Physics
CONG LIANLI, Earth Sciences
GUO SHICANG, Earth Sciences
GUO XIAOJIANG, Mathematics
GUO YUQI, Mathematics
HE DAMING, Earth Sciences
HE XIANGPANG, Mathematics
HU JIAFU, Earth Sciences
HU WENGUO, Physics
JU JIANHUA, Earth Sciences
LI JIANPIN, Mathematics
LI YAOTANG, Mathematics
LI YONGKUN, Mathematics
LIN LIZHONG, Physics
LIU ZHENGRONG, Mathematics
LUO YAOHUANG, Physics
MEI DONGCHENG, Physics
PENG KUANGDING, Physics
PENG SHOULI, Physics
TANG XINGHUA, Mathematics
TIEN XINSHI, Physics
WANG WEIGUO, Earth Sciences
WEN XIAOMIN, Physics
WU XINGHUI, Material Sciences
XIE YINGQI, Atmospheric Science, Mathematics
YAN GUANGXIONG, Mathematics
YAN HUASHENG, Earth Sciences
YANG DEQING, Physics
YANG HUAKANG, Mathematics
YANG XUESHENG, Earth Sciences
YANG YU, Material Sciences
ZHANG LI, Physics
ZHANG ZHONGMIN, Physics
ZHAO XIAOHUA, Mathematics
ZHENG BAOZHONG, Material Sciences
ZHENG XIYIN, Mathematics
ZHOU QING, Physics

School of Tourism and Business Administration (tel. (871) 5034561):
GUANG NINGSHEN, Tourism Administration
LI HAO, Tourism Administration
LIU XUEYU, Business Management
TIAN WEIMING, Tourism Administration
WANG JIANPIN, Econometrics
XUE QUNHUI, Tourism Administration
YANG GUIHUA, Tourism Administration
ZHANG MINGAN, Business Management
ZHANG XIAOPIN, English

YUNNAN UNIVERSITY OF FINANCE AND ECONOMICS

237 Longquan Rd, 650221 Kunming
Telephone: (871) 5122394
E-mail: sjxx@ynufe.edu.cn
Internet: www.ynufe.edu.cn

Founded 1981, current name adopted 2006

Pres.: Prof. SHUXIN XIONG
Vice-Pres.: YANG XIAO
Vice-Pres.: WANG XIAO-PING

Library: 1.6m. vols
Number of teachers: 1,400

Number of students: 16,000

Publications: *Foreign Economic Theory and Administration*, *Journal*

YUNNAN UNIVERSITY OF NATIONALITIES

134 Yi Er Yi Ave, 650031 Kunming

Telephone: (871) 5154308

Internet: www.ynni.edu.cn

Founded 1951 as Yunan Institute for the Nationalities, current name adopted 2003

State control

Schools of chemistry and biotechnology, economics, foreign languages, int. education, law, management, mathematics and computer science, physics and electronic–electrical information engineering, Southeast and South Asian languages and cultures

Academic year: September to July

Pres.: ZHANG YINGJIE

Vice-Pres.: HE SHAOYING

Vice-Pres.: MA LIJUAN

Vice-Pres.: WANG DEQIANG

Vice-Pres.: ZHANG QIAOGUI

Library of 430,000 vols, 28 special collns

Number of teachers: 1,314

Number of students: 23,000

ZHEJIANG GONGSHANG UNIVERSITY

18 Xuezheng St, 310038 Hangzhou

Telephone: (571) 28877323

E-mail: international@mail.zjgsu.edu.cn

Internet: www.zjgsu.edu.cn

Founded 1911 as Hangzhou Business School, current name adopted 2004

Pres.: Prof. ZHANG RENSHOU

Vice-Pres.: DAI WENZHAN

Library: 2.5m. vols, 3,000 journals and newspapers

Number of teachers: 1,472

Number of students: 33,400

DEANS

College of Further Education: Prof. JIA BAOHUA

Hangzhou College of Commerce: Prof. FU YUYING

School of Accounting: Prof. XU YONGBIN

School of Art and Design: Prof. ZHANG JIANCHUN

School of Business Administration: Prof. HAO YUNHONG

School of Computer Science and Information Engineering: Prof. LING YUN

School of Economics: Prof. HE DA'AN

School of Environmental Science and Engineering: Prof. YANG CHUNPING

School of Finance: Prof. QIAN SHUITU

School of Food Science and Biotechnology: Prof. DENG SHAOPING

School of Foreign Languages: Prof. LIU FAGONG

School of Humanities: Prof. GAO WANLONG

School of Information and Electronic Engineering: Prof. WANG WEIMING

School of Japanese Language and Culture: Prof. WANG BAOPING

School of Law: Prof. TAN SHIGUI

School of Marxism Studies: Prof. WANG LAIFA

School of Public Administration: Prof. CHEN SHENGYONG

School of Statistics and Mathematics: Prof. QIAN XUEYA

School of Tourism and City Administration: Prof. TANG DAIJIAN

Zhang Naiqi Honors College: Prof. XU FENG

ZHEJIANG UNIVERSITY

38 Zheda Rd, Hangzhou 310027, Zhejiang Province

Telephone: (571) 87951846

E-mail: zupo@zju.edu.cn

Internet: www.zju.edu.cn

Founded 1897, merged with Hangzhou Univ., Zhejiang Agricultural Univ. and Zhejiang Medical Univ. 1998

State control

Languages of instruction: Chinese, English

Academic year: September to June

Pres.: Prof. PAN YUNHE

Exec. Vice-Pres.: Prof. NI MINGJIANG

Vice-Pres.: Prof. BU FANXIAO

Vice-Pres.: Prof. CHU, JIAN

Vice-Pres.: Prof. HU JIANMIAO

Vice-Pres.: Prof. LAI MAODE

Vice-Pres.: Prof. SI, JIANMIN

Vice-Pres.: Prof. ZHU, JUN

Dir for Int. Programmes Office: Prof. QIU JIZHEN

Librarian: ZHU HAIKANG

Number of teachers: 3,285

Number of students: 90,475 (43,222 full-time, 30,571 part-time, 16,682 distance learning)

Publications: *Applied Mathematics of Chinese Universities* (in Chinese and English), *Applied Psychology* (in Chinese), *China Higher Medical Education* (in Chinese), *Engineering Design* (in Chinese), *Journal of Zhejiang University (Agricultural and Life Sciences)* (in Chinese), *Journal of Zhejiang University (Humanities and Social Science)* (in Chinese), *Journal of Zhejiang University (Medicine)* (in Chinese), *Journal of Zhejiang University (Natural Science)* (in Chinese), *Journal of Zhejiang University (Sciences)* (in Chinese and English), *Materials Science and Engineering* (in Chinese), *Management Engineering* (in Chinese), *Population and Eugenics* (in Chinese), *Practical Oncology* (in Chinese), *Spatial Structures* (in Chinese)

ZHEJIANG UNIVERSITY OF TECHNOLOGY

District 6, Zhaohui Xincun, Hangzhou 310032, Zhejiang Province

Telephone: (571) 88320114

E-mail: webmaster@zjut.edu.cn

Internet: www.zjut.edu.cn

Founded 1953

Academic year: September to July

Pres.: Prof. SHEN YINCHU

Vice-Pres.: Prof. MA CHUN'AN

Vice-Pres.: Prof. XIAO RUIFENG

Vice-Pres.: Prof. XUAN YONG

Vice-Pres.: Prof. ZHANG LIBIN

Librarian: Prof. HE LIMIN

Library of 1,002,000 vols

Number of teachers: 2,600

Number of students: 18,000

Publication: *Journal* (separate edns for natural sciences and social sciences, each 6 a year)

DEANS

College of Architecture and Civil Engineering: Prof. ZHENG JIANJUN

College of Arts and Humanities: Prof. SUN LIPING

College of Biological and Environmental Engineering: Prof. CHEN JIANMENG

College of Business Administration: Prof. CHENG HUIFANG

College of Chemical Engineering: Prof. JI JIANBING

College of Electrical and Mechanical Engineering: Prof. CHAI GUOZHONG

College of Foreign Languages: Prof. LIAO FEI

College of Information Engineering: Prof. CAI JIAMEI

College of Law: Prof. ZHANG XU

College of Pharmaceutical Sciences: Prof. QIAN JUNQING

College of Sciences: Prof. CHENG CHENG

College of Vocational and Technical Education: Prof. DU SHIGUI

ZHENGZHOU UNIVERSITY

100 Kexue St, Zhengzhou 450001, Henan Province

Telephone: (371) 7763036

E-mail: headmaster@zzu.edu.cn

Internet: www.zzu.edu.cn

Founded 1956

provincial control

Academic year: September to July

Pres.: SHEN CHANGYU

Vice-Pres.: GAO DANYING

Vice-Pres.: JIAO LIUCHENG

Vice-Pres.: SONG MAOPING

Vice-Pres.: XU ZHENLU

Vice-Pres.: ZHENG YULING

Head of Graduate Dept: ZHU CHENGSHEN

Librarian: ZHANG LEISHUN

Library of 3,900,000 vols

Number of teachers: 2,200

Number of students: 44,000

Publication: *Journal* (edns: science, natural sciences, 4 a year; philosophy and social science, medical science, 6 a year)

DEANS

College of Chemical Engineering: WEI XINLI

College of Nursing: (vacant)

College of Public Health: HU DONGSHENG

Department of Bioengineering: KANG QIAOZHEN

Department of Chemistry: LIU HONGMIN

Department of History and Archaeology: JIANG JIANSHE

Department of Management Engineering: (vacant)

Department of Mathematics: CHEN SHAOCHUN

Department of Music: GONG WEI

Institute of Physical Science and Technology: WANG ZHONGYONG

School of Applied Technology: LI SHUXIN

School of Basic Medical Science: DONG ZIMING

School of Civil Engineering: LIU LIXIN

School of Economics: DU SHUYUN

School of Education: WANG ZONGMIN

School of Electrical Engineering: CHEN TIEJUN

School of Environment and Water Conservancy: WANG FUMING

School of Foreign Languages: SHEN NANA

School of Information Management: KE PING

School of Journalism and Communication: DONG GUANGAN

School of Law: TIAN TUCHENG

School of Liberal Arts: ZHANG HONGSHENG

School of Materials Science and Engineering: GUAN SHAOKANG

School of Mechanical Engineering: ZHANG LUOMING

School of Physical Education: WU LANYING

School of Pharmacy: RAO YAOGANG

School of Physical Science and Technology: LI YUXIAO

School of Public Administration: (vacant)

School of Tourism Management: MAO ANFU

PROFESSORS

AN, GUOLOU, History and Archaeology

AN, YUHUI, Basic Medical Science

CAO, SHAOKUI, Materials Science and Engineering

CEN, SHAOCHENG, Mechanical Engineering

CHAN, JIE, Basic Medical Science

CHEN, HUAI, Civil Engineering
CHEN, JINGBO, Materials Science and Engineering
CHEN, JINZHOU, Materials Science and Engineering
CHEN, TAN, Public Health
CHEN, TIEJUN, Electrical Engineering
CHEN, YILANG, Chemical Engineering
CHENG, BAOSHAN, Law
CUI, JING, Basic Medical Science
CUI, JINGBIN, Basic Medical Science
CUI, LIUXIN, Public Health
CUI, XIULING, Chemistry
DONG, GUANGAN, Journalism and Culture
DONG, MINGMIN, Bioengineering
DONG, QIWU, Chemical Engineering
DONG, ZIMING, Basic Medical Science
DU, CHENXIA, Chemistry
DU, SHUYUN, Economic School
DU, XIANTANG, Bioengineering
DUAN, GUANGCAI, Public Health
FAN, MING, Information Engineering
FAN, XIQING, Physical Science and Technology
FAN, YAOTING, Chemistry
FANG, WENJI, Chemical Engineering
FENG, DONGQING, Electrical Engineering
FENG, LIYUN, Public Health
FU, CHUNJING, Basic Medical Science
FU, RUNFANG, Basic Medical Science
GAO, JIANHUA, Chemistry
GAO, JINFENG, Electrical Engineering
GAO, XIAOQUN, Basic Medical Science
GAO, ZHENGYAO, Physical Science and Technology
GONG, JUNFANG, Chemistry
GUAN, HUILING, Mechanical Engineering
GUAN, SHAOKANG, Materials Science and Engineering
GUAN, XINXIN, Chemistry
GUO, SHILING, Chemical Engineering
GUO, XIANJI, Chemistry
GUO, YANCHUN, Chemistry
GUO, YINGJIAN, Foreign Languages
GUO, YIQUN, Chemistry
GUO, YUANCHENG, Civil Engineering
HAN, GUOHE, History and Archaeology
HAN, JIE, Mechanical Engineering
HAN, QIAO, Chemistry
HAN, WEICHENG, Chemistry
HE, ZHANHANG, Chemistry
HOU, HONGWEI, Chemistry
HOU, ZONGYUAN, Law
HU, DONGSHENG, Public Health
HU, JIANLI, Chemistry
HUA, SHAOJIE, Mechanical Engineering
HUO, YUPING, Physical Science and Technology
JIA, HANDONG, Chemistry
JIA, XIAOLIN, Materials Science and Engineering
JIANG, DENGGAO, Chemical Engineering
JIANG, JIANCHU, Law
JIANG, JIANSHE, History and Archaeology
JIANG, MAYUN, Education
JIANG, YUANLI, Chemical Engineering
KE, PING, Information Management
LI, DAWANG, Civil Engineering
LI, GANG, Chemistry
LI, HAIMEI, Materials Science and Engineering
LI, JIANJUN, Chemistry
LI, JIANKE, Bioengineering
LI, LIMIN, Chemistry
LI, TIAN, Civil Engineering
LI, WENJIE, Public Health
LI, XIAOWEN, Basic Medical Science
LI, XINFA, Materials Science and Engineering
LI, YINGDAN, Public Health
LI, YUEBAI, Basic Medical Science
LI, YUXIAO, Physical Science and Technology
LI, ZHIMIN, Public Health
LI, ZHONGJUN, Chemistry
LIANG, ERJUN, Physical Science and Technology
LIANG, FENGRONG, Law
LIAO, XINCHENG, Chemistry
LIN, LIN, Chemistry
LIU, DAZHUANG, Chemical Engineering
LIU, DEFA, Law
LIU, GUOJI, Chemical Engineering
LIU, HONGMIN, Chemistry
LIU, HONGXIA, Chemistry
LIU, HUALIAN, Public Health
LIU, JINDUN, Chemical Engineering
LIU, JINXIA, Chemistry
LIU, LIXIN, Civil Engineering
LIU, MINYING, Materials Science and Engineering
LIU, PU, Chemistry
LIU, SHOUCHANG, Chemistry
LIU, XIANGWEN, Law
LIU, XIANLIN, Electrical Engineering
LIU, XINTIAN, Materials Science and Engineering
LIU, YUNBO, Foreign Languages
LU, MEIYI, History and Archaeology
LU, SONGYUE, Law
LU, TAIFENG, Law
LU, WENGE, Public Health
LU, XINGUANG, Materials Science and Engineering
LU, ZUHUI, Physical Science and Technology
LUO, DAPENG, Public Health
MA, SHENGGANG, Mechanical Engineering
MA, XIAOJIAN, Chemical Engineering
MAO, LUYUAN, Materials Science and Engineering
MIAO, HUIQING, Economic School
MIAO, LIANYING, Law
NING, JINCHENG, Law
NING, ZHENHUAN, Physical Science and Technology
NIU, YUNYIN, Chemistry
PEI, BINGNAN, Information Engineering
PEI, YINGXIN, Public Health
QI, YUANMING, Bioengineering
QIAO, HAILING, Basic Medical Science
QIN, GUANGYONG, Physical Science and Technology
QU, CHUANZHI, Basic Medical Science
QU, LINGBO, Chemistry
RAO, YAOGANG, Pharmacy
REN, BAOZENG, Chemical Engineering
REN, CUIPING, Chemistry
SHEN, GUIMING, Law
SHEN, KAIJU, Law
SHEN, NANA, Foreign Languages
SHEN, NINGFU, Materials Science and Engineering
SHEN, XIANZHANG, Electrical Engineering
SHEN, XIAOCHENG, Bioengineering
SHI, JIE, Chemistry
SHI, MAOSHENG, Law
SHI, QIUZHI, Chemistry
SHI, XUEZHONG, Public Health
SHUI, TINGLIANG, Chemical Engineering
SONG, MAOPING, Chemistry
SU, JINGXIANG, Information Engineering
SU, YUNLAI, Chemistry
SUN, PEIQIN, Chemical Engineering
SUN, YUFU, Materials Science and Engineering
TAN, XINMIN, Education
TANG, KEYONG, Materials Science and Engineering
TANG, MINGSHENG, Chemistry
TAO, JINGCHAO, Chemistry
TIAN, TUCHENG, Law
TONG, LIPING, Civil Engineering
WANG, DONGWEI, Civil Engineering
WANG, FENG, Law
WANG, FUAN, Chemical Engineering
WANG, GUANGLONG, Chemical Engineering
WANG, GUOLING, Education
WANG, HONGXING, Chemistry
WANG, HONGYING, Materials Science and Engineering
WANG, JIE, Electrical Engineering
WANG, JINGWU, Materials Science and Engineering
WANG, LIANFENG, Law
WANG, LIDONG, Bioengineering
WANG, MINCAN, Chemistry
WANG, MINGCHEN, Basic Medical Science
WANG, XIANGYU, Chemistry
WANG, XIKE, Materials Science and Engineering
WANG, XINGGUANG, History and Archaeology
WANG, XINLING, Civil Engineering
WANG, YAN, Chemical Engineering
WANG, YUDONG, Materials Science and Engineering
WANG, YUNZHI, History and Archaeology
WANG, ZHONGQUAN, Basic Medical Science
WANG, ZHONGYONG, Information Engineering
WEI, XINLI, Chemical Engineering
WU, FENG, Basic Medical Science
WU, MIN, Public Health
WU, MINGJIAN, Chemical Engineering
WU, XIAOLING, Mechanical Engineering
WU, YANGJIE, Chemistry
WU, YIMING, Public Health
WU, YOULIN, Physical Science and Technology
XIAO, GUOXING, Law
XIAO, QIANGANG, Law
XU, HAISHENG, Chemical Engineering
XU, QILOU, Civil Engineering
XU, QUN, Materials Science and Engineering
XU, SHUN, Chemistry
XU, XIUCHENG, Chemical Engineering
XU, YAN, Chemistry
XU, YOULI, History and Archaeology
XUE, CHANGGUI, Basic Medical Science
XUE, LEXUN, Bioengineering
YAN, SUQING, Public Health
YANG, CHANGCHUN, Chemistry
YANG, GUANYU, Chemistry
YANG, JIUJUN, Materials Science and Engineering
YANG, SHENGLI, Basic Medical Science
YANG, TIANYU, History and Archaeology
YANG, YUANHUI, Electrical Engineering
YE, BAOXIAN, Chemistry
YE, YANGDONG, Information Engineering
YU, XIANGDONG, History and Archaeology
YU, YANGUANG, Information Engineering
YUAN, SIGUO, Chemical Engineering
YUAN, ZULIANG, History and Archaeology
ZENG, ZHIPING, Chemical Engineering
ZHANG, AFANG, Materials Science and Engineering
ZHANG, BAOLIN, Chemical Engineering
ZHANG, BINGLIN, Physical Science and Technology
ZHANG, GUOSHUO, History and Archaeology
ZHANG, HAOQIN, Chemical Engineering
ZHANG, HENG, Mechanical Engineering
ZHANG, HONGQUAN, Public Health
ZHANG, HONGYUN, Chemistry
ZHANG, JIANMIN, Chemistry
ZHANG, LINNA, Mechanical Engineering
ZHANG, MINFU, History and Archaeology
ZHANG, PING, Basic Medical Science
ZHANG, QIAN, Basic Medical Science
ZHANG, QINXIAN, Basic Medical Science
ZHANG, RUI, Materials Science and Engineering
ZHANG, RUIQIN, Chemistry
ZHANG, SHUSHENG, Chemistry
ZHANG, SHUYUAN, Chemistry
ZHANG, XIUQUAN, Law
ZHANG, XUHUA, History and Archaeology
ZHANG, YADONG, Chemical Engineering
ZHANG, ZHAO, Basic Medical Science
ZHANG, ZHIHONG, Information Engineering
ZHAO, JIANWEN, Law
ZHAO, QINGXIANG, Materials Science and Engineering
ZHAO, WENEN, Chemical Engineering
ZHAO, XINGTAI, Education
ZHAO, YUFEN, Chemistry
ZHENG, YONGFU, History and Archaeology
ZHOU, CAIRONG, Chemical Engineering
ZHOU, CHUXIAN, Chemistry
ZHOU, DAPENG, Chemistry
ZHOU, PENG, Information Engineering

ZHOU, QINGLEI, Information Engineering
ZHOU, YUANFANG, Public Health
ZHU, CHENGSHEN, Materials Science and Engineering
ZHUANG, LEI, Information Engineering
ZHUANG, YINFENG, Materials Science and Engineering

ZHONGNAN UNIVERSITY OF ECONOMICS AND LAW

114 Wuluo Rd, Wuhan 430064, Hubei Province
Telephone: (27) 88044332
E-mail: xz@znufe.edu.cn
Internet: www.znufe.edu.cn
Founded 1948
Academic year: September to July
Pres.: WU HANDONG
Vice-Pres.: LI HANCHANG
Vice-Pres.: TAN YOUTU
Vice-Pres.: ZHANG ZHONGHUA
Vice-Pres.: ZHAO LINGYUN
Head of Graduate Dept: ZHU YANFU
Librarian: HU YUANMIN
Number of teachers: 1,173
Number of students: 35,200
Publications: *Journal* (6 a year), *Studies in Law and Business* (6 a year)

DEANS

School of Accounting: LUO FEI
School of Banking and Insurance: ZU XINGRONG
School of Business Administration: ZHANG XINGUO
School of Economics: LU XIANXIANG
School of Finance and Public Administration: YANG CANMING
School of Foreign Languages: XIE QUN
School of Humanities: WANG YUCHEN
School of Information Science: YANG YUNYAN
School of Journalism and Mass Media: YIN XIULIN
School of Law: QI WENYUAN
School of Public Administration: ZHAO MAN
School of Public Security: YANG ZONGHUI

PROFESSORS

CAI, HONG, Law
CAI, LING, Economics
CAO, SHIQUAN, Law
CHAO, LONGQI, Banking and Insurance
CHEN, CHIBO, Business Administration
CHEN, DAJIE, Finance and Public Administration
CHEN, GUANGYAN, Finance and Public Administration
CHEN, JINLIANG, Law
CHEN, XIAOJUN, Law
CHENG, LIHUA, Humanities
CHENG, QIZHI, Economics
CHENG, QUANMING, Finance and Public Administration
CUI, MINGXIA, Law
DAI, WUTANG, Economics
DU, XINGCHAI, Economics
DUAN, NINGHUA, Information Science
FAN, ZHONGXI, Law
FANG, SHIRONG, Law
GU, YUANQING, Economics
GUO, DAOYANG, Accounting
HU, XIANSHUN, Information Science
HUANG, SHIPING, Humanities
JIA, QIYU, Information Science
JIANG, HAISU, Business Administration
KU, KEJIAN, Business Administration
LEI, XINGHU, Law
LI, CHANGQING, Banking and Insurance
LI, DAMING, Finance and Public Administration
LI, DAORONG, Humanities
LI, GEFEI, Banking and Insurance
LI, GUANGZHONG, Accounting
LI, JIANXUN, Public Security
LI, MAONIAN, Information Science
LI, NAINZHAO, Banking and Insurance
LI, QINGZHI, Public Security
LI, WEINING, Economics
LI, XIANPEI, Business Administration
LI, XUANJU, Information Science
LIANG, YUXIA, Law
LIN, HANCHUAN, Economics
LIU, DAHONG, Law
LIU, KEFENG, Humanities
LIU, LIELONG, Economics
LIU, LUANSHENG, Humanities
LIU, MAOLIN, Law
LIU, SIHUA, Economics
LIU, TENGHONG, Information Science
LIU, XIANFAN, Humanities
LU, XIANXIANG, Economics
LU, ZHONGMEI, Law
LUO, FEI, Accounting
LUO, SHENGBAO, Business Administration
MEI, ZIHUI, Banking and Insurance
MOU, BINGHUA, Information Science
NI, PINGSONG, Finance and Public Administration
NIE, HUAMING, Banking and Insurance
OUYANG, XUCHU, Business Administration
PANG, FENGXI, Finance and Public Administration
PENG, XINGLV, Business Administration
PENG, YONGXING, Information Science
PENG, ZHENGHUI, Law
QI, WENYUAN, Law
QIN, YOUTU, Law
QIU, JIAWU, Information Science
QU, GUANGQIN, Law
SHEN, BENZHU, Law
SHONG, QINGHUA, Banking and Insurance
SU, SHAOZHI, Economics
SUN, XIAOFU, Law
SUN, XIAOMEI, Humanities
TANG, GUOPING, Accounting
TANG, WEIBEN, Economics
TANG, WUYUN, Economics
TONG, ZHIWEI, Law
WAN, HOUFEN, Business Administration
WANG, FULIN, Humanities
WANG, JUNPING, Public Security
WANG, QUANXIN, Law
WANG, SHOU'AN, Information Science
WANG, XINGYUAN, Information Science
WU, GUANGBING, Economics
WU, HANGDONG, Law
WU, JUNPEI, Finance and Public Administration
WU, LIANLIAN, Humanities
WU, YIJUN, Business Administration
WU, ZHIZHONG, Law
XIA, CHENGCAI, Accounting
XIA, XINYUAN, Economics
XIA, YONG, Law
XIONG, SHENGXU, Business Administration
XU, DUNKAI, Economics
XU, GUOXIN, Economics
XU, JIANGUO, Finance and Public Administration
XU, RENZHANG, Finance and Public Administration
YAN, DEYU, Accounting
YAN, LIDONG, Business Administration
YAN, QIZHONG, Business Administration
YAN, RICHU, Information Science
YANG, CANMING, Finance and Public Administration
YANG, JIAZHI, Economics
YANG, KAIHAN, Information Science
YANG, YUNYAN, Economics
YANG, ZONGHUI, Public Security
YAO, HUIYUAN, Economics
YAO, LI, Law
YE, QING, Finance and Public Administration
YU, XIYAN, Business Administration
YU, ZONGQI, Humanities
YUAN, JICHENG, Humanities
ZENG, QINGWEI, Information Science
ZHAN, CAILI, Accounting
ZHANG, CHAOQUN, Finance and Public Administration
ZHANG, FULIN, Humanities
ZHANG, HUAIFU, Finance and Public Administration
ZHANG, LONGPING, Accounting
ZHANG, SHIJING, Humanities
ZHANG, SHUZHEN, Law
ZHANG, YU, Public Security
ZHANG, YUANHUANG, Public Security
ZHANG, ZHENGLING, Humanities
ZHAO, LINGYU, Economics
ZHAO, MAN, Finance and Public Administration
ZHENG, ZHUJUN, Law
ZHOU, JUN, Banking and Insurance
ZHU, HAIFANG, Accounting
ZHU, YANFU, Economics
ZOU, LIGANG, Law
ZU, XINGRONG, Banking and Insurance

HONG KONG

The Higher Education System

Hong Kong Island was ceded to the United Kingdom under the terms of the Treaty of Nanking (Nanjing) in 1842. The Kowloon Peninsula was acquired by the Convention of Peking (Beijing) in 1860. The New Territories were leased from China in 1898 for a period of 99 years. Among the institutions of higher education established during Hong Kong's period under British control were the University of Hong Kong (the country's oldest tertiary establishment, founded 1912), the Hong Kong Polytechnic University (founded 1937 as the Government Trade School) and the Hong Kong Baptist University (founded 1956 as the Hong Kong Baptist College). On 1 July 1997, upon the expiry of the lease on the New Territories, China regained sovereignty over the whole of Hong Kong. As a Special Administrative Region of China, Hong Kong enjoys a high degree of autonomy, except in matters of defence and foreign affairs. The Hong Kong Education Bureau is responsible for education at all levels. Higher education is provided by universities, polytechnics, technical institutes and institutions of professional education. In 2010/11 enrolment at the eight institutions of higher education funded by the University Grants Committee (UGC) totalled 164,857 students. In the same year 12,918 students were enrolled at the country's 16 post-secondary colleges, 62,094 students were enrolled at the Institute of Vocational Education (founded 1999), 20,196 students were enrolled at the Open University of Hong Kong (founded 1989 as the Open Learning Institute of Hong Kong) and 245,787 students were enrolled at the 2,344 adult education institutions. In 2011/12 figures given by the Education Bureau estimated that a total of 296,800 students were enrolled across all types of higher education institutes (incl. non-local courses). The Government provides loans and grants for needy students through the Student Financial Assistance Agency.

Following recent changes to the education system, admission to higher education is now based on achievement in the Hong Kong Diploma of Secondary Education. Selection is on a competitive basis. Undergraduate programmes offered include the Associate degree, which takes three years and is available in a wide range of subjects, and the Bachelors degree, which has been increased from three years to four years of study. At postgraduate level, in addition to the certificates and diplomas on offer, students may undertake a one- to two-year Masters course following the Bachelors. The highest level of university-level education is the Doctorate, a research-based degree which normally last for a minimum of three years and requires the submission of a thesis. Entry requirements for the doctoral programme vary between institutions.

Technical and vocational education (in the form of various diplomas) is provided by private institutions, universities and other higher education institutions offering sub-degree level qualifications, and by the 12 member institutions of the Vocational Training Council (VTC), which was founded in 1982; the largest of the VTC member institutions is the Institute of Vocational Education. The Higher Diploma, which takes two to three years, is considered to be equivalent to an Associate degree.

The Hong Kong Council for Accreditation of Academic and Vocational Qualifications is a statutory body, which was established in 2007 to replace the Hong Kong Council for Academic Accreditation and to provide for the implementation of the Qualifications Framework. The Council provides quality assurance and assessment services to education and training institutions, continuing education providers and the general public. In addition to the allocation of public funds, the UGC promotes and supports quality assurance and monitors the academic standards of its member institutions: City University of Hong Kong, Hong Kong Baptist University, Lingnan University, the Chinese University of Hong Kong, the Hong Kong Institute of Education (founded 1994), the Hong Kong Polytechnic University, the Hong Kong University of Science and Technology, and the University of Hong Kong. In 2007 the UGC set up the semi-autonomous Quality Assurance Council, which was to strengthen quality assurance measures in UGC-funded institutions. The Joint Quality Review Committee was established in 2005 by the Heads of the Universities Committees of the UGC-funded institutions, to provide quality assurance processes for self-financed sub-degree programmes offered at continuing education units and community colleges, or other departments of these institutions.

Regulatory and Representative Bodies

GOVERNMENT

Education Bureau: 15th Fl., Wu Chung House, 213 Queen's Rd E, Wan Chai; tel. (852) 28910088; e-mail edbinfo@edb.gov.hk; internet www.edb.gov.hk; Sec. for Education EDDIE NG HAK-KIM; Permanent Sec. for Education TSE LING KH-CHING.

Leisure and Cultural Services Department: Leisure and Cultural Services HQ, 1–3 Pai Tau St, Sha Tin; tel. (852) 24145555; e-mail enquiries@lcsd.gov.hk; internet www.lcsd.gov.hk; attached to Home Affairs Bureau; Dir BETTY FUNG CHING SUK-YEE; Deputy Dir for Cultural Services CYNTHIA LIU CHIU-FUN; Deputy Dir for Leisure Services BOBBY CHENG KAM-WING.

ACCREDITATION

Hong Kong Council for Accreditation of Academic & Vocational Qualifications: 10 Siu Sai Wan Rd, Chai Wan; tel. (852) 36580000; e-mail info@hkcaavq.edu.hk; internet www.hkcaavq.edu.hk; f. 1990; Chair. MARTIN LIAO; Exec. Dir Prof. YIU-KWAN FAN.

NATIONAL BODIES

Heads of Universities Committee: The Hong Kong Polytechnic Univ., Hung Hom, Kowloon; tel. (852) 27665168; e-mail pphucom@polyu.edu.hk; internet www.polyu.edu.hk; Convenor Prof. WAY KUO.

Hong Kong Examinations and Assessment Authority: Southorn Centre, 12th–14th Fl., 130 Hennessy Rd, Wan Chai; tel. (852) 36288833; e-mail tsa1@hkeaa.edu.hk; internet www.hkeaa.edu.hk; Chair. EDDIE NG HAK-KIM; Deputy Chair. HUI CHIN-YIM; Sec.-Gen. Dr FRANCIS CHEUNG.

University Grants Committee: 7th Fl., Shui On Centre, 6–8 Harbour Rd, Wan Chai; tel. (852) 25243987; e-mail ugc@ugc.edu.hk; internet www.ugc.edu.hk; f. 1965; Chair. Hon. LAURA M. CHA; Sec.-Gen. MICHAEL V. STONE.

Vocational Training Council: VTC Tower, 27 Wood Rd, Wan Chai; tel. (852) 28361000; e-mail vtcmailbox@vtc.edu.hk; internet www.vtc.edu.hk; f. 1982; Chair. Hon. ANDREW LEUNG KWAN-YUEN; Exec. Dir Dr CARRIE WILLIS.

Learned Societies

GENERAL

Royal Asiatic Society Hong Kong Branch: POB 3864, Central; tel. (852) 65907523; e-mail membership@royalasiaticsociety.org.hk; internet www.royalasiaticsociety.org.hk; f. 1847, re-established 1959; encourages history, arts, science and literature in relation to Asia, particularly Hong Kong and China and their cultures; lectures and social activities; 600 mems (incl. 100 overseas mems); library of 5,500 books, 140,000 index cards; Pres. MICHAEL BROOM; Hon. Sec. DAVID MCKELLAR; publ. *Journal of the Hong Kong Branch of the Royal Asiatic Society* (1 a year).

BIBLIOGRAPHY, LIBRARY SCIENCE AND MUSEOLOGY

Hong Kong Library Association: POB 10095, Gen. Post Office Hong Kong; e-mail hkla@hkla.org; internet www.hkla.org; f. 1958; promotes librarianship; offers professional growth, networking and community service; devt of policies promoting provision of information and library services in Hong Kong; 623 mems; Pres. HAIPENG LI; Hon. Sec CHRISTOPHER CHAN; Hon. Treas. RYUN LEE; publ. *Journal* (irregular).

University of Hong Kong Museum Society: Univ. Museum and Art Gallery, Univ. of Hong Kong, 94 Bonham Rd, Pokfulam; tel. (852) 22415500; e-mail info@hkums.com; internet www.hkums.com; f. 1988; attached to Univ. of Hong Kong; supports the Univ. of Hong Kong Museum and Art Gallery; promotes Chinese arts and antiquities; sponsors art and educational programmes in the community; 500 mems; Chair. BONNIE KWAN HUO; Vice-Chair. YVONNE CHOI; Sec. WINNIE TONG; Treas. AUDY MAK; publ. *MVSE News* (5 a year).

ECONOMICS, LAW AND POLITICS

Hong Kong Institute of Certified Public Accountants: 37th Fl., Wu Chung House, 213 Queen's Rd E, Wan Chai; tel. (852) 22877228; e-mail hkicpa@hkicpa.org.hk; internet www.hkicpa.org.hk; f. 1973, fmrly Hong Kong Soc. of Accountants; registers and grants practising certificates to Certified Public Accountants in Hong Kong; mems earn description Certified Public Accountant and designatory letters CPA; assures the quality of entry into the profession through its postgraduate CPA Qualification Programme; promulgates financial reporting, auditing and ethical standards in Hong Kong; 28,000 mems; Pres. WILSON FUNG; Chief Exec. and Registrar WINNIE C. W. CHEUNG; publs *APlus* (12 a year), technical bulletin, guides and other publs online.

Hong Kong Management Association: 14th Fl., Fairmont House, 8 Cotton Tree Dr., Central; tel. (852) 25266516; e-mail hkma@hkma.org.hk; internet www.hkma

.org.hk; f. 1960; offers management training courses, management consultancy services, library information, seminars, forums, awards and competitions; 12,000 mems; Chair. Hon. DAVID K. P. LI; Deputy Chair. Dr DENNIS SUN; Deputy Chair. HENRY H. L. FAN; Deputy Chair. Dr IAN FOK; Dir-Gen. Dr ELIZABETH S. C. SHING; publ. *The Hong Kong Manager* (4 a year).

The Law Society of Hong Kong: 3rd Fl., Wing On House, 71 Des Voeux Rd, Central; tel. (852) 28460500; e-mail sg@hklawsoc.org.hk; internet www.hklawsoc.org.hk; f. 1907; professional assn for solicitors in Hong Kong; ensures compliance by solicitors with relevant laws, codes, regulations and practice directions; supports and protects the character, status and interests of solicitors; 6,122 mems; Pres. HUEN WONG; Vice-Pres. JUNIUS K. Y. HO; Vice-Pres. DIETER YIH; Sec.-Gen. RAYMOND C. K. HO; Deputy Sec.-Gen. HEIDI K.P. CHU; publ. *Hong Kong Lawyer*.

LANGUAGE AND LITERATURE

Alliance Française: 1st and 2nd Fl., 123 Hennessy Rd, Wan Chai; tel. (852) 25277825; e-mail afinfo@alliancefrancaise.com.hk; internet www.alliancefrancaise.com.hk; f. 1953; offers courses and examinations in French language and culture and promotes cultural exchange with France; Pres. R. A. V. RIBERO; Dir-Gen. JEAN-PIERRE DUMONT; Treas. THIERRY MÉQUILLET; publ. *Paroles*.

British Council: 3 Supreme Court Rd, Admiralty; tel. (852) 29135100; e-mail enquiries@britishcouncil.org.hk; internet www.britishcouncil.org.hk/index.asp; f. 1948; offers courses and examinations in English language and British culture and promotes cultural exchange with the UK; Dir RUTH GEE; Deputy Dir of Teaching Centre GEORGINA PEARCE.

Goethe-Institut: 14th Fl., Hong Kong Arts Centre, 2 Harbour Rd, Wan Chai; tel. (852) 28020088; e-mail info@hongkong.goethe.org; internet www.goethe.de/hongkong; f. 1963; offers courses and examinations in German language and culture and promotes cultural exchange with Germany; library of 7,400 vols, incl. audiovisual materials; Dir MICHAEL MÜLLER-VERWEYEN; Deputy Dir and Head of Language Courses MARTIN BODE; Head of Library and Information Service GABRIELE SANDER.

Hong Kong Chinese Speaking PEN Centre: Flat F, 4th Fl., Tower 6, Jubilant Pl. 99, Paucheung St, Kowloon; f. 1955; 92 mems; library of 1,600 vols; Pres. YU HOI FU; Sec. S. B. TENG; publ. *PEN News* (52 a year, in Chinese).

MEDICINE

Hong Kong Medical Association: Duke of Windsor Social Service Bldg, 5th Fl., 15 Hennessy Rd; tel. (852) 25278285; e-mail hkma@hkma.org; internet www.hkma.org; f. 1920, fmrly Hong Kong Chinese Medical Assn; promotes welfare and protects the lawful interests of the medical profession; promotes cooperation with nat. and int. medical socs; works for the advancement of medical science; 8,400 mems; Pres. Dr TSE HUNG HING; Vice-Pres. Dr ALVIN CHAN YEE SHING; Vice-Pres. Dr CHIN CHOW PAK; Hon. Sec. Dr ERNIE LO CHI FUNG; Hon. Treas. Dr CHI CHU LEUNG; Chief Exec. YVONNE LEUNG; publs *HKMA CME Bulletin* (12 a year), *Hong Kong Medical Journal* (6 a year), *HKMA News* (12 a year).

Research Institutes

MEDICINE

Institute of Chinese Medicine: 2nd and 3rd Fl., Science Centre E Block, Chinese Univ. of Hong Kong, Sha Tin, New Territories; tel. (852) 31634370; internet www.icm.cuhk.edu.hk/icm/en; f. 2000, fmrly Chinese Medicinal Material Research Centre; attached to Chinese Univ. of Hong Kong; conducts scientific research to modernize, commercialize and promote Chinese medicine; sections in clinical trials, drug devt, standardization and safety of Chinese medicine, natural products; Chair. Prof. JACK CHENG; Dir Prof. P. C. LEUNG; Dir Prof. K. P. FUNG.

NATURAL SCIENCES

Hong Kong Observatory: 134A Nathan Rd, Kowloon; tel. (852) 29268200; e-mail mailbox@hko.gov.hk; internet www.hko.gov.hk; f. 1883, renamed Royal Observatory, Hong Kong 1912, original name restored 1997; attached to the Govt of the Hong Kong Special Administrative Region; operates weather forecasting, cyclone warning and other meteorological and geophysical services; library of 40,000 vols; Dir Dr BOO-YING LEE; publs *Daily Weather Chart*, *Hong Kong Observatory Almanac* (1 a year), *Hong Kong Observatory Calendar*, *Hong Kong Tide Tables* (1 a year), *Monthly Weather Summary*, *Occasional papers* (irregular), *Summary of Meteorological Observations in Hong Kong* (1 a year), *Technical Notes* (irregular), *Technical Notes (local)* (irregular), *Tropical Cyclones* (1 a year).

Libraries and Archives

Hong Kong

Hong Kong Central Library: 66 Causeway Rd, Causeway Bay; tel. (852) 31501234; e-mail hkcl_ref@lcsd.gov.hk; internet www.hkpl.gov.hk; f. 2001; attached to Hong Kong Public Libraries, Leisure and Cultural Services Dept; depository library for publs of Asian Devt Bank, EU, ILO, Int. Maritime Org., UN, UNESCO, World Bank, World Trade Org. and World Food Programme; 2.5m. vols, incl. books, audiovisual materials, newspapers, periodicals, CD-ROM databases, online databases, ebooks, microforms and maps; Chief Librarian ROCHELLE LAU.

Hong Kong Public Libraries: c/o Hong Kong Central Library, Moreton Terrace, Causeway Bay; tel. (852) 29210208; e-mail enquiries@lcsd.gov.hk; internet www.hkpl.gov.hk; f. 1962; attached to Leisure and Cultural Services Dept; promotes literary arts and literary research in Hong Kong; cultivates public interest in creative writing and literary research; encourages literary writing and cultural exchange; central reference library of 6 subject depts; toy library; a young adult library; exhibition gallery and lecture theatre; provides a network of 66 br. libraries and 10 mobile libraries; 12.47m. items, incl. books, audiovisual materials, newspapers, periodicals, CD-ROM databases, microforms and maps.

Pao Yue-kong Library—Hong Kong Polytechnic University: Hung Hom, Kowloon; tel. (852) 27666863; e-mail lbinf@polyu.edu.hk; internet www.lib.polyu.edu.hk; f. 1972 as The Univ. Library, current name adopted 1995; inter-library loan and document delivery services; reference and personal information consultancy services, information skills workshops, online information literacy programmes; 2,663,242 vols, 844,875 monographs, 249,022 serials bound vols, 419 e-databases, 49,272 ejournal titles, 475,362 ebooks, 462,372 audiovisual items, 400,438 microform items; PolyU Institutional Repository, Examination Paper Database, Course Scheme Database, Electronic Theses Database, Newspaper Clippings Image Database; video-on-demand and online audio libraries; Univ. Librarian Dr SHIRLEY WONG; publ. *Directory of Professional Associations and Learned Societies in Hong Kong*.

Public Records Office: 3rd Fl., Hong Kong Public Records Bldg, 13 Tsui Ping Rd, Kwun Tong, Kowloon; tel. (852) 21957700; e-mail proinfo@grs.gov.hk; internet www.info.gov.hk/pro; f. 1972; attached to Govt Records Service (f. 1997); 22,000 Hong Kong Govt publs; newspapers colln, photographs colln, map colln; 800,000 archival records and library items.

University Library System: Librarian's Office, 7/F Tin Ka Ping Bldg, Sha Tin New Territories; tel. (852) 39437305; e-mail library@cuhk.edu.hk; internet www.lib.cuhk.edu.hk; f. 1963; attached to Chinese Univ. of Hong Kong; coordinates the collns and services of the Univ. Library (f. 1965) and the 7 br. libraries; spec. collns: Careers colln; CUHK theses submitted since 1967; Chinese Overseas colln; History of Medicine of Hong Kong, China and the Asia-Pacific region; Hong Kong Govt documents; Hong Kong Studies; Instructional Materials colln; Modern Chinese Drama colln; rare Chinese books from the Yuan to the Qing dynasties; 2,573,000 vols incl. 1,068,250 vols of books and bound journals in East Asian languages, 1,350,820 vols of books and bound journals in Western languages, more than 10,070 active print serials, 109,700 ejournals, 2.28m. ebooks, 755 e-databases; Univ. Librarian Dr COLIN STOREY; Exec. Officer CHERIE YIP; publ. *Annotated Bibliography of Rare Books in the CUHK Libraries*.

University of Hong Kong Libraries: Main Library, Univ. of Hong Kong Hong Kong; tel. (852) 28592203; e-mail hkulref@hkucc.hku.hk; internet lib.hku.hk; f. 1912; 2,960,414 print vols in E Asian and W languages, 6,639 current print journals, 55,484 ejournals, 3,502,923 ebooks, 118,558 audiovisual items and 1,584,944 materials in microform; spec. collns incl. Hong Kong Colln, Morrison Colln, UN and WHO Depository Collns, Hong Kong Tourist Asscn Colln, Republic of China govt publs, Taiwan Studies, Univ. of Hong Kong theses; Univ. Librarian PETER E. SIDORKO; Deputy Univ. Librarian Dr Y. C. WAN.

Museums and Art Galleries

Hong Kong

Art Museum: Institute of Chinese Studies, Chinese Univ. of Hong Kong, Sha Tin, New Territories; tel. (852) 26097416; e-mail artmuseum@cuhk.edu.hk; internet www.cuhk.edu.hk/ics/amm; f. 1971; attached to Institute of Chinese Studies, Chinese Univ. of Hong Kong; collects, preserves, researches and exhibits artefacts representing the rich art and cultural heritage of ancient and pre-modern China; promotes Chinese culture and heritage; facilitates academic exchange between China and the West; collaborates with univ. dept of Fine Arts for practice in museology and teaching in art history.

Hong Kong Film Archive: 50 Lei King Rd, Sai Wan Ho; tel. (852) 27392139; e-mail hkfa@lcsd.gov.hk; internet www.filmarchive.gov.hk; f. 1993; attached to Leisure and Cultural Services Dept; acquires and conserves films made in Hong Kong; catalogues and maintains archival colln; provides information related to cinema and the Hong Kong film industry; organizes thematic retrospectives, exhibitions, symposia and seminars on cinema; publ. *Oral History Series*.

Hong Kong Heritage Museum: 1 Man Lam Rd, Sha Tin; tel. (852) 21808188; e-mail hkhm@lcsd.gov.hk; internet www.heritagemuseum.gov.hk; attached to Leisure and Cultural Services Dept; colln of local history relics, natural history relics, performing art relics, folk art and popular culture artefacts (toys and comics); art colln: contemporary art, design and Chinese fine art (Chinese paintings, calligraphy and Chinese antiquities); 6 permanent galleries: Orientation Theatre, New Territories Heritage Hall, Cantonese Opera Heritage Hall, T. T. Tsui Gallery of Chinese Art, Chao Shao-an Gallery, Children's Discovery Gallery and 6 thematic galleries; 3 br. museums: Hong Kong Railway Museum (Tai Po), Sam Tung Uk Museum (Tsuen Wan), Sheung Yiu Folk Museum (Sai Kung); Chief Curator BELINDA WONG.

Hong Kong Maritime Museum: Ground Fl., Murray House, Stanley Plaza, Stanley; tel. (852) 28132322; e-mail info@hkmaritimemuseum.org; internet www.hkmaritimemuseum.org; stimulates public interest in ships and the sea particularly the S China coast and adjacent seas; promotes the growth of Hong Kong as a major port and int. maritime centre; 2 galleries: ancient and modern displaying c. 500 exhibits incl. ceramics, ships models, paintings, trade goods and ships manifests; Chair. ANTHONY J. HARDY; Dir Dr STEPHEN DAVIES; Exec. Man. and Curator CATALINA CHOR.

Hong Kong Museum of Art: 10 Salisbury Rd, Tsim Sha Tsui, Kowloon; tel. (852) 27210116; e-mail enquiries@lcsd.gov.hk; internet www.lcsd.gov.hk/hkma; f. 1962, present bldg 1991; attached to Leisure and Cultural Services Dept; 15,000 art objects; Chinese antiquities, incl. the Henry Yeung colln; historical paintings, prints and drawings of Hong Kong, Macao and China, incl. Chater, Sayer, Law and Ho Tung collns; contemporary works by local artists; Chinese paintings and calligraphy, incl. the Xubaizhai Colln; 1 br. museum: Museum of Tea Ware; Chief Curator CHRISTINA CHU.

Branch Museum:

Museum of Tea Ware: 10 Cotton Tree Dr., Central; tel. (852) 28690690; f. 1984; displays famous Yixing teapots; conducts tea gatherings and lecture programmes to promote ceramic art and Chinese tea drinking culture.

Hong Kong Museum of History: 100 Chatham Rd South, Tsimshatsui, Kowloon; tel. (852) 27249042; e-mail hkmh@lcsd.gov.hk; internet hk.history.museum; f. 1962 as City Museum and Art Gallery, present status and name 1975, present location 1998; attached to Leisure and Cultural Services Dept; archaeology, ethnography, natural history and history of Hong Kong; historical photographs and documents; postal history and numismatics colln; brs at Lei Cheng Uk Han Tomb Museum, Law Uk Folk Museum, Hong Kong Museum of Coastal Defence, Dr Sun Yat-sen Museum and Fireboat Alexander Grantham Exhibition Gallery; permanent exhibition: 'The Hong Kong Story'; Chief Curator ESA LEUNG KIT-LING.

Branch Museums:

Dr Sun Yat-sen Museum: 7 Castle Rd, Central; tel. (852) 23676373; e-mail sysm@lcsd.gov.hk; internet hk.drsunyatsen.museum; f. 2006; life and career of Dr Sun Yat-sen; Hong Kong's role in reform movements and revolutionary activities in the 19th–20th centuries; 2 permanent exhibitions display historical artefacts.

Fireboat Alexander Grantham Exhibition Gallery: Quarry Bay Park; tel. (852) 23677821; displays unique fire fighting artefacts; documents marine rescue work in Hong Kong.

Hong Kong Museum of Coastal Defence: 175 Tung Hei Rd, Shau Kei Wan; tel. (852) 25691500; e-mail hkmcd@lcsd.gov.hk; internet hk.coastaldefence.museum; f. 2000, fmrly the Lei Yue Mun Fort; preserves and presents 600-year history of coastal defence in Hong Kong.

Law Uk Folk Museum: 14 Kut Shing St, Chai Wan; tel. (852) 28967006; 18th-century Hakka village house.

Lei Cheng Uk Han Tomb Museum: 41 Tonkin St, Sham Shui Po, Kowloon; tel. (852) 23862863; e-mail hkmh@lcsd.gov.hk; f. 1988 declared as gazetted monument, tomb discovered 1955; tomb closed to public; displays pottery and bronze wares excavated from the tomb, texts, graphics, photos, maps, video cassettes, models of the tomb; 2 exhibitions 'Lei Cheng Uk Han Tomb' and 'Han Culture in S China'.

Hong Kong Science Museum: 2 Science Museum Rd, Tsim Shat Tsui E, Kowloon; tel. (852) 27323232; e-mail enquiries@hk.science.museum; internet hk.science.museum; f. 1991; attached to Leisure and Cultural Services Dept; 500 exhibits on permanent display; spec. thematic exhibitions; education and extension activities; lecture hall and spec. rental exhibition hall; Chief Curator MICHAEL HING-IAN WONG; Sr Man. MARIANNE YUEN-MAN KWOK.

Hong Kong Space Museum: 10 Salisbury Rd, Tsim Sha Tsui, Kowloon; tel. (852) 27210226; e-mail spacem@space.lcsd.gov.hk; internet hk.space.museum; f. 1980; attached to Leisure and Cultural Services Dept; promotes interest in astronomy and related sciences by exhibitions, lectures, films, Omnimax and sky shows; 100 staff; library of 1,700 vols, also films and video cassettes; Curator CHAN KI HUNG; publ. *Astrocalendar* (1 a year).

Hong Kong Visual Arts Centre: 7A Kennedy Rd, Central; tel. (852) 25213008; internet www.lcsd.gov.hk/ce/museum/apo/en/vac.html; f. 1992; attached to Art Promotion Office, Leisure and Cultural Services Dept; provides studios for trained artists practising in the fields of sculpture, printmaking and ceramics; organizes art activities incl. workshops, exhibitions, demonstrations, lectures and artist-in-residence programmes.

Ping Shan Tang Clan Gallery and Heritage Trail Visitors Centre: Hang Tau Tsuen, Ping Shan, Yuen Long, New Territories; tel. (852) 26171959; e-mail amo@lcsd.gov.hk; internet www.lcsd.gov.hk/ce/museum/monument/en/ping_shan.php; f. 1993 as Ping Shan Heritage Trail, present name and staus 2007, converted from the Old Ping Shan Police Station built in 1899; attached to Antiquities and Monuments Office, Leisure and Cultural Services Dept; displays various relics belonging to members of the Tang Clan who personally relate their history, customs and cultural life; introduces monuments and bldgs along the Ping Shan Heritage Trail; spec. thematic exhibitions on history and culture of the New Territories.

University Museum and Art Gallery: Univ. of Hong Kong, 94 Bonham Rd, Pokfulam; tel. (852) 22415500; e-mail museum@hkusua.hku.hk; internet www.hku.hk/hkumag/main.html; f. 1953 as Fung Ping Shan Museum of Chinese Art and Archaeology, present name and bldg 1996; attached to Univ. of Hong Kong; 1,000 items of Chinese antiquities, ceramics, bronzes and paintings; colln incl. items dating from the Neolithic period to the Qing dynasty; bronze colln incl. works from the Shang to the Tang dynasties; largest colln of Yuan dynasty Nestorian crosses in the world; carvings in jade, wood and stone; colln of Chinese oil paintings; attached tea gallery promotes Chinese tea culture; Dir YEUNG CHUN-TONG; Curator for Art TINA YEE-WAN PANG; Curator for History ANITA YIN-FONG WONG.

Universities

CHINESE UNIVERSITY OF HONG KONG

Sha Tin, New Territories
Telephone: (852) 39437000
E-mail: cpr@cuhk.edu.hk
Internet: www.cuhk.edu.hk

Founded 1963
State control
Languages of instruction: English, Chinese
Academic year: August to July

Chancellor: CHIEF EXEC. OF THE HONG KONG SPEC. ADMIN. REGION
Chair. of Ccl: VINCENT H. C. CHENG
Vice-Chancellor and Pres.: Prof. JOSEPH J. Y. SUNG
Pro-Vice-Chancellor and Provost: Prof. BENJAMIN W. WAH
Pro-Vice-Chancellor and Vice-Pres.: Prof. PAK-CHUNG CHING
Pro-Vice-Chancellor and Vice-Pres.: Prof. TAI-FAI FOK
Pro-Vice-Chancellor and Vice-Pres.: Prof. KIT-TAI HAU
Pro-Vice-Chancellor and Vice-Pres.: Prof. MICHAEL K. M. HUI
Pro-Vice-Chancellor and Vice-Pres.: Prof. FANNY M. C. CHEUNG
Dean of Students: Prof. DENNIS K. P. NG
Bursar: CHAN LAM YUET-PING SALOME
Registrar: ERIC S. P. NG
Sec.: JACOB S. K. LEUNG
Treas.: ROGER K. H. LUK
Librarian: LOUISE JONES

Library of 2,530,764 vols
Number of teachers: 1,623
Number of students: 18,698

Publications: *Asian Anthropology* (1 a year), *Asian Economic Journal* (4 a year), *Asian Journal of Counselling* (2 a year), *Asian Journal of English Language Teaching* (1 a year), *Asian Journal of Mathematics* (4 a year), *Chinese Academic Journal* (every 2 years), *Chinese Journal of Communication* (4 a year), *Comparative Literature and Culture* (1 a year), *Communication and Society* (4 a year), *Communications in Information and Systems* (4 a year), *Crosslinks in English Language Teaching* (every 2 years), *Education Journal* (2 a year), *Education Journal in Chinese* (2 a year), *Educational Research Journal* (2 a year), *Geographic Information Sciences* (2 a year), *Global Chinese Journal on Computers in Education* (2 a year), *Journal of Basic Education* (2 a year), *Journal of Chinese Philosophy and Culture* (2 a year), *Journal of Chinese Studies* (2 a year), *Journal of Chinese Literature* (irregular), *Journal of Contemporary Chinese Education* (2 a year), *Journal of General and Liberal Education* (1 a year), *Journal of Phenomenology and Contemporary Philosophy* (1 a year), *Journal of Phenomenology and the Human Sciences* (1 a year), *Journal of Translation History* (1 a year), *Journal of Translation Studies* (2 a year),

Methods and Application of Analysis (4 a year), *Phenomenology and the Human Sciences* (1 a year), *Renditions* (2 a year), *Southeast Asia Bulletin of Mathematics* (6 a year), *Studies in Chinese Language* (3 a year), *The China Review* (2 a year), *Twenty-first Century* (6 a year)

DEANS

Faculty of Arts: Prof. LEUNG YUEN-SANG
Faculty of Business Administration: Prof. VERNON N. HSU
Faculty of Education: Prof. ALVIN S. M. LEUNG
Faculty of Engineering: Prof. C. P. WONG
Faculty of Law: Prof. CHRISTOPHER GANE
Faculty of Medicine: Prof. FRANCIS K. L. CHAN
Faculty of Science: Prof. HENRY N. C. WONG
Faculty of Social Science: Prof. PAUL S. N. LEE
Graduate School: Prof. WONG WING-SHING

PROFESSORS

AHUJA, A., Imaging and Interventional Radiology
CHAN, A., Clinical Oncology
CHAN, C., Medicine and Therapeutics
CHAN, H., Mathematics/Institute of Mathematical Sciences
CHAN, H., Physiology
CHAN, J., Journalism and Communication
CHAN, K., Orthopaedics and Traumatology
CHAN, L., Medicine and Therapeutics
CHAN, N., Statistics
CHAN, W., Biomedical Sciences
CHANG,
CHEN, H., Psychology
CHEN, P., Chinese Language and Literature
CHEN, Z.
CHENG, C., Orthopaedics and Traumatology
CHEUNG, F., Psychology
CHING, P., Electronic Engineering
CHIU, D., Information Engineering
CHIU, F., Psychiatry
CHIU, W.
CHO, C., Pharmacology
CHUNG, K., Obstetrics and Gynaecology
FAURE, D., History
FOK, T., Paediatrics
FOURNIER, C., Social Science
FUNG, K., Biochemistry
GIN, T., Anaesthesia and Intensive Care
HAINES, S., English
HAU, K., Educational Psychology
HSIUNG, P., History
HSU, V., Decision Sciences and Managerial Economics
HUANG, J., Mechanical and Automation Engineering
HUANG, Y., Biomedical Sciences
HUI, K., Marketing
HUI, S., Medicine and Therapeutics
JACKSON, B.
JIANG, L.
KUNG, H., Biomedical Sciences/Stanley Ho Centre for Emerging Infectious Diseases
KWAN, T., Philosophy
LAGERWEY, J., Chinese Studies
LAM, C.
LAN, H., Biomedical Sciences
LAU, K., Mathematics
LAU, N., Geography and Resource Management
LAU, W., Surgery
LAU, Y., Surgery
LAW, S., Management
LEE, L., Chinese Culture
LEE, S., Infectious Diseases
LEE, T., Nursing
LEE, V., Pharmacy
LEUNG, K., Orthopaedics and Traumatology
LEUNG, K., Computer Science and Engineering
LEUNG, N.
LEUNG, P.
LEUNG, Y., Geography and Resource Management
LI, D., Systems Engineering and Engineering Management
LI, S., Information Engineering
LIU, T.
LIU, P.
LO, V., Journalism and Communication
LO, Y., Chemical Pathology
LUI, C., Computer Science and Engineering
MAK, F., Electronic Engineering/Mechanical and Automation Engineering
MAK, T., Chemistry
MAKINO, S.
MIRRLEES, J., Finance/Economics
MOK, S., Clinical Oncology
MUNDELL, R., Economics
NG, H., Anatomical and Cellular Pathology
NG, K., Mathematics/Mathematical Sciences
NG, P., Paediatrics
NG, T., Biomedical Sciences
NG, Y., Architecture
NGAN, K., Electronic Engineering
PANG, C., Ophthalmology and Visual Sciences
POO, M., History
POON, W., Surgery
SHAO, Q.
SO, J., Fine Arts
TAM, L., Mathematics/Mathematical Sciences
TOMLINSON, B., Medicine and Therapeutics
VAN HASSELT, C., Otorhinolaryngology, Head and Neck Surgery
WANG, S., Government and Public Administration
WANG, W., Linguistics and Modern Languages/Electronic Engineering/Centre for East Asian Studies
WATT, J., Fine Arts/Chinese Studies
WEI, J., Mathematics
WING, Y., Psychiatry
WOLFF, L., Law
WOO, J., Medicine
WONG, K., Medicine and Therapeutics
WONG, T., Accountancy
WONG, T.
WONG, T.
WONG, W., Humanities
WONG, W., Information Engineering
WU, C., Chemistry
WYER, JR, R., Marketing
XIA, K.
XIE, Z., Chemistry
XIN, Z., Mathematics/Mathematical Sciences
XU, G., Institute of Space and Earth Information Science
XU, L., Computer Science and Engineering
XU, Y., Mechanical and Automation Engineering
YANG, C., Office of Distinguished Professor-at-Large
YAO, A., Computer Science and Engineering/Mathematical Sciences
YAO, X., Biomedical Sciences
YAU, S., Office of Distinguished Professor-at-Large
YEUNG, W., Information Engineering
YEW, T., Biomedical Sciences
YU, C., Chemistry
YU, C., Medicine and Therapeutics
YU, C.
YU, J.
YUM, P., Information Engineering
ZEE, C., Jockey Club School of Public Health and Primary Care
ZHANG, J., Economics
ZHANG, J., Life Sciences
ZHAO, G., Microbiology
ZHAO, Z., Chinese Language and Literature/Translation/Centre for East Asian Studies
ZHOU, X., Systems Engineering and Engineering Management
ZOU, J.

CITY UNIVERSITY OF HONG KONG

83 Tat Chee Ave, Kowloon
Telephone: (852) 34427654
E-mail: webmaster@cityu.edu.hk
Internet: www.cityu.edu.hk

Founded 1984 as City Polytechnic of Hong Kong, present name and status 1994
public control
Language of instruction: English
Academic year: September to August

Pres.: Prof. WAY KUO
Provost: Prof. ARTHUR B. ELLIS
Vice-Pres. for Devt and External Relations: Prof. RODERICK S. C. WONG
Vice-Pres. for Research and Technology: Prof. JIAN LU
Vice-Pres. for Student Affairs: Prof. HORACE H. S. IP
Vice-Pres. for Admin.: SUNNY W. K. LEE
Chief of Staff: Prof. PAUL K. S. LAM

Library of 1,247,800 vols
Number of teachers: 1,275 full-time
Number of students: 20,143 (16,804 full-time, 3,399 part-time)

Publications: *CityU Today* (3 a year), *Linkage* (4 a year)

DEANS

Chow Yei Ching School of Graduate Studies: Prof. JIAN LU
College of Business: Prof. HOUMIN YAN
College of Liberal Arts and Social Sciences: Prof. XIAOWEI ZANG
College of Science and Engineering: Prof. HONG YAN (acting)
School of Creative Media: Prof. JEFFREY SHAW
School of Energy and Environment: Prof. JOHNNY C. L. CHAN
School of Law: Prof. FENG LIN (acting)

HONG KONG BAPTIST UNIVERSITY

Kowloon Tong, Kowloon
Telephone: (852) 34117400
E-mail: aaco@hkbu.edu.hk
Internet: www.hkbu.edu.hk

Founded 1956
State control
Languages of instruction: English, Chinese
Academic year: September to May

Pres. and Vice-Chancellor: Prof. ALBERT C. CHAN
Vice-Pres. for Academic Affairs: Prof. FRANKLIN T. LUK
Vice-Pres. for Admin. and Sec.: ANDY S. C. LEE
Vice-Pres. for Research and Devt: Prof. RICK W. K. WONG
Academic Registrar: Dr K. S. SO
Librarian: Dr HAIPENG LI

Library of 1,153,322 vols, 142,201 audiovisual materials and microforms, 285,159 ebooks, 40,258 ejournals, 3,064 serials
Number of teachers: 667 (full-time)
Number of students: 8,266

Publications: *Contemporary Historical Review* (4 a year), *Journal of the History of Christianity in Modern China* (1 a year), *Journal of Physical Education and Recreation* (2 a year), *Sino Humanitas* (2 a year)

DEANS

Academy of Visual Arts: Prof. WAN QINGLI
Faculty of Arts: Prof. CHUNG LING
Faculty of Science: Prof. TAO TANG
Faculty of Social Sciences: Prof. ADRIAN BAILEY
Graduate School: Prof. RICK W. K. WONG
School of Business: Prof. STEPHEN Y. L. CHEUNG
School of Chinese Medicine: Prof. AIPING LU

School of Communication: Prof. RINGO MA (acting)
School of Continuing Education: SIMON C. H. WONG

HONG KONG POLYTECHNIC UNIVERSITY

Yuk Choi Rd, Hung Hom, Kowloon
Telephone: (852) 27665116
E-mail: polyu.international@polyu.edu.hk
Internet: www.polyu.edu.hk

Founded 1937 as Govt Trade School, became Hong Kong Technical College 1947 and Hong Kong Polytechnic 1972, present name and status 1994
autonomous control
Language of instruction: English
Academic year: September to August

Chancellor: CHIEF EXEC. OF THE HONG KONG SPEC. ADMIN. REGION
Pres.: Prof. TIMOTHY W. TONG
Deputy Pres. and Provost: Prof. PHILIP C. H. CHAN
Exec. Vice-Pres.: NICHOLAS W. YANG
Vice-Pres. for Institutional Advancement and Partnership: Prof. ANGELINA YUEN
Vice-Pres. for Int. and Exec. Education: Prof. JUDY TSUI
Vice-Pres. for Research Devt: Prof. ALBERT S.C. CHAN
Univ. Librarian: SHIRLEY WONG

Library: see under Libraries and Archives
Number of teachers: 1,200
Number of students: 32,000

Publications: *PolyU Milestones* (2 a year), *University Calendar* (1 a year)

DEANS

College of Professional and Continuing Education: Prof. PETER P. YUEN
Faculty of Applied Science and Textiles: Prof. K. Y. WONG
Faculty of Business: Prof. EDWARD CHENG
Faculty of Construction and Land Use: Prof. JIN-GUANG TENG
Faculty of Engineering: Prof. H. C. MAN
Faculty of Health and Social Sciences: Prof. MAURICE YAP
Faculty of Humanities: Prof. CHU-REN HUANG
School of Design: Prof. CEES DE BONT
School of Hotel and Tourism Management: Prof. KAYE CHON

HONG KONG UNIVERSITY OF SCIENCE AND TECHNOLOGY

Clear Water Bay, Kowloon
Telephone: (852) 23586000
E-mail: webmaster@www.ust.hk
Internet: www.ust.hk

Founded 1988
State control
Language of instruction: English
Academic year: September to July

Chancellor: CHIEF EXEC. OF THE HONG KONG SPEC. ADMIN. REGION
Pres.: Prof. Dr TONY F. CHAN
Vice-Pres. for Academic Affairs: Prof. Dr WEI SHYY
Vice-Pres. for Admin. and Business: Prof. Dr YUK-SHAN WONG
Vice-Pres. for Institutional Advancement: Dr EDEN WOON
Vice-Pres. for Research and Graduate Studies: Prof. Dr JOSEPH HUN-WEI LEE
Univ. Librarian: DIANA CHAN

Library of 687,000 print vols, 357,000 microforms, 36,000 audiovisual items, 165,000 ebooks, 26,100 ejournals, 317 databases
Number of teachers: 627
Number of students: 12,596

Publications: *Academic Calendar*, *HKUST Facts and Figures*

DEANS

Business and Management: Prof. LEONARD K. CHENG
Engineering: Prof. KHALED BEN LETAIEF
HKUST Fok Ying Tung Graduate School: Prof. LIONEL M. NI
Humanities and Social Science: Prof. JAMES Z. LEE
Science: Prof. NANCY YUK-YU IP
Undergraduate Education: KAR YAN TAM

PROFESSORS

ADAVAL, R., Marketing
ALTMAN, M., Physics
ARYA, S., Computer Science and Engineering
AU, O., Electronic and Computer Engineering
BAARK, E., Environment
BAARK, E., Social Science
BANFIELD, D., Biology
BARFORD, J., Chemical and Biomolecular Engineering
BEN LETAIEF, K., Electronic and Computer Engineering
BENSAOU, B., Computer Science and Engineering
BERMAK, A., Electronic and Computer Engineering
CAI, L., Mechanical Engineering
CAI, N., Industrial Engineering and Logistics Management
CAI, Y., Social Science
CAO, X., Electronic and Computer Engineering
CHAN, A., Biochemistry
CHAN, C., Chemical and Biomolecular Engineering
CHAN, C., Civil and Environmental Engineering
CHAN, C., Environment
CHAN, C., Humanities
CHAN, C., Physics
CHAN, G., Computer Science and Engineering
CHAN, H., Physics
CHAN, K., Finance
CHAN, K., Humanities
CHAN, K., Mathematics
CHAN, M., Electronic and Computer Engineering
CHAN, T., Computer Science and Engineering
CHAN, T., Mathematics
CHANG, C., Civil and Environmental Engineering
CHANG, H., Mathematics
CHAO, C., Mechanical Engineering
CHAO, M., Management
CHASNOV, J., Mathematics
CHATTOPADHYAY, P., Management
CHAU, Y., Chemical and Biomolecular Engineering
CHEN, B., Mathematics
CHEN, G., Chemical and Biomolecular Engineering
CHEN, G., Civil and Environmental Engineering
CHEN, J., Humanities
CHEN, K., Accounting
CHEN, K., Electronic and Computer Engineering
CHEN, K., Mathematics
CHEN, L., Computer Science and Engineering
CHEN, L., Humanities
CHEN, P., Accounting
CHEN, P., Electronic and Computer Engineering
CHEN, S., Economics
CHEN, T., Accounting
CHEN, Y., Social Science
CHENG, J., Civil and Environmental Engineering
CHENG, L., Economics
CHENG, R., Electronic and Computer Engineering
CHENG, S., Computer Science and Engineering
CHENG, S., Mathematics
CHEUNG, K., Information Systems, Business Statistics and Operations Management
CHEUNG, M., Civil and Environmental Engineering
CHEUNG, S., Computer Science and Engineering
CHEUNG, S., Humanities
CHEUNG, Z., Biochemistry
CHEW, S., Economics
CHIANG, Y., Mathematics
CHIGRINOV, V., Electronic and Computer Engineering
CHIN, R., Computer Science and Engineering
CHO, H., Social Science
CHOI, C., Biology
CHOI, D., Finance
CHONG, J., Social Science
CHONG, K., Humanities
CHOW, K., Biology
CHUNG, A., Computer Science and Engineering
CHUNG, K., Biochemistry
CLARK, T., Information Systems, Business Statistics and Operations Management
COOK, D., Economics
DAI, W., Chemistry
DALTON, A., Marketing
DASGUPTA, S., Finance
DING, C., Computer Science and Engineering
DING, F., Finance
DING, X., Social Science
DU, D., Finance
DU, S., Physics
DUCLOS, R., Marketing
FARH, L., Management
FENG, W., Biochemistry
FOREMAN, B., Physics
FU, F., Humanities
FUNG, J., Environment
FUNG, J., Mathematics
FUNG, P., Electronic and Computer Engineering
FUNG, Y., Humanities
GALLI, M., Marketing
GAN, J., Environment
GAN, J., Finance
GAN, J., Mathematics
GAO, F., Chemical and Biomolecular Engineering
GAO, Y., Mechanical Engineering
GEORGE, E., Management
GHIDAOUI, M., Civil and Environmental Engineering
GOLIN, M., Computer Science and Engineering
GONG, Y., Management
GOONETILLEKE, R., Industrial Engineering and Logistics Management
GOYAL, V., Finance
GU, L., Computer Science and Engineering
GUO, L., Marketing
GUO, Z., Chemistry
HA, A., Information Systems, Business Statistics and Operations Management
HAMDI, M., Computer Science and Engineering
HAN, L., Social Science
HAN, Y., Physics
HARRISON, P., Environment
HAYNES, R., Chemistry
HE, J., Management
HE, W., Social Science
HE, X., Mathematics
HELSEN, K., Marketing
HILARY, G., Accounting
HO, S., Biology
HO, V., Humanities
HOLZ, C., Social Science
HONG, J., Industrial Engineering and Logistics Management
HONG, J., Marketing

HORNER, A., Computer Science and Engineering
HOSSAIN, T., Economics
HSIEH, C., Accounting
HSING, I., Chemical and Biomolecular Engineering
HSU, C., Accounting
HSU, C., Mechanical Engineering
HU, I., Information Systems, Business Statistics and Operations Management
HU, J., Mathematics
HUA, X., Economics
HUANG, A., Accounting
HUANG, H., Electronic and Computer Engineering
HUANG, J., Mathematics
HUANG, P., Biology
HUANG, X., Chemistry
HUANG, Z., Management
HUI, D., Chemical and Biomolecular Engineering
HUI, K., Accounting
HUI, K., Information Systems, Business Statistics and Operations Management
HUNG, C., Humanities
IP, N., Biochemistry
JAISINGH, J., Information Systems, Business Statistics and Operations Management
JAMES, L., Information Systems, Business Statistics and Operations Management
JIA, G., Chemistry
JIANG, W., Industrial Engineering and Logistics Management
JING, B., Mathematics
JONEJA, A., Industrial Engineering and Logistics Management
JU, N., Finance
KARHADE, P., Information Systems, Business Statistics and Operations Management
KATAFYGIOTIS, L., Civil and Environmental Engineering
KI, W., Electronic and Computer Engineering
KIKKERT, G., Civil and Environmental Engineering
KIM, J., Mechanical Engineering
KIM, K., Economics
KIM, S., Computer Science and Engineering
KO, R., Biochemistry
KU, A., Social Science
KUANG, J., Civil and Environmental Engineering
KUNG, J., Social Science
KURSUN, V., Electronic and Computer Engineering
KWOK, H., Electronic and Computer Engineering
KWOK, J., Computer Science and Engineering
KWOK, Y., Mathematics
LAI, E., Economics
LAI, K., Biochemistry
LAM, D., Mechanical Engineering
LAM, H., Chemical and Biomolecular Engineering
LAM, J., Chemistry
LAU, A., Civil and Environmental Engineering
LAU, A., Environment
LAU, A., Mathematics
LAU, D., Biology
LAU, K., Electronic and Computer Engineering
LAU, S., Biology
LAU, V., Electronic and Computer Engineering
LEA, C., Electronic and Computer Engineering
LEE, C., Industrial Engineering and Logistics Management
LEE, D., Computer Science and Engineering
LEE, J., Social Science
LEE, K., Biology
LEE, N., Industrial Engineering and Logistics Management
LEE, O., Biology
LEE, R., Mechanical Engineering
LEE, Y., Mechanical Engineering
LENG, Y., Mechanical Engineering
LENNOX, C., Accounting
LEUNG, C., Civil and Environmental Engineering
LEUNG, P., Physics
LEUNG, S., Economics
LEUNG, S., Mathematics
LEUNG, W., Chemistry
LI, B., Computer Science and Engineering
LI, J., Management
LI, J., Mathematics
LI, K., Mathematics
LI, N., Biology
LI, Q., Information Systems, Business Statistics and Operations Management
LI, W., Mathematics
LI, X., Chemistry
LI, Y., Information Systems, Business Statistics and Operations Management
LI, Z., Civil and Environmental Engineering
LI, Z., Electronic and Computer Engineering
LI, Z., Mechanical Engineering
LIANG, C., Biochemistry
LIN, F., Computer Science and Engineering
LIN, N., Physics
LIN, Y., Social Science
LIN, Z., Chemistry
LING, S., Mathematics
LIU, G., Humanities
LIU, H., Biology
LIU, H., Environment
LIU, L., Finance
LIU, Q., Industrial Engineering and Logistics Management
LIU, T., Humanities
LIU, Y., Computer Science and Engineering
LO, A., Information Systems, Business Statistics and Operations Management
LO, H., Civil and Environmental Engineering
LO, I., Civil and Environmental Engineering
LOCHOVSKY, F., Computer Science and Engineering
LORTZ, R., Physics
LOY, M., Physics
LU, Z., Humanities
LUI, F., Economics
LUO, Q., Computer Science and Engineering
LUONG, H., Electronic and Computer Engineering
MA, J., Humanities
MA, J., Social Science
MCKAY, G., Chemical and Biomolecular Engineering
MCKAY, M., Electronic and Computer Engineering
MACKAY, P., Finance
MAK, B., Computer Science and Engineering
MAK, H., Industrial Engineering and Logistics Management
MARKLE, A., Management
MENG, G., Mathematics
MI, Y., Chemical and Biomolecular Engineering
MILLER, A., Biology
MOK, P., Electronic and Computer Engineering
MOW, W., Electronic and Computer Engineering
MOY, A., Mathematics
MU, M., Mathematics
MUKHOPADHYAY, A., Marketing
MUPPALA, K., Computer Science and Engineering
MURCH, R., Electronic and Computer Engineering
MUTHUKRISHNAN, A., Marketing
NASON, E., Management
NG, C., Civil and Environmental Engineering
NG, K., Chemical and Biomolecular Engineering
NG, K., Humanities
NG, S., Information Systems, Business Statistics and Operations Management
NG, T., Physics
NG, W., Computer Science and Engineering
NI, L., Computer Science and Engineering
NI, S., Finance
NOVOSELOV, K., Accounting
PALOMAR, D., Electronic and Computer Engineering
PAPADIAS, D., Computer Science and Engineering
PATCHELL, G., Environment
PATCHELL, G., Social Science
PENG, H., Biology
PING GAO, P., Chemical and Biomolecular Engineering
PONG, T., Computer Science and Engineering
POON, A., Electronic and Computer Engineering
POON, R., Biochemistry
QI, R., Biochemistry
QI, X., Industrial Engineering and Logistics Management
QIAN, P., Biology
QIAN, T., Mathematics
QIU, H., Mechanical Engineering
QIU, L., Electronic and Computer Engineering
QU, H., Computer Science and Engineering
QU, J., Electronic and Computer Engineering
QUAN, L., Computer Science and Engineering
RENNEBERG, R., Chemistry
SANDER, P., Computer Science and Engineering
SAUTMAN, B., Social Science
SEASHOLES, M., Finance
SEN, R., Finance
SENGUPTA, J., Marketing
SHANG, C., Civil and Environmental Engineering
SHAO, Q., Mathematics
SHARIF, N., Social Science
SHEN, H., Computer Science and Engineering
SHEN, V., Computer Science and Engineering
SHENG, P., Physics
SHI, B., Electronic and Computer Engineering
SHI, L., Electronic and Computer Engineering
SHIMOKAWA, S., Social Science
SHUM, S., Information Systems, Business Statistics and Operations Management
SIN, J., Electronic and Computer Engineering
SIN, R., Information Systems, Business Statistics and Operations Management
SING, M., Social Science
SO, A., Social Science
SO, M., Information Systems, Business Statistics and Operations Management
SO, R., Industrial Engineering and Logistics Management
SOU, I., Physics
STAM, W., Management
SULLIVAN, B., Management
SUN, J., Humanities
SUN, Q., Mechanical Engineering
SZETO, K., Physics
TAI, C., Computer Science and Engineering
TAKEUCHI, R., Management
TAM, K., Information Systems, Business Statistics and Operations Management
TAM, K., Social Science
TAM, W., Physics
TANAKA, M., Economics
TANG, B., Chemistry
TANG, C., Computer Science and Engineering
TANG, K., Mechanical Engineering
TANG, Z., Physics
THONG, J., Information Systems, Business Statistics and Operations Management
TONG, P., Physics
TSANG, D., Electronic and Computer Engineering
TSANG, S., Biochemistry
TSENG, M., Industrial Engineering and Logistics Management
TSIM, K., Biology
TSUI, C., Electronic and Computer Engineering

TSUNG, F., Industrial Engineering and Logistics Management
TU, J., Social Science
TUNG, Y., Civil and Environmental Engineering
VISARIA, S., Economics
WAN, J., Biochemistry
WAN, X., Information Systems, Business Statistics and Operations Management
WANG, G., Civil and Environmental Engineering
WANG, H., Management
WANG, J., Civil and Environmental Engineering
WANG, J., Physics
WANG, N., Physics
WANG, P., Economics
WANG, S., Accounting
WANG, S., Economics
WANG, W., Biology
WANG, X., Humanities
WANG, X., Mathematics
WANG, X., Physics
WANG, Y., Civil and Environmental Engineering
WANG, Y., Economics
WEI, K., Finance
WEI, Z., Biochemistry
WEN, W., Physics
WEN, Z., Biochemistry
WILLIAMS, I., Chemistry
WONG, A., Electronic and Computer Engineering
WONG, E., Management
WONG, G., Physics
WONG, J., Biology
WONG, K., Physics
WONG, L., Humanities
WONG, M., Electronic and Computer Engineering
WONG, M., Mathematics
WONG, M., Physics
WONG, R., Computer Science and Engineering
WONG, R., Social Science
WONG, S., Humanities
WONG, W., Biochemistry
WONG, Y., Biochemistry
WONG, Y., Biology
WU, D., Computer Science and Engineering
WU, H., Chemistry
WU, J., Mechanical Engineering
WU, L., Mathematics
WU, X., Social Science
WU, Y., Chemistry
WU, Z., Biochemistry
XIA, J., Biochemistry
XIANG, Y., Marketing
XIANG, Y., Mathematics
XIE, D., Economics
XIE, Y., Biology
XIJUN HU, X., Chemical and Biomolecular Engineering
XU, B., Chemistry
XU, C., Computer Science and Engineering
XU, J., Economics
XU, J., Electronic and Computer Engineering
XU, K., Mathematics
XU, S., Information Systems, Business Statistics and Operations Management
XU, Y., Information Systems, Business Statistics and Operations Management
XUE, H., Biochemistry
YAN, M., Mathematics
YAN, Y., Chemistry
YANG, H., Civil and Environmental Engineering
YANG, Q., Computer Science and Engineering
YANG, S., Chemistry
YANG, Z., Physics
YAO, S., Mechanical Engineering
YE, W., Mechanical Engineering
YEE, A., Humanities
YEUNG, D., Computer Science and Engineering
YEUNG, K., Chemical and Biomolecular Engineering
YI, K., Computer Science and Engineering
YIK, M., Social Science
YIP, K., Humanities
YIU, C., Humanities
YOU, H., Accounting
YU, J., Chemistry
YU, J., Environment
YU, M., Information Systems, Business Statistics and Operations Management
YU, S., Information Systems, Business Statistics and Operations Management
YU, T., Mechanical Engineering
YU, W., Electronic and Computer Engineering
YUAN, G., Electronic and Computer Engineering
YUEN, M., Mechanical Engineering
ZANG, A., Accounting
ZENG, B., Electronic and Computer Engineering
ZHANG, C., Computer Science and Engineering
ZHANG, C., Finance
ZHANG, G., Accounting
ZHANG, H., Information Systems, Business Statistics and Operations Management
ZHANG, J., Industrial Engineering and Logistics Management
ZHANG, L., Civil and Environmental Engineering
ZHANG, M., Accounting
ZHANG, M., Biochemistry
ZHANG, M., Humanities
ZHANG, M., Information Systems, Business Statistics and Operations Management
ZHANG, N., Computer Science and Engineering
ZHANG, Q., Computer Science and Engineering
ZHANG, R., Industrial Engineering and Logistics Management
ZHANG, T., Mechanical Engineering
ZHANG, X., Civil and Environmental Engineering
ZHANG, Y., Accounting
ZHANG, Z., Physics
ZHAO, J., Civil and Environmental Engineering
ZHAO, T., Mechanical Engineering
ZHAO, Y., Marketing
ZHENG, R., Information Systems, Business Statistics and Operations Management
ZHENG, S., Information Systems, Business Statistics and Operations Management
ZHOU, R., Marketing
ZHU, G., Biochemistry
ZHU, J., Management
ZHU, K., Industrial Engineering and Logistics Management
ZHU, T., Economics
ZHU, X., Humanities
ZHU, Y., Mathematics
ZHU, Y., Social Science
ZWEIG, D., Social Science

LINGNAN UNIVERSITY

8 Castle Peak Rd, Tuen Mun, New Territories
Telephone: (852) 26168888
E-mail: ocpa@ln.edu.hk
Internet: www.ln.edu.hk

Founded 1888 as Christian College in China, as Lingan College Co Ltd 1967, self-accrediting status 1998, current name adopted 1999
Academic year: September to August

Chancellor: Hon CHUN-YING LEUNG
Pres.: Prof. CHAN YUK-SHEE
Vice-Pres.: Prof. SEADE JESÚS
Assoc. Vice-Pres. and Comptroller: HERDIP SINGH
Assoc. Vice-Pres. for Student Affairs: Prof. LEE HUNG-KAI
Assoc. Vice-Pres. and Registrar: Prof. WILLIAM LEE
Librarian: RACHEL CHEUNG

Library of 495,922 vols
Number of teachers: 188
Number of students: 2,701

DEANS

Faculty of Arts: Prof. STEPHEN CHAN
Faculty of Business: Prof. DEAN TJOSVOLD
Faculty of Social Sciences: Prof. XIANGDONG WEI

OPEN UNIVERSITY OF HONG KONG

30 Good Shepherd St, Homantin, Kowloon
Telephone: (852) 27112100
E-mail: infoctr@ic.ouhk.edu.hk
Internet: www.ouhk.edu.hk

Founded 1989 as Open Learning Institute of Hong Kong, present location 1996, present name and status 1997
public control

Chancellor: Hon. CHIEF EXEC. OF THE HONG KONG SPEC. ADMIN. REGION
Pres.: Prof. JOHN LEONG CHI-YAN
Vice-Pres. for Academic Affairs: Prof. DANNY WONG
Vice-Pres. for Technology and Devt: Prof. LEUNG CHUN-MING
Registrar: LEE SHU WING
Librarian: MOK WONG WAI-MAN

Library of 500,000 vols, 133,000 printed and multimedia items, 20,200 ebooks, 980 printed serials, 18,200 electronic serials
Number of teachers: 590 full-time, 1,060 part-time
Number of students: 17,000 (full-time and distance learning)

DEANS

School of Arts and Social Sciences: Prof. TAM KWOK-KAN
School of Business and Administration: Prof. IP YIU-KEUNG
School of Education and Languages: YVONNE FUNG SHI YUK-HANG
School of Science and Technology: Prof. HO KIN CHUNG

UNIVERSITY OF HONG KONG

Pokfulam, Hong Kong
Telephone: (852) 28592111
E-mail: cpao@hku.hk
Internet: www.hku.hk

Founded 1912
Language of instruction: English
Academic year: September to June

Chancellor: Dr The Hon. CHUN-YING LEUNG
Pro-Chancellor: Dr The Hon. Sir DAVID LI KWOK PO
Chair. of the Ccl: CHE HUNG LEONG
Vice-Chancellor and Pres.: Prof. PETER MATHIESON
Deputy Vice-Chancellor and Provost: Prof. ROLAND T. CHIN
Exec. Vice-Pres. for Admin. and Finance: Prof. STEVEN J. CANNON
Pro-Vice-Chancellor and Vice-Pres. for Research: Prof. PAUL TAM KWONG HANG
Pro-Vice-Chancellor and Vice-Pres. for Univ. Relations: Prof. SHEW-PING CHOW
Dean for Student Affairs: Dr ALBERT WAI LAP CHAU
Treas.: Dr MARGARET KO MAY YEE LEUNG (acting)
Registrar: HENRY WAI WING KUN
Librarian: PETER E. SIDORKO

Library of 2,960,414 vols
Number of teachers: 6,094 (full-time)
Number of students: 27,005

Publication: *Journal of Oriental Studies* (2 a year)

DEANS

Faculty of Architecture: Prof. CHRIS WEBSTER
Faculty of Arts: Prof. DOUGLAS WILLIAM FRERE KERR
Faculty of Business and Economics: Prof. ERIC C. CHANG
Faculty of Dentistry: Prof. EDWARD C.M. LO LO
Faculty of Education: Prof. STEPHEN J. ANDREWS
Faculty of Engineering: Prof. NORMAN C. TIEN
Faculty of Law: Prof. JOHANNES CHAN MAN MUN
Faculty of Medicine: Prof. GABRIEL M LEUNG
Faculty of Science: Prof. KWOK SUN
Faculty of Social Sciences: Prof. JOHN P. BURNS

PROFESSORS

ANDREWS, S. J., Education
ARNER, D. W., Law
AU, F. T. K., Civil Engineering
AU, T. K. F., Psychology
BACON-SHONE, J. H., Social Sciences
BIDDLE, G. C., Business
BRAY, T. M., Education
BURNS, J. P., Social Sciences
CARLESS, D. R., Education
CARROLL, J. M., History
CARTY, J. A., Law
CHAN, C. K. K., Education
CHAN, C. L. W., Social Work and Social Administration
CHAN, D. T. M., Medicine
CHAN, G. C. F., Paediatrics and Adolescent Medicine
CHAN, G. K. Y., Chemistry
CHAN, J. C. W., Politics and Public Administration
CHAN, J. M. M., Law
CHAN, L. C., Pathology
CHAN, L. S., Earth Sciences
CHAN, S. C., Electrical and Electronic Engineering
CHAN, S. C., Surgery
CHAN, S. S. C., Nursing
CHAN, W. K., Chemistry
CHAN, Y. S., Physiology
CHAN, Y. Y., Journalism
CHANG, E. C., Business and Economics
CHANG, E. C., Economics and Finance
CHAU, K. T., Electrical and Electronic Engineering
CHAU, K. W., Real Estate and Construction
CHAU, H. F., Physics
CHAU, P. Y. K., Business
CHE, C. M., Chemistry
CHEAH, K. S. E., Biochemistry
CHEN, A. H. Y., Law
CHEN, E. Y. H., Psychiatry
CHEN, G., Chemistry
CHENG, C., Psychology
CHENG, K. M., Education
CHENG, K. S., Physics
CHENG, S. W. K., Surgery
CHEUNG, A. N. Y., Pathology
CHEUNG, A. S. C., Chemistry
CHEUNG, A. S. Y., Law
CHEUNG, B. M. Y., Medicine
CHEUNG, D. W. L., Computer Science
CHEUNG, G. S. P., Dentistry
CHEUNG, K. M. C., Orthopaedics and Traumatology
CHEUNG, L. K., Dentistry
CHEUNG, P. Y. S., Electrical and Electronic Engineering
CHEUNG, R. T. F., Medicine
CHEUNG, W. S., Mathematics
CHEUNG, Y. F., Paediatrics and Adolescent Medicine
CHEW, W. C., Electrical and Electronic Engineering
CHIM, J. C. S., Medicine
CHIN, F. Y. L., Computer Science
CHIN, T. H. R., Computer Science
CHIU, P., Chemistry
CHIU, P. K. Y., Orthopaedics and Traumatology
CHIU, R. L. H., Urban Planning and Design
CHOW, B. K. C., Biological Sciences
CHOW, K. W., Mechanical Engineering
CHOW, T. W., Dentistry
CHU, K. M., Surgery
CHU, S. C. K., Mathematics
CHUA, D. K. L., Music
CHUNG, S. K., Anatomy
CHYE, M. L., Biological Sciences
CI, J., Philosophy
CLARKE, D. J., Fine Arts
CORBET, E. F., Dentistry
CORKE, H., Biological Sciences
DHAMMAJOTI, K. L., Buddhism
DIKOTTER, F., History
DUDGEON, D., Biological Sciences
EDWARDS, L. P., Modern China Studies
ENRIGHT, M. J., Business
FANG, H. H. P., Civil Engineering
FARHOOMAND, A. F., Business
FIELDING, R., Behavioural Sciences
FU, H., Law
FUNG, S. H. Y., Physics
FUNG, T. W. K., Statistics and Actuarial Science
GAO, J., Physics
GLOFCHESKI, R. A., Law
GOO, S. H., Law
GORN, G. J., Business
GUAN, X., Clinical Oncology
GUAN, Y., Public Health
HAO, Q., Physiology
HAYWARD, W. G., Psychology
HILL, D. J., Electrical and Electronic Engineering
HO, C. S. H., Psychology
HO, E. Y. L., English
HO, L. K. S., Law
HO, P. C., Obstetrics and Gynaecology
HO, S. L., Medicine
HOLLIDAY, I. M., Politics and Public Administration
HSU, B. F. C., Real Estate and Construction
HUANG, G. Q., Industrial and Manufacturing Systems Engineering
HUI, C., Business
HUI, S. Y. R., Electrical and Electronic Engineering
HUNG, Y. S., Electrical and Electronic Engineering
HUTTON, C. M., English
HYLAND, K. L., English
IP, M. S. M., Medicine
IRWIN, M. G., Anaesthesiology
JAWORSKI, A., English
JIAO, J. J. J., Earth Sciences
JIM, C. Y., Geography
JIN, D., Biochemistry
JIN, L., Dentistry
JUNG, H. S., Dentistry
KAO, C. M., Computer Science
KERR, D. W. F., English
KHONG, P. L., Diagnostic Radiology
KHOO, U. S., Pathology
KUMARASWAMY, M. M., Civil Engineering
KUTNICK, P. J., Education
KWAN, A. K. H., Civil Engineering
KWOK, S., Science
KWOK, Y. K., Electrical and Electronic Engineering
KWONG, D. L. W., Clinical Oncology
KWONG, Y. L., Medicine
LAI, C. L., Medicine
LAI, J. S. M., Ophthalmology
LAI, L. W. C., Real Estate and Construction
LAI, P. T., Electrical and Electronic Engineering
LAIDLER, K. A., Sociology
LAM, C. L. K., Family Medicine and Primary Care
LAM, C. W., Pathology
LAM, J., Mechanical Engineering
LAM, K. S. L., Medicine
LAM, S. S. K., Business
LAM, T. W., Computer Science
LAM, T. H., Community Medicine
LAM, T. P., Family Medicine and Primary Care
LAM, W. F., Politics and Public Administration
LAU, A. H., Business
LAU, F. C. M., Computer Science
LAU, S. H., Economics and Finance
LAU, W. C. S., Medicine
LAU, Y. L., Paediatrics and Adolescent Medicine
LAU, A. S. Y., Paediatrics and Adolescent Medicine
LAW, N. W. Y., Education
LAW, S. Y. K., Surgery
LAW, W. L., Surgery
LEE, E. W. Y., Politics and Public Administration
LEE, S. M. S., Statistics and Actuarial Science
LEE, S. P., Medicine
LEE, T. M. C., Psychology
LEE, W. W. M., Biological Sciences
LEUNG, A. Y. H., Medicine
LEUNG, F. C. C., Biological Sciences
LEUNG, F. K. S., Education
LEUNG, G. M., Community Medicine
LEUNG, J. C. B., Social Work and Social Administration
LEUNG, K. C. A., Humanities and Social Sciences
LEUNG, S. Y., Pathology
LEUNG, W. K., Dentistry
LEUNG, W. K., Medicine
LEUNG, Y. C., Mechanical Engineering
LI, R. A., Medicine
LI, V. O. K., Electrical and Electronic Engineering
LI, W. K., Statistics and Actuarial Science
LI, X. Y., Civil Engineering
LI, Y., Mechanical Engineering
LIM, C. L., Law
LIN, G. C. S., Geography
LIU, A. M. M., Real Estate and Construction
LO, C. M., Surgery
LO, E. C. M., Dentistry
LO, S. H., Civil Engineering
LOO, B. P. Y., Geography
LOUIE, K. H., Arts
LU, J., Mathematics
LU, L., Pathology
LU, W. W., Orthopaedics and Traumatology
LUI, T. L., Sociology
LUK, K. D. K., Orthopaedics and Traumatology
LUNG, D. P. Y., Architecture
LUNG, M. L., Clinical Oncology
MAK, K. L., Industrial and Manufacturing Systems Engineering
MAMOULIS, N., Computer Science
MAN, R. Y. K., Pharmacology and Pharmacy
MARCHETTI, G., Comparative Literature
MASTERS, R. S. W., Human Performance
MCGRATH, C. P. J., Dentistry
MCPHERSON, D. B., Education
MOK, N., Mathematics
NG, C. O., Mechanical Engineering
NG, E. H. Y., Obstetrics and Gynaecology
NG, I. O. L., Pathology
NG, J. K. F., Anaesthesiology
NG, K. W., Statistics and Actuarial Science
NG, T. S., Electrical and Electronic Engineering
NG, T. S. T., Civil Engineering
NGAN, A. H. W., Mechanical Engineering
NGAN, H. Y. S., Obstetrics and Gynaecology
NICHOLLS, J. M., Pathology
PARK, C. W., Business
PEIRIS, J. S. M., Public Health
PHILLIPS, D. L., Chemistry
POON, R. T. P., Surgery

POSTIGLIONE, G. A., Education
QIU, L. D., Economics and Finance
RAO, N., Education
REYES, A. T., Law
ROWLINSON, S. M., Real Estate and Construction
SABINE, M. A., History
SADOVY, Y. J., Biological Sciences
SAMARANAYAKE, L. P., Dentistry
SAMMAN, N., Dentistry
SAUNDERS, R. M. K., Biological Sciences
SHAH, N., Biological Sciences
SHAM, P. C., Medicine
SHEN, J., Chinese Medicine
SHEN, S., Physics
SHUM, D. K. Y., Biochemistry
SO, K. F., Anatomy
SONG, F. M., Economics and Finance
SRIVASTAVA, G., Pathology
SUEN, W. C., Economics and Finance
SUN, H., Chemistry
SUN, M., Earth Sciences
SZE, K. Y., Mechanical Engineering
TAM, P. K. H., Surgery
TAN, K. C. B., Medicine
TAN, L., Linguistics
TAN, S. T., Mechanical Engineering
TANG, B. S., Urban Planning and Design
TANG, F., Physiology
TANG, G. W. K., Obstetrics and Gynaecology
TANG, S. C. W., Medicine
TAO, Z., Business
THAM, L. G., Civil Engineering
THOMAS, G. M., Fine Arts
TIEN, N. C., Engineering
TILBURY, M. J., Law
TIWARI, A. F. Y., Nrusing
TOLLEFSON, J. W., Education
TSANG, K. M., Mathematics
TSAO, G. S. W., Anatomy
TSE, D. K. C., Business
TSE, H. F., Medicine
TSE, S. K., Education
TSE, T. H., Computer Science
TSUI, A. B. M., Education
VEITCH, T. S., Law
WANG, J., Physics
WANG, L., Mechanical Engineering
WANG, M., Mechanical Engineering
WANG, W. J., Architecture
WANG, W. P., Computer Science
WANG, Z., Physics
WEEKES, B. S., Education
WHITEHILL, T. L., Education
WILKINSON, R. M., Professional Legal Education
WILLIAMS, G. A., Biological Sciences
WONG, A. O. L., Biological Sciences
WONG, D. S. H., Ophthalmology
WONG, I. C. K., Pharmacology and Pharmacy
WONG, K. P., Economics and Finance
WONG, R. Y. C., Economics and Finance
WONG, S. C., Civil Engineering
WONG, V. C. N., Paediatrics and Adolescent Medicine
WOO, P. C. Y., Microbiology
WU, E. X., Electrical and Electronic Engineering
WU, S. S., Biological Sciences
WU, W., Anatomy
XIE, M. H., Physics
XU, A., Medicine
XU, C., Economics and Finance
XU, G., History
YAM, V. W. W., Chemistry
YANG, D., Chemistry
YANG, H., Statistics and Actuarial Science
YANG, R., Education
YEH, A. G. O., Urban Planning and Design
YEUNG, L. K., Electrical and Electronic Engineering
YEUNG, W. S. B., Obstetrics and Gynaecology
YIM, B. C. K., Business
YIP, P. S. F., Social Work and Social Administration
YIU, C. K. Y., Dentistry
YIU, E. M. L., Education
YOUNG, B., Civil Engineering
YOUNG, S. N. M., Law
YU, G., Law
YU, J., Mathematics
YU, Y., Computer Science
YUEN, K. C., Statistics and Actuarial Science
YUEN, K. Y., Microbiology
YUEN, R. M. F., Medicine
ZANG, W., Mathematics
ZHANG, D., Geography
ZHANG, F., Physics
ZHANG, L. F., Education
ZHANG, X. C., Law
ZHANG, Z., Chinese Medicine
ZHENG, B., Microbiology
ZHOU, K. Z., Business
ZHOU, M. F., Earth Sciences
ZHOU, Y., Business
ZONG, Y., Earth Sciences
ZWAHLEN, R. A., Dentistry

Colleges

Chung Chi College: Taipo Rd, New Territories; tel. (852) 26098009; e-mail ccc@cuhk.edu.hk; internet www.cuhk.edu.hk/ccc; f. 1951, present location 1956, present status 1963; attached to Chinese Univ. of Hong Kong; depts of arts, business admin., education, engineering, law, medicine, science and social science; 2,807 students; Head Prof. YUEN-SANG LEUNG; Dean of Gen. Education Prof. KWOK-NAM LEUNG; Dean of Students Prof. WING-PING FONG; Librarian KEVIN LEUNG; publs *Chung Chi Alumni* (4 a year, electronic), *Chung Chi Campus Newsletter*.

Hong Kong Academy for Performing Arts: 1 Gloucester Rd, Wan Chai; tel. (852) 25848500; e-mail aso@hkapa.edu; internet www.hkapa.edu; f. 1984, present status 1992; schools of dance, drama, film and television, music, theatre and entertainment arts and Chinese traditional theatre; library: 18,000 vols of Chinese books, 48,000 vols of English books, 1,900 books in other languages, 25,000 music scores, 36,000 audiovisual items, 329 printed journals, 2,100 titles in archives, 600 slide sets and kits, 7,400 electronic plays, 5,200 ebooks, 1,300 ejournal titles, 40 reference and aggregator databases; 453 teachers (79 full-time, 374 part-time); 749 students; Pres. CHIEF EXEC. OF THE HONG KONG SPEC. ADMIN. REGION; Dir Prof. KEVIN THOMPSON; Assoc. Dir for Admin. and Registrar Dr HERBERT HUEY; Assoc. Dir for Operations PHILIP SODEN; Librarian LING WAI-KING; publ. *Dramatic Arts* (1 a year).

Hong Kong Design Institute: Planning Team Office, Room 735, VTC Tower, 27 Wood Rd, Wan Chai; tel. (852) 28361912; e-mail hkdi@vtc.edu.hk; internet www.hkdi.edu.hk; f. 2007; attached to Vocational Training Ccl; depts of designs, engineering, fashion and textiles, printing and digital media, toy design and multimedia exhibition design; at present all programmes are delivered at IVE campuses; new HKDI campus at Tiu Keng Leng opens in 2010–11; Exec. Dir Dr CARRIE WILLIS; publ. *D. I. Winners*.

Hong Kong Institute of Education: 10 Lo Ping Rd, Tai Po, New Territories; tel. (852) 29488888; e-mail info@ied.edu.hk; internet www.ied.edu.hk; f. 1994 by merger of four colleges of education and the Institute of Language in Education, present location 1997, self-accrediting status 2004; faculties of arts and sciences, education studies, languages; library: 605,914 vols; 412 teachers; 7,153 students; Pres. Prof. ANTHONY B. L. CHEUNG; Vice-Pres. for Academic Affairs Prof. LEE WING ON; Vice-Pres. for Admin. Prof. CHRIS MONG CHAN; Vice-Pres. for Research and Devt Prof. CHENG YIN CHEONG; publs *Education Focus, Education Matters, Joy of Learning* (bilingual magazine).

IVE Morrison Hill: 6 Oi Kwan Rd, Wan Chai; tel. (852) 25745321; e-mail csivemh@vtc.edu.hk; internet www.vtc.edu.hk/ti/mhti/homepage/english; f. 1969, fmrly Morrison Hill Technical Institute; attached to Vocational Training Ccl; depts of business administration, construction, information and communications technology, real estate and facilities management; library: 50,000 books, 200 periodicals; 300 full-time teachers; 6,260 students; Prin. DANIEL KWOH KAI HING.

Maritime Services Training Institute: 23 Castle Peak Rd, Tai Lam Chung, Tuen Mun, New Territories; tel. (852) 24583833; e-mail msti@vtc.edu.hk; internet www.vtc.edu.hk/vtc/web/template/about_the_centr.jsp?fldr_id=498; f. 1988; attached to Vocational Training Ccl; programmes for new entrants and professionals in marine-related and shore-based industry.

New Asia College: Sha Tin, New Territories; tel. (852) 26097609; e-mail nac@cuhk.edu.hk; internet www3.cuhk.edu.hk/na; f. 1949 as Asia Evening College of Arts and Commerce, current name adopted 1950, present status and location 1973; attached to Chinese Univ. of Hong Kong; 2,800 students; Head Prof. HENRY WONG; Dean of Gen. Education Prof. S. O. CHAN; Dean of Students Prof. MARIA S. M. TAM; publs *Ch'ien Mu Lectures in History and Culture* (monograph series), *New Asia College Academic Bulletin*, *New Asia Life Monthly*.

Shaw College: LG1, Wen Lan Tang; tel. (852) 26097363; e-mail shaw-college@cuhk.edu.hk; internet www5.cuhk.edu.hk/shaw; f. 1990; attached to Chinese Univ. of Hong Kong; Head Prof. JOSEPH J. Y. SUNG; Dean of Gen. Education Prof. HO PUI-YIN; Dean of Students Prof. FREEDOM Y. K. LEUNG; publs *Shaw Link*, *Shaw Net*.

United College: 2nd Fl., Tsang Shiu Tim Bldg, Chinese Univ. of Hong Kong, Sha Tin, New Territories; tel. (852) 26097575; e-mail unitedcollege@cuhk.edu.hk; internet www2.cuhk.edu.hk/uc; f. 1956 by merger of five colleges: Canton Overseas, Kwang Hsia, Wah Kiu, Wen Hua and Ping Jing College of Accountancy, present status 1959, present location 1971; attached to Chinese Univ. of Hong Kong; faculties of arts, business admin., education, engineering, law, medicine, science and social science; 2,931 students; Head Prof. FUNG KWOK-PUI; Dean of Gen. Education Prof. JIMMY C. M. YU; Dean of Students Prof. STEPHEN H. S. WONG; Librarian YIFENG WU; publs *United Bulletin*, *United College Alumni Newsletter* (4 a year), *United We Advance*.

MACAO

The Higher Education System

Established by Portugal in 1557 as a permanent trading post with China, Macao became a Portuguese Overseas Province in 1951. A new statute, promulgated in February 1976, redefined Macao as a 'Special Territory' under Portuguese jurisdiction, but with a great measure of administrative and economic independence. Macao became a 'special administrative region' (SAR) of the People's Republic of China on 20 December 1999. Macao was thus to have the same status as that agreed (with effect from 1997) for Hong Kong, and was to enjoy autonomy in most matters except defence and foreign policy. As prescribed by the Basic Law of Macao, the Government formulates policies on education, including policies regarding the educational system and its administration, the language of instruction, the allocation of funds, the examination system, the recognition of educational qualifications and the system of academic awards. There are currently some 10 public and private universities, polytechnic institutes and research centres, including the University of Macao (founded 1981 as the University of East Asia), which is the country's largest higher education institution (with more than 8,600 students), the Macao Polytechnic Institute (founded 1991) and the Macao University of Science and Technology (founded 2000 and currently has seven faculties). The University of Macao has six research faculties in the fields of business administration, health sciences, social sciences, arts and humanities, science and technology, law and education, as well as the Institute of Chinese Medical Sciences and Honours College. The University of Macao is administered by a Chancellor, a University Council and a Rector. Total enrolment in the higher education sector stood at 32,312 students in 2009/10. Substantial numbers of students choose to pursue their further education abroad. The language of instruction for higher education programmes is normally English or Chinese (or a combination of both). Portuguese is also used for certain subjects, such as law, Portuguese language and translation.

Undergraduate courses include the three-year Higher Diploma (Bacharelato) and the Bachelors degree (Licenciatura), which takes at least four years. Entrance to these undergraduate programmes, which are available at both universities and institutes, is based on the successful completion of secondary education and entrance examinations offered by individual institutions. At postgraduate level, the Masters degree programmes (entailing coursework and research) are normally of two to three years' duration and require the submission of a thesis. Some universities also offer one-year Postgraduate Certificate/Diploma programmes, which only contain the first part of the Masters (the coursework element). Doctoral courses generally take three to five years following the Masters. Postgraduate programmes are mainly offered by universities.

Regulatory Body

NATIONAL BODY

Gabinete de Apoio ao Ensino Superior (Tertiary Education Services Office): Av. do Dr Rodrigo Rodrigues No 614A–640, Edif. Long Cheng, 5° a 7° andares; tel. (853) 28345403; e-mail info@gaes.gov.mo; internet www.gaes.gov.mo; f. 1992; govt dept in charge of higher education affairs under the leadership of the Sec. for Social Affairs and Culture; formulates policies for the devt of higher education; helps in the evaluation of higher education instns; Dir SOU CHIO FAI; Deputy Dir SÍLVIA RIBEIRO OSÓRIO HO; publ. *Macao Higher Education Magazine* (4 a year, in Chinese, English and Portuguese, print and online).

Learned Societies

GENERAL

Fundação Macau (Macao Foundation): Avda. de Almeida Ribeiro, No 39, 7 andar; tel. (853) 28966777; e-mail info@fm.org.mo; internet www.fmac.org.mo; conducts research on cultural, social, economic, educational, scientific, academic, philanthropic activities for the promotion of Macao; Pres. CHUI SAI ON; Pres. for Admin. ZHILIANG WU.

ARCHITECTURE AND TOWN PLANNING

Architects Association of Macau: tel. (853) 28703458; e-mail info@macaoarchitects.com; internet www.macaoarchitects.com; f. 1980 as Macau Association of Architects in Private Practice, present name 1988; Dir EDDIE Y. K. WONG; Gen. Sec. JOY TIN TIN CHOI.

ECONOMICS, LAW AND POLITICS

Associação de Ciências Sociais de Macau (Macao Association of Social Sciences): Estrada Adolfo Loureiro 3A, Edif. Tak On, 3rd Floor A, POB 957; tel. (853) 28319880; f. 1985; 40 mems; Pres. LIU BOLONG; publ. *Huo Keng* (2 a year).

FINE AND PERFORMING ARTS

Instituto Cultural do Governo da R. A. E. de Macau (Cultural Affairs Bureau): Praça do Tap Seac, Edif. do Instituto Cultural; tel. (853) 83996699; e-mail postoffice@icm.gov.mo; internet www.icm.gov.mo; f. 1982, fmrly Cultural Institute of Macao, reorganized to present status 1994; cultural studies; classes for music, drama and ballet; promotion of cultural events; also oversees the Macao Historical Archives, the Macao Central Library and the Macao Museum; Pres. Dra HEIDI HO; publ. *Revista de Cultura* (4 a year, in Chinese, English, and Portuguese).

LANGUAGE AND LITERATURE

Alliance Française: 4/F Travessa do Bom Jesus R/C; tel. (853) 28965342; e-mail info.macao@afchine.org; internet www.alliancefrancaise.org.mo; f. 1987; offers courses and examinations in French language and culture and promotes cultural exchange with France; 11 mems; Pres. JOAQUIM JORGE PERESTRELO NETO VALENTE; Dir (vacant); Head of Studies PATRICIA BERTONECHE.

MEDICINE

Nurses Association of Macao: Ave Macao 1-1B, E Sunrise House, Block 2-D; tel. (853) 28525614; e-mail naom@macau.ctm.net; internet www.naom.org.mo; f. 1986; improves professional standards of care and promotes basic rights of nurses; 650 mems; Pres. LI XUE-PING; Vice-Pres. SHU-CHEN HUANG; Chair. TIAN JIE BING; Sec.-Gen. MAO XIAONI.

Research Institutes

GENERAL

Macau Ricci Institute/Instituto Ricci de Macau: Ave Cons. Ferreira de Almeida 95-E; tel. (853) 28532536; e-mail info@riccimac.org; internet www.riccimac.org; f. 1999; fosters mutual understanding between China and the world community; library of 19,800 vols incl. 11,400 Chinese books, 8,400 Western books; Dir ARTUR WARDEGA; Vice-Dir LUÍS SEQUEIRA; Gen. Sec. JERÓNIMO HUNG; publs *Humanitas Publications Series*, *Jesuitas Publications Series*, *Macau Ricci Institute Studies Series*.

ECONOMICS, LAW AND POLITICS

Social, Economic and Public Policy Research Centre: Rua de Luís Gonzaga Gomes; tel. (853) 85996267; e-mail cepes@ipm.edu.mo; internet www.ipm.edu.mo/cepes; f. 2007; attached to Macao Polytechnic Institute; research areas incl. gambling industry of Macao, devt of economy, society, govt and public policy in Macao; provides consultancy services to Macao Spec. Admin. Region Govt; Exec. Deputy Dir Prof. CHEN QINGYUN.

MEDICINE

Institute of Chinese Medical Sciences: c/o Univ. of Macao, Ave Padre Tomás Pereira SJ, Taipa; tel. (853) 83974698; e-mail icms.enquiry@umac.mo; internet www.umac.mo/icms; f. 2002; attached to Univ. of Macao; develops postgraduate education; trains management and scientific research professionals in medical science; researches in medicine and pharmacology; networks with int. instns and orgs; promotes traditional Chinese medicine; Dir YITAO WANG.

Macao Institute for Applied Research in Medicine and Health: Macao Univ. of Science and Technology, Ave Wai Long, Taipa; tel. (853) 88972633; e-mail miar@must.edu.mo; internet www.mustf-miar.org.mo; attached to Macao Univ. of Science and Technology; provides educational service, clinical practice and various biological research and devt for the Faculty of Chinese Medicine (Macao Univ. of Science and Technology); also provides a platform in Macao for biotechnology industrialization, modernization and internationalization of Chinese medicine; Dir Dr TIMOTHY MING WAI CHAN; Deputy Dir Dr BRAD W. C. LAU.

Libraries and Archives

Macao

Arquivo Histórico de Macau (Macao Historical Archives): Praca do Tap Seac, Edif. do Instituto Cultural; tel. (853) 28592919; e-mail info.ah@icm.gov.mo; internet www.archives.gov.mo; f. 1952 as Macao Gen. Archives, renamed and restructured 1979; attached to Instituto Cultural do Governo da R.A.E. de Macau (Cultural Affairs Bureau); promotes research; holds govt gazettes, original records, microfilms of rare works on Macao's history and Portugal's relations with the Far East; 7,000 vols; Dir MARIE IMELDA MACLEOD; publ. *Boletim do Arquivo Histórico de Macau*.

Biblioteca Central de Macau (Macao Central Library): No 3, Largo de Sto. Agostinho, Macao; tel. (853) 28371623; e-mail inf.bc@icm.gov.mo; internet www.library.gov.mo; f. 1895; attached to Cultural Affairs Bureau of the Macao SAR Govt; public network of main library and 6 brs; gen. colln; Chinese Books (Sir Robert Ho Tung); highlights traditional culture and encourages leisure reading through reading activities, exhibitions and lectures; participates in Library Week; 900,000 vols, incl. 5,000 Chinese and 20,000 Western ancient books; Dir OPHELIA TANG; Sec. CATHERINE LO.

Biblioteca da Ilha Verde (Ilha Verde Library): Ave de Concórdia 281, 4th Floor, Edif. 'May Fair Garden' II Fase; tel. (853) 28225783; internet www.library.gov.mo/pt/general/library_3.aspx; f. 1995; attached to Macao Central Library; cultural and educational centre for dissemination of entertainment and information; 34,000 vols of monographs, 2,400 multimedia material, 72 newspaper titles and 435 journals.

Biblioteca de Coloane (Library of Coloane): Rua de 5 de Outubro, Coloane; tel. (853) 28882254; internet www.library.gov.mo/pt/general/library_5.aspx; f. 1983; attached to Macao Central Library; 8,700 vols of monographs, 16 newspaper titles and 59 magazine titles.

Biblioteca de Mong Há (Mong Ha Library): Bairro de Mong Há, near the Pavilion de Mong Ha; tel. (853) 28317288; internet www.library.gov.mo/pt/general/library_4.aspx; f. 1988; attached to Macao Central Library; 21,000 vols incl. monographs, 51 journal titles and 229 magazines.

Biblioteca do Edificio do IACM (IACM Building Library): Ave de Almeida Ribeiro 163, Edif. do IACM; tel. (853) 28572233; internet www.library.gov.mo/pt/general/library_6.aspx; f. 1929 fmrly Biblioteca do Leal Senado; attached to Macao Central Library; spec. collns incl. historical and scholarly works on China and Portuguese rule in the Far East and Africa; 30,000 vols, 19,000 monographs, 22 journals, 99 newspapers.

Biblioteca Sir Robert Ho Tung (Sir Robert Ho Tung Library): Largo do Sto. Agostinho 3; tel. (853) 28377117; internet www.library.gov.mo/pt/general/library_2.aspx; f. 1958; attached to Macao Central Library; largest public library in Macao; 100,000 vols, incl. 5,000 ancient Chinese books, 79,924 other books, 4,925 multimedia materials, 74 journals, 732 magazines, 23 newspaper titles; Librarian SAM CHAN FAI; publ. *Boletim Bibliográfico de Macau*.

Museums and Art Galleries

Macao

Macao Tea Culture House: Lou Lim Ieoc Garden, Ave do Conselheiro Ferreira de Almeida; tel. (853) 28827103; e-mail dic@iacm.gov.mo; internet www.iacm.gov.mo/museum; f. 2005; attached to Civic and Municipal Affairs Bureau; represents China's tea culture; Macao's role in the history of Chinese tea propagation and trade.

Macao Maritime Museum: 1 Largo do Pagode da Barra; tel. (853) 28595481; e-mail museumaritimo@marine.gov.mo; internet www.museumaritimo.gov.mo; f. 1987, present bldg 1990; focuses on the maritime activities of Macao, China and Portugal; collns divided into themes presenting evolution and seafaring accomplishments; library of 3,485 vols.

Museu das Comunicações (Communications Museum): Estrada D. Maria II 7; tel. (853) 28718570; e-mail info@macao.communications.museum; internet macao.communications.museum; f. 2006; stimulates interest in philatelic colln, stamp colln; promotes Macao philately and scientific and technical knowledge of telecommunications.

Museu de Arte de Macau (Macao Museum of Art): Centro Cultural de Macau, Ave Xian Xing Hai s/n Nape; tel. (853) 287919814; e-mail mam@iacm.gov.mo; internet www.mam.gov.mo; f. 1999; attached to Civil and Municipal Affairs Bureau; collns incl. Shi Wan ceramics, Chinese painting and calligraphy, historical pictures, Macao contemporary art, ceramics and stoneware excavated from Heisha in Macao, seal cutting from Guangdong, Western historical paintings, poster design, photographic works; attached auditorium and library; Dir CHAN HOU SENG.

Museu de Macau (Museum of Macao): Praceta do Museu de Macau 112; tel. (853) 28357911; e-mail info.mm@icm.gov.mo; internet www.macaumuseum.gov.mo; f. 1998; attached to Instituto Cultural do Governo da R.A.E. de Macau; promotes understanding and interest in Macao's history and cultural heritage; creates and develops collns related to archaeology, history, natural history, ethnography and ethnology; serves as a centre for learning through research and study; preserves and records materials of historical and cultural significance; library of 3,000 vols; Dir CHAN IENG HIN; publ. *Museum of Macao* (magazine).

Nature and Agriculture Museum: Seac Pai Van Park, Coloane Island; tel. (853) 28870277; e-mail decn@iacm.gov.mo; internet nature.iacm.gov.mo.

Temporary Exhibition Gallery of the Civic and Municipal Affairs Bureau (IACM): Ave Almeida Ribeiro 163, 'Leal Senado' Bldg; tel. (853) 89884100; internet www.iacm.gov.mo/museum; f. 1985; attached to Civic and Municipal Affairs Bureau; housed in historically significant 'Leal Senado' bldg; exhibits works of local and Chinese artists.

Universities

UNIVERSIDADE DE CIÊNCIA E TECNOLOGIA DE MACAU
(Macao University of Science and Technology)

Ave Wai Long, Taipa, Macao
Telephone: (853) 28881122
E-mail: enquiry@must.edu.mo
Internet: www.must.edu.mo
Founded 2000
Private control
Languages of instruction: English, Putonghua
Academic year: September to August
Chancellor: Dr CHAK WAN LIU
Rector: Prof. LIU LIANG
Vice-Rector: Prof. ZHANG SHUGUANG
Vice-Rector: Prof. CHEN XI
Vice-Rector: Prof. TONG KA LOK
Dir for Institutional Devt: Dr KEITH MORRISON
Univ. Librarian: Prof. DAI LONG JI
Library of 140,000 vols, 1.2m. ebooks, 950 hard copy periodicals, 56,311 ejournals
Number of teachers: 498
Number of students: 10,393
Publication: *Journal of Macau University of Science and Technology*

DEANS

Faculty of Chinese Medicine: (vacant)
Faculty of Health Sciences: Prof. MANSON FOK
Faculty of Hospitality and Tourism Management: Prof. MICHAEL HITCHCOCK
Faculty of Humanities and Arts: Prof. YU QIU YU
Faculty of Information Technology: Prof. TSOI AH CHUNG
Faculty of Law: SHEN SI BAO
Faculty of Management and Administration: Prof. CHAN LAI KOW
School of Continuing Studies: AMY CHU OI MEI (Head)

UNIVERSIDADE DE MACAU
(University of Macao)

Ave Padre Tomás Pereira, Taipa
Telephone: (853) 28831622
E-mail: info@umac.mo
Internet: www.umac.mo
Founded 1981 as Univ. of East Asia, current name adopted 1991
State control
Languages of instruction: Chinese, Portuguese, English
Academic year: September to June
Chancellor: CHIEF EXEC. OF MACAO SPEC. ADMIN. REGION
Rector: Prof. WEI ZHAO
Vice-Rector for Academic Affairs: Prof. XITAO FAN
Vice-Rector for Admin.: Dr ALEX LAI IAT LONG
Vice-Rector for Research: Prof. RUI PAULO DA SILVA MARTINS
Vice-Rector for Student Affairs: Prof. HAYDN H. D. CHEN
Librarian: Dr PAUL POON WAH TUNG
Library: 3m. vols, 300,000 periodicals, 13,000 vols old Chinese edns, 1m. ebooks, 35,000 online journals
Number of teachers: 481

Number of students: 8,600

Publication: *Journal of Macau Studies* (6 a year)

DEANS

Faculty of Arts and Humanities: Prof. MARTIN MATHEW MONTGOMERY

Faculty of Business Administration: Prof. JACKY YUK CHOW SO

Faculty of Education: Prof. XITAO FAN

Faculty of Health Sciences: Prof. GE WEI

Faculty of Law: Prof. JOHN SHIJIAN MO

Faculty of Science and Technology: Prof. PHILIP CHEN CHUN LUNG

Faculty of Social Sciences: Prof. HAO YUFAN

Honours College: Prof. MOK KAI MENG

Institute of Chinese Medical Sciences: Prof. WANG YITAO

Colleges

Instituto de Formação Turística (Institute for Tourism Studies): Colina de Mong-Há; tel. (853) 28561252; e-mail iftpr@ift.edu.mo; internet www.ift.edu.mo; f. 1995, governed by Sec. for Social Affairs and Culture of the Macao Spec. Admin. Region Govt; offers degree programmes in heritage, hospitality, tourism, tourism events and tourism retail, marketing management; Pres. Prof. FANNY VONG.

Instituto Polytécnico de Macau (Macao Polytechnic Institute): Rua Luis Gonzaga Gomes; tel. (853) 28578722; e-mail webadmin@ipm.edu.mo; internet www.ipm.edu.mo; f. 1991; programmes in Chinese–English translation and interpretation, Chinese–Portuguese translation and interpretation, accounting and finance, computer studies, design, e-commerce, management, music, nursing and biomedical science, public administration, physical education and sports, social work, visual arts; 500 teachers; 2,800 students; Pres. Prof. LEI HEONG IOK; Vice-Pres. Prof. YIN LEI; Sec.-Gen. RAYMOND CHAN; publs *Journal of MPI* (4 a year, in Chinese and English), *Journal of Sino-Western Cultural Studies* (2 a year).

COLOMBIA

The Higher Education System

The Roman Catholic Church pioneered higher education in Colombia, with the establishment of the Pontificia Universidad Javeriana in 1623, and remained the driving force behind universities until the 1930s. The tertiary education system is regulated by a legal framework laid down by the 1991 Constitution. In 1994 the General Educational Law (No. 115) put the Ministry of National Education in charge of public and private education. In 2011 there were some 288 higher education institutes in Colombia, of which 208 were private. In that year a total of 1,849,500 students were enrolled in higher education; some 45% of these students were attending private institutions. Tertiary education providers are classified into the four following types: universidades (universities), instituciones universitarias (university institutions), instituciones técnicas profesionales (professional technical institutions) and instituciones tecnológicas (technological institutions). In 2011 the Government allocated funds equivalent to 0.98% of GDP for tertiary education. This figure was predicted to have risen to 1.4% by 2014.

Admission to higher education is on the basis of the secondary school certificate (Bachillerato) and the Examen de Estado para Ingreso a la Educación Superior (State Examination for Admission to Higher Education). The two-stage examination is conducted by the Instituto Colombiano para el Fomento de Educación Superior (ICFES, Colombian Institute for the Promotion of Higher Education). The basic university degree structure consists of Licenciado (equivalent to Bachelors), Maestría/Magister (Masters) and Doctorado (Doctorate) degrees. Undergraduates study for four to seven years for the Licenciado or Título Profesional (professional title). Most courses last for five years and require the submission of a thesis or professional placement in the final year. Since 2002 a credit system has been applied to undergraduate degree programmes. At postgraduate level the Diploma de Especialización (Diploma of Specialization) requires one to four years of study following the Licenciado, usually in a professional or applied discipline. The Diploma accounts for around 90% of total enrolment in postgraduate courses and most of such degrees are offered at private institutions. The Maestría/Magister is awarded after two years of full-time study beyond the Licenciado, while a Doctorado requires two to three years of study in an area of specialization after the Maestría/Magister and is based on the submission and defence of a thesis.

In 2011 there were 39 professional technical institutions (of which 30 were private) and 54 technological institutions (of which 42 were private). Approximately 30% of all tertiary students were enrolled in one of these institutions in 2011. The Servicio Nacional de Aprendizaje (SENA, National Apprenticeship Service) is responsible for the provision of technical and vocational education at all levels. There are currently three types of vocational certificate offered by SENA: the Certificado de Aptitud Profesional (CAP), the Título de Técnico Profesional and the Título de Tecnólogo. The minimum requirements for entry into the operative level of CAP (which lasts around six months) are Grade 5 or Grade 7 of school, depending on the trade, and Grade 9 for entry into the technician level (which lasts about one year). Candidates are also required to have completed Grade 9 of secondary education for admission into Técnico Profesional courses, which entail around 18 months of study. The Título de Tecnólogo is the highest level of qualification offered by SENA. Tecnólogo programmes are generally two years in duration and require the Bachillerato or a Título de Técnico Profesional in a similar field for entry.

The current system of higher education accreditation in Colombia was established in accordance with the 1992 Higher Education Law (No. 30) with the creation of the Consejo Nacional de Acreditación (CNA, National Council for Accreditation). The foundation of the CNA marked a shift in focus from state control of institutions to state support of institutional autonomy. Institutions must demonstrate that they meet minimum quality standards through a mandatory process overseen by the Consejo Nacional de Aseguramiento de la Calidad de la Educación Superior (National Council for the Quality Assurance of Higher Education), created in 2003. In addition, institutions or individual undergraduate courses can apply, on a voluntary basis, for an Acreditación de Alta Calidad (Accreditation of Excellence) co-ordinated by the CNA. In 2011 it was estimated that only 13% of undergraduate programmes and 21% of higher education institutions had attained accreditation at this level. At postgraduate level, Maestría/Magister courses must be accredited by the Consejo Nacional de Maestrías y Doctorados (CNMD, National Council on Masters and Doctorates), a department within the CNA.

In March 2011 the Government set forth its proposed Higher Education Reform Project (as an amendment to the 1992 Higher Education Law), which included controversial plans to allow higher education institutions to operate on a 'for-profit' basis, a practice outlawed hitherto. The stated aims of the proposed reforms were to increase enrolment in higher education (from some 37% of students in the relevant age group in 2011 to 50% by 2014), to enhance the quality of provision, to make the system relevant to the needs of the economy and more competitive abroad and to improve governance and transparency within the sector. The proposals, which were loosely based on the Brazilian model of tertiary education, attracted intense criticism, with opponents claiming that privatizing much of the sector would lead to lower educational standards and would exclude students from poor backgrounds. In November, following mass protests and strikes by students, the Government withdrew the draft legislation from congressional consideration and announced that a wide-ranging consultation on the issue would be launched in 2012.

Regulatory and Representative Bodies

GOVERNMENT

Ministry of Culture: Carrera 8, No 8–55, Bogotá, DC; tel. (1) 3424100; e-mail servicioalcliente@mincultura.gov.co; internet www.mincultura.gov.co; Minister MARIANA GARCÉS CÓRDOBA.

Ministry of National Education: Calle 43, No 57–14, Centro Administrativo Nacional (CAN), Bogotá, DC; tel. (1) 2222800; e-mail despachoministra@mineducacion.gov.co; internet www.mineducacion.gov.co; Minister MARÍA FERNANDA CAMPO SAAVEDRA.

ACCREDITATION

Consejo Nacional de Acreditación (National Council for Accreditation): Calle 19, No 6–68 17°, Bogotá, DC; tel. (1) 3411050; e-mail cna@cna.gov.co; internet www.cna.gov.co; f. 1992; implements Nat. Policy on higher education accreditation; 16 mems; Coordinator ALVARO ZAPATA DOMINGUEZ.

FUNDING

Instituto Colombiano de Crédito Educativo y Estudios Técnicos en el Exterior (ICETEX) (Colombian Institute for Educational Loans and Advanced Studies Abroad): Carrera 3, No 18–32, Bogotá, DC; tel. (1) 4173535; internet www.icetex.gov.co; f. 1950; provides undergraduate and postgraduate grants; selects Colombian students for foreign scholarships, and finances foreign postgraduate students in Colombia; information and documentation centres; library of 15,000 vols; Pres. Dr FERNANDO RODRÍGUEZ CARRIZOSA; Sec. Gen. AURA YINETH CORREA NIÑO.

NATIONAL BODIES

Asociación Colombiana de Universidades (Colombian Universities Association): Calle 93, No 16–43, Bogotá, DC; tel. (1) 6231580; e-mail ascun@ascun.org.co; internet www.ascun.org.co; f. 1957; encourages integration of the academic community; represents and serves as an interlocutor to all Colombian univs; Exec. Dir Dr CARLOS HERNANDO FORERO ROBAYO; Sec. Gen. Dr XIOMARA ZARUR MIRANDA.

Instituto Colombiano para el Fomento de la Educación Superior (ICFES) (Colombian Institute for the Promotion of Higher Education): Calle 17, No 3–40, Bogotá, DC; tel. (1) 3077008; e-mail faxciudadano@icfes.gov.co; internet www.icfes.gov.co; f. 1992; attached to Min. of Nat. Education; assesses the Colombian educational system at all levels; implements policies to promote higher education and assessment; promotes the devt of research in HEIs; Dir Gen. Dra MARGARITA MARÍA PEÑA BORREREO; Sec. Gen. GIOCONDA PIÑA ELLES.

Learned Societies

GENERAL

Academia Colombiana de la Lengua (Colombian Academy of Language): Sede Carrera 3 No 17–34, Apdo Aereo 13922, Bogotá, DC; tel. (1) 3341190; e-mail comlinguistica@gmail.com; internet academiacolombianadelalengua.co; f. 1871; corresp. of the Real Academia Española (Madrid); publishes 3 reference books, incl. the *Diccionario de la Lengua Española*; 62 mems (25 corresp., 25 full-time, 12 hon.); library of 40,000 vols; Dir JAIME POSADA DÍAZ; Exec. Sec. SANTIAGO DÍAZ PIEDRAHITA; Librarian JUAN MENDOZA VEGA; publ. *Vigía del Idioma* (2 a year).

AGRICULTURE, FISHERIES AND VETERINARY SCIENCE

Sociedad de Agricultores de Colombia (Colombian Farmers' Society): Carrera 7, No 24–89, Edif. Colpatria, Of. 4402, Bogotá, DC; tel. (1) 2410035; e-mail presidencia@sac.org.co; internet www.sac.org.co; f. 1871; consultative body for the Govt; promotes nat. agricultural devt and welfare of peasants; represent the interests of rural farmers; 400 mems; library of 5,500 vols, 435 periodical titles; Pres. RAFAEL MEJIA LÓPEZ; Sec. Gen. LUIS FERNANDO FORERO GÓMEZ; publs *Documentos Independientes*, *El Editorial Agrario* (irregular), *Revista Nacional de Agricultura* (4 a year).

BIBLIOGRAPHY, LIBRARY SCIENCE AND MUSEOLOGY

Centro Regional para el Fomento del Libro en América Latina y el Caribe (CERLALC) (Regional Centre for the Promotion of Books in Latin America and the Caribbean): Calle 70, No 9–52, Bogotá, DC; tel. (1) 5402071; e-mail libro@cerlalc.org; internet www.cerlalc.org; f. 1971; promotes production and circulation of books; devt of libraries; provides training; promotes protection of copyright; 21 mem. countries; library of 5,600 documents, 100 periodicals; Dir FERNANDO ZAPATA LÓPEZ; Sec. Gen. ALBA DOLORES LÓPEZ HOYOS; publs *El Libro en América Latina y el Caribe* (4 a year), *Pensar el Libro*.

Colegio Colombiano de Bibliotecología ASCOLBI (Colombian Association of Librarians): Calle 21 No 6–58, Of. 404, Bogotá, DC; tel. (1) 2823620; internet www.ascolbi.org; f. 1942 as Asociación Colombiana de Bibliotecarios (ASCOLBI); represents interests of librarians; coordinates and organizes professional devt activities with other nat. orgs; 1,200 mems; Pres. EDGAR ALLAN DELGADO.

Fundación para el Fomento de la Lectura (FUNDALECTURA) (Foundation for the Promotion of Reading): Dg 40A Bis No 16–46, Bogotá, DC; tel. (1) 3201511; e-mail contactenos@fundalectura.org.co; internet www.fundalectura.org; f. 1990; library of 20,000 vols, 6,000 spec. vols for children and juveniles, 540 titles of nat. and int. journals; Exec. Dir CARMEN BARVO; publs *Nuevas Hojas de Lectura* (3 a year, print and online, www.nuevashojasdelectura.com), *Revista Latinoamericana de Literatura Infantil y Juvenil* (2 a year, online).

ECONOMICS, LAW AND POLITICS

Academia Colombiana de Jurisprudencia (Colombian Academy of Jurisprudence): Carrera 9 No 74–08, Of. 203, Bogotá; tel. (1) 2124315; f. 1894; 50 mems; Pres. HERNANDO MORALES M.; publ. *Revista* (2 a year).

Sociedad Colombiana de Economistas (Colombian Society of Economists): Carrera 20 No 36–41, Bogotá, DC; tel. (1) 2852527; e-mail contactenos@economistascolombia.org; internet www.economistascolombia.org; f. 1958; 5,500 mems; library of 105 vols; Pres. Dr LILIA BEATRIZ SANCHEZ SALAMANCA; publs *Biblioteca Digital Latinoamericana* (online), *Revista* (6 a year).

HISTORY, GEOGRAPHY AND ARCHAEOLOGY

Academia Boyacense de Historia (Boyaca Academy of History): Casa del Fundador, Tunja, Boyacá; f. 1905; publication and encouragement of historical, literary and anthropological studies in Boyaca; 30 mems; library of 1,000 vols, 600 MSS from the period 1539–1860; Pres. JAVIER OCAMPO LOPEZ; Sec. RAMÓN CORREA; publ. *Repertorio Boyacense* (2 a year).

Academia Colombiana de Historia (Colombian Academy of History): Calle 10 No 8–95, Apdo Aéreo 14428, Bogotá, DC; tel. (1) 3413615; e-mail contacto@academiadehistoria.org.co; internet www.academiahistoria.org.co; f. 1902; 40 mems, excluding Colombian and foreign corresp. mems; library of 45,000 vols; Pres. JUAN CAMILO RODRÍGUEZ GÓMEZ; Sec. LUIS HORACIO LÓPEZ DOMÍNGUEZ; Library Coordinator ROGER PITA PICO; publ. *Boletín de Historia y Antigüedades* (print and online, boletin.academiahistoria.org.co).

Academia de la Historia de Cartagena de Indias (Academy of History of Cartagena de Indias): Palacio de la Inquisición, Plaza Bolívar, Cartagena, Bolívar; tel. (5) 6643930; e-mail info@academiadelahistoriadecartagenadeindias.org; internet academiadelahistoriadecartagenadeindias.org; f. 1918; spec. collns on history of Cartagena and Colombia; 24 mems, 7 hon. mems, 64 Colombian corresp. mems, 10 foreign corresp. mems; library of 10,000 vols; Pres. LEON TRUJILLO VELEZ; Sec. JORGE PÉREZ VILLA; publ. *Boletín Historial* (4 a year).

Sociedad Bolivariana de Colombia (Colombian Bolivarian Society): Avda Calle 20 No 5–17 este, Bogotá, DC; tel. (1) 2431166; e-mail s.bolivariana@etb.net.co; internet www.sociedadbolivarianadecolombia.org; f. 1924; 20 hon. mems; library of 1,000 vols, specialized bibliography on Simón Bolívar; Pres. Dr MIGUEL SANTAMARÍA DÁVILA; Sec. Dr GERMÁN VELANDIA PELÁEZ; Sec. Dr GUSTAVO ALTAMAR LAYSECA; Treas. Dr FELIPE ZAPATA CAYCEDO; publ. *Revista Bolivariana* (3 a year).

Sociedad Geográfica de Colombia (Colombian Geographical Society): Calle 44 No 45–67, Bloque C, Módulo 1, Of. 602, Bogotá, DC; tel. (1) 3150747; internet www.sogeocol.com.co; f. 1903; br. socs in Barranquilla, Medellín, Pasto, Sibundoy, Tunja; 60 mems (31 full-time, 29 corresp.); Pres. Dr EUFRASIO BERNAL DUFFO; Sec. Dr RODOLFO LLINÁS RIVERA; Treas. Dr MARIANO OSPINA RODRÍGUEZ; publ. *Cuadernos de Geografía Colombiana*.

LANGUAGE AND LITERATURE

Alliance Française/Alianza Francesa: Carrera 11, No 93–40, Apdo Aereo 5064, Bogotá; tel. (1) 2563197; e-mail bogota@alianzafrancesa.org.co; internet www.alianzafrancesa.org.co; offers courses and examinations in French language and culture and promotes cultural exchange with France; attached teaching offices in Armenia, Barranquilla, Bogatá-Centro, Bucuramanga, Cali, Cartagena, Cúcuta, Manizales, Medellín, Pereira, Popayán and Santa Marta.

British Council: Carrera 9, No 76–49, 5°, Bogotá, DC; tel. (1) 3259090; e-mail servicioalcliente@britishcouncil.org.co; internet www.britishcouncil.co; offers courses and examinations in English language and British culture and promotes cultural exchange with the UK; separate teaching centre in Bogotá and Medellin; library of 7,500 vols, 60 periodicals; Dir CHRIS RAWLINGS.

Goethe-Institut: Carrera 11A, No 93–52, Apdo 25 08 65, Bogotá, DC; tel. (571) 6018600; e-mail info@bogota.goethe.org; internet www.goethe.de/bogota; courses and examinations in German language and culture; promotes cultural exchange with Germany; Dir KATJA KESSING.

Instituto Caro y Cuervo (Caro and Cuervo Institute): Calle 10, No 4–69, Bogotá; tel. (1) 3422121; e-mail contactenos@caroycuervo.gov.co; internet www.caroycuervo.gov.co; f. 1942; attached to Min. of Culture; Hispanic philology and literature; library of 102,491 vols, 102,000 vols of periodicals; Dir JOSE LUIS ACOSTA H.; Sec. Gen. LILIANA RIVERA ORJUELA; Library Dir LUZ CLEMENCIA MEJÍA MUÑOZ; publs *Aguas Vivas*, *Archivo Epistolar Colombiano*, *Atlas Lingüístico-Etnográfico de Colombia*, *Biblioteca de Publicaciones del Instituto*, *Biblioteca Colombiana*, *Biblioteca 'Ezequiel Uricoechea'*, *Clásicos Colombianos*, *Cuadernos del Seminario Andrés Bello*, *Diccionario de Construcción y Régimen de la Lengua Castellana*, *Filólogos Colombianos*, *La Granada Entreabierta*, *Litterae*, *Poesia Rescatada*, *Thesaurus* (3 a year).

PEN Internacional, Colombia: Calle 88, 11A-20, Apdo 302, Bogotá, DC; tel. (1) 6919627; e-mail presidencia@pencolombiadeescritores.com; internet pencolombiadeescritores.com; f. 1936; 50 mems; library of 1,000 vols; Pres. CÁRLOS VÁSQUEZ ZAWADSKY; Sec. Gen. GABRIELA SANTA ARCINIEGAS; publ. *Ecos: Revista Literaria y Cultural* (2 a year).

MEDICINE

Academia Nacional de Medicina de Colombia (Colombian National Academy of Medicine): Carrera 7, No 69–11, Bogotá, DC; tel. (1) 3458890; e-mail info@anmdecolombia.org.co; internet anmdecolombia.net; f. 1873;

557 mems; library of 10,000 vols; Pres. Dr FERNANDO SANCHEZ TORRES; Permanent Sec. Dr HERNANDO GROOT LIÉVANO; Sec. Gen. Dr HERMAN ESGUERRA VILLAMIZAR; Treas. Dr GERMÁN GAMARRA HERNÁNDEZ; publs *Medicina* (4 a year), *Temas Médicos* (1 a year).

Asociación Colombiana de Facultades de Medicina—ASCOFAME (Colombian Association of Medical Faculties): Carrera 14, No 101–53, Barrio Rincón de Chicó, Bogotá, DC; tel. (1) 7425380; e-mail ascofame@ascofame.org.co; internet www.ascofame.org.co; f. 1959; furthers higher education and research in medicine; divs of education, evaluation, health and social security, information; 46 medical faculties (institutional mems), 4,500 individuals, 7 affiliated mems; library of 3,500 vols, 100 periodicals and audiovisual materials; Pres. Dr JORGE JULIAN OSORIO GÓMEZ; Sec. Dra LUZ MARINA CORSO MORALES; Exec. Dir Dr RICARDO HUMBERTO ROZO URIBE; publs *Boletín del Centro de Etica Médica y Bioética*, *Boletín de Medicamentos y Terapéutica* (4 a year), *Cuadernos de Actualización Médica Permanente*, *Gaceta Médica*, *Revista de ASCOFAME*.

Asociación Colombiana de Fisioterapía (Colombian Association of Physiotherapy): Carrera 7A, No 64–44, Of. 101, Bogotá, DC; tel. (1) 8043865; internet www.ascofi.org.co; f. 1953; promotes research in physiotherapy in accordance with est. policies at nat., regional and local levels; 950 mems; library of 300 vols; Pres. VICTORIA EUGENIA MOLINA ARBELAÉZ; Sec. Gen. GLORIA AMPARO POSADA RODRIGUEZ; publ. *Revista* (1 a year).

Asociación Colombiana de Psiquiatría (Colombian Association of Psychiatry): Carrera 18, No 84–87, Of. 404, Bogotá, DC; tel. (1) 2561148; e-mail vicepresidencia@psiquiatria.org.co; internet www.psiquiatria.org.co; f. 1961; devt of psychiatry through teaching, dissemination and research; promotes practice of professional speciality; 854 mems; Pres. Dr JUAN CARLOS ROJAS FERNÁNDEZ; publs *Cuadernos de Psiquiatría Enlace* (4 a year), *Revista Colombiana de Psiquiatría* (4 a year).

Asociación Colombiana de Radiología (Colombian Academy of Radiology): Carrera 43 No 33–57, Bloque 5, Of. 220, Medellín, Antioquia; tel. (4) 2626978; e-mail asoar@une.net.co; internet www.acronline.org; f. 1945 as Sociedad Colombiana de Radiología, current name adopted 1993; 400 mems; library of 3,000 vols, collns of journals; Pres. Dr GABRIEL ENRIQUE DIB DIAZGRANADOS; Sec. Dr JAIME ALFONSO MADRID JARAMILLO; publ. *Revista Colombiana de Radiología* (4 a year).

Asociación Colombiana de Sociedades Científicas (Colombian Association of Scientific Societies): Carrera 16A, No 80-65, Of. 602, Edif. Oval, Bogotá, DC; tel. (1) 7034681; e-mail sociedadsc@col.net.co; internet www.sociedadescientificas.com; f. 1956, current name adopted 1970; health sciences; 3,692 mems, 61 mem. asscns; Pres. Dr CARLOS FRANCISCO FERNANDEZ RINCON; Sec. Dr SAUL RUGELES QUINTERO.

Federación Colombiana de Obstetricia y Ginecología (Colombian Federation of Obstetrics and Gynaecology): Carrera 15 No 98–42, Of. 204, Bogotá, DC; tel. (1) 6016622; e-mail fecolsog@fecolsog.org; internet www.fecolsog.org; f. 1943; 300 mems; library of 1,000 vols; Pres. Dr JUAN DIEGO VILLEGAS ECHEVERRI; Sec. Gen. Dr LUIS ALFONSO LÓPEZ JIMÉNEZ; Treas. Dra AMPARO RAMÍREZ CORREDOR; publ. *Revista Colombiana de Obstetricia y Ginecología* (4 a year).

Federación Médica Colombiana (Colombian Medical Federation): Carrera 7, No 82–66, Of. 218/219, Bogotá, DC; internet www.federacionmedicacolombiana.com; f. 1934; Pres. SERGIO ISAZA VILLA; Sec. GENTIL GÓMEZ MEJÍA; publ. *Directorio Médico Asistencial* (1 a year).

Instituto Nacional de Medicina Legal y Ciencias Forenses (National Institute of Legal Medicine and Forensic Sciences): Calle 7A, No 12A–51, Bogotá, DC; tel. (1) 4069944; e-mail cdivulgacion@medicinalegal.gov.co; internet www.medicinalegal.gov.co; f. 1914; library of 30,000 vols; Dir-Gen. CARLOS EDUARDO VALDÉS; publs *Colombia Forense*, *Revista*.

Sociedad Colombiana de Cardiología (Colombian Cardiological Society): Avda Calle 127 No 16A–76, Of. 502, Bogotá, DC; tel. (1) 5230012; e-mail secretaria@scc.org.co; internet scc.org.co; f. 1943; 245 mems; Pres. EFRAIN GÓMEZ LÓPEZ; Sec. GUSTAVO RESTREPO; Treas. JUAN MANUEL, SR; publ. *Revista SCC* (4 a year, print and online, revcolcard.org.scc.org.co).

Sociedad Colombiana de Cirugía Ortopédica y Traumatología (Colombian Society of Orthopaedic Surgery and Traumatology): Calle 134 No 7B-83, Of. 201, Bogotá, DC; tel. (1) 6257445; e-mail secretaria@sccot.org.co; internet www.sccot.org.co; f. 1946; 1,300 mems; Pres. Dr JUAN CARLOS LÓPEZ T.; Sec. Gen. Dr JOSÉ GABRIEL RÚGELES O.; publs *Carta de Ortopédica* (12 a year), *Revista Cientifica Sociedad Colombiana de Ortopedia y Traumatologia* (4 a year).

Sociedad Colombiana de Patología (Colombian Society of Pathology): Dpto de Patología, Universidad del Valle, Calí, Valle del Cauca; tel. (4) 3269266; e-mail socopat2008@gmail.com; f. 1955; 155 mems; Pres. Dr MARCO ALFONSO NIETO; Sec. Dra MARÍA DEL PILAR RÍOS BERNAL; Treas. Dr OSCAR RUIZ AMBRA.

Sociedad Colombiana de Pediatría (Colombian Paediatrics Society): Carrera 19A No 84–14, Of. 304, Calí, Valle del Cauca; tel. (1) 5300757; e-mail info@scp.com.co; internet www.scp.com.co; f. 1917 Sociedad Pediátrica de Bogotá, current name adopted 1944; 150 mems; library of 2,300 vols; Pres. Dra ANA CRISTINA MARIÑO DREWS; Sec. Dr NICOLÁS IGNACIO RAMOS RODRÍGUEZ; publs *Acta Pedriatrica Colombiana*, *Pediatría* (4 a year).

NATURAL SCIENCES

General

Academia Colombiana de Ciencias Exactas, Físicas y Naturales (Colombian Academy of Exact, Physical and Natural Sciences): Carrera 28A, No 39A–63, Apdo Aéreo 44763, Bogotá, DC; tel. (1) 2683290; e-mail info@accefyn.org.co; internet www.accefyn.org.co; f. 1933; promotes research, teaching and dissemination of science; 40 active mems (106 corresp., 8 hon.); Pres. JAIME RODRIGUEZ LARA; Sec. JOSÉ A. LOZANO IRIARTE; publ. *Revista* (4 a year, print and online, www.accefyn.org.co/revista).

Biological Sciences

Asociación Colombiana de Ciencias Biológicas (Colombian Association of Biological Sciences): Calle 22 Norte No 19–68, Armenia, Quindío; e-mail info@asociacioncolombianadecienciasbiologicas.org; internet www.asociacioncolombianadecienciasbiologicas.org; f. 1965; Pres. RAMÓN FAYAD NAFFAH; publ. *Revista ACCB*.

Mathematical Sciences

Sociedad Colombiana de Matemáticas (Colombian Society of Mathematics): Apdo Aéreo 2521, Bogotá, DC; tel. (1) 2216795; e-mail scm@scm.org.co; internet www.scm.org.co; f. 1955; 800 mems; library of 7,000 vols; Pres. CARLOS H. MONTENEGRO; publs *Lecturas Matemáticas*, *Revista Colombiana de Matemáticas* (2 a year).

Physical Sciences

Sociedad Colombiana de Ciencias Químicas (Colombian Society of Chemical Sciences): Univ. Nacional de Colombia, sede, Unidad Camilo Torres, Bloque C Modulo 7, Of. 202, Bogotá, DC; tel. (1) 2216920; e-mail socolquim@gmail.com; internet www.socolquim.com; f. 1941; promotes chemical research in Colombia; upholds professional ethical standards; serves as an advisory body for public and private orgs, to maintain relations with similar instns at home and abroad; 350 mems; Pres. LUIS ALFONSO CAICEDO MESA; Vice-Pres. and Treas. NOHORA VEGA CASTRO; Sec. JULIAN PINO FAJARDO; publ. *Química e Industria* (2 a year).

TECHNOLOGY

Asociación Colombiana de Industrias Gráficas (Colombian Association of Graphic Industries): Carrera 4A No 26A–20, Bogotá, DC; tel. (1) 2819611; e-mail andigraf@andigraf.com.co; internet www.andigraf.com.co; f. 1975; 200 company mems; Pres. JOSE GRANADA RODRIGUEZ; publs *Boletín Informativo* (12 a year), *Colombia Gráfica* (1 a year).

Sociedad Antioqueña de Ingenieros y Arquitectos (Society of Engineers and Architects of Antioquia): Carrera 81 A No 48B–44, Medellín, Antioquia; tel. (4) 2640832; e-mail sai@sai.org.co; internet www.sai.org.co; f. 1913; 950 mems; library of 3,000 vols; Pres. DIEGO ZAPATA GÓMEZ; Technical Sec. HUGO ALONSO CARMONA RIOS; Exec. Dir ANA MARIA GAVIRIA DUQUE; publs *Noti SAI* (irregular), *Revista Técnica SAI* (4 a year).

Sociedad Colombiana de Ingenieros (Colombian Society of Engineers): Carrera 4, No 10–41, Bogotá, DC; tel. (1) 7052780; e-mail presidenciasci@sci.org.co; internet www.sci.org.co; f. 1887; 2,000 mems; library of 5,000 vols; Pres. Ing. DIANA MARÍA ESPINOSA BULA; Exec. Dir Ing. PIEDAD NIETO PABÓN; publ. *Anales de Ingeniería* (4 a year).

Research Institutes

GENERAL

Departamento Administrativo de Ciencia, Tecnología e Innovación (COLCIENCIAS) (Department of Administration of Science, Technology and Innovation): Transversal 9A No 133–28, Apdo Aéreo 051580, Bogotá, DC; tel. (1) 6258480; e-mail contacto@colciencias.gov.co; internet www.colciencias.gov.co; f. 1968; promotes scientific and technical devt; coordinates and finances projects; library of 15,000 vols, 225 periodicals, 10,000 databases; Dir-Gen. PAULA MARCELA ARIAS PULGARÍN; Sec. Gen. ARLEYS CUESTA SIMANCA; publs *Carta de Colciencias* (12 a year), *Colombia Ciencia y Tecnología* (4 a year).

AGRICULTURE, FISHERIES AND VETERINARY SCIENCE

Instituto Colombiano Agropecuario (Colombian Agricultural and Livestock Institute): Carrera 41, No 17–81, Bogotá, DC; tel. (1) 3323700; e-mail gerencia@ica.gov.co; internet www.ica.gov.co; f. 1962; promotes, coordinates and carries out research, teaching and devt in agriculture and animal husbandry; areas of research: analysis and diagnostics, fishing and aquaculture, frontier protection, plant and animal protection; library: see under Libraries and Archives;

Dir-Gen. LUIS FERNANDO CAICEDO LINCE; publ. *Informe Anual*.

ECONOMICS, LAW AND POLITICS

Departamento Administrativo Nacional de Estadística (National Administrative Department of Statistics): Transversal 45 No 26–70 Interior 1 CAN, Apdo Aéreo 80043, Bogotá, DC; tel. (1) 5978300; e-mail dane@dane.gov.co; internet www.dane.gov.co; f. 1953; produces and disseminates strategic statistical information; regulates nat. statistical system; library of 12,000 vols, 850 periodicals received; Dir-Gen. MAURICIO PERFETTI DEL CORRAL; publs *Atlas Sociodemigráfico de Colombia*, *Bases de Contabilidad*, *Colombia Estadística*, *DIVIPOLA*.

EDUCATION

Centro de Investigación y Educación Popular (Centre for Research and Popular Education): Carrera 5 No 33B-02, Bogotá, DC; tel. (1) 2456181; e-mail cinep@cinep.org.co; internet www.cinep.org.co; f. 1972; private, non-profit org. specializing in social sciences education and analysis of the Colombian system; library of 25,000 vols; Deputy Dir Dr LUIS GUILLERMO GUERRERO GUEVARA; publs *Cien Días* (3 a year), *Controversia* (2 a year), *Noche y Niebla* (2 a year).

Instituto Colombiano para la Evaluación de la Educación (Colombian Institute for Educational Evaluation): Calle 17 No 3–40, Bogotá, DC; tel. (1) 3077008; e-mail faxciudadano@icfes.gov.co; internet www.icfes.gov.co; f. 1968; attached to Min. of Nat. Education; govt body supervising the running of higher education; coordinates the country's distance education system; library: documentation centre specializing in higher, distance and 'open' education, and nat. film colln: 9,200 vols, 2,500 documents, 2,527 periodicals, 1,015 films, audiovisual items and video cassettes; Dir-Gen. Dra MARGARITA MARÍA PEÑA BORRERO; publs *Estadísticas de la Educación Superior*, *Memorias de Eventos Científicos*, *Revista ICFES* (irregular).

HISTORY, GEOGRAPHY AND ARCHAEOLOGY

Instituto Colombiano de Antropología e Historia (Colombian Institute of Anthropology and History): Calle 12 No 2–41, Bogotá, DC; tel. (1) 4440544; e-mail quejasyreclamos@icanh.gov.co; internet www.icanh.gov.co; f. 1941; research in fields of history, archaeology and anthropology; oversees cultural, archaeological and anthropological patrimony of Colombia; administers nat. archaeological parks; publishes edns of 'Flora of the Botanic Expedition' of the New Kingdom of Granada; library of 30,000 vols; open to public; Dir FABIÁN SANABRIA SÁNCHEZ; publs *Fronteras de la Historia* (2 a year), *Revista Colombiana de Antropología* (2 a year).

Instituto Geográfico 'Agustín Codazzi' (Agustín Codazzi Geographic Institute): Carrera 30, No 48–51, Bogotá, DC; tel. (1) 3694000; e-mail cig@igac.gov.co; internet www.igac.gov.co; f. 1935; prepares topographical, cadastral, sectional, nat., and agricultural maps of the country, and geophysical, cadastral and geodetic surveys; prepares geographical studies of Colombia; library of 10,000 vols; Dir JUAN ANTONIO NIETO ESCALANTE.

MEDICINE

Instituto Nacional de Cancerología (National Cancer Institute): Calle 1, No 9–85, Bogotá, DC; tel. (1) 3341111; e-mail contactenos@cancer.gov.co; internet www.cancer.gov.co; f. 1934; diagnosis, therapy, control, teaching and research in cancer; adviser instn to Min. of Health and Social Protection, designs and implements nat. policies and programmes to control cancer; library of 26,000 vols; Dir-Gen. RAÚL HERNANDO MURILLO MORENO; publ. *Revista Colombiana de Cancerología* (4 a year).

Instituto Nacional de Salud (National Institute of Health): Avda Calle 26, No 51–20, Zona 6 CAN, Bogotá, DC; tel. (1) 2207700; e-mail contactenos@ins.gov.co; internet www.ins.gov.co; f. 1968, current name adopted 1975; attached to Min. of Health and Social Protection; library of 10,000 vols, 500 periodicals; Dir Dr MOISES WASSERMAN; publs *Biomédica* (4 a year, print and online, www.revistabiomedica.org), *Informe Quincenal de Casos y Brotes de Enfermedades* (26 a year).

NATURAL SCIENCES

Biological Sciences

Instituto de Ciencias Naturales (Institute of Natural Sciences): Universidad Nacional de Colombia Apdo 7945, Bogotá, DC; Universidad Nacional de Colombia, Ciudad Universitaria, Entrada Calle 53, Edif. 425, Bogotá, DC; tel. (1) 3165305; e-mail inscien_bog@unal.edu.co; internet www.icn.unal.edu.co; f. 1936; library of 8,000 vols; Dir Dr JAIME AGUIRRE; publs *Biblioteca José Jerónimo Triana*, *Caldasia* (2 a year), *Colombia Diversidad Biotica*, *Fauna de Colombia*, *Flora de Colombia*.

Instituto de Investigaciones Marinas y Costeras 'José Benito Vives de Andreis' (INVEMAR) (José Benito Vives de Andreis Institute of Marine and Coastal Research): Apdo Aéreo 1016, Santa Marta, Magdalena; Calle 25, No 2–55, Playa Salguero, Santa Marta, Magdalena; tel. (5) 4328600; e-mail njinvemar@invemar.org.co; internet www.invemar.org.co; f. 1963; attached to Min. of Environment; aims to study and preserve the marine wildlife of the Colombian Caribbean; library of 8,850 vols; Dir-Gen. Dr FRANCISCO ARMANDO ARIAS ISAZA; publ. *Boletín de Investigaciones Marinas y Costeras* (2 a year, print and online, www.invemar.org.co/boletin).

Physical Sciences

Observatorio Astronómico Nacional (National Astronomical Observatory): Carrera 8, Calle 8, Apdo Aéreo 2584, Bogotá, DC; tel. (1) 3165222; e-mail obsan_fcbog@unal.edu.co; internet www.observatorio.unal.edu.co; f. 1803; attached to National Univ. of Colombia; research areas: gravitation and cosmology, extragalactic astronomy (active galactic nuclei) and stellar astronomy; 2 working and 1 legacy telescopes; library of 3,000 vols; Dir Prof. MARIO ARMANDO HIGUERA GARZÓN; publs *Anuario del Observatorio*, occasional publications.

TECHNOLOGY

Instituto Colombiano del Petróleo (Colombian Petroleum Institute): El Limonal km 12 Autopista Piedecuesta, Bucaramanga, Santander; tel. (7) 6445420; e-mail portafolioicp@ecopetrol.com.co; f. 1985; exploration and devt of oil reserves; 20 laboratories; library of 27,162 vols, 145 periodical titles, 1,800 audiovisual items; Dir JAIME CADAVID CALVO; publ. *Ciencia, Tecnología y Futuro*.

Instituto Colombiano de Normas Técnicas y Certificación (ICONTEC) (Colombian Institute for Technical Standards and Certification): Carrera 37, No 52–95, Edif. ICONTEC, Bogotá, DC; tel. (1) 6078888; e-mail direccion@icontec.org; internet www.icontec.org; f. 1963; 1,200 mems; library of 800,000 vols; Exec. Dir Ing. FABIO TOBÓN; Admin. Dir RICARDO TOBO; publ. *Normas y Calidad* (4 a year).

Servicio Geológico Colombiano (Colombian Geological Service): Diagonal 53, No 34–53, Bogotá, DC; tel. (1) 2221811; e-mail cliente@sgc.gov.co; internet www.sgc.gov.co; f. 1940 as Nat. Geological Survey, current name adopted 2011; library of 6,000 vols, 104 current periodicals, 2,400 technical reports; Dir Dr MARTA LUCIA CALVACHE; publs *Revista Ingeominas al Día* (4 a year), *Revista Sucesos* (4 a year).

Libraries and Archives

Barranquilla

Biblioteca Pública Departamental Meira Delmar (Meira Delmar Public Library): Calla 38B, No 38–21, Barranquilla, Atlántico; tel. (5) 3402015; e-mail mnoriega@gobalt.gov.co; f. 1922, current name adopted 1998; 40,000 vols; Dir MYRIAM NORIEGA DIAZ.

Bello

Biblioteca del Marco Fidel Suárez (Marco Fidel Suárez Library): Calle 52A No 51–00, Bello, Antioquia; tel. (4) 2758249; e-mail bibliomfs@une.net.co; f. 1951; public library and regional centre; 25,000 vols; spec. collns on local heritage and municipal documents; Dir GUILLERMO AGUIRRE.

Bogotá

Archivo General de la Nacion Colombia (National General Archive of Colombia): Calle 24 No 5–60, 4°, Bogotá, DC; tel. (1) 3282888; e-mail contacto@archivogeneral.gov.co; internet www.archivogeneral.gov.co; f. 1868; annexe archives, colonial archives, gen. collns, govt archives, notaries, maps and plans; 40,600 vols and 3,135 m of documents; Dir Gen. CARLOS ALBERTO ZAPATA CÁRDENAS; publs *Catálogos*, *Revista*.

Biblioteca Agropecuaria de Colombia (Colombian Agricultural Library): Inst. Colombiano Agropecuario, Apdo Aéreo 240142, Santafé de Bogotá, DC; tel. (1) 4227300; e-mail bac@corpoica.org.co; internet www.corpoica.org.co; f. 1954; 46,000 vols on agriculture and livestock, 46,300 pamphlets, 1,900 journals, 29,560 documents, 170 maps, 150 audiovisual titles, 497 audio cassettes; Dir FRANCISCO SALAZAR ALONSO.

Biblioteca Alfonso Borrero Cabal, S. J. (Alfonso Borrero Cabal Library): Carrera 7A, No 41–00, Bogotá, DC; tel. (1) 3208320; e-mail biblioteca@javeriana.edu.co; internet www.javeriana.edu.co/biblos; f. 1931; attached to Pontifical Xavierian University; 287,000 vols, 3,500 rare and old books; Dir SILVIA PRADA FORERO.

Biblioteca 'Luis-Angel Arango' (Luis-Angel Arango Library): Calle 11, No 4–14, La Candelaria, Bogotá, DC; tel. (1) 3431224; e-mail wbiblio@banrep.gov.co; internet www.banrepcultural.org/blaa; f. 1932; attached to Banco de la República (Bank of the Republic); incl. Museo Botero and Museo de Artes del Banco de la Republica; 1,050,000 vols, 23,000 periodicals, 14,000 maps, 102,000 slides, 4,000 original works of art, 25,000 sound recordings, 9,000 video recordings; Dir Dr ALEXIS HJALMAR ALBERTO DE GREIFF ACEVEDO; publ. *Boletín Cultural y Bibliográfico* (3 a year).

Biblioteca Nacional de Colombia (National Library): Calle 24, No 5–60, Bogotá, DC; tel. (1) 3816464; e-mail bnc@mincultura.gov.co; internet www.bibliotecanacional.gov.co; f. 1777; 800,000 vols, 70,000 antique and rare vols, 35,000 digitized items, 22,000 periodicals, 90 incunabula; spec. Bible colln, private papers and collns, repository of publs of the Org. of American States (OAS) and the 6 organs of UN; Dir CONSUELO GAITÁN; publs *A Contratiempo; Revista de Musica en la Cultura* (2 a year, online), *Conservamos*.

Biblioteca Seminario Conciliar de San José (Library of the San José Seminary): Carrera 7 No 94–80, Bogotá, DC; tel. (1) 6440405; e-mail semmayorbogota@hotmail.com; internet www.seminariobogota.org; f. 1581; 40,000 vols specializing in philosophy and theology; Dir Rev. CESAR BARACALDO VEGA.

Dirección de Bibliotecas—Sede Bogotá, Universidad Nacional de Colombia: Carrera 30, No 45–03, Campus Universitario, Área Administrativa, Bogotá, DC; tel. (1) 3165000; e-mail bibteca_bog@unal.edu.co; internet www.biblioteca.unal.edu.co; f. 1867; 11 spec. libraries and 1 central library; 1.5m. vols; Dir JENNIFER SÁNCHEZ SALAZAR.

División de Documentación (Documentation Division): Calle 43 No 57-14, Bogotá, DC; tel. (1) 222800; e-mail njaramillo@mineducacion.gov.co; attached to Min. of Nat. Education; coordinates the Educational Documentation and Information Sub-system, the School Libraries National Programme and runs the National Educational Documentation Centre; 11,563 vols, 300 pamphlets, 6,000 documents, 300 periodicals; Dir MARY LUZ ISAZA; publs *Correo Educativo, Memorias del Ministro de Educación al Congreso Nacional* (1 a year).

Calí

Biblioteca del Centenario (The Centenary Library): Avda Colombia Calle 4 Oeste 1–16 B/El Peñón, Calí, Valle del Cauca; tel. (2) 8932908; f. 1910; 22,000 vols; Dir ORIETTA LOZANO.

Biblioteca Departamental 'Jorge Garcés Borrero' (Jorge Garcés Borrero Departmental Library): Calle 5 No 24A–91, Calí, Valle del Cauca; tel. (2) 6200400; internet www.bibliovalle.gov.co; 54,000 vols; Dir ELISA INÉS ARBOLEDA MAYORK.

Cartagena

Centro de Información y Documentación/Biblioteca Fernández de Madrid (Information and Documentation Centre): Centro Carrera 6, No 36–100, Cartagena, Bolívar; tel. (5) 6600682; e-mail biblioteca@unicartagena.edu.co; internet www.unicartagena.edu.co/index.php/biblioteca; f. 1827; attached to Univ. of Cartagena; 3 satellite libraries and 1 central library; 50,000 vols; Dir RAQUEL MIRANDA AVENDAÑO.

Manizales

Biblioteca Central, Universidad de Caldas (Central Library, University of Caldas): Calle 65 No 26-10, Manizales, Caldas; tel. (6) 8781500; e-mail ucaldas@ucaldas.edu.co; internet biblio.ucaldas.edu.co; f. 1958; 53,000 vols, 5,500 documents, 1,300 periodicals; Dir CARLOS AUGUSTO JARAMILLO PARRA.

Biblioteca Pública Municipal (Municipal Public Library): Calle 22, No 19–07, 2°, Manizales, Caldas; tel. (6) 8844495; e-mail bibliomunicipal@ctm.gov.co; f. 1931; 8,100 vols; Librarian LUISA FERNANDA ZULUAGA GÓMEZ.

Medellín

Biblioteca de la Universidad Pontificia Bolivariana (Library of the Pontifical Bolivarian University): Circular 1, No 70–01 Bloque 15, Ciudad Universitaria, Medellín, Antioquia; tel. (4) 3544582; internet bibliotecas.medellin.upb.edu.co; f. 1936; 139,000 vols, 3,000 periodicals, 12,779 pamphlets, 150,000 audiovisual records; Librarian Lic. OLGA BEATRIZ BERNAL LONDOÑO.

Biblioteca Pública Piloto de Medellín para América Latina (Medellín Pilot Public Library for Latin America): Carrera 64, No 50–32, Medellín, Antioquia; tel. (4) 4600590; e-mail comunicaciones@bibliotecapiloto.gov.co; internet www.bibliotecapiloto.gov.co; f. 1952; 85,000 vols; spec. collns: Antioquia and Antioquian authors, UNESCO depository; Dir-Gen. GLORIA INÉS PALOMINO LONDOÑO.

Sistema de Bibliotecas, Universidad de Antioquia: Calle 67 No 53–108, Bloque 8, Ciudad Universitaria, Medellín, Antioquia; tel. (4) 2195151; e-mail comunicaciones@biblioteca.udea.edu.co; internet biblioteca.udea.edu.co; f. 1935; 16 br. libraries; 758,621 vols, 127,720 ebooks and ejournals; Coordinator for Libraries RAÚL PALMA ARANGO; publs *Ex-Libris* (4 a year), *Leer y Releer* (4 a year).

Popayán

División de Bibliotecas, Universidad del Cauca (Division of Libraries, University of Cauca): Carrera 2A, No 3N–111, Popayán, Cauca; tel. (2) 8209900; e-mail biblios@unicauca.edu.co; internet biblio.unicauca.edu.co; f. 1827; 140,000 vols, 250 titles of periodicals; microfiche, dissertations and theses, maps, cassettes, CD-ROMs, photographs; Dir MIRYAM TORRES LONDONO; publs *Boletín Bibliográfico, Boletín del Comité de Investigaciones Científicas, Cuadernos de Medicina, Revista Cátedra*.

Tunja

Universidad Pedagógica y Tecnológica de Colombia, Biblioteca Central 'Jorge Palacios Preciado' (Jorge Palacios Preciado Central Library, Pedagogical and Technological University of Colombia): Apdo Aéreo 1234, Tunja, Boyacá; tel. (8) 7424020; e-mail adquisiciones.biblioteca@uptc.edu.co; f. 1932; 68,000 vols, 1,800 periodical titles; spec. collns: theses, Fondo E. Posada, rare books, learned works; Dir LUZ ELIANA MARQUEZ BARRERA.

Museums and Art Galleries

Bogotá

Casa Museo 'Jorge Eliécer Gaitán' (Jorge Eliécer Gaitán Memorial Museum): Calle 42, No 15–52, Barrio Santa Teresita, Bogotá; tel. (1) 6044747; e-mail casagaitan@unal.edu.co; f. 1948; attached to National Univ. of Colombia since 2005; colln on history of Bogotá; Dir GLORIA GAITÁN.

Casa Museo Quinta de Bolívar (Bolívar House-Museum): Calle 20, No 2–91 Este, Bogotá; tel. (1) 3366419; e-mail quintabolivar@mincultura.gov.co; internet www.quintadebolivar.gov.co; f. 1919; exhibits relics of Simon Bolivar and his epoch; Dir DANIEL CASTRO BENÍTEZ.

Jardín Botánico de Bogotá 'José Celestino Mutis' (José Celestino Mutis Botanical Gardens of Bogotá): Avda Calle 63, No 68–95, Bogotá, DC; tel. (1) 4377060; e-mail contactenos@jbb.gov.co; internet www.jbb.gov.co; f. 1955; research and conservation of biodiversity in the Andean ecosystem; library of 6,500 vols; Dir LUIS OLMEDO MARTÍNEZ ZAMORA; Librarian OSCAR MAURICIO OVALLE NAVARRO; publ. *Pérez-Arbelaezia* (2 a year).

Museo Colonial (Colonial Museum): Carrera 6, No 9–77, Bogotá, DC; tel. (1) 3416017; e-mail museocolonial@mincultura.gov.co; internet www.museocolonial.gov.co; f. 1942; paintings, sculpture, furniture, gold and silver work, drawings of the Spanish colonial period; library of 1,000 vols in education dept; Dir CONSTANZA TOQUICA CLAVIJO; Curator JUAN PABLO CRUZ; publ. *Cuadernos de Estudio* (1 a year).

Museo del Oro del Banco de la República (Gold Museum): Carrera 6 No 15-88, Parque de Santander, Bogotá, DC; tel. (1) 3432222; e-mail wmuseo@banrep.gov.co; internet www.banrepcultural.org/museo-del-oro; f. 1939; 50,000 pre-Columbian gold objects representing the gods, myths and customs of the Quimbaya, Muisca, Tairona and other native Indian cultures of ancient Colombia; Dir MARÍA ALICIA URIBE VILLEGAS.

Museo Nacional de Colombia (National Museum of Colombia): Carrera 7, No 28–66, Bogotá, DC; tel. (1) 3816470; e-mail info@museonacional.gov.co; internet www.museonacional.gov.co; f. 1823; archaeology, art, ethnology, history since Spanish conquest; collns of portraits, arms, banners, medals, coins, ceramics, fine arts; theatre; exhibition gallery; Dir MARÍA VICTORIA DE ANGULO DE ROBAYO.

Medellín

Museo de Ciencias Naturales del Colegio de San José (Natural Science Museum): Calle 54A No 30–01, Medellín, Antioquia; tel. (4) 4600727; e-mail museodecienciasnaturales@itm.edu.co; f. 1913; natural history in general, zoology, botany, mineralogy, anthropology; library of 500 vols and 1,000 periodicals; Dir LUIS ALBERTO ZAMUDIO D.; publs *Avancemos* (12 a year), *Boletín Cultural* (4 a year).

Museo Filatélico del Banco de la República (Philatelic Museum of the Bank of the Republic): Edif. Banco de la República, Parque de Berrió, Medellín, Antioquia; tel. (4) 5767400; e-mail grincogo@banrep.gov.co; f. 1977; collns of Colombian postage stamps, and stamps from other countries; Dir GONZALO RINCÓN GÓMEZ; publ. *Revista*.

Museo Universitario (University Museum): Apdo Aéreo 1226, Medellín, Antioquia; Calle 67 No 53–108, Bloque 15, Medellín, Antioquia; tel. (4) 2195180; e-mail museo@quimbaya.udea.edu.co; internet museo.udea.edu.co; f. 1970 by merging Museo de Ciencias Naturales (f. 1942) and Museo de Antropología (f. 1943); sections: anthropology, natural sciences, univ. history, visual arts; interactive exhibition; Dir BAIRO ALBERTO MARTÍNEZ PARRA; publ. *Códice* (3 a year).

Roldanillo

Museo Rayo/Museo de Dibujo y Grabado Latinoamericano (Rayo Museum): Calle 8, No 8–53, Roldanillo, Valle del Cauca; tel. (92) 2298623; e-mail info@museorayo.co; internet www.museorayo.co; f. 1976, opened 1981; run by Fundación Museo Rayo; specializes in modern works on or with paper, generally graphic art and design, by Latin American artists or those working in Latin America; spec. colln of Omar Rayo; library of 2,003 vols; Dir AGUEDA PIZARRO RAYO; Curator MIGUEL GONZALEZ; publ. *Ediciones Embalaje*.

Universities

PONTIFICIA UNIVERSIDAD JAVERIANA
(Pontifical Javierian University)

Carrera 7 No 40–62, Bogotá, DC
Telephone: (1) 3208320
E-mail: puj@javeriana.edu.co
Internet: www.javeriana.edu.co

Founded 1622, re-established 1931, current name adopted 1937
Academic year: January to November (2 semesters)

Grand Chancellor: Fr ADOLFO NICOLÁS
Vice-Grand Chancellor: Fr FRANCISCO DE ROUX
Rector: Fr JOAQUÍN EMILIO SÁNCHEZ GARCÍA
Vice-Rector for Academic Affairs: Fr VICENTE DURÁN CASAS
Vice-Rector for Admin.: Ing. ROBERTO ENRIQUE MONTOYA VILLA
Vice-Rector for Extension: LUIS FERNANDO ÁLVAREZ LONDOÑO
Vice-Rector for Research: URIBE MALLARINO
Vice-Rector for Univ. Affairs: ANTONIO JOSÉ SARMIENTO NOVA
Rector for Calí Section: Fr JOAQUÍN SÁNCHEZ
Sec. Gen.: JAIRO HUMBERTO CIFUENTES MADRID

Library: see under Libraries and Archives
Number of teachers: 3,958
Number of students: 28,611

Publications: *Ambiente y Desarrollo* (2 a year), *Cuadernos de Administración* (2 a year), *Cuadernos de Desarrollo Rural* (2 a year), *Cuadernos de Literatura* (2 a year), *Ingeniería y Universidad* (2 a year), *International Law* (2 a year), *Memoria y Sociedad* (2 a year), *Papel Político* (2 a year), *Revista de la Maestría en Derecho Económico* (1 a year), *Revista Iberolatinoamericana de Seguros* (2 a year), *Signo y Pensamiento* (2 a year), *Theologica Xaveriana* (2 a year), *Universitas Canonica* (1 a year), *Universitas Humanistica* (2 a year), *Universitas Médica* (4 a year), *Universitas Odontologica* (2 a year), *Universitas Philosophica* (2 a year), *Universitas Psychologica* (3 a year), *Universitas Scientiarum* (3 a year), *Vniversitas: Revista de Ciencias Juridicas* (2 a year)

DEANS

Faculty of Architecture and Design: GIOVANNI FERRONI DEL VALLE
Faculty of Arts: LEONOR CONVERS
Faculty of Canon Law: Dr ISMAEL ARTURO GARCERANTH RAMOS
Faculty of Communication and Language: JOSÉ VICENTE ARISMENDI
Faculty of Dentistry: Dr DANIEL HENAO PÉREZ
Faculty of Economic and Administrative Sciences: GUSTAVO TOBÓN LONDOÑO
Faculty of Economic and Administrative Sciences (in Calí): Dr BERNARDO BARONA
Faculty of Education: CARLOS GAITÁN RIVEROS
Faculty of Engineering: Ing. JORGE LUIS SÁNCHEZ TÉLLEZ
Faculty of Engineering (in Calí): Dr JORGE FRANCISCO ESTELA
Faculty of Environmental and Rural Studies: LUIS ALBERTO VILLA DURÁN
Faculty of Humanities and Social Sciences (in Calí): Dr ESTEBAN OCAMPO
Faculty of Law: Fr CARLOS IGNACIO JARAMILLO JARAMILLO
Faculty of Medicine: Dra MARY BERMÚDEZ GÓMEZ
Faculty of Nursing: LUZ STELLA MEDINA MATALLANA
Faculty of Philosophy: DIEGO PINEDA
Faculty of Political Sciences and International Relations: Fr EDWIN MURILLO AMARIS
Faculty of Psychology: BLANCA PATRICIA BALLESTEROS DE VALDERRAMA
Faculty of Sciences: INGRID SCHULER
Faculty of Social Sciences: GERMÁN MEJÍA PAVONY
Faculty of Theology: Fr HERMANN RODRÍGUEZ OSORIO
Department of Languages: Dra NELLY ESPERANZA TORRES

UNIVERSIDAD AUTÓNOMA DE BUCARAMANGA
(Autonomous University of Bucaramanga)

Avda 42, No 48–11, Bucaramanga, Santander
Telephone: (7) 6436111
Internet: www.unab.edu.co

Founded 1952
Private control
Language of instruction: Spanish
Academic year: January to November

Pres.: Dr ALBERTO MONTOYA PUYANA
Vice-Pres. for Academic Affairs: Dra EULALIA GARCÍA BELTRÁN
Vice-Pres. for Admin.: Dr GILBERTO RAMÍREZ VALBUENA
Dir of Int. Relations: MARIA T. CAMARGO
Librarian: ELENA UVAROVA

Library of 65,700 vols, 3,100 journals
Number of teachers: 500
Number of students: 7,400

Publications: *Revista Colombiana de Computación* (2 a year), *Revista Colombiana de Marketing* (2 a year), *Revista Cuestiones*, *Revista Estr@do* (2 a year, online), *Revista Medunab* (3 a year), *Revista Prospectiva*, *Revista Reflexión Política* (2 a year), *Revista Temas Socio-Jurídicos* (2 a year)

DEANS

Faculty of Business Administration: JUAN CARLOS HEDERICH MARTÍNEZ
Faculty of Communication and Audiovisual Arts: SANTIAGO HUMBERTO GOMEZ MEJIA
Faculty of Economics and Accountancy: FERNANDO CHAPARRO GARCIA
Faculty of Education: ALHIM ADONAI VERA SILVA
Faculty of Engineering Management: LUZ STELLA RUEDA CADENA
Faculty of Health: LUZ MARINA CORSO MORALES
Faculty of Law: JORGE EDUARDO LAMO GOMEZ
Faculty of Mechanical and Electronic Engineering: GERMAN OLIVEROS VILLAMIZAR
Faculty of Music: MAGNOLIA SANCHEZ MEJIA
Faculty of Systems Engineering: WILSON BRICEÑO PINEDA
Faculty of Technical and Technological Studies: YANETH ROCIO ORELLANA HERNANDEZ

UNIVERSIDAD AUTÓNOMA LATINOAMERICANA
(Latin American Autonomous University)

Carrera 55, No 49–51, Medellín, Antioquia
Telephone: (4) 5112199
E-mail: vicerectoria@unaula.edu.co
Internet: www.unaula.edu.co

Founded 1966
Private control
Language of instruction: Spanish
Academic year: February to November

Pres.: Dr ORLANDO GÓMEZ GÓMEZ
Rector: Dr JOSÉ RODRIGO FLÓREZ RUIZ
Vice-Rector for Academic Affairs: Dr RICARDO ANÍBAL VÉLEZ MUÑOZ
Vice-Rector for Admin.: Dr ALFONSO TITO MEJÍA RESTREPO
Sec. Gen.: Dr ÁLVARO VELÁSQUEZ ORTIZ
Librarian: Dr ALONSO GUILLERMO MERINO G.

Number of teachers: 250
Number of students: 2,000

Publications: *Actividad Contable* (1 a year), *Apuntes de Economía* (1 a year), *Círculo de Humanidades* (4 a year), *Ratio Juris* (2 a year), *Revista Unaula* (1 a year), *Sociología* (1 a year), *Visión Autónoma* (2 a year)

DEANS

Faculty of Accountancy: Dr JORGE ALBERTO SÁNCHEZ GIRALDO
Faculty of Economics: Dr ÁLVARO JAVIER CORREA VÉLEZ
Faculty of Education and Social Sciences: Dr FERNANDO CORTÉS GUTIÉRREZ
Faculty of Engineering: Dr LUIS ALBERTO HERRERA RODRÍGUEZ
Faculty of Law: Dr FERNANDO SALAZAR MEJÍA
Faculty of Postgraduate Studies: Dr HÉCTOR ORTIZ CAÑAS (Dir)

UNIVERSIDAD CATÓLICA DE MANIZALES
(Catholic University of Manizales)

Carrera 23 No 60–63, Manizales, Caldas
Telephone: (6) 8782900
E-mail: direxco@ucm.edu.co
Internet: www.ucm.edu.co

Founded 1954
Private control
Language of instruction: Spanish
Academic year: February to November (2 semesters)

Rector: Sis. GLORIA DEL CARMEN TORRES BUSTAMANTE
Vice-Rector for Academic Affairs: CARLOS EDUARDO GARCÍA LÓPEZ
Vice-Rector for Admin. and Finance: Sis. MARÍA JARAMILLO LÓPEZ
Vice-Rector for Univ. Welfare: GABRIEL ANDRÉS CIFUENTES GALLO
Dir for Finance: DIEGO ÁLVAREZ LEÓN
Dir for Human Resources: Sis. MARIELA HERNÁNDEZ GUZMÁN
Dir for Planning: CAROLINA OLAYA ALZATE
Sec. Gen.: Sis. ANA BELÉN PRADA MACÍAS
Library Coordinator: GRISEL RAMOS PINEDA

Number of teachers: 250
Number of students: 2,600

Publications: *Protocolo*, *Revista de Investigaciones*

DEANS

Faculty of Education: Sis. LUZ MERY CHAVERRA RODRÍGUEZ
Faculty of Engineering and Architecture: JHON JAIRO ANGEL HERNÁNDEZ
Faculty of Health Sciences: Sis. GLORIA ESTELA ROLÓN DÍAZ
Faculty of Humanities, Social Sciences and Administration: Sis. MARÍA AMANDA TANGARIFE RODRÍGUEZ

UNIVERSIDAD CATÓLICA DE PEREIRA
(Catholic University of Pereira)

Carrera 21 No 49–95, Avda de las Américas, Pereira, Risaralda
Telephone: (6) 3124000
E-mail: ucpr@ucpr.edu.co
Internet: www.ucp.edu.co

Founded 1975
Private control
Language of instruction: Spanish
Academic year: January to November

Rector: Fr ALVARO EDUARDO BETANCUR JIMÉNEZ

Vice-Rector for Academic Affairs: LUIS EDUARDO PELÁEZ VALENCIA
Dir for Admin. and Finance: CLAUDIA MILENA RODAS CADAVID
Sec. Gen.: JOSÉ FREDY ARISTIZABAL
Library Dir: JUDITH GÓMEZ GÓMEZ
Number of teachers: 300
Number of students: 2,300
Publication: *Páginas de la UCPR* (5 a year)

DEANS
Faculty of Architecture and Design: MIGUEL ÁNGEL VELA ROCERO
Faculty of Basic Sciences and Engineering: JUAN LUIS ARIAS VARGAS
Faculty of Economics and Business Administration: NELSON LONDOÑO PINEDA
Faculty of Humanities, Social Sciences and Education: OLGA PATRICIA BONILLA

UNIVERSIDAD CENTRAL
(Central University)

Carrera 5, No 21–38, Bogotá, DC
Telephone: (1) 3239868
E-mail: webpage@ucentral.edu.co
Internet: www.ucentral.edu.co
Founded 1966
Private control
Language of instruction: Spanish
Academic year: January to December
Rector: Dr RAFAEL SANTOS CALDERÓN
Vice-Rector for Academic Affairs: Dr LIGIA ECHEVERRI ÁNGEL
Vice-Rector for Admin. and Finance: Dr NELSON GNECCO IGLESIAS
Sec. Gen.: Dr FABIO RAÚL TROMPA AYALA
Library Dir: YOLANDA GARCÍA
Number of teachers: 700
Number of students: 12,000
Publications: *Cuadernos del Cine Club* (2 a year), *Hojas Universitarias* (2 a year), *Magazin Mercadológico* (2 a year), *Nómadas* (2 a year), *NotiCentral* (4 a year)

DEANS
Faculty of Administrative Sciences, Economics and Accounting: GERMÁN UMAÑA MENDOZA
Faculty of Engineering: JULIO MARIO RODRÍGUEZ DEVIS
Faculty of Social Sciences, Humanities and Arts: GLORIA ALVARADO FORERO

UNIVERSIDAD DE ANTIOQUIA
(University of Antioquia)

Calle 70, 52–21, Apdo Aéreo 1226, Medellín, Antioquia
Telephone: (4) 2195000
E-mail: rectoria@udea.edu.co
Internet: www.udea.edu.co
Founded 1803
State control
Languages of instruction: English, French, German, Spanish
Academic year: January to November
Rector: ALBERTO URIBE CORREA
Gen. Vice-Rector: JOHN JAIRO ARBOLEDA CÉSPEDES
Vice-Rector for Academic Affairs: JUAN CARLOS AMAYA CASTRILLÓN
Vice-Rector for Admin.: RUBÉN ALBERTO AGUDELO GARCÍA
Vice-Rector for Extension: MARÍA HELENA VIVAS LÓPEZ
Vice-Rector for Research: FANOR MONDRAGÓN PÉREZ
Sec. Gen.: LUQUEGI GIL NEIRA
Librarian: MARÍA TERESA ARBELAEZ GARCES
Library: see under Libraries and Archives
Number of teachers: 6,512
Number of students: 37,752 (35,360 undergraduate, 2,006 postgraduate, 386 doctoral)
Publications: *Diálogos de Derecho y Política* (3 a year), *Estudios de Literatura Colombiana* (2 a year), *Iatreia* (4 a year), *Lecturas de Economia* (2 a year, in Spanish and English), *Revista Estudios de Derecho* (2 a year), *Revista Facultad de Ingeniería* (4 a year), *Revista Interamericana de Bibliotecología* (3 a year), *Revista Universidad de Antioquia* (4 a year), *Versiones* (2 a year)

DEANS
Faculty of Agricultural Sciences: LUIS GUILLERMO PALACIO BAENA
Faculty of Arts: CLARA MÓNICA ZAPATA JARAMILLO
Faculty of Communications: DAVID HERNÁNDEZ GARCÍA
Faculty of Dentistry: Dra CLARA EUGENIA ESCOBAR GÜENDICA
Faculty of Economics: RAMÓN JAVIER MESA CALLEJAS
Faculty of Education: CARLOS ARTURO SOTO LOMBANA
Faculty of Engineering: CARLOS ALBERTO PALACIO TOBÓN
Faculty of Exact and Natural Sciences: NORA EUGENIA RESTREPO SÁNCHEZ
Faculty of Law and Political Science: CLEMENCIA URIBE RESTREPO
Faculty of Medicine: ELMER GAVIRIA RIVERA
Faculty of Nursing: SANDRA CATALINA OCHOA MARÍN
Faculty of Pharmaceutical Chemistry: JUAN CARLOS ALARCÓN PÉREZ
Faculty of Social and Human Sciences: GLORIA PATRICIA PELÁEZ JARAMILLO
Institute of Philosophy: Dr FRANCISCO (Dir)
Institute of Physical Education and Sports: GLORIA MARIA CASTEÑADA CLAVIJO (Dir)
Institute of Political Studies: Profa ADRIANA MARÍA GONZÁLEZ GIL (Dir)
Institute of Regional Studies: CLAUDIA PATRICIA PUERTA SILVA (Dir)
Inter-American School of Librarianship: MARIA TERESA ARBELÁEZ GARCÉS (Dir)
National Faculty of Public Health: MARÍA PATRICIA ARBELÁEZ MONTOYA
School of Languages: JOHN JAIRO GIRALDO ORTIZ (Dir)
School of Microbiology: LILIANA MARCELA OCHOA GALEANO (Dir)
School of Nutrition and Dietetics: BERTA LUCÍA GAVIRIA GÓMEZ (Dir)

UNIVERSIDAD DE BOGOTÁ 'JORGE TADEO LOZANO'
(Jorge Tadeo Lozano University of Bogotá)

Apdo Aéreo 34185, Carrera 4, No 22–61, Bogotá, DC
Telephone: (1) 2427030
E-mail: btadeo12@andinet.lat.net
Internet: www.utadeo.edu.co
Founded 1954
Private control
Language of instruction: Spanish
Academic year: February to December (2 semesters)
Pres.: GUILLERMO RUEDA MONTAÑA
Rector: CECILIA MARÍA VÉLEZ WHITE
Vice-Rector for Academic Affairs: DIÓGENES CAMPOS ROMERO
Vice-Rector for Admin.: NOHEMY ARIAS OTERO
Sec. Gen.: CARLOS SÁNCHEZ GAITÁN
Dir for Research, Creativity and Innovation: RAFAEL ORDUZ MEDINA
Library Dir: MARIA CONSUELO MONCADA
Library of 132,647 vols
Number of teachers: 1,000
Number of students: 11,500
Publications: *Agenda Cultural*, *Ecotropica*, *La Tadeo*, *Tadeísta*

DEANS
Faculty of Arts and Design: ALBERTO SALDARRIAGA ROA
Faculty of Economic and Administrative Sciences: SALOMÓN KALMANOVITZ KRAUTER
Faculty of Natural Sciences and Engineering: ISAAC DYNER REZONZEW
Faculty of Social Sciences: JORGE ORLANDO MELO GONZÁLEZ

UNIVERSIDAD DE CALDAS
(University of Caldas)

Calle 65 No 26–10, Apdo Aéreo 275, Manizales, Caldas
Telephone: (6) 8781500
E-mail: ucaldas@ucaldas.edu.co
Internet: www.ucaldas.edu.co
Founded 1943
State control
Languages of instruction: English, Spanish
Academic year: February to December (2 semesters)
Rector: RICARDO GÓMEZ GIRALDO
Vice-Rector for Academic Affairs: LUZ AMALIA RIOS VASQUEZ
Vice-Rector for Admin.: FABIO HERNANDO ARIAS OROZCO
Vice-Rector for Community Relations: FANNY OSORIO GIRALDO
Vice-Rector for Research and Postgraduate Affairs: CARLOS EMILIO GARCÍA DUQUE
Sec. Gen.: FERNANDO DUQUE GARCÍA
Librarian: HECTOR MARIO CASTILLO
Library: see under Libraries and Archives
Number of teachers: 488
Number of students: 3,620
Publications: *Agronomía* (2 a year, print and online, agronomia.ucaldas.edu.co), *Altamira* (1 a year), *Biosalud* (1 a year, print and online, biosalud.ucaldas.edu.co), *Boletín Científico Museo de Historia* (1 a year), *Cuadernos Filósofos Literarios* (1 a year), *Cultura y Droga* (1 a year, print and online, culturaydroga.ucaldas.edu.co), *Revista Colombiana de las Artes Escénicas* (2 a year), *Revista Luna Azul* (2 a year), *Revista Vector* (1 a year, print and online, vector.ucaldas.edu.co), *Virajes: Revista e Antropología ySociología* (1 a year, print and online, virajes.ucaldas.edu.co)

DEANS
Faculty of Agricultural Sciences: CARLOS ALBERTO PARRA SALINAS
Faculty of Arts and Humanities: ORLANDO LONDOÑO BETANCOURT
Faculty of Engineering: Dr CARLOS ALBERTO RUIZ VILLA
Faculty of Exact and Natural Sciences: WILLIAM ARISTIZÁBAL BOTERO
Faculty of Health Sciences: Dr DOLLY MAGNOLIA GONZALEZ HOYOS
Faculty of Juridical and Social Sciences: Dra JAVIER GONZAGA VALENCIA HERNÁNDEZ

UNIVERSIDAD DE CARTAGENA
(University of Cartagena)

Apdo Aéreo 1382, Cartagena, Bolívar
Telephone: (59) 654480
E-mail: comunicaciones@unicartagena.edu.co
Internet: www.unicartagena.edu.co
Founded 1827
State control
Language of instruction: Spanish
Academic year: February to December
Rector: Dr GERMÁN ARTURO SIERRA ANAYA
Vice-Rector for Academic Affairs: Dr EDGAR PARRA CHACÓN

Vice-Rector for Admin.: Dr Robinson Mena Robles
Vice-Rector for Research: Jesús Tadeo Olivero Verbel
Sec. Gen.: Marly Mardini Llamas
Central Library Dir: Raquel Miranda Avendaño

Library: see under Libraries and Archives
Number of teachers: 600
Number of students: 4,300

Publications: *Prospecto Universidad*, *Revista Ciencia*, *Revista Facultad de Economía*, *Revista Facultad de Medicina*, *Tecnología y Educación*

DEANS

Faculty of Dentistry: Dra Luisa Leonor Arevalo Tovar
Faculty of Economics: Dr Raúl Quejada Pérez
Faculty of Engineering: Dr Ramón Torres Ortega
Faculty of Exact and Natural Sciences: Dr Rafael Galeano Andrades
Faculty of Humanities: Dr Federico Gallego Vásquez
Faculty of Law and Political Science: Dra Josefina Quintero Lyons
Faculty of Medicine: Dra Elizabeth López Rivas
Faculty of Nursing: Dra Amparo Montalvo Prieto
Faculty of Pharmaceutical Science: Dr Gabriel Acevedo del Río
Faculty of Social Sciences and Education: Dra Ana Pombo Gallardo

UNIVERSIDAD DE CÓRDOBA
(University of Córdoba)

Carrera 6 No 76–103, Montería, Córdoba
Telephone: (4) 7860151
E-mail: contacto@unicordoba.edu.co
Internet: www.unicordoba.edu.co

Founded 1964
State control
Language of instruction: Spanish
Academic year: February to December

Rector: Dra Alba Manuela Durango Villadiego
Vice-Rector for Academic Affairs: Dr Omar Pérez Sierraz
Sec.: Dra María Virginia Lorduy Villarreal
Library Dir: Julio Alvarez

Number of teachers: 900 (400 full-time, 500 part-time)
Number of students: 11,355

Publications: *Revista Facultad Ciencias de la Salud*, *Revista MVZ Córdoba* (3 a year, print and online, revistas.unicordoba.edu.co/revistamvz), *Revista Temas Agrarios* (2 a year, print and online, revistas.unicordoba.edu.co/rta), *Rio* (print and online, www.unicordoba.edu.co/revistas/revistario)

DEANS

Faculty of Agricultural Sciences: Dr Juan Jaraba Navas
Faculty of Basic Sciences: Dr Nicolás de la Espriella Vélez
Faculty of Education and Humanities: Dr Felix Santana Lobo
Faculty of Engineering: Dr Daniel José Salas Álvarez
Faculty of Health Sciences: Dra Hiltony Villa Dangond
Faculty of Veterinary Medicine and Animal Husbandry: Dr Lázaro Reza García

UNIVERSIDAD DE CUNDINAMARCA
(University of Cundinamarca)

Diagonal 18 No 20–29, Fusagasugá, Cundinamarca
Telephone: (91) 8732512
E-mail: unicundi@mail.unicundi.edu.co
Internet: www.unicundi.edu.co

Founded 1969
State control
Language of instruction: Spanish
Academic year: April to June

Rector: Dr Adolfo Miguel Polo Solano
Vice-Rector for Academic Affairs: Dr Rogelio Rigual Collado
Vice-Rector for Admin. and Finance: Ing. Reinaldo Camacho Castellanos
Dir for Institutional Planning: Dr Efrain Cruz Fiscal
Sec. Gen.: Adriano Muñoz Barrera
Library Coordinator: Ana Milena Cobos Rodríguez

DEANS

Faculty of Agricultural Sciences: Marco Eduardo Pachón Suarez
Faculty of Business Administration, Economics and Accountancy: Hernán José Romero Rincón
Faculty of Education: Cesar Julio Zabala Archila
Faculty of Engineering: Jorge Luis Reales Sánchez
Faculty of Health Sciences: Rogelio Rigual Collado
Faculty of Social Sciences, Humanities and Political Science: Gonzalo Escobar Reyes
Faculty of Sports Sciences: Edwin Alzate Baron
School of Postgraduate Studies: José del Carmen Correa Alfonso

UNIVERSIDAD DE LA AMAZONIA
(University of the Amazon)

Carrera 3F, Barrio Porvenir, Florencia, Caquetá
Telephone: (8) 4358786
E-mail: rectoria@uniamazonia.edu.co
Internet: www.uniamazonia.edu.co

Founded 1971 as Instituto Tecnológico Universidad Surcolombiana, current name and status 1982
State control
Language of instruction: Spanish

Rector: Leonidas Rico Martínez
Vice-Rector for Academic Affairs: Edwin Eduardo Millán Rojas
Vice-Rector for Admin.: Alicia Correa Hurtado
Vice-Rector for Research and Postgraduate Affairs: Alberto Fajardo Oliveros
Sec. Gen.: Juan Carlos Galindo Alvarado
Librarian: Liliana María Pérez Sierra
Number of students: 4,000

DEANS

Faculty of Accountancy, Economics and Administration: Diana Ali Garcia Capdevilla
Faculty of Agricultural Sciences: Gustavo Adolfo Celis Parra
Faculty of Basic Sciences: Marco Aurelio Múnera
Faculty of Education: Silvio Muñoz Cuéllar
Faculty of Engineering: Angelica Maria Antia Solano
Faculty of Law and Political Sciences: Elizabeth Meza Areiza

UNIVERSIDAD DE LA GUAJIRA
(University of the Guajira)

Km 5, Vía Maicao, Riohacha, La Guajira
Telephone: (5) 7282729
Internet: www.uniguajira.edu.co

Founded 1976
State control
Academic year: February to July, August to November

Rector: Ing. Carlos Arturo Robles Julio
Vice-Rector: Rosalba Cuesta López
Chief Admin. Officer: Cristóbal Vega Gutiérrez
Librarian: Marinela Mengual Meza

Number of teachers: 107
Number of students: 1,258

Publications: *Revista Universidad de La Guajira*, *WOUMMAINPA*

DEANS

Faculty of Basic and Applied Sciences: Geomar Enrique Molina Bolivar
Faculty of Economics and Business Administration: Edilma Frias Acosta
Faculty of Education: José Clemente Martínez
Faculty of Engineering: Jairo Salcedo Davila
Faculty of Social Sciences: Erotida Mejía Curiel

UNIVERSIDAD DE LA SABANA
(Sabana University)

Km 7, Autopista Norte de Bogotá D.C., Apdo Aéreo 53753, Chía, Cundinamarca
Telephone: (1) 8615555
E-mail: universidad.de.la.sabana@unisabana.edu.co
Internet: www.unisabana.edu.co

Founded 1979
Private control
Languages of instruction: English, Spanish
Academic year: February to November

Faculties of communication, education, engineering, law and political science, medicine, nursing and rehabilitation, philosophy and humanities, psychology; international business management school

Chancellor: Javier Echevarría Rodríguez
Rector: Obdulio Velásquez Posada
Vice-Rector for Academic Affairs: María Clara Quintero Laverde
Vice-Rector for Outreach and Devt: Mauricio Rojas Pérez
Vice-Rector for Teachers and Students: Liliana Ospina de Guerrero
Sec.-Gen.: Rolando Roncancio Rachid

Library of 110,895 vols, 131,539 ebooks, 775 periodical titles, 1,335 audiovisual items
Number of teachers: 500
Number of students: 8,900

Publications: *Pensamiento y Cultura* (1 a year), *Persona y Bioética* (1 a year)

UNIVERSIDAD DE LA SALLE
(La Salle University)

Carrera 5 No 59A–44, Bogotá, DC
Telephone: (1) 3488000
E-mail: relainter@lasalle.edu.co
Internet: www.lasalle.edu.co

Founded 1964
Private control
Language of instruction: Spanish
Academic year: February to May

Rector: Carlos Gómez Restrepò
Vice-Rector for Academic Affairs: Carlos Enrique Carvajal Costa
Vice-Rector for Admin.: Dr Eduardo Ángel Reyes
Vice-Rector for Promotion and Human Devt: Bro. Frank Leonardo Ramos Baquero
Vice-Rector for Research and Transfer: Dr Luis Fernando Ramírez Hernández
Librarian: Dr Napoleón Muñoz Neda

Number of teachers: 1,000
Number of students: 15,120 (14,420 undergraduate and 700 postgraduate)
Publications: *Ciencia Animal*, *Ensayo en Administración*, *Reflejos*

DEANS

Faculty of Administrative Sciences and Accountancy: Dr GONZALO TRUJILLO ECHEVERRI
Faculty of Agricultural Sciences: Dra CLAUDIA AIXA MUTIS BARRETO
Faculty of Economic and Social Sciences: Dr ADRIANA PATRICIA LÓPEZ VELÁSQUEZ
Faculty of Educational Sciences: Dra LUZ AMPARO MARTÍNEZ R.
Faculty of Engineering: Ing. CARLOS R. COSTA POSADA
Faculty of Health Sciences: JAIRO GARCÍA TOUCHIE
Faculty of Housing Sciences: LILIANA GIRALDO ARIAS
Faculty of Philosophy and Humanities: MERY CASTILLO

UNIVERSIDAD DEL ATLÁNTICO
(University of Atlántico)

Km 7 Vía Puerto Colombia, Barranquilla, Atlántico
Telephone: (5) 3599458
E-mail: rector@mail.uniatlantico.edu.co
Internet: www.uniatlantico.edu.co
Founded 1941
Rector: ANA SOFÍA MESA DE CUERVO
Vice-Rector for Admin. and Finance: FREDDY A. DÍAZ MENDOZA
Sec. Gen.: ROBERTO NORIEGA
Librarian: EDUARDO PINZON
Number of teachers: 845
Number of students: 17,910
Publications: *Cuadernos de Literatura del Caribe e Hispanoamérica*, *Economía*, *Historia Caribe*

DEANS

Faculty of Architecture: WILSON ANNICHIARICCO
Faculty of Economics: FERNANDO CABARCAS CHARRIS
Faculty of Education: JANETH TOVAR GUERRA
Faculty of Fine Arts: GUILLERMO CARBO RONDEROS
Faculty of Law and Political Science: GUILLERMO CARBO RONDEROS
Faculty of Nutrition and Dietetics: SONIA SAAVEDRA ARENAS
Faculty of Pharmacy and Chemistry: CLARA FAY VARGAS LASCARRO

UNIVERSIDAD DEL CAUCA
(University of Cauca)

Claustro de Santo Domingo, Calle 5 No 4–70, de Popayán, Cauca
Telephone: (2) 8209900
E-mail: rectoria@ucauca.edu.co
Internet: www.unicauca.edu.co
Founded 1827
State control
Language of instruction: Spanish
Academic year: January to December
Rector: Dr JUAN DIEGO CASTRILLÓN ORREGO
Vice-Rector for Academic Affairs: Dr EDUARDO ROJAS PINEDA
Vice-Rector for Admin.: Dr LUIS CARLOS AYALA CALDAS
Vice-Rector for Culture and Welfare: Mag. TERESA ELIZABETH MUÑOZ ÑÁÑEZ
Vice-Rector for Research: Dr HUGO ALDEMAR COSME VARGAS
Sec. Gen.: LAURA ISMENIA CASTELLANOS VIVAS
Library Dir: MIRYAM TORRES LONDONO
Library: see under Libraries and Archives
Number of teachers: 600
Number of students: 7,000
Publications: *Consentido* (2 a year, print and online, www.consentido.unicauca.edu.co), *Revista Novedades Colombianas* (irregular, print and online, museo.unicauca.edu.co/revistas)

DEANS

Faculty of Accountancy Sciences, Economics and Administration: Mag. ALEJANDRA MILLER RESTREPO
Faculty of Agricultural Sciences: Dr JOSÉ MANUEL TOBAR MESA
Faculty of Arts: GERMÁN ANTONIO TEJEDA PUENTES
Faculty of Civil Engineering: Dr JULIO CÉSAR DIAGO FRANCO
Faculty of Electronic Engineering and Telecommunications: Ing. OSCAR JOSUÉ CALDERÓN CORTÉS
Faculty of Health Sciences: Dr JOSÉ LUIS DIAGO FRANCO
Faculty of Humanities and Social Sciences: Dr ALFONSO RAFAEL BUELVAS GARAY
Faculty of Law, Social and Political Sciences: Dr ROBERTO RODRÍGUEZ FERNÁNDEZ
Faculty of Natural Sciences, Exact and Education: Dr WILLIAM GARCÍA BRAVO

UNIVERSIDAD DEL MAGDALENA
(University of Magdalena)

Carrera 32 No 22–08, Santa Marta, Magdalena
Telephone: (57) 4301692
E-mail: vicedocencia@unimagdalena.edu.co
Internet: www.unimagdalena.edu.co
Founded 1958
State control
Language of instruction: Spanish
Academic year: February to December (2 semesters)
Rector: Dr RUTHBER ESCORCIA CABALLERO
Vice-Rector for Academic Affairs: PEDRO ESLAVA ELJAIEK
Vice-Rector for Extension and Social Projection: PABLO VERA
Vice-Rector for Research: JOSE HENRY ESCOBAR ACOSTA
Sec. Gen.: MERCEDES DE LA TORRE HASBÚN
Library Dir: MARTHA LUCIA RUIZ ARANGO
Library of 67,500 vols
Number of teachers: 800
Number of students: 9,200
Publications: *Revista Agronómica*, *Revista Duazary*, *Revista Económica*, *Revista Facultad Ingeniería Pesquera*, *Revista Oraloteca* (1 a year, print and online, oraloteca.unimagdalena.edu.co)

DEANS

Faculty of Basic Sciences: JAVIER RODRÍGUEZ BARRIOS
Faculty of Education: ROLANDO ESCORCIA CABALLERO
Faculty of Engineering: JUAN CARLOS DE LA ROSA
Faculty of Health Sciences: GUILLERMO TROUT GUARDIOLA
Faculty of Humanities: ALEJANDRA MARÚ MOLINARES
Faculty of Managerial Sciences and Economics: EDWIN CHACÓN VELASQUEZ

UNIVERSIDAD DEL NORTE
(University of the North)

Km 5 Via Puerto Colombia, Barranquilla, Atlántico
Telephone: (5) 3509509
E-mail: aroa@uninorte.edu.co
Internet: www.uninorte.edu.co
Founded 1966
Private control
Languages of instruction: English, Spanish
Academic year: January to December
Rector: JESÚS FERRO BAYONA
Vice-Rector for Academic Affairs: ALBERTO ROA VARELO
Vice-Rector for Admin.: ALMA LUCÍA DIAZ GRANADOS
Dean for Students: GINA PEZZANO
Dir for Int. Cooperation and Devt: CARMEN H. JIMENEZ DE PEÑA
Librarian: LUIS ALBERTO TARAZONA
Library of 89,200 vols, 1232 periodicals
Number of teachers: 900
Number of students: 10,700
Publications: *Derecho* (2 a year), *Eidos* (2 a year), *Ingenieria y Desarollo* (2 a year), *Investigacion y Desarrollo* (4 a year), *Memorias* (2 a year), *Pensamiento y Gestion* (2 a year), *Psicología Desde el Caribe* (2 a year), *Revista de Economía del Caribe* (2 a year), *Revista Salud Uninorte* (2 a year), *Zona Próxima* (2 a year)

DEANS

Division of Administrative Sciences: DIEGO CARADONA MADARIAGA
Division of Basic Sciences: JOACHIM HAHN
Division of Engineering: JAVIER PAEZ SAAVEDRA
Division of Health Sciences: HERNANDO BAQUERO LATORRE
Division of Humanities and Social Sciences: JOSE AMAR AMAR
Division of Law: SILVIA GLORIA DE VIVO
Institute of Studies in Education: LEONOR JARAMILLO DE CERTAIN (Dir)

UNIVERSIDAD DE LOS ANDES
(University of the Andes)

Carrera 1, No 18A–12, Bogotá, DC
Telephone: (1) 3394949
E-mail: infofcom@uniandes.edu.co
Internet: www.uniandes.edu.co
Founded 1948
Private control
Languages of instruction: English, Spanish
Academic year: January to December
Pres.: DIEGO PIZANO
Rector: PABLO NAVAS SANZ DE SANTAMARÍA
Vice-Rector for Academic Affairs: JOSÉ RAFAEL TORO GÓMEZ
Vice-Rector for Admin. and Finance: JAVIER SERRANO RODRÍGUEZ
Vice-Rector for Advancement and Alumni: MAURICIO SANZ DE SANTAMARÍA SAMPER
Vice-Rector for Research: CARL LANGEBAEK RUEDA
Sec. Gen.: MARÍA TERESA TOBÓN RUBIO
Registrar: ALEJANDRO RICO
Librarian: ANGELA MARÍA MEJÍA
Library of 376,500 vols, 37,770 audiovisuals, 64,470 periodicals
Number of teachers: 1,320
Number of students: 15,500
Publications: *Colombia Internacional* (4 a year), *Hipótesis* (2 a year), *Historia Crítica* (2 a year), *Nota Uniandina* (3 a year), *Revista de Estudios Sociales* (2 a year), *Revista de Ingeniería* (2 a year)

DEANS

Faculty of Administration: JAVIER YÁÑEZ ARENAS
Faculty of Architecture and Design: ALBERTO MIANI URIBE
Faculty of Arts and Humanities: CLAUDIA MONTILLA VARGAS
Faculty of Economics: ANA MARÍA IBÁÑEZ
Faculty of Engineering: EDUARDO BEHRENTZ VALENCIA
Faculty of Law: HELENA ALVIAR GARCÍA

Faculty of Medicine: Luis Andres Sarmiento Rodríguez
Faculty of Sciences: Silvia Restrepo Restrepo
Faculty of Social Sciences: Hugo Fazio Vengoa

UNIVERSIDAD DE LOS LLANOS
(University of Los Llanos)

Km 12 Vía Puerto López, Villavicencio, Meta
Telephone: (98) 6616800
E-mail: contacto@unillanos.edu.co
Internet: www.unillanos.edu.co
Founded 1974 as Universidad Tecnológica de Los Llanos Orientales, current name adopted 1992
State control
Language of instruction: Spanish
Academic year: February to December
Rector: Oscar Domínguez González
Vice-Rector for Academic Affairs: Eduardo Castillo González
Vice-Rector for Human Resources: Hernando Parra Cuberos
Sec. Gen.: Hernando Parra Cuberos
Library of 45,000 vols
Number of teachers: 350
Number of students: 6,000
Publications: *Catálogo*, *Revista Orinoquia*

DEANS
Faculty of Agricultural Sciences and Natural Resources: José Myray Saavedra Alvarez
Faculty of Basic Sciences and Engineering: Elvis Miguel Pérez Rodríguez
Faculty of Economics: Charles Robin Arosa Carrera
Faculty of Health Sciences: Blanca Stella Piñeros Serrada
Faculty of Humanities and Education: Manuel Eduardo Hozman Mora

UNIVERSIDAD DEL PACÍFICO
(University of the Pacific)

Avda Simón Bolívar 54a–10, Buenaventura, Valle del Cauca
Telephone: (92) 2439789
E-mail: info@unipacifico.edu.co
Internet: www.unipacifico.edu.co
Founded 1988
State control
Language of instruction: Spanish
Rector: Dr Omar Barona Murillo
Sec. Gen.: Dra Maria Carmela Quiñonez

UNIVERSIDAD DEL QUINDÍO
(University of Quindío)

Carrera 15, Calle 12n, Armenia, Quindío
Telephone: (6) 7359300
E-mail: uq@uniquindio.edu.co
Internet: www.uniquindio.edu.co
Founded 1960
State control
Language of instruction: Spanish
Academic year: February to November
Rector: Alfonso Londoño Orozco
Vice-Rector for Academic Affairs: Orlando Salazar Salazar
Vice-Rector for Admin.: Clara Ines Aristizabal Roa
Vice-Rector for Research: Patricia Landazury
Sec. Gen.: Franceline Barrero Rendón
Librarian: Lic. Miryam Garcia
Library of 26,250 vols
Number of teachers: 800
Number of students: 12,300
Publications: *Revista de Investigaciones* (2 a year, print and online, www.uniquindio.edu.co/uniquindio/revistainvestigaciones), *Revista de la Universidad del Quindío*, *Revista Disertaciones*, *Revista Educación Matemática* (print and online, revistamatematicas.uniquindio.edu.co), *Revista Facultad de Formación Avanzada e Investigaciones*

DEANS
Faculty of Agroindustrial Sciences: Magda Ivonne Pinzón Fandiño
Faculty of Basic and Technological Sciences: Lic. Eduardo Arango Posada
Faculty of Economics and Administration: Fabiola Restrepo Sánchez
Faculty of Education: Lic. Arles López Espinosa
Faculty of Engineering: Ing. José Fernando Echeverry Murillo
Faculty of Health Sciences: Roberto Estefan Chehab
Faculty of Humanities and Fine Arts: William García Rodríguez

UNIVERSIDAD DEL ROSARIO/ COLEGIO MAYOR DE NUESTRA SEÑORA DEL ROSARIO
(Our Lady of the Rosary University)

Calle 12c No 6–25, Bogotá, DC
Telephone: (1) 4225321
E-mail: orelaint@urosario.edu.co
Internet: www.urosario.edu.co
Founded 1653
Private control
Languages of instruction: English, Spanish
Academic year: February to November
Rector: Dr Hans-Peter Knudsen Quevedo
Vice-Rector: Alejandro Venegas Franco
Sec. Gen.: Catalina Lleras Figueroa
Library Dir: Dra Margarita Lisowska
Library of 119,000 vols, 100 databases
Publications: *Anuario Colombiano de Derecho Internacional* (1 a year), *Avances en Psicología Latinoamericana* (2 a year), *Desafíos* (2 a year), *Revista Ciencias de la Salud* (3 a year), *Revista de Economía del Rosario* (2 a year), *Revista Desafíos*, *Revista Estudios Socio-Jurídicos* (2 a year), *Revista Universidad & Empresa* (2 a year), *Territorios* (2 a year)

DEANS
Faculty of Economics: Hernán Jaramillo Salazar
Faculty of Human Sciences: Stephanie Lavaux
Faculty of International Relations: Eduardo Barajas Sandoval
Faculty of Law: Antonio Aljure Salame
Faculty of Medicine and Health Sciences: Dr Leonardo Palacios Sánchez
Faculty of Political Science: Eduardo Barajas Sandoval
Faculty of Natural Sciences and Mathematics: Mauricio Linares Porto
School of Management: Dr Fernando Locano Botero

UNIVERSIDAD DEL TOLIMA
(University of Tolima)

Barrio Santa Helena Parte Alta, Apdo Aéreo 546, Ibagué, Tolima
Telephone: (8) 2771212
E-mail: contactenos@ut.edu.co
Internet: www.ut.edu.co
Founded 1945
State control
Language of instruction: Spanish
Academic year: January to December
Rector: Dr José Herman Muñoz Ñungo
Vice-Rector for Academic Affairs: David Benitez M.
Vice-Rector for Admin.: Juan Fernando Reinoso Lastra
Vice-Rector for Human Resources: Libardo Vargas Celemin
Registrar: Luis Guillermo Melo
Librarian: Cielo Urueña Lozano
Number of teachers: 240
Number of students: 30,800
Publication: *Revista Panorama Universitario*

DEANS
Faculty of Agricultural Engineering: José Aldemar Muñoz Hernandez
Faculty of Economics and Business Administration: Carlos Eduardo Montealegre Hernández
Faculty of Educational Science: Dr Andrés Felipe Mosquera Velásquez
Faculty of Forestry Engineering: Luís Alfredo Lozano Botache
Faculty of Health Sciences: Juan Carlos Ferrero Otero
Faculty of Science: Luis Fernando Rodriguez Herrera
Faculty of Technology: Laureano Emilio Hernandez Bonilla
Faculty of Veterinary Medicine and Zootechnics: Libia Elsy Guzmán Osorio
Institute of Distance Education: Luis Alberto Malagón Plata (Dir)

UNIVERSIDAD DEL VALLE
(University of Valle)

Ciudad Universitaria, Meléndez, Calle 13 No 100-00, Calí, Valle del Cauca
Telephone: (2) 3212100
E-mail: directorio@correounivalle.edu.co
Internet: www.univalle.edu.co
Founded 1945
State control
Academic year: January to December
Rector: Iván Enrique Ramos Calderón
Vice-Rector for Academic Affairs: Héctor Cadavid Ramírez
Vice-Rector for Admin.: Javier Fong Lozano
Vice-Rector for Research: Carolina Isaza de Lourido
Vice-Rector for Univ. Welfare: Jesús Maria Sánchez Ordoñez
Sec. Gen.: Luis Alberto Herrera Ramírez
Library Dir: Carlos Armando Rodríguez
Library of 267,656 vols
Number of teachers: 962
Number of students: 14,640 (9,640 full-time; 5,000 part-time)
Publications: *Colombia Médica* (4 a year, print and online, colombiamedica.univalle.edu.co), *Cuadernos de Administración*, *Heurística*, *Historia y Espacio* (2 a year), *Humboltia*, *Fin de Siglo*, *La Palabra*, *Lenguaje*, *Matemáticas: Enseñanza Universitaria* (2 a year, print and online, revistaerm.univalle.edu.co), *Planta Libre*, *Pliegos Administrativos*, *Poligramas*, *Praxis Filosófica* (2 a year, print and online, praxis.univalle.edu.co), *Revista de Ciencias* (1 a year, print and online, revistaciencias.univalle.edu.co), *Revista Estomatología*, *Revista Universidad del Valle*, *Sociedad y Economía* (2 a year)

DEANS
Faculty of Administrative Science: Carlos Eduardo Cobo Oliveros
Faculty of Economics and Social Sciences: Beatríz Castro Carvajal
Faculty of Engineering: Edgar Quiroga Rubiano
Faculty of Exact and Natural Science: Dr Jaime Ricardo Cantera Kintz
Faculty of Health: Julián Alberto Herrera Murgueitio

Faculty of Humanities: GLADYS STELLA LÓPEZ JIMÉNEZ
Faculty of Integrated Arts: MARITZA LÓPEZ DE LA ROCHE
Institute of Education and Pedagogy: RENATO RAMÍREZ RODRIGUEZ (Dir)
Institute of Psychology: INGRID CAROLINA GOMEZ BARRIOS (Dir)

UNIVERSIDAD DE MEDELLÍN (University of Medellín)

Carrera 87, No 30–65, Medellín, Antioquia
Telephone: (4) 3405555
E-mail: udem@guayacan.udem.edu.co
Internet: www.udem.edu.co
Founded 1950
Private control
Language of instruction: Spanish
Academic year: February to December
Rector: NÉSTOR HINCAPIÉ VARGAS
Vice-Rector for Academic Affairs: ALBA LUZ MUÑOZ RESTREPO
Vice-Rector for Admin. and Finance: STELLA SABA LÓPEZ
Vice-Rector for Extension: CARLOS TULIO MONTOYA HERRERA
Vice-Rector for Research: LUZ DORIS BOLÍVAR YEPES
Sec. Gen.: ESPERANZA RESTREPO DE ISAZA
Dir for Libraries: SANDRA MILENA DUQUE MUÑETÓN
Library of 98,791 vols, incl. 74,108 gen. vols, 2,312 reference books, 806 periodical titles, 14,230 theses, 380 audiovisual items, 3,023 CD-ROMs, 3,486 DVDs
Number of teachers: 804
Number of students: 12,863 (11,496 undergraduate, 1,367 postgraduate)
Publications: *Colombian Accounting Journal*, *Con-Textos* (2 a year), *Opinión Jurídica* (2 a year), *Revista Universidad de Medellín* (2 a year), *Semestre Económico* (2 a year)

DEANS
Faculty of Communication: LUIS MARIANO GONZALEZ AGUDELO
Faculty of Economic and Administrative Sciences: MARTA CECILIA BENÍTEZ TRUJILLO
Faculty of Engineering: CARLOS EDUARDO LÓPEZ BERMEO
Faculty of Law: JUAN CARLOS VASQUEZ RIVERA

UNIVERSIDAD DE NARIÑO (University of Nariño)

Ciudad Universitaria Torobajo, Calle 18 Carrera 50, San Juan de Pasto, Nariño
Telephone: (2) 7311449
E-mail: rectoria@udenar.edu.co
Internet: www.udenar.edu.co
Founded 1827 as Colegio Provincial by General Francisco de Paula Santander, current name adopted 1964
Rector: Dr JOSÉ EDMUNDO CALVACHE LÓPEZ
Vice-Rector for Academic Affairs: LUZ STELLA LAGOS MORA
Vice-Rector for Admin.: GERMAN ARTEAGA MENESES
Vice-Rector for Research, Postgraduates and Int. Relations: FREDY VILLALOBOS
Sec. Gen.: FERNANDO GUERRERO FARINANGO
Library Dir: FERNANDO SOTO AGREDA
Library of 10,000 vols; agronomy library of 15,000 vols
Number of teachers: 700
Number of students: 8,000
Publications: *Awarca*, *Docencia, Investigación e Innovación* (online), *Foro Universitario*, *Revista de Ciencias* (1 a year), *Revista de Ciencias Agrícolas* (2 a year), *Revista de Investigaciones*, *Revista de Zootecnia*, *Revista Historia de la Educación Colombiana* (1 a year, print and online, akane.udenar.edu.co/siweb/rudecolombia), *Revista Latinoamericana de Etnomatemática* (2 a year), *Tendencias* (2 a year, print and online, tendencias.udenar.edu.co)

DEANS
Faculty of Agroindustrial Engineering: ANDRES MAURICIO HURTADO BENAVIDES
Faculty of Agronomy: TULIO CESAR LAGOS BURBANO
Faculty of Animal Science: HECTOR FABIO VALENCIA RIOS
Faculty of Arts: LUIS ALFONSO CAICEDO RODRIGUEZ
Faculty of Economics and Administration: JESUS HUMBERTO MARTINEZ BETANCOURT
Faculty of Education: ROBERTO RAMIREZ BRAVO
Faculty of Engineering: NELSON ANTONIO JARAMILLO ENRIQUEZ
Faculty of Exact and Natural Sciences: PABLO FERNANDEZ IZQUIERDO
Faculty of Health Sciences: CASTULO FERNANDO CISNEROS RIVERA
Faculty of Human Sciences: MANUEL ENRIQUE MARTINEZ RIASCOS
Faculty of Law: LEONARDO A. ENRIQUEZ MARTINEZ

UNIVERSIDAD DE PAMPLONA (University of Pamplona)

Ciudad Universitaria 'El Buque', Pamplona, Santander del Norte
Telephone: (7) 5685303
E-mail: rectoria@unipamplona.edu.co
Internet: www.unipamplona.edu.co
Founded 1960, univ. status 1970
State control
Language of instruction: Spanish
Academic year: February to December
Rector: ELIO DANIEL SERRANO VELASCO
Vice-Rector for Academic Affairs: VÍCTOR MANUEL GÉLVEZ ORDOÑEZ
Vice-Rector for Admin. and Finance: ÁLVARO ENRIQUE PAZ MONTES
Vice-Rector for Research: ARIEL REY BECERRA BECERRA
Dir for Social Interaction: JORGE ALBERTO GALLEGO HERNÁNDEZ
Dir for Univ. Welfare: GERMÁN GRANADOS VILLAMIZAR
Sec. Gen.: CLARA LILIANA PARRA ZABALA
Dir for Library: JOAQUÍN ANTONIO JARAMILLO HURTADO
Publications: *Bistua* (2 a year), *Faria* (2 a year), *Zulima* (2 a year)

DEANS
Faculty of Agricultural Sciences: ALFONSO EUGENIO CAPACHO MOGOLLÓN
Faculty of Arts and Humanities: ANTONIO STALIN GARCÍA RÍOS
Faculty of Basic Sciences: FREDDY SOLANO ORTEGA
Faculty of Economics and Business: SERGIO AUGUSTO JIMÉNEZ RAMÍREZ
Faculty of Education: OLGA BELÉN CASTILLO DE CUADROS
Faculty of Engineering and Architecture: WILLIAM MAURICIO ROJAS CONTRERAS
Faculty of Health: ELIANA ELIZABETH RIVERA

UNIVERSIDAD DE SAN BUENAVENTURA (University of San Buenaventura)

Carrera 9 No 123–76, Of. 602–603, Bogotá, DC
Telephone: (1) 6295955
E-mail: rector.general@usb.edu.co
Internet: www.usb.edu.co
Founded 1708, present status 1961
Private control
Language of instruction: Spanish
Academic year: February to November
Rector Gen.: Fr HERNANDO ARIAS RODRÍGUEZ
Sec. Gen.: Fr ERNESTO LONDOÑO OROZCO.

CAMPUSES

Bogotá, DC Campus

Carrera 8H No 172–20, Bogotá, DC
Telephone: (1) 6671090
E-mail: informacion@usbbog.edu.co
Internet: www.usbbog.edu.co
Rector: Fr PABLO CASTILLO NOVA
Academic Dir: Dr MAURICIO MALAVET
Admin. Dir: Dr EVA JANETT PRADA
Librarian: MARIA ELIZABETH COY
Publications: *Criterios* (2 a year), *Franciscanum* (2 a year), *Ingenium* (2 a year), *Itinerario* (2 a year), *Psychologia* (2 a year)

DEANS
Faculty of Business Sciences: Ing. EDGAR EMIRO RODRIGUEZ
Faculty of Education: Dr MARCO FIDEL CHICA
Faculty of Engineering: Ing. WILSON SOTO
Faculty of Law and Political Science: Dr HERNANDO URIBE
Faculty of Philosophy: Dr MIGUEL ANGEL VILLAMIL
Faculty of Psychology: Dr NOHELIA HEWITT
Faculty of Theology: Fr HUGO MARTINEZ

Calí Campus

Avda 10 de Mayo, La Umbría, Vía a Pance, Calí, Valle del Cauca
Telephone: (2) 4882222
E-mail: informacion@usbcali.edu.co
Internet: www.usbcali.edu.co
Rector: Fr ÁLVARO CEPEDA VAN HOUTEN
Vice-Rector for Academic Affairs: JUAN CARLOS FLÓREZ BURITICÁ
Vice-Rector for Admin. and Finance: FELIX RODRÍGUEZ BALLESTEROS
Sec.: JUAN DE LA CRUZ CASTELLANOS ALARCÓN
Librarian: CICILIA LIBREROS
Publications: *Architectura*, *Derecho* (2 a year), *Economía* (2 a year), *Educación* (2 a year), *Contaduria* (2 a year), *Ingeniería de Sistemas* (2 a year)

DEANS
Faculty of Architecture, Art and Design: Arq. JUAN MARCO DUQUE RECIO
Faculty of Economics: Ing. JAIME CAMPO RODRIGUEZ
Faculty of Education: Dr WALTER MENDOZA BORRERO
Faculty of Engineering: Ing. MARIO JULIÁN MORA CARDONA
Faculty of Law and Political Sciences: Dra ALBA LILIANA SILVA DE ROA
Faculty of Psychology: Dra CARMEN ELENA URREA BENÍTEZ

Cartagena Campus

Calle Real de Ternera, Diagonal 32 No 30–966, Cartagena, Bolívar
Telephone: (5) 6535530
E-mail: rectoria@usbcartagena.edu.co
Internet: www.usbcartagena.edu.co
Rector: Fr NELSON ANTONIO PÉREZ CANO
Vice-Rector for Academic Affairs: RAFAEL ACOSTA FEGALI
Vice-Rector for Admin.: CHRISTIAN AYOLA ESCALLÓN
Sec.: Fr HUMBERTO ÁVILA GÓME

DEANS
Faculty of Administration and Accountancy: SANDRA PORTO ARROLLO

Faculty of Education, Humanities and Social Sciences: KAREN POSADA PARDO
Faculty of Engineering, Architecture, Arts and Design: LEOPOLDO VILLADIEGO CONEO
Faculty of Health Sciences: LOURDES BENÍTEZ PEÑA
Faculty of Law and Political Sciences: JHON ERIC RHENALS TURRIAGO

Medellín Campus

Carrera 56C No 51–110, Centro, Medellín, Antioquia
Telephone: (4) 5145600
Internet: www.usbmed.edu.co

Rector: Fr JOSÉ WILSON TÉLLEZ CASAS
Vice-Rector for Academic Affairs: Fr FRANCISCO LOTERO MATIZ
Vice-Rector for Admin. and Finance: JORGE ALBEIRO HERRERA BUILES
Sec.: Fr HERNANDO MEZA MEDINA

Number of teachers: 250
Number of students: 2,600

DEANS
Faculty of Business Science: LUIS FERNANDO AGUDELO HENAO
Faculty of Education: SANDRA EUGENIA POSADA HERNÁNDEZ
Faculty of Engineering: MARTA CECILIA MEZA PELÁEZ
Faculty of Integrated Arts: CARLOS ALBERTO PINTO SANTA
Faculty of Law: (vacant)
Faculty of Psychology: BEATRIZ MARÍN LONDOÑO

UNIVERSIDAD DE SUCRE
(University of Sucre)

Apdo Aéreo 406, Carrera 28, No 5-267, Sincelejo, Sucre
Telephone: (5) 2821240
E-mail: atencionalciudadano@unisucre.edu.co
Internet: www.unisucre.edu.co

Founded 1977
State control
Language of instruction: Spanish
Academic year: February to December

Rector: VICENTE PERIÑÁN PETRO
Vice-Rector for Academic Affairs: IVÁN NÚÑEZ OROZCO
Vice-Rector for Admin.: ANTONIO JOSÉ HERRERA SUCCAR
Sec. Gen.: JEINY EMILIANI RUIZ
Chief Planning Officer: LUIS RAMOS BADEL
Librarian: OSWALDO SUÁREZ MILANÉS

Library of 12,000 vols
Number of teachers: 65
Number of students: 910

DEANS
Faculty of Agricultural Sciences: ORLANDO NAVARRO MEJÍA
Faculty of Economic Sciences and Administration: PEDRO MANUEL HERRERA GUTIÉRREZ
Faculty of Education and Science: CARMEN PAYARES PAYARES
Faculty of Engineering: HERALDO ALVIZ SANTOS
Faculty of Health Sciences: MARÍA LUCY HERNÁNDEZ CHADID

UNIVERSIDAD DISTRITAL 'FRANCISCO JOSÉ DE CALDAS'
(Francisco José De Caldas City University)

Carrera 7, No 40B–53, Bogotá, DC
Telephone: (1) 3239300
E-mail: admisiones@udistrital.edu.co
Internet: www.udistrital.edu.co

Founded 1950
State control
Language of instruction: Spanish

Rector: INOCENCIO BAHAMÓN CALDERÓN
Vice-Rector for Academic Affairs: BORIS BUSTAMANTE BOHORQUEZ
Vice-Rector for Admin. and Finance: ROBERTO VERGARA PORTELA
Sec. Gen.: LEONARDO GÓMEZ PARIS

Number of teachers: 600
Number of students: 7,200

DEANS
Faculty of Arts: ELIZABETH GARAVITO LÓPEZ
Faculty of Engineering: OCTAVIO JOSÉ SALCEDO PARRA
Faculty of Environment and Natural Resources: LUIS JAIRO SILVA HERRERA
Faculty of Science and Education: WILLIAM FERNANDO CASTRILLÓN CARDONA
Faculty of Technology: PABLO EMILIO GARZÓN CARREÑO

UNIVERSIDAD EAFIT
(Eafit University)

Avda Las Vegas, Carrera 49 No 7 Sur-50, Medellín
Telephone: (4) 2619600
E-mail: contacto@eafit.edu.co
Internet: www.eafit.edu.co

Founded 1960
Private control
Language of instruction: Spanish
Academic year: January to December

Rector: JUAN LUIS MEJÍA ARANGO
Vice-Rector: JULIO ACOSTA ARANGO
Sec. Gen.: HUGO ALBERTO CASTAÑO ZAPATA
Dir for Admin. and Finance: PAULA ANDREA ARANGO GUTIÉRREZ
Dir for Planning: ALBERTO JARAMILLO JARAMILLO
Dir for Research: FÉLIX LONDOÑO GONZÁLEZ
Dir for Teaching: GABRIEL JAIME ARANGO VELÁSQUEZ
Library Dir: MARTHA SENN

Library of 40,000 vols

Publications: *AD Minister* (2 a year), *Cuadernos de Investigación*, *Eafitense* (12 a year), *Ecos de Economía* (2 a year), *Lúdica*, *Nuevo Foro Penal* (3 a year), *Revista Universidad Eafit* (4 a year), *Ruido Blanco* (2 a year), *Yesca y Pedernal* (4 a year)

DEANS
School of Administration: FRANCISCO LÓPEZ GALLEGO
School of Economics and Finances: JUAN FELIPE MEJÍA MEJÍA
School of Engineering: ALBERTO RODRÍGUEZ GARCÍA
School of Law: HUGO ALBERTO CASTAÑO ZAPATA
School of Sciences and Humanities: JORGE ALBERTO GIRALDO RAMIREZ

UNIVERSIDAD EXTERNADO DE COLOMBIA
(Externado University of Colombia)

Calle 12, No 1–17 Este, Bogotá, DC
Telephone: (1) 3537000
E-mail: sitioweb@uexternado.edu.co
Internet: www.uexternado.edu.co

Founded 1886
Private control
Language of instruction: Spanish
Academic year: February to December

Rector: Dr JUAN CARLOS HENAO
Sec. Gen.: Dra MARTA HINESTROSA
Library Dir: Dra LINA ESPITALETA DE VILLEGAS

Library of 162,160 vols, 1,269 journal titles

Publications: *Boletín Tiempo y Turismo*, *Colección de Estudios en Derecho Penal—Cuadernos de Conferencias y Artículos* (3 a year), *Contexto* (4 a year), *Derecho del Estado* (2 a year), *Derecho Económico*, *Derecho Penal y Criminología* (3 a year), *Derecho y Vida*, *Documentos para la Historia del Constitucionalismo Colombiano* (2 a year), *Filosofía del Derecho* (4 a year), *Lúdica*, *Oasis—Observatorio de Análisis de los Sistemas Internacionales*, *Revista de Derecho Privado* (2 a year), *Revista de Economía Institucional*, *Revista Zero*, *Temas de Derecho Público* (4 a year)

DEANS
Faculty of Administration and Business Studies: ALEJANDRO BELTRÁN DUQUE
Faculty of Economics: MAURICIO PÉREZ SALAZAR
Faculty of Education: Dra MIRYAM OCHOA PIEDRAHITA
Faculty of Finance, Government and International Relations: Dr ROBERTO HINESTROSA
Faculty of Furniture Restoration: Dra HELENA WIESNER
Faculty of Hotel Management and Tourism: Dr LUIS CARLOS CRUZ CORTÉS
Faculty of Law: Dr FERNANDO HINESTROSA
Faculty of Public Finance: JUAN MANUEL GUERRERO JIMÉNEZ
Faculty of Social Communication and Journalism: LUZ AMALIA CAMACHO VELÁSQUEZ
Faculty of Social Sciences and Humanities: Dra LUCERO ZAMUDIO

UNIVERSIDAD FRANCISCO DE PAULA SANTANDER
(Francisco de Paula Santander University)

Avda Gran Colombia 12E–96, Barrio Colsag, San José de Cúcuta, Norte de Santander
Telephone: (7) 5776655
E-mail: oficinadeprensa@ufps.edu.co
Internet: www.ufps.edu.co

Founded 1962
State control
Language of instruction: Spanish

Rector: HÉCTOR MIGUEL PARRA LÓPEZ
Vice-Rector for Academic Affairs: JESÚS ERNESTO URBINA CÁRDENAS
Vice-Rector for Admin.: SERGIO IVÁN QUINTERO AYALA
Vice-Rector for Univ. Welfare: MAWENCY VERGEL ORTEGA
Sec. Gen.: CLAUDIA ELIZABETH TOLOZA MARTÍNEZ
Librarian: GLORIA MATILDE MELO SALCEDO

Library of 5,000 vols
Number of teachers: 350
Number of students: 6,500

DEANS
Faculty of Agricultural and Environmental Sciences: EVARISTO CARVAJAL VALDERRAMA
Faculty of Basic Sciences: SANDRA ORTEGA SIERRA
Faculty of Business Studies: ESMERALDA CONTRERAS
Faculty of Education, Arts and Humanities: DANIEL VILLAMIZAR JAIMES
Faculty of Engineering: NELSON BELTRÁN GÁLVIZ
Faculty of Health Sciences: LUZ MARINA BAUTISTA RODRIGUEZ

UNIVERSIDAD ICESI
(ICESI University)

Calle 18, 122–135, Calí, Valle del Cauca
Telephone: (2) 5552334
E-mail: comunicaciones@icesi.edu.co
Internet: www.icesi.edu.co

Founded 1979
Private control
Language of instruction: Spanish
Rector: FRANCISCO PIEDRAHITA PLATA
Sec. Gen.: MARÍA CRISTINA NAVIA K.
Head Librarian: ANDRÉS SANTIAGO LONDOÑO
Library of 64,452 vols, 640 journal titles, 255 ebooks, 39,425 ejournal titles
Number of teachers: 375
Number of students: 4,831 (4,012 undergraduate, 819 postgraduate)
Publications: *Ciencias Sociales* (2 a year), *Estudios Gerenciales* (3 a year), *Papel de Colgadura* (2 a year), *Precedente* (3 a year), *Revista Interacción* (3 a year), *Sistemas y Telemática* (52 a year), *Trans-pasando Fronteras* (2 a year)

DEANS

Faculty of Administration and Economics: HÉCTOR OCHOA DÍAZ
Faculty of Engineering: GONZALO ULLOA
Faculty of Health: Dra YURI TAKEUUCHI
Faculty of Law and Social Sciences: Dr JERÓNIMO BOTERO
Faculty of Natural Sciences: ZAIDA LENTINI

UNIVERSIDAD INCCA DE COLOMBIA
(INCCA University of Colombia)

Carrera 13 No 24–15, Bogotá, DC
Telephone: (2) 4442000
E-mail: rectoria@unincca.edu.co
Internet: www.unincca.edu.co
Founded 1955
Private control
Language of instruction: Spanish
Academic year: January to December
Faculties of engineering, administration and basic sciences, judicial and state sciences, pedagogical, human and social sciences; postgraduate school; technological institute
Pres. and Rector: Dr ENRIQUE CONTI BAUTISTA
Gen. Vice-Rector: Dr ALFREDO GARCIA MONSALVE
Vice-Rector for Academic Affairs: NELSON HURTADO PENAGOS
Sec. Gen.: Dr HÉCTOR MANUEL RODRIGUEZ CORTÉS
Library Dir: GLORIA MARIA BASTOS P.
Publication: *Revista Científica de UNINCCA* (2 a year)

UNIVERSIDAD INDUSTRIAL DE SANTANDER
(Industrial University of Santander)

Apdo Aéreo 678, Bucaramanga, Santander
Carrera 27, Calle 9, Bucaramanga, Santander
Telephone: (7) 6344000
E-mail: rectoria@uis.edu.co
Internet: www.uis.edu.co
Founded 1948
State control
Language of instruction: Spanish
Academic year: February to December
Rector: Dr ÁLVARO RAMÍREZ GARCÍA
Vice-Rector for Academic Affairs: JANETH AIDE PEREA VILLAMIL
Vice-Rector for Admin.: LUIS EDUARDO BECERRA ARDILA
Sec. Gen.: ADRIANA CASTILLO PICO
Dir for Int. Relations: VIATCHESLAV KAFAROV
Library Dir: CARLOS TRIVINO MUNOZ
Number of teachers: 500
Number of students: 10,000
Publications: *Anuario de Historia Regional y de las Fronteras* (1 a year), *Boletín de Geología* (2 a year), *Revista Filosofía UIS* (2 a year), *Revista Integración* (2 a year), *Revista Ion* (2 a year), *Revista Médicas UIS* (3 a year), *Revista Salud* (3 a year), *Revista UIS Humanidades* (2 a year), *Revista UIS Ingenierías* (2 a year)

DEANS

Faculty of Health: CLARA INES VARGAS CASTELLANOS
Faculty of Human Sciences: ALVARO ACEVEDO TARAZONA
Faculty of Physical/Chemical Engineering: SONIA AZUCENA GIRALDO DUARTE
Faculty of Physical/Mechanical Engineering: RICARDO ALFREDO CRUZ HERNANDEZ
Faculty of Sciences: GERMAN MORENO ARENAS

UNIVERSIDAD LA GRAN COLOMBIA
(La Gran Colombia University)

Carrera 6, No 13–40, Bogotá, DC
Telephone: (1) 3276999
E-mail: rectorjg@colomsat.net.co
Internet: www.ugc.edu.co
Founded 1953
Private control
Language of instruction: Spanish
Academic year: January to November (2 semesters)
Rector: JOSÉ GALAT NOUMER
Vice-Rector for Academic Affairs: MARÍA EUGENIA CORREA OLARTE
Vice-Rector for Admin.: RICARDO NÚÑEZ PINZÓN
Sec. Gen.: CARLOS ALBERTO PULIDO BARRANTES
Dir for Planning: VIVIANA KATHERINE USGAME PEÑA
Library Dir: JOHN ELIECER GARZÓN

DEANS

Faculty of Accountancy: GERARDO CARDOZO ROJAS
Faculty of Architecture: FRANCISCO BELTRÁN RAPALINO
Faculty of Civil Engineering: JAIME SALAMANCA LEÓN
Faculty of Economics and Administration: ADRIANA ROJAS MARTÍNEZ
Faculty of Education: ANA CECILIA OSORIO CARDONA
Faculty of Law: GLORIA INÉS QUICENO FRANCO
Faculty of Postgraduate Courses and Continuing Education: ANA CECILIA OSORIO CARDONA

UNIVERSIDAD LIBRE
(Free University)

Calle 8A No 5–80, Bogotá, DC
Telephone: (1) 3821000
E-mail: ori@unilibrebog.edu.co
Internet: www.unilibre.edu.co
Founded 1923
Private control
Language of instruction: Spanish
Campuses in Barranquilla, Calí, Cartagena, Cúcuta, Pereira, Socorro
Nat. Rector: NICOLÁS ENRIQUE ZULETA HINCAPIÉ
Publications: *Advocatus* (2 a year), *Avances* (2 a year, print and online, www.revistaavances.co), *Entramado* (2 a year), *Libre Empresa* (2 a year), *Revistas Criterio Libre* (2 a year), *Verba Iuris* (2 a year)

DEANS

Faculty of Economics: CLARA INÉS CAMACHO ROA
Faculty of Engineering: Ing. JORGE RENÉ SILVA LARROTTA
Faculty of Law: JESÚS HERNANDO ÁLVAREZ MORA
Faculty of Philosophy: RUBÉN ALBERTO DUARTE CUADROS

UNIVERSIDAD LIBRE, SECCIONAL DE PEREIRA
(Free University, Pereira Section)

Belmonte Avenida Las Américas, Pereira, Risaralda
Telephone: (6) 3155600
Internet: www.unilibrepereira.edu.co
Founded 1971
Private control
Language of instruction: Spanish
Academic year: February to December
Rector: GLORIA MARÍA ATEHORTÚA RADA
Sec.: GIOVANI ARIAS
Academic Sec.: CARLOS ALBERTO DUQUE
Dir for Planning: DANIEL LEONARDO PERDOMO GAMBOA
Library Dir: ADRIANA PATRICIA OYUELA LÓPEZ
Publication: *Memorando de Derecho* (1 a year)

DEANS

Faculty of Economics, Administration and Accounting: EDUARD MURILLO CÓRDOBA
Faculty of Engineering: JORGE ENRIQUE RAMÍREZ RINCÓN
Faculty of Health Sciences: MARÍA TERESA RODRÍGUEZ LUGO
Faculty of Law: IVÁN GIRALDO HENAO

UNIVERSIDAD MILITAR NUEVA GRANADA
(Nueva Granada Military University)

Carrera 11 No 101–80, Bogotá, DC
Telephone: (1) 6343200
E-mail: rectoria@unimilitar.edu.co
Internet: www.umng.edu.co
Founded 1982
State control
Language of instruction: Spanish
Academic year: January to December
Rector: EDUARDO ANTONIO HERRERA BERBEL
Gen. Vice-Rector: ALBERTO BRAVO SILVA
Vice-Rector for Academic Affairs: Dra MARHA BAHAMON JARA
Vice-Rector for Admin.: EDGAR CEBALLOS
Vice-Rector for Research: Dr JOSE RICARDO CURE HAKIM
Number of teachers: 270
Number of students: 15,400

DEANS

Faculty of Basic Sciences: Dr FERNANDO CANTOR
Faculty of Economics and Business Administration: Dra MARTHA ELENA CASTAÑEDA
Faculty of Engineering: Dr ERNESTO VILLAREAL
Faculty of Law: Dr BERNARDO VANEGAS
Faculty of Medicine: Dr JUAN MIGUEL ESTRADA

UNIVERSIDAD NACIONAL ABIERTA Y A DISTANCIA
(National Open and Distance University)

Calle 14 Sur No 14–23, Bogotá, DC
Telephone: (1) 3443700
E-mail: atencionalusuario@unad.edu.co
Internet: www.unad.edu.co
Founded 1981 as Unidad Universitaria del Sur de Bogotá; present name and status 1997
State control
Language of instruction: Spanish
Academic year: February to December
Rector: Dr JAIME LEAL AFANADOR
Vice-Rector for Academic Affairs and Research: Mag. CONSTANZA ABADÍA GARCÍA
Vice-Rector for Educational Media and Communications: GLORIA C. HERRERA SÁNCHEZ

Vice-Rector for Int. Relations: NICOLAI ROSSIASCO PIRAJAN
Vice-Rector for Regional Projection and Community Devt: Mag. EDGAR GUILLERMO RODRÍGUEZ DÍAZ
Vice-Rector for Students and Alumni: Mag. MIGUEL ROBERTO HERNÁNDEZ SAAVEDRA
Sec. Gen.: Mag. LEONARDO SÁNCHEZ TORRES

DEANS

School of Administrative Sciences, Economics and Accountancy: Mag. GONZALO EDUARDO JIMÉNEZ BERMÚDEZ
School of Agricultural Sciences, Livestock and the Environment: Mag. PRISCILA REY VÁSQUEZ
School of Basic Sciences, Technology and Engineering: GUSTAVO VELÁSQUEZ QUINTANA
School of Health Sciences: LEONARDO YUNDA PERLAZA
School of Sciences and Education: Mag. CLARA ESPERANZA PEDRAZA GOYENECHE
School of Social Sciences, Arts and Humanities: Mag. SANDRA MILENA MORALES MANTILLA

UNIVERSIDAD NACIONAL DE COLOMBIA
(National University of Colombia)

Ciudad Universitaria, Apdo Aéreo 14490, Bogotá, DC
Telephone: (1) 3165000
E-mail: secgener@unal.edu.co
Internet: www.unal.edu.co
Founded 1867
Academic year: February to December
Campuses in Manizales, Medellín, Palmira
Rector: IGNACIO MANTILLA PRADA
Gen. Vice-Rector: JORGE IVÁN BULA ESCOBAR
Vice-Rector for Academic Affairs: JUAN MANUEL TEJEIRO SARMIENTO
Vice-Rector for Research and Extension: ALEXANDER GÓMEZ
Vice-Rector for Bogotá Campus: DIEGO FERNANDO HERNÁNDEZ LOSADA
Vice-Rector for Manizales Campus: GERMAN ALBEIRO CASTAÑO DUQUE
Vice-Rector for Medellín Campus: CARLOS ALFREDO SALAZAR MOLINA
Vice-Rector for Palmira Campus: RAÚL MADRIÑAN MOLINA
Sec. Gen.: CATALINA RAMÍREZ GÓMEZ
Library: see under Libraries and Archives
Publications: *Acta Bibliográfica, Agronomía Colombiana, Alimentos, Anuario Colombiano de Historia, Anuario del Observatorio Astronómico Nacional, Boletín de Matemáticas, Caldasia, Cuadernos de Economía, Forma y Función, Geografía Geología Colombiana, Ideas y Valores, Ingeniería e Investigación, Lozania, Maguaré, Mutisia, Revistas*

DEANS

Faculty of Agronomy: VÍCTOR JULIO FLÓREZ RONCANCIO
Faculty of Arts: RODRIGO MARCELO CORTÉS SOLANO
Faculty of Dentistry: MANUEL ROBERTO SARMIENTO LIMAS
Faculty of Economics: JOSÉ GUILLERMO GARCÍA ISAZA
Faculty of Engineering: JOSÉ ISMAEL PEÑA REYES
Faculty of Humanities: SERGIO BOLAÑOS CUELLAR
Faculty of Law and Political and Social Sciences: GENARO ALFONSO SÁNCHEZ MONCALEANO
Faculty of Medicine: RAÚL ESTEBAN SASTRE CIFUENTES
Faculty of Nursing: RENATA VIRGINIA GONZÁLEZ CONSUEGRA
Faculty of Sciences: JESÚS SIGIFREDO VALENCIA RIOS
Faculty of Veterinary Medicine and Animal Husbandry: CLAUDIA JIMÉNEZ ESCOBAR

OTHER CAMPUSES

Manizales Campus: Carrera 27 No 64–60, Manizales, Caldas

DEANS

Faculty of Administration: JUAN MANUEL CASTAÑO MOLANO
Faculty of Engineering and Architecture: CAMILO YOUNES VELOSA
Faculty of Exact and Natural Sciences: FABIÁN FERNANDO SERRANO SUÁREZ

Medellín Campus: Calle 59A No 63–20, Medellín, Antioquia

DEANS

Faculty of Architecture: EDGAR ARROYO CASTRO
Faculty of Agricultural Sciences: JAIRO ALEXANDER OSORIO SARAZ
Faculty of Humanities and Economics: YOBENJ AUCARDO CHICANGANA BAYONA
Faculty of Mining: JOHN WILLIAM BRANCH BEDOYA
Faculty of Sciences: LUIS ALFONSO VÉLEZ MORENO

Palmira Campus: Carrera 32 No 12–00, Chapinero, Vía Candelaria, Palmira, Valle del Cauca

DEANS

Faculty of Engineering and Administration: CARLOS HUMBERTO MORA BEJARANO
Faculty of Stockbreeding: NORA CRISTINA MESA COBO

UNIVERSIDAD PEDAGÓGICA NACIONAL
(National Pedagogic University)

Calle 72 No 11–86, Bogotá, DC
Telephone: (1) 5941894
E-mail: informacion_upn@pedagogica.edu.co
Internet: www.pedagogica.edu.co
Founded 1955
State control
Languages of instruction: English, Spanish
Academic year: January to December (2 semesters)
Rector: Dr JUAN CARLOS OROZCO CRUZ
Vice-Rector for Academic Affairs: Dr EDGAR ALBERTO MENDOZA PARADA
Vice-Rector for Admin. and Finance: Dr GUILLERMO ANTONIO TAMAYO SÁNCHEZ
Vice-Rector for Univ. Management: VICTOR MANUEL RODRÍGUEZ SARMIENTO
Chief Librarian: OLGA LUCÍA SALINAS SALINAS
Number of teachers: 1,000
Number of students: 10,000
Publications: *Bio-grafia* (2 a year), *Nodos y Nudos* (2 a year), *Pedagogica y Saberes* (2 a year), *Revista Colombiana de Educación* (2 a year), *Revista Folios* (2 a year)

DEANS

Faculty of Education: OLGA CECILIA DIÁZ
Faculty of Fine Arts: CARLOS HERNANDO DUEÑAS MONTAÑO
Faculty of Humanities: ADOLFO LEÓN ATEHORTÚA CRUZ
Faculty of Physical Education: JOSÉ ALFONSO MARTÍN REYES
Faculty of Science and Technology: LUIS EDUARDO ESPITIA SUPELANO
National Pedagogical Institute: YOLANDA LADINO OSPINA (Dir)

UNIVERSIDAD PEDAGÓGICA Y TECNOLÓGICA DE COLOMBIA
(Pedagogical and Technological University of Colombia)

Avda Central del Norte 39–115, Tunja, Boyacá
Telephone: (8) 7405626
E-mail: rectoria@uptc.edu.co
Internet: www.uptc.edu.co
Founded 1953
State control
Language of instruction: Spanish
Academic year: February to December
Rector: GUSTAVO ORLANDO ÁLVAREZ ÁLVAREZ
Vice-Rector for Academic Affairs: CELSO ANTONIO VARGAS GÓMEZ
Vice-Rector for Admin.: FRANCISCO MANOSALVA CERON
Sec. Gen.: SULMA LILIANA MORENO GÓMEZ
Librarian: BARBARÁ MARTÍN MARTÍN
Number of teachers: 600
Number of students: 16,000
Publications: *Acción Pedagógica* (2 a year), *Agenda P & G* (2 a year), *Agrodesarrollo* (2 a year), *Anuario de Investigaciones* (1 a year), *Apuntes del Cenes* (2 a year), *Boletín de Acuerdos* (2 a year), *Ciencia en Desarrollo* (2 a year), *Ciencia y Agricultura* (2 a year), *Cuadernos de Lingüística Hispánica* (1 a year), *Cuadernos de Psicopedagogía* (1 a year), *EPG Geografía* (2 a year), *Matemáticas y Educación* (2 a year), *Observatorio Urbano* (3 a year), *Pensamiento y Acción* (2 a year), *Perspectiva Geográfica* (2 a year), *Perspectiva Salud y Enfermedad* (2 a year), *Revista Metalurgia y Ciencia de Materiales* (2 a year), *Terra Nostra* (4 a year)

DEANS

Faculty of Agricultural Sciences: HUGO EDUARDO CASTRO FRANCO
Faculty of Basic Sciences: CARLOS NORBERTO GÓMEZ GÓMEZ
Faculty of Distance Education: JAVIER EMIGDIO PARRA ARIAS
Faculty of Economics and Administration: JOSÉ DEL CARMEN OVIEDO BARRERA
Faculty of Education: OLGA NAJAR SÁNCHEZ
Faculty of Engineering: JORGE HUMBERTO SAAVEDRA
Faculty of Health Sciences: LUCÍA CARLOTA RODRÍGUEZ BARRETO
Faculty of Law and Social Sciences: LEONEL ANTONIO VEGA PÉREZ
Sectional Faculty, Chiquinquirá: OSCAR ORLANDO REINA VERA
Sectional Faculty, Duitama: ADÁN BAUTISTA MORANTES
Sectional Faculty, Sogamoso: LUIS ALEJANDRO FONSECA PÁEZ

UNIVERSIDAD PONTIFICIA BOLIVARIANA
(Pontifical Bolivarian University)

Circular 1, No 70–01, Medellín, Antioquia
Telephone: (4) 4488388
E-mail: secretaria@logos.upb.edu.co
Internet: www.upb.edu.co
Founded 1936
Private control
Language of instruction: Spanish
Academic year: January to December
Chancellor: Mgr RICARDO ANTONIO TOBÓN RESTREPO
Rector: Fr JULIO JAIRO CEBALLOS SEPÚLVEDA
Vice-Rector for Academic Affairs: JORGE IVÁN RAMÍREZ AGUIRRE
Vice-Rector for Admin. and Finance: GABRIEL JAIME ÁNGEL FARACO
Vice-Rector for Pastoral Affairs: Mgr DIEGO ALONSO MARULANDA DÍAZ

Sec. Gen.: CLEMENCIA RESTREPO POSADA
Library Coordinator: MARICELA GÓMEZ VARGAS
Library: see under Libraries and Archives
Publications: *Administración UPB* (1 a year), *Boletín de Programación de Radio Bolivariana* (6 a year), *Comunicación Social UPB* (1 a year), *Cuestiones Teológicas y Filosóficas* (2 a year), *Escritos* (irregular), *Pensamiento Humanista* (1 a year), *Revista Contaminación Ambiental* (2 a year), *Revista de la Facultad de Derecho y Ciencias* (1 a year), *Revista de Medicina UPB* (2 a year), *Revista Universidad Pontificia Bolivariana* (2 a year)

DEANS

School of Architecture and Design: Arq. FELIPE BERNAL HENAO
School of Education and Pedagogy: Mgr ADRIANA ALVAREZ CORREA
School of Engineering: Dra PIEDAD GAÑÁN ROJO
School of Health Sciences: MÓNICA URIBE RÍOS
School of Law and Political Sciences: Dr LUIS FERNANDO ALVAREZ JARAMILLO
School of Social Sciences: Dr ERIKA JAILLIER CASTRILLÓN
School of Strategic Sciences: JUAN GONZALO ARBOLEDA ARBOLEDA
School of Theology, Philosophy and Humanities: Fr GUILLERMO LEON ZULETA SALAS

UNIVERSIDAD POPULAR DEL CÉSAR
(Popular University of César)

Balneario Hurtado Via a Patillal, Valledupar, César
Telephone: (5) 5842472
E-mail: rectoria@unicesar.edu.co
Internet: www.unicesar.edu.co
Founded 1973 as Instituto Tecnológico Universitario del César; present name and status 1976
State control
Language of instruction: Spanish
Academic year: February to December (2 semesters)
Rector: Dr JESUALDO HERNÁNDEZ MIELES
Vice-Rector for Academic Affairs: ROBERTO DAZA SUÁREZ
Vice-Rector for Admin.: WILFRIDO GODOY RAMÍREZ
Vice-Rector for Research: RAÚL BERMÚDEZ MÁRQUEZ
Sec. Gen.: IVÁN JESÚS MORÓN CUELLO
Library Dir: JAIME FAUSTO MORENO
Library of 17,000 vols

DEANS

Faculty of Administration, Accountancy and Economics: VÍCTOR ECHEVERRY GÓMEZ
Faculty of Education: JAIME MAESTRE APONTE
Faculty of Engineering: CLARIBEL PARRA DITTA
Faculty of Fine Arts: EFRAÍN QUINTERO MOLINA
Faculty of Health: NANCY HERNÁNDEZ
Faculty of Political and Social Sciences: NÉSTOR QUIROZ MORENO

UNIVERSIDAD SANTIAGO DE CALÍ
(Santiago de Calí University)

Calle 5 No 62-00, Barrio Pampalinda, Calí, Valle del Cauca
Telephone: (2) 5183000
E-mail: secgener@usaca.edu.co
Internet: www.usc.edu.co
Founded 1958
Private control
Languages of instruction: English, Spanish
Academic year: January to December
Faculties of communication and advertising, economics, engineering; see also under Deans
Rector: Dr CARLOS ANDRÉS PEREZ GALINDO
Vice-Rector: ARTURO HERNAN ARENAS FERNANDEZ
Dir for Extension: JORGE OLAYA GARCERA
Sec. Gen.: FORTUNATO GARCÍA WALLIS
Finance and Admin. Man.: HUMBERTO SALAZAR GRAJALE
Welfare Man.: OSCAR ALBEIRO GALLEGO GOMEZ
Library Dir: JAVIER SALDARRIAGA ARANGO
Publication: *Revista INGENIUM*

DEANS

Faculty of Basic Sciences: CARLOS ANDRÉS PÉREZ
Faculty of Education: JAMES RUIZ MORALES
Faculty of Health: JEFFERSON OCORO MONTAÑO
Faculty of Law: HEBERTH ARMANDO RIOS QUINTANA

UNIVERSIDAD SANTO TOMÁS
(Saint Thomas University)

Carrera 9, No 51–11, Bogotá, DC
Telephone: (1) 5878797
E-mail: comunicaciones@usantotomas.edu.co
Internet: www.usta.edu.co
Founded 1580, restored 1965
Private control
Language of instruction: Spanish
Academic year: February to December
Campuses in Bucaramanga and Tunja
Rector: Fr CARLOS MARIA ALZATE MONTES
Vice-Rector for Academic Affairs: Fr EDUARDO GONZÁLEZ GIL
Vice-Rector for Admin. and Finance: Fr JAIME MONSALVE TRUJILLO
Dir for Research: HENRRY BORJA OROZCO
Sec. Gen.: HÉCTOR FABIO JARAMILLO SANTAMARIA
Dir-Gen. for Library: Fr JORGE FERDINANDO RODRÍGUEZ
Library of 69,800 vols
Publications: *Análisis*, *Cuadernos de Filosofía Latinoamericana*, *Educación y Pedagogía* (2 a year), *Revista Activos*, *Revista Ciencia, Tecnología y Ambiente* (2 a year), *Revista CIFE*, *Revista de Psicología*, *Revista Interamericana de Investigación* (2 a year)

DEANS

Faculty of Administration and Business Studies: ROCIO DEL PILAR HINCAPIE
Faculty of Civil Engineering: MÓNICA YASMIN RUEDA PINTO
Faculty of Economics: JIN ANTONY COTRINO SOSSA
Faculty of Education: MARTA OSORIO DE SARMIENTO
Faculty of Electronic Engineering: ADRIANA CECILIA PAEZ PINO
Faculty of Environmental Engineering: DUVAN JAVIER MESA FERNANDEZ
Faculty of Government and International Relations: EDITH ROSINA CAMERANO FUENTES
Faculty of Graphic Design: PIEDAD GOMEZ CASTILLO
Faculty of Industrial Engineering: CARLOS EDUARDO NAVARETTE SÁNCHEZ
Faculty of International Business: MAURICIO DIAGAMA DURÁN
Faculty of Law: MARÍA CRISTINA PATIÑO GONZÁLEZ
Faculty of Marketing: RICARDO HOYOS BALLESTEROS
Faculty of Mechanical Engineering: ELVER JOFRE CARVAJAL BONILLA
Faculty of Philosophy and Letters: FREDDY ORLANDO SANTAMARIA VELASCO
Faculty of Physical Culture, Entertainment and Sports: JESÚS ASTOLFO ROMERO GARCÍA
Faculty of Psychology: LIGIA SUSANA GOMEZ VILLEGAS
Faculty of Public Accounting: CARLOS ARTURO GOMEZ
Faculty of Science and Technology: CARLOS FERNANDO LATORRE BARRAGAN
Faculty of Social Communication: MARÍA LIGIA HERRERA NAVARRO
Faculty of Sociology: RICARDO ARTURO ARIZA LÓPEZ
Faculty of Statistics: HUGO ANDRES GUTIERREZ ROJAS
Faculty of Telecommunications Engineering: MIGUEL EUGENIO ARIAS FLÓREZ

UNIVERSIDAD SURCOLOMBIANA
(South Colombian University)

Avda Pastrana Borrero, Carrera 1, Neiva, Huila
Telephone: (8) 8754753
E-mail: contactenos@usco.edu.co
Internet: www.usco.edu.co
Founded 1970
State control
Language of instruction: Spanish
Academic year: February to December
Rector: EDUARDO PASTRANA BONILLA
Vice-Rector for Academic Affairs: HIPOLITO CAMACHO COY
Vice-Rector for Admin.: DIANA PATRICIA PEREZ CASTAÑEDA
Vice-Rector for Research and Social Projection: JAIRO ANTONIO RODRÍGUEZ RODRÍGUEZ
Sec. Gen.: JUAN PABLO BARBOSA OTÁLORA
Library Dir: LUIS ALFREDO PINTO
Number of teachers: 450
Number of students: 4,500
Publications: *Ingeniería y Región* (1 a year, print and online, www.ingenieriayregion.com), *Periódico Institucional Digital Suregion* (online, www.suregion.com.co)

DEANS

Faculty of Economics and Administration: MYRIAM LOZANO ANGEL
Faculty of Education: NIDIA GUZMAN DURAN
Faculty of Engineering: ERVIN ARANDA ARANDA
Faculty of Exact and Natural Sciences: RUBEN DARIO VALBUENA VILLARREAL
Faculty of Health: HÉCTOR HERNÁN ZAMORA CAICEDO
Faculty of Law: MARTHA CECILIA ABELLA DE FIERRO
Faculty of Social Sciences and Humanities: JUAN CARLOS ACEBEDO RESTREPO

UNIVERSIDAD TECNOLÓGICA DEL CHOCÓ 'DIEGO LUIS CÓRDOBA'
(Diego Luis Córdoba Technological University of Chocó)

Carrera 2A, No 25–22, Quibdó, Chocó
Telephone: (4) 6726565
E-mail: contactenos@utch.edu.co
Internet: www.utch.edu.co
Founded 1972 as Instituto Politécnico 'Diego Luis Córdoba'; current name adopted 1975
State control
Language of instruction: Spanish
Academic year: January to November
Rector: EDUARDO GARCÍA VEGA
Vice-Rector for Admin.: ECEHOMO LEDEZMA DENIS
Vice-Rector for Extension: GILBERTO PANESSO
Vice-Rector for Research: ROSA EMILIA MOSQUERA
Vice-Rector for Teaching: LUCY MARISOL RENTERIA
Sec. Gen.: ICAR JAIR SERNA

Librarian: ZAHILY SARRAZOLA MARTINEZ

Number of teachers: 125
Number of students: 1,500

Publications: *Obras Literarias*, *Revista Investigacion Biodiversidad Y Desarrollo*

DEANS

Faculty of Basic Sciences: ALICIA MENA MARMOLENO
Faculty of Education: GUILLERMO ALBERTO AMPUDIA PEREA
Faculty of Engineering: DAVID EMILIO MOSQUERA VALENCIA
Faculty of Humanities and Arts: VICTOR RAFAEL FRANCISCO VALENCIA ABADIA
Faculty of Law: DORTON PINO SERNA

UNIVERSIDAD TECNOLÓGICA DE PEREIRA
(Technological University of Pereira)

Apdo Aéreo 97, Pereira, Risaralda
Telephone: (6) 3137300
E-mail: contactenos@utp.edu.co
Internet: www.utp.edu.co

Founded 1958
State control
Language of instruction: Spanish
Academic year: February to December

Rector: LUIS ENRIQUE ARANGO JIMÉNEZ
Vice-Rector for Academic Affairs: WILLIAM ARDILA URUEÑA
Vice-Rector for Admin.: FERNANDO NOREÑA JARAMILLO
Sec. Gen.: CARLOS ALFONSO ZULUAGA ARANGO
Librarian: MARGARITA FAJARDO

Library of 30,000 vols, 1,400 periodicals
Number of teachers: 700

Publications: *Revista de Ciencias Humanas* (2 a year), *Revista Médica de Risaralda* (2 a year), *Scientia et Technica* (3 a year)

DEANS

Faculty of Basic Sciences: HUGO ARMANDO GALLEGO BECERRA
Faculty of Education: Dra MARÍA TERESA ZAPATA SALDARRIAGA
Faculty of Engineering: Ing. JOSÉ GILBERTO VARGAS CANO
Faculty of Environmental Sciences: Dr JHONIERS GUERRERO ERAZO
Faculty of Fine Arts and Humanities: JUAN HUMBERTO GALLEGO RAMÍREZ
Faculty of Health Sciences: Dr JUAN CARLOS MONSALVE BOTERO
Faculty of Industrial Engineering: Ing. WILSON ARENAS VALENCIA
Faculty of Mechanical Engineering: Ing. EDUCARDO RONCANCIO HUERTAS
Faculty of Technology: Ing. JOSÉ REINALDO MARÍN BETANCOURTH

Schools of Art and Music

Conservatorio del Tolima (Conservatory of Tolima): Carrera 1, Calle 9, No 1–18, Ibagué, Tolima; tel. (8) 2618526; e-mail info@conservatoriodeltolima.edu.co; internet www.conservatoriodeltolima.edu.co; f. 1906, current name adopted 1920; faculties of arts, education and music; library: 3,200 vols, 100 DVDs, 35 LDs, 150 CDs, 200 cassettes, 1,700 LPs, 150 video cassettes; 121 teachers; 2,135 students; Rector Dr JAMES ENRIQUE FERNÁNDEZ CÓRDOBA; Sec. Gen. Dr JAIRO BERNAL GUARNIZO.

Conservatorio de Música (Conservatory of Music): Dpto de Música, Facultad de Artes, Universidad Nacional, Carrera 30 No 45–03, Edif. 303, Bogotá, DC; tel. (1) 3165000; e-mail proinde_fabog@unal.edu.co; internet www.facartes.unal.edu.co/conservatorio; f. 1882 as Academia Nacional de Música, current name adopted 1910; 60 teachers; 900 students; library: 11,000 vols, scores and records; Dir MARIO ALBERTO SARMIENTO RODRÍQUEZ.

Institución Universitaria Bellas Artes y Ciencias de Bolívar (University Institute of Fine Arts and Sciences of Bolívar): Centro, San Diego, Carrera 9 No 39–12, Cartagena, Bolívar; tel. (5) 6600391; e-mail info@unibac.edu.co; internet www.unibac.edu.co; f. 1890 as Instituto Musical en Cartagena, current name adopted 2000; depts of fine arts, graphic design, music, performing arts; library: 1,500 vols; Rector SACRA NADER DAVID; Vice-Rector for Academic Affairs ESTELA BARRETO ÁLVAREZ; Vice-Rector for Admin. LUDYS MOLINA JIMENEZ; Sec. Gen. ELZIE TORRES ANAYA; publ. *Ojo al Arte*.

COMOROS

The Higher Education System

The Comoros declared their independence from France in 1975. French is one of the official languages, along with Comorian and Arabic. For many years higher education in the Comoros was limited to a number of programmes in teacher training, agriculture and health sciences at colleges and schools (including the M'Vouni School for Higher Education, which was established near the capital, Moroni, in 1981). Many students left the Comoros to study abroad; the World Bank estimated that 1,000 students did so in 1995. The Government provided scholarships for these students, but relied on funds from international donors to do so. The islands' first university, the Université des Comores, opened in Moroni in December 2003 and 2,600 students were enrolled there in 2005/06; by 2010 this figure had risen to 5,419. The university consists of four faculties, institutes of technology and educational training and research, a school of medicine and public health and a centre for continued education. The university adopted the Licence/Maîtres/Doctorat (LMD) system of degree awards in 2005. In 2008/09 a total of 3,457 students were enrolled in tertiary education in the Comoros.

Technical and vocational training is carried out at three institutions: L'Ecole Nationale Technique Polyvalente which awards the Brevet d'Etudes Professionnelles in electrical, mechanical, building and plumbing professions; the Ecole Nationale de Pêche which trains students in the fishing industry; and the Centre National Horticole which provides instruction in horticultural practices over two years for those who have left school without any qualifications.

Illiteracy, especially among females, poses considerable difficulties for the Comoros (as in many African countries). According to UNESCO, the adult literacy rate in 2009 was 74.2% (males 79.7%; females 68.7%). The development of higher education is hampered by inadequacies in the primary and secondary education system, although enrolment rates have increased notably in recent years. According to UNESCO estimates, enrolment at primary schools in 2006/07 included 87% of children in the relevant age-group, while enrolment at secondary schools in 2004/05 was equivalent to 46% of children in the relevant age-group.

Regulatory and Representative Bodies

GOVERNMENT

Ministry of National Education, Research, Culture and the Arts: BP 73, Moroni; tel. 7744180; Minister ABDOULKARIM MOHAMED.

Research Institute

AGRICULTURE, FISHERIES AND VETERINARY SCIENCE

Institut National de la Recherche pour L'Agriculture, La Pêche et l'Environnement (INRAPE): Moroni; tel. 7644549; e-mail inrape@yahoo.fr; f. 1995; agricultural and environmental research; adaptation of agriculture to climate change; environmental biodiversity; navy biology emergent animal illnesses; Dir-Gen. ASNAOUI MOHADJI.

Library

Moroni

Centre National de Documentation et de Recherche Scientifique (CNDRS): BP 169, Moroni; tel. 744187; e-mail cndrscomores@yahoo.fr; internet www.cndrs-comores.org; f. 1979; incorporates the nat. library and archives, nat. museum and research centre (human and natural sciences); Dir Dr DJAFFAR MMADI.

University

UNIVERSITÉ DES COMORES

route de la corniche, BP 2585, Moroni

Telephone: 734227

E-mail: univ_com@snpt.km

Internet: www.univ-comores.com

Founded 2003

State control

Pres.: MOHAMED RACHADI

DEMOCRATIC REPUBLIC OF THE CONGO

The Higher Education System

Prior to independence from Belgium in 1960, the country was known as Belgian Congo. Following independence it became the Democratic Republic of the Congo, and then Zaire in 1971; in 1997 the name reverted to Democratic Republic of the Congo. The oldest university is the Université de Kinshasa (formerly Université Lovanium), which was founded in 1954 by the Université Catholique de Louvain (Belgium). Between 1971 and 1981 the Université de Kinshasa was merged with the Université de Kisangani (formerly the Protestant-run Université Libre du Congo, founded 1963) and the Université de Lubumbashi (founded 1955) to form the National University of Zaire (UNAZA). Since 1981 these three state-run universities have reverted to autonomous institutions. There are also private universities, including ones at Kinshasa, Mbuji-Mayi, Bas-Congo, Bakavu, Butembo and Goma. Other institutions of higher education include technical institutes and teaching institutes. The medium of instruction is French. Although the number of private institutions in the higher education sector has increased substantially in recent years, many of them offer poor quality teaching and do not have official accreditation. As a result of the prolonged civil conflict in the late 1990s and early 2000s, government funding for education was effectively suspended, contributing to a drastic decline in enrolment; the number of students enrolled at higher education establishments was estimated to have fallen by some 80%. In 2002 an emergency programme for education, at an estimated cost of US $101m., was introduced to restore access to basic education. The number of students enrolled in higher education rose considerably following the signing of a peace agreement in 2003; in 2008/09 there were an estimated 379,867 students in tertiary education, compared with only some 60,341 in 2002/03.

Administration of higher education is split between government ministries: the Ministry of Finance controls budget allocation; the Ministry of the Civil Service controls personnel; and the Ministry of Planning oversees the use of human resources. Senior administrative and academic figures, such as the Rector and heads of department, are appointed by the President and/or the Minister of Higher and University Education and Scientific Research.

The Diplôme d'Etat d'Etudes Secondaires du Cycle Long is required for admission to university education. University degree programmes are divided into three cycles. The first cycle lasts three years and leads to the award of the Diplôme de Graduat; the second cycle lasts two to three years and results in the award of the Licence, although programmes in the fields of medicine and veterinary medicine require longer and lead to the award of the Diplôme de Doctorat followed by the Diplôme de Spécialiste; and the third cycle is generally a two-year programme of postgraduate study resulting in either the award of a Diplôme d'Etudes Spéciales (DES) or the Diplôme d'Etudes Approfondies (DEA). Holders of the DES or the DEA are eligible to undertake a further three to five years' study (including the writing of a thesis) leading to the award of a Doctorat. In 2010 there were reports that the Government was planning to introduce the European Bologna system of higher education in order to enable the country's universities to meet the challenges of globalization.

Technological and teaching-training institutes attached to universities provide three-year courses of higher vocational education, leading to the award of the Gradué. The entry requirement to such programmes is completion of upper secondary education. In 2008/09 there was a total of 616,992 students enrolled at technical and vocational institutes.

In an attempt to regulate and improve the quality of teaching at tertiary level, in October 2009 the Minister of Higher and University Education appointed a commission to carry out an organizational audit and inquiry into the state of the country's higher education sector (both public and private); any institutions that did not prove 'viable' were to be penalized or closed down (by November 2010 a total of 98 higher education institutions—the majority of which were privately operated—had been closed down in five provinces). In May 2010 the United Nations Development Programme signed an agreement with seven Congolese higher education institutions, including the Université de Kinshasa, to promote higher education for women (with particular priority being given to female postgraduate students). From the academic year 2011/12 the Government planned to extend the use of English at tertiary-level educational institutions to make it the country's second language of higher education after the French language, for which a project was also in place in association with the Services pour l'Education, les Savoirs et l'Appui à la Maîtrise et à l'usage du français (SESAM).

Regulatory Bodies

GOVERNMENT

Ministry of Higher and University Education and Scientific Research: Kinshasa; Minister CHELO LOTSIMA.

Ministry of Primary and Secondary Education and Professional Training: Enceinte de l'Institut de la Gombe, BP 3163, Kinshasa-Gombe; tel. (12) 30098; e-mail info@eduquepsp.cd; internet www.eduquepsp.cd; Minister MAKER MWANGU FAMBA.

Ministry of Youth, Sport, Culture and the Arts: 77 ave de la Justice, BP 8541, Kinshasa 1; tel. (12) 31005; Minister BANZA MUKALAYI NSUNGU.

Learned Societies

GENERAL

UNESCO Office Kinshasa: Immeuble Losonia, Blvd du 30 juin, POB 7248, Kinshasa; tel. 8848253; e-mail kinshasa@unesco.org; Head of Office CATHERINE OKAI.

BIBLIOGRAPHY, LIBRARY SCIENCE AND MUSEOLOGY

Association des Archivistes, Bibliothécaires et Documentalistes: BP 805, Kinshasa 11; f. 1973.

HISTORY, GEOGRAPHY AND ARCHAEOLOGY

Société des Historiens: BP 7246, Lubumbashi; f. 1974; attached to Min. of Higher Education and Univ.; brings about a better understanding of the nation's past; organizes meetings, etc. for historians; preserves the national archives, works of art, and archaeological remains; Pres. Prof. NDAYWELÈ NZIEM; Sec. Gen. Prof. Dr TSHIBANGU MUSAS KABET; publs *Etudes d'Histoire Africaine* (1 a year), *Likundoli* (2 a year).

LANGUAGE AND LITERATURE

Alliance Française: 11, Ave Lubefu, Commune de la Gombe, BP 5404, Kinshasa 10; tel. 8803221; offers courses and exams in French language and culture and promotes cultural exchange with France; attached teaching centres in Boma, Bukavu, Kananga, Kikwit, Kisangani, Lubumbashi and Matadi.

Research Institutes

GENERAL

Centre de Recherche en Sciences Humaines (CRSH): BP 3474, Kinshasa-Gombe; e-mail bourses@sshrc-crsh.gc.ca; f. 1985 by fusion of IRS and ONRD; administration, economics, education, history, law, linguistics, literature, philosophy, psychology, social sciences, sociology; library of

4,000 vols and 12,000 periodicals; Dir-Gen. MAKWALA MA MAVAMBU YE BEDA; publs *Cahier Zaïrois de Recherche en Sciences Humaines* (4 a year), *IRS—Information*.

AGRICULTURE, FISHERIES AND VETERINARY SCIENCE

Institut National pour l'Etude et la Recherche Agronomique (INERA): BP 2037, Kinshasa 1; tel. (1) 32332; internet www.inera-drc.org; f. 1933; 2,250 staff; library of 38,428 vols; Pres. Dr Ir. MASIMANGO NDYANABO; publs *Bulletin Agricole du Zaïre* (2 a year), *Bulletin Agroclimatologique* (1 a year), *Info-INERA* (12 a year), *Programme d'Activités* (1 a year).

HISTORY, GEOGRAPHY AND ARCHAEOLOGY

Institut Géographique: 106 Blvd du 30 Juin, BP 3086, Kinshasa-Gombe; f. 1949; geodetic, topographical, photogrammetric and cartographic studies; small library; Dir-Gen. Major LUBIKU LUSIENSE BELANI.

MEDICINE

Institut de Médecine Tropicale: BP 1697, Kinshasa; e-mail info@itg.be; f. 1899; clinical laboratory serving Hôpital Mama Yemo with reference laboratory functions for other medical services in Kinshasa; Dir Dr DARLY JEANTY.

NATURAL SCIENCES

Biological Sciences

Institut Congolais pour la Conservation de la Nature: BP 868, Kinshasa 1; tel. 31401; f. 1925; 2,295 staff; library of 2,500 vols; Man. Dir EULALIE BASHIGE; publ. *Revue Leopard*.

TECHNOLOGY

Bureau de Recherches Géologiques et Minières (BRGM): BP 1974, Kinshasa 1; copper mining; see main entry under France; Dir G. VINCENT.

Centre de Recherches Géologiques et Minières: 44 Ave des Huileries, BP 898, Kinshasa 1; tel. 9928982; e-mail crgm@cedesurk.refer.org; f. 1939; staff of 120 undertake mineral exploration and geological mapping; library of 7,305 vols; Dir-Gen. Prof. NTOMBI MUEN KABEYA; publ. *Revue* (52 a year).

Commissariat Général à l'Energie Atomique: BP 868-184, Kinshasa XI; f. 1959; 140 staff; library of 3,000 vols; Commissary Gen. Prof. MALU WA KALENGA; publs *Bulletin d'Information Scientifique et Technique* (4 a year), *Rapport de Recherche* (1 a year).

Libraries and Archives

Kinshasa

Archives Nationales: BP 3428, 42A Ave de la Justice, Commune de la Gombe, Kinshasa; tel. 31083; f. 1947; 3,000 vols; Curator ANTOINE KIOBE LUMENGA-NESO.

Bibliothèque Centrale de l'Université de Kinshasa: BP 125, Kinshasa 11; e-mail bibliotheques@unikin.ac.cd; internet koha .unikin.cd; f. 1954; 300,000 vols; Chief Librarian (vacant); publs *Liste des Acquisitions, Nouvelles du Mont Amba* (52 a year).

Bibliothèque Publique: BP 410, Kinshasa; f. 1932; 24,000 vols; Librarian B. MONGU.

Kisangani

Bibliothèque Centrale de l'Université de Kisangani: BP 2012, Kisangani; tel. 2948; f. 1963; 90,000 vols; Chief Librarian MUZILA LABEL KAKES.

Lubumbashi

Bibliothèque Centrale de l'Université de Lubumbashi: POB 2896, Lubumbashi; f. 1955; 300,000 vols, 1,000 periodicals, 500,000 microfiches and microfilms; Librarian MUBADI SULE MWANANSUKA; publs *Cahiers Philosophiques Africains* (6 a year), *Lettres*, *Likundoli* (irregular), *Séries A*.

Museums and Art Galleries

Kananga

Musée National de Kananga: 160 Ave Kinkole, BP 612, Kananga.

Kinshasa

Musée National de Kinshasa: BP 4249, Kinshasa.

Lubumbashi

Musée National de Lubumbashi: BP 2375, Lubumbashi.

Universities

UNIVERSITÉ DE KINSHASA

BP 127, Kinshasa 11
Telephone: 30123
Internet: www.unikin.cd
Founded 1954 as the Université Lovanium by the Université Catholique de Louvain in collaboration with the Govt; reorganized 1971 and 1981
Language of instruction: French
Academic year: October to July
Rector: JEAN BERCHMANS LABANA LASAY'ABAR
Sec. Gen. for Admin.: JOSEPH KATANGA KABALEVI
Library: see under Libraries and Archives
Number of teachers: 536
Number of students: 5,800
Publications: *Annales* (2 a year), *Cahiers Economiques et Sociaux* (4 a year)

DEANS

Faculty of Economics: KINTAMBO MAFUKU
Faculty of Law: Prof. NYABIRUNGU MWENE NSONGA
Faculty of Medicine: Dr NGALA KENDA
Faculty of Pharmacy: MULUMBA BIPI
Faculty of Sciences: MUKANA WA MURANA
Polytechnic Faculty: ANDRE DE BOECK

ATTACHED RESEARCH INSTITUTES

Centre de Cardiologie: .

Centre de Recherches pour le Développement: .

Centre de Recherche pour l'Exploitation de l'Energie Renouvelable (CREER): .

Centre de Recherche Interdisciplinaire pour le Droit de l'Homme: .

Centre Interdisciplinaire d'Etudes et de Documentation Politiques (CIE-DOP): .

Centre Interdisciplinaire pour le Développement et l'Education Permanente (CIDEP): BP 2307, Kinshasa 1; training courses in management; brs at Kisangani, Lubumbashi and Karanga; politics and administration, commerce, social sciences, applied education, applied technology; 1,785 students; Sec. Gen. MBULAMOKO ZENGE MOVOAMBE.

Institut d'Etudes et de Recherche Historique du Temps Présent: .

Institut de Recherches Economiques et Sociales (IRES): BP 257, Kinshasa 11; Dir ILUNGA ILUKAMBA.

Institut des Sciences et Techniques de l'Information (ISTI): BP 14.998, Kinshasa 1; first degrees and doctorates; 15 staff; 103 students; Dir-Gen. MALEMBE TAMANDIAK.

Institut Supérieur d'Arts et Métiers (ISAM): BP 15.198, Kinshasa 1; f. 1968; management training for the clothing industry; 18 staff, 101 students; Dir OMONGA OKAKO DENEWADE.

Institut Supérieur de Commerce, Kinshasa: BP 16.596, Kinshasa 1; 37 staff; 600 students; Dir-Gen. PANUKA D'ZENTEMA.

Institut Supérieur des Bâtiments et Travaux Publics (IBTP): BP 4.731, Kinshasa 2; 83 staff; 916 students; Dir-Gen. BUTASNA BU NIANGA.

Institut Supérieur de Techniques Appliquées (ISTA): BP 6593, Kinshasa 31; tel. 20727; f. 1971; technical training; 513 staff; 5,814 students; library of 3,443 vols, 2,486 periodicals, 2,789 dissertations; Dir-Gen. Prof. MUKANA WA MUANDA.

Institut Supérieur des Techniques Médicales (ISTM): BP 774, Kinshasa 11; tel. 22113; f. 1981; 80 staff, 1,005 students; Dir-Gen. Dr PHAKA MBUMBA.

Laboratoire d'Analyses des Médicaments et des Aliments:

UNIVERSITÉ DE KISANGANI

BP 2012, Kisangani
Telephone: 2152
Internet: www.unikis.ac.cd
Founded 1963, present name 1981
State control
Language of instruction: French
Academic year: October to July (3 terms)
Faculties of administration, medicine, political science, science, social sciences
Rector: MWABILA MADELA
Admin. Sec.: GUDIJIGA A. GIKAPA
Academic Sec.: BOKULA MOISO
Budget Administrator: LINDONGA TEMELE-ZEMAKA
Library: see under Libraries and Archives
Number of teachers: 216
Number of students: 2,439
Publication: *Le Cahier du CRIDE*.

ATTACHED RESEARCH INSTITUTES

Bureau Africain des Sciences de l'Education (BASE): BP 14, Kisangani; Dir A. S. MUNGALA.

Centre de Recherche Interdisciplinaire pour le Développement de l'Education (CRIDE): BP 1386, Kisangani; Dir KALALA NKUDI.

Institut Facultaire des Sciences Agronomiques (IFA): BP 1232, Kisangani; f. 1973; first degrees and doctorates in agriculture; 38 teachers; 683 students; library of 7,141 vols, 14,574 periodicals; Rector Dr Ir Prof. MAMBANI BANDA; publ. *Annales*.

Institut Supérieur de Commerce, Kisangani: BP 2.012, Kisangani; Dir KABAMBI MULAMBA.

Institut Supérieur d'Etudes Agronomiques de Bengamisa: BP 202, Kisangani; 31 staff; 328 students; Dir-Gen. LUMPUNGU KABAMBA

UNIVERSITÉ DE LUBUMBASHI

BP 1825, Lubumbashi
Telephone: 225285

E-mail: unilu@unilu.net
Internet: www.unilu.ac.cd
Founded 1955, reorganized 1971 and 1981
Language of instruction: French
sstate control
Academic year: October to February, March to July
Rector: Prof. KAUMBA LUFUNDA
Sec. Gen. for Academic Affairs: Prof. HUIT MULONGO
Sec. Gen. for Admin.: CHABU MUMBA
Chief Librarian: SUKA MUBADI
Number of teachers: 442
Number of students: 13,158
Publications: *Cahiers Philosophiques Africains*, *Cahiers d'Etudes Politiques et Sociales* (2 a year), *Etudes d'Histoire Africaine* (2 a year), *Likundoli* (2 a year), *Mitunda* (African cultures, 2 a year), *Prospective et Perspective* (2 a year), *Recherches Linguistiques et Littéraires* (2 a year), various faculty publs

DEANS
Faculty of Agricultural Science: Prof. MICHEL NGONGO LUHEMBWE
Faculty of Economics: Prof. KASANGANA MWALABA
Faculty of Law: Prof. MALEMBA M. N'SAKILA
Faculty of Letters: Prof. KASHALA KAPALOWA
Faculty of Medicine: Prof. MUTETA WA PA MANDA
Faculty of Psychology and Pedagogy: (vacant)
Faculty of Sciences: Prof. BYAMUNGU BIN RUSANGIZA
Faculty of Social, Administrative and Political Sciences: Prof. ELENGESA NDUNGUNA
Faculty of Veterinary Medicine: Prof. KASHALA KAPAWOLA
Polytechnic Faculty: Prof. KALENGA NGOY

AFFILIATED RESEARCH INSTITUTES
Ecole Supérieur de Commerce (ESC): Dir Prof. KIZOBO O'OBWENG O.
Ecole Supérieure d'Ingénieur (ESI): Dir Prof. NGOIE NSENGA.
Institut Supérieur d'Etudes Sociales de Lubumbashi: BP 825, Lubumbashi 1; tel. 4315; f. 1956; 18 full-time staff, 785 students; Dir KITENGE YA.
Institut Supérieur de Statistique (ISS): BP 2471, Lubumbashi (Shaba); tel. 3905; f. 1967; 72 staff, 700 students; library of 3,000 vols, 10 periodicals; Dir-Gen. Prof. Dr MBAYA KAZADI; Sec.-Gen. for Academic Affairs Prof. Dr ANYENYOLA WELO; Sec. Gen. for Admin. Lic. BIHINI YANKA; publ. *Annales*.
Institut Supérieur des Techniques Médicales: Dir Prof. MALONGA KAJ

UNIVERSITÉ DE MBUJIMAYI

80 Ave de l'Université, BP 225, Mbuji-Mayi
Telephone: 99713112
E-mail: univmayi@yahoo.fr
Internet: um-rdc.org
Founded 1990
Private control
Language of instruction: French
Academic year: November to July
Faculties of applied sciences, economics, law, medicine
Rector: Prof. GHISLAIN DISASHI NTUMBA
Sec. Gen.: Prof. CHARLES TSHULA
Number of teachers: 130
Number of students: 900

UNIVERSITÉ KONGO

BP 202, Mbanza-Ngungu, Bas-Congo
Telephone: (99) 8208474
E-mail: info@universitekongo.org
Internet: www.universitekongo.org
Founded 1990 as Univ. de Bas-Zaïre
Private control
Language of instruction: French
Rector: Prof. JEAN NSONSA VINDA
Sec. Gen.for Academic Affairs: Prof. JOSE LAMI NZUNZU
Sec. Gen. for Admin.: LIEVIN MBUNGU TSENDE
Number of teachers: 292
Number of students: 4,098

DEANS
Faculty of Agronomy: Prof. JULES ALONI KOMANDA
Faculty of Economics and Management: Prof. ANTONIE KAMIANTAKO MIYAMWENI
Faculty of Law: Prof. HONORE MVIOKI BABUTANA
Faculty of Literature and Social Communication: Prof. MABASI BAKABANA
Faculty of Medicine: Prof. Dr NAZAIRE NSEKA MANGANI
Polytechnic Faculty: Prof. MULAPI WALUMENGE

Colleges

Académie des Beaux-Arts (ABA): BP 8249, Kinshasa 1; tel. (1) 261494; 250 students; Dir BEMBIKA NKUNKU.
Institut National des Arts (INA): BP 8332, 1 Ave du Commerce, Zone en Gombé, Kinshasa 1; 72 staff; 147 students; Dir Prof. BAKOMBA KATIK DIONG.

REPUBLIC OF THE CONGO

The Higher Education System

Higher education was established while the Republic of the Congo was under French administration (it was then part of French Equatorial Africa), through the foundation of an Institute for Advanced Studies and a Centre for Advanced Administrative and Technical Studies. Following independence in 1960 the Fondation de l'Enseignement Supérieur en Afrique Centrale was created, which comprised several centres and schools. It was dissolved in 1971 and in the same year the Université de Brazzaville was inaugurated; in 1977 it adopted its current name, the Université Marien-Ngouabi. In 2000 there were some 20,000 students enrolled at the Université Marien-Ngouabi, which is the only state university. In 2002/03 the total number of students in further and higher education was estimated at 12,456; in 2011 the French Ministry of Foreign Affairs estimated student numbers at 21,841. Public education exists at two levels: university and non-university. The latter category includes the Christian Polytechnic and Professional Institute of Arts, the Institute of Business and Economical Development and the Mondongo Higher Institute of Agricultural Sciences. The Ministry of Higher Education is primarily in charge of higher education, although more specific courses are overseen by the relevant government ministry. Private initiatives are increasingly moving into the higher education system, providing mainly technical and professional training in subjects such as business management. The Université Libre du Congo (Brazzaville) is a private university with a Faculty of Law, and three institutes specializing in food science, commercial and international management, and nursing sciences; it offers both short (three-year) and long (five-year) qualifications. Some Congolese students attend further education establishments abroad. In September 2004 the World Bank approved a grant of US $20m. to assist with the reconstruction of the country's educational sector, which had been severely damaged by years of civil conflict.

The four types of higher educational establishment—public and private universities, training schools and institutions of continuing education—are stipulated in the 1990 law related to education, which was modified by the November 1995 law (008/90) defining the organizational structures of the Congolese educational system. This law also stipulates a number of depositions, among them equality in access, free public education, the Government's responsibility for the organization of education and the recognition of the private sector.

Admissions to the Université Marien-Ngouabi, which comprises five faculties, three institutes and three schools, are determined by ministerial decree. Generally, the university accepts candidates of Congolese nationality and foreigners holding a high school degree (baccalauréat) or its equivalent in return for an application fee. A number of the university's faculties, schools and institutes (including the Faculty of Medicine) also hold a competitive entrance examination for potential new students. University-level qualifications are divided into two cycles: first, either the Diplôme Universitaire d'Études Littéraires (DUEL) in arts and humanities or the Diplôme Universitaire d'Études Scientifiques (DUES) in the sciences is awarded after two years of study; second, the Licence is awarded after an additional one year of study after DUEL/DUES, with an option of studying for a further two years for the Diplôme des Études Supérieures (DES). Medical degrees, however, entail seven years of study, during which there is no intermediate degree. There are also a number of professional institutes and schools that award the DES, usually after two-year courses of study. In 2004/5 the Ecole Supérieure de Gestion et d'Administration des Entreprises was the first institution to introduce the Licence-Master-Doctorat (LMD) degree system. In 2011 it hosted approximately 2,500 national and foreign students. In 2011 the Université Marien-Ngouabi was also in the process of implementing the LMD degree system across all of its faculties.

Following a large increase in the number of candidates applying to gain a place at the Université Marien-Ngouabi in 2009, the Government looked into expanding the intake capacity of the university. Furthermore, in an attempt better to meet the economic requirements of the country, students were encouraged to undertake science and technology courses rather than arts and humanities options.

Regulatory Bodies

GOVERNMENT

Ministry of Culture and the Arts: BP 20480, Brazzaville; tel. 81-02-35; Minister JEAN-CLAUDE GAKOSSO.

Ministry of Higher Education: Ancien Immeuble de la Radio, BP 169, Brazzaville; tel. 81-08-15; Minister GEORGES MOYEN.

Ministry of Scientific Research and Technological Innovation: Ancien Immeuble de la Radio, Brazzaville; tel. 81-03-59; internet www.mrsit-congo.net; Minister BRUNO JEAN-RICHARDS ITOUA.

Ministry of Technical Education, Vocational Training and Employment: BP 2076, Brazzaville; tel. 81-17-27; e-mail metp_cab@yahoo.fr; Minister SERGE BLAISE ZONIABA.

Learned Societies

GENERAL

Union Panafricaine de la Science et de la Technologie (UPST) (Pan-African Union of Science and Technology): Ave E. P. Lumumba, BP 2339, Brazzaville; tel. 83-65-35; f. 1987; coordinates research into scientific and technological devt; 409 mem. instns (asscns, academies, socs and research institutes); Pres. Prof. EDWARD S. AYENSU; publ. *Nouvelles de l'UPST* (4 a year).

LANGUAGE AND LITERATURE

PEN Centre of Congo: BP 2181, Brazzaville; tel. 81-36-01; Pres. E. B. DONGALA.

Research Institutes

GENERAL

Direction Générale de la Recherche Scientifique et Technique: BP 2499, Brazzaville; tel. 81-06-07; f. 1966; spec. commissions for industrial and technological sciences, medical science, natural sciences, social sciences and agricultural sciences; library of 4,500 vols; Dir-Gen. Prof. MAURICE ONANGA; publ. *Sciences et Technologies*.

Institut de Recherche pour le Développement (IRD): BP 1286, Zone Industrielle, Pointe-Noire; tel. 94-02-38; f. 1950; biological and physical oceanography, botany, nematology, pedology, plant ecology, plant physiology; library; see main entry under France; Dir LAURENT VEYSSEYRE.

Institut de Recherche pour le Développement (IRD–DGRST): BP 181, Brazzaville; tel. 83-26-80; f. 1947; bioclimatology, botany, demography and sociology, entomology, hydrology, medical epidemiology, microbiology, nutrition, phytopathology, soil science; see main entry under France; library of 16,000 vols; Dir C. REICHENFELD.

AGRICULTURE, FISHERIES AND VETERINARY SCIENCE

Centre de Recherche Forestière du Littoral: BP 764, Pointe-Noire; tel. 53-73-84; e-mail centreforestier@yahoo.fr; f. 1997; Dir Dr MAURICE DIABANGOUAYA.

Centre d'Etudes sur les Resources Végétales (CERVE): BP 1249, Brazzaville; tel. 81-55-24; e-mail cervedgrst@yahoo.fr; f. 1985; attached to Min. of Scientific Research; catalogues plant species of the Congo; promotes traditional phytotherapy; develops indigenous and exotic fodder plants; library of 100 vols; Dir Prof. LAURENT TCHISSAMBOU.

Station Fruitière du Congo: BP 27, Loudima; f. 1963; Dir C. MAKAY.

HISTORY, GEOGRAPHY AND ARCHAEOLOGY

Centre de Recherche Géographique et de Production Cartographique: Ave de l'OUA, BP 125, Brazzaville; tel. 81-07-80; e-mail cergec2@yahoo.fr; f. 1945; attached to Min. of Scientific Research and Technical Innovation; library of 2,786 vols; Dir F. ELONGO.

MEDICINE

Direction de la Médecine Préventive: BP 236, Brazzaville; tel. 81-43-51; f. 1978; attached to Ministry of Health and Social Affairs; responsible for carrying out policy on endemo-epidemic illnesses; 98 staff; Dir Dr RÉNÉ CODDY-ZITSAMELE; publ. various reports and research papers.

TECHNOLOGY

Centre de Recherche et d'Initiation des Projets de Technologie (CRIPT) (Centre for Research and Technology Project Initiation): BP 97, Brazzaville; tel. 13-34-72; e-mail criptdgrst@yahoo.fr; f. 1986; attached to Min. of Scientific Research and Technical Innovation; develops farming and forestry, promotes industry, sets up projects concerned with industrial science and technology, and adapts imported technology for local requirements; Dir Dr LÉON-VOUMBO MATOUMONA.

Libraries and Archives

Brazzaville

Bibliothèque Nationale Populaire (National People's Library): BP 1489, Brazzaville; tel. 83-34-85; f. 1971; 15,000 vols (7,000 in brs); Dir PIERRE MAYOLA.

Bibliothèque des Sciences de la Santé et Centre de Documentation/AFRO Health Sciences Library and Documentation Centre: BP 6, Brazzaville; tel. 241-39425; f. 1952; 7,000 vols; Librarian MARIE-PAULE KABORE.

Bibliothèque Universitaire, Université Marien-Ngouabi: BP 2025, Brazzaville; tel. 83-14-30; f. 1992; 78,000 vols; Chief Librarian INNOCENT MABIALA; publs *Cahiers congolais d'anthropologie et d'histoire*, *Cahiers de la Jurisprudence*, *Congolaise de Droit*, *Revue*.

Centre d'Information des Nations Unies: BP 7248, Kinshasa; tel. 23-34-31; e-mail unickinshasa@undp.org; f. 1983; attached to UN Dept of Information in New York; 4,378 vols (mostly NGO publs); Dir ISMAEL A. DIALLO.

Museums and Art Galleries

Brazzaville

Musée National: BP 994, Brazzaville; tel. 81-03-30; f. 1965; ethnographic colln and nat. history; library of 285 vols; Dir JEAN GILBERT JULES KOULOUFOUA.

Kinkala

Musée Régional André Grenard Matsoua: BP 85, Kinkala; tel. 85-20-14; f. 1978; under the Min. of Culture and the Arts; ethnography; library; Curator BIVINGOU-NZEINGUI.

Pointe Noire

Musée Régional Ma-Loango Diosso: BP 1225, Pointe-Noire; tel. 94-15-79; f. 1982; attached to Min. of Culture and the Arts; collects historical, ethnographical, scientific, artistic materials as a source of information on Congolese culture; Curator JOSEPH KIMFOKO-MADOUNGOU.

University

UNIVERSITÉ MARIEN-NGOUABI

BP 69, Brazzaville
Telephone: 81-01-41
E-mail: unimariengouabi@yahoo.fr

Founded 1961 as Fondation de l'Enseignement Supérieur en Afrique Centrale, became Université de Brazzaville 1971, present name 1977

State control

Language of instruction: French

Rector: Prof. ARMAND MOYIKOUA

Library: see under Libraries and Archives

Number of teachers: 595

Number of students: 20,259

Publications: *Annales de l'Université Marien Ngouabi*, *Revue médicale du Congo* (6 a year)

DEANS

Faculty of Arts and Humanities: DIEUDONNÉ TSOKINI

Faculty of Economics: HERVÉ DIATA

Faculty of Health Sciences: JEAN ROSAIRE IBARA

Faculty of Law: PLACIDE MOUDOUDOU

Faculty of Science: JEAN-MAURILLE OUAMBA

ATTACHED INSTITUTES

Institut du Développement Rural (IDR): BP 69, Brazzaville; f. 1976; Dir FULBERT AKOUANGO.

Institut Supérieur d'Education Physique et Sportive (ISEPS): BP 1100, Brazzaville; f. 1976; Dir PIERRE BAZOLO.

Institut Supérieur de Gestion (ISG): BP 2469, Brazzaville; f. 1976; Dir FILA HYACINTHE DEFOUNDOUX

Colleges

Collège d'Enseignement Technique Agricole: BP 30, Sibiti; f. 1943; Dir JEAN BOUNGOU.

Collège Technique, Commercial et Industriel de Brazzaville (et Centre d'Apprentissage): Brazzaville; f. 1959; Dir HUBERT CUOPPEY.

Ecole Supérieure Africaine des Cadres des Chemins de Fer et de Gestion des Transports: POB 13225, Brazzaville; tel. 71-20-47; f. 1977; management and technical courses.

COSTA RICA

The Higher Education System

The Universidad de Costa Rica is the oldest institution of higher education in Costa Rica. It was founded in 1843 by the Roman Catholic Church as Universidad de Santo Tomás, closed in the 1880s and refounded under its current name in 1940. The Ministry of Public Education controls the formal education system under the aegis of the Consejo Superior de Educación (Higher Council of Education). The supervisory body of public universities is the Consejo Nacional de Rectores (National Council of Rectors). Private universities are under the control of the Consejo Nacional de Educación Superior de Universidades Privadas (National Council of Higher Education for Private Universities). In 2013 there were five state universities—the most recent being the Universidad Técnica Nacional (National Technical University)—and 52 private universities. The Sistema Nacional de Acreditación (SINAES—National University Accreditation System) in 2010 became the legal accreditation body for universities and para-universities. In 2004/05 there were 110,717 students enrolled in higher education; in 2012/13 there were 195,364 students, 51.8% of whom were enrolled in private universities and 47.6% in state universities.

The administrative structure of a university consists of an Asamblea General (legislative body), Consejo Universitario (board of directors), Rectoría (president) and Vicerectorías (vice-presidents). Faculties are the top academic divisions, and are subdivided into departments. There are also attached research centres and institutes.

Entry to higher education institutions is primarily based on the Título de Bachiller; applicants may also be required to sit an entrance examination, particularly for admittance into the public universities. The Bachillerato Universitario is the main undergraduate qualification, for which a student is required to accrue 120–144 credits over four to five years. The Licenciatura may either be awarded following the Bachillerato Universitario or it may be a single qualification with entrance based on the Título de Bachiller or equivalent; this depends on whether a Bachillerato Universitario is available in the field of study. A minimum total of 150 credits are needed for the Licenciatura, including the credits obtained for the Bachillerato Universitario if this has been undertaken. The Licenciatura also requires the completion of a dissertation and is more specialized than the Bachillerato Universitario. At postgraduate level, following the Bachillerato Universitario, a Maestría (of which there are two types: the Maestría Académica and the Maestría Profesional) is awarded after at least two years of study and the attainment of 60–72 credits. For both types of course students must have a working knowledge of a foreign language. Finally, the Doctorado, entrance to which course is generally limited to those holding a Maestría, requires a minimum of two years of study and entails the defence of a thesis.

Technical and vocational education is offered by public and private 'para-universities' of which in 2013 there were two and 28 respectively. Courses last for two to three years and lead to the award of the Diplomado or Técnico Superior. The higher education system has been undergoing fundamental reform since 2006 and a new national Plan Nacional de la Educatión Superior Universitaria Estatal was in place for 2011–15.

Regulatory and Representative Bodies

GOVERNMENT

Ministry of Culture and Youth: Avdas 3 y 7, Calles 11 y 15, frente al parque España, San José; tel. 2221-3806; e-mail culturayjuventudtica@gmail.com; internet www.mcj.go.cr; Minister MANUEL OBREGÓN LÓPEZ.

Ministry of Public Education: Apdo 10087-1000, San José; Edif. Rofas, frente al Hospital San Juan de Dios, San José; tel. 2258-3745; e-mail contraloriaservicios@mep.go.cr; internet www.mep.go.cr; Minister Dr LEONARDO GARNIER RÍMOLO.

Ministry of Science and Technology: Apdo 5589-1000, San José; Calles 19 y 17, Avda Segunda, San José 1000; tel. 2248-1515; e-mail micit@micit.go.cr; internet www.micit.go.cr; Minister ALEJANDRO CRUZ MOLINA.

ACCREDITATION

Sistema Nacional de Acreditación de la Educación Superior (SINAES) (National System of Accreditation in Higher Education): Apdo 1174-1200, San José; Edif. 'Dr Franklin Chang Díaz', de la Embajada de los Estados Unidos de América, Pavas, San José; tel. 2519-5700; e-mail sinaes@sinaes.ac.cr; internet www.conare.ac.cr; f. 1999; attached to Consejo Nacional de Rectores; Dir ROSA ADOLIO CASCANTE; Sec. JENNIFFER SEQUEIRA DUARTE.

NATIONAL BODY

Consejo Nacional de Rectores (CONARE) (National Council of Rectors): Apdo 1174-1200, San José; Edif. 'Dr. Franklin Chang Díaz', de la Embajada de los Estados Unidos de América, Pavas, San José; tel. 2519-5700; e-mail conare@conare.ac.cr; internet www.conare.ac.cr; f. 1974; coordinates decision-making regarding the state univ. education system; composed of rectors of Universidad de Costa Rica, Instituto Tecnológico de Costa Rica, Universidad Nacional and Universidad Estatal a Distancia; Pres. LUIS GUILLERMO CARPIO MALAVASI.

Learned Societies

GENERAL

Asociación Costarricense de Gestores de Recursos Humanos (Costa Rican Association of Human Resource Managers): Curridabat, de la Pops 300 sur y 150 oeste, frente Condominios Ana Catalina, San José; tel. 2280-1785; e-mail info@acgrh.net; internet acgrh.net; f. 2003; Pres. RANDALL GONZÁLEZ; Sec. MARLEN MONTERO SOLÍS.

Oficina de la UNESCO en San José (Office of UNESCO in San José): Apdo 1003-1007, Centro Colón, San José; Paseo Colon, Avda 1 bis, Calle 28, Casa Esquinera 2810, San José; tel. 2010-3800; e-mail san-jose@unesco.org; internet www.unesco.org/sanjose; f. 1986; designated Cluster Office for Costa Rica, El Salvador, Guatemala, Honduras, Mexico, Nicaragua and Panama; Dir JORGE GRANDI (acting).

HISTORY, GEOGRAPHY AND ARCHAEOLOGY

Academia de Geografía e Historia de Costa Rica (Academy of Geography and History of Costa Rica): Apdo 4499-1000, San José; Edif. de Patrimonio Nacional, Avda central, No 293, Entre Calles primera y tercera, San José; tel. 2234-7629; e-mail info@academiaghcr.com; internet www.academiaghcr.com; f. 1940; 40 mems; Pres. Dra MARÍA EUGENIA BOZZOLI VARGAS; Sec. Dra EUGENIA IBARRA ROJAS; publ. *Anales*.

LANGUAGE AND LITERATURE

Academia Costarricense de la Lengua (Costa Rican Academy of Language): Casa de las Academias, Avda central, No 140, Calles 1 y 3, San José; tel. 2248-4894; e-mail acladministracion@acl.ac.cr; internet www.acl.ac.cr; f. 1923; corresp. of the Real Academia Española (Madrid); 20 mems; Pres. ESTRELLA CARTÍN DE GUIER; Sec. MARIO PORTILLA CHAVES.

Alliance Française: Apdo 10195-1000, San José; Avda 7, Calle 5, San José; tel. 2222-2283; e-mail info@afsj.net; internet www.afsj.net; offers courses and exams in French language and culture and promotes cultural exchange with France; Dir MATHILDE VANMANSART.

MEDICINE

Colegio de Médicos y Cirujanos de Costa Rica (College of Physicians and Surgeons of Costa Rica): Sabana, San José; tel. 2210-2200; e-mail info@medicos.sa.cr; internet www.medicos.sa.cr; f. 1857; promotes devt of medical profession through medical research, interchange between mem. asscns and cooperation with nat. and int. medical authorities; 50 mem. asscns; Pres. Dr MARINO RAMÍREZ CARRANZA; Sec. DANIELA UMAÑA MARÍN; publs *Acta Médica Costarricense* (4 a year), *Medicine, Vida y Salud*.

Member Associations:

Asociación Costarricense de Cardiología (Costa Rican Cardiology Association): Apdo 527, San José; Del ICE Sabana 300 m oeste, Edif. Gran Campo, 2°, local No 5 (frente a Restaurante El Chicote), San José; tel. 2291-3148; e-mail asocar@medicos.cr; internet www.acc.co.cr; f. 1978; 40 mems; library of 50 vols; Pres. Dr LUIS FERNANDO VALERIO SOTO; Sec. Dr ESTEBAN COTO VALLDEPERAS.

Asociación Costarricense de Cirugía (Costa Rican Surgery Association): POB 548–1000, San José; tel. 2231-0301; e-mail info@acc.cr; internet www.acc.cr; f. 1954; 150 mems; Pres. Dr GUSTAVO JIMÉNEZ RAMÍREZ; Sec. Dra GRACIELA CORTÉS RAMOS.

Asociación Costarricense de Medicina Interna (Costa-Rican Association of Internal Medicine): Hospital San Juan de Díos, San José; tel. 2257-5252; internet www.medicinainternacr.com; Pres. Dr RODOLFO LEAL VEGA.

Asociación Costarricense de Pediatría (Costa Rican Association of Paediatrics): Apdo 7034–1000, San José; Calle 20 Avda 2–4 HNN, San José; tel. 2256-4060; e-mail info@acopecr.com; internet www.acopecr.com; f. 1951; organizes nat. conf. annually in October; 370 mems; Pres. Dra JULIA FERNÁNDEZ MONGE; Sec. Dra MARCELA MÉNDEZ MATA; publ. *Acta Pediátrica Costarricense*.

Asociación de Obstetricia y Ginecología de Costa Rica (Association of Obstetrics and Gynaecology of Costa Rica): Apdo 1011–1116, La Y Griega, San José; tel. 2220-0181; e-mail info@aogcr.com; internet www.aogcr.com; f. 1956; organizes nat. congress, meetings and regional activities; 220 mems; Chair. Dra CAM LIM BADILLA APUY; Sec. Dra ANGÉLICA VARGAS CAMPOS.

Research Institutes

GENERAL

Consejo Nacional para Investigaciones Científicas y Tecnológicas (CONICIT) (National Council for Scientific and Technological Research (CONICIT)): Apdo 10318-1000, San José; 100 m este de la Rotonda de las Garantías Sociales, Zapote, San José; tel. 2224-4172; e-mail conicit@conicit.go.cr; internet www.conicit.go.cr; f. 1973; promotes devt of science and technology; provides funds for research; works in cooperation with the Min. of Nat. Planning and Economic Policy, and Min. of Science and Technology; library of 3,500 vols; spec. colln: UNISIST programme; Pres. WALTER FERNÁNDEZ ROJAS; Exec. Sec. MAX LÓPEZ CERDAS.

AGRICULTURE, FISHERIES AND VETERINARY SCIENCE

Centro Agronómico Tropical de Investigación y Enseñanza (CATIE) (Tropical Agronomic Centre for Research and Education (CATIE)): Sede Central, CATIE 7170, Cartago, Turrialba 30501; tel. 2558-2000; e-mail comunica@catie.ac.cr; internet www.catie.ac.cr; f. 1973 by the IICA and the Costa Rican govt; non-profit-making scientific and educational asscn for research and graduate education in devt, conservation and the sustainable use of natural resources in Belize, Colombia, Costa Rica, Dominican Republic, El Salvador, Guatemala, Honduras, Mexico, Nicaragua, Panama and Venezuela; library of 92,000 vols, 5,000 current periodicals; Dir-Gen. JOSÉ JOAQUÍN CAMPOS; publs *Revista Agroforestería en las Américas*, *Revista Forestal Centroamericana*, *Revista Manejo Integrado de Plagas* (4 a year).

ECONOMICS, LAW AND POLITICS

Instituto Latinoamericano de las Naciones Unidas para la Prevención del Delito y Tratamiento del Delincuente (ILANUD) (UN Latin American Institute for Prevention of Crime and Treatment of Offenders): Apdo 10071-1000, San José; Edif. Plaza de la Justicia, 3°, San José; tel. 2257-5826; e-mail ilanud@ilanud.or.cr; f. 1975 as a UN regional agency; training, advice and research in the fields of law and criminology, crime prevention and treatment of offenders; specialized library and data bank for int. use; arranges symposia, ministerial meetings; projects incl. standardization of criminal statistics, human rights in the admin. of justice, female and juvenile crime, 'white-collar' crime; Dir Dr ELÍAS CARRANZA; publ. *ILANUD* (2 a year).

Instituto Nacional de Estadística y Censos (National Institute of Statistics and Censuses): Apdo 10163-1000, San José; De la Rotonda de La Bandera, 450 m oeste, Calle Los Negritos, Edif. Ana Lorena, Mercedes de Montes de Oca, San José; tel. 2280-9280; e-mail informacion@inec.go.cr; internet www.inec.go.cr; f. 1883; 250 mems; library of 10,000 vols; Pres. JACQUELINE CASTILLO RIVAS; Dir CATHALINA GARCÍA SANTAMARÍA; publs *Cifras Básicas sobre Fuerza de Trabajo* (1 a year), *Cifras Básicas sobre Pobreza e Ingresos* (1 a year), *Costa Rica: Cálculo de Población por Provincia, Cantón y Distrito* (2 a year), Costo de la Canasta Básica de Alimentos (12 a year), Encuesta de Hogares de Propósitos Múltiples, Módulo de Empleo (1 a year), Indicadores Demográficos (1 a year), Mortalidad Infantil y Evolución Reciente (2 a year).

EDUCATION

Fundación Omar Dengo (Omar Dengo Foundation): Apdo 1032-2050, San José; Barrio Francisco Peralta, Avdas 10 y 12, Calle 25, San José; tel. 2527-6001; e-mail info@fod.ac.cr; internet www.fod.ac.cr; f. 1987; promotes economic, social and human devt of Costa Rica, improves quality of education; Pres. ALFONSO GUTIÉRREZ; Sec. GUILLERMO VARGAS; Exec. Dir Dr LEDA MUÑOZ; publ. *Estado de la Nación* (irregular).

MEDICINE

Instituto Costarricense de Investigación y Enseñanza en Nutrición y Salud (Costa Rican Institute for Research and Teaching on Nutrition and Health): Apdo 4, Tres Ríos, Cartago; La Unión, Cartago; tel. 2279-9911; e-mail msolis@inciensa.sa.cr; internet www.inciensa.sa.cr; f. 1977; attached to Min. of Health; prevention and control of public health problems; laboratory-based surveillance, laboratory monitoring, quality assurance and research and teaching; library of 4,500 vols; Dir-Gen. Dra LISSETTE NAVAS ALVARADO.

NATURAL SCIENCES

Biological Sciences

Organization for Tropical Studies: Apdo 676-2050, San Pedro; tel. 2524-0607; e-mail oet@ots.ac.cr; internet www.ots.ac.cr; f. 1963; promotes education, research and responsible use of natural resources in the tropics; operates 3 biological stations: Las Cruces, incorporating Wilson Botanical Garden (premontane forest), Palo Verde (dry forest) and La Selva (tropical wet forest); consortium of 58 univs and research instns in the USA, Latin America and Australia; library of 10,000 vols, 50 current periodicals; Pres. and CEO ELIZABETH LOSOS; Sec. CYNTHIA SAGERS; publ. *Liana* (2 a year, Spanish and English).

Centro Científico Tropical (Tropical Science Centre): Apdo 83870-1000, San José; tel. 2253-3267; e-mail info@cct.or.cr; internet www.cct.or.cr; f. 1962; private non-profit asscn; research and training in tropical science; consultation on tropical ecology, land use capability and planning, environmental assessments; biological reserve and field station at Monteverde Cloud Forest; library of 7,000 vols; Exec. Dir JULIO CALVO ALVARADO; publ. *Occasional Paper Series* (irregular).

Physical Sciences

Instituto Meteorológico Nacional (National Meteorological Institute): Apdo 5583-1000, San José; Barrio Aranjuez, Avda 9 y Calle 17, frente a costado Noroeste del Hospital Calderón Guardia, San José; tel. 2222-5616; e-mail imn@imn.ac.cr; internet www.imn.ac.cr; f. 1888; climatology, hydrometeorology, agrometeorology, synoptic and aeronautical meteorology; Dir JUAN CARLOS FALLAS S.; publ. *Tópicos Meteorológicos y Oceanográficos* (2 a year).

TECHNOLOGY

Comisión de Energía Atómica de Costa Rica (National Atomic Energy Commission of Costa Rica): Apdo 6681-1000, San José; San Francisco de Goicoechea de la Escuela Claudio Cortés, 25 m al oeste, Edif. Solar de la Abadía, 2°, Local 4, San José 1000; tel. 2248-1591; e-mail info@cea.go.cr; internet www.cea.go.cr; f. 1969; Pres. Ing. MARIO CONEJO SOLÍS; Dir LILLIANA SOLÍS DÍAZ.

Libraries and Archives

San José

Archivo Nacional de Costa Rica (National Archive of Costa Rica): Apdo 41-2020, Zapote, San José; 900 m sur y 150 oeste de Plaza del Sol Curridabat, San José; tel. 2283-1400; e-mail ancost@ice.co.cr; internet www.archivonacional.go.cr; f. 1881; 5,000 vols, 18 kms of archives; Dir-Gen. Lic. VIRGINIA CHACÓN ARIAS; publs *Cuadernillos del Archivo Nacional* (irregular), *Revista del Archivo Nacional* (1 a year).

Biblioteca Instituto Diplomático 'León Fernández Bonilla' (Diplomatic Institute Library 'Leon Fernandez Bonilla'): Apdo 10027-1000, San José; tel. 2223-7555; e-mail biblioteca@rree.go.cr; internet www.rree.go.cr; f. 1989, current name adopted 1995; attached to Min. of Foreign Relations; int. affairs, diplomacy, foreign policy, law; 20,000 vols historical memories, official diary, texts; Librarian LUIS GONZÁLEZ CALVO; publ. *Revista Costarricense de Política Exterior*.

Biblioteca 'Mark Twain'—Centro Cultural Costarricense-Norteamericano ('Mark Twain' Library—Costa Rican-North American Cultural Centre): Apdo 1489-1000, San José; tel. 2207-7574; e-mail bibmarktwain@centrocultural.cr; internet www.centrocultural.cr; f. 1945; locations in San Pedro, La Sabana, Cartago, Heredia and Alajuela; 18,000 vols and documents; Librarian ANDREA SOLIS; publ. *CCCNoticias* (6 a year).

Biblioteca Nacional Miguel Obregón Lizano (National Library Miguel Obregón Lizano): Apdo 10008-1000, San José; Calles 15 y 17, Avda 3 y 3B, costado norte del Parque Nacional, Edif. Biblioteca Nacional, San José; tel. 2221-2436; e-mail bibliotecanacional@sinabi.go.cr; f. 1888; 270,000 vols; Dir YAMILETTE SOLANO NAVARRO; publ. *Bibliografía Nacional*.

Centro de Información 'Alvaro Castro Jenkins' (Information Centre 'Alvaro Castro Jenkins'): Avda Central y Primera, Calles 2 y 4, San José; tel. 2243-4460; e-mail centroinf@bccr.fi.cr; f. 1950; attached to the Central Bank; specializes in economics, finance, accounting, computer science, project management, talent management, risks; 44,000 vols; Librarian DEYANIRA VARGAS DE BONILLA.

Departamento de Servicios Bibliotecarios, Documentación e Información de la Asamblea Legislativa (Department of Library, Documentation and Information of the Legislative Assembly): Apdo 75-1013, San José; Barrio Francisco Peralta Avda 8 Calle 33, San José 10104; tel. 2243-2230; e-mail sitiobiblioteca@asamblea.go.cr; f. 1953; 40,000 vols, 800 periodicals; Dir EDITH PANIAGUA HIDALGO; publs *C. R. Leyes, Decretos* (12 a year), *Revista Parliamentaria* (4 a year).

Sistema de Bibliotecas, Documentación e Información (Libraries, Documentation and Information System): Apdo 11501-2060, San José; Ciudad Universitaria Rodrigo Facio, San Pedro de Montes de Oca, San José; tel. 2253-6152; e-mail mbriceno@sibdi.ucr.ac.cr; internet sibdi.ucr.ac.cr; f. 1946; attached to Univ. de Costa Rica; 450,000 vols, 13,425 periodicals, 48,059 theses, 23,212 audiovisual items, 5,615 maps and atlases; Dir Licda MARY EUGENIA BRICEÑO MEZA.

Museums and Art Galleries

Alajuela

Museo Histórico Cultural Juan Santamaría (Cultural Historical Museum Juan Santamaria): Apdo 785-4050, Alajuela; Avda tercera, Calle central y segunda (una cuadra al norte del parque central), Alajuela; tel. 2441-4775; e-mail mhcjscr@racsa.co.cr; f. 1974; attached to Min. of Culture and Youth; 19th-century colln; library of 2,000 vols; Dir Prof. RAÚL AGUILAR PIEDRA; publ. *11 de Abril: Cuadernos de Cultura*.

Museo Regional de San Ramón (San Ramon Regional Museum): Costado norte del parque de San Ramón, Avdas 1 y 3, Calles 0 y 2, Alajuela; tel. 2447-7137; f. 1977; attached to Univ. de Costa Rica; Dir ROXANA SALAZAR BONILLA.

Heredia

Museo de Cultura Popular (Museum of Popular Culture): Santa Lucia de Barva, Heredia; tel. 2260-1619; e-mail mcp@una.cr; internet www.museo.una.ac.cr; f. 1994; attached to Escuela de Historia, Univ. Nacional; Dir MAYELA SOLANO QUIRÓS.

San José

Galería Nacional (National Gallery): Apdo 10303-1000, San José; Calle 4, Avda 9, San José; tel. 2258-4929; e-mail galerianacional@museocr.org; internet www.museocr.org/index.php?cccc=galeria-nacional-centro-costarricense-de-ciencia-y-cultura; f. 1994; attached to Centro Costarricense de Ciencia y Cultura; nat. and int. art exhibitions; exhibitions with techniques such as painting, sculpture, installations, fused glass, photography, graphic and digital art.

Museo de Arte Costarricense (Costa Rican Art Museum): Apdo 378-1009, San José; Parque Metropolitano de La Sabana, contiguo a la estatua de León Cortés, San José; tel. 2256-1281; e-mail macprensa@musarco.go.cr; internet www.musarco.go.cr; f. 1977; attached to Min. of Culture and Youth; collects and exhibits representative works of Costa Rican art; promotes artistic work through workshops and grants; supervision and preservation of state art collns; library of 5,000 vols; Dir ELIZABETH BARQUERO.

Museo de Arte y Diseño Contemporáneo (Museum of Contemporary Art and Design): Centro Nacional de la Cultura, Antigua Fábrica Nacional de Licores. Avda 3, Calle 15, San José; tel. 2257-7202; e-mail info@madc.cr; internet www.madc.cr; f. 1994; colln of paintings, sculptures, engravings, drawings; Dir FIORELLA RESENTERRA.

Museo de Ciencias Naturales La Salle (Natural Science Museum La Salle): Sabana Suroeste, San José; tel. 2232-1306; f. 1960; attached to Colegio de La Salle; 65,000 zoology, palaeontology, archaeology and mineralogy specimens; Dir-Gen. FRANCISCO VELÁSQUEZ SIMÓN.

Museo de los Niños (Children's Museum): Apdo 10303-1000, San José; Calle 4, Avda 9, San José; tel. 2258-4929; e-mail info@museocr.org; internet www.museocr.org/index.php?cccc=museo-de-los-ninos-centro-costarricense-de-ciencia-y-cultura; f. 1994; attached to Centro Costarricense de Ciencia y Cultura; interactive museum.

Museos del Banco Central (Central Bank Museums): Apdo 12388-1000, San José; Avda Central y 2, Calle 5, Plaza de la Cultura, San José 1000; tel. 2243-4221; e-mail museoro@racsa.co.cr; internet www.museosdelbancocentral.org; f. 1950; permanent exhibitions of pre-Columbian gold and colonial coins, temporary exhibitions of fine arts; Exec. Dir VIRGINIA VARGAS MORA.

Museo del Jade (Jade Museum): Planta Baja, Of. Centrales Instituto Nacional de Seguros, Avda 7, Calle 9 y 11, San José; tel. 2287-6034; e-mail museodeljade@ins-cr.com; f. 1977, current name adopted 1980; pre-Columbian gold objects, jade artefacts.

Museo Nacional de Costa Rica (National Museum of Costa Rica): Apdo 749-1000, San José; Avda Central y 2, costado este Plaza de la Democracia, San José; tel. 2257-1433; e-mail informacion@museocostarica.go.cr; internet www.museocostarica.go.cr; f. 1887; pre-Columbian art, colonial and republican history, nat. herbarium, natural history, culture; library of 70,000 vols; Pres. HAZEL CÓRDOBA SOTO; Dir CHRISTIAN KANDLER RODRÍGUEZ; Sec. MARLEN ROJAS OVARES; publs *Brenesia, Trees and Seeds from the Neotropics, Vínculos* (2 a year).

Affiliated Museums:

Museo de Insectos (Museum of Insects): Faculty of Agricultural Sciences, Univ. de Costa Rica, San José, San Pedro; internet www.miucr.ucr.ac.cr; f. 1962; 1m. specimens of butterflies and other insects.

Museo de Zoología (Museum of Zoology): Escuela de Biología, Univ. de Costa Rica, San José, San Pedro; tel. 2511-4468; e-mail museo@biologia.ucr.ac.cr; internet museo.biologia.ucr.ac.cr; mammals, herpetology, fish; small library.

Universities

ESCUELA DE AGRICULTURA DE LA REGIÓN TROPICAL HÚMEDA/ UNIVERSIDAD EARTH
(School of Agriculture of the Tropical Humid Region)

Apdo 4442-1000, San José
Telephone: 2713-0000
E-mail: admision@earth.ac.cr
Internet: www.earth.ac.cr

Founded 1986
Private control
Languages of instruction: English, Spanish
Academic year: January to December

Rector: Dr JOSÉ A. ZAGLUL
Provost: Dr DANIEL SHERRARD
Vice-Pres. for Admin. and Finance: Ing. LUIS CÉSAR ACOSTA SALAZAR
Librarian: Lic. JOSÉ RUPERTO ARCE

Library of 51,000 vols
Number of teachers: 50
Number of students: 500

Publication: *Tierra Tropical: Sostenibilidad, Ambiente y Sociedad*

INSTITUTO TECNOLÓGICO DE COSTA RICA
(Technological Institute of Costa Rica)

Apdo 159-7050, Cartago
Telephone: 2552-5333
E-mail: infoportal@tec.ac.cr
Internet: www.tec.ac.cr

Founded 1971
public control
Language of instruction: Spanish
Academic year: February to December

Schools of agricultural engineering, agricultural management engineering, agronomy, architecture and town planning, biology, business administration, chemistry, communication, computer science, construction engineering, culture and sport, electromechanical engineering, electronic engineering, forestry engineering, industrial design, industrial production engineering, materials science and engineering, mathematics, physics; safety and hygiene at work, social sciences

Rector: Dr JULIO CALVO ALVARADO
Vice-Rector for Academic Affairs: Ing. LUIS PAULINO MENDEZ
Vice-Rector for Academic Services and Students: Dra CLAUDIA MADRIZOVA
Vice-Rector for Admin.: WILLIAM VIVES BRENES
Vice-Rector for Research and Extension: Dr MILTON VILLARREAL CASTRO
Librarian: CRISTINA GÓMEZ MOLINA

Library of 54,000

Publications: *Espacio Virtual de la Física, Investiga.TEC* (3 a year), *Revista Comunicación* (2 a year), *Revista Forestal Mesoamericana Kurú* (2 a year), *Revista Virtual Matemática Educación e Internet, TEC Empresarial* (3 a year), *Tecnología en Marcha* (3 a year)

UNIVERSIDAD ADVENTISTA DE CENTRO AMÉRICA
(Adventist University of Central America)

Apdo 138-4050, Alajuela
1.5 km al Norte de los Tribunales de Justicia, La Ceiba, Alajuela
Telephone: 2436-3300
E-mail: mercadeo@unadeca.net
Internet: www.unadeca.ac.cr

Founded 1927, current name and status 1987
Private control

Language of instruction: Spanish
Academic year: March to November

Rector: Dra Herminia Perla
Asst Rector: Lic. Yessica Caballero

UNIVERSIDAD AMERICANA
(American University)

Barrio Los Yoses, frente a KFC, San José
Telephone: 2207-7000
E-mail: matricula@uam.cr
Internet: www.uam.ac.cr
Founded 1997
Private control
Language of instruction: Spanish
Academic year: March to November
Faculties of communication, economic sciences, education, engineering, health, social sciences
Rector: Rosa Ma. Monge Monge
Vice-Rector: Luis Diego Guillén Martinez

UNIVERSIDAD AUTÓNOMA DE CENTRO AMERICA
(Autonomous University of Central America)

Apdo 7637-1000, San José
Campus Los Cipreses, 1 km al norte del Servicentro La Galera, San José, Curridabat
Telephone: 2272-9100
E-mail: info@uaca.ac.cr
Internet: www.uaca.ac.cr
Founded 1976
Private control
Language of instruction: Spanish
Academic year: January to December (3 terms)
Rector: Lic. José Guillermo Malavassi Vargas
Gen. Sec.: Lisette Martínez
Chancellor: Gonzalo Gallegos J.
Vice-Chancellor: William Ramirez Salas
Registrar: Roxinia Castillo
Librarian: Julissa Méndez Marín
Number of teachers: 500
Number of students: 3,000
Publications: *Acta Académica* (2 a year), *Ordenanzas y Anuario Universitario*

DEANS
Faculty of Architecture: Manuel Gutiérrez Rojas
Faculty of Engineering: Ing. Luis Javier Villalobos Cordero
Faculty of Health Sciences: Dr Francisco. Echeverría Batalla
Faculty of Human Sciences: William Ramírez Salas
Faculty of Social Sciences: Lic. Alvis González Garita

UNIVERSIDAD AUTÓNOMA DE MONTERREY
(Autonomous University of Monterrey)

Apdo 3510-1000, San José
Telephone: 2283-7853
E-mail: info@unam.ac.cr
Internet: www.unamcr.com
Founded 1958
Private control
Language of instruction: Spanish
Academic year: March to November
Rector: Lic. Oscar Sáenz Aguilar

DEANS
Faculty of Administrative Sciences: Licda Ana Eugenia Barrantes Gamboa
Faculty of Public Accounting: Lic. William Carazo Gutiérrez
Faculty of Social Sciences: Lic. Marco Ortega Guevara

UNIVERSIDAD BÍBLICA LATINOAMERICANA
(Latin American Biblical University)

Apdo 901-1000, San José
Telephone: 2283-8848
E-mail: registro@ubila.net
Internet: www.ubila.net
Founded 1923
Private control
Language of instruction: Spanish
Academic year: March to November
Schools of biblical studies, theological studies
Rector: Dr Edwin José Mora Guevara
Dean: Elizabeth Cook
Library: collns from Latin American Church, periodicals, bibliographies

UNIVERSIDAD BRAULIO CARRILLO
(Braulio Carrillo University)

Apdo 5635-1000, San José
Paseo Colón, de Pizza Hut, San José
Telephone: 2222-6780
E-mail: admin@universidadbrauliocarrillo.com
Internet: www.universidadbrauliocarrillo.com
Founded 1994
Private control
Language of instruction: Spanish
Academic year: March to November
Rector: Dr Juan Manuel Gómez Solera

UNIVERSIDAD CATÓLICA DE COSTA RICA
(Catholic University of Costa Rica)

Apdo 519-2100, San José
600 este, 200 norte y 100 este de la Iglesia Católica de Moravia, Paso Ancho, Seminario Central, Moravia, San José
Telephone: 2240-7272
E-mail: info@ucatolica.ac.cr
Internet: www.ucatolica.ac.cr
Founded 1993
Private control
Language of instruction: Spanish
Academic year: March to November
Rector: Fernando Muñoz Mora
Publication: *Revista Humanitas*

UNIVERSIDAD CENTRAL
(Central University)

Detrás de la Iglesia Santa Teresita en Barrio Escalante, diagonal al Banco de Costa Rica, San José
Telephone: 2212-0400
E-mail: mercadeo@universidadcentral.com
Internet: www.universidadcentral.com
Founded 1989
Private control
Language of instruction: Spanish
Academic year: March to November
Faculties of economic sciences, education sciences, engineering sciences, social sciences
Rector: Lic. Sergio Mata Navarro

UNIVERSIDAD CENTROAMERICANA DE CIENCIAS SOCIALES (UCACIS)
(Central American University of Social Sciences)

San Pedro de Montes de Oca, el Cantón Universitario de Costa Rica, En la Calle principal de San Pedro, de almacenes Casa Blanca 600 m sur, San José
Telephone: 2280-5310
E-mail: info@ucacis.ac.cr
Internet: www.ucacis.ac.cr
Founded 1986
Private control
Language of instruction: Spanish
Academic year: March to November
Rector: Maribel Soto Arguedas
Library of 2,000 vols

UNIVERSIDAD CONTINENTAL DE LAS CIENCIAS Y LAS ARTES
(Continental University of the Sciences and the Arts)

300 m este del Museo Nacional, Barrio la California, diagonal a INTACO, San José
Telephone: 2256-7944
E-mail: info@uccart.com
Internet: www.uccart.com
Founded 1999
Private control
Language of instruction: Spanish
Academic year: March to November
Rector: Leonardo Villegas
Registrar: Laura Ramírez
Publication: *Revista Cultural Anamorfosis*

UNIVERSIDAD CREATIVA
(Creative University)

Montes de Oca, Mercedes, de la Farmacia la Paulina 100 este, 100 norte y 250 este Residencial Guaymi, Calle B, lote 19, San José
Telephone: 2528-5095
E-mail: info@ucreativa.com
Internet: www.ucreativa.com
Founded 1995
Private control
Language of instruction: Spanish
Academic year: March to November
Rector: Dr Luis Montoya Salas

UNIVERSIDAD CRISTIANA DEL SUR
(Southern Christian University)

50 m sur de Pizza Hut, Paseo Colón, Oficentro Grano de Oro Of. No 1000, San José
Telephone: 2222-5303
E-mail: info@educacion.ac.cr
Internet: www.educacion.ac.cr
Founded 1997
Private control
Language of instruction: Spanish
Academic year: March to November
Schools of business administration, law
Rector: Dra Sonia Romero Mora
Vice-Rector: Lic. Freddy Ramos Corea
Exec. Dir: Danny Aguilar Espinoza

UNIVERSIDAD DE CIENCIAS MEDICAS
(University of Medical Sciences)

Sabana oeste, 400 m oeste del MAG, San José
Telephone: 2549-0000
E-mail: info@ucimed.com
Internet: www.ucimed.com
Founded 1976
Private control
Language of instruction: Spanish
Academic year: March to November
Rector: Dr Pablo Guzmán Stein

DEANS
Faculty of Medicine: Dr Oscar Montero Jiménez
Faculty of Microbiology: Dr Mario Chaves Villalobos
Faculty of Nutrition: Dra Jeanette Zúñiga Quesada

Faculty of Pharmacy: Dr JORGE ALBERTO LOPEZ MORA
Faculty of Physiotherapy: Licda GLORIA VENEGAS OVIEDO
Graduate Studies: Dr JOSÉ GUILLERMO JIMÉNEZ MONTERO

UNIVERSIDAD DE COSTA RICA
(University of Costa Rica)

Universidad de Costa Rica Sede 'Rodrigo Facio Brenes', Montes de Oca, San José 2060
Telephone: 2511-0000
E-mail: consultas.odi@ucr.ac.cr
Internet: www.ucr.ac.cr
Founded 1843, refounded 1940
public control
Language of instruction: Spanish
Academic year: March to November
Rector: Dr HENNING JENSEN PENNINGTON
Vice-Rector for Admin.: Dr CARLOS ARAYA LEANDRO
Vice-Rector for Research: Dra ALICE LORENA PÉREZ SÁNCHEZ
Vice-Rector for Social Action: ROBERTO SALOM ECHEVERRÍA
Vice-Rector for Teaching: Dr BERNAL HERRERA MONTERO
Librarian: Lic. AURORA ZAMORA GONZÁLEZ (acting)
Library: see under Libraries and Archives

DEANS
Faculty of Agrifood: Dr LUIS FELIPE ARAUZ CAVALLINI
Faculty of Arts: Dra ANNETTE CALVO SHADID
Faculty of Dentistry: MADELINE HOWARD MORA
Faculty of Economics: CARLOS PALMA RODRÍGUEZ
Faculty of Education: Dr ANA LUPITA CHAVES SALAS
Faculty of Engineering: EDWIN SOLÓRZANO CAMPOS
Faculty of Fine Arts: M. M. EDDIE MORA BERMÚDEZ
Faculty of Law: Dr ERICK ALFREDO CHIRINO SÁNCHEZ
Faculty of Medicine: Dr LUIS BERNARDO VILLALOBOS SOLANO
Faculty of Microbiology: Dr FERNANDO CHAVES MORA
Faculty of Pharmacy: LIDIETTE FONSECA GONZÁLEZ
Faculty of Science: Dr JAVIER TREJOS ZELAYA
Faculty of Social Sciences: FRANCISCO ENRÍQUEZ SOLANO (acting)
Graduate Studies: Dra CECILIA DÍAZ OREIRO

REGIONAL CENTRES
Centro Regional del Atlántico (Atlantic Regional Centre): e-mail alvaroz@sa.ucr.ac.cr; internet turrialba.sa.ucr.ac.cr; Dir Dr ALEX MURILLO FERNÁNDEZ.
Centro Regional de Caribe (Caribbean Regional Centre): internet www.srl.ucr.ac.cr; Dir Lic. RICARDO WING ARGÜELLO.
Centro Regional de Guanacaste (Regional Centre of Guanacaste): e-mail sede.guanacaste@ucr.ac.cr; internet www.sedeguanacaste.ucr.ac.cr; Dir Dr RAZZIEL ACEVEDO ÁLVAREZ.
Centro Regional del Occidente (Western Regional Centre): internet www.so.ucr.ac.cr; Dir Dr FRANCISCO RODRÍGUEZ CASCANTE.
Centro Regional del Pacífico (Pacific Regional Centre): internet www.srp.ucr.ac.cr; Dir M. L. MARJORIE JIMÉNEZ CASTRO

UNIVERSIDAD DE IBEROAMÉRICA
(University of Ibero-America)

200 m este del ICE de Tibás, San José
Telephone: 2297-2242
E-mail: info@unibe.ac.cr
Internet: www.unibe.ac.cr
Founded 1995
Private control
Language of instruction: Spanish
Chancellor: Dr ISRAEL HERNÁNDEZ
Vice-Chancellor: Dra SHIRLEY BENAVIDEZ VINDAS
Publications: *Revista de Farmacéutica UNIBE*, *Revista de la Facultad de Medicina de la Universidad de Iberoamérica*

DEANS
Faculty of Medicine: Dr RAFAEL LAMAS ALFONSO
Faculty of Nursing: Dra PATRICIA ROBLES
Faculty of Pharmacy: Dra LISSETTE RODRIGUEZ
Faculty of Psychology: Dra ERIKA COTO

UNIVERSIDAD DE LA SALLE (ULASALLE)
(University of La Salle)

Apdo 536-1007, Centro Colón, San José
Sabana sur 100 m al este, 150 m al sur del Colegio de Médicos, San José
Telephone: 2290-1010
E-mail: info@ulasalle.ac.cr
Internet: www.ulasalle.ac.cr
Founded 1995
Private control
Language of instruction: Spanish
Academic year: March to November
Rector: OSCAR AZMISTIA BARRANCO
Vice-Rector for Academic Affairs: Dr RAFAEL ÁNGEL PÉREZ CÓRDOBA
Vice-Rector for Academic Affairs: Dra XINIA CERDAS ARAYA
Vice-Rector for Admin. Affairs: Dra ROSA ESPINOZA LAÍN
Vice-Rector for Training and Human Devt: Lic. JUAN CARLOS CANALES PÁEZ
Gen. Sec.: Licda ANA MARCELA CARMONA GUILLÉN

DEANS
Faculty of Administration: ORLANDO SABORÍO ELIZONDO
Faculty of Education: Dra XINIA CERDAS ARAYA
Faculty of Law: Dra VILMA ALPÍZAR MATAMOROS
Faculty of Psychology: WENDY OBANDO LELVA

UNIVERSIDAD DE LAS CIENCIAS Y EL ARTE DE COSTA RICA
(University of Science and Arts of Costa Rica)

250 m sur de la Corte Suprema de Justicia, San José
Telephone: 2207-9714
Internet: www.udelascienciasyelarte.ac.cr
Founded 1997, became ind. from Panamerican Univ. 1996
Private control
Language of instruction: Spanish
Academic year: March to November
Faculties of economic sciences, fine arts, health sciences, social sciences; schools of architecture, art and design, education, law, management, nursing
Rector: FRANCISCO JIMÉNEZ VILLALOBOS

UNIVERSIDAD DE SAN JOSÉ
(University of San José)

Apdo 7446-1000, San José
San Francisco de Dos Rios, de la Iglesia de San Francisco de Dos Rios, 400 este y 150 sur, San José 10106
Telephone: 2218-0747
E-mail: info@universidadsanjosecr.com
Internet: www.universidadsanjosecr.com
Founded 1976 as Colegio Académicum; present name and status 1992
Private control
Language of instruction: Spanish
Academic year: January to December (3 terms)
Schools of business administration, computer science, education and psychology, humanities, international trade, law, social science; international postgraduate school
Rector: MANUEL SANDI MURILLO
Registrar: Lic. RÓGER SEGNINI ESQUIVEL
Librarian: JOSÉ SEGNINI
Publication: *Revista Universitaria*

UNIVERSIDAD DEL DISEÑO/ FACULTAD DE ARQUITECTURA Y ESTUDIOS AMBIENTALES
(University of Design)

100 m oeste del Hipermás, Heredia
Telephone: 2562-7333
E-mail: info@unidis.ac.cr
Internet: www.unidis.ac.cr
Founded 1993
Private control
Language of instruction: Spanish
Academic year: March to November
Rector: Lic. ADOLFO ENRIQUE BONILLA LEIVA

UNIVERSIDAD DEL TURISMO
(Tourism University)

Apdo 215-1007, Paseo Colón, San José
Edif. Centro Colón, San José
Telephone: 2258-6290
E-mail: info@utur.ac.cr
Internet: www.utur.ac.cr
Founded 1996
Private control
Language of instruction: Spanish
Academic year: March to November
Rector: Lic. RAMÓN MADRIGAL LEÓN
Vice-Rector: PABLO HERNÁNDEZ B

UNIVERSIDAD DEL VALLE
(University of Valle)

100 m este de Pollos Fritos Kentucky en barrio la California, San José
Telephone: 2280-8308
E-mail: info@udelvalle.com
Internet: www.udelvalle.com
Private control
Language of instruction: Spanish
Academic year: March to November
Rector: Lic. MIGUEL ÁNGEL ALFARO RODRÍGUEZ

DEANS
Faculty of Industrial Engineering: Ing. RANDY CHAVARRIA BRICEÑO
Faculty of Information Engineering: Licda RAQUEL CORDOBA SANABRIA
Faculty of Law: Lic. ALLAN SALAZAR CASCANTE
Faculty of Psychology: GRETTEL BARRIENTOS SOLANO
Faculty of Social Sciences: Licda GIORGA ACON WONG

UNIVERSIDAD EMPRESARIAL DE COSTA RICA
(Business University of Costa Rica)

Apdo 12640-1000, San José
Zapote Residencial, Monte Alegre, San José
Telephone: 2217-8931
E-mail: info@unem.edu.pl
Internet: www.unem.edu.pl
Founded 1992 as Int. Postgraduate School affiliated with Universidad de San José, present name and status 1997
Private control
Languages of instruction: Spanish, English
Academic year: January to December
Faculties of administrative sciences, biological sciences, education and humanities, psychology and behavioural sciences, social sciences, postgraduate studies; school of languages
Rector: Lic. WILLIAM ZAMORA GONZÁLEZ
Registrar: ELAINE PÉREZ
Librarian: RODOLFO MARTÍNEZ
Publication: *Gazetta Empresarial*

UNIVERSIDAD EN CIENCIAS ADMINISTRATIVAS SAN MARCOS
(University of Administrative Sciences San Marcos)

Apdo 1515-1250, San José, Escazu
100 m este del Parque Morazán, Avda 3, Calle 11, San José
Telephone: 2257-8715
E-mail: info@usam.ac.cr
Internet: www.usam.ac.cr
Founded 1996
Private control
Language of instruction: Spanish
Academic year: March to November
Rector: JOAQUÍN BRIZUELA ROJAS
Dir-Gen. for Academic Affairs: CARLOS ZÚÑIGA

ESCUELA LIBRE DE DERECHO UNIVERSIDAD
(Free School of Law University)

75 m al oeste del Registro Nacional, Zapote, San José
Telephone: 2283-5533
E-mail: info@uescuelalibre.cr
Internet: www.uescuelalibre.ac.cr
Founded 1978
Private control
Language of instruction: Spanish
Academic year: March to November
Rector: Lic. RICARDO GUERRERO PORTILLA
Vice-Rector for Academic Affairs: CARLOS GÓMEZ RODAS
Vice-Rector for Admin. Affairs: AÍDA MELÉNDEZ ARAYA
Dir: Lic. SERGIO DONATO CALDERÓN
Publications: *Revista Historica*, *Revista Tribuna Libre*

UNIVERSIDAD ESTATAL A DISTANCIA
(State Distance University)

Apdo 474-2050, San José
De la Rotonda la Betania 500 m al este, Carretera a Sabanilla Mercedes de Montes de Oca, San José
Telephone: 2527-2000
E-mail: informacion@uned.ac.cr
Internet: www.uned.ac.cr
Founded 1977
public control
Language of instruction: Spanish
Academic year: March to November
28 Regional centres; schools of business administration, education, exact and natural sciences, social and humanities
Rector: LUIS GUILLERMO CARPIO MALAVASI
Academic Vice-Rector: KATYA CALDERÓN HERRERA
Exec. Vice-Rector: ANA CRISTINA PEREIRA GAMBOA
Vice-Rector for Planning: Dr EDGAR CASTRO MONGE
Dir of IT and Communications: MSc VIGNY ALVARADO CASTILLO
Librarian: RITA LEDEZMA

UNIVERSIDAD EVANGÉLICA DE LAS AMÉRICAS (UNELA)
(Evangelical University of the Americas)

Costado oeste de la Clínica Bíblica, Torre Omega 9°, San José
Telephone: 2221-7870
E-mail: info.unela@gmail.com
Internet: www.unela.ac.cr
Founded 1992
Private control
Language of instruction: Spanish
Academic year: March to November
Rector: Dr ENRIQUE GUANG
Registrar: LUIS HERBOZO

DEANS

School of Ecclesiastical Resource Management: RONALD VÁSQUEZ
School of Theology: HUMBERTO DEL CASTILLO

UNIVERSIDAD FIDELITAS
(Fidelitas University)

Apdo 8063-1000, San José
Del Colegio de Ingenieros y Arquitectos en Curridabat, Santa Marta, San José, San Pedro
Telephone: 2253-0262
E-mail: informacion@ufidelitas.ac.cr
Internet: www.ufidelitas.ac.cr
Founded 1980 as Collegium Fidélitas; current name adopted 1994
Private control
Language of instruction: Spanish
Rector: ANA ISABEL SOLANO BRENES

DEANS

Faculty of Economics and Social Sciences: JOSE EDUARDO ARAYA MOLINA
Faculty of Engineering: ALFREDO ABARCA ROJAS

UNIVERSIDAD FLORENCIO DEL CASTILLO
(Florencio del Castillo University)

100 m sur de la Esq. sureste de los Tribunales de Justicia, Cartago
Telephone: 2591-4750
E-mail: info@uca.ac.cr
Internet: www.uca.ac.cr
Founded 1996
Private control
Language of instruction: Spanish
Academic year: March to November
Rector: Lic. CHRISTIAN CHINCHILLA MONGE
Vice-Rector: FRANCISCO BOLAÑOS RODRIGUEZ
Sec.: DAHIANNA ROJAS MAROTO

UNIVERSIDAD FUNDEPOS ALMA MATER
(Fundepos Alma Mater University)

3° del Edif. San José 2000, a un costado del puente Juan Pablo II en La Uruca, San José
Telephone: 2231-5855
E-mail: matricula@fundepos.ac.cr
Internet: www.fundepos.ac.cr
Founded 2003
Private control
Language of instruction: Spanish
Academic year: March to November
Rector: Dr LUIS ALBERTO CHAVES MONGE
Library of 7,500 vols

UNIVERSIDAD HISPANOAMERICANA
(Spanish American University)

Llorente de Tibás, San José
Telephone: 2241-9090
E-mail: info@uhispanoamericana.ac.cr
Internet: www.uhispanoamericana.ac.cr
Founded 1981 as Sapientia College; univ. status 1991
Private control
Language of instruction: Spanish
Academic year: March to November
Campuses in Barrio Aranjuez, Barrio Escalante, Heredia, Puntarenas
Rector: Lic. ÁNGEL MARÍN ESPINOZA
Vice-Rector: Ing. JOSÉ RAÚL PINO ALEA
Vice-Rector for Student Life and Welfare: CARLO MAGNO ARROYO
Publication: *Sapiencia* (1 a year)

UNIVERSIDAD INDEPENDIENTE DE COSTA RICA
(Independent University of Costa Rica)

Apdo 414-2400, San José
Desamparados, 50 m este de la esquina noreste del Cementerio, San José
Telephone: 2259-1038
E-mail: info@uindependiente.ac.cr
Internet: www.uindependiente.ac.cr
Founded 1996
Private control
Language of instruction: Spanish
Academic year: March to November
Faculties of education science and humanities, social and administrative sciences
Rector: Dra SONIA ABARCA MORA

UNIVERSIDAD INTERNACIONAL DE LAS AMERICAS
(International University of the Americas)

Apdo 1447-1002, San José
Barrio Aranjuez, Calle 23 (Avdas 7 y 7bis), El Carmen, San José
Telephone: 2212-5500
E-mail: info@uia.ac.cr
Internet: www.uia.ac.cr
Founded 1986
Private control
Library of 25,000 vols
Schools of administration, advertising, computer engineering, dentistry, education, electromechanical engineering, industrial engineering, international business, international relations, journalism, languages, law, medicine, pharmacy, public finance, tourism
Rector: Dr MÁXIMO SEQUEIRA ALEMÁN

UNIVERSIDAD INTERNACIONAL SAN ISIDRO LABRADOR
(International University St Isidore the Labourer)

300 m sur de la Escuela Morazán, Barrio Morazán, San Isidro de El General, Pérez Zeledón, San José 11901
Telephone: 2771-6767
E-mail: info@uisil.com
Internet: www.uisil.com

Founded 1995
Private control
Language of instruction: Spanish
Academic year: March to November

Rector: OLGA MONTERO CECILIANO

Publication: *Revista el Labrador*

UNIVERSIDAD JUAN PABLO II
(John Paul II University)

Curridabat Centro de la Iglesia, Esq. noreste 50 norte, San José
Telephone: 2272-5901
E-mail: admision@ujpii.ac.cr
Internet: ujpii.ac.cr
Private control
Language of instruction: Spanish
Academic year: March to November

Schools of business administration, human sciences, social doctrine of the church

Rector: EMILIO GARREAUD INDACOCHEA

UNIVERSIDAD LATINA DE COSTA RICA
(Latin University of Costa Rica)

Apdo 1561-2050, San José, San Pedro Lourdes de Montes de Oca, San José
Telephone: 2224-1920
E-mail: internacional@ulatina.cr
Internet: www.ulatina.ac.cr
Founded 1979
Private control

Campuses in Cañas, Grecia, Guápiles, Limón, Palmares, Paso Canoas, Puntarenas, San Isidro del General, Santa Cruz, Turrialba

Rector: CLOTILDE FONSECA
Vice-Rector for Academic Affairs: RONALD ALVAREZ

DEANS

Faculty of Business Studies: YORLENY ZAVALA
Faculty of Engineering: DIÓGENES ÁLVAREZ
Faculty of Health Studies: NESTOR AZOFEIFA
Faculty of Hospitality: BENITO AVILÉS
Faculty of Social Sciences: LAURA RAMÍREZ
Graduate Studies: JOSÉ ÁNGEL CHACÓN

UNIVERSIDAD LATINOAMERICANA DE CIENCIA Y TECNOLOGIA (ULACIT)
(Latin American University of Science and Technology)

Apdo 10235-1000, San José
100 m sur del Periódico La República, Barrio Tournón, San José
Telephone: 2523-4000
E-mail: info@ulacit.ac.cr
Internet: www.ulacit.ac.cr
Founded 1987
Private control
Languages of instruction: English, Spanish
Academic year: January to December

Schools of advertising and marketing, business and accounts, English, health, law, psychology, safety and environment

Rector and Pres.: Dr SILVIA CASTRO
Vice-Rector for Academic Affairs: Dr ILEANA CONTRERAS
Vice-Rector for Admin.: WILLY VILLALOBOS
Vice-Rector for External Affairs: GABRIELA TIJERINO
Vice-Rector for Research and Devt: EDGAR SALGADO
Vice-Rector for Student Services: MARIANELA NÚÑEZ
Vice-Rector for Technology Management: ALLAN MADRIGAL
Registrar: Lic. MITZI MADRIGAL
Dir of Library: FANNY CHINCHILLA

Library of 25,000 vols
Number of teachers: 300
Number of students: 3,000

DEANS

Faculty of Business Administration: LAURA BRAVO
Faculty of Engineering: JOHANNA MADRIGAL
Faculty of Dentistry: Dr MARIELA PADILLA
Faculty of Information Technology: FAWSY BENDECK
Faculty of Social Sciences: YORLENI ROMERO

UNIVERSIDAD LIBRE DE COSTA RICA
(Free University of Costa Rica)

Avda Central 25 y 2, Calle San José, San José
Telephone: 2258-0033
E-mail: info@ulicori.ac.cr
Internet: www.ulicori.ac.cr
Founded 1993
Private control
Language of instruction: Spanish
Academic year: March to November

Schools of business administration, criminology, education, graduate studies, medical records and health information systems, music, physical therapy, political science and foreign trade, social work and social development

Rector: Dr CARLOS PANIAGUA VARGAS

UNIVERSIDAD MAGISTER
(Magister University)

Apdo 352-1300, San José
Estamos Ubicados de la Facultad de Derecho de la Universidad de Costa Rica 100 m oeste, Barrio Dent, San José, Montes de Oca, San Pedro
Telephone: 2234-0435
E-mail: info@umagister.com
Internet: www.umagister.com
Founded 1981
Private control
Language of instruction: Spanish

Rector: VIVIAN GONZÁLEZ TREJOS

UNIVERSIDAD METROPOLITANA CASTRO CARAZO
(Castro Carazo Metropolitan University)

Apdo 325-1005, San José
Avda primera, Entre las Calles 5 y 7, San José
Telephone: 2542-0300
E-mail: info@umca.net
Internet: www.umca.net
Founded 1936
Private control
Language of instruction: Spanish
Academic year: March to November

Faculties of accounting, computer engineering, education, law, management

Rector: ESTRELLA PORRAS Z.
Vice-Rector for Student Services: MARVIN VILLALOBOS PALMA

UNIVERSIDAD NACIONAL
(National University)

Apdo 86-3000, Heredia
Campus Omar Dengo, Avda 1, Calle 9, Heredia
Telephone: 2277-3000
E-mail: registro@una.ac.cr
Internet: www.una.ac.cr
Founded 1973
public control
Language of instruction: Spanish
Academic year: February to November

Rector: Lic. SANDRA LEÓN COTO
Vice-Rector for Academic Affairs: FRANCISCO GONZÁLEZ ALVARADO
Vice-Rector for Devt: DINIA FONSECA OCONOR
Vice-Rector for Student Affairs: Lic. NELLY OBANDO ÁLVAREZ
Library Dir: Lic. MARGARITA GARCÍA

Publications: *ABRA* (2 a year), *Economía y Sociedad* (2 a year), *ISTMICA* (1 a year), *Letras* (2 a year), *MHSalud* (2 a year), *Relaciones Internacionales* (4 a year), *Repertorio Americano* (2 a year), *Revista Bibliotecas* (2 a year), *Revista Ciencias Ambientales*, *Revista Ciencias Veterinarias*, *Revista de Historia* (2 a year), *Revista Geográfica de América Central*, *Revista Latinoamericana de Derechos Humanos*, *Revista Ciencias Marinas y Costeras*, *REVMAR*, *Siwo Revista de Teología*, *Temas de Nuestra América*, *Revista de Estudios Latinoamericanos* (2 a year), *Uniciencia* (2 a year), *Universidad en Diálogo*, *Vida Silvestre Neotropical* (2 a year)

DEANS

Centre of General Studies: Lic. ENRIQUE MATA RIVERA
Centre for Research and Teaching in Education: Dra ILEANA CASTILLO CEDEÑO
Centre for Research, Teaching and Extension in Fine Arts: FLORIVETTE RICHMOND CANTILLO
Faculty of Earth and Sea Sciences: Dr MARCO VINICIO HERRERO ACOSTA
Faculty of Exact and Natural Sciences: ALBERTO SEGURA GUTIÉRREZ
Faculty of Health Sciences: ANTONIETA CORRALES ARAYA
Faculty of Philosophy and Arts: Dr ALBINO CHACÓN GUTIÉRREZ
Faculty of Social Sciences: CARLOS A. BUEZO CRUZ

UNIVERSIDAD PARA LA COOPERACIÓN INTERNACIONAL
(University for International Cooperation)

Apdo 504-2050, San José
De la Rotonda El Farolito, 200 m este y 150 m norte, Barrio Escalante, San José
Telephone: 2283-6464
E-mail: info@uci.ac.cr
Internet: www.uci.ac.cr
Founded 1994
Private control
Language of instruction: Spanish
Academic year: March to November

Faculties of environment and development, health sciences

Rector: Dr EDUARD MÜLLER CASTRO
Gen. Sec.: Dr FRANKLIN MARÍN

DEANS

Faculty of Economics, Business and Technology: BERNARDO LÓPEZ GONZÁLEZ
Faculty of Legal and Social Sciences: Dr CARLOS MANAVELLA
Faculty of Project Management: RAMIRO FONSECA

UNIVERSIDAD SAN JUAN
(St John's University)

San Pablo de Heredia, 100 m al norte del Palacio Municipal, Heredia, San Pablo
Telephone: 2237-4622
E-mail: info@universidadsanjuan.com
Internet: www.universidadsanjuan.com
Private control
Language of instruction: Spanish
Academic year: March to November

Pres.: FERNANDO TREJOS CASTRO

Rector: GUILLERMO ELADIO QUIRÓS ALVAREZ
Publication: *Vida y Salud*

UNIVERSIDAD SANTA LUCIA
(Santa Lucia University)

100 m este del Cine Omni, San José
Telephone: 2257-4552
E-mail: recepcion@usl.ac.cr
Internet: www.usl.ac.cr
Private control
Language of instruction: Spanish
Rector: LIGIA MENESES SANABRIA

UNIVERSIDAD SANTA PAULA
(Santa Paula University)

Apdo 67-2050, San José, Montes de Oca, San Pedro
Autopista Florencio del Castillo, Lomas de Ayarco Sur, primera entrada, 25 m sur, Curridabat, San José
Telephone: 2272-7123
E-mail: info@uspsantapaula.com
Internet: www.uspsantapaula.com
Private control
Language of instruction: Spanish
Academic year: March to November
Schools of audiology, occupational therapy, physical therapy, respiratory therapy, speech therapy
Rector: Licda ROCÍO VALVERDE GALLEGOS
Publication: *Terapéutica*

UNIVERSIDAD TECNOLÓGICA COSTARRICENSE
(Costa Rican Technological University)

Avda Central, Calle 1 de la librería Universal 50 m este y 25 norte, San José
Telephone: 2223-1124
E-mail: info@utccr.com
Internet: www.utccr.com
Private control
Language of instruction: Spanish
Academic year: March to November
Rector: CARLOS CASTRO QUESADA

UNIVERSIDAD VERITAS
(Veritas University)

Apdo 1380-1000, San José
1 km al oeste de Casa Presidencial, Edif. Veritas, Zapote, San José
Telephone: 2246-4600
E-mail: info@veritas.cr
Internet: www.uveritas.ac.cr
Founded 1968
Private control
Academic year: January to December (3 semesters)
Faculties of architecture, art, design
Exec. Pres.: RONALD SASSO R.
Rector: Ing. JOSÉ JOAQUIN SECO AGUILAR
Vice-Pres.: LUIS DIEGO BOLAÑOS
Dean for Academic Affairs: OSCAR PAMIO

Colleges

Colegio Universitario de Cartago (CUC) (University College of Cartago (CUC)): Barrio El Molino, de la Funeraria La Última Joya, 300 m sur, Cartago; tel. 2591-3363; internet www.cuc.ac.cr; f. 1976; Dean MARIO MORALES GAMBOA; Dir for Academic Affairs YAMILETH JENKINS ALVARADO; Dir for Admin. and Finance ISRAEL AMADOR TENORIO.

INCAE Business School: Apdo 960-4050, Alajuela; 2 km W from Vivero PROCESA 1, La Garita, Alajuela; tel. 2437-2200; internet www.incae.edu; f. 1964 in Nicaragua (see also under Nicaragua); Costa Rica campus opened 1983; library: 32,600 vols; Pres. Dr ARTURO CONDO; Librarian Lic. THOMAS BLOCH.

Instituto Centroamericano de Administración Pública (ICAP) (Central American Institute of Public Administration): Apdo 10025-1000, San José; 100 sur, 75 oste de la Heldería Pop's, Curridabat, San José; tel. 2234-1011; e-mail info@icap.ac.cr; internet www.icap.ac.cr; f. 1954 as Escuela Superior de Administración Pública (ESAPAC) by a jt project of the govts of Costa Rica, El Salvador, Guatemala, Honduras and Nicaragua (Panama incl. 1961); Centre for Information Technology; Dir Dr HUGO ZELAYA CÁLIX; publ. *Revista Centroamerica de Administración Pública* (2 a year).

CÔTE D'IVOIRE

The Higher Education System

Côte d'Ivoire was a province in French West Africa before gaining its independence in 1960. The Université de Cocody in Abidjan is the oldest university, founded in 1958 as the Centre d'Enseignement Supérieur d'Abidjan; in 1964 it became the Université Nationale de Côte d'Ivoire, and it acquired its current name in 1995. There are also two other state universities, one at Abobo-Adjamé (also in Abidjan) and the other at Bouaké. In 2006 there was total of 18 private universities and 120 private grandes écoles in Côte d'Ivoire. The country's first Islamic university, the Université Musulmane de Côte d'Ivoire, was opened in 2009. Some 156,772 students were enrolled at tertiary-level institutions in 2006/07. The Ministry of Higher Education and Scientific Research oversees the universities. There are also two administrative bodies, the Council of Higher Education Teaching and the Standing Board of Higher Education Teaching.

The Baccalauréat is the secondary school qualification required for admission to university. After the first two years of undergraduate studies, a diploma is awarded based on the academic path being followed: arts and humanities (Diplôme Universitaire d'Études Littéraires—DUEL), sciences (Diplôme Universitaire d'Études Scientifiques—DUES), law (Diplôme Universitaire d'Études Juridiques—DUEJ), economics (Diplôme Universitaire d'Études Économiques Générales—DUEEG) or general studies (Diplôme d'Études Universitaires Générales—DEUG). After the Diplôme, a further one to two years of study lead to the award of the Licence. However, four years of study are required for the Diplôme d'Agronomie générale and five years for the Diplôme d'Ingénieur. In medicine, the title of Docteur en Médecine is awarded after six to seven years of study. The grandes écoles offer five-year post-secondary courses which lead to the award of professional diplomas that are of a higher standard than the Licence. At postgraduate level, the Maîtrise is awarded following one year of study after the Licence. A further year of study (including completion of a thesis) leads to the Diplôme d'Études Approfondies (DEA). A final one year of postgraduate study results in the award of the Diplôme d'Études Supérieures (in science, law or economics) and a final three years of research after the Maîtrise leads to the award of the Doctorat de Spécialité de Troisième Cycle. Higher awards, of Diplôme de Docteur Ingénieur and Doctorat d'Etat, are given following several more years of research. The Doctorat d'Université is awarded to foreign students. In 2012/13 reforms were being undertaken to introduce the Licence–Master–Doctorat three-cycle system of degree qualifications, awarded after three, five and eight years of further study.

Vocational and technical education is provided by various schools and institutes. The Brevet de Technicien Supérieur is awarded upon completion of a two- to three-year course. Two-year post-secondary courses leading to the Diplôme Universitaire de Technologie are offered by the instituts universitaires de technologie.

Regulatory Bodies

GOVERNMENT

Ministry of Culture and Francophone Affairs: 22Eétage, Tour E, Tours Administratives, BP V39, Abidjan; tel. 20-21-83-94; e-mail culture.ci@ci.refer.org; internet www.culture.gouv.ci; Minister MAURICE KOUAKOU BANDAMA.

Ministry of Higher Education and Scientific Research: 20Eétage, Tour C, Tours Administratives, BP V151, Abidjan; tel. 20-33-54-64; internet www.enseignement.gouv.ci; Minister IBRAHIMA CISSÉ BACONGO.

Ministry of National and Technical Education: 28Eétage, Tour D, Tours Administratives, BP V120, Abidjan; tel. 20-21-85-27; e-mail menfb@ci.refer.org; internet education-ci.org; Minister KANDIA KAMISSOKO CAMARA.

Learned Societies

LANGUAGE AND LITERATURE

Alliance Française: AFI N'Gokro, BP 1899, Yamoussoukro; tel. 30-64-25-30; e-mail afi_yakro@yahoo.fr; offers courses and exams in French language and culture; promotes cultural exchange with France; attached teaching offices in Abengourou, Korhogo and San Pedro.

Goethe-Institut Côte d'Ivoire: Cocody, rue C2708, BP 982 Abidjan 08, Abidjan; tel. 22-40-01-60; e-mail verw@abidjan.goethe.org; internet www.goethe.de/af/abi/deindex.htm; f. 1970; offers courses and exams in German language and culture; promotes cultural exchange with Germany; library of 7,750 vols; Dir HENRIKE GROHS.

Research Institutes

GENERAL

Institut de Recherche pour le Développement (IRD): rue du Chevalier de Clieu, Zone 4, 15 BP 917, Abidjan 15; tel. 21-24-37-79; internet www.ird.ci; f. 1946; health education, economic devt, environmental management; see main entry under France; Rep. ALAIN MORLIÈRE.

AGRICULTURE, FISHERIES AND VETERINARY SCIENCE

Centre de Co-opération Internationale en Recherche Agronomique pour le Développement (CIRAD): see entry in Burkina Faso.

Centre National de Recherche Agronomique (CNRA) (National Centre for Agricultural Research): Adiopodoumé, KM17 Route de Dabou, 01 POB 1740, Abidjan 01; tel. 23-47-24-24; e-mail info@cnra.ci; internet www.cnra.ci; f. 1998; 140 mems; Dir-Gen. Dr KOFFI SIE; publ. *CNRA-Info* (4 a year).

ECONOMICS, LAW AND POLITICS

Centre Ivoirien de Recherches et d'Etudes Juridiques: Blvd Latrille, opp. Eglise St Jean, Cocody 01, BP 3811, Abidjan; tel. 22-44-60-54; f. 1973; strategic research into problems affecting the judiciary in Côte d'Ivoire; Dir KOMENAN ZAPKA.

Centre de Recherche et d'Action pour la Paix (CERAP): 08 BP 2088, Abidjan 08; tel. 22-40-47-20; e-mail iddh@cerap-inades.org; internet www.cerap-inades.org; f. 1962; promotes devt of newly ind. countries; research and training in human rights, peace, politics, economics; library of 50,000 vols, 230 periodicals; Gen. Dir Dr HYACINTHE LOUA; publs *Débats: Courrier d'Afrique de l'Ouest* (12 a year), *La Lettre de l'IDDH, Bulletin sur les Droits de l'homme en Afrique de l'Ouest* (4 a year).

MEDICINE

Institut Pasteur de Côte d'Ivoire: 01 BP 490, Abidjan 01; tel. 23-45-33-92; e-mail pasteur@pasteur.ci; f. 1972; research laboratories for the study of viral diseases, including yellow fever, poliomyelitis, rabies, influenza, hepatitis, HIV/AIDS; clinical analysis laboratories used by the Centre Hospitalier Univ., Cocody; small library in process of formation; Dir MIREILLE DOSSO.

Institut Pierre Richet: BP1500, Bouaké; tel. 30-63-37-46; f. 1973; research into tropical endemic diseases, incl. malaria, sleeping sickness, dengue fever and yellow fever; part of l'Organisation de Co-opération et de Coordination de la Lutte contre les Grandes Endémies en Afrique de l'Ouest (OCCGE); training on 2 levels: technician in medical entomology, and medical entomologist; missions and field studies carried out as required by member countries of OCCGE; library containing spec. colln and field data; Dir P. CARNEVALE.

NATURAL SCIENCES

General

Centre de Recherches Océanographiques: 29 rue des Pêcheurs, BP V18, Abidjan; tel. 21-35-50-14; e-mail abe@cro.ird.ci; internet www.refer.ci/ivoir_ct/rec/cdr/cro/accueil.htm; f. 1958; biological oceanography, hydrobiology, physics and chemistry; library of 30,000 vols; Dir Dr JACQUES ABE; publs *Archives Scientifiques*, *Journal Ivoirien d'Océanologie et de Limnologie*.

Physical Sciences

Station Géophysique de Lamto: BP 31, N'Douci; tel. 31-62-90-95; e-mail lamtogeo@aviso.ci; f. 1962; atmospherical and climatological, seismological, infrared studies; Dir Prof. MAMADOU FOFANA.

TECHNOLOGY

Société pour le Développement Minier de la Côte d'Ivoire (SODEMI): 01 BP 2816, 31 Blvd des Martyrs, Abidjan 01; tel. 22-44-29-95; e-mail sodemi@sodemi.ci; internet www.sodemi.ci; f. 1962; geological and geophysical minerals prospecting; mineral mining; library of 5,435 vols, 28 current periodicals, 2,556 geological or prospecting reports, 3,500 topographic and geological maps; Dir-Gen. J. N'ZI.

Libraries and Archives

Abidjan

Archives de Côte d'Ivoire: BP V126, Abidjan; tel. 20-32-41-58; f. 1913.

Bibliothèque Centrale de la Côte d'Ivoire: BP 6243, Abidjan-Treichville; f. 1963; attached to Min. of National Education; public lecture service; 14,000 vols; Librarian P. ZELLI ANY-GRAH.

Bibliothèque Centrale de l'Université de Cocody: BP V34, Abidjan 01; tel. 22-44-08-47; f. 1963; 95,000 vols, 1,650 periodicals; Librarian FRANÇOISE N'GORAN.

Bibliothèque de l'Institut Français de Côte d'Ivoire: 01 BP 3995, 01 Abidjan; tel. 20-22-24-36; 38,415 vols, 5,000 vols in African Documentation section, 57 periodicals and reviews; Dir CHRISTIAN OQUET; Librarian BLAISE CAMARA.

Bibliothèque Nationale de Cote d'Ivoire: BP V180, Abidjan; tel. 47-24-86-28; internet www.bnci.ci; f. 1968; 75,000 vols and 135 current periodicals; Dir COFFIE TIBURCE; publ. *Bibliographie de la Côte d'Ivoire* (1 a year).

Museum

Abidjan

Musée des Civilisations: BP 1600, Abidjan 01; fmrly Musée de la Côte d'Ivoire; exhibits of ethnographical, sociological, artistic and scientific nature; attached to Centre des Sciences Humaines; Dir MEMEL SILVIE KASSI.

Universities

UNIVERSITÉ D'ABOBO-ADJAMÉ

BP 801, Abidjan 02

Telephone: 22-37-81-22
E-mail: abobo-adj@abobo.edu.ci
Internet: www.abobo.edu.ci

Founded 1957 as Centre d'Enseignement Supérieur; became part of Univ. Nationale de Côte d'Ivoire 1964; ind. status and current name adopted 1992

State control

Units of basic sciences, food technology and higher education; school of health sciences; centres for advanced training and ecology

Pres.: ETIENNE EHOUAN EHILÉ

Library of 14,000 vols
Number of teachers: 50
Number of students: 5,000

UNIVERSITÉ DE BOUAKÉ

BP V 18, Bouaké 01

Telephone: 30-63-48-57
Internet: www.refer.ci/ivoir_ct/edu/sup/uni/bke/accueil.htm

Founded 1960, became part of Univ. Nationale de Côte d'Ivoire 1964, present status 1994

State control

Units of communication, environment and society, economics and development, higher education, law, administration and development and medical sciences; centres for development research and lifelong education

Pres.: FRANÇOIS KOUAKOU N'GUESSAN
Sec. Gen.: GERMAIN ADJA-DIBY

UNIVERSITÉ FÉLIX HOUPHOUËT-BOIGNY

01 BP V34, Abidjan

Telephone: 22-48-48-41
E-mail: info@ufrseg.info
Internet: ufrseg.info

Founded 1958 as the Centre d'Enseignement Supérieur d'Abidjan; became part of Univ. Nationale de Côte d'Ivoire 1964; fmrly Univ. of Cocody (f. 1995), current name adopted 2012

State control
Language of instruction: French
Academic year: September to July

Pres.: CÉLESTIN TÉA GOKOU
Gen. Sec.: JÉRÔME TOTO BALOUBI
Librarian: FRANÇOISE N'GORAN

Number of teachers: 1,081
Number of students: 37,500

Publications: *En-Quête* (Humanities), *Repères* (Humanities), *Revues Médicales* (4 a year), *Revues Sociales* (2 a year)

DEANS

Faculty of Biosciences: VALENTIN N'DOUBA
Faculty of Construction Engineering and Technology: MARIE-CHANTAL KOUASSI-GOFFRI
Faculty of Criminology: ZÉPHIRIN BOLIGA
Faculty of Earth Sciences and Mining Resources: JEAN BIENI
Faculty of Economic Sciences: GILBERT-MARIE AKE NGBO
Faculty of Human and Social Sciences: IGNACE ZASSELI BIAKA
Faculty of Information, Art and Communication: AUGUSTE AGHI BAHI
Faculty of Language, Literature and Civilization: FRANÇOIS ASSI ADOPO
Faculty of Law: DJEDRO MELEDJE
Faculty of Mathematics and Computer Science: KONIN KOUA
Faculty of Medicine: ISIDORE MOHÉNOU DIOMANDE
Faculty of Odontostomatology: SIAKA TOURÉ
Faculty of Pharmacy: ANGLADE KLA MALAN

PROFESSORS

Faculty of Biosciences:

ACHY SEKA, A., Atmospheric Physics
AIDARA, D.
ASSA, A.
BOKRA, Y.
DEGNY, E.
DJAKOURE, A. L.
EBBY, N.
EHILE, E. E.
HONENOU, P.
KAMENAN, A.
KOPOH, K.
KOUAKOU, G.
KOUASSI, N., Zoology
KRA, G.
LOROUGNON, G.
N'DIAYE, A. S., Cell Biology
NEZIT, P., Mathematics
N'GUESSAN, Y. T., Organic Chemistry
OFFOUMOU, A. M.
SERI, B.
TOURE, S., Mathematics
TOURE, V., Organic Chemistry

Faculty of Economic Sciences:

ATSAIN, A.
ALLECHI, M.
KOULIBALY, M.

Faculty of Language, Literature and Civilization:

ANO, N., Oral Literature
BOKA, M., The African Novel in French
DIBI, K., Metaphysical Philosophy
HAUHOUOT, A., Geography
KODJO, N., History
KOMENAN, A. L., Philosophy
KONATE, Y., Philosophy
KONE BONI, T., Philosophy
LEZOU, D. G., The Francophone African Novel South of the Sahara, Semiotics
M'BRA, E., History
N'DA, P., The Francophone Novel
NIAMKET, K., Philosophy
NIANGORAN, B., Ethnology
SEMI-BI, Z., History
TANO, J., Differential Psychology

Faculty of Law:

BLEOU, D. M., Public Law
DEGNI-SEGUI, R., Public Law
ISSA, S., Private Law
SARASSORO, H., Private Law
WODIE, V. F., Public Law
YAO-N'DRE, P., Public Law

Faculty of Medicine:

ANDOH, J.
ATTIA, Y. R.
BAMBA, M.
BEDA, Y. B.
BOUHOUSSOU, K. M.
COULIBALY, O. A.
DAGO, A. B. A.
DJEDJE, M.
DOSSO, B. M.
EHOUMAN, A.
GADEGBEKU, A. S.
KADIO, A.
KANGA, J. M.
KANGA, M.
KEITA, A. K.
KONE, N.
KOUAKOU, N. M.
KOUAME, K. J.
LAMBIN, Y.
MOBIOT, M. L.
N'DORI, R.
N'DRI, K. D.
N'GUESSAN, K. G.
NIAMKET, E. K.
ODEHOURI, K. P.
ODI, A. M.
ROUX, C.
SANGARE, A.
SANGARE, I. S.
SOMBO, M. F.
TIMITE ADJOUA, M.
WAOTA, C.
WELFFENS-EKRA, C.

Faculty of Odontostomatology:

ANGOA, Y.
BAKAYOKO, L. R.
BROU, K. E.
EGNANKOU, K.
ROUX, H.
TOURE, S.

Faculty of Pharmacy:

BAMBA, M.
KONE, M.
MARCY, R.
OUATTARA, L.
YAPO, A. E.

DIRECTORS

Institute of African History of Art and Archaeology: ZAN SEMI-BI
Institute of African Literature and Aesthetics: (vacant)
Institute of Applied Linguistics: ASSY ADOPO
Institute of Ethnosociology: (vacant)
Institute of Teacher-training and Teaching Research: ADOU AKA
Centre for Architectural and Urban Research: (vacant)
Centre for Communication Teaching and Research: REGINA SERIE TRAORE
University Centre for French Studies: N'GUESSAN KOUASSI

Colleges

Académie Régionale des Sciences et Techniques de la Mer: BP V158, Abidjan; tel. 20-37-18-23; f. 1975 by 17 African countries; merchant shipping, training for radio officers, marine management; library; Dir-Gen. AKA ADOU.

Ecole Nationale d'Administration: BP V 20, Abidjan; tel. 22-41-52-25; e-mail ena@globe.access.net; f. 1960; 954 students; library: 11,676 vols, 15 periodicals; Dir GUILLAUME KOUACOU DJAH.

Ecole Nationale des Postes et Télécommunications: BP 1501, Abidjan; tel. 21-25-54-94.

Ecole Nationale Supérieure de Statistique et d'Economie Appliquée: Cnr blvd François Mitterand and blvd des Grandes Ecoles, Campus Universitaire de Cocody, 08 BP3, Abidjan 08; tel. 22-44-08-40; e-mail ensea@ensea.ed.ci; internet www.ensea.refer.ci; f. 1961; 20 teachers; 120 students; library: 13,268 vols; Dir KOFFI N'GUESSAN.

Ecole Nationale Supérieure des Travaux Publics: BP 1083, Yamoussoukro; tel. 30-64-01-00; f. 1963; comprises l'Ecole Préparatoire, l'Ecole Nationale Supérieure des Ingénieurs, le Centre de Formation Continue, l'Ecole Nationale des Techniciens Supérieurs; library: 60,000 vols; 97 teachers; 567 students; Dir SYLVAIN KACOU.

Ecole Supérieure d'Agronomie: BP 1313, Yamoussoukro; tel. 30-64-07-70; e-mail esayakro@africaonline.ci; f. 1965; training of agricultural managers; research into agricultural production; 75 teachers; 600 students; library: 6,000 vols; Dir Dr KAMA BERTÉ.

Ecole Supérieure Interafricaine de l'Electricité/Interafrican Electrical Engineering College: BP 311, Bingerville; tel. 22-40-33-12; f. 1979; bilingual (English and French) training to graduate level in electrical engineering for students sponsored by power-supply authorities or private companies from all over Africa; Dir-Gen. ABDOU KARIM DIAGNE.

Institut National Polytechnique Félix Houphouët-Boigny: BP 1093, Yamoussoukro; tel. 30-64-05-41; f. 1975; technical and vocational training; comprises l'Ecole de Formation Continue et de Perfectionnement des Cadres, l'Ecole Supérieure d'Agronomie, l'Ecole Supérieure de Commerce et d'Administration d'Entreprises, l'Ecole Supérieure d'Industrie, l'Ecole Supérieure des Travaux Publics; library: 20,000 vols; 350 teachers; 3,500 students; Dir-Gen. ADO GOSSAN; publs *Akounda* (1 a year), *Leader* (4 a year).

CROATIA

The Higher Education System

Before gaining independence in 1991 Croatia was a federal republic of the former Yugoslavia. The oldest university is Sveučilište u Zagreb (University of Zagreb), which was founded in 1669. Higher education is administered according to the Higher Education Law of 1996, and is the responsibility of the Ministry of Science, Education and Sports. In 2010/11 a total of 148,616 students were enrolled at 133 institutions of higher education in Croatia, including nine universities (in Zagreb, Rijeka, Osijek, Zadar, Pula, Dubrovnik and Split).

Higher education institutions set their own admissions requirements, with the approval of the Ministry of Science, Education and Sport. Students are usually required to possess the requisite secondary school qualifications and sit an entrance exam. In 2001 Croatia signed up to the Bologna Process, began its implementation in the academic year 2005/06 and aimed to have carried out most prescribed changes (including the replacement of the existing two-cycle system with a three-cycle system, the introduction of quality assurance and the implementation of the European Credit Transfer and Accumulation System—ECTS) by 2011; the traditional undergraduate degrees, the Vise Obrazovanje (two to three years' study) and Visoko Obrazovanja (four to six years' study), have been phased out in favour of the Baccalaureus (Bachelors—three to four years and 180 ECTS credits). Study for a Magistar (Masters degree, 60–120 credits) in either arts or science subjects lasts for one to two years and includes a magistarski rad (Masters thesis). The Doktorat (Doctorate) is the highest postgraduate qualification, study for which usually takes three to four years and includes the research and defence of a doktorski rad (doctoral thesis). ECTS credits are also assigned in the third cycle, but at the discretion of the individual higher education institution. All graduates automatically receive diploma supplements free of charge, in Croatian and English.

Tertiary-level technical and vocational education consists of one- to four-year programmes in industrial, trade and craft occupations. Students who complete a postgraduate course in art at a polytechnic may attain the professional title of Master of Arts in accordance with a separate law. In 2012 the Agency for Vocational Education and Training was undertaking a complete reform of the vocational teaching and qualification system.

Both higher education institutions and study programmes must undergo an evaluation process in order to be accredited for operation in Croatia. The request for accreditation is submitted to the Ministry of Science, Education and Sport, which then requests a recommendation from the National Council for Higher Education.

Regulatory and Representative Bodies

GOVERNMENT

Ministry of Culture: Runjaninova 2, HR-10000 Zagreb; tel. (1) 4866-666; e-mail kabinet@min-kulture.hr; internet www.min-kulture.hr; Minister ANDREA ZLATAR VIOLIĆ.

Ministry of Science, Education and Sports: Donje Svetice 38, HR-10000 Zagreb; tel. (1) 4569-000; e-mail ministar@mzos.hr; internet public.mzos.hr; Minister Dr ŽELJKO JOVANOVIĆ.

ACCREDITATION

ENIC/NARIC Croatia: Croatian ENIC/NARIC Office, Donje Svetice 38/5, HR-10000 Zagreb; tel. (1) 6274-888; e-mail enic@azvo.hr; internet www.azvo.hr/index.php/hr/medunarodne-aktivnosti/ured-enic; f. 2004; information centre for academic mobility and recognition of foreign higher education qualifications; part of European Network of nat. information centres on recognition and mobility; Head of Office KATARINA ŠIMIĆ JAGUNIĆ.

NATIONAL BODIES

Agencija za znanost i visoko obrazovanje (Agency for Science and Higher Education): Donje Svetice 38/5, HR-10000 Zagreb; tel. (1) 6274-800; e-mail ured@azvo.hr; internet www.azvo.hr; f. 2004; autonomously and independently performs activities within the scope and authorities determined under the Scientific Activity and Higher Education Act, the Act on Quality Assurance in Higher Education and Science, the Act on Recognition of Foreign Educational Qualifications; quality assurance and improvement in higher education and science; full mem. of Int. Network for Quality Assurance Agencies in Higher Education since 2006; Pres Prof. Dr MILE DŽELALIJA; Dir Prof. Dr JASMINA HAVRANEK (acting).

Hrvatska akademska i istraživačka mreža (CARNet) (Croatian Academic and Research Network): Josipa Marohnića 5, HR-10000 Zagreb; tel. (1) 6661-616; e-mail ured@carnet.hr; internet www.carnet.hr; f. 1991; attached to Min. of Science, Education and Sports; develops advanced information technology and infrastructure for the academic and research community to improve higher education and to promote design, introduction and implementation of new technologies in Croatia; 241 mem. instns in 432 locations; Chair. of the Board TOMISLAV VRAČIĆ; CEO ZVONIMIR STANIĆ.

Rektorski zbor (Rectors' Conference): Sveučilište u Zagrebu, Zvonimirova 8, HR-10000 Osijete; tel. (1) 4698-109; e-mail unizginfo@unizg.hr; internet www.unizg.hr/o-sveucilistu/rektorski-zbor; funding of science and higher education; Pres. Prof. Dr VESNA VRTIPRAH; Sec. Gen. Prof. PAULA PAVLETIĆ.

Vijeće Veleučilišta i Visokih škola Hrvatske (Croatian Council of Universities and University Colleges of Applied Sciences): Veleučilište 'Marko Marulić' u Kninu, Krešimirova 30, HR-22300 Knin; tel. (22) 664-450; e-mail dekan@veleknin.hr; internet www.azvo.hr/index.php/hr/vijee-veleuilita-i-visokih-kola; f. 2002, current name adopted 2003; promotes common interests of colleges, integration of vocational studies, student mobility; 44 mems (incl. 15 polytechnics, 29 colleges); Pres. Prof. Dr MARKO JELIĆ.

Learned Societies

GENERAL

Društvo za Proučavanje i Unapredenje Pomorstva (Society for Research and Promotion of Maritime Science and Sport): Riva 16/V, POB 301, HR-51000 Rijeka; tel. (51) 334-210; e-mail dpuprh@inet.hr; f. 1962; research divided into 9 sections: economics, ethnology, history, law, literature, medicine, natural sciences, nautical sciences, technology; 323 elected mems; Pres. Prof. Dr BLANKA KESIĆ; Sec. Dr DUŠAN VRUS; publ. *Pomorski Zbornik. Annals of Maritime Studies* (1 a year).

Hrvatska Akademija Znanosti i Umjetnosti (Croatian Academy of Sciences and Arts): Zrinski Trg 11, HR-10000 Zagreb; tel. (1) 4895-111; e-mail kabpred@hazu.hr; internet www.hazu.hr; f. 1861; promotes and organizes scientific research, applications of the findings; develops artistic and cultural activities; promotes nat. cultural heritage throughout the world; depts of fine arts, literature, mathematical sciences, medical sciences, music and musicology, natural sciences, philological sciences, physical and chemical sciences, social sciences, technical sciences; 16 scientific ccls and 13 cttees; 160 full mems, 100 assoc. mems, 160 corresponding mems; library: see under Libraries and Archives; Pres. Prof. Dr ZVONKO KUSIĆ; Sec. Gen. Prof. Dr PAVAO RUDAN; publs *Ljetopis Hrvatske Akademije Znanosti i Umjetnosti*, *Rad* (Memoirs).

BIBLIOGRAPHY, LIBRARY SCIENCE AND MUSEOLOGY

Hrvatsko Knjižničarsko Društvo (Croatian Library Association): c/o Nacionalna i sveučilišna knjižnica, Hrvatske bratske zajednice 4, HR-10000 Zagreb; tel. (1) 6159-320; e-mail hkd@hkdrustvo.hr; internet www.hkdrustvo.hr; f. 1940; promotes library services and the profession of librarianship; organizes professional meetings; creates library legislation; promotes devt of libraries and general literacy; raises awareness on preservation of cultural heritage; 1,200 mems; Pres. MARIJANA MIŠETIĆ; Sec. DUNJA HOLCER; publs *HKD Novosti* (4 a year, online, www.hkdrustvo.hr/hkdnovosti), *Vjesnik Bibliotekara Hrvatske* (irregular).

Hrvatsko Muzejsko Društvo (Croatian Museum Association): c/o Muzej za umjetnost i obrt, Trg Maršala Tita 10, HR-10000 Zagreb; tel. (1) 553-669; e-mail hmd@hrmud.hr; internet www.hrmud.hr; f. 1946 as Asscn of the Employees and Assocs of Museums, Galleries and Conservation Institutes in People's Republic of Croatia, current name adopted 1998; promotes growth and advancement of museum profession and protects the common interests of museum workers; 500 mems; Pres. MILVANA ARKO-PIJEVAC; Sec. SLAĐANA LATINOVIĆ; publ. *Vijesti Muzealaca i Konzervatora* (News of Museum Custodians and Conservators, 4 a year).

EDUCATION

Hrvatski pedagoško-književni zbor (Croatian Pedagogic-Literary Association): Trg Maršala Tita 4, HR-10000 Zagreb; tel. (1) 4855-713; e-mail hpkzbor@gmail.com; internet www.hpkz-napredak.hr; f. 1871; develops pedagogical and educational life; brs in Slavonski Brod, Križevci, Vukovar, Dubrovnik, Split, Petrinja, Sibenik and Zagreb; 2,000 mems; Pres. Prof. Dr NEVIO ŠETIĆ; Vice-Pres. Prof. JELENA PAVIÈIÆ VUKIÆEVIÆ; Sec. ALBINO CRNOBORI; publ. *Napredak* (4 a year).

HISTORY, GEOGRAPHY AND ARCHAEOLOGY

Hrvatsko geografsko društvo (Croatian Geographical Society): Marulićev Trg 19, HR-10000 Zagreb; tel. (1) 4895-402; e-mail geografija.hr@gmail.com; internet www.hagede.hr; f. 1897, current name adopted 1992; promotes geography as a profession and teaching of science subjects; organizes confs, scientific meetings, methodical and professional seminars, field training, study tours; 600 mems; library of 6,550 vols; Pres. ALEKSANDAR LUKIĆ; publs *Acta Geographica Croatica*, *Geoadria* (2 a year), *Geografski horizont* (4 a year), *Hrvatski Geografski Glasnik* (1 a year).

Hrvatsko Numizmatičko Društvo (Croatian Numismatic Society): Margaretska 3, HR-10000 Zagreb; tel. (1) 4920-520; e-mail hr.numiz.drus@zg.htnet.hr; internet www.hrvatskonumizmatickodrustvo.hr; f. 1928; 500 mems; library of 5,800 vols; Pres. DAMIR KOVAČ; Sec. EDGAR FABRY; publs *Numizmatičke Vijesti* (1 a year), *Numizmatika*, *OBOL / Bilten HND* (1 a year).

LANGUAGE AND LITERATURE

Alliance Française: Ante Kovačića 4, HR-10000 Zagreb; tel. (1) 4818-292; e-mail alliance-francaise@zg.t-com.hr; internet www.alliance-francaise.hr; f. 1952, current name adopted 1991; offers courses and examinations in French language and culture; promotes cultural exchange with France; attached offices in Dubrovnik, Rijek and Split; Chair. Prof. JAGODA LUKAVAC.

British Council: Palmotićeva 60/I, HR-10000 Zagreb; tel. (1) 4899-508; e-mail exams@britishcouncil.hr; internet www.britishcouncil.hr; offers courses and examinations in English language and British culture; promotes cultural exchange with the UK; library of 7,500 vols, 60 periodicals; Dir JAMES HAMPSON.

Goethe-Institut: Ulica Grada Vukovara 64, HR-10000 Zagreb; tel. (1) 6195-000; e-mail info@zagreb.goethe.org; internet www.goethe.de/zagreb; offers courses and examinations in German language and culture; promotes cultural exchange with Germany; library of 10,000 vols, 20 periodicals; Dir KATRIN OSTWALD-RICHTER.

MEDICINE

Hrvatsko Farmaceutsko Društvo (Croatian Pharmaceutical Society): Masarykova 2, HR-10000 Zagreb; tel. (1) 4872-849; e-mail hfd-fg-ap@zg.t-com.hr; internet www.hfd-fg.hr; f. 1858, current name adopted 1946; sections of community pharmacy, drug analysis, health ecology, history of pharmacy, hospital pharmacy, junior pharmacists, medical plants, pharmaceutical technology, pharmacy information, pharmacy owners; organizes professional and scientific events; cooperation with health instns, Croatian Pharmaceutical Chamber and other asscns; 6 regional brs; 1,000 mems; library of 2,000 vols; Chair. KREŠIMIR RUKAVINA; Sec. Gen. MAJA JAKŠEVAC MIKŠA; publs *Acta Pharmaceutica* (4 a year, in English), *Farmaceutski Glasnik* (12 a year).

Hrvatskog Liječničkog Zbor (Croatian Medical Association): Šubićeva 9, HR-10000 Zagreb; tel. (1) 4693-300; e-mail tajnistvo@hlz.hr; internet www.hlz.hr; f. 1874; helps in professional devt; 18 brs; 3,556 mems; Pres. Prof. Dr ŽELJKO METELKO; Sec. Prof. Dr TOMISLAV BOŽEK; publs *Acta Stomatologica Croatica*, *Liječničke Novine*, *Liječnički Vjesnik*.

NATURAL SCIENCES

General

Hrvatsko Prirodoslovno Društvo (Croatian Society of Natural Sciences): Frankopanska 1/I, POB 258, HR-10001 Zagreb; tel. (1) 4831-224; e-mail hpd@hpd.hr; internet www.hpd.hr; f. 1885; organizes meetings and scientific platforms for the promotion of natural sciences; Pres. Prof. Dr MLADEN JURAČIĆ; Sec. Dr NENAD JUDAŠ; publs *Periodicum Biologorum* (6 a year, online (biologorum.irb.hr/index.php/biologorum)), *Priroda* (Nature, 12 a year, online (www.hpd.hr/priroda/index.html)).

TECHNOLOGY

Hrvatski Savez Građevinskih Inženjera (Croatian Association of Civil Engineers): Berislavićeva 6, HR-10000 Zagreb; tel. (1) 4872-498; e-mail dgiz@zg.t-com.hr; internet www.hsgi.org; f. 1970; promotes scientific research work in the field of architecture; organizes lectures, confs and symposia; 3,017 mems; library of 5,000 vols; Pres. JOSIP ŠVENDA; Sec. ŽELJKA ŠARIĆ; publ. *Časopis Građevinar* (print and online (www.casopis-gradjevinar.hr)).

Research Institutes

GENERAL

Zavod za Povijest i Filozofiju Znanosti u Zagrebu (Institute for the History and Philosophy of Science in Zagreb): Ante Kovačića 5, HR-10000 Zagreb; tel. (1) 4698-231; e-mail zavodzd@hazu.hr; internet info.hazu.hr/zavod_za_povijest_i_filozofiju_znanosti; f. 1992 by merger of the Institute for History of Natural, Mathematical and Medical Sciences (f. 1960) and Institute for the Philosophy of Science and Peace; attached to Croatian Acad. of Sciences and Arts; depts of history of natural and mathematical sciences, philosophy of science, history of medical sciences; incorporates Institute of the History of Pharmacy of the Croatian Pharmaceutical Soc., Institute for the History of Medicine, Medical Faculty, Univ. of Zagreb, Cabinet for the History of Veterinary Medicine, Museum of the Soc. of Physicians of Croatia and Institute for the Philosophy of Sciences; fosters research into the history of science; library of 12,000 vols, 1,295 periodicals; Dir Prof. Dr ŽARKO DADIĆ; publ. *Rasprave i Gradja za Povijest Nauka* (1 a year).

Zavod za Znanstveni i Umjetnički rad u Splitu (Institute for Scientific and Artistic Work in Split): Trg Braće Radića 7, HR-21000 Split; tel. (21) 348-599; e-mail hazusplit@hazu.hr; internet info.hazu.hr/zavod_za_znanstveni_i_umjetnicki_rad_u_splitu; f. 1981; attached to Croatian Acad. of Sciences and Arts; focuses on navigation, historical sciences and the arts; maritime colln; organizes exhibitions, lectures, annual scientific and cultural manifestations; library of 12,000 vols, 1,295 periodicals; Hon. Dir Prof. Dr DAVORIN RUDOLF; publ. *Adrias*.

AGRICULTURE, FISHERIES AND VETERINARY SCIENCE

Institut za oceanografiju i ribarstvo (Institute of Oceanography and Fisheries): Šetalište Ivana Meštrovića 63, HR-21000 Split; tel. (21) 408-000; e-mail office@izor.hr; internet www.izor.hr; f. 1930; conducts research in aquaculture, geology, hydrography, ichthyology, mariculture and fishery technology, marine biology, marine fisheries, oceanography, sedimentology; postgraduate study in fisheries; incl. hatchery and research vessel; 8 laboratories; library of 15,000 vols; Dir Dr IVONA MARASOVIĆ; publs *Acta Adriatica*, *Notes*.

Poljoprivredni Institut Osijek (Osijek Agricultural Institute): Južno Predgrade 17, HR-31001 Osijek; tel. (31) 515-501; e-mail institut@poljinos.hr; internet www.poljinos.hr; f. 1916; agricultural and scientific research into breeding of wheat, barley, corn, soybeans, sunflowers and alfalfa; depts of agricultural technique and melioration, agrochemical laboratory, basic seed production, forage crops, fruit-growing, industrial plants, maize, seed production and processing, small cereal crops; 160 mems; library of 5,380 vols; Dir Dr ZVONIMIR ZDUNIĆ; publ. *Poljoprivreda* (Agriculture, 2 a year).

ARCHITECTURE AND TOWN PLANNING

Kabinet za Arhitekturu i Urbanizam, Arhiv za Likovne Umjetnosti Hrvatske Akademije Znanosti i Umjetnosti (Cabinet for Architecture and Urban Planning, Fine Arts Archives): Hebrangova 1, Gundulićeva 24, HR-10000 Zagreb; tel. (1) 4825-406; e-mail arlikum@hazu.hr; internet info.hazu.hr/the_cabinet_for_architecture_and_urban_planning; f. 1952; attached to Croatian Acad. of Sciences and Arts; scientific study of the history of architecture and town planning and methods of protection, conservation and presentation of monuments; holds seven collns: catalogue colln, author files, exhibition files, periodicals colln, artist's correspondence, personal archives, archives of art socs and photograph colln; 5 mems; library of 40,000 vols, 1,295 periodicals; Hon. Dir VELIMIR NEIDHARDT; publ. *Rad JAZU* (irregular).

BIBLIOGRAPHY, LIBRARY SCIENCE AND MUSEOLOGY

City of Zagreb, City Institute for the Conservation of Cultural and Natural Heritage: Kuševićeva 2, HR-10000 Zagreb; tel. (1) 6101-970; e-mail zastita.spomenika@

zagreb.hr; f. 1991; attached to City of Zagreb Govt; tasks related to cultural and natural heritage and cultural property; research on architectural heritage, analysing, assessing or reassessing bldgs of artistic and historical interest; initiates projects, incl. measures for conservation-restoration of movable and immovable cultural heritage, monitors and evaluates restorative and reconstructive interventions related to art objects; approves architectural plans and documentation in the process of issuing bldg permits; issues permits for export of cultural goods; catalogues private collns; protects natural environment and natural values, nature parks, forest parks, monuments of park architecture, important landscapes, prescribes nature protection measures and conditions; library of 1,400 vols; Prin. SILVIJE NOVAK; publ. *Godišnjak zaštite spomenika kulture Hrvatske* (Yearbook of Protection of Croatian Cultural Monuments).

Hrvatski restauratorski zavod (Croatian Conservation Institute): Nike Grškovića 23, HR-10000 Zagreb; tel. (1) 4684-599; e-mail uprava@h-r-z.hr; internet www.h-r-z.hr; f. 1997 by merger of Institute for Restoration of Works of Art (f. 1948) and Conservation Institute of Croatia (f. 1966); restoration of and research into the conservation of paintings, historic architecture, wooden sculpture, furniture, stucco, stone, mosaics, wall paintings, architectural monuments, paper and leather, textiles, metal and other archaeological finds; underwater archaeological research; Dir MARIO BRAUN; publ. *Portal* (1 a year).

Regionalni zavod za zaštitu spomenika kulture (Regional Institute for the Protection of Historic Monuments): Poljudsko šetalište 15, POB 191, HR-21000 Split; tel. (21) 342-327; f. 1854; library of 12,000 vols and periodicals, 130,000 photographs and negatives; Dir Dr JOŠKO BELAMARIĆ; Sec. NEIRA STOJANAC; publ. *Prilozi povijesti umjetnosti u Dalmaciji*.

ECONOMICS, LAW AND POLITICS

Institut za Međunarodne Odnose (Institute for Development and International Relations): Ulica Ljudevita Farkaša Vukotinovića 2, POB 303, HR-10000 Zagreb; tel. (1) 4877-460; e-mail ured@irmo.hr; internet www.imo.hr; f. 1963 as Africa Research Institute, present name and status 1996; attached to Min. of Science, Education and Sports; interdisciplinary study of devt processes and economic and int. relations and cooperation in the field of economics, culture, science, environmental protection and politics; organizes seminars, int. confs and specialist training programmes; library of 9,000 vols, 100 periodicals, 10,000 monographs; Dir Dr SANJA TIŠMA; publs *Croatian International Relations Review* (2 a year, in English), *Culturelink* (3 a year).

Jadranski zavod (Adriatic Institute): Šenoina 4, HR-10000 Zagreb; tel. (1) 4920-733; e-mail jz@hazu.hr; internet info.hazu.hr/jadranski_zavod; f. 1945, present status 1948, current name adopted 1994; attached to Croatian Acad. of Sciences and Arts; collects, studies, and analyses data related to Croatian and foreign legislation and to judicial and arbitration practice in maritime and sea law; maritime and sea law, with particular emphasis on the carriage of goods by sea, maritime safety, insurance, protection of the marine environment and maritime delimitations; library of 30,000 vols; Dir Prof. Emeritus VLADIMIR-DJURO DEGAN; publ. *Usporedno pomorsko pravo* (Comparative Maritime Law, 1 a year, in Croatian and English).

LANGUAGE AND LITERATURE

Leksikografski Zavod Miroslav Krleza (Miroslav Krleza Institute of Lexicography): Frankopanska 26, HR-10000 Zagreb; tel. (1) 4800-398; e-mail lzmk@lzmk.hr; internet www.lzmk.hr; f. 1950; collects and processes MSS for encyclopaedic, lexicographic, bibliographic, monographic and other scientific edns; publishes results of research and cooperates with similar institutions abroad; 10,000 contributors, specialists in all fields; library of 50,000 vols, 1,300 periodicals; Dir-Gen. Dr ANTUN VUJIC; Dir Dr BRUNO KRAGIC; publ. *Studia Lexicographica*.

Staroslavenski institut (Old Church Slavonic Institute): Demetrova 11, HR-10000 Zagreb; tel. (1) 4851-380; e-mail info@stin.hr; internet www.stin.hr; f. 1902 as Old Church Slavonic Academy, current name adopted 1952; research of the Croatian Glagolitic heritage: language, literature and palaeography; library of 25,000 vols, 511 periodicals; Dir. Dr MARICA ČUNČIĆ; publ. *Slovo* (1 a year).

MEDICINE

Institut za medicinska istraživanja i medicinu rada (Institute for Medical Research and Occupational Health): Ksaverska cesta 2, POB 291, HR-10001 Zagreb; tel. (1) 4682-500; e-mail uprava@imi.hr; internet www.imi.hr; f. 1947 as Institute of Occupational Hygiene, present status 1958, current name adopted 1959; attached to Min. of Science, Education and Sports; conducts research on working and living environment, hygiene, health and dissemination of knowledge on industrial hygiene, environmental pollution and radiation; seeks to implement research results in industry and runs a number of projects of nat. interest; units of analytical toxicology and mineral metabolism, animal breeding, biochemistry and organic analytical chemistry, environmental hygiene, mutagenesis, occupational and environmental medicine, radiation dosimetry and radiobiology, radiation protection, toxicology; incl. poison control centre; library of 8,000 vols, 75 periodicals; Dir Dr ANA LUCIĆ VRDOLJAK; publ. *Arhiv za higijenu rada i toksilologiju* (Archives of Industrial Hygiene and Toxicology, 4 a year, in Croatian and English).

NATURAL SCIENCES

General

Institut Rudjer Bošković (Rudjer Bošković Institute): Bijenička cesta 54, HR-10000 Zagreb; tel. (1) 4561-111; e-mail info@irb.hr; internet www.irb.hr; f. 1950; research in physics (biophysics, experimental, material, medical, nuclear and atomic, theoretical), chemistry (biochemistry, material, organic and physical), electronics, environment, molecular biology, molecular medicine; marine research centres in Rovinj and Zagreb; 82 laboratories; library of 23,000 vols, 16,000 periodicals; Dir-Gen. Dr TOME ANTIČIĆ.

Biological Sciences

Državni zavod za zaštitu prirode (State Institute for Nature Protection): Trg Mažuranića 5, HR-10000 Zagreb; tel. (1) 5502-900; e-mail info@dzzp.hr; internet www.dzzp.hr; f. 2002; Dir Dr MATIJA FRANKOVIĆ.

Physical Sciences

Državni hidrometeorološki zavod (Meteorological and Hydrological Service): Grič 3, HR-10000 Zagreb; tel. (1) 4565-666; e-mail dhmz@cirus.dhz.hr; internet meteo.hr; f. 1947; climatology, ecological studies, hydrology, meteorology; maintains Marine Meteorological Centre in Split; library of 7,000 vols, 45 periodicals; Dir IVAN CACIČ; publs *Bilten* (12 a year), *Croatian Meteorological Journal* (1 a year).

RELIGION, SOCIOLOGY AND ANTHROPOLOGY

Institut za Društvena Istraživanja u Zagreb (Institute for Social Research in Zagreb): Amruševa 11/II, HR-10000 Zagreb; tel. (1) 4810-264; e-mail idiz@idi.hr; internet www.idi.hr; f. 1964; attached to Univ. of Zagreb; research in all fields of sociology, social anthropology, psychology; library of 16,400 vols (incl. books and periodicals); Dir. Dr BRANISLAVA BARANOVIĆ; publs *Revija za Sociologiju* (Sociology Review), *Sociology and Space* (4 a year).

Institut za etnologiju i folkloristiku (Institute of Ethnology and Folklore Research): Šubićeva 42, HR-10000 Zagreb; tel. (1) 4596-700; e-mail institut@ief.hr; internet www.ief.hr; f. 1948 as Institute of Folk Art, present name and status 1991; conducts research in the disciplines of ethnology, cultural anthropology, folklore research, literary studies, theatre studies, history, linguistics, ethnomusicology, ethnochoreology, ethno-theatre studies, art history, cultural studies in field, archive and theoretical research of contemporary and historical phenomena and processes in traditional culture; 185,000 items of archives and documentation; spec. colln of ethnographic materials: 1,990 text collns and music annotations, 19 dance collns, 374 kinetograms, 57 drawing collns with 2,000 panels, 3,910 audio cassette recordings (music recordings and narratives); record library (1,044 sound recordings); photographic and slide library (61,883 items); 1,533 video cassettes and 51 films; library of 28,100 vols, 9,100 periodicals; Dir Dr TVRTKO ZEBEC; Sec. SANJA LESIĆ; publ. *Narodna Umjetnost* (2 a year).

Libraries and Archives

Dubrovnik

Znanstvena knjižnica Dubrovnik (Scientific Library of Dubrovnik): Cvijete Zuzorić 4, HR-20000 Dubrovnik; tel. (20) 323-911; e-mail dubrovacke-knjiznice@dkd.hr; internet www.dkd.hr/du_znan.html; f. 1975; 267,000 vols, 7,000 periodicals, 77 incunabula, 928 MSS, 10,490 books belonging to the Republic of Dubrovnik up to 1808 (Old Ragusina), colln of 14,000 vols (New Ragusina); Dir VESNA CUCIC.

Pula

Sveucilisna knjiznica u Puli (University Library of Pula): Herkulov prolaz 1, HR-52100 Pula; tel. (52) 213-888; e-mail skpu@unipu.hr; internet www.skpu.hr; f. 1949 as Scientific Library, current status 1994, current name 1995; publicly accessible central library for the Juraj Dobrila Univ. of Pula; Antonio Smareglia memory room; spec. colln of the Istrian Area; marine library; colln of Eduard Calić; Mijo Mirkovic memory room; Biblioteca Provinciale; music colln; graphic colln; 320,000 vols, 6,602 periodicals; spec. collns: the Istrian area 15,000 monographic vols, Austro-Hungarian Naval Library (20,000 vols); Marine Library: 20,731 vols (31,716 monographs, 6,655 journals, annals and newspapers); 200 vols of incunabula and books from the 16th and 17th centuries; 2,400 audio recordings, 541 maps, postcards and plaques; Univ. Library Man. TIJANA BARBIC-DOMAZET; publ. *Nova Istra* (4 a year).

Rijeka

Sveučilišna knjižnica Rijeka (University Library Rijeka): Dolac 1, POB 132, HR-51000 Rijeka; tel. (51) 336-911; e-mail ravnatelj@svkri.hr; internet www.svkri.uniri.hr; f. 1949 as Scientific Library of Rijeka, present status 1979; legal deposit library; spec. collns of material on the Primorsko-Goranska region and on the Glagolitic script; repository of Univ. of Rijeka publs and dissertations; 400,000 vols, heritage colln: 100,000 vols; Dir SENKA TOMLJANOVIĆ.

Split

Sveučilišna knjižnica u Splitu (Split University Library): Ruđera Boškovića 31, HR-21000 Split; tel. (21) 434-800; e-mail svkst@svkst.hr; internet www.svkst.hr; f. 1903; 400,000 vols, 12,000 periodicals, 700 MSS, 5,000 rare books, maps and atlases, sheet music, sound recordings and graphic material; Dir Prof. KROLO PETAR.

Varaždin

Gradska knjižnica i čitaonica 'Metel Ožegović' ('Metel Ožegović' Varaždin Public Library): Trg Slobode 8A, HR-42000 Varaždin; tel. (42) 212-767; e-mail info@knjiznica-vz.hr; internet knjiznica-vz.hr; f. 1838, current name adopted 1990; 190,000 vols; Dir MARIO SOŠTARIĆ.

Zadar

Znanstvena knjižnica Zadar (Research Library of Zadar): Ante Kuzmanića 3, HR-23000 Zadar; tel. (23) 211-365; e-mail zkzd@zkzd.hr; internet www.zkzd.hr; f. 1855 as Biblioteca Comunale Paravia, current name adopted 1992; 884,000 vols (incl. 20,000 vols Dalmatica), 372 parchments, 34 incunabula, 1,140 MSS, 1,470 rare books, 300 Masters and Doctoral theses, 2,398 photographs and 700 negatives on glass plates, 2,688 maps and atlases, 4,263 music scores; Dir MIRO GRUBIĆ; publ. *Knjižno blago Naučne biblioteke u Zadru continued as Knjižno blago Znanstvene knjižnice Zadar*.

Zagreb

Hrvatski državni arhiv (Croatian State Archives): Marulićev Trg 21, HR-10000 Zagreb; tel. (1) 4801-999; e-mail hda@arhiv.hr; internet www.arhiv.hr; f. 1643; records of central govt archives, other public instns and nat. cinematographic production; incl. 24,000 linear m of records since 10th century, on the history of Croatia; 20,000 km of film; 160,000 vols, 90,000 books, 70,000 magazines and newspapers, 1,500,000 photographs; Dir Dr VLATKA LEMIĆ; publ. *Fontes: Izvori za hrvatsku povijest* (Fontes: Sources for Croatian history).

Knjižnica Hrvatske akademije znanosti i umjetnosti (Library of the Croatian Academy of Sciences and Arts): Strossmayerov trg 14, HR-10000 Zagreb; tel. (1) 4895-114; e-mail library@hazu.hr; internet knjiznica.hazu.hr; f. 1867; 400,000 vols, 1,000 periodicals; spec. colln: 15,000 vols of old and rare books, colln of Burgenland literary heritage, digital colln; Dir VEDRANA JURIČIĆ.

Knjižnice Grada Zagreba (Zagreb City Libraries): Starčevićev Trg 6, HR-10000 Zagreb; tel. (1) 4572-300; e-mail kgz@kgz.hr; internet www.kgz.hr; f. 1967 by merger of City Library of Zagreb (f. 1907) and Silvije Strahimir Kranjčević Library; network of public libraries; comprises the City Library of Zagreb and the Božidar Adžija Library (f. 1927) holding the largest collns, Tin Ujević Library (f. 1947), the County Research and Devt Dept, 12 br. libraries with a network of 31 attached brs in 45 locations; bookmobile service; 2,260,011 vols, 1,072 periodicals; Dir DAVORKA BASTIĆ; publ. *Književni petak* (Literary Friday).

Nacionalna i sveučilišna knjižnica u Zagrebu (National and University Library in Zagreb): ul. Hrvatske bratske zajednice 4, POB 550, HR-10000 Zagreb; tel. (1) 6164-111; e-mail nsk@nsk.hr; internet www.nsk.hr; f. 1611, current name adopted 1874, present bldg 1995; generates and organizes Croatian nat. colln of library holdings and supervises acquisition of publs on the nat. level and on behalf of the Univ. of Zagreb; acts as the nat. bibliographic office; keeps and renews/updates the library's holdings in accordance with int. programme; performs bibliographic and information activities, incl. inter-library lending; performs scientific research in the area of librarianship and information science; 3,000,000 vols, 3,625 periodicals; Dir-Gen. DUNJA SEITER-SVERKO; publs *Hrvatska bibliografija* (Croatian Bibliography, 12 a year), *The Voice of NUL* (4 a year).

Museums and Art Galleries

Dubrovnik

Dubrovacki muzeji (Dubrovnik Museums): Pred dvorom 3, HR-20000 Dubrovnik; tel. (20) 321-422; internet www.mdc.hr/dubrovnik; f. 1872 as the Dubrovnik Regional Museum, present status 1940; manages 6 museums; Head Dir PAVICA VILAC.

Attached Museums:

Archäologisches Museum (Archaeological Museum): Brace Andrijica 7, Dubrovnik; tel. (20) 324-041; e-mail dubrovacki.muzeji1@du.t-com.hr; internet www.mdc.hr/dubrovnik/nj/arheoloski/index.html; f. 1991; reference library; museums holdings divided into the prehistoric, antique, early medieval collns, colln from 13th century to the 1667 earthquake, Egyptian, vase and coin collns; Dir and Sr Curator ROMANA MENALO.

Etnographisches Museum—Museum 'Rupe' (Ethnographic Museum—the 'Rupe' Museum): Od Rupa 3, Dubrovnik; tel. (20) 412-545; internet www.mdc.hr/dubrovnik/nj/etnografski/index.html; f. 1991; 5,000 exhibits on permanent display of traditional folk costumes, folklore, textiles, lace; Dir MIRJANA ZEC.

Geburtshause von Marin Drzic (Marin Drzic House): Siroka ul. 7, Dubrovnik; tel. (20) 420-490; internet www.mdc.hr/dubrovnik/nj/marindrzic/index.html; f. 1989; theatrical museum, scientific-documentary institute and exhibition space; collns of posters, programmes and photographs of Marin Drzic's plays in Croatia and abroad; display of post-modern installations reconstructing the Renaissance period during which Drzic lived; puppets, posters and stage props; Dir IVANA JASIĆ.

Kulturgeschichtliches Museum (Cultural Historical Museum): Knežev dvor 1, HR-20000 Dubrovnik; tel. (20) 321-422; internet www.mdc.hr/dubrovnik/eng/kulturnopovijesni/index.html; f. 1950; Rector's palace: seat of govt and residence of the Prince (Rector) of the Dubrovnik Republic; colln of paintings, ceramics, icons, metalwork, textiles, furniture, glassware, photography, postcards, documents, instruments, clocks and watches; Sr Curator LJILJANA IVUSIĆ; Sr Curator RENATA ANDJUS.

Museum Für Zeitgenössische Geschichte (Modern History Museum): ul. Brace Andrijica 7, Dubrovik; tel. (20) 429-461; e-mail msp@dumus.hr; internet www.mdc.hr/dubrovnik/nj/suvremenapovijest/index.html; f. 1956; colln of documents from the Second World War, memoirist writings on the Croatian Homeland War; do not have permanent premises for exhibitions; Dir and Sr Curator Prof. VARINA JURICA TURK; publ. *The City-That is you*.

Schiffahrts Museum (Maritime Museum): St John's Fortress, HR-20000 Dubrovnik; tel. (20) 323-904; e-mail pomorski@dumus.hr; internet www.mdc.hr/dubrovnik/nj/pomorski/index.html; f. 1941, present status 1987; 4,000 exhibits; Dubrovnik's maritime past; ship models from the 17th, 18th and 19th centuries; flags, cannons and other weapons, figureheads, nautical instruments and log books; library of rare books and archival materials; library of 10,027 vols; Dir Prof. ĐIVO BAŠIĆ.

Muzej Srpske Pravoslavne Crkve (Museum of the Serbian Orthodox Church): Od Puća 2, HR-20000 Dubrovnik; f. 1953; colln of portraits, 170 icons from Serbia, Crete, Corfu, Venice, Russia, Greece, Dubrovnik, Boka-Kotorska; the palace that houses the colln is also of historical interest; library of 25,000 vols.

Umjetnička Galerija Dubrovnik (Museum of Modern and Contemporary Art Dubrovnik): Frana Supila 23, HR-20000 Dubrovnik; tel. (20) 426-590; e-mail info@ugdubrovnik.hr; internet www.ugdubrovnik.hr; f. 1945; exhibitions of modern and contemporary art and exhibitions from its rich holdings of modern and contemporary art; 2,541 works of art; library of 1,157 vols; Dir VESNA DELIC GOZZE.

Rijeka

Muzej Moderne i Suvremente Umjetnosti, Rijeka (Museum of Modern and Contemporary Art of Rijeka): Dolac 1/II, HR-51000 Rijeka; tel. (51) 492-611; e-mail mmsu-rijeka@ri.t-com.hr; internet www.mmsu.hr; f. 1948; colln of paintings, sculptures, prints, posters, photographs, installations, new media from Croatia and other countries; colln of 5,000 artworks, covering periods from the end of the 19th century to present day; library of 20,000 vols of books and catalogues; Dir Dr SLAVEN TOLJ; publ. *Arhitektura u Rijeci*.

Prirodoslovni Muzej Rijeka (Natural History Museum Rijeka): Lorenzov Prolaz 1, HR-51000 Rijeka; tel. (51) 553-669; e-mail info@prirodoslovni.com; internet www.prirodoslovni.com; f. 1876; permanent exhibition of geological history of the Adriatic; inorganic, zoological and botanical collns (90,000 specimens); library of 4,024 vols; Dir MILVANA ARKO-PIJEVAC.

Slavonski Brod

Brlić House (Ivana Brlić-Mažuranić Memorial): Titov Trg 8, HR-55000 Slavonski Brod; f. 1933; private family house containing archives, furniture showing the evolution of a Croatian middle-class family over 300 years; Ivana Brlić (1874–1938) was a writer and first female mem. of the Yugoslav Acad. of Sciences and Arts; library of 8,000 vols; Curator VIKTOR RUŽIĆ.

Split

Arheološki muzej u Splitu (Archaeological Museum in Split): Zrinjsko-Frankopanska 25, HR-21000 Split; tel. (21) 329-340; e-mail info@armus.hr; internet www.mdc.hr/split-arheoloski; f. 1820, present bldg 1914; prehistoric collns, relics from the Greek colonies on the east shore of the Adriatic

Sea; Roman and Christian relics from Salonae and Dalmatia; Croatian medieval monuments from 9th to 13th centuries; numismatic colln; library of 50,000 vols, (incl. 8 incunabula, 170 16th-century books); Dir DAMIR KLIŠKIĆ; Curator JELENA JOVANOVIĆ.

Etnografski muzej Split (Ethnographical Museum of Split): Iza Vestibula 4, HR-21000 Split; tel. (21) 344-164; e-mail etnografski-muzej-st@st.t-com.hr; f. 1907; 19,500 artefacts of nat. costumes, jewels, weapons, traditional technological objects from Dalmatia, Dinaric Alps area and other neighbouring regions; illustrations section; library of 3,000 vols; Dir Dr SILVIO BRAICA.

Galerija umjetnina Split (Split Art Gallery): ul. kralja Tomislava 15, HR-21000 Split; tel. (21) 350-110; e-mail galerija-umjetnina@galum.hr; internet www.galum.hr; f. 1931; 2,300 paintings and sculptures (ancient and modern); library of 14,000 vols; Dir JOSIP BOTTERI; Sr Curator IRIS SLADE; Sr Curator JASMINKA BABIĆ.

Muzeji Ivana Meštrovića (Ivan Mestrovic Museums): Setaliste Ivana Mestrovica 46, HR-21000 Split; tel. (21) 340-800; e-mail mim@mestrovic.hr; internet www.mestrovic.hr; f. 1991 as Ivan Meštrović Foundation, current name and status 2007; protects and promotes Ivan Meštrović's life and work; permanent exhibition of sculptures of Ivan Meštrović (1883–1962); Dir ANDRO KRSTULOVIĆ OPARA; Sr Curator DANICA PLAZIBAT.

Attached Museums:

Church of the Most Holy Redeemer: HR-22322 Otavice; tel. (98) 407-538; e-mail mim@mestrovic.hr; f. 1931, donated to public 1952; Ivan Meštrović's family vault and mausoleum; permanent display of stone reliefs carved in the altar and lateral niches and on lateral walls, bas-relief of religious themes; spec. wall display: *Annunciation with the Archangel Gabriel and Virgin Mary, Eternally Crucified, Evangelists, Lamentation, Nativity, Soul of the Deceased*; Curator ZORANA JURIC SABIC.

Meštrović Atelier: Mletacka 8, HR-10000 Zagreb; tel. (1) 485-1123; e-mail mim@mestrovic.hr; f. 1959; works from first 4 decades of Meštrović's artistic life incl. portraits with the recurring theme of mother and child, female nudes, religious and mythological themes, monuments and historical figures; sculptures in marble, stone, wood and bronze; drawings and graphics; Museum Advisor LJILJANA ČERINA; Sr Curator DANICA PLAZIBAT.

Mestrovic Gallery: Setaliste I. Mestrovica 46, HR-21000 Split; tel. (21) 340-800; e-mail mim@mestrovic.hr; internet www.mestrovic.hr; f. 1952; colln of 192 sculptures, 583 drawings, 4 paintings, 291 architectonic plans made by Ivan Meštrović (1898–1961), 2 furniture sets based on Meštrović's sketches; documentation relating to Meštrović's life and work; Dir ANDRO KRSTULOVIĆ OPARA; Sr Curator MAJA SEPAROVIC PALADA.

Meštrovic's Crikvine-Kaštilac: Setaliste Ivana Mestrovica 39, HR-21000 Split; tel. (21) 340-800; e-mail mim@mestrovic.hr; internet www.mestrovic.hr; f. 1952; fmr summerhouse of the Capogrosso family built in the early 16th century; bought by Ivan Meštrović in 1939; on display in the Holy Crucifix Church: reliefs and artwork inspired by the life of Christ made by Meštrović between 1916 and 1950; Dir ANDRO KRSTULOVIC OPARA.

Muzej grada Splita (Split City Museum): Papalićeva 1, HR-21000 Split; tel. (21) 360-171; e-mail muzej-grada-st@st.htnet.hr; internet www.mgst.net; f. 1946; political and cultural history, urban devt of Split; library of 8,000 vols; Dir ELVIRA ŠARIĆ KOSTIĆ; publ. *Editions*.

Prirodoslovni muzej i zoološki vrt (Museum of Natural Sciences and Zoo): Kolombatovićevo šetalište 2, HR-21000 Split; tel. (21) 322-988; e-mail prirodoslovni@prirodoslovni.hr; internet www.prirodoslovni.hr; f. 1924; contains more than 130,000 exhibits of mineralogical, palaeontological, botanical and zoological specimens from Dalmatia and the Adriatic Sea; collns of minerals, fossils, Coleoptera, marine invertebrates and vertebrates, plants, mammals, reptiles and birds (mostly Dalmatian); library of 7,000 vols; Dir Prof. NEDILJKO ŽEVRNJA; publs *Museum of Natural Sciences, Zoological Garden*.

Zagreb

Arheološki muzej u Zagrebu (Archaeological Museum in Zagreb): Trg Nikole Šubića Zrinskog 19, POB 13, HR-10000 Zagreb; tel. (1) 4873-101; e-mail amz@amz.hr; internet www.amz.hr; f. 1846; archaeological finds from neolithic times to 13th century, incl. paleolithic colln, Egyptian colln, Greek, Roman and medieval collns, numismatic colln; Lapidarium in courtyard, featuring stone monuments from Roman era; colln of nearly 400,000 varied artefacts and monuments; library of 45,000 vols; Dir and Sr Curator Prof. Dr JACQUELINE BALEN; Sec. MLADEN KRŠNJAVI; publ. *Vjesnik Arheološkog Muzeja u Zagrebu* (1 a year).

Etnografski Muzej Zagreb (Ethnographic Museum Zagreb): Trg Mažuranićev 14, HR-10000 Zagreb; tel. (1) 4826-220; e-mail emz@emz.hr; internet www.emz.hr; f. 1919; exhibitions, cultural traditions of the 3 ethnographic regions of Croatia: Pannonic, Dinaric, Adriatic; dept of world cultures; collns of folks costumes, small decorated wood items, pottery and wickerwork, house inventory items, musical instruments, traditional adornments, textiles, traditional economy and items related to customs and beliefs; library of 20,000 vols; Dir DAMODAR FRLAN; publ. *Ethnographic Researches* (1 a year).

Glyptothèque HAZU: Medvedgradska ul. 2, HR-10000 Zagreb; tel. (1) 4686-060; e-mail gliptoteka@hazu.hr; internet gliptoteka.mdc.hr; f. 1937; attached to Croatian Academy of Sciences and Arts; colln of medieval frescos and plaster casts of ancient, medieval and modern sculptures and architecture; originals of Croatian sculptures since 19th century; Dir Prof. ARIANA KRALJ; Sec. MILENA RUMIHA KANIŽAJ.

Hrvatski muzej naivne umjetnosti (Croatian Museum of Naïve Art): Sv. Cirila i Metoda 3, Gornji grad, HR-10000 Zagreb; tel. (1) 4851-911; e-mail info@hmnu.org; internet hmnu.org; f. 1952 as the Peasant Art Gallery, current name 1994; 1,875 works of art, paintings, sculptures, drawings and prints; permanent display: *Naive Art as a Segment of Modern Art*; works of ind. Croatian artists and artists from the Hlebine School; Dir Prof. VLADIMIR CRNKOVIC; Museum Sec. KSENIJA PAVLINIC-TOMAŠEGOVIC.

Hrvatski povijesni muzej (Croatian History Museum): Matoševa 9, HR-10000 Zagreb; tel. (1) 4851-900; e-mail hismus@hismus.hr; internet www.hismus.hr; f. 1846; history of Croatia; 200,000 artefacts arranged into stone monuments, paintings, prints and sculptures, 20th century fine art, religious artefacts, objects from everyday life, flags and uniforms, heraldry and sphragistics, decorations, plaques, medals and badges, edged weapons and fire-arms, maps, first and second documentary, varia and photographs, films and negatives; library of 20,000 vols; Dir Prof. ANKICA PANDŽIĆ.

Hrvatski prirodoslovni muzej (Croatian Natural History Museum): Demetrova 1, HR-10000 Zagreb; tel. (1) 4851-700; e-mail info@hpm.hr; internet www.hpm.hr; f. 1846; depts of botany, geology and palaeontology, mineralogy and petrography, zoology; library of 40,000 vols; Dir Dr TATJANA VLAHOVIĆ; publ. *Natura Croatica* (2 a year).

Hrvatski školski Muzej (Croatian School Museum): Trg m. Tita 4, HR-10000 Zagreb; tel. (1) 4855-716; e-mail hsm@hsmuzej.hr; internet www.hsmuzej.hr; f. 1901; history of the school system and education in Croatia; collns of teaching aids, teaching materials and school equipment, student and teacher writings, textbooks and handbooks, school regulations, archival colln of documents, colln of photographs and a record file on schools; library of 37,500 vols; Dir and Sr Curator Prof. BRANKA MANIN; publ. *Anali za Povijest Odgoja* (1 a year).

Kabinet Grafike (Department of Prints and Drawings): A. Hebrangova 1, HR-10000 Zagreb; tel. (1) 4895-390; e-mail kabgraf@hazu.hr; internet www.kabinet-grafike.hazu.hr; f. 1916 as Arts dept of the fmr Yugoslav Acad. of Sciences and Arts, present status 1951; attached to Croatian Acad. of Sciences and Arts; 17,500 inventory units divided into 4 collns: old colln of drawings and prints (15th–19th centuries), colln of 20th and 21st centuries (drawings and prints), colln of posters, chalcographic plates; Dir SLAVICA MARKOVIĆ.

Moderna Galerija (Gallery of Modern Art): Andrije Hebranga 1, HR-10000 Zagreb; tel. (1) 6041-040; e-mail moderna-galerija@zg.t-com.hr; internet www.moderna-galerija.hr; f. 1905; Croatian arts since 19th century; collns of painting, sculpture and graphic arts; 1,945 medals; library of 5,922 vols; Dir BISERKA RAUTER PLANČIĆ.

Muzej Grada Zagreba (Zagreb City Museum): Opatička 20, HR-10000 Zagreb; tel. (1) 4851-361; e-mail mgz@mgz.hr; internet www.mgz.hr; f. 1907; exhibits on Zagreb since prehistoric times; 5 collns: prehistoric archaeology, medieval archaeology, colln and flat of the architect Viktor Kovačić, Bela and Miroslav Krleža memorial space, Dr Ivan Ribar and Cata Dujšin-Ribar colln; library of 11,000 vols; Dir Prof. VINKO IVIĆ; Sec. KAMILO ČOKL; publ. *Iz starog i novog Zagreba* (from Old and New Zagreb, irregular).

Muzej Suvremene Umjetnosti Zagreb (Museum of Contemporary Art Zagreb): Ave Dubrovnik 17, HR-10000 Zagreb; tel. (1) 6052-700; e-mail msu@msu.hr; internet www.msu.hr; f. 1954; collns of drawings, graphics, prints and art on paper, 456 films and video cassettes, photographs after the 1950s developed at the Centre for Photography, Film and Television (CEFFT); sculpture colln of 561 artworks, 1,200 works by Croatian and int. artists; Tošo Dabac archive: 200,000 negatives, 2,000 enlargements, photography equipment, newspaper clippings; Seissel Donation: paintings and architectural designs by Josip Seissel; Richter colln: 182 works of art by Vjenceslav Richter dating 1964–2002; Benko Horvat colln: 611 paintings, graphic art dating 15th–18th centuries; library of 12,500 vols; Dir and Sr Curator SNJEŽANA PINTARIĆ.

Muzej za umjetnost i obrt (Museum of Arts and Crafts): Trg maršala Tita 10, HR-10000 Zagreb; tel. (1) 4882-111; e-mail muo@muo.hr; internet www.muo.hr; f. 1880; colln of fine and applied arts since 14th century;

furniture, textiles, ceramics, glass, metalwork, sculpture, paintings, photography, costumes, clocks and watches, ivory, architecture, design and posters; library of 65,000 vols; Dir Prof. MIROSLAV GAŠPAROVIĆ.

Strossmayerova galerija starih majstora (Strossmayers' Gallery of Old Masters): Trg Nikole Šubića Zrinskog 11, HR-10000 Zagreb; tel. (1) 4895-115; e-mail sgallery@hazu.hr; internet www.hazu.hr/strossmayerova_galerija_starih_m.html; f. 1884; about 3,000 works of art (paintings, prints and sculptures) from 14th to 19th centuries; library of 40,000 vols, 400 journals; Dir Prof. IVA PASINI TRŽEC; publs *HAZU, Informatica Museologica* (2 a year, in Croatian and English), *Muzeologija* (1 a year, in Croatian and English), *Razreda za likovne umjetnosti*.

Tehnički muzej Zagreb (Zagreb Technical Museum): Savska cesta 18, HR-10000 Zagreb; tel. (1) 4844-050; e-mail info@tehnicki-muzej.hr; internet www.tehnicki-muzej.hr; f. 1954, present bldg 1959; colln of over 5,000 exhibits pertaining to various technical fields; depts of planetarium, cabinet Nikola Tesla, energy transformation, firemen, fundamentals of farming with Apijarijem, mining, geology and oil, surveying and cadastre, famous personalities of Croatian science and technology, transport; library of 12,000 vols; Dir MARKITA FRANULIĆ.

Universities

HRVATSKOG KATOLIČKOG SVEUČILIŠTA
(Croatian Catholic University)

Ilica 242, POB 272, HR-10001 Zagreb
Telephone: (1) 3706-600
E-mail: info@unicath.hr
Internet: www.unicath.hr
Founded 2006
Private control
Language of instruction: Croatian
Academic year: October to June (2 semesters)
Depts of history, psychology, sociology
Rector: Prof. Dr ŽELJKO TANJIĆ
Library Dir: TOMISLAV MURATI

MEĐUNARODNO SVEUČILIŠTE U DUBROVNIKU
(Dubrovnik International University)

Svetog Dominika 4, HR-20000 Dubrovnik
Telephone: (20) 414-111
E-mail: diu@diu.hr
Internet: www.diu.hr
Private control
Language of instruction: English
Academic year: September to May (2 semesters)
Pres.: Prof. Dr MIOMIR ŽUŽUL
Rector: Prof. Dr JANICE MCCORMICK
Vice-Pres.: IVANA ŽUŽUL
Provost: Prof. Dr STJEPAN KRASIC
Provost for Science and Scientific Research: Prof. Dr VLATKO SILOBRČIĆ
Dean of Students: NADA RAIČ
Number of students: 100

DEANS

School of International Business and Economics: Prof. Dr MICHAEL GARY O'CALLAGHAN
School of International Relations and Diplomacy: Prof. Dr CYNTHIA P. SCHNEIDER

SVEUČILIŠTE JOSIPA JURJA STROSSMAYERA U OSIJEKU
(Josip Jurja Strossmayer University of Osijek)

Trg sv. Trojstva 3, POB 716, HR-31000 Osijek
Telephone: (31) 224-125
E-mail: rektorat@unios.hr
Internet: www.unios.hr
Founded 1975
State control
Academic year: October to June (2 semesters)
Rector: Prof. Dr GORDANA KRALIK
Vice-Rector for Education and Students: Prof. Dr DRAGO ŽAGAR
Vice-Rector for Devt Strategy and Spatial Planning: Prof. Dr RUDOLF EMERT
Vice-Rector for Financial and Business Affairs: Prof. Dr VLADMIR SIGMUND
Vice-Rector for Science, Technology, Projects and Int. Cooperation: Prof. Dr IVAN SAMARDŽIĆ
Librarian: DRAGUTIN KATALENAC
Number of teachers: 523
Number of students: 13,214
Publications: *Ekonomski vjesnik* (Economic Courier), *Medicinski vjesnik* (Medical Courier), *Poljoprivreda* (Agriculture), *Pravni vjesnik* (Law Courier), *Tehnički vjesnik* (Technical Courier)

DEANS

Catholic Faculty of Theology: Prof. Dr PERO ARAČIĆ
Faculty of Agriculture: Prof. Dr VLADO GUBERAC
Faculty of Civil Engineering: Dr DAMIR MARKULAK
Faculty of Economics: Prof. Dr ŽELJKO TURKALJ
Faculty of Education: Prof. Dr ANĐELKA PEKO
Faculty of Electrical Engineering: Prof. Dr GALIĆ RADOSLAV
Faculty of Food Technology: Prof. Dr DRAGO ŠUBARIĆ
Faculty of Humanities and Social Sciences: Prof. Dr ANA PINTARIĆ (acting)
Faculty of Law: Dr IGOR BOJANIĆ
Faculty of Mechanical Engineering (Slavonski Brod): Prof. Dr DRAŽAN KOZAK
Faculty of Medicine: Prof. Dr ALEKSANDAR VČEV

PROFESSORS

Faculty of Agriculture (Petra Svačića 1D, HR-31000 Osijek; tel. (31) 554-800; e-mail nastava@suncokret.pfos.hr; internet www.pfos.hr):

BERTIĆ, B., Agrochemistry, Fertilizers
BUKVIĆ, Ž., Mechanization in Livestock Farming and Crop Production
EMERT, R., Agricultural Machinery and Maintenance
GUBERAC, V., Plant Breeding, Seed Science
IVEZIĆ, M., Entomology with Phytopharmacy and Plant Protection, Nematology
JOVANOVAC, S., General Livestock, Genetics of Domestic Animals
JURIĆ, I., Principles of Agriculture, Tropical Agriculture
JURKOVIĆ, D., Plant Protection, Phytopharmacy
KALINOVIĆ, I., Storage and Technology of Agricultural Products
KNEŽEVIĆ, I., Cattle Breeding
KNEŽEVIĆ, M., Botany
KOVAČEVIĆ, V., Cereal Crop Production
KRALIK, G., Husbandry of Swine, Poultry and Fur-bearing Animals
KRISTEK, A., Industrial Crops
MADJAR, S., Agricultural Improvement, Irrigation
MILAKOVIĆ, Z., Microbiology
RASTIJA, T., General Cattle and Horse Raising
SENČIĆ, Đ., Pig Breeding, Livestock Breeding
STEINER, Z., Nutrition of Domestic Animals
STJEPANOVIĆ, M., Forage Crops
VUKADINOVIĆ, V., Plant Physiology, Agricultural Mechanization
ZIMMER, R., Mechanization in Farming, Processing Technology and Storing
ŽUGEC, I., General Crop Production, Alternative Agriculture

Faculty of Civil Engineering (Drinska 16A, HR-31000 Osijek; tel. (31) 274-377; e-mail dekan@gfos.hr; internet www.gfos.unios.hr):

ANIČIĆ, D., Surveying, Earthquake Engineering
MEDANIĆ, B., Construction Management
SIGMUND, V., Construction Stability and Dynamics, Resistance of Materials
TAKAČ, S., Wooden Buildings, Bricklaying

Faculty of Economics (Gajev Trg 7, HR-31000 Osijek; tel. (31) 224-400; internet www.efos.unios.hr):

BOROZAN, D., Macroeconomics
BRANIMIR, M., Finance
NOVAK, B., Managerial Finance
CRNJAC, M., Mathematics, Economics
CRNKOVIC, L., Economics, Accounting
FERENCAK, I., Economic Theory
HOCENSKI-DREISEIDL, M., Economy
HORVAT, JASNA, Measurement Instruments, CADAC Methods, Multivariate Statistics, Public Opinion
JELINIĆ, S., Commercial Law, Company Law
KARIĆ, M., Microeconomics, Cost Management
LAMZA-MARONIĆ, M., Management and Information Systems
LAUC, A., Sociology of Management
LEKO-SIMIC, M., Marketing
MASEK, A., Economy
MATIC, BRANKO, Finance, Banking
MELER, M., Marketing
NOVAC, B., Finance Management, Financial Markets
PFEIFER, S., Management, Entrepreneurship
PROKLIN, P., Accounting, Financial Analysis
RUZIC, D., Marketing
SEGETLIJA, Z., Business Logistics, Retail Business, Retail Marketing
SINGER, S., Entrepreneurship, Corporate Entrepreneurship, Strategic Management
SUNDALIC, A., Sociology, Sociology of Management
TURKALJ, Ž., Business Organization, Work Organization, Fundamentals of Organization

Faculty of Education (L. Jägera 9, HR-31000 Osijek; tel. (31) 200-602; e-mail helpdesk@ufos.hr; internet www.ufos.hr):

BABIĆ, N., Pre-School Education, Teaching Methods in Pre-School Education, Education Communication

Faculty of Electrical Engineering (Knezá Trpimira 2B, HR-31000 Osijek; tel. (31) 224-600; e-mail etf@etfos.hr; internet www.etfos.hr):

CRNKOVIĆ, I., Computer and Software Engineering
HOCENSKI, Z., Computer and Software
JOZSA, L., Power Engineering
MARTINOVIĆ, G., Computer and Software Engineering
MRČELA, T., Common Objects
NIKOLOVSKI, S., Power Engineering
RADOSLAV, G., Common Objects
RIMAC-DRLJE, S., Communications
ŠVEDEK, T., Communications
ZAGAR, D., Communications

Faculty of Food Technology (Franje Kuhača 20, HR-31000 Osijek; tel. (31) 224-300; e-mail office@ptfos.hr; internet www.ptfos.unios.hr):

MANDIĆ, M., Quality Control, Sensor Analyses, Fundamentals of Food Technology, Food Science
PILIŽOTA, V., Raw Materials in Food Industry, Technology of Fruit and Vegetable Preserving and Processing
ŠERUGA, M., Physical Chemistry, Packing Materials, Methods of Analysis by Instrument
UGARČIĆ-HARDI, Ž, Raw Materials in Food Industry, Flour Production and Processing

Faculty of Humanities and Social Sciences (Lorenza Jägera 9, HR-31000 Osijek; tel. (31) 211-400; internet www.ffos.unios.hr):

APARAC-JELUŠIĆ, T., Library Science, Informatics and Communication
BRLENIĆ-VUJIĆ, B., Comparative Literature
JERKOVIĆ, J., Conducting, Choir
MARIJANOVIĆ, S., Croatian Literature
NIKČEVIĆ, M., Methodology of Scientific Work, Methodics of Literature Teaching
OBAD, V., German Literature
ŽIVKOVIĆ, P., Medieval History

Faculty of Law (S. Radića 13, HR-31000 Osijek; tel. (31) 224-500; e-mail office@pravos.hr; internet www.pravos.unios.hr):

BABAC, B., Administrative Law, Administrative Science
BELAJ, V., Civil Law
BOSANAC, N.
JELINIĆ, S., Commercial Law, Social Law, Copyright
LAUC, Z., Constitutional Law
LJUBANOVIĆ, V., Criminal Procedural Law

Faculty of Mechanical Engineering (Trg Ivane Brlić-Mažuranić 2, HR-35000 Slavonski Brod; tel. (35) 446-188; internet www.sfsb.unios.hr):

ARAČIĆ, S., Welding and Surface Protection
BUDIĆ, I., Casting and Deformation
GRIZELJ, B., Casting and Deformation
KATALINIĆ, B., Automation, Flexible Systems
KLADARIĆ, H., Materials and Heat Treatment
KLJAJIN, M., Machine Elements and Design
KRUMES, D., Tribology and Surface Engineering
MARUŠIĆ, V., Tribology and Surface Engineering
MATEJIČEK, F., Mechanics and Strength
RAOS, P., Machine Maintenance and Polymer Processing
SAMARDŽIĆ, I., Welding and Surface Protection
ŠIMUNOVIĆ, G., Preparation and Production Management
STOIĆ, ANTUN, Machine Maintenance and Polymer Processing
ŽIVIĆ, M., Energy

Faculty of Medicine (Josipa Huttlera 4, POB 392, HR-31000 Osijek; tel. (31) 512-800; e-mail ured@mefos.hr; internet www.mefos.unios.hr):

BALEN, S., Internal Medicine, History of Medicine and Medical Ethics
BELOVARI, T., Histology and Embryology
BILIĆ, A., Internal Medicine, History of Medicine and Medical Ethics
BIRUŠ, M., Medical Chemistry, Biochemistry and Clinical Chemistry
BUŠIĆ, Z., Surgery and War Surgery
ĆULO, F.
ĐANIĆ, D., Otorhinolaryngology and Maxillofacial Surgery
DMITROVIĆ, B., Pathological Anatomy and Forensic Medicine
DOBRIĆ, I., Dermatology
DRENJANČEVIĆ, I., Physiology and Immunology
DUMIĆ, M., Medical Chemistry, Biochemistry and Clinical Chemistry
FAJDIĆ, J., Surgery and War Surgery
FILAKOVIĆ, P., Psychiatry and Psychology
GALIĆ, J., Urology
GLAVAŠ-OBROVAC, L., Medical Chemistry, Biochemistry and Clinical Chemistry
HAS, B., Surgery and War Surgery
HEFFER, M., Medical Biology
JOVANOVIĆ, S., Orthopedic, Physical and Rehabilitation Medicine
KADOJIĆ, D., Neurology
KARNER, I., Pathophysiology
KLAPAN, I., Otorhinolaryngology and Maxillofacial Surgery
KOSTOVIĆ-KNEŽEVIĆ, L., Histology and Embryology
KURBEL, S., Physiology and Immunology
MARCIKIĆ, M., Pathological Anatomy and Forensic Medicine
NEMET, D., Internal Medicine, History of Medicine and Medical Ethics
PRIMORAC, D., Paediatrics
PUNTARIĆ, D., Public Health
RADIĆ, R., Anatomy and Neuroscience
RUDAN, P., Anatomy and Neurosciences
ŠAMIJA, M., Oncology and Radiology
ŠAKIĆ-ZDRAVČEVIĆ, K., Anaesthesiology, Reanimation and Intensive Care
ŠESTO, M., Internal Medicine, History of Medicine and Medical Ethics
SOLDO, I., Infectious Diseases
SOLDO, S. B., Neurology
TURINA, M., Surgery and War Surgery
VČEV, A., Internal Medicine, History of Medicine and Medical Ethics
VUKIĆ, M., Neurosurgery
VUKŠIĆ, Z., Psychiatry and Psychology
ZAPUTOVIĆ, L., Internal Medicine, History of Medicine and Medical Ethics

Department of Mathematics (Trg Lj. Gaja 6, HR-31000 Osijek; tel. (31) 224-800; e-mail math@mathos.hr; internet www.mathos.hr):

BUTKOVIĆ, D., Linear Algebra
SCITOVSKI, R., Numerical Mathematics, Computer Exercises II
SVRTAN, D., Theoretical Mechanics, Discrete Mathematics
VOLENEC, V., Geometry Models, Metric Geometry

SVEUČILIŠTE JURJA DOBRILE U PULI
(Juraj Dobrila University of Pula)

Zagrebačka 30, HR-52100 Pula
Telephone: (52) 377-000
E-mail: ured@unipu.hr
Internet: www.unipu.hr
Founded 2006
public control
Languages of instruction: Croatian, Italian, English
Academic year: September to June

Depts of economics and tourism, educational sciences, humanities, Italian studies, music; centre for cultural and historical analysis of socialism

Rector: Prof. Dr ROBERT MATIJASIĆ
Vice-Rector for Financial and Business Affairs: Prof. Dr LOVRE BOZINA
Vice-Rector for Int. Cooperation: Prof. Dr IVAN JURKOVIĆ
Vice-Rector for Science and Research: Prof. Dr MARLI GONAN BOZAC
Vice-Rector for Teaching and Student Affairs: Prof. ĐENI DEKLEVA RADAKOVIĆ

Library: see under Libraries and Archives
Number of teachers: 230
Number of students: 3,000

SVEUČILIŠTE U DUBROVNIKU
(University of Dubrovnik)

Branitelja Dubrovnika 29, HR-20000 Dubrovnik
Telephone: (20) 445-700
E-mail: rektorat@unidu.hr
Internet: www.unidu.hr
Founded 2003
State control
Languages of instruction: Croatian, English
Academic year: October to September

Depts of aquaculture, art and restoration, communication, economics and business, electrical engineering and computer science, professional studies

Rector: Prof. Dr VESNA VRTIPRAH
Vice-Rector for Int. Cooperation and Science: Prof. Dr VLATKO LIPOVAC
Vice-Rector for Teaching and Student Affairs: Dr ŽELJKO KURTELA
Sec.-Gen.: DALIBOR IVUŠIĆ
Academic Sec.: BRANKO PUTICA
Head Librarian: MARIS SJEKAVICA

Library of 14,000 vols, 50 periodicals
Number of teachers: 266
Number of students: 2,700

Publications: *Ekonomska misao i praksa* (Economic Thought and Practice, in Croatian and English), *Naše more* (Our Sea, 3 a year), *Punkt*, *Sveučilišni Godišnjak* (University Yearbook, 1 a year)

SVEUČILIŠTE U RIJECI
(University of Rijeka)

Trg braće Mažuranića 10, HR-51000 Rijeka
Telephone: (51) 406-500
E-mail: ured@uniri.hr
Internet: www.uniri.hr
Founded 1973
State control
Language of instruction: Croatian
Academic year: October to June (2 semesters)

Rector: Prof. Dr PERO LUČIN (acting)
Vice-Rector for Business and Integration Processes: Dr TONČI MIKAC
Vice-Rector for Community Collaboration, Economy and Student Employability: Dr PAVAO KOMADINA
Vice-Rector for Int. Cooperation: Dr DAMIR ZEC
Vice-Rector for Science and Devt: Prof. Dr NEVENKA OŽANIĆ
Vice-Rector for Teaching and Student Affairs: Prof. Dr SNJEŽANA PRIJIĆ-SAMARŽIJA
Sec.-Gen.: ROBERTA HLAČA MLINAR
Library Dir: SENKA TOMLJANOVIĆ

Library of 300,000 vols
Number of teachers: 928
Number of students: 19,139

Publications: *Gaudeamus* (irregular), *Sveučilišni vodič* (1 a year)

DEANS

Academy of Applied Arts: Prof. Dr ANTE VLADISLAVIĆ
Faculty of Civil Engineering: Prof. Dr ALEKSANDRA DELUKA-TIBLJAS
Faculty of Economics: Prof. Dr HERI BEZIĆ
Faculty of Engineering: Prof. Dr GORAN TURKALJ
Faculty of Humanities and Social Sciences: Dr PREDRAG ŠUSTAR
Faculty of Law: Prof. Dr MIOMIR MATULOVIĆ
Faculty of Maritime Studies: Prof. Dr SERDO KOS
Faculty of Medicine: Prof. Dr ALAN ŠUSTIĆ
Faculty of Teacher Education: Prof. Dr JASNA KRSTOVIĆ

SVEUČILIŠTE U SPLITU
(University of Split)

Livanjska 5, HR-21000 Split
Telephone: (21) 558-200
E-mail: rektorat.office@unist.hr
Internet: www.unist.hr

Founded 1974
State control
Languages of instruction: Croatian, English
Academic year: October to June (2 semesters)

Rector: Prof. Dr IVAN PAVIĆ
Vice-Rector for Finance and Accounting: Prof. Dr BRANKA RAMLJAK
Vice-Rector for Information Technology, Logistics and Technical Devt: Prof. Dr TOMISLAV KILIĆ
Vice-Rector for Legal, Human Resources and Gen. Issues: Prof. Dr DRAGAN BOLANCA
Vice-Rector for Science, Int. and Interinstitutional Relations: Prof. Dr ROKO ANDRICEVIĆ
Sec.-Gen.: PAULA VUČEMILOVIĆ ŠIMUNOVIĆ

Library of 400,000 vols, 12,000 periodicals
Number of teachers: 1,500
Number of students: 23,000

Publications: *Sveučilišni godišnjak*, *Universitas* (12 a year)

DEANS

Academy of Arts: Prof. Dr BRANKO MATULIĆ
Faculty of Catholic Theology: Prof. Dr ANTE VUČKOVIĆ
Faculty of Chemistry and Technology: Dr NENAD KUZMANIĆ
Faculty of Civil Engineering and Architecture: Prof. Dr ALEN HARAPIN
Faculty of Economics: Prof. Dr ŽELJKO GARAČA
Faculty of Electrical Engineering, Mechanical Engineering and Naval Construction: Prof. Dr SRDJAN PODRUG
Faculty of Kinesiology: Prof. Dr BORIS MALEŠ
Faculty of Law: Dr BORIS BUKLIJAŠ
Faculty of Medicine: Prof. Dr DRAGAN LJUTIĆ
Faculty of Natural Sciences, Mathematics and Education: Prof. Dr MARKO ROSIĆ
Faculty of Philosophy: Prof. Dr MARKO TROGRLIĆ
Maritime Faculty: Prof. Dr ROSANDA MULIĆ

PROFESSORS

Academy of Arts (Glagoljaška bb, POB 545, HR-21000 Split; tel. (21) 342-801; e-mail office@umas.hr; internet www.umas.hr):

IVANČIĆ, N., Painting
LEROTIĆ, T., Visual Communication and Design
LISTEŠ, G., String Instruments and Guitar
MIJIĆ, M., Sculpture
JOKIĆ, S., Film and Video
SIRIŠČEVIĆ, M., Music Theory and Composition
SUNKO, V., Music Pedagogy
ZRNIĆ, V., Film and Video

Faculty of Chemistry and Technology (Teslina 10, HR-21000 Split; tel. (21) 329-420; e-mail dekanat@ktf-split.hr; internet www.ktf-split.hr):

ANDRIČIĆ, B., Organic Technology
KATALINIĆ, V., Food Technology and Biotechnology
KLARIĆ, I., Organic Technology
KLIŠKIĆ, M., Electrochemistry and Protection Materials
KROLO, P., Inorganic Technology
MARTINAC, V., Thermodynamics
MASTELIĆ, J., Organic Chemistry
MILOŠ, M., Biochemistry
PERIĆ, J., Environmental Engineering
RADIĆ, N., Analytical Chemistry
RUŠIĆ, D., Chemical Engineering
SVILOVIĆ, S., Chemical Engineering
ZELIĆ, J., Inorganic Technology

Faculty of Civil Engineering and Architecture (Matice Hrvatske 15, HR-21000 Split; tel. (21) 303-333; e-mail dekan@gradst.hr; internet www.gradst.hr):

BONACCI, O., Hydrology
DAMJANIĆ, F., Technical Mechanics
JOVIĆ, V., Hydromechanics
MARGETA, J., Water Supply
MAROVIĆ, P., Strength of Materials, Testing of Structures
MIHANOVIĆ, A., Mechanics, Stability and Dynamics of Structures
MILIČIĆ, J., Construction and Construction Machines
ŠESTANOVIĆ, S., Geology and Petrology
ŠKOMRLJ, J., Technology and Organization of Construction
STOJIĆ, P., Hydrotechnical Systems
VOJNOVIĆ, J., Building Construction
VRDOLJAK, B., Mathematics

Faculty of Economics (Matice Hrvatske 31, HR-21000 Split; tel. (21) 430-600; e-mail dekanat@efst.hr; internet www.efst.hr):

ALFIREVIĆ, N., Management
ALJINOVIĆ, Z., Quantitative Methods
ANDRIJIĆ, S., Macroeconomics, Econometrics
BABIĆ, Z., Quantitative Methods
BAKOTIĆ, D., Management
BILIĆ, I., Management
BOGDANOVIĆ, M., Management
BUBLE, M., Organization Design, Job Evaluation
BULOG, I., Management
DOMANČIĆ, P., International Finance
DULČIĆ, A., Economics of Trade and Tourism
GOIĆ, S., Management
GRUBIŠIĆ, D., Management
JELAVIĆ, A., Business Economics
JURUN, E., Quantitative Methods
KORDIĆ, L., National Economy
KRUŽIĆ, D., Management
LOVRINČEVIĆ, M., Management
LUKŠIĆ, B., Business Economics
MARASOVIĆ, B., Quantitative Methods
MIKULIĆ, D., National Economy
MRNJAVAC, Z., National Economy
PETRIĆ, L., National Economy
PIVAC, S., Quantitative Methods
PIVČEVIĆ, S., National Economy
POKLEPOVIĆ, T., Quantitative Methods
PRANIĆ, L., National Economy
ROZGA, A., Quantitative Methods
ŠIMUNDIĆ, B., National Economy
ŠKRABIĆ, B. P., Quantitative Methods
ŠTAMBUK, D., Regional Economics
TOMIĆ-PLAZIBAT, N., Quantitative Methods
DULČIĆ, Z., Management

Faculty of Electrical Engineering, Mechanical Engineering and Naval Construction (Ruđera Boškovića bb, HR-21000 Split; tel. (21) 305-777; e-mail dekanat@fesb.hr; internet www.fesb.hr):

BAJIĆ, D., Mechanical Engineering Technology
BARBIR, F., Mechanical Engineering and Naval Architecture
BARLE, J., Mechanical Engineering Technology
BEGUŠIĆ, D., Electronics
BEROŠ, S. M., Electronics
BILIĆ, B., Mechanical Engineering Technology
BONKOVIĆ, M., Electronics
CECIĆ, M., Electronics
DOMAZET, Z., Mechanical Engineering and Naval Architecture
DUPLANČIĆ, I., Mechanical Engineering Technology
GOTOVAC, S., Electronics
JAJAC, B., Power Engineering
JELASKA, D., Mechanical Engineering and Naval Architecture
KRSTULOVIĆ-OPARA, L., Mechanical Engineering and Naval Architecture
LOZINA, Z., Mechanical Engineering and Naval Architecture
MAGAZINOVIĆ, G., Mechanical Engineering and Naval Architecture
MARASOVIĆ, J., Electronics
MARKOVINA, R., Mechanical Engineering and Naval Architecture
MATELJAN, I.
MEDIĆ, I., Power Engineering
MILUN, S., Power Engineering
MIŠINA, N., Mechanical Engineering Technology
NIKŠA, K., Power Engineering
OŽEGOVIĆ, J., Electronics
PAPIĆ, V., Electronics
PAVAZZA, R., Mechanical Engineering and Naval Architecture
PULJAK, I., Mathematics and Physics
RINO, L., Power Engineering
STIPANIČEV, D., Electronics
TERZIĆ, B., Power Engineering
VEŽA, I., Mechanical Engineering Technology
VUČINA, D., Mechanical Engineering and Naval Architecture
VUJEVIĆ, S., Power Engineering
ŽIVKOVIĆ, D., Mechanical Engineering Technology
ZULIM, I., Electronics

Faculty of Law (Domovinskog rata 8, HR-21000 Split; tel. (21) 393-500; e-mail dekanat@pravst.hr; internet www.pravst.hr):

BILIĆ, I., Political Economy
BORKOVIĆ, I., Administrative Law
BOSNIĆ, P., International Private Law
CARIĆ, A., Criminal Law
CVITAN, O., Administrative Sciences
DUJIĆ, A., Modern Political Systems
GRABOVAC, I., Maritime and Transport Law
PETRIĆ, I., Economic Politics
PETRINOVIĆ, I., History of Political Theories
RUDOLF, D., International Public Law
SMID, V., Civil Law
VISKOVIĆ, N., Theory of State and Law

Faculty of Natural Sciences, Mathematics and Education (Teslina 12/III, HR-21000 Split; tel. (21) 385-133; e-mail dekanat@pmfst.hr; internet www.pmfst.hr):

BEZIĆ, N., Biology
BORAS, V., Polytechnic
GRANIĆ, A., Informatics
KRSTULOVIĆ, A., Polytechnic
MATIĆ, T., Polytechnic
PUIZINA, J., Biology
ROSIĆ, M., Informatics
ŠANTIĆ, M., Biology
STANKOV, S., Informatics

Maritime Faculty (Zrinsko-Frankopanska 38, HR-21000 Split; tel. (21) 380-762; e-mail studentska.sluzba@pfst.hr; internet www.pfst.hr):

BIĆANIĆ, Z., Nautical Engineering
KASUM, J.
KEZIĆ, D., Maritime Electrotechnical and Information Technology
MULIĆ, R.

SVEUČILIŠTE U ZADRU
(University of Zadar)

ul. Mihovila Pavlinovića bb, HR-23000 Zadar
Telephone: (23) 200-555
E-mail: info@unizd.hr
Internet: www.unizd.hr

Founded 2002
State control
Language of instruction: Croatian
Academic year: October to June (two semesters)

Depts of agronomy and aquaculture, archaeology, classical philology, Croatian and Slavic studies, ecology, economics, English, ethnology and cultural anthropology, French and Iberoromance studies, geography, German studies, health studies, history, history of art, information sciences, Italian studies, linguistics, maritime studies, pedagogy, philosophy, psychology, sociology, teachers' and preschool teachers' education, tourism and communication studies

Rector: Prof. Dr ANTE UGLEŠIĆ
Vice-Rector for Mobility and Projects: Prof. Dr LEONARDO MARUŠIĆ
Vice-Rector for Org., Human Resources, Publishing and Quality Assurance: Prof. Dr JOSIP FARIČIĆ
Vice-Rector for Science, Technology, Devt and Material Resources: Prof. Dr DIJANA VICAN
Vice-Rector for Teaching and Student Affairs: Dr ROBERT BACALJA
Sec.-Gen.: ANTONELLA LOVRIĆ
Librarian: MIRTA MATOŠIĆ

Library of 122,000 vols, 25,000 periodicals
Number of teachers: 411
Number of students: 5,945

Publications: *Acta Iadertina*, *Archaeologia Adriatica*, *Ars Adriatica*, *Croatica et Slavica Iadertina*, *Geoadria*, *Hieronymus*, *Libellarium*, *Liburna*, *Magistra Iadertina*, *Oeconomica Iadertina*, *[sic]* (online)

SVEUČILIŠTE U ZAGREBU
(University of Zagreb)

Trg maršala Tita 14, POB 407, HR-10002 Zagreb
Telephone: (1) 4564-111
E-mail: unizginfo@unizg.hr
Internet: www.unizg.hr

Founded 1669
State control
Language of instruction: Croatian
Academic year: October to June (2 semesters)

Rector: Prof. Dr ALEKSA BJELIŠ
Vice-Rector for Financial Management: Prof. Dr VESNA VAŠIČEK
Vice-Rector for Legal Issues and Int. Cooperation: Prof. Dr KSENIJA TURKOVIĆ
Vice-Rector for Master Planning and Inter-Institutional Cooperation: Prof. Dr BOJAN BALETIĆ
Vice-Rector for Research and Technology: Prof. Dr MELITA KOVACEVIĆ
Vice-Rector for Students and Study Programmes: Prof. Dr BLAŽENKA DIVJAK
Academic Sec.: LGA ŠARLOG BAVOLJAK

Number of teachers: 5,250
Number of students: 50,000

Publication: *Sveučilišni vjesnik* (University Herald)

DEANS

Academy of Dramatic Arts: Prof. BORNA BALETIĆ
Academy of Fine Arts: Prof. PERUŠKO BOGDANIĆ
Academy of Music: Prof. MLADEN JANJANIN
Catholic Faculty of Theology: Prof. Dr TONČI MATULIĆ
Faculty of Agriculture: Prof. Dr TATJANA KRIČKA
Faculty of Architecture: Prof. BORIS KORUŽNJAK
Faculty of Chemical Engineering and Technology: Prof. Dr STANISLAV KURAJICA
Faculty of Civil Engineering: Prof. Dr VESNA DRAGČEVIĆ
Faculty of Education and Rehabilitation Sciences: Prof. Dr LJILJANA MIKŠAJ-TODOROVIĆ
Faculty of Electrical Engineering and Computing: Prof. Dr NEDJELJKO PERIĆ
Faculty of Food Technology and Biotechnology: Prof. Dr DAMIR JEŽEK
Faculty of Forestry: Prof. Dr MILAN ORŠANIĆ
Faculty of Geodesy: Prof. Dr MIODRAG ROIĆ
Faculty of Geotechnical Engineering (Varaždin): Prof. Dr JOSIP MESEC
Faculty of Graphic Arts: Prof. Dr DIANA MILČIĆ
Faculty of Kinesiology: Prof. Dr IGOR JUKIĆ
Faculty of Law: Prof. Dr ZORAN PARAĆ
Faculty of Mechanical Engineering and Naval Architecture: Prof. Dr IVAN JURAGA
Faculty of Metallurgy (Sisak): Prof. Dr FARUK UNKIĆ
Faculty of Mining, Geology and Petroleum Engineering: Prof. Dr BILJANA KOVAČEVIĆ-ZELIĆ
Faculty of Organization and Informatics (Varaždin): Prof. Dr VJERAN STRAHONJA
Faculty of Pharmacy and Biochemistry: Prof. Dr KARMELA BARIŠIĆ
Faculty of Philosophy: Prof. Dr DAMIR BORAS
Faculty of Political Science: Dr NENAD ZAKOŠEK
Faculty of Science: Prof. Dr AMIR HAMZIĆ
Faculty of Teacher Education: Prof. Dr IVAN PRSKALO
Faculty of Textile Technology: Prof. Dr SANDRA BISCHOF
Faculty of Transport and Traffic Engineering: Prof. Dr ERNEST BAZIJANAC
Faculty of Veterinary Medicine: Prof. Dr TOMISLAV DOBRANIĆ
Graduate School of Economics and Business: Prof. Dr TONĆI LAZIBAT
School of Dental Medicine: Prof. Dr HRVOJE BRKIĆ
School of Medicine: Prof. Dr DAVOR MILIČIĆ

Colleges

Američka visoka škola za management i tehnologiju (American College of Management and Technology): Don Frana Bulića 6, HR-20000 Dubrovnik; tel. (20) 433-000; e-mail american.college@acmt.hr; internet www.acmt.hr; f. 1995; undergraduate programmes in service management and information technology; postgraduate programmes in human resource development and service leadership and innovation; 1,500 students; Pres. and Dean DON HUDSPETH.

Evanđeoski teološki fakultet (Evangelical Theological Seminary): Cvjetkova 32, POB 370, HR-31103 Osijek; tel. (31) 494-200; e-mail info@evtos.hr; internet www.evtos.hr; f. 1972; library: 85,000 vols; 240 (40 full-time, 200 part-time) students; Rector Prof. Dr PETER KUZMIČ; Academic Dean Dr ALEKSANDAR BIRVIS.

Inter-University Centre Dubrovnik: Don Frana Bulića 4, HR-20000 Dubrovnik; tel. (20) 413-627; e-mail iuc@iuc.hr; internet www.iuc.hr; f. 1972; courses in comparative media systems, diversity in Europe, European constitutionalism and beyond, patriarchalism scanning in contemporary Europe, philosophy of science, archaeology, history; library: 10,000 vols; Dir-Gen. Prof. KRUNOSLAV PISK; Deputy Dir-Gen. Prof. PETER KAMPITS.

Međunarodna diplomska škola za poslovno upravljanje—Zagreb (International Graduate Business School—Zagreb): Trg J .F. Kennedy 7, Zagreb; tel. (1) 2314-990; e-mail mba@igbs.hr; internet igbs.hr; f. 2003; courses in business analytics, business ethics, business law, corporate finance, entrepreneurship, European economic policy, financial accounting, financial intermediation, human resources, international financial strategy, international macro economics, investments, leadership skills, managerial accounting, managerial economy, marketing management, new product management, operations management, retail management, strategic management; Dean Dr ZLATAN FRÖHLICH.

RRiF Visoka škola za financijski menadžment (RRiF University College of Financial Management): Martićeva 29, Zagreb; tel. (1) 4699-735; e-mail visoka-skola@rrif.hr; internet www.visoka-skola-rrif.hr; f. 2006; offers Bachelors of Economics degrees in accounting and finance; Dean ĐURĐICA JURIĆ.

Teološki fakultet 'Matija Vlačić Ilirik' s pravom javnost (Theological Faculty 'Matija Vlačić Ilirik'): Radićeva 34, HR-10000 Zagreb; tel. (1) 4828-915; e-mail teoloski-fakultet@tfmvi.hr; internet www.tfmvi.hr; f. 1976 by Lutheran Church and Baptist Union; courses in 5 areas of theology incl. Old Testament, New Testament, history of the church and theology, systematic theology, practical theology; Dean Prof. Dr VITOMIR BELAJ; Vice-Dean Dr LIDIJA MATOŠEVIĆ; Sec. ENOH ŠEBA.

Utilus Visoka poslovna škola za turistički i hotelski menadžment (Utilus Business School for Tourism and Hotel Management): ul. Grada Mainza 21, HR-10000 Zagreb; tel. (1) 2442-595; e-mail utilus@utilus.hr; internet www.utilus.hr; f. 2004; Dean Dr BORIS VUKONIĆ; Vice-Dean Dr KSENIJA KEČA.

Visoka novinarska škola (College of Journalism): Iblerov trg 10, Importanne Galleria, 1. kat LP, Zagreb; tel. (1) 5555-080; e-mail info@nclstudij.com; internet www.nclstudij.com; attached to 'VERN' Polytechnic; Dean Prof. Dr MATE GRANIĆ.

Visoka policijska škola (Police College): Avenija Gojka Suška 1, HR-10000 Zagreb; tel. (1) 2426-304; e-mail vps@fkz.hr; internet www.policija.hr; professional, graduate and supplementary courses in criminology; Dean Dr JOŠKO VUKOSAV; Sec. DUŠAN MILIVOJEVIĆ.

Visoka Politehnička škola u Zagrebu (Zagreb Polytechnic College): Baštijanova bb, Zagreb; tel. (1) 3666-629; e-mail tajnistvo@politehnika.hr; internet politehnika.hr/tehnicki; programmes in construction, economics, electrical engineering, film, television and new media, technical management; Dean Prof. Dr PAVAO REBIĆ.

Visoka poslovna škola 'Libertas' ('Libertas' Business College): Trg J. F. Kennedy 6B, HR-10000 Zagreb; tel. (1) 2323-377; e-mail poslovna.skola@libertas.hr; internet www.vps-libertas.hr; f. 2004; programmes in business economics, management of internal and international trade, management of finances, banking and insurance; 1,000 students; Dean Prof. Dr DUŠKO PAVLOVIĆ; Vice-Dean for Tuition Dr DAVOR PERKOV.

Visoka poslovna škola 'Minerva' ('Minerva' Business College): Sv. Duje 8/a, HR-21204 Dugopolje; tel. (21) 493-100; e-mail info@vps-minerva.hr; internet www.vps-minerva.hr; f. 2007; education in management information systems; programmes in accounting and finance, computer science, foreign languages, general economics, law, management, psychology, statistics; Dean Dr ANTE CORKALO.

Visoka poslovna škola s pravom javnosti, Višnjan (Business Administration College, Višnjan): Istarska 23, HR-52463 Višnjan; tel. (52) 449-500; e-mail info@vpsvisnjan.hr; internet www.vpsvisnjan.hr; f. 2000; bachelors and masters programmes in tourism management; Dean Prof. Dr ZDENKO TOMČIĆ; Sec. DESANKA ĐULABIĆ.

Visoka poslovna škola Zagreb (Business School Zagreb): ul. grada Vukovara 68, HR-

10000 Zagreb; tel. (1) 6310-844; e-mail vpsz@vpsz.hr; internet www.vpsz.hr; f. 2006; courses in communications management, marketing management; Dean Dr GORAN POPOVIĆ (acting); Vice-Dean for Education Dr TOMISLAV IVANČEVIĆ; Vice-Dean for Research and Devt ZORAN NAJDANOVIĆ; Sec. MARIJA BARIČEVIĆ.

Visoka škola međunarodnih odnosa i diplomacije 'Dag Hammarskjöld' (University College of International Relations and Diplomacy 'Dag Hammarskjöld'): Ilica 242, HR-10000 Zagreb; tel. (1) 3700-826; e-mail tajnistvo@diplomacija.hr; internet www.diplomacija.hr; Dean Prof. IVO ŠLAUS; Vice-Dean Dr GORAN BANDOV.

Visoka škola tržišnih komunikacija Agora (College of Agora): Trnjanska cesta 114, HR-10000 Zagreb; tel. (1) 2225-700; e-mail tajnistvo@vsa.hr; internet www.vsa.hr; f. 2003; programmes in communication management, creative market communication management, market communication design; Dean Prof. Dr SAVA BOGDANOVIĆ.

Visoka škola za ekonomiju, poduzetnistvo i upravljanje 'Nikola Šubić Zrinski' (Nikola Šubić Zrinski University College of Economics, Entrepreneurship and Management): Selska cesta 119, HR-10110 Zagreb; tel. (1) 3695-706; internet www.zrinski.org/nikola; courses in business, economics, entrepreneurship, management; Dean ZDRAVKO TKALEC; Vice-Dean for Devt and Int. Cooperation MARTINA FERK; Vice-Dean for Education Dr ALJOŠA ŠESTANOVIĆ; Sec. VLATKA KOVAČ; Librarian ANA LOVRIĆ.

Visoka škola za informacijske tehnologije (College of Information Technology): Klaićeva 7, HR-10000 Zagreb; tel. (1) 3764-007; e-mail dekanat@vsite.hr; internet www.vsite.hr; f. 2006; Dean MILORAD NIKITOVIĆ.

Visoka škola za inspekcijski i kadrovski menadžment (College for Inspection and Human Resource Management in Maritime Sciences): Brigade HV 114, HR-21000 Split; tel. (21) 645-375; e-mail dekan@vsikm.hr; internet vsikm.hr; Dean Prof. Dr ĐORĐE NADRLJANSKI.

Visoka škola za menadžment i dizajn Aspira (University College of Management and Design Aspira): Domovinskog rata 65, HR-21000 Split; tel. (21) 339-170; e-mail info@aspira.hr; internet www.aspira.hr; Dean Prof. Dr SLOBODAN DRAGIČEVIĆ.

Visoka škola za menadžment u turizmu i informatici u Virovitici (College of Tourism and Information Technology in Vitrovitica): Matije Gupca 78, HR-33000 Virovitica; tel. (33) 721-099; internet www.vsmti.hr; programmes in enterprise services, IT management, management in rural tourism, rural entrepreneurship; Dean Prof. Dr VESNA BEDEKOVIĆ; Vice-Dean Dr OLIVER JUKIĆ; Librarian Prof. IVANA VIDAK; publ. *Časopis Praktični menadžment* (Journal of Practical Management).

Visoka škola za odnose s javnošću i studij medija 'Kairos' ('Kairos' College for Public Relations and Media Studies): Ilica 242, Zagreb; tel. (1) 3706-240; e-mail vskairos@vskairos.hr; internet www.vskairos.hr; Dean Dr BRANKO HEBRANG.

Visoka škola za poslovanje i upravljanje 'Baltazar Adam Krčelić' ('Baltazar Adam Krčelić' College of Business and Management): Vladimira Novaka 23, HR-10290 Zaprešić; tel. (1) 4002-782; e-mail dekan@vspu.hr; internet www.vspu.hr; f. 2001; programmes in business economics and finance, communications management, cultural management, financial management, office management, project management; 3,000 students; Dean Prof. Dr MILAN JURINA; Vice-Dean for Finance and Devt VINKO MOROVIĆ; Vice-Dean for Study Affairs Dr DRAGUTIN FUNDA.

Visoka škola za primijenjeno računarstvo (University College for Applied Computer Engineering): Ilica 242, HR-10000 Zagreb; tel. (1) 2222-182; e-mail info@racunarstvo.hr; internet www.racunarstvo.hr; f. 2008; depts of computer networks, general courses, information systems, IT security, operating systems, software engineering; 200 students; Dean MISLAV BALKOVIĆ; Vice-Dean for Education Prof. SILVIJA GRGIĆ.

Visoka škola za sigurnost s pravom javnosti (University College of Applied Sciences in Safety): ul. I. Lučića 5, HR-10000 Zagreb; tel. (1) 6168-143; e-mail tajnistvo@vss.hr; internet www.vss.hr; f. 1997; courses in professional study of safety; Dean Prof. Dr SLAVKO SEVER; Sec. Prof. NEDA ČUS-BOGDAN.

Visoka tehnička škola u Bjelovaru (Technical College in Bjelovar): Trg Eugena Kvaternika 4, Bjelovar; tel. (43) 241-201; e-mail referada@vtsbj.hr; internet www.vtsbj.hr; programmes in mechatronics and nursing; Dean Dr ANTE ČIKIĆ (acting); Vice-Dean for Education and Devt TATJANA BADROV.

Visoko Gospodarsko Učilište u Križevcima (College of Agriculture at Križevci): Milislava Demerca 1, HR-48260 Križevci; tel. (48) 681-597; e-mail dekan@vguk.hr; internet www.vguk.hr; f. 1860; graduate and professional programmes in farm management, plant production and zoology; library: 10,000 vols; Dean Dr MARIJANA IVANEK-MARTINCIC (acting); Vice-Dean Prof. Dr TATJANA JELEN.

Visoko učilište Effectus—Visoka škola za financije i pravo (Effectus—University College for Law and Finance): Trg J. F. Kennedy 2, HR-10000 Zagreb; tel. (1) 6117-777; e-mail referada@vsfp.eu; internet www.effectus-uciliste.eu; depts of general economics, finance, law, interdisciplinary courses; Dean Prof. Dr ROBERT KOPAL; Vice-Dean for Education NATAŠA TROJAK; Vice-Dean for Int. Relations VESNA CIGAN; Sec. GORAN TRBOJEVIĆ.

Zagrebačke škole ekonomije i managementa (Zagreb School of Economics and Management): Jordanovac 110, HR-10000 Zagreb; tel. (1) 2354-010; e-mail tajnistvo@zsem.hr; internet www.zsem.hr; f. 2002; depts of accounting, economics, finance, foreign languages, information and communication technology, legal disciplines, management, marketing and communication, mathematics and statistics; Dean Dr ĐURO NJAVRO; Man. Dir ZORAN BARAC.

Zdravstveno veleučilište Zagreb (University of Applied Health Sciences): Mlinarska cesta 38, HR-10000 Zagreb; tel. (1) 5495-800; internet www.zvu.hr; f. 1966 as Advanced School of Nursing and Health Technicians; programmes in environmental health engineering, environmental sanitation, management in nursing, medical laboratory diagnostics, midwifery, nursing, occupational therapy, physiotherapy, public health, radiological technology; Dean Prof. Dr MLADEN HAVELKA; Vice-Dean Prof. Dr ŽELJKO ROMIĆ; Sec.-Gen. NENAD MOJSOVIĆ.

Polytechnics

Međimursko veleučilište u Čakovcu (Međimurje University of Applied Sciences in Čakovec): Bana Josipa Jelačića 22A, HR-40000 Čakovec; tel. (40) 396-990; e-mail veleuciliste@mev.hr; internet www.mev.hr; programmes in computer engineering, management, sustainable development; Dean Dr NEVENKA BRESLAUER; Library Man. Prof. MAJA BRATKO; publ. *Zbornik Međimurskog veleučilišta* (2 a year).

Politehnika Pula, visoka tehničko—poslovna škola: Riva 6, HR-52100 Pula; tel. (52) 381-412; internet www.politehnika-pula.hr; f. 2002; courses on technical knowledge, business economics, management, computer science and social sciences; 50 teachers; 500 students; Dean Prof. Dr LUCIANO DELBIANCO; publ. *Techne-časopis za politehničku obrazovnu teoriju i praksu* (2 a year).

Tehničko veleučilište u Zagrebu (Technical Polytechnic in Zagreb): Vrbik 8, HR-10000 Zagreb; tel. (1) 5603-900; e-mail tvz@tvz.hr; internet www.tvz.hr; f. 1998; programmes incl. computing, civil engineering, electrical engineering, information technologies, mechtronics; 5,400 students; Dean Prof. Dr SLAVICA ĆOSOVIĆ BAJIĆ; Vice-Dean for Devt Ing. GORAN BELAMARIĆ; Vice-Dean for Education and Students Prof. Dr PREDRAG VALOŽIĆ; Vice-Dean for Science and Int. Cooperation Prof. Dr IVO ČALA.

Veleučilište 'Hrvatsko zagorje' Krapina ('Hrvatsko zagorje' Polytechnic, Krapina): Šetalište Hrvatskog narodnog preporoda 6, HR-49000 Krapina; tel. (49) 382-125; e-mail info@vhzk.hr; internet www.vhzk.hr; f. 2005, present name and status 2011; conducts studies in informatics, operational management, transport logistics; library: 25,000 vols, 600 periodicals; 1,500 students; Dean Prof. Dr ANTUN PRESEČKI; Vice-Dean for Education and Science Ing. NENAD SIKIRICA; Vice-Dean for Organization and Finances MIROSLAV FLEGO; Vice-Dean for Int. Relations and Cooperation Prof. Dr HUSEIN PAŠAGIĆ.

Veleučilište 'Lavoslav Ružička' u Vukovaru ('Lavoslav Ružička' Polytechnic in Vukovar): Županijska 50, HR-32000 Vukovar; tel. (32) 444-688; e-mail dekanat@vevu.hr; internet www.vevu.hr; programmes in administration, business, physiotherapy; library: 3,300 vols; Dean Prof. Dr GORDANA BUJIŠIĆ; Vice-Dean for Teaching SANDRA MRVICA MAĐARAC.

Veleučilište 'Marko Marulić' u Kninu (Marko Marulić Polytechnic in Knin): Petra Krešimira IV 30, HR-22300 Knin; tel. (22) 664-450; e-mail info@veleknin.hr; internet www.veleknin.hr; f. 2005; depts of agriculture, food technology, innovation centre, trade with enterprises; professional studies in commercial business, crop production, food technology, livestock; Dean Prof. Dr MIRKO GUGIĆ.

Veleučilište 'Nikola Tesla' u Gospiću (University of Applied Sciences 'Nikola Tesla' Gospić): Bana Ivan Karlovic 16, HR-53000 Gospić; tel. (53) 676-321; e-mail velegs@gs.t-com.hr; internet www.velegs-nikolatesla.hr; f. 2006; programmes in administrative studies, economic studies, entrepreneurship, road traffic, safety; 16 teachers; Dean Prof. BRANISLAVA ŠUTIĆA.

Veleučilište u Karlovcu (Karlovac University of Applied Sciences): *Campus 1*: Ivana Meštrovića 10, HR-47000 Karlovac; *Campus 2*: Josipa Jurаja Strossmayera 9, HR-47000 Karlovac; tel. (47) 843-500; e-mail dekanat@vuka.hr; internet www.vuka.hr; f. 1997; depts of business administration, food processing technology, gamekeeping and environmental protection, mechanical engineering, mechatronics, nursing, safety and protection, textile technology; Dean Dr BRANKO WASSERBAUER; Vice-Dean for Education MARINA TEVČIĆ; Vice-Dean for Finances Dr ANTE PAVIĆ; Vice-Dean for Int. Cooperation Dr JOVAN VUČINIĆ; Vice-Dean for Professional and Scientific Work and

Relations with Economy Dr DARKO VYROUBAL; Sec. MILAN VIGNJEVIĆ.

Veleučilište u Požegi (Požega Polytechnic): Vukovarska 17, HR-34000 Požega; tel. (34) 271-018; e-mail ured@vup.hr; internet www.vup.hr; f. 1998; depts of agriculture, social sciences; library: 2,660 vols, 20 periodicals; 2,000 students; Dean Dr DOMAGOJ MATIJEVIĆ (acting); Sec.-Gen. JASMINA SMOLČIĆ; Librarian Prof. ANTONIJA VALEŠIĆ.

Veleučilište u Rijeci (Polytechnic of Rijeka): Trpimirova 2/V, HR-51000 Rijeka; tel. (51) 321-300; e-mail ured@veleri.hr; internet www.veleri.hr; f. 1998; depts of agriculture, business, occupational safety, transport; brs in Porec, Pula, Pazin, Ogulin; library: 3,600 vols, 34 periodicals; 148 teachers; 1,300 students; Dean Prof. Dr DUŠAN RUDIĆ; Vice-Dean SAŠA HIRNIG; Vice-Dean for Int. Cooperation Prof. Dr DAMIR ŠEKULJA; Sec. BORIS SERGOVIĆ; Chief Librarian Dr SANJA GRAKALIĆ PLENKOVIĆ.

Veleučilište u Šibeniku (Šibenik Polytechnic): Trg Andrije Hebranga 11, Šibenik; tel. (22) 311-060; internet www.vus.hr; depts of administration, management and traffic studies.

Veleučilište u Slavonskom Brodu (Slavonskom Brod Polytechnic): Dr Mile Budaka 1, HR-35000 Slavonski Brod; tel. (35) 492-800; internet www.vusb.hr; f. 2005; depts of agriculture, social sciences, technology; Dean Prof. Dr ANTUN STOIĆ; Vice-Dean for Education Dr KRUNOSLAV MIROSAVLJEVIĆ; Vice-Dean for Devt MLADEN BOŠNJAKOVIĆ.

Veleučilište u Varaždinu (Polytechnic of Varaždin): Križanića 33/6, HR-42000 Varaždin; tel. (42) 493-338; e-mail tajnistvo@velv.hr; internet www.velv.hr; f. 2001; programmes in automation, construction, electrical engineering, multimedia, design and application, nursing, production engineering, technical and economic logistics; 3,000 students; Dean Prof. Dr MARIN MILKOVIĆ; Vice-Dean for Devt Dr GORAN KOZINA; Vice-Dean for Scientific Research and Int. Relations Dr VLADO TROPŠA; Vice-Dean for Teaching Affairs Prof. Dr DAMIR VUSIĆ.

Veleučilište Velika Gorica (Velika Gorica University of Applied Sciences): Zagrebačka cesta 5, HR-10410 Velika Gorica; tel. (1) 6222-501; e-mail info@vvg.hr; internet www.vvg.hr; professional programmes in aircraft maintenance, computer systems maintenance, crisis management, eye optics, motor vehicle maintenance; spec. programmes in crisis management, information systems, logistics; 150 teachers; 920 students; Dean Prof. IVAN TOTH.

Veleučilište 'VERN' ('VERN' University of Applied Sciences): Trg bana J. Jelačića 3, HR-10000 Zagreb; tel. (1) 4825-927; e-mail vuv@vern.hr; internet www.vern.hr; f. 1990, present name and status 2007; depts of applied mathematics and IT, economy and marketing, entrepreneurship and management, finance, accounting and law, languages and culture, psychology and communications, tourism; Dean OZREN JUREKOVIĆ (acting); Vice-Dean for Int. Cooperation and Lifelong Learning AIDA LIHA; Vice-Dean for Research and Devt MIRA LENARDIĆ; Vice-Dean for Study Programmes VIŠNJA GROZDANIĆ; Sec. DOLORES RADOVČIĆ.

CUBA

The Higher Education System

The oldest university is the Universidad de la Habana, which was founded in 1728 while Cuba was governed by Spain. Control of the island was ceded to the USA in 1898 and independence was gained in 1902. Most universities have been founded since 1959, when guerrilla forces led by Dr Fidel Castro Ruz seized control of government. State education in Cuba is universal and free to Cuban citizens at all levels; foreign students pay tuition fees (although state subsidies are provided to foreign nationals under specific programmes). Education is based on Marxist-Leninist principles and combines study with manual work. According to Law 1307 of 29 July 1976, higher education institutions consist of universities, centros universitarios (university centres), institutos superiores politécnicos (higher polytechnic institutes), institutos superiores (higher institutes), sedes universitarias (university headquarters), filiales universitarias (affiliated universities), escuelas latinoamericana o escuelas internacionales (Latin American and international tertiary institutes) and facultades independientes de ciencias médicas (independent faculties of medical sciences). The universities are administered by the Ministry of Higher Education, while the institutos superiores, which provide training for those who wish to become specialists in specific areas, are under the control of various relevant ministries. Workers attending university courses receive a state subsidy to provide for their dependants. Courses at intermediate and higher levels lay an emphasis on technology, agriculture and teacher training. In 2010/11 there were an estimated 473,309 students in tertiary education. Due to restrictions in government spending, in 2012 the National Statistical Office reported that student enrolment had been reduced by over 25% to 351,116 students, with the largest group (118,914) studying medical sciences.

Admission to higher education is based on the completion of upper secondary education in either the pre-university or polytechnic stream and on the results of the national competitive entrance examination. The main undergraduate qualification is the Licenciatura, which is awarded after five years of study. Courses may also lead to a professional title, such as Ingeniero (Engineer), Contador (Accountant), Estomatólogo (Dentist), Doctor (medical or veterinary) or Arquitecto (Architect). In 1993 a system of Cuban postgraduate qualifications was established by law under the Reglamento de la Educación Posgrado de la República de Cuba. During the 1990s a cumulative credit system was established in order to standardize workloads at postgraduate level. There are four general types of academic postgraduate qualification available: Maestría (Masters, taking two to three years), Especialidad de Posgrado (Postgraduate Specialization, awarded on completion of a professional programme), Doctorado (Doctorate, taking three to four years and leading to the award of the title Doctor en Ciencias de Determinada Especialidad—Doctor of Sciences in a Determined Specialism) and Posdoctorado (Postdoctorate, resulting in the award of the title Doctor en Ciencias—Doctor of Sciences). There are currently more than 20 research institutes that offer education (mainly of a scientific nature) at postgraduate level. The operations of each research institute are overseen by a government ministry. Technical and vocational education is offered at the secondary level and higher.

The Junta de Acreditación Nacional (JAN) was established in 1999 as the national umbrella organization responsible for quality assurance, accreditation and evaluation of all tertiary institutions and programmes.

Regulatory and Representative Bodies

GOVERNMENT

Ministry of Culture: Calle 2, No 258, Entre 11 y 13, Plaza de la Revolución, Vedado, Havana 10400; tel. (7) 838-2246; e-mail atención@cubarte.cult.cu; internet www.min.cult.cu; Minister RAFAEL BERNAL ALEMANY.

Ministry of Education: Calle 17, Esq. O, Vedado, Havana; tel. (7) 838-2930; e-mail despacho@mined.rimed.cu; internet www.cubaeduca.cu; Minister ENA ELSA VELÁZQUEZ COBIELLA.

Ministry of Higher Education: Calle 23, No 565, Esq. F, Vedado, Plaza de la Revolución, Havana; tel. (7) 838-2314; e-mail sitio_mes@reduniv.edu.cu; internet www.mes.edu.cu; Minister RODOLFO ALARCON ORTIZ.

Ministry of Science, Technology and the Environment: Calle M No 260, Entre 21 y 19, Vedado, Plaza de la Revolución, Havana; tel. (7) 835-5566; e-mail comunicacion@citma.cu; Minister ELBA ROSA PÉREZ MONTOYA.

NATIONAL BODY

Consejo Nacional de Universidades (National University Council): Ministerio de Educación Superior, Ciudad Libertad, Havana 1; f. 1960; coordinating body for educational and scientific activities and for the admin. of the 4 nat. univs; Pres. JOSÉ RAMÓN FERNÁNDEZ; Sec. Ing. MIGUEL MARRERO VALLET.

Learned Societies

GENERAL

Academia de Ciencias de Cuba (Cuban Academy of Sciences): Industria y San José, Capitolio Nacional, Habana Vieja, 12400 Havana; tel. (7) 862-6545; e-mail alejandro@academiaciencias.cu; internet www.academiaciencias.cu; f. 1861; attached research institutes: see under Research Institutes; Nat. Archive: see under Libraries and Archives; Pres. Dr ISMAEL CLARK; publs *Actas Botánicas Cubanas* (1 a year), *Anuario L. L. sobre estudios Lingüísticos*, *Anuario L. L. sobre estudios Literarios*, *Boletín Climática* (1 a year), *Boletín del Archivo Nacional* (1 a year), *Boletín de Síntesis*, *Boletín Meteorológico Marino* (3 a year), *Boletín Oficial de la ONIITEM* (1 a year), *Boletín Señal* (52 a year), *Cablegráfica* (12 a year), *Datos Astronómicos para Cuba* (1 a year), *Datos Astronómicos para el Caribe* (2 a year), *Directorio Biotec* (1 a year), *Estudios de Historia de la Ciencia y la Tecnología* (1 a year), *Estudios de Politica Científica y Tecnología* (1 a year), *Físicas y Matemáticas* (2 a year), *Poeyana* (1 a year), *Resumen Climático de Cuba* (1 a year), *Revista Ciencias Biológicas* (2 a year), *Revista Ciencia de la Información* (4 a year), *Revista Ciencias de la Tierra y del Espacio* (2 a year), *Revista Ciencias Técnicas*, *Revista Cubana de Ciencias Sociales* (2 a year), *Revista Cubana de Meteorología* (2 a year), *Tablas de Mareas* (1 a year).

Ateneo de La Habana (Havana Athenaeum): San Martín 258, Havana; f. 1902; Sec. Dr JOSÉ ENRIQUE HEYMANN Y DE LA GÁNDARA.

Casa de las Américas (House of the Americas): Calle 3ra Esq. a G, El Vedado, Havana 10400; tel. (7) 838-2706; e-mail presidencia@casa.cult.cu; internet www.casadelasamericas.org; f. 1959; cultural instn supporting Latin American literature, art and science; organizes festivals, exhibitions, conferences; maintains the 'José Antonio Echeverría' public library; documentary centre; Pres. ROBERTO FERNÁNDEZ RETAMAR; publs *Anales del Caribe* (1 a year), *Boletín de Música* (2 a year), *Casa de las Américas* (3 a year), *Conjunto* (4 a year), *Criterios* (1 a year).

EDUCATION

UNESCO Office Havana and Regional Bureau for Culture in Latin America and the Caribbean: Calzada 551–Esq. a D, Vedado, Havana; tel. (7) 32-2840; e-mail habana@unesco.org; internet www.unesco.org.cu; f. 1950; designated Cluster Office for Cuba, Dominican Republic and Haiti; Dir FRANCISCO JOSÉ LACAYO PARAJON.

LANGUAGE AND LITERATURE

Academia Cubana de la Lengua (Cuban Academy of Language): Centro Cultural Dulce María Loynaz, Calle E 502, entre calles 17 y 19, Vedado, 10400 Havana; tel. (7) 835-2732; e-mail acadcuba@cenyai.inf.cu; f. 1926; corresp. of the Real Academia Española (Madrid); Dir ROBERTO FERNÁNDEZ RETAMAR; Sec. MARLEN DOMÍNGUEZ HERNÁNDEZ.

Alliance Française: Calle J N° 302 esq. a 15 Vedado, Havana; tel. (7) 833-3370; e-mail dgafcuba@enet.cu; offers courses and exams in French language and culture and promotes cultural exchange with France; attached office in Santiago; Prin. ANDRE DE UBEDA.

British Council: 7ma Avda, e/ Calle 34 y 36, Miramar, Havana; tel. (7) 207-9605; e-mail information@cu.britishcouncil.org; internet www.britishcouncil.org/cuba; offers courses and exams in English language and British culture and promotes cultural exchange with the UK; Dir JENNY WHITE.

Unión de Escritores y Artistas de Cuba (Writers' and Artists' Union of Cuba): Calle 17 No 351, Vedado, Havana; tel. (7) 53-5081; internet www.uneac.com; f. 1961; 4,589 mems; Pres. CARLOS MARTÍ BRENES; Exec. Sec. MARTIZA HERNANDEZ; publs *Ediciones Unión* (12 a year), *La Gaceta de Cuba* (4 a year), *Literatura Cubana* (2 a year).

MEDICINE

Sociedad Cubana de Historia de la Medicina (Cuban Society for the History of Medicine): Calle L No 406 esq. 23 y 25, Vedado, Havana 4; e-mail amaro@abril.sld.cu; Pres. Dr RUBÉN RODRÍGUEZ GAVALDÁ; Sec. Dra MARÍA DEL CARMEN AMARO CANO; publ. *Cuadernos*.

Sociedad Cubana de Imagenología (Cuban Imagenology Society): Calle L 406 esq. 23 y 25, Vedado, 10400 Havana; tel. (7) 876-1150; e-mail jrxdigestivo@hha.sld.cu; internet www.sld.cu/sitios/imagenologia; f. 2007; 600 mems; Pres. Prof. ORLANDO VALLS PÉREZ; Sec. Prof. MIGUEL A. RODRÍGUEZ ALLENDE.

Research Institutes

AGRICULTURE, FISHERIES AND VETERINARY SCIENCE

Centro de Investigaciones Apícolas (Beekeeping Research Centre): Arroyo Arenas, El Cano, La Lisa, Havana 19190; tel. (7) 202-0027; e-mail eeapi@eeapi.cu; f. 1982; tropical beekeeping research; bee selection; honey flora; hive products; beekeeping economy; library of 2,550 vols; Dir ADOLFO M. PÉREZ PIÑEIRO; Research Dir JUAN CARLOS PÉREZ MORALES; publs *Apiciencia* (3 a year), *Boletín Apiciencia* (4 a year).

Centro de Investigaciónes para el Mejoramiento Animal (Research Centre for the Improvement of Livestock): Carretera Central km 21½, Loma de Tierra, Cotorro, 14000 Havana; tel. (7) 57-9408; f. 1970; library of 4,600 vols; Dir JOSÉ R. MORALES; publ. *Revista Cubana de Reproducción Animal* (2 a year).

Centro de Investigaciones Pesqueras (Fisheries Research Centre): Barlovento, Santa Fé, Playa, Havana; tel. (2) 09-7875; f. 1959; research on fisheries, marine aquaculture, fish-processing technology; training courses; library of 4,230 vols, 1,500 periodicals; Gen. Dir Dr TIZOL CORREA RAFAEL; publs *Ciencia y Tecnología Pesquera* (4 a year), *Revista Cubana de Investigaciones Pesqueras*.

Instituto Cubano de Investigaciones de los Derivados de la Caña de Azúcar (ICIDCA) (Cuban Institute for Research on Sugar Cane By-Products): Vía Blanca y Carretera Central 804, Apdo 4026, San Miguel del Padrón, Havana; tel. (7) 55-7015; e-mail icidca@ceniai.inf.cu; internet www.icidca.cu; f. 1963; library of 7,000 vols; Dir LUIS O. GÁLVEZ TAUPIER; publ. *Sobre los derivados de la Caña de Azúcar* (4 a year).

Instituto de Investigaciones Agropecuarias 'Jorge Dimitrov' (Jorge Dimitrov Livestock Research Institute): Carretera a Manzanillo km 16½, Gaveta Postal 2140, Bayamo, Granma; tel. (23) 5239; e-mail dimitrov@dimitrov.granma.inf.cu; attached to Cuban Acad. of Sciences; Dir Dr ISMAEL LEONARD ACOSTA.

Instituto de Investigaciones Avícolas (Poultry Research Institute): Gaveta Postal 1, 17200 Santiago de las Vegas, Havana; tel. (7) 683-9040; e-mail viiacan@ceniai.inf.cu; internet www.iia.cu; f. 1976; Dir Dr SAÚL AMIGO DELGADO; publ. *Revista Cubana de Ciencia Avícola* (2 a year).

Instituto de Investigaciones de Sanidad Vegetal (Plant Health Research Institute): Calle 110 No 514 entre 5ta B y 5ta F, Miramar, Playa, CP 11600 Havana; tel. (7) 202-2516; e-mail administrador@inisav.cu; internet www.inisav.cu; f. 1970; Dir Dr EMILIO FERNANDEZ DIR GONZALVES; publ. *Fitosanidad* (4 a year).

Instituto de Investigaciones en Viandas Tropicales (Research Institute for Tropical Vegetables): Apdo 6, Santo Domingo 53000, Villa Clara; tel. (42) 40-3103; e-mail inivit@ip.etecsa.cu; f. 1967; library of 14,439 vols; Dir Dr SERGIO RODRIGUEZ MORALES; publ. *Agrotecnia de Cuba*.

Instituto de Investigaciones Forestales (Institute of Forestry Research): Calle 174 No 1723 e/ 17-B y 17-C, Siboney, Playa, Havana; tel. (7) 208-2189; e-mail direccion@forestales.co.cu; f. 1969; attached to Cuban Acad. of Sciences; library of 10,000 vols; Dir HUMBERTO GARCÍA CORRALES; publ. *Revista Forestal Baracoa* (2 a year).

Instituto de Investigaciones Fundamentales en Agricultura Tropical 'Alejandro de Humboldt' (Alexander von Humboldt Institute of Basic Research in Tropical Agriculture): Calle 2, esq. a 1, Santiago de las Vegas, 17200 Havana; tel. (7) 57-9010; e-mail yamiletrst@inifat.esihabana.cu; f. 1904; library of 2,600 vols; Dir Dr ADOLFO RODRÍGUEZ NODALS; publ. *Agrotecnia de Cuba*.

Instituto de Investigaciones Porcinas (Pig Research Institute): Carretera del Guatao km 5½, Punta Brava, Bauta, Havana; e-mail iip00@ceniai.inf.cu; internet www.iip.co.cu; f. 1972.

HISTORY, GEOGRAPHY AND ARCHAEOLOGY

Instituto de Geografía Tropical (Institute of Tropical Geography): Calle 13 No 409 esq. F. Vedado, Plaza de la Revolución, 10400 Havana; tel. (7) 832-4295; internet www.geotech.cu; f. 1962; attached to Min. of Science, Technology and the Environment; Dir Dra MARLEN MARTHA PALET RABAZA.

LANGUAGE AND LITERATURE

Instituto de Literatura y Lingüística 'José Antonio Portuondo Valdor' (José Antonio Portuondo Valdor Institute of Literature and Linguistics): Ave Salvador Allende 710 e/ Soledad y Castillejo, Centro, 10300 Havana; tel. (7) 878-6486; e-mail ill@ceniai.inf.cu; internet www.ill.cu; f. 1965; attached to Min. of Science, Technology and the Environment; Dir Dra NURIA GREGORI TORADA; publs *Anuario* (linguistics edn, 1 a year), *Anuario* (literature edn, 1 a year).

MEDICINE

Centro Ingeniería Genética y Biotecnología de Cuba (Centre for Genetic Engineering and Biotechnology of Cuba): Ave 31E 160 y 190, Rpto Cubanacán, Playa, Havana; internet www.cigb.edu.cu; f. 1986; research, devt, production and commercial applications of biotechnology; vaccine research; Dir-Gen. Dr LUIS HERRERA MARTINEZ; publ. *Biotecnología Aplicada*.

Centro Nacional de Información de Ciencias Médicas (CNICM) (National Centre for Information on Medical Science): Calle E No 454 e/ 19 y 21, El Vedado, 10400 Havana; tel. (7) 32-2004; e-mail webmaster@infomed.sld.cu; internet www.sld.cu/cnicm.html; Dir Dr JEREMÍAS HERNÁNDEZ OJITO; publ. *Revista Cubana de Medicina*.

Instituto Nacional de Higiene, Epidemiología y Microbiología (National Institute of Hygiene, Epidemiology and Microbiology): Infanta 1158 e/ Llinás y Clavel, Centro, 10300 Havana; tel. (7) 870-5723; internet www.sld.cu/webs/epidem; f. 1943; attached to Min. of Public Health; library of 3,000 vols; Dir Dr MARIANO BONET.

Instituto Nacional de Oncología y Radiobiología de La Habana (National Institute of Oncology and Radiobiology in Havana): Calle 29 y F, Vedado, 10400 Havana; tel. (7) 55-2577; e-mail dinor@infomed.sld.cu; f. 1961; library of 2,700 vols; Dir Dr ALBERTO CÉSPEDES CARRILLO; publ. *Revista Cubana de Oncología*.

NATURAL SCIENCES

General

Centro Nacional de Investigaciones Científicas (National Centre for Scientific Research): Ave 25 No 15202 esq. 158, Reparto Cubanacán, Playa, 12100 Havana; tel. (7) 271-4453; internet www.cnic.edu.cu; f. 1969; natural, biomedical and technological sciences, devt of medicines and medical equipment; postgraduate education; library of 100,000 vols; Dir Dr CARLOS GUTIERREZ CALZADO; publs *Revista CENIC Ciencias Biológicas* (3 a year), *Revista CENIC Ciencias Químicas* (3 a year).

Instituto de Oceanología (Institute of Oceanology): Ave 1ra. No 18406 entre 184 y 186, Rpto. Flores, Playa, 11600 Havana; tel. (7) 271-6008; e-mail oceano@oceano.inf.cu; internet www.oceanologia.cu; f. 1965; attached to Min. of Science, Technology and the Environment; Dir Dra SANDRA LOZA-ALVAREZ; Scientific Deputy Dir Dra LILIAM ARRIAZA; publs *Avicennia*, *Serie Oceanológica* (print and online, oceanologia.redciencia.cu).

Biological Sciences

Centro Nacional de Producción de Animales de Laboratorio (CENPALAB) (National Centre for the Production of Laboratory Animals): Carretera El Cacahual km 2½ AP 3, Bejucal, La Habana; e-mail ccalidad@cenpalab.inf.cu; f. 1982; attached to Cuban Acad. of Sciences; Dir Dr LEONARDO CABEZAS RODRÍGUEZ.

Mathematical Sciences

Centro de Estudios de Población y Desarrollo (CEPDE) (Centre for Population and Development Studies): Oficina Nacional de Estadísticas, Paseo 60 e/ 3ra y 5ta, Vedado, Plaza de la Revolución, 10400 Havana; tel. (7) 830-0053; e-mail oneweb@

one.gov.cu; attached to Nat. Statistical Office; Dir Dr JUAN CARLOS ALFONSO FRAGA.

Physical Sciences

Centro de Investigaciones para la Industria Minero-Metalúrgica (Research Centre for Mining and Metallurgy): Finca la Luisa, Carretera Varona 12028, Boyeros, A. P. 8067, Havana; tel. (7) 644-2315; e-mail cipimm@cipimm.minbas.cu; f. 1967; attached to Min. of Basic Industry; research in geology, mining, chemical analysis, metallurgy; Dir Dr EDUARDO ACEVEDO DEL MONTE.

Centro Nacional de Investigaciones Sismológicas (CENAIS) (National Centre for Seismological Research): Ministerio de Ciencia Tecnología y Medio Ambiente, Calle 17 No 61 e/ 4 y 6, Vista Alegre, 90400 Santiago de Cuba; tel. (22) 653958; e-mail director@cenais.cu; internet www.cenais.cu; f. 1992; Dir Dr BLADIMIR MORENO TOIRÁN.

Instituto de Cibernética, Matemática y Física (ICIMAF) (Institute of Cybernetics, Mathematics and Physics): Calle 15 No 551 e/ C y D, Vedado, Havana; tel. (7) 832-7764; e-mail icimaf@icmf.inf.cu; internet www.icmf.inf.cu; f. 1964; attached to Cuban Acad. of Sciences; Dir Ing. RAIMUNDO FRANCO PARELLADA.

Instituto de Geofísica y Astronomía (Institute of Geophysics and Astronomy): Calle 212 No 2906, Marianao, Havana; tel. (7) 271-4331; e-mail lpalacio@iga.cu; internet www.iga.cu; f. 1974; attached to Min. of Science, Technology and the Environment; library of 1,000 vols; Dir Dra LOURDES PALACIO SUÁREZ; publ. *Datos Astronómicos para Cuba* (1 a year).

Instituto de Meteorología (INSMET) (Institute of Meteorology): Apdo 17032, Loma de Casablanca, Regla, 11700 Havana; tel. (7) 61-7500; e-mail meteoro@met.inf.cu; internet www.met.inf.cu; attached to Min. of Science, Technology and the Environment; Dir Dr TOMÁS GUTIERREZ PÉREZ; publs *Boletín Meteorológico Marino* (2 a year), *Revista Cubana de Meteorología* (2 a year).

PHILOSOPHY AND PSYCHOLOGY

Instituto de Filosofía (Institute of Philosophy): Calzada No 251 esq. J., Vedado, 10400 Havana; tel. (7) 832-1887; e-mail instituto@filosofia.cu; internet www.filosofia.cu; f. 1966; attached to Cuban Acad. of Sciences; library of 3,000 vols; Dir Dra CONCEPCIÓN NIEVES AYÚS; publs *Revista Cubana de Ciencias Sociales* (2 a year), *Revista Cubana de Filosofía* (3 a year, online).

RELIGION, SOCIOLOGY AND ANTHROPOLOGY

Centro de Antropología (Centre for Anthropology): Calzada de Buenos Aires 111 e/ Agua Dulce y Diana, Cerro, 10600 Havana; tel. (7) 33-5514; e-mail antropol@ceniai.inf.cu; attached to Min. of Science, Technology and the Environment; Dir Dra LOURDES SERRANO PERALTA.

Centro de Investigaciones Psicológicas y Sociológicas (CIPS) (Centre for Research in Psychology and Sociology): Calle B No 352 esq. 15, Vedado, Havana; tel. (7) 830-1451; internet www.cips.cu; attached to Min. of Science, Technology and the Environment; undertakes sociopsychological surveys which relate to social politics in Cuba and the means of ensuring the participation of workers in the different levels of social planning; Dir Lic. ANGELA CASAÑAS MATA.

TECHNOLOGY

Centro de Desarrollo Científico de Montañas (Centre for the Scientific Development of Mountainous Regions): Matazón, Sabaneta, El Salvador, Guantanamo; tel. (21) 9-9230; attached to Cuban Acad. of Sciences; Dir Ing. FRANCISCO VELÁZQUEZ RODRÍGUEZ.

Centro de Desarrollo de Equipos e Instrumentos Científicos (CEDEIC) (Centre for the Development of Scientific Equipment and Instruments): c/o Academia de Ciencias de Cuba, Industria y San José, 12400 Havana; tel. (7) 862-6545; e-mail alejandro@academiaciencias.cu; attached to Cuban Acad. of Sciences; laser technology and its application in medicine, nutrition and electronics; Dir Ing. LUIS EMILIO GARCÍA MAGARINO.

Centro de Diseño de Sistemas Automatizados de Computación (CEDISAC) (Centre for the Design of Automated Computer Systems): Avda 47E/18A y 20, Aptdo Postal 604, Miramar, 11300 Havana; tel. (7) 23-5153; e-mail cdisac@ceniai.inf.cu; attached to Cuban Acad. of Sciences; Dir Dra BEATRIZ ALONSO BECERRA.

Centro de Investigaciones de Energía Solar (Centre for Research into Solar Energy): Micro 3 Reparto 'Abel Santamaría', Santiago de Cuba 90800; tel. (226) 7-1131; e-mail arecio@cies.ciges.inf.cu; f. 1986; attached to Min. of Science, Technology and the Environment; Dir Ing. ORLANDO LASTRES DANGUILLECOURT.

Centro de Investigaciones para la Industria Minero Metalúrgica (Research Centre of the Metal-Mining Industry): Finca 'La Luisa' km 1½, Carretera Varona No. 12028, Apdo 8067, Boyeros, Havana; tel. (7) 57-8082; internet www.camaracuba.cu; f. 1967; library of 4,000 vols; Dir Dr EDUARDO ACEVEDO; publs *Resenas*, *Revista Tecnológica* (3 a year).

Libraries and Archives

Havana

Archivo Nacional de Cuba (Cuban National Archive): Compostela 906 esq. a San Isidro, 10100 Havana; tel. (7) 862-9436; e-mail arnac@ceniai.inf.cu; internet www.ceniai.inf.cu/ciencia/citma/aid/archivo; f. 1840; 25,000 linear metres of archive material; 12,834 vols, 675 periodicals; Dir Dra BERARDA SALABARRÍA ABRAHAM.

Biblioteca Central 'Rubén Martínez Villena' de la Universidad de la Habana (Rubén Martínez Villena Central Library of the University of Havana): Calle San Lázaro y L, Municipio Plaza de la Revolución, Havana; tel. (7) 78-1230; e-mail susan@dict.uh.cu; internet www.dict.uh.cu; f. 1728; 945,000 vols; Dir Lic. BÁRBARA SUSANA SÁNCHEZ VIGNAU; publs *Revista Cubana de Educación Superior* (3 a year), *Revista Cubana de Física* (2 a year), *Revista Cubana de Psicología* (3 a year), *Revista Debates Americanos* (2 a year), *Revista de Biología* (1 a year), *Revista de Ciencias Matemáticas* (2 a year), *Revista de Investigaciones Marinas* (3 a year), *Revista del Jardín Botánico Nacional* (1 a year), *Revista Economía y Desarrollo* (2 a year), *Revista Investigación Operacional* (3 a year), *Revista Universidad de la Habana* (2 a year).

Biblioteca del Instituto Pre-universitario de La Habana (Library of the Havana Pre-University Institute of Education): Zuleta y San José, Havana; f. 1894; 32,000 vols, newspaper library; Dir JOSÉ MANUEL CASTELLANOS RODILES.

Biblioteca 'Fernando Ortiz' del Instituto de Literatura y Lingüística (Fernando Ortiz Library of the Institute of Literature and Linguistics): Salvador Allende 710 entre Soledad y Castillejo, 10300 Havana; tel. (7) 878-5405; e-mail ill@ceniai.inf.cu; f. 1793; 1m. items; Librarian Lic. Ma. ELOISA DÍAZ FAURE.

Biblioteca Histórica Cubana y Americana 'Francisco González del Valle' (Francisco González del Valle Library of Cuban and American History): Obispo/Mercaderes y San Ignacio, Havana; tel. (7) 864-8960; e-mail biblioteca@patrimonio.ohc.cu; internet www.ohch.cu; f. 1938; Deputy Dir TAMARA YANES ALONSO.

Biblioteca 'José Antonio Echeverría' ('José Antonio Echeverría' Library): G y 3ra, Havana; tel. (7) 838-2706; e-mail biblioservicios@casa.cult.cu; internet biblio.casadelasamericas.org; f. 1959; Caribbean and Latin American books; 150,000 vols, 8,500 journals; Dir ERNESTO SIERRA.

Biblioteca 'Manuel Sanguily' (Manuel Sanguily Library): Cuchillo de Zanja 19, Primer Piso, entre Rayo y San Nicolás, Centro Havana; tel. (7) 63-3232; f. 1960; 29,512 vols, 3,200 periodicals; Dir ESTRELLA GARCÍA.

Biblioteca Nacional 'José Martí' (José Martí National Library): Apdo 6670, Avda de Independencia e/20 de Mayo y Aranguren, Plaza de la Revolución José Martí, Havana; tel. (7) 881-2428; e-mail direccion@bnjm.cu; internet www.bnjm.cu; f. 1901; 4,242,936 items; Dir ELIADES ACOSTA MATOS; publs *Bibliografía Cubana* (1 a year), *Bibliotecas: Anales de Investigación*, *Catálogo Cuba en Publicaciones Extranjeras*, *Indice General de Publicaciones Periódicas Cubanas*, *Revista de la Biblioteca Nacional José Martí*.

Biblioteca Provincial 'Rubén Martínez Villena' (Rubén Martínez Villena Provincial Library): Plaza de Armas, Centro Histórico, La Habana Vieja, Havana; tel. (7) 862-9035; e-mail database@bpvillena.ohc.cu; internet www.bpvillena.ohc.cu; f. 1960; spec. braille colln; 94,328 vols; Dir Lic. ANA MARÍA SÁNCHEZ RODRÍGUEZ.

Centro de Información Bancaria y Económica, Banco Central de Cuba (Banking and Economic Information Centre, Central Bank of Cuba): Cuba 410 e/ Amargua y Lamparilla, 10100 Havana; tel. (7) 62-8318; e-mail cibe@bc.gov.cu; internet www.bc.gov.cu; f. 1950; 33,000 vols; Man. ARACELIS CEJAS RODRÍGUEZ; Library Dept Chief JORGE FERNÁNDEZ PÉREZ; publs *Cuba: Half Yearly Economic Report*, *Economic Report* (1 a year), *Revista del Banco Central* (Journal of the Central Bank of Cuba).

Centro de Información y Documentación Agropecuario (Livestock Information and Documentation Centre): Gaveta postal 4149, Havana 4; tel. (7) 81-8808; f. 1971; 20,000 vols, 1,400 journals; Dir Dr DAVID WILLIAMS CANTERO.

Instituto de Información Científica y Tecnológica (IDICT) (Institute of Scientific and Technical Information): Apdo postal 2213, 10200 Havana; Capitolio de La Habana, Prado entre Dragones y San José, La Habana Vieja, Havana; tel. (7) 862-6531; e-mail tere@idict.cu; internet www.idict.cu; f. 1963; attached to Min. of Science, Technology and the Environment; 150,000 vols, 8,000 journals; Gen. Dir CARMEN SÁNCHEZ ROJAS; publs *Ciencia, Innovación y Desarrollo* (4 a year), *Ciencias de la Información* (4 a year).

Santiago

Biblioteca Central de la Universidad de Oriente (Central Library of the University of Oriente): Avda Patricio Lumumba s/n, 90500 Santiago de Cuba; tel. (226) 3-1973; f. 1947; 42,000 vols; Librarian Lic. MAURA GONZÁLEZ PÉREZ; publs *Revista Cubana de Química*, *Revista Santiago*.

Biblioteca Provincial 'Elvira Cape' ('Elvira Cape' Provincial Library): Calle Heredia 258 e/ Pío Rosado y Hartman, 90100 Santiago de Cuba; tel. (22) 65-4836; e-mail bpcape@lib.cultstgo.cult.cu; internet www.cultstgo.cult.cu/biblioteca/index.htm; f. 1899; 169,000 vols, 1,760 periodicals; Dir DAYMA SERPA LÓPEZ.

Museums and Art Galleries

Camagüey

Museo Ignacio Agramonte (Ignacio Agramonte Museum): Camagüey; tel. (32) 28-2425; e-mail cmqcppatrimonia@pprincips.cult.cu; f. 1955; paintings, furniture, textiles and relics from the colonial period; Dir YOLANDA GUTIÉRREZ CAMPOS.

Cárdenas

Museo Municipal 'Oscar M. de Rojas' ('Oscar M. de Rojas' Muncipal Museum): Calle Calzada 4 e/ Echeverría y Martí, Cárdenas; f. 1903; exhibits relating to Martí and other aspects of Cuban history, malacology, insects, butterflies and colonial weaponry; library; Curator OSCAR M. DE ROJAS Y CRUZAT.

Havana

Acuario Nacional de Cuba (National Aquarium of Cuba): Ave 1ra y Calle 60, Miramar, Playa, Havana 11300; tel. (7) 203-6401; e-mail comercial@acuarionacional.cu; internet www.acuarionacional.cu; f. 1960; attached to Min. of Science, Technology and the Environment; library of 3,000 vols; Dir Lic. GUILLERMO GARCÍA MONTERO.

Archivo Histórico Municipal (Muncipal Historical Archive): Tacón 1 e/ Obispo y O'Reilly, Havana; tel. (7) 861-5001; e-mail archivo@patrimonio.ohch.cu; internet www.ohch.cu; f. 1938; historical items since 1550.

Jardín Botánico Nacional de Cuba (National Botanical Garden of Cuba): Carretera del Rocío km 3.5, CP 19230, Calabazar, Boyeros, Havana; tel. (7) 697-9309; e-mail leivajbn@rect.uh.cu; internet www.uh.cu/centros/jbn; f. 1968; attached to Univ. de la Habana; 200,000 specimens in herbarium; Cuban flora colln: fungi, pteridophytes, gymnosperms and angiosperms; postgraduate training on vegetal anatomy, morphology and systematics; library of 4,459 vols, 1,130 periodicals; Dir-Gen. Dra ANGELA LEIVA SÁNCHEZ; Scientific Dir Dra ROSA RANKIN RODRÍGUEZ; publs *Bissea* (4 a year), *Revista del Jardín Botánico Nacional* (1 a year).

Museo Antropológico Montané (Montané Anthropological Museum): Edif. Felipe Poey, Plaza Ignacio Agramonte, Colina Universitaria, Havana; tel. (7) 879-3488; f. 1903; colln of pre-Columbian artefacts; library of 5,000 vols; Dir Dr ANTONIO J. MARTÍNEZ FUENTES.

Museo Casa Natal José Martí (House Museum of José Martí): Calle Leonor Pérez 314 e/ Calles Egido y Picota, Havana; internet www.cnpc.cult.cu/cnpc/museos/marti; f. 1925; relics of José Martí and his works; Curator MARIA DE LA LUZ RAMIREZ ESTRADA.

Museo de Arte Colonial de la Habana (Havana Museum of Colonial Art): San Ignacio 61, Plaza de la Catedral, Havana; tel. (7) 862-6440; e-mail colonial@bp.patrimonio.ohc.cu; internet www.ohch.cu; f. 1969; housed in mansion built 1720; Dir MARGARITA SUÑAREZ GARCÍA.

Museo de Historia Natural 'Felipe Poey' (Felipe Poey Museum of Natural History): Facultad de Biología, Universidad de La Habana, Calle 25 e/J e I, Vedado, 10400 Havana; tel. (7) 879-3488; e-mail museopoey@fbio.uh.cu; internet www.uh.cu/museos/poey/index.html; f. 1842; library of 80,520 vols; Dir Dr ALEJANDRO BARRO CAÑAMERO.

Museo Ernest Hemingway (Ernest Hemingway Museum): Finca Vigía, San Francisco de Paula, 19180 Havana; tel. (7) 91-0809; f. 1962; house, library and personal items of Ernest Hemingway who lived at the address 1939–60; Dir DANILO M. ARRATE HERNÁNDEZ.

Museo Municipal de Guanabacoa (Guanabacoa Muncipal Museum): Calle Martí 108 e/ Versalles y San Antonio, Guanabacoa, Havana; tel. (7) 797-9117; e-mail musgbcoa@cubarte.cult.cu; f. 1964; popular Cuban religions of African origin; Dir MARIA CRISTINA PEÑA REIGOSA.

Museo Nacional y Palacio de Bellas Artes (National Museum and Palace of Fine Arts): Trocadero entre Zulueta y Monserrate, 10200 Havana Vieja; tel. (7) 63-9042; e-mail musna@cubarte.cult.cu; internet www.museonacional.cult.cu; f. 1913; ancient Egyptian, Greek and Roman art, 16th- to 19th-century European art, Cuban art from the colonial period to the present; Dir MORAIMA CLAVIJO COLOM.

Attached Museums:

Castillo de la Real Fuerza de la Havana (Castle of the Royal Garrison of Havana): O'Reilly entre Avda del Puerto y Tacón, Plaza de Armas, 10100 Havana Vieja; tel. (7) 61-6130; f. 1977; modern ceramic exhibits housed in a 16th-century fortification; Dir ALEJANDRO G. ALONSO.

Museo de Artes Decorativas (Museum of Decorative Arts): Calle 17, No 502 entre D y E, Vedado, 10100 Havana; tel. (7) 32-0924; f. 1964; European and Oriental decorative art since 17th century; Dir KATIA VARELA.

Museo Napoleónico (Napoleonic Museum): San Miguel 1159 esq. Ronda, Plaza de la Revolución, Havana; tel. (7) 79-1460; e-mail musnap@cubarte.cult.cu; internet www.cnpc.cult.cu; f. 1961; historical objects and works of art of Revolutionary and Imperial France; specialized library.

Museo Numismático (Numismatic Museum): Obispo 305 e/ Aguiar y Habana, Havana 1; tel. (7) 861-5811; e-mail numismatica@cultural.ohch.cu; internet www.ohch.cu; f. 1975; coins, banknotes, medals and decorations; library; Dir INÉS MORALES GARCÍA.

Parque Zoológico Nacional (National Zoological Garden): Carretera de Varona km $3^1/_2$, Boyeros, Havana; tel. (7) 44-7616; e-mail pzn@ceniai.inf.cu; f. 1984; attached to Min. of Science, Technology and the Environment; library of 1,300 vols; Dir TOMÁS ESCOBAR HERRERA; publ. *Revista Cubazos.*

Matanzas

Museo Provincial de Matanzas (Matanzas Provincial Museum): Palacio de Junco, Calle Milanés e/ Magdalena y Ayllón, Plaza de la Vigía, Matanzas; tel. (52) 24-3195; f. 1959; history, natural history, decorative arts, weaponry, archaeology and ethnology; library of 1,000 vols; Dir Lic. GONZALO DOMÍNGUEZ CABRERA; publ. *Museo* (2 a year).

Remedios

Museo de Remedios 'José Maria Espinosa' (José Maria Espinosa Museum in Remedios): Maceo 32, Remedios; f. 1933; history, science, art; Dir. ALBERTO VIGIL Y COLOMA.

Santiago

Museo Emilio Bacardi Moreau (Emilio Bacardi Moreau Museum): Pío Rosado esq. Aguilera, 90100 Santiago; tel. (7) 62-8402; e-mail cppatrim@cultstgo.cult.cu; f. 1899; history, art; Curator JOSÉ A. AROCHA ROVIRA; Curator FIDELIA PÉREZ GONZÁLEZ.

Universities

UNIVERSIDAD DE CAMAGÜEY
(Camaguey University)

Carretera de Circunvalación Norte km $5^1/_2$, 74650 Camagüey
Telephone: (32) 28-1363
E-mail: dri@reduc.edu.cu
Internet: www.reduc.edu.cu
Founded 1967 as br. of Univ. of Havana, present name 1974
State control
Academic year: September to July
Rector: Dra C. LIANET GOYAS CÉSPEDES
Vice-Rector for Academic Affairs: Dra ANGELA PALACIOS HIDALGO
Vice-Rector for Admin. and Services: MSc FRANCISCO PRÉSTAMO
Vice-Rector for Extension: Ing. PEDRO RODRÍGUEZ
Vice-Rector for Financial Affairs: Dra ANA FERNÁNDEZ
Vice-Rector for Research and Postgraduate Affairs: Dra HILDA OQUENDO
Registrar: Lic. RAÚL GARRIGA CORZO
Librarian: Lic. SARA ARTILES VISBAL
Number of teachers: 450
Number of students: 3,200
Publications: *Revista de Producción Animal, Revista La Nueva Gestión Organizacional, Revista Retos de la Dirección*

DEANS

Faculty of Animal Sciences: Dr JOSÉ BERTOT
Faculty of Communication: MSc TEL PINO SOSA
Faculty of Computer Science: Dr LUIS CORRALES BARRIOS
Faculty of Construction: Dr ELIO PÉREZ
Faculty of Economics and Business: Dra ANA DE DIOS
Faculty of Electromechanics: Dr LUIS CORRALES BARRIOS
Faculty of Food Chemistry: Dr PABLO GALINDO
Faculty of Languages: NORMA MOREDO
Faculty of Law: Dra MARÍA ELENA PRADO
Faculty of Social and Humanistic Sciences: Dra FLOR DE MARÍA FERNÁNDEZ FIFONTES

UNIVERSIDAD DE CIEGO DE AVILA
(University of Ciego de Avila)

km 9 Carretera de Ciego de Avila a Morón, 69450 Ciego de Ávila
Telephone: (33) 22-4544
E-mail: webmaster@rect.unica.cu
Internet: www.unica.cu
Founded 1978 as Instituto Superior Agrícola de Ciego de Avila, current name and status since 1996
Faculties of agronomy, computer science, economics, engineering, humanities
Rector: Dr MARIO ARES SÁNCHEZ
Library Dir: JORGE ANTONIO GÓMEZ CORDERO
Library of 41,963 vols
Number of teachers: 1,451
Number of students: 6,061
Publication: *Fidelia* (4 a year)

UNIVERSIDAD DE CIENFUEGOS 'CARLOS RAFAEL RODRÍGUEZ'
(University of Cienfuegos 'Carlos Rafael Rodríguez')

Carretera de Rodas km 4, Cuatro Caminos, Cienfuegos 59430
Telephone: (432) 2-1521
E-mail: rector@ucfinfo.ucf.edu.cu
Internet: www.ucf.edu.cu

Founded 1979 as Instituto Superior Técnico de Cienfuegos; univ. status 1994; current name adopted 1998
State control

Rector: JUAN BAUTISTA COGOLLOS MARTÍNEZ
Vice-Rector for Academic Affairs: VÍCTOR MILLO CARMENATE
Vice-Rector for Admin.: FRANK HERNANDEZ GONZÁLEZ
Vice-Rector for Research and Postgraduates: NEREYDA MOYA PADILLA
Vice-Rector for Standardization of Higher Education: LOURDES POMARES CASTELLÓN
Sec.-Gen.: Lic. BLAS JUANES RAMÍREZ
Librarian: RAQUEL ZAMORA FONSECA

Library of 50,000 vols
Number of teachers: 363
Number of students: 2,600

Publication: *Anuarios Científico* (1 a year)

DEANS

Faculty of Agrarian Science: ENRIQUE PARETS SELVA
Faculty of Economics and Business: Prof. GUILLERMO LOPEZ CARVAJAL
Faculty of Engineering: JUAN GABRIEL NOA AGUILA
Faculty of Physical Culture and Sport: OVEL PÉREZ MENA
Faculty of Social Sciences: ADIANEZ FERNÁNDEZ BERMÚDEZ

PROFESSORS

Faculty of Agrarian Science:

ABREU JIMENEZ, M., Agronomics
ALBELO HERNANDEZ, E., Agronomics
BETANCOURT AGUILAR, C., Chemistry
CASANOVAS COSIO, E., Animal Production Technology
CASTELLANOS GONZALEZ, L., Agronomics
CONCEPCION GUTIERREZ, I., Agronomics
CUELLAR VALERO, E., Biology
DIAZ CABO, J., Agronomics
DIAZ PEÑA, M., Industrial Engineering
FRESNEDA QUINTANA, C., Agronomics
MARTINEZ GUZMAN, R., Forestry Agronomy
MESA REYNALDO, J., Agronomics
NODARSE CASTILLO, M., Biology
PADRON PADRON, W., Agronomics
PARETS SELVA, E., Agronomics
PEREZ ARMAS, R., Agronomics
RAJADEL ACOSTA, O., Education
REYNA REYES, R., Veterinary
RIVERO CASANOVA, C., Biology
RODRIGUEZ TORRES, I., Education
ROMERO JIMENEZ, A., Microbiology
SANCHEZ IZNAGA, A., Mechanical Engineering
SOCARRAS ARMENTEROS, Y., Agronomics
SOCORRO CASTRO, A., Agronomics
SOSA RODRIGUEZ, F., Agronomics
VEGA MARRERO, G., Agronomics
YERA MOSQUERA, Y., Agronomics

Faculty of Economics and Business:

ACEA DEL SOL, D., Industrial Engineering
ALONSO GARCIA, Y., Industrial Engineering
ALONSO HERNANDEZ, I., Economics
ALVAREZ SANCHEZ, Y., Accounting
ALZURI ESTRADA, S., Law
ARGUDIN SOTO, Y., Industrial Engineering
BALBIS MOREJON, M., Economics
BARRERA GARCIA, A., Industrial Engineering
BARRIZONTE CASTELLANOS, O., Industrial Engineering
BECERRA LOIS, F., Economics
BRITO BRITO, A., Industrial Engineering
CABRERA GONZALEZ, A., Accounting
CAPOTE LEON, G., Industrial Engineering
CARRERA MARTINEZ, V., Economics
CASTILLO COTO, A., Economics
CASTILLO PADRON, Y., Accounting
CHAPIS CABRERA, E., Accounting
CORREA SANCHEZ, A., Accounting
CORREA SOTO, J., Industrial Engineering
COVAS VARELA, D., Industrial Engineering
CURBELO HERNANDEZ, M., Industrial Engineering
CURBELO MARTINEZ, D., Industrial Engineering
CURBELO MARTINEZ, M., Industrial Engineering
DE LEON LAFUENTE, L., Economics
DELGADO ALVAREZ, N., Industrial Engineering
DIAZ GISPERT, L., Economics
DIAZ MONZON, R., Accounting
DIAZ RODRIGUEZ, A., Industrial Engineering
DIEZ VALLADARES, O., Economics
DOMINGUEZ DOMINGUEZ, M., Economics
FEITO CESPON, M., Industrial Engineering
FERNANDEZ RANGEL, L., Accounting
FUENTES DIAZ, D., Accounting
GARCIA LORENZO, D., Accounting
GODOY COLLADO, M., Accounting
GOMEZ ALFONSO, E., Accounting
GONZALEZ ALVAREZ, R., Industrial Engineering
GONZALEZ CAPOTE, D., Economic
GONZALEZ HERNANDEZ, G., Physics
GONZALEZ MORALES, V., Economics
GONZALEZ ORTIZ, K., Economics
HERNANDEZ CASTILLO, D., Economics
HERNANDEZ DEL SOL, J., Economics
JUANES RAMIREZ, B., Accounting
LEYVA PADRON, E., Economics
LOPEZ BASTIDA, E., Chemistry
LOPEZ CARVAJAL, G., Economics
LOPEZ RODRIGUEZ, I., Economics
LOPEZ TOLEDO, M., Economics
MALDONADO MARTIN, M., Economics
MARTINEZ CALDERIN, L., Accounting
MARTINEZ CURBELO, G., Industrial Engineering
MATA VARELA, M., Economics
MAZAIRA RODRIGUEZ, Z., Economics
MENDEZ TERRY, M., Economics
OROPESA VARENS, M., Industrial Engineering
PEREZ DE ARMAS, M., Industrial Engineering
PEREZ FALCO, G., Accounting
PEREZ FERNANDEZ, D., Industrial Engineering
PEREZ GUEVARA, D., Tourism
PEREZ PEREZ, D., Education
PINO ALONSO, J., Social Sciences
POMA GARCIA, Y., Accounting
POMARES CASTELLON, L., Economics
PORTELA PEÑALVER, L., Economics
QUEVEDO DELFIN, A., Economic
QUEVEDO REYES, Y., Economics
QUINTERO RODRIGUEZ, J., Economics
RAMOS ALVAREZ, A., Accounting
REYES HERNANDEZ, R., Accounting
RICARDO CABRERA, H., Industrial Engineering
RIVERO ALONSO, K., Industrial Engineering
RODRIGUEZ DOMINGUEZ, L., Education
RODRIGUEZ GARCIA, N., Industrial Engineering
RODRIGUEZ HERNANDEZ, M., Economics
RODRIGUEZ PEREZ, B., Industrial Engineering
RODRIGUEZ VARELA, D., Economics
RUIZ DOMINGUEZ., R., Economics
SANCHEZ VALLADARES, O., Education
SARDUY AVALOS, L., Education
SARRIA PABLO, Y., Economics
SILVA LOPEZ, C., Accounting
SOSA GONZALEZ, M., Economics
SUAREZ DEL VILLAR LAVASTIDA, A., Industrial Engineering
SUAREZ GONZALEZ, Y., Accounting
TARRIO MESA, K., Sociology
TARTABULL CONTRERA, Y., Economic
URQUIOLA SANCHEZ, O., Accounting
VALDES GARRIDO, Y., Economics
VALDES GUADA, A., Education
VARENS ALBELO, V., Accounting
ZAMORA FONSECA, R., Information Sciences
ZULUETAS TORRES, O., Industrial Engineering

Faculty of Engineering:

ACEVEDO CARDOSO, D., Computer Science
AGUILA CUDEIRO, S., Education
ALEJO MACHADO, O., Computer Science
ALFONSO RODRIGUEZ, R., Electrical Engineering
ALVAREZ ACOSTA, H., Computer Science
ALVAREZ BETANCOURT, Y., Computer Science
ALVAREZ BRAVO, C., Computer Science
ALVAREZ CANCIOBELLO, R., Mechanical Engineering
ALVAREZ-GUERRA PLASENCIA, M., Mechanical Engineering
ARANZOLA RODRIGUEZ, M., Mechanical Engineering
ARCIS CARABALLO, A., Computer Science
ARENCIBIA RODRIGUEZ DEL REY, Y., Computer Science
BELTRAN RODRIGUEZ, W., Physics
BERMUDEZ RAMOS, G., Computer Science
BERNAL CASTILLO, J., Physics
BORGGIANO MIKULENKO, N., Mechanical Engineering
BOTANA BELTRAN, L., Education
BRAVO ESTEVEZ, M., Education
BRAVO HIDALGO, D., Mechanical Engineering
BRITO ACUÑA, K., Computer Science
CABELLO ERAS, J., Mechanical Engineering
CABRERA ALVAREZ, E., Economics
CABRERA SANCHEZ, J., Mechanical Engineering
CARRERA MARTINEZ, V., Mechanical Engineering
CARRILLO RAMOS, A., Computer Science
CASTELLANOS HERNANDEZ, J., Computer Science
CASTILLO MORALES, G., Mechanical Engineering
CASTRO PERDOMO, N., Chemistry
CHANG HERNANDEZ, L., Computer Science
CHOU RODRIGUEZ, E., Chemistry
CHOU RODRIGUEZ, R., Mechanical Engineering
COGOLLOS MARTINEZ, J., Mechanical Engineering
CONCEPCION MORALES, E., Applied Mathematics
CORDOVES DELGADO, G., Computer Science
CORTES CORTES, M., Mathematics
CRESPO SANCHEZ, G., Chemistry
CURBEIRA HERNANDEZ, D., Education
DE ARMAS DIAZ, J., Computer Science
DE ARMAS VALDIVIA, G., Education
DE LEON RODRIGUEZ, N., Mathematics
DEL RISCO CABRERA, L., Physics
DELGADO CASTILLO, R., Chemistry
DELGADO RIVERO, C., Computer Science
DIAZ TORRES, Y., Chemistry
DOMINGUEZ DIAZ, Y., Computer Science
ECHEVARRIA CARTAYA, Y., Computer Science
ENJAMIO RODRIGUEZ, Y., Physics
ESTEPA FERNANDEZ, N., Computer Science
FERNANDEZ BERMUDEZ, A., Education
FERNANDEZ CURBELO, L., Computer Science
FERNANDEZ PIEDRA, O., Physics
FIGUEREDO NORIS, L., Mechanical Engineering

FRANCISCO MARTIN, W., Chemistry
FUENTES GARI, E., Applied Mathematics
FUENTES VEGA, J., Mechanical Engineering
FUNDORA BELTRAN, P., Mechanical Engineering
GARCIA DIAZ, M., Education
GARCIA MARTINEZ, Y., Chemistry
GESSA GALVEZ, M., Education
GOMEZ SARDUY, J., Electrical Engineering
GONZALEZ PAZ, A., Computer Science
GONZALEZ PEREZ, F., Mechanical Engineering
HECTOR ORTIZ, K., Computer Science
HERNANDEZ ABREUS, R., Mathematics
HERNANDEZ FERREIRA, A., Physics
HERNANDEZ GONZALEZ, F., Mechanical Engineering
HERNANDEZ PENA, R., Mechanical Engineering
HERRERA MARTINEZ, N., Psychology
HURTADO REYES, S., Computer Science
JIMENEZ CORREA, J., Education
JIMENEZ SANTANA, Y., Nuclear Physics
JULVES ALVAREZ, M., Sociology
JUSTAFRE GARCIA, L., Education
LABAÑINO SUBARNABA, P., Computer Science
LAPIDO RODRIGUEZ, M., Mechanical Engineering
LEON RODRIGUEZ, A., Computer Science
LEYVA BRAVO, J., Computer Science
LINARES AMADO, E., Computer Science
LLODY GARCIA, Y., Mechanical Engineering
LOPEZ EXPOSITO, J., Mechanical Engineering
LOPEZ LOPEZ, G., Computer Science
MADRAZO DE LA ROSA, K., Computer Science
MARTELL ALONSO, L., Education
MARTIN BLANCO, J., Chemistry
MARTINEZ DIAZ, V., Mechanical Engineering
MARTINEZ PEREZ, S., Law
MARTINEZ ROQUE, A., Computer Science
MAZAIRA FERNANDEZ, J., Mathematics
MEDERO RUIZ, M., Computer Science
MEDINA MENDIETA, J., Computer Science
MENCIAS HOURRUITINER, V., Education
MENDOZA FERNANDEZ, A., Mechanical Engineering
MENENDEZ CLAVIJO, J., Computer Science
MILLO CARMENATE, V., Mechanical Engineering
MIRABAL PEREZ, J., Education
MIRANDA PEREZ, R., Economics
MIRANDA TORRES, V., Law
MOLINA YERA, O., Education
MONTEAGUDO YANES, J., Mechanical Engineering
MONTELIER HERNANDEZ, S., Mechanical Engineering
MONTERO HERRERA, L., Computer Science
MONZON CARDENAS, M., Chemistry
MORALES DIAZ, Y., Mathematics
MOREJON VIZCAINO, A., Computer Science
MUÑOZ GONZALEZ, O., Mathematics
NOA AGUILA, J., Mechanical Engineering
OLIVERT FERNANDEZ, N., History
PACHECO GONZALEZ, V., Chemistry
PADILLA RODRIGUEZ, R., Mechanical Engineering
PADRON PADRON, E., Electrical Engineering
PEÑA ACCION, J., Mechanical Engineering
PEÑA MATOS, M., Telecommunication
PEREZ CAÑEDO, B., Computer Science
PEREZ FERNANDEZ, A., Computer Science
PEREZ GOMEZ, Y., Mechanical Engineering
PIEDRA SARRÍA, A., History
PISCH VIDAL, L., Education
PUERTAS FERNANDEZ, J., Mechanical Engineering
QUINTERO BARRIZONTE, J., Computer Science
REYES CALVO, R., Automatic
RIVERO LAZA, F., Education
RIVERO PEREZ, J., Computer Science
RODRIGUEZ CEPERO, A., Computer Science
RODRIGUEZ HERNANDEZ, C., Computer Science
RODRIGUEZ LEON, C., Computer Science
ROQUE ESTRADA, A., Computer Science
RUIZ PORTELA, S., History
SAGASTUME GUTIERREZ, A., Mechanical Engineering
SANCHEZ ARCE, M., Mathematics
SANTANA JUSTIZ, M., Mathematics
SOSA LOPEZ, D., Computer Science
SOSA NUÑEZ, F., Mathematics
SOUSA SANTOS, V., Electrical Engineering
SUAREZ MONZON, N., Chemistry
SUAREZ SURI, P., Mathematics
TOLEDO DIAZ, L., Computer Science
TOLEDO DORREGO, A., Computer Science
TOLEDO GUERRA, Y., Computer Science
TOLEDO RIVERO, V., Mathematical Cybernetics
TORRES DEL TORO, M., Mathematics
VALDIVIA NODAL, Y., Electrical Engineering
VALLADARES PEREZ, D., Automatic
VEGA LARA, B., Automatic
VELAZQUEZ TORRES, D., Chemistry
VIEGO FELIPE, P., Electrical Engineering

Faculty of Physical Culture and Sport:
ABAD SAINZ, M., Education
ADAY JUAN, D., Education
AGUERO PEÑA, L., Education
AGUILA CUDEIRO, B., Automatic
AGUILA HURTADO, R., Law
AGUILAR SARDUY, B., Education
ALFONSO PADRON, G., Education
ALONSO HIDALGO, Y., Education
ALPIZAR FIGUEREDO, V., Physical Culture and Sport
ARGUELLES CANTERO, M., Accounting
BARROSO LOPEZ, I., Education
BASULTO MARRERO, B., Education
BELTRAN RODRIGUEZ, C., Computer Science
BERMUDEZ QUINTANA, Y., Education
BUENO FERNANDEZ, E., Physical Education
CABEZA SOSA, I., Cultural Studies
CABRERA PEREZ, A., Education
CARTAYA SARMIENTO, Y., Cultural Studies
CUELLAR VEGA, J., Education
CURBELO ENTENZA, A., Education
DE ARMAS VALDIVIA, D., Chemistry
DE LA CRUZ PEÑA, I., Education
DELGADO MOYA, M., Physical Education
DIAZ RUIZ, Y., Education
DIAZ TORRES, A., Mechanical Engineering
DIAZ ZUÑET, L., Education
ECHEVARRIA CARTAYA, F., Mathematics
ECHEVARRIA CHONGO, Y., Physical Education
ENJAMIO RODRIGUEZ, M., Mathematics
ESCOBAR ESCOBAR, L., Education
ESPINOSA SOSA, M., Education
FERNANDEZ BERMUDEZ, D., Automatic
FERNANDEZ CORDERO, A., Education
FERNANDEZ MORERA, M., Education
FERRER ENTEZA, A., Education
FLEITES GARCIA, M., Education
FONSECA VEGA, A., Education
FUENTES JOVA, I., Education
FURONES RODRIGUEZ, M., Education
GARCIA AGUILERA, R., Education
GARCIA MARTINEZ, M., Mathematics
GARCIA MOLINA, M., Physical Education
GARCIA MORENO, L., Education
GARCIA RIVERO, M., Physical Culture and Sport
GARCIA RODRIGUEZ, A., Social Communication
GARCIA VEGA, J., Education
GOMEZ ESPINOSA, R., Physical Education
GOMEZ MOLINA, L., Education
GOMEZ MOLINA, L., Physical Culture and Sport
GONZALEZ CARDOSO, A., Education
GONZALEZ DIAZ, L., Education
GONZALEZ GONZALEZ, M., Education
GONZALEZ REYES, J., Education
GONZALEZ RODRIGUEZ, O., Physical Culture and Sport
GRANADO MEJIAS, A., Physical Education
HERNANDEZ AGUILA, A., Education
HERNANDEZ MESA, M., Education
HERRERA MARTINEZ, A., Computer Science
JIMENEZ GONZALEZ, J., Physical Culture and Sport
JIMENEZ SANTANA, D., Computer Science
JULVES ALVAREZ, L., Computer Science
JUSTAFRE GARCIA, N., Chemistry
LAMOTHE MATOS, S., Education
LEE LOPEZ, D., Education
LEE PUELLO, D., Chemistry
LEON HIDALGO, R., Education
LEON LEON, A., Education
LLANES GRANDE GRANDE, S., Education
LLANES ROBAINA, L., Chemistry
LOPEZ ARAÑA, O., Education
LOPEZ ARISTICA, M., Psychology
LOPEZ HERRERA, M., Psychology
LOPEZ MENDEZ, A., Mechanical Engineering
LOPEZ MILIAN, A., Education
LOPEZ MILIAN, A., Agronomics
LOPEZ SUAREZ, D., Education
MACHADO TRELLES, V., Electrical Engineering
MADRUGA TRIANA, M., Psychology
MARCHENA LEYVA, G., Education
MARTINEZ GOITIZOLO, C., Education
MARTINEZ OLMO, Y., Education
MARTINEZ PEREZ, P., Electrical Engineering
MARTINEZ SABINA, B., Education
MENA MENDEZ, D., Social Comunication
MENDOZA DOMINGUEZ, I., Education
MESA CUBA, D., Law
MIGUEL LEAL, W., Education
MIRABAL PEREZ, M., Mathematics
MIRANDA TORRES, Y., Electrical Engineering
MIYAR BATISTA, L., Education
MOLINA SOTO, G., Education
MOLINA TORRES, M., Education
MONTES DE OCA HERNANDEZ, Y., Education
MORALES PEREZ, P., Education
MORALES SOSA, Y., Physical Culture and Sport
MUJICA CAICOYA, C., Education
MUÑOZ GONZALEZ, L., Education
NAVARRO RÍOS, R., Physical Culture and Sport
NIEBLAS RODRIGUEZ, L., Education
NOVELLA FERNANDEZ, I., Education
NUÑEZ GONZALEZ, M., Education
OLIVERT FERNANDEZ, V., Mathematical Cybernetics
PADILLA JORGE, A., Education
PELLON LIMA, R., Education
PEREZ GARCIA, P., Social Sciences
PEREZ GOMEZ, A., Computer Science
PEREZ GONZALEZ, S., Education
PÉREZ MENA, O., Physical Culture and Sport
PIEDRA SARRÍA, Y., Computer Science
QUIÑONES CHAPIS, M., Education
RABASSA PUERTO, R., Education
RAMIREZ RODRIGUEZ, Y., Education
RAMOS MIRANDA, F., Chemistry
RANGEL DIAZ, C., Education
ROCHE ARIZ, F., Education
RODRIGUEZ AGUILA, J., Physical Education
RODRIGUEZ AÑON, C., Education
RODRIGUEZ FERNAND, N., Education
RODRIGUEZ GONZALEZ, Y., Education
ROUCO ALBELLANES, Z., Education
RUIZ PORTELA, P., Mathematics
SAEZ MONROY, A., Education
SANABRIA SANABRIA, E., Education
SANCHEZ QUINTANA, A., Education
SESMONDE RODRIGUEZ, T., Physical Culture and Sport
STUAR RIVERO, A., Physical Culture and Sport
SUAREZ GUARDADO, G., Education
SUAREZ SUAREZ, G., Education

Tamame Molina, A., Education
Terry Garcia, R., Education
Toledo Amat, S., Economics
Toledo Guerra, S., History
Tornes Hurtado, I., Education
Valdes Montero, C., English Language
Valdez Hidalgo, A., Education
Varens Santos, S., Physical Education
Vega Suarez, A., Cultural Studies
Yera Jacomino, D., Education
Yera Jacomino, A., Accounting

Faculty of Social Sciences:

Abad Consuegra, R., Cultural Studies
Abreus Gonzalez, A., English Language
Acevedo Rodriguez, C., Cultural Studies
Acosta Chongo, Y., Education
Acosta Morales, Y., Economy
Aguero Contreras, F., Education
Aguila Cudeiro, L., Psychology
Aguila Cudeiro, Y., Economy
Aguilera Mojena, A., English Language
Alfonso Alverde, C., Sociology
Alfonso Gallegos, Y., Cultural Studies
Alfonso Garcia, A., Psychology
Alfonso Pacio, P., Education
Alpizar Fernandez, R., Education
Alvarez Beovidez, M., Education
Alvarez Gonzalez, A., Education
Alvarez Migueles, M., Education
Aparicio Aloma, M., Law
Arias Cardulis, I., Education
Armentero Reboredo, A., Teaching English
Baute Alvarez, L., Education
Baute Rosales, M., Education
Beltran Alonso, H., History
Bravo Lopez, G., Education
Brito Delgado, J., Physics
Brunet Herrera, L., Cultural Studies
Bruno Diaz, D., Design
Cabrera Fernandez, X., Education
Cabrera Perez, Y., Cultural Studies
Carballosa Gonzalez, A., Education
Carbonell Lemus, A., Education
Casanova Rodriguez, C., Psychology
Cedeño Solis, S., Cultural Studies
Chang Ramirez, J., Education
Chaviano Suarez, D., Cultural Studies
Cima Mesa, D., English Language
Cordero Guerra, G., Cultural Studies
Davila Lorenzo, M., Education
De Armas Valdivia, Y., Education
Delgado Cabrera, M., Psychology
Díaz Bacallao, A., Law
Diaz Gonzalez, D., Philosophy
Diaz Machado, K., Cultural Studies
Dominguez Fonseca, L., Education
Dorticos Torriente, Y., Education
Dueñas Fragoso, J., Law
Espinosa Requesens, I., Philosophy
Fernandez Bermudez, A., Cultural Studies
Fernandez Bermudez, Y., Social Comunication
Fernandez Hernandez, T., Education
Fernandez Peiso, L., Law
Ferrer Garcia, M., Education
Ferriol Morales, M., History
Figuera Marante, L., Cultural Studies
Fumero Roldan, L., Cultural Studies
Garcia Fernandez, I., English Language
Garcia Placeres, P., English Language
Garcia Sanchez, G., Education
Garcias Dueñas, R., Cultural Studies
Gessa Pacheco, H., Education
Gonzalez Rodriguez, M., Cultural Studies
Graña Fuentes, R., English Language
Guardado Stuart, Y., History
Hernandez Fraga, K., Law
Hernandez Garcias, M., History
Hernandez Moreno, E., Education
Herrera Hernandez, Y., English Language
Herrera Machado, D., Law
Herrera Martinez, Y., Cultural Studies
Ibañez Terry, J., History
Iglesias Leon, M., Education
Jacomino Ruiz, A., Cultural Studies
Julves Alvarez, Y., History
Justafre Garcia, Y., Law
Lara Diaz, L., Education
Lopez Diaz, C., Education
Lopez Saavedra, L., Sociology
Lopez Verdecia, Y., Cultural Studies
Losada Bermejo, L., English Language
Machado Trelles, Y., Cultural Studies
Madrazo Elizarde, D., Philology
Madruga Torreira, E., Education
Mainegra Rodriguez, O., Education
Martin Brito, L., Philology
Martinez Iglesias, M., Education
Martinez Perez, Y., Economy
Matos Reyes, E., Education
Medina Garcia, A., Cultural Studies
Medina Hernandez, O., Cultural Studies
Medina Marin, M., Education
Mena Fernandez, I., Economy
Mendoza Otero, J., Education
Mirabal Perez, Y., Cultural Studies
Miranda Molina, M., Teaching English
Miranda Torres, Y., Education
Molina Martinez, A., Teaching English
Molina Montero, A., Education
Molina Perez, M., French Language
Monzon Bruguera, Y., Law
Morales Calatayud, M., Philosophy
Moya Padilla, N., Philosophy
Muñiz Garcia, G., Cultural Studies
Nicolas Dominguez, M., History
Olivert Fernandez, Y., Education
Pardo Cordero, J., Law
Paredes Marin, A., English Language
Peña Maranges, J., English Language
Perez Calderon, G., Education
Perez Cruz, I., Education
Perez Lanza, C., Cultural Studies
Perez Navarro, L., Cultural Studies
Perez Novo, E., Education
Perez Padron, S., Social Communication
Perez Rosado, F., Philosophy
Piedra Sarría, Y., Cultural Studies
Pino Bermudez, D., Cultural Studies
Prendes Rey, C., Education
Prieto Rodriguez, J., Sociology
Pulido Cardenas, M., Education
Ramirez Jimenez, J., History
Ripoll Salcines, R., Law
Rizo Rabelo, N., Philosophy
Rodriguez Becerra, I., Psychology
Rodriguez Blandino, D., Teaching English
Rodriguez Leyva, M., Cultural Studies
Rodriguez Orrego, V., History
Rojas Cabrera, A., Cultural Studies
Roman Corella, L., Cultural Studies
Rosales Delgado, J., Education
Rovira Novo, A., Teaching English
Ruiz Martinez, E., Cultural Studies
Ruiz Portela, Y., Cultural Studies
Salas Placeres, M., Psychology
Sampedro Muñoz, N., History
Sanchez Arce, L., Education
Sanchez Galvez, S., History
Sanchez Quintero, M., Sociology
Senra Perez, N., Psychology
Stivens Portela, A., History
Suarez Diaz, N., History
Tamayo Volmey, J., Education
Varona Santiago, V., Law
Vazquez Cedeño, A., Education
Vazquez Cedeño, S., Education
Yanes Rodriguez, G., Education
Zamora Martell, S., Law

ATTACHED RESEARCH INSTITUTES

Centre de Estudios de Didáctica y Dirección de la Educación Superior (CEDDES): e-mail mcaceres@rectorado.ucf.edu.cu; Dir Dra Maritza Cáceres Mesa.

Centro de Estudios de Energía y Medio Ambiente (CEEMA): e-mail marmas@fmec.ucf.edu.cu; Dir Dr Marcos de Armas Teira.

Centro de Estudio Para la Transformación Agraria Sostenible (CETAS): e-mail asocorro@fmec.ucf.edu.cu; Dir Dr Alejandro Rafael Socorro Castro.

Centro de Estudio Socioculturales de Cienfuegos (CESOC): e-mail lmartin@fmec.ucf.edu.cu; Dir Dra Lilian Martín Brito.

Grupo de Estudios Avanzados: Universidad de Cienfuegos, Cienfuegos; e-mail opavel@ucf.edu.cu; State control; Dir Dr Owen Fernández Piedra

UNIVERSIDAD DE GRANMA
(University of Granma)

Carretera de Manzanillo km 17.5, Bayamo, Granma
Telephone: (23) 9-2130
E-mail: antonia@udg.granma.inf.cu
Internet: www.udg.co.cu
Founded 1967
State control
Faculties of accountancy and finance, agriculture, engineering, social and human sciences, veterinary medicine
Rector: Dra Antonia María Castillo Ruíz
Number of teachers: 316
Number of students: 2,300

UNIVERSIDAD AGRARIA DE LA HABANA
(Agricultural University of Habana)

Autopista Nacional y Carretera de Tapaste San José de las Lajas, La Habana
Telephone: (64) 6-3014
E-mail: rector@main.isch.edu.cu
Internet: www.isch.edu.cu
Founded 1976
Faculties of agronomy, mechanization of agricultural production and veterinary science; department of Marxism-Leninism; campus on Isla de la Juventud
Rector: Dr Julián Rodríguez Rodríguez
Number of teachers: 447
Number of students: 2,300

UNIVERSIDAD DE LA HABANA
(University of Habana)

c/o Zarezka Martínez Remigio, Gen. Sec., Havana
Telephone: (7) 879-1313
E-mail: webmaster@uh.cu
Internet: www.uh.cu
Founded 1728, reorganized 1976
Academic year: September to July
Rector: Dr Gustavo Cobreiro Suárez
Gen. Sec.: Dra Zarezka Martínez Remigio
Library: see under Libraries and Archives
Number of teachers: 2,974
Number of students: 27,537
Publications: *Universidad de la Habana*, various scientific and technical publs

DEANS

Faculty of Accounting and Finance: Dra Maricela Victoria Reyes Espinosa
Faculty of Arts and Letters: Dr José Antonio Baujín
Faculty of Biology: Dra Alicia Otazo Sánchez
Faculty of Chemistry: Dr José Manuel Nieto Villar
Faculty of Communication: Francisco González García
Faculty of Distance Education: Antonio Miranda Justiniani
Faculty of Foreign Languages: Dr Roberto Espí Valero
Faculty of Geography: Dra Nancy Pérez Rodríguez

Faculty of Law: Dr José Luis Toledo Santander
Faculty of Mathematics and Computing: Dr Luis Ramiro Piñeiro Diaz
Faculty of Philosophy and History: Dr José Carlos Vázquez López
Faculty of Physics: Dra Maria Sánchez Colina
Faculty of Planning for the National Economy: Dra Vilma Hidalgo de los Santos
Faculty of Psychology: M.Sc. Karelyn López Sánchez
Faculty of Tourism: Dra Lourdes Cisneros Mustelier
Institute of Pharmacy and Food: Dr Oscar Ros López
San Gerónimo de la Habana School: Félix Julio Alfonso López
Spanish Language for Non-Spanish Speakers: Dra Hilda León Castellanos

UNIVERSIDAD DE HOLGUÍN 'OSCAR LUCERO MOYA'
(University of Holguin 'Oscar Lucero Moya')

Avda 20 Aniversario, Nuevo Holguín, Gaveta Postal 57, 80100 Holguín
Telephone: (24) 48-1302
E-mail: acristina@ict.uho.edu.cu
Internet: www.uho.edu.cu

Founded 1976 as Centro Universitario de Holguín; became Instituto Superior Técnico de Holguín 1982; current name and status 1995

Rector: Dr Segundo Pacheco Toledo
Librarian: Matilde Riveron Hernández

Library of 90,980 vols
Number of teachers: 376
Number of students: 3,276

Publications: *Ambito* (4 a year), *Diéresis* (1 a year)

DEANS

Faculty of Engineering: Manuel Vega Almaguer
Faculty of Economics: Miguel Torres Perez

UNIVERSIDAD CENTRAL 'MARTA ABREU' DE LAS VILLAS
(Central University 'Marta Abreu' of Las Villa)

Carretera a Camajuaní Km $5\frac{1}{2}$, 54830 Santa Clara, Villa Clara
Telephone: (42) 28-1519
E-mail: rector@uclv.edu.cu
Internet: www.uclv.edu.cu

Founded 1952
Academic year: September to July

Rector: Dr José Ramón Saborido Loidi
Vice-Rector for Academic Affairs: Dra Miriam Nicado Gracia
Vice-Rector for Admin. Affairs: Dr Osvaldo Fernández Martínez
Vice-Rector for Economic and Financial Management: Dr José Ramón Castellanos Castillo
Vice-Rector for Extension: Dr Juan José Hernández Santana
Vice-Rector for Research and Postgraduate Affairs: Dr Angel Rubio González
Gen. Sec.: Dr Samuel Rodríguez García
Librarian: Ing. José Rivero Díaz

Library of 386,000 vols
Number of teachers: 1,187
Number of students: 5,132

Publications: *Biotecnología Vegetal* (4 a year), *Centro Agrícola*, *Centro Azúcar*, *Islas* (4 a year)

DEANS

Faculty of Agricultural Sciences: Dr Andrés Castro Alegría
Faculty of Building: Dr Gilberto Quevedo Sotolongo
Faculty of Chemistry and Pharmacy: Dr Ronaldo Santos Herrero
Faculty of Economics: Dr Inocencio Raul Sánchez
Faculty of Electrical Engineering: Dr Félix Álvarez Paliza
Faculty of Humanities: Ana Iris Díaz Martínez
Faculty of Industrial Engineering and Tourism: Dr Hugo Granela Martín
Faculty of Information Science and Education: M.Sc. Roberto Vicente Rodríguez
Faculty of Law: Dr Yadira García Rodriguez
Faculty of Mathematics, Computing and Physics: Dra Yanet Rodríguez Sarabia
Faculty of Mechanical Engineering: Dr Angel Silvio Machado Rodríguez
Faculty of Psychology: Dra Osana Molerio Pérez
Faculty of Social Sciences: Dra Mely del Rosario González Aróstegui

UNIVERSIDAD DE MATANZAS 'CAMILO CIENFUEGOS'
(University of Matanzas 'Camilo Cienfuegos')

Autopista a Veradero km 3, Matanzas
Telephone: (53) 52-62222
E-mail: info@umcc.cu
Internet: www.umcc.cu

Founded 1972

Library of 80,000 vols
Number of teachers: 381
Number of students: 3,020

Rector: Ing. Jorge Rodríguez Pérez
Vice-Rector for Admin. and Services: Ing. José R. Díaz
Vice-Rector for Research and Postgraduate Studies: Dr Roberto Vizcón Toledo
Vice-Rector for Teaching: Ing. Miguel Sarraf González

Publications: *Revista de Investigaciones Turísticas*, *Revista Pastos y Forrajes*

DEANS

Faculty of Agronomy: Dr Sergio Rodríguez Jiménez
Faculty of Chemistry and Mechanics: Dr Roberto Vizcón Toledo
Faculty of Computer Science: Dr Julio Telot González
Faculty of Economics and Industry: Lic. Benita N. García Gutiérrez
Faculty of Physical Education: Lic. Félix Moya
Faculty of Social Sciences and Humanities: Lic. Zoe Dominguez García

ATTACHED RESEARCH INSTITUTES

Centro de Estudios de Anticorrosión y Tensioactivos (CEAT): Dir Carlos A. Echeverría Lage.

Centro de Estudios de Combustión y Energía (CECYEN): e-mail barroso@quimec.umcc.cu; Dir Jorge Ángel Barroso Estébanez.

Centro de Estudio y Desarrollo Educacional (CEDE): e-mail gerardo.ramos@umcc.cu; Dir Dr Gerardo Ramos Serpa.

Centro de Estudios de Medioambiente (CEMAN): Dir Dra Juana Zoila Junco Horta

UNIVERSIDAD DE ORIENTE
(University of East)

Avda Patricio Lumumba s/n, 90500 Santiago de Cuba
Telephone: (22) 63-1860
E-mail: marcosc@rect.uo.edu.cu
Internet: www.uo.edu.cu

Founded 1947
Academic year: September to July

Rector: Dr Marcos Cortina Vega
Vice-Rector: MSc Elio Castellanos
Vice-Rector: Dra Zaida Valdés Estrada
Vice-Rector: Dr Sergio Cano Ortiz
Vice-Rector: Dr Juan Bory Reyes
Vice-Rector: Dr Pedro A. Beatón Soler
Sec. Gen.: Arq. Sonia Quesada
Librarian: Dr Bayardo Dupotey Ribas

Library: see under Libraries and Archives
Number of teachers: 842
Number of students: 24,500 (5,500 undergraduate, 19,000 postgraduate and continuing education)

Publications: *Revista Cubana de Química* (3 a year), *Revista Santiago* (2 a year), *Tecnología Química* (3 a year)

DEANS

Faculty of Building Construction: MSc Alejandro Fajardo
Faculty of Chemical Engineering: Dra Ana Sánchez del Campo Laffita
Faculty of Computing Sciences and Mathematics: MSc Alejandro Garcés Calvelo
Faculty of Distance Learning: Dra Rosario León Robaina
Faculty of Economics: MSc Ulises Pacheco Feria
Faculty of Electrical Engineering: MSc Emilio Soto Morlá
Faculty of Humanities: Dra Etna Sanz
Faculty of Law: Dra Josefina Méndez
Faculty of Mechanical Engineering: Dr Roberto Zagaró Zamora
Faculty of Natural Sciences: Dr Pedro Muné Bandera
Faculty of Social Sciences: Dra María Julia Jiménez Fiol

UNIVERSIDAD DE PINAR DEL RÍO

Calle J. Martí 272 esq. a 27 de Noviembre, Pinar del Río 20100
Telephone: (48) 77-9353
E-mail: mfdez@vrect.upr.edu.cu
Internet: www.upr.edu.cu

Founded 1972
State control
Language of instruction: Spanish
Academic year: September to July

Library of 29,872 vols

Rector: Dr Andrés Erasmo Ares Rojas
Vice-Rector for Admin.: Dr Carlos María Lazo Vento
Vice-Rector for Community Relations: Dra Mayra Carmona González
Vice-Rector for Research: Dra Marisela González Pérez
Vice-Rector for Teaching: Dra José Manuel González Abréu
Vice-Rector for Univ. Extension and Internationalization: Dra Yorki Mayor Hernández
Dir for Int. Relations: Dra María Elena Fernández Hernández
Sec. Gen.: Magalys González Hernández
Librarian: María del Carmen Martínez

Number of teachers: 707
Number of students: 9,117

Publications: *Journal in Forest Science* (2 a year), *Journal of Cooperative and Development* (2 a year), *Student Scientific Journal in Forestry and Environment* (2 a year)

DEANS

Faculty of Agronomy and Forestry: Dr LUÍS WILFREDO MARTÍNEZ BECERRA

Faculty of Economics: YOSVANY BARRIOS HERNÁNDEZ

Faculty of Humanities: Dr JUAN SILVIO CABRERA ALBERT

Faculty of Mountain Agronomy: Dr JOSÉ REYNALDO DÍAZ

Faculty of Technical Sciences: Dr WILFREDO FALCÓN URQUIAGA

Faculty of Telecommunications and Informatics: Dr WILFREDO FALCÓN URQUIAGA

AFFILIATED INSTITUTES

Centre of Agroecology: Universidad de Pinar del Río, Facultad de Forestal y Agronomía, Pinar del Río; tel. (48) 75-5452; e-mail mariol@af.upr.edu.cu; Dir Dra MARIOL MOREJÓN.

Centre for Forestry Sciences: e-mail betancourt@af.upr.edu.cu; Dir Dr YNOCENTE BETANCOURT FIGUERAS.

Centre for Higher Education Research: e-mail tdiaz@vrect.upr.edu.cu; Dir Dra TERESA DE LA C. DÍAZ.

Centre for Management and Tourism Studies: e-mail diana@eco.upr.edu.cu; Dir Dra DIANA DE LA NUEZ HERNÁNDEZ.

Centre of Natural Resources and the Environment: e-mail mcasas@eco.upr.edu.cu; Dir Dra MAYRA CASAS VILARDELL.

Centre for the Study of Co-operatives: e-mail arivera@eco.upr.edu.cu; Dir Dr CLAUDIO A. RIVERA

Colleges

Instituto Superior de Ciencias Médicas de Camagüey: Carretera Central Oeste esquina a Madame Curie, Camagüey; tel. (32) 9-2100; e-mail romulo@finlay.cmw.sld.cu; f. 1981 from medical faculty of Univ. of Camagüey; schools of dentistry, medicine, nursing; biomedical, clinical and sociomedical research; 587 teachers; 3,500 students; Rector Dr RÓMULO RODRÍGUEZ RAMOS; publ. *Revista de Ciencias Médicas de Camagüey* (2 a year).

Instituto Superior de Relaciones Internacionales 'Raul Roa García': Calle Calzada 308 esq. H, Vedado, Havana 10400; tel. (7) 831-9495; e-mail isri@isri.minrex.gov.cu; internet www.isri.cu; f. 1971; spec. colln containing the personal library of Dr Raúl Roa García; library: 14,000 vols; 61 teachers; Rector Embajadora Lic. ISABEL ALLENDE KARAM; Gen. Sec. Dr RENÉ OCHOA FÚNEZ.

Instituto Superior Politécnico 'José Antonio Echeverría': Calle 114 No 11901 entre 119 y 127, CUJAE, Marianao, CP 19390, Havana; tel. (7) 261-4932; e-mail rosy@tesla.cujae.edu.cu; internet www.cujae.edu.cu; f. 1976, fmrly Faculty of Technology of Univ. of Havana; faculties of architecture, chemical engineering, civil engineering, electrical engineering, industrial engineering, information engineering, mechanical engineering; advanced education centre, biomedical engineering centre, hydraulic research centre, innovation and maintenance study centre, management techniques study centre, microelectronic research centre, process engineering centre, renewable energy technology study centre, systems engineering study centre, tropical architecture and construction centre; library: 157,370 vols; 1,012 teachers; 5,299 students; Rector Dr GUSTAVO COBREIRO SUÁREZ; Sec. Ing. RAÚL CAPETILLO ALVAREZ; publs *Arquitectura y Urbanismo* (3 a year), *Ingeniería Electrónica, Automática y Telecomunicaciones* (3 a year), *Ingeniería Energética* (3 a year), *Ingeniería Hidráulica y Ambiente* (3 a year), *Ingeniería Industrial* (3 a year), *Ingeniería Mecanica* (3 a year).

Schools of Art and Music

Academia Nacional de Bellas Artes 'San Alejandro' (National Academy of Fine Arts): Avda 31 y Calle 100 No. 10006, Obelisco de Marianao, 11400 Havana; tel. (7) 260-9234; e-mail sanalejandro@cubarte.cult.cu; internet www.sanalejandro.cult.cu; f. 1818 as Academia de San Alejandro; fmrly Escuela de Pintura, organized by the French painter Jean Baptiste Vermay; 800 students; Dir DOMINGO RAMOS ENRÍQUEZ.

Conservatorio Alejandro García Caturla: Avda 31 y Calle 82, Marianao, Havana.

Conservatorio de Música Amadeo Roldán: Rastro y Lealtad, Havana.

CYPRUS

The Higher Education System

Cyprus was governed by the United Kingdom from 1878 until it achieved independence in 1960, following a guerrilla campaign by Greek Cypriots seeking unification (Enosis) with Greece. Government was subsequently on the basis of a power-sharing agreement between the Greek and Turkish communities, but in 1963 the Turks withdrew from central government. In 1974, after Greek officers of the Cypriot National Guard had staged a coup, the Turkish army occupied the northern third of the island, where Turkish Cypriots subsequently established a de facto Government and, in 1975, declared a Turkish Federated State of Cyprus (TFSC). In 1983 the TFSC unilaterally declared an independent Turkish Republic of Northern Cyprus (TRNC). The Greek Cypriot administration, meanwhile, claims to be the Government of all Cyprus, and is generally recognized as such. Until 1965 each community in Cyprus managed its own schooling through a Communal Chamber. On 31 March of that year, however, the Greek Communal Chamber was dissolved and a Ministry of Education (now Ministry of Education and Culture) was established to take its place. Inter-communal education has been placed under this Ministry.

Cyprus:

There are three public universities in Cyprus. The University of Cyprus, in Nicosia, was founded in 1989 (and admitted its first students in 1992); in 2010/11 4,691 undergraduate and 1,549 postgraduate students were admitted into seven faculties (incl. Graduate School). The Open University of Cyprus was established in 2003 and is dedicated entirely to distance learning within the EU Lifelong Learning initiative. The Cyprus University of Technology was established in 2004 and began teaching in 2007; with the exception of the Faculty of Health Sciences which is based in Nicosia, its other four faculties are based in Limassol. Three private universities were granted an initial licence to operate in 2007 following the implementation of Law 109 (I)/2005, which regulates the establishment and operation of private universities; in 2010 a fourth began operating. In 2012 the University of Central Lancashire, Cyprus (UCLan Cyprus) and the University of East London, Cyprus (UEL Cyprus) commenced operations in the country. There are a number of public institutions of specialized tertiary education, including the Cyprus Forestry College and the School for Tourist Guides. The Mediterranean Institute of Management is the only non-university level public institution that awards a one-year postgraduate diploma in Business Administration and Public Administration. In 2009/10 32,233 students (including 11,138 foreign pupils) were enrolled in tertiary education, while a total of 20,051 students from the Greek Cypriot area were studying at universities abroad, mainly in Greece, the USA and the United Kingdom.

Students must hold the main secondary school qualification (Apolytirion) and sit a competitive entrance examination to gain admission to higher education. Cyprus became a signatory to the Bologna Process in 2001, and a three-tier Bachelors/Masters/Doctorate degree system (together with the European Credit Transfer and Accumulation System—ECTS) has been implemented; the transition was facilitated by the fact that Cyprus's existing university education structure was on a three-tier basis, so only minor adjustments were needed. The first university degree level is the undergraduate Bachelors degree (Ptychio), which is awarded after four years' study and consists of 240 ECTS credit units. At postgraduate level, the Masters requires three to four semesters of study and consists of 90–120 credit units, while the third-tier qualification, Doctor of Philosophy (Didaktoriko), takes an average of three to four years (with a maximum of eight years permitted) and requires the defence of an original research thesis before a committee of examiners. Non-university higher education consists of one- to three-year Certificate, Diploma and Higher Diploma programmes, offered by the University of Cyprus and around 25 non-university private institutions in professional fields of study. The latter institutions are registered by the Ministry of Education and Culture, in accordance with Law 67 (I)/96, which was introduced in September 1997.

Qualifications awarded by private higher education institutions only have academic standing if the programme of study has been accredited by the Evaluation Committee of Private Universities (in the case of private universities) and by the Council for Educational Evaluation-Accreditation (CEEA) (for private non-university institutions). Institutional registration with the Ministry alone does not mean that courses are accredited. The Cyprus Agency of Quality Assurance and Accreditation in Education, which will cover all higher educational establishments in the country (both private and public), is currently in the process of being set up pending approval of draft legislation required for its creation. The process of implementing a National Qualifications Framework for Cyprus has also been commenced.

Post-secondary technical and vocational education is offered by both public and private institutions and is overseen by the Ministry of Education and Culture.

Turkish Republic of North Cyprus:

The international community, including the UN and EU, does not recognize the TRNC as a separate self-governing country. The Republic of Cyprus is recognized as having *de jure* sovereignty over the whole island. The Greek Cypriot Government, which legally remains the competent authority for all of Cyprus, does not recognize or accredit Turkish Cypriot higher education institutions.

The education system in the TRNC follows the Turkish model, and those institutions recognized by the Turkish Government can be expected to have a comparable standard of education to the Turkish mainland. Since the TRNC is not officially recognized as an independent political entity by any member of the Bologna Process except Turkey, it is not eligible to join the Process.

Cyprus's first university, the Eastern Mediterranean University, which is located near Gazi Mağusa (Famagusta), was opened in 1979 as the Higher Technological Institute and was elevated to full university status under its current name in 1986. A total of 13,255 students attended the university in 2008/09. Other institutions providing university-level higher education in the TRNC are the Near East University in Lefkoşa (Nicosia), the Girne American University, the Middle East Technical University—Northern Cyprus Campus, the European University of Lefke (Levka) and the Cyprus International University. In 2011/12 over 47,000 students were studying at universities in the TRNC (20% were Turkish Cypriots, 62% came from Turkey and 18% from other countries). In 2012 a School of Foreign Languages was opened at the ITU-TRNC Education and Research Campus in Gazi Mağusa (Famagusta), a project initiated by Istanbul Technical University, which aims to develop basic and engineering sciences courses and other undergraduate departments in the near future. All schools and educational institutes are administered by the Ministry of National Education, Youth and Sport (with the exception of private kindergartens, a vocational school of agriculture attached to the Ministry of Agriculture and Natural Resources, a training school for nursing and midwifery attached to the Ministry of Health and a school for hotel catering attached to the Ministry of Economy, Tourism and Culture). Education in the Turkish Cypriot zone is divided into two sections, formal and adult (informal) education. Formal education covers nursery, primary, secondary and higher education. Adult education caters for special training outside the school system. In

1982 an International Institute of Islamic Banking and Economics was opened to provide postgraduate training.

Completion of the Lise Bitirme Diplomasi or equivalent is required for entry to undergraduate courses. In addition, candidates from both Turkey and the TRNC itself must also undertake a central examination. In the case of overseas students, each university has its own regulations for entrance, but all applicants must hold a minimum of 12 years' pre-university education and a Higher Secondary Education Certificate, or its equivalent. The organization of undergraduate degrees is based on the US-style 'credit' and grade-point average (GPA) system. The Lisans Diplomasi (Bachelors degree) lasts eight semesters (four years) and students require at least 120 credits and a GPA of 2.0 to graduate. A two-year Ön-Lisans Diplomasi (Associate degree) course is also available. Yüksek Lisans Diplomasi (Masters) programmes such as the Master of Arts (MA), Master of Business Administration (MBA) and Master of Science (MSc) take 18 months' to two years' study following the Bachelors, and require between 21 (MSc) and 42 (MBA) credits. A Masters (or equivalent) is required for admission onto the Doktora (Doctor of Philosophy—PhD) programme, which is a combination of core coursework and original research; candidates for a PhD must submit a research thesis.

Technical and vocational education is provided by several colleges and institutes, admission to which is dependent upon the Lise Bitirme Diplomasi. These establishments offer courses in the fields of agriculture, hotel management and catering, and nursing and midwifery.

Regulatory and Representative Bodies

GOVERNMENT

Ministry of Economy Tourism, Culture and Sport: Selçuklu Rd, Lefkoşa, TRNC, via Mersin 10, Turkey; tel. 2289629; internet etksb.gov.ct.tr; Minister SERDAR DENKTAŞ.

Ministry of Education and Culture: Kimonos and Thoukididis, 1434 Nicosia; tel. 22800600; e-mail moec@moec.gov.cy; internet www.moec.gov.cy; Minister KYRIAKOS KENEVEZOS.

Ministry of National Education, Youth and Sport: Lefkoşa, TRNC, via Mersin 10, Turkey; tel. 2284505; e-mail info@mebnet.net; internet www.mebnet.net; Minister MUSTAFA Ş. ARABACIOĞLU.

ACCREDITATION

Cyprus Council of Educational Evaluation–Accreditation (CEEA): POB 12592, Latsia, 2251 Nicosia; 50 Leoforos Athalassas, Strovolos, 2023 Nicosia; tel. 22465850; e-mail sekap@cytanet.com.cy; internet www.moec.gov.cy/sekap; f. 1987; an ind. body consisting of a Chair. and 6 other mems, who are appointed for a 5-year term by the Ccl of Ministers on the recommendation of the Min. of Education and Culture; carries out programmatic evaluation and accreditation of private instns of higher education; Chair. Prof. GEORGE PHILOKYPROU.

Cyprus Council for the Recognition of Higher Education Qualifications (KYSATS): POB 12758, 2252 Nicosia; 50 Leoforos Athalassas, First Floor, Strovolos, 2023 Nicosia; tel. 22465850; e-mail info@kysats.ac.cy; internet www.kysats.ac.cy; f. 1996; consists of 7 mems appointed by the Ccl of Ministers on the recommendation of the Min. of Education and Culture; Chair. Prof. MARIOS MAVRONICOLAS.

Evaluation Committee of Private Universities (ECPU): 50 Leoforos Athalassas, Strovolos, 2023 Nicosia; tel. 22465853; e-mail administration@ecpu.ac.cy; internet www.ecpu.ac.cy; f. 2006; composed of 7 mems, who are appointed by the Ccl of Mins on the recommendation of the Min. of Education and Culture and who serve a 5-year term; headed by Chair. of CEEA (*q.v.*); examines applications for the establishment of private univs; Chair. Prof. GEORGE PHILOKYPROU.

Higher Education Planning, Evaluation, Accreditation and Coordination Council TRNC (YÖDAK): 29B Sehit Yusuf Ecvet Cad., Lefkoşa, TRNC, via Mersin 10; tel. 2292340; e-mail yodak@ncyodak.eu; internet www.ncyodak.eu; f. 2005; Pres. Prof. Dr HASAN ALI BIÇAK.

Learned Societies

GENERAL

Etaireia Kypriakon Spoudon (Society of Cypriot Studies): POB 21436, 1508 Nicosia; tel. 22432578; e-mail cypriotstudies@gmail.com; internet www.cypriotstudies.org; f. 1936; colln, preservation and study of material concerning all periods of the history, dialect and folklore of Cyprus; maintains Museum of Cypriot Folk Art (f. 1937); library of Kypria, Cypriot studies; 1,050 mems; library of 5,000 vols; Pres. Dr CHARALAMPOS CHOTZAKOGLOU; Dir ELENI CHRISTOU; Sec. Dr MARIA MICHAEL; publ. *Kypriakai Spoudai* (Cypriot Studies, 1 a year).

BIBLIOGRAPHY, LIBRARY SCIENCE AND MUSEOLOGY

Association of Friends of Museums of Northern Cyprus: c/o Eski Eserler ve Müzeler Dairesi Müdürlüğü, Lefkoşa, TRNC, via Mersin 10, Turkey; tel. 2289345; f. 1975 as Turkish Cypriot Asscn of Friends of Museums and Antiquities; current name adopted 1994.

Kypriake Enose Bivbiothikonomon-Epistemonon Pleroforeses (KEBEP) (Cyprus Association of Librarians-Information Scientists—CALIS): POB 21100, 1501 Nicosia; e-mail kebepcy@gmail.com; internet kebep.eu; f. 1984; promotes library, archival and information science in Cyprus; fortifies and secures the profession of information scientists-librarians; coordinates actions that relate to information science, publishing, open access; advises on planning, org. and operation of Cyprus libraries; participates in governing boards that relate to information science and libraries; 220 mems; Pres. PANAGIOTIS THEMISTOKLEOUS; Treas. ELENI KAMPERI.

HISTORY, GEOGRAPHY AND ARCHAEOLOGY

Association of Cypriot Archaeologists: POB 20058, 1600 Nicosia; tel. 22307315; e-mail acarchaeologists@gmail.com; internet www.cypriotarchaeologists.org.cy; f. 1983; study and research of Cypriot cultural heritage of all periods; protection of archaeological sites and monuments on the island; continuous scientific devt of its mems; organizes lectures, workshops, conferences, and various collaborations with local and foreign instns; Pres. DESPO PILIDES; Sec. VASILIKI LYSANDROU; publ. *Archaeologia Cypria*.

Association for Historical Dialogue and Research: 28 Odos Marcou Dracou, 1102 Nicosia; tel. 22445740; e-mail ahdr.mide@gmail.com; internet www.ahdr.info; f. 2003; advocates advancement of historical understanding among the public and more specifically among children, young people and educators by providing access to learning opportunities; organizes intercommunal confs, exhibitions and teacher-training workshops; opened Home for Cooperation (H4C) in May 2011 as shared space for all Cypriots to engage in historical inquiry and advance mutual understanding and dialogue; maintains library; Pres. KYRIAKOS PACHOULIDES; Sec. RANA ZINCIR CELAL.

Cyprus Geographical Association: POB 23656, Nicosia; tel. 22368981; f. 1968; research and study of the geography of Cyprus; aims to improve the teaching of geography, and safeguard professional interests of geographers; 200 mems; library of 500 vols; Pres. Prof. PANAYIOTIS ARGYRIDES; publ. *The Geographical Chronicles* (1 a year).

LANGUAGE AND LITERATURE

Alliance Française: 20 Ayias Sophias and Dionysou St, 3065 Limassol; tel. 25877784; e-mail aflima@spidernet.com.cy; internet www.aflimassol.org; f. 1963; offers courses and exams in French language and culture and promotes cultural exchange with France; Dir BALDET BERTRAND.

British Council: POB 21175, 1503 Nicosia; 1–3 Aristotelous St, 1011 Nicosia; tel. 22585100; e-mail enquiries@cy.britishcouncil.org; internet www.britishcouncil.org/cyprus.htm; f. 1934; offers courses and exams in English language and British culture and promotes cultural exchange with the United Kingdom; Dir PETER SKELTON.

Research Institutes

GENERAL

Cyprus Research and Publishing Centre: 3B Abdi Cavus, Lefkoşa, TRNC, via Mersin 10, Turkey; tel. 2272592; f. 1984; research in the fields of ethnography, history, language and literature, society; publ. *New Cyprus* (12 a year).

Kentron Epistemonikōn Ereunon Kyprou (Cyprus Research Centre): POB 21952, 1515 Nicosia; 6 Gladstonos, 1095 Nicosia; tel. 22456301; e-mail erevna@moec.gov.cy; internet www.moec.gov.cy/kee; f. 1964; attached to Min. of Education and Culture; promotes scientific research on history and culture of Cyprus; research library; archival collns in the form of MSS, printed matter, CD ROMs and photographic materials; Dir Dr ANNA POURADIER DUTEIL-LOIZIDOU; Sec. SKEVI STAVROPOULOU.

HISTORY, GEOGRAPHY AND ARCHAEOLOGY

Cyprus American Archaeological Research Institute: 11 Andreas Demetriou St, 1066 Nicosia; tel. 22456414; e-mail admin@caari.org.cy; internet www.caari.org; f. 1978; one of the American Schools of Oriental Research; promotes the study of archaeology and related disciplines in Cyprus; encourages communication among scholars interested in Cyprus and provides residence facilities; library of 8,300 books, 110 current periodicals; representative ceramic, geological, lithic, archaeometallurgical and faunal reference collns, slide archive; Dir Dr ANDREW P. MCCARTHY; Librarian EVI KARYDA; publ. *CAARI News* (2 a year).

Libraries and Archives

Girne (Kyrenia)

National Archive and Research Department: 45 Mustafa Çağatay Cad., Girne, TRNC, via Mersin 10, Turkey; tel. 28152156; e-mail infoarsiv@kamunet.net; internet arsiv.kamunet.net; f. 1971; Man. JENNIFER ŞENGÖR.

Larnaca

Larnaca Municipal Library: Stadiou & Gr. Afxentiou, Larnaca; tel. 24654185.

Lefkoşa

Cyprus Turkish National Library: Atatütk Kültür Merkezi, Lefkoşa, TRNC; tel. 22283257; e-mail mkutuphane@mebnet.net; internet mkutup.mebnet.net; f. 1961; 95,000 vols; Chief Librarian UMURE ÖRS.

Limassol

Municipal Library: 352 Agiou Andreou & Karaiskaki, 3035 Limassol; tel. 25362155; f. 1945; 60,000 vols; Librarian A. KYRIAKIDES.

Nicosia

Cyprus Library: Eleftherias Sq., 1011 Nicosia; tel. 22303180; e-mail cypruslibrary@cytanet.com.cy; internet www.cypruslibrary.gov.cy; f. 1987; 155,000 vols, 2,164 CDs and DVDs, 285 video cassettes, 1,352 microforms; spec. colln: Cypriot studies; Dir DIMITRIS NIKOLAOU (acting); publ. *Bulletin of the Cyprus Bibliography* (1 a year).

Cyprus Library Reference Department: 46 Faneromeris St, 1011 Nicosia; tel. 22410171; e-mail louizap@yahoo.com; internet www.cypruslibrary.gov.cy; 33,000 vols; Librarian LOUIZA-MARIA PELEKANOU.

Cyprus Museum Library: POB 22024, Nicosia; tel. 22865848; e-mail antiquitieslibrary@da.mcw.gov.cy; f. 1883, inc. in Dept of Antiquities 1934; 19,834 vols (excl. bound periodicals), 240 periodical titles, Pierides colln of 1,400 vols; Librarian MARIA DEMETRIOU-ECONOMIDOU.

Library of the Cultural Centre of the Archbishop Makarios III Foundation: POB 21269, 1505 Nicosia; tel. 22430008; e-mail info@makariosfoundation.org.cy; internet www.makariosfoundation.org.cy; f. 1983; research library of 65,000 vols relating mostly to Greek, Byzantine and post-Byzantine studies, Christian theology and recent political history of Cyprus; incorporates the library of the Holy Archbishopric of Cyprus, the library of the Society of Cypriot Studies, and the Foundation library; Dir Dr M. STAVROU.

Library of the Pedagogical Institute of Cyprus: POB 12720, 2252 Nicosia; 40 Makedonias Ave, Latsia, 2238 Nicosia; tel. 22402300; e-mail papandreou@cyearn.pi.ac.cy; internet www.pi.ac.cy; f. 1972; 60,000 vols, mainly on education; Dir ANDREAS PAPANDREOU.

Nicosia Municipal Arts Centre Library: POB 21015, 1500 Nicosia; 19 Palias Ilektrikis, 1016 Nicosia; tel. 22797400; e-mail info@nimac.org.cy; internet www.nimac.com.cy; associated with Pierides Foundation; 30,000 vols on history of art.

State Archives of the Republic of Cyprus: Min. of Justice and Public Order, 1461 Nicosia; IBM Centrum Tower, 42–44 Grivas Dhigenis Ave, Agioi Omologites, Nicosia; tel. 22451045; e-mail statearchives@sa.mjpo.gov.cy; internet www.mjpo.gov.cy; f. 1978; place of deposit for public records received from govt depts and other bodies, subject to the State Archives Law of 1991; makes these records publicly available for research; 13,798 vols; 159,000 Secretariat Archives files, 10.8 km of linear shelving of archival holdings; State Archivist EFFY PARPARINOU.

Paphos

Paphos Municipal Library: 28 Plateia Oktovriou, Paphos; tel. 26233847.

Museums and Art Galleries

Ayia Napa

Thalassa Municipal Museum of the Sea: 14 Kriou Nerou St, POB 30707, Ayia Napa; tel. 23816366; e-mail thalassa.museum@agianapa.org.cy; f. 2005; artefacts span some 7,000 years, from Neolithic period to Venetian rule.

Tornaritis-Pierides Municipal Museum of Marine Life: 25 Ayias Mavris St, Ayia Napa; tel. 23721179; internet www.tornaritis.com/tp/marinelife/main.html; f. 1992; natural history and marine environment.

Gazi Mağusa

St Barnabas Icon and Archaeology Museum: Gazi Mağusa, TRNC, via Mersin 10, Turkey; tel. 23648331; f. 1974; St Barnabas monastery dating from 5th century; colln of icons from around 10th century to 20th century; works of art from Neolithic to Roman period; bronze and marble pieces; library of 5,000 vols; Famagusta Dept of Antiquities Dir HASAN TEKEL.

Larnaca

Larnaca District Archaeological Museum: Plateia Kalograion, 6305 Larnaca; tel. 24304169; f. 1969; exhibits incl. artefacts from Neolithic settlements of Choirokitia and Tenta.

Larnaca Municipal Museum of Natural History: Leoforos Grigori Afxentiou, Larnaca; tel. 24652569; collns of local reptiles, insects, birds, animals, fossils and rock formations; marine life and plants from Cyprus and neighbouring countries; colln of insects and endemic plants.

Pierides Museum: 4 Zenonos Kitieou St, Larnaca; tel. 24814555; e-mail pieridesmuseum@bankofcyprus.com; more than 2,500 artefacts chronicle 9,000 years of island's history, incl. maps, glassware and sculptures; Curator PETER ASHDJIAN.

Lefkoşa

Dervish Pasha Mansion and Ethnographical Museum: Belig Pasha St, Lefkoşa, TRNC, via Mersin 10, Turkey; tel. 2281922; f. 1988; colln of Ottoman artefacts.

National Struggle Museum: 7 Kinyras, Old City, Lefkoşa, TRNC, via Mersin 10, Turkey; tel. 22305878; f. 1989; documents, photographs and other memorabilia of the 1955–1959 Nat. Liberation Struggle and from the 1974 Turkish invasion.

Limassol

Cyprus Medieval Museum: Limassol Castle, Richardou & Berengarias, Limassol; tel. 25305419; f. 1987; rich colln of local and imported pottery from the Early Christian, Byzantine and medieval periods; unique collns of medieval tombstones, coats of arms and architectural exhibits from palaces, castles and churches; coins, arms, cannons, etc.

Cyprus Wine Museum: 42 Pafos St cnr, Erimi, Limassol; tel. 25873808; e-mail cypruswinemuseum@cytanet.com.cy; internet www.cypruswinemuseum.com; f. 2004; covers 5,500 years of Cypriot wine-making history; Head of the Board ANASTASIA GUY; Dir FRANCIS-NECTARIOS GUY.

Limassol District Archaeological Museum: Vyronos & Anastasi Sioukri St, 3401 Limassol; tel. 25305157; internet www.limassolmunicipal.com.cy/museum; f. 1948; artefacts from 10th century BC to late Roman period; Archaeological Officer YIANNIS VIOLARIS.

Municipal Folk Art Museum: 253 Agiou Andreou St, Limassol; tel. 25362303; f. 1985; exhibits of 19th- and early 20th-century nat. costumes, tapestry, embroidery, wooden chests, waistcoats, men's jackets, necklaces, a variety of light clothes, town costumes, country tools.

Nicosia

Byzantine Museum and Art Gallery Archbishop Makarios III Foundation: Plateia Archiepiskopou Kyprianou, POB 21269, 1505 Nicosia; tel. 22430008; internet www.makariosfoundation.org.cy; f. 1982; Museum Chair. Archbishop CHRYSOSTOMOS II.

Cyprus Classic Motorcycle Museum: 44 Granikou St, 1010 Nicosia; tel. 22680222; e-mail cyclassicmotorcyclemuseum@cytanet.com.cy; internet agrino.org/motormuseum; exhibits more than 150 motorcycles (mainly British); Administrator ANDREAS NICOLAOU.

Cyprus Folk Art Museum: POB 21436, 1508 Nicosia; tel. 22432578; e-mail cypriotstudies@gmail.com; internet www.cypriotstudies.org; f. 1937; Cyprus arts and crafts from early to recent times; more than 5,000, mainly Cypriot Greek, items; library of 1,600 vols; Dir HELEN CHRISTOU; Sec. MICHAEL GEORGIOU; publ. *Cypriot Studies* (1 a year).

Cyprus Jewellers Museum: 7–9 Odos Praxippou, Laiki Geitonia, Nicosia; tel. 22667278; traditional Cypriot jewellery from end of 19th century to present.

Cyprus Museum (Cyprus Archaeological Museum): POB 22024, Nicosia; tel. 22865888; e-mail antiquitiesdept@da.mcw.gov.cy; internet www.mcw.gov.cy/da; f. 1882; pottery from the Neolithic and Chalcolithic periods to the Graeco-Roman Age; terracotta figures of the Neolithic Age to Graeco-Roman times, including the Ayia Irini group; limestone and marble sculpture from the Archaic to the Graeco-Roman Age; jewellery from the Neolithic period, especially Mycenaean (1400–1200 BC), to early Byzantine times, and coins from the 6th century BC to Roman times; misc. collns, incl. inscriptions (Cypro-Minoan, Phoenician, Cypro-syllabic, Latin, Greek), bronzes, glass, alabaster, bone, etc.; exhibitions of jewellery, seals, coins; reconstructed tombs; extensive reserve collns are available for students; Dir for Antiquities Dr DESPINA PILIDES (acting).

Cyprus Museum of Natural History: POB 12586, 2251 Nicosia; tel. 22585834; e-mail museum.info@ppgroup.com.cy; internet www.natmuseum.org.cy; f. 1996; more than 2,500 exhibits; Administrator THEODORA KORNIOTOU.

Ethnological Museum: 20 Patriarchou Grigoriou St, Nicosia; tel. 22305316; internet www.mcw.gov.cy; f. 1960; 18th-century mansion of dragoman Hadjigeorgakis Kornesios; collns incl. glassware, silverware, ceramics and furniture from the Byzantine, Medieval and Ottoman eras.

Kykkos Monastery Museum: POB 28183, 2091 Nicosia; tel. 22942736; e-mail mimk@cy.net; internet www.kykkos-museum.cy.net; early Christian and Byzantine icons, woodcarvings, embroidery, MSS, frescoes, books, vestments, etc.

Leventis Municipal Museum of Nicosia: 15–17 Ippokratous St, Laiki Geitonia, Nicosia; tel. 22661475; e-mail info@leventismuseum.org.cy; internet www.leventismuseum.org.cy; f. 1989; more than 10,000 exhibits, incl. maps, ceramics, embroidery and silver work; large photographic archive dating from the end of the 19th century to present; small library; Curator LOUKIA LOIZOU HADJIGAVRIEL.

Museum of the History of Cypriot Coinage: POB 21995, 1515 Nicosia; Bank of Cyprus Cultural Foundation, 86–90 Phaneromenis St, 1011 Nicosia; tel. 22128157; e-mail info@cultural.bankofcyprus.com; internet www.boccf.org; f. 1995; more than 500 coins dating from 6th century BC to present; Curator ELENI ZAPITI.

State Gallery of Contemporary Art: Gonia Leoforou Stasinou Ave & Kritis St, Nicosia; tel. 22458228; Cypriot art from the late 19th century to the present day.

Paphos

Paphos District Archaeological Museum: POB 60050, 8100 Paphos; 43 Grivas Dhigenis, Paphos; tel. 26306215; f. 1964; artefacts from Neolithic era to around 1700.

Universities

GREEK CYPRIOT UNIVERSITIES

CYPRUS UNIVERSITY OF TECHNOLOGY

POB 50329, Limassol
Telephone: 25002500
E-mail: administration@cut.edu.tr
Internet: www.cut.ac.cy

Founded 2004
public control
Academic year: September to July (4 semesters)

Faculties of fine and applied arts, engineering and technology, geotechnical sciences and environmental management, communication and media studies, health sciences, and management and economics; language centre; faculty of health sciences located in Nicosia

Pres.: DEMETRIOS KONTIDES
Vice-Pres.: PANICOS LEONIDOU
Dean: ELPIDA KERAVNOU PAPAILIOU
Vice-Rector for Academic Affairs: TULA ONOUFRIOU
Vice-Rector for Finance and Devt: ANDREAS ANAGIOTIS
Registrar: STELLA IOANNOU
Library Dir: MARIOS ZERVAS

DEANS

Faculty of Engineering and Technology: KRISTIS CHRYSOSTOM
Faculty of Geotechnical Sciences and Environmental Management: Prof. VASSILIS GEKAS
Faculty of Management and Economics: Prof. ANDREAS SAVVIDES

PROFESSORS

Faculty of Communication and Media Studies:
- ZOTOS, Y., Communication and Internet Studies

Faculty of Engineering and Technology:
- ANAYIOTOS, A., Mechanical Engineering and Materials Science and Engineering
- KASPARIS, T., Electrical Engineering, Computer Engineering and Informatics
- KELIRES, P., Mechanical Engineering and Materials Science and Engineering
- KERAVNOU PAPAILIOU, E., Electrical Engineering, Computer Engineering and Informatics
- ONOUFRIOU, T., Civil Engineering and Geomatics

Faculty of Geotechnical Sciences and Environmental Management:
- GEKAS, V., Agricultural Sciences, Biotechnology and Food Science
- IOANNOU, N., Agricultural Sciences, Biotechnology and Food Science
- KATSIOTIS, A., Agricultural Sciences, Biotechnology and Food Science
- VAROTSIS, C., Environmental Science and Technology

Faculty of Management and Economics:
- GIATRAKOS, Y., Hotel and Tourism Management
- KONTOGHIORGHES, E., Commerce, Finance and Shipping
- SAVVIDES, A., Commerce, Finance and Shipping
- THEODOSSIOU, P., Commerce, Finance and Shipping

EUROPEAN UNIVERSITY OF CYPRUS

POB 22006, Nicosia
6 Diogenes St, Engomi, 2404 Nicosia
Telephone: 22713000
E-mail: reg@euc.ac.cy
Internet: www.euc.ac.cy

Founded 1961 as Cyprus College; acquired university status 2007
Private control

Pres.: Dr ANDREAS ELEFTHERIADES
Vice-Pres.: Dr CHRISTOFOROS HADJIKYPRIANOU
Rector: Prof. ANDREAS G. ORPHANIDES
Vice-Rector: Prof. KOSTAS GOULIAMOS
Dir for Admin. and Human Resources: EVRIPIDES POLYCARPOU
Librarian: THEODOROS TZITZIMBOUROUNIS

Library of 75,000 vols
Number of students: 4,000

Publication: *Journal of Critical Studies; Cadences* (multilingual, multicommunal literary magazine)

DEANS

School of Arts and Education Sciences: Assoc. Prof. Dr ANDREAS MAKRIS
School of Business Administration: Dr ANDREAS HADJIS
School of Humanities and Social Sciences: Assoc. Prof. Dr NORA LIASSIS
School of Sciences: Prof. Dr NICOS TEREZOPOULOS

PROFESSORS

School of Arts and Education Sciences:
- KOLIADES, E., Educational Psychology and Special Education
- PAPOULIA, P., Greek Language Instruction
- PYRGIOTAKIS, I., Education Sciences

School of Business Administration:
- ELEFTHERIADES, A., Marketing/Management
- GOULIAMOS, K., Marketing and Public Relations

School of Humanities and Social Sciences:
- FARSEDAKIS, I., Criminology
- ORPHANIDES, A., Social Sciences

School of Sciences:
- APOSTOLIDOU, S., Nursing
- KOTZAMBASSAKI, S., Nursing
- POULIS, A., Physiotherapy
- POULIS, S., Physiotherapy
- TEREZOPOULOS, N., Natural Sciences
- VASSILIADOU, A., Nursing

FREDERICK UNIVERSITY

POB 24729, 1303 Nicosia
7 Y. Frederickou St, Pallouriotissa, 1036 Nicosia
Telephone: 22431355
E-mail: info@frederick.ac.cy
Internet: www.frederick.ac.cy

Founded 1965 as the Nicosia Technical and Economics School; became Frederick Institute of Technology 1975; acquired univ. status 2007
Private control

Comprises Frederick Institute of Technology (see under Colleges) and the following six schools: architecture, fine and applied arts; education; engineering and applied sciences; economic sciences and administration; health sciences; and humanities and social sciences; campus in Limassol

Pres.: MICHAEL FREDERICKOU
Rector: Dr DIMITRIOS TOMBAIDES (acting)
Librarian: DAPHNOS ECONOMOU

NEAPOLIS UNIVERSITY PAPHOS

2 Danais Ave, 8042 Paphos
Telephone: 26843300
E-mail: info@nup.ac.cy
Internet: www.nup.ac.cy

Founded 2007
Private control

Undergraduate programmes cover: architecture, assessment and property development, business administration, banking, accounting and finance, law and psychology

Rector: Prof. ELIAS DINENIS

OPEN UNIVERSITY OF CYPRUS

POB 12794, 2252 Nicosia
Telephone: 22411600
E-mail: info@ouc.ac.cy
Internet: www.ouc.ac.cy

Founded 2003
public control
Languages of instruction: Greek, English
Academic year: September to June

Faculties of humanities and social sciences, pure and applied sciences, and economics and management

Chair.: Prof. COSTAS CHRISTOU
Vice-Chair.: YIANNIS IOANNOU
Vice-Chair.: COSTAS PROCOPIOU
Dir for Admin. and Finance: Prof. CHRISTOPHER CHRISTODOULIDES
Librarian: PANAGIOTIS THEMISTOCLEOUS

Library of 7,400 vols, 102 int. databases
Number of teachers: 155

Number of students: 3,574

UCLAN CYPRUS (UNIVERSITY OF CENTRAL LANCASHIRE, CYPRUS)

12–14 University Ave, Pyla, 7080 Larnaca
Telephone: 24812121
E-mail: admissions@uclancyprus.ac.cy
Internet: www.uclancyprus.ac.cy
Founded 2012
Private control
Language of instruction: English
Offers joint UK and Cypriot Bachelors and Masters degree programmes
Rector: Dr LEE CHATFIELD
Financial Controller: CHRISTOS ELEFTHERIOU
Head of Admissions: CHRISTOS CHRISTOU
Library/IT Man.: ANNETTE CHRYSOSTOMOU

DEANS

School of Business and Management: Prof. PANIKOS POUTZIOURIS
School of Law: Dr TIM POTIER#

UNIVERSITY OF CYPRUS

Univ. House 'Anastasios G. Leventis', POB 20537, 1678 Nicosia
Telephone: 22894000
E-mail: info@ucy.ac.cy
Internet: www.ucy.ac.cy
Founded 1989
State control
Languages of instruction: Greek, Turkish
Academic year: September to June
Rector: Prof. CONSTANTINOS CHRISTOFIDES
Vice-Rector for Academic Affairs: Prof. ATHANASIOS GAGATSIS
Vice-Rector for Int. Affairs, Finance and Admin.: Prof. MARIOS MAVRONICOLAS
Dir for Library: PHILIPPOS TSIMPOGLOU
Library of 324,000 vols, 192,000 ebooks, 30,000 ejournals
Number of teachers: 302
Number of students: 7,051

DEANS

Faculty of Economics and Management: Prof. HARIDIMOS TSOUKAS
Faculty of Engineering: Prof. PANOS PAPANASTASIOU
Faculty of Humanities: NIYAZI KIZILYÜREK
Faculty of Letters: Prof. MICHALIS PIERIS
Faculty of Pure and Applied Sciences: Prof. GEORGE PAPADOPOULOS
Faculty of Social Sciences and Education: Prof. STELIOS N. GEORGIOU

PROFESSORS

Faculty of Economics and Management:
- CHARITOU, A., Accounting and Finance
- HADJINICOLAS, G., Public and Business Administration
- LEONIDOU, L. C., Public and Business Administration
- MAMUNEAS, T., Economics
- MICHAEL, M. S., Economics
- MICHAELIDES, A., Accounting and Finance
- NISHIOTIS, G., Accounting and Finance
- PASHARDES, P., Economics
- PISSARIDES, C., Economics
- SOTERIOU, A., Public and Business Administration
- TRIGEORGIS, L., Accounting and Finance
- TSOUKAS, H., Public and Business Administration
- VAFEAS, N., Accounting and Finance
- VLADIMIROS, H., Public and Business Administration
- ZENIOS, S., Accounting and Finance

Faculty of Engineering:
- ALEXANDROU, A., Mechanical and Manufacturing Engineering
- CHARALAMBOUS, C., Electrical and Computer Engineering
- DOUMANIDIS, C., Mechanical and Manufacturing Engineering
- GIAPINTZAKIS, I., Mechanical and Manufacturing Engineering
- HADJICOSTIS, C., Electrical and Computer Engineering
- PANTAZOPOULOU, S., Civil and Environmental Engineering
- PETROU, M., Civil and Environmental Engineering
- POLYCARPOU, M., Electrical and Computer Engineering

Faculty of Humanities:
- IOANNOU, Y., French Studies and Modern Languages
- KIZILYÜREK, N., Turkish and Middle Eastern Studies
- PAPAPAVLOU, A., English Studies
- STEPHANIDES, S., English Studies
- STROHMEIER, M., Turkish and Middle Eastern Studies
- THEOCHARIDES, I., Turkish and Middle Eastern Studies

Faculty of Letters:
- AGAPITOS, P., Byzantine and Modern Greek Studies
- IACOVOU, M., History and Archaeology
- KASSIANIDOU, V., History and Archaeology
- MICHAELIDES, D., History and Archaeology
- PANAYOTOU–TRIANTAPHYLLOPOULOU, A., Classics and Philosophy
- PIERIS, M., Byzantine and Modern Greek Studies
- SCHABEL, C., History and Archaeology
- VOUTOURIS, P., Byzantine and Modern Greek Studies

Faculty of Pure and Applied Sciences:
- ALLEXANDROU, C., Physics
- CHRISTOFIDES, C., Physics
- CHRISTOFIDES, T., Mathematics and Statistics
- CONSTANTINOU, A., Biological Sciences
- DAMIANOU, P., Mathematics and Statistics
- DELTAS, C., Biological Sciences
- EFSTATHIOU, A. M., Chemistry
- FOKIANOS, K., Mathematics and Statistics
- GEORGIOU, G., Mathematics and Statistics
- KARAGEORGHIS, A., Mathematics and Statistics
- KOSTRIKIS, L., Biological Sciences
- KOUMANDOS, S., Mathematics and Statistics
- KYRIAZIS, G., Mathematics and Statistics
- LEONTIDIS, E., Chemistry
- OTHONOS, A., Physics
- PANAGOPOULOS, H., Physics
- PAPARODITIS, E., Mathematics and Statistics
- PATRICKIOS, C. S., Chemistry
- RAZIS, P., Physics
- SAPATINAS, T., Mathematics and Statistics
- SMYRLIS, Y-S., Mathematics and Statistics
- SOPHOCLEOUS, C., Mathematics and Statistics
- STYLIANOPOULOS, N., Mathematics and Statistics
- THEOCHARIS, C. R., Chemistry
- TSERTOS, H., Physics
- VIDRAS, A., Mathematics and Statistics

Faculty of Social Sciences and Education:
- CHRISTOU, C., Education
- CONSTANTINIDOU, F., Psychology
- CONSTANTINOU, C., Education
- CONSTANTINOU, C. M., Social and Political Sciences
- DEMETRIOU, K., Social and Political Sciences
- GAGATSIS, A., Education
- GEORGIOU, S., Psychology
- IOANNIDES KOUTSELINI, M., Education
- JOSEPH, J. S., Social and Political Sciences
- KAPARDIS, A., Law
- KATSIKIDES, S., Social and Political Sciences
- RAFTOPOULOS, A., Psychology

Medical School:
- ADAM, A.
- ZACHARIOU, Z.
- ZERRIS, V. A.

UNIVERSITY OF NICOSIA

POB 24005, Nicosia
46 Makedonitissas Ave, 1700 Nicosia
Telephone: 22841500
E-mail: info@unic.ac.cy
Internet: www.unic.ac.cy
Founded 1980 as Intercollege; univ. status 2007
Private control
Schools of business, education, sciences, and humanities, social sciences and law
Pres.: Dr NICOS PERISTIANIS
Exec. Vice-Pres. for Admin.: Dr EMILIOS SOLOMOU
Vice-Pres. for Enrolment Management: Dr PAVLOS PAVLOU
Vice-Pres. for Finance: GEORGE SOLEAS
Rector: Dr MICHALIS ATTALIDES
Sr Vice-Rector: Dr ANDREAS POLEMITIS
Vice-Rector and Dir for Academic Affairs: Dr PHILIPPOS POUYIOUTAS
Registrar: SKEVI IOANNOU
Dir for Communications: JOHN MAVRIS
Dir for Library: KOULLA PERISTIANI
Head of Student Affairs: MYRIA THRASSOU
Number of students: 4,000 in Nicosia, 1,000 on Limassol and Larnaca campuses
Publication: *Cyprus Review* (2 a year)

TURKISH CYPRIOT UNIVERSITIES

The international community, including the UN and EU, does not recognize the TRNC as a separate self-governing country. The Republic of Cyprus is recognized as having *de jure* sovereignty over the whole island. The Greek Cypriot Government, which legally remains the competent authority for all of Cyprus, does not recognize or accredit Turkish Cypriot higher education institutions.

CYPRUS INTERNATIONAL UNIVERSITY

Haspolat, Lefkoşa, TRNC, via Mersin 10, Turkey
Telephone: 26711111
E-mail: info@ciu.edu.tr
Internet: www.ciu.edu.tr
Founded 1997
Private control
Accredited by the Higher Education Council of Turkey (YÖK)
Language of instruction: English
Academic year: September to June
Pres.: Prof. Dr MEHMET ALI YÜKSELEN
Vice-Pres.: Prof. Dr NÜKET SARACEL

Gen. Sec.: Asst Prof. Dr MURAT TÜZÜNKAN
Dir for Admissions: ÖZGÜR YILMBAŞAR
Dir for Campus: MEHMET ÇOBANOĞLU
Dir for Library: GÜLTEN LAYSALA
Dir for Student Devt and Counselling Centre: ERINÇ AYDINOVA

DEANS

Faculty of Agriculture: Prof. Dr AHMET AKER
Faculty of Arts and Sciences: Prof. Dr METIN KARADAĞ
Faculty of Communication: Prof. Dr HIKMET SEÇIM
Faculty of Economics and Administrative Sciences: Prof. Dr NÜKET SARACEL
Faculty of Education: Prof. Dr OĞUZ KARAKARTAL
Faculty of Engineering: Prof. Dr A. TÜLAY TULUN
Faculty of Fine Arts: Prof. Dr ATILLA YÜCEL
Faculty of Health Services: Prof. Dr ZEHRA GÜNAY SARIYAR
Faculty of Law: Prof. Dr PERVIN SOMER
Faculty of Pharmacy: Prof. Dr TURAY YARDIMCI

PROFESSORS

Faculty of Agriculture:

AKER, A.

Faculty of Arts and Sciences:

KARADAĞ, M.
KARAKAŞ, S.
KÜÇÜK, S.
ÖZÜNLÜ, U.
RÜSTEMLI, A.

Faculty of Communication:

SEÇIM, H.

Faculty of Economics and Administrative Sciences:

SARACEL, N.

Faculty of Education:

ANKAY, A.
DEĞIRMENCIOĞLU, C.
DEMIREL, O.
ERIPEK, S.
GÜRKAN, T.
IŞMAN, A.
KARAKARTAL, O.
KÖMLEKSIZ, M.
ÖNDER, A.
SARP, N.
SÖNMEZ, V.

Faculty of Engineering:

AKGIRAY, O.
ÇELIK, T.
TAYANÇ, M.
TULUN, T.
YÜKSELEN, M.

Faculty of Fine Arts:

AYIRAN, N.
YÜCEL, A.

Faculty of Law:

ÖZCAN, M.
SOMER, P.
SONSUZOĞLU, P.

Faculty of Pharmacy:

ÖZDEMIR, O.
SARIYAR, Z.
SUMNU, M.
YARDIMCI, T.

DIRECTORS

Institute of Graduate Studies and Research: Prof. Dr HIKMET SEÇIM
School of Applied Sciences: Asst Prof. Dr SALIH KARANFIL
School of Foreign Languages: Assoc. Prof. Dr MEHMET ALI YAVUZ
School of Justice: Asst Prof. Dr SALIH ÖNDER YEŞILTEPE
School of Tourism and Hotel Management: Asst Prof. Dr ALI ÖZTÜREN
Vocational High School of Health Services: Prof. Dr ZEHRA GÜNAY SARIYAR
Vocational School: Asst Prof. Dr MEHMEDALI EGEMEN

EASTERN MEDITERRANEAN UNIVERSITY

POB 95, Gazi Mağusa, TRNC, via Mersin 10, Turkey
Telephone: 23654444
E-mail: info@emu.edu.tr
Internet: www.emu.edu.tr

Founded 1979 as Higher Technological Institute; univ. status 1986
State control
Language of instruction: English
Academic year: September to June (2 semesters)

Accredited by the Higher Education Council of Turkey

Rector: Prof. Dr ABDULLAH Y. ÖZTOPRAK
Vice-Rector for Academic Affairs: Prof. Dr OSMAN YILMAZ
Vice-Rector for Int. and Admin. Affairs: Prof. Dr MAJID HASHEMIPOUR
Vice-Rector for Promotion and Devt: Prof. Dr HALIL NADIRI
Vice-Rector for Student Affairs and Information: Assoc. Prof. Dr MUSTAFA K. UYGUROĞLU
Vice-Rector for Student Services and Social-Cultural Affairs: Prof. Dr ULKER VANCI OSAM
Gen. Sec.: GÜROL ÖZKAYA
Registrar: HÜSEYIN ÜNSAL YETİNER
Librarian: OSMAN SOYKAN

Library of 150,000 vols, 600 periodical subscriptions and 25 electronic networks
Number of teachers: 641 full-time, 141 part-time
Number of students: 14,256
Publications: *EMU Tourism Research Journal* (in English), *Journal of Cyprus Studies* (in English), *Review of Social, Economic and Business Studies* (in English), *Woman 2000* (in English)

DEANS

Faculty of Architecture: Prof. Dr ŞEBNEM ÖNAL HOŞKARA
Faculty of Arts and Sciences: Prof. Dr REZA BASHIROV
Faculty of Business and Economics: Prof. Dr CEM TANOVA
Faculty of Communication and Media Studies: Prof. Dr SÜLEYMAN İRVAN
Faculty of Education: Prof. Dr HALIL İBRAHIM YALIN
Faculty of Engineering: Prof. Dr HASAN AMCA
Faculty of Health Sciences: Prof. Dr HÜLYA HARUTOĞLU
Faculty of Law: Prof. Dr METIN GÜRKANLAR
Faculty of Medicine: Prof. Dr NAHIDE GÖKÇORA
Faculty of Pharmacy: Prof. Dr İLKAY ERDOĞAN ORHAN
Faculty of Tourism: Prof. Dr MEHMET ALTINAY

EUROPEAN UNIVERSITY OF LEFKE

Gemıkonağı, Lefke, TRNC, via Mersin 10, Turkey
Telephone: 26602000
E-mail: webmaster@eul.edu.tr
Internet: www.lefke.edu.tr

Founded 1990 by Cyprus Science Foundation; accredited by Higher Education Ccl of Turkey
State control
Languages of instruction: English, Turkish
Academic year: October to June

Rector: Prof. Dr AHMET BÜLEND GÖKSEL
Vice-Rector for Accreditation and Academic Affairs: Assoc. Prof. Dr AKIN CELLATOĞLU
Gen. Sec.: MEHMET YALÇIN
Registrar: HÜSEYIN ESER
Library Man.: ALEV LORT

Library of 30,000 vols, 70 periodicals
Number of teachers: 120
Number of students: 4,500
Publication: *Laü'nün Sesi Journal* (6 a year)

DEANS

Faculty of Agricultural Sciences and Technologies: Prof. Dr KAZIM ABAK
Faculty of Architecture and Engineering: Prof. Dr K. BALASUBRAMANIAN
Faculty of Arts and Sciences: Prof. Dr GÜNAY KARAAĞAÇ
Faculty of Communication Sciences: Prof. Dr FARUK KALKAN
Faculty of Economics and Administrative Sciences: Prof. Dr AHMET ŞINASI AKSOY (acting)
Faculty of Education: Prof. Dr ÜLKÜ KÖYMEN
Faculty of Health Sciences: Prof. Dr NILGÜN SARP

PROFESSORS

Faculty of Agricultural Sciences and Technologies:

DERICI, R., Horticultural Production and Marketing, and Agribusiness Management
SÖZEN, N., Horticultural Production and Marketing, Agribusiness Management, and Landscape Architecture
TÜRKMAN, A., Agribusiness Management
TUZCU, O., Horticultural Production and Marketing

Faculty of Architecture and Engineering:

DEMIRKAN, M., Interior Architecture
KHASHMAN, A., Electrical and Electronic Engineering, and Electronics and Communication Engineering
OĞUZ, H., Computer Engineering and Software Engineering
ÖZDENIZ, M., Architecture
TÜRKMAN, F., Civil Engineering

Faculty of Economics and Administrative Sciences:

ŞAYLAN, G., Public Administration

Faculty of Education:

SARP, N., Pre-school Teaching

Faculty of Health Sciences:

ŞEYLAN, G., Social Work
TABAK, R., Health Management, and Nutrition and Dietetics

Faculty of Law:

DEMIR, F.
ERTAŞ, S.
GÜNUĞUR, H.

DIRECTORS

English Preparatory School: FIGEN ARKIN
Institute of Science and Humanities: Dr MEHMET HASGÜLER
School of Applied Sciences: Asst Prof. Dr UMUT ARIK
School of Tourism Management and Information Services: Prof. Dr AYŞEN TÜRKMAN

GIRNE AMERICAN UNIVERSITY

University Dr., Girne, TRNC, via Mersin 10, Turkey
Telephone: 26502000
E-mail: info@gau.edu.tr
Internet: www.gau.edu.tr

Founded 1985
Private control

Overseas campus in Canterbury, UK
Chancellor: SERHAT AKPINAR
Vice-Chancellor: ASIM VEHBI
Rector: Prof. Dr YILDIRIM ÖNER
Vice-Rector for Academic Affairs: SADIK ULKER
Library of 25,000 50 periodical/journal subscriptions, 2m. e-books, 13,000 ejournals
Number of teachers: 300
Number of students: 7,700
Publication: *GAU Journal of Social and Applied Science*

DEANS

Faculty of Architecture, Design and Fine Arts: Asst Prof. Dr HOSSAIN SADRI (acting)
Faculty of Business and Economics: Prof. Dr ISMAIL SILA (acting)
Faculty of Communication: Prof. Dr ALPAY ATAOL
Faculty of Education: Prof. Dr TANJU GÜRKAN
Faculty of Engineering: Assoc. Prof. Dr ZAFER AĞDELEN
Faculty of Humanities: Prof. Dr NESRIN KALE
Faculty of Law: Prof. Dr SELÇUK DEMIRBULAK

PROFESSORS

Faculty of Architecture, Design and Fine Arts:
AYAN, M.
Faculty of Business and Economics:
KOSTIN, A., Management Information Systems
ÖNER, Y., Management and Organizations
TURGAY, T., Strategic Management
Faculty of Communication:
AYDIN, E.
Faculty of Engineering:
ABIYEV, A., Electrical-Electronics Engineering
ZEKI, A., Electrical-Electronics Engineering

MIDDLE EAST TECHNICAL UNIVERSITY, NORTH CYPRUS CAMPUS

Kalkanlı, Güzelyurt, TRNC, via Mersin 10, Turkey
Telephone: 26612000
E-mail: ncc@metu.edu.tr
Internet: www.ncc.metu.edu.tr
Founded 2000
Private control
Language of instruction: English
Offers a range of undergraduate and graduate programmes covering business administration, computer education, economics, engineering, political science and international relations, and psychology
Pres.: Prof. Dr TURGUT TÜMER
Vice-Pres.: Prof. Dr EROL TAYMAZ
Sec.-Gen: LEVENT KÜPELI
Dir for Admin. Affairs: ECEVIT MERT
Dir for Construction and Technical Services: TOLGA TOGAN TORUN
Dir for Financial Affairs: SERVET SADIK HIRKA
Dir for Human Resources: AYSEL ARIFOGLU GUNSEL
Dir for Information and Communication Technologies: DORUK NEZIR
Dir for Institutional Relations and Communication: HABIBE MUHTAROĞLU
Dir for Library and Documentation: ZUHAL TOPALOĞLU
Dir for Social and Cultural Affairs: NAZILE KÜPELI
Dir for Sports and Recreation: METIN GEZGIN (acting)
Dir for Student Affairs and Registrar: ÖZCAN KASAL (acting)
Library of 25,000 vols, 54,700 ejournals and 90,800 ebooks through 145 online databases
Number of teachers: 130
Number of students: 1,850

NEAR EAST UNIVERSITY (Yakın Doğu Üniversitesi—YDÜ)

Near East Blvd, Nicosia, TRNC, via Mersin 10, Turkey
Telephone: (392) 6802000
E-mail: info@neu.edu.tr
Internet: www.neu.edu.tr
Founded 1988
Private control
Founding Rector: Dr SUAT İ. GÜNSEL
Rector: Prof. Dr ÜMIT HASSAN
Vice-Rector: Prof. Dr FAHREDDIN M. SADIKOĞLU
Vice-Rector: Prof. Dr ŞENOL BEKTAŞ
Vice-Rector: Prof. Dr HÜSEYIN GÖKÇEKUŞ
Vice-Rector: Prof. Dr JOUNI SUISTOLA
Dir for Public Relations: Dr ERDOĞAN SARACOĞLU
Dir for Foreign Students' Affairs: OKAN DONANGIL
Registrar: ÜMIT SERDAROĞLU
Gen. Sec.: Dr YETER TABUR
Dir for Grand Library: TÜMER GARIP
Library of 500,000 vols, 50,000 ejournals and 6,500 DVDs
Number of students: 20,000

DEANS

Faculty of Architecture: Prof. HARUN ÖZER
Faculty of Arts and Sciences: Prof. Dr İLKAY SALIHOĞLU
Faculty of Communication: Prof. Dr ORHAN ÇIFTÇI
Faculty of Dentistry: Prof. Dr MUTAHHAR ULUSOY
Faculty of Divinity: Asst Prof. Dr YUSUF SUIÇMEZ
Faculty of Economics and Administrative Sciences: Prof. Dr AYKUT POLATOĞLU
Faculty of Education: Prof. Dr İ. KAYA ÖZKIN
Faculty of Engineering: Prof. Dr FAHREDDIN M. SADIKOĞLU
Faculty of Health Sciences: Prof. Dr SEVINÇ YÜCECAN
Faculty of Law: Prof. Dr YILDIRIM ULER
Faculty of Maritime Studies: Prof. Dr MUSTAFA ALTUNÇ
Faculty of Medicine: Prof. Dr GAMZE MOCAN KUZEY
Faculty of Performing Arts: Prof. Dr BOZKURT KURUÇ
Faculty of Pharmacy: Prof. Dr RÜMEYSA DEMIRDAMAR
Faculty of Veterinary Medicine: Prof. Dr ÖMER MEMDUH ESENDAL

PROFESSORS

Faculty of Arts and Science:
DERZINEVESI, H.
KORMUSHIN, I.
ÖZKIN, I.
Faculty of Communication:
ABISEL, N., Public Relations and Publicity
CIGDEM, A.
DEMIRALP, Ü., Journalism
HUDAOGLU, G., Journalism
KOKER, E.
KOKER, L.
OZBEK BOSTANCIOĞLU, M.
Faculty of Dentistry:
BERBEROGLU, A., Periodontology
CETINER, S., Paediatric Dentistry
ORHAN, K., Oral and Maxillofacial Radiology
SOLAK, H., Restorative Odontotherapy
TÜZÜM, S., Oral and Maxillofacial Diseases and Surgery
ULUSOY, M., Prosthetic Dentistry and Orthodontics
ULUSOY, N., Restorative Dentistry and Endodontics
Faculty of Divinity:
AKYÜZ, A., Hadith
ALTUNDAĞ, M., Interpretation
ATAR, F., Law of Islam
AYBAKAN, B., Law of Islam
BÜYÜKKARA, M., History of Islam Creeds
ÇELEBI, İ., Kelâm (Verse)
ÇIÇEK, Y., Interpretation
DEMIRCI, M., Interpretation
ERDOĞAN, M., Law of Islam
HARMAN, Ö., History of Religions
KÖSE, A., Religious Psychology
ÜSTÜN, İ., History of Islam
YÜCEL, A., Hadith
YURDAGUR, M., Kelâm (Verse)
Faculty of Economics and Administrative Sciences:
ARUOBA, Ç.
HASSAN, Ü.
SUISTOLA, J.
Faculty of Education (Ataturk Faculty of Education):
BASKAN, G.
BIROL, C., Pre-school Teaching
DERZINEVESI, H.
ERDOGDU, M.
ILHAN, A.
KESER, H.
KOKER, L.
UZUNBOYLU, H., Computer and Instructional Technologies
Faculty of Engineering:
ABIYEV, R., Computer Engineering
AKAY, D., Biomedical Engineering
AMIRCANOV, A.
ATUN, A.
BEKTAS, S.
DINCER, S.
GOKCEKUS, H., Civil Engineering
IKHDAIR, S.
KHASHMAN, A.
SAVAS, M.
Faculty of Fine Arts and Design:
AYKÜZ, U.
ATALAY, C., Plastic Arts
EMRALI, R., Plastic Arts and Graphic Design
SÖNMEZ, N., Plastic Arts and Graphic Design
Faculty of Health Sciences:
YURTTAGÜL, M.
Faculty of Law:
ARUOBA, Ç., International Law
AYBAY, R., International Law
CAN, C., Sociology of Law and Jurisprudence
DERZINEVESI, H., Documentation and Terminology of Ottoman Law
ERDEM, M., International Criminal Law and International Law
ERTAŞ, Ş., Private Law, Law of Succession and Law of Obligations
GÜREL, Ş.
HASSAN, Ü., Law History and General Public Law
HAVATÇU, A., Civil Law
KARAMUSTAFAOĞLU, T., Constitutional Law
KARAN, H., Trade Law
KOÇ, N., Civil Law and Law of Obligations
KOCAMAN, A., Civil Law and Law of Obligations
KOCAMAN, B., Public Finance
KÖKER, E.
KÖKER, L., General Public Law
KUMRULU, A., Tax Law

ÖZKAN, I., Private International Law and European Community Law
PAZARCI, H., International Law
SAĞLAM, F., Constitutional Law and Human Rights
SANCAR, M., Public Law
ŞEKER, M., Philosophy of Law and Sociology of Law
SOYER, P., Business Law and Social Security Law
TAHIROĞLU, B., Roman Law
TEZCAN, D., International Law and Law of Criminal Procedures
TURANBOY, A., Trade Law
ULER, Y., Administrative Law

Faculty of Maritime Studies:

SALIHOGLU, I.

Faculty of Medicine:

ÇELEBI, L.
ÇETIN, A.
ILGI, S.
ÖZER, N.
SERAKINCI, N., Medical Biology and Genetics
TARHAN, E.

Faculty of Performing Arts:

DERZINEVESI, H., Turkish Language and Literature, and Folk Sciences Studies
GULIYEV, C., Acting
TUNCAY, M., Acting and Drama Writing

Faculty of Pharmacy:

ÇALIŞ, I., Pharmacognosy
ERDOĞAN, H., Pharmaceutical Chemistry
MEHMETÇIK, G., Biochemistry
ONUR, R., Pharmacology
ÖZKUM, D.
SAYGI, S., Toxicology

Faculty of Veterinary Medicine:

AKAN, M.
ALTUNAY, H.
ALTUNTAŞ, A.
DAĞALP, S.
EMRE, M.
ERGÜM, A.
HAZIROĞLU, M.
İZGÜR, M.
KÜPLÜLÜ, Ö.
ÖZCAN, Z.
PIŞKIN, İ.
SALMANOĞLU, B.
SEL, T.
ŞIRELI, U.
SULU, N.
UYSAL, H.
YALÇIN, S.
YARDIMCI, H.
YILDIZ, G.

DIRECTORS

Graduate School of Health Sciences: Prof. Dr İHSAN ÇALIŞ
Graduate School of Social Sciences: Prof. Dr A. AYKUT POLATOĞLU

Colleges

Americanos College: POB 22425, 1521 Nicosia; 2–3 Omirou Ave, Nicosia; tel. 22661122; e-mail college@ac.ac.cy; internet www.ac.ac.cy; f. 1975; Dir Dr MARIOS AMERICANOS; Dir for Admissions Dr ADONIS AMERICANOS; Dir for Student Affairs ANDRI VIOLANDI; Librarian ANTHI AMERICANOS.

CDA College: POB 21972, 1515 Nicosia; 2 Evagorou Ave, Eleftherias Sq., Nicosia; tel. 22661104; e-mail cdaadm@spidernet.com.cy; internet www.cdacollege.ac.cy; f. 1976; Private control; Bachelors degrees in business administration and in travel and tourism management; programmes in information and communication technology, interior design, beauty therapy, travel and tourism administration, office administration, executive secretarial studies and secretarial studies; brs in Limassol and Larnaca; 800 students; Prin. D. A. CHRISTOFOROU.

College of Tourism and Hotel Management: POB 20281, 2150 Nicosia; Larnaca Rd, Aglangia, Nicosia; tel. 22462846; e-mail info@cothm.ac.cy; internet www.cothm.ac.cy; f. 1987; Diploma, Bachelors, Masters and Postgraduate Diploma programmes; library: 10,000 vols; Pres. ANTONIS CHARALAMBIDES; Dir SAVVAS ADAMIDES; Registrar ANDROULA KOTSONI; Librarian ANNA DARBINIAN.

CTL Eurocollege: POB 51938, 3509 Limassol; 118 Spyros Kyprianou Ave, 3077 Limassol; tel. 25736501; e-mail college@ctleuro.ac.cy; internet www.ctleuro.ac.cy; f. 1991; Bachelors degree, Masters degree and Diploma programmes in business, office administration, computing, hospitality and tourism, law.

Cyprus College: POB 22006, 1516 Nicosia; 6 Diogenous St, Engomi, Nicosia; tel. 22713000; e-mail reg@cycollege.ac.cy; internet www.cycollege.ac.cy; f. 1961; 2-year assoc. degree courses, 3- and 4-year Bachelors degree courses in social sciences, business administration, computer science, MBA programme; 2 campuses: Nicosia and Limassol; library: 35,000 vols; 51 teachers; 3,500 students; Dir NICOS ANASTASIOU; Head Librarian THEODOROS TZITZIMBOUROUNIS; publ. *Journal of Business and Society*.

Cyprus College of Art: 6 Eleftherias St, Lempa, 8260 Paphos; tel. 25341387; e-mail enquiries@artcyprus.org; internet www.artcyprus.org; f. 1969; one-year foundation courses in art and design; undergraduate degree programmes in asscn with partner orgs in the United Kingdom; postgraduate courses in fine art; br/studio location in Larnaca; opened the Cornaro Institute in Larnaca in 2010; 8 teachers; 40 students; Prin. Dr STASS PARASKOS; Dir Dr MICHAEL PARASKOS.

Cyprus International Institute of Management: POB 20378, 2151 Nicosia; 21 Akademias Ave, Aglandjia, 2107 Nicosia; tel. 22462246; e-mail ciim@ciim.ac.cy; internet www.ciim.ac.cy; f. 1990; accredited by Cyprus Council of Educational Evaluation–Accreditation (CEEA); 1-year full-time and 2-year part-time courses leading to MBA and MPSM degrees and Advanced Diploma; MSc in management, finance and banking, and human resource management and organizational behaviour; executive programmes; campus in Limassol; library: 5,000 vols; Dir Dr THEODORE PANAYOTOU; Dir for Admissions THEODORA PETASI; Registrar MARIA IOANNOU.

Frederick Institute of Technology: 7 Y. Frederickou St, Pallouriotisa, 1036 Nicosia; tel. 22431355; e-mail info@fit.ac.cy; internet www.fit.ac.cy; f. 1965; campus in Limassol; diploma programmes in business, secretarial studies, audiovisual communication, computer studies, design, nursery education, and aesthetics and beauty care; Masters degree in business administration and BA degree in audiovisual communication.

Global College: 245 Eleonon St, Strovolos, 2048 Nicosia; tel. 22814555; e-mail gic@cytanet.com.cy; internet www.globalcollege.ac.cy; f. 1972; secretarial studies, engineering, business administration, hospitality management, computer studies and security management; Gen. Dir GEORGE KRITICOS.

Intercollege (International College): 46 Makedonitissas Ave, POB 24005, 1700 Nicosia; tel. 22841500; e-mail info@intercollege.ac.cy; internet www.intercollege.ac.cy; f. 1980; affiliated to the Univ. of Nicosia; instruction in English and Greek; undergraduate and postgraduate courses lead to qualifying examinations for local, British and US degrees and diplomas; also campuses at Limassol and Larnaca; library: 70,000 vols; 203 teachers (112 full-time, 91 part-time); 5,000 students (incl. 613 at Limassol and 566 at Larnaca); Rector Dr VAN COUFOUDAKIS; Exec. Dir Dr STYLIANOS MAVROMOUSTAKOS; publ. *Cyprus Review* (2 a year).

KES College: 5 Kallipolis Ave, 1055 Nicosia; tel. 22875737; e-mail info@kes.ac.cy; internet www.kes.ac.cy; f. 1971; programmes in office admin. and secretarial studies, journalism and public relations, computer studies, business studies, travel and tourism management, hotel management, food preparation and culinary arts, beauty therapy and medical representatives courses; Dir THEO P. STYLIANOU.

PA College: Larnaca; tel. 24021555; e-mail information@pacollege.ac.cy; internet www.pacollege.ac.cy; f. 1983; BA degrees in business administration, banking and accounting; BSc in business computing; library: 5,578 vols, 428 journals, 4,000 e-journals; Dir Dr ANDREAS Z. PATSALIDES; publ. *Cyprus International Journal of Management* (2 a year).

Philips College: POB 28008, Strovolos, 2090 Nicosia; 4–6 Lamias St, 2001 Nicosia; tel. 22441860; e-mail info@philips.ac.cy; internet www.thephilipscollege.com; f. 1978; accounting and finance, business studies, economics and management, telecommunications, languages, journalism, computing and information systems, public relations, law and social studies; Prin. Prof. PHILIPPOS CONSTANTINOU; Rector Prof. DEMETRIOS NATSOPOULOS; Registrar EVI PAPACHRISTOFOROU; Librarian MARIOS SOCRATOUS.

REA College: POB 50625, 3608 Limassol; 2 Pasikratous St, 3085 Nicosia; tel. 25381095; e-mail info@reacollege.ac.cy; f. 1986; BSc degrees in aesthetics, dietetics, nutrition.

Susini College: POB 51147, 3502 Limassol; 10 Tagmatarchou Pouliou St, 3020 Limassol; tel. 25366196; e-mail susini@spidernet.com.cy; internet www.susini.ac.cy; f. 1982; aesthetics and beauty therapy; br. in Nicosia; Dir for Studies PHANIE ANTONIADOU-POUPOUTSI.

Vladimiros Kafkarides School of Drama: Nicosia; tel. 2421609; Dir DEMETRIOS LAZARIDES.

Schools of Art and Music

Arte Music Academy: POB 21207, 1504 Nicosia; 34–36 Leonidou, 1097 Nicosia; tel. 22676823; e-mail academy@artemusic.org; internet www.artemusic.org; f. 2002; Bachelors degree in music; Dir PITSA SPYRIDAKI; Artistic Dir MARTINO TIRIMO; Academic Registrar KLERI AGGELIDOU; Librarian ANTRI SPYRIDAKI.

Cyprus Academy of Music: 75A Agiou Andreou Ave, 1040 Nicosia; tel. 22432665; f. 1956; offers 10-year Professional Diploma of Musical Arts.

CZECH REPUBLIC

The Higher Education System

Higher education institutions predate the foundation of the former Czechoslovakia in 1918, with the oldest being Univerzita Karlova, which was founded in 1348. In 1990, following the removal of the communist Government, which had been in power since 1948, Czechoslovakia was replaced by the Czech and Slovak Federative Republic (CzSFR). In turn, the CzSFR was dissolved in 1993 and the Czech Republic and Slovakia became independent, sovereign states. Higher education reforms in both states were initiated under Act 172, passed in 1990; the Higher Education Act of 1998 (amended 2001 and 2006) and a new education law (implemented in 2005) have also come into force. During the first decade of the 21st century the number of students at private higher education institutions in the Czech Republic has increased almost 30-fold. In 2009/10 some 389,231 students attended 73 higher education institutions (around two-thirds of which were in the private sector); in 2010/11 there were 72 universities attended by 396,307 students and 182 higher professional schools attended by 29,800 students. Public higher education is free (up to the age of 26 years) and is financed by the Ministry of Education, Youth and Sports.

The secondary school leaving certificate (Maturita) is the main requirement for admission to higher education. Precise entry requirements vary among institutions, and students may have to sit an entrance examination. Legislation passed in 1998, and amended in 2001, brought the Czech Republic into line with the Bologna Process. The new law essentially established three levels of study programme, introduced the European Credit Transfer and Accumulation System (ECTS), as well as stating that all students were to be awarded a Diploma Supplement upon request. The Bakalár (Bachelors) is the main undergraduate degree (180–240 credit units), and normally lasts for three years (four years for a number of courses). The first postgraduate degree, Magistr (Masters, 60–180 credit units), is awarded after one to three years' study following the Bakalár. Some disciplines involve integrated undergraduate and postgraduate programmes lasting five to six years (300–360 credit units), leading to professional qualifications; these include engineering, architecture and medicine. Holders of the Magistr can upgrade their degree by passing an advanced Masters ('rigorózní') state examination in the same field and defending a thesis. Finally, following Magistr, doctoral studies take three to four years and result in the award of the title Doktor.

Post-secondary technical and vocational education dates from the establishment of vyšší odborná škola (tertiary technical schools) in 1992. Since 1995 these schools have operated under the School Act. In 2010/11 there were 1,107 such establishments offering education and training to 393,852 students in many different vocational fields (e.g. economics and management, health care and music). The normal requirement for admission is completed secondary education (general or vocational), although an entrance examination may be set by the director of the school. The period of study is two to three-and-a-half years, and students who pass the Absolutorium examination are awarded the Diplomovaný Specialista. In recent years the tertiary technical schools have been introducing a modular system of curriculum together with a credit allocation system.

The quality of higher education is overseen by the Accreditation Commission.

Regulatory and Representative Bodies

GOVERNMENT

Ministry of Culture: Maltéské nám. 1, 118 11 Prague 1; tel. 257085111; e-mail epodatelna@mkcr.cz; internet www.mkcr.cz; Minister JIŘÍ BALVÍN.

Ministry of Education, Youth and Sports: Karmelitská 7, 118 12 Prague 1; tel. 234811111; e-mail info@msmt.cz; internet www.msmt.cz; Minister DALIBOR ŠTYS.

ACCREDITATION

Akreditační komise (Accreditation Commission): Min. of Education, Youth and Sports, Higher Education Dept, Karmelitská 7, 118 12 Prague 1; tel. 234811488; e-mail smrckaj@msmt.cz; internet www.akreditacnikomise.cz; f. 1990; evaluates teaching, scholarly, scientific, research, devt and innovative, artistic and other creative activities of higher education instns; 21 mems (academic and professional experts); Chair. Prof. Dr VLADIMÍRA DVOŘÁKOVÁ; Sec. Dr JIŘÍ SMRČKA.

ENIC/NARIC Czech Republic: U Dvou Srpů 2024/2, 15 000 Prague 5; tel. 257011335; e-mail skuhrova@csvs.cz; internet www.naric.cz; Head ŠTEPÁNKA SKUHROVÁ.

NATIONAL BODIES

Česká konference rektorů (Czech Rectors' Conference): Masarykova univerzita, Žerotínovo nám. 9, 601 77 Brno; tel. 549491121; e-mail crc@muni.cz; internet crc.muni.cz; Pres. Prof. Dr VÁCLAV HAMPL; Gen. Sec. Dr MARIE FOJTÍKOVÁ.

Rada vysokých škol (Council of Higher Education Institutions): José Martího 31, 162 52 Prague 6; tel. (2) 20560221; e-mail arvs@ftvs.cuni.cz; internet www.radavs.cz.

Learned Societies

GENERAL

Akademie věd České republiky AV ČR (Academy of Sciences of the Czech Republic): Národní tř. 3, 117 20 Prague 1; tel. 221403111; e-mail kavcr@kav.cas.cz; internet www.avcr.cz; f. 1992; network of 60 autonomous research institutes which conduct theoretical and applied research in three broad sections: chemical and life sciences (Dir Prof. HELENA ILLNEROVÁ), humanities and social sciences (Dir Dr VILÉM HEROLD), mathematics, physics and earth sciences (Dir Dr KAREL JUNGWIRTH); attached research institutes: see under Research Institutes; library: see under Libraries and Archives; Pres. Prof. JIŘÍ DRAHOŠ; Pres. of Scientific Council Prof. Dr JIŘÍ ČTYŘOKÝ.

Rada vědeckých společností České republiky (Council of Scientific Societies of the Czech Republic): Středisko společných činností Akademie věd ČR, Národní tř. 3, 117 20 Prague; tel. 221403478; e-mail rvs@kav.cas.cz; internet www.cas.cz/rvs; coordinates 70 scientific socs, representing natural science, medicine and the social and technical sciences; 34,000 mems; Pres. Prof. Dr IVO HÁNA.

AGRICULTURE, FISHERIES AND VETERINARY SCIENCE

Česká Akademie Zemědělských Věd (Czech Academy of Agricultural Sciences): Těšnov 65/17, 117 05 Prague 1; tel. 222320582; e-mail cazv@cazv.cz; internet www.cazv.cz; f. 1924; sections of agricultural engineering, energy and devt, animal production, economics, management, sociology and information technology, food technology and technique, forestry, human nutrition and food quality, plant production, plant protection, soil science, veterinary medicine, water management; agricultural research, devt and education; 624 mems; Pres. Mgr JAN LIPAVSKÝ; Vice-Pres. Prof. Ing. JAN HRON; Sec. Ing. VÁCLAV HRUBÝ; publs *Agricultural Economics* (12 a year), *Czech Journal of Animal Science* (12 a year), *Czech Journal of Food Sciences* (6 a year), *Czech Journal of Genetics and Plant Breeding* (4 a year), *Horticultural Science* (4 a year), *Journal of Forest Science* (12 a year), *Plant Protection Science* (4 a year), *Plant, Soil and Environment* (12 a year), *Research in Agricultural Engineering* (4 a year), *Soil and Water Research* (4 a year), *Veterinary Medicine* (12 a year).

ARCHITECTURE AND TOWN PLANNING

Obec architektů (Society of Architects): Revoluční 23, 110 00 Prague 1; tel. (2) 57535025; e-mail obecarch@architekt.cz; internet www.architekt.cz; f. 1989; 1,000 mems; Pres. JIŘÍ MOJŽÍŠ; publ. *Architekt* (12 a year).

ECONOMICS, LAW AND POLITICS

Česká Společnost Ekonomická (Czech Economic Society): Politických vězňů 7, 110 00 Prague 1; e-mail cse@cse.cz; internet www.cse.cz; f. 1962; 180 mems; Pres. PETR JAKUBIK.

Česká Společnost pro Mezinárodní Právo (Czech Society for International Law): Národní tř. 18, 116 91 Prague 1; tel. 224933494; e-mail sturma@prf.cuni.cz; internet www.cyil.eu; f. 1969 as Czechoslovak Soc. of Int. Law, present status 1993; attached to Acad. of Sciences of the Czech Republic; non-profit org. of academics and professionals in the field of int. law; cooperates with the Czech br. of the Int. Law Assn and with foreign socs of int. law; represents, through its mems, the Czech doctrine of int. law in int. scientific orgs; organizes lectures and discussions, research confs and publishes non-periodical books and periodicals; 101 mems; Pres. Prof. Dr PAVEL STURMA; Scientific Sec. Dr VERONIKA BÍLKOVÁ; First Vice-Pres. Prof. Dr MONIKA PAUKNEROVÁ; publs *Bulletin of CSMP/CSIL* (www.csmp-csil.org), *Czech Yearbook of Public & Private International Law*.

Česká Společnost pro Politické Vědy (Czech Association for Political Sciences): Nám. W. Churchilla 4, 130 67 Prague 3; tel. (2) 24095204; e-mail cabada@kap.zcu.cz; internet www.cspv.cz; f. 1964; 160 mems; Pres. Assoc. Prof. LADISLAV CABADA; Sec. Dr HELENA HRICOVÁ; Sec. LINDA PIKNEROVÁ; publ. *Politologická Revue* (2 a year).

EDUCATION

Česká komise pro UNESCO (Czech Commission for UNESCO): Rytirska 31, 110 00 Prague 1; tel. 221610126; e-mail unesco@mzv.cz; internet www.mzv.cz/unesco; f. 1994, as part of Min. of Foreign Affairs, subsidiary advisory body of govt; Sec. Gen. Ing. MILAN KUNA.

Česká pedagogická společnost (Czech Pedagogical Society): Poříčí 31, 603 00 Brno; tel. 549493645; e-mail sekretar@cpds.cz; internet www.cpds.cz; f. 1964; 240 mems; Pres. Dr TOMÁŠ CECH; Sec. Dr MARTA RYBIČKOVÁ; publ. *Pedagogická orientace* (4 a year).

FINE AND PERFORMING ARTS

Asociace hudebních umělců a vědců (Association of Musicians and Musicologists): Radlická 99, 150 00 Prague 5; tel. 251553996; e-mail ahuv@seznam.cz; internet www.ahuv.cz; f. 1990; 1,200 mems; Pres. Prof. JIŘÍ HLAVÁČ; Exec. Sec. MARCELA POSEJPALOVÁ; publ. *Hudební rozhledy* (12 a year).

Česká hudební společnost (Czech Music Society): Radlická 99, 150 00 Prague 5; tel. 251552453; e-mail mila.smetackova@volny.cz; f. 1973; 5,000 mems; Pres. MÍLA SMETÁČKOVÁ; Sec. Gen. EVA STRAUSOVÁ; publs *ČHS News* (2 a year), *Josef Suk Society News* (2 a year), *Vítězslav Novák Society News* (1 a year).

Český filmový a televizní svaz (FITES) (Czech Film and Television Association): Pod Nuselskými schody 1721/3, 120 00 Prague 2; tel. 222562331; e-mail info@fites.cz; internet www.fites.cz; f. 1966; 720 mems; Pres. MARTIN SKYBA; publ. *Synchron* (6 a year).

Český spolek pro komorní hudbu (Czech Chamber Music Society): c/o Česká filharmonie Rudolfinum, 1, Alšovo nábřeží 12, 110 00 Prague; tel. 227059343; e-mail cskh@cfmail.cz; internet www.ceskafilharmonie.cz; f. 1894; 3,500 mems; Chair. Ing. IVAN ENGLICH.

Divadelní ústav (Theatre Institute): Celetná 17, 110 00 Prague 1; tel. 224809132; e-mail redakce@divadlo.cz; internet www.divadlo.cz; f. 1956; research and documentation on Czech theatre; Czech centre of the International Theatre Institute (ITI); library of 100,000 vols; Dir ONDŘEJ ČERNÝ; publs *Divadelní noviny* (24 a year), *Divadelní revue* (4 a year), *Informační servis Divadelního ústavu* (12 a year), *Loutkář* (10 a year), *Ročenka českých divadel* (1 a year), *Theatre Czech* (1 a year).

Společnost Pro Estetiku (Society for Aesthetics): Dept of Aesthetics, Faculty of Arts, Charles Univ., Celetna 20, 116 42 Prague 1; tel. 221619620; e-mail estetikaspol@estetikaspol.cz; internet www.estetikaspol.cz; f. 1968; mem. of the Ccl of Scientific Socs of the Czech Republic; 65 mems; Pres. Dr ONDREJ DADEJIK; Sec. KATERINA NOVOTNÁ.

Unie výtvarných umělců (Union of Creative Artists): Masarykovo nábř. 250, 110 00 Prague 1; tel. 541213555; e-mail uvucr@uvucr.cz; internet www.uvucr.cz; f. 1990; supports the professional interests of visual artists; acts as an information centre and coordinates the activities of its members; keeps a register of professional visual artists working in the Czech Republic; 3,000 mems; Pres. VÁCLAV KUBÁT; Exec. Vice-Pres. VÍT WEBER; publs *Art Folia* (1 a year), *Atelier* (26 a year), *Technologia Artis* (1 a year), *Výtvarné umění* (4 a year).

HISTORY, GEOGRAPHY AND ARCHAEOLOGY

Česká archeologická společnost (Czech Archaeological Society): Letenská 4, 118 01 Prague 1; tel. 224317913; e-mail zuzana.blahova@ff.cuni.cz; internet www.archaeology.cz/cas; f. 1919; organizes annual colloquia, publs, lectures, excursions about new archaeological excavations; 580 mems; Pres. Dr KAREL SKLENÁŘ; Sec. Dr ONDŘEJ CHVOJKA; publs *Archeologie Moravy a Slezska* (Archaeology of Moravia and Silesia, 1 a year), *Studia Hercynia* (1 a year).

Česká demografická společnost (Czech Demographic Society): Albertov 6, 128 43 Prague 2; tel. 221951418; e-mail demodept@natur.cuni.cz; internet www.natur.cuni.cz/~demodept/cds; f. 1964; 450 mems; Pres. JITKA RYCHTAŘÍKOVÁ; Sec. FELIX KOSCHIN.

Česká geografická společnost (Czech Geographical Society): Albertov 6, 128 43 Prague 2 Czechia; tel. 221951383; e-mail perlin@natur.cuni.cz; internet www.geography.cz; f. 1894; 500 mems; Pres. Prof. TADEUSZ SIWEK; Scientific Sec. Dr RADIM PERLÍN; Sec. Dr DANA FIALOVÁ; publs *Geografické rozhledy* (Geographical perspective, 5 a year), *Geografie* (Geography, scientific journal, 4 a year), *Informace CGS* (2 a year).

Matice Moravská (Moravian Society of History and Literature): Arne Nováka 1, 602 00 Brno; tel. 549493552; e-mail matice@phil.muni.cz; internet www.matice-moravska.cz; f. 1849; 560 mems; Pres. Prof. Dr JIŘÍ L. MALÍŘ; Sec. Dr BRONISLAV CHOCHOLÁČ; publ. *Časopis Matice Moravské* (2 a year).

LANGUAGE AND LITERATURE

Alliance Française: c/o French Embassy in the Czech Republic, Štěpánská 35, 111 21 Prague 1; tel. 221401063; e-mail michel.wattremez@diplomatie.gouv.fr; internet www.alliancefrancaise.cz; offers courses and exams in French language and culture and promotes cultural exchange with France; attached offices in Brno, České Budějovice, Hradec Králové, Kladno, Kroměříž, Liberec, Louny, Ostrava, Pardubice, Plzeň, Pribram, Ústí nad Labem and Zlín; General Coordinator MICHEL WATTREMEZ.

British Council: Bredovský dvůr, Politických vězňů 13, 110 00 Prague 1; tel. 221991160; e-mail info.praha@britishcouncil.cz; internet www.britishcouncil.cz; teaching centre; offers courses and exams in English language and British culture and promotes cultural exchange with the UK; attached teaching centre in Pilsen; Dir NIGEL BELLINGHAM; Deputy Dir STEVE OXLEY.

Český esperantský svaz (Czech Union of Esperantists): c/o Pavel Polnicky, Na Vinici 110/10, 290 01 Podebrady; tel. 325615651; internet www.esperanto.cz; f. 1969; 800 mems; Pres. JANA MELICHÁRKOVÁ; Sec. PAVEL POLNICKÝ; publ. *Starto* (4 a year).

Czech Centre of International PEN: POB 123, 110 00 Prague 1; Klementinum 190 (Nat. Library Bldg), 5 Fl., 110 00 Prague; tel. (2) 24234343; e-mail centrum@pen.cz; internet www.pen.cz; f. 1924; Writers in Prison Cttee; regular authors' readings, exhibitions, spring and autumn literary festivals, discussions with writers in schools, clubs and civic facilities; awards Karel Čapek Prize and PEN Club Lifetime Achievement Prize every 2 years; 197 mems, incl. 13 hon. mems; Pres. Mgr JIRI DĚDEČEK; Dir Ing. LIBUŠE LUDVIKOVÁ; Sec. DANA MOJŽÍŠOVÁ.

Goethe-Institut: Masarykovo nábřeží 32, 110 00 Prague 1; tel. 221962111; e-mail info@prag.goethe.org; internet www.goethe.de/ins/cz/pra/; offers courses and exams in German language and culture and promotes cultural exchange with Germany; library of 14,000 vols; Dir Dr STEPHAN NOBBE.

Literárněvědná společnost (Literary Society): Katedra slavistiky PF Univerzity Hradec Králové, Rokitanského 62, 500 03 Hradec Králové; tel. 493331360; e-mail oldrich.richterek@uhk.cz; f. 1934; 285 mems; Pres. Prof. Dr OLDŘICH RICHTEREK.

Obec spisovatelů (Society of Czech Writers): Železná 18, 110 00 Prague 1; tel. 224234060; e-mail obecspis@volny.cz; internet www.obecspisovatelu.cz; f. 1989; seminars, debates and confs; 600 mems; Hon. Pres. VÁCLAV HAVEL; Pres. TOMÁŠ MAGNUSEK; publ. *Dokořán* (4 a year).

MEDICINE

Česká Imunologická Společnost (Czech Society for Immunology): Vídeňská 1083, 142 20 Prague 4; e-mail cis@biomed.cas.cz; internet www.biomed.cas.cz/cis/; f. 1986; 600 mems; Pres. Prof. Dr ALEŠ MACELA; Sec. Dr MARTIN BILEJ; publ. *Imunologický Zpravodaj* (3 a year).

Česká lékařská společnost J. E. Purkyně (J. E. Purkyně Czech Medical Association): Sokolská 31, 120 26 Prague 2; tel. 224266201; e-mail cls@cls.cz; internet www.cls.cz; f. 1947; 34,500 mems; Pres. Prof. Dr JAROSLAV BLAHOŠ; Scientific Sec. Prof. Dr JIŘÍ HOMOLKA; publs *Acta Chirurgiae Plasticae* (in English, 4 a year), *Anesteziologie a intenzivní medicína* (Anaesthesiology and Intensive Critical Care Medicine, 6 a year), *Časopis lékařů českých* (Journal of Czech Physicians, 12 a year), *Česká a slovenská farmacie* (Czech and Slovak Pharmacy, 6 a year), *Česká a slovenská gastroenterologie a hepatologie* (Czech and Slovak Gastroenterology and Hepatology, 6 a year), *Česká a slovenská neurologie a neurochirurgie* (Czech and Slovak Neurology and Neurosurgery, 6 a year), *Česká a slovenská oftalmologie* (Czech and Slovak Ophthalmology, 6 a year), *Česká a* *slovenská psychiatrie* (Czech and Slovak Psychiatry, 8 a year), *Česká gynekologie* (Czech Gynaecology, 6 a year), *Česká radiologie* (Czech Radiology, 6 a year), *Česká revmatologie* (Czech Rheumatology, 4 a year), *Česká stomatologie a Praktické zubní lékařství* (Czech Stomatology and Practical Dentistry, 6 a year), *Česko-slovenská dermatologie* (Czech-Slovak Dermatology, 6 a year), *Česko-slovenská patologie a Soudní lékařství* (Czech-Slovak Pathology and Forensic Medicine, 4 a year), *Česko-slovenská pediatrie* (Czech-Slovak Paediatrics, 12 a year), *Československá fyziologie* (Czechoslovak Physiology, 4 a year), *Epidemiologie, mikrobiologie, imunologie* (Epidemiology, Microbiology, Immunology, 4 a year), *Hygiena* (Hygiene, 4 a year), *Klinická biochemie a metabolismus* (Clinical Biochemistry and Metabolism, 4 a year), *Klinická onkologie* (Clinical Oncology, 6 a year), *Lékař a technika* (Physician and Technology, 6 a year), *Otorinolaryngologie a foniatrie* (Otorhinolaryngology and Phoniatrics, 4 a year), *Pracovní lékařství* (Occupational Medicine, 4 a year), *Praktický lékař* (The Generalist, 12 a year), *Rehabilitace a fyzikální lékařství* (Rehabilitation and Physical Medicine, 4 a year), *Rozhledy v chirurgii* (Surgical Review, 12 a year), *Vnitřní lékařství* (Internal Medicine, 12 a year), *Revizní a posudkové lékařství* (Health Insurance and Medical Revision, 4 a year), *Endoskopie* (Endoscopy, 4 a year), *Transfuze a hematologie dnes* (Transfusion and Haematology Today, 4 a year).

NATURAL SCIENCES

General

Český Svaz Vědeckotechnických Společností (Czech Association of Scientific and Technical Societies): Novotného lávka 5, 116 68 Prague 1; tel. 221082247; e-mail poriz@csvts.cz; internet www.csvts.cz; f. 1990; promotes professional interests of mems; organizes educational programmes, training courses in technical and general fields of education, and congresses, confs, workshops and seminars; 136,000 mems; Pres. Doc. Ing. Jaromir Volf; Exec. Sec. Ing. Vladimir Poriz; publs *Bio Prospect* (irregular), *Chemical Papers (Prague)* (6 a year), *Glass Paper* (irregular), *Plant Physician* (4 a year), *Reporter* (4 a year), *Silicate Reporter* (irregular).

Společnost pro dějiny věd a techniky (Society of the History of Sciences and Technology): Ovocny trh 3, 116 36 Prague; tel. 224491468; e-mail milada.sekyrkova@ruk.cuni.cz; internet sdvt.cz; f. 1965; 200 mems; Pres. Prof. Petr Svobodny; Sec. Dr Milada Sekyrková; publs *Acta historiae rerum naturalium necnon technicarum* (1 a year), *Dějiny věd a techniky* (4 a year), *Práce z dějin techniky a přívodních věd* (Treatise on the History of Technology and Sciences, irregular).

Biological Sciences

Česká botanická společnost (Czech Botanical Society): Benátská 2, 128 01 Prague 2; tel. 221951664; e-mail botspol@natur.cuni.cz; internet www.natur.cuni.cz/cbs; f. 1912; 680 mems; library of 3,000 vols, 1,400 periodicals; Chair. Dr Lubomír Hrouda; Sec. Dr J. Štěpánek; publs *Bryonora* (2 a year), *Preslia* (4 a year), *Zprávy ČBS* (irregular).

Česká parazitologická společnost (Czech Society for Parasitology): c/o Institute of Postgraduate Medical Education, 10, Ruská 85, 100 05 Prague; tel. 271019254; e-mail fajfrlik@fnplzen.cz; internet www.parazitologie.cz; f. 1993; 199 mems; Pres. Dr Libuse Kolářová; Sec. Dr Karel Fajfrlík; publ. *Zprávy České parazitologické společnosti* (4 a year).

Česká Společnost Bioklimatologická (Czech Society for Bioclimatology): Kroftova 43, 616 67 Brno; tel. 267103321; e-mail jstr@ig.cas.cz; internet www.cbks.cz; f. 1965; 75 mems; Pres. Dr J. Rožnovský; Sec. J. Střeštík; publ. *Digests of Science Reports* (1 a year).

Česká společnost entomologická (Czech Entomological Society): Vinicna 7, 128 00 Prague 2; tel. 224923535; e-mail klapagenda@centrum.cz; internet www.entospol.cz; f. 1904; 750 mems; library of 20,500 vols; Pres. Dr Josef Jelinek; Sec. Dr Klara Farkacova; publ. *Klapalekiana* (2 a year).

Česká společnost histo- a cytochemická (Czech Society for Histo- and Cytochemistry): Kamenice 3, 625 00 Brno; tel. 549493701; e-mail pdubovy@med.muni.cz; internet www.med.muni.cz/hcspol; f. 1962; associated with the International Federation of Societies for Histochemistry and Cytochemistry; 120 mems; Pres. Prof. Dr Petr Dubový; Sec. Prof. Dr Svatopluk Čech.

Česká společnost pro biomechaniku (Czech Society for Biomechanics): FTVS–Katedra anatomie a biomechaniky, J. Martiho 31, 160 00 Prague 6; tel. 220560225; e-mail otahal@ftvs.cuni.cz; internet biomech.ftvs.cuni.cz/csb; f. 1990; 168 mems; Pres. Prof. Stanislav Otáhal; Sec. Asst Prof. Miroslav Sochor.

Česká společnost zoologická (Czech Zoological Society): Viničná 7, 128 44 Prague; tel. 221951860; e-mail vohralik@natur.cuni.cz; internet www.zoospol.cz; f. 1927; 230 mems; library of 18,250 vols; Pres. Dr Václav Pižl; Sec. Dr M. Skuhravá; Sec. Dr M. Švátora; publ. *Acta Societatis Zoologicae Bohemicae* (4 a year).

Česká vědecká společnost pro mykologii (Czech Scientific Society for Mycology): POB 106, 111 21 Prague 1; tel. 533435238; e-mail cvsm@natur.cuni.cz; internet www.natur.cuni.cz/cvsm; f. 1946; voluntary org. for professional and amateur mycologists; organizes mycological lectures for the public, mycological excursions (mushroom-picking, micromycetes), seminar meetings; 200 mems; library of 900 vols, 135 journals; Pres. Dr Vladimír Antonín; Sec. Dr Alena Kubátová; publs *Czech Mycology* (2 a year, in English), *Mykologické Listy* (4 a year, in Czech with English summary).

Československá Biologická Společnost (Czechoslovak Biological Society): Kamenice 5, 625 00 Brno; tel. 549495589; e-mail renata.hezova@gmail.com; internet www.icsbs.cz; f. 1922; 400 mems; Pres. Prof. Dr Vojtěch Mornstein; Sec. Prof. Dr Roman Janisch; publ. *Zpravodaj Čs. Biologické Společnosti* (2 a year).

Československá Společnost Mikrobiologická (Czechoslovak Society for Microbiology): Vídeňská 1083, 142 20 Prague 4; tel. 296442494; e-mail gabriel@biomed.cas.cz; internet www.cssm.info; f. 1928; organizes int. and nat. conferences in the field of basic and applied microbiology, molecular biology and genetics; undergraduate and postgraduate courses; 1,000 mems from Czech Republic and Slovakia; Pres. Dr Jiri Gabriel; Sec. Gen. Dr Jiri Holatko; publ. *Folia Microbiologica* (English, 6 a year).

Mathematical Sciences

Jednota českých matematiků a fyziků (Union of Czech Mathematicians and Physicists): Žitná 25, 117 10 Prague 1; tel. 222211100; e-mail predseda@jcmf.cz; internet www.jcmf.cz; f. 1862; 2,100 mems; Pres. Josef Kubát; Sec. Jiri Fiala; publs *Matematika-Fyzika-Informatika* (12 a year), *Pokroky matematiky, fyziky a astronomie* (4 a year), *Rozhledy matematicko-fyzikální* (4 a year), *Učitel matematiky* (4 a year).

Physical Sciences

Česká astronomická společnost (Czech Astronomical Society): Královská obora 233, 170 21 Prague 7; tel. (2) 33377204; e-mail info@astro.cz; internet www.astro.cz; f. 1917; 700 mems; Pres. Dr Jiří Borovička; Sec. Dr Miloslav Zejda; publ. *Kosmické rozhledy* (irregular).

Česká geologická společnost (Czech Geological Society): V Holešovičkách 41, 182 09 Prague 8; tel. 266009323; e-mail budil@cgu.cz; internet www.geologickaspolecnost.cz; f. 1923; 500 mems; Pres. Dr Petr Budil; Sec. Blanka Čizková; publ. *Journal* (4 a year).

Česká meteorologická společnost (Czech Meteorological Society): Na Šabatce 17, 143 06 Prague; tel. 221912514; e-mail tomas.halenka@mff.cuni.cz; internet www.cmes.cz; f. 1958; provides information on meteorology and climatology, history of meteorology, and meteorological bibliography and terminology; 215 mems; Pres. Doc. Dr Tomáš Halenka; Sec. Dr Milan Šálek; Treas. Petr Skalak.

Česká společnost chemická (Czech Chemical Society): Novotneho lavka 5, 116 68 Prague 1; tel. 221082383; e-mail csch@csch.cz; internet www.csch.cz; f. 1866; 3,480 mems; Pres. Prof. Dr Jitka Ulrichová; publ. *Chemické Listy* (12 a year).

Spektroskopická společnost J. Marca Marci (J. Marcus Marci Spectroscopic Society): Thákurova 7, 166 29 Prague 6; Masarykova univerzita, Přírodovědecká fakulta, Kotlářská 2, 611 37 Brno; tel. (54) 9491436; e-mail immss@spektroskopie.cz; internet www.spektroskopie.cz; f. 1949; 970 mems; Chair. Prof. Dr Viktor Kanický; Scientific Sec. Prof. Dr Jan Hála.

Vědecká společnost pro nauku o kovech (Metals Science Society): Ke Karlovu 5, 121 16 Prague 2; tel. 221911362; e-mail vsnk@met.mff.cuni.cz; f. 1966; 120 mems; Pres. Prof. Vladimír Cíhal; Sec. Prof. Vladimír Šíma.

PHILOSOPHY AND PSYCHOLOGY

Filozofický ústav Akademie věd České republiky (Institute of Philosophy of the Czech Academy of Sciences): Jilská 1, 110 00 Prague 1; tel. 222220099; e-mail flusekr@site.cas.cz; internet www.flu.cas.cz; f. 1990; 250 mems; Dir Dr Pavel Baran; publs *Acta Comeniana* (in English, French and German), *Filosofický časopis* (Philosophical Journal, 6 a year, summaries in English and German), *Teorie vedy* (Theory of Science, 4 a year, in Czech and English).

RELIGION, SOCIOLOGY AND ANTHROPOLOGY

Česká národopisná společnost (Czech Ethnological Society): Národní třída 3, 117 20 Prague 1; e-mail narodopis@narodopisnaspolecnost.cz; internet www.narodopisnaspolecnost.cz; f. 1893; has 2 spec. comms: Comm. for Folk Architecture and Comm. for Folk Customs; assen of professionals working in the fields of ethnology and cultural anthropology; 250 mems; Chair. Dr Daniel Drápala; publs *Národopisný věstník* (1 a year), *Zpravodaj České národopisné společnosti* (3 a year).

Česká společnost antropologická (Czech Anthropological Society): Viničná 7, 128 44 Prague 2; internet anthropology.cz; f. 1964; 180 mems; Pres. Dr J. Jelínek; Sec. Doc. Dr V. Novotný; publ. *Zprávy* (4 a year).

Masarykova Česká Sociologická Společnost (Masaryk Czech Sociological Association): Husova 4, 110 00 Prague 1; tel. 222220631; e-mail mcss@seznam.cz; internet www.ceskasociologicka.org; f. 1964; supports devt of Czech sociology on nat. and regional level; 311 mems; Pres. Doc. Dr JIŘÍ BURIÁNEK; Sec. JIRI VINOPAL.

TECHNOLOGY

Česká společnost pro kybernetiku a informatiku (Czech Society for Cybernetics and Informatics): Pod Vodárenskou věží 2, 182 07 Prague 8; tel. 266053901; e-mail cski@utia.cas.cz; internet www.cski.cz; f. 1966; 297 mems; Pres. Prof. OLGA ŠTĚPÁNKOVÁ; Sec. DAGMAR HARMANCOVÁ; publs *Kybernetika* (6 a year, in English), *Zpravodaj* (12 a year).

Česká společnost pro mechaniku (Czech Society for Mechanics): Dolejškova 5, 182 00 Prague 8; tel. 266053045; e-mail csm@it.cas.cz; internet www.csm.cz; f. 1966; 580 individual mems, 18 organizational mems; Pres. Prof. Ing. MILOSLAV OKROUHLÍK; Sec. Ing. JITKA HAVLÍNOVÁ.

Česká společnost pro vědeckou kinematografii (Czech Society for Scientific Cinematography): Zemědělská 1665/1, 613 00 Brno-Černá Pole; tel. 545135021; e-mail rygl@mendelu.cz; f. 1923; 150 mems; Pres. Ing. V. BOUČEK; Sec. Ing. L. RYGL; publ. *Bulletin* (1 a year).

Research Institutes

ARCHITECTURE AND TOWN PLANNING

ABF—Nadace pro rozvoj architektury a stavitelství (Architecture and Building Foundation): Václavské nám. 833/31, 110 00 Prague 1; tel. 224225001; e-mail fibiger@abf-nadace.cz; internet www.abf-nadace.cz; f. 1991; incl. Česká stavební akademie (Czech Bldg Acad.); organizes 2 evaluative competitions: Stavba roku (Bldg of the year) and Vyrok-technologie roku (Product-technology of the year); organizes spec. exhibitions; library of 10,000 vols; Dir Dr JAN FIBIGER; Sec. PETRA PROKOPOVA; publs *ABF Forum* (4 a year), *Building Products Review* (1 a year), *Forum of Architecture and Building* (12 a year).

ECONOMICS, LAW AND POLITICS

CERGE-EI: POB 882, Politických vězňů 7, 111 21 Prague 1; tel. 224005123; e-mail office@cerge-ei.cz; internet www.cerge-ei.cz; f. 1991; attached to Acad. of Sciences of the Czech Republic and to Charles Univ.; conducts US-style PhD programme in economics; library of 100,000 vols; depository for World Bank publs; Dir Dr Ing. MICHAL KEJAK; publs *CERGE-EI Working Papers*, *Working Papers* (12 a year).

Ústav státu práva AV ČR (Institute of State and Law AS CR): Národní 18, 116 91 Prague 1; tel. 221990711; e-mail ilaw@ilaw.cas.cz; internet www.ilaw.cas.cz; attached to Acad. of Sciences of the Czech Republic; library of 40,000 vols, 100 periodicals; Dir Dr JAROSLAV ZACHARIÁŠ; publ. *Právník* (12 a year).

FINE AND PERFORMING ARTS

Ústav dějin umění AV ČR, v.v.i. (Institute of Art History AS CR, v.v.i.): Husova 4, 110 00 Prague 1; tel. 222222144; e-mail arthist@site.cas.cz; internet www.udu.cas.cz; f. 1953; attached to Acad. of Sciences of the Czech Republic; Dir Dr LUBOMIR KONEČNÝ; publs *Estetika: The Central European Journal of Aesthetics* (2 a year), *Fontes Historiae Artium* (book series, irregular), *Studia Rudolphina* (1 a year), *Umění* (6 a year).

HISTORY, GEOGRAPHY AND ARCHAEOLOGY

Archeologický ústav AV ČR, Brno (Archaeological Institute AS CR, Brno): Královopolská 147, 612 64 Brno; tel. 541514101; e-mail archeo@iabrno.cz; internet www.iabrno.cz; attached to Acad. of Sciences of the Czech Republic; Dir Dr PAVEL KOUŘIL; publs *Fontes Archeologicae Moravicae* (irregular), *Studie Archeologického ústavu* (2 a year).

Archeologický ústav AV ČR, Praha (Archaeological Institute AS CR, Prague): Letenská 4, 118 01 Prague 1; tel. 257530922; e-mail jiran@arup.cas.cz; internet www.arup.cas.cz; f. 1919; attached to Acad. of Sciences of the Czech Republic; Dir Dr LUBOŠ JIRÁŇ; publs *Archeologické rozhledy* (4 a year), *Památky archeologické* (2 a year).

Historický ústav AV ČR (Institute of History AS CR): Prosecká 76, 190 00 Prague 9; tel. 286887513; e-mail bucharova@hiu.cas.cz; internet www.hiu.cas.cz; f. 1921; attached to Acad. of Sciences of the Czech Republic; Dir Dr MILOSLAV POLÍVKA; publs *Český časopis historický* (4 a year), *Folia Historica Bohemica* (irregular), *Historia Europae Centralis* (1 a year), *Historica* (Historical Sciences in the Czech Republic, 1 a year), *Historická geografie* (every 2 years), *Mediaevalia Historica Bohemica* (1 a year), *Moderní dějiny* (1 a year), *Slovanské historické studie* (1 a year), *Slovanský přehlad* (4 a year).

Kabinet pro klasická studia FLÚ AV ČR, v.v.i. (Institute for Classical Studies AS CR): Na Florenci 3, 110 00 Prague 1; tel. 222828303; e-mail uks@ics.cas.cz; internet www.ics.cas.cz; f. 1953; attached to Acad. of Sciences of the Czech Republic; researches classical traditions and impact of ancient civilizations on cultural life of Bohemia since its beginning to 21st century; library of 60,000 vols; Head Dr JIŘÍ BENEŠ; publs *Eirene, Studia Graeca et Latina* (on classical studies, 1 a year), *Listy filologické, Folia philologica* (Folia Philologica, 2 a year).

Orientální ústav AV ČR (Oriental Institute AS CR): Pod vodárenskou věží 4, 182 08 Prague 8; tel. 266053111; e-mail orient@orient.cas.cz; internet www.orient.cas.cz; f. 1922; attached to Acad. of Sciences of the Czech Republic; research in history, religious and philosophical systems, languages, literatures and cultures of Asia and Africa; library of 210,000 vols; Dir Dr STANISLAVA VAVROUŠKOVÁ; Sec. PAVEL HONS; publ. *Archiv orientální* (4 a year).

Slovanský ústav AV ČR (Institute of Slavonic Studies AS CR): Valentinská 1, 110 00 Prague 1; tel. 224800251; e-mail slu@slu.cas.cz; internet www.slu.cas.cz; f. 1922; attached to Acad. of Sciences of the Czech Republic; Dir Dr HELENA ULBRECHTOVÁ; publs *Byzantinoslavica* (2 a year), *Germanoslavica* (2 a year), *Slavia* (4 a year).

Ústav pro soudobé dějiny AV ČR v.v.i. (Institute of Contemporary History AS CR v.v.i.): Vlašská 9, 118 40 Prague 1; tel. 257286362; e-mail usd@usd.cas.cz; internet www.usd.cas.cz; f. 1990; attached to Acad. of Sciences of the Czech Republic; Czech and Slovak history from 1938–2000; library of 35,000 vols; Dir Dr OLDŘICH TŮMA; publ. *Soudobé dějiny*.

Výzkumný ústav geodetický, topografický a kartografický (VUGTK) (Research Institute of Geodesy, Topography and Cartography): 250 66 Zdiby 98; tel. 284890351; e-mail vugtk@vugtk.cz; internet www.vugtk.cz; f. 1954; library of 70,000 vols; Dir Dr Ing. VÁCLAV SLABOCH; publ. *Proceedings of Research Works* (every 2 years).

LANGUAGE AND LITERATURE

Ústav pro českou literaturu AV ČR (Institute of Czech Literature AS CR): Na Florenci 3/1420, 110 00 Prague 1; tel. 234612111; e-mail literatura@ucl.cas.cz; internet www.ucl.cas.cz; f. 1947; attached to Acad. of Sciences of the Czech Republic; library of 130,000 vols; Dir Dr PAVEL JANOUŠEK; publ. *Česká literatura* (6 a year).

Ústav pro jazyk český AV ČR (Czech Language Institute AS CR): Letenská 4, 118 51 Prague 1; tel. 257533756; e-mail ujc@ujc.cas.cz; internet www.ujc.cas.cz; f. 1911; attached to Acad. of Sciences of the Czech Republic; Dir Dr KAREL OLIVA; publs *Acta Onomastica* (1 a year), *Bibliografie české lingvistiky* (1 a year), *Časopis pro moderní filologii* (2 a year), *Linguistica Pragensia* (2 a year), *Naše řeč* (5 a year), *Slovo a slovesnost* (4 a year).

MEDICINE

Farmakologický ústav AV ČR (Institute of Pharmacology AS CR): 4–Krč, Vídeňská 1083, 142 20 Prague; tel. 261710024; e-mail fkuavcr@biomed.cas.cz; internet www.cas.cz; attached to Acad. of Sciences of the Czech Republic; Dir Dr EVŽEN BUCHAR.

Ústav experimentální medicíny AV ČR v.v.i. (Institute of Experimental Medicine AS CR v.v.i): Vídeňská 1083, 142 20 Prague 4; tel. 241062230; e-mail uemavcr@biomed.cas.cz; internet uem.avcr.cz/institute; f. 1975; attached to Acad. of Sciences of the Czech Republic; Dir Prof. EVA SYKOVÁ.

NATURAL SCIENCES

General

Ústav geoniky AV ČR (Institute of Geonics AS CR): Poruba, Studentská 1768, 708 00 Ostrava; tel. 596979352; e-mail geonics@ugn.cas.cz; internet www.ugn.cas.cz; f. 1982; attached to Acad. of Sciences of the Czech Republic; Dir Prof. RADIM BLAHETA; Librarian EVA DUDKOVA; publ. *Moravian Geographical Report* (4 a year).

Biological Sciences

Biofyzikální ústav AV ČR (Institute of Biophysics AS CR): Královopolská 135, 612 65 Brno; tel. 541517111; e-mail ibp@ibp.cz; internet www.ibp.cz; f. 1955; attached to Acad. of Sciences of the Czech Republic; Dir Dr STANISLAV KOZUBEK.

Botanický ústav AV ČR, v.v.i. (Institute of Botany AS CR): Zámek 1, 252 43 Průhonice; tel. 271015233; e-mail ibot@ibot.cas.cz; internet www.ibot.cas.cz; attached to Acad. of Sciences of the Czech Republic; Dir Dr JAN KIRSCHNER; publs *Folia Geobotanica* (4 a year), *Index Seminum et Plantarum* (1 a year).

Biologické centrum AV ČR, v.v.i., Entomologický ústav (Biology Centre AS CR v.v.i., Institute of Entomology): Branišovská 1160/31, 370 05 České Budějovice; tel. 385310350; e-mail entu@entu.cas.cz; internet www.entu.cas.cz; f. 1962, part of Biology Centre AS CR since 2006; attached to Acad. of Sciences of the Czech Republic; basic and applied research on insects as models for biological research or as pests or species important for environment monitoring; Dir Prof. Dr FRANTIŠEK SEHNAL; Head Dr JAN ŠULA; publ. *European Journal of Entomology* (4 a year).

Fyziologický Ústav AV CR, v.v.i. (Institute of Physiology AS CR): Videnska 1083, 142 20 Prague 4; tel. 241062424; e-mail fgu@fgu.cas.cz; internet www.fgu.cas.cz; f. 1954;

attached to Acad. of Sciences of the Czech Republic; Dir Dr LUCIE KUBÍNOVÁ; publ. *Physiological Research* (6 a year).

Hydrobiologický Ústav AV ČR (Hydrobiological Institute AS CR): Na sádkách 7, 370 05 České Budějovice; tel. 387775881; e-mail hbu@hbu.cas.cz; internet www.hbu.cas.cz; attached to Acad. of Sciences of the Czech Republic; Dir Dr JOSEF MATĚNA.

Mikrobiologický ústav AV ČR (Institute of Microbiology AS CR): Vídeňská 1083, 142 20 Prague 4; tel. 244472272; e-mail mbu@biomed.cas.cz; internet www.biomed.cas.cz/mbu; f. 1962; attached to Acad. of Sciences of the Czech Republic; Dir Prof. RNDr BLANKA ŘÍHOVÁ; publ. *Folia Microbiologica* (6 a year).

Parazitologický ústav AV ČR (Institute of Parasitology AS CR): Branišovská 31, 370 05 České Budějovice; tel. 387775403; e-mail paru@paru.cas.cz; internet www.paru.cas.cz; f. 1962; attached to Acad. of Sciences of the Czech Republic; Dir Dr TOMÁŠ SCHOLZ; publ. *Folia Parasitologica* (4 a year).

Ústav biologie obratlorců AV ČR, v.v.i. (Institute of Vertebrate Biology AS CR, v.v.i.): Květná 8, 603 65 Brno; tel. 543422538; e-mail ubo@ivb.cz; internet www.ivb.cz; f. 1954; 90 mems; attached to Acad. of Sciences of the Czech Republic; library of 37,358 vols of zoology, population biology; Dir Dr Ing. MARCEL HONZA; publs *Biennial Report IVB*, *Folia Zoologica* (4 a year).

Ústav experimentální botaniky AV ČR (Institute of Experimental Botany AS CR): Rozvojová 263, 165 02 Prague 6; tel. 225106453; e-mail zazimalova@ueb.cas.cz; internet www.ueb.cas.cz; f. 1962; attached to Acad. of Sciences of the Czech Republic; Dir Asst Prof. Doc. EVA ZAŽÍMALOVÁ; publs *Biologia Plantarum* (irregular), *Photosynthetica* (irregular).

Ústav fyziky plazmatu AV ČR (Institute of Plasma Physics AS CR): Za Slovankou 3, 182 21 Prague 8; tel. 266052052; e-mail ipp@ipp.cas.cz; internet www.ipp.cas.cz; f. 1959; attached to Acad. of Sciences of the Czech Republic; Dir Prof. Dr Ing. PAVEL CHRÁSKA.

Ústav molekulární biologie rostlin AV ČR, v.v.i. (Institute of Plant Molecular Biology AS CR, v.v.i.): Branišovská 31, 370 05 České Budějovice; tel. 385310357; e-mail umbr@umbr.cas.cz; internet www.umbr.cas.cz; f. 1991; attached to Biology Centre, Acad. of Sciences of the Czech Republic; Dir Prof. Dr J. ŠPAK.

Ústav Molekulární Genetiky AV ČR, v.v.i. (Institute of Molecular Genetics AS CR, v.v.i.): Vídeňská 1083, 142 20 Prague 4; tel. 241063215; e-mail office@img.cas.cz; internet www.img.cas.cz; f. 1961 as Institute of Experimental Biology and Genetics; joined with several biochemical laboratories of the Institute of Organic Chemistry and Biochemistry and renamed Institute of Molecular Genetics 1977; public research instn 2007; attached to Acad. of Sciences of the Czech Republic; basic and applied research in molecular biology and genetics and in cell biology, incl. molecular and cellular immunology, functional genomics and bioinformatics, virology, oncogene biology, apoptosis, molecular biology of devt, mechanisms of receptor signalling and cell differentiation, biology of cytoskeleton, epigenetic mechanisms, genome stability and structural biology; Dir Prof. VÁCLAV HOŘEJŠÍ.

Ústav organické chemie a biochemie AV ČR (Institute of Organic Chemistry and Biochemistry AS CR): Flemingovo nám. 2, 166 10 Prague 6; tel. 220183333; e-mail uochb@uochb.cas.cz; internet www.uochb.cas.cz; f. 1950; attached to Acad. of Sciences of the Czech Republic; Dir Dr ZDENĚK HAVLAS; publ. *Collection of Czechoslovak Chemical Communications* (12 a year).

Ústav půdní biologie AV ČR (Institute of Soil Biology AS CR): Na sádkách 7, České Budějovice; tel. 385310134; e-mail upb@upb.cas.cz; internet www.upb.cas.cz; f. 1979; attached to Acad. of Sciences of the Czech Republic; Dir Dr VÁCLAV PIŽL.

Ústav živočišné fyziologie a genetiky AV ČR (Institute of Animal Physiology and Genetics AS CR): Rumburská 89, 277 21 Liběchov; tel. 206639511; e-mail uzfg@iapg.cas.cz; internet www.iapg.cas.cz/uzfg; attached to Acad. of Sciences of the Czech Republic; Dir Prof. Dr IVAN MÍŠEK.

Mathematical Sciences

Český Statistický Úřad (Czech Statistical Office): Na padesátém 81, 100 82 Prague 10; tel. 274054070; internet www.czso.cz; f. 1899; library of 27,500 vols; Pres. JAN FISCHER; publs *CZSO Monthly Statistics*, *Selected Economic and Social Indicators of the Czech Republic* (4 a year), *Statistical Bulletin* (4 a year).

Matematický Ústav AV ČR (Institute of Mathematics AS CR): Žitná 25, 115 67 Prague 1; tel. 222090711; e-mail mathinst@math.cas.cz; internet www.math.cas.cz; f. 1947; attached to Acad. of Sciences of the Czech Republic; Dir Dr PAVEL KREJČÍ; publs *Applications of Mathematics* (6 a year), *Czechoslovak Mathematical Journal* (4 a year), *Mathematica Bohemica* (4 a year).

Physical Sciences

Astronomický ústav AV ČR (Astronomical Institute AS CR): Fricova 298, 251 65 Ondřejov; tel. 323620113; e-mail sekretariat@asu.cas.cz; internet www.asu.cas.cz; f. 1950; attached to Acad. of Sciences of the Czech Republic; Dir Dr PETR HEINZEL; publs *Scripta Astronomica* (irregular), *Time and Latitude* (4 a year).

Česká geologická služba (Czech Geological Survey): 118 21 Prague 1, Klárov 3; tel. 257089500; e-mail secretar@cgu.cz; internet www.geology.cz; f. 1919; library: see under Libraries and Archives; Dir Mgr ZDENĚK VENERA; publs *Bulletin of Geosciences* (4 a year), *Geological Bibliography of the Czech Republic* (1 a year), *Geoscience Research Reports* (1 a year), *Journal of Geological Sciences* (1 a year), *Special Papers* (1 a year).

Fyzikální ústav AV ČR (Institute of Physics AS CR): Na Slovance 2, 182 21 Prague 8; tel. 266053111; e-mail secretary@fzu.cz; internet www.fzu.cz; f. 1954; attached to Acad. of Sciences of the Czech Republic; Dir Dr KAREL JUNGWIRTH; publs *Československý časopis pro fyziku* (6 a year), *Czechoslovak Journal of Physics* (12 a year), *Jemná mechanika a optika* (Fine Mechanics and Optics, 12 a year).

Geofyzikální ústav AV ČR, v.v.i. (Geophysical Institute AS CR): Boční II/1401, 141 31 Prague; tel. 267103111; e-mail gfu@ig.cas.cz; internet www.ig.cas.cz; f. 1953; attached to Acad. of Sciences of the Czech Republic; scientific research in the fields of geophysical sciences; establishes and operates geophysical observatories and participates in the int. exchange of geophysical data; acquires, processes and disseminates scientific information and issues scientific publs; provides scientific assessments, professional opinions and recommendations, consulting and advisory services; organizes scientific meetings, conferences and seminars; Dir Dr PAVEL HEJDA; publs *Bulletin of the Czechoslovak Seismological Stations* (1 a year), *Studia Geophysica et Geodaetica* (4 a year), *Travaux Géophysiques* (irregular).

Geologický ústav AV ČR, v.v.i. (Institute of Geology AS CR, v.v.i.): Rozvojová 269, 165 00 Prague 6; tel. 233087111; e-mail inst@gli.cas.cz; internet www.gli.cas.cz; f. 1957; attached to Acad. of Sciences of the Czech Republic; geology, esp. basin analysis and tectonics, environmental geology and geochemistry, karstology, mineralogy, palaeontology, pedology, petrology; library of 10,000 vols; Dir Dr VÁCLAV CÍLEK; publs *Geolines* (2 a year), *Institute Research Reports* (1 a year).

Společná laboratoř chemie pevných látek AV ČR a Univerzity Pardubice (Joint Laboratory of Solid State Chemistry of the Institute of Macromolecular Chemistry AS CR and Pardubice University): Studentská 84, 532 10 Pardubice; tel. 466036150; e-mail slchpl@upce.cz; internet www.upce.cz/en/fcht/slchpl.html; f. 1986; attached to Acad. of Sciences of the Czech Republic and Univ. of Pardubice; solid state chemistry: non-graphite intercalation compounds metal phosphonates thermoelectric materials chalcogenide glasses; Head Dr VITEZSLAV ZIMA.

Státní úřad pro jadernou bezpečnost (State Office for Nuclear Safety): Senovážné nám. 9, 110 00 Prague 1; tel. 221624111; e-mail podatelna@sujb.cz; internet www.sujb.cz; f. 1993; regulatory activities in nuclear safety, radiation protection, inspection of materials and technologies of dual use for nuclear, biological and chemical weapons; Chair. DANA DRÁBOVÁ.

Ústav analytické chemie AV ČR (Institute of Analytical Chemistry AS CR): Veveří 97, 602 00 Brno; tel. 532290182; e-mail uiach@iach.cz; internet www.iach.cz/uiach; f. 1956; attached to Acad. of Sciences of the Czech Republic; research in analytical chemistry, devt of theory, methodology, and instrumentation for analytical chemistry; Head Prof. LUDMILA KRIVANKOVA; publ. *Research Activities and Future Trends* (irregular).

Ústav anorganické chemie AV ČR, v.v.i. (Institute of Inorganic Chemistry AS CR, v.v.i.): 250 68 Husinec-Řež; tel. 220940158; e-mail sekretar@iic.cas.cz; internet www.iic.cas.cz; f. 1959; attached to Acad. of Sciences of the Czech Republic; basic and applied research, preparation of inorganic compounds and materials and their applications in the field of inorganic chemistry; brs of inorganic chemistry, incl. physical chemistry, solid state physics, polymer chemistry, and ecology; bio-inorganic chemistry; attached laboratories of inorganic materials and low temperatures located in Prague; Dir Ing. JANA BLUDSKÁ; publs *Bulletin* (1 a year), *Ceramics–Silikáty* (6 a year).

Ústav chemických procesů AV ČR (Institute of Chemical Process Fundamentals AS CR): Rozvojová 135, 165 02 Prague; tel. 220390111; e-mail icecas@icpf.cas.cz; internet www.icpf.cas.cz; f. 1960; attached to Acad. of Sciences of the Czech Republic; Dir Prof. JIŘÍ DRAHOŠ.

Ústay Fyzikální Chemie J. Heyrovského AV ČR, v.v.i. (J. Heyrovský Institute of Physical Chemistry AS CR, v.v.i.): Dolejškova 3, 182 23 Prague 8; tel. 286583014; e-mail director@jh-inst.cas.cz; internet www.jh-inst.cas.cz; f. 1972; attached to Acad. of Sciences of the Czech Republic; research in physical chemistry, electrochemistry, chemical physics; library of 18,000 vols, 200 current periodical titles; Dir Prof. Dr ZDENĚK SAMEC; Sec. VLADIMIRA BERGEROVA; publs *Journal of American Chemical Society*, *Journal of Chemical Physics*, *Journal of Physical Chemistry*.

Ústav Fyziky Atmosféry AV ČR, v.v.i. (Institute of Atmospheric Physics AS CR, v.v.i.): 4, Boční II/1401, 141 31 Prague; tel. 272016011; e-mail iap@ufa.cas.cz; internet www.ufa.cas.cz; f. 1964; attached to Acad. of Sciences of the Czech Republic; research in aeronomy, climatology, ionospheric and magnetospheric physics, meteorology, space physics, wind energy and atmospheric pollution; library of 7,284 vols; Dir Doc. ZBYNĚK SOKOL; Head of Library EVA SMITKOVA.

Ústav fyziky materiálů AV ČR (Institute of the Physics of Materials AS CR): Žižkova 22, 616 62 Brno; tel. 541212286; e-mail secretar@ipm.cz; internet www.ipm.cz; f. 1956; attached to Acad. of Sciences of the Czech Republic; Dir Assoc. Prof. Dr PETR LUKÁŠ; publs *Engineering Mechanics* (6 a year), *Metallic Materials* (6 a year).

Ústav jaderné fyziky AV ČR (Nuclear Physics Institute AS CR): 250 68 Řež; tel. 220941147; e-mail ujf@ujf.cas.cz; internet www.ujf.cas.cz; f. 1955; attached to Acad. of Sciences of the Czech Republic; research in nuclear physics and related fields; operated by Nuclear Research Institute Řež plc; library of 50,000 vols; Dir Dr PETR LUKÁŠ; Scientific Sec. Dr VLADIMÍR WAGNER.

Ústav jaderného výzkumu Řež a.s. (Nuclear Research Institute Řež): Husinec-Řež 130, 250 68 Řež; tel. 266172000; e-mail ujv@ujv.cz; internet www.ujv.cz/web/ujv/clenstvi-v-organizacich; f. 1955; nuclear safety and reliability; integrity and technical engineering; project and engineering services; waste management and fuel cycle chemistry; laboratories; radio pharmaceuticals; library of 50,000 vols; Gen. Dir ALES JOHN.

Ústav makromolekulární chemie AV ČR (Institute of Macromolecular Chemistry AS CR): Heyrovský nám. 2, 162 06 Prague 6; tel. 296809111; e-mail office@imc.cas.cz; internet www.imc.cas.cz; f. 1959; attached to Acad. of Sciences of the Czech Republic; Dir FRANTIŠEK RYPÁČEK.

Ústav pro hydrodynamiku AV ČR, v.v.i. (Institute of Hydrodynamics AS CR, v.v.i.): Pod Patankou 30/5, 166 12 Prague 6; tel. 233109011; e-mail ih@ih.cas.cz; internet www.ih.cas.cz; f. 1953; attached to Acad. of Sciences of the Czech Republic; research in hydromechanics, rheology and hydrology; Dir Dr ZDENEK CHARA; publs *Engineering Mechanics* (6 a year), *Journal of Hydrology and Hydromechanics* (6 a year).

Ústav struktury a mechaniky hornin AV ČR (Institute of Rock Structure and Mechanics AS CR): V Holešovičkách 41, 182 09 Prague 8; tel. 266009111; e-mail irsm@irsm.cas.cz; internet www.irsm.cas.cz; f. 1958; attached to Acad. of Sciences of the Czech Republic; library of 28,000 vols; Dir Ing. KAREL BALIK; publs *Acta Montana, Series A: Geodynamics* (in English, irregular), *Acta Montana, Series B: Fuel, Carbon, Mineral Processing* (in English, irregular), *Acta Montana, Series AB: Geodynamics, Fuel, Carbon, Mineral Processing* (in English and Czech, irregular).

Ústav termomechaniky AV ČR (Institute of Thermomechanics AS CR): Dolejškova 5, 182 00 Prague 8; tel. 286890383; e-mail secr@it.cas.cz; internet www.it.cas.cz; f. 1954; attached to Acad. of Sciences of the Czech Republic; library of 12,000 vols; Dir Dr JIRI PLESEK; publs *Acta Technica CSAV* (4 a year), *Engineering Mechanics* (6 a year).

PHILOSOPHY AND PSYCHOLOGY

Centrum pro teoretická studia Univerzita Karlova (Centre for Theoretical Study at Charles University): Jilská 1, 110 00 Prague 1; tel. 222220671; e-mail office@cts.cuni.cz; internet www.cts.cuni.cz; attached to Acad. of Sciences of the Czech Republic; Dir Doc. DAVID STORCH.

Filozofický ústav AV ČR (Institute of Philosophy AS CR): Jilská 1, 110 00 Prague; tel. 222220124; e-mail flusekr@site.cas.cz; internet www.flu.cas.cz; f. 1990; attached to Acad. of Sciences of the Czech Republic; Dir Dr PAVEL BARAN; publs *Acta Comeniana* (irregular), *Filosofický časopis* (Philosophical Review, 6 a year), *Teorie vědy* (4 a year).

Psychologický ústav AV ČR (Institute of Psychology AS CR): Veveří 97, 602 00 Brno; tel. 532290270; e-mail cermak@psu.cas.cz; internet www.psu.cas.cz; f. 1967; attached to Acad. of Sciences of the Czech Republic; Dir Doc. Dr IVO ČERMÁK; publs *Československá psychologie* (6 a year), *Zprávy* (irregular).

RELIGION, SOCIOLOGY AND ANTHROPOLOGY

Etnologický ústav AV ČR, v.v.i. (Institute of Ethnology AS CR, v.v.i.): Na Florenci 3, 110 00 Prague; tel. 222828503; e-mail office@eu.cas.cz; internet www.eu.cas.cz; f. 1954; attached to Acad. of Sciences of the Czech Republic; library of 80,000 vols; Dir Dr ZDENĚK UHEREK; publs *Český lid: Etnologický časopis / Český lid Ethnological* (4 a year), *Hudební věda* (4 a year).

Sociologický ústav AV ČR (Institute of Sociology AS CR): Jilská 1, 110 00 Prague; tel. 222221753; e-mail socmail@soc.cas.cz; internet www.soc.cas.cz; f. 1990; attached to Acad. of Sciences of the Czech Republic; Dir Dr MARIE ČERMÁKOVÁ; publs *Historická demografie* (1 a year), *Sociologický časopis* (Czech Sociological Review, 6 a year).

TECHNOLOGY

Laboratoř anorganických materiálů (Laboratory of Inorganic Materials): Institute of Rock Structure and Mechanics V, Holešovičkách 41, 182 09 Prague 8; tel. 220445191; e-mail lubomir.nemec@vscht.cz; internet www.vscht.cz/sls; f. 1961; attached to Acad. of Sciences of the Czech Republic and Institute of Chemical Technology; Dir Prof. LUBOMÍR NĚMEC.

SVUSS Praha, s.r.o.: Na Harfě 336/9, 190 00 Prague 9–Vysočany; tel. (2) 66035661; e-mail suchanek@svuss.cz; internet www.svuss.cz; f. 1998; technical studies in engineering, heat transfer and the power industry; carries out tests and research in the field of thermodynamics; library of 10,000 vols; Dir Ing. MIROSLAV SUCHANEK (acting).

Ústav fotoniky a elektroniky AV ČR (Institute of Photonics and Electronics AS CR): Chaberská 57, 182 51 Prague 8; tel. 284681804; e-mail ufe@ufe.cz; internet www.ure.cas.cz; f. 1955 as Ústav radiotechniky a elektroniky AV ČR, present name 2007; attached to Acad. of Sciences of the Czech Republic; research and devt in photonics, optoelectronics, and signals and systems; library of 16,500 vols, 390 periodicals; Dir Dr Ing. VLASTIMIL MATĚJEC.

Ústav Informatiky AV ČR, v.v.i. (Institute of Computer Science AS CR, v.v.i.): Pod Vodárenskou věží 2, 182 07 Prague 8; tel. 266052083; e-mail ics@cs.cas.cz; internet www.cs.cas.cz; f. 1975; attached to Acad. of Sciences of the Czech Republic; library of 8,000 vols; Dir Dr MICHAL CHYTIL; publ. *Neural Network Word*.

Ústav přístrojové techniky AV ČR, v.v.i. (Institute of Scientific Instruments AS CR, v.v.i.): Královopolská 147, 612 64 Brno; tel. 541514111; e-mail institute@isibrno.cz; internet www.isibrno.cz; f. 1957; attached to Acad. of Sciences of the Czech Republic; methodology in selected areas of chemistry, physics, technology, main programs: bioinformatics, coherence optics, electron optics and microscopy, magnetic resonance, vacuum technologies; Dir Dr LUDĚK FRANK.

Ústav teoretické a aplikované mechaniky AV ČR (Institute of Theoretical and Applied Mechanics AS CR): Prosecká 76, 190 00 Prague 9; tel. 286882121; e-mail itam@itam.cas.cz; internet www.itam.cas.cz; attached to Acad. of Sciences of the Czech Republic; Dir Dr MILOŠ DRDÁCKÝ; publ. *Engineering Mechanics* (6 a year).

Ústav teorie informace a automatizace AV ČR (Institute of Information Theory and Automation AS CR): POB 18, 182 08 Prague 8; Pod Vodárenskou věží 4, 182 08 Prague 8; tel. 266053111; e-mail utia@utia.cas.cz; internet www.utia.cas.cz; f. 1959; attached to Acad. of Sciences of the Czech Republic; Dir Prof. Dr JAN FLUSSER; publ. *Kybernetica* (6 a year).

Ústav termomechaniky AV ČR, v.v.i. (Institute of Thermomechanics AS CR, v.v.i.): Dolejškova 1402/5, 182 00 Prague 8; tel. 266052021; e-mail secr@it.cas.cz; internet www.it.cas.cz; f. 1953, merged with the Institute of Electrical Engineering in 2006; attached to Acad. of Sciences of the Czech Republic; basic research in fluid dynamics, thermodynamics, dynamics of mechanical systems, solid mechanics, interactions of fluids and solids, environmental aerodynamics, biomechanics, mechatronics, electrophysics, electrical machines, drives and electronics and material diagnostics; Dir Dr JIRI PLESEK; Deputy Dir Dr MIROSLAV CHOMAT; publs *Acta Technica* (4 a year), *Engineering Mechanics* (6 a year).

VÚTS Liberec a.s. (Research Institute for Textile Machines, Liberec Co.): U jezu 4, 461 19 Liberec 4; tel. 485301111; e-mail vuts@vuts.cz; internet www.vuts.cz; f. 1951; library of 10,000 vols; 154 mems; Gen. Dir Prof. Ing. MIROSLAV VÁCLAVÍK.

Libraries and Archives

Brno

Moravská zemská knihovna (Moravian Library): Kounicova 65A, 601 87 Brno; tel. 541646111; e-mail mzk@mzk.cz; internet www.mzk.cz; f. 1808; 3,850,000 vols, 4,300 periodicals; Dir Dr J. KUBÍČEK.

Ústřední knihovna a informační středisko Veterinární a farmaceutické univerzity (Central Library and Information Centre of the University of Veterinary and Pharmaceutical Sciences): Palackého 1–3, 612 42 Brno; tel. 541562080; e-mail gect@vfu.cz; internet sis.vfu.cz; f. 1919; 174,126 vols; Chief Librarian TOMÁŠ GEC; publ. *Acta veterinaria Brno* (4 a year).

České Budějovice

Státní vědecká knihovna (State Research Library): Na Sadech 26-27, Lidická 1, 370 59 České Budějovice; tel. 386111211; e-mail library@cbvk.cz; internet www.cbvk.cz; f. 1885; 1,500,000 vols; Dir Dr KVETA CEMPIRKOVA.

Hradec Králové

Studijní a vědecká knihovna (Research Library): Pospíšilova 395, POB 7, 500 03 Hradec Králové; tel. 495514871; e-mail knihovna@svkhk.cz; internet www.svkhk.cz; f. 1949; 1,189,172 vols; Dir Mgr EVA SVOBODOVÁ.

Liberec

Krajská vědecká knihovna v Liberci (Research Library in Liberec): Rumjancevova 1362/1, 460 53 Liberec; tel. 482412111; e-mail library@kvkli.cz; internet www.kvkli.cz; f. 1945; 760,000 books, 1,600 periodicals, 29,000 vols of standards, 380,000 vols of patents, 27,000 vols of printed music, 9,000 sound recordings, 3,500 vols of maps, 600 CD-ROMs; Dir PAVEL HARVÁNEK; publ. *Světlík* (World of the Liberec Region Libraries, 6 a year).

Olomouc

Vědecká knihovna v Olomouci (Research Library in Olomouc): Bezručova 3, 779 11 Olomouc; tel. 585223441; e-mail info@vkol.cz; internet www.vkol.cz; f. 1566; 2,034,000 vols, 1,448 MSS, 1,800 incunabula, 70,000 old prints; Dir JITKA HOLÁSKOVÁ; publ. *Krok* (4 a year).

Ostrava

Moravskoslezská Vědecká Knihovna v Ostravě (Moravian-Silesian Research Library in Ostrava): Prokešovo nám. 9, 728 00 Ostrava; tel. 596118881; e-mail msvk@svkos.cz; internet www.svkos.cz; f. 1951; 1,110,656 vols, 609,085 books, 3,774 newspapers and journals, 10,748 sound documents, 64,139 standards, 284,635 patents; Dir Ing. LEA PRCHALOVÁ.

Ústřední knihovna Vysoké školy báňské-Technické univerzity Ostrava (Central Library of the VSB-Technical University of Ostrava): 17 listopadu 15, 708 33 Ostrava-Poruba; tel. 596991278; e-mail knihovna@vsb.cz; internet www.knihovna.vsb.cz; f. 1849; 380,000 vols; Dir DANIELA TKAČÍKOVÁ; publ. *Sborník vědeckých prací Vysoké školy báňské—Technické univerzity Ostrava* (Transactions, irregular).

Plzeň

Studijní a vědecká knihovna Plzeňského kraje (Education and Research Library of Pilsener Region): Smetanovy sady 2, 305 48 Plzeň; tel. 377224249; e-mail svk@svkpl.cz; internet www.svkpl.cz; f. 1950; 791,000 books, 1,700 current periodicals, 793,000 documents; Dir Dr JAROSLAV VYČICHLO; publs *Přírůstky zahraniční literatury* (foreign accessions, 4 a year), *Západni Čechy v tisku* (West Bohemia in Print).

Prague

Knihovna Akademie věd České republiky (Library of the Academy of Sciences of the Czech Republic): Národní 3, 115 22 Prague 1; tel. 221403260; e-mail infoknav@lib.cas.cz; internet www.knav.cz; f. 1952; HQ of the network of information centres and spec. libraries of academic institutes; 1m. vols, 2,102 periodicals; Dir MARTIN LHOTÁK.

Knihovna Archeologického Ústavu AV ČR, Praha, v.v.i. (Library of the Archaeological Institute of the Academy of Sciences of the Czech Republic): Letenská 4, 118 01 Prague; tel. (2) 57014318; e-mail knihovna@arup.cas.cz; internet www.arup.cas.cz; f. 1919; 40,281 vols; Chief Librarian ALZBETA DANIELISOVA; publs *Archeologické Rozhledy* (4 a year), *Castellologica Bohemica* (irregular), *Castrum Pragense* (irregular), *Mediaevalia Archaeologica* (irregular), *Památky Archeologické* (1 a year), *Památky Archeologické-Supplementum* (irregular), *Výzkumy v Čechách* (irregular).

Knihovna České geologické služby (Library of the Czech Geological Survey): Klárov 3, 118 21 Prague 1; tel. 257089411; e-mail breit@cgu.cz; internet www.geology.cz; f. 1924; archive of 60,000 vols; 168,000 vols; Head of Library RNDr HANA BREITEROVÁ; publs *Geological Bibliography of the Czech Republic* (1 a year), *Library of the Geological Survey* (irregular).

Knihovna Evangelické teologické fakulty Univerzity Karlovy (Library of the Protestant Theological Faculty of the Charles University): Černá 9, 115 55 Prague 1; tel. 221988104; e-mail kis-l@bojar.ruk.cuni.cz; internet kis.is.cuni.cz; f. 1919; 190,000 vols, 185 current periodicals; Dir BARBORA DROBÍKOVÁ; publs *Communio Viatorum* (3 a year), *Teologická reflexe* (2 a year).

Knihovna Národní Galerie (Library of the National Gallery): Národní galerie v Praze, Staroměstské nám. 12, 110 15 Prague; Hradčanské nám. 15, 119 04 Prague 1; tel. 220515458; e-mail library@ngprague.cz; internet www.ngprague.cz; f. 1880; 105,000 vols; Dir Dr MARTINA HORÁKOVÁ; Librarian MARIE RUMÍŠKOVÁ.

Knihovna Národního Muzea (Library of the National Museum): Václavské nám. 68, 115 79 Prague 1; tel. 224497111; e-mail jarmila_kucerova@nm.cz; internet www.nm.cz; f. 1818; 3.6m. vols; Dir Mgr Dr MARTIN SEKERA; Librarian Dr JARMILA KUCEROVA; publ. *Sborník Národního Muzea, Řada C–Literární Historie*.

Knihovna Národního technického muzea (Library of the National Technical Museum): Kostelní 42, 170 78 Prague 7; tel. 220399187; e-mail knihovna@ntm.cz; internet www.ntm.cz; f. 1833; 200,000 vols; Chief Librarian Mgr LUCIE CHRASTOVA.

Knihovna Orientálního Ústavu Akademie věd České Republiky (Library of the Oriental Institute of the Academy of Sciences of the Czech Republic): Pod vodárenskou věží 2, 182 08 Prague; tel. 266053950; e-mail jan.luffer@orient.cas.cz; internet www.orient.cas.cz; f. 1929; 210,000 vols, 'Lu Xun' Chinese library of 67,000 vols, Korean library of 3,500 vols, Tibetan colln of Kanjur and Tanjur; Head of Library Dr JAN LUFFER; publs *Archiv Orientální* (4 a year), *Nový Orient* (4 a year).

Knihovna Uměleckoprůmyslového musea (Museum of Decorative Arts Library): 17 listopadu 2, 110 01 Prague 1; tel. 251093135; e-mail knihovna@upm.cz; internet www.knihovna.upm.cz; f. 1885; 175,000 vols; Dir Dr JARMILA OKROUHLÍKOVÁ; publ. *Acta UPM* (irregular).

Masarykův ústav a Archiv AV ČR, v.v.i. (Masaryk Institute and Archives ASCR, v.v.i.): Gabčíkova 2362/10, 182 00 Prague 8; tel. 286010110; e-mail mua@mua.cas.cz; internet www.mua.cas.cz; f. 1953; attached to Acad. of Sciences of the Czech Republic; 60,000 vols; Dir Dr LUBOŠ VELEK; publs *Práce z Archivu Akademie věd* (Studies of the Archives of the Acad. of Sciences, 1 a year), *Práce z dějin Akademie věd* (Studies on the History of the Academy of Sciences, 2 a year), *Práce z dějin věd* (Studies on the History of Sciences and the Humanities, 2 a year), *Studia historiae academiae scientiarum—Práce z dějin akademie věd* (Studies on the History of the Academy of Sciences, 1 a year), *Studie o rukopisech* (Codicological Studies, 1 a year).

Městská knihovna v Praze (Municipal Library of Prague): Mariánské nám. 1, 115 72 Prague 1; tel. 222113306; e-mail knihovna@mlp.cz; internet www.mlp.cz; f. 1891; central library, 42 brs and 2 mobile libraries; 2,291,359 vols, incl. books, journals, maps, CDs, DVDs, MP3s, reproductions; Dir Dr TOMÁŠ ŘEHÁK.

Národní knihovna České republiky (National Library of the Czech Republic): Klementinum 190, 110 00 Prague 1; tel. 221663111; e-mail sekret.ur@nkp.cz; internet www.nkp.cz; f. 1366; 6,800,000 vols, 18,707 MSS, 3,500 incunabula, 200,000 early printed books; Dir-Gen. Ing. TOMÁŠ BÖHM; publs *Knihovna-knihovnická revue*, *Miscellanea oddělení rukopisů a starých tisků* (1 a year), *Národní knihovna* (4 a year).

Branch Library:

Slovanská knihovna (Slavonic Library): Klementinum 190, 110 00 Prague; tel. 221663356; e-mail sluzby.sk@nkp.cz; internet www.nkp.cz/slk; f. 1924; 775,000 vols; Dir Dr LUKÁŠ BABKA.

Národní lékařská knihovna (National Medical Library): Nové Město, Sokolská 54, 121 32 Prague 2; tel. 296335911; e-mail nml@nlk.cz; internet www.nlk.cz; f. 1949; 335,000 vols, 1,500 current periodicals, 6,000 doctoral theses; WHO documentation centre; oversees translation of MeSH into Czech; operates union catalogue of medical literature; Dir HELENA BOUZKOVA; publs *Bibliographia medica čechoslovaca* (12 a year), *Referátový výběr* (series of 4 abstracts journals, 4 or 6 a year).

Národní pedagogická knihovna Komenského (Comenius National Library of Education): Mikulandská 5, 116 74 Prague 1; tel. 221966402; e-mail library@npkk.cz; internet www.npkk.cz; f. 1919; youth br. (Suk Library) of 58,000 vols (since 1790); 471,000 vols; Dir ALICE KOŠKOVÁ.

Státní technická knihovna (State Technical Library): Mariánské nám. 5, POB 206, 110 01 Prague 1; tel. 2221663111; e-mail informace@stk.cz; internet www.stk.cz; f. 1718; 1,501,632 vols, 1,524 periodicals, 31 databases; Dir Ing. MARTIN SVOBODA.

Univerzita Karlova, Pedagogická fakulta, Ústřední knihovna (Charles University Faculty of Education, Central Library): M. D. Rettigove 4, 116 39 Prague 1; tel. 296242420; e-mail knihovna@pedf.cuni.cz; internet www.pedf.cuni.cz/ustredniknihovna; f. 1948; 211,302 vols, 177 periodicals; Dir Mgr JITKA BÍLKOVÁ; Librarian ZUZANA MARSICKOVA.

Úřad Průmyslového Vlastnictví (Industrial Property Office): Antonína Čermáka 2A, 160 68 Prague 6-Bubeneč; tel. 220383111; e-mail objednavky@upv.cz; internet www.upv.cz; 30m. documents; Dir for Patent Information Dept Ing. MIROSLAV PACLÍK.

Ústav dějin Univerzity Karlovy a Archiv Univerzity Karlovy (Institute of the History of Charles University and Archive of Charles University): Ovocný trh 5, 116 36 Prague 1; tel. 224491463; e-mail udauk@ruk.cuni.cz; internet udauk.cuni.cz; focuses on history of education and schooling in Czech lands (spec. focus on Charles Univ.); 49,000 vols, 6 km of archival material; Dir PETR SVOBODNÝ; Librarian Dr JIŘINA URBANOVÁ; Archivist Dr MAREK ĎURČANSKÝ; publ. *Acta Universitatis Carolinae—Historia Universitatis Carolinae Pragensis*.

Ústav Vědeckých Informací 1. Lékařské Fakulty, Univerzita Karlova (Institute of Scientific Information, First Medical Faculty, Charles University): U Nemocnice 4, 121 08 Prague 2; tel. 224965600; e-mail knihovna@lf1.cuni.cz; internet uvi.lf1.cuni.cz; f. 1949; 450,512 vols, 712 current periodicals; Dir Dr HANA SKÁLOVÁ; Sec. BĚLA ČERNÁ; publs *Acta Universitatis Carolinae Medica*, *Folia Biologica*, *Prague Medical Report*, *Proceedings of the Scientific Conferences*, *Sborník Lékařský*.

Ústav zemědělských a potravinářských informací (Institute of Agricultural and Food Information): Londýnská 55, 120 21 Prague 2; tel. 224256387; e-mail knihovna@uzpi.cz; internet www.knihovna.uzpi.cz; f. 1993; 1.2m. vols; Dir Ing. C. PERLÍN; publs *Genetika a šlechtění* (Genetics and Plant Breeding, 4 a year), *Lesnictví* (Forest Science, 12 a year), *Ochrana rostlin* (Plant Protection Science, 4 a year), *Potravinářské vědy* (Food Science, 6 a year), *Rostlinná výroba* (Plant Production, 12 a year), *Veterinární medicína* (Veterinary Medicine, 12 a year), *Zahradnictví* (Horticulture, 4 a year), *Zemědělská ekonomika* (Agricultural Economics, 12 a year), *Zemědělská technika* (Agricultural Engineering, 4 a year), *Živočišná výroba* (Journal of Animal Science, 12 a year).

Ústřední tělovýchovná knihovna (Central Library of Physical Training): José Martiho 31, 162 52 Prague 6; tel. 220172158; e-mail utk@ftvs.cuni.cz; internet www.ftvs.cuni.cz/knihovna; f. 1927; 300,000 vols; Dir Dr JANA BĚLÍKOVÁ; publ. *Acta Universitatis Carolinae Kinanthropologica*.

Ústřední zemědělská knihovna (Central Agricultural Library): Slezská 7, POB 39, 120 56 Prague 2; tel. 227010111; e-mail uzpi@uzpi.cz; internet www.uzpi.cz; f. 1926; a section of the Institute of Agricultural and Food Information; 1.1m. vols; Dir Dr BAŠEK VÁCLAV; publ. *Seznam časopisů* (List of Periodicals, 1 a year).

Ústí nad Labem

Severočeská Vědecká Knihovna (North Bohemian Research Library): POB 134, W. Churchilla 3, 401 34 Ústí nad Labem; tel. 475209126; e-mail library@svkul.cz; internet www.svkul.cz; f. 1945; inter library loan; 823,000 vols; Dir ALEŠ BROŽEK; publ. *Výběr Kulturních Výročí* (online, www.svkul.cz/o-knihovne/publikace/vyber-kulturnich-vyroci).

Museums and Art Galleries

Brno

Moravská galerie v Brně (Moravian Gallery in Brno): Husova 18, 662 26 Brno; tel. 532169111; e-mail info@moravska-galerie.cz; internet www.moravska-galerie.cz; f. 1873; mostly European fine and applied art of all periods; library of 130,000 vols; Dir MAREK POKORNÝ; Head of Library JUDITA MATĚJOVÁ.

Moravské zemské muzeum (Moravian Provincial Museum): Zelný trh 6, 659 37 Brno; tel. 533435220; e-mail mzm@mzm.cz; internet www.mzm.cz; f. 1817; history, natural history, geology, arts, anthropology, horticulture; library of 260,000 vols; Dir Dr MARTIN REISSNER; publs *Acta Musei Moraviae–Scientiae Biologicae* (2 a year), *Acta Musei Moraviae–Scientiae Geologicae* (2 a year), *Acta Musei Moraviae–Scientiae Sociales* (2 a year), *Anthropologie* (3 a year), *Folia Ethnografica* (2 a year), *Folia Mendeliana* (2 a year), *Folia Numismatica* (2 a year).

Muzeum města Brna (Brno Municipal Museum): Špilberk 1, 662 24 Brno; tel. 542123611; e-mail muzeum.brno@spilberk.cz; internet www.spilberk.cz; f. 1904; history of Brno and Špilberk Castle; art gallery; Dir Dr PAVEL CIPRIAN.

Technické muzeum v Brně (Technical Museum in Brno): Purkyňova 105, 612 00 Brno; tel. 541421411; internet www.technicalmuseum.cz; f. 1961; library of 42,000 vols; Dir Ing. VLASTIMIL VYKYDAL; publs *Archeologia technica* (1 a year), *Muzejní noviny*, *Nožířské listy* (1 a year), *Sborník z konzervátorského a restaurátorského semináře* (1 a year).

České Budějovice

Jihočeské muzeum v Českých Budějovicích (South Bohemian Museum in České Budějovice): Dukelská 1, 370 51 České Budějovice; tel. 387929311; e-mail muzeumcb@muzeumcb.cz; internet www.muzeumcb.cz; f. 1877; history, archaeology, natural history, arts; Dir PAVEL ŠAFR; publs *Archeologické výzkumy v jižních Čechách* (archaeology, 1 a year), *Jihočeský sborník historický* (history, 1 a year), *Sborník Přírodní vědy* (nature, 1 a year), *Výběr Časopis pro historii a vlastivědu jižních Čech* (regional and cultural history, 4 a year).

Cheb

Krajské muzeum Cheb (Cheb Regional Museum): nám. Krále Jiřího z Poděbrad 493/4, 350 11 Cheb; tel. 739322499; e-mail sekretariat@muzeumcheb.cz; internet www.muzeumcheb.cz; f. 1874; history, local ceramics; library of 25,000 vols, 7,000 regional publs, 300 old and rare books and 25 MSS; Dir Dr EVA DITTERTOVÁ; publ. *Sborník chebského muzea* (1 a year).

Chrudim

Muzeum loutkářských kultur v Chrudim (Chrudim Puppet Museum): Břetislavova 74, 537 60 Chrudim; tel. 469620310; e-mail puppets@puppets.cz; internet www.puppets.cz; f. 1972; Dir Mgr SIMONA CHALUPOVÁ.

Harrachov

Muzeum skla (Glass Museum): Harrachov 95, 512 46 Harrachov; tel. 481528141; e-mail obchod@sklarnaharrachov.cz; internet www.sklarnaharrachov.cz; f. 1972; Dir K. PIPEK.

Hluboká nad Vltavou

Alšova jihočeská galerie (Aleš South Bohemian Gallery): Zámak è. 144, 373 41 Hluboká nad Vltavou; tel. 387967041; e-mail ajg@ajg.cz; internet www.ajg.cz; f. 1953; Czech art since 13th century, 16th–18th century European art, Czech and world ceramics since early 20th century; library of 12,950 vols; Dir Dr HYNEK RULÍŠEK.

Hradec Králové

Muzeum východních Čech, Hradec Králové (Museum of East Bohemia, Hradec Králové): Eliščino nábřeží 465, 500 01 Hradec Králové 1; tel. 495512391; e-mail info@muzeumhk.cz; internet www.muzeumhk.cz; f. 1879; natural sciences, history, archaeology, education; 1866 War Memorial; library of 70,000 vols; Dir Dr NADA MACHKOVA PRAJZOVA; publs *Acta* (irregular), *Fontes* (irregular), *Historická fotografie* (irregular), *Královéhradecko* (irregular), *Zpravodaj muzea v Hradci Králové* (irregular).

Hukvaldy

Památník Leoše Janáčka (Leos Janacek Museum): Smetanova 14, Brno; tel. 606033100; e-mail info@mzm.cz; internet www.mzm.cz; f. 1933; renovated original house of Leos Janacek; exhibits life and work of Leos Janacek; audiovisual hall; Head Mgr SIMONA ŠINDLÁŘOVÁ.

Jablonec nad Nisou

Muzeum skla a bižuterie (Museum of Glass and Jewellery): Muzea 398/4, 466 01 Jablonec nad Nisou; tel. 483369011; e-mail info@msb-jablonec.cz; internet www.msb-jablonec.cz; f. 1961; Bohemian glass, Jablonec jewellery; library of 15,000 vols; Dir Ing. VALEČKOVÁ MILADA.

Karlovy Vary

Galerie umění Karlovy Vary (Karlovy Vary Art Gallery): Goethova stezka 6, 360 01 Karlovy Vary; tel. 353224387; e-mail info@galeriekvary.cz; internet www.galeriekvary.cz; f. 1953; 20th-century Czech art; Dir JAN SAMEC.

Karlovarské muzeum (Karlovy Vary Museum): Nová louka 23, 360 01 Karlovy Vary; tel. 226252253; e-mail sekretariat@kvmuz.cz; internet www.kvmuz.cz; f. 1870; history, natural history, arts; Dir LENKA ZUBAČOVÁ.

Zlatý klíč muzeum (Golden Key Museum): Lázeňská 3, 360 01 Karlovy Vary; tel. 353223888; f. 1960; art nouveau paintings; Dir MARIE GULGOVÁ.

Kolín

Regionální muzeum v Kolíně (Kolín Regional Museum): Brandlova 35, 280 02 Kolín; tel. 321723841; e-mail muzeum@kolin.cz; f. 1895; local history; open-air museum at Kouřim; library of 49,500 vols; Dir JARMILA VALENTOVÁ.

Kopřivnice

Technické muzeum Tatra (Tatra Cars Museum): Záhumenní 367/1, 742 21 Kopřivnice; tel. 556808421; internet www.tatramuseum.cz; f. 1947; Tatra cars, trucks, railway carriages, aircraft, engines and chassis, history of Tatra production; Dir LUMÍR KAVÁLEK.

Kutná Hora

České muzeum stříba (Czech Silver Museum): Hrádek, Barborská 28, 284 01 Kutná Hora; tel. 327512159; e-mail info@cms-kh.cz; internet www.cms-kh.cz; f. 1877; medieval castle, medieval silver mine, Gothic town house, town life in 17th–19th centuries; Dir SVĚTLANA HRABÁNKOVÁ.

Liberec

Oblastní galerie v Liberci (Liberec Regional Art Gallery): U Tiskárny 81/1, 460 01 Liberec 5; tel. 485106325; e-mail oblgal@ogl.cz; internet www.ogl.cz; f. 1873; 16th- to 18th-century Dutch and Flemish painting, 19th-century French landscapes, 20th-century Czech art; Dir Mgr JAN RANDÁČEK.

Severočeské muzeum v Liberci (North Bohemian Museum in Liberec): Masarykova tř. 11, 460 01 Liberec; tel. 485246111; e-mail muzeumlb@muzeumlb.cz; internet www.muzeumlb.cz; f. 1873; European and Bohemian applied arts, regional history, natural history; collections of glass, ceramics, porcelain, textiles, tapestries, jewellery, metal objects, furniture, posters, archaeological artefacts; library of 35,000 vols; Dir JIŘÍ KŘÍŽEK; publ. *Sborník Severočeského musea* (every 2 years).

Lidice

Památník Lidice (Lidice Memorial Museum): Kladno district, 273 54 Lidice; tel. 312253088; e-mail muzeum@lidice-memorial.cz; internet www.lidice-memorial.cz; f. 1948; attached to Min. of Culture; history of the destruction of the village of Lidice in the Second World War; gallery of painting and sculptures devoted to Lidice; Dir MILOUŠ CERVENCL.

Litoměřice

Severočeská galerie výtvarného umění v Litoměřicích (North Bohemian Gallery of Fine Art in Litoměřice): Michalská 7, 412 01 Litoměřice; tel. 416732382; e-mail info@galerie-ltm.cz; internet www.galerie-ltm.cz; f. 1958; European art since the 12th century; Czech art from 13th century to present time; spec. colln of naive art; library of 16,000 vols; Dir Dr JAN ŠTÍBR.

Mariánské Lázně

Městské muzeum Mariánské Lázně (Mariánské Lázně Municipal Museum): Goethovo nám. 11, 353 01 Mariánské Lázně; tel. 354622740; e-mail muzeum@goethe-haus

.cz; f. 1887; history, geology; open-air geological park; Dir Ing. JAROMÍR BARTOŠ.

Mladá Boleslav

Škoda Auto Museum (Škoda Auto Museum): Tř. Václava Klementa 294, 293 60 Mladá Boleslav; tel. 326832038; e-mail museum@skoda-auto.cz; internet muzeum.skoda-auto.cz; f. 1974; Dir MARGIT ČERNÁ.

Opava

Slezské zemské muzeum (Silesian Museum): Tyršova 1, 746 01 Opava; tel. 553622999; e-mail szmred@szmo.cz; internet www.szmo.cz; f. 1814; attached to Min. of Culture; history, natural history, social sciences, arts; arboretum at Nový Dvůr; botanic garden; library of 280,000 vols; Dir Dr JAROMÍR KALUS; Chief Librarian Mgr JITKA STERBOVA; publs *Casopis Slezskeho zemskeho muzea* (natural sciences and historical sciences series, each 3 a year), *Slezsky sbornik* (3 or 4 a year), *Vlastivědné listy Slezska a severní Moravy* (2 a year).

Pardubice

Východočeské muzeum v Pardubicich (Museum of Eastern Bohemia): Zámek č. 2, 530 02 Pardubice; tel. 466799240; e-mail vcm@vcm.cz; internet www.vcm.cz; f. 1880; history, natural history, arts; library of 45,000 vols; Dir Dr FRANTISEK ŠEBEK; publs *Panurus* (1 a year), *Východočeský sborník historický* (1 a year), *Východočeský sborník přírodovědný* (1 a year).

Plzeň

Západočeská galerie v Plzni (West Bohemian Gallery in Plzeň): Pražská 13, 301 00 Plzeň; tel. 377 908 511; e-mail info@zpc-galerie.cz; internet www.zpc-galerie.cz; f. 1954; Czech art from the 14th century to the contemporary period; Dir Dr JANA POTUŽÁKOVÁ.

Západočeské muzeum v Plzni (West Bohemian Museum in Plzeň): Kopeckého sady 2, 301 00 Plzeň; tel. 377329380; e-mail info@zcm.cz; internet www.zcm.cz; f. 1878; history, natural history, arts; Dir Dr FRANTIŠEK FRÝDA; publs *Folia Musei Rerum Naturalium Bohemiae Occidentalis* (separate series for zoology, geology and botany, each 2 a year), *Sborník* (*Příroda*, 5 a year; *Historie*, 1 a year).

Prace u Brna

Mohyla míru (Peace Monument): 664 58 Prace u Brna; tel. 544244724; f. 1910; battle of Slavkov (Austerlitz); Dir Mgr ANTONÍN REČEK.

Prague

České muzeum výtvarných umění v Praze (Czech Museum of Fine Arts in Prague): Husova 19/21, 110 00 Prague 1; tel. 222220218; e-mail muzeum@cmvu.cz; internet www.cmvu.cz; f. 1963; temporary exhibitions of modern and contemporary art; Dir Dr IVAN NEUMANN.

Galerie hlavního města Prahy (City Gallery Prague): Staroměstské Náměstí 13, 110 00 Prague; tel. (2) 33325330; e-mail office@ghmp.cz; internet www.ghmp.cz; f. 1963; Pragensia, works by Czech artists since 19th century; library of 2,000 vols; Dir Dr. MAGDALENA JUŘÍKOVÁ.

Muzeum hlavního města Prahy (Central Museum of the City of Prague): Na Poříčí 52, 110 00 Prague 1; tel. 224223696; e-mail muzeum@muzeumprahy.cz; internet www.muzeumprahy.cz; f. 1881; history of Prague, archaeology, fine art; library of 17,000 vols; Dir Dr ZUZANA STRNADOVÁ; publ. *Archeologica pragensia* (1 a year).

Národní galerie v Praze (National Gallery in Prague): Staroměstské nám. 12, 110 15 Prague 1; tel. 222329331; e-mail genreditel@ngprague.cz; internet www.ngprague.cz; f. 1796; art of all periods; library of 90,000 vols; Dir-Gen. (vacant).

Národní muzeum (National Museum): Central Bldg, Václavské nám. 68, 115 79 Prague 1; tel. 224497111; e-mail nm@nm.cz; internet www.nm.cz; f. 1818; expositions, spec. exhibitions, lecturing and teaching, pubs; collns of natural history, prehistory, history of Czech and foreign provenance, especially in the field of ancient history of the Near E and Africa, anthropology, Asian culture, bibliology, botanics, classical archaeology, Czech history, entomology, ethnography, geology, history of physical education and sport, history of theatre, hydrobiology, medieval archaeology, micology, mineralogy, musicology, non-European ethnography, numismatics, palaeontology, petrology, prehistory, zoology; library: see under Libraries and Archives; Dir-Gen. Dr MICHAL LUKEŠ; publs *Casopis Národního muzea* (Journal of the National Museum, 2 a year), *Museum* (2 a year), *Numismatické listy* (Numismatic Papers, 4 a year), *Sborník Národního muzea v Praze* (Acta Musei Nationalis Pragae, 2 a year).

Constituent Museums:

České muzeum hudby (Czech Museum of Music): Karmeliská 2, 118 00 Prague 1; tel. 257257777; e-mail c_muzeum_hudby@nm.cz; internet www.nm.cz; f. 1936; incl. Dvořák (Prague 2, Ke Karlovu 20), Smetana (Prague 1, Novotného lávka 1), musical instruments (Prague 1, Karmeliská 2); library, sound archives; Dir Dott. EMANUELE GADALETA.

Historické muzeum (Historical Museum): Václavské nám. 68, 115 79 Prague 1; tel. 224497276; e-mail pavel_dousa@nm.cz; internet www.nm.cz; f. 1964; history of Czech Republic, history of money, ethnography of the Czech Republic, sport, Czech theatre; Dir Dr PAVEL DOUŠA; publs *Casopis Národního muzea. Řada historická* (2 a year), *Fontes archaeologici Pragenses* (irregular), *Muzeum: Muzejní a vlastivědná práce* (2 a year), *Numismatické listy* (4 a year), *Shornik Národního Muzea v Praze, řada A - Historie* (2 a year).

Náprstkovo muzeum asijských, afrických a amerických kultur (Náprstek Museum of Asian, African and American Cultures): Betlémské nám. 1, 110 01 Prague 1; tel. 224497500; e-mail naprstek@nm.cz; internet www.nm.cz; f. 1862; research into Asian, African, American, Australian and Oceanian cultural heritage; permanent and temporary exhibitions, public lectures and cultural events; library of 250,000 vols; Dir Dr EVA DITTERTOVÁ; publ. *Annals* (1 a year).

Přírodovědecké muzeum (Natural History Museum): Václavské nám. 68, 115 79 Prague; tel. 224497111; e-mail jiri.litochleb@nm.cz; internet www.nm.cz; f. 1964; Dir Dr JIŘÍ LITOCHLEB; publs *Acta Entomologica* (irregular), *Journal of the National Museum, Natural History Series* (1 a year), *Lynx* (1 a year), *Sborník Národního muzea, řada B* (Acta Musei Nationalis Pragae, Series B).

Národní Pedagogické Muzeum a Knihovna J. A. Komenského (National Pedagogical Museum and Library of J. A. Comenius): Valdštejnská 20, 118 00 Praha 1; tel. 257533455; e-mail pedagog@npmk.cz; internet www.npmk.cz; f. 1892; documents illustrating the devt of nat. education and the life and work of Comenius; pedagogical and educational literature; library of 500,000 vols; Dir Dr MARKÉTA PÁNKOVÁ.

Národní technické muzeum (National Technical Museum): Kostelní 42, 170 78 Prague 7; tel. 220399111; e-mail info@ntm.cz; internet www.ntm.cz; f. 1908; attached to Min. of Culture; library: see under Libraries and Archives; Dir KAREL KSANDR; publs *Bibliografie a prameny Národního technického muzea, Rozpravy Národního technického muzea, Sborník Národního technického muzea v Praze.*

Národní zemědělské muzeum (National Museum of Agriculture): Kostelní 44, 170 00 Prague 7; tel. 220308200; e-mail nzm.praha@nzm.cz; internet www.nzm.cz; f. 1891; exhibition of agriculture and food industry located in Kačina Castle near Kutná Hora; exhibition of agricultural machinery located in Čáslav; exhibition of forestry, hunting and fisheries in Ohrada Castle nr České Budějovice; exhibition of horticulture in Valtice near Břeclav; library of 120,000 vols, photographic archive; Dir for NMA Čáslav Ing. VLADIMÍR MICHÁLEK; Dir for NMA Hunting Lodge Ohrada Mgr. MARTIN SLABA; Dir for NMA Kačina Chateau Dr PAVEL NOVÁK; Dir for NMA Valtice Ing. VILÉM KŘEČEK; publs *Acta Museorum agriculturae*, *Prameny a studie* (Sources and Studies), *Vědecké práce ZM* (Scientific Studies).

Památník národního písemnictví (Museum of Czech Literature): Strahovské nádvoří 1/132, 118 38 Prague 1; tel. 220517285; e-mail post@pamatnik-np.cz; internet www.pamatniknarodnihopisemnictvi.cz; f. 1953; literary archives containing 6m. objects; collns showing devt of literature and literary culture in historical Czech lands, incl. documents on life, work, and legacy of important figures of Czech literature and literary culture from 18th century until present and colln of works of visual art; library of 600,000 vols; Dir Mgr ZDENĚK FREISLEBEN; publ. *Literární archiv* (1 a year).

Poštovní muzeum (Postal Museum): Nové mlýny 2, 110 00 Prague 1; tel. 222312006; e-mail postovni.muzeum@cpost.cz; internet www.ceskaposta.cz/cz/muzeum; f. 1918; Dir Dr JAN GALUŠKA.

Uměleckoprůmyslové museum v Praze (Museum of Decorative Arts): 17 listopadu 2, 110 00 Prague 1; tel. 251093111; e-mail info@upm.cz; internet www.upm.cz; f. 1885; applied art from ancient times to the present; library of 150,000 vols; Dir Dr HELENA KOENIGSMARKOVÁ.

Vojenský historický ústav Prahay (Military History Institute, Prague): U. Památníku 2, 130 05 Prague-Žižkov 3; tel. 973204900; e-mail museum@army.cz; internet www.vhu.cz; f. 1919; library of 250,000 vols books, magazines, historical maps; Dir Mgr ALEŠ KNÍŽEK.

Constituent Museums:

Armádní muzeum Žižkov (Army Museum): U. Památníku 2, 130 05 Prague 3; tel. 220204924.

Letecké muzeum Kbely (Aviation Museum, Kbely): Kbely, Mladoboleslavská ul., 197 00 Prague 3; tel. 220207513; e-mail info@militarymuseum.cz.

Vojenské technické muzeum (Museum of Military Technology): Krhanice, Prague; tel. 317702130.

Židovské muzeum v Praze (Jewish Museum in Prague): Staré školy 1, 3, 110 00 Prague 1; tel. 222749211; e-mail office@jewishmuseum.cz; internet www.jewishmuseum.cz; f. 1906; consists of the Maisel Synagogue, the Spanish Synagogue, the Pinkas Synagogue, the Old Jewish Cemetery, the Klausen Synagogue and the Ceremonial Hall; provides detailed commentary on Judaism and Jewish history, as well as the history of the Jews in Bohemia and Moravia; Dir Dr LEO PAVLÁT; publ. *Judaica Bohemiae* (1 a year).

Rožnov pod Radhoštěm

Valašské muzeum v přírodě (Wallachian Open-Air Museum): Palackého 147, 756 61 Rožnov pod Radhoštěm; tel. 571757111; e-mail muzeum@vmp.cz; internet www.vmp.cz; f. 1925; open-air museum consisting of a wooden town, Wallachian village and mill valley; methodological centre for open-air museums; library of 15,000 vols; Dir Ing. VÍTĚZSLAV KOUKAL.

Slavkov u Brna

Zámek Slavkov—Austerlitz (Chateau Slavkov—Austerlitz): Palackého nám. 1, 684 01 Slavkov u Brna; tel. 544221204; e-mail info@zamek-slavkov.cz; internet www.zamek-slavkov.cz; f. 1949; Napoleonic wars (particularly the Battle of Austerlitz), 17th- and 18th-century paintings, chapel of the Holy Cross; library colln on Napoleon; Dir Ing. ALEŠ SILHÁNEK.

Tábor

Husitské Muzeum (Hussite Museum): Nám. Mikuláše z Husi 44, 390 01 Tábor; tel. 381252242; e-mail tabor@husmuzeum.cz; internet www.husitskemuzeum.cz; f. 1878; Hussite movement; library of 40,000 vols; Dir MILOŠ DRDA; publ. *Husitský Tábor* (1 a year).

Teplice

Regionální muzeum v Teplicích (Teplice Regional Museum): Zámecké nám. 14, 415 01 Teplice; tel. 417537869; e-mail info@muzeum-teplice.cz; internet www.muzeum-teplice.cz; f. 1897; history, natural history, arts; library of 80,000 vols; Dir Dr DUŠAN SPIČKA; publs *Archeologický výzkum* (archaeological research, irregular), *Zprávy a studie* (local history and natural history, every 2 years).

Terezín

Památník Terezín (Terezín Memorial): Principova Alej 304, 411 55 Terezín; tel. 416782225; e-mail pamatnik@pamatnik-terezin.cz; internet www.pamatnik-terezin.cz; f. 1947; museums of the Small Fortress (resistance and political persecution 1940–45) and the wartime Jewish ghetto of Terezín; Art Exhibition of the Terezín Memorial; Terezín 1780–1939; the Litoměřice concentration camp; library of 11,000 vols; Dir Dr JAN MUNK; publ. *Terezínské listy* (1 a year).

Uherské Hradiště

Slovácké muzeum v Uherském Hradišti (Slovácko Museum in Uherské Hradiště): Smetanovy sady 179, 686 01 Uherské Hradiště; tel. 572551370; e-mail info@slovackemuzeum.cz; internet www.slovackemuzeum.cz; f. 1914; collns focus on archaeology, ethnography, history and visual art; library of 30,000 vols; Dir Dr IVO FROLEC; publ. *Slovácko* (1 a year).

Uherský Brod

Muzeum J. A. Komenského v Uherském Brodě (Uherský Brod J. A. Comenius Museum): Ul. Přemysla Otakara II 37, 688 12 Uherský Brod; tel. 572632288; e-mail muzeum@mjakub.cz; internet www.mjakub.cz; f. 1898; life, work and heritage of Protestant bishop and educational reformer, J. A. Comenius (1592–1670); history and ethnology of the Uherskobrodsko region; library of 40,000 vols; Dir Dr PAVEL POPELKA; publ. *Studia Comeniana et historica* (2 a year).

Zlín

Muzeum jihovýchodní Moravy (Museum of South-Eastern Moravia): Soudní 1, 762 57 Zlín; tel. 577004633; e-mail info@muzeum.zlin.cz; internet www.muzeum.zlin.cz; f. 1953; social science (archaeology, history, ethnography), natural history (botany, entomology, geology), shoe museum; library of 25,220 vols; Dir Dr ANTONIN SOBEK; publs *Acta Carpathica Occidentalis*, *Acta Musealia*.

Obuvnické muzeum (Footwear Museum): Tř. Tomáše Bati 1970, POB 175, 762 57 Zlín; tel. 577004618; e-mail m.stybrova@seznam.cz; internet www.muzeum.zlin.cz/obuvmuz.htm; f. 1959; library of 3,000 vols; Dir MIROSLAVA ŠTÝBROVÁ.

Universities

ČESKÉ VYSOKÉ UČENÍ TECHNICKÉ V PRAZE
(Czech Technical University in Prague)

Zikova 4, 166 36 Prague 6

Telephone: 224351111
E-mail: jiri.bila@fs.cvut.cz
Internet: www.cvut.cz

Founded 1707; reorganized 1806, 1863, 1920, 1960
State control
Languages of instruction: Czech, English
Academic year: September to June

Rector: Prof. Ing. VÁCLAV HAVLÍČEK
Vice-Rector for Construction and Investment: Prof. Ing. MILOSLAV PAVLÍK
Vice-Rector for Devt: Prof. Ing. PETR MOOS
Vice-Rector for External Relations: Prof. Ing. JIŘÍ BÍLA
Vice-Rector for Int. Relations: Prof. Dr VOJTĚCH PETRÁČEK
Vice-Rector for Science and Research: Doc. L. MUSÍLEK
Vice-Rector for Studies and Student Affairs: Doc. Ing. JOSEF JETTMAR
Registrar: Dr JAN GAZDA

Number of teachers: 1,750
Number of students: 24,000

Publications: *Acta Polytechnica* (6 a year, in English), *Pražská Technika* (6 a year, in Czech)

DEANS

Faculty of Architecture: Prof. Ing. ZDENĚK ZAVŘEL
Faculty of Biomedical Engineering: Prof. JOZEF ROSINA
Faculty of Civil Engineering: Prof. Ing. ALENA KOHOUTKOVÁ
Faculty of Electrical Engineering: Prof. Ing. PAVEL RIPKA
Faculty of Information Technology: Prof. Ing. PAVEL TVRDIK
Faculty of Mechanical Engineering: Prof. Ing. FRANTIŠEK HRDLIČKA
Faculty of Nuclear Science and Physical Engineering: Doc. Ing. MIROSLAV ČECH
Faculty of Transportation Sciences: Prof. Ing. MIROSLAV SVÍTEK

ATTACHED INSTITUTES

Centre for Radiochemistry and Radiation Chemistry: Dir Doc. Ing. J. JOHN.

Computing and Information Centre: Dir Doc. Ing. L. OHERA.

Institute of Biomedical Engineering: Dir Prof. Ing. M. VRBOVÁ.

Institute of Experimental and Applied Physics: tel. 224359391; internet www.utef.cvut.cz/en/index.php?ns=1; Dir Ing. STANISLAV POSPÍŠIL.

Klokner (Building) Institute: e-mail klok@klok.cvut.cz; Dir Dr Ing. JIRI KOLISKO.

Masaryk Institute of Advanced Studies: Dir Doc. Ing. J. PETR.

Research Institute for Industrial Heritage: e-mail vcpd@vcpd.cvut.cz; Dir Dr B. FRAGNER.

Technology Innovation Centre: Plzeňská 130/221, 15000 Prague 5; tel. 257199913; e-mail office@tic.cvut.cz; internet www.tic.cvut.cz/l=en; Dir Dr MILAN PRESS

ČESKÁ ZEMĚDĚLSKÁ UNIVERZITA V PRAZE
(Czech University of Life Sciences, Prague)

Kamýcká 129, 165 21 Prague 6–Suchdol

Telephone: 224381111
Internet: www.czu.cz

Founded 1906
State control
Language of instruction: Czech
Academic year: September to August

Rector: Prof. Dr JOSEF KOZÁK
Pro-Rector: Prof. Dr JIŘÍ BALÍK
Pro-Rector: Prof. Dr PAVEL KOVÁŘ
Pro-Rector: Prof. Dr VÁCLAV SLAVÍK
Pro-Rector: Prof. Dr MIROSLAV SVATOŠ
Registrar: Dr MILOŠ FRÝBORT
Librarian: Dr IVAN HAUZNER

Library of 225,000 vols
Number of teachers: 429
Number of students: 5,000

Publications: *Agricultura tropica et subtropica* (1 or 2 a year), *Scientia Agriculturae Bohemica* (4 a year), *Scientific Papers*

DEANS

Faculty of Agricultural Economics and Management: Prof. Dr JAN HRON
Faculty of Agronomy: Prof. Dr KAREL VOŘÍŠEK
Faculty of Forestry: Prof. Dr JOSEF GROSS
Technical Faculty: Prof. Dr KAREL POKORNÝ
Institute of Applied Ecology: Dr ZDENĚK LIPSKÝ (Vice-Dean)
Institute of Tropical and Subtropical Agriculture: Prof. Dr BOHUMIL HAVRLAND

JIHOČESKÁ UNIVERZITA V ČESKÝCH BUDĚJOVICÍCH
(University of South Bohemia in České Budějovice)

Branišovská 31, 370 05 České Budějovice

Telephone: 389031111
E-mail: rektorat@jcu.cz
Internet: www.jcu.cz

Founded 1991
State control
Academic year: September to June

Rector: Prof. Ing. FRANTIŠEK STŘELEČEK
Vice-Rector for Foreign Relations: Doc. Dr MILAN STRAŠKRABA
Vice-Rector for Science: Doc. Ing. MARTIN KŘÍŽEK
Vice-Rector for Study Programmes: Doc. Dr JIŘÍ DIVÍŠEK
Vice-Rector for Univ. Devt: Prof. Ing. VÁCLAV ŘEHOUT

Number of teachers: 418
Number of students: 5,500

Publications: *Memorial Volume of the Faculty of Agriculture–Economics* (2 a year), *Memorial Volume of the Faculty of Agriculture–Phytotechnics* (2 a year), *Memorial Volume of the Faculty of Agriculture–Zootechnics* (2 a year), *Opera historica* (1 a year)

DEANS

Faculty of Agriculture: Prof. Ing. JAN FRELICH

Faculty of Biological Sciences: Doc. Dr ZDENĚK BRANDL

Faculty of Education: Doc. Dr FRANTIŠEK MRÁZ

Faculty of Health and Social Studies: Doc. Dr VLADIMÍR VURM

Faculty of Theology: Prof. Dr KAREL SKALICKÝ

MASARYKOVA UNIVERZITA V BRNĚ
(Masaryk University in Brno)

Žerotínovo nám. 9, 601 77 Brno

Telephone: 549491011

E-mail: info@muni.cz

Internet: www.muni.cz

Founded 1919

State control

Language of instruction: Czech

Academic year: September to August

Rector: Prof. Dr PETER FIALA

Vice-Rector for Academic Affairs: Prof. Dr ZUZANA BRÁZDOVÁ

Vice-Rector for Research and Devt: Prof. Dr JANA MUSILOVÁ

Vice-Rector for Social Affairs of Students and External Relations: Assoc. Prof. Ing. ANTONÍN SLANÝ

Library of 1,544,000 vols

Number of teachers: 3,072

Number of students: 26,681

Publications: *Archivum mathematicum* (8 a year), *MUNI.CZ* (10 a year), *Scripta Medica* (6 a year), *Universitas* (4 a year)

DEANS

Faculty of Arts: Dr JAN PAVLÍK

Faculty of Economics and Administration: Assoc. Prof. Dr IVAN MALÝ

Faculty of Education: Assoc. Prof. Dr VLADISLAV MUŽÍK

Faculty of Informatics: Prof. Dr JIŘI ZLATUŠKA

Faculty of Law: Assoc. Prof. Dr JAN SVATOŇ

Faculty of Medicine: Assoc. Prof. Dr JAN ŽALOUDÍK

Faculty of Science: Assoc. Prof. Dr MILAN GELNAR

Faculty of Sports Studies: Dr MICHAL CHARVÁT

School of Social Studies: Assoc. Prof. Dr LADISLAV RABUŠIC

PROFESSORS

Faculty of Arts (Arna Nováka 1, 660 80 Brno; tel. 549491511; e-mail dekan@phil.muni.cz; internet www.phil.muni.cz):

BÁTORA, J., Archaeology
BLAŽEK, V., Comparative Indo-European Linguistics
CEJPEK, J., Library Studies
FIALA, J., Czech Literature
GAJDOŠ, J., Theory and History of Theatre
HORÁK, P., Philosophy
HORYNA, B., Study of Religion
HROCH, J., Philosophy
KARLÍK, P., Czech Language
KRČMOVÁ, M., Czech Language
KROUPA, J., History of Arts
KURFÜRST, P., Musicology
MALÍŘ, J., Czech History
MĚŘÍNSKÝ, Z., Archaeology
MUNZAR, J., German Literature
NECHUTOVÁ, J., Classics
NEKUDA, V., Slavonic Archaeology
OSLZLÝ, P., Theatre and Film Studies
PLESKALOVÁ, J., Czech Language
POSPÍŠIL, I., History of Russian Literature
RUSÍNOVÁ, Z., Czech Language
SLAVÍČEK, L., History of Art
ŠMAJS, J., Philosophy
ŠTĚDROŇ, M., Musicology
STEHLÍKOVÁ, E., Theatre and Film Studies
STŘÍTECKÝ, J., Philosophy
SVOBODA, M., Psychology
ZOUHAR, J., Philosophy

Faculty of Economics and Administration (Lipová 41A, 659 79 Brno; tel. 549491710; e-mail dekan@econ.muni.cz; internet www.econ.muni.cz):

BLAZEK, L., Theory of Management
IVÁNEK, L., Economics
LANČA, J., Economics and Corporate Management
MÁŠA, M., Management
ONDRČKA, P., Finance
ŠEJBAL, J., Finance
ŽÁK, M., Economics

Faculty of Education (Poříčí 7, 603 00 Brno; tel. 549493050; e-mail dekan@ped.muni.cz; internet www.ped.muni.cz):

CHALUPA, P., Geography
CHVALINA, J., Mathematics
HLADKÝ, J., English Language
HOROVÁ, I., Mathematics
KOŠUT, M., Teaching of Music
MAŇÁK, J., Education
MAREČKOVÁ, M., History
NOVÁK, V., Mathematics
ŠVEC, V., Education
VÍTKOVÁ, M., Special Education

Faculty of Informatics (Botanická 68A, Brno; tel. 549491810; e-mail dekan@fi.muni.cz; internet www.fi.muni.cz):

BUZEK, V., Informatics
DOKULIL, M., Philosophy
GRUSKA, J., Informatics
HŘEBÍČEK, J., Company Information Systems
MATERNA, P., Logic
NOVOTNÝ, M., Mathematics and Informatics
SERBA, I., Informatics
ZEZULA, P., Informatics
ZLATUŠKA, J., Informatics

Faculty of Law (Veveří 70, 611 80 Brno; tel. 549491211; e-mail dekan@law.muni.cz; internet www.law.muni.cz):

BEJČEK, J., Economic Law
FILIP, J., Constitutional Law and Political Science
HAJN, P., Economic Law
HRUŠÁKOVÁ, M., Civil Law
HURDÍK, J., Civil Law
JÍLEK, D., International Public Law
MALENOVSKÝ, J., International Public Law
ROZEHNALOVÁ, N., International Private Law
TELEC, I., Civil Law
VÁGNER, I., Economics
VLČEK, E., History of State and Law

Faculty of Medicine (Komenského nám. 2, 662 43 Brno; tel. 549491111; e-mail dekan@med.muni.cz; internet www.med.muni.cz):

ADAM, Z., Internal Medicine
BEDNAŘÍK, J., Neurology
BENDA, K., Radiology
BRÁZDOVÁ, Z., Social Medicine
BRHEL, P., Occupational Medicine
BRYCHTA, P., Surgery
BUČEK, J., Pathology
ČECH, S., Histology
ČEŠKOVÁ, E., Psychiatry
DAPECI, A., Stomatology
DÍTĚ, P., Internal Medicine
DRTÍLKOVÁ, I., Psychiatry
DUBOVÝ, P., Anatomy
DVOŘÁK, K., Pathology
FAKAN, F., Anatomy
FIŠER, B., Pathology and Physiology
GÁL, P., Surgery
HADAŠOVÁ, E., Pharmacology
HEP, A., Internal Medicine
HOLČÍK, J., Social Medicine
HONZÍKOVÁ, N., Pathology and Physiology
HORKÝ, D., Histology
HRUBÁ, D., Social Medicine
JANISCH, R., Biology
KADAŇKA, Z., Neurology
KOSTŘICA, R., Otorhynolaryngology
KUBEŠOVÁ, H., Internal Medicine
KUKLETA, M., Medical Physiology
KUKLETOVA, M., Stomatology
LITZMAN, J., Immunology
LOKAJ, J., Immunology
LUKÁŠ, Z., Anatomy
MALÝ, Z., Gynaecology and Obstetrics
MAYER, J., Internal Medicine
MELUZÍN, J., Internal Medicine
MUNZAROVÁ, M., Internal Medicine
PÁČ, L., Anatomy
PAČÍK, D., Surgery
PENKA, M., Internal Medicine
PETŘEK, M., Immunology
ŘEHŮŘEK, J., Ophthalmology
REJTHAR, A., Pathology
REKTOR, I., Neurology
ROZTOČIL, A., Gynaecology and Obstetrics
SEMRÁD, B., Internal Medicine
ŠEMRÁDOVÁ, V., Dermatovenereology
ŠEVČÍK, P., Anaesthesiology
SIEGLOVÁ, J., Functional Diagnostics and Rehabilitation
ŠMRČKA, V., Surgery
ŠPINAR, J., Internal Medicine
ŠULCOVÁ, A., Pharmacology
ŠVESTKA, J., Psychiatry
SVOBODA, A., Biology
TOMAN, J., Internal Medicine
VÁCHA, J., Pathological Physiology
VÁLEK, V., Radiology
VANĚK, J., Stomatology
VAŠKŮ, A., Pathological Physiology
VENTRUBA, P., Gynaecology and Obstetrics
VESELÝ, J., Surgery
VÍTOVEC, J., Internal Medicine
VLKOVÁ, E., Ophthalmology
VOMELA, J., Surgery
VORLÍČEK, J., Internal Medicine
WECHSLER, J., Surgery
WENDSCHE, P., Surgery
ŽÁHEJSKÝ, J., Dermatovenereology
ŽALOUDÍK, J., Surgery
ZEMAN, K., Internal Medicine

Faculty of Science (Kotlářská 2, 611 37 Brno; tel. 549491411; e-mail dekan@sci.muni.cz; internet www.sci.muni.cz):

BARTŮSEK, M., Analytical Chemistry
BRÁZDIL, R., Physical Geography
BRZOBOHATÝ, R., Palaeontology
DOŠKAŘ, J., Molecular Biology and Genetics
DOŠLÁ, Z., Mathematics
DOŠLÝ, O., Mathematical Analysis
GAISLER, J., Zoology
GLOSER, J., Plant Physiology
HÁLA, J., Inorganic Chemistry
HAVEL, J., Analytical Chemistry
HOLÍK, M., Physical Chemistry
HOLOUBEK, I., Environmental Chemistry
HOLÝ, V., Physics of Condensed Materials
HORSKÝ, J., Theoretical Physics
HUMLÍČEK, J., Physics
JANČA, J., Physics
JONAS, J., Organic Chemistry
KANICKÝ, V., Analytical Chemistry
KAPIČKA, V., Physics
KNOZ, J., Biology
KOČA, J., Organic Chemistry
KOLÁŘ, I., Algebra and Geometry
KOMÁREK, J., Analytical Chemistry
KOTYK, A., Biochemistry
KUČERA, I., Biochemistry
LENC, M., General Physics and Mathematical Physics
MALINA, J., Archaeology
MUSILOVÁ, J., Physics
NOVÁK, M., Geology
NOVÁK, V., Mathematics
NOVOTNÝ, J., Physics

OHLÍDAL, I., Quantum Electronics and Optics
POTÁČEK, M., Organic Chemistry
PŘICHYSTAL, A., Geology
PROŠEK, P., Physical Geography
RELICHOVÁ, J., Genetics
ROSICKÝ, J., Mathematics
ROZKOŠNÝ, R., Entomology
SCHMIDT, E., Physics
SKLENÁŘ, V., Physical Chemistry
ŠIMEK, M., Animal Physiology
SKULA, L., Mathematics
SLOVÁK, J., Geometry
STANĚK, J., Mineralogy and Petrography
UNGER, J., Anthropology
VAŇHARA, J., Zoology
VELICKÝ, B., Theoretical Physics
VETTERL, J., Physical Electronics
VICHEREK, J., Botany
VŘEŠŤÁL, J., Physical Chemistry
ŽÁK, Z., Inorganic Chemistry
ZIMA, J., Zoology

School of Social Studies (Gorkého 7, 602 00 Brno; tel. 549491911; e-mail dekan@fss.muni.cz; internet www.fss.muni.cz):

FIALA, P., Politology
KELLER, J., Sociology
LIBROVÁ, H., Sociology
MACEK, P., Social Psychology
MAREŠ, P., Sociology
MOŽNÝ, I., Sociology
RABUŠIC, L., Sociology
SIROVÁTKA, T., Social Policy and Social Work
ŠMAUSOVÁ, G., Sociology
SMÉKAL, V., Psychology
STRMISKA, M., Political Science

MENDELOVA UNIVERZITA V BRNĚ
(Mendel University in Brno)

Zemědělská 1, 613 00 Brno
Telephone: 545131111
E-mail: info@mendelu.cz
Internet: www.mendelu.cz
Founded 1919, by State Law
State control
Languages of instruction: Czech, English
Academic year: September to June (2 semesters)
Rector: J. HLUŠEK
Pro-Rector: L. GREGA
Pro-Rector: M. HAVLÍČEK
Pro-Rector: J. NERUDA
Pro-Rector: R. POKLUDA
Chief Admin. Officer: V. SEDLÁŘOVÁ
Chief Librarian: VERA SVOBODOVÁ
Library of 400,000 vols
Number of teachers: 450
Number of students: 11,200 (10,000 full-time, 1,200 part-time)
Publications: *Acta Universitatis Agriculturae et Silviculturae Mendelianae Brunensis* (6 a year, www.acta.mendelu.cz), *Europeane Countryside* (www.degruyter.com/view/j/euco), *Folia Universitatis Agriculturae et Silviculturae Mendelianae Brunensis*

DEANS

Faculty of Agronomy: L. ZEMAN
Faculty of Business and Economics: J. STÁVKOVÁ
Faculty of Forestry and Wood Technology: P. HORÁČEK
Faculty of Horticulture: ROBERT POKLUDA
Faculty of Regional Development and International Studies: IVA ŽIVĚLOVÁ

OSTRAVSKÁ UNIVERZITA V OSTRAVĚ
(University of Ostrava)

Dvořákova 7, 701 03 Ostrava
Telephone: 597091111
E-mail: info@osu.cz
Internet: www.osu.cz
Founded 1991
State control
Rector: Dr JIŘÍ MOČKOŘ
Vice-Rector for Devt and Information Management: Dr Ing. CYRIL KLIMEŠ
Vice-Rector for Research and External Relations: Prof. Dr JAN LATA
Vice-Rector for Study: Doc. Dr IVA MÁLKOVÁ
Library of 230,000 vols
Number of teachers: 583
Number of students: 9,470

DEANS

Faculty of Arts: Dr ZBYNĚK JANÁČEK
Faculty of Fine Arts: Dr ALEŠ ZÁŘICKÝ
Faculty of Science: Dr DANA KRIČFALUŠI
Faculty of Social Studies: Dr OLDŘICH CHYTIL
Medico-Social Faculty: Dr JAROSLAV HORÁČEK
Pedagogical Faculty: Dr TOMÁŠ JARMARA

SLEZSKÁ UNIVERZITA V OPAVĚ
(Silesian University in Opava)

Na Rybníčku 626/1, 746 01 Opava
Telephone: 553684621
E-mail: rektorat@slu.cz
Internet: www.slu.cz
Founded 1991
State control
Language of instruction: Czech
Academic year: October to September
Rector: Doc. Dr RUDOLF ŽÁČEK
Bursar: Ing. JAROSLAV KANIA
Library of 165,581 vols, 295 periodicals
Number of teachers: 400
Number of students: 9,000
Publications: *Acta Academia Karviniensia, Acta Historica*

DEANS

Faculty of Business Administration: Dr BOHUMIL FIALA
Faculty of Philosophy and Science: Prof. ZDENĚK STUCHLÍK
Faculty of Public Policies: Doc. Dr DUŠAN JANÁK
Institute of Mathematics: Prof. JAROSLAV SMÍTAL

TECHNICKÁ UNIVERZITA V LIBERCI
(Technical University of Liberec)

Studentská 2, 461 17 Liberec
Telephone: 485351111
E-mail: rektor@tul.cz
Internet: www.tul.cz
Founded 1953
State control
Languages of instruction: Czech, English
Academic year: September to June
Rector: Prof. ZDENĚK KŮS
Vice-Rector: Prof. JIŘÍ KRAFT
Vice-Rector: Assoc. Prof. ONDŘEJ NOVÁK
Vice-Rector: Assoc. Prof. JANA DRAŠAROVÁ
Registrar: VLADIMÍR STACH
Librarian: NAĎA HAŠČÁKOVÁ
Library of 185,000 vols
Number of teachers: 750
Number of students: 9,800
Publications: *Economics and Management* (7 a year), *Sborník vědeckých prací Technické univerzity* (Annals of Scientific Research)

DEANS

Faculty of Arts and Architecture: Prof. BOŘEK SIPEK
Faculty of Economics: Assoc. Prof. OLGA HASPROVA
Faculty of Education: Assoc. Prof. MIROSLAV BRZEZINA
Faculty of Mechanical Engineering: Assoc. Prof. MIROSLAV MALÝ
Faculty of Mechatronics and Interdisciplinary Engineering Studies: Prof. VÁCLAV KOPECKÝ
Faculty of Textile Engineering: Prof. ALEŠ LINKA

PROFESSORS

BAKULE, V., Finance and Credit
BENEŠ, S., Construction of Machines and Appliances
BEROUN, S., Transport Machines
CYHELSKÝ, L., Statistics
DUCHOŇ, B., Management Technology in Transport
EHLEMAN, J., Information Management
EXNER, J., Mechanical Engineering Technology
FOUSEK, J., Electromechanical Properties of Dielectrics
HAJNIŠ, K., Physical Education
HANUŠ, B., Control Engineering
HES, L., Textile Valuation
HINDLS, R., Insurance, Statistics
HONCŮ, J., Machine Design
HÝČA, M., Applied Mechanics
IBRAHIM, S., Textile Technology
JANOVEC, V., Electromechanical Properties of Dielectrics
JIRSÁK, O., Textile Technology
KAŇOKOVÁ, J., Statistics
KARGER, A., Mathematics, Economics, Topology
KONOPA, V., Technical Cybernetics
KOPKA, J., Teaching of Mathematics
KOŠEK, M., Technical Cybernetics
KOVÁŘ, R., Textile Technology
KOVÁŘ, Z., Combustion Engines
KRAFT, J., Enterprise Economics, Management
KRATOCHVÍL, P., Materials Engineering
KRYŠTŮFEK, J., Textile Technology
KVAČEK, R., Czech History
LANDOROVÁ, A., Financing
LUKÁŠ, D., Textile Technology
MILITKÝ, J., Textile Technology
NECKÁŘ, B., Structure of Textiles
NOSEK, J., Physics
NOSEK, S., Textile Machines
NOUZA, J., Technical Cybernetics
NOVÁ, I., Engineering Metallurgy
NOVÁK, O., Technical Cybernetics
OLEHLA, J., Machines and Devices Construction
OLEHLA, M., Production Systems and Processes
PŘIVRATSKÁ, J., Physics
ŠKALLA, J., Servodrivers and Automation
ŠKALOUD, M., Mechanics
ŠKLÍBA, J., Applied Mechanics
ŠODOMKA, L., Applied Physics
ŠPATENKA, P., Mechanical Engineering Technology
STIBOR, I., Organic Chemistry
STRAKOŠ, Z., Technical Cybernetics
STŘÍŽ, B., Elasticity and Strength
SUCHOMEL, J., Architecture and Design
ULIČNÝ, O., Czech Language
URSÍNY, P., Textile Technology
VÁGNEROVÁ, M., Psychology
VAVERKA, J., Building Engineering
VĚCHET, V., Technical Cybernetics
VOKURKA, K., Applied Physics
VOSTATEK, J., Finance
ZELINKA, B., Mathematical Informatics and Theoretical Cybernetics

UNIVERZITA HRADEC KRÁLOVÉ
(University of Hradec Králové)

Rokitanského 62, 500 03 Hradec Králové
Telephone: 493331111
Internet: www.uhk.cz

Founded 1959 as Institute of Education, present status 2000
State control
Rector: Prof. Dr JOSEF HYNEK
Vice-Rector for Int. Affairs and Science: Prof. Dr ANTONÍN SLABÝ
Vice-Rector for Internal Affairs: Dr PETR GRULICH
Vice-Rector for Strategy and Devt: Dr MONIKA ŽUMÁROVÁ
Librarian: Mgr ZDENKA JEŽKOVÁ
Number of teachers: 416
Number of students: 8,778

DEANS

Faculty of Arts: Mgr Dr PETR GRULICH
Faculty of Education: Doc. Ing. VLADIMÍR JEHLIČKA
Faculty of Informatics and Management: Doc. Ing. VÁCLAV JANEČEK
Faculty of Science: Dr PAVEL TROJOVSKÝ
Institute of Social Work: MIROSLAV MITLÖHNER

UNIVERZITA JANA EVANGELISTY PURKYNĚ V ÚSTÍ NAD LABEM (Jan Evangelista Purkyně University in Ústí nad Labem)

Hoření 13, 400 96 Ústí nad Labem
Telephone: 475282111
E-mail: rektor@rek.ujep.cz
Internet: www.ujep.cz
Founded as Pedagogical Faculty in Ústí nad Labem; univ. status 1991
State control
Rector: Dr Dr STANISLAV NOVÁK
Librarian: Dr IVO BROŽEK
Library of 250,000 vols
Number of teachers: 375
Number of students: 6,000

DEANS

Faculty of Art and Design: Dr VLADIMÍR ŠVEC
Faculty of Education: Dr ZDENĚK RADVANOVSKÝ
Faculty of Environmental Studies: Dr Ing. JOSEF SEJÁK
Faculty of Science: Dr Dr STANISLAV NOVÁK
Faculty of Social and Economic Studies: Prof. Ing. PAVLIK

UNIVERZITA KARLOVA V PRAZE (Charles University in Prague)

Ovocný trh 5, 116 36 Prague 1
Telephone: 224491111
E-mail: sekretariat@ruk.cuni.cz
Internet: www.cuni.cz
Founded 1348
State control
Language of instruction: Czech
Academic year: September to June
Chancellor: RNDr TOMÁŠ JELÍNEK
Rector: Prof. VACLAV HAMPL
Vice-Rector: Prof. Dr IVAN JAKUBEC
Vice-Rector: Prof. Dr JAN SKRHA
Vice-Rector: Doc. MARTIN PRUDKY
Vice-Rector: Doc. Dr MICHAL SOBR
Vice-Rector: Prof. MILAN TICHY
Vice-Rector: Prof. PETR VOLF
Vice-Rector: Doc. Dr STANISLAV STECH
Vice-Rector: Prof. SYLVIE OPATRNA
Quaestor: Ing. JOSEF KUBÍČEK
Library: see under Libraries and Archives
Number of teachers: 4,048
Number of students: 53,000
Publications: *Acta Universitatis Carolinae—series: Mathematica et Physica*, *Biologica* (4 a year), *Environmentalica* (1 a year), *Folia Pharmaceutica Universitatis Carolinae*, *Geographica* (2 a year), *Geologica* (4 a year), *Historia Universitatis Carolinae Pragensis*, *Iuridica* (4 a year), *Kinanthropologica* (2 a year), *Medica* (1 a year), *Novitates Botanicae Universitatis Carolinae* (1 a year), *Oeconomica* (2 a year), *Philologica* (10 a year), *Philosophica et Historica* (10 a year), *Prague Bulletin of Mathematical Linguistics*, *Psychologie v ekonomické praxi* (2 a year), *Sborník lékařský* (4 a year)

DEANS

Faculty of Catholic Theology: Lic. PROKOP BROZ
Faculty of Education: Doc. Dr RADKA WILDOVA
Faculty of Evangelical Theology: Doc. JINDRICH HALAMA
Faculty of Humanities: Doc. Dr LADISLAV BENYOVSZKY
Faculty of Hussite Theology: Prof. JAN B. LASEK
Faculty of Law: Prof. Dr ALES GERLOCH
Faculty of Mathematics and Physics: Prof. ZDENEK NEMECEK
1st Faculty of Medicine: Prof. TOMAS ZIMA
2nd Faculty of Medicine: Prof. ONDREJ HRUSAK
3rd Faculty of Medicine: Prof. MICHAL ANDEL
Faculty of Medicine in Hradec Králové: Prof. MIROSLAV CERVINKA
Faculty of Medicine in Plzeň: Doc. Dr BORIS KREUZBERG
Faculty of Pharmacy in Hradec Králové: Prof. Dr ALEXANDR HRABALEK
Faculty of Philosophy: Doc. Dr MICHAL STEHLIK
Faculty of Physical Education and Sport: Doc. Dr VLADIMIR SÜSS
Faculty of Sciences: Dr BOHUSLAV GAS
Faculty of Social Sciences: Dr JAKUB KONCELIK

PROFESSORS

Faculty of Catholic Theology (6, Thákurova 3, 160 00 Prague; tel. 220181600; e-mail dekan@kft.cuni.cz; internet www.ktf.cuni.cz):

MATĚJKA, J., Practical Theology
POLC, J., Church History
SLABÝ, A., Pastoral Medicine
SOUSEDÍK, S., History of Philosophy
WOLF, V., Systematic Theology
ZEDNÍČEK, M., Canon Law

Faculty of Education (M. D. Rettigové 4, Prague; tel. 221900111; e-mail pavel.vasak@pedf.cuni.cz; internet www.pedf.cuni.cz):

BENEŠ, P., Chemistry
BRABCOVÁ, R., Czech Language
CORNES, P., History
HEJNÝ, M., Mathematics
HELUS, Z., Pedagogical Psychology
HERDEN, J., Music Education
JELÍNEK, S., Russian Language
KOMAN, M., Mathematics
KOTÁSEK, J., Education
PARIZEK, V., Education
PEŠKOVÁ, J., Philosophy
PIŤHA, P., Philosophy
POLEDŇÁK, K., Music Education
VULTERIN, J., Analytical Chemistry

Faculty of Evangelical Theology (1, Černá 9, 115 55 Prague; tel. 221988216; e-mail filipi@ftf.cuni.cz; internet www.ftf.cuni.cz):

FILIPI, P., Practical Theology
POKORNÝ, P., New Testament
REJCHRTOVÁ, N., Church History
TROJAN, J., Social Ethics

Faculty of Humanities (5, V. Kříže 10, 150 00 Prague; tel. 251080111; e-mail sokol@fhs.cuni.cz; internet www.fhs.cuni.cz):

BENYOVSZKY, L., Philosophy
BOUZEK, J., Archaeology, Classical Philology
BYSTŘICKÝ, J., Philosophy, Media
ČEŠKA, J., Philosophy, Literature
DOHNALOVÁ, M., Economics
GABRIŠKOVÁ, L., Languages
HALBICH, M., Anthropology
HAVELKA, M., Sociology, Social History
HAVELKOVÁ, H., Gender Studies
HAVLÍČEK, Anthropology, Ethnology
HAVRDOVÁ, Z., Social Psychology
HORSKÝ, J., History, Historical Anthropology
HOZÁKOVÁ, J., Sociology
HROCH, M., History
KAČÍREK, M., Law
KRUŽÍK, J., Philosophy
MATOUŠEK, V., Anthropology, Archaeology
MORAVCOVÁ, M., Ethnology
MULLER, K., Sociology
NOVÁK, A., Philosophy
PINC, Z., Philosophy
PRUDKÝ, L., Sociology
RYNDA, I., Human Ecology
SELIGOVÁ, M., History
SHANAHAN, D., Languages, Film
ŠKOVAJSA, M., Political Philosophy
ŠKVAŘILOVÁ, B., Anthropology
SOKOL, J., Anthropology, Philosophy
SOUKUPOVÁ, B., Social History
SVATOŇ, O., Sociology
SVOBODA, A., Art, Design
TURKOVÁ, M., Ethnology
VANČÁT, J., Theory of Art
VANČATOVÁ, M., Ethnology
VOPĚNKA, P., Logic, Mathematics
ZIMA, P., Languages, Sociolinguistics

Faculty of Hussite Theology (4, Pacovská 350/4, 140 21 Prague; tel. 241733131; e-mail jligus@htf.cuni.cz; internet www.htf.cuni.cz):

HAŠKOVCOVÁ, H., Medical Ethics
HOLETON, D. R., Liturgics
KUČERA, Z., Systematic Theology
LIGUŠ, J., Philosophy of Communication
SÁZAVA, Z., Biblical Theology

Faculty of Law (1, nám. Curieových 7, 116 40 Prague; tel. 221005111; e-mail dekan@ius.prf.cuni.cz; internet www.prf.cuni.cz):

BAKEŠ, M., Financial Law
BELINA, M., Labour Law
BOGUSZAK, J., Theory of State and Law
CÍSAŘOVÁ, D., Criminal Law
GERLOCH, A., Theory, Philosophy and Sociology of Law
HENDRYCH, D., Administrative Law
KŘÍŽ, J., Civil Law
KUČERA, Z., International Law
MALÝ, K., History of State and Law
NOVOTNÝ, O., Criminal Law
PAVLÍČEK, V., Constitutional Law and Civic Sciences
ŠVESTKA, J., Civil Law
TICHÝ, L., European Law
WINTEROVÁ, A., Civil Law
ZOULÍK, FR., Civil Law

Faculty of Mathematics and Physics (2, K. Karlovu 3, 121 16 Prague; tel. 221951111; e-mail dekan@dekanat.mff.cuni.cz; internet www.mff.cuni.cz):

ANDĚL, J., Mathematics and Statistics
BARVÍK, I., Physics
BEDNÁŘ, J., Physics
BENEŠ, V., Mathematics
BIČÁK, J., Theoretical Physics
BICAN, L., Mathematics
BIEDERMAN, H., Macromolecular Physics
ČÁPEK, V., Theoretical Physics
CIPRA, T., Mathematics
DUPAČOVÁ, J., Mathematics and Statistics
FEISTAUER, M., Mathematics
FORMÁNEK, J., Theoretical Physics
HAJČOVÁ, E., Information Science
HÁLA, J., Physics
HASLINGER, J., Physics
HORÁČEK, J., Theoretical Physics
HOŘEJŠÍ, J., Nuclear Physics
HÖSCHL, P., Physics

HRACH, R., Electronic Physics
HUŠEK, M., Mathematics
HUŠKOVÁ, M., Mathematics
ILAVSKÝ, M., Macromolecular Physics
JUREČKOVÁ, J., Probability and Statistics
KAKGER, A., Mathematics
KEPKA, T., Mathematics
KOWALSKI, O., Mathematics
KVASIL, J., Experimental Physics
LUKEŠ, J., Mathematical Analysis
MARTINEC, Z., Physics and Geophysics
MATOLÍN, V., Electronic Physics
MATOUŠEK, J., Informatics
NEŠETŘIL, J., Mathematics
NETUKA, I., Mathematics
NOVÁK, B., Mathematics
PANEVOVÁ, J., Information Science
PLÁŠIL, F., Informatics
POKORNÝ, J., Informatics
PULTR, A., Mathematics
ROHN, J., Mathematics
SECHOVSKÝ, V., Physics
SIMON, P., Mathematics
SKÁLA, L., Physics
SOUČEK, V., Mathematics
ŠTĚPÁN, J., Mathematics
STĚPÁNEK, P., Mathematics
SVOBODA, E., Theoretical Physics
TICHÝ, M., Physics
TROJANOVÁ, Z., Electronic Physics
VALVODA, V., Physics
VELICKÝ, B., Physics
VIŠŇOVSKÝ, Š., Physics
ZAJÍČEK, L., Mathematics
ZIMMERMANN, K., Information Science

1st Faculty of Medicine (2, Kateřinská 32, 121 08 Prague; tel. 224961111; e-mail stepan.svacina@lf1.cuni.cz; internet www.lf1.cuni.cz):

ASCHERMANN, M., Internal Medicine
BENCKO, V., Hygiene
BETKA, J., Otorhinolaryngology
BROULÍK, P., Internal Medicine
DVOŘÁČEK, J., Urology
ELIŠKA, O., Anatomy
ELLEDER, M., Pathology
FARGHALL, H. M., Pharmacology
FUČÍKOVÁ, T., Immunology and Allergology
HÁJEK, Z., Gynaecology
HORKÝ, K., Internal Medicine
HYNIE, S., Pharmacology
KLENER, P., Oncology
KRAML, J., Biochemistry
LAŠTOVKA, M., Otorhinolaryngology
MAREČEK, Z., Internal Medicine
MAREK, J., Internal Medicine
MARTÍNEK, J., Histology and Embryology
NEČAS, E., Normal and Pathological Physiology
NEVŠÍMALOVÁ, S., Neurology
PAFKO, P., Surgery
PETROVICKÝ, P., Anatomy
POKORNY, J., Physiology
POVÝŠIL, C., Pathological Anatomy
RABOCH, J., Psychiatry
RACEK, J., Stomatology
RYBKA, V., Orthopaedic Surgery
ŠKRHA, J., Internal Medicine
SOSNA, A., Surgery
ŠTĚPÁN, J., Biochemistry
STÍPEK, S., Biochemistry
STREJC, P., Forensic Medicine
TERŠÍP, K., Surgery
TESAŘ, V., Internal Medicine
TOPINKOVÁ, E., Social Medicine
TROJAN, S., Medical Physiology
VANĚK, J., Surgery
VÍTEK, F., Biophysics
VYMĚTAL, J., Clinical Psychology
ZEMAN, J., Paediatrics
ZEMAN, M., Surgery
ZIMA, T., Medical Chemistry
ŽIVNÝ, J., Gynaecology and Obstetrics

2nd Faculty of Medicine (5, Vúvalu 84, 150 06 Prague; tel. 224431111; e-mail josef.koutecky@lfmotol.cuni.cz; internet www.lf2.cuni.cz):

BOUŠKA, I., Forensic Medicine
BROŽEK, G., Physiology
DRUGA, R., Anatomy
GOETZ, P., Biology
HERGET, J., Pathological Physiology
HOŘEJŠÍ, J., Gynaecology and Obstetrics
KODET, R., Pathological Anatomy
KONRÁDOVÁ, V., Histology and Embryology
KOUTECKY, J., Oncology
MATOUŠOVIC, K., Internal Medicine
PELOUCH, V., Medical Chemistry and Biochemistry
SEEMANOVÁ, E., Genetics
SNAJDAUF, J., Surgery
SVIHOVEC, J., Pharmacology
VÍZEK, M., Pathological Physiology
VOJÁČEK, J., Internal Medicine

3rd Faculty of Medicine (10, Ruská 87, 100 00 Prague; tel. 267102111; e-mail michal.andel@lf3.cuni.cz; internet www.lf3.cuni.cz):

ANDĚL, M., Internal Medicine
CIKRT, M., Hygiene
GREGOR, P., Internal Medicine
HORÁK, J., Internal Medicine
HÖSCHL, C., Psychiatry
JELÍNEK, R., Histology and Embryology, Anatomy
KRŠIAK, M., Pharmacology
KUCHYNKA, P., Ophthalmology
LENER, J., Hygiene
MALINA, L., Dermatology
PROVAZNÍK, K., Hygiene
RAŠKA, I., Medical Biology
ROKYTA, R., Pathological Physiology
SCHINDLER, J., Microbiology
STEFAN, J., Forensic Medicine
STINGL, J., Anatomy

Faculty of Medicine in Hradec Králové (Šimkova 870, 500 38 Hradec Králové; tel. 495816111; e-mail dekan@lfhk.cuni.cz; internet www.lfhk.cuni.cz):

DOMINIK, J., Surgery
FIXA, B., Internal Medicine
HEJZLAR, M., Microbiology
HRNČÍŘ, Z., Internal Medicine
HYBÁŠEK, I., Otorhinolaryngology
KRÁL, B., Internal Medicine
KVASNIČKA, J., Internal Medicine
MALÝ, J., Internal Medicine
MARTÍNKOVÁ, J., Pharmacology
NĚMEČEK, S., Histology and Embryology
PIDRMAN, V., Internal Medicine
ROZSÍVAL, P., Ophthalmology
ŠPAČEK, J., Pathological Anatomy
ŠRB, V., Hygiene
ŠTEINER, I., Pathological Anatomy
STRANSKY, P., Biophysics
VOBOŘIL, Z., Surgery
VODIČKA, I., Biophysics
ZADÁK, Z., Internal Medicine

Faculty of Medicine in Plzeň (Husova 13, 306 05 Plzeň; tel. 377593400; e-mail dekan@lfp.cuni.cz; internet www.lfp.cuni.cz):

AMBLER, Z., Neurology
FAKAN, F., Pathological Anatomy
MICHAL, M., Pathological Anatomy
OPATRNÝ, K., Internal Medicine
RACEK, J., Biochemistry
RESL, V., Dermatovenereology
SKÁLOVÁ, A., Pathology
TĚŠÍNSKÝ, P., Ophthalmology
TOPOLČAN, O., Internal Medicine
TŘEŠKA, V., Surgery

Faculty of Pharmacy in Hradec Králové (Heyrovskiho tř. 1203, 501 65 Hradec Králové; tel. 495067111; e-mail dusek@faf.cuni.cz; internet www.faf.cuni.cz):

DRŠATA, J., Biochemistry
FENDRICH, Z., Pharmacology
JAHODÁR, L., Pharmacognosy
KARLÍČEK, R., Analytical Chemistry
KVASNIČKOVÁ, E., Biochemistry
LÁZNÍČEK, M., Radiopharmacy
VIŠŇOVSKÝ, P., Pharmacology
WAISSER, K., Organic Chemistry

Faculty of Philosophy (1, nám. J. Palacha 2, 116 38 Prague; tel. 221619111; e-mail dekan@ff.cuni.cz; internet www.ff.cuni.cz):

BLÁHOVÁ, M., Auxiliary Historical Sciences
BOUZEK, J., Classical Archaeology
ČERMÁK, F., Czech Language
DOHALSKÁ, M., Phonetics
HALÍK, T., Sociology
HILSKY, M., English Literature
HLEDÍKOVÁ, Z., Auxiliary Historical Sciences
HORYNA, M., History of Art
KÖNIGOVÁ, M., Information and Librarianship
KROPÁČEK, L., History and Culture of Africa and Asia
KUČERA, K., Czech Language
KUKLÍK, J., Czech History
MACUROVÁ, A., Czech Language
MAUR, E., Czech History
OPATRNÝ, J., General History
PALEK, B., General Linguistics
PALKOVÁ, Z., Phonetics and Phonology
SKŘIVAN, A., General History
SLÁMA, J., Archaeology
SLAVICKÝ, M., Music Studies
STEHLÍKOVÁ, E., History and Theory of Theatre
ULIČNÝ, O., Czech Language
VACEK, J., Sanskrit and Tamil Philosophy
VERNER, M., Egyptology

Faculty of Physical Education and Sport (6, José Martiho 31, 162 52 Prague; tel. 220562459; e-mail karger@ftvs.cuni.cz; internet www.ftvs.cuni.cz):

BLAHUŠ, P., Kinanthropology
BUNC, V., Kinanthropology
DYLEVSKÝ, I., Anatomy
HOUDEK, V., Theory of Physical Culture
KOVÁŘ, R., Kinanthropology
OTAHAL, S., Biomechanics and Bionics
RYCHTECKÝ, A., Kinanthropology
SLEPIČKA, P., Kinanthropology
SVOBODA, B., Sports Education
TEPLÝ, Z., Human Movement

Faculty of Sciences (2, Albertov 6, 128 43 Prague; tel. 222112111; e-mail stulik@prfdec.natur.cuni.cz; internet www.natur.cuni.cz):

BOUBLÍK, T., Physical and Macromolecular Chemistry
BOUŠKA, V., Geological Mineralogy
BUCHAR, J., Zoology
ČEPEK, P., Geology
ČERNÝ, M., Organic Chemistry
CHLUPÁČ, I., Geology
DROBNÍK, J., Biotechnology
FELTL, L., Analytical Chemistry
GARDAVSKÝ, V., Regional Geography
HAMPL, M., Regional Geography
HŮRKA, K., Zoology
KALVODA, J., Physical Geography
KLINOT, J., Organic Chemistry
KOŘÍNEK, V., Biology
MAREK, F., Geology
MAREŠ, S., Geophysics
MATOLÍN, M., Geophysics
MEJSNAR, J., Biology
NÁTR, M., Plant Physiology
NEUBAUER, Z., Philosophy of Natural Sciences
NOVOTNÝ, I., Biology and Physiology of Animals
PAVLÍK, Z., Demography
PERTOLD, Z., Geology
PEŠEK, J., Geology
PODLAHA, J., Inorganic Chemistry
RIEDER, M., Geology
SMOLÍKOVÁ, L., Physical and Macromolecular Chemistry
STEHLÍK, E., Mathematics

ŠTEMPROK, M., Geology
ŠTRUNECKÁ, A., Biology
ŠTULIK, A., Analytical Chemistry
ŠTYS, P., Entomology
TICHÁ, M., Biochemistry
VÁŇA, J., Botany
VÁVRA, J., Parasitology
ZADRAŽIL, S., Genetics and Microbiology

Faculty of Social Sciences (1, Smetanavo nábřezí 6, 110 00 Prague; tel. 222112111; e-mail mlcoch@mbox.fsv.cuni.cz; internet www.fsv.cuni.cz):

HLAVÁČEK, Economics
KOUBA, K., Political Economy
KRAUS, J., Mass Communication
KŘEN, J., Czechoslovak History
MESSTŘÍK, M., Economics
MLČOCH, L., Economics
PEŠEK, J., Modern History
PETRUSEK, M., Sociology
POTŮČEK, M., Sociology
REIMAN, M., History and Politics of Russia and Eastern Europe
SOJKA, M., Economic Theory
TURNOVEC, F., Economics
URBAN, L., Political Economy

UNIVERZITA PALACKÉHO V OLOMOUCI
(Palacký University)

Křížkovského 8, 771 47 Olomouc
Telephone: 585631001
E-mail: kancler@upol.cz
Internet: www.upol.cz

Founded 1573, reopened 1946
State control
Language of instruction: Czech, English, German
Academic year: September to July

Rector: Prof. Dr MIROSLAV MAŠLÁŇ
Vice-Rector for Communication and Further Education: Dr MICHAL MALACKA
Vice-Rector for Information Technology: Prof. Dr VIT VOŽENÍLEK
Vice-Rector for Int. Relations: Mgr JAKUB DÜRR
Vice-Rector for Int. Org.: Dr MONIKA HORÁKOVÁ
Vice-Rector for Regional Devt: Prof. Dr LUBOMÍR DVOŘÁK
Vice-Rector for Science and Research: Prof. Dr JITKA ULRICHOVÁ
Vice-Rector for Study: Doc.Mgr VIT ZOUHAR
Registrar: Ing. HENRIETA CRKOŇOVÁ
Librarian: Dr DANA LOŠŤÁKOVÁ

Library of 600,000 vols
Number of teachers: 1,800
Number of students: 23,000

Publication: *Acta Universitatis Palackianae* (4 a year)

DEANS

Faculty of Education: Prof. LIBUŠE LUDÍKOVÁ
Faculty of Health Sciences: Doc. JANA MAREČKOVÁ
Faculty of Law: Prof. MILANA HRUŠÁKOVÁ
Faculty of Medicine and Dentistry: Prof. ZDERNĚK KOLÁŘ
Faculty of Philosophy: Prof. Doc. JIŘÍ LACH
Faculty of Physical Culture: Doc. ZBYNĚK SVOZIL
Faculty of Science: Prof. JURAJ ŠEVČÍK
Sts Cyril and Methodius Faculty of Theology: Dr IVANA GABRIELA VLKOVÁ

PROFESSORS

Faculty of Education (Žižkovo nám. 5, 771 40 Olomouc; tel. 585635088; e-mail jelenka .navratilova@upol.cz):

CHRÁSKA, M., Theory of Education
GRECMANOVÁ, H., Education
HANZEL, P., Mathematics
KLAPIL, P., Music Theory
LUDÍKOVÁ, L., Special Needs Education
LUSKA, J., Music Theory
NELEŠOVSKÁ, A., Theory of Elementary Education
ODALOŠ, P., Czech Language and Literature
POTMĚŠIL, M., Special Needs Education
STEINMETZ, K., Music Theory
STOFFOVÁ, V.
VALENTA, M., Special Needs Education

Faculty of Health Sciences (Tř. Svobody 8, 771 11 Olomouc; tel. 585632852; e-mail romana.schneeweissova@upol.cz):

KAMÍNEK, M., Radiology

Faculty of Law (Tř. 17 Listopadu 8, 771 11 Olomouc; tel. 585637509; e-mail dekanat.pf@ upol.cz):

DAVID, V., International Law
FIALA, J., Civic Law
HRUŠÁKOVÁ, M., Civic Law
JELÍNEK, J., Criminal Law
MAREČKOVÁ, M., History
MECL, J., Theory of Law
PORADA, V., Criminal Law
SLÁDEČEK, V., Law
TELEC, I., Civic Law
VLČEK, E., Theory of Law

Faculty of Medicine and Dentistry (Tř. Svobody 8, 771 26 Olomouc; tel. 585632009; e-mail klosova@tunw.upol.cz):

DLOUHÝ, M., Surgery
DUDA, M., Surgery
EBER, M., Stomatology
EHRMANN, J., Internal Diseases
HÁLEK, J., Electronics and Medical Procedures
HEŘMAN, M., Radiology
HOLIBKA, V., General Anatomy
HOUDEK, M., Neurosurgery
INDRÁK, K., Internal Diseases
JANOUT, V., Epidemiology
JAROŠOVÁ, M., Medical Genetics
JEZDINSKÝ, J., Pharmacology
JIRAVA, E., Stomatology
KAMÍNEK, M., Stomatology
KAŇOVSKÝ, P., Neurology
KLEIN, J., Surgery
KLENER, P., Paediatry
KOĎOUSEK, R., Pathological Anatomy
KOLÁŘ, M., Microbiology
KOLÁŘ, Z., Pathology
KOLEK, V., Internal Diseases
KOPŘIVA, F., Paediatry
KRÁL, V., Surgery
KRČ, I., Internal Diseases
KUDELA, M., Gynaecology
LATA, J., Microbiology
LICHNOVSKÝ, V., Histology and Embryology
LUKL, J., Internal Diseases
MAČÁKOVÁ, J., Pathological Physiology
MACHÁČEK, J., Radiology
MELICHAR, B., Oncology
MIHÁL, V., Paediatry
MÍŠEK, I., Paediatry
NEKULA, J., Radiology
PAZDERA, J., Stomatology
PEŠÁK, J., Medical Biophysics
PETŘEK, J., Physiology
PETŘEK, M., Immunology
ŘÍHOVÁ, B., Paediatry
ŠEDLÁČEK, R., Paediatry
ŠANTAVÝ, J., Medical Genetics
ŠČUDLA, V., Internal Diseases
ŠEVČÍK, P., Anaesthesiology
SIMÁNEK, V., Medical Chemistry
STÁREK, I., Othorhinolaryngology
ULRICHOVÁ, J., Medical Chemistry and Biochemistry
URBÁNEK, K., Neurology
VAVERKOVÁ, H., Internal Diseases
VESELÝ, J., Pathological Physiology
WEIGL, E., Immunology

Faculty of Philosophy (Křížkovského 10, 771 80 Olomouc; tel. 585631111; e-mail dekan.ff@ upol.cz):

ANDERŠ, J., Slavonic Studies
ASSENZA, G., Political Science
BARTEČEK, I., History
BLECHA, I., Philosophy
BUREŠOVÁ, A., Theory of Music
BUREŠOVÁ, J., History
ČERNÝ, J., Linguistics
DANIEL, L., History of Visual Arts
FIALA, J., History of Czech Literature
FIALOVÁ, I., History of German Literature
FLÍDROVÁ, H., Russian Language
FLOSS, P., History of Philosophy
HECHT, L., Jewish Studies
HLOBIL, T., History of Visual Arts
GERŠLOVÁ, J., Economics
JAŘAB, J., American Literature
KOŘENSKÝ, J., Slavonic Studies
LOTKO, E., Czech Language
MACHÁČEK, J., English Studies
MAREK, P., Czech History
NOVOTNÝ, J., History of Visual Arts
PEPRNÍK, J., English Language
PLHÁKOVÁ, A., Psychology
SEHNAL, J., Theory of Music
SOBOTKOVÁ, M., History of Czech Language
SPÁČILOVÁ, L., German Language
ŠVOBODA, M., Psychology
ŠIMEK, D., Sociology
ŠRÁMEK, J., French Literature
ŠTĚPÁN, J., Philosophy
ŠTĚPÁNEK, P., History of Visual Arts
ŠVÁCHA, R., History of Visual Arts
ŠVORCOVÁ, Z., Japan Studies
TÁRNYIKOVÁ, J., English Studies
TOGNER, M., History of Visual Arts
TRAPL, M., Czech and Slovak History
ULIČNÝ, O., Czech Studies
UNGER, J., History
VÁCLAVEK, L., History of German Literature
VIČAR, J., Theory of Music
ZAHRÁDKA, M., Russian Literature

Faculty of Physical Culture (Tř. Míru 115, 771 11 Olomouc; tel. 585636009; e-mail dekanat.ftk@upol.cz):

FRÖMEL, K., Kinanthropology
HODAŇ, B., Theory of Physical Culture
JANURA, M., Biomechanics
OPAVSKÝ, J., Neurology
OŠŤÁDAL, O., Internal Diseases
RIEGEROVÁ, J., Kinanthropology
VÁLKOVÁ, H., Kinanthropology
VAVERKA, F., Kinanthropology

Faculty of Science (Tř. 17, Listopadu 1192/ 12, 77146 Olomouc; tel. 585634060; e-mail dekanat.prf@upol.cz):

ANDRÉS, J., Mathematical Analysis
BAJER, J., Optics and Optoelectronics
BIČÍK, V., Zoology
BĚLOHLÁVEK, R., Informatics
BOUCHAL, Z., Optics and Optoelectronics
BRABEC, V., Physics
BUREŠ, S., Zoology
CHAJDA, I., Algebra and Geometry
DUŠEK, M., Quantum Optics
DVOŘÁK, L., Biophysics
DVOŘÁK, Z., Cell Biology
FRÉBORT, I., Biochemistry
HALAŠ, R., Algebra and Geometry
HOBZA, P., Physical chemistry
HRABOVSKÝ, M., Optics
HRADIL, P., Organic chemistry
HRADIL, Z., Optics and Optoelectronics
HUBA, M., Development Studies
KAMENÍČEK, J., Inorganic Chemistry
KOTOUČEK, M., Analytical Chemistry
KRAHULEC, F., Botany
KRUPKOVÁ, O., Mathematical Physics
KUBÁČEK, L., Mathematical Statistics
KULHÁNEK, P., Optics
LASOVSKÝ, J., Physical Chemistry

LEBEDA, A., Botany
LEMR, K., Analytical Chemistry
MAŠLÁŇ, M., Applied Physics
MIKEŠ, J., Geometry and Topology
NAUŠ, J., Biophysics
NAVRÁTIL, M., Biology
NEZVALOVÁ, D., Pedagogy
OPATRNÝ, T., Mathematical Physics
PASTOREK, R., Inorganic Chemistry
PEČ, P., Biochemistry
PEŘINA, J., Optoelectronics
PEŘINOVÁ, V., Mathematical Physics
POSPÍŠIL, J., Experimental Physics
POULÍČKOVÁ, A., Botany
RACHŮNEK, J., Algebra
RACHŮNKOVÁ, I., Mathematical Analysis
ŠARAPATKA, B., Landscape Engineering
ŠEBELA, M., Biochemistry
ŠEVČÍK, J., Analytical Chemistry
SLOUKA, J., Organic Chemistry
STANĚK, S., Mathematical Analysis
ŠTĚRBA, O., Ecology
STRÁNSKÝ, Z., Analytical Chemistry
STRNAD, M., Plant Physiology
TKADLEC, E., Ecology
TRÁVNÍČEK, Z., Inorganic Chemistry
VOŽENÍLEK, V., Geography
ZAPLETAL, J., Geology

Sts Cyril and Methodius Faculty of Theology (Univerzitní 22, 771 11 Olomouc; tel. 585637111; e-mail dekanat.cmtf@upol.cz):

AMBROS, P., Theology
GÓRECKI, E., Education
HALAS, F., History
KARFÍKOVÁ, L., Evangelical Theory
KUNETKA, F., Liturgical Theology
POJSL, M., History of Christian Arts
POMPEY, H., Christian Social Work
TICHÝ, L., Theology

UNIVERZITA PARDUBICE
(University of Pardubice)

Studentská 95, 532 10 Pardubice
Telephone: 466036111
E-mail: promotion@upce.cz
Internet: www.upce.cz

Founded 1950 as Vysoká Škola Chemicko-Technologická v Pardubicích; present name and status 1994
State control
Languages of instruction: Czech, English
Academic year: September to August

Rector: Prof. Ing. MIROSLAV LUDWIG
Vice-Rectors: Doc. Ing. JIŘÍ CAKL, Doc. Ing. JAROSLAV JANDA, Doc. Ing. JIŘÍ MÁLEK
Bursar: Ing. MILAN BUKAČ
Librarian: IVA PROCHÁSKOVÁ

Library of 180,000 vols
Number of teachers: 381
Number of students: 4,794

Publications: *Scientific Papers* (1 a year), *Zpravodaj Univerzity Pardubice* (4 a year)

DEANS

Faculty of Chemical Technology: Doc. Ing. PETR MIKULÁŠEK
Faculty of Economics and Administration: Doc. Ing. JAN ČAPEK
Faculty of Humanities: Prof. MILENA LENDEROVÁ
Jan Perner Faculty of Transport: Prof. Dr Ing. KAREL ŠOTEK

ATTACHED RESEARCH INSTITUTES

Institute of Health Studies: Průmyslová 395, 530 03 Pardubice; Dir Prof. Dr ARNOŠT PELLANT.

Institute of Informatics: Studenská 95, 532 10 Pardubice; Dir Doc. Ing. SIMEON KARAMAZOV

UNIVERZITA TOMÁŠE BATI VE ZLÍNĚ
(Tomas Bata University in Zlín)

Náměstí T. G. Masaryka 5555, 760 01 Zlín
Telephone: 576038120
E-mail: rektor@utb.cz
Internet: www.utb.cz

Founded 2001
State control
Languages of instruction: Czech, English
Academic year: September to August

Rector: Prof. PETR SÁHA
Vice-Rector for Int. Relations: Assoc. Prof. ALEŠ GREGAR
Vice-Rector for Pedagogical Activities: Assoc. Prof. ZDENKA PROKOPOVÁ
Vice-Rector for Research and Devt: Assoc. Prof. VLADIMIR SEDLARIK
Vice-Rector for Social Affairs: Assoc. Prof. DAVID TUČEK

Number of teachers: 500
Number of students: 12,000

DEANS

Faculty of Applied Informatics: Prof. MILAN ADÁMEK
Faculty of Humanities: Assoc. Prof. ANEŽKA LENGÁLOVÁ
Faculty of Logistics and Crisis Management: Prof. IVO BARTEČEK
Faculty of Management and Economics: Prof. DRAHOMÍRA PAVELKOVÁ
Faculty of Multimedia Communications: Assoc. Prof. JANA JANÍKOVÁ
Faculty of Technology: Assoc. Prof. ROMAN ČERMÁK

ATTACHED RESEARCH INSTITUTE

University Institute: e-mail ondrackova@uni.utb.cz; internet www.uni.utb.cz; Dir Ing. JINDŘIŠKA ONDRÁČKOVÁ

VETERINÁRNÍ A FARMACEUTICKÁ UNIVERZITA BRNO
(University of Veterinary and Pharmaceutical Sciences Brno)

Palackého 1–3, 612 42 Brno
Telephone: 541562000
E-mail: rektor@vfu.cz
Internet: www.vfu.cz

Founded 1918
State control
Languages of instruction: Czech, English
Academic year: September to August

Rector: Prof. Dr VLADIMIR VEČEREK
Pro-Rector for Education and Vice-Rector: Prof. Dr IVA STEINHAUSEROVÁ
Pro-Rector for Scientific Research and Foreign Relations: Doc. MILOSLAVA LOPAŤÁŘOVÁ
Pro-Rector for Univ. Devt: Prof. Dr Ing. PAVEL SUCHÝ
Registrar: Mgr DANIELA NĚMCOVÁ
Librarian: Mgr JANA SLÁMOVÁ

Library: see under Libraries and Archives
Number of teachers: 301
Number of students: 2,951

Publication: *Acta Veterinaria Brno* (4 a year)

DEANS

Faculty of Pharmacy: Doc. Dr MILAN ŽEMLIČKA
Faculty of Veterinary Hygiene and Ecology: Doc. Dr LADISLAV STEINHAUSER
Faculty of Veterinary Medicine: Doc. Dr ALOIS NEČAS

PROFESSORS

Faculty of Pharmacy (tel. 541562801; e-mail dekanfaf@vfu.cz; internet faf.vfu.cz):

CSÖLLEI, J., Pharmaceutical Chemistry
KVĚTINA, J., Pharmacology and Toxicology
SUCHÝ, J., Pharmacognosy
VÍTOVEC, J., Pharmacology and Toxicology

Faculty of Veterinary Hygiene and Ecology (tel. 541562795; e-mail fvhe@vfu.cz; internet ww.vfu.cz):

BARANYIOVÁ, E., Behaviour Problems in Animals, Methodology of Scientific Work
BEKLOVÁ, M., Ecology
DVOŘÁK, P., Physics, Veterinary Biophysics, Radiobiology of Food
LITERÁK, I., Biology and Genetics
PAVLÍK, I., Tuberculosis, Paratuberculosis and Mycobacterioses
PIKULA, J., Ecology, Game Animal Diseases
STRAKOVÁ, E., Farm Animal Nutrition
SUCHÝ, P., Animal Nutrition and Dietetics
ŠUCMAN, E., Veterinary Chemistry and Biochemistry
SVOBODOVÁ, Z., Veterinary Toxicology and Ecotoxicology
VÁVROVÁ, M., Chemistry and Technology of Environment Protection
VEČEREK, V. A., Veterinary Public Health
VORLOVÁ, L., Food Chemistry, Hygiene and Technology

Faculty of Veterinary Medicine (tel. 541562440; e-mail dekanfvl@vfu.cz; internet www.vfu.cz):

CELER, V., Veterinary Microbiology
ČÍŽEK, A., Veterinary Microbiology
DVOŘÁK, R., Diseases of Farm Animals
HALOUZKA, R., Veterinary Morphology
HANÁK, J., Equine Diseases
HERA, A., Veterinary Pharmacology
HOŘÍN, P., Animal Genetics
KNOTEK, Z., Diseases of Small Animals
KOUDELA, B., Veterinary Parasitology
KOVÁŘŮ, F., Physiology
MÍŠEK, I., Veterinary Morphology
NEČAS, A., Veterinary Surgery and Orthopaedics
POSPÍŠIL, Z., Epizootiology
SMOLA, J., Microbiology
SVOBODA, M., Diseases of Small Animals
SVOBODOVÁ, V., Veterinary Parasitology
TICHÝ, F., Histology and Embryology
TOMAN, M., Veterinary Immunology
TREML, F., Epizootiology

VYSOKÁ ŠKOLA BÁŇSKÁ – TECHNICKÁ UNIVERZITA OSTRAVA
(Technical University of Ostrava)

17 Listopadu 15, 708 33 Ostrava-Poruba
Telephone: 596991111
E-mail: vaclav.roubicek@vsb.cz
Internet: www.vsb.cz

Founded 1716
State control
Academic year: September to August

Rector: Prof. Ing. VÁCLAV ROUBÍČEK
Vice-Rector for Devt: Prof. Ing. PETR WYSLYCH
Vice-Rector for Education: Prof. Ing. JAROMÍR POLÁK
Vice-Rector for Finance and Org.: Prof. Ing. MIROSLAV NEJEZCHLEBA
Vice-Rector for Research and Devt and Int. Affairs: Prof. Ing. TOMÁŠ ČERMÁK
Registrar: Ing. STANISLAV DZIOB
Librarian: Mgr DANIELA TKAČÍKOVÁ

Number of teachers: 812
Number of students: 14,579

Publications: *Akademik* (6 a year), *Sborník vědeckých prací VŠB-TU Ostrava* (irregular)

DEANS

Faculty of Civil Engineering: Prof. Ing. JINDŘICH CIGÁNEK
Faculty of Economics: Prof. Ing. JIŘÍ KERN
Faculty of Electrical Engineering and Informatics: Doc. Ing. KAREL CHMELÍK

Faculty of Mechanical Engineering: Prof. Ing. PETR HORYL
Faculty of Metallurgy and Material Engineering: Prof. Ing. LUDOVIT DOBROVSKÝ
Faculty of Mining and Geology: Prof. Ing. JAROSLAV DVOŘÁČEK

PROFESSORS

Faculty of Civil Engineering (tel. 596991316; e-mail dekan.fast@vsb.cz):

ALDORF, J., Mine Construction and Geotechnics
CIGANEK, J., Mine Construction and Geotechnics

Faculty of Economics (1, Sokolská tř. 33, 701 21 Ostrava):

HALÁSEK, D., Macroeconomics
JUREČKA, V., General Economics
KALUŽA, J., Informatics in Economics
KERN, J., Macroeconomics
NEJEZCHLEBA, M., Finance
POLÁCH, J., Finance
SMOLÍK, D., Environmental Protection and Reclamation
ŠNAPKA, P., Mining Economics and Management

Faculty of Electrical Engineering and Informatics (tel. 596995252):

BLAHETA, R., Applied Mathematics
BLUNÁR, K., Communications Technology
BRANDŠTETTER, P., Electrical Machines, Apparatus and Drives
ČERMÁK, T., Electrical Drives
DIVIŠ, Z., Transport and Infrastructure
DOSTÁL, Z., Applied Mathematics
HASLINGER, J., Applied Mathematics
HRADÍLEK, Z., Electrical Power Engineering
LITSCHMANN, J., Engineering Cybernetics
NEVŘIVA, P., Technical Cybernetics
PALEČEK, J., Electrical Power Engineering
POKORNÝ, M., Measurement and Control Technology
RUSEK, S., Electrical Power Engineering
SANTARIUS, Electrical Power Engineering
SOKANSKÝ, K., Electrical Power Engineering
VONDRÁK, I., Computer Science

Faculty of Mechanical Engineering (tel. 597321216):

ANTONICKÝ, S., Transportation and Technology
BAILOTTI, K., Transportation and Preparation Equipment
DANĚK, A., Transportation and Technology
DANĚK, J., Transportation and Technology
DEJL, Z., Machine Parts and Mechanisms
FUXA, J., Applied Mechanics
GONDEK, H., Mining Machinery
JANALÍK, J., Hydraulic Machines and Mechanisms
KOLAT, P., Thermal and Nuclear Power Engineering
KOUKAL, J., Engineering Technology
LENERT, J., Mechanics
MAKURA, P., Applied Mechanics
NOSKIEVIČ, P., Power Engineering
ONDROUCH, J., Technical Mechanics
PETRUŽELKA, M., Mechanical Technology
POLÁK, J., Transportation and Manipulation Technology
TŮMA, J., Automation of Machines and Technological Processes
VÍTEČEK, A., Automation of Machines and Technological Processes

Faculty of Metallurgy and Material Engineering (tel. 596995374; e-mail jiri.kliber@vsb.cz):

ADOLF, Z., Steel-making
BAŽAN, J., Steel-making
DOBROVSKÝ, L., Chemical Metallurgy
FILIP, P., Materials Engineering
HAŠEK, P., Thermal Engineering in Industry
HYSPECKÁ, L., Physical Metallurgy
JELÍNEK, P., Casting
JONŠTA, Z., Physical Metallurgy
KALOČ, M., Technology of Fuels
KLIBER, J., Materials Forming
KLIKA, Z., Geochemistry, Mineralogy and Technology
KRAUSOVÁ, E., Economics and Management of Metallurgy
KURSA, M., Metallurgical Technology
LEŠKO, J., Chemical Metallurgy
MICHALEK, K., Metallurgical Technology
NENADÁL, J., Quality Management
OBROUČKA, K., Thermal Engineering
PETŘÍKOVÁ, R., Quality and Safety of Technical Systems
PŘÍHODA, M., Thermal Engineering
ROUBÍČEK, V., Technology of Fuels
SCHINDLER, J., Metallurgical Technology
SOMMER, B., Metal Forming
STRNADEL, B., Materials Engineering
TOŠENOVSKÝ, J., Industrial Process
TVRDÝ, M., Materials Engineering
VROŽINA, M., Automation of Metallurgical Processes
WICHTERLE, K., Chemical Engineering

Faculty of Mining and Geology (tel. 596995456):

DIRNER, V., Environmental Protection and Reclamation
DVOŘÁČEK, J., Economics of Mining
FIGALA, J., General Ecology, Chronobiology
GRYGÁREK, J., Underground Mining
KRYL, V., Mining
LÁNÍČEK, J., Mathematics
LEMBÁK, M., Geotechnics and Underground Civil Engineering
MÁDR, V., Physics
NOVÁČEK, J., Mineral Processing and Ecotechnology
PALAS, M., Economic Geology
PETROŠ, V., Underground Mining
PIŠTORA, J., Applied Physics
PROKOP, P., Mine Ventilation
SCHEJBAL, C., Economic Geology
SCHENK, J., Geodesy and Mine Surveying
SIVEK, M., Economic Geology
STRAKOŠ, V., Automation in Mining
VAŠÍČEK, Z., Geology
VIDLÁŘ, J., Mineral Processing
WYSLYCH, P., Applied Physics
ZAMARSKÝ, V., Geology and Mineralogy

VYSOKÁ ŠKOLA CHEMICKO-TECHNOLOGICKÁ V PRAZE (Institute of Chemical Technology, Prague)

Technická 5, 166 28 Prague 6
Telephone: 220444144
E-mail: rektorat@vscht.cz
Internet: www.ict-prague.eu

Founded 1807
State control
Language of instruction: Czech
Academic year: September to June

Rector: Assoc. Prof. JOSEF KOUBEK
Vice-Rector for Devt and Building: Assoc. Prof. JAN STANĚK
Vice-Rector for Education: Prof. PAVEL HASAL
Vice-Rector for Research and Devt: Prof. MILAN POSPÍŠIL
Registrar: Ing. IVANA CHVÁLNÁ
Librarian: Dr ANNA SOUČKOVÁ

Library of 225,000 vols
Number of teachers: 470
Number of students: 3,500

DEANS

Faculty of Chemical Engineering: Assoc. Prof. DANIEL TURZÍK
Faculty of Chemical Technology: Assoc. Prof. ALEŠ HELEBRANT
Faculty of Environmental Engineering: Prof. GUSTAV SEBOR
Faculty of Food and Biochemical Technology: Assoc. Prof. KAREL MELZOCH

PROFESSORS

BASAŘOVÁ, G., Fermentation Chemistry and Biotechnology
BENDA, V., Biochemistry and Microbiology
BENEŠ, P., Social Sciences
BUBNÍK, Z., Cereal Chemistry and Technology
BURYAN, P., Gas, Coke and Air Protection
ČERVENÝ, L., Organic Technology
ČURDA, D., Food Preservation
DAVÍDEK, J., Food Chemistry and Technology
DEMNEROVÁ, K., Biochemistry and Microbiology
DEYL, Z., Analytical Chemistry
DOHÁNYOS, M., Water Technology and Environmental Engineering
DUCHÁČEK, V., Polymers
ECKERT, E., Chemical Engineering
GROS, J., Economics and Management of the Chemical Industry
HAJŠLOVÁ, J., Food Chemistry and Analysis
HANIKA, J., Organic Technology
HLAVÁČ, J., Silicate Technology
HORÁK, J., Organic Technology
HUDEC, L., Technology of Materials for Electronics
JANDA, V., Water Technology and Environmental Engineering
JIRKŮ, V., Fermentation Chemistry and Biotechnology
JURSÍK, F., Inorganic Chemistry
KADLEC, P., Sugar Technology
KÁŠ, J., Biochemistry
KLÍČ, A., Mathematics
KODÍČEK, M., Biochemistry and Microbiology
KRÁLOVÁ, B., Biochemistry and Microbiology
KRATOCHVÍL, B., Solid-state Chemistry
KUBÍČEK, M., Mathematics
KURAŠ, M., Environmental Engineering
LABÍK, S., Physical Chemistry
LIŠKA, F., Organic Chemistry
MALIJEVSKÝ, A., Physical Chemistry
MAREK, M., Chemical Engineering
MATĚJKA, Z., Power Engine
MATOUŠEK, J., Silicate Technology
NĚMEC, L., Inorganic Materials Laboratory
NOVÁK, J., Physical Chemistry
NOVÁK, P., Chemical Metallurgy and Corrosion Engineering
PÁCA, J., Fermentation Chemistry and Biotechnology
PALEČEK, J., Organic Chemistry
PALETA, O., Organic Chemistry
PAŠEK, J., Organic Technology
PECKA, K., Petroleum Technology and Petrochemistry
PITTER, P., Water Technology and Environmental Engineering
POKORNÝ, J., Food Chemistry and Technology
PORUBSKÝ, S., Mathematics
PROCHÁZKA, A., Computing and Control Engineering
RAUCH, P., Biochemistry
RODA, J., Polymers
RUML, T., Biochemistry and Microbiology
RŮŽIČKA, V., Physical Chemistry
RYCHTERA, M., Fermentation Chemistry and Biotechnology
SCHMIDT, O., Automated Control Systems
ŠEBOR, G., Petroleum Technology and Petrochemistry
SLÁDEČKOVÁ, A., Water Technology and Environmental Engineering
STIBOR, I., Organic Chemistry
SUCHANEK, M., Analytical Chemistry
SVOBODA, J., Organic Chemistry
ŠVORČÍK, V., Materials Science
VELÍŠEK, J., Food Chemistry and Technology
VOLKA, K., Analytical Chemistry

WANNER, J., Water Technology and Environmental Engineering
ZÁBRANSKÁ, J., Water Technology and Environmental Engineering

VYSOKÁ ŠKOLA EKONOMICKÁ V PRAZE
(University of Economics, Prague)

Nám. W. Churchilla 4, 130 67 Prague 3
Telephone: 224095799
E-mail: brazdova@vse.cz
Internet: www.vse.cz
Founded 1919
State control
Languages of instruction: Czech, English
Academic year: September to May
Rector: Prof. JAROSLAVA DURČÁKOVÁ
Vice-Rector: Prof. IGOR ČERMÁK
Vice-Rector: Prof. BRONISLAVA HOŘEJŠÍ
Vice-Rector: Prof. VOJTĚCH KREBS
Vice-Rector: Prof. JIŘÍ PATOČKA
Vice-Rector: Prof. ZBYNĚK REVENDA
Bursar: JIŘÍ KŘÍŽ
Number of students: 14,000
Publications: *Acta Economica Pragensia* (2 a year), *Politická Ekonomie* (6 a year), *Prague Economic Papers* (4 a year)

DEANS
Business Administration: Prof. JIŘÍ KLEIBL
Economics and Public Administration: Prof. JIŘÍ SCHWARZ
Finance and Accounting: Prof. BOJKA HAMERNÍKOVÁ
Informatics and Statistics: Prof. RICHARD HINDLS
International Relations: Prof. DANA ZADRAŽILOVÁ
Management: Prof. PAVEL PUDIL

VYSOKÉ UČENÍ TECHNICKÉ V BRNĚ
(Brno University of Technology)

Antonínská 1, 601 90 Brno
Telephone: 541145111
E-mail: rektor@ro.vutbr.cz
Internet: www.vutbr.cz
Founded 1899
State control
Language of instruction: Czech
Academic year: September to July
Rector: Prof. Dr Ing. JAN VRBKA
Pro-Rector: Asst Prof. PETR DUB
Pro-Rector: Prof. Dr JOSEF JANČÁŘ
Pro-Rector: Prof. Ing. JIŘÍ KAZELLE
Pro-Rector: Asst Prof. LADISLAV ŠTĚPÁNEK
Registrar: JAROMÍR PĚNČÍK
Dir for Public Relations and Admin.: Mgr JITKA VANÝSKOVÁ
Librarian: NATAŠA JURSOVÁ
Number of teachers: 1,026
Number of students: 15,090
Publication: *Události na VUT v Brně* (12 a year)

DEANS
Faculty of Architecture: Asst Prof. Ing. JOSEF CHYBÍK
Faculty of Business and Management: Asst Prof. Ing. KAREL RAIS
Faculty of Chemistry: Prof. Ing. MILAN DRDÁK
Faculty of Civil Engineering: Asst Prof. Ing. JAROSLAV PUCHRÍK
Faculty of Electrical Engineering and Communication: Prof. Ing. RADIMÍR VRBA
Faculty of Fine Arts: Prof. Dr JAN SEDLÁK
Faculty of Information Technology: Prof. Ing. TOMÁŠ HRUŠKA
Faculty of Mechanical Engineering: Prof. Ing. JOSEF VAČKÁŘ

PROFESSORS
Faculty of Architecture (Poříčí 5, 639 00 Brno; tel. 541146600; e-mail chybik@ucit.fa.vutbr.cz; internet www.fa.vutbr.cz):
GREGORČÍK, J., Urban Studies
RULLER, I., Public Constructions
VAVERKA, J., Building Construction
ZEMÁNKOVÁ, H., Industrial Architecture

Faculty of Business and Management (Technická 2, 616 69 Brno; tel. 541141111; e-mail dean@fbm.vutbr.cz; internet www.fbm.vutbr.cz):
DVOŘÁK, J., Economy and Management
KONEČNÝ, M., Economy and Management
MEZNÍK, I., Mathematics
NĚMEČEK, P., Economy and Management

Faculty of Chemistry (Purkyňova 118, 612 00 Brno; tel. 541149111; e-mail drdak@fch.vutbr.cz; internet www.fch.vutbr.cz):
BRANDŠTETR, J., Chemistry of Materials
DRDÁK, M., Food Science and Biotechnology
FRIEDL, Z., Chemistry and Technology of Environmental Protection
JANČA, J., Chemistry
JANČÁŘ, J., Chemistry of Materials
KUČERA, M., Chemistry of Materials
NEŠPŮREK, S., Chemistry
OMELKA, L., Chemistry
PELIKÁN, P., Chemistry
RYCHTERA, M., Food Science and Biotechnology
SCHAUER, F., Environmental Chemistry and Technology
SOMMER, L., Chemistry and Technology of Environmental Protection
WEIN, O., Chemistry

Faculty of Civil Engineering (Veveří 95, 662 37 Brno; tel. 541147111; e-mail dekan@fce.vutbr.cz; internet www.fce.vutbr.cz):
ADÁMEK, J., Structural Materials and Testing Methods
DROCHYTKA, R., Technology of Building Materials and Components
FIXEL, J., Geodesy
KOČÍ, J., Building Construction
KOKTAVÝ, B., Physics
MELCHER, J., Metal and Timber Structures
MYSLÍN, J., Building Construction
NEVOSÁD, Z., Geodesy
ŠÁLEK, J., Water Resources Management
STRÁSKÝ, J., Concrete and Masonry Structures

Faculty of Electrical Engineering and Communication (Údolní 53, 602 00 Brno; tel. 541141111; e-mail dekan@feec.vutbr.cz; internet www.feec.vutbr.cz):
AUTRATA, R., Electrical and Electronic Technology
BIOLEK, D., Telecommunications
BRZOBOHATÝ, J., Microelectronics
CHVALINA, J., Mathematics
DIBLÍK, J., Mathematics
DOSTÁL, T., Radioelectronics
HAVEL, V., Mathematics
HONZÍKOVÁ, N., Biomedical Engineering
HRUŠKA, K., Physics
JAN, J., Biomedical Engineering
KAZELLE, J., Electrical and Electronic Technology
MELKES, F., Mathematics
MUSIL, V., Microelectronics
PIVOŇKA, P., Automation
POSPÍŠIL, J., Radioelectronics
PROCHÁZKA, P., Electrical Engineering
ŘÍČNÝ, V., Radioelectronics
ŠEBESTA, V., Radioelectronics
ŠIKULA, J., Physics
SKALICKÝ, J., Power Electrical and Electronic Engineering
SMÉKAL, Z., Telecommunications
SVAČINA, J., Radioelectronics
TOMÁNEK, P., Physics
VALSA, J., Electrical Engineering
VAVŘÍN, P., Automation and Measurement Engineering
VOMELA, J., Biomedical Engineering
VRBA, K., Telecommunications
VRBA, R., Microelectronics

Faculty of Fine Arts (Rybářská 13, 603 00 Brno; tel. 543146850; e-mail dekan@ffa.vutbr.cz; internet www.ffa.vutbr.cz):
NAČERADSKÝ, J., Painting
RONAI, P., Figure Painting
SEDLÁK, J., History of Art

Faculty of Information Technology (Božetěchova 2, 612 66 Brno; tel. 541141139; e-mail info@fit.vutbr.cz; internet www.fit.vutbr.cz):
ČEŠKA, M., Intelligent Systems
DVOŘÁK, V., Computer Systems
HONZÍK, J., Information Systems
HRUŠKA, T., Information Systems
SERBA, I., Computer Graphics and Multimedia

Faculty of Mechanical Engineering (Technická 2, 616 00 Brno; tel. 541141111; e-mail dekan@fme.vutbr.cz; internet www.fme.vutbr.cz):
BABINEC, F., Process Engineering
BOHÁČEK, F., Machine Design
BUMBÁLEK, B., Technology
CHMELA, P., Optics and Fine Mechanics
CIHLÁŘ, J., Ceramics
DRUCKMÜLLER, M., Stochastics, Teaching of Mathematics
FILAKOVSKÝ, K., Aircraft Design
FOREJT, M., Snagging Technology
HLAVENKA, B., Production Engineering
JANÍČEK, P., Mechanics of Solids
JÍCHA, M., Heat and Nuclear Power
KAČUR, J., Mathematics
KADRNOŽKA, J., Heat and Nuclear Power
KAVIČKA, F., Heat and Nuclear Power
KOCMAN, K., Production Engineering
KOHOUTEK, J., Process Engineering
KOMRSKÁ, J., Physics
KRATOCHVÍL, O., Mechanics of Solids
KULČÁK, L., Aerospace Engineering
LIŠKA, M., Physics
MATAL, O., Heat and Nuclear Power
MEDEK, J., Process Engineering
NOVÁK, V., Mathematics
PÍŠTĚK, A., Aerospace Engineering
PÍŠTĚK, V., Combustion Engines and Motor Vehicles
POCHYLÝ, F., Heat and Nuclear Power
POKLUDA, J., Physics
PTÁČEK, L., Materials Engineering
RUSÍN, K., Foundry Engineering
SCHNEIDER, P., Process Engineering
ŠEDLÁČEK, B., Aerospace Engineering
ŠLAPAL, J., Mathematics, Teaching of Mathematics
SLAVÍK, J., Mechanics of Solids
ŠTEHLÍK, P., Process Engineering
ŠTĚPÁNEK, M., Automation and Computer Science
ŠTRÁNSKÝ, K., Materials Engineering
ŠVEJCAR, J., Materials Engineering
VAČKÁŘ, J., Quality and Metrology
VLK, F., Combustion Engines and Motor Vehicles
VRBKA, J., Mechanics of Solids
ŽENÍŠEK, A., Mathematics

ZÁPADOČESKÁ UNIVERZITA
(University of West Bohemia)

Univerzitní 8, 306 14 Plzeň
Telephone: 377631111
E-mail: rektor@rek.zcu.cz
Internet: www.zcu.cz
Founded 1949 as Plzeň Institute of Technology, present name 1991
State control
Language of instruction: Czech

Academic year: September to June
Chancellor: Dr HELENA HEJDOVÁ
Rector: Doc. Ing. JOSEF PRŮŠA
Vice-Rector: Doc. Dr FRANTIŠEK JEŽEK
Vice-Rector: Dr EVA PASÁČKOVÁ
Vice-Rector: Dr Ing. JAN RYCHLÍK
Vice-Rector: Doc. Ing. JAN HOREJC
Registrar: Ing. ANTONÍN BULÍN
Librarian: Dr MILOSLAVA FAITOVÁ
Librarian: Mgr ALENA SCHOŘOVSKÁ
Library of 437,342 vols
Number of teachers: 1,218
Number of students: 18,898
Publications: *Stady* (univ. papers, 12 a year), *Trojúhelník* (univ. journal, 4 a year)

DEANS

Faculty of Applied Sciences: Prof. Ing. JIŘÍ KŘEN
Faculty of Economics: Doc. Dr MIROSLAV PLEVNÝ
Faculty of Education: Doc. Dr JANA COUFALOVÁ
Faculty of Electrical Engineering: Doc. Ing. JIŘÍ HAMMERBAUER
Faculty of Health Care Studies: Dr ILONA MAURITZOVÁ
Faculty of Law: Dr JIŘÍ POSPÍŠIL
Faculty of Mechanical Engineering: Doc. Ing. JIŘÍ STANĚK
Faculty of Philosophy and Arts: Doc. Dr PAVEL VAŘEKA

PROFESSORS

Faculty of Applied Sciences (Univerzitní 22, 306 14 Plzeň; tel. 377632000; internet www.fav.zcu.cz):

DRÁBEK, P., Mathematics
KŘEN, J., Continuum Mechanics, Biomechanics
KUČERA, M., Mathematics
KUFNER, A., Mathematics
KUNEŠ, J., Applied Physics
LAŠ, V., Mechanics
MAREK, P., Mechanics
MATOUŠEK, V., Man–Machine Communication
MÍKA, S., Mathematics
MUSIL, J., Applied Physics
NOVÁK, P., Geodesy
PLÁNIČKA, F., Mechanics
PŘIKRYL, P., Mathematics
PSUTKA, J., Cybernetics
ROSENBERG, J., Mechanics
RYJÁČEK, Z., Mathematics
ŠAFAŘÍK, J., Informatics and Computing
SCHLEGEL, M., Cybernetics
SKALA, V., Computer Graphics
ŠESTÁK, J., Mechanics
ŠIMANDL, M., Cybernetics
ŠŤASTNÝ, M., Mechanics
VLČEK, J., Applied Physics
ZEMAN, V., Mechanics

Faculty of Economics (Husova 11, 306 14 Plzeň; tel. 377633000; internet www.fek.zcu.cz):

KŘIKAČ, K., Organization and Management of Engineering Production
MACEK, J., Statistics in Economics
MACH, M., Business Economics
SEMENIUK, P., Marketing, Trade and Services

Faculty of Education (Sedláčkova 38, 306 14 Plzeň; tel. 377636000; internet www.fpe.zcu.cz):

HÖPPNEROVÁ, V., German Language
JÍLEK, T., Teaching of History
KRAITR, M., Teaching of Chemistry
KUMPERA, J., Teaching of History
MEHNERT, E., Teaching of German Language
NOVÁK, J., Teaching of Chemistry
PILOUS, V., Materials Engineering
RYCHTECKÝ, A., Physical Training
SCHUPPENER, G., German Language
VIKTORA, V., Czech Language

Faculty of Electrical Engineering (Univerzitní 26, 306 14 Plzeň; tel. 377634000; internet www.fel.zcu.cz):

BARTOŠ, V., Electrical Machines and Apparatus
BENEŠOVÁ, Z., Theory of Electrical Engineering
DOLEŽEL, I., Theory of Electrical Engineering
HALLER, R., Electric Power Engineering
JERHOT, J., Electronics and Vacuum Technology
KOŽENÝ, J., Electric Power Engineering
KŮS, V., Electrical Drives and Power Electronics
MAYER, D., Theory of Electrical Engineering
MENTLÍK, V., Electrical Technology
MÜHLBACHER, J., Electric Power Engineering
PINKER, J., Electronic Systems
ŠKORPIL, J., Engineering Ecology
ŠTORK, M., Analog and Digital Circuitry
VONDRÁŠEK, F., Electrical Drives and Power Electronics
VOSTRACKÝ, Z., Electric Power Engineering

Faculty of Law (Sady Pětatřicátníků 14, 306 14 Plzeň; tel. 377637000; internet www.fpr.zcu.cz):

ADAMOVÁ, S., History of the State and Law
BALÍK, S., History of the State and Law
ELIÁŠ, K., Commercial Law
GERLOCH, A., Theory of Law
HRDINA, A., History of Law
HRONCOVÁ, J., Social Pathology
KOPAL, V., International Law
KUČERA, Z., International Law
PAUKNEROVÁ, M., International Law
RŮŽIČKA, K., International Law
RYBÁŘ, M., Criminology
ŠÁMAL, P., Criminal Law
VÁLKOVÁ, H., Criminal Law
WOKOUN, R., Public Service

Faculty of Mechanical Engineering (Univerzitní 22, 306 14 Plzeň; tel. 377638000; internet www.fst.zcu.cz):

BASL, J., Computer Integrated Production Systems
DVOŘÁKOVÁ, L., Financial and Management Accounting
FIALA, J., Physics of Solids
HOSNEDL, S., Machine Design
JANDEČKA, K., Technology of Metal Cutting
KOTT, J., Design of Power Machines and Equipment
LEEDER, E., Computer Integrated Production Systems
LINHART, J., Power System Engineering
MAREŠ, R., Thermomechanics
MAŠEK, B., Materials Science and Metallography
PFROGNER, F., Materials Science and Metallography
ZRNÍK, J., Materials Science and Metallography

Faculty of Philosophy and Arts (Sedláčkova 38, 306 14 Plzeň; tel. 377635000; internet www.ff.zcu.cz):

BLAŽEK, V., Anthropology
BUDIL, I., Anthropology
DOUBRAVOVÁ, J., Philosophy
FUNDA, O., Philosophy
JEŘÁBEK, H., Sociology
NEÚSTUPNÝ, E., Archaeology
SKŘIVAN, A., History
VOPĚNKA, P., Philosophy

Institute of Art and Design:

BARTA, J., Animation
BERÁNEK, J., Sculpture
GAJDOŠ, J., Drama Theory and Criticism
JIRKŮ, B., Drawing and Art of Painting
MATASOVÁ-TEISINGEROVÁ, A., Intermediary Production
NOVÁK, Jewellery Craft
ŠERÁK, V., Ceramic Design
ZIEGLER, Z., Graphic Design

ATTACHED RESEARCH INSTITUTES

Institute of Art and Design: tel. 377636700; e-mail mistera@uud.zcu.cz; internet www.uud.zcu.cz; Dir Doc., Akad. mal. JOSEF MIŠTERA.

New Technologies Research Centre: tel. 377634700; e-mail rosen@ntc.zcu.cz; internet www.ntc.zcu.cz; Dir Prof. Ing. JOSEF ROSENBERG

Schools of Art and Music

Akademie múzických umění v Praze (Prague Academy of Performing Arts): Malostranské nám. 12, 118 00 Prague 1; tel. 234344514; e-mail info@amu.cz; internet www.amu.cz; f. 1945; languages of instruction: Czech, English; academic year October to June; Rector IVO MATHÉ; Vice-Rector ZDENĚK KIRSCHNER; Vice-Rector MIROSLAV KLÍMA; Registrar TAMARA ČUŘÍKOVÁ; library: 161,374 vols; 338 teachers; 1,178 students; publs *Acta Academica Informatorium* (10 a year), *Disk* (4 a year).

Akademie výtvarných umění v Praze (Prague Academy of Fine Arts): U Akademie 4, 170 22 Prague 7; tel. 220408200; e-mail avu@avu.cz; internet www.avu.cz; f. 1799; languages of instruction: Czech, English; academic year October to July; Rector Prof. JIŘÍ SOPKO; Pro-Rector Prof. EMIL PŘIKRYL; Pro-Rector Doc. JIŘÍ LINDOVSKÝ; Registrar Ing. VLADIMÍR KALUGIN; library: 75,000 vols; 58 teachers; 265 students; publs *Almanach*, *Exhibition Catalogues*.

Janáčkova Akademie Múzických Umění v Brnì (Janáček Academy of Music and Performing Arts in Brno): Beethovenova 2, 662 15 Brno; tel. 542591111; e-mail rektor@jamu.cz; internet www.jamu.cz; f. 1947; languages of instruction: Czech, English; academic year September to June; Rector Prof. VÁCLAV CEJPEK; Vice-Rector Prof. Dr LEOŠ FALTUS; Vice-Rector Doc. Dr MIROSLAV PLEŠÁK; Registrar Dr LENKA VALOVÁ; library: 100,000 vols; special collns of printed music and records; 118 teachers; 580 students.

Janáčkova konzervatoř a Gymnázium v Ostravě: Českobratrská 40, 702 00 Ostrava-Moravská; tel. 596112007; e-mail info@jko.cz; internet www.jko.cz; f. 1953; 145 teachers; 376 students; library: 23,000 vols, 7,000 records; Dir MILAN BÁCHOREK.

Konzervatoř, Brno (Conservatoire in Brno): třída Kpt. Jaroše 45, 662 54 Brno; tel. 545215568; e-mail reditel@konzervatorbrno.cz; internet www.konzervatorbrno.eu; f. 1919; music and drama depts; 124 teachers; 360 students; library: 7,000 vols, 29,900 scores, 1,600 records; Dir Mgr E. ZÁMEČNÍK.

Konzervatoř P. J. Vejvanovského, Kroměříž (P. J. Vejvanovského Conservatory, Kromeriz): Pilařova 7, 767 01 Kroměříž; tel. 573339501; e-mail konzervator@konzkm.cz; internet www.konzkm.cz; f. 1949; 55 teachers; 190 students; library: 16,000 vols, 4,600 records; Dir M. SIŠKA.

Konzervatoř, Pardubice (Pardubice Conservatory): Sukova třída 1260, 530 02 Pardubice; tel. 466513503; e-mail reditelstvi@konzervatorpardubice.cz; internet www.konzervatorpardubice.cz; f. 1978; 79 teachers; 172 students; library: 2,200 books, 7,500

vols of music, 1,100 records; Dir Mgr JAROMÍR HÖNIG.

Konzervatoř, Plzeň: Kopeckého sady 10, 301 00 Plzeň; tel. 377226325; e-mail sekretariat@konzervatorplzen.cz; internet www.konzervatorplzen.cz; f. 1961; 78 teachers; 158 students; library: 1,500 books, 1,400 records and CDs, 7,000 scores; Dir MIROSLAV BREJCHA.

Konzervatoř, Teplice: Hudba a Zpěv, Českobratrská 15, 415 01 Teplice; tel. 417538425; e-mail studijni@konzervatorteplice.cz; internet www.konzervatorteplice.cz; f. 1971; 80 teachers; 200 students; library: 10,000 vols, 800 records; Dir Mgr MILAN KUBÍK.

Pražská konzervatoř: Na Rejdišti 1, 110 00 Prague 1; tel. 222319102; e-mail conserv@prgcons.cz; internet www.prgcons.cz; f. 1808; 254 professors; 600 students; library: 85,000 vols, 19,000 records; Dir Mgr PAVEL TROJAN; Chief of Library (Archives) MILOSLAV RICHTER.

Taneční konzervatoř Praha (Prague Conservatory of Dance): Křižovnická 7, 110 00 Prague 1; tel. 222319145; e-mail taneckonzpr@volny.cz; internet www.balet.cz/tkpraha; f. 1945; languages of instruction: Czech, English; 60 teachers; 200 students; Dir Mgr JAROSLAV SLAVICKÝ; publ. *Taneční listy* (Dance Review).

Vysoká Škola Uměleckoprůmyslová (Academy of Art, Architecture and Design): nám. Jana Palacha 80, 116 93 Prague 2; tel. 251098111; e-mail pr@vsup.cz; internet www.vsup.cz; f. 1885; 55 teachers; 400 students; Rector Dr JIŘÍ PELCL; Vice-Rector for Int. and Public Relations Dr MARTINA PACHMANOVÁ; Vice-Rector for Study Dr PAVLA PEČINKOVÁ; Registrar Ing. LUBOŠ KVAPIL.

DENMARK

The Higher Education System

Københavns Universitet (founded 1479) is the oldest university in Denmark. In basic terms, the country's higher education institutions can be grouped into two different sectors: the university sector (offering long-cycle research-based courses) and the college sector (offering professionally orientated short- and medium-cycle courses). The university sector includes eight universities, both multi-faculty universities and institutions specializing in specific fields, and a number of specialist university-level institutions in architecture, art, music, etc. Following the passage of a parliamentary act in 2000, institutions offering medium-cycle higher education merged into more comprehensive university colleges (CVUs), of which there were 10 in 2011. In accordance with the 1998 reform of short-cycle higher education, the majority of vocational colleges have formed vocational academies (erhvervsakademier), which offer courses mainly within the commercial, IT and technical fields. There is also a university in the Faroe Islands, as well as colleges there and in Greenland.

The higher education system is financed by the State and most European students pay no tuition fees (in addition, all Danish students are offered monthly state financial aid); since 2001 the Ministry of Higher Education and Science has been responsible for higher education. (However, the Ministry of Culture oversees arts and cultural education programmes, and the Ministry of Children and Education is responsible for short- and medium-cycle higher education.) The Act on the Universities (1992) extended the traditional academic freedom and autonomy enjoyed by the universities, but the Ministries still dictate regulations on, inter alia, admissions, curricula, quality assurance and appointments of academic staff. Tuition fees for foreign students from outside the European Union and the European Economic Area were introduced in 2006. Quality assurance in the public higher education institutions is overseen by the Danish Evaluation Institute, which incorporated the former Centre for Quality Assurance and Evaluation of Higher Education. Private higher education institutions must submit to an accreditation process run by the Danish Educational Support Agency, a body of the Ministry of Children and Education. The quality assurance system was supplemented by the establishment of a national accreditation system for higher education in 2007 and an accreditation body called ACE Denmark (Akkrediteringsinstitutionen).

To attend university, students must possess one of the secondary school leaving certificates (or equivalent qualification), namely studentereksamen (University Preparatory Examination), højere forberedelseseksamen (Higher Preparatory Examination), højere handelseksamen (Higher Business Examination) or højere teknisk eksamen (Higher Technical Examination). The number of available places each year is stipulated by the Minister of Children and Education and the admission process is organized by the Coordinated Enrolment System. Since the introduction of legislation in 1993, reform of the higher education system of qualifications has broadly brought Denmark into line with the Bologna Process, and the standard degree system consists of Bachelors, Masters (candidatus/candidata) and Doctorate. The European Credit Transfer and Accumulation System was introduced nationally in 2001 and since 2003 only European Bologna-style degrees have been offered. The Bachelors undergraduate degree takes three to three-and-a-half years and must be research-based. The Masters degree, a major part of which is the speciale (Masters thesis), requires two to three-and-a-half years of study following the Bachelors, and a Doctorate (PhD) is awarded following at least eight years of higher education. In 2009 some 128,376 students were enrolled in the university sector, with many more in other centres of higher education. According to the European Commission's Eurostat by 2010 the number of students in tertiary education had risen to 241,000, with the two largest groups studying social sciences, business and law (32%) and health and welfare (21%).

There are 15 short-cycle, professionally orientated programmes (erhvervsakademiuddannelser) offered by the erhvervsakademier (vocational academies), which last two years, and 20 medium-cycle programmes offered by CVUs, lasting three to four years and leading to the award of the title of professionsbachelor (Professional Bachelors). Adult and continuing education was reformed under Act No. 488 (2000), which created three levels of qualifications: Videregående voksenuddannelse (advanced adult education—comparable to a short-cycle higher education level), Diplomuddannelse (Diploma programmes—comparable to a medium-cycle level) and Masteruddannelse (Masters programmes—comparable to a long-cycle level). Most programmes of study last two years (part-time). The admission requirements are a relevant prior qualification and at least two years of professional experience.

Technical and vocational education consists of erhvervsuddannelser (vocational education and training programmes), grundlæggende social- og sundhedsuddannelser (basic social and health education programmes) and other programmes in different fields. These courses are offered by tekniske skoler (technical colleges), handelsskoler (business colleges), landbrugsskoler (agricultural colleges) and social- og sundhedsskoler (social and health care colleges). There are a total of 85 main programmes of vocational education, which are of between two and five years' duration. Normally the sole requirement for admission to a technical/vocational programme is that the applicant has completed compulsory education.

Regulatory and Representative Bodies

GOVERNMENT

Ministry of Children and Education: Frederiksholms Kanal 21, 1220 Copenhagen K; tel. 33-92-50-00; e-mail uvm@uvm.dk; internet www.uvm.dk; Minister CHRISTINE ANTORINI.

Ministry of Culture: Nybrogade 2, 1203 Copenhagen K; tel. 33-92-33-70; e-mail kum@kum.dk; internet www.kum.dk; Minister MARIANNE JELVED.

Ministry of Higher Education and Science: POB 2135, 1015 Copenhagen K; Slotsholmsgade 10, 1216 Copenhagen K; tel. 33-92-97-00; e-mail ufm@ufm.dk; internet ufm.dk; Minister SOFIE CARSTEN NIELSEN.

ACCREDITATION

Danish Agency for Universities and Internationalisation: Bredgade 36, 1260 Copenhagen K; tel. 33-95-12-00; e-mail ui@ui.dk; internet www.en.iu.dk; attached to Min. of Science, Innovation and Higher Education; aims to facilitate more and better knowledge in the form of research, education, knowledge dissemination and public-sector services; promotes internationalization of study programmes, intercultural understanding and integration; Chair. for Internationalisation HANS PETER JENSEN.

Danmarks Akkrediteringsinstitution (Denmark's Accreditation Institution): Bredgade 38, 1260 Copenhagen K; tel. 33-92-69-00; e-mail akkr@akkr.dk; internet www.akkr.dk; f. 2007; Exec. Dir ANETTE DØRGE.

Danmarks Evalueringsinstitut (EVA) (Danish Evaluation Institute): Østbanegade 55, 3rd Fl., 2100 Copenhagen Ø; tel. 35-55-01-01; e-mail eva@eva.dk; internet www.eva.dk; f. 1992 as Danish Centre for Quality Assurance and Evaluation of Higher Education, current name and status 1999; Exec. Dir MIKKEL HAARDER.

FUNDING

Styrelsen for Statens Uddannelsesstøtte (Danish Educational Support Agency): Danasvej 30, 1780 Copenhagen V; tel. 33-26-86-00; e-mail vus@vus.dk; internet www.su.dk; attached to Min. of Science, Innovation and Higher Education; prepares amendments of the scheme, registers applications, pays out grants and loans, offers guidance and information to the educational institutions, deals with complaints and appeals (which are decided by a Board of Appeal), draws up budgets and collects statistics for the use of the min.; Dir LARS MORTENSEN.

NATIONAL BODIES

Danske Universiteter (Universities Denmark): Fiolstraede 44, 1. th, 1171 Copenhagen K; tel. 33-36-98-05; e-mail dkuni@dkuni.dk; internet www.dkuni.dk; f. 1967; org. of the 8 Danish univs to enhance their cooperation, visibility and impact; Pres. JOHN DUE; Vice-Pres. NILS STRANDBERG PEDERSEN; Sec. SUSANNE BJERREGAARD.

Folkeuniversitetet I Danmark (People's University): c/o Syddansk Universitet, Campusvej 55, 5230 Odense M; tel. 65-50-27-27; e-mail mail.sei@fu.dk; internet www.folkeuniversitet.dk; f. 1898; Chair. INGOLF CHRISTENSEN; Rector Dr SOREN EIGAARD.

Styrelsen for Forskning og Innovation (Danish Agency for Science, Technology and Innovation): Bredgade 40, 1260 Copenhagen K; tel. 35-44-62-00; e-mail fi@fi.dk; internet www.fi.dk; f. 1968; attached to Min. of Science, Innovation and Higher Education; provides secretariat services to and supervises scientific research ccls which allocate funds for ind. research, for strategic research and for innovation and which advises the political system; promotes int. research and innovation partnerships; Dir-Gen. HANS MÜLLER PEDERSEN.

Attached Councils:

Danmarks Forskningspolitiske Råd (Danish Council for Research Policy): Bredgade 40, 1260 Copenhagen K; tel. 25186638; e-mail fi@fi.dk; internet en.fi.dk/councils-commissions/the-danish-council-for-research-policy; f. 1996; attached to Min. of Science, Innovation and Higher Education; promotes devt of Danish research; advises Min. on present and future needs of research at the global level; Chair. and Sr. Dir CLAUS HVIID CHRISTENSEN; Vice-Pres. Prof. MARIE-LOUISE NOSCH.

Dansk Radet for Teknologi og Innovation (Danish Council for Technology and Innovation): Bredgade 40, 1260 Copenhagen K; tel. 35-44-62-00; e-mail fi@fi.dk; internet en.fi.dk/councils-commissions/the-danish-council-for-technology-and-innovation; administers the initiatives given to the ccl by the Min.; provides advice for the Min. of Science, Technology and Innovation about technology and innovation policies; Chair. CONNI SIMONSEN; Vice-Chair. ANNETTE TOFT.

Det Frie Forskningsråd (The Danish Council for Independent Research): Bredgade 40, 1260 Copenhagen K; tel. 35-44-62-00; e-mail fi@fi.dk; internet en.fi.dk/councils-commissions/the-danish-council-for-independent-research; f. 1968; provides scientific advice and funds for research activities; promotes int. research collaboration; 5 scientific research ccls: humanities, medical sciences, natural sciences, social sciences, technology and production sciences; Dir. HANS MÜLLER PEDERSEN.

Det Strategiske Forskningsråd (Danish Council for Strategic Research): Bredgade 40, 1260 Copenhagen; tel. 35-44-62-00; e-mail fi@fi.dk; internet fivu.dk/en/dsf; f. 2004; promotes strategic research in welfare, wealth and science; Pres. Prof. PETER OLESEN; Vice-Pres. METTE THUNØ.

Learned Societies

GENERAL

Det Kongelige Danske Videnskabernes Selskab (Royal Danish Academy of Sciences): H. C. Andersens Blvd 35, 1553 Copenhagen V; tel. 33-43-53-00; e-mail kdvs@royalacademy.dk; internet www.royalacademy.dk; f. 1742; works to strengthen the position of science in Denmark; promotes interdisciplinary understanding; 500 mems (250 Danish, 250 foreign); Pres. Prof. Dr KIRSTEN HASTRUP; Sec. and Treas. Prof. MOGENS HØGH JENSEN; publs *Scientia Danica, Series B, Biologica* (irregular), *Scientia Danica, Series H. Humaniora 4* (irregular), *Scientia Danica, Series H. Humaniora 8* (irregular), *Scientia Danica, Series M. Mathematica et Physica* (irregular).

AGRICULTURE, FISHERIES AND VETERINARY SCIENCE

Dansk Skovforening (Danish Forestry Society): Amalievej 20, 1875 Frederiksberg C; tel. 33-24-42-66; e-mail info@skovforeningen.dk; internet www.skovforeningen.dk; f. 1888; promotes the commercial and professional interests of Danish forestry; supports conservation of natural values of the Danish forests; Chair. NIELS IUEL REVENTLOW; Vice-Chair. NIELS OTTO LUNDSTEDT; publs *Dansk Skovbrugs Tidsskrift* (4 a year), *Skoven* (11 a year), *Skoven Nyt* (22 a year).

Dansk Veterinærhistorisk Samfund (Danish Veterinary History Society): Hoejskolelunden 3C, 6630 Roedding; tel. 74-84-24-76; e-mail oldvet@rnet.dk; f. 1934; annual European tour and seminar on the history of veterinary medicine; 320 mems; library of 44 vols; Pres. Dr CARL ANTON HENRIKSEN; publ. *Dansk Veterinærhistorisk Årbog* (every 2 years).

Foreningen af Mejeriledere og Funktionærer (Association of Dairy Managers): Munkehatten 28, Tornbjerg, 5220 Odense SE; tel. 66-12-40-25; e-mail fmf@maelkeritidende.dk; internet www.mejerileder.dk; f. 1887; 823 mems; Pres. SØREN STEEN JENSEN; publs *Danish Dairy and Food Industry* (1 a year), *Maelkeritidende* (23 a year).

Jordbrugsakademikernes (JA) (Danish Federation of Graduates in Agriculture, Horticulture, Forestry and Landscape Architecture): Emdrupvej 28A, 2100 Copenhagen Ø; tel. 33-21-28-00; e-mail post@ja.dk; internet www.ja.dk; f. 1976, current name adopted 2007; 5,000 mems; works for skills and career devt for mems; highlights the academic and policy issues within the mems disciplines; develops networks and peer cohesion among mems; Pres. JAKOB SVENDSEN-TUNE; Sec. FLEMMING BO PETERSEN; publs *Jord og Viden* (8 a year), *moMentum+* (4 a year).

Kongelige Danske Landhusholdningsselskab (Royal Danish Agricultural Society): c/o Landbrug and Fodevarer, Axelborg, Axeltorv 3, 1609 København V; tel. 33-39-42-20; e-mail jsl@lf.dk; internet www.1769.dk; f. 1769; provides a forum for debate on sustainable use of the open land and its resources for the benefit of agriculture, soc. and environment; organizes confs; Pres. FREDERIK LÜTTICHAU; Vice-Pres. STEFFEN HUSTED DAMSGAARD; Sec. JETTE LETHBRIDGE; publ. *Tidsskrift for Landøkonomi* (Journal of Rural Economy, 1 a year).

ARCHITECTURE AND TOWN PLANNING

Akademisk Arkitektforening (Danish Architects' Association): Strandgade 27A, 1401 Copenhagen K; tel. 30-85-90-00; e-mail mail@arkitektforeningen.dk; internet www.arkitektforeningen.dk; f. 1879; promotes quality of planning and design of Danish physical environment and improves and develops conditions for the architect's profession; 7,000 mems; Chair. NATALIE MOSSIN; Dir for the Secretariat JANE SANDBERG; publs *Arkitekten*, *Arkitektur*.

Dansk Byplanlaboratorium (Danish Town Planning Institute): Nørregade 36, 1165 Copenhagen K; tel. 33-13-72-81; e-mail db@byplanlab.dk; internet www.byplanlab.dk; f. 1921; ensures that current town planning issues and questions attract interest; promotes new knowledge and ideas for town planning; library of 6,000 vols; Chair. MAY GREEN; Vice-Chair. MAI-BRITT JENSEN; Vice-Chair. THORKILD AERO; Dir ANNE SKOVBRO; publ. *Dansk Byplanlaboratorium*.

BIBLIOGRAPHY, LIBRARY SCIENCE AND MUSEOLOGY

Danmarks Biblioteksforening (Danish Library Association): Farvergade 27D, 2nd Fl., 1463 Copenhagen K; tel. 33-25-09-35; e-mail db@db.dk; internet www.db.dk; f. 1905; advances the devt of the public library system; 432 mems; Pres. VAGN YTTE LARSEN; First Vice-Pres. HANNE PIGONSKA; Second Vice-Pres. KIRSTEN BOELT; Dir MICHEL STEEN-HANSEN; publ. *Biblioteksvejviser* (1 a year).

Dansk Biblioteks Center AS: Tempovej 7–11, 2750 Ballerup; tel. 44-86-77-77; e-mail dbc@dbc.dk; internet www.dbc.dk; f. 1991; provides Danish libraries with bibliographic data, a union catalogue, databases and online products; Chair. JØRN LEHMANN PETERSEN; Vice-Chair. KIM ØSTRUP; Man. Dir. MOGENS BRABAND JENSEN; Sec. ANNI JACOBSEN; publ. *DBC Avisen*.

Danske Fag-, Forsknings- og Uddannelsesbiblioteker (Danish Industry, Research and Education Libraries): DF Secretariat, Statsbiblioteket, Tangen 2, 8200 Aarhus N; tel. 89-46-22-07; e-mail df@statsbiblioteket.dk; internet www.dfdf.dk; f. 1978; promotes initiatives for benefit of academic and research libraries and collective library system; forum for consideration and discussions of subjects on library issues and library politics; 700 personal, 145 institutional mems; Pres. MICHAEL COTTA-SCHØNBERG; Treas. LILIAN MADSEN; publ. *REVY* (4 a year).

Kulturstyrelsen: H. C. Andersens Blvd 2, 1553 Copenhagen V; tel. 33-73-33-73; e-mail post@kulturstyrelsen.dk; internet www.kulturstyrelsen.dk; f. 2012 by merger of 3 fmr agencies; Arts Council, Heritage Agency and the Danish Agency for Libraries and Media; attached to Min. of Culture; aims to strengthen interaction between art, heritage, libraries and media; improve coordination of state and municipal cultural action; promotes devt and utilization of digitization of cultural and media landscape; develops new services and forms of communication to strengthen int. cultural cooperation in all fields; Dir LONE RAVEN; publ. *Bibliotek og Medier* (4 a year).

Organisationen Danske Museer (Association of Danish Museums): Vartov Farvergade 27D, 2. sal, 1463 Copenhagen; tel. 49-14-39-66; e-mail info@dkmuseer.dk; internet www.dkmuseer.dk; f. 2005 by merger of

Foreningen af Danske Kunstmuseer and Dansk Kulturhistorisk Museums Forening; promotes Danish Museums and protects their interests through nat. and int. activities; develops museums as active instns in soc. to influence public debate and to further the museums' interests in relation to public authorities; establishes a cooperative forum for all professional groups affiliated with Danish museums; disseminates information about museum affairs both to museums and public; contributes to further education and training of museum staff and to instigate learning activities at museums; 180 mems; Chair. CHRISTINE BUHL ANDERSEN; Dir for Secretariat NILS M. JENSEN.

ECONOMICS, LAW AND POLITICS

Danmarks Jurist- og Økonomforbund (Danish Association of Lawyers and Economists): Gothersgade 133, 1123 Copenhagen K; tel. 33-95-97-00; e-mail djoef@djoef.dk; internet www.djoef.dk; f. 1972; works towards improving the working conditions of students and employees within the fields of admin., communication, economics, education, law, political and social science, research and state governance; 75,000 mems; Fed. Pres. FINN BORCH ANDERSEN; Sec. LENA CARLSSON; Dir BRITTA BORCH EGEVANG; publs *DJØF Efteruddannelse* (2 a year), *Juristen* (6 a year), *Ledelse and Erhvervsøkonomi* (4 a year), *Samfundsøkonomen* (6 a year).

Dansk Selskab for Europaforskning (Danish Society for European Studies): c/o Centre for European Studies, University of Southern Denmark, Campusvej 55, 5230 Odense M; tel. 65-50-22-17; e-mail ecsa-dk@sam.sdu.dk; internet www.ecsa.dk; f. 1976; promotes Danish academic study, research and teaching of the administrative, legal, economic, political and social aspects of European integration by means of seminars and publs; 100 mems; Pres. Prof. DEREK BEACH; Vice-Pres. DORTE MARTINSEN; Sec. RENS VAN MUNSTER; Treas. Assoc. Prof. HENRIK PLASCHKE.

International Law Association—Danish Branch: Kromann Reumert Sundkrogsgade 5, 2100 Copenhagen O; e-mail elf@kromannreumert.com; internet www.ila-hq.org; f. 1925; promotes the study, clarification and devt of int. law, both public and private, and furthers int. understanding and respect for int. law; 63 mems; Pres. HENRIK THAL JANTZEN; Sec. and Treas. EVA LE FEVRE.

Nationalekonomisk Forening (Danish Economic Society): Danmarks Nationalbank, Havnegade 5, 1093 Copenhagen K; tel. 33-63-63-63; internet www.econ.ku.dk/nf; f. 1873; organizes lectures, discussions and encourages int. cooperation with similar asscns in the Nordic and other countries to disseminate and debate on economic issues in Denmark; 1,000 mems; Pres. Prof. PEDER ANDERSEN; Sec. CHRISTIAN ANDERSEN HELBO; Treas. ULRIKKE EKELUND; publs *Abonnement på Nationaløkonomisk Tidsskrift, Nationaloekonomisk Tidsskrift* (1 a year).

Udenrigspolitiske Selskab (Danish Foreign Policy Society): Amaliegade 40A, 1256 Copenhagen K; tel. 33-14-88-86; e-mail udenrigs@udenrigs.dk; internet www.udenrigs.dk; f. 1946; studies, debates, publs and confs on int. affairs; 1,000 individual mems, 200 corporate mems; library of 100 vols; Chair. Dr LYKKE FRIIS; Dir KLAUS CARSTEN PEDERSEN; Sec. BRITA V. ANDERSEN; publs *Lande i Lommeformat, Udenrigs* (3 a year).

EDUCATION

Danmark-Amerika Fondet (Denmark-America Foundation): Nørregade 7A, 1165 Copenhagen K; tel. 35-32-45-45; e-mail advising@daf-fulb.dk; internet www.wemakeithappen.dk; f. 1914; provides grants to study in the USA; advises about univ. education in the USA; Pres. STEN SCHEIBYE; Treas. PETER HØJLAND.

Mellemfolkeligt Samvirke (MS ActionAid Denmark): Fælledvej 12, 2200 Copenhagen N; tel. 77-31-00-00; e-mail ms@ms.dk; internet www.ms.dk; f. 1944; open membership org.; supports long-term devt work, education programmes and campaigns; mem. of the International Movement ActionAid; 8,000 mems; library of 40,000 vols on third world issues, immigrants and refugees in Denmark, 600 periodicals, 1,300 films; Chair. TRINE PERTOU MACH; Vice-Chair. ARVID AAGAARD; Sec. Gen. LARS UDSHOLT; Treas. DINES JUSTESEN; publs *Etcetera* (8 a year), *FOCUS Kontakt* (6 a year), *Kontakt Globalt Magasin* (6 a year), *ZAPP Jorden Rundt* (6 a year).

FINE AND PERFORMING ARTS

Billedkunstnernes Forbund (Danish Visual Artists): Vingårdstræde 2, 1, 1070 Copenhagen K; tel. 33-12-81-70; e-mail bkf@bkf.dk; internet www.bkf.dk; f. 1969; influences current policies to enhance economic and social security for visual artists; enhances use of, and respect for, visual art; protects artistic freedom; 1,300 mems; Chair. BJARNE W. SØRENSEN; publ. *Billedkunstneren* (4 a year).

Choral Denmark: Niels Græsholm, Aalandsgade 49, 3.t. v, 2300 Copenhagen S; tel. 24-45-44-21; e-mail formand@danskekorledere.dk; internet www.wscm8.com; promotes Danish choral culture, performers, scores and recordings in an int.context; Chair NIELS GRÆSHOLM.

Dansk Billedhuggersamfund (Danish Sculptors' Society): c/o Mogens Lund 'Sundhuset', Clarasvej 2, 8700 Horsens; tel. 76-28-20-10; e-mail mnl@billedhuggersamfundet.dk; internet www.skulptur.dk; f. 1905; improves sculptors' opportunities to display and then be able to sell their work; outdoor exhibits of particularly larger works; 120 mems; Pres. SOREN SCHAARUP; Treas. HENRIK VIOLENCE.

Dansk Komponist Forening (Danish Composers' Society): Gråbrødretorv 16, 1st Fl., 1154 Copenhagen K; tel. 33-13-54-05; e-mail dkf@komponistforeningen.dk; internet www.komponistforeningen.dk; f. 1913; supports composers and sound artists in their artistic potential; 220 mems; Chair. NIELS ROSING-SCHOW; Sec. KIRSTEN WREM; Sec. TINA SCHELLE; Sec. KATRINE GREGERSEN DAL.

Dansk Korforening (Danish Choral Society): Absalonsgade 3, 4180 Sorø; f. 1911; 27 mems; Pres. ASGER LARSEN.

Danske Kunsthåndværkere (Danish Arts and Crafts Association): Bredgade 66, 1260 Copenhagen K; tel. 33-15-29-40; e-mail mail@dkkh.dk; internet www.dkkh.dk; f. 1976; represents Danish craft professionals at political level; arranges exhibitions; professional advice for schools, museums; 5 regional groups of artist-craftsmen; 500 mems; Pres. HANNE LANGE HOULBERG; Man. Dir NICOLAI GJESSING; publ. *KUNSTUFF–Danish Crafts and Design* (4 a year).

Edition•S–music¬sound¬art: Gråbrødrestræde 18, 1156 Copenhagen K; tel. 33-13-54-45; e-mail sales@edition-s.dk; internet www.edition-s.dk; f. 1871 as The Soc. for the Publ of Danish Music, present status 2007; publishes art music for the classical and experimental music scene; CEO KLAUS IB JØRGENSEN; Chair. SVEND HVIDTFELT NIELSEN.

Kunstforeningen GL STRAND (GL STRAND Gallery of Modern and Contemporary Art): Gammel Strand 48, 1202 Copenhagen K; tel. 33-36-02-60; e-mail info@glstrand.dk; internet www.glstrand.dk; f. 1825; Dir HELLE BEHRNDT; publ. *Medlemsnyt* (4 a year).

Kunstnerforeningen af 18. November (Artists' Association of the 18th November): Frederiksgade 8, 4 tv, 1265 Copenhagen K; tel. 33-15-96-14; internet www.18nov.dk; f. 1842; asscn of architects, dancers, graphic artists, musicians, professional painters, sculptors, writers; art colln, concerts, exhibitions, lectures, movies, workshop; 200 mems; library of 300 vols; Chair. NIELS WAMBERG; Sec. MOGENS KISCHINOVSKY; Treas. EVA NEDERGAARD.

Ny Carlsbergfondet (New Carlsberg Foundation): Brolæggerstræde 5, 1211 Copenhagen K; tel. 33-11-37-65; e-mail sekretariatet@nycarlsbergfondet.dk; internet www.ny-carlsbergfondet.dk; f. 1902; supports the Ny Carlsberg Glyptotek (see Museums and Art Galleries, Copenhagen), and other Danish art museums; promotes the study of art and art history; annual awards; Chair. KARSTEN OHRT.

Sammenslutningen af Danske Kunstforeninger (Association of Danish Art Societies): c/o Mogens Christiansen, Cikorievej 1, 4300 Holbæk Copenhagen K; tel. 59-44-19-08; e-mail mc@mckunst.dk; internet www.sdkunst.dk; f. 1942; arranges touring art exhibitions with govt support; 15,000 mems; Pres. FINN MIKKELSEN; Vice-Pres. HENRY ROSSLE; Sec. HANS-JØRGEN HØJVÆLDE; Treas. MOGENS CHRISTIANSEN.

HISTORY, GEOGRAPHY AND ARCHAEOLOGY

Arktisk Institut (Danish Arctic Institute): Strandgade 102, 1401 Copenhagen K; tel. 32-31-50-50; e-mail arktisk@arktisk.dk; internet www.arktiskinstitut.dk; f. 1954; information, scientific and historic activities related to the Arctic; library of 35,000 vols, incl. 26,000 books, 9,000 pamphlets and 750 periodicals; archives of Arctic expeditions, diaries, and more than 150,000 photographs, mainly of Greenland; Chair. LEO BJØRNSKOV; Dir Dr BENT NIELSEN.

Dansk Selskab for Oldtids- og Middelalderforskning (Danish Society for Research of Ancient and Medieval Times): Nationalmuseet, Frederiksholms Kanal 12 1220 Copenhagen K; tel. 33-47-31-36; e-mail else.rasmussen@natmus.dk; f. 1934; 130 mems; Pres. MICHAEL ANDERSEN; Sec. ELSE MATHORNE RASMUSSEN.

Danske Historiske Forening (Danish Historical Association): Univ. of Copenhagen, SAXO-Institute, Karen Blixens Vej 4, 2300 Copenhagen S; tel. 51-29-98-32; e-mail histtid@hum.ku.dk; internet www.historisktidsskrift.dk; f. 1839; 1,200 mems; Chair. Assoc. Prof. CARSTEN DUE-NIELSEN; Treas. ANDERS MONRAD MØLLER; publ. *Historisk Tidsskrift* (2 a year).

Jysk Arkaeologisk Selskab Nordjylland (Jutland Archaeological Society, North Jutland): Moesgård, 8270 Højbjerg; tel. 87-16-11-51; e-mail moesgaard@hum.au.dk; internet www.jyskarkaeologiskselskab.dk; f. 1951 as Aalborg Archaeological Soc., merged with Jutland Archaeological Soc. Moesgaard 2010, present name and status 2010; lectures and publs of primary archaeological and ethnological investigations; 120 mems; Pres. LARS CHRISTIAN NØRBACH; Treas. PETER VAN HAUEN; publs *Handbooks* (irregular), *KUML* (1 a year).

Jysk Selskab for Historie (Jutland Historical Society): Historisk Institut, Århus Universitet, 8000 Århus C; tel. 89-42-20-23; f. 1866; promotes interest in and study of historical topics; 500 mems; Pres. HENRIK FODE; Treas. ERIK STRANGE PETERSEN; publs *Historie* (2 a year), *Nyt fra Historien* (2 a year).

Kongelige Danske Geografiske Selskab (Royal Danish Geographical Society): Øster Voldgade 10, 1350 Copenhagen K; tel. 35-32-25-00; e-mail rdgs@geo.ku.dk; internet www.rdgs.dk; f. 1876; furthers interest in geographical science; organizes meetings, expeditions and research projects; 450 mems; Pres. HRH CROWN PRINCE FREDERIK; Vice-Pres. Rear-Admiral NILS WANG; Vice-Pres. Prof. CHRISTIAN WICHMANN MATTHIESSEN; Man. Dir PETER AUGUSTINUS; Sec. Gen. Prof. HENRIK BREUNING-MADSEN; Treas. Assoc. Prof. BIRGER U. HANSEN; publ. *Geografisk Tidsskrift* (Danish Journal of Geography).

Kongelige Danske Selskab for Fædrelandets Historie (Royal Danish Society for National History): c/o Erik Goebel, Kingosvej 16, 4600 Koge; e-mail bestil@danskeselskab.dk; internet www.danskeselskab.dk; f. 1745; publishes sources related to country's history; contributes to Danish history research promotion; 65 mems, 20 foreign corresps; Chair. NIELS-KNUD LIEBGOTT; Sec. ERIK GØBEL; Treas. Dr ANDERS MONRAD MØLLE; publ. *Danske Magazin*.

Det Kongelige Nordiske Oldskriftselskab (Royal Society of Northern Antiquaries): Frederiksholms Kanal 12, 1220 Copenhagen K; tel. 41-20-61-66; e-mail oldskriftselskabet@natmus.dk; internet www.oldskriftselskabet.dk; f. 1825 as Nordiske Oldskriftselskab; supports and raises awareness of Denmark and other Nordic culture in ancient and medieval times; publishes books and journals; organizes excursions and lectures; 675 mems; library: in the Nat. Museum; Dir NIELS-KNUD LIEBGOTT; Sec. PETER VANG PETERSEN; Treas. GEORG LETT; publs *Aarbøger for Nordisk Oldkyndighed og Historie*, *Nordiske Fortidsminder*.

Selskabet for Dansk Kulturhistorie (Society for the History of Danish Culture): Rosenborg Castle, Øster Voldgade 4A, 1350 Copenhagen K; tel. 33-15-32-86; e-mail jh@dkks.dk; f. 1936; promotes study of Danish cultural history, esp. after 1500; 50 mems; Pres. STEFFEN HEIBERG; Sec. JØRGEN HEIN; publ. *Cultural Monuments*.

LANGUAGE AND LITERATURE

Alliance Française: Christiansholms Tværvej 19, 2930 Klampenborg, Copenhagen; tel. 55-66-04-950; e-mail internet@prebenhansen.dk; internet www.alliancefrancaise.dk; f. 1884; offers courses and exams in French language and culture and promotes cultural exchange with France; attached offices in Aarhus and Abyhoj; Chair. PETER PREBEN HANSEN; Vice-Chair. ROLF MEURS-GERKEN.

British Council: c/o Republikken, Vesterbroggade 24B, 1620 Copenhagen V; tel. 33-36-94-00; e-mail denmark.enquiries@britishcouncil.org; internet www.britishcouncil.org/denmark; activities in 3 regional programme strands: climate change, intercultural dialogue and creative cities; Country Dir. DORTE FRIIS.

Dansk Forfatterforening (Danish Authors' Society): Strandgade 6 St, 1401 Copenhagen K; tel. 32-95-51-00; e-mail df@danskforfatterforening.dk; internet www.danskforfatterforening.dk; f. 1894; aims to improve conditions for creative artists in general and for mems of the soc. in particular; organized in five professional groups: children's and youth literature, fiction, non-fiction, poetry, translation; 1,300 mems; Chair. JO HERMANN (acting); Sec. NENA WIINSTEDT; Treas. LISE BIDSTRUP; publ. *Forfatteren* (8 a year).

Danske Sprog- og Litteraturselskab (Society for Danish Language and Literature): Christians Brygge 1, 1219 Copenhagen K; tel. 33-13-06-60; e-mail sekretariat@dsl.dk; internet www.dsl.dk; f. 1911; reissues Danish language and literary works; publishes bibliographies and scientifically based dictionaries; builds electronic language resources; 95 mems; Pres. CHR. GORM TORTZEN; Sec. MARIA KROGH LANGNER.

Goethe-Institut: Frederiksborggade 1, 2 th, 1360 Copenhagen K; tel. 33-36-64-64; e-mail info@kopenhagen.goethe.org; internet www.goethe.de/ins/dk/kop; f. 1961; offers exams in German language and culture and promotes cultural exchange with Germany; Dir ANNE-SUSANNE FACKLER.

Íslenzka fræðafélag (Icelandic Literary Society): Helsevej 21, 3400 Hillerød; f. 1912; Sec. P. JÓNASSON; publ. *Skírnir*.

MEDICINE

Danmarks Farmaceutiske Selskab (Danish Pharmaceutical Society): Rygårds Allé 1, 2900 Hellerup; tel. 39-46-36-00; e-mail pd@pharmadanmark.dk; internet www.farmaceutisk-selskab.dk; f. 1912; 765 mems; Pres. Dr SOREN ILSØE-KRISTENSEN; Treas. Dr DITTE MARIA KARPF.

Dansk Knoglemedicinsk Selskab (Danish Bone Medical Society): Læge Morten Frost Nielsen Odense Universitets Hospital, Endokrinologisk Afd., M. Søndre Blvd 29, 5000 Odense C; e-mail indkommende_post@dkms.dk; internet www.dkms.dk; f. originally known as Danish Society for Bone and Dental Research; promotes and coordinates bone and calcium research; organizes scientific meetings and publishes materials about the treatment of bone diseases; Pres. Prof. Dr BO ABRAHAMSEN; Sec. Prof. Dr MORTEN FROST MUNK NIELSEN.

Kræftens Bekæmpelse (Danish Cancer Society): Strandboulevarden 49, 2100 Copenhagen Ø; tel. 35-25-75-00; e-mail info@cancer.dk; internet www.cancer.dk; f. 1904; CEO LEIF VESTERGAARD PEDERSEN.

Lægeforeningen (Danish Medical Association): Kristianiagade 12, 2100 Copenhagen Ø; tel. 35-44-85-00; e-mail dadl@dadl.dk; internet www.laeger.dk; f. 1857; protects and promotes the interests of the medical profession; serves as the body through which the influence of the medical profession may be exercised; 24,972 mems; Pres. MADS KOCH HANSEN; Man. Dir BENTE HYLDAHL FOGH; publs *Bibliotek for Læger* (history of medicine, 4 a year), *Danish Medical Journal* (5 a year), *Lægeforeningens Medicinfortegnelse (Physicians Desk Reference)* (every 2 years), *Ugeskrift for Læger* (52 a year).

Lægevidenskabelige Selskaber (Organization of Medical Sciences Companies): Kristianiagade 12, 2100 Copenhagen Ø; tel. 35-44-81-32; e-mail dms@dadl.dk; internet www.selskaberne.dk; f. 1919; umbrella org. for the medical companies in Denmark; aims to promote the interests of mem. socs; arranges an annual meeting with a scientific topic of general interest; provides financial support for scientific meetings arranged by mem. socs; supports publication of Danish doctoral dissertations; awards the annual August Krogh Prize to a Danish scientist; 23,153 mems represented through 121 scientific socs; Chair. Prof. Dr PETER SCHWARZ; Vice-Chair. Prof. Dr NIELS QVIST; Sec. KARIN EWALD; publ. *The Danish Medical Bulletin*.

Medicinhistorisk Selskab for Jylland og Fyn (Medicine Historical Society of Jutland and Funen): c/o Steno Museet, C.F, Møllers Alle 2, Universitetsparken, 8000 Århus C; tel. 87-15-54-15; internet www.jmhs.dk; promotes interest in the study of medicine and related sciences history; meetings held at the Steno Musem; Chair. Prof. Dr OLE SONNE; Deputy Chair. SOREN HESS; Sec. HANNE TEGLHUS; publ. *Dansk Medicinhistorisk Årbog* (Danish Medical History Yearbook).

Medicinske Selskab i København (Medical Society of Copenhagen): Kristianiagade 12, 2100 Copenhagen Ø; tel. 35-44-84-01; e-mail kms@dadl.dk; internet www.dmsk.dk; f. 1772; provides financial support for travel medical scientific use and for young researchers, medical projects; recommends on various awards and scholarships; 2,755 mems; Pres. Dr JACOB ROSENBERG; Sec. BITTEN DAHLSTORM.

Osteoporoseforeningen (Osteoporosis Society): Park Allé 5, POB 5069, 8100 Arhus C; tel. 86-13-91-11; e-mail info@osteoporose-f.dk; internet osteoporose-f.dk; f. 1992; supports research, prevention projects, lectures on the disease; participates in fairs and exhibitions to create awareness; Chair. ULLA KNAPPE; publs *Apropos* (4 a year), *Osteoporosis Society* (4 a year).

Pharmadanmark (Pharma Denmark): Rygårds Alle 1, 2900 Hellerup; tel. 39-46-36-00; e-mail pd@pharmadanmark.dk; internet www.pharmadanmark.dk; f. 1873; spreads awareness of the preconditions for growth and devt of pharmaceuticals; library of 16,000 vols; 3,205 mems; Chair. ANTJE MARQUARDSEN; publ. *Pharma* (12 a year).

Tandlægeforeningen (Danish Dental Association): Amaliegade 17, 1256 Copenhagen K; tel. 70-25-77-11; e-mail info@tandlaegeforeningen.dk; internet www.tandlaegeforeningen.dk; f. 1873; 6,345 mems; Pres. FREDDIE SLOTH-LISBJERG; publ. *Tandlaegebladet*.

NATURAL SCIENCES

General

Selskabet for Naturlærens Udbredelse (Society for the Promotion of Natural Science): c/o DTU Mathematics and Computer Science, Matematiktorvet, Bldg 303B, 2800 Kongens Lyngby; tel. 21-26-03-50; e-mail snu@naturvidenskab.net; internet www.naturvidenskab.net; f. 1824; organizes visits and lectures on new scientific discoveries in physics, chemistry and technology; awards H. C. Ørsted Medal and Kirstine Meyer Award; 200 mems; Pres. Prof. Dr DORTE OLESEN; Sec. CECILIE K. PEDERSEN; publ. *KVANT/Tidsskrift for Fysik og Astronomi* (4 a year).

Biological Sciences

Danmarks Naturfredningsforening (Danish Society for Nature Conservation): Masnedøgade 20, 2100 Copenhagen Ø; tel. 39-17-40-00; e-mail dn@dn.dk; internet www.dn.dk; f. 1911; 133,000 mems; Pres. ELLA MARIA BISSCHOP-LARSEN; Dir GUNVER BENNEKOU; publ. *Tidsskriftet natur og miljø* (4 a year).

Dansk Botanisk Forening (Danish Botanical Society): Sølvgade 83, 1307 Copenhagen K; tel. 33-14-17-03; e-mail dbotf@mail.tele.dk; internet www.botaniskforening.dk; f. 1840; 1,400 mems; Pres. JAKOB HERMANN; Vice-Pres. PAUL MØLLER PEDERSEN; Treas. KARIN RAVN-JONSEN; publ. *URT* (4 a year).

Dansk Entomologisk Forening (Danish Entomological Society): c/o Zoological Museum, Universitetsparken 15, 2100, Copenhagen Ø; e-mail def@entoweb.dk;

internet www.entoweb.dk/def/english.php; f. 1868; works to strengthen the conservation of insect habitats; promotes integration of entomology and insect habitats in nature conservation and in plans, policies and projects at all levels; 800 mems; Pres. MICHAEL KAVIN; Sec. CARSTEN HVIID; publ. *Entomologiske Meddelelser* (4 a year).

Dansk Naturhistorisk Forening (Danish Natural History Society): c/o The Natural History Museum, Univ. of Copenhagen, University Park 15, 2100 Copenhagen; tel. 35-32-11-20; e-mail dnf@zmuc.ku.dk; internet snm.ku.dk/dnf; f. 1833; promotes interest in all aspects of natural history, particularly zoology; conducts meetings, excursions and travel; 300 mems; Pres. Assoc. Prof. Dr NADJA MØBJERG; Vice-Pres. Assoc. Prof. NIELS BONDE; Treas. Dr LARS VILHELMSEN; Sec. JYTTE FREDSKOV; publs *Årsskrift for Dansk Naturhistorisk Forening* (1 a year), *Danmarks Fauna* (irregular).

Dansk Ornithologisk Forening (Danish Ornithological Society): Vesterbrogade 140, 1620 Copenhagen V; tel. 33-28-38-00; e-mail dof@dof.dk; internet www.dof.dk; f. 1906; 13 local brs; conservation org. with a special focus on birds; 16,000 mems; Chair. EGON OSTERGAARD; Vice-Chair. MARCO BRODDE; Vice-Chair. NIELS RIIS; Dir JAN EJLSTED; publs *Dansk Ornitologisk Forenings Tidsskrift* (4 a year), *DOF-Nyt* (4 a year), *Fugle i Felten* (4 a year), *Fugle og Natur* (4 a year).

Physical Sciences

Astronomisk Selskab (Astronomical Society): Schæffergaardsvej 4, 2820 Gentofte; tel. 25-71-65-35; e-mail hn@astronomisk.dk; internet www.astronomisk.dk; f. 1916; 600 mems; organizes lectures and observing events; Chair. HENRY NØRGAARD; Treas. STEEN TRABERG-BORUP; publ. *Kvant* (jtly with Danish Physical Soc., 4 a year).

Dansk Fysisk Selskab (Danish Physical Society): c/o Ian Bearden, Niels Bohr Institutet Københavns, Universitet Blegdamsvej 17, 2100 Copenhagen Ø; tel. 45-35-32-53-23; e-mail bearden@nbi.dk; internet www.dfs.nbi.dk; f. 1972; promotes Danish research on physics through meetings and lectures; represents the physicists in Denmark to the European Physical Soc.; 700 mems; Pres. IAN BEARDEN; Vice-Pres. JOHN ANDERSON; Treas. HELGE KNUDSEN; publ. *Kvant* (jtly with Astronomical Soc., 4 a year).

Dansk Geologisk Forening (Geological Society of Denmark): Øster Voldgade 10, 1350 Copenhagen K; tel. 35-32-23-54; e-mail dgfemail@gmail.com; internet 2dgf.dk; f. 1893; organizes lectures, discussions; excursions; administers 2 prizes; 600 mems; Chair. Dr LARS NIELSEN; Deputy Chair. MARTIN SØNDERHOLM; Treas. GUNVER K. KRARUP PEDERSEN; publs *Dansk Geologisk Forening Årsskrift* (online), *Geologisk Tidsskrift* (2 a year).

Dansk Matematisk Forening (Danish Mathematical Society): c/o Bjarne Toft, IMADA, Univ. of Southern Denmark, 5230 Odense M; tel. 65-50-23-23; e-mail dmf@mathematics.dk; internet www.mathematics.dk; f. 1873; 300 mems; Pres. Prof. BJARNE TOFT; Vice-Pres. and Sec. Prof. VAGN LUNDSGAARD HANSEN; publs *Mathematica Scandinavica*, *Nordisk Matematisk Tidskrift*.

Kemisk Forening (Danish Chemical Society): Universitetsparken 5, 2100 Copenhagen Ø; tel. 35-32-01-55; e-mail secretary@chemsoc.dk; internet www.chemsoc.dk; f. 1879; 870 mems; Pres. Assoc. Prof. STEFAN VOGEL; Vice-Pres. Prof. PETER WESTH; Sec. Asst Prof. MICHAEL PITTELKOW; publ. *Dansk Kemi* (12 a year).

PHILOSOPHY AND PSYCHOLOGY

Dansk Psykolog Forening (Danish Psychological Association): Stockholmsgade 27, 2100 Copenhagen Ø; tel. 35-26-99-55; e-mail dp@dp.dk; internet www.dp.dk; f. 1947; professional union and representative body for psychologists in Denmark; 9,139 mems; Chair. EVA SECHER MATHIASEN; Vice-Chair. RIE RASMUSSEN; Dir ARNE GRØNBORG JOHANSEN; Sec. METTE GORSKI; publ. *Psykolog Nyt* (26 a year).

RELIGION, SOCIOLOGY AND ANTHROPOLOGY

Danske Bibelselskab (Danish Bible Society): Frederiksborggade 50, 1360 Copenhagen K; tel. 33-12-78-35; e-mail bibelselskabet@bibelselskabet.dk; internet www.bibelselskabet.dk; f. 1814; editing and distributing Bibles and other biblical scriptures; Pres. PETER SKOV-JAKOBSEN; Chair. Dr CAI FRIMODT-MØLLER; Gen. Sec Dr MORTEN THOMSEN HØJSGAARD (acting); publs *Bibelen og Verden* (4 a year), *Bibliana* (2 a year).

Grønlandske Selskab (Greenlandic Society): Strandgade 102, 1401 Copenhagen K; tel. 61-60-53-31; e-mail dgs@groenlandselskab.dk; internet www.groenlandselskab.dk; f. 1905; informs about and builds relations with Greenland; strengthens public knowledge about Greenland and its people, the Arctic region as a whole; supports Danish-Greenlandic cooperation; 850 mems; Chair. EINAR LUND JENSEN; Sec. LISBETH VALGREEN; publ. *Grønland* (4 a year).

Orientalsk Samfund (Nordic Institute of Asian Studies): Leifsgade 33.3, 2300 Copenhagen S; tel. 35-32-95-00; e-mail sec@nias.ku.dk; internet www.nias.ku.dk; f. 1968; attached to Univ. of Copenhagen; Nordic research and resource centre, focuses on modern Asia from a predominantly social sciences perspective; library of 38,000 vols of books and journals; Chair. LARS BILLE; Sec. GEIR HELGESEN; publ. *nytt—Asia Insights* (3 a year).

TECHNOLOGY

Akademiet for de Tekniske Videnskaber (Danish Academy of Technical Sciences): Lundtoftevej 266, 2800 Kgs. Lyngby; tel. 45-88-13-11; e-mail atvmail@atv.dk; internet www.atv.dk; f. 1937; aims at a scientific basis to promote technical and scientific research; works to increase value creation and welfare in Danish society; 650 mems; Pres. Prof. MARTIN P. BENDSØE; Vice-Pres. BJERNE STEFFEN CLAUSEN; Chief Sec. LISE THURMANN; Acad. Dir LIA LEFFLAND.

Byggecentrum (Building Centre): Hindsgavl Allé 2, 5500 Middelfart; tel. 70-12-36-00; e-mail info@byggecentrum.dk; internet www.byggecentrum.dk; f. 1956; acts as centre for construction information; bookshop, database services, postgraduate training, exhibitions, training centre; Man. Dir JOERN VIBE ANDREASEN; publ. *BYGGEDATA*.

Dansk Husflidsselskab (Danish Society of Domestic Crafts): Gedskovvej 3, 5300 Kerteminde; tel. 63-32-20-96; e-mail dansk@husflid.dk; internet www.husflid.dk; f. 1873; 4,000 local mems, 140 local orgs; Pres. ELSE MARIE SCHJERNING; Vice-Pres. BODIL NIELSEN; Treas. AGNES STENSGAARD; Sec. for Management BENTE FOREST MACHHOLM; publ. *Husflid* (6 a year).

Elektroteknisk Forening (Society of Danish Electrotechnicians): Kronprinsensgade 28, 5000 Odense C; tel. 40-56-01-48; e-mail info@dkef.dk; internet www.dkef.dk; f. 1903; divided into 5 sections, organizes visits, lectures and field trips to establish networks across the industry; 1,300 mems; Nat. Chair. BENT CRAMER; Sec. Gen. ANDERS EBBESEN JENSEN; Treas CLAUS FRØS LUND; publ. *Elteknik* (10 a year).

Højteknologifonden (Danish National Advanced Technology Foundation): Holbergsgade 14 3, 1057 Copenhagen K; tel. 33-63-72-80; e-mail info@hoejteknologifonden.dk; internet hoejteknologifonden.dk; f. 2004; offers funds and framework to private companies and univs for developing new technologies; Chair. JØRGEN MADS CLAUSEN; Vice-Chair. Prof. KLAUS BOCK; Dir CARSTEN ORTH GAARN-LARSEN; Vice-Dir TRINE AABO ANDERSEN.

Ingeniørforeningen i Danmark (IDA) (Danish Society of Engineers): Kalvebod Brygge 31–33, 1780 Copenhagen V; tel. 33-18-48-48; e-mail ida@ida.dk; internet www.ida.dk; f. 1937; divided into 8 geographical regions; brs in Aalborg, Århus, Copenhagen and Odense; 88,000 mems; Pres. FRIDA FROST; Exec. Sec. NINA SEIERUP VON AHNEN; Vice-Pres. LASSE GRØNBECH; publ. *Ingeniøren* (52 a year).

Research Institutes

GENERAL

Carlsberg Laboratory: Gamle Carlsberg Vej 10, 2500 Copenhagen V; tel. 33-27-52-21; e-mail carlslab@crc.dk; internet www.carlsberglab.dk; f. 1876; attached to Carlsberg Foundation; ind.unit of the Research Centre run by Carlsberg Limited; research in biochemistry, biotechnology and chemistry; library of 15,000 vols, 300 periodicals; Dir Prof. OLE HINDSGAUL; Sec. ANNETTE PETTERSSON.

Danish Meat Research Institute: Maglegaardsvej 2, 4000 Roskilde; tel. 72-20-20-00; e-mail dmri@teknologisk.dk; internet www.dti.dk; attached to Danish Technological Institute; aims to find methods and technologies for efficient production of safe meat products; Man. Dir LARS LEOPOLD HINRICHSEN; Dir LARS HINRICHSEN.

Danish Obesity Research Centre: c/o Institute of Preventive Medicine Frederiksberg, Hospital Nordre Fasanvej 57, 2000 Frederiksberg; tel. 38-16-30-25; e-mail ta@ipm.regionh.dk; internet www.danorc.dk; f. 2007; investigates effects of the nutritional components: industrial fatty acids, ruminant fatty acids and milk protein on the devt of overweight and obesity—ind. of their calorific value; Centre Leader Prof. Dr THORKILD I. A. SØRENSEN; Sr Dir Prof. HENRIK JØRGEN JØRGEN; Exec. Vice-Pres. Dr HENRIK DALBØGE.

DTU Fødevareinstituttet (National Food Institute): Mørkhøj Bygade 19, 2860 Søborg; tel. 35-88-70-00; e-mail food@food.dtu.dk; internet www.food.dtu.dk; f. 1959, present status 2007; attached to Technical Univ. of Denmark; conducts research into the entire food chain, from primary agricultural production and industrial processing to final preparation in the home of the consumer; provides education and gives advice on nutrition, food safety, food technology, environment and health; Dir JØRGEN SCHLUNDT.

Nationale Forskningscenter for Arbejdsmiljø (National Research Centre for the Working Environment): Lersø Park Allé 105, 2100 Copenhagen Ø; tel. 39-16-52-00; e-mail nfa@arbejdsmiljoforskning.dk; internet www.arbejdsmiljoforskning.dk; f. 2003; attached to Min. of Employment; monitors, analyses and explores conditions in the working environment affecting health, safety and work role functioning; acts as a gateway to working environment knowledge for enterprises through the Working Environment Information Centre; Chair. Prof. KJELD MØLLER PEDERSEN; Dir-Gen. Dr PALLE ØRBÆK; Deputy Dir-Gen. ULLA W. SKJØTH.

Rockwool Fondens Forskningsenhed (Rockwool Foundation Research Unit): Sølvgade 10, 2. tv., 1307 Copenhagen K; tel. 33-34-48-00; e-mail forskningsenheden@rff.dk; internet www.rff.dk; f. 1987; attached to The Rockwool Foundation; produces new, empirically based analyses related to current problems of modern soc. within the areas of labour market conditions and of the functions, stability and legitimacy of the welfare state; Pres. ELIN SCHMIDT; Chair. TOM KÄHLER; Deputy Chair. LARS NØRBY JOHANSEN; Research Dir Prof. TORBEN TRANÆS; Sec. MAI-BRITT SEJBERG.

AGRICULTURE, FISHERIES AND VETERINARY SCIENCE

DTU Veterinærinstituttet (National Veterinary Institute DTU): Bülowsvej 27, 1870 Frederiksberg C; tel. 35-88-60-00; e-mail vet@vet.dtu.dk; internet www.vet.dtu.dk; f. 1908, present status and name 2007; attached to Technical Univ. of Denmark; conducts research on infectious diseases in livestock and makes diagnoses in diseased animals; advises public authorities and cooperates with them on the Danish veterinary contingency plan; Dir KRISTIAN MØLLER; Deputy Dir KIRSTEN FLAGSTAD; Exec. Sec. TINA VALDIMARSSON.

Hedeselskabet (Danish Land Development Service): Klostermarken 12, POB 91, 8800 Viborg; tel. 87-28-11-33; e-mail hedeselskabet@hedeselskabet.dk; internet www.hedeselskabet.dk; f. 1866; forestry, forest nurseries, shelter belts, soil improvement, environmental protection, environmental engineering, land reclamation, drainage, irrigation, hydrology and research; specialists carry out practical assignments and research; technical projects designed and administered for farmers, foresters, industry, government authorities in Denmark and abroad; CEO OVE KLOCH; Chair. FRANTS COUNT BERNSTORFF-GYLDENSTEEN; Man. Dir SVEND AAGE LINDE; publ. *Vækst* (6 a year).

Nationalt Center for Fødevarer og Jordbrug (Danish Centre for Food and Agriculture): Aarhus Univ., Blichers Allé 20, POB 50, 8830 Tjele; tel. 87-15-60-00; e-mail dca@au.dk; internet agrsci.au.dk; f. 2011; attached to Aarhus Univ.; provides advice and cooperation within the fields of food and agriculture; depts of agroecology, animal science, engineering, food science and molecular biology and genetics; Dir JØRGEN B. JESPERSEN.

ECONOMICS, LAW AND POLITICS

Danmarks Statistik (Statistics Denmark): Sejrøgade 11, 2100 Copenhagen Ø; tel. 39-17-39-17; e-mail dst@dst.dk; internet www.dst.dk; f. 1849; central instn for all Danish statistics; library: see under Libraries and Archives; Dir-Gen. JAN PLOVSING; publs *Statistisk Årbog* (1 a year), *Statistisk Månedsoversigt* (12 a year), *Statistisk Tiårsoversigt* (statistical 10-year survey, 1 a year).

Dansk Center for Internationale Studier og Menneskerettigheder (Danish Centre for International Studies and Human Rights): Strandgade 56, 1401 Copenhagen K; tel. 32-69-86-86; e-mail dcism@dcism.dk; internet www.dcism.dk; f. 2003; undertakes research and analysis concerning foreign security and devt policy; conflict and genocide and human rights in Denmark and abroad; library of 115,000 books and reports, 1,000 journals and yearbooks; Chair. OLE LØNSMANN POULSEN; Treas. HANNE ERBS.

Constituent Institutes:

Dansk Institut for Internationale Studier (DIIS) (Danish Institute for International Studies (DIIS)): Østbanegade 117, 2100 Copenhagen K; tel. 32-69-87-87; e-mail diis@diis.dk; internet www.diis.dk; f. 2003; research areas: foreign policy global transformations in finance, migration and aid international security natural resources and development peace, risk and violence; Dir NANNA HVIDT.

Dansk Institut for Menneskerettigheder (Danish Institute for Human Rights): Strandgade 56, 1401 Copenhagen K; tel. 32-69-88-88; e-mail center@humanrights.dk; internet www.humanrights.dk; f. 2002; promotes and develops knowledge about human rights on a nat., regional and int. basis predicated on the belief that human rights are universal, mutually interdependent and interrelated; Dir JONAS CHRISTOFFERSEN.

EDUCATION

Sino-Danish Center for Education and Research (SDC): Niels Jensens Vej 2, Bldg 1190, 8000 Aarhus C; tel. 87-15-25-97; e-mail contact@sinodanishcenter.dk; internet www.sinodanishcenter.com; f. 2008; promotes and strengthens collaboration between Danish and Chinese research and learning environments for the benefit of both countries; Exec. Dir Prof. HANS GREGERSEN.

HISTORY, GEOGRAPHY AND ARCHAEOLOGY

Danske Komité for Historikernes Internationale Samarbejde (Danish Committee for International Historical Cooperation): Copenhagen Univ., 2300 Copenhagen S; f. 1926; 43 mems; Chair. Prof. NIELS STEENSGARD.

MEDICINE

CCBR's Clinical Research Center: Telegrafvej 4, 2750 Ballerup; tel. 44-52-54-00; e-mail info-ccbr@ccbr.com; internet www.ccbr.com; f. 1992 as QAC CCBR, present status and name 1998; operates clinical-trial sites; has 22 offices around the world; CEO HANS CHRISTIAN HOECK; Dir for Clinical Operations ANETTE VIERNING.

Center for Integrated Molecular Brain Imaging: Rigshospitalet, Section 9201, Blegdamsvej 9, 2100 Copenhagen Ø; tel. 35-45-67-12; e-mail cimbi@cimbi.dk; internet www.cimbi.dk; f. 2006; researches on the neural bases of personality dimensions that predispose individuals to affective and substance use disorders; Dir Prof. GITTE MOOS KNUDSENS.

Center of Functionally Integrative Neuroscience: Aarhus University Hospital—Århus Sygehus, Nørrebrogade 44, Bldg 10G, 5th Fl., 8000 Arhus C; Bldg 10G, 5th Fl., Nørrebrogade 44, 8000 Arhus C; tel. 89-49-43-98; e-mail mai@cfin.dk; internet www.cfin.au.dk; f. 2000; attached to Danish Nat. Research Foundation; researches to understand the ability of the human brain; Head LEIF ØSTERGAARD.

Danish Cancer Society Research Center: Strandboulevarden 49, 2100 Copenhagen Ø; tel. 35-25-75-00; e-mail info@cancer.dk; internet www.cancer.dk/research; f. 1949; attached to Danish Cancer Soc.; Dir Prof. JØRGEN H. OLSEN; Sec. LAILA FISCHER; publ. *Report* (every 2 years, in English).

Dansk Center for Aldringsforskning (Danish Ageing Research Center): Institute of Public Health—Epidemiology, J. B. Winsløwsvej 9B, st. t. v., 5000 Odense C; tel. 65-50-40-88; e-mail uiversen@health.sdu.dk; internet www.sdu.dk/en/om_sdu/institutter_centre/darc; f. 1996; attached to Univ. of Southern Denmark; conducts research in human ageing processes from a range of different angles; combines ageing research from the molecular level, to the individual and finally to the entire population; Head Prof. Dr KAARE CHRISTENSEN; Centre Sec. ULLA IVERSEN.

Dansk Psykiatrisk Biobank (Danish Psychiatric Biobank): Psykiatrisk Center Sct, Hans ForksningInstituttet for Biologisk Psykiatri, Boserupvej 2, 4000 Roskilde; tel. 46-33-49-68; e-mail kontakt@psykiatriskbiobank.dk; internet www.ribp.dk; f. 2001; ensures long lasting and stable scientific devts that could involve running and integrating new and relevant scientific disciplines in basic and clinical psychiatric research; collaboration with 11 European and American research centres; Research Dir Dr THOMAS WERGELAND; Centre Man. HENRIK LUBLIN.

Finsen Laboratory: Rigshospitalet, Copenhagen Biocenter, Jagtvej 124, 2200 Copenhagen N; Rigshospitalet, Copenhagen Biocenter, Ole Maaloes Vej 5, Bldg 3, 3rd Fl., 2200 Copenhagen N; tel. 35-45-60-22; e-mail finsenlab@finsenlab.dk; internet www.finsenlab.dk; f. 1896; attached to Rigshospitalet, Copenhagen Univ. Hospital; cancer research unit; performs basic cancer research; Head of Laboratory BO PORSE.

Hagedorn Research Institute: Niels Steensens Vej 6, 2820 Gentofte; tel. 44-44-88-88; internet www.hagedorn.dk; f. 1989; attached to Novo Nordisk; researches to find a cure for diabetes and its complications; Corporate Vice-Pres. and Dir for Research Prof. ALLAN ERTMANN KARLSEN.

Kennedy Centret (Kennedy Center): Gamle Landevej 7, 2600 Glostrup; tel. 43-26-01-00; e-mail kennedy@kennedy.dk; internet www.kennedy.dk; f. 2004; nat. research and advisory centre for genetics, visual impairment and mental retardation; Pres. BIRGITTE DISSING NAUNTOFTE; Dir Prof. KAREN BRØNDUM-NIELSEN.

Wilhelm Johannsen Centre for Functional Genome Research: Bldg 24.4, Blegdemsvej 3, 2200 Copenhagen N; tel. 35-32-78-26; e-mail wjc@wjc.ku.dk; internet www.wjc.ku.dk; f. 2001; attached to Univ. of Copenhagen; researches in functional characterization of the human genome by identification of novel human disease genes, novel genetic entities and novel genetic mechanisms; Centre Dir Prof. NIELS TOMMERUP.

NATURAL SCIENCES

General

De Økonomiske Råd (Danish Economic Councils): Amaliegade 44, 1256 Copenhagen K; tel. 33-44-58-00; e-mail dors@dors.dk; internet www.dors.dk; f. 1962; consists of the Danish Economic Ccl and the Danish Environmental Economic Ccl; 26 mems; Dir LARS HAAGEN PEDERSEN; publs *Danish Economy* (2 a year), *Economics and the Environment* (1 a year).

Biological Sciences

Arctic Station, University of Copenhagen: Faculty of Science, Univ. of Copenhagen, Bülowsvej 17, 1870 Frederiksberg C; Arctic Station, POB 504, 3953 Qeqertarsuaq, Greenland; tel. 35-32-42-56; e-mail gin@science.ku.dk; internet www.arktiskstation.ku.dk; f. 1906, research facility at Univ. of Copenhagen 1953; study of Arctic nature; laboratory; research ship 'Porsild'; library of 3,000 vols, colln of journals; Head of Board

Prof. REINHARDT MØBJERG KRISTENSEN; Sec. GITTE HENRIKSEN.

Bioinformatik-centret (Bioinformatics Centre): Dept of Biology, Univ. of Copenhagen, Ole Maaloes Vej 5, 2200 Copenhagen N; tel. 35-32-13-17; e-mail info@binf.ku.dk; internet www.binf.ku.dk; f. 2002, present status 2006; attached to Univ. of Copenhagen; conducts basic research in bioinformatics using probabilistic models and comparative methods; computational analysis of non-coding RNA, gene regulation and protein structure; responsible for MA programme in bioinformatics; Head Prof. ANDERS KROGH; Sec. SIANNY BRANDT.

Biologisk Institut (Institute of Biology): Univ. of Southern Denmark, Campusvej 55, 5230 Odense M; tel. 65-50-27-52; e-mail mj@biology.sdu.dk; internet www.sdu.dk/en/om_sdu/institutter_centre/i_biologi; f. 1973; attached to Univ. of Southern Denmark; focuses research on ecotoxicology and environmental stress, bioacoustics and behaviour, and aquatic ecology; library of 1,000 vols; Head Prof. MARIANNE HOLMER.

DTU Aqua—National Institute of Aquatic Resources: Jægersborg Alle 1, 2920 Charlottenlund; tel. 35-88-33-00; e-mail aqua@aqua.dtu.dk; internet www.aqua.dtu.dk; f. 1995 as Danish Institute for Fisheries Research; attached to Technical Univ. of Denmark; organized into 8 scientific sections; fisheries, aquaculture, marine, freshwater and seafood research; large specialist library of fisheries and biology texts; offers, in collaboration with the Univ. of Copenhagen, MSc programme in aquatic science and technology; Dir FRITZ W. KÖSTER (acting).

Research School of Water Resources (Fiva): c/o Dr Karsten H. Jensen, Dept of Geography and Geology, Univ.of Copenhagen, Øster Voldgade 10, 1350 Copenhagen K; tel. 35-32-24-84; e-mail khj@geo.ku.dk; internet www.fiva.dk; f. 2002; supports and improves research education of PhD students within the field of water resources; formal collaboration between 9 instns in Denmark with expertise within water resources; Dir Prof. Dr KARSTEN H. JENSEN; Scientific Sec. FREDERIK ULDALL.

Statens Serum Institut (State Serum Institute): Artillerivej 5, 2300 Copenhagen S; tel. 32-68-32-68; e-mail serum@ssi.dk; internet www.ssi.dk; f. 1902; responsible for research-based health surveillance, rational use of IT in the Danish health care system and prevention and control of infectious diseases, biological threats and congenital disorders; library of 19,000 vols; Pres. and CEO NILS STRANDBERG PEDERSEN; Dir of Research ERIK JUHL.

Zoologisk Have (Copenhagen Zoo): Roskildevej 38, POB 7, 2000 Frederiksberg; tel. 72-20-02-00; e-mail mst@zoo.dk; internet www.zoo.dk; f. 1859; 3,300 animals of 264 species; participation in nature conservation projects, behaviour, genetics, and veterinary issues worldwide; Man. Dir LARS LUNDING ANDERSEN.

Physical Sciences

Center for Sun-Climate Research: Elektrovej, Bldg 327, 2800 Lyngby Copenhagen OE; tel. 45-25-95-00; e-mail office@space.dtu.dk; internet www.space.dtu.dk/english/research/research_divisions/sun_climate.aspx; f. 2004; attached to Nat. Space Institute, Technical Univ. of Denmark; investigates link between Earth's climate and solar activity through effects of cosmic rays on Earth's cloud cover; Dir HENRIK SVENSMARK; Sec. SUSSANE KNAPPE.

Danmarks Meteorologiske Institut (Danish Meteorological Institute): Lyngbyvej 100, 2100 Copenhagen Ø; tel. 39-15-75-00; e-mail epost@dmi.dk; internet www.dmi.dk; f. 1872; attached to Min. of Climate, Energy and Buildings; meteorology and geophysics; meteorological service for Denmark, Faroe Islands and Greenland; library of 40,000 vols; Dir-Gen. Dr LARS PRAHM; publs *Danmarks Klima* (1 a year), *Magnetic Results* (Godhavn and Thule, Greenland).

De Nationale Geologiske Undersøgelser for Danmark og Grønland (Geological Survey of Denmark and Greenland): Ø. Voldgade 10, 1350 Copenhagen K; tel. 38-14-20-00; e-mail geus@geus.dk; internet www.geus.dk; f. 1995; geological research, mapping, monitoring, data storage and advisory services in connection with the use and protection of geological natural resources within Denmark, Greenland and the Faroe Islands; library of 14,800 vols, incl. scientific journals, books, geological maps; Man. Dir JOHNNY FREDERICIA; publs *Geological Survey of Denmark and Greenland Bulletin*, *Geological Survey of Denmark and Greenland Map Series*.

DHI: Agern Allé 5, 2970 Hørsholm; tel. 45-16-92-00; e-mail dhi@dhigroup.com; internet www.dhi.dk; f. 2001, present name and status 2005; promotes technological devt and competence building within areas of water, environment and health through research; 29 offices around the globe; CEO ASGER KEJ; Chief Financial Officer PETER RASMUSSEN; Man. Dir. KARSTEN HAVNØ.

Kort & Matrikelstyrelsen (National Survey and Cadastre): Rentemestervej 8, 2400 Copenhagen NV; tel. 70-12-02-11; e-mail info@mim.dk; internet www.kms.dk; f. 1989 by merger of fmr Geodetic Institute, Danish Cadastral Dept and Hydrographic Div.; attached to Min. of Environment; responsible for geodetic survey of Denmark, Faroe Islands and Greenland; topographic survey and mapping of those areas, also nautical charting and issue of nautical publs; cadastral survey, registration, and mapping of Denmark; seismographic service in Denmark, Faroe Islands and Greenland; research and devt within geodesy and seismology; devt of digital maps and charts; Dir JESPER JARMBÆK.

Niels Bohr Institutet: Astronomisk Observatorium, Københavns Universitet, Juliane Maries Vej 30, 2100 Copenhagen Ø; tel. 35-32-59-60; e-mail rimestad@astro.ku.dk; internet www.nbi.dk; f. 1993 by merger of Astronomical Observatory, Ørsted Laboratory, Geophysical Institute and Niels Bohr Institute; astronomy, physics and geophysics; library of 12,000 vols, 100 periodicals; Head of Dept Prof. ROBERT FEIDENHANS'L; Sec. NINA SANDER BECH.

RELIGION, SOCIOLOGY AND ANTHROPOLOGY

Instytut Polsko-Skandynawski/Polsk-Skandinavisk Forskningsinstitut (Polish–Scandinavian Research Institute): POB 2584, 2100 Copenhagen Ø; tel. 39-29-98-26; f. 1985; ind. research institute for Polish–Scandinavian studies; provides support for research in the field of history and biographical science; organizes lectures; 25 mems; library of 1,000 vols; 20 m of archives; Pres. Prof. Dr Hab. E. S. KRUSZEWSKI; Dir Prof. Dr Hab. BOLESLAW HAJDUK; Dir Prof. Dr SVEN EKDAHL.

SFI—Det Nationale Forskningscenter for Velfærd (Danish National Centre for Social Research): Herluf Trolles Gade 11, 1052 Copenhagen K; tel. 33-48-08-00; e-mail sfi@sfi.dk; internet www.sfi.dk; f. 1958; ind. nat. research centre operating under Min. of Social Welfare; carries out commissioned projects in the area of welfare state policies, and disseminates the results; library of 32,500 vols; Man. Dir AGI CSONKA; Chair. Prof. PETER NANNESTAD; publ. *Social Forskning* (4 a year).

TECHNOLOGY

Biotech Research & Innovation Centre: Univ. of Copenhagen, Copenhagen Biocenter, 4th Fl., Ole Maaløes Vej 5, 2200 Copenhagen N; tel. 35-32-56-66; e-mail bric@bric.dk; internet www.bric.ku.dk; f. 2003; attached to Univ. of Copenhagen; establishes strong research education programme; ensures that research results are used for the devt of commercial products; promotes exchange of ideas within the Danish biotech research community; Chair. PETER KRISTENSEN; Dir Prof. KRISTIAN HELIN.

Danish e-Infrastructure Cooperation (DeIC): DeIC Secretariat, DTU, Anker Engelunds Vej 1, Bldg 101A, 2800 Lyngby; tel. 45-25-72-64; e-mail sekretariat@deic.dk; internet www.deic.dk; f. 2012 by merger of Forskningsnettet (Danish Research Network) with Danish Centre for Scientific Computing (DCSC); attached to Min. of Research, Innovation and Higher Education; supports Denmark as an e-Science nation; delivery of e-infrastructure (computing, data storage and network) for research and research-based teaching; Chair. BØRGE OBEL.

Risø Nationallaboratoriet for Bæredygtig Energi (Risø National Laboratory for Sustainable Energy): Frederiksborgvej 399, POB 49, 4000 Roskilde; tel. 46-77-46-77; e-mail risoe@risoe.dk; internet www.risoe.dtu.dk; f. 1958; attached to Danmarks Tekniske Universitet; research and devt in fields of industrial materials, new functional materials, energy systems analysis, renewable energy, and nuclear safety; Dir and Provost HENRIK C. WEGENER (acting); publ. *Risø Report*.

Libraries and Archives

Ålborg

Aalborg Bibliotekerne (Central Library for the County of North Jutland): Rendsburggade 2, 9000 Ålborg; tel. 99-31-43-00; e-mail bibliotek@aalborg.dk; internet www.aalborgbibliotekerne.dk; f. 1895; 15 brs and 3 mobile libraries; 730,000 vols, 1,300 current periodicals; Chief Librarian BODIL HAVE.

Aalborg Universitetsbibliotek (Aalborg University Library): Langagervej 2, POB 8200, 9220 Ålborg Oest; tel. 99-40-94-00; e-mail aub@aub.aau.dk; internet www.aub.aau.dk; f. 1973; open to the public; 710,000 vols (incl. 27,000 ejournals and 160,000 ebooks); Library Dir NIELS-HENRIK GYLSTORFF.

Allerød

Allerød Biblioteker (Allerød Libraries): Skovensvej 4, 3450 Allerød; tel. 48-10-40-10; e-mail info@bibliotek.alleroed.dk; internet www.bibliotek.alleroed.dk/forside; 3,667 vols, colln of CDs, DVDs, films; Librarian ANETTE AALUND.

Århus

Århus Kommunes Biblioteker (Århus Public Libraries): Møllegade 1, 8000 Århus C; tel. 89-40-92-00; e-mail hovedbibliotek@aarhus.dk; internet www.aakb.dk; f. 1934; 18 brs; 1,124,228 vols (incl. audiovisual materials); Chief Librarian KNUD SCHULZ.

Erhvervsarkivet Statens Erhvervshistoriske Arkiv (Danish National Business Archives): Vester Allé 12, 8000 Århus C; tel.

86-12-85-33; e-mail mailbox@ea.sa.dk; internet www.sa.dk/content/us/about_us/danish_business_archives; f. 1948; keeps registers, documents, etc. from companies and orgs in the business sector; also a research institute for economic and social history; material dates back to around 1500; 100,000 vols, 50 km of shelves; Chief Archivist Hon. Dr MICHAEL H. GELTING; publ. *Erhvervshistorisk Årbog* (Business History Yearbook).

Handelshøjskolens Bibliotek (Århus School of Business Library, Business and Social Sciences): Århus Univ., Fuglesangsallé 4, 8210 Århus V; tel. 87-16-40-63; e-mail bibliotek@asb.dk; internet www.lib.asb.dk; f. 1939; attached to Aarhus Univ.; spec. colln: European documentation centre for EU; 177,000 vols, 75,000 ebook titles, 44,000 ejournal titles; Library Dir TOVE BANG.

Statsbiblioteket (State and University Library): Victor Albecks Vej 1, 8000 Århus C; tel. 89-46-20-22; e-mail sb@statsbiblioteket.dk; internet www.statsbiblioteket.dk; f. 1902; attached to Min of Culture; legal deposit library, nat. newspaper colln, nat. media archive, loan centre for public libraries; part of one of the 26 Arhus Univ. Libraries; br. in Copenhagen; 4,850,022 vols; Dir SVEND LARSEN.

Copenhagen

Administrative Bibliotek (Administrative Library): Slotsholmsgade 12, 1216 Copenhagen K; tel. 72-26-98-91; e-mail dab@dab.dk; internet www.dab.dk; f. 1924 as the Library for the Mins of Labour and Social Affairs, present status 1995; attached to Min. of Science, Technology and Innovation; central library and documentation centre for civil servants in central govt; 160,000 vols, spec. colln: Danish governmental publs; Library Dir NIELS HASSELGAARD JENSENIUS.

AU Library, Campus Emdrup (DPB) (National Library of Education): Tuborgvej 164, POB 840, 2400 Copenhagen NV; tel. 87-15-90-96; e-mail dpb@dpu.dk; internet www.dpb.dpu.dk; f. 1887; attached to Dept of Education, Aarhus Univ.; colln incl. material in the field of education, educational systems, educational psychology, psychology of children and adolescents, children's literature; 800,000 vols, 3,057 current periodicals, 600,000 microfiches; Head Librarian JENS BENNEDSEN.

CBS Bibliotek (CBS Library): Solbjerg Plads 3, 2000 Frederiksberg; tel. 38-15-38-15; e-mail library@cbs.dk; internet www.cbs.dk/library; f. 1922; attached to Copenhagen Business School; 224,983 vols; Dir RENÉ STEFFENSEN.

Danmarks Kunstbibliotek (Danish National Art Library): Nyhavn 2, POB 1053, 1007 Copenhagen K; tel. 33-74-48-02; e-mail dkb@kunstbib.dk; internet www.kunstbib.dk; f. 1754; spec. library for the schools of Danish Acad. of Arts, univ. institutes of art history as well as architecture museum; archive and study colln for practising architects, public authorities, and Danish and foreign architecture scholars; 280,000 vols on history of art and architecture, 300,000 architectural drawings, 100,000 photographs, 90,000 slides; Dir Dr PATRICK KRAGELUND.

Danmarks Statistiks Informationsservice og Bibliotek (Statistics Denmark's Information Service and Library): Sejrøgade 11, 2100 Copenhagen Ø; tel. 39-17-30-30; e-mail bib@dst.dk; internet www.dst.dk/da/informationsservice; f. 1850; attached to Danmarks Statistik (see under Research Institutes: Economics, Law and Politics); prin. library for descriptive statistics; 235,000 vols; Head of Communication CARSTEN ZANGENBERG.

Designmuseum Danmark Bibliotek (Designmuseum Danmark Library): Bredgade 68, 1260 Copenhagen K; tel. 33-18-56-50; e-mail bib@designmuseum.dk; internet designmuseum.dk/bibliotek; f. 1890, fmrly Danish Museum of Art & Design; attached to Designmuseum Danmark; reference and research library for design; subject areas incl. applied arts and industrial design: furniture, fashion and costume, glass, ceramics, textiles, metalwork and jewellery, book production, graphic design and posters, and traditional art of Asia; 180,000 vols, 3,000 magazines, 30,000 posters, 50,000 graphics, prints and sketches; Head of Library and Research LARS DYBDAHL.

Det Biovidenskabelige Fakultetsbibliotek (Faculty of Life Sciences Library): Dyrlægevej 10, 1870 Frederiksberg C; tel. 35-33-21-45; e-mail bvfb@life.ku.dk; internet www.bvfb.life.ku.dk; f. 1783, present name and status 2008; attached to Faculty of Life Sciences, Univ. of Copenhagen; 586,000 vols; Chief Librarian FREDE MØRCH.

Det Farmaceutiske Bibliotek, Københavns Universitet (Pharmaceutical Sciences Library, University of Copenhagen): Universitetsparken 4, Second Fl., 2100 Copenhagen Ø; tel. 35-33-63-19; e-mail library@farma.ku.dk; internet www.farma.ku.dk; f. 1892; supports research and teaching at the Institutes of Pharmaceutical Sciences, Faculty of Health and Medical Sciences, Univ. of Copenhagen; 55,000 vols; Faculty Librarian ALICE NØRHEDE.

Forsvarets Bibliotek (Danish Defence Library): Kastellet 46, 2100 Copenhagen Ø; tel. 33-47-95-25; e-mail kgb@mil.dk; internet forsvaret.dk/fak/bibliotek; f. 2010 by merger of Danish Naval Library, Royal Danish Air Force Library and Royal Danish Military Library; attached to Royal Danish Defence College, Danish Defence Acad.; central defence research library; organized under the Defence Academy of Sciences of the Military History and Knowledge Dissemination; 40,000 vols; Librarian ANITA MOUNTAIN ELLEBY.

Frederiksberg Kommunes Bibliotek (Frederiksberg Public Library): Falkoner Plads 3, 2000 Frederiksberg; tel. 38-21-18-00; e-mail biblioteket@frederiksberg.dk; internet www.fkb.dk; f. 1887; 3 brs; also a music library and a spec. genealogy section; 2.5m. vols; 1,000 periodicals; Chief Librarian ANNE MOLLER-RASMUSSEN.

Iva Biblioteket, Det Informationsvidenskabelige Akademi (Library of the Royal School of Library and Information Science): Birketinget 6, 2300 Copenhagen S; tel. 32-58-60-66; e-mail biblioteket@iva.ku.dk; internet iva.ku.dk/bibliotek; f. 1956; attached to Univ. of Copenhagen; specializes in library and information science material; mem. of NORFRI cooperation; 18,000 vols, 73,000 ebooks; Librarian LISBETH RASMUSSEN.

Københavns Biblioteker (Copenhagen Libraries): Biblioteksfaglig Afdeling, Krystalgade 15, 1172 Copenhagen K; tel. 33-73-60-60; e-mail hovadm@kff.kk.dk; internet bibliotek.kk.dk; f. 1885; 1 main library, 19 brs and 2 specialized libraries; 1,702,739 vols; Library Dir JENS STEEN ANDERSEN.

Københavns Stadsarkiv (Copenhagen City Archives): Rådhuset, 1599 Copenhagen V; tel. 33-66-23-70; e-mail stadsarkiv@kff.kk.dk; internet www.kbharkiv.dk; f. before 1563, current name adopted 1936; 40,000 linear m of records, 150,000 maps, 200,000 cards and drawings; Head KRISTIAN BAK; publ. *København. Kultur og Historie* (1 a year).

Kongelige Bibliotek (Royal Library): POB 2149, 1016 Copenhagen K; tel. 33-47-47-47; e-mail kb@kb.dk; internet www.kb.dk; f. 1482 as univ. library, as the King's Library 1648, merged 1989; acts as the Danish Nat. Library and univ. library for the Univ. of Copenhagen; prin. research and univ. library for theology, humanities, law and social sciences, natural and health sciences; nat. archive for MSS and archives of prominent Danes; incl. Danish Museum of Books and Printing, Nat. Museum of Photography, Museum of Danish Cartoon Art; 6.2m. vols, 173,000 MSS, 290,000 sheet music, 1.83m. photos, 325,000 maps, 7.5m. ephemera, digitized online books and serials photo; Dir-Gen. ERLAND KOLDING NIELSEN; publs *Diamantbladet* (4 a year), *Fund og Forskning i Det Kongelige Biblioteks Samlinger* (1 a year), *Magasin fra Det Kongelige Bibliotek* (4 a year).

Library of Architecture, Design, Conservation and Performing Arts: Danneskiold-Samsøes Allé 50, 1434 Copenhagen K; tel. 32-68-68-00; e-mail bibliotek@kadk.dk; internet www.kasb.dk; f. 1929 as Bygningsteknisk Studiearkiv, current name adopted 2011; attached to Royal Danish Acad. of Fine Arts, Schools of Architecture, Design and Conservation; 21,750 vols, 15,000 blueprints; Chief Librarian DITTE JESSING.

Patent- og Varemærkestyrelsens bibliotek (Library of the Danish Patent and Trademark Office): Helgeshoj Allé 81, 2630 Taastrup; tel. 43-50-80-00; e-mail bibliotek@dkpto.dk; internet www.dkpto.dk/soeg-i-online-registre/bibliotek.aspx; f. 1894; 35m. patent specifications; 28,860 vols; Head of Library JON FINSEN; Head of Library LIZZI VESTER; publs *Dansk Brugsmodeltidende* (Danish Utility Models Gazette, 26 a year), *Dansk Mønstertidende* (Danish Design Gazette, 26 a year), *Dansk Patenttidende* (Danish Patent Gazette, 52 a year), *Dansk Varemarketidende* (Danish Trademark Gazette, 52 a year).

Statens Arkiver (Danish State Archives): Rigsarkivet, Rigsdagsgården 9, 1218 Copenhagen K; tel. 33-92-33-10; e-mail mailbox@ra.sa.dk; internet www.sa.dk; f. 1582; comprises 4 individual archives: Danish Nat. Archives, Danish Business Archives, Danish Data Archives and The Filming Centre; Dir ASBJØRN HELLUM; publs *Arkiv*, *Siden Saxo*.

Esbjerg

Esbjerg Kommunes Biblioteker (Esbjerg Public Library): Nørregade 19, 6700 Esbjerg; tel. 76-16-20-00; e-mail biblio@esbjergkommune.dk; internet www.esbjergbibliotek.dk; f. 1897; offers materials in all major languages incl. languages spoken by the local immigrant communities; 9 brs, incl. 2 mobile libraries; 600,000 vols; Chief Librarian ANNETTE BRØCHNER LINDGAARD.

Greve

Greve Bibliotek (Greve Library): Portalen 2, 2670 Greve; tel. 43-95-80-00; e-mail greve@grevebib.dk; internet www.grevebibliotek.dk; 3 brs; 162,750 vols, CDs and magazines; Librarian MARIANNE OLSEN.

Hellerup

Gentofte Bibliotekerne (Public Library): Ahlmanns Allé 6, 2900 Hellerup; tel. 39-98-58-00; e-mail bibliotek@gentofte.dk; internet www.genbib.dk; f. 1918; 5 brs; 546,808 vols; Chief Librarian PIA HANSEN.

Lyngby

Danmarks Tekniske Informationscenter (Technical Information Centre of Denmark):

POB 777, Bldg 101D, Anker Engelunds Vej 1, 2800 Kgs. Lyngby; tel. 45-25-72-00; e-mail dtub@dtic.dtu.dk; internet www.dtic.dtu.dk; f. 1942; attached to Technical Univ. of Denmark; 700,000 vols, 4,000 current periodicals, 11,000 ejournals; Dir MOGENS SANDFÆR.

Odense

Landsarkivet for Fyn (Provincial Archives of Funen): Jernbanegade 36A, 5000 Odense C; tel. 66-12-58-85; e-mail mailbox@lao.sa.dk; internet www.sa.dk/content/us/about_us/provincial_archives/provincial_archives_of_-funen; f. 1893; incl. records of local admin. of Funen and neighbouring islands, and colln of private papers; The Karen Brahe Library, the only nearly complete private Danish library dating from the 17th century; 3,400 vols, 1,153 MSS, approx. 20 km of records; Dir STEEN OUSAGER.

Odense Centralbibliotek (Odense Central Library): Østre Stationsvej 15, 5000 Odense C; tel. 66-13-13-72; e-mail adm-bib@odense.dk; internet www.odensebib.dk; f. 1924; 865,000 vols, 145,000 CDs, audiobooks, video cassettes and DVDs; Library Dir KENT SKOV ANDREASEN; Chief Librarian JYTTE CHRISTENSEN; Chief Librarian PETER THOMSEN.

Syddansk Universitetsbibliotek (University Library of Southern Denmark): Campusvej 55, 5230 Odense M; tel. 65-50-26-11; e-mail sdub@bib.sdu.dk; internet www.sdu.dk/bibliotek; f. 1999 by merger between the research libraries of Odense Univ., Southern Denmark School of Business, Southern Denmark School of Engineering and South Jutland Univ. Centre; economics, engineering, history, languages, literature, medicine, music, natural sciences, philosophy, religion, social sciences; 1,600,000 vols, 2,300 periodicals, 86,400 ejournals; Chief Librarian AASE LINDAHL.

Roskilde

Roskilde Universitetsbibliotek (Roskilde University Library): Universitetsvej 1, POB 258, 4000 Roskilde; tel. 46-74-22-07; e-mail rub@ruc.dk; internet www.rub.ruc.dk; f. 1971, current location 2001; open to gen. public; humanities, social sciences and natural sciences; 853,628 vols, incl. 637,145 books and 216,483 audiovisual items; Dir CLAUS VESTERAGER PEDERSEN.

Silkeborg

Silkeborg Bibliotek (Silkeborg Library): Hostrupsgade 41A, 8600 Silkeborg; tel. 87-22-19-00; e-mail silkeborgbibliotek@silkeborgbib.dk; internet silkeborgbib.dk; f. 1900; 216,000 vols, plus 128,000 in the Children's Dept, 50,000 records and cassettes; Library Dir LARS BORNÆS.

Vejle

Vejle Bibliotekerne (Vejle Public Libraries): Willy Sørensens Plads 1, 7100 Vejle; tel. 76-81-32-00; e-mail vejlebib@vejlebib.dk; internet www.vejlebib.dk; f. 1895; consists of a main library located in Vejle; 4 brs and 1 mobile library; 487,388 vols (incl. audiobooks, CDs and DVDs), 3,922 periodicals; Chief Librarian LONE KNAKKERGAARD.

Viborg

Landsarkivet for Nørrejylland (Provincial Archives of Northern Jutland): Ll. Sct. Hans Gade 5, 8800 Viborg; tel. 86-62-17-88; e-mail mailbox@lav.sa.dk; internet www.sa.dk/content/us/about_us/provincial_archives/provincial_archives_of_northern_jutland; f. 1891 as an archival repository; comprises material from state and local authorities and instns, from private individuals, asscns and orgs, and from the landed estates located in Northern Jutland (1389 until the present day); houses the State Archives Filming Centre; 70 km of shelving; Dir J. THOMASSEN.

Museums and Art Galleries

Ålborg

Kunsten Museum of Modern Art Aalborg: Kong Christians Allé 50, 9000 Aalborg; tel. 99-82-41-00; e-mail kunsten@aalborg.dk; internet www.kunsten.dk; f. 1877, bldg inaugurated 1972; exhibits modern and contemporary art; permanent colln of 1,500 paintings, sculptures and mixed media works dating from 1900 to present day; Fine Art Dept: Danish art since 1900 (painting, sculpture, graphics, sculpture park); Anna and Kresten Krestensen Colln: Danish and int. art 1920–1950; Kirsten and Axel P. Nielsen Colln (art of 1960s and 1970s); Erik Veistrup Colln (art 1906–2006); reference library; library of 13,000 vols; Chair. ANDERS HJULMAND; Dir GITTE ØRSKOU.

Nordjyllands Historiske Museum (North Jutland Museum of History): Algade 48, 9000 Aalborg; tel. 99-31-74-00; e-mail historisk_museum@aalborg.dk; internet www.nordmus.dk; f. 1863; archaeology, ethnology, glass, history, silver, tobacco industry; Dir LARS CHRISTIAN NØRBACH; publ. *Årbog* (1 a year).

Århus

ARoS Århus Kunstmuseum (Århus Art Museum): Aros Allé 2, 8000 Århus C; tel. 87-30-66-00; e-mail info@aros.dk; internet www.aros.dk; f. 1859; Danish art since the 18th century and modern int. art; library of 21,000 vols; Chair. CARSTEN FODE; Dir JENS ERIK SØRENSEN.

Naturhistorisk Museum (Natural History Museum): Universitetsparken, Wilhelm Meyers Allé 210, 8000 Århus C; tel. 86-12-97-77; e-mail nm@nathist.dk; internet www.naturhistoriskmuseum.dk; f. 1921; attached to Min. of Cultural Affairs; Denmark exhibition: natural history of Danish landscapes; Danish Animals exhibition; Animals of the World exhibition; African Savannah exhibition; permanent field laboratory: 'Molslaboratoriet', Femmöller, 8400 Ebeltoft; the museum laboratories are open to scientists, and specialize in terrestrial ecology, limnology, entomology, acarology, mammalogy, ornithology and bio-acoustics; library of 15,000 vols; Dir THOMAS SECHER JENSEN; publs *Natura Jutlandica* (in English), *Natur og Museum* (in Danish).

Auning

Dansk Landbrugsmuseum (Danish Agricultural Museum): Gl. Estrup, Randersvej 4, 8963 Auning; tel. 86-48-34-44; e-mail dansklandbrugsmuseum@gl-estrup.dk; internet www.gl-estrup.dk; f. 1889; exhibitions on the history of country life, agricultural technology and beekeeping; apprx. 70,000 items; colln of pictures and brochures, incl. about 10,000 photos and 10,000 brochures; Chair. KNUD ERIK JENSEN; Dir PETER BAVNSHØJ.

Charlottenlund

Ordrupgaard: Vilvordevej 110, 2920 Charlottenlund; tel. 39-64-11-83; e-mail ordrupgaard@ordrupgaard.dk; internet www.ordrupgaard.dk; f. 1918; French and Danish 19th- and early 20th-century paintings, incl. works by Degas, Delacroix, Gauguin, Hammershøi, Manet, Pissarro and Renoir; Danish arts and crafts of the 19th century; Dir ANNE-BIRGITTE FONSMARK.

Copenhagen

Botanisk Have (Botanical Garden): c/o Natural History Museum of Denmark, Univ. of Copenhagen, Øster Farimagsgade 2B, 1353 Copenhagen K; tel. 35-32-22-22; e-mail snm@snm.ku.dk; internet botanik.snm.ku.dk; f. 1874; attached to Natural History Museum of Denmark, Univ. of Copenhagen; 25 acres of landscape gdn, palm-house and greenhouses; rare trees, plants (12,000 species); colln of living plants and seed and gene bank for plants, dried plants, algae, fungi; library of 50,000 vols, 100,000 issues of periodicals; Head FLEMMING LARSEN.

Danske Filminstitut—Museum og Cinematek (Danish Film Institute—Archive and Cinematheque): Gothersgade 55, 1123 Copenhagen K; tel. 33-74-34-00; e-mail dfi@dfi.dk; internet www.dfi.dk; f. 1997 by merger of 3 instns: Danish Film Institute, Nat. Film Board, Danish Film Museum; attached to Min. of Culture; collns of films, books, posters, documentation; cinemas with daily screenings; nat. agency for film and cinema culture; supports devt, production and distribution of films; runs the nat. archives; library of 70,000 vols, 13,500 scripts, 250 periodicals; Man. Dir and CEO HENRIK BO NIELSEN; publs *FILM* (3 a year), *Kosmorama* (2 a year).

Davids Samling (David Collection): Kronprinsessegade 30, 1306 Copenhagen DK; tel. 33-73-49-49; e-mail museum@davidmus.dk; internet www.davidmus.dk; f. 1945; attached to C. L. David Foundation and Colln; colln of Islamic art, European 18th-century art, Danish early modern art; Dir Dr KJELD VON FOLSACH; Curator Dr PETER WANDEL; publ. *The Journal of the David Collection*.

Designmuseum Danmark (Design Museum Denmark): Bredgade 68, 1260 Copenhagen K; tel. 33-18-56-56; e-mail info@designmuseum.dk; internet www.designmuseum.dk; f. 1890, fmrly The Danish Museum of Art & Design; European applied art from the Middle Ages to modern times, Chinese and Japanese art; library: see under Libraries and Archives; Dir ANNE-LOUISE SOMMER; Sec. HENRIETTE FALKENBERG.

Geologisk Museum (Geological Museum): c/o Natural History Museum of Denmark, Univ. of Copenhagen, Øster Voldgade 5–7, 1350 Copenhagen K; tel. 35-32-23-45; e-mail rcp@snm.ku.dk; internet geologi.snm.ku.dk; f. 1772 as Universitetets Nye Naturaltheater; attached to Natural History Museum of Denmark, Univ. of Copenhagen; centre for Danish geology; minerals, rocks, meteorites and fossils; geology of Denmark and Greenland; origin of man; plate tectonics; volcanoes; salt in the subsoil; part of Natural History Museum of Denmark; Chair. Prof. MINIK THORLEIF ROSING.

Hirschsprung: Stockholmsgade 20, 2100 Copenhagen O; tel. 35-42-03-36; e-mail dhs@hirschsprung.dk; internet www.hirschsprung.dk; f. 1911; showcases Heinrich Hirschsprung's colln of paintings, drawings and sculptures by Danish artists, incl. Skagen painters, Symbolists and Fynboerne; impressionist art colln providing overview of Danish 19th-century art; Dir MARIANNE SAABYE; Curator JAN GORM MADSEN; Curator ANNA SCHRAM VEJLBY.

Københavns Museum (Museum of Copenhagen): Absalonsgade 3, 1658 Copenhagen V; Vesterbrogade 59, 1620 Copenhagen V; tel. 33-21-07-72; e-mail sekr@kff.kk.dk; internet www.copenhagen.dk; f. 1901; history of Copenhagen, incl. pictures, architecture, models; colln of Kierkegaard relics; Dir JETTE SANDAHL; Chair. PIA ALLERSLEV.

Nationalmuseet (National Museum): Prinsens Palæ, Frederiksholms Kanal 12, 1220 Copenhagen K; tel. 33-13-44-11; e-mail nationalmuseet@natmus.dk; internet www.natmus.dk; f. 1807 on basis of the older Royal Collns; consists of 3 divs; colln of archaeological discoveries, royal portraits, coins and medals, Egyptian mummies, Greek vases, Etruscan and Roman glass jewellery; library of 200,000 vols; Dir PER KRISTIAN MADSEN; publ. *Nationalmuseets Arbejdsmark* (1 a year).

Attached Museums:

Frihedsmuseet (Museum of Danish Resistance): Churchillparken 7, 1263 Copenhagen K; tel. 41-20-62-91; e-mail frihedsmuseet@natmus.dk; internet natmus.dk/en/besoeg-museerne/frihedsmuseet; f. 1957; chronological devt of Danish resistance during the Nazi occupation 1940–45, colln of documents related to resistance groups; photo archive with colln of 60,000 pictures; Chief Curator ESBEN KJELDBÆK.

Frilandsmuseet (Open-Air Museum): Kongevejen 100, 2800 Lyngby; tel. 33-13-44-11; e-mail fogf@natmus.dk; internet natmus.dk/en/besoeg-museerne/frilandsmuseet; f. 1897; examples of more than 50 farms, mills and houses from 1650 to 1950, representing virtually every region in Denmark and the Faroe Islands as well as the fmr Danish provinces of southern Sweden and northern Germany; displays of rural crafts; incorporates Brede Works factory community with workmen's and foremen's houses, eating house, orphanage and nursery gdn; archives of drawings, photographs, measurements and historical records concerning the bldgs; Curator and Head PETER HENNINGSEN.

Frøslevlejrens Museum: Lejrvej 83, 6330 Padborg; tel. 74-67-65-57; e-mail froeslevlejrensmuseum@natmus.dk; internet natmus.dk/en/besoeg-museerne/froeslevlejren; f. 1969; internment camp built during the German occupation of Denmark in 1944; documents, photographs and other exhibitions.

Musikmuseet—Musikhistorisk Museum og Carl Claudius' Samling (Music Museum—Musical History Museum and Carl Claudius Collection): Åbenrå 32, 1124 Copenhagen K; tel. 41-20-63-13; e-mail musik@natmus.dk; internet natmus.dk/en/visit-the-museums/the-danish-music-museum; f. 1898; exhibition closed until 2013, library and archive remain open and available to the public; extensive colln of musical instruments from all over the world with spec. emphasis on European instruments from the Renaissance onwards; concerts, library, archives; library of 51,000 vols; Curator Dr LISBET TORP; publ. *Meddelelser* (1 a year).

Ny Carlsberg Glyptotek: Dantes Plads 7, 1556 Copenhagen V; tel. 33-41-81-41; e-mail info@glyptoteket.dk; internet www.glyptoteket.dk; f. 1888; Danish and French sculpture and painting since 19th century; Egyptian, Greek, Roman and Etruscan art, mainly sculpture; 10,000 works of art; library of 50,000 vols; Deputy Dir LOUISE RUE MOOS; Dir FLEMMING FRIBORG; publ. *Meddelelser fra Ny Carlsberg Glyptotek (ny serie)* (1 a year).

Rosenborg Slot (Rosenborg Castle): Øster Voldgade 4A, 1350 Copenhagen K; tel. 33-15-32-86; e-mail museum@dkks.dk; internet dkks.dk; f. 1833; contains 'The Chronological Collns of the Danish Kings', the colln was founded by Frederik III in about 1660, and depicts the history of Danish kings from Frederik II in the mid-16th century to Frederik VII in the 19th century; consists of arms, apparel, jewellery, and furniture from 1470 to 1863; also houses the Royal Regalia and the Crown Jewels; Museum Dir JØRGEN SELMER; Senior Curator JØRGEN HEIN.

Attached Museum:

Amalienborgmuseet (Amalienborg Museum): Christian VIII's Palace, 1257 Copenhagen K; tel. 33-12-21-86; e-mail amalienborgmuseet@dkks.dk; internet www.dkks.dk/amalienborgmuseet; f. 1994; exhibitions cover the reigns of Danish kings, from 1863 to 1972 (Christian IX, Frederik VIII, Christian X and Frederik IX); Dir NIELS-KNUD LIEBGOTT; Curator BIRGIT JENVOLD; Sec. JACOB MADSEN.

Statens Forsvarshistoriske Museum (Civil Defence Historical Museum): Frederiksholms Kanal 29, 1220 Copenhagen K; tel. 33-11-60-37; e-mail sfhm@sfhm.dk; internet www.sfhm.dk; f. 2004 by merger between Royal Arsenal Museum and Royal Naval Museum; attached to Min. of Culture; collns of weapons, vehicles, uniforms and other military and civilian equipment from the period after c. 1200; naval colln of 300 years of maritime technology; historic weapons colln merged with a number of other subject collns related to special army history; Dir OLE LOUIS FRANTZEN.

Statens Museum for Kunst (National Gallery of Denmark): Sølvgade 48–50, 1307 Copenhagen K; tel. 33-74-84-94; e-mail smk@smk.dk; internet www.smk.dk; 700 years of art from early Renaissance to contemporary works; collns incl. European art from 1300-1800; Danish and Nordic art from 1750-1900; French art from 1900–1930 and Danish and int. art after 1900; 10,000 paintings and sculptures; Royal Colln of Graphic Art incl. 240,000 Danish and foreign prints and drawings; Royal Cast Colln contains 2,600 plaster casts; spec. exhibitions and workshops; library of 130,000 vols; Dir KARSTEN OHRT; Exec. Sec. BIRGITTE KANN MØLLER; publ. *SMK Art Journal* (1 a year).

Teatermuseet (Theatre Museum): Christiansborg, Ridebane 18, 1218 Copenhagen K; tel. 33-11-51-76; e-mail info@teatermuseet.dk; internet www.teatermuseet.dk; f. 1912; situated in the old Court theatre; illustrates the devt of the Danish theatre since 18th century; colln of drawings, engravings, paintings, photographs, costumes, set models describing the history of Danish-language theatre from 1700 to present day; Dir PETER CHRISTENSEN TEILMANN; Curator MIKAEL KRISTIAN HANSEN; Curator IDA POULSEN.

Thorvaldsens Museum: Bertel Thorvaldsens Plads 2, 1213 Copenhagen K; tel. 33-32-15-32; e-mail thm@thorvaldsensmuseum.dk; internet www.thorvaldsensmuseum.dk; f. 1848; sculptures and drawings by the Danish sculptor Bertel Thorvaldsen (1770–1844), his collns of contemporary European paintings, drawings and prints and classical antiquities; his library, archives relating to Thorvaldsen's studies and the museum's history; letter archive; library of 8,000 vols; Dir STIG MISS.

Zoologisk Museum (Zoological Museum): c/o Natural History Museum of Denmark, Univ. of Copenhagen, Universitetsparken 15, 2100 Copenhagen Ø; tel. 35-32-11-01; e-mail zm@snm.ku.dk; internet zoologi.snm.ku.dk; f. 1862 by merger of Royal Museum of Natural History with Univ. Zoological Museum; attached to Natural History Museum of Denmark, Univ. of Copenhagen; collns of multicellular animals, which serve as objects for a wide range of int. research projects; research is organized in 3 scientific depts: Vertebrates and Quaternary Zoology; Invertebrates (excl. insects, myriapods and arachnids); and Entomology; public education programmes and school service; library of 15,000 vols, 750 periodicals, 160,000 reprints; Dir MORTEN MELDGAARD; publ. *Steenstrupia* (2 a year).

Dronningmølle

Rudolph Tegners Museum og Statuepark (Rudolph Tegners Museum and Statue Park): Museumsvej 19, 3120 Dronningmølle; tel. 49-71-91-77; e-mail museum@rudolphtegner.dk; internet www.rudolphtegner.dk; f. 1938; devoted to the works and collns of the sculptor Rudolph Tegner (1873–1950); 200 works in plaster, clay, bronze and marble; Dir LUISE GOMARD.

Ebeltoft

Glasmuseet Ebeltoft (Glass Museum Ebeltoft): Strandvejen 8, 8400 Ebeltoft; tel. 86-34-17-99; e-mail glasmuseet@glasmuseet.dk; internet www.glasmuseet.dk; f. 1985; exhibits contemporary, int. glass; organizes lectures, talks, concerts, guided tours, video presentations, workshops and children's activities; colln of the latest trends in contemporary glass art; hot glass studio; Exec. Dir DAGMAR BRENDSTRUP.

Elsinore

Danmarks Tekniske Museum (Danish Museum of Science and Technology): Fabriksvej 25, 3000 Elsinore; tel. 49-22-26-11; e-mail info@tekniskmuseum.dk; internet www.tekniskmuseum.dk; f. 1911, present location 2002; colln of steam engines, electric appliances (incl. Valdemar Poulsen's telegraphone, the forerunner of modern tape recording), bicycles, cars and aircraft; authentic pewter workshop; library of 18,000 vols; Chair. JØRGEN LINDEGAARD; Curator JENS BREINEGAARD.

Kronborg Castle: Kronborg 2C, 3000 Elsinore; tel. 49-21-30-78; e-mail kronborg@slke.dk; internet www.ses.dk/kronborg; f. 1425; fortified royal castle dating from the late 16th century; contains the Royal Apartments (furniture, tapestry, regalia), banqueting hall, chapel; known as 'Hamlet's castle'; Dir LARS HOLST.

M/S Museet for Søfart (Maritime Museum of Denmark): Ny Kronborgvej 1, 3000 Elsinore; tel. 49-21-06-85; e-mail info@mfs.dk; internet www.mfs.dk; f. 1915; Danish shipping since 1400, incl. the Sound Dues, the Napoleonic Wars, trade with China and the fmr Danish colonies in India, navigation and the Lifeboat Service; maritime objects, model ships, paintings, photographs and text boards; depiction of the Danish sailor's life since 16th century; regular temporary exhibitions; library of 30,000 vols; spec. collns of logbooks and photographs; Chair. ERIK ØSTERGAARD; Dir CAMILLA MORDHORST.

Faaborg

Faaborg Museum: Grønnegade 75, 5600 Faaborg; tel. 62-61-06-45; e-mail info@faaborgmuseum.dk; internet www.faaborgmuseum.dk; f. 1910; colln of paintings and sculptures by the circle of Funenite artists; Dir SUSANNE THESTRUP TRUELSEN.

Frederikssund

J. F. Willumsens Museum: Jenriksvej 4, 3600 Frederikssund; tel. 47-31-07-73; e-mail jfw@frederikssund.dk; internet www.jfwillumsensmuseum.dk; f. 1957; colln of J. F. Willumsen's works, his old colln and archive containing photographs, books, letters, diaries; J. F. Willumsen's paintings, drawings, pastels, graphics, ceramics, sculpture, photography and architecture; Dir ANNETTE JOHANSEN; Curator LISBETH LUND.

Hillerød

Nationalhistoriske Museum paa Frederiksborg Slot (Museum of National History at Frederiksborg Castle): Frederiksborg Slot, 3400 Hillerød; tel. 48-26-04-39; e-mail frbmus@frbmus.dk; internet www.dnm.dk; f. 1878; castle built in 1560s, extended 1600–20; contains chronological colln of portraits and paintings illustrating the history of Denmark, each era in a separate room, the furniture and appointments in keeping with the period of the paintings; 10,000 exhibits; picture archive; library of 15,000 vols; Pres. Chamberlain HENNING FODE; Dir METTE SKOUGAARD.

Højbjerg

Moesgård Museum (Moesgaard Museum): Moesgård Allé 20, 8270 Højbjerg; tel. 89-42-11-00; e-mail moesgaard@moesmus.dk; internet www.moesmus.dk; f. 1861, current name adopted 1997; collns of Danish prehistoric antiquities; exhibition of the Grauballe Man (a 2,000 year old bog body) and war sacrifices from Illerup Ådal; research org. in environmental, Danish and Oriental archaeology and ethnology; merged with Odder Museum and responsible for Viking Museum; museum closed till September 2014; Dir JAN SKAMBY MADSEN; Curator NIELS H. ANDERSEN.

Horsens

Horsens Kunstmuseum (Horsens Art Museum): Carolinelundsvej 2, 8700 Horsens; tel. 76-29-23-70; e-mail kunstmuseum@horsens.dk; internet www.horsenskunstmuseum.dk; f. 1906, present status 1984; colln of modern Danish art, paintings and sculptures; works of Bjørn Nørgaard, Kirsten Ortwed, Troels Wörsel, Michael Kvium, Erik A. Frandsen, Nina Steñ-Knudsen, Lars Nørgaard, Christian Lemmerz, Signe Guttormsen, Elmgren og Dragset, Cathrine Raben Davidsen, Anne Marie Ploug, J. G. Dokoupil, Olav Christoffer Jenssen, Ola Billgreen; Dir CLAUS HAGEDORN-OLSEN; Curator LONE SCHUBERT.

Hørsholm

Dansk Jagt- og Skovbrugsmuseet (Danish Museum of Hunting and Forestry): Folehavevej 15–17C, 2970 Hørsholm; tel. 45-86-05-72; e-mail museum@jagtskov.dk; internet www.jagtskov.dk; f. 1942; colln of hunters' and poachers' gear, traps, and home-made weapons that illustrate Danish forestry after the Enlightenment era; colln of specimens of deformities, abnormalities and diseases in animals, decoy colln; organizes workshops and tours; Pres. OLE ROED JACOBSEN; Dir JETTE BAAGØE; Curator HELLE SERUP.

Humlebæk

Louisiana Museum of Modern Art: Gl. Strandvej 13, 3050 Humlebæk; tel. 49-19-07-19; e-mail mail@louisiana.dk; internet www.louisiana.dk; f. 1958; more than 3,000 works; colln incl. artists such as Picasso, Giacometti, Dubuffet, Yves Klein, Andy Warhol, Rauschenberg, Henry Moore, Louise Bourgeois, Philip Guston, Morris Louis, Jorn, Baselitz, Polke, Kiefer and Per Kirkeby; Chair. LARS HENRIK MUNCH; Exec. Dir POUL ERIK TØJNER; Curator HELLE CRENZIEN; publs *Louisiana Magasin* (2 a year), *Louisiana Revy* (2 a year).

Ishoj

Arken Museum for Moderne Kunst (Arken Museum of Modern Art): Skovvej 100, 2635 Ishøj; tel. 43-54-02-22; e-mail reception@arken.dk; internet www.arken.dk; f. 1996; over 300 works of art; colln of Danish, Nordic and int. contemporary art, from 1990 onwards; interactive installations; photographic and graphic idioms; paintings and sculptures; Chair. OLE BJØRSTORP; Dir CHRISTIAN GETHER; Chief Curator STINE HØHOLT; publs *ARKEN Bulletin* (irregular), *KLUB ARKEN* (3 a year).

Kolding

Museet på Koldinghus (Museum of Koldinghus): Markdanersgade 11, POB 91, 6000 Kolding; tel. 76-33-81-00; e-mail museum@koldinghus.dk; internet www.koldinghus.dk; f. 1992; colln of Danish fine arts, Danish crafts and decorative art from c. 1550 to c. 1940; colln of silverware and jewellery from Renaissance to present day; Dir POUL DEDENROTH-SCHOU.

Trapholt: Æblehaven 23, 6000 Kolding; tel. 76-30-05-30; e-mail kunstmuseum@trapholt.dk; internet www.trapholt.dk; f. 1988; colln of Danish furniture design; modern Danish visual art and sculpture; Richard Mortensen exhibition; ceramics, textiles and product design (mainly sets); sculpture park, with works by Danish contemporary artists; Arne Jacobsen's Cube-flex summer cottage; temporary exhibitions of art, design and handicraft; Pres. OLE F. RASMUSSEN; Dir KAREN GRØN (acting).

Niva

Nivaagaards Malerisamling (Nivaagaard Picture Gallery): Gl. Strandvej 2, 2990 Nivå; tel. 49-14-10-17; e-mail info@nivaagaard.dk; internet www.nivaagaard.dk; f. 1908; colln of artworks from Italian and Northern European Renaissance, Dutch Baroque and the Danish Golden Age in the form of portrait, landscape painting and religious motif; Chair. EBBE SIMONSEN; Museum Dir and Board Sec. MICHAEL BJØRN NELLEMANN.

Odense

Kunsthallen Brandts: Brandts Torv 1, 5000 Odense C; tel. 65-20-70-00; e-mail info@brandts.dk; internet www.brandts.dk/en/kunsthallen-brandts-en/udstillinger-2; f. 1987, fmrly Kunsthallen Brandts Klædefabrik; exhibits contemporary Danish and int. art that incl. visual art, decorative art, performance, design, architecture and video art; Dir LARS GRAMBYE.

Mediemuseum (Media Museum): Brandts Torv 1, 5000 Odense C; tel. 65-20-70-52; e-mail info@mediemuseum.dk; internet www.brandts.dk/en/mediamuseum/udstillinger-4; f. 1984 as Danmarks Grafiske Museum; over 150,000 artefacts, records, photos, movies, graphs, films, printing machines, radios and television sets covering Danish media history; colln of newspapers and magazines; library of 10,000 vols; Dir ERVIN NIELSEN; Curator FLEMMING STEEN NIELSEN; Curator CHRISTIAN HVIID MORTENSEN; publ. *Petit Grafiana*.

Museet for Fotokunst (Museum of Photo Art): Brandts Torv 1, 5000 Odense C; tel. 65-20-70-00; e-mail info@brandts.dk; internet www.brandts.dk/en/museet-for-fotokunst-en/udstillinger-3; f. 1984, moved into renovated bldg and became an approved museum in 1987; colln of 9,000 photographic works focusing on photographic art from 1945; archive of artists and of works; individual spec. collns and reference library for int. photography of the past 50 years; Chair. JØRGEN BRANDT; Dir INGRID FISCHER JONGE; Curator CHARLOTTE PRÆSTEGAARD SCHWARTZ; Curator JENS FRIIS; publ. *KATALOG* (3 a year).

Odense Bys Museer (Odense City Museums): Overgade 48, 5000 Odense C; tel. 65-51-46-01; e-mail museum@odense.dk; internet museum.odense.dk; f. 1860; Dir Dr TORBEN GRØNGAARD JEPPESEN; Chief Curator DONALD MYRTUE; publs *Anderseniana* (1 a year), *Fynske Fortællinger* (1 a year), *Fynske Minder* (1 a year), *Fynske Studier* (1 a year).

Selected Museums:

Carl Nielsen Museet (Carl Nielsen Museum): Claus Bergs Gade 11, 5000 Odense C; tel. 65-51-46-01; e-mail museum@odense.dk; internet www.museum.odense.dk/museer/carl-nielsen-museet.aspx; f. 1980; devoted to the life and works of Carl Nielsen and his wife Anne Marie Carl-Nielsen; Curator EJNAR ASKGAARD.

Fyns Kunstmuseum (Funen Art Museum): Jernbanegade 13, 5000 Odense C; tel. 65-51-46-01; e-mail museum@odense.dk; internet www.museum.odense.dk/museer/fyns-kunstmuseum.aspx; f. 1880 as a smaller version of the Statens Museum for Kunst; art gallery; colln contains works since 1750; specializes in concrete art which is an art form that is dedicated to shape, line, geometry and colours; Curator ANNE CHRISTIANSEN.

Fynske Landsby (Funen Village): Sejerskovvej 20, 5260 Odense S; tel. 65-51-46-01; e-mail museum@odense.dk; internet www.museum.odense.dk/museer/den-fynske-landsby.aspx; open-air museum recreating the time of the era of Hans Christian Andersen (1805–75); concerts and musical theatre; Curator MYRTUE ANDERS.

Hans Christian Andersens Hus (Hans Christian Andersen Museum): Bangs Boder 29, 5000 Odense C; e-mail museum@odense.dk; internet www.museum.odense.dk/museer/hc-andersens-hus.aspx; f. 1905; devoted to the writer's life (1805–75) and work; Curator EJNAR ASKGAARD; Curator HENRIK LÜBKER; publ. *Anderseniana*.

H. C. Andersens Barndomshjem i Munkemøllestræde (Hans Christian Anderson's Childhood Home in Munkemøllestræde): Munkemøllestræde 3-5, 5000 Odense C; tel. 65-51-46-01; e-mail museum@odense.dk; internet www.museum.odense.dk/museer/hc-andersens-barndomshjem/hc-andersens-barndomshjem.aspx; f. 1930; 2 small rooms converted into a museum; 1 was the setting for Hans Christian's childhood.

Odense City Museum—Møntergården: Overgade 48, 5000 Odense C; tel. 65-51-46-01; e-mail museum@odense.dk; internet www.museum.odense.dk/museer/moentergaarden.aspx; local cultural history, coins and medals, archaeology; Curator KARSTEN KJER MICHAELSEN; Curator ANDERS MYRTUE.

Randers

Randers Kunstmuseum (Museum of Danish Art): Stemannsgade 2, 2. Kulturhuset, 8900 Randers; tel. 86-42-29-22; e-mail info@randerskunstmuseum.dk; internet www.randerskunstmuseum.dk; f. 1887; colln of 4,000 paintings, sculptures and graphics; Danish art from 19th and 20th centuries; int. art from second half of 20th century; Musuem Dir LISE JEPPESEN; Curator CHRISTINA RAUH OXBØLL.

Roskilde

Museet for Samtidskunst (Museum of Contemporary Art): Stændertorvet 3D, 4000 Roskilde; tel. 46-31-65-70; e-mail info@samtidskunst.dk; internet samtidskunst.dk; f. 1991; colln consists of sound art, video art, intermedia art, installation art, media art and documentation from 1950 up to today; Chair. FRANK BIRKEBÆK; Dir SANNE KOFOD OLSEN.

Vikingeskibsmuseet i Roskilde (Viking Ship Museum): Vindeboder 12, 4000 Roskilde; tel. 46-30-02-00; e-mail museum@vikingeskibsmuseet.dk; internet www.vikingeskibsmuseet.dk; f. 1969; exhibits the 5 Viking ships found at Skuldelev in 1962; promotes research in ship-building history in gen.; research on maritime subjects is carried out in cooperation with the Nat. Museum of Denmark and other nat. and int. research instns; Chair. JOY MORTENSEN; Dir TINNA DAMGÅRD-SØRENSEN.

Rungsted Kyst

Karen Blixen Museet (Karen Blixen Museum): Rungsted Strandvej 111, 2960 Rungsted Kyst; tel. 45-57-10-57; e-mail karen-blixen@blixen.dk; internet www.karen-blixen.dk; f. 1991; documentary exhibition about Karen Blixen's life and work; gallery with Karen Blixen's drawings and paintings; a small cinema; spec. exhibition room; Dir CATHERINE LEFEBVRE; Curator ANNE SOFIE TIEDEMANN DAL.

Silkeborg

KunstCentret Silkeborg Bad (Art Centre Silkeborg Bad): Gjessøvej 40, 8600 Silkeborg; tel. 86-81-63-29; e-mail reception@silkeborgbad.dk; internet www.silkeborgbad.dk; f. 1992; colln of sculptures in the park area; displays contemporary Danish and foreign art; Silkeborg Bunker Museum is located within the park, in a personnel bunker belonging to the Second World Warr; Dir IBEN FROM; publ. *Nyt*.

Skagen

Skagens Museum: Brøndumsvej 4, 9990 Skagen; tel. 98-44-64-44; e-mail museum@skagensmuseum.dk; internet www.skagensmuseum.dk; f. 1908; displays works from the end of the 19th century; Chair. HANS JØRGEN KAPTAIN; Dir LISETTE VIND EBBENSEN.

Vejen

Vejen Kunstmuseums (Vejen Art Museum): Østergade 4, 6600 Vejen; tel. 75-36-04-82; e-mail museum@vejenkom.dk; internet www.vejenkunstmuseum.dk; f. 1924; colln of Danish symbolism from the late 19th century; exhibits works of sculptor and ceramist Niels Hansen Jacobsen; Chair. PETER BREDSTEN; Dir TERESA NIELSEN.

Vejle

Vejle Kunstmuseums (Vejle Museum of Art): Flegborg 16-18, 7100 Vejle; tel. 76-51-31-00; e-mail museerne@vejle.dk; internet www.vejlekunstmuseum.dk; f. 1901; collns of Danish art from early 20th century to present, from classic modernism and pre-COBRA until today; 15,000 items of Danish prints and drawings; Dir NINA DAMSGAARD; Curator SIGNE JACOBSEN; Curator MARIANNE SØRENSEN.

Universities and Technical Universities

AALBORG UNIVERSITET (Aalborg University)

Fredrik Bajers Vej 5, POB 159, 9100 Ålborg
Telephone: 99-40-99-40
E-mail: aau@aau.dk
Internet: www.aau.dk
Founded 1974 as Aalborg Univ. Centre, current name adopted 1994
State control
Academic year: September to July

Rector: PER MICHAEL JOHANSEN
Vice-Rector: INGER ASKEHAVE
Univ. Dir: PETER PLENGE
Library Dir: NIELS-HENRIK GYLSTORFF

Library: see under Libraries and Archives
Number of teachers: 2,000
Number of students: 16,000

Publication: *Studieguide* (1 a year)

DEANS

Faculty of Engineering and Science: Prof. ESKILD HOLM NIELSEN
Faculty of Humanities: LONE DIRCKINCK-HOLMFELD
Faculty of Medicine: Prof. EGON TOFT
Faculty of Social Sciences: HANNE KATHRINE KROGSTRUP

AARHUS UNIVERSITET

Nordre Ringgade 1, 8000 Aarhus C
Telephone: 87-15-00-00
E-mail: au@au.dk
Internet: www.au.dk
Founded 1928
State control
Languages of instruction: Danish, English
Academic year: September to June

Rector: LAURITZ B. HOLM-NIELSEN
Pro-Rector: SØREN E. FRANDSEN
Chair.: MICHAEL CHRISTIANSEN
Deputy Chair.: PEDER TUBORGH
Univ. Dir: JØRGEN JØRGENSEN
Deputy Dir: OLE OLSEN

Number of teachers: 4,114 (full-time and part-time)
Number of students: 42,000

Publications: *AU-gustus* (4 a year), *CAMPUS* (22 a year)

DEANS

Faculty of Arts: METTE THUNØ
Faculty of Health: ALLAN FLYVBJERG
Faculty of Science and Technology: BRIAN BECH NIELSEN
School of Business and Social Sciences: SVEND HYLLEBERG

PROFESSORS

Faculty of Health (Vennelyst Blvd 9, 8000 Aarhus C; tel. 87-15-00-00; e-mail health@au.dk; internet health.au.dk):

AALKJAER, C., General Physiology
ANDERSEN, J. P., Molecular Physiology
ASTRUP, J., Neurosurgery
AUTRUP, H. N., Environment and Occupational Medicine
BEK, T., Ophthalmology
BLACK, F. T., Medicine
BOLUND, L., Clinical Genetics
BONDE, J. P., Clinical Occupational Medicine
BÜNGER, C., Experimental Orthopaedic Surgery
CHRISTENSEN, B., General Medicine
CHRISTENSEN, E. I., Structural Cell Biology
CHRISTIANSEN, G., Medical Molecular Biology
CLAUSEN, T., Physiology
DAHL, R., Lung Diseases and Allergology
DANSCHER, G., Neurobiology
DJURHUUS, J. C., Surgery
EHLERS, N., Ophthalmology
ESMANN, M., Biophysics
FALK, E., Ischaemic Heart Disease
FOLDSPANG, A., Health Service Research
FRØKIER, J., Clinical Psychology and Nuclear Medicine
FUGLSANG-FREDERIKSEN, A., Neurophysiology
GJEDDE, A., Positron Tomography
GLIEMANN, J., Biochemistry
GREGERSEN, H., Gastrointestinal Sensory Motor Function
GREGERSEN, M., Forensic Medicine
GREGERSEN, N., Medical Molecular Biology
GUNDERSEN, H. J., Stereology
GYLDENSTED, C., X-ray Diagnostics
HAMILTON-DUTOIT, S., Pathology
HASENKAM, J. M., Heart Surgery
HOKLAND, P., Experimental Clinical Research
HÖLLSBERG, P., Virology
HVID, I., Experimental Orthopaedics
ISIDOR, F., Prosthetics
JAKOBSEN, J. K., Neurology
JENSEN, P. H., Medical Biochemistry
JENSEN, T. S., Pain Research
JENSENIUS, J. C. T., Immunology
JØRGENSEN, T. M., Urology
KARRING, T., Periodontology
KILIAN, M., Microbiology and Immunology
KIRKEVOLD, M., Clinical Nursing Science
KØLVRAA, S., Clinical Genetics
LAMBERT, J. D. C., Physiology
LARSEN, M. J., Endodontics
LAURBERG, P., Endocrinology
LAURITZEN, T., General Practice
LEDET, T., Biochemical Pathology
MAASE, H. VON DER, Oncology
MAUNSBACH, A., Anatomy
MELSEN, B., Orthodontics
MOESTRUP, S. K., Medical Biochemistry
MOGENSEN, C. E. S., Medicine
MOGENSEN, S. C., Virology and Immunology
MØLLER, J. V., Biophysics
MORS, N. P. O., Experimental Clinical Research
MOSEKILDE, L., Bone Diseases
MULVANY, M., Cardiovascular Pharmacology
MUNK-JØRGENSEN, P., Psychiatry
NEXOE, E., Clinical Biochemistry
NIELSEN, S., Structural Cell Biology and Pathophysiology
NIELSEN, T. T., Cardiology
NYGAARD, H., Biomedical Engineering
OLSEN, J., Social Medicine
ØRNTOFT, T. F., Molecular Cancer Diagnostics
OVERGAARD, J., Experimental Cancer Research
OVESEN, T., Experimental Clinical Research
PAASKE, W., Cardiovascular Surgery
PAKKENBERG, B., Neurostereology
PAULSEN, P. K., Surgery
PEDERSEN, F. S., Molecular Oncology
PEDERSEN, J. C. M., Microbiology and Immunology
POULSEN, S., Paediatric Dentistry
RICHELSEN, B., Clinical Nutrition
ROSENBERG, R., Psychiatry
SABROE, S., Health Sciences
SCHIØTZ, P. O., Paediatrics
SCHMITZ, O., Clinical Pharmacology
SCHØNHEYDER, H., Clinical Microbiology
SIGSGAARD, T., Occupational Medicine
SØBALLE, K., Experimental Orthopaedic Surgery
SØRENSEN, F. B., Pathology
SØRENSEN, H. T., Clinical Epidemiology
STENGARD-PEDERSEN, K., Rheumatology
SVENSSON, P., Oral Physiology
THOMSEN, P. H., Psychiatry for Children and Adolescents
TOENNESEN, E., Anaesthesiology
VESTERBY, C. A., Forensic Medicine
VESTERGAARD, P., Psychiatry
VÆTH, M., Biostatistics
VILSTRUP, H., Hepatology
WEEKE, J., Medical Endocrinology
WENZEL, A., Oral Radiology

Faculty of Science and Technology (Ny Munkegade, Bygning 520, 8000 Aarhus C; tel. 89-42-31-88; e-mail nat@au.dk; internet au.dk/nat):

ANDERSEN, H. H., Mathematics

ANDERSEN, J. U., Experimental Physics
ASMUSSEN, S., Mathematics
BALSLEV, H., Biology
BESENBACHER, F., Experimental Solid State Physics
BOLS, M., Chemistry
BØDKER, S., Computer Science
BØTTIGER, J., Materials Science
CHRISTENSEN, K. R., Biological Oceanography
CHRISTENSEN, N. E., Theoretical Solid State Physics
CHRISTENSEN-DALSGAARD, J., Astronomy
CHRISTIANSEN, F. V. B., Population Biology
CLARK, B., Chemistry
FIELD, D., Experimental Molecular Physics
GRONBAK, K. G., Computer Science
HANSEN, T. I., Sports Medicine
IVERSEN, B., Materials Chemistry
JACOBSEN, H. J., Chemistry
JANTZEN, J. C., Mathematics
JENSEN, J. L., Mathematical Statistics
JENSEN, K., Computer Science
JØRGENSEN, K. A., Organic Chemistry
JØRGENSEN, P., Theoretical Chemistry
KJEMS, J., Molecular Biology
KORSTGÅRD, J. A., Structural Geology and Basin Tectonics
KRAGH, H., History of Science
KRISTENSEN, M., Nanophotonics
LOESCHKE, V., Biology
MACINTOSH, D. J., Biology
MADSEN, I. H., Mathematics
MADSEN, O. L., Computer Science
MØLMER, K., Physics
NIELSEN, J. A., Mathematical Finance
NIELSEN, M., Theoretical Computer Science
NIELSEN, N. C., Solid State NMR
ODGAARD, B. V., Palynology
OGILBY, P. R., Chemistry
PETERSEN, J. S., Chemistry
PIETROWSKI, J., Quaternary Geology
RATTAN, S. I. S., Molecular Biology
REVSBECH, N. P., Microbial Ecology
SKRYDSTRUP, T., Chemistry
STENSGAARD, I., Experimental Solid State Physics
VEDEL, E. B., Mathematical Statistics
WEBER, R. E., Zoophysiology

School of Business and Social Sciences (Nordre Ringgade 1, 8000 Aarhus C; tel. 87-15-00-00; e-mail bss@au.dk; internet bss.au.dk):

AGERVOLD, M., Psychology
ANDERSEN, T. M., Economic Planning
BASSE, E. M., Jurisprudence
BLOM-HANSON, J., Political Science
CHRISTENSEN, B. J., Economic Planning
CHRISTENSEN, J. G., Political Science
CHRISTENSEN, J. P., Jurisprudence
DALBERG-LARSEN, J. V., Jurisprudence
DAMGAARD, E., Political Science
DANIELSEN, J. H., Jurisprudence
ELKLIT, A., Psychology
ELKLIT, J., Political Science
EVALD, J., Jurisprudence
GENEFKE, J., Economic Planning
GERMER, P., Jurisprudence
HALDRUP, N., National Economy
HOEGH-OLESEN, H., Psychology
HYLLEBERG, S. A. F., National Economy
IVERSEN, B. O., Jurisprudence
IVERSEN, T., Jurisprudence
JØRGENSEN, P. L., Economics
KRISTENSEN, L. H., Jurisprudence
KVALE, S., Psychology
MADSEN, O. Ø., Economic Planning
MADSEN, P. B., Jurisprudence
MAMMEN, J., Psychology
MOLS, N. P., Management
MORTENSEN, P. B., Register-based Research
NANNESTAD, P., Political Science
NIELSEN, G. T., Jurisprudence
NØRGAARD, I. M., Jurisprudence
NØRGAARD, O., Political Science
NYBORG, H., Psychology
OVERGAARD, P. B., Economic Planning
PALDAM, N. M., Economic Planning
PEDERSEN, J., Jurisprudence
PEDERSEN, P. J., Economics
REVSBECH, K., Jurisprudence
RISBJERG THOMSEN, S., Political Science
ROSHOLM, M., National Economy
SOERENSEN, G., Political Science
SOMMER, D., Psychology
SVENDSEN, G. T., Political Science
SVENSSON, P., Political Science
THOMSEN, H. H. B., Jurisprudence
TOGEBY, L., Political Science
VASTRUP, C., Economics
VEDSTED-HANSEN, J., Jurisprudence
ZACHARIAS, B., Psychology

DANMARKS TEKNISKE UNIVERSITET
(Technical University of Denmark)

Anker Engelunds Vej 1, Bldg 101A, 2800 Kgs. Lyngby
Telephone: 45-25-25-25
E-mail: dtu@dtu.dk
Internet: www.dtu.dk

Founded 1829 as College of Advanced Technology, current name adopted 1994
Pres.: Dr ANDERS OVERGAARD BJARKLEV
Provost and Exec. Vice-Pres.: Dr HENRIK C. WEGENER
Univ. Dir and Exec. Vice-Pres.: CLAUS NIELSEN
Dean for Graduate Studies and Int. Affairs: Prof. Dr MARTIN P. BENDSØE
Dean for Undergraduate Studies and Student Affairs: Prof. Dr MARTIN VIGILD
Dir for Private and Public Sectors Services: Dr NIELS AXEL NIELSEN

Library: see under Libraries and Archives
Number of teachers: 1,464
Number of students: 7,597

Publication: *DTU in profile* (1 a year)

PROFESSORS

ADLER-NISSEN, J. L., Biotechnology
AHRING, B. K., Biotechnology
ALTING, L., Mechanical Engineering
ANDERSEN, M. A. E., Power Electronics
ANDRAESEN, M. M., Product Development
ANDREANI, P., Analogue Integrated Systems
ARVIN, E., Water Supply Engineering
BAY, N., Materials Processing
BENDSØE, M., Applied Functional Analysis
BJARKLEV, A. O., Optical Communication
BJERG, P. L., Environmental Geochemistry
BJERRUM, N., Chemical Engineering
BJØRNER, D., Computer Science
BLANKE, M.
BOHR, H., Biomolecular Structure and Function
BOHR, J., Physics
BOHR, T., Theoretical Physics
BRUNAK, S., Bio-informatics
BRUUN, K. E., Analogue Electronics
BRUUN, P., Industrial Management
BRØNS, M., Mathmematics
BUCHHAVE, P., Optics
CARLSEN, H., Energy Engineering
CHIFFRE, DE, L., Process Technology, Geometrical Metrology
CHORKENDORFF, I., Heterogeneous Catalysis
CHRISTENSEN, C. J. H., Heterogeneous Catalysis
CHRISTENSEN, E. L., Microwave Systems
CHRISTENSEN, TH. H., Environmental Engineering
CHRISTIANSEN, P. L., Non-linear Dynamics
CLAUSEN, J., Mathematic Optimization
CONRADSEN, K., Statistical Image Analysis
DAM-JOHANSEN, K., Combustion and Chemical Reaction Engineering
DAU, T., Hearing Aid Audiology and Acoustics
DITLEVSEN, O. D., Actions on Structures and Structural Reliability
EMMITT, S., Innovation and Management in Building
FANGER, P. O., Heating and Air Conditioning
FOGED, N., Geotechnical Engineering
FREDSØE, J., Marine Hydraulics
GAARSLEV, A., Construction Management
GANI, R., Systems Design
GIMSING, N. J., Structural Engineering
HAMMER, K., Microbiology
HANSEN, E. H., Analytical Chemistry
HANSEN, H. N., Microtechnical Production
HANSEN, L. K., Digital Signal Processing
HANSEN, P. C., Scientific Computing
HANSEN, P. F., Safety Assessment of Marine Systems
HANSEN, V. L., Mathematics
HASSAGER, O.
HEIN, L., Engineering Design Methodology
HENZE, M., Waste-water Engineering
HVAM, J. M., Optoelectronics
HVILSTED, S.
JACOBI, O. I., Geoinformatics and Photogrammetry
JACOBSEN, K. W., Physics
JAUHO, A.-P., Theoretical Nanotechnology
JENSEN, J. A., Biomedical Signal Processing
JENSEN, J. J., Marine Structures
JENSEN, O. M., Building Materials
JENSEN, P. L., Technology and Working Life, Working Environment
JEPPESEN, P., Optical Communication
JOHNSSON, J. E., Chemical Reaction Engineering
JØRGENSEN, S. B., Technical Chemistry
JUSTESEN, J., Error-Correcting Codes, Information Theory
KLEMM, P., Applied Microbiology
KLIT, P., Machine Elements and Lubrication Theory
KNUDSEN, L. R., Cryptology
KNUDSEN, S., Experimental and Computational Gene Expression Analysis
KRENK, S., Structural Mechanics
KRISTENSEN, M., Glass Components
KROZER, V., Microwave Electronics
LARSEN, P. S., Fluid Mechanics
LELEUR, S., Decision Support Systems and Planning
LIND, M., Control Systems
LUNDT, I.
LYNGAAE-JOERGENSEN, J., Polymer Technology
MADSEN, H.
MADSEN, J., Computer Systems
MADSEN, K., Numerical Analysis
MADSEN, O. G., Transport Optimization
MADSEN, P., Hydrodynamics
MADSEN, S. N.
MARKVORSEN, S., Differential Geometry
MENON, A., Microsystems Technology
MOLIN, S., Applied Microbiogenetics
MØLLER, P., Corrosion and Surface Technology
MOLLERUP, J., Chromatography and Thermodynamics
MØLTOFT, J., Reliability Engineering
MØRK, J., Active Semiconductor Components for Optical Communication Systems
MØRUP, S., Physics of Nanostructures
NIELSEN, J. B., Fermentation Physiology
NIELSEN, M. P., Structural Analysis
NIELSEN, O. A., Transport Planning
NIELSON, F., Computer Science
NIELSON, H. R., Programming Language Technology and Secure IT Systems
NILSSON, J. F., Computer Science
NØRSKOV, J. K., Theoretical Physics
OLESEN, B. W., Indoor Environment and Energy
PAUL, J., Refrigeration
PEDERSEN, N. F.
PEDERSEN, P., Structural Mechanics

PEDERSEN, P. T., Strength of Materials
POLACK, J., Acoustics
QVALE, B., Mechanical Engineering
REITZEL, E., Form-finding of Minimal Structures
ROENNE-HANSEN, J., Electric Power Engineering
SKOU, N., Radar and Radiometer Systems
SKOUBY, K. E., Economy and Regulation of Telecommunication
SKRIVER, H. L.
SOMERS, M. A., Physical Metallurgy
SPLIID, H., Applied Statistics: Statistical Practice and Consulting
STENBY, H. E., Applied Thermodynamics and Separation Processes
STUBKJAER, K. E.
SUNDELL, J.
SVENDSEN, SV. AA. HØJGAARD, Energy Technology in Buildings
SVENSSON, B., Food Protein Biochemistry
TANNER, D., Organic Chemistry
TELLEMAN, P., Biochemical Microsystems
THOMASSEN, C., Mathematics
TØNNESEN, O., Experimental High Voltage Technique
TROMBORG, B., Optoelectronics
TVERGAARD, V., Mechanics of Materials
ULSTRUP, J., Inorganic Chemistry
VESTERAGER, J., Product Development
VILLADSEN, J., Biotechnology
VILLUMSEN, A., Geology
WANHEIM, T., Machine Engineering

HANDELSHØJSKOLEN I KØBENHAVN
(Copenhagen Business School)

Solbjerg Plads 3, 2000 Frederiksberg
Telephone: 38-15-38-15
E-mail: cbs@cbs.dk
Internet: www.cbs.dk
Founded 1917, present status 1965
Private control
Languages of instruction: Danish, English
Academic year: September to July
Chair.: PETER SCHÜTZE
Deputy Chair.: EVA BERNEKE
Pres.: PER HOLTEN-ANDERSEN
Univ. Dir: HAKON IVERSEN
Exec. Sec.: HELLE GRUNNET-JEPSEN
Library: see under Libraries and Archives
Number of teachers: 1,286 (566 full-time, 720 part-time)
Number of students: 19,264
Publications: *ARK*, *CEBAL*, *SPRINT*

DEANS

Faculty of Education: JAN MOLIN
Faculty of Research: ALAN IRWIN

IT-UNIVERSITETET I KØBENHAVN
(IT University of Copenhagen)

Rued Langgaards Vej 7, 2300 Copenhagen S
Telephone: 72-18-50-00
E-mail: itu@itu.dk
Internet: www.itu.dk
Founded 1999, ind. univ. status 2003, present status and name 2003
State control
Academic year: September to June
Vice-Chancellor: Dr MADS TOFTE
Provost: Prof. Dr JØRGEN STAUNSTRUP
Univ. Dir: GEORG DAM STEFFENSEN
Chair. of the Board: JØRGEN LINDEGAARD
Number of teachers: 257
Number of students: 2,067

KØBENHAVNS UNIVERSITET
(University of Copenhagen)

Nørregade 10, 1165 Copenhagen K
Telephone: 35-32-26-26
E-mail: ku@ku.dk
Internet: www.ku.dk
Founded 1479
State control
Languages of instruction: Danish, English
Academic year: September to August (2 terms)
Rector: Prof. RALF HEMMINGSEN
Pro-Rector: Prof. THOMAS BJØRNHOLM
Pro-Rector: LYKKE FRIIS
Univ. Dir: JØRGEN HONORÉ
Univ. Librarian: MICHAEL COTTA-SCHØNBERG
Number of teachers: 4,823 (f.t.e.)
Number of students: 40,866 (23,473 undergraduate, 17,393 graduate)

DEANS

Faculty of Health and Medical Sciences: Prof. Dr ULLA WEWER
Faculty of Humanities: ULF HEDETOFT
Faculty of Law: Prof. Prof. JACOB GRAFF NIELSEN
Faculty of Science: JOHN RENNER HANSEN
Faculty of Social Sciences: Assoc. Prof. TROELS ØSTERGAARD SØRENSEN
Faculty of Theology: KIRSTEN BUSCH NIELSEN

PROFESSORS

Faculty of Health and Medical Sciences (3B, Blegdamsvej, 2200 Copenhagen N; tel. 35-32-79-00; e-mail email@sund.ku.dk; internet healthsciences.ku.dk):

ASMUSSEN, E., Dental Materials
BENDIXEN, G., Internal Medicine
BOCK, E. M., Cellular Biology
BOCK, J. E., Obstetrics and Gynaecology
BOLWIG, T. G., Psychiatry
BOYSEN, G., Neurology
BRETLAU, P., Otorhinolaryngology
BUUS, S., Basic Immunology
CHRISTENSEN, N. J., Internal Medicine
CHRISTOFFERSEN, P., Pathological Anatomy
DABELSTEEN, S. E., Oral Diagnosis
DEURS, B. G., Structural Cell Biology
DIRKSEN, A., Internal Medicine
GALBO, H., Physiopathology
GJERRIS, F. O., Neurosurgery
GYNTELBERG, F., Occupational Medicine
HALD, T., Surgery
HAUNSØ, S., Internal Medicine
HEMMINGSEN, R. P., Psychiatry
HENRIKSEN, J. H., Clinical Physiology
HJØRTING-HANSEN, E., Oral and Maxillofacial Surgery
HOLLNAGEL, H., General Practice
HOLMSTRUP, P., Periodontology
HØIBY, N., Microbiology
HOLST, J. J., Medical Physiology
HORNSLET, A., Virology
HULTBORN, H., Neurophysiology
KEHLET, N., Surgery
KEIDING, N., Statistics
KRASILNIKOFF, P. A., Paediatrics
KRASNIK, A., Social Medicine
KREIBORG, S., Paedodontics
LARSEN, J. F., Obstetrics and Gynaecology
LARSEN, S., Pathological Anatomy
LORENZEN, I., Internal Medicine
LUND, B., Surgery
LUND-ANDERSEN, H., Eye Diseases
MELLERGÅRD, M. J., Psychiatry
MENNÉ, T., Dermatology
MICHELSEN, N., Clinical Social Medicine
MOGENSEN, J. V., Anaesthesiology
MORLING, N., Forensic Genetics
NIELSEN, J. O., Epidemic Diseases
NORÉN, O., Biochemistry
OLESEN, J., Neurology
ØLGAARD, K., Internal Medicine
OTTESEN, B., Obstetrics and Gynaecology
ÖWALL, B., Prosthodontics
PAULSON, O. B., Neurology
PETERSEN, P. E., Community Dentistry and Postgraduate Education
PETTERSON, G., Thorax Surgery
PHILIP, J., Obstetrics and Gynaecology
POULSEN, H. E., Clinical Pharmacology
PRAUSE, J. U., Eye Diseases
QUISTOR, F. F., Biochemistry
REHFELD, J. F., Clinical Chemistry
REIBEL, J., Oral Pathology and Oral Medicine
RØRTH, M., Clinical Oncology
ROSTGAARD, J., Normal Anatomy
ROVSING, H. C., Radiology
SCHOU, J., Pharmacology
SCHROEDER, T. V., Surgery
SCHROLL, M., Geriatrics
SCHWARTZ, T. W., Molecular Pharmacology
SIGGAARD-ANDERSEN, O., Clinical Chemistry and Laboratory Technique
SIMONSEN, J., Forensic Pathology
SJÖSTRÖM, H., Biochemistry
SKAKKEBÆK, N., Paediatrics
SKINHØJ, P., Epidemic Diseases
SKOUBY, F., Paediatrics
SOLOW, B., Orthodontics
SØRENSEN, T. I. A., Clinical Epidemiology
STADIL, F. W., Surgery
SVEJGAARD, A., Clinical Immunology
THYLSTRUP, A., Cardiology
TOMMERUP, N., Medical Genetics
TOS, M., Otorhinolaryngology
VEJLSGAARD, G., Dermato-venereology
WULF, H. C., Dermato-venereology
WULFF, H. R., Clinical Decision Theory and Ethics

Faculty of Humanities (Njalsgade 80, 2300 Copenhagen S; tel. 35-32-88-11; e-mail hum-fak@hum.ku.dk; internet humanities .ku.dk):

BOLVIG, A., History
BONDEBJERG, I., Film Studies
COLLIN, F., Philosophy
DUNCAN, R., American Studies
EKSELL, K., Semitic Philosophy
ELBRO, C., Linguistics
FLOTO, I., History
FORTESQUE, M., Linguistics
GABRIELSEN, V., Ancient History
HARDER, P., English Literature
HJARVARD, S., Film Studies
HØJRUP, T., Ethnology
HOV, L., Theatre
JENSEN, K. B., Media Studies
JØRGENSEN, J. N., Danish Language
LIND, G., History
LUND, N., History
RANDSBORG, K., Archaeology
RUUS, H., Danish Language
SCHWAB, H., Music
VILLAUME, P., History
ZERLANG, M., Comparative Literature

Faculty of Law (Studiestraede 6, 1455 Copenhagen K; tel. 35-32-26-26; e-mail jurfak@jur.ku.dk; internet jura.ku.dk):

BALVIG, F., Legal Sociology and Sociology of Law
BLUME, P., Legal Informatics
BONDESON, U., Criminology
BRYDE ANDERSEN, M., Private Law, Computer Law
DUE, O., European Union Law
FOIGEL, I., Law of Taxation
GREVE, V., Criminal Law
KETSCHER, K., Social Law
KOKTVEDGAARD, M., Law of Competition, Intellectual Property Law
KRARUP, O., Public Law
LOOKOFSKY, J., Law of Contracts and Torts, Private International Law
NIELSEN, L., Family Law
RASMUSSEN, H., International Law and European Union Law
RØNSHOLDT, S., Administrative Law
SMITH, E., Legal Procedure
TAKSØE-JENSEN, F., Family Law, Law of Wills and Succession
TAMM, D., History of Law
VON EYBEN, B., Law of Property

ZAHLE, H., Jurisprudence

Faculty of Social Sciences (Øster Farimagsgade 5, Bldg 12, 1st Fl. 1353 Copenhagen K; tel. 35-32-35-46; e-mail samf-fak@samf.ku.dk; internet socialsciences.ku.dk):

ANDERSEN, E., Economics
ANDERSEN, E. B., Theoretical Statistics
BERTILSSON, M., Sociology
ESTRUP, H., Economics
GRODAL, B. K., Economics
GØRTZ, E., Social Description
GUNDELACH, P., Sociology
HASTRUP, K., Anthropology
HEURLIN, B., Political Science
HJORTH-ANDERSEN, C., Economics
JØRGENSEN, T. B., Political Science
JUSELIUS, K., Economics
KEIDING, H., Economics
KNUDSEN, T., Political Science
PEDERSEN, O. K., International Politics
PEDERSEN, O. K., Political Science
SCHULTZ, C., Economics
SJØBLOM, B. G., Political Science
SØRENSEN, P. B., Economics
THYGESEN, N. C., Economics
VIND, K., Economics

Faculty of Theology (Købmagergade 44–46, POB 2164, 1150 Copenhagen K; tel. 35-32-39-61; e-mail dtf@fak.teol.ku.dk; internet www.teol.ku.dk):

GLEBE-MØLLER, J., Dogmatics
GRANE, L., Church History
GRØN, A., Ethics and Philosophy of Religion
HANSEN, H. B., Church History
HYLDAHL, N. C., New Testament Exegesis
JØRGENSEN, T., Dogmatics
KJELDGAARD-PEDERSEN, S., Church History, History of Dogma
LAUSTEN, M. S., Theology, Danish Church History
LEMCHE, N. P., Old Testament Exegesis
MÜLLER, M., New Testament Exegesis
THOMPSON, T. L., Old Testament Exegesis

ROSKILDE UNIVERSITET
(Roskilde University)

Universitetsvej 1, POB 260, 4000 Roskilde
Telephone: 46-74-20-00
E-mail: ruc@ruc.dk
Internet: www.ruc.dk

Founded 1970 as Roskilde Univ. Centre, current name adopted 2008
State control
Academic year: September to July (2 semesters)

Rector: Prof. Dr IB POULSEN
Pro-Rector: Prof. Dr HANNE LETH ANDERSEN
Chair.: CHRISTIAN S. NISSEN
Univ. Dir: PETER LAURITZEN
Dir for Library: CLAUS VESTERAGER PEDERSEN

Library of 853,628 vols, incl. 216,483 audiovisual media
Number of teachers: 500
Number of students: 9,500

PROFESSORS

Humanities:

BRASK, P., Science of Texts, Theory and Methodology of Literary Analysis
BRYLD, C., History
DENCIK, L., Social Psychology
ELLE, B., Educational Psychology
HELTOFT, L., Danish
ILLERIS, K., Educational Research
KAMPMANN, J., Educational Research
KJØRUP, S., Philosophy and Communication
MCGUIRE, B. P., History
MORTENSEN, A. T., Philosophy and Communication
NISSEN, G., History
OLESEN, H. S., Educational Psychology
PEDERSEN, S., Philosophy
POULSEN, IB., Danish
POULSEN, J., Journalism
PREISLER, B., English
SCHRØDER, K. CHR., Communication
SIMONSEN, B., Educational Research
WEBER, K., Educational Research
WUCHERPHENNIG, W. P., German

Natural Sciences:

AGGER, P., Environmental Planning
ANDERSEN, O., Environmental Science
BRANDT, J., Geography
DYRE, J. C., Physics
FORBES, V. E., Environmental Biology
GALLAGHER, J. P., Computer Science
HANSEN, P. E., Chemistry
ILLERIS, S., Geography
LØBNER-OLESEN, A., Molecular Biology
NIELSEN, L. K., Transport and Environment
NISS, M., Mathematics
PRÆSTGAARD, E., Chemistry
SCHROLL, H., Environmental Assessment
SIMONSEN, K. F., Geography
SØRENSEN, B. E., Physics
THULSTRUP, E., Chemistry
WESTH-ANDERSEN, P., Chemistry

Social Sciences:

AAGE, H., Political Economy
ANDERSEN, J., Social Sciences
BOGASON, P., Public Administration
BOJE, TH. P., Social Sciences
DAVIS, J. D., Political Economy
FRAMKE, W., Tourism Planning
GREVE, B., Public Administration
JESPERSEN, J., Welfare State Studies
LAURIDSEN, L. S., International Development
MARCUSSEN, H. S., Institutional Aspect of Natural Resource Management
MATTSON, J., Business Administration
NIELSEN, K., Industrial Theory
NIELSEN, K. A., Technological and Organizational Development of Enterprises
OLSEN, O. J., Planning
SCHEUER, S., Social Sciences
SUNDBO, J., Business Administration
TORFING, J., Social Sciences
WHISTON, TH. G., Environmental Regulation

SYDDANSK UNIVERSITET
(University of Southern Denmark)

Campusvej 55, 5230 Odense M
Telephone: 65-50-10-00
E-mail: sdu@sdu.dk
Internet: www.sdu.dk

Founded 1998 by merger of Odense Univ., Southern Denmark School of Business and Engineering and South Jutland Univ. Centre, fmrly Odense Univ. (f. 1966)
State control
Languages of instruction: Danish, English
Academic year: September to June (2 semesters)

Vice-Chancellor: JENS ODDERSHEDE
Pro-Vice-Chancellor: BJARNE GRAABECH SØRENSEN
Univ. Dir: JACOB SCHMIDT
Chief Librarian: AASE LINDAHL

Library: see under Libraries and Archives
Number of teachers: 747
Number of students: 20,000

Publication: *Ny Viden* (12 a year)

DEANS

Faculty of Business and Social Sciences: Prof. Dr JESPER STRANDSKOV
Faculty of Engineering: PER MICHAEL JOHANSEN
Faculty of Health Sciences: Prof. OLE SKØTT
Faculty of Humanities: Dr FLEMMING G. ANDERSEN
Faculty of Science: Prof. HENRIK PEDERSON

PROFESSORS

Faculty of Health Sciences (J. B. Winsløws Vej 19, 3, 5000 Odense C; tel. 65-50-39-03; e-mail fac@health.sdu.dk; internet www.sdu.dk/om_sdu/fakulteterne/sundhedsvidenskab.aspx):

ANDERSEN, K. E., Dermato-venereology
BAKKETEIG, L., Epidemiology
BARINGTON, T., Clinical Immunology
BECK-NIELSEN, H., Medical Endocrinology
BENDIX, T., Biomechanics
BIE, P., Physiology
BINDSLEV-JENSEN, C., Dermatological Allergology
BRO, F., General Practice
BRØSEN, K., Clinical Pharmacology
CHRISTENSEN, K., Ageing and Longevity
DITZEL, H., Biomedicine
DOBBELSTEIN, M., Biomedicine
FENGER, C., Pathology
FINSEN, B., Biomedicine
GRANDJEAN, P. A., Environmental Medicine
GREEN, A., Clinical Epidemiology
HAGHFELT, T., Cardiology
HALLAS, J., Clinical Pharmacology
HØILUND-CARLSEN, P., Clinical Physiology
HOLMSKOV, U., Biomedicine
HØRDER, M., Clinical Chemistry
HUSBY, S., Paediatrics
JAKOBSON, A., Cancer Therapy
JENSEN, W. A., Biomedicine
JUNKER, P., Rheumatology
KASSEM, M., Biomedicine
KOLMOS, H. J., Microbiology
KRAGH-SØRENSEN, P., Psychiatry
LOUS, J., General Practice
MANNICHE, C., Biomechanics
OWENS, T., Biomedicine
PEDERSEN, C., Infectious Medicine
PETERSEN, S., Asthma and Allergy in Childhood
RASMUSSEN, J. Z., Anatomy
RITSKES-HOITINGA, M., Comparative Medicine and Laboratory Animal Science
SAHLIN, K., Exercise Physiology
SCHAFFALITZKY DE MUCKADELL, O. B., Medical Gastroenterology
SCHRØDER, H. D., Neuropathology and Neuromuscular Biology
SJØLIE, A. K., Ophthalmology
SKØTT, O., Physiology
SØRENSEN, T., Psychiatry
THOMSEN, J., Forensic Medicine
TOFT, P., Anaesthesiology
VACH, W., Medical Statistics
VAUPEL, J. W., Demographic Studies
WALTER, S., Surgery
WESTERGAARD, J. G., Obstetrics

Faculty of Humanities (Campusvej 55, 5230 Odense M; tel. 65-50-10-00; e-mail humfak@sdu.dk; internet www.sdu.dk/om_sdu/fakulteterne/humaniora.aspx):

BACHE, C., English Language and Literature
BASBØLL, H., Scandinavian Language
BORGNAKKE, K., General Pedagogy
DROTNER, K., Media Studies and Media Culture
HAMMER, O., Religious Studies and Comparative Religion
HOLM, P., Maritime and Regional History
JAKOBSEN, H. G., Scandinavian Language
JENSEN, B., Slavic Studies
JESPERSEN, K. J. V., History
JOHANSEN, J. D., Comparative Literature
JUST, F., History
KLAWONN, E. G., Philosophy
MAI, A.-M., Danish Literature
MORTENSEN, F. H., Scandinavian Language and Literature

NIELSEN, H. F., Historical and Comparative Germanic Linguistics
NYE, D., American Studies
QVORTRUP, L., Multimedia
ROBERING, K., Humanistic Information Science
SAUERBERG, L. O., English Language and Literature
SINHA, C. G., Language and Cognitive Linguistics

Faculty of Science (Campusvej 55, 5230 Odense M; tel. 65-50-20-99; e-mail anc@sdu.dk; internet www.sdu.dk/om_sdu/fakulteterne/naturvidenskab.aspx):

ANGELOV, C. K., Software Engineering
BERNSEN, N. O., Natural Interactive Systems
BJERREGAARD, P., Biology
BUUR, J., User-oriented Product Development
CANFIELD, D., Biology
DOUTHWAITE, S. R., Molecular Biology
DYBKJÆR, L., Natural Interactive Systems
GERDES, K., Molecular Microbiology
HAAGERUP, U., Mathematics
ISSINGER, O., Biochemistry
JENSEN, J. B., Computer Science
JENSEN, O. N., Protein Mass Spectrometry
JØRGENSEN, B., Statistics
KNUDSEN, J., Biochemistry
KORNERUP, P., Computer Science
KRISTENSEN, B. B., Software Engineering
KRISTIANSEN, K., Eukaryotic Molecular Biology
LARSEN, K. S., Computer Science
LUND, H. H., Information Technology
MCKENZIE, C. J., Nanobioscience
MANN, M., Molecular Biology
MICHELSEN, A., Biology
MOURITSEN, O. G., Physics
NIELSEN, H. T., Chemistry
ØSTERGARD, J. E., Physics and Technology
PEDERSEN, H., Mathematics
PERRAM, J. W., Applied Mathematics
PETERSEN, H. G., Applied Mathematics
ROEPSTORFF, P., Molecular Biology
RØRDAM, M., Mathematics
RUBAHN, H.-G., Physics and Technology
SIGMUND, H. P., Physics
TOWN, R. M., Chemistry
VALENTIN-HANSEN, P., Molecular Biology
WENGEL, J., Chemistry
WIIL, U. K., Software Engineering
WILLATZEN, H., Mathematical Modelling

University-level Institutions

Danmarks Medie-og Journalisthøjskole (Danish School of Media and Journalism): Olof Palmes Alle 11, 8200 Aarhus N; tel. 89-44-04-40; e-mail info@dmjx.dk; internet www.dmjx.dk; offers courses on photo journalism, media law, journalism, social media, print media and more; Rector JENS OTTO KJAER HANSEN; Pro-Rector LARS POULSEN.

Den Frie Lærerskole (Independent Academy for Free School Teaching): Svendborgvej 15, Ollerup, 5762 Vester Skerninge; tel. 62-24-10-66; e-mail dfl@dfl-ollerup.dk; internet dfl-ollerup.dk; f. 1949; provides training for teachers for a method of traditional schooling that focuses on the individual.

Diakonhøjskolen (Diaconal College of Aarhus): Lyseng Alle 15, 8270 Højbjerg; tel. 86-27-41-22; e-mail info@diakonhojskolen.dk; internet www.diakonhojskolen.dk; f. 1920, current name adopted 1928; provides education on 'Diaconia'; offers BA degrees on courses about Christianity; 10 teachers; 200 students; Prin. JENS PEDERSEN MAIBOM.

Erhvervsakademi Arhus (Business Academy Aarhus): Sønderhøj 30, 8260 Viby J; tel. 72-28-60-00; e-mail info@baaa.dk; internet www.baaa.dk; offers Acad. Profession (AP) and BA degree programmes; Rector CHRISTIAN MATHIASEN.

Erhvervsakademi Dania (Dania-Danish Academy of Business and Technology): Minervavej 63, 8960 Randers; tel. 87114400; e-mail eadania@eadania.dk; internet www.eadania.dk; f. 2009; academic profession degrees in Hospitality and Tourism Management, Marketing Management and IT Technology; BA in International Hospitality Management; 1,800 full-time students; Rector LIS RANDA.

Erhvervsakademi Kolding (International Business Academy): Skamlingvejen 32, 6000 Kolding; tel. 72-24-18-00; e-mail iba@iba.dk; internet iba.dk; f. 2004 by merger of Kolding Business School, Fredericia (2002) and Aabenraa (2004); degree-level study programmes; study exchange programmes; 6,000 students.

Erhvervsakademiet Lillebælt (Lillebælt Academy of Professional Higher Education): Munke Mose Allé 9, 5000 Odense C; tel. 70-10-58-00; e-mail eal@eal.dk; internet www.eal.dk; f. 2009; campuses in Odense and Vejle; offers courses in Danish business, technology, economics, trade, nutrition and hospitality; 1,200 students; Chair. PETER ZINCK; Vice-Chair. TORBEN MØLGAARD ANDERSEN; Prin. JENS MEJER PEDERSEN.

Gotvedskolen (Godvet School of Gymnastics): Vodroffsvej 51, 1900 Frederiksberg C; tel. 35-35-20-19; e-mail kontor@gotvedskolen.dk; internet www.gotvedskolen.dk; f. 1958; Dir SOREN EKMAN.

Ingeniørhøjskolen i København (Copenhagen University College of Engineering): Lautrupvang 15, 2750 Ballerup; tel. 44-80-50-88; e-mail int@ihk.dk; internet www.ihk.dk; f. 1881; applied sciences; awards BSc in engineering; library: 32,900 vols; 250 teachers; 2,300 students; Rector FLEMMING KROGH.

Niels Brock-Copenhagen Business School: Nørre Voldgade 34, 1358 Copenhagen; tel. 33-41-91-00; e-mail brock@brock.dk; internet www.brock.dk; f. 1881 as FUHU Grocery Skole, current name adopted 1991; 25,000 students; Dir ANYA ESKILDSEN; Deputy Dir MORTEN S. PETERSEN.

Paul Petersens Idrætsinstitut (Paul Petersen Sports Science Institute): Tietgensgade 65, 1704, Copenhagen V; tel. 33-29-80-25; e-mail jss@ppkbh.dk; internet paulpetersen.dk; f. 1878; provides gymnastics training; theoretical training; Dir CARL EMMANUEL LARSEN.

Pharmakon (Danish College of Pharmacy Practice): Milnersvej 42, 3400 Hillerød; tel. 48-20-60-00; e-mail info@pharmakon.dk; internet www.pharmakon.dk; f. 1970; works to educate, develop and advise upon pharmaceutical practices; trains pharmacy technicians; Prin. JANNE ALBERTSEN.

Professionshojskolen Kobenhaven (University College Copenhagen): Buddinge Hovedgade 80, 2860 Søborg; tel. 41-89-70-00; e-mail ucc@ucc.dk; internet www.ucc.dk; f. 2007; provides education in teacher and social education, nursing, physiotherapy, psychomotor therapy, textile and handicraft design and sign language interpretation; research and devt within the Nordic and European educational instns; 600 teachers; 16,500 (10,000 full-time, 6,500 part-time) students; Rector LAUST JOEN JAKOBSEN; Pro-Rector HENRIK PEDERSEN.

Professionshojskolen Lillebaelt (University College Lillebaelt): Rømersvej 3, 5200 Odense V; tel. 63-18-31-14; e-mail international@ucl.dk; internet ucl.dk; f. 2008; provides education for social educators, teachers, nurses, radiographers, physiotherapists, occupational therapists, biomedical laboratory scientists, public administrators and social workers; 7,000 students; Rector ERIK KNUDSEN; Dir for Acad. Affairs Dr JØRGEN PETER NIELSEN THORSLUND; Dir for Planning and Resources ALLAN KJÆR HANSEN; Dir for Research and Devt STEFFEN SVENDSEN.

Professionshøjskolen Metropol (Metropolitan University College): Tagensvej 18, 2200 Copenhagen N; tel. 72-48-75-00; e-mail info@phmetropol.dk; internet www.phmetropol.dk; provides training and courses for teachers; Rector STEFAN HERMANN; Vice-Rector for Research and Devt NICHOLAS LUBANSKI.

Professionshøjskolen Nordjylland (University College Nordjylland): POB 38, 9100 Aalborg; tel. 72-69-00-00; e-mail ucn@ucn.dk; internet www.ucn.dk; schools of business, education, health, nursing, social studies, technology; 600 teachers; 10,005 students; Rector NIELS HORSTED.

Professionshøjskolen Syddanmark (University College South Denmark): Degnevej 16, 6705 EsbjergØ; tel. 72-66-20-00; e-mail ucsyd@ucsyd.dk; internet ucsyd.dk; offers study programmes in the fields of education, health, science, social science and science communication; campuses in Haderslev, Esbjerg, Kolding, Aabenraa and Sønderborg; 6,500 students; Rector BIRTHE FRIIS MORTENSEN.

Rudolf Steiner Børnehaveseminariet: Johannevej 20, 2920 Charlottenlund; tel. 39-63-21-37; e-mail steinerseminar@mail.tele.dk; internet www.steinerseminar.dk.

Skolen for Holistisk Afspænding (School for Holistic Relaxation): c/o Røder Bartholinsgade 5, 2. tv., 1356 København K; tel. 24-26-03-07; e-mail post@holisterne.dk; internet holisterne.dk; f. 1976.

Syddansk Erhvervsskole (SDE College): Munke Mose Allé 9, 5000 Odense C; tel. 70-10-99-00; e-mail sde@sde.dk; internet www.sde.dk; f. 2008 by merger of Odense Technical College (Odense Tekniske Skole, f. 1844) with Vejle Technical College (Vejle Tekniske Skole, f. 1855); 45 programmes under vocational education divided into 10 basic fields; professional higher education; upper secondary technical education in Grindsted, Odense and Vejle; 5,000 students; Dir NIELS HENNING OLSEN.

University College Zealand: Slagelsevej 7, 4180 Soroe; tel. 72-48-10-00; internet ucsj.dk; f. 2007; offers courses in teaching, social education and social work, leisure management, nursing, nutrition and health physiotherapy, occupational therapy and biomedical laboratory science; 4 campuses: Roskilde, Slagelse, Næstved, Storstrøm; 11,000 students; Rector ULLA KOCH; Pro-Rector LENA VENBORG PEDERSEN.

VIA University College: Skejbyvej 1, 8240 Risskov; tel. 87-55-00-00; e-mail viauc@viauc.dk; internet www.viauc.dk; f. 2008 by merger of Alpha Centre for Higher Education, the Mid-West Centre for Higher Education, the Vita Centre for Higher Education, the University College Jutland, Vitus Bering Denmark and TEKO; faculties of education and social studies, health sciences, performing arts; school of technology and business; library: 500,000 vols, 17,000 ejournals; 2,100 teachers; 17,000 students; Rector HARALD MIKKELSEN; Vice-Rector PETER FRIESE; Univ. College Dir ASBJØRN CHRISTENSEN.

Voksen Pædagogisk Center (Adult Educational Centre): Artillerivej 126, 4th Fl.,

2300, Copenhagen S; tel. 32-68-73-33; e-mail vpc@vpckk.dk; internet www.vpckk.dk; offers courses and training for people who want to work as managers, employees and board memrs in voluntary asscns and within public education frameworks; Chair. CLAUS MICHAELSEN.

Colleges, Schools of Art and Music

Århus Kunstakademi (Aarhus Art Academy): Vestergade 29, 8000 Aarhus C; tel. 86-13-81-44; e-mail info@aarhuskunstakademi.dk; internet www.aarhuskunstakademi.dk; f. 1963; offers 4-year programme of artistic training; 1,210 students; Rector ESBEN KULLBERG.

Arkitektskolen i Århus (Århus School of Architecture): Nørreport 20, 8000 Århus C; tel. 89-36-00-00; e-mail a@aarch.dk; internet aarch.dk; f. 1965; attached to Min. of Culture; offers courses in architectural design, planning, furniture and industrial design; library: 44,000 vols, 170 journals; 160 teachers; 850 students; Rector TORBEN NIELSEN; Pro-Rector CHARLOTTE BUNDGAARD; publs *Skolehåndbogen* (1 a year), *Virksomhedsregnskab* (1 a year).

Danske Filmskole (National Film School of Denmark): Theodor Christensens Plads 1, 1437 Copenhagen K; tel. 32-68-64-00; e-mail infoz@filmskolen.dk; internet www.filmskolen.dk; f. 1966; attached to Min. of Culture; films, television, script writing and animation direction; 100 students; Dir POUL NESGAARD.

Danske Musicalakademi har Fredericia (Danish Academy of Musical Theatre, Fredericia): Kongensgade 107, 7000 Fredericia; tel. 75-91-53-30; e-mail mail@musicalakademiet.dk; internet www.musicalakademiet.dk; f. 2000; offers full-time courses in singing, dancing and acting; Chair. Prof. ERIK KALTOFT; Vice-Chair. Prof. JOHN BECH HANSEN; Vice-Chancellor HELGE REINHARDT; Dir GEIR SVEAASS.

Designskolen Kolding (Kolding Design School): Ågade 10, 6000 Kolding; tel. 76-30-11-00; e-mail dk@designskolenkolding.dk; internet www.designskolenkolding.dk; f. 1967 as Kunsthåndværkerskole (Arts and Crafts School), current name adopted 1998, current status 2010; attached to Min. of Science, Innovation and Higher Education; offers courses in graphic design, illustration design, fashion design, textile design, industrial design, interactive design; library: 20,000 vols, 60 periodicals; 390 students; Rector ELSEBETH GERNER NIELSEN.

Forfatterskolen (Author School): Peder Skrams Gade 2A, 1, 1054 Copenhagen K; tel. 28-51-36-00; e-mail forfatterskolen@forfatterskolen.dk; internet www.forfatterskolen.dk; f. 1987; offers a 2-year artistic education, which is based on each student's artistic potential; literary writing techniques, general knowledge of literature, and the authors' terms and conditions; Rector PABLO LLAMBIAS.

Fynske Kunstakademi (Funen Art Academy): Brandts Torv 1, 4th Fl., POB 1213, 5100 Odense C; tel. 66-11-12-88; e-mail info@detfynskekunstakademi.dk; internet www.funenartacademy.com; f. 1944 as Odense Drawing and Painting School, current name adopted 1954; offers 5-year higher education in contemporary visual arts; Rector MERETE JANKOWSKI.

Jyske Kunstakademi (Jutland Art Academy): Mejlgade 32-34, 8000 Århus C; tel. 86-13-69-19; e-mail djk@djk.nu; internet www.djk.nu; offers 5-year educational programme in contemporary art; Chair. Prof. Dr LENE TORTZEN BAGER; Rector JESPER RASMUSSEN.

Jyske Musikkonservatorium (Royal Academy of Music): Skovgaardsgade 2C, 8000 Århus C; tel. 72-26-74-00; e-mail mail@musikkons.dk; internet www.musikkons.dk; f. 2010 by merger of Northern Acad. of Music (f. 1927) in Aalborg and Royal Acad. of Music (f. 1930) in Aarhus; attached to Min. of Culture; 3 main areas of study: classical music, rhythmic music and electronic music; Prin. THOMAS WINTHER; Admin. Dir KIRSTEN PRÆSTEGAARD.

KaosPilots: Mejlgade 35, 8000 Aarhus C; tel. 86-12-95-22; e-mail kaos@kaospilot.dk; internet www.kaospilot.dk; f. 1991; focuses on business and strategy devt, innovation-process design and consultation, organizational work, marketing and product devt, event and project management; Programme Dir JON TANGEN.

Københavns Mode-og Design Skole (Copenhagen Academy of Fashion Design): Noerrebrogade 45, First Fl., 2200 Copenhagen N; tel. 33-32-88-10; e-mail info@modeogdesignskolen.dk; internet www.modeogdesignskolen.dk; f. 1983; advanced course in fashion and design; Prin. MARIANNE DUCHWAIDER.

Kongelige Danske Kunstakademis Skoler for Arkitektur, Design og Konservering-Arkitektskolen (Royal Danish Academy of Fine Arts, Schools of Architecture, Design and Conservation, School of Architecture): Philip de Langes Allé 10, 1435 Copenhagen K; tel. 32-68-60-00; e-mail info@kadk.dk; internet www.karch.dk; f. 1754 as The Royal Danish Painting, Sculpture and Building Acad., merger between the Royal Danish Acad. of Fine Arts, School of Architecture and the Danish Design School and the Royal Danish Acad. of Fine Arts, School of Conservation 2011, current name adopted 2011; offers Bachelors and Masters courses in architectural design and restoration, urban and landscape planning, and industrial, graphic and furniture design; library: see under Libraries and Archives; 1,100 students; Rector LENE DAMMAND LUND; Pro-Rector SVEND LAWAETZ.

Kongelige Danske Musikkonservatorium (Royal Danish Academy of Music): Rosenørns Allé 22, 1970 Frederiksberg C; tel. 72-26-72-26; e-mail dkdm@dkdm.dk; internet www.dkdm.dk; f. 1867, present status 1948; pedagogical training with a view to professional music teaching; specialized courses in the fields of music teaching, composition, conducting and church music, as well as recording direction; library: 50,000 vols; 170 teachers; 400 students; Prin. BERTEL KRARUP; Admin. Dir CARSTEN RUBY; Librarian MUSSE MAGNUSSEN SVARE.

Løgumkloster Kirkemusikskole (Løgumkloster Church Music School): Vestergade 9-13, 6240 Løgumkloster; tel. 74-74-40-70; e-mail lkms@km.dk; internet www.kirkemusikskole.dk; f. 1979; choir and organ training education; library: 5,000 vols on organ music and music for mixed choir, with emphasis on music history and organ literature; Rector HANS CHRISTIAN HEIN; Man. Dir MINNA B. SØNDERGAARD.

Margrethe-Skolen (Scandinavian Academy of International Fashion and Design): Aps Østergade 53-55, 1100 Copenhagen; tel. 33-13-09-26; e-mail info@margrethe-skolen.dk; internet www.margrethe-skolen.dk; provides training for fashion and design courses; Dir CHRISTINA BECKMAN.

Rytmisk Musikkonservatorium (Rhythmic Music Conservatory): Leo Mathisens Vej 1, Holmen, 1437 Copenhagen K; tel. 32-68-67-00; e-mail rmc@rmc.dk; internet www.rmc.dk; f. 1986; attached to Min. of Culture; degree programmes in the field of contemporary music—music performance, music education, music and movement education, music technology and music management; 30 teachers; 196 students; Chair HENRIK DALDORPH.

Sjællands Kirkemusikskole (Zealand Church Music School): Allehelgensgade 8, 4000 Roskilde; tel. 46-32-03-08; e-mail sjkms@km.dk; internet www.kirkemusikskole.dk/sjaelland; f. 1993; trains organists, church singers and church choir leaders on base and competency levels; offers regular short courses for church employees; Rector OLE BRINTH.

Statens Scenekunstskole (Danish National School of Performing Arts): Per Knutzons Vej 5, 1437 Copenhagen K; tel. 41-72-20-00; e-mail post@teaterskolen.dk; internet www.teaterskolen.dk; attached to Min. of Culture; trains actors, directors, scenographers, stage managers, production managers, sound and lighting technicians, contemporary dancers, choreographers and dance partnership students; 120 students; Rector SVERRE RØDAHL; Vice-Rector HENNING SPROGØE.

Syddansk Musikkonservatorium and Skuespillerskole (Southern Academy of Music and Dramatic Arts (SMKS)): Island St 2, 5000 Odense C.; tel. 63-11-99-00; e-mail info@smks.dk; internet www.smks.dk; f. 2010 by merger of Acad. of Music, Carl Nielsen Acad. of Music and Nat. School of Acting at Odense Theatre; attached to Min. of Culture; music and performing arts programmes; library: 2 library brs in Odense and Esbjerg; 50 teachers; 300 students; Chair. BIRGIT BERGHOLT; Rector AXEL MOMME.

Tekstilhåndværkerskolen i Aalborg (Textile Crafts School in Aalborg): Nørregade 31, 9000 Aalborg; tel. 98-16-82-83; e-mail post@tekstil-hs.dk; internet www.tekstil-hs.dk; f. 1980; clothing design and model construction with emphasis on the craft skills.

Vestervig Kirkemusikskole (Vestervig Church Music School): Skindbjerg High 1, 7770 Vestervig; tel. 97-94-16-85; e-mail vvkms@km.dk; internet www.kirkemusikskole.dk/vestervig; f. 1980; offers training and courses for organists, church singers, priests and other employees of the church; library: 5,000 vols; Rector IVAR MÆLAND.

FAROE ISLANDS

The Higher Education System

The Faroe Islands have been under Danish administration since Queen Margrethe I of Denmark inherited Norway in 1380 (although they were briefly occupied by the United Kingdom during the Second World War). Under the Home Rule Act of 1948 the Faroe Islands became a self-governing community in the Kingdom of Denmark. According to the Act, so-called Joint Matters (the judiciary, defence and foreign affairs) are under the authority of the Danish Government, whereas Special Matters (financial, economic and cultural matters, industry, foreign trade and natural resources in the subsoil) are under the control of the Faroese Government. Education-related issues were originally classified as matters of joint interest, which often led to unclear administrative processes. In the late 1990s, administration of the entire Faroese education sector was finally transferred to the Faroese Government. The education system in the Faroe Islands mainly follows the same model as the Danish system; however, the study content and quality assurance is organized locally. The Ministry of Education, Research and Culture is responsible for all levels of education. The country's only university—the state-run University of the Faroe Islands—was established in 1965 in the capital, Tórshavn.

The University comprises two faculties: Humanities, Social Sciences and Education, and Natural and Health Sciences, all of which offer Bachelors, Masters and doctoral courses. The University has also recently incorporated the Faroe Islands' Teacher Training College (founded 1870), which offers courses lasting three-and-a-half or four years, the School of Nursing (which was founded in 1960, offers four-year courses and is recognized by the Danish health authorities) and the Nursery Teacher Training College, which offers three-year courses. It was planned that in the near future these three institutions would offer Bachelors degree programmes. The language of instruction is Faroese and there are currently around 600 students enrolled at the newly expanded University. The University works closely with the University of Copenhagen and the University of Greenland in research projects. The University's operating costs are covered by an annual allocation from the Faroese national budget. Other higher education institutions include the Centre of Maritime Studies and Engineering and the Fire-fighting Training Centre, which together form a single administrative unit; and several colleges and institutes offering basic vocational courses in the fields of business, technology, commerce, fisheries and health education. A number of apprenticeship training programmes in a variety of fields are also available in the Faroes. A significant number of Faroese students study abroad, mainly in Denmark, but in recent years increasingly in other countries, such as the United Kingdom. The Government pays the tuition fees of Faroese students who undertake their further education outside the Nordic countries.

The general access requirement to higher education in the Faroe Islands is the completion of 12 years of school education, including the secondary school leaving examination or comparable qualification. In line with a regulation issued in 2003, all degrees offered at the University of the Faroe Islands now comply with the objectives of the Bologna Process. At undergraduate level, all Bachelors degree programmes take three years to complete, while, at postgraduate level, Masters degrees take a further two years. The University also offers courses leading to award of the Doctorate, which usually takes four years.

New legislation on courses organized within technical apprenticeship training was passed in 2004. The Vocational Education Board, which consists of employers and public authorities, authorizes the establishment of new training courses when required. However, the Board itself cannot set up new courses.

Regulatory and Representative Bodies

GOVERNMENT

Ministry of Education, Research and Culture: Hoyvíksvegur 72, POB 3279, FO110 Tórshavn; tel. 306500; e-mail mmr@mmr.fo; internet www.mmr.fo; Minister BJØRN KALSØ.

Learned Societies

GENERAL

Faroe Islands Art Society: c/o Listasavn Føroya, POB 1141, FO110 Tórshavn; tel. 313579; e-mail info@art.fo; internet art.fo/en/listafelag_foroya.php; f. 1941; attached to Faroe Islands Art Museum; encourages and helps educate about pictorial art forms; Chair. MALAN MARNERSDÓTTIR; Sec. JÓANNES LAMHAUGE; Treas. HILMAR HØGENNI.

Føroya Fróðskaparfelag/Societas Scientiarum Faeroensis (Faroese Society of Science and Letters): POB 209, FO110 Tórshavn; tel. 322074; e-mail fff@frodskaparfelag.fo; internet www.frodskaparfelag.fo; f. 1952; procures scientific and scholarly literature and promotes research work; 170 mems; Pres. Dr ANDRAS MORTENSEN; publs *Fróðskaparrit* (1 a year), *Supplementa*.

Føroysk Myndlistafólk (Faroese Society of Visual Arts): POB 120, FO110 Tórshavn; e-mail mynd@mynd.fo; internet www.mynd.fo; f. 1981; attached to Faroe Islands Art Museum; increases cooperation amongst Faroese artists; improves the circumstances and situation of Faroese visual arts; holds an annual spring exhibition; 40 mems; Chair. OLE WICH; Sec. VÍGDIS PEDERSEN; Treas. SIGRUN GUNNARSDÓTTIR NICLASEN.

HISTORY, GEOGRAPHY AND ARCHAEOLOGY

Føroya Forngripafelag (Faroese Archaeological Society): POB 1173, FO110 Tórshavn; tel. 340500; e-mail savn@savn.fo; f. 1898; attached to Føroya Fornminnissavn (Historical Museum); works in conjunction with the Nat. Museum of Antiquities; Pres. MORTAN WINTHER POULSEN.

LANGUAGE AND LITERATURE

Rithøvundafelag Føroya (Faroese Writers' Association): Lützenstrøð 4, FO100 Tórshavn; e-mail rit@rit.fo; internet www.rit.fo; f. 1957; promotes the growth of Faroese literature and protects authors' rights; 117 mems; Pres. HELLE THEDE JOHANSEN.

Research Institutes

AGRICULTURE, FISHERIES AND VETERINARY SCIENCE

Havstovan (Faroe Marine Research Institute): Nóatún 1, POB 3051, FO110 Tórshavn; tel. 353900; e-mail hav@hav.fo; internet www.hav.fo; f. 1951; attached to Govt of the Faroe Islands; depts of environment, fisheries and technology; Dir EILIF GAARD; publ. *Fiskirannsóknir* (irregular).

Heilsufrøðiliga Starvsstovan (Faroese Food and Veterinary Agency): Falkavegur 6, 2 hædd, FO100 Tórshavn; tel. 556400; e-mail hfs@hfs.fo; internet www.hfs.fo; f. 1975; research, services, quality control and inspection in the fish and food industry and in the environment; govt dept; Dir BARÐUR ENNI.

Libraries and Archives

Tórshavn

Býarbókasavnið (Tórshavn Public Library): Niels Finsens Gøtu 7, POB 358, FO110 Tórshavn; tel. 302030; e-mail bbs@bbs.fo; internet www.bbs.fo; f. 1969; 74,958 vols; City Librarian ARNBJØRN ÓLAVSSON DALSGARÐ.

Føroya Landsbókasavn (National Library of the Faroe Islands): J. C. Svabosgøtu 16, POB 61, FO110 Tórshavn; tel. 340525; e-mail flb@savn.fo; internet www.flb.fo; f. 1828; attached to Govt of the Faroe Islands; responsible for 15 public and 11 school libraries; 173,000 vols; Exec. Dir ERHARD JACOBSEN; Nat. Deputy Librarian ANNIKA SMITH; publ. *Føroyskur Bókalisti* (list of Faeroese publs, 1 a year).

Landsskjalasavnið (Faroese National Archives): V. U. Hammershaimbsgøta 24, FO100 Tórshavn; tel. 340540; e-mail fararch@savn.fo; internet www.lss.fo; f. 1932; medieval documents (1298–1599), archives of parliament and central and local admin. (1615–1980); Dir SÁMAL T. F. JOHANSEN; Archivist JOHN KJÆR.

Museums and Art Galleries

Gøtu

Gøtu Fornminnissavn (Gøta Museum): POB 25, FO510 Gøta; tel. 222717; e-mail blasastova@blasastova.fo; internet www.blasastova.fo; aspects of Gøta's history seen through 4 exhibits: Blásastova, Hjá Glyvra Hanusi, Hjá Peri, Jákupsstova.

Tórshavn

Føroya Fornminnissavn (National Museum of Archaeology and Cultural History): Kúrdalsvegur 15, POB 1155, FO110 Tórshavn; tel. 340500; e-mail savn@savn.fo; internet www.fornminni.fo; f. 1898, taken over by State 1952; archaeology, ethnology, inspection of ancient monuments; Dir ANDRAS MORTENSEN; Museum Curator ERLAND VIBERG JOENSEN.

Føroya Náttúrugripasavn (Natural History Museum): V. U. Hammershaimbsgøtaa 13, FO100 Tórshavn; tel. 340500; e-mail ngs@savn.fo; internet www.ngs.fo; f. 1955; attached to Min. of Education, Research and Culture; researches and collects to create awareness about Faroese natural history through exhibits; Dir Dr DORETE BLOCH.

Listasavn Føroya (Faroe Islands Art Museum): Gundadalsvegur 9, POB 1141, FO110 Thorshavn; tel. 313579; e-mail info@art.fo; internet art.fo; f. 1989; modern and early Faroese pictorial art; Chair. MARTIN NÆS; Dir NILS OHRT; Curator MORTAN OLASON VANG.

Savnið 1940–45 (Faroe-British Museum): POB 362, FO110 Tórshavn; tel. 312074; f. 1983; military and civilian artefacts from British occupation during Second World War (1939–45).

University

FRÓDSKAPARSETUR FØROYA/ UNIVERSITAS FÆROENSIS (University of the Faroe Islands)

J. C. Svabos Gøta 14, POB 272, FO100 Tórshavn
Telephone: 352500
E-mail: setur@setur.fo
Internet: setur.fo
Founded 1965
Language of instruction: Faroese
Academic year: August to June
Faculties of humanities, social sciences and education, natural and health sciences
Rector: JÓAN PAULI JOENSEN
Vice-Rector: SÚSANNA M. MORTENSEN
Univ. Dir and Sec.-Gen.: RÚNA HJELM
Chair.: HERÁLVUR JOENSEN
Number of teachers: 65
Number of students: 475

PROFESSORS

ANDREASSEN, E., Oral Literature
BLOCH, D., Zoology
BROWN, R. J., Geophysics
HANSEN, B., Oceanography
JOENSEN, J. P., History and Ethnology
MARNERSDÓTTIR, M., Literature
SIGURDARDÓTTIR, T., Literature
SPARRE ANDERSEN, M., Geophysics

GREENLAND

The Higher Education System

Greenland first came under Danish rule in 1380. In the revision of the Danish Constitution in 1953, Greenland became part of the Kingdom of Denmark. In 1975 the Minister for Greenland appointed a commission to devise terms for Greenland home rule, and its proposals were approved in a referendum among the Greenland electorate in January 1979. From that year the island gradually assumed full administration of its internal affairs. At another referendum held in Greenland on 25 November 2008 the Act on Greenland Self-rule was approved by the electorate and entered into force the following year. Responsibility for foreign affairs, defence, rulings by the Danish Supreme Court and policies regarding currency remains with the Danish Government.

The educational system closely follows that of Denmark, except that the main language of instruction is Greenlandic. Danish is, however, widely used. Greenland's only university—the state-funded University of Greenland—was established in the capital, Nuuk, in 1974. The University, which had an enrolment of around just 150 students in 2007, comprises three departments: learning, nursing and health sciences, and Ilimmarfik. The University awards Bachelors degrees in all four departments and Masters degrees in all departments except for Theology. A small number of students also undertake Doctorate programmes leading to the award of a PhD. Most courses at the University are taught in Danish and only a few in Greenlandic. The small enrolment rate is due in part to the Government's policy of providing students a free university education anywhere in Europe or North America; the majority of Greenlandic students choose to pursue their further education in Denmark. There is also a teacher training college (Ilinniarfissuaq) in Nuuk, which was established in 1845 and has an enrolment of around 130 students and a Business School (Niuernermik Ilinniarfik). The Agency of Industry, Labour Market and Vocational Education and Training (AoILVET) is responsible for education in Greenland.

The general access requirement to higher education in Greenland is the completion of 12 years of school education, including the secondary school leaving examination or comparable qualification. Three levels of degree are awarded at the University of Greenland: a Bachelors degree after three years, a Masters after an additional two and a PhD after about a further four years (the number of students undertaking the doctoral course, however, is very limited).

There are a number of vocational schools offering courses over two years providing trainee-level workers. Alternatively, students can continue at school for an additional two years and take a Journeyman examination. The schools cover a variety of areas including construction, engineering, fishing, navigation, sheep farming and the food industry.

In 2006 the Greenlandic Parliament adopted the Greenland Education Programme (2006–20) (GEP), in order to improve levels of academic attainment in Greenland. The GEP aimed to ensure that two-thirds of the working population had academic qualifications or vocational skills by 2020. The second phase of the programme (2013–20) was to focus on higher education.

Regulatory Body

GOVERNMENT

Ministry of Education, Church, Culture and Gender Equality: POB 1029, 3900 Nuuk; tel. (299) 345000; e-mail iiknn@nanoq.gl; Minister NICK NIELSEN.

Learned Societies

GENERAL

Grønlandske Selskab (The Greenland Society): see under Denmark.

Nunani Avannarlerni Piorsarsimassutsikkut Attaveqaat (NAPA)/Nordens Institut i Grønland (The Nordic Institute of Greenland): Imaneq 21, POB 770, 3900 Nuuk; tel. 324733; e-mail napa@napa.gl; internet www.napa.gl; f. 1987; Dir (vacant); Chair. VIVIAN MOEN; Deputy Chair. KIM LARSEN; Man. LEISE JOHNSEN.

BIBLIOGRAPHY, LIBRARY SCIENCE AND MUSEOLOGY

NUKAKA–Nunatsinni Katersugaasiviit Kattuffiat/Sammenslutningen af museer i Grønland (Association of Museums in Greenland): c/o Nunatta Katersugaasivia Allagaateqarfialu, POB 145, 3900 Nuuk; tel. 322611; e-mail bo@natmus.gl; internet www.nukaka.gl; f. 1993; supports the interests and devt of archives, local and spec. museums; Chair. CAR-ERIK HOLM; Sec. BO ALBRECHTSEN; Treas. OLE G. JENSEN.

EDUCATION

Center for Vejledning i Grønland (Centre for Guidance in Greenland): Jagtvej 40, POB 1038, 3900 Nuuk; tel. 523639; e-mail cvg@ninuuk.gl; internet www.vejledning.gl; f. 2002; offers counselling degrees; competence devt for counselling groups; support for counsellors in urban and rural sectors; Centre Leader and Lecturer BETH KROGH.

FINE AND PERFORMING ARTS

'Simerneq' (Artists' Society): POB 1009, 3900 Nuuk; f. 1979; Sec. INGER HAUGE.

LANGUAGE AND LITERATURE

Kalaallit Atuakkiortut/Den Grønlandske Forfatterforening (Greenlandic Authors' Society): c/o ICC, Dronning Ingridsvej 1, POB 25, 3900 Nuuk; tel. 323632; e-mail kalatu@greennet.gl; internet www.atuakkiortut.gl; f. 1975; copyrights for authors and translators; writing workshops and poetry festivals fostering interest in poetry among the youth; 80 mems; Pres. HANS A. LYNGE; Chair. AQQALUK LYNGE; Sec. KARL ELIAS OLSEN; Treas. T. P. POULSEN; publ. *Kalaaleq* (magazine).

Research Institutes

AGRICULTURE, FISHERIES AND VETERINARY SCIENCE

Forsøgsstationen 'Upernaviarsuk' (Upernaviarsuk Agricultural Research Station): POB 152, 3920 Qaqortoq; tel. (299) 649303; e-mail hh@nunalerineq.gl; govt instn carrying out experiments in sheep rearing, fodder crops, tree planting and gardening in a polar environment.

MEDICINE

Greenland Institute for Circumpolar Health Research: Peqqissaannermik Ilinniarfik, POB 1499, 3900 Nuuk; e-mail gihr@peqqik.gl; internet www.pi.gl/da/greenland_institute_f_circumpolar_health_research; f. 2008; attached to Peqqissaannermik Ilinniarfik; enhances cooperation between researchers from other countries and health professionals in Greenland; develops, exchanges, disseminates and applies scientific knowledge; creates nat. and int. networks; Chair. KARIN LADEFOGED; Vice-Chair. and Sec. GERT MULVAD; Research Dir Prof. PETER BJERREGAARD; Treas. SUZANNE MØLLER.

NATURAL SCIENCES

General

Kommissionen for Videnskabelige Undersøgelser i Grønland (Commission for Scientific Research in Greenland): Centre for Strategic Research and Growth, Bredgade 40, 1260 Copenhagen K, Denmark; tel. 35446200; e-mail fi@fi.dk; internet www.fi.dk/raad-og-udvalg/kommissionen-for-videnskabelige-undersoegelser-i-groenland; f. 1878; attached to Danish Agency for Science, Technology and Innovation; Chair. Prof. MINIK T. ROSING; Deputy Chair. DANIEL THORLEIFSEN; publ. *Grønlandsforskning historie og perspektiver*.

Biological Sciences

Arctic Station, University of Copenhagen: see under Denmark.

Grønlands Naturinstitut/Pinngortitaleriffik (Greenland Institute of Natural Resources): POB 570, 3900 Nuuk; tel. 361200; e-mail info@natur.gl; internet www.natur.gl; applied research in natural resources, environmental protection and biodiversity; depts of birds and mammals, fish and shrimp, marine ecology and climate impact; Dir KLAUS HOYER NYGAARD.

Physical Sciences

Danmarks Meteorologiske Institut (Danish Meteorological Institute): see under Denmark.

Greenland Climate Research Centre (GCRC): c/o Greenland Institute of Natural Resources, Kivioq 2, POB 570, 3900 Nuuk; tel. 361200; e-mail gcrc@natur.gl; internet www.natur.gl/en/climate-research-centre; f. 2009; concerned with the expected impacts of climate change on Arctic marine, limnic and terrestrial environments and on Greenlandic soc.; incl. adaptation and prevention strategies; Head of Centre SØREN RYSGAARD; Deputy Head of Centre PETER SCHMIDT MIKKELSEN.

Libraries

Nuuk

Groenlandica (Greenlandic National Library): Manutooq 1, POB 1074, 3900 Nuuk; tel. 3385630; e-mail groenlandica@katak.gl; internet www.groenlandica.gl; f. 2008; attached to Nunatta Atuagaateqarfia Central and Public Library of Greenland); collects, records and stores all Greenlandic literature and publs; colln of foreign literature and information about Inuit and the Arctic area; nat. colln; spec. collns: Samuel Petrus Kleinschmidts Reference Library and Archive, The Oldendow Colln, Svend Frederiksen's Archive, The Jonathan Petersen Colln, The Frederik Nielsen (Faré) Colln; 90,637 items incl. books, MSS and photographs; Head CHARLOTTE D. ANDERSON; Librarian SISSEL GRAM; Librarian KIRSTEN HEILMANN.

Nunatta Atuagaateqarfia/Grønlandske Landsbibliotek (National Library of Greenland): Imaneq 26, POB 1011, 3900 Nuuk; tel. 321156; e-mail nalib@katak.gl; internet www.katak.gl; 70,426 vols; Dir ELISA JEREMIASSEN; Librarian KIRSTEN BIRKEFOSS.

Museums

Aasiaat

Aasiaat Museum: Niels Egedesvej 2, 3950 Aasiaat; tel. 894762; e-mail aasmus@qaasuitsup.gl; internet www.aasiaatmuseum.gl; f. 1978, current location 2000; promotes the historic cultural heritage of the town; art, artefacts, domestic crafts, photo exhibitions.

Ilulissat

Ilulissat Museum: Nuisariannguaq 9, POB 99, 3952 Ilulissat; tel. 943643; e-mail ilumus@ilulissat.gl; f. 1979; local, cultural and natural history; cultural history of the N Greenlandic sledgedog and the Sermermiut settlement; library and archive of photographs and materials on Knud Rasmussen; Curator and Head of Museum Mag. KIRSTEN STRANDGAARD.

Kangilinnguit

Ivittuut Mine- og Mineralmuseum (Ivittuut Mining and Mineral Museum): 3930 Kangilinnguit; tel. 691077; e-mail museum.ivittuut@sermersooq.gl; f. 2006; Pres. PER NUKAARAQ HANSEN; Curator and Man. ANE BONDE ROLSTED.

Nuuk

Nunatta Katersugaasivia Allagaateqarfialu/Grønlands Nationalmuseum og Arkiv (Greenland National Museum and Archive): Hans Egedesvej 8, POB 145, 3900 Nuuk; tel. 322611; e-mail nka@natmus.gl; internet www.natmus.gl; f. 1966; collns cover the 4,500 years of history in Greenland; collns: Inuit Archaeological Collns, Norse Collns, Gustav Holm Colln (Ammassalik c. 1880), Inughuit and Polareskimos (c. 1900), kayaks; arts, handicrafts and photographic colln; Dir DANIEL THORLEIFSEN; Deputy Dir GEORG NYGAARD; Curator AVIAAJA ROSING JAKOBSEN.

Nuuk Kunstmuseum/Nuup Katersugaasivii (Nuuk Artmuseum): Kissarneqqortuunnguaq 5, POB 1005, 3900 Nuuk; tel. 327733; e-mail kunstm@greennet.gl; internet www.nuukkunstmuseum.gl; f. 2005 by Svend and Helen Junge; displays Svend and Helen Junge's 45-year colln of 300 pictures, paintings, drawings and graphics, 400 sculptures made of soapstone, tooth and wood, colln of 150 paintings by Emanuel A. Petersen (1894–1948).

Qaqortoq

Qaqortoq Museum: Torvevej B-29, POB 154, 3920 Qaqortoq; tel. 641080; e-mail oljn@kujalleq.gl; Dir OLE G. JENSEN.

Qasigiannguit

Qasigiannguit Katersugaasiviat/Qasigiannguit lokalmuseum (Qasigiannguit Museum): Poul Egedesvej 24, POB 130, 3951 Qasigiannguit; tel. 911477; e-mail qasmus@qaasuitsup.gl; Dir ANNE METTE OLSVIG.

Upernavik

Upernaviup Katersugaasivia (Upernavik Museum): Niuertup Ottup Aqq. B-12, POB 93, 3962 Upernavik; tel. 961085; e-mail inussuk@greennet.gl; f. c. 1950; colln of photographs, historical objects, items representing Greenland's hunting culture; Upernavik Retreat: artists' residence.

University

ILISIMATUSARFIK/GRØNLANDS UNIVERSITET
(University of Greenland)

Manutooq 1, POB 1061, 3905 Nuuk
Telephone: 362300
E-mail: mail@uni.gl
Internet: www.uni.gl

Founded 1984, fmrly Inuit Institut, current name and univ. status 1989
State control
Languages of instruction: Danish, English, Greenlandic

Dept of nursing and health sciences, learning, Ilimmarfik Institute that incl. journalism, language, literature and media, social and cultural history, social science, social work, theology, translation and interpretation

Rector: TINE PARS
Pro-Rector: UFFE JAKOBSEN
Pres.: MINIK ROSING
Univ. Dir: ESTRID JANUSSEN
Chair. for the Board: TOVE SØVNDAHL PEDERSEN
Pro-Vice-Chancellor: KAREN LANGGÅRD
Univ. Librarian: BOLETHE OLSEN

Library of 33,000 vols, 90 journals
Number of teachers: 64
Number of students: 635

Publication: *Grønlandsk Kultur- og Samfundsforskning* (Greenlandic Culture and Society Research, 1 a year)

Colleges

Arctic Technology Centre (ARTEK): Sanaartornermik Ilinniarfik, POB 1001, 3911 Sisimiut; tel. 864488; e-mail hahi@sanilin.gl; internet www.arktiskcenter.gl; f. 2000 as a collaboration between Sanaartornermik Ilinniarfik (the Building and Construction School) in Sisimiut and the Technical Univ. of Denmark (DTU); educates engineers and carries out research and innovation projects in Arctic technology; activities are anchored both in Greenland and in Denmark at DTU; is organizationally part of the dept of Civil Engineering (DTU BYG); Head of Centre CARL EGEDE BØGGILD.

Eqqumiitsuliornermik Ilinniarfik/Kunstskolen (School of Arts): c/o KIIIP, POB 286, 3900 Nuuk; tel. 322640; e-mail kunst@greennet.gl; f. 1973; Dir ARNANNGUAQ HØEGH.

Ilinniarfissuaq/Grønlands Seminarium (Greenlands Teacher-Training College): C. E. Jansensvej 2, POB 1026, 3900 Nuuk; tel. 321191; e-mail ilinnia@teachnet.gl; internet www.ilinniarfissuaq.gl; f. 1845; attached to Univ. of Greenland; pedagogical, social and administrative education and in-service training; 25 teachers; 163 students; Rector TINE PARS; Vice-Rector UFFE JAKOBSEN; Dir ESTRID JANUSSEN; Chair. TOVE SØVNDAHL PEDERSEN; Librarian LIDA LORENTZEN.

Niuernermik Ilinniarfik/Grønlands Handelsskole (Greenland Business College): Aqqusinersuaq 18, POB 1038, 3900 Nuuk; tel. 323099; e-mail ninuuk@ninuuk.gl; internet www.ninuuk.gl; f. 1979; courses and in-service training in journalism, interpreting and mercantile matters, also technical mercantile training; library: 8,000 vols, 27 journal titles on finance, IT, management, marketing, personnel and sales; 15 full-time teachers; 250 full-time students; Dir BO NÓRRESLET; Librarian MALENE MUURMANN.

Oqaatsinik Pikkorissarfiup (Greenland Language School): Siimuup Aqq. 32, POB 3019, 3911 Sisimiut; tel. 866700; e-mail sprogcenter@oqaatsit.gl; internet www.oqaatsit.gl; Dir ANNE GOUL FROBERG (acting).

Peqqissaanermik Ilinniarfik (Centre for Health Studies): Centre for Sundhedsuddannelser, POB 1499, 3900 Nuuk; tel. 349950; e-mail cfspost@nanoq.gl; internet www.pi.gl; f. 1993; attached to Min. of Education, Research and Nordic Cooperation; 40 students; Superintendent LISA EZEKIASSEN; Dir for Nursing Education SUZANNE MILLER; Librarian HANNE KRISTOFFERSEN.

Socialpædagogisk Seminarium/Grønlands Socialpædagogiske Seminarium: POB 519, 3952 Ilulissat; tel. 946430; e-mail pi.sps@attat.gl; internet www.pi.sps.gl; attached to Perorsaanermik Ilinniarfik; Rector NUKA KLEEMANN; Deputy Man. and Head of Education ANDREAS EJLERSEN; Librarian REBEKAH ENØ FLIGHTS.

DJIBOUTI

The Higher Education System

Higher education in Djibouti is modelled after the French system. The sole university in Djibouti, the Université de Djibouti, was founded in 2006 to replace the Pôle Universitaire de Djibouti (which was established in 2000) and had 3,159 students in 2008/09 and more than 6,000 at the beginning of the 2012/13 academic year. The University has three faculties—law, economics and administration; arts, languages and social sciences; science—and an Institute of Technology. Higher education is the responsibility of the Ministry of Higher Education and Research.

The University offers undergraduate and postgraduate courses, and admission is on the basis of secondary school qualifications, including the Baccalauréat de l'Enseignement Secondaire, the Baccalauréat Technologique or the Baccalauréat Professionnel. Higher education degrees are divided into three cycles: the Licence is awarded after two to three years' study; and the Maîtrise requires a further two years of study. Currently, however, the third cycle—the Doctorat—is not available at the University. The mediums of instruction are French and Arabic.

Regulatory Bodies

GOVERNMENT

Ministry of Higher Education and Research: Djibouti; Minister Dr NABIL MOHAMMED AHMED.

Ministry of Islamic Affairs, Culture and Endowments: BP 32, 1 rue de Moscou, Djibouti; Minister ADEN HASSAN ADEN.

Ministry of National Education and Professional Training: BP 16, Cité Ministérielle, Djibouti; tel. 350997; e-mail menfop@education.gov.dj; internet www.education.gov.dj; Minister Dr DJAMA ELMI OKIEH.

Learned Society

LANGUAGE AND LITERATURE

Alliance Française: BP 56, Djibouti; tel. 353091; e-mail alliance-francaise@intnet.dj; offers courses and examinations in French language and culture and promotes cultural exchange with France.

Research Institute

GENERAL

Institut Supérieur d'Études et de Recherches Scientifiques et Techniques (ISERT): BP 486, Djibouti; tel. 352795; Dir NABIL MOHAMED.

Library

Djibouti

Assemblée Nationale, Service de la Bibliothèque: BP 138, Djibouti; tel. 350172; f. 1977; 2,000 vols; Librarian ILTIREH DJAMA GUIREH.

University

UNIVERSITÉ DE DJIBOUTI

Ave Georges Clemenceau, BP 1904, Djibouti

Telephone: 250459

Internet: www.univ.edu.dj

Founded 2000 as Pôle Universitaire de Djibouti, present name adopted 2006

Rector: AIDID ADEN GUEDI

Sec.-Gen.: PHILIPPE RIBIERE

Librarian: SAFIA ALI SAID

Number of teachers: 96

Number of students: 6,000

DIRECTORS

Faculty of Languages, Literature and Human Sciences: ABDOULMALIK IBRAHIM ZEID

Faculty of Law, Economics, Management and Tertiary Technological Procedures: Mag. TEEREY IBRAHIM

Faculty of Sciences and Industrial Technological Procedures: IBRAHIM SOULEIMAN GUILLEM

DOMINICA

The Higher Education System

The main provider of higher education is the Dominica State College, which was established in 2002 by merging four publicly owned tertiary education institutions (including a teacher-training college, a sixth-form college and a nursing school). In 2009 there were around 2,500 students enrolled at the college. There is also a centre of the University of the West Indies (UWI), and the Ross University School of Medicine in Dominica (affiliated to the Ross University School of Medicine, NJ, in the USA). In 2006/07 there were 218 students enrolled at the UWI Open Campus in Dominica.

At the Dominica State College the President is the chief academic and administrative officer. The other senior college officials are: the Vice-President for Academic Affairs, the Registrar, the Bursar and the Deans of the four Faculties. The daily administration of the college is vested in the Registrar. The Vice-President for Academic Affairs oversees the academic operations of each faculty. The College awards Associate degrees (equivalent to 60 credits) in its four faculties of arts and science, applied arts and technology, education, and health sciences; students may then transfer to one of the international universities (mainly American) with which the College has agreements to complete a further two years education to Bachelors degree level.

Admission to higher education is based on the Caribbean Examinations Council Secondary Education Certificate or GCE A-levels and O-levels. Students may also be required to sit an entrance examination. The University of the West Indies offers courses leading to the award of various certificates and diplomas, as well as undergraduate Bachelors and postgraduate Masters degrees.

Regulatory Bodies

GOVERNMENT

Ministry of Culture, Youth and Sports: Second Fl., Govt HQ, Kennedy Ave, Roseau; tel. 2663548; e-mail culture@dominica.gov.dm; internet culture.gov.dm; Minister JUSTINA CHARLES.

Ministry of Education and Human Resource Development: Second Fl., Govt HQ, Kennedy Ave, Roseau; tel. 2663256; e-mail education@dominica.gov.dm; Minister PETTER SAINT-JEAN.

Learned Society

LANGUAGE AND LITERATURE

Alliance Française: Elmshall Rd, Bath Estate Bridge, POB 251, Roseau; tel. 4484557; offers courses and examinations in French language and culture and promotes cultural exchange with France.

Library

Roseau

Library of the House of Assembly: Victoria St, Roseau; tel. 2663291; e-mail houseofassembly@dominica.gov.dm; f. 1968; 300 vols of parliamentary reports, Proceedings of the House, speeches, ministerial statements, debates, legislation.

Museum

Roseau

Dominica Museum: Bay Front, Roseau; tel. 4488923; exhibits on Dominica's geology, history, archaeology, economy and culture, including its pre-Columbian population and the slave trade.

University

ROSS UNIVERSITY SCHOOL OF MEDICINE IN DOMINICA

POB 266, Portsmouth
Telephone: 4455355
E-mail: admissions@rossu.edu
Internet: www.rossu.edu

New York Office: 460 West 34th St, 12th Floor, New York, NY 10001, USA
Telephone: (212) 279-5500 (New York)
Internet: www.rossmed.edu.dm

Attached to Ross University School of Medicine, NJ (USA)

Library of 5,000 books, 190 current journals, 100 audiovisual items, 30 multimedia programmes

College

University of the West Indies, Dominica Centre: University Centre, POB 82, Roseau; tel. 4483182; e-mail uwi@cwdom.dm; internet www.cavehill.uwi.edu/bnccde/dominica.

DOMINICAN REPUBLIC

The Higher Education System

The Universidad Autónoma de Santo Domingo, founded by Papal Bull in 1538, claims to be the oldest university in the Americas. Other universities in the Republic were all founded during the 20th century. There are 31 higher education institutions recognized by the Consejo Nacional de Educación Superior, Ciencia y Tecnologia (National Council for Higher Education, Science and Technology—CONESCYT). Higher education in the public sector is fully government funded and there is a possibility of part funding for private institutions. In 2001 Law no. 139-01 brought about a fundamental reform of the higher education system. Higher education institutions were classified into technical institutes, specialized institutes of higher education and universities, and a system of credits was established. In 2003/04 there were 293,565 students enrolled in higher education.

The secondary school qualification (Bachillerato) is the main requirement for admission to higher education. For the Licenciado a minimum of 140 credits are required. Some disciplines (architecture, law, dentistry, pharmacy, veterinary medicine and engineering) require a minimum of four years' study (200 credits), and medicine requires a minimum of five years' study. Postgraduate degrees include the Epecialidad, the Maestría, Master or Magíster, and the Doctorado, which is now awarded only for research-based theses. Both universities and technological institutes offer technical and vocational education. Courses last for two to three years (85 credits) and students gain the title Técnico. In 2009/10 there were 38,002 students enrolled in vocational studies.

In 2010 the Government agreed a US $100m. loan with the Inter-American Development Bank for school improvements as part of its 10-year plan for education.

Regulatory and Representative Bodies

GOVERNMENT

Ministry of Culture: A Centro de Eventos y Exposiciones, Avda George Washington, Esq. Presidente Vicini Burgos, Santo Domingo; tel. 221-4141; e-mail accesoainfo@sec.gob.do; internet www.cultura.gob.do; Minister JOSÉ ANTONIO RODRÍGUEZ.

Ministry of Education: Avda Máximo Gómez, Esq. Santiago No 02, Gazcue, Distrito Nacional, 10205 Santo Domingo; tel. 688-9700; e-mail mlibreacceso@see.gob.do; internet www.minerd.gob.do; Minister CARLOS AMARANTE BARET.

Ministry of Higher Education, Science and Technology: Avda Máximo Gómez 31, Esq. Pedro Henríquez Ureña, 11903 Santo Domingo, DN; tel. 731-1100; e-mail info@seescyt.gov.do; internet www.seescyt.gov.do; Minister LIGIA AMADA DE MELO.

NATIONAL BODY

Asociación Dominicana de Rectores de Universidades (Dominican Association of University Presidents): Apdo 2465, Santo Domingo, DN; Calle Juan Paradas Bonilla 5, Apto 3, tercer Nivel, Ensanche Naco, 11093 Santo Domingo; tel. 683-0003; e-mail adru@verizon.net.do; internet www.adru.org; f. 1980, present status 1981; 18 mem. univs and higher education institutes; Exec. Dir Ing. JOSÉ JORGE GOICO GERMOSÉN.

Learned Societies

GENERAL

Instituto de Cultura Dominicana: Biblioteca Nacional, César Nicolás Penson, 11903 Santo Domingo; f. 1971; promotes cultural tradition of the country, encourages artistic creation and the expression of the spirit of the Dominican people; Pres. ENRIQUE APOLINAR HENRÍQUEZ; Sec. PEDRO GIL ITURBIDES.

BIBLIOGRAPHY, LIBRARY SCIENCE AND MUSEOLOGY

Asociación Dominicana de Bibliotecarios, Inc. (Librarians' Association): c/o Biblioteca Nacional, Plaza de la Cultura, César Nicolás Penson 91, 11903 Santo Domingo; tel. 688-4086; f. 1974; develops library services in the Republic; increases the standing of the profession and encourages the training of its mems; 90 mems; Pres. PRÓSPERO J. MELLA CHAVIER; Sec. Gen. V. REGÚS; publ. *El Papiro* (4 a year).

Sociedad Dominicana de Bibliófilos: Calle Las Damas 106, 11903 Santo Domingo; internet bibliofilos.org.do; f. 1973; promotes culture and dissemination of works and productions; library of 13,951 vols; Pres. MARIANO MELLA; Sec. OCTAVIO AMIAMA; Treas. TOMÁS W. FERNÁNDEZ.

HISTORY, GEOGRAPHY AND ARCHAEOLOGY

Academia Dominicana de la Historia (Dominican Academy of History): Casa de las Academias, Calle Mercedes 204, Ciudad Colonial, 10210 Santo Domingo; tel. 689-7907; e-mail academiahis@codetel.net.do; internet www.academiahistoria.org.do; f. 1931; promotes knowledge and study of the past in gen. and esp. of the Dominican nation; 24 mems, 36 nat. corresp. mems, 210 foreign corresp. mems; Pres. Dr EMILIO CORDERO MICHEL; Admin. Man. VERONICA CASS; Exec. Sec. TESSIE BRENS; publ. *Clio* (2 a year).

LANGUAGE AND LITERATURE

Academia Dominicana de la Lengua (Dominican Academy of Letters): Casa de las Academias, Calle Mercedes 204, 11903 Santo Domingo; tel. 687-9197; e-mail info@academia.org.do; internet www.academia.org.do; f. 1927; Corresp. of the Real Academia Española (Madrid); studies and encourages the devt of the culture and language of Dominican Republic; 68 mems; library of 50,000 vols; Dir Dr BRUNO ROSARIO CANDELIER; Sec. MANUEL NÚÑEZ.

Alliance Française: Horacio Vicioso 103, Centro de los Heroes, 11903 Santo Domingo; tel. 532-2935; e-mail alianza.francesa@afsd.net; internet www.afsd.net; f. 1914; offers courses and examinations in French language and culture; promotes cultural exchange with France; attached offices in Higuey, Mao, Monte Cristi, San Francisco de Macoris and Santiago de los Caballeros; Hon. Pres. Pozzo Di Borgo S. E. CÉCILE; Pres. MARIO TOLENTINO DIPP; Vice-Pres. JOSEFINA PIMENTEL BOVES; Treas. SANTIAGO COLLADO CHASTEL.

MEDICINE

Asociación Médica de Santiago (Santiago Medical Association): Apdo 445, Santiago de los Caballeros; f. 1941; library of 1,500 vols; 65 mems; Pres. Dr RAFAEL FERNÁNDEZ LAZALA; Sec. Dr JOSÉ COROMINAS P.; publ. *Boletín Médico* (4 a year).

Asociación Médica Dominicana (Dominican Medical Association): Apdo 1237, 11903 Santo Domingo; f. 1941; 1,551 mems; Pres. Dr ANGEL S. CHAN AQUINO; Sec. Dr CARLOS LAMARCHE REY; publ. *Revista Médica Dominicana*.

Research Institutes

AGRICULTURE, FISHERIES AND VETERINARY SCIENCE

Instituto Azucarero Dominicano (Dominican Sugar Institute): Avda Jiménez Moya, Apdo 667, 11903 Santo Domingo; tel. 532-5571; e-mail inst.azucar2@verizon.net.do; internet www.inazucar.gov.do; f. 1965; promotes enhancement and improvement of products derived from the sugar industry; market studies; assists in promotion and removing trade barriers; domestic marketing by setting formalities; supervises policies; Exec. Dir FAUSTINO JIMENEZ.

HISTORY, GEOGRAPHY AND ARCHAEOLOGY

Instituto Cartográfico Militar de las Fuerzas Armadas (Military Cartographic Institute): Base Naval 27 de Febrero, 11903 Santo Domingo; tel. 686-2954; internet www.secffaa.mil.do/icm.htm; f. 1950; photogrammetry, cartography, geodesy, hydrography, photographic laboratory; sells all kinds of speciality maps of the country; Dir Capt. DOMINGO GÓMEZ.

Libraries and Archives

Baní

Biblioteca 'Padre Billini': Calle Baní 6, 31000 Duarte; f. 1926; 38,000 vols; Dir Lic. FERNANDO HERRERA.

Moca

Biblioteca Municipal 'Gabriel Morillo': Calle Antonio de la Maza esq. Independencia, 83000 Moca; f. 1942; 6,422 vols; Dir Lic. ADRIANO MIGUEL TEJADA.

San Pedro de Macorís

Biblioteca del Ateneo de Macorís (Library of the Athenaeum of Macorís): 21000 San Pedro de Macorís; f. 1890; 6,274 vols; Pres. Lic. JOSÉ A. CHEVALIER.

Santiago de los Caballeros

Biblioteca de la Sociedad Amantes de la Luz: España esq. Avda Central, Santiago de los Caballeros; f. 1874; public library of cultural society; 18,000 vols; Dir Lic. BERENI ESTRELLA DE INOA.

Santo Domingo

Archivo General de la Nación: Calle Modesto Diaz 2, Zona Universitaria, 10103 Santo Domingo; f. 1935, present status 2000; attached to Secretariat of State for Culture; documents dating from the founding of the Republic and others that were inherited from the colonial era; documents of public and private interest; 16,000 vols; Dir-Gen. Dr ROBERTO CASSÁ; Sub-Dir Dr LUÍS MANUEL PUCHEU; publs *Boletín AGN* (4 a year), *Proceedings of Quisqueya* (4 a year).

Biblioteca de la Secretaría de Estado de Relaciones Exteriores (Library of the Secretariat of State for Foreign Affairs): Estancia Ramfis, Santo Domingo; spec. collns relating to int. law; Dir Dr PRÓSPERO J. MELLA CHAVIER.

Biblioteca de la Universidad Autónoma de Santo Domingo (Library of Santo Domingo University): Ciudad Universitaria, Apdo 1355, Santo Domingo; 104,441 vols (Dominicana, historical archives, prints, maps, microfilms, etc.), 782,795 reviews (chiefly foreign, relating to the different faculties), gramophone records; Dir Dra MARTHA MARÍA DE CASTRO COTES; publ. *Boletín de Adquisiciones*.

Biblioteca Municipal de Santo Domingo (Municipal Library of Santo Domingo): Padre Billini 18, Santo Domingo; f. 1922; Librarian LUZ DEL CARMEN RAPOZO.

Biblioteca Nacional Pedro Henríquez Ureña: César Nicolás Penson 91, 20711 Santo Domingo; tel. 688-4086; f. 1971; collects government publs; houses Nat. Bibliography; exhibits, confs, research and documentation; 153,955 vols; Dir Lic. ROBERTO DE SOTO.

Biblioteca República Dominicana: Dr Delgado esq. Avda Francia, Santo Domingo; tel. 686-0028; e-mail biblioteca_rd@yahoo.com; f. 1989, present bldg a chapel of the Dominican Order dating from 1729; promotes culture; collns of periodicals; also contains a students' reading room, textbooks, maps; over 30,000 vols, of which Dominican authors comprise 700; Dir JOSÉ RIJO.

Centro Nacional de Conservación de Documentos, Secretaría de Estado de Cultura (Library and Documentation Section): Archivo General de la Nación, Calle Modesto Díaz No. 2, Zona, 10210 Universitaria, Santo Domingo; tel. 532-2508; f. 1976, current name adopted 2000; offers services in environmental health; restoration; digital restoration; consultancy; workshops (technical training); Dir Lic. ELIDA JIMÉNEZ.

Museums and Art Galleries

Santo Domingo

Amber World Museum: Arz. Meriño 452, esq. Restauración, Zona Colonial, 10210 Santo Domingo; tel. 682-3309; internet www.ambermuseum.com; f. 1996; historical and scientific data of the creation of amber; exhibitions and workshops; Pres. JORGE CARIDAD.

Galería Nacional de Bellas Artes (National Fine Arts Gallery): Santo Domingo; f. 1943; contains the later paintings and sculptures previously exhibited in the Museo Nacional; controlled by the Dirección Gen. de Bellas Artes (Fine Arts Ccl); Dir Dr JOSÉ DE J. ALVAREZ VALVERDE.

Larimar Museum: Isabel La Catolica St No. 54, Zona Zolonial, Santo Domingo; tel. 686-5700; e-mail info@larimarfactory.com; internet www.larimarmuseum.com; f. 1996; educational unit of Amabar Nacional; facts and scientific explanations about blue pectolite or larimar; Pres. JORGE CARIDAD; Pres. ARELIS DE CARIDAD.

Museo Alcázar de Colón: la Plaza España, Zona Colonial, 10210 Santo Domingo; tel. 682-4750; historical colln of over 800 pieces of furniture, carpets, ceramics, sculptures and paintings dating from the 12th century; research and conservation; Dir VICKY JAQUEZ.

Museo Bellapart (Bellapart Museum): Avda JF Kennedy Esq. Dr Lembert Peguero, Edif. Honda 5to Nivel, Santo Dominigo; tel. 541-7721; e-mail info@museobellapart.com; internet www.museobellapart.com; f. 1999; Dominican art; paintings from the 1890s to the 1990s; covers all styles and artistic movements of the 20th century to the present; incl. paintings, sculptures, prints and drawings; library of 1,000 vols, offers World Art, Caribbean and Dominican Art reference books; Pres. JUAN JOSE BELLAPART; Dir MYRNA GUERRERO VILLALONA.

Museo Casa de Tostado: Calle Arzobispo Meriño, esq. Padre Billini, Ciudad Colonial, 10210 Santo Dominigo; tel. 689-5000; e-mail casadetostado@cultura.gov.do; f. 1973; museum of the Dominican family; preserves information of nat. and foreign history; traditions and customs since mid-19th century; exhibits major colln of decorative arts; Dir EVA CAMILO.

Museo de Arte Moderno (Museum of Modern Art): Avda Pedro Henríquez Ureña, Plaza de la Cultura 'Juan Pablo Duarte' 10204 Santo Domingo; tel. 685-2153; e-mail museo_de_arte_moderno@yahoo.com; f. 1976 as Gallery of Modern Art, current name adopted 1992; attached to Secretaria de Estado de Cultura; state controlled; modern art of nat. and foreign artists; permanent and exchange exhibitions; organizes lectures, confs, films and children's workshops; library: art library of 2,047 vols, children's library of 2,050 vols; Dir Lic. MARÍA ELENA DITRÉN; publs *Boletín mensual de actividades* (12 a year), *Revista especializada*.

Museo de las Atarazanas Reales: Calle Colón, No. 4, Ciudad Colonial, 10210 Santo Domingo; tel. 682-5834; conserves, exhibits and distributes underwater archaeological heritage on nat. art.

Museo de las Casas Reales (Museum of the Royal Houses): Calle Las Mercedes esq. Damas, Ciudad Colonial, Apdo 2664, 10210 Santo Domingo; tel. 682-4202; e-mail museodelacasar@verizon.net.do; f. 1511, present status 1973, officially opened 1976; bldgs were HQs of the colonial govt (houses Palace of the Governor General and the Royal Court and Accounts); exhibition of items from 1492–1821; arms and armour, ceramics and items from shipwrecks; library of 17,700 vols; Dir ANA YEE DE CURY; publ. *Casas Reales* (3 a year).

Museo del Hombre Dominicano (Museum of Dominican Man): Plaza de la Cultura Juan Pablo Duarte, Calle Pedro Henríquez Ureña, Santo Domingo; tel. 687-3622; e-mail info@museodelhombredominicano.org.do; internet www.museodelhombredominicano.org.do; f. 1973 as Museo Nacional; 19,000 exhibits: Pre-Columbian (Indian archaeological, anthropological and ethnographical exhibits; ceramics, wooden objects, idols, amulets, charms, weapons and tools, pots, osseous remains); Colonial (weapons and armour, parts of ships, Spanish religious objects, ceramics, bells); educational confs. and workshops; offers specialized courses in social science with emphasis on social research, archaeology and socio-cultural anthropology; library of 4,000 vols; Dir Dr CARLOS HERNÁNDEZ SOTO; publ. *Serie Investigaciones Antropológicas*.

Museo Faro a Colón: Avda Bulv. del Faro, Villa Duarte, 11602 Santo Dominigo; tel. 591-1492; dedicated to the memory and houses the remains of Admiral Don Cristobal Colón; researches, exhibits, preserves and disseminates the history and the int. heritage related to the discovery, colonization and evangelization of the Americas.

Museo Nacional de Historia Natural (National Museum of Natural History): Calle César Nicolás Penson, Plaza de la Cultura, 10204 Santo Domingo; tel. 689-0106; e-mail c.mir@mnhn.gov.do; internet www.mnhn.gov.do; f. 1974; conserves, researches, exhibits and disseminates nat. natural heritage; geology, palaeontology, zoology; library of 3,000 vols, 10 periodicals; Dir CELESTE MIR; publs *Hispaniolana* (journal, irregular), *Novitates Caribaea* (irregular).

Museo Nacional de Historia y Geografía (National Museum of History and Geography): Calle Pedro Henríquez Ureña, Plaza de la Cultura Juan Pablo Duarte, Santo Domingo; tel. 686-6668; e-mail museohistoriard@yahoo.com; f. 1982; history, geographical features and phenomena of the island of Santo Domingo; Dir HECTOR LUIS MARTINEZ; publ. *Revista de Historia y Geografía*.

Oficina de Patrimonio Cultural: Las Atarazanas 2, Santo Domingo; tel. 682-4750; f. 1967; Dir Arq. MANUEL E. DEL MONTE URRACA.

Attached Museums:

Alcázar de Colón (Columbus Palace): Plaza Spain, Ciudad Colonial, 10210 Santo Domingo; tel. 682-4750; f. museum 1957; the castle, built in 1510, was the residence of Don Diego Columbus, son of Christopher Columbus, and Viceroy of the island; period furniture and objects, paintings, musical instruments, ceramics, and the most important colln of tapestries in the Caribbean.

Casa-Fuerte de Ponce de León (Ponce de León's Fort): San Rafael del, Yuma, Higüey; tel. 551-0118; f. 1972; the residence of Juan Ponce de León, who discovered Florida and Puerto Rico; authentic furniture and household items from a 16th-century house.

Fortaleza de San Felipe (St Philip's Fortress): West End Malecon, 57000 Puerto Plata; tel. 261-6043; f. 1972; 16th-century fort; archaeological objects found during restoration; disseminates information about military life of the 18th and 19th centuries.

Museo de la Familia Dominicana Siglo XIX (Museum of the Dominican Family): Casa de Tostado, Calle Arzobispo Meriño, Santo Domingo; f. 1973, built in 1503; a 16th-century house displaying household items of a noble family of the 19th century.

Sala de Arte Prehispánico: Avda San Martín 279, POB 723, Santo Domingo; tel. 540-7777; e-mail saladearte@embodom.com; f. 1973; run by the García Arévalo Foundation; studies and exhibits culture of pre-Hispanic times; library of 6,000 vols on anthropology and the history of Santo Domingo and the Caribbean; Dir MANUEL ANTONIO GARCÍA ARÉVALO; publs *Caney*, *Salida Semestral*.

Universities

PONTIFICIA UNIVERSIDAD CATÓLICA MADRE Y MAESTRA

Autopista Duarte, Santiago de los Caballeros

Telephone: 580-1962

E-mail: anunez@pucmmsti.edu.do

Internet: www.pucmmsti.edu.do

Founded 1962, present bldg 1967

Private control

Academic year: August to May (2 semesters) and a session May to July

Campuses in Santo Domingo, Puerto Plata, Bonao

Rector: Mgr AGRIPINO NÚÑEZ COLLADO

Acad. Vice-Rector: Ing. NELSON GIL

Exec. Vice-Rector: Lic. SONIA GUZMÁN DE HERNÁNDEZ

Registrar: Lic. DULCE RODRÍGUEZ DE GRULLÓN

Librarian: Lic. ALTAGRACIA PEÑA

Number of teachers: 755

Number of students: 9,918

Publications: *Boletín de Noticias*, *Revista de Ciencias Jurídicas*

DEANS

Faculty of Engineering: Ing. VICTOR COLLADO

Faculty of Health Sciences: Dr RAFAEL FERNANDEZ LAZALA

Faculty of Humanities and Sciences: Lic. DAVID ALVAREZ MARTÍN

UNIVERSIDAD ABIERTA PARA ADULTOS

Apdo postal 1238, Avda Hispanoamérica, Urb. Thomén, Santiago de los Caballeros

Telephone: 724-0266

E-mail: univ.adultos@uniabierta.edu.do

Internet: www.uapa.edu.do

Founded 1991, present status 1995

Academic year: January to December

Rector: Dr ÁNGEL HERNÁNDEZ

Vice-Chancellor for Academics: RAFAEL ESPINAL

Vice-Chancellor for Finance: Dr MIRIAN ACOSTA

Vice-Rector for International Relations: MAGDALENA CRUZ

Pres.: Lic. RUBEN HERNANDEZ

Treas.: CORINA MONTERO

Sec.: FRANCISCO SANTOS

Publications: *Boletin UAPA Informa* (newsletter), *Revista Educación Superior*

UNIVERSIDAD ADVENTISTA DOMINICANA

Au. Duarte km 74 1/2, Monsignor Nouel, Bonao, Sonador

Telephone: 525-7533

E-mail: info@unad.edu.do

Internet: www.unad.edu.do

Founded 1947, present bldg 1976

Private control

Language of instruction: Spanish

Academic year: September to May

Rector: Dr FELIBERTO MARTÍNEZ PÁEZ

Vice-Rector for Academics: ALFA RIGEL SUERO MORETA

Library of 30,000 vols

DEANS

Faculty of Administrative Sciences: Dr DANIEL MOLINA

Faculty of Engineering: Ing. GABRIEL NINA BRITO

Faculty of Health: Dr ARELIS TREJO

Faculty of Humanities: Dr JAIRO UTATE

Faculty of Theology: Dr CARLOS REYES

UNIVERSIDAD APEC

Avda Máximo Gómez 72, El Vergel, Apdo 2867, Santo Domingo

Telephone: 686-0021

E-mail: univ.apec@codetel.net.do

Internet: www.unapec.edu.do

Founded 1965

Academic year: July to June

Pres.: Dr ROBERTO RODRIGUEZ UREÑA

Rector: Lic. DENNIS R. SIMÓ

Vice-Rector for Academics: CARLOS SANGIOVANNI

Vice-Rector for Admin.: Lic. CÉSAR REYNOSO

Vice-Rector for Int. Affairs: Lic. INMACULADA MADERA

Librarian: GIOVANNA RIGGIO

Library of 37,525 vols

Number of teachers: 658

Number of students: 9,000

Publications: *Boletín Trimestral* (4 a year), *Coloquios Jurídicos*, *Investigación y Ciencia*

DEANS

Art and Communication: ANDRÉS HERNÁNDEZ

Economics and Business: Dra AIDA ROCA

Engineering and Computer Science: Dr WILLIAM CAMILO

Gen. Studies: Dr ANDRÉS L. MATEO

Graduate Studies: Dra DALMA CRUZ

Law: Dr ALEJANDRO MOSCOSO

Tourism: Lic. LUIS FELIPE AQUINO

UNIVERSIDAD AUTÓNOMA DE SANTO DOMINGO

Ciudad Universitaria, Apdo 1355, Santo Domingo

Telephone: 535-8273

E-mail: info@uasd.edu.do

Internet: www.uasd.edu.do

Founded 1538 by Papal Bull of Paul III, closed 1801–15; reopened as a lay institution in 1815, reorganized in 1914, present status 1961, oldest univ. in the Americas

Academic year: January to December

Rector: Dr JULIO RAVELO ASTACIO

Vice-Rector for Academic Affairs: Lic. RAMÓN CAMACHO JIMÉNEZ

Vice-Rector for Admin. Affairs: Lic. JULIO URBÁEZ

Sec.-Gen.: MARIO SURIEL

Personnel Dir: Lic. JULIO CÉSAR RODRÍGUEZ

Number of teachers: 1,665

Number of students: 26,040

Publications: *Ciencia*, *Derecho y Política*

DEANS

Faculty of Agronomy and Veterinary Science: Ing. Agr. FRANK M. VALDÉZ

Faculty of Economic and Social Sciences: Dr EDILBERTO CABRAL

Faculty of Engineering and Architecture: Ing. MIGUEL ROSADO MONTES DE OCA

Faculty of Humanities: Lic. ANA DOLORES GUZMÁN DE CAMACHO

Faculty of Law and Politics: Lic. ROBERTO SANTANA

Faculty of Medicine: Dr CÉSAR MELLA MEJÍAS

Faculty of Sciences: Lic. PLÁCIDO CABRERA

UNIVERSIDAD CATÓLICA NORDESTANA (UCNE)

Los Arroyos, POB 239, San Francisco de Macorís

Telephone: 588-3505

E-mail: rectoria@ucne.edu

Internet: www.ucne.edu

Founded 1978

Private control

Language of instruction: Spanish

Academic year: January to December (3 semesters)

Rector: Rev. Dr RAMÓN ALFREDO DE LA CRUZ BALDERA

Great Chancellor: Mgr FAUSTO RAMÓN MEJÍA VALLEJO

Vice-Rector: Dr LUIS ELÍAS ESMURDOC

Academic Vice-Rector: ZAMIRA ASILIS

Admin. and Financial Vice-Rector: Dr YANY ALTAGRACIA ALMÁNZAR

Vice-Pres. for Projects: Dr FREDDY ARTURO MARTINEZ

Librarian: Lic. VICTOR BELÉN

Library of 24,519 vols

Number of teachers: 323

Number of students: 4,022

Publications: *Ciencia y Humanismo* (3 a year), *Gaceta Jurídica* (3 a year), *Innovación Académica* (4 a year)

DEANS

Faculty of Architecture: Arq. MANUEL ORTEGA

Faculty of Economic and Social Sciences: Lic. JUAN CASTILLO

Faculty of Education: Lic. LUZ ESPERANZA FRANCISCO

Faculty of Engineering: Ing. MARTIN PANTALEON

Faculty of Health Sciences: Dr BRUNEL SANTOS

Faculty of Law: Dr MARTIN ORTEGA THEN

Faculty of Modern Languages: Lic. EMELDA RAMOS

Faculty of Tourism: Lic. LISA RODRIGUEZ GATÓN

School of Dentistry: DAYSI ROMERO (Dir)

School of Medicine: Dr RAMONA MERCEDES (Dir)

School of Systems and Computing Engineering: Ing. CRISTOPHER BELLO (Dir)

UNIVERSIDAD CATÓLICA SANTO DOMINGO

Calle Santo Domingo No 3, Ens. La Julia, POB 2733, Santo Domingo

Telephone: 544-2812

E-mail: egresados@ucsd.edu.do

Internet: www.ucsd.edu.do

Founded 1982

Private control

Language of instruction: Spanish

Academic year: January to December

Pres.: NICOLÁS DE JESÚS CARDENAL LÓPEZ RODRÍGUEZ

Sec.: Lic. ALLAN RAMOS

Deputy Sec.: Lic. LUÍS GARCÍA DUBUS

Treas.: Sr DON ANTONIO NAJRI

Vice-Treas.: Dr JUAN J. GASSÓ PEREYRA
Rector: Rev. Fr Dr P. RAMÓN ALONSO
Vice-Rector for Academics: Licda ROSA KRANWINKEL
Vice-Rector for Admin.: Ing. ANGEL MENA
Vice-Rector for Planning: Lic. FRANCISCO CRUZ PASCUAL
Number of teachers: 350
Number of students: 6,000
Publication: *Revista UCSD* (3 a year)

DEANS
Faculty of Health Sciences: Dr JESÚS ANT. FIALLO
Faculty of Humanities and Education: Licda CARMEN MILDRED LÓPEZ
Faculty of Legal and Political Sciences: Dr MANUEL RAMÓN PEÑA CONCE
Faculty of Religious Science: SOCORRO ALVÁREZ
Faculty of Science and Technology: Ing. ROBERTO MOREL

UNIVERSIDAD CATÓLICA TECNOLÓGICA DEL CIBAO

Avda Universitaria, esq. Pedro A. Rivera, Apdo 401, La Vega
Telephone: 573-1020
E-mail: uteci@codetel.net.do
Internet: www.ucateci.edu.do
Founded 1983, current name adopted 2002, present status 2006
Academic year: January to December
Rector: Rev. Dr FAUSTO RAMON MEJIA VALLEJO
Pres.: HUGO ALVAREZ VALENCIA
Vice-Pres.: JESUS RUBEN GOMEZ
Sec.: HILDA PEREZ PICHARDO
Treas.: PEDRO ANT RIVERA TORRES

DEANS
Faculty of Health Sciences: Dr JOSE N. PIMENTEL
Faculty of Humanities: JOSE RAFAEL ABREU

UNIVERSIDAD CENTRAL DEL ESTE

Avda Francisco, Alberto Caamaño Deñó, San Pedro de Macorís
Telephone: 529-3562
E-mail: info@uce.edu.do
Internet: www.uce.edu.do
Founded 1970
Private control
Academic year: January to December (3 semesters)
Pres. and Rector: Dr JOSÉ E. HAZIM FRAPPIER
Exec-Rector: Lic. RICHARD PEGUERO
Vice-Rector for Academics: Lic. ISMENIA JIMÉNEZ ABUD
Vice-Rector for Admin.: Lic. DOLORES MONTALVO
Sec. Gen.: Lic. PIEDAD L. NOBOA MEJÍA
Registrar: Lic. PIEDAD L. NOBOA MEJÍA
Librarian: Lic. LIXONDER CAÑAS
Library of 150,000 vols
Number of teachers: 677
Number of students: 6,700
Publications: *Anuario Científico*, *Publicaciones Periódicas*, *UCE*

DEANS
Faculty of Administration and Systems: Lic. JESÚS STERLING
Faculty of Engineering and Natural Resources: Ing. MARÍA CRISTINA TEJADA
Faculty of Law: Dr JUANA OZUNA
Faculty of Medicine: Dr JOSÉ GUILLERMO WAZAR
Faculty of Science and Technology: Dr FERMÍN MERCEDES
Faculty of Sciences and Humanities: Lic. LEÓN ALBERTO

UNIVERSIDAD CENTRAL DOMINICANA DE ESTUDIOS PROFESIONALES

Avda Independencia, km 9, Colegio San Gabriel, Apdo Postal 1263, Santo Domingo
Telephone: 508-3279
E-mail: info@ucdep.edu.do
Founded 1975
Private control
Rector: Dr DULCÍLIDO VÁSQUEZ
Vice-Rector for Admin.: Lic. XIOMARA PÉREZ
Vice-Rector for Planning and Devt: Lic. CARLOS HERNÁNDEZ
Exec. Vice-Rector: Ing. MARIO BONILLA M.
Sec. Gen.: Lic. JUDITH J. VÁZQUEZ

DEANS
Faculty of Health Sciences: CHARLOTTE KING
Faculty of Humanities and Social Sciences: FÉLIX SÁNCHEZ
Faculty of Technology and Natural Resources: RAFAEL LEBRON

UNIVERSIDAD DE LA TERCERA EDAD

Calle Camila Henríquez Ureña, esq. Jesús Maestro, Mirador Norte, Santo Domingo
Telephone: 482-7093
E-mail: tercera.edad@codetel.net.do
Internet: www.ute.edu.do
Founded 1989, present status 1992
State control
Academic year: January to December (2 semesters)
Rector: Dr JOSÉ NICOLÁS ALMÁNZAR GARCÍA
Vice-Rector for Academics: Lic. ALTAGRACIA NÚÑEZ
Vice-Rector for Admin. and Devt: Dra FANNY POLANCO JORGE

SUBJECT COORDINATORS
Design: Lic. ALICIA ARBAJE
Economics and Administration: Lic. RAFAEL OVIEDO JIMÉNEZ
Education: Lic. CARMEN PEÑA
Law: Lic. RHINA DE LOS SANTOS
Psychology: Lic. GERMANIA MORALES
Public Relations and Social Communication: Lic. RAFAEL PARADELL DÍAZ

UNIVERSIDAD DEL CARIBE

Autopista 30 de Mayo km 7½, POB 67-2, Santo Domingo
Telephone: 616-1616
E-mail: univ.delcaribe@codetel.net.do
Internet: www.unicaribe.edu.do
Founded 1995
Rector: MIGUEL ROSADO
Vice-Rector for Admin.: ARTURO MENDÉZ

UNIVERSIDAD DOMINICANA O&M

Apdo postal 509, Avda Independencia 200, Santo Domingo
Telephone: 533-7733
E-mail: info@udoym.edu.do
Internet: www.udoym.edu.do
Founded 1966
Academic year: January to December
Faculties of continuing education, economics and administration, engineering and technology, humanities and social science, and law; campuses in La Romana, Moca, Puerto Plata, San José de Ocoa, and Santiago
Rector: Dr JOSÉ RAFAEL ABINADER
Number of students: 28,000

UNIVERSIDAD EUGENIO MARÍA DE HOSTOS

Apdo Postal 2694, Santo Domingo
Telephone: 532-2495
E-mail: vrauniremhos@gmail.com
Internet: www.uniremhos.edu.do
Founded 1981
Private control
Rector: Lic. CARMEN MARÍA CASTILLO SILVA
Vice-Rector for Academics: Lic. CARMEN ROSA MARTÍNEZ V.
Vice-Rector for Admin.: Rev. RAFAEL MARCIAL SILVA
Gen. Admin.: Dr JORGE DÍAZ VARGAS

DIRECTORS
Faculty of Health Sciences: Dr JOSÉ RODRÍGUEZ SOLDEVILLA
School of Computer Studies: Lic. SANDY SANTOS
School of Law: Lic. CECILIO GÓMEZ PÉREZ
School of Marketing Studies: Lic. PEDRO MELO
School of Medicine: Dr RAÚL ALVAREZ STURLA
School of Nursing: Lic. AMANDA PEÑA DE SANTANA
School of Oral Medicine: Dr CÉSAR LINARES IMBERT
School of Public Health: Dr MANUEL TEJADA BEATO
School of Veterinary Medicine: Dr TULIO S. CASTAÑOS VÉLEZ
Campus in Ozama: Lic. GUILLERMO DÍAZ
Campus in San Cristóbal: Lic. EMILIANO DE LA ROSA

UNIVERSIDAD EXPERIMENTAL 'FELIX ADAM'

Calle Plaza de la Cultura 151, El Millón, Santo Domingo
Telephone: 683-3121
E-mail: universidadunefa@unefa.edu.do
Internet: www.unefa.edu.do
Founded 1996
Chair.: Dr ANDRÉS MATOS SENA
Rector: Dr BRITO JOSE RAMON HOLGUIN
Number of teachers: 36

UNIVERSIDAD FEDERICO HENRÍQUEZ Y CARVAJAL

Isabel Aguiar No 100 casi esq. Guarocuya, Herrera, Santo Domingo Oeste
Telephone: 531-1000
E-mail: info@ufhec.edu.do
Internet: www.ufhec.edu.do
Depts of dentistry, humanities, nursing, sciences

UNIVERSIDAD IBEROAMERICANA

Apdo Postal 22-333, Avda Francia 129, Gazcue, 10205 Santo Domingo
Telephone: 689-4111
E-mail: admisiones@unibe.edu.do
Internet: www.unibe.edu.do
Founded 1982
Academic year: September to August
Rector: Dr JULIO AMADO CASTAÑOS
Academic Dean: NEY ARIAS SCHEKER
Library of 20,000 vols
Publications: *Aretha* (journal of social sciences and economics), *Baka*, *Informa UNIBE*, *Revista UNIBE de Ciencia y Cultura* (3 a year), *Scientia* (science magazine)

DEANS
Faculty of Health Sciences: Dr JULIO CASTAÑOS

Faculty of Law and Politics: Dr GUILLERMO MORENO

DIRECTORS

Faculty of Economics and Social Sciences:

School of Business Administration: Lic. MIGUELINA FRANCO

School of Hotel Management and Tourism: Lic. PILAR CONSTANZO

School of Marketing: Lic. ZAYENKA MARTÍNEZ ROA

Faculty of Health Sciences:

School of Dentistry: Dr JACQUELINE RODRIGUEZ RAMIREZ

Faculty of Human Sciences:

School of Advertising and Communication: Lic. RAFAEL RINCÓN M.

School of Architecture: Arq. VENCIAN BEN

School of Design: SANDRA GÓMEZ

School of Education: LAURA SARTORI

School of Psychology: Lic. FRANCESCA HERNÁNDEZ

UNIVERSIDAD INTERAMERICANA

Apdo postal 20687, C/Dr Baez 2 y 4, Gazcue, 10205 Santo Domingo

Telephone: 685-6562

E-mail: unica@codetel.net.do

Internet: www.unica.edu.do

Founded 1977

Private control

Rector: Lic. GABRIEL READ

Pres.: Dr ZORAIDA HALL VDA. SUNCAR

Vice-Chancellor for Academics: PARMENIO RAUL DIAZ

Vice-Chancellor of Planning and Devt: MIGUEL CIPRIAN

Dean of Faculty and Students: NESTOR MELENCIANO

DEANS

Faculty of Science and Technology: MAX MENDEZ

Faculty of Social Sciences and Humanities: MARY FRANCES CARABALLO

DIRECTORS

Experimental College: Licda JUAN CACERES

School of Accountancy and Business Administration: HENRY JEROME

School of Advertising: FEDERICO SANCHEZ

School of Dental Technology: Dr WALTER SUERO MENDEZ

School of Education: Licda ALTAGRACIA CABRERA

School of Informatics: NARCISO RAMIREZ

School of Law: RODOLFO JIMENEZ

School of Marketing: RODOLFO JIMENEZ

School of Social Communication and Public Relations: ADRIANO DE LA CRUZ

UNIVERSIDAD NACIONAL EVANGÉLICA

San Carlos, Calle Libertador No. 18, esq. Emilio Prud'Homme, Santo Domingo

Telephone: 221-6786

E-mail: rectoria@unev.edu.do

Internet: www.unev-rd.edu.do

Founded 1986

Private control

Pres: Dr PETER GOMEZ

Vice-Pres: Rev. JUAN CARLOS INFANTE, Dr ANA INES POLANCO

Sec.: PABLO VENTURA

Treas.: HOMER BERG

Rector: Lic. SALUSTIANO BOLIVAR MOJICA RIJO

Vice-Rector for Academics: Lic. FÉLIX MIGUEL URENA

Vice-Rector for Admin.: Ing. EPIFANIO GONZALEZ MINAYA

DEANS

Faculty of Health Sciences: Dr WILFREDO MANON ROSSI

Faculty of Humanities: SANTOS GUZMAN

Faculty of Rural Development: Dr CESAR LOPEZ

UNIVERSIDAD NACIONAL 'PEDRO HENRÍQUEZ UREÑA'

Avda John F. Kennedy km 6½, Santo Domingo

Telephone: 562-6601

E-mail: info@unphu.edu.do

Internet: www.unphu.edu.do

Founded 1966, present status 1967

Private control

Languages of instruction: Spanish, English

Academic year: September to August (3 semesters)

Rector: Arq. MIGUEL R. FIALLO

Vice-Rector for Academic Affairs: Lic. DANIELA FRANCO DE GUZMÁN

Vice-Rector for Admin. Affairs: Lic. JOSE RAFAEL ESPAILLAT

Vice-Rector for Postgraduate Studies: Lic. LOURDES CONCEPCION

Registrar: Lic. JEANNE MENA

Librarian: Dra ELOISA MARRERO

Library of 80,000 vols

Number of teachers: 759

Number of students: 8,000

Publications: *Aula*, *Biblionotas*, *Cuadernos de Filosofía*, *Cuadernos Jurídicos*

DEANS

Faculty of Agronomy and Veterinary Science: Dr JOSE ESPAILLAT

Faculty of Architecture and Arts: Arq. OMAR RANCIER

Faculty of Economics and Social Sciences: Lic. LUIS MARTINEZ SILFA

Faculty of Engineering and Technology: Ing. CARLOS TRONCOSO

Faculty of Health Science: Dr JOSE J. ASILIS

Faculty of Humanities: Lic. DIANA FRANCO DE GUZMAN

Faculty of Law and Politics: Dr MANUEL BERGÉS CHUPANI

Faculty of Postgraduate Studies: Dr LOURDES CONCEPCION

Faculty of Science: Ing. CARLOS TRONCOSO

UNIVERSIDAD NACIONAL TECNOLÓGICA

Calle Dr Delgado 103, Gazcue, 10205

Telephone: 731-3200

E-mail: info@unnatec.edu.do

Internet: www.insutec.edu.do

Founded 2003

Private control

Academic year: January to December (3 trimesters)

Pres.: CIELO REYNOSO DE REYES

Dir of Business Admin.: MAESTRA YSAMNA M. MONTERO T

UNIVERSIDAD ODONTOLÓGICA DOMINICANA

Avda 27 de Febrero esq. Calle ira. Las Caobas, 10905 Santo Domingo

Telephone: 338-7461

Internet: www.uod.edu.do

Founded 1983

Rector: DESCHAMPS VILMA BAEZ

UNIVERSIDAD PSICOLOGÍA INDUSTRIAL DOMINICANA

Calle 1era. No 27 Urb. KG km 6½, Carretera Sánchez, Linea

Telephone: 533-7141

E-mail: psicologiadom@codetel.net.do

Internet: www.upid.edu.do

Founded 1976 as Industrial Psychology Dominicana, present status 2001

Private control

Rector: Lic. MILDRED DÍAZ ÁLVAREZ

Vice-Rector for Academics: Lic. MILDRED DÍAZ ÁLVAREZ

Vice-Rector for Admin.: Lic. SORAIMA E. REYES GÓMEZ

UNIVERSIDAD TECNOLÓGICA DE SANTIAGO (UTESA)

Avda Estrella Sadhalá, esq. Av. Circunvalación, Apdo 685, Santiago de los Caballeros

Telephone: 582-7156

E-mail: utesa@codetel.net.do

Internet: www.utesa.edu

Founded 1974

Private control

Academic year: January to December

Faculties of architecture and engineering, health sciences, sciences and humanities, secretarial sciences, social and economic sciences

Rector: Dr PRIAMO RODRÍGUEZ CASTILLO

Asst Rector: JOSELINA TAVAREZ

Vice-Rector for Academics: Mag. ARNALDO PEÑA VENTURA

Vice-Rector for Admin.: MARÍA ESTHER U.

Vice-Rector for Campus Premises: Mag. RAMÓN ANÍBAL CASTRO

Sec.-Gen.: Mag. JOSEFINA CRUZ

Registrar: Lic. ANDRÉS VIVAS

Librarian: Mag. ILUMINADA DE LA HOZ

Library of 157,976 vols

Number of teachers: 1,027

Number of students: 35,742

Publications: *Ciencias y Tecnología*, *Revista Universitas*

UNIVERSIDAD TECNOLÓGICA DEL SUR

Avda Enriquillo 1, Mejoramiento Social, Azua de Compostela

Telephone: 521-3785

E-mail: info@utesur.edu.do

Internet: www.utesur.edu.do

Founded 1978

Rector: ALTAGRACIA MILAGROS GARRIDO DE SÁNCHEZ

Pres.: JUAN VALERIO SÁNCHEZ

Colleges

Barna Business School: Avda John F. Kennedy 34, Ens. Naco; tel. 683-4461; e-mail barna@barna.edu.do; internet www.barna.edu.do; offers programmes in credit risk management, executive development, financial management, general management, marketing management; MBA and MBA intensive.

Centros APEC de Educación a Distancia: Avda San Martin No 147, Villa Juana, 10412 Santo Domingo; tel. 472-1155; e-mail cenapec@cenapec.edu.do; internet www.cenapec.edu.do; f. 1972; offers low-cost educational programmes by means of distance education system; 525 teachers; 31,800 students; Pres. LUIS TAVERAS AZAR; Exec. Dir JUAN MIGUEL PEREZ; Academic Dir ANA

BELKIS AVILA; Admin. Dir Lic BELKIS SANTANA; Treas. JAIME R. FERNANDEZ; Sec. SONIA VILLANUEVA DE BROUWER.

El Domínico–Americano: Avda Abraham Lincoln 21, Santo Domingo; tel. 535-0665; internet www.icda.edu.do; f. 1947; promotes English as a foreign language; broadening relationships between the Dominican Republic and the USA; conducts exchange programmes; library: 13,300 vols; Dir Lic. ELIZABETH DE WINDT; Gen. Academic Dir Lic. THELMA CAMARENA; Pres. ENGRACIA FRANJUL DE ABATE; Sec. ELLEN DUCY DE PÉREZ; Treas. ERNESTO L. BETANCOURT.

Instituto Politécnico Loyola: Calle Padre Angel Arias 1, 91000 San Cristóbal; tel. 528-4010; internet www.ipl.edu.do; f. 1966; offers industrial engineering, network and telecommunications engineering, professional devt and training; library: 20,000 vols; Rector P. FRANCISCO ESCOLÁSTICO H.; Vice-Rector for Academics Lic. MARINO BRITO GUILLÉN.

Instituto Superior de Agricultura (Higher Institute of Agriculture): Avda 166, Av. Antonio Guzmán Fdez, km 51/2, La Herradura, 51000 Santiago; tel. 247-2000; internet www.isa.edu.do; f. 1962; ind. instn but operates joint programme in agriculture with the Universidad Católica Madre y Maestra; training in agricultural sciences at high school and undergraduate level; offers courses in admin., agrarian reform, agricultural economics, agricultural engineering, animal production, aquaculture, biotechnology, epidemiology, food technology, forestry, horticulture, irrigation, veterinary medicine and animal husbandry; library: 15,000 vols; Rector BENITO FERREIRAS; Pres. ACHILLES BERMDEZ; Treas. FLIX GARCA.

Instituto Tecnológico de Santo Domingo: Avda de los Próceres, Galá, Apdo 342-9, Santo Domingo; tel. 567-9271; e-mail desarrollo@mail.intec.edu.do; internet www.intec.edu.do; f. 1972, present status 1973; depts of basic sciences and environment, business, engineering, health, social sciences and humanities; library: 44,000 books, 1,400 periodicals; 2,300 students; Rector Dr MICHAEL J. SCALE; Acad. Vice-Rector Lic. ALTAGRACIA LÓPEZ; Man. EMIL PELLETIER; Librarian Lic. LUCERO ARBOLEDA DE ROA; publs *Ciencia y Sociedad* (4 a year), *Documentos Intec* (1 a year), *Indice de Publicaciones de Universidades* (1 a year).

Instituto Tecnológico del Cibao Oriental: Avda Universitaria 100, Sanchez Ramirez, Cotuí; tel. 585-2291; e-mail iteco@verizon.net.do; internet www.iteco.edu.do; f. 1982, present status 1983; courses in agricultural engineering, bioanalysis, business, civil engineering, education, geology, law, and mines; Rector Lic. ESCLARECIDA NÚÑEZ DE ALMONTE; Pres. Lic. JULIO TEJEDA; Vice-Pres. Dr LUIS GARCÍA SANTOS; Sec. Dr MANUEL DE JESÚS BRITO O.

Schools of Art and Music

Dirección General de Bellas Artes (Fine Arts Council): Máximo Gómez esq. Avda Independencia, Santo Domingo; tel. 687-0504; e-mail dgba.do@hotmail.com; internet www.bellasartes.gov.do; f. 1940; Dir-Gen. FRANKLIN DOMINGUEZ.

Controls:

Academias de Música (Academies of Music): Villa Consuelo and Villa Francisca, Santo Domingo; also 19 provincial towns.

Conservatorio Nacional de Música (National Conservatoire of Music): Santo Domingo.

Escuela de Arte Escénico (School of Scenic Art): Santo Domingo.

Escuela de Artes Plásticas (School of Plastic Arts): Santiago.

Escuela de Bellas Artes (School of Fine Arts): San Francisco de Macorís.

Escuela de Bellas Artes (School of Fine Arts): San Juan de la Maguana.

Escuela Nacional de Bellas Artes (National School of Fine Arts): Santo Domingo.

ECUADOR

The Higher Education System

The Universidad de San Fulgencio, founded in 1586, was one of the first universities established in the Americas. In 1826 it merged with the Seminario de San Luis y San Gregorio Magno (founded in 1651) and the Universidad de Santo Tomás de Aquino (founded in 1681) to form the Universidad Central del Ecuador. During the 19th century higher education, which had previously been accessible only to Ecuadoreans of pure Spanish ancestry, became available to mestizo and indigenous citizens. In 1895 universities came under the sole control of the state, although this situation was reversed in 1946 when the Catholic church was allowed to participate once again in the higher education system, establishing its first modern private university, the Pontificia Universidad del Ecuador. In 2007/08 there were 534,500 students in higher education, of whom some 35% were enrolled at private institutions. As well as at universities, higher education is also offered at polytechnics (escuelas politécnicas). There were 71 universities and polytechnics in 2011, with total enrolment of 71,995 students in 2012. Both types of institution can be classified in one of the following three categories: public, private but partly financed by the State (particular cofinanciada) or private and self-financed (particular autofinanciada). Universities and polytechnics provide both undergraduate and postgraduate degree courses. Until 2010 higher education was administered by the Consejo Nacional de Educación Superior (CONESUP, National Council for Higher Education); however, following the introduction of the Ley Orgánica de Educación Superior in October 2010 it was replaced by the Secretaría Nacional de Educación Superior, Ciencia, Tecnología e Innovación (SENESCYT). As the newly created governmental higher education authority, the organization was charged with putting in place a number of reforms concerning the administration, funding and accreditation of tertiary institutions. The general aims of the changes were to broaden access to higher education, particularly for disadvantaged socio-economic groups, and to prevent the 'deepening of the process of privatization and mercantilization of higher education' in accordance with the goals set out in the National Development Plan 2009–13. More specifically, there was to be a new admissions test for public universities, and a requirement for better qualified teaching staff (by 2017 university professors would be expected to hold at least a Master's degree, and preferably a Doctorate). In addition, under the new law a number of specialized tertiary institutions were permitted to operate and several conservatories offering programmes in the arts gained official recognition.

Admission to higher education is on the basis of the Bachillerato, the main secondary school qualification; some universities also set entrance examinations. A credit system was introduced, as a means of measuring the volume of study in both undergraduate and postgraduate degrees, which is now used at a number of institutions. The main undergraduate degree is the Licenciatura, which generally requires four years of study. (A professional title can also be awarded.) Degrees in a number of professional subjects, including engineering and architecture, are five years in duration, while degrees in law, pharmacy, psychology, medicine and dentistry last for six years. There are four types of postgraduate qualifications: the Diplomado Superior, which requires the completion of professional/specialist courses (in areas such as tourism management, IT, communications and planning) worth around 15 credits and taking about six months; the Especialización degree, which is normally a one-year programme requiring the completion of courses worth a total of 30 credits and the writing of a short thesis; the Maestría, which is a two-year programme and requires the completion of courses worth a total of 60 credits and the submission and defence of a dissertation; and the Doctorado, which is awarded after an average of three years of study following a Licenciatura or other postgraduate qualification. The Doctorado also requires the submission and defence of a thesis. Not all institutions offer doctorate programmes.

There are two levels of post-secondary vocational qualification: the Técnico (technician), which is awarded after two years of study and the Tecnólogo (technologist) after three. These courses are offered at institutos técnicos superiores (higher technical institutes), of which there were a nation-wide total of 293 in 2011. A credit system means that successful students may gain credit transfer when progressing to a Licenciatura in a related subject. The Junta Nacional de Defensa del Artesano offers apprenticeship programmes and craft certification for individuals employed in various trades. Apprenticeship training, which requires the Bachillerato for entry, generally lasts for three years and leads to the Título de Maestro en la Rama Artesenal or the Título de Maestro de Taller. Students who do not hold the Bachillerato but have seven or more years' experience in a particular trade may be eligible for the award after passing a practical examination.

In accordance with the Ley Orgánica de Educación Superior, introduced in 2010, the Consejo Nacional de Evaluación y Acreditación (CONEA, National Council for Evaluation and Accreditation) was replaced by the Consejo de Educación Superior. By 2015 every institute of higher education was required to have complied with the assessment and accreditation system of the Consejo de Evaluación, Acreditación y Aseguramiento de la Calidad de la Educación Superior (CEAACES, Council for the Evaluation, Accreditation and Quality Assurance of Higher Education). In 2012 a total of 26 universities were deemed to be at risk of suspension and possibly closure, following an evaluation of all university institutions conducted by CEAACES in the previous year. Further investigations were to be undertaken with sanctions expected against those institutions that did not meet the new assessment criteria.

Regulatory and Representative Bodies

GOVERNMENT

Ministry of Culture and Heritage: Avda Colón E5-34 y Juan León Mera, Quito; tel. (2) 381-4550; e-mail comunicacion@ministeriodecultura.gov.ec; internet www.culturaypatrimonio.gob.ec; Minister FRANCISCO VELASCO ANDRADE.

Ministry of Education: Avda Amazonas N34-451 y Avda Atahualpa, Quito; tel. (2) 396-1300; e-mail info@educacion.gob.ec; internet www.educacion.gob.ec; Minister AUGUSTO X. ESPINOSA A.

ACCREDITATION

Consejo de Educación Superior (CES) (Higher Education Council): Avda República E7-226 y Diego de Almagro, Quito; tel. (2) 394-7820; e-mail comunicacion@ces.gob.ec; internet www.ces.gob.ec; f. 1982; responsible for coordination, regulation of univs, technological institutes and academic programmes; Pres. RENÉ RAMÍREZ GALLEGOS; Gen. Sec. Dr MARCELO CALDERÓN VINTIMILLA; publs *Investigación Universitaria* (2 a year), *Planinformativo*.

Learned Societies

GENERAL

Casa de la Cultura Ecuatoriana 'Benjamín Carrión' (House of Ecuadorian Culture 'Benjamin Carrion'): Apdo 67, Avda 6 de Diciembre 794, Quito; tel. 223-391; internet www.casadelacultura.gob.ec; f. 1944;

attached museums: see under Museums and Art Galleries; library: see under Libraries and Archives; 700 mems; Pres. RAÚL PÉREZ TORRES (acting); Gen. Sec. Dr MARCO PLACENCIA; publs *Letras de Ecuador* (2 a year), *Línea Imaginaria* (1 a year).

UNESCO Office Quito and Regional Bureau for Communication and Information: Veintimilla E9-53 entre Plaza y Tamayo, Quito; tel. (2) 252-8911; e-mail quito@unesco.org; internet www.unesco.org/quito; designated Cluster Office for Bolivia, Colombia, Ecuador, Peru and Venezuela; Dir GUSTAVO LÓPEZ OSPINA.

LANGUAGE AND LITERATURE

Academia Ecuatoriana de la Lengua (Ecuadorian Academy of Language): Apdo 17-07-9699, Vicente Ramón Roca E9-60 y Tamayo, 170109 Quito; tel. (2) 543-234; e-mail academiaecuat@andinanet.net; internet www.academiaec.org; f. 1875; 20 mems; Corresp. of the Real Academia Española (Madrid); library of 3,000 vols; Dir Dra SUSANA CORDERO; Sec. CLAUDIO MENA VILLAMAR; publs *Horizonte Cultural* (12 a year), *Memorias* (1 a year).

Alliance Française: Avda Eloy Alfaro N32-468 y Rusia, Casilla 17-11-6275, Quito; tel. (2) 224-6589; e-mail informa@afquito.org.ec; internet www.afquito.org.ec; offers courses in French; promotes French culture and cultural exchange with France; attached teaching offices in Cuenca, Guayaquil, Loja and Portoviejo; Dir MARCEL TAILLEFER.

MEDICINE

Academia Ecuatoriana de Medicina (Ecuadorian Academy of Medicine): Abel Gilbert N34-13 y Antonio Flores Jijon, Bellavista, Quito; tel. (2) 244-7356; e-mail jmalvear@uio.satnet.net; f. 1958; 120 mems; Pres. Dr. REINALDO PÁEZ ZUMÁRRAGA; Permanent Sec. Dr JOSÉ MIGUEL ALVEAR; publs *Archivos de la Academia Ecuatoriana de Medicina*, *Historia de la Academia Ecuatoriana de Medicina*, *Publicacion Homenaje a Academico Ecuatoriano*.

Federación Médica Ecuatoriana (Medical Federation of Ecuador): Avda Naciones Unidas E2-17 e Iñaquito, Quito; tel. (2) 245-2660; e-mail federacion11@hotmail.com; internet www.federacionmedicaecuatoriana.info; f. 1942; 1,500 mems; Pres. Dr ALBERTO NARVÁEZ O.; Gen. Sec. Dr CARLOS FIGUEROA F.

Sociedad Ecuatoriana de Pediatría (Paediatrics Society of Ecuador): Avda Naciones Unidas E2-17 e Iñaquito, Quito; tel. (2) 226-2881; e-mail info@pediatria.org; internet www.pediatria.org.ec; f. 1945; scientific extension courses and lectures; Pres. Dra ROSA ROMERO; Sec. Dra ASTRID LEÓN MONAR; publ. *Revista Ecuatoriana de Pediatría*.

Research Institutes

GENERAL

Institut de Recherche pour le Développement (IRD) (Institute of Research for Development): Apdo 17-12-857, Quito; Whymper 442 y Coruña, Quito; tel. (2) 250-4856; e-mail docquito@ird.fr; internet www.ecuador.ird.fr; f. 1974; agronomy, botany and vegetal biology, economics, geography, geology, human sciences, hydrology, pedology; see main entry under France; library of 550 vols, 400 periodicals, 80 extracts; Rep. JEAN-YVES COLLOT.

AGRICULTURE, FISHERIES AND VETERINARY SCIENCE

Instituto Nacional Autónomo de Investigaciones Agropecuarias (Autonomous National Institute of Agricultural Research): Apdo 17-17-1362, Quito; Avda Eloy Alfaro 30-350 y Avda Amazonas, Edif. MAG (4°), Quito; tel. (2) 256-5963; e-mail iniap@iniap.gob.ec; internet www.iniap.gob.ec; f. 1959; Dir Gen. JULIO CÉSAR DELGADO ARCE; publ. *Revista* (4 a year).

Instituto Nacional de Pesca (National Fishery Institute): Letamendi 102 y La Ría, Guayaquil; tel. (2) 401-773; e-mail direccion_inp@inp.gob.ec; internet www.inp.gob.ec; f. 1960; library of 20,000 vols; Dir Gen. MONCAYO CALDERERO EDWIN FERNANDO; Sec. SEMINARIO SOTOMAYOR ROSA ESTELA; publ. *Revista Científica de Ciencias Marinas y Liminología*.

ECONOMICS, LAW AND POLITICS

Friedrich-Ebert-Stiftung Instituto Latinoamericano de Investigaciones Sociales (FES-ILDIS) (Latin American Institute of Social Research): Casilla 17-03-367, Quito; Avda República 500 y Diego de Almagro, Edif. Pucará, 4°, Of. 404, Quito; tel. (2) 256-2103; e-mail info@fes.ec; internet www.fes-ecuador.org; f. 1974; affiliated to the Friedrich-Ebert Foundation; research in economics, political science and education, sociology; library of 15,000 vols; Dir Dr REINHART WETTMANN.

Instituto Nacional de Estadística y Censos (National Institute for Statistics and Census): Juan Larrea N15-36 y José Riofrío, Quito; tel. (2) 254-4326; e-mail inec@inec.gob.ec; internet www.ecuadorencifras.gob.ec; f. 1976; library of 6,500 vols; Exec. Dir JOSÉ ROSERO MONCAYO; Gen. Sec. JORGE SANDOVAL ATAPUMA; publ. Indice de Precios al Consumidor Urbano, Indice de Precios al Productor, Indice de Precios de Materiales, Equipo y Maquinaria de la Construcción.

HISTORY, GEOGRAPHY AND ARCHAEOLOGY

Instituto Geográfico Militar (Military Geographical Institute): Apdo 17-01-2435, Quito;; tel. (2) 397-5100; internet www.igm.gob.ec; f. 1928; attached to Min. of Defence; provides cartographic and geographic documentation for nat. devt and security; formulates disaster and land information systems; library of 10,500 vols; Dir Ing. PEDRO CABEZAS GALLEGOS; publs *Indices Toponímicos*, *Revista Geográfica* (2 a year).

MEDICINE

Instituto Nacional de Higiene y Medicina Tropical 'Leopoldo Izquieta Pérez' (National Institute of Hygiene and Topical Medicine): Julian Coronel 905 y Esmeraldas, Guayaquil; tel. (4) 281-542; f. 1941; library of 5,600 vols; Dir Dra ROSARIO ZAMBRANO BONILLA; publ. *Revista Ecuatoriana de Higiene y Medicina Tropical*.

NATURAL SCIENCES

General

Instituto Oceanográfico de la Armada (Naval Oceanographic Institute): Avda 25 de Julio Vía Puerto Marítimo, Base Naval Sur, Guayaquil; tel. (4) 248-1300; e-mail inocar@inocar.mil.ec; internet www.inocar.mil.ec; f. 1972; library of 2,500 vols; Dir BYRON SANMIGUEL MARÍN (acting); publ. *Acta Oceanográfica del Pacífico* (1 a year).

Biological Sciences

Charles Darwin Research Station: Casilla 17-01-3891, Quito; Puerto Ayora, Isla Santa Cruz, Galapagos; tel. (5) 252-6147; e-mail cdrs@fcdarwin.org.ec; internet www.darwinfoundation.org; f. 1964; maintains meteorological stations, herbarium, zoological museum and marine laboratory; breeding programme for endangered reptiles; studies and preserves flora and fauna of the archipelago; library of 4,000 vols, 12,000 separates, 105 current periodicals, slides, aerial photographs, maps; Pres. Dr DENNIS GEIST; Sec. BARBARA WEST; publ. *Noticias de Galápagos* (2 a year).

Physical Sciences

Instituto Nacional de Meteorología e Hidrología (National Institute of Meteorology and Hydrology): Iñaquito 36–14 y Corea, Quito; tel. (2) 397-1100; e-mail inamhi@inamhi.gob.ec; internet www.inamhi.gob.ec; f. 1961; library of 6,500 vols; Exec. Dir Ing. CARLOS PÁEZ PÉREZ; publs *Anuario Hidrológico*, *Anuario Meteorológico*.

Observatorio Astronómico de Quito (Quito Astronomical Observatory): Apdo 17-01-165, Quito; Avda Gran Colombia s/n y Avda 10 de Agosto, Interior del parque La Alameda, Quito; tel. (2) 257-0765; e-mail observatorio.astronomico@epn.edu.ec; internet oaq.epn.edu.ec; f. 1873; astronomy, astrophysics, meteorology and archaeoastronomy, seismology; library of 5,000 vols; Dir Dr ERICSON LÓPEZ IZURIETA.

TECHNOLOGY

Comisión Ecuatoriana de Energía Atómica (Atomic Energy Commission of Ecuador): Juan Larrea N15-36 y Riofrío, Quito; tel. (2) 222-5166; e-mail comecen1@comecenat.gov.ec; f. 1958; 40 mems; research in nuclear physics, radioisotopes, radiobiology, chemistry, medicine; library of 5,000 vols; Exec. Dir Dr MARCOS BRAVO SALVADOR; publ. *Noticias Trimestrales*.

Libraries and Archives

Cuenca

Biblioteca Panamericana (Pan-American Library): Apdo 57, Cuenca; tel. (7) 826-130; f. 1912; 64,000 vols; Dir LADY LISSETH MONAR CADENA.

Biblioteca Pública Municipal de Cuenca (Public Municipal Library of Cuenca): Apdo 202, Cuenca; tel. (6) 924-0403; e-mail biblioteca@cuenca.es; f. 1927; 50,000 vols; Dir JUAN TAMA MÁRQUEZ.

Centro de Documentación Regional 'Juan Bautista Vázquez' de la Universidad de Cuenca (Juan Bautista Vázquez Regional Documentation Centre): Avda 12 de Abril y Agustín Cueva, Cuenca; tel. (7) 405-1000; e-mail biblioteca.ucuenca@hotmail.com; internet biblioteca.ucuenca.edu.ec; f. 1882; 250,000 vols; Dir ROCÍO CAMPOVERDE.

Guayaquil

Biblioteca 'Angel Andrés García' de la Universidad 'Vicente Rocafuerte' ('Angel García Andrés' Library of Vicente Rocafuerte University): Avda de las Américas frente al Cuartel Modelo, Apdo 1133, Guayaquil; f. 1847; 13,000 vols; Dir SONIA MORETA.

Biblioteca de Autores Nacionales 'Carlos A. Rolando' (Library of Ecuadorian Writers): Apdo 6069, Guayaquil; 10 de Agosto entre Chile y Pedro Carbo Palacio Municipal, Guayaquil; tel. (4) 515-738; f. 1913; 12,000 vols, 15,000 pamphlets, 17,000 leaflets, 3,000 MSS relating to Ecuadorian authors and foreign works about Ecuador; Dir (vacant).

Biblioteca General de la Universidad de Guayaquil (Library of the University of

Guayaquil): Ciudadela Universitaria Salvador Allende, Malecón del Salado entre Avda Fortunato Safadi y Avda Kennedy, Guayaquil; tel. (4) 282-440; f. 1901; 50,000 vols; Dir Lic. LEONOR VILLAO DE SANTANDER; publs *El Universitario*, *Revista*.

Biblioteca Municipal 'Pedro Carbo' (Public Library 'Pedro Carbo'): Avda 10 de Agosto entre Pedro Carbo y Chile, Guayaquil; tel. (4) 524-100; e-mail dcpc_bib@hotmail.com; f. 1862; 550,000 vols; Dir NANCY PALACIOS DE MEDINA.

Quito

Archivo-Biblioteca de la Función Legislativa (Archive-Library of the Legislative Branch): Avda 10 de Agosto y Briceño, Quito; f. 1886; scientific and cultural; information on law, politics and history; 27,000 vols; Dir Lic. RAFAEL A. PIEDRA SOLÍS; publs *Clave de la Legislación Ecuatoriana*, *Diario de Debates de la Legislatura*.

Archivo Nacional de Ecuador (National Archives of Ecuador): 10 de Agosto N11-539 y Santa Prisca, Quito; tel. (2) 228-0431; e-mail archivonacionalec@andinanet.net; internet www.ane.gob.ec; f. 1938; 2,500 vols; colonial documents from the 16th to 19th century; Dir ROCÍO PAZMIÑO ACUÑA; Sec. JUAN R. FREKE-GRANIZO; publ. *Arnahis*.

Biblioteca de la Universidad Central del Ecuador (Central University of Ecuador Library): Avda América s/n, Ciudadela Universitaria, Hall del Teatro Universitario, Quito; tel. (2) 250-5859; e-mail bgeneral@ac.uce.edu.ec; internet www.uce.edu.ec/web/biblioteca-general; f. 1826; 170,000 vols; Dir ALONSO ALTAMIRANO; publ. *Bibliografía Ecuatoriana*.

Biblioteca Economica del Banco Central del Ecuador (Economic Library of the Central Bank of Ecuador): Apdo 17150029-C, Quito; Avda 10 de Agosto, entre Pasaje Carlos Ibarra y Sta Prisca, Edif. Alameda, Quito; tel. (2) 257-2522; e-mail ccartagenova@bce.ec; internet biblioteca.bce.ec; f. 1993; 15,000 vols, 3,500 periodicals, specializes in economics, admin., banking and finance, social sciences; Dir CARLOS CARTAGENOVA.

Biblioteca Ecuatoriana 'Aurelio Espinosa Pólit' ('Aurelio Espinosa Pólit' Ecuadorian Library): Apdo 17-01-160, Quito; José Nogales y Francisco Arcos, Cotocollao, Quito; tel. (2) 249-1157; e-mail director@beaep.org.ec; internet www.beaep.org.ec; f. 1929; Ecuadorian art and history museum; 300,000 vols; Librarian JULIAN G. BRAVO.

Biblioteca Municipal (Municipal Library): García Moreno 882 y Sucre, Quito; tel. (2) 222-8418; e-mail bibmuni@yahoo.com; internet www.centrocultural-quito.com; f. 1886; 12,500 vols, 300 MSS, 4 incunabula; Dir ESTELLA RODRIGO.

Biblioteca Nacional del Ecuador (National Library of Ecuador): 12 de Octubre 555, Apdo 67, Quito; tel. (2) 290-2272; e-mail bibliotecanacionalecuador@gmail.com; f. 1792; 70,000 vols of which 7,000 date from the 16th to 18th centuries; Dir LAURA DE CRESPO; Sec. PATRICIA PALACIOS.

Attached Library:

Biblioteca de la Casa de la Cultura Ecuatoriana (Library of Ecuadorian Culture): Apdo 67, Avda Colombia, Quito; tel. (2) 222-3391; e-mail biblioteca@cce.org.ec; f. 1944; 12,000 vols and over 20,000 periodicals; incl. the 'Laura de Crespo' Room of Nat. Authors; Dir LUCY MALDONADO.

Museums and Art Galleries

Guayaquil

Museo Antropológico del Banco Central (Anthropological Museum of the Central Bank): Avda de las Américas 1100 y Avda Juan Tanca Marengo, Guayaquil; tel. (4) 285-800; internet www.bce.fin.ec/contenido.php?cnt=arb0000393; f. 1974; archaeology of the Ecuadorian coast; gallery of contemporary Latin American art; research; library of 7,500 vols; Dir FREDDY OLMEDO R.; publ. *Miscelánea Antropológica Ecuatoriana*.

Museo Municipal de Guayaquil (Municipal Museum of Guayaquil): Calle Sucre entre Chile y Pedro Carbo, Guayaquil; tel. (4) 259-9100; e-mail info@museodeguayaquil.com; internet www.museodeguayaquil.com; f. 1862; historical, ethnographical, palaeontological, geological exhibits; colonial period and modern paintings and numismatics (also see under Libraries and Archives); Dir VICTOR HUGO ARELLANO PAREDES.

Quito

Museo de Arte Colonial (Colonial Art Museum): Cuenca St and Mejía St, Quito; tel. (2) 228-2297; e-mail gestion.museos@casadelacultura.gob.ec; f. 1914; attached to Casa de la Cultura Ecuatoriana 'Benjamín Carrión'; pieces from the Escuela Quiteña of the colonial epoch (17th and 18th centuries); Dir JUAN CARLOS FERNÁNDEZ-CATALÁN.

Museo de Artes Visuales e Instrumentos Musicales: Avda 12 de Octubre 555 y Patria, Quito; tel. (2) 222-3392; attached to Casa de la Cultura Ecuatoriana 'Benjamín Carrión'; art from Ecuador and Latin America since 19th century.

Museo de Ciencias Naturales de la Escuela Militar 'Eloy Alfaro' (Museum of Natural Sciences of 'Eloy Alfaro' Military School): Avda Orellana y Amazonas, Quito; f. 1937; geological specimens and fauna from the Galapagos Islands; taxidermy and anatomy illustrated, especially of mammals and birds; Taxidermist LUIS ALFREDO PÉREZ VACA; publ. *Revista Anual del Plantel*.

Museo Jacinto Jijón y Caamaño (Jacinto Jijón y Caamaño Museum): Edif. de la Biblioteca General de la PUCE 3°, Avda 12 de Octubre 1076 y Roca, Quito; tel. (2) 299-1242; e-mail jmjaramillo@puce.edu.ec; internet www.puce.edu.ec/index.php?pagina=museojjc; f. 1969; archaeology, art, ethnography; library of 2,000 vols; Dir ERNESTO SALAZAR.

Museo Municipal de Arte e Historia 'Alberto Mena Caamaño' (Municipal Museum of Art and History 'Alberto Mena Caamano'): Espejo 1147 y Benalcázar, Pichincha, Quito; tel. (2) 214-018; e-mail info@centrocultural-quito.com; f. 1959; archaeology, colonial art, 19th-century art, items of historical interest; history archive (1583–1980), information library; Dir ALFONSO ORTIZ CRESPO.

Universities

PONTIFICIA UNIVERSIDAD CATÓLICA DEL ECUADOR
(Pontifical Catholic University of Ecuador)

Apdo 17-01-2184, Quito
Avda 12 de Octubre 1076 y Roca, Quito

Telephone: (2) 299-1700
E-mail: webmaster@puce.edu.ec
Internet: www.puce.edu.ec

Founded 1946
Private control
Language of instruction: Spanish
Academic year: August to July

Co-financed

Grand Chancellor: FAUSTO TRÁVEZ TRÁVEZ
Vice-Grand Chancellor: GILBERTO FREIRE YÁNEZ
Rector: Dr MANUEL CORRALES PASCUAL
Vice-Rector: Ing. PABLO ITURRALDE PONCE
Gen. Sec.: Dr SANTIAGO JARAMILLO HERDOIZA
Librarian: OSWALDO ORBE CORTEZ

Number of teachers: 1,900
Number of students: 13,200

Publications: *Economía y Humanismo* (4 a year), *Nuestra Ciencia*, *Revista PUCE* (2 a year)

DEANS

Faculty of Accounting and Administrative Sciences: Ing. PAULINA CADENA VINUEZA
Faculty of Architecture, Design and Arts: Arq. ALEXIS MOSQUERA RIVERA
Faculty of Communication, Linguistics and Literature: Dra LUCÍA LEMOS SILVA
Faculty of Economics: MÓNICA MANCHENO KAROLYS
Faculty of Education Sciences: JOSÉ LUIS FERNANDEZ GRACIA
Faculty of Engineering: Ing. DIEGO ANDRADE STACEY
Faculty of Human Sciences: Dr JUAN HIDALGO AGUILERA
Faculty of Jurisprudence: Dr SANTIAGO GUARDERAS IZQUIERDO
Faculty of Medicine: Dr EDISON CHAVES ALMEIDA
Faculty of Natural Sciences: Dr HUGO NAVARRETE
Faculty of Nursing: NELLY SARMIENTO SARMIENTO
Faculty of Philosophical and Theosophical Sciences: FERNANDO BARREDO HEINERT
Faculty of Psychology: MARIE-FRANCE MERLYN SACOTO

REGIONAL CAMPUSES

Ambato Campus: Apdo 18-01-662, Ambato;Avda Manuelita Sáenz Sector El Tropezón, Ambato; tel. (3) 258-6016; e-mail pucesa@puce.edu.ec; internet www.pucesa.edu.ec; Pro-Rector Dr CÉSAR ENRIQUE GONZÁLEZ LOOR.

Esmeraldas Campus: Apdo 08-01-0065, Esmeraldas;Calle Espejo y Santa Cruz s/n, Esmeraldas; tel. (6) 272-6613; e-mail prorrector@pucese.net; internet www.pucese.net; Pro-Rector AITOR URBINA GARCÍA DE VICUÑA.

Ibarra Campus: Apdo 10-10-34, Ibarra;Avda Aurelio Espinosa Pólit, Cdla. 'La Victoria', Ibarra; tel. (2) 264-1786; e-mail prorect@pucei.edu.ec; internet www.pucei.edu.ec; Pro-Rector Dr MARÍA JOSÉ RUBIO GÓMEZ.

PUCE—Manabí: *Campus Portoviejo*: Ciudadela 1° de Mayo, Calle Eudoro Loor s/n y 25 de Diciembre, Portoviejo; *Campus Chone*: Via Chone-El Carmen, km 11, Chone; *Campus Bahía de Caráquez*: Vía Bahía-Chone, km 8; tel. (5) 263-7300; e-mail pucemanabi@hotmail.com; Pro-Rector Rev. HOMERO FUENTES VERA.

PUCE—Santo Domingo de los Colorados: Apdo 17-24-539, Santo Domingo de los Tsáchila;Vía Chone km 2 y San Cristóbal, Santo Domingo de los Tsáchila; tel. (2) 370-2860; e-mail sprorrectorado@pucesd.edu.ec; Pro-Rector Dr MARGALINA FONT ROIG

UNIVERSIDAD AGRARIA DEL ECUADOR
(Agricultural University of Ecuador)

Apdo 09-01-1248, Guayaquil
Avda 25 de Julio y Pio Jaramillo, Via Puerto Maritimo, Guayaquil
Telephone: (4) 243-9995
E-mail: info@uagraria.edu.ec
Internet: www.uagraria.edu.ec
Founded 1992
public control
Language of instruction: Spanish
Rector: Ing. MARTHA RINA BUCARAM LEVERONE
Vice-Rector: Ing. RICARDO MARQUEZ

DEANS
Faculty of Agricultural Science: Ing. JAVIER DEL CIPPO
Faculty of Veterinary Medicine: Dr MANUEL PULIDO

UNIVERSIDAD ANDINA SIMÓN BOLÍVAR ECUADOR
(Simon Bolivar Andean University)

Apdo 17-12-569, Quito
Toledo N22-80 (Plaza Brasilia), Quito
Telephone: (2) 322-8085
E-mail: uasb@uasb.edu.ec
Internet: www.uasb.edu.ec
Founded 1992
public control
Language of instruction: Spanish
Academic year: October to September
Campuses in Sucre (Bolivia) and Caracas (Venezuela); offices in Bogotá (Colombia) and La Paz (Bolivia)
Rector: ENRIQUE AYALA MORA
Gen. Sec.: VIRGINIA ALTA PERUGACHI
Librarian: ENRIQUE ABAD ROA
Publications: *Comentario Internacional: Revista del Centro Andino de Estudios Internacionales*, *Foro: Revista de Derecho*, *Kipus: Revista Andina de Letras*, *Procesos: Revista Ecuatoriana de Historia*

DIRECTORS
Arts: ARIRUMA KOWII
Business: ALFONSO TROYA
Communication: JOSÉ LASO
Education: MARIO CIFUENTES
Health Studies: JAIME BREILH
History: GUILLERMO BUSTOS
Law: CÉSAR MONTAÑO
Management: WILSON ARAQUE
Social and Global Studies: CÉSAR MONTÚFAR

ATTACHED RESEARCH INSTITUTES
Centro Andino de Estudios Internacionales (Andean Centre for International Studies): tel. (4) 256-0945; e-mail dctena@hoy.net; Coordinator. MICHEL LEVI.
Programa Andino de Derechos Humanos (Andean Human Rights Programme): tel. (4) 255-6403; e-mail gina.benavides@uasb.edu.ec; Coordinator GINA BENAVIDES

UNIVERSIDAD CASA GRANDE
(University Casa Grande)

Frente a la Puerta 6 del C.C. Albán Borja, Guayaquil
Telephone: (4) 220-2180
E-mail: relacionespublicas@casagrande.edu.ec
Internet: www.casagrande.edu.ec
Founded 1992
Private control
Language of instruction: Spanish
Self-financed
Rector: MARCIA GILBERT LEONOR BAQUERIZO
Vice-Rector: LETICIA ORCÉS
Dir Gen.: MARÍA TIBAU
Gen. Sec.: KATIA SAN MARTÍN
Librarian: WENDY MATEO

DEANS
Faculty of Administration and Political Sciences: MODESTO CORREA SAN ANDRÉS
Faculty of Communication 'Monica Herrera': ENRIQUE ROJAS
Faculty of Human Ecology, Education and Development: LUCILA PERÉZ

UNIVERSIDAD CATÓLICA DE CUENCA
(Catholic University of Cuenca)

Apdo 01-01-1937, Cuenca
Humboldt y Avda de las Américas, Cuenca
Telephone: (7) 842-606
E-mail: uccsis@etapa.com.ec
Internet: www.ucacue.edu.ec
Founded 1970
Private control
Language of instruction: Spanish
Academic year: October to July (3 semesters)
Co-financed
Rector: Dr CÉSAR CORDERO MOSCOSO
Vice-Rector for Academic Affairs: Dr ENRIQUE POZO CABRERA
Vice-Rector for Admin. Affairs: Ing. GERARDO ARÉVALO IDROVO
Vice-Rector for Extension: Dr HUGO ORTIZ SEGARRA
Gen. Sec.: Dr RODRIGO CISNEROS AGUIRRE
Dean for Communications, Radio and Television Channel 2: Ing. JHONNY PERALTA IZQUIERDO
Dean for Extension Univ. at Azogues: Dr MARCO VICUÑA DOMÍNGUEZ
Dean for Extension Univ. at Cañar: Dr BOLÍVAR CABRERA BERREZUETA
Dean for Extension Univ. at Macas: JOSÉ MERINO V.
Dean for Extension Univ. at Méndez: Dr JORGE CÁRDENAS ESPINOZA
Dean for Extension Univ. at San Pablo, Troncal: REMIGIO VÁZQUEZ LÓPEZ
Librarian: Prof. ANGEL LÓPEZ VÁZQUEZ
Library of 8,000 vols
Number of teachers: 850
Number of students: 12,000
Publications: *Diálogo*, *Estudios*, *Panoramas*, *Presencia*, *Retama*

DEANS
Bilingual Secretarial School: OSCAR CALLE MASACHE
Faculty 'Cardenal Echeverría': PATRICIO BONILLO
Faculty of Agricultural Engineering, Mining, Veterinary Science and Ecology: Ing. HUMBERTO SALAMEA CARPIO
Faculty of Chemical and Industrial Engineering: Ing. SANTIAGO GÓMEZ LIVISACA
Faculty of Civil Engineering and Architecture: GERARDO AREVALO IDROVO
Faculty of Commercial Engineering, Management and Accounting: Ing. SIXTO SANCHEZ PERALTA
Faculty of Distance Learning: Dr HUGO ORTIZ SEGARRA
Faculty of Economics: Dr HUGO ORTIZ SEGARRA
Faculty of Ecotourism: JUANA CATALINA JARAMILLO
Faculty of Education and Psychology: Dr ENRIQUE CAMPOVERDE CAJAS
Faculty of Electrical Engineering: Dr EDUARDO CORONEL DÍAZ
Faculty of Enterprise Engineering: RAMIRO CARANGUI CÁRDENAS
Faculty of Informatics Systems: Dr EDUARDO CORONEL DIAZ
Faculty of Law and Social Sciences: Dr ENRIQUE POZO CABRERA
Faculty of Medicine and Health Sciences: Dr CARLOS DARQUEA LOPEZ
Faculty of Odontology: Dr CARLOS MORALES VILLAVICENCIO
Faculty of Systems, Electrical and Electronics: Ing. DIEGO CORDERO G.
Institute of Languages: Ing. RAÚL CAMPOVERDE CAJAS
Institute of Nursing: Dra MARÍA FERNANDA ORTIZ HINOJOSA
Postgraduate Cttee: Dr MARCO VICUNA DOMÍNGUEZ
School of Drama and Aerobics: Dr CARLOS EFRAÍN CRESPO
School of Journalism and Communications: Dr IVÁN CULCAY VILLAVICENCIO
School of Physical Education: Dr ROLANDO CORONEL DÍAZ
School of Social Service: LEONOR MASACHE MALDONADO

UNIVERSIDAD CATÓLICA DE SANTIAGO DE GUAYAQUIL
(Catholic University of Santiago de Guayaquil)

Avda Carlos Julio Arosemena km $1\frac{1}{2}$ Vía Daule, Guayaquil
Telephone: (4) 220-6950
E-mail: vinculacion.rrii@cu.ucsg.edu.ec
Internet: www2.ucsg.edu.ec
Founded 1962
Private control
Language of instruction: Spanish
Academic year: May to April
Co-financed
Rector: LINO MAURO TOSCANINI SEGALE
Vice-Rector: ALFREDO ESCALA MACAFERRI
Vice-Rector for Admin. Affairs: LUIS FERNANDO HIDALGO PROAÑO
Vice-Rector for Academic Affairs: MARIA CECILIA LOOR DUEÑAS DE TAMARIZE
Gen. Sec.: GUILLERMO VILLACRES SMITH
Dir for Library: JEFFERSON STALYN ALEJANDRO DOMINGUEZ
Library of 32,974 vols
Number of teachers: 1,200
Number of students: 15,000
Publications: *Revista Alternativas*, *Revista Medicina*

DEANS
Faculty of Architecture: Arq. FLORENCIO COMPTE GUERRERO
Faculty of Arts and Humanities: Dra MARIA DE LOURDES ESTRADA RUIZ
Faculty of Business: SERVIO CORREA
Faculty of Economics: Ing. HUGO FERNANDEZ MACAS
Faculty of Engineering: LILA VALAREZO MORENO
Faculty of Law: JOSÉ MIGUEL GARCÍA BAQUERIZO
Faculty of Medical Sciences: Dr GUSTAVO RAMIREZ AMAT
Faculty of Philosophy: ELBA BERMUDEZ REYES
Faculty of Technical Education for Development: Ing. MANUEL ROMERO PAZ

UNIVERSIDAD CENTRAL DEL ECUADOR
(Central University of Ecuador)

América Avda and Universitaria, Quito
Telephone: (2) 226-080
E-mail: rectorado@uce.edu.ec
Internet: www.uce.edu.ec
Founded 1586 as Univ. de San Fulgencio, became Real y Pontificia Univ. de San Gregorio in 1622, Univ. de Santo Tomás de Aquino in 1688, then Univ. Central del Sur

de la Gran Colombia, current name adopted 1826
public control
Language of instruction: Spanish
Academic year: September to July

Rector: EDGAR GUALBERTO SAMANIEGO ROJAS
Vice-Chancellor for Academic and Investigation: CLÍMACO RODRIGO EGAS ARROYO
Vice-Chancellor for Admin. and Financial Affairs: JOSÉ LEONARDO VILLAVICENCIO ROSERO
Dir Gen. Academic: Dr EDMUNDO ESTÉVEZ MONTALVO
Gen. Sec.: RUBÉN DARÍO MORENO SUQUILANDA

Library of 54,000 vols
Number of teachers: 1,800
Number of students: 51,000

Publications: *Anales*, *Cifras*

DEANS

Faculty of Administrative Sciences: Dr WELLINGTON RÍOS
Faculty of Agricultural Sciences: MARCELO CALVACHE
Faculty of Architecture and Urbanism: Arq. MIGUEL ANGEL HERNÁNDEZ CARRIÓN
Faculty of Arts: JOSÉ ANGEL P. CELA
Faculty of Chemical Engineering: LUIS CALLE GUADALUPE
Faculty of Chemistry: WILSON PARRA
Faculty of Dentistry: Dr ALEJANDRO FARFÁN
Faculty of Economics: MARCO POSSO
Faculty of Engineering in Geology, Mines, Petroleum and Environmental Studies: VÍCTOR HUGO AGUIRRE
Faculty of Engineering, Physics and Mathematics: Dra Ing. TERESA AYABACA CAZAR
Faculty of Law and Political and Social Sciences: Dr WALTER MARTÍNEZ VELA
Faculty of Medical Sciences: Dr MILTON TAPIA CALVOPIÑA
Faculty of Philosophy, Literature and Science Education: Dr EDGAR HERRERA MONTALVO
Faculty of Physical Culture: GUIDO CHALÉN GARZON
Faculty of Psychological Sciences: Dr PABLO PICERNO
Faculty of Social Communication: JOSÉ VILLAMARÍN CARRASCAL
Faculty of Veterinary Medicine: Dr BOLÍVAR RICAURTE

UNIVERSIDAD DE CUENCA
(University of Cuenca)

Avda 12 de Abril s/n y Agustín Cueva, Cuenca
Telephone: (7) 405-1000
Internet: www.ucuenca.edu.ec

Founded 1867
State control
Language of instruction: Spanish
Academic year: September to July

Rector: Ing. FABIÁN CARRASCO CASTRO
Vice-Rector: Ing. SILVANA LARRIVA GONZÁLEZ

Number of teachers: 1,075
Number of students: 14,404

Publications: *MASKANA*, *PUCARA*

DEANS

Faculty of Agriculture: Dr ROMEO SANCHEZ M.
Faculty of Architecture: FERNANDO PAUTA CALLE
Faculty of Arts: Dr CARLOS ROJAS
Faculty of Chemistry: Dra SILVANA DONOSO
Faculty of Dentistry: Dr GONZALO MONTESINOS
Faculty of Economics: VICTOR AGUILAR
Faculty of Engineering: Ing. PATRICIO GUERRERO (acting)
Faculty of Hospitality Sciences: Dr SANTIAGO CARPIO
Faculty of Jurisprudence: Dr CARLOS CASTRO RIERA
Faculty of Medical Sciences: Dr PABLO CORDERO
Faculty of Philosophy: MARÍA AUGUSTA VINTIMILLA
Faculty of Psychology: MARCO MUÑOZ

UNIVERSIDAD DE GUAYAQUIL
(University of Guayaquil)

Ciudadela Universitaria Salvador Allende, Avda Kennedy y Avda Delta, Guayaquil
Telephone: (4) 229-3598
E-mail: ugrector@ug.edu.ec
Internet: www.ug.edu.ec

Founded 1867
public control
Language of instruction: Spanish
Academic year: April to February (2 semesters)

Rector: CARLOS CEDENO NAVARRETE
Gen. Vice-Rector: OSWALDO PACHECO GIL
Vice-Rector for Academic Affairs: JOSÉ LIZARDO APOLO PINEDA
Vice-Rector for Admin. Affairs: CÉSAR ROMERO VILLAGRÁN
Librarian: Licda LEONOR V. DE SANTANDER

Number of teachers: 2,222
Number of students: 83,448

Publication: *Revista Ciencias Médicas*

DEANS

Faculty of Administrative Sciences: Ing. MARCO SURATY MOLESTINA
Faculty of Agricultural Sciences: CÉSAR PACHECO MONROY (acting)
Faculty of Architecture: JORGE CABELLO FARAH
Faculty of Chemical Engineering: FERNANDO QUIROZ PÉREZ
Faculty of Chemistry: CÉSAR MUÑOZ ITURRALDE
Faculty of Economics: WASHINGTON AGUIRRE GARCÍA
Faculty of Industrial Engineering: ALFREDO BUCARAM ORTIZ
Faculty of Law, Social Sciences and Politics: ALFREDO RUIZ GUZMÁN
Faculty of Mathematics and Physics: Ing. FERNANDO ABAD MONTERO (acting)
Faculty of Medicine: Dr GONZALO MAITTA MENDOZA
Faculty of Natural Sciences: Dr CARMITA BONIFAZ DE ELAO
Faculty of Odontology: Dr WASHINGTON ESCUDERO DOLTZ
Faculty of Philosophy, Literature and Education: FERNANDO CHUCHUCA BASANTES
Faculty of Psychological Sciences: CECILIA BASTIDAS BOLAÑOS
Faculty of Physical Education, Sports and Recreation: ENRIQUE N. GAMBOA ABRIL
Faculty of Social Communication: HÉCTOR CHÁVEZ VILLAO
Faculty of Veterinary Medicine: MARÍO COBO CEDEÑO (acting)

UNIVERSIDAD DE ESPECIALIDADES TURÍSTICAS
(University of Tourism Specialties)

Avda Machala OE6-160 y Avda Occidental, Quito
Telephone: (2) 602-0788
E-mail: universidad@uct.edu.ec
Internet: www.uct.edu.ec

Founded 2000
Private control
Language of instruction: Spanish
Academic year: March to August

Schools of graduate studies, hospitality, tourism

Rector: MARIA DE LOURDES JARRIN
Vice-Rector: MARÍAMPARO MORENO

UNIVERSIDAD DE LAS AMERICAS
(University of the Americas)

Avda de los Granados E12-41 y Colimes Esq., 170125 Quito
Telephone: (2) 398-1000
E-mail: admision@udla.edu.ec
Internet: www.udla.edu.ec

Founded 1995
Private control
Language of instruction: Spanish
Academic year: September to August

Campuses in Colón and Granados

Rector: Dr CARLOS LARREÁTEGUI
Vice-Rector for Academic Affairs: GONZALO MENDIETA

DEANS

Biomedical Research Institute: CÉSAR PAZ-Y-MIÑO
Faculty of Architecture: JOSÉ ORDÓÑEZ
Faculty of Communication: JOSÉ VELÁSQUEZ
Faculty of Economics and Administrative Sciences: VINCENTE ALBORNOZ
Faculty of Engineering and Agricultural Sciences: TOMÁS VILLÓN
Faculty of General Education: DIEGO CHAUVIN
Faculty of Health Sciences: ALFREDO BORRERO
Faculty of Law: ALEXANDRA VELA
Faculty of Medicine: RAUL JERVIS
Faculty of Odontology: EDUARDO FLORES
Faculty of Social Sciences: MAURICIO MONTALVO
Institute of Graduate Studies: GIUSEPPE MARZANO

UNIVERSIDAD DE LOS HEMISFERIOS
(University of the Hemispheres)

POB 023-828-670, Quito
Paseo de la Universidad No 300 y Juan Díaz (Urb. Iñaquito Alto), Quito
Telephone: (2) 246-6666
E-mail: info@uhemisferios.edu.ec
Internet: www.uhemisferios.edu.ec

Founded 2004
Private control
Language of instruction: Spanish

Rector: Ing. ALEJANDRO RIBADENEIRA ESPINOSA

DEANS

Faculty of Arts and Humanities: DIEGO ALEJANDRO JARAMILLO
Faculty of Business and Economics: HERNÁN LÓPEZ AGUIRRE
Faculty of Communication: IVÁN RODRIGO MENDIZÁBAL (Director)
Faculty of Graduate Studies: GERÓNIMO GANDO GARZÓN (Director)
Faculty of Law: Dr RENÉ BEDÓN GARZÓN

UNIVERSIDAD DE OTAVALO
(University of Otavalo)

Cdla. Imbaya, Avda de los Sarances s/n y Pendoneros, Otavalo
Telephone: (6) 292-0461
E-mail: info@uotavalo.edu.ec
Internet: www.uotavalo.edu.ec

Founded 2002
Private control
Language of instruction: Spanish

Schools of graphic design, international trade and finance, law, management and business development, marketing and international tourism, social development

Rector: Dra SUSANA CORDERO AGUILAR

Vice-Rector for Academic Affairs: Ing. LUIS ALBERTO ACOSTA
Gen. Sec.: Dr TITO VILLEGAS
Librarian: JESSICA RAMOS
Publication: *Sarance N° 27*

UNIVERSIDAD DEL AZUAY
(University of Azuay)

Apdo 01 01 981, Cuenca
Avda 24 de Mayo 7-77 y Hernán Malo, Cuenca
Telephone: (7) 409-1000
E-mail: webmaste@uazuay.edu.ec
Internet: www.uazuay.edu.ec
Founded 1968, present status 1990
public control
Language of instruction: Spanish
Academic year: October to July
Co-financed; school of management science
Rector: Dr CARLOS CORDERO DÍAZ
Vice-Rector: Ing. MIRIAM BRIONES GARCÍA
Gen. Sec: Dra XIMENA MEJIA MOSCOSO
Library of 46,000 vols
Publication: *Marginalia* (2 a year)

DEANS
Faculty of Administration: OSWALDO MERCHÁN MANZANO
Faculty of Design: FABIÁN LANDIVAR LARA
Faculty of Law: Dr REMIGIO AUQUILLA LUCERO
Faculty of Medicine: Dr HERNAN SACOTO AGUILAR
Faculty of Philosophy: CARLOS DELGADO ÁLVAREZ
Faculty of Science and Technology: Ing. GERMÁN ZÚÑIGA CABRERA
Faculty of Theology: Fr ANTONIO ALONSO MARTÍNEZ

UNIVERSIDAD DEL PACIFICO—ESCUELA DE NEGOCIOS
(Pacific University—School of Business)

Km 7 1/2 Vía a la Costa (a 1 km de Riocentro Los Ceibos), Guayaquil
Telephone: (04) 287-3387
Internet: www.upacifico.edu.ec
Founded 1997
Private control
Language of instruction: Spanish
Self-financed; campuses in Quito, Guayaquil and Cuenca
Rector: Dra SONIA ADELINA ROCA DE CASTRO
Number of teachers: 134

UNIVERSIDAD ESTATAL AMAZÓNICA
(Amazonica State University)

Km 2 1/2 Via Napo (Paso Lateral), El Puyo, Puyo-Pastaza
Telephone: (3) 288-8118
E-mail: info@uea.edu.ec
Internet: www.uea.edu.ec
Founded 2002
public control
Language of instruction: Spanish
Schools of agricultural engineering, agroindustrial engineering, environmental engineering, tourism
Rector: Ing. JULIO CÉSAR VARGAS BURGOS
Vice-Rector: Ing. NELLY NARCISA MANJARREZ FUENTES
Gen. Sec.: Dr LENIN ERNESTO ANDRADE CERDÁN

UNIVERSIDAD ESTATAL DE BOLÍVAR
(Bolivar State University)

Avda Ernesto Che Guevara s/n y Avda Dr. Gabriel Secaira, Guaranda
Telephone: (3) 220-6059
E-mail: info@ueb.edu.ec
Internet: www.ueb.edu.ec
Founded 1989
public control
Language of instruction: Spanish
Rector: Ing. DIÓMEDES NÚÑEZ MINAYA
Vice-Rector for Academic Affairs: Lic. FRANCISCO MORENO DEL POZO
Vice-Rector for Admin. and Finance: Ing. ANGEL GRACIA
Librarian: Lic. CATINA ESPINOZA G.
Number of teachers: 190
Number of students: 5,900
Publication: *Enlace Universitario*

DEANS
Faculty of Administrative Sciences, Business Management and Informatics: EDGAR PATRICIO RIVADENEIRA
Faculty of Agriculture, Natural Resources and Environment: Ing. NELSON ARTURO MONAR GAVILANES
Faculty of Education, Social Sciences, Philosophy and Humanistic Sciences: Dr JORGE ANDRADE SANTAMARIA
Faculty of Health Sciences: Ing. OSWALDO LÓPEZ
Faculty of Jurisprudence and Political Sciences: Dr ULISES BARRAGAN

UNIVERSIDAD ESTATAL DE MILAGRO
(Milagro State University)

Cdla. Universitaria km $1\frac{1}{2}$, Vía km 26, Los Rios
Telephone: (4) 297-4319
E-mail: unemi@hotmail.com
Internet: www.unemi.edu.ec
Founded 2001
public control
Language of instruction: Spanish
Schools of administration and commercial sciences, engineering sciences, health sciences, science education and communication
Rector: JAIME OROZCO HERNÁNDEZ
Vice-Rector for Academics and Research: Ing. FABRICIO GUEVARA VIEJÓ
Vice-Rector for Admin.: Dra CATALINA BARZOLA MORÁN
Gen. Sec.: Lic. DIANA PINCAY CANTILLO
Dir of Library: DIOCONDA GAVILÁNEZ

UNIVERSIDAD ESTATAL DEL SUR DE MANABÍ
(State University of Southern Manabi)

Complejo Universitario, Ciudadela 10 de Agosto, Vía a Noboa, Jipijapa
Telephone: (5) 260-0229
E-mail: unesum@hotmail.com
Internet: unesum.edu.ec
Founded 2001
public control
Language of instruction: Spanish
Schools of administrative sciences and economics, computer science and system, forestry, environmental and agricultural sciences, health sciences
Rector: Ing. BLANCA INDACOCHEA DE ÁLVAREZ
Gen. Sec.: Dr ANTONIO GONZÁLEZ VASQUEZ
Publication: *Alcance*

UNIVERSIDAD ESTATAL PENÍNSULA DE SANTA ELENA
(State University of Santa Elena Peninsula)

Avda Principal La Libertad, La Libertad
Telephone: (4) 278-1732
E-mail: unipen@interactive.net.ec
Internet: www.upse.edu.ec
Founded 1998
public control
Language of instruction: Spanish
Academic year: May to February
Rector: Ing. JIMMY CANDELL SOTO
Vice-Rector: GEORGE CLEMENTE

DEANS
Faculty of Administrative Sciences: Ing. FREIRE RENDÓN MERCEDES ENEDINA
Faculty of Agricultural Sciences: Ing. MORA ALCÍVAR ANTONIO ULDEMAR
Faculty of Industrial Engineering: Ing. ELIO RODRÍGUEZ QUIMI

UNIVERSIDAD INTERNACIONAL DEL ECUADOR
(International University of Ecuador)

Simón Bolívar Avda Jorge Fernández SN, Quito
Telephone: (02) 298-5600
Internet: www.uide.edu.ec
Founded 1992
Private control
Language of instruction: Spanish
Self-financed; campuses in Eloy Alfaro, Galapagos, Loja
Rector: MARCELO FERNÁNDEZ SÁNCHEZ
Vice-Rector: Ing. XAVIER FERNÁNDEZ ORRANTIA
Dir Gen. Academic: Dr GUSTAVO VEGA
Gen. Sec.: Dr ÉDGAR VELASCO
Publication: *Erasmus*

DEANS
Faculty of Administrative Sciences: RAMIRO CANELOS
Faculty of Architecture: Arq. DIEGO ARTETA
Faculty of Automotive Engineering: Ing. DIEGO PÉREZ
Faculty of Basic Sciences: Dr ÉDGAR VELASCO
Faculty of Jurisprudence 'Andres F. Cordova': Dra MARIA PAULA ROMO
Faculty of Medical Sciences and Health: Dr BERNARDO SANDOVAL C.
Faculty of Social Sciences and Communication: GONZALO ORTIZ CRESPO

UNIVERSIDAD INTERNACIONAL SEK
(International University SEK)

El Calvario s/n y Francisco Compte, Guápolo, Quito
Telephone: (2) 398-4800
Internet: www.uisek.edu.ec
Founded 1993
Private control
Language of instruction: Spanish
Self-financed; two campuses in Quito
Pres.: Dr JORGE SEGOVIA BONET
Rector: Dr RODOLFO CEPRIÁN MOLINA
Vice-Rector for Academic Affairs: Dr JOSÉ MARÍA DELGADO M.
Gen. Sec.: Dra CAROLINA VILLAGOMEZ M.
Publication: *Anuario UISEK* (1 a year)

DEANS
Faculty of Architecture and Urbanism: OSWALDO PÁEZ
Faculty of Communication Sciences: ROSA SOLÓRZANO
Faculty of Economics, Management and Tourism: IVÁN MARTÍNEZ

Faculty of Environmental Science: KATTY CORAL
Faculty of Law and Social Sciences: PATRICIA ALVEAR
Faculty of Mechanical Engineering: JULIO VALLEJO
Faculty of Occupational Safety and Health: PABLO SUASNAVAS
Faculty of Psychology: VERÓNICA GARCIA
Faculty of Systems and Telecommunications: JHONNY BARRERA

UNIVERSIDAD ISRAEL
(Israel University)

Fco. Pizarro E4–142 y Avda Orellana (Diagonal al Colegio Militar), Quito
Telephone: (2) 255-5741
E-mail: info@uisrael.edu.ec
Internet: www.uisrael.edu.ec
Founded 1999
Private control
Language of instruction: Spanish
Self-financed
Rector: RENÉ CORTIJO JACOMINO
Vice-Rector: FREDDY ÁLVAREZ SUBÍA

UNIVERSIDAD LAICA 'ELOY ALFARO' DE MANABÍ
(Secular University 'Eloy Alfaro' of Manabi)

Via San Mateo s/n Manta, Manta
Telephone: (5) 262-3740
E-mail: uleam@uleam.edu.ec
Internet: www.uleam.edu.ec
Founded 1985
public control
Language of instruction: Spanish
Rector: Dr MEDARDO MORA SOLORZANO
Vice-Rector for Academic Affairs: LEONARDO MOREIRA DELGADO
Gen. Sec.: CARLOS SAN ANDRÉS CEDEÑO

DEANS

Faculty of Administrative Sciences: Ing. MARIO MOREIRA
Faculty of Agricultural Sciences: Ing. RICARDO TUBAY LOOR
Faculty of Architecture: Arq. RICARDO AVILA AVILA
Faculty of Communication Science: ROCIO SALTOS CARVAJAL
Faculty of Economics: Dr ANDRÉS VENEREO BRAVO
Faculty of Education Sciences: AMALIA REYES MOREIRA
Faculty of Engineering: Ing. FREDDY MACHUCA QUIRÓZ
Faculty of Foreign Trade and International Business: Arq. JORGE ALAVA FAGGIONI
Faculty of Hospitality and Tourism: JOUBER AZÚA VÁSQUEZ
Faculty of Industrial Engineering: Ing. LEONOR VIZUETE GAIBOR
Faculty of Information Sciences: Ing. JOSÉ ARTEAGA VERA
Faculty of Jurisprudence: Dr CESAR PALMA ALCÍVAR
Faculty of Languages: SALVADOR ACEBO CHANCAY
Faculty of Management, Development and Executive Secretariat: DIVINA INTRIAGO DURÁN
Faculty of Marine Sciences: Dr LUIS AYALA CASTRO
Faculty of Medicine: Dr RODDY MATA MOREIRA
Faculty of Naval Mechanics: Ing. LUISR CHALLA HASING
Faculty of Nursing: YUBAGNI REZABALA DE MONROY
Faculty of Physical Education, Sports and Recreation: Dr PEDRO AZÚA GUILLEN
Faculty of Public Accounting and Auditing: Dr JUSTO CEVALLOS MERO
Faculty of Social Work: OLGA VÉLEZ DE MENDOZA
Faculty of Specialities in Areas of Health: Dr HERNÁN RODRÍGUEZ BARCIA

UNIVERSIDAD LAICA 'VICENTE ROCAFUERTE' DE GUAYAQUIL
('Vicente Rocafuerte' Secular University of Guayaquil)

Apdo 1133, Guayaquil
Avda de las Américas frente al Cuartel Modelo, Guayaquil
Telephone: (4) 228-7200
Internet: www.ulvr.edu.ec
Founded 1847, univ. status 1966
Private control
Language of instruction: Spanish
Academic year: April to January
Faculties of administration, architecture, civil engineering, economics, education, journalism, jurisprudence and social sciences; schools of accountancy, child education, design, foreign trade, languages, marketing, publicity, secretarial administration, co-financed
Rector: Dr JORGE TORRES PRIETO
Gen. Vice-Rector and Gen. Sec.: ALFREDO AGUILAR ALAVA
Vice-Rector for Academic Affairs: ALFONSO SÁNCHEZ GUERRERO
Librarian: CECILIA RODRÍGUEZ GRANDA
Library of 8,000 vols
Number of teachers: 400
Number of students: 9,400

UNIVERSIDAD NACIONAL DE CHIMBORAZO
(National University of Chimborazo)

Avda Eloy Alfaro y 10 de Agosto, Riobamba
Telephone: (3) 262-8155
E-mail: contactos@unach.edu.ec
Internet: www.unach.edu.ec
Founded 1995
public control
Language of instruction: Spanish
Academic year: October to July (2 semesters)
Rector: Dra MARIA ANGÉLICA BARBA MAGGI
Vice-Rector for Academic Affairs: Dra ANITA CECILIA RÍOS
Vice-Rector for Admin. Affairs: Dr VINICIO MEJÍA

DEANS

Faculty of Education Sciences: SUSANA PONCE
Faculty of Engineering: Ing. EDMUNDO CABEZAS
Faculty of Health Sciences: Dr MIGUEL CARDOSO
Faculty of Political Science: MARÍA EUGENIA BORJA

UNIVERSIDAD NACIONAL DE LOJA
(National University of Loja)

Casilla letra 'S', Loja
Ciudad Universitaria Guillermo Falconí Espinosa 'La Argelia', Loja
Telephone: (7) 254-7252
E-mail: rector@unl.edu.ec
Internet: www.unl.edu.ec
Founded 1859 as the Junta Universitaria, univ. status 1943
public control
Language of instruction: Spanish
Academic year: October to July
Schools of agriculture and renewable natural resources, education, art and communication, energy industries and non-renewable natural resources, human health, law, society and administration
Rector: Dr GUSTAVO ENRIQUE VILLACÍS RIVAS
Vice-Rector: Dr ERNESTO RAFAEL GONZÁLEZ PESANTES
Gen. Sec.: Dr ERNESTO ROLDÁN JARA
Librarian: Col Dra MARTHA ESTHER REYES
Library of 3,500 vols
Number of teachers: 846
Number of students: 14,000
Publications: *Estudios Universitarios*, *Revista Científica*

UNIVERSIDAD POLITÉCNICA SALESIANA
(Salesian Polytechnic University)

Calle Vieja 12-30 y Elia Liut, Cuenca
Telephone: (7) 286-2213
E-mail: svicerrectorcue@ups.edu.ec
Internet: www.ups.edu.ec
Founded 1994
Private control
Language of instruction: Spanish
Co-financed
Rector: Lic. JAVIER HERRÁN GÓMEZ
Vice-Rector: Dr EDGAR LOYOLA ILLESCAS
Vice-Rector for Academic Affairs: FERNANDO PESÁNTEZ
Gen. Sec.: Dr JEFFREY ZUÑIGA RUILOVA
Publications: *Alteridad* (2 a year), *La Granja* (2 a year), *Retos* (2 a year), *Sophia* (2 a year), *Ingenius* (2 a year), *Universitas* (2 a year)

DEANS

Faculty of Administration and Economics: Ing. TANIA ALEXANDRA CHICAIZA VILLALBA
Faculty of Education: Lic. MARÍA SOL VILLAGÓMEZ RODRÍGUEZ
Faculty of Life Sciences: PACO FERNANDO NORIEGA RIVERA
Faculty of Reason and Faith: Lic. ARMANDO ROMERO ORTEGA
Faculty of Sciences: Ing. JACK BRAVO TORRES
Faculty of Science and Technology: Ing. DIEGO PEÑALOZA RIVERA
Faculty of Social Science sand Human Behaviour: RUBÉN DARIO BRAVO CASTILLO

UNIVERSIDAD REGIONAL AUTÓNOMA DE LOS ANDES
(Autonomous Regional University of the Andes)

Km 5 ½ Via Baños, Ambato
Telephone: (3) 274-8182
Internet: www.uniandesonline.edu.ec
Founded 1997
Private control
Language of instruction: Spanish
Self-financed; extensions in Babahoyo, Ibarra, Quevedo, Puyo, Riobamba, Santo Domingo, Tulcán
Rector: Dra EMPERATRIZ CORONA GÓMEZ ARMIJOS
Vice-Rector for General Affairs: Ing. GABRIELA MENA
Gen. Sec: Dr LUIS FERNANDO LATORRE

DEANS

Faculty of Business Administration: EDWIN VÁSQUEZ ERAZO
Faculty of Education Sciences: EDWIN VÁSQUEZ
Faculty of Jurisprudence: Dr MARIO ZAVALA HOYOS
Faculty of Medicine: Dr OCTAVIO MIRANDA
Faculty of Systems and Information: Dra MÓNICA MAYORGA

UNIVERSIDAD SAN FRANCISCO DE QUITO
(San Francisco University of Quito)

POB 17-1200-841, Quito
Avda Diego de Robles y Vía Interoceánica, Quito
Telephone: (2) 297-1700
Internet: www.usfq.edu.ec
Founded 1988
Private control
Language of instruction: Spanish
Self-financed; campuses in Quito and San Cristobal
Rector: Dr. Santiago Emilio Gangotena González
Number of teachers: 300
Number of students: 6,000
Publications: *Avances en Ciencias e Ingenierías* (2 a year), *IurisDictio*, *Liberarte*, *The Panchonomist* (4 a year)

DEANS

College of Administrative Development: Magdalena Barreiro
College of Architecture and Interior Design: Diego Oleas
College of Biological and Environmental Sciences: Stella de la Torre
College of Communication and Contemporary Arts: Hugo Burgos
College of Health Sciences: Gonzalo Mantilla
College of Hospitality, Culinary Arts and Tourism: Mauricio Cepeda
College of Jurisprudence: Dr Luis Parraguez
College of Music: Esteban Molina
College of Science and Engineering: Santiago Gangotena
College of Social Sciences and Humanities: Carmen Fernández Salvador
Graduate College: Arq. Jorge Alava Fagioni

UNIVERSIDAD SAN GREGORIO DE PORTOVIEJO
(University of San Gregorio de Portoviejo)

Avda Metropolitana No 2005 y Avda Olimpica, Portoviejo
Telephone: (5) 293-5002
Internet: www.sangregorio.edu.ec
Founded 2000
Private control
Language of instruction: Spanish
Self-financed; depts of architecture, audit and accounting, business management, communication sciences, dentistry, early education, finance and trade relations, graphic design, law, marketing, production and direction of radio and television
Rector: Dr Marcelo Iván Farfán Intriago
Vice-Rector for Academic Affairs: Arq. Jaime Alfredo Alarcón Zambrano
Vice-Rector for Admin. Affairs: Ricardo Rafael Alarcón Cobeña
Dir Gen. Academics: Dra Lyla Luz Alarcón Ramírez
Gen. Sec.: Ábner Arturo Bello Molina
Librarian: Dayana Bernat Morales
Publication: *San Gregorio*

UNIVERSIDAD TÉCNICA DE AMBATO
(Technical University of Ambato)

Casilla 18-01-334, Ambato
Telephone: (3) 853-905
Internet: www.uta.edu.ec
Founded 1969
public control
Language of instruction: Spanish
Schools of accounting and audit, design, architecture and arts, jurisprudence and social sciences
Rector: Ing. Luis Amoroso Mora
Vice-Rector for Academic Affairs: Dr Galo Naranjo López
Vice-Rector for Admin. Affairs: Dr Jorge Leon
Gen. Sec.: Dr Patricio Poaquiza
Librarian: Elsa Naranjo
Number of teachers: 400
Number of students: 7,200

DEANS

Faculty of Administrative Sciences: Ing. Luis Velásquez Medina
Faculty of Agricultural Engineering: Ing. Hernán Zurita Vásquez
Faculty of Civil and Mechanical Engineering: Ing. Francisco Pazmiño G.
Faculty of Health Sciences: Dr Marco Alvarez
Faculty of Humanities and Education: Ing. Wilma Gavilanes
Faculty of Science and Engineering in Food: Ing. Gladys Cecilia Navas Miño
Faculty of Systems Electronics and Industrial Engineering: Ing. Edison Alvarez

UNIVERSIDAD TÉCNICA DE BABAHOYO
(Technical University of Babahoyo)

Apdo 66, Babahoyo
Vía Flores, Babahoyo
Telephone: (5) 730-646
E-mail: blupera@utb.edu.ec
Internet: www.utb.edu.ec
Founded 1971
public control
Language of instruction: Spanish
Rector: Dr Rafael Falconi Montalvan
Vice-Rector for Admin. Affairs: Dr Zoila Sánchez de Torres
Gen. Sec.: Alberto Bravo Medina
Librarian: Miguel Bastidas
Number of teachers: 450
Number of students: 5,000

DEANS

Faculty of Administration, Finance and Informatics: Ausberto Colina Gonzalvo
Faculty of Agriculture: Otto Ordeñana Burnhan
Faculty of Health Sciences: Dr César Noboa Aquino
Faculty of Social Sciences and Education: Dr Jacinto Muñoz Muñoz

UNIVERSIDAD TÉCNICA DE COTOPAXI
(Technical University of Cotopaxi)

Campus Universitario, Avda Simón Rodríguez s/n Barrio El Ejido, Sector San Felipe, Latacunga
Telephone: (3) 225-2205
E-mail: info@utc.edu.ec
Internet: www.utc.edu.ec
Founded 1995
public control
Language of instruction: Spanish
Academic units of administrative sciences and humanities, agricultural sciences and natural resources, engineering and applied sciences
Rector: Ing. Hernán Yánez Ávila
Vice-Rector: Ing. Guido Yauli
Gen. Sec.: Dr Lucas Guanoquiza
Publications: *Alma Mater*, *Gestión*, *Desafios*

UNIVERSIDAD TÉCNICA DE ESMERALDAS 'LUIS VARGAS TORRES'
(Technical College of Esmeraldas 'Luis Vargas Torres')

Avda Kennedy 704 entre Hilda Padilla y Calle H, Esmeraldas
Telephone: (6) 246-0700
E-mail: utelvt@utelvt.edu.ec
Internet: www.utelvt.edu.ec
Founded 1970
public control
Language of instruction: Spanish
Rector: Luis Felipe Pacheco Luque
Vice-Rector for Academic Affairs: Dr César Saavedra Bustos
Vice-Rector for Admin. Affairs: Ing. Guillermo Mosquera Quintero
Gen. Sec.: Abog. Voltaire Realpe
Librarian: Solanda Gobea
Number of teachers: 200
Number of students: 800

DEANS

Faculty of Administration and Economics: Dr Marlon Gruezo Estacio
Faculty of Agricultural and Environmental Sciences: Ing. Alfredo Lajones
Faculty of Engineering and Technology: Ing. Franklin Reina
Faculty of Science and Education: Marino Chavez
Faculty of Social Sciences and Development Studies: Dr Gonzalo Salazar

UNIVERSIDAD TÉCNICA DE MACHALA
(Technical University of Machala)

Avda Panamerica km 5 1/2 via a Pasaje, Machala
Telephone: (7) 298-3362
E-mail: utmachala@utmachala.edu.ec
Internet: www.utmachala.edu.ec
Founded 1969
public control
Language of instruction: Spanish
Academic year: March to January
Rector: Ing. César Javier Quezada Abad
Vice-Rector for Academic Affairs: Ing. Laura Amarillis Borja Herrera
Vice-Rector for Admin. Affairs: Jorge Ramiro Ordoñez Morejon
Gen. Sec.: José Antonio Romero Tandazo
Librarian: María Unda Serrana de Barrezueta
Library of 5,000 vols
Number of teachers: 600
Number of students: 10,000
Publication: *Revista de la Facultad de Agronomía y Veterinaria*

DEANS

Faculty of Agriculture: Dr Jose Roberto Paladines Romero
Faculty of Agronomy and Veterinary Science: Max Iñiguez
Faculty of Business Administration and Accountancy: Danilo Pico
Faculty of Chemical Sciences and Health: Alberto Game
Faculty of Civil Engineering: Luis Ordóñez Jaramillo
Faculty of Social Sciences: Ramiro Ordoñez
Institute of Languages: Laura León de Astudillo (Director)
School of Nursing: Daysi Espinoza de Ramírez (Director)

UNIVERSIDAD TÉCNICA DE MANABÍ
(Technical University of Manabi)

Apdo 82, Portoviejo
Avda Urbina y Che Guevara, Portoviejo
Telephone: (5) 263-2677
E-mail: webmaster@utm.edu.ec
Internet: www.utm.edu.ec
Founded 1954
public control
Language of instruction: Spanish
Academic year: May to January (2 semesters)
Rector: Ing. VINCENTE FÉLIX VÉLIZ BRIONES
Vice-Rector for Academic Affairs: Ing. MARA MOLINA DE LOZANO
Gen. Sec.: GARY LOOR FERNÁNDEZ
Librarian: MERCEDES PLÚA VÉLEZ
Number of teachers: 500
Number of students: 8,000
Publication: *Revista*

DEANS

Faculty of Administrative Sciences and Economics: GUILLERMO HINOSTROZA GARCIA
Faculty of Agricultural Engineering: Ing. CÉSAR ALFREDO JARRE CEDEÑO
Faculty of Agronomy: Ing. JULIO VALDANO TORO GARCÍA
Faculty of Arts and Education: Dr KLEVER MAXIMILIANO TORO GARCIA
Faculty of Chemistry, Mathematics and Physics: Ing. VINCENTE HERNÁN NIETO CASTRO
Faculty of Health Sciences: Dr JOSÉ BOSCO BARBERÁN MERA
Faculty of Humanistic and Social Sciences: FLOR MARÍA MENDOZA MORA
Faculty of Information Science: Ing. CARLOS ALBERTO INTRIAGO ZAMBRANO
Faculty of Veterinary Sciences: Dr TITO RAMÓN PALACIOS MOLINA
Faculty of Zootechnology: Dr MARIO MARTI MATA MOREIRA

UNIVERSIDAD TÉCNICA DEL NORTE
(North Technical University)

Apdo 199, Ibarra
Ciudadela Universitaria 'El Olivo', Avda 17 de Julio 5–12, Ibarra
Telephone: (6) 299-7800
E-mail: info@utn.edu.ec
Internet: www.utn.edu.ec
Founded 1986
public control
Language of instruction: Spanish
Rector: Dr MIGUEL NARANJO TORO
Vice-Rector for Academic Affairs: Dra MARIA DE LA PORTILLA VERA
Vice-Rector Admin. Affairs: Ing. NEY MORA GRIJALVA
Gen. Sec.: HUGO REALPE LOPEZ

DEANS

Faculty of Administrative Sciences and Economics: Dra SORAYA RHEA GONZALEZ
Faculty of Agricultural Engineering and Environmental Sciences: Dr BOLIVAR BATALIAS BEDÓN
Faculty of Education Science and Technology: Dr HUGO RENÉ ANDRADE JARAMILLO
Faculty of Engineering and Applied Sciences: Ing. MILTON GAVILÁNEZ VILLALOBOS
Faculty of Health Sciences: Dra MARIANA ELENA OLEAS GALEAS
Institute of Graduate Studies: Dr FERNANDO CAICEDO CAICEDO (Director)

UNIVERSIDAD TÉCNICA ESTATAL DE QUEVEDO
(Quevado State Technical University)

Casilla 73, Quevedo
Avda Quito km 1 1/2 Vía a Santo Domingo de los Tsachilas, Quevedo
Telephone: (5) 275-1430
E-mail: rector@uteq.edu.ec
Internet: www.uteq.edu.ec
Founded 1984
public control
Language of instruction: Spanish
Rector: Ing. ROQUE LUIS VIVAS MOREIRA
Vice-Rector: Ing. GUADALUPE MURILLO DE LUNA
Vice-Rector: Ing. WILLIAMS BURBANO MONTECÉ
Librarian: Ing. ARIOSTO VICUÑA
Number of teachers: 200
Number of students: 3,000
Publication: *Ciencia y Tecnología* (2 a year)

DEANS

Faculty of Agricultural Sciences: Ing. FELIX VALVERDE
Faculty of Animal Science: Dr DÉLSITO ZAMBRANO GRACIA
Faculty of Distance Education: ROGER YELA BURGOS
Faculty of Engineering: Ing. BYRON OVIEDO BAYAS
Faculty of Enterprise Science: JOHN BOZA VALLE
Faculty of Environmental Science: Ing. GARY RAMIREZ HUILA
Faculty of Law: Dr COLÓN BUSTAMANTE

UNIVERSIDAD TÉCNICA PARTICULAR DE LOJA
(Private Technical University of Loja)

Apdo 11-01-608, Loja
San Cayetano Alto, Loja
Telephone: (7) 257-0275
E-mail: utpl_ects@utpl.edu.ec
Internet: www.utpl.edu.ec
Founded 1971
Private control
Language of instruction: Spanish
Academic year: October to August (2 semesters)
Co-financed; depts of administrative sciences, agricultural and food sciences, architecture and art, chemistry, communication sciences, computer science and electronics, economics, education sciences, finance and accounting, geology, mines and civil engineering, health sciences, law and social sciences, modern languages and literature, natural sciences
Rector-Chancellor: JOSÉ BARBOSA CORBACHO
Vice-Chancellor: SANTIAGO ACOSTA AIDE
Gen. Sec.: Ing. GABRIEL ULPIANO GARCÍA TORRES
Dir of Open and Distance Education: Dra MARÍA JOSÉ RUBIO GÓMEZ
Librarian: Lic. AMADA JARAMILLO LOJÁN
Library of 25,000 vols
Number of teachers: 200
Number of students: 2,200
Publications: *El Reloj* (12 a year), *Universidad* (12 a year), *Universidad Técnica Particular de Loja* (1 a year)

UNIVERSIDAD TECNOLÓGICA EMPRESARIAL DE GUAYAQUIL
(Business Technological University of Guayaquil)

Urdesa Central, Guayacanes 520 y la 5ta, Guayaquil
Telephone: (4) 288-4833
E-mail: admision@uteg.edu.ec
Internet: www.uteg.edu.ec
Founded 2000
Private control
Language of instruction: Spanish
Self-financed
Rector: GALO CABANILLA GUERRA
Vice-Rector for Academic Affairs: Ing. MARA CABANILLA GUERRA
Gen. Sec.: MERCEDES LEÓN SOLIS
Publication: *Ciencia y Tecnología* (2 a year)

UNIVERSIDAD TECNOLÓGICA EQUINOCCIAL
(Technical University of the Equinox)

CP 17-01-2764, Quito
Bourgeois N34-102 y Rumipamba, Quito
Telephone: (2) 244-6233
E-mail: info@ute.edu.ec
Internet: www.ute.edu.ec
Founded 1986
Private control
Language of instruction: Spanish
Co-financed; campuses in Santo Domingo and Santa Elena
Rector: JOSÉ JULIO CEVALLOS GÓMEZ
Vice-Rector for Gen. and Academic Affairs: Dra LOURDES ARMENDÁRIZ GALARZA
Gen. Sec.: Dr VINCENTE ARCOS ZAPATA
Publications: *Eidos* (1 a year), *Enfoqute* (2 a year)

DEANS

Faculty of Architecture, Arts and Design: Arq. AGUSTÍN OLEAS CARRILLO
Faculty of Economics and Business: MANUEL ESTRELLA EGAS
Faculty of Engineering Sciences: Ing. JORGE VITERI MOYA
Faculty of Health Sciences 'Eugenio Espejo': Dr JOSÉ RICARDO HIDALGO OTTOLENGHI
Faculty of Social Sciences and Communication: NELSON REINOSO VILLAVICENCIO
Faculty of Tourism and Environmental Preservation, Hospitality and Food: JOSÉ VELASCO CORONEL

UNIVERSIDAD TECNOLÓGICA INDOAMÉRICA
(Indo-American Technological University)

Bolívar 20-35 y Guayaquil, Ambato
Telephone: (3) 242-1452
E-mail: indoamerica@uti.edu.ec
Internet: www.uti.edu.ec
Founded 1998
Private control
Language of instruction: Spanish
Self-financed
Rector: Ing. SAÚL LARA PAREDES
Vice-Rector for Gen. Affairs: DIEGO GUDBERTO LARA PAREDES
Gen. Sec.: BETTY MARILYN MERIZALDE RECALDE

Other Higher Educational Institutes

Centro Internacional de Estudios Superiores de Comunicación para América Latina (International Centre for Advanced Studies in Communications for Latin America): Apdo 17-01-584, Quito; Avda Diego de Almagro N32-113 y Andrade Marín, Quito; tel. (2) 254-8011; e-mail info@ciespal.net; internet www.ciespal.net; f. 1959; training, documentation and research in fields of information science, radio and television; library: 2,000 vols, 20,700 documents; Dir-Gen. FERNANDO CHECA; Gen. Sec. ALEXIS AMÉZQUITA; publ. *Chasqui* (4 a year).

Facultad Latinoamericana de Ciencias Sociales—FLACSO (Latin American Faculty of Social Sciences—FLACSO): La Pradera E7-174 y Avda Diego de Almagro, Quito; tel. (2) 323-8888; e-mail flacso@flacso.org.ec; internet www.flacso.org.ec; f. 1956.

Instituto de Altos Estudios Nacionales (National Institute of Advanced Studies): Avda Rio Amazonas N37–271 y Villalengua Esq., Quito; tel. (2) 382-9900; e-mail infoiaen@iaen.edu.ec; internet iaen.edu.ec; f. 1972.

Polytechnic Schools

Escuela Politécnica del Ejercito (Army Polytechnic School): POB 171-5-231B, Sangolquí; Campus Politécnico, Avda El Progreso s/n Avda Gen. Rumiñahui s/n Sangolquí, Sangolquí; tel. (2) 398-9400; e-mail urci@espe.edu.ec; internet www.espe.edu.ec; f. 1922, current name adopted 1977; public control; language of instruction: Spanish; Rector ROQUE APOLINAR MOREIRA CEDEÑO; Vice-Rector Academic Affairs WILLIAM ROBERTO ARAGÓN C.

Escuela Politécnica Nacional (National Polytechnic School): CP 17-01-2759, Quito; Ladrón de Guevara E11–253, Quito; tel. (2) 250-7126; e-mail dri@epn.edu.ec; internet www.epn.edu.ec; f. 1984; public control; faculties of administrative science, chemical and agroindustrial engineering, civil and environmental engineering, electrical engineering and electronics, geology and petroleum, mechanical engineering, science, systems engineering; Rector Ing. ALFONSO ESPINOSA RAMÓN; Vice-Rector Ing. ADRIÁN PEÑA IDROVO.

Escuela Superior Politécnica Agropecuaria de Manabí (Agricultural Polytechnic School of Manabi): Calceta, 10 de Agosto No 82 y Granda Centeno, Manabi; tel. (5) 268-5134; e-mail espam@espam.edu.ec; internet www.espam.edu.ec; f. 1999; public control; Rector Ing. FÉLIX LÓPEZ LEONARDO; Vice-Rector for Academic Affairs Ing. LORENA CARREÑO MENDOZA; Gen. Sec. LYA VILLAFUERTE VÉLEZ.

Escuela Superior Politécnica de Chimborazo (Polytechnic School of Chimborazo): Panamericana Sur km 1½, 060155, Riobamba; tel. (3) 299-8200; internet www.espoch.edu.ec; f. 1972; public control; Rector Dr ROMEO RODRÍGUEZ CÁRDENAS; Vice-Rector for Academic Affairs Ing. ROSA ELENA PINOS; Vice-Rector for Research and Devt Ing. FAUSTO MARCELO DONOSO; publ. *GACETA* (4 a year).

Escuela Superior Politécnica del Litoral (Coastal Polytechnic School): Km 30.5 Via Perimetral, CP 09-01-5863, Guayaquil; tel. (4) 226-9269; e-mail httpd@espol.edu.ec; internet www.espol.edu.ec; f. 1991; public control; faculties of economics and business, electrical and computer engineering, engineering and earth sciences, humanities and social sciences, maritime, ocean and natural resources engineering, mechanical and production sciences engineering; schools of business administration, design and visual communication; institutes of chemical and environmental sciences, mathematics, physical sciences; Rector SERGIO FLORES; Provost CECILIA PAREDES; publs *FENopina*, *Investigación y Desarrollo* (1 a year), *Matemática* (2 a year), *Tecnológica de la ESPOL* (4 a year).

Schools of Art and Music

Conservatorio de Música 'José María Rodríguez' (Conservatory of Music 'José María Rodríguez'): Cuenca; f. 1938; Dir Prof. RAFAEL SOJOS JARAMILLO.

Conservatorio Superior Nacional de Música (National Music Conservatory): Casilla 17-01-3358, Quito; Manuel de Abascal y Cochapata E12-56, Quito; tel. (2) 226-3988; e-mail direccion@conamusi.edu.ec; internet www.conamusi.edu.ec; f. 1900; library: 14,000 vols; 120 teachers; 800 students; Rector RAÚL ERNESTO ESCOBAR GUEVARA; Vice Rector RICARDO MONTEROS TELLO; Gen. Sec. CHAMORRO GONZALEZ OSCAR GONZALO; publ. *Conservatorio*.

EGYPT

The Higher Education System

The higher education system in Egypt consists of Islamic and secular sectors. The Islamic sector is based upon Al-Azhar University in Cairo, founded in AD 970 as an adjunct to Al-Azhar mosque. Cairo University, the first secular university, was founded in 1908, and in 1925 it became a public institution. The Ministry of Higher Education governs secular higher education under the aegis of the Supreme Council of Universities (established in 1950), while the Central Administration of Al-Azhar Institutes, a department of the Supreme Council of Al-Azhar Institutes, controls Islamic higher education. The Government is constitutionally required to provide free higher education to all, but students also pay small enrolment fees. Prior to 1993 there were only two private higher education institutions in Egypt—the American University in Cairo (AUC) and the Arab Academy for Science and Technology (both of which had foreign ownership). Following the passage of a new law in 1993, Egyptian private higher education institutions were established from 1996. In 2007/08 there were an estimated 2,488,434 students enrolled in higher education; the figure had increased by 2010 to an estimated 4 million. In the same year there were 18 public universities, 64 Al-Azhar faculties, 18 private universities and 100 higher education institutions, 134 private higher institutions with an enrolment of 364,493 students, and 11 private intermediate institutions with a total enrolment of 21,429. In the non-university higher educational institutions there were 95,427 students enrolled in eight technical colleges, comprising of 45 technical institutes.

Students intending to attend higher education must hold the General Secondary School Certificate (or the Technical Secondary School Certificate); exact entry requirements vary between institutions and faculties. Islamic or Al-Azhar higher education requires the student successfully to complete Al-Azhar secondary school, otherwise applicants must take a preparatory year of Arabic and Koranic studies. Al-Azhar higher education offers similar courses to those offered by secular universities; however, all courses have a pronounced Islamic focus and students are required to dedicate at least five hours a week to religious study. The AUC, founded in 1919, is independent of the Egyptian higher education system but its degrees are recognized as equivalent to those awarded by Egyptian universities. Competition to gain places at the AUC is extremely fierce and candidates need to achieve higher-than-average results in their school leaving examinations. The AUC is regionally accredited by the Middle States Association of Colleges and Schools.

The main undergraduate degree is the Bachelors, which is usually awarded after four years, but in some disciplines may take five (architecture, dentistry, engineering, pharmacy, veterinary medicine) or six years (medicine). The language of instruction at private universities is mostly a foreign language (English, French or German). Instruction at public universities is generally in Arabic, except in dentistry, engineering, medicine, pharmacy, science and veterinary medicine, for which it is in English. The first postgraduate degree is the Diploma, which lasts for one year full-time or two years part-time and leads to the award of the Diploma in Higher Studies, Diploma of Graduate Studies or simply the Diploma. The next postgraduate degree, the Masters, generally requires two years of full-time study (including the writing of a thesis). Finally, the Doctor of Philosophy (PhD) degree, admission to which requires a minimum grade of 'good' in the Masters, entails a three- to four-year course, based entirely on research.

Technical and vocational training is available at intermediate vocational institutes, higher technical institutes and as non-formal education. Intermediate technical institutes specialize in post-secondary, two-year practically orientated courses mainly in the fields of commerce, health and industry leading to the award of the Technical Institute Diploma; higher technical institutes focus on advanced courses in technical education across a wide range of subjects, leading to either the Diploma (two years) or Bachelors degree (four to five years). Non-formal education consists of refresher courses, evening classes and on-the-job training. The majority of the intermediate vocational institutes are certified by the Ministry of Higher Education, while several are affiliated to or endorsed by other appropriate government ministries.

In 2007 a National Authority for Quality Assurance and Accreditation of Education (NAQAAE) was established by presidential decree to oversee the country's 50,000 educational institutes and prepare them for accreditation. The NAQAAE planned to make it compulsory for each establishment to supply an annual report on the quality of its academic programmes. The NAQAAE would then complete an external report on each institution every five years, on the basis of which accreditation would be granted. At 2010, however, this process was still in its early stages and very few programmes had actually been accredited.

In recent years the Government has accorded significant priority to improving the burgeoning higher education sector. In particular, efforts have been made to move away from the highly centralized system by offering more autonomy to individual institutions, thereby increasing accountability. In mid-2011, in response to widespread student protests, the Egyptian Government pledged to replace the incumbent heads of public universities and college deans who were allegedly linked to the former regime of the ousted President, Muhammad Hosni Mubarak. According to new arrangements, the presidents of public universities were to be selected by an electoral college, while deans of colleges and department heads were to be chosen through direct voting.

Regulatory and Representative Bodies

GOVERNMENT

Ministry of Culture: 2 Sharia Shagaret el-Dor, Cairo (Zamalek); tel. (2) 27486957; e-mail ecm.gov@gmail.com; internet www.ecm.gov.eg; Minister Dr MUHAMMAD SABER ARAB.

Ministry of Education: 12 Sharia el-Falaky, Cairo; tel. (2) 27947363; e-mail minister@moe.gov.eg; internet www.moe.gov.eg; Minister MAHMOUD MOHAMED MAHMOUD ABO EL-NASR.

Ministry of Higher Education: 101 Sharia Qasr el-Eini, Cairo; tel. (2) 27920323; e-mail mohe.info@gmail.com; internet www.egy-mhe.gov.eg; Minister of Higher Education HOSSAM ESSA.

ACCREDITATION

National Authority for Quality Assurance and Accreditation of Education (NAQAAE): Bldg of the Telecom Institute, 5 Mahmoud Elmeligy St, 6th Dist., Nasr City; tel. (2) 22630672; e-mail nagdy@naqaae.org; internet www.naqaae.org; f. 2007; board of 15 mems; Chair. Dr MAGDY KASSEM.

NATIONAL BODY

Supreme Council of Universities: 96 Ahmed Orabi, Mohandsen, Giza; tel. (2) 33029271; e-mail scu@mailer.eun.eg; internet www.scu.eun.eg; f. 1950; delineates gen. policy of univ. education and scientific research in order to attain nat. objectives in social, economic, cultural and scientific devt plans; determines admission numbers, fields of specialization and equivalences; the Egyptian Univs Network links univ. computer centres and research institutes throughout Egypt, and is the Egyptian gateway to the internet, and provides information services and online learning facilities; 33 mem. univs and private institutes; library of 3,300 vols (English and Arabic); Pres. THE MINISTER OF HIGHER EDUCATION AND MINISTER OF STATE FOR SCIENTIFIC RESEARCH; Sec. Gen. Prof. SALWA EL-GHARIB.

Learned Societies

GENERAL

Academy of the Arabic Language: 15 Aziz Abaza St, Zamalek, Cairo; tel. (2) 27362002; e-mail acc@idsc.net.eg; internet www.arabicacademy.org.eg; f. 1932; 40 Egyptian active mems, also corresp. mems, hon. mems and foreign active mems; library of 60,000 vols; Pres. Prof. AHMED SHAWKY DHEIF; Sec. Gen. IBRAHIM ABDEL MEGEED; publ. *Review* (2 a year).

Institut d'Égypte (Egyptian Institute): 13 Sharia Sheikh Rihane, Cairo; f. 1798 by Napoleon Bonaparte; literature, arts and science relating to Egypt and neighbouring countries; 160 mems; library of 160,000 vols; Pres. Dr SILEMAN HAZIEN; Sec. Gen. P. GHALIOUNGUI; publ. *Mémoires*.

AGRICULTURE, FISHERIES AND VETERINARY SCIENCE

Egyptian Society of Dairy Science: National Research Centre, El-Behoth St, Dokki, Cairo, 12622; e-mail mo_salam38@yahoo.com; internet sites.google.com/site/egydairys; f. 1972; Pres. Prof. Dr M. H. ABD EL-SALAM; Sec. Gen. Prof. Dr S. EL-SHIBINY; publ. *Egyptian Journal of Dairy Science* (2 a year, in Arabic and English).

BIBLIOGRAPHY, LIBRARY SCIENCE AND MUSEOLOGY

Supreme Council of Antiquities: 3 Al-Adel Abou Bakr St, Zamalek, Cairo; tel. (2) 27365645; e-mail hawass@sca.gov.eg; internet www.sca.gov.eg; f. 1859; attached to Min. of Culture of Egypt; Dir Dr GABBALLAH ALI GABBALLAH; Sec. Gen. Dr ZAHI HAWASS.

ECONOMICS, LAW AND POLITICS

Egyptian Society of International Law: 16 Sharia Ramses, Cairo; tel. (2) 25743162; f. 1945; to promote the study of int. law and to work for the establishment of int. relations, based on law and justice; lectures; Pres. Dr MOUFEED CHEHAB; Sec. Gen. Dr SALAH AMER; Admin. Dir A. EL MAHROUKY; 800 mems; library of 4,100 books, 120 periodicals, 100,000 documents; publ. *Revue Egyptienne de Droit International* (1 a year).

Egyptian Society of Political Economy, Statistics and Legislation: 16 Sharia Ramses, BP 732, Cairo; tel. (2) 25750797; e-mail espesl@hotmail.com; internet www.espesl.org.eg; f. 1909; 3,018 mems; library of 45,000 vols; Pres. Prof. AHMAD FATHI SOROOR; Gen. Sec. Dr MUSTAFA EL SAID; publ. *L'Egypte Contemporaine* (4 a year, in Arabic, English and French).

FINE AND PERFORMING ARTS

Armenian Artistic Union: 3 Sharia Soliman, el-Halaby, BP 1060, Cairo; tel. (2) 25742282; f. 1920; promotion of Armenian and Arabic culture; 120 mems; Pres. VAHAG DEPOYAN.

L'Atelier: 6 Victor Bassili St, al Pharaana, Azarita, Alexandria; tel. (3) 24860526; e-mail info@atelieralex.com; internet www.atelieralex.com; f. 1935; soc. of artists and writers; 350 mems; library of 5,500 vols; Pres. Dr MOHAMED RAFIK KHALI; Vice-Pres. Dr MOHAMED SALEM.

Institute of Arab Music: 22 Sharia Ramses, Cairo; tel. (2) 22750702; f. 1924; promotion and teaching of Arab music; libraries of records, tapes and scores of Arab music; Chair. of Board HASSAN TAKER MOK; Sec. Gen. FARZY RASHAD.

HISTORY, GEOGRAPHY AND ARCHAEOLOGY

Egyptian Geographical Society: 109 Qasr Al-Aini St, BP 422 Mohamed Farid, Cairo; tel. (2) 27945450; e-mail geoegypt@yahoo.com; internet server2002.net/egs1/n002.html; f. 1875, reorganized 1917; cartography section incl. 15,000 maps; 1,500 mems; library of 50,000 vols; Pres. Prof. M. S. ABULEZZ; Sec. Gen. Prof. S. AL-HOSEINY; Library Dir H. LOTFY; publs *Al-Majallah Al-Jugrafiyah Al-'Arabiyah* (2 a year), *Bulletin of the Egyptian Geographical Society (Bulletin de la Soeiété de Géographie d'Egypte)* (1 a year), *Geographical research series* (24 occasional issues), proceedings of symposia, confs workshops dealing with current geographical issues.

Société Archéologique d'Alexandrie: 6 Mahmoud, Moukhtar St, BP 815, Alexandria 21111; tel. (3) 24820650; e-mail asalex@yahoo.col; f. 1893; 248 mems; Pres. Prof. M. EL ABBADI; Sec. Gen. Prof. M HAGGAG.

Society for Coptic Archaeology: 222 Sharia Ramses, Cairo; tel. (2) 24824252; e-mail bgwassif@yahoo.com; f. 1934; studies Coptic archaeology, linguistics, papyrology, church history, liturgy and art; organizes symposia and confs; 360 mems; library of 16,000 vols; Pres. WASSIF BOUTROS-GHALI; Vice-Pres. Dr PETER GROSSMANN; publ. *Bulletin de la Société Copte d'Archéologie (BSAC)* (1 a year).

LANGUAGE AND LITERATURE

Alliance Française: 4 Aboul Feda St, Port Saïd; tel. (66) 3227431; e-mail allianceportsaid@suezcanal.net; offers courses and examinations in French language and culture and promotes cultural exchange with France; library of 4,000 vols; Dir BERNARD CHAUMONT-GAILLAIRD.

British Council: 192 el Nil St, Agouza, Cairo; tel. (2) 33031514; e-mail information@britishcouncil.org.eg; internet www.britishcouncil.org/egypt; teaching centre; offers courses and examinations in English language and British culture and promotes cultural exchange with the UK; attached offices in Alexandria and Heliopolis (teaching centre); Dir Dr JOHN GROTE; Dir, English Language Services STEVEN MURRELL.

Goethe-Institut: 5 Sharia el-Bustan, Cairo 11518; tel. (2) 25759877; e-mail info@cairo.goethe.org; internet www.goethe.de/ins/eg/kai; offers courses and examinations in German language and culture and promotes cultural exchange with Germany; attached centre in Alexandria; Dir and Regional Man. GABRIELE BECKER.

Instituto Cervantes: 20 Boulos Hann St, Dokki, Cairo; tel. (2) 37601746; e-mail cencai@cervantes.es; internet elcairo.cervantes.es; offers courses and examinations in Spanish language and culture and promotes cultural exchange with Spain and Spanish-speaking Latin and Central America; library of 18,500 vols; Dir LUIS JAVIER RUIZ SIERRA.

MEDICINE

Alexandria Medical Association: 4 G. Carducci St, Alexandria; f. 1921; 1,200 mems; Pres. Prof. H. S. EL BADAWI; Sec. Gen. Prof. TOUSSOUN ABOUL AZI; publ. *Alexandria Medical Journal* (4 a year, in Arabic, English and French).

Egyptian Dental Association: 84A Mat'haf el-Manial St, el-Manial, Cairo; tel. (2) 23658568; e-mail eda@internetegypt.com; internet www.eda-egypt.org; f. 1937, 1960 separated from Egyptian Medical Asscn; Pres. Prof. HATEM ABDEL RAHMAN; Gen. Sec. Dr AHMED FARID SHEHAB; publ. *Egyptian Dental Journal* (4 a year).

Egyptian Medical Association for the Study of Obesity: 14 el Khalil St, el Mohandessin, Giza, Cairo; tel. (2) 33023642; e-mail info@emaso-eg.org; internet www.emaso-eg.org; f. 2003; Pres. SHERIF HAFEZ; Gen. Sec. MOHAMED ABOULGHATE.

Egyptian Orthopaedic Association: 16 Sharia Houda Shaarawi, Cairo 11111; tel. (2) 23930013; e-mail eoa@eoa.org.eg; internet www.eoa.org.eg; f. 1948; scientific and social activities in the field of orthopaedic surgery and traumatology; holds bi-annual scientific meetings, monthly clinical meetings; 1,700 mems; Pres. Prof. KHAMIS H. EL DEEB; Sec. Gen. Prof. ABDEL MOHSEN ARAFA; publ. *Egyptian Orthopaedic Journal* (4 a year).

Ophthalmological Society of Egypt: Dar el Hekma, 42 Sharia Kasr el-Aini, Cairo; e-mail eos@eyegypt.com; f. 1902; 480 mems; Pres. Prof. KHALIL ABOU SHOUSA EL SAID; Hon. Sec. Dr AHMAD EZ EL DIN NAIM.

NATURAL SCIENCES

Biological Sciences

Egyptian Entomological Society: 14 Sharia Ramses, BP 430, Cairo; tel. (2) 25750979; e-mail ees@ees.eg.net; internet www.ees.eg.net; f. 1907; publishes bulletins and economic series; 502 mems; library of 28,000 vols; Pres. Prof. MAHMOUD HAFEZ; Vice-Pres. Prof. MOHAMMAD ALI MOHAMMAD; Sec. Gen. Prof. IBRAHIM MOHAMED.

Egyptian Society of Parasitology: 1 Ozoris St, Tager Bldg, Garden City, Cairo; tel. (2) 22608713; e-mail morsyegypt2000@yahoo.com; internet www.parasitology.eg.net; f. 1967; holds scientific meetings, annual conf.; covers helminthology, medical entomology, protozoology, molluscs, insect control, immuno-diagnosis of parasitic diseases, treatment etc.; 350 mems; Pres. Prof. MAHMOUD HAFEZ; Sec. Gen. Prof. TOSSON A. MORSY; publ. *Journal* (2 a year).

PHILOSOPHY AND PSYCHOLOGY

Egyptian Association for Mental Health: 1 Sharia Ilhami, Qasr al-Doubara, Cairo; internet www.arabpsynet.com/associations/eamh.ass.htm; f. 1948; 630 mems; Pres. Dr JAMEL ABOU ELAZAYEM.

Egyptian Association for Psychological Studies: 1 Osiris St, Tager Bldg, Garden City, Cairo; tel. (2) 33541857; e-mail eapsegypt@hotmail.com; internet www.arabpsynet.com/homepage/psy-ass.htm; f. 1948; 1,200 mems; Pres. Dr ATEF KAMEL; publ. *Yearbook of Psychology*.

RELIGION, SOCIOLOGY AND ANTHROPOLOGY

Institut Dominicain d'Etudes Orientales: Priory of the Dominican Fathers, 1 Sharia Masna al-Tarabish, BP 18, Abbassiah, Cairo 11381; tel. (2) 24825509; e-mail info@ideo-cairo.org; internet www.ideo-cairo.org; f. 1952; library of 140,000 vols; Dir Fr

JEAN-JACQUES PÉRENNÈS; publ. *Mélanges* (every 2 years).

TECHNOLOGY

Egyptian Materials Research Society: 33 Abdel-Khalik Tharwat St, Cairo; tel. (2) 23925997; e-mail contact@egmrs.org; internet www.egmrs.org; f. 1978 as Egyptian Soc. of Solid State Science and Applications (ESSA); present name 2003; 500 mems; Chair Prof. KAMEL ABD EL-HADY; publ. *Egyptian Journal of Solids*.

Egyptian Society of Engineers: 28 Sharia Ramses, Cairo; e-mail ese@rusys.eg.net; internet www.ese.eg.net; f. 1920; Pres. Prof. IBRAHIM ADHAM EL DEMIRDASH; Sec. Dr MOHAMED M. EL HASHIMY.

Research Institutes

GENERAL

Academy of Scientific Research and Technology: 101 Kasr el-Eini St, Cairo 11516; tel. (2) 27921267; e-mail info@asrt.sci.eg; internet www.asrt.sci.eg; f. 1972; promotes the creation of an integrated system of scientific research; encourages female and youth participation in scientific leadership; affiliated instns: Central Metallurgical Research and Devt Institute, Egyptian Nat. Scientific and Technological Information Network, Gen. Directorate of Statistics on Science and Technology, Institute of Astronomy and Geophysics, Institute of Oceanography and Fisheries, Nat. Information and Documentation Centre, Nat. Institute for Standards, Nat. Network for Technology and Devt (UNTD), Nat. Research Centre, Petroleum Research Institute, Remote Sensing Centre, Scientific Instruments Centre, Science Museum; library of 34,000 vols, 50,000 periodicals; Pres. Prof. MOHAMMAD TAREK HUSSEIN.

National Research Centre: Al-Tahrir St, Dokki, Cairo; tel. (2) 33337615; e-mail info@nrc.sci.eg; internet www.nrc.sci.eg; f. 1956; began functioning in 1947 and laboratory work started in 1956; fosters and carries out research in both pure and applied sciences; the 54 laboratories are divided into 13 sections: Textile Industries, Food Industries and Nutrition, Pharmaceutical Industries, Chemical Industries, Engineering, Agriculture and Biology, Medical, Applied Organic and Inorganic Chemistry, Physics, Basic Sciences, Environment, Genetic Engineering and Biotechnology; library of 12,000 vols; Pres. Dr HANY EL NAZER; publ. *NRC News*.

AGRICULTURE, FISHERIES AND VETERINARY SCIENCE

Agricultural Research Centre, Ministry of Agriculture: 9 Gamaa St, Giza; tel. (2) 35720944; e-mail abouhadid@arc.sci.eg; internet www.arc.sci.eg; Pres. Prof. AYMAN FARID ABOU HADID; Vice-Pres. Prof. MOHAMMED MOSTAFA EL GHARY.

Attached Research Institutes:

Agricultural Economics Research Institute: 7 Nadi El Said St, Dokki, Giza; tel. (2) 33354549; e-mail aeri84@hotmail.com; f. 1973; Dir Prof. FAUZY ABD ELAZIZ EL SHAZLY; publ. *Classification of the Agricultural Land Resources according to the Yield of the Most Important Field Crops* (every 5 years).

Agricultural Engineering Research Institute: Nadi El Said St, Dokki, Giza; tel. (2) 37487212; e-mail aenri@aenri.org; internet www.aenri.org; Dir Prof. GAMAL HASSAN EL SAYED; publs *Egyptian Journal of Agricultural Research* (4 a year), *Misr Journal of Agricultural Engineering* (4 a year).

Agricultural Extension and Rural Development Research Institute: tel. (2) 25716301; e-mail aerdri@hotmail.com; f. 1977; Dir Prof. A. G. EL DEIN SAYED MAHMOUD WAHBA.

Agricultural Genetic Engineering Research Institute: e-mail taymourm@ageri.sci.eg; Dir Prof. TAYMOUR MOHAMED NASR EL DIN IBRAHIM.

Animal Health Research Institute: Nadi El Said St, Dokki; tel. (2) 33374856; e-mail ahriegypt@gawab.com; internet www.ahri.gov.eg; f. 1928; Nat. Veterinary Laboratory of the Egyptian Veterinary Services; animal health and safety of food from animal origin; centre of excellence and the point of reference in animal disease diagnosis; Dir Prof. MONA MEHREZ ALY.

Animal Production Research Institute: Nadi El Said St, Dokki, Cairo; tel. (2) 33372934; f. 1938; Dir Prof. Dr FATEN FAHMY MOHAMED ABOU-AMMO.

Animal Reproduction Research Institute: 5 Hadek el Ahram, Giza; tel. (2) 33764325; e-mail arri2002@arabia.com; Dir Prof. ATEF ABEELMONSEF AHMED.

Cotton Research Institute: tel. (2) 35725035; e-mail cri_egypt@yahoo.com; internet arc.claes.sci.eg; f. 1919; Dir Prof. MOHAMED ABD EL MAGEED ABD EL AZIZ.

Field Crops Research Institute: Cairo University St, Giza; tel. (2) 35738425; internet www.fcri-egypt.com; f. 1971; Dir Prof. MOHAMED ABOU ZEID EL NAHRAWY.

Food Technology Research Institute: tel. (2) 35735090; e-mail nlftri@ie-eg.com; f. 1991; Dir Prof. Dr SAEB ABDEL-MONEIM HAFEZ.

Horticultural Research Institute: 9 Cairo University St, Giza; tel. (2) 35720617; e-mail hortinst@yahoo.com; f. 1948; produces new high-yielding early-maturing horticulture crop cultivars; maintains horticulture crop genetic resources; introduces new cultivars and germplasm of certain promising horticulture species; conducts research for optimizing the best cultural practices; implements extension and training programmes to transfer new technologies to farmers nationwide; 695 mems; Dir. Prof. SALAMA EID SALEM SHREIF; publ. *Egyptian Journal of Horticulture* (2 a year).

Plant Pathology Research Institute: tel. (2) 35724893; e-mail nagiabouzeid@link.net; f. 1919; research in various aspects of disease survey: ecology, biology, epidemiology and control measures; 170 research staff; library of 1,098 vols; Dir Prof. NAGI MOHAMED ABOU ZEID; publs *Agricultural Research Review*, *Egyptian Phytopathology*, *Journal of Applied Microbiology*.

Plant Protection Research Institute: 7 Nadi El Said St, Dokki, Giza 12311; tel. (2) 37486163; e-mail ppri@arc.sci.eg; f. 1912; Dir Prof. NAGI MOHAMED ABOU ZEID.

Soil, Water and Environment Research Institute: Cairo University St, Giza; tel. (2) 35720608; e-mail swerisweri@hotmail.com; f. 1969; Dir Prof. HAMDY EL HOUSSANY KHALIFA.

Sugar Crops Research Institute: 9 Cairo University St, Giza; tel. (2) 35735699; e-mail scriare@yahoo.com; Dir Prof. SAMIA SAAD EL SAYED EL MAGHRABY.

Veterinary Serum and Vaccine Research Institute: Abbasia, Cairo; tel. (2) 23421009; e-mail svri@idsc.gov.eg; internet www.vsvri-eg.com; Dir Prof. FEKRIA ABD ELHAFEZ EL BORDENY.

Institute of Oceanography and Fisheries: 101 Kasr El-Aini St, Cairo; tel. (2) 27921342; e-mail soliman@niof.sci.eg; internet www.niof.sci.eg; f. 1931 in connection with the Faculty of Science, Cairo; attached to the Academy of Scientific Research; undertakes oceanographical, environmental and fisheries research at Alexandria, the Red Sea, the Aqaba and Suez Gulfs at Attaka, inland waters and at Kanater (aquaculture); Dir Prof. SOLIMAN HAMED; publ. *Journal of Aquatic Research*.

Attached Institute:

National Oceanographic Data Center: e-mail ahmedmoustafaelnemr@yahoo.com; internet www.nodc-egypt.org; Dir Dr AHMAD EL NEMR.

ARCHITECTURE AND TOWN PLANNING

Housing and Building National Research Centre: BP 1770, Cairo 12311; tel. (2) 33356853; e-mail hbrc@hbrc.edu.eg; internet www.hbrc.edu.eg; attached to the Min. of Housing, Utilities and Urban Devt; carries out basic and applied research work on building materials and means of construction; also provides technical information and acts as consultant to the different authorities concerned with bldg and construction materials; 8 specialized laboratories; Chair. Prof. MOSTAFA EL DEMERDASH.

ECONOMICS, LAW AND POLITICS

Centre d'Etudes et de Documentation Economique, Juridique et Sociale: 2 Sikkat al-Fadl, BP 392, Muhammad Farid, Cairo; tel. (2) 23928711; e-mail cedej@cedej.org.eg; internet www.cedej.org.eg; f. 1969; attached to Sous-direction des Sciences Sociales et Humaines (MAE) and CNRS, Paris; cooperation, documentation and research on an exchange basis between Egypt and France; research on Egypt (19th and 20th century) and the Arab world; univ. exchanges in cooperation with Egyptian Govt; library of 30,000 vols, 8 documentalists scan and classify 40 Egyptian periodicals; Dir MARC LAVERGNE; publs *Egypte—Monde Arabe* (2 a year), *Mutun* (2 a year, in Arabic).

Institute of Arab Research and Studies: BP 229, 1 Tolombat St, Garden City, Cairo; tel. (2) 33551648; f. 1953; studies in contemporary Arab affairs, economics, sociology, history, geography, law, literature, linguistics; library of 77,000 vols, 1,068 periodicals; Dir Prof. AHMED YOUSSEF AHMED; publ. *Bulletin of Arab Research and Studies* (1 a year).

Institute of National Planning: Salah Salem St, Nasr City, Cairo; tel. (2) 22629225; e-mail inplanning@idsc.net.eg; internet www.inplanning.gov.eg; f. 1960; research, training, documentation and information; organized in 11 scientific and technical centres; library of 70,000 vols; Dir Dr OLA SULEIMAN KHALIL YUSUF AL HAKIM; publs *Egyptian Review of Development and Planning*, *Issues in Planning and Development* (irregular).

EDUCATION

National Centre for Educational Research and Development: Waked St, St Republic 12 Downtown, Cairo; tel. (2) 5890980; e-mail ncerd@ncerd.org; internet www.ncerd.org; f. 1972; coordinates current educational policy with that of the National Specialized Councils; exchanges information with like instns throughout the world; provides local and foreign documents on education; Dir Dr A. D. JEHAN KAMAL MOHAMED;

publ. *Contemporary Trends in Education* (2 a year).

HISTORY, GEOGRAPHY AND ARCHAEOLOGY

Deutsches Archäologisches Institut (German Archaeological Institute): 31 Sharia Abu El-Feda, Cairo-Zamalek 11211; tel. (2) 27351460; e-mail sekretariat.kairo@dainst.de; internet www.dainst.org; research in archaeology and related fields; maintains relations with int. scholars; organizes congresses, colloquia and tours; Dir Prof. Dr STEPHAN J. SEIDLMAYER; Sec. IRENE EL KHORAZATY.

Institut Français d'Archéologie Orientale (French Institute of Oriental Archaeology): 37 rue al Cheikh Ali Youssef, BP 11562 Qasr al-Aïny, Cairo 11441; tel. (2) 27971600; e-mail direction@ifao.egnet.net; internet www.ifao.egnet.net; f. 1880; excavations, research, seminars and publs intended to widen knowledge of Egyptian history from the Pharaohs to the Islamic period; library of 82,000 books; Dir BÉATRIX MIDANT-REYNES; publs *Annales Islamologiques* (1 a year), *Bulletin Critique des Annales Islamologiques, Bulletin de l'Institut Français d'Archéologie Orientale* (1 a year), *Cahiers des Annales Islamologiques, Cahiers de la Céramique Égyptienne*.

MEDICINE

Central Health Laboratories: Ministry of Health, 19 Sheikh Rehan St, Abdin, Cairo; tel. (2) 27947371; e-mail centralhealthlabs@yahoo.com; internet www.healthlabs.net; f. 1885; Dir-Gen. Dr ABDEL MONEIM EL BEHAIRY; library of 2,000 vols; publs *Bacteriology, Sera and Vaccines Production, Virology*.

Giza Memorial Institute for Ophthalmic Research: Sharia Al-Ahram, Giza, Cairo; tel. (2) 35724442; e-mail portal@mohealth.gov.eg; internet www.mohp.gov.eg; f. 1925; attached to Min. of Public Health; library of 2,800 vols; Dir Dr ABDEL MEGID ABDEL RAHMAN.

National Hepatology and Tropical Medicine Research Institute: 10 Sharia Kasr el-Aini, Cairo; tel. (2) 23642494; e-mail info@nhtmri.org; internet www.nhtmri.org; f. 1932; depts of biochemistry, clinical pharmacy, dermatology and andrology, haematology, microbiology, paediatrics, parasitology, pathology, public health epidemiology, radiology, tropical and liver surgery, tropical medicine; library of 4,000 vols; Dir-Gen. Prof. Dr WAHEED DOSS.

National Nutrition Institute: Min. of Health, 16 Kasr El-Aini St, Cairo; tel. (2) 23646413; e-mail admin@nni.org.eg; internet www.nni.org.eg; f. 1955; research, analysis, training and education in nutrition science; 469 staff; Dir Dr AZZA GOHAR.

National Organization for Drug Control and Research: 6 Abou Hazem St, Giza; tel. (2) 27480472; e-mail pharinfo@pharmaco.sti.sci.eg; f. 1976; Chair. Dr ALI HIGAZI.

Theodor Bilharz Research Institute: Warak el Hadar, Embaba, BP 30, Giza 12411; tel. (2) 35401019; e-mail info@tbri.sci.eg; internet www.tbri.sci.eg; f. 1979; for the control, diagnosis and treatment of endemic diseases, especially urinary and hepatic schistosomiasis; Dir Prof. JEHAN G. EL FENDI; publs *Egyptian Journal of Shistosomiosis, TBRI Biomedical Bulletin, TBRI Today*.

VACSERA Holding Company for Biological Products and Vaccines: 51 Sharia Wezarat El-Zeraa, Agouza, Giza 22311; tel. (2) 37611111; e-mail ceo@vacsera.com; internet www.vacsera.com; Chair. Dr MOHAMED RABIE.

NATURAL SCIENCES

General

UNESCO Office Cairo and Regional Bureau for Science and Technology in the Arab States: 8 Abdel Rahman Fahmy St, Garden City, Cairo 11511; tel. (2) 27945599; e-mail cairo@unesco.org; internet www.unesco.org/cairo; f. 1947; designated Cluster Office for Egypt, Sudan and Yemen; Dir TAREK SHAWKI.

Physical Sciences

Egyptian Mineral Resources Authority: BP 11511 Ataba, Cairo; e-mail info@egsma.gov.eg; internet www.egsma.gov.eg; f. 1896; regional geological mapping, mineral prospecting, evaluation of mineral deposits, and granting mineral exploration and exploitation rights; cartography laboratory; 763 research workers; library of 82,000 vols; Chair. HUSSEIN HAMOUDA.

National Authority for Remote Sensing and Space Sciences: BP 1564, Alf Maskan, Cairo; tel. (2) 26225801; e-mail info@narss.sci.eg; internet www.narss.sci.eg; f. 1972; covers agriculture, engineering, environment, geology, geophysics, hydrogeology, mineral and energy resources, photogrammetry, physics and soils; operates advanced digital data processing facility for satellite and aircraft data, also Beechcraft King-Air aeroplane with most advanced remote sensing equipment; design and implementation of nat. space scientific and technical activities; library of 2,500 books; Chair. Prof. AYMAN EL DESSOUKI IBRAHIM; publ. *Journal* (1 a year).

National Research Institute of Astronomy and Geophysics: BP 11421, Helwan, Cairo; tel. (2) 25549780; e-mail astro@nriag.sci.eg; internet www.nriag.sci.eg; f. 1903; attached to the Academy of Scientific Research and Technology; comprises the Helwan Observatory, the Kottamyia Observatory, the Misallat geomagnetic observatory, seismic stations at Helwan, Aswan, Matrouh, and satellite tracking stations at Helwan and Abu Simbel; library of 10,594 vols; Pres. Prof. ANAS MOHAMED IBRAHIM OSMAN; publs *Journal of Astronomy and Astrophysics, Journal of Geophysics*.

RELIGION, SOCIOLOGY AND ANTHROPOLOGY

Ibn Khaldun Centre for Development Studies: BP 13, Mokatim, Cairo; tel. (2) 25081617; e-mail info@eicds.org; internet www.eicds.org; f. 1988; advancement of applied social sciences with special emphasis on Egypt and the Arab and Third Worlds; the Centre is an associated centre of the Arab Social Science Research network of the Arab Institute for Studies and Communication (ASSR–AISC); Dir Dr SAAD EDDIN IBRAHIM; publ. *Civil Society* (12 a year).

TECHNOLOGY

Central Metallurgical Research and Development Institute: 1 Elfelezat St, Helwan, Cairo 11421; tel. (2) 25010642; e-mail rucmrdi@rusys.eg.net; internet www.cmrdi.sci.eg; f. 1972; attached to the Min. of Scientific Research; extractive metallurgy, ore dressing, technical services, metal-forming and working, welding research; library of 4,000 vols; Chair. Prof. Dr BAHAA ZAGHLOUL.

Egyptian Atomic Energy Authority: 8 Ahmad Elzomor St, Nasr City, Children Village BP, Cairo 11787; tel. (2) 22876033; e-mail hisham_f@frcu.eun.eg; internet www.eaea.org.eg; f. 1957; maintains 22-MW open pool multipurpose reactor at the Inshas site for production of radioisotopes for industrial and medical applications, research on neutron physics and personnel training; employs 850 academic scientists supported by 650 technical staff; Pres. Prof. ALY ISLAM METWALLY ALY.

Attached Research Centres:

National Centre for Radiation Research and Technology (NCRRT): tel. (2) 22746791; internet www.eaea.org.eg/ncrrt.html; f. 1972; main facilities incl. a 400,000 Ci, Co-60 unit and an electron accelerator (under construction); organized in 3 divs: radiation research, industrial irradiation, biotechnology; Chair. Prof. AMIN EL BAHY.

Nuclear Research Centre (NRC): BP 13975, Abu Zabal; tel. (4) 620810; internet www.eaea.org.eg/nrc.html; main facilities incl. a 2-MW ET-RR-1 research reactor, a 2.5 Van de Graaff accelerator, a radioisotope production laboratory, nuclear fuel research and devt laboratory, laboratories for application of radioisotopes, electronic instrumentation laboratory and radiation protection laboratory; organized in 4 divs: basic nuclear sciences, reactors, material and nuclear industry, radioisotope applications; Chair. Prof. NASF CAMSAN.

The Hot Laboratories and Waste Management Centre (HLWMC): BP 13975, Abu Zabal; tel. (2) 44620784; internet www.eaea.org.eg/hlwmc.html; f. 1980; main facilities incl. low and intermediate level liquid waste station, radioisotope production laboratories, radwaste disposal site; organized in 3 divs: radioisotopes, fuel treatment, radwaste treatment.

The National Centre for Nuclear Safety and Radiation Control (NCNSRC): tel. (2) 22728793; internet www.eaea.org.eg/ncnsrc.html; f. 1982; organized in 3 divs: nuclear regulations and emergencies, radiation control, safety of nuclear installations.

Egyptian Petroleum Research Institute: 1 Ahmed el Zomor St, Nasr City, Cairo 11727; tel. (2) 22747847; e-mail research@epri.sci.eg; internet www.epri.sci.eg; f. 1976; organ of the Min. of Higher Education and Scientific Research; jt Board with Egyptian Gen. Petroleum Corporation; 7 research sections, dealing with all aspects of petroleum and energy-related problems; contract research and commercial services to local oil companies; library of 5,000 vols; Dir Prof. AHMED MOHAMMAD AHMED AL SABAGH; publ. *Egyptian Journal of Petroleum*.

Hydraulics Research Institute: POB 13621, Police Station St, Delta Barrage, Cairo; tel. (2) 42188268; e-mail info@hri-egypt.org; internet www.hri-egypt.org; f. 1949; depts of Calibration and Instrumentation, Numerical Modelling, Physical Modelling, Sedimentation and Field Measurements; Dir Prof. FATTHY SAAD HASANAIN AL-GAMAL.

National Institute for Standards: Tersa St, el-Matbaa, el Haram, POB 136, Giza 12211; e-mail shaalan@sit.nis.sci.eg; internet www.nis.sci.eg; f. 1963; attached to the Min. of Higher Education and Scientific Research; 197 staff; responsible for maintenance of nat. standards for physical units and their use for purposes of calibration; research on scientific metrology, to develop new techniques for measurements, calibrations, and devt of new standards; constituent laboratories: electricity, photometry, frequency, thermometry, radiation, acoustics, mass, length metrology, engineering metrology, testing of materials, safety tests and textile testing, ultrasonics, polymer testing, and reference materials; Dir Prof. ALI ABUELEZZ; publ. *Egyptian Journal of Measurement Science and Technology*.

Textile Consolidation Fund: 7 el-Taher St, Abdin, Cairo; tel. (2) 23925521; e-mail tcf_textiles@tcfegypt.org.eg; internet www.tcfegypt.org.eg; f. 1953; incl. textiles quality control centre and textiles devt centre; library of 5,000 vols; Gen. Man. MAGDI EL AREF.

Libraries and Archives

Alexandria

Alexandria Municipal Library: 18 Sharia Menasha Moharrem Bey, BP 138 el Shatby, Alexandria 21526; tel. (3) 24839999; e-mail secretariat@bibalex.org; f. 1892; under control of the Bibliotheca Alexandrina; 22,390 Arabic vols, 35,399 European vols, 4,086 MSS; Chief Librarian BESHIR BESHIR EL SHINDI.

Alexandria University Central Library: Mailbox 233, El-Ibrahimia, Alexandria; 163 El-Horiyah Rd, El-Shatby, Alexandria; tel. (3) 24282928; e-mail auclib@auclib.edu.eg; internet www.clib.alexu.edu.eg; f. 1985; 30,000 books, 31,800 dissertations and thesis, 14,537 microfilm reels, 9,002 periodicals, 1,545 MSS, 31,800 dissertations; Supervisor Prof. SHAWKY SALEM.

Bibliotheca Alexandrina: El Shatby, BP 138, Alexandria 21526; tel. (3) 24839999; e-mail infobib@bibalex.org; internet www.bibalex.org; f. 2001, built as a successor to the ancient Alexandria library; 1,500,000 vols, 100,000 MSS, 50,000 maps, 250,000 audio and audiovisual items; incl. collns from the Sidi Mursi Abul Abbas Mosque and the Al Azhar Religious Institute in Smouha; deposit library for UNESCO, WTO, Red Cross and Ccl of Europe; Dir-Gen. Dr ISMAIL SERAGELDIN.

Library of the Greek Orthodox Patriarchate of Alexandria: BP 2006, Alexandria; tel. (3) 24868595; e-mail patriarxeio.alexandreias@gmail.com; internet www.patriarchateofalexandria.com; f. AD 43; 41,000 vols, 542 MSS, contains 2,241 rare editions; Librarian NICOLAS ALEXOPOULOS.

Assiut

Assiut University Library: Assiut; tel. (88) 2412526; e-mail auslibrarynquiries@yahoo.com; internet www.aun.edu.eg/library/index.htm; 250,000 vols; Dir S. M. SAYED.

Cairo

Al-Azhar University Library: Nasr City, Cairo; tel. (2) 2608652; e-mail library@azhar.edu.eg; internet www.azhar.edu.eg/sp/lib/index.htm; 80,000 vols, incl. 20,000 MSS; Librarian M. E. A. HADY.

American University in Cairo Library: AUC Ave, POB 74, New Cairo 11835; tel. (2) 6153648; e-mail library@aucegypt.edu; internet library.aucegypt.edu; f. 1919; 403,722 vols; Dean for Libraries and Learning Technologies SHAHIRA EL-SAWY.

Arab League Information Centre (Library): Midan al-Tahir, Cairo 11642; tel. (2) 25750511; f. 1945; 30,000 vols, 250 periodicals; Sec. Gen. Dr SAUD ABD AL AZIZ EL ZABIDI.

Cairo University Library: Orman, Giza; tel. (2) 37759743; e-mail sherifshn@cu.edu.eg; internet www.cl.cu.edu.eg; f. 1932; 1,407,000 vols, 30,000 periodicals; Gen. Dir Dr SHERIF KAMEL SHAHEEN.

Egyptian Library: Abdin Palace, Cairo; over 20,000 vols; Dir ABDEL HAMID HOSNI.

Egyptian National Library and Archives: Sharia Corniche el-Nil, Bulaq, Cairo; e-mail info_cent@darelkotob.gov.eg; internet www.darelkotob.gov.eg; f. 1870; 1,500,000 vols (400,000 European); 11 brs with 250,000 vols, incl. fine arts library; Dir-Gen. ALI ABDUL MOHSEN.

Egypt National Agricultural Library: 7 Nadi el Said St, Dokki, Giza; tel. (2) 33351313; e-mail magdy@nile.enal.sci.eg; internet nile.enal.sci.eg; f. 1920; 25,000 vols; Dir Dr MAGDY ABD EL RAHMAN; publ. *Egyptian Journal of Agricultural Research*.

Library of the Ministry of Education: 16 Sharia el-Falaki, Cairo; tel. (2) 38544805; f. 1927; 55,966 vols (European and Arabic); Dir HASSAN ABDEL SHAFI.

Library of the Ministry of Health: Sharia Magles el Shaab, Cairo 11467; over 27,000 vols.

Library of the Ministry of Justice: Midan Lazoghli, Cairo; f. 1929; private library for the use of judges and mems of the Parquet (public prosecution and criminal investigation authority); a centre attached to the library contains the latest texts of local and comparative legislature on Personal Status; over 90,000 vols and periodicals in Arabic, French and English (law and social science); Dir F. ABOU EL KHEIR.

Library of the Ministry of Supply and Internal Trade: 99 Sharia Kasr el-Aini, Cairo; internet msht.tripod.com; over 20,000 vols.

Library of the Ministry of Waqfs: Sharia Sabri Alu Alam, Ean el-Luk, Cairo; f. 1942; 20,219 vols.

Library of the Monastery of St Catherine: 18 Midan El Daher, Cairo; f. 6th century; over 4,000 Greek, Oriental and Slavonic MSS; contains the Codex Sinaiticus Syriacus; Librarian Monk DANIEL; Librarian Monk SYMEON.

Library of the National Research Institute of Astronomy and Geophysics: Helwan, Cairo; internet www.nriag.sci.eg; f. 1903; 11,000 vols; Dir Prof. R. M. KEBEASY.

National Assembly Library: Palace of the Nat. Assembly, Cairo; internet www.parliament.gov.eg/english/publicsec/library; f. 1924; over 61,000 vols; Dir ANTOUN MATTA.

National Research Centre Library: El Buhoth St, Dokki Cairo; tel. (2) 33371362; e-mail info@nrc.sci.eg; internet www.nrc.sci.eg; f. 1955; accumulates and disseminates information in all languages and in all brs of science and technology; 35,600 vols, 2,500 periodicals, UNESCO and WHO spec. collns; Dir WAGLAA MAHMOUD FAHMY.

Damanhour

Damanhour Municipal Library: Damanhour; 13,431 vols.

Mansoura

Mansoura Municipal Library: Mansoura; contains 17,984 vols (Arabic 13,036, European 4,948).

Museums and Art Galleries

Alexandria

Greco-Roman Museum: Museum St, Alexandria; tel. (3) 24865820; e-mail sca3press@yahoo.com; internet www.grm.gov.eg; f. 1892; exhibits from the Greek, Roman and Byzantine eras; library of 15,500 vols, Omar Tousson colln of 4,000 vols; Dir DOREYA SAID; publs *Annuaire du Musée Gréco-Romain*, *Guide to the Alexandrian Monuments*.

National Maritime Museum: Alexandria; Dir Dr MEHREZ EL HUSSEINI.

Aswan

Nubia Museum: el Fanadek St, Aswan; tel. (97) 2319333; e-mail nubiamuseum@numibia.net; internet www.numibia.net/nubia; f. 1997; history of Nubia since prehistoric times to present; library of 200 vols; Dir Dr RAGEH Z. MOHAMED MAHMUD.

Cairo

Agricultural Museum: Al Sawra St, Dokki, Cairo; tel. (2) 33608682; f. 1938; exhibits of ancient and modern Egyptian agriculture and rural life, horticulture, irrigation; botanical and zoological sections; library of 8,885 vols; Dir SAMIR M. SULTAN.

Al-Gawhara Palace Museum: The Citadel, Cairo; tel. (2) 25116187; f. 1954, refurnished 1956; built in 1811 in the Ottoman style, the Palace retains much of its original interior; contains Oriental and French furniture, incl. gilded throne, Turkish paintings, exhibitions of clocks, glass, 19th-century costumes.

Cairo Geological Museum: BP Dawawin, Cairo 11521; Cornish el-Nil, Maadi Rd, Cairo; tel. (2) 23187056; e-mail info@egsma.gov.eg; internet www.egsma.gov.eg/default2.htm; f. 1904; gen. dept of the Egyptian Geological Survey; 50,000 specimens, mostly Egyptian; depts: vertebrates, invertebrates, rocks and minerals; library of 4,200 vols and 6,000 periodicals; Dir-Gen. MOHAMMED AHMED EL BEDAWI.

Cairo Museum of Hygiene: Midan-el-Sakakini, Daher, Cairo; Dir Dr FAWZI SWEHA.

Coptic Museum: Fakhry Abd el Nour St, Abbassia, Cairo; tel. (2) 23639742; f. 1910; sculpture and frescoes, MSS, textiles, icons, ivory and bone, carved wood, metalwork, pottery and glass; library of 6,587 vols; Dir Dr MAHAR SALIB.

Cotton Museum: Gezira, Cairo; tel. (2) 33608682; f. 1923; est. by the Egyptian Agricultural Soc.; all aspects of cotton growing, diseases, pests, and methods of spinning and weaving are shown; Dir M. EL BAHTIMI.

Egyptian (National) Museum: Midan-el-Tahrir, Cairo; tel. (2) 25796948; e-mail egyptianmuseum@hotmail.com; f. 1902; exhibits from prehistoric times until the 3rd century AD; excludes Coptic and Islamic periods; est. by decree in 1835 to conserve antiquities; the Antiquities Dept administers the archaeological museums and controls excavations; library of 40,000 vols; Dir MAMDOUH MOHAMED ELDAMATY; publ. *Annals of the Antiquities Service of Egypt*.

Egyptian National Railways Museum: Cairo Station Bldgs, Ramses Sq., Cairo 11669; tel. (2) 25763793; f. 1933; contains models of foreign and Egyptian railways, and technical information and statistics on the evolution and devt of the Egyptian railway services; library of 5,595 vols (Arabic 2,694, European 2,901); Curator IBRAHIM SALEH ALY.

Gayer-Anderson Museum: Beit el-Kretlia, Cairo; f. 1936; private collns of Oriental art objects bequeathed to Egypt by R. G. Gayer-Anderson Pasha in 1936; Curator YOUNES MAHRAN.

Museum of Islamic Art: Ahmed Maher Sq., Bab al-Khalq, Cairo 11638; tel. (2) 23901520; e-mail islam_mus_director@hotmail.com; internet www.islamicmuseum.gov.eg; f. 1881; colln of 86,000 items representing the evolution of Islamic art from the first quarter of the 7th century to 1900; library of 15,000 vols; Dir-Gen. Dr NIMAT M. ABU-BAKR; publs

Islamic Archaeological Studies (1 a year), catalogues on Islamic decorative arts.

Museum of Modern Art: 4 Sharia Kasr el-Nil, Cairo; internet www.modernartmuseum.gov.eg; f. 1920; Chair. AHMED NAWAR.

The Military Museum: The Citadel, Cairo; f. 1947; history of Egyptian army; 220 paintings of military battles; 250 statues and busts; library of 6,000 vols.

Universities

AIN SHAMS UNIVERSITY

Elkhalifa Elmaamoon St, Abbassia, Cairo 11566
Telephone: (2) 26831231
E-mail: vpce@asunet.shams.edu.eg
Internet: net.shams.edu.eg
Founded 1950
Languages of instruction: Arabic, English, French
Academic year: October to June
Pres.: Prof. MAGED MOHAMMED ALI KHALIL EL-DEEB
Vice-Pres. for Community and Environment: Prof. GAMAL SAMY ALI MAHMOUD
Vice-Pres. for Education and Student Affairs: Prof. ATEF MOHAMMED AWAD EL AWAM
Vice-Pres. for Postgraduate Studies and Research: Prof. MOHAMMED SAID SALAMA ALI
Sec. Gen.: Prof. HASSAN ABD EL AZEEZ AMMAR
Chief Librarian: SOHAIR HASSAN SOMIDA
Library of 15,786 vols (3,318 Arabic, 12,468 English), 63 periodicals, 133,000 theses (30,000 Arabic, 103,000 English)
Number of teachers: 7,297
Number of students: 185,000

DEANS

Faculty of Agriculture: Prof. ESAM OSMAN FAYED
Faculty of Al-Alsun: Prof. ABDEL KADER ATTIA MOHAMMED ABO EL-ANIN
Faculty of Arts: Prof. MAMDOUH MOHAMMED GAD EL-DMATY
Faculty of Commerce: Prof. HUSSEIN MOHAMMED AHMED EID
Faculty of Computer and Information Sciences: Prof. MOHAMED ESAAM KHALIFA
Faculty of Dentistry: Prof. TAREK SALAH EL-DIN HUSSEIN
Faculty of Education: Prof. SUZAN MOHAMMED SALAH EL-DIN FOUAD
Faculty of Engineering: Prof. HADIA MOHAMMED SAID EL-HANAWY
Faculty of Law: Prof. EL SAID EID NAIL
Faculty of Medicine: Prof. AHMED IBRAHIM NASAR
Faculty of Nursing: Prof. SABAH SAAD EL SAID EL SHARKAWY
Faculty of Pharmacy: Prof. NAHED DAWOOD MORTADA
Faculty of Science: Prof. ADEL RAMDAN MOSTFA EL SAYED AHMED
Faculty of Specific Education: Prof. NADIA EL SAYED EL HOSENY
Faculty of Women: Prof. WAFAA MOHAMMED AHMED IBRAHIM
Institute of Childhood Studies: Prof. KHALID HUSSEIN MOSTAFA TAMAN
Institute of Environmental Studies and Research: Prof. AHMED MUSTAFA HUSSIEN EL ATIK

AL-AZHAR UNIVERSITY

Cairo 11751
Telephone: (2) 22623278
E-mail: azhar@azhar.eun.eg
Internet: www.azhar.edu.eg
Founded AD 970, modernized and expanded 1961
Academic year: September to June
Rector: AHMAD AL TAYIB
Vice-Rector: Prof. SAMA GAD
Vice-Rector: Prof. TAHA ABU KREISHA
Library: see under Libraries and Archives
Number of teachers: 9,000
Number of students: 185,000 (on several campuses)

DEANS

Faculty of Agriculture: Prof. AMIN YOUSSEF
Faculty of Arabic and Islamic Studies: Prof. MAHMOUD EL SAIED SHAIKHOON
Faculty of Arabic Studies: Prof. ABDULLAH HELLAL
Faculty of Commerce: Prof. ABDEL-HAMID RABEE
Faculty of Education: MUHAMMAD ABDEL SAMEE OTHMAN
Faculty of Engineering: Prof. ABDEL-WAHID AHMAD
Faculty of Islamic Jurisprudence and Law: Prof. MOHAMMAD RAFAT OTHMAN
Faculty of Islamic Theology: Prof. ABDEL-MOUTI MOHAMMAD BAYOMI
Faculty of Language and Translation: Prof. AHMAD BASEM ABDEL-GHAFFAR
Faculty of Medicine: Prof. ISMAEEL KHALAF
Faculty of Science: Prof. ABDEL-WAHAB AL SHARKAWI
Islamic Women's College: Prof. KAWTHAR KAMEL

ALEXANDRIA UNIVERSITY

El-Guish Rd, El-Shatby Alexandria
Telephone: (3) 5921675
E-mail: iddsc@alexu.edu.eg
Internet: www.alexu.edu.eg
Founded 1942
State control
Languages of instruction: Arabic, English, French
Academic year: October to June
Pres.: Prof. OSAMA IBRAHIM SAYED AHMED
Vice-Pres. for Community Devt and Environmental Affairs: Prof. MAHMOUD EL KHISHEN
Vice-Pres. for Damanhour Br.: Prof. MOHAMED AHMED BAUOMY
Vice-Pres. for Education and Students Affairs: Prof. ROUCHDY ZAHRAN
Vice-Pres. for Graduate Studies and Research: Prof. SEDDIK ABD-EL SALAM TAWFIK
Sec. Gen.: METWALLY ABD-EL SALAM
Chief Librarian: SOHER GAMAL
Library: see under Libraries and Archives
Number of teachers: 6,272
Number of students: 118,906

DEANS

Faculty of Agriculture: Prof. MOHAMED GAMAL MOHAMED EL-TORKY
Faculty of Agriculture (Saba Basha): Prof. AHMED KAMAL KHALIL MOURAD
Faculty of Arts: Prof. ASHRAF AHMED GABER FARAG
Faculty of Commerce: Prof. SAID ABD EL AZIZ ALY OSSMAN
Faculty of Dentistry: Prof. IHAB ADEL MOHAMED HAMAD
Faculty of Education: Prof. MOHAMED ISMAIL ABDEL-MAKSOUD ANBISY
Faculty of Engineering: Prof. FAHMY ALY IBRAHIM FATHELBAB
Faculty of Fine Arts: Prof. MOHAMED HESHAM SEOUDI KAMEL
Faculty of Law: Prof. AHMED AWAD ABD EL MAGED HINDY
Faculty of Medicine: Prof. MOHAMED ASHRAF SAAD GALAL
Faculty of Nursing: Prof. FATEN EZZ EL-DINE FIKRY
Faculty of Pharmacy: Prof. MOHAMED IBRAHIM AHMED ABOU SHEAR
Faculty of Physical Education for Girls: Prof. MAGDA MOHAMED SALAH EL-SHAZLY
Faculty of Specific Education: Prof. FATEN MOUSTAFA KAMAL LOUTFY
Faculty of Sport Education for Men: Prof. NADER MOHAMED MOHAMED MORGAN
Faculty of Tourism and Hotels: Prof. HANAN SAAD ABD EL-HALEEM KATARA
Faculty of Veterinary Medicine: Prof. YEHIA ZAKARIA ATEFEY
High Institute of Public Health: Prof. IBRAHIM FAHMY KHARBOUSH
Institute of Graduate Studies and Research: Prof. MOUKHTAR IBRAHIM YOUSSEF
Medical Research Institute: Prof. GAMAL EL-DINE AHMED AMIN EL-SAWAF

AMERICAN UNIVERSITY IN CAIRO

Tahrir Sq. Campus, BP 2511, 113 Sharia Kasr el Aini, Cairo 11511
New Cairo Campus, BP 74, Cairo 11835
American Office: 3rd Fl., 420 Fifth Ave, New York, NY 10018-2729, USA
Telephone: (2) 27942964
Internet: www.aucegypt.edu
Founded 1919
Private control
Language of instruction: English
Academic year: September to June
Pres.: DAVID A. ARNOLD
Provost: LISA ANDERSON
Vice-Provost: ALI HADI
Vice-Pres. and Exec. Sec. of Board of Trustees: MARY CORRARINO
Vice-Pres. for Continuing Education: EDWARD SIMPSON
Vice-Pres. for Finance: ANDREW SNAITH
Vice-Pres. for Institutional Advancement: JAMES L. BULLOCK
Vice-Pres. for Planning and Admin.: PAUL DONOGHUE
Vice-Pres. for Student Affairs: ASHRAF EL FIQI
Dean of Libraries: SHAHIRA EL SAWY
Library: see under Libraries and Archives
Number of teachers: 303
Number of students: 5,577
Publications: *Alif* (English and Arabic poetry), *Cairo Papers in Social Science*

DEANS

School of Business, Economics and Communications: D. O'CONNOR
School of Humanities and Social Sciences: A. M. LESCH
School of Sciences and Engineering: M. HAROUN

ATTACHED UNITS

Centre for Adult and Continuing Education: non-credit study programme for 30,000 students a year; offers courses and post-secondary and postgraduate career programmes in Arabic/English, Arabic/French translation, English language, business and secretarial skills, and computing; Dean Dr HARRY MILLER.

Desert Development Centre: research to improve the social and economic well-being of new desert settlers, integrating agriculture, renewable energy and community research; Dir Dr RICHARD TUTWILER.

Social Research Centre: e-mail src@aucegypt.edu; current research projects on demography and human resettlement; Dir Dr HODA RASHAD

ASSIUT UNIVERSITY

Assiut Governorate, Assiut Univ. POB, Assiut 71515
Telephone: (88) 2357007
E-mail: info@aun.eun.eg
Internet: www.aun.edu.eg

Founded 1957
State control
Languages of instruction: Arabic, English
Academic year: September to June

Rector: Prof. MOSTAFA MOHAMAD KAMAL
Deputy-Rector for Community Services and Environmental Devt: Prof. MOHAMED AHMED SHANAWANY
Deputy-Rector for Postgraduate Studies and Research Affairs: Prof. MOHAMED RAGAB BAYOUMI
Deputy-Rector for Student Affairs and Education: Prof. SAID AHMED IBRAHIM
Sec. Gen.: MOHAMED MAHMOUD OMAR
Chief Librarian: SAMIA ALI ISMAIL

Library of 40,000 vols, abstracts covering all educational and research fields, 35,000 full text periodicals, 28,000 ebooks; 28 br. libraries
Number of teachers: 3,975
Number of students: 79,140

Publications: *Assiut Journal of Agricultural Sciences, Assiut Medical Journal, Assiut University Bulletin for Environmental Researches, Assiut University Journal of Computer Science, Assiut University Journal of Geology, Assiut University Journal of Mathematics, Assiut University Journal of Zoology, Assiut Veterinary Medical Journal, Bulletin of Faculty of Physical Education, Bulletin of Pharmaceutical Sciences, Egyptian Sugar Journal, Journal of Engineering Sciences, Journal of Faculty of Education, Journal of Law Studies* (Arabic)

DEANS

Faculty of Agriculture: Prof. MOHAMED ABD EL WAHAB ABO NOHOUL
Faculty of Arts: Prof. NASEEF SHAKER SAYED
Faculty of Commerce: Prof. ADEL RAYAN MOHAMED RAYAN
Faculty of Education: Prof. SALAH EL DEEN HUSSIEN EL SHARIEF
Faculty of Education (New Valley Branch): Prof. AHMED SAYED MOHAMED IBRAHIM
Faculty of Engineering: Prof. IBRAHIM M. ISMAIL SALEH
Faculty of Information and Computer and Information Sciences: Prof. HOSSNI MOHAMED IBRAHIM (acting)
Faculty of Law: Prof. ESSAM MOHAMED AHMED ZANNATI
Faculty of Medicine: Prof. MAHER ABDEL SALAM EL ASSAL
Faculty of Nursing: Prof. IKRAM ALI HASHIM SOLIMAN
Faculty of Pharmacy: Prof. GAMAL AHMED S. ABD-ELAAL
Faculty of Physical Education: Prof. TAREQ MOHAMED MOHAMED ABDEL AZIZ
Faculty of Science: Prof. AHMED YEHYA ABDEL-MALEK
Faculty of Social Service: Prof. NABIEL IBRAHIM AHMED
Faculty of Specific Education: Prof. MOHAMED SALAH EL-DIN YOUSSEF (acting)
Faculty of Veterinary Medicine: Prof. MOSTAFA KHALIL MOSTAFA

ATTACHED RESEARCH INSTITUTES

South Egypt Cancer Institute: El-Methaq St, Mansheit El-Omara Sq., POB 171516, Assiut; tel. (88) 2337670; e-mail seci@seci.info; f. 1997 as part of the Faculty of Medicine, present status 1999; depts of anaesthesia, biostatistics, cancer biology, cancer epidemiology, clinical pathology, ICU and pain relief, medical oncology, paediatric oncology, radiology, radiotherapy and nuclear medicine, surgical oncology; Dean Prof. MAHMOUD MOHAMED MOSTAFA.

Sugar Technology Research Institute: Assiut Univ. Old Bldg; tel. (88) 2313713; e-mail sugar@acc.aun.edu.eg; internet www.aun.edu.eg/suger/general.html; language of instruction: English; teaching, training, devt and research in the Egyptian sugar industry; offers postgraduate diplomas; depts of sugar industry, industrial engineering and management, chemical and pharmaceutical industries, materials and applications, advanced agricultural technology, environmental sciences and pollution treatment; Dean Prof. ABDEL AZIZ AHMED SAID.

There are 46 attached university centres and special units

CAIRO UNIVERSITY

BP 12611, Orman, Giza, Cairo
Telephone: (2) 35729584
E-mail: info@main-scc.cairo.edu.eg
Internet: www.cu.edu.eg

Founded 1908
State control
Language of instruction: Arabic, English, French
Academic year: October to June

Pres.: Prof. HOSSAM KAMEL
Vice-Pres. for Beni-Suef Br.: Prof. MOHAMED ANAS KASEM GAFAR
Vice-Pres. for Community Services and Environmental Affairs: Prof. ABDALLA ABDEL FATTAH ELTATAWY
Vice-Pres. for Fayoum Branch: Prof. GALAL MOSTAFA SAEED
Vice-Pres. for Postgraduate Studies and Research: Prof. MOTAZ MOHAMED HOSNY KHORSHED
Vice-Pres. for Undergraduate Studies: Prof. HAMED TAHER HASSANEEN FOAD
Sec. Gen.: FAYZA MEGAHED
Librarian: AHMED SHOAB

Library: see under Libraries and Archives
Number of teachers: 7,066
Number of students: 202,167

DEANS

Faculty of Agriculture: Prof. SALWA BAYOUMY MOHAMED EL MAGHOULY
Faculty of Agriculture (in Fayoum): Prof. ABDALLA MOHAMED ABDEL RAHMAN MOUSA
Faculty of Arabic and Islamic Studies (in Fayoum): Prof. MOHAMED SALAH EL DEEN MOSTAFA
Faculty of Archaeology: Prof. OLA MOHAMED ABD EL AZIZ ELAGEZY
Faculty of Archaeology (in Fayoum): Prof. MOHAMED ABDEL HALIM NOUR ELDIN (acting)
Faculty of Arts: Prof. AHMED MAGDY HEGAZY
Faculty of Arts (in Beni-Suef): Prof. MOHAMED MAHRAN RASHWAN (acting)
Faculty of Commerce: Prof. AHMED FARGHALY MOHAMED HASSAN
Faculty of Commerce (in Beni-Suef): Prof. KAWSSAR ABDEL FATTAH MAHAMED ALABAGY
Faculty of Computer and Information Science: Prof. Dr ALY ALY MOHAMED FAHMY
Faculty of Dar el Oloum: Prof. AHMED MOHAMED ABD EL AZIZ KESHK
Faculty of Dar el Oloum (in Fayoum): Prof. IBRAHIM MOHAMED IBRAHIM SAKR
Faculty of Dentistry: Prof. MAHMOUD IBRAHIM FAHMY EL REFAAY
Faculty of Economics and Political Science: Prof. KAMAL MAHMOUD EL MENOUFY
Faculty of Education (in Beni-Suef): Prof. MOSTAFA HASSAN MOHAMED EL NASHAR
Faculty of Education (in Fayoum): Prof. MOHAMED ABD EL RAHMAN EL SHARNOBY
Faculty of Engineering: ALY ABDEL RAHMAN YOUSEF
Faculty of Engineering (in Fayoum): Prof. SAMY EL BADAWY YEHYA
Faculty of Kindergartens: Prof. MONA MOHAMED ALY GAD
Faculty of Law: Prof. AHMED ELSAYED SAWY
Faculty of Law (in Beni-Suef): Prof. Dr REDA IBRAHIM EBEID
Faculty of Mass Communication: Prof. MAGY EL HALAWANY
Faculty of Medicine: Prof. MADIHA MOAHMOUD KHATAB
Faculty of Medicine (in Beni-Suef): Prof. MOHAMED ELSAYED EL BATANOUNY
Faculty of Medicine (in Fayoum): Prof. KAMAL ELBASYOUNY
Faculty of Nursing: Prof. BASAMAT OMAR AHMED
Faculty of Pharmacy: Prof. AHMED ATTEIA MOHAMED SEADA
Faculty of Pharmacy (in Beni-Suef): Prof. AHMED ABDEL BARY ABDEL RAHMAN
Faculty of Physiotherapy: Prof. KAMAL EL SAYED MOHAMED SHOKRY
Faculty of Science: Prof. HAMDY MAHMOUD HASSANEN ELSAYED
Faculty of Science (in Beni-Suef): Prof. AHMED HAFEZ HUSSEIN EL GHANDOUR
Faculty of Science (in Fayoum): Prof. KAMAL AHMED MOHAMED HASSAN DEEB
Faculty of Social Service (in Fayoum): Prof. AHMED MAGDY HEGAZY MAHMOUD (acting)
Faculty of Specific Education: Prof. ALY MOHAMED ALY ELMELEGY
Faculty of Specific Education (in Fayoum): Prof. AHMED GALAL EWIES ELAWA
Faculty of Tourism and Hotels (in Fayoum): Prof. AWAD ABBAS RAGAB
Faculty of Urban Planning: Prof. MAHER MOHEB ISTENO AFANDY
Faculty of Veterinary Medicine: Prof. MOHAMED IBRAHIM MOHAMED DESOUKY
Faculty of Veterinary Medicine (in Beni-Suef): Prof. SHAWKY SOLIMAN IBRAHIM SOLIMAN
Institute of African Studies and Research: Prof. EL SAYED ALY FLEEFEL
Institute of Educational Studies and Research: Prof. MOSTAFA ABDEL SAMIAA
Institute of Statistical Studies and Research: Prof. ABDEL GHANI MOHAMED ABDEL GHANI IBRAHIM
National Institute of Laser Science: Prof. HUSSIEN MOSTAFA MUSA KHALED
National Institute of Tumours: Prof. MOHAMED ABDEL HARETH MOHAMED ABDELRAHMAN

HELWAN UNIVERSITY

Ain Helwan, Helwan, Cairo
Telephone: (2) 25590000
E-mail: info@helwan.edu.eg
Internet: www.helwan.edu.eg

Founded 1975, incorporating existing institutes of higher education
State control
Languages of instruction: Arabic, English
Academic year: September to June

Pres.: Prof. ABD ALLAH BARAKAT
Vice-Pres. for Community Service and Environmental Devt: ABLA HANAFY
Vice-Pres. for Postgraduate Studies and Research: Prof. AHMAD ABD EL KAREEM SALAMA
Vice-Pres. for Undergraduate Studies and Student Affairs: MOHAMMAD HAZEM FATHALLAH
Sec.-Gen.: SEKINA HANAFY MAHMOUD MOHAMED
Librarian: MAHMOUD QATR

Library of 34,795 vols, 425 journals, 9,379 theses
Number of teachers: 2,179
Number of students: 95,567

Publications: *Journal of Economic and Legal Studies* (2 a year), *Journal of Educational and Social Studies*, *Journal of Engineering Research* (6 a year), *Journal of Research on Art Education* (3 a year), *Journal of Studies on Social Work and Humanities*, *Journal of the Faculty of Arts* (2 a year), *Journal of the Science and Art of Sport* (2 a year), *Science and Art of Music* (2 a year), *Scientific Journal of Commercial Studies and Research* (4 a year), *Scientific Journal of Physical Studies* (4 a year)

DEANS

Faculty of Applied Arts: Prof. ADEL HEFNAWY
Faculty of Art Education: Prof. MOHAMMAD LABEEB NADA
Faculty of Arts: Prof. MOHAMED YEHIA MOHAMED
Faculty of Commerce and Business Administration: Prof. MOHAMED AMIN ABDALLA AMIN KAED
Faculty of Education: Prof. ABD EL-MOTTELEB AL KORETY
Faculty of Engineering (Mataria): Prof. TAHANY YOUSSEF
Faculty of Engineering and Technology (Helwan): Prof. OMAR HANAFY
Faculty of Fine Arts: Prof. MOHAMMAD TAWFEEK
Faculty of Home Economics: Prof. ABD EL RAHMAN ATIA
Faculty of Information and Computer Sciences: Prof. YEHIA KAMAL HELMY
Faculty of Law: Prof. MOHAMED ELSHAHAT ELGENDY
Faculty of Music Education: Prof. AMERA FARAG
Faculty of Pharmacy: Prof. MOHAMED MOHY ELDIN ELMAZAR
Faculty of Physical Education (Men): Prof. SOBHY HASANEIN
Faculty of Physical Education (Women): Prof. HANAN ROSHDY
Faculty of Science: Prof. MOHAMMAD EL SAYYED
Faculty of Social Work: Prof. MOHAMED REFAAT KASSEM ABDEL RAHMAN
Faculty of Tourism and Hotel Management: Prof. DOHA MOUSTAFA

MANSOURA UNIVERSITY

60 Elgomhoria St, Mansoura
Telephone: (50) 347900
E-mail: info@mans.edu.eg
Internet: www.mans.eun.eg

Founded 1973 from the Mansoura br. of Cairo Univ.
State control
Languages of instruction: Arabic, English
Academic year: October to June

Pres.: Prof. AHMED GAMAL ELDIN ABDEL FATTAH MOUSA
Vice-Pres. for Community Services and Environmental Affairs: Prof. MOHAMED AHMED GABALLA YOSSEF
Vice-Pres. for Postgraduate Studies and Research: Prof. MAGDY MOHAMED ABOU RAYAAN
Vice-Pres. for Undergraduate Studies: Prof. MOHAMED SUIELM MOHAMED ELBASUONY
Sec. Gen.: MAGDY AHMED MAHMOUD SALEH
Chief Librarian: ABDALLA HUSSIEN

Number of teachers: 2,230
Number of students: 107,022

Publications: *Egyptian Journal for Commercial Studies* (4 a year), *Journal of the Faculty of Arts* (2 a year), *Journal of Veterinary Medical Research* (1 a year), *Mansoura Dental Journal* (4 a year), *Mansoura Engineering Journal* (4 a year), *Mansoura Faculty of Education Journal* (3 a year), *Mansoura Journal of Forensic Medicine and Clinical Toxicology* (2 a year), *Mansoura Journal of Pharmaceutical Sciences* (2 a year), *Mansoura Medical Journal* (2 a year), *Mansoura Science Bulletin* (2 a year), *Mansoura University Journal of Agriculture* (12 a year), *Revue des Recherches Juridiques et Economiques* (2 a year)

DEANS

Faculty of Agriculture: Prof. HESHAM NAGY ABDEL MAGEED
Faculty of Commerce: Prof. NABIL AL HUSSINI AL NAGGAR
Faculty of Computer and Information Science: FATMA ABOU-CHADI
Faculty of Medicine: Prof. AMR SARHAN
Faculty of Nursing: Prof. FARDOS RAMADAN
Faculty of Science: Prof. TAHA ZAKI NABAWY SOKKAR
Faculty of Science (in Damiatta): Prof. MOHAMED R. MOSTAFA
Faculty of Veterinary Medicine: Prof. MOHAMED MOHAMED FOUDA

MINIA UNIVERSITY

Menia Governorate, Menia
Telephone: (86) 361443
E-mail: man.prt@miniauniv.edu.eg
Internet: www.minia.edu.eg

Founded 1976, incorporating existing faculties of Assiut Univ.
Languages of instruction: Arabic, English
Academic year: October to June

Pres.: Prof. ABD EL MONIEM ABD EL HAMID EL BASSIOUNY
Vice-Pres. for Community Services and Environmental Affairs: Prof. ABD EL GHAFAR FARIED ABD EL GHAFAR
Vice-Pres. for Postgraduate Studies and Research: Prof. MOHAMED SAIED MOHAMED ALY
Vice-Pres. for Undergraduate Studies: Prof. MAHER GABER MOHAMED AHMED
Sec. Gen.: LAILA AHMED IBRAHIM SOROOR
Chief Librarian: NABELA EL SAWY

Number of teachers: 1,288
Number of students: 36,906

DEANS

Faculty of Agriculture: Prof. MOHAMED ATEF FAHMY AHMED KESHK
Faculty of al Alsun (Languages): Prof. AMAL MOSTAFA KAMAL MOHAMED
Faculty of Arts: Prof. MOHAMED NAGEEB AHMED MOHAMED
Faculty of Computer and Information Science: (vacant)
Faculty of Dar al Olum: Prof. MOHY ELDIN OTHMAN RASHDAN
Faculty of Dentistry: Prof. HANY HUSSIEN MOHAMED AMIN
Faculty of Education: Prof. ATTA TAHA ZEDAN SHEHATA
Faculty of Engineering: Prof. MOHAMED MONESS ALY AHMED
Faculty of Fine Arts: Prof. WAFAA OMAR ABD ELHALEEM
Faculty of Medicine: Prof. MOHAMED IBRAHIM BASUONY
Faculty of Nursing: Prof. GALAL MOHAMED SHAWKY HAMED
Faculty of Pharmacy: Prof. MOHAMED MONTASER ABD ELHAKIM
Faculty of Physical Education (Female): (vacant)
Faculty of Physical Education (Male): Prof. BAHY ELDIN IBRAHIM SALAMA
Faculty of Science: Prof. ABD ELRAHMAN ABD ELAZIZ AHMED
Faculty of Specific Education: Prof. ABD ELAZEEM ABD ELSALAM ELFERGANY
Faculty of Tourism and Hotel Management: Prof. ABD ELBARY AHMED ALY DAWOOD

MINUFIYA UNIVERSITY

Gamal Abd el Nasser St, BP 32511, Shebeen el Kam
Telephone: (48) 222170
E-mail: menofia@menofia.edu.eg
Internet: www.menofia.edu.eg

Founded 1976
State control
Languages of instruction: Arabic, English
Academic year: September to July

Pres.: Prof. MOHAMED A. IZZULARAB
Vice-Pres. for Community and Environmental Devt: Prof. ABD EL ALEEM MOHAMMED ABD EL KHALIK EL DERAEE
Vice-Pres. for Graduate Studies and Research: Prof. THABET ABD EL RAHAMAN EDRESE
Vice-Pres. for Sadat Br.: Prof. AHMED HAMED ZAGHLOL
Vice-Pres. for Undergraduate Education: Prof. MOSTAFA ABD EL RAHMAN
Sec. Gen.: MOSTAFA SADAK KHALIL
Librarian: HAMDY EL SHAMY

Number of teachers: 2,928
Number of students: 71,225

Publications: *Minoufiya Journal of Electronic Engineering Research* (2 a year), *Minoufiya Medical Journal* (2 a year), *Scientific Journal of the Faculty of Science* (1 a year)

DEANS

Faculty of Agriculture: Prof. ALI IBRAHIM FARAG
Faculty of Arts: Prof. AHMED ABD EL KADER EL SHATHLY
Faculty of Commerce: Prof. GAMAL EL DIN MOHAMED EL MORSEY
Faculty of Commerce (Sadat Br.): Prof. HASANIEN SAYED TAHA
Faculty of Computers and Information: Prof. MOHIEY MOHAMED HADHOUD
Faculty of Education: Prof. ALI MOHAMED SHUAIB
Faculty of Education (Sadat Br.): Prof. ABD EL AAL AGWA
Faculty of Electronic Engineering: Prof. ATEF EL SAYED ABOU EL AZM
Faculty of Engineering: Prof. ADEL ALI ABOU EL ALA
Faculty of Home Economics: Prof. FATMA EL ZAHRAA EL SHERIEF
Faculty of Hotels and Tourism: (vacant)
Faculty of Law: Prof. MOHAMED SAMY EL SHAWA
Faculty of Law (Sadat Br.): Prof. ABD EL HADEY MOHAMED EL ASHREY
Faculty of Medicine: Prof. SAID SHALABY IBRAHIM
Faculty of Nursing: Prof. MAGDA MOAWAD
Faculty of Physical Education: Prof. ESAM EL DIN METWALY ALI
Faculty of Science: Prof. GAMALAT YOUSEF OSMAN
Faculty of Special Education: Prof. ALI BADAWI MAHROUS
Faculty of Veterinary Medicine: Prof. SALAH EL SAYED IBRAHIM
Genetic Engineering and Biotechnology Research Institute: (vacant)
Institute of Desert Environment Research: Prof. MUBARAK HASSANY ALI
National Liver Research Institute: Prof. EMAM ABD EL LATIEF EMAM

MISR UNIVERSITY FOR SCIENCE AND TECHNOLOGY (MUST)

BP 77, Sixth of October City
Telephone: (2) 38354686
E-mail: must@must.edu
Internet: www.must.edu

Founded 1996
Private control
Language of instruction: English
Academic year: October to July

Chancellor: KHALED M. EL-TOUKHY
Pres.: Prof. MOHAMED RAAFAT MAHMOUD
Vice-Pres. for Community Service: Prof. FAROUK ABU-ZAID
Vice-Pres. for Int. Cooperation and Quality Assurance: Prof. MOSTAFA M. KAMEL
Registrar: ASHRAF ABDULLAH
Librarian: Prof. KAMAL ARAFAT

Library of 70,000 vols
Number of teachers: 533
Number of students: 12,348

DEANS

College of Applied Medical Sciences: FATIMA AL-SHARQAWI
College of Archaeology and Tourist Guidance: MOHAMMED IBRAHIM BAKR
College of Biotechnology: Prof. ALI Z. ABDUL-SALAM
College of Business: Prof. MOHAMMED H. AZZAZI
College of Dental Medicine: Prof. TAREK M. AL-SHARKAWI
College of Engineering: Prof. MOHAMMED K. BEDEEWI
College of Foreign Languages and Translation: Prof. MOHSEN ABU-SEDA
College of Information Technology: MOHAMMED S. ABDUL-WAHHAB
College of Mass Media: Prof. FAROUK ABU-ZIED
College of Medicine: Prof. MAJED GAMAL ZAYED
College of Pharmacy: Prof. MOHAMMED F. AL-MELEEGI
College of Physical Therapy: Prof. BASEM AL-NAHHAS

SOUTH VALLEY UNIVERSITY

Qena Governorate, Qena
Telephone: (96) 5211277
E-mail: info@svu.edu.eg
Internet: www.svu.edu.eg

Founded 1995
State control
Languages of instruction: Arabic, English
Academic year: September to June

Campuses in Aswan, Hurghada, Luxor

Pres.: Prof. ABBAS MOHAMED MOHAMED MANSOUR
Vice-Pres. for Aswan Campus: Prof. MANSOUR MOHAMED KAPPASH
Vice-Pres. for Community Services and Environmental Affairs: Prof. MAHMOUD KHODARI MA'LA
Vice-Pres. for Postgraduate Studies and Research: Prof. MAHMOUD KHODARI MA'LA
Vice-Pres. for Undergraduate Studies: Prof. MOHAMED THARWAT KAPPASH
Chief Librarian: AWATEF YASSIEN ALQADI

Number of teachers: 1,092
Number of students: 44,178

DEANS

Faculty of Agriculture: Prof. MOHAMMAD ALI
Faculty of Archaeology: Prof. ABDULLAH K. MOUSA
Faculty of Arts: Prof. ABUELFADL M. M. BADRAN
Faculty of Commerce: Prof. JAMAL IBRAHIM
Faculty of Education: Prof. SAMEH A. M. JAFAR
Faculty of Education (Hurghada): Prof. KAREEMA KHATAAB
Faculty of Engineering: Prof. AREF M. SULAIMAN
Faculty of Fine Arts (Luxor): Prof. MOHAMED ORABY
Faculty of Hotel and Tourism: Prof. SALEH ABDELMU'TI
Faculty of Law: Prof. THARWAT M. ABDEL-'AAL
Faculty of Medicine: Prof. MANSOUR KABBASH
Faculty of Nursing: Prof. SAYED TAHA
Faculty of Physical Education: Prof. EMAD ABU-ELQASEM
Faculty of Science: Prof. SAYED O. AL-KHATEEB
Faculty of Social Work: Prof. ALI A. DANDARAWI
Faculty of Specific Education: Prof. HIFNI ISMAIEL
Faculty of Veterinary Medicine: Prof. ABDEL-LATIF S. SHAKER

DEANS (ASWAN CAMPUS)

Faculty of Arts: Prof. AHAMD SUKRANO ABDEL-HAFEZ (acting)
Faculty of Education: Prof. NADY K. AZIZ
Faculty of Energy Engineering: Prof. JABER SHABIB
Faculty of Engineering: Prof. ABD-ALLAH IBRAHIM
Faculty of Science: Prof. ALI K. KHALAF-ALLAH

SUEZ CANAL UNIVERSITY

el Shikh Zayed, Ismailia
Telephone: (64) 3297020
E-mail: president_office@suez.edu.eg
Internet: scuegypt.edu.eg

Founded 1976
State control
Languages of instruction: Arabic, English
Academic year: October to June

Pres.: Prof. FAROUK MAHMOUD ABD EL KADER
Vice-Pres. for Community Services and Environmental Affairs: Prof. ALY IBRAHIM ELSAYED IBRAHIM BADR
Vice-Pres. for Port Said: MOHAMED ELSAYED ALY RAHEEM
Vice-Pres. for Postgraduate Studies and Research: Prof. MOSTAFA KAMEL MOHAMED MOSBAH
Vice-Pres. for Undergraduate Studies: Prof. IBRAHIM ASHOUR IBRAHIM BADR
Sec. Gen.: NAINAA MOHAMED MOHAMED KHALIFA
Librarian: KAMILIA ALHOSARY

Number of teachers: 1,466
Number of students: 47,488

DEANS

El Arish:

- Faculty of Agricultural and Environmental Sciences: Prof. MOHAMED RAGAB ABDO HUMOS
- Faculty of Education: Prof. NASSEF BEDEER IBRAHIM ELAASY

Ismailia:

- Faculty of Agriculture: Prof. MOHAMED SAMIR MOHAMED ATTEYA ELSHAZLY
- Faculty of Commerce: Prof. MOSTAFA ALY MAHMOUD ELBAZ
- Faculty of Computers and Information Science: Prof. MOHAMED HELMY MAHRAN
- Faculty of Dentistry: Prof. MOHAMED ELHUSSEINY MOHAMED MEKY
- Faculty of Education: Prof. MAHMOUD ABBASS MAHMOUD ABDEIN
- Faculty of Medicine: Prof. SOLIMAN HAMED SOLIMAN ELKAMASH
- Faculty of Pharmacy: Prof. SALAH ELDIN MOHAMED ABDALLA
- Faculty of Science: Prof. ELSAYED HUSSEIN MOSTAFA ELTAMNY
- Faculty of Tourism and Hotels: Prof. ABD EL RAHMAN ABD EL FATTAH MOHAMED
- Faculty of Veterinary Medicine: Prof. MOHAMED ELSAYED ANANY

Port Said:

- Faculty of Commerce: Prof. MOHAMED ABD EL RAHMAN ELAADY
- Faculty of Education: FAKRY IBRAHIM KHALIL KHALAF
- Faculty of Engineering: Prof. AHMAD KAMAL ABD-EL KHALEK
- Faculty of Nursing: Prof. HODA WADEEA TAWFEK
- Faculty of Physical Education (Male): Prof. SAYED ABDEL GAWAD ELSAYED AHMED
- Faculty of Specific Education: Prof. MOHAMED SAYED AHMED SALEH

Suez:

- Faculty of Commerce: Prof. MAHMOUD SAYED AHMED SALEM
- Faculty of Education: Prof. BELAL AHMED SOLIMAN AHMED
- Faculty of Industrial Education: Prof. AHMED ESSA GAMEA ELNEKHILY
- Faculty of Petroleum and Mining Engineering: Prof. SHUHDY EL MAGHRABY ELALFY SHALABY

TANTA UNIVERSITY

El Geish St, Tanta
Telephone: (40) 3317928
E-mail: president@tanta.edu.eg
Internet: www.tanta.edu.eg

Founded 1972
State control
Languages of instruction: Arabic, English
Academic year: October to June

Pres.: Prof. ABDELFATTAH A. SADAKAH
Vice-Pres. for Community Service and Environment Devt: Prof. MOHAMED MOSAAD NASSAR
Vice-Pres. for Education and Student Affairs: Prof. AZIZ MAHFOUZ KAFAFY
Vice-Pres. for Graduate Studies and Research: Prof. MOHAMED ADEL KHALIFAA
Sec. Gen.: RAWIA SOLIMAN GAD
Chief Librarian: ADEL YASSIEN

Number of teachers: 2,042
Number of students: 109,037

DEANS

Faculty of Agriculture: Prof. HELMY ALI ANBAR
Faculty of Arts: Prof. ZAIN EL DEIN MOSTAFA
Faculty of Commerce: Prof. SAID LEBDA
Faculty of Dentistry: Prof. SHWKRIA MOHAMMED ESMAIL
Faculty of Education: Prof. MOHAMMED AMIN ATWA
Faculty of Engineering: Prof. ABDEL-WAHED ASAR
Faculty of Law: Prof. HUSIEN MOHAMMED FATHY
Faculty of Medicine: Prof. SHAWKI ABD-ELAZIZ EL ABD
Faculty of Nursing: Prof. Dr HELMY HAMAD AHMED SHALABY
Faculty of Pharmacy: Prof. MOKHTAR MOHAMMED MABROUK
Faculty of Physical Education: Prof. REYAD ZAKRIA EL MENSHAWY
Faculty of Science: Prof. EBRAHIM KAMEL EL SHORBAGY
Faculty of Specific Education: Prof. HUSIEN MOHAMMED FATHY (acting)

ZAGAZIG UNIVERSITY

Sharkia Governorate, Zagazig
Telephone: (55) 238470
E-mail: info@zu.edu.eg
Internet: www.zu.edu.eg

Founded 1974, incorporating existing faculties of Ain-Shams Univ.
State control
Languages of instruction: Arabic, English
Academic year: October to June

Pres.: Prof. MAHER MOHAMED ALI EL DOMIATY
Vice-Pres. for Education and Student Affairs: Prof. AHMED ELREFAAY BAHGAT EL AZIZY
Vice-Pres. for Environmental Affairs: Prof. TAREK YOUSSEF GAAFAR
Vice-Pres. for Postgraduate Studies: Prof. MOHAMED BAHGAT AWAD
Sec. Gen.: MOHAMMED MOHAMMED HASHEM
Chief Librarian: RAMADAN ALY OTHMAN

Number of teachers: 4,250
Number of students: 151,091

DEANS

Faculty of Agriculture: Prof. MOHAMMED BASSEM ASHOUR
Faculty of Arts: Prof. HASSAN MOHAMMED HAMMAD
Faculty of Commerce: Prof. IBRAHIM MOUSSA ABD ELFATAH
Faculty of Computer and Information Science: Prof. D MOHAMMED ABBAS SHOUMAN
Faculty of Education: Prof. HAMDY HASSAN ELMAHROUKY
Faculty of Engineering: Prof. ASHRAF MOHAMMED ELSHEIHY
Faculty of Law: Prof. ATEF HASSAN MAHMOUD ELNOKALY
Faculty of Medicine: Prof. SAAD SABRY ELOSH
Faculty of Nursing: Prof. NAGWA AHMED ELSHAFEEY
Faculty of Pharmacy: Prof. MOHAMMED NAGUIB MOHAMMED ZAKARIA
Faculty of Physical Education (Female): Prof. NABILA ABDALLA MOHAMED OMRAN
Faculty of Physical Education (Male): Prof. ABD ELAZEEM ABD ELHAMID ELSAYED
Faculty of Science: Prof. MOHAMMED GAMAL HELMY ABD ELWAHED
Faculty of Specific Education: Prof. ADEL EBRAHIM ELBAZ
Faculty of Veterinary Medicine: Prof. ALAA ELDEEN MOHAMMED MORSHEDY
Higher Institute of Ancient Near East Civilizations: Prof. MAHMOUD OMAR MOHAMED
Higher Institute of Asian Research and Studies: Prof. BAYOUMI AWAD ALLAH TARTOUR
Higher Institute of Productive Efficiency: Prof. MOHAMMED NAGY ELGAAFRY

University-Level Institute

BENHA HIGHER INSTITUTE OF TECHNOLOGY

New Benha, el Kaludia, Benha City 13512
Telephone: (13) 3229263
E-mail: ahuzayyin@gmx.net
Internet: www.bhit-buni.edu.eg

Founded 1988
State control

Depts of basic sciences, civil engineering, electrical engineering and mechanical engineering

Dean: AHMED SOLIMAN HUZAYYIN
Vice-Dean for Postgraduates: ADEL ALAM EL DIN
Vice-Dean for Students: MAHMOUD FATHY M. HASSAN

Library of 8,100 vols

Number of teachers: 275
Number of students: 1,530

Colleges

Arab Academy for Science, Technology and Maritime Transport: Gamal Abdel Naser St, BP 1029, Miami, Alexandria; tel. (3) 5622366; internet www.aast.edu; f. 1972; colleges of computer and information technology, engineering and technology, fisheries technology and aquaculture, graduate school of business, international transport and logistics, language and communication, management and technology, and maritime transport and technology; campuses in Cairo, South Valley, Port Said and Smart Village; library: 36,000 vols, 350 periodicals; 490 teachers; 4,000 students; Pres. Dr ISMAIL ABDEL GHAFFAR.

Higher Institute of Public Health: 165 el Horreya Ave, el Hadra, Alexandria; tel. (3) 4285575; e-mail hiph.adv@gmail.com; internet www.hiph-egypt.net; f. 1956; an autonomous unit of the Univ. of Alexandria; undertakes fundamental teaching and applied public health research; 81 staff mems and 50 instructors; depts of biostatistics, epidemiology, family health, microbiology, nutrition, occupational and environmental health, public health administration, tropical health; library: 10,000 vols; Dean Prof. MOUSRAFA I. MOURAD; Vice-Dean for Postgraduate Studies and Research Prof. NIHAD I. DABBOUS; Vice-Dean for Community Service and Environmental Affairs Prof. MOHAMED A. EL BARRAWY.

Sadat Academy for Management Sciences: Kernish el Nile el Maadi, BP 2222, Cairo; tel. (2) 23787628; e-mail info@sadatacademy.edu.eg; internet www.sadatacademy.edu.eg; f. 1981; prin. governmental org. for management devt in Egypt; activities carried out through 10 academic depts: accountancy, administrative law, business administration, computer and information systems, economics, insurance and quantitative analysis, languages, personnel and organizational behaviour, production, public administration; also consists of 4 professional centres: Training, Consultation, Research and Local Admin.; and Faculty of Management (undergraduate) and Nat. Institute of Management Devt (postgraduate); library: 32,000 vols, 250 periodicals; 124 teachers; 4,948 students; Pres. Prof. AHMED MAHMOUD YOUSSEF; Vice-Pres. for Education and Research Prof. SHERIEF HASSAN; Vice-Pres. for Training and Consultation Prof. ABDELHAMED MOSTAFA ABO NAAM; Vice-Pres. for Postgraduate Studies and Research Prof. MOHAMED ZAKY EID; publ. *Magalet Al-Behouth Al Edaria* (Administrative Research Review, 4 a year, in Arabic and English).

Branches:

Alexandria Branch: 59 Menshya Moharram Bak St, Alexandria; tel. (3) 3931515; e-mail alex-sams@sadatacademy.edu.eg; Dir Dr BADEAA ELDIN RESHO.

Assyot Branch: Mogamaa al Masaleh, Assyot; tel. (88) 2310499; e-mail asiut-sams@sadatacademy.edu.eg; Dir Dr ABDEL MOHAMMED.

Dekkernes Branch: Korneish el Bahr St, Dekernes; tel. (50) 7472521; e-mail dekernes-sams@sadatacademy.edu.eg; Dir SALAH ABD EL HAY.

Port Said Branch: Abdel-Salam Arif St, Port Said; tel. (66) 3351396; e-mail portsaid-sams@sadatacademy.edu.eg; Dir Prof. SAFWAT ALI HMEDA.

Ramsis Branch (Faculty of Management): 14 Ramsis St, Cairo; tel. (2) 225764337; e-mail ramsis-sams@sadatacademy.edu.eg; Dir MOHAMMED MOUSSA.

Tanta Branch: Sedkee St, Tanta; tel. (40) 3302083; e-mail tanta-sams@sadatacademy.edu.eg; Dir Prof. SAYED ABD EL MOULA.

Schools of Art and Music

Academy of Arts: el Afghany St, off Alharam Ave, Giza; tel. (2) 35850727; e-mail aoarts@idsc.gov.eg; f. 1959; comprises 8 institutes of univ. status; Pres. Prof. FAWZY FAHMY AHMED; Dir for Public Relations AWAD KAMEL FAHMI; publ. *Alfann Almuasir* (4 a year).

Constituent Institutes:

Higher Institute of Arab Music: Cairo; tel. (2) 24851561; f. 1967; depts of instrumentation, singing, theory of composition; postgraduate studies; library of 11,000 vols; 125 teachers; 280 students; Dean Dr SAID HAIKUL.

Higher Institute of Art Criticism: Cairo; library of 2,500 vols; 8 teachers; 90 students; Dean Dr NAHIL RACHAB.

Higher Institute of Ballet: Cairo; tel. (2) 35853999; f. 1958; 2 brs in Alexandria and Ismailia; depts of classical ballet, choreography, postgraduate studies; library of 3,500 vols; 21 teachers; 21 students; Dean Dr MAGDA EZZ.

Higher Institute of Child Arts: Cairo; tel. (2) 35850727; f. 1990; postgraduate studies.

Higher Institute of Cinema: Cairo; tel. (2) 35850291; f. 1959; depts of animation, cartoons, directing, editing, photography and camerawork, scenery design, scriptwriting, sound production; postgraduate studies; library of 5,000 vols; 90 teachers; 450 students; Dean Dr SHAWKY ALY MOHAMED.

Higher Institute of Folklore: Cairo; tel. (2) 35851230; f. 1981; dept of postgraduate studies; library of 6,000 vols; 25 teachers; 60 students; Dean Dr ALYAA SHOUKRY.

Higher Institute of Music (Conservatoire): Cairo; tel. (2) 35853451; f. 1959; depts of composition and theory, musicology, percussion, piano, singing, solfa and music education, string instruments, wind instruments; postgraduate studies; library of 24,000 vols, 3,000 records; 90 teachers; 78 students; Dean Prof. NIBAL MOUNIB.

Higher Institute of Theatre Arts: Cairo; tel. (2) 35853233; f. 1944; depts of acting and directing, drama and criticism, scenic and stage design; postgraduate studies; library of 15,500 vols; 90 teachers; 330 students; Dean Dr SANAA SHAFIE.

EL SALVADOR

The Higher Education System

The state-controlled Universidad de El Salvador, founded in 1841, was the only university until the mid-1960s, since when several private universities have been established. The Ministry of Education oversees higher education. Other institutions of higher education include colleges and technical institutes. There is currently a total of around 52 higher education institutions, the majority of which are privately operated. In 2010/11 there were 160,374 students enrolled in tertiary education.

Entrance to higher education is achieved on the basis of obtaining the main secondary school qualification, the Bachillerato, and success in an entrance examination. In 2004 a new higher education law was passed that fundamentally reformed the higher education system and at the same time introduced a system of credits. The first qualification is the Técnico awarded after two years' study and is regarded as a technical or professional qualification in the sciences or humanities areas. At university level, which is considered to offer career-orientated and multidisciplinary education, the Tecnólogo is awarded after a minimum of four years' study or the equivalent of 128 credits, the Licenciado, Ingeniero or Arquitecto after a minimum of five years' study (160 credits). The postgraduate Maestría is awarded after a further three years, and the Doctorado is available in some subjects.

El Sistema de Supervisión y Mejoramiento de la Calidad de las Instituciones de Educación Superior (System of Quality Supervision and Improvement for Higher Education Institutes) was created by the Ministry of Education in 1997 to oversee a three-stage quality assurance process—qualification, evaluation and accreditation—for both public and private higher education institutions. All institutions are required by the Ministry of Education to undergo the first two stages of the quality assurance process, while the final stage—accreditation—is voluntary. El Consejo de Educación Superior (Higher Education Council) is the consultative body which authorizes and evaluates both institutes and programmes. The Comisión de Acreditación de la Calidad de la Educaciòn Superior (Commission for the Accreditation of Quality in Higher Education) accredits higher education establishments that volunteer to have the quality of their degree programmes recognized.

Regulatory and Representative Bodies

GOVERNMENT

Ministry of Education: Edif. A, Plan Maestro, Centro de Gobierno, Alameda Juan Pablo II y Calle Guadalupe, San Salvador; tel. 2537-2122; e-mail educacion@mined.gob.sv; internet www.mined.gob.sv; Minister FRANZI HASBÚN BARAKE.

ACCREDITATION

Comisión de Acreditación de Calidad de la Educación Superior (Commission for the Accreditation of Quality in Higher Education): Alameda Juan Pablo II y Calle Guadalupe, Plan Maestro, Centro de Gobierno, Edif. A2, San Salvador; tel. 2281-0282; e-mail cda_dnes@mined.gob.sv; attached to Min. of Education; awards accredited status to univs and other higher education instns; 7 mems; Pres. Dr HÉCTOR LINDO FUENTES; Exec. Dir Lic. MARÍA DE LOS ÁNGELES DE SALGUERO.

Learned Societies

GENERAL

Academia Salvadoreña de la Lengua (Salvadoran Academy of Language): Casa de las Academias, 9A Avda Norte y Alameda Juan Pablo II, San Salvador; e-mail casadeacademia@asl.org.sv; internet www.asl.org.sv; f. 1875; corresp. of the Real Academia Española (Madrid); 18 mems; library of 200 vols; Dir Dr RENÉ FORTÍN MAGAÑA; Sec. ANA MARÍA NAFRÍA.

HISTORY, GEOGRAPHY AND ARCHAEOLOGY

Academia Salvadoreña de la Historia (Salvadoran Academy of History): Alameda Juan Pablo II y Novena Avda Norte 425, San Salvador; tel. 2557-3180; e-mail academia@historia.org.sv; internet www.historia.org.sv; f. 1925; corresp. of the Real Academia de la Historia (Madrid); 18 mems; library of 9,000 vols; Dir PEDRO ANTONIO ESCALANTE; Sec. EUGENIA LÓPEZ VELÁSQUEZ.

LANGUAGE AND LITERATURE

Alliance Française: Col. y Calle la Mascota N° 547 y psje 2, San Salvador; tel. 2264-4141; e-mail secretaria@afelsalvador.com; internet www.afelsalvador.com; f. 1951; offers courses and examinations in French language and culture, and promotes cultural exchange with France; Pres. OSCAR DURÁN VIZCARRA; Sec. SAMUEL HUMBERTO LEIVA JOYA.

MEDICINE

Asociación de Ginecología y Obstetricia de El Salvador (Association of Gynaecology and Obstetrics of El Salvador): Colegio Médico de El Salvador, Final Pasaje 10, Col. Miramonte, San Salvador; tel. 2235-3432; e-mail asogoes@hotmail.com; f. 1947; 150 mems; library of 2,000 vols; Pres. Dr MIGUEL ANTONIO GUIDOS SERRANO; Sec. Dra MIRNA ELIZABETH ROLDAN DE RIVAS.

Colegio Médico de El Salvador (Medical College of El Salvador): Final Psje N° 10, Col. Miramonte, San Salvador; tel. 2205-4500; e-mail juntadirectiva@colegiomedico.org.sv; internet www.colegiomedico.org.sv; f. 1943; 2,000 mems; Chair. Dr MIGUEL MAJANO; Sec. Dra SANDRA DEL CARMEN LEAL; publ. *Mundo Medico Salvadoreño* (3 a year).

Research Institutes

AGRICULTURE, FISHERIES AND VETERINARY SCIENCE

Centro Nacional de Tecnología Agropecuaria y Forestal (National Centre of Agricultural and Forestry Technology): Km 33½ Carretera a Santa Ana, Municipio de Ciudad Arce, La Libertad; tel. 2302-0200; e-mail comunicaciones@centa.gob.sv; internet www.centa.gob.sv; f. 1942; library of 11,000 vols, 134 current periodicals; Exec. Dir Ing. ALIRIO EDMUNDO MENDOZA; publs *Agricultura en El Salvador* (irregular), *Circular* (irregular).

ECONOMICS, LAW AND POLITICS

Dirección General de Estadística y Censos (Department of Statistics and Censuses): Apdo 2670, San Salvador; Avda Juan Bertis 79, Delgado, San Salvador; tel. 2590-2100; f. 1881; Dir-Gen. Lic. JOSUÉ SAMUEL HERNÁNDEZ; publs *Anuario Estadístico* (1 a year), *Encuesta de Hogares de Propósitos Múltiples* (1 a year), *Encuesta Económica* (1 a year), *IPC* (12 a year).

NATURAL SCIENCES

Physical Sciences

Servicio Meteorológico Nacional (National Meteorological Service): Km 5½ Carretera a Nueva San Salvador, Avda Las Mercedes, San Salvador; tel. 2267-9522; internet www.snet.gob.sv; f. 1889; library of 2,000 vols; Dir LUIS GARCÍA GUIROLA; publs *Almanaque Climatológico*, *Almanaque Marino Costero*.

Libraries and Archives

San Salvador

Archivo General de la Nación (General Archive of the Nation): Palacio Nacional, Avda Cuscatlán y 2ª, Calle Poniente, San Salvador; tel. 2222-9418; e-mail archivo.general@cultura.gob.sv; f. 1948; 2,000 vols; Dir Lic. GERARDO MONTERROSA; publ. *Repositorio*.

Biblioteca Dr José Gustavo Guerrero (Dr José Gustavo Guerrero Library): Edif. 2 4to. Nivel, Complejo de Oficinas del Ministerio de Relaciones Exteriores, Calle El Pedregal, Final Blvd Cancillería, Antiguo Cuscatlán; tel. 2231-1186; f. 1961; attached to Instituto Especializado de Educación

Superior para la Formación Diplomática, Ministry of Foreign Affairs; incl. legislation colln, newspaper colln, Salvadoran colln; 10,000 vols; Librarian ARIADNA BERENICE MORALES.

Biblioteca Nacional de El Salvador 'Francisco Gavidia' (National Library of El Salvador 'Francisco Gavidia'): 4ta Calle Oriente y Avda Monseñor Oscar A. Romero N° 124, San Salvador; tel. 2221-6312; e-mail biblioteca.nacional@cultura.gob.sv; internet www.binaes.gob.sv; f. 1870; spec. collns: old books, titles on int. orgs, Braille colln; 150,000 vols; Dir MANLIO ARGUETA.

Sistema Bibliotecario de la Universidad de El Salvador (Library System of the University of El Salvador): Apdo 2923, San Salvador; Final 25 Avda Norte, Ciudad Universitaria, San Salvador; tel. 2225-0278; e-mail sb@biblio.ues.edu.sv; internet biblioteca.ues.edu.sv; f. 1847; 44,000 vols; Dir CARLOS R. COLINDRES.

Museums and Art Galleries

San Salvador

Museo de Historia Natural de El Salvador (Natural History Museum of El Salvador): Barrio San Jacinto, Final de Calle Los Viveros, Col. Nicaragua, San Salvador; tel. 2270-9228; e-mail eecheverria@cultura.gob.sv; f. 1883; Dir Lic. EUNICE ECHEVERRÍA.

Museo Nacional de Antropología 'David J. Guzmán' (National Museum of Anthropology 'David J. Guzman'): Avda la Revolución, Col. San Benito, San Salvador; tel. 2243-3927; f. 1883; Dir Arq. EDUARDO GÓCHEZ; publs *Anales*, *Colección Antropología e Historia*, *El Xipe*, *La Cofradía*.

Attached Museums:

Museo Arqueológico del Sitio San Andrés (Archaeological Site Museum San Andrés): Parque Arqueológico San Andrés, km 32, Carretera Panamericana, Ciudad Arce; tel. 2221-4419; e-mail direcciondepatrimonio@concultura.gob.sv; internet www.cultura.gob.sv; f. 1996; museum at major archaeological site of San Andrés, occupation of which spans c. 2,000 years; Head of Cultural Heritage Dr SONIA BAIRES.

Museo Arqueológico del Sitio Tazumal (Archaeological Site Museum Tazumal): Diagonal 5ª, Calle Oriente, Calle al Cuje, Chalchuapa; tel. 2444-0010; f. 1951.

Parque Zoológico Nacional (National Zoological Park): Final Calle Modelo, San Salvador; tel. 2270-0828; e-mail zoologiconacional@cultura.gob.sv; internet cultura.presidencia.gob.sv/zoo; f. 1953; recreation, environmental education and research, conservation; library of 1,800 vols; Dir Dr RICARDO ALFONSO ESCOBAR.

Universities

UNIVERSIDAD ALBERT EINSTEIN
(Albert Einstein University)

Urb. Lomas de San Francisco, Antiguo Cuscatlán, San Salvador
Telephone: 2212-7600
E-mail: infouae@uae.edu.sv
Internet: www.uae.edu.sv

Founded 1973
Private control
Language of instruction: Spanish
Faculties of architecture, business studies, engineering

Rector: Arq. JUANA SALAZAR ALVARENGA DE PACHECO
Vice-Rector: Arq. ROSA MARÍA ZÚNIGA CLARA
Gen. Sec.: Arq. IVO OSEGUEDA JIMÉNEZ
Library of 10,317 vols
Number of teachers: 13 (10 full-time, 3 part-time)
Number of students: 620

UNIVERSIDAD AUTÓNOMA DE SANTA ANA
(Autonomous University of Santa Ana)

Autopista sur Poniente km 63 1/2, Santa Ana
Telephone: 2440-0245
Internet: unasa.edu.sv

Founded 1982
Private control
Language of instruction: Spanish
Faculties of health sciences, social sciences

Rector: Ing. SERGIO ERNESTO CARRANZA VEGA
Library of 5,640 vols
Number of teachers: 81 (21 full-time, 60 part-time)
Number of students: 1,202
Publication: *INFOCIENCIA* (1 a year)

UNIVERSIDAD CAPITÁN GENERAL GERARDO BARRIOS
(Captain General Gerardo Barrios University)

Calle Las Flores y Avda Las Magnolias Col. Escolán, San Miguel
Telephone: 2645-6500
E-mail: nuevoingresosm@ugb.edu.sv
Internet: www.ugb.edu.sv

Founded 2006
Private control
Language of instruction: Spanish

Rector: Ing. RAÚL RIVAS QUINTANILLA
Vice-Rector: Lic. SIRHAN RAÚL RIVA
Library of 22,167 vols
Number of teachers: 59 (58 full-time, 1 part-time)
Number of students: 3,979

DEANS

Faculty of Business Studies: Lic. CARLOS E. MENDOZA MORENO
Faculty of Engineering and Architecture: Ing. TELMA NOEMÍ GARCÍA VENTURA
Faculty of Legal Sciences: Licda YANET CAMPOS DE RIVAS
Faculty of Science and Humanities: Lic. JOSÉ SALVADOR ALVARENGA RIVERA
Faculty of Science and Technology: Licda AZUCENA GUEVARA DE URBINA

UNIVERSIDAD CATÓLICA DE EL SALVADOR
(Catholic University of El Salvador)

25 Calle Oriente y 25 Avda Sur, Santa Ana
Telephone: 2447-8785
E-mail: catolica@catolica.edu.sv
Internet: www.catolica.edu.sv

Founded 1982, current name adopted 2008
Private control
Language of instruction: Spanish
Academic year: February to December

Rector: Mgr Lic. FRAY ROMEO TOVAR ASTORGA
Vice-Rector for Gen. Affairs: Dr MOISÉS ANTONIO MARTINÉZ ZALDIVÁR
Vice-Rector for Academic Affairs: ROBERTO ANTONIO LÓPEZ
Gen. Sec.: CÁSTULO AFRANIO HERNÁNDEZ ROBLES
Dir of Admin.: RICARDO MORALES
Dir of Academics: MARCO MARROQUÍN
Dir of Library: MAURICIO EDGARDO MENENDÉZ LEMUS
Library of 37,409 vols
Number of teachers: 75
Number of students: 3,782

DEANS

Faculty of Business Studies: CENIA PATRICIA ORELLANA DE RAMÍREZ
Faculty of Engineering and Architecture: Ing MAURICIO ERNESTO VELÁSQUEZ SORIANO
Faculty of Health Sciences: Dra MARTA VIEYTEZ
Faculty of Regional Multidisciplinary Centre, Ilobasco: JUAN ALFONSO TRIGUEROS CHÁVEZ
Faculty of Science and Humanities: JAIME OSMÍN TRIGUEROS CHÁVEZ

ATTACHED INSTITUTES

Departamento de Educación a Distancia: promotes teacher training courses.

Instituto de Desarrollo Rural: promotes extra-curricular activities in the rural sphere, projects on agricultural devt, training courses for the rural population, technical analysis for agricultural cooperatives and environmental health and hygiene projects.

Instituto de Promoción Humana: promotes courses in administration, administration for rural cooperatives, nutrition, administration for small businesses

UNIVERSIDAD CENTROAMERICANA 'JOSÉ SIMEÓN CAÑAS'
(Central American University 'José Simeón Cañas')

Apdo 01-168, San Salvador
Blvd Los Próceres, San Salvador
Telephone: 2210-6600
E-mail: ofi-com@uca.edu.sv
Internet: www.uca.edu.sv

Founded 1965
Private control
Language of instruction: Spanish
Academic year: March to December

Rector: Ing. ANDREU OLIVA DE LA ESPERANZA
Vice-Rector for Academics: Ing. CELINA PÉREZ RIVERA
Vice-Rector for Finance: Ing. AXEL SÖDERBERG
Sec. Gen.: Lic. RENÉ ALBERTO ZELAYA
Librarian: JACQUELINE MORALES DE COLOCHO
Library of 355,000 vols
Number of teachers: 544
Number of students: 9,650
Publications: *Comunica* (15 a year, online), *De Legibus* (2 a year), *El Salvador en la Mira* (24 a year, online), *En Plural* (2 a year), *Estudios Centroamericanos ECA* (irregular), *La Casa de Todos: Revista de Arquitectura y Urbanismo* (3 a year), *Realidad: Revista de Ciencias Sociales y Humanidades* (4 a year), *Revista Carta a las Iglesias* (12 a year), *Revista Contabilidad y Empresa* (3 a year), *Revista de Administración y Empresas* (2 a year), *Revista Latinoamericana de Teología* (3 a year)

DEANS

Faculty of Economics: JOSÉ MEJÍA HERRERA
Faculty of Engineering: CARLOS CAÑAS
Faculty of Human and Natural Sciences: Dr SILVIA AZUCENA DE FERNÁNDEZ
Faculty of Postgraduate Studies: LIDIA SALAMANCA

UNIVERSIDAD CRISTIANA DE LAS ASAMBLEAS DE DIOS
(Christian University of the Assemblies of God)

27 Calle Oriente No 134, Barrio San Miguelito, Entre el Teatro de Cámara y la Cascada, San Salvador
Telephone: 2225-5046
E-mail: informatica@ucad.edu.sv
Internet: www.ucad.edu.sv
Founded 1983
Private control
Language of instruction: Spanish
Rector: Dr AUGUSTO FERRUFINO AGUILAR
Sec. Gen.: Lic. ORLANDO OVIDIO CAMBARA
Dir for Student Assistance: Licda ANA ISABEL DE MUNGUÍA
Library of 6,010 vols
Number of teachers: 12 (11 full-time, 1 part-time)
Number of students: 724

DEANS
Faculty of Economics: Lic. RAÚL JONATHAN CORTÉS MOLINA
Faculty of Law and Social Sciences: Dr JUAN ARMANDO MATA ELÍAS
Faculty of Sciences and Humanities: Licda EMILIA ARTOLA
Faculty of Theology: Lic. OSCAR ARMANDO DURÁN

UNIVERSIDAD DE EL SALVADOR
(University of El Salvador)

Apdo 3110, San Salvador
Final 25 Avda, Ciudad Universitaria, San Salvador
Telephone: 2225-8826
E-mail: mirsalva@navegante.com.sv
Internet: www.ues.edu.sv
Founded 1841
public control
Language of instruction: Spanish
Academic year: February to December
Rector: Ing. MARIO ROBERTO NIETO LOVO
Vice-Rector for Academics: ANA MARÍA GLOWER DE ALVARADO
Sec. Gen.: ANA LETICIA DE AMAYA
Library Dir: JOSEFINA ROQUE
Library of 148,610 vols
Number of teachers: 2,117 (1414 full-time, 703 part-time)
Number of students: 43,159
Publications: *Aquí Odontología* (12 a year), *Búho Dilecto* (6 a year), *Derecho Público*, *El Quehacer Científico* (1 a year), *El Salvador: Coyuntura Económica* (4 a year), *Enfoque Tecnológico* (2 a year), *Revista Electrónica de la Facultad de Medicina* (2 a year), *Revista Ciencia Política*

DEANS
Faculty of Agricultural Sciences: Ing. JUAN ROSA QUINTANILLA
Faculty of Chemistry and Pharmacy: Licda ANABEL DE LOURDES AYALA DE SORIANO
Faculty of Dentistry: Dr MANUEL DE JESÚS JOYA ÁBREGO
Faculty of Economics: Lic. ROGER ARMANDO ARIAS
Faculty of Engineering and Architecture: Ing. FRANCISCO ALARCÓN
Faculty of Jurisprudence and Social Sciences: Dr JULIO OLIVO GRANADINO
Faculty of Medicine: Dr ARNULFO HERRERA
Faculty of Natural and Mathematical Sciences: MARTÍN GUERRA
Faculty of Sciences and Humanities: Lic. RAYMUNDO CALDERÓN
Multidisciplinary Faculty of the Oriental Region: Lic. CRISTÓBAL HERNÁN RÍOS BENÍTEZ
Multidisciplinary Faculty of the Paracentral Region: Ing. ISIDRO VARGAS
Multidisciplinary Faculty of the Western Region: Lic. RAÚL ERNESTO AZCÚNAGA

UNIVERSIDAD DE ORIENTE
(University of East)

4ta Calle Poniente N° 705, San Miguel
Telephone: 2668-3700
E-mail: info@univo.edu.sv
Internet: www.univo.edu.sv
Founded 1981
Private control
Language of instruction: Spanish
Rector: Dr PEDRO FAUSTO ARIETA VEGA
Pres.: RENÉ FERNANDO CESTÓNI PARDICCI
Vice-Rector for Academic Affairs: Lic. MARIA LUISA SEVILLANO
Vice-Rector for Gen. Affairs: EVER ISRAEL MARTÍNEZ REYES
Sec. Gen.: ROGELIO CISNEROZ LAZO
Library of 18,741 vols
Number of teachers: 41 (39 full-time, 2 part-time)
Number of students: 3,576

DEANS
Faculty of Agriculture: Ing. HUGO FLORES CÓRDOVA
Faculty of Economics: Lic. JOSÉ OSCAR LOZANO CASTRO
Faculty of Engineering and Architecture: Ing. ROBERTO ALFREDO HERRERA LARIN
Faculty of Health Sciences: Dr JOSÉ LUIS CASTRO CISNEROS
Faculty of Law: Lic. RÓMULO REYES
Faculty of Science and Humanities: Lic. YASMIN MABEL FLORES

UNIVERSIDAD DE SONSONATE (USO)
(University of Sonsonate)

29 Calle Oriente y Avda Central Final Col. 14 de Diciembre, Sonsonate
Telephone: 2429-9503
E-mail: informacion@usonsonate.edu.sv
Internet: www.usonsonate.edu.sv
Founded 1982
Private control
Language of instruction: Spanish
Rector: Ing. JESÚS ADALBERTO DÍAZ PINEDA
Vice-Rector: Dr FRANCISCO CARLO ARÉVALO HERRERA
Sec. Gen.: Licda ANA MARÍA DE LOS ÁNGELES RODRÍGUEZ SALAZAR
Library of 9,287 vols
Number of teachers: 16
Number of students: 2,360

DEANS
Faculty of Economics and Social Sciences: Lic. RICARDO ALFONSO CRUZ MENJIVAR
Faculty of Engineering and Natural Sciences: Arq. MIREYA ANNABELLA POCASANGRE DE DÍAZ
Faculty of Legal Sciences: Licda SILVIA YOLANY LÓPEZ DE CRUZ

UNIVERSIDAD DON BOSCO
(Don Bosco University)

Apdo 1874, San Salvador
Calle Plan del Pino, Cantón Venecia, Soyapango, San Salvador
Telephone: 2251-8200
E-mail: rectoria@udb.edu.sv
Internet: www.udb.edu.sv
Founded 1986
Private control
Language of instruction: Spanish
Dept of basic science; schools of aeronautics, technology studies
Rector: Ing. FEDERICO MIGUEL HUGUET RIVERA
Vice-Rector for Academic Affairs: Dr JOSÉ HUMBERTO FLORES MUÑOZ
Vice-Rector for Science and Technology: REINA ELIZABETH DURÁN DE ALVARADO
Dir for Social Projection: Licda SONIA KARINA SALGUERO
Library of 46,267 vols
Number of teachers: 138 (132 full-time, 6 part-time)
Number of students: 3,625
Publications: *Científica* (1 a year), *Diá-logos* (2 a year), *Puntos, Teoría y Praxis* (4 a year)

DEANS
Faculty of Economics: HERBERT HUMBERTO BELLOSO FUNES
Faculty of Engineering: Ing. GODOFREDO GIRÓN
Faculty of Rehabilitation Sciences: JOSÉ ROLANDO MARTÍNEZ PANAMEÑO
Faculty of Science and Humanities: Lic. EDSON ALBERTO OSORIO VALLES

UNIVERSIDAD DR ANDRÉS BELLO
(Dr Andrés Bello University)

1a Calle Poniente y 39 Avda Norte N° 2128, Col. Flor Blanca, San Salvador
Telephone: 2510-7400
E-mail: informacion@unab.edu.sv
Internet: www.unab.edu.sv
Founded 1991
Private control
Language of instruction: Spanish
Pres.: Lic. GUILLERMO ESCOBAR HERNÁNDEZ
Rector: Lic. MARCO TULIO MAGAÑA ESCALANTE
Vice-Rector: Licda ANA MARTA MORENO DE ARAUJO
Library of 29,880 vols
Number of teachers: 71
Number of students: 5,401

DEANS
Faculty of Economics: Licda ANA MARTA MORENO DE ARAUJO
Faculty of Health Sciences: Licda IRMA YOLANDA DE LANDOS
Faculty of Humanities: Lic. LUIS ALONSO REYES BENÍTEZ

UNIVERSIDAD 'DR JOSÉ MATÍAS DELGADO'
('Dr José Matías Delgado' University)

Km 8½ Carretera a Santa Tecla, Ciudad Merliot
Telephone: 2212-9400
E-mail: informacion@ujmd.edu.sv
Internet: www.ujmd.edu.sv
Founded 1977
Private control
Language of instruction: Spanish
Academic year: January to December (2 semesters)
Rector: Dr DAVID ESCOBAR GALINDO
Vice-Rector: JOSÉ ENRIQUE SORTO CAMPBELL
Vice-Rector for Academics: Dr FERNANDO BASILIO CASTELLANOS
Library Dir: SARA ESCOBAR DE GONZÁLEZ
Library of 44,477 vols
Number of teachers: 176 (118 full-time, 58 part-time)
Number of students: 6,503

DEANS
Faculty of Agriculture and Agricultural Research: MARÍA GEORGIA GÓMEZ DE REYES

Faculty of Economics, Business and Enterprise: Ing. ROBERTO ALEJANDRO SORTO FLETES
Faculty of Engineering: Ing. SILVIA BARRIOS DE FERREIRO
Faculty of Graduate and Continuing Education: Lic. JUAN CARLOS FERNÁNDEZ SACA
Faculty of Health Sciences: Dr JOSÉ NICOLÁS ASTACIO
Faculty of Jurisprudence and Social Sciences: Dra MIRNA VICTORIA QUINTEROS DE QUINTANILLA
Faculty of Sciences and Arts: Arq. LUIS SALAZAR RETANA
School of Architecture: Arq. LUIS SALAZAR RETANA (Dir)
School of Communication Sciences: Lic. RICARDO CHACÓN (Dir)
School of Planning, Business Administration and Marketing: Lic. ANA PATRICIA LINARES (Dir)

UNIVERSIDAD EVANGÉLICA DE EL SALVADOR
(Evangelical University of El Salvador)

Prolongación Alameda Juan Pablo II, Calle El Carmen, San Antonio Abad, San Salvador
Telephone: 2275-4000
Internet: www.uees.edu.sv
Founded 1981
Private control
Language of instruction: Spanish
Pres.: Lic. MAURICIO ANTONIO BARRIENTOS
Rector: Lic. CÉSAR EMILIO QUINTEROS
Vice-Rector for Academic Affairs: Dra CRISTINA DE AMAYA
Sec.: Dr MARIO ERNESTO PALENCIA TREJO
Library of 29,304 vols
Number of teachers: 157 (77 full-time, 80 part-time)
Number of students: 2,798

DEANS
Faculty of Business Science and Economics: MANUEL DE JESÚS RIVERA LÓPEZ
Faculty of Dentistry: Dr RUTH ELIZABETH FUENTES DE SERMEÑO
Faculty of Engineering: CORINA QUIJANO DE GARCÍA
Faculty of Legal Sciences: Licda ROMMY DE ESTRADA
Faculty of Medicine: Dr MIRNA GARCÍA DE GONZÁLEZ
Faculty of Social Sciences: Lic. RICARDO ERNESTO RIVAS

UNIVERSIDAD FRANCISCO GAVIDIA
(Francisco Gavidia University)

Col. Flor Blanca, Calle el progreso N° 2748, San Salvador
Telephone: 2249-2700
Internet: www.ufg.edu.sv
Founded 1981
Private control
Language of instruction: Spanish
Rector: Ing. MARIO ANTONIO RUIZ RAMÍREZ
Library of 73,881 vols
Number of teachers: 195
Number of students: 11,263

DEANS
Faculty of Economics: ADALBERTO ELÍAS CAMPOS BATRES
Faculty of Engineering and Architecture: ELBA PATRICIA CASTANEDO DE UMAÑA
Faculty of Law: JANNETH CAROLINA BRITO CENTENO
Faculty of Social Sciences: ZOILA ROMERO

UNIVERSIDAD LUTERANA SALVADOREÑA
(Salvadoran Lutheran University)

Intesección NorOriente Carretera a Los Planes de Renderos y Autopista a Comalapa, km No 3, Bo., San Jacinto, San Salvador
Telephone: 2133-2600
E-mail: uls@uls.edu.sv
Internet: www.uls.edu.sv
Founded 1991
Private control
Language of instruction: Spanish
Rector: Lic. FIDEL NIETO LAÍNEZ
Vice-Rector: Lic. DAGOBERTO GUTIÉRREZ
Sec. Gen.: Licda ANA DE SALOMONE
Library of 14,388 vols
Number of teachers: 24 (10 full-time, 14 part-time)
Number of students: 1,370

DEANS
Faculty of Human and Natural Sciences: Dr ROLANDO MARTÍNEZ
Faculty of Theology and Humanities: Licda MARITZA RIVAS

UNIVERSIDAD MODULAR ABIERTA
(Modular Open University)

1ª Calle Poniente No 2817, San Salvador
Telephone: 2260-5320
E-mail: informacion@uma.edu.sv
Internet: www.uma.edu.sv
Founded 1981
Private control
Language of instruction: Spanish
Rector: Licda JUDITH VIRGINIA MENDOZA DE DÍAZ
Sec. Gen.: Lic. JULIO EDUARDO MELÉNDEZ NÚÑEZ
Library of 27,548 vols
Number of teachers: 34
Number of students: 4,385

DEANS
Faculty of Economics: Licda VILMA ANABELLA MARTÍNEZ FLAMENCO
Faculty of Law and Social Sciences: Lic. MAURICIO ANTONIO VÁSQUEZ LÓPEZ
Faculty of Science and Humanities: Licda BLANCA LUZ GUZMÁN DE DUARTE

UNIVERSIDAD MONSEÑOR OSCAR ARNULFO ROMERO
(Monseñor Oscar Arnulfo Romero University)

Carretera a Chalatenango km 52.5, Chalatenango
Telephone: 2347-7912
E-mail: info@umoar.edu.sv
Internet: www.umoar.edu.sv
Founded 1993
Private control
Language of instruction: Spanish
Rector: Lic. JUAN JOSÉ SOLÓRZANO ARRIOLA
Vice-Rector: Lic. ROMÁN HONORIO MEJÍA FIGUEROA
Sec. Gen.: Licda CARMEN NAVAS ESCOBAR DE MEJÍA
Librarian: SERGIO SANTIAGO AVILÉS
Library of 4,599 vols
Number of teachers: 7 (6 full-time, 1 part-time)
Number of students: 1,173

DEANS
Faculty of Agricultural Sciences and Forestry: Ing. ALCIDES DEL CARMEN SANTAMARIA VAQUERO

Faculty of Business Studies and Economics: Lic. JOSÉ ANTONIO RAMOS HENRIQUEZ
Faculty of Law and Social Sciences: Lic. EUGENIO ANTONIO ALEGRIA
Faculty of Science and Humanities: Lic. ALFREDO ANTONIO LOBO ACOSTA

UNIVERSIDAD NUEVA SAN SALVADOR
(Nueva San Salvador University)

Alameda Roosevelt y 41 Avda Sur, San Salvador
Telephone: 2526-4500
Internet: www.unssa.edu.sv
Founded 1981
Private control
Language of instruction: Spanish
Schools of chemistry and pharmacy, dentistry, humanities
Rector: Dr RAFAEL HERNÁN CONTRERAS RODRÍGUEZ
Vice-Rector: Ing. ERICK ROBERTO TADEO SALGUERO
Sec. Gen.: Ing. JORGE EDUARDO AFANE SALUME
Library of 4,311 vols
Number of teachers: 57 (17 full-time, 40 part-time)
Number of students: 566

DEANS
Faculty of Economics: Licda PATRICIA DAGMAR MENJIVAR DE PALACIOS
Faculty of Health Sciences: Dr CARLOS ERNESTO GODINES VALENCIA
Faculty of Law and Social Sciences: Dr OVIDIO RAMIREZ CUELLA

UNIVERSIDAD PANAMERICANA DE EL SALVADOR
(Pan American University of El Salvador)

Calle Progreso 234 a 60 m de Avda Bernal, Col. Miramonte Poniente, San Salvador
Telephone: 2527-2000
E-mail: informacionss@upan.edu.sv
Internet: www.upan.edu.sv
Founded 1989
Private control
Language of instruction: Spanish
Rector: Dr OSCAR MORÁN FOLGAR
Vice-Rector: NUBIA ADALILA MENDOZA FIGUEROA
Sec. Gen.: CELINA DEL CARMEN LÓPEZ URÍAS
Registrar: ALMA ARACELY POZAS DE IBARRA
Librarian: RAQUEL HERNÁNDEZ
Library of 18,536 vols
Number of teachers: 18
Number of students: 2,055

DEANS
Faculty of Economics: Licda JASMÍN DEL CARMEN AGUILAR MEMBREÑO
Faculty of Jurisprudence: Lic. ERICK ROMMEL ORELLANA OSORIO
Faculty of Science and Humanities: Licda EVELYN PATRICIA LÓPEZ AGUILAR

UNIVERSIDAD PEDAGÓGICA DE EL SALVADOR DR LUIS ALONSO APARICIO
(Dr Luis Alonso Aparicio Pedagogical University of El Salvador)

Diagonal Dr Arturo Romero y 25 Avda Norte, San Salvador
Telephone: 2226-4081
E-mail: info@pedagogica.edu.sv
Internet: www.pedagogica.edu.sv
Founded 1982
Private control

Language of instruction: Spanish
Rector: Ing. LUIS MARIO APARICIO
Vice-Rector for Academic Affairs: Licda CATALINA MACHICA DE MERINO
Library of 38,953 vols
Number of teachers: 46
Number of students: 2,949
Publication: *Uperspectiva* (2 a year)

DEANS

Faculty of Education: Lic. JORGE ALBERTO ESCOBAR
Faculty of Economics: Lic. MANUEL ORTEGA

UNIVERSIDAD POLITÉCNICA DE EL SALVADOR
(Polytechnic University of El Salvador)

Boulevard Tutunichapa y 5ta Avda Norte, Frente a redondel Jose Marti (Don Rua), San Salvador
Telephone: 2225-7810
Internet: www.upes.edu.sv
Founded 1979
Private control
Language of instruction: Spanish
Rector: Ing. ROBERTO LÓPEZ MEYER
Vice-Rector for Academics: Ing. ROBERTO ANTONIO ARGUETA QUAN
Vice-Rector for Admin.: Lic. ORLANDO ALFONSO RIVAS PAZ
Sec. Gen.: Ing. JULIO CÉSAR RICO
Library of 7,169 vols
Number of teachers: 16 (13 full-time, 3 part-time)
Number of students: 875

DEANS

Faculty of Economics: Lic. WILBER EVENOR GÓMEZ RIVAS
Faculty of Engineering and Architecture: Ing. RAÚL ALBERTO GARCÍA AQUINO
Faculty of Law: Licda SANDRA ROMERO DE GARAY

UNIVERSIDAD SALVADOREÑA 'ALBERTO MASFERRER'
('Alberto Masferrer' Salvadorean University)

Apdo 2053, San Salvador
19 Avda Norte, Entre 3A Calle Poniente y Alameda Juan Pablo II, San Salvador
Telephone: 2231-9600
E-mail: informacion@mail.usam.edu.sv
Internet: www.usam.edu.sv
Founded 1979
public control
Language of instruction: Spanish
Academic year: January to December
Rector: Dr CÉSAR AUGUSTO CALDERÓN
Vice-Rector: Licda DAYSI CAROLINA DE GÓMEZ
Sec. Gen.: JULIO ALFREDO RIVAS HERNÁNDEZ
Registrar: ANA LORENA DE MELÉNDEZ
Dir: Lic. JOSÉ LUIS CASTRO
Librarian: XIMENA TIZNADO
Library of 11,733 vols
Number of teachers: 300
Number of students: 2,846
Publication: *Revista Somos* (4 a year)

DEANS

Faculty of Chemistry and Pharmacy: Licda LUISA RAQUEL ARAYA DE CORNEJO
Faculty of Dentistry: Dr ARMANDO RAFAEL MARTÍNEZ
Faculty of Law and Social Sciences: Lic. JULIO ALFREDO RIVAS HERNÁNDEZ
Faculty of Medicine: Dra CARMEN J. CABEZAS DE SÁNCHEZ
Faculty of Veterinary Medicine: Dr NERY RAFAEL MATA

UNIVERSIDAD TÉCNICA LATINOAMERICANA
(Latin American Technical University)

3ª Avda Norte y 7ª Calle Oriente No 2-6, Santa Tecla, La Libertad
Telephone: 2228-4775
E-mail: informacion@utla.edu.sv
Internet: www.utla.edu.sv
Founded 1981
Private control
Language of instruction: Spanish
Faculties of economics, engineering
Rector: Ing. ROSENDO MAURICIO SERMEÑO PALACIOS
Vice-Rector: Ing FRANCISCO ALFREDO CARRILLO LARREYNAGA
Sec. Gen.: Ing. ROOSEVELT ADOLFO OSORIO
Librarian: JOSÉ MAURICIO AGUILAR M.
Library of 4,050 vols
Number of teachers: 50
Number of students: 422

DEANS

Faculty of Economic Sciences: Lic. ÁLVARO LEMUS MARTÍNEZ
Faculty of Engineering: Ing. MAURICIO ANTONIO AGUIRRE ORELLANA

UNIVERSIDAD TECNOLÓGICA DE EL SALVADOR
(Technological University of El Salvador)

Calle Arce y 17 Avda Norte, N° 116, San Salvador
Telephone: 2275-8888
Internet: www.utec.edu.sv
Founded 1981
Private control
Language of instruction: Spanish
Academic year: January to December
Pres.: JOSÉ MAURICIO LOUCEL FUNES
Rector: NELSON ZÁRATE
Vice-Rector for Academic Affairs: JOSÉ MODESTO VENTURA
Vice-Rector for Admin.: DANILO DÍAZ
Vice-Rector for Educational Devt: JOSÉ ADOLFO ARAUJO
Vice-Rector for Research: Licda NORIS ISABEL LÓPEZ GUEVARA
Vice-Rector for Social Projection: JUAN CARLOS CERNA
Registrar: Dr JOSÉ ENRIQUE BURGOS
Dean of Student Affairs: Lic. CARLOS ALFREDO LOUCEL
Dir of Library: ARACELY PÉREZ DE HERNÁNDEZ
Library of 82,106 vols
Number of teachers: 400
Number of students: 16,078
Publications: *Revista de Aniversario*, *Revista Enlaces*, *Revista Entorno*, *Revista Redes*, *Revista Tecno-lógica*

DEANS

Faculty of Business Science: Licda LISSETTE CRISTALINA CANALES DE RAMÍREZ
Faculty of Graduate Studies: Lic. RAFAEL RODRÍGUEZ LOUCEL
Faculty of Information and Applied Science: Ing. FRANCISCO ARMANDO ZEPEDA
Faculty of Law: Lic. EDGARDO VELÁSQUEZ
Faculty of Social Sciences: Licda ARELY VILLALTA DE PARADA

Colleges

Escuela de Comunicación Mónica Herrera (Monica Herrera School of Communications): Avda Manuel Gallardo 3-3, Nueva San Salvador, Santa Tecla; tel. 2523-6500; e-mail info@monicaherrera.edu.sv; internet www.monicaherrera.com; f. 1995; library: 5,087 vols; 9 teachers (7 full-time, 2 part-time); 370 students; Dir TERESA PALACIOS DE CHÁVEZ.

Escuela Especializada en Ingeniería ITCA-FEPADE (Specialized School in Engineering ITCA-FEPADE): Km 11 Carretera a Santa Tecla, La Libertad; tel. 2132-7400; internet www.itca.edu.sv; f. 1969, current name adopted 2008; library: 27,305 vols; 140 teachers (138 full time, 2 part time); 5,766 students; Rector Lic. ELSY ESCOLAR; publ. *Revista Tecnológica* (1 a year).

Escuela Nacional de Agricultura 'Roberto Quiñónez' (National School of Agriculture 'Roberto Quinonez'): Km 33½ Carretera a Santa Ana, San Andrés Ciudad Arce, La Libertad, San Salvador; tel. 2366-4800; e-mail ena@ena.edu.sv; internet ena.edu.sv; f. 1956; library: 8,800 vols; 15 teachers; 354 students; Dir-Gen. Ing. LUIS ALONSO IBARRA PÉREZ.

Escuela Superior de Economía y Negocios—ESEN (College of Economics and Business): Km 12 ½ Carretera al Puerto de La Libertad, Calle nueva a Comasagua, Santa Tecla, La Libertad; tel. 2234-9292; e-mail admision@esen.edu.sv; internet www.esen.edu.sv; f. 1994; library: 10,003 vols; 25 teachers; 674 students; Rector Ing. RICARDO POMA; Dir-Gen. Lic. JOSÉ EVERARDO RIVERA BONILLA; Sec. Lic. CARLOS ERNESTO BOZA.

Escuela Superior Franciscana Especializada/ESFE Agape (Franciscana Specialized College): Km 63 Carretera San Salvador, Sonsonate; e-mail esfe@agape.edu.sv; internet esfe.agape.edu.sv; f. 1981, current name adopted 2009; library: 3,043 vols; 655 students; Rector Ing. RAMÓN ALBERTO VEGA CALVO; Vice-Rector DINORA ARIAS.

Instituto Americano de Educación Superior (American Institute of Higher Education): Calle Loma Linda No 258, Col. San Benito, San Salvador; tel. 2535-7888; internet www.americancollege.net; f. 1978; library: 4,275 vols; Dir-Gen. ALESSANDRA LEPPO DE CASSAÚS.

Instituto Especializado de Educacion Superior de Profesionales de la Salud de El Salvador (Specialized Institute of Higher Education of Health Professionals of El Salvador): 37ª Avda sur y 12 Calle Poniente No 566, Col. Flor Blanca, San Salvador; tel. 2298-9325; internet www.ieproes.edu.sv; f. 1995; library: 12,412 vols; 193 teachers (64 full-time, 129 part-time); 2,277 students; Dir Gen. ZOILA MARINA TORRES DE GUADRÓN.

Instituto Especializado de Educación Superior 'El Espíritu Santo' ('The Holy Spirit' Specialized Institute of Higher Education): Urb. Jardines de Merliot, Avda El Boqueron y Calle Chiltiupan, polígono O No 5, Ciudad Merliot, La Libertad; tel. 2278-6683; e-mail info@ieeses.edu.sv; internet www.ieeses.edu.sv; f. 1953, current name adopted 1995; school of pedagogy incl. depts of Christian education, research, professional practice, psychopedagogy, social projection, teaching, centre of learning resources; library: 7,012 vols; 10 teachers (8 full-time, 2 part-time); 504 students; Rector ELSA AMÉRICA MENDOZA MEJÍA; Vice-Rector JOSÉ ISRAEL RIVERA PÉREZ; Sec. Gen. DORA ALICIA POSADA.

Instituto Especializado de Educación Superior para la Formación Diplomática (Specialized Institute of Higher Education for Diplomatic Training): Calle El Pedregal, Blvd Cancillería, Antiguo Cuscatlán, La Libertad; tel. 2231-1343; e-mail iesesford@rree.gob.sv; internet www.iesford.edu.sv; f. 2003; attached to Min. of Foreign Affairs; library: 1,348 vols; Rector FRANCISCO

SALVADOR FONSECA SALGADO; Sec. Gen. NELLY CUELLAR DE YAMAGIWA.

Instituto Especializado de Nivel Superior Centro Cultural Salvadoreño Americano (Specialized Institute of Higher Level of the Salvadoran American Cultural Centre): Calle Sisimiles frente a Metrocentro Norte, San Salvador; tel. 2239-8000; e-mail adireccion@ccsa.edu.sv; internet www.iensccsa.edu.sv; f. 2008; library: 9,710 vols; Rector Dra MARÍA ERLINDA HERNÁNDEZ DE MORAS; Sec. Gen. Licda MARGARITA RODRIGUEZ.

Instituto Especializado de Nivel Superior Escuela Militar 'Capitán General Gerardo Barrios' (Specialized Institute of Higher Level Military School 'Captain General Gerardo Barrios'): Final Avda Jerusalén y Calle Chiltiupan, Antiguo Cuscatlán; e-mail correo@mail.escmilitar.edu.sv; internet www.escmilitar.edu.sv; f. 1999; library: 22,724 vols; 30 teachers; 414 students; Dir FÉLIX EDGARDO NÚÑEZ ESCOBAR.

Instituto Superior de Economía y Administración de Empresas (ISEADE-FEPADE) (Institute of Economics and Business Administration): Calle El Pedregal y Calle de Acceso a Escuela Militar, Antiguo Cuscatlán, La Libertad; tel. 2212-1700; e-mail contacto@iseade.edu.sv; internet www.iseade.edu.sv; f. 1988 as Fundación Empresarial para el Desarrollo Educativo FEPADE, current name adopted 1997; library: 2,747 vols; Rector JOAQUÍN SAMAYOA; Sec. Gen. Lic. JUAN VALIENTE; publ. *Revista Empresa* (2 a year).

Instituto Tecnológico de Chalatenango (Technological Institute of Chalatenango): Km 75 Carretera hacia Chalatenango frente a Estadio Municipal Gregorio Martínez, Cantón Upatoro, Chalatenango; tel. 2347-1500; internet www.itcha.edu.sv; f. 1981; library: 2,565 vols; 604 students; Pres. Ing. RAMÓN ALBERTO VEGA CALVO; Dir-Gen. Ing. JOAQUÍN ERNESTO GUILLÉN MÉNDEZ; Sec. Ing. SALVADOR ZEPEDA CARRILLO.

Instituto Tecnológico de Usulután (ITU) (Technological Institute of Usulutan): 800 m al sur sobre Calle a San Dionisio, contiguo al 'CENTA', Usulután; tel. 2624-1992; internet www.itu.edu.sv; f. 1982; library: 1,821 vols; 10 teachers; 279 students; Dir RAÚL FRANCISCO DIAZ MENDOZA; publ. *ITU Calidad*.

EQUATORIAL GUINEA

The Higher Education System

Equatorial Guinea has been independent for just over four decades, of which two were dominated by a brutal dictatorship. Its intellectual and cultural traditions were determined by colonial values rather than by its own cultural values, although it is slowly redressing this situation. Despite the fact that, at 93% in 2010, the adult literacy rate is the highest in sub-Saharan Africa, the universally poor condition of general education (Equatorial Guinea has very limited resources) has an adverse affect on higher education, with students arriving having had very little access to books, and with an education based almost entirely on recitation. This naturally limits the level and type of coursework that may be offered. That the language of instruction is mainly Spanish while the majority of good jobs require English also presents difficulties. Many students elect to study abroad; this is supported by scholarships from foreign countries or agencies, administered by the Government. Equatorial Guinea has no national programme of scholarship for foreign study. In 1999/2000 there were 1,003 pupils in higher education. Since 1979 assistance in the development of the educational system has been provided by Spain. The French Government also provides considerable financial assistance. The Universidad Nacional de Guinea Ecuatorial (UNGE), founded in 1995, is Equatorial Guinea's only university. Two higher education campuses (which together comprise the Colegio Nacional Enrique Nvó Okenve), at Bata and Malabo, are administered by the Spanish Universidad Nacional de Educación a Distancia. The College was originally established—as the Colegio Laboral La Salle—in 1959 under Spanish colonial administration and was renamed after independence in 1968. There is also a vocational college, the Escuela Nacional de Agricultura, in Malabo.

Regulatory Bodies

GOVERNMENT

Department of Culture and Tourism: Malabo; Minister GUILLERMINA MOKUY MBA OBONO.

Ministry of Education and Science: Malabo; Minister LUCAS NGUEMA ESONO MBANG.

Learned Societies

LANGUAGE AND LITERATURE

Centro Cultural Hispano-Guineano: Malabo; f. 1982; maintains library; organizes cultural events; publs *Africa 2000* (3 a year), *Ediciones del Centro Cultural Hispano-Guineano* (series dedicated to Equatoguinean writers).

Institut Culturel d'Expression Française (ICEF): BP 936, Malabo; tel. 92660; e-mail directeur@icef-malabo.org; internet www.institutfrancais-malabo.org; f. 1984; offers courses and examinations in French language and culture and promotes cultural exchange with France; Dir VINCENT BRACK.

Research Institute

NATURAL SCIENCES

Biological Sciences

Bioko Biodiversity Protection Program: c/o Univ. Nacional de Guinea Ecuatorial, Carretera Luba s/n, Malabo; tel. 286768; e-mail butynski@bioko.org; internet www.bioko.org; part of academic partnership between Arcadia Univ. (USA, *q.v.*) and Univ. Nacional de Guinea Ecuatorial (*q.v.*); conservation of Bioko Island's biodiversity, especially its critically endangered primates and nesting sea turtles, through devt of economically sustainable educational programmes, research programmes and conservation activities; maintains wildlife research centre at Moka; Co-Dir GAIL HEARN; Co-Dir WAYNE MORRA; Research Dir CLAUDIO POSA BOHOME.

Universities

UNIVERSIDAD NACIONAL DE EDUCACIÓN A DISTANCIA (UNED), EQUATORIAL GUINEA BRANCH

Edif. Poveda, c/o Amanecer de África s/n, Barrio de Ela Nguema, Malabo

Telephone: 92911

E-mail: unedmalabo@yahoo.es

Founded 1993

Language of instruction: Spanish

Part of Universidad Nacional de Educación a Distancia (Spain); br. in Bata (tel. 82277)

Dir: PILAR MONTES PALOMINO

Dir for Studies: Dr ANDRÉS ESONO ONDÓ

Library of 10,000 vols

UNIVERSIDAD NACIONAL DE GUINEA ECUATORIAL (UNGE)

Carretera Luba s/n, Malabo

Telephone: 91644

E-mail: proeqg@intnet.gq

Founded 1995

State control

Language of instruction: English, French, Spanish

Schools of administration (Malabo), agriculture, arts and social sciences (Malabo), engineering and technology (Bata), fisheries and forestry, medicine (Bata), nursing (Bata) teacher training (Malabo, with br. in Bata)

Rector: CARLOS NSE NSUGA

Library of 7,500 vols

Number of teachers: 100

Number of students: 1,200

ERITREA

The Higher Education System

From 1962 to 1993 Eritrea was a de facto province of Ethiopia. Independence was achieved in 1993 following a 33-year war of secession. Since independence Eritrea has been rebuilding its infrastructure, economy and government. The University of Asmara (UOA, the only university) was founded by the Camboni Sisters Missionary Institute in 1958 and was originally known as the Santa Famiglia University Institute. In 1960 the Institute was accredited by the Superior Council of the Institute of Italian Universities and in 1968 it achieved university status under its current name; an English section was opened in the same year. In 2004/05 there were some 5,500 students enrolled on Bachelors degree courses at the UOA, which was under the control of the Ministry of Education. Masters degrees were offered from the beginning of that academic year.

The UOA closed in September 2006. Higher education was subsequently provided by six newly established technical institutes, each associated with a relevant government ministry. The institutes provide education in the fields of nursing and health sciences, technology (the Eritrea Institute of Technology–EIT), business and economics, arts and social sciences, agriculture and marine biology. The UOA administration remains on the site and it is believed that the university will start operating again in 2012, with students being transferred from the EIT in Mai Nefhi, about 20 km south-west of Asmara. It has recently been reported that the university infrastructure is undergoing extensive renovation.

Regulatory Body

GOVERNMENT

Ministry of Education: POB 5610, Asmara; tel. (1) 113044; Minister SEMERE RUSOM.

Learned Societies

LANGUAGE AND LITERATURE

Alliance Française: POB 209, Asmara; tel. (1) 126599; internet www.afasmara.org.er; offers courses and examinations in French language and culture and promotes cultural exchange with France.

British Council: 175-11, St No 23, POB 997, Asmara; tel. (1) 123415; e-mail information@britishcouncil.org.er; internet www.britishcouncil.org/africa; f. 1971; offers courses and examinations in English language and British culture; promotes cultural exchange with the UK; 1,500 mems; library of 7,000 vols; Information and Knowledge Centre Man. MICHAEL TEKIE.

Libraries and Archives

Asmara

Asmara Public Library: 82 Felket Ave 173, Asmara; tel. (1) 127044; f. 1959; 32,400 vols; br. library with 11,000 vols in N Asmara; Dir EFREM MATHEWOS KAHSAY.

Massawa

Massawa Municipal Library: POB 17, Massawa; tel. (1) 552407; f. 1997; 10,000 vols; Chief Librarian MUHAMMAD NUR SAID.

Museum

Asmara

National Museum of Eritrea: St Mariam Ghimbi H., Asmara; tel. (1) 122389; e-mail yozuky@gmail.com; internet www.mrieka.com; f. 1992; archaeology, ethnography, medieval period, natural history and militaria, paleontology; oversees excavations and preservation of the national archaeological heritage; Dir-Gen. Dr YOSIEF LIBSEQAL.

ESTONIA

The Higher Education System

From 1940 until 1991 Estonia was a Soviet Socialist Republic within the USSR. Higher education was based on the Soviet system, but following independence the Estonian Education Act of 1992 identified the development of Estonian language and culture as one of the main aims of education. The higher education system is regulated primarily by the Universities Act, the Institutions of Professional Higher Education Act and the Private Schools Act. Estonia implemented the Bologna Process at undergraduate level in 2002 and at postgraduate level in 2005; this has led to the establishment of a two-tier Bachelors and Masters degree system (with exceptions in certain subjects). The language of instruction for the majority of courses is Estonian. In 2011 there were six public universities, including the University of Tartu (founded in 1632) and Tallinn University, one private university, the Estonian Business School, 22 professional higher education institutions, and two vocational education institutions with authority to provide professional higher education programmes; in the same year there were some 67,600 students enrolled in higher education. The Ministry of Education and Research is responsible for higher education, and until 2008 several organizations were also involved in administrative and academic oversight; these included the Higher Education Advisory Chamber (HEAC), the Research and Development Council, the Estonian Science Council, the Estonian Innovation Fund and the Higher Education Quality Assessment Council (QAC). In January 2009 the Higher Education Quality Agency (HEQA) took over from the HEAC and QAC as an autonomous and independent quality assessment agency. From 2009 to 2011 all higher education institutions were to be required to go through the external quality assessment organized by the HEQA. By 2012 no institute was to be eligible to operate without being accredited by the HEQA. Estonian public universities have significantly more autonomy than applied higher education institutions. In addition to organizing academic life, public universities have the power to draw up new curricula, establish admission terms and conditions, approve their budgets and development plans, elect their rector and make decisions (albeit limited) in matters concerning assets.

The Ministry of Education and Research sets requirements for admission to higher education, which generally consist of the Secondary Education Leaving Certificate (Gümnaasiumi lõputunnistus) and performance in national entrance examinations (Riigieksamitunnistus). Public university admissions are determined by the State, which sets enrolment quotas, although universities may take additional paying students once the quotas have been met. Specialist institutions may also set specific admissions criteria. Under the Bologna Process, higher education qualifications consist of Bachelors, Masters and Doctoral degrees. The Bakalaureusekraad (Bachelors) is the main undergraduate degree, consisting of three to four years of study (180 European Credit Transfer and Accumulation System—ECTS—credit units) and the defence of a thesis. However, some degrees leading to professional qualifications require five years of study; this is particularly the case in medicine, veterinary medicine, pharmacy, architecture, civil engineering and teacher training. The first postgraduate degree is the Magistrikaad (Masters—300 to 360 ECTS credit units), which lasts two years (or one year following a four-year Bachelors) and is dependent on attainment of the Bakalaureusekraad. The second level of postgraduate qualification (and final university degree) is the Doktorikraad; studies at this level last four years (240 ECTS credit units) and are completed with the defence of a thesis. Both the Magistrikaad and Doktorikraad may be either academic or professional qualifications.

Since their introduction in 1999, the main institutions of post-secondary vocational and technical education are the rakenduskõrgkool (applied higher education institutes), which offer three- to four-and-a half-year Diplom degrees. Between 180 and 270 ECTS credit units are required to complete a Diplom.

Regulatory and Representative Bodies

GOVERNMENT

Ministry of Culture: Suur-Karja St 23, 15076 Tallinn; tel. 6282250; e-mail min@kul.ee; internet www.kul.ee; Minister URVE TIIDUS.

Ministry of Education and Research: Munga St 18, 50088 Tartu; tel. 7350222; e-mail hm@hm.ee; internet www.hm.ee; Minister JAAK AAVIKSOO.

ACCREDITATION

ENIC/NARIC Estonia: Academic Recognition Information Centre, Archimedes Foundation, L. Koidula 13A, 10125 Tallinn; tel. 6979215; e-mail enic-naric@archimedes.ee; internet www.archimedes.ee/enic; evaluates foreign qualifications; provides information about foreign and Estonian higher education systems; Head GUNNAR VAHT.

Sihtasutus Archimedes, Eesti Kõrghariduse Kvaliteediagentuur (Archimedes Foundation, Estonian Higher Education Quality Agency): Toompuiestee 30, 10149 Tallinn; tel. 6400455; e-mail ekka@archimedes.ee; internet www.ekka.archimedes.ee; f. 2009; conducts institutional accreditation and quality assessment of study programme groups in Estonian HEIs and develops principles and procedures for such assessments; represents Estonia in issues concerning quality of higher and vocational education; 8 mems; Dir HELI MATTISEN.

NATIONAL BODY

Rektorite Nõukogu (Estonian Rectors' Conference): Ülikooli 18, 50090 Tartu; tel. 7376516; e-mail ern@ern.ee; internet www.ern.ee; f. 2000; contributes to nat. educational, scientific and cultural life by discussion and making recommendations; 6 public univs as mems; Chair. Prof. ALAR KARIS; Sec. Gen. HANNA KANEP.

Learned Societies

GENERAL

Eesti Kodu-uurimise Selts (Society of Estonian Areal Studies): Kohtu 6, 10130 Tallinn; tel. 6440475; e-mail ekus@ekus.ee; internet www.ekus.ee; f. 1939; attached to Estonian Acad. of Sciences; develops and organizes scientific investigation; organizes cultural activities; 223 mems; Chair. Dr ANDRUS RISTKOK.

Eesti Teaduste Akadeemia (Estonian Academy of Sciences): Kohtu 6, 10130 Tallinn; tel. 6442129; e-mail akadeemia@akadeemia.ee; internet www.akadeemia.ee; f. 1938; advances scientific research and represents Estonian science nationally and internationally; provides science-policy advice; communicates and disseminates knowledge; divs of astronomy and physics, biology, geology and chemistry, humanities and social sciences, informatics and engineering; 90 mems (75 ordinary, 15 foreign); Pres. Prof. Dr RICHARD VILLEMS; Sec. Gen. Prof. Dr LEO MÕTUS; publs *Acta Historica Tallinnensia*, *Linguistica Uralica*, *Oil Shale*, *Toimetised* (Proceedings: physics and mathematics, engineering, chemistry, Estonian Journal of Earth Sciences; biology/ecology), *Trames*.

FINE AND PERFORMING ARTS

Eesti Muusikateaduse Selts (Estonian Musicological Society): Rävala pst. 16, 10143 Tallinn; tel. 5299117; e-mail emts@hot.ee; internet www.muusikateadus.ee; f. 1992; attached to Estonian Acad. of Sciences; promotes and supports research in the field of music; holds 2 symposia a year; organizes confs, seminars, courses; Chair. TOOMAS SIITAN; publ. *Res musica* (yearbook).

HISTORY, GEOGRAPHY AND ARCHAEOLOGY

Eesti Geograafia Selts (Estonian Geographical Society): Kohtu 6, 10130 Tallinn; tel. 6199828; e-mail geograafiaselts@gmail.com; internet www.egs.ee; f. 1845; works towards the propagation of knowledge in the area of geography both in Estonian and in foreign languages; 409 mems; Pres. Dr MIHKEL KANGUR; Scientific Sec. Dr TIIT VAASMA.

LANGUAGE AND LITERATURE

Alliance Française: Liivaluite 5, 11214 Tallinn; tel. 6722013; e-mail hellemichelson@hot.ee; offers courses and examinations in French language and culture; promotes cultural exchange with France.

British Council: Veerenni 24, 10135 Tallinn; tel. 6257790; e-mail info@britishcouncil.ee; internet www.britishcouncil.ee; offers examinations in English; introduces British culture and promotes cultural exchange with the UK; library of 6,000 vols; Dir URSULA ROOSMAA.

Eesti Kirjanduse Seltsi (Estonian Literary Society): Vanemuise 19, 51014 Tartu; tel. 7427079; e-mail eks@kirjandus.ee; internet www.kirjandus.ee; f. 1907; promotes literature, scholarship and arts; supports and coordinates research, educational activities; supports and establishes libraries, archives, museums; Chair. TOOMAS LIIVAMÄGI; Academic Sec. MARJA UNT.

Eesti Semiootika Selts (Estonian Semiotics Association): Jakobi 2–318, 50410 Tartu; tel. 7375933; e-mail ess@semiootika.ee; internet www.semiootika.ee; f. 1998; attached to Estonian Acad. of Sciences; provides a forum to discuss issues related to semiotics; organizes scientific events; 63 mems; Chair. PEETER TOROP; publ. *Acta Semiotica Estica* (in Estonian with abstracts in English, online, www.semiootika.ee/acta).

Emakeele Selts (Estonian Mother Tongue Society): Roosikrantsi 6, 10119 Tallinn; tel. 6449331; e-mail es@eki.ee; internet www.emakeeleselts.ee; f. 1920; promotes and maintains interest in the Estonian language; coordinates language research and devt; systematic research into Estonian dialects; language-planning and modern literary language research; arranges language days outside Estonia; also focuses on the modern literary language, loan-words in Estonian and the Estonian dialectal landscape; 366 mems (348 ordinary, 12 hon.); library of 6,364 vols; Chair. Prof. HELLE METSLANG; Academic Sec. KILLU PALDROK; publs *Emakeele Seltsi aastaraamat* (1 a year), *Oma Keel* (2 a year).

Goethe-Institut: Suurtüki 4B, 10133 Tallinn; tel. 6276960; e-mail info@tallinn.goethe.org; internet www.goethe.de/tallinn; offers courses and examinations in German language and culture, and promotes cultural exchange with Germany; library of 9,000 vols, 25 periodicals; Dir Dr RALF EPPENEDER.

NATURAL SCIENCES

General

Estonian Union of the History and Philosophy of Science: Ülikooli 18, 50090 Tartu; tel. 7421514; e-mail erki@zbi.ee; f. 1967; attached to Estonian Acad. of Sciences; 93 mems; Chair. JAAK AAVIKSOO; Scientific Sec. ERKI TAMMIKSAAR.

Biological Sciences

Eesti Inimesegeneetika Ühing (Estonian Society of Human Genetics): Riia 23, 51010 Tartu; tel. 7375029; e-mail estshg@ebc.ee; internet www.estshg.ebc.ee; Pres. ANDRES METSPALU.

Estonian Naturalists' Society: Struve 2, 51003 Tartu; tel. 7341935; e-mail elus@elus.ee; internet www.elus.ee; f. 1853; attached to Estonian Acad. of Sciences; promotes environmental preservation and education by aiding study of Estonian nature; 21 scientific and environmental sections; organizes scientific studies, confs, seminars and discussions, tours and nature observations, projects; 763 mems; library of 160,056 vols; Pres. Dr TÕNU VIIK; Research Sec. IVAR OJASTE; publs *Folia Cryptogamica Estonica, Schola Biotheoretica.*

Physical Sciences

Eesti Keemia Selts (Estonian Chemical Society): Akadeemia tee 15, 12618 Tallinn; tel. 6202816; internet ecs.kbfi.ee; f. 1919; attached to Estonian Acad. of Sciences; organizes and promotes interests of chemists and chemical engineers; sponsors Estonian Chemistry Confs; Pres. Prof. MARGUS LOPP; Sec. Dr ELVI MUKS.

RELIGION, SOCIOLOGY AND ANTHROPOLOGY

Eesti Akadeemiline Usundiloo Selts (Estonian Society for the Study of Religions): Ülikooli 16, 51003 Tartu; tel. 7375227; internet www.eaus.ee; f. 2006; promotes academic study of religions; organizes confs, meetings; 55 mems; Pres. MADIS ARUKASK.

Research Institutes

AGRICULTURE, FISHERIES AND VETERINARY SCIENCE

Eesti Maaülikool Põllumajandus- ja Keskkonnainstituut (Institute of Agricultural and Environmental Sciences): Kreutzwaldi 5, 51014 Tartu; tel. 7313820; internet pk.emu.ee; f. 2005; attached to Estonian Univ. of Life Sciences; monitors and organizes studies on horticulture, agronomy, production and marketing of agricultural products, applied hydrology, nature tourism, landscape conservation and maintenance, ornamental gardening and landscape architecture; has 3 centres and 11 depts; Dir ARET VOOREMÄE; publ. *Agraarteadus/Journal of Agricultural Sciences*; publ. *Agronomy Research* (2 a year).

Eesti Maaülikooli Veterinaarmeditsiini ja Loomakasvatuse Instituut (Institute of Veterinary Medicine and Animal Sciences of the Estonian University of Life Sciences): Kreutzwaldi 62, 51014 Tartu; tel. 7313706; e-mail vl@emu.ee; internet vl.emu.ee; f. 2005; performs teaching and research activities in the field of animal nutrition, animal production, incl. aquaculture, animal genetics and breeding, reproductive biology, biotechnology, normal and pathological morphology, animal health, infectious and invasive diseases, therapy, food hygiene, food technology; Dir Dr ANDRES ALAND; Sec. MALLE PABSTEL.

Eesti Maaviljeluse Instituut (Estonian Research Institute of Agriculture): Teaduse 13, 75501 Saku; tel. 6711542; e-mail info@eria.ee; internet www.eria.ee; f. 1994; attached to Min. of Agriculture; depts of agricultural engineering, agricultural products, plant biotechnology, plant sciences; Dir TAAVI VÕSA.

Jõgeva Sordiaretuse Instituut (Jõgeva Plant Breeding Institute): J. Aamisepa 1, 48309 Jõgeva; tel. 7766901; e-mail jogeva@jpbi.ee; internet www.sordiaretus.ee; f. 1920; attached to Min. of Agriculture; variety breeding of agricultural crops; applied research on agrotechnical aspects and seed production of agricultural crops; basic research in genetics and heritability of valuable traits, selection and description of genetic resources; Dir MATI KOPPEL; Sec. MAARIKA ÕUNAPUU.

ECONOMICS, LAW AND POLITICS

Eesti Konjunktuuriinstituut (Estonian Institute of Economic Research): Rävala 6, 401B, 19080 Tallinn; tel. 6881242; e-mail eki@ki.ee; internet www.ki.ee; f. 1934; gathers, processes and analyses socioeconomic data; undertakes specific research of prevailing economic problems; Dir MARJE JOSING; Sec. PIIA JÕEKALDA; publs *Baltic Facts* (1 a year), *Economic Indicators of Estonia* (10 a year), *Economic Survey of Baltic States* (4 a year), *Konjunktuur* (4 a year).

Eesti Maaülikooli Majandus- ja Sotsiaalinstituut (Institute of Economics and Social Sciences of Estonian University of Life Sciences): Kreutzwaldi 1A, 51014 Tartu; tel. 7313014; e-mail mst@emu.ee; internet ms.emu.ee; f. 1969; conducts research on agricultural economics and policy, agricultural market and marketing, agricultural accounting and finance, rural sociology, cooperation, rural entrepreneurship and environmental economics; Dir Prof. Dr RANDO VÄRNIK.

Eesti Tuleviku-uuringute Instituut (Estonian Institute for Futures Studies): Lai 34, 10133 Tallinn; tel. 6411165; e-mail eti@eti.ee; internet www.eti.ee; f. 1991; attached to Tallinn Univ.; organizes formulation and discussions on futures scenarios; conducts analyses, expert studies, empirical research, scenarios to provide aid in the formulation of devt strategies; Dir ERIK TERK.

HISTORY, GEOGRAPHY AND ARCHAEOLOGY

Institute of History: Rüütli St 6, 10130 Tallinn; tel. 6836451; e-mail ai@tlu.ee; f. 1947; attached to Tallinn Univ.; conducts research, devt and training activities; carries out archaeological excavations, preservation and maintenance; library of 20,000 vols; Dir ERKI RUSSOW; Research Sec. MAIE PIHLAMÄGI; publs *Acta Historica Tallinnensia* (1 a year), *Eesti Arheoloogia Ajakiri* (1 a year).

LANGUAGE AND LITERATURE

Institute of the Estonian Language: Roosikrantsi 6, 10119 Tallinn; tel. 6177500; e-mail eki@eki.ee; internet www.eki.ee; f. 1947 as Institute of Language and Literature, present name and status 1993; depts of linguistics and language technology, dictionary, Finno-Ugric languages and dialects, terminology and language planning; Dir Dr URMAS SUTROP; publ. *Eesti Keele Instituudi Toimetised* (irregular).

Underi ja Tuglase Kirjanduskeskus (Under and Tuglas Literature Centre): Roosikrantsi St 6, 10119 Tallinn; tel. 6443147; e-mail utkk@utkk.ee; internet www.utkk.ee; f. 1993; attached to Estonian Acad. of Sciences; studies Estonian literature and the local written culture in historical and theoretical perspectives, within the context of historically multilingual Baltic space and as world literature; Dir Dr JAAN UNDUSK.

MEDICINE

Pärnu Institute of Health Resort Treatment and Medical Rehabilitation: Kuuse 4, 40012 Pärnu; tel. 4425900; Dir ENDEL VEINPALU.

Technomedicum: Ehitajate tee 5, 19086 Tallinn; Akadeemia tee 1, 12618 Tallinn; tel. 6202200; e-mail tm@cb.ttu.ee; internet www

.ttu.ee/asutused/tehnomeedikum; f. 2006 by merging Dept of Biomedical Engineering, Dept of Clinical Medicine and Centre of Cardiology; attached to Tallinn Univ. of Technology; conducts research and degree studies in medicine, technology and biomedicine; Dir KALJU MEIGAS.

Tervise Arengu Instituut (National Institute for Health Development): Hiiu 42, 11619 Tallinn; tel. 6593900; e-mail tai@tai.ee; internet www.tai.ee; f. 2003 by merger of Institute of Experimental and Clinical Medicine, Estonian Health Education Center, Public Health and Social Training Center; attached to Min. of Social Affairs; evaluates and assesses population health and health determinants; organizes public health services and social services; provides consultations on health policy; Dir MARIS JESSE.

NATURAL SCIENCES

General

Eesti Mereinstituut (Estonian Marine Institute): Mäealuse 14, 12618 Tallinn; tel. 6718901; e-mail meri@sea.ee; internet www.sea.ee; f. 1992; attached to Univ. of Tartu; biology and ecology of freshwater and marine fish, population and community dynamics; long-term dynamics and basic mechanisms of Baltic Sea ecosystem; effect of temporal and spatial variability of coastal processes on the biological and functional diversity; optics and remote sensing of coastal and inland waters; investigations on dynamics and regularities of devt of ecological subsystems in the NE Baltic, Gulfs of Finland and Rīga; modelling of the Baltic Sea and Estonian large lakes ecosystems and composing of the operational forecasting models; effect of aquatic invasive species on ecosystems; effect of human induced eutrophication processes on coastal ecosystems of the Baltic Sea; Dir Prof. TOOMAS SAAT; Sec. ESTER ARGEL; publ. *Estonian Marine Institute Report Series* (irregular).

Biological Sciences

Eesti Maaülikooli Metsandus- ja Maaehitusinstituut (Estonian University of Life Sciences, Institute of Forestry and Rural Engineering): Kreutzwald 5, 51014 Tartu; tel. 7313156; e-mail met@emu.ee; internet mi.emu.ee; f. 1920; attached to Estonian Univ. of Life Sciences; depts of geomatics, rural building, water management, forest biology, silviculture, forest management, forest industry, ecophysiology; Dir Dr TOOMAS TIMMUSK; publ. *Forestry Studies/Metsanduslikud Uurimused* (2 a year).

Estonian Biocentre: Riia 23B, 51010 Tartu; tel. 7375063; e-mail biokeskus@ebc.ee; internet www.ebc.ee; f. 1986; promotes research and technological devt of gene and cell technologies; Dir Prof. RICHARD VILLEMS.

Institute of Ecology: Uus-Sadama 5, 10120 Tallinn; tel. 6199800; e-mail eco@tlu.ee; f. 1992; attached to Tallinn Univ.; studies structural and functional organization of terrestrial ecosystems and their responses to changing environmental conditions; Dir MIHKEL KANGUR.

International Centre for Environmental Biology: Mustamäe tee 4, 10621 Tallinn; tel. 6115804; Dir JÜRI MARTIN.

Meresüsteemide Instituut (Marine Systems Institute): Akadeemia 15A, 12618 Tallinn; tel. 6204300; e-mail msi@msi.ttu.ee; internet www.msi.ttu.ee; f. 2002; attached to Tallinn Univ. of Technology; conducts research on physical oceanography, turbulence and wave studies, marine optics and remote sensing, marine ecology, ice studies, operational oceanography, monitoring and modelling methods, marine geology and sediment dynamics, marine meteorology; Dir JÜRI ELKEN.

Physical Sciences

Eesti Geoloogiakeskus (Geological Survey of Estonia): Kadaka tee 82, 12618 Tallinn; tel. 6720094; e-mail egk@egk.ee; internet www.egk.ee; attached to Min. of the Environment; investigation of terrestrial and aquatic areas of Estonia, compilation, maintenance and delivery of geological data; geological mapping, identification and inventory of ground water and mineral resources, environmental problems; Chair. AGNES VILLMANN.

Estonian Meteorological and Hydrological Institute: Mustamäe tee 33, 10616 Tallinn; tel. 6660901; e-mail jalmar.mandel@emhi.ee; internet www.emhi.ee; issues weather forecasts; gathers, treats and stores the results of meteorological and hydrological measurements; climatological survey of Estonia; attached to Min. of the Environment; Dir-Gen. JALMAR MANDEL.

Keemilise ja Bioloogilise Füüsika Instituut (National Institute of Chemical Physics and Biophysics): Akadeemia tee 23, 12618 Tallinn; tel. 5132288; e-mail kbfi@kbfi.ee; internet www.kbfi.ee; f. 1979; conducts fundamental and applied research and devt of material sciences, gene and biotechnology, environmental technology and computer science; Dir RAIVO STERN; Scientific Sec. JÜRI SIIGUR.

Oil Shale Research Institute: Järveküla tee 12, 30328 Kohtla-Järve; tel. 3344550; f. 1958; library of 100,000 vols; Dir RICHARD JOONAS.

Tartu Observatoorium (Tartu Observatory): Tõravere, 61602 Tartu; tel. 7410265; e-mail aai@aai.ee; internet www.aai.ee; f. 1802, present status 1947; attached to Min. of Education and Research; depts of astrophysics, cosmology, remote sensing, space technology; library of 100,000 vols; Dir Dr ANU REINART; Scientific Sec. MARE RUUSALEPP; publ. *Tartu Tähetorni Kalender* (1 a year, in Estonian).

Tartu Ülikool Füüsika Instituut (Institute of Physics of University of Tartu): Riia 142, 51014 Tartu; tel. 7374602; e-mail dir@fi.tartu.ee; internet www.fi.ut.ee; f. 1973; research in materials science, laser physics, theoretical physics, biophysics, environmental physics, plasma physics and medical physics; library of 30,000 vols, 50 periodicals; Dir Dr TOOMAS PLANK (acting); Sec. LIIVIA SILDOS.

TTÜ Geoloogia Instituut (Institute of Geology at Tallinn University of Technology): Ehitajate tee 5, 19086 Tallinn; tel. 6203010; e-mail gi@ttu.ee; internet www.gi.ee; f. 1947; conducts research in the fields of paleontology, sedimentology, geochemistry; Dir Dr ATKO HEINSALU; Sec. MAARJA MÄRSS; publ. *Proceedings* (4 a year).

RELIGION, SOCIOLOGY AND ANTHROPOLOGY

Estonian Interuniversity Population Research Centre: POB 3012, 10504 Tallinn; Uus-Sadama 5, Tallinn; tel. 6454125; e-mail asta@ekdk.estnet.ee; internet www.popest.ee; evaluates research proposal and implementation reports, incl. annual research and financial reports; Chair. TIIT TAMMARU; Dir ALLAN PUUR; publ. *EKDK RY* (series A, B, C and D, all irregular).

Institute of International and Social Studies: Uus-Sadama 5, 10120 Tallinn; tel. 6199860; e-mail rasi@tlu.ee; f. 1988; attached to Tallinn Univ.; depts of ethnosociology and political studies, social stratification, centre for lifestyle studies, gender studies and civil society research and devt; Dir AIRI-ALINA ALLASTE.

TECHNOLOGY

Eesti Maaülikool Tehnikainstituut (Institute of Technology of Estonian University of Life Sciences): Fr. R. Kreutzwaldi 56, 51014 Tartu; tel. 7313332; internet te.emu.ee; f. 2005; depts of agricultural and production engineering, applied physics and mathematics, energy engineering, husbandry engineering and ergonomics; Dir MARGUS ARAK.

Estonian Energy Research Institute: Paldiski maantee 1, 10137 Tallinn; tel. 6622028; e-mail eeri@eeri.ee; Dir ÜLO RUDI.

TTÜ Küberneetika Instituut (Institute of Cybernetics at Tallinn University of Technology): Akadeemia tee 21, 12618 Tallinn; tel. 6204150; e-mail dir@ioc.ee; internet www.ioc.ee; f. 1960; conducts research in computer science, control systems, mechanics, speech technology, systems biology, wave engineering; library of 8,000 vols; Dir Prof. ANDRUS SALUPERE.

Libraries and Archives

Narva

Narva Linnaarhiivi (Narva City Archives): Linda tn. 4, 20308 Narva; tel. 3591140; e-mail arhiiv@narva.ee; Dir ANDRES KUSTOLA.

Tallinn

Academic Library of Tallinn University: Rävala Ave 10, 15042 Tallinn; tel. 6659439; e-mail tlulib@tlulib.ee; internet www.tlulib.ee; f. 1946; 2,600,000 vols; Dir ANDRES KOLLIST.

Eesti Rahvusraamatukogu (National Library of Estonia): Tõnismägi 2, 15189 Tallinn; tel. 6307611; e-mail nlib@nlib.ee; internet www.nlib.ee; f. 1918, nat. library status 1988, parliamentary library 1989; nat. and parliamentary library with public access; nat. ISBN, ISSN and ISMN agency; research library for the humanities and social sciences; professional devt centre; cultural centre for book and art exhibitions, concerts, confs; 3,411,404 vols; Dir-Gen. JANNE ANDRESOO; publs *Eesti Rahvusraamatukogu Toimetised* (Acta Bibliothecae Nationalis Estoniae), *Raamatukogu* (The Library, 6 a year).

Tallinna Linnaarhiivi (Tallinn City Archives): Tolli 6, 10133 Tallinn; tel. 6457401; e-mail linnaarhiiv@tallinnlv.ee; internet www.tallinn.ee/arhiivindus; f. 1883, current name adopted 1989; contains 1,286 archives; 456,104 archival items incl. documents from the 13th century up to 2010.

Tartu

Eesti Maaülikooli Raamatukogu (Library of Estonian University of Life Sciences): Kreutzwaldi 1A, 51014 Tartu; tel. 7313062; e-mail library@emu.ee; internet library.emu.ee; f. 1952; 295,391 vols (incl. 263,049 books, 9,876 journals); Head of Library TIINA TOHVRE.

Rahvusarhiiv (National Archives of Estonia): J. Liivi 4, 50409 Tartu; tel. 7387505; e-mail rahvusarhiiv@ra.ee; internet www.ra.ee; f. 1999; incl. Historical Archives, State Archives, Film Archives and 4 regional depts in Haapsalu, Kuressaare, Rakvere, Valga; colln of 8.8m. records, 10m. digital images on web, 9.5m. metres of film recordings, 100,000 maps, 2,200 seals, 1,500 parchments; State Archivist PRIIT PIRSKO; Dir for Research and Publishing Bureau TÕNU TANNBERG; publ.

Tuna (Past, 4 a year, in English and Russian).

Tartu Ülikooli Raamatukogu (University of Tartu Library): W. Struve 1, 50091 Tartu; tel. 7375702; e-mail library@utlib.ee; internet www.utlib.ee; f. 1802; European Union Documentation Centre; 3,700,000 vols, 34,090 MSS; Dir MARTIN HALLIK (acting).

Museums and Art Galleries

Narva

Narva Museum: St-Peterburi mnt. 2, 20308 Narva; tel. 3599230; e-mail info@narvamuuseum.ee; internet www.narvamuuseum.ee; colln showing history of Narva during medieval period, Swedish authority, Russian empire; incl. Narva castle and town, art gallery; library of 21,000 vols; Man. ANDRES TOODE.

Tallinn

Eesti Ajaloomuuseum (Estonian History Museum): Pirita tee 56, 10127 Tallinn; tel. 6228600; e-mail post@ajaloomuuseum.ee; internet www.ajaloomuuseum.ee; f. 1802, current name adopted 1989; incl. Great Guild Hall, Maarjamae Palace, Park of Monuments, Film Museum; research and colln on archeology, medieval and near history, numismatics and cultural history; 282,669 artefacts; temporary exhibits, concerts, lectures, publs; library of 11,000 vols; Dir SIRJE KARIS.

Eesti Arhitektuurimuuseum (Museum of Estonian Architecture): Arts centre, Rotermann's Salt Storage, Ahtri 2, 10151 Tallinn; tel. 6257000; e-mail info@arhitektuurimuuseum.ee; internet www.arhitektuurimuuseum.ee; f. 1991; colln of materials of 20th-century architecture; maps of towns and other settlements, architectural drawings and projects, textual materials connected with them, models, papers on architecture and town bldg; 30,000 prints and drawings; architects' personal collns; colln of 200 models; furniture colln; Dir LEELE VÄLJA.

Eesti Kunstimuuseum (Art Museum of Estonia): Weizenbergi 34, Valge 1, 10127 Tallinn; tel. 6026001; e-mail muuseum@ekm.ee; internet www.ekm.ee; f. 1919; incl. Adamson-Eric Museum, Kadriorg Art Museum, Kumu Art Museum, Mikkel Museum, Niguliste Museum; colln of fine and applied art; art exhibitions; 60,000 works of art; library of 39,416 vols of books and periodicals, 138 video recordings, 26 CD-ROMs; Dir-Gen. SIRJE HELME; Sec. KLARIKA KURE.

Eesti Teatri- ja Muusikamuuseum (Estonian Theatre and Music Museum): Müürivahe 12, 10146 Tallinn; tel. 6446407; e-mail info@tmm.ee; internet www.tmm.ee; f. 1924, present status 1941; collects, preserves, studies and introduces the Estonian theatre and musical life; organizes exhibitions, concerts and discussions; library of 50,000 vols; Dir TANEL VEEREMAA; publ. *AegiKiri* (1 a year).

Eesti Vabaohumuuseum (Estonian Open Air Museum): Vabaõhumuuseumi tee 12, 13521 Tallinn; tel. 6549100; e-mail evm@evm.ee; internet www.evm.ee; f. 1957; architectural and ethnographical objects from 18th–20th centuries; collns of 56,815 museum objects; Dir MERIKE LANG.

Tallinna Linnamuuseum (Tallinn City Museum): Vene St 17, POB 77, 10123 Tallinn; tel. 6155183; e-mail info@linnamuuseum.ee; internet www.linnamuuseum.ee; f. 1937; connects 9 museums around the city; 154,000 artefacts; collns of archaeology, ceramics, cultural history, documents, glass, art, seals, decorative leather, bricks, photographs and negatives, toy, furniture, badges and medals, numismatics, weapons, textiles, precious metals; library of 6,300 vols; Dir MARUTA VARRAK; Sec. MARIANNE LEIS.

Tartu

Eesti Kirjandusmuuseum (Estonian Literary Museum): Vanemuise 42, 51003 Tartu; tel. 7377700; e-mail kirmus@kirmus.ee; internet www.kirmus.ee; f. 1909, present name and status 1940; attached to Min. of Education and Research; comprises Archival Library (incl. bibliography dept), Estonian Folklore Archives, Estonian Cultural History Archives, folklore dept and ethnomusicology dept; Dir Mag. JANIKA KRONBERG; publs *Folklore/Electronic Journal of Folklore* (4 a year), *Maetagused* (4 a year), *Paar sammukest* (Some Small Steps, 1 a year), *Pro Folkloristika: Estonian Folklore Archives* (1 a year).

Eesti Rahva Muuseum (Estonian National Museum): Veski 32, 51014 Tartu; tel. 7350400; e-mail erm@erm.ee; internet www.erm.ee; f. 1909; ethnology and culture of the Estonian and Finno-Ugric people; library of 34,750 vols; Dir TÕNIS LUKAS (acting); publs *Eesti Rahva Muuseumi Aastaraamat* (1 a year), *Eesti Rahva Muuseumi Sari* (1 a year), *Journal of Ethnology and Folkloristics* (2 a year).

Tartu Kunstimuuseum (Tartu Art Museum): Raekoja plats 18, 51003 Tartu; tel. 7441080; e-mail tartmus@tartmus.ee; internet www.tartmus.ee; f. 1940; Estonian and European art since 19th century; colln of paintings, drawings, graphic arts, sculpture, watercolour paintings, photographs and video cassettes; library of 20,734 vols; Dir REET MARK.

Tartu Ulikooli Kunstimuuseum (University of Tartu Art Museum): Ülikooli St 18, 50090 Tartu; tel. 7375384; e-mail kunstimuuseum@ut.ee; internet www.ut.ee/artmuseum; f. 1803; colln of plaster casts of ancient sculpture, gems and coins, graphic art from 15th–19th centuries, Russian icons, applied art, Greek and Roman antiquities; Dir INGE KUKK.

Universities

EESTI EVANGEELSE LUTERLIKU KIRIKU USUTEADUSE INSTITUUT
(Institute of Theology of the Estonian Evangelical Lutheran Church)

Pühavaimu 6, 10123 Tallinn
Telephone: 6117400
E-mail: ui@eelk.ee
Internet: www.ui.eelk.ee

Founded 1946
Private control

Faculty of theology; depts of continuing education, church music

Rector: OVE SANDER
Head of Library: JANA LAHE

Library of 70,000 vols
Number of students: 120

EESTI KUNSTIAKADEEMIA
(Estonian Academy of Arts)

Teatri väljak 1, 10143 Tallinn
Telephone: 6267301
E-mail: artun@artun.ee
Internet: www.artun.ee

Founded 1914 as Tallinn Industrial Art School, present name and status 1995
State control

Rector: Prof. SIGNE KIVI
Vice-Rector for Academic Affairs: ANDRES TALI
Vice-Rector for Research: Prof. MART KALM
Library Man.: ELVIRA MUTT

Library of 92,813 vols, 1,737 audiovisual materials
Number of teachers: 160
Number of students: 1,200

DEANS

Faculty of Architecture: Prof. TOOMAS TAMMIS
Faculty of Art and Culture: Prof. MART KALM
Faculty of Design: LYLIAN MEISTER
Faculty of Fine Arts: ANDRES TALI
Open Academy: VEIKO TAMMJÄRV (Head)

EESTI MAAÜLIKOOL
(Estonian University of Life Sciences)

Kreutzwaldi 1, 51014 Tartu
Telephone: 7313001
E-mail: info@emu.ee
Internet: www.emu.ee

Founded 1951 as Estonian Agricultural Univ., current name adopted 2005
State control
Languages of instruction: English, Estonian
Academic year: September to June

Comprises 5 research institutes (see under Research Institutes), 1 college and 2 research centres

Rector: Prof. MAIT KLAASSEN
Vice-Rector for Research: Dr ÜLLE JAAKMA
Vice-Rector for Studies: PAAVO KAIMRE
Library Man.: TIINA TOHVRE

Library: see under Libraries and Archives
Number of teachers: 410
Number of students: 4,269

Publication: *Eesti Maaülikooli Teaduslike Tööde Kogumik*

EESTI MUUSIKA- JA TEATRIAKADEEMIA
(Estonian Academy of Music and Theatre)

Rävala pst. 16, 10143 Tallinn
Telephone: 6675700
E-mail: ema@ema.edu.ee
Internet: www.ema.edu.ee

Founded 1919 as Tallinn Higher Music School, present status 1996
State control

Depts of cultural management and humanities, piano, strings, brass and woodwind, vocal, chamber music, conducting, composition, musicology, jazz music; institutes of interpretation pedagogics, music education; drama school

Rector: Prof. PEEP LASSMANN
Vice-Rector for Academic Affairs and Research: Prof. MARGUS PÄRTLAS
Vice-Rector for Devt: Prof. HELENA TULVE
Chief Librarian: ILVI RAUNA

Library of 204,011 vols of books, 159,301 scores, 2,711 theses and works of research, 24,088 audio recordings, 3,155 video recordings, 117 periodicals
Number of teachers: 283, (122 full-time)
Number of students: 751

Publication: *Res Musica* (1 a year)

ESTONIAN BUSINESS SCHOOL

Lauteri 3, 10114 Tallinn
Telephone: 6651325
E-mail: info@ebs.ee

Internet: www.ebs.ee
Founded 1988
Private control
Languages of instruction: English, Estonian, Russian
Academic year: August to June (2 semesters)
Offers Bachelors, Masters and Doctoral degrees in international business administration
Rector: Prof. Dr ARNO ALMANN
Vice-Rector for Admin. and Finance: TÕNU KÜTTMAA
Vice-Rector for Research: Prof. Dr RUTH ALAS
Vice-Rector for Studies and Devt: Dr HEIKKI PÄEVA
Academic Sec.: MAARJA MURUMÄGI
Head of Library: EDA PIHU
Library of 8,273 vols, 45 periodicals
Number of students: 1,500
Publication: *Journal of Management and Change* (2 a year)

TALLINNA TEHNIKAÜLIKOOL
(Tallinn University of Technology)

Ehitajate tee 5, 19086 Tallinn
Telephone: 6202002
E-mail: info@ttu.ee
Internet: www.ttu.ee
Founded 1918, current status 1936, current name adopted 1938
State control
Languages of instruction: English, Estonian, Russian
Academic year: September to June
Incl. Tallinn College, Tartu College, Virumaa College and Kuressaare College
Rector: Prof. ANDRES KEEVALLIK
Vice-Rector for Academic Affairs: Prof. KALLE TAMMEMÄE
Vice-Rector for Innovation and Internationalization: ALAR KOLK
Vice-Rector for Research: Prof. ERKKI TRUVE
Academic Sec.: KAI AVIKSOO
Dir for Library: JÜRI JÄRS
Library of 740,000 vols
Number of teachers: 613
Number of students: 14,151

DEANS

Faculty of Chemical and Materials Technology: Prof. ANDRES ÖPIK
Faculty of Civil Engineering: Prof. ROODE LIIAS
Faculty of Information Technology: Prof. ENNU RÜSTERN
Faculty of Mechanical Engineering: Prof. TAUNO OTTO
Faculty of Power Engineering: Prof. ARVI HAMBURG
Faculty of Science: Prof. TÕNIS KANGER
Faculty of Social Sciences: Prof. SULEV MÄELTSEMEES
Tallinn School of Economics and Business Administration: Prof. ÜLLAS EHRLICH

PROFESSORS

Faculty of Chemical and Materials Technology (Ehitajate tee 5, 19086 Tallinn; tel. 6203525; e-mail k@ttu.ee):
- CHRISTJANSON, P., Polymer Technology
- KALLAVUS, U., Materials Research
- KAPS, T., Woodworking
- MELLIKOV, E., Semiconductor Materials Technology
- MUNTER, R., Environmental Technology
- OJA, V., Chemical Engineering
- ÖPIK, A., Physical Chemistry
- PAALME, T., Food Science and Technology
- SOONE, J., Environmental Technology
- TRIKKEL, A., Physical Chemistry
- VIIKNA, A., Textile Technology
- VOKK, R., Food Science

Faculty of Civil Engineering (Ehitajate tee 5, 19086 Tallinn; tel. 6203521; e-mail e@ttu.ee):
- AAVIK, A., Road Construction
- ENGELBRECHT, J., Applied Mechanics
- IDNURM, S., Steel Structures
- KLAUSON, A., Structural Mechanics
- KÕIV, T. A., Heating and Ventilation
- KOPPEL, T., Hydrodynamics
- LAVING, J., Traffic and Transportation Engineering
- LIIAS, R., Construction Economics and Management
- LILL, I., Building Technology
- RAADO, L.-M., Building Materials
- RANDLEPP, A., Geodesy
- SALUPERE, A., Solid Mechanics
- SOOMERE, T., Hydrodynamics
- SUTT, J., Construction Economics and Management

Faculty of Information Technology (Raja tn. 15, 12618 Tallinn; tel. 6203528; e-mail i@ttu .ee):
- BULDAS, A., Information Security
- KALJA, A., Systems Programming
- KUKK, V., Circuit and Systems Theory
- KUUSIK, R., Informatics
- LOSSMANN, E., Telecommunications
- MIN, M., Electronic Measurement
- MÕTUS, L., Real Time Systems
- ÕUNAPUU, E., IT Systems
- PENJAM, J., Theoretical Computer Science
- RANG, T., Electronics Design
- RÜSTERN, E., Automatic Control and Systems Analysis
- TAKLAJA, A., Microwave Engineering
- TAMMET, T., Network Software
- TEPANDI, J., Applied Artificial Intelligence
- UBAR, R.-J., Computer Engineering and Diagnostics
- VAIN, J., Formal Methods

Faculty of Mechanical Engineering (Ehitajate tee 5, 19086 Tallinn; tel. 6203480; e-mail m@ttu.ee):
- AJAOTS, M., Fine Mechanics
- EERME, M., Computer-aided Design and Manufacturing
- KIITAM, A., Quality Engineering
- KULU, P., Materials Science
- KÜTTNER, R., Computer-aided Design and Manufacturing
- LAANEOTS, R., Metrology and Measurement Techniques
- LAVRENTJEV, J., Automotive Engineering
- MELLIKOV, E., Semiconductor Materials Technology
- PAIST, A., Thermal Power Engineering
- PAPPEL, T., Machine Mechanics
- PAPSTEL, J., Production Engineering
- ROOSIMÖLDER, L., Product Development
- SIIRDE, A., Thermal Power Equipment
- TAMRE, M., Mechatronics

Faculty of Power Engineering (Ehitajate tee 5, 19086 Tallinn; tel. 6203763; e-mail a@ttu .ee):
- JARVIK, J., Electrical Machines
- LAUGIS, J., Electrical Drives and Electricity Supply
- LEHTLA, T., Robotics
- MELDORF, M., Transfer in Power Systems
- TAMMOJA, H., Electrical Power Engineering
- VALGMA, I., Rock Engineering

Faculty of Science (Ehitajate tee 5, IV-208, 19086 Tallinn; tel. 6202997; e-mail y@ttu.ee):
- ELKEN, J., Oceanography
- JÄRVEKÜLG, L., Molecular Diagnostics
- KALJURAND, M., Analytical Chemistry
- KARELSON, M., Molecular Technology
- KRUSTOK, J., Applied Physics
- LIPPING, T., Radiophysics
- LOPP, M., Organic Chemistry
- MEIGAS, K., Biomedical Technology
- PAAL, E., Algebra and Geometry
- PALUMAA, P., Genomics and Proteomics
- PUUSEMP, P., Algebra and Geometry
- SAMEL, N., Bio-organic and Natural Products Chemistry
- TAMM, T., Inorganic and Gen. Chemistry
- TAMMERAID, L., Mathematical Analysis
- TIMMUSK, T., Molecular Biology
- TRUVE, E., Gene Technology
- VILU, R., Biochemistry

Tallinn School of Economics and Business Administration (Akadeemia tee 3, 12618 Tallinn; tel. 6203945; e-mail t@ttu.ee):
- AASMA, A., Economic Mathematics
- ALVER, J., Accounting
- ALVER, L., Financial Accounting
- KEREM, K., Economic Theory
- KILVITS, K., Economic Policy
- KOLBRE, E., Management Economics
- KUKRUS, A., Economic Law and Regulation
- LEIMANN, J., Organization and Management
- LISTRA, E., Finance and Banking
- SAAT, M., Business Administration
- TEDER, J., Small Businesses
- TINT, P., Working Environment and Safety

TALLINNA ÜLIKOOL
(Tallinn University)

Narva mnt 25, 10120 Tallinn
Telephone: 6409101
E-mail: tlu@tlu.ee
Internet: www.tlu.ee
Founded 2005 by merger of Tallinn Pedagogical Univ., Estonian Academic Library, Estonian Institute of Humanities and Institute of History
State control
Language of instruction: Estonian
Academic year: September to June
Comprises 19 institutes and 6 colleges for 6 disciplines: arts, educational sciences, health sciences, humanities, natural sciences, social sciences
Rector: Prof. TIIT LAND
Vice-Rector for Academic Affairs: Prof. PRIIT REISKA
Vice-Rector for Devt: Dr EVE EISENSCHMIDT
Vice-Rector for Research: Prof. KATRIN NIGLAS
Dir for Library: ANDRES KOLLIST
Library: see under Libraries and Archives
Number of teachers: 532
Number of students: 10,500

TARTU ÜLIKOOL
(University of Tartu)

Ülikooli 18, 50090 Tartu
Telephone: 7375100
E-mail: info@ut.ee
Internet: www.ut.ee
Founded 1632
State control
Language of instruction: Estonian
Academic year: September to June
Rector: Prof. Dr VOLLI KALM (acting)
Vice-Rector for Academic Affairs: MARTIN HALLIK
Vice-Rector for Devt: ERIK PUURA
Vice-Rector for Research: MARCO KIRM
Dir for Admin.: ANDRES LIINAT
Academic Sec.: IVAR-IGOR SAARNIIT
Dir for Library: MARTIN HALLIK (acting)
Library: see under Libraries and Archives
Number of teachers: 1,800
Number of students: 17,000
Publications: *Acta et Commentationes Universitatis Tartuensis* (44 series), *Universitas Tartuensis* (12 a year)

DEANS

Faculty of Economics and Business Administration: Prof. Dr MAAJA VADI
Faculty of Exercise and Sports Sciences: Prof. MATI PÄÄSUKE
Faculty of Law: Prof. JAAN GINTER
Faculty of Mathematics and Computer Science: Prof TÕNU KOLLO
Faculty of Medicine: Prof. Dr JOEL STARKOPF
Faculty of Philosophy: Dr MARGIT SUTROP
Faculty of Physics and Chemistry: Prof. J. JÄRV
Faculty of Science and Technology: Dr PEETER BURK
Faculty of Social Sciences and Education: Prof. Dr JAANUS HARRO
Faculty of Theology: Prof. Dr RIHO ALTNURME

PROFESSORS

Faculty of Economics and Business Administration:

EAMETS, R., Macroeconomics
HALDMA, T., Accounting
KALDARU, H., Microeconomics
METS, T., Entrepreneurship
PAAS, T., Econometrics
RAJU, O., Economic Theory
REILJAN, J., International Economics
SEPP, J., Economic Policy
VADI, M., Management
VARBLANE, U., International Business

Faculty of Exercise and Sport Sciences:

JÜRIMÄE, J., Coaching
JÜRIMÄE, T., Sport Pedagogy
ÖÖPIK, V., Exercise Physiology
PÄÄSUKE, M., Kinesiology and Biomechanics
RAUDSEPP, L., Sport Psychology

Faculty of Law:

BACHMANN, T., Cognitive Psychology and Psychology of Law
GINTER, J., Criminology
KULL, I., Civil Law
LUTS-SOOTAK, M., Legal History
MERUSK, K., Constitutional and Administrative Law
NARITS, R., Comparative Jurisprudence
PISUKE, H., Intellectual Property Law
SAAR, J., Criminology
SOOTAK, J., Criminal Law
TRUUVÄLI, E., Theory of Law
VARUL, P., Civil Law

Faculty of Mathematics and Computer Science:

ABEL, M., Geometry and Topology
BULDAS, A., Cryptography
DUMAS MENJIVAR, M., Software Equipment
KAARLI, K., Universal Algebra
KILP, M., Algebra
KOIT, M., Speech Technology
KOLLO, T., Mathematical Statistics
LEIGER, T., Mathematical Analysis
LELLEP, J., Theoretical Mechanics
OJA, E., Functional Analysis
PÄRNA, K., Probability Theory
PEDAS, A., Differential and Integral Equations
VAINIKKO, E., Distributed Systems
VENE, V., Programming Languages Semantics
VILO, J., Bioinformatics

Faculty of Medicine:

ALTRAJA, A., Pulmonology
AREND, A., Histology and Embryology
ASSER, T., Neurosurgery
EHA, J., Cardiology
EVERAUS, H., Haematology and Oncology
KAASIK, A., Molecular Toxicology
KARRO, H., Obstetrics and Gynaecology
KIIVET, R., Health Care Management
KÕKS, S., Ship of Physiological Genomics
LEMBER, M., Propaedeutics of Internal Medicine
LUTSAR, I., Medical Microbiology and Virology
MAAROOS, H., Polyclinic and Family Medicine
MAAROOS, J., Sports Medicine and Rehabilitation
MIKELSAAR, A., Human Biology and Genetics
MIKELSAAR, M., Medical Biotechnology
PEETSALU, A., Surgical Diseases
SEPPET, E., Pathological Physiology
SILM, H., Dermatology and Venerology
STARKOPF, J., Anaesthesiology and Intensive Care
TAMM, A., Laboratory Medicine
TEESALU, P., Ophthalmology
TILLMANN, V., Paediatrics
UIBO, R., Immunology
UUSKÜLA, A., Epidemiology
VÄLI, M., Forensic Medicine
VASAR, E., Physiology
VASAR, V., Psychiatry
VESKI, P., Pharmaceutical Technology and Biopharmaceutics
ZILMER, M., Medical Biochemistry
ŽARKOVSKI, A., Pharmacology and Toxicology

Faculty of Philosophy:

COHNITZ, D., Theoretical Philosophy
DULITŠENKO, A., Slavic Languages and Literature
EHALA, M., Didactics of Estonian and Applied Linguistics
ELKEN, J., Painting
HUUMO, T., Finnish Language and Culture
KIRSS, T., Estonian Literature
KISSELJOVA, L., Russian Literature
KRIISKA, A., Laboratory Archaeology
KULL, K., Biosemiotics
KÜLMOJA, I., Russian Language
KUUTMA, K., Cultural Research
LANG, V., Archaeology
LAUR, M., Modern History
LEETE, A., Ethnology
LILL, A., Classical Philology
MAISTE, J., Art History
MATJUS, Ü., History of Estonian Philosophy
MEDIJAINEN, E., Contemporary History
METSLANG, H., Modern Estonian
MUST, A., Archival Studies
PAJUSALU, K., History and Dialects of Estonian Language
PAJUSALU, R., General Linguistics
ROSENBERG, T., Estonian History
SUTROP, M., Practical Philosophy
SUTROP, U., Anthropological and Ethnolinguistics
TALVET, J., Comparative Literature
TOROP, P., Semiotics of Culture
VALK, Ü., Estonian and Comparative Folklore
VALLIKIVI, A., Liberal Arts
VIHALEMM, R., Philosophy of Science
VOGELBERG, K., English Language and Literature

Faculty of Science and Technology:

AABLOO, A., Technology of Polymeric Materials
AHAS, R., Human Geography
BURK, P., Chemical Physics
FREIBERG, A., Biophysics and Plant Physiology
HEINARU, A., Genetics
HÕRAK, P., Animal Physiological Ecology
JAAGUS, J., Climatology
JÄRV, J., Organic Chemistry
KALM, V., Applied Geology
KARELSON, M., Molecular Technology
KÄRNER, J., General Zoology
KIKAS, J., Disordered Systems Physics
KIRSIMÄE, K., Geology and Mineralogy
KIVISAAR, M., Bacterial/Microbial genetics
KÕLJALG, U., Mycology
KURG, A., Molecular Biotechnology
LAAN, M., Biotechnology
LANGEL, Ü., Molecular Biotechnology
LEITO, I., Analytical Chemistry
LÕHMUS, K., Applied Ecology
LUST, E., Physical Chemistry
LUŠTŠIK, A., Solid State Physics
MAIMETS, T., Cell Biology
MANDER, Ü., Physical Geography and Landscape Ecology
MEIDLA, T., Palaeontology and Stratigraphy
MERISTE, M., Technology of Proactive Systems
MERITS, A., Applied Virology
METSPALU, A., Biotechnology
NOOLANDI, J., Polymer Physics
OJA, T., Geoinformatics and Cartography
PAAL, J., Plant Ecology
PÄRTEL, M., Botany
POOGA, M., Chemical Biology
RANNIKMÄE, M., Science Education
REMM, M., Bioinformatics
REMME, J., Molecular Biology
RINKEN, A., Bio-organic Chemistry
RÕÕM, R., Meteorology
SAARI, P., Wave Optics
SAMMELSELG, V., Inorganic Chemistry
SARAPUU, T., Educational Technology in Science
SEDMAN, J., General and Microbial Biochemistry
TAMMARU, T., Integrative Zoology
TAMMELO, R., Field Theory
TENSON, T., Technology of Anti-microscopic Substances
USTAV, M., Biomedical Technology
VILLEMS, R., Archaegenetics
ZOBEL, K., Ecological Plant Ecology
ZOBEL, M., Plant Ecology

Faculty of Social Sciences and Education:

ALLIK, J., Experimental Psychology
BERG, E., International Relations Theory
HARRO, J., Psychophysiology
KASEKAMP, A., Baltic Politics
LAUK, E., Journalism
LAURISTIN, M., Social Communication
NÄÄTÄNEN, R., Cognitive Neuroscience
PETTAI, V., Comparative Politics
TULVISTE, P., Cultural Psychology
TULVISTE, T., Developmental Psychology
VIHALEMM, P., Media Studies

Faculty of Theology:

ALTNURME, R., Church History
KULL, A., Systematic Theology
KULMAR, T., Comparative Religion
KÄMMERER, T., Ancient Near-Eastern Languages
LEHTSAAR, T., Psychology of Religion

Other Higher Educational Institutes

Arvutikolledž (Computer Science College): Erika 7A, 10416 Tallinn; tel. 6603149; e-mail info@iati.ee; internet www.iati.ee/collage; f. 2000; Bachelors degrees in computer graphics, programming; Rector ALEKSANDR BOTIN.

Eesti–Ameerika Äriakadeemia (Estonian–American Business Academy): Punane 29, 13611 Tallinn; tel. 6054100; e-mail info@eaba.ee; internet www.eaba.ee; f. 1989; courses in management, economics, international tourism, public relations, IT management and journalism; library: 25,900 vols; Rector HELENA GUSSAROVA (acting).

Eesti Ettevõtluskõrgkool Mainor (Estonian Entrepreneurship University of Applied Sciences): Suur-Sõjamäe 10A, 11415, Tallinn; tel. 6101908; e-mail eek@eek.ee; internet www.eek.ee; f. 1992, current name adopted 2010; Bachelors and Masters degrees in entrepreneurship, management, information technology, design for creative entrepreneurship; 2,300 students; Rector Dr KRISTA TUULIK; Vice-Rector for Academic and Financial Affairs TAUNO ÕUNAPUU; Librarian ANNE SAAGPAKK.

Eesti Infotehnoloogia Kolledž (Estonian Information Technology College): Raja 4C, 12616 Tallinn; tel. 6285800; e-mail info@itcollege.ee; internet www.itcollege.ee; f. 2000; Bachelors degree in IT systems development, IT systems admin., information systems analysis, technical communication; 52 teachers; 800 students; Rector TIIT ROOSMAA; Vice-Rector TOOMAS LEPIKULT; Head of Academic Affairs INGA VAU; Sec. MALLE TRAGON.

Eesti Lennuakadeemia (Estonian Aviation Academy): Lennu 40, Reola, 61707 Ülenurme; tel. 7448100; e-mail eava@eava.ee; internet www.lennuakadeemia.ee; f. 1993 as Tartu Aviation College, current name adopted 2008; depts of aircraft maintenance training, air traffic services training, aviation management, communication and navigation, flying training; Rector JAAN TAMM; Vice-Rector for Studies ANTS AAVER; Librarian LILIA INGEL.

Eesti Mereakadeemia (Estonian Maritime Academy): Kopli 101, 11712 Tallinn; tel. 6135500; e-mail eesti.mereakadeemia@emara.ee; internet www.emara.ee; f. 1991; Rector HEIKI LINDPERE; Vice-Rector for Academic Affairs TIINA PUUSALU; Vice-Rector for Finances and Admin. AIVO LIND; Library Man. PILLE TOOL; publ. *Meremees*.

Euroakadeemia (Euroacademy): Mustamäe tee 4, 10621 Tallinn; tel. 6115801; e-mail euro@euroakadeemia.ee; internet www.euroakadeemia.ee; f. 1997 as EuroUniversity, current name adopted 2009; faculties of business management, design, environmental protection, international relations, translation and interpretation; Rector JÜRI MARTIN; Pro-Rector PEETER KARING; Head of Library ANNIKA OJA.

Institute of Economics and Management: Erika 7A, 10416 Tallinn; tel. 6487722; e-mail info@ecomen.eu; internet www.ecomen.eu; f. 1993, current name adopted 2005; courses in business economics and business management; 600 students; Rector Prof. Dr HANON BARABANER; Pro-Rector Dr ANGELA MELIKHOVA; Pro-Rector for Economic and Admin. Affairs LJUDMILLA BARABANER; Pro-Rector for Research, Teaching and Studies and Quality Assurance ALEKSANDER LUKJANOV; Library Man. SIRJE PRATKA.

Kaitseväe Ühendatud Õppeasutused (Estonian National Defence College): Riia 12, 51013 Tartu; tel. 7176110; e-mail oppeasutused@mil.ee; internet www.ksk.edu.ee; f. 1998; Bachelors and Masters programmes in officers training; Commandant Col. AARNE ERMUS.

Sisekaitseakadeemia (Estonian Academy of Security Sciences): Kase Str. 61, 12012 Tallinn; tel. 6965402; e-mail international@sisekaitse.ee; internet www.sisekaitse.ee; f. 1992; colleges of correction, police and border guard, rescue, taxation and customs; 1,400 students; Rector LAURI TABUR.

Tallinna Majanduskool (Tallinn School of Economics): Tammsaare tee 147, 12915 Tallinn; tel. 6507850; e-mail info@tmk.edu.ee; internet www.tmk.edu.ee; f. 1911; library: 22,000 vols; 100 teachers; 1,700 students; Dir RAIVO TÄHT.

Tartu Teoloogia Akadeemia (Tartu Academy of Theology): Ujula 1A, 51008 Tartu; tel. 7420958; e-mail info@teoloogia.ee; internet www.teoloogia.ee; f. 1992; offers Bachelors in pastoral counselling, Christian media, Christian youth work and ministerial-pastoral training; Pres. EENOK HAAMER; Vice-Pres. for Academic Affairs SIIMON HAAMER.

ETHIOPIA

The Higher Education System

Addis Ababa University is the oldest university in the country. It was originally founded in 1950 as University College of Addis Ababa, became known as Haile Selassie University in 1961 and adopted its current name in 1975. There have been efforts to establish higher education institutions in outlying areas of Ethiopia; however, most institutions are located in the central, north and north-western parts of the country (mostly Addis Ababa, Bahir Dar, Mekelle, Alemaya, Awassa and Jimma). Higher education is offered at universities (both public and private), university colleges and specialized institutions, all of which are the responsibility of the Ministry of Education. A total of 264,822 students were enrolled in university-level higher education in 2007/08, according to government statistics. By 2007 there were 15,000 students enrolled in Addis Ababa University alone. The number of higher education establishments (particularly public universities) has expanded notably in recent years and several teacher training colleges and university colleges have been upgraded to university status. By 2010 there were 22 public universities and in August 2009 the Government announced plans to construct 10 new universities in different parts of the country in the near future. Partly owing to this rapid expansion, higher education in the public sector is no longer fully subsidized by the Government. The private higher education sector in Ethiopia has also grown at a considerable rate. From practically zero in 1998, enrolment in privately owned higher education institutions had grown to 39,691 in 2005/06 and to 79,314 in 2010/11; total enrolment for that year in all higher education institutions (both public and private) was 467,843 students, as reported by the Ministry of Education. By 2010 there were more than 60 accredited higher education institutions in the private sector.

Higher education is financed by the Government, and the budget of each university is supervised by its Board. The University Senate is the managerial body of a University; the Academic Commission is the main academic body. The Academic Commission controls all aspects regarding the structure of degree programmes, certification and student issues. Heads of Department chair Department Councils, which are subordinate to the Academic Commission, and which make recommendations on matters of study, research, staff recruitment, pedagogy and examinations. The Ministry of Education appoints senior university officers, such as the President and Vice-Presidents. Heads of Department are either appointed by Deans of Faculty or elected by Department Councils.

The centrally controlled Ethiopian Higher Education Entrance Qualification Certificate Examination is the main requirement for admission to higher education. The grade actually needed for admission may vary according to institution and on a yearly basis depending upon the number of places available. A policy of positive discrimination in favour of females and students from schools with poor facilities in certain regions has been applied at a number of institutions. The primary undergraduate degree is the Bachelors, which takes three to four years, although some professional subjects require longer (five years for engineering, law and pharmacy; six years for medicine and veterinary medicine). The first postgraduate degree is the Masters, which lasts for two years, and the second postgraduate degree is the Doctor of Philosophy, which is awarded at least three years after the Masters and requires the submission of a thesis. The majority of Masters courses are provided by the country's oldest public universities—Addis Ababa University and Haramaya University.

Technical and vocational education at tertiary level consists of a two-year Diploma and a three-year Advanced Diploma, both of which require the Ethiopian Higher Education Entrance Qualification Certificate for entry and are offered at universities and colleges. The Diploma covers a variety of applied fields, including accounting, management, secretarial studies and computing, while the Advanced Diploma is offered only in engineering and technological fields. Total enrolment in the technical and vocational sector rose from 191,151 in 2006/07 to 371,347 in 2010/11 in 496 public and private institutions; also in that year female students accounted for 46% of the total student intake.

In an effort to improve the quality of higher education in Ethiopia a new bill was approved in June 2009 that built upon the 2003 Higher Education proclamation to oversee both state-controlled and private higher educational institutions. The Higher Education Proclamation 351 (Ethiopian Federal Ministry of Education, 2003) made provision for the creation of the Higher Education Relevance and Quality Agency (HERQA) and this was established in 2003 with the aim of safeguarding and enhancing the quality and relevance of higher education. The responsibilities of the HERQA include the pre-accreditation and accreditation of programmes at private higher education institutions; the conduct of external quality audits in all public and some private institutions; the development of draft benchmarks for selected subjects; and the establishment of courses that are of appropriate quality and relevance to employment and the development needs of the country. Although programme accreditation by HERQA is not mandatory, between 2006 and 2008 a total of 185 programmes at private institutions were granted pre-accreditation permits and 190 programmes were granted full accreditation.

Regulatory Bodies

GOVERNMENT

Ministry of Culture and Tourism: POB 2183, Addis Ababa; tel. (11) 5512310; e-mail info@tourismethiopia.org; internet www.tourismethiopia.gov.et; Minister Amin Abdulkadir.

Ministry of Education: POB 1367, Addis Ababa; tel. (11) 1553133; e-mail moe.heducation@yahoo.com; internet www.moe.gov.et; Minister Shiferaw Shigutie Wolassa.

Ministry of Science and Technology: POB 2490, Addis Ababa; tel. (11) 4661867; e-mail most@ethionet.et; internet www.most.gov.et; Minister Demitu Hambissa.

Learned Societies

GENERAL

UNESCO Office Addis Ababa: POB 1177, Addis Ababa; ECA Bldg, Menelik Ave, Addis Ababa; tel. (11) 5513953; e-mail addis@unesco.org; Dir Firmin E. Matoko.

AGRICULTURE, FISHERIES AND VETERINARY SCIENCE

Association for the Advancement of Agricultural Sciences in Africa: POB 30087, Addis Ababa; tel. (11) 5443536; f. 1968; promotes the devt and application of agricultural sciences and the exchange of ideas, encourages Africans to enter training, and holds seminars annually in different African countries; 1,200 mems (individual and institutional); library of 5,000 vols; Admin. Sec. Gen. Prof. M. El-Fouly (acting); publ. *African Journal of Agricultural Sciences*.

BIBLIOGRAPHY, LIBRARY SCIENCE AND MUSEOLOGY

Ethiopian Library and Information Association: POB 30530, Addis Ababa; tel. (11) 5518020; f. 1961; promotes the interests of libraries, archives, documentation centres, etc.; 200 mems; Pres. Tamirat Mota; Sec. Zinabie Mekonnen.

LANGUAGE AND LITERATURE

Alliance Française: Wavel St, POB 1733, Addis Ababa; tel. (11) 1550213; e-mail aef@allianceaddis.org; internet www.allianceaddis.org; offers courses and examinations in French language and culture and promotes cultural exchange with France; attached teaching centre in Dire Dawa.

British Council: POB 1043, Comoros St, Addis Ababa; tel. (11) 6620388; e-mail information@et.britishcouncil.org; internet www.britishcouncil.org/africa; offers courses and examinations in English language and British culture; promotes cultural exchange with the UK; library of 25,000 vols; Dir BARBARA WICKHAM.

Goethe-Institut: POB 1193, Addis Ababa; tel. (11) 1242345; e-mail vl@telecom.net.et; internet www.goethe.de/af/add/enindex.htm; f. 1962; offers courses and examinations in German language and culture and promotes cultural exchange with Germany; 1,500 mems; library of 4,000 vols, 10 periodicals; Head YONAS TAREKEGN.

MEDICINE

Ethiopian Medical Association: POB 2179, Addis Ababa; tel. (11) 5533742; e-mail ema.emj@telecom.net.et; f. 1961; Pres. Dr TELAHUM TEKA; publ. *Ethiopian Medical Journal* (4 a year).

Ethiopian Public Health Association: Dembel City Centre, POB 7117 Addis Ababa; tel. (11) 5540391; e-mail epha@ethionet.et; internet www.epha.org.et; f. 1989; promotes public health, prevention of diseases, timely treatment of the sick and rehabilitation of the disabled; Pres. Dr DAMEN HAILEMARIAM; Exec. Sec. Dr GETNET MITIKE; publ. *Ethiopian Journal of Health Development*.

NATURAL SCIENCES

Physical Sciences

Geophysical Observatory: Faculty of Science, Addis Ababa Univ., POB 1176, Addis Ababa; tel. (11) 1239477; internet www.sc.aau.edu.et/geophysical; f. 1958; research in seismology, gravity, tectonics, crustal deformation, geomagnetic observation and geodesy; library of 100 vols and 10 periodicals; Sec. Assoc. Prof. LAIKE M. ASFAW; publ. *Seismological Bulletin* (2 a year).

Research Institutes

AGRICULTURE, FISHERIES AND VETERINARY SCIENCE

Awasa Agriculture Research Centre: c/o Awasa Agricultural College, POB 6, Awasa; tel. (46) 2200224; e-mail arc@padis.gn.apc.org; f. 1967; soil and water management, crop protection, horticulture, field crops, agronomy and crop physiology, agricultural economics and farming systems, livestock, forestry; library of 2,300 vols, 28 journals; Man. DANIEL DAURO.

Ethiopian Institute of Agricultural Research: POB 2003, Addis Ababa; tel. (11) 6460137; e-mail infocom@eiar.gov.et; internet www.eiar.gov.et; f. 1966; agricultural mechanization, agronomy and crop physiology, animal feeds and nutrition, animal health, animal production, biotechnology, crop protection, field crops, forestry, horticulture, post-harvest technologies, soil and water management; financial aid provided by the Ethiopian govt and other sources; 50 research centres and stations nationally; library of 150,000 vols; Deputy Dir-Gen. Dr SOLOMON ASEFA; publs *Ethiopian Journal of Agricultural Economics, Ethiopian Journal of Agricultural Science, Ethiopian Journal of Animal Production, Pest Management Journal of Ethiopia*.

HISTORY, GEOGRAPHY AND ARCHAEOLOGY

Archaeological Institute: POB 76, Addis Ababa; Dir Dr BERHANOU ABBÉBÉ; publ. *Annales d'Ethiopie*.

Ethiopian Mapping Agency: POB 597, Addis Ababa; tel. (11) 5518445; e-mail ema@ethionet.net.et; internet www.ema.gov.net; f. 1955; attached to Min. of Economic Devt and Cooperation; conducts land surveying, mapping, remote sensing and geographical research; library of 3,000 vols; Dir-Gen. SULTAN MOHAMMED; publ. *Geo-Information Bulletin of Ethiopia* (2 a year).

NATURAL SCIENCES

Biological Sciences

Desert Locust Control Organization for Eastern Africa (DLCO EA): POB 4255, Addis Ababa; tel. (11) 6461477; e-mail dlc@telecom.net.et; f. 1962; library of 2,000 vols; Dir PETER ONYANGO ODIYO.

Institute of Biodiversity Conservation and Research: POB 30726, Addis Ababa; tel. (11) 6612244; e-mail bioresearch@telecom.net.et; internet www.telecom.net.et/~ibcr; f. 1998; promotes and carries out research into the devt and sustainable use of the country's biodiversity; Gen. Man. Dr ABEBE DEMISSIE.

National Herbarium: Biology Dept, Addis Ababa University, POB 3434, Addis Ababa; tel. (11) 1236760; e-mail info@bio.aau.edu.et; f. 1959; Keeper Prof. SEBSEBE DEMISSEW; Curator Dr ENSERMU KELBESSA; publ. *Flora of Ethiopia and Eritrea* (10 a year).

Physical Sciences

Geological Survey of Ethiopia: POB 2302, Addis Ababa; tel. (11) 6464482; e-mail geology.institute@telecom.net.et; internet www.geology.gov.et; f. 1968 as a Department within the Ministry of Mines; as Ethiopian Institute of Geological Surveys 1984; library of 66,877 vols; Gen. Man. MASRESHA GEBRESILASSIE; Chief Geologist HUNDE MELKA.

RELIGION, SOCIOLOGY AND ANTHROPOLOGY

Institute of Ethiopian Studies: Addis Ababa University, POB 1176, Addis Ababa; tel. (11) 1119469; e-mail ies.aau@telecom.net.et; internet www.ies-ethiopia.org; f. 1963; conducts, promotes and coordinates research and publication on Ethiopian Studies with special emphasis on the humanities and cultural studies; operates an advanced study and documentation centre and an ethnological-historical museum: see under Museums and Art Galleries; library: see under Libraries and Archives; Dir ELIZABETH W. GIORGIS (acting); publs *IES Bulletin* (4 a year), *Journal of Ethiopian Studies* (2 a year).

Libraries and Archives

Addis Ababa

Addis Ababa University Libraries: POB 1176, Addis Ababa; tel. (11) 1239720; internet www.aau.edu.et/index.php/academics/aau-libraries; f. 1950; consists of the main University library and six br. libraries: the Science Library, Technology North Library (Amist Kilo campus), Technology South Library (Lideta Campus), Faculty of Business and Economics Library, Central Medical Library and Law Library; 500,000 vols, 632 microfiches, 3,000 serial titles and an electronic journals database, colln incl. 90,000 vols on Ethiopia; Librarian Dr TAYE TADESSE.

British Council Knowledge and Learning Services: POB 1043, Artistic Bldg, Adwa Ave, Addis Ababa; tel. (11) 1550022; e-mail kls@et.britishcouncil.org; f. 1959; 51,000 vols, 137 periodicals; Librarian Ato MULUGETA HUNDE.

Ethiopia National Archives and Library Agency: POB 717, Addis Ababa; tel. (11) 5516532; e-mail nale@ethionet.et; internet www.nale.gov.et; f. 1944; incl. archives repository and research, Ethiopian studies and MSS division, legal deposit and copyright registration, microfilm and microfiche library, reference, documentation and periodical div.; 164,000 vols; Dir-Gen. ATIKILT ASSEFA.

Institute of Ethiopian Studies Library: Addis Ababa University, POB 1176, Addis Ababa; tel. (11) 1550844; e-mail girmajem@ies.aau.edu.et; internet www.ies-ethiopia.org/indexf.htm; f. 1963; colln of printed and non-printed materials on Ethiopia, Somalia, Djibouti, Red Sea, Indian Ocean, Sudan; 110,000 vols, 9,000 MSS; Librarian GIRMA JEMANEH.

Museums and Art Galleries

Addis Ababa

Museum of the Institute of Ethiopian Studies: Univ. of Addis Ababa, POB 1176, Addis Ababa; tel. (11) 1550844; e-mail ies.aau@telecom.net.et; internet www.ies-ethiopia.org; f. 1963; Curator AHMED ZEKARIA.

National Museum of Ethiopia: POB 76, Addis Ababa; tel. (11) 1119113; collns of early hominid fossils, incl. 'Lucy', a nearly complete skeleton of *Australopithecus afarensis*; Dir MAMITU YILMA.

Universities

ADDIS ABABA UNIVERSITY

POB 1176, Addis Ababa
Telephone: (11) 1239800
Internet: www.aau.edu.et
Founded 1950 as Univ. College of Addis Ababa, present status 1961, current name adopted 1975
State control
Language of instruction: English
Academic year: September to July

Pres.: Prof. ANDREAS ESHETÉ
Vice-Pres. for Business and Devt: Ato MOHAMMED HABIB
Assoc. Vice-Pres. for Academic Affairs and External Relations Officer: Dr BUTTE GOTU
Assoc. Vice-Pres. for Continuing and Distance Education Programmes: Dr MEKONEN DISASA
Assoc. Vice-Pres. for Research and Graduate Programmes: Prof. ENDASHAW BEKELE
Registrar: Dr ZEMEDE ASFAW
Librarian: Dr TAYE TADESSE

Library of 493,000 vols
Number of teachers: 948
Number of students: 15,364

Publications: *Ethiopian Journal of Development Research, Ethiopian Journal of Education, Register of Current Research on Ethiopia and the Horn of Africa, SINET: An Ethiopian Journal of Science*

DEANS

College of Social Sciences: Dr BEKELE GUTEMA
Faculty of Business and Economics: Dr MULAT DEMEKE
Faculty of Education: Ato AKALU GETANEH
Faculty of Informatics: Ato GETACHEW JEMANEH
Faculty of Law: Ato GETACHEW ABERA
Faculty of Medicine: Dr ZUFAN LAKEW
Faculty of Science: Prof. GEZAHEGN YIRGU
Faculty of Technology: Dr ABEBE DINKU
Faculty of Veterinary Medicine: Dr MERGA BEKANA
Institute of Language Studies: Dr GEREMEW LEMU
School of Pharmacy: Dr TSIGE GEBREMARIAM

BAHIR DAR UNIVERSITY

POB 79, Bahir Dar
Telephone: (58) 2200137
E-mail: infobdu@gmail.com
Internet: www.bdu.edu.et
Founded 2000 by merger of Bahir Dar Teachers' College and Bahir Dar Polytechnic Institute
public control
Language of instruction: English
Academic year: September to June
Pres.: Assoc. Prof. BAYLIE DAMTIE
Vice-Pres. for Academic Affairs: Asst Prof. FIREW TEGEGNE
Vice-Pres. for Business and Devt: Assoc. Prof. G. EGZIABHER KAHSAY
Vice-Pres. for Information and Strategic Communication: Asst Prof. FANTAHUN AYELE
Number of teachers: 1,314
Number of students: 34,972
Publications: *Journal of Law*, *Journal of Social Science*, *The Ethiopian Journal of Science and Technology*

DEANS

College of Agriculture and Environmental Science: Assoc. Prof. ZELEKE MEKURIAW
College of Business and Economics: TESFAYE MELAKU
College of Medical and Health Science: Asst Prof. WORKU BELAY
College of Science: Asst Prof. ASSEFA SERGAWE

HARAMAYA UNIVERSITY

POB 138, Dire Dawa
Telephone: (25) 5530319
E-mail: talamirew@haramaya.edu.et
Internet: www.haramaya.edu.et
Founded 1952, university status 1985
State control
Language of instruction: English
Academic year: September to June
Pres.: Prof. BELAY KASSA
Vice-Pres. for Academic Affairs: Dr TENA ALAMIREW
Vice-Pres. for Admin. and Student Affairs: Dr BELAINEH LEGESSE
Vice-Pres. for Research: Dr NIGUSSIE DECHASA
Registrar: Dr DESSALEGNE CHEMEDA
Librarian: YARED MAMO
Number of teachers: 960
Number of students: 31,119 (13,548 full-time, 17,571 evening, distance-education, summer in-service)
Publications: *Alemaya Annual Research Report*, *East African Journal of Sciences*, *The Alemayan*

DEANS

College of Agriculture and Environmental Sciences: Dr KINDIE TESFAYE
College of Computing and Informatics: ADEM KEDIR
College of Continuing and Distance Education: Dr TEGEGN SINISHAW
College of Economics and Business: MULUGETA DEMIE
College of Health Sciences: BIFTU GEDA
College of Law: GIZACHEW ADMASU
College of Medical Sciences: TEKABE ABDOSH
College of Natural and Computational Sciences: Dr ABI TADESSE
College of Social Sciences and Humanities: JEYLAN WOLIYE
College of Veterinary Medicine: Dr DESTA BEYENE
Institute of Technology: Dr SOLOMON WORKU
School of Graduate Studies: Dr YOSEF MEKASHA

HAWASSA UNIVERSITY

POB 5, Hawassa
Telephone: (46) 2200221
E-mail: info@hu.edu.et
Internet: hu.edu.et
Founded 2000 as Debub Univ. by merger of Hawassa College of Agriculture, Dilla College of Teachers' Education and Health Science and Wondo Genet College of Forestry, current name adopted 2006
State control
Faculties of business and economics, hotel management and tourism, law, medicine, natural sciences, public health, social sciences, technology, veterinary medicine; colleges of agriculture, forestry, health sciences, teachers' education
Pres.: Dr ADMASU TSEGAYE
Library of 200,000 vols
Number of teachers: 963
Number of students: 20,000

JIMMA UNIVERSITY

POB 378, Jimma
Telephone: (47) 1112202
E-mail: ero@ju.edu.et
Internet: www.ju.edu.et
Founded 1999 through merger of Jimma College of Agriculture (f. 1952) and Jimma Institute of Health Sciences (f. 1983)
Pres.: Asst Prof. DAMTEW MARIAM
Vice-Pres. for Academics and Research: Asst Prof. SOLOMON MOGUS
Vice-Pres. for Admin. and Devt: KORA TUSHUNE
Vice-Pres. for Training and Health Services: ABRAHAM AMLAK
Dean of Students: EWNETU SEID
Registrar: Dr SOLOMON GENET
Head of External Relations Office: Assoc. Prof. CHALLI JIRA
Head of Library and Documentation Service: GETACHEW BAYISA
Number of teachers: 370
Number of students: 16,279

DEANS

College of Agriculture, Ambo: EYLACHEW ZEWDIE
College of Agriculture, Jimma: BERHANU BELAY
Faculty of Business: Asst Prof. SOLOMON ALEMU
Faculty of Education: ZELALEM TESHOME
Faculty of Medical Sciences: Asst Prof. MINAS TSADIK
Faculty of Public Health: Asst Prof. KIFLE MIKAEL
Faculty of Science and Liberal Arts: TAREKEGN BIRHANU
Faculty of Technology: ADMASSU SHIMELES
School of Graduate Studies: Prof. MEKONNEN ASSEFA

UNIVERSITY OF MEKELLE

POB 231, Mekelle, Tigray Region
Telephone: (34) 4407500
Adi-Haqi Campus: POB 451, Mekelle, Tigray Region
Telephone: (34) 4407600
Aider Campus: POB 1871 Mekelle, Tigray Region
Telephone: (34) 4416690
E-mail: mekelle.university@telecom.net.et
Internet: www.mu.edu.et
State control
Founded 2000
Library of 200,000 vols, 18 periodical titles
Pres.: Prof. MITUKU HAILE
Vice-Pres. for Academics: Dr KINDEYA GEBREHIWOT
Vice-Pres. for Research and Community Service: Dr ABDELKADIR KEDIR
Vice-Pres. for Support Services: Dr YASIN IBRAHIM
Librarian: Dr HAGOS
Number of teachers: 1,119
Number of students: 16,470
Publications: *Journal of Drylands* (2 a year), *Momona Ethiopian Journal of Science* (2 a year)

DEANS

College of Business and Economics: Dr ZAID NEGASH
College of Dry Land Agriculture and Natural Resources: Dr GIRMAY TESFAY
College of Engineering: Dr GEBREMESKEL KAHSAY
College of Law and Governance: FANA HAGOS
College of Medicine: Dr ABDELKADIR M.SEID
College of Natural and Computational Sciences: Dr ALEM ABREHA
College of Social Science and Languages: Dr ASSEFA ABEGAZ
College of Veterinary Science: Dr GEBREHIWOT TADESSE

College

Yared Music School: POB 30097, Addis Ababa; tel. (11) 1550166; f. 1967; attached to Addis Ababa Univ.; 130 students; Head TEKLE YOHANES ZIKE.

FIJI

The Higher Education System

The supra-national University of the South Pacific maintains two of its 14 campuses in Fiji (one in the capital, Suva, and the other in Labasa on the northern island of Vanua Levu). In 2014 there were 20,437 students at the university and its extension centres. The privately owned University of Fiji was established in Lautoka on the western side of Viti Levu in 2004; the University, which offers a variety of courses up to postgraduate level, has four centres of excellence and is governed by the University of Fiji Council. In January 2010 six public higher education institutions—the Fiji Institute of Technology, the Fiji School of Medicine, the Fiji School of Nursing, the Fiji College of Advanced Education, the Lautoka Teachers College and the Fiji College of Agriculture—merged to form the Fiji National University (FNU). In early 2011 the Training and Productivity Authority of Fiji was also incorporated into the new university. The campuses of the FNU, which is the largest university in Fiji, are located in various towns around the country and offer a wide range of programmes (mainly orientated towards technical and vocational training) from certificate to postgraduate degrees. In 2009 there were 69 vocational and technical institutions (with 2,387 enrolled students). In the same year Fiji had four teacher-training colleges (with 633 students).

The Fiji School Leaving Certificate and Form Seven Examination are the main criteria for admission to higher education. The undergraduate Bachelors degree usually lasts for three years (although the medicine course is of six years' duration), the postgraduate Masters degree for one to two years and the Doctorate for at least two years following award of the Masters. Post-secondary vocational and technical training is offered by the country's three universities and by several other institutes of professional training and vocational education. The main qualifications are the Certificate and Diploma.

Following the implementation of the Higher Education Promulgation law in 2008, a six-member Higher Education Commission was appointed by the Minister of Education in January 2010. From that date any new higher education institution was required to seek the recognition of the Commission in order officially to be registered. By 2012 65 institutes of higher education were recognized by the Commission. Also in 2012 the Fiji Qualifications Framework was put into place.

Regulatory Body

GOVERNMENT

Ministry of Education, National Heritage, Culture and Arts: Marela House, Thurston St, PMB, Suva; tel. 3314477; internet www.education.gov.fj; Minister FILIPE BOLE.

ACCREDITATION

Fiji Higher Education Commission: Red Cross Bldg, 22 Gorrie St, Suva; tel. 3100031; internet www.fhec.gov.fj; f. 2010; devt and promotion of higher education in Fiji; advises the Min. of Education; regulates the operation of higher education institutions; establishes nat. standards for different qualifications; Dir SALOTE RABUKA; Registrar RAJENDRA PRASAD.

Learned Societies

GENERAL

Gandhi-Tappoo Centre for Writing, Ethics and Peace Studies: PMB, Saweni, Lautoka; tel. 6640600; internet www.unifiji.ac.fj/gandhi; attached to Univ. of Fiji; teaches writing, ethics and peace studies; funding from individuals, asscns, instns, org, foundations, govts to carry out the activities of the centre through research, writing, public lectures, publs, seminars, confs and community involvement; promotes civic education and welfare of women and children through cross-cultural research and intercultural communication; Chair. SURESH LAL TAPPOO; Dir SATENDRA PRATAP NANDAN.

ECONOMICS, LAW AND POLITICS

Citizens' Constitutional Forum: POB 12584, Suva; 23 Denison Rd, Suva; tel. 3308379; e-mail ccf@kidanet.net.fj; internet www.ccf.org.fj; f. 1987; community education and advocacy on Fiji's constitution, democracy, human rights and multiculturalism; Chair. TESSA MACKENZIE; CEO Rev. AKUILA YABAKI.

Ecumenical Centre for Research Education and Advocacy: GPOB 15473, Suva; tel. 3307588; e-mail info@ecrea.org.fj; internet www.ecrea.org.fj; f. 1990 as Fiji Institute of Contextual Theology, current name adopted 2001; addresses social, religious, economic and political issues that confront Fiji; conducts programmes on 3 issues: economic justice, faith and society and youth peace and devt; Exec. Dir JOSEPH CAMILLO.

LANGUAGE AND LITERATURE

Alliance Française: POB 14548, Suva; tel. 3313802; e-mail info@af-fiji.org.fj; internet www.af-fiji.org.fj; f. 1987; offers courses and exams in French language and culture; promotes cultural exchange with France; br. in Saweni, Univ. of Fiji; Dir ERIC DAVIAS; Pres. MALINI RAGHWAN.

MEDICINE

Fiji Medical Association: POB 1116, Suva; 304 Waimanu Rd, Suva; tel. 3315388; e-mail fma@unwired.com.fj; internet www.fijimedassoc.webnode.com; f. 1953; holds confs and seminars; collective voice of medical practitioners; 215 mems; Pres. Dr IFEREIMI WAQAINABETE; Sec. Dr REAPI MATAIKA; Treas. Dr AKUILA NAQASIMA; publ. *Fiji Medical Journal* (4 a year).

Research Institutes

AGRICULTURE, FISHERIES AND VETERINARY SCIENCE

Sugar Research Institute of Fiji: POB 3560, Lautoka; tel. 7761839; e-mail sanjayn@srif.org.fj; internet www.srif.net.fj; f. 2006; Finance and Admin. Man. SANJAY PRAKASH.

NATURAL SCIENCES

Physical Sciences

Centre for Climate Change, Environment, Energy and Sustainable Development (CEESD): PMB, Lautoka; tel. 6640600; internet www.unifiji.ac.fj/centres.htm; attached to Univ. of Fiji; research and analysis of emerging issues in renewable energy and climate change; assists govts in key areas such as fulfilling reporting obligations under regional and int. environment conventions and treaties; offers postgraduate programmes and research opportunities in strategic areas incl. natural resource management and climate change; Dir MAHENDRA KUMAR.

SPC Applied Geoscience and Technology Division (SOPAC): PMB, GPO, Suva; 241 Mead Rd, Nabua, Suva; tel. 3381377; e-mail director@sopac.org; internet www.sopac.org; f. 2011; Dir RUSSELL HOWORTH.

Libraries and Archives

Lautoka

Western Regional Library: POB 150, Lautoka; 270 Tavewa Ave, Lautoka; tel. 6660091; f. 1964.

Suva

Library Service of Fiji: POB 2526, Govt Bldgs, Suva; 64 Ratu Sukuna Rd, Nasese, Suva; tel. 3315344; internet www.education.gov.fj/core_7.aspx; f. 1964; attached to Min. of Education; public spec. and school library service; 12 e-community learning centres, 1 mobile library, 28 school media centres, 40 govt dept libraries; operates free library services in Lautoka, Rakiraki, Tavua, Labasa and Savusavu; 1.5m. vols; Dir SOKOVETI TUIMOALA.

National Archives of Fiji: POB 2125, Govt Bldgs, Suva; 25 Carnarvon St, Suva; tel. 3304144; e-mail archives@govnet.gov.fj; internet www.info.gov.fj/archives.html; f.

1954 as the Central Archives of Fiji and the Western Pacific High Comm., current name adopted 1970; attached to Min. of Information; official repository for permanent records of Govt of Fiji and of materials printed or published in Fiji; govt records since 1871; Anglican and Methodist church records since 1835; 1m.; 15,000 vols of monographs on the S Pacific, files on local newspapers since 1869, Fiji official publs since 1874, 3,800 reels of microfilm; Prin. Archivist SETAREKI TALE; Librarian SALESIA IKANIWAI.

Suva City Library: POB 176, Suva; tel. 3313433; f. 1909, fmrly Carnegie Library, current name adopted 1953; 77,000 vols (48,000 in children's library, 29,000 in adults' library), 25 periodicals; Chief Librarian HUMESH PRASAD.

Museum

Suva

Fiji Museum: POB 2023, Govt Bldgs, Suva; tel. 3315944; e-mail fijimuseum@kidanet.net.fj; internet www.fijimuseum.org.fj; f. 1904; archaeological, ethnological and historical collns of Fiji; archives of Fijian oral traditions; photographic archives; Chair. IQBAL JANNIF; Dir SAGALE BUADROMO; publ. *Domodomo* (2 a year).

Universities

FIJI NATIONAL UNIVERSITY

POB 7222, Nasinu
Kings Rd, Nasinu
Telephone: 3394000
E-mail: vc@fnu.ac.fj
Internet: www.fnu.ac.fj

Founded 2009 by merger of Fiji Institute of Technology, Fiji School of Medicine, Fiji School of Nursing, Fiji College of Advanced Education, Lautoka Teachers College, Fiji College of Agriculture and Training and Productivity Authority of Fiji
State control
Language of instruction: English
Academic year: January to December

Vice-Chancellor: Dr GANESH CHAND
Chief Librarian: TANVEER HAIDER NAQVI

Library of 30,000 vols in College of Medicine Nursing and Health Sciences Library

DEANS

College of Agriculture, Fisheries and Forestry: Prof. PARAS NATH
College of Business, Hospitality and Tourism Studies: Dr MAHENDRA REDDY
College of Engineering, Science and Technology: Dr JOSUA T. K. MATAIKA (acting)
College of Humanities and Education: Dr ECI NABALARUA
College of Medicine, Nursing and Health Sciences: Prof. IAN ROUSE

UNIVERSITY OF FIJI

PMB, Saweni, Lautoka
Telephone: 6640600
E-mail: info@unifiji.ac.fj
Internet: www.unifiji.ac.fj

Founded 2004
Private control
Language of instruction: English
Academic year: February to November

Chancellor: RATU EPELI NAILATIKAU
Pro-Chancellor: ANIL TIKARAM (acting)
Vice-Chancellor: Prof. RICHARD COLL (acting)
Registrar: KAMLESH ARYA
Univ. Librarian: JOSE A. POULOSE

Library of 18,000 vols
Number of teachers: 80
Number of students: 1,300

Publications: *Asia-Pacific Journal of Education, Business and Society*, *The University of Fiji Law Journal*

DEANS

School of Business and Economics: (vacant)
School of Humanities and Arts: Dr WAHAB ALI
School of Law: SALVIN NAND
School of Science and Technology: (vacant)
Umanand Prasad School of Medicine: Prof. ALTAISAIKHAN KHASAG

UNIVERSITY OF THE SOUTH PACIFIC

Laucala Campus, Suva
Telephone: 3231000
E-mail: studentinfo@usp.ac.fj
Internet: www.usp.ac.fj

Founded 1968
State control
Language of instruction: English
Academic year: February to November (2 semesters)

Pro Chancellor: FIAME NAOMI MATA'AFA
Vice-Chancellor and Pres.: Prof. RAJESH CHANDRA
Deputy Vice-Chancellor for Admin. and Regional Campuses: Dr ESTHER WILLIAMS (acting)
Deputy Vice-Chancellor for Learning, Teaching and Student Services: Prof. Dr SUSAN A. KELLY
Pro-Vice-Chancellor for Planning and Quality: Dr MICHAEL GREGORY
Pro-Vice-Chancellor for Research and Int. Affairs: Prof. JOHN BYTHELL
Registrar: WALTER FRASER
Librarian: SIN JOAN YEE

Library: 1m. vols, 30,000 full text titles
Number of teachers: 1,159
Number of students: 20,437 (948 postgraduate)

Publications: *Alafua Agricultural Bulletin*, *Directions: Journal of Educational Studies*, *Journal of Pacific Studies*, *MANA*, *South Pacific Journal of Natural and Applied Sciences* (1 a year), *SSED Review* (4 a year)

DEANS

Faculty of Arts, Law and Education: Dr AKANISI KEDRAYATE
Faculty of Business and Economics: Prof. BIMAN CHAND PRASAD
Faculty of Science, Technology and Environment: Dr ANJEELA JOKHAN

PROFESSORS

BHASKARA, R., Economics
CAMPBELL, I., History and Politics
GASKELL, I., Literature and Language
HASSALL, G., Governance
HUGHES, R., Law
MEAKINS, R., Biology
NUNN, P., Oceanic Geoscience
OMLIN, C., Computer Science
ONWOBOLU, G., Engineering
PATHAK, R., Management
PETERSON, R., Banking
SHARMA, M. D., Banking
SOTHEESWARAN, S., Organic Chemistry
SUBRAMANI, Literature and Language
THAMAN, R., Pacific Island Biogeography
WHITE, M., Accounting and Financial Management
ZANN, L., Marine Studies

FINLAND

The Higher Education System

The higher education system consists of two parallel systems, universities and ammattikorkeakoulut (AMKs, polytechnics or, as they are sometimes termed in English, universities of applied sciences): universities focus on academic teaching and research while polytechnics specialize in professional and vocational training. The structure of the degree system is the same in both sectors. There are 14 universities and 25 polytechnics. The oldest university is the Kuvataideakatemia (Academy of Fine Arts), which was founded in 1848. In 2009 student enrolments were as follows: polytechnics 135,033; universities 168,475. In 2010 a total of 303,554 students were enrolled in tertiary education.

All universities are state-owned and are administered by the Ministry of Education and Culture's Department for Higher Education and Science Policy. University-level education is currently free but students may be required to pay for extraneous services, such as health care and compulsory membership of the Student's Union. Under the 1997 Universities Act, universities are obliged to promote free research and provide free education. However, the Organisation for Economic Cooperation and Development suggested in 2010 that students be charged tuition fees as part of a number of reforms to help Finland out of economic recession. Other suggestions include replacing grants with repayable loans and speeding up the admissions system by standardizing university entrance requirements. Universities have enjoyed relative autonomy in decision-making, based on three-year performance agreements with the Ministry of Education and Culture. Government funding used to account for about 64% of university budgets, with the rest coming from the Academy of Finland, the Technology Development Centre Tekes, business enterprises, the European Union (EU) and other public bodies. The amended Universities Act of July 2009 (which came into effect in January 2010) further extended the autonomy of universities by giving them an independent legal personality, either as a public corporation or as a foundation under private law, with university staff no longer being employed by the State. The Government would continue to provide core funding (in the form of monthly payments to be managed by the universities themselves), with the universities responsible for acquiring additional finance. In addition, the new legislation required at least 40% of university board members to be appointed from outside the universities and ruled that university rectors, who had previously been elected by the professors, other staff and students, would in future be appointed by the board. Furthermore, the amended Act saw the creation of the new Aalto University through a merger between three existing institutions (further mergers were envisaged in the near future), and, controversially, permitted universities to charge tuition fees for students from outside the EU and European Economic Area.

The current polytechnic system was established during the 1990s to create a non-university higher education sector and was in place by 2000. The polytechnics were founded through mergers of institutions that had previously provided higher vocational training and, in contrast to the government-funded and -controlled university sector, AMKs are municipal or private institutions authorized by the Government. Funding of public polytechnics is shared between central government and local government, although they may also have other sources of external funding. Polytechnics follow three-year performance agreements made with the Ministry of Education and Culture.

Admission to both universities and polytechnics is on the basis of completed secondary education and entrance examinations. University admission is subject to the Universities Decree (115/1998), while admission to polytechnics is governed by the Polytechnic Studies Act (351/2003). In 2005 a two-tier Bachelors and Masters degree system was formally introduced in both universities and polytechnics, in accordance with the Bologna Process (although a two-tier system had been in place since 1993). The traditional Finnish credit system was replaced with the European Credit Transfer System (ECTS) in 2005. The university Bachelors degree lasts for three years and students must accrue 180 ECTS credits; the university Masters degree is a two-year course following completion of the Bachelors and requiring at least 120 ECTS credits. The polytechnic Bachelors requires 180–240 ECTS credits over three-and-a-half to four years, and the polytechnic Masters 60–90 ECTS credits in one to one-and-a-half years. (Admission to the polytechnic Masters requires a polytechnic Bachelors and at least three years' professional experience.) In dentistry and medicine the old-style degree system remains in place. In these subject areas the first degree is the Lisensiaatti or Licentiate, which requires 300–360 ECTS credits and takes five to six years. Students who have received the Masters may take the Tohtori or Doctorate, which lasts at least four years. In certain subjects, particularly the sciences, the Bachelors gives direct access to doctoral programmes. Students of medicine and dentistry can begin their doctoral studies directly after completion of the Lisensiaatti/Licentiate.

The entire Finnish system of vocational education and training was reformed in the late 1990s. In addition to the technical and vocational education offered by polytechnics there is also an apprenticeship scheme combining workplace and classroom learning.

The Finnish Higher Education Evaluation Council (FINHEEC), which operates under the auspices of the Ministry of Education and Culture, is responsible for carrying out audits of the quality assurance systems of the country's higher education institutions. The audits are performed on a registration basis. Many institutions have already been accredited and FINHEEC aimed to audit all institutions by 2012.

Regulatory and Representative Bodies

GOVERNMENT

Department for Higher Education and Science Policy: POB 29, 00023 Helsinki; tel. (29) 5330004; e-mail kirjaamo@minedu.fi; internet www.minedu.fi/opm/ministerioe_ja_hallinnonala/osastot_ja_yksikoet/korkeakoulu_ja_tiedepolitiikan_osasto/index.html?lang=en; f. 1809; attached to Min. of Education and Culture; divs of higher education policy, science policy, information management; responsible for matters relating to univs, polytechnics and research; Dir-Gen. TAPIO KOSUNEN; Sec. SATU SALONEN.

Ministry of Education and Culture: POB 29, 00023 Helsinki; Meritullinkatu 10, 00170 Helsinki; tel. (9) 5330004; e-mail kirjaamo@minedu.fi; internet www.minedu.fi; Minister of Culture and Housing PIA VIITANEN; Minister of Education and Science KRISTA KIURU.

Tutkimus ja Innovaationeuvosto (Research and Innovation Council): POB 29, 00023 Helsinki; Meritullinkatu 10, 00171 Helsinki; tel. (29) 5330381; e-mail tin@minedu.fi; internet www.minedu.fi/opm/tiede/tutkimus-_ja_innovaationeuvosto/?lang=en; f. 2009; Chair. THE PRIME MINISTER OF FINLAND; Sec.-Gen. ANSSI MÄLKKI.

ACCREDITATION

ENIC/NARIC Finland: Opetushallitus/Utbildningsstyrelsen, Finnish Nat. Board of Education, Hakaniemenranta 6, POB 380, 00531 Helsinki; tel. (29) 5331000; e-mail recognition@oph.fi; internet www.oph.fi/recognition; Counsellor of Education, Head of Unit Dr CARITA BLOMQVIST.

FUNDING

Tekes/Teknologian ja Innovaatioiden Kehittämiskeskus (Finnish Funding Agency for Technology and Innovation): POB 69, 00101 Helsinki; Kyllikinportti 2, Länsi-Pasila, 00101 Helsinki; tel. (29) 5055000; e-mail kirjaamo@tekes.fi; internet www.tekes.fi; f. 1983; funding org. for research and devt projects run by private enterprise, research institutes and univs; encourages cooperation between differing fields of technology; assists companies in research; has technology devt depts at 14 regional Employment and Economic Devt Centres (known as the TE Centres); offices in Beijing, Brussels, Tokyo, Silicon Valley, Shanghai and Washington, DC; Dir-Gen. PEKKA SOINI.

NATIONAL BODIES

Arene ry/Ammattikorkeakoulujen rehtorineuvosto (Rectors' Conference of Finnish Universities of Applied Sciences): Pohjoinen Makasiinikatu 7 A 2, 00130 Helsinki; tel. (9) 61299230; internet www.arene.fi; represents all the rectors of the Finnish Univs of Applied Sciences; aims to strengthen the dual system and professional higher education in Finland; Exec. Dir TIMO LUOPAJÄRVI.

CIMO Kansainvälisen liikkuvuuden ja yhteistyön keskus (Centre for International Mobility): POB 343, 00531 Helsinki; Hakaniemenranta 6, 00531 Helsinki; tel. (9) 5338500; e-mail cimoinfo@cimo.fi; internet www.cimo.fi; f. 1991; attached to Min. of Education and Culture; administers scholarship and exchange programmes; responsible for implementing EU education, training, culture and youth programmes in Finland; offers training, information, advisory services and publs; promotes and organizes int. trainee exchanges; Dir-Gen. PASI SAHLBERG.

Korkeakoulujen arviointineuvosto (KKA) (Finnish Higher Education Evaluation Council (FINHEEC)): POB 133, Meritullinkatu 1, 00171 Helsinki; tel. (29) 5330072; e-mail finheec@minedu.fi; internet www.finheec.fi; f. 1995; assists higher education instns and the Min. of Education and Culture in evaluation; carries out audits of higher education instns and other evaluations; Sec.-Gen. Dr HELKA KEKÄLÄINEN.

Opetushallitus Utbildningsstyrelsen (Finnish National Board of Education): POB 380, 00531 Helsinki; Hakaniemenranta 6, 00530 Helsinki; tel. (29) 5331000; e-mail kirjaamo@oph.fi; internet www.oph.fi; f. 1991 by merger of Nat. Board of General Education and Nat. Board of Vocational Education; responsible for the devt of education in Finland; draws up core curricula for basic and upper secondary education, and the framework for vocational qualifications and competence-based qualifications; evaluates learning results and improves the efficiency of training; Dir-Gen. AULIS PITKÄLÄ.

Suomen yliopistot UNIFI ry (Universities Finland UNIFI): Pohjoinen Makasiinikatu 7 A 2, 00130 Helsinki; tel. (50) 5229421; e-mail unifi@unifi.fi; internet www.unifi.fi; f. 1969 as Finnish Ccl of Univ. Rectors, current name adopted 2010; promotes cooperation between univs and helps them to achieve their common strategic goals; works with political decision makers, nat. authorities, mins and central interest groups to advance research and higher education; strengthens role of univs as key partners in social and political discussion; promotes int. cooperation between univs, esp. in the Nordic countries, Europe and Asia; 15 mems; Exec. Dir Dr LEENA TREUTHARDT.

Learned Societies

GENERAL

Elintarviketieteiden Seura ry (Finnish Society of Food Science and Technology): POB 115, 00241 Helsinki; Pasilankatu 2, 00241 Helsinki; tel. (9) 5474700; e-mail info@ets.fi; internet www.ets.fi; f. 1947; promotes and develops scientific and technological research and education on the food chain; 1,200 mems; Pres. EILA JÄRVENPÄÄ; Sec. ANNA KOJO; publ. *Kehittyvä Elintarvike* (6 a year).

Liikuntatieteellinen Seura (Finnish Society of Sport Sciences): Olympiastadion, Eteläkaarre, 00250 Helsinki; tel. (10) 7786600; e-mail toimisto@lts.fi; internet www.lts.fi; f. 1933; attached to Min. of Education and Culture; promotes Finnish sports, health and wellbeing through physical sciences; disseminates information pertaining to sport; holds seminars and discussion events; carries out surveys and compiles summaries; 903 individual mems, 15 institutional mems; Pres. Prof. ANTTI UUTELA; Exec. Dir Dr KARI L. KESKINEN; publ. *Motion-Sport in Finland* (2 a year).

Mevi ry/Eliisa Vainikka (Finnish Association for Media and Communication Studies): c/o Univ. of Tampere, Virta 320, 33014 Tampere; tel. (50) 3589218; internet www.uta.fi/jarjestot/toy/yhteystiedot.php; 500 mems; Pres. SINIKKA TORKKOLA; Sec. and Treas. ELIISA VAINIKKA; publ. *Media & viestintä* (4 a year).

Societas Scientiarum Fennica/Suomen Tiedeseura (Finnish Society of Sciences and Letters): Fabianinkatu 4 B 16, 2nd Fl., 00130 Helsinki; tel. (9) 633005; e-mail societas@scientiarum.fi; internet www.scientiarum.fi; f. 1838; promotes science and the humanities by arranging public lectures, seminars and symposia; publishing scientific literature; awarding grants and prizes; promoting contacts within the scientific community; offering mems possibilities for interdisciplinary contacts; 357 mems; Chair. Prof. MARIANNE STENIUS; Permanent Sec. Prof. CARL G. GAHMBERG; Treas. Prof. DAN-OLOF RISKA; publs *Commentationes Humanarum Litterarum*, *Commentationes Scientiarum Socialium*, *Sphinx-Årsbok-Vuosikirja* (1 a year).

Suomalainen Tiedeakatemia (Finnish Academy of Science and Letters): Mariankatu 5, 00170 Helsinki; tel. (9) 636800; e-mail acadsci@acadsci.fi; internet www.acadsci.fi; f. 1908; promotes scientific and scholarly research; organizes lectures, discussions, meetings; awards grants; publishes scientific papers; 866 mems (incl. 687 ordinary mems, 179 foreign mems); Chair. JORMA SIPILÄ; Sec.-Gen. OLLI MARTIO; Treas. PEKKA ILMAKUNNAS; publs *Annales Academiae Scientiarum Fennicae* (Mathematica, Geologica-Geographica and Humaniora), *Folklore Fellows' Communications*.

Suomen Aktuaariyhdistys ry (Actuarial Society of Finland): Valliuksenkatu 8, 21100 Naantali; e-mail secretary@actuary.fi; internet www.actuary.fi; f. 1922; promotes insurance sciences and actuarial mathematics; 300 mems; Pres. LAURI SARASTE; Sec. SARI ROPPONEN.

Suomen Arkkitehtiliiton (Finnish Association of Architects): Runeberginkatu 5, 00100 Helsinki; tel. (9) 584448; e-mail safa@safa.fi; internet www.safa.fi; f. 1892; supervises professional standards; works to influence architectural legislation; 3,100 mems; Chair. ESKO RAUTIOLA; Sec.-Gen. PAULA HUOTELIN; publs *ark—Finnish Architectural Review* (6 a year), *Journal of Architectural Competitions* (irregular).

Suomen Kaupunkitutkimuksen Seura (Finnish Society for Urban Studies): Tieteiden talo, Kirkkokatu 6, 00170 Helsinki; e-mail skts@kaupunkitutkimuksenseura.fi; internet www.kaupunkitutkimuksenseura.fi; f. 1999; promotes interdisciplinary urban research; functions as an academic forum for scholars; increases appreciation of urban studies; organizes symposia, confs and public discussions; cooperation with foreign univs and clubs; 85 mems; Pres. ANJA KERVANTO NEVANLINNA; Sec. MATTI HANNIKAINEN.

Suomen Naistutkimuksen Seura (Association for Women's Studies in Finland): Univ. of Helsinki, POB 59, 00014 Helsinki; e-mail maiju.parviainen@uef.fi; internet www.nt-suns.org; f. 1988; attached to Univ. of Helsinki; promotes and supports women's studies; organizes seminars, confs; 600 mems; Chair. TUIJA PULKKINEN; Sec. VENLA OIKKONEN; publ. *Naistutkimus—Kvinnoforskning* (4 a year, in Finnish and Swedish).

Suomen Rakennusinsinöörien Liitto (Finnish Association of Civil Engineers): Töölönkatu 4, 1st Fl., 00100 Helsinki; tel. (20) 7120600; e-mail ril@ril.fi; internet www.ril.fi; f. 1934; org. for civil engineering with MSc and univ. students of civil engineering; 6,200 mems; Chair. RISTO VAHANEN; Vice-Pres. HARRI TANSKA; Vice-Pres. TOPI TISSARI; publs *Building magazine* (52 a year), *Rakennustekniikka* (4 a year).

Suomen Tähtitieteilijäseura ry (Finnish Astronomical Society): Univ. of Helsinki, POB 64, (Gustaf Hällströminkatu 2A), 00014 Helsinki; tel. (9) 19150600; e-mail stt.seura@gmail.com; f. 1969; organizes scientific meetings and consultations; maintains contacts with foreign astronomers, int. orgs; liaises with govt; 100 mems; Pres. ELIZAVETA RASTORGUEVA; Vice-Pres. MIKA JUVELA.

Tieteellisten seurain valtuuskunta/Vetenskapliga Samfundens Delegation (Federation of Finnish Learned Societies): Mariankatu 5, 00170 Helsinki; tel. (9) 228691; e-mail tsv@tsv.fi; internet www.tsv.fi; f. 1899; promotes scholarly publishing, scientific information, scientific cooperation and science policy; houses the Exchange Centre for Scientific Literature and a meeting and conf. centre; 260 mem. socs; Pres. Prof. ILKKA NIINILUOTO; Exec. Dir Prof. AURA KORPPI-TOMMOLA; publs *Catalogue* (every 5 years), *Tieteessä tapahtuu* (Science Now, 8 a year, online, www.tieteessatapahtuu.fi).

Vapaan Sivistystyön ry/Samverkande Bildningsorganisationerna (Finnish Adult Education Association): Annankatu 12 A 18, 00120 Helsinki; tel. (50) 5466038; e-mail toimisto@vsy.fi; internet www.vsy.fi; f. 1969; umbrella org. for non-formal adult education; 8 mem. orgs; Exec. Dir AARO HARJU.

AGRICULTURE, FISHERIES AND VETERINARY SCIENCE

Suomen Eläinlääkäriliitto (Finnish Veterinary Association): Aleksis Kiven katu 52–54, 00510 Helsinki; tel. (9) 77454810; internet www.sell.fi; f. 1892; promotes veterinary science and the practice of veterinary medicine; 2,400 mems; Pres. KIRSI SARIO; Chief Exec. MARJATTA VEHKAOJA; publ. *Suomen Eläinlääkärilehti* (Finnish Veterinary Journal, 10 a year).

Suomen Maataloustieteellinen Seura ry (Scientific Agricultural Society of Finland): c/o MTT Agrifood Research Finland, Myllytie 1, 31600 Jokioinen; tel. (3) 41883689; e-mail tiedotus@smts.fi; internet www.smts.fi; f. 1909; acts as a link between research scientists and other bodies utilizing scientific information about agriculture; organizes Agricultural Sciences meeting twice a year;

500 mems; Chair. Prof. MARKKU OLLIKAINEN; Sec. ARI RAJALA; publ. *Agricultural and Food Science* (irregular).

Suomen Meijeritieteellinen Seura ry (Finnish Society for Dairy Science): Dept of Food Technology, POB 30, 00039 Valio; e-mail emmi.martikainen@valio.fi; internet pro.tsv.fi/mts; f. 1938; promotes research work and cooperation in the field of dairy science; organizes meetings, lectures, discussion sessions; 200 mems; Chair. Prof. TAPANI ALATOSSAVA; Sec. EMMI MARTIKAINEN; publ. *Meijeritieteellinen Aikakauskirja* (Finnish Journal of Dairy Science).

Suomen Metsätieteellinen Seura (Finnish Society of Forest Science): POB 18, 01301 Vantaa; tel. (10) 2112144; e-mail sms@helsinki.fi; internet www.metsatieteellinenseura.fi; f. 1909; encourages forest research and wood science in Finland; organizes seminars, workshops, excursions, and distributes grants; 500 mems; library: see under Libraries and Archives; Chair. Prof. TIMO TOKOLA; Sec.-Gen. Dr PEKKA NYGREN; publs *Dissertationes Forestales* (irregular, online, www.metla.fi/dissertationes), *Metsätieteen aikakauskirja* (in Finnish, online, www.metla.fi/aikakauskirja), *Silva Fennica* (in English, online, www.silvafennica.fi).

Suomen Vesiyhdistys ry (Water Association Finland): POB 721, 00101 Helsinki; tel. (50) 5884237; internet www.vesiyhdistys.fi; f. 1969, as Water Asscn; disseminates information on hydrology, limnology, aquatic ecology, fisheries, water supply, civil engineering, water conservation, water management and water areas of law; organizes professional seminars, study tours and publishing; 500 mems, incl. 20 institutional mems; Pres. Prof. RIKU VAHALA; Sec. Dr JARI KOSKIAHO.

Suoseura ry (Finnish Peatland Society): Tilanhoitajankaari 22 C 55, 00790 Helsinki; tel. (40) 5242486; internet www.suoseura.fi; f. 1949; encourages study and research of peat and peatlands and their sustainable and socio-economic use; organizes meetings and excursions; takes part in nat. and int. working groups; operates Int. Peat Society and Finnish Nat. Cttee; 400 mems; Chair. RIITTA KORHONEN; Sec. JENNI SIMKIN; publ. *SUO (Mires and peat)* (4 a year).

BIBLIOGRAPHY, LIBRARY SCIENCE AND MUSEOLOGY

Suomen Kirjastoseura/Finlands biblioteksförening (Finnish Library Association): Runeberginkatu 15 A 6, 00100 Helsinki; tel. (44) 5222941; e-mail info@fla.fi; internet www.suomenkirjastoseura.fi; f. 1910; organizes campaigns for the libraries; provides decision makers with expert information on the subject; 2,000 mems; Pres. JUKKA RELANDER; Sec.-Gen. SINIKKA SIPILÄ; publ. *Kirjastolehti* (Bulletin, 4 a year).

Suomen museoliitto/Finlands museiförbund (Finnish Museums Association): Annankatu 16 B 50, 00120 Helsinki; tel. (9) 58411700; e-mail info@museoliitto.fi; internet www.museoliitto.fi; f. 1923; devt of museum sector; dissemination of information on museums; training and spec. information for mems; 200 mem. socs; library of 2,000 vols; Chair. Gov. PIRJO ALA-KAPEE; Sec.-Gen. KIMMO LEVÄ; publ. *Museo* (4 a year).

Suomen Tieteellinen Kirjastoseura ry (Finnish Research Library Association): POB 217, Kirkkokatu 6 (Tieteiden talo), 00171 Helsinki; tel. (9) 19122138; internet pro.tsv.fi/stks; f. 1929; promotes the role of libraries in research and education; 700 mems; Chair. KIMMO TUOMINEN; Sec. IRIS KARPPINEN; publ. *Signum* (journal, 6 a year).

ECONOMICS, LAW AND POLITICS

Ekonomiska Samfundet i Finland (Economic Society of Finland): c/o Hanken Svenska handelshögskolan, POB 479, 00101 Helsinki; tel. (40) 5116825; internet www.ekonomiskasamfundet.fi; f. 1894; promotes the interest of economic science and a wider application of this science; provides forum for economic debate; 806 mems; Chair. KIM LINDSTRÖM; Sec. JOHAN WIKSTRÖM (acting); publ. *Ekonomiska Samfundets Tidskrift* (Economic Society Journal, 3 a year).

Hallinnon Tutkimuksen Seura ry/Sällskapet för Förvaltningsforskning (Finnish Association for Administrative Studies): c/o Dr Vuokko Niiranen, Univ. of Eastern Finland, Kuopio Campus, POB 1627, 70211 Kuopio; tel. (40) 5504801; e-mail vuokko.niiranen@uef.fi; internet hallinnontutkimus.fi; f. 1981; attached to Univ. of Helsinki; promotes and develops admin. research in Finland; participates in int. cooperation in admin. studies and science; 660 individual mems, 4 organizational mems; Pres. Dr VUOKKO SYVÄJÄRVI; Sec. ALISA PUUSTINEN; publ. *Hallinnon Tutkimus* (Administrative Studies Journal, 4 a year).

International Law Association, Finnish Branch: POB 4, 00014 Abo; internet www.ila-hq.org/en/branches/index.cfm/bid/16; f. 1946; 105 mems; Pres. GUSTAF MOLLER; Sec. KATJA KARJALAINEN; Treas. UWE UUSITALO.

Ius Gentium (Finnish Society of International Law): POB 208, 00171 Helsinki; tel. (9) 19122468; e-mail iusgentium@iusgentium.fi; internet www.iusgentium.fi; f. 1983; research on int. law and legal theory; organizes seminars and lectures on topics relating to int. law and legal theory; 100 mems; Chair. KRISTIAN WOHLSTRÖM; Sec. ANNIKA NASKILA; publs *Acta Societatis Fennicae Iuris Gentium*, *Finnish Yearbook of International Law* (1 a year), *Kansainoikeus/Ius Gentium*, A, B and C series.

Suomalainen Lakimiesyhdistys ry (Finnish Lawyers' Society): Kasarmikatu 23A 17, 00130 Helsinki; tel. (9) 6120300; e-mail toimisto@lakimiesyhdistys.fi; internet www.lakimiesyhdistys.fi; f. 1898; 2,500 mems; Pres. Prof. JAANA NORIO-TIMONEN; Sec. TEEMU JUUTILAINEN; publs *Lakimies-aikakauskirja* (8 a year), *Oikeustiede-Jurisprudentia* (1 a year), *Suomalaisen Lakimiesyhdistyksen Julkaisuja* (series A, B, C, D and E).

Suomen Asianajajaliitto (Finnish Bar Association): POB 194, 00101 Helsinki; Simonkatu 12 B 16, 2nd Fl., 00101 Helsinki; tel. (9) 6866120; e-mail info@barassociation.fi; internet www.asianajajat.fi; f. 1862; regulates and supervises the legal profession; promotes quality of legal services and devt of legal environment; 2,000 mems; Pres. MIKA ILVESKERO; Sec.-Gen. MARKKU YLÖNEN.

Suomen Kriminalistiyhdistys—Kriminalistföreningen i Finland ry (Finnish Association of Criminologists): c/o Petri Danielsson, Nat. Research Institute of Legal Policy, POB 444, 00531 Helsinki; tel. (2) 95665375; internet www.kriminalistiyhdistys.fi; f. 1934; promotes research, organizes debates on topical criminological policy subjects; 240 mems; Chair. VILLE HINKKANEN; Sec. PETRI DANIELSSON; Treas. DAN HELENIUS; publ. *Nordisk Tidskrift for Kriminalividenskab* (4 a year).

Suomen Taloushistoriallinen Yhdistys/Ekonomisk-Historiska föreningen i Finland (Finnish Economic History Association): Dept of History and Ethnology, POB 35 (V), 40014 Jyväskylä; tel. (14) 2601248; e-mail juhamart@jyu.fi; internet groups.jyu.fi/taloushistoria; f. 1952; attached to Univ. of Jyväskylä; studies economic and social history; 100 mems; Chair. Prof. Dr ILKKA NUMMELA; Sec. Prof. Dr JARI OJALA; Exec. Dir JUUSO MARTTILA; publs *Scandinavian Economic History Review* (in cooperation with other Scandinavian socs for the advancement of the study of economic history), *Suomen talouselämän vaikuttajat* (in cooperation with Finnish Literature Soc.).

Suomen Tilastoseura/Statistiska Samfundet i Finland (Finnish Statistical Society): c/o Statistics Finland, POB 3A, 00022 Helsinki; tel. (9) 173413769; e-mail sihteeri@tilastoseura.fi; internet www.tilastoseura.fi; f. 1920; promotes devt of theoretical and applied statistics; unites statisticians working in various fields; promotes statistical education and research; 330 mems; Pres. JYRKI MÖTTÖNEN; Sec. KAISA MÄNTYSAARI; publ. *Scandinavian Journal of Statistics* (4 a year, published with other Nordic statistical asscns).

Suomen Väestötieteen Yhdistys (Finnish Demographic Society): c/o Univ. of Helsinki, Dept of Social Research, POB 59 (Unioninkatu 38), 00014 Helsinki; tel. (9) 19124753; internet blogit.helsinki.fi/svy; f. 1973; attached to Univ. of Helsinki; fosters research and promotes interaction between scholars in the field of population studies; organizes meetings and seminars for researchers; 101 mems; Chair. Prof. PEKKA MARTIKAINEN; Sec. JESSICA NISÉN; publ. *Finnish Yearbook of Population Research* (published in collaboration with The Population Research Institute).

Suomen Ympäristöoikeustieteen Seura/Miljörättsliga Sällskapet i Finland (Finnish Society of Environmental Law): POB 1225, 00101 Helsinki; tel. (9) 27091890; e-mail sys@sysry.fi; internet www.sysry.fi; f. 1980; supports and promotes legal and admin. research of environmental problems; promotes cooperation between researchers and authorities; 350 mems; Chair. Prof. ERKKI J. HOLLO; Vice-Pres. TIMO KOTKASAARI; publ. *Ympäristöjuridiikka-Miljöjuridik* (Journal of Environmental Law, 4 a year).

Taloustieteellinen Yhdistys (Finnish Economic Association): HECER, POB 17, Arkadiankatu 7, 00014 Helsinki; tel. (44) 3818674; e-mail sihteeri@taloustieteellinenyhdistys.fi; internet www.taloustieteellinenyhdistys.fi; f. 2009 by the merger of People's Economic Asscn and Soc. for Economic Research; attached to Univ. of Helsinki; supports economic research and promotion of economic and political debate; 845 mems; Pres. Prof. Dr PANU KALMI; Sec. EMMI MARTIKAINEN; publs *Finnish Economic Papers* (2 a year), *Kansantaloudellinen aikakauskirja* (National Economic Journal, 4 a year).

Valtiotieteellinen Yhdistys (Finnish Political Science Association): c/o Dept of Political and Economic Studies, POB 54, 00014 Helsinki; tel. (9) 19124955; e-mail valtiotieteellinen.yhdistys@gmail.com; internet www.vty.fi; f. 1935; attached to Univ. of Helsinki; promotes political science in Finland; 590 mems; Chair. HANNA WASS; Sec. JENNI RINNE; publ. *Politiikka* (4 a year).

FINE AND PERFORMING ARTS

Suomen Etnomusikologinen Seura ry (Finnish Society for Ethnomusicology): c/o Musiikkitiede, POB 59, 00014 Helsinki; tel. 19124777; e-mail ses-list@helsinki.fi; internet www.etnomusikologia.fi; f. 1974; promotes ethnomusicology research and disseminates information on world music cultures; culturally sensitive attitude of music study; organizes seminars, lectures, concerts; 151 mems; Pres. Dr JARKKO NIEMI; Sec.

SAMPSA HEIKKILÄ; publ. *Musiikin suunta* (4 a year).

Suomen Musiikkitieteellinen Seura ry/ Musikvetenskapliga Sällskapet i Finland rf (Finnish Musicological Society): Kaivokatu 12, 20014 Turun; tel. (14) 2601397; e-mail mts.toimisto@gmail.com; internet mtsnet.wordpress.com; f. 1911; attached to Univ. of Helsinki; encourages musicological research; encourages int. exchanges; 200 mems; Chair. MARKUS MANTERE; Sec. SINI MONONEN; publs *Acta Musicologica Fennica*, *Musiikki* (4 a year).

Suomen Näytelmäkirjailijat ja Käsikirjoittajat—Finlands Dramatiker och Manusförfattare ry (Finnish Playwrights and Screenwriters Guild): Meritullinkatu 33 G 6, 00170 Helsinki; tel. (9) 1356796; e-mail info@sunklo.fi; internet www.sunklo.fi; f. 1921; serves the needs of Finnish and Swedish authors and promotes Finnish drama; protects the professional, copyright and financial interests of its individual mems; handles the rights of properties owned by other controlling bodies; 500 mems; Chair. HEINI JUNKKAALA; Sec. MINNA SIRNÖ.

Suomen Säveltäjät ry/Finlands Tonsättare rf (Society of Finnish Composers): Runeberginkatu 15 A 11, 00100 Helsinki; tel. (9) 445589; e-mail saveltajat@composers.fi; internet www.composers.fi; f. 1945; 190 mems; Pres. TAPIO TUOMELA; Exec. Dir JARI ESKOLA.

Suomen Taideyhdistys (Finnish Art Society): c/o Kunsthalle Helsinki, Nervanderinkatu 3, 00100 Helsinki; tel. (45) 77314315; e-mail info@suomentaideyhdistys.fi; internet www.suomentaideyhdistys.fi; f. 1846; arranges exhibitions, presents awards and grants; 1,700 mems; Chair. LASSE SAARINEN; Treas. HANNU HOKKA.

Suomen Taiteilijaseura/Konstnärsgillet i Finland (Artists' Association of Finland): Iso Roobertinkatu 3–5 A 22, 00120 Helsinki; tel. (40) 7752715; e-mail aaf@artists.fi; internet www.artists.fi; f. 1864; promotes social and professional interests of artists and holds an annual exhibition; 3,000 mems; Chair. HANNA OJAMO; Exec. Dir PETRA HAVU; publs *Taide* (Art), *Taiteilija-lenti* (4 a year).

Taidehistorian seura ry/Föreningen för konsthistoria ry (Society for Art History in Finland): Univ. of Helsinki, POB 3, 00014 Helsinki; e-mail pinja.metsaranta@helsinki.fi; internet www.taidehistorianseura.fi; f. 1973; promotes research in art history; 483 mems; Chair. JOHANNA VAKKARI; Sec. PINJA METSÄRANTA; publ. *Taidehistoriallisia tutkimuksia/Konsthistoriska studier* (Studies in Art History, 1 a year).

Turun Soitannollinen Seura (Musical Society of Turku): Sibelius Museum, Piispankatu 17, 20500 Turku; tel. (2) 2313789; internet www.musisoi.net; f. 1790; 655 mems; Chair. EMILIE GARDBERG; Sec. INKA-MARIA PULKKINEN.

HISTORY, GEOGRAPHY AND ARCHAEOLOGY

Ethnos—Suomen Kansatieteilijöiden Yhdistys (Ethnos—The Association of Finnish Ethnologists): c/o Tieteiden talo, Kirkkokatu 6, 00170 Helsinki; tel. (50) 5597676; e-mail sihteeri@ethnosry.org; internet www.ethnosry.org; f. 1972; organizes seminars, trips, book clubs, publs to raise awareness on ethnology research; Pres. KATRIINA SIIVONEN; Sec. SARI KATAINEN; publ. *Ethnologia Fennica* (in English and German).

Historian Ystäväin Liitto (Society of the Friends of History): Tieteiden talo, Kirkkokatu 6, 00170 Helsinki; tel. (9) 22869351; e-mail toimisto@historianyst.fi; internet www.historianyst.fi; f. 1926; 1,500 mems; Chair. JANNE VIRKKUNEN; Sec. JULIA BURMAN; publs *Historiallinen Aikakauskirja* (Finnish Historical Review, 4 a year), *Historiallinen Kirjasto* (irregular), *Historian Aitta* (irregular), *Historian Ystävä*.

Metsähistorian Seura ry (Finnish Forest History Society): c/o Lusto, Suomen Metsämuseo, 58450 Punkaharju; tel. (15) 3451030; e-mail metsahistorian.seura@lusto.fi; internet www.lusto.fi/seura; f. 1994; research, documentation and public attention of forest history and tradition; arranges meetings, seminars and study tours; 329 mems and 11 supporting mems; Chair. TAPANI TASANEN; Sec. LEENA PAASKOSKI; publ. *Vuosilusto* (every 2 years).

Suomen Arkeologinen Seura ry (The Archaeological Society of Finland): c/o The House of Sciences and Letters, Kirkkokatu 6, 00170 Helsinki; e-mail miikka.tallavaara@helsinki.fi; internet www.sarks.fi; f. 1982; maintains contacts among archaeologists in various capacities; Chair. Dr TEEMU MÖKKÖNEN; Sec. MIIKKA TALLAVAARA; publs *Fennoscandia archaeologica* (1 a year), *Muinaistutkija* (4 a year, in Finnish, online, www.sarks.fi/mt/etusivu.html).

Suomen Historiallinen Seura/Finska Historiska Samfundet (Finnish Historical Society): Tieteiden talo, Kirkkokatu 6, 00170 Helsinki; tel. (9) 22869351; e-mail shs@histseura.fi; internet www.histseura.fi; f. 1875; 807 mems; Chair. Prof. KARI TERÄS; Exec. Dir and Sec. JULIA BURMAN; publs *Bibliotheca Historica* (Historical studies in Finnish, English and German), *Historiallinen Aikakauskirja* (4 a year), *Historiallinen Arkisto* (Historical Archives), *Historiallisia Tutkimuksia* (Historical Researches), *Studia Fennica: Historica*, *Studia Historica* (Historical studies in German, French and English), *Suomen historian lähteitä* (Sources of the History of Finland).

Suomen Kartografinen Seura (Cartographic Society of Finland): c/o Annamaija Krannila National Land Survey of Finland, POB 84, 00521 Helsinki; tel. (40) 0373522; e-mail sihteeri@kartogra.fi; internet www.kartogra.fi; f. 1957; organizes meetings, lectures, exhibitions and visits to mapping orgs; promotes the discipline and profession of cartography and geoinformatics; represents Finnish cartographers as a nat. cttee of the Int. Cartographic Asscn; 140 mems; Pres. Dr ANTTI JAKOBSSON; Sec. ANNAMAIJA KRANNILA.

Suomen Kirkkohistoriallinen Seura/ Finska Kyrkohistoriska Samfundet (Finnish Society of Church History): Dept of Church History, Univ. of Helsinki, 00014 Helsinki; tel. (9) 19122055; internet www.skhs.fi; f. 1891; scientific publs; public lectures; historical archive collns; 600 mems; Chair. Dr TUIJA LAINE; Vice-Chair. Dr ANDRE SWANSTRÖM; Sec. SINI MIKKOLA.

Suomen Maantieteellinen Seura/Geografiska Sällskapet i Finland (Geographical Society of Finland): c/o Univ. of Helsinki, POB 64 (Gustaf Hällströmin k. 2), 00014 Helsinki; tel. (9) 19151215; e-mail maija.taka@helsinki.fi; internet www.geography.fi; f. 1888; promotes research in geography and related sciences at home and abroad; 900 mems; library of 56,000 vols; Pres. Dr SANNA MÄKI; Sec. MAIJA TAKA; publs *Fennia* (2 a year), *Terra* (4 a year).

Suomen Muinaismuistoyhdistys/Finska Fornminnesföreningen (Finnish Antiquarian Society): POB 913, 00101 Helsinki; tel. (9) 40509287; internet www.muinaismuistoyhdistys.fi; f. 1870; 600 mems; Pres. MIKA LAVENTO; Vice-Pres. RENJA SUOMINEN-KOKKONEN; Sec. INKERI HAKAMIES; publs *Iskos*, *Kansatieteellinen Arkisto*, *Suomen Muinaismuistoyhdistyksen Aikakauskirja—Finska Fornminnesföreningens Tidskrift*, *Suomen Museo ja Finskt Museum*.

Suomen Sukututkimusseura/Genealogiska Samfundet i Finland (Genealogical Society of Finland): Liisankatu 16A, 00170 Helsinki; tel. (10) 3877901; e-mail jasenrekisteri@genealogia.fi; internet www.genealogia.fi; f. 1917; promotes Finnish genealogy; 6,000 mems; library of 45,000 vols; Chair. TEPPO YLITALO; CEO P. T. KUUSILUOMA; publs *Genos* (4 a year), *Sukutieto* (4 a year), *Vuosikirja—Årsskrift* (irregular).

LANGUAGE AND LITERATURE

British Council: POB 297, 00101 Helsinki; Hub Helsinki, Annankatu 31–33 C, 00100 Helsinki; tel. (9) 7743330; e-mail info@britishcouncil.fi; internet www.britishcouncil.fi; promotes cultural exchange with the UK; Country Dir ANTTI KARJALAINEN; Programme Dir HANNA KLINGE.

Finlands svenska författareförening (Society of Swedish Authors in Finland): Urho Kekkonens gata 8 B 14, 00100 Helsinki; tel. (9) 446266; e-mail forfattarna@kaapeli.fi; internet www.forfattarna.fi; f. 1919; monitors Finnish–Swedish writers' union and copyright interests; 200 mems; Pres. PETER SANDSTRÖM; Sec.-Gen. and Treas. MERETE JENSEN.

Goethe-Institut: Salomonkatu 5B, 00100 Helsinki; tel. (44) 7222710; e-mail info@helsinki.goethe.org; internet www.goethe.de/ins/fi/hel/knt; offers courses and examinations in German language and culture and promotes cultural exchange with Germany; library of 2,800 vols, 30 periodicals; Dir MIKKO FRITZE.

Kirjallisuudentutkijain Seura (Finnish Literary Research Society): c/o Univ. of Helsinki, Kotimainen kirjallisuus, Suomen kielen ja kotimaisen kirjallisuuden laitos, POB 3 (Fabianinkatu 33), 00014 Helsinki; e-mail kts@uta.fi; internet pro.tsv.fi/skts; f. 1927; advances the study of literature; promotes general interest in literary research; organizes annual research seminar; 170 mems; Chair. Dr RIIKKA ROSSI; Sec. ANTTI AHMALA; publ. *Avain—Finnish Review of Literary Studies* (4 a year).

Klassillis-filologinen yhdistys (Society for Classical Philology): c/o World Cultures Dept, Classical Philology, POB 24, 00014 Helsinki; e-mail antiquitas@lists.utu.fi; internet www.helsinki.fi/hum/kla/kfy/esittely.html; f. 1879; attached to Univ. of Helsinki; promotes study of classical philology and classical antiquity in gen.; 100 mems; Pres. Prof. OLLI SALOMIES; Sec. and Treas. KATJA VARAKAS; publ. *Arctos: Acta Philologica Fennica* (1 a year).

Kotikielen Seura (Society for the Study of Finnish): POB 3 (Fabianinkatu 33), 00014 Helsinki; e-mail seura@kotikielenseura.fi; internet www.kotikielenseura.fi; f. 1876; attached to Univ. of Helsinki; Finnish linguistics; organizes meetings and symposia; awards annual prizes and scholarships; 700 mems; Pres. Prof. Dr TIINA ONIKKI-RANTAJÄÄSKÖ; Sec. RIITTA JUVONEN; publ. *Virittäjä* (4 a year).

Suomalais-Ugrilainen Seura (Finno-Ugrian Society): POB 320, Mariankatu 7, 00171 Helsinki; tel. (9) 662149; internet www.sgr.fi; f. 1883; promotes research of Uralic and Altaic languages, ethnography of their speakers and its historical and prehistorical past; 800 mems; Pres. Prof. Dr ULLA-MAIJA FORSBERG; Sec. ULRIIKKA PUURA; publs *Finnisch-Ugrische Forschungen* (every 2 years), *Journal de la Société Finno-Ougrienne* (every

2 years), *Mémoires de la Société Finno-Ougrienne* (irregular), *Uralica Helsingiensia*.

Suomalaisen Kirjallisuuden Seura/ Finska Litteratursällskapet (Finnish Literature Society): Hallituskatu 1, POB 259, 00171 Helsinki; tel. (20) 1131231; e-mail sks@finlit.fi; internet www.finlit.fi; f. 1831; promotes study of folklore, ethnology, literature and Finnish language; incl. literary archives on Finnish literature and literary culture; 3,052 mems; library: see under Libraries and Archives; Chair. Prof. AILI NENOLA; Dir and Sec.-Gen. TUOMAS M. S. LEHTONEN; publs *Hiidenkivi* (6 a year), *Studia Fennica: Ethnologica, Studia Fennica: Folkloristica, Studia Fennica: Historica, Studia Fennica: Linguistica* (1 a year), *Studia Fennica: Litteraria*.

Suomen Englanninopettajat ry (Association of Teachers of English in Finland): Rautatieläisenkatu 6A, 00520 Helsinki; tel. (9) 145414; e-mail english@suomenenglanninopettajat.fi; internet www.suomenenglanninopettajat.fi; f. 1948; 3,000 mems; Pres. JAAKKO MÄKI; publ. *Tempus* (8 a year).

Suomen Kirjailijaliitto (Union of Finnish Writers): Runeberginkatu 32, C 28, 00100 Helsinki; tel. (9) 445392; e-mail info@suomenkirjailijaliitto.fi; internet www.suomenkirjailijaliitto.fi; f. 1897; allied to the Scandinavian Authors' Council and European Writers' Congress; 660 mems; Pres. TUULA-LIINA VARIS; Exec. Dir SUVI OINONEN; publs *Suomalaiset kertojat, Suomen Runotar*.

Svenska Litteratursällskapet i Finland (Society of Swedish Literature in Finland): Riddareg. 5, 00170 Helsinki; tel. (9) 618777; e-mail info@sls.fi; internet www.sls.fi; f. 1885; preserves, develops and mediates Swedish cultural heritage in Finland; 1,000 mems; library: see under Libraries and Archives; Pres. Prof. MAX ENGMAN; Sec. Prof. MARIKA TANDEFELT; publ. *Skrifter* (irregular).

Uusfilologinen Yhdistys ry (Modern Language Society): c/o Univ. of Helsinki, POB 24 (Unioninkatu 40), 00014 Helsinki; tel. (44) 0702943; e-mail ufy-sihteeri@helsinki.fi; internet www.helsinki.fi/jarj/ufy; f. 1887; 240 mems; Pres. Prof. JUHANI HÄRMÄ; Hon. Sec. Dr MARIANNA HINTIKKA; publ. *Mémoires de la Société Néophilologique* (irregular).

MEDICINE

Brain Research Society of Finland: POB 63 (Hartmaninkatu 8), 00290 Helsinki; e-mail tiina-kaisa.kukko-lukjanov@utu.fi; internet www.brsf.org; f. 1973; organizes lectures and courses for scientists; works to improve brain research opportunities; 220 mems; Chair. IRMA HOLOPAINEN; Sec. TIINA-KAISA KUKKO-LUKJANOV.

Cancer Society of Finland: Pieni Roobertinkatu 9, 00130 Helsinki; tel. (9) 135331; e-mail society@cancer.fi; internet www.cancer.fi; f. 1936; 130,000 mems; Chair. Prof. TEUVO TAMMELA; Sec.-Gen. Dr SAKARI KARJALAINEN; publs *Focus Oncologie* (1 a year), *Syöpä—Cancer* (5 a year).

Finska Läkaresällskapet (Medical Society of Finland): POB 82, 00251 Helsinki; Johannesbergsvägen 8, 00251 Helsinki; tel. (9) 47768090; e-mail kansliet@fls.fi; internet www.fls.fi; f. 1835; 1,000 mems; library of 35,000 vols; Pres. Prof. TOM BÖHLING; Sec. ULLA WIKLUND; Treas. Prof. BJÖRN EKLUND; publ. *Finska Läkaresällskapets Handlingar*.

Lääketieteellinen Radioisotooppiyhdistys (Finnish Society of Nuclear Medicine): Helsingin Diakonissalaitos, Isotooppilaboratorio, Alppikatu 2, 00530 Helsinki; tel. (9) 77507218; e-mail eeva.boman@kuh.fi; internet www.fsnm.org; f. 1959; promotes devt and application of nuclear medicine; acts as a link between field practitioners and the public sector; organizes meetings, lectures and training sessions; maintains relationships with int. socs of nuclear medicine, ind. laboratories in Finland; supplies equipment and radiopharmaceuticals; 300 mems; Chair. MARKO SEPPÄNEN; Sec. Dr TOMMI NOPONEN; publ. *Tuiketiedote* (2 a year).

Lääketieteellisen Fysiikan ja Tekniikan Yhdistys ry (Finnish Society for Medical Physics and Medical Engineering): Department of Applied Physics, Univ. of Eastern Finland, POB 1627, 70211 Kuopio; tel. (40) 3552369; e-mail secretary@lfty.fi; internet www.lfty.fi; f. 1968; maintains interest towards medical physics, medical engineering and biophysics; strengthens devt of research, education and industry in the field; 140 mems; Chair. Prof. JARI VIIK; Sec. JUHO VÄISÄNEN.

Sosiaalilääketieteen Yhdistys ry (Society for Social Medicine in Finland): c/o Riikka Lämsä, Terveyden ja hyvinvoinnin laitos, POB 30, 00271 Helsinki; tel. (9) 7886296; e-mail sihteeri@socialmedicine.fi; internet www.socialmedicine.fi; f. 1968; promotes factors contributing to social medical research; organizes seminars, lectures, presentations, courses, symposia; publishes, supports research in the field; gives opinions on matters of social medicine and maintains relations with foreign sector orgs; 700 mems; Chair. Dr TEA LALLUKKA; Sec. PEIJA HAARAMO; publ. *Sosiaalilääketieteellinen Aikakauslehti* (4 a year).

Suomalainen Lääkäriseura Duodecim (Finnish Medical Society Duodecim): Kalevankatu 11A, POB 713, 00100 Helsinki; tel. (9) 618851; e-mail central@duodecim.fi; internet www.duodecim.fi; f. 1881; 20,000 mems and 100 mem. asscns; library of 22,500 vols; Pres. Prof. Dr MARKKU MUSTONEN; Sec. Dr MATTI RAUTALAHTI; publ. *Duodecim* (Medical Journal, 26 a year).

Suomen Farmakologiyhdistys (Finnish Pharmacological Society): Univ. of Oulu, Dept of Pharmacology and Toxicology, POB 5000, 90014 Oulu; tel. (8) 5375235; e-mail jukka.hakkola@oulu.fi; internet www.sfy.fi; f. 1948; supports the devt of Finnish Pharmacology; organizes nat. and int. scientific meetings; 400 mems; Pres. Prof. JUKKA HAKKOLA; Vice-Pres. Prof. ULLAMARI PESONEN.

Suomen Farmaseuttinen Yhdistys/ Farmaceutiska Föreningen i Finland (Finnish Pharmaceutical Society): Fredrikinkatu 61, 2 kerros, 00100 Helsinki; tel. (9) 19159159; internet pro.tsv.fi/finpharmsociety; f. 1887; promotes pharmaceutical sciences, pharmaceutical research and its applications; 300 mems; Pres. Prof. NIKLAS SANDLER; Sec. Dr LEENA PELTONEN; Treas. TIIA KUURANNE.

Suomen Hammaslääkäriseura Apollonia (Finnish Dental Society Apollonia): Bulevardi 30 B 5, 00120 Helsinki; tel. (9) 6803120; e-mail toimisto@apollonia.fi; internet www.apollonia.fi; f. 1892; 6,700 mems; Pres. Prof. SATU LAHTI; Sec.-Gen. Dr VESA POHJOLA.

Suomen Kardiologinen Seura (Finnish Cardiac Society): Isokatu 47, 90100 Oulu; tel. (10) 5481000; e-mail fcs@fincardio.fi; internet www.fincardio.fi; f. 1967; supports cardiac research; awards yearly grants for research; 760 mems, 38 industrial mems; Pres. JYRI LOMMI; Sec. Dr MAIJA KAARTINEN; publ. *Sydänääni* (5 a year).

Suomen Sairaanhoitajaliitto ry (Finnish Nurses Association): Asemamiehenkatu 2, 00520 Helsinki; tel. (10) 3213320; e-mail info@sairaanhoitajaliitto.fi; internet www.sairaanhoitajaliitto.fi; f. 1925; offers learning and networking opportunities to nurses; 50,000 mems; Pres. MERJA MERASTO; Vice-Pres. MARIANNE SIPILÄ; publs *Sairaanhoitaja* (12 a year), *Premissi* (6 a year), *Tutkiva Hoitotyö* (4 a year).

Suomen Toksikologiyhdistys (Finnish Society of Toxicology): c/o Juha Laakso, Finnish Safety and Chemicals Agency, POB 66, 00521 Helsinki; tel. (40) 4893369; internet www.toksikologit.fi; f. 1979; organizes annual scientific meetings and promotes cooperation in toxicology with nat. and int. socs; 300 mems; Chair. KIRSI VÄHÄKANGAS; Sec. JUHA LAAKSO; Treas. KIRSI MYÖHÄNEN.

NATURAL SCIENCES

Biological Sciences

Birdlife Finland: Annankatu 29 A 16, 00101 Helsinki; tel. (9) 41353300; e-mail office@birdlife.fi; internet www.birdlife.fi; f. 1973; protection of birds, promotes biodiversity conservation and sustainable devt; 30 nat. assoc. orgs; affiliated to BirdLife Int.; 11,000 mems; Chair. JARI KÅRLUND; Dir AKI ARKIOMAA; publs *Linnut-lehti* (Birds, 4 a year), *Linnut-vuosikirja* (1 a year), *Ornis Fennica* (4 a year), *Tiira-lehti* (4 a year).

Kasvinsuojeluseura ry (Plant Protection Society): Raitamaantie 8A (Kannelmäki), 00420 Helsinki; tel. (10) 4394770; internet www.kasvinsuojeluseura.fi; f. 1931; research and protection from diseases, pests and weeds; arranges meetings and excursions, awards grants to researchers; 1,500 mems; Pres. IRMELI MARKKULA; Sec. SATU RANTALA; publ. *Kasvinsuojelulehti* (Plant Protection Magazine, 4 a year).

Societas Amicorum Naturae Ouluensis/ Oulun Luonnonystäväin Yhdistys ry (Natural History Society of Oulu): Dept of Biology (Botany), 90570 Univ. Oulu; tel. (8) 5531546; f. 1925; 436 mems; Pres. Prof. P. LAHDESMAKI; Chair. JAAKKO LUMME; Sec. S. KONTUNEN-SOPPELA; publs *Aquilo ser. botanica* (1 a year), *Aquilo ser. zoologica* (1 a year).

Societas Biochemica, Biophysica et Microbiologica Fenniae (Biochemical, Biophysical and Microbiological Society of Finland): c/o Univ. of Helsinki, Meilahti Clinical Proteomics Core Facility, POB 63, 00014 Helsinki; tel. (9) 19125202; e-mail saara.tikka@helsinki.fi; internet www.biobio.org; f. 1945; divs of biochemistry, biophysics, microbiology, virology, food science, plant molecular biology, peptide, glycoscience and proteomics; 900 mems; Pres. Dr MARC BAUMANN; Sec. Dr SAARA TIKKA; Treas. Prof. MARKUS LINDER.

Societas Biologica Fennica Vanamo ry/ Suomen Biologian Seura Vanamo: c/o Univ. of Hesinki, Kasvimuseo, POB 7 (Unioninkatu 44), 00014 Helsinki; tel. (40) 8498808; e-mail annina.launis@helsinki.fi; internet www.vanamo.fi; f. 1896; works as a link between biologists; promotes biological research; 1,500 mems; Pres. Prof. JOUKO RIKKINEN; Sec. ANNINA LAUNIS; publs *Atlas Florae Europaeae, Luonnon Tutkija* (The Naturalist, 5 a year).

Societas Entomologica Fennica/Suomen Hyönteistieteellinen Seura ry (Entomological Society of Finland): c/o Univ. of Helsinki, Finnish Museum of Natural History, 00014 Helsinki; tel. (9) 19158662; internet www.suomenhyonteistieteellinenseura.org; f. 1935; serves as a link between researchers and entomology enthusiasts; Pres. ILPO MANNERKOSKI; Sec. Dr NINA LAURENNE; publ. *Entomologica Fennica* (4 a year).

Societas pro Fauna et Flora Fennica: c/o Univ. of Helsinki, Dept of Biosciences, POB 65, (Viikinkaari 1), 00014 Helsinki; tel. (9) 19159824; internet www.societasfff.fi; f. 1821; promotes zoological and botanical research; nature conservation activities; 1,041 mems; library of 44,000 vols; Pres. Prof. CARL-ADAM HÆGGSTRÖM; Hon. Sec. Dr HENRY PIHLSTRÖM; publ. *Memoranda Societatis pro Fauna et Flora Fennica* (3 a year).

Physical Sciences

Geofysiikan Seura/Geofysiska Sällskapet (Geophysical Society of Finland): c/o Kati Suhonen, Dept of Physics, Div. of Geophysics and Astronomy, POB 64, 00014 Helsinki; tel. (8) 44330335; internet www.geofysiikanseura.fi; f. 1926; advances geophysical research and serves as a link between those involved in it; 225 mems and 12 corporate mems; Chair. Dr KIRSTI KAURISTIE; Sec. KATI SUHONEN; publ. *Geophysica* (1 a year, in English).

Suomen Geologinen Seura r y/Geologiska Sällskapet i Finland (Geological Society of Finland): Geological Survey of Finland, POB 96, 02151 Espoo; tel. (20) 5502299; e-mail sihteeri@geologinenseura.fi; internet www.geologinenseura.fi; f. 1886; promotes geological and mineralogical research; 1,200 mems; Chair. PETRI LINTINEN; Sec. MAARIT SARESMA; publ. *Geologi* (6 a year).

Suomen Kemian Seura/Kemiska Sällskapet i Finland (Association of Finnish Chemical Societies): Urho Kekkosen katu 8 C 31, 00100 Helsinki; tel. (10) 4256300; e-mail toimisto@kemianseura.fi; internet www.kemianseura.fi; f. 1970; organizes annual Finnish Chemical Congress; acts as link between the three mem. socs, promotes research in chemistry, chemical education, chemical industry; library of 800 vols; Chair. JUSSI KIVIKOSKI; publs *Acta Chemica Scandinavica*, *Kemia-Kemi* (8 a year).

Constituent Societies:

Finska Kemistsamfundet/Suomen Kemistiseura (Finnish Society of Chemistry): Urho Kekkonen gata 8 C 31, 00100 Helsinki; tel. (44) 5394125; e-mail toimisto@kemianseura.fi; internet www.finskakemistsamfundet.fi; f. 1891; 300 mems; Pres. TRIIN GYLLENBERG; Sec. MARIA WEINTRAUB.

Kemiallisteknillinen Yhdistys/Kemisktekniska Forening ry (Finnish Society of Chemical Engineers): Urho Kekkosen katu 8 C 31, 00100 Helsinki; tel. (9) 4542040; e-mail office@kemianseura.fi; internet www.kty.fi; f. 1970; 816 mems; Pres. RISTO HAKULINEN; Sec. VALENTINA LISKI.

Suomalaisten Kemistien Seura (Finnish Chemical Society): Urho Kekkosen katu 8 C 31, 00100 Helsinki; tel. (10) 4256302; e-mail heleena.karrus@kemianseura.fi; internet suomalaistenkemistienseura.fi; f. 1919; 3,480 mems; Pres. Prof. Dr KIMMO HIMBERG; Sec.-Gen. HELEENA KARRUS.

Suomen Limnologinen yhdistys (Finnish Limnological Society): c/o Heidi Holmroos, Univ. of Helsinki, Dept of Environmental Sciences, Aquatic Sciences, POB 65, (Viikinkaari 1), 00014 Helsinki; tel. (41) 5403314; e-mail sly.sihteeri@gmail.com; internet www.suomenlimnologinenyhdistys.fi; f. 1950; preservation and management of aquatic systems; fosters Finnish limnological research; provides information and a discussion forum for experts in this field; 180 mems; Chair. Prof. JUKKA HORPPILA; Sec. HEIDI HOLMROOS; publ. *Boreal Environment Research* (6 a year).

Suomen Luonnonsuojeluliitto (Finnish Association for Nature Conservation): Kotkankatu 9, 00510 Helsinki; tel. (9) 228081; e-mail eero.yrjo-koskinen@sll.fi; internet www.sll.fi; f. 1938; works for environmental protection and nature conservation; incl. 15 dist. orgs; 30,000 mems; Pres. RISTO SULKAVA; Exec. Dir EERO YRJÖ-KOSKINEN; publs *Luonnonsuojelija* (5 a year), *Suomen Luonto* (10 a year).

Suomen Matemaattinen Yhdistys (Finnish Mathematical Society): c/o Univ. of Helsinki, Dept of Mathematics and Statistics, POB 68 (Gustaf Hällströmin katu 2B), 00014 Helsinki; tel. (9) 19151501; e-mail hanne.kekkonen@helsinki.fi; internet matemaattinenyhdistys.fi; f. 1868; supports research and education in mathematics; improves awareness about mathematics in general; organizes int. visitor programme, annual Mathematics Day event; 319 mems; Pres. Prof. MATTI LASSAS; Sec. Dr HANNE KEKKONEN; publ. *Arkhimedes*.

Suomen Sammalseura ry (Finnish Bryological Society): c/o Univ. of Helsinki, POB 7, (Unioninkatu 44), 00014 Helsinki; tel. (9) 1912442; e-mail xhe@mappi.helsinki.fi; internet pro.tsv.fi/sammalseura; f. 1987; promotes bryological research; supports cooperation of bryologists; 78 mems; Chair. SINIKKA PIIPPO; Sec. XIOLAN HE-NYGRÉN; publ. *Bryobrothera* (irregular).

Ympäristötieteellinen Seura ry (Finnish Society for Environmental Science): c/o Finnish Environment Institute SYKE, Ecotoxicology and Risk Assessment, Survontie 9A, 40500 Jyväskylä; tel. (29) 5251368; e-mail matti.t.leppanen@ymparisto.fi; internet www.fses.fi; f. 1987; encourages environmental scientific research and spreads information about protecting environment; organizes seminars, workshops, confs; 84 mems; Chair. Prof. Dr TUULA TUHKANEN; Sec. and Treas. MATTI LEPPÄNEN.

PHILOSOPHY AND PSYCHOLOGY

Suomen Estetiikan Seura ry (Finnish Society for Aesthetics): c/o Univ. of Helsinki, Dept of Philosophy, History, Culture and Art Studies, Aesthetics, POB 3, 00014 Helsinki; tel. (9) 19124158; internet www.estetiikka.fi; f. 1972; promotes research in aesthetics; creates contacts between arts and sciences; encourages discussions on aesthetic values; organizes annual seminars; 100 mems; Chair. Prof. ARTO HAAPALA; Sec. VEERA LAUNIS; publ. *Synteesi* (1 a year).

Suomen Filosofinen Yhdistys (Philosophical Society of Finland): c/o Univ. of Helsinki, Dept of Philosophy, POB 24 (Unioninkatu 40A), 00014 Helsinki; tel. (29) 5335136; e-mail risto.vilkko@helsinki.fi; internet www.helsinki.fi/jarj/sfy; f. 1873; promotes study of philosophy and related disciplines; 399 mems; Pres. Prof. ILKKA NIINILUOTO; Sec. Dr RISTO VILKKO; publs *Acta Philosophica Fennica* (irregular), *Ajatus* (1 a year).

Suomen Psykiatriyhdistys (Finnish Psychiatric Association): Fredrikinkatu 71 A 4, 00100 Helsinki; tel. (9) 4770660; e-mail psy@psy.fi; internet www.psy.fi; f. 1913; promotes scientific psychiatry and occupational functioning, and mental health work; organizes meetings and training; participates in int. activities; 1,348 mems; Pres. Prof. MINNA VALKONEN-KORHONEN; Sec.-Gen. Dr TARJA MELARTIN.

Suomen Psykologinen Seura ry (Finnish Psychological Society): Liisankatu 16 A 1 krs, 00170 Helsinki; tel. (9) 2782122; e-mail psykologinenseura@psykologia.fi; internet www.psykologia.fi; f. 1952; supports and develops psychological research and publs activities; practical operation of the link between psychology and applied psychology between reps of Finland; 1,600 mems; Pres. Prof. JARKKO HAUTAMÄKI; Scientific Sec. TAINA SCHAKIR; publs *Acta Psychologica Fennica* (irregular), *Psykologia* (6 a year).

RELIGION, SOCIOLOGY AND ANTHROPOLOGY

Suomalainen Teologinen Kirjallisuusseura (Finnish Theological Literature Society): c/o Univ. of Helsinki, POB 4 (Vuorikatu 3, 2.krs), 00014 Helsinki; tel. (45) 1390879; e-mail stksj@pro.tsv.fi; internet pro.tsv.fi/stksj; f. 1891; promotes scientific research in theology; publishes theological texts and translations of classics; 850 mems; Chair. Prof. RISTO SAARINEN; Sec. AILI NYMAN; Sec. JONAH SALMINEN.

Suomen Antropologinen Seura/Antropologiska Sällskapet i Finland (Finnish Anthropological Society): Univ. of Helsinki, POB 59, 00014 Helsinki; tel. (9) 19123094; e-mail info@suomenantropologinenseura.fi; internet www.antropologinenseura.fi; f. 1975; promotes research in the fields of anthropology and related disciplines; organizes meetings, lectures, public events, seminars and confs; 400 mems; Pres. Dr LAURA HUTTUNEN; Sec. VILLE LAAKKONEN; Treas. PAULIINA LUKINMAA; publ. *Suomen Antropologi/Antropologi i Finland* (Journal of the Finnish Anthropological Society, 4 a year).

Suomen Itämainen Seura (Finnish Oriental Society): c/o Univ. of Helsinki, Dept of World Cultures, POB 59 (Unioninkatu 38B), 00014 Helsinki; tel. (9) 19122224; internet www.suomenitamainenseura.org; f. 1917; promotes research in Oriental cultures and knowledge of Finland; 210 mems; Pres. Prof. SAANA SVÄRD; Sec. JOUNI HARJUMÄKI; publ. *Studia Orientalia*.

Suomen Kansantietouden Tutkijain Seura ry (Finnish Folklore Researcher's Society): c/o Cultural Research, Univ. of Eastern Finland, POB 111, 80101 Joensuu; tel. (9) 4452119; internet www.kansantietoudentutkijat.fi; f. 1937; promotes knowledge of the disciplines of folklore and research; organizes seminars, meetings, tours and photographic competition; 145 mems; Chair. SINIKKA VAKIMO; Sec. TANJA LEHIKOINEN; publ. *Elore* (2 a year).

Suomen Kirkkohistoriallinen Seura (Finnish Society of Church History): c/o Univ. of Helsinki, Dept of Church History, POB 33, 00014 Helsinki; e-mail info@skhs.fi; internet www.skhs.fi; f. 1887; colln of the sources of nat. church history; publishes monographs, other work related to church; organizes excursions to historically interesting places; Chair. and Treas. Dr MIKKO KETOLA; Sec. Rev. Dr SINI MIKKOLA; publ. *Yearbook*.

TECHNOLOGY

Akustinen Seura ry (Acoustical Society of Finland): c/o Aalto Univ., Dept of Signal Processing and Acoustics, POB 13000, 00076 Aalto; tel. (50) 3661341; e-mail sihteeri@akustinenseura.fi; internet www.acoustics.hut.fi/asf; f. 1943; ties together acousticians and people interested in acoustics; research and publishing; organizes nat. conf.; 220 mems; 20 supporting companies; Chair. TAPIO LOKKI; Sec. MARKO HIIPAKKA.

Ilmansuojeluyhdistys ry (Finnish Air Pollution Prevention Society): POB 136, 00251 Helsinki; tel. (45) 1335989; e-mail sihteeri@isy.fi; internet www.isy.fi; f. 1976; air and climate protection; research and devt; 400

mems; Pres. KAARLE KUPIAINEN; Sec. KERTTU KOTAKORPI; publ. *Ilmansuojelu* (Air Care Magazine, 4 a year).

Maanmittaustieteiden seura ry (Finnish Society of Surveying Sciences): POB 60, 00521 Helsinki; tel. (9) 1481900; e-mail sihteeri@maanmittaustieteidenseura.fi; internet mts.fgi.fi; f. 1926; 602 mems; Pres. KIRSIKKA NIUKKANEN; Sec. JUHANA HIIRONEN; publs *Maanmittaus aikakauskirja*, *Nordic Journal of Surveying and Real Estate Research* (2 a year).

Rakenteiden Mekaniikan Seura (Finnish Association for Structural Mechanics): c/o Aalto Univ. School of Engineering, Dept of Civil and Structural Engineering, Rakentajanaukio 4A, POB 12100, 00076 Aalto; tel. (9) 47022264; internet rmseura.tkk.fi; f. 1970; promotes research and exchange of knowledge on engineering materials; structural mechanics and design; 222 individual mems, 10 collective mems; Chair. JOUNI FREUND; Sec. SAMI PAJUNEN; publ. *Rakenteiden Mekaniikka* (Journal of Structural Mechanics, 4 a year).

Suomen Aerosolitutkimusseura ry (Finnish Association for Aerosol Research): c/o Hanna Vehkamäki, Dept of Physics, POB 64 (Gustaf Hällströmin katu 2), 00014 Helsinki; tel. (9) 19150710; internet www.atm.helsinki.fi/faar; f. 1983; attached to Univ. of Helsinki; acts as a link between researchers in various institutes and univs; organizes meetings and confs; 180 mems; Chair. Prof. HANNA VEHKAMÄKI; Sec. Dr KATRIANNE LEHTIPALO; publ. *Report Series in Aerosol Science*.

Suomen Atomiteknillinen Seura/Atomtekniska Sällskapet i Finland (Finnish Nuclear Society): POB 78, 02151 Espoo; tel. (40) 1591156; e-mail sihteeri@ats-fns.fi; internet www.ats-fns.fi; f. 1966; promotes knowledge and devt of nuclear technology in Finland; exchanges information on int. level; 819 mems, 18 corporate mems; Pres. LIISA HEIKINHEIMO; Sec. ANNA NIEMINEN; publ. *ATS Ydintekniikka* (ATS Nuclear Engineering, 4 a year).

Suomen Automaatioseura ry (Finnish Society of Automation): Asemapäällikönkatu 12B, 00520 Helsinki; tel. (20) 1981220; e-mail office@automaatioseura.fi; internet www.automaatioseura.com; f. 1953; promotes automation technology, theory and applications; operates a process, factory and building automation industry; organizes exhibitions, confs, meetings, courses, provides publs in the field; formulates opinions, makes suggestions and proposals; Chair. HARRI HAPPONEN; Exec. Dir ANTTI KUISMA; publ. *Automaatioväylä-lehti* (7 a year).

Suomen Operaatiotutkimusseura ry (Finnish Operations Research Society): POB 702, 00101 Helsinki; e-mail sihteeri@operaatiotutkimus.fi; internet www.operaatiotutkimus.fi; f. 1973; promotes and advances operations research; organizes seminars, excursions, training courses, confs; 180 mems; Chair. Prof. MARKKU KUULA; Sec. JOUNI POUSI.

Suomen Tekoälyseura (Finnish Artificial Intelligence Society): Kuusitie 4 B 66, 00270 Helsinki; tel. (40) 5665832; e-mail office@stes.fi; internet www.stes.fi; f. 1986; promotes public knowledge about artificial intelligence; offers channel for discussion; 200 mems; Chair. JUKKA KORTELA; Vice-Chair. TAPANI RAIKO.

Suomen Tribologiayhdistys ry (Finnish Society for Tribology): c/o Pekka Salonen, STADIA, Tekniikka ja liikenne, POB 4201, 00099 Helsinki; e-mail pekka_salonen@kolumbus.fi; internet www.tribologysociety.fi; f. 1977; supports research, technical devt and education of tribology; maintains int. cooperation to foreign tribology socs; 111 mems; Chair. PEKKA SALONEN; Sec. JUSSI LEHTIÖ; publ. *Tribologia* (4 a year).

Svenska Tekniska Vetenskapsakademien i Finland (Swedish Academy of Engineering Sciences in Finland): Pohjoisesplanadi 33A, 00100 Helsinki; tel. (40) 7225711; e-mail stv@stvif.fi; internet www.stvif.fi; f. 1921; promotes research in engineering sciences; 175 mems; Pres. JARL-THURE ERIKSSON; Sec. Dr ÅSA LINDBERG; publ. *Förhandlingar* (Proceedings).

Tekniikan Akateemisten Liitto TEK ry (Academic Engineers and Architects in Finland—TEK): Ratavartijankatu 2, 00520 Helsinki; tel. (9) 229121; internet www.tek.fi; f. 1896; negotiates and concludes collective agreements regarding salaries and work conditions for mems; serves as link between engineers and architects; regional offices in Espoo, Tampere, Oulu, Lappeenranta and Turku; 73,500 mems; Exec. Dir HEIKKI KAUPPI; publ. *TEK Member Magazine* (9 a year).

Tekniikan edistämissäätiö (Finnish Foundation for Technology Promotion): c/o Työ ja elinkeinoministeriö, POB 32 (Aleksanterinkatu 4), 00023 Helsinki; tel. (9) 5063523; internet www.tekniikanedistamissaatio.fi; f. 1949; provides yearly fellowships for the advancement of technology; Pres. JORMA ELORANTA; Sec.-Gen. KARI MÄKINEN.

Teknillisten Tieteiden Akatemia/Akademin för Tekniska Vetenskaper ry (Finnish Academy of Technology): Teknillisten Tieteiden Akatemia, Pohjoisesplanadi 33A, 00100 Helsinki; tel. (9) 6818090; internet www.ttatv.fi; f. 1957; promotes technical-scientific research; 440 mems; Pres. ASKO SAARELA; Sec.-Gen. PANU NYKÄNEN.

Tekniska Föreningen i Finland (Engineering Society in Finland): Banvaktsg. 2A, 00520 Helsinki; tel. (9) 4767718; e-mail kansli@tfif.fi; internet www.tekniska.fi/tfif; f. 1880; 4,300 mems; Chair. MIKAELA RUNEBERG; Dir BRITTA SUNDE; publ. *Forum för ekonomi och teknik*.

Tietojenkäsittelytieteen Seura ry (Finnish Society for Computer Science): c/o Päivi Majaranta, Univ. of Tampere, School of Information Sciences, 33014 Tampere; tel. (50) 3185879; e-mail sihteeri@tkts.fi; internet www.tkts.fi; f. 1982; forum for researchers in the area of computer science; promotes computer science research, applications and the publ. of research results; arranges discussions and courses; nat. and int. cooperation; organizes annual computer science event; 400 mems; Chair. MARKKU TUKIAINEN; Sec. PÄIVI MAJARANTA; publ. *Tietojenkäsittelytiede*.

Research Institutes

GENERAL

Finnish Centre of Excellence in Historical Research: c/o Univ. of Tampere, School of Social Sciences and Humanities, 33014 Tampere; Main Campus, Pinni B, 3rd Fl., Room B3087, Kanslerinrinne 1, 33014 Tampere; tel. (50) 5242284; internet www.uta.fi/yky/coehistory; attached to Univ. of Tampere; studies the history of Finland from the late middle ages (1400) to present day; research about structural history of power, everyday life and perceptions; Dir Prof. PERTTI HAAPALA.

Kuluttajatutkimuskeskus (National Consumer Research Centre): POB 5 (Kaikukatu 3), 00531 Helsinki; tel. (10) 6059000; e-mail kirjaamo@kuluttajatutkimuskeskus.fi; internet www.kuluttajatutkimuskeskus.fi; f. 1990; attached to Min. of Employment and the Economy; investigates change and risk factors in consumer behaviours; Dir Dr PÄIVI TIMONEN.

Multidimensional Tourism Institute: Viirinkankaantie 1, 96300 Rovaniemi; internet tourism.luc.fi; f. as Lapland Institute for Tourism Research and Education, present name 2012; attached to Univ. of Lapland; promotes cooperation between product devt, innovation, tourism research and tourism education; Dir Dr JOHAN EDELHEIM.

Suomen Akatemia (Academy of Finland): Hakaniemenranta 6, POB 131, 00531 Helsinki; tel. (29) 5335000; e-mail kirjaamo@aka.fi; internet www.aka.fi; f. 1969; promotes and provides funding for research; library of 30,000 vols, 290 periodicals, journals and newsletters; Pres. Prof. HEIKKI MANNILA; Vice-Pres. for Research Prof. MARJA MAKAROW; publs *A propos* (12 a year, in Finnish), *ProAcademia* (2 a year, in English).

AGRICULTURE, FISHERIES AND VETERINARY SCIENCE

Elintarviketurvallisuusvirsato—Evira (Finnish Food Safety Authority—Evira): Mustialankatu 3, 00790 Helsinki; tel. (29) 5300400; e-mail info@evira.fi; internet www.evira.fi; f. 2006; food control supervision and guidance, laboratory operations, risk assessments and scientific research; Dir-Gen. MATTI AHO.

Laboratory Animal Centre: c/o Univ. of Oulu, POB 5000, 90014 Oulu; Aapistie 5D, 90220 Oulu; tel. (8) 5375070; internet www.oulu.fi/keks; attached to Univ. of Oulu; responsible for laboratory animals and laboratory animal services; conducts environmental research; provides the provision of advice for animal testing activities; Dir HANNA-MARJA VOIPIO.

Maa-ja elintarviketalouden tutkimuskeskus (MTT Agrifood Research Finland): 31600 Jokioinen; tel. (29) 5300700; internet www.mtt.fi; f. 1898, present name and status 2001; consists of 4 research units, 2 research programmes; Dir-Gen. Prof. ERKKI KEMPPAINEN; publs *Agricultural and Food Science* (Journal), *Finnish Agriculture and Rural Industries* (1 a year).

Research Units:

Biotekniikka-ja elintarviketutkimus (Biotechnology and Food Research): 31600 Jokioinen; tel. (3) 41881; Head Dr EEVA-LIISA RYHÄNEN.

Kasvintuotannon tutkimus (Plant Production Research): 31600 Jokioinen; tel. (3) 41881; Head Prof. HARRI HUHTA.

Kotieläintuotannon tutkimus (Animal Production Research): 31600 Jokioinen; tel. (3) 41881; Head JUTTA SIIVONEN.

Taloustutkimus (Economic Research): Latokartanonkaari 9, 00790 Helsinki; tel. (20) 772004; Dir Dr SARI FORSMAN-HUGG.

Metsäntutkimuslaitos (Metla) (Finnish Forest Research Institute): Jokiniemenkuja 1, POB 18, 01301 Vantaa; tel. (29) 5322111; e-mail kirjaamo@metla.fi; internet www.metla.fi; f. 1917; promotes through research, economical, ecological, and socially sustainable management and use of forests; maintains 9 research units; library of 45,000 vols; Dir-Gen. Prof. LEENA PAAVILAINEN; publs *Finnish Forest Sector Economic Outlook* (1 a year), *Metsätieteellinen aikakauskirja* (4 a year), *Metsätieteen aikakauskirja*, *Silva Fennica* (4 a year), *Working Papers of Metla* (online).

Riista ja Kalatalouden Tutkimuslaitos (Finnish Game and Fisheries Research Institute): Viikinkaari 4, POB 2, 00791 Helsinki; tel. (20) 57511; e-mail julkaisumyynti@rktl.fi; internet www.rktl.fi; f. 1971; attached to Min. of Agriculture and Forestry; assesses, forecasts and compiles statistics on fish and game resources; Dir-Gen. Prof. Dr EERO HELLE.

BIBLIOGRAPHY, LIBRARY SCIENCE AND MUSEOLOGY

Museovirasto (National Board of Antiquities): POB 913, 00101 Helsinki; tel. (9) 40501; e-mail museovirasto.kirjaamo@nba.fi; internet www.nba.fi; f. 1884; attached to Min. of Education and Culture; directs and supervises Finland's admin. of antiquities; researches cultural heritage, preserves artefacts, bldgs and sites of cultural and historical value; maintains the Nat. Museum and other museums; closed for relocation; library of 180,000 vols and 1,000 periodicals; Dir-Gen. HELENA EDGREN.

ECONOMICS, LAW AND POLITICS

Elinkeinoelämän Tutkimuslaitos (ETLA) (Research Institute of the Finnish Economy): Lönnrotinkatu 4B, 00120 Helsinki; tel. (9) 609900; e-mail info@etla.fi; internet www.etla.fi; f. 1946; research in economics, business economics and social policy; 3 research units, 1 forecasting unit; Chair. JORMA OLLILA; Man. Dir Dr VESA VIHRIÄLÄ.

Tilastokeskus (Statistics Finland): 00022 Statistics Finland; Työpajankatu 13, 00580 Helsinki; tel. (9) 17341; e-mail kirjaamo@stat.fi; internet www.stat.fi; f. 1865; library: see under Libraries and Archives; Dir-Gen. MARJO BRUUN; publs *Bulletin of Statistics* (4 a year), *Official Statistics of Finland*, *Statistical Yearbook of Finland* (1 a year).

Ulkopoliittenen Instituutti (Finnish Institute of International Affairs): POB 400, 00161 Helsinki; Kruunuvuorenkatu 4, 00160 Helsinki; tel. (9) 4327000; e-mail kirjaamo@fiia.fi; internet www.fiia.fi; f. 1961; conducts research, organizes seminars, publishes reports on int. relations and the EU; library of 23,500 vols, 200 periodicals; Chair. ANTTI TANSKANEN; Dir Dr TEIJA TIILIKAINEN; publs *Finnish Foreign Policy Papers*, *Ulkopolitiikka* (Finnish Journal of Foreign Affairs, 4 a year).

Valtion Taloudellinen Tutkimuskeskus (Government Institute for Economic Research): POB 1279, 00101 Helsinki; Arkadiankatu 7, 00101 Helsinki; tel. (29) 5519400; e-mail viestinta@vatt.fi; internet www.vatt.fi; analyses public finances and evaluates economic reforms; Dir-Gen. JUHANA VARTIAINEN; publ. *Finnish Economy—Structural Indicators* (every 2 years).

EDUCATION

Suomen Kasvatustieteellinen Seura/ Samfundet för Pedagogisk Forskning (Finnish Educational Research Association): POB 35, 40014 Univ. of Jyväskylä; e-mail kaisa.kiuttu@jyu.fi; internet www.kasvatus.net; f. 1967; Chair. MARJATTA LAIRIO; Sec. JUHANI TÄHTINEN; publ. *Kasvatus* (Finnish Journal of Education, 5 a year).

MEDICINE

BioMediTech—Institute of Biosciences and Medical Technology: Biokatu 10, First Fl., 33520 Tampere; e-mail info@biomeditech.fi; internet www.biomeditech.fi; attached to Tampere Univ. of Technology and Univ. of Tampere; research activities incl. biomaterials, stem cells, cancer, immunology, biosensors, imaging, computational methods; aims to develop personalized medicine via new diagnostic and treatment methods; Dir HANNU HANHIJÄRVI.

Minerva Foundation Institute for Medical Research: Biomedicum Helsinki 2U, Tukholmankatu 8, 00290 Helsinki; tel. (9) 19125700; internet www.helsinki.fi/minerva; f. 1959; basic and experimental biomedical, genetic and nutritional research; library of 4,000 vols; Chair. VESA OLKKONEN; Sec. CIA OLSSON.

Terveyden ja Hyvinvoinnin Laitos (National Institute for Health and Welfare): POB 30, 00271 Helsinki; Mannerheimintie 166, 00271 Helsinki; tel. (29) 5246000; e-mail info@thl.fi; internet www.thl.fi; f. 2009 by merger of Nat. Research and Devt Centre for Welfare and Health and National Public Health Institute; statutory statistical authority in health and welfare; divs of health and social services, health protection, welfare and health policies, welfare and health promotion; library of 35,000 vols, 300 journals, 7,000 ejournals; Dir-Gen. PEKKA PUSKA; publs *Dialogi* (6 to 8 a year in Finnish, 1 a year in English), *Nordisk alkohol- & narkotikatidskrift* (Nordic Studies on Alcohol and Drugs), *THL Magazine*, *Yhteiskuntapolitiikka*.

NATURAL SCIENCES

Physical Sciences

Geodeettinen laitos/Geodetiska Institutet (Finnish Geodetic Institute): POB 15, 02431 Masala; Geodeetinrinne 2, 02430 Masala; tel. (9) 295550; e-mail info@fgi.fi; internet www.fgi.fi; f. 1918; research in geodesy, geodynamics, remote sensing, photogrammetry, navigation, geoinformatics, cartography; library of 25,000 vols; Dir-Gen. Prof. Dr JARKKO KOSKINEN; publs *Suomen Geodeettisen laitoksen julkaisuja* (Publications of the Finnish Geodetic Institute), *Suomen Geodeettisen laitoksen tiedonantoja* (Reports of the Finnish Geodetic Institute), *Tiedote*.

Geologian Tutkimuskeskus/Geologiska Forskningscentralen (Geological Survey of Finland): POB 96, Betonimiehenkuja 4, 02151 Espoo; tel. (29) 5030000; e-mail info@gtk.fi; internet www.gtk.fi; f. 1885; works on assessment, research and sustainable use of earth resources; library of 182,000 vols; Chair. TARMO TUOMINEN; Dir-Gen. Dr ELIAS EKDAHL; publ. *Special Paper*.

Ilmatieteen Laitos/Meteorologiska Institutet (Finnish Meteorological Institute): POB 503, 00101 Helsinki; Erik Palménin aukio 1, 00560 Helsinki; tel. (29) 5392200; internet www.fmi.fi; f. 1838; provides information about the atmosphere above and around Finland; ensures public safety relating to atmospheric and airborne hazards; provides satisfying requirements for specialized meteorological products; library of 37,000 vols; Dir-Gen. Dr PETTERI TAALAS; Dir MIKKO ALESTALO; publ. *Suomen meteorologinen vuosikirja* (Meteorological Yearbook of Finland, in English and Finnish).

Mittatekniikan Keskus (Centre for Metrology and Accreditation): Tekniikantie 1 POB 9, 02151 Espoo; tel. (29) 5054000; internet www.mikes.fi; SI system measurement units, metrological research, developing measuring applications; Dir-Gen. Dr TIMO HIRVI; Exec. Sec. TAINA SARVIKAS.

Säteilyturvakeskus (STUK)/Strålsäkerhetscentralen (Radiation and Nuclear Safety Authority): POB 14, 00881 Helsinki; Laippatie 4, 00880 Helsinki; tel. (9) 759881; e-mail stuk@stuk.fi; internet www.stuk.fi; f. 1958; govt authority for radiation protection and nuclear safety, incl. inspection and research in the field; library of 30,000 vols; Dir-Gen. Prof. PETTERI TIIPPANA.

Suomen Ympäristökeskus (Finnish Environment Institute): POB 140, 00251 Helsinki; Mechelininkatu 34A, Töölö, 00251 Helsinki; tel. (20) 610123; e-mail kirjaamo.syke@ymparisto.fi; internet www.environment.fi/syke; f. 1995; research on changes in the environment and ways to control these changes through long-term environmental monitoring; library of 60,000 vols, 14,000 electronic journals, 800 journals; Dir-Gen. LEA KAUPPI; publ. *Ympäristö-lehti* (8 a year).

RELIGION, SOCIOLOGY AND ANTHROPOLOGY

Donnerska institutet för religionshistorisk och kulturhistoriskforskning/ Steinerbiblioteket (Donner Institute for Research in Religious and Cultural History): POB 70, 20501 Turku; Piispankatu 13, 20500 Turku; tel. (20) 7861451; e-mail donner.institute@abo.fi; internet www.abo.fi/donnerinstitute; f. 1959; promotes research in religious and cultural history; organizes Nordic conf. on comparative religion every 3 years; library of 90,000 vols, 600 journals; Chair. Prof. ULRIKA WOLF-KNUTS; Dir Dr RUTH ILLMAN; publs *Approaching Religion* (online, www.abo.fi/approachingreligion), *Scripta Instituti Donneriani Aboensis* (online, www.abo.fi/scripta).

Kotimaisten Kielten Keskus (Research Institute for the Languages of Finland): Vuorikatu 24, 00100 Helsinki; tel. (29) 5333200; internet www.kotus.fi; nat. research centre and expert institution for linguistic studies; library of 70,000 vols; Dir Prof. PIRKKO NUOLIJÄRVI; publs *Hiidenkivi*, *Kielikello* (4 a year), *Språkbruk* (in Swedish).

TECHNOLOGY

VTT Technical Research Centre of Finland: Vuorimiehentie 5, POB 1000, 02044 VTT; tel. (20) 722111; e-mail info@vtt.fi; internet www.vtt.fi; f. 1942; provides multitechnological applied research, devt testing and information services to the public sector, companies and int. orgs; technological focus on applied materials, biotechnology and chemistry processes, energy, information and communication technologies, industrial systems management, microtechnologies and electronics, technology in the community; Pres. and CEO ERKKI LEPPÄVUORI; Sec. ANNELI KARTTUNEN; publs *VTT Impulse* (Technology Magazine), *VTT Research Highlights*, *VTT Review*, *VTT Science*, *VTT Symposium*, *VTT Tiedotteita—Research Notes* (Technology Magazine).

Libraries and Archives

Aalto

Aalto-yliopiston Kirjasto (Aalto University Library): POB 31000, 00076 Aalto; tel. (50) 4066916; e-mail kirjasto-toolo@aalto.fi; internet lib.aalto.fi; f. 1849, present status 2010; Arabia campus library: art and design, Otaniemi campus library: science and technology, Töölö campus library: business and economics, 20 institutional libraries in science and technology in Otaniemi campus; 770,000 vols, 56,000 ejournals, 253 MSS, 15,500 theses, 3,067 printed music titles, 586,200 microforms, 4,500 sound recordings, 11,900 print periodicals, 336,214 ebooks, 150,000 govt documents, 64 maps, 24,530 audiovisual materials, 410 databases; Chief Librarian Dr EEVA-LIISA LEHTONEN.

Åbo

Åbo Akademis Bibliotek (Åbo Akademi University Library): Domkyrkogatan 2–4, 20500 Åbo; tel. (2) 2154180; e-mail biblioteket@abo.fi; internet www.abo.fi/bibliotek/en; f. 1919; 2m. vols (excluding pamphlets and MSS); Chief Librarian Dr PIA SÖDERGÅRD; publ. *Skrifter utgivna av Åbo Akademis bibliotek.*

Espoo

Espoon Kaupunginkirjasto/maakuntakirjasto (Espoo City Library/Regional Central Library): Kamreerintie 3C, POB 36, 02070 Espoo; tel. (9) 8165011; f. 1869; 14 br. libraries, 2 in hospitals and instns, 2 mobile units; 1m. vols; spec. collns Uusimaa-Nylandica (provincial colln), Norwegian colln; Chief Librarian ULLA PACKALÉN.

Helsinki

Celia Library: POB 20, IIRIS, 00030 Helsinki; Marjaniementie 74 (Iiris Centre), 2nd Fl., Helsinki; tel. (9) 229521; e-mail palvelut@celia.fi; internet www.celia.fi; f. 1890; state-owned specialist library; provides talking books, ebooks and Braille books for print-disabled people; 40,000 vols; Dir MARKETTA RYÖMÄ.

Deutsche Bibliothek (German Library): Pohjoinen Makasiinikatu 7, 00130 Helsinki; tel. (9) 669363; e-mail deutsche.bibliothek@kolumbus.fi; internet www.deutsche-bibliothek.org; f. 1881; 36,000 vols; spec. collns incl. Fennica colln; Dir GABRIELE SCHREY-VASARA; Librarian MARJA IMMONEN; publ. *Jahrbuch für Englisch-deutsche Literaturbeziehungen* (1 a year).

Eduskunnan kirjasto (Library of Parliament): 00102 Helsinki; Main Post Office Bldg, Asema-aukio 5H, 4th Floor, 00100 Helsinki; tel. (9) 4323432; e-mail library@parliament.fi; internet lib.eduskunta.fi/resource.phx/library/index.htx; f. 1872; reference and archival services, information service, interlibrary loans service, e-services, electronic resources, the Finnish parliamentary glossary, archive of parliament, parliamentary photographic archive, information management training; 500,000 vols on parliamentary information, legal information, social and political information, admin.; Dir SARI PAJULA; publs *Bibliographia Iuridica Fennica 1982–1993*, *Eduskunnan kirjaston tutkimuksia ja selvityksiä* (Library of Parliament Studies and Reports), *Valtion virallisjulkaisut* (Govt Publs in Finland, 1961–1996).

Hanken Svenska Handelshögskolans Bibliotek (Library of the Hanken School of Economics): Arkadiagatan 22, POB 479, 00101 Helsinki; tel. (40) 3521265; e-mail lanedisk@hanken.fi; internet www.hanken.fi/library; f. 1909; 61,500 vols of printed books, 118 journals, 95,000 ebooks, 33,500 ejournals; Library Dir TUA HINDERSSON-SÖDERHOLM.

Helsingin Kaupunginkirjasto (Helsinki City Library): POB 4100, 00099 Helsinki; Rautatieläisenkatu 8, 00520 Helsinki; tel. (9) 3108511; e-mail city.library@hel.fi; internet www.lib.hel.fi; f. 1860; 35 br. libraries, 2 mobile libraries and 11 institutional libraries; 1,900,366 vols (incl. 1,589,549 books, 28,796 sheets of music, 221,149 recordings, 3,647 CDs and DVDs, 4,637 vols of subscribed journals); Library Dir TUULA HAAVISTO.

Helsingin Yliopiston Kirjasto (Helsinki University Library): POB 53 (Fabianinkatu 32), 00014 Helsinki; tel. (9) 19123920; e-mail library@helsinki.fi; internet www.helsinki.fi/library; attached to Univ. of Helsinki; 4 brs: City Centre campus, Kumpula campus, Viikki campus, Meilahti campus Library Terkko; became ind. institute of Univ. in 2010; 2.3m. vols, 26,500 ejournals, 81 shelf kms, 339,000 ebooks; Univ. Librarian Dr KIMMO TUOMINEN.

Kansallisarkisto (National Archives of Finland): Rauhankatu 17, POB 258, 00171 Helsinki; tel. (29) 5337000; e-mail arkisto@narc.fi; internet www.arkisto.fi; f. 1869; central office for public archives; controls seven Provincial Archives at Hämeenlinna, Joensuu, Jyväskylä, Mikkeli, Oulu, Turku, and Vaasa; holds historical documents and archives of the Govt, Supreme Court and other court records, and private papers of statesmen and politicians; the Provincial Archives contain documents relating to regional and local admin.; 87,345 vols, 102,607 m of shelvable archival material, 1,005,660 cartographical items; Dir-Gen. Dr JUSSI NUORTEVA.

Attached Archive:

Helsingin Kaupunginarkisto (Helsinki City Archives): POB 5510, 00099 Helsinki; Eläintarhantie 3F, 00099 Helsinki; tel. (9) 31043571; e-mail kaupunginarkisto@hel.fi; internet www.hel.fi/hki/tieke/en/city+archives; f. 1945; central archive repository for City Admin.; private archives; Dir JUSSI JÄÄSKELÄINEN; City Archivist EEVA-KAISA PEURANEN (acting).

Kansalliskirjasto (National Library of Finland): c/o Univ. of Helsinki, POB 15, 00014 Helsinki; Unioninkatu 36, 00014 Helsinki; tel. (9) 19123196; e-mail kk-palvelu@helsinki.fi; internet www.nationallibrary.fi; f. 1640 in Turku (Åbo), moved to Helsinki 1828; nat. library of Finland and research library of arts and humanities; comprehensive colln of books printed in Finland, large foreign colln, incl. the Slavonic library and the American resource centre; Nordenskiöld colln (cartography), Finnish historical newspaper library, spec. collns; web archive, nat. electronic library; 3m. vols, 670,000 MSS and 410 incunabula, 108,000 m of shelving; Dir Prof. KAI EKHOLM; publ. *The National Library of Finland Bulletin.*

Kansalliskirjasto, Slaavilainen Kirjasto (National Library of Finland, Slavonic Library): POB 15 (Fabianinkatu 35), 00014 Helsinki; tel. (2) 94124066; e-mail kk-slav@helsinki.fi; internet www.nationallibrary.fi/services/kokoelmat/slaavilainenkirjasto.html; f. 1843; held a legal deposit right to all publs printed in Russia from 1828–1917; acquires literature in arts, humanities and social science for Russian and E European studies; colln in Slavonic languages; 470,000 vols; Librarian IRMA REIJONEN.

Sibelius-Akatemian Kirjasto/Sibelius-Akademins bibliotek (Sibelius Academy Library): POB 86, 00251 Helsinki; Töölönlahdenkatu 16C, 00100 Helsinki; tel. (40) 7104223; e-mail sibakirjasto@siba.fi; internet lib.siba.fi/en; f. 1885; 19,000 vols, 75,000 scores, 34,000 recordings, 1,100 video recordings and a colln of periodicals, complete works and anthologies; Chief Librarian IRMELI KOSKIMIES.

Suomalaisen Kirjallisuuden Seuran Kirjasto (Library of the Finnish Literature Society): POB 259, 00171 Helsinki; Hallituskatu 1, 00170 Helsinki; tel. (20) 1131272; e-mail kirjasto@finlit.fi; internet www.finlit.fi/english/library; f. 1831; 230,000 vols of Finnish literature, literary studies, cultural research, other fields of the humanities; Chief Librarian Dr Phil. CECILIA AF FORSELLES.

Attached Libraries:

Suomalaisen Kirjallisuuden Seuran Kansanrunousarkisto (Folklore Archives of the Finnish Literature Society): Hallituskatu 1, POB 259, 00171 Helsinki; tel. (20) 1131240; e-mail kansanrunousarkisto@finlit.fi; internet www.finlit.fi; f. 1934; 600 shelf m of MSS, audio recordings, video cassettes and photographs on Finnish folklore and oral history; Dir LAURI HARVILAHTI.

Suomalaisen Kirjallisuuden Seuran Kirjallisuusarkisto (Literary Archives of the Finnish Literature Society): Mariankatu 19E, Hallituskatu 1, POB 259, 00171 Helsinki; tel. (20) 1131262; e-mail kirjallisuusarkisto@finlit.fi; internet www.finlit.fi; f. 1831; 1,300 shelf m of MSS, correspondence, recordings and photographs on Finnish literature, history and language; 2,000 private archives by Finnish writers, scholars and functionaries; Chief Archivist ULLA-MAIJA PELTONEN.

Svenska litteratursällskapet i Finland, arkiv och bibliotek (Archives and library): Riddaregatan 5, 00170 Helsinki; tel. (9) 61877466; e-mail info@sls.fi; internet www.sls.fi; f. 1885; 2,200 collns, 300,000 photographs; 50,000 vols; Librarian MARTIN GINSTRÖM; publs *Folklivsstudier*, *Källan*, *Meddelanden från Folkkultursarkivet.*

Tilastokirjasto (Library of Statistics): Library of Statistics, POB 2B, Statistics Finland, 00022 Helsinki; Työpajankatu 13B, Second Fl., 00022 Helsinki; tel. (9) 17342220; e-mail info@stat.fi; internet www.stat.fi/tup/tilastokirjasto; f. 1865; service centre for Finnish and int. statistics; 330,000 vols, 4,203 periodicals, 35,000 microfiches, 20,100 electronic publs; Dir for Information Services SARI PALÉN.

Joensuu

Joensuun seutukirjasto—Pohjois-Karjalan maakuntakirjasto (Joensuu Regional Library—Central Library of North Karelia): POB 114, Koskikatu 25, 80101 Joensuu; tel. (13) 2677111; e-mail kirjasto@jns.fi; internet www.jns.fi/resource.phx/sivut/sivut-kirjasto; f. 1862; spec. colln of N Karelia; 500,000 vols; Dir for Libraries REBEKKA PILPPULA.

Jokioinen

MTT (Maa ja elintarviketalouden tutkimuskeskus) kirjasto (MTT Agrifood Research Finland Library): Datum, Second Floor, 31600 Jokioinen; tel. (29) 5300700; e-mail kirjasto@mtt.fi; internet www.mtt.fi; f. 1935; 80,000 vols, 600 periodicals; Information Specialist SIRPA SUONPÄÄ; Information Specialist NINA-MARI SALMINEN.

Jyväskylä

Jyväskylän Yliopiston Kirjasto (Jyväskylä University Library): POB 35, 40014 Jyväskylä; Seminaarinkatu 15, Bldg B, 40014 Jyväskylä; tel. (14) 2601211; e-mail jykneuvonta.kirjasto@library.jyu.fi; internet kirjasto.jyu.fi; f. 1912; attached to Univ. of Jyväskylä; depository library for Finnish prints and audiovisual material; European Documentation Centre for EU resources; 1.8m. vols, 7,500 journals, 20,000 ejournals; Dir ARI MUHONEN; publs *Jyväskylä Studies in Biological and Environmental Science*, *Jyväskylä Studies in Business and Economics*, *Jyväskylä Studies in Computing*, *Jyväskylä Studies in Education, Psychology and Social Research*, *Jyväskylä Studies in Humanities*, *Studies in Sport, Physical Education and Health.*

Kuopio

Itä-Suomen yliopiston kirjasto (University of Eastern Finland Library): Snellmania Yliopistonranta 1E, POB 1627, 70211 Kuopio; tel. (29) 4458400; e-mail library@uef.fi; internet www.uef.fi/en/kirjasto; f. 2010 by merger of fmr Joensuu and Kuopio Univ. Libraries; 3 campus libraries in Joensuu, Kuopio and Savonlinna; 1,000,000 vols, 300,000 ebooks, 600 printed journals, 36,000 ejournals; Dir Dr JARMO SAARTI.

Kuopion kaupunginkirjasto (Kuopio City Library): Maaherrankatu 12, POB 157, 70101 Kuopio; tel. (17) 182111; e-mail kirjasto.kut@kuopio.fi; internet www.kuopio.fi/kirjasto; f. 1872; 10 br. libraries and 2 mobile libraries; 700,000 vols; Library Dir. MARJA-TIITTANEN SAVOLAINEN; Chief Librarian HILKKA KOTILAINEN.

Varastokirjasto (National Repository Library): Päivärannantie 10, POB 1710, 70421 Kuopio; tel. (17) 2646000; e-mail varkirja@nrl.fi; internet www.varastokirjasto.fi; f. 1989; repository to be shared by all libraries in Finland; 1,300,000 vols, 80,000 periodicals, 500,000 dissertations; Dir PENTTI VATTULAINEN.

Oulu

Oulun yliopiston kirjasto (Oulu University Library): POB 7500, 90014 Oulu; tel. (8) 5531011; e-mail kirjasto@oulu.fi; internet www.oulu.fi/kirjasto; f. 1959; depository library; European Documentation Centre; spec. collns incl. material concerning N and Arctic research; 1,212,700 vols of printed books, 1,500 journals and 327,500 e-books; Library Dir PÄIVI KYTÖMÄKI; publ. *Acta Universitatis Ouluensis*.

Pori

Porin kaupunginkirjasto—Satakunnan maakuntakirjasto (Pori Public Library—Regional Library of Satakunta): POB 200, 28101 Pori; Gallen-Kallela St 12, 28100 Pori; tel. (2) 6215800; e-mail kirjasto@pori.fi; internet www.pori.fi/kirjasto; f. 1858; centre of Hungarian literature; 506,339 vols; Librarian ASKO HURSTI.

Tampere

Tampereen kaupunginkirjasto—Pirkanmaan maakuntakirjasto (Tampere City Library—Pirkanmaa Regional Library): Pirkankatu 2, POB 152, 33101 Tampere; tel. (3) 565611; e-mail tampereen.kaupunginkirjasto@tampere.fi; internet kirjasto.tampere.fi; f. 1861; provides regional library services to 22 municipalities in the Tampere Region; 1,021,635 vols, 142,682 audiovisual materials and 122 newspapers; spec. collns: Poland, Pirkanmaa region; Dir of Libraries TUULA HAAVISTO.

Tampereen teknillisen yliopiston kirjasto (Tampere University of Technology Library): Korkeakoulunkatu 10, POB 537, 33101 Tampere; tel. (40) 1981500; e-mail kirjasto@tut.fi; internet www.tut.fi/library; f. 1956; 237,000 vols, 305 printed periodicals, 25,000 ejournals, 150,000 ebooks; Library Dir RIITTA LÄHDEMÄKI.

Tampereen yliopiston kirjasto (Tampere University Library): Kalevantie 5, POB 617, 33014 Tampere; tel. (40) 1909696; e-mail kirjasto@uta.fi; internet www.uta.fi/kirjasto; f. 1925; 522,465 vols, 373,163 ebooks, 35,769 ejournals; Chief Librarian Dr MIRJA IIVONEN.

Turku

Turun kauppakorkeakoulun kirjastotietopalvelu (Turku School of Economics, Library and Information Services): c/o Univ. of Turku, Discipline Specific Library Anthropos, Economics Library, 20014 Turku; Rehtorinpellonkatu 3, 20500 Turku; tel. (2) 3339161; e-mail tsekirjasto@utu.fi; f. 1950; attached to Univ. of Turku; 110,000 vols; Dir ULLA NYGRÉN.

Turun yliopiston pääkirjasto (University of Turku Main Library): University Hill, 20014 Turku; tel. (2) 3336176; e-mail library@utu.fi; internet library.utu.fi; f. 1921, present location 1954; colln of old Finnish literature; first European Documentation Centre of Finland; jt ICT library of Univ. of Turku, Åbo Akademi Univ. and Turku Univ. of Applied Sciences; incl. European Documentation Centre; 2.8m. vols; Library Dir ULLA NYGRÉN; publ. *Annales Universitatis Turkuensis*.

Museums and Art Galleries

Espoo

Gallen-Kallelan Museo (Gallen-Kallela Museum): Gallen-Kallelan tie 27, 02600 Espoo; tel. (9) 8492340; e-mail tarvaspaa@gallen-kallela.fi; internet www.gallen-kallela.fi; f. 1961; home and studio of Finland's nat. artist Akseli Gallen-Kallela; features his life and works; Dir TUIJA WAHLROOS.

Helsinki

Amos Andersonin taidemuseo (Amos Anderson Art Museum): POB 14, 00101 Helsinki; Yrjönkatu 27, 00100 Helsinki; tel. (9) 6844460; e-mail museum@amosanderson.fi; internet www.amosanderson.fi; f. 1965; private art museum in Finland; colln of modern art incl. art primarily from the 20th century; Dir KAI KARTIO; Sr Curator KAJ MARTIN.

Arkkitehtuurimuseo (Museum of Finnish Architecture): Kasarmikatu 24, 00130 Helsinki; tel. (9) 85675100; e-mail mfa@mfa.fi; internet www.mfa.fi; f. 1956; nat. specialist museum; 500,000 drawings, 85,000 photographs, 30,000 pictures; library of 33,000 vols, Fennica colln of 9,000 vols, 100 periodicals; Dir JUULIA KAUSTE.

Ateneumin Taidemuseo (Ateneum Art Museum): Kaivokatu 2, 00100 Helsinki; tel. (9) 4500401; e-mail ainfo@ateneum.fi; internet www.ateneum.fi; f. 1888; Finnish art from mid-18th century to 1950s; int. art; colln of paintings and sculptures, paints and drawings; Dir MAIJA TANNINEN-MATTILA.

Designmuseo/Designmuseet (Design Museum): Korkeavuorenkatu 23, 00130 Helsinki; tel. (9) 6220540; e-mail info@designmuseum.fi; internet www.designmuseum.fi; f. 1873; history and devt of Finnish design; 75,000 objects, 40,000 drawings and 100,000 images; library of 10,000 vols; Dir JUKKA SAVOLAINEN.

Didrichsen Taidemuseo (Didrichsen Art Museum): Kuusilahdenkuja 1, 00340 Helsinki; tel. (10) 2193970; e-mail office@didrichsenmuseum.fi; internet www.didrichsenmuseum.fi; f. 1965; Finnish art from the 20th century; modern int. art; oriental art and Finland's only pre-Columbian art colln; Dir PETER DIDRICHSEN; Chief Curator MARIA DIDRICHSEN.

Helsingin Kaupunginmuseo/Helsingfors Stadsmuseum (Helsinki City Museum): Sofiankatu 4, POB 4300, 00099 Helsinki; tel. (9) 31036630; e-mail kaupunginmuseo@hel.fi; internet www.helsinkicitymuseum.fi; f. 1911; cultural history museum; main exhibition on the history of Helsinki; spec. exhibitions to highlight various features of the city's past; colln of 200,000 objects; documentation and inventory pertaining to different eras; photographic archive with photographs from 1860s to the present; Helsinki landscape paintings and graphics; library of 15,000 vols; Dir TIINA MERISALO; publs *Memoria*, *Narinkka*, *Sofia* (2 a year).

Kiasma—Museum of Contemporary Art: Mannerheiminaukio 2, 00100 Helsinki; tel. (9) 173361; e-mail info@kiasma.fi; internet www.kiasma.fi; f. 1998; museum of contemporary art under Finnish Nat. Gallery; 8,000 works of art; Dir PIRKKO SIITARI; publ. *Kiasma magazine*.

Luonnontieteellinen Keskusmuseo/Naturhistoriska Centralmuseet (Finnish Museum of Natural History): c/o Univ. of Helsinki, Pohjoinen Rautatiekatu 13, POB 17, 00014 Helsinki; tel. (9) 1911; e-mail luonnontieteellinenmuseo@helsinki.fi; internet www.luomus.fi; f. 1925; attached to Univ. of Helsinki; Dir LEIF SCHULMAN; publs *Delectus Seminum* (every 2 years), *Lutukka* (4 a year), *Norrlinia*, *Sahlbergia* (2 a year).

Attached Museums:

Eläinmuseo/Zoologiska Museet (Zoological Museum): c/o Univ. of Helsinki, P. Rautatiekatu 13, POB 17, 00014 Helsinki; tel. (9) 19150034; e-mail luonnontieteellinenmuseo@helsinki.fi; internet www.luomus.fi/elaintiede; f. 1923; Dir AINO JUSLÉN.

Geologian Museo/Geologiska Museet (Geological Museum): c/o Univ. of Helsinki, Arkadiankatu 7, POB 17, 00014 Helsinki; tel. (9) 19128745; e-mail luonnontieteellinenmuseo@helsinki.fi; internet www.luomus.fi/geologia; attached to Univ. of Helsinki; 50,000 mineral and rock samples, 600 meteorite and 44,000 fossils, bone and soil samples; Superintendent Dr ARTO LUTTINEN.

Kasvitieteellinen puutarha ja Kasvimuseo (Botanical Garden and Herbarium): c/o Univ. of Helsinki, Unioninkatu 44, POB 7, 00014 Helsinki; tel. (9) 19124456; e-mail luonnontieteellinenmuseo@helsinki.fi; internet www.luomus.fi/kasvitiede; f. 2009 after the Botanical Museum and Botanical Gardens were merged to form a part of the Museum; 7,050 different origin of the crop, 4,230 of taxon incl. trees, shrubs, annual and perennial plants; Dir MARKO HYVÄRINEN.

Mannerheim-museo/Mannerheim-museet (Mannerheim Museum): Kalliolinnantie 14, 00140 Helsinki; tel. (9) 635443; e-mail info@mannerheim-museo.fi; internet www.mannerheim-museo.fi; f. 1951; fmr home of Baron G. Mannerheim (1867–1951), Marshal of Finland and Pres. of the Republic (1944–46); exhibitions related to his life and to the history of Finland; Dir VERA VON FERSEN.

Postimuseo (Postal Museum): Häkiläpolku 3, 33100 Tampere; tel. (400) 806909; e-mail info@postimuseo.fi; internet www.postimuseo.fi/en; f. 1926; 10,000 artefacts, 30,000 photographs, 350,000 negatives and slides, 2,100 posters, 28,000 postcards, 1,500 video films; library of 30,000 vols; Dir KIMMO ANTILA; publ. *Tabellarius* (1 a year).

Sinebrychoffin Taidemuseo (Sinebrychoff Art Museum): Blvd 40, 00120 Helsinki; tel. (294) 500460; e-mail leena.hannula@fng.fi; internet www.sinebrychoffintaidemuseo.fi; f. 1921; foreign art; 20 private collns and Paul Sinebrychoff's letters archive; concerts, museum education, workshops; Dir KIRSI ESKELINEN; Chief Curator MINERVA KELTANEN.

Sotamuseo (Military Museum): Maurinkatu 1, POB 266, 00170 Helsinki; tel. (29) 9530241; e-mail sotamuseo@mil.fi; f. 1929; central museum of defence forces; over 200,000 artefacts and 200,000 photographs and images; Dir HARRI HUUSKO; Curator RIITTA BLOMGREN.

Suomen kansallismuseo/Finlands nationalmuseum (National Museum of Finland): POB 913, 00101 Helsinki; Mannerheimintie 34, 00101 Helsinki; tel. (9) 401286469; e-mail kansallismuseo@nba.fi; internet www.nba.fi/fi/kansallismuseo; f. 1893; archaeology, ethnography, ethnology, history, numismatics; several museums throughout Finland; Dir-Gen. Dr HELENA EDGREN.

Suomen Valokuvataiteen Museo (Finnish Museum of Photography): Tallberginkatu 1C 85, 00180 Helsinki; The Cable Factory, Tallberginkatu 1G, 00180 Helsinki; tel. (9) 68663621; e-mail fmp@fmp.fi; internet www.valokuvataiteenmuseo.fi; f. 1969; nat. specialist museum; 3.7m. prints and negatives; Dir ELINA HEIKKA.

Valtion Taidemuseo/Statens Konstmuseum (Finnish National Gallery): Kaivokatu 2, 00100 Helsinki; tel. (9) 173361; e-mail kirjaamo@fng.fi; internet www.fng.fi; f. 1887 as the Ateneum, re-organized as the Finnish National Gallery in 1990; comprises Ateneum Art Museum, Museum of Contemporary Art Kiasma, Sinebrychoff Art Museum, Central Art Archives; library of 50,000 vols; Dir-Gen. RISTO RUOHONEN.

Hyvinkää

Hyvinkää Taidemuseo (Hyvinkää Art Museum): Hämeenkatu 3D, 05800 Hyvinkää; tel. (40) 4801644; e-mail taidemuseo@hyvinkaa.fi; internet www.hyvinkaantaidemuseo.fi; f. 1982; domestic and foreign contemporary art and art history; Dir SANNA TEITTINEN (acting); Sec. ERJA HOLOPAINEN.

Suomen Rautatiemuseo (Finnish Railway Museum): Hyvinkäänkatu 9, 05800 Hyvinkää; tel. (30) 725241; e-mail info@rautatie.org; internet www.rautatie.org; f. 1898, present location 1974; nat. specialist museum; 20,000 artefacts, 150,000 photographs; library of 16,000 vols; Dir ELINA HOLOPAINEN.

Jyväskylä

Alvar Aalto Museo (Alvar Aalto Museum): POB 461, 40101 Jyväskylä; Alvar Aallon katu 7, 40600 Jyväskylä; tel. (14) 2667113; e-mail museum@alvaraalto.fi; internet www.alvaraalto.fi; f. 1966; 1,600 objects; 120,000 drawings and sketches; 20,000 letters; 20,000 photographs; library of 3,000 vols; Dir and Chief Curator KAARINA MIKONRANTA (acting).

Jyväskylän Yliopiston Museo (Jyväskylä University Museum): POB 35, 40014 Jyväskylä; tel. (40) 5272802; internet www.jyu.fi/erillis/museo; f. 1900; collects, preserves, researches and exhibits material related to univ. history; sections of cultural history and natural history; collns incl. 36,000 items and 27,000 photographs; 250,000 scientific samples of wild animals; Dir Prof. JANNE VILKUNA.

Kuopio

Kuopion Taidemuseo (Kuopio Art Museum): Kauppakatu 35, 70100 Kuopio; tel. (17) 182633; e-mail taidemuseo.kut@kuopio.fi; internet taidemuseo.kuopio.fi; f. 1980; 6,700 art works; Finnish art from end of 19th century; emphasis on local painters; central theme is nature and the environment; Dir AIJA JAATINEN.

Oulu

Pohjois-Pohjanmaan Museo (Northern Ostrobothnia Museum): Ainolan Puisto, POB 26, 90015 Oulu; tel. (50) 3166497; e-mail ppm@ouka.fi; internet www.ouka.fi/ppm; f. 1896; specializes in historical-ethnological research on N Ostrobothnia; focus on the city of Oulu; Dir PASI KOVALAINEN.

Parola

Pansasarimuseo (Tank Museum): POB 31, 13721 Parola; Hattulantie 334, 13720 Parola; tel. (40) 5681186; e-mail toimisto@panssarimuseo.fi; internet www.panssarimuseo.fi; f. 1961; military historical museum; Dir TIMO TERÄSVALLI; publ. *Armour Magazine*.

Pietarsaari

Nanoq-museon (Arctic Museum Nanoq): Pörkenäsintie 60, 68620 Pietarsaari; tel. (6) 7293679; e-mail info@nanoq.fi; internet www.nanoq.fi; f. 1991; colln of Goichman's paintings, soapstone sculptures; Dir PENTTI KRONQVIST; Curator JOHANNA ENROTH.

Pori

Porin Taidemuseo (Pori Art Museum): Eteläranta, 28100 Pori; tel. (2) 6211080; e-mail taidemuseo@pori.fi; internet www.poriartmuseum.fi; f. 1981; 2,800 works of Finnish art and int. contemporary art; library of 2,711 vols, 6,166 exhibition catalogues; Dir ESKO NUMMELIN.

Satakunta Museo (Satakunta Museum): Hallituskatu 11, 28100 Pori; tel. (2) 6211078; e-mail satakunnanmuseo@pori.fi; internet www2.pori.fi/smu/sivut; f. 1888; 80,000 archaeological and historical exhibits; 300,000 photographs relating to the history of Satakunta province; library of 13,115 vols in reference library and 9,228 old books; Dir JUHANI RUOHONEN; publ. *Sarka* (1 a year).

Attached Museum:

Rosenlew-Museo (Rosenlew Museum): Kuninkaanlahdenkatu 14, 28100 Pori; tel. (2) 6211865; e-mail rosenlew-museo@pori.fi; f. 2003; presents the history and products of the Rosenlew Company (industrial co in Finland).

Rauma

Lönnströmin Taidemuseo (Lönnström Art Museum): Valtakatu 7, 26100 Rauma; tel. (2) 83874700; e-mail info@lonnstromintaidemuseo.fi; internet www.lonnstromintaidemuseo.fi; f. 1993; contemporary and traditional art; Dir JENNY NYBOM.

Riihimäki

Riihimäen Taidemuseo (Riihimäki Art Museum): Temppelikatu 8, 11100 Riihimäki; tel. (19) 7584124; e-mail riihimaen.taidemuseo@riihimaki.fi; internet www.riihimaki.fi/riihimaki/taidemuseo; f. 1994; Finnish art, foreign art, antiquities; Curator HELENA LINDSTÉN.

Tampere

Museokeskus Vapriikki (Museum Centre Vapriikki): Alaverstaanraitti 5, 33101 Tampere; tel. (3) 56566966; e-mail vapriikki@tampere.fi; internet www.tampere.fi/vapriikki; colln of 367,000 objects; Dir TOIMI JAATINEN.

Component Museums:

Amurin Työläismuseokortteli (Amuri Museum of Workers' Housing): Satakunnankatu 49, POB 487, 33101 Tampere; tel. (3) 56566690; e-mail amuri@tampere.fi; internet www.tampere.fi/amuri; f. 1974; showcases devt of workers' housing 1880–1970, with authentic bldgs; Dir TOIMI JAATINEN.

Hämeen Museo (Häme Museum): POB 487, 33101 Tampere; tel. (3) 31465306; f. 1904; prehistory and folk art of the cultural district of Tampere and the old Häme province; closed for renovation during 2010.

Sara Hildénin Taidemuseo (Sara Hildén Art Museum): Laiturikatu 13, Särkänniemi, 33230 Tampere; tel. (3) 56543500; e-mail sara.hilden@tampere.fi; internet www.tampere.fi/sarahilden; f. 1979; exhibition centre for the works of the Sara Hildén Foundation colln (f. 1962 when Sara Hildén donated all her art works to it); 4,500 collns, modern art, with emphasis on Finnish and foreign art of the 1960s and 1970s; library of 9,000 vols; Dir RIITTA VALORINTA.

Tampereen Taidemuseo (Tampere Art Museum): Puutarhakatu 34, POB 487, 33101 Tampere; tel. (3) 56566577; e-mail tamu@tampere.fi; internet www.tampere.fi/taidemuseo; f. 1931; 7,000 works incl. paintings, prints, drawings and sculptures; Finnish art since early 19th century; Dir TAINA MYLLYHARJU.

Attached Museum:

Moominvalley of the Tampere Art Museum: Hämeenpuisto 20, POB 487, 33101 Tampere; tel. (3) 56566578; e-mail muumi@tampere.fi; internet muumilaakso.tampere.fi/museo; f. 1987; based on the Moomin books by Tove Jansson; 2,000 works.

Turku

Aboa Vetus & Ars Nova Historian ja Nykytaiteen Museo (Aboa Vetus & Ars Nova, Museum of History and Contemporary Art): Itäinen Rantakatu 4–6, 20700 Turku; tel. (20) 7181640; e-mail info@aboavetusarsnova.fi; internet www.aboavetusarsnova.fi; f. 1995; private museum; focuses on Finnish middle ages and contemporary art; Matti Koivurinta Foundation art colln; archaeological excavations in Aboa Vetus; Dir JOHANNA LEHTO-VAHTERA; publ. *Aboa Vetus & Ars Nova Magazine*.

Sibeliusmuseum/Sibelius-museo (Sibelius Museum): Biskopsgatan 17, 20500 Turku; tel. (2) 2154494; e-mail sibeliusmuseum@abo.fi; internet www.sibeliusmuseum.abo.fi; f. 1926; archive and library, instrument colln and an exhibition section; archives and library contain material related to Jean Sibelius and Finnish music; instrument colln incl. 2,000 musical instruments; associated with the musicological research dept of Åbo Akademi Univ.; Dir and Curator Dr INGER JAKOBSSON-WÄRN.

Turun Maakuntamuseo/Åbo Landskapsmuseum (Turku Provincial Museum): POB 286, 20101 Turku; tel. (2) 330000; e-mail museokeskus@turku.fi; internet www.museumcentreturku.fi; f. 1881; consists of the Castle of Turku with the collns of Turku Historical Museum, Luostarinmäki Handicrafts Museum, Pharmacy Museum and the Qwensel House, Kylämäki Village of living history, Turku Biological Museum, furniture, paintings, costumes, textiles, porcelain, glass, silver, copper, firearms, uniforms, weapons, coins and medals; Dir IMMONEN OLLI; publ. *Raportteja* (Studies).

Turun Taidemuseo/Åbo Konstmuseum (Turku Art Museum): Aurakatu 26, 20100 Turku; tel. (2) 2627100; e-mail info@turuntaidemuseo.fi; internet www.turuntaidemuseo.fi; f. 1891; 6,000 works of art; paintings, sculpture, prints and drawings, mainly of Finnish and Scandinavian art since early 19th century; Dir KARI IMMONEN.

Wäinö Aaltosen Museo (Wäinö Aaltonen Museum of Art): POB 286, 20101 Turku; Itäinen Rantakatu 38, 20810 Turku; tel. (2) 2620850; e-mail wam@turku.fi; internet www.wam.fi; f. 1967; Wäinö Aalto's work; recent focus on sculpture; library of 8,000 works collected by Wäinö Aalto; Dir IMMONEN OLLI.

Universities

AALTO-YLIOPISTO (Aalto University)

POB 11000, 00076 Aalto
Telephone: (9) 47001
E-mail: president@aalto.fi
Internet: www.aalto.fi
Founded 2010 by merger of Helsingin kauppakorkeakoulu (f. 1911), Teknillinen korkeakoulu (f. 1908), Taideteollinen korkeakoulu (f. 1871)
Languages of instruction: English, Finnish, Swedish
Academic year: September to May
Pres.: Prof. Dr TUULA TEERI
Deputy Pres. for Academic Affairs: Prof. Dr ILKKA NIEMELÄ
Vice-Pres. for Academic Affairs: Prof. MARTTI RAEVAARA
Vice-Pres. for Knowledge Networks: Dr HANNU SERISTÖ
Dir for Finance: MARIANNA BOM
Library Dir: Dr EEVA-LIISA LEHTONEN
Library: see under Libraries and Archives
Number of teachers: 350
Number of students: 19,750

DEANS

School of Arts, Design and Architecture: Prof. ANNA VALTONEN
School of Business: Prof. Dr INGMAR BJÖRKMAN
School of Chemical Technology: Prof. OUTI KRAUSE
School of Electrical Engineering: Prof. Dr TUIJA PULKKINEN
School of Engineering: Prof. Dr PETRI VARSTA
School of Science: Prof. Dr KIMMO KASKI

PROFESSORS

School of Arts, Design and Architecture:
CEDERSTRÖM, E., Motion Picture, Documentary
DEAN, P., New Media
DIAZ-KOMMONEN, L., New Media, Design for Systems of Representations
GRÖNDAHL, L., Scenography, Stage Design
HAKURI, M., Environmental Art
HEIKKILÄ, S., Furniture Design
HEINÄNEN, T., Motion Picture, Filming
HIRVONEN, P., Fashion Design
HYVÖNEN, H., Textile Design
ITKONEN-TOMASZEWSKI, L., Graphic Design
JACUCCI, G., Industrial Design
JULIN-ARO, J., Functional Materials and Design
KÄÄRIÄINEN, P., Textile Design
KAREOJA, P., Spatial Design
KEINONEN, T., Industrial and Strategic Design
KELLY, P., International Design and Production
KORVENMAA, P., Design and Culture
KOSKINEN, I., Industrial and Strategic Design
KUPIAINEN, R., Visual Culture, Theory
LAAKSO, H., Visual Culture
LAKANEN, A., Motion Picture, Editing
LAMPELA, J., Motion Picture, Directing
LEINONEN, T., New Media
LEVANTO, I., Art History
MCGRORY, P., Industrial and Strategic Design
MÄENPÄÄ, M., Media Production
MAJA, A., Scenography, Film and Television
MÄKI, T., Fine Arts
MIETTINEN, E., Industrial Design
NIEMINEN, E., Design, Material Research
NIKKANEN, R., Industrial Design
PARANTAINEN, J., Photography
POHJAKALLIO-KOSKINEN, P., Art Pedagogy
PRIHA, P., Textile Design
RAEVAARA, M., Art Education, Visual Knowledge Building
RITALAHTI, R., Motion Picture, Production
RYYNÄNEN, M., Visual Culture, Theory
SALLI, T., Product Design
SALO, M., Photography
SEDERHOLM, M., Art Education
SONVILLA-WEISS, S., e-Pedagogy Design, Visual Knowledge Building
SOTAMAA, Y., Design and Innovation
SUOMINEN, J., Mass Customization in Design
TÖYRY, M., Journalism
VAPAASALO, T., Graphic Design and Communication
VARTO, J., Art Education, Research
VIENO, J., Motion Picture, Screenwriting
VIHMA, S., Design Semiotics
VON BAGH, P., Motion Picture, History and Theory
YLI-VIKARI, T., Ceramics Design

School of Science
Faculty of Chemistry and Materials Sciences:
ALOPAEUS, V., Chemical Engineering and Plant Design
DAHL, O., Chemical Pulping and Environmental Technology
FORSEN, O., Laboratory of Corrosion and Material Chemistry
FRANSSILA, S., Materials Science
GANE, P., Paper Technology
GASIK, M., Materials Processing and Powder Metallurgy
HANNULA, S., Processing and Heat Treatment of Materials
HEISKANEN, K., Mechanical Process and Recycling Technology
HUGHES, M., Wood Technology
HURME, M., Chemical Engineering and Plant Design
JÄMSÄ-JOUNELA, S., Laboratory of Process Control and Automation
JOKELA, R., Laboratory of Organic Chemistry
KAIRI, M., Wood Technology
KARPPINEN, M., Laboratory of Inorganic and Analytical Chemistry
KIVIVUORI, S., Processing and Heat Treatment of Materials
KONTTURI, K., Laboratory of Physical Chemistry
KORHONEN, A., Department of Materials Science and Engineering
KOSKINEN, A., Laboratory of Organic Chemistry
KOSKINEN, J., Department of Materials Science and Engineering
KRAUSE, O., Laboratory of Industrial Chemistry
KULMALA, S., Laboratory of Inorganic and Analytical Chemistry
LAAKSO, S., Laboratory of Biochemistry
LAINE, J., Forest Products Chemistry
LEISOLA, M., Laboratory of Bioprocess Engineering
MALONEY, T., Paper Technology
NORDSTRÖM, K., Laboratory of Biochemistry and Microbiology
PALTAKARI, J., Wood Technology
PAULAPURO, H., Paper Technology
ROJAS, O.
SEPPÄLÄ, J., Laboratory of Polymer Technology
SIXTA, H., Chemical Pulping and Wood Refinery
TASKINEN, P., Department of Materials Science and Engineering
VAN HEININGEN, A., Forest Products Chemistry
VIITANIEMI, P., Wood Technology
VUORINEN, T., Forest Products Chemistry
WINTER, S.
YAMAUCHI, H.

Faculty of Electronics, Communications and Automation:
AALTO, S., Teletraffic Theory
ALKU, P., Acoustics and Audio Signal Processing
ARKKIO, A., Electromechanics
ARO, M., Power Systems and High Voltage Engineering
ESKELINEN, P., Radio Science and Engineering
HAARLA, L., Electromechanics
HÄGGMAN, S., Communications and Networking
HALLIKAINEN, M., Space Technology
HALME, A., Automation Technology
HALONEN, K., Electronic Circuit Design
HALONEN, L., Lighting Technology
HÄMMÄINEN, H., Communications and Networking
HONKANEN, S., Photonics, Micro and Nano Sciences
IKONEN, E., Metrology Research Institute
KANTOLA, R., Communications and Networking
KARJALAINEN, M., Acoustics and Audio Signal Processing
KOIVO, H., Systems Technology
KOIVUNEN, V., Signal Processing
KUIVALAINEN, P., Electron Physics
KYYRÄ, J., Power Systems and High Voltage Engineering
LAINE, U., Acoustics and Audio Signal Processing
LEHTONEN, M., Power Systems and High Voltage
LIPSANEN, H., Nanotechnology
LUOMI, J., Electromagnetics
NIKOSKINEN, K., Electromagnetics
ÖSTERGÅRD, P., Information Theory, Discrete Mathematics and Algorithms
OVASKA, S., Power Electronics
PAKANEN, J., Lighting Technology
PAULASTO-KRÖCKEL, M., Electronics
RÄISÄNEN, A., Radio Science and Engineering
RICHTER, A., Signal Processing
RYYNÄNEN, J., Electronic Circuit Design
SEPPONEN, R., Applied Electronics
SIHVOLA, A., Electromagnetics
SIMOVSKI, C., Radio Science and Engineering
SKYTTÄ, J., Signal Processing
TIRKKONEN, O., Communications and Networking
TITTONEN, I., Metrology Research Institute
TRETYAKOV, S., Radio Science
VAINIKAINEN, P., Radio Science
VÄLIMÄKI, V., Acoustics and Audio Signal Processing
VALTONEN, M., Circuit Theory
WICHMAN, R., Signal Processing

Faculty of Engineering and Architecture:
AALTO, J., Structural Mechanics
AALTONEN, K., Production Engineering
ACHE, P., Urban and Regional Planning
AHTILA, P., Energy Economics and Power Plant Engineering
AIRILA, M., Machine Design
EKMAN, K., Machine Design
EKROOS, A., Law
ERNVALL, T., Transportation Engineering
FOGELHOLM, C., Energy Engineering and Environmental Protection
HAGGREN, H., Photogrammetry and Remote Sensing
HÄKKINEN, P., Ship Laboratory
HÄNNINEN, H., Engineering Materials
HARRIS, T., Urban Design
HEDMAN, M., Architecture
HEIKKINEN, P., Wood Program
HUOVINEN, S., Structural Engineering and Building Physics
JOLMA, A., Cartography and Geoinformatics
JUHALA, M., Automotive Engineering

JUTILA, A., Bridge Engineering
KAILA, J., Waste Management Technology
KANKAINEN, J., Construction Economics and Management
KARVONEN, T., Water Resources
KIIRAS, J., Construction Economics and Management
KOMONEN, M., Public Building Design
KUOSMANEN, P., Machine Design
LAMPINEN, M., Applied Thermodynamics
LAPINTIE, K., Urban and Regional Planning
LARMI, M., Internal Combustion Engine Laboratory
LEVÄINEN, K., Real Estate Studies
LOUKOLA-RUSKEENIEMI, K., Rock Engineering
LUTTINEN, T., Transportation Engineering
MÄKELÄINEN, P., Steel Structures
MATUSIAK, J., Ship Laboratory
NISKANEN, A., History of Architecture
NYKÄNEN, P., Industrial History
ORKAS, J., Foundry Engineering
PAAVILAINEN, S., Basics and Theory of Architecture
PAAVOLA, J., Structural Mechanics
PELLINEN, T., Highway Engineering
PELTONIEMI, M., Rock Engineering
PENTTALA, V., Building Materials Technology
PIETOLA, M., Machine Design
PIRILÄ, P., Energy Economics and Power Plant Engineering
PURSULA, M., Transportation Engineering
PUTTONEN, J.
RAUTAMÄKI, M., Landscape Planning
RAVASKA, O., Soil Mechanics and Foundation Engineering
SAARELA, O., Aeronautical Engineering
SÄRKKÄ, P., Rock Engineering
SEPPÄNEN, O., Heating Ventilating and Air-Conditioning
SIIKALA, A., Building Technology
SIIKONEN, T., Applied Thermodynamics
SIITONEN, T., Housing Design
SIREN, K., Heating Ventilating and Air-Conditioning
SOINNE, E., Aeronautical Engineering
TALVITIE, A.
TUHKURI, J., Mechanics of Materials
VAHALA, R., Water and Wastewater Engineering
VAKKILAINEN, P., Water Resources Engineering
VARSTA, P., Ship Laboratory
VEPSÄLÄINEN, P., Soil Mechanics and Foundation Engineering
VERMEER, M., Geodesy
VIITANEN, K., Real Estate Studies
VILJANEN, M., Structural Engineering and Building Physics
VIRRANTAUS, K., Cartography and Geoinformatics
VITIKAINEN, A., Real Estate Studies
WECK, T., Building Structures

Faculty of Information and Natural Sciences:
ALA-NISSILÄ, T., Physics
ALAVA, M., Physics
ARTTO, K., Industrial Management
AURA, T., Media Technology
AURELL, E., Information and Computer Science
AUTERE, J., Software Business
EHTAMO, H., System Analysis
EIROLA, T., Mathematics
ELORANTA, E., Industrial Management
FRIBERG, A., Optical Physics
GRIPENBERG, G., Mathematics
HÄMÄLÄINEN, M., Computer and Information Science
HÄMÄLÄINEN, R., Applied Mathematics
HELJANKO, K., Information and Computer Science
HOLMSTRÖM, J., Industrial Management
HYVÖNEN, E., Media Technology
IKKALA, O., Applied Physics
ILMONIEMI, R., Applied Physics
JÄÄSKELÄINEN, I., Cognitive Systems
JAATINEN, M., Business Processes and Services in Digital Networks
JÄRVENPÄÄ, E., Work Psychology and Leadership
JÄRVENPÄÄ, S., Networked Business Processes and Business Models
JAUHO, A., Applied Physics
KAIVOLA, M., Applied Physics
KARHUNEN, J., Information and Computer Science
KASKI, K., Computational Engineering
KASKI, S., Information and Computer Science
KAUPPINEN, E., Physics
KAUPPINEN, M., Software Business
KAURANEN, I., Development and Management in Industry
KEIL, T., Strategic Management
KERTÉSZ, J., Computational Complex Systems
KINNUNEN, J., Mathematics
KOSKELAINEN, A., Applied Physics
LAAMANEN, T., Strategic Management
LÄHDESMÄKI, H., Information and Computer Science
LAINE, J., Software Business
LAMBERG, J., Strategic Management
LAMPINEN, J., Computational Engineering
LASSENIUS, C., Computer Science
LILLRANK, P., Quality Management
LIPPONEN, J., Work Psychology and Leadership
LUND, P., Applied Physics
MALMI, L., Information Processing Science
MANNILA, H., Information and Computer Science
MÄNNISTÖ, T., Software Business
MÄNTYLÄ, M., Computer and Information Science
MAULA, M., Venture Capital
MERILÄINEN, P., Applied Physics
NEVANLINNA, O., Mathematics
NIEMELÄ, I., Information and Computer Science
NIEMINEN, M., Software Business and Engineering
NIEMINEN, R., Physics
NYBERG, K., Information and Computer Science
OITTINEN, P., Media Technology
OJA, E., Information and Computer Science
ORPONEN, P., Information and Computer Science
PITKÄRANTA, J., Mathematics
PUOLAMÄKI, K., Virtual Techniques
PUSKA, M., Physics
RAUSCHECKER, J., Systems Neuroscience
RUOKOLAINEN, J., Applied Physics
SAARINEN, E., System Analysis
SAIKKONEN, H., Computer Science and Engineering
SALO, A., System Analysis
SALOMAA, R., Applied Physics
SAMS, M., Cognitive Systems
SAVIOJA, L., Media Technology
SIMULA, O., Information and Computer Science
SMEDS, R., Business and Service Processes in Digital Networks
SOISALON-SOININEN, E., Software Technology
STENBERG, R., Mechanics
SULONEN, R., Software Business and Engineering
TAKALA, T., Telecommunication Software and Multimedia
TANSKANEN, K., Logistics
TARHIO, J., Information Processing Science
TÖRMÄ, P., Applied Physics
TULKKI, J., Computational Science
VALKEILA, E., Mathematics
VAN DIJKEN, S., Physics
VARTIAINEN, M., Work Psychology and Leadership
VUORIMAA, P., Multimedia Technology
WALLENIUS, H., Economics
YLÄ-JÄÄSKI, A., Telecommunications Software and Multimedia

ÅBO AKADEMI
(Åbo Akademi University)

Tuomiokirkontori 3, 20500 Turku
Telephone: (2) 21531
E-mail: information@abo.fi
Internet: www.abo.fi

Founded 1918
State control
Language of instruction: Swedish
Academic year: August to July

Depts of biosciences, chemical engineering, information technologies, law, natural sciences, political science, psychology and logopedics, social sciences; faculties of arts, education, theology; school of business and economics

Chancellor: JARL-THURE ERIKSSON
Rector: JORMA MATTINEN
First Vice-Rector: Prof. CHRISTINA NYGREN-LANDGÄRDS
Second Vice-Rector: Prof. MIKKO HUPA
Third Vice-Rector: Prof. MALIN BRÄNNBACK
Head of Admin.: ULLA ACHRÉN
Chief Librarian: PIA SÖDERGÅRD

Library: 2m. vols, 300,000 ebooks, 17,000 ejournals
Number of teachers: 700
Number of students: 8,350

Publications: *Acta Academiae Aboensis*, *Årsberättelse* (Annual Review)

PROFESSORS

Department of Biosciences:
BONSDORFF, E., Marine Ecology
ERIKSSON, J., Cell Biology
JOHNSON, M., Biochemistry
LINDSTRÖM, K., Ecology and Environmental Biology
SISTONEN, L., Cell and Molecular Biology
SLOTTE, J. P., Biochemistry
TÖRNQUIST, K., Biology
VUORELA, P., Pharmacy

Department of Chemical Engineering:
FAGERVIK, K., Chemical Engineering
FARDIM, P., Fibre and Cellulose Technology
HUPA, M., Inorganic Chemistry
IVASKA, A., Analytical Chemistry
LEWENSTAM, A., Analytical Chemistry
MIKKOLA, J-P, Industrial Chemistry and Reaction Engineering
MURZIN, D., Industrial Chemistry and Reaction Engineering
PELTONEN, J., Paper Coating and Converting
SALMI, T., Industrial Chemistry and Reaction Engineering
SAXÉN, H., Thermal and Flow Engineering
TOIVAKKA, M., Paper Coating and Converting
WÄRNÅ, J., Industrial Chemistry and Reaction Engineering
WESTERLUND, T., Process Design and Systems Engineering
WIKSTRÖM, K., Industrial Management
WILÉN, C.-E., Polymer Technology
WILLFÖR, S., Wood and Paper Chemistry
ZEVENHOVEN, R., Thermal and Flow Engineering

Department of Information Technologies:
BACK, B., Information Systems
BACK, R.-J., Computer Science
CARLSSON, C., Information Systems
LILIUS, J., Computer Engineering
PETRE, I., Computer Science
PORRES PALTOR, I., Computer Engineering

SERE, K., Computer Science
TOIVONEN, H., Computer Engineering
WALDEN, P., Information Systems
WESTERHOLM, J., Computer Engineering

Department of Law:

HONKA, H., Commercial Law
PIRJATANNIEMI, E., Public International Law
SUKSI, M., Public Law
WETTERSTEIN, P., Private Law

Department of Natural Sciences:

CORANDER, J., Mathematics and Statistics
EHLERS, C., Geology and Mineralogy
HÖGNÄS, G., Mathematics
HOTOKKA, M., Physical Chemistry
LEINO, R., Organic Chemistry
LINDBERG, M., Physics
ÖSTERBACKA, R., Physics
SALMINEN, P., Mathematics
SJÖHOLM, R., Organic Chemistry
STAFFANS, O., Mathematics

Department of Political Science:

ANCKAR, C., Political Science
DJUPSUND, G., Political Science
JOAS, M., Public Administration
KARVONEN, L., Political Science

Department of Psychology and Logopedics:

LAINE, M., Psychology
SANDNABBA, K., Psychology
SANTTILA, P., Psychology
TUOMAINEN, J., Logopedics

Department of Social Sciences:

BJÖRKQVIST, K., Developmental Psychology
EKLUND, E., Rural Studies
ERIKSSON, K., Caring Science
FINNÄS, F., Demograhy
HURME, H., Developmental Psychology
JAKOBSSON, G., Social Policy
LAGERSPETZ, M., Sociology
LINDSTRÖM, U., Caring Science
SILIUS, H., Women's Studies
SUNDBACK, P., Sociology

Faculty of Arts:

AHLUND, C., Comparative Literature
ANDERSSON, E., Swedish Language
ÅSTROM, A.-M., Nordic Ethnology
BERGGREN, L., Art History
BRUSILA, J., Musicology
GUSTAFSSON, M., Philosophy
HAAPAMÄKI, S., Swedish Language
LARJAVAARA, M., French Language and Literature
LÖNNQVIST, B., Russian Language and Literature
NIKANNE, U., Finnish Language and Literature
NEUENDORFF, D., German Language
NYNÄS, P., Comparative Religion
RINGBOM, A., Art History
SELL, R., English Language and Literature
VILLSTRAND, N. E., Nordic History
VIRTANEN-ULFHIELM, T., English Language
WOLF-KNUTS, U., Nordic Folklore

Faculty of Education:

BJÖRKQVIST, O., Didactics of Mathematics and Sciences
GRÖNHOLM, M., Didactics of Languages and the Humanities
ITKONEN, T., Special Education
LINDAHL, M., Early Childhood Education
NYGREN-LANDGÅRDS, C., Pedagogics in Sloyd Education
SALO, P., Adult Education
SJÖHOLM, K., Didactics of Languages and the Humanities
ULJENS, N., General Education

Faculty of Theology:

AF HÄLLSTRÖM, G., Dogmatics
DAHLBACKA, I., Church History
KURTÉN, T., Theological Ethics
LAATO, A., Old Testament Exegesis and Jewish Studies
SUNDKVIST, B., Practical Theology
SYREENI, K., New Testament Exegetics

School of Business and Economics:

BRÄNNBACK, M., International Marketing
HASSEL, L., Accounting
JÄNTTI, M., Economics
KRISTENSSON UGGLA, B., Organization and Management
ÖSTERMARK, R., Accounting
REHN, A., Business Administration
TÖRNROOS, J.-Å., Management Science
WIDÉN, G., Information Studies
WILLNER, J., Economics

HELSINGIN YLIOPISTO/ HELSINGFORS UNIVERSITET (University of Helsinki)

POB 33 (Yliopistonkatu 4), 00014 Helsinki
Telephone: (9) 1911
E-mail: admissions@helsinki.fi
Internet: www.helsinki.fi/university

Founded 1640 Turku (Åbo), 1828 Helsinki
State control
Languages of instruction: Finish, Swedish
Academic year: September to May (2 terms)

Chancellor: Prof. Dr ILKKA NIINILUOTO
Rector: Prof. Dr THOMAS WILHELMSSON
Vice-Rector for Academic Quality Assurance and Int. Affairs: Prof. Dr ULLA-MAIJA FORSBERG
Vice-Rector for Education and Lifelong Learning: Prof. Dr JUKKA KOLA
Vice-Rector for Research and Innovation: Prof. Dr JOHANNA BJÖRKROTH
Vice-Rector for Social Interaction and Fundraising: Prof. Dr KIMMO KONTULA
Dir of Admin.: ESA HÄMÄLÄINEN
Univ. Librarian: KAISA SINIKARA

Library: see under Libraries and Archives
Number of teachers: 1,694
Number of students: 35,258

DEANS

Faculty of Agriculture and Forestry (Viikki Campus): Prof. MARKETTA SIPI
Faculty of Arts: Prof. ANNA MAURANEN
Faculty of Behavioural Sciences: Prof. PATRIK SCHEININ
Faculty of Biological and Environmental Sciences (Viikki Campus): Prof. JARI NIEMELÄ
Faculty of Law: Prof. KIMMO NUOTIO
Faculty of Medicine (Meilahti Campus): Prof. RISTO RENKONEN
Faculty of Pharmacy (Viikki Campus): Prof. JOUNI HIRVONEN
Faculty of Science: Prof. KEIJO HÄMÄLÄINEN
Faculty of Social Sciences: Prof. LIISA LAAKSO
Faculty of Theology: Prof. AILA LAUHA
Faculty of Veterinary Medicine (Viikki Campus): Prof. ANTTI SUKURA
Swedish School of Social Science: HENRIK HÄGGLUND (Rector)

PROFESSORS

Faculty of Agriculture and Forestry (Viikki Campus) (POB 62 (Viikinkaari 11), 00014 Helsinki; tel. (9) 19158247; e-mail mmtdk-international@helsinki.fi; internet www.helsinki.fi/mmtdk):

AHOKAS, J. M., Agricultural Engineering
ALATOSSAVA, J. T., Dairy Technology
DAHLIN, S. B., Logistics
HARI, P. K. J., Forest Ecology
HARTIKAINEN, H. H., Soil and Environment Chemistry
HATAKKA, A., Environmental Biotechnology
HEINONEN, I. M., Functional Food
HELENIUS, J. P., Agroecology
HELIÖVAARA, K. T., Forest Zoology
HOKKANEN, H. M. T., Agricultural Zoology
HYVÖNEN, L. E. T., Food Technology
HYVÖNEN, S. M., Marketing
JAAKKOLA, A. O., Agricultural Chemistry and Physics
JUSLIN, H. J., Forest Products Marketing
KANGAS, A., Forest Mensuration and Management
KOLA, J. T. S., Agricultural Politics
KOSKELA, M. O., Food Economics
KUULUVAINEN, J. T. M., Social Economics of Forestry
LAASASENAHO, J. E., Forest Mensuration and Management
LUUKKANEN, M. O., Silviculture in Developing Countries
MAKAROW, M. T., Applied Biochemistry
MÄKELÄ, P. S. A., Crop Production
MÄKINEN, V.-P. J., Agricultural Entrepreneurship
MIKKONEN, E. U. A., Logging and Utilization of Forest Products
MUTANEN, M. L., Nutrition Physiology
NÄSI, J. M., Animal Nutrition
OJALA, M. J., Animal Breeding
OLLIKAINEN, M. M. O., Environmental Economics
PEHKONEN, A. I., Agricultural Engineering
PIIRONEN, V. I., Food Chemistry
PUOLANNE, T. E. J., Meat Technology
PUTTONEN, P. K., Silviculture
RÄSÄNEN, L. K., Nutrition
SALKINOSA-SALONEN, M. S., Microbiology
SALOVAARA, H. O., Cereal Technology
SARIS, P.-E. J., Food Microbiology
SIPI, M. H., Forest Technology
SJÖBERG, A.-M. K., Technology of Households and Institutions
SUMELIUS, J. H., Agricultural Economics
TEERI, T. H., Plant Production
TENKANEN, T. M., Chemistry of Bioproduction
TERVO, M. J., Forest Product Marketing
TOKOLA, T. E., Geoinformatics
TUORILA, H. M., Food Technology
VALKONEN, P. T., Plant Pathology
VALSTA, L., Business Economics of Forestry
VANHATALO, A. O., Animal Science
WESTERMARCK, H. E., Extension Education
WESTMAN, C. J. V., Forest Soil Science
YLÄTALO, E. M. O., Agricultural Economics

Faculty of Arts (Fabianinkatu 33, Second Floor, POB 3, 00014 Helsinki; e-mail hum-info@helsinki.fi; internet www.helsinki.fi/hum):

APO, S.-K., Folklore
BACON, G. H. A., Film and Television Research
BREUER, U. M., German Philology
CARLSON, L. H., Language Theory and Translation
CHESTERMAN, A. P. C., Multilingual Communication
CLARK, P. A., Urban History
GOTHONI, R. R., Study of Religions
HAAPALA, A. K., Aesthetics
HAKULINEN, A. T., Finnish Language
HÄMEEN-ANTTILA, J. M., Arabic Language and Islamic Research
HÄRMÄ, J., Romance Philology
HARVIAINEN, J. M. T., Semitic Languages
HELKKULA, M., French Language
HENRIKSSON, M. J., American Studies
HIETARANTA, P. S., English Language
HURSKAINEN, A. J., African Languages and Cultures
HYVÄRINEN, I. K., German Philology
JANHUNEN, J.-A., East Asian Languages and Cultures
KALLIOKOSKI, J. T., Finnish Language
KARLSSON, F. G., General Linguistics
KONTTINEN, K. P. R., Art History
KORHONEN, J. A., German Philology
KOSKENNIEMI, K. M., Computer Linguistics
KOSKI, P. K. M., Theatre Science and Drama Literature
KOURI, E. I., General History

KULONEN, U.-M., Finno-Ugrian Philology
LAITINEN, L. M., Finnish Language
LARJAVAARA, M. E. T., Finnish Philology
LAVENTO, M. T., Archaeology
LEHTINEN, A. T., Finnish Philology
LEHTONEN, J. U. E., Finno-Ugrian Ethnology
LEINO, P. A., Finnish Language
LINDSTEDT, J. S., Slavonic Philology
LYYTIKÄINEN, P. R., Finnish Literature
MAZZARELLA, S. M., Scandinavian Literature
MEINANDER, C. H., History
MUSTAJOKI, A. S., Russian Language and Literature
NENOLA, A. A., Women's Studies
NEVALAINEN, T. T. A., English Philology
NIINILUOTO, I. M. O., Theoretical Philosophy
NIKULA, R. K., Arts History
NUMMI, J. T., Finnish Literature
ÖSTMAN, J.-O. I., English Philology
PARPOLA, S. K. A., Assyriology
PEKKILÄ, E. O., Musicology
PESONEN, P. J., Russian Literature
PETTERSSON, B. J. O., American Literature
PYRHÖNEN, H. M., General Literature and Aesthetics
RAUD, R., Japanese Languages and Culture
RIIHO, T. T., Iberian Languages and Romanian
RIIKONEN, H. K., General Literature
SAARI, M. H., Scandinavian Languages
SAARINEN, H. K., General History
SALOMIES, O. I., Latin Language and Roman Literature
SANDU, N.-G., Theoretical Philosophy
SIIKALA, A. A.-L., Folklore
SILTALA, J. H., Finnish History
SUOMELA-HÄRMÄ, M. E., Italian Philology
TAAVITSAINEN, I. A. J., English Philology
TARASTI, E. A. P., Musicology
VEHMAS-LEHTO, R. L. I., Russian Language
VENTOLA, E. M., English Philology
VIHAVAINEN, T. J., Russian Studies
VON PLATO, J., Philosophy

Faculty of Behavioural Sciences (POB 9, 00014 Helsinki
Siltavuorenpenger 5A, Second Floor, 00014 Helsinki; tel. (9) 19120509; e-mail behav-int@helsinki.fi; internet www.helsinki.fi/behav):

ÅHLBERG, M. K., Biology Pedagogics
ALHO, K. A., Psychology
BUCHBERGER, A.-I. V., Pedagogics of Mother Tongue Teaching
ENGESTRÖM, Y. H. M., Adult Education
HAUTAMÄKI, J. J., Special Pedagogics
HYTÖNEN, J. M. K., Pedagogics
IIVONEN, A. K., Phonetics
KALLIONIEMI, A. J. V., Theological Pedagogy
KAUKINEN, L. K., Crafts
KELTIKANGAS-JÄRVINEN, A.-L., Applied Psychology
KLIPPI, A. M. K., Logopaedics
KRAUSE, M. C., Cognitive Science
KROKFORS, L. M., Pedagogics
LAVONEN, J. M. J., Pedagogy of Physics and Chemistry
NIEMI, H. M., Pedagogics
NYMAN, G. S., Psychology
OJALA, M. O., Pre-school and Early Childhood Education
PEHKONEN, E. K., Pedagogy of Mathematics and Computer Science
SCHEININ, P. M., Pedagogics
SIMOLA, H. J., Pedagogics
SUMMALA, K. H. I., Psychology
TANI, S. H., Pedagogy of Geography and the Environment
TELLA, S. K., Pedagogics
TUOMI-GRÖHN, T. T., Home Economics
TURKKI, K. M., Home Economics
UUSIKYLÄ, K. T., Pedagogics
VIRKKUNEN, R. J. T., Developmental Work Research
VIRSU, V. V. E., Neuropsychology
VUORINEN, R. H. E., Applied Psychology

Faculty of Biological and Environmental Sciences (Viikki Campus) (POB 56 (Viikinkaari 9), 00014 Helsinki; tel. (9) 1911; e-mail bio-sci@helsinki.fi; internet www.helsinki.fi/bio):

BAMFORD, D. H., General Microbiology
DONNER, K. K., Zoology
ELORANTA, P. V., Limnology
GAHMBERG, C.-G., Biochemistry
HÄNNINEN, H. J. P., Zoology
HANSKI, I. A., Morphology and Ecology
HOLM, L. U. T., Bioinformatics
HYVÖNEN, J. T., Botany
KAILA, K. K., Physiological Zoology
KAIRESALO, T. A., Freshwater Ecology
KANGASJÄRVI, J. S., Plant Biology
KAUPPI, P. E., Environmental Protection
KEINÄNEN, K. P., Molecular Biology
KOKKO, H. M., Veterinary Ecology
KORHOLA, A. A., Arctic Global Change
KORHONEN, T. K., General Microbiology
KUIKKA, O. S., Fisheries Biology
KUOSA, H. J., Baltic Sea Research
KUPARINEN, J. S., Marine Biology
LEHTONEN, H. V. T., Fisheries Science
MERILÄ, J. K. K., Population Biology
NIEMELÄ, J. K., Urban Ecology
PALVA, E. T., Genetics
RANTA, E. J., Zoology
RIKKINEN, J. K., Zoology
ROMANTSCHUK, M. L., Environmental Biotechnology
SCHRÖDER, J. P., Genetics
STRÖMMER, R. H., Soil Ecology
SUNDSTRÖM, L. B., Evolution Biology
VIHKO, P., Biochemistry
VOIPIO, J. T. I., Electrophysiology

Faculty of Law (POB 4 (Yliopistonkatu 3), 00014 Helsinki; tel. (9) 1911; internet www.helsinki.fi/oik/tdk):

AUREJÄRVI, E. I., Civil Law
FRÄNDE, D. G., Criminal Law and Judicial Procedure
HALILA, H. J., Sports Law
HAVANSI, E. E. T., Judicial Procedure
HEIMONEN, M. O., Economics
HEMMO, M. A., Insurance and Tort Law
HOLLO, E. J., Environmental Law
KALIMA, K.-E. K., Financial Law
KANGAS, U. P. A., Civil Law
KEKKONEN, J. T., Judicial History and Roman Law
KONSTARI, T. T., Administrative Law
KOSKENNIEMI, M. A., International Law
KOSKINEN, P. T., Criminal Law
LAHTI, R. O. K., Criminal Law
LAPPALAINEN, J. A., Judicial Procedure
MÄENPÄÄ, O. I., Administrative Law
MAJAMAA, V. V., Environmental Law
MAJANEN, M. I., Criminal Law
MIKKOLA, M. L. A., Labour Law
RISSANEN, K. K., Commercial Law
RYYNÄNEN, O. J., Public Law
SISULA-TULOKAS, L. M., Civil Law
TEPORA, J. K., Civil Law
TIITINEN, K.-P., Labour Law
TIKKA, K. S., Financial Law
TUORI, K. H., Administrative Law
WILHELMSSON, T. K. J., Private and Commercial Law

Faculty of Medicine (Meilahti Campus) (Tukholmankatu 8B, 5th and 6th Fl., POB 20, 00014 Helsinki; tel. (9) 1911; e-mail med-studentaffairs@helsinki.fi; internet www.med.helsinki.fi):

ALALUUSUA, A. S. K., Dentistry
ALMQVIST, S. F., Child Psychiatry
ANDERSSON, L. C. L., Pathological Anatomy
BROMMELS, M. H., Health Care Administration
HAAHTELA, T. M. K., Clinical Allergology
HARJULA, A. L. J., Surgery
HÄYRY, P. J., Transplantation Surgery and Immunology
HERNESNIEMI, J. A., Neurosurgery
HIETANEN, J. H. P., Dentistry
HÖCKERSTEDT, K. A. V., Surgery
HOLMBERG, P. E., Physics
HUUSKONEN, M. S., Occupational Health
IKONEN, E. M., Cell and Tissue Biology
JÄNNE, O. A., Physiology
JOENSUU, H. T., Radiotherapy and Oncology
KALIMO, H. O., Applied Neuropathology
KALSO, E. A., Internal Medicine
KAPRIO, J. A., Public Health Service
KARLSSON, H. E., Psychiatry
KARMA, P. H., Otorhinolaryngology
KARPPANEN, H. O., Pharmacology
KARVONEN, J. M., Applied Dermatology and Venereology
KASTE, K. A. M., Neurology
KEKKI, P. V., General Practice and Primary Health Care
KESKI-OJA, J. K., Cell Biology
KINNULA, V. L., Pulmonary Medicine
KINNUNEN, P. K. J., Chemistry
KIVILAAKSO, E. O., Surgery
KIVISAARI, M. L., Diagnostic Radiology
KLOCKARS, M. L. G., General Practice
KNIP, J. M., Paediatrics
KÖNÖNEN, M. H. O., Stomatognatic Physiology and Prosthetic Dentistry
KONTTINEN, Y. T., Oral Medicine
KONTULA, K. K., Molecular Medicine
KORPI, E. R., Pharmacology
KORTTILA, K. T., Anaesthesiology and Intensive Care
LAHELMA, E. T., Public Health Science
LAITINEN, L. A. I., Tuberculosis and Pulmonary Medicine
LEHTO, V. P., Pathological Anatomy
LEIRISALO-REPO, T. K. M., Rheumatology
LEPÄNTALO, M. J. A., Vascular Surgery
LINDQVIST, J. C., Oral and Maxillofacial Surgery
LÖNNQVIST, J. K., Psychiatry
MÄKELÄ, T. P., Biochemistry and Cell Biology
MAURY, C. P. J., Internal Medicine
MERI, S. K., Immunology
MEURMAN, J. H., Dentistry
MURTOMAA, H. T., Oral Public Health
NEUVONEN, P. J., Clinical Pharmacology
NIEMINEN, M. S., Cardiology
NILSSON, C.-G. D., Obstetrics and Gynaecology
PAAKKARI, A. T. I., Pharmacology
PAAVONEN, J. A., Obstetrics and Gynaecology
PANULA, P. A. J., Biomedicine
PELTOLA, H. O., Infectious Diseases
PELTOMÄKI, P. T., Medical Genetics
PELTONEN-PALOTIE, L. P. M., Medical Genetics
PERTOVAARA, A. Y., Physiology
RANKI, P. A., Dermatology and Venereology
REPO, H., Internal Medicine
RINTALA, R. J., Child Surgery
ROSENBERG, P. H., Anaesthesiology
RUUTU, M. L., Urology
SAJANTILA, A. J., Genetic Forensic Medicine
SALASPURO, M. P. J., Alcohol and Narcotics Medicine
SANTAVIRTA, S. S., Orthopaedics and Traumatology
SARNA, S. J., Biometry
SIIMES, M. A., Paediatrics
SINTONEN, H. P., Health Economics
SKURNIK, M., Bacteriology
SOVIJÄRVI, A. R. A., Clinical Physiology
STENMAN, U.-H. E., Clinical Chemistry
TASKINEN, M.-R., Internal Medicine

TERVO, T. M. T., Applied Ophthalmology
TIKKANEN, M. J., Internal Medicine
TILVIS, R. S., Geriatrics
TUOMILEHTO, J. O. J., Public Health Science
UITTO, V. V.-J., Oral Biology
VIRKKUNEN, M. E., Forensic Psychiatry
VIRTANEN, I. T., Anatomy
VON WENDT, L. O. W., Child Neurology
VUORI, E. O., Forensic Chemistry
WAHLBECK, K. L. R., Psychiatry
YKI-JÄRVINEN, H., Internal Medicine
YLIKORKALA, R. O., Obstetrics and Gynaecology

Faculty of Pharmacy (Viikki Campus) (POB 56 (Viikinkaari 9), 00014 Helsinki; tel. (9) 1911; e-mail ftdk-hallinto@helsinki.fi; internet www.helsinki.fi/farmasia):

AIRAKSINEN, M. S. A., Social Pharmacy
ELO, H. O., Pharmacological Chemistry
HILTUNEN, R. V. K., Pharmacognosy
HIRVONEN, J. T., Pharmaceutical Technology
KOSTIAINEN, R. K., Pharmaceutical Chemistry
MÄNNISTÖ, P. T., Pharmacology and Drug Development
MARVOLA, M. L. A., Biopharmacy
TASKINEN, J. A. A., Pharmaceutical Chemistry
TUOMINEN, R. K., Pharmacology and Toxicology
VUORELA, H. J., Pharmacognosy
YLIRUUSI, J. K., Pharmaceutical Technology

Faculty of Science (POB 44 (Jyrängöntie 2), 00014 Helsinki; tel. (9) 19150058; e-mail sci-info@helsinki.fi; internet www.helsinki.fi/facultyofscience):

AHLGREN, T. J., Physics
AHONEN-MYKA, A. H., Computer Science
ANNILA, A. J., Biophysics
ARJAS, E., Biometry
ASTALA, K. O., Mathematics
BECKMANN, A. H.-T., Geophysics
CHAICHIAN, M., High Energy Physics
ENQVIST, K.-P., Cosmogony
ERONEN, M. J., Geology and Palaeontology
FORTELIUS, H. L. M., Evolution Palaeontology
GYLLENBERG, M. A. G., Applied Mathematics
HALONEN, L. O., Physical Chemistry
HÄMÄLÄINEN, K. J., Physics
HÄMERI, K. J., Aerosol Physics
HOYER, P. G., Elementary Particle Physics
ILLMAN, S. A., Mathematics
KAJANTIE, K. O., Theoretical Physics
KARHU, J. A., Geology and Mineralogy
KASKI, S. J. I., Computer Science
KEINONEN, J., Applied Physics
KILPELÄINEN, I. A., Organic Chemistry
KIVINEN, J. T., Computer Science
KOSKINEN, H. E. J., Space Physics
KOSONEN, M. E., Planning Geography
KOTIAHO, A. A. T., Environmental Chemistry and Analytics
KULMALA, M. T., Physics
KUPIAINEN, A. J., Mathematics
LAHTINEN, O. A., Applied Mathematics
LEPPÄRANTA, M. J., Geophysics
LESKELÄ, M. A., Inorganic Chemistry
LÖYTÖNEN, M. K., Cultural Geography
LUMME, K. A., Astronomy
MARTIO, O. T., Mathematics
MATTILA, P. E. J., Mathematics
MATTILA, V. A. K., Astronomy
MAUNU, S.-L., Polymer Chemistry
MICHELSSON, J. A., Mathematics
NORDLUND, K. H., Aerosol Physics
NUMMELIN, E., Applied Mathematics
OIVANEN, M. T., Organic Chemistry
ORAVA, R. O., Experimental Particle Physics
PAAKKI, J. P., Computer Science
PÄIVÄRINTA, L. J., Applied Mathematics
PELLIKKA, P. K. E., Geoinformatics
PESONEN, L. J., Geophysics
PYYKKÖ, V. P., Chemistry
RAATIKAINEN, K. E. E., Computer Science
RÄISÄNEN, J. A., Physics
RÄMØ, O. T., Geology and Mineralogy
RÄSÄNEN, M. O., Physical Chemistry
RIEKKOLA, M.-L., Analytical Chemistry
RISKA, D.-O. W., Physics
RITALA, M. K., Inorganic Chemistry
SAARIKKO, H. M. T., Physics
SAARINEN, H. S. S., Chemistry
SALONEN, V.-P., Environmental Geology
SAVIJÄRVI, H. I., Meteorology
SEPPÄLÄ, M. K., Computer-applied Mathematics
SEPPÄLÄ, M. K., Geography
SERIMAA, R. E., Physics
SIPPU, S. S., Computer Science
SUOMINEN, J. K., Mathematics
TALMAN, P. K., Geography
TENHU, H. J., Polymer Chemistry
TIKKANEN, M. J., Geography
TIRRI, H. R., Computer Science
TOIVONEN, H. T. T., Computer Science
TOPPILA, O. S., Mathematics
TÖRNROOS, R. F., Geology and Mineralogy
TUKIA, P. P., Mathematics
UKKONEN, E. J., Computer Science
VÄÄNÄNEN, J. A., Mathematics
VERKAMO, A. I., Software Engineering
VESALA, T. V., Meteorology
VIITALA, P. J., Planning Geography
WÄHÄLÄ-HASE, K., Organic Chemistry
WESTERHOLM, J. O., Geography

Faculty of Social Sciences (POB 54 (Unioninkatu 37), 00014 Helsinki; tel. (9) 1911; e-mail soc-sci@helsinki.fi; internet www.helsinki.fi/socialsciences):

ÅBERG, L. E. G., Communication
AIRAKSINEN, T., Practical Philosophy
ALAPURO, R. S., Sociology
ARMSTRONG, K. V., Cultural Anthropology
AULA, P. S., Communication
BLOMBERG-KROLL, H. K., Social Policy
ERÄSAARI, R. O., Social Policy
GYLLING, H. A., Applied Ethics
HAILA, A.-K. E., Social Policy
HAUTAMÄKI, A. A., Social Psychology and Psychology
HÄYRINEN-ALESTALO, M. G., Science and Technology and Research
HELKAMA, K. E., Social Psychology
HENTILÄ, S. J., Political History
HJERPPE, R. T., Economic History
HONKAPOHJA, S. M. S., Economics
HUOTARI, K. H., Social Work
JALLINOJA, R. I., Family Sociology
KANNIAINEN, V. L., Economics
KARISTO, A. O., Social Policy
KARVINEN-NIINIKOSKI, S. M. E., Social Policy
KETTUNEN, P. T., Political History
KIVIKURU, U., Journalism
KOPONEN, M. J., Development Studies
KOSKELA, E. A., Economics
KULTTI, K. K., Economics
LIEBKIND-ORMALA, K. R., Social Psychology
MASSA, J. K., Environmental Politics
MORING, T. A., Communication
NIEMI, H. O., Statistics
NYLUND, M., Social Work
PALOKANGAS, T. K., Economics
PATOMÄKI, H. O., Political Science
PEKONEN, K. J., Political Science
PELTONEN, M. T., Social History
PERÄKYLÄ, A. M., Sociology
PIRTTILÄ-BACKMAN, A.-M., Social Psychology
RISKA, E. K., Sociology
ROOS, J. P., Social Policy
SAIKKONEN, P. J., Statistics
SASSI, S. S., Communication
SATKA, M. E. A., Social Policy
SIIKALA, J. J. T., Sociology
SJÖBLOM, S. M., Municipal Administration
SULKUNEN, P. J., Sociology
SUNDBERG, J. H., Political Science
TARKKONEN, L. J., Statistics
TÖRRÖNEN, L. M., Social Work
TUOMELA, R. H., Practical Philosophy
VÄLIVERRONEN, E. T., Mass Communication
VALKONEN, Y. T., Sociology
VARTIA, Y. O., Economics
VIRTANEN, T. I., Political Science

Faculty of Theology (POB 4 (Vuorikatu 3), 00014 Helsinki; tel. (09) 1911; e-mail teol-hallinto@helsinki.fi; internet www.helsinki.fi/teol):

AEJMELAEUS, L. J. T., Exegetics
HALLAMAA, J. I., Social Ethics
HEIKKILÄ, M. K. J., Practical Theology
HEININEN, S. K. M., General Church History
HELANDER, E. M., Church Sociology
KNUUTTILA, S. J. I., Theological Ethics and Philosophy of Religion
KOTILA, H. T., Practical Theology
LAUHA, A. M., Church History
PENTIKÄINEN, J. Y., Study of Religions
RÄISÄNEN, H. M., New Testament Exegetics
RUOKANEN, M. M., Doctrinal Theology
SAARINEN, R. J., Ecumenics
SOLLAMO, R. T., Biblical Languages
TIRRI, K. A. H., Theological Pedagogy
TYÖRINOJA, R. J., Systematic Theology
VEIJOLA, T. K., Old Testament Exegetics

Faculty of Veterinary Medicine (Viikki Campus) (POB 66, 00014 Helsinki
Agnes Sjöbergin katu 2, 00014 Helsinki; tel. (9) 1911; internet www.vetmed.helsinki.fi):

ANDERSSON, C. M., Animal Breeding
BJÖRKROTH, K. J., Food Hygiene
HÄNNINEN, M. L., Veterinary Environmental Hygiene
JÄRVINEN, A.-K., Pet Diseases
KATILA, M. T. H., Animal Breeding
KORKEALA, H. J., Food Hygiene
LINDBERG, L.-A., Anatomy
PALVA, A., Veterinary Microbiology
POHJANVIRTA, R. K., Toxicology
PÖSÖ, A. R., Veterinary Physiology
PYÖRÄLÄ, S. H. K., Veterinary Medicine
SALONIEMI, H., Animal Hygiene
SNELLMAN, P. M., Diagnostic Radiology
SPILLMANN, T., Veterinary Internal Medicine
SUKUNA, A. K. K., Veterinary Pathology
TULAMO, R.-M., Veterinary Surgery
VAINIO-KIVINEN, O. M., Pharmacology
VAPAATALO, O. P., Virology

ITÄ-SUOMEN YLIOPISTO
(University of Eastern Finland)

Joensuu Campus: Yliopistokatu 2, POB 111, 80101 Joensuu
Telephone: (45) 1111
Kuopio Campus: Yliopistonranta 1, POB 1627, 70211 Kuopio
Telephone: (294) 451111
E-mail: kirjaamo@uef.fi
Internet: www.uef.fi
Founded 2010 by merger of Univ. of Joensuu and Univ. of Kuopio
State control
Languages of instruction: English, Finnish
Academic year: August to June
Rector: Prof. Dr PERTTU VARTIAINEN
Academic Rector: Prof. Dr JUKKA MÖNKKÖNEN
Dir for Admin.: TUOMO MERILÄINEN
Library Dir: JARMO SAARTI
Library: see under Libraries and Archives
Number of teachers: 2,596
Number of students: 15,012

DEANS

Faculty of Health Sciences: Prof. HILKKA SOININEN
Faculty of Science and Forestry: Prof. TIMO JÄÄSKELÄINEN
Faculty of Social Sciences and Business Studies: Prof. JUHA KINNUNEN
Philosophical Faculty: Prof. MARKKU FILPPULA

JYVÄSKYLÄN YLIOPISTO (University of Jyväskylä)

POB 35, 40014 Jyväskylä
Telephone: (14) 2601211
E-mail: tiedotus@jyu.fi
Internet: www.jyu.fi
Founded 1863 as Teacher Training School, present status 1966
Languages of instruction: English, Finnish
State control
Academic year: September to July (3 terms)
Rector: Prof. Dr MATTI MANNINEN
Vice-Rector: Prof. Dr HELENA RASKU-PUTTONEN
Vice-Rector: Prof. KAISA MIETTINEN
Admin. Dir: KIRSI MOISANDER
Chief Librarian: KIMMO TUOMINEN
Library: 1.5m. vols incl. 7,500 printed journals; Finnish and foreign database and over 20,000 ejournals
Number of teachers: 800
Number of students: 15,000
Publications: *Jyväskylä Studies in the Arts, Jyväskylä Studies in Biological and Environmental Science, Jyväskylä Studies in Business and Economics, Jyväskylä Studies in Communication, Jyväskylä Studies in Computing, Jyväskylä Studies in Education, Psychology and Social Research, Jyväskylä Studies in Humanities, Jyväskylä Studies in Languages, Jyväskylä Studies in Sport, Physical Education and Health, Kasvatus* (Finnish Journal of Education), *Studia Historica Jyväskyläensia, Studia Philologica Jyväskyläensia*

DEANS

Faculty of Education (incl. Dept of Teacher Training): Prof. Dr MARJATTA LAIRIO
Faculty of Humanities: Prof. PETRI KARONEN
Faculty of Information Technology: Prof. Dr PEKKA NEITTAANMÄKI
Faculty of Mathematics and Science: Prof. HENRIK KUNTTU
Faculty of Social Sciences: Prof. Dr TIMO AHONEN
Faculty of Sport and Health Sciences: Prof. LASSE KANNAS
School of Business and Economics: Prof. Dr JUKKA PELLINEN

PROFESSORS

Faculty of Education (POB 35 (Viveca), 40014 Jyväskylä
Rautpohjankatu 8 (Bldg Viveca), 40014 Jyväskylä; tel. (14) 2601211; e-mail ktk.tdk@edu.jyu.fi; internet www.jyu.fi/edu):

ALANEN, L., Early Childhood Education
HAKALA, J., Education
HÄNNIKÄINEN, M., Early Childhood Education
KAIKKONEN, P., Foreign Language Education
KAUPPINEN, A., Finnish Language Education
KORPINEN, E., Education
LAURINEN, L., Education
MÄÄTTÄ, P., Special Education
POIKKEUS, A.-M., Early Childhood Education
PUOLIMATKA, T., Education
RASKU-PUTTONEN, H., Educational Psychology
SALOVIITA, T., Special Education
VIIRI, J., Pedagogy of Mathematics and Science

Faculty of Humanities (Athenaeum, POB 35, 40014 Jyväskylä
Seminaarinkatu 15, Bldg A, Room 201, 40014 Jyväskylä; tel. (40) 8053404; e-mail humtdk@jyu.fi; internet www.jyu.fi/hum):

ERKKILÄ, J., Music Therapy
HANKA, H., Art History
KALAJA, P., English Language
KARONEN, P., History
KIRSTINÄ, L., Literature
KOSKIMAA, R., Digital Culture
KUNNAS, T., Literature
LAHDELMA, T., Hungarology
LEPPÄNEN, S., English Language
LOUHIVUORI, J., Musicology
LUUKKA, M.-R., Finnish Language
MARTIN, M., Finnish Language
MERISALO, O., Romance Philology
MIELIKÄINEN, A., Finnish Language
MUITTARI, V., Scandinavian Philology
NUMMELA, I., History
PIIRAINEN-MARSH, A., English Philology
RAHKONEN, M., Scandinavian Philology
SALLINEN, A., Speech Communication
SALOKANGAS, R., Journalism
SALO-LEE, L., Intercultural Communication
SIHVOLA, J., History
STARK, L., Ethnology
TOIVIAINEN, P., Musicology
VAINIO, M., Musicology
VALO, M., Speech Communication
VANHALA-ANISZEWSKI, M., Russian Language and Literature
VESTERINEN, I., Cultural Anthropology
VON BONSDORFF, P., Art Education
WAENERBERG, A., Art History
ZETTERBERG, S., History

Faculty of Information Technology (POB 35 (Agora), 40014 Jyväskylä
Agora, Mattilanniemi 2, 40100 Jyväskylä; tel. (14) 2601211; internet www.jyu.fi/it):

HÄMÄLÄINEN, T., Information Technology: Telecommunications
HEIKKILÄ, J., Information Systems and Electronic Business
JOUTSENSALO, J., Information Technology: Telecommunications
KÄRKKÄINEN, T., Software Engineering
LYYTINEN, K., Information Systems
MÄKINEN, R. A. E., Applied Mathematics
NEITTAANMÄKI, P., Mathematical Information Technology
PUURONEN, S., Information Systems
ROSSI, T., Software Technology
SAARILUOMA, P., Cognitive Science
SAKKINEN, M., Software Production
SALMINEN, A., Information Technology
TIIHONEN, T., Mathematical Information Technology
TYRVÄINEN, P., Digital Media
VEIJALAINEN, J., Software Production

Faculty of Mathematics and Science (POB 35 (YK), 40014 Jyväskylä; e-mail pylvanai@jyu.fi; internet www.jyu.fi/science):

AHLSKOG, M., Physics
ALATALO, R., Ecology
ALÉN, R., Applied Chemistry
ÄYSTÖ, J., Physics
BAMFORD, J., Molecular Biology
GEISS, S., Stochastics
HOIKKALA, A., Evolutionary Genetics
JÄRVENPÄÄ, E., Mathematics
JONES, R. I., Limnology
JULIN, R., Physics
KARJALAINEN, J., Fish Biology and Fisheries
KATAJA, M., Physics
KILPELÄINEN, T., Mathematics
KNUUTINEN, J., Applied Chemistry
KOLEHMAINEN, E., Organic Chemistry
KORPPI-TOMMOLA, J., Chemistry
KOSKELA, P., Mathematics
KUITUNEN, M., Environmental Sciences
KUNTTU, H., Physical Chemistry
KUUSALO, T., Mathematics
LEINO, M., Physics
LESKINEN, E., Statistics
MAALAMPI, J., Physics
MANNINEN, M., Physics
MAPPES, J., Ecology and Environmental Management
MÖNKKÖNEN, M., Applied Ecology
NÄKKI, R., Mathematics
NYBLOM, J., Statistics
OIKARI, A., Environmental Sciences
OKER-BLOM, C., Biotechnology
PENTTINEN, A., Statistics
RINTALA, J., Environmental Sciences
RISSANEN, K., Chemistry
SAKSMAN, E., Mathematics
SILLANPÄÄ, R., Chemistry
TIMONEN, J., Applied Physics
TÖRMÄ, P., Physics
VALKONEN, J., Chemistry
VIRTANEN, J., Nanoscience
VUENTO, M., Biochemistry
WHITLOW, H., Physics
YLÄNNE, J., Cell Biology

Faculty of Social Sciences (POB 35, 40014 Jyväskylä
Ylistönmäentie 33, 40014 Jyväskylä; tel. (14) 2601211; internet www.jyu.fi/ytk):

AHONEN, T., Psychology
HEISKALA, R., Social Policy
JÄRVELÄ, M., Social Policy
JYRKÄMÄ, J., Social Gerontology
KANGAS, A., Cultural Policy
KORHONEN, T., Psychology
LYYTINEN, H., Developmental Neuropsychology
MÄNTYSAARI, M., Social Work
NURMI, J.-E., Psychology
PALONEN, K., Political Science
PULKKINEN, T., Political Science and Women's Studies
SIISIÄINEN, M., Sociology
WAHLSTRÖM, J., Psychology

Faculty of Sport and Health Sciences (POB 35 (L), 40014 Jyväskylä
Keskussairaalantie 4, 40014 Jyväskylä; tel. (14) 2602001; internet www.jyu.fi/liikunta):

HÄKKINEN, K., Sport Coaching and Fitness Testing
HEIKINARO-JOHANSSON, P., Physical Education
HEINONEN, A., Physiotherapy
ITKONEN, H., Sport Sociology
KAINULAINEN, H., Sport Physiology
KANNAS, L., Health Education
KUJALA, U., Sport Medicine
LAAKSO, L., Physical Education
LINTUNEN, T., Sports Psychology
MÄLKIÄ, E., Physiotherapy
RANTANEN, T., Gerontology and Public Health
RINTALA, P., Applied Physical Education
SILVENNOINEN, M., Physical Education
SUOMINEN, H., Sports Gerontology

School of Business and Economics (POB 35, 40014 Jyväskylä
Ylistö Ohjelmakaari 10, 40014 Jyväskylä; tel. (14) 2601211; e-mail jsbe-info@jyu.fi; internet www.jyu.fi/jsbe):

AALTIO, J., Management and Leadership
KOIRANEN, M., Entrepreneurship
NIITTYKANGAS, H., Entrepreneurship
PEHKONEN, J., Economics
PELLINEN, J., Accounting
PESONEN, H.-L., Corporate Environmental Management
TAKALA, T., Management and Leadership
TERVO, H., Economics
UUISTALO, O., Marketing
VIRTANEN, A., Accounting

LAPIN YLIOPISTO
(University of Lapland)

POB 122, 96101 Rovaniemi
Yliopistonkatu 8, 96300 Rovaniemi
Telephone: (16) 341341
E-mail: tiedotus@ulapland.fi
Internet: www.ulapland.fi
Founded 1979, present name and status 1991
State control
Languages of instruction: English, Finnish
Academic year: August to July
Rector: Prof. Dr MAURI YLÄ-KOTOLA
Vice-Rector for Admin.: Prof. Dr JUKKA MÄKELÄ
Vice-Rector for Education: Prof. Dr KAARINA MÄÄTTÄ
Vice-Rector for Research: Prof. Dr MINNA UOTILA
Library Dir: SUSANNA PARIKKA
Library of 385,000 vols, 4,757 periodicals, 578,000 ebooks, 40,674 ejournals
Number of teachers: 349
Number of students: 4,600

DEANS

Arctic Centre: Prof. Dr PAULA KANKAANPÄÄ
Faculty of Art and Design: Prof. TIMO JOKELA
Faculty of Education: Prof. Dr PÄIVI NASKALI
Faculty of Law: Prof. Dr JUHA KARHU
Faculty of Social Sciences: Prof. Dr JUHA PERTTULA
Multidimensional Tourism Institute: Dr JOHAN EDELHEIM

PROFESSORS

Arctic Centre (POB 122, 96101 Rovaniemi; tel. (16) 341341):
- FORBES, B., Global Change
- KOIVUROVA, T., Environmental and Minority Law
- MOORE, J., Climate Change
- STAMMLER, F., Arctic Anthropology
- TENNBERG, M., Sustainable Development

Faculty of Art and Design (POB 122, 96101 Rovaniemi; tel. (16) 341341):
- BRUSILA, R., Graphic Design
- ERKKILÄ, J., Fine Arts
- GRANÖ, P., Art Education
- HÄKKILÄ, J., Industrial Design
- HÄNNINEN, K., Textile Design
- HAUTALA-HIRVIOJA, T., Art History
- HEIKKILÄ-RASTAS, M., Fashion and Clothing Design
- JOKELA, T., Art Education
- MIETTINEN, S., Industrial Design
- UOTILA, M., Design Research
- YLÄ-KOTOLA, M., Audiovisual Media Studies

Faculty of Education (POB 122, 96101 Rovaniemi; tel. (16) 341341):
- KURTAKKO, K., Education
- MÄÄTTÄ, K., Educational Psychology
- NASKALI, P., Gender Studies
- POIKELA, E., Education
- RAJALA, R., Education
- RUOKAMO, H., Media Education

Faculty of Law (POB 122, 96101 Rovaniemi; tel. (16) 341341; e-mail lawinter@ulapland.fi):
- HUSA, J., Comparative Law and Institutional Law
- JUANTO, J., Financial Law
- KARHU, J., Law of Obligations
- KORHONEN, R, Legal Informatics
- KUUSIKKO, K., Administrative Law
- LINNA, T., Procedural Law
- MIKKOLA, T., Private International Law and Comparative Law
- NYSTÉN-HAARALA, S., Commercial Law
- SAARENPÄÄ, A., Privacy Law, Family and Inheritance Law
- TAMMI-SALMINEN, E., Property Law
- VIIKARI, L, Public International Law

Faculty of Social Sciences (POB 122, 96101 Rovaniemi; tel. (16) 341341):
- HAAHTI, A., Tourism Research
- KINNUNEN, M., Sociology
- LAITINEN, M., Social Work
- MERILÄINEN, S., Management
- PERTTULA, J., Psychology
- POHJOLA, A., Social Work
- REID, J., International Relations
- RONKAINEN, S., Research Methodology
- SEPPÄNEN, M., Social Work
- TUOMINEN, M., Cultural History
- VEIJOLA, S., Cultural Studies of Tourism
- VIERU, M., Accounting

LAPPEENRANNAN TEKNILLINEN KORKEAKOULU
(Lappeenranta University of Technology)

POB 20, 53851 Lappeenranta
Skinnarilankatu 34, 53850 Lappeenranta
Telephone: (294) 462111
E-mail: info@lut.fi
Internet: www.lut.fi
Founded 1969
State control
Languages of instruction: English, Finnish
Academic year: August to July (2 terms)
Rector: Prof. Dr ILKKA PÖYHÖNEN
Vice-Rector for Education: Prof. Dr HANNU RANTANEN
Vice-Rector for Int. Affairs: Dr KIRSIMARJA BLOMQVIST
Vice-Rector for Research: Prof. Dr VELI-MATTI VIROLAINEN
Dir for Admin.: JUHA-MATTI SAKSA
Librarian: TUULA HEIKKANEN-VAINIKKA
Library of 145,000 vols, 600 journals
Number of teachers: 915
Number of students: 5,000

DEANS

Faculty of Technology: ESA MARTTILA
Faculty of Technology Management: VESA HARMAAKORPI
School of Business: JAANA SANDSTRÖM

PROFESSORS

- AALTIO, I., Management and Organization
- HANDROOS, H., Machine Automation
- KÄLVIÄINEN, H., Information Processing
- KÄSSI, T., Industrial Economics
- KERTTULA, E., Telematics
- KOSKELAINEN, L., Power Plant Engineering
- KYLÄHEIKO, K., Economics
- LARJOLA, J., Heat Transfer and Fluid Dynamics
- LEHTOMAA, A., Entrepreneurship in Technology
- LINDSTRÖM, M., Physical Chemistry
- LIUHTO, J., International Operations
- LUKKA, A., Logistics (esp. Transport), Inventories, Purchasing
- LUKKA, M., Applied Mathematics
- LUUKKO, A., Physics
- MANNER, H., Paper Technology
- MARQUIS, G., Steel Structures
- MARTIKAINEN, J., Welding Technology
- MARTIKKA, H., Design of Machine Elements
- MARTTILA, E., Environmental Engineering
- MIKKOLA, A., Virtual Engineering
- MINKKINEN, P., Inorganic and Analytical Chemistry
- NAOUMOV, V., Data Communications
- NIEMI, M., Civil Law
- NYSTRÖM, L., Process Technology
- NYSTRÖM, M., Membrane Technology
- PAATERO, E., Chemical Technology
- PARTANEN, J., Electrical Systems
- PIRTTILÄ, T., Industrial Engineering and Management (esp. Logistics)
- PITKÄNEN, S., Engineering and Technology Management
- PORRAS, J., Data Communications
- PÖYHÖNEN, I., Wood Technology
- PYRHÖNEN, J., Electrical Machines and Drives
- PYRHÖNEN, O., Control Engineering
- RANTANEN, H., Industrial Engineering
- SARKOMAA, P., Technical Thermodynamics
- TARJANNE, R., Energy Management and Economics
- TIUSANEN, T., International Operations of Industrial Firms
- TOIVANEN, P., Information Processing
- TUOMINEN, M., Industrial Engineering and Management
- TURUNEN, I., Process Systems Engineering
- VERHO, A., Structural Design of Machinery
- VORACEK, J., Information Processing
- ZAMANKHAN, P., Computational Heat and Fluid Dynamics

OULUN YLIOPISTO
(University of Oulu)

Pentti Kaiteran Katu 1, POB 8000, 90014 Oulu
Telephone: (294) 480000
Internet: www.oulu.fi
Founded 1958
State control
Language of instruction: Finnish
Academic year: September to May (2 terms)
Rector: Prof. Dr LAURI LAJUNEN
Vice-Rector for Education: Dr OLLI SILVÉN
Vice-Rector for Research: Dr TAINA PIHLAJA-NIEMI
Dir for Academic Affairs: EVA MARIA RAUDASOJA
Admin. Dir: HANNU PIETILÄ
Librarian: PÄIVI KYTÖMÄKI
Library: see under Libraries and Archives
Number of teachers: 1,679
Number of students: 15,864

DEANS

Faculty of Economics and Business Administration: Prof. Dr PETRI SAHLSTRÖM
Faculty of Education: Prof. RIITTA-LIISA KORKEAMÄKI
Faculty of Humanities: Prof. TIMO LAUTTAMUS
Faculty of Medicine: Prof. KARI MAJAMAA
Faculty of Science: Prof. JOUNI PURSIAINEN
Faculty of Technology: Prof. KAUKO LEIVISKÄ

PROFESSORS

Faculty of Economics and Business Administration (POB 4600, 90014 Oulu; tel. (8) 5532905; e-mail international.tatk@oulu.fi; internet www.taloustieteet.oulu.fi):
- ALAJOUTSIJÄRVI, K., Marketing
- JUGA, J., Logistics
- KALLUNKI, J. P., Accounting
- KOIVUMÄKI, T., Electronic Commerce
- PELTONEN, T., Management and Organization
- PERTTUNEN, J., Finance
- PUHAKKA, M., Economics
- RAHIALA, M., Econometrics
- SVENTO, R., Economics

Faculty of Education (POB 2000, 90014 Oulu; tel. (8) 5531011; e-mail studentaffairs.ktk@oulu.fi; internet www.oulu.fi/edu):
- FREDRIKSON, M., Music Education
- HAKKARAINEN, P., Early Childhood Education
- JÄRVELÄ, S., Education
- JÄRVIKOSKI, T., Social Science
- JÄRVILEHTO, T., Psychology
- KALAOJA, E., Didactics
- KERANTO, T., Mathematics and Science Education
- KORKEAMÄKI, R.-L., Education

LUUKKONEN, J., Education
MÄKINEN, K., Didactics of Foreign Languages
RUISMÄKI, H., Music Education
SILJANDER, P., Education
SOINI, H., Educational Psychology
SUORTTI, J., Education
SYRJÄLÄ, L., Education
VARIS, M., Didactics of Finnish Language and Literature
YLI-LUOMA, P., Education

Faculty of Humanities (POB 1000, 90014 Oulu; tel. (8) 5533221; e-mail hutkwww@oulu.fi; internet www.oulu.fi/hutk):

BLUHM, L., German Language and Literature
FÄLT, O. K., History
HUHTALA, L., Literature
JOHNSON, A., English
KORPILAHTI, P., Logopaedics
LAUTTAMUS, T., English
LEHTIHALMES, M., Logopaedics
LEHTOLA, V.-P., Saami Culture
MANNINEN, J., History of Science and Ideas
MANTILA, H., Finnish
NUÑES GARCES, M., Archaeology
PENNANEN, J., Cultural Anthropology
ROSSI, P., Scandinavian Languages
SAMMALLAHTI, P., Saami (Lapp) Language and Culture
SORVALI, I., Scandinavian Languages
SULKALA, H., Finnish
SUOMI, K., Phonetics
VAHTOLA, J., Finnish and Scandinavian History

Faculty of Medicine (POB 5000, 90014 Oulu; tel. (8) 5375011; internet www.medicine.oulu.fi):

AIRAKSINEN, P. J., Ophthalmology
ALAHUHTA, S., Anaesthesiology
ALA-KOKKO, L., Medical Biochemistry
HALLMAN, H., Paediatrics
HAUSEN, H., Dentistry
HILLBOM, M., Neurology
HUIKURI, H., Internal Medicine
ISOHANNI, M., Psychiatry
ISOLA, A., Nursing Science
JAAKKOLA, M., Pulmonary Disease
JALOVAARA, P., Surgery
JÄMSÄ, T., Medical Technology
JANHONEN, S., Nursing Didactics
JÄRVELIN, M.-R., Public Health Science
JOUKAMAA, M., Psychiatry
JUVONEN, T., Surgery
KAPRIO, J., Public Health Science
KEINÄNEN-KIUKAANNIEMI, S., General Practice
KESÄNIEMI, A., Internal Medicine
KNUUTTILA, M., Dentistry
KOIVUKANGAS, J., Neurosurgery
KOPONEN, H., Psychiatry
KORTELAINEN, M., Forensic Medicine
LARMAS, M., Dentistry
MÄKELÄ, J., Gastroenterological Surgery
MOILANEN, I., Child Psychiatry
MYLLYLÄ, V., Neurology
NIKKILÄ, J., Health Administration
OIKARINEN, A., Dermatology and Venereology
OIKARINEN, K., Dentistry
PAAVONEN, T., Pathological Anatomy
PELKONEN, O., Pharmacology
PELTONEN, J., Anatomy
PIHLAJANIEMI, T., Medical Biochemistry
PYHTINEN, J., Diagnostic Radiology
RAJANIEMI, H., Anatomy
RÄSÄNEN, P., Psychiatry
RAUSTIA, A., Dentistry
RISTELI, J., Clinical Chemistry
RUOKONEN, A., Clinical Chemistry
RUSKOAHO, H., Molecular Pharmacology
RYYNÄNEN, M., Obstetrics and Gynaecology
SALO, T., Oral Pathology
SAVOLAINEN, M., Internal Medicine
SORRI, M., Otorhinolaryngology
STENBÄCK, F., Pathology
SURAMO, I., Diagnostic Radiology
TAPANAINEN, J., Obstetrics and Gynaecology
TUULONEN, A., Ophthalmology
UHARI, M., Paediatrics
VAINIO, O., Clinical Microbiology
VAINIO, S., Developmental Biochemistry
VIROKANNAS, H., Occupational Health
VUOLTEENAHO, O., Physiology

Faculty of Science (POB 3000, 90014 Oulu; tel. (8) 5531011; internet www.science.oulu.fi):

AKSELA, H., Physics
AKSELA, S., Physics
ALAPIETI, T., Geology and Mineralogy
HÄGGMAN, H., Plant Physiology
HANSKI, E., Geochemistry
HEIKKINEN, O., Geography
HEISKANEN, A., Information Processing Science
HILTUNEN, K., Biochemistry
HOHTOLA, A., Plant Physiology
HOHTOLA, E., Zoology
HOLMSTRÖM, L., Applied Mathematics
HORMI, O., Chemistry
HUTTUNEN, S., Botany
IIVARI, J., Information Processing Science
JÄRVILEHTO, M., Animal Physiology
JAUHIAINEN, J., Applied Geography and Regional Planning
JOKISAARI, J., Physics
KAIKKONEN, P., Geophysics
KAITALA, A., Zoology
KARJALAINEN, P. T., Geography
KINNUNEN, J., Mathematics
KUUTTI, K., Information Processing Science
LAAJOKI, K., Geology and Mineralogy
LÄÄRÄ, E., Statistics
LAASONEN, K., Chemistry
LAITINEN, R., Chemistry
LAJUNEN, L., Inorganic Chemistry
LUNKKA, J. P., Surficial Geology
MUOTKA, T., Zoology
MURSULA, K., Physics
MUSTONEN, V., Mathematics
MYLLYLÄ, R., Biochemistry
NORDSTRÖM, K., Statistics
NYGRÉN, T., Physics
OINAS-KUKKONEN, H., Information Processing Science
OIVO, M., Information Processing Science
OKSANEN, J., Plant Ecology
ORELL, M., Zoology
PAASI, A., Geography
PAMILO, P., Genetics
PERÄMÄKI, P., Inorganic Chemistry
PEURANIEMI, V., Surficial Geology
POUTANEN, J., Astronomy
PULLI, P., Information Processing Science
PURSIAINEN, J., Chemistry
RAHIALA, M., Econometrics
RUDDOCK, L., Protein Science
RUMMUKAINEN, K., Theoretical Physics
RUSANEN, J., Geoinformatics
SAARINEN, J., Geography
SARANEN, J., Applied Mathematics
SAUKKONEN, S., Information Processing Science
SAVOLAINEN, O., Genetics
SEPPÄNEN, V., Information Processing Science
SIMILÄ, J., Information Processing Science
TERVONEN, I., Information Processing Science
THUNEBERG, E., Theoretical Physics
TUOMI, J., Botany
VÄÄNÄNEN, K., Mathematics
WECKSTRÖM, M., Biophysics
WIERENGA, R., Biochemistry

Faculty of Technology (Linnanmaa, POB 4000, 90014 Oulu; tel. (8) 5532001; e-mail international.ttk@oulu.fi; internet www.ttk.oulu.fi):

BRONER-BAUER, K., Architecture
GLISIC, S., Telecommunication
HAAPASALO, H., Industrial Engineering and Management
HÄRKKI, J., Metallurgy
HENTILÄ, H., Planning and Urban Design
HEUSALA, H., Electronics
IINATTI, J., Telecommunications
JUNTTI, M., Telecommunications
KARHU, S., Radio Technology
KARHUNEN, J., Machine Design
KARJALAINEN, J., Production Engineering
KARJALAINEN, P., Physical Metallurgy
KEISKI, R., Mass and Heat Transfer Processes
KESS, P., Industrial Engineering and Management
KLØVE, B., Water Management
KOISO-KANTTILA, J., Architecture
KORTELA, U., Control and Systems Engineering
KOSTAMOVAARA, J., Electronics
LAHDELMA, S., Machine Condition Diagnostics
LAKSO, E., Environment Engineering
LANTTO, V., Material Physics
LAPPALAINEN, K., Production Engineering
LATVA-AHO, M., Telecommunications
LEIVISKÄ, K., Process Engineering
LEPPÄNEN, P., Telecommunications
MÄÄTTÄ, K., Electronics
MAHLAMÄKI, R., Architecture
MÄNTYLÄ, P., Mechanical Metallurgy
MYLLYLÄ, R., Optoelectronics and Electronic Measurement Technology
NEUBAUER, P., Bioprocess Engineering
NEVALA, K., Mechatronics
NIINIMÄKI, J., Mechanical Process Engineering
NISKANEN, J., Machine Construction
OJALA, T., Computer Engineering
PIETIKÄINEN, M., Computer Technics
PRAMILA, A., Technical Mechanics
RAHKONEN, T., Electronics
RIEKKI, J., Software Architecture for Embedded Systems
RÖNING, J., Embedded Systems
RUOTSALAINEN, K., Mathematics
SALONEN, E., Radio Technology
SAUVOLA, J., Multimedia Systems
SEIKKALA, S., Applied Mathematics
SEPPÄNEN, T., Biomedical Technology
SILVÉN, O., Signal Processing
SJÖLIND, S., Engineering Mechanics
TARUMAA, A., Planning and Urban Design
TASA, J., Architecture
TUPPURAINEN, Y., Architecture
VÄHÄKANGAS, J., Electronics Production Technology
VÄYRYNEN, S., Work Science

SVENSKA HANDELSHÖGSKOLAN
(Hanken School of Economics)

POB 479, 00101 Helsinki
Arkadiagatan 22, Main Bldg, 00101 Helsinki
Telephone: (9) 431331
E-mail: info@hanken.fi
Internet: www.hanken.fi

Founded 1909
State control
Languages of instruction: English, Swedish
Academic year: August to July

Depts of accounting and commercial law, economics, finance and statistics, management and organization, marketing

Rector: Prof. Dr EVA LILJEBLOM
Vice-Rector: Prof. Dr LARS-JOHAN LINDQVIST
Vice-Rector: Prof. Dr KAREN SPENS
Vice-Rector: Prof. Dr RUNE STENBACKA
Admin. Dir: MAUNO LINDROOS
Library Dir: TUA HINDERSSON-SÖDERHOLM

Library of 62,500 vols of printed books, 49 printed journals, 112,000 ebooks and 32,300 ejournals

Number of teachers: 127
Number of students: 2,362
Publications: *Economics and Society*, *Hanken Magazine*, *Research Reports*, *Working Papers*

PROFESSORS

Department of Accounting and Commercial Law:

BRUUN, N., Commercial Law
KUKKONEN, M., Commercial Law
LEE, N., Commercial Law
MÄNTYSAARI, P., Commercial Law
MARTIKAINEN-PELTOLA, M., Accounting
TROBERG, P., Accounting

Department of Economics:

BERGLUND, T.
BRUNILA, A.
STENBACKA, R.

Department of Finance and Statistics:

AHLGREN, N., Finance
HÖGHOLM, K., Finance
KNIF, J., Finance
KORKEAMÄKI, T., Finance
LILJEBLOM, E., Finance
LÖFLUND, J., Finance
MAIO, P., Finance

Department of Management and Organization:

ARENIUS, P., Entrepreneurship and Management
BJÖRK, B.-C., Information System Science
DEN HOND, F., Management and Organization
HEARN, J., Management and Organization
KOCK, S., Entrepreneurship and Management
MANTERE, S., Management and Organization
VAARA, E., Management and Organization

Department of Marketing:

GRÖNROOS, C., Marketing
HOLMLUND-RYTKÖNEN, M., Marketing
KOVACS, G., Supply Chain Management and Corporate Geography
LILJANDER, V., Marketing
SPENS, K., Supply Chain Management and Corporate Geography
STRANDVIK, T., Marketing

Centre for Languages and Business Communication:

TANDEFELT, M.

TAIDEYLIOPISTO/ KONSTUNIVERSITETET
(University of the Arts Helsinki)

POB 1, 00097 Helsinki
Telephone: (9) 72580000
E-mail: kirjaamo@uniarts.fi
Internet: www.uniarts.fi
Founded 2003 by merger of Finnish Academy of Fine Arts (f. 1848), Sibelius Academy (f. 1882), Theatre Academy Helsinki (f. 1979)
State control
Rector: Prof. Dr TIINA ROSENBERG
Number of teachers: 600 (f.t.e.)
Number of students: 2,100

TAMPEREEN TEKNILLINEN YLIOPISTO
(Tampere University of Technology)

POB 527, 33101 Tampere
Korkeakoulunkatu 10, 33720 Tampere
Telephone: (3) 311511
Internet: www.tut.fi
Founded 1965 as a subsidiary of Helsinki Univ. of Technology, present name 1972
State control
Language of instruction: Finnish
Academic year: September to May
Pres.: Prof. MARKKU KIVIKOSKI
Vice-Pres. for Education: Prof. MATTI PENTTI
Vice-Pres. for Research, Postgraduate Education and Quality Assurance: Prof. PAUL H. ANDERSSON
Dir of Admin.: TIINA ÄIJÄLÄ
Library Dir: MINNA NIEMI-GRUNDSTRÖM
Library: see under Libraries and Archives
Number of teachers: 412
Number of students: 10,400

DEANS

Faculty of Business and Built Environment: Prof. MIKA HANNULA
Faculty of Computing and Electrical Engineering: Prof. ULLA RUOTSALAINEN
Faculty of Engineering Sciences: Prof. JOUKO HALTTUNEN
Faculty of Natural Sciences: Prof. MARTTI KAURANEN

PROFESSORS

AITTOMÄKI, A., Refrigeration Technology
ASTOLA, J., Digital Signals Processing
AUMALA, O., Metrology
ERIKSSON, J.-T., Electrodynamics and Magnetism
GABBOUJ, M., Information Technology
HAIKALA, I., Computer Science
HARJU, J., Telecommunications
HARTIKAINEN, J., Soil Mechanics and Foundation Engineering
JAAKKOLA, H., Information Technology
JALLINOJA, R., Architectural Theory
JARSKE, P., Telecommunications
KALLBERG, H., Transport
KALLI, S., Information Technology
KÄRNÄ, J., Electrical Power Engineering
KARVINEN, R., Fluid Dynamics and Heat Transfer
KATAINEN, J., Architectural Design
KAUNONEN, A., Control Engineering
KIVIKOSKI, M., Industrial Electronics
KORPINEN, L., Electrical Power Engineering
KOSKI, J., Structural Mechanics
KURKI-SUONIO, R., Computer Science and Engineering
LAKSO, T., Production Engineering
LAUTALA, P., Control Engineering
LEMMITYINEN, H., Chemistry
LEPISTÖ, T., Mathematics
LINDBERG, R., Structural Engineering
MÄKILÄ, P., Automation Technology
MALMIVUO, J., Bioelectronics
MATTILA, M., Occupational Safety Engineering
MAULA, J., Urban Planning
NOUSIAINEN, P., Textile Technology
NYBERG, T., Paper Machine Automation
OTALA, M., Industrial Management
PESSA, M., Semiconductor Technology
PUHALKA, J., Environmental Biotechnology
RENFORS, M., Telecommunications Engineering
RIIHELÄ, S., Construction Economics and Management
RIITAHUHTA, A., Machine Design
RISTALAINEN, E., Electronics
SAARIKORPI, J., Industrial Management and Engineering
SAARINEN, J., Signal Processing Laboratory
SARAMAKI, T., Signal Processing
SAVOLAINEN, A., Process Engineering
SIEKKINEN, V., Maintenance Technology
SIIKANEN, U., Architectural Construction
TALLQVIST, T., History of Architecture
TIANEN, T., Materials Engineering
TOMBERG, J., Information Technology
TÖRMÄLÄ, P., Plastics Technology
TORVINEN, S., Production Automation
TUHKANEN, T., Environmental Engineering
TUOKKO, R., Automation Technology
TUOMALA, M., Structural Mechanics
UUSI-RAUVA, E., Industrial Management and Engineering
VANHARANTA, H., Industrial Management and Engineering
VILENIUS, M., Hydraulic Machines

TAMPEREEN YLIOPISTO
(University of Tampere)

Kalevantie 4, 33014 Tampere
Telephone: (3) 355111
E-mail: kirjaamo@uta.fi
Internet: www.uta.fi
Founded 1925 as a Civic College in Helsinki
State control
Languages of instruction: English, Finnish
Academic year: September to May
Chancellor: Dr KRISTA VARANTOLA
Rector: Prof. KAIJA HOLLI
First Vice-Rector: Prof. PERTTI HAAPALA
Second Vice-Rector: Prof. HARRI MELIN
Admin. Dir: PETRI LINTUNEN
Chief Librarian: Dr MIRJA IIVONEN
Library: see under Libraries and Archives
Number of teachers: 1,084
Number of students: 15,200
Publication: *Acta Universitatis Tamperensis*

DEANS

Institute of Biomedical Technology: Prof. HANNU HANHIJÄRVI
School of Communication, Media and Theatre: HEIKKI HELLMAN
School of Education: TIINA KUJALA
School of Health Sciences: Prof. PEKKA RISSANEN
School of Information Sciences: Prof. KARI-JOUKO RÄIHÄ
School of Language, Translation, and Literary Studies: Prof. JUKKA HAVU
School of Management: Prof. MARKKU SOTARAUTA
School of Medicine: Prof. MATTI LEHTO
School of Social Sciences and Humanities: Prof. RISTO KUNELIUS

TURUN YLIOPISTO
(University of Turku)

20014 Turku
Telephone: (2) 33351
E-mail: international@utu.fi
Internet: www.utu.fi
Founded 1920
State control
Languages of instruction: English, Finnish
Academic year: August to July (2 semesters)
Chancellor: Prof. Dr PEKKA PUSKA
Rector: Prof. KALERVO VÄÄNÄNEN
Vice-Rector: Prof. KALLE-ANTTI SUOMINEN
Vice-Rector: Prof. RIITTA PYYKKÖ
Vice-Rector: Prof. TAPIO REPONEN
Chief Librarian: ULLA NYGRÉN
Library: see under Libraries and Archives
Number of teachers: 810
Number of students: 17,925
Publication: *Annales Universitatis Turkuensis*

DEANS

Faculty of Education: Prof. MARJA VAURAS
Faculty of Humanities: Prof. EIJA SUOMELA-SALMI
Faculty of Law: Prof. JUKKA MÄHÖNEN
Faculty of Mathematics and Natural Sciences: Prof. REIJO LAHTI
Faculty of Medicine: Prof. TAPANI RÖNNEMAA
Faculty of Social Sciences: Prof. Dr KIMMO RENTOLA
Turku School of Economics: Prof. MARKUS GRANLUND (Dir)

PROFESSORS

Faculty of Education (tel. (2) 3338803; e-mail education@utu.fi; internet www.edu.utu.fi):

HAKKARAINEN, K., Education
HUSU, J., Education
JAUHIAINEN, A., Education
KESKINEN, S., Education
KIVIRAUMA, J., Education
KOSKENSALO, A., Teaching of Foreign Languages
LEHTINEN, E., Teacher Training
NIEMI, P., Education
RINNE, R., Adult Education
SARMAVUORI, K., Teaching of Mother Tongue
SOININEN, M., Didactics
VAURAS, M., Education (Learning and Teaching)
VIRTA, A., Teaching of History and Social Sciences

Faculty of Humanities (tel. (2) 3335201; e-mail hum-info@utu.fi; internet www.hum.utu.fi):

AHOKAS, P., Comparative Literature
ANTTONEN, V., Comparative Religion
DE ANNA, L., Italian Language, Culture and Translation
GAMBIER, Y., French Translation Studies
HAKAMIES, P., Folkloristics
HÄKKINEN, K., Finnish Language
HÄYRYNEN, M., Landscape Studies
HELASVUO, M.-L., Finnish Language
HELIN, I., German Translation Studies
HILTUNEN, R., English
HIRVONEN, I., Scandinavian Philology
HUUMO, T., Finnish Language
ITKONEN, E., General Linguistics
JOHANSSON, M., French Studies
KEINÄSTÖ, K., German Philology
KOSTIAINEN, A., Gen. History
KUORTTI, J., English
KUUSAMO, A., Art History
LAPPALAINEN, P., Finnish Literature
LILJESTRÖM, M., Gender Studies
MYLLYNTAUS, T., Finnish History
PIETILÄ, P., English
PYYKKÖ, R., Russian Language and Culture
RICHARDSON, J., Musicology
ROJOLA, L., Finnish Literature
SAARINEN, S., Finno-Ugric Languages
SALMI, H., Cultural History
SIHVONEN, J., Media Studies
STEINBY, L., Comparative Literature
SUNDMAN, M., Scandinavian Languages
SUOMELA-SALMI, E., French Language and Culture
SUOMINEN, J., Digital Culture
SYRJÄMAA, T., Gen. History
TAAVITSAINEN, J.-P., Archaeology
TUOMI-NIKULA, O., Cultural Heritage Studies
VAAHTERA, J., Classical Languages and Culture
VAINIO-KORHONEN, K.-M., Finnish History
VIRTANEN, K., Cultural History
WIDE, C., Scandinavian Languages

Faculty of Law (tel. (2) 3335502; e-mail oikanslia@utu.fi; internet www.law.utu.fi):

BJÖRNE, L., Roman, Law and Legal History
HELIN, M., Private Law
JOKELA, A. T., Procedural Law
KAIRINEN, M., Labour Law
KULLA, H., Admin. Law
KUMPULA, A., Environmental Law
MÄHÖNEN, J., Civil Law
NOUSIAINEN, K., Jurisprudence
OSSA, J., Financial Law
SAARNILEHTO, A., Civil Law
SILTALA, R., Jurisprudence
TUOMISTO, J., Civil Law
VILJANEN, P., Criminal and Procedural Law
VILJANEN, V.-P., Constitutional Law
WIKSTRÖM, K., Financial Law

Faculty of Mathematics and Natural Sciences (tel. (2) 3336576; e-mail info-ml@utu.fi; internet www.sci.utu.fi):

ANDERSSON, H., Human Geography
ARO, E.-M., Plant Physiology
GLOOS, K., Physics
HAAPAKKA, K., Analytical Chemistry
HARJU, T., Mathematics
HEIKKONEN, J., Information Technology
HEINO, J., Biochemistry
HIETARINTA, J., Theoretical Physics
HÖLSÄ, J., Inorganic Chemistry
HONKALA, I., Mathematics
HUOPALAHTI, R., Food Chemistry
ISOAHO, J., Electronics and Information Technology
JAUHIAINEN, J., Regional Devt
KALLIO, H., Food Chemistry
KALLIOLA, R., Physical Geography
KANKARE, J., Analytical Chemistry
KARHUMÄKI, J., Mathematics
KARI, J., Mathematics
KAUPPINEN, R., Optics and Spectroscopy
KÄYHKÖ, J., Geography
KNUUTILA, T., Computer Science
KORPIMÄKI, E., Ecology
KUKK, E., Physics
KVARNSTRÖM, C., Materials Chemistry
LAHDELMA, R., Information Systems Science
LAHTI, R., Biochemistry
LEIPÄLÄ, T., Applied Mathematics
LÖNNBERG, H., Organic Chemistry
LÖVGREN, T., Biotechnology
LUKKARI, J., Physical Chemistry
MÄKELÄ, M., Applied Mathematics
NEVALAINEN, O., Computer Science
NIEMELÄ, P., Biodiversity Research
NIKINMAA, M., Animal Physiology
NORRDAHL, K., Ecology
OKSANEN, L., Plant Ecology
PETTERSSON, K., Biotechnology
PIHLAJA, K., Physical Chemistry
PRIMMER, C., Genetics
RÄSÄNEN, M., Quaternary Geology
RINTAMÄKI, E., Plant Physiology
SAARINEN, T., Geology and Mineralogy
SALAKOSKI, T., Computer Science
SALMINEN, J.-P., Organic Chemistry
SALMINEN, S., Food Devt
SAVILAHTI, H., Genetics
SOLIN, O., Radiochemistry
SUNDBLAD, K., Geology and Mineralogy
SUOMINEN, K.-A., Physics
TAPANINEN, U., Maritime Logistics Research (Centre for Maritime Studies)
TENHUNEN, H., Nanoelectronics
TUOMINEN, A., Electronics
VALTAOJA, E., Astronomy
VALTONEN, M., Astronomy
VÄYRYNEN, J., Physics
VUORINEN, M., Mathematics
YLINEN, K., Mathematics

Faculty of Medicine (tel. (2) 33351; e-mail intmedi@utu.fi; internet www.med.utu.fi):

AIRAKSINEN, J., Cardiology
ARO, H., Orthopaedics and Traumatology
ARONEN, P., Diagnostic Radiology
CARPÉN, O., Pathology
DEAN, P., Diagnostic Radiology
ELENIUS, K., Medical Biochemistry
GRÉNMAN, R., Otorhinolaryngology
HÄNNINEN, P., Medical Physics
HAPPONEN, R.-P., Oral Surgery
HÄRKÖNEN, P., Cell Biology
HARTIALA, J., Clinical Physiology and Nuclear Medicine
HIETALA, J., Psychiatry
HUOVINEN, P., Bacteriology
HUUPPONEN, R., Pharmacology
ISOLAURI, E., Paediatrics
JALKANEN, S., Immunology
JALONEN, J., Anaesthesiology
KÄHÄRI, V.-M., Dermatology and Venereal Diseases
KANERVA, L., Synthetic Drug Chemistry
KEMPPAINEN, P., Stomatognathic Physiology
KIVELÄ, S.-L., General Practice
KÖNÖNEN, E., Dentistry
KORKEILA, J., Psychiatry
KOTILAINEN, P., Infectious Diseases
KOULU, M., Drug Devt
LAUNIS, V., Medical Ethics
LEINO-KILPI, H., Nursing Science
LEIVO, I., Pathology
MÄKINEN, J., Obstetrics and Gynaecology
MÖTTÖNEN, T., Rheumatology
NÄRHI, T., Dental Prosthetics
NUUTILA, P., Internal Medicine
OLKKOLA, K., Anaesthesiology
PELLINIEMI, L., Electron Microscopy
PELTONEN, J., Anatomy
PIHA, J., Child Psychiatry
PUOLAKKAINEN, P., Surgery
PYRHÖNEN, S., Oncology and Radiotherapy
RAITAKARI, O., Cardiovascular Medicine
ROBERTS, P. J., Surgery
ROINE, R., Neurology
RÖNNEMAA, T., Internal Medicine
SAARIJÄRVI, S., Psychiatry
SALOKANGAS, R., Psychiatry
SALANTERÄ, S., Clinical Nursing Science
SALMI, M., Medical Biochemistry
SAUKKO, P., Forensic Medicine
SAVOLAINEN, J., Clinical Allergology
SCHEININ, M., Biomaterial Technology
SCHEININ, M., Clinical Pharmacology
SIMELL, O. G., Paediatrics
SYRJÄNEN, S., Oral Pathology and Radiology
TENOVUO, J. O., Cardiology
TOPPARI, J., Physiology
TUOMINEN, R., Public Health
VÄÄNÄNEN, K., Cell Biology
VAHTERA, J., Public Health
VÄLIMÄKI, M., Nursing Science
VALLITTU, P., Prosthetic Dentistry and Biomaterials Science
VARRELA, J., Oral Devt and Orthodontics
VESTI, E., Ophthalmology
VIIKARI, J., Internal Medicine
VIITANEN, M., Geriatrics

Faculty of Social Sciences (tel. (2) 3335362; e-mail soc@lists.utu.fi; internet www.soc.utu.fi):

ERVASTI, H., Social Policy
FORSSÉN, K., Social Work
HÄMÄLÄINEN, H., Psychology
KIVINEN, O., Sociology of Education
KOISTINEN, O., Theoretical Philosophy
KORPILAHTI, P., Logopaedics
LAGERSPETZ, E., Practical Philosophy
NIEMI, P., Psychology
NURMI, H., Political Science
RÄIHÄ, H., Psychology
RENTOLA, K., Contemporary History
RITAKALLIO, V.-M., Social Policy
SALMIVALLI, C., Psychology
SOIKKANEN, T., Contemporary History
UUSIPAIKKA, E., Statistics
VOGT, H., Political Science
WIBERG, M., Political Science

Turku School of Economics (tel. (2) 33351; internet www.tse.fi):

ALVAREZ, L., Quantitative Methods in Management
GRANLUND, M., Management Accounting
HALINEN-KAILA, A., Marketing
IMMONEN, R., Business Law
KAUPPI, H., Economics
KOVALAINEN, A., Women's Studies
LÄHTEENMÄKI, S., Management and Organization
LAURILA, J., Management and Organization
LIUHTO, K., Marketing Int. Business, Pan-European Institute

LUKKA, K., Management Accounting
MARJANEN, H., Economic Geography
NUMMELA, N., Int. Business
OJALA, L., Logistics
OLKKONEN, R., Marketing
PAASIO, A., Business and Innovation Devt, Business
RÄSÄNEN, P., Economic Sociology
REPONEN, T., Information Systems Science
SALONEN, H., Economics
SCHADEWITZ, H., Accounting and Finance
SILLANPÄÄ, M., Commercial Law
STENBERG, E., Int. Marketing
SUOMI, R., Information Systems Science
VARTIAINEN, H., Public Economics
VIRÉN, N., Economics

VAASAN YLIOPISTO
(University of Vaasa)

POB 700, 65101 Vaasa
Wolffintie 34, 65200 Vaasa
Telephone: (6) 3248111
E-mail: information@uva.fi
Internet: www.uva.fi

Founded 1966 as School of Economics and Business Administration, present name and status 1991
State control
Languages of instruction: English, Finnish, Swedish
Academic year: September to May
Rector: Prof. Dr MATTI JAKOBSSON
Vice-Rector for Enterprise and Economic Relations: Prof. ERKKI ANTILA
Vice-Rector for Research: Prof. VESA SUUTARI
Vice-Rector for Teaching and Educational Operations: Prof. HANNU KATAJAMÄKI
Dir for Academic Affairs: ANJA BRITSCHGI
Head of Library Services: MARITA AHOLA
Library of 120,000 vols
Number of teachers: 296
Number of students: 4,978
Publication: *Acta Wasaensia*

DEANS

Faculty of Business Studies: Prof. VESA SUUTARI
Faculty of Philosophy: Prof. HANNU KATAJAMÄKI
Faculty of Technology: Prof. ERKKI ANTILA

PROFESSORS

Faculty of Business Studies:
ÄIJÖ, J., Accounting and Finance
ANNOLA, V., Business Law
GABRIELSSON, P., Management and Organization
KALMI, P., Economics
KOHTAMÄKI, M., Management and Organization
LAAKSONEN, M., Marketing
LAAKSONEN, P., Marketing
LAITINEN, E., Accounting and Finance
LAITINEN, T., Accounting and Finance
LARIMO, J., Marketing
LEHTONEN, A., Law
LUOMALA, H., Marketing
NIKKINEN, J., Accounting and Finance
PIEKKOLA, H., Economics
ROTHOVIUS, T., Accounting and Finance
ROUTAMAA, V., Management and Organization
SUUTARI, V., Management and Organization
VÄHÄMAA, S., Accounting and Finance
VESALAINEN, J., Management and Organization
VIITALA, R., Management and Organization

Faculty of Philosophy:
AALTONEN, S., English Language
BJÖRKLUND, S., Language Immersion
HYYRYLÄINEN, E., Public Admin.
KATAJAMÄKI, H., Regional Studies
KOSKELA, M., Applied Linguistics
LEHTINEN, E., Modern Finnish
LÖNNROTH, H., Swedish
MÄKINEN, E., Public Admin.
NUOPPONEN, A., Applied Linguistics
PARRY, C., German Language
PILKE, N., Swedish
PORTER, G., English Language
SALMINEN, A., Public Admin.
SKOG-SÖDERSVED, M., German Language
VARTIAINEN, P., Public Admin.
VIRKKALA, S., Regional Studies

Faculty of Technology:
ALANDER, J., Production Automation
HASSI, S., Mathematics
HELO, P., Logistics
KANTOLA, J., Industrial Management
KAUHANIEMI, K., Electrical Engineering
NIEMI, S., Electrical Engineering
PYNNÖNEN, S., Statistics
SOTTINEN, T., Business Mathematics
TAKALA, J., Production Economics
VEKARA, T., Electrical Engineering
WANNE, M., Information Technology

Universities of Applied Sciences

Arcada-Nylands Svenska Yrkeshögskola (Arcada University of Applied Sciences): Jan-Magnus Janssonin aukio 1, 00550 Helsinki; tel. (20) 7699699; e-mail information@arcada.fi; internet www.arcada.fi; f. 1996; depts of business, information technology and media, energy and materials technology, health and welfare; library: 22,797 vols, 52,000 ebooks, 266 journals, 10,713 ejournals; 170 teachers; 2,700 students; Rector HENRIK WOLFF; Vice-Rector CAMILLA WIKSTRÖM-GROTELL; Vice-Rector Dr TOM LIND; Head of Library MARIA VON HERTZEN.

Centria Ammattikorkeakoulun Koulutustarjonta (Centria University of Applied Sciences): Talonpojankatu 2, 67100 Kokkola; tel. (6) 8250000; e-mail info@centria.fi; internet web.centria.fi; f. 1991, current name adopted 2012; business and administration, catering and domestic services, communication and transport, culture, health and sports, humanities and education, natural sciences, social sciences, social services, technology, tourism; postgraduate programmes in business administration and technology; 246 teachers; 3,300 students; Rector MARJA-LIISA TENHUNEN.

Diakonia-Ammattikorkeakoulu (Diaconia University of Applied Sciences): POB 12, 00511 Helsinki; Sturenkatu 2, 00510 Helsinki; tel. (20) 690431; e-mail international.office@diak.fi; internet www.diak.fi; f. 1996; degree programmes in education, nursing, social welfare, sign language interpretation and media; library: 150,000 vols, periodicals and audiovisual items; 3,000 students; Rector and Exec. Dir Dr JORMA NIEMALÄ; Vice-Rector PIRJO HAKALA; Head of Library Services SUSANNA KINNARI.

HAAGA-HELIA Ammattikorkeakoulu (HAAGA-HELIA University of Applied Sciences): Ratapihantie 13, 00520 Helsinki; tel. (9) 229611; e-mail admissions@haaga-helia.fi; internet www.haaga-helia.fi; bachelors programmes in business administration, hospitality management, journalism, sport and leisure; campuses in Haaga, Malmi, Pasila, Provoo (two), Vierumäki, Villila; 600 teachers; 10,500 students; Man. Dir and Pres. RITVA LAAKSO-MANNINEN.

Hämeen Ammattikorkeakoulu (HAMK University of Applied Sciences): POB 230, 13101 Hämeenlinna; Visamäentie 35A, 13100 Hämeenlinna; tel. (3) 6464503; e-mail hamk@hamk.fi; internet www.hamk.fi; f. 1996; culture, natural resources and the environment, natural sciences, social sciences, business and administration, social services, health and sports technology, communication and transport tourism, catering and domestic services and vocational teacher education; library: 120,000 vols, 450 periodicals in Finnish, 350 in other languages; 403 teachers; 8,161 students; Rector and Pres. PERTTI PUUSAARI; Vice-Rector for Education RISTO SALMINEN; Vice-Rector for RDI and System Devt JANNE SALMINEN; Admin. Sec. KATI ANKKURI.

Helsinki Metropolia University of Applied Sciences: POB 4000, Blvd 31, 00079 Metropolia; tel. (20) 7835000; e-mail admissions@metropolia.fi; internet www.metropolia.fi; f. 2008 by merger of EVTEK Univ. of Applied Sciences and Helsinki Polytechnic Stadia; courses in culture, business, healthcare, social services and technology; 16,700 students; Pres. and Man. Dir RIITTA KONKOLA; Vice-Pres. VESA TAATILA; Dir for Academic Services PEKKA KORHONEN; Dir for Finance and Admin. JORMA UUSITALO; Head of Library and Information Services HAKALA HELLEVI.

HUMAK Humanistinen Ammattikorkeakoulu (HUMAK University of Applied Sciences): Annankatu 12 A 17, 00120 Helsinki; tel. (20) 7621300; e-mail humak@humak.fi; internet www.humak.fi; f. 1998; programmes in civic activities and youth work, cultural management and production, sign language interpreting; 120 teachers; 1,300 students; Pres. and Man. Dir TAPIO HUTTULA.

Jyväskylän Ammattikorkeakoulu (JAMK University of Applied Sciences): Rajakatu 35, 40200 Jyväskylä; tel. (20) 7438100; e-mail admissions@jamk.fi; internet www.jamk.fi; incl. School of Business and Services Management, School of Health and Social Studies, School of Technology, Teacher Education College; 600 teachers; 8,000 students; Rector and Pres. JUSSI HALTTUNEN; Vice-Rector HEIKKI MALINEN; Dir for Admin. PEKKA JÄÄSKÖ; Library Dir MAKKONEN TEEMU.

Kajaanin Ammattikorkeakoulu (Kajaani University of Applied Sciences): POB 52, 87101 Kajaani; Ketunpolku 3, 87100 Kajaani; tel. (8) 618991; e-mail kajaanin.amk@kajak.fi; internet www.kajak.fi; f. 1992; schools of business, engineering, health and sports, tourism; library: 27,000 vols, 350 periodicals; 120 teachers; 2,000 students; Pres. TURO KILPELÄINEN; Head of Academic Affairs SISSALA AINOMARJA; Dir for Library KARJALAINEN RIITTA-LIISA.

Karelia Ammattikorkeakoulu (Karelia University of Applied Sciences): Tikkarinne 9, 80200 Joensuu; tel. (13) 260600; e-mail info@karelia.fi; internet www.karelia.fi; f. 1992; courses in culture, social sciences, business and administration, natural sciences, natural resources and the environment, tourism, catering and domestic services, social services, health and sports, technology, communication and transport; 400 teachers; 4,000 students; Pres. PETRI RAIVO; Vice-Rector PEKKA AUVINEN; Dir for Library KARI TIAINEN.

Kemi-Tornion Ammattikorkeakoulu (Kemi-Tornio University of Applied Sciences): POB 505, 94101 Kemi; tel. (10) 38350; e-mail ktamk@tokem.fi; internet www.tokem.fi; f. 1992; business admin., business and data-processing, cultural and media arts, health care, social services, technology;

library: 100,000 vols, 6,300 ejournals, 37,000 ebooks; 260 teachers; 2,900 students; Rector Dr REIJO TOLPPI; Vice-Rector HANNELE KERÄNEN; Head of the Library PUUSTINEN MARJATTA.

Kymenlaakson Ammattikorkeakoulu (Kymenlaakson University of Applied Sciences): POB 9, 48401 Kotka; tel. (44) 7028888; e-mail admissions@kyamk.fi; internet www.kyamk.fi; f. 1992; courses in business and administration, culture, natural resources and the environment, natural sciences, social health and physical education, social sciences, technology and transport; library: 100,000 vols, 500 periodicals; 220 teachers; 4,500 students; Rector and Pres. Dr PETTERI IKONEN; Vice-Rector Dr MIRJA TOIKKA; Library Man. IIRIS KUUSINEN.

Lahden Ammattikorkeakoulu (Lahti University of Applied Sciences): Paasikivenkatu 7A, POB 214, 15101 Lahti; tel. (3) 82818; e-mail lamk@lamk.fi; internet www.lamk.fi; f. 1991; faculties of business studies, design and fine arts, music and drama, social and health care, technology, tourism and hospitality; 250 teachers; 5,000 students; Pres. Dr OUTI KALLIOINEN; Vice-Pres. HELENA KARENTO.

Laurea Ammattikorkeakoulu (Laurea University of Applied Sciences): Ratatie 22, Fifth Floor, 01300 Vantaa; tel. (9) 88687150; internet www.laurea.fi; courses in culture, natural resources and the environment, natural sciences, social sciences, business and administration, social services, health and sports, tourism, catering and domestic services, hotel and restaurant studies, and correctional services; library: 115,300 vols, 10,000 ejournals; 8,000 students; Pres. MAARIT FRÄNTI; Vice-Pres. JOUNI KOSKI; Dir of Admin. and Finance KIMMO HANNONEN; Chief Librarian HANNA LAHTINEN.

Mikkelin Ammattikorkeakoulu (Mikkeli University of Applied Sciences): Tarkkampujankuja 1, POB 181, 50101 Mikkeli; tel. (15) 35561; e-mail mamk@mamk.fi; internet www.mamk.fi; studies in business management, environmental engineering, information technology, double degree programmes; 200 teachers; 4,453 students; CEO and Rector HEIKKI SAASTAMOINEN; Vice-Rector KALEVI NIEMI; Head of Library and Information Services MARJA-LEENA SAARINEN.

Novia Yrkeshögskolan (Novia University of Applied Sciences): POB 6, 65201 Vaasa; Tehtaankatu 1, 65100 Vaasa; tel. (6) 3285000; e-mail admissions@novia.fi; internet www.novia.fi; f. 2008 by merger of Svenska Yrkeshögskolan and Yrkeshögskolan Sydväst; courses in culture, healthcare, social welfare, technology, and communications; 5 campuses in Jakobstad, Vaasa (Seriegatan and Wolffskavägen), Raseborg and Turku; 4,000 students; Pres. Dr ÖRJAN ANDERSSON; Vice-Pres. BIRGITTA FORSSTRÖM; Chief Librarian GUNILLA JANSSON.

Oulun Seudun Ammattikorkeakoulu (Oulu University of Applied Sciences): POB 222, 90101 Oulu; Kiviharjunlenkki 1B, 90220 Oulu; tel. (10) 2721030; e-mail international@oamk.fi; internet www.oamk.fi; f. 1992; schools of business and information management, engineering, health and social care, music, dance and media, renewable natural resources, vocational teacher education; 800 teachers; 9,000 students; Rector JOUKO PAASO; Vice-Rector RISTO KIMARI; Dir for Library MINNA KOISTINEN.

Rovaniemen Ammattikorkeakoulu (Rovaniemi University of Applied Sciences): Jokiväylä 11C, 96300 Rovaniemi; tel. (20) 7984000; e-mail polytechnic@ramk.fi; internet www.ramk.fi; f. 1996; courses in business and administration, forestry and rural industries, health care and social services, sports and leisure, technology, tourism and hospitality management; 3,000 students; Rector MARTTI LAMPELA.

Saimaan Ammattikorkeakoulu (Saimaa University of Applied Sciences): Skinnarilankatu 36, 53850 Lappeenranta; tel. (20) 4966411; e-mail info@saimia.fi; internet www.saimia.fi; 260 teachers; 2,700 students; Rector ANNELI PIRTTILÄ; publ. *Puhuri*.

Satakunnan Ammattikorkeakoulu (Satakunta University of Applied Sciences): Tiedepuisto 3, 28600 Pori; tel. (2) 6203000; e-mail info@samk.fi; internet www.samk.fi; f. 1997; 450 teachers; 6,300 students; Pres. and Man. Dir Dr JUHA KÄMÄRI; Vice-Pres. Dr ANNE POHJUS; Vice-Pres. Dr CIMMO NURMI; Head of Library Services JUSSI KÄRKI; publ. *AGORA* (4 a year).

Savonia Ammattikorkeakoulu (Savonia University of Applied Sciences): POB 6, 70201 Kuopio; Microkatu 1, 70201 Kuopio; tel. (17) 2556000; e-mail savonia@savonia.fi; internet portal.savonia.fi/amk; f. 1992; courses in business and administration, catering and domestic services, communication and transport, culture, health and sports technology, natural resources and the environment, natural sciences, social sciences, social services, tourism; campuses in Kuopio, Iisalmi and Varkaus; 350 teachers; 7,000 students; Pres. VELI-MATTI TOLPPI; Head of Library and Information Services TUULA SNICKER.

Seinäjoen Ammattikorkeakoulu (Seinäjoki University of Applied Sciences): POB 412, 60101 Seinäjoki; tel. (20) 1245000; e-mail seamk@seamk.fi; internet www.seamk.fi; f. 1996; courses in business and administration, catering and domestic services, communication and transport, culture, health and sports, natural resources and the environment, natural sciences, social sciences, social services, technology, tourism; 220 teachers; 4,800 students; Pres. TAPIO VARMOLA; Dir for Library TARJA KOSKIMIES.

Tampereen Ammattikorkeakoulu (Tampere University of Applied Sciences): Kuntokatu 3, 33520 Tampere; tel. (3) 2452111; e-mail viestinta@tamk.fi; internet www.tamk.fi; f. 1996, merged with PIRAMK Univ. of Applied Sciences and TAMK Univ. of Applied Sciences 2010; Bachelors-level degrees in art and media, business economics and technology, environmental engineering, international business; teacher education centre; library: 100,000 vols, 650 journals, audiovisual material, final theses, 15,000 sheet music titles; 400 full-time teachers, 700 part-time; 10,000 students; Pres. MARKKU LAHTINEN; Vice-Pres. MARJA SUTELA; Vice-Pres. MIKKO NAUKKARINEN; Vice-Pres. PÄIVI KARTTUNEN; Head of Library and Information Services KAISA RISSANEN.

Turun Ammattikorkeakoulu (Turku University of Applied Sciences): Joukahaisenkatu 3A, 20520 Turku; tel. (2) 263350; e-mail ammattikorkeakoulu@turkuamk.fi; internet www.turkuamk.fi; f. 1992; faculties of arts academy, health care, life sciences and business, technology, environment and business, telecommunication and e-business, well being services; library: 134,000 vols of books, 800 journals, 11,000 electronic journals; 850 teachers; 9,500 students; Rector JUHA KETTUNEN; Vice-Rector Dr JUHANI SOINI; Vice-Rector OLLI MERTANEN; Vice-Rector SAARA LAMPELO.

Vaasan Ammattikorkeakoulu (Vaasa University of Applied Sciences): Wolffintie 30, 65200 Vaasa; tel. (20) 7663300; e-mail info@puv.fi; internet www.puv.fi; f. 1996; 147 teachers; 3,400 students; Rector TAUNO KEKÄLE; Vice-Rector ELISABETH MALKA.

ÅLAND ISLANDS

The Higher Education System

For geographical and economic reasons, the Åland Islands were traditionally associated closely with Sweden. In 1809, when Sweden was forced to cede Finland to Russia, the islands were incorporated into the Finnish Grand Duchy. However, following Finland's declaration of independence from the Russian Empire in 1917, the Ålanders demanded the right to self-determination and sought to be reunited with Sweden, with support from the Swedish Government. In 1920 Finland granted the islands autonomy but refused to acknowledge their secession. The Åland Islands are governed according to the Autonomy Act, which was introduced in 1920 and revised in 1951 and 1993. The Act provides for independent rights of legislation in internal affairs (including education) and for autonomous control over the islands' economy.

The education system is similar to that of Finland, except that Swedish is the language of instruction and Finnish an optional subject. The only provider of degree-level higher education in the Åland Islands is the Åland University of Applied Sciences, which was founded in the capital, Mariehamn, in 1997 by the Åland Provincial Government as a cooperative network for vocational higher education certified with a polytechnic diploma. In 2003 the University became permanent following its merger with Åland Open University. The main language of instruction at the University, which had an enrolment of 600 students in 2012, is Swedish; however, increasing numbers of courses are taught partly in English. As in Finland, the higher education system of the Åland Islands has been amended according to the Bologna Process, including the adoption of the European Credit Transfer and Accumulation System (ECTS). The University offers seven Bachelors degree programmes in: business administration, electrical engineering, health and caring services, hospitality management, information technology, marine engineering and navigation. The Bachelors courses last between three-and-a-half to four-and-a-half years and require the accumulation of between 210 and 270 ECTS credit units. In addition, in its capacity as an open university, the Åland University of Applied Sciences offers academic courses, further education, as well as lectures and seminars.

In 2011 a total of 812 people were undertaking post-secondary vocational education in the Åland Islands.

Regulatory and Representative Body

GOVERNMENT

Department for Education and Culture: Självstyrelsegården, POB 1060, AX-22111 Mariehamn; tel. (18) 25000; internet www.regeringen.ax/utbildning_kultur/kontaktinformation.pbs; Minister JOHAN EHN.

Learned Societies

LANGUAGE AND LITERATURE

Nordens Institut på Åland (Nordic Institute on Åland): Köpmansgatan 4, AX-22100 Mariehamn; tel. (18) 25000; internet www.nipa.ax; f. 1985; attached to Nordic Council of Mins; cultural instn; strengthens cultural life through contacts with other Nordic countries; Dir ÅSA JUSLIN; Sec. HARRIET LUNDELL.

RELIGION, SOCIOLOGY AND ANTHROPOLOGY

Ålands Kulturstiftelse r.s. (Åland Cultural Foundation): POB 172, AX-22101 Mariehamn; tel. (18) 19535; internet www.kulturstiftelsen.ax; f. 1950; promotes scientific research of Åland history and cultural life in the islands; engages and supports publishing; Chair. LARS INGMAR JOHANSSON; Vice-Pres. AGNETA ERIKSSON-SPRUCE; Sec. HELENA BLOMQVIST; publs *Det åländska folkets historia* (The History of the Åland People), *Internationella avtal och dokument rörande Åland, läs dem direkt på internet*, *Meddelanden från Ålands kulturstiftelse* (Communications), *Skrifter utgivna av Ålands kulturstiftelse* (Papers), *Urkundssamlingen* (The Tract Collection).

MEDICINE

Ålands Cancerförening (Ålands Cancer Association): Nyfahlers, Skarpansvägen 30, AX-22100 Mariehamn; tel. (18) 22419; e-mail info@cancer.ax; internet www.cancer.ax; f. 1986; organizes support groups and rehabilitation courses for cancer patients and their families; Chair. ANDERS MATTSSON; Vice-Chair. GUN-MARI LINDHOLM; Gen. Man. HELKA ANDERSSON.

Ålands Hälso–och Sjukvård (Ålands Health): POB 1091, AX-22111 Mariehamn; Doktorsvägen 1, AX-22100 Mariehamn; tel. (18) 5355; e-mail info@ahs.ax; internet www.ahs.ax; health services; provides safe working environment for health professionals; Chair. BARBRO SUNDBACK; Vice-Chair. ROGER JANSSON; Medical Dir DICK SJOGREN (acting).

Research Institutes

ECONOMICS, LAW AND POLITICS

Ålands Emigrantinstitut (Åland Islands' Emigrant Institute): Norra Esplanadgatan 5, AX-22100 Mariehamn; tel. (18) 13325; e-mail emi.inst@aland.net; internet www.eminst.net; f. 1994; attached to Åland Islands Emigrant Institute Soc.; promotes research into Ålandic emigration; collects, catalogues and distributes material connected with Ålandic emigration; Chair. BERTIL LINDQVIST; Vice-Chair. CHRISTINA H. BOMAN; Treas. MAJVOR SÖDERBERG.

Ålands Fredsinstitut (Åland Islands Peace Institute): Hamngatan 4, POB 85, AX-22101 Mariehamn; tel. (18) 15570; e-mail peace@peace.ax; internet www.peace.ax; f. 1992; conducts projects and research into peace and conflict issues with regard to Ålands and spec. status of Ålands under int. law; library: holds material on peace and conflict issues, minorities, autonomy and human rights; Chair. BARBRO SUNDBACK; Dir SIA SPILIOPOULOU ÅKERMARK; Head for Library and Archive JOHN KNIGHT; publ. *Rapport från Ålands fredsinstitut* (Report from the Åland Islands Peace Institute, 3–5 a year).

Libraries and Archives

Mariehamn

Ålands Landskapsarkiv (Provincial Archives of Åland): Självstyrelsegården, Strandgatan, POB 1060, AX-22100 Mariehamn; tel. (18) 25344; e-mail arkivet@regeringen.ax; internet www.arkivet.ax; f. 1978; archives incl. older documents from parishes and rural districts, documents from asscns, businesses, foundations, individuals, farms and village communities; archives belonging to the State of Finland pertaining to Åland Islands.

Mariehamns Stadsbibliotek—Central-Bibliotek för Åland (Mariehamn City Library—Central Library of Åland): POB 76, AX-22101 Mariehamn; Strandgatan 29, AX-22100 Mariehamn; tel. (18) 531411; e-mail biblioteket@mariehamn.ax; internet www.bibliotek.ax; f. 1890 as Åland lending library, present bldg 1989, current name adopted 1987; Ålandica colln (works relating to the islands); 120,008 vols, incl. 99,175 books, 7,819 CDs and cassettes, 1,820 DVDs and video cassettes, 259 magazine subscriptions and 19 newspapers; Chief Librarian EVA GUSTAFSSON-LINDVALL; Cultural Dir TOM ECKERMAN.

Sund

Sunds Bibliotek: Sundsvägen 1158, Finby, AX-22530 Sund; tel. (18) 45978; e-mail sundsbibliotek@aland.net; internet www.sund.ax/bibliotek.pbs; Librarian SONJA BERGLUND.

Museums and Art Galleries

Eckerö

Ålands Jakt och Fiskemuseum (Åland Hunting and Fishing Museum): Fiskeläge 37, AX-22270 Eckerö; tel. (18) 38299; e-mail jakt-fiske.museum@aland.net; internet www.jaktfiskemuseum.ax; f. 1995; mounted birds and animals; activities such as pearl digging and pewter casting.

Geta

Dånö hembygdsmuseum (Dånö Homestead Museum): AX-22340 Geta; tel. (40) 7685782; e-mail kgk@aland.net; attached to Dånö Museum Assoc.; inventories from the pilot crofter's holding as well as household items and hand tools.

Kastelholm

Ålands Fotografiska Museum (Åland's Camera Museum): Bastövägen 7, AX-22310 Pålsböle Åland; tel. (18) 43964; e-mail alands.fotografiska.museum@aland.net; internet www.aland.com/se/fotografiskamuseum; colln of cameras, accessories and photographic equipment; spec. exhibitions.

Lappo

Skärgårdsmuseet i Lappo (Archipelago Museum in Lappo): AX-22840 Lappo; tel. (400) 529462; internet lappo.net/museum; f. 1982; traditional island and fishing culture; blacksmith's workshop with colln of old utensils; colln of 10 traditional rural boats; photographic exhibition; short films of life in the Finnish archipelago.

Mariehamn

Ålands Konstmuseum (Åland Art Museum): Storagatan 1, AX-22100 Mariehamn; tel. (18) 25426; e-mail konst.info@regeringen.ax; internet www.museum.ax/museum/konstmuseum.pbs; f. 1963; attached to Museibyrån; local artists since 19th century; promotes artistic activity and disseminates knowledge about art; Art Curator SUSANNE PROCOPÉ ILMONEN.

Ålands Museum: POB 1060, AX-22111 Mariehamn; tel. (18) 25000; e-mail museum.info@regeringen.ax; internet www.museum.ax; f. 1934; attached to Museibyrån; prehistoric, historic and ethnological material; permanent exhibition of cultural history; spec. exhibitions; library of 11,000 vols; Curator ANNIKA DAHLBLOM; publs *Åländsk odling* (1 a year), *Sevärt* (series).

Ålands Sjöfartsmuseum (Åland Maritime Museum): Hamngatan 2, AX-22100 Mariehamn; tel. (18) 19930; e-mail info@sjofartsmuseum.ax; internet www.sjofartsmuseum.ax; f. 1935, opened to public 1954; collns and exhibitions focusing on Ålands's maritime heritage; ships' documents, model ships and figureheads; world's last sailing ships owned by Gustaf Erikson; rare 18th-century pirate's flag; also responsible for the museum admin. of the Pommern, owned by Mariehamn town; library: collns of nautical literature, archives incl. muster rolls, log books, colln of clippings, photographs, drawings and charts; Pres. JAN

LIMNELL; Dir Dr HANNA HAGMARK; publ. *Sjöhistorisk Årsskrift för Åland* (1 a year).

Fängelsemuseet Vita Björn (Fängelsemuseet Vita Björn): c/o Aland Board of Antiquities, POB 1060, AX-22111 Mariehamn; tel. (18) 25000; internet www.museum.ax/museum/vitabjorn.pbs; f. 1985; exhibitions concerning events that took place between 1700 and 1950.

Museibyrån (Åland Board of Antiquities): POB 1060, AX-22111 Mariehamn; tel. (18) 25000; e-mail museum.info@regeringen.ax; internet www.museum.ax; administers Åland's antiquities, researches its cultural heritage, preserves artefacts, bldgs and sites of cultural and historical value; maintains Ålands museum and Konstmuseum; responsible for other museums located on the islands; library of 11,000 vols; Curator VIVEKA LÖNDAHL; publs *Åländsk odling* (1 a year), *Sevärt* (series).

Önningebymuseet (Önningeby Colony): Jonesasgatan 3, Önningeby, AX-22140 Mariehamn; tel. (18) 33710; e-mail kjell.ekstrom@aland.net; internet www.visitaland.com/onningebymuseum; f. 1992; historical art and cultural museum; arranges exhibitions with contemporary art, programme evenings with music, poetry and songs.

University

HÖGSKOLAN PÅ ÅLAND (Åland University of Applied Sciences)

POB 1010, AX-22111 Mariehamn
Telephone: (18) 537000
E-mail: info@ha.ax
Internet: www.ha.ax

Founded 2003 by merger with Åland Open Univ., current name adopted 2003
State control
Language of instruction: Swedish

Faculties of business admin., electrical engineering, health and caring sciences, hospitality management, information technology, marine engineering, navigation, Open Univ.; degrees awarded by the Univ. of Åland are equal to the corresponding BA degrees in Finland

Rector: EDVARD JOHANSSON
Vice-Rector: SVEN SCHAUMAN
Head of Open Univ.: BRITTMARI WIKSTROM
Chief Librarian: SUZANNE DONNER

Number of teachers: 35
Number of students: 600

FRANCE

The Higher Education System

The French higher education system was restructured following the student-led unrest of 1968. The Loi de l'Orientation d'Education was enacted (it was reconfirmed in 1989) and greater autonomy was granted to institutions. However, ultimate responsibility for determining the curricula and teaching methods remains with the Ministries of Education (the Ministry of National Education, Youth and Community Life, and the Ministry of Higher Education and Research). France and the French Overseas Regions and Departments (French Guiana, Guadeloupe, Martinique, Réunion and, since 2011, Mayotte) are divided into 30 educational districts, called Académies, each responsible for the administration of education, from primary to higher levels, in its area. In 2009/10 there were 79 universities under the Ministries of Education, including universities in French Overseas Regions and Departments; these institutions are: Université des Antilles et de la Guyane (French Guiana, Guadeloupe, Martinique), Université de la Réunion (Réunion) and Centre Universitaire de Formation et de Recherche de Mayotte (founded in 2011). In the same year there was a total of 4,312 other higher education institutions. Since higher education is funded by the State, tuition fees are very low. Furthermore, students from low-income families can apply for scholarships, pay nominal sums for tuition and textbooks, and are eligible to receive a monthly stipend. The main accreditation agency for higher education in France is the Ministry of National Education, Youth and Community Life.

Students must have achieved the Baccalauréat, the main secondary school qualification, to gain admission to higher education. Some institutions may set additional entrance examinations, and the grandes écoles (as well as some of the specialist institutions) require students to undertake two to three years' additional preparatory study at a lycée prior to sitting competitive entrance examinations. Since 2002 France has gradually implemented the Bologna Process and by 2007 all universities offered the Licence–Master–Doctorat (LMD) qualifications. The standard undergraduate degree is the three-year Licence (equivalent to Bachelors and requiring the attainment of 180 European Credit Transfer and Accumulation System—ECTS—credit units). Following the Licence, students may take the Masters, which is awarded after two years (and the accumulation of a further 120 ECTS credit units) and replaces the range of pre-Bologna five-year degrees. There are two Masters tracks, Research or Professional. The Research Masters is required for entry to Doctoral studies, and the Doctorate is awarded after at least three years of study. Alternatively, medical students are required to study for a total of seven years for the Doctoral degree of Diplôme d'État de Docteur en Médecine and five years for the award of the Diplôme d'État de Docteur en Chirurgie Dentaire. (However, the medical courses—covering general medicine, dentistry and pharmacy—are currently undergoing comprehensive reform in order to bring them into line with the Bologna Process.)

In addition to universities and instituts universitaires de technologie, other public institutions offering higher education include instituts universitaires professionnalisés and grandes écoles (including the distinguished écoles normales supérieures). There are also professional schools for engineering, business and management, political sciences and veterinary sciences. Instituts universitaires de technologie were first established in 1966 and offer specialist two-year programmes leading to the award of Diplôme Universitaire de Technologie. Instituts universitaires professionnalisés have been established since 1992 and train senior executives in the fields of engineering, business and management, general administration, information and communication. Courses last for three years, including a six-month work placement, and culminate in the award of the Maîtrise degree. Grandes écoles are regarded as the most prestigious establishments for graduates wishing to enter high-level public service or business. The most prominent grandes écoles are the écoles normales supérieures; courses last for four years and students are awarded the Diplôme d'Études Approfondies. In 2009/10 a total of 2,316,100 students were enrolled in higher education; this figure rose to 2,347,800 at the beginning of the 2011/12 academic year.

Technical and vocational education is broken down into five levels, Niveau V to Niveau I, and is offered by secondary and post-secondary institutions. Broadly speaking, Niveaux III–I cover the post-secondary level, and lead to the award of a title such as Brevet de Technicien Supérieur, Diplôme d'État de Technicien, or Diplôme Universitaire de Technologie.

In August 2007, under the administration of Nicolas Sarkozy, the Higher Education Minister, Valérie Pécresse, proposed a law concerning the 'freedom and responsibilities of the universities' (la loi relative aux libertés et responsabilités des universités—LRU). Under the LRU law, universities were to be reformed within a year, and were all to become fully autonomous by 2012. University Presidents, elected by an Administrative Council including representatives of industry, were to have more control over how research staff divided their time between research and teaching, and how students were recruited. Publication quotas were to be imposed on researchers and faculties were to become more competitive and productive in terms of the professional market, and were to be free to acquire funding by working more closely with industry. Furthermore, universities were to be encouraged to create 'clusters' with other higher education and research institutions. Another stage of the reform was the devolution of property ownership from the State to the universities. The overall intention was for universities to function much like successful commercial enterprises.

However, the reform project met with considerable resistance amongst the student and researcher populations who saw it as an attack on the traditional republican value of freedom to education, and as undermining fundamental research in favour of applied research. A growing social movement of protest within the academic world was launched at the end of 2008 and persisted until mid-2009. Strikes at a number of universities that year endangered the end-of-year examinations and the Government eventually sent in security forces to evict students. Despite the staunch opposition, by January 2011 73 universities were autonomous and the remaining 11 would have to follow suit by August 2012.

The new Socialist administration under François Hollande on taking power in 2012 almost immediately put into place a public concertation on the higher education and research system (les Assises de l'Enseignement Supérieur et de la Recherche). The concertation was to be declined on a national and territorial basis and followed by the pilot group's report to the Ministry in December. At the beginning of 2013 a new project of law would be presented to replace the LRU.

Regulatory and Representative Bodies

GOVERNMENT

Ministry of Culture and Communication: 3 rue de Valois, 75033 Paris Cedex 01; tel. 1-40-15-80-00; e-mail point-culture@culture.gouv.fr; internet www.culturecommunication.gouv.fr; Minister AURÉLIE FILIPPETTI.

Ministry of Higher Education and Research: 1 rue Descartes, 75231 Paris Cedex 05; tel. 1-55-55-90-90; e-mail secretariat-communication@recherche.gouv.fr; internet www.enseignementsup-recherche.gouv.fr; Minister GENEVIÈVE FIORASO.

Ministry of National Education: 110 rue de Grenelle, 75357 Paris Cedex 07; tel. 1-55-55-10-10; e-mail mediateur@education.gouv.fr; internet www.education.gouv.fr; Minister VINCENT PEILLON.

ACCREDITATION

Comité national d'évaluation (CNE): 43 rue de la Procession, 75015 Paris; tel. 1-55-55-60-97; e-mail sgcne@cne-evaluation.fr; internet www.cne-evaluation.fr; f. 1984; govt org. with authority over all instns of higher education in France; evaluation of quality of main 'missions of public service' of each such instn; First Vice-Pres. MICHEL HOFFERT.

Commission des Titres d'Ingénieur (CTI): Greffe de la CTI, Direction Générale de l'Enseignement Supérieur, 110 rue de Grenelle, 75357 Paris 07 SP; tel. 1-55-55-67-25; e-mail greffe-cti@education.gouv.fr; internet www.cti-commission.fr; f. 1934; quality assurance and accreditation for engineers; Pres. BERNARD REMAUD.

ENIC/NARIC France: Centre international d'études pédagogiques (CIEP), 1 rue Descartes, 75231 Paris Cedex 05; tel. (1) 55-55-04-28; internet www.ciep.fr/enic-naricfr; Dir FRANÇOISE PROFIT.

NATIONAL BODIES

Conférence des Directeurs des Ecoles Françaises d'Ingénieurs (CDEFI): 151 blvd de l'Hôpital, 75013 Paris; tel. 1-44-24-64-49; e-mail cdefi@cdefi.fr; internet www.cdefi.fr; f. 1976; Exec. Dir ALEXANDRE RIGAL.

Conférence des Présidents d'Université: 103 blvd Saint-Michel, 75005 Paris; tel. 1-44-32-90-00; e-mail contact@cpu.fr; internet www.cpu.fr; f. 1971; consultative body at the disposition of the Min. of Nat. Education, Youth and Community Life; also studies questions of interest to all univs and coordinates the activities of various commissions on all aspects of education; 109 mems; Pres. LIONEL COLLET.

Conférence des Recteurs Français (French Rectors' Conference): Chancellerie des universités de Paris, 47 rue des Ecoles, 75005 Paris; f. 1967; establishes personal and permanent links between mems; encourages the discussion of professional problems; establishes relations with nat. and int. bodies concerned with education, science and culture; the Rectors are Chancellors of the state univs in their admin. area; Pres. Rector ALI SAÏB (Acad. d'Aix-Marseille); Vice-Pres. Rector BÉATRICE GILLES (Acad. de Nancy-Metz).

Fédération Interuniversitaire de l'Enseignement à Distance (FIED): Université Pierre et Marie Curie, 75252 Paris; tel. 4-42-95-34-80; e-mail secretariat@fied.fr; internet www.fied.fr; f. 1987; promotes distance learning by encouraging cooperation between French and int. univs and instns; 35 mems; Pres. Prof. PIERRE JARRAUD; Sec. Dr PATRICK BOIRON; Treas. Dr ANTOINE RAUZY.

Office national d'information sur les enseignements et les professions (ONISEP) (National Office for Information on Study and the Professions): 12 mail Barthélémy Thimonnier, 77437 Marne la Vallée Cedex 2; tel. 1-64-80-35-00; e-mail service_clients@onisep.fr; internet www.onisep.fr; attached to Min. of Nat. Education, Youth and Community Life; produces careers information for schools, colleges and careers centres; website helps students to search for a course by field, level of study and instn; Dir HERVÉ DE MONTS DE SAVASSE.

Union des Établissements d'Enseignement Supérieur Catholique (UDESCA) (Union of Catholic Higher Education Establishments): 21 rue d'Assas, 75270 Paris Cedex 06; tel. 1-70-64-29-76; e-mail delegue@univ-cathofrance.fr; internet www.udesca.fr; f. 1973; comprises the 5 Catholic institutes and univs at Angers, Lille, Lyon, Paris and Toulouse, and represents them in dealings with state instns; Pres. Prof. PHILIPPE BORDEYNE.

Union des Professeurs de Spéciales (Mathématiques et Sciences Physiques): 3 rue de l'École Polytechnique, 75005 Paris; tel. 1-43-26-97-92; e-mail ups@prepas.org; internet www.prepas.org/ups; f. 1927; 2,500 mems; Pres. BRUNO JEAUFFROY; Sec. ERIC MERLE; publ. *Bulletin* (4 a year).

Learned Societies

GENERAL

Académie des Jeux Floraux: Hotel d'Assézat, 31000 Toulouse; tel. 5-61-21-22-85; e-mail jeux.floraux@free.fr; internet jeux.floraux.free.fr; f. 1323; human sciences; composed of 40 'mainteneurs' and 25 'Maîtres ès Jeux Floraux'; Permanent Sec. JEAN NAYRAL DE PUYBUSQUE; publ. *Recueil* (1 a year).

Académie des Sciences, Agriculture, Arts et Belles-Lettres d'Aix: 2A rue du 4 Septembre, 13100 Aix-en-Provence; tel. 4-42-38-38-95; e-mail musee.arbaud@dbmail.com; f. 1829; collns of ceramics, paintings, sculptures; 40 fellows, 50 assoc. mems; library of 60,000 journals and plates, 10,000 books, 5,000 biographical MSS, 2,000 MSS related to local history, 1,200 portraits and 60 paintings of the Aix-en-Provence region; Pres. ROGER BOOT; Perm. Sec. JEAN LUC KIEFFER; publ. *Bulletin*.

Académie des Sciences, Arts et Belles-Lettres de Dijon: 5 rue de l'Ecole-de-Droit, 21000 Dijon; tel. 3-80-54-22-93; e-mail acascia@orange.fr; internet www.acascia-dijon.fr; f. 1740; library, symposiums, communications; 550 mems; Pres. PIERRE BODINEAU; Sec. MARTINE CHAUNEY-BOUILLOT; publs *Mémoires de l'Académie* (every 2 years), *Mémoires de la Commission des Antiquités de la Côte d'Or* (every 2 years).

Académie des Sciences, Belles-Lettres et Arts de Lyon: Palais Saint-Jean, 4 ave Adolphe Max, 69005 Lyons; tel. 4-78-38-26-54; e-mail secretariat@academie-sbla-lyon.fr; internet www.academie-sbla-lyon.fr; f. 1700; weekly meetings, annual grant for researchers in nuclear physics, medicine (oncology), literature, poetry; 52 elected mems; library of 60,000 vols; Pres. Prof. GÉRARD PAJONK; Chancellor Prof. JACQUES R. FAYETTE; publ. *Mémoires* (1 a year).

Académie des Sciences d'Outre-mer: 15 rue La Pérouse, 75116 Paris; tel. 1-47-20-87-93; e-mail vbenichou@academiedoutremer.fr; internet www.academiedoutremer.fr; f. 1922; sections on economics and sociology, education, geography, law, politics and administration, science and medicine; 275 mems (incl. 100 corresp., 50 assoc., 25 free mems); library of 80,000 vols and 3,000 periodicals; Permanent Sec. PIERRE GENY; publs *Hommes et Destins*, *Mondes et Cultures* (1 a year).

Académie Goncourt: Société de Gens de Lettres, c/o Drouant, Place Gaillon, 75002 Paris; internet www.academie-goncourt.fr; f. 1896 by Edmond de Goncourt; comprises 10 writers in the French language; each year they compile a shortlist of the most noteworthy fiction written in French and award 'le prix Goncourt' to the author of the work judged the best; Pres. FRANÇOIS NOURISSIER; Sec.-Gen. DIDIER DECOIN.

Agence de la Francophonie: 28 rue de Bourgogne, 75007 Paris; tel. 1-44-11-12-50; e-mail oif@francophonie.org; internet www.francophonie.org; f. 1970; an intergovernmental organization of French-speaking countries for cooperation in the fields of education, culture, science, technology, and in any other ways to bring the peoples of those countries closer together; 47 mems; Dir CHRISTIAN VALANTIN.

Alliance Française Paris Ile-de-France: 101 Blvd Raspail, 75270 Paris Cedex 06; tel. 1-42-84-90-00; e-mail info@alliancefr.org; internet www.alliancefr.org; f. 1883; French language school for foreigners; ind. instn; centre for training of teachers of French as a foreign language; Pres. GOÉRY DELACÔTE; Dir for the School PASCALE DE SCHUYTER HUALPA.

Comité des Travaux Historiques et Scientifiques: 110 rue de Grenelle, 75357 Paris Cedex 7; tel. 1-55-95-89-10; e-mail secretariat.general@cths.fr; internet www.cths.fr; f. 1834; attached to Min. of Higher Education and Research; research and publs in the fields of archaeology, geography, history, human sciences, life sciences, natural sciences; organizes annual nat. congress of learned socs; 255 mems; Pres. Prof. M. CLAUDE MORDANT; Gen. Sec. CATHERINE GROS; publ. *Actes du Congrès national des Sociétés savantes*.

Euskaltzaindia/Académie de la Langue Basque: Plaza Barria 15, 48005 Bilbao; tel. 9-44-155-81-55; e-mail webmaster@euskaltzaindia.net; internet www.euskaltzaindia.net; See also Spain chapter, under Learned Societies.

Institut de France: 23 quai de Conti, 75270 Paris Cedex 06; tel. 1-44-41-44-41; e-mail com@institut-de-france.fr; internet www.institut-de-france.fr; f. 1795; 623 mems; Chancellor PIERRE MESSMER; Dir of Services ERIC PEUCHOT.

Constituent Academies:

Académie des Beaux-Arts: 23 quai Conti, 75270 Paris Cedex 06; tel. 1-44-41-43-20; internet academie-des-beaux-arts.fr; f. 1648; sections of painting, sculpture, architecture, engraving, musical composition, free members, artistic creation (cinema and audiovisual arts); 126 mems (55 ordinary, 55 corresp., 16 foreign assocs); Pres. JEAN PRODROMIDÈS; Permanent Sec. ARNAUD D'HAUTERIVES; publ. *La Lettre de l'Académie des Beaux-Arts* (4 a year).

Académie des Inscriptions et Belles-Lettres: 23 quai Conti, 75270 Paris Cedex 06; tel. 1-44-41-43-10; e-mail secretaireperpetuel@aibl.fr; internet www.aibl.fr; f. 1663; 195 mems (55 academicians, 40 foreign assocs, 50 French and 50 foreign corresp.); Pres. Prof. JEAN-MARIE DENTZER; Permanent Sec. Prof. MICHEL ZINK; Gen. Sec. HERVÉ DANESI; publs *Comptes Rendus des Séances* (4 a year), *Journal des Savants* (2 a year), *Monu-*

ments et Mémoires de la Fondation Eugène Piot (1 a year).

Académie des Sciences: 23 quai Conti, 75270 Paris Cedex 06; tel. 1-44-41-44-41; internet www.academie-sciences.fr; f. 1666; sections of the first div.: mathematics, mechanical engineering and informatics, physics, sciences of the universe; sections of the second div.: chemistry, genomics, human biology and medical sciences, integrative biology, molecular and cellular biology; inter-section; 250 mems, at most 140 foreign assocs, 143 corresp. mems; Pres. ALAIN CARPENTIER; Vice-Pres. PHILIPPE TAQUET; Permanent Secs CATHERINE BRECHIGNAC (Sciences of the Universe and their Applications), JEAN-FRANÇOIS BACH (Chemical, Biological and Medical Sciences and their Applications); publs *Comptes Rendus Biologies* (12 a year), *Comptes Rendus Chimie* (12 a year), *Comptes Rendus Geoscience* (12 a year), *Comptes Rendus Mathématique* (12 a year), *Comptes Rendus Mécanique* (12 a year), *Comptes Rendus Palevol* (8 a year, palaeontology and evolution), *Comptes Rendus Physique* (10 a year).

Académie des Sciences Morales et Politiques: 23 quai Conti, 75270 Paris Cedex 06; tel. 1-44-41-43-26; e-mail kerbrat@asmp.fr; internet www.asmp.fr; f. 1795; sections of philosophy, moral and sociological sciences, legislation, public law and jurisprudence, political economy, statistics and finance, history and geography, general interest; 122 mems (50 ordinary, 60 corresp., 12 foreign assocs); Pres. BERTRAND COLLOMB; Permanent Sec. XAVIER DARCOS.

Académie des Technologies: Grand Palais des Champs Elysées, Porte C, ave Franklin D. Roosevelt, 75008 Paris; tel. 1-53-85-44-44; e-mail secretariat@academie-technologies.fr; internet www.academie-technologies.fr; f. 2000; analyses and publicizes academic studies on technology and its impact on society; ensures that society benefits from technological progress; 218 mems; Pres. BRUNO REVELLIN-FALCOZ; Dir SYLVIE GOUGON.

Académie Française: 23 quai Conti, 75270 Paris Cedex 06; tel. 1-44-41-43-00; e-mail contact@academie-francaise.fr; internet www.academie-francaise.fr; f. 1635; 40 mems; Permanent Sec. HÉLÈNE CARRÈRE D'ENCAUSSE.

AGRICULTURE, FISHERIES AND VETERINARY SCIENCE

Académie d'Agriculture de France: 18 rue de Bellechasse, 75007 Paris; tel. 1-47-05-10-37; e-mail aaf@paris.inra.fr; internet www.academie-agriculture.fr; f. 1761; 420 mems (120 full-time, 60 foreign, 180 corresp., 60 foreign corresp.); Pres. ANDRÉ FROUIN; Permanent Sec. GEORGES PÉDRO; library of 80,000 vols, 500 periodicals; publ. *Comptes rendus* (4 a year).

Académie Vétérinaire de France: 34 rue Bréguet, 75011 Paris; tel. 1-53-36-16-19; e-mail academie@veterinaire.fr; internet www.academie-veterinaire-france.fr; f. 1844; 44 mems; Pres. PIERRE LARVOR; Sec.-Gen. CLAUDE MILHAUD.

Association Centrale des Vétérinaires: 10 place Léon Blum, 75011 Paris; tel. 1-43-56-21-02; e-mail acveto@orange.fr; internet asso-acv.veterinaire.fr; f. 1889; 1,700 mems; Pres. Dr B. WILMET.

Association Française pour l'Etude du Sol: INRA, CS40001, 2163 ave de la Pomme de Pin, Ardon 45075 Orléans Cedex 2; tel. 2-38-41-48-23; e-mail afretsol@orleans.inra.fr; internet www.afes.fr; f. 1934; pedology, agronomy; 800 mems; Pres. Dr JEAN-PAUL LEGROS; publ. *Etude et Gestion des Sols* (4 a year).

Société Française d'Economie Rurale: 19 Av. du Maine, 75732 Paris Cedex 15; tel. 1-45-49-88-40; e-mail sfer@engref.fr; internet www.sfer.asso.fr/sfer; f. 1949; 2 study sessions a year; 400 mems; Pres. LUCIEN BOURGEOIS; Sec.-Gen. DENIS HAIRY; publ. *Economie Rurale* (6 a year).

Société Nationale d'Horticulture de France (SNHF): 84 rue de Grenelle, 75007 Paris; tel. 1-44-39-78-78; e-mail info@snhf.org; internet www.snhf.asso.fr; f. 1827; 8,000 mems, 120,000 affiliated mems; library of 16,000 vols; Pres. JEAN PUECH; Gen. Sec. (vacant); publ. *Jardins de France* (10 a year).

Société Vétérinaire Pratique de France: 10 Pl. Léon Blum, 75011 Paris; tel. 6-36-19-64-57; e-mail veterinaire-pratique@club-internet.fr; internet www.svpf.fr; f. 1879; 750 mems; Pres. PATRICK PERRIN; Sec.-Gen. MICHEL BERNADAC; publ. *Bulletin* (4 a year).

ARCHITECTURE AND TOWN PLANNING

Académie d'Architecture: 9 place des Vosges, 75004 Paris; tel. 1-48-87-83-10; internet www.archi.fr/aa; f. 1840 as Société Centrale des Architectes, name changed 1953; 100 elected mems; Pres. AYMERIC ZUBLENA; Gen. Sec. JEAN-MARIE VALENTIN.

Association Nationale pour la Protection des Villes d'Art: 39 ave de La Motte-Picquet, 75007 Paris; tel. 1-47-05-37-71; e-mail florence.rouxcourtois@orange.fr; f. 1963; an asscn of local societies in 40 cities for the protection and restoration of historic and artistic buildings; Pres. PAULE ALBRECHT.

Cité de l'Architecture et du Patrimoine: Palais de Chaillot, 1 pl. du Trocadéro, 75116 Paris; tel. 1-58-51-52-00; e-mail info@citechaillot.org; internet www.citechaillot.org; f. 1980; funded by Min. of Culture and Communication; contemporary French architecture and architectural heritage; library of 10,000 vols, 70 periodicals; Pres. FRANÇOIS DE MAZIÈRES; publs *Archiscopie* (12 a year), *Colonnes* (2 a year).

Compagnie des Experts-Architectes près la Cour d'Appel de Paris: 24 rue Bezout, 75014 Paris; tel. 1-43-27-59-69; e-mail info@ceacap.org; internet www.ceacap.org; f. 1928; 125 mems; Pres. MICHEL AUSTRY; Gen. Sec. ROBERT LEGRAS.

Conseil National de l'Ordre des Architectes: Tour Maine Montparnasse, 33 ave du Maine, BP 154, 75755 Paris Cedex 15; tel. 1-56-58-67-00; e-mail info@cnoa.com; internet www.architectes.org; f. 1977; official regulating body for the architectural profession; Pres. of Conseil LIONEL CARLI; Vice-Pres. FRÉDÉRIC DENISART; Vice-Pres. BÉRENGÈRE PY-RODRIGUES DE SA; publ. *d'Architectures* (12 a year).

Office Général du Bâtiment et des Travaux Publics: 55 ave Kléber, 75784 Paris Cedex 16; tel. 1-40-69-51-00; internet www.ogbtp.com; f. 1918; combines the majority of societies, unions and federations of architects and contractors; Pres. YVES TOULET.

Société Française des Architectes: 247 rue St Jacques, 75005 Paris; tel. 1-56-81-10-25; e-mail contact@sfarchi.org; internet www.sfarchi.org; f. 1877; cultural asscn; 1,000 mems; Pres. PABLO KATZ; publs *Le Visiteur* (1 a year), *Tribune d'Histoire et d'Actualité de l'Architecture*.

Société pour la Protection des Paysages et de l'Esthétique de la France: 39 ave de la Motte-Picquet, 75007 Paris; e-mail sppef@wanadoo.fr; internet sppef.free.fr; f. 1901; protection and promotion of towns and landscapes; 4,000 mems; Pres. P. ALBRECHT; publ. *Sites et Monuments* (4 a year).

BIBLIOGRAPHY, LIBRARY SCIENCE AND MUSEOLOGY

Association des Archivistes Français: 9 rue Montcalm, 75018 Paris Cedex 03; tel. 1-46-06-39-44; e-mail secretariat@archivistes.org; internet www.archivistes.org; f. 1904; 700 mems; Pres. HENRI ZUBER; Sec. AGNÈS DEJOB; publ. *La Gazette des Archives* (4 a year).

Association des Bibliothécaires Français: 31 rue de Chabrol, 75010 Paris; tel. 1-55-33-10-30; e-mail abf@abf.asso.fr; internet www.abf.asso.fr; f. 1906; 2,500 mems; Pres. GILLES EBOLI; Gen. Sec. DANIEL LE GOFF; publ. *ABF Bulletin d'Informations* (4 a year).

Association des Professionnels de l'Information et de la Documentation (ADBS): 25 rue Claude Tillier, 75012 Paris; tel. 1-43-72-25-25; e-mail adbs@adbs.fr; internet www.adbs.fr; f. 1963; 5,000 mems; organizes annual congress with Groupement français de l'industrie de l'information; Pres. CAROLINE WIEGANDT; publ. *Documentaliste—sciences de l'information* (6 a year).

Association Générale des Conservateurs des Collections Publiques de France: 6 ave du Mahatma Gandhi, 75116 Paris; tel. 1-44-17-60-00; internet www.agccpf.com; f. 1922; promotes and improve museums and museums' curatorship; 1,000 mems; Pres. JACQUES MAIGRET; publ. *Musées et Collections Publiques de France* (4 a year).

Centre d'Archives et de Documentation Politiques et Sociales: 86 blvd Haussmann, 75008 Paris; f. 1949; Dir Dr G. ALBERTINI; publs *Est et Ouest* (12 a year), *Informations Politiques et Sociales* (52 a year in France, Africa and Asia), *Le Monde des Conflits* (12 a year).

ECONOMICS, LAW AND POLITICS

Association d'Etudes et d'Informations Politiques Internationales: 86 blvd Haussmann, 75008 Paris; f. 1949; Dir G. ALBERTINI; publs *Documenti sul Comunismo* (Rome), *Est & Ouest* (Paris, 26 a year), *Este y Oeste* (Caracas).

Fondation Nationale des Sciences Politiques: 27 rue Saint Guillaume, 75337 Paris Cedex 07; tel. 1-45-49-50-50; internet www.sciences-po.fr; f. 1945; administers the Institut d'Etudes Politiques de Paris (*q.v.*); promotes research centres and social science studies, documentation service; library of 620,000 vols; Pres. RENÉ RÉMOND; Admin. R. DESCOINGS; publs *Critique Internationale*, *Mots* (4 a year), *Revue de l'OFCE* (4 a year), *Revue Economique* (6 a year), *Revue Française de Science Politique* (6 a year), *Vingtième Siècle*.

Institut des Actuaires Français: 4 rue Chauveau-Lagarde, 75008 Paris; tel. 1-44-51-72-72; e-mail info@actuaires-paris.com; internet www.institutdesactuaires.com; f. 1890; 600 mems; library of 5,000 vols; Pres. DANIEL BLANCHARD; publ. *Bulletin* (4 a year).

Institut d'Histoire Sociale: 4 ave Benoît-Frachon, 92023 Nanterre Cedex; tel. 1-46-14-09-29; e-mail bibliotheque@souvarine.fr; internet www.souvarine.fr; f. 1935; study of Communist and Soviet activities; library of 40,000 vols specializing in political sciences and history of workers' movements since beginning of 19th century, trade union periodicals and political reviews; Pres. EMMANUEL LE ROY LADURIE; Librarian VIRGINIE HÉBRARD; publ. *Histoire & Liberté* (4 a year).

Institut Français des Relations Internationales: 27 rue de la Procession, 75740

Paris Cedex 15; tel. 1-40-61-60-00; e-mail ifri@ifri.org; internet www.ifri.org; f. 1979; studies foreign policy, economy, defence and strategy; 560 mems; library of 32,000 vols; Dir-Gen. THIERRY DE MONTBRIAL; Sec.-Gen. VALÉRINE GENIN; publs *Cahiers d'Asie*, *Etudes de l'Ifri*, *Notes de l'IFRI*, *Notes du Cerfa* (12 a year), *Notes du CFE*, *Nouvelles de Chine* (12 a year), *Policy Papers*, *Politique Etrangère* (4 a year), *Travaux et Recherches*.

Société d'Economie et de Science Sociales: 20 rue Notre-Dame-de-Nazareth, 75003 Paris; tel. 1-40-29-96-29; e-mail socsciencesociale@free.fr; internet www.science-sociale.org; f. 1856; concerned with social reforms and sociology; 300 mems; library of 3,000 vols, including collection 'La Réforme Sociale'; Pres. EDOUARD SECRETAN; Sec. Prof. ANTOINE SAVOYE; publ. *Les Etudes Sociales* (2 a year).

Société de Législation Comparée: 28 rue St Guillaume, 75007 Paris; tel. 1-44-39-86-23; e-mail slc@legiscompare.com; internet www.legiscompare.com; f. 1869; comparative law; publishes books on comparative and foreign law; 600 mems (400 French, 200 overseas); library of 100,000 vols; Pres. EMMANUEL PIWNICA; Gen. Sec. BÉNÉDICTE FAUVARQUE-COSSON; publ. *Revue Internationale de Droit Comparé* (4 a year).

Société d'Etudes Jaurésiennes: 21 blvd Lefebvre, 75015 Paris; tel. 1-48-28-25-89; internet www.jaures.info/welcome/index.php; f. 1959; promotes all aspects of the life and works of Jean Jaurès; promotes the publication or re-edition of his speeches and writings; 500 mems; Pres. MADELEINE REBERIOUX; Sec.-Gen. GILLES HEURÉ; publs *Cahiers Jean Jaurès* (4 a year), *Cahiers Trimestriels* (4 a year).

Société d'Histoire du Droit: Université de Paris II, 12 place du Panthéon, 75005 Paris; e-mail societe_histoire_droit@yahoo.fr; f. 1913; 550 mems; Pres. Prof. OLIVIER GUILLOT; Sec. A. LEFEBVRE.

Société Française de Statistique: c/o Institut Henri Poincaré, 11 rue Pierre et Marie Curie, 75231 Paris Cedex 05; tel. 1-44-27-66-60; e-mail sfds@ihp.jussieu.fr; internet www.sfds.asso.fr; f. 1997; 1,100 mems; library of 60,000 vols; Pres. AVNER BAR-HEN; Gen. Sec. JEAN-MICHEL MARIN; publs *Journal de la Société Française de Statistique* (4 a year), *Revue de Statistique Appliquée* (4 a year).

EDUCATION

Association Francophone d'Education Comparée (AFEC): c/o Abdel-Rahamane Baba-Moussa, Université de Caen Basse-Normandie, Esplanade de la Paix, 14032 Caen Cedex; e-mail afec-bureau@hotmail.fr; internet www.afec-info.org; f. 1973; promotes comparative education among francophone teachers and educationalists; organizes one seminar a year and participates in meetings of the Comparative Education Soc. in Europe and the World Ccl of Comparative Educational Socs; 100 mems; Pres. Dr ABDEL RAHAMANE BABA-MOUSSA; Vice-Pres. MOUSSA DAFF; Sec.-Gen. EVE COMANDÉ; publs *Bulletin de liaison et d'information* (3 a year), *Education comparée—nouvelle série* (2 a year).

Centre Culturel Calouste Gulbenkian: 39, blvd de la Tour Mauboung, 75007 Paris; tel. 1-53-85-93-93; e-mail calouste@gulbenkian-paris.org; internet www.gulbenkian-paris.org; f. 1965; attached to Calouste Gulbenkian Foundation in Lisbon (Portugal); non-profit-making; exhibitions, lectures, seminars, concerts; awards grants in the fields of education, art, science and charity; library of 80,000 vols; Dir JOÃO CANAÇA.

Fondation Biermans-Lapôtre: 9A blvd Jourdan, 75014 Paris Cedex 14; tel. 1-40-78-72-00; e-mail admin@fbl-paris.org; internet www.fbl-paris.org; f. 1924; attached to Fondation Universitaire (see Belgium chapter); house for Belgian and Luxembourg students; promotes academic and scientific exchanges between France and Belgium; offers grants; Dir JOS AELVOET; Dir Adjunct CLAUDE GONFROID.

Office National d'Information sur les Enseignements et les Professions: 12 mail B. Thimonnier, BP 86 Lognes, 77423 Marne la Vallée, Cedex 02; tel. 1-64-80-35-00; internet www.onisep.fr; f. 1970; Dir MICHEL VALDIGUIÉ; publs *Avenirs*, *Bulletin d'Information* (12 a year), *Les Cahiers de l'ONISEP*, *ONISEP Communiqué* (6 a year), *Réadaptation* (12 a year).

FINE AND PERFORMING ARTS

Association Française d'Action Artistique: 1 bis, ave de Villars, 75007 Paris; tel. 1-53-69-83-00; e-mail info@afaa.asso.fr; internet www.afaa.asso.fr; f. 1922; offers international cultural exchanges; assists in the development of the performing arts, visual arts, architecture, heritage and cultural projects in France; Pres. ROBERT LION.

Association du Salon d'Automne: Grand Palais, Porte H, 75008 Paris; tel. 1-43-59-46-07; e-mail contact@salon-automne-paris.com; internet www.salon-automne-paris.com; f. 1903; sections: painting, engraving, mural and decorative art, sculpture, photography; Pres. JEAN-FRANÇOIS LARRIEU.

Jeunesses Musicales de France: 20 rue Geoffroy l'Asnier, 75004 Paris; tel. 1-44-61-86-86; e-mail info@lesjmf.org; internet www.lesjmf.org; f. 1944; encourages young audiences, promotes concerts, festivals; 320 delegates in 450 towns; Pres. J. L. TOURNIER; Dir BRUNO BOUTLEUX.

Société de l'Histoire de l'Art Français: 2 rue Vivienne, 75084 Paris Cedex 02; tel. 1-40-20-50-77; f. 1873; 1,000 mems; Pres. DANIEL ALCOUFFE; Gen. Sec. ELIZABETH FOUCART-WALTER; publs *Annuels*, *Archives de l'Art Français*, *Bulletin*.

Société des Amis du Louvre: Palais du Louvre, 75058 Paris Cedex 01; tel. 1-40-20-53-34; e-mail contact@amis-du-louvre.org; internet www.amis-du-louvre.org; f. 1897; 70,000 mems; Pres. MARC FUMAROLI; Sec.-Gen. SERGE-ANTOINE TCHEKHOFF; publs *Bulletin Trimestriel* (4 a year), *Chronique*.

Société des Artistes Décorateurs (SAD): Grand Palais, Porte C, ave Franklin D. Roosevelt, 75008 Paris; tel. 1-43-59-66-10; f. 1901; promotes modern art; 400 mems; Pres. CLAUDE MOLLARD.

Société des Artistes Français: Grand Palais, Porte C, ave Franklin Roosevelt, 75008 Paris; tel. 1-43-59-52-49; internet www.lesalon-artistesfrancais.com; f. 1882; 5,000 mems; organizes the annual Salon des Artistes Français (open to French and foreign artists); Pres. CHRISTIAN BILLET; publ. *Bulletin*.

Société des Artistes Indépendants: Grand Palais, Porte C, ave Franklin D. Roosevelt, 75008 Paris; tel. 1-45-63-39-15; e-mail indep@club-internet.fr; internet www.artistes-independants.fr; f. 1884; 2,500 members; supports modern artists; annual exhibition of paintings, sculpture, tapestry; Salon des Artistes Indépendants since 1884; Pres. ALAIN COLLIARD; Sec.-Gen. FRANÇOISE LE GOFF.

Société des Auteurs, Compositeurs et Editeurs de Musique: 225 ave Charles-de-Gaulle, 92528 Neuilly sur Seine Cedex; tel. 1-47-15-47-15; e-mail communication@sacem.fr; internet www.sacem.fr/eptic; f. 1851; 120,000 mems; deals with colln and distribution of performing rights; Pres. LAURENT PETITGIRARD; Chair. BERNARD MIYET.

Société d'Histoire du Théâtre: BnF, 58 rue de Richelieu, 75084 Paris Cedex 02; tel. 1-42-60-27-05; e-mail info@sht.asso.fr; internet www.sht.asso.fr; f. 1933; performing arts library; 650 mems; library of 15,000 vols; Dir DELAUNAY LÉONOR; Sec.-Gen. ROSE MARIE MOUDOUÈS; publ. *Revue d'Histoire du Théâtre* (4 a year).

Société Française de Musicologie: 2 rue Louvois, 75002 Paris; tel. 1-53-79-88-45; e-mail sfmusico@club-internet.fr; internet www.sfm.culture.fr; f. 1917; 650 mems; Pres. FLORENCE GÉTREAU; Sec.-Gen. GUY GOSSELIN; publ. *Revue de Musicologie* (2 a year).

Société Française de Photographie: 71 rue de Richelieu, 75002 Paris; tel. 1-42-60-05-98; internet www.sfp.photographie.com; f. 1854; 430 mems; library of 10,000 vols, and 25,000 old photographs; Pres. MICHEL POIVERT; publs *Bulletin* (4 a year), *Etudes photographiques* (2 a year).

Société Nationale des Beaux-Arts: 11 rue Berryer, 75008 Paris; tel. 1-43-59-47-07; e-mail snba.berryer@libertysurf.fr; f. 1890; organizes art exhibitions; 900 mems; Pres. ETIENNE AUDFRAY; Gen. Sec. GUY PERRON.

HISTORY, GEOGRAPHY AND ARCHAEOLOGY

Association de Géographes Français: 191 rue Saint-Jacques, 75005 Paris; tel. 1-44-32-14-00; e-mail assogeo@wanadoo.fr; f. 1920; 200 mems; Pres. R. POURTIER; Sec. Y. BOQUET; publ. *Bibliographie géographique annuelle* (1 a year).

Association des Amis de la Revue de Géographie de Lyon: 18 rue Chevreul, 69362 Lyons Cedex 07; tel. 4-78-78-75-44; e-mail buisson@univ-lyon3.fr; internet www.geocarrefour.org; f. 1923; Pres. NICOLE COMMERÇON; publ. *Revue de Géographie de Lyon* (4 a year).

Centre International d'Etudes Romanes: 7 pl. des Arts, 71700 Tournus; tel. 3-85-32-54-45; e-mail info@art-roman.org; internet www.art-roman.org; f. 1952; 400 mems; Hon. Pres. HUBERT BLANC; Vice-Pres. and Sec.-Gen. MARGUÉRITE THIBERT; publ. *Bulletin* (every 2 or 3 years).

Comité National Français de Géographie: 191 rue Saint-Jacques, 75005 Paris; internet cnfg.univ-paris1.fr; co-ordinates French geographical activity and participates in the work of the International Geographical Union; 400 mems; Pres. ALAIN MIOSSEC; Sec.-Gen. P. ARNOULD; publ. *Bibliographie Géographique Internationale* (published jointly with the International Geographical Union).

Comité Scientifique du Club Alpin Français: 24 ave de Laumière, 75019 Paris; tel. 1-53-72-87-13; internet www.clubalpin.com; f. 1874; 90,000 mems; Dir J. MALBOS.

Demeure Historique: Hôtel de Nesmond, 57 quai de la Tournelle, 75005 Paris; tel. 1-55-42-60-00; internet www.demeure-historique.org; f. 1924; study, research and conservation of historic bldgs, châteaux, etc.; 3,000 mems; Pres. JEAN DE LAMBERTYE; publ. *La Demeure Historique* (4 a year).

Fédération Française de Spéléologie: 28 rue Delandine, 75011 Paris; tel. 4-72-56-09-63; e-mail secretariat@ffspeleo.fr; internet ffspeleo.fr; f. 1963; speleology; 12,000 mems; library of 2,000 vols, 600 periodicals; Pres. LAURENCE TANGUILLE; Sec.-Gen. HENRY VAUMORON; publs *Bulletin Bibliographique Spéléologique*, *Karstologia* (2 a year),

Karstologia Mémoires, *Spelunca* (4 a year), *Spelunca Mémoires*.

Institut Français d'Etudes Byzantines: 21 rue d'Assas, 75006 Paris; tel. 1-44-39-52-24; e-mail bibliotheque.vernon.ifeb@icp.fr; internet www.icp.fr; f. 1897; Byzantine research, particularly on sources of ecclesiastical history; library of 50,000 vols; publ. *Revue des Etudes Byzantines* (1 a year).

Institut Français d'Histoire Sociale: Centre de documentation et de recherche, Archives Nationales, 60 rue des Francs-Bourgeois, 75141 Paris Cedex 03; tel. 1-40-27-64-49; f. 1948; 57 mems; library of 11,000 vols, 50,000 pamphlets, large colln of periodicals, MSS and illustrated documents; Pres. JEAN-PIERRE CHALINE.

Société de Biogéographie: 57 rue Cuvier, 75231 Paris Cedex 05; f. 1924; 350 mems; Pres. C. SASTRE; Sec.-Gen. M. SALOMON; publs *Biogeographica*, *Mémoires hors série*.

Société de Géographie: 184 blvd St-Germain, 75006 Paris; tel. 1-45-48-54-62; e-mail socgeo@socgeo.org; internet www.socgeo.org; f. 1821; 850 mems; library of 40,000 vols, 120,000 photographs at Bibliothèque Nationale de France, 58 rue de Richelieu, 75084 Paris Cedex 02 (Librarian JEAN-YVES SARAZIN); Pres. Prof. JEAN-ROBERT PITTE; Sec.-Gen. MICHEL DAGNAUD; publs *Bulletin de liaison des membres de la Société de Géographie*, *La Géographie* (4 a year).

Société de Géographie Humaine de Paris: 8 rue Roquépine, 75008 Paris; f. 1873; Pres. JACQUES AUGARDE; library of 2,000 vols; publ. *Revue Economique Française* (4 a year).

Société de l'Histoire de France: 60 rue des Francs-Bourgeois, 75003 Paris; e-mail info@erudist.net; internet www.shfrance.org; f. 1834; publishes a series of French historical texts and documents; gives public lectures on French history; 250 mems; Pres. Prof. CLAUDE GAUVARD; Sec. Prof. MARC H. SMITH; publ. *Annuaire-Bulletin* (1 a year).

Société d'Emulation du Bourbonnais: 93 rue de Paris, 03000 Moulins; tel. 4-70-34-08-13; e-mail emulation.bourbonnais@orange.fr; internet www.societedemulationdubourbonnais.com; f. 1845; activities in the fields of history, science, arts and literature; 400 mems; library of 30,000 vols; Pres. SYLVIE VILATTE; publ. *Bulletin* (4 a year).

Société des Océanistes: Musée du Quai Branly, 222 rue de l'Université, 75343 Paris Cedex 7; tel. 1-56-61-71-16; e-mail sdo@quaibanrly.fr; internet www.oceanistes.org/oceanie; f. 1945; 560 mems; Pres. MAURICE GODLIER; Sec.-Gen. PHILIPPE PELTIER; publs *Journal* (2 a year), *Publications*.

Société d'Ethnographie de Paris: 6 rue Champfleury, 75007 Paris; f. 1859; 400 mems; publ. *L'Ethnographie* (2 a year).

Société d'Ethnologie Française: Maison de l'ethnologie et de l'archéologie, 21 allée de l'Université, 92203 Nanterre Cedex; tel. 1-44-17-60-00; e-mail contact.sef@culture.gouv.fr; holds annual nat. conf. and study sessions; 100 mems; Pres. T. BARTHÉLÉMY; Sec.-Gen. G. RAVENEAU; publ. *Ethnologie Française* (4 a year).

Société d'Etude du XVIIe Siècle: c/o Université de Paris-Sorbonne, Occident Moderne, 1 rue Victor-Cousin, 75230 Paris Cedex 05; f. 1948; 1,250 mems; Pres. JEAN-ROBERT ARMOGATHE; Sec. JEAN-LOUIS QUANTIN; publ. *XVIIe Siècle* (4 a year).

Société d'Histoire Générale et d'Histoire Diplomatique: 13 rue Soufflot, 75005 Paris; tel. 1-43-54-05-97; f. 1887; history and diplomatic relations; 400 mems; publ. *Revue d'Histoire Diplomatique*.

Société d'Histoire Moderne et Contemporaine: Bureau 114, 56 rue Jacob, 75006 Paris; tel. 1-45-45-11-11; e-mail rhmc@ens.fr; internet www.rhmc.fr; f. 1901; early modern and modern French, European and world history; 600 mems; Pres. Prof. DANIEL ROCHE; Sec.-Gen. Prof. PHILIPPE MINARD; publ. *Revue d'Histoire Moderne & Contemporaine*.

Société Française d'Archéologie: Musée National des Monuments Français, Palais de Chaillot, 1 place du Trocadéro, 75116 Paris; tel. 1-42-73-08-07; e-mail sfa.sfa@wanadoo.fr; internet www.sfa-monuments.fr; f. 1834; mem. of CSSF; 1,500 mems; Pres. MARIA PAULA ARNAULD; publs *Bulletin Monumental* (4 a year), *Congrès Archéologique de France* (1 a year).

Société Française d'Egyptologie: Collège de France, pl. Marcelin-Berthelot, 75231 Paris Cedex 05; tel. 1-40-46-94-31; e-mail s.f.e@orange.fr; internet www.egypt.edu; f. 1923; 850 mems; Pres. D. VALBELLE; Sec. MARIE-CLAIRE CUVILLIER; publs *Bulletin* (3 a year), *Revue d'Egyptologie* (1 a year).

Société Française de Numismatique: Bibliothèque Nationale de France, Département des Monnaies, Médailles et Antiques, 58 rue de Richelieu, 75002 Paris; tel. 1-53-79-86-26; e-mail secretariat@sfnum.asso.fr; internet www.sfnum.asso.fr; f. 1865; 700 mems; Pres. GEORGES GAUTIER; Gen. Sec. ANDRÉ RONDE; publs *Bulletin de la S. F. N.* (12 a year), *Revue Numismatique* (1 a year).

Société Française d'Histoire d'Outre-Mer: 15 rue Catulienne, 93200 Saint Denis; tel. 6-07-30-04-22; e-mail sfhom4@yahoo.fr; internet www.sfhom.com; f. 1913; 420 mems; Pres. HÉLÈNE D'ALMEIDA-TOPOR; Sec.-Gen. JOSETTE RIVALLAIN; publ. *Outre-Mers* (history, 2 a year).

Société Historique, Archéologique et Littéraire de Lyon: Archives Municipales de Lyon, 1 place des Archives, 69002 Lyon; e-mail shallyon@cegetel.net; f. 1807; 78 mems; Pres. PHILIPPE DUFIEUX; Sec. PAUL CHOPELIN; publ. *Bulletin* (1 a year).

Société Nationale des Antiquaires de France: Palais du Louvre, Pavillon Mollien, 75058 Paris Cedex 01; f. 1804; history, philology and archaeology of Antiquity, Middle Ages and Renaissance; 435 mems, 10 hon. mems, 10 hon. foreign corresps, 42 resident mems; Pres. ELISABETH TABURET-DELAHAYE; Vice-Pres. MICHEL SOT; Sec.-Gen. ANNIE CAUBET; publ. *Mémoires de la Société Nationale des Antiquaires de France* (irregular).

Vieilles Maisons Françaises: 93 rue de l'Université, 75007 Paris; tel. 1-40-62-61-71; internet www.vmf.net; f. 1958; seeks to bring together all those who own buildings of historical interest and those who help to preserve them; 16,000 mems; Pres. PHILIPPE TOUSSAINT; publ. *Vieilles Maisons Françaises*.

LANGUAGE AND LITERATURE

Association des Ecrivains de Langue Française (ADELF) (French Language Writers Association): 14 rue Broussais, 75014 Paris; tel. 1-43-21-95-99; e-mail contact@adelf.fr; f. 1926 as 'Société des romanciers et auteurs coloniaux français'; awards 10 literary prizes; brings together writers of all nationalities whose works are published in French; 1,000 mems in 79 countries; library of 2,500 vols; Pres. JACQUES CHEVRIER; Sec.-Gen. MARIE-NEIGE BERTHET; publs *Collection des Colloques*, *Lettres et Cultures de langue française* (2 a year).

Association Française des Professeurs de Langues Vivantes: 19 rue de la Glacière, 75013 Paris; e-mail aplv.lm@gmail.com; f. 1902; 3,000 mems; Pres. JEAN-MARC DELAGNEAU; Gen. Sec. LAURE PESKINE; publs *Le Polyglotte* (4 a year), *Les Langues Modernes*.

Association Guillaume Budé: 95 blvd Raspail, 75006 Paris; e-mail info@bude.asso.fr; internet www.bude.asso.fr; f. 1917; 3,000 mems; publishes ancient Greek, Latin and Byzantine texts, classical texts with French translations and studies on history, philology and archaeology, which are published by the Société d'éditions 'Les Belles Lettres' at the same address; Pres. JACQUES JOUANNA; Vice-Pres. BERNARD DEFORGE, ALAIN MICHEL; publ. *Bulletin* (2 a year).

British Council: 9 rue de Constantine, 75340 Paris Cedex 07; tel. 1-49-55-73-00; e-mail projects@britishcouncil.fr; internet www.britishcouncil.fr; teaching centre; offers courses and exams in English language and British culture and promotes cultural exchange with the UK; Dir JOHN TOD.

Centre National du Livre: 53 rue de Verneuil, 75343 Paris Cedex 07; tel. 1-49-54-68-68; e-mail secretariat@centrenationaldulivre.fr; internet www.centrenationaldulivre.fr; f. 1946, present name 1993, to uphold and encourage the work of French writers; gives financial help to writers, editors and public libraries; promotes translation into French; Pres. BENOIT YVERT; Sec.-Gen. MARC-ANDRE WAGNER; publ. *Lettres*.

Espéranto-Jeunes (JEFO): 4 bis rue de la Cerisaie, 75004 Paris; tel. 1-42-78-68-86; internet esperanto-jeunes.org; f. 1969; promotes Esperanto among young people; 145 mems; Pres. BERTRAND HUGON; publs *JEFO informas* (4 a year), *Koncize* (4 a year).

Fondation Saint-John Perse: Cité du Livre, 10 rue des Allumettes, 13098 Aix-en-Provence Cedex 2; tel. 4-42-91-98-85; e-mail fondation.saint.john.perse@wanadoo.fr; internet www.up.univ-mrs.fr/~wperse; f. 1975; colln of 16,000 documents comprising all MSS, books, correspondence, private library and personal belongings of Saint-John Perse (Nobel Prize for literature 1960); organizes annual exhibition and symposium; 500 mems; Pres. YVES-ANDRÉ ISTEL; Dir BEATRICE COIGNET; publs *Cahiers Saint-John Perse* (irregular), *Souffle de Perse* (irregular).

Goethe-Institut: 17 Ave d'Iéna, 75116 Paris; tel. 1-44-43-92-30; e-mail kallies@paris.goethe.org; internet www.goethe.de/fr/par/deindex.htm; offers courses and exams in German language and culture and promotes cultural exchange with Germany; attached centres in Bordeaux, Lille, Lyons, Nice and Toulouse; library of 25,000 vols; Dir MARION HAASE.

Instituto Cervantes: 7 rue Quentin Bauchart, 75008 Paris; tel. 1-40-70-92-92; e-mail cenpar@cervantes.es; internet paris.cervantes.es; offers courses and exams in Spanish language and culture and promotes cultural exchange with Spain and Spanish-speaking South and Central America; attached centres in Bordeaux and Lyon; library of 42,000 vols, 100 periodicals; Dir AUGSTÍN VERA LUJÁN.

La France Latine—Revue d'Études d'Oc: c/o Prof. Philippe Blanchet, Université de Rennes 2, Place du Recteur le Moal, C524307, 35043 Rennes Cedex; e-mail philippe.blanchet@univ-rennes2.fr; internet www.prefics.org/credilif/flreo.html; f. 1957; studies romance languages, cultures and literatures in S France in all its forms mainly in the 'Langues d'Oc' (Occitan); library of 157 vols; Scientific Dir Prof. PHILIPPE BLANCHET; Scientific Dir Prof. SUZANNE THIOLIER-MÉJEAN; publ. *Revue* (2 a year).

Maison de Poésie (Fondation Emile Blémont): 11 bis rue Ballu, 75009 Paris; tel. 1-40-23-45-99; e-mail lamaisondepoesie@gmail.com; f. 1928; annual prizes: Grand Prix de la Maison de Poésie, Prix Arthur Rimbaud, Prix Edgar Poe, Prix Emile Verhaeren, Prix Louis Maudin, Prix Paul Verlaine, Prix Philippe Chahaneix; library of 16,000 vols; Pres. JACQUES CHARPENTREAU; Sec. BERNARD PLIN; publ. *Le Coin de Table* (4 a year).

PEN International (Centre français): 6 rue François-Miron, 75004 Paris; tel. 1-42-77-37-87; e-mail penfrancais@aol.com; internet www.penclub.fr; f. 1921; 550 mems; Pres. SYLVESTRE CLANCIER; Sec.-Gen. PHILIPPE PUJAS; publ. *La Lettre du PEN Club français* (6 a year).

Société de Linguistique de Paris: Ecole Pratique des Hautes Etudes, 4E section, Sorbonne, 47 rue des Ecoles, 75005 Paris; internet www.slp-paris.com; f. 1864; 800 mems; Pres. A. BORILLO; Sec. M. A. LEMARECHAL; publs *Bulletin*, *Collection Linguistique*, *Mémoires* (1 a year).

Société des Anciens Textes Français: 19 rue de la Sorbonne, 75005 Paris; f. 1875; 125 mems; Pres. Prof. RICHARD TRACHSLER; Dir Prof. PIERRE-YVES BADEL; Gen. Sec. Dr GÉRALDINE VEYSSEYRE.

Société des Auteurs et Compositeurs Dramatiques: 11 bis rue Ballu, 75442 Paris Cedex 09; tel. 1-40-23-44-44; e-mail infosacd@sacd.fr; internet www.sacd.fr; f. 1777; protects the rights of authors of theatre, radio, cinema, television and multimedia; Pres. CHRISTINE MILLER; publ. *La Revue de la SACD*.

Société des Etudes Latines: 1 rue Victor-Cousin, 75230 Paris Cedex 05; e-mail societe-etudes-latines@listes.paris-sorbonne.fr; internet www.societedesetudeslatines.com; f. 1923; Admin. Prof. JACQUELINE CHAMPEAUX; publ. *Revue des Etudes Latines* (1 a year).

Société des Gens de Lettres: Hôtel de Massa, 38 rue du Faubourg St Jacques, 75014 Paris; tel. 1-53-10-12-00; e-mail sgdl@sgdl.org; internet www.sgdl.org; f. 1838; defends the moral and social rights of authors and writers; Pres. ALAIN ABSIRE; Gen. Sec. DOMINIQUE LE BRUN; publ. *Lettre*.

Société d'Histoire Littéraire de la France: 112 rue Monge, 75005 Paris; tel. 1-45-87-23-30; f. 1894; 400 mems; Pres. M. FUMAROLI; Dir S. MENANT; publ. *Revue d'Histoire Littéraire de la France* (6 a year).

MEDICINE

Académie Nationale de Chirurgie: 'Les Cordeliers', 15 rue de l'Ecole de Médecine, 75006 Paris; tel. 1-43-54-02-32; e-mail ac.chirurgie@bhdc.jussieu.fr; internet www.biusante.parisdescartes.fr/acad-chirurgie; f. 1731; promotes debates on latest scientific devts on 12 specialities of surgery; fosters discussions on ethical and legal implications of surgery; 500 mems; library of 5,000 vols; Pres. Prof. JACQUES BAULIEUX; Vice-Pres. Prof. FRANÇOIS RICHARD; Sec.-Gen. Dr HENRI JDET; publs *Académie de Chirurgie Magazine* (4 a year), *e-Memoires* (4 a year, online).

Académie Nationale de Médecine: 16 rue Bonaparte, 75272 Paris Cedex 06; tel. 1-42-34-57-70; e-mail administration@academie-medecine.fr; internet www.academie-medecine.fr; f. 1820 by Louis XVIII; library of 400,000 vols; 130 mems attached to sections on medicine, surgery, hygiene, biological sciences, social sciences, veterinary medicine, pharmacy; Pres. CLAUDE BOUDÈNE; Perm. Sec. JACQUES-LOUIS BINET; publ. *Bulletin de l'Académie nationale de médecine* (9 a year).

Académie Nationale de Pharmacie: 4 ave de l'Observatoire, 75006 Paris; tel. 1-43-25-54-49; e-mail info@acadpharm.org; internet www.acadpharm.org; f. 1803; 440 mems; Pres. FRANÇOIS CHAST; Gen. Sec. J.-P. CHIRON; publ. *Annales Pharmaceutiques Françaises*.

Association des Morphologistes: 624 rue des Grèzes, 34070 Montpellier; tel. 4-67-03-03-00; e-mail info@morphologistes.fr; internet www.morphologistes.fr; f. 1899; 1,005 mems; Chief Editor BERTRAND MACE; publ. *Morphologie* (4 a year).

Association Française d'Urologie: Colloquium, 12 rue de la Croix Faubin, 75577 Paris Cedex 11; tel. 1-44-64-15-15; e-mail contact@urofrance.org; internet www.urofrance.org; f. 1896; 1,027 mems; Pres. PASCAL RISCHMANN; Sec.-Gen. Dr PATRICK COLOBY; publ. *Progrès en Urologie* (6 a year).

Association Scientifique des Médecins Acupuncteurs de France (ASMAF): 2 rue du Général de Larminat, 75015 Paris; tel. 1-42-73-37-26; e-mail jm.stephan@meridiens.org; internet www.meridiens.org; f. 1945 as Société d'Acupuncture; 1,500 mems; Sec.-Gen. Dr JEAN-MARC STÉPHAN; publ. *Méridiens* (4 a year).

Centre d'Etude de l'Expression: Centre hospitalier Sainte-Anne, 100 rue de la Santé, 75014 Paris; tel. 1-45-89-21-51; e-mail cee75@orange.fr; internet www.centre-etude-expression.fr; f. 1973; exhibitions of artworks from Sainte-Anne's colln and contemporary artists; develops psychological studies of various forms of expression: plastic, verbal, mimic, dance-movement, musical, theatrical; Pres. JEAN-PIERRE LIMOUSIN; Sec.-Gen. Dr ANNE-MARIE DUBOIS.

Comité National contre les Maladies Respiratoires: 66 blvd Saint-Michel, 75006 Paris; tel. 1-46-34-58-80; e-mail contact@lesouffle.org; internet www.lesouffle.org; f. 1916; research, information, health education, assistance for the handicapped; Pres. GERARD HUCHON; publ. *La Lettre du Souffle* (4 a year).

Confédération des Syndicats Médicaux Français: 79 rue de Tocqueville, 75017 Paris; tel. 1-43-18-88-00; e-mail csmf@csmf.org; internet www.csmf.org; f. 1930; 16,000 mems; Pres. Dr MICHEL CHASSANG; Sec.-Gen. Dr WANNEPAIN.

Fédération des Gynécologues et Obstétriciens de Langue Française: Hôpital St-Antoine, 184 rue du Fg St-Antoine, 75012 Paris; tel. 1-49-28-28-76; e-mail jmilliez@sat.ap-hop-paris.fr; f. 1950; 600 mems; Pres. Prof. ULYSSE GASPARD (Liège); Sec.-Gen. Prof. JACQUES MILLIEZ (Paris); publ. *Journal de Gynécologie Obstétrique et Biologie de la Reproduction* (8 a year).

Fédération Nationale des Médecins Radiologues: 62 blvd de Latour Maubourg, 75007 Paris Cedex 07; tel. 1-53-59-34-00; e-mail fnmr@fnmr.org; internet www.fnmr.org; f. 1907; 4,800 mems; Pres. Dr DENIS AUCANT; Secs-Gen. Dr JACQUES NINEY, Dr LAURENT VERZAUX.

Société de Médecine de Strasbourg: Faculté de Médecine, 4 rue Kirschleger, 67085 Strasbourg Cedex; tel. 3-88-11-62-59; f. 1919; organizes medical confs; 450 mems; Pres. Prof. E. QUOIX; Sec.-Gen. Prof. E. ANDRÈS; publ. *Journal de Médecine de Strasbourg* (12 a year).

Société de Médecine Légale et de Criminologie de France: 2 place Mazas, 75012 Paris; tel. 1-43-43-42-54; e-mail dgosset@adm.univ-lille2.fr; internet www.smlc.asso.fr; f. 1868; Pres. Prof. MICHEL PENNEAU; Sec. DIDIER GOSSET; publ. *Médecine légale-droit médical*.

Société de Neurophysiologie Clinique de Langue Française: Hôpital Sainte Anne, 1 rue Cabanis, 75674 Paris Cedex 14; tel. 1-40-48-82-03; f. 1948; 520 mems; Pres. Dr LUIS GARCIA-LARREA; Sec.-Gen. Dr S. S. LEFAUCHER; publ. *Neurophysiologie Clinique* (6 a year).

Société de Pathologie Exotique: 20 rue Ernest Renan, 75015 Paris Cedex 15; tel. 1-45-66-88-69; e-mail socpatex@pasteur.fr; internet www.pathexo.fr; f. 1908; 500 mems; library of 2,000 vols, 125 periodicals; Pres. JEAN DELMONT; Sec.-Gen. Dr SIXTE BLANCHY; publ. *Bulletin* (5 a year).

Société de Pneumologie de Langue Française: 66 blvd Saint-Michel, 75006 Paris; tel. 1-46-34-03-87; e-mail splf@splf.org; internet www.splf.org; Pres. M. FOURNIER; Secs-Gen. J. F. CORDIER, J. P. GRIGNET, B. HOUSSET, E. LEMARIÉ; publ. *Revue des Maladies Respiratoires*.

Société d'Histoire de la Pharmacie: 4 ave de l'Observatoire, 75270 Paris Cedex 06; tel. 1-53-73-97-37; f. 1913; 1,000 mems; Pres. Prof. OLIVIER LAFONT; Sec. B. BONNEMAIN; publ. *Revue d'Histoire de la Pharmacie* (4 a year).

Société d'Ophtalmologie de Paris: 108 rue du Bac, 75007 Paris; f. 1888; Sec.-Gen. Dr JEAN-PAUL BOISSIN; publ. *Bulletin* (12 a year).

Société Française d'Allergologie et d'Immunologie Clinique: Institut Pasteur, 28 rue du Dr Roux, 75724 Paris Cedex 15; tel. 1-45-68-82-41; internet www.sfaic.com; f. 1947; 860 mems; Pres. Prof. D. VERVLOET; publ. *Revue Française d'Allergologie et d'Immunologie clinique* (5 a year).

Société Française d'Anesthésie et de Réanimation: 74 rue Raynouard, 75016 Paris; tel. 1-45-25-82-25; e-mail contact@sfar.org; internet www.sfar.org; f. 1934; 4,298 mems; Pres. LAURENT JOUFFROY; Sec.-Gen. DAN BENHAMOU; publ. *Annales françaises d'Anesthésie et de Réanimation* (12 a year).

Société Française d'Angéiologie: 153 ave Berthelot, 69007 Lyons; tel. 4-78-72-38-98; e-mail dr.pmeicler@wanadoo.fr; internet www.sfa-online.com; f. 1947; 450 mems; Pres. Dr FRANÇOIS ANDRÉ ALLAERT; Sec.-Gen. Dr MICHÈLE CAZAUBON; publ. *La revue Angéiologie* (4 a year).

Société Française de Biologie Clinique: 194 Ave de Strasbourg, 54000 Nancy Cedex; tel. 3-83-35-36-25; e-mail sfbc@orange.fr; internet www.sfbc.asso.fr; Pres. ALAIN LEGRAND; Sec.-Gen. NELLY JACOB.

Société Française de Chirurgie Orthopédique et Traumatologique: Secrétariat: 56 rue Boissonade, 75014 Paris; tel. 1-43-22-47-54; e-mail sofcot@sofcot.com.fr; internet www.sofcot.com.fr; 1,950 mems; Pres. J. M. THOMINE; publs *Bulletin des Orthopédistes Francophones* (2 a year), *Revue de Chirurgie Orthopédique*.

Société Française de Chirurgie Pédiatrique: 149 rue de Sèvres, 75015 Paris; tel. 4-91-38-66-82; e-mail webmaster-sfcp@chirpediatric.fr; internet www.chirpediatric.fr; f. 1959; 350 mems; Pres. Prof. PAUL MITROFANOFF; Sec.-Gen. Prof. J. L. CLAVERT; publ. *European Journal of Paediatric Surgery* (6 a year).

Société Française de Chirurgie Plastique, Reconstructive et Esthétique: 26 rue de Belfort, 92400 Courbevoie; tel. 1-46-67-74-85; e-mail sofcpre@wanadoo.fr; internet www.plasticiens.fr; f. 1953; 628 mems; Pres. Prof. V. DARSONVAL; Sec.-Gen. Prof. M. REVOL; publ. *Annales de Chirurgie Plastique et Esthétique* (6 a year).

Société Française de Chirurgie Thoracique et Cardio-vasculaire: 56 blvd Vincent Auriol, 75013 Paris; tel. 1-42-16-42-10; e-mail sfctcv@sfctcv.net; internet www.fstcvs.org; f. 1948; 643 mems; studies problems linked with thoracic and cardiovascular surgery; Pres. Prof. ALAIN PAVIE; Sec.-Gen. Dr R. NOTTIN; publ. *Journal de Chirurgie Thoracique et Cardiovasculaire* (4 a year).

Société Française de Gynécologie: 36 rue de Toqueville, 75017 Paris; tel. 1-42-27-95-59; e-mail jean.belaisch@wanadoo.fr; internet www.sfgynecologie.org; 582 mems; Pres. J. P. WOLFF; Sec.-Gen. ANDRÉ GORINS; publ. *Gynécologie* (6 a year).

Société Française de Médecine Aérospatiale: Laboratoire de Médecine Aérospatiale du Centre d'Essais en Vol, 91228 Brétigny sur Orge Cedex; tel. 1-69-88-23-80; internet www.soframas.asso.fr; f. 1960; publishes papers on experimental and clinical studies; 1,100 mems; Pres. Dr M.-P. CHARETTEUR; Sec.-Gen. Prof. G. SOLIGNAC; publ. *Médecine Aérospatiale* (4 a year).

Société Française de Mycologie Médicale: 191 rue de Vaugirard, 75015 Paris; tel. 1-43-06-68-72; e-mail sfmm1@orange.fr; internet pagesperso-orange.fr/sfmm; f. 1956; 250 mems; Pres. CLAUDE GUIGUEN; Deputy Sec.-Gen. Dr MARIE-ELISABETH BOUGNOUX; publ. *Journal de Mycologie Médicale* (4 a year).

Société Française d'Endocrinologie: c/o Sylvia Delplanque, 88 rue de la Roquette, 75011 Paris; tel. (1) 40-24-02-72; e-mail sfesecret@wanadoo.fr; internet www.sf-endocrino.net; f. 1939; 850 mems; Pres. Prof. VINCENT ROHMER; Sec.-Gen. Prof. HERVÉ LEFEBVRE; Treas. Prof. LAURENCE LEENHARDT; publ. *Annales d'Endocrinologie* (6 a year).

Société Française de Neurologie: Service de Neurologie 1, Clinique Paul Castaigne, Hôpital de la Salpêtrière, 47 blvd de l'Hôpital, 75651 Paris Cedex 13; tel. 1-42-16-18-28; internet www.sf-neuro.org; f. 1899; 550 mems; library of 22,000 vols; Sec.-Gen. Prof. C. PIERROT-DESEILLIGNY; publ. *Revue Neurologique* (12 a year).

Société Française de Pédiatrie: Hôpital Trousseau, 26 ave du Dr Arnold Netter, 75571 Paris Cedex 12; tel. 1-49-28-92-96; e-mail sfpediatrie@orange.fr; internet www.sfpediatrie.com; f. 1929; 1,500 mems; Pres. Prof. ALAIN CHANTEPIE; Sec.-Gen. Prof. PACTRICK TOUNIAN; publ. *Archives de Pédiatrie* (12 a year).

Société Française de Phlébologie: 46 rue Saint-Lambert, 75015 Paris; tel. 1-45-33-02-71; e-mail sfphlebo@club-internet.fr; internet www.sf-phlebologie.org; f. 1947; 2,000 mems; Pres. M. PERRIN; Sec.-Gen. F. VIN; publ. *Phlébologie—Annales Vasculaires* (4 a year).

Société Française de Phytiatrie et de Phytopharmacie: CNRA, Route de Saint Cyr, 78000 Versailles; tel. 1-49-50-75-22; f. 1951; 1,000 mems.

Société Française de Radiologie: 20 ave Rapp, 75007 Paris; tel. 1-53-59-59-69; e-mail sfr@sfradiologie.org; internet www.sfrnet.org; f. 1909; 8,100 mems; Pres. LAURENT VERZAUX; Gen. Sec. JEAN-PIERRE PRUVO; publ. *Journal de Radiology* (12 a year).

Société Française de Santé Publique: BP 7, 2 rue Doyen Jacques-Parisot, 54501 Vandoeuvre lès Nancy Cedex; tel. 3-83-44-39-17; internet www.sfsp.fr; f. 1877; 750 mems; Pres. Dr FRANÇOIS BOURDILLON; publ. *Santé publique* (6 a year).

Société Française d'Histoire de la Médecine: c/o Dr Jean-Jacques Ferrandis, 6 rue des Impressionnistes, 91210 Draveil; tel. 6-18-46-72-49; e-mail jj.ferrandis@orange.fr; internet www.bium.univ-paris5.fr/sfhm; f. 1902; 700 mems; Pres. Prof. GUY PALLARDY; Gen. Sec. Dr JEAN-JACQUES FERRANDIS; publ. *Histoire des Sciences médicales* (4 a year).

Société Française d'Hydrologie et de Climatologie Médicales: 15 ave Charles de Gaulle, 73100 Aix-les-Bains; tel. 4-79-35-14-87; internet www.soc-hydrologie.org; f. 1853; 320 mems; Pres. Prof. MICHEL BOULANGÉ; Sec.-Gen. Dr ROMAIN FORESTIER; publ. *La Presse Thermale et Climatique* (1 a year).

Société Française d'Ophtalmologie: Maison de l'Ophtalmologie, 17 Villa d'Alésia, 75014 Paris; tel. 1-44-12-60-50; e-mail sfo@sfo.asso.fr; internet www.sfo.asso.fr; f. 1883; annual conference; 7,200 mems; Pres. Dr J. L. ARNÉ; Sec.-Gen. Dr J. P. RENARD; publ. *Journal Français d'Ophtalmologie* (10 a year).

Société Française d'Oto-Rhino-Laryngologie et de Pathologie Cervico-Faciale: 9 rue Villebois-Mareuil, 75017 Paris; internet orl-france.org; f. 1880; 1,500 mems; Pres. Dr R. BATISSE; Sec. Prof. CHARLES FRECHE; publ. *Comptes Rendus and Rapports Discutés au Congrès*.

Société Française du Cancer: Hôpital St Louis, 1 Ave Claude Vellefaux, 75475 Paris; tel. 1-17-44-70-76; e-mail info@sfc.asso.fr; internet www.sfc.asso.fr; f. 1906; 440 mems; offers grants to doctors from abroad or French doctors for work abroad; quarterly meetings, annual symposium; Pres. MICHEL MARTY; Sec.-Gen. JEAN-FRANÇOIS BERNAUDIN.

Société Médicale des Hôpitaux de Paris: Hôpital Hôtel-Dieu, 1, place du Parvis Notre-Dame, 75181 Paris Cedex 04; e-mail smhp@wanadoo.fr; internet www.smhp.fr; f. 1849; Sec. Prof. CLAIRE LE JEUNNE; publ. *Annales de Médecine Interne*.

Société Médico-Psychologique: 14/16 ave Robert Schuman, 92100 Boulogne; e-mail secretairegeneral.smp@hotmail.fr; f. 1852; 675 mems; Pres. Prof. JEAN-FRANÇOIS ALLILAIRE; Sec.-Gen. Dr MARC LUC MASSON; publ. *Annales médico-psychologiques* (10 a year).

Société Nationale Française de Gastro-Entérologie: CHU Reims, rue Serge Kochman, 51092 Reims Cedex; tel. 3-26-35-94-31; e-mail secretariat.reims@snfge.org; internet www.snfge.org; f. 1947; 1,800 mems; Pres. Dr ALEX PARIENTE; Sec.-Gen. Prof. GUILLAUME CADIOT; publs *Gastroentérologie Clinique et Biologique*, *Hepato-Gastro et Oncologie Digestive*.

Société Odontologique de Paris: 6 rue Jean Hugues, 75116 Paris; tel. 1-42-09-29-13; internet www.sop.asso.fr; 2,500 mems; Pres. PHILIP SAFAR; Man. PHILIPPE CHALANSET; publs *Journal de la Société Odontologique de Paris*, *Revue d'Odonto-Stomatologie* (4 a year).

Société Scientifique d'Hygiène Alimentaire: 16A rue de l'Estrapade, 75005 Paris; tel. 1-43-25-11-85; e-mail isa@ssha.asso.fr; internet www.ssha.asso.fr; f. 1904; 1,182 mems; Pres. Dr GUY EBRARD.

NATURAL SCIENCES

General

Comité National Français des Recherches Arctiques et Antarctiques: c/o Antenne parisienne des TAAF, 47 Blvd de Sébastopol, 75004 Paris; tel. 1-40-79-37-56; e-mail info@cnfra.org; f. 1958; Pres. J.-C. HUREAU.

Fédération Française des Sociétés de Sciences Naturelles: 57 rue Cuvier, 75231 Paris Cedex 05; tel. 1-40-79-34-95; e-mail faunedefrance@laposte.net; f. 1919; natural sciences and nature conservation; groups 175 socs; Pres. J. LESCURE; Gen. Sec. J. FRETEY; publ. *Revue de la FFSSN* (1 a year).

Biological Sciences

Les Naturalistes Parisiens: 45 rue de Buffon, 75005 Paris; f. 1904; undertakes research in natural history and deepens the scientific knowledge of its mems; 600 mems; Pres. C. DUPUIS; publs *Bulletin* (4 a year), *Cahiers des Naturalistes*.

Société Botanique de France: rue J. B. Clément, 92296 Châtenay-Malabry Cedex; tel. 1-46-83-55-20; e-mail sbfsecretariat@yahoo.fr; internet www.bium.univ-paris5.fr/sbf; f. 1854; 800 mems; Pres. ANDRÉ CHARPIN; Sec. ELISABETH DODINET; publs *Acta Botanica Gallica* (6 or 7 a year), *Le Journal de Botanique* (4 a year).

Société de Biologie: Université Pierre et Marie Curie, CP 2A, 7 quai St Bernard, 75252 Paris Cedex 05; tel. 1-44-27-35-50; e-mail societe.biologie@snv.jussieu.fr; internet www.societedebiologie.com; f. 1848; organizes meetings about innovative biological research; 260 mems (incl. 140 hon. mems and 120 elected mems); Pres. Dr WILLIAM ROSTÈNE; Sec.-Gen. Dr CLAUDE JACQUEMIN; publ. *Biologie Aujourd'hui* (4 a year, online, www.biologie-journal.org).

Société d'Etudes Ornithologiques de France: Muséum National d'Histoire Naturelle, 55 rue Buffon, CP 51, 75231 Paris Cedex 05; tel. 1-40-79-38-34; e-mail seof@mnhn.fr; internet www.seofalauda.wix.com/seof; f. 1993; scientific study of wild birds and their protection; publishes monographs, national and regional ornithological lists, atlases, CDs; 800 mems; library of 23,500 vols; Pres. P. NICOLAU-GUILLAUMET; Sec.-Gen. J. PH. SIBLET; Librarian E. BREMOND-HOSLET; publ. *Alauda* (4 a year).

Société Entomologique de France: 45 rue Buffon, 75005 Paris; tel. 1-40-79-33-84; e-mail secretaire-general@lasef.org; internet www.lasef.org; f. 1832; 650 mems; library of 12,000 vols, 80 periodicals; Gen. Sec. H. PIGUET; publs *Annales* (4 a year), *Bulletin* (5 a year), *L'Entomologiste* (6 a year).

Société Française de Biologie Végétale: 4 place Jussieu, 75252 Paris Cedex 05; tel. 1-44-27-59-18; e-mail sfbv.cordillot@wanadoo.fr; internet sfbv.snv.jussieu.fr; f. 1955; 600 mems; Pres. P. MOREAU; Sec.-Gen. A. ZACHOWSKI; publ. *Plant Physiology and Biochemistry* (12 a year).

Société Française d'Ichtyologie: 43 rue Cuvier, 75231 Paris Cedex 05; tel. 1-40-79-37-49; e-mail keith@mnhn.fr; internet www.mnhn.fr/sfi; f. 1976; fish culture, biology and systematics of fish, sea and freshwater fisheries; 320 mems; library of 5,000 vols, 800 periodicals; Pres. M. GAYET; Sec. P. KEITH; publ. *Cybium* (4 a year).

Société Mycologique de France: 20 rue Rottembourg, 75012 Paris; tel. 1-44-67-96-90; e-mail smf@mycofrance.org; internet mycofrance.org; f. 1884; 1,800 mems; Pres. M. BUYCK; Sec.-Gen. M. CHALANGE; publ. *Bulletin Trimestriel*.

Société Nationale de Protection de la Nature: 9 rue Cels, 75014 Paris; tel. 1-43-20-15-39; e-mail snpn@wanadoo.fr; internet www.snpn.com; f. 1854; 4,000 mems; Pres. FRANÇOIS RAMADE; Gen. Sec. MICHEL ECHAUBARD; publs *La Terre et la Vie* (4 a year), *Le Courrier de la Nature* (7 a year), *Zones Humides Infos* (4 a year).

Société Zoologique de France: 195 rue St Jacques, 75005 Paris; tel. 1-40-79-31-10; e-mail dhondt@mnhn.fr; internet www.snv.jussieu.fr/zoologie; f. 1876; zoology, evolution; 600 mems; Pres. Prof. J. DAGUZAN; Gen. Sec. Dr J. L. D'HONDT; publs *Bulletin* (4 a year), *Mémoires* (irregular).

Mathematical Sciences

Société Mathématique de France: Institut Henri Poincaré, 11 rue Pierre et Marie Curie, 75231 Paris Cedex 05; tel. 1-44-27-67-96; e-mail smf@dma.ens.fr; internet smf.emath.fr; f. 1872; 2,000 mems; Pres. MARC PEIGNÉ; Gen. Sec. CLAIRE ROPARTZ; publs *Annales Scientifiques de l'Ecole Normale Supériure* (6 a year), *Astérisque* (12 a year), *Cours Spécialisés* (2 a year), *Gazette des Mathématiciens* (4 a year), *Mémoires* (4 a year), *Revue d'Histoire des Mathématiques* (2 a year).

Physical Sciences

Association Française d'Observateurs d'Etoiles Variables: Observatoire Astronomique, 11 rue de l'Université, 67000 Strasbourg; tel. 3-85-89-09-78; e-mail afoev@astro.u-strasbg.fr; internet www.astro.u-strasbg.fr/afoev; f. 1921; observations (visual, photographic, PEP, CCD) of variable stars; 110 mems; Pres. M. VERDENET; Sec.-Gen. J. GUNTHER; Sec.-Gen. D. PROUST; publ. *Bulletin de l'AFOEV* (4 a year).

Association Française pour l'Etude du Quaternaire: Maison de la Géologie, 79 rue Claude Bernard, 75005 Paris; e-mail pierre.antoine@cnrs-bellevue.fr; internet www.afeq.cnrs-bellevue.fr; f. 1962 to prepare scientific publications and exchange information on the Quaternary; 600 mems; Pres. Dr D. LEFÈVRE; Sec. Dr C. FERRIER; publ. *Quaternaire* (4 a year).

Association Scientifique et Technique pour l'Exploitation des Océans: Immeuble Ile de France, La Défense 9, 4 place de la Pyramide, 92070 Paris La Défense Cedex 33; tel. 1-47-67-25-32; f. 1967; oil technology and allied activities, pollution control, polymetallic nodules, sand and gravel workings, fishing technology and fish farming; 80 mem. industries; Chair. PIERRE JACQUARD; Man. Dir B. E. DIMONT; publ. *Annuaire Technique et Industriel*.

Fédération Française pour les sciences de la Chimie: 28 rue Saint-Dominique, 75007 Paris; tel. 1-53-59-02-10; e-mail pascale.bridou@wanadoo.fr; internet www.ffc-asso.fr; f. 2005; 4,000 mems; Pres. Prof. MAURICE LEROY.

Société Astronomique de France: 3 rue Beethoven, 75016 Paris; tel. 1-42-24-13-74; e-mail ste.astro.france@wanadoo.fr; internet www.saf-lastronomie.com; f. 1887; 2,200 mems; Pres. PHILIPPE MOREL; Sec.-Gen. FRANCIS OGER; publs *L'Astronomie* (12 a year), *Les Ephémérides* (1 a year), *Observations et Travaux* (3 a year).

Société des Experts-Chimistes de France: 23 rue Saint-Dominique, 75007 Paris; tel. 1-53-59-02-16; e-mail contact@chimie-experts.org; internet www.chimie-experts.org; f. 1912; 300 mems; Pres. JEAN-PIERRE DAL PONT; Sec.-Gen. THÉRÈSE GIBERT; publ. *Annales des Falsifications de l'Expertise Chimique et Toxicologique*.

Société Française de Biochimie et Biologie Moléculaire: 45 rue des Saints-Pères, 75270 Paris Cedex 06; tel. 1-42-86-33-77; e-mail sfbbm@cep.u-psud.fr; internet coli.polytechnique.fr/sfbbm; f. 1914; 1,320 mems; Pres. E. WESTHOF; Gen. Sec. P. DESSEN; publs *Biochimie, Regard sur la Biochimie*.

Société Française de Chimie: 250 rue St Jacques, 75005 Paris; tel. 1-40-46-71-60; e-mail sfc@sfc.fr; internet www.sfc.fr; f. 1857; 4,600 mems; Pres. ARMAND LATTES; Sec.-Gen. JEAN-CLAUDE BRUNIE; publs *Analusis* (10 a year), *Journal de Chimie physique* (10 a year), *L'Actualité chimique* (12 a year).

Société Française de Minéralogie et de Cristallographie: 4 place Jussieu, casier 83, 75252 Paris Cedex 05; tel. 1-44-27-60-24; e-mail sfmc@ccr.jussieu.fr; internet www.sfmc-fr.org; f. 1878; 600 mems; Pres. JEAN-ROBERT KIENAST; Gen. Sec. DANIEL NEUVILLE; publs *Bulletin de Liaison*, *European Journal of Mineralogy*.

Société Française de Physique: 33 rue Croulebarbe, 75013 Paris; tel. 1-44-08-67-10; e-mail sfp@sfpnet.org; internet sfp.in2p3.fr; f. 1873; 2,500 mems; Pres. EDOUARD BREZIN; Gen. Sec. JEAN VANNIMENUS; publs *Annales de Physique*, *Bulletin*, *Catalogue de l'Exposition de Physique*, *Colloques*, *Journal de Physique*.

Société Géologique de France: 77 rue Claude-Bernard, 75005 Paris; tel. 1-43-31-77-35; e-mail accueil@geosoc.fr; internet www.geosoc.fr; f. 1830; 1,500 mems; library of 65,000 vols, 500 periodicals; Pres. ISABELLE COJAN; Exec. Dir FRANÇOISE PEIFFER-RANGIN; Sec. DANIELE GROSHENY; Sec. CAROLINE MEHL; publs *Géochronique* (4 a year, co-edited with BRGM), *Géologie de la France* (co-edited with BRGM, online), *Géologues* (4 a year), *Mémoires* (irregular), *Terra Nova* (co-edited with EUG and Sociétés Géologiques Européennes).

Union des Professeurs de Physique et de Chimie: 42 rue Saint Jacques, 75005 Paris Cedex 06; tel. 1-40-46-83-80; e-mail secretariat.national@udppc.asso.fr; internet www.udppc.asso.fr; f. 1906; 4,000 mems; Pres MICHELINE IZBICKI; publ. *Le Bup physique-chimie* (12 a year).

PHILOSOPHY AND PSYCHOLOGY

Association pour la Diffusion de la Pensée Français: 6 rue Ferrus, 75683 Paris Cedex 14; tel. 1-43-13-11-00; f. 1946; aims to promote the French language and Francophone culture worldwide; 600 overseas mems; Pres. JACQUES BLOT.

Société Française de Philosophie: c/o 45 rue d'Ulm, 75320 Paris Cedex 005; e-mail listesfp-subscribe@sofrphilo.fr; f. 1901; 200 mems; Pres. DIDIER DELEULE; Sec.-Gen. ANNE BAUDART; publs *Bulletin*, *Revue de Métaphysique et de Morale* (4 a year).

Société Française de Psychologie: 71 ave Edouard-Vaillant, 92774 Boulogne Cedex; tel. 1-55-20-58-32; e-mail sfp@psycho.univ-paris5.fr; internet www.sfpsy.org; f. 1901; 1,000 mems; Pres. JACQUES PY; Sec.-Gen. ALAIN PAINEAU; publs *La Lettre de SFP*, *Pratiques Psychologiques*, *Psychologie Française*.

Société Française d'Etudes des Phénomènes Psychiques: Centre Gabriel Delanne, 22 rue Paulin Méry, 75013 Paris; tel. 1-45-88-30-25; e-mail contact@sfepp.org; internet sfepp.org; f. 1893; conducts experiments in psychic clairvoyance and undertakes research to prove the immortality of the soul; conducts courses in meditation and yoga; Pres. JEAN-MARIE CODRON.

RELIGION, SOCIOLOGY AND ANTHROPOLOGY

Association Française des Arabisants: Collège de France, 52 rue du Cardinal Lemoine, 75005 Paris; e-mail afda@afda.asso.fr; internet www.afda.asso.fr; f. 1973; promotes Arabic studies; studies questions of doctrine and practice relative to teaching and research in Arabic; keeps its members informed of ideas and activities of interest to teachers, researchers and students of Arabic; 450 mems; Pres. JEAN-YVES L'HOPITAL; Sec. ABDELLATIF IDRISSI; publs *Actes des journées d'études arabes* (irregular), *Annuaire des Arabisants* (every 2 years), *L'Arabisant* (every 2 years), *Lettre d'Information* (2 a year).

Société Asiatique: Palais de l'Institut, 23 quai de Conti, 75006 Paris; tel. 1-44-41-43-14; internet www.aibl.fr/fr/asie/home.html; f. 1822; 725 mems; library of 90,000 vols; Pres. JEAN-PIERRE MAHÉ; publs *Cahiers*, *Journal Asiatique* (2 a year).

Société d'Anthropologie de Paris: Musée de l'Homme, 17 place du Trocadéro, 75116 Paris; tel. 1-45-59-53-31; e-mail secretairegeneral@sapweb.fr; internet www.sapweb.fr; f. 1859; biological anthropology; 310 mems; Pres. OLIVIER DUTOUR; Sec.-Gen. ALAIN FROMENT; publ. *Bulletins et Mémoires* (4 a year).

Société de l'Histoire du Protestantisme Français: 54 rue des Saints-Pères, 75007 Paris; tel. 1-45-48-62-07; e-mail shpf@libertysurf.fr; f. 1852; library of 150,000 vols, 12,000 MSS, 2,000 periodical titles; Pres. THERRY DU PASQUIER; Sec.-Gen. JEAN-HUGUES CARBONNIER; publs *Bulletin*, *Cahiers de Généalogie Protestante* (4 a year).

Société de Mythologie Française: 3 rue St-Laurent, 75010 Paris; tel. 1-42-05-30-57; e-mail phparrain@mythofrancaise.asso.fr; internet www.mythofrancaise.asso.fr; f. 1950; 200 mems; Pres. BERNARD SERGENT; publ. *Mythologie Française* (4 a year).

Société des Africanistes: Musée de l'Homme, 17 place du Trocadéro, 75116 Paris; tel. 1-47-27-72-55; e-mail africanistes@wanadoo.fr; internet www.mae.u-paris10.fr/africanistes; f. 1931; 400 mems; Pres. PHILIPPE LABURTHE-TOLRA; Sec. FRANÇOIS GAULME; publ. *Journal des Africanistes* (2 a year).

Société des Américanistes: Maison René Ginouvès, 21 allée de l'Université, 92023 Nanterre Cedex; tel. 1-46-69-26-34; e-mail jsa@mae.u-paris10.fr; f. 1895; 500 mems; Pres. PHILIPPE DESCOLA; Gen. Sec. DOMINIQUE MICHELET; publ. *Journal* (2 a year).

Société d'Histoire Religieuse de la France: 26 rue d'Assas, 75006 Paris; internet www.enc.sorbonne.fr/shrf; f. 1910; 560 mems; Pres. CATHERINE VINCENT; Sec.-Gen. OLIVIER PONCET; publ. *Revue d'Histoire de l'Eglise de France* (2 a year).

Société Française de Sociologie: 59/61 rue Pouchet, 75849 Paris Cedex 17; tel. 1-40-25-12-63; e-mail afs@iresco.fr; internet www.iresco.fr/societes/afs; f. 1962; Pres. DANIEL BERTAUX; Sec. MICHÈLE VINAUGER.

TECHNOLOGY

Académie de marine: CC 11, 75398 Paris Cedex 08; 21 pl. Joffre, 75007 Paris; tel. 1-44-42-82-02; e-mail academiedemarine@wanadoo.fr; internet www.academiedemarine.com; f. 1752; sections on history, literature and arts, law and economics, mercantile marine, military affairs, naval equipment, navigation and oceanic sciences, yachting and fishing; 109 mems; Pres. Prof. JEAN-PIERRE QUÉNEUDEC; Vice-Pres. ANDRÉ RAVIER; Sec.-Gen. VERONIQUE DE LONGEVIALLE; publ. *Communications et Mémoires* (3 a year).

Association Aéronautique et Astronautique de France (AAAF): 61 ave du Château, 78480 Verneuil-sur-Seine; tel. 1-39-79-75-15; internet www.aaafasso.fr; f. 1972; 1,800 mems; formed by merger of Asscn Française des Ingénieurs de l'Aéronautique et de l'Espace and Société Française d'Astronautique; Pres. MICHEL SCHELLER; Sec.-Gen. ROBERT DUBOST; publ. *La Nouvelle Revue d'Aéronautique et d'Astronautique* (4 a year).

Association des Anciens Elèves de l'Ecole Nationale Supérieure des Industries Agricoles et Alimentaires: 9–11 ave Franklin D. Roosevelt, 75008 Paris; tel. 1-42-25-92-48; internet www.uniagro.fr/gene/

main.php?base=1141&url_assoc=y; 1,500 mems; Pres. JEAN-LOUIS TIXIER; Sec.-Gen. MICHEL MERY; publ. *Industries Alimentaires et Agricoles* (12 a year).

Association Française des Sciences et Technologies de l'Information: 4 place Jussieu, 75252 Paris Cedex 05; tel. 3-83-59-20-51; e-mail asti.asso@lri.fr; internet www.asti.asso.fr; f. 1998; 25 mem. orgs; Pres. JEAN-PAUL HATON; Sec.-Gen. CLAUDE GIRAULT; publ. *Hebdo*.

Association Française du Froid: 17 rue Guillaume Apollinaire, 75006 Paris; tel. 1-45-44-52-52; e-mail a.f.f@wanadoo.fr; internet www.aff.asso.fr; f. 1908; 1,000 mems; Pres. LOUIS LUCAS; Sec.-Gen. JEAN LETEINTURIER-LAPRISE; publs *Bulletin: Kryos*, *Revue Générale du Froid* (10 a year).

Association Nationale de la Recherche Technique: 41 Blvd des Capucines, 75002 Paris; tel. 1-55-35-25-50; e-mail com@anrt.asso.fr; internet www.anrt.asso.fr; f. 1953; promotes technical research and organizations; fosters contact with technical research institutions abroad; Pres. JEAN-FRANÇOIS DEHECQ; publ. *La lettre Européenne du Progrès Technique* (10 a year).

Conseil National des Ingénieurs et des Scientifiques de France: 7 rue Lamennais, 75008 Paris; tel. 1-44-13-66-88; internet www.cnisf.org; f. 1848; Pres. NOËL CLAVELLOUX; Sec. MONIQUE MONIN; publ. *I.D.*.

Société de l'Electricité, de l'Electronique, et des Technologies de l'Information et de la Communication (SEE): 17 rue de l'Amiral Hamelin, 75783 Paris Cedex 16; tel. 1-56-90-37-00; e-mail see@see.asso.fr; internet www.see.asso.fr; f. 1883; Pres. ALAIN BRAVO; Sec. PATRICK MORO; publs *3EI—Enseigner l'Electrotechnique et l'Electronique Industriel* (4 a year), *e-STA—Revue des Sciences et Technologies de l'Automatique* (online), *Revue de l'Electricité et de l'Electronique* (10 a year).

Société d'Encouragement pour l'Industrie Nationale: 4 place Saint-Germain-des-Prés, 75006 Paris; e-mail adm@industrienationale.fr; internet www.industrienationale.fr; f. 1801; Dir BERNARD MOUSSON; publ. *L'Industrie Nationale*.

Société Française de Métallurgie et de Matériaux (SF2M): 250 rue Saint Jacques, 75005 Paris; tel. 1-46-33-08-00; e-mail sfmm@wanadoo.fr; internet www.sf2m.asso.fr; f. 1945; 1,200 mems; Pres. ANNICK PERCHERON-GUEGAN; Sec. PAUL V. RIBOUD.

Société Française de Photogrammétrie et de Télédétection: 2 ave Pasteur, 94165 St Mandé Cedex; tel. 1-64-15-32-86; e-mail sfpt@ensg.ign.fr; internet www.ign.fr/sfpt; f. 1959; photogrammetry and remote sensing; 615 mems; Pres. G. BEGNI; Sec.-Gen. I. VEILLET; publ. *Bulletin* (4 a year).

Société Française des Microscopies: Case 243, Université Pierre et Marie Curie, 4 pl. Jussieu, 75252 Paris Cedex 05; tel. 1-44-27-26-21; e-mail sfmu@sfmu.fr; internet www.sfmu.fr; f. 1959; all types of microscopy, electronic optics and electronic diffraction, optics, spectroscopy, microprobe, x-ray; physics, chemistry, biology; 470 mems; Pres. VIRGINIE SERIN; Sec. VIVES PATRICIA; publs *Biology of the Cell* (9 a year), *European Physical Journal: Applied Physics* (6 a year).

Société Hydrotechnique de France: 25 rue des Favorites, 75015 Paris; tel. 1-42-50-91-03; e-mail shf@shf.asso.fr; internet www.shf.asso.fr; f. 1912; fluid mechanics, applied hydraulics, geophysical hydraulics and water conservation; 600 mems; Pres. DANIEL LOUDIERE; Pres. for Scientific Cttee PIERRE-LOUIS VIOLLET; Gen. Dir JEAN-GEORGES PHILIPPS; publs *Journées de l'Hydraulique* (1 a year), *La Houille Blanche—Revue Internationale de l'Eau* (6 a year), *Proceedings*, guides on hydroelectricity and flood forecasts, research documents.

Research Institutes

GENERAL

Centre National de la Recherche Scientifique (CNRS): 3 rue Michel-Ange, 75794 Paris Cedex 16; tel. 1-44-96-40-00; internet www.cnrs.fr; f. 1939; coordinates and promotes scientific research, and proposes to the Govt means of doing research and how to allocate funds; makes grants-in-aid to scientific bodies and to individuals to enable them to carry out research work; subsidizes or sets up laboratories for scientific research; is split into 40 sections, covering all scientific fields; funds 11,600 researchers, 14,400 engineers and 4,000 technicians and admin. staff; depts of chemistry, engineering, environment and sustainable development, human and social sciences, life sciences, mathematics, physics, planet and universe; Pres. CATHÉRINE BRÉCHIGNAC; Dir-Gen. ARNOLD MIGUS; Sec.-Gen. JACQUES BERNARD.

AGRICULTURE, FISHERIES AND VETERINARY SCIENCE

Centre de Co-opération Internationale en Recherche Agronomique pour le Développement (CIRAD): 42 rue Scheffer, 75116 Paris; tel. 1-53-70-20-00; internet www.cirad.fr; (laboratories: BP 5035, 34032 Montpellier Cedex 1; tel. 4-67-61-58-00); f. 1970, current name adopted 1986; state-owned; research and devt within the framework of French scientific and technical cooperation with developing countries; stations in over 50 countries; library of 134,000 vols, 3,300 scientific periodicals; Dir-Gen. GÉRARD MATHERON; Sec.-Gen. HERVÉ DEPERROIS.

Research Departments:

Département d'Amélioration des Méthodes pour l'Innovation Scientifique (CIRAD-AMIS): 2477 ave Agropolis, TA 40/02, 34398 Montpellier Cedex 5; tel. 4-67-61-58-00; e-mail amis@cirad.fr; plant modelling, food production, agronomy, crop protection, biotechnology and plant genetic research, economics, policy and marketing; Dir JACQUES MEUNIER; publ. *Sésame bulletin*.

Département d'Élevage et de Médecine Vétérinaire (CIRAD-EMVT): Campus international de Baillarguet, BP 5035, 34398 Montpellier Cedex 5; tel. 4-67-59-37-10; e-mail valo.emvt@cirad.fr; f. 1948; research and missions to countries of Africa, Asia and South America; Dir EMMANUEL CAMUS; publ. *Revue d'Elevage et de Médecine Vétérinaire des Pays Tropicaux* (4 a year).

Département des Cultures Annuelles (CIRAD-CA): 2477 ave Agropolis, BP 5035, 34398 Montpellier Cedex 5; tel. 4-67-61-58-00; e-mail dirpersyst@cirad.fr; f. 1992; experts stationed in Benin, Brazil, Burkina Faso, Burundi, Cameroon, CAR, Chad, Colombia, Costa Rica, Côte d'Ivoire, Dominica, Gabon, Ghana, Guinea, Honduras, Laos, Madagascar, Mali, Niger, Paraguay, Philippines, Senegal, Thailand, Togo, Turkey, Viet Nam; Dir MARCO WOPEREIS; publ. *Agriculture et développement* (4 a year, abstracts in French, English and Spanish).

Département des Cultures Pérennes (CIRAD-CP): Blvd de la Lirondem, TA 80/PS3, 34398 Montpellier Cedex 5; tel. 4-67-61-58-00; e-mail dircp@cirad.fr; f. 1992; research and technical assistance relating to cocoa, coconuts, coffee, oil palm and rubber; Dir DOMINIQUE BERRY; publ. *Plantations, recherche, développement* (in French and English or Spanish).

Département des Territoires, Environnement et Acteurs (CIRAD-TERA): 73 rue Jean-François Breton, TA 60/15, 34398 Montpellier Cedex 5; tel. 4-67-61-58-00; e-mail tera@cirad.fr; smallholder farming, land and resources, savannah and irrigated systems, humid tropics; Dir ROLLAND GUIS.

Département Forestier (CIRAD-Forêt): Campus international de Baillarguet, BP 5035, 34398 Montpellier Cedex 5; tel. 4-67-59-37-10; e-mail forets@cirad.fr; forestry; Dir BERNARD MALLET; publ. *Bois et forêts des tropiques*.

INRA–Jouy-en-Josas: Domaine de Vilvert, 78352 Jouy-en-Josas Cedex; tel. 1-34-65-21-21; e-mail communication@jouy.inra.fr; internet www.jouy.inra.fr; f. 1950; scientific research on livestock production and health, human nutrition, animal biology, microbiology, applied mathematics and bioinformatics, animal models for human and animal health; library of 6,000 vols, 2,200 periodicals; Pres. Dr NURIEL MAMBRINI-DOUDET.

Institut d'Immunologie Animale et Comparée: Ecole Nationale Vétérinaire d'Alfort, 7 ave du Général de Gaulle, 94704 Maisons-Alfort Cedex; tel. 1-43-68-98-82; f. 1981; organizes courses; research in immunostimulation, clinical immunology, immunopathology; Dir Prof. CH. PILET.

Institut National de la Recherche Agronomique (INRA): 147 rue de l'Université, 75338 Paris Cedex 07; tel. 1-42-75-90-00; internet www.inra.fr; f. 1946; agricultural research, incl. agricultural and food industries, rural economics and sociology, plant and animal production and forestry; administers and subsidizes a large number of centres, laboratories and experimental farms in France; Pres. and Dir-Gen. MARION GUILLOU; publs *Agronomy for Sustainable Development* (10 a year), *Animal Research* (6 a year), *Annales des Sciences Forestières* (6 a year), *Apidologie* (6 a year), *Archorales: Les Métiers de la Recherche* (online), *Bulletin des Technologies* (1 a year), *Cahiers d'Economie et Sociologie rurales* (4 a year), *Courrier de l'Environnement* (online), *Genetics Selection Evolution* (6 a year), *INRA Sciences Sociales* (6 a year), *Le Lait* (6 a year), *Production Animales* (3 a year), *Reproduction Nutrition Development* (6 a year), *Veterinary Research* (6 a year).

Laboratoire Central de Recherches Vétérinaires: BP 67, 22 rue Pierre Curie, 94703 Maisons-Alfort Cedex; tel. 1-49-77-13-00; f. 1901; 140 mems; study of contagious diseases in domestic and wild animals; supervises sanitary regulations for import and export of livestock; Dir Dr ERIC PLATEAU.

ECONOMICS, LAW AND POLITICS

Centre d'Etudes de l'Emploi: Le Descartes I, 29 promenade Michel Simon, 93166 Noisy-le-Grand Cedex; tel. 1-45-92-68-00; internet www.cee-recherche.fr; attached to Min. of Employment and Min. of Education; for the study and research of changes in the field of employment; research units: age and work, employment and social security, employment markets and instns, workers and orgs; Dir PIERRE RALLE; publs *CEE.INFO* (3 a year), *Connaisance de l'Emploi* (12 a year).

Centre d'Etudes Prospectives et d'Informations Internationales: 113 rue de Grenelle, 75007 Paris; tel. 1-53-68-55-00; e-mail cepiiweb@cepii.fr; internet www.cepii.fr; f. 1978 by the Govt, under the aegis of Centre d'Analyse Strategique; aids public and private decision-makers in the int. economic field by conducting synthetic studies of the global economic environment in the mid-term (5–10 years), constructing economic models and databases, and by providing a coherent statistical information system of the world economy and its major participants; 50 mems; library of 30,000 vols, 500 periodicals; Dir SÉBASTIEN JEAN; publs *CEPII Working Papers* (12 a year), *CHELEM Data Bank: bilingual DVD and internet* (1 a year), *Economie Internationale* (4 a year), *La Lettre du CEPII* (11 a year), *L'Economie mondiale* (1 a year), *Modelling International Relationships in Applied General Equilibrium: MIRAGE*.

Institut de Recherches Economiques et Sociales: 16 blvd du Mont d'Est, 93192 Noisy-Le-Grand Cedex; tel. (1) 48-15-18-93; e-mail contact@ires-fr.org; internet www.ires-fr.org; f. 1982 by the main French trade unions in association with the French Govt to meet the economic and social research needs of trade unions; central research areas: employment patterns, industrial relations, wage patterns, work patterns; Pres. PIERRETTE CROSEMARIE; Dir JACKY FAYOLLE; publs *La Chronique Internationale* (6 a year), *La Lettre de l'IRES* (4 a year), *La Revue de L'IRES* (3 a year).

Institut de Sciences Mathématiques et Economiques Appliquées: 59 blvd Vincent Auriol-TD 022, 75703 Paris; tel. 1-44-97-25-15; e-mail perroux@univ-mlv.fr; internet www.ismea.org; f. 1944; int. cooperation and links with Third World univs; library of 14,500 vols; Chair. Prof. ROLANDE BORRELLY; publs *Economie Appliquée* (4 a year), *Economies et Sociétés* (12 a year).

Institut National de la Statistique et des Etudes Economiques: 18 blvd Adolphe Pinard, 75675 Paris Cedex 14; tel. 1-41-17-50-50; e-mail insee-contact@insee.fr; internet www.insee.fr; f. 1946; statistical research: population census, economic indices and forecasts, economic and social studies; library: see under Libraries and Archives; Dir-Gen. JEAN-PHILIPPE COTIS; publs *Annuaire Statistique de la France* (1 a year, free online), *Bulletin Statistique* (online), *Economie et Statistique* (12 a year, free online), *Informations Rapides* (370 a year), *Insee Méthodes*, *Insee Première* (60 a year), *Insee Résultats*, *La Commerce en France (Collection Références)*, *La France des Services (Collection Références)*, *La France et ses Régions*, *Les salaires en France (Collection Références)*, *L'industrie en France (Collection Références)*, *Note de Conjoncture* (4 a year), *Tableaux de l'économie Française* (1 a year).

Institut National d'Etudes Démographiques: 133 blvd Davout, 75980 Paris Cedex 20; tel. 1-56-06-20-00; e-mail enquetes@ined.fr; internet www.ined.fr; f. 1945; library of 40,000 vols; Dir FRANÇOIS HÉRAN; publs *Classiques de l'Economie et de la Population* (2 or 3 a year), *Les Cahiers de l'INED* (4–6 a year), *Population* (4 a year), *Population et Sociétés* (12 a year).

EDUCATION

Centre International d'Etudes Pédagogiques de Sèvres: 1 ave Léon Journault, BP 75, 92318 Sèvres Cedex; tel. 1-45-07-60-00; internet www.ciep.fr; f. 1945; research and studies in comparative education; training overseas teachers in French as a foreign language; 170 mems; Dir M. LÉOUTRE; publ. *Revue Internationale d'Education*.

Institut National de Recherche Pédagogique: 19 Mail de Fontenay, BP 17424, 69347 Lyons Cedex 07; tel. 4-72-76-61-71; e-mail contact@inrp.fr; internet www.inrp.fr; f. 1879; develops and promotes research into teaching and education; library: see under Libraries and Archives; Dir EMMANUEL FRAISSE; publs *Aster* (2 a year), *Didaskalia* (2 a year), *Etapes de la Recherche*, *Histoire de l'Education* (4 a year), *Perspectives Documentaires* (3 a year), *Recherche et Formation* (3 a year), *Repères* (2 a year), *Revue Française de Pédagogie* (4 a year).

FINE AND PERFORMING ARTS

Institut de Recherche et Co-ordination Acoustique et de la Musique: Centre National d'Art et de Culture Georges-Pompidou, 1 pl. Igor-Stravinsky, 75004 Paris Cedex 04; tel. 1-44-78-48-43; internet www.ircam.fr; attached to Centre National d'Art et de Culture Georges-Pompidou; interdisciplinary research centre for musicians and scientists; data processing, electroacoustics, instrumental and vocal research; Dir FRANK MADLENER.

Institut National d'Histoire de l'Art (INHA): 2 rue Vivienne, 75002 Paris; tel. 1-47-03-86-04; e-mail inha@inha.fr; internet www.inha.fr; f. 2001; library: Bibliothèque d'art et d'archéologie Jacques Doucet; Dir-Gen. ANTOINETTE LE NORMAND-ROMAIN.

HISTORY, GEOGRAPHY AND ARCHAEOLOGY

Centre de Recherches Historiques: Ecole des Hautes Etudes en Sciences Sociales, UMR 8558, 54 blvd Raspail, 75006 Paris; tel. 1-49-54-24-42; e-mail crh@msh-paris.fr; internet www.ehess.fr; f. 1950; joint research in economic, social, cultural and political history; 126 mems; Dir GÉRARD BÉAUR; Dir PAUL-ANDRÉ ROSENTAL; Dir JUDITH LYON-CAEN; publs *Annales* (history, social sciences, 6 a year), *Cahiers* (2 a year), *Entreprises et Histoire* (4 a year), *Histoire et Mesure* (4 a year), *1900* (1 a year).

Centre d'Études Supérieures de la Renaissance: 59 rue Néricault-Destouches, BP 11328, 37013 Tours Cedex 1; tel. 2-47-36-77-60; e-mail cesr@univ-tours.fr; internet www.cesr.univ-tours.fr; f. 1956; library of 58,000 vols; Dir Prof. PHILIPPE VENDRIX; Head Librarian CLAIRE DAVID.

Fondation et Institut Charles de Gaulle: 5 rue de Solférino, 75007 Paris; tel. 1-44-18-66-77; e-mail contact@charles-de-gaulle.org; internet www.charles-de-gaulle.org; f. Institute 1971, Foundation f. 1992; assembles material related to the life and work of Charles de Gaulle for the purpose of scholarship; library of 4,500 vols, periodicals, documents, cuttings, 4,000 photographs, recorded interviews, audiovisual material; Pres. YVES GUÉNA.

Institut Géographique National: 73 ave de Paris, 94165 Saint-Mandé; tel. 1-43-98-80-00; internet www.ign.fr; f. 1940; satellite-image, aerial and ground surveys, map printing; nat. map and aerial photograph library, scientific library; administers Ecole Nat. des Sciences Géographiques *(q.v.)*; Pres. MICHEL FRANC; Dir-Gen. JEAN POULIT; publ. *Bulletin d'Information* (4 a year).

Sous-Direction de l'Archéologie: 4 rue d'Aboukir, 75002 Paris; tel. 1-40-15-77-81; e-mail jean-francois.texier@culture.gouv.fr; f. 1964; library of 4,500 vols, 47 periodicals; Dir JEAN-FRANÇOIS TEXIER.

MEDICINE

Institut Alfred-Fournier: 25 blvd Saint-Jacques, 75014 Paris; internet www.institutfournier.org; research into sexually transmitted diseases; f. 1923; Dir Dr P. BARBIER.

Institut Arthur-Vernes: 36 rue d'Assas, 75006 Paris; tel. 1-44-39-53-00; internet www.institut-vernes.fr; f. 1981; Pres. J. C. SERVAN-SCHREIBER; Gen. Man. CATHERINE RAUCHE.

Institut Gustave-Roussy: 39 rue Camille Desmoulins, 94805 Villejuif Cedex; tel. 1-42-11-42-11; e-mail roussy@igr.fr; internet www.igr.fr; f. 1921; diagnosis and treatment of cancer, research, and training in oncology (affiliated with Univ. Paris-Sud for teaching purposes); library of 11,000 vols, with spec. collns on cancerology; Dir Prof. GILBERT LENOIR.

Institut National de la Santé et de la Recherche Médicale (INSERM): 101 rue de Tolbiac, 75654 Paris Cedex 13; tel. 1-44-23-60-00; internet www.inserm.fr; f. 1941 as Institut National d'Hygiène, renamed 1964; assisted by scientific commissions and the Scientific Council; 270 research units throughout France; Pres. MONIQUE CAPRON; Dir-Gen. Prof. CHRISTIAN BRÉCHOT; publs *Annuaire des laboratoires*, *rapport d'activité*, *INSERM Actualités*, Collections, etc.

Institut Pasteur: 25–28 rue du Dr Roux, 75015 Paris; tel. 1-45-68-80-00; e-mail info@pasteur.fr; internet www.pasteur.fr; f. 1887; Pres. ALICE DAUTRY; Sec. AGNÈS LABIGNE; publs *Annales: Actualités*, *Annales Research in Virology*, *Bulletin* (4 a year), *Immunology and Microbiology* (16 a year).

NATURAL SCIENCES

General

Institut de Recherche pour le Développement (IRD): 44 Blvd de Dunkerque, 13002 Marseille; tel. 4-91-99-92-00; e-mail dic@ird.fr; internet www.ird.fr; f. 1944; public corpn charged to aid developing countries by means of research, both fundamental and applied, in the non-temperate regions, with spec. application to human environment problems, food production and tropical diseases; 35 centres in Africa, Asia, the Pacific, S America and French overseas territories; library and documentation centre; Pres. DICHEL LAURENT; publ. *Sciences au Sud* (5 a year).

Maintains the Following Services:

Antenne IRD de Bouaké: BP 1434, Bouaké, Côte d'Ivoire; tel. 31-63-95-43; e-mail cote-ivoire@ird.fr; internet www.ird.ci; f. 1976; jt research project with l'Institut des Savanes; studies of dams for agricultural irrigation, social mobility and sexually transmitted diseases, production and distribution of foodstuffs in the central region of Côte d'Ivoire.

Centre IRD de Bondy: 32 ave Henri Varagnat, 93143 Bondy Cedex; tel. 1-48-02-55-00; e-mail bondy@ird.fr; internet www.bondy.ird.fr; f. 1945; applied computer science, entomology, geodynamics, geophysics, social sciences; scientific information (cartography, documentation, audiovisual); Dir GEORGES DE NONI.

Centre IRD de Bretagne: BP 70, 29280 Plouzané Cedex; tel. 2-98-22-45-01; e-mail brest@ird.fr; internet www.brest.ird.fr; f. 1975; oceanography; Dir CLAUDE ROY.

Centre IRD de Montpellier: BP 64501, 34394 Montpellier Cedex 5; tel. 4-67-41-61-00; e-mail montpellier@ird.fr; internet www.mpl.ird.fr; agrarian research, applied zoology, genetics, geology, hydrobiology and oceanography, hydrology, medical entomology, nutrition, phytopathology, phytovirology, soil biology; Dir YVES DUVAL.

Centre IRD d'Orléans: Technoparc, 5 rue du Carbone, 45072 Orléans Cedex 2; tel. 2-38-49-95-00; e-mail orleans@ird.fr; internet www.orleans.ird.fr; human adaptation to tropical environments, environmental dynamics between forests, agriculture and biodiversity, valorization of vegetal biodiversity; Dir YVELINE PONCET.

Centre IRD de Sète: CRHMT, Ave Jean Monnet, BP 171, 34203 Sète Cedex; tel. 4-99-57-32-34; e-mail philippe.cury@ird.fr; Dir-Gen. MICHEL LAURENT.

Institut Français de l'Environnement: 5 route d'Olivet, BP 16105, 45061 Orléans Cedex 2; tel. 2-38-79-78-78; e-mail cgdd-soes-orleans@developpement-durable.gouv.fr; internet www.ifen.fr; f. 1991; attached to Min. of Town and Country Planning and the Environment; collects and disseminates statistical information about the environment; focal point in France for European Environment Agency.

Biological Sciences

Institut de Biologie Physico-chimique: 13 rue Pierre et Marie Curie, 75005 Paris; tel. 1-58-41-50-00; e-mail ifr550@ibpc.fr; internet www.ibpc.fr; f. 1927; Dir Dr J.-P. HENRY; Dirs of Laboratories J.-P. HENRY (Molecular and Cell Biology of Secretion), F.-A. WOLLMAN (Molecular and Membrane Physiology of the Chloroplast), J.-L. POPOT (Molecular Physical Chemistry of Biological Membranes), M. SPRINGER (Regulation of Microbial Gene Expression), R. LAVERY (Theoretical Biochemistry).

Institut de Biologie Structurale (IBS): 41 rue Jules Horowitz, 38027 Grenoble Cedex 1; tel. 4-38-78-95-50; internet www.ibs.fr; jointly financed by the Commissariat à l'Energie Atomique (CEA) and the CNRS; Dir Prof. EVA PEBAY-PEYROULA.

Station Biologique de Roscoff: Place Georges-Teissier, 29680 Roscoff Cedex; tel. 2-98-29-23-23; e-mail guyard@sb-roscoff.fr; internet www.sb-roscoff.fr; f. 1872; attached to Univ. Pierre et Marie Curie and CNRS; chemical and biological oceanography, plankton research, microbiology, biology of hydrothermal vent fauna, cell cycle and developmental biology, cell and molecular biology on macroalgae, population genetics, marine genomics; library of 7,000 vols, 380 periodicals; Dir Prof. BERNARD KLOAREG; Librarian NICOLE GUYARD; publ. *CBM-Cahiers de Biologie marine* (4 a year).

Physical Sciences

Association Nationale pour l'Etude de la Neige et des Avalanches (ANENA): 15 rue Ernest Calvat, 38000 Grenoble; tel. 4-76-51-39-39; e-mail info@anena.org; internet www.anena.org; f. 1971; promotes knowledge and advises about avalanches and safety in snowy, mountainous terrain; library of 2,000 vols; publ. *Neige et Avalanches* (4 a year).

Bureau de Recherches Géologiques et Minières (BRGM): 3 ave Claude Guillemin, BP 6009, 45060 Orléans Cedex 2; tel. 2-38-64-34-34; internet www.brgm.fr; f. 1959; publicly owned industrial and trading org.; study and devt of underground resources in France and abroad; library of 22,000 vols, 4,000 scientific journals, 55,000 maps; Dir-Gen. Y. LE BARS; publs *Chronique de la Recherche minière* (4 a year), *Géochronique* (4 a year, published with Société géologique de France), *Géologie de la France* (4 a year), *Hydrogéologie* (4 a year), geological maps, bibliographies, SDI and retrospective searches.

Bureau des Longitudes: Palais de l'Institut, 3 Quai de Conti, 75006 Paris; tel. 1-43-26-59-02; e-mail contact@bureau-des-longitudes.fr; internet www.bureau-des-longitudes.fr; f. 1795 by Convention Nationale; Pres. NICOLE CAPITAINE; Vice-Pres. PIERRE BAÜER; Sec. PASCAL WILLIS; publs *Cahier des Sciences de l'Univers*, *Connaissance des Temps*, and supplements to *Connaissance des Temps* (1 a year), *Ephémérides Astronomiques*, *Ephémérides Nautiques*.

Centre de Recherches Atmosphériques: 8 route de Lannemezan, 65300 Campistrous; tel. 5-62-40-61-00; e-mail campistrous@free.fr; internet campistrous.free.fr; f. 1960; cloud physics, atmospheric chemistry, planetary boundary layer; library of 2,000 vols; Dir R. DELMAS; publ. *Atmospheric Research* (4 a year).

Centre International pour la Formation et les Echanges en Géosciences (CIFEG): 3 ave Claude Guillemin, BP 36517, 45065 Orléans Cedex 2; tel. 2-38-64-33-67; e-mail m.laval@cifeg.org; internet www.cifeg.org; f. 1981; geoscientific information networking; documentation centre on earth sciences of Africa and SE Asia; exchanges between developed and developing countries; library of 3,500 vols, 65 periodicals, 400 maps; Pres. J. GIRI; Dir M. LAVAL; publ. *PANGEA* (2 a year).

Centre National de Recherches Météorologiques: 42 ave G. Coriolis, 31057 Toulouse Cedex; tel. 5-61-07-93-70; internet www.cnrm.meteo.fr; f. 1946; meteorological research; 250 staff; Dir ERIC BRUN.

Commissariat à l'Energie Atomique (CEA): Centre d'Etudes de Saclay, 91191 Gif sur Yvette Cedex 15; tel. 1-64-50-10-00; internet www.cea.fr; f. 1945; basic and applied nuclear research, energy generator studies; 5 affiliated civil research centres; Pres. of Atomic Energy Cttee the Prime Minister; library; Man. Dir YANNICK D'ESCATHA; publs *CEA-Technologies*, *Clefs CEA*, *Les Défis du CEA*.

Attached Research Centres:

Centre CEA/Cesta (Gironde): BP 2, 33114 Le Barp; tel. 5-57-04-40-00; internet www-dam.cea.fr; production of nuclear arms.

Centre CEA/DAM Ile de France (Essonne): Bruyères-le-Châtel, 91297 Arpajon Cedex; tel. 1-69-26-40-00; internet www-dam.cea.fr; computerized research into nuclear explosions; monitoring of global seismic activity.

Centre CEA de Cadarache (France-Bouches-du-Rhone): 13108 St-Paul-lez-Durance Cedex; tel. 4-42-25-70-00; e-mail wwwcad@dircad.cea.fr; internet www-cadarache.cea.fr; f. 1959; nuclear reactor devt (fission and fusion); research and development on new energies: biofuels, hydrogen or solar, nuclear safety and environmental protection; fundamental research; industrial innovation; Dir CHRISTIAN BONNET.

Centre CEA de Fontenay-aux-Roses (Hauts-de-Seine): BP 6, 92265 Fontenay-aux-Roses Cedex; tel. 1-46-54-70-80; f. 1945; first French reactor; Zoé natural uranium, heavy water moderated; work in life sciences; research in: emerging diseases, environmental toxicology, neurovirology and radiobiology; research and devt in biomedical imaging and health technologies; cognitics, robotics for nuclear, industrial and medical needs; Dir MALGORZATA TKATCHENKO.

Centre CEA de Grenoble (Isère): 17 rue des Martyrs, 38054 Grenoble Cedex 9; tel. 4-76-78-44-00; f. 1957; applied nuclear research on heat transfer studies and on behaviour of nuclear fuels; fundamental research on biology, chemistry, materials science, physics; advanced technologies: heat exchangers, instrumentation, life sciences, materials, microelectronics, optronics and tracer studies; library of 31,000 vols; Dir GEORGES CAROLA.

Centre CEA de la Marcoule (Gard): BP 171, 30207 Bagnols-sur-Cèze Cedex; tel. 4-66-79-60-00; internet www-marcoule.cea.fr; f. 1982; fuel cycle research and devt: uranium isotopic enrichment, spent fuel processing, waste conditioning, dismantling, fast reactors; Dir JEAN-YVES GUILLAMOT.

Centre CEA de Saclay (Essonne): 91191 Gif-sur-Yvette Cedex; tel. 1-69-08-90-32; e-mail internet.saclay@cea.fr; internet www-centre-saclay.cea.fr; f. 1949; laboratories specializing in research on astrophysics, biology, condensed-matter physics, earth sciences, electronics, elementary particle physics, nuclear metallurgy and chemistry, nuclear physics, radioactivity measurement and reactors; library of 48,000 vols, 400,000 reports; Dir ELIANE LOQUET.

Centre CEA de Valduc: 21120 Is-sur-Tille; tel. 3-80-23-40-00; e-mail webdam@cea.fr; internet www-dam.cea.fr; f. 1996; nuclear materials used in arms production.

Institut Curie: 26 rue d'Ulm, 75248 Paris Cedex 05; tel. 1-44-32-40-00; internet www.curie.fr; f. 1978 (fmrly Fondation Curie—Inst. du Radium); treatment, research and teaching in cancer; library of 7,000 vols; two sections: Research (Dir M. BORNENS), Medicine (Dir P. BEY); Pres. CLAUDE HURIET; Dir PHILIPPE KOURILSKY.

Institut Français de Recherche pour l'Exploitation de la Mer (IFREMER): 155 rue J. Jacques Rousseau, 92138 Issy-les-Moulineaux Cedex; tel. 1-46-48-21-00; e-mail grh@ifremer.fr; internet www.ifremer.fr; f. 1984; research in all fields of oceanography and ocean technology; CEO JEAN-YVES PERROT; publs *Aquatic Living Resources* (6 a year), *Oceanologica Acta* (6 a year).

Attached Institutes:

Centre IFREMER de Brest: BP 70, 29280 Plouzane; tel. 2-98-22-40-40; e-mail egiordma@ifremer.fr; internet www.ifremer.fr/brest; f. 1968; Dir FRANÇOIS LE VERGE.

Centre IFREMER de Nantes: BP 21105, 44311 Nantes Cedex 03; tel. 2-40-37-40-43; internet www.ifremer.fr/nantes; Dir ROBERT POGGI.

Centre IFREMER de Toulon: BP 330, 83507 La Seyne sur Mer; tel. 4-94-30-48-00; internet www.ifremer.fr/toulon; Dir GUY HERROUIN.

Centre IFREMER Océanologique du Pacifique: BP 7004, 98719 Taravao, Tahiti French Polynesia; tel. 54-60-00; internet www.ifremer.fr/cop/tahiti.htm; f. 1972; devt of ocean resources: minerals, fishing and aquaculture in French S Pacific territories; library of 200 vols; Dir DOMINIQUE BUESTEL.

Institut Polaire Français Paul Emile Victor: Technopôle Brest-Iroise, BP 75, 29280 Plouzané; tel. 2-98-05-65-00; e-mail infoipev@ipev.fr; internet www.institut-polaire.fr; f. 1992 by merger of Mission de Recherche des Terres Australes et Antarctiques Françaises and Expéditions Polaires Françaises; conducts and supports scientific research in polar regions (Arctic, Antarctic, Subantarctic) and oceanography on V/R Marion Dufresne; Dir Dr YVES FRENOT.

Laboratoire d'Astronomie de Lille 1: 1 impasse de l'Observatoire, 59000 Lille; tel. 3-20-52-44-24; internet lal.univ-lille1.fr; f. 1934; astronomy, celestial mechanics; Dir ALAIN VIENNE.

Météo-France: 1 quai Branly, 75340 Paris Cedex 07; tel. 1-45-56-71-71; internet www.meteofrance.com; f. 1945; Dir JEAN-PIERRE BEYSSON; publs *Atmospheriques* (3 a year), *Bibliographies*, *Bulletin Climatique* (12 a year), *Cours et Manuels* (irregular), *Données et Statistiques*, *La Météorologie* (3 a year), *METEO-HEBDO* (52 a year), *Met Mar* (3 a year), *Monographies*, *Notes techniques*, *Phénomènes Remarquables* (irregular).

Observatoire Astronomique de Marseille–Provence: 38 rue Frédéric Joliot-Curie, 13388 Marseilles Cedex 13; tel. 4-95-04-41-00; e-mail oampdirection@oamp.fr; internet www.oamp.fr; library of 5,000 vols; Dir OLIVIER LE FÈVRE.

Observatoire Astronomique de Strasbourg: 11 rue de l'Université, 67000 Strasbourg; tel. 3-90-24-24-10; internet astro.u-strasbg.fr; f. 1882; specializes in astronomical data and information, galactic evolution, cosmology, high-energy astrophysics; houses the Strasbourg Astronomical Data Centre (CDS); library of 16,000 vols; Dir JEAN-MARIE HAMEURY; publ. *Publications de l'Observatoire* (irregular).

Observatoire de Bordeaux: Université de Bordeaux I, CNRS, 2 rue de l'Observatoire, BP 89, 33270 Floirac; tel. 5-57-77-61-00; internet www.obs.u-bordeaux1.fr; f. 1879; astrodynamics, astrometry, helioseismology, planetary atmosphere, radio aeronomy, radioastronomy, solar physics; library of 3,700 vols; Dir A. CASTETS.

Observatoire de la Côte d'Azur: Blvd de l'Observatoire, CS 34229, 06304 Nice Cedex 4; tel. 4-92-00-30-11; internet www.oca.eu; f. 1881; astronomy and astrophysics, earth science; library of 21,000 vols, 250 periodicals; Dir FARROKH VAKILI.

Observatoire de Lyon: 9 ave Charles-André, 69561 Saint-Genis-Laval Cedex; tel. 4-78-86-85-34; e-mail accueil@obs.univ-lyon1.fr; internet www-obs.univ-lyon1.fr; f. 1880; specializes in two-dimensional photometry and infra-red imagery; library of 20,000 vols; Dir BRUNO GUIDERDONI.

Observatoire de Paris: 61 ave de l'Observatoire, 75014 Paris; tel. 1-40-51-22-21; internet www.obspm.fr; f. 1667; research and training in astronomy, astrophysics and related sciences; library of 60,000 vols; Pres. Prof. C. CATALA.

Attached Stations:

Observatoire de Paris, Site de Meudon: 5 pl.Jules Janssen, 92195 Meudon Principal Cedex; tel. 1-45-07-75-30; administered by the Observatoire de Paris; f. 1875; astrophysics; Dir M. COMBES.

Station de Radioastronomie de Nançay: 18330 Nançay; tel. 2-48-51-82-41; e-mail communication@obs-nancay.fr; administered by the Observatoire de Paris; f. 1953; study of the sun, comets, planets and radio sources; radio telescopes; Dir M. COMBES.

Observatoire de Physique du Globe de Clermont-Ferrand: 24 ave des Landais, 63171 Aubière Cedex; tel. 4-73-40-73-80; e-mail p.bachelery@opgc.univ-bpclermont.fr; internet www.obs.univ-bpclermont.fr; f. 1871; atmospheric physics, cloud systems, earth sciences, and geophysical surveillance; Dir Prof. PATRICK BACHELERY.

Observatoire des Sciences de l'Univers de Besançon: BP 1615, 41 bis ave de l'Observatoire, 25010 Besançon Cedex; tel. 3-81-66-69-00; e-mail direction@obs-besancon.fr; internet www.obs-besancon.fr; f. 1882; a research unit of the Université de Franche-Comté; library of 15,000 vols; Dir Prof. FRANÇOIS VERNOTTE.

Observatoire Midi-Pyrénées: Headquarters: 14 ave E. Belin, 31400 Toulouse; tel. 5-61-33-29-29; internet www.omp.obs-mip.fr; library of 50,000 vols; solar, planetary, stellar, galactic and extragalactic astrophysics, atmospheric physics and chemistry, physical oceanography, surface sciences, earth sciences; Dir DOMINIQUE LE QUEAU.

RELIGION, SOCIOLOGY AND ANTHROPOLOGY

Centre Européen de Recherches sur les Congrégations et les Ordres Religieux (CERCOR): 35 rue du 11 Novembre, Bâtiment M, 42023 Saint-Etienne Cedex 2; tel. 4-77-42-16-70; e-mail cercor@univ-st-etienne.fr; internet cercor.univ-st-etienne.fr; f. 1982; a research group of CNRS (*q.v.*); studies the history of the monastic and religious institutions in Western and Eastern Christianity of Christian antiquity to the 20th century; coordinates and promotes research (confs, etc.); runs a specialized documentation service; publishes texts; library of 7,000 vols; Dir THIERRY PÉCOUT; publ. *Revue Mabillon*.

Fondation Maison des Sciences de l'Homme: 54 blvd Raspail, 75270 Paris Cedex 06; tel. 1-49-54-20-00; internet www.msh-paris.fr; f. 1963, supports research and int. cooperation in the social sciences; library of 155,000 vols, 2,000 current periodicals; Administrator ALAINE D'IRIBARNE; publ. *Lettre d'informations* (4 a year).

Institut d'Ethnologie du Muséum National d'Histoire Naturelle: Musée de l'Homme, Palais de Chaillot, Place du Trocadéro, 75116 Paris; tel. 1-44-05-73-45; e-mail diff.pub@mnhn.fr; f. 1925; archaeology, linguistics, social anthropology; Dir M. PANOFF; publs *Collections Travaux et Mémoires*, *Mémoires*.

Institut d'Etudes Augustiniennes: 3 rue de l'Abbaye, 75006 Paris; tel. 1-43-54-80-25; e-mail claudine.croyere@paris-sorbonne.fr; f. 1943; research into life, thought and times of St Augustine; library of 53,000 vols, 2,000 early printed books, 19 incunabula; Dir V. ZARINI; publs *Recherches Augustiniennes* (irregular), *Revue des Etudes Augustiniennes* (2 a year).

Institut du Monde Arabe: 1 rue des Fossés Saint Bernard, Place Mohammed-V, 75236 Paris Cedex 05; tel. 1-40-51-38-38; internet www.imarabe.org; f. 1980 by France and 21 Arab countries to promote knowledge of Arab culture and civilization; aims to encourage cultural exchanges, communication and co-operation between France and the Arab world, particularly in the fields of science and technology; int. library and documentation centre of 60,000 vols, 1,200 periodicals; museum of Arab-Islamic civilization from 7th–19th century; exhibitions of Arab contemporary art; audiovisual centre; Pres. YVES GUÉNA; Dir MOKHTAR TALEB-BENDIAB; publs *Al-Moukhtarat*, *Qantara* (4 a year).

Institut International d'Anthropologie: 1 place d'Iéna, 75116 Paris; tel. 1-47-93-09-73; internet www.multimania.com/anthropa; f. 1920; 400 mems; affiliated to Ecole d'Anthropologie (*q.v.*); incorporates intercultural documentation centre; Pres. Dr A. PAJAULT; Sec.-Gen. Dr B. HUET; publ. *Nouvelle Revue Anthropologique* (irregular).

Institut Kurde de Paris (Kurdish Institute): 106 rue La Fayette, 75010 Paris; tel. 1-48-24-64-64; internet www.institutkurde.org; f. 1983; research into Kurdish language, culture and history; Kurdish language teaching and publication of textbooks, maps, music cassettes, video films in Kurdish; library of 10,000 vols (accessible to the public); Pres. KENDAL NEZAN; publs *Etudes Kurdes* (2 a year), *Information Bulletin* (12 a year), *Kurmancî* (2 a year).

Maison des Sciences de l'Homme-Alpes: BP 47, 38040 Grenoble Cedex 9; tel. 4-76-82-73-00; internet www.msh-alpes.fr; f. 1998; supports research in the social sciences; Pres. MICHEL AUDIFFREN.

TECHNOLOGY

Association Française pour la Protection des Eaux: 67 rue de Seine, 94140 Alfortville; tel. 1-43-75-84-84; e-mail president@anpertos.org; internet www.anpertos.org; f. 1960; brings to public notice the necessity of protecting and preserving the quality and quantity of water-supplies, studies problems of water pollution and its prevention; 800 mems; Pres. P. L. TENAILLON; publ. *TOS*.

Centre National d'Etudes Spatiales (CNES): 2 place Maurice Quentin, 75001 Paris; internet www.cnes.fr; f. 1961; prepares national programmes of space research, provides information, promotes international co-operation; Pres. YANNICK D'ESCATHA; Dir-Gen. MICHEL LEFÈVRE.

France Telecom R & D: 38–40 rue du Général Leclerc, 92131 Issy les Moulineaux; tel. 1-45-29-44-44; internet www.rd.francetelecom.com; f. 1944; engaged in the devt of future communications systems; responsible for according official approval for telecommunications equipment; 3,700 staff; library of 2,500 vols, 1,000 periodicals; CEO THIERRY BRETON; publs *Annales des Télécommunications* (6 a year), *Bulletin Signalétique des Télécommunications* (12 a year), *Innovation Telecom* (12 a year), *L'Echo des Recherches* (4 a year), *Networks*.

IFP Energies Nouvelles (IFPEN): 1 et 4 ave de Bois-Préau, 92852 Rueil-Malmaison Cedex; tel. 1-47-52-60-00; internet www.ifpenenergiesnourvelles.com; f. 1945; scientific and technical org. for the purpose of research, devt and industrialization, training specialists at the IFP School, information and documentation, int. technical assistance in different fields of the oil, gas and automotive engineering industries; library of 275,000 vols; Chair. and CEO O. APPERT; publ. *Oil and Gas Science and Technology*.

Institut d'Hydrologie et de Climatologie: Faculté de Médecine, Pitié-Salpétrière, 91 blvd de l'Hôpital, 75013 Paris; tel. 1-45-83-69-92; 5 main laboratories in Paris, and further laboratories at the principal spas; Gen. Sec. Prof. G. OLIVE.

Institut Laue-Langevin (ILL): BP 156, 38042 Grenoble Cedex 9; tel. 4-76-20-71-11; e-mail welcome@ill.fr; internet www.ill.fr; f. 1967 by France and Fed. Republic of Germany, UK became third equal partner in 1973; associated scientific members are Spain (1987), Switzerland (1988), Austria (1990), Russia (1996), Italy (1997) and Czech Republic (1999); research on fundamental and nuclear physics, solid state physics, metallurgy, chemistry and biology by using reactor neutrons; receives 1,500 guest scientists a year and carries out experiments on 25 ILL-funded instruments and several instruments funded by collaborating research groups; central facility is high flux beam reactor producing maximum flux of

$1.5 \times 10^{15} n/cm^2/s$; library of 11,000 vols, 250 periodicals; Dir Dr C. CARLILE.

Institut National de l'Audiovisuel: 4 ave de l'Europe, 94366 Bry-sur-Marne Cedex; tel. 1-49-83-23-67; internet www.ina.fr; f. 1975; 2 research depts: Recherche Prospective (research combining telecommunications, computer science and audiovisual science); Groupe de Recherches Musicales (numerical devt of synthesis and treatment of sound psychoacoustics and musical perception, technology of electroacoustical instruments); library of 3,000 vols; Pres. EMMANUEL HOOG; publ. *Dossiers Audiovisuels* (6 a year).

Institut National de l'Environnement Industriel et des Risques (INERIS) (National Institute for Environmental Technology and Hazards): Parc Technologique ALATA, BP 2, 60550 Verneuil-en-Halatte; tel. 3-44-55-66-77; e-mail ineris@ineris.fr; internet www.ineris.fr; f. 1990; library of 28,000 vols; Dir-Gen. GEORGES LABROYE; publ. *INERIS Magazine* (5 a year).

Institut National de Recherche en Informatique et en Automatique (INRIA): Domaine de Voluceau, Rocquencourt, BP 105, 78153 Le Chesnay Cedex; tel. 1-39-63-55-11; e-mail communication@inria.fr; internet www.inria.fr; f. 1967; 8 research units; library of 45,000 vols; Pres. and Dir-Gen. MICHEL COSNARD; publs *Les conférences et supports de cours INRIA*, *Rapports d'activités scientifiques*, *Rapports de recherche et thèses*.

Institut National des Sciences et Techniques Nucléaires (INSTN) (National Institute of Nuclear Science and Technology): CEA-Saclay, 91191 Gif-sur-Yvette Cedex; internet www-instn.cea.fr; f. 1956; provides courses in nuclear engineering, robotics and computer-integrated manufacturing (CIM) and, in cooperation with the univs, postgraduate courses in reactor physics, dynamics of structures, analytical chemistry, radiochemistry, metallurgy, data processing, robotics, radiobiology, energy management, the use of radioisotopes in medicine and pharmacy; Dir JEAN-PIERRE LE ROUX; Pres. BERNARD BIGOT.

Laboratoire de Biotechnologie de l'Environnement: Ave des Etangs, 11100 Narbonne; tel. 4-68-42-51-51; internet www.montpellier.inra.fr/narbonne; f. 1895; attached to INRA; research in microbiological wastewater treatment; library of 5,000 vols; Dir JEAN-PHILIPPE DELGENÈS; publ. *Water Research*.

Office International de l'Eau (International Office for Water—IOW): 21 rue de Madrid, 75008 Paris; tel. 1-44-90-88-60; e-mail cnide@oieau.fr; internet www.oieau.fr; f. 1991; documentation centre on water problems and management; library of 37,000 vols and 180,000 articles; Pres. M. ROUSSEL; Dir D. PREUX; publs *AquaVeille* (52 a year, e-newsletter), *Information Eaux* (24 a year).

Office National d'Etudes et de Recherches Aérospatiales (ONERA): 29 ave de la Division-Leclerc, 92322 Châtillon; tel. 1-46-73-40-40; internet www.onera.fr; f. 1946 to develop, direct, and coordinate scientific and technical research in the field of aeronautics and space; library of 40,000 vols, 150,000 reports, 11,000 microfiches, 850 periodicals; Pres. MICHEL DE GLINIASTY; publ. *Aerospace Science and Technology* (8 a year, in English).

Libraries and Archives

Abbeville

Bibliothèque Municipale: Hôtel d'Emonville, place Clemenceau, BP 20010, 80101 Abbeville Cedex; tel. 3-22-24-95-16; e-mail bibliotheque-municipale@ville-abbeville.fr; internet www.ville-abbeville.fr/equipculturels.htm; f. 1643; 140,000 vols; Librarian P. HAZEBROUCK.

Aix-en-Provence

Bibliothèque Méjanes: 8–10 rue des Allumettes, 13090 Aix-en-Provence; tel. 4-42-91-98-88; e-mail citedulivre-stage@mairie-aixenprovence.fr; internet www.citedulivre-aix.com; f. 1810; 590,000 vols; Dir GILLES EBOLI.

Bibliothèque de l'Université d'Aix-Marseille III: 3 ave Robert-Schuman, 13626 Aix-en-Provence Cedex 1; tel. 4-42-17-24-40; internet infobu.u-3mrs.fr; 156,000 vols, 273,000 periodicals, 86,000 theses; Librarian J. C. RODA.

Albi

Mediathèque Pierre Amalric: ave Charles de Gaulle, 81000 Albi; tel. 5-63-38-56-10; e-mail mediatheque@albi.fr; internet www.mediatheque-albi.fr; f. during the French Revolution; 300,000 vols of monographs and 500 MSS; Librarian MATTHIEU DESACHY.

Amiens

Bibliothèques d'Amiens Métropole: 50 rue de la République, BP 60542, 80005 Amiens Cedex 1; tel. 3-22-97-10-10; internet bibliotheques.amiens.fr; f. 1826; 800,000 vols, 2,500 MSS, 300 incunabula; Dir SÉVERINE MONTIGNY; Sec. GISÈLE LAMENDIN.

Bibliothèque de l'Université de Picardie Jules Verne: 15 placette Lafleur, BP 446, 80004 Amiens Cedex 01; tel. 3-22-82-71-65; internet www.bu.u-picardie.fr; f. 1966; 330,000 vols, 3,900 periodicals; Dirs F. MONTBRUN, B. LOCHER.

Angers

Bibliothèque Municipale: 49 rue Toussaint, 49100 Angers; tel. 2-41-24-25-50; e-mail bibliotheque@ville.angers.fr; internet www.bm.angers.fr; 400,000 vols, 2,120 MSS, 111 incunabula; Librarian JEAN-CHARLES NICLAS.

Bibliothèque Universitaire d'Angers: 5 rue Le Nôtre, 49045 Angers Cedex; tel. 2-41-22-64-00; e-mail bu@univ-angers.fr; internet bu.univ-angers.fr; f. 1970; Dir OLIVIER TACHEAU.

Avignon

Bibliothèque Universitaire: 74 rue Louis Pasteur, 84018 Avignon Cedex 1; tel. 4-90-16-27-60; e-mail bu@univ-avignon.fr; internet www.bu.univ-avignon.fr; f. 1968; 100,000 books, 1,200 periodicals, 3,000 electronic periodicals; Dir FRANÇOISE FEBVRE.

Médiathèque Ceccano: 2 bis rue Laboureur, BP 349, 84025 Avignon Cedex 1; tel. 4-90-85-15-59; internet www.avignon.fr/fr/pratique/biblio/ceccano.php; f. 1810; 300,000 vols, 7,000 MSS, 700 incunabula, 2,700 musical scores, 40,000 engravings and maps, 30,000 coins; Chief Librarian CÉCILE FRANC.

Besançon

Bibliothèque de l'Université de Franche-Comté: 32 rue Mégevand, BP 1057, 25001 Besançon Cedex; tel. 3-81-66-53-50; internet scd.univ-fcomte.fr; f. 1880; Dir SOPHIE DESSEIGNE.

Bibliothèques Municipales: 1 rue de la Bibliothèque, BP 09, 25012 Besançon Cedex; tel. 3-81-87-81-40; e-mail bibliotheques@besancon.fr; internet www.besancon.com/biblio/francais/bm1.htm; f. 1694; 350,000 vols, 3,800 MSS, 1,000 incunabula; Dir HENRY FERREIRA-LOPES.

Bordeaux

Bibliothèque Municipale: 85 cours du Maréchal Juin, 33075 Bordeaux Cedex; tel. 5-56-10-30-00; e-mail bibli@mairie-bordeaux.fr; internet www.mairie-bordeaux.fr/bibliotheque/bibintro.htm; f. 1736; 900,000 vols, 4,200 MSS, 333 incunbula, 1,000 current periodicals; Chief Librarian PIERRE BOTINEAU.

Service Interétablissements de Co-opération Documentaire des Universités de Bordeaux: 4 ave des Arts, 33607 Pessac Cedex; tel. 5-56-84-86-86; e-mail sicod@bu.u-bordeaux.fr; internet www.montesquieu.u-bordeaux.fr/presentation/sicod.html; 3.2m. vols; Dir GÉRARD BRIAND.

Brest

Service Commun de Documentation: 10 ave Victor-Le-Gorgeu, BP 91342, 29213 Brest Cédex 1; tel. 2-98-01-64-04; e-mail scd@univ-brest.fr; internet www.univ-brest.fr; f. 1968; Dir NICOLAS TOCQUER.

Caen

Bibliothèque de Caen: Place Louis-Guillouard, 14053 Caen Cedex; tel. 2-31-30-47-00; e-mail bibliotheque.caen@agglo-caen.fr; internet www.caenlamer.fr/bibliothequecaen; f. 1809; 693,000 vols, 6,055 periodicals, 12,000 pre-1800 printed items, 6,000 slides, 5,700 video cassettes, 70,000 CDs, 7,500 talking books for the visually impaired, 1,900 software disks for microcomputer and CD-ROMs; spec. Normandy colln; Librarian NOËLLA DU PLESSIS.

Bibliothèque de l'Université de Caen: Esplanade de la Paix, 14032 Caen Cedex; tel. 2-31-56-58-70; e-mail bibliotheque@unicaen.fr; internet scd.unicaen.fr; f. 1955; Dir DANIÈLE VERDY.

Cambrai

Bibliothèque Municipale Classée: 37 rue St Georges, BP 179, 59403 Cambrai Cedex; tel. 3-27-82-93-93; e-mail admin@media-cambrai.com; f. 1791; 130,000 vols, 1,400 MSS, 600 incunabula; Librarian BÉNÉDICTE TÉROUANNE.

Carpentras

Bibliothèque Inguimbertine et Musées de Carpentras: 234 blvd Albin-Durand, 84200 Carpentras; tel. 4-90-63-04-92; e-mail jf.delmas@carpentras.fr; f. 1745; 265,000 vols, 3,126 MSS; Librarian JEAN-FRANÇOIS DELMAS.

Châlons-sur-Marne

Bibliothèque Municipale à Vocation Régionale Georges Pompidou: 68 rue Léon-Bourgeois, 51038 Châlons-en-Champagne Cedex; tel. 3-26-26-94-30; e-mail bibliotheque.mairie@chalons-en-champagne.net; internet www.chalons-en-champagne.net/bmvr; f. 1803; 330,000 vols, 2,000 MSS, 120 incunabula; Librarian RÉGIS DUTRÉMÉE.

Chambéry

Bibliothèque de l'Université de Savoie (SCDBU, Service commun de la documentation et des bibliothèques universitaires): Direction et Service centraux, Domaine universitaire de Jacob-Bellecombette, Bât. 15, BP 1104, 73011 Chambéry Cedex; tel. 4-79-75-91-13; e-mail contact-scd@univ-savoie.fr; internet www.scd.univ-savoie.fr; f. 1962; 199,950 vols,

1,928 periodicals, 50,000 e-periodicals; Dir ALAIN CARACO.

Clermont-Ferrand

Bibliothèque Municipale et Interuniversitaire: 1 blvd Lafayette, BP 27, 63001 Clermont-Ferrand Cedex 01; tel. 4-73-40-62-40; e-mail bmiu@univ-bpclermont.fr; internet bmiu.univ-bpclermont.fr; f. 1902; 682,437 vols, 2,587 current periodicals; Dir LIVIA RAPATEL.

Colmar

Bibliothèque de la Ville de Colmar: 1 place des Martyrs de la Résistance, BP 509, 68021 Colmar Cedex; tel. 3-89-24-48-18; e-mail bibliotheque@ville-colmar.com; f. 1803; 400,000 vols, 1,300 MSS, 2,500 incunabula; Chief Librarian FRANCIS GUETH.

Dijon

Bibliothèque de l'Université de Bourgogne: 7 blvd du Docteur Petitjean, 21078 Dijon; tel. 3-80-39-64-63; e-mail emmanuelle.ashta@u-bourgogne.fr; internet scd.u-bourgogne.fr; Dir F. HAGENE.

Bibliothèque Municipale: 3–7 rue de l'Ecole-de-Droit, 21000 Dijon; tel. 3-80-44-94-14; e-mail bmdijon@ville-dijon.fr; internet bm-dijon.fr; f. 1701; 460,000 vols; Chief Librarian ANDRÉ-PIERRE SYREN.

Douai

Bibliothèque Municipale: rue de la Fonderie, 59500 Douai; tel. 3-27-97-88-51; e-mail bibliotheque@biblio.ville-douai.fr; internet www.ville-douai.fr/culture/bibliot/accueil.htm; f. 1770; 250,000 vols, 2,000 MSS, 300 incunabula, 200 periodicals; Librarian MICHELE DEMARCY.

Grenoble

Bibliothèque Municipale d'Etude et d'Information: 12 blvd Maréchal Lyautey, BP 1095, 38021 Grenoble Cedex 1; tel. 4-76-86-21-00; e-mail info@bm-grenoble.fr; internet www.bm-grenoble.fr; f. 1772; 600,000 vols, 654 incunabula, 20,980 MSS, 81,000 prints, 2,575 maps; spec. colln: local history; Dir CATHERINE POUYET.

Service de Co-opération Documentaire Sciences-Médecine: BP 66, 38402 St Martin d'Hères; tel. 4-76-51-42-84; internet www.ujf-grenoble.fr/bus; linked with university science and medical libraries; Dir MARIE-FRANCE ROCHARD.

Service Interétablissements de Co-opération Documentaire: Domaine universitaire BP 85, 38402 St Martin d'Hères Cedex; tel. 4-76-82-61-61; e-mail sicd2admin@upmf-grenoble.fr; internet odyssee.upmf-grenoble.fr; f. 1880; Dir MARIE-NOËLLE ICARDO.

Haguenau

Musée Historique et Archives Municipales: 9 rue du Maréchal Foch, BP 40 261, 67504 Haguenau Cedex; tel. 3-88-90-29-39; e-mail musees-archives@ville-haguenau.fr; f. 1899; 8,000 vols; Dir PIA WENDLING; publ. *Etudes Haguenoviennes* (1 a year).

La Rochelle

Médiathèque Michel Crépeau: Communauté de Villes, ave Marillac, 17042 La Rochelle Cedex 1; tel. 5-46-45-71-71; e-mail mediatheque@agglo-larochelle.fr; f. 1750; 360,000 vols; Librarian BRUNO CARBONE.

Le Havre

Bibliothèque Municipale: 17 rue Jules Lecesne, 76600 Le Havre; tel. 2-32-74-07-40; e-mail biblio@ville-lehavre.fr; internet www.ville-lehavre.fr/quotidien/culture/bibliotheque/cadre.htm; f. 1796; public borrowing, reference, record library; 389,237 vols, 1,449 periodicals, 1,020 MSS; Librarian PATRICIA DOULERS.

Le Mans

Bibliothèque de l'Université du Maine: ave Olivier Messiaen, 72085 Le Mans Cedex 09; tel. 2-43-83-30-48; e-mail bu@univ-lemans.fr; internet scd.univ-lemans.fr; 140,000 vols, 800 periodicals; Dir MICHÈLE NARDI.

Lille

Bibliothèque de l'Université des Sciences et Technologies de Lille: Service commun de la documentation de Lille I: ave Henri Poincaré, BP 155, 59653 Villeneuve d'Ascq Cedex; tel. 3-20-43-44-10; e-mail jean-bernard.marino@univ-lille1.fr; internet www.univ-lille1.fr/bustl; economics, humanities, technology, science; 160,000 books, 60,000 theses; Chief Librarian JEAN-BERNARD MARINO.

Bibliothèque Municipale: 32–34 rue Edouard Delesalle, 59043 Lille Cedex; tel. 3-20-15-97-20; e-mail bmlille@mairie-lille.fr; internet www.bm-lille.fr; f. 1726; 650,000 vols; Head Librarian ISABELLE DUQUENNE; Librarian LAURE DELRUE-VANDENBULCKE.

Service Commun de la Documentation de Lille II: (Secteur Médecine/Pharmacie and Secteur Droit/Gestion): 1 place Déliot, BP 179, 59017 Lille Cedex; tel. 3-20-90-76-50; internet www.scd.univ-lille2.fr; f. 1993; Chief Librarian BRIGITTE MULETTE.

Service Commun de la Documentation de l'Université de Lille III—Charles de Gaulle: Domaine universitaire du Pont-de-bois, BP 99, 59652 Villeneuve d'Ascq Cedex; tel. 3-20-41-70-00; internet www.univ-lille3.fr/portail/index.php?page=scd; Dir JEAN-PAUL CHADOURNE.

Limoges

Bibliothèque de l'Université de Limoges: 39C rue Camille-Guérin, 87031 Limoges Cedex; tel. 5-55-43-57-00; internet www-scd.unilim.fr; f. 1965; 100,000 vols; Dir ODILE ROHOU.

Bibliothèque Francophone Multimédia: 2 pl. Aimé Césaire, 87032 Limoges Cedex; tel. 5-55-45-96-00; e-mail francophonie@bm-limoges.fr; internet www.bm-limoges.fr; f. 1804; 530,000 vols, 900 periodicals, 14,000 video cassettes, 32,000 records; spec. collns incl. enamels, ceramics, porcelain; Librarian FRANÇOISE DIET-ESCARFAIL; Librarian CHANTAL DE GRANDPRÉ.

Lyons

Bibliothèque Interuniversitaire de Lettres et Sciences Humaines: 5 parvis René-Descartes, BP 7000, 69342 Lyon; tel. 4-37-37-65-00; e-mail biu@ens-lsh.fr; internet biu.ens-lsh.fr/biu; Dir CHARLES MICOL.

Bibliothèque Municipale: 30 blvd Vivier-Merle, 69431 Lyon Cedex 03; tel. 4-78-62-18-00; e-mail bm@bm-lyon.fr; internet www.bm-lyon.fr; f. 1565; 2.4m. vols, 12,449 MSS, 1,157 incunabula, 130,000 prints, 12,399 periodicals, 172,000 records, 59,883 photographs; Dir PATRICK BAZIN.

Marseilles

Bibliothèque de l'Université d'Aix-Marseille: Campus Timone, 27 blvd Jean Moulin, 13385 Marseille Cedex 05; tel. 4-91-32-45-37; e-mail anne.dujol@univ-amu.fr; internet bu.univ-amu.fr; f. 2012 by merger of 3 ancient univs of Aix-Marseille; multidisciplinary network of 60 libraries in Aix, Marseille, Gap, Digne and Arles; 1.2m. documents, collns incl. rare books and periodicals in humanities, law, medicine; Dir ANNE DUJOL.

Bibliothèque et Archives, Chambre de Commerce et d'Industrie Marseille-Provence: La Canebière, Palais de la Bourse, BP 21856, 13221 Marseilles; tel. 4-91-39-33-21; e-mail sylvie.drago@ccimp.com; internet www.marseille-provence.cci.fr; f. 1872; agriculture, business, commerce, economics, geography, history, industry, law, marine, overseas, Provence; online information service; 60,000 vols, 60,000 brochures, 3,000 periodicals; Dir PATRICK BOULANGER; Librarian SYLVIE DRAGO.

Bibliothèque Municipale: 23 rue de la providence, 13001 Marseilles; tel. 4-91-55-90-00; e-mail accueil-bmvr@mairie-marseille.fr; internet www.bmvr.mairie-marseille.fr; f. 1800; 750,000 vols; Dir FRANÇOIS LARBRE.

Metz

Bibliothèque Municipale: 1 cour Elie Fleur, 57000 Metz; tel. 3-87-55-53-33; e-mail mediatheque@mairie-metz.fr; internet bm.mairie-metz.fr/metz; f. 1811; 400,000 vols, 1,195 MSS, 5,000 engravings, 463 incunabula; video cassettes, slides; Chief Librarian PIERRE LOUIS.

Service Commun de Documentation de l'Université Paul Verlaine–Metz: Ile du Saulcy, 57045 Metz Cedex 1; tel. 3-87-31-50-80; e-mail colinmaire@scd.univ-metz.fr; internet www.scd.univ-metz.fr; f. 1972; 250,000 vols, 1,100 periodicals; Dir HERVÉ COLINMAIRE.

Montpellier

Bibliothèque Interuniversitaire: Administration: 60 rue des Etats généraux, 34965 Montpellier Cedex 2; tel. 4-67-13-43-50; e-mail biu.secretariat@univ-montp1.fr; internet www.biu.univ-montp1.fr; f. 1890; Chief Librarian PIERRE GAILLARD.

Médiathèque Centrale d'Agglomération Emile Zola: 240 rue de l'Acropole, 34000 Montpellier; tel. 4-67-34-87-10; e-mail accueil.mca@montpellier-agglo.com; internet services.mediathequed.montpellier-agglo.com; f. during the French Revolution; 1,000,000 vols; Dir M. G. GUDIN DE VALLERIN.

Mulhouse

Bibliothèque de l'Université et de la Société Industrielle de Mulhouse (Section Histoire industrielle, Histoire des Sciences et des techniques): 16 rue de la Fonderie, 68093 Mulhouse; tel. 3-89-56-82-79; e-mail scdmulhouse@uha.fr; internet www.scd.uha.fr; f. 1826; 20,000 vols, 800 (and 20 current) periodicals; Dir ANNIE SCHALLER.

Université de Haute Alsace, Service Commun de Documentation: 8 rue des Frères Lumière, 68093 Mulhouse; tel. 3-89-33-63-60; e-mail scdmulhouse@uha.fr; internet www.scd.uha.fr; f. 1977; Dir PHILIPPE RUSSELL.

Nancy

Bibliothèque Municipale: 43 rue Stanislas, CS 64230, 54042 Nancy Cedex; tel. 3-83-37-38-83; e-mail bmnancy@mairie-nancy.fr; f. 1750; 500,000 vols; Chief Librarian ANDRÉ MARKIEWICZ.

Service Commun de Documentation: 30 rue Lionnois, 54000 Nancy; tel. 3-83-68-22-00; e-mail webscd@scd.uhp-nancy.fr; internet scd.uhp-nancy.fr; 356,000 vols, 4,100 periodicals; Chief Librarian SEBASTIEN BOGAERT.

Nantes

Bibliothèque Municipale: 15 rue de l'Hermonière, BP 44113, 44041 Nantes Cedex 01;

tel. 2-40-41-95-95; e-mail bm@mairie-nantes.fr; internet www.bm.nantes.fr; f. 1753; 900,000 vols; Chief Librarian AGNÈS MARCETTEAU.

Bibliothèque Universitaire de Nantes: Chemin de la Censive du Tertre, BP 32211, 44322 Nantes Cedex 03; tel. 2-40-14-12-30; internet www.bu.univ-nantes.fr; f. 1962; 260,000 vols, 5,000 periodicals; Chief Librarian MICHELLE GUIOT.

Nice

Bibliothèque de l'Université de Nice-Sophia Antipolis: Parc Valrose, BP 2053, 06101 Nice Cedex 02; tel. 4-92-07-60-00; e-mail sabu@unice.fr; internet www.unice.fr/bu; f. 1963; 260,000 vols, 4,400 periodicals; Dir LOUIS KLEE.

Bibliothèque Municipale à Vocation Régionale de Nice: 1 ave Saint-Jean-Baptiste, 06364 Nice Cedex 4; tel. 4-97-13-48-00; e-mail bmvr@ville-nice.fr; internet www.bmvr-nice.com.fr; f. 1802; network of 15 br. libraries; 1m. vols, 208,700 compact discs, records and cassettes, 17,002 video cassettes, 519 CD-ROMs; spec. colln on Michel Butor; Chief Librarian FRANÇOISE MICHELIZZA.

Nîmes

Carré d'Art Bibliothèques: Mairie, Place de l'Hôtel de Ville, 30033 Nîmes Cedex 9; tel. 4-66-76-70-01; e-mail webmaster@ville-nimes.fr; internet bibliotheque.nimes.fr; f. 1803; 323,000 vols, 590 periodicals, 800 MSS, 40,000 ancient books, 19,000 CDs; Chief Librarian J.-M. MASSADAU; publ. *Journal Carré d'Art* (3 a year).

Orléans

Médiathèque d'Orléans: 1 pl. Gambetta, 45043 Orléans Cedex 1; tel. 2-38-68-45-45; e-mail bibliotheques@ville-orleans.fr; internet www.bm-orleans.fr; f. 1714; 420,000 vols, 2,600 MSS; Librarian JEAN-MICHEL AUZANNEAU.

Service Commun de la Documentation de l'Université d'Orléans: Domaine de la Source, 6 rue de Tours, 45072 Orléans Cedex 02; tel. 2-38-41-71-84; e-mail secretariat.scd@univ-orleans.fr; internet scd.univ-orleans.fr; f. 1965; 400,000 vols and theses, 3,300 periodicals; Dir CATHERINE MOREAU.

Paris

American Library in Paris: 10 rue du Général Camou, 75007 Paris; tel. 1-53-59-12-60; e-mail alparis@americanlibraryinparis.org; internet americanlibraryinparis.org; f. 1920; organizes lectures, talks, book signings, exhibits, concerts and performances; 113,000 vols, 250 periodicals, 2,500 online periodicals; Chair. MARY LEE TURNER; Dir CHARLES TRUEHEART.

Archives de France: 56 rue des Francs-Bourgeois, 75141 Paris Cedex 03; tel. 1-40-27-60-00; internet www.archivesdefrance.culture.gouv.fr; f. 1790; 480 km documents; Dir HERVE LEMOINE.

Attached Units:

Archives Nationales du Monde du Travail: 78 blvd du Général Leclerc, BP 405, 59057 Roubaix Cedex 1; tel. 3-20-65-38-00; f. 1993; Chief Curator FRANÇOISE BOSMAN.

Centre des Archives Contemporaines: 2 rue des Archives, 77300 Fontainebleau; tel. 1-64-31-73-00; e-mail cac.fontainebleau@culture.gouv.fr; Chief Curator CHRISTINE PETILLAT.

Centre des Archives d'Outre-Mer: 29 chemin du Moulin-Detesta, 13090 Aix-en-Provence; tel. 4-42-93-38-50; e-mail anom.aix@culture.gouv.fr; f. 1962; Chief Curator MARTINE CORNEDE.

Centre Historique des Archives Nationales: 60 rue des Francs-Bourgeois, 75003 Paris; e-mail anparis@culture.gouv.fr; Chief Curator GÉRARD ERMISSE.

Centre National du Microfilm: Domaine d'Espeyran, 30800 St-Gilles-du-Gard; tel. 4-66-87-30-09; e-mail cnmn@culture.gouv.fr; Chief Curator ANNE DEBANT.

Bibliothèque Administrative de la Ville de Paris: Hôtel de Ville, 75196 Paris Cedex 04; tel. 1-42-76-48-87; e-mail bavp@paris.frr; f. 1872; 550,000 vols (reports, studies, statistics, official texts, budgets, etc.), 3,200 periodicals, 8,000 photographs, 2,700 MSS, 12,000 architectural designs, 40,000 microfiches, 2,000 microfilms covering areas of French and foreign local admin., French legislation, economic, political and social history, ex-French colonies and gen. biography; Chief Librarian PIERRE CASSELLE.

Bibliothèque Centrale de l'Ecole Polytechnique: Plateau de Saclay, 91128 Palaiseau Cedex; tel. 1-69-33-40-76; e-mail bibliotheque@polytechnique.fr; internet www.bibliotheque.polytechnique.fr; f. 1794; 300,000 vols, 1,700 periodicals; Chief Librarian MADELEINE DE FUENTES.

Bibliothèque Centrale du Conservatoire National des Arts et Métiers: 292 rue St-Martin, 75141 Paris Cedex 03; tel. 1-40-27-27-03; e-mail mireille.le_van_ho@cnam.fr; internet bibliotheque.cnam.fr; f. 1794; 150,000 vols, 3,600 periodicals on science, technology, political economy; spec. collns: exhibition catalogues, Bartholdi, Organum; Dir MIREILLE LE VAN HO.

Bibliothèque Centrale des Musées Nationaux: Palais du Louvre, 2 quai François Mitterrand, Porte des arts and 14 quai F. Mitterrand, Porte des Lions, 75001 Paris Cedex 01; tel. 1-40-20-52-66; e-mail sbadg.dmf@culture.gouv.fr; internet ccbmn.culture.fr; f. 1848; books and MSS connected with the Louvre and the Nat. Museums (Egyptology colln, Oriental antiquities, Graeco-Roman antiquities, drawings, paintings and sculptures); open only to curators and authorized persons; 180,000 vols, 1,800 periodicals; Librarian FRANÇOISE PETITOU.

Bibliothèque Centrale du Muséum National d'Histoire Naturelle: 38 rue Geoffroy-Saint-Hilaire, 75005 Paris; tel. 1-40-79-36-27; e-mail milenoir@mnhn.fr; internet mussi.mnhn.fr; f. 1635; 580,500 vols, 10,000 MSS, 23,334 periodicals; Chief Librarian MICHELLE LENOIR.

Bibliothèque de Documentation Internationale Contemporaine: Centre Universitaire, 6 allée de l'Université, 92001 Nanterre Cedex; tel. 1-40-97-79-00; e-mail courrier@bdic.fr; internet www.bdic.fr; f. 1914; history of the 2 World Wars and int. relations since beginning of 20th century, social and revolutionary movements, political emigrations; over 1m. vols, 90,000 series of periodicals; Dir GENEVIÈVE DREYFUS-ARMAND; publs *Journal* (irregular), *Matériaux pour l'Histoire de Notre Temps* (3 a year).

Bibliothèque de Géographie—Sorbonne: 191 rue Saint-Jacques, 75005 Paris; tel. 1-44-32-14-63; e-mail bibgeo@univ-paris1.fr; internet www.univ-paris1.fr; f. 1927; geography; 92,000 vols, 4,600 periodicals, 100,000 maps, 40,000 photographs, 500 other media; Librarian RACHEL CREPPY.

Bibliothèque de l'Académie Nationale de Médecine: 16 rue Bonaparte, 75272 Paris Cedex 06; tel. 1-46-34-60-70; e-mail bibliotheque@academie-medecine.fr; internet www.bibliotheque.academie-medecine.fr; f. 1820; archives of the Académie Royale de Chirurgie (1731–93), Société Royale de Médecine (1776–93), Société de l'Ecole de Médecine (1800–21), Comité Central de Vaccine (1803–23) and Académie de Médecine (since 1820); portraits, medals and sculptures; 450,000 vols, 113 incunabula, 4,000 periodicals (500 current), 7,000 biographical dossiers; Librarian JÉRÔME VAN WIJLAND; Sec. FRANÇOISE SLAVIERO.

Bibliothèque de la Cour des Comptes: 13 rue Cambon, 75100 Paris Cedex; tel. 1-42-98-97-12; f. 1807 by Napoleon I; 50,000 vols on finance, law and economy; Librarian (vacant).

Bibliothèque de l'Arsenal: 1 rue de Sully, 75004 Paris; tel. 1-42-77-44-21; e-mail arsenal@bnf.fr; internet www.bnf.fr/fr/la_bnf/anx_autres_sites/a.arsenal_salle_lecture.html; f. 1756, by the Marquess of Paulmy, public library in 1797; inc. Bibliothèque Nat. 1934; open to scholars; houses performing arts colln of the Bibliothèque Nationale (2.5m. vols and other items); incl. archives of the Bastille; 1m. vols, 15,000 MSS, autographs, 100,000 prints, 18th-century maps; Dir BRUNO BLASSELLE; Deputy Dir EVE NETCHINE.

Bibliothèque de la Sorbonne: 13 rue de la Sorbonne, 75257 Paris Cedex 05; tel. 1-40-46-30-27; e-mail info@biu.sorbonne.fr; internet www.bibliotheque.sorbonne.fr/biu; f. 1762; 22m. vols, 13,000 periodicals; Chief Librarian PHILIPPE MARCEROU; publ. *Mélanges de la Bibliothèque de la Sorbonne*.

Bibliothèque de l'Ecole Nationale Supérieure des Mines: 60 blvd Saint-Michel, 75272 Paris Cedex 06; tel. 1-40-51-90-56; e-mail bib@bib.ensmp.fr; internet bib.ensmp.fr; f. 1783; 300,000 vols, 3,820 periodicals, 30,000 maps; Chief Librarian LAURENCE TARIN.

Bibliothèque de l'Ecole Normale Supérieure: 45 rue d'Ulm, 75230 Paris Cedex 05; internet halley.ens.fr; f. 1810; 500,000 vols; Chief Librarian LAURE LÉVEILLÉ.

Bibliothèque de l'Institut de France: 23 quai Conti, 75006 Paris; tel. 1-44-41-44-10; e-mail mireille.pastoureau@institut-de-france.fr; internet www.bibliotheque-institutdefrance.fr; f. 1795; research and heritage library; comprises 5 acads: Académie française, Académie des Inscriptions et Belles-Lettres, Académie des Sciences, Académie des Beaux-Arts, Académie des Sciences morales et politiques; 1m. vols, 8,000 periodicals, 10,000 MSS; Chief Curator Dr MIREILLE PASTOUREAU.

Bibliothèque de l'Institut National de la Statistique et des Etudes Economiques: 18 blvd Adolphe Pinard, 75675 Paris Cedex 14; tel. 1-41-17-53-43; e-mail dg75-bibliotheque-service-public@insee.fr; internet www.insee.fr/fr/insee-statistique-publique/default.asp?page=bibliotheque/bibliotheque.htm; f. 1946; 100,000 vols, 5,000 periodicals; current and historical publs on french statistics and economics; regional publs; official publs on int. statistics and economics and publs of statistical offices around the world; Chief Librarian and Head of Documentation PHILIPPE PINÇON.

Bibliothèque de l'Institut National de Recherche Pédagogique: 5 parvis René Descartes, 69342 Lyons Cedex 07; tel. 1-37-37-66-10; e-mail soula@inrp.fr; internet www.inrp.fr; f. 1879; educational research; 550,000 vols, 5,000 periodicals, 100,000 textbooks; Chief Librarian MARIE-LOUISE SOULA.

Bibliothèque de l'Institut National d'Histoire de l'Art—Collections Jacques Doucet: 2 rue Vivienne, 75002 Paris; 58 rue de Richelieu, 75083 Paris Cedex 02; tel. 1-47-03-76-23; e-mail bibliotheque@inha.fr;

internet www.inha.fr; f. 1918; 450,000 vols, 6,674 periodicals; Chief Librarian MARTINE POULAIN.

Bibliothèque des Avocats à la Cour d'Appel: Palais de Justice, 75001 Paris; f. 1708, confiscated during the Revolution, but refounded in 1810; not open to the public; 160,000 vols; Librarian MICHEL BRICHARD.

Bibliothèque du Ministère des Affaires Etrangères: 3 rue Suzanne Masson, La Courneuve, 93126 Paris; tel. 1-43-17-42-61; e-mail biblio.archives@diplomatie.gouv.fr; internet www.diplomatie.gouv.fr; f. 1680; 500,000 vols; Head Librarian ISABELLE LEFORT; Librarian LIONEL CHENÉDÉ.

Bibliothèque du Sénat: Palais du Luxembourg, 15 rue de Vaugirard, 75291 Paris Cedex 06; tel. 1-42-34-35-39; f. 1818; open to members of Parliament; 450,000 vols, chiefly on history and law, 1,343 MSS and 45,000 prints; Dir PHILIPPE MARTIAL.

Bibliothèque du Service Historique de la Marine: Château de Vincennes, BP 122, 00481 Armées; tel. 1-43-28-81-50; e-mail contact@servicehistorique.marine.defense.gouv.fr; internet www.servicehistorique.marine.defense.gouv.fr; f. 1919; 300,000 vols on naval history; Chief Curator ALAIN MORGAT.

Bibliothèque du Service Historique de l'Armée de Terre: Château de Vincennes, BP 107, 00481 Armées; tel. 1-41-93-34-62; f. c.1800; 16th- to 20th-century science and military history, French history, cartography; over 600,000 vols; Librarian RAPHAËL MASSON.

Bibliothèque et Archives du Conseil d'Etat: Place du Palais-Royal, 75100 Paris 01 SP; tel. 1-40-20-81-31; internet www.conseil-etat.fr; f. 1871; 100,000 vols on jurisprudence, admin. science, political science and legislation; Librarian SERGE BOUFFANGE.

Bibliothèque Forney: 1 rue du Figuier, 75004 Paris; tel. 1-42-78-14-60; e-mail bibliotheque.forney@paris.fr; f. 1886; art library; reference library; wallpapers, posters, ephemera; 250,000 vols, 20,000 periodicals (chiefly on arts and crafts), 38,000 posters, 5,000 wallpapers, 1.5m. postcards; Librarian Conservateur Gen. FRÉDÉRIC CASIOT.

Bibliothèque Georges-Duhamel: 44 ave de Paris, 95290 L'Isle-Adam; tel. 1-34-69-41-99; f. 1797; encyclopaedic library; permanent exhibitions in Georges Duhamel picture gallery; 88,882 vols; record library: 6,400 records, 1,500 compact discs; Dir PAUL JOLAS; publ. *Rencontres Artistiques et Littéraires*.

Bibliothèque Gustav Mahler: 11 bis rue Vézelay, 75008 Paris; tel. 1-53-89-09-10; internet www.bgm.org; f. 1986; reference colln for musicians, students, researchers; 30,000 vols, 35,000 musical scores, 6,000 reviews, 70,000 records; archives: MSS, letters, photos, etc. on Mahler's life and works; also 16,000 dossiers on contemporary composers, autographs and MSS of 19th- and 20th-century musicians; Pres. PIERRE BERGÉ; Librarian ALAIN GALLIARI; publ. *Bulletin d'information de la BMGM* (1 a year).

Bibliothèque Historique de la Ville de Paris: 24 rue Pavée, 75004 Paris; tel. 1-44-59-29-40; f. 1871; 650,000 vols, 15,000 MSS on history of Paris; Curator JEAN DERENS.

Bibliothèque Interuniversitaire Cujas de Droit et Sciences Economiques: 2 rue Cujas, 75005 Paris; tel. 1-44-07-79-87; e-mail cujasdir@univ-paris1.fr; internet www-cujas.univ-paris1.fr; f. 1876; 1m. vols; Chief Librarian DOMINIQUE ROCHE.

Bibliothèque Interuniversitaire de Santé: 12 rue de l'Ecole-de-Médecine, 75270 Paris Cedex 06; tel. 1-76-53-19-51; e-mail info-med@biusante.parisdescartes.fr; internet www.biusante.parisdescartes.fr; f. 1733; 1m. vols, 30,000 pre-1800 books and theses, 109 incunabula, 20,000 periodicals (2,300 current); Chief Librarian GUY COBOLET.

Bibliothèque Interuniversitaire de Santé: 4 ave de l'Observatoire, 75270 Paris Cedex 06; tel. 1-53-73-95-23; e-mail info-pharma@biusante.parisdescartes.fr; internet www.biusante.parisdescartes.fr; f. 1570; centre for the acquisition and dispersion of scientific and technical information (CADIST) on beauty care; 280,000 vols, 945 periodicals, archives of Parisian apothecaries; Dir GUY COBOLET (acting).

Bibliothèque Mazarine: 23 quai de Conti, 75006 Paris; tel. 1-44-41-44-06; e-mail contact@bibliotheque-mazarine.fr; internet www.bibliotheque-mazarine.fr; f. 1643, present status 1945; attached to Institut de France; 600,000 vols, 5,000 MSS, 2,370 incunabula, 180,000 books published before 1801; Dir YANN SORDET.

Bibliothèque-Musée de l'Opéra: 8 rue Scribe, 75009 Paris; tel. 1-53-79-37-40; internet www.bnf.fr; f. 1875; a service of Bibliothèque Nationale, music dept; 200,000 vols, 30,000 scores, 80,000 libretti, 100,000 drawings, 40,000 lithographs, 100,000 photographs, 2,000 periodicals; Dir ODILE DUPONT; Curator ROMAIN FEIST.

Bibliothèque Nationale de France: quai François Mauriac, 75013 Paris; tel. 1-53-79-53-79; internet www.bnf.fr; f. 14th century; specialized depts: printed books (11m. vols), periodicals (350,000 titles), maps and plans (890,000), prints and photographs (11m.), MSS (350,000 bound vols), coins, medals and antiques (580,000 items), music (incl. Bibliothèque-Musée de l'Opéra *(q.v.)*), sound archive and audiovisual aids (1m. discs and tape recordings, 20,000 films, 40,000 video materials), performing arts (3m. items), Bibliothèque de l'Arsenal *(q.v.)*; Pres. JEAN-NOËL JEANNENEY; Dir-Gen. AGNÈS SAAL; publs *Bibliographie nationale Française* (52 a year), *Chronique de la Bibliothèque Nationale de France* (6 a year).

Bibliothèque Publique d'Information: Centre Georges-Pompidou, 75197 Paris Cedex 04; tel. 1-44-78-12-33; e-mail bpi-info@bpi.fr; internet www.bpi.fr; f. 1977; 400,000 books, 2,722 periodicals, 2,425 films, 10,000 music records; Dir PATRICK BAZIN.

Bibliothèque Sainte-Geneviève: 10 pl. du Panthéon, 75005 Paris; tel. 1-44-41-97-97; e-mail bsgmail@univ-paris1.fr; internet www-bsg.univ-paris1.fr; f. 1624 by Cardinal F. de La Rochefoucauld as library of the Abbaye Sainte-Geneviève; collns on arts and recreation, computer science, general works, geography, history, information, languages, literature, philosophy and psychology, religion, science and mathematics, social sciences, technology and applied science; interlibrary loan; guided tours; online databases; 1.3m. vols, 14,000 periodicals, 120,000 early printed books, 1,500 incunabula and 4,200 MSS, 50,000 prints; encyclopaedic library; spec. colln: Bibliothèque Nordique (160,000 vols, 3,500 periodicals), Estonian colln (1,000 vols), 3,800 current serial titles; Dir YVES PEYRÉ.

Bibliothèques de l'Institut Catholique de Paris: c/o Bibliothèque de Fels, 21 rue d'Assas, 75270 Paris Cedex 06; tel. 1-44-39-52-30; e-mail bibliotheque.de.fels@icp.fr; internet www.icp.fr; f. 1875; history, literature, pedagogy, philosophy, psychology, theology; 600,000 vols, incl. 450,000 books, 623 current periodicals, 6,000 other periodicals; Dir for Libraries CHRISTOPHE LANGLOIS.

Attached Library:

Bibliothèque Jean de Vernon: 21 rue d'Assas, 75006 Paris; tel. 44-39-52-32; e-mail bibliotheque.de.vernon@icp.fr; internet ipac.icp.fr; 100,000 vols, 400 periodicals; biblical exegesis, archaeology and languages of the ancient Near E, Orthodox Church instns, history of the Byzantine Empire; Dir for Library MARIE-FRANÇOISE PAPE.

Bibliothèque Thiers: 27 pl. Saint-Georges, 75009 Paris; tel. 1-48-78-14-33; e-mail bibliotheque.thiers@free.fr; internet www.institut-de-france.fr; f. 1906; attached to Institut de France; 150,000 vols, 3,000 MSS and 30,000 engravings on 19th century-history; Dir SYLVIE BIET.

Bibliothèque Universitaire des Langues et Civilisations: 65 rue des Grands Moulins, 75013 Paris; tel. 1-81-69-18-96; e-mail contact@bulac.fr; internet www.bulac.fr; f. 1868; languages and cultures of countries in Asia, Africa, Central and Eastern Europe, and Middle Eastern, Oceanian and Amerindian languages; 660,000 vols, 8,695 periodicals; Dir MARIE-LISE TSAGOURIA.

CÉDIAS—Musée Social: 5 rue Las-Cases, 75007 Paris; tel. 1-45-51-66-10; e-mail bibliotheque@cedias.org; internet www.cedias.org; f. 1894; social information and documentation; public library; 100,000 vols; Dir JEAN-YVES BARREYRE; publ. *Vie Sociale* (4 a year).

Centre de Documentation Economique de la Chambre de Commerce et d'Industrie de Paris: 16 rue de Châteaubriand, 75008 Paris; tel. 1-55-65-72-72; f. 1821; economics, business information, management, market surveys, companies; economic data bank (DELPHES); 300,000 vols, 750 periodicals; Dir GÉRARD FALCO.

Centre de Documentation et d'Information Scientifique pour le Développement (CEDID): 209 rue La Fayette, 75010 Paris; tel. 1-48-03-75-95; f. 1985 by ORSTOM; 70,000 documents on devt and North-South co-operation, world environment, tropical agriculture, health, evolving societies, and women in third world countries; 200 general and scientific reviews, press cuttings, database, etc.; open to the public.

Direction des Services d'Archives de Paris: 18 blvd Sérurier, 75019 Paris; tel. 1-53-72-41-23; f. 1872; collns of various kinds of documents relating to the history of Paris, urbanization and architecture; 34,000 vols specializing in history of Paris and admin. publs, 1,200 periodicals; Dir AGNÈS MASSON.

Institut François-Mitterrand: 10 rue Charlot, 75003 Paris; tel. 1-44-54-53-93; e-mail ifm@mitterrand.org; internet www.mitterrand.org; f. 1996; archives documents relevant to the history of the second half of the 20th century.

Service de la Bibliothèque et des Archives de l'Assemblée Nationale: Palais Bourbon, 126 rue de l'Université, 75007 Paris; tel. 1-40-63-64-74; e-mail archives@assemblee-nationale.fr; internet www.assemblee-nationale.fr; f. 1796; open to deputies, staff members, secretaries of political groups, civil servants of the Assembly; 700,000 vols, 1,870 MSS, and 80 incunabula, 3,000 periodicals, 50,000 microfiches, 2,500 microfilms, mainly on history, political science, law, economy; Dir ELIANE FIGHIERA; publs *Sélection d'Articles de Périodiques*, *Sélection d'Ouvrages Récemment Acquis* (8 a year).

Service Documentaire de l'Ecole Ponts et ParisTech: 6 et 8 ave Blaise Pascal, Cité Descartes, Champs sur Marne, 77455 Marne-la-Vallée Cedex 2; tel. 1-64-15-36-90; e-mail bibliotheque@enpc.fr; internet www.enpc.fr; f. 1747; 200,000 vols on bldg, civil engineering, urban and regional planning, and transport, 3,200 MSS, 3,000 maps, 10,000 photographs 1850–1900, 10 libraries; Dir ISABELLE GAUTHERON.

Société Historique et Littéraire Polonaise—Bibliothèque Polonaise de Paris (Polish Historical and Literary Society—Polish Library in Paris): 6 quai d'Orléans, 75004 Paris; tel. 1-55-42-83-83; e-mail b.borkowska@bplp.fr; internet www.bibliotheque-polonaise-paris-shlp.fr; f. 1854; resources centre specializes in 19th- and 20th-century history, literature and art; organizes cultural meetings, confs and colloquia, musical events, temporary exhibitions; administered by the Polish Historical and Literary Society (Société Historique et Littéraire Polonaise); 200,000 vols, 3,000 MSS (archives of 19th- and 20th-century Polish emigration to France), 1,000 magazines, 90,000 brochures, 1,000 posters, 1,420 paintings, 25,000 drawings and engravings, 350 sculptures, 600 medals and coins, 4,000 maps (16th to 20th centuries), 5,000 old photographs; Pres. C. PIERRE ZALESKI; Dir DANUTA DUBOIS.

UNESCO Library: UNESCO, 7 pl. de Fontenoy, 75007 Paris; tel. 1-45-68-03-56; e-mail library@unesco.org; internet www.unesco.org/library; f. 1946; reference and information services, incl. online searches, for the org. as a whole, as well as for the gen. public with an interest in UNESCO's fields of competence; manages multilingual UNESCO Thesaurus; 150,000 vols, 800 periodicals; Reference Librarian PETRA VAN DEN BORN.

Pau

Bibliothèque de l'Université de Pau et des Pays de l'Adour: Campus universitaire, 64000 Pau; tel. 5-59-92-33-60; internet www.univ-pau.fr/scd; f. 1962; 142,000 vols, 2,067 periodicals; Dir SYLVAINE FREULON.

Bibliothèque Square Paul Lafond: Rue Mathieu Lalanne, 64000 Pau; tel. 5-59-27-15-72; e-mail mial@agglo-pau.fr; internet mediatheques.agglo-pau.fr; f. 1803; 350,000 vols; includes municipal archives; spec. collns on Henri IV and Béarn; Librarian OLIVIER CAUDRON.

Périgueux

Bibliothèque Municipale: 12 ave Georges Pompidou, 24000 Périgueux; tel. 5-53-45-65-45; e-mail bibliotheque@perigueux.fr; f. 1809; 170,000 vols; Librarian J. L. GLÉNISSON.

Perpignan

Bibliothèque Universitaire: BP 59939, Moulin à Vent, 52 ave Paul Alduy, 66962 Perpignan Cedex 9; tel. 4-68-66-22-99; e-mail secdirbu@univ-perp.fr; internet www.univ-perp.fr/scms/bu/buweb.htm; f. 1962; 183,000 vols, 103,000 theses; spec. collns: Catalan, Mexican studies, history of Pyrénées-Orientales, renewable energy, materials science, geology of N Africa; Dir JOËL MARTRES.

Poitiers

Bibliothèque Universitaire de Poitiers: BP 605, 86022 Poitiers Cedex; tel. 5-49-45-33-11; e-mail bu@univ-poitiers.fr; internet www.scd.univ-poitiers.fr; f. 1879; 452,000 vols, 5,830 periodicals; spec. collns: 30,000 early printed vols, Fonds Dubois (16th–19th centuries, economics, politics, social history), Argenson family archives; Dir STÉPHANE BASSINET.

Médiathèque François-Mitterrand: 4 rue de l'Université, BP 619, 86022 Poitiers Cedex; tel. 5-49-52-31-51; e-mail mediatheque@mairie-poitiers.fr; internet www.bm-poitiers.fr; f. 1803; 750,000 vols, 550 current periodicals; Dir AGNÈS MACQUIN; publ. *Programme* (5 a year).

Reims

Bibliothèque de l'Université de Reims: Ave François Mauriac, 51095 Reims Cedex; tel. 3-26-91-39-28; e-mail carine.elbekri@univ-reims.fr; internet www.univ-reims.fr/bu; f. 1970; 400,000 vols, 4,278 periodicals; Dir CARINE EL BEKRI.

Bibliothèque Municipale: 2 rue des Fuseliers, 51095 Reims Cedex; tel. 3-26-35-68-00; e-mail cathedrale@bm-reims.fr; internet www.bm-reims.fr; f. 1809; 800,000 vols, 3,000 MSS; Librarian DELPHINE QUÉREUX-SBAÏ; publ. *Ouvrez les guillemets* (12 a year).

Rennes

Bibliothèque de l'Université de Rennes I: BP 90404, 35704 Rennes Cedex 7; tel. 2-23-23-34-18; e-mail scd-contact@listes.univ-rennes1.fr; internet www.scd.univ-rennes1.fr; f. 1855; 550,000 vols; Dir GHYSLAINE DUONG-VINH.

Bibliothèque de l'Université de Rennes II: Place du Recteur Henri Le Moal, 35043 Rennes Cedex; tel. 2-99-14-12-55; internet www.uhb.fr/scd; Librarian E. LEMAU.

Bibliothèque Municipale: 1 rue de La Borderie, 35042 Rennes Cedex; tel. 2-23-62-26-42; e-mail bm@bm-rennes.fr; internet www.bm-rennes.fr; f. 1803; 650,000 vols; Chief Librarian MARINE BEDEL.

Rouen

Bibliothèque de l'Université de Rouen: Anneau central, rue Lavoisier, 76821 Mont-Saint-Aignan Cedex; tel. 2-35-14-81-75; internet www.univ-rouen.fr; 400,000 vols; Dir YANNICK VALIN.

Bibliothèque Municipale: 3 rue Jacques-Villon, 76043 Rouen Cedex 1; tel. 2-35-71-28-82; e-mail bibliotheque@rouen.fr; f. 1791; 500,000 vols incl. 600 incunabula, 6,000 MSS; Chief Librarian F. LEGENDRE.

St-Etienne

Bibliothèque de l'Université Jean-Monnet: 1 rue Tréfilerie, 42023 St-Etienne Cedex 2; tel. 4-77-42-16-99; e-mail achard@univ-st-etienne.fr; internet www.univ-st-etienne.fr/scdoc; Dir MARIE-CLAUDE ACHARD.

Strasbourg

Bibliothèque Nationale et Universitaire: 5 rue du Maréchal Joffre, BP 51029, 67070 Strasbourg Cedex; tel. 3-88-25-28-00; e-mail quid@bnu.fr; internet www.bnu.fr; f. 1871; 3.5m. vols; 1.1m. documents, books, newspapers, reviews, 7,000 MSS and 300 incunabula; Admin. ALBERT POIROT; Sec. Gen. LAURENT MASSON; publ. *La Revue de la BNU*.

Toulon

Bibliothèque de l'Université de Toulon et du Var: BP 10122, 83957 La Garde Cedex; tel. 4-94-14-23-26; internet bu.univ-tln.fr; f. 1971; general library; Dir J. KERIGUY.

Toulouse

Bibliothèque de Toulouse: 1 rue de Périgord, BP 7092, 31506 Toulouse Cedex 7; tel. 5-62-27-40-05; internet www.bibliotheque.toulouse.fr; f. 1782; 20 brs; 914,000 vols, 3,700 periodicals; Chief Librarian LIDWINE HARIVEL (acting).

Bibliothèque Universitaire de l'Arsenal (Toulouse 1): 11 rue des Puits-Creusés, BP 7093, 31070 Toulouse Cedex 7; tel. 5-34-45-61-11; internet www.ut-capitole.fr/bu; f. 1879; 900,000 vols; spec. collns: Fonds Pifteau (books printed in Toulouse, books on regional history and geography), Fonds Chabaneau (18th-century books), Fonds Claude Perroud (French Revolution), Fonds Liguge (Spanish history), Fonds Montauban (History of Protestantism); Dir MARCEL MARTY; Chief Librarian BRUNO VAN DOOREN.

Tours

Bibliothèque Municipale: 2 bis ave André Malraux, 37042 Tours Cedex; tel. 2-47-05-47-33; e-mail contact@bm-tours.fr; internet www.bm-tours.fr; f. 1791; original library destroyed in 1940; 550,000 vols, 1,800 periodicals, 1,634 MSS; Dir RÉGIS RECH.

Service Commun de la Documentation de l'Université de Tours: 5 rue des Tanneurs, 37041 Tours Cedex (Letters); tel. 2-47-36-64-86 Parc de Grandmont, 37200 Tours (Sciences and Pharmacy); 2 bis blvd Tonnellé, 37032 Tours Cedex (Medicine); 50 ave Portalis, 37206 Tours Cedex 3 (Law); tel. 2-47-36-11-24 6 place Jean-Jaurès, 41000 Blois (Blois section); internet www.scd.univ-tours.fr; Dir GIL-FRANÇOIS EUVRARD.

Troyes

Médiathèque de l'Agglomération Troyenne: 7 rue des Filles-Dieu, BP 602, 10088 Troyes Cedex; tel. 3-25-43-56-20; e-mail contact@mediatheque-agglo-troyes.fr; internet www.mediatheque-agglo-troyes.fr; f. 1651; 400,000 vols; Librarian THIERRY DELCOURT.

Valence

Médiathèque Publique et Universitaire: Place Charles Huguenel, 26000 Valence; tel. 4-75-79-23-70; e-mail medieval@wanadoo.fr; internet sicd2.upmf-grenoble.fr/bu/valence; f. 1775; 100,000 vols, 650 periodicals; Librarian JOHANN BERTI.

Valenciennes

Bibliothèque Municipale: 2–6 rue Ferrand, BP 282, 59300 Valenciennes Cedex; tel. 3-27-22-57-00; e-mail mpdion@ville-valenciennes.fr; internet www.bibliotheque.valenciennes.fr; f. 1598; 400,000 vols, also incl. 80,000 prints, photographs, maps; Dir MARIE-PIERRE DION.

Vandoeuvre-lès-Nancy

Institut de l'Information Scientifique et Technique (INIST-CNRS): 2 allée du Parc de Brabois, 54514 Vandoeuvre-lès-Nancy Cedex; tel. 3-83-50-46-00; e-mail infoclient@inist.fr; internet www.inist.fr; f. 1988; collects, processes and distributes int. research findings; produces 2 databases: PASCAL (Sciences, Technology, Medicine) and FRANCIS (Humanities, Social Sciences, Economics); 10,000 vols, 26,000 serial titles, 60,000 scientific reports, 62,000 conf. proceedings, 110,000 doctoral theses; Dir-Gen. RAYMOND DUVAL.

Versailles

Bibliothèque Municipale: 5 rue de l'Indépendance Américaine, 78000 Versailles; tel. 1-39-07-13-20; e-mail bibliotheque@versailles.fr; internet www.bibliotheques.versailles.fr/statique; f. 1803; 800,000 vols, 900 periodicals; Chief Librarian SOPHIE DANIS.

Museums and Art Galleries

Agen

Musée des Beaux-Arts: Place du Docteur Esquirol, 47916 Agen Cedex 9; tel. 5-53-69-47-23; e-mail musee@ville-agen.fr; internet www.ville-agen.fr/musee; f. 1876; local, Roman and medieval archaeology; paintings by Corneille de Lyon, de Troy, Drouais, Nattier, Goya, the Impressionists, Roger Bissière and François-Xavier Lalanne; ceramics; Chinese art; Curator MARIE-DOMINIQUE NIVIÈRE.

Aix-en-Provence

Musée Granet: pl. St Jean de Malte, 13100 Aix-en-Provence; tel. 4-42-52-88-32; internet www.museegranet-aixenprovence.fr; f. 1765; Egyptian, Greek, Celto-Ligurian, Roman and Gallo-Roman archaeology; pictures of Cézanne and the French Schools, with spec. emphasis on Provence; Italian, Spanish, Flemish, Dutch and German Schools; modern painting; sculpture; furniture of 16th, 17th and 18th centuries; Curator BRUNO ELY.

Alençon

Musée des Beaux-Arts et de la Dentelle: Cour Carrée de la Dentelle, 61000 Alençon; tel. 2-33-32-40-07; e-mail musee@mairie-calais.fr; internet www.musee.calais.fr; f. 1857; French, Dutch and Flemish paintings from 17th–19th centuries; French, Italian and Dutch drawings from 16th–19th centuries; French, Flemish, Italian and Eastern European lace since 16th century; French and British prints from 16th–19th centuries; ethnological items from Cambodia; Curator AUDE PESSEY-LUX.

Amboise

Musée de l'Hôtel de Ville: rue François I, BP 247, 37402 Amboise; tel. 2-47-23-47-42; e-mail a.champion-guenand@ville-amboise.fr; internet www.ville-amboise.fr; f. 1970; colln incl. tapestries, statues and paintings relating to the history of Amboise; Curator AGATHE CHAMPION-GUENAND.

Amiens

Musée de Picardie: 48 rue de la République, 80000 Amiens; tel. 3-22-97-14-00; e-mail musees-amiens@amiens-metropole.com; internet w2.amiens.com/museedepicardie; f. 1854; fine colln of paintings of Northern and French Schools; murals by Puvis de Chavannes and Sol Le Witt; Egyptian, Greek and Roman antiquities; prehistoric, Iron and Bronze age collns; objets d'art of Middle Ages and Renaissance; 19th-century sculpture; 20th-century paintings; Chief Curator SABINE CAZENAVE.

Angers

Musée des Beaux-Arts: 14 rue du Musée, 49100 Angers; tel. 2-41-05-38-00; e-mail musees@ville.angers.fr; internet www.angers.fr/mba; f. 1797; housed in 15th-century 'logis Barrault'; paintings of 18th-century French School and 17th-century Dutch and Flemish Schools; sculpture, incl. busts by Houdon; Dir PATRICK LE NOUËNE.

Affiliated Museums:

Galerie David d'Angers: 33 bis rue Toussaint, 49100 Angers; tel. 2-41-05-38-90; e-mail musees@ville.angers.fr; internet www.angers.fr/musees; f. 1984; sited in restored Gothic church; almost all the sculptor's work; Dir and Curator PATRICK LE NOUËNE.

Musée Jean Lurçat et de la Tapisserie Contemporaine: 4 blvd Arago, 49100 Angers; tel. 2-41-24-18-45 (Musée Jean Lurçat); tel. 2-41-24-18-48 (Musée de la Tapisserie Contemporaine); occupies 12th-century Hôpital Saint-Jean; paintings of Jean Lurçat and tapestry.

Musée Pincé: 32 bis rue Lenepveu, 49100 Angers; tel. 2-41-88-94-27; f. 1889; Greek, Roman, Etruscan and Egyptian antiquities; Chinese and Japanese art.

Antibes

Musée Picasso: Château Grimaldi, 06600 Antibes; tel. 4-92-90-54-20; e-mail musee.picasso@ville-antibes.fr; internet www.antibes-juanlespins.com/fr/culture; f. 1948; 230 works by Picasso; colln of modern and contemporary art: Atlan, Miró, Calder, Richier, Ernst, Hartung and others; Nicolas de Staël room with works from Antibes period; sculpture garden; Dir MAURICE FRÉCHURET; publ. catalogues.

Arras

Musée des Beaux-Arts d'Arras: Ancienne Abbaye Saint-Vaast, 22 rue Paul Doumer, 62000 Arras; tel. 3-21-71-26-43; e-mail musee.arras@ville-arras.fr; internet www.musenor.com/gm/gmarras.htm; f. 1825; medieval sculpture, 17th- and 19th-century paintings, porcelain, Gallo-Roman archaeology; Chief Curator STEPHANIE DESCHAMPS.

Arromanches

Exposition Permanente du Débarquement (Permanent Exhibition of the Landings): Place du 6 Juin, 14117 Arromanches; tel. 2-31-22-34-31; e-mail info.arromanches@normandy1944.com; internet www.normandy1944.com; f. 1954; exhibition of the Normandy landings of D-Day, 6th June 1944; comprises artificial harbour and museum of relief maps, working models, photographs, diorama and films.

Avignon

Musée Calvet: 65 rue Joseph Vernet, 84000 Avignon; tel. 4-90-86-33-84; e-mail musee.calvet@wanadoo.fr; internet www.musee-calvet-avignon.com; f. 1810; fine art since 16th century; Dir SYLVAIN BOYER; Curator for Archaeology ODILE CAVALIER.

Musée du Petit Palais: pl. du Palais des Papes, 84000 Avignon; tel. 4-90-86-44-58; e-mail musee.petitpalais@mairie-avignon.com; internet www.petit-palais.org; f. 1976; medieval and Renaissance paintings of the Avignon and Italian Schools, medieval sculpture from Avignon; Curator DOMINIQUE VINGTAIN.

Musée Lapidaire: 27 rue de la République, 84000 Avignon; tel. 4-90-85-75-38; internet www.avignon.fr/fr/culture/musees/lapidaire.php; f. 1933; ancient Egyptian, Greek and Gallo-Roman sculpture; Curator ODILE CAVALIER.

Bayonne

Musée Basque et de l'histoire Bayonne: 37 quai des Corsaires, 64100 Bayonne; tel. 5-59-59-08-98; internet www.musee-basque.com; f. 1922; 4 sections covering the history and folklore of the town of Bayonne, the French Basque country, the Spanish Basque country, and the Basques in the New World; library of 30,000 vols; Dir RAFAEL ZULAIKA; Curator OLIVIER RIBETON; publ. *Bulletin* (2 a year).

Besançon

Musée des Beaux-Arts et d'Archéologie: 1 place de la Révolution–place du Marché, 25000 Besançon; tel. 3-81-87-80-49; e-mail musee-beaux-arts-archeologie@besancon.fr; internet www.musee-arts-besancon.org; f. 1694, moved to present bldgs 1843; Danish (pre- and proto-historic), Egyptian, Greek, Etruscan and Roman antiquities; regional (pre- and proto-historic, Gallo-Roman, early medieval) antiquities; medieval objets d'art; 15th- to 20th-century European paintings (esp. French 18th- to 19th- century), sculpture, ceramics and objets d'art; 15th- to 20th-century drawings in temporary exhibitions; Curator F. SOULIER-FRANÇOIS; Curator F. THOMAS-MAURIN; Curator P. LAGRANGE.

Biot

Musée National Fernand Léger: Chemin du Val de Pome, 06410 Biot; tel. 4-92-91-50-30; internet www.musee-fernandleger.fr; permanent exhibition of paintings, drawings, ceramics.

Blérancourt

Musée Franco-Américain du Château de Blérancourt: Château de Blérancourt, 33 place du Général Leclerc, 02300 Blérancourt; tel. 3-23-39-60-16; e-mail musee.blerancourt@culture.gouv.fr; internet www.museefrancoamericain.fr; f. 1924 to contain collns presented to the State by Mrs Anna Murray Dike, Miss Anne Morgan, and other French and American benefactors, relating to the history of Franco-American relations; the castle, fmrly the ancestral home of the Ducs de Gesvres, is classed as an historical monument; library of 6,500 vols; Curator ANNE DOPFFER; Curator MATHILDE SCHNEIDER.

Bordeaux

CAPC Musée d'Art Contemporain de Bordeaux: Entrepôt Lainé, 7 rue Ferrère, 33000 Bordeaux; tel. 5-56-00-81-50; e-mail capc@mairie-bordeaux.fr; internet www.capc-bordeaux.fr; f. 1984, by 'Capc' assn (f. 1974); temporary exhibitions; permanent collns; education dept for children; library of 60,000 vols, mostly catalogues; Dir Dr CHARLOTTE LAUBARD; publs *Cultural Programme* (4 a year), *Exhibition Catalogue* (4 a year), *RosaB* (2 a year, online).

Musée d'Aquitaine: 20 cours Pasteur, 33000 Bordeaux; tel. 5-56-01-51-00; e-mail musaq@mairie-bordeaux.fr; internet www.mairie-bordeaux.fr; f. 1987; regional prehistory, history and ethnology; ethnographical collection of pieces from Africa and Oceania; library of 20,000 vols; Curator HÉLÈNE LAFONT-COUTURIER.

Musée des Beaux-Arts: Jardin de la Mairie, 20 cours d'Albret, 33000 Bordeaux; tel. 5-56-10-20-56; e-mail musbxa@mairie-bordeaux.fr; internet www.culture.fr/culture/bordeaux; f. 1801; permanent colln of 2,300 paintings, 504 sculptures, 2,370 drawings; archive; library of 25,000 vols, not open to public; Curator GUILLAUME AMBROISE.

Caen

Musée de Normandie: Château de Caen, 14000 Caen; tel. 2-31-30-47-60; e-mail mdn@ville-caen.fr; internet www.musee-de-normandie.caen.fr; f. 1946; history, archaeology and ethnology of Normandy; Dir J.-Y. MARIN; publs *Annales de Normandie* (4 a year), *Publications* (irregular).

Carnac

Musée de Préhistoire: 10 pl. de la Chapelle, 56340 Carnac; tel. 2-97-52-22-04; e-mail contact@museedecarnac.fr; internet www.museedecarnac.com; f. 1881; municipal museum; local prehistory and archaeology; collns from megalithic period; research library; photographic archive (3,000 items); Dir ANNE-ELISABETH RISKINE.

Chantilly

Musée et Château de Chantilly (Musée Condé): Château de Chantilly, 60500 Chantilly; tel. 3-44-27-31-80; e-mail daniele.clergeot@fondationdechantilly.org; internet www.chateaudechantilly.com; f. 1898; paintings, miniatures, furniture, drawings, 70,000 books, 3,000 MSS, etc.; Curator OLIVIER BOSC; publ. *Le Musée Condé* (1 a year).

Compiègne

Musée National du Château de Compiègne: 60200 Compiègne; tel. 3-44-38-47-

02; e-mail chateau.compiegne@culture.gouv.fr; internet www.musee-chateau-compiegne.fr; royal palace of the first kings of France, reconstructed under Louis XV and Louis XVI and partly redecorated under the 1st Empire; furniture of 18th and 19th centuries, mostly 1st Empire period; tapestries of 18th century; collns from the 2nd Empire period; souvenirs of the Empress Eugénie; Chief Curator EMMANUEL STARCKY.

Affiliated Museum:

Musée National de la Voiture et du Tourisme: Palais de Compiègne, 60200 Compiègne; tel. 3-44-38-47-00; e-mail palais.compiegne@culture.gouv.fr; internet www.musee-chateau-compiegne.fr; f. 1927 with the cooperation of the Touring Club de France; old carriages, sedan chairs, survey of devt of the bicycle and the automobile; 180 vehicles; Chief Curator JACQUES PEROT.

Dijon

Musée des Beaux-Arts: Palais des Etats, Cour de Bar, 21000 Dijon; tel. 3-80-74-52-70; e-mail museedesbeauxarts@ville-dijon.fr; internet www.ville-dijon.fr; f. 1787 and housed in the Palace of the Dukes of Burgundy and the Palace of the States of Burgundy; Swiss primitives; paintings of Franco-Flemish School of 15th century and of other French and foreign schools; prints and drawings; sculptures from tombs of the Dukes of Burgundy; marble, ivory, armour; modern art; Granville colln; Chief Curator EMMANUEL STARCKY.

Musée Magnin: 4 rue des Bons-Enfants, 21000 Dijon; tel. 3-80-67-11-10; e-mail musee.magnin@culture.gouv.fr; internet www.musee-magnin.fr; Italian and French paintings from 16th–19th centuries; Curator RÉMI CARIEL.

Fontainebleau

Château de Fontainebleau: 77300 Château de Fontainebleau; tel. 1-60-71-50-70; e-mail contact.chateau-de-fontainebleau@culture.fr; internet www.chateaudefontainebleau.fr; bldgs from 12th–19th centuries; paintings, interior decoration and furniture of the Renaissance, 17th and 18th centuries, 1st and 2nd Empires and 19th century; Dir BERNARD NOTARI.

Giverny

Claude Monet Foundation: 84 rue Claude Monet, 27620 Giverny; tel. 2-32-51-28-21; e-mail contact@fondation-monet.com; internet www.fondation-monet.com; f. 1980 after restoration; consists of Monet's house and garden where he lived from 1883 to 1926; contains Monet's collection of Japanese engravings; Curator GERALD VAN DER KEMP; Sec.-Gen. Mme C. LINDSEY.

Grenoble

Musée de Grenoble: 5 pl. Lavalette, BP 326, 38010 Grenoble Cedex 01; tel. 4-76-63-44-44; e-mail musee-de-grenoble@ville-grenoble.fr; internet www.museedegrenoble.fr; f. 1796; art and antiquities; library of 50,000 vols; Dir GUY TOSATTO.

Langeais

Château de Langeais: 37130 Langeais; tel. 2-47-96-72-60; e-mail contact@chateau-de-langeais.com; internet www.chateau-de-langeais.com; built in 15th century by Louis XI, given to the Institut de France in 1904; furniture and tapestries from the 13th–15th centuries and 15th-century architecture; Admin. SANDRINE DURAND.

Le Havre

Musée des Beaux-Arts 'André Malraux'—MuMa Le Havre: 2 blvd Clemenceau, 76600 Le Havre; tel. 2-35-19-62-62; e-mail contact-muma@lehavre.fr; internet www.muma-lehavre.fr; f. 1845; permanent colln from 14th to 20th century (Boudin, Impressionists, Dufy); Dir ANNETTE HAUDIQUET.

Affiliated Museums:

Espace Maritime et Portuaire du Havre: Quai Frissard, 76600 Le Havre; tel. 2-35-24-51-00; e-mail musees.histoire@ville-lehavre.fr; internet www.ville-lehavre.fr; Le Havre maritime and port history since 1830; Dir C. MAUBANT.

Musée de l'Hôtel Dubocage de Bléville: Rue Jérôme Bellarmato, 76600 Le Havre; tel. 2-35-42-27-90; e-mail musees.histoire@ville-lehavre.fr; internet www.musees-haute-normandie.fr; f. 2010, fmrly Musée de l'Ancien Havre; drawings and documents on the history of Le Havre from 1517 to the present; reserves colln; Dir ELISABETH LEPRÊTRE.

Musée du Prieuré de Graville: Rue Elisée Reclus, 76600 Le Havre; tel. 2-35-24-51-00; e-mail musees.histoire@ville-lehavre.fr; internet www.ville-lehavre.fr; f. 1926; sculpture from the 12th to 18th century; models of old houses; Dir ELIZABETH LEPRÊTRE.

Le Mans

Musée Automobile de la Sarthe: Circuit des 24 Heures du Mans, BP 29254, 72009 Le Mans Cedex 1; tel. 2-43-72-72-24; e-mail musee.automobile.lemans@wanadoo.fr; internet www.sarthe.com/sport/museeauto.htm; f. 1961; cars, cycles and motorcycles; Dir FRANCIS PIQUERA.

Musée de la Reine Bérengère: 9–13 rue de la Reine Bérengère, 72000 Le Mans; tel. 2-43-47-38-51; e-mail musees@ville-lemans.fr; 16th-century architecture, folklore, ceramics, local history; Curator FRANÇOISE CHASERANT.

Musée de Tessé: 2 ave de Paderborn, 72000 Le Mans; tel. 2-43-47-38-51; fine arts, paintings and sculpture, archaeology, Egyptology; Curator FRANÇOISE CHASERANT.

Les Eyzies de Tayac

Musée National de Préhistoire: 1 rue du Musee, BP 7, 24620 Les Eyzies de Tayac; tel. (5) 53-06-45-45; e-mail reservation.prehistoire@culture.gouv.fr; internet www.musee-prehistoire-eyzies.fr; f. 2004; 18,000 exhibited objects, incl. prehistoric carvings; permanent exhibitions on human evolution and the prehistoric people of the Périgord region; Dir JEAN-JACQUES CLEYET-MERLE.

Lille

Palais des Beaux-Arts de Lille (Museum of Fine Arts of Lille): 18 bis rue de Valmy, 59000 Lille; tel. 3-20-06-78-00; e-mail cvilliers@mairie-lille.fr; internet www.pba-lille.fr; f. 1801, closed for renovation in 2006; paintings of Flemish, Italian, Spanish, German, French and Dutch Schools; exceptional colln of drawings; sculpture, ceramics and archaeological exhibits; colln of over 4,000 Art Brut pieces; Chief Curator ALAIN TAPIÉ.

Limoges

Musée Municipal de l'Evêché: Place de la Cathédrale, 87000 Limoges; tel. 5-55-45-98-10; e-mail museveche@ville-limoges.fr; internet www.ville-limoges.fr; f. 1912; paintings, drawings, engravings, sculptures, Limoges enamels, metalwork; Egyptian colln; archaeological and lapidary colln; enamels research centre; library of 7,000 vols; Curator VÉRONIQUE NOTIN.

Musée National Adrien Dubouché: Place Winston Churchill, 87000 Limoges; tel. 5-55-33-08-50; e-mail contact.musee-adriendubouche@culture.gouv.fr; internet www.musee-adriendubouche.fr; f. 1900; ceramics and glass; Curator CHANTAL MESLIN-PERRIER.

Lyons

Musée des Beaux-Arts: 20 place des Terreaux, 69001 Lyons; tel. 4-72-10-17-40; internet www.mba-lyon.fr; f. 1801 and housed in the former Benedictine Abbey of the Dames de Saint-Pierre, built in 1659; the important colln contains paintings of French, Flemish, Dutch, Italian and Spanish Schools, and sections devoted to local painters, modern art, and murals by Puvis de Chavannes; ancient, medieval and modern sculpture; French, Italian, Oriental and Hispano-Moorish ceramics; drawings, prints, furniture, numismatic colln; Egyptian, Greek, Roman and Near and Middle Eastern antiquities; library of 50,000 vols; Chief Curator SYLVIE RAMOND; publs *Cahiers du Musée des Beaux-Arts de Lyon* (1 a year), illustrated guides.

Magny-les-Hameaux

Musée National de Port-Royal des Champs: Route des Granges, 78114 Magny-les-Hameaux; tel. 1-39-30-72-72; e-mail musee.port-royal@culture.gouv.fr; internet www.port-royal-des-champs.eu; f. 1952; history of Port-Royal and Jansenism; ruins of the Abbey of Port-Royale; presented in the house of 'Petites Ecoles' where Racine studied; Curator PHILIPPE LUEZ.

Maisons-Laffitte

Château de Maisons-Laffitte: 78600 Maisons-Laffitte; tel. 1-39-62-01-49; internet www.maisonslaffitte.net; château dates from 1642; contains paintings, sculptures, tapestries; Curator FLORENCE DE LA RONCIÈRE.

Marseilles

Musée Cantini: 19 rue Grignan, 13006 Marseilles; tel. 4-91-54-77-75; e-mail dgac-musee-cantini@mairie-marseille.fr; internet www.mairie-marseille.fr/vivre/culture/musees/cantini.htm; f. 1936; modern art (1900–60); library of 20,000 vols on 20th-century art; Curators NICOLAS CENDO, OLIVIER COUSINOU.

Musée d'Archéologie Méditerranéenne: 2 rue de la Charité, 13002 Marseilles; tel. 4-91-14-58-80; internet www.mairie-marseille.fr/vivre/culture/musees/archeo.htm; f. 1863; Egyptian, Greek, Cypriot, Celto-Ligurian, Etruscan, Roman and Gallo-Roman antiquities; library of 4,500 vols; Curators ANNIE PHILIPPON, BRIGITTE LESCURE.

Affiliated Museum:

Musée des Docks Romains: 28 place Vivaux, 13002 Marseilles; tel. 4-91-91-24-62; internet www.culture.gouv.fr/culture/archeosm/fr/fr-act-mus4.htm; f. 1963; ancient commerce; exhibits include amphorae, ingots and marine archaeology; Curator AGNÈS DURAND.

Musée des Beaux-Arts: Palais Longchamp, Aile Gauche, 7 rue Edouard Stephan, 13004 Marseilles; tel. 4-91-14-59-30; e-mail dgac-musee-beauxarts@mairie-marseille.fr; internet www.mairie-marseille.fr/vivre/culture/musees/boart.htm; f. 1802; paintings (French, Italian, Flemish and German schools); murals by French artists, incl. Corot, Courbet, Daubigny, Daumier, Millet and Puvis de Chavannes; colln of paintings and sculptures by Puget; sculptures by

Daumier and Rodin; Curator MARIE-PAULE VIAL.

Musée de la Marine et de l'Economie de Marseille: Chambre de Commerce et d'Industrie Marseille-Provence, Palais de la Bourse, La Canebière, CS 21856, 13221 Marseille Cedex 1; tel. 4-91-39-33-21; e-mail patrick.boulanger@ccimp.com; internet www.ccimp.com; f. 1932; history of Marseilles and Mediterranean shipping; models of ships, paintings, drawings, plans; 25,000 tape recordings; Nossof, Cantelar and Grimard collns (history of steam ships); Archivist, Chief of Cultural Heritage Dept PATRICK BOULANGER.

Metz

Metz, Musées de La Cour d'Or: 2 rue du Haut Poirier, 57000 Metz; tel. 3-87-68-25-00; e-mail musee@metzmetropole.fr; internet musee.metzmetropole.fr; f. 1839; prehistory, protohistory, arts and popular traditions of northern Lorraine, and natural history collns (not open to public); architecture; fine arts (since 15th century); archaeology and history; military collns (not open to public); library of 5,000 vols, 100 periodicals; Dir CLAUDE VALENTIN.

Montpellier

Musée Atger: Faculté de Médecine, 2 rue de l'Ecole de Médecine, 34000 Montpellier; tel. 4-34-43-35-80; e-mail bu.medecine@montpellier.fr; internet www.biu-montpellier.fr; f. 1813; drawings and paintings of French, Italian and Flemish schools, 16th–18th centuries (Fragonard, Rubens, Tiepolo); Curator HÉLÈNE LORBLANCHET.

Musée Fabre: 13 rue Montpelliéret, 34000 Montpellier; tel. 4-67-14-83-00; e-mail musee.fabre@montpellier-agglo.com; internet museefabre.montpellier-agglo.com; f. 1825 by the painter François-Xavier Fabre; paintings of French (Bazille, Courbet, Delacroix, Géricault, Greuze), Italian, Spanish, Dutch and Flemish Schools; drawings, sculpture (Houdon), furniture, tapestries, porcelain, silver; Dir MICHEL HILAIRE.

Mulhouse

Cité de l'Automobile—Musée National, Collection Schlumpf: 15 rue de l'Epée, 68051 Mulhouse; tel. 3-89-33-23-23; e-mail message@collection-schlumpf.com; internet www.citedelautomobile.com; f. 1982; history of the motor car since 1878; 424 vehicles on display, incl. an important colln of Bugattis; library of 4,500 vols; Dir MARTIN BIJU-DUVAL.

Musée de l'Impression sur Etoffes: 14 rue Jean-Jacques Henner, BP 1468, 68072 Mulhouse; tel. 3-89-46-83-00; e-mail accueil@musee-impression.com; internet www.musee-impression.com; f. 1955; 18th–20th century printed textiles; Curator JAQUELINE JACQUÉ; publ. *L'Imprimé* (2 a year).

Nancray

Musée de Plein Air des Maisons Comtoises: 25360 Nancray; tel. 3-81-55-29-77; e-mail musee@maisons-comtoises.org; internet www.maisons-comtoises.org; f. 1984; folklore of Franche-Comté; 60,000 illustrations of rural architecture; Dir CATHERINE LOUVRIER; publs *Barbizier*, *Revue Régionale d'Ethnologie Comtoise* (1 a year).

Nancy

Musée des Beaux-Arts: Place Stanislas, 54000 Nancy; tel. 3-83-85-30-72; e-mail mbanancy@mairie-nancy.fr; internet www.mairie-nancy.fr; f. 1793; paintings, sculpture, drawings, prints and glass from 15th–20th centuries; Curator BLANDINE CHAVANNE.

Nantes

Musée des Beaux-Arts: 10 rue Georges-Clemenceau, 44000 Nantes; tel. 2-51-17-45-00; e-mail contact@nantes.fr; internet www.nantes.fr/culture/musees-nantais/musee-des-beaux-arts.html; f. 1800; 2,200 paintings; library of 10,000 vols; Curator JEAN AUBERT.

Nice

Direction des Musées de Nice: Palais Masséna, 65 rue de France, 06050 Nice Cedex 1; tel. 4-93-88-11-34; f. 1935; Dir JEAN FRANÇOIS MOZZICONACCI.

Comprises:

Galerie de la Marine: 59 quai des Etats-Unis, 06300 Nice; tel. 4-93-62-37-11; Curator ANNE-MARIE VILLERI.

Galerie des Ponchettes: 77 quai des Etats-Unis, 06300 Nice; tel. 4-93-62-31-24; Curator ANNE-MARIE VILLERI.

Musée d'Archéologie: 160 ave des Arènes de Cimiez, 06000 Nice; tel. 4-93-81-59-57; f. 1989; Curator Mlle D. MOUCHOT.

Musée d'Art et d'Histoire: Palais Masséna, 65 rue de France, 06050 Nice Cedex 1; tel. 4-93-88-11-34; f. 1921; art and history; Dir LUC THEVENON.

Musée d'Art Moderne et d'Art Contemporain: Promenade des Arts, 06300 Nice; tel. 4-93-62-61-62; e-mail mamac@ville-nice.fr; internet www.mamac-nice.org; f. 1990; colln 'Nice à partir des années 60'; nouveaux réalistes, pop art, fluxus, colour field painting; Dir GILBERT PERLEIN.

Musée de Paléontologie–Terra Amata: 25 blvd Carnot, 06300 Nice; tel. 4-93-55-59-93; f. 1976; Curator Mme M. GOUDET.

Musée des Beaux-Arts: 33 ave des Baumettes, 06000 Nice; tel. 4-93-44-50-72; internet www.musee-beaux-arts-nice.org; f. 1928; 18th- and 19th-century painting and sculpture, (Impressionists, Van Dongen); works of Jules Chéret; Dir BÉATRICE DEBRABANDÈRE-DESCAMPS.

Muséum d'Histoire Naturelle: 60 bis blvd Risso, 06300 Nice; tel. 4-97-13-46-80; f. 1823; Curator ALAIN BIDAR.

Musée du Vieux-Logis: 59 ave Saint Barthélémy, 06100 Nice; tel. 4-93-84-44-74; f. 1937; medieval furniture and sculpture; Curator LUC THEVENON.

Musée International d'Art Naïf Anatole Jakovsky: Château Ste Hélène, ave Val-Marie, 06200 Nice; tel. 4-93-71-78-33; f. 1982; Dir ANNE DEVROYE-STILZ.

Musée Matisse: 164 ave des Arènes de Cimiez, 06000 Nice; tel. 4-93-81-08-08; e-mail matisse@nice-coteazur.org; internet www.musee-matisse-nice.org; f. 1963; collns of paintings and sculptures by Henri Matisse; Curator MARIE-THÉRÈSE PULVÉNIS DE SELIGNY.

Musée Naval: Tour Bellanda, Colline du Château, 06300 Nice; tel. 4-93-80-47-61; Curator JEAN WURSTHORN.

Palais Lascaris: 15 rue Droite, 06300 Nice; tel. 4-93-62-72-40; e-mail palais.lascaris@ville-nice.fr; f. 1970; 17th- and 18th-century frescoes, furniture and art; Curator SYLVIE LECAT.

Musée National Message Biblique Marc Chagall: ave du Dr Ménard, 06000 Nice; tel. 4-93-53-87-20; e-mail museecie@rmn.fr; internet www.musee-chagall.fr; f. 1973; permanent colln of the artist's biblical works; library of 3,000 vols; Curator JEAN LACAMBRE.

Nîmes

Carré d'Art-Musée d'Art Contemporain: pl. de la Maison Carrée, 30000 Nîmes Cedex; tel. 4-66-76-35-70; e-mail info@carreartmusee.com; internet carreartmusee.nimes.fr; f. 1993; Dir JEAN-MARC PRÉVOST.

Musée Archéologique: 13 blvd Amiral-Courbet, 30000 Nîmes; tel. 4-66-76-74-80; internet musees.nimes.fr; f. 1823; protohistoric and Gallic and Roman archaeology; library of 6,000 vols; Curator DOMINIQUE DARDE.

Musée d'Histoire Naturelle: 13 blvd Amiral-Courbet, 30033 Nîmes Cedex 9; tel. 4-66-76-73-45; e-mail museum@ville-nimes.fr; internet musees.nimes.fr; f. 1892; library of 3,000 vols; Dir LUC GOMEL.

Musée du Vieux Nîmes: Place aux Herbes, 30000 Nîmes Cedex; tel. 4-66-76-73-70; e-mail musee.vieux-nimes@ville-nimes.fr; internet musees.nimes.fr; f. 1921; local history, folklore and traditional crafts; Curator MARTINE NOUGARÈDE.

Orléans

Musée des Beaux-Arts: 1 rue Fernand Rabier, 45000 Orléans; tel. 2-38-79-21-55; e-mail vgalliot-rateau@ville-orleans.fr; internet www.orleans.fr; f. 1823; sculpture since 16th century; Dutch, Flemish, French, German, Italianand Spanish paintings and pastels (esp. of 18th century); Max Jacob and Gaudier-Brzeska room; French paintings and sculptures from 17th to 19th century; library of 30,000 vols; Curator and Dir BÉNÉDICTE DE DONKER.

Attached Museum:

Musée Historique et Archéologique de l'Orléanais: Hôtel Cabu, Place Abbé Desnoyers, 45000 Orléans; tel. (2) 38-79-21-55; e-mail vgalliot-rateau@ville-orleans.fr; internet www.ville-orleans.fr; f. 1855; Gallo-Roman bronzes from Neuvy-en-Sullias; 17th to 19th century Orléans arts and crafts; the old port and river traffic; Orléans' factories of porcelain, vinegar, sugar, printed calico and imagery; Renaissance sculpture; rooms devoted to Joan of Arc and 19th- century's architectural patrimony drawn by Charles Pensée; Curator BÉNÉDICTE DE DONKER; Muséum Asst CATHERINE LETELLIER-GORGET.

Paris

Centre des Monuments Nationaux (Monum): Hôtel Béthune-Sully, 62 rue Saint-Antoine, 75004 Paris; tel. 1-44-61-21-54; e-mail courrier@monuments-nat.fr; internet www.monum.fr; Dir CHRISTOPHE VALLET.

Cité des Sciences et de l'Industrie: 30 ave Corentin Cariou, 75930 Paris Cedex 19; tel. 1-40-05-70-00; internet www.cite-sciences.fr; f. 1986; located in La Villette complex; permanent exhibitions: the universe, the earth, the environment, space, life, communication, etc.; multimedia public library (300,000 vols, 2,700 periodicals, 4,000 films, 1,300 educational software discs), history of science multimedia library, the Louis Braille room for the visually handicapped, Science Newsroom; Pres. GÉRARD THÉRY.

Galerie Nationale du Jeu de Paume: 1 pl. de la Concorde, 75008 Paris; tel. 1-47-03-12-50; e-mail accueil@jeudepaume.org; internet www.jeudepaume.org; f. 1991; devoted to temporary exhibitions of contemporary art; Dir DANIEL ABADIE.

Galeries Nationales du Panthéon Bouddhique: 19 ave d'Iéna, 75116 Paris; tel. 1-40-73-88-00; Chinese and Japanese art; Curator JEAN-FRANÇOIS JARRIGE.

Les Arts Décoratifs: 107 rue de Rivoli, 75001 Paris; tel. 1-44-55-57-50; e-mail webmaster@lesartsdecoratifs.fr; internet www.lesartsdecoratifs.fr; f. 1864; library of 120,000 vols, 2,000 periodicals, 40,000 sale catalogues since 18th century; Pres. HÉLÈNE DAVID-WEILL; Gen. Man. SOPHIE DURRLEMAN; Dir of Museums BÉATRICE SALMON.

Affiliated Museums:

Musée de la Mode et du Textile: Les Arts Décoratifs, 107 rue de Rivoli, 75001 Paris; tel. 1-44-55-57-50; e-mail webmaster@lesartsdecoratifs.fr; internet www.lesartsdecoratifs.fr; f. 1985; fashion, textiles and accessories; Dir BÉATRICE SALMON.

Musée de la Publicité: Les Arts Décoratifs, 107 rue de Rivoli, 75001 Paris; tel. 1-44-55-57-50; e-mail webmaster@lesartsdecoratifs.fr; internet www.lesartsdecoratifs.fr; non-permanent exhibitions of posters, television, film and radio commercials; interactive multimedia library; Dir BÉATRICE SALMON.

Musée des Arts Décoratifs: Les Arts Décoratifs, 107 rue de Rivoli, 75001 Paris; tel. 1-44-55-57-50; e-mail webmaster@lesartsdecoratifs.fr; internet www.lesartsdecoratifs.fr; f. 1883; colln from Middle Ages to the present: woodwork, sculpture, tapestries, textiles, jewels, ceramics, furniture, painting, gold and silver work, glass; library of 100,000 vols, 1,500 periodicals; Dir BÉATRICE SALMON.

Musée Nissim de Camondo: Les Arts Décoratifs, 63 rue de Monceau, 75008 Paris; tel. 1-53-89-06-40; e-mail webmaster@lesartsdecoratifs.fr; internet www.lesartsdecoratifs.fr; bequeathed by Count Moïse de Camondo, who collected unique 18th-century objects in his Hôtel Parc Monceau; Dir BÉATRICE SALMON; Chief Curator SYLVIE LEGRAND-ROSSI.

Maison de Balzac: 47 rue Raynouard, 75016 Paris; tel. 1-55-74-41-80; internet www.balzac.paris.fr; f. 1960; documents relating to life and work of Honoré de Balzac; first edns and autographed letters; comprehensive range of work from the romantic period; library of 15,000 vols; Curator YVES GAGNEUX.

Maison de Victor Hugo: 6 place des Vosges, 75004 Paris; tel. 1-42-72-10-16; e-mail maisonsvictorhugo@paris.fr; internet www.musee.hugo.paris.fr; f. 1903; personal belongings, correspondence, first editions, drawings by Victor Hugo; library of 10,000 vols, 6,000 pamphlets; Curator DANIELLE MOLINARI.

Musée Astronomique de l'Observatoire de Paris: 61 ave de l'Observatoire, 75014 Paris; f. 1667; astronomical instruments of the 16th, 17th, 18th and 19th centuries; statues and pictures of celebrated astronomers.

Musée Carnavalet—Histoire de Paris: 23 rue de Sévigné, 75003 Paris; tel. 1-44-59-58-58; internet www.carnavalet.paris.fr; f. 1880; Paris and its history from prehistoric times; depts of archaeology, graphic arts, furniture, numismatics, painting, architectural models, sculpture; Chief Curator JEAN-MARC LÉRI.

Musée Cernuschi: 7 ave Vélasquez, 75008 Paris; tel. 1-53-96-21-50; internet www.cernuschi.paris.fr; f. 1896; Asian art; Dir CHRISTINE SHIMIZU.

Musée Cognacq-Jay: 8 rue Elzévir, 75003 Paris; tel. 1-40-27-07-21; internet www.cognacq-jay.paris.fr; f. 1929; 18th century works of art, French and English paintings, pastels, sculptures, porcelain, furniture, etc.; Dir and Curator ROSE-MARIE MOUSSEAUX.

Musée d'Art Moderne de la Ville de Paris: 9 rue Gaston de Saint-Paul, 75116 Paris; located at: 11 ave du Président Wilson, 75116 Paris; tel. 1-53-67-40-00; internet www.mam.paris.fr; f. 1961; modern and contemporary art; Curator FABRICE HERGOTT.

Musée d'Ennery: 59 ave Foch, 75116 Paris; tel. 1-45-53-57-96; f. 1903; 17th- to 19th-century Far East decorative arts; closed for renovation; Curator JEAN-FRANÇOIS JARRIGE.

Musée d'Histoire Contemporaine: Hôtel National des Invalides, 129 rue de Grenelle, 75007 Paris; tel. 1-44-42-42-44; e-mail mhc@bdic.fr; internet www.bdic.fr/page.php?id_page=125; f. 1914; attached to Bibliothèque de Documentation Internationale Contemporaine (*q.v.*); 400,000 documents (paintings, engravings, posters, cartoons, etc.); 800,000 photographs and postcards; Curator LAURENT GERVEREAU.

Musée d'Orsay: 62 rue de Lille, 75343 Paris; tel. 1-40-49-48-00; internet www.musee-orsay.fr; f. 1986; works from the second half of the 19th century and early 20th century: paintings and pastels, sculptures, art objects, photographs, also plans, sketches, etc.; audiovisual information, database, cultural service, exhibitions and dossier-exhibitions, cinema, lectures, concerts; Pres. SERGE LEMOINE.

Musée de l'Air et de l'Espace: BP 173, Aéroport du Bourget, 4 93352 Le Bourget Cedex; tel. 1-49-92-71-99; internet www.mae.org; f. 1919; aeronautics, representative colln of aircraft; library of 40,000 vols; Dir-Gen. GERARD FELDZER; publ. *Pégase* (4 a year).

Musée de l'Armée: Hôtel des Invalides, 129 rue de Grenelle, 75007 Paris; tel. 1-44-42-38-77; e-mail accueil-ma@invalides.org; internet www.invalides.org; f. 1905; collns of artillery, arms, armour, uniforms, flags; history of French Army from its origin to present day; Napoleon's tomb; Second World War; library of 50,000 vols, 60,000 prints, 74,400 photographs; Dir B. DEVAUX; publ. *Revue de la Société des Amis du Musée de l'Armée* (2 a year).

Musée de l'Histoire de France: Centre historique des Archives nationales, 60 rue des Francs-Bourgeois, 75141 Paris Cedex 03; tel. 1-40-27-60-96; e-mail infomusee.archivesnationales@culture.gouv.fr; f. 1867; frequent exhibitions showing original documents from the Nat. Archives tracing the principal events in the history of France; also historical objects and iconography; Dir ISABELLE NEUSCHWANDER; Curator PIERRE FOURNIÉ.

Musée de l'Homme: Palais de Chaillot, place du Trocadéro, 75116 Paris; tel. 1-44-05-72-03; e-mail koukoua@mnhn.fr; internet www.museedelhomme.fr; f. 1878; attached to the Muséum National d'Histoire Naturelle (*q.v.*); ethnography, anthropology, prehistory; also a research and education centre; library of 400,000 vols, 5,000 periodicals, 1,000 microfiches; Profs BERNARD DUPAIGNE, ANDRÉ LANGANEY, HENRY DE LUMLEY.

Musée de l'Orangerie: Jardin des Tuileries, 75001 Paris; tel. 1-44-50-43-00; e-mail musee.orangerie@culture.gouv.fr; internet www.musee-orangerie.fr; f. 1927; permanent exhibition of the 'Nymphéas' (Water Lilies) murals by Claude Monet, and Jean Walter et Paul Guillaume colln (Cézanne, Renoir, Rousseau, Picasso, Matisse, Derain, Modigliani, Soutine, Utrillo); Dir EMMANUEL BRÉON.

Musée de la Marine: Palais de Chaillot, 17 place du Trocadéro, 75116 Paris; tel. 1-53-65-69-69; internet www.musee-marine.fr; f. 1827; colln of models and paintings of the navy; oceanographic research; library: 50,000 documents, 190,000 photographs; Dir Rear-Adm. GEORGES PRUD'HOMME; publs *Neptunia* (4 a year), catalogues.

Musée de la Monnaie: Monnaie de Paris, 11 quai de Conti, 75270 Paris Cedex 06; tel. 1-40-46-55-60-10; e-mail musee@monnaiedeparis.fr; internet www.monnaiedeparis.fr; f. 1771; closed since July 2010; visits to manufacturers' workshops closed; collns of coins, medals, drawings, paintings, old machines, engravings and stained glass windows.

Musée de la Poste: 34 blvd de Vaugirard, 75015 Paris; tel. 1-42-79-24-24; e-mail reservation.dnmp@laposte.fr; internet www.ladressemuseedelaposte.fr; f. 1971; colln incl. material on historic postal services and transport; Curator CHAPPE.

Musée des Arts et Métiers: 292 rue St Martin, 75141 Paris Cedex 03; 60 rue Réaumur, 75003 Paris; tel. 1-53-01-82-00; e-mail musee@cnam.fr; internet www.arts-et-metiers.net; f. 1794; evolution of industrial technology from 16th century to the present; Dir SERGE CHAMBAUD.

Musée des Monuments Français: Palais de Chaillot, 1 place du Trocadéro, 75116 Paris; tel. 1-44-05-39-10; internet www.citechaillot.fr/musee.php; f. 1882; casts of portions of monuments and sculptures from beginning of Christianity to 20th century; architectural models; library of 10,000 works on history of art, 200,000 photographs, colln of scale reproductions of murals of the Middle Ages and materials connected with building and decoration; Dir GUY COGEVAL; publ. *Guides*.

Musée des Plans-Reliefs: Hôtel National des Invalides, 75007 Paris; tel. 1-45-51-95-05; internet www.museedesplansreliefs.culture.fr; f. 1668; Dir MAX POLONOVSKI.

Musée du Louvre: 75058 Paris Cedex 01; tel. 1-40-20-50-50; e-mail info@louvre.fr; internet www.louvre.fr; f. 1793; Gen. Dir HENRI LOYRETTE; depts and curators: Oriental antiquities (ANNIE CAUBET), Egyptian antiquities (CHRISTIANE ZIEGLER), Greek, Etruscan and Roman antiquities (ALAIN PASQUIER), Islamic art (FRANÇIS RICHARD), sculpture (JEAN-RENÉ GABORIT), objets d'art (DANIEL ALCOUFFE), paintings (VINCENT POMAREDE), drawings and prints (FRANÇOISE VIATTE).

Musée du Luxembourg: 19 rue de Vaugirard, 75006 Paris; tel. 1-43-54-87-71; e-mail info@museeduluxembourg.fr; internet www.museeduluxembourg.fr; f. 1750; hosts temporary exhibitions, according to a programme decided by the Min. of Culture and Communications and the Senate; Pres. of Senate CHRISTIAN PONCELET.

Musée du Petit Palais: 5 ave Dutuit, 75008 Paris; ave Winston Churchill, 75008 Paris; tel. 1-53-43-40-00; internet petitpalais.paris.fr; f. 1902; paintings, sculptures and works of art from antiquity to 1925; organizes visits, concerts, lectures, literary events, screenings, shows; Dir GILLES CHAZAL.

Musée Gustave Moreau: 14 rue de la Rochefoucauld, 75009 Paris; tel. 1-48-74-38-50; e-mail info@musee-moreau.fr; internet www.musee-moreau.fr; f. 1903 from a bequest by the painter Gustave Moreau of his house and contents, including paintings, watercolours, sketches, wax sculptures and designs; Curator GENEVIÈVE LACAMBRE.

Musée Jacquemart-André: 158 blvd Haussmann, 75008 Paris; tel. 1-45-62-11-59; e-mail message@musee-jacquemart-andre.com; internet www.musee-jacquemart-andre.com; f. 1912; painting, sculpture, ceramics, tapestry and furniture from Renaissance to 18th century; Dir ALAIN SCHIEDÉ.

Musée Marmottan: 2 rue Louis Boilly, 75016 Paris; tel. 1-44-96-50-33; e-mail marmottan@marmottan.com; internet www.marmottan.com; f. 1932; Primitives, Renaissance, Empire and Impressionists; Wildenstein Colln of medieval miniatures; permanent exhibition 'Monet et ses Amis'; affiliated to the Académie des Beaux-Arts-Fondation Rouart; Dir JEAN-MARIE GRANIER.

Musée National d'Art Moderne: 75191 Paris Cedex 04; tel. 1-44-78-12-33; internet www.centrepompidou.fr; attached to Centre National d'Art et de Culture Georges-Pompidou; painting since beginning of 20th century, sculpture, architecture, design, new media, drawings, photographs, art films; Dir ALFRED PACQUEMENT.

Muséum National d'Histoire Naturelle: see under State Colleges and Institutes.

Musée National de la Légion d'Honneur et des Ordres de Chevalerie: Hôtel de Salm, 2 rue de la Légion d'Honneur, 75007 Paris; tel. 1-40-62-84-25; e-mail musee.gclh@free.fr; internet www.legiondhonneur.fr; f. 1925; contains histories of National Orders from the Middle Ages until the present and Awards of all countries: unique colln of decorations, costumes, arms, documents, etc.; also colln and documents relating to Napoleon I; Centre de Documentation Int. de l'Histoire des Ordres et des Décorations; Dir-Curator ANNE DE CHEFDEBIEN.

Musée National des Arts Asiatiques Guimet: 6 pl. d'Iéna, 75116 Paris; tel. 1-56-52-53-00; internet www.guimet.fr; f. 1889; Asiatic Dept of Nat. Museums; art, archaeology, religions, history and music of India, Central Asia, Tibet, Afghanistan, China, Korea, Japan, Cambodia, Thailand, Burma, Viet Nam, Indonesia; library of 100,000 vols; Chief Curator Prof. SOPHIE MAKARIOU; Head Librarian CRISTINA CRAMEROTTI; publs *Annales*, *Arts Asiatiques*.

Musée National des Arts d'Afrique et d'Océanie: 293 ave Daumesnil, 75012 Paris; tel. 1-44-74-84-80; f. 1931 as Musée des Colonies, 1935 Musée de la France d'Outre-Mer, current name adopted 1960; exhibits from Maghreb, Africa and the Pacific Islands; tropical aquarium; temporary exhibitions; library: c. 5,000 vols, 160 periodicals; Dir GERMAIN VIATTE.

Musée National des Arts et Traditions Populaires: 6 ave du Mahatma Gandhi, 75116 Paris; tel. 1-44-17-60-00; f. 1937; 142,000 objects; library: 90,000 books, 2,000 periodicals; 281,000 photographic documents, 70,000 tape records; Curator MICHEL COLARDELLE; publs *Architecture rurale française*, *Archives d'Ethnologie Française*, *Catalogues des Expositions*, *Ethnologie française* (4 a year), *Guides Ethnologiques*, *Mobilier traditionnel français*, *Récits et contes populaires*.

Musée National du Moyen Âge/Musée de Cluny: 6 pl. Paul Painlevé, 75005 Paris; tel. 1-53-73-78-00; e-mail contact.musee-moyenage@culture.gouv.fr; internet www.musee-moyenage.fr; f. 1843; everyday life and fine and decorative arts of the Middle Ages; medieval art; sculptures, illuminated MSS, stained-glass panels, goldsmith work, furniture and tapestries; Lady and the Unicorn tapestries set; Dir ELISABETH DELAHAYE.

Musée Picasso: 5 rue de Thorigny, 75003 Paris; tel. 1-42-71-25-21; internet www.musee-picasso.fr; f. 1985 from a colln begun in 1979; traces the evolution of Picasso's art; 251 paintings, 160 sculptures, 107 ceramics, 1,500 drawings and engravings; library: c. 2,000 vols on Picasso and his world; Dir ANNE BALDASSARI; Chief Curator GÉRARD RÉGNIER; publs catalogues, guides.

Musée Rodin: Hôtel Biron, 79 rue de Varenne, 75007 Paris; tel. 1-44-18-61-10; internet www.musee-rodin.fr; f. 1919; sculpture and drawings by Rodin and objects from his collns; Dir CATHERINE CHEVILLOT.

Palais de la Découverte: ave Franklin D. Roosevelt, 75008 Paris; tel. 1-56-43-20-21; internet www.palais-decouverte.fr; f. 1937 as a scientific centre for the popularization of science; depts of mathematics, astronomy, physics, chemistry, biology, medicine, earth sciences; also incl. a Planetarium and cinema; library of 7,000 vols; Dir JACK GUICHARD; publ. *Revue*.

Palais du Cinéma: Palais de Tokyo, 24 rue Hamelin, 75116 Paris; tel. 1-45-53-74-74; exhibitions concerning motion pictures; motion picture theatres; library and film archive; Dir XAVIER NORTH.

Palais Galliera Musée de la Mode de la Ville de Paris: 10 ave Pierre Ier de Serbie, 75116 Paris; tel. 1-56-52-86-46; e-mail dominique.revellino@paris.fr; internet www.palaisgalliera.paris.fr; f. 1977; temporary exhibitions of French costumes and accessories from 1725 to the present day; library of 10,000 vols; Dir OLIVIER SAILLARD; Librarian DOMINIQUE REVELLINO.

Pavillon de l'Arsenal: 21 blvd Morland, 75004 Paris; tel. 1-42-76-33-97; e-mail infopa@pavillon-arsenal.com; internet www.pavillon-arsenal.com; f. 1988; information and documentation centre on urban planning and architecture; permanent exhibition on Paris; temporary exhibitions, photo library, educational facilities, etc.; Dir Mme DOMINIQUE ALBA; publ. catalogues.

Pau

Musée Bernadotte: 8 rue Tran, 64000 Pau; tel. 5-59-27-48-42; internet musee.ville-pau.fr/infospratiques/liens/bernadotte; f. 1935; pictures and documents tracing the career of Jean Baptiste Bernadotte, Marshal under Napoleon, later King of Sweden; Swedish pictures; Curator PH. COMTE; publ. *Bulletin* (1 a year).

Musée des Beaux-Arts: rue Mathieu Lalanne, 64000 Pau; tel. 5-59-27-33-02; e-mail museedesbeauxarts.pau@laposte.net; internet musee.ville-pau.fr; f. 1864; pictures from French, Flemish, Dutch, English, Italian and Spanish schools; contemporary artists; sculptures, engravings and drawings; numismatic collections; Curator GUILLAUME AMBROISE.

Musée National du Château de Pau: 64000 Pau; tel. 5-59-82-38-02; e-mail olivier.pouvreau@culture.gouv.fr; internet www.musee-chateau-pau.fr; f. 1927; 16th- and 17th-century colln of tapestries; state apartments of Louis-Philippe I and Napoleon III; exhibition on the reign of King Henry IV; engravings, drawings; library and research facility (Centre Jacques de Laprade) for students of history, literature and history of art; Curator PAUL MIRONNEAU; publ. *Bulletin* (4 a year).

Musée Régional Béarnais: 64000 Pau; tel. 5-59-27-07-36; a colln relating to the Bearnese country.

Perpignan

Casa Pairal, Musée Catalan des Arts et Traditions Populaires: Mairie de Perpignan, BP 931, 66931 Perpignan Cedex; located at: Le Castillet, Place de Verdun, 66000 Perpignan; tel. 4-68-35-42-05; internet www.mairie-perpignan.fr; f. 1963; ethnography, folklore and anthropology of the Catalan region; Curator JACQUES-GASPARD DELONCLE.

Poitiers

Conservation des Musées de Poitiers: 3 bis rue Jean-Jaurès, 86000 Poitiers; tel. 5-49-41-07-53; e-mail musees.poitiers@alienor.org; internet www.musees-poitiers.org; f. 1794; library of 10,000 vols, 50 periodicals; Curator MARIE-CHRISTINE PLANCHARD; Curator MARYSE REDIEN; Curator MICHEL REROLLE; Curator PHILIPPE BATA.

Attached Museums:

Baptistère Saint-Jean: rue Jean-Jaurès, 86000 Poitiers; c/o Office de Tourisme de Poitiers, 45 pl. Charles De Gaulle, 86009 Poitiers; tel. 5-49-41-21-24; e-mail accueil@ot-poitiers.fr; internet www.ot-poitiers.fr; f. 1836; Merovingian archaeology.

Hypogée des Dunes: 101 rue du Père de la Croix, 86000 Poitiers; f. 1909; 7th–8th-century Merovingian archaeology.

Musée Rupert de Chièvres: 9 rue Victor Hugo, 86000 Poitiers; tel. 5-49-41-07-53; f. 1887; reconstruction of a 19th-century collector's private house; pre-1800 paintings, furniture, objets d'art.

Musée Sainte-Croix: 3 bis rue Jean-Jaurès, 86000 Poitiers; tel. 5-49-41-07-53; e-mail musees@mairie-poitiers.fr; f. 1974; fine arts, history of Poitou (archaeological, ethnographical collections, sculpture and paintings post 1800).

Reims

Musée des Beaux-Arts: 8 rue Chanzy, 51100 Reims; tel. 3-26-35-36-00; e-mail sylvie.leibel@mairie-reims.fr; internet www.ville-reims.fr/fr/culture/a-visiter/musee-des-beaux-arts; f. 1795; paintings (esp. French School, 17th-century Le Nain, and 19th-century Corot–Delacroix), and Cranach drawings; 15th- and 16th-century 'Toiles Peintes'; colln of ceramics; Curator DAVID LIOT.

Musée Saint-Remi: 53 rue Simon, 51100 Reims; tel. 3-26-35-36-30; internet www.ville-reims.fr/fr/culture/a-visiter/musee-saint-remi; the old Abbey of St Remi (12th to 18th centuries); Prehistoric, Celtic, Gallo-Roman, Romanesque and Gothic antiquities and sculptures; tapestries of St-Remi life (1530); old weapons; Chief Curator MARC BOUXIN.

Rennes

Musée de Bretagne: 46 blvd Magenta, CS 51138, 35011 Rennes Cedex; tel. 2-23-40-66-70; internet www.musee-bretagne.fr; f. 1960; geology, prehistory, Armorica at the Roman period, medieval art, historical documents, popular art, furniture, 19th-century costumes, contemporary regional art and history; Dir PASCAL AUMASSON.

Musée des Beaux-Arts: 20 quai Emile Zola, 35000 Rennes; tel. 2-99-28-55-85; e-mail museebeauxarts@ville-rennes.fr; internet www.mbar.org; f. 1799; paintings, drawings, engravings, sculpture of French and foreign Schools from the 15th century; archaeology; library of 35,000 vols; Curator FRANCIS RIBEMONT.

Rouen

Musées de la Ville de Rouen: 1 pl. Restout, 76000 Rouen; tel. 2-35-71-28-40; e-mail musees@rouen.fr; internet www.rouen-musees.com.

Attached Museums:

Musée de la Céramique: 1 rue Faucon, 76000 Rouen; tel. 2-35-07-31-74; f. 1983; 16th–19th-century ceramics.

Musée de la Ferronnerie: rue Jacques Villon, 76000 Rouen; tel. 2-35-88-42-92; f. 1922; 3rd–19th-century ironwork; Curator MARIE PESSIOT.

Musée des Beaux-Arts: Esplanade Marcel Duchamp, 76000 Rouen; tel. 2-35-71-28-40; f. 1801; paintings, drawings, sculpture, decorative art; Dir LAURENT SALOMÉ.

Rueil-Malmaison

Musée National des Châteaux de Malmaison et de Bois-Préau: 92500 Rueil-Malmaison; tel. 1-41-29-05-55; internet www.chateau-malmaison.fr; f. 1906; historical colln of Napoleon I and Joséphine; Dir AMAURY LEFEBURE.

St-Denis

Musée d'art et d'histoire: 22 bis rue Gabriel Péri, 93200 St-Denis; tel. 1-42-43-05-10; e-mail musee@ville-saint-denis.fr; internet www.musee-saint-denis.fr; f. 1901; located in a disused 17th-century Carmelite monastery; collns: medieval archaeology and ceramics; history and memorabilia from the monastery and Madame Louise; the Paris Commune; paintings by Albert André; Paul Eluard and Francis Jourdain collns; remains of the old hospital; documentation room for researchers and students; Curator SYLVIE GONZALEZ.

St-Etienne

Musée d'Art et d'Industrie: pl. Louis Comte, 42000 St-Etienne; tel. 4-77-49-73-00; e-mail museemai@mairie-st-etienne.fr; internet www.mairie-st-etienne.fr; f. 1833, at Palais des Arts since 1850; armaments, fabrics, bicycles; Curator NADINE BESSE.

Attached Museums:

Musée d'Art Moderne de Saint-Etienne Métropole: La Terrasse, BP 80241 42006 St-Etienne, Cedex 1; tel. 4-77-79-52-52; e-mail mam@agglo-st-etienne.fr; internet www.mam-st-etienne.fr; f. 1987; colln of modern and contemporary art; temporary exhibitions; library of 40,000 vols; Gen. Dir Dr LORAND HEGYI.

Musée de la Mine: 3 blvd Franchet d'Esperey, 42000 St-Etienne; tel. 4-77-43-83-23; e-mail museemin@mairie-st-etienne.fr; mining and industrial museum on the site of a former working mine.

St-Germain-en-Laye

Musée des Antiquités Nationales: Château, BP 3030, 78103 St-Germain-en-Laye Cedex; tel. 1-39-10-13-00; internet www.musee-antiquitesnationales.fr; f. 1862; prehistoric, Bronze Age, Celtic, Gallo-Roman and Merovingian antiquities, comparative archaeology; library of 25,000 vols; Dir PATRICK PÉRIN; publ. *Antiquités nationales* (1 a year).

St-Malo

Musée de St-Malo: Château de St-Malo, 35400 St-Malo; tel. 2-99-40-71-57; e-mail musee@ville-saint-malo.fr; f. 1950; history of Saint-Malo and temporary exhibitions; Curator PH. PETOUT.

Attached Museum:

Musée International du Long Cours Cap-Hornier: Tour Solidor, St-Servan, 35400 St-Malo; tel. 2-99-40-71-58; e-mail musee@ville-saint-malo.fr; f. 1969; int. history of sailing around the world since 16th century; Curator PH. PETOUT.

St-Paul-de-Vence

Fondation Maeght: 06570 St-Paul-de-Vence; tel. 4-93-32-81-63; e-mail contact@fondation-maeght.com; internet www.fondation-maeght.com; f. 1964; modern paintings and sculpture incl. Bonnard, Braque, Giacometti, Miró and Calder; work by contemporary artists; library of 40,000 vols on modern arts and daily films on art and artists; Dir ISABELLE MAEGHT.

St-Tropez

Annonciade, Musée de St-Tropez: pl. Georges Grammont, 83990 St-Tropez; tel. 4-94-17-84-10; e-mail annonciade@ville-sainttropez.fr; internet www.amis-annonciade.fr; f. 1955; French paintings 1890–1950 Pointillism, nabi, fauvism and independant art during the two world wars; Curator JEAN-PAUL MONERY.

Saumur

Château Musée: Hôtel de Ville, 49408 Saumur Cedex; tel. 2-41-40-24-40; e-mail chateau.musee@ville-saumur.fr; internet www.ville-saumur.fr; f. 1829, and reorganized 1960; local archaeology, the Comte Charles Lair colln of decorative arts, incl. tapestries, furniture, wood carvings, liturgical ornaments; fine porcelain of 16th–18th centuries; Curator JACQUELINE MONGELLAZ.

Sceaux

Parc et musée de l'Ile de France: Château de Sceaux, Domaine de Sceaux, 92330 Sceaux; tel. 1-41-87-29-50; e-mail museeidf@cg92.fr; internet www.chateau-sceaux.fr; f. 1935; old and modern paintings, sculpture, engravings, furniture, decorative art, tapestries, history and drawings of the environs of Paris; documentation centre on the Paris region; educational services; multimedia centre; annexes: Orangerie and Pavillon de l'Aurore, les Ecuries (Parc de Sceaux); Dir DOMINQUE BREME.

Sèvres

Musée National de Céramique: place de la Manufacture, 92310 Sèvres; tel. 1-41-14-04-20; e-mail musee.sevres@culture.gouv.fr; f. 1824; ancient and modern ceramic art; Curator ANTOINETTE HALLÉ; publ. *Revue de la Société des Amis du Musée National de Céramique* (1 a year).

Soissons

Musée Municipal: 2 rue de la Congrégation, 02200 Soissons; tel. 3-23-93-30-50; e-mail musee@ville-soissons.fr; internet www.musee-soissons.org; f. 1857; antiquities, medieval sculpture, paintings since 17th century, local history and protohistory; archaeology of the Aisne Valley from Neolithic to Middle Ages; Curator DOMINIQUE ROUSSEL.

Attached Museum:

Musée Arsenal: Site de l'abbaye Saint-Jean-des-Vignes, rue Saint Jean, 02200 Soissons; tel. 3-23-53-42-40; e-mail musee@ville-soissons.fr; internet www.musee-soissons.org; temporary exhibition space in the Arsenal; Dir DOMINIQUE ROUSSEL.

Strasbourg

Palais Rohan: 2 pl. du Château, 67076 Strasbourg Cedex; tel. 3-88-52-50-00; internet www.musees-strasbourg.org.

Attached Museums:

Musée Archéologique: c/o Palais Rohan, 2 pl. du Château, 67000 Strasbourg; tel. 3-88-52-50-00; f. 1856; prehistoric, Celtic, Gallo-Roman and Merovingian collns; results of excavations in Alsace; Curator BERNADETTE SCHNITZLER.

Musée des Arts Décoratifs et Appartements Historiques: c/o Palais Rohan, 2 place du Château, 67076 Strasbourg Cedex; tel. 3-88-52-50-00; f. 1883; furniture from 18th and early 19th centuries; French paintings; ceramics; silver objects; musical instruments; wrought-iron and tin; Curator ETIENNE MARTIN.

Musée des Beaux-Arts: c/o Palais Rohan, 2 pl. du Château, 67000 Strasbourg; tel. 3-88-52-50-00; internet www.musees.strasbourg.eu/index.php?page=musee-des-beaux-arts; f. 1801; French and foreign paintings: Old Masters, art from 14th–19th centuries, Italian, Spanish, Flemish, Dutch and French schools; Chief Curator DOMINIQUE JACQUOT.

Toulouse

Musée des Augustins: 21 rue de Metz, 31000 Toulouse; tel. 5-61-22-21-82; e-mail augustins@mairie-toulouse.fr; internet www.augustins.org; f. 1793 and housed in the former Augustine Convent, of which parts date from the 14th and 15th centuries; Roman and Gothic sculptures, 16th–19th-century local and foreign paintings; Curator ALAIN DAGUERRE DE HUREAUX.

Tours

Musée de la Société Archéologique de Touraine: Hôtel Gouin, 25 rue du Commerce, 37000 Tours; tel. 2-47-66-22-32; Gallic and Roman archaeology, medieval and 16th century sculptures, prehistoric artefacts; iconography of Tours, 18th- to 19th- century pottery.

Musée des Beaux-Arts: 18 place François-Sicard, 37000 Tours; tel. 2-47-05-68-73; e-mail musee-beauxarts@ville-tours.fr; internet www.musees.regioncentre.fr; f. 1793 and moved in 1910 to the fmr Archbishop's palace; paintings by Mantegna, Rembrandt, Rubens, Vignon, Lancret, Boucher, Delacroix, Degas, Debré; sculpture by Le Moyne, Houdon, Bourdelle, Davidson, Calder; furniture, tapestries and objets d'art; library of 15,000 vols; Curator SOPHIE JOIN-LAMBERT.

Affiliated Museums:

Château d'Azay-le-Ferron: 36290 Azay-le-Ferron; tel. 2-54-39-20-06; e-mail contact@chateau-azay-le-ferron.com; bldgs, objets d'art and furniture of the 15th–19th centuries; Curator PHILIPPE LE LEYZOUR.

Musée Saint-Martin: 3 rue Rapin, 37000 Tours; tel. 2-47-64-48-87; e-mail museebeauxarts-secretariat@ville-tours.fr; internet www.mba.tours.fr; f. 1990; contains colln of souvenirs of St Martin; carved marbles, fragments from the tomb inscription as it was in the construction raised c. 470 by Perpetuus, Romanesque wall painting; Curator SOPHIE JOIN-LAMBERT.

Musée des Vins de Touraine: 16 rue Nationale (parvis Saint-Julien), 37000 Tours; tel. 2-47-61-07-93; f. 1975; Curator LAURENT BASTARD.

Musée du Compagnonnage: 8 rue Nationale, 37000 Tours; tel. 2-47-61-07-93; e-mail museecompagnonnage@ville-tours.fr; f. 1968; archives and historical masterpieces; Curator LAURENT BASTARD.

Ungersheim

Ecomusée d'Alsace: BP 71, 68190 Ungersheim; tel. 3-89-74-44-74; e-mail contact@ecoparcs.com; internet www.ecomusee-alsace.com; f. 1984 by the Asscn Maisons Paysannes d'Alsace to safeguard the rural architecture of Alsace; an open-air museum comprising a reconstituted village of 70 cottages, showing life in olden days with a baker, an oil-mill, a blacksmith, a clogmaker, and a sawmill working on site; nature walks, seminars; library of 950 vols, 4,000 drawings and reliefs, 25,000 photographs, video cassettes; Pres. MARC GRODWOHL.

Vaison-la-Romaine

Musée Archéologique Théo Desplans: Colline de Puymin, 84110 Vaison-la-Romaine; tel. 4-90-36-50-48; e-mail reservegroupe@vaison-la-romaine.com; internet www.vaison-la-romaine.com; f.

1920, present site 1975; archaeological colln from excavations at Vaison; Curator CHRISTINE BEZIN.

Valenciennes

Musée des Beaux-Arts: blvd Watteau, 59300 Valenciennes; tel. 3-27-22-57-20; e-mail mba@ville-valenciennes.fr; internet www.valenciennes.fr; painting, sculpture, archaeology, etc.; Dir E. DELAPIERRE.

Vallauris

Musée National Picasso 'La Guerre et la Paix': place de la Libération, 06220 Vallauris; tel. 4-93-64-71-83; internet www.musee-picasso-vallauris.fr; f. 1959; works by Picasso incl. *La Guerre et la Paix* in 12th-century chapel; Curator JEAN-MICHEL FORAY.

Verdun

Centre Mondial de la Paix, des Libertés et des Droits de l'Homme: Palais Episcopal, BP 183, 55100 Verdun; tel. 3-29-86-55-00; e-mail cmpaix@wanadoo.fr; f. 1994; exhibition on the First World War; and 'From War to Peace', an interactive exhibition, which depicts the origins of war in Europe, attempts at peacekeeping and punishment of war crimes, the history of European cooperation and the EU, the UN, and the nature and application of human rights; meetings, confs and roleplay situations for students; Dir JEAN-LUC DEMANDRE.

Versailles

Musée et Domaine National du Château de Versailles: Château de Versailles, place d'Armes, RP 834, 78000 Versailles; tel. 1-30-83-78-00; e-mail direction.public@chateauversailles.fr; internet www.chateauversailles.fr; f. 1623 by Louis XIII; historical painting and sculpture, furniture of the 17th to 19th centuries; Grand Trianon, Petit Trianon châteaux, Hameau de la Reine, park; Man. Dir BÉATRIX SAULE (acting).

Vizille

Musée de la Révolution Française: Domaine de Vizille, 38220 Vizille; tel. 4-76-68-07-35; e-mail musee.revolution@cg38.fr; internet www.domaine-vizille.fr; f. 1984; relics, art and library connected with the French Revolution of 1789; library of 20,000 vols, 25,000 microfiches; Dir ALAIN CHEVALIER.

State Universities

CENTRE UNIVERSITAIRE DE FORMATION ET DE RECHERCHE JEAN-FRANÇOIS CHAMPOLLION

pl. de Verdun, 81012 Albi Cedex 9
Telephone: 5-63-48-17-17
E-mail: contact.albi@univ-jfc.fr
Internet: www.univ-jfc.fr

Areas of study: arts, computer science, economics, humanities, languages, law, literature, management, sport, science, social science

Pres.: JEAN-LOUIS DARRERON
Vice-Pres. for Admin.: MICHEL ROUSTAN
Vice-Pres. for Science and Education Ccl: PIERRE LAGARRIGUE
Dir: HERVÉ PINGAUD
Sec.-Gen.: PASCAL GUERRIN
Librarian: FLORENCE LUNARDI

Number of teachers: 80
Number of students: 2,600

INSTITUT NATIONAL POLYTECHNIQUE DE GRENOBLE

46 ave Félix Viallet, 38031 Grenoble Cedex 1
Telephone: 4-76-57-45-00
E-mail: contact@grenoble-inp.fr
Internet: www.grenoble-inp.fr

Founded 1907

29 Research laboratories, 6 constituent schools

Pres.: PAUL JACQUET
Vice-Pres. for Admin. Ccl: DIDIER GEORGES
Vice-Pres. for Industry Partnership: CHRISTIAN VOILLOT
Vice-Pres. for Int. Relations: JEAN-LUC KONING
Vice-Pres. for Scientific Ccl: FRANÇOIS WEISS
Vice-Pres. for Studies and Univ. Life: NADINE GUILLEMOT
Sec.-Gen.: JEAN-FRANÇOIS PICQ

Number of teachers: 350
Number of students: 5,076

Publication: *Ingénieurs INPG* (52 a year).

CONSTITUENT SCHOOLS

Ecole Internationale du Papier de la Communication Imprimée et des Biomatériaux (PAGORA): 461 rue de la Papeterie, BP 65, 38402 Saint Martin d'Hères Cedex; tel. 4-76-82-69-00; e-mail contact.pagora@grenoble-inp.fr; internet pagora.grenoble-inp.fr; f. 2008, fmrly l'Ecole Française de Papeterie et des Industries Graphiques (EFPG); Dir BERNARD PINEAUX.

Ecole Nationale Supérieure de Physique, Electronique, Matériaux (PHELMA): 3 Parvis Louis Néel, BP 257, 38016 Grenoble Cedex 1; tel. 4-56-52-91-00; e-mail scolarite@phelma.grenoble-inp.fr; internet phelma.grenoble-inp.fr; f. 2008 by merger of Ecole Nationale Supérieure de Physique de Grenoble (ENSPG), Ecole Nationale Supérieure d'Electricité et de Radioelectricité (ENSERG) and Ecole Nationale Supérieure d'Electrochimie et d'Electrométallurgie de Grenoble (ENSEEG); Dir PIERRE BENECH.

Ecole Nationale Supérieure des Systèmes Avancés et Réseaux (ESISAR): 50 rue Barthélémy de Laffemas, BP 54, 26902 Valence Cedex 9; tel. 4-75-75-94-00; e-mail direction@esisar.grenoble-inp.fr; internet esisar.grenoble-inp.fr; Dir Prof. CHANTAL ROBACH.

Ecole Nationale Supérieure d'Informatique, de Mathématiques Appliquées et de Télécommunications (ENSIMAG): 681 rue de la Passerelle, BP 72, 38402 Saint Martin d'Hères Cedex; tel. 4-76-82-72-00; e-mail webmestre.ensimag@imag.fr; internet ensimag.grenoble-inp.fr; f. 2008 by merger of Ecole Nationale Supérieure d'Informatique et de Mathématiques Appliquées de Grenoble (ENSIMAG) and INP Grenoble TELECOM; Dir BRIGITTE PLATEAU.

Ecole Nationale Supérieure d'Ingénieurs pour l'Energie, l'Eau et l'Environnement (ENSE3): rue de la Houille Blanche, BP 46, 38402 Saint Martin d'Hères Cedex; tel. 4-76-82-62-00; e-mail direction.ense3@grenoble-inp.fr; internet ense3.grenoble-inp.fr; f. 2008 by merger of Ecole Nationale Supérieure d'Ingénieurs Electriciens de Grenoble (ENSIEG) and Ecole Nationale Supérieure d'Hydraulique et de Mécanique de Grenoble (ENSHMG).

Génie Industriel: 46 ave Félix Viallet, 38031 Grenoble Cedex 1; tel. 4-76-57-46-01; e-mail corinne.mairot@grenoble-inp.fr; internet genie-industriel.grenoble-inp.fr; f. 2008 by merger of Ecole Nationale Supérieure de Génie Industriel (ENSGI) and part of the Ecole Nationale Supérieure d'Hydraulique et de Mécanique de Grenoble (ENSHMG); Dir JEANNE DUVALLET

INSTITUT NATIONAL POLYTECHNIQUE DE LORRAINE

2 ave de la Forêt de Haye, BP 3, 54501 Vandoeuvre
Telephone: 3-83-59-59-59
E-mail: inpl@inpl-nancy.fr
Internet: www.inpl-nancy.fr

Founded 1970
Language of instruction: French

28 Research laboratories; 7 constituent schools

Pres.: FRANÇOIS LAURENT
Vice-Pres. for Admin.: CHRISTINE ROIZARD
Vice-Pres. for Scientific Ccl: PIERRE ARCHAMBAULT
Vice-Pres. for Studies and Univ. Life: DOMINIQUE PETITJEAN
Sec.-Gen.: JEAN-YVES RIVIÈRE

Number of teachers: 560
Number of students: 4,000.

CONSTITUENT SCHOOLS

Ecole Européenne d'Ingénieurs en Génie des Matériaux (EEIGM): 6 rue Bastien Lepage, BP 630, 54010 Nancy Cedex; tel. 3-83-36-83-00; e-mail eeigm@eeigm.inpl-nancy.fr; internet www.eeigm.inpl-nancy.fr; f. 1991; 191 students; Dir ISABELLE HENROT.

Ecole Nationale Supérieure d'Agronomie et des Industries Alimentaires (ENSAIA): 2 ave de la Forêt de Haye, BP 172, 54505 Vandoeuvre Cedex; tel. 3-83-59-58-51; e-mail ensaia@ensaia.inpl-nancy.fr; internet www.ensaia.inpl-nancy.fr; f. 1970; 58 teachers; 436 students; library of 7,500 vols; Dir MICHEL FICK; Dean of Study FRANTZ FOURNIER; publ. *Bulletin Scientifique* (1 a year).

Ecole Nationale Supérieure d'Electricité et de Mécanique (ENSEM): 2 ave de la Forêt de Haye, 54516 Vandoeuvre; tel. 3-83-59-55-43; e-mail ensem@ensem.inpl-nancy.fr; internet www.ensem.inpl-nancy.fr; f. 1990; 50 teachers; 379 students; Dir YVES GRANJON.

Ecole Nationale Supérieure de Géologie (ENSG): rue du Doyen Marcel Roubault, BP 40, 54501 Vandoeuvre lès Nancy; tel. 3-83-59-64-02; e-mail com@ensg.inpl-nancy.fr; internet www.ensg.inpl-nancy.fr; f. 1908; 36 teachers; 300 students; Dir JEAN-MARC MONTEL.

Ecole Nationale Supérieure des Industries Chimiques (ENSIC): 1 rue Grandville, 54001 Nancy; tel. 3-83-17-50-00; e-mail ensic@ensic.inpl-nancy.fr; internet www.ensic.inpl-nancy.fr; f. 1887; 65 teachers; 462 students; Dir BERNARD VITOUX.

Ecole Nationale Supérieure des Mines de Nancy (ENSMN): Parc de Saurupt, CS 14234, 54042 Nancy Cedex; tel. 3-83-58-42-32; e-mail ensmn@mines.inpl-nancy.fr; internet www.mines.inpl-nancy.fr; f. 1919; 803 students; library of 37,500 vols, 180 periodicals; Dir MICHEL JAUZEIN.

Ecole Nationale Supérieure en Génie des Systèmes et de l'Innovation (ENSGSI): 8 rue Bastien Lepage, BP 90647, 54010 Nancy Cedex; tel. 3-83-19-32-32; e-mail ensgsi@ensgsi.univ-lorraine.fr; internet www.ensgsi.univ-lorraine.fr; f. 1993; 25 teachers; 340 students; Dir Prof. PASCAL LHOSTE

INSTITUT NATIONAL POLYTECHNIQUE DE TOULOUSE

6 allée Emile Monso, BP 34038, 31029 Toulouse Cedex 4
Telephone: 5-34-32-30-00
E-mail: inp@inp-toulouse.fr
Internet: www.inp-toulouse.fr

Founded 1970
State control
Languages of instruction: English, French
Academic year: September to July

4 Constituent schools and 19 research laboratories; 3 attached institutes

Pres.: Dr OLIVIER SIMONIN
Vice-Pres. for Research and Valorisation: Dr CATHERINE XUEREB
Vice-Pres. for Studies and Student Life: Dr MARITXU GUIRESSE
Dir-Gen.: GILLES BOUCHER
Librarian: SANDRINE MALOTAUX

Number of teachers: 900
Number of students: 6,200

Publication: *INP Communique*.

CONSTITUENT SCHOOLS

Ecole Nationale d'Ingénieurs de Tarbes (ENIT): 47 ave d'Azereix, BP 1629, 65016 Tarbes Cedex; tel. 5-62-44-27-00; e-mail directeur@enit.fr; internet www.enit.fr; f. 1963; Dir TALAL MASRI.

Ecole Nationale Supérieure Agronomique de Toulouse (ENSAT): ave de l'Agrobiopole, BP 32607, Auzeville-Tolosane, 31326 Castanet-Tolosan Cedex; tel. 5-34-32-39-00; e-mail sandrine.audran@ensat.fr; internet www.ensat.fr; f. 1909 as Institut Agricole de Toulouse; Dir GRÉGORY DECHAP-GUILLAUME.

Ecole Nationale Supérieure d'Electrotechnique, d'Electronique, d'Informatique et d'Hydraulique et des Télécommunications (ENSEEIHT): 2 rue Charles Camichel, BP 7122, 31071 Toulouse Cedex 7; tel. 5-34-32-20-00; e-mail ric@enseeiht.fr; internet www.enseeiht.fr; Dir ALAIN AYACHE.

Ecole Nationale Supérieure des Arts Chimiques et Technologiques (ENSIACET): 4 allée Emile Monso, BP 44362, 31030 Toulouse Cedex 4; tel. 5-34-32-33-00; e-mail directeur@ensiacet.fr; internet www.ensiacet.fr; f. 2001; Dir JEAN-MARC LE LANN; 105 teachers; 750 students

UNIVERSITÉ DE PROVENCE—AIX-MARSEILLE I

3 pl. Victor Hugo, 13331 Marseilles Cedex 03
Telephone: 4-13-55-00-00
E-mail: presidence@univ-provence.fr
Internet: www.univ-provence.fr

Founded 1970; attached to PRES Aix-Marseille Université

Univ. restructured in 2009 into 9 research units, an engineering school, an institute of technology, and a Masters institute based on campuses in Aix, Marseille, Aubagne, Lambesc, Salon de Provence, Arles, Digne, and Avignon

Pres.: JEAN-PAUL CAVERNI
Vice-Pres. for Admin.: JEAN-CLAUDE LORAUD
Vice-Pres. for Science Ccl: DENIS BERTIN
Vice-Pres. for Studies and Univ. Life: CATHERINE VIRLOUVET
Sec.-Gen.: FATHIE BOUBERTEKH
Librarian: Mme GACHON

Library: see under Libraries and Archives
Number of teachers: 1,087
Number of students: 22,334.

TEACHING AND RESEARCH UNITS

Centre de Formation des Musiciens Intervenants (CFMI): 29 ave Robert Schuman, 13621 Aix-en-Provence Cedex 01; tel. 4-42-95-32-40; e-mail cfmi@univ-provence.fr; Dir PHILIPPE BOIVIN.

Centre Interuniversitaire de Mécanique (UNIMECA): 60 rue Joliot-Curie, 13453 Marseilles Cedex 13; tel. 4-91-11-38-00; internet artemmis.univ-mrs.fr/im2; Dir PATRICK VIGLIANO.

Département Environnement Technologie et Société (DENTES): 3 pl. Victor Hugo, Case 75, 13331 Marseilles Cedex 03; tel. 4-91-10-63-28; Dir RÉMI CHAPPAZ.

Département Métiers de l'Image et du Son (SATIS): 9 blvd Lakanal, 13400 Aubagne; tel. 4-13-55-18-88; e-mail satis@univ-provence.fr; internet sites.univ-provence.fr/satis; Dir JACQUES SAPIEGA.

École Polytechnique Universitaire de Marseille: 60 rue Joliot-Curie, 13453 Marseilles Cedex 13; tel. 4-91-11-26-56; e-mail direction@polytech.univ-mrs.fr; internet www.polytech-marseille.com; Dir DAVID E. ZEITOUN.

Institut de la Francophonie: tel. 4-42-95-35-53; internet sites.univ-provence.fr/francophonie; Dir ROBERT CHAUDENSON.

Institut Universitaire de Formation des Maîtres (IUFM) de l'Académie d'Aix-Marseille: 33 rue Eugène Cas, 13248 Marseilles Cedex 04; tel. 4-91-10-75-75; internet www.aix-mrs.iufm.fr; Dir JACQUES GINESTIÉ.

IUT de Provence (Arles): rue Raoul Follereau, BP 90178, 13637 Arles Cedex; tel. 4-90-52-24-10; e-mail iut-arles@up.univ-mrs.fr; Dir ROBERT PUJADE.

IUT de Provence (Digne-les-Bains): 19 blvd Saint-Jean Chrysostome, 04000 Digne-les-Bains; tel. 4-92-30-23-70; internet sites.univ-provence.fr/iutdigne; Dir YVES ALPE.

Maison Méditerranéenne des Sciences de l'Homme (MMSH): 5 rue du Château de l'Horloge, BP 647, 13094 Aix-en-Provence Cedex 02; internet www.mmsh.univ-aix.fr; Dir BRIGITTE MARIN.

Observatoire Astronomique de Marseille-Provence (OAMP): see Research Institutes.

UFR Civilisations et Humanités: 29 ave Robert Schuman, 13621 Aix-en-Provence Cedex 01; tel. 4-42-95-32-90; e-mail elisabeth.malamut@univ-provence.fr; Dir XAVIER LAFON.

UFR de Psychologie, Sciences de l'Éducation: 29 ave Robert Schuman, 13621 Aix-en-Provence Cedex 01; tel. 4-42-95-37-09; e-mail thierry.ripoll@univ-provence.fr; internet sites.univ-provence.fr/wpse; Dir THIERRY RIPOLL.

UFR Études Romanes, Latino-américaines, Orientales et Slaves (ERLAOS): 29 ave Robert Schuman, 13621 Aix-en-Provence Cedex 01; tel. 4-42-95-34-46; internet www.univ-provence.fr/erlaos; Dir PASCAL GANDOULPHE.

UFR Langue Anglo-saxonnes et Germaniques–Langues Étrangères Appliquées (LAG–LEA): 29 ave Robert Schuman, 13621 Aix-en-Provence Cedex 01; tel. 4-42-95-36-42; Dir DOMINIQUE BATOUX.

UFR Lettres, Arts, Communications et Sciences du langage (LACS): 29 ave Robert Schuman, 13621 Aix-en-Provence Cedex 01; internet sites.univ-provence.fr/lacs; Dir HENRIETTE STOFFEL.

UFR Mathématiques, Informatique, Mécanique (MIM): 39 rue Joliot-Curie, 13453 Marseilles Cedex 13; tel. 4-13-55-11-11; e-mail denis.lugiez@univ-provence.fr; internet gsite.univ-provence.fr; Dir DENIS LUGIEZ.

UFR Sciences de la Matière (SM): ave Escadrille-Normandie-Niemen, service 411, entrée BJ4, 13397 Marseilles Cedex 20; tel. 4-91-28-90-40; e-mail ufrsm@up.univ-mrs.fr; internet sites.univ-provence.fr/~ufrsm; Dir ANDRÉ THEVAND.

UFR Sciences de la Vie, de la Terre et de l'Environnement (SVTE): 3 pl. Victor Hugo, Case 82, 13331 Marseilles Cedex 03; tel. 4-13-55-11-25; Dir JACQUES MARVALDI.

UFR Sciences Géographiques et de l'Aménagement: 29 ave Robert Schuman, 13621 Aix-en-Provence Cedex 01; tel. 4-42-95-38-44; internet sites.univ-provence.fr/wgeo; Dir JEAN-LUC BONNEFOY

UNIVERSITÉ DE LA MÉDITERRANÉE—AIX-MARSEILLE II

58 blvd Charles Livon, 13284 Marseilles Cedex 07
Telephone: 4-91-39-65-00
E-mail: service-communication@univmed.fr
Internet: www.univmed.fr

Founded 1973
Language of instruction: French
Academic year: October to June

Univs of Aix-en-Provence consist of three univs in Aix-en-Provence; economic science and information technology are the principal subjects of instruction here

Pres.: Prof. YVON BERLAND
Vice-Pres. for Admin. Council: DIDIER LAUSSEL
Vice-Pres. for Communication: PATRICE VANELLE
Vice-Pres. for Education and Student Life: THIERRY PAUL
Vice-Pres. for Int. Relations: PIERRE FUENTES
Vice-Pres. for Science Council: PIERRE CHIAPPETTA
Sec.-Gen.: DAMIEN VERHAEGHE

Number of teachers: 1,500
Number of students: 22,000.

TEACHING AND RESEARCH UNITS

Ecole Supérieure d'Ingénieurs de Luminy (ESIL): 163 ave de Luminy, Case 925, 13288 Marseilles Cedex 9; tel. 4-91-82-85-00; e-mail contact@esil.univmed.fr; internet www.esil.univmed.fr; Dir HENRI KANOUI.

Ecole Universitaire de Maïeutique Marseille Mediterranée (EU3M): Site de la Faculté de Médecine Nord, blvd Pierre Dramard, 13344 Marseilles Cedex 15; tel. 4-91-24-32-00; Dir ANNE DEMEESTER.

Ecole de Journalisme et de Communication de Marseille: 21 rue Virgile Marron, 13392 Marseilles Cedex 05; tel. 4-91-24-32-00; e-mail ejcm@ejcm.univmed.fr; internet www.ejcm.univ-mrs.fr; Dir LIONEL FLEURY.

Faculté de Médecine: 27 blvd Jean Moulin, 13385 Marseilles Cedex 5; tel. 4-91-32-43-00; e-mail medecine-admin@univ-amu.fr; internet www.timone.univ-mrs.fr/medecine; Dean GEORGES LEONETTI.

Faculté de Pharmacie: 27 blvd Jean Moulin, 13385 Marseilles Cedex 5; tel. 4-91-83-55-00; e-mail pharmacie-doyen@univ-amu.fr; internet www.pharmacie.univ-mrs.fr; Dean PATRICE VANELLE.

Faculté des Sciences (Luminy): 163 ave de Luminy, 13288 Marseilles Cedex 09; tel. 4-91-82-90-00; internet www.sciences.univmed.fr; Dean CHENG-CAI ZHANG.

Faculté des Sciences Economiques et de Gestion: 14 ave Jules Ferry, 13621 Marseilles; tel. 4-42-91-48-00; e-mail webscol@sceco.univmed.fr; internet sceco.univ-aix.fr; Dean PIERRE GRANIER.

Faculté des Sciences du Sport: 163 ave de Luminy, Case 910, 13288 Marseilles Cedex 9; tel. 4-91-17-04-12; internet www.staps.univ-mrs.fr; Dean ERIC BERTON.

Faculté d'Odontologie: 27 blvd Jean Moulin, 13385 Marseilles Cedex 5; tel. 4-86-13-68-68; internet www.univmed.fr/odontologie; Dean JACQUES DEJOU.

ATTACHED INSTITUTES

Centre de Recherche pour l'Enseignement des Mathématiques (IREM): Faculté des Sciences de Luminy, 163 ave de Luminy, 13288 Marseilles Cedex 9; tel. 4-91-26-90-91; research into the teaching of mathematics; Dir ROBERT ROLLAND.

Centre d'Océanologie de Marseille: Campus de Luminy, 163 ave de Luminy, 13288 Marseilles Cedex 9; tel. 4-91-82-93-00; internet www.com.univ-mrs.fr; Dean M. IVAN DEKEYSER.

Centre International de Formation et de Recherche en Didactique (CIFORD): Faculté des Sciences de Luminy, 163 ave de Luminy, 13288 Marseilles Cedex 9; tel. 4-91-26-90-30; Dir PAUL ALLARD.

Centre Universitaire Régional d'Etudes Municipales (CURET): 191 rue Breteuil, 13006 Marseilles; tel. 4-91-37-61-62; courses in local government administration; Dir M. FOUCHET.

Institut de Mécanique de Marseille: 60 rue Joliot Curie, 13453 Marseilles; tel. 4-91-11-38-02; internet artemmis.univ-mrs.fr/unimecafr; Dir PATRICK VIGLIANO.

Institut Régional du Travail: 12 traverse St Pierre, 13100 Aix-en-Provence; tel. 4-42-17-43-11; e-mail irt@univmed.fr; internet irt.univmed.fr; Dir MARIO CORREIA.

Institut Universitaire Professionnalisé (IUP) Affaires et Finances: Faculté des Sciences Economiques, 14 ave Jules Ferry, 13621 Aix-en-Provence Cedex; tel. 4-42-33-48-70; course on business and finance.

Institut Universitaire de Technologie d'Aix-en-Provence: 413 ave Gaston Berger, 13625 Aix-en-Provence Cedex 1; tel. 4-42-93-90-00; internet www.iut.univ-aix.fr; Dir CLAUDE FIORE

UNIVERSITÉ PAUL CEZANNE—AIX-MARSEILLE III

3 ave Robert Schuman, 13628 Aix-en-Provence Cedex 1
Telephone: 4-42-17-28-00
Internet: www.univ-amu.fr

Founded 1973 as Univ. d'Aix-Marseille III (Univ. de Droit, d'Economie et des Sciences)

Academic year: September to June

Univs of Aix-en-Provence consist of 3 univs in Aix-en-Provence; law, economics and foundation science are the principal subjects of instruction here

Pres.: MARC PENA
Vice-Pres. for Admin.: BRUNO HAMELIN
Vice-Pres. for Science Ccl: PIERRE MULLER
Vice-Pres. for Studies and Univ. Life: DOMINIQUE VIRIOT-BARRIAL
Sec.-Gen.: THÉRÈSE CHETAIL
Librarian: DOMINIQUE JACOBI

Number of teachers: 1,133
Number of students: 22,800

Publications: *Interface* (12 a year), *L'Inter Cours* (12 a year), annual research reports.

TEACHING AND RESEARCH UNITS

Faculté de Droit et de Science Politique: 3 ave Robert Schuman, 13628 Aix-en-Provence; tel. 4-42-17-28-05; e-mail secretariat.sridroit@univ-cezanne.fr; internet www.facdedroit.univ-cezanne.fr; Dean GILBERT ORSONI.

Faculté d'Economie Appliquée: 3 ave Robert Schuman, 13628 Aix-en-Provence; tel. 4-42-17-29-85; internet www.fea-upcam.fr; Dean JEAN-PIERRE CENTI.

Faculté des Sciences et Techniques: ave Escadrille Normandie-Niemen, 13397 Marseilles Cedex 20; tel. 4-91-28-84-46; e-mail sec-doyen.fst@univ-cezanne.fr; internet www.fst.univ-cezanne.fr; Dean JEAN-MARC PONS.

Institut d'Administration des Entreprises: chemin de la Quille, Puyricard, CS 30063, 13089 Aix-en-Provence Cedex 2; tel. 4-42-28-08-08; internet www.iae-aix.com; Dir PATRICK ROUSSEAU.

Institut d'Etudes Françaises pour Etudiants Etrangers: 23 rue Gaston de Saporta, 13100 Aix-en-Provence; tel. 4-42-21-70-90; e-mail institut.iefee@univ-cezanne.fr; internet www.iefee.com; Dir CARINE FERRADOU.

Institut d'Etudes Politiques: 25 rue Gaston de Saporta, 13625 Aix-en-Provence; tel. 4-42-17-01-60; e-mail directeur@sciencespo-aix.fr; internet www.sciencespo-aix.fr; Dir CHRISTIAN DUVAL.

Institut de Management Public et Gouvernance Territoriale: 21 rue Gaston de Saporta, 13625 Aix-en-Provence Cedex 1; tel. 4-42-17-05-50; internet www.impgt.univ-amu.fr; Dir OLIVIER KERAMIDAS.

Institut Universitaire de Technologie: 142 Traverse Charles Susini, 13013 Marseilles Cedex 13; tel. 4-91-28-93-00; internet iutmrs.univ-cezanne.fr; Dir MICHEL GAUCH

UNIVERSITÉ D'ANGERS

40 rue de Rennes, BP 73532, 49035 Angers Cedex
Telephone: 2-41-96-23-23
E-mail: presidence@univ-angers.fr
Internet: www.univ-angers.fr

Founded 1971; fmrly Centre Universitaire d'Angers

Pres.: DANIEL MARTINA
Vice-Pres.: GÉRARD MOGUEDET
Sec.-Gen.: HENRI-MARC PAPAVOINE
Librarian: OLIVIER TACHEAU

Number of teachers: 959
Number of students: 18,514

Publications: *Journal of the Short Story in English, Plantes médicinales et phytothérapie, Publications du Centre de Recherche en Littérature et Linguistique de l'Anjou et des Bocages*

DEANS

Faculty of Law, Economic Sciences and Business Sciences: MICHÈL FAVREAU,
Faculty of Letters and Human Sciences: DIDIER LE GALL
Faculty of Medicine: JEAN-PAUL SAINT-ANDRE
Faculty of Pharmacy: OLIVIER DUVAL
Faculty of Science: DANIEL SCHAUB

ATTACHED INSTITUTES

Etudes Supérieures de Tourisme et Hôtellerie d'Angers (ESTHUA): 7 allée François Mitterrand, BP 40455, 49004 Angers; tel. 2-41-96-21-99; Dir M. BONNEAU.

Institut des Sciences et Techniques de l'Ingénieur d'Angers (ISTIA): 62 ave Notre-Dame du Lac, 49000 Angers; tel. 2-41-22-65-00; e-mail istia@contact.univ-angers.fr; Dir C. ROBLEDO.

Institut Universitaire de Technologie (IUT): 4 blvd Lavoisier, BP 42018, 49016 Angers Cedex; tel. 2-41-73-52-52; e-mail scolarite.iut@univ-angers.fr; Dir Y. MEIGNEN

UNIVERSITÉ D'ARTOIS

9 rue du Temple, BP 10665, 62030 Arras Cedex
Telephone: 3-21-60-37-00
E-mail: sio-arras@univ-artois.fr
Internet: www.univ-artois.fr

Founded 1991

Pres.: CHRISTIAN MORZEWSKI (acting)
Sec.-Gen.: MARIE-PAULE DEJONGHE
First Vice-Pres.: ROMÉO CECCHELLI
Librarians: CORINNE LEBLOND (Arras), CHANTAL DUBOIS (Béthune), FRÉDÉRIC WATRELOT (Douai), VIRGINIE JUSTIN-LABONNE (Lens), GHISLAINE HEYER (Liévin)

Number of teachers: 850
Number of students: 14,500

Publication: *Interpôles Artois* (8 a year).

TEACHING AND RESEARCH UNITS

Faculté de Droit Alexis de Tocqueville: rue d'Esquerchin, 59500 Douai; tel. 3-27-94-50-50; e-mail nathalie.sammartino@univ-artois.fr; internet www.univ-artois.fr; Dean TANGUY LE MARC'HADOUR.

Faculté d'Économie, Gestion, Administration et Sciences Sociales: 9 rue du Temple, BP 10665, 62030 Arras Cedex; tel. 3-21-60-37-62; e-mail fegass@univ-artois.fr; Dir NICOLAS BLONDEL.

Faculté d'Histoire et Géographie: 9 rue du Temple, BP 10665, 62030 Arras Cedex; e-mail richard.chapelet@univ-artois.fr; Dir STÉPHANE CURVEILLER.

Faculté de Langues et Civilisations Étrangères: 9 rue du Temple, BP 10665, 62030 Arras Cedex; tel. 3-21-60-37-45; e-mail langues@univ-artois.fr; Dir AHMED EL KALADI.

Faculté de Lettres et Arts: 9 rue du Temple, BP 10665, 62030 Arras Cedex; tel. 3-21-60-49-54; e-mail lettres@univ-artois.fr; Dir JEAN-MARC VERCRUYSSE.

Faculté des Sciences Appliquées: Technoparc Futura, 62400 Béthune Cedex; tel. 3-21-64-71-23; e-mail patrick.bonnel@univ-artois.fr; Dir HERVÉ ROISSE.

Faculté des Sciences Jean Perrin: rue Jean Souvraz, SP 18, 62307 Lens Cedex; tel. 3-21-79-17-00; e-mail aurore.atmania@univ-artois.fr; Dir PASQUALE MAMMONE.

Faculté des Sports et de l'Education Physique: Chemin du Marquage, 62800 Béthune Cedex; tel. 3-21-45-85-00; e-mail facdessports@univ-artois.fr; Dir NICOLAS BLONDEL.

Institut Universitaire de Formation des Maîtres: 365 bis rue Jules Guesde, BP 50458, 59658 Villeneuve d'Ascq Cedex; tel. 3-20-79-86-00; e-mail webmaster@lille.iufm.fr; internet www.lille.iufm.fr; Dir DOMINIQUE-GUY BRASSART.

ATTACHED RESEARCH INSTITUTES

Institute Universitaire de Technologie de Béthune: 1230 rue de l'Université, BP 819, 62408 Béthune Cedex; tel. 3-21-63-23-00; Dir PATRICK MARTIN.

Institute Universitaire de Technologie de Lens: rue de l'université, SP 16, 62307 Lens Cedex; tel. 3-21-79-32-32; e-mail contact@iut-lens.univ-artois.fr; Dir NATASHA LACROIX

UNIVERSITÉ D'AUVERGNE (CLERMONT-FERRAND I)

49 blvd F. Mitterrand, BP 32, 63001 Clermont-Ferrand Cedex
Telephone: 4-73-17-79-79
E-mail: president@udamail.fr
Internet: www.u-clermont1.fr

Founded 1976; present status 1985
Pres.: PHILIPPE DULBECCO
Vice-Pres.: MICHEL MADESCLAIRE
Sec.-Gen.: MARTINE HENAULT
Librarian: Mlle SART
Number of teachers: 650
Number of students: 15,000.

TEACHING AND RESEARCH UNITS

Dentistry: 11 blvd Charles de Gaulle, 63000 Clermont-Ferrand Cedex; tel. 4-73-17-73-00; internet webodonto.u-clermont1.fr; Dean Prof. THIERRY ORLIAGUET.

Economic and Social Sciences: 41 blvd F. Mitterrand, BP 54, 63002 Clermont-Ferrand; tel. 4-73-43-42-00; internet www.ecogestion.u-clermont1.fr; Dir Prof. MARY-FRANÇOISE RENARD.

IPAG: 26 ave Léon-Blum, 63000 Clermont-Ferrand; tel. 4-73-17-77-50; internet www.u-clermont1.fr/institut-de-preparation-a--l-administration-generale; Dir FRANÇOIS CHOUVEL.

Law and Politics: 41 blvd F. Mitterrand, BP 38, 63002 Clermont-Ferrand; tel. 4-73-17-75-74; e-mail ufr-droit@droit.u-clermont1.fr; internet www-droit.u-clermont1.fr; Dean Prof. JEAN-PIERRE JARNEVIC.

Medicine: 28 place Henri Dunant, BP 38, 63001 Clermont-Ferrand; tel. 4-73-17-79-00; e-mail doyen.medecine@u-clermont1.fr; internet medecine.u-clermont1.fr; Dean Prof. PATRICE DETEIX.

Pharmacy: 28 place Henri Dunant, BP 38, 63001 Clermont-Ferrand; tel. 4-73-17-79-00; e-mail doyen.pharmacie@udamail.fr; internet pharmacie.u-clermont1.fr; Dean Prof. JOSEPH FIALIP.

University Institute of Technology (Clermont-Ferrand): Ensemble universitaire des Cézeaux, BP 86, 63172 Aubière; tel. 4-73-17-70-01; internet iutweb.u-clermont1.fr; Dir Prof. JEAN-MARC LAVEST.

University Professional Institute of Business Management: Pôle Tertiaire et Technologique, 26 ave Léon-Blum, 63000 Clermont-Ferrand; tel. 4-73-17-77-00; internet iup-management.net; Dir Prof. MAURICE CHENEVOY

UNIVERSITÉ D'AVIGNON ET DES PAYS DE VAUCLUSE

74 rue Louis Pasteur, 84029 Avignon Cedex 1
Telephone: 4-90-16-25-00
E-mail: presidence@univ-avignon.fr
Internet: www.univ-avignon.fr

Founded 1303; closed in 1793 after French Revolution; reopened in 1963; univ. status since 1984
State control
Language of instruction: French
Academic year: September to June

Pres.: Prof. EMMANUEL ETHIS
Dir-Gen.: LUÇAY SAUTRON
Librarian: ISABELLE DIMONDO

Library of 155,600 vols, 73 online databases, 8,311 periodical titles
Number of teachers: 357
Number of students: 7,125

Publications: *Culture et Musée*, *Ecologia Mediterranea*, *Etudes Vauclusiennes*.

TEACHING AND RESEARCH UNITS

Faculté des Arts, Lettres et Langues: 74 rue Louis Pasteur, 84029 Avignon Cedex 1; tel. 4-90-16-26-64; e-mail secretariat-pedagogique-lettres@univ-avignon.fr; Dir ALAIN SERVEL.

Faculté de Droit, Economie et Gestion: 74 rue Louis Pasteur, 84029 Avignon Cedex 1; tel. 4-90-16-27-41; e-mail dir-droit@univ-avignon.fr; Dean PIERRE FRESSOZ.

Faculté des Sciences Humaines et Sociales: 74 rue Louis Pasteur, 84029 Avignon Cedex 1; tel. 4-90-16-27-18; e-mail sla@univ-avignon.fr; Dir PIERRE-LOUIS SUET.

Faculté des Sciences et Technologies: 33 rue Louis Pasteur, 84000 Avignon Cedex 1; tel. 4-90-14-40-00; e-mail sciences@univ-avignon.fr; Dir PASCAL LAURENT.

ATTACHED RESEARCH INSTITUTES

Centre d'Enseignement et de Recherche en Informatique (CERI): 339 Chemin des Meinajaries, 84911 Avignon Cedex 9; tel. 4-90-84-35-00; e-mail ceri-info@univ-avignon.fr; Dir MARC EL-BÈZE.

Institut Universitaire de Technologie (IUT): 337 Chemin des Meinajaries, BP 1207, 84911 Avignon Cedex 9; tel. 4-90-84-14-00; e-mail info-sg-iut@univ-avignon.fr; internet www.iut.univ-avignon.fr; Dir HÉLÈNE DOMINGUEZ

UNIVERSITÉ BLAISE PASCAL

34 ave Carnot, BP 185, 63006 Clermont-Ferrand Cedex 1
Telephone: 4-73-40-63-63
E-mail: president@univ-bpclermont.fr
Internet: www.univ-bpclermont.fr

Founded 1810, present status 1984 as Université de Clermont-Ferrand II—Université Blaise Pascal

Pres.: NADINE LAVIGNOTTE
Vice-Pres: BETTINA ABOAB, MARIE-JOSEPH BIACHE, PASCALE DUCHÉ
Sec.-Gen.: HERVÉ COMBAZ
Librarian: L. RAPATEL

Number of teachers: 970
Number of students: 14,400

Publication: *Journal de l'Université Blaise-Pascal* (3 a year).

TEACHING AND RESEARCH UNITS

Ecole Nationale Supérieure de Chimie de Clermont-Ferrand (ENSCCF—National Higher School of Chemistry): Campus des Cézeaux, 24 ave des Landais, BP 10187, 63174 Aubière Cedex; tel. 4-73-40-71-45; e-mail scolarite@ensccf.fr; internet ensccf.univ-bpclermont.fr; Dir SOPHIE COMMEREUC.

Institut Supérieur d'Informatique de Modélisation et de leurs Applications (ISIMA—Graduate Engineering School focused on Computing): Campus des Cézeaux, BP 10125, 63173 Aubière Cedex; tel. 4-73-40-50-00; e-mail secretariat@isima.fr; internet www.isima.fr; Head Prof. VINCENT BARRA.

Institut Universitaire de Formation des Maîtres d'Auvergne (IUFM—University Institute for Teacher Training): 36 ave Jean Jaurès, CS 20001, 63407 Chamalières Cedex; tel. 4-73-31-71-50; e-mail elsa.graive@univ-bpclermont.fr; internet www.auvergne.iufm.fr; Dir DIDIER JOURDAN.

Institut Universitaire de Technologie d'Allier de Montluçon (MONIUT—University Institute of Technology): ave Aristide Briand, BP 2235, 03107 Montluçon Cedex; tel. 4-70-02-20-00; e-mail secretariat.geii@moniut.univ-bpclermont.fr; internet www.moniut.univ-bpclermont.fr; Dir CÉCILE CHARASSE.

Langues appliquées, Commerce et Communication (LACC—Applied Language, Business and Communication): 34 ave Carnot, 63037 Clermont-Ferrand Cedex; tel. 4-73-40-64-05; e-mail eric.agbessi@univ-bpclermont.fr; internet www.lacc.univ-bpclermont.fr; Dir ERIC AGBESSI.

Lettres, Langues et Sciences Humaines (Literature, Languages and Human Sciences): 29 blvd Gergovia, 63037 Clermont-Ferrand Cedex; tel. 4-73-34-65-04; e-mail secretariat.lettres@univ-bpclermont.fr; internet www.lettres.univ-bpclermont.fr; Dir MATHIAS BERNARD.

Observatoire de Physique du Globe de Clermont-Ferrand (OPGC): Campus des Cézeaux, 24 ave des Landais, BP 80026, 63177 Aubière Cedex; tel. 4-73-40-73-80; e-mail g.delcampo@opgc.univ-bpclermont.fr; internet www.opgc.univ-bpclermont.fr; Dir PATRICK BACHÈLERY.

Polytech Clermont-Ferrand: 24 ave des Landais, BP 20206, 63174 Aubière Cedex; tel. 4-73-40-75-00; e-mail claude-gilles.dussap@polytech.univ-bpclermont.fr; internet www.cust.univ-bpclermont.fr; Dir CLAUDE-GILLES DUSSAP.

Psychologie, Sciences sociales, Sciences de l'éducation (Psychology, Social Sciences and Educational Science): 34 ave Carnot, 63037 Clermont-Ferrand Cedex; tel. 4-73-40-64-63; e-mail scolarite.psycho@univ-bpclermont.fr; internet www.psycho.univ-bpclermont.fr; Dir DELPHINE MARTINOT.

Sciences et Techniques des Activités Physiques et Sportives (STAPS—Science and Engineering in Physical Education and Sport): Campus des Cézeaux, 24 ave des Landais, BP 104, 63172 Aubière Cedex; tel. 4-73-40-75-35; e-mail secretariat.staps@univ-bpclermont.fr; internet www.staps.univ-bpclermont.fr; Dir ÉRIC DORÉ.

Sciences et Technologies (Science and Technology): 24 ave des Landais, BP 80026, 63171 Aubière Cedex; tel. 4-73-40-70-02; e-mail secretariat.sciences@univ-bpclermont.fr; internet www.sciences.univ-bpclermont.fr; Dir GILLES BOURDIER

UNIVERSITÉ DE BORDEAUX I

351 cours de la Libération, 33405 Talence Cedex
Telephone: 5-40-00-60-00
E-mail: communication@u-bordeaux1.fr
Internet: www.u-bordeaux1.fr

Pres.: ALAIN BOUDOU
Vice-Pres. for Admin.: JEAN-BAPTISTE VERLHAC
Vice-Pres. for Curriculum and Univ. Life: ACHILLE BRAQUELAIRE
Vice-Pres. for Int. Relations: JEAN-MICHEL BAUDERON
Vice-Pres. for Science: DEAN LEWIS
Sec.-Gen.: ERIC DUTIL

Number of teachers: 1,000
Number of students: 11,150.

TEACHING AND RESEARCH UNITS

Faculté de Chimie: 351 cours de la Libération, 33405 Talence Cedex; tel. 5-40-00-61-45; e-mail sec-ufrchimie@adm.u-bordeaux1.fr; Dir ALAIN FRITSCH.

Faculté de Mathématiques et Informatique: 351 cours de la Libération, 33405 Talence Cedex; tel. 5-40-00-64-21; e-mail direction@ufr-mi.u-bordeaux1.fr; internet www.u-bordeaux1.fr/ufr/math-info; Dir CHARLES-HENRI BRUNEAU.

Faculté de Physique: 351 cours de la Libération, 33405 Talence Cedex; tel. 5-40-00-62-17; e-mail sec@crphy.u-bordeaux1.fr; internet www.ufr-physique.u-bordeaux1.fr; Dir GENEVIÈVE DUCHAMP.

Faculté des Sciences Biologiques: ave des Facultés, 33405 Talence Cedex; tel. 5-40-00-87-00; e-mail ufr-biologie@adm.u-bordeaux1.fr; internet www.u-bordeaux1.fr/biologie; Dir JEAN-PIERRE RENAUDIN.

Faculté des Sciences de la Terre et de la Mer: ave des Facultés, 33405 Talence Cedex; tel. 5-40-00-88-79; e-mail ufr-termer@adm.u-bordeaux1.fr; internet www.u-bordeaux1.fr/terre_mer; Dir PASCAL LECROART.

UNIVERSITY PROFESSIONAL INSTITUTES

University Professional Institute of Computer-Assisted Management: tel. 5-40-00-89-49; internet miage.u-bordeaux.fr; Dir NICOLE BIDOIT.

University Professional Institute of Electrical Engineering and Industrial Informatics: tel. 5-40-00-28-30; internet www.creea.u-bordeaux.fr; Dir YVES DANTO.

University Professional Institute of Industrial Systems Engineering—Aircraft Maintenance: tel. 5-56-13-31-58; internet www.u-bordeaux1.fr/ima; Dir CHRISTIAN BOUILLE.

University Professional Institute of Mechanical Engineering: tel. 5-40-00-65-15; internet www.u-bordeaux1.fr/iup_gm; Dir MICHEL NOUILLANT.

ATTACHED INSTITUTES

École Nationale Supérieure de Chimie et de Physique de Bordeaux (ENSCPB): 16 ave Pey Berland, 33607 Pessac Cedex; tel. 5-40-00-65-65; e-mail admin@enscpb.fr; internet www.enscpb.fr; Dir BERNARD CLIN.

École Nationale Supérieure d'Électronique et de Radiocommunication de Bordeaux (ENSERB): 1 ave du Dr Albert Schweitzer, 33402 Talence Cedex; tel. 5-56-84-65-00; e-mail direction@enseirb-matmeca.fr; internet www.enserb.u-bordeaux.fr; Dir PHILIPPE MARCHEGAY.

Institut de Chimie de la Matière Condensée de Bordeaux (ICMCB): tel. 5-40-00-62-96; internet www.icmcb-bordeaux.cnrs.fr; Dir CLAUDE DELMAS.

Institut Européen de Chimie et Biologie (IECB): tel. 5-40-00-22-16; internet www.iecb-polytechnique.u-bordeaux.fr; Dir JEAN-JACQUES TOULMÉ.

Institut de Mathématiques de Bordeaux (IMCB): tel. 5-40-00-60-70; e-mail institut@math.u-bordeaux1.fr; internet www.math.u-bordeaux.fr/maths; Dir PHILIPPE CASSOUNOGUES.

Institut de Physique Fondamentale (IPF): tel. 5-40-00-83-13; internet www.u-bordeaux1.fr/ipf; Dir ERIC FREYS.

Institut de Recherche pour l'Enseignement des Mathématiques (IREM): tel. 5-40-00-89-74; Dir PIERRE DAMEY.

Institut des Sciences et Techniques d'Alimentation de Bordeaux (ISTAB): tel. 5-40-00-87-53; e-mail scolarite@istab.u-bordeaux1.fr; internet www.u-bordeaux1.fr/istab; Dir FRANÇOIS RIBOULET.

Institut du Pin (IP): tel. 5-40-00-64-20; e-mail ipin@ipin.u-bordeaux1.fr; internet www.u-bordeaux1.fr/ipin; Dir JEAN BARANGER.

Institut Universitaire de Technologie: Domaine Universitaire, 33405 Talence Cedex; tel. 5-56-84-57-02; internet www.iut.u-bordeaux1.fr; Dir PIERRE LAFON.

Observatoire: 2 rue de l'Observatoire, 33270 Floirac; tel. 5-57-77-61-63; internet www.obs.u-bordeaux1.fr; Dir THIERRY JACQ

UNIVERSITÉ BORDEAUX II (VICTOR SEGALEN)

146 rue Léo-Saignat, 33076 Bordeaux Cedex
Telephone: 5-57-57-10-10
E-mail: info@u-bordeaux2.fr
Internet: www.u-bordeaux2.fr
Founded 1970
Languages of instruction: English, French
Academic year: September to July

Pres.: MANUEL TUNON DE LARA
Vice-Pres. for Ccl of Admin.: Prof. ANTOINE DE DARUVAR
Vice-Pres. for Int. Relations: Prof. VINCENT DOUSSET
Vice-Pres. for Scientific Ccl: Prof. PIERRE DOS SANTOS
Vice-Pres. for Studies and Univ. Life: Prof. NICOLE RASCLE
Sec.-Gen.: CORINNE DUFFAU
Librarian: ANNE-MARIE BERNARD

Number of teachers: 1,000
Number of students: 22,000

Publication: *Anima* (4 a year)

UNIVERSITÉ BORDEAUX III (MICHEL DE MONTAIGNE)

Domaine Universitaire, 33607 Pessac Cedex
Telephone: 5-57-12-44-44
E-mail: accueil@u-bordeaux3.fr
Internet: www.u-bordeaux3.fr; attached to PRES Université de Bordeaux

Pres.: PATRICE BRUN
Vice-Pres. for Admin.: JEAN-PAUL JOURDAN
Vice-Pres. for Science Ccl: PATRICK BAUDRY
Vice-Pres. for Studies and Univ. Life: JEAN-YVES COQUELIN
Sec.-Gen.: THOMAS RAMBAUD
Librarian: ANITA LARGOUET

Number of teachers: 646
Number of students: 15,200

Publications: *Annales du Midi*, *Aquitania*, *Bulletin hispanique*, *Cahier d'outre-mer*, *Communication et organisation*, *Revue des études anciennes*, *Sud-Ouest européen*.

TEACHING AND RESEARCH UNITS

Institut de Journalisme Bordeaux Aquitaine (IJBA): 1 rue Jacques Ellul, 33080 Bordeaux Cedex; tel. 5-57-12-20-20; e-mail journalisme@ijba.u-bordeaux3.fr; Dir MARIA SANTOS-SAINZ.

Faculté des Humanités: Maison des Pays Ibériques, Domaine Universitaire, 33607 Pessac Cedex; tel. 5-57-12-46-38; e-mail accueil-ufr-humanites@u-bordeaux3.fr; Dir MARIE-BERNADETTE DUFOURCET-HAKIM.

Faculté des Langues et Civilisations: Bâtiment A, 1er étage, Domaine Universitaire, 33607 Pessac Cedex; tel. 5-57-12-44-71; e-mail accueil-ufr-langues@u-bordeaux3.fr; Dir STEPHAN MARTENS.

Faculté des Sciences des Territoires et de la Communication: Domaine Universitaire, 33607 Pessac Cedex; tel. 5-57-12-62-80; e-mail accueil-ufr-stc@u-bordeaux3.fr; Dir HÉLÈNE VELASCO-GRACIET.

Institut Environnement, Géo-ingénierie et Développement (EGID): 1 allée Daguin, 33607 Pessac Cedex; tel. 5-57-12-10-10; e-mail administration@egid.u-bordeaux.fr; Dir JEAN-MARIE MALEZIEUX.

Institut Universitaire de Technologie: Quartier Sainte Croix, 1 rue Jacques Ellul, 33080 Bordeaux Cedex; tel. 5-57-12-20-44; e-mail direction@iut.u-bordeaux3.fr; internet www.iut.u-bordeaux3.fr; Dir CLOTILDE DE MONTGOLFIER

PROFESSORS

ABECASSIS, A., Philosophy
AGOSTINO, M., Contemporary History
AGUILA, Y., Spanish
AUGUSTIN, J.-P., Geography
BARAT, J.-C., English
BART, F., Geography
BAUDRY, P., Sociology
BECHTEL, F., Physics applied to Archaeology
BERIAC, F., Medieval History
BERTIN-MAGHIT, J.-P., Cinema
BESSE, M. G., Portuguese Literature
BOHLER, D., Medieval Languages and Literature
BOST, J.-P., Ancient History
BOUCARUT, M., Petrography
BRAVO, F., Spanish
BRESSON, A., Medieval History
CABANES, J.-L., Contemporary French Literature
CAMBRONNE, P., Latin
CHAMPEAU, G., Spanish
CHARRIE, J.-P., Geography
COCULA, A.-M., Modern History
COCULA, B., French Language
CORZANI, J., Contemporary French Literature
COSTE, D., Comparative Literature
DEBORD, P., Ancient History
DE CARVALHO, P., Latin
DECOUDRAS, P. M., Land and Society in Tropical Environments
DEPRETTO, C., Russian
DESCAT, R., Greek History
DESCHAMPS, L., Latin
DES COURTILS, J., History of Art
DESVOIS, J.-M., Spanish
DI MÉO, G., Geography
DOTTIN ORSINI, M., Comparative Literature
DUBOIS, C., French
DUCASSE, R., Information Science
DURRUTY, S., English
DUTHEIL, F., Italian
DUVAL, G., English
FONDIN, H., Information and Communication Science
FOURTINA, H., English
FRANCHET D'ESPEREY, H., Latin
GARMENDIA, V., Spanish
GAUTHIER, M., American English
GILBERT, B., English
GORCEIX, P., German
GOZE, M., Urban Planning
GRANDJEAT, Y., North American Civilization
GUILLAUME, P., Modern History
GUILLAUME, S., Modern History
HOTIER, H., Information and Communication Science
HUMBERT, L., Geology
JARASSE, D., History of Modern Art
JOLY, M., Image Analysis
JOUVE, M., English
LACHAISE, B., Modern History
LACOSTE, J., History of Art
LAMORE, J., Spanish
LANGHADE, J., Arabic
LARRERE, C., Philosophy
LAVAUD, C., Philosophy
LAVEAU, P., German
LEBIGRE, J.-M., Physical Geography, Biogeography
LEPRUN-PIÉTON, S., Art, Plastic Arts
LERAT, C., English
LOPEZ, F., Spanish
LOUISE, G., Medieval History
LOUPES, P., History
LY, A., Spanish
MAILLARD, J.-C., Geography
MALEZIEUX, J.-M., Geology
MALLET, D., Arabic
MANTION, J.-R., 18th-century French Literature
MARIEU, J., Urban Planning and Projects
MARQUETTE, J.-B., History
MARTIN, D., French Language and Literature
MATHIEU, M., Contemporary Francophone Literature
MAZOUER, C., Contemporary French Literature
MONDOT, J., German
MORIN, S., Tropical Geography
MOULINE, L., Theatre
MULLER, C., General Linguistics
NAVARRI, R., French Language and Literature

NOTZ, M.-F., Medieval Language and Literature
OLLIER, N., English
ORPUSTAN, J.-B., Basque
PAILHE, J., Geography
PELLETIER, N., German
PERRIN-NAFFAKH, A.-M., Contemporary Language and Literature
PERROT, M., Information and Communications Science
PEYLET, G., Contemporary Language and Literature
PICCIONE, M.-L., Contemporary Language and Literature
PONCEAU, J.-P., Medieval Language and Literature
PONTET, J., Modern History
PORTINE, H., Teaching French as a Foreign Language
POUCHAN, P., Geology
RABATE, D., Contemporary French Literature
RAMOND, C., Philosophy
REYNIER-GIRARDIN, C., English
RIBEIRO, M., Portuguese
RICARD, M., Tropical Pacific Phytoplankton
RIGAL-CELLARD, B., English
RITZ, R., English
ROCHER, A., Japanese
RODDAZ, J.-M., Ancient History
ROSSI, G., Geography
ROUCH, M., Italian
ROUDIE, P., Geography
ROUYER, M.-C., English
ROUYER, P., Plastic Art
RUIZ, A., German
SALOMON, J.-N., Geography
SCHVOERER, M., Physics applied to Archaeology
SENTAURENS, J., Spanish
SEVESTRE, N., Music and History of Music
SHEN, J., Applied Mathematics
SHUSTERMAN, R., English
SINGARAVELOU, Geography
TAILLARD, C., History of Modern Art
TERREL, J., Philosophy
VADE, Y., Contemporary Language and Literature
VAGNE-LEBAS, M., Social Communication
VIGNE, M.-P., English
VITALIS, A., Information and Communication Science
VLES, V., Urban Planning
ZAVIALOFF, N., Russian

UNIVERSITÉ BORDEAUX IV (MONTESQUIEU)

ave Léon-Duguit, 33608 Pessac Cedex
Telephone: 5-56-84-85-86
E-mail: umb4@montesquieu.u-bordeaux.fr
Internet: www.u-bordeaux4.fr

Founded 1995 from units fmrly within the Univ. of Bordeaux I

State control; attached to PRES Université de Bordeaux

7 Establishments at Bordeaux, Agen and Périgeux; 3 doctoral schools, 12 research units, 2 technology institutes, 1 business management institute, 1 political science institute

Pres.: YANNICK LUNG
Vice-Pres. for Admin. and Finance: CLAUDE DUPUY
Vice-Pres. for Education: GÉRARD BORDENAVE
Vice-Pres. for Research: DANIEL BOURMAUD
Sec.-Gen.: MARLÈNE BARBOTIN
Librarian: DOMINIQUE MONTBRUN-ISRAËL

Number of teachers: 690 incl. researchers
Number of students: 18,700.

TEACHING AND RESEARCH UNITS

Faculté de Droit et Science Politique: Dean JEAN-FRANÇOIS BRISSON.

Faculté d'Économie, Gestion et AES: Dir BERTRAND BLANCHETON.

Institut d'Administration des Entreprises (IAE): 35 ave Abadie, 33072 Bordeaux Cedex; tel. 5-56-00-45-67; internet www.iae-bordeaux.fr; Dean SERGE EVRAERT.

Institut Universitaire de Formation des Maîtres d'Aquitaine (IUFM): 160 ave de Verdun, BP 90152, 33705 Mérignac; tel. 5-56-12-67-60; e-mail relations_internationales@iufm.u-bordeaux4.fr; internet iufm.u-bordeaux4.fr; f. 1991; in 2008 became Univ. School; Dean Prof. PHILIPPE GIRARD; Sec.-Gen. Prof. LUDOVIC CANÉ.

Institut Universitaire de Technologie Bordeaux Montesquieu: 35 ave Abadie, 33072 Bordeaux Cedex; tel. 5-56-00-96-05; e-mail directeur-iutbxm@u-bordeaux4.fr; internet www.iut.u-bordeaux4.fr; Dir ANNIE LESPINASSE.

Institut Universitaire de Technologie Périgueux Bordeaux IV: 39 rue Paul Mazy, 24019 Périgueux Cedex; tel. 5-53-02-58-58; e-mail iutpxbx4@u-bordeaux4.fr; internet www.perigueux.u-bordeaux4.fr; Pres. PATRICK MONTFORT.

ATTACHED INSTITUTE

Institut d'Etudes Politiques: 11 allée Ausone, 33607 Pessac Cedex; tel. 5-56-84-42-52; e-mail direction@sciencespobordeaux.fr; internet www.sciencespobordeaux.fr; Dir VINCENT HOFFMANN-MARTINOT

UNIVERSITÉ DE BOURGOGNE

Maison de l'Université, Esplanade Erasme, BP 27877, 21078 Dijon Cedex
Telephone: 3-80-39-50-00
E-mail: presidente@u-bourgogne.fr
Internet: www.u-bourgogne.fr

Founded 1722 as Dijon Faculty of Law

Pres.: SOPHIE BÉJEAN
Vice-Pres.: ALAIN BONNIN
Sec.-Gen.: JEAN NARVAEZ
Librarian: NATALIE CÊTRE

Number of teachers: 1,500
Number of students: 27,400

Publications: *Journal d'Information, Livret de la recherche, Publications de l'Université* (irregular series of monographs).

TEACHING AND RESEARCH UNITS

Faculté de Droit et de Science Politique: tel. 3-80-39-54-26; e-mail estelle.mielle@u-bourgogne.fr; internet ufr-juridique.u-bourgogne.fr; Dean LAURENCE RAVILLON.

Faculté de Langues et Communication: 2 blvd Gabriel, 21000 Dijon; tel. 3-80-39-55-00; Dir SYLVIE INIESTA.

Faculté de Lettres et Philosophie: 2 blvd Gabriel, 21000 Dijon; tel. 3-80-39-56-01; e-mail seclphi@u-bourgogne.fr; internet ufr-lettres-philosophie.u-bourgogne.fr; Dean PHILIPPE MONNERET.

Faculté de Médecine: 7 blvd Jeanne d'Arc, BP 87900, 21079 Dijon; tel. 3-80-39-32-00; internet medecine.u-bourgogne.fr; Dean FRÉDÉRIC HUET.

Faculté de Science Economique et Gestion: 7 blvd Jeanne d'Arc, BP 87900, 21079 Dijon; tel. 3-80-39-54-00; e-mail edlisit@u-bourgogne.fr; internet ufr-economique.u-bourgogne.fr; Dean STÉPHANE TIZIO.

Faculté des Sciences de la Vie, de la Terre et de l'Environnement: Batiment Gabriel, 6 blvd Gabriel, 21079 Dijon; tel. 3-80-39-50-30; e-mail direction-ufrsvte@u-bourgogne.fr; internet ufr-svte.u-bourgogne.fr; Dir MICHEL NARCE.

Faculté des Sciences du Sport: Campus Universitaire Montmuzard, BP 27 877, 21078 Dijon; tel. 3-80-39-67-01; e-mail tania.carnet@u-bourgogne.fr; Dir JEAN-PIERRE REY.

Faculté des Sciences et Techniques: Bâtiment Mirande, 9 ave Alain Savary, BP 47870, 21078 Dijon; tel. 3-80-39-67-01; e-mail thierry.grison@u-bourgogne.fr; internet sciences-techniques.u-bourgogne.fr; Dir THIERRY GRISSON.

Faculté des Sciences Humaines: 2 blvd Gabriel, 21000 Dijon; e-mail carine.lausseur@u-bourgogne.fr; internet sciences-humaines.u-bourgogne.fr; Dir DANIEL DURNEY.

Faculté des Sciences Pharmaceutiques et Biologiques: 7 blvd Jeanne d'Arc, BP 87900, 21079 Dijon; tel. 3-80-39-33-00; e-mail secretariat.doyen.pharmacie@u-bourgogne.fr; internet pharmacie.u-bourgogne.fr; Dir Prof. EVELYNE KOHLI

PROFESSORS

Arts Faculties:
ABDI, Psychology
ALI BOUACHA, French Linguistics
BASTIT, Philosophy
BAVOUX, Geography
BENONY, Psychology
BERCOT, Modern Literature
CHAPUIS, Geography
CHARRIER, Geography
CHARUE, German
CHARUE, German
CHEVIGNARD, American English
CHIFFRE, Geography
COMANZO, English
COURTOIS, Comparative Literature
DOBIAS, Classical Literature
DUCHENE, History
DUCOS, Classical Literature
DURIX, English
DURU, Education
FAYARD, Modern History
FAYOL, Psychology
FERRARI, Philosophy
FOYARD, French Philology
GARNOT, Modern History
HAAS, French Linguistics
IMBERTY, Italian
JACOBI, Information and Communication Science
JOLY, Latin
LAMARRE, Geography
LARRAZ, Romance Languages
LAVAUD, Spanish
LAVAUD, Spanish
MCCARTHY, English
MORDANT, Protohistory
NOUHAUD, Spanish
PELLAN, English
PERARD, Geography
PERROT, Philosophy
PIROELLE, English
PITAVY, English
PITAVY, English
POURKIER, Greek
QUILLIOT, Philosophy
RATIE, English
REFFET, German
RONSIN, Modern History
SADRIN, English
SADRIN, French Literature
SAINT-DENIS, Medieval History
SAURON, Audiology
SOUILLER, Comparative Literature
SOUTET, Linguistics, Phonetics
TABBAGH, Medieval Archaeology
TAVERDET, French Philology
TUROWSLI, History of Art
VINTER, Psychology
WOLIKOW, History and Civilization
WUNENBURGER, Philosophy
ZAGAR, Psychology

Faculties of Law and Economic Science:
BALESTRA, Economic Sciences
BART, Law, Roman Law
BAUMONT, Economics
BODINEAU, History of Law
BOLARD, Private Law
BROUSSOLLE, Public Law
CASIMIR, Management
CHADEFAUX, Management
CHAPPEZ, Public Law
CHARREAUX, Management
CLERE, History of Law
COURVOISIER, Political Sciences
DE MESNARD, Economics
DESBRIÈRES, Economics
DOCKES, Private Law
DUBOIS, Public Law
FILSER, Management Sciences
FORTUNET, History of Law
FRITZ, Political Sciences
GADREAU, Economics
HURIOT, Economic Sciences
JACQUEMONT, Management
JOBERT, History of Law
KORNPROBST, Public Law
LOQUIN, Private Law
MARTIN-SERF, Private Law
MATHIEU, Public Law
MICHELOT, Economics, Mathematics
PAUL, Economics of Education
PERREUR, Economic Sciences
PICHERY, M. C., Economics
PIERI, History of Law
PIERI, Private Law
PIZZIO, Private Law
ROUGET, Economics
SALMON, Political Economy
SIMON, Public Law

Faculties of Medicine and Pharmacy:
ARTUR, Physical Biochemistry
AUTISSIER, Anatomy
AUTISSIER, Physical Chemistry
BEDENNE, Gastroenterology
BELON, Pharmacology
BESANCENOT, Internal Medicine
BINNERT, Radiology
BLETTERY, Resuscitation
BONNIN, Parasitology
BRALET, Physiology
BRENOT, Vascular Surgery
BRON, Ophthalmology
BROSSIER, Physical Chemistry
BRUN, Endocrinology
BRUNOTTE, Biophysics
CAMUS, Pneumology
CARLI, Haematology
CASILLAS, Rehabilitation
CHAILLOT, Pharmacy
CHAVANET, Infectious Diseases
COUGARD, Surgery
CUISENIER, Surgery
DAVID, Thoracic and Cardiac Surgery
DELCOURT, Pharmacy
DIDIER, Rehabilitation
DUBOIS-LACAILLE, Pharmacognosy
DUMAS, Neurology
DUMAS, Pharmacology
DUSSERRE, Biostatistics
ESCOUSSE, Clinical Pharmacology
FAIVRE, Gastroenterology
FANTINO, Physiology
FAVRE, General Surgery
FELDMAN, Gynaecology and Obstetrics
FREYSZ, Anaesthesiology
GAMBERT, Biochemistry
GIRARD, Anaesthesiology
GIROUD, Neurology
GISSELMANN, Epidemiology
GOUYON, Paediatrics
GRAMMONT, Orthopaedic Surgery and Traumatology
GUERRIN, Oncology
HILLON, Hepatology, Gastroenterology
HORIOT, Radiotheraphy
HUICHARD, Pharmaceutical Law
JEANNIN, Pneumology
JUSTRABO, Pathological Anatomy
KAZMIERCZAK, Bacteriology, Virology
KRAUSE, Radiology
LAMBERT, Dermatology
LORCERIE, Internal Medicine
LOUIS, Cardiology
MABILLE, S. P., Radiology
MACK, Biochemistry
MALKA, Stomatology and Maxillofacial Surgery
MARTIN, F., Immunology
MOURIER, Neurosurgery
NEEL, Biochemistry
NIVELON, Paediatrics
PADIEU, Biological Chemistry
PFITZEMEYER, Internal Medicine
PIARD, Pathological Anatomy
PORTIER, Infectious and Tropical Diseases
POTHIER, Bacteriology
POURCELOT, Pharmacy
RAT, General Surgery
RIFLE, Nephrology
ROCHAT, Pharmacy
ROCHETTE, Pharmacy
ROMANET, Otorhinolaryngology
ROUSSET, Bacteriology
SAGOT, Gynaecology
SAUTREAUX, Neurosurgery
SCHREIBER, Pharmacy
SMOLIK, Occupational Medicine
SOLARY, Haematology
TAVERNIER, Rheumatology
TEYSSIER, Cytogenetic Histology
THEVENIN, Pharmacy
THIERRY, Neurosurgery
TRAPET, Adult Psychiatry
TROUILLOUD, Orthopaedic Surgery and Anatomy
VERGES, Endocrinology of Metabolic Diseases
WEILLER, Radiology
WILKENING, Anaesthesiology
WOLF, Cardiology
ZAHND, Embryology

Higher Institute of Transport and the Car:
AIVAZZADEH, S., Mechanics
LESUEUR, Mechanics
VERCHERY, Mechanics

Higher National School of Applied Biology:
BELIN, Alimentary Biotermology
BESNARD, Physiology of Nutrition
DIVIES, Microbiology
GERVAIS, Process Engineering
LE MESTE, Physical Chemistry of Food
L'HUGUENOT, Biochemistry
MOLIN, Mathematics
TAINTURIER, Organic Chemistry
VOILLEY, Biology, Biochemistry

Physical Education and Sport:
MORLON, B., Biophysics
VANHOECKE, J., Physical Education and Sport

Science Faculties:
ANDREUX, Geochemistry
BELLEVILLE, J., Animal Physiology
BERGER, Physics
BERTRAND, Chemistry
BESANÇON, Chemistry
BOBIN, Physics
BONNARD, Mathematics
BOQUILLON, Physics
CAMPY, Geology
CEZILLY, Ecology
CHABRIER, Computer Sciences
CHAMPION, Physics
CLOUET, Animal Physiology
COLSON, Chemistry
CONNAT, Animal Biology
COQUET, Physics
CORTET, Mathematics
DEMARQUOY, Animal Physiology
DEREUX, Physics
DOLECKI, Mathematics
DORMOND, Chemistry
DULIEU, Animal Physiology
FANG, Mathematics
FLATO, Mathematics
FRANGE, Chemistry
FROCHOT, B., Ecology
GAUTHERON, B., Chemistry
GOUDONNET, Physics
GUILARD, R., Mathematics
GUIRAUD, Geology
JANNIN, Physics
JANNOT, Physics
JAUSLIN, Physics
JOUBERT, Mathematics
KUBICKI, Chemistry
LALLEMANT, Chemistry
LANG, J., Geology
LANGEVIN, Mathematics
LARPIN, Physical Chemistry
LASSALE, Mathematics
LATRUFFE, Biochemistry
LAURIN, Geology
LENOIR-ROUSSEAU, Zoology
LINES, Mathematics
LOETE, Physics
LOREAU, Geology
MARCUARD, Statistical Probability
MARNIER, Physics
MARTY, Plant Biology
MATVEEV, Mathematics
MAUME, B., Biochemistry
MEUNIER, Chemistry
MICHELOT, Physics
MICHON, Mathematics
MILAN, Electronics
MILLOT, Physics
MOÏSE, C., Chemistry
MOUSSU, Mathematics
MUGNIER, Chemistry
NIEPCE, J.-CL., Chemistry
PAINDAVOINE, Automatics
PALLO, Informatics
PAUL, Plant Biology
PAUTY, Physics
PERRON, Mathematics
PIERRE, Physics
PINCZON, Mathematics
PRIBETICH, Electronics
PUGIN, Biochemistry
RACLIN, Mechanics
REMOISSENET, Physics
ROUSSARIE, Mathematics
SCHMITT, Mathematics
SEMENOV, Mathematics
SIEROFF, Neurophysiology
SIMON, Mathematics
STEINBRUNN, Chemistry
THIERRY, Geology
TOURNEFIER, Biology
VALLADE, Plant Biology
WABNITZ, Physics
YETONGNON, Informatics

University Institute of Technology:
BELEY, Biology, Applied Biochemistry
BERLIÈRE, Contemporary History
BERNARD, Physiology and Nutrition
BESSIS, Botany
BIZOUARD, M., Thermodynamics
BUGAUT, Biochemistry
CHANUSSOT, Physics
DIOU, Industrial Computer Science
GORRIA, Computer Engineering
GREVEY, Materials
POISSON, Biochemistry
SACILOTTI, Physics
TRUCHETET, Computer Engineering

University Professional Institute of Management in Education, Training and Culture:
JAROUSSE, J.-P., Education
PATRIAT, C., Informatics and Communication
SOLAUX, A., Education

Viticulture and Oenology Experimental Centre:

CHARPENTIER, O., Oenology
FEUILLAT, M., Oenology

UNIVERSITÉ DE BRETAGNE OCCIDENTALE

Site 1–3, rue des Archives, BP 808, 29285 Brest Cedex
Telephone: 2-98-01-60-03
E-mail: secretariat.general@univ-brest.fr
Internet: www.univ-brest.fr

Pres.: PASCAL OLIVARD
Vice-Pres.: GEORGES TYMEN
Sec.-Gen.: STÉPHANE CHARPENTIER
Librarian: ALAIN SAINSOT

Number of teaching staff: 820
Number of students: 20,000.

TEACHING AND RESEARCH INSTITUTES

Faculté de Droit, Économie et Gestion: 12 rue de Kergoat, CS 93837, 29238 Brest Cedex 3; tel. 2-98-01-60-23; e-mail directeur .deg@univ-brest.fr; internet www.univ-brest .fr/ufr-droit-economie; Dean BÉATRICE THOMAS-TUAL.

Faculté de Lettres et Sciences Humaines: 20 rue Duquesne, CS 93837, 29238 Brest Cedex 3; tel. 2-98-01-67-98; e-mail scolarite.lettres@univ-brest.fr; internet www.faculte-lettres-shs-brest.fr; Dir MARIE-ARMELLE BARBIER.

Faculté de Médecine et Sciences de la Santé: 22 rue Camille Desmoulins, CS 93837, 29238 Brest Cedex 3; tel. 2-98-01-64-73; e-mail doyen.medecine@univ-brest.fr; internet www.faculte-medecine-brest.fr; Dean Prof. MARC DE BRAEKELEER.

Faculté d'Odontologie: 22 rue Camille Desmoulins, CS 93837, 29238 Brest Cedex 3; tel. 2-98-01-64-89; e-mail alain.zerilli@ univ-brest.fr; Dean ALAIN ZERILLI.

Faculté des Sciences et Techniques: 6 ave Victor Le Gorgeu, CS 93837, 29238 Brest Cedex 3; tel. 2-98-01-61-22; e-mail directeur .sciences@univ-brest.fr; internet www .faculte-sciences-brest.fr; Dir CORINNE TARITS.

Faculté de Sport et Éducation Physique: 6 ave Victor Le Gorgeu, CS 93837, 29238 Brest Cedex 3; tel. 2-98-01-71-47; e-mail secrestaps@univ-brest.fr; internet www .univ-brest.fr/ufr-sport; Dir GILLES KERMARREC.

ATTACHED RESEARCH INSTITUTES

École Supérieure de Microbiologie et Sécurité Alimentaire de Brest (ESMISAB): Technopôle Brest-Iroise, 29280 Plouzané; tel. 2-98-05-61-00; e-mail esmisab@ univ-brest.fr; internet www.univ-brest.fr/ esmisab; Dir YVES TIRILLY.

Institut de Recherche sur l'Enseignement des Mathématiques (IREM): 6 ave Victor Le Gorgeu, 29238 Brest Cedex 3; tel. 2-98-01-65-44; e-mail irem@univ-brest.fr; Dir (vacant).

Institut des Sciences Agro-alimentaires et du Monde Rural: 2 rue de l'université, 29334 Quimper Cedex; tel. 2-98-90-85-48; Dir ADRIEN BINET.

Institut de Synergie des Sciences de la Santé: Site CHU Morvan, 29609 Brest Cedex; tel. 2-98-01-81-30; internet www .univ-brest.fr/i3s; Dir CLAUDE FEREC.

Institut Universitaire Européen de la Mer (IUEM): place Nicolas Copernic, 29280 Plouzané; tel. 2-98-49-86-00; e-mail direction .iuem@univ-brest.fr; internet www .univ-brest.fr/iuem; Dir PAUL TREGUER

UNIVERSITÉ DE BRETAGNE-SUD

BP 92116, 56321 Lorient Cedex
Telephone: 2-97-01-70-89
E-mail: communication@univ-ubs.fr
Internet: www.univ-ubs.fr

Founded 1995

Pres.: OLIVIER SIRE
Vice-Pres. for Admin.: IOANA GALLERON
Vice-Pres. for Int. Relations: GEOFFREY WILLIAMS
Vice-Pres. for Science Ccl: PIERRE-FRANÇOIS MARTEAU
Vice-Pres. for Studies and Univ. Life: GILBERT LE BOUAR
Sec.-Gen.: CHRISTIAN BILY
Librarian: ANNIE COISY

Number of teachers: 427
Number of students: 8,576.

TEACHING AND RESEARCH UNITS

École Nationale Supérieure d'Ingénieurs de Bretagne Sud: 2 rue le Coat Saint-Haouen, BP 92116, 56321 Lorient Cedex; tel. 2-97-88-05-59; e-mail ensibs .scol@listes.univ-ubs.fr; internet www-ensibs .univ-ubs.fr; Dir JEAN-LUC PHILIPPE.

Faculté de Droit, des Sciences Economiques et de Gestion: 1 rue de la Loi, 56000 Vannes; tel. 2-97-01-26-00; e-mail dseg@univ-ubs.fr; Dir PATRICK LE MESTRE.

Faculté de Lettres Langues Sciences Humaines et Sociales: 4 rue Jean Zay, BP 92116, 56321 Lorient Cedex; tel. 2-97-87-29-67; e-mail helene.tanguy@univ-ubs.fr; Dir ERIC LIMOUSIN.

Faculté des Sciences et Sciences de l'Ingénieur: 2 rue Coat Saint-Haouen, BP 92116, 56321 Lorient Cedex; tel. 2-97-88-05-50; e-mail helene.tanguy@univ-ubs.fr; Dir VIRGINIE DUPONT.

Institut Universitaire et Technologique de Lorient: 10 rue Jean Zay, 56325 Lorient Cedex; tel. 2-97-87-28-03; e-mail iutlo.dir@ listes.univ-ubs.fr; internet www-iutlorient .univ-ubs.fr; Dir JEAN VERGER.

Institut Universitaire et Technologique de Vannes: 8 rue Montaigne, BP 561, 56017 Vannes Cedex; tel. 2-97-62-64-64; e-mail iutva.com@listes.univ-ubs.fr; internet www .iu-vannes.fr; Dir PATRICE KERMORVANT

UNIVERSITÉ DE CAEN BASSE-NORMANDIE

Esplanade de la Paix, BP 5186, 14032 Caen Cedex 5
Telephone: 2-31-56-55-00
E-mail: presidence@unicaen.fr
Internet: www.unicaen.fr

Founded 1432; reorganized 1985

Pres.: JOSETTE TRAVERT
Vice-Pres: RÉGIS CARIN, DOMINIQUE KERVADEC
Sec.-Gen.: HÉLÈNE BROCHET-TOUTIRI
Librarian: BERNARD VOUILLOT

Number of teachers: 1,364
Number of students: 24,244.

TEACHING AND RESEARCH UNITS

Faculté de Droit et Sciences Politiques: Esplanade de la paix, BP 5186, 14032 Caen Cedex 5; e-mail droit.direction@unicaen.fr; internet www.unicaen.fr/droit; Dean Prof. JEAN-FRANÇOIS AKANDJI-KOMBE.

Faculté de Géographie: Esplanade de la paix, BP 5186, 14032 Caen Cedex 5; tel. 2-31-56-54-64; e-mail geographie.direction@ unicaen.fr; internet www.unicaen.fr/ geographie; Dir STÉPHANE COSTA.

Faculté des Langues Vivantes Etrangères: Esplanade de la paix, BP 5186, 14032 Caen Cedex 5; tel. 2-31-56-57-77; e-mail lve.secretariat@unicaen.fr; internet www.unicaen.fr/lve; Dir ERIC GILBERT.

Faculté de Médecine: ave de la Côte de Nacre, 14000 Caen Cedex 5; tel. 2-31-56-57-77; internet www.unicaen.fr/medecine; Dean Prof. JEAN-LOUIS GERARD.

Faculté de Psychologie: Esplanade de la paix, BP 5186, 14032 Caen Cedex 5; tel. 2-31-56-57-61; e-mail dominique.bour@unicaen.fr; internet www.unicaen.fr/psychologie; Dir JOËLLE LEBREUILLY.

Faculté de Sciences: blvd Maréchal Juin, 14032 Caen Cedex; tel. 2-31-56-73-10; e-mail sciences@unicaen.fr; internet www.unicaen .fr/sciences; Dir MARC LEVALOIS.

Faculté des Sciences de l'Homme: Esplanade de la paix, BP 5186, 14032 Caen Cedex 5; tel. 2-31-56-54-51; e-mail sciences .homme@unicaen.fr; internet www.unicaen .fr/sc-homme; Dir YINSU VIZCARRA.

Faculté des Sciences Economiques et de Gestion: 19 rue Claude Bloch, BP 1586, 14000 Caen Cedex; tel. 2-31-56-55-27; e-mail sciences.economiques.scolarite@unicaen.fr; internet www.unicaen.fr/sc-eco; Dir BONIFACE MBIH.

Faculté des Sciences et Techniques des Activités Physiques et Sportives: blvd Maréchal Juin, 14032 Caen Cedex; tel. 2-31-56-60-00; e-mail catherine.garncarzyk@ unicaen.fr; internet www.unicaen.fr/staps; Dir CATHERINE GARNCARZYK.

Faculté des Sciences Pharmaceutiques: blvd Becquerel, 14032 Caen Cedex; tel. 2-31-56-60-00; e-mail pharmacie.administration@ unicaen.fr; internet www.unicaen.fr/ pharmacie; Dean JEAN-MARIE GAZENGEL.

Faculté d'Histoire: Esplanade de la paix, BP 5186, 14032 Caen Cedex 5; tel. 2-31-56-58-30; e-mail histoire.secretariat@unicaen.fr; internet www.unicaen.fr/ufr/histoire; Dir JEAN QUELLIEN.

ATTACHED INSTITUTES

Ecole Nationale Supérieure d'Ingénieurs de Caen: 6 blvd Maréchal Juin, 14050 Caen Cedex; tel. 2-31-45-27-50; e-mail scolarite@ensicaen.fr; internet www .ensicaen.fr; Dir D. GUERREAU.

Institut Universitaire de Formation des Maîtres: 186 rue de la Délivrande, 14053 Caen Cedex 04; tel. 2-31-46-70-80; internet www.caen.iufm.fr; Dir JEAN MARC GUEGUENIAT

UNIVERSITÉ DE CERGY-PONTOISE

33 blvd du Port, 95011 Cergy-Pontoise Cedex
Telephone: 1-34-25-60-00
Internet: www.u-cergy.fr

Founded 1991

Pres.: FRANÇOISE MOULIN CIVIL
Vice-Pres.: ANNE-SOPHIE BARTHEZ
Sec.-Gen.: BERNARD FRADIN

Number of teachers: 833
Number of students: 17,000

UNIVERSITÉ DE CORSE PASQUALE PAOLI/UNIVERSITÀ DI CORSICA

BP 52, 22 ave Jean-Nicoli, 20250 Corti
Telephone: 4-95-45-00-00
Internet: www.univ-corse.fr

Founded 1976, opened 1981
Language of instruction: French
Academic year: September to July

Pres.: PAUL-MARIE ROMANI
Sec.-Gen.: FABIENNE PALMARO
Chief Librarian: MARIE-PAULE PEREZ

Library of 80,000 vols
Number of students: 4,400

DEANS

Faculty of Law, Economics and Management: JEAN-YVES COPPOLANI
Faculty of Literature, Languages, Arts and Human Sciences: PASCAL OTTAVI
Faculty of Sciences and Techniques: VANINA PASQUALINI
University Institute of Technology: CHRISTIAN CRISTOFARI
University Trainees Training Centre: CHRISTOPHE STORAI

ATTACHED RESEARCH INSTITUTES

Centre de Recherche Corse Méditerranée (CRCM): tel. 4-95-45-00-77; Dir PHILIPPE PESTEIL.

Institut de Développement des Iles Méditerranéennes (IDIM): tel. 4-95-45-00-18; Dir JEAN YVES COPPOLANI.

Institut d'Études Scientifiques de Cargèse: 20130 Cargèse; internet cargese.univ-corse.fr; Dir ELISABETH DUBOIS-VIOLETTE.

'Lieux, Identités, eSpaces et Acitvités': tel. 4-95-45-01-78; Dir MARIE-ANTOINETTE MAUPERTUIS.

'Sciences pour l'environnement': SPE UMA 6134, Quartier Grossetti, BP 52, 20250 Corte; tel. 4-95-45-01-65; e-mail spe@univ-corse.fr; internet spe.univ-corse.fr; Dir PAUL BISGAMBIGLIA

UNIVERSITÉ D'ÉVRY-VAL D'ESSONNE

blvd F. Mitterrand, 91025 Évry Cedex
Telephone: 1-69-47-70-00
E-mail: olivier.emery@univ-evry.fr
Internet: www.univ-evry.fr
Pres.: RICHARD MESSINA
First Vice-Pres.: ALIAN ZOZIME
Second Vice-Pres.: GÉRARD PORCHER
Sec.-Gen.: HAKIM KHELLAF
Number of teachers: 473
Number of students: 10,000.

TEACHING AND RESEARCH UNITS

Faculté de Droit: 335 Bâtiment Ile-de-France, 91025 Évry Cedex; tel. 1-69-47-70-97; e-mail nadine.bonnet@univ-evry.fr; Dir FRANÇOIS COLLY.

Faculté de Langues, Arts et Musique: B104 bis Bâtiment 1° cycles, 1° étage, 91025 Évry Cedex; tel. 1-69-47-74-44; e-mail secretariat.art@univ-evry.fr; Dir BRIGITTE GAUTHIER.

Faculté des Sciences Fondamentales et Appliquées: Bâtiment Maupertuis, rue du Père André Jarlan, 91025 Évry Cedex; tel. 1-69-47-74-44; e-mail ufrsfa@univ-evry.fr; Dir ANNIE CHAUSSE.

Faculté des Sciences Sociales et Gestion: 2 rue du Facteur Cheval, 91025 Évry Cedex; tel. 1-69-47-78-90; e-mail corinne.garault@univ-evry.fr; Dir EMMANUEL QUENSON.

Faculté des Sciences et Technologie: 40 rue du Pelvoux, 91020 Évry Cedex; tel. 1-69-47-75-24; e-mail ufrst@univ-evry.fr; Dir GÉRARD PORCHER.

ATTACHED RESEARCH INSTITUTE

Institut Universitaire de Technologie (IUT): 22 allée Jean Rostand, 91025 Évry Cedex; tel. 1-69-47-72-00; e-mail f.quemener@iut.univ-evry.fr; internet www.iut.univ-evry.fr; Dir PAUL DEMAREZ

UNIVERSITÉ DE FRANCHE-COMTÉ

1 rue Claude Goudimel, 25030 Besançon Cedex
Telephone: 3-81-66-66-66
E-mail: dri@univ-fcomte.fr
Internet: www.univ-fcomte.fr
Founded 1423 at Dôle, 1691 at Besançon
Pres.: CLAUDE CONDÉ
Vice-Pres.: DANIEL SECHTER
Vice-Pres.: JACQUES BAHI
Vice-Pres.: OUSSAMA BARAKATT
Sec.-Gen.: LOUIS BÉRION
Library: see under Libraries and Archives
Number of teachers: 1,400
Number of students: 19,519
Publications: *En Direct, Tout l'U.*

TEACHING AND RESEARCH INSTITUTES

Faculté des Sciences du Langage, de l'Homme et de la Société: 30 rue Mégevand, 25030 Besançon Cedex; tel. 3-81-66-53-10; internet slhs.univ-fcomte.fr; Dir ANDRÉ MARIAGE.

Faculté des Sciences et Techniques: 16 route de Gray, 25030 Besançon Cedex; tel. 3-81-66-69-51; e-mail webst@univ-fcomte.fr; internet sciences.univ-fcomte.fr; Dir ABDERRAZZAK KADMIRI.

Faculté des Sciences Juridiques, Economiques, Politiques et de Gestion: 45D ave de l'Observatoire, 25030 Besançon Cedex; tel. 3-63-08-25-47; e-mail catherine.tirvaudey@univ-fcomte.fr; internet sjepg.univ-fcomte.fr; Dir CATHERINE TIRVAUDEY.

Faculté des Sciences Médicales et Pharmaceutiques: place Saint-Jacques, 25030 Besançon Cedex; tel. 3-81-66-55-05; e-mail webmaster-smp@univ-fcomte.fr; internet medecine-pharmacie.univ-fcomte.fr; Dir Prof. EMMANUEL SAMAIN.

Faculté des Sciences, Techniques et Gestion de l'Industrie: Campus Universitaire, 4 place Tharradin, BP 71427, 25211 Montbéliard Cedex; tel. 3-81-99-46-62; e-mail ufr-stgi@univ-fcomte.fr; internet stgi.univ-fcomte.fr; Dir ABDERRAZZAK KADMIRI.

Unité de Promotion, de Formation et de Recherche des Sports: 31 chemin de l'Épitaphe, 25000 Besançon Cedex; tel. 3-81-66-67-90; e-mail u-sports@univ-fcomte.fr; internet ufrstaps.univ-fcomte.fr; Dir ERIC PREDINE

UNIVERSITÉ DE GRENOBLE I (UNIVERSITÉ JOSEPH FOURIER)

BP 53, 38041 Grenoble Cedex 9
Telephone: 4-76-51-46-00
E-mail: service.communication@ujf-grenoble.fr
Internet: www.ujf-grenoble.fr
Founded 1339
Academic year: September to June
Pres.: Prof. PATRICK LÉVY
Vice-Pres.: PIERRE BACONNIER
Vice-Pres.: Prof. JEAN-CLAUDE FERNANDEZ
Vice-Pres.: MICHAEL KLASEN
Vice-Pres.: YASSINE LAKHNECH
Vice-Pres.: Prof. ANNE MILLET
Vice-Pres.: Prof. ISABELLE OLIVIER
Vice-Pres.: Prof. KONSTANTIN PROTASSOV
Vice-Pres.: JEAN-GABRIEL VALAY
Sec.-Gen.: JEAN-LUC ARGENTIER
Number of teachers: 1,500
Number of students: 17,000
Publications: *La Pie* (12 a year), *Les Dépêches de l'UJF* (10 a year), *Papyrus* (2 a year).

ATTACHED INSTITUTES

Collège des Ecoles Doctorales: tel. 4-76-51-45-08; Dir PATRICK WITOMSKI.

Département Licence Sciences et Technologies: 480 Ave centrale, 38400 St Martin d'Hères; tel. 4-76-51-45-63; internet dlst.ujf-grenoble.fr; Dir YVES MARKOWICZ.

Département Université Joseph Fourier Valence: BP 2, 26901 Valence Cedex 9; tel. 4-56-52-11-11; e-mail contact.valence@ujf-grenoble.fr; internet valence.ujf-grenoble.fr; Dir JEAN-PIERRE JULIEN.

Ecole de Physique des Houches: La Côte des Chavants, 74310 Les Houches; tel. 4-50-54-40-69; e-mail secretariat.houches@ujf-grenoble.fr; internet houches.ujf-grenoble.fr; Dir LETICIA CUGLIANDOLO.

Ecole Polytechnique—Polytech'Grenoble: 28 Ave Benoît Frachon, 38400 St Martin d'Hères; tel. 4-76-82-79-02; e-mail polytech@ujf-grenoble.fr; internet www.polytech-grenoble.fr; Dir RENÉ-LOUIS INGLEBERT.

Floralis–Filiale de la Valorisation de la Recherche de l'UJF: 6 allée de Bethléem, 38610 Gières; tel. 4-76-00-70-30; e-mail contact@floralis.fr; internet www.floralis.fr; Dir ERIC LARREY.

Formation Continue: 2 ave de Vignate, 38610 Gières; tel. 4-56-52-03-29; e-mail formation-continue@ujf-grenoble.fr; Dir JEAN-GABRIEL VALAY.

Institut Universitaire de Formation des Maîtres: 30 ave Marcelin Berthelot, 38100 Grenoble; tel. 4-56-52-07-00; internet iufm.ujf-grenoble.fr; Dir PATRICK MENDELSON.

Institut Universitaire de Technologie: 151 rue de la Papeterie, 38402 St Martin d'Hères; tel. 4-76-82-53-00; e-mail administration.iut@ujf-grenoble.fr; internet www-iut.ujf-grenoble.fr; Dir JEAN-MICHEL TERRIEZ.

Observatoire des Sciences de l'Univers Grenoble: 414 rue de la Piscine, 38400 St Martin d'Hères; tel. 4-76-51-49-81; e-mail obs-dir@ujf-grenoble.fr; internet www.obs.ujf-grenoble.fr/osug; Dir HENRI-CLAUDE NATAF.

Service Commun des Enseignements Transversaux: Dir JEAN-PIERRE HENRY

UNIVERSITÉ DE GRENOBLE II (UNIVERSITÉ PIERRE MENDÈS-FRANCE)

BP 47X, 38040 Grenoble Cedex
Telephone: 4-76-82-54-00
E-mail: presidence@upmf-grenoble.fr
Internet: www.upmf-grenoble.fr
Founded 1970
Academic year: September to June
Pres.: ALAIN SPALANZANI
Vice-Pres. for Admin.: MARCEL-RENÉ TERCINET
Vice-Pres. for Continuing Education and Educational ICT: LIONEL FILIPPI
Vice-Pres. for Curriculum and University Life: ALAIN FERNEX
Vice-Pres. for Devt: THIERRY MENISSIER
Vice-Pres. for Finance and Capital: CLAUDE BENOIT
Vice-Pres. for Information System: DOMINIQUE RIEU
Vice-Pres. for Intervarsity: THÉOPHILE OHLMANN
Vice-Pres. for Int. Relations: JACQUES FONTANEL
Vice-Pres. for Science Ccl: RENÉ FAVIER
Vice-Pres. for Student Body: SOUHAIL MANAI
Sec.-Gen.: FRANCK LENOIR
Library: see under Libraries and Archives
Number of teachers: 718
Number of students: 19,531
Publication: *Intercours.*

TEACHING AND RESEARCH UNITS

Faculté de Droit: BP 47, 38040 Grenoble Cedex 9; tel. 4-76-82-55-01; e-mail chantal.fayen@upmf-grenoble.fr; internet www

.facdroit-grenoble.org; Dean SÉBASTIEN BERNARD.

Faculté de l'Economie de Grenoble: 1241 rue des Résidences, Domaine Universitaire, BP 47, 38040 Grenoble Cedex 9; tel. 4-76-82-55-01; e-mail accueil.ese@upmf-grenoble.fr; internet ese.upmf-grenoble.fr; Dir MICHEL ROCCA.

Faculté des Sciences de l'Homme et de la Société: 1251 ave Centrale, Domaine Universitaire, BP 47, 38040 Grenoble Cedex 9; tel. 4-76-82-59-00; e-mail sonia.rocton@upmf-grenoble.fr; internet shs.upmf-grenoble.fr; Dir RÉMI KOUABENAN.

Faculté des Sciences Humaines: 1281 ave Centrale, Domaine Universitaire, BP 47, 38040 Grenoble Cedex 9; tel. 4-76-82-73-50; e-mail philippe.saltel@upmf-grenoble.fr; internet sh.upmf-grenoble.fr; Dir PHILIPPE SALTEL

PROFESSORS

ALBOUY, M., Management
ANTONIADIS, A., Mathematics
ARNAUD, P., Sociology
BAILLE, J., Education
BARREYRE, P.-Y., Management
BELLISSANT, C., Computer Science
BERNARD, J.-P., Political Science
BIAYS, J. P., Political Science
BILLAUDOT, B., Economics
BORRELLY, R., Economics
BOUTOT, A., Philosophy
BRECHON, P., Political Science
CHATELUS, M., Economics
CHIANEA, G., History of Law
COURTIN, J., Informatics
COVIAUX, C., Private Law
CROISAT, M., Political Science
D'ARCY, F., Political Science
DESTANNE DE BERNIS, G., Economics
DIDIER, P., History of Law
DROUET D'AUBIGNY, G., Mathematics
EUZEBY, A., Economics and Management
EUZEBY, C., Economics
FOUCHARD, A., History
FRANCILLON, J., Private Law
GIROD, P., Management
GLEIZAL, J.-J., Public Law
GOUTAL, J.-L., Private Law
GRANGE, D., History
GRELLIERE, V., Law
GROC, B., Computer Science
GUILHAUDIS, M., Public Law
HOLLARD, M., Economics
JOLIBERT, A., Management
LARGUIER, J., Private Law
LESCA, H., Management
LE STANC, C., Law
MAISONNEUVE, B., Mathematics
MARIGNY, J., History
MARTIN, C., Management
N'GUYEN XUAN DANG, M.
OHLMANN, T., Psychology
PAGE, A., Management
PARAVY, P., History
PASCAL, G., Philosophy
PATUREL, R., Management
PECCOUD, F., Computer Science
PETIT, B., Private Law
PIETRA, R., Philosophy
POUSSIN, G., Psychology
POUYET, B., Public Law
RENARD, D., Political Science
RICHARD, A., Economics
ROMIER, G., Applied Mathematics
ROUSSET, M., Public Law
SALVAGE, PASCALE, Law
SALVAGE, PHILIPPE, Law
SCHNEIDER, C., Public Law
SEGRESTIN, D., Industrial Engineering
SIRONNEAU, J.-P., Sociology
SOLE, J., History
SOULAGE, B., Political Science
TERCINET, M., Public Law
TESTON, G.
TIBERGHIEN, G., Psychology
TRAHAND, J., Management
VALETTE-FLORENCE, P.
VERNANT, D., Philosophy

ATTACHED INSTITUTE

Institut d'Études Politiques: 1030 ave Centrale, Domaine Universitaire, 38400 Saint-Martin-d'Hères; tel. 4-76-82-60-00; e-mail accueil@iep-grenoble.fr; internet www-sciences-po.upmf-grenoble.fr; Dir OLIVIER IHL

UNIVERSITÉ DE GRENOBLE III (UNIVERSITÉ STENDHAL)

BP 25, 38040 Grenoble Cedex 9
1180 ave Centrale, 38400
Telephone: 4-76-82-43-00
E-mail: presidence@u-grenoble3.fr
Internet: www.u-grenoble3.fr
Founded 1970
Pres.: LISE DUMASY
Vice-Pres.: ELISABETH LAVAULT-OLLÉON
Vice-Pres.: FRANCIS GROSSMANN
Vice-Pres.: FRANÇOIS MANGENOT
Vice-Pres.: ISABELLE PAILLIART
Vice-Pres.: LAURENCE GARINO-ABEL
Sec.-Gen.: MARTINE PEVET
Number of teachers: 330
Number of students: 12,000.

TEACHING AND RESEARCH INSTITUTES

Département Sciences du Langage et Français Langue Etrangère–UFR LLASIC: Bâtiment B, 1180 ave Centrale, 38400 Grenoble Cedex 9; tel. 4-76-82-77-25; e-mail agnes.tutin@u-grenoble3.fr; internet www.u-grenoble3.fr/version-francaise/presentation/services-et-composantes/les-ufr-et-structures-pedagogiques/departement-sciences-du-langage-et-francais-langue-etrangere-fle–69276.kjsp?rh=u3fr_docu0241; Dir JEAN-PIERRE CHEVROT.

Faculté d'Etudes Anglophones: Bâtiment C, 1180 ave Centrale, 38400 Grenoble Cedex 9; tel. 4-76-82-41-93; e-mail christine.morenas@u-grenoble3.fr; Dir DONNA ANDRÉOLLE.

Faculté de Langues, Littératures et Civilisations Etrangères: Bâtiment G, 1381 rue des résidences, 38400 Grenoble Cedex 9; tel. 4-76-82-43-54; e-mail jacques.rambert@u-grenoble3.fr; Dir ALMUDENA DELAGADO-LARIOS.

Faculté des Lettres et Arts: Bâtiment B, 1180 ave Centrale, 38400 Grenoble Cedex 9; tel. 4-76-82-43-15; e-mail gisele.nesta@u-grenoble3.fr; Dir BRIGITTE COMBE.

Faculté des Sciences de la Communication: Institut de la Communication et des Médias, 11 ave du 8 mai 1945, BP 337, 38434 Grenoble Cedex 9; tel. 4-56-52-87-17; Dir FABIENNE MARTIN-JUCHAT

DIRECTORS OF DEPARTMENTS

Languages, Literature and Foreign Civilizations:
- Applied Foreign Languages: (vacant)
- German and Dutch Studies: JEAN-FRANÇOIS MARILLIER
- Iberian and Spanish-American Studies: ANNE CAYUELA
- Italian and Romanian Studies: ENZO NEPPI
- Oriental Studies: RITA MAZEN
- Russian and Slav Studies: ISABELLE DESPRES
- Trilingual Law and Economics: SUZAN BERTHIER

Modern and Classical Literature:
- Classical Studies: BENOÎT GOIN
- Comparative Literature: FLORENCE GOYET
- Languages, Literatures and French Civilization: BRIGITTE COMBE

Sciences of Language:
- French as a Foreign Language: VIOLAINE DE NUCHÈZE, JEAN EMMANUEL LE BRAY

UNIVERSITÉ DE HAUTE-ALSACE

2 rue des Frères Lumière, 68093 Mulhouse Cedex
Telephone: 3-89-33-63-00
E-mail: presidence@uha.fr
Internet: www.uha.fr
Founded 1975
State control
Languages of instruction: English, French
Academic year: September to June
Pres.: Prof. Dr ALAIN BRILLARD
Sec.-Gen.: SAMUEL BITSCH
Librarian: ANNE-MARIE SCHALLER
Library of 150,000 vols
Number of teachers: 580
Number of students: 7,967

DEANS

Faculty of Arts, Languages and Humanities: Dr YANN KERDILÈS
Faculty of Economics, Social Sciences and Law: Dr GÉRALD COHEN
Faculty of Science and Technology: Dr CHRISTOPHE KREMBEL

UNIVERSITÉ DU HAVRE

25 rue Philippe Lebon, BP 1123, 76063 Le Havre Cedex
Telephone: 2-32-74-40-00
E-mail: presidence@univ-lehavre.fr
Internet: www.univ-lehavre.fr
Founded 1984
State control
Academic year: September to July
Pres.: CAMILLE GALAP
Vice-Pres. for Admin.: PASCAL REGHEM
Vice-Pres. for Science Ccl: MOULAY AZIZ ALAOUI
Vice-Pres. for Studies and Univ. Life: ELAINE TALBOT
Sec.-Gen.: JEAN CLARISSE
Librarian: PIERRE-YVES CACHARD
Number of teachers: 399
Number of students: 7,040.

TEACHING AND RESEARCH UNITS

Centre de Formation des Apprentis: 25 rue Philippe Lebon, BP 1123, 76063 Le Havre Cedex; tel. 2-32-74-44-67; e-mail cfa@univ-lehavre.fr; Dir STÉPHANE LAUWICK.

Faculté des Affaires Internationales: 25 rue Philippe Lebon, BP 420, 76057 Le Havre Cedex; tel. 2-32-74-41-00.

Faculté des Lettres et Sciences Humaines: 25 rue Philippe Lebon, 76086 Le Havre Cedex; tel. 2-32-74-42-00; e-mail lsh@univ-lehavre.fr; Dir ELISABETH ROBERT-BARZMAN.

Faculté des Sciences et Techniques: 25 rue Philippe Lebon, BP 540, 76058 Le Havre Cedex; tel. 2-32-74-43-00; e-mail ufr-st@univ-lehavre.fr.

Institut Supérieur d'Etudes Logistiques: Ecole d'Ingénieurs, Quai Frissard, BP 1137, 76063 Le Havre Cedex; tel. 2-32-74-49-00; e-mail isel@univ-lehavre.fractiver; internet www.isel-logistique.fr; Dir EDOUARD REPPERT.

Institut Universitaire de Technologie: pl. Robert Schuman, BP 4006, 76610 Le Havre Cedex; tel. 2-32-74-46-63; e-mail christian.delaruelle@univ-lehavre.fr; internet www-iut.univ-lehavre.fr; Dir CHRISTIAN DELARUELLE.

Service Formation Continue: tel. 2-32-74-44-50; e-mail formation.continue@univ-lehavre.fr; Dir STÉPHANE LAUWICK

UNIVERSITÉ DE LILLE I (UNIVERSITÉ DES SCIENCES ET TECHNOLOGIES DE LILLE)

Cité Scientifique, 59655 Villeneuve d'Ascq Cedex

Telephone: 3-20-43-43-43
E-mail: presidence@univ-lille1.fr
Internet: www.univ-lille1.fr

Founded 1855 as Faculty of Sciences, present status 1971
Languages of instruction: English, French
Academic year: September to July

Pres.: PHILIPPE ROLLET
Vice-Pres.: JEAN-CHRISTOPHE CAMART
Vice-Pres.: JEAN-PHILIPPE CASSAR
Vice-Pres.: JAMAL EL KHATTABI
Vice-Pres.: GUILBERT FRANCIS
Vice-Pres.: SEYS FRANÇOIS-OLIVIER
Vice-Pres.: NINA HAUTEKEETE
Vice-Pres.: MICHÈLE HOCHEDEZ
Vice-Pres.: SALAH MAOUCHE
Vice-Pres.: PHILIPPE MATHIEU
Vice-Pres.: JEAN-FRANÇOIS PAUWELS
Vice-Pres.: NICOLAS POSTEL
Vice-Pres.: JEOFFREY RICHE
Sec.-Gen.: PATRICE SERNICLAY

Number of teachers: 1,500
Number of students: 20,000

DEANS

College of Technology: MOULAY-DRISS BENCHIBOUN
Faculty of Biology: DIDIER VIEAU
Faculty of Chemistry: ALAIN RIVES
Faculty of Computer Science and Electronics: NOUR-EDDINE OUSSOUS
Faculty of Earth Science: JEAN-LUC PODEVIN
Faculty of Economics: LAURENT CORDONNIER
Faculty of Geography and Urbanism: PHILIPPE MENERAULT
Faculty of Mathematics: GUOTING CHEN
Faculty of Management: PASCAL PHILIPPART
Faculty of Marine Biology: SEBASTIEN LEFEBVRE
Faculty of Physics: DOMINIQUE DEROZIER
School of Engineering: GUY REUMONT
School of Telecommunication: NARENDRA JUSSIEU

PROFESSORS

BOILLY, B., Biology
BONNELLE, J.-P., Chemistry
BREZINSKI, C., Computer Sciences
BRUYELLE, P., Geography
CHAMLEY, H., Geotechnics
CONSTANT, E., Electronics
CORDONNIER, V., Calculus and Information Science
DAUCHET, M., Theoretical Computing
DEBOURSE, J.-P., Management Science
DEBRABANT, P., Engineering
DEGAUQUE, P., Electronics
DHAINAUT, A., Biology
DORMARD, S., Economics
DOUKHAN, J.-C., Engineering
DUPOUY, J.-P., Biology
DYMENT, A., Mathematics
ESCAIG, B., Solid State Physics
FOCT, J., Chemistry
FOURET, R., Physics
FRONTIER, S., Biology
GLORIEUX, P., Physics
GOSSELIN, G., Sociology
GOUDMAND, P., Energy Generation
GRUSON, L., Pure and Applied Mathematics
GUILBAULT, Biology
LABLACHE-COMBIER, A., Organic Chemistry
LAVEINE, J.-P., Palaeobotany
LEHMANN, D., Geometry
LENOBLE, Atmospheric Optics
LOMBARD, J., Sociology
LOUCHEUX, C., Macromolecular Chemistry
MACKE, B., Physics
MAILLET, P., Economic and Social Sciences
MICHEAUX, P., Mechanical Engineering
PAQUET, J., Applied Geology
PORCHET, M., Biology
PROUVOST, J., Mineralogy
RACZY, L., Computer Sciences
SALMER, G., Electronics
SCHAMPS, J., Physics
SEGUIER, G., Electro-Technology
SIMON, M., Economic and Social Sciences
SLIWA, H., Chemistry
SPIK, G., Biology
STANKIEWICZ, F., Economic Sciences
TOULOTTE, J.-M., Computer Sciences
TURREL, G., Chemistry
VERNET, P., Biology of Populations and Ecosystems
VIDAL, P., Automation
ZEYTOUNIAN, R., Mechanics

UNIVERSITÉ DE LILLE II (DROIT ET SANTÉ)

42 rue Paul Duez, 59000 Lille

Telephone: 3-20-96-43-43
E-mail: sg@univ-lille2.fr
Internet: www.univ-lille2.fr

Founded 1969
State control
Language of instruction: French
Academic year: October to June

Pres.: Prof. CHRISTIAN SERGHERAERT
Vice-Pres.: CLAIRE DAVAL
Vice-Pres.: IRÈNE LAUTIER
Vice-Pres.: LARBI AIT HENNANI
Vice-Pres.: Prof. MARIE-HÉLÈNE FOSSE-GOMEZ
Vice-Pres.: PATRICK PELAYO
Vice-Pres.: Prof. RÉGIS MATRAN
Vice-Pres.: RÉMY PAMART
Vice-Pres.: Prof. SALEM KACET
Vice-Pres.: Prof. VÉRONIQUE DEMARS
Vice-Pres.: Prof. XAVIER VANDENDRIESSCHE
Sec.-Gen.: GUY BAILLIEUL

Number of teachers: 1,198
Number of students: 28,330

DEANS

Faculty of Biological and Pharmaceutical Sciences: Prof. LUC DUBREUIL
Faculty of Dentistry: Prof. PIERRE HUBERT DUPAS
Faculty of Finance, Banking and Accountancy: Dir: PASCAL GRANDIN
Faculty of Legal, Political and Social Sciences: Prof. BERNARD BOSSU
Faculty of Medical Engineering and Management: Dir: Prof. ALAIN DUROCHER
Faculty of Medical Sciences: Prof. DIDIER GOSSET
Faculty of Physical Education and Sport: Dir: Prof. PATRICK PELAYO

ATTACHED INSTITUTE

Institut d'Études Politiques: 84 rue de Trévise, 59000 Lille; tel. 3-20-90-48-40; e-mail directeur@iep.univ-lille2.fr; internet www.sciencespo-lille.eu; Dir PIERRE MATHIOT

UNIVERSITÉ DE LILLE III, CHARLES DE GAULLE (SCIENCES HUMAINES, LETTRES ET ARTS)

Domaine Universitaire du Pont de Bois, BP 60149, 59653 Villeneuve d'Ascq Cedex

Telephone: 3-20-41-60-00
E-mail: valerie.souilleux@univ-lille3.fr
Internet: www.univ-lille3.fr

Founded 1560, present status 1985

Pres.: JEAN-CLAUDE DUPAS
Sec.-Gen.: EMMANUEL PARISIS
Librarian: JEAN-PAUL CHADOURNE

Number of teachers: 830
Number of students: 18,500

Publications: *Bien dire, bien apprendre*, *Cahiers de Recherches de l'institut de Papyrologie et d'Egyptologie*, *Etudes Irlandaises* (2 a year), *Germanica* (1 or 2 a year), *Graphé*, *Lexique* (1 a year), *Revue des Sciences Humaines* (4 a year), *Revue du Nord* (history, 5 a year), *Roman 20–50* (2 a year), *Uranie*

TEACHING AND RESEARCH UNITS

Applied Foreign Languages: Dir: HEROGUEL ARMAND
Arts and Culture: (vacant)
Classical Languages and Culture: Dir: ALAIN DEREMETZ
Education: Dir: CORA COHEN-AZRIA
English Language, Literature and Civilization: Dir: JEAN-LUC SWITALSKI
German and Scandinavian Studies: Dir: DOMINIQUE HERBET
History, Art and Politics: Dir: LAURIANNE SÈVE
INFOCOM: Dir: BERNARD DELFORCE
Information, Documentation and Scientific and Technical Information: Dir: JOACHIM SCHOPFEL
IUP—Artistic and Cultural Professions: Dir: PIERRE DELCAMBRE
IUP—Information Communication: Dir: OLIVIER CHANTRAINE
Mathematics, Economics and Social Sciences: Dir: LAURENCE BROZE
Modern Literature: Dir: THIERRY CHARNAY
Philosophy: Dir: PHILIPPE SABOT
Psychology: Dir: Mme S. DE BOSSCHER
Romance, Slav and Oriental Studies: Dir: CONSTANTIN BOBAS
Training Centre for Accompanying Musicians: Dir: PASCAL HAMEAUX
University Institute of Technology B: Dir: BRUNO TRINEL (acting)

PROFESSORS (1ST CLASS AND EXCEPTIONAL)

Classics:
BOULOGNE, J., Greek Language and Literature
DUMONT, J.-CHR., Social History of the Roman Republic

English Studies:
BECQUEMONT, D., History of Ideas, Phonetics and Phonology
DUPAS, J. C., Anglo-Saxon Language and Literature
DURAND, R., North American Literature and Civilization
ESCARBELT, B., Anglo-Saxon Language and Literature
GOURNAY, J.-F., 19th-century Literature and Civilization
SYS, J., British Civilization, History of Ideas

French Linguistics and Literature:
ALLUIN, B., Modern and Contemporary Language and Literature
BONNEFIS, PH., 19th-century Literature
BRASSEUR, A., Medieval Language and Literature
BUISIRE, A., French Language and Literature
CORBIN, D., French Language
GARY-PRIEUR, M. N., French Language
GUILLERM, J.-P., 19th-century Literature
GUILLERM-CURUTCHET, L., French Language and Literature
HORVILLE, R., 17th-century Literature
LESTRINGANT, FR., 16th-century Literature
MALANDAIN, P., Modern and Contemporary Language and Literature

German Studies:
COLONGE, P., 19th- and 20th-century Literature and Civilization
ROUSSEAU, A., Dutch Linguistics

VAN DE LOUW, G., Dutch
VAYDAT, P., Anglo-German Relations: 1870–1914

History, Art and Politics:

CHADEAU, E., Contemporary History
DELMAIRE, B., Medieval History
DELMAIRE, R., Ancient Roman History
GUIGNET, PH., Modern History
ROSSELLE, D., Modern Economic and Social History
VALBELLE, D., Egyptology

Mathematics, Economics, Social Sciences:

CELEYRETTE, J., Mathematics

Philosophy:

KINTZLER, C., General Philosophy and Aesthetics
KIRSCHER, G., Modern and Contemporary Philosophy
MACHEREY, P., Aesthetics and History of Philosophy

Psychology:

LECONTE, P., Experimental Psychology
VERQUERRE, R., Psychology

Romance, Slav, Semitic and Hungarian Studies:

ALLAIN, A., Russian

Other Professors:

LOSFELD, G., Information Science
REUTER, Y., Teaching of French

UNIVERSITÉ DE LIMOGES

33 rue François Mitterrand, BP 23204, 87032 Limoges Cedex 01
Telephone: 5-55-14-91-00
Internet: www.unilim.fr

Founded 1968
Academic year: September to June

Pres.: JACQUES FONTANILLE
Sec.-Gen.: DANIEL POUMÉROULY
Librarian: JOËLLE CARTIGNY

Library: see under Libraries and Archives
Number of teachers: 1,050
Number of students: 14,109

DEANS

Faculty of Arts and Humanities: PHILIPPE ALLÉE
Faculty of Law and Economic Sciences: PASCALE TORRE
Faculty of Medicine: DENIS VALLEIX
Faculty of Pharmacy: JEAN-LUC DUROUX
Faculty of Science and Technology: ANNE-MERCEDES BELLIDO

PROFESSORS

Faculty of Arts and Humanities (39E rue Camille Guérin, 87036 Limoges Cedex; tel. 5-55-43-56-00; e-mail jacques.migozzi@unilim.fr; internet www.flsh.unilim.fr):

BALABANIAN, O., Geography and Development
BARRIÈRE, B., Medieval Archaeological History
BEDON, R., Ancient Language and Literature
BEHAR, P., Germanic and Scandinavian Language and Literature
CAPDEBOSCQ, A. M., Romance Language and Literature
CARON, P., Modern and Contemporary French Language and Literature
CHANDES, G., Middle Age to Renaissance French Language and Literature
DUMONT, J., Ancient World Archaeological History
EL GAMMAL, J. M., World Medieval Archaeological History
FILTEAU, C., Modern and Contemporary French Language and Literature
FONTANILLE, J., Language Sciences
GENDREAU-MASSALOUX, Romance Language and Literature
GRASSIN, J.-M., Comparative Literature
GRASSIN, M., Anglo-Saxon English Language and Literature
LECLANCHE, J.-L., Middle Age to Renaissance French Language and Literature
LEMOINE, B., Anglo-Saxon English Language and Literature
LEVET, J.-P., Ancient Language and Literature
MOREAU, J.-P., Anglo-Saxon English Language and Literature
NOUHAUD, M., Ancient Language and Literature
RAMBAUX, C., Ancient Language and Literature
VALADAS, B., Economic and Regional Geography
VERDON, J., World Medieval Archaeological History

Faculty of Law and Economic Sciences (5 rue Félix Eboué, BP 3127, 87031 Limoges Cedex 1; tel. 5-55-34-97-03; e-mail helene.pauliat@unilim.fr; internet www.fdse.unilim.fr):

ALAPHILIPPE, F., Private Law and Criminology
ARCHER, R., Economics
CAVAGNAC, M., Economics
DARREAU, P., Economics
FLANDIN-BLETY, P., Legal and Institutional History
KARAQUILLO, J.-P., Private Law and Criminology
LENCLOS, J.-L., Public Law
MARGUENAUD, J.-P., Private Law
MOULY, J., Private Law
PAULIAT, H., Public Law
PRIEUR, M., Public Law
SAUVIAT, A., Economics
TARAZI, A., Economics
TEXIER, P., Legal and Institutional History
VAREILLE, B., Private Law

Faculty of Medicine (2 rue du Docteur Marcland, 87025 Limoges Cedex; tel. 5-55-43-58-00; e-mail doyen.medecine@unilim.fr; internet www.unilim.fr/medecine):

ADENIS, J.-P., Ophthalmology
ALAIN, L., Infantile Surgery
ALDIGIER, J.-C., Cardiology
ARCHAMBEAUD, F., Clinical Medicine
ARNAUD, J. P., Orthopaedics, Traumatology, Plastic Surgery
BARTHE, D., Histology, Embryology
BAUDET, J., Obstetrics and Gynaecology
BENSAID, J., Clinical Cardiology
BERTIN, P., Therapeutics
BESSEDE, J.-P., Otorhinolaryngology
BONNAUD, F., Pneumo-Phthisiology
BONNETBLANC, J.-M., Dermatology, Venereology
BOULESTEIX, J., Paediatrics and Medical Genetics
BOUQUIER, J.-J., Clinical Paediatrics
BOUTROS, T. F., Epidemiology
BRETON, J.-C., Biochemistry
CATANZANO, G., Pathological Anatomy
COLOMBEAU, P., Urology
CUBERTAFOND, P., Digestive Surgery
DARDE, M. L., Parasitology
DE LUMLEY-WOODYEAR, L., Paediatrics
DENIS, F., Bacteriology, Virology
DENIZOT, N., Anaesthesiology
DESCOTTES, B., Anatomy
DUDOGNON, P., Occupational Therapy
DUMAS, J. PH., Urology
DUMAS, M., Neurology
DUMONT, D., Occupational Medicines
DUPUY, J.-P., Radiology
FEISS, P., Anaesthesiology
GAINANT, A., Digestive Surgery
GAROUX, R., Child Psychiatry
GASTINNE, H., Resuscitation
HUGON, J., Histology, Embryology
LABROUSSE, C., Occupational Therapy
LASKAR, M., Thoracic and Cardiovascular Surgery
LAUBIE, B., Endocrinology, Metabolism, Nutrition
LEGER, J.-M., Adult Psychiatry
LEROUX-ROBERT, C., Nephrology
MENIER, R., Physiology
MERLE, L., Pharmacology
MOREAU, J.-J., Neurosurgery
MOULIES, D., Infantile Surgery
PECOUT, C., Orthopaedics, Traumatology, Plastic Surgery
PICHON BOURDESSOULE, D., Haematology
PILLEGAND, B., Hepatogastroenterology
PIVA, C., Forensic Medicine and Toxicology
PRA LORAN, V., Haematology
RAVON, R., Neurosurgery
RIGAUD, M., Biochemistry
ROUSSEAU, J., Radiology
SAUVAGE, J.-P., Otorhinolaryngology
TABASTE, J.-L., Gynaecology, Obstetrics
TREVES, R., Rheumatology
VALLAT, J.-M., Neurology
VALLEIX, D., Anatomy
VANDROUX, J.-C., Biophysics
WEINBRECK, P., Tropical Medicine

Faculty of Pharmacy (2 rue du Docteur Marcland, 87025 Limoges Cedex; tel. 5-55-43-58-00; e-mail doyen.pharmacie@unilim.fr; internet www.facpharmacie.unilim.fr):

BERNARD, M., Physical Chemistry and Pharmaceutical Technology
BOSGIRAUD, C., Biology
BROSSARD, C., Physical Chemistry and Pharmaceutical Technology
BUXERAUD, J., Pharmacology
CARDOT, PH., Physical Chemistry and Pharmaceutical Technology
CHULIA, A., Pharmacology
CLEMENT-CHULIA, D., Physical Chemistry and Pharmaceutical Technology
DELAGE, C., Physical and Mineral Chemistry
GHESTEM, A., Botany
HABRIOUX, G., Biochemistry
OUDART, N., Pharmacology

Faculty of Science and Technology (123 ave Albert Thomas, 87060 Limoges Cedex; tel. 5-55-45-72-00; e-mail directeur.sciences@unilim.fr; internet www.sciences.unilim.fr):

BARONNET, J.-M., Energetics
BERLAND, R., Electronics, Electrotechnology and Automatics
BESSON, J.-L., Dense Media and Materials
CAPERAA, S., Civil Engineering
CARON, A., Information Processing
CATHERINOT, A., Energetics
COLOMBEAU, B., Optics
COUDERT, J. F., Methodology, Plasma and Automation
DECOSSAS, J. L., Electronics, Electrotechnology and Automatics
DESCHAUX, P., Physiology
DESMAISON, J., Mineral Chemistry
DUVAL, D., Mathematics
FAUCHAIS, P., Energetics
FRAY, C., Electronics, Electrotechnology and Automatics
FRIT, B., Mineral Chemistry
GAUDREAU, B., Mineral Chemistry
GLANDUS, J.-C., Mechanics, Mechanical Engineering and Civil Engineering
GOURSAT, P., Mineral Chemistry
GUILLON, P., Electronics, Electrotechnology and Automatics
JECKO, B., Electronics, Electrotechnology and Automatics
JECKO, F., Electronics, Electrotechnology and Automatics
JULIEN, R., Biochemistry
KRAUSZ, P., Organic, Analytical and Industrial Chemistry
LABBE, J.-C., Chemistry of Materials
LAUBIE, F., Mathematics

MALAISE, M., Mechanics, Mechanical Engineering and Civil Engineering
MARCOU, J., Electronics, Electrotechnology and Automatics
MARTIN, C., Energetics
MAZET, M., Organic, Analytical and Industrial Chemistry
MERCURIO, D., Mineral Chemistry
MERCURIO, J.-P., Mineral Chemistry
MOLITON, A., Optics
MOLITON, J. P., Electronics, Electrotechnology and Automatics
MORVAN, H., Biology
NARDOU, F., Physical Chemistry
OBREGON, J., Electronics, Electrotechnology and Automatics
PLATON, F., Mechanics, Mechanical Engineering and Civil Engineering
QUERE, R., Electronics, Electrotechnology and Automatics
QUINTARD, P., Dense Media and Materials
RATINAUD, M. M., Biochemistry and Biology
SABOURDY, G., Geology
THERA, M., Mathematics

AFFILIATED INSTITUTES

ENSIL (Limoges Engineering School): 16 rue d'Atlantis, parc ESTER, 87068 Limoges Cedex; tel. 5-55-42-36-70; e-mail direction@ensil.unilim.fr; internet www.ensil.unilim.fr; Dir PATRICK LEPRAT.

GEIST Institute ('Genetics, Environment, Immunity, Health and Therapy'): Faculty of Medecine, 2 rue du Docteur Marcland, 87000 Limoges; tel. 5-55-43-58-48; e-mail michel.cogne@unilim.fr; Dir MICHEL COGNÉ.

Higher National School of Industrial Ceramics: 47–73 ave Albert Thomas, 87065 Limoges Cedex; tel. 5-55-45-22-22; e-mail directin@ensci.fr; internet www.ensci.fr; Dir CHRISTIAN GAULT.

IAE (Institute of Business Administration): 3 rue François Mitterrand, 87031 Limoges; tel. 5-55-14-90-32; e-mail alain.rivet@unilim.fr; internet www.iae.unilim.fr; Dir ALAIN RIVET.

Institute of Life and Health Sciences: 123 ave Albert Thomas, 87060 Limoges Cedex; tel. 5-55-45-76-76; Dir RAYMOND JULIEN.

Institute of the Environment and Water: 123 ave Albert Thomas, 87060 Limoges Cedex; tel. 5-55-45-74-69; Dir JEAN-CLAUDE BOLLINGER.

IPAG (Institute of Preparation for General Administration/Institut de Préparation à l'Administration Générale): 32 rue Turgot, 87000 Limoges; tel. 5-55-34-97-44; e-mail ipag@unilim.fr; internet www.ipag.unilim.fr; Dir CHRISTIAN MOULINARD.

IPAM 'Processes Applied to Materials' Research Institute: Faculty of Sciences and Technology, 123 ave Albert Thomas, 87060 Limoges Cedex; tel. 5-55-45-76-70; e-mail armelle.vardelle@unilim.fr; Dir ARMELLE VARDELLE.

IUFM (Institute for Teacher Training): 209 blvd de Vanteaux, 87000 Limoges; tel. 5-55-01-76-86; internet www.limousin.iufm.fr; Dir VALÉRIE LEGROS.

IUT (University Institute of Technology (Limousin)): Allée Andrés Maurois, 87065 Limoges Cedex; tel. 5-55-43-43-55; e-mail dir.iut@unilim.fr; internet www.iut.unilim.fr; Dir GILLES BROUSSAUD.

Science, Technology, Health: 13 Rue de Genève, 87065 Limoges Cedex; tel. 5-55-45-76-74; e-mail ed-sts@unilim.fr; internet www.unilim.fr/edsts; Dir ABBAS CHAZAD MOVAHHEDI.

SHS Institute of Human and Social Sciences: Faculty of Law and Economics, 5 rue Félix Eboué, BP 3127, 87031 Limoges Cedex; tel. 5-55-14-92-10; e-mail alain.sauviat@unilim.fr; Dir ALAIN SAUVIAT.

University Professional Institute: 2 Rue du Docteur Marcland, 87025 Limoges Cedex; tel. 5-55-43-59-15; e-mail iup@unilim.fr; Dir JEAN-FRANÇOIS NYS.

XLIM Mixed Research Unit: Faculty of Sciences and Technology, 123 ave Albert Thomas, 87060 Limoges Cedex; tel. 5-55-45-72-50; e-mail dominique.cros@unilim.fr; internet www.xlim.fr; Dir DOMINIQUE CROS

UNIVERSITÉ DU LITTORAL CÔTE D'OPALE

Services Centraux, 1 pl. de l'Yser, BP 1022, Général-De-Gaulle, 59375 Dunkerque Cedex 1
Telephone: 3-28-23-73-73
E-mail: web-ulco@univ-littoral.fr
Internet: www.univ-littoral.fr
Founded 1991
Campuses in Boulogne, Calais, Dunkerque and St-Omer; areas of study: economics, fine and performing arts, humanities, languages, law, literature, management, natural sciences, social sciences, sport, technology
Pres.: ROGER DURAND
Sec.-Gen.: CATHERINE SION
Vice-Pres. for Admin.: FAUSTIN AISSI
Vice-Pres. for Science Ccl: ROBIN BOQUET
Vice-Pres. for Studies and Univ. Life: SABINE DUHAMEL
Librarian: MIREILLE CHAZAL
Library of 100,000 vols, 900 periodical subscriptions; CD-ROM databases; spec. collns: Centre de Documentation Européenne, Relais INSEE (statistics), science fiction, cartoons, theses
Number of students: 11,000

UNIVERSITÉ DE LYON

Caserne Sergent Blandan, 37 rue du Repos, 69361 Lyon
Telephone: 4-37-37-26-70
E-mail: contact@universite-lyon.fr
Internet: www.universite-lyon.fr
Founded 2007 by merger of 9 founding mems and 11 assoc. mems
State control
Pres.: MICHEL LUSSAULT
Number of teachers: 11,500
Number of students: 120,000.

FOUNDING MEMBER INSTITUTIONS

Ecole Centrale de Lyon

36 ave Guy de Collongue, 69134 Ecully Cedex
Telephone: 4-72-18-60-00
Internet: www.ec-lyon.fr
Cultural, scientific and technical training for engineers in all brs of industry
Pres.: CHRISTIAN MARI
Vice-Pres.: FRANÇOIS VIDAL
Dir: PATRICK BOURGIN
Deputy Dir: PIERRE DREUX
Dir of Studies: MARIE-ANNICK GALLAND
Dir of Research: JEAN-PIERRE BERTOGLIO
Sec.-Gen.: PHILIPPE WISLER
Library of 15,000 vols
Number of students: 900

DIRECTORS

Communication, Languages, Business and Sport: Dir: JACQUELINE VACHERAND-REVEL
Electronics: Dir: FRANÇOIS BURET
Fluid Mechanics, Acoustics and Energy: Dir: GILLES ROBERT
Mathematics and Computer Science: Dir: LIMING CHEN
Solid Mechanics and Mechanical and Civil Engineering: Dir: FABRICE THOUVEREZ
Surface Science and Materials: Dir: YVES ROBACH

Ecole Nationale des Mines de Saint-Etienne

158 cours Fauriel, 42023 Saint-Étienne Cedex 2
Telephone: 4-77-42-01-23
E-mail: inform@emse.fr
Internet: www.mines-stetienne.fr
Founded 1816
Dir: Prof. PHILIPPE JAMET
Sec.-Gen.: RACHEL VITANI
Number of teachers: 220
Number of students: 1,700

Institut National des Sciences Appliquées de Lyon

20 ave Albert Einstein, 69621 Villeurbanne Cedex
Telephone: 4-72-43-83-83
E-mail: accueil@insa-lyon.fr
Internet: www.insa-lyon.fr
Founded 1957
Library of 80,000 vols
Biochemistry, computer science, civil, electrical, energetics, production and mechanical engineering, material science
Dir: Prof. ALAIN STORCK
Number of teachers: 500
Number of students: 5,400

DIRECTORS

Business Relations: Dir: Prof. JEAN-MARIE PINON
Fondation Partenariale de l'INSA de Lyon: Dir: ALEXIS MÉTÉNIER
Human Resources: Dir: CLAUDE GUÉDAT
Information Systems: Dir: YVES CONDEMINE
Internal Relations: Dir: CORINNE SUBAÏ
Int. Relations: Dir: MARIE-PIERRE FAVRE
Research: Dir: Prof. JEAN-MARIE REYNOUARD
Training: Dir: Prof. CHRISTOPHE ODET

Université Jean Monnet de Saint-Etienne

10 rue Tréfilerie, CS 82301, 42023 Saint-Etienne Cedex 2
Telephone: 4-77-42-17-00
Internet: www.univ-st-etienne.fr
Founded 1969 as Université de Saint-Étienne; present name 1991
State control
Language of instruction: French
Academic year: October to June
Pres.: KHALED BOUABDALLAH
Vice-Pres: JEAN-YVES COTTIN (Scientific Ccl), MARIE-HÉLÈNE LAFAGE-PROUST (Ccl of Admin.), AGNÈS MORINI (Studies and Univ. Life)
Sec.-Gen.: EVELYNE SARMEJEANNE
Librarian: BRIGITTE RENOUF
Number of teachers: 592
Number of students: 13,684
Publications: *L'Université communique* (52 a year), and various institute bulletins

DEANS

Arts, Letters and Languages: Dir: YVES CLAVARON (acting)
Humanities and Social Sciences: Dir: JEAN FRANÇOIS BRUN
Institut d'Administration des Entreprises: Dir: BERNARD BOUREILLE
Institut du Travail: Pres.: DOMINIQUE TERRAT
Law: Dean: NATACHA VIGNE
Medicine: Dean: Prof. FABRICE ZENI

Sciences: Dir: ALAIN TROUILLET
Télécom Saint-Etienne: Dir: LAURENT CARRARO
University Institute of Technology: Dir: J. MAZERAN

Université Lyon I (Université Claude-Bernard)

43 blvd du 11 Novembre 1918, 69622 Villeurbanne Cedex
Telephone: 4-72-44-80-00
E-mail: secretariat.presidence@univ-lyon1.fr
Internet: www.univ-lyon1.fr
Founded 1970
State control
Language of instruction: French
Academic year: October to June
Pres.: FRANÇOIS-NOËL GILLY
Vice-Pres. for Admin.: HAMDA BEN HADID
Vice-Pres. for Research: GERMAIN GILLET
Vice-Pres. for Studies: GILLES GAY
Sec.-Gen.: ALAIN HELLEU
Number of teachers: 2,630
Number of students: 36,000
Publications: *Annuaire sur la Recherche* (1 a year), *Lettre FLASH/INFO* (4 a year), *Livret de l'Etudiant* (1 a year).

TEACHING AND RESEARCH UNITS

Faculté de Médecine Lyon Est: 8 ave Rockefeller, 69373 Lyon Cedex 08; tel. 4-78-77-70-00; Dean Prof. JÉRÔME ETIENNE.

Faculté de Médecine et de Maïeutique Lyon Sud—Charles Mérieux: 165 chemin du Petit Revoyet, BP 12, 69921 Oullins Cedex 08; tel. 4-26-23-59-05; e-mail wwwsud@univ-lyon1.fr; Dean Prof. FRANÇOIS-NOËL GILLY.

Faculté d'Odontologie: 11 rue Guillaume Paradin, 69372 Lyon Cedex 08; tel. 4-78-77-86-78; internet odontologie.univ-lyon1.fr; Dean Prof. DENIS BOURGEOIS

Université Lyon 2 (Université Louis Lumière)

86 rue Pasteur, 69635 Lyon Cedex 07
Telephone: 4-78-69-70-00
Internet: www.univ-lyon2.fr
Pres.: ANDRÉ TIRAN
First Vice-Pres. for Ccl of Admin.: MARIE ANAUT
Vice-Pres. for Culture and Student Life: JACQUES GERSTENKORN
Vice-Pres. for Finance and Capital: GÉRARD KLOTZ
Vice-Pres. for Human Resources: MICHEL GUILLOT
Vice-Pres. for Int. Relations: CHRISTIAN MONTÈS
Vice-Pres. for Scientific Ccl: NATHALIE FOURNIER
Vice-Pres. for Studies and Univ. Life: JACQUES BONNIEL
Sec.-Gen.: BERNARD FRADIN
Number of teachers: 976
Number of students: 28,322
Publication: *Le Rayon Vert* (10 a year)

DEANS

Faculty of Anthropology and Sociology: ALI CHEIBAN
Faculty of Economics and Business Studies: LUC BAUMSTARK
Faculty of Geography, History, History of Art and Tourism: JEAN-LUC LAMBOLEY
Faculty of Law and Political Science: MARIE-ODILE NICOUD
Faculty of Literature, Science of Language and Arts: PIERRE SABY
Faculty of Modern Languages: JOSIANE PACCAUD-HUGUET

DIRECTORS

Institute of Communication: ALAIN GIROD
Institute of Labour: PATRICK ROZENBLATT
Institute of Political Studies: GILLES POLLET
Institute of Psychology: ISABELLE TAPIERO
Institute of Teacher Training: ALAIN KERLAN
Institute of Trade Union Training: JEAN-FRANÇOIS PAULIN
Institut Universitaire de Technologie Lumière: MICHEL LE NIR

Université Lyon 3 (Université Jean Moulin)

1 rue de l'Université, BP 0638, 69239 Lyon Cedex 02
Telephone: 4-78-78-77-78
E-mail: webmaster@univ-lyon3.fr
Internet: www.univ-lyon3.fr
Founded 1973
Pres.: HUGUES FULCHIRON
Vice-Pres. for Ccl of Admin.: PIERRE SERVET
Vice-Pres. for Information Systems and New Technologies: LAÏD BOUZIDI
Vice-Pres. for Research: JACQUES COMBY
Vice-Pres. for Science Ccl: CYRIL NOURISSAT
Vice-Pres. for Studies and Univ. Life: SABINE DANA-DEMARET
Sec.-Gen.: BERNARD PASCAL
Number of teachers: 650
Number of students: 23,137
Publication: *Lyon 3 Infos* (12 a year)

DEANS

Faculty of Languages: DENIS JAMET
Faculty of Law: LOUIS-AUGUSTIN BARRIERE
Faculty of Letters and Civilizations: NICOLE GONTHIER
Faculty of Philosophy: DENIS FOREST
School of Management: JÉRÔME RIVE
Institut Universitaire de Technologie: SYLVAIN CORNIC

UNIVERSITÉ DU MAINE

ave Olivier Messiaen, 72085 Le Mans Cedex 9
Telephone: 2-43-83-30-00
E-mail: webmaster@univ-lemans.fr
Internet: www.univ-lemans.fr
Founded 1977
Pres.: YVES GUILLOTIN
Vice-Pres. for Admin.: RACHID EL GUERJOUMA
Vice-Pres. for Science Ccl: JEAN-YVES BUZARÉ
Vice-Pres. for Studies and Univ. Life: DANIEL LUZZATI
Sec.-Gen.: ANNE-MARIE RIOU
Librarian: MICHÈLE NARDI
Number of teachers: 628
Number of students: 10,308

DEANS

Faculty of Law, Economic Science and Management: LAURENT PUJOL
Faculty of Letters, Languages and Human Sciences: DOMINIQUE AMIARD
Faculty of Sciences and Technology: MICHEL PEZERIL

ATTACHED INSTITUTES

Higher National School of Engineering: rue Aristote, 72085 Le Mans Cedex 09; tel. 2-43-83-35-93; e-mail ensim@univ-lemans.fr; internet ensim.univ-lemans.fr.

University Institute of Technology (Laval): 52 rue des docteurs Calmette et Guérin, BP 2045, 53000 Laval Cedex 09; tel. 2-43-59-49-05; e-mail webmaster@univ-lemans.fr; internet www.iut-laval.univ-lemans.fr.

University Institute of Technology (Le Mans): ave Olivier Messiaen, 72085 Le Mans Cedex 09; tel. 2-43-83-34-01; e-mail iut-lemans@univ-lemans.fr; internet iut.univ-lemans.fr

UNIVERSITÉ DE MARNE-LA-VALLÉE

5 blvd Descartes, Champs/Marne, 77454 Marne-la-Vallée Cedex 2
Telephone: 1-60-95-75-00
E-mail: com@univ-mlv.fr
Internet: www.univ-mlv.fr
Founded 1991
Pres.: FRANCIS GODARD
Sec.-Gen.: SOPHIE JULIEN
Librarian: CHRISTELLE OTIN
Number of teachers: 400
Number of students: 11,000

TEACHING AND RESEARCH UNITS

Economic Sciences and Management: MURIEL JOUGLEUX
Engineering: DOMINIQUE REVUZ
Francilien Institute of Applied Sciences: MICHEL MADON
Francilien Institute of Engineering Services: CHRISTIAN BOURRET
French Institute of Town Planning: CHRISTIAN LEFEVRE
Gaspard Monge Institute of Electronics and Computing: JEAN-MARC LAHEURTE
Humanities and Social Sciences: FREDÉRIC MORET
Languages and Civilization: CLAUDIE TERRASSON
Letters, Arts, Communication and Technology: PASCALE ALEXANDRE
Mathematics: DANIEL LAMBERTON
Sports Science: ERIC LEVET-LABRY
University Institute of Technology: JACQUES DESARMENIEN

UNIVERSITÉ MONTPELLIER I

Service Communication, 5 Blvd Henri IV, CS 19044, 34967 Montpellier Cedex 2
Telephone: 4-67-41-74-00
E-mail: presidence@univ-montp1.fr
Internet: www.univ-montp1.fr
Founded 1970
State control
Language of instruction: French
Academic year: September to June
Pres.: PHILIPPE AUGÉ
Vice-Pres. for Admin.: JEAN MARTINEZ
Vice-Pres. for Science Ccl: JACQUES MERCIER
Vice-Pres. for Studies and Univ. Life: CHANTAL MARION
Gen. Sec.: PASCAL BEAUREGARD
Librarian: HÉLÈNE LORBLANCHET
Number of teachers: 829
Number of students: 18,538
Publications: *Cadran*, *Journal de Médecine*, *L'Economie Méridionale*, *Le Ligament*, *Revue de la Société d'Histoire du Droit*.

TEACHING AND RESEARCH UNITS

Faculté d'Administration Économique et Sociale: Ave Raymond Dugrand, CS 59640, 34960 Montpellier Cedex 2; tel. 4-67-15-84-60; Dir PATRICE N'DIAYE.

Faculté de l'Economie: Ave de la Mer, CS 79606, 34960 Montpellier Cedex 2; tel. 4-67-15-84-50; Dir CHRISTIAN LAGARDE.

Faculté du Droit et Science Politique: 39 rue de l'Université, 34960 Montpellier Cedex 2; tel. 4-67-61-54-00; Dir MARIE ELISABETH ANDRÉ.

Faculté de Médecine: 2 rue Ecole de Médecine, CS 59001, 34960 Montpellier Cedex 2; tel. 4-67-60-10-00; Dir JACQUES BRINGER.

Faculté d'Odontologie: 545 Ave du Prof. J. L. Viala, 34193 Montpellier Cedex 5; tel. 4-

67-10-44-70; Administrative Dir PHILIPPE HERNANDEZ.

Faculté de Pharmacie: 15 Ave Charles Flahault, BP 14491, 34093 Montpellier Cedex 2; tel. 4-67-54-80-00; Dir LAURENCE VIAN.

Faculté des Sciences du Sport: 700 Ave du Pic Saint-Loup, 34090 Montpellier Cedex 2; tel. 4-67-41-57-00; Dir DENIS DELIGNIÈRES.

Institut de Préparation à l'Administration Générale: Espace Richter, rue Vendémiaire, Bâtiment B, CS 19519, 34960 Montpellier Cedex 2; tel. 4-67-15-85-46; Dir ETIENNE DOUAT.

Institut des Sciences de L'Entreprise et du Management: Espace Richter, rue Vendémiaire, Bâtiment B, CS 19519, 34960 Montpellier Cedex 2; tel. 4-67-13-02-00; Dir MONIQUE LACROIX

UNIVERSITÉ DE MONTPELLIER II (SCIENCES ET TECHNIQUES DU LANGUEDOC)

pl. Eugène Bataillon, 34095 Montpellier Cedex 5

Telephone: 4-67-14-30-30

E-mail: presidence@univ-montp2.fr

Internet: www.univ-montp2.fr

Pres.: DANIÈLE HÉRIN

Vice-Pres. for Ccl of Admin.: ERIC BUFFENOIR

Vice-Pres. for Ccl of Studies and Univ. Life: CHRISTOPHE IUNG

Vice-Pres. for Scientific Ccl: CHRISTIAN PERIGAUD

Sec.-Gen.: PHILIPPE PAILLET

Librarian: MIREILLE GALCERAN

Number of teachers: 797

Number of students: 15,878

Publications: *Cahiers de Mathématiques*, *Naturalia Monspelianesia*, *Paléobiologie Continentale—Paléovertebrata*.

TEACHING AND RESEARCH UNITS

Faculté des Sciences: pl. Eugène Bataillon, 34095 Montpellier Cedex 5; tel. 4-67-14-30-34; e-mail facsciences@univ-montp2.fr; internet www.ufr.univ-montp2.fr; Dir GILLES HALBOUT.

Institut d'Administration des Entreprises: pl. Eugène Bataillon, 34095 Montpellier Cedex 5; tel. 4-67-14-38-65; e-mail secretariat.direction.iae@univ-montp2.fr; internet www.iae.univ-montp2.fr; Dir ERIC STEPHANY.

Institut Universitaire de Formation des Maîtres: 2 pl. Marcel Godechot, 34092 Montpellier Cedex 5; tel. 4-67-61-83-00; e-mail iufm-direction@univ-montp2.fr; internet www.montpellier.iufm.fr; Dir PATRICK DEMOUGIN.

Institut Universitaire de Technologie de Béziers: 3 pl. du 14 Juillet, BP 50438, 34505 Béziers Cedex; tel. 4-67-11-60-00; e-mail iut-beziers-direction@univ-montp2.fr; internet www.iutbeziers.univ-montp2.fr; Dir PHILIPPE PUJAS.

Institut Universitaire de Technologie de Montpellier: 99 ave d'Occitanie, 34296 Montpellier Cedex 5; tel. 4-99-58-50-40; e-mail iut-montpellier-direction@univ-montp2.fr; internet www.iutmontp.univ-montp2.fr; Dir PHILIPPE PEIROT.

Institut Universitaire de Technologie de Nîmes: 8 rue Jules-Raimu, 30907 Nîmes Cedex; tel. 4-66-62-85-00; e-mail ut-nimes-direction@univ-montp2.fr; internet www.iut-nimes.fr; Dir SALAM CHARAR.

Observatoire de Recherche Méditerranéen de l'Environnement (OSI—OREME): Bâtiment 22, CC 060, pl. Eugène Bataillon, 34095 Montpellier Cedex 5; tel. 4-67-14-40-85; e-mail oreme@univ-montp2.fr; internet www.oreme.univ-montp2.fr; Dir NICOLAS ARNAUD.

Polytech' Montpellier: pl. Eugène Bataillon, 34095 Montpellier Cedex 5; tel. 4-67-14-31-60; e-mail polytech-direction@univ-montp2.fr; internet www.polytech.univ-montp2.fr; Dir SERGE PRAVOSSOUDOVITCH

UNIVERSITÉ DE MONTPELLIER III (UNIVERSITÉ PAUL VALÉRY)

route de Mende, BP 5043, 34199 Montpellier Cedex 5

Telephone: 4-67-14-20-00

E-mail: communication@univ-montp3.fr

Internet: www.univ-montp3.fr

Founded 1970

State control

Language of instruction: French

Academic year: September to July

Pres.: ANNE FRAÏSSE

Vice-Pres. for Ccl of Admin.: YANN BISIOU

Vice-Pres. for Int. Relations: BURGHART SCHMIDT

Vice-Pres. for Scientific Ccl: PATRICK GILLI

Vice-Pres. for Studies and Univ. Life: CÉCILE POUSSARD

Sec.-Gen.: YVES CHAIMBAULT

Librarian: JEAN-FRANCOIS FOUCAUD

Number of teachers: 486

Number of students: 15,117

Publication: 68 research periodicals

TEACHING AND RESEARCH UNITS

Economic, Mathematical and Social Sciences: Dir: PATRICE SÉÉBOLD

Human and Environmental Sciences: Dir: Prof. DAVID LEFÈVRE

Languages and Foreign and Regional Cultures: Dir: MARIE-PAULE MASSON

Letters, Arts, Philosophy and Psychoanalysis: Dir: CHRISTIAN BELIN

Science of Society: Dir: RENÉ PRY

UNIVERSITÉ DE NANCY I (HENRI POINCARÉ)

24–30 rue Lionnois, BP 60120, 54003 Nancy Cedex

Telephone: 3-83-68-20-00

E-mail: info@uhp-nancy.fr

Internet: www.uhp-nancy.fr

Founded 1970

Pres.: JEAN-PIERRE FINANCE

Vice-Pres. of the Ccl of Admin.: BRUNO LEHEUP

Vice-Pres. of the Scientific Ccl: PIERRE MUTZENHARDT

Vice-Pres. of Studies and Univ. Life: CHRISTINE ATKINSON

Sec.-Gen.: LUC ZIEGLER

Librarian: ANNE-PASCALE PARRET

Number of teachers: 1,703

Number of students: 17,928

Publication: *Transversales* (3 a year)

TEACHING AND RESEARCH UNITS

Dental Surgery: Dean: PIERRE BRAVETTI

Higher School of Computing and its Applications: Dir: ANDRÉ SCHAFF

Higher School of the Science and Technology of Engineering: Dir: ARNAUD DELEBARRE

Higher School of the Science and Technology of the Wood Industry: Dir: JEAN-MICHEL LEBAN

Medicine: Dean: HENRY COUDANE

Pharmacy: Dean: FRANCINE PAULUS

Science and Technology: Dir: PIERRE STEINMETZ

Sport: Dean: ALAIN PIZZINATO

University Institute of Teacher Training (Lorraine): Dir: FABIEN SCHNEIDER

University Institute of Technology (Longwy): Dir: ANTOINE DI SANO

University Institute of Technology (Nancy-Brabois): Dir: EDDY BAJIC

University Institute of Technology (Saint Dié): Dir: PATRICE NUS

UNIVERSITÉ DE NANCY II

25 rue Baron Louis, BP 454, 54001 Nancy Cedex

Telephone: 3-83-34-46-00

Internet: www.univ-nancy2.fr

Founded 1970

State control

Language of instruction: French

Academic year: October to May

Pres.: MARTIAL DELIGNON

Vice-Pres. of Ccl of Admin.: PASCALE FADE

Vice-Pres. of Scientific Ccl: MATTIEU PETRISSANS

Vice-Pres. of Studies and Univ. Life: CHICOT EBOUÉ

Sec.-Gen.: FRANÇOIS NOËL

Librarian: FLORENCE BOUCHET

Library: see under Libraries and Archives

Number of teachers: 531

Number of students: 22,000

Publications: *Autrement dire*, *Etudes d'archéologie classique*, *La Revue française d'études américaines*, *Les Annales de l'Est*, *Revue Géographique de l'Est*, *Verbum*

TEACHING AND RESEARCH UNITS

Arts: Dir: MARCEL PAUL-CAVALLIER

History, Geography and Musicology: Dir: EMMANUEL CHIFFRE

Human Sciences: Dir: CHRISTINE BOCEREAN

Languages and Foreign Culture: Dir: ELSA CHAARANI

Science of Languages: Dir: RICHARD DUDA

UNIVERSITÉ DE NANTES

1 quai de Tourville, BP 13522, 44035 Nantes Cedex 1

Telephone: 2-40-99-83-83

E-mail: president@president.univ-nantes.fr

Internet: www.univ-nantes.fr

Founded 1962

State control

Pres.: Prof. YVES LECOINTE

Vice-Pres. for Admin.: GWENAËLLE LE DREFF

Vice-Pres. for Business Relations: JEAN-CHARLES CADIOU

Vice-Pres. for Capital: MARC JOYAU

Vice-Pres. for Culture and Initiatives: DANIELLE PAILLER

Vice-Pres. for Int. Relations: FRANÇOISE LEJEUNE

Vice-Pres. for Science Ccl: JACQUES GIRARDEAU

Vice-Pres. for Studies and Univ. Life: VINCENT LANG

Librarian: HÉLÈNE GROGNET

Number of teachers: 1,569

Number of students: 33,182

Publication: *Prisme* (6 a year)

TEACHING AND RESEARCH UNITS

Arts and Languages: FRÉDÉRIC LE BLAY

Dentistry: Dean: OLIVIER LABOUX

History, Art History and Archaeology: JEAN-NOËL GUYODO

Institute of Economy and Management (Nantes): BERNARD FIOLEAU

Institute of Geography and Planning: PAUL FATTAL

Institute of Preparatory Administrative Studies: THIBAUT DE BERRANGER

Institute for Research and Training in French as a Foreign Language: LOIC FRAVALO
Institute of Technology (Nantes): JEAN-PIERRE CITEAU
Institute of Technology (Roche-sur-Yon): THIERRY GUINET
Institute of Technology (St-Nazaire): Prof. RONALD GUILLÉN
International Language Centre: HERVÉ QUINTIN
Law and Political Sciences: GILLES DUMONT
Medicine: JEAN-MICHEL ROGEZ
Observatory of the Sciences of the Universe: PATRICK LAUNEAU
Pharmacology and Biology: ALAIN PINEAU
Polytech'Nantes: l'Ecole d'ingénieurs de l'Université: RENÉ LE GALL
Psychology: MOHAMMED BERNOUSSI
Science and Technology: MICHEL EVAIN
Sociology: RÉMY LE SAOUT
Sports Science: BRUNO PAPIN
Teacher Training: MICHEL HEICHETTE

UNIVERSITÉ DE NICE SOPHIA ANTIPOLIS

Grand Château, 28 ave Valrose, BP 2135, 06103 Nice Cedex 2
Telephone: 4-92-07-60-60
E-mail: presidence@unice.fr
Internet: www.unice.fr

Founded 1965
State control
Language of instruction: French

Pres.: ALBERT MAROUANI
First Vice-Pres.: PIERRE COULLET
Vice-Pres.: ELIANE KOTLER
Vice-Pres.: JEAN-MARC LARDEAUX
Vice-Pres.: LUDOVIC ARNAULT
Sec.-Gen.: ALAIN MIAOULIS
Librarian: LOUIS KLEE

Number of teachers: 1,311
Number of students: 26,196.

TEACHING AND RESEARCH UNITS

École Polytech'Nice-Sophia: 930 route des Colles, BP 145, 06903 Sophia Antipolis Cedex; e-mail communication@polytech.unice.fr; internet www.polytech.unice.fr; Dir PHILIPPE GOURBESVILLE.

Faculté de Chirurgie Dentaire: 24 ave des Diables Bleus, 06357 Nice Cedex 4; tel. 4-92-00-11-11; e-mail doyen-odonto@unice.fr; internet odontologie.unice.fr; Dean Prof. MARC BOLLA.

Faculté de Droit et Science Politique: ave Doyen L. Trotabas, 06050 Nice Cedex 1; tel. 4-92-15-70-00; e-mail sec-doyen-droit@unice.fr; internet droit.unice.fr; Dean CHRISTIAN VALLAR.

Faculté Espaces et Cultures: 98 blvd Edouard Herriot, BP 3209, 06204 Nice Cedex 3; tel. 4-93-37-53-59; e-mail gaed@unice.fr; internet unice.fr/gaed; Dir HLIMI TOURIA.

Faculté des Lettres, Arts et Sciences Humaines: 98 blvd Edouard Herriot, BP 3209, 06204 Nice Cedex 3; tel. 4-93-37-53-53; e-mail doyen-lash@unice.fr; internet lettres.unice.fr; Dean JEAN-YVES BOURSIER.

Faculté de Médecine: 28 ave de Valombrose, 06107 Nice Cedex 2; tel. 4-93-37-76-02; e-mail sfaure@unice.fr; internet medecine.unice.fr; Dean Prof. DANIEL BENCHIMOL.

Faculté des Sciences: 28 ave Valrose, 06108 Nice Cedex 2; tel. 4-92-07-69-96; e-mail direction-sciences@unice.fr; internet sciences.unice.fr; Dir FRÉDÉRIQUE VIDAL.

Faculté des Sciences du Sport: 261 route de Grenoble, 06205 Nice Cedex 3; tel. 4-92-29-65-00; e-mail dir-staps@unice.fr; internet staps.unice.fr; Dir JEAN-MARIE GARBARINO.

Institut d'Administration des Entreprises: 24 ave des Diables Bleus, 06357 Nice Cedex 4; tel. 4-92-00-11-39; e-mail sylvie.thiery@unice.fr; internet www.iae-nice.fr; Dir JACQUES SPINDLER.

Institut du Droit de la Paix et du Développement (IDPD): ave Doyen L. Trotabas, 06050 Nice Cedex 1; tel. 4-92-15-71-94; e-mail cammarer@unice.fr; internet idpd.unice.fr; Dean ALAIN PIQUEMAL.

Institut Supérieur d'Economie et de Management: 24 ave des Diables Bleus, 06300 Nice Cedex; tel. 4-92-00-12-22; e-mail isem@unice.fr; internet unice.fr/isem; Dir (vacant).

Institut Universitaire de Formation des Maîtres (IUFM): 89 ave George V, 06046 Nice Cedex 1; tel. 4-93-53-75-28; e-mail mohamed.najmi@unice.fr; internet www.iufm.unice.fr; Dir MOHAMED NAJMI.

Institut Universitaire de Technologie: 41 blvd Napoléon III, 06206 Nice Cedex 3; tel. 4-97-25-82-34; internet iut.unice.fr; Dir HENRI ALEXIS.

Service Commun en Langues: 98 blvd Edouard Herriot, BP 3209, 06204 Nice Cedex 3; tel. 4-93-37-54-10; e-mail scl@unice.fr; internet www.unice.fr/scl; Dir LAURENT ROUVEYROL

UNIVERSITÉ DE NÎMES

rue du Docteur Georges Salan, 30021 Nîmes Cedex 1
Internet: www.unimes.fr

Pres.: JACQUES MARIGNAN
Vice-Pres. for Admin. and Finance: EMMANUEL ROUX
Vice-Pres. for Research: CATHERINE BERNIÉ-BOISSARD
Vice-Pres. for Support, Training and Student Life: ERIC AUZIOL
Sec.-Gen.: STÉPHANIE MENSAH
Librarian: VALÉRIE TRAVIER

Number of teachers: 85
Number of students: 3,618

UNIVERSITÉ D'ORLÉANS

Château de la Source, ave du Parc Floral, BP 6749, 45067 Orléans Cedex 2
Telephone: 2-38-41-71-71
E-mail: contact@univ-orleans.fr
Internet: www.univ-orleans.fr

Founded 1961
Language of instruction: French
Academic year: September to June

Pres.: YOUSSOUFI TOURÉ
Vice-Pres.: ANNE LAVIGNE
Vice-Pres.: FLORIAN BOITEUX
Vice-Pres.: ISABELLE RANNOU
Vice-Pres.: PHILIPPE FAURE
Vice-Pres.: PIERRE ALLORANT
Sec.-Gen.: ANDRÉ PILLOT
Librarian: Mme DESBORDES

Number of teachers: 1,106
Number of students: 16,001

Publications: *Plaquette en direction des entreprises* (1 a year), research catalogue.

TEACHING AND RESEARCH UNITS

Ecole Polytechnique: 12 rue de Blois, BP 6744, 45067 Orléans Cedex 2; tel. 2-38-41-70-50; e-mail concours.polytech@univ-orleans.fr; internet www.univ-orleans.fr/polytech; Pres. RICHARD ROZIECKI.

Faculté de Droit, d'Economie et de Gestion (Faculty of Law, Economics and Business): rue de Blois, BP 6739, 45067 Orléans Cedex; tel. 2-38-41-70-31; e-mail rsa.deg@univ-orleans.fr; internet www.univ-orleans.fr/deg; Dean Prof. DOMINIQUE BESSIRE.

Faculté des Lettres, Langues et Sciences Humaines: 10 rue de Tours, BP 46527, 45065 Orléans Cedex 2; tel. 2-38-49-25-00; Dir ALAIN DAVESNE.

Faculté des Sciences: 1 rue de Chartres, BP 6759, 45067 Orléans Cedex 2; tel. 2-38-41-71-71; e-mail directeur.sciences@univ-orleans.fr; Dir NIRINA ANDRIANARIVELO.

Faculté des Sciences et Techniques des Activités Physiques et Sportives: allée du château, BP 6237, 45062 Orléans Cedex 2; tel. 2-38-41-71-78; e-mail infos.staps@univ-orleans.fr; Dir RÉGIS DE REYKE.

Institut Universitaire de Formation des Maîtres (Centre Val de Loire): 72 rue du Faubourg de Bourgogne, 45044 Orléans Cedex 2; tel. 2-38-49-26-00; e-mail directeur.iufm@univ-orleans.fr; Dir JEAN-MARIE GINESTA.

ATTACHED RESEARCH INSTITUTES

Institut Universitaire de Technologie de Bourges: 63 ave de Lattre de Tassigny, 18020 Bourges Cedex; tel. 2-48-23-80-80; e-mail irection@bourges.univ-orleans.fr; internet www.bourges.univ-orleans.fr/iut; Dir GÉRARD POISSON.

Institut Universitaire de Technologie de Chartres: 1 place Roger Joly, 28000 Chartres; tel. 2-37-91-83-00; e-mail monique.guerin@univ-orleans.fr; internet www.univ-orleans.fr/iut-chartres/iut.

Institut Universitaire de Technologie de l'Indre: 2 ave F. Mitterrand, 36000 Chateauroux; tel. 2-54-08-25-50; e-mail gerard.guillaume@univ-orleans.fr; internet www.univ-orleans.fr/composantes/iut-indre/iut-indre-new; Dir JEAN-CHRISTOPHE BARDET.

Institut Universitaire de Technologie d'Orléans: 16 rue d'Issoudun, BP 16729, 45067 Orléans Cedex 2; tel. 2-38-49-44-00; e-mail scolarite.iut45@univ-orleans.fr.

Observatoire des Sciences de l'Univers en région Centre (OSUC): Campus Géosciences, 1A rue de la Férolerie, 45071 Orléans Cedex 2; tel. 2-38-49-49-45; e-mail dir-osuc@univ-orleans.fr; Dir ELISABETH VERGÈS

UNIVERSITÉ PARIS I (PANTHÉON-SORBONNE)

12 pl. du Panthéon, 75231 Paris Cedex 05
Telephone: 1-44-07-77-04
E-mail: cabpresi@univ-paris1.fr
Internet: www.univ-paris1.fr

Founded 1971
State control
Language of instruction: French
Academic year: September to June

Pres.: JEAN-CLAUDE COLLIARD
Vice-Pres. for Admin.: JEAN DA SILVA
Vice-Pres. for Science Ccl: YVONNE FLOUR
Vice-Pres. for Studies and Univ. Life: GRÉGOIRE LOISEAU
Sec.-Gen.: FRANÇOIS RIOU
Librarian: ANNE MAGNAUDET

Number of teachers: 1,603
Number of students: 39,234

TEACHING AND RESEARCH UNITS

Business Law: Dir: Prof. JEAN-JACQUES DAIGRE (acting)
Business Management and Economics: Dir: PIERRE MEDAN
Economic and Social Administration, Labour and Social Studies: Dir: SABINE MONNIER
Economics: Dir: JEAN-CLAUDE BERTHÉLEMY
Geography: Dir: Prof. BERNARD TALLET (acting)
History: Dir: Prof. JEAN-MARIE BERTRAND (acting)
History of Art and Archaeology: Dir: Prof. MICHEL POIVERT

International and European Studies: Dir: Prof. PIERRE MICHEL EISEMANN
Legal Studies: Dir: Prof. EMMANUEL JEULAND (acting)
Mathematics and Computer Science: Dir: PASCAL GOURDEL (acting)
Philosophy: Dir: JACQUES DUBUCS
Plastic Arts and Science of Art: Dir: JOSÉ MOURE (acting)
Political Science: Dir: Prof. FRANÇOIS BASTIEN (acting)
Public Administration and Public Law: Dir: Prof. GÉRALDINE CHAVRIER (acting)

INSTITUTES

French Institute of Communication: Pres.: MATHIEU GALLET
Institute of Business Administration: Dir: PIERRE-LOUIS DUBOIS
Institute of Demography: Dir: MARLÈNE LAMY (acting)
Institute of Economic and Social Development Studies: Dir: Prof. ANFRÉ GUICHAOUA (acting)
Institute of Insurance: Dirs: VINCENT HEUZE, JÉRÔME KULLMANN
Institute of Labour Social Sciences: Dir: JEAN-MARIE MONNIER
Institute of Legal Studies: Dir: FRANÇOIS-XAVIER LUCAS
Institute of Tourism Research and Higher Study: (vacant)

DEPARTMENTS

Applied Modern Languages, Economics and Law: Dir: L. THOMPSON (acting)
Applied Modern Languages, Humanities: Dir: A. HAKKAK (acting)
Social Sciences: Dir: Mme YOTTE

PROFESSORS

Applied Modern Languages, Economics and Law (12 place du Panthéon, 75005 Paris; tel. 1-44-07-78-33; e-mail seglas@univ-paris1.fr):

BULLIER, A.-J., Legal English Studies
KERSAUDY, F., English for Economists

Business Law (tel. 1-44-07-77-35; e-mail ufr05@univ-paris1.fr):

AYNES, L., Private and Civil Law
BOULOC, B., Criminal Law
CADIET, L., Civil Procedure
CHAPUT, Y., Commercial Law—Insolvency
DAIGRE, J. J., Business Law
DAVID, C., Tax Law
DELEBECQUE, P., Civil Law
FLOUR, Y., Civil Law
GAUDU, F., Labour Law
GIUDICELLI, G., Criminal Law
GUTMANN, D., Insurance Law
HEUZE, V., Insurance Law
JOURDAIN, P., Civil Law
LABRUSSE, C., Civil Law
LE CANNU, P., Business Law
LE NABASQUE, H., Business Law
LIBCHABER, R., Civil Law
LUCAS DE LEYSSAC, C., Commercial Law
MENJUCQ, M., International Corporate Law
MUIR-WATT, H., Civil Law and International Civil Law
PARLEANI, G., Business Law
POLLAUD-DULIAN, F., Artistic and Literary Copyright Law
THIREAU, J. L., History of Law
VINEY, G., Civil Law

Business Management and Economics (17 rue de la Sorbonne, 75005 Paris Cedex 05; tel. 1-40-46-27-77; e-mail ufr06@univ-paris1.fr):

AMADIEU, J. F., Human Resources Management
BAETCHE, A., Scientific Methods Applied to Marketing
CHIROLEU-ASSOULINE, M., Macroeconomics
COT, A., Economics
COURET, A., Business Law
DE LA BRUSLERIE, H., Finance
DESAIGUES, B., Environmental Economics
GOFFIN, R., Finance
GREGORY, P., Marketing
IPSOMER, I., Marketing
LAURENT, P., Business Law
MUCHIELLI, J.-L., Industrial Economics
PEYRARD, M., International and European Business
PONCET, P., Finance
RAIMBOURG, P., Finance
RAY, J.-E., Labour Law
ROJOT, J., Organization Theory and Human Resources Management
ROLLAND, C., Computer Science
ROURE, F., Finance
STEYER, A., Speculative Methods in Marketing

Economic and Social Administration, Labour and Social Studies (1 rue d'Ulm, Bureau 14, 75005 Paris; tel. 1-44-07-79-28; e-mail dirufr12@univ-paris1.fr):

CHAPOULIE, Sociology
COUTURIER, G., Labour Law
GAZIER, B., Labour Economy
LENOIR, R., Sociology
PIGENET, Sociology
RODIÈRE, P., Labour Law
TSIKOUNAS, History

Economic and Social Development (Centre de Nogent-sur-Marne, 45 bis ave de la Belle-Gabrielle, 94736 Nogent-sur-Marne Cedex; tel. 1-43-94-72-15; e-mail iedes@univ-paris1.fr):

GRELLET, G., Economic Development
HAUBERT, M., Social Development
LAUTIER, B., Economic and Social Development

Economics (Centre P.M.F., 90 rue de Tolbiac, 75634 Paris Cedex 13; tel. 1-44-07-88-88; e-mail ufr02@univ-paris1.fr):

ANDREFF, W., Economy of the Transition
ARCHAMBAULT, E., Accountancy and Social Economics
BERTHELEMY, J. C., International Economics
BORDES, C., Money and Macroeconomics
CHAUVEAU, TH., Money and Finance
DE BOISSIEU, C., Monetary Economics
ENCAOUA, D., Industrial Economics
FARDEAU, M., Health Economics, Social Economics
FAU, J., Economic Analysis
FONTAGNE, L., International Economics
GARDES, F., Econometrics
GREFFE, X., Political Economy
HAIRAULT, J. O., Macroeconomics
HENIN, P., Macroeconomics
KEMPF, H., Macroeconomics
KOPP, P., Microeconomics
LAFAY, J. D., Public Economy
LAFFARGUE, J. P., International Economics
LANTNER, R., Economics and Industrial Politics
LAPIDUS, A., History of Economic Thought
LEVY-GARBOUA, L., Microeconomics
MASSON-D'AUTUME, A., Macroeconomics
MEIDINGER, C., Microeconomics
MENARD, C., Theory of Organization
PRADEL, J., Statistics
SCHUBERT, K., Macroeconomics
SOFER, C., Microeconomics
SOLLOGOUB, M., Microeconomics
VERNIÈRES, M., Economic Analysis
WIGNIOLLE, B., Macroeconomics
ZAGAME, P., Macroeconomics

Geography (191 rue St Jacques, 75231 Paris Cedex 05; tel. 1-44-32-14-00; e-mail geo1@univ-paris1.fr):

BECKOUCHE, P., Economic Geography
BOUINOT, J., Planning and Economic Geography
BRUN, J., Social Geography
CAZES, G., Geography of Tourism
CHALÉARD, J. L., Geography of Developing Countries
FRUIT, J. P., Rural Geography
KAISER, B., Geomorphology
LE COEUR, C., Natural Resources, Geomorphology
MALEZIEUX, J., Regional Geography, Land Use
MERLIN, P., Urban Geography
PECH, P., Environment
POURTIER, R., Tropical Geography
PREVELAKIS, G., Geopolitics
PUMAIN, D., Urban Geography
SAINT-JULIEN, TH., Human Geography, Statistics
SOPPELSA, J., Geopolitics
TABEAUD, M., Climatology

History (17 rue de la Sorbonne, 75005 Paris Cedex 05; tel. 1-40-46-27-88; e-mail hist1@univ-paris1.fr):

BALARD, M., Mediterranean Medieval History
BENOÎT, P., Modern History
BERTRAND, J. M., Ancient History
BOULÈGUE, J.-M., History of Black Africa
BOURIN, M., Medieval History
CABANTOUS, A., Modern History
CHARLE, C., Contemporary History
CHARPIN, D., Near Eastern History
CHRISTOL, M., Roman History
CORBIN, A., Contemporary History
CORSI, P., Modern History
D'ALMEIDA-TOPOR, H., Contemporary History
DAVID, J. M., Ancient History
FRANK, R., Contemporary History
GAUVARD, C., Medieval History
GENET, J. P., Medieval History
GUERRA, F., History of Latin America
KAPLAN, M., Byzantine Medieval History
KASPI, A., History of North America
LEMAITRE, N., Modern History
MARSEILLE, J., Economic and Social History
MARTIN, J. C., Modern History
MICHAUD, C., Modern History
MICHEAU, F., Medieval History
MICHEL, B., History of Eastern Europe
ORY, P., Contemporary History
PARISSE, M., Medieval History
REY, M. P., Contemporary History
RIVET, D., Contemporary History
ROBERT, J. L., Contemporary History
SCHMITT, P., Ancient History
WORONOFF, D., Economic and Social History
ZYLBERBERG, M., Modern History

History of Art and Archaeology (3 rue Michelet, 75006 Paris Cedex 06; tel. 1-53-73-71-11; e-mail ufr03sec@univ-paris1.fr):

BURNOUF, J., Medieval Archaeology
CROISSANT, F., Greek Archaeology
DAGEN, P., Contemporary Art
DARRAGON, E., Contemporary Art
DEMOULE, J.-P., Protohistory
DENTZER, J. M., Oriental Archaeology
DUMASY, F., Classical Archaeology
GILI, J., Cinema
HUOT, J. L., Oriental Archaeology
LICHARDUS, M., Protohistory
MONNIER, G., History of Contemporary Art
MOREL, P., Modern Art
PIGEOT, N., Archaeology and Protohistory
POLET, J., African Art and Archaeology
PRESSOUYRE, L., Medieval Art and Archaeology
PRIGENT, C., Medieval Art
RABREAU, D., Modern Art
SCHNAPP, A., Greek Archaeology
SODINI, J. P., Byzantine Archaeology
TALADOIRE, E., Meso-American Archaeology
TREUIL, R. A., Archaeology and Protohistory

VANCI, M., Contemporary Art
VAN DER LEEUW, S., Archaeology and Protohistory
VOLFOVSKY, C., Preservation of Cultural Heritage

Institute of Business Administration (21 rue Broca, 75240 Paris Cedex 05; tel. 1-53-55-27-47; e-mail iae@univ-paris1.fr; internet www.iae-paris.com):

ALLOUCHE, J., Human Resources Management
GIARD, V., Operations Management
HELFER, J.-P., Marketing and Strategy
HOARAU, C., Finance and Control
LE FLOCH, P., Business Law
MAILLET, P., Finance
PAUCELLE, J. L., Information Systems
TRIOLAIRE, G., Management

Institute of Demography (i DUP, Centre PMF, 90 rue de Tolbiac, 75013 Paris Cedex 13; tel. 1-44-07-86-46; e-mail idup@univ-paris1.fr):

DITTGEN, A., Socio-Demography
GROSSAT, B., Socio-Demography
LAMY-FESTY, M., Social Demography
NORVEZ, A., Socio-Demography

Institute of Social Sciences (tel. 1-45-36-16-40; e-mail patrick.diez@univ-paris1.fr):

FREYSSINET, J., Economics
OFFERLE, M., Political Science
PAULRE, B., Economics
PIOTEL, F., Sociology

International and European Studies (12 pl. du Panthéon, Bureau 304, 75005 Paris; tel. 1-44-07-77-33; e-mail ufr07@univ-paris1.fr):

BARAV, A., European Community Law
BERLIN, D., European Community Law
BURDEAU, G., International Public Law
CARREAU, D., Economic Public Law
DAUDET, Y., International Public Law
DELMAS-MARTY, M., Penal Law
EISEMAN, P. M., International Public Law
HUDAULT, J., History of Law
IDOT, L., European Community Law
JUILLARD, P., International Economic Law
LAGARDE, P., International Private Law
LEGRAND, P., Comparative Law
LE ROY, E., Legal Anthropology
LOVISI, C., History of Law
MANIN, P., European Community Law
MASCLET, J. C., European Community Law
MAYER, P., International Private Law
RENOUX-ZAGAMÉ, M. F., History of Law
RUIZ FABRI, H., Constitutional Law
SIRINELLI, P., Private Law
SOREL, J. M., International Public Law
STERN, B., International Public Law

Mathematics and Computer Science (Centre Pierre Mendès-France, 14ème étage, Bureau C 14-03, 90 rue de Tolbiac, 75013 Paris; tel. 1-44-07-89-84):

ABDOU, J., Game Theory
AUSLENDER, A., Optimization
BALASKO, Y., Mathematical Economics
BONNISSEAU, J.-M., Mathematics and Economics
CORNET, B., Mathematics and Economics
COTTRELL, M., Probability, Statistics and Neural Networks
GIRE, F., Computer Science
GUYON, X., Probability and Statistics
HADDAD, G., Differential Equations and Functional Analysis
JOUINI, E., Mathematics and Economics

Philosophy (90 rue de Tolbiac, 75013 Paris; tel. 1-44-07-88-32; e-mail philo1@univ-paris1.fr):

BLONDEL, E., Moral and Political Philosophy
BONARDEL, F., Philosophy of Religion
BRAGUE, R., History of Philosophy
CHAUVIRÉ, C., American Philosophy and Anthropology
CHEDIN, O., History of Philosophy
GRAS, A., Social Philosophy
KAMBOUCHNER, D., History of Philosophy
KERVEGAN, J. F., Philosophy of Law
MICHAUD, Y., Political Philosophy
MOEGLIN-DELCROIX, A., Aesthetics
MOSCONI, J., Philosophy of Mathematics
PINTO, E., Aesthetics
POLITIS, H., History of Philosophy
RIVENC, F., Philosophy of Logic
SALEM, J., History of Philosophy

Plastic Arts and Science of Art (Centre Saint Charles, 47 rue des Bergers, 75015 Paris; tel. 1-44-07-84-40; e-mail raufr04@univ-paris1.fr):

BAQUE, P., Visual Arts
CHATEAU, D., Aesthetics
CHIRON, E., Visual Arts
CLANCY, G., Aesthetics
CONTE, R., Visual Arts
DARRAS, B., Culture and Communication
DUGUET, A. N., Video and Media
FRENAULT-DERUELLE, P., Semiotics
HUYGHE, P. D., Visual Arts and Aesthetics
JIMENEZ, M., Aesthetics
LANCRI, J., Visual Arts
LEBENSZTEJN, J. C., History of Art
MIEREANU, C., Musicology
NOGUEZ, D., Cinema and Audiovisual Arts
SERCEAU, D., Cinema and Audiovisual Arts
SICARD, N., Visual Arts

Political Science (17 rue Cujas, 75005 Paris; tel. 1-40-46-28-04; e-mail raufr11@univ-paris1.fr):

BIRNBAUM, P., Political Sociology
BRAUD, P., Political Sociology
COLLIARD, J. C., Comparative Government
COTTERET, J.-M., Political Communication
FRANÇOIS, B., Constitutional Law
GAXIE, D., Political Sociology
GRESLE, F., Sociology
KLEIN, J., International Relations
LAGROYE, J., Political Ideology
LESAGE, M., Theory of Organizations
SFEZ, L., Communication
ZORGBIBE, C., International Relations

Public Administration and Public Law (12 pl. du Panthéon, 75005 Paris; tel. 1-44-07-77-38; e-mail ufr01@univ-paris1.fr):

BRECHON-MOULÈNES, C., Public Economic Law
CASTAGNEDE, B., Public Finance
DURUPTY, M., Public Law
FATOME, E., Administrative Law
FRIER, P., Public Law
GICQUEL, J., Public Law
JEGOUZO, Y., Administrative Law
LE MIRE, P., Public Law
MAISL, H., Administrative Law
MARCOU, G., Administrative Law
MATHIEU, B., Constitutional Law
MODERNE, F., Administrative Law
MORABITO, M., History of Law
MORAND-DEVILLER, J., Administrative Law
PFERS MANN, O., Comparative Public Law
PICARD, E., Administrative Law
RICHER, L., Administrative Law
TIMSIT, G., Public Law

UNIVERSITÉ DE PARIS II (UNIVERSITÉ PANTHÉON-ASSAS)

12 place du Panthéon, 75005 Paris Cedex 05
Telephone: 1-44-41-55-01
E-mail: presidence@u-paris2.fr
Internet: www.u-paris2.fr

Founded 1970

Pres.: LOUIS VOGEL
Vice-Pres. for Admin.: Prof. JEAN-DIDIER LECAILLON
Vice-Pres. for Science Ccl: JEAN COMBACAU
Vice-Pres. for Studies and Univ. Life: CHRISTA VALTCHEVA
Sec.-Gen.: SYLVIE TORAILLE
Librarian: GENEVIÈVE SONNEVILLE

Number of teachers: 1,547
Number of students: 17,900

TEACHING AND RESEARCH UNITS

Centre for Human Resources Training: Dir: F. BOURNOIS
Centre for Studies and Research in Construction and Housing: Dir: Prof. P. MALINVAUD
Economic and Social Administration (First and Second cycles): Dir: MARTINE PELE
Economics: ANTOINE BILLOT
Higher Institute for Defence Studies: Dir: Prof. YVES CARO
Image and Communication Institute: Dir: Prof. C. TUAL
Information Sciences (French Press Institute): Dir: Prof. NADINE TOUSSAINT-DESMOULINS
Institute for Administration Training: Dir: JEAN-MICHEL DE FORGES
Institute of Advanced International Studies: Dirs: C. LEBEN, P.-MARIE DUPUY
Institute of Business Law: Dir: Prof. MICHEL GERMAIN
Institute of Comparative Law: Dir: Prof. LOUIS VOGEL
Institute of Criminology: Dir: Prof. JACQUES-HENRI ROBERT
Institute of Judicial Studies: Dir: Prof. S. GUINCHARD
IUP–Management: Dir: Prof. RAYMOND TRÉMOLIÈRES
Law (First cycle): Dir: PIERRE CROCQ
Law (Second cycle) and Political Science: Dir: M. COMBACAU
Law (Third cycle) and Political Science: Dir: LAURENT LEVENEUR

PROFESSORS

ALLAND, D., Public Law
ALPHANDERY, E., Economic Sciences
AMSELEK, P., Public Law
ANCEL, D., Private Law
AUBY, J. B., Public Law
AUDIT, B., Private Law
AVRIL, P., Political Science
BALLE, F., Political Science
BALLOT, G., Economic Sciences
BARRAT, J., Information Sciences
BÉAUD, O., Public Law
BENZONI, L., Economic Sciences
BERNARD, M., Education Sciences
BETBEZE, J.-P., Economic Sciences
BETTATI, M., Public Law
BIENVENU, J. J., Public Law
BILLOT, A., Economic Sciences
BLAISE, J.-B., Private Law
BLUMANN, C., Public Law
BOISIVON, J.-P., Management Science
BONET, G., Private Law
BONNEAU, T., Private Law
BOURNOIS, F., Management Science
BRESSON, G., Economic Sciences
BURDEAU, F., History of Law
BUREAU, D., Private Law
CARBASSE, J. M., History of Law
CARO, J.-Y., Economic Sciences
CARTIER, M.-E., Private Law
CASTALDO, A., History of Law
CATALA, N., Private Law
CAZENAVE, P., Economic Sciences
CHAGNOLLAUD, D., Political Science
CHAMPENOIS, G., Private Law
CHARPIN, F., Economic Sciences
CHEVALLIER, J., Public Law
CHRISTIN, Y., Economic Sciences
COCATRE-ZILGIEN, P., History of Law
COHEN-JONATHAN, G., Public Law
COMBACAU, J., Public Law
CROCQ, P., Private Law
DECOCQ, A., Private Law
DELVOLVE, P., Public Law

DERIEUX, E., Information Sciences
DESNEUF, P., Economic Sciences
DESPLAS, M., Economic Sciences
DIBOUT, P., Public Law
DIDIER, P., Private Law
DISCHAMPS, J. C., Management Science
DONIO, J., Computing
DRAGO, G., Public Law
DUBOIS, P.-M., Public Law
DUPUY, G., Public Law
DURRY, G., Private Law
DUTHEIL DE LA ROCHÈRE, J., Public Law
FACCARELLO, G., Economic Sciences
FEYEL, G., History
FOUCHARD, P., Private Law
FOYER, J., Private Law
GAUDEMET, Y., Public Law
GAUDEMET-TALLON, H., Private Law
GAUTIER, P. Y., Private Law
GERMAIN, M., Private Law
GHOZI, A., Private Law
GJIDARA, M., Public Law
GOYARD, C., Public Law
GRIMALDI, M., Private Law
GUINCHARD, S., Private Law
HAROUEL, J.-L., History of Law
HUET, J., Private Law
HUMBERT, M., History of Law
JAHEL, S., Private Law
JARROSON, C., Private Law
JAUFFRET-SPINOSI, C., Private Law
JAVILLIER, J.-C., Private Law
JOUET, J., Information Sciences
LABROUSSE, C., Economic Sciences
LAFAY, G., Economic Sciences
LAINGUI, A., History of Law
LAMARQUE, J., Public Law
LARROUMET, C., Private Law
LEBEN, C., Public Law
LEFEBVRE-TEILLARD, A., History of Law
LE GALL, J.-P., Private Law
LEMENNICIER-BUCQUET, B., Economic Sciences
LEMOYNE DE FORGES, J. M., Public Law
LEQUETTE, Y., Private Law
LEVENEUR, L., Private Law
LOMBARD, M., Public Law
LOMBOIS, C., Private Law
LUBOCHINSKY, C., Economic Sciences
MALINVAUD, P., Private Law
MARTINEZ, J. C., Public Law
MAYAUD, Y., Private Law
MAZEAU, D., Private Law
MERLE, P., Private Law
MOLFESSIS, N., Private Law
MONCONDUIT, F., Political Science
MORANGE, J., Public Law
MOREAU, J., Public Law
MOURGUES, M. DE, Economic Sciences
NÊME, C., Economic Sciences
OLIVIER, J. M., Private Law
OTTAYJ, L., Private Law
PELÉ, M., Management Science
PERINET-MARQUET, H., Private Law
PONDAVEN, C., Economic Sciences
PORTELLI, H., Political Science
QUENET, M., History of Law
RAYNAUD, P., Political Science
REDSLOB, A., Economic Sciences
RIALS, S., Public Law
RIEFFEL, R., Information Sciences
RIGAUDIERE, A., History of Law
ROBERT, J.-H., Private Law
ROUGEMONT, M. DE, Computing
SCANNAVINO, A., Economic Sciences
SCHWARTZENBERG, R. G., Public Law
SUR, S., Public Law
SYNVET, H., Private Law
TERRÉ, F., Private Law
TEYSSIÉ, B., Private Law
THERY, P., Private Law
TOUSSAINT-DESMOULINS, N., Information Sciences
TREMOLIÈRES, R., Management Science
TRUCHET, D., Public Law
TUAL, C., English
VEDEL, C., Economic Sciences
VERPEAUX, M., Public Law
VITRY, D., Economic Sciences
VOGEL, L., Private Law
ZOLLER, E., Public Law

UNIVERSITÉ DE PARIS III (SORBONNE-NOUVELLE)

17 rue de la Sorbonne, 75230 Paris Cedex 05
Telephone: 1-40-46-28-84
E-mail: presidence@univ-paris3.fr
Internet: www.univ-paris3.fr

Founded 1970
State control
Language of instruction: French
Academic year: October to June

Pres.: Prof. MARIE-CHRISTINE LEMARDELEY
Vice-Pres. for Admin.: CARLE BONAFOUS-MURAT
Vice-Pres. for Science Ccl: PIERRE CIVIL
Vice-Pres. for Studies and Univ. Life: ANNE SALAZAR ORVIG
Sec.-Gen.: VINCENT GAILLOT

Number of teachers: 680
Number of students: 18,307

TEACHING AND RESEARCH UNITS

Arts and Media: Dir: BRUNO PÉQUIGNOT (acting)
Higher School of Interpreters and Translators: Dir: CLARE DONOVAN
Institute for the Advanced Study of Latin America: Dir: GEORGES COUFFIGNAL
Languages, Literature, Culture and Foreign Societies: Dir: JEAN-PATRICK GUILLAUME (acting)
Literature, Linguistics and Language Instruction: Dir: JEAN-LOUIS CHISS

UNIVERSITÉ DE PARIS IV (PARIS-SORBONNE)

1 rue Victor-Cousin, 75230 Paris Cedex 05
Telephone: 1-40-46-22-11
E-mail: president@paris-sorbonne.fr
Internet: www.paris-sorbonne.fr

Founded 1970
State control
Language of instruction: French
Academic year: October to June

Pres.: GEORGES MOLINIÉ
Vice-Pres. for Admin.: DENIS LABOURET
Vice-Pres. for Science Ccl: BARTHÉLÉMY JOBERT
Vice-Pres. for Studies and Univ. Life: ARIANE BUISSON
Sec.-Gen.: SYLVIE N'GUYEN
Librarian: JOËLLE CLAUD

Number of teachers: 1,300
Number of students: 23,271

TEACHING AND RESEARCH UNITS

Applied Foreign Languages: Dir: Prof. LILIANE GALLET-BLANCHARD
English: Dir: Prof. PIERRE COTTE
French and Comparative Literature: Dir: Prof. DIDIER ALEXANDRE
French Language: Dir: Prof. OLIVIER SOUTET
Geography and Planning: Dir: Prof. GUY CHEMLA
Germanic Studies: Dir: Prof. MARTINE DALMAS
Greek: Dir: Prof. ALAIN BILAUT
History: Dir: Prof. A. TALLON
History of Art and Archaeology: Dir: Prof. THIBAUT WOLVESPERGES
Iberian and Latin-American Studies: Dir: Prof. SADI LAKHDARI
Institute for the Research of the Civilizations of the Modern Western World: Dir: Prof. DENIS CROUZET
Institute of Applied Humanities: Dir: Prof. CLAUDE MONTACIÉ
Italian and Romanian: Dir: Prof. ANDREA FABIANO
Latin Language and Literature: Dir: Prof. GÉRARD CAPDEVILLE
Music and Musicology: Dir: Prof. FRÉDÉRIC BILLIET
Philosophy and Sociology: Dir: Prof. STÉPHANE CHAVIER
Slavonic Studies: Dir: Prof. LAURE TROUBETZKOY

DIRECTORS OF GRADUATE SCHOOLS

Ancient and Medieval Worlds: Prof. PAUL DEMONT
Civilization, Cultures, Literature and Societies: GÉRARD RAULET
Concepts and Languages: Prof. JEAN-PIERRE BARTOLI
French and Comparative Literatures: Prof. BERTRAND MARCHAL
Graduate School of Geography, Paris: space, society and planning: Prof. CHRISTIAN GRATALOUP
History of Art and Archaeology: Prof. MARIANNE GRIVEL
Modern and Contemporary History: Prof. JACQUES-OLIVIER BOUDON

UNIVERSITÉ PARIS V (DESCARTES)

12 rue de l'École de Médecine, 75270 Paris Cedex 06
Telephone: 1-40-46-16-16
E-mail: secretaire.general@parisdescartes.fr
Internet: www.parisdescartes.fr

Founded 1970
Academic year: October to July

Pres.: AXEL KAHN
Vice-Pres. for Admin.: ARNAUD DUCRUIX
Vice-Pres. for Science Ccl: BRUNO VARET
Vice-Pres. for Studies and Univ. Life: MARIE-HÉLÈNE JEANMERET-CRETTEZ
Sec.-Gen.: FRANÇOIS PAQUIS
Librarian: JERÔME KALFON

Number of teachers: 2,177
Number of students: 38,000

Publication: *Diologues de Descartes* (4 a year).

TEACHING AND RESEARCH UNITS

Faculté Biomédicale: 45 rue des Saints-Pères, 75006 Paris Cedex 06; tel. 1-42-86-22-33; e-mail responsable-administratif@biomedicale.univ-paris5.fr; Dir DANIEL JORE.

Faculté de Chirurgie Dentaire: 1 rue Maurice Arnoux, 92120 Montrouge; tel. 1-58-07-67-00; e-mail gerard.levy@parisdescartes.fr; Dean GÉRARD LÉVY.

Faculté de Droit: 10 ave Pierre Larousse, 92240 Malakoff; tel. 1-41-17-30-00; internet www.droit.univ-paris5.fr; Dean JEAN-PIERRE MACHELON.

Faculté de Mathématique et Informatique: 45 rue des Saints-Pères, 75006 Paris; tel. 1-42-86-40-41; e-mail scolarite@mi.parisdescartes.fr; Dir CHRISTINE GRAFFIGNE.

Faculté de Médecine: 15 rue de l'école de médecine, 75270 Paris Cedex 06; tel. 1-53-10-46-00; e-mail scolarite@mi.parisdescartes.fr; Dir PATRICK BERCHE.

Faculté des Sciences Humaines et Sociales: rue des Saints-Pères, 75270 Paris Cedex 06; tel. 1-53-10-50-60; e-mail accueil@shs.parisdescartes.fr; Dean SYLVETTE MAURY.

Faculté des Sciences Pharmaceutiques et Biologiques: 4 ave de l'Observatoire, 75006 Paris; tel. 1-53-73-95-95; e-mail martine.aiach@parisdescartes.fr; Dean MARTINE AIACH.

Faculté des Sciences et Techniques des Activités Physiques et Sportives: 1 rue Lacretelle, 75015 Paris; tel. 1-56-56-12-00;

e-mail bertrand.during@parisdescartes.fr; Dir BERTRAND DURING.

Institut de Psychologie: Centre Henri Piéron, 71 ave Edouard Vaillant, 92774 Boulogne-Billancourt Cedex; tel. 1-55-20-58-58; e-mail communication@psychologie.parisdescartes.fr.

Institut Universitaire de Technologie: 143 ave de Versailles, 75016 Paris; tel. 1-42-86-47-00; e-mail iut@iut.univ-paris5.fr; Dir GUILLAUME BORDRY

UNIVERSITÉ DE PARIS VI (PIERRE ET MARIE CURIE)

4 place Jussieu, 75005 Paris
Telephone: 1-44-27-44-27
E-mail: dag@upmc.fr
Internet: www.upmc.fr

Founded 1971

Pres.: JEAN-CHARLES POMEROL
Vice-Pres. for Int. Relations: SERGE FDIDA
Vice-Pres. for Medicine: BRUNO RIOU
Vice-Pres. for Research: JEAN CHAMBAZ
Vice-Pres. for Resources and Means: MAURICE RENARD
Vice-Pres. for Training and Professional Integration: PATRICK PORCHERON
Sec.-Gen.: CLAUDE RONCERAY

Number of teachers: 3,250
Number of students: 29,570

TEACHING AND RESEARCH UNITS

Apprenticeship Training Centre (CFA): DENIS POULAIN
Biology: DANIEL VERGÉ
Chemistry: DIDIER DEVILLIERS
Earth Sciences, Environment and Biodiversity: LUC ABBADIE
Engineering: JEAN DEVARS
Henri Poincaré Institute: CÉDRIC VILLANI
Institute of Astrophysics, Paris (IAP): LAURENT VIGROUX
Institute of Doctoral Training (IFD): PHILIPPE DENOULET
Institute of Statistics (ISUP): MICHEL DELECROIX
Mathematics: HERVÉ LE DRET (Dean)
Medicine: SERGE UZAN (Dean)
Oceanological Observatory, Banyuls: PHILIPPE LEBARON
Oceanological Observatory, Roscoff: BERNARD KLOAREG
Oceanological Observatory, Villefranche-sur-Mer: FAUZI MANTOURA
Physics: PATRICK BOISSÉ
Polytech'Paris-UPMC: JEAN-MARIE CHESNEAUX

UNIVERSITÉ DE PARIS VII (DENIS DIDEROT)

2 place Jussieu, 75251 Paris Cedex 05
Telephone: 1-44-27-44-27
E-mail: mmtx@sigu7.jussieu.fr
Internet: www.diderotp7.jussieu.fr

Founded 1970

Pres.: VINCENT BERGER
Vice-Pres. for Admin.: LAURE ELIE
Vice-Pres. for Cultural Life and Univ. Integration: BERNADETTE BRICOUT
Vice-Pres. for Int. Relations: FRÉDÉRIC OGEE
Vice-Pres. for Projects and Building Planning: FRANÇOIS MONTARRAS
Vice-Pres. for Science Ccl: RICHARD LAGANIER
Vice-Pres. for Studies and Univ. Life: JEAN-LOUIS COLLIN
Sec.-Gen.: DENIS GUILLAUMIN

Number of teachers: 1,400
Number of students: 26,000

TEACHING AND RESEARCH UNITS

Anthropology, Ethnology and Religious Studies: Dir: P. DESHAYES
Biochemistry: Dir: PATRICK VICART
Biology and Natural Sciences: Dir: CLAUDE LAMOUR-ISNARD
Chemistry: Dir: JEAN AUBARD
Clinical Human Sciences: Dir: PAUL-LAURENT ASSOUN
Computer Studies: Dir: GUY COUSINEAU
Dental Surgery: Dir: MARIE-LAURE BOY-LEFEVRE
Earth and Physical Sciences: Dir: YVES GAUDEMER
Eastern Asian Languages and Literature: Dir: CÉCILE SAKAI
Film, Communication and Information Studies: Dir: BAUDOIN JURDANT
Geography, History and Social Sciences: Dir: JEAN-PIERRE VALLAT
Institute of English: Dir: PHILIPPE JAWORSKI
Institute of Haematology: Dir: FRANÇOIS SIGAUX
Intercultural Studies in Applied Languages: Dir: JOHN HUMBLEY
Linguistic Research: Dir: ALAIN ROUVERET
Mathematics: Dir: PIERRE VOGEL
Medicine (Lariboisière-Saint-Louis): Dir: ALAIN LE DUC
Medicine (Xavier-Bichat): Dir: J. M. DESMONTS
Physics: Dir: LUC VALENTIN
Sciences of Texts and Documents: Dir: PIERRE CHARTIER
Social Sciences: Dir: ETIENNE TASSIN
University Institute of Technology: Dir: ALAIN JUNGMAN

UNIVERSITÉ DE PARIS VIII—VINCENNES À ST-DENIS

2 rue de la Liberté, 93526 St Denis Cedex 02
Telephone: 1-49-40-67-89
E-mail: presidence@univ-paris8.fr
Internet: www.univ-paris8.fr

Founded 1969
State control
Language of instruction: French

Pres.: PASCAL BINCZAK
Vice-Pres. for Admin.: CHRISTINE BOUISSOU
Vice-Pres. for Science Ccl: ELISABETH BAUTIER
Vice-Pres. for Studies and Univ. Life: JEAN-MARC MEUNIER
Sec.-Gen.: BERNARD FRADIN
Librarian: CAROLE LETROUIT

Number of teachers: 1,047
Number of students: 21,815

Publications: *Extrême-Orient/Extrême-Occident, Marges, Médiévales, Recherches linguistiques de Vincennes, Théorie, Littérature, Epistémologie*

TEACHING AND RESEARCH UNITS

Arts, Philosophy and Aesthetics: Dir: ERIC LECERF
Culture and Communication: Dir: MARTINE POUPON-BOUFFIERE
Economy and Management: Dir: PATRICK BOULOGNE
Educational Science, Psychoanalysis and French as a Foreign Language: Dir: JEAN-LOUIS LEGRAND
French Institute of Geopolitics: Dir: BARBARA LOYER
Institute of Distance Learning: Dir: GILLES BERNARD
Institute of European Studies: Dir: MIRELLE AZZOUG
Languages and Foreign Cultures: Dir: ANNICK ALLAIGRE
Law: Dir: JEAN-YVES ROCHEX
Mathematics, Computer Studies, Technology and ICT: Dir: ARAB BEN ALI CHÉRIF
Psychology: Dir: MARIE CARMEN CASTILLO
Science of Language: Dir: ANNE ZRIBI HERTZ
Territory, Environment and Societies: Dir: ANTOINE DA LAGE
Texts and Society: Dir: MARTINE CREACH
University Institute of Technology (Montreuil): Dir: ANDRÉ-MAX BOULANGER
University Institute of Technology (Tremblay): Dir: GORGUI SEYE

UNIVERSITÉ DE PARIS IX (PARIS-DAUPHINE)/UNIVERSITÉ PARIS DAUPHINE

place du Maréchal de Lattre de Tassigny, 75775 Paris Cedex 16
Telephone: 1-44-05-44-05
E-mail: service.communicationping@dauphinepong.fr
Internet: www.dauphine.fr

Founded 1968
State control
Language of instruction: French

Pres.: LAURENT BATSCH
Vice-Pres. for Int. Relations: ARNAUD RAYNOUARD
Vice-Pres. for Science Ccl: ELYÈS JOUINI
Vice-Pres. for Studies and Univ. Life: DOMINIQUE DAMAMME
Head of Secretariat: MAGALI ALZRAA

Library of 170,000 vols, 9,000 current periodicals

Number of teachers: 400
Number of students: 8,867

DIRECTORS

Teaching and Research Units:
- Analysis and Systems Modelling for Decision Mathematics (LAMSADE): VANGÉLIS PASCHOS
- Cultural Identity and Speciality Languages (CICLaS): MARTINE PIQUET
- Decision Mathematics (CEREMADE): (vacant): ERIC SÉRÉ
- Economics (LEDa): PATRICE GEOFFRON
- Law (L2D): JOËL MONÉGER
- Management (DRM): ISABELLE HUAULT
- Social Sciences (IRISSO): DOMINIQUE DAMAMME

University Professional Institutes:
- Institute of Finance (IFD): ELYÈS JOUINI
- Institute for the Management of Research and Innovation (IMRI): MICHEL POIX

PROFESSORS

ALTER, N., Sociology
ARNOLD, V., Mathematics
AUBIN, J.-P., Mathematics
BENSOUSSAN, A., Applied Mathematics
BERLIOZ-HOUIN, B., Business Law
BERTHET, CH., Computer Studies
BIENAYME, A., Industrial Economics
BLONDEL, D., Economics
BOUQUIN, H., Finance
BRUNET, A., Civil Law
CAREY-ABRIOUX, C.
CAZES, P., Statistics
CHAITIN-CHATELIN, F., Mathematics
CHAVENT, G., Mathematics
CHEDIN, G., English Language
CHEVALIER, J.-M., Economics
CLAASSEN, E., Economics
COHEN, E., Finance
COLASSE, B., Finance
COTTA, A., Business Organization
COUSOT, P., Computer Studies
DANA, R.
DE MONTMORILLON, B., Finance
DESMET, P.
DIDAY, E., Computer Studies
DOSS, H., Mathematics
EKELAND, I., Mathematics
ETNER, F., Economics
FLORENS, D., Mathematics
FRISON-ROCHE, M. A., Civil Law

Gauvin, C., English Language
Geman, H., Finance
Ghozi, A., Civil Law
Giovannangeli, J.-L., English Language and Literature
Gourieroux, C., Mathematics
Grelon, B., Civil Law
Guillaume, M., Economics
Guillochon, B., Economics
Haddad, S., Computer Studies
Hamon, J., Finance
Hess, C., Mathematics
Jomier, G., Computer Studies
Larnac, P.-M., Economics
Lena, H., Public Law
Le Pen, C., Economics
Le Tallec, P., Mathematics
Levy, E., Economics
Levy, G., Computer Studies
Lions, P.-L., Mathematics
Liu, M., Sociology
Lombard, M., Public Law
Lorenzi, J.-H., Economics
Mailles, D., Computer Studies
Manin, A., Public Law
Mariet, F., Education
Mathis, J., Finance
Metais, J., Economics
Meyer, Y., Mathematics
Michalet, C., Economics
Morel, J.-M., Mathematics
Nussenbaum, M., Finance
Palmade, J., Sociology
Parly, J.-M., Economics
Paschos, V., Computer Studies
Piganiol, B., Management
Pilisi, D., Economics
Pinson, S., Computer Studies
Piquet, M., English Language and Literature
Pras, B., Finance
Richard, J., Finance
Rigal, J.-L., Computer Studies
Rives-Lange, J. L., Civil Law
Romelaer, P., Finance
Roux, D., Business Economics
Roy, B., Scientific Methods of Management
Salin, P., Monetary Economics
Schmidt, C., Sociology
Simon, Y., Finance
Siroen, J.-M., Economics
Sulzer, J.-R., Finance
Terny, G., Public Economics
Thietart, R., Finance
Tolla, P., Computer Studies
Trinh-Hebreard, S., Sociology
Vallee, C., Public Law

UNIVERSITÉ DE PARIS X (PARIS-NANTERRE)

200 ave de la République, 92001 Nanterre Cedex
Telephone: 1-40-97-72-00
E-mail: service.communication@u-paris10.fr
Internet: www.u-paris10.fr

Pres.: Bernadette Madeuf
Vice-Pres. for Capital: Colette Vallat
Vice-Pres. for Ccl of Admin. and Training: Philippe Guttinger
Vice-Pres. for Int. Devt and the Foreign Language Policy: Danielle Leeman
Vice-Pres. for Resources and the Steering Committee: Sébastien Kott
Vice-Pres. for Science Ccl: Bernard Laks
Vice-Pres. for Studies and Univ. Life: Cornelius Crowley
Sec.-Gen.: Didier Ramond
Librarian: Evelyne Dieckhoff

Number of teachers: 1,500
Number of students: 36,500

TEACHING AND RESEARCH UNITS

Economic Sciences, Management, Maths and Computer Science: Dir: Françoise Labre
Industrial Systems and Communication Technology: Dir: Alain Priou
Institute of Technology (Ville d'Avray): Dir: Jacky Barraud
Languages and Foreign Cultures: Dir: Sylvaine Hughes
Law and Political Science: Dir: Matthieu Conan
Literature, Languages and Philosophy: Dir: Jean-François Balaude
Psychology and Education Sciences: Dir: Pascal Mallet
Science and Techniques of Physical and Sporting Activities: Dir: Tarak Driss
Social Science and Administration: Dir: Bernard Bazin

UNIVERSITÉ DE PARIS XI (PARIS-SUD)

15 rue G. Clémenceau, 91405 Orsay Cedex
Telephone: 1-69-41-67-50
E-mail: secretariat@presidence.u-psud.fr
Internet: www.u-psud.fr
Founded 1970
State control
Language of instruction: French
Academic year: September to June

Pres.: Guy Couarraze
Vice-Pres. for Admin.: Jean-Jacques Girerd
Vice-Pres. for Science Ccl: Jacques Bittoun
Vice-Pres. for Studies and Univ. Life: Colette Voisin
Sec.-Gen.: Christine Arnulf-Koechlin
Librarian: Françoise Meignien

Number of teachers: 1,800
Number of students: 30,000

Publications: *Aspects de la recherche* (1 a year), *Plein-Sud* (6 a year).

TEACHING AND RESEARCH UNITS

Faculté de Droit, Economie et Gestion (Sceaux): 54 blvd Desgranges, 92331 Sceaux Cedex; tel. 1-40-91-17-00; Dean Jérôme Fromageau.

Faculté de Médecine (Kremlin-Bicêtre): 63 rue Gabriel Péri, 94276 Le Kremlin-Bicêtre Cedex; tel. 1-49-59-67-67; Dean Serge Bobin.

Faculté de Pharmacie (Châtenay-Malabry): 5 rue Jean-Baptiste Clément, 92296 Châtenay-Malabry Cedex; tel. 1-46-83-57-89; Dean Dominique Porquet.

Faculté des Sciences (Orsay): 15 rue Georges Clémenceau, 91405 Orsay Cedex; tel. 1-69-15-74-08; e-mail doyen.sciences@u-psud.fr; Dir Philippe Masson.

Faculté des Sciences et Techniques des Activités Physiques et Sportives (Orsay): Bâtiment 335, 91405 Orsay Cedex; tel. 1-69-15-61-57; e-mail christine.le-scanff@u-psud.fr; Dir Christine Le Scanff.

UNIVERSITY INSTITUTES

Instituts Universitaires de Technologie de Génie Électrique, Informatique Industrielle, Génie Mécanique et Productique (Cachan): 9 ave de la Division Leclerc, 94234 Cachan Cedex; tel. 1-41-24-11-00; e-mail direction.iut-cachan@u-psud.fr; Dir Souhil Megherbi.

Instituts Universitaires de Technologie de Gestion et Commerce (Sceaux): 8 ave Cauchy, 92330 Sceaux Cedex; tel. 1-40-91-24-99; e-mail gea1.iut-sceaux@u-psud.fr; Dir Jean-Gilles Mbianga.

Instituts Universitaires de Technologie d'Informatique, Mesures Physiques et Chimie (Orsay): Plateau du Moulon, BP 127, 91400 Orsay Cedex; tel. 1-69-33-60-00; e-mail directeur.iut-orsay@u-psud.fr; Dir Nelly Bensimon.

Polytech'Paris-Sud: Bâtiment 620, 91405 Orsay Cedex; tel. 1-69-33-86-13; e-mail communication@polytech.u-psud.fr; Dir François Aguillon

UNIVERSITÉ DE PARIS XII (PARIS-VAL-DE-MARNE)

61 ave du Général de Gaulle, 94010 Créteil Cedex
Telephone: 1-45-17-10-00
E-mail: sgp12@u-pec.fr
Internet: www.univ-paris12.fr
Founded 1970
Academic year: October to July

Pres.: Simone Bonnafous
Vice-Pres. for Admin.: Suzanne Pontier
Vice-Pres. for Information Systems: Didier Nicolle
Vice-Pres. for Institutional Relations: Jean-François Dufeu
Vice-Pres. for Science Ccl: Luc Hittinger
Vice-Pres. for Studies and Univ. Life: Christian Regnaut
Sec.-Gen.: Pascale Saint-Cyr
Librarian: Sophie Mazens

Number of teachers: 1,200
Number of students: 32,000.

TEACHING AND RESEARCH UNITS

Faculté d'Administration et Echanges Internationaux: tel. 1-45-17-18-79; e-mail marie.berrous@u-pec.fr; Dean Josiane Attuel.

Faculté de Droit: 83–85 ave du Général de Gaulle, 94000 Créteil Cedex; tel. 1-56-72-60-02; e-mail secdoyen-droit@u-pec.fr; Dean Prof. Jean-Jacques Israel.

Faculté des Lettres, Langues et Sciences Humaines: tel. 1-45-17-11-92; e-mail com-llsh@u-pec.fr; Dean Jeanne-Marie Boivin.

Faculté de Médecine: tel. 1-49-81-36-20; e-mail conseilmed@u-pec.fr; Dir Prof. Jean-Luc Dubois-Randé.

Faculté des Sciences Économiques et de Gestion: tel. 1-41-78-46-34; e-mail sophie .pointereau@u-pec.fr; Dean Philippe Adair.

Faculté de Sciences de l'Education, Sciences Sociales et STAPS: SESS, Immeuble Pyramide, 80 ave du Général de Gaulle, 94009 Créteil Cedex;STAPS, Centre Duvauchelle, 27 rue Magellan, 94000 Créteil Cedex; e-mail sess-staps@u-pec.fr.

Faculté des Sciences et Technologie: tel. 1-45-17-13-35; e-mail doyen.sciences@u-pec .fr; Dean Dr Jacques Moscovici

UNIVERSITÉ DE PARIS XIII (PARIS-NORD)

99 ave Jean-Baptiste Clément, 93430 Villetaneuse
Telephone: 1-49-40-30-00
E-mail: cab-pres@upn.univ-paris13.fr
Internet: www.univ-paris13.fr
Founded 1970
Academic year: September to June

Pres.: Jean-Loup Salzmann
Vice-Pres. for Admin.: Ariane Desporte
Vice-Pres. for Science Ccl: Charles Desfrançois
Vice-Pres. for Studies and Univ. Life: André Tardieu
Sec.-Gen.: Rémy Gicquel
Librarian: Dominique Baudin

Number of teachers: 1,181
Number of students: 22,000

Publications: *Annales du CESER*, *Cahiers de Linguistique Hispanique Médiévale*, *Psychologie clinique*.

TEACHING AND RESEARCH UNITS

Faculté de Droit et des Sciences Politiques et Sociales: 99 ave Jean-Baptiste Clément, 93430 Villetaneuse; tel. 1-49-40-32-97; e-mail magali.marante@univ-paris13.fr; internet www.univ-paris13.fr/dsps; Dir DIDIER GUEVEL.

Faculté des Lettres, Sciences de l'Homme et des Sociétés: 99 ave Jean-Baptiste Clément, 93430 Villetaneuse; tel. 1-49-40-32-11; e-mail sec-ufrl@univ-paris13.fr; internet www.univ-paris13.fr/lshs; Dir ELISABETH BELMAS.

Faculté de Santé, Médecine et Biologie Humaine: 74 rue Marcel Cachin, 93017 Bobigny Cedex; tel. 1-48-38-73-18; e-mail f.boullay_rollin@smbh.univ-paris13.fr; internet www.smbh.univ-paris13.fr; Dir JEAN-LUC DUMAS.

Faculté des Sciences de la Communication: 99 ave Jean-Baptiste Clément, 93430 Villetaneuse; tel. 1-49-40-44-78; e-mail sec-ufrc@univ-paris13.fr; internet www.univ-paris13.fr/communication; Dir VINCENT BRULOIS.

Faculté des Sciences Économiques et de Gestion: 99 ave Jean-Baptiste Clément, 93430 Villetaneuse; tel. 1-49-40-35-38; e-mail arbia.kefi@univ-paris13.fr; internet www.univ-paris13.fr/ecogestion; Dir PHILIPPE BARBET.

Institut Galilée: 99 ave Jean-Baptiste Clément, 93430 Villetaneuse; tel. 1-49-40-36-65; e-mail secretariat1.direction.galilee@univ-paris13.fr; internet www-galilee.univ-paris13.fr; Dir JEAN-PIERRE ASTRUC.

Institut Universitaire de Technologie (Bobigny): L'Illustration, 1 rue de Chablis, 93017 Bobigny Cedex; tel. 1-48-38-88-36; e-mail diriut@iutb.univ-paris13.fr; internet www.iut-bobigny.univ-paris13.fr; Dir DANIEL VERBA.

Institut Universitaire de Technologie (Saint-Denis): place du 8 Mai 1945, 93206 Saint-Denis Cedex; tel. 1-49-40-61-00; e-mail diriut@iutb.univ-paris13.fr; internet www.iutsd.univ-paris13.fr; Dir JEAN-MARIE GOURDON.

Institut Universitaire de Technologie (Villetaneuse): 99 ave Jean-Baptiste Clément, 93430 Villetaneuse; tel. 1-49-40-30-28; e-mail secrdir@iutv.univ-paris13.fr; internet www.iutv.univ-paris13.fr; Dir PASCAL COUPEY

UNIVERSITÉ DE PAU ET DES PAYS DE L'ADOUR

ave de l'Université, BP 576, 64012 Pau Cedex
Telephone: 5-59-40-70-00
E-mail: communication@univ-pau.fr
Internet: www.univ-pau.fr
Founded 1970
State control
Pres.: JEAN-LOUIS GOUT
Vice-Pres. for Admin.: JEAN GOURDOU
Vice-Pres. for Development and Technological Tranfer: MICHEL MAGOT
Vice-Pres. for Int. Relations: DAVID BESSIÈRES
Vice-Pres. for Property: ALAIN GRACIAA
Vice-Pres. for Relations with the Territorial Collectivities: VINCENT VLES
Vice-Pres. for Resources and Budget: DAVID CARASSUS
Vice-Pres. for Science Ccl: MOHAMED AMARA
Vice-Pres. for Studies and Univ. Life: MICHEL BRAUD
Sec.-Gen.: JEAN-LOUIS FOURCAUD
Librarian: MARIE-ANNICK CAZAUX
Number of teachers: 693
Number of students: 11,401

TEACHING AND RESEARCH UNITS

Faculty of Law, Economics and Management: Dean: JEAN-JACQUES LEMOULAND
Faculty of Letters, Languages and Human Sciences: Dean: JEAN-PIERRE BARRAQUÉ
Faculty of Science and Technical Studies (la Côte Basque): Dean: CLAUDE MOUCHÈS
Faculty of Science and Technical Studies (Pau): Dean: VÉRONIQUE LAZZERI-PORDOY
Multidisciplinary Faculty (Bayonne Anglet Biarritz): Dean: PHILIPPE ZAVOLI

UNIVERSITÉ PAUL VERLAINE—METZ

Ile du Saulcy, BP 80794, 57012 Metz Cedex 1
Telephone: 3-87-31-50-50
E-mail: com@univ-metz.fr
Internet: www.univ-metz.fr
Founded 1970
Pres.: LUC JOHANN
Vice-Pres. for Admin.: ANDRÉ PETITJEAN
Vice-Pres. for Science Ccl: PHILIPPE BURG
Vice-Pres. for Studies and Univ. Life: GÉRARD MICHAUX
Sec.-Gen.: HÉLÈNE TIXIER
Librarian: SYLVIE DEVILLE
Number of teachers: 786
Number of students: 14,231.

TEACHING AND RESEARCH UNITS

Faculté de Droit, Economie et Administration: Ile du Saulcy, 57045 Metz Cedex 1; tel. 3-87-31-50-51; e-mail mangematin@univ-metz.fr; Dir YAHN MANGEMATIN.

Faculté des Etudes Supérieures de Management: 1 rue Augustin Fresnel BP 15100, 57073 Metz Cedex 1; tel. 3-87-37-84-80; e-mail accueil@esm.univ-metz.fr; Dir GUY SOLLE.

Faculté de Lettres et Langues: Ile du Saulcy, 57045 Metz Cedex 1; tel. 3-87-31-52-53; e-mail clerc@univ-metz.fr; Dir KATHIE BIRAT.

Faculté de Mathématiques, Informatique et Mécanique: Ile du Saulcy, 57045 Metz Cedex 1; tel. 3-87-31-53-54; e-mail rollin@univ-metz.fr; Dir NIDHAL REZG.

Faculté des Sciences Fondamentales et Appliquées: Rue du Général Delestraint, 57070 Metz Cedex 1; tel. 3-87-37-86-00; e-mail gasser@univ-metz.fr; Dir JEAN-GEORGES GASSER.

Faculté de Sciences Humaines et Arts: tel. 3-87-54-72-03; e-mail lanfranchi@univ-metz.fr; Dir JEAN-BAPTISTE LANFRANCHI

UNIVERSITÉ DE PERPIGNAN

52 ave Paul Alduy, 66860 Perpignan Cedex
Telephone: 4-68-66-20-00
E-mail: webmaster@univ-perp.fr
Internet: www.univ-perp.fr
Founded 1971
Pres.: JEAN BENKHELIL
Vice-Pres. for Admin.: MARTIN GALINIER
Vice-Pres. for Science Ccl: OLIVIER PANAUD
Vice-Pres. for Studies and Univ. Life: FABRICE LORENTE
Sec.-Gen.: PAUL TAVERNER
Librarian: JOËL MARTRES
Number of teachers: 450
Number of students: 10,500

TEACHING AND RESEARCH UNITS

Comparative Law and Francophone States: Dir: D. BAISSET
Exact and Experimental Sciences: Dir: L. ASPART
Legal and Economic Science: Dir: Y. PICOD
Letters and Humanities: Dir: N. MARTY
Sports, Tourism and the International Hotel Industry: Dir: J. M. HOERNER

PROFESSORS

Exact and Experimental Sciences:
AMOUROUX, M., Applied Physics and Computer Science
BAILLY, J. R., Biochemistry
BERÇOT, P., Applied Organic Synthesis
BLAISE, P., Chemistry
BODIOT, D., Mineral Chemistry and Thermochemistry
BOMBRE, F., Solid State Physics
BONNARD, M., Algebraic Topology
BOURGAT, R., General Biology
BRUNET, S., Applied Physics and Computer Science
BRUSLE, J., Marine Biology
CAUVET, A. M., Plant Biology and Physiology
CHOU, C. C., Functional Analysis
CODOMIER, L., Biology and Chemistry of Marine Plants (Research)
COMBES, C., Animal Biology
CROZAT, G., Physics
DAGUENET, M., Thermodynamics and Energetics
DUPOUY, J., General Biology
EL JAÏ, A., Computer Science
FABRE, B., Thermology
FOUGERES, A., Mathematics
GIRESSE, P., Marine Sedimentology Research Centre
GONZALEZ, E., Organic Chemistry
GOT, H., Sedimentology and Marine Geochemistry
HENRI-ROUSSEAU, O., Theoretical Chemistry
HILLEL, R., Chemistry
HORVATH, C., Mathematics
HUYNH, V. C., Atomic and Molecular Physics
JUPIN, H., Plant Biology
MARTY, R., Mathematics applied to Human Sciences
MEYNADIER, CHR., Thermodynamics and Energetics
PENON, P., Plant Physiology
SOULIER, J., Organic Chemistry
SOURNIA, A., Atomic and Molecular Physics
SPINNER, B., Mineral Chemistry and Thermochemistry
VIALLET, P., Physical Chemistry

Humanities, Legal, Economic and Social Sciences

Humanities:
ANDIOC, R., Romance Languages and Literature
AUBAILLY, J.-C., French
BELOT, A., Romance Languages and Literature
BROC, N., Geography
DAUGE, Y., Classics
DELEDALLE, G., Philosophy
DENJEAN, A., English Language and Anglo-Saxon Literature
HOLZ, J. M., Geography
HUGUET, L., Germanic and Scandinavian Languages and Literature
ISSOREL, J., Spanish
LEBLON, B., Romance Languages and Literature
MEYER, J., Contemporary History
RETHORE, J., Literature
SAGNES, J., History

Law and Economics:
BLANC, F. P., History of Law
BREJON DE LAVERGNEE, N., Economic Dynamics
CONSTANS, L., Public Law
Mme DONAT, J., Private Law and Criminology
DOUCHEZ, M.-H., Administrative Law
HUNTZINGER, J., International Law
PEROCHON, F., Law
RUDLOFF, M., Economics

SAINT-JOURS, Y., Private Law and Criminology
SERRA, Y., Private Law
University Institute of Technology:
AZE, D., Mathematics
BARRIOL, R., Mechanical Engineering
BARUSSEAU, J. P., Marine Sedimentology
COMBAUT, G., Marine Chemistry
COSTE, C., Industrial Chemistry
FARINES, M., Organic Chemistry
GRELLET, P., Biochemistry, Applied Biology
MASSE, J., Organic Chemistry
MASSON, PH., Animal Husbandry

UNIVERSITÉ DE PICARDIE JULES VERNE

chemin du Thil, 80025 Amiens Cedex 01
Telephone: 3-22-82-72-72
Internet: www.u-picardie.fr
Founded 1965
Academic year: October to June
Pres.: GEORGES FAURÉ
Vice-Pres. for Admin.: JEANNINE RICHARD-ZAPPELLA
Vice-Pres. for Science Ccl: SAID KAMEL
Vice-Pres. for Studies and Univ. Life: GÉRARD BRÛLÉ
Sec.-Gen.: LAURENT ANNE
Librarian: DESSAIVRE LOUISE
Number of teachers: 800
Number of students: 23,000.

TEACHING AND RESEARCH UNITS

Faculté des Arts: 30 rue des Teinturiers, 80000 Amiens Cedex 01; tel. 3-22-22-43-43; Dir Prof. SERGE BISMUTH.

Faculté de Droit et de Science Politique: 10 placette Lafleur, BP 2716, 80027 Amiens Cedex 01; tel. 3-22-82-71-52; Dir BENOIT MERCUZOT.

Faculté d'Economie et de Gestion: 10 placette Lafleur, BP 2716, 80027 Amiens Cedex 01; tel. 3-22-82-71-28; Dir Prof. JEAN-PIERRE GIRARD.

Faculté d'Histoire et de Géographie: chemin du Thil, 80025 Amiens Cedex 01; tel. 3-22-82-73-29; Dir Prof. PHILIPPE NIVET.

Faculté de Langues et Cultures Etrangères: chemin du Thil, 80025 Amiens Cedex 01; tel. 3-22-82-73-73; Dir Prof. WOLFGANG SABLER.

Faculté des Lettres: chemin du Thil, 80025 Amiens Cedex 01; tel. 3-22-82-73-85; Dir MARIE-FRANCOISE MONTAUBIN.

Faculté de Médecine: 3 rue des Louvels, 80036 Amiens Cedex 01; tel. 3-22-82-77-45; Dir Prof. DANIEL LE GARS.

Faculté de Pharmacie: 1 rue des Louvels, 80037 Amiens Cedex 01; tel. 3-22-82-77-54; Dir GILLES DUVERLIE.

Faculté de Philosophie et Sciences Humaines et Sociales: Bâtiment E, chemin du Thil, 80025 Amiens Cedex 01; tel. 3-22-82-74-04; Dir Prof. PHILIPPE MONCHAUX.

Faculté des Sciences: 33 rue Saint-Leu, 80039 Amiens Cedex 01; tel. 3-22-82-75-22; Dir Prof. F. ROPEZ.

Faculté des Sciences du Sport: allée Paul Grousset, 80025 Amiens Cedex 01; tel. 3-22-82-73-74; Dir Prof. ARNAUD JAILLET.

University Campus at Beauvais: 52 blvd Saint-André, 60000 Beauvais Cedex; tel. 3-44-06-88-00; Administrator LAURENT SEGUIN

UNIVERSITÉ DE POITIERS

15 rue de l'Hôtel Dieu, 86034 Poitiers Cedex
Telephone: 5-49-45-30-00
E-mail: webmaster@univ-poitiers.fr
Internet: www.univ-poitiers.fr
Founded 1431
Pres.: JEAN-PIERRE GESSON
Sec.-Gen.: BERNARD CONTAL
Librarian: MYRIAM MARCIL
Number of teachers: 870
Number of students: 24,000
Publications: *La Licorne, Les Cahiers de Civilisation Médiévale, Les Cahiers Forell, Migrinter, Revue Norois.*

TEACHING AND RESEARCH INSTITUTES

Faculté des Sciences du Sport: Bâtiment C6, 8 allée Jean Monnet, 86000 Poitiers; tel. 5-49-45-33-43; e-mail ufr.scsport@univ-poitiers.fr; internet scsport.univ-poitiers.fr; Dir LAURENT BOSQUET.

Faculté de Droit et Sciences Sociales: Bâtiment A1, 2 rue Jean Carbonnier, 86022 Poitiers; tel. 5-49-45-31-35; e-mail ufr.droit@univ-poitiers.fr; internet droit.univ-poitiers.fr; Dean JOËL MONNET.

Faculté de Lettres et Langues: Bâtiment A3, 1 rue Raymond Cantel, BP 613, 86022 Poitiers; tel. 5-49-45-32-71; e-mail ufr.ll@univ-poitiers.fr; internet ll.univ-poitiers.fr; Dir JEAN-LOUIS DUCHET.

Faculté de Médecine et Pharmacie: Bâtiment D1, 6 rue de la Miletrie, BP 199, 86034 Poitiers; tel. 5-49-45-43-43; e-mail faculte.medecine@univ-poitiers.fr; internet medphar.univ-poitiers.fr; Dean MICHEL MORICHAU BEAUCHANT.

Faculté des Sciences Économiques: Bâtiment A1, 2 rue Jean Carbonnier, 86022 Poitiers; tel. 5-49-45-31-35; e-mail ufr.sceco@univ-poitiers.fr; internet sceco.univ-poitiers.fr; Dean CHRISTIAN AUBIN.

Faculté des Sciences Fondamentales et Appliquées: Bâtiment B5, 9 rue C. C. Chenou, BP 633, 86022 Poitiers; tel. 5-49-45-30-00; e-mail ufr.sfa@univ-poitiers.fr; internet sfa.univ-poitiers.fr; Dean YVES BERTRAND.

Faculté des Sciences Humaines et Arts: 8 rue René Descartes, 86022 Poitiers; tel. 5-49-45-45-45; e-mail ufr.sha@univ-poitiers.fr; internet sha.univ-poitiers.fr; Dir YVES JEAN

UNIVERSITÉ DE REIMS CHAMPAGNE-ARDENNE

9 blvd de la Paix, 51097 Reims Cedex
Telephone: 3-26-05-30-00
E-mail: presidence@univ-reims.fr
Internet: www.univ-reims.fr
Founded 1548
Pres.: RICHARD VISTELLE
Vice-Pres. for Admin.: COLLETTE PADET
Vice-Pres. for Science Ccl: YANNICK REMION
Vice-Pres. for Studies and Univ. Life: GUILLAUME GELLE
Sec.-Gen.: ISABELLE TERRAIL
Library: see under Libraries and Archives
Number of teachers: 1,106
Number of students: 22,163
Publications: *Cahiers de l'Institut du Territoire et de l'Environnement de l'Université de Reims* (1 a year), *Cahiers du Centre de Recherches sur la Décentralisation Territoriale* (1 a year), *Etudes Champenoises* (1 a year), *Imaginaires, Jurisprudence Cour d'appel* (4 a year).

TEACHING AND RESEARCH UNITS

Faculté de Droit et de Science Politique: 57 rue Pierre Taittinger, 51096 Reims Cedex; tel. 3-26-91-38-44; e-mail aurelien.patit@univ-reims.fr; Dean OLIVIER DUPERON.

Faculté de Lettres et Sciences Humaines: 57 rue Pierre Taittinger, 51096 Reims Cedex; tel. 3-26-91-36-38; Dean M. BOULANGER.

Faculté de Médecine: 51 rue Cognacq Jay, 51095 Reims Cedex; tel. 3-26-91-81-83; e-mail scolmed@univ-reims.fr; Dean JACQUES MOTTE.

Faculté d'Odontologie: 2 rue du Général Koenig, 51100 Reims Cedex; tel. 3-26-91-34-55; e-mail nathalie.antoni@univ-reims.fr; Dean LOUIS-FRÉDÉRIC JACQUELIN.

Faculté de Pharmacie: 51 rue Cognacq Jay, 51095 Reims Cedex; tel. 3-26-91-81-82; e-mail scol.pharmacie@univ-reims.fr; Dean MATTHIEU KALTENBACH.

Faculté des Sciences Economiques, Sociales et de Gestion: e-mail info.seg@univ-reims.fr; Dir MARTINE GUILLEMIN.

Faculté des Sciences Exactes et Naturelles: e-mail scolarite.sciences@univ-reims.fr.

Faculté des Sciences et Techniques des Activités Physiques et Sportives: chemin des Rouliers, 51682 Reims Cedex; tel. (3) 26-91-31-61; Dean Dr PASCAL LEGRAIN

UNIVERSITÉ DE RENNES I

2 rue du Thabor, CS 46510, 35065 Rennes Cedex
Telephone: 2-23-23-35-35
E-mail: sai@listes.univ-rennes1.fr
Internet: www.univ-rennes1.fr
Academic year: September to May
Pres.: GUY CATHELINEAU
Vice-Pres. for Admin.: DAVID ALIS
Vice-Pres. for Science Ccl: CLAUDE LABIT
Vice-Pres. for Studies and Univ. Life: NATHALIE PAYELLE
Sec.-Gen.: MARTINE RUOUD
Number of teachers: 1,601
Number of students: 23,884.

TEACHING AND RESEARCH UNITS

Ecole Nationale Supérieure des Sciences Appliquées et de Technologie: 6 rue de Kérampont, BP 80518, 22305 Lannion Cedex; tel. 2-96-46-90-00; e-mail accueil@enssat.fr; internet www.enssat.fr; Dir JEAN-CHRISTOPHE PETTIER.

Ecole Supérieure d'Ingénieur de Rennes: e-mail gwenaelle.merel@univ-rennes1.fr; internet www.esir.univ-rennes1.fr; Dir CHRISTOPHE WOLINSKI.

Faculté de Droit et Science Politique: 9 rue Jean Macé, CS 54203, 35042 Rennes Cedex; tel. 2-23-23-76-76; Dean Prof. EDOUARD VERNY.

Faculté de Médecine: 2 rue du Professeur Léon Bernard, CS 34317, 35043 Rennes Cedex; tel. 2-23-51-13-96; Dean Prof. PHILIPPE DELAVAL.

Faculté de Pharmacie: 2 rue du Professeur Léon Bernard, CS 34317, 35043 Rennes Cedex; tel. 2-23-23-44-30; e-mail doyen.pharmacie@univ-rennes1.fr; internet www.pharma.univ-rennes1.fr; Dean Prof. JEAN DEUFF.

Faculté des Sciences Economiques: 7 place Hoche, CS 86514, 35065 Rennes Cedex; tel. 2-23-23-35-45; e-mail eco-scol@univ-rennes1.fr; Dean Prof. ISABELLE CADORET.

Faculté d'Odontologie: 2 rue du Professeur Léon Bernard, CS 34317 Rennes Cedex; tel. 2-23-23-43-41; Dean Dr ANNE DAUTEL-MORAZIN.

Institut de Formation Supérieure en Informatique et Communication: Campus de Beaulieu, 35042 Rennes Cedex; tel. 2-99-84-74-02; e-mail istic-contact@univ-rennes1.fr; Dir GILLES LESVENTES.

Institut de Gestion de Rennes: 11 rue Jean Macé, CS 70803, 35708 Rennes Cedex 7; tel. 2-23-23-77-77; e-mail igriae@

univ-rennes1.fr; internet www.igr.univ-rennes1.fr; Dir LAURENT BIRONNEAU.

Institut de Préparation à l'Administration Générale: 106 blvd de la Duchesse Anne, 35700 Rennes Cedex; tel. 2-23-23-78-93; e-mail ipag@univ-rennes1.fr; internet www.ipag.univ-rennes1.fr; Dir GILLES GUIHEUX.

Institut Universitaire de Technologie de Lannion: rue Edouard Branly, BP 30219, 22302 Lannion Cedex; tel. 2-96-46-93-00; e-mail scol.iutlan@univ-rennes1.fr; internet www.iut-lannion.fr; Dir DIDIEU DEMIGNY.

Institut Universitaire de Technologie de Rennes: 3 rue du Clos-Courtel, BP 90422, 35704 Rennes Cedex 7; tel. 2-23-23-40-00; e-mail iutren-contact@listes.univ-rennes1.fr; internet www.iutren.univ-rennes1.fr; Dir JACQUES MIRIEL.

Institut Universitaire de Technologie de St Brieuc: 18 rue Henri Wallon, BP 406, 22004 St Brieuc Cedex 1; tel. 2-96-60-96-60; e-mail iut-st-brieuc@univ-rennes1.fr; internet www.iutsb.univ-rennes1.fr; Dir JACQUES BERTHOUX.

Institut Universitaire de Technologie de St-Malo: rue de la Croix Desilles, CS 51713, 35417 St-Malo Cedex 1; tel. 2-99-21-95-00; e-mail iutsm-scolarite@univ-rennes1.fr; internet www.iutsm.univ-rennes1.fr; Dir Prof. JEAN-JACQUES MONTOIS.

Observatoire des Sciences de l'Univers de Rennes: Campus de Beaulieu, Bâtiment 15 303-2, 263 ave du Général Leclerc, 35042 Rennes Cedex; tel. 2-23-23-52-22; internet osur.univ-rennes1.fr; Dir P. DAVY.

UFR Mathématiques: 263 rue du Général Leclerc, CS 74205, 35042 Rennes Cedex; tel. 2-23-23-59-51; e-mail andre.rebour@univ-rennes1.fr; Dir BERNARD DELYON.

UFR Philosophie: 263 rue du Général Leclerc, CS 74205, 35042 Rennes Cedex; tel. 2-23-23-63-02; e-mail sophie.rabaux@univ-rennes1.fr; Dir PIERRE JORAY.

UFR Sciences de la Vie et de l'Environnement: Bât. 13, Campus Scientifique de Beaulieu, 263 rue du Général Leclerc, 35042 Rennes Cedex; tel. 2-23-23-61-12; Dir Prof. HUBERT LERIVRAY.

UFR Sciences et Propriétés de la Matière: 263 rue du Général Leclerc, CS 74205 Rennes Cedex; tel. 2-23-23-62-44; e-mail spm-administration@listes.univ-rennes1.fr; Dir PATRICIA BÉNARD-ROCHERULLÉ.

ATTACHED INSTITUTE

Institut d'Études Politiques: 104 blvd de la Duchesse-Anne, 35700 Rennes; tel. 2-99-84-39-39; e-mail scolarite@sciencespo-rennes.fr; internet www.sciencespo-rennes.fr; Dir PATRICK LE FLOCH

UNIVERSITÉ RENNES II—HAUTE BRETAGNE

pl. du Recteur Henri Le Moal, CS 24307, 35044 Rennes Cedex

Telephone: 2-99-14-10-00

E-mail: martine.autret@univ-rennes2.fr

Internet: www.uhb.fr

Founded 1969

Pres.: JEAN EMILE GOMBERT

First Vice-Pres.: RAYMONDE SECHET (Scientific Ccl)

Second Vice-Pres.: ALAIN ABELHAUSER (Studies and Univ. Life)

Third Vice-Pres.: DANIELLE CHARLES-LE BIHAN (Ccl of Admin.)

Sec.-Gen.: AMINE AMAR

Librarian: ELISABETH LEMAU

Number of teachers: 643

Number of students: 17,004.

TEACHING AND RESEARCH UNITS

Faculté des Activités Physiques et Sportives: tel. 2-99-14-17-65; e-mail evelyne.delanoe@univ-rennes2.fr; Dir PAUL DELAMARCHE.

Faculté des Arts, Lettres et Communication: tel. 2-99-14-15-01; e-mail francois-xavier.rouxel@univ-rennes2.fr; Dir YVES HELIAS.

Faculté des Langues: tel. 2-99-14-16-01; e-mail dominique.colin@univ-rennes2.fr; Dir FRANÇOISE DUBOSQUET.

Faculté des Sciences Humaines: tel. 2-99-14-19-02; e-mail elisabeth.garnier@univ-rennes2.fr; Dir LOÏC BRÉMAUD.

Faculté des Sciences Sociales: tel. 2-99-14-17-82; e-mail pierrette.mauger@univ-rennes2.fr; Dir JACQUELINE SAINCLIVIER

UNIVERSITÉ DE LA ROCHELLE

Technoforum, 23 ave Albert Einstein, 17071 La Rochelle Cedex 9

Telephone: 5-46-45-91-14

E-mail: webmestre@univ-lr.fr

Internet: www.univ-larochelle.fr

Founded 1993

Pres.: GÉRARD BLANCHARD

Vice-Pres. for Admin.: MATHIAS TRANCHANT

Vice-Pres. for Science Ccl: FRANCIS ALLARD

Vice-Pres. for Studies and Univ. Life: PIERRE COURTELLEMONT

Sec.-Gen.: PHILIPPE BÉZAGU

Librarian: OLIVIER CAUDRON

Number of teachers: 471

Number of students: 7,444.

TEACHING AND RESEARCH UNITS

Faculté de Droit, Science politique et Gestion: 45 rue François de Vaux de Foletier, 17024 La Rochelle Cedex 1; tel. 5-46-45-85-20; e-mail contact_droit@univ-lr.fr; Dir ANDRÉ GIUDICELLI.

Faculté des Lettres, Langues, Arts et Sciences Humaines: 1 Parvis Fernand Braudel, 17042 La Rochelle Cedex 1; tel. 5-46-45-68-00; e-mail contact_flash@univ-lr.fr; Dir CHARLES ILLOUZ.

Faculté des Sciences Fondamentales et Sciences pour l'Ingénieur: ave Michel Crepeau, 17042 La Rochelle Cedex 1; tel. 5-46-45-82-59; e-mail sci_direction@univ-lr.fr; Dir CHRISTIAN INARD.

Institut Universitaire de Technologie: 15 rue François de Vaux de Foletier, 17026 La Rochelle Cedex 1; tel. 5-46-51-39-00; e-mail kaszewski@univ-lr.fr; Dir PATRICE JOUBERT

UNIVERSITÉ DE ROUEN

1 rue Thomas Becket, Secrétariat-Général, 76821 Mont-Saint-Aignan Cedex

Telephone: 2-35-14-60-00

E-mail: communication@univ-rouen.fr

Internet: www.univ-rouen.fr

Founded 1966

Academic year: September to June

Pres.: CAFER ÖZKUL

First Vice-Pres. for Admin.: JOËL ALEXANDRE

Vice-Pres.: NICOLE ORANGE

Vice-Pres.: SABINE MÉNAGER

Vice-Pres. for Admin.: DANIÈLE CARRICABURU

Vice-Pres. for Science Ccl: LAURENCE VILLARD

Vice-Pres. for Studies and Univ. Life: LAURENT YON

Sec.-Gen.: (vacant)

Librarian: LAURENCE BOITARD

Number of teachers: 1,371

Number of students: 24,044.

TEACHING AND RESEARCH UNITS

Faculté de Droit, Sciences Economiques et Gestion: 3 Ave Pasteur, 76186 Rouen Cedex; tel. 2-32-76-98-98; Dean GUY QUITAINE.

Faculté de Lettres et Sciences Humaines: rue Lavoisier, 76821 Mont-Saint-Aignan Cedex; tel. 2-35-14-64-00; Dir J. MAURICE.

Faculté de Médecine et Pharmacie: 22 blvd Gambetta, 76183 Rouen Cedex; tel. 2-35-14-85-55; Dean PIERRE FREGER.

Faculté des Sciences de l'Homme et de la Société: rue Lavoisier, 76821 Mont-Saint-Aignan Cedex; Dir R. WEIL.

Faculté des Sciences du Sport et Education Physique: blvd Siegfried, 76821 Mont-Saint-Aignan Cedex; Dean ALAIN LORET.

Faculté des Sciences et Techniques: pl. Emile Blondel, 76821 Mont-Saint-Aignan Cedex; e-mail doyen.sciences@univ-rouen.fr; Dean JEAN-PAUL DUPONT.

Institut d'Administration des Entreprises: 3 ave Pasteur, 76100 Rouen Cedex 1; tel. 2-32-76-95-84; e-mail iae@univ-rouen.fr; Dir CHRISTIAN HURSON.

Institut de Préparation à l'Administration Générale: 3 ave Pasteur, 76186 Rouen Cedex 1; tel. 2-32-76-98-46; e-mail ipag76@univ-rouen.fr; Dir CECILE-ANNE SIBOUT.

Institut Universitaire de Formation des Maîtres: 2 rue du Tronquet, BP 18, 76131 Mont-Saint-Aignan Cedex; tel. 2-32-82-30-40; internet www.rouen.iufm.fr; Dir BRUNO MAHEU.

Institut Universitaire de Technologie (Evreux): 55 rue Saint Germain, 27000 Evreux Cedex; tel. 2-32-19-15-00; e-mail direction.iutevreux@univ-rouen.fr; Dir BRUNO QUERRÉ.

Institut Universitaire de Technologie (Rouen): rue Lavoisier, 76821 Mont-Saint-Aignan Cedex; tel. 2-35-14-62-03; e-mail iut.rouen@univ-rouen.fr; internet www.univ-rouen.fr/iutrouen; Dir MOULAY ABDELGHANI IDRISSI

PROFESSORS

Behavioural and Educational Sciences:

ABALLERA, F., Sociology
ASTOLFI, J. P., Educational Sciences
DURAND, J., Sociology
GATEAUX, J., Educational Sciences
HOUSSAYE, J., Educational Sciences
KOKOSOWSKI, A., Educational Sciences
LEMOINE, CL., Psychology
MALANDAIN, CL., Psychology
MARBEAUX-CLEIRENS, B., Psychology
MELLIER, D., Psychology

Law and Economics:

BADEVANT, B., Law
BRAS, J. P., Public Law
CAYLA, O., Public Law
CHRÉTIEN, P., Public Law
COURBE, P., Private Law
DAMMAME, D., Political Science
EPAULARD, A., Economics
GOY, R., Public Law
KULLMANN, J., Private Law
LEHMANN, P., Economics
MONNIER, L., Economics
PORTIER, F., Economics
RENOUX, M. F., Law
SASSIER, Y., Law
TAVERNIER, P., Public Law
TEBOUL, G., Public Law
TONNEL, M., Economics
VATTEVILLE, E., Administration and Management
VESPERINI, J.-P., Economics

Letters and Humanities:

ARNAUD, J. C., Geography

BALAN, B., Epistemology
BENAY, J., German
BERGER, PH., Spanish
CAITUCOLI, C., Linguistics
CAPET, A., English
COIT, K., English
CORTES, J., Linguistics
CYMERMAN, C., Spanish
DELAMOTTE, R., Linguistics
GARDIN, B., Linguistics
GRANIER, J., Philosophy
GUERMOND, Y., Geography
HUSSON, G., Greek
LE BOHEC, S., Ancient History
LECLAIRE, J., English
LECLERC, Y., French
LEGUAY, J.-P., Medieval History
LEMARCHAND, G., Modern History
LESOURD, M., Geography
MAQUERLOT, J. P., English
MAURICE, J., French
MAZAURIC, C., Modern History
MERVAUD, C., French
MERVAUD, M., Russian
MILHOU, A., Spanish
MORTIER, D., Comparative Literature
NIDERST, A., French
NOISETTE DE CRAUZAT, CL., Musical History
PASTRE, J. M., German
PHILONENKO, A., Philosophy
PICHARDIE, J. P., English
PIERROT, J., Modern French Literature and Language
PIGENET, M., Contemporary History
POINSOTE, J. L., Classics
PUEL, M., English
RAVY, G., German
RETAILLE, B., Geography
ROUDAUT, F., French
SALAZAR, B., Spanish
SOHNA, R., Modern History
THELAMON, F., Ancient History
TREDE, M., Classics
VAN DER LYNDEN, A. M., Spanish
WALLE, M., German
WILLEMS, M., English
ZYLBERBER, G. M., Modern History

Medicine and Pharmacy:

ANDRIEU-GUTTRANCOURT, J., Otorhinolaryngology
AUGUSTIN, P., Neurology
BACHY, B., Infantile Surgery
BENOZIO, E., Radiology
BERCOFF, E., Internal Medicine
BESANÇON, P., Chemistry
BESSOU, J. P., Surgery
BEURET, F., Rehabilitation
BIGA, N., Orthopaedics
BLANQUART, F., Rehabilitation
BONMARCHAND, G., Resuscitation
BONNET, J. J., Pharmacology
BRASSEUR, G., Ophthalmology
BRASSEUR, P. H., Bacteriology
CAILLARD, J.-F., Industrial Medicine
CAPRON, R., Biophysics
COLIN, R., Gastroenterology
COLONNA, L., Psychiatry
COMOY, D., Biochemistry
COSTENTIN, J., Pharmacology
COURTOIS, H., Internal Medicine
CRIBIER, A., Cardiology
CZERNICHOW, P., Epidemiology
DEHESDIN, D., Otorhinolaryngology
DENIS, P., Physiology
DUCROTTE, P., Hepatology
DUVAL, C., Clinical Obstetrics
FESSARD, C., Paediatrics
FILLASTRE, J. P., Nephrology
FREGER, P., Anatomy
GARNIER, J., Botany and Cryptogamy
GODIN, M., Nephrology
GRISE, PH., Urology
HECKETSWEILER, P., Hepatology
HEMET, J., Pathological Anatomy
HUMBERT, G., Tropical and Infectious Diseases
JANVRESSE, C., Hygiene
JOLY, P., Dermatology
JOUANY, M., Toxicology
KUHN, J. M., Endocrinology
LAFONT, O., Organic Chemistry
LAURET, P., Dermatology
LAVOINNE, D., Biochemistry
LECHEVALLIER, J., Infantile Surgery
LEDOSSEUR, P., Radiology
LEFUR, R., Cancerology
LELOET, X., Rheumatology
LEMELAND, J. F., Hygiene
LEMOINE, J. P., Gynaecology
LEREBOURS, E., Nutrition
LEROY, J., Therapeutics
LETAC, B., Cardiology
MACE, B., Histology
MAITROT, B., Biochemistry
MALLET, E., Biology
MARCHAND, J., Chemical Pharmacology
MATRAY, F., Medical Biochemistry
METAYER, J., Anatomy
MICHOT, F., Digestive Tract Surgery
MIHOUT, B., Neurology
MITROFANOFF, P., Infantile Surgery
MONCONDUIT, M., Haematology
MUIR, J. F., Pneumology
NOUVET, G., Pneumology
ORECCHIONI, A.-M., Pharmacology
PASQUIS, P., Physiology
PEILLON, C., Orthopaedic and Traumatological Surgery
PERON, J. M., Stomatology
PETIT, M., Psychiatry
PIGUET, H., Immuno-haematology
PROTAIS, P., Physiology
PROUST, B., Forensic Medicine
SAOUDI, N., Cardiology
SORIA, C., Pharmaceutical Biochemistry
SOYER, R., Thoracic Surgery
TADIE, M., Neurosurgery
TENIÈRE, P., General Surgery
TESTART, J., Clinical Surgery
THIEBOT, J., Radiology
THOMINE, M., Orthopaedic and Traumatological Surgery
THUILLIEZ, C., Therapeutics
TILLY, H., Haematology
TRON, F., Immunology
TRON, P., Paediatrics
VANNIER, J. P., Paediatrics
WATELET, J., General Surgery
WINCKLER, C., Anaesthesiology
WOLF, L., Therapeutic Internal Medicine

Sciences and Technology:

ANTHORE, R., Physics
ATTIAS, J., Biochemistry
AUGER, P., Physics
BALANGE, P., Biochemistry
BANEGE, A., Physics
BARBEY, G., Chemistry
BLANCHARD, D., Mechanics
BLAVETTE, D., Physics
BOISARD, J., Vegetal Biology
BORGHI, R., Mechanics
BOUAZIZ, R., Chemistry
BRISSET, J. L., Chemistry
CAGNON, M., Physics
CALBRIX, J., Mathematics
CARLES, D., Electronics
CARPENTIER, J. M., Chemistry
CASTON, J., Biology
CAZIN, L., Biology
CHAMPRANAUD, J. M., Computer Sciences
CHARPENTIER, J., Physiology
CHERON, B., Thermodynamics
COMBRET, C., Chemistry
COTTEREAU, M. J., Thermodynamics
DAVOUST, D., Chemistry
DEBRUCQ, D., Electronics
DERRIDJ, M., Mathematics
DE SAM LAZARO, J., Mathematics
DESBENE, A., Chemistry
DESBENE, P., Chemistry
DONATO, P., Mathematics
DOSS, H., Mathematics
DUHAMEL, P., Chemistry
DUVAL, J.-P., Computer Sciences
DUVAL, P., Physics
FOUCHER, B., Biochemistry
FRILEUX, P. N., Biology
GALLOT, J., Physics
GAYOSO, J., Chemistry
GORALCIK, P., Computer Sciences
GRENET, J., Physics
GUESPIN, J., Microbiology
HANNOYER, B., Physics
HANSEL, G., Mathematics
HUSSON, A., Biology
LAMBOY, M., Geology
LANERY, E., Mathematics
LANGE, C., Chemistry
LECOURTIER, Y., Electronics
LEDOUX, M., Thermodynamics
LENGLET, M., Chemistry
LOPITAUX, J., Chemistry
MAHEU, B., Thermodynamics
MENAND, A., Physics
METAYER, M., Chemistry
MEYER, R., Geology
MICHON, J. F., Computer Sciences
OZKUL, C., Physics
PAULMIER, C., Chemistry
PEREZ, G., Chemistry
PETIPAS, C., Physics
POIRIER, J. M., Chemistry
QUEGUINNER, G., Chemistry
RIPOLL, C., Biochemistry
SELEGNY, E., Chemistry
STRELCYN, J. M., Mathematics
SURIN, A., Mathematics
TEILLET, J., Physics
UNANUE, A., Chemistry
VAILLANT, R., Animal Physiology
VAUTIER, C., Physics
VERCHERE, J. F., Chemistry
VIGER, C., Electronics
VIGIER, P., Physics
WEILL, M., Thermodynamics

UNIVERSITÉ DE SAVOIE (CHAMBÉRY)

BP 1104, 73011 Chambéry Cedex
27 rue Marcoz, 73000 Chambéry
Telephone: 4-79-75-85-85
E-mail: guide@univ-savoie.fr
Internet: www.univ-savoie.fr

Founded 1970
Academic year: October to July

Pres.: GILBERT ANGÉNIEUX
Vice-Pres. for Admin.: DENIS VARASCHIN
Vice-Pres. for Int. Relations: ERIC BRUNAT
Vice-Pres. for Science Ccl: LUC FRAPPAT
Vice-Pres. for Studies and Univ. Life: PASCAL MOUILLE
Sec.-Gen.: GILLES STOLL
Dir of Libraries: ALAIN CARACO

Number of teachers: 412
Number of students: 11,500

Publications: *Annales* (1 a year), *Présences* (12 a year).

TEACHING AND RESEARCH UNITS

Centre Interdisciplinaire Scientifique de la Montagne: Bâtiment Belledonne, Campus scientifique, 73376 Le Bourget du Lac Cedex; tel. 4-79-75-81-29; e-mail secretariat.montagne@univ-savoie.fr; internet www.cism.univ-savoie.fr; Dir THIERRY VILLEMIN.

Faculté de Droit et d'Economie: BP 1104, 73011 Chambéry Cedex; tel. 4-79-75-84-30; e-mail secretariat.fde@univ-savoie.fr; internet www.fde.univ-savoie.fr; Dir MICHEL JULIEN.

Faculté des Lettres, Langues and Sciences Humaines: route du Sergent Revel, 73000 Jacob-Bellecombette Cedex; tel. 4-79-75-84-79; internet www.llsh.univ-savoie.fr; Dir OLIVIER DESRICHARD.

Faculté des Sciences Fondamentales et Appliquées: Campus scientifique, 73376, Le Bourget du Lac Cedex; tel. 4-79-75-87-01; e-mail sfa-contact@univ-savoie.fr; internet www.sfa.univ-savoie.fr; Dir PATRICE ORRO.

ATTACHED INSTITUTES

Annecy National College of Engineering: BP 806, 74016 Annecy Cedex;5 chemin de Bellevue, 74016 Annecy-Le-Vieux; tel. 4-50-09-66-00; e-mail etudes@esia.univ-savoie.fr; internet www.esia.univ-savoie.fr; Dir LAURENT FOULLOY.

Chambéry National College of Engineering: 73376 Le Bourget du Lac Cedex; tel. 4-79-75-88-06; internet www.esigec.univ-savoie.fr; Dir PIERRE BATTISTI.

Institute of Technology Annecy: 9 rue de l'Arc-en-Ciel, BP 240, 74942 Annecy-Le-Vieux; tel. 4-50-09-22-22; internet www.iut.univ-savoie.fr; Dir GILLES HEIDSIECK.

Institute of Technology Chambéry: Savoie Technolac, 73376 Le Bourget du Lac Cedex; tel. 4-79-75-81-75; internet src-serveur2.univ-savoie.fr; Dir NICOLE ALBEROLA

UNIVERSITÉ DE STRASBOURG

4 rue Blaise Pascal, CS 90032, 67081 Strasbourg Cedex
Telephone: 3-68-85-00-00
E-mail: president@unistra.fr
Internet: www.unistra.fr
Founded 2009 by merger of Universités de Strasbourg I (Université Louis Pasteur), II (Université Marc Bloch, Sciences Humaines) and III (Université Robert Schuman)
State control
Pres.: ALAIN BERETZ
First Vice-Pres.: MICHEL DENEKEN
Vice-Pres. for Basic and Continuing Education: FRÉDÉRIQUE GRANET
Vice-Pres. for Business Partnerships: JEAN-MARC JELTSCH
Vice-Pres. for Digital Policy and Information Systems: CATHERINE MONGENET
Vice-Pres. for Heritage: YVES LARMET
Vice-Pres. for Human Resources and Social Policy: HUGUES DREYSSÉ
Vice-Pres. for Int. Relations: ANNE KLEBES-PÉLISSIER
Vice-Pres. for Research and Doctoral Studies: ÉRIC WESTHOF
Vice-Pres. for Social Sciences: BERNARD ANCORI
Vice-Pres. for Univ. Life: CLEMENT RAUSCHER
Library: 1.2m. vols
Number of teachers: 2,676
Number of students: 42,448.

TEACHING AND RESEARCH UNITS

Centre d'Etudes Internationales de la Propriété Intellectuelle: 11 rue du Maréchal Juin, BP 68, 67046 Strasbourg Cedex; tel. 3-68-85-88-00; e-mail ceipi@ceipi.edu; Dir CHRISTOPHE GEIGER.

Centre Universitaire d'Enseignement du Journalisme: 11 rue du Maréchal Juin, CS 10068, 67046 Strasbourg Cedex; tel. 3-68-85-83-00; e-mail nicole.gauthier@cuej.unistra.fr; Dir NICOLE GAUTHIER.

Ecole Européenne de Chimie, Polymères et Matériaux: 25 rue Becquerel, 67087 Strasbourg Cedex 2; tel. 3-68-85-26-00; e-mail daniel.guillon@unistra.fr; Dir DANIEL GUILLON.

Ecole de Management Strasbourg: 61 ave de la Forêt Noire, 67085 Strasbourg Cedex; tel. 3-68-85-80-00; e-mail contact@em-strasbourg.eu; Dir MICHEL KALIKA.

Ecole Nationale Supérieure de Physique: Parc d'Innovation, blvd Sébastien Brant, BP 10413, 67412 Illkirch Cedex; tel. 3-68-85-43-32; e-mail eric.fogarassy@unistra.fr; Dir ERIC FOGARASSY.

Ecole et Observatoire des Sciences de la Terre: 5 rue René Descartes, 67084 Strasbourg Cedex; tel. 3-68-85-00-29; e-mail michel.granet@eost.u-strasbg.fr; Dir MICHEL GRANET.

Ecole Supérieure de Biotechnologie: Parc d'Innovation, blvd Sébastien Brant, BP 10413, 67412 Illkirch Cedex; tel. 3-68-85-43-32; e-mail claude.kedinger@unistra.fr; Dir CLAUDE KEDINGER.

Faculté des Arts: Bâtiment Le Portique, 14 rue René Descartes, BP 80010, 67084 Strasbourg Cedex; tel. 3-68-85-63-46; e-mail arts@unistra.fr; Dir FRANCIS GAST.

Faculté de Chimie: 1 rue Blaise Pascal, 67008 Strasbourg Cedex; tel. 3-68-85-16-60; e-mail planeix@unistra.fr; Dir JEAN-MARC PLANEIX.

Faculté de Chirurgie Dentaire: 1 pl. de l'Hôpital, 67000 Strasbourg Cedex; tel. 3-88-85-39-01; e-mail dentaire@unistra.fr; Dean Prof. YOUSSEF HAIKEL.

Faculté de Droit, de Sciences Politiques et de Gestion: 1 pl. d'Athènes, BP 66, 67045 Strasbourg Cedex; tel. 3-68-85-81-00; e-mail j.poughon@unistra.fr; Dean JEAN-MICHEL POUGHON.

Faculté de Géographie et d'Aménagement: 3 rue de l'Argonne, 67083 Strasbourg Cedex; tel. 3-68-85-08-91; e-mail geographie@unistra.fr; Dean JOËL HUMBERT.

Faculté des Langues et Sciences Humaines Appliquées: Bâtiment Le Patio, 22 rue René Descartes, 67084 Strasbourg Cedex; tel. 3-68-85-67-51; e-mail lsha@unistra.fr; Dir NATHALIE HILLENWECK.

Faculté des Langues Vivantes: Bâtiment Le Patio, 22 rue René Descartes, 67084 Strasbourg Cedex; tel. 3-68-85-65-72; e-mail languesvivantes@unistra.fr; Dean BERNARD GENTON.

Faculté des Lettres: Bâtiment Le Portique, 14 rue René Descartes, BP 80010, 67081 Strasbourg Cedex; tel. 3-68-85-64-03; e-mail revol@unistra.fr; Dean THIERRY REVOL.

Faculté de Mathématique et d'Informatique: 7 rue René Descartes, 67084 Strasbourg Cedex; tel. 3-88-85-02-03; e-mail noot@unistra.fr; Dir RUTGER NOOT.

Faculté de Médecine: 4 rue Kirschleger, 67085 Strasbourg Cedex; tel. 3-88-85-35-20; e-mail medecine@unistra.fr; Dean BERTRAND LUDES.

Faculté de Pharmacie: 74 route du Rhin, BP 60024, 67401 Illkirch Cedex; tel. 3-88-85-42-87; e-mail doyen.pharma@unistra.fr; Dean JEAN-YVES PABST.

Faculté de Philosophie: Bâtiment Le Portique, côté Campus, 14 rue René Descartes, BP 80010, 67084 Strasbourg Cedex; e-mail jchiroll@unistra.fr; Dir JEAN-CLAUDE CHIROLLET.

Faculté de Physique et Ingénierie: 3–5 rue de l'Université, 67084 Strasbourg Cedex; tel. 3-88-85-06-72; e-mail phi-contact@unistra.fr; Dir ABDELMJID NOURREDDINE.

Faculté de Psychologie: 12 rue Goethe, 67000 Strasbourg Cedex; tel. 3-68-85-19-45; e-mail kelche@unistra.fr; Dean CHRISTIAN KELCHE.

Faculté des Sciences Economiques et de Gestion: Pôle européen de gestion et d'économie, 61 ave de la Forêt Noire, 67085 Strasbourg Cedex; tel. 3-68-85-20-58; e-mail heraud@unistra.fr; Dean JEAN-ALAIN HÉRAUD.

Faculté des Sciences de l'Education: 7 rue de l'Université, 67000 Strasbourg Cedex; tel. 3-68-85-06-18; e-mail pascal.marquet@unistra.fr; Dean PASCAL MARQUET.

Faculté des Sciences Historiques: Palais Universitaire, 9 pl. de l'Université, 67084 Strasbourg Cedex; tel. 3-68-85-68-61; e-mail jeanmarie.husser@unistra.fr; Dir JEAN MARIE HUSSER.

Faculté des Sciences Sociales, Pratiques Sociales et Développement: Bâtiment Le Patio, 22 rue René Descartes, 67084 Strasbourg Cedex; tel. 3-68-85-60-26; e-mail sciencessociales@unistra.fr; Dir JACQUELINE IGERSHEIM.

Faculté des Sciences du Sport: Bâtiment Le Portique, 14 rue René Descartes, BP 80010, 67084 Strasbourg Cedex; tel. 3-68-85-64-41; e-mail staps@unistra.fr; Dir GILLES ERB.

Faculté des Sciences de la Vie: 28 rue Goethe, 67083 Strasbourg Cedex; tel. 3-68-85-66-88; e-mail gauer@unistra.fr; Dean FRANÇOIS GAUER.

Faculté de Théologie Catholique: Palais Universitaire, 9 pl. de l'Université, BP 90020, 67084 Strasbourg Cedex; tel. 3-68-85-68-22; e-mail theo-catho@unistra.fr; Dean JEAN-PIERRE WAGNER.

Faculté de Théologie Protestante: Palais Universitaire, 9 pl. de l'Université, BP 90020, 67084 Strasbourg Cedex; tel. 3-68-85-68-34; e-mail theoprot@unistra.fr; Dean REMI GOUNELLE.

Institut d'Etudes Politiques: 47 ave de la Forêt Noire, 67082 Strasbourg Cedex; tel. 3-68-85-84-00; e-mail scolarite.iep@unistra.fr; internet www-iep.u-strasbg.fr; Dir SYLVAIN SCHIRMANN.

Institut des Hautes Etudes Européennes: 10 rue Schiller, 67081 Strasbourg Cedex; tel. 3-68-85-82-00; e-mail ihee@unistra.fr; Dir ERIC MAULIN.

Institut de Préparation à l'Administration Générale: 47 ave de la Forêt Noire, 67082 Strasbourg Cedex; tel. 3-68-85-85-00; e-mail ipag@unistra.fr; Dir FRANCESCO DE PALMA.

Institut du Travail: 39 ave de la Forêt Noire, 67000 Strasbourg Cedex; tel. 3-68-85-87-00; e-mail institut.travail@unistra.fr; Dir FABIENNE MULLER.

Institut Universitaire de Formation des Maîtres: 141 ave de Colmar, 67100 Strasbourg Cedex; tel. 3-88-43-82-07; e-mail jean-claude.bove@iufm.unistra.fr; internet www.alsace.iufm.fr; Dir FRANÇOIS WERCKMEISTER.

Institut Universitaire de Technologie (Haguenau): 30 rue du Maire André Traband, 67500 Haguenau Cedex; tel. 3-88-05-34-00; e-mail iuthag-contact@unistra.fr; Dir FRANCIS BRAUN.

Institut Universitaire de Technologie (Louis Pasteur): 1 allée d'Athènes, 67300 Schiltigheim Cedex; tel. 3-88-85-25-26; e-mail violaine.delarchand@unistra.fr; Dir PASCALE BERGMANN.

Institut Universitaire de Technologie (Robert Schuman): 72 route du Rhin, BP 10315, 67411 Illkirch Cedex; tel. 3-88-85-89-00; e-mail iutrs@unistra.fr; Dir BERNARD LICKEL.

Observatoire Astronomique: 11 rue de l'Université, 67000 Strasbourg Cedex; tel. 3-88-85-24-45; e-mail herve.wozniak@astro.unistra.fr; Dir HERVÉ WOZNIAK

UNIVERSITÉ DU SUD TOULON VAR

ave de l'Université, BP 20132, 83957 La Garde Cedex
Telephone: 4-94-14-20-00
E-mail: inscriptions@univ-tln.fr
Internet: www.univ-tln.fr
Founded 1970
Academic year: September to July
Pres.: PHILIPPE TCHAMITCHIAN
Vice-Pres.: (vacant)
Sec.-Gen.: FRANÇOISE VILLEVAL
Librarian: DANIEL EYMARD
Number of teachers: 380
Number of students: 10,700

TEACHING AND RESEARCH UNITS

Business Administration: PIERRE GENSSE
Economic Sciences and Management: PHILIPPE GILLES
Letters and Humanities: GILLES LEYDIER
Law: JEAN JACQUES PARDINI
Media and Information Technology Institute: FRANCK RENUCCI
Sciences and Technology: SERGE DESPIAU
Sports: PIERRE FONTANARI
School of Engineering: OLIVIER LE CALVÉ
University Institute of Technology: ROBERT CHANU

UNIVERSITÉ DE TECHNOLOGIE DE BELFORT-MONTBÉLIARD

90010 Belfort Cedex
Telephone: 3-84-58-30-00
E-mail: contact@utbm.fr
Internet: www.utbm.fr
Founded 1999 as a result of merger of Ecole Nationale d'Ingénieurs de Belfort and Institut Polytechnique de Sévenans
State control
Dir: CHRISTIAN LERMINIAUX

UNIVERSITÉ DE TECHNOLOGIE DE COMPIÈGNE

Centre Pierre Guillaumat BP 60319, 60203 Compiègne Cedex
Telephone: 3-44-23-44-23
E-mail: accueil@utc.fr
Internet: www.utc.fr
Founded 1972
State control
Language of instruction: French
Academic year: September to August (2 semesters)
Pres.: Dr ALAIN STORCK
Gen. Sec.: SOLANGE BONNEAUD
Librarian: ANNIE BERTRAND
Number of teachers: 450
Number of students: 4,450
Publication: *Interactions* (6 a year)

DIRECTORS

Dept of Biological Engineering: CÉCILE LEGALLAIS
Dept of Chemical Engineering: PIERRE GUIGON
Dept of Computer Science: AZIZ MOUKRIM
Dept of Mechanical Engineering: MICHÈLE GUIGON
Department of Mechanical Engineering Systems: BENOÎT EYNARD
Dept of Technology and Human Sciences: FRANÇOIS SEBBAH
Dept of Urban Engineering Systems: JEAN-PASCAL FOUCAULT

UNIVERSITÉ DE TECHNOLOGIE DE TROYES

12 rue Marie Curie, BP 2060, 10010 Troyes Cedex
Telephone: 3-25-71-76-00
E-mail: infos@utt.fr
Internet: www.utt.fr
Founded 1994
State control
Academic year: September to June
Pres.: Prof. CHRISTIAN LERMINIAUX
Vice-Pres: PHILIPPE ADNOT, BRUNO GUELORGET
Librarian: GILLES-FRANÇOIS EUVRARD
Library of 10,000 vols
Number of teachers: 165
Number of students: 2,500 (of which 180 are postgraduate)

UNIVERSITÉ DE TOULOUSE I (SCIENCES SOCIALES)

2 rue du Doyen-Gabriel-Marty, 31042 Toulouse Cedex 9
Telephone: 5-61-63-35-00
E-mail: sercom@ut-capitole.fr
Internet: www.univ-tlse1.fr
Founded 1229
State control
Pres.: BRUNO SIRE
Vice-Pres. for Admin.: CHRISTIAN LAVIALLE
Vice-Pres. for Science Ccl: HUGUES KENFACK
Vice-Pres. for Studies and Univ. Life: GÉRARD JAZOTTES
Sec.-Gen.: CÉCILE CHICOYE
Librarians: BRUNO VAN DOOREN
Number of teachers: 554
Number of students: 18,267
Publications: *Annales*, *Livre de la Recherche*

TEACHING AND RESEARCH UNITS

Administration and Communication: Dir: FRANCIS BESTION
Economics: Dir: MARIE-FRANÇOISE CALMETTE
Information Science: Dir: CHANTAL SOULE-DUPUY
Law: Dir: BERNARD BEIGNIER

ATTACHED INSTITUTES

Centre Universitaire d'Albi: 2 ave Franchet d'Espérey, 81011 Albi Cedex 09; tel. 5-63-48-19-79; e-mail scolarite.generale@ut-capitole.fr; Dir O. DEVAUX.

Centre Universitaire de Montauban: 116 blvd Montauriol, 82017 Montauban Cedex; tel. 5-63-63-32-71; e-mail scolarite.generale@ut-capitole.fr; Dir B. MARIZ.

Ecole Supérieure Universitaire de Gestion: 2 rue Albert Lautmann, 31042 Toulouse Cedex; tel. 5-61-21-55-18; Dir P. SPITERI.

Institut d'Etudes Politiques: 2 ter rue des Puits-creusés, BP 88562, 31685 Toulouse Cedex 6; tel. 5-61-11-02-60; e-mail contact@sciencespo-toulouse.fr; internet www.sciencespo-toulouse.fr; Dir PHILIPPE RAIMBAULT.

Institut Universitaire Technologique de Rodez: 33 ave du 8 mai 1945, 12000 Rodez; tel. 5-65-77-10-80; e-mail scolarite.generale@ut-capitole.fr; Dir B. ALLAUX

UNIVERSITÉ DE TOULOUSE II (LE MIRAIL)

5 allées Antonio Machado, 31058 Toulouse Cedex 9
Telephone: 5-61-50-42-50
Internet: www.univ-tlse2.fr
Pres.: DANIEL FILATRE
Vice-Pres. for Admin.: PIERRE-YVES BOISSAU
Vice-Pres. for Science Ccl: MARIE CHRISTINE JAILLET
Vice-Pres. for Studies and Univ. Life: MARIE-HÉLÈNE GARELLI
Number of teachers: 1,095
Number of students: 23,117
Publications: *Anglophonia* (2 a year), *Caravelle* (2 a year), *Cinémas d'Amérique Latine* (1 a year), *Clio* (2 a year), *Criticón* (3 a year), *Homo* (1 a year), *Kairos* (2 a year), *Littératures* (2 a year), *Pallas* (2 a year), *Science de la Société* (3 a year), *Sud/Ouest Européen*.

TEACHING AND RESEARCH UNITS

Faculté d'Histoire, Arts et Archéologie: tel. 5-61-50-41-98; Dir JEAN-MICHEL MINOVEZ.

Faculté de Langues, Littératures et Civilisations Etrangères: tel. 5-61-50-38-20; e-mail ufrlangu@univ-tlse2.fr; Dir ALAIN COZIC.

Faculté de Langues, Littératures et Civilisations Etrangères: tel. 5-61-50-37-91; e-mail ufrlettr@univ-tlse2.fr; Dir VALÉRIE VISA-ONDARCHUHU.

Faculté de Psychologie: tel. 5-61-50-49-50; e-mail accueil.psycho@univ-tlse2.fr; internet ufr-psycho.univ-tlse2.fr; Dir PIERRE LARGY.

Faculté des Sciences, Espaces, Sociétés: tel. 5-61-50-38-44; e-mail ufrses@univ-tlse2.fr; Dir RÉGIS GUILLAUME

UNIVERSITÉ TOULOUSE III (PAUL SABATIER)

118 route de Narbonne, 31062 Toulouse Cedex 9
Telephone: 5-61-55-66-11
E-mail: contactweb@cict.fr
Internet: www.ups-tlse.fr
Founded 1969
State control
Academic year: September to June
Pres.: GILLES FOURTANIER
Vice-Pres. for Admin.: MARC REVERSAT
Vice-Pres. for Science Ccl: ALAIN MILON
Vice-Pres. for Studies and Univ. Life: Prof. JEAN-LUC ROLS
Sec.-Gen.: Mme A. VERDAGUER
Librarian: Mme HEUSSE
Number of teachers: 2,784
Number of students: 28,451.

TEACHING AND RESEARCH UNITS

Faculté de Chirurgie Dentaire: 3 chemin des Maraîchers, 31062 Toulouse Cedex 9; tel. 5-62-17-29-29; e-mail secdenta@adm.ups-tlse.fr; internet dentaire.ups-tlse.fr; Dir Prof. MICHEL SIXOU.

Faculté des Langues Vivantes: 118 route de Narbonne, 31062 Toulouse Cedex 9; tel. 5-61-55-83-60; e-mail reslv@adm.ups-tlse.fr; internet langues.ups-tlse.fr; Dir JEAN-BERNARD HISLEN.

Faculté de Mathématiques, Informatique et Gestion: 118 route de Narbonne, 31062 Toulouse Cedex 9; tel. 5-61-55-67-73; e-mail secmig@adm.ups-tlse.fr; internet www.ufr-mig.ups-tlse.fr/index; Dir JEAN-PAUL BAHSOUN.

Faculté de Médecine Purpan: 37 allées Jules Guesde, 31062 Toulouse Cedex 9; tel. 5-61-14-59-07; e-mail respurpa@adm.ups-tlse.fr; internet www.medecine.ups-tlse.fr; Dir Prof. JEAN-PIERRE VINEL.

Faculté de Médecine Rangueil: 33 route de Narbonne, 31062 Toulouse Cedex 9; tel. 5-62-88-90-05; e-mail resrangu@adm.ups-tlse.fr; internet www.medecine.ups-tlse.fr; Dir Prof. DANIEL ROUGÉ.

Faculté de Physique et Chimie Automatique: 118 route de Narbonne, 31062 Toulouse Cedex 9; tel. 5-61-55-68-28; e-mail dirpca@adm.ups-tlse.fr; internet pca3w.ups-tlse.fr/inter/index; Dir Prof. JEAN-MARC BROTO.

Faculté des Sciences Pharmaceutiques: 35 chemin des Maraîchers, 31062 Toulouse Cedex 9; tel. 5-62-25-68-04; e-mail respharm@adm.ups-tlse.fr; internet www.pharmacie.ups-tlse.fr; Dir Prof. RAYMOND BASTIDE.

Faculté des Sciences et Techniques des Activités Physiques et Sportives: 118 route de Narbonne, 31062 Toulouse Cedex 9; tel. 5-61-55-66-34; e-mail resstaps@adm.ups-tlse.fr; internet www.ufrstaps.ups-tlse.fr; Dir Prof. GÉRARD AUNEAU.

Faculté des Sciences de la Vie et de la Terre: 118 route de Narbonne, 31062 Toulouse Cedex 9; tel. 5-61-55-69-30; e-mail dirsvt@adm.ups-tlse.fr; internet ufrsvt.ups-tlse.fr; Dir Prof. BERNARD KNIBIEHLER

UNIVERSITÉ DE TOURS (UNIVERSITÉ FRANÇOIS-RABELAIS)

60 rue du plat d'Etain, BP 12050, 37020 Tours Cedex 01
Telephone: 2-47-36-66-00
E-mail: moip@univ-tours.fr
Internet: www.univ-tours.fr

Founded 1970
State control
Languages of instruction: English, French
Academic year: September to June

Pres.: LOÏC VAILLANT
Vice-Pres. for Admin.: ALAIN RONCINI
Vice-Pres. for Int. Relations: ARNAUD GIACOMETTI
Vice-Pres. for Science Ccl: MICHEL ISINGRINI
Vice-Pres. for Studies and Univ. Life: NADINE IMBAULT
Sec.-Gen.: PIERRE GABETTE
Librarian: CORINNE TOUCHELAY

Library of 600,000 vols, 5,600 periodical titles
Number of teachers: 1,300
Number of students: 22,000.

TEACHING AND RESEARCH UNITS

Centre d'Etudes Supérieures de la Renaissance: 59 rue Néricault-Destouches, BP 11328, 37013 Tours Cedex 01; tel. 2-47-36-77-60; e-mail cesr@univ-tours.fr; internet cesr.univ-tours.fr; Dir VENDRIX PHILIPPE.

Ecole d'ingénieurs Polytechnique: 64 Ave Jean Portalis, 37200 Tours Cedex 01; tel. 2-47-36-14-14; e-mail polytech@univ-tours.fr; internet polytech.univ-tours.fr; Dir CHRISTIAN PROUST.

Faculté des Arts et Sciences Humaines: 3 rue des Tanneurs, 37041 Tours Cedex 01; tel. 2-47-36-68-36; e-mail secrtash@univ-tours.fr; internet ash.univ-tours.fr; Dir BERNARD BURON.

Faculté de Droit, d'Economie et des Sciences Sociales: 50 Ave Jean Portalis, BP 0607, 37206 Tours Cedex 03; tel. 2-47-36-10-92; e-mail fac-droit@univ-tours.fr; internet droit.univ-tours.fr; Dean Prof. CLAUDE OPHELE.

Faculté de Lettres et Langues: 3 rue des Tanneurs, 37041 Tours Cedex 01; tel. 2-47-36-68-35; e-mail jean-michel.fournier@univ-tours.fr; internet lettres.univ-tours.fr; Dir JEAN-MICHEL FOURNIER.

Faculté de Médecine: 10 Blvd Tonnellé, BP 3223, 37032 Tours Cedex 01; tel. 2-47-36-60-04; e-mail dominique.perrotin@univ-tours.fr; internet med.univ-tours.fr; Dean DOMINIQUE PERROTIN.

Faculté de Pharmacie: 31 Ave Monge, 37200 Tours Cedex 01; tel. 2-47-36-71-42; e-mail ufrpharmacie@univ-tours.fr; internet pharma.univ-tours.fr; Dir ALAIN GUEIFFIER.

Faculté des Sciences: Parc Grandmont, 37200 Tours Cedex 01; tel. 2-47-36-70-30; e-mail scosciences@univ-tours.fr; internet sciences.univ-tours.fr; Dir ALAIN VERGER.

Institut Universitaire de Technologie (Blois): 15 rue de la Chocolaterie, CS 2903, 41000 Tours Cedex 02; tel. 2-54-55-21-33; e-mail isabelle.laffez@univ-tours.fr; internet iut-blois.univ-tours.fr; Dir ISABELLE LAFEZ

UNIVERSITÉ DE VALENCIENNES ET DU HAINAUT-CAMBRESIS

Le Mont Houy, BP 311, 59304 Valenciennes Cedex
Telephone: 3-27-14-12-34
E-mail: uvhc@univ-valenciennes.fr
Internet: www.univ-valenciennes.fr

Founded 1964
State control
Language of instruction: French
Academic year: September to June

Pres.: MOHAMED OURAK
Vice-Pres. for Admin.: J. M. FLAMME
Vice-Pres. for Science Ccl: A. ARTIBA
Vice-Pres. for Studies and Univ. Life: A. KABILA
Sec.-Gen.: P. CHABASSE
Librarian: FRANÇOISE TRUFFERT

Library of 180,000 vols
Number of teachers: 650
Number of students: 10,300

TEACHING AND RESEARCH UNITS

Higher Industrial Institute: Dir: FRANÇOIS VERHEYDE
Higher National School of Engineering and Computer Science: Dir: DANIEL COUTELLIER
Institute of Business Administration: Dir: PATRICK LELEU
Institute of General of Administrative Studies: Dir: EMMANUEL CHERRIER
Institute of Science and Technology: Dir: CLAUDINE FOLLET
Institute of Technology: Dir: JEAN-PIERRE ROUZÉ
Law, Economics and Management: Dean: ALEXANDRE BONDUELLE
Letters, Languages, Arts and Humanities: Dir: SERGE GOUAZÉ
School of Continuing Education and Social and Economic Promotion: Dir: D. WILLAEYS
Sport Science: Dir: FRANCK BARBIER

UNIVERSITÉ DE VERSAILLES SAINT-QUENTIN-EN-YVELINES

55 ave de Paris, 78035 Versailles Cedex
Telephone: 1-39-25-78-00
E-mail: secretariat@ilei.uvsq.fr
Internet: www2.uvsq.fr

Founded 1991

Pres.: SYLVIE FAUCHEUX
Vice-Pres. for Admin.: JEAN-LUC VAYSSIÈRE
Vice-Pres. for Science Ccl: GÉRARD CAUDAL
Vice-Pres. for Studies and Univ. Life: SONJA DENOT-LEDUNOIS
Sec.-Gen.: NICOLAS MIGNAN
Librarian: CHRISTOPHE PÉRALES

Number of teachers: 1,360
Number of students: 18,000.

TEACHING AND RESEARCH UNITS

Faculté de Droit et de Science Politique: 43 rue de la Division Leclerc, 78280 Guyancourt Cedex; tel. 1-39-25-53-13; e-mail doyen@droit.uvsq.fr; Dean Prof. SANDRINE CLAVEL.

Faculté des Sciences: 45 ave des Etats-Unis, 78035 Versailles; tel. 1-39-25-41-12; e-mail dominique.barth@uvsq.fr; Dir DOMINIQUE BARTH.

Fafculté des Sciences de la Santé: Bâtiment François Rabelais, 9 blvd d'Alembert, 78280 Guyancourt; tel. 1-39-25-57-40; e-mail djillali.annane@uvsq.fr; Dean DJILLALI ANNANE.

Faculté des Sciences Sociales: 47 blvd Vauban, 48047 Guyancourt Cedex; tel. 1-39-25-51-01; e-mail direction.ufr-scs@uvsq.fr; Dir MARYSE BRESSON.

Institut d'Etudes Culturelles: Bâtiment Vauban, 47 blvd Vauban, 78047 Guyancourt Cedex; tel. 1-39-25-50-02; e-mail christian.delporte@uvsq.fr; Dir CHRISTIAN DELPORTE.

Institut des Langues et des Etudes Internationales: Bâtiment Vauban, 47 blvd Vauban, 78280 Guyancourt Cedex; tel. 1-39-25-52-70; e-mail secretariat@ilei.uvsq.fr; Dir LAURENT BAZIN.

Institut des Sciences et Techniques des Yvelines: 10–12 ave de l'Europe, 78140 Vélizy; tel. 1-39-25-38-50; e-mail directeur@isty.uvsq.fr; Dir PIERRE BLAZEVIC.

Institut Supérieur de Management: Bâtiment Vauban, 47 blvd Vauban, 78047 Guyancourt Cedex; tel. 1-39-25-55-34; e-mail secretariat.ism@uvsq.fr; Dir PHILIPPE HERMEL.

Institut Universitaire de Technologie (Mantes-en-Yvelines): 7 rue Jean Hoët, 78200 Mantes-la-Jolie; tel. 1-30-98-13-62; e-mail directeur@iut-mantes.uvsq.fr; Dir SAMIR ALLAL.

Institut Universitaire de Technologie (Vélizy): 7 rue Jean Hoët, 78200 Mantes-la-Jolie; tel. 1-39-25-48-33; e-mail iut@iut-velizy.uvsq.fr; Dir STÉPHANE DELAPLACE

State Colleges and Institutes

GENERAL

Collège de France: 11 pl. Marcelin Berthelot, 75231 Paris Cedex 05; tel. 1-44-27-12-11; e-mail message@college-de-france.fr; internet www.college-de-france.fr; f. 1530 by François I; library: 85,000 vols; 54 professors; Administrator PIERRE CORVOL.

Ecole des Hautes Etudes en Sciences Sociales: 190–198 ave de France, 75244 Paris Cedex 13; tel. 1-49-54-25-25; internet www.ehess.fr; f. 1947; 300 teachers; 3,000 students; Pres. FRANÇOIS WEIL.

Ecole Pratique des Hautes Etudes: 46 rue de Lille, 75007 Paris; tel. 1-53-63-61-20; e-mail nicole.daire@ephe.sorbonne.fr; internet www.ephe.sorbonne.fr; f. 1868; library: 50,000 vols; 300 teachers; 4,000 students; Pres. JEAN-CLAUDE WAQUET; Sec.-Gen. NICOLE DAIRÉ.

Divisions:

Department of History and Philology: 190 ave de France, 75013 Paris; tel. 1-49-54-83-59; e-mail danielle.jacquart@ephe.sorbonne.fr; f. 1868; Dean DANIELLE JACQUART; publ. *Annuaire*.

Department of Life and Earth Science: 46 rue de Lille, 75007 Paris; tel. 1-53-63-61-95; e-mail michel.veuille@mnhn.fr; f. 1868; Dean MICHEL VEUILLE; publ. *Annuaire*.

Department of Religious Studies: 46, rue de Lille, 75007 Paris; tel. 153-63-61-96; e-mail hubert.bost@ephe.sorbonne.fr; f. 1886; Dean HUBERT BOST; publ. *Annuaire*.

Attached Institutes:

Institut Européen en Sciences des Religions: 14 rue Ernest Cresson, 75014 Paris; tel. 1-40-52-10-00; e-mail iesr@ephe.sorbonne.fr; internet www.iesr.fr; Dir ISABELLE SAINT-MARTIN.

Institut Transdisciplinaire d'Etude du Vieillissement: Université Montpellier II, Bâtiment 24, pl. Eugène Bataillon, CC 105, 34095 Montpellier Cedex 5; tel. 6-70-53-84-05; e-mail verdier@univ-montp2.fr; Dir JEAN-MICHEL VERDIER.

Pôle Universitaire Léonard de Vinci: 92916 Paris La Défense Cedex; 12 ave Léonard de Vinci, 92400 Courbevoie, Hauts-de-Seine; tel. 1-41-16-70-00; e-mail contact@devinci.fr; internet www.devinci.fr; f. 1995 by the Gen. Ccl of the Hauts-de-Seine Département; depts: economics and social sciences, languages, gen. culture, personal devt, sport; library: 80,000 books, reports, memoirs, market research reports, 400 journals, 1,000 CD-ROM and DVD titles, 20 online databases; 6,418 students; Pres. CHARLES PASQUA.

ADMINISTRATION

Ecole Nationale d'Administration: 2 ave de l'Observatoire, 75272 Paris Cedex 06; tel. 1-44-41-85-00; internet www.ena.fr; f. 1945 to provide training for the higher ranks of the civil service; 600 teachers; 2,050 students; library: 25,000 vols; Dir BERNARD BOUCAULT.

Groupe ESC Clermont: 4 blvd Trudaine, 63037 Clermont-Ferrand Cedex 01; tel. 4-73-98-24-24; e-mail info@esc-clermont.fr; internet www.esc-clermont.fr; f. 1919; dependent on the Direction de l'Enseignement Supérieur du Ministre de l'Education; library: 9,000 vols, Chamber of Commerce library of 12,000 vols; 200 teachers; 600 students; Dir DAVID MARKER; publs *Développements* (3 a year), *Point Zéro* (6 a year).

AGRICULTURE, FORESTRY, VETERINARY SCIENCE

AgroParisTech: 16 rue Claude Bernard, 75231 Paris Cedex 05; tel. 1-44-08-168-50; e-mail marie-pierre.quessette@agroparistech.fr; internet www.agroparistech.fr; f. 2007 by a merger of Ecole Nationale Supérieure des Industries Agricoles et Alimentaires, f. 1893, the Institut National Agronomique Paris-Grignon, f. 1971, and Ecole Nationale du Génie Rural, des Eaux et des Forêts, f. 1965.; library: 50,000 vols and 1,700 periodicals; 230 teachers; 2,000 students; Dir-Gen. REMI TOUSSAIN.

Attached Institute:

AgroParisTech—Grignon Energie Positive: Ferme expérimentale AgroParisTech, 78850 Thiverval-Grignon; tel. 1-30-54-57-40; e-mail grignonenergiepositive@agroparistech.fr; internet www.agroparistech.fr/energiepositive; f. 1979; library: c. 1,000 vols; Dir OLIVIER LAPIERRE; publ. *Sols* (3 or 4 a year).

Ecole Nationale Supérieure du Paysage: 10 rue du Maréchal-Joffre, 78000 Versailles; tel. 1-39-24-62-00; e-mail b.welcomme@versailles.ecole-paysage.fr; internet www.ecole-paysage.fr; f. 1975; architecture, ecology, humanities, landscaping, plastic arts, rural development, town planning; library: 6,000 vols, 75 periodicals; Dir M. BERNARD; publ. *Les Carnets du Paysage* (4 a year).

Ecole Nationale Vétérinaire d'Alfort: 7 ave Général de Gaulle, 94704 Maisons Alfort; tel. 1-43-96-71-00; e-mail web-direction@vet-alfort.fr; internet www.vet-alfort.fr; f. 1765; library: 150,000 vols; 80 teachers; 700 students; Dean Prof. JEAN-PAUL MIALOT; publ. *Le Recueil de Médecine Vétérinaire*.

Ecole Nationale Vétérinaire de Nantes: Atlanpole-La Chantrerie, BP 40706, 44307 Nantes Cedex 03; tel. 2-40-68-77-77; e-mail direction@vet-nantes.fr; internet www.oniris-nantes.fr; f. 1979; 73 teachers; 634 students; Dir-Gen. PIERRE SAÏ.

Ecole Nationale Vétérinaire de Toulouse: 23 chemin des Capelles, BP 87614, 31076 Toulouse Cedex 3; tel. 5-61-19-38-00; e-mail direction@envt.fr; internet www.envt.fr; f. 1828; library: 50,000 vols; 75 teachers; 570 students; Dir Prof. ALAIN MILON; Sec.-Gen. JEAN-CLAUDE BRETHES; Librarian Prof. GAËLLE JAN; publ. *Revue de Médecine Vétérinaire* (12 a year).

Institut Supérieur des Sciences Agronomiques, Agroalimentaires, Horticoles et du Paysage: 65 rue de Saint-Brieuc, CS 84215, 35042 Rennes Cedex; tel. 2-23-48-50-00; e-mail dircom@agrocampus-ouest.fr; internet www.agrocampus-ouest.fr; f. 2008 by the merger of the Institut National d'Enseignement Supérieur et de Recherche Agronomique et Agro-alimentaire in Rennes and the Institut National d'Horticulture et de Paysage in Angers, f. 1874; campuses in Angers, Beg-Meil and Rennes; library: 19,000 vols; 135 teachers; 1,880 students; Dir-Gen. Prof. GRÉGOIRE THOMAS.

Montpellier SupAgro/Centre International d'Etudes Supérieures en Sciences Agronomiques: 2 pl.Viala, 34060 Montpellier Cedex 2; tel. 4-99-61-22-00; e-mail contact@supagro.inra.fr; internet www.supagro.fr; f. 2007 by the merger of Ecole Nationale Supérieure Agronomique de Montpellier, f. 1872, the Centre National d'Etudes Agronomiques des Régions Chaudes, f. 1902, the Département Industries Agroalimentaires Régions Chaudes de l'Ecole Nationale Supérieure des Industries Agricoles et Alimentaires, f. 1893, and the Centre d'Expérimentations Pédagogiques de Florac, f. 1970; library: 100,000 vols, 1,400 periodicals; 100 teachers; 1,250 students; Dir-Gen. ETIENNE LANDAIS; Sec.-Gen. PHILIPPE DE CORNELISSEN.

Attached Institutes:

Centre d'Expérimentations Pédagogiques de Florac: 9 rue Célestin Freinet, BP 35, 48400 Florac; tel. 4-66-65-65-65; e-mail admin.cep@educagri.fr; internet www.cep.educagri.fr; Dir PATRICK AUMASSON.

Institut des Hautes Etudes de la Vigne et du Vin: e-mail ihev@supagro.inra.fr; Dir HERVÉ HANNIN.

Institut des Régions Chaudes: 1101 ave Agropolis, BP 5098, 34093 Montpellier; tel. 4-67-61-70-00; e-mail fabrice.dreyfus@supagro.inra.fr; internet www.supagro.fr/irc; Dir FABRICE DREYFUS.

VetAgro Sup (Institut d'Enseignement Supérieur et de Recherche en Alimentation, Santé Animale, Sciences Agronomiques et d'Environnement): 1 ave Bourgelat, BP 83, 69280 Marcy L'Etoile; tel. 4-78-87-25-25; internet www.vet-lyon.fr; f. 2010 by the merger of Ecole Nationale Vétérinaire de Lyon, f. 1762, Ecole Nationale d'Ingénieurs des Travaux Agricoles de Clermont-Ferrand, f. 1984, and Ecole Nationale des Services Vétérinaires, f. 1973; library: 10,000 vols; 120 teachers; 1,200 students.

Attached Institute:

Ecole Nationale des Services Vétérinaires: tel. 4-78-87-25-45; e-mail ensv@ensv.vetagro-sup.fr; internet blanc.vet-lyon.fr; Dir Dr OLIVIER FAUGÈRE.

ARCHITECTURE

Ecole d'Architecture de Lille et des Régions Nord: 2 rue Verte, quartier de l'Hôtel de Ville, 59650 Villeneuve d'Ascq; tel. 3-20-61-95-50; internet www.lille.archi.fr; f. 1755 as Ecole d'Architecture, reorganized 1968; library: 15,000 vols; 127 teachers; 700 students; Dir JEAN MARC ZURETTI.

Ecole Nationale Supérieure d'Architecture de Paris-La Villette: 144 ave de Flandre, 75019 Paris; tel. 1-44-65-23-00; e-mail directeur@paris-lavillette.archi.fr; internet www.paris-lavillette.archi.fr; f. 1969, current name adopted 1982; attached to Min. of Culture and Communications; library: 25,000 vols; 80 teachers; 2,300 students; Dir GILLES ENRIQUEZ.

Ecole Spéciale d'Architecture: 254 blvd Raspail, 75014 Paris; tel. 1-40-47-40-47; e-mail info@esa-paris.fr; internet www.esa-paris.fr; f. 1865; library: 7,000 vols; 80 teachers; 675 students; Pres. FRANÇOIS BORDRY.

ECONOMICS, LAW AND POLITICS

Centre Français de Droit Comparé: 28 rue Saint-Guillaume, 75007 Paris; tel. 1-44-39-86-23; e-mail cfdc@legiscompare.com; internet www.centrefdc.org; f. 1951; library: 100,000 vols; Pres. JACQUES ROBERT; Sec.-Gen. DIDIER LAMÈTHE; publ. *Revue Internationale de Droit Comparé* (4 a year).

Ecole Nationale de la Magistrature: 10 rue des Frères Bonie, 33080 Bordeaux Cedex; tel. 5-56-00-10-10; e-mail initiale@enm_magistrature.fr; internet www.enm.justice.fr; f. 1958; library: 50,000 vols; 450 students; Dir JEAN-FRANÇOIS THONY; publ. *Les Cahiers de la Jusitice* (2 a year).

Ecole Nationale de la Statistique et de l'Administration Economique (ENSAE): 3 ave Pierre Larousse, 92245 Malakoff Cedex; tel. 1-41-17-65-25; e-mail info@ensae-paristech.fr; internet www.ensae.fr; f. 1942; attached to the Institut National de la Statistique et des Etudes Economiques (see under Research Institutes); economics, statistics, finance; 344 students; Dir SYLVIANE GASTALDO.

Ecole Nationale de la Statistique et de l'Analyse de l'Information (ENSAI): Campus de Ker Lann, rue Blaise Pascal, 35170 Bruz; tel. 2-99-05-32-32; e-mail communication@ensai.fr; internet www.ensai.com; f. 1942; attached to the Institut National de la Statistique et des Etudes Economiques (see Research Institutes); statistics and information processing at Masters level; 21 teachers; 335 students; Dir LAURENT DI CARLO (acting).

Institut d'Etudes Politiques de Paris: 27 rue Saint-Guillaume, 75337 Paris Cedex 07; tel. 1-45-49-50-50; internet www.sciences-po.fr; f. 1945 as successor to l'Ecole Libre des Sciences Politiques; attached to Fondation Nationale des Sciences Politiques; seven campuses in France: Dijon, Le Havre, Menton, Nancy, Paris, Poitiers and Reims; library: 700,000 vols; 10,000 students; Dir RICHARD DESCOINGS.

EDUCATION

Ecole Normale Supérieure: 45 rue d'Ulm, 75230 Paris Cedex 05; tel. 1-44-32-30-00; e-mail communication@ens.fr; internet www.ens.fr; f. 1794 by the Nat. Convention; graduate and postgraduate studies in humanities, social sciences and science; library: see under Libraries and Archives; 800 teachers; 2,300 students; Dir MONIQUE CANTO-SPERBER; Sec.-Gen. CORALIE WALUGA;

Librarian PIERRE PETITMENGIN; publ. *Annales Scientifiques de l'Ecole Normale Supérieure*.

Ecole Normale Supérieure de Cachan: 61 ave du Président Wilson, 94235 Cachan Cedex; tel. 1-47-40-20-00; e-mail webmaster@ens-cachan.fr; internet www.ens-cachan.fr; f. 1912 as Ecole Normale de l'Enseignement Technique; became Ecole Normale Supérieure in 1985; library: 55,000 vols; 145 teachers; 1,150 students; Dir YANN BARBAUX.

Ecole Normale Supérieure de Lyon: 15 parvis René Descartes, BP 7000, 69342 Lyon Cedex 07; tel. 4-37-37-60-00; e-mail webmaster@ens-lyon.fr; internet www.ens-lyon.fr; f. 2010 by the merger of Ecole Normale Supérieure Lettres et Sciences Humaines (fmrly Ecole Normale Supérieure de Fontenay/Saint-Cloud) with Ecole Normale Supérieure de Lyon; library: 1,200,000 vols; 230 teachers; 2,000 students; Pres. JACQUES SAMARUT; Dir-Gen. OLIVIER FARON; Sec.-Gen. YVES QUINTEAU; Librarian CHRISTINE ANDRÉ.

GEOGRAPHY

Ecole Nationale des Sciences Géographiques: 6 et 8 ave Blaise Pascal, Cité Descartes, Champs-sur-Marne, 77455 Marne-la-Vallée Cedex 2; tel. 1-64-15-30-01; e-mail info@ensg.ign.fr; internet www.ensg.ign.fr; f. 1941; administered by Institut Géographique National; library: 36,000 vols, 950,000 maps, 1.1m. aerial photographs; 30 teachers; 300 students, 2,000 trainees; Dir MICHEL KASSER.

HISTORY

Ecole Nationale des Chartes: 19 rue de la Sorbonne, 75005 Paris; tel. 1-55-42-75-00; e-mail secretariat@enc.sorbonne.fr; internet www.enc.sorbonne.fr; f. 1821, reorganized 1846; library: 150,000 vols; 170 students; Dir JACQUES BERLIOZ; Librarian ISABELLE DIU; publs *Etudes et Rencontres*, *Matériaux pour l'Histoire*, *Mémoires et Documents*, *Positions des thèses* (1 a year).

Institut National du Patrimoine: Galerie Colbert, 2 rue Vivienne, 75002 Paris; tel. 1-44-41-16-41; e-mail webmaster@inp.fr; internet www.inp.fr; f. 1990; trains curators of museums, archives and historical monuments; Dir ERIC GROSS; Sec.-Gen. SOPHIE SEYER.

LANGUAGE AND LITERATURE

Institut National des Langues et Civilisations Orientales (INALCO): 2 rue de Lille, 75343 Paris Cedex 07; tel. 1-49-23-26-00; e-mail secretariat.general@inalco.fr; internet www.inalco.fr; f. 1669; 228 teachers; 10,500 students; Pres. JACQUES LEGRAND; Sec.-Gen. JEAN BAYLE.

Research Centres:

Centre d'Etudes Japonaises: 49 bis ave de la Belle Gabrielle, 75012 Paris; tel. 1-80-51-95-00; e-mail anne.bayard-sakai@inalco.fr; internet inalcocej.free.fr; Dir ANNE BAYARD-SAKAI.

Centre d'Etudes et de Recherche sur les Littératures et les Oralités du Monde: 49 bis ave de la Belle Gabrielle, 75012 Paris; tel. 1-80-51-95-00; e-mail gilles.delouche@inalco.fr; internet www.cerlom.fr; Dir GILLES DELOUCHE.

Centre de Recherches Europes-Eurasie: 49 bis ave de la Belle Gabrielle, 75012 Paris; tel. 1-80-51-95-00; e-mail marie.vrinat-nikolov@inalco.fr; internet inalcocej.free.fr; comprises Centre d'Etudes Balkaniques, Centre d'Etude de l'Europe Médiane and Centre de Recherches Russes et Euro-Asiatique.; Dir MARIE VRINAT NIKOLOV.

Centre de Recherches Linguistiques sur l'Asie Orientale: c/o EHESS, 54 blvd Raspail, 75006 Paris; tel. 1-80-51-95-00; e-mail djamouri@ehess.fr; internet crlao.ehess.fr; Dir REDOUANE DJAMOURI.

Centre de Recherche Moyen-Orient et Méditerranée: 49 bis ave de la Belle Gabrielle, 75012 Paris; tel. 1-80-51-95-00; e-mail cermom@gmail.com; Dir MASHA ITZHAKI.

Equipe Asies: 49 bis ave de la Belle Gabrielle, 75012 Paris; tel. 1-80-51-95-00; e-mail isabelle.rabut@inalco.fr; comprises Centre d'Etudes Chinoises, Centre d'Etudes Coréennes, Centre de Recherche sur l'Océan Indien Occidental et le Monde Austronésien, Centre Asie du Sud et du Sud-Est and Littérature et société: Tibet, Népal, Mongolie.; Dir ISABELLE RABUT.

Equipe de Recherche en Textes, Informatique, Multilinguisme: 49 bis ave de la Belle Gabrielle, 75012 Paris; tel. 1-80-51-95-00; e-mail crim@inalco.fr; internet www.crim.fr; Dir VALETTE MATHIEU.

Histoire Sociétés et Territoires du Monde: 49 bis ave de la Belle Gabrielle, 75012 Paris; tel. 1-80-51-95-00; e-mail robert.ziavoula@inalco.fr; Dir ROBERT ZIAVOULA.

Langage, Langues et Cultures d'Afrique Noire: UMR 8135 du CNRS, 7 rue Guy Môquet, BP 8, 94801 Villejuif; tel. 1-49-58-38-46; e-mail llacan@vjf.cnrs.fr; internet llacan.vjf.cnrs.fr; Dir MARTINE VANHOVE.

Langues et Cultures du Nord de l'Afrique et Diasporas: 49 bis ave de la Belle Gabrielle, 75012 Paris; tel. 1-80-51-95-00; e-mail abounf@inalco.fr; comprises Centre de Recherche Berbère, Centre de Recherche et Etudes en Arabe Maghrébin and Langues et Cultures Juives du Maghreb et de la Méditerranée Occidentale.; Dir ABDELLAH BOUNFOUR.

Mondes Iranien et Indien: 27 rue Paul Bert, 94204 Ivry-sur-Seine; tel. 1-49-60-40-05; e-mail iran-inde@ivry.cnrs.fr; internet www.iran-inde.cnrs.fr; Dir POLLET SAMVELIAN.

Pluralité des Langues et des Idendités en Didactique: Acquisition, Médiations: 49 bis ave de la Belle Gabrielle, 75012 Paris; tel. 1-80-51-95-00; e-mail gzarate@inalco.fr; internet www.plidam.fr; Dir GENEVIÈVE ZARATE.

LIBRARIANSHIP

Ecole Nationale Supérieure des Sciences de l'Information et des Bibliothèques (ENSSIB): 17–21 blvd du 11 Novembre 1918, 69623 Villeurbanne Cedex; tel. 4-72-44-43-43; e-mail enssib@enssib.fr; internet www.enssib.fr; f. 1963 as Ecole Nationale Supérieure de Bibliothécaires; library: 17,000 vols and 585 periodicals, also audiovisual items; 12 teachers; 300 students; Dir ANNE-MARIE BERTRAND; publ. *Bulletin des Bibliothèques de France* (6 a year).

MEDICINE

Ecole des Hautes Etudes en Santé Publique (EHESP): ave du Professeur Léon-Bernard, CS 74312, 35043 Rennes Cedex; tel. 2-99-02-22-00; internet www.ehesp.fr; f. 1945; post-univ. courses; library: 15,000 vols; 60 full-time teachers; 500 full-time students; 4,000 part-time students; Dir Prof. ANTOINE FLAHAULT.

Ecole du Val-de-Grâce: 1 pl. Alphonse Laveran, 75230 Paris Cedex 05; tel. 1-40-51-69-69; internet www.ecole-valdegrace.sante.defense.gouv.fr; f. 1850 as Ecole d'Application du Service de Santé des Armées (name changed as above in 2005); mainly two-year graduate courses; library: 40,000 vols and 2,067 periodicals; Dir MGI DE SAINT-JULIEN; publ. *Médecine et Armées*.

SCIENCES

Ecole Nationale de la Météorologie: 42 ave Gaspard Coriolis, 31057 Toulouse Cedex 1; tel. 5-61-07-94-19; e-mail enm.fr@meteo.fr; internet www.enm.meteo.fr; f. 1948; attached to INP de Toulouse; library: 4,000 vols; 35 teachers; 230 students; Dir FRANÇOIS LALAURETTE.

Institut National des Sciences Appliquées de Lyon (INSA Lyon): 20 ave Albert Einstein, 69621 Villeurbanne Cedex; tel. 4-72-43-83-83; e-mail accueil@insa-lyon.fr; internet www.insa-lyon.fr; f. 1957; Dir Prof. ALAIN STORCK.

Institut National des Sciences Appliquées de Rennes (INSA Rennes): 20 ave des Buttes de Coësmes, CS 70839, 35708 Rennes Cedex 7; tel. 2-23-23-82-00; internet www.insa-rennes.fr; f. 1961; civil engineering and town planning, communications systems, computer science, electronic engineering, mechanical engineering and control, physical and materials science; 150 teachers; 1,700 students; Dir M'HAMED DRISSI.

Institut National des Sciences Appliquées de Rouen (INSA Rouen): ave de l'Université, 76801 Saint-Etienne-du-Rouvray Cedex; tel. 2-32-95-97-00; e-mail insa@insa-rouen.fr; internet www.insa-rouen.fr; f. 1985; chemistry, mathematics, energy, mechanical engineering, technology and applied sciences; library: 15,000 vols, 200 periodicals; 141 teachers; 1,546 students; Dir Prof. JEAN-LOUIS BILLOËT.

Institut National des Sciences Appliquées de Strasbourg (INSA Strasbourg): 24 blvd de la Victoire, 67084 Strasbourg Cedex; tel. 3-88-14-47-00; e-mail secretariat.direction@insa-strasbourg.fr; internet www.insa-strasbourg.fr; f. 1875 and rejoined the INSA group in 2003; 1,300 students; Dir MARC RENNER.

Institut National des Sciences Appliquées de Toulouse (INSA Toulouse): 135 ave de Rangueil, 31077 Toulouse Cedex 4; tel. 5-61-55-95-13; e-mail webmaster@insa-toulouse.fr; internet www.insa-toulouse.fr; 10,000 students; Dir DIDIER MARQUIS.

Muséum National d'Histoire Naturelle: Jardin des Plantes, 57 rue Cuvier, 75005 Paris Cedex 05; tel. 1-40-79-56-01; e-mail webaccueil@mnhn.fr; internet www.mnhn.fr; f. 1635 as the Jardin Royal des Plantes Médicinales (current organization adopted in 1793); teaching and research in natural history; administers the Zoological Garden, the Musée de l'Homme and several other natural history depts and institutions; Dir Prof. BERTRAND-PIERRE GALEY; Librarian MONIQUE DUCREUX.

TECHNOLOGY

Conservatoire National des Arts et Métiers: 292 rue St-Martin, 75141 Paris Cedex 03; tel. 1-40-27-20-00; internet www.cnam.fr; f. 1794; 55 regional centres, diploma and doctorate courses; library: see under Libraries and Archives; 470 teachers; 100,000 students (full- and part-time); Pres. GÉRARD MESTRALLET.

Ecole Centrale des Arts et Manufactures/Ecole centrale Paris: Grande Voie des Vignes, 92295 Châtenay-Malabry Cedex; tel. 1-41-13-10-00; e-mail direction@ecp.fr; internet www.ecp.fr; f. 1829; higher degrees in multiple disciplines of engineering; library: 60,000 vols and 340 periodicals; 224 teachers (full-time); 1,589 students; Dir HERVÉ BIAUSSER; publ. *Centraliens* (12 a year).

Ecole Centrale de Lille: Cité Scientifique, BP 48, 59651 Villeneuve d'Ascq Cedex; tel. 3-20-33-53-53; e-mail renseignements@ec-lille.fr; internet www.ec-lille.fr; f. 1872; 6 research laboratories; library: 10,000 vols; 100 teachers; 1,400 students; Dir Prof. ETIENNE CRAYE.

Ecole Nationale de l'Aviation Civile: 7 ave Edouard-Belin, BP 54005, 31055 Toulouse Cedex 4; tel. 5-62-17-40-00; internet www.enac.fr; f. 1948; training of civil aviation personnel; advanced studies in engineering; library: 30,000 vols; 400 teachers and researchers; 2,000 students; Dir M. HOUALLA.

Ecole Nationale du Génie de l'Eau et de l'Environnement de Strasbourg: 1 quai Koch, BP 61039, 67070 Strasbourg Cedex; tel. 3-88-24-82-82; e-mail engees@engees.u-strasbg.fr; internet www-engees.u-strasbg.fr; f. 1960; 450 students; Dir CLAUDE BERNHARD.

Ecole Nationale de la Photographie: 16 rue des Arènes, BP 149, 13200 Arles Cedex; tel. 4-90-99-33-33; e-mail communication@enp-arles.com; internet www.enp-arles.com; f. 1982; under auspices of Min. of Culture and Communications; 3-year course; library: 10,000 vols; 7 teachers; 75 students; Dir RÉMY FENZY.

Ecole Nationale Supérieure des Arts et Industries Textiles (ENSAIT): 2 allée Louise et Victor Champier, BP 30329, 59056 Roubaix Cedex 01; tel. 3-20-25-64-64; e-mail xavier.flambard@ensait.fr; internet www.ensait.fr; f. 1883; library: 3,844 vols; 50 teachers; 210 students; Dir XAVIER FLAMBARD.

Ecole Nationale Supérieure d'Arts et Métiers ParisTech: 151 blvd de l'Hôpital, 75013 Paris; tel. 1-44-24-62-99; e-mail alex.remy@ensam.eu; internet www.ensam.eu; comprises 11 Centres d'Enseignement et de Recherche in Aix-en-Provence, Angers, Bastia, Bordeaux-Talence, Châlon-en-Champagne, Châlon-sur-Saône, Chambéry, Cluny, Lille, Metz and Paris; f. 1871 as Ecole Nationale des Arts et Métiers (current structure adopted in 2007).

Ecole Nationale Supérieure de Céramique Industrielle: 12 rue Atlantis, 87068 Limoges Cedex; tel. 5-87-50-23-00; e-mail direction@ensci.fr; internet www.ensci.fr; f. 1893; library: 4,000 vols; 23 teachers; 190 students; Dir AGNES SMITH; publ. *Annuaire*.

Ecole Nationale Supérieure de l'Electronique et de ses Applications (ENSEA): 6 ave du Ponceau, 95014 Cergy-Pontoise Cedex; tel. 1-30-73-66-66; e-mail directeur@ensea.fr; internet www.ensea.fr; f. 1952; postgraduate courses in electrical engineering, computing and telecommunications; library: 6,000 vols, 150 periodicals; 90 teachers and researchers; 700 students; Dir PIERRE POUVIL.

Ecole Nationale Supérieure de Mécanique: see under University of Nantes.

Ecole Nationale Supérieure du Pétrole et des Moteurs: 228–232 ave Napoléon Bonaparte, 92852 Rueil-Malmaison Cedex; tel. 1-47-52-64-57; e-mail info-ifpschool@ifp.fr; internet www.ifp-school.com; f. 1954 by the merger of Ecole Nationale Supérieure du Pétrole et des Combustibles Liquides and Ecole Nationale des Moteurs à Combustion et à Explosion; successor to the Institut Français du Pétrole, f. 1944; 5 centres: economics and management; geological or geophysical exploration; internal combustion engines; petroleum engineering and project management; refining, petrochemicals, gas; 400 students; Dir JEAN-LUC KARNIK.

Ecole Nationale Supérieure de Techniques Avancées (ENSTA ParisTech): 32 blvd Victor, 75739 Paris; tel. 1-45-52-54-01; e-mail secretariat-general@ensta.fr; internet www.ensta-paristech.fr; f. 1741, refounded 1970; chemical engineering, electronics, information technology, mechanics, naval architecture, nuclear techniques, oceanology, systems engineering; 3-year curriculum; undergraduate and postgraduate studies; library: 10,000 vols; 180 permanent teachers, 650 visiting; 480 students (not incl. doctoral candidates); Dir YVES DEMAY.

Ecole Nationale des Travaux Publics de l'Etat: 3 rue Maurice Audin, 69518 Vaulx en Velin Cedex; tel. 4-72-04-70-70; e-mail webmaster@entpe.fr; internet www.entpe.fr; f. 1953 in Paris, moved 1975; library: 14,000 vols; 689 teachers (full-time and part-time); 614 students; Dir JEAN-BAPTISTE LESORT.

Ecole Polytechnique: 91128 Palaiseau Cedex; tel. 1-69-33-33-33; internet www.polytechnique.fr; f. 1794; library: 300,000 vols; 660 teachers; 2,700 students; Dir-Gen. XAVIER MICHEL.

Ecole des Ponts ParisTech: 6–8 ave Blaise Pascal, Cité Descartes, Champs-sur-Marne, 77455 Marne-la-Vallée Cedex 2; tel. 1-64-15-30-30; e-mail brigitte.millard@enpc.fr; internet www.enpc.fr; f. 1747; civil and mechanical engineering, town and country planning, transport; library: 85,000 vols, 2,500 periodicals, 37,000 18th-century MSS, 900 maps, 30,000 photographs; 1,700 students; Dir PHILIPPE COURTIER.

Ecole Supérieure de Physique et de Chimie Industrielles de la Ville de Paris (ParisTech): 10 rue Vauquelin, 75231 Paris Cedex 5; tel. 1-40-79-44-00; e-mail direction@espci.fr; internet www.espci.fr; f. 1882; training of research engineers; 20 research laboratories; library: 5,000 vols; 67 teachers; 75 to 80 students per year; Pres. JEAN-LOUIS MISSIKA.

ENILIA-ENSMIC, Lycée de l'Alimentation: ave François Mitterrand, BP 49, 17700 Surgères; tel. 5-46-27-69-00; e-mail epl.surgeres@educagri.fr; internet www.enilia-ensmic.fr; f. 2010 by the merger of Ecole Nationale d'Industrie Laitière et des Industries Agroalimentaires (f. 1906 as Ecole Professionnelle de Laiterie) and Ecole Nationale Supérieure de Meunerie et des Industries Céréalières (f. 1924 as Ecole Française de Meunerie); 230 students; Dir CHRISTIANE MAZEL; publ. *Industries des Céréales* (6 a year).

Groupe des Ecoles des Mines: 60 blvd St-Michel, 75272 Paris Cedex 06; e-mail jcontact@gemtech.fr; internet www.gemtech.fr; f. 1783; library: 200,000 vols, 350 periodicals; 1,000 teachers; 6,200 students.

Campuses:

Ecole des Mines d'Albi-Carmaux: Campus Jarlard, 81013 Albi Cedex 09; tel. 5-63-49-30-00; e-mail ecole@enstimac.fr; internet www.enstimac.fr; Dir BRUNO VERLON.

Ecole des Mines d'Alès: internet www.mines-ales.fr; Dir ALAIN DORISON.

Ecole des Mines de Douai: 91 rue Charles Bourseul, BP 838, 59508 Douai Cedex; e-mail jean-claude.duriez@mines-douai.fr; internet www2.mines-douai.fr; Dir JEAN-CLAUDE DURIEZ.

Ecole des Mines de Nancy: Parc De Saurupt, CS 14234, 54042 Nancy Cedex; tel. 3-83-58-42-32; e-mail ensmn@mines.inpl-nancy.fr; internet www.mines.inpl-nancy.fr; Dir MICHEL JAUZEIN.

Ecole des Mines de Nantes: La Chantrerie 4, rue Alfred Kastler, BP 20722, 44307 Nantes Cedex 03; tel. 2-51-85-81-00; e-mail stephane.cassereau@emn.fr; internet www.mines-nantes.fr; Dir STÉPHANE CASSEREAU.

Ecole des Mines de Saint-Etienne: 158 cours Fauriel, 42023 Saint-Etienne Cedex 02; tel. 4-77-42-01-23; e-mail webmaster@emse.fr; internet www.emse.fr; Dir PHILIPPE JAMET.

Mines ParisTech: 60 blvd St-Michel, 75272 Paris Cedex 06; tel. 1-40-51-90-00; e-mail benoit.legait@mines-paristech.fr; internet www.mines-paristech.fr; Dir BENOÎT LEGAIT.

Groupe ENI (Ecoles Nationales d'Ingénieurs): 1 route d'Ars Laquenexy, CS 65820, 57078 Metz Cedex 3; tel. 3-87-34-42-61; internet www.ingenieur-eni.fr; comprises five schools in Brest, Metz, Saint-Etienne, Tarbes and Val de Loire.

Schools:

Ecole Nationale d'Ingénieurs de Brest (ENIB): Site de la pointe du Diable, Technopôle Brest-Iroise, 29280 Plouzané; tel. 2-98-05-66-00; e-mail secretariat@enib.fr; internet www.enib.fr; Dir JACQUES TISSEAU.

Ecole Nationale d'Ingénieurs de Metz (ENIM): 1 route d'Ars Laquenexy, CS 65820, 57078 Metz Cedex 3; tel. 3-87-34-69-03; e-mail enim@enim.fr; internet www.enim.fr; Dir PIERRE PADILLA.

Ecole Nationale d'Ingénieurs de Saint-Etienne (ENISE): 58 rue Jean Parot, 42100 St-Etienne; tel. 4-77-43-84-84; e-mail secretariat.etudes@enise.fr; internet www.enise.fr; Dir ROLAND FORTUNIER.

Ecole Nationale d'Ingénieurs de Tarbes (ENIT): 47 ave d'Azereix, BP 1629, 65016 Tarbes Cedex; tel. 5-62-44-27-00; e-mail directeur@enit.fr; internet www.enit.fr; 60 teachers; 850 students; library of 4,000 vols; Dir TALAL MASRI.

Ecole Nationale d'Ingénieurs de Val de Loire (ENIVL): rue de la Chocolaterie, BP 3410, 41034 Blois Cedex; tel. 2-54-55-84-00; e-mail scolarite@enivl.fr; internet www.enivl.fr; Dir ROMUALD BONÉ.

Institut des Hautes Etudes Scientifiques: Le Bois-Marie, 35 route de Chartres, 91440 Bures-sur-Yvette; tel. 1-60-92-66-00; internet www.ihes.fr; f. 1958; advanced research in mathematics, theoretical physics; library: 4,000 vols, 125 periodicals; Dir JEAN PIERRE BOURGUIGNON; publ. *Publications Mathématiques* (2 a year).

Institut Polytechnique de Bordeaux: 1 ave du Dr Albert Schweitzer, BP 99, 33402 Talence Cedex; tel. 5-40-00-37-26; e-mail direction@ipb.fr; internet www.ipb.fr; f. 2009; comprises 5 schools; Dir-Gen. FRANÇOIS CANSELL.

Schools:

Ecole Nationale Supérieure de Chimie, de Biologie et de Physique: 16 ave Pey-Berland, 33607 Pessac Cedex; tel. 5-40-00-65-65; internet www.enscpb.fr; 60 teachers; 550 students; Dir JEAN-MARC HEINTZ.

Ecole Nationale Supérieure de Cognitique: 146 rue Léo Saignat, Case 40, 33076 Bordeaux Cedex; tel. 5-57-57-17-00; internet www.ensc.fr; Dir BERNARD CLAVERIE.

Ecole Nationale Supérieure d'Electronique, Informatique, Télécommunications, Mathématiques et Mécanique de Bordeaux: 1 ave du Dr Albert Schweitzer, BP 99, 33402 Talence Cedex; tel. 5-56-84-65-00; e-mail direction@enseirb-matmeca.fr; internet www.enseirb-matmeca.fr; f. 2009 by the merger of Ecole Nationale Supérieure d'Electronique et de Radioélectricité de Bordeaux and Ecole d'Ingénieurs en Modélisation Mathématique et Mécanique; Dir MARC PHALIPPOU.

Ecole Nationale Supérieure en Environnement, Géoressources et Ingénierie du Développement Durable: 1 allée F. Daguin, 33607 Pessac Cedex; tel. 5-57-12-10-00; e-mail direction@ensegid.fr; internet www.ensegid.fr; f. 2011; Dir J. M. MALÉZIEUX.

Ecole Nationale Supérieure de Technologie des Biomolécules de Bordeaux: 146 rue Léo Saignat, 33076 Bordeaux Cedex; tel. 5-57-57-10-44; e-mail enstbb@ipb.fr; internet www.enstbb.ipb.fr; Dir MARC BONNEU.

Institut Supérieur de l'Aéronautique et de l'Espace (ISAE): 10 ave Edouard Belin, BP 54032, 31055 Toulouse Cedex 4; tel. 5-61-33-80-80; e-mail communication@isae.fr; internet www.isae.fr; f. 2007 by the merger of Ecole Nationale Supérieure de l'Aéronautique et de l'Espace (f. 1909) and Ecole Nationale Supérieure d'Ingénieurs de Constructions Aéronautiques (f. 1945); library: 10,000 vols; 106 teachers; 4,277 students; Dir-Gen. OLIVIER FOURURE.

Supméca Paris—Institut Supérieur de Mécanique de Paris: 3 rue Fernand Hainaut, 93407 St-Ouen Cedex; tel. 1-49-45-29-00; e-mail informations@supmeca.fr; internet www.supmeca.fr; f. 1948; library: 3,000 vols; 400 students; Dir ALAIN RIVIÈRE; publ. *La Lettre de l'ISMCM-CESTI* (2 a year).

Supméca Toulon—Institut Supérieur de Mécanique de Toulon: Maison des Technologies, pl. Georges Pompidou, Quartier Mayol, 83000 Toulon; tel. 4-94-03-88-00; e-mail informations@toulon.supmeca.fr; internet www.supmeca.fr; f. 1994; training of engineers, applied research in automation and industrial engineering; 30 teachers; 150 students; Dir PASCALE AZOU-BRIARD.

Télécom Bretagne—Ecole Nationale Supérieure des Télécommunications de Bretagne: Technopôle Brest-Iroise, CS 83818, 29238 Brest Cedex 3; tel. 2-29-00-11-11; internet www.enst-bretagne.fr; f. 1977; attached to Min. of Technology, Information and Posts; 108 full-time teachers; 1,217 students; Dir PAUL FRIEDEL.

TÉLÉCOM ParisTech—Ecole Nationale Supérieure des Télécommunications: 46 rue Barrault, 75634 Paris Cedex 13; tel. 1-45-81-77-77; e-mail communication@telecom-paristech.fr; internet www.telecom-paristech.fr; f. 1878; attached to France Télécom; Dir YVES POLLANE.

Télécom SudParis—Télécom Ecole de Management: 9 rue Charles Fourier, 91011 Evry Cedex; tel. 1-60-76-40-40; e-mail webmaster@it-sudparis.eu; internet www.it-sudparis.eu; f. 1979; attached to Min. of Finance, Industry and the Economy; mem. of Conférence des Grandes Ecoles; engineering and business schools; 150 full-time teachers; 1,000 students; Dir SÉBASTIEN CAUWET.

Catholic Colleges and Institutes

INSTITUT CATHOLIQUE DE PARIS

21 rue d'Assas, 75270 Paris Cedex 06
Telephone: 1-44-39-52-00
E-mail: contact@icp.fr
Internet: www.icp.fr

Founded 1875
Academic year: October to June

Chancellor: Mgr ANDRÉ VINGT-TROIS
Rector: JOSEPH MAÏLA
Vice-Rector: Sr GENEVIÈVE MEDEVIELLE
Gen. Sec.: FRANÇOIS ARDONCEAU
Dir of Communication: FRANÇOISE GARDERE-CREAC'H
Librarian: ODILE DUPONT

Library: see under Libraries and Archives
Number of teachers: 847
Number of students: 15,000 (excluding affiliated schools)

Publications: *Guide des Études* (1 a year), *Transversalités: Revue de l'Institut Catholique de Paris* (4 a year)

DEANS

Biblical and Systematic Theology: Abbé JESUS ASURMENDI
Doctoral Studies: P. HERVÉ LEGRAND
Faculty of Canon Law: Père JEAN-PAUL DURAND
Faculty of Letters: NATHALIE NABERT
Faculty of Philosophy: Abbé P. CAPELLE
Faculty of Theology: Abbé HENRI-JÉRÔME GAGEY
Higher Institute of Ecumenical Studies: Abbé YVES-MARIE BLANCHARD
Higher Institute of Liturgy: Frère PATRICK PRÉTOT
Higher Institute of Pastoral Catechetics and University Extension: DENIS VILLEPELET
Higher Institute of Pedagogy: FRANÇOISE CHEBAUX
Institute for French Language and Culture and University Summer School: MURIEL CORDIER
Institute of Music and Liturgical Music: E. BELLANGER
Institute of Sacred Art: GENEVIÈVE HEBERT
Institute of Science and Theology of Religions: R. P. PAUL COULON
Institute of Social Sciences and Economics: JOSEPH MAÏLA
School of Ancient Oriental Languages: FLORENCE MALBRAN-LABAT

AFFILIATED SCHOOLS AND INSTITUTES

Centre de Formation Pédagogique Emmanuel Mounier: 78A rue de Sèvres, 75341 Paris Cedex 07; Dir R. MOREAU.

Ecole de Bibliothécaires-Documentalistes: Paris; Dir D. VIGNAUD.

Ecole de Formation Psycho-Pédagogique: Paris; Dir M. C. DAVID.

Ecole de Psychologues-Praticiens: Paris; Dir J. P. CHARTIER.

Ecole Supérieure de Chimie Organique et Minérale: 95000 Cergy; Dir G. SANTINI.

Ecole Supérieure des Sciences Economiques et Commerciales: 95000 Cergy; Dir P. TAPIE.

Institut Géologique Albert-de-Lapparent: 95000 Cergy; Dir C. CHOMAT.

Institut Libre d'Education Physique Supérieure: 95000 Cergy; Dir F. HELAINE.

Institut Polytechnique Saint-Louis: 95000 Cergy.

Constituent Schools:

Ecole de Biologie Industrielle: 95000 Cergy; Dir F. DUFOUR.

Ecole d'Electricité, de Production et des Méthodes Industrielles: 95000 Cergy; e-mail contact@epmi.fr; Dir M. DARCHERIF.

Institut d'Agro-Développement International: 95000 Cergy; Dir S. LAMY.

Institut Supérieur Agricole de Beauvais: Rue Pierre Waguet, 60000 Beauvais and 95000 Cergy; f. 1855; Dir M. P. CHOQUET.

Institut Supérieur d'Electronique de Paris: Dir M. CIAZYNSKI.

Institut Supérieur d'Interprétation et de Traduction: Paris; Dir M. MERIAUD

INSTITUT CATHOLIQUE DE TOULOUSE

31 rue de la Fonderie, BP 7012, 31068 Toulouse Cedex 7
Telephone: 5-61-36-81-00
E-mail: documentation@ict-toulouse.asso.fr
Internet: www.ict-toulouse.asso.fr

Founded 1877 and administered by a Ccl of Bishops of the region
Academic year: October to June

Chancellor: HE Mgr ROBERT LE GALL (Archbishop of Toulouse)
Rector: Père PIERRE DEBERGÉ
Registrar: MONIQUE DELCROIX
Librarian: MAGALI HURTREL-PIZARRO (acting)

Library of 250,000
Number of teachers: 238
Number of students: 6,334

Publications: *Bulletin de Littérature ecclésiastique* (4 a year), *Revue Purpan* (4 a year)

DEANS

Faculty of Canon Law: B. DU PUY-MONTBRUN
Faculty of Law: A. MASSART
Faculty of Letters: B. BILLEREY
Faculty of Philosophy: B. HUBERT
Faculty of Theology: P. MOLAC

INSTITUT DE SCIENCES ET THÉOLOGIE DES RELIGIONS

11 Impasse Flammarion, 13001 Marseilles
Telephone: 4-91-50-35-50
E-mail: istr@cathomed.cef.fr
Internet: cathomed.cef.fr

Founded 1991 by the Diocese of Marseilles

Rector: CHRISTIAN SALENSON

Library of 500 vols
Number of teachers: 30
Number of students: 250

Publication: *Chemins de Dialogue* (every 2 years)

UNIVERSITÉ CATHOLIQUE DE LILLE

60 blvd Vauban, BP 109, 59016 Lille Cedex
Telephone: 3-20-13-40-00
E-mail: saio@icl-lille.fr
Internet: www.univ-catholille.fr

Founded 1875 as Faculty of Law, became univ. instn in 1877
Private (Roman Catholic) control

Rector: Mme TH. LEBRUN
Vice-Rectors: Père B. CAZIN, O. TRANCHANT, J. C. CAILLIEZ
Admin. Officer: B. MAELFAIT
Librarian: D. PENEZ

Library: nearly 500,000 vols
Number of teachers: 3,284
Number of students: 20,186

Publications: *Catho Actualités*, *Encyclopédie Catholicisme*, *La Lettre de la Catho*, *Mélanges de Science Religieuse* (3 a year), *Mémoires et Travaux*, *Repères*, *Vie et Foi*, *Vues d'ensemble*

DEANS

Faculty of Economic Sciences: D. VANPETEGHEM
Faculty of Law: A. MASSART
Faculty of Letters and Human Sciences: J. HEUCLIN
Faculty of Medicine: G. FORZY
Faculty of Science: J. C. CAILLIEZ
Faculty of Theology: J. Y. BAZIOU

FEDERATED INSTITUTES

Centre de Recherches Economiques, Sociologiques et de Gestion (CRESGE): Rue du Port, 59000 Lille; tel. 3-20-54-58-92; e-mail cresge@univ-catholille.fr; f. 1964; Dir L. AUBREE.

Ecole de Hautes Etudes Commerciales du Nord (EDHEC): 58 rue du Port, 59046 Lille Cedex; tel. 3-20-15-45-00; e-mail contact@edhec.edu; f. 1920; 1,886 students; Dirs-Gen. O. OGER, J.-L. TURRIÈRE.

Branch:

EDHEC Nice: 393 Promenade des Anglais, BP 116, 06202 Nice Cedex; tel. 4-93-18-99-66; e-mail contact@edhec.edu; 736 students; EDHEC Paris; 131 students.

Ecole des Hautes Etudes Industrielles (HEI): 13 rue de Toul, 59046 Lille Cedex; tel. 3-28-38-48-58; e-mail contact@hei.fr; f. 1885; civil engineering, chemistry and electrical engineering; 1,676 students; Dir J. M. IDOUX.

Ecole de Sages-Femmes (ESF): Campus Saint Raphaël, 59000 Lille; tel. 3-20-13-47-36; f. 1882; 109 students; Dir CHRISTIANE ROUX.

Ecole Supérieure de Management et l'Entreprise (ESPEME): 23 rue Delphin Petit, 59046 Lille Cedex; tel. 3-20-15-45-00; f. 1988; 912 students; Dir A. F. MALVACHE.

Branch:

ESPEME Nice: 393 Promenade des Anglais, BP 116, 06202 Nice Cedex; tel. 4-93-18-99-66; 912 students; Dir BERNARD BOTTERO.

Ecole Supérieure de Traducteurs, Interprètes, et de Cadres du Commerce Extérieur (ESTICE): 83 blvd Vauban, BP 109, 59016 Lille Cedex; tel. 3-20-54-90-90; f. 1961; 113 students; Dir O. TRANCHANT.

Ecole Supérieure Privée d'Application des Sciences (ESPAS): 83 blvd Vauban, 59000 Lille; tel. 3-20-57-58-71; f. 1988; 88 students; Dir O. TRANCHANT.

IFsanté (Ecole d'aides soignants IFAS + école de puéricultrices ECPUER + école de formation aux soins infirmiers IFSI): Campus Saint Raphaël, 59000 Lille; tel. 3-28-36-10-10; e-mail contact@ifsante.fr; f. 1927; 499 students; Dir BERNADETTE MIROUX.

Institut Catholique d'Arts et Métiers (ICAM): 6 rue Auber, 59046 Lille Cedex; tel. 3-20-22-61-61; f. 1898; 850 students; Dir-Gen. G. CARPIER; Dir PH. CARPENTIER.

Institut de Communication Médicale: 83 blvd Vauban, 59000 Lille Cedex; tel. 3-20-57-58-71; e-mail icm@univ-catholille.fr; f. 1988; 20 students; Dir MARC DENEUCHE.

Institut d'Economie Scientifique et de Gestion (IESEG): 3 rue de la Digue, 59800 Lille; tel. 3-20-54-58-92; e-mail ieseg@ieseg.fr; f. 1964; 1,702 students; Dir J. P. AMMEUX.

Institut de Formation d'Animateurs de Catéchèse pour Adultes (IFAC): 60 blvd Vauban, 59016 Lille Cedex; tel. 3-20-57-69-33; f. 1980; 113 students; Dir J.M. BEAURENT.

Institut de Formation en Kinésithérapie, Pédicurie et Podologie: 10 rue J. B. de la Salle, 59000 Lille; tel. 3-20-92-06-99; f. 1964; 798 students; Dirs M. PAPAREMBORDE, D. VENNIN.

Institut de Formation Pedagogique (IFP): 236 rue du Fg de Roubaix, 59041 Lille Cedex; tel. 3-20-13-41-20; e-mail contact@ifp-npdc.fr; f. 1962; 584 students; Dir E. THEVENIN.

Institut des Stratégies et Techniques de Communication (ISTC): 83 blvd Vauban, 59800 Lille; tel. 3-20-54-32-32; f. 1991; 262 students; Dir CLAUDE DOGNIN.

Institut Social Lille (ISL): 83 Blvd Vauban, BP 12, 59004 Lille Cedex; tel. 3-20-21-93-93; e-mail isl@institut-social-lille.fr; f. 1932; 527 students; Dir E. PRIEUR.

Institut Supérieur d'Agriculture (ISA): Blvd Vauban, 59046 Lille Cedex; tel. 3-28-38-48-48; f. 1963; agricultural, agro-engineering; five-year course; 952 students; Dir P. CODRON.

Institut Supérieur d'Electronique du Numérique (ISEN): 41 Blvd Vauban, 59046 Lille Cedex; tel. 3-20-30-40-50; internet www.isen.fr; f. 1956; electronics engineering; 80 teachers; 750 students; Dir ANDREAS KAISER.

Institution Saint Jude: 18/22 rue Larmartine, 59820 Cambria; tel. 3-20-77-10-49; 82 students; Dir N. CARLIER.

Lycée privé commercial 'De la Salle': 2 rue Jean Le Vasseur, 59046 Lille Cedex; tel. 3-20-93-50-11; 267 students; Dir GUY MICHEL MAHIEU.

Lycée privé La Sagesse: 7 rue du temple, 59400 Cambria; tel. 3-27-82-28-28; 188 students; Dir B. DUMORTIER.

Lycée privé Notre-Dame de Grâce: Quai des Nerviens, BP 127, 59602 Maubeuge Cedex; tel. 3-27-53-00-66; 82 students; Dir JEAN-PIERRE LAMQUET.

Lycée privé Saint-Joseph: 26 route de Calais, 62200 Saint-Martin-lez-Boulogne; tel. 3-21-99-06-99; 274 students; Dir MICHEL DUFAY.

Lycée privé Saint Paul: 25 bis rue Colbert, 59000 Lille Cedex; tel. 3-20-55-10-20; 168 students; Dir JEAN-CLAUDE PONTHIER.

Lycée Technologique OZANAM: 50 rue Saint Gabriel, 59000 Lille; tel. 3-20-21-96-50; e-mail secretariat.direction@ozanam-lycee.fr; 384 students; Dir R. PRIESTER

UNIVERSITÉ CATHOLIQUE DE L'OUEST

3 place André Leroy, BP 808, 49008 Angers Cedex 01
Telephone: 2-41-81-67-55
E-mail: ucobn@uco.fr
Internet: www.uco.fr

Founded 1875, under the patronage of the Bishops of the western region of France
Academic year: September to June

Rector: Dr ROBERT ROUDDEAU
Vice-Rectors: LUC PASQUIER PATRICK GILLET
Sec.-Gen.: BERNARD FLOURIOT
Librarian: Y. LE GALL

Library of 200,000 vols and periodicals
Number of students: 12,500
Publications: *Annuaire*, *Impacts* (4 a year)

DEANS

Applied Ecology Institute: P. GILLET
Applied Mathematics Institute: J. M. MARION
Basic and Applied Research Institute: J. P. BOUTINET
Education and Communication Institute: CATHERINE NAFTI-MALHERBE
Faculty of Theology: LOUIS MICHEL RENIER
Institute of Applied Psychology and Sociology: PATRICK MARTIN
International Centre for French Studies (for Foreign Students): MARC RELIN
Literature and History Institute: B. HAM
Modern Languages Institute: D. STAQUET
Teacher Training Institute: R. MARTIN

AFFILIATED SCHOOLS

Ecole Supérieure d'Electronique de l'Ouest: 4 rue Merlet de la Boulaye, 49000 Angers; f. 1956; Dir M. V. HAMON.

Ecole Supérieure des Sciences Commerciales d'Angers: 1 rue Lakanal, 49000 Angers; Dir M. POTE.

Ecole Technique Supérieure de Chimie de l'Ouest: 50 rue Michelet, 49000 Angers; Dir B. DAVID.

Institut Supérieur d'Action Internationale et de Production: 18 rue du 8 Mai 1945, 49124 St Barthélemy; Dir J. Y. BIGNONET.

Institut Supérieur des Métiers: 91 rue Haute Follio, 53000 Laval; Dir EMMANUEL ROUSSEAU.

Maison de L'Initiative: Campus de la Tour, d'Auvergne, 37 rue du Maréchal Foch, 22204 Guingamp Cedex; Dir C. NAFTI-MALHERBE.

Université Catholique de l'Ouest Bretagne Nord: Campus de la Tour, d'Auvergne, 37 rue du Maréchal Foch, 22204 Guingamp Cedex; Dir MICHEL DORVEAUX.

Université Catholique de l'Ouest Bretagne Sud: Le Vincin, BP 17, 56610 Arradon; Dir SYLVIE MURZEAU

UNIVERSITÉ CATHOLIQUE DE LYON

25 rue du Plat, 69288 Lyons Cedex 02
Telephone: 4-72-32-50-12
Internet: www.univ-catholyon.fr

Founded 1875

Rector: MICHEL QUESNEL
Vice-Rector: DENISE LE LOUP
Sec.-Gen.: PATRICK BORDET
Librarian: Mlle BEHR

Library of 240,000 vols
Number of teachers: 300
Number of students: 7,422

Publications: *Bulletin*, *Cahiers*

DEANS

Faculty of Law: PASCALE BOUCAUD
Faculty of Letters: HENRI BRENDERS
Faculty of Philosophy: PIERRE GIRE
Faculty of Science: J. M. EXBRAYAT
Faculty of Theology: JEAN-PIERRE LEMONON

Independent Institutes

GENERAL

American University of Paris: 31 ave Bosquet, 75007 Paris; tel. 1-40-62-06-00; e-mail admissions@aup.edu; internet www.aup.edu; f. 1962; language of instruction: English; mem. of Middle States Assn of Colleges and Schools; 4-year arts and sciences undergraduate courses; 2 summer sessions; adult education programmes; large computer science laboratory; technical writing programme; library: 100,000 vols; 100 teachers; 800 students; Pres. Dr MICHAEL K. SIMPSON.

Groupe IPAC: e-mail info@ipac-france.com; internet www.ipac-france.com; private control; accredited by the state for studies up to Masters level; courses in management, consulting, design, health, social and environmental studies, business; attached institute IFALPES offers French as a foreign language for adults; Pres. JEAN-MICHEL DELAPLAGNE.

Campuses:

IPAC Albertville: 542 rue Louis Armand Za du Chiriac, 73200 Albertville; tel. 4-79-37-14-01; Dir JÉRÔME BAPTENDIER.

IPAC Annecy: 42 chemin de la Prairie, 74000 Annecy; tel. 4-50-45-13-91; Dir PAUL TARDIVEL.

IPAC Chambéry: L'Axiome, 44 rue Charles Montreuil, 73000 Chambéry; tel. 4-79-69-65-91; Dir ISABELLE DELIÈGE.

IPAC Geneva: 58 Rue du Grand pré, 1201 Geneva, Switzerland; tel. 22-340-42-00.

IPAC Genvois–Léman: 15 rue Montréal, 74100 Ville la Grand; tel. 4-50-37-14-32; Dir GÉRARD PONT.

IPAC Thonon: 5F ave du Général de Gaulle, Centre commercial de l'Etoile, 74200 Thonon les Bains; tel. 4-50-70-72-43.

IPAC Vallée de l'Arve: Espace Scionzier, Bâtiment 3, 560 ave des Lacs, 74950 Scionzier; tel. 4-50-96-13-00; Dir RÉGIS DUVAL.

Schiller International University—France: (For general information, see entry for Schiller International University in Germany chapter).

Campuses:

Schiller International University—Paris Campus: 32 blvd de Vaugirard, 75015 Paris; tel. 1-45-38-56-01; e-mail info-schiller@schillerparis.com; internet www.paris-schiller.com; Dir SOUHA AKIKI.

Schiller International University—Strasbourg Campus: Château du Pourtalès, 161 rue Mélanie, 67000 Strasbourg; tel. 3-88-45-84-64; e-mail blasiush@aol.com; internet www.schillerstrasbourg.com.

AGRICULTURE

Ecole Supérieure d'Agriculture de Purpan: 75 voie du Toec, 31076 Toulouse Cedex 3; tel. 5-61-15-30-30; e-mail malummer@esa_purpan.fr; internet www.esa_purpan.fr; f. 1919; 5-year diploma course; Masters degrees in agriculture, management and technology in the food industry, agricultural economics and management, environment and regional devt; library: 20,000 vols, 1,100 periodicals; 100 teachers (37 full-time); 700 students; Dir MICHEL ROUX; publ. *Purpan* (4 a year).

Esitpa—Ecole d'Ingénieurs en Agriculture: 3 rue du Tronquet, BP 40118, 76134 Mont-Saint-Aignan Cedex; tel. 2-32-82-92-00; e-mail webmaster@esitpa.org; internet www.esitpa.org; f. 1919; 5-year diploma courses for agricultural engineers; Dir P. DENIEUL.

Groupe ESA—Ecole Supérieure d'Agriculture d'Angers: 55 rue Rabelais, BP 30748, 49007 Angers Cedex 01; tel. 2-41-23-55-55; e-mail webmaster@groupe-esa.com; internet www.groupe-esa.com; f. 1898; library: 45,000 vols, 520 periodicals; 600 students; Dir AYMARD HONORÉ; publs *Bibliographie Agricole et Rurale* (5 a year), *Cahiers Agriscope* (3 a year).

COMMERCE, BUSINESS ADMINISTRATION AND STATISTICS

Audencia Nantes Ecole de Management: 8 route de la Jonelière, BP 31222, 44312 Nantes Cedex 3; tel. 2-40-37-34-34; internet www.audencia.com; f. 1900; library: 13,000 vols, 450 periodicals; 343 teachers (43 full-time, 300 part-time); 1,200 students; Pres. JEAN-FRANÇOIS MOULIN; Dir-Gen. and Dean AÏSSA DERMOUCHE.

Centre Européen d'Education Permanente (CEDEP) (European Centre for Executive Development): blvd de Constance, 77305 Fontainebleau Cedex; f. 1971; management development courses in business administration for member companies (6 French, 2 Danish, 3 British, 1 Swedish, 2 Belgian, 1 Indian, 2 Dutch, 5 European); associated with the Institut Européen d'Administration des Affaires; Gen. Dir MITCHELL KOZA.

CERAM Business School: Rue Dostoïevski, BP 085, 06902 Sophia Antipolis Cedex; tel. 4-89-88-98-24; e-mail info@ceram.fr; internet www.ceram.edu; f. 1978 by Nice Chamber of Commerce; library: 16,000 vols; 220 teachers (100 full-time, 120 part-time); 750 students, plus 100 on Masters course; Dir MAXIME CRENER.

Ecole de Management de Normandie: 30 rue de Richelieu, 76087 Le Havre Cedex; tel. 2-32-92-59-99; e-mail info@ecole-management-normandie.fr; internet www.ecole-management-normandie.fr; f. 1871; campuses in Caen, Cherbourg and Deauville; courses in business administration, tourism and leisure management; library: 37,050 vols, 39 databases; 37 teachers; 1,302 students; Dir-Gen. JEAN GUY BERNARD.

Ecole du Chef d'Entreprise (ECE): 24–26 rue Hamelin, 75116 Paris; f. 1944; business administration; 50 teachers; Pres. M. Y. CHOTARD; Dir C. GOURDAIN; Sec.-Gen. M. JANNOR.

Ecole Nouvelle d'Organisation Economique et Sociale—Groupe ENOES: 62 rue de Miromesnil, 75008 Paris; internet www.enoes.com; f. 1937; courses in transport and logistics, business administration and accountancy; Pres. GILLES DE COURCEL; Gen. Sec. MICHEL OHAYON.

Ecole Supérieure de Commerce de Montpellier: 2300 ave des Moulins, 34185 Montpellier Cedex 4; tel. 4-67-10-25-00; e-mail info@supco-montpellier.fr; internet www.supdeco-montpellier.com; f. 1897; 250 teachers; 1,750 students; 3-year courses in business administration and management sciences; Dir Dr DIDIER JOURDAN.

Ecole Supérieure des Sciences Economiques et Commerciales (ESSEC Business School—Paris): Ave Bernard Hirsch, BP 50105, 95021 Cergy-Pontoise Cedex; tel. 1-34-43-30-00; e-mail indigo@essec.fr; internet www.essec.com; f. 1907; 4-year, 3-year, 2-year and 1-year degree courses; Masters degree in business administration and management; MSc in agribusiness management, finance, information and decision systems, international law and management, international supply management, logistics, marketing, strategy and management of international business, and urban management; MBA programmes in hospitality, luxury-brand management; Exec. MBA and other executive education courses; doctoral and BBA programmes; library: 49,000 vols, 1,500 periodicals; 370 teachers (100 full-time, 270 part-time); 3,700 students; Pres. PIERRE TAPIE.

EDHEC Business School: 58 rue du Port, 59046 Lille Cedex; tel. 3-20-15-45-00; internet www.edhec.com; f. 1906; MBA programmes; Dir-Gen. OLIVIER OGER.

EMLYON Business School: 23 ave Guy de Collongue, 69134 Ecully Cedex; tel. 4-78-33-78-00; e-mail info@em-lyon.com; internet www.em-lyon.com; f. 1872; library: 12,927 vols; 80 teachers; 1,250 students; Dir-Gen. PATRICK MOLLE.

ESC Bretagne Brest: 2 ave de Provence, CS23812, 29238 Brest Cedex 3; tel. 2-98-34-44-44; e-mail info@esc-bretagne-brest.com; internet www.esc-brest.fr; f. 1962; library: 5,000 vols, 150 periodicals; 110 teachers; 533 students; Dir C. MONIQUE.

ESC Pau—Groupe Ecole Supérieure de Commerce de Pau: 3 rue Saint John Perse, Campus Universitaire BP 7512, 64075 Pau Cedex; tel. 5-59-92-64-64; e-mail info@esc-pau.fr; internet www.esc-pau.fr; f. 1970 by the Chamber of Commerce; library: 5,000 vols; 136 teachers (16 full-time, 120 part-time); 500 students; Dir LAURENT HUA.

ESCP-EAP European School of Management: 79 ave de la République, 75543 Paris Cedex 11; tel. 1-49-23-20-00; e-mail info@escp-eap.net; internet www.escp-eap.net; f. 1999 by merger of Groupe ESCP and Ecole Européenne des Affaires (EAP); 120 teachers in 5 countries; 3,000 students in 5 countries; campuses in Paris (France), London (UK), Berlin (Germany), Madrid (Spain) and Turin (Italy); postgraduate degree programmes, executive education; 5 research centres; Dean JEAN-LOUIS SCARINGELLA.

ESC Bordeaux: 680 cours de la Libération, 33405 Talence Cedex; tel. 5-56-84-55-55; e-mail info@bem.edu; internet www.bem.edu; f. 1874 by Chamber of Commerce; library: 17,000 vols; 74 teachers; 1,800 students; Dir GEORGES VIALA.

ESCEM—Groupe Ecole Supérieure de Commerce et de Management: 1 rue Léo Delibes, BP 0535, 37205 Tours Cedex 3; tel. 2-47-71-71-71; e-mail com@escem.fr; internet www.escem.fr; f. 1961; graduate management degree programme, Masters and int. MBA degree programmes, continuing education and distance learning in management; courses in accountancy, economics, finance, international business, management information systems, marketing; Masters degrees in business administration and information systems; library: 13,000 vols; 405 teachers (55 full-time, 350 part-time); 1,600 students; Dir GUY LE BOUCHER; publ. *Les Cahiers de Recherche de l'ESCEM* (2 a year).

Branch campus:

Groupe ESCEM Campus Poitiers: 11 rue de l'Ancienne Comédie, BP 5, 86001 Poitiers Cedex; tel. 5-49-60-58-00; internet www.escem.fr.

ESIDEC—Ecole Supérieure Internationale de Commerce de Metz: 3 place Edouard Branly, BP 95090, 57073 Metz Cedex 3; tel. 3-87-56-37-37; e-mail gregory.marongio@icn-groupe.fr; internet www.esidec.fr; f. 1988; run by the Moselle Chamber of Commerce and Industry; courses in management, logistics, marketing, finance, law, trade, purchasing; 40 teachers; 210 students; Dir THIERRY JEAN.

Groupe CPA—Centre de Perfectionnement aux Affaires: 14 ave de la Porte de Champerret, 75017 Paris; tel. 1-44-09-34-00; f. 1930; gen. management courses for top executives; establishing close links with Groupe HEC (Hautes Etudes Commerciales); see entry for HEC School of Management for details of br. institutions; Dir JEAN-LOUIS SCARINGELLA.

Groupe EAC—Ecole Supérieure d'Economie, d'Art et de Communication: 33 rue de La Boétie, 75008 Paris; tel. 1-47-70-23-83; e-mail paris@groupeeac.com; internet www.groupeeac.com; f. 1987; library: 500 vols; 70 teachers; 350 students; Dir CLAUDE VIVIER.

Groupe ESC Lille—Ecole Supérieure de Commerce de Lille: Ave Willy Brandt, 59777 Euralille; tel. 3-20-21-59-62; internet www.esc-lille.fr; f. 1892; library: 3,700 vols, 270 periodicals; 1,000 students; Dir JEAN-PIERRE DEBOURSE.

HEC School of Management: 78351 Jouy-en-Josas Cedex; tel. 1-39-67-70-00; e-mail hecinfo@hec.fr; internet www.hec.edu; f. 1881; sponsored by the Paris Chamber of Commerce and Industry; incorporates CPA (Centre de Perfectionnement aux Affaires); degree courses in fields of management; executive development programmes; library: 60,000 vols; 589 teachers (104 full-time, 450 part-time, 35 visiting); 2,500 students; Dean BERNARD RAMANANTSOA; Dir of CPA JEAN-MARC DE LEERSNYDER.

CPA Sites:

CPA Grand Sud-Ouest: 20 blvd Lascrosses, 31000 Toulouse; tel. 5-61-29-49-91; Dir ALAIN MAINGUY.

CPA Lyon: 93 chemin des Mouilles, 69130 Ecully Cedex; tel. 4-78-33-52-12; Dir CHARLES AB-DER-HALDEN.

CPA Madrid: Calle Serrano 208, 28012 Madrid, Spain; tel. 91-538-37-59; Dir TEODORO AGUADO DE LOS RÍOS.

CPA Méditerranée: c/o CERAM II, 60 rue Dostoïevski, 06902 Sophia Antipolis; tel. 4-92-96-96-95; Dir ADRIEN CORBIÈRE-MÉDECIN.

CPA Nord: 551 rue Albert Bailly, 59700 Marcq-en-Baroeul; tel. 3-20-25-97-53; Dir JEAN-CLAUDE VACHER.

CPA Paris: 14 ave de la Porte de Champerret, 75017 Paris; tel. 1-44-09-34-00.

INSEAD: Blvd de Constance, 77305 Fontainebleau; tel. 1-60-72-40-00; internet www.insead.fr; f. 1958; postgraduate MBA programme; PhD programme; executive development programmes; 100 professors; library: 40,000 vols; Chair. Board of Govs CLAUDE JANSSEN; Dean Prof. GABRIEL HAWAWINI.

Reims Management School: 59 rue Pierre-Taittinger, 51100 Reims Cedex; tel. 3-26-77-47-47; e-mail service.com@reims-ms.fr; internet www.reims-ms.fr; f. 1928; schools and subject areas: Cesem (International School of Management), MBA (part- and full-time), Sup de Co (new economy), Sup TG (sales and administration), Tema (management school with emphasis on technology); 62 full-time teachers; 2,600 students; Dir DOMINIQUE WAQUET.

LAW AND POLITICAL SCIENCE

American Graduate School of International Relations and Diplomacy: 6 rue de Lubeck, 75116 Paris; tel. 1-47-20-00-94; e-mail info@agsird.edu; internet www.agsird.edu; f. 1994; MA and PhD programmes; 11 teachers; 90 students (50 full-time, 40 part-time); Dir Dr MARCIA A. GRANT.

Ecole des Hautes Etudes Internationales: 107 rue de Tolbiac, 75013 Paris; tel. 1-45-70-73-37; e-mail contact@hep-hei-esj.net; internet www.hep-hei-esj.net; f. 1904; Pres. M. SCHUMANN; Dir P. CHAIGNEAU.

Ecole de Notariat d'Amiens: 44 square des 4 Chênes, 80000 Amiens; tel. 3-22-92-61-26; e-mail ecolenotariat-amiens@wanadoo.fr; internet www.cr-picardie.notaires.fr/front/actualites/ecolenotariat.asp; f. 1942; Dir ALAIN DORÉ.

Ecole de Notariat de Paris: 9 rue Villaret-de-Joyeuse, 75017 Paris; tel. 1-43-80-87-62; f. 1896; Dir M. P. MATHIEU.

Ecole Supérieure de Journalisme: 107 rue Tolbiac, 75013 Paris; tel. 1-45-70-73-37; e-mail contact@hep-hei-esj.net; internet www.hep-hei-esj.net; f. 1899; Pres. M. CAZENEUVE; Dir P. CHAIGNEAU.

Institut International des Droits de l'Homme (International Institute of Human Rights): 2 Allée René Cassin, 67000 Strasbourg; tel. 3-88-45-84-45; e-mail administration@iidh.org; internet www.iidh.org; f. 1969 by René Cassin; postgraduate teaching in international and comparative law of human rights; annual study session during July; annual 2-week course in June on refugee law, organized in collaboration with the UN High Commr for Refugees (in French); 50 teachers; 350 students; Pres. GÉRARD COHEN-JONATHAN; Sec.-Gen. JEAN-FRANÇOIS FLAUSS..

Attached Centre:

International Centre for University Human Rights Teaching: Strasbourg; f. 1973 at the request of UNESCO; 2-week courses for univ. teachers; 2 teachers; 40 students; Sec.-Gen. Prof. JEAN-FRANÇOIS FLAUSS.

MEDICINE

Ecole Dentaire Française: 1 bis 3 rue de l'Est, 75020 Paris; tel. 1-47-97-77-81; e-mail edf@lesmetiersdelasante.com; internet www.ecole-dentaire.fr; f. 1886; Dir R. J. CACHIA.

Institut et Centre d'Optométrie: 134 route de Chartres, 91440 Bures-sur-Yvette; tel. 1-64-86-12-13; e-mail ico.direction@wanadoo.fr; internet www.ecole-optometrie.fr; f. 1917; 40 teachers; 350 students; Dir JEAN-PAUL ROOSEN.

RELIGION

Faculté Libre de Théologie Protestante de Paris: 83 blvd Arago, 75014 Paris; tel. 1-43-31-61-64; e-mail secretariat@iptheologie.fr; internet www.iptheologie.fr; f. 1877; religious history, Old and New Testament, ecclesiastical history, systematic theology, philosophy, practical theology, Hebrew, Greek, German, English; library: 60,000 vols; 12 professors, 180 students; Dean JACQUES-NOËL PÉRÈS.

Institut Européen des Sciences Humaines: Centre de Bouteloin, 58120 Saint-Léger-de-Fougeret; tel. 3-86-79-40-62; internet www.iesh.org; f. 1990; Muslim theology; library: 5,000 vols; 8 teachers; 200 students; Dir ZUHAIR MAHMOOD.

Institut Orthodoxe Français de Paris Saint-Denys: 96 blvd Auguste-Blanqui, 75013 Paris; tel. 6-89-32-25-38; e-mail institut.saintdenys@club-internet.fr; internet institutdetheologie.free.fr; f. 1944; faculties of theology and philosophy; library: 5,000 vols; 20 professors; 125 students; Rector BERTRAND-HARDY (Bishop Germain of Saint Denis); publ. *Présence Orthodoxe*.

Institut de Théologie Orthodoxe Saint-Serge: 93 rue de Crimée, 75019 Paris; tel. 1-42-01-96-10; e-mail ito@saint-serge.net; internet www.saint-serge.net; f. 1925; library: 30,000 vols; 15 professors; 50 students; Dean Rev. Fr BORIS BOBRINSKOY; publ. *Pensée Orthodoxe* (every 2 years).

Séminaire Israélite de France (Ecole Rabbinique): 9 rue Vauquelin, 75005 Paris; tel. 1-47-07-21-22; f. 1829; Talmud, Bible, Jewish history and philosophy, Hebrew language and literature studies, rabbinical law; library: 60,000 vols; 6 teachers; 15 students; Dir Chief Rabbi MICHEL GUGENHEIM.

SCIENCES

Ecole d'Anthropologie: 1 place d'Iéna, 75116 Paris; tel. 1-47-93-09-73; e-mail institutanthropologie@hotmail.fr; internet www.multimania.com/anthropa; f. 1876; anthropotechnics, biology, biometeorology, criminology, demography, ethnography, ethnology, genetics, immunology, physical anthropology, prehistory, psychology, third-world problems; Dir Prof. BERNARD J. HUET; publ. *Nouvelle revue anthropologique* (irregular).

Institut de Paléontologie Humaine: 1 rue René Panhard, 75013 Paris; tel. 1-43-31-62-91; e-mail iph@mnhn.fr; f. 1910; geochronology, palaeo-anthropology, palynology, prehistory, quaternary geology, sedimentology, vertebrate palaeontology; library: 25,000 vols; 107 students; Dir HENRY DE LUMLEY; publs *Archives*, *Etudes Quaternaires*, *L'Anthropologie*.

Institut Edouard Toulouse: 1 rue Cabanis, 75014 Paris; tel. 1-45-65-81-36; f. 1983; teaching, training and research in psychiatry, seminars on psychoanalysis; Pres. Dr JEAN AYME; Sec. Dr MARCEL CZERMAK; publ. *Cahiers de l'Hôpital Henri Rousselle*.

Institut Océanographique: 195 rue Saint Jacques, 75005 Paris; tel. 1-44-32-10-70; e-mail institut@oceano.org; internet www.oceano.org; f. 1906 by Prince Albert I of Monaco; education, scientific research, museology, publishing; library: 30,000 vols; Pres. JEAN CHAPON; Dir LUCIEN LAUBIEN; Sec. C. BEAUVERGER; publ. *Oceanis* (4 a year).

Attached Museum:

Musée Océanographique: see under Monaco.

SOCIAL AND ECONOMIC SCIENCES

Collège Libre des Sciences Sociales et Economiques: 184 blvd Saint-Germain, 75006 Paris; f. 1895; composed of 6 sections: social, economic, international and public relations; evening and correspondence courses; diplomas conferred after 2 or 3 years' study, and submission of theses on some aspect of applied economics; Pres. J. RUEFF; Dir L. DE SAINTE-LORETTE.

Ecole de Hautes Etudes Sociales: 107 rue Tolbiac, 75013 Paris; tel. 1-45-70-73-37; e-mail contact@hep-hei-esj.net; internet www.hep-hei-esj.net; f. 1899; Pres. M. SCHUMANN; Dir P. CHAIGNEAU.

Faculté des Lettres et Sciences Sociales: BP 800, 29200 Brest; tel. 2-98-80-19-87; f. 1960; library: 18,000 vols; 105 teachers; 2,752 students; Pres. and Dean Prof. MICHEL QUESNEL.

IFG-CNOF: 37 quai de Grenelle, 75015 Paris; tel. 1-40-59-30-30; internet www.ifgcnof.com; f. 1926; provides executive, managerial and administrative training.

Institut Européen des Hautes Etudes Internationales (IEHEI): 10 ave des Fleurs, 06000 Nice; tel. 4-93-97-93-70; e-mail iehei@wanadoo.fr; internet www.iehei.org; f. 1964; library: 4,000 vols; 20 teachers; 35 students; Pres. VLAD CONSTANTINESCO; Dir CLAUDE NIGOUL.

TECHNOLOGY

Ecole Catholique d'Arts et Métiers (ECAM): 40 montée Saint-Barthélemy, 69321 Lyons Cedex 05; tel. 4-72-77-06-00; e-mail info@ecam.fr; internet www.ecam.fr; f. 1900; courses in mechanical engineering, materials science, electrical and electronic engineering, automation, information technology, production engineering; library: 5,000 vols; 525 students; Dir BERNARD PINATEL; publ. *Bulletin* (4 a year).

Ecole de Thermique: 3 rue Henri Heine, 75016 Paris; tel. 1-44-30-41-00; teaching centre for the Institut Français de l'Energie (IFE); Dir (vacant).

Ecole Généraliste d'Ingénieurs de Marseille (EGIM): Technopôle de Château-Gombert, 38 rue Joliot Curie, 13451 Marseilles Cedex 20; tel. 4-91-05-45-45; e-mail sdei@egim-mrs.fr; internet www.egim-mrs

.fr; f. 1891; specialist courses in civil engineering, information and communications technology, marine engineering, mechanical and materials engineering, mechatronics, microelectronics design, systems engineering, thermal systems engineering; 70 teachers; 778 students; Dir JEAN-PAUL FABRE.

Ecole Spéciale des Travaux Publics, du Bâtiment et de l'Industrie: 57 blvd Saint-Germain, 75005 Paris; tel. 1-44-41-11-18; e-mail information@adm.estp.fr; internet www.estp.fr; f. 1891; civil engineering training programmes at undergraduate and graduate levels; continuing education courses; library: 10,000 vols; 700 teachers; 2,000 students; Dir S. EYROLLES.

Ecole Supérieure d'Optique et Institut d'Optique: Centre Scientifique d'Orsay, Bât. 503, 91403 Orsay Cedex; tel. 1-69-35-88-88; e-mail international@iota.u-psud.fr; internet www.institutoptique.fr; f. 1920; attached to Univ. Paris XI; optical engineering, optics and photonics at postgraduate level; 60 teachers (20 full-time, 40 assoc.); 240 students; Dir Prof. ANDRÉ DUCASSE.

Ecole Supérieure de Fonderie et de Forge: 44 ave de la division Leclerc, 92310 Sèvres; tel. 1-55-64-04-40; e-mail contact@esff.fr; internet www.esff.fr; f. 1923; library: 2,150 vols; Dir G. CHAPPUIS.

Ecole Supérieure des Industries du Vêtement: 73 blvd Saint-Marcel, 75013 Paris; tel. 1-40-79-92-60; e-mail info@esiv.fr; internet www.esiv.fr; f. 1946; 14 teachers; 70 students; Dir ANNE STEFANINI.

Ecole Supérieure des Industries Textiles d'Epinal: 85 rue d'Alsace, 88025 Epinal Cedex; tel. 3-29-35-50-52; e-mail esite@wanadoo.fr; f. 1905; training of industrial textile engineers; library: 1,500 vols; Dir J. TIERCET.

Ecole Supérieure des Techniques Aéronautiques et de Construction Automobile: 34 rue Victor Hugo, 92300 Levallois-Perret; tel. 1-41-27-37-00; e-mail infos@estaca.fr; internet www.estaca.fr; f. 1925; private school offering 5-year courses in aeronautical, automotive, railway and space engineering; Masters course in safety of transportation systems (taught in English); EUROMIND, European Masters in design and technology of advanced vehicle systems (taught in English); 1,000 students; Dir ERIC PARLEBAS.

Ecole Supérieure du Bois: rue Christian Pauc, BP 10605, 44306 Nantes Cedex 3; tel. 2-40-18-12-12; e-mail contact@ecolesuperieuredubois.com; internet www.ecolesuperieuredubois.com; f. 1934; training of engineers and management for wood industry; 33 teachers (13 full-time, 20 external); 250 students; Dir X. MARTIN.

Ecole Supérieure du Soudage et de ses Applications (Advanced Postgraduate Welding Engineering School): BP 50362, 95942 Roissy CDG Cedex; tel. 1-49-90-36-27; e-mail m.d.jols@institutdesoudure.com; internet www.institutdesoudure.com; f. 1930; 55 teachers; 30 students; Dir MICHEL DIJOLS.

Ecole Technique Supérieure du Laboratoire: 95 rue du Dessous-des Berges, 75013 Paris; tel. 1-45-83-76-34; e-mail mail@etsl.fr; internet www.etsl.fr; f. 1934; Pres. J. CHOMIENNE; Dir F. LAISSUS.

EFREI—Ecole Française d'Electronique et d'Informatique: 30–32 ave de la République, 94815 Villejuif; tel. 1-46-77-64-67; e-mail admission@efrei.fr; internet www.efrei.fr; f. 1936; courses in telecommunications, electronic engineering and computer science; 50 teachers; 1,170 students; Dir ERIC PARLEBAS.

EPF—Ecole d'Ingénieurs: 3 bis rue Lakanal, 92330 Sceaux; tel. 1-41-13-01-51; internet www.epf.fr; f. 1925; engineering training; Pres. Dr ALAIN JENEVEAU.

ESIEE Paris: Cité Descartes, BP 99, 93162 Noisy-le-Grand Cedex; tel. 1-45-92-65-00; e-mail admissions@esiee.fr; internet www.esiee.fr; f. 1962; computer science, automation, telecommunications, signal processing, microelectronics; library: 18,000 vols; 100 teachers; 1,000 students; Dir ALAIN CADIX.

ESME Sudria: 38 rue Molière, 94200 Ivry-sur-Seine; 51 blvd de Brandenbourg, 94200 Ivry-sur-Seine; tel. 1-56-20-62-00; e-mail contact@esme.fr; internet www.esme.fr; f. 1905; training in electrical engineering, electronics, telecommunications and computer engineering; Dir-Gen. HERVÉ LABORNE.

European Institute of Technology: 8 rue Saint Florentin, 75001 Paris; tel. 1-40-15-05-69; f. 1988 to strengthen industrial research and development, and to increase the contribution of technological innovation to economic growth in Europe; Sec.-Gen. JOHN M. MARCUM.

IFOCA—Institut National de Formation et d'Enseignement Professionnel du Caoutchouc: 60 rue Auber, 94408 Vitry-sur-Seine Cedex; tel. 1-49-60-57-57; e-mail info@ifoca.com; internet www.ifoca.com; f. 1941; 8 teachers; 35 students; Dir GÉRARD GALLAS.

Institut Français Textile—Habillement: ave Guy de Collongue, 69134 Ecully Cedex; tel. 4-72-86-16-00; e-mail information@ifth.org; internet www.ifth.org; f. 1946; library: 255 vols and documents; Dir M. BEDEAU.

Institut Textile et Chimique de Lyon (ITECH): 87 chemin des Mouilles, 69134 Ecully Cedex; tel. 4-72-18-04-80; e-mail info@itech.fr; internet www.itech.fr; f. 1899; diploma courses in leather technology, painting and adhesives technology; plastics, textiles; 120 teachers; 360 students; Dir JEAN-PIERRE GALLET; Dean CHRISTIANE BASSET.

International Space University: Parc d'Innovation, 1 rue Jean Dominique Cassini, 67400 Illkirch-Graffenstaden; tel. 3-88-65-54-30; e-mail info@isu.isunet.edu; internet www.isunet.edu; f. 1987; offers Master of Space Studies and Master of Space Management degree programmes, introductory space course and a summer session programme; 6 full-time, 6 part-time and 100 visiting teachers; 150 students; Pres. Dr MICHAEL SIMPSON.

Supélec—Ecole Supérieure d'Electricité: Plateau du Moulon, 3 rue Joliot-Curie, 91192 Gif-sur-Yvette Cedex; tel. 1-69-85-12-12; internet www.supelec.fr; campuses at Gif, Metz and Rennes; f. 1894; attached to Univ. Paris XI; 2- or 3-year courses in electrical engineering, radio engineering, information science, electronics and computer science; 120 permanent teachers; 1,200 students; Dir-Gen. J. J. DUBY; Dir of Studies F. MESA; Gen. Sec. A. POTONNIER.

SUPINFO—Ecole Supérieure d'Informatique: 23 rue du Château Landon, 75010 Paris; tel. 1-53-35-97-00; e-mail paris@supinfo.com; internet www.supinfo.com; f. 1965; 90 teachers; 1,000 students; Dir LEO ROZENTALIS; publ. *Dossiers de l'Association pour la Promotion de l'Ecole Supérieure d'Informatique*.

Schools of Art and Music

Conservatoire à Rayonnement Régional de Boulogne-Billancourt—Centre Georges-Gorse: 22 rue de la Belle-Feuille, 92100 Boulogne-Billancourt; tel. 1-55-18-45-85; internet www.bb-cnr.com; f. 1959 as Conservatoire de Boulogne-Billancourt; achieved nat. school status as Conservatoire National de Région de Musique et de Danse de Boulogne-Billancourt in 1979; present name and status 2007; library: 7,000 books, 40 periodicals, 20,000 scores, 6,000 records, 600 audiovisual and multimedia items; 90 teachers; 1,650 students; Dir ALAIN LOUVIER.

Conservatoire National de Région de Musique et de Danse de Lyon: 4 montée Cardinal Decourtray, 69321 Lyons; tel. 4-78-25-91-39; e-mail communication@conservatoire-lyon.fr; internet www.conservatoire-lyon.fr; f. 1872; library: 2,600 vols, 40,000 scores, 4,500 records, 2,000 orchestral scores; 190 teachers; 2,900 students; Dir ALAIN JACQUON.

Conservatoire National Supérieur d'Art Dramatique: 2 bis rue du Conservatoire, 75009 Paris; tel. 1-42-46-12-91; e-mail communication@cnsad.fr; internet www.cnsad.fr; f. 1786; library: 23,500 vols; 55 teachers; 100 students; Dir DANIEL MESGUICH.

Conservatoire National Supérieur de Musique et de Danse de Paris: 209 ave Jean Jaurès, 75019 Paris; tel. 1-40-40-45-45; e-mail cnsmdp@cnsmdp.fr; internet www.cnsmdp.fr; f. 1795; 386 teachers; 1,413 students; Dir ALAIN POIRIER.

Conservatoire National Supérieur Musique et Danse de Lyon: 3 quai Chauveau, CP 120, 69266 Lyons Cedex 09; tel. 4-72-19-26-26; e-mail cnsmd@cnsmd-lyon.fr; internet www.cnsmd-lyon.fr; f. 1980; library: 42,000 vols; 170 teachers; 550 students; Dir HENRY FOURÈS.

Ecole du Louvre: Palais du Louvre, Porte Jaujard, Place du Carrousel, 75038 Paris Cedex 01; tel. 1-55-35-18-00; internet www.ecoledulouvre.fr; f. 1882; library: 40,000 vols; 1,700 students; Prin. PH. DUREY; Sec.-Gen. M. C. DEVEVEY.

Ecole Nationale Supérieure des Arts Décoratifs (ENSAD): 31 rue d'Ulm, 75240 Paris Cedex 05; tel. 1-42-34-97-00; e-mail info@ensad.fr; internet www.ensad.fr; f. 1766; visual arts and design; library: 15,000 vols and spec. collns; 164 teachers; 600 students; Dirs ELIZABETH FLEURY PATRICK RAYNAUD; publs *Catalogue des Projets de Fin d'Etudes* (2 a year), *Journal des Arts-Déco* (3 a year).

Ecole Nationale Supérieure des Beaux-Arts: 14 rue Bonaparte, 75272 Paris Cedex 06; tel. 1-47-03-50-00; f. 1648 as Académie Royale de Peinture et de Sculpture, and in 1671 as Académie Royale d'Architecture; library: 120,000 vols; 75 teachers; 650 students; Dir (vacant); publs *Beaux-Arts Histoire*, *Ecrits d'Artistes*, *Espaces de l'art*.

Ecole Supérieure d'Art Clermont Communauté: 142 ave Jean Mermoz, 63100 Clermont-Ferrand; tel. 4-73-91-43-86; e-mail erba@ville-clermont-ferrand.fr; internet www.ecoledart.ville-clermont-ferrand.fr; f. 1882; library: 7,000 vols and spec. collns; 17 teachers; 130 students; Dir SYLVAIN LIZON.

Ecole Supérieure des Beaux-Arts de Marseille: 184 ave de Luminy, 13288 Marseilles Cedex 9; tel. 4-91-82-83-10; e-mail fballongue@mairie-marseille.fr; internet www.esbam.fr; f. 1710; library: 15,000 vols; 420 students; Dir NORBERT DUFFORT; publ. *Verba Volant* (2 a year).

Schola Cantorum: 269 rue St Jacques, 75005 Paris; tel. 1-43-54-15-39; e-mail info@schola-cantorum.com; internet www.schola-cantorum.com; f. 1896 by Vincent d'Indy; music, dance and dramatic art; Dir MICHEL DENIS.

FRENCH GUIANA

The Higher Education System

French occupation of the land that is now French Guiana commenced in 1604. After brief periods of Dutch, English and Portuguese rule, fuelled by rumours of potential gold and diamond reserves, the territory was finally confirmed as French in 1817. The colony, hitherto known as Cayenne, became an Overseas Department of France in 1946, with the same laws and administration as a department of metropolitan France. In 1974 French Guiana was granted regional status, as part of France's governmental reorganization, thus acquiring greater economic autonomy. In March 2003 a constitutional amendment conferred the status of Overseas Region (Région d'outre-mer) on French Guiana.

Education in French Guiana is modelled on the French system and, as such, is compliant with the Bologna Process. Successful completion of the Baccalauréat is required for entrance into tertiary institutions. Higher education in law, administration and French language and literature is provided by a branch of the Université des Antilles et de la Guyane (UAG), an institution whose roots date back to 1880, but which was formally established in 1970 and granted full university status in 1982. It has campuses in Cayenne and Korou, as well as branches in Guadeloupe (where its headquarters are located) and in Martinique. In 2011 the Institut Universitaire de Formation des Maîtres (IUFM—French Guiana University Institute for Teacher Training) was incorporated into the French Guiana branch of the UAG. The Licence (Bachelors degree) is required for admission into the IUFM. The programme at this institute lasts two years, the first for further specialization in a discipline and the second for teacher training in that discipline. The general administration of the UAG, which is divided into divisions, departments and offices, comes under the overall authority of the President of the University and is managed on a day-to-day basis by a Secretary-General. There are also three governing boards : the Board of Directors, the Scientific Council and the Board of Studies and University Life. The UAG offers a range of courses, including, at undergraduate level, certificates, diplomas, Associate and Bachelors degrees, and, at postgraduate level, Masters and Doctorate degrees. The University is accredited by the French Ministry of Higher Education and Research. In addition to the UAG, there is also a technical institute at Kourou and an agricultural college. A musicology programme is offered at the Community College of French Guiana and is available to students of Guadeloupe and Martinique via distance learning. In 2011/12 a total of 2,720 students were enrolled in higher education in French Guiana, of whom 1,943 were studying at the UAG campus in Cayenne. Many students undertake their further education in France or in the French West Indies.

Vocational education is the responsibility of the Department of Work, Employment and Educational Training, which is responsible for setting educational standards.

Regulatory Bodies

GOVERNMENT

Council of Culture, Education and Environment: 66 ave du Général de Gaulle, 97300 Cayenne; tel. 5-94-25-66-84; e-mail ccee@cr-guyane.fr; internet www.cr-guyane.fr/institution-region/organisation-politique/le-ccee; Pres. JEAN-PIERRE BACOT.

Learned Societies

LANGUAGE AND LITERATURE

Alliance Française: 2 pl. du marché, 97300 Cayenne; tel. 5-94-30-98-72; e-mail administration@af-cayenne.com; internet www.af-cayenne.com; f. 2007; offers courses and exams in French language; Pres. LAËTITIA COPIN.

Research Institutes

GENERAL

Centre National de la Recherche Scientifique (National Centre for Scientific Research): 2 ave Gustave Charlery, 97300 Cayenne; tel. 5-94-35-27-99; e-mail ups2561@cnrs-dir.fr; internet www.guyane.cnrs.fr; f. 2000; devt of regional research on Amazonian ecosystem; conducts research in science, technology and humanities; Dir ANNE CORVAL; Sec. JOSIANE PAUCHONT; publ. *Année* (1 a year).

Institut de Recherche pour le Développement (Institute of Research for Development): 275 route de Montabo, BP 165, 97323 Cayenne; tel. 5-94-29-92-92; e-mail guyane@ird.fr; internet www.guyane.ird.fr; f. 1949; researches on plant biodiversity, forest ecosystems, relationship between man and environment, languages and cultures of Amazonian environment, migration and cross-border mobility; see main entry under France; library of 7,000 vols; Rep. PATRICK SEYLER; publ. *L'Homme et la Nature en Guyane*.

Unité Mixte de Recherche Ecologie des Forêts de Guyane (Joint Research Unit Ecology of Guiana Forests): Campus Agronomique de Kourou, BP 316, 97310 Kourou; tel. 5-94-32-93-00; e-mail eft@ecofog.gf; internet www.ecofog.gf; researches relations between diversity and ecosystem functioning, effects of exploitation, anthropic pressure and global change; innovations to valorize forest resources; Dir ERIC MARCON.

EDUCATION

Institut de Recherche sur l'Enseignement en Mathématiques (Institute for Research in Mathematics Education): Cayenne; tel. 5-90-48-30-43; e-mail irem.antilles-guyana@univ-ag.fr; internet www.univ-ag.fr/fr/institution/instituts/irem.html; research in mathematics education; training; Dir RÉGIS BLACHE.

MEDICINE

Institut Pasteur de la Guyane (Pasteur Institute of French Guiana): 23 ave Pasteur, BP 6010, 97306 Cayenne; tel. 5-94-29-26-00; internet www.pasteur-cayenne.fr; f. 1940, fmrly Institut d'Hygiène et de Prophylaxie; medical and biological research; Dir PHILIPPE QUENEL.

Libraries and Archives

Cayenne

Archives Départementales (Departmental Archives): 1, pl. Léopold Héder, BP 5021, 97300 Cayenne; tel. 5-94-29-52-70; internet www.cg973.fr/archives-departementales; f. 1983; history of French Guiana; classification; storage; research; Dir SANDRA MONTABORD.

Bibliothèque Alexandre Franconie: 1 ave du Général de Gaulle, 97300 Cayenne; tel. 5-94-29-59-16; e-mail bibliotheque.franconie@cg973.fr; internet bibliotheques.cg973.fr; f. 1885; attached to Bibliothèques du Conseil Général de la Guyane (Library of the Gen. Council of Guiana); 50,000 vols; Dir MARIE-ANNICK ATTICOT.

Service Commun de la Documentation (Bibliothèques de la Guyane) (Common Documentation Service (Library of French Guiana)): Campus St-Denis, BP 1179, 97346 Cayenne; tel. 5-94-29-40-46; e-mail nicole.clementmartin@guyane.univ-ag.fr; internet buag.univ-ag.fr; f. 1984; attached to Université des Antilles et de la Guyane; 36,000 vols, 240 periodicals; Dir of French Guiana Br. NICOLE CLÉMENT-MARTIN.

Museums

Cayenne

Musée Départemental Alexandre-Franconie (Alexandre Franconie Departmental Museum): 1 ave du Général de Gaulle, 97300 Cayenne; tel. 5-94-29-59-13; e-mail musee@cg973.fr; internet musee.cg973.fr; f. 1901; flora and fauna of Guiana; entomology; historical documents; ethnography; Guiana's penal colony (Devil's Island); library of 300 vols; Dir DAVID CARITA; Sec. ROBERTE STANISLAS.

Musée des Cultures Guyanaises (Museum of Guianese Cultures): 78 rue Mme Payé, 97300 Cayenne; tel. 5-94-31-41-72; e-mail mcg87@wanadoo.fr; f. 1998; exhibitions and documentation centre on social history and culture of French Guiana; housed in a typical Guianese house built over 100 years ago; incl. an indoor garden with aromatic and medicinal plants; Dir. MARIE-PAULE JEAN-LOUIS.

University

UNIVERSITÉ DES ANTILLES ET DE LA GUYANE
(University of the French West Indies and Guiana)

Campus de Saint-Denis, BP 1179, 97346 Cayenne
Telephone: 5-94-29-40-16
E-mail: charge.communication@guyane.univ-ag.fr
Internet: www.univ-ag.fr
Founded 1970, current name adopted 1982
State control
(See also under Guadeloupe and Martinique)
Pres.: CORINNE MENCE-CASTER
Vice-Pres. (French Guiana): M. ANTOINE PRIMEROSE
Library: see under Libraries and Archives
Number of students: 1,692

Other Higher Educational Institutes

Institut d'Enseignement Supérieur de la Guyane (Institute of Higher Education of French Guiana): N°2091 Rte de Baduel, BP 792, 97337 Cayenne; tel. 5-94-29-92-10; internet www.univ-ag.fr/fr/institution/instituts/iesg.html; f. 1991; attached to Univ. des Antilles et de la Guyane; depts of arts, languages and humanities, law and economics, science and technology; 1,800 students; Dir RENÉ DORVILLE.

Institut Universitaire de Technologie (University Institute of Technology): ave Bois Chaudat, BP 725, 97310 Kourou; tel. 5-94-32-80-00; internet iut.univ-ag.fr; f. 1986, opened 1988; attached to Univ. des Antilles et de la Guyane; offers Bachelors and Masters courses in electrical engineering and industrial computing, network and telecommunication, marketing techniques, administration and network securities, marketing; 200 students; Dir OLLIVIER TAMARIND.

FRENCH POLYNESIA

The Higher Education System

Tahiti, the largest of the Society Islands, and the other island groups were annexed by France in the late 19th century. The islands were governed from France under a decree of 1885 until 1946, when French Polynesia became an Overseas Territory administered by a Governor in the capital, Papeete (from 1977 the islands were administered by a High Commissioner). In March 2004 French Polynesia was formally designated as an Overseas Country (Pays d'outre-mer) of France. Its status is that of an Overseas Collectivity (Collectivité d'outre-mer). Although French Polynesia has gradually attained greater autonomy over the years, France continues to control various important spheres of government, including defence, foreign diplomacy and justice.

The country's only university was established in 1987 as the French University of the Pacific (Université de la Polynésie Française), with two centres, one in the French Polynesian capital of Papeete and the other in New Caledonia. In 1997 the decision was made to split the two parts into separate universities; accordingly, in 1999 the University of French Polynesia (Université de la Polynésie Française) and the University of New Caledonis (Université de la Nouvelle Calédonie) were formed. In 2008/09 the Pacific Institute for Teacher Training (Institut Universitaire de Formation des Maîtres, IUFM du Pacifique) was incorporated into the University of French Polynesia. In 2011/12 a total of 3,211 students were enrolled there. The University offers courses in business, economics, health, languages, law, literature, political science, sciences and teacher training, social sciences. The qualifications available include certificates, diplomas, Bachelors, Masters and Doctorates. As in France, the degree programmes are compliant with the Bologna Process.

Technical and professional education includes eight technical institutions, a tourism training programme, preparation for entrance to the metropolitan Grandes Ecoles, a National Conservatory for Arts and Crafts, and training centres for those in the construction industry, health services, traditional handicrafts, primary school teaching and social work. Technical/professional education is supported by state funds. There are, in addition, a number of privately operated institutions.

Regulatory Bodies

GOVERNMENT

Ministry of Education, Higher Education, Youth and Sports: Immeuble Papineau, 6ème étage, BP 2551, 98713 Papeete; tel. 478383; e-mail secretariat@education.min.gov.pf; Minister MICHEL LEBOUCHER.

Ministry of Tourism (MTE), Ecology, Culture and Air Transport: Bâtiment du GIE Tahiti Tourisme, Quai des paquebots, BP 2551, 98713 Papeete; tel. 508860; e-mail contact@tourisme.min.gov.pf; Minister GEFFRY TAHIATA SALMON.

Learned Societies

GENERAL

Société des Etudes Océaniennes (Society for Oceanian Studies): BP 110, 98713 Papeete, Tahiti; tel. 419603; e-mail seo@archives.gov.pf; internet etudes-oceaniennes.com; f. 1917; study of archeology, anthropology, ethnography, natural sciences, philosophy, history, customs and traditions of Polynesia; 450 mems; library of 7,000 vols; Pres. CHONG FASAN DIT JEAN; Vice-Pres. GHEHENNEC CONSTANT; Sec. MICHEL BAILLEUL; Treas. YVES BABIN; publ. *Bulletin de la Société des Etudes Océaniennes* (3 a year).

Te Fare Tauhiti Nui/Maison de la Culture: 646 blvd Pomaré, BP 1709, 98713 Papeete; tel. 544544; e-mail secretariat@maisondelaculture.pf; internet www.maisondelaculture.pf; f. 1971 as Maison des Jeunes–Maison de la Culture, present name and status 1998; promotes culture locally and abroad; sponsors many public and private cultural events; library of 13,000 vols; Dir HEREMOANA MAAMAATUAIATAPU (acting); Sec. CHRISTIANE BROTHERSON BALDERANIS.

LANGUAGE AND LITERATURE

Fare Vana'a/Académie Tahitienne: BP 2609, 98713 Papeete, Tahiti; tel. 501550; e-mail farevanaa@mail.pf; internet www.farevanaa.pf; f. 1972; 20 mems; Dir JOHN TAROANUI DOOM; Chancellor RAYMOND VANAGA PIETRI; Sec. ETIENNE CHIMIN; Treas. PATUA COULIN.

NATURAL SCIENCES

Biological Sciences

Société d'Ornithologie de Polynésie (Ornithological Society of Polynesia): BP 7023, 98719 Taravao, Tahiti; tel. 521100; e-mail sop@manu.pf; internet www.manu.pf; f. 1990; attached to BirdLife Int.; protects birds, their habitats and biodiversity; works with the people through sustainable management of natural resources; Pres. PHILIPPE RAUST; Sec. GEORGE SANFORD; Treas. ALAIN SCOUPPE.

Research Institutes

GENERAL

Institut de Recherche pour le Développement (IRD) Centre de Tahiti: BP 529, 98713 Papeete, Tahiti; tel. 474200; e-mail dirpapet@ird.pf; internet www.polynesie.ird.fr; f. 1964; researches on biodiversity and sustainable use of natural resources (see main entry under France); library of 7,000 vols; Rep. PHILIPPE LACOMBE.

AGRICULTURE, FISHERIES AND VETERINARY SCIENCE

Centre IFREMER du Pacifique: BP 7004, 98719 Taravao, Tahiti; tel. 546000; e-mail dir.cop@ifremer.fr; internet www.ifremer.fr/cop; f. 1972; part of IFREMER (*q.v.*); research in aquaculture (crustacea, fish, shellfish); Dir MARC TAQUET; Sec. LOIC GOURMELEN.

FINE AND PERFORMING ARTS

Institut de la Communication Audiovisuelle: BP 4469, 98713 Papeete, Tahiti; tel. 506750; internet www.ica.pf; attached to Min. of Tourism (MTE), Ecology, Culture, and Air Transport; collects, preserves and restores audiovisual heritage of Polynesia; produces television programmes and documentaries; collns incl. video recordings, local television broadcasts and feature films; colln of images and sounds on the archipelagos of French Polynesia (Australes, Tuamotu, Gambier, Marquises, Société); library of 34,000 vols.

MEDICINE

Institut Louis Malardé: BP 30, 98713 Papeete, Tahiti; tel. 416465; internet www.ilm.pf; f. 1949 as Institute of Medical Research of the French Est. in Oceania, present bldg 1950, current name adopted 2001; chemistry of natural products, emerging infectious diseases, marine biotoxins, medical entomology; library of 1,000 vols, 9,185 periodicals; Dir Dr PATRICK HOWELL; Exec. Sec. MARIE SOLIGNAC.

NATURAL SCIENCES

Biological Sciences

Te mana o te moana: BP 1374, 98729 Papetoai, Moorea; tel. 564011; e-mail temanaotemoana@mail.pf; internet www.temanaotemoana.org; f. 2004; Pres. CÉCILE GASPAR; Sec. and Treas. RICHARD BAILEY.

Archive

Papeete

Service des Archives Territoriales: BP 9063, 98715 Papeete, Tahiti; tel. 419601; e-mail service.archives@archives.gov.pf; Head of Service PIERRE MORILLON.

Museums and Art Galleries

Papeari

Musée Paul Gauguin: BP 7029, 98727 Papeari, Tahiti; tel. 571058; e-mail museegauguin@mail.pf; f. 1964; 1,000 documents on the life and work of the artist Paul Gauguin (1848–1903), who spent the last part of his life in Tahiti and other parts of the S Pacific; library of unpublished documents; colln of paintings by Buffet, R. Delaunay, S. Delaunay and others; 20 original works by Gauguin (paintings, sculptures, watercolours); Curator G. ARTUR.

Papeete

Robert Wan Pearl Museum: BP 850, blvd Pomare, Papeete; tel. (689) 461554; e-mail museedelaperle@mail.pf; internet www.robertwan.com/museum.php; f. 1975; cultured pearls, spec. colln Tahitian Black Pearl.

Tamanu

Te Fare Manaha/Musée de Tahiti et des Iles: Pointe des Pêcheurs 'Nu'uroa, Punaauia, BP 380 354, 98718 Tamanu; tel. 548435; e-mail secretariat@museetahiti.pf; internet www.museetahiti.pf; f. 1974, fmrly as Musée de Tahiti et des Iles–Te Fare Iamanaha, current name adopted 2005; collects, conserves and appreciates Polynesian cultural heritage; Dir and Curator THÉANO JAILLET; Librarian VAIREA TEISSIER.

University

UNIVERSITÉ DE LA POLYNÉSIE FRANÇAISE
(University of French Polynesia)

BP 60056, 98702 Faa'a, Tahiti
Telephone: 866400
E-mail: scd@upf.pf
Internet: www.upf.pf

Founded 1999 from the French Polynesia centre of the fmr Université Française du Pacifique (f. 1987)
State control
Academic year: September to June

Depts of humanities, languages and social studies; law, economics and management; and sciences

Pres.: Prof. ERIC CONTE
Vice-Pres. for Admin. Ccl: PATRICK CAPOLSINI
Vice-Pres. for Scientific Ccl: ALBAN GABILLON
Vice-Pres. for Student Life: VINCENT DROPSY
Library Dir: ISABELLE HEUTTE

Library of 80,000 books, 260 periodicals, 700 audiovisual items
Number of teachers: 95
Number of students: 3,211

Publication: *Comparative Law Journal of the Pacific—Revue Juridique Polynésienne* (1 a year)

College

Conservatoire artistique de Polynésie française 'Te Fare Upa Rau': BP 463, 98713 Papeete, Tahiti; tel. 501414; e-mail conserv.artist@mail.pf; internet www.conservatoire.pf; f. 1979; attached to Min. of Tourism (MTE), Ecology, Culture, and Air Transport; conserves and promotes Polynesian culture; provides theoretical and practical training in fine and performing arts; 40 teachers; 1,693 students; Dir FABIEN DINARD; Registrar FABIOLA TEAHUI; Sec. JEANNINE TAAE CHAVEZ.

GUADELOUPE

The Higher Education System

Guadeloupe was first occupied by the French in 1635, and has remained French territory, apart from a number of brief occupations by the British in the 18th and early 19th centuries. It gained departmental status in 1946, was granted the status of a Region in 1974 and was designated an Overseas Region (Région d'outre-mer) in 2003. In 2007 the dependencies of Saint-Barthélemy and the French part of Saint-Martin seceded from Guadeloupe to become Overseas Collectivities (Collectivités d'outre-mer).

Higher education in Guadeloupe is modelled on the metropolitan French system and, as such, is compliant with the Bologna Process. Successful completion of the Baccalauréat is required for entrance into tertiary institutions. There is a branch of the Université des Antilles et de la Guyane (UAG, which was established in 1970 and was granted full university status in 1982), located at two campuses—one at Pointe-à-Pitre (Grande-Terre) and the other at St Claude (Basse-Terre). The Guadeloupe branch of the UAG (which has other branches in French Guiana and Martinique) comprises faculties of law and economics, natural sciences, medical sciences, science and technology, sports science, and arts and humanities; it also has a Doctoral School and a Department of Continuing Education. In 2011 the Guadeloupe University Institute for Teacher Training (Institut Universitaire de Formation des Maîtres, IUFM) was incorporated into the Guadeloupe branch of the UAG. The Licence (Bachelors degree) is required for admission into the IUFM. The programme at this institute lasts two years, the first for further specialization in a discipline and the second for teacher training in that discipline. The general administration of the UAG, which is divided into divisions, departments and offices, comes under the overall authority of the President of the University and is managed on a day-to-day basis by a Secretary-General. There are also three governing boards: the Board of Directors, the Scientific Council and the Board of Studies and University Life. The UAG offers a range of courses, including, at undergraduate level, certificates, diplomas, Associate and Bachelors degrees, and, at postgraduate level, Masters and Doctorate degrees. The University is accredited by the French Ministry of Higher Education and Research.

Besides the UAG, higher education on Guadeloupe is also provided by colleges of agriculture, fisheries, hotel management, nursing, midwifery and child care. In addition, continuing education and training is offered at the National Centre for Distance Education (Centre National d'Enseignement à Distance). In 2011/12 there was a total of 9,113 students in higher education. Many students undertake their further education in France or in the French West Indies.

Research Institutes

AGRICULTURE, FISHERIES AND VETERINARY SCIENCE

CIRAD Guadeloupe: Station de Neufchâteau, Sainte-Marie, 97130 Capesterre-Belle-Eau; tel. 5-90-86-30-21; e-mail cecile.gaume@cirad.fr; internet www.cirad.fr/guadeloupe; Regional Dir PHILIPPE GODON; Head of Caribbean Regional Cooperation DOMINIQUE POLTI.

INRA Antilles-Guyane: Domaine Duclos, Prise d'Eau, 97170 Petit Bourg; tel. 5-90-25-59-00; e-mail xande@antilles.inra.fr; internet www.antilles.inra.fr; f. 1949 as Centre de Recherches des Antilles et de la Guyane; attached to Min. of Higher Education and Research and Min. of Agriculture, Food, Fisheries, Rural Affairs and Planning (see main entry under France); animal science, forestry, plant science, rural economy and sociology, soil science, technology transfer, zoology and biological control; controls 5 research units, 3 experimental farms and a documentation service; Pres. DANIELLE CÉLESTINE-MYRTIL-MARLIN.

MEDICINE

Institut Pasteur de la Guadeloupe: BP 484, 97183 Abymes Cedex; tel. 5-90-89-69-40; internet www.pasteur-guadeloupe.fr; f. 1948; medical and microbiological analysis laboratories; int. vaccination centre; Public Health Dept certified laboratories for water and food analysis (chemical and microbiological); mycobacteria and environmental health research units; small library; Dir Dr ANTOINE TALARMIN; Exec. Sec. Dr HENRIETTA DESIREE; publ. *Archives* (1 a year).

Libraries and Archives

Basse-Terre

Département de la Guadeloupe Archives Départementales: BP 74, 97102 Basse-Terre Cedex; tel. 5-90-81-13-02; e-mail info@cg971.fr; internet www.cg971.fr/archives; f. 1951; 10,000 vols; Dir ANNE LEBEL; publ. *Bulletin de la Société d'Histoire de la Guadeloupe* (3 a year).

Pointe-à-Pitre

Bibliothèque Universitaire Antilles-Guyane: Campus de Fouillole, BP 32, 97159 Pointe-à-Pitre Cedex; tel. 5-96-48-90-01; internet buag.univ-ag.fr; f. 1972; 65,000 vols, 750 periodicals, 2,200 electronic journals; Dir, Guadeloupe Br. JACQUES FAULE.

Museums and Art Galleries

Basse-Terre

Historical Museum of Guadeloupe: Fort Delgrès, 97100 Basse-Terre; tel. 5-90-81-37-48.

Pointe-à-Pitre

Musée Municipal Saint John Perse: 9 rue Noziéres, 97110 Pointe-à-Pitre; tel. 5-90-90-01-92; e-mail musee.st-john-perse@wanadoo.fr; f. 1987; 2-storey 19th-century colonial house: colln of accounts from life of poet St John Perse; exhibits incl. MSS and personal items; attached library and videotheque.

Musée Victor Schoelcher: 24 rue Peynier, 97110 Pointe-à-Pitre; tel. 5-90-82-08-04; e-mail musee.schoelcher@cg971.fr; f. 1883; Dir H. PETITJEAN ROGET.

Affiliated Museums:

Ecomusée de Marie-Galante: Habitation Murat, 97112 Grand Bourg, Marie Galante; tel. 5-90-97-94-41; internet www.cg971.fr/musees/ecomusee/index_ecomuse.htm; f. 1980; local arts, history and traditions and history of sugar cane; medicinal herb garden in the fmr animal enclosure; library of 400 vols; Dir C. MOMBRUN.

Musée Edgar Clerc: La Rosette, 97160 Le Moule; tel. 5-90-23-57-57; internet www.cg971.fr; f. 1984; library of 800 vols; Curator SUSANA GUIMARAES.

Musée Fort Fleur d'Epée: Bas du Fort, 97190 Gosier; tel. 5-90-90-94-61; internet www.cg971.fr/musees/fleurdepee/index_epee.htm; f. 1759; military history; art gallery; coin colln.

Parc Archéologique des Roches Gravées: Bord de mer, 97114 Trois-Rivières; tel. 5-90-92-91-88; internet www.cg971.fr/musees/parc/index_roche.htm; f. 1970; 1 ha, containing tropical vegetation, volcanic rocks and stones bearing marks made by Arawak Indians, the original inhabitants of the island.

Vieux-Habitants

Musée du Café: Le Bouchu, 97119 Vieux-Habitants; tel. 5-90-98-54-96; e-mail cafe.chaulet@wanadoo.fr; internet www.in-west-indies.com/site-museums-musee-du-cafe–cafe-chaulet-909.htm; history of coffee from 1721 to present-day Guadeloupe; production and processing techniques of picking, roasting and converting coffee beans into a beverage.

University

UNIVERSITÉ DES ANTILLES ET DE LA GUYANE

Fouillole, BP 250, 97157 Pointe-à-Pitre Cedex

Telephone: 5-90-48-30-30

Internet: www.univ-ag.fr

Founded 1982

public control

Pres.: CORINNE MENCE-CASTER

Vice-Pres. for Guadeloupe: EUSTADE JANKY

Vice-Pres. for Martinique: PHILIPPE SAINT-CYR

Vice-Pres. for Guyana: ANTOINE PRIMEROSE

Librarian: SYLVAIN HOUDEBERT

Library: see under Libraries and Archives

Number of teachers: 233

Number of students: 5,728

TEACHING AND RESEARCH UNITS

Arts and Humanities: Dean: CORINNE MENCE-CASTER

Exact and Natural Sciences: Dean: HUBERT TREFLE

Law and Economics: Dir: EMMANUEL JOS

Medicine: Dir: Prof. PASCAL BLANCHET

Sports: Dir: CLAUDE HERTOGH

MARTINIQUE

The Higher Education System

Martinique has been a French possession since 1635. The island became a Department of France in 1946 and in 1974 Martinique, together with Guadeloupe and French Guiana, was given regional status as part of France's governmental reorganization. In March 2003 the status of Overseas Region (Région d'outre-mer) was conferred on Martinique by constitutional amendment.

Higher education in Martinique is modelled on the metropolitan French system and, as such, is compliant with the Bologna Process. Successful completion of the Baccalauréat is required for entrance into tertiary institutions. There is a branch of the Université des Antilles et de la Guyane (UAG, which was established in 1970 and was granted full university status in 1982), located at Schoelcher. The Martinique branch of the UAG (which has other branches in French Guiana and Guadeloupe) comprises a faculty of law and economics, a faculty of arts and humanities, an inter-faculty science department and an institute of legal studies. During 2011/12 some 4,629 students were enrolled at the University in Martinique. In 2011 the Martinique University Institute for Teacher Training (Institut Universitaire de Formation des Maîtres, IUFM) was incorporated into the Martinique branch of the UAG. The Licence (Bachelors degree) is required for admission into the IUFM. The programme at this institute lasts two years, the first for further specialization in a discipline and the second for teacher training in that discipline. The general administration of the UAG, which is divided into divisions, departments and offices, comes under the overall authority of the President of the University and is managed on a day-to-day basis by a Secretary-General. There are also three governing boards: the Board of Directors, the Scientific Council and the Board of Studies and University Life. The UAG offers a range of courses, including, at undergraduate level, certificates, diplomas, Associate and Bachelors degrees, and, at postgraduate level, Masters and Doctorate degrees. The University is accredited by the French Ministry of Higher Education and Research.

In addition to the UAG, higher education on Martinique is also provided by a number of vocational and technical colleges. In 2011/12 there was a total of 7,941 students in higher education. Many students undertake their further education in France or in the French West Indies.

Learned Society

AGRICULTURE, FISHERIES AND VETERINARY SCIENCE

Martinique Billfish Association: Chevalier de Ste-Marthe, 97200 Fort-de-France; tel. 5-96-55-26-73; e-mail referencement@pixellweb.com; internet www.martinique-billfish.org; f. 1993; devt and practice of fishing; study of ecosystems, wildlife and underwater biological balance; Pres. JOSÉ ZÉCLER.

Research Institutes

AGRICULTURE, FISHERIES AND VETERINARY SCIENCE

Institut de Recherche pour le Développement (IRD)—Centre IRD Martinique-Caraïbe: BP 8006, 97259 Fort de France Cedex; tel. 5-96-39-77-39; e-mail martinique@ird.fr; internet www.mq.ird.fr; f. 1958, fmrly ORSTOM; soil science, nematology; see main entry under France; library of 1,700 vols; Dir and Rep. MARC MORELL.

Martinique Agricultural Research Pole: BP 214, 97285 Le Lementin; tel. 5-90-42-30-00; e-mail dir-reg.martinique@cirad.fr; internet www.cirad.fr; attached to CIRAD Agricultural Research for Devt; cultivation of bananas, pineapples, fruit-producing trees and intensive farming; Rep. CHRISTIAN CHABRIER.

MEDICINE

Laboratoire Départemental d'Analyses: 35 blvd Pasteur, BP 628, 97261 Fort de France Cedex; tel. 5-96-71-34-52; e-mail lda@cg972.fr; internet lda97.com; f. 1977; attached to Le Conseil Général de la Martinique; hygiene research and analysis of human blood and food and water; entomology; immunology of parasitic diseases; Pres. of Gen. Ccl CLAUDE LISE; Dir Dr J. M. P. LAFAYE.

Libraries and Archives

Fort-de-France

Archives Départementales de la Martinique: 19 ave Saint-John-Perse, BP 649, 97263 Fort-de-France Cedex; tel. 5-96-55-43-43; e-mail archives@cg972.fr; f. 1949; 12,000 vols; Dir DOMINIQUE TAFFIN.

Bibliothèque Schoelcher: 1 rue de la Liberté, BP 640, 97264 Fort-de-France Cedex; tel. 5-96-70-26-67; e-mail bibliotheque.schoelcher@cg972.fr; internet www.cg972.fr/biblio_schoelcher/html/default.htm; f. 1883; attached to Le Conseil Général de la Martinique; promotes study and research in heritage and modernity, literary and scientific culture of the city; 226,000 vols; Dir ANIQUE SYLVESTRE; Adjoint Dir LUCIEN PAVILLA.

Schoelcher

Bibliothèques de l'Université des Antilles et de la Guyane, Service Commun de la Documentation: BP 7210, 97275 Schoelcher Cedex; tel. 5-96-72-75-30; e-mail sylvain.houdebert@univ-ag.fr; internet buag.univ-ag.fr; f. 1972; HQ for the 10 libraries of the Univ. in Martinique, French Guiana, Guadeloupe; 300,000 vols incl. print books, 2,700 print periodicals and 15,000 ejournals, 30 ebooks; Dir of SCD UAG SYLVAIN HOUDEBERT; Dir of Martinique Br. NATHALIE ERNY.

Museums and Art Galleries

Anse-Turin

Gauguin Art Centre and Museum: Anse-Turin; tel. 5-96-78-22-66; historical site; art and history museum; art of famous painter Gauguin.

Fort-de-France

Musée Départemental d'Archéologie Précolombienne et de Préhistoire de la Martinique: 9 rue de la Liberté, 97200 Fort-de-France; tel. 5-96-71-57-05; e-mail musarc@cg972.fr; f. 1971; prehistory of Martinique; archaeological colls; Dir JOSEPH-MOUROSE ROSE-COLETTE.

Musée Régional d'Histoire et d'Ethnographie: 10 blvd du Général de Gaulle, 97200 Fort-de-France; tel. 5-96-72-81-87; e-mail cr.972.musees@wanadoo.fr; internet www.cr-martinique.fr; f. 1999; attached to Conseil Régional Martinique; displays furnishings, antiques, a gallery of traditional costumes and jewellery, as well as numerous paintings and engravings (18th and 19th centuries) retracing briefly the historical milestones of the island and the history of Saint-Pierre and Fort-de-France; attached library specializing in works on slavery; Curator LYNE-ROSE BEUZE.

Riviere-Pilote

L'Ecomusée (The Living Museum): Anse Figuier, 97211 Riviere-Pilote; tel. 5-96-62-79-14; internet www.cr-martinique.fr; f. 1993 by Assen Martiniquaise de Promotion et de Protection des Arts et Traditions Populaires; attached to Conseil Régional Martinique; displays prehistory to present-day Native America; beginnings of French colonialism; economy-oriented cultures of cotton, tobacco and indigo; slave-period crops of sugar cane, coffee, and cocoa; central factories; advent of the banana economy; Conservateur LYNE-ROSE BEUZE.

Trois-Ilets

La Savane des Esclaves: Quartier La Ferme, 97229 Trois-Ilets; tel. 5-96-68-33-91; e-mail lasavanedesesclaves@wanadoo.fr; restored habitat that displays the way of life of slaves who fled the plantations to seek refuge in nature.

Maison De La Canne (House of Cane): Quartier Valable, 97229 Trois-Ilets; tel. 5-96-68-31-68; internet www.cr-martinique.fr; f. 1987; attached to Conseil Régional Martinique; history and devt of sugar cane products;

Conservator LYNE-ROSE BEUZE; Documentalist MARIE-JOSÉ SYLVESTRE.

University

UNIVERSITÉ DES ANTILLES ET DE LA GUYANE

Campus de Choelcher, BP 7209, 97275 Schoelcher Cedex

Telephone: 5-90-48-91-98
Internet: www.univ-ag.fr
Public control
(See also under French Guiana and Guadeloupe)
Pres.: CORINNE MENCE-CASTER
Vice-Pres. for Martinique: PHILIPPE SAINT CYR
Library: see under Libraries and Archives
Number of teachers: 158
Number of students: 4,629

DEANS
Arts and Humanities: CORINNE MENCE-CASTER
Law and Economics: JUSTIN DANIEL

NEW CALEDONIA

The Higher Education System

New Caledonia became a French possession in the 19th century, when the island was annexed as a dependency of Tahiti. It became an Overseas Territory of the French Republic in 1946 and was designated as an Overseas Country (Pays d'outre-mer) in 1999. New Caledonia's unique status of Collectivité spécifique was conferred following a constitutional revision in 2003. A gradual transfer of power from metropolitan France to local institutions was to be effected over a period of between 15 and 20 years under the terms of the Nouméa Accord, which was approved by referendum in November 1998. New Caledonia's education system remains closely modelled on the French system, and the primary language of instruction at all levels is French. The New Caledonia Educational Authority for Primary, Secondary and Higher Education, which is based in the capital, Nouméa, is a decentralized government department that oversees the educational system in New Caledonia.

Admission to higher education is dependent on the successful completion of the three-year upper-secondary school programme. There are currently five institutions of higher education in New Caledonia, the most important of which is the University of New Caledonia (UNC, Université de la Nouvelle-Calédonie). This institution dates back to 1987 when the French University of the Pacific (Université Française du Pacifique) was established, with two centres, one in French Polynesia and the other in New Caledonia. In 1997 it was decided to split the two parts into separate universities; consequently, in 1999 the UNC and the University of French Polynesia (UFP) were created. In 2009 the University Institute for Teacher Training (Institut Universitaire de Formation des Maîtres), which was established in 1990, was incorporated into the UNC. The University, which is located on two campuses—Nouville and Magenta, in 2011/12 had an enrolment of 2,392 students. The main language of instruction at the UNC is French. The UNC comprises a multidisciplinary doctoral school (linked to the UFP), the teacher-training institute and four departments (law, economy and management; literature, languages and humanities; science and technology; and continuing education). As in France, the UNC has adopted the Bologna-style three-tier degree system (Licence/Master/Doctorat—LMD) and the European Credit Transfer and Accumulation System (ECTS). The University offers a range of diplomas as well as Bachelors and Masters degrees. It also provides preparatory courses for the competitive entrance examinations for medical school and the teachers' college, and offers distance learning for off-campus students with the participation of the French National Centre for Distance Education (Centre National d'Enseignement á Distance). Furthermore, the UNC is the location for five research teams (recognized by the French Ministry of Higher Education and Research)—the Centre for New Studies on the Pacific Region, the Computer Studies and Mathematics Research Team, Laboratory of Economic and Legal Studies, the Island Laboratory of Life Sciences and the Environment and the Multidisciplinary Centre for Earth Sciences and the Environment. Many students from New Caledonia attend universities in France.

Regulatory Bodies

GOVERNMENT

Department of Culture, Women Affairs and Citizenship: 21 bis rue Georges Clémenceau, BP T5, 98852 Nouméa; tel. 26-97-60; e-mail dccfc@gouv.nc; internet www.gouv.nc/portal/page/portal/gouv/annuaire_administration/administration/dccfc; Minister EPÉRI DÉWÉ GORODEY.

Directorate of Education of New Caledonia: 19 ave Foch, Immeuble Foch, BP 1933-98846 Nouméa Sud; tel. 23-96-00; e-mail denc@gouv.nc; internet www.denc.gouv.nc; Dir CHRISTIAN PRALONG.

Department of Vocational Training: 19 ave du Maréchal Foch, BP 110, 98845 Nouméa; tel. 24-66-22; e-mail dfpc@gouv.nc; internet www.dfpc.gouv.nc; Minister SYLVIE ROBINEAU; Dir PIERRE-HENRI CHARLES.

Learned Societies

GENERAL

Groupe de Recherche en Histoire Océanienne Contemporaine (GRHOC) (Research Group for the Modern History of Oceania): BP R4, 98845 Nouméa; tel. 26-58-58; e-mail angleviel@univ-nc.nc; f. 1996; historical and anthropological research; devt of regional research; 10 mems; Pres. (vacant); publs *101 Mots pour Comprendre* (1 a year), *Annales d'Histoire Calédonienne* (1 a year).

HISTORY, GEOGRAPHY AND ARCHAEOLOGY

Société d'Etudes Historiques de la Nouvelle-Calédonie (New Caledonia Society for Historical Studies): BP 63, 98845 Nouméa; tel. 76-71-55; e-mail seh-nc@lagoon.nc; internet www.seh-nc.com; f. 1969; heritage conservation; publishes books and periodicals on history, prehistory, Melanesian society; contact with univs of Pacific area; archives; 200 mems; Pres. GABRIEL JACK; Vice-Pres. MAXWELL SHEKLETON.

LANGUAGE AND LITERATURE

Association des Ecrivains de Nouvelle-Calédonie (Writers' Association of New Caledonia): Eight rue Paul Monchovet, Pointe Brunelet, 98800 Nouméa; e-mail contact@ecrivains-nc.net; internet www.ecrivains-nc.net; f. 1996; exchanges ideas and promotes writing in all its forms; 27 mems; Pres. CLAUDINE JACQUES; Vice-Pres. NICOLAS KURTOVITCH; Treas. MARC BOUAN; Sec. CLAUDE MAILLAUD.

Research Institutes

GENERAL

Institut de Recherche pour le Développement (IRD) (Research Institute for Development): 101 Promenade Roger Laroque, Anse Vata BP A5, 98848 Nouméa; tel. 26-10-00; e-mail infocom-noumea@ird.fr; internet www.nouvelle-caledonie.ird.fr; f. 1946; archaeology, botany and plant ecology, geology, geophysics, microbiology, pharmacology, applied zoology, physical and biological oceanography; library of 12,500 vols, 800 periodicals; Pres. MICHEL LAURENT; Dir GILLES FÉDIÈRE; publs *Earth Sciences*, *Life Sciences*, *Sea Sciences*, *Science in the south*, *Social Sciences*.

AGRICULTURE, FISHERIES AND VETERINARY SCIENCE

Institut Agronomique néo-Calédonien (New Caledonian Agronomic Institute): BP 35, Paita; tel. 43-74-15; internet www.iac.nc; f. 1999; promotes rural devt in New Caledonia by research activities in agriculture, forestry, food and livestock; develops relationships of scientific, technical, economic and financial institutions with French and foreign counterparts and in partnership with private sector; Dir-Gen. THIERRY MENNESSON.

EDUCATION

Centre de documentation pédagogique de Nouvelle-Calédonie (New Caledonia Centre for Pedagogic Documentation): Immeuble Flize, Rez de chaussée, BP 215, 98845 Nouméa; tel. 24-28-28; e-mail librairie@cdp.nc; internet www.cdp.nc; f. 1978, fmrly Centre Territorial de Recherche et de Documentation Pédagogiques de Nouvelle-Calédonie; research in education; library of 13,000 vols, 800 video cassettes, 2,200 slide serials; Pres. IVES MELET; Dir CHRISTIAN LUCIEN; Sec.-Gen. HENRI TOURNACHE.

MEDICINE

Institut Pasteur de Nouvelle Calédonie (Pasteur Institute of New Caledonia): 9–11 ave Paul Doumer, BP 61, 98845 Nouméa; tel. 27-26-66; e-mail direction@pasteur.nc; internet www.institutpasteur.nc; f. 1913 as Institut de Microbiologie de Nouvelle-Calédonie, name changed to Institut Pasteur de Nouméa 1954, present name 1990; medical analysis laboratory; research laboratory: dengue fever, leptospirosis, tuberculosis; library of 1,080 vols; Dir Prof. DOMINIQUE BAUDON; Exec. Sec. SIDAVY SABOT; publ. *Rapport technique* (1 a year).

RELIGION, SOCIOLOGY AND ANTHROPOLOGY

Coordination pour l'Océanie des Recherches sur les Arts, les Idées et les Littératures (CORAIL): BP 2448, 98846 Nouméa; f. 1987; studies francophone and anglophone literatures and civilizations of the S Pacific; annual themed conference; Pres. VÉRONIQUE FILLIOL; Sec. JACQUES VERNAUDON; publ. *Actes du Colloque* (1 a year).

Libraries and Archives

Nouméa

Bibliothèque Bernheim (Bernheim Library): BP G1, 98848 Nouméa; tel. 24-20-90; e-mail bernheim@bernheim.nc; internet www.bernheim.nc; f. 1901; public library (adults and children); record library; historical, ethnological collns of 2,500 vols dealing with New Caledonia and the Pacific Islands; associated with Bibliothèque Nationale de France for colln of legal deposit; 141,000 vols, 28,500 vols of children's books, 85 periodicals; Curator and Dir CHRISTOPHE AUGEAN.

Secretariat of the Pacific Community Library: 95 Promenade Roger Laroque, Anse Vata, BP D5, 98848 Nouméa; tel. 26-20-00; e-mail library@spc.int; internet www.spc.int/library; f. 1947; SPC Nouméa reference library: collns on health, women, youth, statistics, demography, cultural policy, agriculture, forestry, fisheries, and economic and social devt in the Pacific Islands; brs: Suva, Fiji and SPC Nouméa (HQ): holds 6 collns serving forestry regional office, maritime programme, community education centre, regional media centre, agriculture and adolescent reproductive health; 40,000 regional and int. publs in French, English and other Pacific languages; Librarian ELEANOR KLEIBER; Archivist ROBERT APPEL.

Service des Archives de Nouvelle Calédonie (New Caledonia Archive Service): POB 525 98845 Nouméa; 3 rue Félix Raoul Thomas, Nouville, Nouméa; tel. 26-60-20; e-mail archives@gouv.nc; internet www.archives.gouv.nc; f. 1987; collects and preserves the archives produced by State of New Caledonia, provinces, municipalities, notaries, corpns, asscns and individuals; 7,000 vols, 5,196 linear m of archives; Dir JACQUES ANCEY (acting).

Museums and Art Galleries

Nouméa

Musée de l'Histoire Maritime (Museum of Maritime History): 11 ave James Cook, BP 1755, 98845 Nouméa; tel. 26-34-43; e-mail mdhm@canl.nc; internet www.patrimoine-maritime.asso.nc; f. 1999; attached to Patrimoine Maritime de Nouvelle Calédonie; preserves and displays collns from archaeological underwater excavations carried out by Fortunes de Mer Calédoniennes and Assn Salomon.

Musée de la Ville de Nouméa: 39 rue Jean Jaurès, pl. des Cocotiers, 98800, Nouméa; tel. 26-28-05; e-mail mairie.musee@ville-noumea.nc; internet www.noumea.nc/musee-de-la-ville; f. 1874; colln incl. artefacts from First World War, Second World War and history of New Caledonia; originally housed colonial-style town hall of Nouméa from 1880 to 1975; Curator VERONIQUE DEFRANCE.

Musée de Nouvelle-Calédonie (Museum of New Caledonia): BP 2393, 98846 Nouméa; 45 ave du Maréchal Foch, Nouméa; tel. 27-23-42; e-mail smp@gouv.nc; f. 1971; colln of 4,500 items; emblematic wooden sculptures, masks, ritual dance costumes, jewellery, pottery and other objects reflecting cultural practices and religious beliefs; Dir MARIE-SOLANGE NEAOUTYINE.

University

UNIVERSITÉ DE LA NOUVELLE-CALÉDONIE
(University of New Caledonia)

BP R4, 98851 Nouméa Cedex
Telephone: 29-02-90
E-mail: president@univ-nc.nc
Internet: www.univ-nc.nc

Founded 1999 from New Caledonia centre of fmr Université Française du Pacifique
State control
Academic year: February to November (2 semesters)

Depts of arts, economics and management, languages and humanities, law, science and technology

Pres.: JEAN-MARC BOYER
Vice-Pres. for Scientific Ccl for Research: MICHEL ALLENBACH
Vice-Pres. for Student Affairs: PIERRE MESTRE
Sec.-Gen.: ODILE BOYER
Registrar: CHRISTIAN CABOTTE
Library Dir: PHILIPPE BESNIÉ

Library of 70,000 vols, 410 journals, 350 periodicals
Number of teachers: 100
Number of students: 3,000
Publication: *UNC-Info* (12 a year)

College

Conservatoire National des Arts et Métiers (National Conservatory of the Arts and Crafts): 15 bis rue de Verdun, Immeuble CCI, 2ième étage, BP 3562, 98846 Nouméa; tel. 28-37-07; e-mail noucnam@offratel.nc; internet cnam.nc; f. 1794; attached to the Conservatoire National des Arts et Métiers in Paris; higher technical education; 20 teachers; 500 students; Pres. JEAN BEGAUD; Rector CHRISTIAN FOREST; Dir BERNARD SCHALL; Dir for Teaching HENRI CHARLES.

RÉUNION

The Higher Education System

Réunion was first occupied by France in 1642, and was ruled as a colony until 1946, when it received full departmental status. In 1974 it became an Overseas Department (Département d'outre-mer) with the status of a region.

Education is modelled on the French system, and, as such, is compliant with the Bologna Process. The island's only university is the University of La Réunion (Université de La Réunion), which was established (as the University Centre of Réunion) in the capital, Saint-Denis, in 1970 and was granted full university status (under its present name) in 1982. Successful completion of the Baccalauréat is required for entrance into tertiary institutions. The University comprises five faculties, four institutes (including an institute of teacher training), a school of engineering, an observatory of science of the universe and an apprentice training centre. It offers a range of courses (covering the three broad areas of arts and humanities; law, economics and management; and science, technology and health) including vocational and professional programmes, Bachelors/Licence and Masters degrees and Doctorates. The University, which is located across six campuses, is administered by a President, a Board of Directors, a Scientific Council and a Board of Studies and Academic Life. In 2011/12 there were 11,593 students enrolled at the University.

There is also a wide range of vocational and technical courses and apprenticeships available at a number of institutions in Réunion (including the Chamber of Trades and Crafts and the Chamber of Commerce and Industry), and in 2011/12 a total of 4,188 students were enrolled in non-university higher education.

Learned Societies

GENERAL

Académie de la Réunion: 24 ave Georges Brassens, Le Moufia, 97702 St-Denis Messag. Cedex 9; tel. 2-62-48-10-10; e-mail communication.secretariat@ac-reunion.fr; internet www.ac-reunion.fr; f. 1913; 25 mems; Rector MOSTAFA FOURAR; Deputy Rector BERNARD ZIER; Sec.-Gen. EUGÈNE KRANTZ; publ. *Bulletin*.

HISTORY, GEOGRAPHY AND ARCHAEOLOGY

Association Historique Internationale de l'Océan Indien: c/o Archives Départementales de la Réunion, 4 rue Marcel Regnol, 97490 St-Denis; f. 1960; 86 mems; Pres. CL. WANQUET; Sec.-Gen. B. JULLIEN; publ. *Bulletin de Liaison et d'Information* (2 a year).

NATURAL SCIENCES

Association Réunionnaise de Développement de l'Aquaculture: Z. I. Les Sables, BP 16, 97427 Etang-Salé; tel. 2-62-26-50-82; e-mail arda.reunion@wanadoo.fr; internet www.arda.fr; f. 1991 by the Conseil Régional de La Réunion; inland and marine aquaculture; study and devt of aquatic environments.

Research Institutes

AGRICULTURE, FISHERIES AND VETERINARY SCIENCE

CIRAD la Réunion: Station de la Bretagne, BP 20, 97408 St-Denis Messag. Cedex 9; tel. 2-62-52-80-00; e-mail dir-reg.reunion@cirad.fr; internet www.cirad.fr/reunion; f. 1962; attached to CIRAD Agricultural Research for Devt (France); agronomic research, mainly on sugar cane, fruit, vegetables, maize and fodder crops; water management and prevention of soil erosion; 181 staff, 55 researchers; 6 research stations; 1,180 publs; library of 5,000 vols; Regional Dir GILLES MANDRET; Dir for Environmental Risk, Agriculture and Integrated Management of Resources PAUL FALLAVIER; Dir for Plant Protection BERNARD REYNAUD; Dir for Quality of Agricultural and Tropical Food Production ERIC CARDINALE.

ECONOMICS, LAW AND POLITICS

Institut National de la Statistique et des Études Économiques—Direction Régionale de la Réunion (National Institute of Statistics and Economic Studies–Regional Directorate of Réunion): Parc Technologique, BP 13, 97408 St-Denis Menage Cedex 9; tel. 2-62-48-89-00; e-mail dr974_dir@insee.fr; internet www.insee.fr/fr/insee_regions/reunion/home/home_page.asp; f. 1966; attached to INSEE, Paris (see main entry in chapter on France); produces statistical data, economic studies; database with 10,000 bibliographical references on the region, database with 2,000 chronological series; Dir VALÉRIE ROUX; publs *L'Economie de la Réunion* (4 a year), *Tableau Economique de la Réunion* (1 a year).

HISTORY, GEOGRAPHY AND ARCHAEOLOGY

CRESOI Centre d'Histoire de l'Université de la Réunion Histoire, Politique et Patrimoine (CRESOI Centre of History University of Réunion Island History, Politics and Heritage): Univ. of La Réunion, Rue René Cassin, 97400 St-Denis; e-mail cresoi@centre-histoire-ocean-indien.fr; internet www.centre-histoire-ocean-indien.fr; f. 2001; attached to Univ. de La Réunion; researches colonization, decolonization, heritage, history of slavery, industrial tourism, political and cultural history, tourism; Dir Prof. YVAN COMBEAU; publ. *Revue Historique de l'Océan Indien*.

Libraries and Archives

St-Denis

Bibliothèque Centrale de Prêt de la Réunion: 1 pl. Joffre, 97400 St-Denis; tel. 2-62-21-03-24; e-mail bdp@cg974.fr; f. 1956; 100,000 vols; Dir ELISABETH DÉGON.

Bibliothèque Départementale de la Réunion: 52 rue Roland Garros, 97400 St-Denis; tel. 2-62-21-13-96; e-mail bdr@cg974.fr; f. 1855; 95,000 vols; Dir ALAIN VAUTHIER.

Service Commun de la Documentation (Bibliothèque Universitaire): Université de la Réunion, 15 ave René Cassin, BP 7152, 97715 St-Denis Cedex 9; tel. 2-62-93-83-79; e-mail scd@univ-reunion.fr; internet bu.univ-reunion.fr; f. 1971; attached to Univ. de la Réunion; arts, economics, human sciences, law, management, medicine, politics, social sciences, science; 171,252 vols, 1,495 current periodicals, 3,000 online periodicals; special colls on the Indian Ocean islands; Library Dir ANNE-MARIE BLANC.

St-Pierre

Mediathèque Raphaël Barquissau: rue du Collège Arthur, BP 396, 97458 St-Pierre Cedex; tel. 2-62-96-71-96; e-mail ksl@mediatheque-saintpierre.fr; internet www.mediatheque-saintpierre.fr; f. 1967; 130,000 vols, 190 periodicals, more than 530 ancient books, 12,000 CDs, 2,500 video cassettes; Dir and Chief Librarian LINDA KOO SEEN LIN.

Ste-Clotilde

Archives Départementales de La Réunion: 4 rue Marcel Pagnol, Champ-Fleuri, 97490 Ste-Clotilde; tel. 2-62-94-04-14; f. 1946; public and private sources of history on Bourbon Island and Réunion French dept; some Mauritius island archives on microfilms from French period; 5,000 vols, 163,000 items in public and private archives; Dir NADINE ROUAYROUX.

Museums and Art Galleries

St-Denis

Musée Léon-Dierx: 28 rue de Paris, 97400 St-Denis; tel. 2-62-20-24-82; e-mail musee.dierx@cg974.fr; internet www.cg974.fr/culture; f. 1911, old bldg destroyed 1963, museum reopened to the public 1965, colln and reserves reinstated 1970; fine arts; colln of contemporary art, installations and video cassettes; library: literature on featured artists, history of art, catalogues, monographs, essays and articles; Curator LAURENCE LECIEUX.

Muséum d'Histoire Naturelle: Jardin de l'Etat, 97400 St-Denis; tel. 2-62-20-02-19; e-mail museum@cg974.fr; internet www.cg974.fr; f. 1855, fmrly the Legislative Palace built by the East India Co, present status 1855; zoology and mineralogy; permanent colln of rocks, minerals, wildlife from the Indian Ocean region; library of 12,000 vols; Dir Dr SONIA RIBES-BEAUDEMOULIN.

St-Gilles-les-Hauts

Musée Historique de Villèle: Domaine Panon-Desbassyns, 97435 St-Gilles-les-Hauts; tel. 2-62-55-64-10; e-mail musee.villele@cg974.fr; internet www.cg974.fr/index.php/culture-et-sport/les-musees/musee-historique-de-villele.html; f. 1974; 18th century plantation house and adjoining properties; French East India Co. furniture and china, prints, models, weapons, documents; Curator JEAN BARBIER.

St-Leu

Musée Stella Matutina: 6 allée des Flamboyants, 97424 St Leu; tel. 2-62-34-16-24; e-mail com.seml@wanadoo.fr; f. 1991 as museum, fmr sugar cane factory built 1855, closed 1978, bought and restored by Réunion Island dept 1986; dedicated to sugar cane production and other agricultural products incl. coffee, spices and vanilla; a laboratory that teaches the art of smelling and creating fragrances.

University

UNIVERSITÉ DE LA RÉUNION

15 ave René Cassin, BP 7151, 97715 St-Denis Messag. Cedex 9

Telephone: 2-62-93-80-80

E-mail: contact@univ-reunion.fr

Internet: www.univ-reunion.fr

Founded 1970, present status 1982

Pres.: Prof. MOHAMED ROCHDI

Vice-Pres. for Ccl of Admin.: Prof. HARRY BOYER

Vice-Pres. for External Relations and Professional Integration: Dr FRÉDÉRIC MIRANVILLE

Vice-Pres. for Int. Relations: Prof. LAURENT SERMET

Vice-Pres. for Scientific Ccl: Prof. DOMINIQUE STRASBERG

Vice-Pres. for Students: NICAISE GONTHIER

Vice-Pres. for Studies and Univ. Life: Dr FABRICE LEMAIRE

Librarian: JEAN-CLAUDE MIRÉ

Library: see under Libraries and Archives

Number of teachers: 1,310

Number of students: 12,000

DEANS

Faculty of Arts and Humanities: Prof. GUY FONTAINE

Faculty of Health: Prof. PASCAL GUIRAUD

Faculty of Human and Environmental Science: PIERRE LEROYER

Faculty of Law and Economics: Prof. PASCAL PUIG

Faculty of Science and Technology: Prof. JEAN-PIERRE CHABRIAT

Colleges

Ecole Supérieure d'Ingénieurs Réunion Océan Indien: ESIROI-IDAI, Parc Technologique Universitaire, 2 rue Joseph Wetzell, 97490 Ste-Clotilde; tel. 2-62-48-33-44 ESIROI-CODE, 117 rue du Général Ailleret, 97430 Le Tampon; tel. 2-62-57-91-60 ESIROI-STIM, 15 ave René Cassin, BP 7151, 97715 St-Denis Messag. Cedex 9; tel. 2-62-52-89-06; e-mail secretariat.stim@univ-reunion.fr; internet esiroi.univ-reunion.fr; attached to Univ. de La Réunion; depts of integrated agri-food innovation and development (IDAI), sustainable construction and environment (CODE), telecommunications services, computer and multimedia (STIM); Dir for Integrated Agri-Food Innovation and Development (ESIROI-IDAI) Dr MIREILLE FOUILLAUD.

Institut d'Administration des Entreprises de La Réunion: 24–26 ave de la Victoire, BP 7151, 97715 St-Denis Messag. Cedex 9; tel. 2-62-21-16-26; e-mail iae@univ-reunion.fr; internet www.iae-reunion.fr; f. 1998; attached to Univ. de La Réunion; industry research; devt of science and management techniques; Dir Prof. MICHEL BOYER; Exec. Sec. VERONIQUE ROCHE.

Institut Universitaire de Technologie: 40 ave de Soweto, Terre Ste, BP 373, 97410 St-Pierre; tel. 2-62-96-28-70; e-mail iut.contact@univ-reunion.fr; internet www.univ-reunion.fr/universite/composantes/iut.html; attached to Univ. de la Réunion; depts of biological engineering, business management and administration, civil engineering, network telecommunications; Dir FRANCK LUCAS.

GABON

The Higher Education System

Gabon gained its independence from France in 1960, and the higher education system still reflects its French heritage; many students also go to France to attend university or receive technical training. The first institutions of higher education were a polytechnic institute and law school associated with the Central African Higher Education Foundation, created in 1961 by the heads of state of the former French Equatorial Africa. Université Omar Bongo, the first university, was founded in Libreville in 1970 and adopted its current name in 1978. The other three universities are Université des Sciences et Techniques de Masuku (founded 1986 in Franceville), Université des Sciences de la Santé (founded 2002 in Owendo) and Université des Sciences de l'Éducation. Higher education is highly centralized and controlled mostly by the State, which subsidizes each student for about 95% of the cost of education and provides financial aid equivalent to 40% of the total budget allocation for higher education. Student fees represent only 3% of income. In 1998/99 there were some 7,473 students enrolled in tertiary education.

Admission to higher education is dependent upon award of the Baccalauréat, the main secondary-school qualification, and passing the competitive entrance examination (le concours). According to the existing, pre-Bologna system of higher education, university-level degrees are divided into three cycles. The first cycle lasts for two years and leads to the award of Diplôme Universitaire d'Études Littéraires, Diplôme Universitaire d'Études Scientifiques, Diplôme Universitaire d'Études Juridiques, Diplôme Universitaire d'Études Économiques (these four diplomas may now come under the general title of Diplôme Universitaire d'Études Générales) or Diplôme Universitaire de Technologie. A further year of study (three in total) leads to the award of the Licence; alternatively, a further two years (four in total) leads to the Maîtrise; these degrees comprise the second cycle. Some professional titles, such as Diplôme d'Ingénieur and the Doctorat en Médecine, are awarded after five to six years of study. Finally, the third cycle consists of diploma programmes offered by professional institutions, admission to which is conditional on the Maîtrise. As in many other Francophone countries in Africa, a number of higher education institutions in Gabon are in the process of implementing the Bologna-style Licence/Master/Doctorat (LMD) system. This will involve a Licence, requiring six semesters of study, a Master, requiring four semesters of study after the Licence, and a Doctorat, requiring six semesters of study following the Master.

Higher vocational education is offered by professional schools and institutes. Students may also undertake apprenticeships. The École Nationale de Commerce provides courses in financial and commercial administration and accounting, which lead to the award of the Diplôme de l'École Nationale de Commerce. In 2009 a five-year Public Services Higher Education and Vocational Training Support Project was launched to aid efforts to enhance technical skills in potential growth sectors.

In 2010 at the États Généraux de l'Éducation de la Recherche et de l'Adéquation Formation-Emploi a new law was proposed to replace the 1996 law on education, training and research; a ten-year plan also was put into place to reform fundamentally the education system at all levels in Gabon; to consolidate the LMD system throughout the country (before 2020), to create the Conseil National de l'Enseignement, de la Formation et de la Recherche to oversee higher education and research institutes, to build a further three universities and to modernize the existing universities, with a large project planned at Université Omar Bongo. The scientific and research centres were also to be restructured and refinanced.

Regulatory Bodies

GOVERNMENT

Ministry of National Education, Higher and Technical Education, Professional Training, Culture, Youth and Sports: BP 6, Libreville; tel. (1) 72-44-61; Minister SÉRAPHIN MOUNDOUNGA.

Learned Societies

GENERAL

UNESCO Office Libreville: BP 2183, Libreville; Cité de la Démocratie, bâtiment 6, Libreville; tel. (1) 762879; designated Cluster Office for the Republic of the Congo, the Democratic Republic of the Congo, Equatorial Guinea, Gabon, São Tomé e Príncipe; Dir MAKHILY GASSAMA.

LANGUAGE AND LITERATURE

Alliance Française: BP 1371, Port Gentil; tel. (2) 565941; e-mail alliance.francogab@inet.ga; offers courses and exams in French language and culture and promotes cultural exchange with France.

Research Institutes

GENERAL

Centre National de la Recherche Scientifique et Technologique (CENAREST): BP 13354, Libreville; tel. (1) 732578; e-mail infos@cenarestgabon.com; internet www.cenarest.org; f. 1976; principal research body; designs and operates research programmes into human sciences, tropical ecology, agronomy, medicinal plants and plant biotechnology; consists of 5 research institutes: l'Institut de Pharmacopée et de Médecine Traditionnelles; l'Institut de Recherches Agronomiques et Forestières; l'Institut de Recherche en Ecologie Tropicale; l'Institut de Recherches en Sciences Humaines; and l'Institut de Recherches Technologiques; Dir SAMUEL MBADIGA.

AGRICULTURE, FISHERIES AND VETERINARY SCIENCE

Centre Technique Forestier Tropical, Section Gabon: BP 149, Libreville; f. 1958; silviculture, technology, genetic improvement; library of 500 vols; Dir J. LEROY DEVAL.

Institut de Recherches Agronomiques et Forestières (IRAF): BP 2246, Libreville; tel. (1) 732375; e-mail angoye@assala.com; internet www.cenarest.org/instituts/iraf; f. 1977; attached to Centre National de la Recherche Scientifique et Technologique (CENAREST); research into agronomy, silviculture and forestry; Dir ALFRED NGOYE.

MEDICINE

Centre International de Recherches Médicales de Franceville: BP 769, Franceville; tel. (2) 677096; e-mail faxcirmf@cirmf.sci.ga; f. 1979; undertakes basic and applied research in medical parasitology (e.g. malaria, filariosis, trypanosomiasis) and viral diseases (incl. HIV/AIDS, Ebola); library of 1,800 vols, 72 periodicals, 20,000 microfiches; Dir-Gen. Prof. PHILIPPE BLOT.

Institut de Pharmacopée et de Médecine Traditionnelles (IPHAMETRA): BP 1935, Libreville; tel. (1) 734786; internet www.cenarest.org/instituts/iphametra; f. 1976; attached to Centre National de la Recherche Scientifique et Technologique (CENAREST); Dir Dr HENRI PAUL BOUROBOU.

NATURAL SCIENCES

Biological Sciences

Institut de Recherche en Ecologie Tropicale (IRET): BP 13354, Makokou; tel. (1) 443319; e-mail agnesgras@yahoo.fr; internet www.cenarest.org/instituts/iret; f. 1979; attached to Centre National de la Recherche Scientifique et Technologique (CENAREST); Dir PAUL POSSO.

RELIGION, SOCIOLOGY AND ANTHROPOLOGY

Institut de Recherches en Sciences Humaines (IRSH): BP 846, Libreville; tel. (1) 734719; internet www.cenarest.org/

instituts/irsh; f. 1976; attached to Centre National de la Recherche Scientifique et Technologique (CENAREST); Dir Dr MAGLOIRE MOUNGANGAI.

TECHNOLOGY

Bureau de Recherches Géologiques et Minières (BRGM): BP 175, Libreville; f. 1960; see main entry under France; Dir M. BERTUCAT.

Institut de Recherches Technologiques (IRT): BP 14070, Libreville; tel. (1) 733089; internet www.cenarest.org/instituts/irt; f. 1976; attached to Centre National de la Recherche Scientifique et Technologique (CENAREST); Dir Dr JEAN DANIEL MBEGAI.

Libraries and Archives

Libreville

Direction Générale des Archives Nationales, de la Bibliothèque Nationale et de la Documentation Gabonaise (DGABD): BP 1188, Libreville; tel. (1) 736310; f. 1969 (Nat. Archives and Nat. Library), 1980 (Gabonese Documentation); 29,000 vols, 2,000 periodical titles, 2 linear km archives, 639 microfilms, 666 maps and plans, 1,712 archive photographs; Archives Dir JÉRÔME ANGOUME-NGOGHE; Nat. Library Dir JEAN MICHEL NOUDODO; Documentation Dir JEAN PAUL MIFOUNA; Dir-Gen. RENÉ GEORGES SONNET-AZIZE.

Museum

Libreville

Musée National des Arts et Traditions du Gabon: BP 4018, Libreville; tel. (1) 761456; e-mail museegabon@numibia.net; nat. museum; thematic exhibition on Gabonese masks; public library on arts from Gabon; Dir Prof. PAUL ABA'A NDONG.

Universities

UNIVERSITÉ DES SCIENCES DE LA SANTÉ

BP 18231, Owendo, Libreville
Telephone: (1) 702028
E-mail: rectorat@uss-univ.com

Founded 2002
State control
Courses in health sciences

Rector: ANDRÉ MOUSSAVOU-MOUYAMA

UNIVERSITÉ DES SCIENCES ET TECHNIQUES DE MASUKU
(University of Science and Technology of Masuku)

BP 901, Franceville
Telephone: (2) 677449
E-mail: webmaster@univ-masuku.ga
Internet: www.univ-masuku.ga

Founded 1986
State control
Language of instruction: French

Rector: Dr ISSAC MOUARAGADJA
Vice-Rector for Academic Affairs and Research: Prof. RAPHAEL BILL BIKANGA
Vice-Rector for Admin. Affairs and Inter-university Cooperation: Prof. BENOIT BOUKILA
Sec.-Gen.: Dr JEAN JACQUES YAMA
Librarian: GEORGE NGALO

Library of 11,000 vols
Number of students: 3,000

DEANS

Faculty of Sciences: Dr LÉON NGADI
National Higher Institute of Agronomy and Biotechnology: Prof. ALAIN SOUZA (Dir)
Polytechnic School of Masuku: Dr GASTON NTCHAYI MBOUROU (Dir)

UNIVERSITÉ OMAR BONGO

BP 13 131, blvd Léon M'Ba, Libreville
Telephone: (1) 732045
E-mail: uob@internetgabon.com
Internet: www.uob.ga

Founded 1970, renamed 1978
State control
Language of instruction: French
Academic year: October to July

Rector: JEAN-ÉMILE MBOT
Vice-Rector for Academic Affairs and Research: JÉRÔME KWENZI-MAKALA
Vice-Rector for Admin. and Inter-university Cooperation: JÉRÔME NDZOUNGOU
Sec.-Gen.: GUY ROSSATANGA-RIGNAULT
Librarian: FERDINAND NGOUNGOULOU

Library of 12,000 vols
Number of teachers: 300
Number of students: 4,800

Publications: *Cahiers d'Histoire et d'Archéologie, Cahiers Gabonais d'Anthropologie, Exchorésis, Gabonica, Kilombo, Psychologie et Culture, Revue Gabonaise des Sciences de l'Homme, Revue Gabonaise des Sciences du Langage, Waves*

DEANS

Faculty of Law and Economics: Prof. JEAN JACQUES EKOMIE
Faculty of Letters and Sciences: GUY SERGE BIGNOUMBA

ATTACHED RESEARCH INSTITUTES

Centre d'Études en Littérature Gabonaise: Dir HÉMERY-HERVAIS SIMA EYI.

Centre d'Études et de Recherches d'Histoire Économique, Administrative et Financière (CERHEAF): BP 13131, Libreville; Dir Prof. PIERRE NDOMBI.

Centre d'Études et de Recherches du Monde Anglophone (CERMA): Dir DANIEL RENÉ AKENDENGUE.

Centre d'Études et de Recherches Philosophiques (CERP): Dir GILBERT ZUE NGUEMA.

Centre de Recherches Afro-Hispaniques (CRAHI): Dir GISÈLE AVOME MBA.

Centre de Recherches et d'Études en Psychologie (CREP): Dir THÉODORE KOUMBA.

Groupe de Recherches en Langues et Cultures Orales (GRELACO): Dir Prof. JAMES DUPLESSIS EMEJULU.

Institut Cheikh Anta Diop (ICAD): Dir GRÉGOIRE BIYOGO NANG.

Laboratoire d'Analyse Spatiale et des Environnements Tropicaux (LANASPET): Dir GALLEY YAWO.

Laboratoire de Graphique et de Cartographie (LAGRAC): Dir Dr JULES DJEKI.

Laboratoire National d'Archéologie (LANA): Dir MICHEL ATHANASE LOCKO.

Laboratoire Universitaire de la Tradition Orale (LUTO): Dir Prof. FABIEN OKOUE-METOGO.

Politiques et Développement des Espaces et Sociétés de l'Afrique Subsaharienne (CERGEP): Dir MARC LOUIS ROPIVIA

Colleges

Institut Africain d'Informatique: BP 2263, Libreville; tel. (1) 720005; e-mail info@iai.ga; internet www.iai.ga; f. 1971 by mem. states of OCAM to train computer programmers, computer science engineers and analysts; small library; 8 permanent teachers; 281 students; Dir FABIEN MBALLA.

THE GAMBIA

The Higher Education System

Higher education, in the sense of an institution offering Bachelors, Masters and Doctorate degrees, did not exist in The Gambia until 1995. Prior to this, Gambians wishing to pursue higher education could either study abroad or enrol at one of a small number of post-secondary technical/vocational institutions. A University Extension Programme was established in 1995 as a collaborative effort between the Government and the Nova Scotia Gambia Association (NSGA), a Canadian NGO, and Saint Mary's University (located in Halifax, Nova Scotia). The first university, the University of The Gambia, was opened in Banjul in 1999, with the assistance of Saint Mary's University. The higher education sector in The Gambia is administered and funded by the Government. Some 1,591 students were enrolled at tertiary establishments in 1994/95, but by 2007 the number had risen to 8,373. In 2009/10 2,842 students were enrolled at the University of The Gambia. In addition to the tertiary institutions, there are about 100 registered Skills Training Centres providing courses towards local and external certificates and diplomas in a variety of professional fields. These are mainly privately operated centres. In January 2011 The Gambia's first private university—the American International University West Africa—opened in Banjul. The university comprises the following: a College of Dentistry, College of Health Professionals, College of Medicine, College of Nursing and College of Pharmacy. The university was reported to be the first university in Africa to provide programmes based on a curriculum modelled on major professional schools in the USA.

Admission to university is on the basis of the West African Senior School Certificate or equivalent qualification. The University of The Gambia (comprising nine Schools) offers Bachelors degrees, which are awarded following four years; however, the Bachelors of Medicine and of Surgery take seven years to complete. Initially, there were no postgraduate degree courses, but since 2007 the following two-year Masters degree programmes have been introduced: Master of Arts in African History, Master of Arts in French and Master of Science in Public Health. Admission to the Masters courses is based on the holding of the Bachelors. The University of The Gambia also offers a number of undergraduate programmes at pre-Bachelors level. These include the Higher Certificate and Higher Diploma in Agriculture and a Paralegal Certificate and Diploma.

Technical and vocational education is offered by the Gambia College (founded 1978 and composed of four Schools covering the areas of agriculture, education, nursing and midwifery, and public health), the Management Development Institute (founded 1982), the Rural Development Institute in Mansa Konko (founded 1979), the Gambia Technical Training Institute (founded 1980) and the Institute of Travel and Tourism (founded 1979 as the Gambia Hotel School). The main qualifications are the Diploma and Certificate. The National Training Authority (NTA), which was established in 2002, is responsible for regulating vocational education and training. In 2006 the NTA launched the Gambia Skills Qualifications Framework and it is currently developing a quality assurance mechanism to be used for the registration and accreditation of private vocational providers and programmes. It is also drawing up regulations and curricula for apprenticeship training.

A higher education policy is being developed following the establishment of a Ministry of Higher Education, Research, Science and Technology in early 2007. In the interim, the tertiary and higher education component of the Education Policy 2004–2015, prepared by the Ministry of Basic and Secondary Education, is being used to guide the activities of the new Ministry.

Regulatory Bodies

GOVERNMENT

Ministry of Basic and Secondary Education: Willy Thorpe Bldg, Banjul; tel. 4228235; e-mail info@mobse.gov.gm; internet www.mobse.gov.gm; Minister Hon. FATOU LAMIN FAYE.

Ministry of Higher Education, Research, Science and Technology: Bertil Hardway, Kotu; tel. 4465752; e-mail info@moherst.gov.gm; internet www.moherst.gov.gm; Minister MAMBURY NJIE.

Ministry of Tourism and Culture: The Quadrangle, Banjul; tel. 4222376; e-mail info@motc.gov.gm; internet www.motc.gov.gm; Minister FATOU MAS JOBE-NJIE.

Learned Society

LANGUAGE AND LITERATURE

Alliance Franco-Gambienne: Kairaba Ave, Kanifing, POB 2930, Serrekunda, Banjul; tel. 4375418; e-mail alliancefg@hotmail.com; internet www.alliancefranco.gm; offers courses and exams in French language and culture and promotes cultural exchange with France.

Research Institutes

MEDICINE

Medical Research Council Unit, The Gambia: POB 273, Banjul; Atlantic Blvd, Fajara; tel. 4496715; e-mail aoffong@mrc.gm; internet www.mrc.gm; f. 1947; laboratory research, field research and clinical studies aimed at reducing illness and death from tropical infectious diseases; research on viral diseases, bacterial diseases and malaria; a nutrition research group is based at the MRC Keneba Field Site; Unit Dir Prof. UMBERTO D'ALESSANDRO.

Medical Research Council Dunn Nutrition Unit, Keneba: Keneba, West Kiang; f. 1974; field station of the Dunn Nutrition Unit laboratory in Cambridge, UK; research on maternal undernutrition, including work on paediatric gastroenterology and nutrition, and the physiological adaptation of mothers to pregnancy and lactation; maternal vitamin and mineral requirements; research into long-term effects of antenatal and early postnatal nutrition; research on growth deficiency and the role of economic status on malnutrition; calorimetry research on comparisons of energy expenditure between Gambians and Europeans; Head RITA WEGMULLER; Deputy Head LANDING JARJOU.

Library

Banjul

Gambia National Library: Department Mail Bag, Reg Pye Lane, Banjul; tel. 4228312; e-mail national.library@qanet.gm; f. 1946 by British Ccl, taken over by Govt 1962, autonomous 1985; serves as a public and nat. library; nat. deposit library; 115,400 vols, 85 periodicals; spec. colln of Gambiana; Dir ABDOU WALLY MBYE; publs *National Bibliography*, *Wax Taani Xalel Yi* (children's magazine).

Museum

Banjul

Gambia National Museum: PMB 151, Independence Dr., Banjul; tel. 4226244; e-mail hceesay@gmail.com; internet www.ncac.gm; library of 645 vols; f. 1982; wide network of museums in the country explaining aspects of Gambian culture and history; provides Nat. Museum services: cultural programmes, literary programmes, children's programmes, research and documentation; Curator HASSOUM CESSAY.

University

UNIVERSITY OF THE GAMBIA

Administration Bldg, Kanifing, POB 3530, Serrekunda
Telephone: 4372213
E-mail: unigambia@qanet.gm
Internet: www.unigambia.gm
Founded 1999
State control
Academic year: October to July (2 semesters)
Vice-Chancellor: Prof. DONALD E. U. EKONG
Registrar: E. J. AKPAN
Student Affairs: LAMIN S. JAITEH
Senate: LANG SAJO MUSTAPHA JADAMA
Council: MOMODOU LAMIN TARRO
Number of teachers: 99 (78 full-time, 21 part-time)
Number of students: 1,356

DEANS

Faculty of Economics and Management Sciences: SULAYMAN M. B. FYE
Faculty of Humanities and Social Sciences: Prof. EDRIS MAKWARD
Faculty of Medicine and Allied Health Sciences: Prof. ETIM M. ESSIEN
Faculty of Science and Agriculture: Prof. FELIXTINA JONSYN-ELLIS (acting)

College

Gambia College: Brikama Campus, POB 144, Banjul; tel. 4484812; e-mail gcollege@qanet.gm; f. 1978; library: 23,000 vols; 57 teachers; 400 students; Pres. A. B. SENGHORE; Registrar N. S. MANNEH.

GEORGIA

The Higher Education System

Georgia was formerly a constituent republic of the USSR, from which it gained its independence in 1999. Most institutions were founded during the Soviet period and consequently reflected Soviet practices, but since independence there have been numerous reforms and ongoing projects. The Laws on Higher and General Education adopted in 2004 and 2005, respectively, laid out further plans for the reform of secondary and higher education, including implementation of the Bologna Process. The various reforms have focused on reviewing and improving the content of study programmes, increasing the autonomy of institutions, modernizing teaching methodologies and implementing quality assurance procedures. In addition to state institutions, many private institutions of higher education were opened after 1991; there were 108 in 2009/10. In that year there was a total of 102,710 students enrolled at institutions of higher education (including universities)—of these, 74,056 were attending state establishments and 28,654 private establishments. There are three different types of higher education institutions in Georgia: universities, teaching universities and colleges. Colleges offer professional higher education programmes and first-cycle courses to Bachelors level. Teaching universities offer courses to Masters level and only universities are authorized to offer all three cycles of education up to Doctorate level. In 2012 there were five colleges, 27 teaching universities and 25 universities accredited by the Ministry of Education and Science, which is the administrative body for higher education.

Higher education admissions are generally determined on the basis of performance in the Unified National University Entry Examinations, administered by the National Assessment and Examinations Centre. Students take a range of compulsory and voluntary subjects relevant to their intended path of study. A number of universities set their own entrance requirements. In May 2005 Georgia signed up to the Bologna Process. Georgia's new degree structure consists of Bachelors, Masters and Doctorate degrees, and the European Credit Transfer System (ECTS) has been adopted to facilitate student transfers. The Bachelors is the main undergraduate degree and is awarded after fours years' study (240 ECTS credits). Since 2010 old-style one-cycle undergraduate programmes (lasting five to six years) are no longer offered by any institutions, with the exception of medical degrees. A Masters degree is awarded after the Bachelors following two years of study (120 ECTS credits). The third tier of the new higher education system is the doctoral degree, which requires three years of study (180 ECTS credits) following the Masters and the presentation and defence of a thesis. All higher education institutions issue Diploma Supplements free of charge—either automatically or upon request.

In addition to the three-tier degree system, short-cycle vocational/professional tertiary programmes have been introduced, which normally last two to three years (120–180 ECTS credits) and culminate in the award of certified specialist. Credits accumulated for the award of certified specialist can be transferred to the relevant Bachelors courses. Reform of the vocational education system commenced in 2007 and an Education Reform Strategy was adopted from 2009 to 2012 in order to bring the Georgian system into line with European and international practices; in 2010 a National Qualifications Framework was approved.

The National Centre for Educational Quality Enhancement was established in September 2010 to replace the National Centre for Educational Accreditation. As a result of amendments made to educational legislation in that month, mandatory licensing and institutional accreditation were substituted by the authorization procedure. Authorization (the instrument for the external evaluation of the compatibility of an institution with standards, certifying internal (self) evaluation) is now a mandatory procedure for educational institutions, whilst accreditation (a type of external evaluation mechanism, which determines the compatibility of an educational programme with standards) is generally a voluntary one. State funding, however, is allocated only to accredited programmes. Accreditation is mandatory for doctoral programmes and regulated professions as well as for programmes covering the Georgian language and liberal arts.

Regulatory and Representative Bodies

GOVERNMENT

Ministry of Culture and Monument Protection: 0105 Tbilisi, Sanapiro St 4; tel. (32) 293-22-55; e-mail pr@culture.gov.ge; internet www.mcs.gov.ge; Minister GURAM ODISHARIA.

Ministry of Education and Science: 0102 Tbilisi, D. Uznadze N52; tel. (32) 220-02-20; e-mail pr@mes.gov.ge; internet www.mes.gov.ge; Minister TAMAR SANIKIDZE.

ACCREDITATION

ENIC/NARIC Georgia: Div. of Academic Recognition and Mobility, Min. of Education and Science, 0102 Tbilisi, D. Uznadze 52; tel. (32) 95-75-23; e-mail mobility_division@yahoo.com; Head Dr IRAKLI MACHABELI.

Learned Societies

GENERAL

Georgian National Academy of Sciences: 0108 Tbilisi, 52 Rustaveli Ave; tel. (32)299-61-42; e-mail academy@science.org.ge; internet www.science.org.ge; f. 1941; depts of agricultural science problems, applied mechanics, biology, chemistry and chemical technology, earth sciences, linguistics and literature, machine building and control processes, mathematics and physics, physiology and experimental medicine, and social sciences; 195 mems (64 academicians, 41 corresp.); library: see under Libraries and Archives; Pres. Prof. Dr GIORGI KVESITADZE; publs *Academy of Sciences* (3 a year, in Georgian and English), *Metsnierba da Technika* (12 a year), *Metsnierba da Technologiebi* (12 a year).

HISTORY, GEOGRAPHY AND ARCHAEOLOGY

Georgian Geographical Society: 0107 Tbilisi, Ketskhoveli 11; attached to Georgian Acad. of Sciences; Chair. V. SH. DZHAOSHVILI.

LANGUAGE AND LITERATURE

British Council: 0108 Tbilisi, Pr. Rustaveli 34; tel. (32) 25-04-07; e-mail office@ge.britishcouncil.org; internet www.britishcouncil.org.ge; offers courses and examinations in English language and British culture and promotes cultural exchange with the UK; Dir JO BAKOWSKI; Librarian TAMUNA KVACHADZE.

Goethe-Institut: 0108 Tbilisi, ul. Sandukeli 16; tel. (32) 293-89-45; e-mail info@tbilissi.goethe.org; internet www.goethe.de/ins/ge/tif/deindex.htm; offers courses and examinations in German language and culture and promotes cultural exchange with Germany; library of 3,500 vols; Dir Dr STEPHAN WACKWITZ.

MEDICINE

Georgian Neuroscience Association: c/o Beritashvili Institute of Physiology, 0160 Tbilisi, Gotua St 14; tel. (32) 37-21-50; e-mail nodmit@biphysiol.ge; internet www.itic.org.ge/gena; f. 1996; 105 mems; Pres. Prof. SIMON KHECHINASHVILI; Exec. Sec. Prof. Dr NODAR MITAGVARIA.

NATURAL SCIENCES

Biological Sciences

Georgian Botanical Society: 0107 Tbilisi, Kodzhorskoe shosse; attached to Georgian Acad. of Sciences; Pres. G. SH. NAKHUTSRISHVILI.

Georgian Society of Geneticists and Selectioners: 0160 Tbilisi, ul. L. Gotua 3; tel. (32) 37-42-27; attached to Georgian Acad. of Sciences; Pres. T. G. CHANISHVILI.

Georgian Society of Parasitologists: 0179 Tbilisi, Pr. Chavchavadze 31; tel. (32) 22-33-53; attached to Georgian Acad. of Sciences; f. 1958; 83 mems; Pres. Prof. B. E. KURASHVILI; Sec. K. G. NIKOLAISHVILI; publ. *Actual Problems of Parasitology in Georgia*.

Physical Sciences

Georgian Geological Society: 0108 Tbilisi, Pr. Rustaveli 52; tel. (32) 99-64-45; e-mail gageosociety@gmail.com; f. 1933; attached to Georgian Acad. of Sciences; 500 mems; Chair. IRAKLI P. GAMKRELIDZE.

Georgian National Speleological Society: 0193 Tbilisi, M. Aleksidze 8; tel. (32) 33-74-49; f. 1980; attached to Georgian Acad. of Sciences; 75 mems; Chair. Z. K. TATASHIDZE; publ. *Caves of Georgia* (irregular).

PHILOSOPHY AND PSYCHOLOGY

Georgian Philosophy Society: 0108 Tbilisi, Pr. Rustaveli 29; attached to Georgian Acad. of Sciences; Pres. DEVON BELCHER; Sec. RAYMOND WOLLER.

Research Institutes

GENERAL

Kutaisi Scientific Centre: 4600 Kutaisi, Abashidze 22; tel. (331) 7-77-77; attached to Georgian Acad. of Sciences; Dir R. ADAMAI.

AGRICULTURE, FISHERIES AND VETERINARY SCIENCE

Gulisashvili, V. Z., Institute of Mountain Forestry: 0186 Tbilisi, E. Mindeli 9; tel. (32) 30-34-66; e-mail postmaster@forest.acnet.ge; f. 1945; attached to Georgian Acad. of Sciences; Dir G. N. GIGAURI.

Scientific Research Centre of the Biological Basis of Cattle-Breeding: 0162 Tbilisi, Paliashvili 87; tel. (32) 29-40-03; f. 1991; attached to Georgian Acad. of Sciences; Dir A. DOLMAZASHVILI.

Water Management Institute of Georgian Technical University: 0162 Tbilisi, Ave I. Chavchavadze 60; tel. (32) 222-40-94; e-mail gwmi1929@gmail.com; internet gwmi.ge; f. 1929; attached to Georgian Min. of Education and Science; library of 32,000 vols; Dir Prof. Dr GIVI GAVARDASHVILI; publs *Recent Problems of Water Management, Environmental Protection, Transactions of International Conferences*.

ARCHITECTURE AND TOWN PLANNING

Kiriak Zavriev Institute of Structural Mechanics and Earthquake Engineering: 0193 Tbilisi, M. Aleksidze 8; tel. (32) 33-59-28; e-mail info@ismee.ge; internet ismee.ge; f. 1947; attached to Georgian Acad. of Sciences; Dir Prof. P. REKVAVA.

BIBLIOGRAPHY, LIBRARY SCIENCE AND MUSEOLOGY

Kekelidze, K. S., Institute of Manuscripts: 0193 Tbilisi, Merab Aleksidze St, Korp. 3; tel. (32) 36-24-54; e-mail manuscript@iatp.org.ge; internet www.acnet.ge/manuscr.htm; f. 1958; attached to Georgian Acad. of Sciences; Dir Z. ALEKSIDZE; publ. *Mravaltavi* (Philology and History, 1 a year).

ECONOMICS, LAW AND POLITICS

Gugushvili, P. V., Institute of Economics: 0105 Tbilisi, ul. Kikodze 22; tel. (32) 99-68-53; e-mail root@econom.acnet.ge; f. 1944; attached to Georgian Acad. of Sciences; Dir G. TSERETELI.

Institute of Political Science: 0162 Tbilisi, Paliashvili 87; tel. (32) 22-41-04; e-mail politic@gw.acnet.ge; f. 2000; attached to Georgian Acad. of Sciences; Dir V. KESHELAVA.

Institute of State and Law: 0105 Tbilisi, ul. Kikodze 14; tel. (32) 98-32-45; e-mail root@stlow.acnet.ge; f. 1957; attached to Georgian Acad. of Sciences; Dir (vacant).

FINE AND PERFORMING ARTS

Chubinashvili, G. N., Institute of History of Georgian Art: 0108 Tbilisi, Pr. Rustaveli 52; tel. (32) 99-05-88; f. 1941; attached to Georgian Acad. of Sciences; Dir T. SAKVARELIDZE; publ. *Ars Georgica*.

HISTORY, GEOGRAPHY AND ARCHAEOLOGY

Ivane Javakhishvili Institute of History and Ethnology: 0179 Tbilisi, ul. Melikishvili 10; tel. (32) 99-06-82; e-mail histend55@yahoo.com; f. 1941; attached to Ivane Javakhishvili Tbilisi State Univ.; scientific research in ancient and modern history; confs, seminars; library of 55,000 vols; Dir Prof. Dr VAZHA I. KIKNADZE; Vice-Dir GURAM NIKOLASHVILI; publ. *Proceedings of the Institute of History and Ethnology* (1 a year).

Lordkipanidze Centre for Archaeological Studies: 0102 Tbilisi, D. Uznadze 14; tel. (32) 95-97-65; attached to Georgian Acad. of Sciences.

Mtskheta Institute of Archaeology: 3300 Mtskheta; f. 1994; attached to Georgian Acad. of Sciences; Dir A. APAKIDZE; publ. *Mtskheta*.

Vakhushti Bagrationi Institute of Geography: 0193 Tbilisi, M. Aleksidze 1 (Bl. 8); tel. (32) 33-74-49; e-mail geograf@gw.acnet.ge; f. 1933; attached to Georgian Acad. of Sciences; library of 68,000 vols; Dir ZURAB TATASHISZE; publ. *Caves of Georgia* (irregular).

LANGUAGE AND LITERATURE

Chikobava, A. S., Institute of Linguistics: 380002 Tbilisi, P. Ingorokva St 8; tel. (32) 93-29-21; internet www.acnet.ge/ike.htm; e-mail root@ike.acnet.ge; f. 1941; attached to Georgian Acad. of Sciences; Dir G. KVARATSKHELIA; publs *Dialectological Studies, Etymological Studies, Iberian-Caucasian Linguistics, Problems of Georgian Language Structure, Problems of Georgian Literary Norms, Problems of Modern General Linguistics*.

Shota Rustaveli Institute of Georgian Literature: 0108 Tbilisi, Kostava St 5; tel. (32) 99-53-00; e-mail litinst@litinstituti.ge; internet www.litinstituti.ge; f. 1932; attached to Georgian Acad. of Sciences; Dir Prof. IRMA RATIANI; Deputy Dir Prof. MAKA ELBAKIDZE; publs *Literary Researches* (1 a year), *Litinfo* (electronic), *Sjani* (1 a year, peer-reviewed int. journal of literary theory and comparative literature).

Tsereteli, G. V., Institute of Oriental Studies: 0103 Tbilisi, ul. G. Tsereteli 3; tel. (32) 23-23-72; e-mail root@orient.acnet.ge; f. 1960; attached to Georgian Acad. of Sciences; Dir T. GAMKRELIDZE.

MEDICINE

Beritashvili Institute of Physiology: 0160 Tbilisi, ul. Gotua 14; tel. (32) 37-12-31; e-mail info@biphysiol.ge; internet www.biphysiol.ge; f. 1935 as Academic Research Institute; attached to Min. of Education and Science; library of 48,000 vols; Dir Dr M. G. TSAGARELI; Sec. N. EMUKHVARI.

Eliyava Institute of Bacteriophage, Microbiology and Virology: 0160 Tbilisi, ul. L. Gotua 3; tel. (32) 37-42-27; e-mail chanish@kheta.ge; f. 1923; attached to Georgian Acad. of Sciences; Dir T. CHANISHVILI.

Institute of Medical Biotechnology: 0159 Tbilisi, Chiaureli 2; tel. (32) 54-07-25; e-mail imb_admin@caucasus.net; internet www.imb.org.ge; f. 1991; attached to Min. of Education and Science; Dir TEIMURAZ TOPURIA; Head of Scientific Board Assoc. Prof. IA PANTSULAIA.

Institute of Pharmaceutical Chemistry: 0159 Tbilisi, P. Sarajishvili 36; tel. (32) 52-98-50; e-mail root@pharmac.acnet.ge; f. 1932; attached to Georgian Acad. of Sciences; library of 3,500 vols, 40 periodicals; Dir Prof. ETHER P. KEMERTELIDZE.

Natishvili, A. N., Institute of Experimental Morphology: 0159 Tbilisi, Chiaureli 2; tel. (32) 52-09-06; f. 1946; attached to Georgian Acad. of Sciences; Dir N. A. JAVAKHISHVILI.

Research Institute of Clinical Medicine: 0112 Tbilisi, Tevdore Mgvdeli St 13; tel. (32) 294-02-89; e-mail radiologymedicine@yahoo.com; f. 1991; Dir Prof. FRIDON TODUA; publ. *Georgian Journal of Radiology* (4 a year).

Research Institute of Skin and Venereal Diseases: 0112 Tbilisi, ul. Ninoshvili 55; tel. (32) 95-35-64; f. 1935; library of 23,800 vols; Dir Dr BADZI CHLAIDZE; publ. *Trudy* (Proceedings, 1 a year).

Scientific Research Centre for Radiobiology and Radiation Ecology: 0103 Tbilisi, Telavi 51; tel. (32) 94-20-17; e-mail kiazo@gw.acnet.ge; internet www.acnet.ge/radiobio; f. 1990; attached to Georgian Acad. of Sciences; Dir K. SH. NADAREISHVILI; publs *Biomedical Techniques* (2 a year), *Problems of Ecology* (2 a year), *Radiation Studies* (2 a year).

Virsaladze Institute of Medical Parasitology and Tropical Medicine: 0112 Tbilisi, D. Agmashenebeli 139; tel. (32) 95-92-26; e-mail medpari@yahoo.com; internet geoparasitology.dsl.ge; f. 1924; Dir NORA KOKAIA; Deputy Dir and Admin. Man. NINO IASHVILI.

Zhordania Institute of Human Reproduction: 0109 Tbilisi, Kostava 43; tel. (32) 99-61-97; e-mail archil@list.ru; Dir Prof. A. KHOMASSURIDZE.

NATURAL SCIENCES

Biological Sciences

Batumi Botanical Gardens: Mtsvane Kontskhi, Makhinjauri, Batumi; e-mail bbg@bbg.ge; internet www.bbg.ge; f. 1912; library of 22,000 vols; Dir TAMAZ DARCHIDZE.

Davitashvili, L. Sh., Institute of Palaeobiology: 0108 Tbilisi, Niagvris 4; tel. (32) 93-12-82; e-mail guram@paleobi.acnet.ge; f. 1957; attached to Georgian Acad. of Sciences; Dir G. A. MCHEDLIDZE.

Durmishidze Institute of Plant Biochemistry: 0102 Tbilisi, D. Agmashenebeli 10; tel. (32) 95-81-45; e-mail postmaster@biochem.acnet.ge; f. 1971; attached to Georgian Acad. of Sciences; library of 72,000 vols; Dir Prof. Dr G. I. KVESITADZE.

Institute of Molecular Biology and Biological Physics: 0160 Tbilisi, ul. L. Gotua 14; tel. (32) 37-17-33; e-mail admin@biophys

.org.ge; f. 1986; attached to Georgian Acad. of Sciences; Dir Dr Malkhaz Zaalishvili.

Institute of Zoology: 0179 Tbilisi, Pr. Chavchavadze 31; tel. (32) 22-01-64; f. 1941; attached to Georgian Acad. of Sciences; Dir I. Eliyava.

Ketskhoveli, N., Institute of Botany: 0105 Tbilisi, Kojori 1; tel. (32) 99-74-48; e-mail nakhutsrishvili@yahoo.com; f. 1933; attached to Georgian Acad. of Sciences; Dir G. Nakhutsrishvili.

National Botanical Garden of Georgia: 0114 Tbilisi, Botanikuri 1; tel. (32) 272-43-06; e-mail tavartkm@gmail.com; f. 1845; attached to Georgian Acad. of Sciences; scientific research, horticulture, plant conservation, education; Dir Maia Tavartkiladze.

Mathematical Sciences

A. Razmadze Mathematical Institute of I. Javakhishvili Tbilisi State University: 0177 Tbilisi, Tamarashvili St 6; tel. (32) 39-56-26; e-mail ninopa@rmi.ge; internet www .rmi.tsu.ge; f. 1935; attached to Ivane Javakhishvili Tbilisi State Univ.; library of 95,690 vols; Dir Prof. Nino Partsvania; publs *Georgian Mathematical Journal* (4 a year, in English), *Memoirs on Differential Equations and Mathematical Physics* (3 a year, in English).

N. Muskhelishvili Institute of Computational Mathematics of Georgian Technical University: 0160 Tbilisi, 10, Kvernadze str.; tel. (32) 33-24-38; e-mail bachanabc@yahoo.com; internet www .compmath.ge; f. 1956; attached to Georgian Technical Univ.; research in mathematics and computer science; library of 98,000 vols of books and journals; Dir Prof. Vakhtang Kvaratskhelia; Scientific Sec. Dr George Giorgobiani; publs *Computational Mathematics and Programming*, *Mathematical and Technical Cybernetics*.

Physical Sciences

Abastumani Astrophysical Observatory: 0301 Abastumani, Kanobili Mountain; tel. (32) 95-53-67 0179 Tbilisi, ul. Kazbegi 2a; tel. (32) 37-63-03; e-mail roki@gw.acnet.ge; f. 1941; attached to Georgian Acad. of Sciences; Dir R. Kiladze.

Andronikashvili Institute of Physics: 0162 Tbilisi, ul. Tamarashvili 6; e-mail aiphysics@aiphysics.ge; f. 1950; attached to Georgian Acad. of Sciences; Dir G. A. Kharadze.

Dzanelidze, A. I., Geological Institute: 0193 Tbilisi, M. Aleksidze 1 Bldg 9; tel. (32) 29-39-41; e-mail geolog@gw.acnet.ge; f. 1925; attached to Georgian Acad. of Sciences; Dir Prof. Mirian Topchishvili.

Ferdinand Tavadze Institute of Metallurgy and Materials Science: 1060 Tbilisi, Al. Kazbegi Ave 15; tel. (32) 37-02-67; e-mail info@mmi.ge; internet mmi.ge; f. 1945; attached to Georgian Acad. of Sciences; conducts research on metallurgical processes, new materials and technologies, materials science and powder metallurgy; library of 152,953 vols; Dir Prof. Dr Giorgi F. Tavadze.

Institute of Hydrometeorology: 0112 Tbilisi, D. Agmashenebeli 150a; tel. (32) 95-10-47; e-mail root@hydmet.acnet.ge; f. 1953; attached to Georgian Acad. of Sciences; Dir G. G. Svanidze; publ. *Transactions*.

Institute of Inorganic Chemistry and Electrochemistry: 0186 Tbilisi, Mindeli 11; tel. (32) 54-15-59; e-mail iice@caucasus .net; internet www.iice-eng.myweb.ge; f. 1956; attached to Georgian Acad. of Sciences; conducts research on chemical physics, electrochemistry, inorganic chemistry, physical chemistry; Dir Grigor Tatishvili.

Ferdinand Tavadze Institute of Metallurgy and Materials Science: 1060 Tbilisi, Al. Kazbegi Ave 15; tel. (32) 37-02-67; e-mail info@mmi.ge; internet mmi.ge; f. 1945; attached to Georgian Acad. of Sciences; conducts research on metallurgical processes, new materials and technologies, materials science and powder metallurgy; library of 152,953 vols; Dir Prof. Dr Giorgi F. Tavadze.

M. Nodia Institute of Geophysics: 0171 Tbilisi, M. Alexidze 1; tel. (32) 236-37-93; e-mail tamaz.chelidze@gmail.com; internet www.ig-geophysics.ge; f. 1933; attached to Ivane Javakhishvili Tbilisi State Univ.; library of 40,000 vols; Dir Dr Nugzar Ghlonti; publ. *Journal of Georgian Geophysical Society* (Series A: Solid Earth Physics and Series B: Physics of Atmosphere, Ocean and Space Plasma, 1 a year).

Melikishvili, P. G., Institute of Physical and Organic Chemistry: 0186 Tbilisi, V. Jikia 5; tel. (32) 99-88-23; f. 1929; attached to Georgian Acad. of Sciences; Dir T. Andronikashvili.

Transcaucasian Hydrometeorological Research Institute: 0112 Tbilisi, D. Agmashenebeli 150a; tel. (32) 63-74-01.

PHILOSOPHY AND PSYCHOLOGY

Tsereteli Institute of Philosophy: 0108 Tbilisi, Pr. Rustaveli 29; tel. (32) 99-52-62; e-mail root@philos.acnet.ge; attached to Georgian Acad. of Sciences; f. 1946; Dir T. Buachidze.

Uznadze, D. N., Institute of Psychology: 0105 Tbilisi, ul. Iashvili 22; tel. (32) 93-24-54; e-mail root@psycho.acnet.ge; f. 1943; attached to Georgian Acad. of Sciences; Dir Sh. Nadirashvili.

RELIGION, SOCIOLOGY AND ANTHROPOLOGY

Abuserisdze Tbeli Batumi Scientific Research Institute: 6016 Batumi, Ninoshvili 23; tel. (222) 3-29-01; e-mail isac@batumi .net; f. 1958; attached to Georgian Acad. of Sciences; Dir Dr Iuri Bibileishvili; publs *Culture and Life in South-Western Georgia* (1 a year), *Economic Problems in South-Western Georgia* (1 a year), *Folklore of South-Western Georgia* (1 a year), *Monuments of South-Western Georgia* (1 a year).

Institute of Demography and Sociological Studies: 0105 Tbilisi, ul. Pushkina 5; tel. (32) 93-36-93; internet www.acnet.ge/ demograph; f. 1990; attached to Georgian Acad. of Sciences; Dir Dr L. L. Chikava; publ. *Demography* (4 a year).

TECHNOLOGY

Eliashvili Institute of Control Systems: 0160 Tbilisi, K. Gamsakhurdia 34; tel. (32) 37-20-44; e-mail postmaster@contsys.acnet .ge; f. 1956; attached to Georgian Acad. of Sciences; library of 10,000 vols; Dir M. Salukvadze; publs *Language Processors and Speech Recognition* (1 a year), *Theory and Devices of Automatic Control* (1 a year).

G. Tsulukidze Mining Institute: 0186 Tbilisi, Mindelli 7; tel. (32) 32-47-16; e-mail im_mod@mining.org.ge; internet www .mining.org.ge; f. 1957; attached to Min. of Defence; underground structures construction and underground mining; open-cast operations and blast technologies; rock properties and in-massif physical processes research; special transport, reliability and diagnostics; mineral dressing, high-tech materials and mining wastes processing; Dir Dr Nikoloz Chikhradze.

Institute of Hydrogeology and Engineering Geology: 0188 Tbilisi, Rustaveli Ave 31; tel. (32) 52-72-19; e-mail bguram@gw .acnet.ge; internet www.acnet.ge/ hydrogeology_eng.htm; f. 1958; attached to Georgian Acad. of Sciences; Dir G. Buachidze; publ. *Problems of Hydrogeology and Engineering Geology*.

Institute of Machine Mechanics: 0186 Tbilisi, Mindeli 10; tel. (32) 32-11-65; e-mail rdimmg@yahoo.com; internet www.imm.ge; f. 1953; attached to Georgian Acad. of Sciences; Dir Tamaz Natriashvili.

Sukhumi I. N. Vekua Institute of Physics and Technology: 0108 Tbilisi, Pr. Rustaveli 52; tel. (32) 99-69-13; e-mail sipt@ sipt.org; internet www.sipt.org; f. 1945; attached to Georgian Acad. of Sciences; Dir V. Kashia.

Tbilisi Scientific-Industrial Institute 'Analizkhelsatsko': 0190 Tbilisi, Georgia Kakheti 36; tel. (32) 77-68-22; e-mail ninodzagania@yahoo.com; f. 1956; attached to Georgian Acad. of Sciences; Dir-Gen. Tamaz Dzagania.

Vladimer Chavchanidze Institute of Cybernetics of the Georgian Technical University: 0186 Tbilisi, ul. S. Euli 5; tel. (32) 30-30-49; e-mail ic@cybernet.ge; internet cybernet.ge; f. 1960; attached to Georgian Acad. of Sciences; conducts research on mathematical, physical, chemical and biological aspects of information technologies and informatics; Dir Dr Tamaz Sulaberidze; Scientific Sec. Dr Giorgi Mumladze.

Libraries and Archives

Tbilisi

Central Library of the Georgian Academy of Sciences: 0193 Tbilisi, M. Aleksidze 1–4; tel. (32) 36-34-13; e-mail acadlibrary@ gw.acnet.ge; f. 1941; 3,200,000 vols; Dir M. Zaalishvili.

Ivane Javakhishvili Tbilisi State University Library: 0128 Tbilisi, Pr. Chavchavadze 1; tel. (32) 22-10-32; internet www.tsu .edu.ge; f. 1918; 3,000,000 vols; Dir S. Apakidze.

National Library of Georgia: 0107 Tbilisi, Gulisashvili 5; tel. (32) 99-80-95; f. 1846; 6,000,000 vols, 24,000 periodicals; Dir Levan Berdzenishvili.

Museums and Art Galleries

Kutaisi

N. A. Berdzenishvili, Kutaisi State Historical Museum (N. A. Berdzenishvili, Kutaisi State Historical Museum): 4600 Kutaisi, 18 Pushkin St; tel. (431) 2-45-691; e-mail omarilanchava@gmail.com; internet www.histmuseum.ge; f. 1912; attached to Min. of Culture and Monument Protection of Georgia; library of 25,000 vols; Dir Dr Omar Lanchava; publ. *Works of Kutaisi State Historical Museum* (1 a year).

Sokhumi

Sokhumi Botanical Garden: 6600 Sokhumi, ul. Chavchavadze 20; tel. (122) 2-44-58; attached to Georgian Acad. of Sciences; Dir (vacant).

State Museum of the Abkhazian Autonomous Republic: 6600 Sokhumi, ul. Lenina 22; f. 1915; Dir A. A. Argun.

Tbilisi

Georgian National Museum: 0105 Tbilisi, 3 Rustaveli Ave; tel. (32) 99-80-22; e-mail info@museum.ge; internet www.museum.ge;

f. 1852; attached to Georgian Acad. of Sciences; library of 250,000 vols; Gen. Dir Acad. DAVID LORDKIPANIDZE.

Georgian National Museum—National Gallery: 0108 Tbilisi, Rustaveli Ave 11; tel. (32)215-73-00; e-mail info@museum.ge; internet www.museum.ge; f. 1920, merged with Georgian National Museum in 2007; collns of modern Georgian art (painting, drawing, sculpture, applied art); exhibitions, educational programmes and cultural actions; Dir-Gen. Prof. DAVID LORDKIPANIDZE; Admin. Man. LANA KARAIA.

Georgian State Art Museum: 0107 Tbilisi, ul. Gulisashvili 1; tel. (32) 99-66-35; f. 1920; Dir NODAR LOMOURI.

Georgian State Museum of Oriental Art: 0100 Tbilisi, ul. Azizbekova 3; Dir G. M. GVISHIANI.

State Museum of Georgian Literature: 0108 Tbilisi, Giorgi Chanturia 10; tel. (32) 99-86-67; f. 1930; library of 11,893 vols; Dir I. A. ORDZHONIKIDZE; publ. *Literary Chronicle*.

Tbilisi State Museum of Anthropology and Ethnography: 0100 Tbilisi, Pr. Komsomolskii 11; library of 150,000 vols; Dir A. V. TKESHELASHVILI.

Universities

AKAKI TSERETELI STATE UNIVERSITY

4600 Kutaisi, Tamar Mepe St 59
Telephone: (431) 24-57-84
E-mail: atsu@atsu.edu.ge
Internet: www.atsu.edu.ge
Founded 1933
public control
Academic year: September to July
Rector: Prof. GEORGE GAVTADSE
Librarian: GIORGI CHICHINADZE
Library of 975,080 vols and 114 periodicals
Number of teachers: 463
Number of students: 8,224

DEANS

Agrarian Faculty: Prof. RAMAZ KILADZE
Faculty of Arts: Assoc. Prof. IRMA KIPIANI
Faculty of Business, Law and Social Sciences: Assoc. Prof. AKAKI BAKURADZE
Faculty of Exact and Natural Sciences: Assoc. Prof. DAVID LEKVEISHVILI
Faculty of Maritime Transport: Assoc. Prof. AMIRAN BREGVADZE
Faculty of Medicine: Assoc. Prof. GIORGI GABUNIA
Faculty of Pedagogics: Assoc. Prof. KAKHA ADEISHVILI
Faculty of Social Sciences: Assoc. Prof. AKAKI BAKURADZE
Faculty of Technical Engineering: Prof. FRIDON GOGIASHVILI
Faculty of Technological Engineering: Prof. MERAB SHALAMBERIDZE

BATUMI ART TEACHING UNIVERSITY

6000 Batumi, 16 Pirosmani St
Telephone: (22) 24-43-59
E-mail: info@batu.edu.ge
Internet: www.batu.edu.ge
Founded 1995
State control
Academic year: September to May
Faculties of art research, ballet, cinema, drama, fine arts, musical disciplines, television and radio journalism
Rector: Prof. Dr ERMILE MESKHIA (acting)
Vice-Rector: Prof. ZAZA KHALVASHI
Library of 150 vols
Number of teachers: 135
Number of students: 203

BATUMI 'RUSTAVELI' STATE UNIVERSITY

6010 Batumi, Ninoshvili 35
Telephone: (222) 7-17-80
E-mail: info@bsu.edu.ge
Internet: bsu.edu.ge
Founded 1935
State control
Faculties of biology, economics, education, foreign languages, geography, history, initial military education and physical culture, medicine, philology, physics and mathematics
Rector: NUGZAR MGELADZE

GEORGIAN ACADEMY OF PHYSICAL EDUCATION

0179 Tbilisi, Pr. Chavchadze 49
Telephone: (32) 22-31-60
Founded 1938
State control
Rector: OMAR GOGIASHVILI

GEORGIAN STATE ACADEMY OF ANIMAL HUSBANDRY AND VETERINARY MEDICINE

0114 Tbilisi, Krtsanisi
Telephone: (32) 72-04-49
Founded 1932
State control
Rector: JEMAL GUGUSHVILI
Vice-Rector: ROMAN TSAGAREISHVILI

GEORGIAN TECHNICAL UNIVERSITY

0171 Tbilisi, ul. M. Kostava 77
Telephone: (32) 44-11-66
E-mail: intrelgu@yahoo.com
Internet: www.gtu.edu.ge
Founded 1990
State control
Languages of instruction: English, Georgian, Russian
Academic year: September to June
Rector: Prof. R. KHURODZE
Vice-Rector: Prof. ARCHIE PRANGISHVILI
Head of Foreign Affairs: TARIEL TAKTAKISHVILI
Head of Teaching and Methodology: O. ZUMBURIDZE
Librarian: V. PAPASKIRI
Number of teachers: 2,050
Number of students: 28,000
Publication: *Agmshenebeli* (newspaper)

DEANS

Faculty of Architecture: G. MIKIASHVILI
Faculty of Aviation: S. TEPNADZE
Faculty of Basic Sciences: T. DADIANI
Faculty of Chemical Engineering: N. KUTSLAVA
Faculty of Civil Engineering: C. LAGUNDARIDZE
Faculty of Communication: A. ROBITACHVILI
Faculty of Humanities: K. KOKRASHVILI
Faculty of Hydraulic Engineering: L. GOGELIANI
Faculty of Information Technology: Z. TSVERAIDZE
Faculty of Mechanics and Machine-building: A. TAVKHELIDZE
Faculty of Metallurgy: N. TSERETELI
Faculty of Mining and Geology: A. ABSHILAVA
Faculty of Power Engineering: G. ARABIDZE
Faculty of Transport: O. GEBASHVILI

GORI STATE UNIVERSITY

1400 Gori, Chavchavadze 53
Telephone: (370) 7-29-97
E-mail: gori@ip.osgf.ge
Founded 1935
State control
Depts of auditing, accountancy and statistics, business and management, correspondence learning, finance and commerce, foreign languages, history and law, international economic relations, nature and philology, pedagogics and medicine
Rector: GEDEVAN KHELAIA
Vice-Rector for Admin.: JEMALI DZIDZIGURI
Library of 200,000 vols

'ILIA CHAVCHAVADZE' STATE UNIVERSITY

0179 Tbilisi, Pr. I. Chavchavadze 32
Telephone: (32) 29-41-97
E-mail: uni@iliauni.edu.ge
Internet: www.iliauni.edu.ge
Founded 2006 by merger of Tbilisi 'Ilia Chavchavadze' State Univ. of Language and Culture and Tbilisi 'Sulkhan-Saba Orbeliani' State Pedagogical Univ.
State control
Rector: Prof. GIGI TEVZADZE
Admin. Dir: SERGO RATIANI

DEANS

Faculty of Education: IVANE KALADZE
Faculty of Humanities and Cultural Studies: SHUKIA APRIDONIDZE
Faculty of Life Sciences: GIORGI NAKHUTSRISHVILI
Faculty of Philology of Foreign Languages: MZIA BAKRADZE
Faculty of Philosophy and Social Sciences: Prof. GIGI TEVZADZE
Faculty of Physics and Mathematics: JUANSHER CHKAREULI

PROFESSORS

Faculty of Education (depts of correctional pedagogy and pre-school pedagogy, education economics and management, education psychology, general pedagogy, specific methods):
- IMEDADZE, NATELA
- KALADZE, IVANE
- KORINTELI, REVAZ
- MALAZONIA, DAVID
- MAQASHVILI, KETEVAN
- SHAVERDASHVILI, EKATERINE

Faculty of Humanities and Cultural Studies (depts of culture, history, linguistics, literary studies):
- APRIDONIDZE, SHUKIA
- GHAGHANIDZE, MERAB
- KOBALAVA, IZABELA
- KOCHLAMAZASHVILI, TAMAZ
- LADARIA, NODAR
- PITSKHELAURI, KONSTANTINE

Faculty of Life Sciences (dept of biology):
- BADRIDZE, IASON, Ecology of Behaviour
- GEGELASHVILI, GIORGI, Molecular and Cellular Biochemistry
- KOPALIANI, NATIA, Zoology, Conservative Biology
- NAKHUTSRISHVILI, GIORGI, Botany, Ecology
- SHATIRISHVILI, AIVENGO, Genetics, Evolutionary Biology
- SOLOMONIA, REVAZ, Biochemistry, Physiology
- TARKHNISHVILI, DAVID, Ecology, Evolutionary Biology

Faculty of Philology of Foreign Languages (depts of American/English studies, comparative literary studies, Germanic studies, linguoculturology, Oriental studies, Romance studies, Slavic studies):

BAKRADZE, MZIA
DOKHTURISHVILI, MZAGHO
GAJIEV, VALEKH
GOGOLADZE, TEIMURAZ
GVENTSADZE, MZIA
JASHI, KETEVAN
LEBANIDZE, GURAM VAKHTANG
MARSAGISHVILI, REZO
MIKADZE, MZIA
PIRTSKHALAVA, NINO

Faculty of Philosophy and Social Sciences (depts of economics, international relations and security studies, journalism, philosophy, politology, psychology, sociology and demography):

BERIASHVILI, MAMUKA
DARCHIASHVILI, DAVID
IMEDADZE, IRAKLI
NODIA, GIORGI
SURGULADZE, REVAZ
TEVZADZE, GIGI
TEVZADZE, GURAM
TSULADZE, GIOGI

Faculty of Physics and Mathematics (depts of mathematics, physics):

CHKAREULI, JUANSHER
JANGVELADZE, TEMUR
KHARAZISHVILI, ALEXANDRE
KHIMSHIASHVILI, GIORGI
MURUSIDZE, IVANE
SVANADZE, MERAB
TSIBAKHASHVILI, NELI

IVANE JAVAKHISHVILI TBILISI STATE UNIVERSITY

0179 Tbilisi, Pr. Chavchavadze 1
Telephone: (32) 222-56-79
E-mail: international@tsu.ge
Internet: www.tsu.edu.ge

Founded 1918
public control
Language of instruction: Georgian
Academic year: September to June

Chancellor: DAVID CHOMAKHIDZE
Rector: Prof. ALEXANDER KVITASHVILI
Vice-Rector: Dr LEVAN ALEKSIDZE
Vice-Rector: MARINE CHITASHVILI
Head of the Scientific Library: ZURAB GAIPARASHVILI

Library: see under Libraries and Archives
Number of teachers: 3,000
Number of students: 21,000

Publications: *Proceedings* (4 a year, in 2 series), *Tbilisi University* (52 a year)

DEANS

Faculty of Economics and Business: TEIMURAZ BERIDZE
Faculty of Exact and Natural Sciences: RAMAZ BOTCHORISHVILI
Faculty of Humanities: DAREJAN TVALTVADZE
Faculty of Law: IRAKLI BURDULI
Faculty of Medicine: ALEXANDER TSISKARIDZE
Faculty of Social and Political Sciences: NANA MATCHARASHVILI

SOKHUMI STATE UNIVERSITY

0186 Tbilisi, ul. Anna Politkovskaya 9
E-mail: info@sou.edu.ge
Internet: www.sou.edu.ge

Founded 1932 as Sokhumi Pedagogical Institute, renamed 1979, current name adopted 2007
State control

Faculties of economics and business, education, humanities, law, mathematics and computer sciences, natural sciences and health care, social sciences and political sciences
Number of students: 3,800

Rector: JONI APAKIDZE
Head of Admin.: SHOTA AKHALAIA
Head of Library: RAISA NIZHARADZE

TBILISI STATE INSTITUTE OF CULTURE

0102 Tbilisi, D. Agmashenebeli 40
Telephone: (32) 95-10-50

Founded 1992
State control

Faculties of choreography, fine and applied arts, humanities and musicology

Rector: TEMUR ZHGENTI
Vice-Rector: VLADIMER KIRVALISHVILI

TBILISI STATE MEDICAL UNIVERSITY

0177 Tbilisi, Vazha-Pshavela 33
Telephone: (32) 54-24-50
E-mail: iad@tsmu.edu
Internet: www.tsmu.edu

Founded 1930
State control
Languages of instruction: English, Georgian
Academic year: September to June

Rector: Prof. ZURAB VADACHKORIA

Library of 500,000 vols
Number of teachers: 1,000
Number of students: 6,000

Publications: *Annals of Biomedical Research and Education* (4 a year), *Georgian Medical News* (12 a year), *Research* (1 a year)

DEANS

Faculty of Medicine: Prof. TINATIN CHIKOVANI
Faculty of Pharmacy: Prof. DALI BERASHVILI
Faculty of Physical Medicine and Rehabilitation: Prof. KAKHA CHELIDZE
Faculty of Public Health: Prof. BIDZINA ZURASHVILI
Faculty of Stomatology: Prof. SAMSON MGEBRISHVILI

TBILISI STATE UNIVERSITY OF ECONOMIC RELATIONS

0144 Tbilisi, Ketevan Tsamebuli 55
Telephone: (32) 94-28-83
E-mail: rectori@internet.ge

Founded 1992
State control

Rector: AVTANDIL CHUTLASVILI
Vice-Rector: GURAM TAVARTKILADZE

Library of 29,000
Number of students: 1,811

DEANS

Business Administration: Prof. GELA ALADASHVILI
Law: Prof. VENEDI BENIDZE

TELAVI 'I. GOGEBASHVILI' STATE UNIVERSITY

2200 Telavi, Universitetis 1
Telephone: (35) 07-15-33
E-mail: office_teasu@grena.ge
Internet: www.tesau.edu.ge

Founded 1939
State control
Academic year: September to June

Rector: GEORGE GOTSIRIDZE
Head of Admin.: HAMLET RAZMADZE
Head of Quality Assurance Office: TINATIN ZURABISHVILI
Head of Library: NANA KARAULASHVILI

Library of 148,000 vols; 3 periodical titles
Number of teachers: 212
Number of students: 1,652

DEANS

Faculty of Actuarial and Natural Sciences: TEA MCHEDLURI
Faculty of Agriculture and Food Processing: NIKO SULKHANISHVILI
Faculty of Humanities: MALKHAZ TCIRIKIDZE
Faculty of Medicine: LALI MEKOKISHVILI
Faculty of Pedagogical Sciences: NINO NAKHUTSRISHVILI
Faculty of Social Sciences, Business and Law: IRMA SHIOSHVILI

PROFESSORS

BERTLANI, A., Russian Philology
BOKHASHVILI, I., Law
BURDULI, M., Medicine
CHACHANIDZE, G., Informatics
CHANTURIA, E., Law
CHIBURDANIDZE, L., Economics
CHICHIASHVILI, E., Foreign Languages
CHIKADZE, R., Georgian Philology
CHKHARTISHVILI, N., Viticulture
DOGONADZE, N., Pedagogical Sciences
ELANIDZE, V., History of Georgia
ELIZBARASHVILI, E., Geography
FARSADANISHVILI, A., History of Diplomacy
GELDIASHVILI, N., Georgian Philology
GIGASHVILI, K., Georgian Philology
GIORGADZE, G., Law
GOGOCHURI, N., Georgian Philology
GOTSIRIDZE, G., World History
IANVARASHVILI, L., Philosophy and Social Sciences
JACHVADZE, E., World History
JANASHIA, L., Pedagogical Sciences
JANGULASHVILI, E., Pedagogical Sciences
JAVAKHISHVILI, A., Economics
JAVAKHISHVILI, G., Georgian Philology
JAVAKHISHVILI, M., Chemistry and Technology
KATSITADZE, N., Physical Culture
KHOSITASHVILI, M., Wine Making
KOKILASHVILI, V., Physics and Mathematics
KURATASHVILI, A., Economics
KVASHILAVA, A., Law
MALATSIDZE, V., Medicine
MAMUKELASHVILI, E., Political Studies
MCHEDLISHVILI, D., Physics and Mathematics
MIKELADZE, M., Georgian Philology
MODEBADZE, N., Physics and Mathematics
NADIRADZE, T., Biology and Ecology
NANOBASHVILI, K., Informatics
RAINAULI, Z., Medicine
RCHEULISHVILI, G., History of Georgia
ROSTOMASHVILI, N., Physics and Mathematics
SHALVASHVILI, L., Georgian Philology
SHIOSHVILI, I., Philosophy and Social Sciences
VAKHTANGISHVILI, T., History of Georgia
ZURABISHVILI, T., Philosophy and Social Sciences
ZUROSHVILI, L., Biology and Ecology

TSKHINVALI PEDAGOGICAL INSTITUTE–GEORGIAN SECTOR

Shida Qartli, 1400 Gori, Chavchavadze 57
Telephone: (370) 2-19-35

Founded 1932
State control

Faculties of biology, chemistry and physical training, education, teaching and methods, foreign languages, Georgian language and literature, history and philology, mathematics and physics, natural sciences

Rector: VAHTANG AHALAIA
Vice-Rector: V. BURCHULADZE

Other Higher Educational Institutes

Georgian 'S. Rustaveli' State Institute of Theatre and Cinematography: 0108 Tbilisi, Pr. Rustaveli 17; tel. (32) 99-94-11; e-mail eliso@geo.net.ge; f. 1939; drama, film, television, stage management, archive management, art history; library: 50,000 vols; 150 teachers; 800 students; Rector Prof. GIGA LORDKIPHANIDZE.

Georgian State Agrarian University: 0131 Tbilisi, D. Agmashenebeli 13-km, Dighomi; tel. (32) 95-71-47; e-mail agrdig@geointer.net.ge; f. 1929 as Georgian Agricultural Institute; present name and status 1991; faculties of agricultural electrification and automation, agricultural mechanization, agronomy, economics and humanities, forestry, hydromelioration and engineering ecology, technology and viticulture; library: 747,600 vols; 583 teachers; 7,500 students; Rector Prof. Dr NAPOLEON KARKASHADZE.

Georgian State Institute of Subtropical Agriculture: 4600 Kutaisi, Pr. Chavchavadze 13; tel. (331) 7-06-14; e-mail ssmsi@sanet.net.ge; faculties of agri-business, agricultural engineering, agriculture and food technology, economics; library: 90,000 vols; Rector GURAM KILASONIA.

Kutaisi 'N. I. Muskhelishvili' Technical University: 4614 Kutaisi, Akhalgazrdobis Gamziri 98; tel. (331) 2-06-90; e-mail vg@posta.ge; f. 1973; institutes of automobile and transport, cybernetics, electrical engineering, food and chemical industry, humanities and economics, mechanical engineering, technology and design; library: 250,000 vols, 300 periodicals; 360 teachers; 5,600 students; Rector AMIRAN HVADAGIANI.

Tbilisi State Academy of Arts: 0108 Tbilisi, ul. Griboedova 2; tel. (32) 93-69-59; e-mail nanniashuili@posta.ge; f. 1922; faculties of architecture, art history and theory, design, fine arts; library: 42,000 vols; 355 teachers; 1,600 students; Rector Prof. IOSEB KOIAVA; publ. *Works* (1 a year).

Tbilisi 'V. Saradzhishvili' State Conservatoire: 0108 Tbilisi, ul. Griboedova 8; tel. (32) 99-91-44; e-mail tbil_conservatory@hotmail.com; f. 1917; courses in choral conducting, composition, musicology, orchestral instruments, piano, singing; library: 100,000 vols; 205 teachers; 700 students; Rector Prof. MANANA DOIJASHVILI.

GERMANY

The Higher Education System

During 1949–90 Germany was divided between the sovereign states of the Federal Republic of Germany (FRG) and the German Democratic Republic (GDR). Both states developed their own higher education systems. In the FRG, the Grundgesetz (Basic Law) of 1949 stated that the majority of aspects of the administration and legislation of the education system were the responsibility of the Länder (States). Following reunification in 1990, the former GDR was incorporated into the Federal structure, and adopted the higher education standards already implemented in the FRG. Higher education thus remains the responsibility of the 16 Länder, and is overseen by the national Kultusministerkonferenz (Standing Conference of the Ministers of Education and Cultural Affairs of the Länder). Higher education is divided between Hochschulen and Fachhochschulen. Hochschulen encompass various types of classical university: standard universities (Universität), technical universities (Technische Hochschulen/Universität), combined Hochschulen-Fachhochschulen (Universität-Gesamthochschulen), teacher-training institutes (Pädagogische Hochschulen), theological universities (Theologische Hochschulen), art universities (Kunsthochschulen) and music universities (Musikhochschulen). Fachhochschulen are universities of applied science specializing in technical vocation education and training. In 2011/12 there was a total of 421 Hochschulen of which 108 were universities and 210 Fachhochschulen. Statistics for 2011 gave that 1,460,658 students were enrolled in higher education (non-university) institutions and 2,380,974 were enrolled in universities and equivalent institutions. In late 2012 only five of the 16 Länder charged tuition fees at state-funded higher education institutions, while in the other 11 tuition was provided free of charge. Students from poorer backgrounds are eligible for a student loan, repayment of which is income-linked.

Admission to Hochschulen is based on performance in Zeugnis der Allgemeinen Hochschulreife/Abitur or Fachgebundene Hochschulreife, and admission to Fachhochschulen depends on Fachhochschulreife, Zeugnis der Allgemeinen Hochschulreife or Fachgebundene Hochschulreife. From 1998 Germany has gradually implemented the Bologna Process and introduced a two-tier Bachelors and Masters degree system to replace the traditional German degrees in Hochschulen. The Bachelors lasts three to four years (at least 180 European Credit Transfer and Accumulation System—ECTS credit units) and the Masters a further one to two years (60–120 ECTS credit units). The Masters also requires the submission of a thesis as part of the final examination. Doctoral studies, lasting two to four years, follow the Masters. In Fachhochschulen, the traditional Fachhochschuldiplom (four years) has been retained as, unlike the Bachelors, it involves a large element of practical training; however, both the Bachelors and Masters degrees have also been introduced in Fachhochschulen, parallel to the traditional Diplom. However, unlike the Hochschulen, Fachhochschulen are not permitted to offer courses leading to the award of doctoral qualifications.

Mixed academic and vocational training (in economics, technical subjects and social sciences) is also offered by Berufsakademien or Studienakademien, which were first established in Baden-Württemberg in 1974; they are not present in every Land. Admission to these institutions is based on any university entrance award in conjunction with a training contract. Students are awarded the Berufsakademien Diplom after a three-year course. In addition, the Berufsakademien have started to offer three-year Bachelors degree courses.

Technical and vocational education is offered by different types of institution in addition to the degree-level programmes offered by the Fachhochschulen and the Berufsakademien. An estimated two-thirds of German students of the relevant age attend Berufsschulen, which combine classroom-based instruction and practical experience in a three-year course. Berufsfachschulen specialize in two- to three-year occupational training courses, leading to the award of the titles Facharbeiterbrief (Skilled Worker Certificate), Kaufmannsgehilfenbrief (Clerical Assistant Certificate) and Gesellenbrief (Craftsman Certificate). Berufsoberschulen are only available in some Länder and allow those who have completed secondary education and have acquired at least five years of professional experience (or undertaken two years of vocational training) to study for the Fachgebundende Hochschulreife, which confers eligibility to enter Hochschulen and Fachhochschulen (but only for specific subjects). Fachschulen/Fachakademie provide one- to three-year courses for those who already have previous vocational education and professional experience and who are looking to gain middle management skills.

Since 2002 all new degree-type programmes have to be accredited by one of several accreditation bodies (of which there were 11 in March 2011). The Akkreditierungsrat (national accreditation council), which was established in 2005, keeps records of all accredited programmes and regulates the individual accreditation bodies.

Regulatory and Representative Bodies

GOVERNMENT

Federal Ministry of Education and Research: Heinemannstr. 2, 53175 Bonn; tel. (228) 99570; e-mail information@bmbf.bund.de; internet www.bmbf.de; Federal Min. JOHANNA WANKA.

Gemeinsame Wissenschaftskonferenz (Joint Science Conference): Friedrich-Ebert-Allee 38, 53113 Bonn; tel. (228) 54020; e-mail gwk@gwk-bonn.de; internet www.gwk-bonn.de; f. 1970 as Bund-Länder Commission for Educational Planning (Bund-Länder-Kommission für Bildungsplanung) by agreement between the Federal and Länder govts; granted additional functions in 1975 by the Skeleton Agreement on Research Promotion; present name and status 2008; intergovernmental comm.; permanent forum for discussion of all questions of education and research promotion that are of common interest to the Fed. and Länder govts; makes recommendations to the Heads of the Fed. and Länder govts on educational planning and research promotion; cooperates closely with the various Conferences of Länder Ministers; Chair. Prof. Dr E. JÜRGEN ZÖLLNER; Deputy Chair. Prof. Dr ANNETTE SCHAVAN; Sec.-Gen. Dr HANS-GERHARD HUSUNG.

Kultusministerkonferenz/Ständige Konferenz der Kultusminister der Länder in der Bundesrepublik Deutschland (Standing Conference of the Ministers of Education and Cultural Affairs of the Länder): Taubenstrabe 10, 10117 Berlin; tel. (30) 25418499; e-mail poststelle@kmk.org; internet www.kmk.org; f. 1948; conf. of ministers and senators of the 16 Länder whose portfolios encompass culture, education, research and training; maintains offices in Berlin; Pres. STEPHAN DORGERLOH; Vice-Pres. SYLVIA LÖHRMANN; Vice-Pres. BRUNHILD KURTH; Vice-Pres. TIES RABE; Gen. Sec. UDO MICHALLIK.

ACCREDITATION

Agentur für Qualitätssicherung und Akkreditierung kanonischer Studiengänge in Deutschland eV (Agency for Quality Assurance and Accreditation of Canonical Programmes of Studies in Germany): Kapuzinergasse 2, 85072 Eichstätt; tel. (8421) 931128; e-mail sekretariat@akast.info; internet www.akast.info; accredits canonical study programmes; advances Catholic theological faculties and schools and assures quality of canonical study programmes; Chair. Prof. Dr ALFRED E. HIEROLD; Sec. MONIKA STIERSTORFER.

Akkreditierungs-, Certifizierungs- und Qualitätssicherungs-Instituts (ACQUIN) (Accreditation, Certification and Quality Assurance Institute): Brandenburger Str. 2, 95448 Bayreuth; tel. (921) 53039050; e-mail sekr@acquin.org; internet www.acquin.org; f. 2001; member-based, non-profit org.; licensed by the Akkreditierungsrat (*q.v.*) to award its quality seal to study programmes that have successfully undergone accreditation; accreditation of German Bachelors and Masters study programmes in all subject fields based on the expertise of Standing Expert Cttee mems; evaluation and accreditation of selected int. study programmes; int. cooperation and networking; organizes projects and workshops with nat. and int. partners; develops new quality assurance methods; pilot project: 'Process Quality in Teaching and Learning'; Chair. Prof. Dr Ing. GERD ZIMMERMAN; Dir THOMAS REIL; Sec. URSULA HAMMON.

Akkreditierungsagentur für Studiengänge der Ingenieurwissenschaften, der Informatik, der Naturwissenschaften und der Mathematik—ASIIN eV (Accreditation Agency for Degree Programmes in Engineering, Informatics, Natural Sciences and Mathematics): c/o VDI, POB 10 11 39, 40002 Düsseldorf; Robert-Stolz-Str. 5, 40470 Düsseldorf; tel. (211) 9009770; e-mail info@asiin.de; internet www.asiin.de; f. 1999 as ASII, merged with Akkreditierungsagentur für die Studiengänge Chemie, Biochemie und Chemieingenieurwesen an Universitäten und Fachhochschulen (A-CBC) and current name adopted 2002; accredited by Akkreditierungsrat since 2002, full member of ENQA since 2007, accepted into EQAR since 2009; not-for-profit br. of ASIIN, official accreditation in Germany since 2002; the only German accreditation agency to be explicitly specialized in accrediting degree programmes in engineering, informatics, natural sciences and mathematics; accredited by Akkreditierungsrat (*q.v.*); represents competence in agronomy, architecture, business informatics, chemistry, city and spatial planning, civil engineering, computer science, electrical engineering, geosciences, industrial engineering, informatics, information systems, IT, landscape architecture, life sciences, materials and processes, mathematics, mechanical engineering, nutritional science, physical technologies, physics, process engineering, surveying as well as in quality management and quality assurance in higher education; also incl. system accreditation and institutional reviews/accreditation; 40 mems; Chair. Dr Ing. HANS-HEINZ ZIMMER; Deputy Chair. Prof. Dr Ing. JÖRG STEINBACH; Man. Dir Dr IRING WASSER; Sec. KARIN BERG.

Akkreditierungsagentur im Bereich Gesundheit und Soziale (AHPGS) (Accreditation Agency in Health and Social Sciences): Sedanstr. 22, 79098 Freiburg; tel. (761) 2085330; e-mail ahpgs@ahpgs.de; internet www.ahpgs.de; f. 2001; promotes quality and transparency of German univ. study courses for health and social professionals; works to guarantee uniform and internationally comparable quality standards in the new Bachelors and Masters degrees through accreditation procedures; operates continual information exchange with other nat. and int. accreditation agencies as well as univ. representatives, practitioners' orgs and asscns; mems incl. the dean conference nursing science (33 univs), the assemblies of the depts of social work (73 univs) and remedial education (8 univs) as well as the German Coordinating Agency for Public Health; accredited by the Akkreditierungsrat (*q.v.*); Chair. Prof. Dr JÜRGEN VON TROSCHKE; CEO GEORG RESCHAUER; Sec. GABRIELE KRAUSE.

Akkreditierungsrat (Accreditation Council): Adenauerallee 73, 53113 Bonn; tel. (228) 3383060; e-mail akr@akkreditierungsrat.de; internet www.akkreditierungsrat.de; f. 1999 by Kultusministerkonferenz (*q.v.*) and Hochschulrektorenkonferenz (*q.v.*); attached to Stiftung zur Akkreditierung von Studiengängen in Deutschland (Foundation for the Accreditation of Study Programmes in Germany); acts on behalf of Länder to accredit accreditation agencies and degree programmes leading to Bakkalaureus/Bachelors and Magister/Masters degrees; internal quality assurance systems for HEIs; financed by Stifterverband für die Deutsche Wissenschaft (*q.v.*); Chair. Prof. Dr REINHOLD R. GRIMM; Man. Dir Dr OLAF BARTZ.

AQAS eV/Agentur für Qualitätssicherung durch Akkreditierung von Studiengängen: Hohenstaufenring 30–32, 50674 Köln; tel. (221) 9950060; e-mail info@aqas.de; internet www.aqas.de; f. 2002; accredited by Akkreditierungsrat (*q.v.*); 85 mems; Chair. Prof. Dr EBERHARD MENZEL; Deputy Chair. Prof. Dr KONRAD WOLF; Man. Dir Dr VERENA KLOETERS; Dir for Strategy, Process, Int. Affairs DORIS HERRMANN.

ENIC/NARIC Germany: Central Office for Foreign Education, Secretariat of the Standing Conference of the Ministers of Education and Cultural Affairs, POB 2240, 53012 Bonn; Graurheindorfer Str. 157, 53117 Bonn; tel. (228) 501264; e-mail zab@kmk.org; internet www.kmk.org/zab; f. 1905; attached to Kultusministerkonferenz (*q.v.*); Head of Dept BARBARA BUCHAL-HÖVER.

Evaluationsagentur Baden-Württemberg (evalag) (Evaluation Agency Baden-Württemberg): Postfach 100961, 68009 Mannheim; M7, 9A–10, 68161 Mannheim; tel. (621) 12854510; e-mail evalag@evalag.de; internet www.evalag.de; accredits focusing on internal quality assurance system of higher education instns in areas of teaching and learning; CEO Dr ANKE RIGBERS; Chair. Prof. Dr HANS WEDER; Deputy Chair. Prof. Dr STEFAN HORNBOSTEL; Sec. BÄRBEL BENDER.

Foundation for International Business Administration Accreditation (FIBAA): Berliner Freiheit 20–24, 53111 Bonn; tel. (228) 2803560; e-mail brackmann@fibaa.org; internet www.fibaa.org; f. 1994; accredits Bachelors, Masters and Diploma courses in fields such as economics, business computing, engineering and business admin., business psychology, business law, etc., in Germany, Austria and Switzerland; provides information and advice on Bachelors and Masters courses to univs, students and private enterprises; maintains offices in Zürich (Switzerland); Man. Dir DAISUKE MOTOKI; Man. Dir HANS-JÜRGEN BRACKMANN.

Zentrale Evaluations- und Akkreditierungsagentur (Central Evaluation and Accreditation Agency): Lilienthalstrabe 1, 30179 Hannover; tel. (511) 54355701; internet www.zeva.org; f. 1995; evaluates and accredits study and system programmes at univs, univs of applied sciences and univs of cooperative education; higher education governance and management; Academic Dir Prof. Dr RAINER KÜNZEL; Man. Dir HERMANN REUKE; Sec. SANJA PETERSEN.

FUNDING

Deutscher Akademischer Austausch Dienst eV (DAAD) (German Academic Exchange Service): POB 20 04 04, 53134 Bonn; Kennedyallee 50, 53175 Bonn; tel. (228) 8820; e-mail postmaster@daad.de; internet www.daad.de; f. 1925 as Academic Exchange Service, current name adopted 1931; br. office in Berlin; foreign brs in Beijing, Brussels, Cairo, Hanoi, Jakarta, London, Mexico City, Moscow, Nairobi, New Delhi, New York, Paris, Rio de Janeiro, Tokyo, Warsaw; awards scholarships and grants, largely funded from Federal budget, to promote academic and cultural exchange between German and foreign students and thereby encourage closer relations between Germany and other countries; exchange of professors, lecturers in German for foreign univs, IAESTE—student-trainees, scholarships for German and foreign students and graduates; 234 mem. univs, 124 students; Pres. Prof. Dr SABINE KUNST; Vice-Pres. Prof. Dr MAX G. HUBER; Sec.-Gen. Dr DOROTHEA RÜLAND; publ. *Change by Exchange* (image brochure and flyers).

NATIONAL BODIES

Deutsche Hochschulverband (DHV) (German Association of University Professors and Lecturers): Rheinallee 18, 53173 Bonn; tel. (228) 9026666; e-mail dhv@hochschulverband.de; internet www.hochschulverband.de/cms1; f. 1920 as German Asscn of Univs, dissolved in 1936, refounded 1950; 24,000 mems; Pres. Prof. Dr BERNHARD KEMPEN; Man. Dir Dr MICHAEL HARTMERE; Deputy Man. Dir Dr HUBERT DETMER.

Deutscher Volkshochschul-Verband eV (German Adult Education Association): Obere Wilhelmstr. 32, 53225 Bonn; tel. (228) 9756920; e-mail info@dvv-vhs.de; internet www.dvv-vhs.de; f. 1953; 16 regional asscns of 1,000 Volkshochschulen with 4,000 brs; Pres. Prof. Dr RITA SÜSSMUTH; Chair. Dr ERNST-DIETER ROSSMANN; Dir ULRICH AENGENVOORT; Deputy Dir GUNDULA FRIELING; publs *Adult Education and Development* (2 a year, in English, French and Spanish), *DVV magazin dis.kurs* (4 a year).

Hochschulrektorenkonferenz (HRK) (German Rectors' Conference): Ahrstr. 39, 53175 Bonn; tel. (228) 8870; internet www.hrk.de; f. 1949; central voluntary body representing the univs and higher education instns; 258 mem instns; Pres. Prof. Dr MARGRET WINTERMANTEL; Sec.-Gen. Dr Ing. THOMAS KATHÖFER.

Katholischer Akademischer Ausländer-Dienst (Catholic Academic Foreigner Service): Hausdorffstr. 151, 53129 Bonn; tel. (228) 917580; e-mail zentrale@kaad.de; internet www.kaadbonn.de; f. 1954; coordinates activities of Catholic orgs concerned with foreign students in Germany and grants scholarships; Pres. Prof. Dr ALBERT FRANZ; Gen. Sec. Dr HERMANN WEBER; publ. *Jahresakademie* (1 a year).

Learned Societies

GENERAL

Akademie der Künste (Academy of Arts): POB 210250, 10502 Berlin; Pariser Pl. 4, 10117 Berlin; tel. (30) 200571000; e-mail info@adk.de; internet www.adk.de; f. 1696; sections of fine art, architecture, music, literature, performing arts, film and media arts; 400 mems; Pres. Prof. KLAUS STAECK; Vice-Pres. NELE HERTLING; publ. *Sinn und Form* (6 a year).

Akademie der Wissenschaften zu Göttingen (Göttingen Academy of Sciences and Humanities): Theaterstr. 7, 37073 Göttingen; tel. (551) 395362; e-mail adw@gwdg.de; internet www.adw-goe.de; f. 1751; attached to Univ. of Göttingen; sections of philology and history, mathematics and physics; 381 mems and corresp. mems; Pres. Prof. Dr

STEFAN TANGERMANN; Vice-Pres. Prof. Dr THOMAS KAUFMANN; Vice-Pres. Prof. Dr KURT SCHOENHAMMER; publs *Abhandlungen Neue Folge*, *Göttingische Gelehrte Anzeigen*, *Jahrbuch*.

Akademie der Wissenschaften und der Literatur Mainz (Mainz Academy of Sciences, Humanities and Literature): Geschwister Scholl-Str. 2, 55131 Mainz; tel. (6131) 5770; e-mail generalsekretariat@adwmainz.de; internet www.adwmainz.de; f. 1949; 250 mems; Pres. Prof. Dr ELKE LÜTJEN-DRECOLL; Vice-Pres. for Literature Prof. Dr NORBERT MILLER; Vice-Pres. for Mathematics and Natural Sciences Dr REINER ANDERL; Vice-Pres. for Philosophy and Social Sciences Prof. Dr GERNOT WILHELM; Sec.-Gen. Prof. Dr CLAUDIUS GEISLER; publs *Abhandlungen*, *Forschungsreihen*.

Bayerische Akademie der Wissenschaften (Bavarian Academy of Sciences and Humanities): Alfons-Goppel-Str. 11, 80539 Munich; tel. (89) 230310; e-mail info@badw.de; internet www.badw.de; f. 1759; sections of mathematics and natural sciences (Secs Prof. Dr GOTTFRIED SACHS, Prof. Dr HORST KESSLER) and philosophy and history (Secs Prof. Dr ARNOLD PICOT, Prof. Dr THOMAS O. HÖLLMANN); 172 mems; Pres. Prof. Dr KARL-HEINZ HOFFMANN; Gen. Sec. BIANCA MARZOCCA.

Berlin-Brandenburgische Akademie der Wissenschaften (Berlin-Brandenburg Academy of Sciences and Humanities): Jaegerstr. 22/23, 10117 Berlin; tel. (30) 203700; e-mail bbaw@bbaw.de; internet www.bbaw.de; f. 1700, refounded 1992/93; sections of humanities, social sciences, mathematics and natural sciences, biological and medical sciences, engineering sciences; 307 mems (166 ordinary, 69 extraordinary, 70 emeriti, 2 hon.); Pres. Prof. Dr GÜNTER STOCK; Vice-Pres. Prof. Dr JÜRGEN KOCKA; Vice-Pres. Prof. Dr KLAUS LUCAS; publs *Berichte und Abhandlungen* (irregular), *Gegenworte—Zeitschrift für den Disput über Wissen*, *Jahrbuch* (1 a year).

Goethe-Gesellschaft in Weimar eV: Burgpl. 4 99423 Weimar; POB 2251, 99403 Weimar; tel. (3643) 202050; e-mail info@goethe-gesellschaft.de; internet www.goethe-gesellschaft.de; f. 1885; literature, art and history of Goethe's time; 3,000 mems; Pres. Dr Hab. JOCHEN GOLZ; Dir Dr PETRA OBERHAUSER; publs *Goethe-Jahrbuch*, *Schriften der Goethe-Gesellschaft* (irregular).

Goethe-Institut: Dachauer Str. 122, 80637 Munich; tel. (89) 159210; e-mail info@goethe.de; internet www.goethe.de; f. 1951; 147 institutes globally, 13 in Germany; promotes German language and fosters cultural cooperation with other countries; sets internationally recognized standards in the teaching and learning of German as a foreign language; Pres. Prof. Dr KLAUS-DIETER LEHMANN; Sec.-Gen. Dr HANS-GEORG KNOPP; Business Dir JÜRGEN MAIER; publs *Fikrun wa fann* (2 a year, in Arabic, English and Persian), *Goethe-Institut aktuell* (4 a year), *Humboldt* (2 a year, in Portuguese and Spanish), *Willkommen*, *Yearbook*.

Heidelberger Akademie der Wissenschaften (Heidelberg Academy of Sciences and Humanities): Karlstr. 4, 69117 Heidelberg; tel. (6221) 543265; e-mail haw@adw.uni-heidelberg.de; internet www.haw.uni-heidelberg.de; f. 1909; sections of mathematics and natural sciences (Sec. Prof. Dr WOLFGANG SCHLEICH), philosophy and history (Sec. Prof. Dr SILKE LEOPOLD); Pres. Prof. Dr HERMANN H. HAHN; Man. Dir GUNTHER JOST.

Institut für Auslandsbeziehungen (IFA) (Institute for Foreign Cultural Relations): POB 102463, 70020 Stuttgart; Charlottenpl. 17, 70173 Stuttgart; tel. (711) 22250; e-mail info@ifa.de; internet www.ifa.de; f. 1917; promotes artistic exchange and dialogue between civil societies; provides information about foreign cultural policy; library of 450,000 vols; Pres. URSULA SEILER-ALBRING; Gen. Sec. RONALD GRÄTZ; Librarian GUDRUN CZEKALLA; publs *Ifa//dokumente*, *Ifa-Edition Kultur und Außenpolitik*, *Ifa//literaturrecherchen*, *Kulturaustausch*, *Reihe Dokumentation*.

Leopoldina—Nationale Akademie der Wissenschaften (German Academy of Sciences Leopoldina): POB 110543, 06019 Halle (Saale); Emil-Abderhalden-Str. 37, 06108 Halle (Saale); tel. (345) 472390; e-mail leopoldina@leopoldina.org; internet www.leopoldina.org; f. 1652, present status 2008; attached to Nationale Akademie der Wissenschaften; br. in Berlin; advises govt, parliament, public on socially relevant scientific issues; represents German scientists in int. acad. circles and maintains links with scientific instns in other European and non-European countries; supports training of junior scientists; promotes cooperation among researchers by organizing meetings, symposia, biennial confs, assemblies, monthly lectures, seminars on history of science; 1,300 mems; library: see under Libraries and Archives; Pres. Prof. Dr JÖRG HACKER; Sec.-Gen. Prof. Dr JUTTA SCHNITZER-UNGEFUG; Sec. for Medicine Prof. Dr INGO HANSMANN; publs *Acta Historica Leopoldina*, *Jahrbuch* (1 a year), *Nova Acta Leopoldina*.

Nordrhein-Westfälische Akademie der Wissenschaften und der Künste (North Rhine-Westphalia Academy of Sciences and Humanities): Palmenstr. 16, 40217 Düsseldorf; tel. (211) 617340; e-mail awk@awk.nrw.de; internet www.akdw.nrw.de; f. 1950, present status 1970, present name 1993; sections of natural, engineering and economic sciences, philosophy; 356 mems (225 full, 131 corresp.); Pres. Prof. Dr Hab. HANNS HATT; Vice-Pres. Prof. Dr Ing. Hab. HELMUT ERMERT; Vice-Pres. Prof. Dr PETER M. LYNEN; Vice-Pres. Prof. Dr WOLFGANG DIETER LEBEK; publs *Abhandlungen*, *Jahrbuch* (Yearbook), *Sitzungsberichte*.

Prinz-Albert-Gesellschaft eV (Prince Albert Society): Seidmannsdorfer Str. 5, 96450 Coburg; tel. (921) 554190; e-mail prinz-albert-gesellschaft@uni-bayreuth.de; internet www.prinz-albert-gesellschaft.uni-bayreuth.de; f. 1981; encourages research into Anglo-German relations in spheres of scholarship, culture and politics; Chair. Prof. Dr DIETER WEISS; Exec. Chair. MICHAEL ECKSTEIN; Sec. SILVIA BÖCKING; publs *Prinz Albert Forschungen* (Prince Albert Research, Series), *Prinz-Albert-Studien* (Prince Albert Studies, Series).

Sächsische Akademie der Wissenschaften zu Leipzig (Saxony Academy of Sciences in Leipzig): POB 100440, 04004 Leipzig; Karl-Tauchnitz Str. 1, 04107 Leipzig; tel. (341) 7115350; e-mail sekretariat@saw-leipzig.de; internet www.saw-leipzig.de; f. 1846; about 30 research projects; 221 mems (142 ordinary, 79 corresp.); Pres. Prof. Dr PIRMIN STEKELER-WEITHOFER; Vice-Pres. Prof. Dr HEINER KADEN; Sec.-Gen. Dr UTE ECKER; Head of Mathematics and Natural Sciences Section Prof. Dr DIETER MICHEL; publs *Abhandlungen*, *Denkströme* (www.denkstroeme.de), *Jahrbuch* (every 2 years), *Sitzungsberichte*.

Union der Deutschen Akademien der Wissenschaften (Union of the German Academies of Sciences and Humanities): Geschwister-Scholl-Str. 2, 55131 Mainz; tel. (6131) 2185280; e-mail info@akademienunion.de; internet www.akademienunion.de; f. 1973; consists of academies of sciences and humanities in Berlin, Düsseldorf, Göttingen, Heidelberg, Leipzig, Mainz and Munich; deals with research projects common to the academies and coordinates the work of their mems; Pres. Prof. Dr GÜNTER STOCK; Vice-Pres. Prof. Dr ELKE LÜTJEN-DRECOLL; Gen. Sec. Dr DIETER HERRMANN.

AGRICULTURE, FISHERIES AND VETERINARY SCIENCE

Agrarsoziale Gesellschaft eV (ASG): POB 1144, 37001 Göttingen; Kurze Geismarstr. 33, 37073 Göttingen; tel. (551) 497090; e-mail info@asg-goe.de; internet www.asg-goe.de; f. 1947; works for improvement of living conditions in rural areas; 330 mems, plus 130 corporate mems; library of 6,000 vols; Chair. Dr MARTIN WILLE; Man. Dir. Dr DIETER CZECH; Sec. KARIN SCHÄFER; publs *Arbeitsbericht der ASG*, *Kleine Reihe der ASG*, *Ländlicher Raum* (4 a year), *Materialsammlung der ASG*, *Schriftenreihe für ländliche Sozialfragen*.

Dachverband Wissenschaftlicher Gesellschaften der Agrar-, Forst-, Ernährungs-, Veterinär- und Umweltforschung eV: Eschbormer Landstr. 122, 60489 Frankfurt am Main; tel. (69) 24788321; e-mail a.schaffner@dlg.org; internet www.agrarforschung.de; f. 1973; advancement and coordination of research; information; contacts; representation; 34 mem instns; Pres. Prof. Dr OLAF CHRISTEN; Man. Dir Dr ACHIM SCHAFFNER.

Deutsche Landwirtschafts-Gesellschaft eV (German Agricultural Society): Eschborner Landstr. 122, 60489 Frankfurt; tel. (69) 247880; e-mail info@dlg.de; internet www.dlg.org; f. originally 1885, refounded 1947; 22,000 mems; Pres. CARL-ALBRECHT BARTMER; Dir Dr REINHARD GRANDKE; publs *Agrifuture* (4 a year, in English, for European farmers), *Entwicklung und ländlicher Raum* (12 a year, in English, German and French), *Journal of International Agriculture* (4 a year), *Mitteilungen* (1 a year), *Zeitschrift für Agrargeschichte und Agrarsoziologie* (4 a year).

Deutsche Veterinärmedizinische Gesellschaft (German Veterinary Medical Society): Friedrichstr. 17, 35392 Gießen; tel. (641) 24466; e-mail info@dvg.net; internet www.dvg.net; f. 1949; 5,000 mems; Chair. Prof. Dr VOLKER MOENNIG; Man. Dir. Dr SUSANNE ALLDINGER; publ. *Kongressbericht* (every 2 years).

Deutscher Forstwirtschaftsrat (German Forestry Council): Claire-Waldoff-Str. 7, 10117 Berlin; tel. (30) 31904560; e-mail info@dfwr.de; internet www.dfwr.de; f. 1950; 67 mems; Pres. GEORG SCHIRMBECK; Vice-Pres. NORBERT LEBEN; Man. Dir Dr MARKUS ZIEGELER.

Verband Deutscher Landwirtschaftlicher Untersuchungs- und Forschungsanstalten eV (VDLUFA) (Association of German Agricultural, Analytical and Research Institutes): c/o LUFA Speyer, Obere Langgasse 40, 67346 Speyer; tel. (6232) 136121; e-mail info@vdlufa.de; internet www.vdlufa.de; f. 1888; devt of methods and quality assurance in agricultural analytical sector; provides bases for a standardized evaluation of test results; initiates and advances applied agricultural research; 550 mems; Pres. Prof. Dr FRANZ WIESLER; Vice-Pres. for Animals Prof. Dr HANS SCHENKEL; Vice-Pres. for Plants Prof. Dr THOMAS EBERTSEDER; Exec. Sec. Dr HANS-GEORG BROD; publs *Handbuch der landwirtschaftlichen Versuchs- und Untersuchungsmethodik (VDLUFA-Methodenbuch)*,

VDLUFA-Mitteilungen, *VDLUFA-Schriftenreihe*.

ARCHITECTURE AND TOWN PLANNING

DAI–Verband Deutscher Architekten- und Ingenieurvereine eV: Salzufer 8, 10587 Berlin; tel. (30) 21473174; e-mail kontakt@dai.org; internet www.dai.org; f. 1871; 5,500 mems; Pres. Prof. Dr Ing. CHRISTIAN BAUMGART; publ. *DAI-Verbandszeitschrift BAUKULTUR*.

Deutscher Verband für Wohnungswesen, Städtebau und Raumordnung eV (German Federation for Housing and Planning): Littenstr. 10, 10179 Berlin; tel. (30) 20613250; e-mail info@deutscher-verband.org; internet www.deutscher-verband.org; f. 1946; independent research in housing; urban and country planning; 700 mems; Pres. GERNOT MITTLER; Vice-Pres. HELMUT RAUSCH; Vice-Pres. Dr JOSEF MEYER; Sec.-Gen. CHRISTIAN HUTTENLOHER.

Stiftung Bauhaus Dessau (Bauhaus Dessau Foundation): Gropiusallee 38, 06846 Dessau; tel. (340) 6508-0; e-mail service@bauhaus-dessau.de; internet www.bauhaus-dessau.de; f. 1994; preserves and conveys the historic heritage of Bauhaus and contributes ideas and solutions to the problems of design in the contemporary environment; library: public research and reference library with particular reference to urban design, architecture and living; archive of 25,000 items from collns and legacies of Bauhaus teachers and students; Dir Prof. PHILIPP OSWALT.

Attached College:

Bauhaus Kolleg: Gropiusallee 38, 06846 Dessau; tel. (340) 6508403; e-mail goegel@bauhaus-dessau.de; f. 1999; 1-year postgraduate programme; language of instruction: English; Man. INA GOEGEL.

BIBLIOGRAPHY, LIBRARY SCIENCE AND MUSEOLOGY

Arbeitsgemeinschaft der Spezialbibliotheken eV: Geschaeftsstelle, c/o Max Planck Institute for Social Law and Social Policy, Bibliothek, Amalienstraße 33, 80799 Munich; tel. (89) 38602462; e-mail geschaeftsstelle@aspb.de; internet www.aspb.de; f. 1946; asscn of specialized libraries in the German-speaking countries; organizes confs; acts as Section 5 (Spec. Libraries) of the German Libraries Asscn; 500 mems; Pres. HENNING FRANKENBERGER; Vice-Pres. Dr. SONJA GRUND; Treas. YVONNE BRZOSKA; publ. *Conference Proceedings (Tagungsband der Arbeits- und Fortbildungstagung)* (every 2 years).

Berufsverband Information Bibliothek eV (Association of Information and Library Professionals): POB 13 24, Gartenstr. 18, 72703 Reutlingen; tel. (7121) 34910; e-mail mail@bib-info.de; internet www.bib-info.de; f. 1949 as Verein der Bibliothekare und Assistentenen, present name 2000; represents the interests of librarians; maintains professional standards; stresses the importance of professional training and salaries that correspond to the level of training; increases public awareness of the social and educational importance of libraries and professional standards; 6,300 mems; Pres. SUSANNE RIEDEL; Sec. MICHAEL REISSER; publs *BuB (Buch und Bibliothek)—Forum Bibliothek und Information* (10 a year), *OPL-Checklisten*.

Deutsche Gesellschaft für Informationswissenschaft und Informationspraxis eV: c/o Leiterin Nadja Strein, Windmühlstr. 3, 60329 Frankfurt am Main; tel. (69) 430313; e-mail mail@dgi-info.de; internet www.dgi-info.de; f. 1948 as Deutsche Gesellschaft für Dokumentation, present name 1999; promotion of information and documentation, information science and practice; 1,100 mems; Pres. Prof. Dr STEFAN GRADMANN; Vice-Pres. Dr LUZIAN WEISEL; publs *Information–Wissenschaft & Praxis-IWP* (6 a year), *Proceedings DGI-Online-Conference / DGI-Connference* (1 a year), *Proceedings Oberhofer Kolloquium* (every 2 years).

Deutscher Museumsbund eV (German Museums Association): In der Halde 1, 14195 Berlin; tel. (30) 84109517; e-mail office@museumsbund.de; internet www.museumsbund.de; f. 1917 to promote museums, their devt and museology; 2,600 mems; Pres. Dr VOLKER RODEKAMP; Dir ANJA SCHALUSCHKE; Deputy Dir Dr HAYAT WIERSCH; publs *Einkaufsführer für Museen* (1 a year), *Museumskunde* (2 a year).

Internationale Vereinigung der Musikbibliotheken, Musikarchive und Musikdokumentationszentren (IVMB) Gruppe Deutschland eV (International Association of Music Libraries, Archives and Documentation Centres—IAML): c/o Universitäts- und Landesbibliothek, 64283 Darmstadt; tel. (6151) 165807; e-mail sekretaerin@aibm.info; internet www.aibm.info; f. 1951; 210 mems; Pres. Dr BARBARA WIERMANN; Vice-Pres. Dr ANDREAS ODENKIRCHEN; Sec. Dr SILVIA UHLEMANN; Treas. PETRA WAGENKNECHT; publs *Fontes Artis Musicae* (4 a year), *Forum Musikbibliothek* (4 a year).

Verein Deutscher Bibliothekare eV (Association of German Academic Librarians): Universitätsbibliothek München Geschwister-Scholl-Pl. 1, 80539 Munich; tel. (89) 21802420; e-mail vdb@ub.uni-muenchen.de; internet www.vdb-online.org; f. 1900, refounded 1948; annual librarians' congress, workshops, seminars; 1,751 mems; Pres. Dr KLAUS-RAINER BRINTZINGER; Sec. Dr ANKE QUAST; publs *Jahrbuch der Deutschen Bibliotheken* (every 2 years), *VDB-Mitteilungen* (2 a year).

Württembergische Bibliotheksgesellschaft (Society of Friends of the Württemberg State Library): POB 105441, 70047 Stuttgart; tel. (711) 2124428; e-mail wbg@wlb-stuttgart.de; internet www.wlb-stuttgart.de/die-wlb/freunde-der-bibliothek; f. 1946; supports the reconstruction of the Württemberg State Library, holds lectures, meetings, exhibitions, etc.; 350 mems; Pres. (vacant); Chair. Prof. Dr WULF D. VON LUCIUS; Sec. CHRISTINE DEMMLER.

ECONOMICS, LAW AND POLITICS

AFW Wirtschaftsakademie Bad Harzburg GmbH (Academy for Distance Study of Economics in Bad Harzburg): An den Weiden 15, 38667 Bad Harzburg; tel. (5322) 90200; e-mail bildung@afwbadharzburg.de; internet www.afwbadharzburg.de; f. as Akademie für Fernstudium (AfF), present name and status 1999; Man. Dr FRANK EDELKRAUT.

Deutsche Aktuarvereinigung eV: Hohenstaufenring 47–51, 50674 Cologne; tel. (221) 9125540; e-mail info@aktuar.de; internet www.aktuar.de; f. 1948; soc. for promotion of actuarial theory in collaboration with the univs; 3,400 mems; Chair. Dr MICHAEL RENZ; Deputy Chair. Dr JOHANNES LÖRPER; publs *Aktuar aktuell* (3 a year), *Blätter der DGVFM* (2 a year), *Der Aktuar* (4 a year).

Deutsche Gesellschaft für Auswärtige Politik eV (German Council on Foreign Relations): Rauchstr. 17–18, 10787 Berlin; tel. (30) 2542310; e-mail info@dgap.org; internet www.dgap.org; f. 1955; discusses and promotes research on problems of int. politics; operates one of the oldest specialized libraries on German foreign policy (open to the public); library of 85,000 vols, 270 periodicals; 2,500 mems; Pres. Dr AREND OETKER; Exec. Vice-Pres. PAUL VON MALTZAHN; Otto Wolff Dir of the Research Institute EBERHARD SANDSCHNEIDER; Deputy Librarian VERENA SCHRADER; publs *IP Internationale Politik* (6 a year), *Internationale Politik* (6 a year).

Deutsche Gesellschaft für Osteuropakunde eV (German Association for East European Studies): Schaperstr. 30, 10719 Berlin; tel. (30) 21478412; e-mail info@dgo-online.org; internet www.dgo-online.org; f. 1913; 850 mems; Pres. Prof. Dr RITA SÜSSMUTH; Exec. Dir Dr HEIKE DÖRRENBÄCHER; publs *Osteuropa* (12 a year), *Osteuropa-Recht* (6 a year), *Osteuropa-Wirtschaft* (4 a year).

Deutsche Statistische Gesellschaft (German Statistic Society): 22039 Hamburg; Holstenhofweg 85, 22043 Hamburg; tel. (40) 65412779; e-mail post@dstatg.de; internet www.dstatg.de; f. 1911; 800 mems; Pres. Prof. Dr WILFRIED SEIDEL; Vice-Pres. Prof. Dr KARL MOSLER; Vice-Pres. JÜRGEN CHLUMSKY; Man. Dir Dr THOMAS SCHUELER; publs *AStA–Advances in Statistical Analysis* (4 a year), *AStA–Wirtschafts- und Sozialstatistisches Archiv*.

Deutsche Vereinigung für Politische Wissenschaft (German Political Science Association): c/o Osnabrück University, FB1-Sozialwissenschaften, 49069 Osnabrück; Seminarstr. 33, 49074 Osnabrück; tel. (541) 9696264; e-mail dvpw@dvpw.de; internet www.dvpw.de; f. 1951; 1,700 mems; Pres. Prof. Dr HUBERTUS BUCHSTEIN; Vice-Pres. Prof. Dr ANDREA LENSCHOW; Vice-Pres. Prof. Dr FRANK NULLMEIER; Dir FELIX W. WURM; publ. *Politische Vierteljahresschrift* (4 a year).

Deutscher Juristentag eV: POB 1169, 53001 Bonn; Sterntorhaus, Oxfordstr. 21, 53111 Bonn; tel. (228) 9839185; e-mail info@djt.de; internet www.djt.de; f. 1860; furthers discussion among jurists; 7,000 mems; Pres. Prof. Dr THOMAS MAYEN; Gen. Sec. Dr ANDREAS NADLER.

Gesellschaft für Öffentliche Wirtschaft (Society for Public Economy): Sponholzstr. 11, 12159 Berlin; tel. (30) 8521045; e-mail goew.dsceep@t-online.de; f. 1951; 70 mems; research and information service and providers of public services; Pres. MICHAEL SCHÖNEICH; Dir WOLF LEETZ; publ. *Zeitschrift für öffentliche und gemeinwirtschaftliche Unternehmen* (4 a year).

Gesellschaft für Rechtsvergleichung eV (Society of Comparative Law): Belfortstr. 16, 79098 Freiburg; tel. (761) 2032126; e-mail gfr@jura.uni-freiburg.de; internet www.rechtsvergleichung.org; f. 1950; 1,000 mems; Chair. Prof. Dr REINHARD ZIMMERMANN; Sec.-Gen. Prof. Dr MARTIN SCHMIDT-KESSEL; publ. *Rechtsvergleichung und Rechtsvereinheitlichung*.

Gesellschaft für Sozial- und Wirtschaftsgeschichte (Society for Social and Economic History): Friedrich-Wilhelms-Universität Bonn, Konviktstr. 11, 53113 Bonn; tel. (228) 735172; e-mail gswg@uni-bonn.de; internet www.gswg.net; f. 1961; 219 mems; Pres. Prof. Dr GÜNTHER SCHULZ; Vice-Pres. Prof. Dr GERHARD FOUQUET; Sec. Prof. Dr RAINER METZ.

Kommission für Geschichte des Parlamentarismus und der Politischen Parteien eV (Commission for History of Parliamentarianism and Political Parties): Schiffbauerdamm 17, 10117 Berlin; tel. (30) 22792572; e-mail info@kgparl.de; internet www.kgparl.de; f. 1952, present location 2006; 27 mems; Pres. Prof. Dr ANDREAS WIRSCHING; Vice-Pres. Prof. Dr HANS-WERNER

HAHN; Man. Prof. Dr ANDREAS SCHULZ; Sec. JUTTA GRAF; publs *Beiträge zur Geschichte des Parlamentarismus und der politischen Parteien, Quellen zur Geschichte des Parlamentarismus und der politischen Parteien.*

EDUCATION

Humboldt Gesellschaft für Wissenschaft, Kunst und Bildung eV (Humboldt Society for Science, Art and Education): Kronberg 6, 35582 Wetzlar; tel. (641) 21424; e-mail erwin.kuntz@puscher.com; internet www.humboldt-gesellschaft.org; f. 1962; 650 mems; Pres. Prof. Dr ERWIN KUNTZ; Vice-Pres. Dr ERICH BAMMEL; Vice-Pres. Dr WOLFGANG SIEGFRIED; Sec. Dr HORST REDLOF; publs *Abhandlungen* (every 2 years), *Mitteilungen* (every 2 years).

FINE AND PERFORMING ARTS

Bayerische Akademie der Schönen Künste (Bavarian Academy of Fine Arts): Max-Joseph-Pl. 3, 80539 Munich; tel. (89) 2900770; e-mail info@badsk.de; internet www.badsk.de; f. 1948; 242 mems; Pres. Prof. Dr DIETER BORCHMEYER; Gen. Sec. Dr KATJA SCHAEFER; publ. *Jahrbuch*.

Deutsche Gesellschaft für Photographie eV (German Society for Photography): Rheingasse 8–12, 50676 Cologne; tel. (221) 9232069; e-mail dgph@dgph.de; internet www.dgph.de; f. 1951; photography, visual media; 1,000 mems; Chair. DITMAR SCHÄDEL; Vice-Chair. Dr CHRISTIANE STAHL; publ. *DGPh-Intern* (4 a year).

Deutsche Mozart-Gesellschaft eV (German Mozart Society): Frauentorstr. 30, 86152 Augsburg; tel. (821) 518588; e-mail deutsche-mozart-gesellschaft@t-online.de; internet www.deutsche-mozart-gesellschaft.de; f. 1951; 3,000 mems; Pres. Dr DIRK HEWIG; publ. *Acta Mozartiana* (1 a year).

Deutscher Komponistenverband eV (German Composers' Association): Kadettenweg 80B, 12205 Berlin; tel. (30) 84310580; e-mail info@komponistenverband.org; internet www.komponistenverband.de; f. 1954; promotes professional interests of German composers; 1,200 mems; Pres. JÖRG EVERS; Vice-Pres. Prof. LOTHAR VOIGTLÄNDER; Man. SABINE BEGEMANN.

Deutscher Verein für Kunstwissenschaft eV (German Society for Studies in Art History): Jebensstr. 2, 10623 Berlin; tel. (30) 3139932; e-mail dvfk@alice.com; internet www.dvfk-berlin.de; f. 1908; support, promotion and publication of research in German art history; 1,000 mems; Chair. Prof. Dr WOLFGANG AUGUSTYN; Sec. Dr JOSEF RIEDMAIER; publ. *Zeitschrift des Deutschen Vereins für Kunstwissenschaft*.

Kestnergesellschaft: Goseriede 11, 30159 Hanover; tel. (511) 701200; e-mail kestner@kestner.org; internet www.kestner.org; f. 1916, refounded 1948; activities concerned with the promotion of modern art; 4,300 mems; Pres. UWE REUTER; Dir Dr VEIT GÖRNER; Man. Dir MAIRI KROLL.

Stiftung Preussischer Kulturbesitz (Prussian Cultural Heritage Foundation): Von-der-Heydt-Str. 16–18, 10785 Berlin; tel. (30) 266412888; e-mail info@hv.spk-berlin.de; internet www.preussischer-kulturbesitz.de; f. 1961; preserves, augments and reunites the Prussian cultural heritage; comprises 17 state museums, the State Library, the State Privy Archives, the Iberian-American Institute and the State Institute for Research in Music with the Museum for Musical Instruments; Pres. Prof. Dr HERMANN PARZINGER; Vice-Pres. Prof. Dr GÜNTHER SCHAUERTE; publ. *Jahrbuch* (1 a year).

Verband Deutscher Kunsthistoriker eV (Association of German Art Historians): Haus der Kultur, Weberstr. 59A, 53113 Bonn; tel. (228) 18034182; e-mail info@kunsthistoriker.org; internet www.kunsthistoriker.org; f. 1948; 2,900 mems; Pres. Prof. Dr KILIAN HECK; Dir. Dr KATHARINA CORSEPIUS; publ. *Kunstchronik* (11 a year).

HISTORY, GEOGRAPHY AND ARCHAEOLOGY

Arbeitsgemeinschaft Historischer Kommissionen und Landesgeschichtlicher Institute (Association of Historic Councils and Regional History Institutes): Schückingstr. 36, 35037 Marburg; tel. (6421) 1840; f. 1898; controls 51 socs and institutes; Pres. Prof. Dr RODERICH SCHMIDT; Man. Dir Dr WINFRIED IRGANG.

Deutsche Akademie für Landeskunde eV (German Academy for Regional Geography): c/o Universität Leipzig, Institut für Geographie, Johannisallee 19A, 04103 Leipzig; tel. (341) 9732792; e-mail kontakt@deutsche-landeskunde.de; internet www.deutsche-landeskunde.de; f. 1882, refounded 1946; study of regional geography, especially of Germany and German-speaking Central Europe; 66 mems; Chair. (Bochum) Prof. Dr HARALD ZEPP; Chair. (Bonn) Prof. Dr WINFRIED SCHENK; publs *Berichte. Geographie und Landeskunde* (4 a year), *Forschungen zur deutschen Landeskunde* (series, 1 or 2 a year).

Deutsche Gesellschaft für Geographie eV (German Geographical Society): c/o Universität Kiel, Ökologie-Zentrum, Olshausenstr. 75, 24118 Kiel; tel. (431) 8803953; internet www.geographie.de; promotes scientific and practical cartography; 25,000 mems; Pres. Prof. Dr HANS-RUDOLF BORK; Vice-Pres. Prof. Dr DIETER BÖHN; Vice-Pres. Dr RUDOLF JUCHELKA; Gen. Sec. Dr ARNO BEYER.

Deutsche Gesellschaft für Kartographie eV (German Cartographic Society): POB 11 14, 01686 Weinböhla; e-mail sekretaer@dgfk.net; internet www.dgfk.net; f. 1951; promotes scientific and practical cartography; 1,600 mems; Pres. Prof. Dr MANFRED WEISENSEE; Vice-Pres. Prof. Dr MANFRED BUCHROITHNER; Vice-Pres. Prof. Dr JOCHEN SCHIEWE; Sec. STEFFEN HILD; publs *Bibliographia Cartographica, Kartographische Nachrichten* (6 a year, print and online, www.kartographische-nachrichten.de).

Deutsche Gesellschaft für Ortung und Navigation eV (German Institute of Navigation): Kölnstr. 70, 53111 Bonn; tel. (228) 201970; e-mail dgon.bonn@t-online.de; internet www.dgon.de; f. 1951 as Ausschuss für Funkortung, present name 1961; promotes research and devt of methods and systems used for navigation; Pres. Prof. Dr HERMANN ROHLING; Man. Dir BERND MARTENS; publ. *European Journal of Navigation* (3 a year, jt publ. of various European navigation instns).

Deutscher Nautischer Verein von 1868 eV (German Nautical Association of 1868): Striepenweg 31, 21147 Hamburg; tel. (40) 79713401; e-mail info@dnvev.de; internet www.dnvev.de; f. 1868; 4,598 mems in 20 local nautical asscns, 47 corporate mems; Pres. REEDER FRANK WESSELS; Vice-Pres. Dr FRITZ FRANTZIOCH; Vice-Pres. and Man. Dir NICOLAI WOELKI; publ. *Kalendar* (1 a year).

Fränkische Geographische Gesellschaft (Frankish Geographical Society): Kochstr. 4/4, 91054 Erlangen; tel. (9131) 8522633; e-mail fgg@geographie.uni-erlangen.de; internet www.fgg.uni-erlangen.de; f. 1954; 830 mems; library of 60,000 vols, 250 current periodicals; Pres. Prof. Dr HORST KOPP; Pres. Ing. HELMUT MAI; Gen. Sec. Dr MANFRED SCHNEIDER; Gen. Sec. Dr UWE TRETER; publs *Erlanger Geographische Arbeiten* (1 a year), *Erlanger Geographische Arbeiten, Sonderband* (irregular), *Mitteilungen der Fränkischen Geographischen Gesellschaft* (1 a year).

Gesamtverein der Deutschen Geschichts- und Altertumsvereine eV (Union of German Historical and Archaeological Societies): Institut für bayerische Geschichte, Ludwigstr. 14, 80539 Munich; tel. (89) 286382800; e-mail wolfgang.schuster@lmu.de; internet www.gesamtverein.de; f. 1852; 238 affiliated asscns; Pres. Prof. Dr HEINZ-GÜNTHER BORCK; Pres. Prof. Dr MANFRED TREML; publ. *Blätter für deutsche Landesgeschichte*.

Gesellschaft für Erdkunde zu Berlin (Geographical Society of Berlin): Arno-Holz-Str. 14, 12165 Berlin; tel. (30) 7900660; e-mail mail@gfe-berlin.de; internet www.gfe-berlin.de; f. 1828 by Heinrich Berghaus, Carl Ritter and other eminent Prussian scientists of the early 19th century, with the support of Alexander von Humboldt; study of geography, geosciences and related disciplines; lectures, seminars, confs and excursions; 300 mems; library of 100,000 vols; Pres. Dr HARTMUT ASCHE; Gen. Sec. Dr CHRISTOF ELLGER; publs *DIE ERDE—Zeitschrift der Gesellschaft für Erdkunde zu Berlin (Journal of the Geographical Society of Berlin)* (4 a year), *Verhandlungen der Gesellschaft für Erdkunde zu Berlin* (1 a year).

Monumenta Germaniae Historica: Ludwigstr. 16, Postfach 34 02 23, 80099 Munich; tel. (89) 286382384; e-mail sekretariat@mgh.de; internet www.mgh.de; f. 1819; library of 130,000 vols; Pres. Prof. Dr CLAUDIA MÄRTL; Sec. Prof. Dr MARTINA HARTMANN; Exec. Sec. Dr HORST ZIMMERHACKL; Librarian Prof. Dr ARNO MENTZEL-REUTERS; publ. *Deutsches Archiv für Erforschung des Mittelalters*.

Verband der Historiker und Historikerinnen Deutschlands (German Historical Association): c/o Goethe-Universität (Campus Westend), Grüneburgplatz 1, 60323 Frankfurt am Main; tel. (69) 79832571; e-mail info@historikerverband.de; internet www.historikerverband.de; f. 1893, refounded 1949; 2,700 mems; Pres. Prof. Dr MARTIN SCHULZE WESSEL; Man. Dir Dr NORA HILGERT.

LANGUAGE AND LITERATURE

British Council: Alexanderpl. 1, 10178 Berlin; tel. (30) 31109955; e-mail info@britishcouncil.de; internet www.britishcouncil.de; projects and activities in the areas of English, the arts and education and society; administers the IELTS examination throughout Germany; Dir JOHN WHITEHEAD; IELTS Man. CAROLINE MURDOCH.

Deutsche Gesellschaft für Sprachwissenschaft (German Linguistic Society): c/o Manfred Sailer Institut für England- und Amerikastudien Goethe-Universität Frankfurt am Main, Grüneburgpl. 1, 60629 Frankfurt am Main; tel. (69) 79832526; e-mail anke.luedeling@rz.hu-berlin.de; internet dgfs.de; f. 1978; 1,180 mems; Pres. Prof. Dr REGINE ECKARDT; Vice-Pres. Dr SEBASTIAN BÜCKING; Sec. Prof. Dr ANKE LÜDELING; Treas. Dr SARAH ZOBEL; publ. *Zeitschrift für Sprachwissenschaft* (2 a year).

Gesellschaft für deutsche Sprache eV (Society for the German Language): Spiegelgasse 13, 65183 Wiesbaden; tel. (611) 999550; e-mail sekr@gfds.de; internet www.gfds.de; f. 1947; 3,000 mems; library of 20,000 vols; Chair. Prof. Dr ARMIN BURKHARDT; Vice-Chair. Prof. Dr PETER SCHLOBINSKI; Man.

Dir Dr ANDREA-EVA EWELS; publs *Der Sprachdienst* (6 a year), *Muttersprache* (4 a year).

Hölderlin-Gesellschaft eV (Hölderlin Society eV): Bursagasse 6, 72070 Tübingen; tel. (7071) 22040; e-mail info@hoelderlin-gesellschaft.de; internet www.hoelderlin-gesellschaft.info; f. 1943, reconstituted 1946; 1,300 mems; Pres. Prof. Dr SABINE DOERING; Vice-Pres. Prof. Dr MICHAEL FRANZ; Dir VALÉRIE LAWITSCHKA; publs *Hölderlin-Jahrbuch* (every 2 years), *Lyrik im Hölderlinturm*, *Schriften der Hölderlin-Gesellschaft* (irregular), *Turm-Vorträge*.

Instituto Cervantes: Rosenstr. 18–19, 10178 Berlin; tel. (30) 2576180; e-mail berlin@cervantes.de; internet www.cervantes.de; f. 2003; offers courses and exams in Spanish language and culture and promotes cultural exchange with Spain and Spanish-speaking Latin and Central America; attached centres in Bremen and Munich; library of 4,500 vols; Dir GASPAR CANO PERAL; Head Librarian CRISTINA BARÓN MARTIN.

Mommsen-Gesellschaft eV (Mommsen Society eV): Geschäftsstelle Jacob-Burckhardt-Str. 5, 79098 Freiburg i.Br.; internet www.mommsen-gesellschaft.de; f. 1950; asscn of univ. teachers of classics, ancient history and archaeology; 620 mems; Pres. Prof. Dr WULF RAECK; Second Pres. Prof. Dr CHRISTIANE REITZ; Man. Dir Dr THOMAS GANSCHOW; Sec. Dr NADIN BURKHARDT.

PEN Zentrum Deutschland (German PEN Centre): Kasinostr. 3, 64293 Darmstadt; tel. (6151) 23120; e-mail pen-germany@t-online.de; internet www.pen-deutschland.de; f. 1951; attached to Int. Asscn of Writers; 705 mems; Pres. JOHANO STRASSER; Man. Dir CLAUDIA C. KRAUßE; Sec.-Gen. HERBERT WIESNER.

MEDICINE

Anatomische Gesellschaft (Anatomical Society): Institut für Anatomie LST II, Friedrich–Alexander–Universität, Universitätstr. 19, 91054 Erlangen; tel. (9131) 8522865; e-mail friedrich.paulsen@anatomie2.med.uni-erlangen.de; internet www.anatomische-gesellschaft.de; f. 1886; 850 mems; Sec. Prof. Dr FRIEDRICH PAULSEN; publs *Annals of Anatomy* (6 a year), Congress abstracts.

Deutsche Dermatologische Gesellschaft (DDG) (German Dermatologic Society): Robert-Koch-Pl. 7, 10115 Berlin; tel. (30) 2462530; e-mail ddg@derma.de; internet www.derma.de; f. 1888; promotes scientific and clinical dermatology, venereology and allergology; disciplines of andrology, phlebology, proctology, dermatologic-oncology, dermatologic radiation therapy, dermatologic microbiology, occupational and environmental dermatology, preventive dermatology/rehabilitation; 3,500 mems; Pres. Prof. Dr THOMAS A. LUGER; Sec.-Gen. Prof. Dr RUDOLF STADLER; Sec.-Gen. Prof. Dr RUDOLF STADLER; publs *Derma News & Views* (4 a year), *Hautarzt* (12 a year), *JDDG (Journal of the German Society of Dermatology)*.

Deutsche Gesellschaft für Anästhesiologie und Intensivmedizin eV (German Society for Anesthesiology and Intensive Care Medicine): Roritzerstr. 27, 90419 Nuremberg; tel. (911) 933780; e-mail dgai@dgai-ev.de; internet www.dgai.de; f. 1953; 10,000 mems; Pres. Prof. Dr GABRIELE NÖLDGE-SCHOMBURG; Vice-Pres. Prof. Dr JÜRGEN SCHÜTTLER; Dir HOLGER SORGATZ; Sec.-Gen. Prof. Dr HUGO VAN AKEN; publ. *Anästhesiologie, Intensivmedizin, Notfallmedizin und Schmerztherapie (AINS)*.

Deutsche Gesellschaft für Angewandte Optik eV (German Society for Applied Optics): c/o Elizabeth Nagel, Coburger Str. 11, 91056 Erlangen; tel. (9131) 758587; e-mail dgao-sekretariat@dgao.de; internet www.dgao.de; f. 1923; 570 individual mems, 28 corporate mems; Pres. Prof. Dr MICHAEL PFEFFER; Vice-Pres. Dr RAINER SCHUHMANN; Sec. Prof. Dr HARTMUT BARTELT; publs *DGaO-Proceedings* (online), *Optik* (12 a year), *Photonik*.

Deutsche Gesellschaft für Chirurgie (German Surgical Society): Luisenstr. 58/59, 10117 Berlin; tel. (30) 28876290; e-mail dgchirurgie@t-online.de; internet www.dgch.de; f. 1872; 6,500 mems; Pres. Prof. Dr AXEL HAVERICH; Sec.-Gen. HARTWIG BAUER; publ. *Langenbecks Archiv für Chirurgie*.

Deutsche Gesellschaft für Endokrinologie (German Society for Endocrinology): c/o EndoScience, Endokrinologie Service GmbH, Mozartstr. 23, 93128 Regenstauf; tel. (9402) 9481112; e-mail dge@endokrinologie.net; internet www.endokrinologie.net; f. 1953; 1,500 mems; Pres. Prof. Dr ANDREAS PFEIFFER; Vice-Pres. Prof. Dr DAGMAR FÜHRER; Vice-Pres. Prof. Dr JÖRG GROMOLL; Sec. Prof. Dr MARTIN GRUßENDORF; publ. *Endokrinologie-Informationen* (6 a year).

Deutsche Gesellschaft für Gynäkologie und Geburtshilfe eV (German Society for Gynaecology and Birth Support): Robert-Koch-Pl. 7, 10115 Berlin; tel. (30) 514883340; e-mail info@dggg.de; internet www.dggg.de; f. 1885; Pres. Prof. Dr KLAUS FRIESE; Vice-Pres. Prof. Dr ROLF KREIENBERG; Vice-Pres. Prof. Dr THOMAS DIMPFL; Sec. Dr CHRISTIAN DANNECKER; Sec. Prof. Dr DIETHELM WALLWIENER.

Deutsche Gesellschaft für Hals-Nasen-Ohren-Heilkunde, Kopf- und Hals-Chirurgie eV (German Society for Otorhinolaryngology, Head and Neck Surgery): c/o Ulrike Fischer, Friedrich-Wilhelm-Str. 2, 53113 Bonn; tel. (228) 9239220; e-mail info@hno.org; internet www.hno.org; f. 1921 by merger of German Asscn of Otorhinolaryngologists and the German Otological Soc., current name adopted 1968; 10 European archives of Otorhinolaryngology; 4,200 mems; Pres. Prof. Dr ROLAND LASZIG; Vice-Pres. Prof. Dr NORBERT STASCHE; Sec.-Gen. Prof. Dr FRIEDRICH BOOTZ; publs *European Archives of Oto-Rhino-Laryngology and Head & Neck* (12 a year, in English), *HNO* (12 a year, in German), *Laryngo-Rhino-Otologie* (12 a year, in German), *ORL–Journal for Oto-Rhino-Laryngology and its Related Specialties* (6 a year).

Deutsche Gesellschaft für Hygiene und Mikrobiologie eV (German Society for Hygiene and Microbiology eV): c/o Medizinische Hochschule Hannover, Institut für Medizinische Mikrobiologie und Krankenhaushygiene, Carl-Neuberg-Str. 1, 30625 Hanover; tel. (511) 5324655; e-mail dghm@mh-hannover.de; internet www.dghm.org; f. 1906; 1,900 mems; Pres. Prof. Dr SEBASTIAN SUERBAUM; Vice-Pres. Prof. Dr HELGE KARCH; Vice-Pres. Prof. Dr STEFFEN STENGER; Sec. Prof. Dr JAN BUER.

Deutsche Gesellschaft für Innere Medizin (German Society for Internal Medicine): Irenenstr. 1, 65189 Wiesbaden; tel. (611) 20580400; e-mail info@dgim.de; internet www.dgim.de; f. 1882; 21,000 mems; Chair. Prof. Dr HENDRIK LEHNERT; Gen. Sec. Prof. Dr HANS-PETER SCHUSTER; Man. Dir MAXIMILIAN GUIDO GUIDO BROGLIE; publ. *Supplementum of Abstracts* (1 a year).

Deutsche Gesellschaft für Kinder- und Jugendmedizin eV (German Society of Pediatrics and Adolescent Medicine): Chausseestr. 128/129, 10115 Berlin; tel. (30) 30877790; e-mail info@dgkj.de; internet www.dgkj.de; f. 1883; 14,000 mems; Pres. Prof. Dr FRED ZEPP; Vice-Pres. Prof. Dr NORBERT WAGNER; Dir Dr GABRIELE OLBRISCH; Sec. SABINE KÜHNE; publ. *Monatsschrift Kinderheilkunde* (12 a year).

Deutsche Gesellschaft für Neurochirurgie (German Society for Neurosurgery): c/o Porstmann Kongresse GmbH, Alte Jakobstr. 77, 10179 Berlin; tel. (30) 28449922; e-mail gs@dgnc.de; internet www.dgnc.de; f. 1950; promotes science, research and practical work in the field of neurosurgery; 244 mems; Chair. Prof. Dr JÜRGEN MEIXENSBERGER; Chair. Prof. Dr GABRIELE SCHACKERT; Sec. Prof. Dr VEIT BRAUN; publ. *Zentralblatt für Neurochirurgie* (4 a year).

Deutsche Gesellschaft für Orthopädie und Orthopädische Chirurgie eV (German Society for Orthopedics and Orthopedic Surgery): Langenbeck-Virchow-Haus, Luisenstr. 58/59, 10117 Berlin; tel. (30) 84712131; e-mail info@dgooc.de; internet www.dgooc.de; f. 1901; Pres. Prof. Dr BERND KLADNY; Gen. Sec. Prof. Dr FRITZ UWE NIETHARD; Treas. Prof. Dr WERNER SIEBERT; publs *Der Orthopäde* (12 a year), *Der Unfallchirurg* (12 a year), *Orthopädie & Unfallchirurgie Mitteilungen & Nachrichten* (6 a year), *Zeitschrift für Orthopädie und Unfallchirurgie* (6 a year).

Deutsche Gesellschaft für Physikalische Medizin und Rehabilitation eV: Messering 8, Haus F, 01067 Dresden; tel. (351) 8975932; e-mail info@dgpmr.de; internet www.dgpmr.de; f. 1886; physical medicine and rehabilitation; 400 mems; Pres. Dr ANETT REIßHAUER; Dir HELFRIED BÖHME; publs *Kurortmedizin* (6 a year), *Physikalische Medizin, Rehabilitationsmedezin*.

Deutsche Gesellschaft für Plastische und Wiederherstellungschirurgie eV (German Society for Plastic and Reconstructive Surgery): Beethoven Str. 12, 04107 Leipzig; tel. (341) 12457114; e-mail geschaeftsstelle@dgpw.de; internet www.dgpw.de; f. 1962; 30 hon. mems, 20 corresp. mems; Gen. Sec. Prof. Dr R. GAHR; publs *German Medical Science e-journal* (online), *Journal* (2 a year).

Deutsche Gesellschaft für Psychiatrie und Psychotherapie, Psychosomatik und Nervenheilkunde (DGPPN) (German Association for Psychiatry, Psychotherapy and Psychosomatics (DGPPN)): Reinhardtstr. 27B, 10117 Berlin; tel. (30) 24047720; e-mail sekretariat@dgppn.de; internet www.dgppn.de; f. 1842; 7,300 mems; Pres. Prof. Dr WOLFGANG MAIER; Man. Dir Dr JULIANE AMLACHER; publs *Nervenarzt*, *Spektrum*.

Deutsche Gesellschaft für Psychoanalyse, Psychotherapie, Psychosomatik und Tiefenpsychologie (DGPT) eV (German Society for Psychoanalysis, Psychotherapy, Psychosomatic and Depth Psychology eV): Johannisbollwerk 20, 20459 Hamburg; tel. (40) 75664990; e-mail psa@dgpt.de; internet www.dgpt.de; f. 1949; 3,400 mems; Pres. ANNE SPRINGER.

Deutsche Gesellschaft für Rechtsmedizin (German Society of Legal Medicine): Alberstr. 9, 79104 Freiburg; tel. (761) 2036854; e-mail legalmed@uniklinik-freiburg.de; internet www.dgrm.de; Pres. Prof. Dr STEFAN POLLAK.

Deutsche Gesellschaft für Sozialmedizin und Prävention (German Society for Social Medicine and Prevention): c/o Institut für Sozialmedizin und Gesundheitsökonomie, Leipziger Str. 44, 39120 Magdeburg; tel. (391) 6724300; internet www.dgsmp.de; f. 1964; 510 mems; Pres. Dr GERT V. MITTEL-

STAEDT; publ. *Das Gesundheitswesen* (12 a year).

Deutsche Gesellschaft für Tropenmedizin und Internationale Gesundheit eV (German Society for Tropical Medicine and International Well-being eV): Bernhard-Nocht-Str. 74, 20359 Hamburg; tel. (40) 42818478; e-mail dtg@bni-hamburg.de; internet www.dtg.org; f. 1907; 870 mems; Pres. Prof. T. LOESCHER; Sec. Dr H. SUDECK.

Deutsche Gesellschaft für Zahn-, Mund- und Kieferheilkunde (German Society for Dental, Oral and Craniomandibular Sciences): Liesegangstr. 17A, 40211 Düsseldorf; tel. (211) 6101980; e-mail dgzmk@dgzmk.de; internet www.dgzmk.de; f. 1859; 10,500 mems; Pres. Prof. Dr HENNING SCHLIEPHAKE; Sec. Dr ULRICH GAA; publs *APW DVD Journal*, *Clinical Oral Investigations*, *Deutsche Zahnärztliche Zeitung* (12 a year), *Oralprophylaxe*, *Zeitschrift für Zahnärztliche Implantologie*.

Deutsche Ophthalmologische Gesellschaft eV: Platenstr. 1, 80336 Munich; tel. (89) 55057680; e-mail geschaeftsstelle@dog.org; internet www.dog.org; f. 1857; 6,500 mems; Pres. Prof. Dr JOHANN ROIDER; Sec. Prof. Dr ANSELM KAMPIK; publs *Der Ophthalmologe* (12 a year), *Graefe's Archive for Clinical Research* (12 a year), *Klinische Monatsblätter für Augenheilkunde* (12 a year).

Deutsche Physiologische Gesellschaft eV (German Society of Physiology): Institut für Physiologie, Universität Rostock, Gertrudenstr. 9, 18057 Rostock; tel. (381) 4948001; e-mail dpg.sekr@uni-rostock.de; internet www.physiologische-gesellschaft.de; f. 1904; 890 mems; Pres. Prof. Dr ARMIN KURTZ; Pres. Prof. Dr ANDREAS DEUBEN; Sec. Prof. Dr RÜDIGER KÖHLING; publ. *Zeitschrift: Physiologie* (2 a year).

Deutsche Psychoanalytische Gesellschaft (German Psychoanalytic Society): Goerzallee 5, 12207 Berlin; tel. (30) 84316152; e-mail geschaeftsstelle@dpg-psa.de; internet www.dpg-psa.de; f. 1910; 500 mems; Pres. Prof. Dr FRANZ WELLENDORF; Pres. Dr JOCHEN HAUSTEIN; Man. Dir Dr THILO EITH; Sec. ERIKA LÜCK; publs *Forum der Psychoanalyse*, *Praxis der Kinderpsychologie und Kinderpsychiatrie*, *Zeitschrift für Psychosomatische Medizin und Psychoanalyse*.

Deutsche Psychoanalytische Vereinigung eV: Körnerstr. 11, 10785 Berlin; tel. (30) 26552504; e-mail geschaeftsstelle@dpv-psa.de; internet www.dpv-psa.de; f. 1950; br. of the Int. Psychoanalytical Asscn; Pres. Prof. Dr MARTIN TEISING; Vice-Pres. Dr CHRISTOPH E. WALKER; Vice-Pres. Dr GERHARD SCHNEIDER; Sec. DANIELA DUTSCHKE.

NATURAL SCIENCES

General

Georg-Agricola Gesellschaft zur Förderung der Geschichte der Naturwissenschaften und der Technik eV: c/o SAXONIA Standortentwicklungs- und -verwaltungsgesellschaft mbH Halsbrücker Str. 34, 09599 Freiberg; tel. (3731) 395040; e-mail tina.zaenssler@saxonia-freiberg.de; internet www.georg-agricola-gesellschaft.de; f. 1926, present location 2007; promotes study of the history of science and technology; organizes annual meetings; 23 mem. asscns; 190 mems; Pres. Prof. REINHARD SCHMIDT; Vice-Pres. ERICH FRITZ; Man. Dir Dr NORMAN POHL; Chair. of the Scientific Bd Prof. Dr HANS-JOACHIM BRAUN; publ. *Die Technikgechichte als Vorbild moderner Technik*.

Gesellschaft Deutscher Naturforscher und Ärzte eV (Association of German Natural Scientists and Physicians): Hauptstr. 5, 53604 Bad Honnef; tel. (2224) 980713; e-mail info@gdnae.de; internet www.gdnae.de; f. 1822; 4,000 mems; Pres. Prof. Dr LUDWIG SCHULTZ; Vice-Pres. Prof. Dr HANS-PETER ZENNER; Vice-Pres. Prof. Dr KLAUS MÜLLEN; Gen. Sec. Prof. Dr JÖRG STETTER; publ. *Verhandlungen der GDNAe* (every 2 years).

Görres-Gesellschaft zur Pflege der Wissenschaft: Adenauerallee 19, 53111 Bonn; tel. (228) 2674371; e-mail verwaltung@goerres-gesellschaft.de; internet www.goerres-gesellschaft.de; f. 1876; 3,290 mems; Pres. Prof. Dr WOLFGANG BERGSDORF; Vice-Pres. Prof. Dr OTTO DEPENHEUER; Man. H. REINARTZ; Gen. Sec. Prof. Dr RUDOLF SCHIEFFER; publs *Historisches Jahrbuch* (1 a year), *Jahrbuch für Volkskunde* (1 a year), *Kirchenmusikalisches Jahrbuch* (1 a year), *Literaturwissenschaftliches Jahrbuch* (1 a year), *Oriens Christianus*, *Philosophisches Jahrbuch* (1 a year), *Portugiesische Forschungen*, *Römische Quartalschrift*, *Spanische Forschungen*, *Vierteljahrsschrift für wissenschaftliche Pädagogik*, *Zeitschrift für medizinische Ethik*.

Naturwissenschaftlicher Verein für Bielefeld und Umgegend eV (Natural History Society for Bielefeld and the Region): c/o Namu, Adenauerpl. 2, 33602 Bielefeld; tel. (521) 172434; e-mail info@nwv-bielefeld.de; internet www.nwv-bielefeld.de; f. 1908; 14 working groups, incl. astronomy, entomology and experimental archaeology; 600 mems; Chair. Prof. Dr PETER FINKE; Vice-Chair. Dr MICHAEL VON TSCHIRNHAUS; Pres. CLAUDIA QUIRINI-JÜRGENS; Pres. Dr MARTIN BÜCHNER; Pres. MATHIAS WENNEMANN; publ. *ILEX* (2 a year).

Wissenschaftsrat (German Council of Science and Humanities): Brohler Str. 11, 50968 Cologne; tel. (221) 37760; e-mail post@wissenschaftsrat.de; internet www.wissenschaftsrat.de; f. 1957 through cooperation of Länder and Federal Govts; advisory and coordinating body for science policy; makes recommendations on the structural and curricular devt of the univs and on the organization and promotion of science and research; 54 nominated mems in 2 commissions (Scientific and Administrative); Chair. Prof. Dr Ing. WOLFGANG MARQUARDT; Sec.-Gen. THOMAS MAY; publ. *Empfehlungen und Stellungnahmen* (1 a year).

Biological Sciences

Bayerische Botanische Gesellschaft eV (Bavarian Botanical Society): Menzinger Str. 67, 80638 Munich; tel. (89) 17861267; e-mail bbg@lrz.uni-muenchen.de; internet www.bbgev.de; f. 1890; research into the flora of Bavaria and adjacent countries; preservation of species and plant communities; 874 mems; library of 20,000 vols; Pres. Prof. Dr SUSANNE RENNER; Pres. Dr PETER DÖBBELER; Sec. Dr EVA FACHER; publ. *Berichte der Bayerischen Botanischen Gesellschaft*.

Botanischer Informationsknoten Bayern (BIB) (Botanical Information Agency of Bavaria): Am Galgenberg 7, 93109 Wiesent; tel. (9482) 90494; e-mail wolfgang.ahlmer@biologie.uni-regensburg.de; internet www.bayernflora.de; collects information and data on flora from regional research institutes; Pres. WOLFGANG AHLMER.

Deutsche Botanische Gesellschaft eV (German Botanical Society): c/o Prof. Dr Rudolf Ehwald, Institut für Biologie, Humboldt-Universität zu Berlin, Invalidenstr. 42, 10115 Berlin; tel. (30) 20938816; e-mail info@deutsche-botanische-gesellschaft.de; internet www.deutsche-botanische-gesellschaft.de; f. 1882; advances scientific botany nationally and internationally; 1,050 mems; Pres. Prof. Dr ULF-INGO FLÜGGE; Gen. Sec. Prof. Dr VOLKER WISSEMANN; publs *Actualia* (3 a year), *Plant Biology* (6 a year).

Deutsche Gesellschaft für Allgemeine und Angewandte Entomologie eV (German Society for General and Applied Entomology): c/o Senckenberg Deutsches Entomologisches Institut, Eberswalder Str. 90, 15374 Müncheberg; tel. (333432) 736983777; e-mail dgaae@dgaae.de; internet www.dgaae.de; f. 1976; 870 mems; Pres. Prof. Dr GERALD BERND MORITZ; Man. ORTRUD TAEGER; Sec.-Gen. Dr PETER LÖSEL; publs *DGaaE Nachrichten* (3–4 a year), *Journal of Applied Entomology*, *Mitteilungen* (every 2 years).

Deutsche Gesellschaft für Züchtungskunde eV (DGfZ) (German Society for Animal Production): Adenauerallee 174, 53113 Bonn; tel. (228) 9144761; e-mail info@dgfz-bonn.de; internet www.dgfz-bonn.de; f. 1905; livestock breeding, animal housing, reproduction, hygiene, nutrition; 650 mems; Pres. Dr OTTO-WERNER MARQUARDT; Vice-Pres. Prof. Dr GEORG ERHARDT; Vice-Pres. Prof. Dr HARALD SIEME; Man. Dir Dr BETTINA BONGARTZ; publ. *Züchtungskunde* (6 a year).

Deutsche Malakozoologische Gesellschaft: Senckenberganlage 25, 60325 Frankfurt am Main; internet www.hausdernatur.de; f. 1868; study of Mollusca; 270 mems; library of 30,000 vols; Pres. Dr VOLLRATH WIESE; publs *Archiv für Molluskenkunde* (2 a year), *Mitteilungen* (1–2 a year).

Deutsche Ornithologen-Gesellschaft eV: c/o Institut f. Vogelforschung, An der Vogelwarte 21, 26386 Wilhelmshaven; tel. (4421) 96890; e-mail info@do-g.de; internet www.do-g.de; f. 1850; 1,900 mems; Pres. Prof. Dr FRANZ BAIRLEIN; publs *Journal of Ornithology* (4 a year), *Vogelwarte* (4 a year).

Deutsche Phytomedizinische Gesellschaft eV (German Phytomedical Society): Messeweg 11/12, 38104 Brunswick; tel. (531) 2993213; e-mail geschaeftsstelle@dpg.phytomedizin.org; internet www.phytomedizin.org; f. 1949; 1,200 mems; Pres. Prof. Dr ANDREAS VON TIEDEMANN; Pres. Dr BERND HOLTSCHULTE; Pres. Dr KLAUS STENZEL; Man. Dir Dr FALKO FELDMANN.

Deutsche Zoologische Gesellschaft eV (German Zoological Society): Corneliusstr. 12, 80469 Munich; tel. (89) 54806960; e-mail dzg@zi.biologie.uni-muenchen.de; internet www.dzg-ev.de; f. 1890; represents zoological sciences in Germany, Austria and Switzerland; promotes zoology as a modern, multi-disciplinary and integrating science and enables the exchange of recent scientific findings; 1,700 mems; Pres. Prof. Dr CONSTANCE SCHARFF; Sec. Dr SABINE GIESSLER; publs *Frontiers in Zoology* (online), *Zoologie—Mitteilungen der Deutschen Zoologischen Gesellschaft*.

Gesellschaft für Biochemie und Molekularbiologie (Society for Biochemistry and Molecular Biology): Mörfelder Landstr. 125, 60598 Frankfurt; tel. (69) 6605670; e-mail info@gbm-online.de; internet www.gbm-online.de; f. 1947; research in molecular life sciences in all its forms, such as biochemistry, molecular biology, molecular medicine; 5,500 mems; Chair. Prof. Dr NIKOLAUS PFANNER; Vice-Pres. Prof. Dr ALFRED WITTINGHOFER; Vice-Pres. Prof. Dr IRMGARD SINNING; Sec. Prof. Dr ULRICH BRANDT; publs *Biological Chemistry* (12 a year), *BIOspektrum* (7 a year).

Gesellschaft für Naturkunde in Württemberg: Rosenstein 1, 70191 Stuttgart; tel. (711) 8936-201; internet www.ges-naturkde-wuertt.de; f. 1844; 653 mems;

Pres. Prof. Dr HANS-DIETER GÖRTZ; publ. *Jahreshefte*.

Münchner Entomologische Gesellschaft e.V. (Munich Entomological Society): c/o Prof. Dr E. G. Burmeister, Zoologische Staatssammlung, Münchhausenstr. 21, 81247 Munich; tel. (89) 81070; e-mail megmail@zsm.mwn.de; internet www.zsm.mwn.de/meg; f. 1904; attached to Library of the Zoological State Colln; 448 mems; library of 15,372 vols, 813 periodicals, 382 running journals, 6,800 separata; Pres. Prof. Dr ERNST-GERHARD BURMEISTER; Sec. JOHANNES SCHUBERTH; publs *Mitteilungen* (1 a year), *Nachrichtenblatt der Bayerischen Entomologen* (2 a year).

Naturhistorische Gesellschaft Hannover (Hanover Society of Natural History): Willy-Brandt-Allee 5, 30169 Hanover; Fössestr. 99, 30453 Hanover; tel. (511) 9807871; e-mail info@n-g-h.org; internet www.n-g-h.org; f. 1797; 501 mems; Pres. Dr DIETER SCHULZ; Pres. Prof. Dr HANSJÖRG KÜSTER; publs *Beihefte*, *Berichte*, *Naturhistorica—Berichte der NGH* (1 a year).

Naturkundeverein Schwäbisch Gmünd eV (Natural History Society of Schwäbisch Gmünd): Münsterpl. 15, 73525 Schwäbisch Gmünd; tel. (7171) 6034130; e-mail vorstand@nkv-gd.de; internet www.nkv-gd.de; f. 1890; works to promote public awareness of and protection of the natural environment; oversees protected sites; Pres. Prof. Dr FRIEDER BAY; Vice-Pres. UDO GEDACK; Sec. MANFRED BONI; publ. *Unicornis*.

Naturwissenschaftlicher und Historischer Verein für das Land Lippe eV (Natural History and Historical Society for the Lippe Region): Willi-Hofmann-Str. 2, 32756 Detmold; tel. (5231) 3033233; e-mail info@nhv-lippe.de; internet www.nhv-lippe.de; f. 1835; 4 groups in Detmold, Bad Salzuflen, Lage and Lemgo; research into natural sciences, prehistory and local folk and art history; 800 mems; Pres. Dr CHRISTIAN REINICKE; Vice-Pres. Prof. Dr JÜRGEN DÖHL; Vice-Pres. Prof. Dr STEFAN BAUMEIER; Sec. Dr RALF FABER; publs *Lippische Mitteilungen aus Geschichte und Landeskunde* (1 a year), *Lippischen Geschichtsquellen*.

Naturwissenschaftlicher Verein der Niederlausitz eV (Natural History Society of Lower Lusatia): POB 101005, 03010 Cottbus; e-mail info@nvn-cottbus.de; internet www.nvn-cottbus.de; f. 1990; research into local natural sciences and protection of nature and the environment; 90 mems; Pres. URSULA STRIEGLER; Pres. CAROLA BUDE.

Naturwissenschaftlicher Verein in Hamburg (Natural History Society of Hamburg): c/o Biozentrum Grindel und Zoologisches Museum, Martin-Luther-King-Pl. 3, 20146 Hamburg; tel. (40) 428385635; e-mail nwv.zoologie@uni-hamburg.de; internet www.biologie.uni-hamburg.de/zim/nwv; f. 1837; 460 mems; Chair. Prof. Dr HARALD SCHLIEMANN.

Naturwissenschaftlicher Verein zu Bremen (Bremen Natural Science Association): c/o Übersee-Museum, Bahnhofspl. 13, 28195 Bremen; tel. (421) 16038153; e-mail info@nwv-bremen.de; internet www.nwv-bremen.de; f. 1864; 400 mems; Chair. Dr HANS-KONRAD NETTMANN; Vice-Chair. Dr JENS LEHMANN; Vice-Chair. Dr MONIKA STEINHOF; publ. *Abhandlungen* (1 a year).

Verein Naturschutzpark eV (Nature Reserves Federation): Niederhaverbeck 7, 29646 Bispingen; tel. (5198) 987030; e-mail vnp-info@t-online.de; internet www.verein-naturschutzpark.de; f. 1909; 4,500 mems; Dir Dr MATHIAS ZIMMERMANN; publ. *Naturschutz- und Naturparke*.

Vereinigung für Angewandte Botanik eV (Association for Applied Botany): Ohnhorststr. 18, 22609 Hamburg; tel. (40) 42816349; e-mail hans.weigel@vti.bund.de; internet www.angewandtebotanik.de; f. 1902; 150 mems; Pres. Prof. Dr HANS-JOACHIM WEIGEL; publ. *Angewandte Botanik* (Journal of Applied Botany and Food Quality, 2 a year).

Mathematical Sciences

Berliner Mathematische Gesellschaft eV (Berlin Mathematical Society): c/o Freie Universität Berlin, Institut für Mathematik, Arnimallee 3, 14195 Berlin; tel. (30) 8544602; e-mail bmg.ev@berlin.de; internet www.berlmathges.de; f. 1901; Pres. Prof. Dr GERHARD PREUß; Vice-Pres. Prof. Dr RUDOLF BAIERL; Sec. Prof. Dr WOLFGANG VOLK; publ. *Sitzungsberichte*.

Deutsche Mathematiker Vereinigung eV (German Mathematical Society): c/o WIAS, Mohrenstr. 39, 10117 Berlin; tel. (30) 20372306; e-mail dmv@wias-berlin.de; internet dmv.mathematik.de; f. 1890; 4,000 mems; Pres. Prof. Dr CHRISTIAN BÄR; Sec. Prof. Dr GÜNTER TÖRNER.

Gesellschaft für Angewandte Mathematik und Mechanik (International Association of Applied Mathematics and Mechanics): c/o Prof. Dr Ing. Hab. Michael Kaliske, Institut für Statik und Dynamik der Tragwerke, Fakultät Bauingenieurwesen, 01062 Dresden; tel. (351) 46333448; e-mail gamm@mailbox.tu-dresden.de; internet www.gamm-ev.de; f. 1922; advancement of scientific work and int. cooperation in applied mathematics, mechanics and physics; 2,300 mems; Pres. Prof. V. MEHRMANN; Vice-Pres. Prof. P. WRIGGERS; Sec. Prof. Dr Ing. Hab. MICHAEL KALISKE.

Gesellschaft für Operations Research eV (GOR) (German Society for Operations Research): Joseph-Sommer-Str. 34, 41812 Erkelenz; tel. (2431) 9026710; e-mail info@gor-ev.de; internet gor.uni-paderborn.de; f. 1998 by merger of Deutsche Gesellschaft für Operations Research and Gesellschaft für Mathematik, Ökonometrie und Operations Research; promotes devt of operations research and encourages coordination of theoretical and practical advances in the area; 1,200 mems; Pres. Prof. Dr STEFAN NICKEL; Man. Dir CHRISTIANE PIENTKA; publs *Mathematical Methods of Operations Research* (6 a year), *OR News* (3 a year), *OR Spectrum* (4 a year).

Physical Sciences

Astronomische Gesellschaft eV: c/o Regina von Berlepsch, Leibniz Institute for Astrophysics Potsdam, An der Sternwarte 16, 14482 Potsdam; tel. (331) 7499348; e-mail info@astronomische-gesellschaft.de; internet www.astronomische-gesellschaft.org; f. 1863, current name adopted 1995; 800 mems; Pres. Prof. Dr ANDREAS BURKERT; Vice-Pres. Prof. Dr MATTHIAS STEINMETZ; Sec. REGINA VON BERLEPSCH; publs *Mitteilungen der Astronomischen Gesellschaft* (1 a year), *Reviews in Modern Astronomy* (1 a year).

Deutsche Bunsen-Gesellschaft für Physikalische Chemie eV (German Bunsen Society for Physical Chemistry): POB 150104, 60061 Frankfurt; Theodor-Heuss Allee 25, 60486 Frankfurt; tel. (69) 7564621; e-mail woehler@bunsen.de; internet www.bunsen.de; f. 1894, present name 1902; promotes research and technical advances in the area of physical chemistry; 1,500 mems; Chair. Prof. Dr MARTIN QUACK; Vice-Chair. Prof. Dr WOLFGANG VON RYBINSKI; Dir Dr FLORIAN AUSFELDER; Sec. ERIKA WÖHLER; publs *Bunsen-Magazin* (6 a year), *Physical Chemistry Chemical Physics* (52 a year, jtly with other learned socs).

Deutsche Geophysikalische Gesellschaft eV (German Geophysical Society): c/o Birger-G, Lühr Helmholtz-Zentrum Potsdam, Deutsches GeoforschungsZentrum, Telegrafenberg, 14473 Potsdam; tel. (331) 2881206; e-mail ase@gfz-potsdam.de; internet www.dgg-online.de; f. 1922; 1,150 mems; Pres. Prof. Dr MICHAEL KORN; Vice-Pres. Prof. Dr EIKO RÄKERS; Exec. Man. BIRGER-G. LÜHR; publs *DGG Mitteilungen* (Red Pages, 3 or 4 a year), *Geophysical Journal International* (12 a year), *GMIT* (2 a year).

Deutsche Gesellschaft für Biophysik eV: c/o Prof. Dr Ulrike Alexiev, Fachbereich Physik, Freie Universität Berlin, Arnimallee 14, 14195 Berlin; tel. (30) 83855157; e-mail ulrike.alexiev@physik.fu-berlin.de; internet www.dgfb.org; f. 1943; 450 mems; Chair. Prof. Dr GERD H. J. GALLA; Vice-Pres. Prof. Dr ULI NIENHAUS; Vice-Pres. Prof. Dr CLAUDIA STEINEM; Sec. Dr ULRIKE ALEXIEV.

Deutsche Gesellschaft für Experimentelle und Klinische Pharmakologie und Toxikologie: Achenbachstr. 43, 40237 Düsseldorf; tel. (211) 60069277; e-mail mitglieder@dgpt-online.de; internet www.dgpt-online.de; f. 1920; 2,500 mems; Pres. Prof. Dr L. HEIN; Man. Dir Dr J. KNOLLMEYER.

Deutsche Gesellschaft für Geowissenschaften (DGG) (German Geological Society): Buchholzer Str. 98, 30655 Hanover; tel. (511) 89805061; e-mail info@dgg.de; internet www.dgg.de; f. 1848; scientific and technical congresses, confs and meetings, several spec. sections (Fachsektionen); 3,000 mems; library of 130,000 vols; Chair. Prof. Dr GERNOLD ZULAUF; Sec. KARIN SENNHOLZ; Treas. Dr HEINZ-GERD RÖHLING; Librarian ANDREAS NIKOLAUS KÜPPERS; publs *Exkursionsführer & Tagungspublikationen (EDGG)* (irregular), *Geowissenschaftliche Mitteilungen* (4 a year), *Schriftenreihe der Deutschen Gesellschaft für Geowissenschaften (SDGG)* (irregular), *Zeitschrift der Deutschen Gesellschaft für Geowissenschaften (ZDGG)* (4 a year).

Deutsche Meteorologische Gesellschaft (German Meteorological Society): c/o Institut für Meteorologie, Freie Universität Berlin, Carl-Heinrich-Becker-Weg 6–10, 12165 Berlin; tel. (30) 79708324; e-mail sekretariat@dmg-ev.de; internet www.dmg-ev.de; f. 1883; 1,750 mems; Pres. Prof. Dr HELMUT MAYER; Sec. Dr DIRK SCHINDLER; publs *Meteorologische Zeitschrift* (6 a year), *Mitteilungen DMG* (4 a year).

Deutsche Mineralogische Gesellschaft (German Mineralogical Society): Institut für Mineralogie und Lagerstättenlehre, RWTH Aachen, 52056 Aachen; tel. (241) 8095774; e-mail info@dmg-home.de; internet www.dmg-home.de; f. 1908; crystallography, petrology, geochemistry, ore minerals, applied mineralogy; 1,300 mems; Pres. Prof. Dr RAINER ALTHERR; Vice-Pres. Prof. Dr FALKO LANGENHORST; Sec. Prof. Dr F. MICHAEL MEYER; publs *Beihefte* (1 a year), *European Journal of Mineralogy (EJM)* (6 a year), *GMit*.

Deutsche Physikalische Gesellschaft eV: Hauptstr. 5, 53604 Bad Honnef; tel. (2224) 92320; e-mail dpg@dpg-physik.de; internet www.dpg-physik.de; f. 1845; 63,000 mems; Pres. Prof. Dr EDWARD G. KRUBASIK; Vice-Pres. Prof. Dr JOHANNA STACHEL; Sec. Dr BERNHARD NUNNER; publs *Physik Journal* (12 a year), *Verhandlungen der DPG* (3 or 6 a year).

Deutscher Zentralausschuss für Chemie: c/o Gesellschaft Deutscher Chemiker,

POB 90 04 40, 60444 Frankfurt am Main; Carl Bosch-Haus, Varrentrappstr. 40–42, 60486 Frankfurt am Main; tel. (69) 7917323; e-mail b.koehler@gdch.de; internet www.gdch.de/gdch/koop/iupac.htm; f. 1952; 7 mems; Pres. Prof. Dr LUTZ FRIEDJAN TIETZE; Man. Dir Prof. Dr WOLFRAM KOCH; publ. *Chemistry International* (6 a year).

Deutsches Atomforum eV (German Forum on Nuclear Energy): Robert-Koch-Pl. 4, 10115 Berlin; tel. (30) 4985550; e-mail info@kernenergie.de; internet www.kernenergie.de; f. 1959; promotes the peaceful uses of atomic energy; Pres. Dr RALF GÜLDNER; Dir DIETER H. MARX.

Geologische Vereinigung eV (Geological Association): Vulkanstr. 23, 56743 Mendig; tel. (2652) 989360; e-mail info@g-v.de; internet www.g-v.de; f. 1910; 1,700 mems; Chair. Prof. Dr RALF LITTKE; Sec. RITA SPITZLEI; publ. *Geologische Rundschau* (International Journal of Earth Sciences, 8 a year).

Gesellschaft Deutscher Chemiker (German Chemical Society): POB 90 04 40, 60444 Frankfurt am Main; Varrentrappstr. 40–42, 60486 Frankfurt am Main; tel. (69) 79170; e-mail gdch@gdch.de; internet www.gdch.de; f. 1946; 29,000 mems; Pres. Prof. Dr MICHAEL DRÖSCHER; Vice-Pres. Prof. Dr BARBARA ALBERT; Vice-Pres. Prof. Dr FRANÇOIS DIEDERICH; Exec. Dir Prof. Dr WOLFRAM KOCH; publs *Analytical and Bioanalytical Chemistry* (24 a year), *Angewandte Chemie* (52 a year, int. edn in English), *ChemBioChem* (12 a year), *Chemie-Ingenieur-Technik* (12 a year), *Chemie in unserer Zeit* (6 a year), *Chemischer Informationsdienst* (52 a year), *Chemistry—A European Journal* (24 a year), *ChemPhysChem* (12 a year), *European Journal of Inorganic Chemistry* (24 a year), *European Journal of Organic Chemistry* (24 a year), *Nachrichten aus der Chemie* (12 a year).

Paläontologische Gesellschaft (Palaeontological Society): Weismüllerstr. 45, 60314 Frankfurt am Main; tel. (69) 400301971; e-mail geschaeftsstelle@palges.de; internet www.palges.de; f. 1912; 1,065 mems; Pres. Dr MICHAEL WUTTKE; Vice-Pres. Prof. Dr RAINER SPRINGHORN; Vice-Pres. Prof. Dr THOMAS MARTIN; Vice-Pres. Dr THOMAS MÖRS; publ. *Paläontologische Zeitschrift* (4 a year).

PHILOSOPHY AND PSYCHOLOGY

Deutsche Gesellschaft für Philosophie eV (DGPhil): c/o Philipps-Universität Marburg, Geschäftsstelle DGPhil, Raum 03B08, Wilhelm-Röpke-Str. 6, 35032 Marburg; tel. (6421) 2824719; e-mail geschaeftsstelle@dgphil.de; internet www.dgphil.de; f. 1948 as Allgemeine Gesellschaft für Philosophie in Deutschland e.V.; holds German Congress for Philosophy every 3 years and Forum for Philosophy in other years; 1,827 mems; Pres. Prof. Dr MICHAEL QUANTE; Dir Prof. Dr ANDREA M. ESSER; Treas. HORST D. BRANDT; publ. *Deutsches Jahrbuch für Philosophie* (Annual Proceedings).

Deutsche Gesellschaft für Psychologie eV (German Psychological Society): POB 42 01 43, 48068 Münster; tel. (2533) 2811520; e-mail geschaeftsstelle@dgps.de; internet www.dgps.de; f. 1904; promotes and disseminates scientific psychology; 3,300 mems; Pres. Prof. Dr JÜRGEN MARGRAF; Vice-Pres. Prof. Dr ANDREA ABELE-BREHM; Vice-Pres. Prof. Dr GERHARD STEMMLER; Sec. Prof. Dr ROLAND DEUTSCH; publ. *Psychologische Rundschau* (4 a year).

Gesellschaft für antike Philosophie eV (Society for Ancient Philosophy eV): c/o Prof. Dr Christoph Horn, Institut für Philosophie, Universität Bonn, Am Hof 1, 53113 Bonn; e-mail philosophie.lfb2@uni-bonn.de; internet www.ganph.de; f. 1999; Pres. Prof. Dr THOMAS BUCHHEIM; Vice-Pres. Prof. Dr CHRISTIAN BROCKMANN; Man. Dir Prof. Dr CHRISTOPH HORN.

Gesellschaft für Geistesgeschichte (Society for the History of Ideas): Am Neuen Markt 8, 14467 Potsdam; tel. (331) 280940; e-mail aludewig@uni-potsdam.de; internet www.geistesgeschichte.net; f. 1958; 80 mems; Pres. Prof. Dr JULIUS H. SCHOEPS; Man. Dir Dr ANNA-DOROTHEA LUDEWIG; publ. *Zeitschrift für Religions- und Geistesgeschichte*.

Gesellschaft für Wissenschaftliche Gerichts- und Rechtspsychologie (Society for Forensic Science and Right Psychology): Rablstr. 45, 81669 Munich; tel. (89) 4481282; e-mail info@gwg.info; internet www.gwg-institut.com; f. 1982; Dir Dr JOSEPH SALZGEBER.

Gottfried-Wilhelm-Leibniz-Gesellschaft: c/o Gottfried Wilhelm Leibniz Bibliothek, Niedersächsische Landesbibliothek, Waterloostr. 8, 30169 Hanover; tel. (511) 1267331; e-mail info@leibnizgesellschaft.de; internet www.gottfried-wilhelm-leibniz-gesellschaft.de; f. 1966; 400 mems; Pres. Prof. ROLF WERNSTEDT; Vice-Pres. Prof. Dr HANS POSER; Vice-Pres. Prof. Dr MICHEL FICHANT; Gen. Sec. Dr WOLFGANG DITTRICH; publs *Studia Leibnitiana*, *Studia Leibnitiana Supplementa / Sonderhefte*, *Supplementa*.

RELIGION, SOCIOLOGY AND ANTHROPOLOGY

Albertus-Magnus-Institut: Adenauerallee 17, 53111 Bonn; tel. (228) 201460; e-mail ami@albertus-magnus-institut.de; internet www.albertus-magnus-institut.de; f. 1931; critical publishing of the works of Albertus Magnus; 8 mems; library of 5,000 vols; Dir Prof. Dr MARC-AEILKO ARIS; Deputy Dir Prof. Dr HANNES MÖHLE; Sec. MONIKA GEYER; publs *Editio Coloniensis*, *Lectio Albertina*, *Subsidia Albertina*.

Berliner Gesellschaft für Anthropologie, Ethnologie und Urgeschichte (Berlin Society for Anthropology, Ethnology and Prehistory): c/o Alix Hänsel, Museum für Vor- und Frühgeschichte, Geschwister-Scholl-Str. 6, 10117 Berlin; tel. (30) 32674817; e-mail kontakt@bgaeu.de; internet www.bgaeu.de; f. 1869; 350 mems; Pres. Dr MARKUS SCHINDLBECK; Vice-Pres. Dr BETTINA JUNGKLAUS; Vice-Pres. Prof. Dr WOLFRAM SCHIER; Sec. Dr ALIX HÄNSEL; publ. *Mitteilungen*.

Deutsche Gesellschaft für Asienkunde eV (German Association for Asian Studies): Rothenbaumchaussee 32, 20148 Hamburg; tel. (40) 445891; e-mail post@asienkunde.de; internet www.asienkunde.de; f. 1967; promotes and coordinates contemporary Asian research; 800 mems; Pres. Dr PETER CHRISTIAN HAUSWEDELL; Exec. Sec. B. SKOWASCH; publ. *ASIEN—The German Journal on Contemporary Asia* (4 a year).

Deutsche Gesellschaft für Soziologie (German Sociological Association): c/o Kulturwissenschaftliches Institut, Goethestr. 31, 45128 Essen; tel. (351) 46337404; e-mail dgs@mailbox.tu-dresden.de; internet www.soziologie.de; f. 1909; 1,600 mems; Pres. Prof. Dr HANS-GEORG SOEFFNER; Man. DANA GIESECKE; publ. *Soziologie—Forum der DGS*.

Deutsche Gesellschaft für Volkskunde eV (German Society for European Ethnology and Folklore Studies): c/o Institut für EE/KW Biegenstr. 9, 35037 Marburg; tel. (6421) 2826514; e-mail geschaeftsstelle@d-g-v.de; internet www.d-g-v.de; f. 1904, current name adopted 1963; confs, scientific publs, network and communications; 1,200 mems; Pres. Prof. Dr KARL BRAUN; Vice-Pres. Dr BEATE SPIEGEL; Vice-Pres. Dr SABINE IMERI; Exec. Sec. CLAUS-MARCO DIETERICH; Sec. MARTIN SCHULTZE; publs *Mitteilungen der Deutschen Gesellschaft für Volkskunde* (4 a year), *Zeitschrift für Volkskunde* (2 a year).

Deutsche Morgenländische Gesellschaft (German Oriental Society): c/o Prof. Dr. Walter Slaje, Seminar für Indologie, Martin-Luther-Universität Halle-Wittenberg, 06099 Halle; tel. (345) 5523650; e-mail walter.slaje@indologie.uni-halle.de; internet www.dmg-web.de; f. 1845; 698 mems; attached research institutes (Orient-Institut) in Beirut and Istanbul: see chapters on Lebanon and Turkey; library of 50,000 vols; Pres. Prof. Dr JENS PETER LAUT; Man. Prof. Dr WALTER SLAJE; Sec. Prof. Dr LESLIE TRAMONTINI; publs *Abhandlungen für die Kunde des Morgenlandes*, *Beiruter Texte und Studien*, *Bibliotheca Islamica*, *Journal of the Nepal Research Centre*, *Verzeichnis der orientalischen Handschriften in Deutschland*, *Wörterbuch der klassischen arabischen Sprache*, *Zeitschrift der Deutschen Morgenländischen Gesellschaft*.

Deutsche Orient-Gesellschaft (German Oriental Society): c/o Institut für Altorientalistik, Hüttenweg 7, 14195 Berlin; tel. (30) 844147925; e-mail dogva@mail.zedat.fu-berlin.de; internet www.orient-gesellschaft.de; f. 1898; 976 mems; Pres. Prof. Dr MARKUS HILGERT; Vice-Pres. Prof. Dr HANS NEUMANN; Sec. Prof. Dr FELIX BLOCHER; publs *Abhandlungen*, *Alter Orient aktuell* (1 a year), *Mitteilungen der DOG* (1 a year), *Wissenschaftliche Veröffentlichungen*.

Gesellschaft für Anthropologie (Society for Anthropology): c/o Dr Christiane Scheffler, Institut für Biochemie und Biologie der Universität Potsdam, FG Humanbiologie, Maulbeerallee 1, 14469 Potsdam; tel. (331) 9771917; e-mail scheffle@rz.uni-potsdam.de; internet www.gfanet.de; f. 1992 by merger of Deutsche Anthropologische Gesellschaft and Gesellschaft für Anthropologie und Humangenetik; Chair. Dr ALBERT ZINK; Sec. Dr BIRGIT GROßKOPF; publ. *Anthropologischer Anzeiger* (4 a year).

Gesellschaft für Evangelische Theologie: Universität Bamberg, Evangelische Theologie, Markuspl. 3, 96045 Bamberg; tel. (951) 8631844; e-mail heinrich.bedford-strohm@ppp.uni-bamberg.de; internet www.gevth.de; f. 1940; c. 800 mems; Pres. Prof. Dr HEINRICH BEDFORD-STROHM; publ. *Verkündigung und Forschung* (2 a year).

GIGA German Institute of Global and Area Studies/Leibniz-Institut für Globale und Regionale Studien: Neuer Jungfernstieg 21, 20354 Hamburg; tel. (40) 42825593; e-mail info@giga-hamburg.de; internet www.giga-hamburg.de; f. 1964, fmrly German Overseas Institute, present name and status 2006; research on political, economic and social devts in Africa, Asia, Latin America, N Africa and the Middle East; 125 mems; library of 170,000 vols, 850 current journals; Pres. Prof. Dr ROBERT KAPPEL; Vice-Pres. Prof. Dr DETLEF NOLTE; publs *Africa Spectrum* (online), *GIGA Focus*, *GIGA Working Papers* (online), *Journal of Current Chinese Affairs—China aktuell* (4 a year), *Journal of Current Southeast Asian Affairs* (4 a year), *Journal of Politics in Latin America* (online), *Korea Yearbook—Politics, Economy and Society* (1 a year).

Rheinische Vereinigung für Volkskunde: Am Hofgarten 22, 53113 Bonn; e-mail d.haverkamp@uni-bonn.de; internet www.rvvb.de; f. 1947; regional ethnology of the Rhineland; 300 mems; Pres. HEINRICH LEONARD COX; Pres. Prof. Dr HELMUT

FISCHER; publs *Bonner Kleine Reihe zur Alltagskultur*, *Rheinisches Jahrbuch für Volkskunde*.

Wissenschaftliche Gesellschaft für Theologie eV: Paulsenstr. 55–56, 12163 Berlin; tel. (30) 82097223; e-mail wgth .berlin@gmx.de; internet www.wgth.de; f. 1973; mems in Germany, Switzerland, Austria, UK, Netherlands, Romania, Czech Republic, Hungary and Scandinavia; 6 sections: Old Testament, New Testament, Church History, Systematic Theology, Practical Theology, Missions and Religion; 700 mems; Pres. Prof. Dr CHRISTOPH SCHWÖBEL; Vice-Pres. Prof. Dr ALBRECHT BEUTEL; Sec. Prof. Dr MICHAEL MEYER-BLANCK; publ. *Veröffentlichungen der Wissenschaftlichen Gesellschaft für Theologie*.

TECHNOLOGY

DECHEMA Gesellschaft für Chemische Technik und Biotechnologie eV (Society for Chemical Engineering and Biotechnology): POB 150104, 60061 Frankfurt am Main; Theodor-Heuss-Allee 25, 60486 Frankfurt am Main; tel. (69) 75640; e-mail info@ dechema.de; internet www.dechema.de; f. 1926; promotes and supports research and technological progress in chemical technology and biotechnology; an interface between science, economy, state and public; organizes ACHEMA summit for chemical technology, environmental protection and biotechnology; 5,500 mems; library of 25,000 vols; Chair. Dr HANS JÜRGEN WERNICKE; Deputy Chair. Prof. Dr FERDI SCHÜTH; Deputy Chair. Dr ALDO BELLONI; Exec. Dir Dr KURT WAGEMANN; publs *Chemie-Ingenieur-Technik* (12 a year), *Materials and Corrosion* (1 a year), *Materialwissenschaft und Werkstofftechnik* (12 a year).

Deutsche Gemmologische Gesellschaft eV (German Gemmological Association): Prof. Schlossmacher Str. 1, 55743 Idar-Oberstein; tel. (6781) 50840; e-mail info@ dgemg.com; internet www.dgemg.com; f. 1932; administers the German Gemmological Training Centre; 1,500 mems; library of 2,500 vols; Dir Dr ULRICH HENN; publ. *Gemmologie* (4 a year, currently as 2 double issues).

Deutsche Gesellschaft für Bauingenieurwesen eV (German Society for Constructional Engineering): Barbarossaplatz 2, 76137 Karlsruhe; f. 1946; 490 mems; Pres. Prof. Dr WILHELM STRICKLER; Sec. Ing. GERHART BOCHMANN.

Deutsche Gesellschaft für Luft- und Raumfahrt—Lilienthal-Oberth eV (DGLR) (German Society for Aeronautics and Astronautics): Godesberger Allee 70, 53175 Bonn; tel. (228) 308050; e-mail info@ dglr.de; internet www.dglr.de; f. 1912; support of aeronautics and astronautics for all scientific and technical purposes; 3,000 mems; Pres. Dr Ing. DETLEF MÜLLER-WIESNER; Vice-Pres Dipl. Ing. CLAUDIA KESSLER; Vice-Pres. Prof. Ing. ROLF HENKE; Sec.-Gen. PETER BRANDT; publs *Aerospace Science and Technology* (1 a year), *DGLR-Mitteilungen* (6 a year), *Luft- und Raumfahrt* (6 a year).

Deutsche Gesellschaft für Materialkunde eV (Materials Science and Engineering): Senckenberganlage 10, 60325 Frankfurt am Main; tel. (69) 75306750; e-mail dgm@dgm.de; internet www.dgm.de; f. 1919; 2,198 mems; Pres. Dr ULRICH HARTMANN; Vice-Pres. Prof. Dr WOLFGANG KAYSSER; Man. Dir Dr Ing. FRANK O. R. FISCHER; publs *Advanced Engineering Materials* (12 a year), *Materialwissenschaft und Werkstofftechnik* (12 a year, in German), *Praktische Metallographie* (Practical Metallography), *Zeitschrift für Metallkunde—International Journal for Materials Research*.

Deutsche Gesellschaft für Photogrammetrie, Fernerkundung und Geoinformation eV (DGPF) (German Society for Photogrammetry, Remote Sensing and Geoinformation): c/o EFTAS GmbH, Oststr. 2–18, 48145 Münster; tel. (251) 133070; e-mail sekretaer@dgpf.de; internet www .dgpf.de; f. 1909, present name 2002; 850 mems; Pres. Prof. Dr CORNELIA GLÄSSER; Vice-Pres. Prof. Dr THOMAS H. KOLBE; Sec. Dr Ing. MANFRED WIGGENHAGEN; publ. *Photogrammetrie-Fernerkundung-Geoinformation* (6 a year).

Deutsche Gesellschaft für Zerstörungsfreie Prüfung eV (DGZfP) (German Society for Non-Destructive Testing): Max-Planck-Str. 6, 12489 Berlin; tel. (30) 678070; e-mail mail@dgzfp.de; internet www.dgzfp.de; f. 1933; confs, training courses and personnel certification; 1,500 mems; Pres. Dr Ing. FRANZISKA AHRENS; CEO MATTHIAS PURSCHKE; publ. *ZfP-Zeitung* (12 a year).

Deutsche Glastechnische Gesellschaft eV (German Society of Glass Technology): Siemensstr. 45, 63071 Offenbach; tel. (69) 9758610; e-mail info@hvg-dgg.de; internet www.hvg-dgg.de; f. 1922; deals with different glass technology problems; promotes knowledge of devts in the field of glass and develops contacts among mems; 1,200 mems; library of 21,500 vols; Pres. Prof. Dr Ing HANSJÜRGEN BARKLAGE-HILGEFORT; Dir Dr Ing. ULRICH ROGER; publ. *dgg journal* (for mems).

Deutsche Keramische Gesellschaft eV (German Ceramic Society): Am Grott 7, 51147 Cologne; tel. (2203) 966480; e-mail info@dkg.de; internet www.dkg.de; f. 1919; promotes ceramics in technical, scientific and artistic point of view; 1,229 mems; Chair. Prof. Dr RAINER TELLE; Deputy Chair. Dr BÄRBEL VOIGTSBERGER; Dir Dr MARKUS BLUMENBERG; publ. *cfi-ceramic forum international/Berichte der DKG* (12 a year).

Deutsche Lichttechnische Gesellschaft eV (German Technical-Scientific Society for Light and Lighting): Burggrafenstr. 6, 10787 Berlin; tel. (30) 26012439; e-mail info@litg .de; internet www.litg.de; f. 1912 as Deutsche Beleuchtungstechnische Gesellschaft; 2,300 mems; Pres. HENNING V. WELTZIEN; Vice-Pres. Prof. Dr Ing. STEPHAN VÖLKER; Man. Dir Dr Ing. MICHAEL L. SEIDL; Sec. REGINA VOIGT; publ. *Licht* (12 a year).

Deutscher Beton- und Bautechnik-Verein eV (German Concrete Association): POB 11 05 12, 10835 Berlin; Kurfürstenstr. 129, 10785 Berlin; tel. (30) 2360960; e-mail info@ betonverein.de; internet www.betonverein .de; f. 1898; quality control, research, standardization and construction advice; 750 mems; Pres. Prof. Dr Ing. MANFRED NUSSBAUMER; Vice-Pres. Dipl. Ing. DIETER STRAUB; Vice-Pres. Dipl. Ing. HENNER MAHLSTEDT; Man. Dir Dr Ing. LARS MEYER; publs *Bemessungsbeispiele*, *Beton-Handbuch*, *Vorträge Betontag*.

Deutscher Kälte- und Klimatechnischer Verein eV (DKV) (German Refrigeration Association): POB 0420, 30004 Hanover; Striehlstr. 11, 30159 Hanover; tel. (511) 8970814; e-mail info@dkv.org; internet www .dkv.org; f. 1909; 5 sections for production and industrial application of refrigeration, food science and technology, storage, transport and air conditioning; 1,300 mems; Pres. Prof. Dr Ing. MICHAEL ARNEMANN; Gen. Man. CARMEN STADTLÄNDER; Vice-Pres. Dr. Ing. JOSEF OSTHUES; publs *DKV-Aktuell* (4 a year), *DKV Arbeitsblätter and kältemaschinenregeln*, *DKV-Forschungsberichte* (irregular), *DKV-Statusberichte* (irregular), *DKV-Tagungsbericht* (1 a year).

Deutscher Markscheider Verein eV (German Association of Mining Surveyors): Shamrockring 1, 44623 Herne; tel. (2323) 154660; e-mail geschaeftsstelle@dmv-ev.de; internet www.dmv-ev.de; assists devt of mining and geotechnical engineering; mountain economy and mining law; participates in education and training in mine surveying; promotes science, research and practice in mine surveying; Pres. Dr Ing. PETER GOERKE-MALLET; Vice-Pres. CARSTEN WEDEKIND; Sec. Prof. Dr Ing. AXEL PREUSSE.

Deutscher Verband für Materialforschung und -prüfung eV (DVM) (German Association for Materials Research and Testing): Unter den Eichen 87, 12205 Berlin; tel. (30) 8113066; e-mail office@dvm-berlin .de; internet www.dvm-berlin.de; f. 1896; organizes conferences, seminars and workshops; 350 mems; Pres. Dr Ing. MANFRED BACHER-HÖCHST; Vice-Pres. Dipl. Ing. LOTHAR KRÜGER; Man. Dir KATHRIN LEERS; publs *DVM-Nachrichten* (news, 3–4 a year), *Materialprüfung* (12 a year).

Deutscher Verband für Schweissen und verwandte Verfahren eV (DVS) (German Welding Society): POB 10 19 65, 40010 Düsseldorf; Aachener Str. 172, 40223 Düsseldorf; tel. (0211) 15910; e-mail verwaltung@dvs-hg.de; internet www .die-verbindungs-spezialisten.de; f. 1947; welding and allied processes; 20,000 mems; Pres. Prof. Dr Ing. H. FLEGEL; Vice-Pres. Dipl. Ing. P. BOYE; Vice-Pres. Dipl. Ing. O. RECKENHOFER; Man. Dir Dr Ing. K. MIDDELDORF; publs *Aufbau und Verbindungstechnik in der Elektronic* (also English edn), *Der Praktiker*, *Die Schweisstechnische Praxis*, *DVS-Berichte*, *DVS-Merkblätter*, *DVS-Richtlinien*, *DVS-Videos*, *Fachbibliographie Schweisstechnik*, *Fachbuchreihe Schweisstechnik*, *Fachwörterbücher*, *Forschungsberichte Humanisierung des Arbeitslebens der Schweisser*, *Referateorgan Schweissen und verwandte Verfahren*, *Schweissen und Schneiden* (also English edn), *Schweisstechnische Forschungsberichte*, *Schweisstechnische Software*.

Deutscher Verband Technisch-wissenschaftlicher Vereine (Federation of Technical and Scientific Associations): Steinpl. 1, 10623 Berlin; tel. (30) 310078386; e-mail info@dvt-net.de; internet www.dvt-net.de; f. 1916; natural science and technology and represents the interests of engineers in relation to science, economics, society, politics and administration; comprises 45 technical and scientific asscns; 45 mems; Chair. Prof. Dr Ing. BRUNO O. BRAUN; Vice-Chair. Dr Ing. WALTER THIELEN; Dir JÖRG MAAS.

Deutscher Verein des Gas- und Wasserfaches eV (DVGW) (German Technical and Scientific Association for Gas and Water): Josef-Wirmer Str. 1–3, 53123 Bonn; tel. (228) 91885; e-mail info@dvgw.de; internet www .dvgw.de; f. 1859 as Asscn of German Gas Experts and Agents of German Gas Works; present name and status 2000; specifications and standardization, testing and certification, research and devt, training, providing consultancy services and information; 13,166 mems; Pres. Prof. Dr MATTHIAS KRAUS; Man. Dir Dr Ing. WALTER THIELEN; publs *DVGW*, *DVGW—Informationen*, *DVGW—Regelwerk*, *DVGW—Schriftenreihen*, *Gas/Erdgas* (Gas/Natural Gas), *GWF—Das Gas- und Wasserfach* (GWF—the Gas and Water Industry), *Wasser/Abwasser* (Water/Wastewater).

DIN Deutsches Institut für Normung eV (German Institute for Standardization): Burggrafenstr. 6, 10787 Berlin; tel. (4930)

26010; e-mail info@din.de; internet www.din .de; f. 1917 as Standards Asscn of German Industry; 1,796 mems; Pres. Prof. Dr Ing. KLAUS HOMANN; Dir Dr Ing. TORSTEN BAHKE; publs *DIN-Catalogue* (1 a year), *DIN Management Letter* (6 a year), *DIN-Mitteilungen* (12 a year).

Fachgebiet Wasserwirtschaft und Hydrosystemmodellierung (Chair of Water Resources Management and Modeling of Hydrosystems): Institut für Bauingenieurwesen, Fakultät VI Planen Bauen, Umwelt, Sekr. TIB1-B14, Gustav-Meyer-Allee 25, 13355 Berlin; tel. (30) 31472308; e-mail reinhard.hinkelmann@wahyd.tu-berlin.de; internet www.wahyd.tu-berlin.de; hydromechanics, hydrology, hydraulic engineering, hydrosystemsmodel, water resources management; Dir Prof. Dr Ing. REINHARD HINKELMANN; Sec. MATA KRISHNA.

Gesellschaft für Informatik eV: Wissenschaftszentrum, Ahrstr. 45, 53175 Bonn; tel. (228) 302145; e-mail gs@gi-ev.de; internet www.gi-ev.de; f. 1969; promotes informatics in research, education, applications; 24,500 mems; Pres. Prof. Dr STEFAN JAEHNICHEN; Man. Dir Dr PETER FEDERER; Exec. Dir CORNELIA WINTER; publs *Informatik Spektrum*, *Künstliche Intelligenz*, *Wirtschaftsinformatik*.

Informationstechnische Gesellschaft im VDE (ITG) (Information Technology Society within VDE): Stresemannallee 15, 60596 Frankfurt am Main; tel. (69) 6308284; e-mail presse@vde.com; internet www.vde .com; f. 1954; 35,000 mems; Pres. Dipl. Ing ALF HENRYK WULF; Vice-Pres. Dr Ing. JOACHIM SCHNEIDER; CEO Dr Ing. HANS HEINZ ZIMMER; Deputy CEO Prof. Dr Ing. HELMUT KLAUSING; publs *AEU International Journal of Electronics*, *Nachrichtentechnische Zeitschrift (NTZ)* (12 a year).

IWL—Institut für gewerbliche Wasserwirtschaft und Luftreinhaltung Dienstleistung und Consulting GmbH (Institute for Commercial Water Supply and the Prevention of Air Pollution): Schillingsrotter Str. 38, 50996 Cologne; tel. (221) 9354623; e-mail schopka-iwl@t-online.de; internet www.iwl-koeln.de; f. 1995; Man. Dir Dr SVERRIR SCHOPKA.

RKW Rationalisierungs- und Innovationszentrum der Deutschen Wirtschaft eV (German Centre for Productivity and Innovation): Kompetenzzentrum, Düsseldorfer Str. 40, 65760 Eschborn; tel. (6196) 4950; e-mail heitzer@rkw.de; internet www.rkw .de; f. 1921; 4,000 mems; Man. Dir W. AXEL ZEHRFELD; Deputy Dir Dr INGRID VOIGT; publ. *RKW-Magazin* (4 a year).

Stahl-Zentrum: Sohnstr. 65, 40237 Düsseldorf; tel. (211) 6707870; e-mail martin .kunkel@stahl-zentrum.de; internet www .stahl-online.de; f. 1998; umbrella org. for Steel Institute VDEh, German Steel Federation, and other orgs and institutes of steel industry; 9,000 mems; library of 120,000 vols; publs *Literaturschau Stahl und Eisen* (26 a year), *MPT Metallurgical Plant and Technology International* (6 a year), *Stahl* (6 a year), *Stahl und Eisen* (12 a year), *Stahlmarkt* (12 a year), *Steel Research (Archiv für das Eisenhüttenwesen)* (12 a year).

VDE Verband der Elektrotechnik Elektronik Informationstechnik eV (VDE Association for Electrical, Electronic & Information Technologies): Stresemannallee 15, 60596 Frankfurt am Main; tel. (69) 63080; e-mail service@vde.com; internet www.vde .com; f. 1893; 35,000 mems; Pres. Dipl. Ing ALF HENRYK WULF; Vice-Pres. Dr Ing. JOACHIM SCHNEIDER; CEO Dr Ing. HANS HEINZ ZIMMER; Deputy CEO Prof. Dr Ing. HELMUT KLAUSING; publs *Dialog VDE-Mitglieder-Information*, *Elektrotechnische Zeitschrift*, *Nachrichtentechnische Zeitschrift*, *VDE-Buchreihe*, *VDE-Fachberichte*, *VDE-Schriftenreihe*, *VDE-Vorschriften*.

Verein der Zellstoff- und Papier-Chemiker und -Ingenieure eV (ZELLCHEMING) (Association of Pulp and Paper Chemists and Engineers): Emilestrasse 21, 64293 Darmstadt; tel. (6151) 33264; e-mail info@zellcheming.de; internet www .zellcheming.com; f. 1905; 2,050 mems; Chair. Dipl. Ing. CLAUS M. PALM; Vice-Chair. Dipl. Ing. THOMAS REIBELT; Exec. Dir Dr Ing. WILHELM BUSSE; publ. *ipw–Das Papier*.

Verein Deutscher Giessereifachleute eV (VDG) (German Foundrymen's Association): POB 10 51 44, 40042 Düsseldorf; Sohnstr. 70, 40237 Düsseldorf; tel. (211) 68710; e-mail info@vdg.de; internet www.vdg.de; f. 1909; 2,600 mems; library of 35,000 vols; Chair. Dr Ing. GOTTHARD WOLF; Sec. GABRIELA BEDERKE; publs *Casting Plant Technology International* (4 a year), *Giesserei* (12 a year), *Giessereiforschung* (4 a year), *Giesserei Jahrbuch*, *VDG aktuell*.

Verein Deutscher Ingenieure eV (VDI) (Association of German Engineers): POB 101139, 40002 Düsseldorf; VDI-Pl. 1, 40468 Düsseldorf; tel. (211) 62140; e-mail kundencenter@vdi.de; internet www.vdi.de; f. 1856; technical and scientific cooperation in 21 engineering sections concerning all fields of technology; training courses for professional engineers; documentation in various brs of engineering and prevention of air pollution and noise; 140,000 mems; Pres. Prof. BRUNO O. BRAUN; Dir Dr WILLI FUCHS; publs *VDI-Verlag: Program: VDI-Nachrichten* (52 a year), technical journals, books, etc.

Research Institutes

GENERAL

Max-Planck-Gesellschaft zur Förderung der Wissenschaften eV (Max Planck Society for the Advancement of Science): POB 101062, 80084 Munich; tel. (89) 21080-0; e-mail webmaster@gv.mpg.de; internet www .mpg.de; f. 1948; funded by the federal and state govts; Pres. Prof. Dr PETER GRUSS; Sec.-Gen. Dr LUDWIG KRONTHALER; publs *Max-PlanckForschung* (4 a year), *MaxPlanckResearch* (4 a year).

Attached Research Institutes:

Bibliotheca Hertziana–Max-Planck-Institut für Kunstgeschichte (Bibliotheca Hertziana—Max Planck Institute for Art History): see Italy chapter.

Friedrich-Miescher-Laboratorium für Biologische Arbeitsgruppen in der Max-Planck-Gesellschaft (Friedrich Miescher Laboratory of the Max Planck Society): POB 2109, 72011 Tübingen; Spemannstr. 39, 72076 Tübingen; tel. (7071) 601800; e-mail herta.soffel@tuebingen .mpg.de; internet www.fml.tuebingen.mpg .de; f. 1969; Man. Dir Dr CHRISTIANE NÜSSLEIN-VOLHARD.

Fritz-Haber-Institut der Max-Planck-Gesellschaft: Faradayweg 4–6, 14195 Berlin; tel. (30) 841330; e-mail fhi@ fhi-berlin.mpg.de; internet www.fhi-berlin .mpg.de; f. 1911; physical chemistry; Exec. Dir Prof. MARTIN WOLF; Vice-Chair. Prof. HANS-JOACHIM FREUND.

Kunsthistorisches Institut in Florenz—Max-Planck-Institut (Art History Institute in Florence—Max Planck Institute): Via Giuseppe Guisti 44, 50121 Florence, Italy; tel. 055-249111; e-mail khi-presse@khi.fi.it; internet www.khi.fi.it; f. 1897, current name adopted 2002; library of 310,000 vols, 2,600 periodicals, 610,000 reproductions, spec. collns incl. art in Italy; Man. Dir Prof. Dr GERHARD WOLF; Dir Prof. Dr ALESSANDRO NOVA; publs *Collana del KHI*, *Deutsche Ausgabe der 'Vite'*, *Die Kirchen von Siena*, *I Mandorli*, *Italienische Forschungen*, *Kleine Schriftenreihe des KHI*, *Mitteilungen des KHI*, *Studi e ricerche*.

Max-Planck-Arbeitsgruppen für strukturelle Molekularbiologie (Max Planck Working Group for Structural Molecular Biology): c/o DESY, Notkestr. 85, Geb. 25B, 22607 Hamburg; tel. (40) 89982801; e-mail office@mpasmb.desy.de; internet www.mpasmb-hamburg.mpg.de; f. 1985; Head Prof. Dr ADA YONATH; Head Prof. Dr ECKHARD MANDELKOW; Head Dr HANS-DIETER BARTUNIK.

Max-Planck-Forschungsstelle für Enzymologie der Proteinfaltung (Max Planck Research Unit for Enzymology of Protein Folding): Weinbergweg 22, 06120 Halle (Saale); tel. (345) 5522801; e-mail user@enzyme-halle.mpg.de; internet www .enzyme-halle.mpg.de; f. 1996; Man. Dir Prof. Dr GUNTER S. FISCHER; Admin. Man. ANGELICA NIEPHAGEN.

Max-Planck-Institut für Astronomie (Max Planck Institute for Astronomy): Königstuhl 17, 69117 Heidelberg; tel. (6221) 5280; e-mail sekretariat@mpia.de; internet www.mpia.de; f. 1967; Man. Dir Prof. Dr THOMAS HENNING; publ. *Sterne und Weltraum* (12 a year).

Max-Planck-Institut für Astrophysik (Max Planck Institute for Astrophysics): POB 1317, 85741 Garching; Karl-Schwarzschild-Str. 1, 85741 Garching; tel. (89) 300000; e-mail info@mpa-garching .mpg.de; internet www.mpa-garching.mpg .de; f. 1958; Man. Dir Prof. Dr WOLFGANG HILLEBRANDT.

Max-Planck-Institut für Ausländisches und Internationales Privatrecht (Max Planck Institute for Comparative and International Private Law): Mittelweg 187, 20148 Hamburg; tel. (40) 419000; e-mail presse@mpipriv .de; internet www.mpipriv.de; f. 1926; library of 500,000 vols; Dir Prof. Dr HOLGER FLEISCHER; Dir Prof. Dr JÜRGEN BASEDOW; Dir Prof. Dr REINHARD ZIMMERMANN; publ. *Rabels Zeitschrift für ausländisches und internationales Privatrecht—The Rabel Journal of Comparative and International Private Law (RabelsZ)* (4 a year).

Max-Planck-Institut für Ausländisches und Internationales Sozialrecht (Max Planck Institute for Foreign and International Social Law): Amalienstr. 33, 80799 Munich; tel. (89) 386020; e-mail beckersek@mpisoc.mpg.de; internet www .mpisoc.mpg.de; f. 1980; Chair. Prof. Dr FRANZ RULAND; Man. Dir Prof. Dr ULRICH BECKER; publ. *Zeitschrift für ausländisches und internationales Arbeits- und Sozialrecht* (4 a year).

Max-Planck-Institut für Ausländisches und Internationales Strafrecht (Max Planck Institute for Foreign and International Criminal Law): Günterstalstr. 73, 79100 Freiburg im Breisgau; tel. (761) 70810; e-mail info@mpicc.de; internet www.mpicc.de; f. 1938; library of 450,000 vols, 1,500 journals and periodicals; Dir Prof. Dr HANS-JÖRG ALBRECHT; Dir Prof. Dr ULRICH SIEBER; publs *eucrim – the european criminal law associations' forum*, *F3—Freedom from fear*, *Monatsschrift für Kriminologie und Strafrechtsre-*

form, Zeitschrift für die gesamte Strafrechtswissenschaft.

Max-Planck-Institut für Ausländisches Öffentliches Recht und Völkerrecht (Max Planck Institute for Comparative Public Law and International Law): Im Neuenheimer Feld 535, 69120 Heidelberg; tel. (6221) 4821; e-mail information@mpil.de; internet www.mpil.de; f. 1924; library of 602,000 vols, 2,680 periodicals; Man. Dir Prof. Dr ARMIN VON BOGDANDY; Dir Prof. Dr RÜDIGER WOLFRUM; publ. *Zeitschrift für ausländisches öffentliches Recht und Völkerrecht*.

Max-Planck-Institut für Bildungsforschung (Max Planck Institute for Human Development): Lentzeallee 94, 14195 Berlin; tel. (30) 824060; e-mail info@mpib-berlin.mpg.de; internet www.mpib-berlin.mpg.de; f. 1963; library of 220,000 vols, 500 print journals; Man. Dir Prof. Dr GERD GIGERENZER.

Max-Planck-Institut für Bioanorganische Chemie (Max Planck Institute for Bioinorganic Chemistry): POB 10 13 65, 45413 Mülheim/Ruhr; Stiftstr. 34–36, 45470 Mülheim/Ruhr; tel. (208) 3064; e-mail mpibac@mpi-muelheim.mpg.de; internet www.mpibac.mpg.de; f. 1958, fmrly Institute for Radiation Chemistry; Dir Prof. Dr WOLFGANG LUBITZ; Dir Prof. Dr KARL WIEGHARDT; Dir Prof. Dr FRANK NEESE; Man. Dir Prof. Dr ROBERT SCHLOEGL.

Max-Planck-Institut für Biochemie (Max Planck Institute for Biochemistry): Am Klopferspitz 18, 82152 Martinsried; tel. (89) 85780; e-mail konschak@biochem.mpg.de; internet www.biochem.mpg.de; f. 1973; Man. Dir Dr RALF TATZEL.

Max-Planck-Institut für Biogeochemie (Max Planck Institute for Biogeochemistry): Hans-Knöll-Str. 10, 07745 Jena; tel. (3641) 5760; e-mail info@bgc-jena.mpg.de; internet www.bgc-jena.mpg.de; f. 1997; Man. Dir Prof. SUSAN TRUMBORE.

Max-Planck-Institut für Biologische Kybernetik (Max Planck Institute for Biological Cybernetics): Spemannstr. 38, 72076 Tübingen; tel. (7071) 601510; e-mail info.kyb@tuebingen.mpg.de; internet www.kyb.tuebingen.mpg.de; f. 1968; works in the elucidation of cognitive processes; Man. Dir Prof. Dr NIKOS K. LOGOTHETIS.

Max-Planck-Institut für Biophysik (Max Planck Institute for Biophysics): Max-von-Laue-Str. 3, 60438 Frankfurt am Main; tel. (69) 63030; e-mail info@biophys.mpg.de; internet www.biophys.mpg.de; f. 1937; Man. Dir Prof. Dr WERNER KÜHLBRANDT.

Max-Planck-Institut für Biophysikalische Chemie (Karl-Friedrich-Bonhoeffer-Institut) (Max Planck Institute for Biophysical Chemistry): Am Fassberg 11, 37077 Göttingen; tel. (551) 2011211; e-mail pr@mpibpc.mpg.de; internet www.mpibpc.gwdg.de; f. 1971; Man. Dir Prof. Dr GREGOR EICHELE; publ. *MPIbpc News*.

Max-Planck-Institut für Chemie (Otto-Hahn-Institut) (Max Planck Institute for Chemistry): POB 30 60, 55020 Mainz; Hahn-Meitner-Weg 1, 55128 Mainz; tel. (6131) 3050; e-mail gfd@mpic.de; internet www.mpic.de; f. 1912, present status 1949; Man. Dir Prof. Dr ULRICH PÖSCHL.

Max-Planck-Institut für Chemische Ökologie (Max Planck Institute for Chemical Ecology): Hans-Knoell-Str. 8, 07745 Jena; tel. (3641) 570; e-mail info@ice.mpg.de; internet www.ice.mpg.de; f. 1996; Chair. Prof. JOHN A. PICKETT; Man. Dir Prof. Dr BILL S. HANSSON.

Max-Planck-Institut für Chemische Physik fester Stoffe (Max Planck Institute for Chemical Physics of Solids): Nöthnitzer Str. 40, 01187 Dresden; tel. (351) 46460; e-mail cpfs@cpfs.mpg.de; internet www.cpfs.mpg.de; f. 1995; Dir Prof. Dr ANDREW P. MACKENZIE; Dir Prof. Dr CLAUDIA FELSER; Dir Prof. JURI GRIN; Dir Prof. Dr LIU HAO TJENG.

Max-Planck-Institut für Demografische Forschung (Max Planck Institute for Demographic Research): Konrad-Zuse-Str. 1, 18057 Rostock; tel. (381) 20810; e-mail info@demogr.mpg.de; internet www.demogr.mpg.de; f. 1996; Exec. Dir Prof. JAMES W. VAUPEL.

Max-Planck-Institut für Dynamik Komplexer Technischer Systeme (Max Planck Institute for Dynamics of Complex Technical Systems): Sandtorstr. 1, 39106 Magdeburg; tel. (391) 61100; e-mail info@mpi-magdeburg.mpg.de; internet www.mpi-magdeburg.mpg.de; f. 1996; Man. Dir Prof. Dr PETER BENNER.

Max-Planck-Institut für Dynamik und Selbstorganisation (Max Planck Institute for Dynamics and Self-Organization): POB 28 53, 37018 Göttingen; Bunsenstr. 10, 37073 Göttingen; tel. (551) 51760; e-mail stephan.herminghaus@ds.mpg.de; internet www.mpisf.mpg.de; f. 1925 as Kaiser Wilhelm Institute for Fluid Dynamics, present name 2004; Man. Dir Prof. Dr STEPHAN HERMINGHAUS.

Max-Planck-Institut für Eisenforschung GmbH (Max Planck Institute for Iron Research): POB 140444, 40074 Düsseldorf; Max-Planck-Str. 1, 40237 Düsseldorf; tel. (211) 67920; e-mail info@mpie.de; internet www.mpie.de; f. 1917; CEO Prof. Dr DIERK RAABE; Vice-CEO Prof. Dr GERHARD DEHM.

Max-Planck-Institut für Entwicklungsbiologie (Max Planck Institute for Developmental Biology): Spemannstr. 35, 72076 Tübingen; tel. (7071) 601350; e-mail mpi.entwicklungsbiologie@tuebingen.mpg.de; internet www.eb.tuebingen.mpg.de; f. 1937; Man. Dir Prof. Dr ELISA IZAURRALDE.

Max-Planck-Institut für Ethnologische Forschung (Max Planck Institute for Social Anthropology): POB 11 03 51, 06017 Halle (Saale); Advokatenweg 36, 06114 Halle (Saale); tel. (345) 29270; e-mail mann@eth.mpg.de; internet www.eth.mpg.de; f. 1998; library: 37,500 monographs, 650 video cassettes, 191 subscribed journals, 4,300 journal vols; Dir Prof. Dr CHRIS HANN; Man. Dir Prof. Dr GÜNTHER SCHLEE; Dir Prof. Dr MARIE-CLAIRE FOBLETS.

Max-Planck-Institut für Europäische Rechtsgeschichte (Max Planck Institute for European Legal History): POB 930227, 60457 Frankfurt am Main; Hausener Weg 120, 60489 Frankfurt am Main; tel. (69) 789780; e-mail duve@rg.mpg.de; internet www.rg.mpg.de; f. 1964; library of 320,000 vols; Man. Dir Prof. Dr THOMAS DUVE; publ. *Jus Commune*.

Max-Planck-Institut für Evolutionäre Anthropologie (Max Planck Institute for Evolutionary Anthropology): Deutscher Pl. 6, 04103 Leipzig; tel. (341) 35500; e-mail info@eva.mpg.de; internet www.eva.mpg.de; f. 1997; Man. Dir Prof. Dr MICHAEL TOMASELLO.

Max Planck-Institut für Evolutionsbiologie (Max Planck Institute for Evolutionary Biology): POB 165, 24302 Plön; August-Thienemann-Str. 2, 24306 Plön; tel. (4522) 7630; e-mail tautz@evolbio.mpg.de; internet www.evolbio.mpg.de; f. 1891 as Biologische Station zu Plön, present name 2007; library of 12,000 vols; Man. Dir Prof. Dr DIETHARD TAUTZ; Librarian BRIGITTE LECHNER.

Max-Planck-Institut für Experimentelle Endokrinologie (Max Planck Institute for Experimental Endocrinology): Feodor-Lynen-Str. 7, 30625 Hanover; tel. (511) 53590; e-mail gottschalk@vw.endo.mpg.de; internet www.endo.mpg.de; f. 1979; Man. Dir Prof. Dr GREGOR EICHELE.

Max-Planck-Institut für Experimentelle Medizin (Max Planck Institute for Experimental Medicine): Hermann-Rein-Str. 3, 37075 Göttingen; tel. (551) 38990; e-mail kraemer@em.mpg.de; internet www.em.mpg.de; f. 1947; molecular biology, neurosciences; library of 60,000 vols; Man. Dir Prof. Dr KLAUS-ARMIN NAVE; Librarian INGEBORG KRAEMER.

Max-Planck-Institut für Extraterrestrische Physik (Max Planck Institute for Extraterrestrial Physics): POB 1312, 85741 Garching; Giessenbachstr., 85748 Garching; tel. (89) 300000; e-mail mpe@mpe.mpg.de; internet www.mpe.mpg.de; f. 1963, present status 1991; Man. Dir Prof. Dr RALF BENDER (acting).

Max-Planck-Institut für Festkörperforschung (Max Planck Institute for Solid State Research): Heisenbergstr. 1, 70569 Stuttgart; tel. (711) 6890; e-mail www@fkf.mpg.de; internet www.fkf.mpg.de; f. 1969; Man. Dir Prof. Dr KLAUS KERN; Man. Dr MICHAEL EPPARD.

Max-Planck-Institut für Gesellschaftsforschung (Max Planck Institute for the Study of Societies): Paulstr. 3, 50676 Cologne; tel. (221) 27670; e-mail info@mpifg.de; internet www.mpifg.de; f. 1984; library of 60,000 vols, 300,000 items in catalogue incl. articles from journals and edited vols, 150 print journals; researches on sociology of markets, institutional change in contemporary capitalism, European liberalization policies, institution building across borders, economic patriotism, governance of global structures, theories and methods; runs the Int. Max Planck Research School on the Social and Political Constitution of the Economy (IMPRS-SPCE), a doctoral programme, with Univ. of Cologne; Man. Dir Prof. Dr JENS BECKERT; Man. Dir Prof. Dr WOLFGANG STREECK; publs *MPIfG Discussion Papers*, *MPIfG Journal Articles*, *MPIfG Working Papers*.

Max-Planck-Institut für Gravitationsphysik (Albert-Einstein-Institut) (Max Planck Institute for Gravitational Physics): Am Mühlenberg 1, 14476 Golm; tel. (331) 56770; e-mail office@aei.mpg.de; internet www.aei.mpg.de; f. 1995; experimental br. in Hanover; library of 7,800 monographs, 140 scientific journals; Man. Dir Prof. Dr GERHARD HUISKEN; Vice-Man. Dir Prof. KARSTEN DANZMANN.

Max-Planck-Institut für Herz- und Lungenforschung (W. G. Kerckhoff-Institut) (Max Planck Institute for Heart and Lung Research): Ludwigstr. 43, 61231 Bad Nauheim; tel. (6032) 7050; e-mail info@mpi-bn.mpg.de; internet www.mpi-hlr.de; f. 1931, present status 1972; Man. Dir Prof. Dr THOMAS BRAUN.

Max-Planck-Institut für Hirnforschung (Max Planck Institute for Brain Research): POB 71 06 62, 60496 Frankfurt; Deutschordenstr. 46, 60528 Frankfurt am Main; tel. (69) 967690; e-mail maja.fricke@vw.mpih-frankfurt.mpg.de; internet www.mpih-frankfurt

.mpg.de; f. 1914 as Kaiser Wilhelm Institute for Brain Research, present name and status 1948; Man. Dir Prof. Dr GILLES LAURENT.

Max-Planck-Institut für Immaterialgüter- und Wettbewerbsrecht (Max Planck Institute for Intellectual Property and Competition Law): Marstallpl. 1, 80539 Munich; tel. (89) 242460; e-mail institut@ip.mpg.de; internet www.ip.mpg.de; f. 1966; Dir Prof. Dr JOSEF DREXL; Dir Prof. Dr RETO M. HILTY.

Max-Planck-Institut für Immunbiologie und Epigenetik (Max Planck Institute for Immunobiology and Epigenetics): Stübeweg 51, 79108 Freiburg; tel. (761) 51080; e-mail presse@immunbio.mpg.de; internet www3.immunbio.mpg.de; f. 1961; Man. Dir Prof. Dr RUDOLF GROSSCHEDL.

Max-Planck-Institut für Infektionsbiologie (Max Planck Institute for Infection Biology): Charitéplatz 1, Campus Charite Mitte, 10117 Berlin; tel. (30) 284600; e-mail sek@mpiib-berlin.mpg.de; internet www.mpiib-berlin.mpg.de; f. 1993; Man. Dir Prof. Dr ARTURO ZYCHLINSKY.

Max-Planck-Institut für Informatik (Max Planck Institute for Informatics): Campus E1 4, 66123 Saarbrücken; tel. (681) 93250; e-mail info@mpi-sb.mpg.de; internet www.mpi-inf.mpg.de; f. 1988; Man. Dir Prof. Dr BERNT SCHIELE.

Max-Planck-Institut für Intelligente Systeme (Max Planck Institute for Metals Research): Heisenbergstr. 3, 70569 Stuttgart; tel. (711) 6890; e-mail info@is.mpg.de; internet www.is.mpg.de; f. 1920; Autonomous Motion Empirical Inference, Low-Dimensional and Metastable Materials, Modern Magnetic Systems, New Materials and Biosystems, Perceiving Systems, Phase Transformations and Theory of Inhomogeneous Condensed Matterinterfaces; Man. Dir Prof. Dr BERNHARD SCHÖLKOPF; publ. *Focus on Intelligent Systems*.

Max-Planck-Institut für Kernphysik (Max Planck Institute for Nuclear Physics): POB 103980, 69029 Heidelberg; Saupfercheckweg 1, 69117 Heidelberg; tel. (6221) 5160; e-mail info@mpi-hd.mpg.de; internet www.mpi-hd.mpg.de; f. 1958; Man. Dir Prof. Dr KLAUS BLAUM.

Max-Planck-Institut für Kognitions- und Neurowissenschaften (Max Planck Institute for Human Cognitive and Brain Sciences): POB 500355, 04303 Leipzig; Stephanstr. 1A, 04103 Leipzig; tel. (341) 994000; e-mail info@cbs.mpg.de; internet www.cbs.mpg.de; f. 2004 by merger of Leipzig Max Planck Institute of Cognitive NeuroScience and Munich Max Planck Institute for Psychological Research; Man. Dir Prof. ARNO VILLRINGER; publ. *MPI Series in Human Cognitive and Brain Sciences*.

Max-Planck-Institut für Kohlenforschung (Max Planck Institute for Coal Research): Kaiser-Wilhelm-Pl. 1, 45470 Mülheim an der Ruhr; tel. (208) 3061; e-mail contact@mpi-muelheim.mpg.de; internet www.kofo.mpg.de; f. 1912 as Kaiser Wilhelm Institut für Kohlenforschung, present name 1949; library of 17,000 vols; research in the catalytic transformation of compounds and materials with the highest degree of chemo-, regio- and stereoselectivity under mild conditions and with an economical use of energy and resources in the following five areas: synthetic organic chemistry, homogeneous catalysis, heterogeneous catalysis, organometallic chemistry and theory; Man. Dir Prof. Dr ALOIS FÜRSTNER.

Max-Planck-Institut für Kolloid- und Grenzflächenforschung (Max Planck Institute for and Interface Research): Am Mühlenberg 1, OT Golm, 14476 Potsdam; tel. (331) 5677814; e-mail andreas.stockhaus@mpikg.mpg.de; internet www.mpikg.mpg.de; f. 1992; research concerned with structures at nano- and micrometer level; Man. Dir Prof. Dr MARKUS ANTONIETTI; Admin. Man. ANDREAS STOCKHAUS.

Max-Planck-Institut für Marine Mikrobiologie (Max Planck Institute for Marine Microbiology): Celsiusstr. 1, 28359 Bremen; tel. (421) 202850; e-mail contact@mpi-bremen.de; internet www.mpi-bremen.de; f. 1992; Dir Prof. Dr RUDOLF AMANN; Sec. ULRIKE TIETJEN.

Max-Planck-Institut für Mathematik (Max Planck Institute for Mathematics): POB 7280, 53072 Bonn; Vivatsgasse 7, 53111 Bonn; tel. (228) 4020; e-mail admin@mpim-bonn.mpg.de; internet www.mpim-bonn.mpg.de; f. 1981; Man. Dir Prof. Dr GERD FALTINGS; Sec. ANDREA KOHLHUBER.

Max-Planck-Institut für Mathematik in den Naturwissenschaften (Max Planck Institute for Mathematics in the Natural Sciences): Inselstr. 22, 04103 Leipzig; tel. (341) 995950; e-mail avanden@mis.mpg.de; internet www.mis.mpg.de; f. 1996; Dir Prof. Dr FELIX OTTO; Dir Prof. Dr JÜRGEN JOST (acting); Dir Prof. Dr WOLFGANG HACKBUSCH.

Max-Planck-Institut für Medizinische Forschung (Max Planck Institute for Medical Research): POB 10 38 20, 69028 Heidelberg; Jahnstr. 29, 69120 Heidelberg; tel. (6221) 4860; e-mail sekr@mpimf-heidelberg.mpg.de; internet www.mpimf-heidelberg.mpg.de; f. 1930 as Kaiser Wilhelm Institute for Medical Research, present name and status 1948; Chair. Dr WINFRIED DENK.

Max-Planck-Institut für Meteorologie (Max Planck Institute for Meteorology): Bundesstr. 53, 20146 Hamburg; tel. (40) 411730; internet www.mpimet.mpg.de; f. 1975; Man. Dir Prof. Dr BJORN STEVENS.

Max-Planck-Institut für Mikrostrukturphysik (Max Planck Institute for Microstructure Physics): Weinberg 2, 06120 Halle; tel. (345) 558250; e-mail hoehl@mpi-halle.de; internet www.mpi-halle.mpg.de; f. 1992; Man. Dir Prof. Dr JÜRGEN KIRSCHNER.

Max-Planck-Institut für Molekulare Biomedizin (Max Planck Institute for Molecular Biomedicine): Röntgenstr. 20, 48149 Münster; tel. (251) 703650; e-mail presse@mpi-muenster.mpg.de; internet www.mpi-muenster.mpg.de; f. 2001; Man. Dir Prof. Dr RALF HEINRICH ADAMS.

Max-Planck-Institut für Molekulare Genetik (Max Planck Institute for Molecular Genetics): Ihnestr. 63–73, 14195 Berlin; tel. (30) 84130; e-mail info@molgen.mpg.de; internet www.molgen.mpg.de; f. 1964; analysis of human genes, their function and evolution; bioinformatics, devt and implementation of new methods for functional genome analysis; library of 50,000 vols; Man. Dir Prof. Dr MARTIN VINGRON.

Max-Planck-Institut für Molekulare Pflanzenphysiologie (Max Planck Institute for Molecular Plant Physiology): Am Mühlenberg 1, 14476 Potsdam-Golm; tel. (331) 56780; e-mail contact@mpimp-golm.mpg.de; internet www.mpimp-golm.mpg.de; f. 1994; Man. Dir Prof. Dr LOTHAR WILLMITZER.

Max-Planck-Institut für Molekulare Physiologie (Max Planck Institute for Molecular Physiology): POB 50 02 47, 44202 Dortmund; Otto-Hahn-Str. 11, 44227 Dortmund; tel. (231) 1330; e-mail roger.goody@mpi-dortmund.mpg.de; internet www.mpi-dortmund.mpg.de; f. present status 1948, present name 1993; Man. Dir Prof. Dr ROGER S. GOODY; Gen. Man. Dr PETER HERTER.

Max-Planck-Institut für Molekulare Zellbiologie und Genetik (Max Planck Institute of Molecular Cell Biology and Genetics): Pfotenhauerstr. 108, 01307 Dresden; tel. (351) 2100; e-mail info@mpi-cbg.de; internet www.mpi-cbg.de; f. 1998; Man. Dir Prof. ANTHONY HYMAN.

Max-Planck-Institut für Neurobiologie (Max Planck Institute for Neurobiology): Am Klopferspitz 18, 82152 Martinsried; tel. (89) 85781; e-mail merker@neuro.mpg.de; internet www.neuro.mpg.de; f. 1917, present name 1998; research on the devt, functions and diseases of the nervous system; molecular developmental biology, cellular and systems studies of neural plasticity, pathology and immunology of the central and peripheral nervous system, information processing in the invertebrate visual system; incl. four depts and several independent research groups; Man. Dir Prof. Dr HARTMUT WEKERLE; Public Relations Officer Dr STEFANIE MERKER.

Max-Planck-Institut für Neurologische Forschung (Max Planck Institute for Neurological Research): POB 41 06 29, 50866 Cologne; Gleueler Str. 50, 50931 Cologne; tel. (221) 47260; e-mail info@nf.mpg.de; internet www.nf.mpg.de; f. 1982; library of 5,200 monographs, 4,800 journals; Dir Prof. Dr U. BENJAMIN KAUPP; Deputy Dir Prof. Dr RUDOLF GRAF.

Max-Planck-Institut für Ökonomik (Max Planck Institute for Economics): Kahlaische Str. 10, 07745 Jena; tel. (3641) 6865; e-mail mader@econ.mpg.de; internet www.econ.mpg.de; f. 1993; library of 25,000 vols, 190 current journals; Exec. Dir Prof. Dr WERNER GÜTH.

Max-Planck-Institut für Ornithologie (Max Planck Institute for Ornithology): Schlossallee 2, 78315 Radolfzell; tel. (7732) 1501740; e-mail apitz@orn.mpg.de; internet www.orn.mpg.de; f. 1998; library of 11,000 journals, 6,000 monographs; Man. Dir Prof. Dr MARTIN WIKELSKI.

Max-Planck-Institut für Pflanzenzüchtungsforschung (Max Planck Institute for Plant Breeding Research): Carl-von-Linné-Weg 10, 50829 Cologne; tel. (221) 50620; e-mail prag@mpipz.mpg.de; internet www.mpiz-koeln.mpg.de; f. 1928; Man. Dir Prof. Dr PAUL SCHULZE-LEFERT.

Max-Planck-Institut für Physik (Werner-Heisenberg-Institut) (Max Planck Institute for Physics): Föhringer Ring 6, 80805 Munich; tel. (89) 323540; e-mail hollik@mpp.mpg.de; internet www.mpp.mpg.de; f. 1917 as Kaiser-Wilhelm-Institut für Physik, present name and status 1948; Man. Dir Prof. Dr WOLFGANG HOLLIK.

Max-Planck-Institut für Physik Komplexer Systeme (Max Planck Institute for Physics of Complex Systems): Nöthnitzer Str. 38, 01187 Dresden; tel. (351) 8710; e-mail info@mpipks-dresden.mpg.de; internet www.mpipks-dresden.mpg.de; f. 1992; Dir Prof. Dr RODERICH MOESSNER.

Max-Planck-Institut für Plasmaphysik (Max Planck Institute for Plasma Physics): Boltzmannstr. 2, 85748 Garching; tel. (89) 329901; e-mail info@ipp.mpg

.de; internet www.ipp.mpg.de; f. 1960; Scientific Dir Prof. Dr SIBYLLE GÜNTER.

Max-Planck-Institut für Polymerforschung (Max Planck Institute for Polymer Research): POB 3148, 55021 Mainz; Ackermannweg 10, 55128 Mainz; tel. (6131) 3790; e-mail info@mpip-mainz.mpg.de; internet www.mpip-mainz.mpg.de; f. 1983; Man. Dir Prof. Dr KLAUS MÜLLEN.

Max-Planck-Institut für Psychiatrie (Deutsche Forschungsanstalt für Psychiatrie) (Max Planck Institute for Psychiatry): Kraepelinstr. 2–10, 80804 Munich; tel. (89) 306221; e-mail holsboer@mpipsykl.mpg.de; internet www.mpipsykl.mpg.de; f. 1917; basic and clinical research, clinical services in psychiatry and neurology; main topics incl. depression, anxiety disorders, multiple sclerosis; Man. Dir Prof. Dr FLORIAN HOLSBOER.

Max-Planck-Institut für Psycholinguistik (Max Planck Institute for Psycholinguistics): see Netherlands chapter.

Max-Planck-Institut für Quantenoptik (Max Planck Institute of Quantum Optics): Hans-Kopfermann-Str. 1, 85748 Garching; tel. (89) 32 9050; e-mail gerhard.rempe@mpq.mpg.de; internet www.mpq.mpg.de; f. 1981; Man. Dir Prof. Dr GERHARD REMPE.

Max-Planck-Institut für Radioastronomie (Max Planck Institute for Radio Astronomy): POB 20 24, 53010 Bonn; Auf dem Hügel 69, 53121 Bonn; tel. (228) 5250; e-mail postmaster@mpifr-bonn.mpg.de; internet www.mpifr-bonn.mpg.de; f. 1966; Man. Dir Dr KARL M. MENTEN.

Max-Planck-Institut für Sonnensystemforschung (Max Planck Institute for Solar System Research): Max-Planck-Str. 2, 37191 Katlenburg-Lindau; tel. (5556) 9790; e-mail presseinfo@mps.mpg.de; internet www.mps.mpg.de; f. 1957 AS Max Planck Institute for Aeronomy, present name 2004; Man. Dir Prof. Dr ULRICH R. CHRISTENSEN.

Max-Planck-Institut für Terrestrische Mikrobiologie (Max Planck Institute for Terrestrial Microbiology): Karl-von-Frisch-Str. 10, 35043 Marburg; tel. (6421) 1780; e-mail office@mpi-marburg.mpg.de; internet www.mpi-marburg.mpg.de; f. 1991; Man. Dir Prof. Dr REGINE KAHMANN.

Max-Planck-Institut für Wissenschaftsgeschichte (Max Planck Institute for History of Science): Boltzmannstr. 22, 14195 Berlin; tel. (30) 226670; e-mail public@mpiwg-berlin.mpg.de; internet www.mpiwg-berlin.mpg.de; f. 1994; library of 65,000 vols; Exec. Dir Prof. Dr LORRAINE DASTON; Dir Prof. Dr JÜRGEN RENN; Dir Prof. Dr HANS-JÖRG RHEINBERGER.

Max Planck-Institut zur Erforschung Multireligiöser und Multiethnischer Gesellschaften (Max Planck Institute for the Study of Religious and Ethnic Diversity): POB 28 33, 37018 Göttingen; Hermann-Föge-Weg 11, 37073 Göttingen; tel. (551) 49560; e-mail info@mmg.mpg.de; internet www.mmg.mpg.de; f. 2007, fmrly Max-Planck-Institut für Geschichte; multidisciplinary study of diversity in historical and contemporary societies particularly concerning ethnic and religious forms and dynamics; library of 121,000 vols; Man. Dir Prof. Dr STEVE VERTOVEC; Head Librarian Dr KRISTIN FUTTERLIEB.

Max-Planck-Institut zur Erforschung von Gemeinschaftsgütern (Max Planck Institute for Research on Collective Goods): Kurt-Schumacher-Str. 10, 53113 Bonn; tel. (228) 914160; e-mail info@coll.mpg.de; internet www.coll.mpg.de; f. 2003; library of 40,000 vols; Dir Prof. Dr CHRISTOPH ENGEL; Dir Prof. Dr MARTIN HELLWIG; Head Librarian REGINA GOLDSCHMITT.

AGRICULTURE, FISHERIES AND VETERINARY SCIENCE

Deutsche Gesellschaft für Holzforschung eV (German Society for Wood Research): Bayerstr. 57–59, 5 Stock, 80335 Munich; tel. (89) 5161700; e-mail mail@dgfh.de; internet www.dgfh.de; f. 1942; Pres. Dipl. Ing. X. HAAS; Man. Dipl.-Ing. AXEL YEUTSCH; publ. *DGfH aktuell* (3 a year).

Gesellschaft für Hopfenforschung eV (Society of Hops Research): Hüll 5 1/3, 85283 Wolnzach; tel. (8442) 3597; e-mail gfh@hopfenforschung.de; internet www.hopfenforschung.de; f. 1926; Chair. Dr MICHAEL MÖLLER; Vice-Chair. Dr BERND SCHMIDT.

Johänn Heinrich von Thünen Institute/ Federal Research Institute for Rural Areas, Forestry and Fisheries: Bundesalle 50, 38116 Braunscweig; tel. (531) 5961003; e-mail info@vti.bund.de; internet www.vti.bund.de; f. 2008, by merger of Federal Research Centre for Fisheries (f. 1948), the Fed. Research Centre for Forestry and Forestry Products and divs of the Federal Agricultural Research Centre; library of 68,500 vols; Pres. Prof. Dr FOLKHARD ISERMEYER; publs *Information on Fishery Research* (1 a year), *Landbauforschung* (4 a year), *Silvae Genetica* (1 a year), *Wissenschaft erleben* (2 a year).

Attached Research Institutes:

Institut für Fischereiökologie (Institute of Fisheries Ecology): Palmaille 9, 22767 Hamburg; tel. (40) 38905290; e-mail foe@vti.bund.de; f. 1885, present name 1993; investigates German marine ecological system and the German fresh waters; Dir Dr REINHOLD HANEL; Deputy Dir Dr THOMAS LANG; Sec. ANNE EBERT.

Institut für Ostseefischerei (Institute for Baltic Sea Fisheries): Alter Hafen Süd 2, 18069 Rostock; tel. (381) 8116102; e-mail osf@vti.bund.de; f. 1991; in charge of fed. tasks of sea research in the Baltic Sea for the Min. of Nutrition, Agriculture and Consumer Protection; conducts research to establish scientific basis for advising in political decision in fisheries; Dir Prof. Dr Hab. CORNELIUS HAMMER; Deputy Dir Dr CHRISTOPHER ZIMMERMAN; Sec. WALTRAUD KLEINFELDT.

Institut für Seefischerei (Institute of Sea Fisheries): Palmaille 9, 22767 Hamburg; tel. (40) 38905178; e-mail sf@vti.bund.de; research on ecological and economic principles underlying sustainable exploitation of natural marine resources; Dir Dr GERD KRAUS; Deputy Dir Dr CHRISTOPH STRANSKY; Sec. KONSTANZE VON SCHUDNAT.

ARCHITECTURE AND TOWN PLANNING

Akademie für Raumforschung und Landesplanung (Academy for Spatial Research and Planning): Hohenzollernstr. 11, 30161 Hanover; tel. (511) 348420; e-mail arl@arl-net.de; internet www.arl-net.de; f. 1946; library of 20,000 vols; Pres. Dr Ing. BERNHARD HEINRICHS; Gen. Sec. Prof. Dr Ing. DIETMAR SCHOLICH; publ. *Raumforschung und Raumordnung* (Spatial Research and Planning, 6 a year, in German with summaries in English).

Deutsche Akademie für Städtebau und Landesplanung (German Academy for Urban and Regional Spatial Planning): Stresemannstr. 90, 10963 Berlin; tel. (30) 23082231; e-mail info@dasl.de; internet www.dasl.de; f. 1922 as Free Acad. of Town Planning; spatial and regional planning, town planning, landscape and open-space planning, transport policy, urban economic devt, protection of built heritage and social policy; library of 5,000 vols; Pres. Prof. Dr Ing. CHRISTIANE THALGOTT; Vice-Pres. Prof. Dr MICHAEL KRAUTZBERGER; Sec. Prof. Ing. JULIAN WÉKEL; publs *Almanach* (1 a year), *Vorbereitende Bericht* (1 or 2 a year).

IKT-Institut für Unterirdische Infrastruktur GmbH (IKT-Institute for Underground Infrastructure): Exterbruch 1, 45886 Gelsenkirchen; tel. (209) 178060; e-mail info@ikt.de; internet www.ikt.de; research related to construction of underground pipes and networks for gas, water and wastewater; Man. Dir Dr Ing. ROLAND W. WANIEK; Research Dir Dr Ing. BERT BOSSELER; publ. *IKT-LinerReports*.

ILS—Institut für Landes- und Stadtentwicklungsforschung GmbH (ILS—Research Institute for Regional and Urban Development): Brüderweg 22–24, 44135 Dortmund; tel. (231) 90510; e-mail poststelle@ils-research.de; internet www.ils-forschung.de; spatial sciences; analyses causes and consequences of new urbanization processes and urban future; library of 44,000 vols, 150 current journals; Dir Prof. Dr RAINER DANIELZYK; publs *ILS-Journal* (3 a year), *ILS-Trends* (3 a year).

Institut für Wohnungswesen, Immobilienwirtschaft, Stadt- und Regionalentwicklung GmbH (InWIS) (Institute of Housing, Real Estate, Urban and Regional Development Ltd): Springorumallee 20, 44795 Bochum; tel. (234) 890340; e-mail info@inwis.de; internet www.inwis.de; attached to Ruhr Univ.; interdisciplinary basic and applied research of housing, real estate, urban and regional science topics; library of 13,000 vols, 85 periodicals; Chair. KLAUS LEUCHTMANN; Dir MICHAEL NEITZEL.

BIBLIOGRAPHY, LIBRARY SCIENCE AND MUSEOLOGY

Internationale Gutenberg-Gesellschaft (International Gutenberg Society): Liebfrauenpl. 5, 55116 Mainz; tel. (6131) 226420; e-mail info@gutenberg-gesellschaft.de; internet www.gutenberg-gesellschaft.de; f. 1901; promotes research into the history of printing and of the book; Pres. THE MAYOR OF THE CITY OF MAINZ; Sec.-Gen. CHRISTINA SCHMITZ.

ECONOMICS, LAW AND POLITICS

Arbeitsgemeinschaft Deutscher Wirtschaftswissenschaftlicher Forschungsinstitut eV (Association of German Economic Science Research Institutes): c/o DIW Berlin, 10108 Berlin; Mohrenstr. 58, 10117 Berlin; tel. (30) 89789211; e-mail arge@diw.de; f. 1949; 29 mem. colleges and institutes; coordinates programmes of the institutes and provides a permanent base for research exchange and cooperation; Chair. Prof. Dr KLAUS F. ZIMMERMANN; Sec.-Gen. RALF MESSER; publ. *Gemeinschaftsdiagnose* (2 a year).

Member Institutes:

Abteilung Wirtschaftswissenschaft im Osteuropa Institut an der Freien Universität Berlin (Economics Department of the East European Institute at the Free University, Berlin): Garystr. 55, 14195 Berlin; tel. (30) 83854008; e-mail schrettl@wiwiss.fu-berlin.de; internet www.oei.fu-berlin.de/wirtschaft; f. 1950; economic research on East European countries; library of 85,000 vols and 95 periodicals; Dir Prof. Dr WOLFRAM SCHRETTL;

publs *Berichte des Osteuropa Instituts/ Reihe Wirtschaft und Recht, Wirtschaftswissenschaftliche Veröffentlichungen*.

BAW Institut für Wirtschaftsforschung GmbH (BAW Economic Research Institute Ltd): Wilhelm-Herbst-Str. 5, 28359 Bremen; tel. (421) 206990; e-mail n.lutzky@baw-bremen.de; f. 1947; library of 20,000 vols; Dir Dr NIKOLAI LUTZKY; publs *BAW-Monatsbericht* (12 a year), *Regionalwirtschaftliche Studien* (irregular).

CESifo Group: Poschingerstr. 5, 81679 Munich; tel. (89) 92241410; e-mail office@cesifo.de; internet www.cesifo-group.de; f. 1999; consists of Centre for Economic Studies (CES), Ifo Institute for Economic Research and CESifo GmbH (Munich Society for the Promotion of Economic Research); empirical economic research; library of 90,000 vols; Pres. Dr HANS-WERNER SINN; publs *CESifo DICE* (4 a year, in English), *CESifo Economic Studies* (in English), *CESifo Forum* (4 a year, in English), *ifo Dresden berichtet* (6 a year), *ifo Schnelldienst* (36 a year), *ifo Wirtschaftskonjunktur* (12 a year).

Deutsches Institut für Wirtschaftsforschung (German Institute for Economic Research): 10108 Berlin; Mohrenstr. 58, 10117 Berlin; tel. (30) 897890; e-mail presse@diw.de; internet www.diw.de; f. 1925; application-oriented economic research and policy advice; Pres. Prof. Dr GERT G. WAGNER; Man. Dir Dr CORNELIUS RICHTER; Vice-Pres. Prof. Dr GEORG WEIZSÄCKER; publs *Economic Bulletin* (12 a year), *Vierteljahrshefte zur Wirtschaftsforschung* (4 a year), *Wochenbericht* (52 a year).

Energiewirtschaftliches Institut an der Universität zu Köln: Alte Wagenfabrik, Vogelsanger Str. 321, 50827 Cologne; tel. (221) 27729100; internet www.ewi.uni-koeln.de; f. 1943; energy economics, environmental economics; library of 12,000 vols, 90 periodicals; Dir Prof. Dr MARC O. BETTZÜGE; publ. *Zeitschrift für Energiewirtschaft* (4 a year).

Forschunginstitut für Wirtschaftspolitik an der Universität Mainz: see under Johannes Gutenberg-Universität.

Forschungsstelle für Allgemeine und Textile Marktwirtschaft an der Universität Münster (Research Institute for General and Textile Economics): Fliednerstr. 21, 48149 Münster; tel. (251) 22939; e-mail 22fatm@wiwi.uni-muenster.de; internet www.wiwi.uni-muenster.de; f. 1941; library of 15,000 vols; Dir Prof. Dr DIETER AHLERT.

Friedrich-Ebert-Stiftung eV: Godesberger Allee 149, 53175 Bonn; tel. (228) 8830; e-mail presse@fes.de; internet www.fes.de; f. 1925; int. cooperation, social democracy, political education, research and consulting; library of 855,000 vols; Chair. Dr PETER STRUCK; Man. Dir Dr ROLAND SCHMIDT.

GfK Verein (GfK Association): Nordwestring 101, 90319 Nuremberg; tel. (911) 3952231; e-mail info@gfk-verein.org; internet www.gfk-verein.de; f. 1934; promotion of market research; carries out research and maintains close cooperation with scientific instns, particularly Friedrich-Alexander Univ. at Erlangen-Nuremberg; supports the education of market researchers, the ongoing training of leadership personnel and participation in commercial ventures; Pres. PETER ZÜHLSDORFF; Vice-Pres. Prof. HUBERT WEILER; Vice-Pres. RALF KLEIN-BÖLTING; Vice-Pres. Prof. Dr NICOLE KOSCHATE; Vice-Pres. Dr RAIMUND WILDNER; publ. *Yearbook of Marketing and Consumer Research*.

Hamburgisches WeltWirtschaftsInstitut gemeinnützige GmbH (HWWI) (Hamburg Institute of International Economics (HWWI)): Heimhuder Str. 71, 20148 Hamburg; tel. (40) 3405760; e-mail info@hwwi.org; internet www.hwwi.org; f. 2005; ind., non-profit research institute; interdisciplinary analysis of key economic and socio-economic trends; provides economically relevant results for business, soc. and policy-making; Dir Prof. Dr THOMAS STRAUBHAAR; publs *Edition HWWI*, *HWWI Insights* (1 a year, in German), *HWWI Policy Papers and Reports*, *HWWI Research Papers*, *HWWI Update*.

Institut der Deutschen Wirtschaft Köln: POB 101863, 50458 Cologne; Konrad-Adenauer-Ufer 21, 50668 Cologne; tel. (221) 49811; e-mail welcome@iwkoeln.de; internet www.iwkoeln.de; f. 1951; education and labour market; economic and social policy; library of 200,000 vols; Pres. Dr HANS-DIETRICH WINKHAUS; Dir Prof. Dr MICHAEL HÜTHER; publ. *iw-trends* (4 a year).

Institut für Angewandte Wirtschaftsforschung eV (Institute for Applied Economic Research): Ob dem Himmelreich 1, 72074 Tübingen; tel. (7071) 98960; e-mail iaw@iaw.edu; internet www.iaw.edu; f. 1957; int. integration and regional devt, labour markets and social security, firm dynamics and structural change; library of 1,250 vols; Chair. Prof. Dr WILHELM RALL; Dir Prof. Dr CLAUDIA M. BUCH; publ. *IAW-News* (4 a year).

Institut für Arbeitsmarkt- und Berufsforschung der Bundesanstur für Arbeit (Institute for Employment Research): Regensburger Str. 104, 90478 Nürnberg; tel. (911) 1790; e-mail info@iab.de; internet www.iab.de; f. 1967; researches the labour market to advise policy-makers at all levels; library of 70,000 vols; Dir Prof. Dr JOACHIM MÖLLER; publ. *Zeitschrift für Arbeitsmarkt Forschung (ZAF)* (4 a year).

Institut für Handelsforschung GmbH: Dürener Str. 401B, 50858 Cologne; tel. (221) 9436070; e-mail info@ifhkoeln.de; internet www.ifhkoeln.de; Dir Dr KAI HUDETZ; Dir BORIS HEDDE.

Institut für Marktanalyse und Agrarhandelspolitik des Johann Heinrich von Thünen-Institut (vTI) (Institute for Market Analysis and Agricultural Trade Policy): Bundesallee 50, 38116 Brunswick; tel. (531) 5965301; e-mail ma@fal.de; internet www.ma.fal.de; f. 1948; Dir Dr MARTIN BANSE (acting); publ. *Agrarwirtschaft* (11 a year).

Institut für Mittelstandsforschung: Maximilianstr. 20, 53111 Bonn; tel. (228) 729970; e-mail post@ifm-bonn.org; internet www.ifm-bonn.org; f. 1957; Pres. Dr JOHANN EEKHOFF; Deputy Dir Dr OLIVER ARENTZ.

Institut für Ökologische Wirtschaftsforschung (IÖW) (Institute for Ecological Economy Research): Potsdamer Str. 105, 10785 Berlin; tel. (30) 8845940; e-mail mailbox@ioew.de; internet www.ioew.de; f. 1985; research for sustainable management; Scientific Dir THOMAS KORBUN; Financial Dir MARION WIEGAND; publ. *Ökologisches Wirtschaften* (Ecological Economy, 24 a year).

Institut für Ost- und Südosteuropaforschung (Institute for East and Southeast European Studies): Landshuter Str. 4, 93047 Regensburg; tel. (941) 9435410; e-mail info@ios-regensburg.de; internet www.ios-regensburg.de; f. 2012 by a merger of the Eastern European Institute (f. 1952) and the Institute for South East European Studies (f. 1930); research into economic and historical devts in E and SE Europe; focus in particular on comparative and transnational perspectives as well as interdisciplinary approaches; regional emphases on SE Europe and the region of the fmr Soviet Union; library of 320,000 vols; Man. Dir Prof. Dr ULF BRUNNBAUER; Dir Prof. Dr JÜRGEN JERGER; publs *Economic Systems* (4 a year), *Südosteuropa: Zeitschrift für Politik und Gesellschaft* (4 a year), *Südost-Forschungen*.

Institut für Seeverkehrswirtschaft und Logistik (Institute of Shipping Economics and Logistics): Universitätsallee 11–13, 28359 Bremen; tel. (421) 220960; e-mail info@isl.org; internet www.isl.org; f. 1954; applied research and devt projects in logistics systems, maritime economics and transport, information logistics/planning and simulation systems; library of 125,000 vols, 230 periodicals and newspapers; Exec. Dir Prof. Dr HANS-DIETRICH HAASIS; publs *ISL Book Series*, *ISL Lectures, Contributions and Presentations*, *Shipping Statistics and Market Review* (figures of shipping, shipbuilding, sea ports and seaborne trade, 10 a year and online (www.infoline.de)).

Institut für Weltwirtschaft an der Universität Kiel: see under Christian-Albrechts Universität.

Institut für Wirtschaftsforschung Halle (IWH) (Halle Institute for Economic Research): POB 11 03 61, 06017 Halle; Kleine Märkerstr. 8, 06108 Halle; tel. (345) 775360; f. 1992; research in macroeconomics, structural change, urban economics; library of 55,000 vols; Pres. Prof. Dr ULRICH BLUM; CEO FROWIN GENSCH; publ. *Wirtschaft im Wandel* (12 a year).

Institut für Wirtschaftspolitik an der Universität zu Köln (Institute for Economic Policy at University of Cologne): Pohligstr. 1, 50969 Cologne; tel. (221) 4705347; e-mail iwp@wiso.uni-koeln.de; internet www.iwp.uni-koeln.de; f. 1950; economic policy, foreign trade policy, EU research; library of 70,000 vols; Dir Prof. Dr JOHANN EEKHOFF; Dir Prof. Dr JÜRGEN B. DONGES; publs *Untersuchungen zur Wirtschaftspolitik*, *Zeitschrift für Wirtschaftspolitik* (3 a year).

Institut zur Zukunft der Arbeit (Institute for the Study of Labour): Schaumburg-Lippe-Str. 5–9, 53113 Bonn; tel. (228) 38940; e-mail iza@iza.org; internet www.iza.org; f. 1998; Pres. Dr KLAUS ZUMWINKEL; Dir Prof. Dr KLAUS F. ZIMMERMANN; Dir for Admin. MARTIN T. CLEMENS; Dir for Labour Policy Dr HILMAR SCHNEIDER; Dir for Research Dr MARCO CALIENDO.

Internationale Wissenschaftliche Vereinigung Weltwirtschaft und Weltpolitik eV (IWVWW): Waltersdorfer Str. 51, 12526 Berlin; tel. (30) 6763387; e-mail iwvww@t-online.de; f. 1989; Pres. Prof. Dr Hab. KARL HEINZ DOMDEY; Man. Dir Prof. Dr H. ENGELSTÄDTER.

Niedersächsische Institut für Wirtschaftsforschung (NIW): Königstr. 53, 30175 Hanover; tel. (511) 12331630; e-mail niw@niw.de; internet www.niw.de; f. 1981; Chair. Prof. Dr JAVIER REVILLA DIEZ; Dir Dr RAINER ERTEL.

Rheinisch-Westfälisches Institut für Wirtschaftsforschung eV (Rhine-Westphalia Institute for Economic Research): Hohenzollernstr. 1–3, 45128 Essen; tel. (201) 81490; e-mail rwi@rwi-essen.de;

internet www.rwi-essen.de; f. 1926; study of the structure and devt of the German (and int.) economy; spec. research facilities, advice on admin. and economics for firms and students; library of 110,000 vols; Pres. Prof. Dr CHRISTOPH M. SCHMIDT; Vice-Pres. Prof. Dr THOMAS K. BAUER; Dir Prof. Dr WIM KÖSTERS; publs *Konjunkturberichte* (Economic Report, 2 a year), *Materialien* (surveys and extensive articles, irregular), *Ruhr Economic Papers* (irregular), *Schriften* (articles on aspects of economic policy, irregular).

Statistisches Bundesamt (Federal Statistical Office): Gustav-Stresemann-Ring 11, 65189 Wiesbaden; tel. (611) 751; e-mail presse@destatis.de; internet www.destatis.de; f. 1950; library of 500,000 vols; Pres. RODERICH EGELER; publs *Datenreport* (2 a year), *Die Bundesländer: Strukturen und Entwicklungen* (2 a year), *Glossar statistischer Fachbegriffe* (irregular), *Kreiszahlen* (1 a year), *Statistik lokal—Daten für die Gemeinden, kreisfreien Städte und Kreise Deutschlands* (1 a year), *Statistik regional—Daten für die Kreise und kreisfreien Städte Deutschlands* (1 a year, database, published in English as *Regional Statistics*), *STATmagazin*, *Wirtschaft und Statistik* (12 a year), *Zahlenkompass—Statistisches Taschenbuch für Deutschland* (1 a year, published in English as *Key Data on Germany*).

Stiftung Marktwirtschaft (Market Economy Foundation): Charlottenstr. 60, 10117 Berlin; tel. (30) 2060570; e-mail info@stiftung-marktwirtschaft.de; internet www.stiftung-marktwirtschaft.com; f. 1982; Dir Prof. Dr BERND RAFFELHÜSCHEN; Dir Prof. Dr MICHAEL EILFORT; publ. *Blickpunkt Marktwirtschaft* (Focus Market Economy, 2 a year).

vTI Johann Heinrich von Thünen-Institut: Bundesallee 50, 38116 Braunschweig; tel. (531) 5961003; e-mail info@vti.bund.de; internet www.vti.bund.de; f. 2008; research areas incl. agriculture and food economy, forestry and wood economy, fisheries and aquaculture; Pres. Prof. Dr FOLKHARD ISERMEYER.

Walter Eucken Institut: Goethestr. 10, 79100 Freiburg im Breisgau; tel. (761) 790970; e-mail wei-freiburg@walter-eucken-institut.de; internet www.walter-eucken-institut.de; f. 1954; centre for regulatory and constitutional economic research; Dir Prof. Dr LARS P. FELD.

Wirtschafts- und Sozialwissenschaftliches Institut in der Hans-Böckler-Stiftung (Economic Research Institute of the Hans Böckler Foundation): Hans-Böckler-Str. 39, 40476 Düsseldorf; tel. (211) 77780; e-mail zentrale@boeckler.de; internet www.boeckler.de; Dir Prof. Dr HEIDE PFARR; publ. *Mitteilungen* (12 a year).

Arnold Bergstraesser Institut für Kulturwissenschaftliche Forschung (ABI): Windausstr. 16, 79110 Freiburg im Breisgau; tel. (761) 888780; e-mail abifr@abi.uni-freiburg.de; internet www.arnold-bergstraesser.de; f. 1960; sociopolitical research particularly on education, admin., political devt, governance, migration and ethnic conflicts in Africa, Asia, Middle East and Latin America; library of 80,000 vols; Dir Prof. Dr REINHART KOESSLER; publ. *International Quarterly for Asian Studies* (2 a year).

Frobenius-Institut an der Johann Wolfgang Goethe-Universität: Grüneburgpl. 1, 60323 Frankfurt am Main; tel. (69) 79833050; internet www.frobenius-institut.de; f. 1898; African, Indonesian and Melanesian cultures and history; library of 114,000 vols; Dir Prof. Dr KARL-HEINZ KOHL; Deputy Dir Prof. Dr MAMADOU DIAWARA; publs *Afrika Archiv*, *Paideuma* (1 a year), *Religionsethnologische Studien*, *Studien zur Kulturkunde*.

Gesellschaft für Deutschlandforschung eV (Society for Research on Germany): c/o Prof. Dr Tilman Mayer, Institut für Politische Wissenschaft und Soziologie, Lennéstr. 25, 53113 Bonn; tel. (228) 735870; e-mail info@gfd-berlin.de; internet www.gfd-berlin.de; f. 1978; contemporary research on Germany; seminars and confs; Pres. Prof. Dr TILMAN MAYER; Vice-Pres. Prof. Dr HANS-JÖRG BÜCKING.

Herder Institute for Historical Research on East Central Europe—Institute of the Leibniz Association: Gisonenweg 5–7, 35037 Marburg; tel. (6421) 1840; e-mail mail@herder-institut.de; internet www.herder-institut.de; f. 1950; historical research on countries and peoples of Eastern Central Europe; library: see under Libraries and Archives; Dir Prof. Dr PETER HASLINGER; publ. *Zeitschrift für Ostmitteleuropa-Forschung* (4 a year).

Institut Finanzen und Steuern eV (Finance and Taxation Institute): Gertraudenstr. 20, 10178 Berlin; tel. (30) 20616774; e-mail info@ifst.de; internet www.ifst.de; f. 1949; Dir Prof. Dr JOHANNA HEY.

Leibniz Institut für Globale und Regionale Studien (German Institute of Global and Area Studies (GIGA)): Neuer Jungfernstieg 21, 20354 Hamburg; tel. (40) 42825593; e-mail info@giga-hamburg.de; internet www.giga-hamburg.de; f. 1964; basic and applied research on political, economic and social devts in Africa, Asia, Latin America, and the Near and Middle East; policy advice to political instns, business community and media; networking within the area studies and comparative area studies community; 4 constituent orgs: Institute of African Affairs (IAA), Institute of Asian Studies (IAS), Institute of Latin American Studies (ILAS), Institute of Middle East Studies (IMES); library of 100,000 vols and 400 periodicals; Dir Prof. Dr ROBERT KAPPEL; publs *GIGA Focus*, *GIGA Journal Family*, *NORD-SÜD aktuell* (4 a year).

Stiftung Wissenschaft und Politik (SWP) (German Institute for International and Security Affairs): Ludwigkirchpl. 3–4, 10719 Berlin; tel. (30) 880070; e-mail swp@swp-berlin.org; internet www.swp-berlin.org; f. 1962; interdisciplinary research in int. affairs and security, computerized information system for fields of int. relations and area studies (660,000 references), publicly available database 'World Affairs On-line'; library of 94,000 vols, 360 periodicals; Pres. Prof. Dr Ing HANS-PETER KEITEL; Dir Prof. Dr VOLKER PERTHES; Dir for Studies Dr BARBARA LIPPERT; Deputy Dir Prof. Dr GÜNTHER MAIHOLD; publs *SWP Comments*, *SWP Research Papers*.

Wissenschaftszentrum Berlin für Sozialforschung (Social Science Research Centre): Reichpietschufer 50, 10785 Berlin; tel. (30) 254910; e-mail wzb@wzb.eu; internet www.wzb.eu; f. 1969; a non-profit org.; conducts int. and interdisciplinary, empirical social science research on 4 research areas: education, work and life chances, markets and politics, society and economic dynamics, civil society, conflicts and democracy; library of 150,000 vols, 450 periodicals (printed), 10,000 periodicals (online access), 80 databases; Pres. Prof. Dr JUTTA ALLMENDINGER; Man. Dir HEINRICH BAßLER; publs *WZB-Bericht* (1 a year), *WZBrief Arbeit*, *WZBrief Bildung*, *WZBrief Zivilengagement*, *WZB-Mitteilungen* (4 a year).

EDUCATION

Deutsches Institut für Internationale Pädagogische Forschung (German Institute for International Educational Research): Schloss-Str. 29, 60486 Frankfurt am Main; tel. (69) 247080; e-mail dipf@dipf.de; internet www.dipf.de; f. 1951; educational information and research; library of 920,000 vols; libraries in Berlin and Frankfurt; Chair. Prof. Dr E. JÜRGEN ZÖLLNER; Deputy Chair. Dr SUSANNE EICKEMEIER; Dir Prof. Dr MARCUS HASSELHORN; Deputy Dir Prof. Dr MARC RITTBERGER; publ. *DIPF informiert* (2 a year).

Gesellschaft für Pädagogik und Information eV: Allee der Kosmonauten 28, 12681 Berlin; tel. (30) 51069333; e-mail mikuszeit@gpi-online.de; internet www.gpi-online.de; f. 1964; promotes research and devt in the field of educational technology and information science; Chair. Prof. Dr GERHARD E. ORTNER; Chair. Dr JOACHIM THOMA; Dir Dr BERND MIKUSZEIT; publs *Pädagogik und Information*, *Schul Praxis—Wirtschaft und Weiterbildung*.

Gesellschaft zur Förderung Pädagogischer Forschung eV (Society for the Promotion of Educational Research): POB 900270, 60442 Frankfurt am Main; Schloss-Str. 29, 60486 Frankfurt am Main; tel. (69) 24708313; e-mail merz@dipf.de; internet www2.dipf.de/gfpf; f. 1950; dissemination of research results, org. of communication processes between educational research and school practice; Pres. BERND FROMMELT; Vice-Pres. Prof. Dr ECKHARD KLIEME; Man. Dr PETER DÖBRICH; publ. *Materialen zur Bildungsforschung* (book series, 2–3 a year).

FINE AND PERFORMING ARTS

Gesellschaft für Musikforschung: c/o Barbara Schumann, Heinrich-Schütz-Allee 35, 34131 Kassel-Wilhelmshöhe; tel. (561) 3105255; e-mail g.f.musikforschung@t-online.de; internet www.musikforschung.de; f. 1946; promotes musicological research in respect with other disciplines; history of music, ethnomusicology and systematic musicology; Pres. Prof. Dr WOLFGANG AUHAGEN; Vice-Pres. Prof. Dr DÖRTE SCHMIDT; publ. *Die Musikforschung* (4 a year).

Staatliches Institut für Musikforschung: Tiergartenstr. 1, 10785 Berlin; tel. (30) 254810; e-mail sim@sim.spk-berlin.de; internet www.sim-berlin.de; f. 1888 as Königliche akademische Hochschule, present name and status 1945; attached to Prussian Cultural Heritage Foundation; collects musicological material, instruments, records, phonograms and tape recordings; conducts research into the devt and history of musicology, incl. acoustics, musical instruments and the style and practice of executing music of the past; archival and documentary research; lectures, concerts and exhibitions; library of 67,000 vols; Dir Dr THOMAS ERTELT; publs *BMS online* (digital successor of the printed *Bibliographie des Musikschrifttums*), *Briefwechsel der Wiener Schule*, *Geschichte der Musiktheorie*, *Klang und Begriff: Perspektiven musikalischer Theorie und Praxis*, *Studien zur Geschichte der Musiktheorie*.

Zentralinstitut für Kunstgeschichte (History of Art): Katharina-von-Bora-Str. 10, 80333 Munich; tel. (89) 28927556; e-mail direktion@zikg.eu; internet www.zikg.eu; f. 1947; 800,000 photographs in image colln; library of 480,000 vols; Dir Prof. Dr WOLF TEGETHOFF; Deputy Dir Prof. Dr WOLFGANG AUGUSTYN; publs *Kunstchronik* (12 a year), *Reallexikon zur Deutschen Kunstgeschichte*, *RIHA Journal*.

HISTORY, GEOGRAPHY AND ARCHAEOLOGY

Deutsches Archäologisches Institut (German Archaeological Institute): Podbielskiallee 69–71, 14195 Berlin; tel. (1888) 77110; e-mail info@dainst.de; internet www.dainst.org; f. 1829; brs in Rome (Prof. Dr DIETER MERTENS), Athens (Prof. Dr WOLF-DIETRICH NIEMEIER), Cairo (Prof. Dr GÜNTER DREYER), Istanbul (Prof. Dr ADOLF HOFFMANN), Madrid (Prof. Dr DIRCE MARZOLI), Middle East (Prof. Dr RICARDO EICHMANN), Sana'a (Dr IRIS GERLACH), Damascus (Dr KARIN BARTL), Eurasia (Prof. Dr SVEND HANSEN) and Tehran; also Römisch-Germanische Kommission, Frankfurt am Main (Prof. Dr SIEGMAR FREIHERR VON SCHNURBEIN), Kommission für Alte Geschichte und Epigraphik, München (Prof. Dr CHRISTOF SCHULER) and Kommission für Allgemeine und Vergleichende Archäologie, Bonn (Dr BURKHARDT VOGT); Pres. Prof. Dr FRIEDERIKE FLESS; Sec.-Gen. Prof. Dr ORTWIN DALLY; publs *Archäologischer Anzeiger*, *Archäologische Berichte aus dem Yemen*, *Athenische Mitteilungen*, *Baghdader Mitteilungen*, *Berichte der Römisch-Germanischen-Kommission*, *Chiron*, *Damaszener Mitteilungen*, *Germania*, *Istanbuler Mitteilungen*, *Madrider Mitteilungen*, *Mitteilungen des DAI Kairo*, *Römische Mitteilungen*, *Teheraner Mitteilungen*, *Zeitschrift für Orient-Archäologie*, *Zeitschrift für Archäologie Außereuropäischer Kulturen*.

Institut für Zeitgeschichte München–Berlin (Institute of Contemporary History Munich and Berlin): Leonrodstr. 46B, 80636 Munich; tel. (89) 126880; e-mail ifz@ifz-muenchen.de; internet www.ifz-muenchen.de; f. 1949; German and European history research since 1918, particularly Weimar Republic, Nat. Socialism and post-1945 history; library of 228,000 vols; Dir Prof. Dr ANDREAS WIRSCHING; Deputy Dir Prof. Dr MAGNUS BRECHTKEN; publs *Biographische Quellen zur Zeitgeschichte*, *Quellen und Darstellungen zur Zeitgeschichte*, *Schriftenreihe der Vierteljahrshefte für Zeitgeschichte* (2 a year), *Studien zur Zeitgeschichte*, *Texte und Materialien zur Zeitgeschichte*, *Vierteljahrshefte für Zeitgeschichte* (4 a year), *Zeitgeschichte im Gespräch*.

Leibniz-Institut für Europäische Geschichte (Leibniz Institute of European History): Alte Universitätsstr. 19, 55116 Mainz; tel. (6131) 3939365; e-mail ieg3@ieg-mainz.de; internet www.ieg-mainz.de; f. 1950; conducts and promotes research on the historical foundations of Europe; cross-cultural projects on European communication and transfer processes; projects on concepts and perceptions of Europe since 1450; research fellowship programme (research, training and int. networking); library of 220,000 vols; Dir for History of Religion Prof. Dr IRENE DINGEL; Dir for Universal History Prof. Dr HEINZ DUCHHARDT; Research Coordinator Dr JOACHIM BERGER; publs *Archiv für Reformationsgeschichte–Literaturbericht* (1 a year), *EGO—Europäische Geschichte Online* (online), *IEG-MAPS* (online), *Veröffentlichungen des Instituts für Europäische Geschichte* (monographs and conf. documentation), *Veröffentlichungen des Instituts für Europäische Geschichte, Beihefte online* (conf. documentation, online).

Vereinigung zur Erforschung der Neueren Geschichte eV (Modern History Research Association): Argelanderstr. 59, 53115 Bonn; tel. (228) 216205; e-mail apw@uni-bonn.de; internet www.pax-westphalica.de; f. 1957; history from 17th century to present day; library of 8,000 vols; Dir Prof. Dr MAXIMILIAN LANZINNER; Vice-Dir Prof. Dr KONRAD REPGEN; Sec. Prof. Dr CHRISTOPH KAMPMANN; publ. *Acta Pacis Westphalicae* (Sources of the Westphalian Peace Conf.).

LANGUAGE AND LITERATURE

Arbeitsstelle für Osterreichische Literatur und Kultur Robert-Musil-Forschung: Universität des Saarlandes, Campus 53/3 *or*, OG/323, 66123 Saarbrücken; tel. (681) 3023334; e-mail fzoelk@mx.uni-saarland.de; internet www.uni-saarland.de/einrichtung/afoelk.html; f. 1970; archives; study programmes, publs, symposia, bibliography; library of 12,000 vols; Dir Prof. Dr RALF BOGNER.

Institut für Deutsche Sprache: POB 10 16 21, 68016 Mannheim; R5 6–13, 68161 Mannheim; tel. (621) 15810; e-mail trabold@ids-mannheim.de; internet www.ids-mannheim.de; f. 1964; scientific study of present-day and historical German; library of 80,000 vols, 500 journals; Dir Prof. Dr LUDWIG M. EICHINGER; publs *Amades-Arbeitspapiere und Materialien zur deutschen Sprache*, *Deutsch im Kontrast*, *Deutsche Sprache* (4 a year), *Phonai*, *Schriften*, *Sprachreport* (4 a year), *Studienbibliographien Sprachwissenschaft*, *Studien zur deutschen Sprache*.

MEDICINE

Bernhard-Nocht-Institut für Tropenmedizin (Bernhard-Nocht-Institute for Tropical Medicine): POB 30 41 20, 20324 Hamburg; Bernhard-Nocht-Str. 74, 20359 Hamburg; tel. (40) 428180; e-mail bni@bni-hamburg.de; internet www.bni-hamburg.de; f. 1900 as Institute for Maritime and Tropical Diseases; tropical medicine and parasitology; Nat. Reference Centre for Tropical Infections; library of 43,000 vols and 48,000 reprints, 160 journals; Chair. Prof. Dr ROLF HORSTMANN; Vice-Chair. Prof. Dr BERNHARD FLEISCHER; Admin. Man. UDO GAWENDA; publ. *Scientific Report* (1 a year).

C. & O. Vogt-Institut für Hirnforschung, Universität Düsseldorf (Brain Research): POB 101007, 40001 Düsseldorf; Universitätsstr. 1, 40225 Düsseldorf; tel. (211) 8112777; e-mail zilles@hirn.uni-duesseldorf.de; internet www.uniklinik-duesseldorf.de/hirnforschung; f. 1937; morphometry, neuroanatomy, immuneohistochemistry, psychopharmacology; neurochemistry; Dir Prof. Dr KARL ZILLES.

Deutsche Gesellschaft für Kardiologie, Herz- und Kreislaufforschung eV (German Cardiac Society): Achenbachstr. 43, 40237 Düsseldorf; tel. (211) 6006920; e-mail info@dgk.org; internet www.dgk.org; f. 1927; Dir KONSTANTINOS PAPOUTSIS; publs *Basic Research in Cardiology* (6 a year), *Clinical Research in Cardiology*, *Herzschrittmachertherapie und Elektrophysiologie*, *Intensiv- und Notfallmedizin*.

Deutsche Gesellschaft für Sexualforschung eV (German Association for Research on Sexuality): Universitätsklinikum Hamburg-Eppendorf, Zentrum für Psychosoziale Medizin, Institut und Poliklinik für Sexualforschung und Forensische Psychiatrie, Martinistr. 52, 20246 Hamburg; tel. (40) 428032225; e-mail briken@uke.uni-hamburg.de; internet www.dgfs.info; f. 1950; Chair. Prof. Dr PEER BRIKEN; Chair. Prof. Dr HERTHA RICHTER-APPELT; Dir ARNE DEKKER; publ. *Zeitschrift für Sexualforschung*.

Deutsche Krebsgesellschaft eV (German Cancer Society): Tiergarten Tower, Str. des 17, Juni 106–108, 10623 Berlin; tel. (30) 32293290; e-mail service@krebsgesellschaft.de; internet www.deutsche-krebsgesellschaft.de; f. 1900; promoting research, treatment and prevention of cancer; Pres. Prof. Dr WERNER HOHENBERGER; Man. Dir Dr DANIELA M. CHRISTMANN; Sec.-Gen. Dr JOHANNES BRUNS; publs *Der Onkologe*, *Forum* (German Cancer Society news, 6 a year), *Journal of Cancer Research and Clinical Oncology* (6 a year).

Geomedizinische Forschungsstelle der Heidelberger Akademie der Wissenschaften (Geomedical Research Office of the Heidelberg Academy of Sciences): Karlstr. 4, 69117 Heidelberg; tel. (6221) 543265; e-mail haw@urz.uni-heidelberg.de; f. 1952; epidemiology of atherosclerotic diseases in Europe and Asia; library of 3,000 vols; Dir Prof. Dr G. SCHETTLER; publs *Geomedical Monographs Series* (6 vols), *World Atlas of Epidemic Diseases* (3 vols 1952–1961), *World Maps of Climatology*, geomedical studies.

Georg-Speyer-Haus, Institut für Tumorbiologie und experimentelle Therapie (Georg-Speyer-Haus, Institute for Tumor Biology and Experimental Therapy): Paul-Ehrlich-Str. 42–44, 60596 Frankfurt am Main; tel. (69) 633950; e-mail kost@gsh.uni-frankfurt.de; internet www.georg-speyer-haus.de; f. 1906; library of 27,664 vols; Dir Prof. Dr FLORIAN GRETEN.

Helmholtz Zentrum München-Deutsches Forschungszentrum für Gesundheit und Umwelt (German Research Centre for Environmental Health): Ingolstädter Landstr. 1, 85764 Neuherberg; tel. (89) 31870; e-mail info@helmholtz-muenchen.de; internet www.helmholtz-muenchen.de; f. 1964; controls 31 institutes; library of 120,000 vols, 350 journals; Scientific and Technical Dir Prof. Dr G. WESS; Admin. Dir Dr N. BLUM.

Herz- und Diabeteszentrum NRW (Heart and Diabetes Center NRW): Georgstr. 11, 32545 Bad Oeynhausen; tel. (5731) 970; e-mail info@hdz-nrw.de; internet www.hdz-nrw.de; f. 1984; cardiology, thoracic and cardiovascular surgery, paediatric cardiology, diabetology, gastroenterology, nuclear medicine, anaesthesiology, radiology, molecular biophysics, radiopharmacy, laboratory and transfusion medicine; library of 3,000 vols and 180 periodicals; CEO WILHELM HECKER; Vice-CEO GÜNTHER WYPPLER; Medical Dir Prof. Dr DIETHELM TSCHÖPE.

Hygiene-Instituts des Ruhrgebiets—Institut für Umwelthygiene und Toxikologie (Institute of Environmental Hygiene and Toxicology): POB 10 12 55, 45812 Gelsenkirchen; Rotthauser str. 21, 45879 Gelsenkirchen; tel. (209) 92420; e-mail info@hyg.de; internet www.hyg.de; f. 1902; attached to Ruhr Univ. Bochum; Chair. Prof. Dr WERNER SCHLAKE; Dir Prof. Dr LOTHAR DUNEMANN.

Institut für Prävention und Arbeitsmedizin der Deutschen Gesetzlichen Unfallversicherung (IPA) (Institute for Prevention and Occupational Medicine of the German Social Accident Insurance): Bürkle-de-la-Camp-Pl. 1, 44789 Bochum; tel. (234) 3024501; e-mail ipa@ipa-dguv.de; internet www.ipa.ruhr-uni-bochum.de; attached to Ruhr Univ.; research areas incl. allergology/immunology, epidemiology, medicine molecular medicine; library of 53,000 vols, 15,000 monographs; Dir Prof. Dr T. BRÜNING.

Institut für Wasserchemie und Chemische Balneologie der Technischen Universität München (Institute for Hydrochemistry and Chemical Balneology at the Technical University of Munich): Marchioninistr. 17, 81377 Munich; tel. (89) 218078231;

e-mail cornelia.popp@ch.tum.de; internet www.ws.chemie.tu-muenchen.de; f. 1951; analytical methods and measurement techniques for biology, chemical engineering, chemistry, geology, physics; Dir Prof. Dr REINHARD NIESSNER.

Leibniz-Institut für Umweltmedizinische Forschung an der Heinrich-Heine-Universität Düsseldorf (Leibniz Research Institute for Environmental Medicine): POB 10 30 45, 40021 Düsseldorf; Auf'm Hennekamp 50, 40225 Düsseldorf; tel. (211) 33890; e-mail krutmann@uni-duesseldorf.de; internet www.iuf.uni-duesseldorf.de; f. 2001; molecular preventive medical research in the field of environmental health; evaluation of risks to human health that result from environmental factors, in order to develop preventive and therapeutic strategies; library of 15,000 vols; Dir Prof. Dr JEAN KRUTMANN.

Max von Pettenkofer-Institut für Hygiene und Medizinische Mikrobiologie (Max von Pettenkofer Institute of Hygiene and Medical Microbiology): Pettenkoferstr. 9A, 80336 Munich; tel. (89) 51605201; e-mail sekretariat@mvp.uni-muenchen.de; internet www.mvp.uni-muenchen.de; Chair. for Bacteriology Prof. Dr JÜRGEN HEESEMANN; Chair. for Virology Prof. Dr ULRICH KOSZINOWSKI.

Paul-Ehrlich-Institut, Bundesamt für Impfstoffe und biomedizinische Arzneimittel (Federal Institute for Serums and Biomedicines): Paul-Ehrlich-Str. 51–59, 63225 Langen; tel. (6103) 770; e-mail pei@pei.de; internet www.pei.de; f. 1896, as Institute for Serum Testing and Serum Research; German and European medicinal product legislation; approval of clinical trials; marketing authorization of biomedicines, vaccines for humans and animals, medicinal products containing antibodies, allergens for therapy and diagnostics, blood and blood products, tissue and medicinal products for gene therapy, somatic cell therapy and xenogenic cell therapy; research in the field of life sciences; divs: allergology, EU cooperation/microbiology, haematology and transfusion medicine, immunology, medicinal biotechnology, safety of medicinal products and medical devices, veterinary medicine, virology; library of 55,000 vols; Pres. Prof. Dr KLAUS CICHUTEK; Vice-Pres. STEFAN VIETHS; publ. *Arbeiten aus dem Paul-Ehrlich-Institut*.

Verein für Wasser-, Boden- und Lufthygiene eV (Society for Water, Soil and Air Purity): POB 10 12 55, 45812 Gelsenkirchen; Rotthauser Str. 19, 45879 Gelsenkirchen; tel. (209) 9242190; e-mail verein@wabolu.de; internet www.wabolu.de; f. 1902; researches and subsidizes int. studies into environmental water and air issues; Chair. Prof. Dr VOLKER HINGST; Vice-Chair. Dr ANDREAS SCHIRMER; Vice-Chair. Dr DIETMAR PETERSOHN; Dir Prof. Dr LOTHAR DUNEMANN.

NATURAL SCIENCES

General

Senckenberg Gesellschaft für Naturforschung (Senckenberg Research Institute and Natural History Museum): Senckenberganlage 25, 60325 Frankfurt; tel. (69) 75420; e-mail info@senckenberg.de; internet www.senckenberg.de; f. 1817; anatomy, botany, distribution, ecology, evolution in zoology, palaeoanthropology, palaeobotany, palaeozoology, marine biology and geology, systematics; Pres. DIETMAR SCHMID; Dir Prof. Dr VOLKER MOSBRUGGER; publs *Abhandlungen der Senckenbergischen Naturforschenden Gesellschaft*, *Archiv für Molluskenkunde*, *Arthropod Systematics & Phylogeny* (3 a year), *Beiträge zur Entomologie—Contributions to Entomology* (2 a year), *Courier Forschungsinstitut Senckenberg*, *Marine Biodiversity*, *Natur und Museum* (6 a year), *Palaeobiodiversity and Palaeoenvironments*, *Senckenbergiana biologica*, *Soil Organisms* (in English), *Vertebrate Zoology*.

Biological Sciences

Alfred-Wegener-Institut für Polar- und Meeresforschung (Alfred Wegener Institute for Polar and Marine Research): POB 120161, 27515 Bremerhaven; tel. (471) 48310; e-mail info@awi.de; internet www.awi.de; f. 1980; conducts research in the Arctic, Antarctic and oceans of high and mid-latitudes; coordinates polar research in Germany; provides major infrastructure to int. scientific community, such as the research icebreaker Polarstern and stations in the Arctic and Antarctica; Dir Prof. Dr KARIN LOCHTE; Admin. Dir Dr HEIKE WOLKE; Deputy Dir Prof. Dr RALF TIEDEMANN; publ. *Berichte zur Polar- und Meeresforschung* (Reports of Polar and Marine Research, irregular).

Constituent Research Units:

Biologische Anstalt Helgoland (Biological Institute Helgoland): POB 180, 27483 Helgoland; Kurpromenade 201, 27498 Helgoland; tel. (4725) 8190; e-mail karen.wiltshire@awi.de; internet www.awi.de; f. 1892; research in marine ecology, esp. in the North Sea; library of 63,000 vols; Dir Prof. Dr KAREN WILTSHIRE; publ. *Helgoländer Meeresuntersuchungen* (Helgoland Marine Research, 4 a year).

Forschungsstelle Potsdam des Alfred-Wegener-Instituts für Polar und Meeresforschung (Potsdam Research Unit of the Alfred Wegener Institute for Polar and Marine Research): POB 60 01 49, 14401 Potsdam; Telegrafenberg A 43, 14473 Potsdam; tel. (331) 2882100; e-mail gabriela.schlaffer@awi.de; internet www.awi.de; f. 1992; terrestrial geoscientific research in the periglacial regions; research into atmospheric processes; Head Prof. Dr HANS-WOLFGANG HUBBERTEN.

Wadden Sea Station Sylt: Hafenstr. 43, 25992 List/Sylt; tel. (4651) 9560; e-mail ragnhild.asmus@awi.de; internet www.awi.de; f. 1924; studies of coastal biological processes and ecosystems and monitoring of coastal changes and their long-term impact; Dir Prof. Dr KAREN WILTSHIRE; Head Dr HARALD ASMUS.

Biozentrum Klein Flottbek (Biocentre Klein Flottbek): Ohnhorststr. 18, 22609 Hamburg; tel. (40) 428160; e-mail sekretariat@botanik.uni-hamburg.de; internet www.biologie.uni-hamburg.de/bzf; f. 1821; research in plant physiology, cell biology, plant systematics, genetics and microbiology, applied plant molecular biology; botanical garden and herbarium comprising 800,000 specimens; library of 45,000 vols and 49,000 reprints; Man. Dir Prof. Dr WOLFGANG STREIT; Man. Dir Prof. Dr DIETER HANELT; publs *Institut für Allgemeine Botanik Hamburg*, *Mitteilungen*.

Deutsche Gesellschaft für Moor- und Torfkunde (German Peat Society): Stilleweg 2, 30655 Hanover; tel. (1523) 1898284; e-mail caspers@dgmtev.de; internet www.dgmtev.de; f. 1970; Pres. Dr G. CASPERS; publ. *TELMA* (1 a year).

Forschungszentrum Borstel Leibniz-Zentrum für Medizin und Biowissenschaften (Borstel Research Centre for Medicine and Biological Sciences): Parkallee 1–40, 23845 Borstel; tel. (4537) 1880; internet www.fz-borstel.de; f. 1947; research in fields of pneumology, infection biology, allergology and inflammation medicine; library of 50,000 vols; Dir Prof. Dr SILVIA BULFONE-PAUS; Dir Prof. Dr PETER ZABEL; Dir Prof. Dr ULRICH SCHAIBLE; Admin. Man. SUSANN SCHRADER.

Institut für Angewandte Botanik (Institute of Applied Botany at Hamburg University): Biozentrum Klein Flottbek und Botanischer Garten der Universität Hamburg, Ohnhorststr. 18, 22609 Hamburg; tel. (40) 428160; e-mail secretariat@botanik.uni-hamburg.de; internet www.biologie.uni-hamburg.de/bzf; f. 1885; research on plant products, agriculture and horticulture; library of 130,000 vols; Man. Dir Prof. Dr WOLFGANG STREIT; Deputy Man. Dir Prof. Dr DIETER HANELT.

Institut für Gerontologie: Evinger Pl. 13, 44339 Dortmund; tel. (231) 7284880; e-mail ffg@post.uni-dortmund.de; internet www.ffg.uni-dortmund.de; attached to Technische Univ.; Dir Prof. Dr GERHARD NAEGELE.

Institut für Vogelforschung 'Vogelwarte Helgoland' (Institute of Avian Research 'Vogelwarte Helgoland'): An der Vogelwarte 21, 26386 Wilhelmshaven; tel. (4421) 96890; e-mail ifv@ifv-vogelwarte.de; internet www.vogelwarte-helgoland.de; f. 1910; research in the fields of bird migration, bird population dynamics, climate change and applied aspects; Dir Prof. Dr FRANZ BAIRLEIN; publ. *Vogelwarte* (4 a year).

Naturforschende Gesellschaft Bamberg eV: Hertzstr. 31, 96050 Bamberg; e-mail nfg@bnv-bamberg.de; internet www.bnv-bamberg.de/home/ba6296; f. 1834; library of 18,000 vols; Dir Dr DIETER BÖSCHE; publ. *Berichte*.

Naturforschende Gesellschaft zu Freiburg im Breisgau: Albertstr. 23B, 79104 Freiburg im Breisgau; tel. (761) 2036484; e-mail naturforschende@geologie.uni-freiburg.de; internet www.naturforschende-gesellschaft.uni-freiburg.de; f. 1821; Chair. Prof. Dr WERNER KONOLD; Vice-Chair. THOMAS UHLENDAHL; Sec. Prof. Dr ALBERT REIF.

Mathematical Sciences

Mathematisches Forschungsinstitut Oberwolfach GmbH (Mathematical Research Institute): Schwarzwaldstr. 9–11, 77709 Oberwolfach-Walke; tel. (7834) 9790; e-mail admin@mfo.de; internet www.mfo.de; f. 1944; library of 75,000 vols; Dir Prof. Dr GERT-MARTIN GREUEL; Vice-Dir Prof. Dr HORST KNÖRRER; Librarian VERENA FRANKE; publs *Oberwolfach Preprints*, *Oberwolfach Reports* (4 a year), *Oberwolfach Seminars*.

Physical Sciences

Astronomisches Rechen-Institut (Astronomical Institute): Mönchhofstr. 12–14, 69120 Heidelberg; tel. (6221) 541845; e-mail direktor@ari.uni-heidelberg.de; internet www.ari.uni-heidelberg.de; f. 1700; attached to Zentrum für Astronomie der Universität Heidelberg; library of 30,000 vols, 102 journals; Dir Prof. Dr EVA GREBEL; Dir Prof. Dr JOACHIM WAMBSGANß; publs *Apparent Places of Fundamental Stars*, *Astronomische Grundlagen für den Kalender*, *Veröffentlichungen*.

Astrophysikalisches Institut und Universitäts-Sternwarte (Astrophysical Institute and University Observatory): Schillergässchen 2–3, 07745 Jena; tel. (3641) 947501; e-mail moni@astro.uni-jena.de; internet www.astro.uni-jena.de; f. 1813; Dir Prof. Dr RALPH NEUHÄUSER.

Bundesamt für Seeschiffahrt und Hydrographie (Federal Maritime and Hydrographic Agency): POB 30 12 20, 20305 Hamburg; Bernhard-Nocht-Str. 78,

20359 Hamburg; tel. (40) 31900; e-mail posteingang@bsh.de; internet www.bsh.de; f. 1945; under the Fed. Min. of Transport; oceanography, tides and currents, geomagnetism, gravimetry, nautical technics, navigating methods, tonnage measurement, hydrographic surveying and nautical geodesy, bathymetry, seabed geology, pollution control, ice information service, nautical charts and publs; hydrographic information service; library of 170,000 vols; Pres. MONIKA BREUCH-MORITZ; Vice-Pres. CHRISTOPH BROCKMANN; publs *Deutsche Hydrographische Zeitschrift* (4 a year), *Nachrichten für Seefahrer* (52 a year).

Bundesanstalt für Geowissenschaften und Rohstoffe (BGR) (Federal Institute for Geosciences and Natural Resources): Stilleweg 2, 30655 Hanover; tel. (511) 6430; e-mail poststelle@bgr.de; internet www.bgr.bund.de; f. 1958; geoscientific investigation, evaluation of mineral resources, environmental protection, geotechnology, seismology, marine and polar research; library of 296,000 vols; Pres. Prof. Dr HANS-JOACHIM KÜMPEL; Vice-Pres. JÖRG HAMMANN; publ. *Zeitschrift fur angewandte Geologie*.

Deutscher Wetterdienst (German Meteorological Service): POB 10 04 65, 63004 Offenbach am Main; Frankfurter Str. 135, 63067 Offenbach am Main; tel. (69) 80620; e-mail info@dwd.de; internet www.dwd.de; f. 1952; central office for the Fed. Republic; library of 179,000 vols; Pres. Prof. Dr GERHARD ADRIAN; Vice-Pres. Dr PAUL BECKER; Chief Librarian BRITTA BOLZMANN; publs *Annalen der Meteorologie*, *Berichte des Deutschen Wetterdienstes*, *Die Grosswetterlagen Europas* (12 a year, online), *Europäischer Wetterbericht* (online), *Geschichte der Meteorologie*, *Klimastatusbericht* (1 a year), *promet-Meteorologische Fortbildung* (4 a year), *Witterungsreport*.

Dr Remeis-Sternwarte Bamberg (Astronomical Institute of the University of Erlangen-Nuremberg): Sternwartstr. 7, 96049 Bamberg; tel. (951) 952220; internet www.sternwarte.uni-erlangen.de; f. 1889; stellar astrophysics; library of 2,000 vols; Chair. Prof. Dr JÖRN WILMS; Chair. Prof. Dr ULRICH HEBER.

Forschungszentrum Jülich GmbH (Jülich Research Centre): 52425 Jülich; Wilhelm-Johnen-Str., 52428 Jülich; tel. (2461) 610; e-mail info@fz-juelich.de; internet www.fz-juelich.de; f. 1956; operated jtly by German fed. Govt (90%) and state of N Rhine-Westphalia (10%); research in information technology and physical basic research, energy (materials and technology), environmental life sciences; library of 600,000 vols, 250,000 microforms, 2,000 journal titles; Pres. Dr KARL EUGEN HUTHMACHER; Chair. Prof. Dr ACHIM BACHEM.

Fraunhofer-Gesellschaft zur Förderung der Angewandten: POB 20 07 33, 80007 Munich; Hansastr. 27C, 80686 Munich; tel. (89) 12050; e-mail info@fraunhofer.de; internet www.fraunhofer.de; f. 1968; inc. GMD–Forschungszentrum Informationstechnik GmbH; research and devt in the fields of engineering science and information technology; 80 research units, incl. 58 Fraunhofer Institutes, at more than 40 locations throughout Germany; 12,500 staff; library of 110,000 vols; Pres. Prof. Dr HANS-JÖRG BULLINGER; publ. *Fraunhofer Magazine*.

Fraunhofer-Institut für Bauphysik (Fraunhofer Institute for Building Physics): POB 80 04 69, 70504 Stuttgart; POB 800469, Nobelstr. 12, 70504 Stuttgart; tel. (711) 97000; e-mail info@ibp.fraunhofer.de; internet www2.ibp.fraunhofer.de; f. 1929; research, devt, testing, demonstration and consulting in the field of building physics; noise control, sound insulation, optimization of audibility conditions in lecture halls, measures for energy economy, lighting technology, new building materials, indoor climate, weathering protection, hygrothermics; Pres. Prof. Dr HANS-JÖRG BULLINGER; Dir Prof. Dr GERD HAUSER; Dir Prof. Dr KLAUS SEDLBAUER; publ. *IBP Report* (building physics research results).

Geologisch-Paläontologisches Institut und Museum, Universität Hamburg (Geological and Palaeontological Institute and Museum): Bundesstr. 55, 20146 Hamburg; tel. (40) 428384999; e-mail christian.betzler@uni-hamburg.de; internet www.uni-hamburg.de/geol_pal; f. 1907; library of 80,000 vols; Man. Dir Prof. Dr CHRISTIAN BETZLER; Deputy Dir Prof. Dr CLAUS-DIETER REUTHER; publ. *Mitteilungen aus dem Geologisch-Paläontologischen Institut der Universität Hamburg* (1 a year).

Hamburger Sternwarte (Hamburg Observatory): Gojenbergsweg 112, 21029 Hamburg; tel. (40) 428388512; e-mail sternwarte@hs.uni-hamburg.de; internet www.hs.uni-hamburg.de; f. 1833; cosmology, exoplanets, stellar physics, model atmospheres; library of 65,000 vols; Dir Prof. P. H. HAUSCHILDT.

Helmholtz-Zentrum Berlin für Materialien und Energie GmbH: Hahn-Meitner-Pl. 1, 14109 Berlin; tel. (30) 80620; e-mail info@helmholtz-berlin.de; internet www.helmholtz-berlin.de; f. 1959 as Hahn-Meitner-Institut Berlin GmbH, merged with BESSY GmbH in 2008; solid state physics, atomic and molecular structures, solar energy (photovoltaic); library of 61,000 vols, 420,000 reports; Chair. Prof. Dr J. TREUSCH; Dir Prof. Dr ANKE KAYSSER-PYZALLA; Dir Dr ULRICH BREUER; Dir Prof. Dr WOLFGANG EBERHARDT.

Institut für Astronomie und Astrophysik Tübingen: Sand 1, 72076 Tübingen; tel. (7071) 2972486; internet www.uni-tuebingen.de; f. 1949; attached to Dept of Mathematics and Physics of Eberhard-Karls Univ. of Tübingen; UV- and X-ray astronomy, optical astronomy, stellar atmospheres, high energy astrophysics; library of 14,153 vols; Head Prof. KLAUS WERNER; Sec. and Librarian HEIDRUN OBERNDÖRFFER.

Institut für Astrophysik Göttingen (Institute of Astrophysics, Göttingen): Friedrich-Hund-Pl. 1, 37077 Göttingen; tel. (551) 395053; e-mail sekr@astro.physik.uni-goettingen.de; internet www.uni-sw.gwdg.de; f. 1750; attached to Georg-August-Univ.; galactic and extragalactic astrophysics, high-energy astrophysics, solar physics, stellar spectroscopy and theoretical astrophysics; houses a modern Cassegrain reflecting telescope with 50 cm mirror diameter and 5 m focal length; Dir Prof. Dr W. KOLLATSCHNY (acting).

Institut für Gefährstoff-Forschung (IGF) (Institute for Research into Dangerous Substances): Waldring 97, 44789 Bochum; tel. (234) 306359; e-mail igf@bgrci.de; internet www.igf-bbg.de; attached to Ruhr Univ.; Dir Dr DIRK DAHMANN.

Institut für Umwelt- und Zukunftsforschung (IUZ) an der Sternwarte Bochum: Blankensteiner Str. 200A, 44797 Bochum; tel. (234) 47711; e-mail info@iuz-bochum.de; internet www.sternwarte-bochum.de; devt and testing of electronic equipment for tracking and reception of satellite data; devt of display and reproduction systems for satellite imagery; photo-interpretation of satellite imagery for geo-scientific and environmental studies; remote sensing; Dir THILO ELSNER.

Karlsruhe Institute of Technology: Kaiserstr. 12, 76131 Karlsruhe; tel. (721) 6080; e-mail info@kit.edu; internet www.kit.edu; f. 2009 by merger of Forschungszentrum Karlsruhe GmbH (f. 1956) and Universität Karlsruhe (f. 1825); energy, nano, micro science and technology, elementary particle and astro-particle physics, climate and environment, computation, mobility systems, optics and photonics, humans and technology, new and applied materials; library of 500,000 vols, 1,600 periodical titles, 587,000 reports; Pres. Prof. Dr HOLGER HANSELKA; publs *clicKIT* (online), *lookKIT*, *KIT dialog*, *KIT Members Magazine*, *KIT Public Magazine*.

Kiepenheuer-Institut für Sonnenphysik (Kiepenheuer-Institute for Solar Physics): Schöneckstr. 6, 79104 Freiburg im Breisgau; tel. (761) 31980; e-mail secr@kis.uni-freiburg.de; internet www.kis.uni-freiburg.de; f. 1942; optical investigation of the solar atmosphere, observatory at Tenerife (Canary Islands); Dir Prof. Dr OSKAR VON DER LÜHE; Deputy Dir Prof. Dr SVETLANA BERDYUGINA.

Landessternwarte Königstuhl (National Observatory Königstuhl): Königstuhl 12, 69117 Heidelberg; tel. (6221) 541700; e-mail postmaster@lsw.uni-heidelberg.de; internet www.lsw.uni-heidelberg.de; f. 1897, present status 2005; attached to Zentrum für Astronomie of Heidelberg Univ.; astronomical scientific research; library of 25,000 vols; Dir Prof. Dr ANDREAS QUIRRENBACH.

Lehrstuhl für Astronomie, Universität Würzburg: Am Hubland, 97074 Würzburg; tel. (931) 8885031; e-mail mannheim@astro.uni-wuerzburg.de; internet www.astro.uni-wuerzburg.de; f. 1967; astronomy, theoretical astrophysics; library of 5,000 vols, 50 journals; Dir Prof. Dr KARL MANNHEIM.

Leibniz-Institut für Analytische Wissenschaften—ISAS—eV (Institute for Analytical Sciences): Bunsen-Kirchhoff-Str. 11, 44139 Dortmund; tel. (231) 13920; e-mail info@isas.de; internet www.isas.de; f. 1952 as Institute of Spectrochemistry and Applied Spectroscopy; focuses on analytical and spectroscopical methods in material sciences and life sciences; Dir Prof. Dr ALBERT SICKMANN; Dir Prof. Dr NORBERT ESSER.

Leibniz-Institut für Arbeitsforschung (IfADo) (Leibniz Research Centre for Working Environment and Human Factors): Ardeystr. 67, 44139 Dortmund; tel. (231) 10840; e-mail gude@ifado.de; f. 1969; attached to Technische Univ.; investigates potentials and risks of modern work on basis of behavioural and life sciences; library of 35,000 vols incl. books, 7,000 online journals; Dir Prof. Dr JAN G. HENGSTLER; Head Librarian SUSANNE LINDEMANN; publ. *EXCLI Journal*.

Universitäts-Sternwarte–Institut für Astronomie und Astrophysik und Observatorium Wendelstein: Scheinerstr. 1, 81679 Munich; tel. (89) 21806001; internet www.usm.uni-muenchen.de; f. 1816; extragalactic astronomy, plasma astrophysics, stellar atmospheres, stellar evolution, cosmochemistry; library of 18,000 vols; Dir Prof. Dr MANFRED HIRT.

UWG Gesellschaft für Umwelt- und Wirtschaftsgeologie GmbH: Wolfener 36, Aufg. K, 12681 Berlin; tel. (30) 23144684; geoscientific and environmental library (books, data, photographs (remote sensing), maps); Dir Dr KLAUS ERLER.

PHILOSOPHY AND PSYCHOLOGY

Institut für Forensische Psychiatrie (Institute for Forensic Psychiatry): Charité-Universitätsmedizin Berlin, Oranienburger

Str. 285, 13437 Berlin; tel. (30) 84451411; e-mail info@forensik-berlin.de; internet www.forensik-berlin.de; f. 1970; studies and research in forensic psychiatry and psychology; weekly interdisciplinary colloquium; annual forensic science conference; library of 21,257 vols, 61 current periodicals, 1,476 special prints, 104 video cassettes; Dir Prof. Dr HANS-LUDWIG KRÖBER.

Institut für Gerichtspsychologie (IfG) (Institute for Forensic Psychology): Gilsingstr. 5, 44789 Bochum; tel. (234) 34091; internet www.gerichtspsychologie-bochum.de; f. 1951; carries out reports on behalf of the courts and solicitors; Dir Dr FRIEDRICH ARNTZEN.

Institut für Philosophie (Institute of Philosophy): Unter den Linden 6, 10099 Berlin; tel. (30) 20932204; e-mail schaume@philosophie.hu-berlin.de; internet www.philosophie.hu-berlin.de; attached to Humboldt Univ.; offers open lectures; Kant archive; Dir Prof. Dr THOMAS SCHMIDT; Sec. ELKE SCHAUM.

Institut für Philosophie Universität Leipzig (Institute of Philosophy at Leipzig University): POB 920, 04009 Leipzig; Beethovenstr. 15, 04107 Leipzig; tel. (341) 9735800; e-mail busch@uni-leipzig.de; internet www.sozphil.uni-leipzig.de/cm/philosophie; attached to Leipzig Univ.; organizes confs and weekly colloquia; Dir Prof. Dr ANDREA KERN; Sec. SEBASTIAN RÖDL; publ. *Leipziger Schriften zur Philosophie*.

Institut für Rechtspsychologie Halle (Saale) (Institute for Forensic Psychology, Halle): Kleine Marktstr. 5, 06108 Halle/Salle; tel. (345) 6140680; e-mail institut@rechtspsychologie-halle.de; internet www.rechtspsychologie-halle.de; f. 1997; Man. BÄRBEL GOLDHAMMER.

RELIGION, SOCIOLOGY AND ANTHROPOLOGY

Arbeitsgemeinschaft Sozialwissenschaftlicher Institute eV (Association of Social Science Institutes): Dreizehnmorgenweg 42, 53175 Bonn; tel. (228) 2281574; e-mail asi@asi-ev.org; internet www.asi-ev.org; f. 1949; Pres. Prof. Dr FRANK FAULBAUM; Man. Dir MATTHIAS STAHL; publs *ASI-Schriftenreihe*, *Soziale Welt* (4 a year).

Bundesinstitut für Bevölkerungsforschung (Federal Institute for Population Research): POB 5528, 65180 Wiesbaden; Friedrich-Ebert-Allee 4, 65185 Wiesbaden; tel. (0611) 752235; e-mail bib@destatis.de; internet www.bib-demografie.de; f. 1973; attached to Statistisches Bundesamt; promotes all fields of demographic research and coordinates research work undertaken by demographers, incl. those in foreign countries; Dir Prof. Dr NORBERT F. SCHNEIDER; publs *Beiträge zur Bevölkerungswissenschaft—Schriftenreihe des BiB* (2–3 a year), *Bevölkerungsforschung Aktuell* (6 a year), *Comparative Population Studies—CPoS, Demographie: Zeitschrift für Bevölkerungswissenschaft* (4 a year).

Forschungsgruppe für Anthropologie und Religionsgeschichte eV (Research Group for Anthropology and History of Religion): Droste-Hülshoff-Str. 9B, 48341 Altenberge; tel. (2505) 1347; e-mail ugarit@uni-muenster.de; internet www.ugarit-verlag.de; f. 1970; research and documentation refer to all fields of religion including interconnections with anthropology, psychology, culture and environment; methodology of research; int. cooperation and exchange; Pres. Prof. Dr M. L. G. DIETRICH; Pres. Prof. Dr R. SCHMITT; publs *Forschungen zur Anthropologie und Religionsgeschichte* (3 a year), *Mitteilungen für Anthropologie und Religionsgeschichte* (1 a year).

GESIS-Leibniz-Institut für Sozialwissenschaften (GESIS-Leibniz-Institute for the Social Sciences): POB 12 21 55, 68072 Mannheim; B2, 1, 68159 Mannheim; tel. (621) 12460; e-mail info@gesis.org; internet www.gesis.org; f. 2007, by merger of Social Science Information Centre (IZ) in Bonn, Central Archive for Empirical Social Research in Cologne (ZA), and Centre for Survey Research and Methodology (ZUMA) in Mannheim; infrastructural services on numerical data, information bases and research methods for social scientists; library of 114,000 vols, 750 journals; Chair. Prof. Dr BERNHARD NAUCK; Pres. Prof. Dr YORK SURE-VETTER; publs *CEWS-publications* (irregular), *GESIS Recherche Spezial* (irregular), *GESIS Series* (irregular), *GESIS Technical Reports* (irregular), *GESIS Working Papers* (irregular), *HSR Historical Social Research* (4 a year), *Informationsdienst Soziale Indikatoren* (2 a year), *Methods, Data, Analysis MDA* (2 a year), *ZA Information* (2 a year).

Institut für Diaspora- und Genozidforschung (Institute of Diaspora and Genocide Studies): Universitätsstr. 150, 44801 Bochum; tel. (234) 3229700; e-mail idg@ruhr-uni-bochum.de; attached to Ruhr Univ.; Dir Prof. Dr MIHRAN DABAG.

Sozialforschungsstelle Dortmund: Evinger Pl. 17, 44339 Dortmund; tel. (231) 85960; e-mail pr@sfs-dortmund.de; internet www.sfs-dortmund.de; f. 1946; research in social sciences; attached to Technische Univ.; Dir Prof. Dr JÜRGEN HOWALDT; Deputy Dir ELLEN HILF.

TECHNOLOGY

Arbeitsgemeinschaft Industrieller Forschungsvereinigungen 'Otto von Guericke' eV (AiF) (AiF—German Federation of Industrial Research Associations): Bayenthalgürtel 23, 50968 Cologne; tel. (221) 376800; e-mail info@aif.de; internet www.aif.de; f. 1954; promotes cooperative research for small and medium-sized industry; Pres. Dr YVONNE PCOPPEST; CEO Prof. Dr MICHAEL STOU.

Bundesanstalt für Materialforschung und -prüfung (Federal Institute for Materials Research and Testing): Unter den Eichen 87, 12205 Berlin; tel. (30) 81040; e-mail info@bam.de; internet www.bam.de; f. 1871; analytical chemistry; reference materials, chemical safety engineering, containment systems for dangerous goods, materials and the environment, materials engineering, materials protection and surface technologies, safety of structures, non-destructive testing, accreditation, quality in testing; library of 80,000 vols; Chair. JÜRGEN MEYER; Pres. Prof. Dr MANFRED HENNECKE; Vice-Pres. Prof. Dr Ing. THOMAS BÖLLINGHAUS; publ. *Amtsblatt* (4 a year).

Clausthaler Umwelttechnik-Institut GmbH (Clausthal Institute of Environmental Technology): Leibnizstr. 21–23, 38678 Clausthal-Zellerfeld; tel. (5323) 9330; e-mail cutec@cutec.de; internet www.cutec.de; f. 1990; wholly owned by state of Lower Saxony; research into waste avoidance, recycling and disposal; Chair. Dr HANS SCHROEDER; Man. Dir Prof. Dr Ing. OTTO CARLOWITZ.

Deutsche Forschungsanstalt für Lebensmittelchemie (German Research Institute for Food Chemistry): Lise-Meitner Str. 34, 85354 Freising; tel. (8161) 712932; e-mail dfa@lrz.tum.de; internet dfa.leb.chemie.tu-muenchen.de; f. 1918; library of 3,000 vols; Dir Prof. Dr PETER SCHIEBERLE; Deputy Dir Prof. Dr PETER KÖHLER.

Deutsche Montan Technologie GmbH (DMT): Am Technologiepark 1, 45307 Essen; tel. (201) 17201; e-mail dmt-info@dmt.de; internet www.dmt.de; f. 1990; specialists in mining; Chair. HEINZ-GERD KÖRNER.

Deutsche Zentrum für Luft- und Raumfahrt eV (DLR) (German Aerospace Centre): Linder Höhe, 51147 Cologne; tel. (2203) 6010; e-mail redaktion@dlr.de; internet www.dlr.de; f. 1969; flight mechanics, guidance and control, fluid mechanics, structures and materials, space flight, telecommunication technology and remote sensing, energetics; library of 400,000 vols; Chair. JOHANN-DIETRICH WÖRNER; Vice-Chair. KLAUS HAMACHER; publs *DLR-Forschungsberichte* (irregular), *DLR-Mitteilungen* (irregular), *DLR-Nachrichten* (4 a year).

Deutsches Textilforschungszentrum Nord-West eV (German Textile Research Centre Northwest eV): Öffentliche Prüfstelle (ÖP), Adlerstr. 1, 47798 Krefeld; tel. (2151) 8430; e-mail info@dtnw.de; internet www2.dtnw.de; f. 1990; research groups incl. biotechnology and catalysis, colloid chemistry and nanotechnology, physical technology and measurement technique, supramolecular and polymer chemistry; Man. Dir Prof. Dr JOCHEN GUTMANN; Deputy Dir Prof. Dr MATHIAS ULBRICHT.

Forschungsinstitut Edelmetalle & Metallchemie (fem) (Research Institute of Precious Metals and Metals Chemistry): Katharinenstr. 17, 73525 Schwäbisch Gmünd; tel. (7171) 10060; e-mail fem@fem-online.de; internet www.fem-online.de; f. 1922; basic and applied research into precious metals science and technology, electrochemical deposition, corrosion, light metals surface technology, plasma surface technology, physical metallurgy, environmental technology and analyses; Dir Dr A. ZIELONKA.

Forschungsinstitut für Wärmeschutz eV München (Thermal Insulation, Testing, Research): Lochhamer Schlag 4, 82166 Gräfelfing; tel. (89) 858000; e-mail info@fiw-muenchen.de; internet www.fiw-muenchen.de; f. 1918; Scientific Dir Dr Ing. MARTIN SPITZNER; Scientific Dir Dr Ing. MARTIN ZEITLER; Scientific Dir Dr ROLAND GELLERT; publ. *Mitteilungen aus dem FIW München* (irregular).

Fraunhofer-Institut für Verfahrenstechnik und Verpackung (Fraunhofer Institute for Process Engineering and Packaging): Giggenhauser Str. 35, 85354 Freising; tel. (8161) 4910; e-mail info@ivv.fraunhofer.de; internet www.ivv.fraunhofer.de; f. 1942; food processing, environmental technology, preservation and packaging, gen. packaging; library of 6,000 vols; Dir Prof. Dr HORST-CHRISTIAN LANGOWSKI; Deputy Dir Dr CLAUDIA SCHÖNWEITZ.

Fraunhofer Institut für Materialfluss und Logistik (Fraunhofer Institute of Liquid Material and Logistics): Joseph-von-Fraunhofer-Str. 2–4, 44227 Dortmund; tel. (231) 97430; e-mail info@iml.fraunhofer.de; internet www.iml.fraunhofer.de; f. 1981; attached to Technische Univ.; Head Prof. Dr AXEL KUHN; Head Prof. Dr MICHAEL TEN HOMPEL; Head Prof. Dr UWE CLAUSEN.

Fraunhofer Institut für Software- und Systemtechnik (ISST) (Fraunhofer Institute for Software and Systems Engineering (ISST)): Emil-Figge-Str. 91, 44227 Dortmund; tel. (231) 976770; e-mail info@isst.fraunhofer.de; internet www.isst.fraunhofer.de; f. 1992; attached to Technische Univ.; br. in Berlin; Dir Prof. Dr JAKOB REHOF; Man. Dir Dr VOLKER ZURWEHN.

GSI Helmholtzzentrum für Schwerionenforschung GmbH (GSI Helmholtz Centre for Heavy Ion Research GmbH):

Planckstr. 1, 64291 Darmstadt; tel. (6159) 710; e-mail info@gsi.de; internet www.gsi.de; f. 1969; carries out basic research with heavy ions in nuclear physics and chemistry, solid state and atomic physics, radiation biology, tumour therapy with ion beams, etc.; heavy ion linear accelerator, synchrotron, storage ring and laboratory; library of 3,000 vols; Chair. Dr BEATRIX VIERKORN-RUDOLPH; Scientific Dir Prof. Dr HORST STÖCKER; publ. *GSI-Scientific Report* (1 a year).

Institut für Angewandte Innovationsforschung eV (Institute for Applied Innovation Research): Buscheypl. 13, 44801 Bochum; tel. (234) 971170; e-mail info@iai-bochum.de; internet www.iai-bochum.de; attached to Ruhr Univ.; Chair. Prof. Dr BERND KRIEGESMANN; Man. Dr HORST KUNHENN; publs *Berichte aus der angewandten Innovationsforschung* (series), *Innovation: Forschung und Management* (series).

Institut für Bauforschung eV (Institute for Building Research): An der Markuskirche 1, 30163 Hanover; tel. (511) 965160; e-mail office@bauforschung.de; internet www.bauforschung.de; f. 1946; research in areas of planning in construction, building materials, construction types, construction and building damage and their causes; Dir Dipl. Ing. HEIKE BÖHMER.

Institut für Erdöl- und Erdgasforschung (Institute for Petroleum Research): Agricolastr. 10, 38678 Clausthal-Zellerfeld; tel. (5323) 722239; e-mail bibliothek@ite.tu-clausthal.de; internet www.ite.tu-clausthal.de; f. 1943; attached to Technische Universität Clausthal; drilling and production technology, gas supply systems, oil and gas recovery, reservoir engineering, refinery technology, research in petroleum products, hydrocarbons and environment; library of 5,000 vols.

Institut für Roboterforschung (Robotics Research Institute): 44221, Dortmund; Otto-Hahn-Str. 8, 44227, Dortmund; tel. (231) 7552634; e-mail uwe.schwiegelshohn@tu-dortmund.de; internet www.irf.tu-dortmund.de; attached to Technische Univ.; Head Prof. Dr Ing. UWE SCHWIEGELSHOHN.

Institut für Textil- und Verfahrenstechnik Denkendorf (Institute for Textile Technology and Process Engineering Denkendorf): Körschtalstr. 26, 73770 Denkendorf; tel. (711) 93400; e-mail itv@itv-denkendorf.de; internet www.itv-denkendorf.de; f. 1921; library of 2,500 vols; Dir Prof. Dr Ing. HEINRICH PLANK; Deputy Dir Dr MICHAEL DOSER.

Landesamt für Natur, Umwelt und Verbraucherschutz Nordrhein-Westfalen (North Rhine-Westphalia State Agency for Nature, Environment and Consumer Protection): Leibnizstr. 10, 45659 Recklinghausen; tel. (2361) 3050; e-mail poststelle@lanuv.nrw.de; internet www.lanuv.nrw.de; f. 2007; research and advice in the fields of air pollution and noise control; prevention of accidental releases; water, wastewater, groundwater and waste management; engineering, circular economy, veterinary issues, food safety and agricultural commodity market; Pres. Dr HEINRICH BOTTERMANN.

Lehr- und Forschungsgebiet Internationale Wirtschaftsbeziehungen (Chair of International Economics): Templergraben 64, 52056 Aachen; tel. (241) 8093931; internet www.iw.rwth-aachen.de; f. 2004; library of 100,000 vols; Dir Prof. Dr OLIVER LORZ; Sec. SUSANNE MOHAMMAD ZADEH; publs *Canadian Journal of Economics*, *Economics Letters*, *Journal of Economic Behavior and Organization*, *Journal of Urban Economics*, *Public Choice*.

Leibniz-Institut für Analytische Wissenschaften—ISAS-eV: Bunsen-Kirchhoff-Str. 11, 44139 Dortmund; tel. (231) 13920; e-mail info@isas.de; internet www.isas.de; f. 1952, present name 2009; attached to Technische Univ.; promotes research in analytical sciences; Dir Prof. Dr NORBERT ESSER; Dir Prof. Dr ALBERT SICKMANN.

Max Rubner-Institut, Bundesforschungsinstitut für Ernährung und Lebensmittel (Max Rubner Institute, Federal Research Institute for Nutrition and Food): Haid-und-Neustr. 9, 76131 Karlsruhe; tel. (721) 66250; e-mail kontakt@mri.bund.de; internet www.mri.bund.de; f. 2008; research instn of the Fed. Min. of Food, Agriculture and Consumer Protection; focuses on health and consumer protection in the food sector, incl. determination and nutritional assessment of food ingredients, investigation of processing procedures, quality assurance of vegetable and animal food, investigation of the motivation of nutritional behaviour, and improvement of nutritional information; library of 300,000 vols; Pres. Prof. Dr GERHARD RECHKEMMER.

Physikalisch-Technische Bundesanstalt (National Metrology Institute): Bundesallee 100, 38116 Brunswick; tel. (531) 5923006; e-mail presse@ptb.de; internet www.ptb.de; f. 1887; divs for mechanics and acoustics, electricity, thermodynamics and explosion protection, optics, precision engineering, ionizing radiation, temperature and synchrotron radiation, and medical physics and information technology; library of 125,000 vols; Pres. Prof. Dr ERNST OTTO GÖBEL; Vice-Pres. Prof. Dr MANFRED PETERS; publs *Maßstäbe* (1 a year), *PTB-Mitteilungen* (4 a year), *PTB news* (3 a year).

Technologie Zentrum Dortmund GmbH (Technology Centre Dortmund GmbH): Emil-Figge-Str. 76–80, 44227 Dortmund; tel. (231) 9742100; e-mail technobox@tzdo.de; internet www.tzdo.de; attached to Technische Univ.; Chair. ERNST PRÜSSE; Man. Dir GUIDO BARANOWSKI; Man. Dir STEFAN SCHREIBER; Man. Dir UDO MAGER.

Zentrum für Konstruktionswerkstoffe, Staatliche Materialprüfungsanstalt Darmstadt–Fachgebiet und Institut für Werkstoffkunde (Centre for Construction Materials, State Material-Testing Foundation-Faculty and Institute of Material Science): Grafenstr. 2, 64283 Darmstadt; tel. (6151) 162351; e-mail oechsner@mpa-ifw.tu-darmstadt.de; internet www.mpa-ifw.tu-darmstadt.de; f. 1927; attached to Technical Univ. of Darmstadt; Dir Prof. Dr Ing. CHRISTINA BERGER; Dir Prof. Dr Ing MATTHIAS OECHSNER.

Libraries and Archives

Aachen

Hochschulbibliothek der RWTH Aachen: Templergraben 61, 52056 Aachen; tel. (241) 8094445; e-mail bth@bth.rwth-aachen.de; internet www.bth.rwth-aachen.de; f. 1870; 2,100,000 vols; Dir Dr ULRIKE EICH.

Stadtbibliothek Aachen (Aachen Public Library): Couvenstr. 15, 52058 Aachen; tel. (241) 47910; e-mail bibliothek@mail.aachen.de; internet stadtbibliothek-aachen.de; f. 1831; gen. information about Aachen and the region, regional history; 511,000 vols, spec. collns incl. folklore, ethnology, archaeology, organ literature; Dir MANFRED SAWALLICH.

Amberg

Staatsarchiv Amberg: Archivstr. 3, 92224 Amberg; tel. (9621) 307270; e-mail poststelle@staam.bayern.de; internet www.gda.bayern.de; f. 1437, present status 1921; 3m. items in archives; 34,400 vols; Co-Dir Dr MARIA RITA SAGSTETTER; Co-Dir R. FRITSCH.

Augsburg

Staatsarchiv Augsburg (Public Archives Augsburg): Salomon-Idler-Str. 2, 86159 Augsburg; tel. (821) 5996330; e-mail poststelle@staau.bayern.de; internet www.gda.bayern.de/augsburg; f. 1830 in Neuburg; 3.05m. items; Dir Dr THOMAS ENGELKE.

Staats- und Stadtbibliothek (State and Municipal Library): Stadt Augsburg, 86143 Augsburg; Schaezlerstr. 25, 86152 Augsburg; tel. (821) 3242739; e-mail bibliothek.stadt@augsburg.de; internet www.sustb.augsburg.de; f. 1537; 536,827 vols, 3,997 MSS, 2,799 incunabula, 20,282 drawings and engravings; Dir Dr HELMUT GIER.

Universitätsbibliothek: Universitätsstr. 22, 86159 Augsburg; tel. (821) 5985300; e-mail dir@bibliothek.uni-augsburg.de; internet www.bibliothek.uni-augsburg.de; f. 1970; 2,122,524 vols, 77,313 theses, 59,418 maps, 394,285 items of audiovisual material and microforms, 1,267 incunabula, 1,546 MSS, 2,295 music MSS; Dir Dr ULRICH HOHOFF.

Aurich

Niedersächsisches Landesarchiv—Staatsarchiv Aurich: Oldersumer Str. 50, 26603 Aurich; tel. (4941) 176660; e-mail aurich@nla.niedersachsen.de; internet www.staatsarchiv-aurich.niedersachsen.de; f. 1872; 20,000 vols; Dir Dr BERNHARD PARISIUS.

Bamberg

Staatsarchiv Bamberg: Hainstr. 39, 96047 Bamberg; tel. (951) 986220; e-mail poststelle@staba.bayern.de; internet www.gda.bayern.de/archive/bamberg; f. 13th century, became Bavarian state archive in 1803; 2.3m. vols; spec. collns: Frankish history, maps, plans, MSS, documents; Dir Dr STEFAN NÖTH.

Staatsbibliothek Bamberg (Bamberg State Library): Neue Residenz, Dompl. 8, 96049 Bamberg; tel. (951) 955030; e-mail info@staatsbibliothek-bamberg.de; internet www.staatsbibliothek-bamberg.de; f. 1803; 521,260 vols, spec. colln of 6,148 MSS, 3,520 incunabula and 80,000 prints and drawings; Dir Prof. Dr WERNER TAEGERT; Deputy Dir Dr STEFAN KNOCH.

Universitätsbibliothek: POB 2705, 96018 Bamberg; Feldkirchenstr. 21, 96052 Bamberg; tel. (951) 8631501; e-mail universitaetsbibliothek@uni-bamberg.de; internet www.uni-bamberg.de/ub; f. 1973; attached to Univ. of Bamberg Press—UBP; 1,630,000 vols; Dir Dr FABIAN FRANKE; publ. *Schriften der Universitätsbibliothek Bamberg*.

Bayreuth

Universitätsbibliothek Bayreuth (University Library Bayreuth): Universität Bayreuth, 95440 Bayreuth; Universitätsstr. 30, 95447 Bayreuth; tel. (921) 553420; e-mail info@ub.uni-bayreuth.de; internet www.ub.uni-bayreuth.de; f. 1973; 1,743,000 vols, 3,500 current periodicals; Dir Dr RALF BRUGBAUER.

Berlin

Akademiebibliothek der Berlin-Brandenburgischen Akademie der Wissenschaften: Jägerstr. 22–23, 10117 Berlin; tel. (30) 20370358; e-mail bib

.benutzung@bbaw.de; internet bibliothek .bbaw.de; f. 1700; 605,000 vols, 630 periodicals, spec. colln of the publs of academies and learned socs; Dir and Head of Library Dr STEFAN WIEDERKEHR; Sec. ANDREA M'BATCHI.

Auswärtiges Amt, Referat 116, Bibliothek und Informationsvermittlung: Werderscher Markt 1, 10117 Berlin; tel. (30) 18172208; e-mail 116-information@ auswaertiges-amt.de; 320,000 vols, 500 journals, 90,000 maps; Head of Dept KAREN SCHMOHL; Librarian ANNETT JUHRIG.

Bibliothek des Deutschen Bundestages: Pl. der Republik 1, 11011 Berlin; tel. (30) 22733073; e-mail bibliothek@bundestag.de; internet www.bundestag.de/htdocs_e/documents/library; f. 1949; 1,400,000 vols. 8,000 periodicals, spec. collns of German and foreign official publs and parliamentary papers; depository library of 10 int. orgs; Dir URSULA FREYSCHMIDT; Librarian ELISABETH MÄRZ; publs *Literaturtipps* (on topical economic and political subjects), *Neue Bücher und Aufsätze in der Bibliothek*, *Schnellinformationen*.

Bibliothek für Bildungsgeschichtliche Forschung des DIPF (Research Library for the History of Education): POB 171138, 10203 Berlin; Warschauer Str. 34–38, 10243 Berlin; tel. (30) 2933600; e-mail bbf@dipf.de; internet www.bbf.dipf.de; f. 1876; holds confs and exhibitions; 726,000 vols, archive colln on the history of education; Head Dr STEFAN CRAMME (acting); publs *Bestandsverzeichnisse zur Bildungsgeschichte* (directory of publications on the history of education, series), *Neuerwerbungsverzeichnisse* (lists of new acquisitions, 12 a year), *Quellen und Dokumente zur Geschichte der Erziehung* (sources and documents on the history of education, series), *Tagungsbände* (conf. papers).

Geheimes Staatsarchiv Preussischer Kulturbesitz (Secret Central Archives of the Prussian Cultural Possession): Dahlem, Archivstr. 12–14, 14195 Berlin; tel. (30) 266447500; e-mail gsta.pk@gsta.spk-berlin .de; internet www.gsta.spk-berlin.de; f. 1598; material and research on history of Prussia and the former Prussian territories since 12th century; 185,000 vols, 2,000 periodicals, 650,000 records and files, 120,000 maps; Dir Prof. Dr JÜRGEN KLOOSTERHUIS; publ. *Veröffentlichungen* (2–3 a year).

Ibero-Amerikanisches Institut Preussischer Kulturbesitz: Potsdamer Str. 37, 10785 Berlin; tel. (30) 266451500; e-mail iai@ iai.spk-berlin.de; internet www.iai.spk-berlin .de; f. 1930; research institute and library dedicated to Latin America, Spain and Portugal; cultural and scientific events; 1,200,000 vols and 870,000 monographs; Dir Dr BARBARA GÖBEL; publs *Bibliotheca Ibero-Americana*, *Biblioteca Luso-Brasileira*, *Estudios Indiana*, *Iberoamericana*, *Indiana*, *Revista Internacional de Linguistica Iberoamericana*.

Kunstbibliothek Staatliche Museen zu Berlin: Matthäikirchpl. 6, 10785 Berlin; tel. (30) 266424101; e-mail auskunft.kb@smb .spk-berlin.de; internet www.smb.museum/ kb; f. 1867; 480,000 vols; spec. collns: ornamental and architectural books, Lipperheidesche Kostumbibliothek, artists' books, posters, photographs, graphic design, drawings; Dir Dr MORITZ WULLEN; Deputy Dir Dr JOACHIM BRAND.

Landesarchiv Berlin (Berlin Regional Archive): Eichborndamm 115–121, 13403 Berlin; tel. (30) 902640; e-mail info@ landesarchiv-berlin.de; internet www .landesarchiv-berlin.de; f. 1948; legal documents, etc. for the Berlin area, and important material on the history of Berlin; 76,000 vols and 5,200 film rolls; Dir Prof. Dr UWE SCHAPER; publ. *Berlin in Geschichte und Gegenwart*.

Politisches Archiv des Auswärtigen Amts (Political Archive of the Foreign Office): Kurstr. 33, 10117 Berlin; tel. (30) 18172159; e-mail 117-r@diplo.de; internet www.auswaertiges-amt.de; f. 1920; Foreign Office archives; documents since 1867; archives of fmr Foreign Min. of the German Democratic Republic; Dir L. BIEWER; publs *Akten zur auswärtigen Politik der Bundesrepublik Deutschland* (series), *Akten zur deutschen auswärtigen Politik 1918–1945* (series), *Biographisches Handbuch des deutschen Auswärtigen Dienstes 1871–1945* (series).

Staatsbibliothek zu Berlin–Preußischer Kulturbesitz: Potsdamer Str. 33, 10785 Berlin; also: Unter den Linden 8, 10117 Berlin; tel. (30) 2660; e-mail info@sbb .spk-berlin.de; internet www .staatsbibliothek-berlin.de; f. 1661; 11,000,000 vols, 25,000 current periodicals and newspapers, 18,400 Occidental MSS, 66,500 musical MSS, 462,300 music prints, 1m. maps, 4,442 incunabula, 321,080 autographs, 1,600 estates, 12,000,000 pictures, 2m. microforms; Mendelssohn archive; Gen. Dir BARBARA SCHNEIDER-KEMPF.

Universitätsbibliothek der Freien Universität Berlin: Garystr. 39, 14195 Berlin; tel. 83851111; e-mail auskunft@ub.fu-berlin .de; internet www.ub.fu-berlin.de; f. 1952; 2,100,000 vols, 1,000 periodicals, 55,000 ejournals, 350,000 theses; 7.7m. vols in departmental libraries; Dir JIŘÍ KENDE; publ. *Universitätsbibliographie*.

Universitätsbibliothek der Humboldt-Universität zu Berlin (University Library of Humboldt University in Berlin): Unter den Linden, 10099 Berlin; Geschwister-Scholl-Str. 1/3, 10117 Berlin; tel. (30) 209399300; e-mail info@ub.hu-berlin.de; internet www .ub.hu-berlin.de; f. 1831; 6.5m. vols, 10,000 current periodicals; Dir Dr ANDREAS DEGKWITZ; Deputy Dir IMMA HENDRIX; Sec. ANNETTE GOLZE; publ. *Schriftenreihe*.

Universitätsbibliothek der Technischen Universität Berlin: Universitätsbibliothek, Fasanenstr. 88, (im Volkswagen-Haus), 10623 Berlin; tel. (30) 31476101; e-mail info@ub.tu-berlin.de; internet www.ub .tu-berlin.de; f. 1884; 2.3m. vols, 2,237 periodicals, 48,053 ejournals, 131,396 architectural drawings; Dir Dr W. ZICK.

Zentral- und Landesbibliothek Berlin (Berlin Central and Provincial Library): Breite Str. 30–36, 10178 Berlin; tel. (30) 90226401; e-mail info@zlb.de; internet www .zlb.de; f. 1901; 3.3m. vols, in print and online; Man. Dir VOLKER HELLER.

Bochum

Stadtbücherei Bochum (Public library Bochum): Gustav-Heinemann Pl. 2–6 (BVZ), 44777 Bochum; tel. (234) 9102496; e-mail stadtbue@bochum.de; internet www.bochum .de/stadtbuecherei; f. 1905; 406,000 vols; Dir HEINZ ALBRECHT.

Universitätsbibliothek (University Library of Bochum): 44780 Bochum; Universitätsstr. 150, 44801 Bochum; tel. (234) 3222788; e-mail direktion-ub@ ruhr-uni-bochum.de; internet www.ub .ruhr-uni-bochum.de; f. 1962; attached to Ruhr-Univ. Bochum; 1,641,948 vols of printed items, 1,182 current journals; 21,366 non-periodical publs, 68,000 full-text journals, 3,843 databases; Univ. Librarian Dr ERDMUTE LAPP; Deputy Librarian GEORG SANDER.

Bonn

Archiv der sozialen Demokratie (Friedrich-Ebert-Stiftung) (Archive of Social Democracy—Friedrich Ebert Foundation): 53170 Bonn; Godesberger Allee 149, 53175 Bonn; tel. (228) 8839046; e-mail archiv .auskunft@fes.de; internet www.fes.de; f. 1969; contains material relating to the Sozialdemokratische Partei Deutschlands (SPD) and the German trade unions; history of German and int. social movement, labour movement, labour problems; 600,000 vols, 3,000 periodicals; Dir for the Archive of Social Democracy Dr ANJA KRUKE; Dir for the Library of the Friedrich-Ebert-Foundation Dr RÜDIGER ZIMMERMANN.

Bibliothek der Hochschulrektorenkonferenz (Library of the University Rectors' Conference): Ahrstr. 39, 53175 Bonn; tel. (228) 887159; e-mail bibliothek@hrk.de; internet www.hrk.de/bibliothek; f. 1954 (Westdeutsche Rektorenkonferenz); 69,000 vols, 800 periodicals, 69,000 monographs, 95,000 records and acts; Head Dr ULRICH MEYER-DOERPINGHAUS; Librarian THOMAS LAMPE.

Bundesamts für Bauwesen und Raumordnung, Wissenschaftliche Bibliothek: POB 210150, 53156 Bonn; tel. (1888) 4012281; e-mail karin.goebel@bbr .bund.de; internet www.bbr.bund.de; f. 1941; 150,000 vols, 450 periodicals; Dir Dr phil. KLAUS SCHLIEBE; publs *Forschungen* (series, irregular), *Informationen zur Raumentwicklung* (12 a year), *Raumforschung und Raumordnung* (5 or 6 issues a year), *Werkstatt: Praxis* (series, irregular).

Stadtarchiv und Stadthistorische Bibliothek Bonn (Bonn City Archive and Historical Library): Berliner Platz 2, 53103 Bonn; tel. (228) 772530; e-mail stadtarchiv@ bonn.de; f. 1899; 140,000 vols; Head Archivist and Librarian Dr NORBERT SCHLOSSMACHER; publs *Bonner Geschichtsblätter* (1 a year), *Studien zur Heimatgeschichte des Stadtbezirkes Bonn-Beuel*, *Veröffentlichungen des Stadtarchivs Bonn*.

Universitäts- und Landesbibliothek (University and Federal State Library): POB 2460, 53014 Bonn; Adenauerallee 39–41, 53113 Bonn; tel. (228) 737350; e-mail ulb@ulb.uni-bonn.de; internet www.ulb .uni-bonn.de; f. 1818; 2,090,000 vols, 6,100 periodicals, 13,500 electronic periodicals, 1,300 incunabula, 880 MSS; Dir Dr RENATE VOGT.

Bremen

Bibliothek/InfoCenter des Instituts für Seeverkehrswirtschaft und Logistik (ISL) (ISL InfoCentre/Library): Universitätsallee GW1 Block A, 28359 Bremen; tel. (421) 2209644; e-mail library@isl.org; internet www.isl.org; f. 1954; centre for maritime information and documentation offering professional services about industries, markets and companies within the areas of maritime industries, transport and logistics; 130,000 vols; Head KATRIN KABITZKE; Librarian ANGELA FEGBEITEL.

Staats- und Universitätsbibliothek: POB 330160, 28331 Bremen; Bibliothekstr., 28359 Bremen; tel. (421) 2182615; e-mail suub@ suub.uni-bremen.de; internet www.suub .uni-bremen.de; f. 1660; 3,297,785 vols, 8,257 current print periodicals, 21,003 online periodicals; Dir MARIA ELISABETH MÜLLER; publ. *Jahresbibliographie Massenkommunikation*.

Staatsarchiv Bremen (Public Archives Bremen): Am Staatsarchiv 1, 28203 Bremen; tel. (421) 3616221; e-mail office@staatsarchiv .bremen.de; internet www .staatsarchiv-bremen.de; f. 1727; Dir Prof. Dr KONRAD ELMSHÄUSER (acting); publs *Kleine*

Schriften des Staatsarchivs Bremen, Veröffentlichungen aus dem Staatsarchiv der Freien Hansestadt Bremen.

Brunswick

Bundesforschungsinstitut für Kulturpflanzen Informationszentrum und Bibliothek (Federal Research Centre for Cultivated Plants Information Centre and Library): Messeweg 11/12, 38104 Braunschweig; tel. (531) 2993397; e-mail julia.schollbach@jki.bund.de; internet www.jki.bund.de; f. 1950; attached to Julius Kühn-Institut; plant protection and related fields; 370,000 vols, 1,200 periodicals, 44,000 reprints, 2,200 microfilms; Head Dr OLAF HERING; publs *Amtliche Pflanzenschutzbestimmungen* (irregular), *Berichte aus der Biologischen Bundesanstalt für Land- und Forstwirtschaft, Nachrichtenblatt des Deutschen Pflanzenschutzdienstes* (12 a year), *Pflanzenschutzmittel-Verzeichnis* (1 a year).

Stadtarchiv (City Archive): Schlosspl. 1, 38100 Braunschweig; tel. (531) 4704711; e-mail stadtarchiv@braunschweig.de; internet www.braunschweig.de/stadtarchiv; f. 1860; 125,000 documents since 1031, municipal records, charters, maps and plans since 1228, spec. collns on the history of the town; spec. historical archive on prominent Brunswick women; Head Dr HENNING STEINFÜHRER.

Stadtbibliothek: POB 3309, 38023 Braunschweig; Schlosspl. 2, 38100 Braunschweig; tel. (531) 4706801; e-mail stadtbibliothek@braunschweig.de; internet www.braunschweig.de/stadtbibliothek; f. 1861; 620,582 vols, medieval MSS, 426 incunabula, 2,500 maps and plans up to 1850; spec. colln on the history of the town; Dir Dr ANETTE HAUCAP-NASS; publs *Braunschweiger Werkstücke, Kleine Schriften* (irregular).

Universitätsbibliothek Braunschweig: Pockelsstr. 13, 38106 Braunschweig; tel. (531) 3915018; e-mail ub@tu-bs.de; internet www.biblio.tu-bs.de; f. 1748; exhibitions; various lectures; Digitale Bibliothek Braunschweig with nearly 11,600 documents; archive of the Technische Universität Braunschweig; 1,460,018 vols, 2,160 printed periodicals, 40,500 online journals, about 126,000 standards, 235,500 printed dissertations; 51,608 microfiches; areas of specialization incl. pharmacy (virtual library), DFG-Sondersammelgebiet, 15th- to 19th-century technology and natural history, children's books since 16th century, archive library of 6 publishing houses; Dir Prof. Dr DIETMAR BRANDES; Deputy Dir Dr BEATE NAGEL.

Bückeburg

Niedersächsisches Landesarchiv, Staatsarchiv Bückeburg: Schlosspl. 2, 31675 Bückeburg; tel. (5722) 967730; e-mail bueckeburg@nla.niedersachsen.de; internet www.nla.niedersachsen.de; f. 1961; archives of old county, later principality, of Schaumburg-Lippe and dist. of Schaumburg; central workshops for restoration and security filming for Lower Saxony; 40,000 vols, 4,100 documents, 35,000 maps; Dir Dr STEFAN BRÜDERMANN; publs *Inventare und kleinere Schriften des Staatsarchivs Bückeburg, Schaumburger Studien.*

Chemnitz

Stadtbibliothek (City Library): Moritzstr. 20, 09111 Chemnitz; tel. (371) 4884222; e-mail information@stadtbibliothek-chemnitz.de; internet www.stadtbibliothek-chemnitz.de; f. 1869; spec. colln of literature on local govt; 500,000 vols; Dir ELKE BEER.

Universitätsbibliothek (University library): 09107 Chemnitz; Str. der Nationen 62, 09111 Chemnitz; tel. (371) 53113100; e-mail sekretariat@bibliothek.tu-chemnitz.de; internet www.bibliothek.tu-chemnitz.de; f. 1836; attached to Chemnitz Univ. of Technology; 1,188,540 vols, 98,000 theses, 1,668 periodicals, 15,282,500 patents; Dir ANGELA MALZ.

Clausthal-Zellerfeld

Universitätsbibliothek der Technischen Universität Clausthal (Library of the Technical University of Clausthal): Leibnizstr. 2, 38678 Clausthal-Zellerfeld; tel. (5323) 722301; e-mail office@ub.tu-clausthal.de; internet www.ub.tu-clausthal.de; f. 1810; 490,000 vols, 660 current print journals, 10,000 ejournals, 805 periodicals, 5,000 geological maps; Dir Dr J. SCHÜLING; Librarian SILKE FRANK.

Coburg

Landesbibliothek (State Library): Schlosspl. 1, 96450 Coburg; tel. (9561) 85380; e-mail geschaeftsstelle@landesbibliothek-coburg.de; internet www.landesbibliothek-coburg.de; f. c. 1550, fmr ducal library of the duchy of Saxe-Coburg (until 1918); 430,000 vols, 600 periodicals; Dir Dr SILVIA PFISTER.

Staatsarchiv Coburg (State Archive of Coburg): Herrngasse 11, 96450 Coburg; tel. (9561) 427070; e-mail poststelle@staco.bayern.de; internet www.gda.bayern.de/archive/coburg; f. 13th century, present title 1939; archives of the duchy and republic of Saxe-Coburg, since 1920 county of Coburg; 380,000 documents; 8,000 vols; Dir JOHANNES HASLAUER.

Cologne

Deutsche Zentralbibliothek für Medizin (German National Library of Medicine): Gleueler Str. 60, 50931 Cologne; tel. (221) 4785600; e-mail info-koeln@zbmed.de; internet www.zbmed.de; f. 1908; virtual library of medicine (www.medpilot.de), virtual library of nutrition, environment and agriculture (www.greenpilot.de), open access journals in medicine (www.egms.de); offers document delivery by post and email; 1,600,000 vols and microforms, 6,000 current periodicals; Dir ULRICH KORWITZ; publs *German Medical Science, ZB MED's medical publishing portal.*

Erzbischöfliche Diözesan- und Dombibliothek mit Bibliothek St Albertus Magnus (Archbishop's Diocesean and Cathedral Library incl. Library St Albertus Magnus): POB 10 11 45, 50451 Cologne; Kardinal-Frings-Str. 1–3, 50668 Cologne; tel. (221) 16423781; e-mail dombibliothek@erzbistum-koeln.de; internet www.dombibliothek-koeln.de; f. 1738; 700,000 vols; Dir Prof. Dr HEINZ FINGER; publ. *Analecta Coloniensia, Libelli Rhenani.*

Historisches Archiv der Stadt Köln: Heumarkt 14, 50667 Cologne; tel. (221) 22122327; e-mail historischesarchiv@stadt-koeln.de; internet www.stadt-koeln.de/historisches-archiv; f. 1322; records since x AD 875; 140,000 vols; Dir Dr BETTINA SCHMIDT-CZAIA; publ. *Mitteilungen.*

Kunst- und Museumsbibliothek mit Rheinischem Bildarchiv (Art and Museum Library of the City of Cologne): Kattenbug 18–24, 50667 Cologne; tel. (221) 22122438; e-mail kmb@stadt-koeln.de; internet www.museenkoeln.de/kmb; f. 1957; 420,000 vols, 792 current journals; Dir Dr ELKE PURPUS.

LVR—Archivberatungs- und Fortbildungszentrum, Abteilung Archivberatung (Archive and Museums Office of the Rhineland, Department of Archive Services): POB 2140, 50250 Pulheim; Ehrenfriedstr. 19, 50259 Pulheim; tel. (2234) 98540; e-mail afz@lvr.de; internet www.rafo.lvr.de; f. 1929; archive of the Landschaftsverband Rheinland with sources of the last 200 years; collns relating to local history; 16,500 vols; Dir Dr ARIE NABRINGS; Sec. SANDRA KASCHUBA; publs *Archivhefte* (archival science in Rheinland), *Inventare nichtstaatlicher Archive* (inventories of non-state archives in Rheinland), *Rheinprovinz* (regional history of Rheinland).

Stiftung Rheinisch-Westfälisches Wirtschaftsarchiv zu Köln (Rheinisch-Westfälisches Foundation Economic Archives Cologne): Unter Sachsenhausen 10–26, 50667 Cologne; tel. (221) 1640800; f. 1906; economic records of the region; research and publ. of research results; lending and reference library of business documents; 35,000 vols; Dir Dr ULRICH S. SOÉNIUS; publ. *Schriften zur rheinisch-westfälischen Wirtschaftsgeschichte.*

Universitäts- und Stadtbibliothek Köln (University and City Library of Cologne): Universitätsstr. 33, 50931 Cologne; tel. (221) 4702374; e-mail eauskunft@ub.uni-koeln.de; internet www.ub.uni-koeln.de; f. 1920; 3.6m vols, 8,500 periodicals; Dir Prof. Dr W. SCHMITZ; Deputy Dir Dr R. THIELE.

Darmstadt

Hessisches Staatsarchiv Darmstadt (State Archive of Hesse): Karolinenpl. 3, 64289 Darmstadt; tel. (6151) 165900; e-mail poststelle@stad.hessen.de; internet www.staatsarchiv-darmstadt.hessen.de; f. 1567; Dir Dr KLAUS-DIETER RACK (acting); publs *Darmstädter Archivdokumente für den Unterricht, Darmstädter Archivenschriften, Geschichte im Archiv.*

Universitäts- und Landesbibliothek Darmstadt (University and State Library Darmstadt): Magdalenenstr. 8, 64289 Darmstadt; tel. (6151) 165850; e-mail info@ulb.tu-darmstadt.de; internet www.ulb.tu-darmstadt.de; f. 1568; 3,900,000 vols, 4,090 MSS, 2,050 incunabula, 17,000 musicalia, 29,000 maps, 4,600,000 German and European patent documents, 425,000 digital documents, 22,000 ejournals; Dir Dr HANS-GEORG NOLTE-FISCHER.

Dessau

Anhaltische Landesbücherei Dessau (Anhalt Library of Dessau): Zerbster Str. 10, 06844 Dessau-Rosslau; tel. (340) 2042048; e-mail bibliothek@dessau-rosslau.de; internet www.bibliothek.dessau.de; f. 1898; 208,209 vols, 133 incunabula, 599 MSS, 205 current periodicals; Dir GABRIELE SCHNEIDER.

Detmold

Landesarchiv Nordrhein-Westfalen-Staats- und Personenstandarchiv Detmold (National archives of North Rhine-Westphalia State and People Condition Archives Detmold): Willi-Hofmann-Str. 2, 32756 Detmold; tel. (5231) 7660; e-mail stadt@lav.nrw.de; internet www.archive.nrw.de; f. 1957 (fmrly Lippisches Landesarchiv, f. 16th century); archives of fmr regions of Lippe (12th century to 1947) and Minden (1815–1947), Dominion of Vianen (Netherlands), Detmold (since 1947); spec. collns: genealogy, French Citizens' Registers, Parish Registers, Jewish and Dissenters' Registers of Westphalia (1808–1874); copies of registers of births, deaths and marriages (1874–1938); 72,000 vols; Dir Dr JUTTA PRIEUR-POHL.

Lippische Landesbibliothek Detmold: Hornsche Str. 41, 32756 Detmold; tel.

(5231) 926600; e-mail llbmail@llb-detmold.de; internet www.llb-detmold.de; f. 1614; 550,000 vols, 10,000 MSS; Dir DETLEV HELLFAIER.

Dortmund

Stadt- und Landesbibliothek Dortmund (City and State Library of Dortsmund): Max-von-der-Gruen-Platz 1–3, 44137 Dortmund; tel. (231) 5023209; e-mail stlb@stadtdo.de; internet www.bibliothek.dortmund.de; f. 1907; spec. colln of MSS and autographs and material on Westphalia; music dept; 1,200,000 vols; Dir ULRICH MOESKE; Librarian HANS-CHRISTIAN WIRTZ; publs *Autographenausstellungen* (irregular), *Mitteilungen* (irregular), *Mitteilungen aus dem Literaturarchiv Kulturpreis der Stadt Dortmund* (every 2 years).

Stiftung Westfälisches Wirtschaftsarchiv (WWA) (Foundation of the Westphalian Economic Archive): Märkische Str. 120, 44141 Dortmund; tel. (231) 5417296; e-mail wwado@dortmund.ihk.de; internet www.archive.nrw.de; f. 1941; records of the economic, social and industrial history of Westphalia and the Ruhr; research; 4,000 shelf-metres of records; 50,000 vols; Dir Dr KARL-PETER ELLERBROCK.

Universitätsbibliothek Dortmund (University Library of Dortmund): 44227 Dortmund; Vogelpothsweg 76, 44227 Dortmund; tel. (231) 7554001; e-mail information@ub.tu-dortmund.de; internet www.ub.tu-dortmund.de; f. 1965; 1.76m. vols, 7,500,000 patents; Dir Dr JOACHIM KREISCHE.

Dresden

Sächsische Landesbibliothek–Staats- und Universitätsbibliothek Dresden (SLUB) (Saxony State and University Library Dresden): 01054 Dresden; Zellescher Weg 18, 01069 Dresden; tel. (351) 4677123; e-mail generaldirektion@slub-dresden.de; internet www.slub-dresden.de; f. 1996; 5,292,235 vols, 147,000 theses, 131,000 maps, 178,000 tapes and records, 3,500,000 photographs, 131,000 standards, 17,577 current periodicals; Dir-Gen. Prof. Dr THOMAS BÜRGER; Deputy Dir-Gen. Dr ACHIM BONTE; Deputy Dir-Gen. MICHAEL GOLSCH; publs *Bibliographie Geschichte der Technik* (1 a year), *BIS:Das Magazin der Bibliotheken in Sachsen* (4 a year), *Sächsische Bibliographie* (1 a year), *SLUB-Kurier* (4 a year).

Sächsisches Staatsarchiv—Hauptstaatsarchiv Dresden (Sächsisches Public Archives—Main public Archives Dresden): POB 100 444, 01074 Dresden; Wilhelm-Buck-Str. 4, 01097 Dresden; tel. (351) 5643740; e-mail poststelle@sta.smi.sachsen.de; internet www.archiv.sachsen.de; f. 1834; 71,000 vols; Dir Dr JÜRGEN RAINER WOLF; publs *Einzelveröffentlichungen*, *Schriftenreihe des Sächsischen Hauptstaatsarchivs* (13 vols).

Städtische Bibliotheken Dresden (Dresden Public Libraries): Freibergerstr. 35, 01067 Dresden; tel. (351) 8648101; e-mail mail@bibo-dresden.de; internet www.bibo-dresden.de; f. 1910; 751,490 vols; Man. Dr AREND FLEMMING; Deputy Man. ROMAN RABE.

Duisburg

Stadtarchiv Duisburg (City Archives of Duisburg): Karmelpl. 5 (Am Innenhafen), 47049 Duisburg; tel. (203) 2832154; e-mail stadtarchiv@stadt-duisburg.de; internet www.archive.nrw.de; f. 12th century; admin., research into local and city history; reference library on local history and customs of Duisburg and Lower Rhine; 60,000 vols; Dir Dr HANS GEORG KRAUME; publs *Duisburger Forschungen*, *Duisburger Geschichtsquellen*.

Stadtbibliothek Duisburg (City Library): Düsseldorfer Str. 5–7, 47049 Duisburg; tel. (203) 2834218; e-mail stadtbibliothek@stadt-duisburg.de; internet www.duisburg.de/micro/stadtbibliothek; f. 1901; 700,000 vols, 1,177 periodicals; Dir Dr JAN-PIETER BARBIAN; publs *Blickpunkt Bibliothek* (26 a year), *Literary Catalogues* (Amerikanische Literatur, Schiller, Heine, Brecht, Böll, Kafka).

Düsseldorf

Bibliotek und Archiv des Heinrich-Heine-Instituts (Heinrich Heine Institute Library and Archives): Bilker Str. 12–14, 40213 Düsseldorf; tel. (211) 8995572; e-mail elena.camaiani@duesseldorf.de; internet www.duesseldorf.de/heineinstitut; f. 1970; exhibitions, readings, lectures; 55,000 vols, literature by/on Heinrich Heine, documents regarding the revolutionary 'Vormärz' era and the Rhineland as well as music and arts in Düsseldorf; MSS collns from 1600 to the present, more than 130 literary, musical and artistic estates, among them the largest colln of autographs by Heinrich Heine, spec. collns of autographs by Clara and Robert Schumann as well as the Düsseldorf School of Painting; Dir Dr SABINE BRENNER-WILCZEK; Librarian ELENA CAMAIANI; publs *Archiv-Bibliothek-Museum* (irregular), *Heine-Studien* (irregular).

Landesarchiv Nordrhein-Westfalen (National archives North Rhine-Westfalen): Graf-Adolf-Str. 67, 40210 Düsseldorf; tel. (211) 1592380; e-mail poststelle@lav.nrw.de; internet www.lav.nrw.de; f. 2004, consists of Zentrale Dienste, Fachbereich Grundsätze, Abteilung Rheinland (f. 1832), Abteilung Westfalen (f. 1829), Abteilung Ostwestfalen-Lippe (f. 1955); Pres. (vacant); publ. *Archivar. Zeitschrift für Archivwesen* (4 a year).

Universitäts- und Landesbibliothek Düsseldorf (University and State Library of Düsseldorf): Universitätsstr. 1, 40225 Düsseldorf; tel. (211) 8112030; e-mail sekretariat@ulb.hhu.de; internet www.ulb.hhu.de; f. 1970; 2,440,755 vols, 27,741 ejournals, 3,534 in print; Dir Dr IRMGARD SIEBERT.

Eichstätt

Universitätsbibliothek Eichstätt-Ingolstadt (University Library of Eichstätt-Ingolstadt): Universitätsallee 1, 85072 Eichstätt; tel. (8421) 9321330; e-mail ub-direktion@ku.de; internet www.ku.de/bibliothek; f. 16th century; developed from fmr Library of Diocesan Seminary and State Library; spec. collns: theology, archives of Asscn of German Catholic Press and of Asscn of Catholic publishers and booksellers, Schlecht music library and MSS, Glossner Oriental and Judaistic library, archives and library of the Inklings Soc.; 1,890,559 vols, 437,855 units of non-book materials, 6,143 MSS, 1,257 incunabula, 2,856 periodicals; Dir Dr MARIA LÖFFLER; publs *Aus den Beständen der Universitätsbibliothek Eichstätt*, *Bibliographien der Universitätsbibliothek Eichstätt*, *Kataloge der Universitätsbibliothek Eichstätt*, *Schriften der Universitätsbibliothek Eichstätt*.

Erfurt

Stadt- und Regionalbibliothek Erfurt: 40.03, 99111 Erfurt; Dompl. 1, 99084 Erfurt; tel. (361) 6551590; e-mail bibliothek@erfurt.de; internet bibliothek.erfurt.de; f. 1897; 526,712 vols (237,312 vols in scientific spec. collns), 500 periodicals; Dir Dr EBERHARD KUSBER.

Universitätsbibliothek Erfurt (University Library Erfurt): POB 900222, 99105 Erfurt; Nordhäuser Str. 63, 99089 Erfurt; tel. (361) 7375800; e-mail information.ub@uni-erfurt.de; internet www.uni-erfurt.de/bibliothek; f. 1994; 1,115,216 vols, 1,950 MSS, 639 incunabula; Dir Dr ECKART GERSTNER.

Erlangen

Universitätsbibliothek Erlangen-Nürnberg (University Library of Erlangen-Nuremberg): 91051 Erlangen; Universitätsstr. 4, 91054 Erlangen; tel. (9131) 8523950; e-mail hb.info@bib.uni-erlangen.de; internet www.ub.uni-erlangen.de; f. 1743; spec. collns on education, science and philosophy; 5,400,000 vols, 895,000 theses, 2,374 MSS, 140 papyri, 2,136 incunabula; Dir KONSTANZE SÖLLNER.

Frankfurt am Main

Bibliothek des Freien Deutschen Hochstifts (Library of the Freies Deutsches Hochstift): Frankfurter Goethe-Haus, Grosser Hirschgraben 23–25, 60311 Frankfurt am Main; tel. (69) 13880262; e-mail jseng@goethehaus-frankfurt.de; internet www.goethehaus-frankfurt.de; f. 1859; 130,000 vols, 40,000 MSS and handwritten letters, 500 paintings and 16,000 prints on public display in the graphic art colln; Dir Dr JOACHIM SENG; Librarian NORA SCHWARZ.

Deutsche Nationalbibliothek (German National Library): Adickesallee 1, 60322 Frankfurt am Main; tel. (69) 15250; e-mail info-f@dnb.de; internet www.dnb.de; f. 1912, present name and status 2006; central archival library and nat. bibliographic centre; collects, permanently archives, documents, records German and German-language publs from 1913 onwards; spec. collns incl. Reichsbibliothek 1848, German exile literature 1933–1945, Anne-Frank-Shoah-Bibliothek; 27m. vols; Dir-Gen. Dr ELISABETH NIGGEMANN; publ. *Deutsche Nationalbibliografie* (online, irregular).

Constituent Libraries:

Deutsche Nationalbibliothek—Deutsches Musikarchiv: Deutscher Pl. 1, 04103 Leipzig; tel. (341) 22710; e-mail info-dma@dnb.de; internet www.dnb.de; f. 1970; 1,740,000 vols; Head of Dept MICHAEL FERNAU.

Deutsche Nationalbibliothek Leipzig: Deutscher Pl. 1, 04103 Leipzig; tel. (341) 22710; e-mail info-1@dnb.de; internet www.dnb.de; f. 1912; 26,160,516 vols; Dir-Gen. Dr ELISABETH NIGGEMANN.

Institut für Stadtgeschichte (Stadtarchiv) (Institute for Urban History (City Archives)): Münzgasse 9, 60311 Frankfurt am Main; tel. (69) 21230142; e-mail michael.fleiter@stadt-frankfurt.de; internet www.stadtgeschichte-ffm.de; f. 1436, fmrly Historical City Archives; municipal records; documents since 9th century, registers since 13th century, deeds since 14th century; records on Frankfurt from other archives; historical records in writings, pictures and sound; 50,000 vols, 750 current periodicals; Dir Dr EVELYN BROCKHOFF.

Universitätsbibliothek Johann Christian Senckenberg: Bockenheimer Landstr. 134–138, 60325 Frankfurt am Main; tel. (69) 79839205; e-mail auskunft@ub.uni-frankfurt.de; internet www.ub.uni-frankfurt.de; f. 1484, current name adopted 2005 following merger of Stadt- und Universitätsbibliothek Frankfurt am Main (StUB) and the Senckenbergische Bibliothek (SeB) 2005; 9.4m. vols; Dir HEINER SCHNELLING; Deputy Dir Dr ANGELA HAUSINGER.

Freiberg im Sachsen

Technische Universität Bergakademie Freiberg Universitätsbibliothek 'Georgius Agricola' (Technical University of

Mountain Academy Freiberg University Library 'Georgius Agricola'): Agricolastr. 10, 09599 Freiberg im Sachsen; tel. (3731) 392959; e-mail unibib@ub.tu-freiberg.de; internet tu-freiberg.de/ze/ub; f. 1765; 717,200 vols, 2,820 autographs, 26,000 standards, 4,470 cards, 71,300 univ. publs; spec. collns: mining and metallurgy, geosciences; Dir KATRIN STUMP; Deputy Dir SABINE ALBANI; publ. *Veröffentlichungen der Bibliothek 'Georgius Agricola' der TU Bergakademie Freiberg* (irregular).

Freiburg im Breisgau

Albert-Ludwigs-Universität Universitätsbibliothek: POB 1629, 79016 Freiburg im Breisgau; Rempartstr. 10–16, 79098 Freiburg im Breisgau; tel. (761) 2033918; e-mail info@ub.uni-freiburg.de; internet www.ub.uni-freiburg.de; f. 1457; 3.1m. vols, incl. dissertations; Dir Dr ANTJE KELLERSOHN.

Deutsches Volksliedarchiv (German Folksong Archive): Rosastraße 17–19, 79098 Freiburg im Breisgau; tel. (761) 7050310; e-mail info@dva.uni-freiburg.de; internet www.dva.uni-freiburg.de; f. 1914; 70,000 vols; Head Dr MICHAEL FISCHER (acting); publs *Deutsche Volkslieder mit ihren Melodien, Historisch-kritisches Liederlexikon 2005ff* (1 a year, online, www.liederlexikon.de).

Stadtarchiv Freiburg im Breisgau (City Archive of Freiburg im Breisgau): Grünwälderstr. 15, 79098 Freiburg im Breisgau; tel. (761) 2012701; e-mail stadtarchiv@stadt.freiburg.de; internet www.freiburg.de; f. 1840; 5 km of records from 12th century to present day; 75,000 vols; Dir Dr ULRICH P. ECKER; publs *Neue Reihe, Schau-ins-Land, Veröffentlichungen aus dem Archiv der Stadt Freiburg*.

Fulda

Hochschul- und Landesbibliothek: Heinrich-von-Bibra-Pl. 12, 36037 Fulda; tel. (661) 96409850; e-mail hlb@hlb.hs-fulda.de; internet www.hs-fulda.de/hlb; f. 1778; 747,000 vols, 3,922 MSS and 431 incunabula; Dir Dr MARIANNE RIETHMÜLLER; Deputy Librarian BERTHOLD WEISS.

Giessen

Universitätsbibliothek Giessen (University Library of Giessen): Otto-Behaghel-Str. 8, 35394 Giessen; tel. (641) 9914032; e-mail auskunft@bibsys.uni-giessen.de; internet www.ub.uni-giessen.de; f. 1612; 3,887,035 vols, 400,197 dissertations, 2,721 MSS, 877 incunabula, 2,841 papyri; Dir Dr PETER REUTER; Librarian CORINA THOMÄ.

Görlitz

Oberlausitzische Bibliothek der Wissenschaften Görlitz (Upper Lusatian Library of Science in Görlitz): Handwerk 2, 02826 Görlitz; tel. (3581) 671350; e-mail olb@goerlitz.de; internet olb.goerlitz.de; f. 1950 (original library 1726 and 1779); scientific, historical and gen. library incl. rare book colln, life and work of Jacob Boehme; 140,000 vols; Librarian MATTHIAS WENZEL.

Gotha

Research Library Gotha: POB 100130, 99851 Gotha; Schloss Friedenstein, 99867 Gotha; tel. (361) 7375530; e-mail bibliothek.gotha@uni-erfurt.de; internet www.uni-erfurt.de/bibliothek/fb; f. 1647; 692,019 vols, 1,062 incunabula, 186,216 maps; Dir Dr KATHRIN PAASCH.

Göttingen

Niedersächsische Staats- und Universitätsbibliothek Göttingen (State and University Library of Gottingen): Platz der Göttinger Sieben 1, 37073 Göttingen; tel. (551) 395212; e-mail sekretariat@sub.uni-goettingen.de; internet www.sub.uni-goettingen.de; f. 1734; 4,275,494 vols, 51,830 electronic publs, 11,695 print periodicals, 27,741 electronic periodicals, 13,680 MSS, 3,109 incunabula, 313,166 map sheets, 1,522,058 microforms; Dir and Head Librarian Prof. Dr NORBERT LOSSAU.

Greifswald

Universitätsbibliothek (University Library): Felix-Hausdorff-Str. 10, 17489 Greifswald; tel. (3834) 861515; e-mail ub@uni-greifswald.de; internet www.ub.uni-greifswald.de; f. 1604; attached to Ernst Moritz Arndt Univ. of Greifswald; 3.2m. vols; Dir Dr PETER WOLFF; Librarian PETRA ZEPERNICK.

Halle am Saale

Bibliothek der Deutschen Akademie der Naturforscher Leopoldina (Library of the German Academy of the Nature Scientists Leopoldina): POB 110543, 06019 Halle/Saale; August-Bebel-Str. 50A, 06108 Halle/Saale; tel. (345) 47239147; e-mail bibliothek@leopoldina.org; internet www.leopoldina.org; f. 1731; 268,000 vols; Dir JOCHEN THAMM.

Universitäts- und Landesbibliothek Sachsen-Anhalt (University and City library of Sachsen-Anhalt): August-Bebel-Str. 13/50, 06108 Halle/Saale; tel. (345) 5522000; e-mail direktion@bibliothek.uni-halle.de; internet bibliothek.uni-halle.de; f. 1696; spec. collns incl. Middle East and N Africa, regional studies and history of Saxony-Anhalt; Ponikau's library; library of the Deutsche Morgenländische Gesellschaft (German Oriental Society); 19 br. libraries; 5.6m. vols, 20,400 periodicals (print and online), 14,600 online journals, 115,200 MSS and autographs; Dir Dr HEINER SCHNELLING; publs *Hercynia, Regionalbibliographie Sachsen-Anhalt* (online), *Schlechtendalia*.

Hamburg

Bibliothek des Max-Planck-Institut für Ausländisches und Internationales Privatrecht (Max-Planck Institute Library for Foreign and International Private Law): Mittelweg 187, 20148 Hamburg; tel. (40) 419000; e-mail knudsen@mpipriv.de; internet www.mpipriv.mpg.de; f. 1926; 460,000 vols, 4,000 periodicals; Dir Prof. Dr HOLGER KNUDSEN.

Commerzbibliothek der Handelskammer Hamburg: Adolphspl. 1, 20457 Hamburg; tel. (40) 36138138; e-mail info@commerzbibliothek.de; internet www.commerzbibliothek.de; f. 1735 by the Commerzdeputation, later Hamburg Chamber of Commerce; historical map series; Hamburg newspapers 1721–1915; 180,000 vols on law, economics and social science; Head DAGMAR GROOTHUIS.

Deutsches Bibel-Archiv (German Bible Archive): Von Melle Park 6, 20146 Hamburg; tel. (40) 428384781; internet www.slm.uni-hamburg.de/berichte97_00/bibel.html; f. 1931; biblical traditions in German literature and art; Bible translations; 8,000 vols; Dir Prof. Dr HEIMO REINITZER; publs *Abhandlungen und Vorträge, Bibel und deutsche Kultur, Naturalis historia bibliae, Vestigia bibliae*.

Staats- und Universitätsbibliothek Hamburg 'Carl von Ossietzky': Von-Melle-Park 3, 20146 Hamburg; tel. (40) 428382233; e-mail auskunft@sub.uni-hamburg.de; internet www.sub.uni-hamburg.de; f. 1479; deposit library for literature published in Hamburg; spec. collns: political science, admin. science, literature on indigenous peoples of Northern America and the Arctic, sea and coastal fishing, literature on Portugal and Spain; 5,238,576 vols, 106,194 maps, music sheets, broadsheets, 736,808 audiovisual material, microforms, 89,087 MSS (incl. autographs, literary remains and 990 papyri), 666,662 electronic entities, 56,853 ejournals; Dir Prof. Dr GABRIELE BEGER; Deputy Dir Dr PETRA BLÖDORN-MEYER; publs *Kataloge der Handschriften, F. G. Klopstock: Werke und Briefe, Publikationen der Staats- und Universitätsbibliothek Hamburg*.

Staatsarchiv der Freien und Hansestadt Hamburg (State Archive of the Free and Hanseatic City of Hamburg): Kattunbleiche 19, 22041 Hamburg; tel. (40) 428313200; e-mail poststelle@staatsarchiv.hamburg.de; internet www.hamburg.de/staatsarchiv; f. 13th century; history of Hamburg; 150,000 books; Dir Dr UDO SCHÄFER; publs *Hamburgisches Urkundenbuch, Veröffentlichungen*.

Hanover

Gottfried Wilhelm Leibniz Bibliothek—Niedersächsische Landesbibliothek (Gottfried Wilhelm Leibniz Library): Waterloostr. 8, 30169 Hanover; tel. (511) 12670; e-mail information@gwlb.de; internet www.gwlb.de; f. 1665; colln of coats of arms and seals; Leibniz archive; 2,000,000 vols, 5,061 periodicals, 4,428 MSS, 80,000 autographs, 395 incunabula; Dir Dr GEORG RUPPELT; Deputy Dir PETER MARMEIN.

Niedersächsisches Landesarchiv (Regional Archive of Lower Saxony): Am Archiv 1, 30169 Hanover; tel. (511) 1206601; e-mail poststelle@nla.niedersachsen.de; internet www.nla.niedersachsen.de; fmrly Hauptstaatsarchiv Hannover, 32,000 m shelf-space; Dir Dr BERND KAPPELHOFF.

Stadtbibliothek (City Library): Hildesheimer Str. 12, 30169 Hanover; tel. (511) 16842169; e-mail stadtbibliothek-hannover@hannover-stadt.de; internet www.stadtbibliothek-hannover.de; f. 1440; gen. information about the city and region; 17 brs; 680,000 vols, 2,000 periodicals; Dir Dr CAROLA SCHELLE-WOLFF; Divisional Dir UWE NIETIEDT.

Technische Informationsbibliothek und Universitätsbibliothek Hannover (TIB/UB) (German National Library of Science and Technology and University Library Hanover): POB 60 80, 30060 Hanover; Welfengarten 1B, 30167 Hanover; tel. (511) 7622268; e-mail auskunft@tib.uni-hannover.de; internet www.tib.uni-hannover.de; f. 1831; German research reports, patent specifications, standards; conf. proceedings; doctoral dissertations and American reports (microforms); spec. emphasis on technical and scientific literature in Eastern and East Asian languages; acts as German Nat. Library of Science and Technology; 9,000,000 vols, 64,000 ejournals, 16,800 specialized journals; Dir UWE ROSEMANN.

Heidelberg

Bibliothek des Max-Planck-Instituts für Ausländisches Öffentliches Recht und Völkerrecht (Library of the Max Planck Institute for Comparative Public Law and International Law): Im Neuenheimer Feld 535, 69120 Heidelberg; tel. (6221) 4821; e-mail library@mpil.de; internet www.mpil.de/ww/de/pub/bibliothek.cfm; f. 1924; 625,000 vols, 2,680 periodicals; Dir Dr HARALD MÜLLER; Deputy Dir RUTH FUGGER.

Universitätsbibliothek (University Library): Plöck 107–109, 69117 Heidelberg; tel. (6221) 542380; e-mail ub@uni-hd.de; internet www.ub.uni-heidelberg.de; f. 1386; 3,000,000 vols, 6,600 MSS, 1,800 incunabula;

Dir Dr VEIT PROBST; publs *Schriften der Universitätsbibliothek*, *Theke* (online).

Jena

Thüringer Universitäts- und Landesbibliothek Jena (Thuringer University and State Library of Jena): POB, 07737 Jena; Bibliothekspl. 2, 07743 Jena; tel. (3641) 940000; e-mail thulb_auskunft@thulb.uni-jena.de; internet www.thulb.uni-jena.de; f. 1558; 3,994,658 vols; Dir Dr SABINE WEFERS; Deputy Dir GABOR KUHLES; Deputy Dir MICHAEL LÖRZER; publ. *Thüringen-Bibliographie* (online).

Karlsruhe

Badische Landesbibliothek (State Library of Baden): POB 1429, 76003 Karlsruhe; Erbprinzenstr. 15, 76133 Karlsruhe; tel. (721) 1752222; e-mail informationszentrum@blb-karlsruhe.de; internet www.blb-karlsruhe.de; f. 1500; 2,394,352 vols, 18,258 current periodicals; 1,363 incunabula; Dir Dr JULIA DAME HILLER GAERTRINGEN; Deputy Dir Dr VOLKER WITTENAUER.

Bibliothek des Bundesgerichtshofs (Library of the Federal Court): Herrenstr. 45A, 76133 Karlsruhe; tel. (721) 1595000; e-mail bibliothek@bgh.bund.de; internet www.bundesgerichtshof.de; f. 1950; law library; 439,000 vols; Deputy Dir Dr MARCUS OBERT.

KIT-Bibliothek: POB 6920, 76049 Karlsruhe; tel. (721) 60843101; e-mail infodesk@bibliothek.kit.edu; internet www.bibliothek.kit.edu; f. 1840; 2,051,000 vols, 70,750 print and electronic periodicals; Dir FRANK SCHOLZE; Librarian SABINE BENZ.

Landesarchiv Baden-Württemberg—Generallandesarchiv Karlsruhe (National Archives Baden-Wurttemberg—General Archives Karlsruhe): Nördliche Hildapromenade 3, 76133 Karlsruhe; tel. (721) 9262206; e-mail glakarlsruhe@la-bw.de; internet www.landesarchiv-bw.de/glak; f. 1803; 79,000 vols on Baden history, 130,000 documents, 42,000 MSS, 3.5m. report files; Dir Prof. Dr WOLFGANG ZIMMERMANN; Archivist Dr PETER EXNER; publ. *Zeitschrift für die Geschichte des Oberrheins* (1 a year).

Kassel

Documenta Archiv: Untere Karlsstr. 4, 34117 Kassel; tel. (561) 7874022; e-mail documentaarchiv@stadt-kassel.de; internet www.documentaarchiv.de; f. 1961; also a research institute; administers the Arnold Bode Estate and the Harry Kramer Estate; 30,000 monographs, 60,000 exhibition catalogues, 150 journals and magazines, 2,000 new acquisitions annually, 2,000 file archives, 250,000 newspaper clippings, 150,000 invitations, 25,000 slides, 3,000 video titles, 450 DVDs, 10,000 photographs, 1,000 Ektachromes, 2,000 artist portraits; Librarian PETRA HINCK; Librarian SABINE FRANKE.

Universitätsbibliothek Kassel-Landesbibliothek und Murhardsche Bibliothek der Stadt Kassel: 34111 Kassel; Diagonale 10, 34127 Kassel; tel. (561) 8042117; e-mail direktion@bibliothek.uni-kassel.de; internet www.uni-kassel.de/ub; f. 1580; 6 departmental libraries; 1,826,710 vols, 30,309 MSS, 28,901 musical scores, 18,127 maps, 20,054 autographs, 3,277 print and 32,884 e-periodicals; Head Librarian Dr AXEL HALLE; Deputy Librarian Dr SALINA BRAUN.

Kiel

Deutsche Zentralbibliothek für Wirtschaftswissenschaften—Leibniz Informationszentrum Wirtschaft (ZBW) (German National Library of Economics—Leibniz Information Centre for Economics): Düsternbrooker Weg 120, 24105 Kiel; tel. (431) 8814555; e-mail info@zbw.eu; internet www.zbw.eu; f. 1919; attached to Leibniz Information Centre for Economics; 4,200,000 vols; Dir Prof. Dr KLAUS TOCHTERMANN; publs *Intereconomics—Review of European Economic Policy* (6 a year), *Wirtschaftsdienst—Zeitschrift für Wirtschaftspolitik* (Journal for Economic Policy, 12 a year).

Schleswig-Holsteinische Landesbibliothek (Schleswig-Holstein Federal State Library): Wall 47–51, 24103 Kiel; tel. (431) 6967733; e-mail landesbibliothek@shlb.de; internet www.shlb.de; f. 1895; culture, civilization, literature, musical scores and pictorial representations of topics concerning Schleswig-Holstein, editors of Schleswig-Holstein Bibliography and Dictionary of Schleswig-Holstein biography; spec. colln on chess; 280,000 vols and literary bequests of about 100 authors and scholars; Dir Dr JENS AHLERS.

Universitätsbibliothek Kiel (Kiel University Library): Leibnizstr. 9, 24118 Kiel; tel. (431) 8804701; e-mail auskunft@ub.uni-kiel.de; internet www.ub.uni-kiel.de; f. 1665; 3 depts and 49 specialist libraries; 4,630,000 vols, 6,600 periodicals, 32,693 ejournals; spec. colln on Scandinavian languages, history and literature; Dir Dr ELSE MARIA WISCHERMANN.

Koblenz

Bundesarchiv (Federal Archives): 56064 Koblenz; Potsdamer Str. 1, 56075 Koblenz; tel. (261) 5050; e-mail koblenz@bundesarchiv.de; internet www.bundesarchiv.de; f. 1952; central archives of the Fed. Republic; 2,174,421 vols; 331,327 m of records of Reich, Federal and GDR Govts, agencies, political parties, private asscns; colln of private papers; 1.1m. documentaries and newsreels (incl. 149,000 feature films), 12.4m. photographs; 81,100 posters, 1.9m. maps and technical drawings, 45,500 audio recordings, 10.3m. files of machine-readable data held at various sites throughout Germany; Pres. Dr MICHAEL HOLLMANN.

Landesbibliothekszentrum Rheinland-Pfalz/Rheinische Landesbibliothek: Bahnhofpl. 14, 56068 Koblenz; tel. (261) 91500101; e-mail info@lbz-rlp.de; internet www.lbz-rlp.de; f. 1987, became part of Landesbibliothekszentrum Rheinland-Pfalz 2004; 649,370 vols, 2,894 periodicals, spec. references to northern part of Rhineland-Palatinate; Central Educational Library of Rhineland-Palatinate; Dir Dr ANNETTE GERLACH; Man. LARS JENDRAL.

Landeshauptarchiv Koblenz (Central State Archive): POB 20 10 47, 56010 Koblenz; tel. (261) 91290; e-mail post@landeshauptarchiv.de; internet www.landeshauptarchiv.de; f. 1832; history of Rhineland Palatinate and fmr territories; 50,000 linear m of archives; Dir Dr ELSBETH ANDRE.

Konstanz

Bibliothek der Universität Konstanz (University of Konstanz Library): Universitätsstr. 10, 78464 Konstanz; tel. (7531) 882871; e-mail information.ub@uni-konstanz.de; internet www.ub.uni-konstanz.de; f. 1965; 2,000,000 vols, 110,000 theses; Dir Dr PETRA HAETSCHER; Vice-Dir OLIVER KOHL-FREY; Librarian EDGAR FIXL.

Landshut

Staatsarchiv Landshut: Burg Trausnitz, 84036 Landshut; tel. (871) 923280; e-mail poststelle@stala.bayern.de; internet www.gda.bayern.de; f. 1753; 34,000 vols; Dir Dr M. RÜTH.

Leipzig

Leibniz-Institut für Länderkunde eV Geographische Zentralbibliothek und Archiv für Geographie (Central Library and Archive of the Leibniz Institute for Regional Geography): Schongauer Str. 9, 04328 Leipzig; tel. (341) 60055129; e-mail bibliothek@ifl-leipzig.de; internet www.ifl-leipzig.de; f. 1896; 220,000 vols, spec. colln of maps and atlases of the 16th–18th centuries, geography archives; Dir Prof. Dr SEBASTIAN LENTZ; Librarian DOROTHEE ZICKWOLFF; Librarian Dr HEINZ PETER BROGIATO; publs *Beiträge zur Regionalen Geographie* (2 a year), *Berichte zur Deutschen Landeskunde* (4 a year), *Europa regional* (4 a year), *Forum IfL*.

Leipziger Städtische Bibliotheken: POB 100927, 04009 Leipzig; Wilhelm-Leuschner-Pl. 10/11, 04107 Leipzig; tel. (341) 1235343; e-mail stadtbib@leipzig.de; internet www.stadtbibliothek.leipzig.de; f. 1677; 1,065,182 vols; Head BIRGIT SPAZIER.

Stadtarchiv (Municipal Archives): 04092 Leipzig; Torgauer Str. 74, 04318 Leipzig; tel. (341) 24290; e-mail stadtarchiv@leipzig.de; internet www.leipzig.de/stadtarchiv; f. c. 1100; Dir Dr BEATE BERGER.

Universitätsbibliothek Leipzig (University Library): Beethovenstr. 6, 04107 Leipzig; tel. (341) 9730516; e-mail auskunft@ub.uni-leipzig.de; internet www.ub.uni-leipzig.de; f. 1543; Hirzel colln contains books and material by and about Johann Wolfgang von Goethe (1749–1832); 23 brs; 5.4m. vols, 7,200 periodicals; Dir Prof. Dr ULRICH JOHANNES SCHNEIDER; Deputy Dir CHARLOTTE BAUER.

Lübeck

Archiv der Hansestadt Lübeck: Mühlendamm 1–3, 23552 Lübeck; tel. (451) 1224152; e-mail archiv@luebeck.de; internet archiv.luebeck.de; f. 1298; municipal archives and documents of the churches, recognized public bodies, instns and private persons; 40,000 vols; Dir Dr JAN LOKERS; Deputy Dir Prof. Dr ROLF HAMMEL-KIESOW.

Bibliothek der Hansestadt Lübeck (Library of the Hanseatic City of Lübeck): Hundestr. 5–17, 23552, Lübeck; tel. (451) 1224114; e-mail stadtbibliothek@luebeck.de; internet www.stadtbibliothek.luebeck.de; f. 1616; 1.1m. vols, 3,686 maps, 39,719 vols of printed music, 11,922 MSS; Dir B. HATSCHER.

Ludwigsburg

Landesarchiv Baden-Württemberg—Staatsarchiv Ludwigsburg: Arsenalpl. 3, 71638 Ludwigsburg; tel. (7141) 186310; e-mail staludwigsburg@la-bw.de; internet www.landesarchiv-bw.de/stal; f. 1868; archives for the admin. dist. of Stuttgart (Nordwürttemberg); 38,000 m of deeds; over 600,000 files from the time of the Third Reich and the time after the Second World War; 43,500 vols; Pres. Prof. Dr ROBERT KRETZSCHMAR; Dir Dr PETER MÜLLER; Deputy Dir Prof. Dr STEPHAN MOLITOR.

Magdeburg

Landeshauptarchiv Sachsen-Anhalt (State Archive of Saxony-Anhalt): POB 4023, 39105 Magdeburg; Hegelstr. 25, 39104 Magdeburg; tel. (391) 598060; e-mail poststelle@lha.mi.sachsen-anhalt.de; internet www.sachsen-anhalt.de; f. 1823; archives of state public record offices; 103,000 vols; 48,000 m of records, 158,000 maps; Dir Dr ULRIKE HÖROLDT.

Stadtbibliothek Magdeburg: Breiter Weg 109, 39104 Magdeburg; tel. (391) 5404880; e-mail stadtbibliothek@magdeburg.de; internet www.magdeburg-stadtbibliothek

.de; f. 1525; 404,000 vols; Dir INES GONSCHORECK.

Mainz

Universitätsbibliothek Mainz (University Library of Mainz): Jakob-Welder-Weg 6, 55128 Mainz; tel. (6131) 3922644; e-mail info@ub.uni-mainz.de; internet www.ub.uni-mainz.de; f. 1946; 3,200,000 vols, 814 MSS; Dir Dr A. BRANDTNER.

Wissenschaftliche Stadtbibliothek: Rheinallee 3B, 55116 Mainz; tel. (6131) 122649; e-mail stb.direktion@stadt.mainz.de; internet www.bibliothek.mainz.de; f. 1477, as University Library, taken over by the City of Mainz in 1805; 683,000 vols, 2,364 incunabula, 1,332 MSS; Dir Dr STEPHAN FLIEDNER (acting); publs *Beiträge zur Geschichte der Stadt Mainz*, *Mainzer Zeitschrift*, *Veröffentlichungen der Bibliotheken der Stadt Mainz*.

Mannheim

Universitätsbibliothek Mannheim (Mannheim University Library): Schloss Schneckenhof West, 68131 Mannheim; tel. (621) 1812948; e-mail zbinfo@bib.uni-mannheim.de; internet www.bib.uni-mannheim.de; 2.2m. vols; Dir CHRISTIAN BENZ; Deputy Librarian ANNETTE KLEIN.

Marbach am Neckar

Deutsches Literatur Archiv Marbach (German Literature Archives of Marbach): Schillerhöhe 8–10, 71672 Marbach; tel. (7144) 8480; e-mail info@dla-marbach.de; internet www.dla-marbach.de; f. 1895; German literature since 1750; 800,000 vols, large colln of autographs and documents, 1,100 legacies; Man. Dir Prof. Dr ULRICH RAULFF; publs *Marbacher Bibliothek* (1 a year), *Marbacher Katalog* (1 a year), *Marbacher Magazin* (4 a year).

Marburg

Deutsches Adelsarchiv (Germany Archive of the Nobility): Schwanallee 21, 35037 Marburg; tel. (6421) 26162; e-mail info@adelsarchiv.de; internet www.vdda.org; f. 1945; genealogy of German nobility; 20,000 vols; Dir Dr CHRISTOPH FRANKE; publ. *Genealogisches Handbuch des Adels*.

Forschungsbibliothek des Herder-Instituts: Gisonenweg 5–7, 35037 Marburg; tel. (6421) 184150; e-mail bibliothek@herder-institut.de; internet www.herder-institut.de; f. 1950; research library specializing in the history and culture of East Central Europe (Poland, Czech Republic, Slovakia, Estonia, Latvia, and Lithuania); 480,000 vols; Chief Librarian Dr JÜRGEN WARMBRUNN; Deputy Librarian Dr JAN LIPINSKY.

Hessisches Staatsarchiv Marburg (Hessiches Public Archives Marburg): Friedrichspl. 15, 35037 Marburg; tel. (6421) 92500; e-mail poststelle@stama.hessen.de; internet www.staatsarchiv-marburg.hessen.de; f. 1870; 150,097 books, 130,120 charts, 330,004 maps and plans, 66 km of records of the Electorate of Hesse-Kassel, the abbeys of Fulda, Hersfeld, the principality of Waldeck; Dir Dr ANDREAS HEDWIG; publs *Repertorien*, *Schriften*.

Universitätsbibliothek (University Library): POB 1920, 35008 Marburg; Wilhelm-Röpke-Str. 4, 35039 Marburg; tel. (6421) 2821319; e-mail verwaltung@ub.uni-marburg.de; internet www.uni-marburg.de/bis; f. 1527; 2,057,493 vols, 716,860 theses, 3,020 MSS; Dir Dr H. NEUHAUSEN; Librarian ANDREAS SEIBEL.

Mönchengladbach

Bibliothek Wissenschaft und Weisheit (Library of Theology and Philosophy): Franziskanerstr. 30, 41063 Mönchengladbach; tel. (2161) 899135; e-mail herbert.schneider.ofm@gmx.de; f. 1929; attached to Zentralbibliothek der Kölnischen Franziskanerprovinz (fmrly Hochsculbibliothek); 70,000 vols; Dir Dr P. HERBERT SCHNEIDER.

Stadtbibliothek (City Library): Blücherstr. 6, 41061 Mönchengladbach; tel. (2161) 256345; e-mail stadtbibliothek@moenchengladbach.de; internet www.stadtbibliothek-mg.de; f. 1904; special colln on social and political questions, library of the 'Volksverein für das katholische Deutschland 1890–1933'; 440,443 vols; Head BRIGITTE BEHRENDT; Head GUIDO WEYER.

Munich

Bayerische Staatsbibliothek: Ludwigstr. 16, 80539 Munich; tel. (89) 286380; e-mail direktion@bsb-muenchen.de; internet www.bsb-muenchen.de; f. 1558; deposit library for Bavaria; 10,062,195 vols, 1.2m. microforms, 97,000 MSS, 63,437 current periodicals, 400,000 maps, 360,000 scores, 88,000 audiovisual items, 2.2m. single sheets and photographs; Dir-Gen. Dr ROLF GRIEBEL; Deputy Dir Dr KLAUS CEYNOWA; publs *Bibliotheksforum Bayern* (4 a year), *Bibliotheksmagazin* (3 a year).

Bayerisches Hauptstaatsarchiv (Bavarian Main State Archives): POB 22 11 52, 80501 Munich; Schönfeldstr. 5–11, 80539 Munich; tel. (89) 286382596; e-mail poststelle@bayhsta.bayern.de; internet www.gda.bayern.de; f. 13th century, reorganized 1978; comprises 5 departments: (1) Ältere Bestände (since 8th century): 278,000 charters, 600,000 documents and vols, 25,000 maps and plans; (2) Neuere Bestände (since 19th century): 5,300 charters, 1,400,000 documents, 180,000 maps and plans; (3) Geheimes Hausarchiv: 10,500 charters, 27,300 documents and vols, 9,900 pictures; (4) Kriegsarchiv: 500,000 documents and vols, 135,000 maps and plans, 110,000 pictures; (5) Nachlässe und Sammlungen: collns of private papers, publs, posters, pictures, etc.; Dir Dr GERHARD HETZER; publs *Archivalische Zeitschrift*, *Archive in Bayern*, *Bayerische Archivinventare*, *Nachrichten aus den Staatlichen Archiven Bayerns*.

Bibliothek des Deutschen Museums: Museumsinsel 1, 80538 Munich; tel. (89) 2179224; e-mail bibliothek@deutsches-museum.de; internet www.deutsches-museum.de/bibliothek; f. 1903; research library for history of science and technology; 946,893 vols; Dir Dr HELMUT HILZ; Deputy Dir CHRISTIAN KNOOP.

Deutsches Bucharchiv München (Institut für Buchwissenschaften) (German Book Archives Munich (Institute for Book Sciences)): Bibliothek und Dokumentationsstelle, Literaturhaus München, Salvatorpl. 1, 80333 Munich; tel. (89) 2919510; e-mail kontakt@bucharchiv.de; internet www.bucharchiv.de; f. 1948; documentation, scientific and technical information about books and periodicals; spec. library for book research; 30,000 vols, 180 periodicals; Dir Prof. Dr LUDWIG DELP.

Deutsches Patent- und Markenamt (German Patent and Trademark Office): Library, 80297 Munich; Zweibrückenstr. 12, 80331 Munich; tel. (89) 21950; e-mail info@dpma.de; internet www.dpma.de; f. 1877; 985,290 vols, 48.7m. patent specifications; Pres. CORNELIA RUDLOFF-SCHÄFFER; Vice-Pres. GÜNTHER SCHMITZ.

Evangelischer Presseverband für Bayern eV (Evangelical Press Society of Bavaria): Birkerstr. 22, 80636 Munich; tel. (89) 121720; e-mail redaktion@epv.de; internet www.epv.de; f. 1963; Pres. Dr ROLAND GERTZ.

Münchner Stadtbibliothek (City Library of Munich): Rosenheimer Str. 5, 81667 Munich; tel. (89) 480983313; e-mail stb.zentraledienste.sekretariat.kult@muenchen.de; internet www.muenchner-stadtbibliothek.de; f. 1843; 3m. vols; Dir Dr WERNER SCHNEIDER.

Staatsarchiv (State Archive): Schönfeldstr. 3, 80539 Munich; tel. (89) 286382525; e-mail poststelle@stam.bayern.de; internet www.gda.bayern.de; f. 1814; 11,295,125 files (records), 9,157 documents (charts), 30,455 maps and plans, 25,000 vols (library); Dir Dr PETER FLEISCHMANN.

Stadtarchiv (City Archives): Winzererstr. 68, 80797 Munich; tel. (89) 2330308; e-mail stadtarchiv@muenchen.de; internet www.muenchen.de/stadtarchiv; f. 1520; 65,000 vols, 78,000 documents, 16m. deeds, 22,000 maps and plans, 1,200,000 photos and postcards, 3,050 soundtracks, 1,500 films, 26,629 posters; Dir Dr MICHAEL STEPHAN; Deputy Dir HANS-JOACHIM HECKER.

Universitätsbibliothek der LMU München: Geschwister-Scholl-Pl. 1, 80539 Munich; tel. (89) 21802428; e-mail direktion@ub.uni-muenchen.de; internet www.ub.uni-muenchen.de; f. 1473; 4,700,000 vols, 3,300 MSS, incl. 650 from the Middle Ages, 179 estates, containing about 55,000 autographs, 475,000 old books published before 1900, rare book colln with around 13,000 vols, ex libris colln, broadsheet and handbill collns; Dir Dr KLAUS-RAINER BRINTZINGER.

Universitätsbibliothek der Technischen Universität (Technical University Library): Arcisstr. 21, 80333 Munich; tel. (89) 28928601; e-mail infocenter@ub.tum.de; internet www.ub.tum.de; f. 1868; 1,859,075 vols; Dir Dr REINER KALLENBORN.

Münster

Landesarchiv Nordrhein-Westfalen Abteilung Westfalen (National Archives North Rhine-Westfalen Department of Westfalen): Bohlweg 2, 48147 Münster; tel. (251) 48850; e-mail westfalen@lav.nrw.de; internet www.archive.nrw.de; f. 1829 as Provinzialarchiv for Westphalia, current name adopted 2008; 30,000 m of documents and 100,000 charters, from 9th century to the present; 180,000 vols; Pres. Prof. Dr WILFRIED REININGHAUS; Dir Dr MECHTHILD BLACK-VELTRUP.

LWL-Archivamt für Westfalen (Landschaftsverband Westfalen-Lippe) (LWL Archives for Westfalen (Landscape Federation of Westfalen-Lippe): Jahnstr. 26, 48133 Münster; tel. (251) 5913890; e-mail lwl-archivamt@lwl.org; internet www.lwl-archivamt.de; f. 1927; non-state archives; training of archivists; 30,000 vols; Dir Dr MARCUS STUMPF; publs *Inventare der nichtstaatlichen Archive Westfalens*, *Westfälische Quellen und Archivpublikationen*, *Archivpflege in Westfalen-Lippe* (Journal, 2 a year), *Texte und Untersuchungen zur Archivpflege*.

Universitäts- und Landesbibliothek (University and State Library): POB 8029, 48043 Münster; Krummer Timpen 3, 48143 Münster; tel. (251) 8324021; e-mail sekretariat.ulb@uni-muenster.de; internet www.ulb.uni-muenster.de; f. 1588, refounded 1902; attached to Univ. of Münster; 2,334,800 vols incl. 305,660 theses, 821 incunabula, 1,406 MSS, 10,000 current periodicals, 3,214 ejournals; Dir Dr BEATE TRÖGER.

Nuremberg

Bibliothek des Germanischen Nationalmuseum: POB 119580, 90105 Nuremberg; Kornmarkt 1, 90402 Nuremberg; tel. (911) 1331151; e-mail bibliothek@gnm.de; internet www.gnm.de; f. 1852; arts, history of civilization, German-speaking regions; special colln of art-history works since AD 800; 650,000 vols, 3,380 MSS, 3,000 16th-century prints, 1,708 current periodicals; Dir Dr EBERHARD SLENCZKA; Librarian Dr JOHANNES POMMERANZ; publs *Anzeiger des Germanischen Nationalmuseums* (1 a year), *Schrifttum zur Deutschen Kunst* (1 a year).

Landeskirchliches Archiv der Evangelisch-Lutherischen Kirche in Bayern: Veilhofstr. 8, 90489 Nürnberg; tel. (911) 588690; e-mail archiv@elkb.de; internet www.archiv-elkb.de; f. 1931; 170,000 vols, 12,000 m of documents; Dir Dr ANDREA SCHWARZ; Archivist Dr JÜRGEN KÖNIG.

Staatsarchiv Nürnberg (State Archive): Archivstr. 17, 90408 Nuremberg; tel. (911) 935190; e-mail poststelle@stanu.bayern.de; f. 1806; archives of middle Franconia since the Middle Ages; incl. Nuremberg trial documents; 50,000 vols; Dir Dr FLEISCHMANN.

Stadtarchiv Nürnberg: Marientorgraben 8, 90402 Nuremberg; tel. (911) 2312770; e-mail stadtarchiv@stadt.nuernberg.de; internet www.stadtarchiv.nuernberg.de; f. 1865; reference library of 50,000 vols; Dir Dr MICHAEL DIEFENBACHER; Librarian WALTER GEBHARDT; publs *Ausstellungskataloge, Nürnberger Werkstücke zur Stadt- und Landesgeschichte, Quellen und Forschungen zur Geschichte und Kultur der Stadt Nürnberg*.

Stadtbibliothek im Bildungscampus Nürnberg: Gewerbemuseumspl. 4, 90403 Nürnberg; tel. (911) 2312790; e-mail stadtbibliothek-nuernberg@stadt.nuernberg.de; internet www.stadtbibliothek.nuernberg.de; f. 1370; 90,000 vols, 3,132 MSS, 2,140 incunabula; Dir ELISABETH STRÄTER.

Universitätsbibliothek Erlangen-Nürnberg, Wirtschafts- und Sozialwissenschaftliche Zweigbibliothek (University Library of Erlangen-Nuremberg, Economics and Social Studies Branch): Lange Gasse 20, 90403 Nuremberg; tel. (911) 5302830; e-mail bibliothek@wiso.uni-erlangen.de; internet www.ub.uni-erlangen.de; f. 1919; 243,000 vols, 1,390 current periodicals; Dir JOACHIM HENNECKE.

Offenbach am Main

Deutscher Wetterdienst Deutsche Meteorologische Bibliothek (German Meteorological Service National Meteorological Library): POB 100465, Frankfurter Str. 135, 63067 Offenbach am Main; tel. (69) 80624276; e-mail bibliothek@dwd.de; internet www.dwd.de/bibliothek; f. 1847; nat. library for meteorology and climatology, inter-library loans; 180,000 vols, 20 incunabula, 14,000 pre-1900, 1,000 current periodicals; Chief Librarian BRITTA BOLZMANN.

Oldenburg

Landesbibliothek: Pferdemarkt 15, POB 3480, 26024 Oldenburg; tel. (441) 7992800; e-mail lbo@lb-oldenburg.de; internet www.lb-oldenburg.de; f. 1792; regional library; 850,434 vols, 95,851 microforms and 1,121 MSS; Dir C. ROEDER; Librarian Dr K.-P. MÜLLER; Librarian M. KLINKOW; Librarian Dr R. FIETZ; publ. *Schriften*.

Niedersächsisches Staatsarchiv in Oldenburg (State Archive of Lower Saxony): Damm 43, 26135 Oldenburg; tel. (441) 9244100; e-mail oldenburg@nla.niedersachsen.de; internet www.staatsarchive.niedersachsen.de; f. before 1615; public record office for the fmr dist. of Oldenburg; record repository with 13,000 m of files; contributes to *Veröffentlichungen der Niedersächsischen Archivverwaltung*; 66,000 vols; Dir Prof. Dr GERD STEINWASCHER; Librarian HANNELORE KLÖCKER.

Osnabrück

Niedersächsisches Landesarchiv—Staatsarchiv Osnabrück (State Archive of Lower Saxony): Schloßstr. 29, 49074 Osnabrück; tel. (541) 331620; e-mail osnabrueck@nla.niedersachsen.de; internet www.staatsarchive.niedersachsen.de; f. 1869; 82,000 vols; Dir Dr BIRGIT KEHNE.

Passau

Staatliche Bibliothek (National Library): Michaeligasse 11, 94032 Passau; tel. (851) 7564400; e-mail sbp_info@staatliche-bibliothek-passau.de; internet www.staatliche-bibliothek-passau.de; f. 1612 as Jesuit library, refounded 1803 as nat. library; spec. collns: philosophy, theology, regional history and literature, emblematic, Jesuitica, printed graphics; 343,000 vols, 151 MSS, 328 incunabula; Dir Dr MARKUS WENNERHOLD.

Universitätsbibliothek (University Library): 94030 Passau; Innstr. 29, 94032 Passau; tel. (851) 5091630; e-mail ubinfo@uni-passau.de; internet www.ub.uni-passau.de; f. 1976; attached to Universität Passau; 2,020,889 vols, 88,000 theses, 2,387 printed journals, 28,367 electronic journals; Dir Dr STEFFEN WAWRA.

Potsdam

Brandenburgisches Landeshauptarchiv in Potsdam (Brandenburg State Central Archive): POB 60 04 49, 14404 Potsdam; Zum Windmühlenberg, 14469 Potsdam; tel. (331) 56740; e-mail poststelle@blha.brandenburg.de; internet www.blha.de; f. 1949; brs at Lübben (Spreewald) and Frankfurt an der Oder; 109,000 vols, 46,000 linear m of files; Dir Dr KLAUS NEITMANN; publs *Brandenburgische Archive* (1 a year), *Quellen, Findbücher und Inventare des Brandenburgischen Landeshauptarchivs, Veröffentlichungen des Brandenburgischen Landeshauptarchivs*.

Stadt- und Landesbibliothek Potsdam (State and City Library of Potsdam): Am Kanal 47, 14467 Potsdam; tel. (331) 2896600; e-mail slb@bibliothek.potsdam.de; internet www.bibliothek.potsdam.de; f. 1969; Brandenburg colln, Gottfried Benn colln; presently located at Friedrich-Ebert-Str. 4 due to renovation at main site; 585,000 vols; Dir MARION MATTEKAT.

Regensburg

Bischöfliche Zentralbibliothek (Central Library of the Diocese of Regensburg): St Petersweg 11–13, 93047 Regensburg; tel. (941) 5972513; e-mail bibliothek@bistum-regensburg.de; internet www.bistum-regensburg.de; f. 1972; incl. the library of St Jacob's Irish monastery and Proske's music library; 314,217 vols, 419 journals, with spec. collns on ascetics and sacred music; Dir PAUL MAI; Librarian ROSEMARIE WEINBERGER.

Staatliche Bibliothek Regensburg: Gesandtenstr. 13, 93047 Regensburg; tel. (941) 6308060; e-mail info@staatliche-bibliothek-regensburg.de; internet www.staatliche-bibliothek-regensburg.de; f. 1816; 350,000 vols, 13,264 maps, 16,302 microforms; spec. colln on regional history; Dir Dr BERNHARD LUEBBERS.

Universitätsbibliothek Regensburg (University Library of Regensburg): 93042 Regensburg; Universitätsstr. 31, 93053 Regensburg; tel. (941) 9433901; e-mail rafael.ball@bibliothek.uni-regensburg.de; internet www.bibliothek.uni-regensburg.de; f. 1964; 3,600,000 vols, 6,824 print periodicals, 21,847 ejournals, 376 databases; all fields of science except technology and agriculture; spec. holdings: Library of the Regensburg Botanical Soc., Prince Thurn and Taxis Court Library and Central Archive, Regensburg Portrait Gallery, Archive of Historical Radio Commercials Int. projects, Scientometrics and Library management; Dir Dr RAFAEL BALL; publ. *Bibliometrie—Praxis und Forschung* (online, www.bibliometrie-pf.de).

Rostock

Universitätsbibliothek (University Library): 18051 Rostock; Albert-Einstein-Str. 6, 18059 Rostock; tel. (381) 4988601; e-mail direktion.ub@uni-rostock.de; internet www.uni-rostock.de/ub; f. 1569; attached to Univ. of Rostock; 2,300,000 vols, 330,000 theses, 1,729 print periodicals, 24,039 e-periodicals, 3,350 MSS, 6,085,000 patents, 49,500 standards, 337 databases; Dir RENATE BÄHKER (acting).

Saarbrücken

Landesarchiv Saarbrücken (State Archive of Saarbrücken): Dudweilerstr. 1, 66133 Saarbrücken; tel. (681) 50100; e-mail landesarchiv@landesarchiv.saarland.de; internet www.landesarchiv.saarland.de; f. 1948; 170 official publs.; 25,000 vols, 14,000 m of archives concerning the Saar; Dir Dr LUDWIG LINSMAYER.

Saarländische Universitäts- und Landesbibliothek (University and State Library of the Saarland): POB 15 11 41, 66041 Saarbrücken; tel. (681) 3022070; e-mail sulb@sulb.uni-saarland.de; internet www.sulb.uni-saarland.de; f. 1950; Medical Library in Homburg, Saar; 1,720,000 vols incl. 375,000 theses; Dir Dr BERND HAGENAU; Librarian MATTHIAS MÜLLER.

Schleswig

Landesarchiv Schleswig-Holstein (National Library of Schleswig-Holstein): Prinzenpalais, 24837 Schleswig; tel. (4621) 861800; e-mail landesarchiv@la.landsh.de; internet www.schleswig-holstein.de/la; f. 1870; 35,000 m of documents since 1059; 450,000 m of documentary film on Schleswig-Holstein; 137,000 vols; Dir Prof. Dr RAINER HERING.

Schwerin im Meckl

Landesbibliothek Mecklenburg-Vorpommern (State Library of Mecklenburg-Vorpommern): Johannes-Stelling-Str. 29, 19053 Schwerin; tel. (385) 58879210; e-mail lb@lbmv.de; internet www.lbmv.de; f. 1779; 650,000 vols; Dir Dr FRANK PILLE.

Sigmaringen

Landesarchiv Baden-Württemberg–Abteilung Staatsarchiv Sigmaringen: POB 1638, 72486 Sigmaringen; Karlstr. 1–3, 72488 Sigmaringen; tel. (7571) 101551; e-mail stasigmaringen@la-bw.de; internet www.landesarchiv-bw.de/stas; f. 1865; archives of Regierungsbezirk Tübingen and Sigmaringen municipal archive; family archives of the princes of Hohenzollern, barons of Stauffenberg, etc.; 19,900 m of archives since 11th century; 67,000 vols; Co-Dir Dr FRANZ-JOSEF ZIWES; Dir Dr VOLKER TRUGENBERGER.

Speyer

Landesarchiv: Otto-Mayer-Str. 9, 67346 Speyer; tel. (6232) 91920; e-mail bibliothek@landesarchiv-speyer.de; internet www.landeshauptarchiv.de/speyer; f. 1817; historical archives of the Palatinate (878–1798), of the French admin. until 1815 and the Bavarian admin. until 1945; current accessions of admins in the Palatinate and Rheinhesse; colln of maps; 60,817 vols; Dir Dr WALTER RUMMEL; Librarian PETRA GREHL.

Landesbibliothekszentrum/Pfälzische Landesbibliothek (Regional Library of Palatinate): Otto-Mayer-Str. 9, 67346 Speyer; tel. (6232) 9006224; e-mail info.plb@lbz-rlp.de; internet www.lbz-rlp.de; f. 1921, part of the Landesbibliothekszentrum Rheinland-Pfalz 2004; 1,096,840 vols on all subjects, with spec. reference to the Palatinate and the Saar, 4,181 periodicals, incl. library of the Historischer Verein der Pfalz; Dir Dr ANNETTE GERLACH; Man. UTE BAHRS.

Stuttgart

Bibliothek der Staatlichen Hochschule für Musik und Darstellende Kunst (Library of the State Academy of Music and Representing Art): Urbanstr. 25, 70182 Stuttgart; tel. (711) 2124664; e-mail bibliothek@mh-stuttgart.de; internet www.mh-stuttgart.de; f. 1857; 21,373 vols, 88,475 musical scores, 3,623 records, 9,802 CDs, 576 DVDs; Chief Librarian CLAUDIA NIEBEL.

Bibliothek des Instituts für Auslandsbeziehungen (Library of Institute for Foreign Relations): POB 10 24 63, 70020 Stuttgart; Charlottenpl. 17, 70173 Stuttgart; tel. (711) 2225147; e-mail bibliothek@ifa.de; internet cms.ifa.de/info/bibliothek; f. 1917; 415,000 vols, 2,300 current periodicals, 11,000 microfilms; Head GUDRUN CZEKALLA; publ. *Kultur-Austausch* (online).

Bibliothek für Zeitgeschichte in der Württembergischen Landesbibliothek: Konrad Adenauer Str. 8, 70173 Stuttgart; tel. (711) 2124516; e-mail bfz@wlb-stuttgart.de; internet www.wlb-stuttgart.de/sammlungen/bibliothek-fuer-zeitgeschichte; f. 1915; contemporary history, political sciences, military sciences, esp. concerning First and Second World Wars, and other conflicts since the beginning of 20th century; 380,000 vols, 450 current periodicals, and special collns (photographs, maps, leaflets, posters, microfiches, etc.); Dir Dr CHRISTIAN WESTERHOFF (acting); publ. *Schriften der Bibliothek für Zeitgeschichte–Neue Folge*.

Fraunhofer-Informationszentrum Raum und Bau (IRB) (Fraunhofer Information Centre for Planning and Building): POB 80 04 69, 70504 Stuttgart; Nobelstr. 12, 70569 Stuttgart; tel. (711) 9702500; internet www.irb.fraunhofer.de; f. 1941; information centre for architecture and town and regional planning in Germany; 117,200 vols and 5,600 research reports, standards, test certificates and licences; Dir THOMAS H. MORSZECK; publs *ARCONIS Wissen zum Planen und Bauen und zum Baumarkt* (4 a year), *Kurzberichte aus der Bauforschung* (6 a year).

Hauptstaatsarchiv Stuttgart: Konrad-Adenauer-Str. 4, 70173 Stuttgart; tel. (711) 2124335; e-mail hstastuttgart@la-bw.de; internet www.landesarchiv-bw.de/hstas; history and regional studies of SW Germany, with particular reference to Württemberg and Baden-Württemberg since 9th century; archives of 107,000 charters, 18,000 m of files and vols, 40,000 maps and plans, 100,000 seals and arms; Dir Dr NICOLE BICKHOFF; Deputy Dir Dr ALBRECHT ERNST.

Rathausbibliothek der Landeshauptstadt Stuttgart (Town Hall Library of the State Capital of Stuttgart): Marktpl. 1, 70173 Stuttgart; tel. (711) 21691212; internet www.stuttgart.de/rathausbibliothek; f. archives 1730; history of Stuttgart and Württemberg, legal history, public admin.; 129,585 vols; spec. collns incl. first editions published in Stuttgart during 18th–19th centuries; Dir GABY VOLLMER.

Universitätsbibliothek (University Library): POB 104941, 70043 Stuttgart; Holzgartenstr. 16, 70174 Stuttgart; tel. (711) 68582222; e-mail sekretariat@ub.uni-stuttgart.de; internet www.ub.uni-stuttgart.de; f. 1829; attached to Univ. of Stuttgart; 1,301,638 vols incl. 451,098 theses, 1,830 print and 22,018 e-periodicals, 122,930 standards, 20,399 e-documents; Dir WERNER STEPHAN; publs *Dissertationen und Hochschulschriften der Universität Stuttgart* (2 a year), *Reden und Aufsätze der Universität Stuttgart* (irregular).

Universitätsbibliothek Hohenheim: Garbenstr. 15, 70599 Stuttgart; tel. (711) 45922096; e-mail ubmail@uni-hohenheim.de; internet ub.uni-hohenheim.de; f. 1818; agriculture, sciences, economics; 500,000 vols; Dir KARL-WILHELM HORSTMANN; Asst Dir Dr CHRISTINE BORKOWSKI.

Württembergische Landesbibliothek (State Library of Württemberg): POB 10 54 41, 70047 Stuttgart; Konrad Adenauerstr. 8, 70173 Stuttgart; tel. (711) 2124454; e-mail direktion@wlb-stuttgart.de; internet www.wlb-stuttgart.de; f. 1765; 5,851,247 vols, 7,087 incunabula; large colln of old Bibles; 15,469 MSS; Hölderlin archive and Stefan George archive; music and ballet colln; Dir Dr HANNSJÖRG KOWARK; Deputy Dir MARTINA LÜLL.

Trier

Bibliothek des Priesterseminars Trier (Library of the Seminar for priests Trier): POB 1330, 54203 Trier; Jesuitenstr. 13, 54290 Trier; tel. (651) 9484141; e-mail bibliothek@bps-trier.de; internet www.bps-trier.de; f. 1805; 490,717 vols on philosophy and theology, 543 theological MSS, and 122 incunabula; Librarian REINHOLD BOHLEN; Librarian PATRICK TRAUTMANN.

Stadtbibliothek und Stadtarchiv Trier (Municipal Library and Archives of Trier): Weberbach 25, 54290 Trier; tel. (651) 7181429; e-mail stadtbibliothek@trier.de; internet cms.trier.de/weberbach; f. Library 1804, Archive in 1894; Library: developed from the fmr Jesuit Library (f. 1560) and Univ. Library (f. 1722); contains considerable parts of the libraries of the dissolved religious instns of the region of Trier (since 1802); contains 2,800 MSS and about 3,000 incunabula; 422,000 younger media; scientific library; colln incl. a Gutenberg Bible, and a page of the *Codex Egberti*; UNESCO world heritage site; archives inc. into the library; contains royal and papal charters since the 8th century for the above named religious instns and (since 1149) for the town, 5 km of younger archive material (originating from the town, the religious instns and from the Counts of Kesselstatt); collns: portraits, maps, photographs; Chief Librarian Prof. Dr MICHAEL EMBACH; Chief Archivist Dr REINER NOLDEN; publs *Ausstellungskataloge Trierer Bibliotheken*, *Landeskundliche Vierteljahrsblätter*, *Ortschroniken des Trierer Landes*, *Rheinland-pfälzische Bibliographie*.

Universitätsbibliothek: Universitätsring 15, 54296 Trier; tel. (651) 2012420; e-mail auskunft@uni-trier.de; internet www.ub.uni-trier.de; f. 1970; attached to Univ. of Trier; open to the public; colln of 803 papyri, colln of Chinese and Japanese woodcuts; 2,210,461 vols; Dir Dr HILDEGARD MÜLLER.

Tübingen

Universitätsbibliothek Tübingen (University Library of Tübingen): POB 2620, 72016 Tübingen; Wilhelmstr. 32, 72074 Tübingen; tel. (7071) 2972846; e-mail sekretariat@ub.uni-tuebingen.de; internet www.ub.uni-tuebingen.de; f. in the last quarter of 15th century; central library of Tübingen Univ.; archive and lending library; platforms and support for e-Learning and online publs for mems of the univ.; 3,672,271 vols, journals, microfilms and microfiches, 2,800,000 vols and journals in faculty libraries, 2,148 incunabula, 8,863 MSS; Dir Dr MARIANNE DÖRR; Deputy Dir Dr EBERHARD PIETZSCH; publ. *Index theologicus (Ixtheo) Zeitschrifteninhaltsdienst Theologie*.

Ulm

Stadtbibliothek Ulm (City Library of Ulm): POB, 89070 Ulm; Vestgasse 1, 89073 Ulm; tel. (731) 1614140; e-mail stadtbibliothek@ulm.de; internet www.stadtbibliothek.ulm.de; f. 1516; 565,187 vols, 490 current periodicals; spec. collns: the arts, regional history; Dir JÜRGEN LANGE; Deputy Dir ALEXANDER ROSENSTOCK; Sec. BRIGITTE KENDEL.

Weimar

Herzogin Anna Amalia Bibliothek: Pl. der Demokratie 1, 99423 Weimar; tel. (3643) 545200; e-mail haab@klassik-stiftung.de; internet www.klassik-stiftung.de/einrichtungen/herzogin-anna-amalia-bibliothek; f. 1691; history of literature, art and music; special collns: German literature of the Classical Period (1750–1850), Faust, Liszt, Nietzsche, Shakespeare; 50,000 vols destroyed by fire September 2004; reopened in 2007; 62,000 destroyed books to be restored by 2016; 1,000,000 vols; Dir Dr MICHAEL KNOCHE; publs *Jugend 1896–1945* (online), *Simplicissimus 1896–1945* (online), *Weimarer Goethe-Bibliographie* (online), *Weimarer Nietzsche-Bibliographie* (online).

Thüringisches Hauptstaatsarchiv Weimar (Central State Archive of Thuringia in Weimar): POB 2726, 99408 Weimar; Marstallstr. 2, 99423 Weimar; tel. (3643) 8700; e-mail weimar@staatsarchive.thueringen.de; internet www.thueringen.de/de/staatsarchive; f. 1547; Dir Dr BERNHARD POST.

Wiesbaden

Bibliothek des Statistischen Bundesamtes (Library of the Federal Statistical Office): 65180 Wiesbaden; Gustav-Stresemann-Ring 11, 65180 Wiesbaden; tel. (611) 754573; e-mail bibliothek@destatis.de; internet www.destatis.de; f. 1948; colln of statistical records, esp. on the economic and demographic devt of all countries; colln of literature for statistical methods, economic science and related topics; 500,000 vols, 1,000 journals; Head of Library HARTMUT RAHM.

Hessisches Hauptstaatsarchiv Wiesbaden (Hesse Main State Archive): Mosbacher Str. 55, 65187 Wiesbaden; tel. (611) 8810; e-mail poststelle@hhstaw.hessen.de; internet www.hauptstaatsarchiv.hessen.de; f. 1963; regional documents since 10th century; Dir Dr KLAUS EILER; publ. *Nassauische Annalen* (1 a year).

Hochschul- und Landesbibliothek RheinMain (University and State Library RheinMain): Rheinstr. 55–57, 65185 Wiesbaden; tel. (611) 94951800; e-mail direktion-hlb@hs-rm.de; internet www.hs-rm.de/bibliothek; f. 1813; 1,065,978 vols, 2,332 current periodicals, 325 MSS and 445 incunabula; Dir Dr MARION GRABKA.

Wolfenbüttel

Herzog August Bibliothek: POB 1364, 38299 Wolfenbüttel; Lessingplatz 1, 38304 Wolfenbüttel; tel. (5331) 8080; e-mail auskunft@hab.de; internet www.hab.de; f.

1572; cultural history from the Middle Ages to the Enlightenment; 902,711 vols, 12,296 MSS, 3,500 incunabula, 3,600 artists' books; Dir Prof. Dr HELWIG SCHMIDT-GLINTZER; Librarian CHRISTIAN HOGREFE; publs *Ausstellungskataloge*, *Kleine Schriften*, *Repertorien zur Erforschung der frühen Neuzeit*, *Wolfenbütteler Abhandlungen zur Renaissance-Forschung*, *Wolfenbütteler Arbeiten zur Barockforschung*, *Wolfenbütteler Barocknachrichten*, *Wolfenbütteler Beiträge*, *Wolfenbütteler Bibliotheks-Informationen*, *Wolfenbütteler Forschungen*, *Wolfenbütteler Hefte*, *Wolfenbütteler Mittelalter-Studien*, *Wolfenbütteler Notizen zur Buchgeschichte*, *Wolfenbütteler Renaissance-Mitteilungen*, *Wolfenbütteler Schriften zur Geschichte des Buchwesens*.

Niedersächsisches Staatsarchiv (State Archive of Lower Saxony): Forstweg 2, 38302 Wolfenbüttel; tel. (5331) 9350; e-mail wolfenbuettel@nla.niedersachsen.de; internet www.staatsarchive.niedersachsen.de; f. 16th century; contains documents and records of the province of Brunswick; 60,000 vols; Dir Dr HORST-RÜDIGER JARCK; Dir Dr BRAGE BEI DER WIEDEN.

Worms

Stadtarchiv im Raschi Haus (Municipal Archive in the Raschi House): Hintere Judengasse 6, 67547 Worms; tel. (6241) 8534700; e-mail stadtarchiv@worms.de; internet www.stadtarchiv.worms.de; Judaic museum; colln of records, documents and maps; Head Archivist Dr GEROLD BOENNEN.

Stadtbibliothek (City Library): Marktpl. 10, 67547 Worms; tel. (6241) 8534209; e-mail stadtbibliothek@worms.de; internet www.stadtbibliothek-worms.de; f. 1881; 324,000 vols, 165 incunabula; spec. collns on Luther, Kant and the Nibelungenlied; Dir Dr BUSSO DIEKAMP; publ. *Der Wormsgau*.

Wuppertal

Stadtbibliothek (City Library): Kolpingstr. 8, 42103 Wuppertal; tel. (202) 5632373; e-mail stadtbibliothek@stadt.wuppertal.de; internet www.wuppertal.de/stadtbib; f. 1852; central library and 9 brs; spec. collns: theology, early socialism; Else Lasker-Schüler-Archiv, Armin T. Wegner-Archiv; 750,000 vols; Dir UTE SCHARMANN.

Würzburg

Staatsarchiv Würzburg (State Archive of Würzburg): Residenz-Nordflügel, 97070 Würzburg; tel. (931) 355290; e-mail poststelle@stawu.bayern.de; internet www.gda.bayern.de/staarin.htm; f. in Middle Ages; 36,000 vols, 6,850,000 documents; archives of Lower Franconia since Middle Ages; Dir Dr WERNER WAGENHÖFER.

Universitätsbibliothek: Am Hubland, 97074 Würzburg; tel. (931) 3185943; e-mail direktion@bibliothek.uni-wuerzburg.de; internet www.bibliothek.uni-wuerzburg.de; f. 1619; spec. Franconian colln; 3,324,306 vols, 225,063 theses, 2,949 incunabula, 2,258 MSS, 73 papyri; Dir Dr KARL SUEDEKUM.

Zweibrücken

Landesbibliothekszentrum/Bibliotheca Bipontina: Bleicherstr. 3, 66482 Zweibrücken; tel. (6332) 16403; e-mail bipontina@lbz-rlp.de; internet www.lbz-rlp.de; f. 1817, became part of the Landesbibliothekszentrum Rheinland-Pfalz 2004; incl. libraries of Historischer Verein Zweibrücken, Pollichia Zweibrücken, Naturwissenschaftlicher Verein Zweibrücken and Verein Deutscher Rosenfreunde; 120,676 vols; Dir Dr ANNETTE GERLACH; Man. Dr SIGRID HUBERT-REICHLING.

Museums and Art Galleries

Aachen

Couven-Museum: Hühnermarkt 17, 52062 Aachen; tel. (241) 4324421; e-mail info@couven-museum.de; internet www.couven-museum.de; f. 1958 in a house built in 1662; 20 rooms showing history of interior design during 18th–19th centuries, featuring the rococo, Louis XVI, Napoleon Empire and Biedermeier periods; incl. reconstructed 'Adler-Apotheke', where chocolate was made for the first time in the city; collns of porcelain and silverware; Dir DAGMAR PREISING.

Internationales Zeitungsmuseum der Stadt Aachen (International Newspaper Museum): Pontstr. 13, 52062 Aachen; tel. (241) 4324910; e-mail izm@mail.aachen.de; internet www.izm.de; f. 1886; 200,000 newspapers; spec. library for press history; Dir ANDREAS DÜSPOHL.

Ludwig Forum für Internationale Kunst (Ludwig Forum for International Art): Jülicher Str. 97–109, 52070 Aachen; tel. (241) 1807104; e-mail info@ludwigforum.de; internet www.ludwigforum.de; f. 1969; modern art since 1960s; spec. collns of graffiti, light sculptures, American pop art and video art; library: Modern art library of 45,000 vols, periodicals and video cassettes; Dir BRIGITTE FRANZEN.

Museum Burg Frankenberg (Burg Museum of Frankenberg): Bismarckstr. 68, 52066 Aachen; tel. (241) 479800; e-mail info@suermondt-ludwig-museum.de; internet www.burgfrankenberg.de; f. 1961, castle dates from 13th century; history of the city from Karl the Great to present; collns of coins, local art; Dir Dr ADAM C. OELLERS.

Suermondt-Ludwig-Museum: Wilhelmstr. 18, 52070 Aachen; tel. (241) 479800; e-mail info@suermondt-ludwig-museum.de; internet www.suermondt-ludwig-museum.de; f. 1882; Gothic art and sculptures; 17th-century paintings (Dutch and Flemish Schools in particular); 10,000 sketches and watercolours, incl. some by Dürer, Rembrandt and Goya; local art since 19th century; library: history of art library of 55,000 vols; Dir ADAM C. OELLERS.

Zollmuseum Friedrichs (Customs Museum): Horbacher Str. 497, 52072 Aachen; tel. (241) 99706015; internet www.zollmuseum-friedrichs.de; 20 rooms and 3,000 exhibits documenting customs practice and history; collns of confiscated materials and smugglers' devices; Dir KURT CREMER.

Baden-Baden

Museum Frieder Burda: Lichtentaler Allee 8B, 76530 Baden-Baden; tel. (7221) 398980; e-mail office@museum-frieder-burda.de; internet www.museum-frieder-burda.de; f. 2004; colln of 1,000 works of modern art with focus on German expressionism, German contemporary art, American abstract expressionism and later works by Picasso; colln is shown in alternation with spec. exhibitions of modern art; Man. Dir ANNETTE SMETANIG.

Staatliche Kunsthalle Baden-Baden (State Art Exhibition Hall): Lichtentaler Allee 8A, 76530 Baden-Baden; tel. (7221) 300763; e-mail info@kunsthalle-baden-baden.de; internet www.kunsthalle-baden-baden.de; f. 1909; int. exhibitions of classical and contemporary art; Dir KAROLA KRAUS (acting); Admin. Dir URSULA EBERHARDT.

Bayreuth

Deutsches Freimaurer Museum in Bayreuth (German Freemasons' Museum in Bayreuth): Im Hofgarten 1, 95444 Bayreuth; tel. (921) 69824; e-mail museum.bayreuth@freimaurer.org; internet museum.freimaurer.org; f. 1902; freemasonry history and practice; library of 25,000 membership records since 1933; incl. sections on Rosicrucians, Illuminati, Templars; Dir THAD PETERSON.

Historisches Museum Bayreuth (Historical Museum of Bayreuth): Habichtweg 11, 95445 Bayreuth; tel. (921) 764010; e-mail museum@historischesmuseum-bayreuth.de; internet www.historischesmuseum-bayreuth.de; f. 1996; covers 1,200 sq. m, 34 exhibition rooms recording history of Bayreuth since 15th century; Dir Dr SYLVIA HABERMANN; Deputy Dir WILFRIED ENGELBRECHT.

Kunst Museum Bayreuth (Art Museum of Bayreuth): Altes Rathaus, Maximilianstr. 33, 95444 Bayreuth; tel. (921) 7645310; e-mail info@kunstmuseum-bayreuth.de; internet www.kunstmuseum-bayreuth.de; f. 1999; art since beginning of 20th century, esp. drawings, watercolours, prints; collns incl. Dr Helmut und Constanze Meyer Kunststiftung and Prof. Dr Klaus Dettmann Kunstsitftung, works of Ackermann, Antes, Beckmann, Bill, 'Brücke' artists, Geiger, Hrdlicka, Hubbuch, Janssen, Lindner, Nay, Rauh, Reuterswärd, Schumacher, Winter; British-American Tobacco colln on history of the tobacco industry; Dir Dr MARINA VON ASSEL.

Richard Wagner Museum mit Nationalarchiv und Forschungsstätte der Richard-Wagner-Stiftung Bayreuth (Richard Wagner Museum with National Archive and Richard Wagner Foundation Research Centre): Wahnfriedstr. 2, 95444 Bayreuth; tel. (921) 757280; e-mail info@wagnermuseum.de; internet www.wagnermuseum.de; f. 1976; closed for renovation until further notice; archives and administration accessible; museum and archive of life and works of Richard Wagner (1813–1883) and of history of Bayreuth festival (early 1870s to late 1940s); Dir Dr SVEN FRIEDRICH; Librarian KRISTINA UNGER.

Berlin

Berlinische Galerie (Berlin Gallery): Alte Jakobstr. 124–28, 10969 Berlin; tel. (30) 78902600; e-mail bg@berlinischegalerie.de; internet www.berlinischegalerie.de; f. 1975; permanent colln of works since beginning of 20th century: paintings and drawings (incl. works by Dix, Grosz and Kirchner), photographs, architectural drawings and models; temporary exhibitions of modern art; library of 65,000 vols, mainly on art since beginning of 20th century; Dir Dr THOMAS KÖHLER; Librarian SABINE SCHARDT.

Botanischer Garten und Botanisches Museum Berlin-Dahlem (Botanic Garden and Botanical Museum Berlin-Dahlem): Königin-Luise-Str. 6–8, 14195 Berlin; tel. (30) 83850100; e-mail zebgbm@bgbm.org; internet www.bgbm.org; f. 1679, Herbarium (f. 1815), Museum (f. 1879); attached to Freie Universität Berlin; plant taxonomy and phytogeography; library of 204,400 vols, 1,300 periodicals, 3.6m. herbaria specimens, 22,000 plant species in culture; Dir Prof. Dr T. BORSCH; publs *Englera* (irregular), *Willdenowia* (3 a year).

Brücke-Museum: Bussardsteig 9, 14195 Berlin; tel. (30) 8312029; e-mail bruecke-museum@t-online.de; internet www.bruecke-museum.de; f. 1967; German expressionism, paintings, sculptures and graphic art of the Brücke group; Dir Prof. Dr MAGDALENA MOELLER; publ. *Brücke Archiv* (1 a year).

Deutsches Historisches Museum (German Historical Museum): Unter den Linden 2, 10117 Berlin; tel. (30) 203040; e-mail info@dhm.de; internet www.dhm.de; f. 1987; German and modern European history; library of 216,000 vols; Pres. Prof. Dr ALEXANDER KOCH.

Haus der Wannsee-Konferenz, Gedenk- und Bildungsstätte (House of the Wannsee Conference, Memorial and Educational Site): Am Grossen Wannsee 56–58, 14109 Berlin; tel. (30) 8050010; e-mail info@ghwk.de; internet www.ghwk.de; f. 1992; memorial and educational site, with permanent exhibition documenting persecution and murder of Jews in Europe 1933–45; educational dept; offers multilingual seminars and study days; library of 30,000 vols, 120 journals; Dir Dr NORBERT KAMPE; Vice-Dir Dr WOLF KAISER.

Käthe-Kollwitz-Museum Berlin: Fasanenstr. 24, 10719 Berlin; tel. (30) 8825210; e-mail info@kaethe-kollwitz.de; internet www.kaethe-kollwitz.de; f. 1986; private museum; permanent exhibition of Käthe Kollwitz's work; temporary exhibitions of artists influenced by Käthe Kollwitz; Dir MARTIN FRITSCH.

Museum für Asiatische Kunst (Asian Art Museum): Lansstr. 8 14195 Berlin-Dahlem; tel. (30) 8301382; e-mail aku@smb.spk-berlin.de; internet www.smb.museum/aku; f. 2006 from merger of Museum of Indian Art (Museum für Indische Kunst) and the Museum of East Asian Art (Museum für Ostasiatische Kunst); art from China (religious bronzes and ceramics), Korea (celadon objects of the 10th- to 14th-century Koryo dynasty) and Japan (Buddhist painting and wood sculpture, Japanese screen painting); art from the Indo-Asian cultural area of 4,000 BC to present, stone sculptures and reliefs, bronze and terracotta figurines from Hinduism, Buddhism and Jainism, metal, ceramics, wood carvings, ivory and jade and precious textiles from Islamic rule in India, Nepal and Tibet represented through fabric painting (thangka), wood sculptures and bronzes; Dir. Prof. Dr KLAAS RUITENBEEK.

Museum für Naturkunde—Leibniz-Institut für Evolutions- und Biodiversitätsforschung (Natural History Museum): Invalidenstr. 43, 10115 Berlin; tel. (30) 20938591; e-mail info@mfn-berlin.de; internet www.naturkundemuseum-berlin.de; f. 1810, east wing of building destroyed 1945 and reopened 2010, present status 2006, current name adopted 2009; attached to Leibniz Institute for Research on Evolution and Biodiversity, Humboldt Univ.; scientific collns incl. mineralogical, geological, palaeontological, zoological specimens; library of 850 vols; Dir Prof. Dr JOHANNES VOGEL; publs *Deutsche Entomologische Zeitschrift*, *Fossil Record*, *Zoosystematics and Evolution*.

Staatliche Museen zu Berlin—Preussischer Kulturbesitz: Stauffenbergstr. 41, 10785 Berlin; tel. (30) 2662610; internet www.smb.museum; f. 1957; supervises museums and collns at the following sites in Berlin: Berlin–Mitte (Museumsinsel), Tiergarten (Kulturforum), Dahlem, Charlottenburg, Köpenick; Gen. Dir Prof. Dr STEFAN WEBER.

Museums:

Ägyptisches Museum und Papyrussammlung (Egyptian Museum and Papyrus Collection): Bodestr. 1–3, 10178 Berlin; tel. (30) 20905101; e-mail aemp@smb.spk-berlin.de; internet www.smb.museum/aemp; f. 1828 as a section of the fmr Royal Art Collection, collns united 1991; Dir Dr FRIEDERIKE SEYFRIED.

Alte Nationalgalerie (Old National Gallery): Bodestr. 1–3, 10178 Berlin; tel. (30) 20905801; e-mail ang@smb.spk-berlin.de; internet www.smb.museum; f. 1861; 19th-century sculpture and painting; Dir UDO KITTELMANN.

Antikensammlung, Pergamonmuseum und Altes Museum (Collection of Classical Antiquties at the Pergamon Museum and the Old Museum): Bodestr. 1–3, 10178 Berlin; tel. (30) 20905201; e-mail ant@smb.spk-berlin.de; internet www.smb.museum/ant; f. 1830; colln also presented in Neues Museum; displays Egyptian and prehistoric objects; Dir Prof. Dr ANDREAS SCHOLL; Deputy Dir Dr MARTIN MAISCHBERGER.

Ethnologisches Museum (Ethnological Museum): Arnimallee 27, 14195 Berlin; tel. (30) 8301438; e-mail md@smb.spk-berlin.de; internet www.smb.museum/em; f. 1829 as the Ethnographic Colln, museum f. 1873; Dir Prof. Dr VIOLA KÖNIG.

Friedrich Christian Flick Collection: Invalidenstr. 50/51, 10557 Berlin; tel. (30) 39783412; e-mail hbf@smb.spk-berlin.de; internet www.smb.museum; 2,000 works, mainly since 1990.

Friedrichswerdersche Kirche (Friedrichswerder Church): Werderscher Markt, Berlin; tel. (30) 2081323; e-mail nng@smb.spk-berlin.de; internet www.smb.museum/fwk; early 19th-century sculpture; Dir UDO KITTELMANN.

Gemäldegalerie (Old Masters' Gallery): Stauffenbergstr. 40, 10785 Berlin; tel. (30) 266424001; e-mail gg@smb.spk-berlin.de; internet www.smb.museum/gg; f. 1830 from collns of The Great Elector (1620–88) and Frederick the Great (1712–86); Dir Prof. Dr BERND LINDEMANN.

Gipsformerei: Sophie-Charlotten-Str. 17–18, 14059 Berlin; tel. (30) 32676911; e-mail gf@smb.spk-berlin.de; internet www.smb.museum/gf; f. 1819; replicas of 6,500 sculptures, from Germany and other European museums; Dir MIGUEL HELFRICH.

Hamburger Bahnhof–Museum für Gegenwart—Berlin (Museum of the Present): Invalidenstr. 50–51, Berlin; tel. (30) 39783411; e-mail hbf@smb.spk-berlin.de; internet www.hamburgerbahnhof.de; f. 1996; art since 1950; Head Dr EUGEN BLUME.

Helmut Newton Stiftung (Helmut Newton Foundation): Jebensstr. 2, 10623 Berlin; tel. (30) 31864856; e-mail info@helmut-newton-stiftung.org; internet www.helmutnewton.com; f. 2003 by the photographer Helmut Newton (1920–2004); preserves and displays Newton's works and those of his wife, June (Alice Springs); temporary exhibitions of work by other photographers; Head Dr MATTHIAS HARDER.

Kunstbibliothek: see under Libraries and Archives.

Kunstgewerbemuseum (Museum of Decorative Arts): Tiergartenstr. 6, 10785 Berlin; tel. (30) 266424336; e-mail kgm@smb.spk-berlin.de; internet www.smb.museum; f. 1867; Dir Dr SABINE THÜMMLER.

Kupferstichkabinett–Sammlung der Zeichnungen und Druckgraphik (Museum of Prints and Drawings): Matthäikirchpl. 8, 10785 Berlin; tel. (30) 266424201; e-mail kk@smb.spk-berlin.de; internet www.kupferstichkabinett.de; f. 1831; colln covers Europe from the Middle Ages to the present and incl. more recent items from the USA; 111,000 drawings, 550,000 prints, illuminated MSS, printed illustrated books, etc.; works by Botticelli, Dürer, Bruegel the Elder, Rembrandt, Schinkel, Menzel, Kirchner, Picasso, Warhol, Hirst; Dir Prof. Dr HEIN-TH. SCHULZE ALTCAPPENBERG.

Münzkabinett der Staatlichen Museen zu Berlin, Stiftung Preussischer Kulturbesitz (Numismatic Collection): Geschwister-Scholl-Str. 6, 10117 Berlin; tel. (30) 266425401; e-mail mk@smb.spk-berlin.de; internet www.smb.museum/ikmk; f. 1868, fmrly Kunstkammer of Prussian Electors (f. 1649); more than 500,000 coins, medals, paper money, seals, models, dies, minting tools: Greek, Roman, Middle Ages to present European, Oriental and Islamic; 4 permanent and 1 additional temporary exhibition gallery in Bode-Museum, additional permanent exhibits at Altes Museum (antiquity) and Neues Museum (antiquity and Middle Ages); library of 20,000 vols, 56 journals; Dir Prof. Dr BERND KLUGE.

Museum Berggruen: Schlossstr. 1, 14059 Berlin Charlottenburg; tel. (30) 266422741; e-mail museum-berggruen@smb.spk-berlin.de; internet www.smb.museum/mb; f. 1996 by the art dealer and collector Heinz Berggruen; colln focusing on Picasso and his contemporaries, incl. Braque, Matisse, Klee, Laurens, Giacometti; Curator FELICIA RAPPE.

Museum Europäischer Kulturen (Museum of European Culture): Im Winkel 6–8, 14195 Berlin; tel. (30) 266426802; e-mail mek@smb.spk-berlin.de; internet www.smb.museum/mek; f. 1999 by merger of the Museum für Volkskunde (Museum of Folklore) and European holdings from the Museum für Völkerkunde (Museum of Ethnology); Dir Dr ELISABETH TIETMEYER.

Museum für Asiatische Kunst (Museum of Asian Art): Takustr. 40, 14195 Berlin; tel. (30) 8301382; e-mail oak@smb.spk-berlin.de; internet www.smb.museum/aku; f. 2006 by merger of Museum of East Asian Art and Museum of Indian Art; Dir Prof. Dr KLAAS RUITENBEEK.

Museum für Fotografie (Museum of Photography): Jebensstr. 2, 10623, Berlin; tel. (30) 266424180; e-mail mf@smb.spk-berlin.de; internet www.smb.museum/mf; f. 2004; preserves, examines and presentes photographic oeuvre of Helmut Newton; history of photography; Head Colln of Photography Dr LUDGER DERENTHAL.

Museum für Islamische Kunst (Museum of Islamic Art): Bodestr. 1–3, 10178 Berlin; Geschwister-Scholl-Str. 6, 10117 Berlin; tel. (30) 266425201; e-mail isl@smb.spk-berlin.de; internet www.smb.museum/isl; f. 1904 as dept of Kaiser Friedrich Museum (now Bodemuseum); Dir Dr STEFAN WEBER.

Museum für Vor- und Frügeschichte (Museum of Pre- and Early History): Bodestr. 1–3, 10178 Berlin; tel. (30) 32674840; e-mail mvf@smb.spk-berlin.de; internet www.neues-museum.de/mvf; f. 1931, colln made independent from the Museum for Ethnology; Dir Prof. Dr MATTHIAS WEMHOFF.

Neue Nationalgalerie (New National Gallery): Potsdamer Str. 50, Berlin; tel. (30) 266424510; e-mail nng@smb.spk-berlin.de; internet www.smb.museum/nng; f. 1968 following merger of collns from the Alte Nationalgalerie and the Gallery of 20th Century Art; painting and sculpture since early 20th century; Dir Dr JOACHIM JÄGER.

Skulpturensammlung und Museum für Byzantinische Kunst (Sculpture Collection and Museum of Byzantine Art): Bodestr. 1–3, 10178 Berlin; tel. (30) 20905601; e-mail sbm@smb.spk-berlin.de; internet www.smb.museum; f. 2000, by merger of Sculpture Colln and Museum of Byzantine Art; Dir Prof. Dr BERND LINDEMANN; Head Dr JULIEN CHAPUIS.

Vorderasiatisches Museum (Museum of Ancient Near East): Bodestr. 1–3, 10178 Berlin; tel. (30) 20905301; e-mail vam@smb.spk-berlin.de; internet www.smb.museum; f. 1899 as Dept of Ancient Near East; Dir Prof. Dr BEATE SALJE; Deputy Dir Dr RALF-B. WARTKE.

Stiftung Stadtmuseum Berlin, Landesmuseum für Kultur und Geschichte Berlins: Poststr. 13–14, 10178 Berlin; tel. (30) 24002150; e-mail info@stadtmuseum.de; internet www.stadtmuseum.de; f. 1874 as Märkisches Museum; illustrates history of Berlin, its culture and its art; library of 112,000 vols; Dir-Gen. Dr FRANZISKA NENTWIG.

Verwaltung der Staatlichen Schlösser und Gärten, West-Berlin (Administration of State Castles and Gardens): Charlottenburg Luisenpl., 10585 Berlin, Schloss; tel. (30) 320911; f. 1927; controls Charlottenburg Castle, Grunewald Hunting Castle (with colln of paintings), Glienicke Castle and Peacock Island (Castle and Park); library of 5,000 vols; Chief Officer Prof. Dr HELMUT BÖRSCH-SUPAN; Chief Officer Prof. Dr JÜRGEN JULIER; Chief Officer Prof. Dr WINFRIED BAER.

Bonn

Beethoven-Haus: Bonngasse 18–26, 53111 Bonn; tel. (228) 981750; e-mail info@beethoven-haus-bonn.de; internet www.beethoven-haus-bonn.de; f. 1889; birthplace of Ludwig van Beethoven (1770–1827); museum and research centre with library; library of 57,000 vols, 125 periodicals, 25,000 music scores (6,000 by Beethoven); Dir Dr MANFRED HARNISCHFEGER; Head of Museums and Curator Dr MICHAEL LADENBURGER.

Kunstmuseum Bonn: Friedrich-Ebert-Allee 2, 53113 Bonn; tel. (228) 776260; e-mail kunstmuseum@bonn.de; internet www.kunstmuseum-bonn.de; f. 1882, restored 1948, new building 1992; colln of 20th-century art; German expressionist painting, with important August Macke colln; contemporary int. graphic art, contemporary German art, photos and video cassettes; library of 47,000 vols; Dir Prof. Dr STEPHAN BERG; Deputy Dir Dr CHRISTOPH SCHREIER.

LVR—LandesMuseum Bonn (LVR State Museum Bonn): Colmantstr. 14–16, 53115 Bonn; tel. (228) 20700; e-mail info.landesmuseum-bonn@lvr.de; internet www.landesmuseum-bonn.lvr.de; f. 1820; prehistoric, Roman and Frankish antiquities of the Rhineland; Rhenish sculpture, painting and applied arts up to the 20th century; Dutch paintings; library of 180,000 vols; Dir Dr GABRIELE UELSBERG; publs *Bonner Jahrbücher des Rheinischen Landesmuseums und des Vereins von Altertumsfreunden im Rheinlande* (1 a year), *Das Rheinische Landesmuseum Bonn* (4 a year).

Zoologisches Forschungsmuseum 'Alexander Koenig' (Zoological Research Museum 'Alexander Koenig'): Adenauerallee 160, 53113 Bonn; tel. (228) 91220; e-mail info.zfmk@uni-bonn.de; internet www.museumkoenig.de; f. 1912; zoology—vertebrates and insects; library of 150,000 vols; Dir Prof. Dr J. W. WÄGELE; publs *Bonner zoologische Beiträge* (4 a year), *Myotis: Mitteilungsblatt für Fledermauskundler* (1 a year).

Bremen

Focke-Museum (District Museum for Art and Culture): Schwachhauser Heerstr. 240, 28213 Bremen; tel. (421) 6996000; e-mail post@focke-museum.de; internet www.focke-museum.de; f. 1900; exhibits from Stone Age to 20th century; library of 40,000 vols, 200 periodicals; Dir Dr FRAUKE VON DER HAAR.

Kunsthalle Bremen—Der Kunstverein in Bremen (Bremen Art Museum): Am Wall 207, 28195 Bremen; tel. (421) 329080; e-mail info@kunsthalle-bremen.de; internet www.kunsthalle-bremen.de; f. 1823; European paintings since 14th century, prints and drawings; sculpture since 16th century; Japanese drawings and books; video art, photography; library of 100,000 vols; Dir Dr CHRISTOPH GRUNENBERG.

Übersee-Museum Bremen (Museum of Overseas Culture, Bremen): Bahnhofspl. 13, 28195 Bremen; tel. (421) 16038101; e-mail office@uebersee-museum.de; internet www.uebersee-museum.de; f. 1896; ethnology, history of commerce, natural history; library of 70,000 vols; Dir Dr WIEBKE AHRNDT; publ. *TenDenZen* (1 a year).

Brunswick

Herzog Anton Ulrich-Museum: Museumstr. 1, 38100 Brunswick; tel. (531) 12250; e-mail info@haum.niedersachsen.de; internet www.haum.niedersachsen.de; f. 1754; colln incl. old pictures, prints and drawings, medieval art, ceramics, 16th-century French enamels, carvings in ivory, bronzes, colln of lace, old clocks, etc.; library: art library of 60,000 vols; Dir Prof. Dr JOCHEN LUCKHARDT.

Städtisches Museum (City Museum): Steintorwall 14 (Am Löwenwall), 38100 Brunswick; tel. (531) 4704505; e-mail staedtisches.museum@braunschweig.de; internet www.braunschweig.de/staedtisches_museum; f. 1861; collns illustrate topography, history and culture of the town; paintings since 19th century; coins and medals (all periods and territories, with about 80,000 pieces); ethnographical collns; Dir Dr CECILIE HOLLBERG; publs *Arbeitsberichte*, *Braunschweiger Werkstücke*, *Miszellen*.

Branch Museum:

Zweigmuseum Altstadtrathaus: Altstadtmarkt 7, 38100 Brunswick; tel. (531) 4704551; e-mail staedtisches.museum@braunschweig.de; f. 1991; bldg dates from late 13th century; history of the city since 9th century.

Cologne

Kölnisches Stadtmuseum: Zeughausstr. 1–3, 50667 Cologne; tel. (221) 22125789; e-mail ksm@museenkoeln.de; internet www.museenkoeln.de; f. 1888; history of Cologne from the Middle Ages to the present day; collns illustrate local culture, economy and everyday life, political history, craftsmen's and merchants' guilds, devotional objects, Judaica, transport, inventions made in the city, paintings by the Berckheyde brothers and Geldorp Gortzius, crafts, early globes, puppet theatre, Eau de Cologne; library of 30,000 vols; Dir Dr MARIO KRAMP; Curator for Graph Dept RITA WAGNER; Curator for Middle Ages Dr BETTINA MOSLER; Librarian BEATRIX ALEXANDER.

Museum für Angewandte Kunst (Museum of Applied Art): An der Rechtschule, 50667 Cologne; tel. (221) 22123860; e-mail makk@stadt-koeln.de; internet www.museenkoeln.de; f. 1888; applied art since Middle Ages; design colln since 1900; library: see under Libraries and Archives; Dir Dr PETRA HESSE.

Museum Ludwig: Heinrich-Böll-Pl., 50667 Cologne; tel. (221) 22126165; e-mail info@museum-ludwig.de; internet www.museum-ludwig.de; f. 1976; paintings, modern sculpture, prints, photos, video cassettes; library; largest colln of Pop Art outside the USA; Russian avant-garde art; several hundred works by Picasso; collns Agfa Foto-Historma: photographs, caricatures and documents; colln of cameras returned to Agfa and Gevaert in Belgium; Dir PHILIPP KAISER; Deputy Dir KATIA BAUDIN.

Museum Schnütgen: Leonhard-Tietz-Str. 10, 50676 Cologne; Cäcilienstr. 29–33, 50667 Cologne; tel. (221) 22122310; e-mail museum.schnutgen@stadt-koeln.de; internet www.museenkoeln.de; f. 1906; 13,000 works of medieval art; houses 11th-century wooden crucifix; library of 20,000 vols; Dir Dr MORITZ WOELK (acting).

Rautenstrauch-Joest-Museum: Cäcilienstr. 29–33, 50667 Cologne; Cäcilienstr. 29–33, 50667 Cologne; tel. (221) 22131356; e-mail rjm@stadt-koeln.de; internet www.museenkoeln.de/rjm; f. 1901; ethnological museum; library of 44,300 vols; Dir Prof. Dr KLAUS SCHNEIDER; Deputy Dir Dr JUTTA ENGELHARD; publ. *Ethnologica*.

Römisch-Germanisches Museum: Roncallipl. 4, 50667 Cologne; tel. (221) 22124438; e-mail roemisch-germanisches-museum@stadt-koeln.de; internet www.museenkoeln.de/roemisch-germanisches-museum; f. 1946; library of 14,000 vols; Dir Dr MARCUS TRIER (acting); publs *Kölner Forschungen*, *Kölner Jahrbuch* (prehistory and early history, 1 a year).

Wallraf-Richartz-Museum & Fondation Corboud: Obenmarspforten (Am Kölner Rathaus), 50667 Cologne; tel. (221) 22121119; e-mail wallraf@museenkoeln.de; internet www.wallraf.museum; f. 1824; paintings, sculpture, prints, drawings dating from the Middle Ages, Baroque period, 18th and 19th centuries; library: see under Libraries and Archives; Dir Dr ANDREAS BLÜHM; Deputy Dir Dr ROLAND KRISCHEL; publ. *Wallraf-Richartz-Jahrbuch*.

Darmstadt

Grossherzoglich-Hessische Porzellansammlung (Grand-Ducal Hessian Porcelain Collection): Schlossgartenstr. 10, Prinz-Georg-Palais, 64289 Darmstadt; tel. (6151) 713233; e-mail info@porzellanmuseum-darmstadt.de; internet www.porzellanmuseum-darmstadt.de; f. 1908; colln consists of a variety of products manufactured by the European porcelain and faience artists of the 18th and 19th centuries; Head ALEXA-BEATRICE CHRIST (acting).

Hessisches Landesmuseum Darmstadt (State Museum of Hesse in Darmstadt): Friedenspl. 1, 64283 Darmstadt; tel. (6151) 165703; e-mail info@hlmd.de; internet www.hlmd.de; f. 1820; archaeology, geology, mineralogy, palaeontology, prehistory, zoology; art collns and cultural history since 9th century, incl. crafts, prints and drawings, stained glass, sculptures, paintings, European art since 1945; library of 55,000 vols; Dir Dr INA BUSCH; Dir Dr THEO JÜLICH; publs *Kaupia–Darmstädter Beiträge zur Naturgeschichte* (2 a year), *Kunst in Hessen und am Mittelrhein* (1 a year).

Museum Jagdschloss Kranichstein: Kranichsteiner Str. 261, 64289 Darmstadt; tel. (6151) 9711180; e-mail museum@schloss-huntingkranichstein.de; internet www.jagdschloss-kranichstein.de; f. 1918; pictures, hunting trophies and weapons, furnished rooms; owned by Stiftung Hessischer Jägerhof; Dir NADINE KRÄMER.

Schlossmuseum Darmstadt (Palace Museum Darmstadt): Residenzschloss, Marktpl. 15, 64283 Darmstadt; tel. (6151) 24035; e-mail info@schlossmuseum-darmstadt.de; internet www.schlossmuseum-darmstadt.de; f. 1924; furnished rooms; paintings, sculptures and handicraft, incl. fine pieces of furniture, tapestry, glass, ceramics, gold and silverware from 16th–20th centuries; guided tours in English, French or Russian; Head ALEXA-BEATRICE CHRIST (acting).

Dortmund

Museum für Kunst und Kulturgeschichte Dortmund (Dortmund Museum of Art and Cultural History): Hansastr. 3, 44137 Dortmund; tel. (231) 5025522; e-mail mkk@stadtdo.de; internet www.museendortmund.de/mkk; f. 1883; collns incl. medieval art and sculpture, furniture since 15th century, design, *objets d'art*, paintings, archaeology; library of 18,000 vols; Dir WOLFGANG E. WEICK.

Dresden

Landesamt für Archäologie mit Landesmuseum für Vorgeschichte (State Office of Archaeology and Museum of Prehistory): Japanisches Palais, Zur Wetterwarte 7, 01109 Dresden; tel. (351) 8926603; e-mail info@archsax.smwk.sachsen.de; f. 1993; preservation of ancient monuments, archaeological research and exhibitions; library of 40,000 vols specializing in prehistory; Dir Dr J. OEXLE; publs *Arbeits- und Forschungsberichte* (1 a year), *Archäologie aktuell im Freistaat Sachsen* (1 a year).

Mathematisch-Physikalischer Salon (Mathematical-Physical Salon): Zwinger, 01067 Dresden; tel. (351) 49140; e-mail besucherservice@skd.museum; internet www.skd.museum; f. 1560; historical watches and clocks, globes, scientific instruments, etc.; library of 7,000 vols; Dir Dr PETER PLAßMEYER.

Militärhistorisches Museum der Bundeswehr (Bundeswehr Museum of Military History): Olbrichtplatz 2, 01099 Dresden; tel. (351) 8232803; e-mail milhistmuseumbweingang@bundeswehr.org; internet www.mhmbw.de; f. 1897; 10,000 exhibits examine violence as a historical, cultural and anthropological phenomenon; encourages creative, open and unbiased discussions and sees itself as a forum for the critical examination of military history and for the dialogue on the role of war and military in the past, present and future; library of 38,591 vols; Dir Col Dr ROGG; publs *Militärhistorisches Museum der Bundeswehr/Ausstellungsführer* (Ausstellungsführer zur Dauerausstellung), *Rechtsextreme Gewalt in Deutschland 1990–2013* (Katalog zur Sonderausstellung 'Rechtsextreme Gewalt in Deutschland 1990–2013'), *Stalingrad-Eine Ausstellung des Militärhistorischen Museums der Bundeswehr* (Katalog zur Sonderausstellung 'Stalingrad'), *Woher?/Wohin?: Bilder vom Abzug der russischen Streitkräfte aus Sachsen* (Katalog zur Sonderausstellung 'Otkuda? Kuda?/Woher? Wohin?').

Municipal Gallery and Art Collection Dresden (Städtische Galerie Dresden-Kunstsammlung): Wilsdruffer Str. 2, 01067 Dresden; tel. (351) 4887301; e-mail sekretariat@museen-dresden.de; internet www.galerie-dresden.de; holds art exhibitions; Dir Dr GISBERT PORSTMANN; Sec. SYLVIA LEUENBERGER.

Museum für Tierkunde Dresden (Dresden Museum of Zoology): Königsbrücker Landstr. 159, 01109 Dresden; tel. (351) 7958414326; e-mail birgit.walker@senckenberg.de; internet www.senckenberg.de; f. 1728; more than 6m. animal specimens; library of 60,000 vols; Dir UWE FRITZ; publs *Entomologische Abhandlungen*, *Faunistische Abhandlungen*, *Malakologische Abhandlungen*, *Reichenbachia Zeitschrift für entomolog. Taxonomie* (1 a year), *Zoologische Abhandlungen*.

Museum Schloss Moritzburg (Museum of Moritzburg Castle): Schloss Moritzburg, 01468 Moritzburg bei Dresden; tel. (35207) 8730; e-mail moritzburg@schloesserland-sachsen.de; internet www.schloss-moritzburg.de; f. 1947; leather hangings, furniture, paintings, statues, porcelain, glasswork, principally of the 18th century; Dir INGRID MÖBIUS.

Staatliche Ethnographische Sammlungen Sachsen: see Staatliche Ethnographische Sammlungen Sachsen, Leipzig.

Staatliche Kunstsammlungen Dresden: POB 12 05 51, 01006 Dresden; Residenzschloss, Taschenberg 2, 01067 Dresden; tel. (351) 491420; e-mail besucherservice@skd.museum; internet www.skd.museum; f. 1560; library of 130,000 vols, housed in the Residenzschloss; Gen. Dir Prof. Dr MARTIN ROTH; publ. *Dresdener Kunstblätter* (6 a year).

Constituent Institutions:

Gemäldegalerie Alte Meister (Old Masters Picture Gallery): Semperbau am Zwinger, Theaterpl. 1, 01067 Dresden; tel. (351) 49146679; e-mail gam@skd.museum; internet www.skd.museum; f. 16th century; Italian Renaissance artists Raffael, Giorgione and Titian; 17th-century Flemish art, Rembrandt, Vermeer, Rubens; old German and Dutch, Jan van Eyck, Dürer, Cranach, Holbein; Spanish and French 17th-century artists Ribera, Murillo, Poussin, Lorrain; Dir Prof. Dr BERNHARD MAAZ.

Gemäldegalerie Neue Meister (New Masters Gallery): Albertinum, Brühlsche Terrasse, 01067 Dresden; tel. (351) 49149731; e-mail gnm@skd.museum; internet www.skd.museum; f. 1960; art since 19th century; collns of German Impressionism and Expressionism; Dir Prof. Dr ULRICH BISCHOFF.

Grünes Gewölbe (Green Vault): Residenzschloss, Taschenberg 2, 01067 Dresden; tel. (351) 49140; e-mail besucherservice@skd.museum; internet www.skd.museum; Renaissance and Baroque artefacts; f. 1723; Dir Prof. Dr DIRK SYNDRAM.

Kunstgewerbemuseum (Museum of Decorative Arts): Schloss Pillnitz, August-Böckstiegel-Str. 2, 01326 Dresden; tel. (351) 26130; e-mail besucherservice@skd.museum; internet www.skd.museum; f. 1876; courtly items incl. textiles and ceramics; Dir Dr PETER PLAßMEYER (acting); Sec. NADJA WENZEL.

Kupferstich-Kabinett (Cabinet of Prints and Drawings): POB 12 05 51, 01006 Dresden; Taschenberg 2, 01067 Dresden; tel. (351) 49143211; e-mail kk@skd.museum; internet www.skd.museum; f. 1720; 50,000 paper works by 11,000 artists since 12th century; Dir Prof. Dr BERNHARD MAAZ.

Münzkabinett (Coin Cabinet): POB 12 05 51, 01006 Dresden; Taschenberg 2, 01067 Dresden; tel. (351) 49143231; e-mail mk@skd.museum; internet www.skd.museum; f. early 16th century; library of 30,000 specialist vols; 300,000 objects, incl. coins, medals, banknotes; Dir Dr RAINER GRUND (acting).

Museum für Sächsische Volkskunst mit Puppentheatersammlung (Museum of Saxon Folk Art with Puppet Theatre Collection): Jägerhof, Köpckestr. 1, 01097 Dresden; tel. (351) 49144502; e-mail elke.wengerek@skd.museum; internet www.skd.museum; f. 1897; items of folk history; costumes; puppet colln; Dir Dr IGOR A. JENZEN.

Porzellansammlung (Porcelain Collection): Zwinger, Glockenspielpavillon, 01067 Dresden; tel. (351) 49146612; e-mail ps@skd.museum; internet www.skd.museum; f. 1717; 20,000 pieces of Meissner, Japanese and Chinese porcelain; Dir Dr ULRICH PIETSCH.

Rüstkammer (Armoury): Semperbau am Zwinger, Theaterpl. 1, 01067 Dresden; tel. (351) 49148591; e-mail gg@skd.museum; internet www.skd.museum; f. 1567; 10,000 chivalric objects, weapons and costumes; Dir Prof. DIRK SYNDRAM.

Skulpturensammlung (Sculpture Collection): Albertinum, Brühlsche Terrasse, 01067 Dresden; tel. (351) 49149741; e-mail skd@skd.museum; internet www.skd.museum; sculptures since 3,000 BC; Dir Dr MORITZ WOELK.

Staatliches Museum für Mineralogie und Geologie (State Museum of Mineralogy and Geology): Königsbrücker Landstr. 159, 01109 Dresden; tel. (351) 7958414403; e-mail ulrike.kloss@senckenberg.de; internet www.senckenberg.de; f. 1728; 400,000 minerals and fossils; library of 35,000 vols; Dir Dr ULF LINNEMANN; Sec. ULRIKE KLOSS; publs *Geologica Saxonica–Abhandlungen* (1 a year), *Schriften* (1–2 a year).

Stadtmuseum Dresden (Dresden City Museum): Wilsdruffer Str. 2, 01067 Dresden; tel. (351) 4887301; e-mail sekretariat@museen-dresden.de; internet www.stadtmuseum-dresden.de; f. 1891; Dresden history and culture; classicist, Late Baroque and Rococo styles, the State House of 1770–75 with architectural colln; colln on the Saxon capital's art and cultural history; promotes research on history of the Saxon art; library of 7,500 vols, 22,500 pictures, 55,000 photographs; Dir Dr ERIKA ESCHEBACH.

Attached Museums:

Kraszewski-Museum: Nordstr. 28, 01099 Dresden; tel. (351) 8044450; e-mail joanna.magacz@museen-dresden.de; internet www.stmd.de; exhibition on Polish history, in particular Józef Ignacy Kraszewski (1812–87), who fought for Polish independence in the 19th century; exhibits in German and Polish; Dir JOANNA MAGACZ.

Kügelgenhaus–Museum der Dresdner Romantik (Museum of German Romanticism): Hauptstr. 13, 01097 Dresden; tel. (351) 8044760; e-mail michaela.hausding@museen-dresden.de; internet www.stmd.de; f. 1981; home to the Museum der Dresdner Romantik; Dir MICHAELA HAUSDING.

Schillerhäuschen (The Schiller House): Schillerstr. 19, 01326 Dresden; tel. (351) 4887372; e-mail joachim.vocke@museen-dresden.de; internet www.stmd.de; dedicated to the poet Friedrich Schiller (1759–1805).

Weber-Museum: Dresdner Str. 44, 01326 Dresden; tel. (351) 2618234; e-mail dorothea.renz@museen-dresden.de; internet www.stmd.de; dedicated to the works of composer Carl Maria von Weber (1786–1826); concert venue; Dir DOROTHEA RENZ.

Verkehrsmuseum Dresden (Transport Museum Dresden): Augustusstr. 1, 01067 Dresden; tel. (351) 86440; e-mail info@verkehrsmuseum-dresden.de; internet verkehrsmuseum-dresden.de; f. 1952; colln of automobiles, motorcycles, bicycles, streetcars, aircraft, model ships and railways; library of 59,000 vols (14,156 vols in spec. colln); Dir JOACHIM BREUNINGER.

Düsseldorf

Aquazoo Löbbecke Museum: Kaiserswertherstr. 380, 40200 Düsseldorf; tel. (211) 8996198; internet www.dusseldorf.de/aquazoo; f. 1904 (museum), 1876 (zoo); zoo and natural science museum; library of 600 vols; Dir Dr W. W. GETTMANN; publs *Aquarius* (2 a year), *Westdeutscher Entomologentag Düsseldorf*.

Kunsthalle Düsseldorf (Arts Centre Dusseldorf): Grabbepl. 4, 40213 Düsseldorf; tel. (211) 8996243; e-mail mail@kunsthalle-duesseldorf.de; internet www.kunsthalle-duesseldorf.de; f. 1967; contemporary art; Chair. DIRK ELBERS; Man. Dir ARIANE BERGER; Man. Dir Dr GREGOR JANSEN; Man. Dir Dr VANESSA JOAN MÜLLER.

Kunstsammlung Nordrhein-Westfalen (North Rhine-Westphalia Art Collection): Grabbepl. 5, 40213 Düsseldorf; tel. (211) 8381204; e-mail service@kunstsammlung.de; internet www.kunstsammlung.de; f. 1961; painting and sculpture since beginning of 20th century, video art and photography; Dir Dr MARION ACKERMANN; publ. *Quartalsprogramm* (4 a year).

Museum Kunstpalast (mit Sammlung Kunstakademie and Glasmuseum Hentrich) (Art Palace Museum (incorporating the Art Academy Collection and Hentrich Glass Museum)): Ehrenhof 4–5, 40479 Düsseldorf; tel. (211) 8990200; e-mail info@smkp.de; internet www.smkp.de; f. 1913; European art and applied art from the Middle Ages to the present day; colln of 19th-century German painting; early Iranian bronzes and ceramics; 6,500 textiles from late antiquity to the 19th century; glass colln, mainly Art Nouveau, Jugendstil and Art Deco; colln of prints and drawings, incl. extensive colln of Italian Baroque drawings; contemporary art; design; library of 80,000 vols; Dir BEAT WISMER.

Essen

Museum Folkwang: Goethestr. 41, 45128 Essen; tel. (201) 8845444; e-mail info@museum-folkwang.essen.de; internet www.museum-folkwang.de; f. 1902; art since 19th century, incl. drawings, prints, posters and photographs; incl. German Poster Museum (Deutsches Plakat Museum) with 340,000 posters; library of 100,000 vols; Dir Dr HARTWIG FISCHER; Deputy Dir Prof. UTE ESKILDSEN.

Flensburg

Museumsberg Flensburg (Mountain Museum Flensburg): Museumsberg 1, 24937 Flensburg; tel. (461) 852956; e-mail museumsberg@flensburg.de; internet www.museumsberg.flensburg.de; f. 1876; contains about 26,000 exhibits, mainly arts and crafts, peasant art, and prehistory of Schleswig; library of 12,000 vols; Dir Dr MICHAEL FUHR; publs *Beiträge zur Kunst- und Kulturgeschichte*, *Nordelbingen*.

Frankfurt am Main

Archäologisches Museum (Archaeological Museum): Karmelitergasse 1, 60311 Frankfurt am Main; tel. (69) 21235896; e-mail info.archaeolmus@stadt-frankfurt.de; internet www.archaeologisches-museum.frankfurt.de; f. 1937; prehistoric, Roman and early medieval objects from the Frankfurt area; Mediterranean and oriental archaeology; Dir Prof. Dr EGON WAMERS.

Deutsches Architekturmuseum (German Architecture Museum): Schaumainkai 43, 60596 Frankfurt am Main; tel. (69) 21238844; e-mail info.dam@stadt-frankfurt.de; internet www.dam-online.de; f. 1979, opened 1984; int. colln of plans, sketches, paintings and models primarily of modern architecture; changing exhibitions, lectures, symposia; library and archive; library of 20,000 vols, 60 current periodicals and yearbooks; Dir Ing. PETER CACHOLA SCHMAL; Deputy Dir Dr Ing. WOLFGANG VOIGT; publ. *German Architecture* (1 a year).

Deutsches Filmmuseum (German Film Museum): Schaumainkai 41, 60596 Frankfurt am Main; tel. (69) 9612200; e-mail info@deutsches-filmmuseum.de; internet www.deutschesfilmmuseum.de; f. 1984; exhibits relating to the German and int. film industry; library: see library and archives of the Deutsches Filminstitut; Dir CLAUDIA DILLMANN.

Freies Deutsches Hochstift, Frankfurter Goethe-Haus Museum (Free German Literature Institute, Frankfurt Goethe-Museum (Goethe House)): Gr. Hirschgraben 23–25, 60311 Frankfurt am Main; tel. (69) 138800; e-mail info@goethehaus-frankfurt.de; internet www.goethehaus-frankfurt.de; f. 1859; birthplace of Johann Wolfgang von Goethe (1749–1832); German literature of the Romantic period and of Goethe's time; selected works since 19th century; 30,000 MSS of German poetry principally from Goethe's time; 400 paintings, 16,000 etchings; library: see under Libraries and Archives; Dir Dr PETRA MAISAK; publ. *Reihe der Schriften*.

Historisches Museum Frankfurt: Saalgasse 19, 60311 Frankfurt am Main; tel. (69) 21235599; e-mail info.historisches-museum@stadt-frankfurt.de; internet www.historisches-museum-frankfurt.de; f. 1878; history of Frankfurt to the present; spec. colln: documents relating to elections of emperors 1562–1792, to the Assembly of Paulskirche 1848–49, and to trade fairs in the 16th–18th centuries; Hoechst Porcelain 1746–96; comic art and caricature; coin colln; children's museum; library of 50,000 vols; Dir Dr JAN GERCHOW; Deputy Dir Dr WOLFGANG CILLEßEN.

Museum für Angewandte Kunst Frankfurt (Museum of Applied Art Frankfurt): Schaumainkai 17, 60594 Frankfurt am Main; tel. (69) 21234037; e-mail info.angewandte-kunst@stadt-frankfurt.de; internet www.angewandtekunst-frankfurt.de; f. 1877; European art craft of 12th to 21st century, design, book art and graphics, Islamic and East Asian art and int. product design; 65,000 exhibits; library of 65,000 vols, 170 current periodicals and yearbooks; Dir Prof. Dr ULRICH SCHNEIDER.

Museum für Kommunikation (Museum for Communication): Schaumainkai 53, 60596 Frankfurt am Main; tel. (49) 6960600; e-mail mfk-frankfurt@mspt.de; internet www.mfk-frankfurt.de; f. 1872; items on history of post and telecommunications; library of 35,000 vols; Dir Dr HELMUT GOLD.

Museum für Moderne Kunst (Museum of Contemporary Art): Domstr. 10, 60311 Frankfurt am Main; tel. (69) 21230447; e-mail mmk@stadt-frankfurt.de; internet www.mmk-frankfurt.de; f. 1991; art since the 1960s; library of 40,000 vols; Dir SUSANNE GAENSHEIMER; Deputy Dir PETER GORSCHLÜTER.

Städel Museum (Barn Museum): Dürerstr. 2, 60596 Frankfurt am Main; Schaumainkai 63, 60596 Frankfurt am Main; tel. (69) 6050980; e-mail info@staedelmuseum.de; internet www.staedelmuseum.de; f. 1816; 2,700 paintings, 100,000 drawings and prints, 600 sculptures spanning 700 years; library of 50,000 vols; Chair. Prof. Dr NIKOLAUS SCHWEICKART; Dir MAX HOLLEIN.

Weltkulturen Museum (World Cultures Museum): Schaumainkai 29–37, 60594 Frankfurt am Main; tel. (69) 21235391; e-mail museum.weltkulturen@stadt-frankfurt.de; internet www.weltkulturenmuseum.de; f. 1904; collns of art and ethnography from all continents, esp. Oceania, SE Asia, Africa, North and South America; spec. colln of contemporary art; library of 43,000 vols, 90 periodicals; Dir Dr CLÉMENTINE DELISS; publ. *Journal-Ethnologie* (online, www.journal-ethnologie.de).

Freiburg im Breisgau

Adelhausermuseum: Gerberau 32, 79098 Freiburg im Breisgau; tel. (761) 2012566; e-mail adelhausermuseum@stadt.freiburg.de; internet www.museen.freiburg.de; f. 1895; native and exotic fauna; herb colln, mineralogy, precious stones, wood types, beekeeping, traditional arts and crafts from Africa, America, Asia and Oceania; social and cultural anthropology; library: ethnology: 4,700 vols, natural history: 5,000 vols; Dir Dr EVA GERHARDS.

Archäologisches Museum Colombischlössle (Archaeological Museum Colombischlossle): Rotteckring 5, 79098 Freiburg im Breisgau; tel. (761) 2012574; e-mail arco-museum@stadt.freiburg.de; internet www.freiburg.de/museen; f. 1936; library of 5,000 vols; Dir Dr HELENA PASTOR BORGOÑÓN.

Augustinermuseum (Augustinian Museum): Augustinerpl., 79098 Freiburg im Breisgau; tel. (761) 2012521; e-mail augustinermuseum@stadt.freiburg.de; internet www.freiburg.de/museen; f. 1923; art and culture of Upper Rhine area from Middle Ages to the 20th century; library of 50,000 vols; Dir Dr TILMANN VON STOCKHAUSEN; Deputy Dir Dr DETLEF ZINKE.

Museum für Neue Kunst (Museum of Modern Art): Marienstr. 10A, 79098 Freiburg im Breisgau; tel. (761) 2012583; e-mail mnk@stadt.freiburg.de; internet www.museen.freiburg.de; f. 1985; German art since 1910; Dir Dr JOCHEN LUDWIG.

Museum für Stadtgeschichte (Museum of City History): Münsterpl. 30, 79098 Freiburg im Breisgau; tel. (761) 2012515; e-mail msg@stadt.freiburg.de; internet www.museen.freiburg.de; city history since 1100; Dir PETER KALCHTHALER.

Giessen

Liebig Museum: Liebigstr. 12, 35390 Giessen; tel. (641) 76392; internet www.liebig-museum.de; exhibition of the life and work of Liebig through documents and pictures; pharmaceutical laboratory and display of chemical analysis since 19th century; Chair. WOLFGANG BERGENTHUM.

Oberhessisches Museum und Gailsche Sammlungen der Stadt Giessen: Brandpl. 2, 35390 Giessen; tel. (641) 3062477; e-mail museum@giessen.de; internet www.giessen.de; f. 1879; palaeolithic colln, first Middle European flint tools; archaeological collns and treasures of Roman-German and Hessian Franconian culture; oil paintings, watercolours and modern copperplate engravings; Dir Dr FRIEDHELM HÄRING.

Comprises:

Altes Schloss: Abteilung Gemäldegalerie und Kunsthandwerk, Brandpl. 2 35390

Giessen; tel. (641) 9609730; e-mail museum@giessen.de; internet www.giessen.de; houses furniture and art in 14th-century bldg; collns of Gothic, Baroque, Renaissance, artefacts since 19th century.

Leib'sches Haus: Abteilung für Stadtgeschichte und Volkskunde, Georg-Schlosser-Str. 2, 35390 Giessen; tel. (641) 3012448; f. 1978; originally the seat of the Junkers of Rodenhausen; now museum of local history and culture; exhibits of material culture of Gießen and surrounding area; portraits, pictures, maps, engravings, textile manufacture and handicraft; furniture, farm implements, costumes, pottery; spec. exhibitions on the political thinkers Georg Büchner and Wilhelm Liebknecht (founder of the German Social Democratic Party).

Wallenfels'sches Haus: Abteilung für Vor- und Frühgeschichte, Archäologie und Völkerkunde mit der Sammlung Heinz Beer, Kirchenpl. 6, 35390 Giessen; tel. (641) 3012037; ethnological museum with artefacts dating from prehistoric times; examples from India, China, Japan, Sri Lanka, Java, East and West Africa, Egypt, New Guinea and Australia.

Gotha

Kommunale Galerien am Hauptmarkt (Local Galleries at the Market): Hauptmarkt 44, 99867 Gotha; tel. (3621) 401101; Dir MARLIES MIKOLAJCZAK.

Münzkabinett (Coin Cabinet): POB 10 03 19, 99867 Gotha; Schloss Friedenstein, 99867 Gotha; tel. (3621) 82340; e-mail service@stiftung-friedenstein.de; internet www.stiftung-friedenstein.de; attached to Castle Museum in Gotha; 130,000 numismatic objects; Dir Dr MARTIN EBERLE.

Museum der Natur Gotha: POB 10 03 19, 99853 Gotha; 99867 Gotha; tel. (3621) 82340; e-mail service@stiftung-friedenstein.de; internet www.stiftung-friedenstein.de; f. 1843; animal and fossil exhibitions, insects, local natural history; Dir Prof. Dr MARTIN EBERLE; publ. *Abhandlungen und Berichte*.

Museum für Kartographie (Museum of Cartography): Schloss Friedenstein, 99867 Gotha; tel. (3621) 854016; e-mail vorstand@stiftungfriedenstein.de; maps, atlases and globes; original copper engraving; Curator JUTTA SIEGERT.

Museum für Regionalgeschichte und Volkskunde (Museum of Regional History and Folklore): Schloss Friedenstein, 99867 Gotha; tel. (3621) 82340; e-mail mrv@stiftungfriedenstein.de; internet www.stiftungfriedenstein.de; f. 1928; exhibition of local history, with *Ekhof-Theater* (baroque theatre); Dir THOMAS HUCK.

Schlossmuseum (Castle Museum): Schloss Friedenstein, 99867 Gotha; tel. (3621) 82340; e-mail schlossmuseum@stiftungfriedenstein.de; internet www.stiftungfriedenstein.de; art collns, historical rooms, coin collns, Egyptological exhibition; Dir Dr MARTIN EBERLE.

Göttingen

Städtisches Museum (Municipal Museum): Ritterplan 7/8, 37073 Göttingen; tel. (551) 4002843; e-mail museum@goettingen.de; internet www.museum.goettingen.de; f. 1889; prehistory and early history, ecclesiastical art, history of Göttingen and the Univ., arts and crafts, etc.; library of 30,000 vols; Dir Dr ERNST BÖHME.

Halle am Saale

Landesamt für Denkmalpflege und Archäologie Sachsen-Anhalt (Landesmuseum für Vorgeschichte) (State Office for Heritage Management and Archaeology—State Museum of Prehistory): Richard-Wagner-Str. 9, 06114 Halle (Saale); tel. (345) 524730; e-mail poststelle@lda.mk.sachsen-anhalt.de; internet www.lda-lsa.de; f. 1882; pre- and medieval history, archaeology, preservation of historic buildings and monuments, restoration, exhibitions; colln of archaeological finds, publishing; library of 130,000 vols; Dir Prof. Dr HARALD MELLER; publs *Archäologie in Sachsen-Anhalt* (1 a year), *Denkmalpflege in Sachsen-Anhalt* (2 a year), *Jahresschrift für mitteldeutsche Vorgeschichte* (1 a year), *Veröffentlichungen* (1 a year).

Hamburg

Altonaer Museum für Kunst und Kulturgeschichte (Altona Museum in Hamburg/North German Regional Museum): POB 50 01 25, 22701 Hamburg; Museumstr. 23, 22765 Hamburg; tel. (40) 42813582; e-mail info@altonaermuseum.de; internet www.altonaer-museum.de; f. 1863; collns on art and cultural history, folk art, shipping and fishing; library of 70,000 vols; Chair. Prof. Dr KIRSTEN BAUMANN; Dir Prof. Dr TORKILD HINRICHSEN; Man. Dir HELMUT SANDER; publs *Altonaer Museum in Hamburg*, catalogues of collns and exhibitions.

Hamburger Kunsthalle (Hamburg Arts Centre): Glockengiesserwall, 20095 Hamburg; tel. (40) 428131200; e-mail info@hamburger-kunsthalle.de; internet www.hamburger-kunsthalle.de; f. 1869; paintings since 14th century, sculpture since 19th century, drawings and engravings since 14th century, Greek and Roman coins, medals since 14th century; library of 167,377 vols; Dir Prof. HUBERTUS GASSNER.

Museum für Hamburgische Geschichte (Museum for History of Hamburg): Holstenwall 24, 20355 Hamburg; tel. (40) 4281322380; e-mail info@hamburgmuseum.de; internet www.hamburgmuseum.de; f. 1839; attached to Stiftung Historische Museen Hamburg; political history of Hamburg, library, coins, handicrafts, models, paintings, history of music, etc.; Chair. Prof. Dr KIRSTEN BAUMANN; Dir Prof. Dr LISA KOSOK; publs *Beiträge zur deutschen Volks- und Altertumskunde*, *Hamburger Beiträge zur Numismatik*, *Numismatische Studien*.

Museum für Kunst und Gewerbe Hamburg (Hamburg Museum of Art and Industry): Steintorpl. 1, 20099 Hamburg; tel. (40) 428134880; e-mail service@mkg-hamburg.de; internet www.mkg-hamburg.de; f. 1877; European sculpture and art since the Middle Ages, ancient art, art of the Near and Far East, European popular art, graphic, photographic and textile collns, contemporary design, historical keyboard instruments; library of 160,000 vols, 450 current periodicals; Dir Prof. Dr SABINE SCHULZE.

Museum für Völkerkunde Hamburg: Rothenbaumchaussee 64, 20148 Hamburg; tel. (40) 428879-0; e-mail sekretariat2@mvhamburg.de; internet www.voelkerkundemuseum.com; f. 1879; ethnological collns from Africa, America, Australia, Indonesia, Europe, Asia and the S Seas; library of 130,000 vols; Dir Prof. Dr W. KÖPKE; publ. *Mitteilungen aus dem Museum für Völkerkunde, N.F.* (1 a year).

Hanover

Historisches Museum Hannover (Historical Museum Hanover): Pferdestr. 6, 30159 Hanover; tel. (511) 16843052; e-mail historisches.museum@hannover-stadt.de; internet www.historisches-museum-hannover.de; f. 1903 as Vaterländisches Museum, 1937–50 Niedersächsisches Volkstumsmuseum, 1950–66 as Niedersächsisches Heimatmuseum; 3 sections: Lower Saxon Folklore, History of the City of Hanover, History of the Kingdom of Hanover up to 1866; library of 20,000 vols; Dir Dr THOMAS SCHWARK.

Museum August Kestner: Trammpl. 3, 30159 Hanover; tel. (511) 16842730; e-mail museum-august-kestner@hannover-stadt.de; internet www.hannover.de/kestner; f. 1889; Egyptian, Greek, Etruscan and Roman art; illuminated MSS, incunabula, applied art and design since the Middle Ages; ancient, medieval and modern coins, medals; library of 40,000 vols, 200 current periodicals; Dir Dr WOLFGANG SCHEPERS; Curator for Classical Archaelogy Dr ANNE VIOLA SIEBERT; Curator for Egyptology Dr CHRISTIAN E. LOEBEN; Curator for Numismatics Dr SIMONE VOGT.

Niedersächsisches Landesmuseum Hannover (Hanover State Museum): Willy-Brandt-Allee 5, 30169 Hanover; tel. (511) 9807686; e-mail info@nlm-h.niedersachsen.de; internet www.landesmuseum-hannover.de; f. 1852; art dating from the Middle Ages to the early 20th century; natural archaeology and ethnology sections; libraries attached to each section; Dir MARTIN SCHMIDT (acting); Operational Dir STEFFEN FÄRBER.

Heidelberg

Kurpfälzisches Museum der Stadt Heidelberg: Hauptstr. 97, 69117 Heidelberg; tel. (6221) 5834020; e-mail kurpfaelzischesmuseum@heidelberg.de; internet www.museum-heidelberg.de; f. 1879; Dir Prof. Dr FRIEDER HEPP.

Hildesheim

Roemer- und Pelizaeus Museum (Roman and Pelizaeus Museum): Am Steine 1–2, 31134 Hildesheim; tel. (5121) 93690; e-mail info@rpmuseum.de; internet www.rpmuseum.de; f. 1844; natural history, applied art, prehistory, ethnography, Egyptian art; library of 35,000 vols; Dir Dr KATJA LEMBKE.

Jena

Goethe-Gedenkstätte (im Inspektorhaus des Botanischen Gartens): Friedrich Schiller Universität Jena, Fürstengraben 26, 07743 Jena; tel. (3641) 931188; e-mail h.huehn@uni-jena.de; internet www.uni-jena.de/gartenhaus_goethe_gedenkstätte.html; f. 1921; Curator Dr BABETT FORSTER; Dir Dr HELMUT HÜHN.

Optisches Museum der Ernst-Abbe-Stiftung Jena (Optical Museum at the Ernst Abbe Foundation): Carl-Zeiss-Pl. 12, 07743 Jena; tel. (3641) 443165; e-mail info@optischesmuseum.de; internet www.optischesmuseum.de; f. 1922; history and devt of optical instruments; vision aids and glasses, cameras and magic lanterns, stereoscopes and magic lantern images, historic workshop of Carl Zeiss; library of 4,000 vols.

Romantikerhaus—Museum der Deutschen Frühromantik (Romantikerhaus—Museum of Early German Romanticism): Unterm Markt 12A, 07743 Jena; tel. (3641) 498249; e-mail romantikerhaus@jena.de; internet www.romantikerhaus.jena.de; f. 1981; Dir KLAUS SCHWARZ.

Stadtmuseum (City Museum): Markt 7, 07743 Jena; tel. (3641) 498261; e-mail stadtmuseum@jena.de; internet www.museen.jena.de; f. 1903; art colln and town historical colln; regional historical literature; library of 30,000 vols; Dir Dr MATIAS MIETH.

Karlsruhe

Badisches Landesmuseum Karlsruhe: Schloss, 76131 Karlsruhe; tel. (721)

9266514; e-mail info@landesmuseum.de; internet www.landesmuseum.de; f. 1919; colln incl. prehistoric, Egyptian, Greek and Roman antiquities, medieval, renaissance and baroque sculpture, works of art from the Middle Ages to the 20th century, weapons, folklore and coins, colln of Turkish trophies; library of 75,000 vols; Dir Prof. Dr HARALD SIEBENMORGEN.

Museum für Literatur am Oberrhein (Museum for Literature at Upper Rhine): Prinz-Max-Palais, Karlstr. 10, 76133 Karlsruhe; tel. (721) 1334087; e-mail info@literaturmuseum.de; internet www.literaturmuseum.de; f. 1965; exhibition of the works, MSS and pictures of various authors; library of 8,000 vols; Pres. Prof. Dr HANSGEORG SCHMIDT-BERGMANN; Sec. MONIKA RIHM; publs *Jahresgabe*, *Mitteilungen*.

Staatliche Kunsthalle: POB 11 12 53, 76062 Karlsruhe; Hans-Thoma-Str. 2–6, 76133 Karlsruhe; tel. (721) 9263359; e-mail info@kunsthalle-karlsruhe.de; internet www.kunsthalle-karlsruhe.de; f. 1846; German, Dutch, Flemish, French paintings and sculpture from the 14th–20th centuries; print room; 90,000 prints and drawings; education service; library of 150,000 vols; Dir Dr PIA MÜLLER-TAMM.

Staatliches Museum für Naturkunde Karlsruhe (State Museum of Natural History, Karlsruhe): Erbprinzenstr. 13, 76133 Karlsruhe; tel. (721) 1752111; e-mail museum@naturkundeka-bw.de; internet www.naturkundemuseum-karlsruhe.de; f. 1785; research and exhibitions in botany, zoology, mineralogy, geology, entomology, palaeontology, vivarium; library of 50,000 vols; Dir Prof. Dr NORBERT LENZ; publs *Andrias*, *Carolinea*, *Exhibition Catalogues* (irregular).

Kassel

Brüder Grimm-Museum Kassel Brüder Grimm-Gesellschaft eV: Brüder Grimm-Platz 4, 34117 Kassel; tel. (561) 103235; e-mail grimmnet@t-online.de; internet www.grimms.de; f. 1959; preservation of works of Jacob, Wilhelm and Ludwig Emil Grimm; colln of works by the brothers; original paintings, autographs, letters, drawings, etchings, int. research projects, travelling exhibitions; Dir Dr BERNHARD LAUER; publ. *Brüder Grimm-Journal, Jahrbuch der Brüder Grimm-Gesellschaft*.

Museumslandschaft Hessen Kassel (State Art Museums): POB 41 04 20, 34066 Kassel; Schloss Wilhelmshöhe, 34131 Kassel; tel. (561) 316800; e-mail info@museum-kassel.de; internet www.museum-kassel.de; f. 18th century; Dir Prof. Dr BERND KÜSTER.

Constituent Museums:

Astronomisch-Physikalisches Kabinett: Karlsaue 20C, Kassel; tel. (561) 31680500; e-mail info@museum-kassel.de; internet www.museum-kassel.de; f. 1992; astronomy and physics colln with history of technology section; planetarium; Dir Dr KARSTEN GAULKE.

Museum Schloss Friedrichstein: Schlossstr., Bad Wildungen; tel. (5621) 6577; e-mail a.scherner@museum-kassel.de; internet www.museum-kassel.de; f. 1980; military and hunting exhibits from 15th–19th centuries; Curator Dr ANTJE SCHERNER.

Museum Schloss Wilhelmshöhe: Schlosspark 1, 34131 Kassel; tel. (561) 316800; e-mail info@museum-kassel.de; internet www.museum-kassel.de; f. 1800; department of classical antiquities, gallery of old master paintings from 15th–18th centuries, collection of drawings and engravings; library of 105,000 vols, 600 journals; Dir Dr MICHAEL EISSENHAUER.

Neue Galerie: Schöne Aussicht 1, Kassel; tel. (561) 316800; e-mail info@museum-kassel.de; internet www.museum-kassel.de; f. 1976; paintings and sculpture of the 19th to 21st century; Dir Prof. Dr BERND KÜSTER.

Konstanz

Archäologisches Landesmuseum (Regional Archaeological Museum): Benediktinerpl. 5, 78467 Konstanz; tel. (7531) 98040; e-mail info@konstanz.alm-bw.de; internet www.konstanz.alm-bw.de; f. 1990; local archaeological artefacts; Dir Dr JÖRG HEILIGMANN.

Bodensee-Naturmuseum (Lake Constance Natural History Museum): Hafenstr. 9, 78462 Konstanz; tel. (7531) 900915; e-mail krothm@stadt.konstanz.de; internet www.konstanz.de/naturmuseum; f. 1967; geology, palaeontology, zoology and botany of Lake Constance; Dir MARTINA KROTH.

Hus-Museum: Hussenstr. 64, 78462 Konstanz; tel. (7531) 29042; e-mail hus-museum@t-online.de; internet www.konstanz.de/tourismus; f. 1965; house of religious thinker, philosopher and reformer, Jan Hus (c. 1369–1415); display by Czech and Slovak artists depicting Hus's life, Ccl of Constance and the Hussite wars; Dir Dr LIBUSE RÖSCH.

Rosgarten Museum: Rosgartenstr. 3–5, 78462 Konstanz; tel. (7531) 900277; internet www.konstanz.de/rosgartenmuseum; f. 1870; central museum for Lake Constance area; prehistoric, early historic colln; arts and crafts from the Middle Ages to 19th century; library of 6,000 vols; Dir Dr TOBIAS ENGELSING.

Leipzig

Deutsches Buch- und Schriftmuseum der Deutschen Nationalbibliothek Leipzig (German Book Museum): Deutscher Pl. 1, 04103 Leipzig; tel. (341) 2271324; e-mail dbsm@dnb.de; internet www.dnb.de; f. 1884; exhibits relate to history of books, writing and paper; library of 172,519 vols, 1,156 incunabula and MSS, 43,127 items of graphic art, 406,597 watermarks, 82,749 printed books since 1501; Dir Dr STEPHANIE JACOBS.

Museum der Bildenden Künste Leipzig (Leipzig Museum of Fine Arts): Katharinenstr. 10, 04109 Leipzig; tel. (341) 2169990; e-mail mdbk@leipzig.de; internet www.mdbk.de; f. 1837; 3,000 paintings; collns of drawings and sculptures; Dir Dr HANS-WERNER SCHMIDT.

Museum für Kunsthandwerk Leipzig, Grassi-Museum (Museum of Applied Arts): Neumarkt 20, 04109 Leipzig; tel. (341) 2133719; e-mail grassimuseum@leipzig.de; internet www.grassimuseum.de; f. 1874; textiles, ceramics, glass, wood, and metal objects; prints and patterns relating to design; Dir Dr EVA M. HOYER.

Staatliche Ethnographische Sammlungen Sachsen, Staatlichen Kunstsammlungen Dresden (State Ethnographical Collection of Saxony): POB 10 09 55, 04009 Leipzig; Museum für Völkerkunde zu Leipzig/Grassimuseum, Johannispl. 5–11, 04103 Leipzig; tel. (341) 9731900; e-mail mvl-grassimuseum@ses.museum; internet www.mvl-grassimuseum.de; f. 2003 by the merger of Museum für Völkerkunde zu Leipzig, Museum für Völkerkunde Dresden and Völkerkundemuseum Herrnhut; Dir Dr CLAUS DEIMEL.

Constituent Museums:

Museum für Völkerkunde Dresden (Ethnographical Museum Dresden): Königsbrücker Landstr. 159, 01109 Dresden; tel. (351) 8926202; e-mail voelkerkunde.dresden@ses.museum; internet www.voelkerkunde-dresden.de; f. 1875; ethnography, physical anthropology; library of 350,000 vols; Dir Dr CLAUS DEIMEL; publs *Abhandlungen und Berichte* (Essays and Records), *Bibliographien Africa 1–3, Oceania 1–3* (irregular), *Dresdner Tagungsberichte* (irregular), *Kleine Beiträge* (irregular).

Museum für Völkerkunde zu Leipzig (Ethnographical Museum in Leipzig): POB 10 09 55, 04009 Leipzig; GRASSI Museum für Völkerkunde zu Leipzig, Johannispl. 5–11, 04103 Leipzig; tel. (341) 9731900; e-mail mvl-grassimuseum@ses.museum; internet www.mvl-grassimuseum.de; f. 1869; ethnographical collns from Asia, Australia, Pacific Islands, Africa, America, Europe; library of 275,000 vols; Dir Dr CLAUS DEIMEL; publ. *Abhandlungen und Berichte*.

Völkerkundemuseum Herrnhut (Ethnographical Museum Herrnhut): Goethestr. 1, 02747 Herrnhut; tel. (35873) 2403; e-mail voelkerkunde.herrnhut@ses.museum; internet www.voelkerkunde-herrnhut.de; f. 1878; ethnography; contains collns made by Moravian Church missionaries; library of 6,000 vols; Curator STEPHAN AUGUSTIN.

Stadtgeschichtliches Museum Leipzig (City history museum Leipzig): Böttchergäßchen 3, 04109 Leipzig; tel. (341) 965130; e-mail stadtmuseum@leipzig.de; internet www.stadtgeschichtliches-museum-leipzig.de; f. 1909; library of 160,000 items; Dir Dr VOLKER RODEKAMP.

Lübeck

Museen für Kunst und Kulturgeschichte (Museums for Art and Cultural History): Düvekenstr. 21, 23552 Lübeck; tel. (451) 1224134; e-mail mkk@luebeck.de; internet www.die-luebecker-museen.de; Dir Dr THORSTEN RODIEK.

Branch Museums:

Katharinenkirche: Königstr. 27, 23552 Lübeck; tel. (451) 1224144; e-mail mkk@luebeck.de; 14th-century bldgs; fmrly Franciscan monasteries church; Dir Dr BETTINA ZÖLLER-STOCK.

Museum Behnhaus Drägerhaus: Königstr. 9–11, 23552 Lübeck; tel. (451) 1224148; e-mail behnhaus@luebeck.de; internet www.die-luebecker-museen.de; f. 1921; museum of 19th-century art located in late 18th-century patrician house; art from Overbeck to Munch; Dir Dr ALEXANDER BASTEK.

Museum Holstentor: Holstentorpl., 23552 Lübeck; tel. (451) 1224129; e-mail mkk@luebeck.de; internet www.die-luebecker-museen.de; built 1464–1478; history of the city and the merchant of Lübeck; Dir Dr THORSTEN RODIEK.

St Annen-Museum und Kunsthalle St Annen (St Annen Museum and Art Gallery): St Annen-Str. 15, 23552 Lübeck; tel. (451) 1224137; e-mail mq@luebeck.de; internet www.die-luebecker-museen.de; f. 1915 (Museum), 2003 (Art Gallery); Late Gothic convent, built 1502–15; medieval ecclesiastical art from Lübeck; domestic art from Lübeck, from Middle Ages to 18th century; modern and contemporary art; Dir Dr BETTINA ZÖLLER-STOCK.

Völkerkundesammlung (Ethnographic Collection): Grosser Bauhof 14, 23552

Lübeck; tel. (451) 1224342; e-mail vks@luebeck.de; internet www.die-luebecker-museen.de; f. 1893; Dir Dr BRIGITTE TEMPLIN.

Magdeburg

Magdeburger Museen: Otto-von-Guericke-Str. 68–73, 39104 Magdeburg; tel. (391) 5403501; e-mail museen@magdeburg.de; internet www.magdeburgermuseen.de; f. 1906; local history colln, art gallery, sculptures, handicrafts, graphics, bibliophilia, costumes, sociology, natural history and prehistory colln; Kulturhistorisches Museum, Kunstmuseum Kloster Unser Lieben Frauen, Museum für Naturkunde, Technikmuseum; library of 50,000 vols; Dir Prof. Dr MATTHIAS PUHLE; publs *Abhandlungen und Berichte Naturkunde und Vorgeschichte*, *Magdeburger Museumshefte* (irregular), *Magdeburger Museumsschriften* (irregular).

Mainz

Gutenberg-Museum: Liebfrauenpl. 5, 55116 Mainz; tel. (6131) 122640; e-mail gutenberg-museum@stadt.mainz.de; internet www.gutenberg-museum.de; f. 1900; world museum of typography; library of 90,000 vols; Dir Dr ANNETTE LUDWIG.

Landesmuseum Mainz (Mainz State Museum): Grosse Bleiche 49–51, 55116 Mainz; tel. (6131) 28570; e-mail landesmuseum-mainz@gdke.rlp.de; internet www.landesmuseum-mainz.de; f. 1803; cultural history and art; Dir Dr ANDREA STOCKHAMMER; Deputy Dir Dr NORBERT SUHR.

Münzsammlung (Coin Collection): Stadtarchiv Mainz, Rheinallee 3B, 55116 Mainz; tel. (6131) 122178; e-mail stadtarchiv@stadt.mainz.de; internet www.stadtarchiv.mainz.de; f. 1784; Dir Dr WOLFGANG DOBRAS.

Naturhistorisches Museum Mainz (Natural History Museum): Reichklarastr. 1, 55116 Mainz; tel. (6131) 122646; e-mail naturhistorisches.museum@stadt.mainz.de; internet www.mainz.de/nhm; f. 1910; mineralogy, geology, palaeontology, zoology and botany of Rheinland-Pfalz and Rwanda; library of 40,000 vols, 60,000 pamphlets; Dir Dr MICHAEL SCHMITZ; Deputy Dir Dr HERBERT LUTZ; publs *Mainzer Naturwissenschaftliches Archiv* (1 a year), *Mainzer Naturwissenschaftliches Archiv, Beihefte*, *Mitteilungen der Rheinischen Naturforschenden Gesellschaft* (1 a year).

Römisch-Germanisches Zentralmuseum–Forschungsinstitut für Vor- und Frühgeschichte (Central Roman-German Museum–Research Museum for Prehistory and Early History): Ernst-Ludwig-Pl. 2, 55116 Mainz; tel. (6131) 9124113; e-mail info@rgzm.de; internet web.rgzm.de; f. 1852; studies in Old World archaeology and prehistory, conservation of prehistoric, Roman and early medieval antiquities; library of 120,000 vols; Gen. Dir Prof. Dr FALKO DAIM; publs *Arbeitsblätter für Restauratoren*, *Archäologisches Korrespondenzblatt*, *Ausstellungskataloge*, *Corpus Signorum Imperii Romani*, *Führer durch die Ausstellungen*, *Kataloge, Restaurierung und Archäologie*, *Studien zu den Anfängen der Metallurgie*, *Vulkanpark-Forschungen*.

Mannheim

Kunsthalle Mannheim (Arts Centre Mannheim): Moltkestr. 9, 68165 Mannheim; Friedrichspl. 4, 68165 Mannheim; tel. (621) 2936452; e-mail kunsthalle@mannheim.de; internet www.kunsthalle-mannheim.eu; f. 1909; 33,000 drawings, water colours and graphics, 1,700 paintings and 600 sculptures; Dir Dr ULRIKE LORENZ; Deputy Dir Dr INGE HEROLD.

Reiss-Engelhorn-Museen Mannheim: POB 10 30 51, 68030 Mannheim; Museum Weltkulturen D5, 68159; tel. (621) 2933150; e-mail reiss-engelhorn-museen@mannheim.de; internet www.rem-mannheim.de; f. 1957 as Reiss-Museum; museum of art, crafts and decorative arts, local theatre history, archaeology and prehistory, ethnology, local history and natural history; colln of historical European musical instruments; Forum Internationale Photgraphie (FIP); library of 120,000 vols; Dir-Gen. Prof. Dr ALFRIED WIECZOREK.

Marburg

Museum für Kunst und Kulturgeschichte (Museum for Art and Cultural History): Biegenstr. 11, 35037 Marburg; tel. (6421) 2822355; e-mail museum@verwaltung.uni-marburg.de; internet www.uni-marburg.de/uni-museum; f. 1927; attached to Philipps-Univ. Marburg; Dir Dr AGNES TIEZE; Sec. MARIA KATZ.

Mettmann

Neanderthal-Museum: Talstr. 300, 40822 Mettmann; tel. (2104) 97970; e-mail museum@neanderthal.de; internet www.neanderthal.de; f. 1996; human evolution since earliest times; library of 4,000 vols; Dir Prof. Dr GERD-C. WENIGER.

Munich

Archäologische Staatssammlung München (Bavarian State Archaeological Collection): Lerchenfeldstr. 2, 80538 Munich; tel. (89) 2112402; e-mail archaeologische.staatssammlung@extern.lrz-muenchen.de; internet www.archaeologie-bayern.de; f. 1885; prehistoric, Roman and early medieval antiquities from Southern Germany, prehistoric archaeology of Mediterranean and Near East; Dir Prof. Dr Hab. RUPERT GEBHARD; Deputy Dir Dr BERND STEIDL; publ. *Kataloge* (irregular).

Bayerische Staatsgemäldesammlungen (Bavarian State Painting Collections): Barerstr. 29, 80799 Munich; tel. (89) 238050; e-mail info@pinakothek.de; internet www.pinakothek.de; medieval to modern art, painting and sculpture; Gen. Dir Prof. Dr KLAUS SCHRENK.

Bayerisches Nationalmuseum (National Bavarian Museum): Prinzregentenstr. 3, 80538 Munich; tel. (89) 2112401; e-mail bay.nationalmuseum@bnm.mwn.de; internet www.bayerisches-nationalmuseum.de; f. 1855; European fine arts, especially sculpture, decorative art and folk art; library of 75,000 vols; Dir Dr RENATE EIKELMANN; publs *Ausstellungskataloge*, *Bestandskataloge*, *Bayerische Blätter für Volkskunde*, *Bildführer*, *Forschungshefte*.

Deutsches Museum von Meisterwerken der Naturwissenschaft und Technik (German Museum of Scientific and Technological Masterpieces): 80306 Munich; Museumsinsel 1, 80538 Munich; tel. (89) 2179213; e-mail information@deutsches-museum.de; internet www.deutsches-museum.de; f. 1903; history of science and technology from its origins to the present day; spec. colln of MSS and autographs, trade literature, plans, pictorial art, films, commemorative medals; research institute for the history of science and technology; 'Kerschensteiner Kolleg' for teacher in-service training; library of 920,000 vols, 3,500 current periodicals; Dir-Gen. Prof. Dr WOLFGANG M. HECKL; publ. *Kultur und Technik* (4 a year).

Affiliated Museums:

Deutsches Museum Bonn (German Museum in Bonn): Ahrstr. 45, 53175 Bonn; tel. (228) 302255; e-mail info@deutsches-museum-bonn.de; internet www.deutsches-museum-bonn.de; f. 1995; science and technology in Germany since 1945; Dir Dr ANDREA NIEHAUS.

Deutsches Museum Flugwerft Schleissheim (German Museum in Flugwerft Schleissheim): Effnerstr. 18, 85764 Oberschleissheim; tel. (89) 3157140; e-mail fws@deutsches-museum.de; f. 1992; aeronautical colln; Dir-Gen. Prof. Dr WOLFGANG M. HECKL.

Deutsches Museum Verkehrszentrum (German Museum—Transport Centre): Am Bavariapark 5, 80339 Munich; tel. (89) 500806762; e-mail verkehrszentrum@deutsches-museum.de; internet www.deutsches-museum.de/verkehrszentrum; f. 2003; traffic museum; Dir Gen. Prof. Dr WOLFGANG M. HECKL.

Neue Sammlung–Staatliches Museum für Angewandte Kunst (State Museum for Applied Arts): POB 34 01 34, 80098 Munich; Türkenstr. 15 (Pinakothek der Moderne), 80333 Munich; tel. (89) 2727250; e-mail info@die-neue-sammlung.de; internet www.die-neue-sammlung.de; f. 1925; modern industrial arts and crafts, architecture, urban planning; industrial and graphic design; Dir Prof. Dr FLORIAN HUFNAGL.

Staatliche Antikensammlungen und Glyptothek (State Antique Collections): Königspl. 1–3, 80333 Munich; tel. (89) 286100; e-mail info@antike-am-koenigsplatz.mwn.de; internet www.antike-am-koenigsplatz.mwn.de; f. 1830; Greek and Etruscan vases and bronzes, Greek and Roman sculpture, terracottas and bronzes, glass, jewellery; Dir Dr FLORIAN KNAUSS; Curator Dr ASTRID FENDT; Curator Dr CHRISTIAN GLIWITZKY; Curator Dr JÖRG GEBAUER.

Staatliche Graphische Sammlung München: Katharina-von-Bora-Str. 10, 80333 Munich; tel. (89) 28927650; e-mail info@sgsm.eu; internet www.sgsm.eu; f. 1758; German, Dutch, French and Italian prints and drawings since 15th century; Dir Dr MICHAEL SEMFF.

Staatliche Münzsammlung (State Coin Collection): Residenzstr. 1, 80333 Munich; tel. (89) 227221; e-mail info@staatliche-muenzsammlung.de; internet www.staatliche-muenzsammlung.de; f. 16th century; coins from different countries and centuries; spec. collns: Greek, Roman and Byzantine coins, German and Italian Renaissance medals, Bavarian coins, precious stones from antiquity, Middle Ages and Renaissance, Japanese lacquer cabinets; library of 26,000 vols; Dir Dr DIETRICH KLOSE.

Staatliche Naturwissenschaftliche Sammlungen Bayerns, München (München Bavarian Natural History Collections): Menzingerstr. 71, 80638 Munich; tel. (89) 17999240; e-mail generaldirektion@snsb.de; internet www.snsb.de; f. 1827; scientific colln of c. 35m. specimens; Gen. Dir Prof. Dr GERHARD HASZPRUNAR.

Subordinate Institutions:

Bayerische Staatssammlung für Paläontologie und Geologie: Richard-Wagner-Str. 10, 80333 Munich; tel. (89) 21806630; e-mail pal.sammlung@lrz.uni-muenchen.de; internet www.palmuc.de/bspg; f. 1759; colln and preservation of fossils and rock materials; library of 120,000 vols; Dir Prof. Dr GERT WÖRHEIDE; publ. *Zitteliana*.

Botanische Staatssammlung München: Menzinger-Str. 67, 80638 Munich; tel. (89) 17861265; e-mail office@

bsm.mwn.de; internet www.botanischestaatssammlung.de; f. 1813; natural history colln of 3m. objects; library of 30,000 vols; Dir Prof. Dr SUSANNE RENNER; publ. *Arnoldia*.

Botanischer Garten München–Nymphenburg: Menzinger Str. 61–65, 80638 Munich; tel. (89) 17861316; e-mail botgart@botmuc.de; internet www.botmuc.de; f. 1914; Dir Prof. Dr SUSANNE RENNER.

Jura-Museum: Willibaldsburg, Burgstr. 19, 85072 Eichstätt; tel. (8421) 2956; e-mail sekretariat@jura-museum.de; internet www.jura-museum.de; f. 1976; natural history; Man. Dir Dr MARTINA KÖLBL-EBERT; publ. *Archaeopteryx*.

Mineralogische Staatssammlung (Mineralogical State Collection Munich): Theresienstr. 41, 80333 Munich; tel. (89) 21804312; e-mail mineralogische.staatssammlung@lrz.uni-muenchen.de; internet www.mineralogische-staatssammlung.de; f. 1823; Dir Prof. Dr WOLFGANG SCHMAHL.

Museum Mensch und Natur (Museum of Man and Nature): Schloss Nymphenburg, Maria-Ward-Str. 1B, 80638 Munich; tel. (89) 1795890; e-mail museum@musmn.de; internet www.musmn.de; f. 1990; modern natural history with interactive exhibition design; permanent exhibitions cover range of subjects from geology and mineralogy to neurobiology, genetics, ecology; temporary exhibitions; Man. Dir MICHAEL APEL; Deputy Man. Dr GILLA SIMON.

Naturkunde-Museum Bamberg: Fleischstr. 2, 96047 Bamberg; tel. (951) 8631249; e-mail info@naturkundemuseum-bamberg.de; internet www.naturkundemuseum-bamberg.de; f. 1790; colln of 200,000 objects from the fields of geology, mineralogy, palaeontology, zoology and botany; Man. Dr MATTHIAS MÄUSER.

Rieskrater-Museum Nördlingen: Eugene-Shoemaker-Pl. 1, 86720 Nördlingen; tel. (9081) 84710; e-mail rieskratermuseum@noerdlingen.de; internet www.rieskratermuseum.de; f. 1990; natural history; Man. Prof. Dr STEFAN HÖLZL.

Staatssammlung für Anthropologie und Paläoanatomie: Karolinenpl. 2A, 80333 Munich; tel. (89) 54884380; e-mail asm.boulesnam@extern.lrz-muenchen.de; internet www.sapm.mwn.de; f. 1886; Dir Prof. Dr GISELA GRUPE; Dir Prof. Dr JORIS PETERS.

Urwelt-Museum Oberfranken: Kanzleistr. 1, 95444 Bayreuth; tel. (921) 511211; e-mail verwaltung@urwelt-museum.de; internet www.urwelt-museum.de; f. 1997; natural history; Man. Dr JOACHIM MARTIN RABOLD.

Zoologische Staatssammlung München: Münchhausenstr. 21, 81247 Munich; tel. (89) 81070; e-mail zsm@zsm.mwn.de; internet www.zsm.mwn.de; f. 1807; more than 25m. zoological objects; library of 92,664 vols (books and serials), 823 running journals, 129,020 separata; Dir Prof. Dr GERHARD HASZPRUNAR; publs *Journal of Zoology*, *Spixiana*, *Spixiana Supplements*.

Staatliches Museum Ägyptischer Kunst (State Museum of Egyptian Art): Arcisstraße 16, 80333 Munich; Hofgartenstr., Munich; tel. (89) 28927630; e-mail info@smaek.de; internet www.aegyptisches-museum-muenchen.de; f. 1966; library: small specialized library; Dir Dr SYLVIA SCHOSKE.

Staatliches Museum für Völkerkunde München (State Museum of Ethnology Munich): Maximilianstr. 42, 80538 Munich; tel. (89) 210136100; e-mail museum.voelkerkunde@mfv.bayern.de; internet www.voelkerkundemuseum-muenchen.de; f. 1862; collns on Asia, America, Africa and the Pacific Islands; library of 100,000 vols, 75 current periodicals; Dir Dr CHRISTINE STELZIG.

Städtische Galerie im Lenbachhaus (Urban Gallery in the Lenbachhaus): Nymphenburger Str. 84, 80636 Munich; Luisenstr. 33, 80333 Munich; tel. (89) 23332000; e-mail lenbachhaus@muenchen.de; internet www.lenbachhaus.de; f. 1929; Munich artists incl. paintings by Kandinsky, Klee and the Blaue Reiter group; int. contemporary art; exhibitions, lectures, performances; library of 65,000 vols; Dir Prof. Dr HELMUT FRIEDEL; Man. KURT LAUBE.

Münster

Landesmuseum für Kunst und Kulturgeschichte (Westphalian Museum of Art and Cultural History): Dompl. 10, 48143 Münster; tel. (251) 590701; e-mail landesmuseum@lwl.org; internet www.lwl-landesmuseum-muenster.de; f. 1908; sculpture, painting, graphic art, goldsmith work since 9th century; engraved portraits, history, numismatics; library of 128,000 vols; Dir Dr WOLFGANG KIRSCH.

Nuremberg

Albrecht-Dürer-Haus: Albrecht-Dürer-Str. 39, 90403 Nuremberg; tel. (911) 2312271; e-mail museen@stadt.nuernberg.de; internet www.museen.nuernberg.de; f. 1828; life and work of the engraver, painter and art theoretician Albrecht Dürer (1471–1528) presented in his home (inhabited 1509–28); library of 8,000 vols; Dir Dr THOMAS SCHAUERTE.

Germanisches Nationalmuseum: Kartäusergasse 1, 90402 Nuremberg; tel. (911) 13310; e-mail info@gnm.de; internet www.gnm.de; f. 1852; German art and culture from prehistoric times to the present, fine art galleries, folk art, public library, archives, print room, musical instruments, arms, toys, etc.; library of 548,000 vols, 1,600 current periodicals; Chief Dir Prof. Dr G. ULRICH GROSSMANN.

Kunsthalle Nürnberg im KunstKulturQuartier (Nuremberg Art Museum): 90317 Nuremberg; Lorenzer Str. 32, 90402 Nuremberg; tel. (911) 2312853; e-mail kunsthalle@stadt.nuernberg.de; internet www.kunsthalle.nuernberg.de; f. 1967; changing exhibitions of int. contemporary art; Dir ELLEN SEIFERMANN.

Stadtmuseum Fembohaus (City Museum Fembohaus): Burgstr. 11, 90403 Nuremberg; tel. (911) 2315418; e-mail museen@stadt.nuernberg.de; internet www.museen.nuernberg.de; f. 1958; art and cultural history of Nuremberg; Dir RUDOLF KÄS.

Offenbach am Main

Klingspor-Museum Offenbach: Herrnstr. 80, 63061 Offenbach am Main; tel. (69) 80652954; e-mail klingspormuseum@offenbach.de; internet www.offenbach.de/klingspor-museum; f. 1953; colln and exhibition of calligraphy, typography, bookbinding, modern book art and private presses; spec. colln of 20th-century calligraphy; library of 73,000 vols; Dir Dr STEFAN SOLTEK; Librarian MARTINA WEISS; Librarian STEPHANIE EHRET.

Pforzheim

Schmuckmuseum Pforzheim im Reuchlinhaus: Jahnstr. 42, 75173 Pforzheim; tel. (7231) 392126; e-mail schmuckmuseum@stadt-pforzheim.de; internet www.schmuckmuseum.de; f. 1938; permanent and temporary exhibitions about jewellery and its history, displaying past 5,000 years; Dir CORNELIE HOLZACH.

Potsdam

Brandenburgisches Landesmuseum für Ur- und Frühgeschichte (Pre- and Early History): Forstweg 1, 14656 Brieselang; tel. (332) 3236940; f. 1953; Dir Prof. Dr J. KUNOW; publs *Forschungen zur Archäologie im Land Brandenburg* (1 a year), *Veröffentlichungen des Brandenburgischen Landesmuseums für Ur- und Frühgeschichte* (1 a year).

Stiftung Preussische Schlösser und Gärten Berlin-Brandenburg (Prussian Palaces and Gardens Foundation of Berlin-Brandenburg): POB 60 14 62, 14414 Potsdam; Allee nach Sanssouci 5, 14471 Potsdam; tel. (331) 9694200; e-mail info@spsg.de; internet www.spsg.de; f. 1995; administers gardens and 150 palaces and other historic bldgs in and around Berlin and Potsdam; more than 30 palaces open to the public; Dir-Gen. Prof. Dr HARTMUT DORGERLOH; Admin. Dir Dr HEINZ BERG.

Recklinghausen

Museen der Stadt Recklinghausen (Recklinghausen City Museums): Grosse-Perdekamp-Str. 25–27, 45657 Recklinghausen; tel. (2361) 501935; e-mail info@kunst-re.de; internet www.kunst-re.de; f. 1950; Dir Dr FERDINAND ULLRICH.

Attached Museums:

Ikonen-Museum (Icon Museum): Kirchpl. 2A, 45657 Recklinghausen; tel. (2361) 501941; e-mail ikonen@kunst-re.de; internet www.kunst-re.de; f. 1956; 3.000 Russian, Byzantine, Greek and Balkan icons, miniatures, metal work, Coptic art and textiles; Dir Prof. Dr FERDINAND ULLRICH; Curator Dr EVA HAUSTEIN-BARTSCH.

Städtische Kunsthalle (City Art Gallery): Recklinghausen; tel. (2361) 501935; e-mail info@kunst-re.de; internet www.kunst-re.de; f. 1950; paintings, drawings, prints and sculptures by contemporary artists; Dir Dr FERDINAND ULLRICH; Dir Dr HANS-JUERGEN SCHWALM.

Vestisches Museum: Hohenzollernstr. 12, 45659 Recklinghausen; tel. (2361) 501946; e-mail info@kunst-re.de; internet www.kunst-re.de; f. 1987; Westphalian arts and crafts, local history, native art; Dir Dr FERDINAND ULLRICH; Dir Dr HANS-JUERGEN SCHWALM.

Schleswig

Stiftung Schleswig-Holsteinische Landesmuseen Schloss Gottorf (Foundation of State Museums in Schleswig-Holstein in Schloss Gottorf): Schloss Gottorf, 24837 Schleswig; tel. (4621) 813222; e-mail info@schloss-gottorf.de; internet www.schloss-gottorf.de; f. 1835; houses archaeological and art and culture museums and the Centre for Baltic and Scandinavian Archaeology; library of 40,000 vols; Dir Prof. Dr CLAUS VON CARNAP-BORNHEIM; Dir Dr JÜRGEN FITSCHEN; publs *Ausgrabungen in Haithabu* (irregular), *Ausgrabungen in Schleswig* (irregular), *Berichte über die Ausgrabungen in Haithabu* (irregular), *Die Funde der älteren Bronzezeit des nordischen Kreises* (irregular), *Offa* (1 a year), *Offa Bücher* (irregular), *Untersuchungen und Materialien zur Steinzeit in Schleswig-Holstein* (irregular).

Affiliated Museums:

Archäologisches Landesmuseum (Provincial Museum of Archaeology): Schloss Gottorf, 24837 Schleswig; tel. (4621) 813222; internet www.schloss-gottorf.de/alm; f. 1835; archaeological and ethnological exhibits.

Eisenkunstgussmuseum Büdelsdorf (Ironwork Museum): Glück-Auf-Allee 4, 24782 Büdelsdorf; internet www.schloss-gottorf.de/ekg; f. 1981; history of ironwork.

Jüdisches Museum Rendsburg (Jewish Museum): Prinzessinstr. 7–8, 24768 Rendsburg; tel. (4331) 25262; e-mail info@jmrd.de; internet www.schloss-gottorf.de/jm; f. 1988.

Landesmuseum für Kunst und Kulturgeschichte (Museum of Art and Culture): Schloss Gottorf, 24837 Schleswig; tel. (4621) 813222; internet www.schloss-gottorf.de/lmkk; artefacts from Middle Ages onwards; colln of 19th-century paintings.

Volkskunde Museum Schleswig (Folklore Museum in Schleswig): Schloss Gottorf, 24837 Schleswig; Suadicanistr. 46–54, 24837 Schleswig; tel. (4621) 96760; e-mail volkskunde@schloss-gottorf.de; internet www.schloss-gottorf.de/vkm; f. 1993; history of local arts and crafts; Dir GUNTRAM TURKOWSKI.

Wikinger Museum Haithabu–Stiftung Schleswig-Holsteinische Landesmuseen Schloss Gottorf (Museum of the Viking-Age settlement Haithabu): Schloss Gottorf, 24837 Schleswig; tel. (4621) 813222; e-mail info@schloss-gottorf.de; internet www.schloss-gottorf.de/wmh; history of the archaeological dig; restored longship on port.

Schwerin

Archäologisches Landesmuseum und Landesamt für Bodendenkmalpflege Mecklenburg-Vorpommern: Domhof 4/5, 19055 Schwerin; tel. (385) 52140; e-mail poststelle@kulturerbe-mv.de; internet www.kulturerbe-mv.de; f. 1953; library of 44,000 vols; Dir Dr FRIEDRICH LÜTH; publs *Archäologie in Mecklenburg-Vorpommern*, *Archäologische Berichte aus Mecklenburg-Vorpommern*, *Beiträge zur Ur- und Frühgeschichte Mecklenburg-Vorpommerns*, *Materialhefte*, *Museumskataloge*.

Speyer

Historisches Museum der Pfalz Speyer (Historical Museum of the Palatinate): Dompl. 4, 67346 Speyer; tel. (6232) 13250; e-mail info@museum.speyer.de; internet www.museum.speyer.de; f. 1869; art and cultural history of the Palatinate, incl. wine museum and diocesan museum; library of 20,000 vols; Dir Dr ALEXANDER KOCH; publs *Mitteilungen des Historischen Vereins* (1 a year), *Pfälzer Heimat* (4 a year).

Stralsund

Kulturhistorisches Museum der Hansestadt Stralsund (Cultural and Historical Museum of Stralsund): Mönchstr. 25–27, 18439 Stralsund; tel. (3831) 253617; e-mail kulturhistorisches-museum@stralsund.de; internet www.stralsund.de; f. 1858; prehistory, ecclesiastical art, folklore, local history, furniture, history of navigation and navy, modern art, handicrafts, 18th-century products; Dir Dr ANDREAS GRÜGER.

Stuttgart

Kunstmuseum Stuttgart (Stuttgart Art Museum): Kleiner Schlosspl. 1, 70173 Stuttgart; tel. (711) 2162188; e-mail info@kunstmuseum-stuttgart.de; internet www.kunstmuseum-stuttgart.de; f. 1924; paintings, drawings, graphics and sculptures by artists since 19th century; Otto Dix colln, Adolf Hölzel colln, Willi Baumeister archive; Dir Dr ULRIKE GROOS; Curator Dr DANIEL SPANKE; Curator Dr SIMONE SCHIMPF.

Landesmuseum Württemberg: Altes Schloss, Schillerpl. 6, 70173 Stuttgart; tel. (711) 89535111; e-mail info@landesmuseum-stuttgart.de; internet www.landesmuseum-stuttgart.de; f. 1862; archaeology, art history and cultural history from prehistoric to medieval times; 4,000 years of glass-making, Swabian sculpture, Renaissance clocks, musical instruments, Württemberg crown jewels; Roman lapidarium; museum for children; Dir Prof. Dr CORNELIA EWIGLEBEN; Chief Curator THOMAS BRUNE.

Linden-Museum Stuttgart, Staatliches Museum für Völkerkunde (Linden Museum Stuttgart, State Museum for Ethnography): Hegelpl. 1, 70174 Stuttgart; tel. (711) 2022456; e-mail sekretariat@lindenmuseum.de; internet www.lindenmuseum.de; f. 1882; ethnographical museum, exhibitions; library of 50,000 vols, 270 current periodicals; Dir Prof. Dr INÉS DE CASTRO; Librarian GÜNTER DARCIS; publ. *Tribus* (1 a year).

Staatliches Museum für Naturkunde Stuttgart (National Museum for Natural History Stuttgart): Rosenstein 1, 70191 Stuttgart; tel. (711) 89360; e-mail museum@smns-bw.de; internet www.naturkundemuseum-bw.de; f. 1791; colln and research in botany, palaeontology, zoology; exhibition (permanent and spec.), education; library of 75,000 vols; Dir Prof. Dr JOHANNA EDER; publs *Stuttgarter Beiträge zur Naturkunde, Serie A: Biologie* (irregular), *Stuttgarter Beiträge zur Naturkunde, Serie C: Wissen für Alle* (2 a year), *Palaediversity, Serie B: Geologie / Paläontologie* (irregular).

Staatsgalerie Stuttgart: POB 10 43 42, 70038 Stuttgart; Konrad-Adenauerstr. 30–32, 70173 Stuttgart; tel. (711) 470400; e-mail info@staatsgalerie.de; internet www.staatsgalerie.de; f. 1843; art since the Middle Ages; colln of prints, drawings and photographs; Oskar Schlemmer Archive, Will Grohmann Archive, Sohm Archive, Adolf Hölzel's art-theoretical writings; library of 120,000 vols; Dir Prof. Dr CHRISTIANE LANGE.

Trier

Rheinisches Landesmuseum Trier (Museum of the Rheinland in Trier): Weimarer Allee 1, 54290 Trier; tel. (651) 97740; e-mail landesmuseum-trier@gdke.rlp.de; internet www.landesmuseum-trier.de; f. 1877; Roman and early medieval exhibits excavated in Trier and the local area; art history from the Middle Ages to the 19th century; numismatic colln; restoration workshops; dendrochronological and archeobotanical analyses; municipal and regional archaeological research; library of 100,000 vols, 3,000 journals; Dir Dr ECKART KÖHNE; publs *Funde und Ausgrabungen im Bezirk Trier* (1 a year), *Schriftenreihe des Rheinischen Landesmuseums Trier* (irregular), *Trierer Grabungen und Forschungen* (irregular), *Trierer Zeitschrift für Geschichte und Kunst* (1 a year).

Ulm

Ulmer Museum (Ulm Museum): Marktpl. 9, 89070 Ulm; tel. (731) 1614300; e-mail info.ulmer-museum@ulm.de; internet www.museum.ulm.de; f. 1924; collns of Ulm and Swabian art from 14th–19th centuries, int. art since beginning of 20th century, archaeological collns, archives of the fmr Ulm School of Design (Hochschule für Gestaltung); Dir Dr GABRIELE HOLTHUIS.

Weimar

Klassik Stiftung Weimar (Classical Period Foundation Weimar): Burgpl. 4, 99423 Weimar; tel. (3643) 545400; e-mail info@klassik-stiftung.de; internet www.klassik-stiftung.de; f. 1953; preserves and researches Weimar's artistic and cultural sites and collns, primarily the classical period in Weimar and modern art in Weimar; administers the Goethe-Nat. Museum (comprises 23 museums and houses connected with Goethe and Schiller, and other bldgs, incl. Liszt's house); also the Nietzsche-Archiv, the Schlossmuseum, the Bauhaus Museum, the Neues Museum, the Goethe- und Schiller-Archiv (800,000 MSS of German writers, artists, composers and scientists) and the Duchess Anna Amalia Bibliothek (850,000 vols); Pres. HELLMUT SEEMANN; Admin. Dir (vacant).

Thüringisches Landesamt für Denkmalpflege und Archäologie (Thuringian Regional Office for the Preservation of Monuments and Archaeology): Humboldtstr. 11, 99423 Weimar; tel. (3643) 818300; e-mail post.weimar@tlda.thueringen.de; internet www.thueringen.de/denkmalpflege; f. 1888; library of 28,000 vols; Pres. Dr Hab. SVEN OSTRITZ; publs *Ausgrabungen und Funde im Freistaat Thüringen*, *Jahresschrift 'Alt-Thüringen'*, *Restaurierung und Museumstechnik*, *Weimarer Monographien zur Ur- und Frühgeschichte*.

Attached Museums:

Museum für Ur- und Frühgeschichte Thüringens (Thuringian Museum for Pre- and Early History): Humboldtstr. 11, 99423 Weimar; tel. (3643) 818331; e-mail museum@tlda.thueringen.de; local history since 400,000 BC.

Steinsburgmuseum: Waldhaussiedlung 8, 98631 Römhild; tel. (36948) 20561; Celtic site and artefacts; Dir Dr M. SIEDEL.

Wittenberg

Lutherhaus, Reformationsgeschichtliches Museum (Museum of the History of the Reformation): Collegienstr. 54, 06886 Lutherstadt Wittenberg; tel. (3491) 4203118; e-mail lutherhaus@martinluther.de; internet www.martinluther.de; f. 1883; portraits, MSS, pictures, woodcuts, copperplates, medallions and original works on the history of the Reformation; library of 60,000 vols; Dir Dr STEFAN RHEIN.

Worms

Museum der Stadt Worms im Andreasstift (Worms City Museum): Weckerlingpl. 7, 67547 Worms; tel. (6241) 946390; e-mail museum@worms.de; internet www.museum.worms.de; f. 1881; archaeology, town history of Worms, spec. colln of glassware, Luther Room (diet of 1521); Dir for Admin. Dr GERALD BOENNEN; publs *Der Wormsgau* (1 a year), *Zeitschrift der Stadt Worms und des Altertumsvereins Worms*.

Museum Heylshof: Stephansgasse 9, 67547 Worms; tel. (6241) 22000; e-mail museum@heylshof.de; internet www.heylshof.de; f. 1923; paintings, sculptures, pottery, porcelains and glass from 15th–19th centuries; Curator CORNELIUS ADALBERT; Curator F. V. HEYL.

Universities

ALBERT-LUDWIGS-UNIVERSITÄT FREIBURG

Fahnenbergpl., 79085 Freiburg im Breisgau
Telephone: (761) 2030
E-mail: info@verwaltung.uni-freiburg.de
Internet: www.uni-freiburg.de

Founded 1457
Academic year: October to July
Rector: Prof. Dr HANS-JOCHEN SCHIEWER
Vice-Rector for Academic Affairs: Prof. Dr HEINER SCHANZ
Vice-Rector for Internationalization and Technology Transfer: Prof. Dr JÜRGEN RÜHE
Vice-Rector for Medicine: Prof. Dr CHARLOTTE NIEMEYER
Vice-Rector for Research: Prof. Dr HERMANN SCHWENGEL
Chancellor: Dr MATTHIAS SCHENEK
Library Dir: ANTJE KELLERSOHN
Library: see under Libraries and Archives
Number of teachers: 5,000
Number of students: 21,622

DEANS

Faculty of Biology: Prof. Dr GUNTHER NEUHAUS
Faculty of Chemistry, Pharmacology and Geosciences: Prof. Dr HARALD HILLEBRECHT
Faculty of Economics and Behavioural Sciences: Prof. Dr DIETER K. TSCHEULIN
Faculty of Engineering: Prof. Dr BERND BECKER
Faculty of Forestry and Environmental Sciences: Prof. Dr JÜRGEN BAUHUS
Faculty of Humanities: Prof. Dr HANS-HELMUTH GANDER
Faculty of Law: Prof. Dr SEBASTIAN KREBBER
Faculty of Mathematics and Physics: Prof. Dr KAY KÖNIGSMANN
Faculty of Medicine: Prof. Dr HUBERT ERICH BLUM
Faculty of Philology: Prof. Dr BERND KORTMANN
Faculty of Theology: Prof. Dr KLAUS BAUMANN

PROFESSORS

Faculty of Applied Sciences:

ALBERS, S., Parallel and Distributed Computing
BASIN, D., Informatics
BECKER, B., Informatics
BERGARD, W., Autonomous Intelligent Systems
BURKHARDT, H., Informatics
HAUSSELT, J., Microsystems Technology
KORVINK, J. G., Microsystems Technology
KUNTZ, Information Technology
LAUSEN, G., Informatics
LEUE, S., Computer Networks
MANOLI, Information Technology
MENZ, W., Microsystems Technology
NEBEL, B., Informatics
OTTMANN, TH., Informatics
PAUL, Information Technology
RAEDT, L. DE, Machine Learning
RÜHE, Information Technology
SCHMIDT-THIEME, L., Computer-Based New Media
SCHNEIDER, G., Communication Systems
SCHOLL, C., Operating Systems
THIEMANN, P., Programming Languages
URBAN, G. A., Microsystems Technology
WILDE, Information Technology
WOIAS, Information Technology
ZAPPE, Information Technology
ZENGERLE, Information Technology

Faculty of Biology:

AERTSEN, A., Neurobiology
BAUER, G., Evolutionary Biology
BAUMEISTER, R., Neurogenetics
BECK, C., Biology
BEYER, P., Cell Biology
BOGENRIEDER, A., Geobotany
DEIL, U., Geobotany
DRIEVER, W., Neurobiology
FISCHBACH, K. F., Biology
FUCHS, G., Microbiology
FUKSHANSKY, L., Botany
GÜNTHER, K., Neurobiology
HAEHNEL, W., Biochemistry
HARTMANN, R., Neurobiology
HERTEL, R., Biology
KLEINIG, H., Cell Biology
MÜLLER, J., Chemical Ecology
NEUBÜSER, A., Neurobiology
NEUHAUS, G., Cell Biology
OELZE, J., Microbiology
PESCHKE, K., Zoology
RESKI, R., Biotechnology
RETH, M., Molecular Immunology
ROSSEL, S., Neurobiology
SCHÄFER, E., Botany
SCHRÖDER, J., Biochemistry
VOGT, K., Neurobiology
WAGNER, E., Botany
WECKESSER, J., Microbiology
WELLMANN, E., Botany

Faculty of Business and Behavioural Sciences:

BLÜMLE, G., Mathematical Economics
FRANCKE, H. H., Financial Economics
FUCHS, R., Sport Science
GEHRIG, T., Economic Development
GIEß-STÜBER, P., Sport Science
GOLLHOFER, A., Sport Science
HAUSER, S., Imperial Economics
HILKE, W., Commercial Economics
KESSLER, W., Business Economics
KNIEPS, G., Political Economy
LANDMANN, O., Economic Theory
RAFFELHÜSCHEN, Financial Economics
REHKUGLER, H., Commercial Economics
SCHAUENBERG, B., Management Economics
SCHOBER, F., Computer Science
SCHULTZ, G., Socio-Political Economics
STRUBE, G., Cognition Science
TSCHEULIN, D., Health Service Economics
VANBERG, V., Political Economics

Faculty of Chemistry, Pharmacology and Geosciences:

BANNWARTH, W., Organic Chemistry
BECHTHOLD, A., Pharmaceutical Biology
BEHRMANN, J., Geology
BREIT, B., Organic Chemistry
BRÜCKNER, R., Organic Chemistry
BUCHER, K., Mineralogy
EBERBACH, W., Biochemistry
FINKELMANN, H., Molecular Chemistry
FRIEDRICH, K., Organic Chemistry
GLAWION, R., Geography
GOSSMANN, H., Geography
GRAPES, R., Geosciences
GRONSKI, W., Macromolecular Chemistry
HENK, A., Geology
HILLEBRECHT, H., Inorganic Chemistry
JANIAK, CH., Inorganic Chemistry
KELLER, J., Mineralogy
KRAMER, V., Crystallography
LEIBUNDGUT, CH., Hydrology
MÄCKEL, R., Geography
MAYER, H., Meteorology
MERFORT, I., Pharmaceutical Biology
MÜHLHAUPT, R., Macromolecular Chemistry
OTTO, H. H., Pharmaceutical Technology
PLATTNER, D., Organic Chemistry
PRINZBACH, H., Organic Chemistry
RÖHR, C., Inorganic Chemistry
RÜCHARDT, C., Organic Chemistry
SCHULZ, G. E., Biochemistry
SCHWESINGER, R., Organic Chemistry
SEITZ, S., Ethnology
STADELBAUER, J., Geography
TIPPER, J. C., Geology
VAHRENKAMP, H., Inorganic Chemistry
WIMMENAUER, W., Geosciences

Faculty of Forestry and Environmental Sciences:

ABETZ, P., Forest Growth
BAUHAUS, J., Silviculture
BECKER, G., Forest Utilization and Work Science
BECKER, M., Forest Policy
BOPPRÉ, M., Forest Zoology
EISFELD, D., Forest Zoology
ESSMANN, H., Environmental Policy
FINK, S., Forest Botany
HILDEBRAND, E. E., Soil Sciences and Forest Nutrition
JAEGER, L., Meteorology
KOCH, B., Land Information Systems
KONOLD, W., Land Use Planning
KRINGS, T., Cultural Geography
LEWARK, S., Forest Utilization and Work Science
MAYER, H., Meteorology
MEIDINGER, E., Forest Management
MITSCHERLICH, G., Forest Growth
OESTEN, G., Forest Management
PELZ, D. R., Biometrics
REIF, A., Silviculture
RENNENBERG, H., Tree Science
ROEDER, A., Forest Management
SCHMIDT, U., Environmental Policy
SCHRÖDER, E.-J., Cultural Geography
SPIECKER, H., Forest Production
VOLZ, K., Forest Policy

Faculty of Law:

BLAUROCK, U., Economic Law
BLOY, R., Penal Law
ESER, A., Penal Law
FRISCH, W., Penal Law
HAEDICKE, M., Civil Law
HAGER, G., International Civil Law
HOHLOCH, G., International Civil Law
HOLLERBACH, A., History of Law, Church Law, Philosophy of Law
KÖBL, U., Social Insurance Law
LEIPOLD, D., Civil, Labour and Procedural Law
LIEBS, D., History of Modern Law
LÖWISCH, M., Civil, Labour, Social Insurance and Commercial Law
MERKT, H., International Civil Law
MURSWIEK, D., State Law
NEHLSEN-VON STRYCK, K., History of Law
PERRON, W., Penal Law
SCHOCH, F., Public Law
SCHWARZE, J., European and International Law
STÜRNER, R., Civil Law
TIEDEMANN, K., Criminal Law and Procedure
VOßKUHLE, A., History of Law, Philosophy of Law
WAHL, R., Administrative Law
WÜRTENBERGER, T., State Law

Faculty of Mathematics and Physics:

BAMBERGER, A., Experimental Physics
BANGERT, V., Mathematics
BLUMEN, A., Theoretical Physics
BRENN, R., Experimental Physics
BRIGGS, J. ST., Theoretical Physics
DZIUK, G., Applied Mathematics
EBBINGHAUS, H.-D., Mathematical Logic
EBERLEIN, E., Stochastics
FLUM, J., Mathematical Logic
GRABERT, H., Theoretical Physics
GROHE, M., Logic
HABERLAND, H., Experimental Physics
HEINZEL, T., Physics
HELM, H., Experimental Physics
HERMES, H., Logic
HERTEN, G., Physics
HONERKAMP, J., Theoretical Physics
JAKOBS, K., Physics
KLAR, H., Physics
KÖNIGSMANN, K., Physics

KRÖNER, D., Applied Mathematics
KUWERT, E., Analysis
LANDGRAF, U., Physics
LUDWIG, J., Physics
POHLMEYER, K., Theoretical Physics
RÖMER, H., Theoretical Physics
RÖPKE, H., Experimental Physics
RÜSCHENDORF, L., Stochastics
RUZICKA, M., Applied Mathematics
SCHMIDT, V., Physics
SCHMITT, H., Experimental Physics
SCHNEIDER, R., Mathematics
SIEBERT, B., Geometry
SOERGEL, W., Algebra
SPILKER, J., Actuarial Mathematics
STROBL, G., Experimental Physics
VAN DER BIJ, J., Theoretical Physics
WAGNER, F., Logic
WEIDEMÜLLER, M., Physics
WITTING, H., Applied Mathematics
WOLKE, D., Mathematics
ZIEGLER, M., Mathematical Logic

Faculty of Medicine:
AKTORIES, K., Pharmacology and Toxicology
BEHRENDS, J., Physiology
BESSLER, W., Immunology
BEYERSDORF, F., Cardiovascular Surgery
BIRNESSER, H., Sports Traumatology
BLUM, H., Gastroenterology
BODE, C., Cardiology
BOGDAN, CH., Microbiology
BORNER, C., Stem Cell Research
BRAND-SABERI, B., Anatomy and Cell Biology
BRANDIS, M., Paediatrics
BRANDSCH, R., Biochemistry
CHRIST, B., Anatomy
DASCHNER, F., Environmental Medicine
DECKER, K., Biochemistry
DICKHUT, H.-H., Rehabilitation and Sports Medicine
FAKLER, Physiology
FROMMHOLD, H., Radiology
FROTSCHER, M., Anatomy
FUNK, J., Eye Hospital
GEIGER, K., Anaesthesiology
GITSCH, G., Gynaecology
GOEPPERT, S., Medical Psychology
GUTTMAN, J., Anaesthesiology
HASSE, J., Surgery
HELLWIG, E., Dentistry
HOFFMAN, H.-D., Anatomy
HOPT, U., General and Visceral Surgery
HUANG, R., Anatomy
JACKISCH, R., Pharmacology and Toxicology
JONAS, P., Physiology
JONAS, J., Dentistry
KECECIOGLU, D., Paediatric Cardiology
KIST, M., Microbiology
KLAR, R., Medicine Informatics
KORINTHENBERG, R., Neurology and Muscular Diseases
KURZ, H., Anatomy
LANGER, M., Radiology
LASZIG, R., Otorhinolaryngology
LEVEN, K.-H., History of Medicine
MERTELSMANN, R., Internal Medicine
MEYER, D. K., Pharmacology and Toxicology
MOSER, E., Radiology
MÜLLER-QUERNHEIM, J., Pneumology
NIERNEYER, C., Paediatric Haemotology and Oncology
NIKKHAH, G., Neurosurgery
OSTERTAG, C., Neurosurgery
PAHL, H., Anaesthesiology
PANNEN, B., Anaesthesiology
PETER, H. H., Rheumatology
PETERS, C., Molecular Medicine
PFANNER, N., Biochemistry
PIRCHER, H., Immunology
POLLAK, S., Forensic Medicine
REICHELT, A., Orthopaedics
ROSPERT, S., Biochemistry
SCHEMPP, W., Cytogenetics
SCHMELZEISEN, R., Oral and Maxillofacial Surgery
SCHÖPF, E., Dermatology
SCHUMACHER, M., Medical Statistics
SIEBERT, F., Biophysics
STARK, B., Plastic and Hand Surgery
STARKE, K., Pharmacology and Toxicology
STRUB, J., Dentistry
SÜDKAMP, N. P., Traumatology
SZABO, B., Pharmacology and Toxicology
TRÖHLER, U., History of Medicine
TROPSCHUG, M., Biochemistry
VOLK, B., Neuropathology
VON TROSCHKE, J., Medical Sociology
VOOS, W., Biochemistry
WALZ, G., Nephrology
WERNER, M., Pathology
WETTERAUER, U., Urology
WOLF, U., Human Genetics and Anthropology
ZENTNER, J. F., General Neurosurgery

Faculty of Philology:
ADAMS, J., American Literature
ANZ, H., Scandinavian Studies
ARNHAMMER, A., German Philology
AUER, P., German Philology
BANNERT, R., Scandinavian Studies
BERG, W. B., Literature
BLANK, W., German Philology
BÖNING, T., German Philology
CHEURÉ, E., Slavonics
DANGEL-PELLOQUIN, E., German Philology
DITTMANN, J., German Philology
DREWS, P., Slavonics
FLUDERNIK, M., English Philology
GÜNTHER, H.-C.
HAHN, U., German Philology
HALFORD, B., Oral Language
HAUSMANN, R., Romance Philology
HERRMANN, H.-P., German Philology
HESS, R., Romance Philology
HOCHBRUCK, W., Literature
JURT, J., Literature
KAISER, G., German Philology
KÄSTNER, H.-J., German Philology
KILIAN, E., Literature
KNOOP, U., German Philology
KOCHENDÖRFER, G., German Philology
KOHL, N., English Literature
KORTE, B., Literature
KORTMANN, B., English Philology
KÜHNE, U., German Philology
KUNZE, K., German Philology
LEFÈVRE, E., Classical Philology
LÖNKER, F., German Philology
MAIR, C., Caribbean Language and Literature
MATTHEWS, R., Linguistics
MAUSER, W., German Philology
MICHEL, W., German Philology
MÜRB, F., German Philology
PIETZCKER, C., German Philology
PILCH, H., English Philology
PÖRKSEN, U., German Philology
PÜTZ, M., English Philology
RAIBLE, W., Romance Philology
RENNER, R., German Philology
RIX, H., Indogermanic Languages
SASSE, G., German Philology
SCHÄFER, E., Latin Philology
SCHMIDT, J., German Philology
SCHOLZ, R., German Philology
SCHWAN, W., German Philology
SIEGERT, R., German Philology
THOMAS, C., German Philology
TICHY, E., Indogermanic Languages
TRISTRAM, H., German Philology
WEIHER, E., Slavonics
ZIMMERMAN, B., German Philology
ZUTT, H., German Philology

Faculty of Philosophy:
ASCHE, R., Modern History
BERGER, C., Music
BRÜGGEMEIER, F.-J., Economic and Social History
DEGELE, N., Sociology
ESSBACH, W., Sociology
FIGAL, G., Philosophy
GEHRKE, H.-J., Ancient History
GREINER, P., Sinology
HINÜBER, O., Indology
JÄGER, W., Political Science
JANHSEN, A., History of Art
KUNTZ, A., Ethnology
KÜSTER, K., Music
LAUT, J.-P., Islamic History
MARTIN, J., Ancient History
MATTER, M., Ethnology
MERTENS, D., Medieval History
MEZGER, W., Ethnology
MORDEK, H., Medieval History
NEUTATZ, D., Modern and East European History
NUBER, H. U., Roman Provincial Archaeology
PALETSCHEK, S., Modern History
PRATER, A., History of Art
REBSTOCK, U., Islamic History
RIESCHER, G., Political History
RÜLAND, J., Political History
SCHLEHE, J., Ethnology
SCHLINK, W., History of Art
SCHMIDT, G., Medieval Latin Philology
SCHNITZLER, G., Modern German Literature and Music
SCHWENGEL, H., Sociology
SEITZ, S., Ethnology
SENGER, H., Sinology
STEIBLE, H., Oriental Philology
STEUER, H., Prehistory
STRAHM, C., Prehistory
STROCKA, V., Classical Archaeology
TRÖHLER, U., History of Medicine
WARLAND, R., Christian Archaeology and Byzantine Art
WINDLER, C., Modern History
WINTERLING, A., Ancient History
ZOTZ, T., Medieval History

Faculty of Theology:
ALBUS, M., Pedagogics and Catechism
ENDERS, M., Philosophy
FRANK, S., Old Church History
GLATZEL, N., Christian Society
HOPING, H., Dogmatics and Liturgical History
IRSIGLER, H., Old Testament
NOTHELLE-WILDFEUER, U., Pastoral Theology
OBERLINNER, L., New Testament Literature
POMPEY, H., Caritas Science and Social Work
RAFFELT, A., Dogmatics
SCHOCKENHOFF, E., Moral Theology
SMOLINSKY, H., New Church History
TZSCHEETZSCH, W., Pedagogics and Catechism
UHDE, B., History
VERWEYEN, H. J., Fundamental Theology
WALTER, P., Dogmatics
WARLAND, R., Christian Archaeology and Art History
WINDISCH, H., Pastoral Theology
ZAPP, H., Church Law

BAUHAUS-UNIVERSITÄT WEIMAR

Geschwister-Scholl-Str. 8, 99421 Weimar
Telephone: (3643) 580
E-mail: international-office@uni-weimar.de
Internet: www.uni-weimar.de

Founded 1860
Academic year: October to June

Rector: Prof. Dr Ing. KARL BEUCKE
Vice-Rector for Academic Affairs: Prof. Dr ANDREA DREYER
Vice-Rector for Research: Prof. Dr Hab. HANS-RUDOLF MEIER

Chancellor: Dr Ing. HEIKO SCHULTZ
Librarian: Dr FRANK SIMON-RITZ
Number of teachers: 83
Number of students: 5,000
Publications: *Der Bogen* (9 a year), *Philosophische Diskurse* (1 a year), *Schriften der Bauhaus-Universität* (2 a year), *Thesis* (6 a year), *VERSO-Architekturtheorie* (1 a year)

DEANS

Faculty of Architecture: Prof. Dipl. Ing. BERND RUDOLF
Faculty of Art and Design: Prof. Dr SIEGFRIED GRONERT
Faculty of Civil Engineering: Prof. Dr Ing. HANS-JOACHIM BARGSTÄDT
Faculty of Media: Prof. Dr ANDREAS ZIEMANN

PROFESSORS

Faculty of Architecture (tel. (3643) 583113; e-mail lars-christian.uhlig@archit.uni-weimar.de; internet www.uni-weimar.de/cms/?297):

BARZ-MALFATTI, H., Design and Settlement Planning I
BÜTTNER-HYMAN, H., Principles of Design
CHRIST, W., Design and Town Planning I
DONATH, D., Information Technology in the Architectural Planning Process
GLEITER, J. H., Design and Architectural Theory
GLÜCKLICH, D., Principles of Ecological Construction
GRASHORN, B., Design and Building Construction
GUMPP, R., Design and Structural Engineering
HASSENPFLUG, D., Sociology and Social History of Towns
KÄSTNER, A., Technology of Building Design
KIEßL, K., Building Ecology and Air-Conditioning
KLEIN, B., Design and Town Planning II
KOPPÁNDY, J., Landscape Architecture
LOUDON, M., Design and Industrial Buildings
NENTWIG, B., Building Industry and Building Management
RIEß, H., Design and Building Construction I
RUDOLF, B., Theory of Building Construction
RUTH, J., Structural Engineering
SCHIRMBECK, E., Design and Interior Design
SCHMITZ, K.-H., Design and Building Construction II
SCHULZ, M., Construction Technology
STAMM-TESKE, W., Design and House-Building
WELCH GUERRA, M., Space Research, Development and Land Planning

Faculty of Art and Design (tel. (3643) 583206; e-mail christa.billing@gestaltung.uni-weimar.de; internet www.uni-weimar.de/gestaltung):

BABTIST, G., Product Design
BACHHUBER, L., Free Art
BARTELS, H., Product Design
BOCK, W., Art Science
FRÖHLICH, E., Free Art
GRONERT, S., Art Science
HINTERBERGER, N. W., Free Art
HOLZWARTH, W., Visual Communication
NEMITZ, B., Free Art
PREIß, A., Art Science
RUTHERFORD, J., Visual Communication
SATTLER, W., Product Design
SCHAWELKA, K., Art Science
STAMM, H., Visual Communication
WEBER, O., Art Science
WENTSCHER, H., Visual Communication

Faculty of Civil Engineering (tel. (3643) 584415; e-mail elke.lindner@bauing.uni-weimar.de; internet www.uni-weimar.de/bauing):

ALFEN, Construction Management
BARGSTÄDT, Construction Site Management
BECKMANN, Waste Management
BERGMANN, Experimental Analysis of Materials and Structures
BEUCKE, Informatics in Construction
BIDLINGMAIER, Waste Management
BRANNOLTE, General Building Materials
BUCHER, Construction Engineering
FREUNDT, Applied Mathematics
GÜRLEBECK, Applied Mathematics
HACK, Preparation of Materials and Recycling
HÜBLER, Information Processing
KAPS, Chemistry for Building
KÖNKE, Building Statistics
KORNADT, Physics of Building
KRANAWETTREISER, Electrical Engineering
LONDONG, Urban Water Management
MÜLLER, Preparation of Materials and Recycling
RAUE, Solid Buildings I
RAUTENSTRAUCH, Wood and Stone Construction
RUTH, Solid Buildings II
SCHANZ, Soil Mechanics
SCHWARZ, Earthquake Centre
SCHWARZ, Surveying
STARK, General Building Materials
TRABERT, Construction Engineering Planning
WERNER, Steel Construction
WITT, Foundation Engineering

Faculty of Media (tel. (3643) 583703; e-mail medien@uni-weimar.de; internet www.uni-weimar.de/medien):

ENGELL, L., Media Philosophy
FRÖHLICH, B., Virtual Reality Systems
GEELHAAR, J., Interface Design
GROSS, T., Computer Supported Cooperative Work
HENNIG-THURAU, T., Marketing and Media
KISSEL, W., Media Events
LEEKER, M., History and Theory of Artificial Worlds
MAIER, M. (acting), Media Management
MINARD, R., Electronic Sound Production
SIEGERT, B., History and Theory of Cultural Technologies
STEIN, B., Content Management and Web Technology
WÜTHRICH, C., Graphical Data Processing

BERGISCHE UNIVERSITÄT WUPPERTAL

42097 Wuppertal
Gaussstr. 20, 42119 Wuppertal
Telephone: (202) 4390
E-mail: kanzler@uni-wuppertal.de
Internet: www.uni-wuppertal.de
Founded 1972
State control
Language of instruction: German
Academic year: October to September
Rector: Prof. Dr LAMBERT T. KOCH
Vice-Rector for Academic Affairs: Prof. Dr ANDREAS FROMMER
Vice-Rector for Finance, Corporate Planning and Information: Prof. Dr HEINZ-REINER TREICHEL
Vice-Rector for Research, External Funding and Advanced Scientific Training: Prof. Dr MICHAEL SCHEFFEL
Vice-Rector for Transfer and Int. Relations: Prof. Dr Ing. PETRA WINZER
Chancellor: Dr ROLAND KISCHKEL
Librarian: UWE STADLER
Number of teachers: 300
Number of students: 17,000

DEANS

Faculty of Architecture, Civil, Mechanical and Safety Engineering: Prof. Dr Ing. EBERHARD SCHMIDT
Faculty of Art and Design: Prof. Dr ULRICH HEINEN
Faculty of Educational and Social Science: Prof. Dr THOMAS HEINZE
Faculty of Electrical, Information and Media Engineering: Prof. Dr Ing. ANTON KUMMERT
Faculty of Humanities: Prof. Dr GERRIT WALTHER
Faculty of Mathematics and Natural Sciences: Prof. Dr WOLFGANG WAGNER
School of Education: Prof. Dr CORNELIA GRÄSEL
Schumpeter School of Business and Economics: Prof. Dr MICHAEL J. FALLGATTER

BRANDENBURGISCHE TECHNISCHE UNIVERSITÄT COTTBUS

POB 10 13 44, 03013 Cottbus
Konrad-Wachsmann-Allee 1, 03046 Cottbus
Telephone: (355) 690
E-mail: intoff@tu-cottbus.de
Internet: www.tu-cottbus.de
Founded 1991
State control
Academic year: October to July
Chancellor: WOLFGANG SCHRÖDER
Pres.: Prof. Dr Hab WALTHER CH. ZIMMERLI
Vice-Pres.: MATTHIAS KOZIOL
Vice-Pres.: Prof. Dr Hab. DIETER SCHMEIßER
Librarian: MAGDALENE FREWER-SAUVIGNY
Library of 577,000 vols, 2,000 periodicals, 80,000 technical standards
Number of teachers: 651
Number of students: 6,400
Publications: *Bodenschutz* (4 a year), *Bodenschutz und Rekultivierung* (10–12 a year), *Energie, Forum der Forschung, Wissenschaftsmagazin der BTU Cottbus* (1 a year), *Lehrstuhl Industriesoziologie* (2 a year)

DEANS

Faculty of Architecture, Civil Engineering and Urban Planning: Prof. Dipl. Ing. HEINZ NAGLER
Faculty of Environmental Sciences and Process Engineering: Prof. Dr GERHARD WIEGLEB
Faculty of Mathematics, Natural Sciences and Computer Science: Prof. Dr WOLFGANG FREUDENBERG
Faculty of Mechanical, Electrical and Industrial Engineering: Prof. Dr Ing. BERND VIEHWEGER

CARL VON OSSIETZKY UNIVERSITÄT OLDENBURG

POB 2503, 26111 Oldenburg
Ammerländer Heerstr. 114–118, 26129 Oldenburg
Telephone: (441) 7980
E-mail: praesidium@uni-oldenburg.de
Internet: www.uni-oldenburg.de
Founded 1973
Academic year: October to September (2 terms)
Pres.: Prof. Dr BABETTE SIMON
Vice-Pres. for Academic Affairs: Prof. Dr GUNILLA BUDDE
Vice-Pres. for Admin. and Finance: Dr HEIDE AHRENS
Vice-Pres. for Research: Prof. Dr KATHARINA AL-SHAMERY

Vice-Pres. for Young Scientists and Quality Management: Prof. Dr BERND SIEBENHÜNER
Library Dir: HANS-JOACHIM WÄTJEN

Library of 1,333,870 vols
Number of teachers: 181
Number of students: 10,688

Publications: *Data Work* (computer sciences, 3 a year), *Einblicke* (research at the University, 2 a year), *Monoculus* (biology, 2 a year)

DEANS

Faculty 1 (School of Educational and Social Sciences): Prof. Dr MANFRED WITTROCK
Faculty 2 (School of Computer Science, Business Admin., Economics and Law): Prof. Dr THORSTEN RAABE
Faculty 3 (School of Linguistics and Cultural Studies): Prof. Dr KAREN ELLWANGER
Faculty 4 (School of Humanities and Social Sciences): Prof. Dr JOHANN KREUZER
Faculty 5 (School of Mathematics and Natural Science): Prof. Dr MARTIN HOLTHAUS

PROFESSORS

Faculty 1 (School of Educational and Social Sciences) (Ammerländer Heerstr. 114–118, 26129 Oldenburg; tel. (441) 7982002; e-mail dekanat.fk1@uni-oldenburg.de; internet www.uni-oldenburg.de/fk1):

Department of Education:

HANFT, A., Adult Education and Continuing Vocational Education
KAISER, A., Elementary Science, Elementary Social Studies
KIPER, H., Theory and Practice in Secondary Education
MEYER, H., General Education, School Teaching
MOSCHNER, B., Teaching and Learning Research
NITSCH, W., Theory of Knowledge
SCHMIDTKE, H.-P., Intercultural Education

Department of Special Needs Education:

ORTMANN, M., Education for the Physically Handicapped
SCHULZE, G. C., Special Education Needs
WITTROCK, M., Education for People with Disturbed Behaviour

Faculty 2 (School of Computer Science, Business Administration, Economics and Law) (Ammerländer Heerstr. 114–118, 26129 Oldenburg; tel. (441) 7984140; internet www.uni-oldenburg.de/fk2):

Business Administration and Education:

BREISIG, T., Organization and Human Resources
LACHNIT, L., Financial and Management Accounting
MOHE, X., Business Consultancy
MÜLLER, M., Production and Environmental Management
PFRIEM, R., General and Environmental Management
RAABE, T., Marketing
REBMANN, K., Vocational and Business Education
SIEBENHÜNER, Ecological Economics

Computer Science:

APPELRATH, H.-J., Information Systems and Databases
BEST, E., Parallel Systems
DAMM, W., Safety Critical Embedded Systems
FATIKOW, S., Microrobotics, Control Engineering
FRÄNZLE, M., Hybrid Systems
HABEL, A., Formal Languages
HASSELBRING, W., Software Engineering
HEIN, A., Automation and Measurement Engineering
JENSCH, P., Image Processing and Process Control
KOWALK, W., Computer Networks and Telecommunications
MÖBUS, C., Learning Environments and Knowledge-Based Systems
NEBEL, W., Embedded Hardware/Software Systems Design
OLDEROG, E.-R., Correct System Design
SONNENSCHEIN, M., Environmental Informatics
STIEGE, G., Graphs and Networks
THEEL, O., System Software and Distributed Systems

Economics:

EBERT, U., Public Finance
LITZ, H.-P., Economic Statistics
SCHEELE, Economic Policy
SCHÜLER, K. W., Econometrics
TRAUTWEIN, H. M., International Economics
WELSCH, H., Economic Theory

Law:

BLANKE, T., Labour Law
FRANK, G., Public Economic Law
SCHIEK, D., European Economic Law
TAEGER, J., Private Law, Business and Economic Law, Legal Informatics

Teaching of Economics and of Technology:

HENSELER, K., Teaching of Technology
KAMINSKI, H., Teaching of Economics
LEWALD, A., Home Economics
REICH, G., Teaching of Technology

Faculty 3 (School of Linguistics and Cultural Studies) (Ammerländer Heerstr. 114–118, 26129 Oldenburg; tel. (441) 7982347; e-mail fk3@uni-oldenburg.de; internet www.uni-oldenburg.de/fk3):

Dutch Studies:

GRÜTTEMEIER, R., Dutch Literature

English Studies:

GELUYKENS, R., Pragmatics, Discourse Analysis, Social Variation
HAMANN, C., Acquisition of First and Second Languages, Bilingualism, Formal Syntax and Semantics
KOEHRING, K., American Literature and Culture

Fine Arts and Visual Communication:

HOFFMANN, D., History of Fine Arts
SPRINGER, P., Theory and History of Art
THIELE, J., Fine Arts and Visual Communication
WENK, S., History of Art, Gender Studies

German Studies:

BRANDES, H., Literature
DOERING, S., Literature
EICHLER, W., Didactics and Linguistics
GLOY, J., Linguistics
KYORA, S., Literature
MEVES, U., Medieval German Literature and Language
STÖLTING, W., German as a Second or Foreign Language

Music:

DINESCU, V., Applied Composition
HOFFMANN, F., Music Education
SCHLEUNING, P., History of Music, Music Teaching
STROH, W. M., Theory of Music and Music Pedagogics

Slavonic Studies:

GRÜBEL, R., Slavonic Literature
HENTSCHEL, G., Linguistics and Slavonic Languages

Visual and Material Culture:

ELLWANGER, K., History of Culture
MÖRSCH, C., Teaching of Material Culture

Faculty 4 (School of Humanities and Social Sciences) (Ammerländer Heerstr. 114–118, 26129 Oldenburg; tel. (441) 7982634; e-mail dekanat.fk4@uni-oldenburg.de; internet www.uni-oldenburg.de/fk4):

Geography:

HAGEN, D., Cartography and Physical Geography

History:

BUDDE, G., 19th- and 20th-century German and European History
ETZEMÜLLER, T., Contemporary History
FREIST, D., Early Modern History
GÜNTHER-ARNDT, H., Teaching of History
HAHN, H.-H., Modern and East European History (esp. History of Poland)
HOLBACH, R., Medieval History
SCHEER, T., Ancient History
VON REEKEN, D., Teaching of History

Philosophy:

GERHARD, M., Philosophy of Nature and of Science, Continental Philosophy
KREUZER, J., Philosophy and History of Philosophy
MÖBUSS, S., Philosophy and Jewish Philosophy
PUSTER, E., Epistemology, Philosophy of Language, Ethics
RUSCHIG, U., Philosophy
SCHULZ, R., Philosophy and History of Science
SUKALE, M., Philosophy and Philosophy of Science

Psychology:

BELSCHNER, W., Psychology
COLONIUS, H., Psychological Methods
HELLMAN, A., Psychological Methods
HÖGE, H., Environmental Psychology and Empirical Aesthetics
LAUCKEN, U., Social Psychology
MEES, U., General Psychology
NACHREINER, F., Applied Psychology
SCHICK, A., Psychological Acoustics and Environmental Psychology
SZAGUN, D., Developmental Psychology
VIEBAHN, P., Educational Psychology
WALCHER, K.-P., Psychology of Personality, Environmental Psychology

Social Sciences:

FLAAKE, K., Women's Studies
GRUNENBERG, A., Political Theory and Political Culture
KRAIKER, G., Social and Political Theory
LOEBER, H.-D., Sociology of Labour and Education
MÜLLER-DOOHM, S., Sociology of the Mass Media
NASSMACHER, K.-H., Comparative Politics
WEISMANN, A., Sociology, Methods of Social Research

Sports Science:

ALKEMEYER, T., Sociology and Philosophy of Sport
LIPPENS, V., Motor Control and Learning
SCHIERZ, M., Sports Science
SCHMÜCKER, B., Sports Science and Sports Medicine

Theology:

GOLKA, F., Jewish Studies, Old Testament
HEUMANN, J., Religious Education
LINK-WIECZOREK, U., Systematic Theology and Religious Education
WEISS, W., New Testament

Faculty 5 (School of Mathematics and Natural Science) (Ammerländer Heerstr. 114–118, 26129 Oldenburg; tel. (441) 7983442; e-mail fk5@uni-oldenburg.de; internet www.uni-oldenburg.de/fk5):

Biology, Earth and Environmental Sciences:

BRUMSACK, H.-J., Geomicrobiochemistry
CYPIONKA, H., Palaeomicrobiology

EBER, W., Botany, Morphology
GIANI, L., Soil Sciences
HAESELER, V., Terrestrial Ecology
HAGEN, D., Cartography and Physical Geography
HOESSLE, C., Biology, School Teaching
JANIESCH, P., Botany, Physiological Ecology
KLEYER, M., Landscape Ecology
KLUMP, G. M., Zoophysiology
KOCH, K.-W., Biochemistry
KRETZBERG, J.
KUMMERER, K., Regional Planning and Development
RICHTER-LANDSBERG, C., Molecular Neurobiology, Neurochemistry
RINKWITZ, S., Neurogenetics
SCHMINKE, H. K., Zoology, Zoosystematics and Morphology
SIMON, U., Biology of Geological Processes
STABENAU, H., Plant Physiology
VARESCHI, E., Aquatic Ecology
WACKERNAGEL, W., Genetics
WEILER, R., Zoology, Neurobiology
WINDELBERG, J., Infrastructure and Environmental Planning

Chemistry:

AL-SHAMERY, K., Physical Chemistry
BECKHAUS, R., Inorganic Chemistry
GMEHLING, J., Industrial Chemistry
KLEINER, T., Physical Chemistry
KÖLL, P., Organic Chemistry
MARTENS, J., Organic Chemistry
METZGER, J. O., Organic Chemistry
POWCHMANN, J., Chemistry, Theory and Practice of School Teaching
RÖSSNER, F., Industrial Chemistry
WICKLEDER, M., Inorganic Chemistry
WITTSTOCK, G., Physical Chemistry

Mathematics:

DEFANT, A., Mathematics, Functional Analysis
HERZBERGER, J., Applied Mathematics, Instrumental Mathematics
KNAUER, U., Mathematics, Algebraic Methods
LEISSNER, W., Mathematics, Geometry
MÜLLER, CH., Mathematics, Stochastics
PFLUG, P., Mathematics, Complex Variables
PIEPER-SEIER, I., Mathematics, Algebra
QUEBBEMANN, H.-G., Mathematics, Number Theory
SCHMALE, W., Mathematics, Dynamic Systems
SCHMIEDER, G., Mathematics, Complex Analysis
SPÄTH, H., Applied Mathematics
VETTER, U., Mathematics, Commutative Algebra

Physics:

BAUER, G. H., Experimental Physics
ENGEL, A., Theoretical Physics
HINSCH, K., Experimental Physics
HOLTHAUS, M., Theoretical Physics
KOLLMEIER, B., Applied Physics
KOLNY, J., Applied Physics
KUNZ-DROLSHAGEN, J., Theoretical Physics, Field Theory
MAIER, K. H., Experimental Physics
MELLERT, V., Applied Physics
MERTINS, A., Applied Physics
PARISI, J., Experimental Physics
PEINKE, J., Experimental Physics
RIESS, F., Teaching of Physics
VERHEY, J., Applied Physics

CHRISTIAN-ALBRECHTS UNIVERSITÄT ZU KIEL

24098 Kiel
Christian-Albrechts-Pl. 4, 24118 Kiel
Telephone: (431) 88000
E-mail: mail@uni-kiel.de
Internet: www.uni-kiel.de
Founded 1665
State control
Academic year: October to July (2 terms)
Pres.: Prof. Dr GERHARD FOUQUET
Vice-Pres.: Prof. Dr FRANK KEMPKEN
Vice-Pres.: Prof. Dr THOMAS BOSCH
Chancellor: FRANK EISOLDT, Prof. Dr. SIEGFRIED WOLFFRAM
Librarian: Dr ELSE M. WISCHERMANN
Number of teachers: 1,700
Number of students: 23,000
Publications: *Christiana Albertina* (2 a year), *Unizeit* (6 a year)

DEANS

Faculty of Agricultural and Nutritional Sciences: Prof. Dr KARIN SCHWARZ
Faculty of Economics and Social Sciences: Prof. Dr BIRGIT FRIEDL
Faculty of Engineering: Prof. Dr REINHARD KNÖCHEL
Faculty of Law: Prof. Dr ALEXANDER TRUNK
Faculty of Mathematics and Natural Sciences: Prof. Dr LUTZ KIPP
Faculty of Medicine: Prof. Dr STEFAN SCHREIBER
Faculty of Philosophy: Prof. Dr MARKUS HUNDT
Faculty of Theology: Prof. Dr HARTMUT ROSENAU

PROFESSORS

Faculty of Agricultural and Nutritional Sciences (Hermann-Rodewald-Str. 4, 24098 Kiel; tel. (431) 8802591; e-mail dekanat@agrar.uni-kiel.de; internet www.agrar.uni-kiel.de):

ABDULAI, A., Food Economics and Food Policy
BRUHN, M., Agricultural Marketing
FOHRER, N., Hydrology and Water Resources Management
HENNING, C., Agricultural Policy
HORN, R., Soil Science
JUNG, C., Plant Breeding and Genetics
KAGE, H., Crop Science
KALM, E., Animal Breeding and Genetics
KRIETER, J., Animal Husbandry, Quality of Products
LATACZ-LOHMANN, U., Farm Management and Production Economics
LOY, J.-P., Agricultural Market Theory
MÜLLER, M. J., Internal Medicine, Human Nutrition
MÜLLER, R. A. E., Agricultural Economics, Information, Innovation
RIMBACH, G., Food Science
ROOSEN, J., Health Economics
ROWECK, H., Landscape Ecology
SATTELMACHER, B., Plant Nutrition
SCHALLENBERGER, E., Animal Husbandry, Hygienics
SCHWARZ, K., Food Technology
SUSENBETH, A., Animal Nutrition
TAUBE, F., Grass and Forage Science, Organic Farming
VERREET, J.-A., Phytopathology, Plant Diseases
WOLFFRAM, S., Animal Nutrition and Nutritional Physiology
WYSS, U., Phytopathology, Biotechnology

Faculty of Economics and Social Sciences (Wilhelm-Seelig-Platz 1, 24098 Kiel; tel. (431) 8802140; e-mail dekanat@bwl.uni-kiel.de; internet www.bwl.uni-kiel.de):

ALBERS, S., Innovation, New Media and Marketing
BRÖCKER, J., Regional Science
DREXL, A., Production Management and Logistics
FRIEDL, B., Controlling
HERWARTZ, H., Econometrics
KLAPPER, D., Marketing
KRAUSE, J., Politics
KRUBER, K.-P., Political and Economic Education
LIESENFELD, R., Statistics and Empirical Economics
LUX, T., Monetary Economics and International Financial Markets
NIPPEL, P., Financial Management
RAFF, H., Industrial Economics
REQUATE, T., Economics of Innovation, Competition and Institutions
SEIDL, C., Public Finance and Choice Theory
SNOWER, D., Economics
VEIT, K.-R., Accounting
WALTER, A., Entrepreneurship and Innovation Management
WOHLTMANN, H.-W., Macroeconomics
WOLF, J., Organization

Faculty of Engineering (Kaiserstr. 2, 24143 Kiel; tel. (431) 8806001; e-mail dekanat@tf.uni-kiel.de; internet www.tf.uni-kiel.de):

BERGHAMMER, R., Computer-Aided Program Development
BROCKS, W., Material Mechanics
DIRKS, H., Electromagnetic Field Theory
FAUPEL, F., Multicomponent Materials
FÖLL, H., General Materials Science
FUCHS, F. W., Power Electronics and Electrical Devices
HACKBUSCH, W., Practical Mathematics
HANUS, M., Programming Languages and Compiler Construction
HEUBERGER, A., Semiconductor Technology
HEUTE, U., Circuits and System Theory
HÖHER, P., Information and Coding Theory Laboratory
JÄGER, W., Centre for Microanalysis
JANSEN, K., Theory of Parallelism
KLINKENBUSCH, I., Computational Electromagnetics Group
KNÖCHEL, R., Microwave Group
KOCH, R., Multimedia Information Processing
LUTTENBERGER, N., Communication Systems
RÖCK, H., Automation and Control Engineering
ROEVER, W. P. DE, Software Technology
ROSENKRANZ, W., Communications
SCHIMMLER, M., Computer Engineering
SCHNEIDER, R., Scientific Computing
SEEGEBRECHT, P., Semiconductor Electronics
SOMMER, G., Cognitive Systems
SRIVASTAV, A., Discrete Optimization
THALHEIM, B., Information Systems Engineering
VON HANXLEDEN, R., Real-Time and Embedded Systems
WEPPNER, W., Sensors and Solid State Ionics
WILKE, T., Theoretical Computer Science

Faculty of Law (Leibnizstr. 4, 24098 Kiel; tel. (431) 8802125; e-mail dekanat@law.uni-kiel.de; internet www.uni-kiel.de/fakultas/jura):

ALEXY, R., Public Law and Legal Philosophy
ECKERT, J., History of German and European Law, Civil Law, Commercial Law
EINSELE, D., Civil Law, Commercial Law, Private International Law, Comparative Law
FISCHER, M., Civil, Commercial and Economic Tax Law
FROMMEL, M., Criminology and Criminal Law
HOYER, A., Penal Law and Procedure
IGL, G., Public Law, Social Law
JICKELI, J., Civil Law, Commercial Law
KRACK, R., Penal Law and Procedure
MEYER-PRITZL, R., Civil Law, Roman Law, History of Law in Modern Times, Comparative Law

Reuter, D., Civil, Commercial and Economic Law
Schack, H., International Civil Law, Private and Civil Trial Law, Copyright Law
Schmidt-Jortzig, E., Public Law
Smid, S., Civil Law and Procedure
Trunk, A., Civil and Civil Trial Law, International Private Law and Comparative Law
von Mutius, A., Public Law and Administration
Zimmermann, A., German and Foreign Public, International, and European Law, and General Theory of the State

Faculty of Mathematics and Natural Sciences (Christian-Albrechts-Platz 4, 24098 Kiel; tel. (431) 8802128; e-mail dekanat@mnf.uni-kiel.de; internet www.uni-kiel.de/fakultas/mathnat):

Alban, S., Pharmaceutical Biology
Bähr, J., Geography
Bauer, T., Ecology
Bayrhuber, H., Teaching Methods of Biology
Bender, H., Mathematics
Bensch, W., Inorganic Chemistry
Bergweiler, W., Mathematics
Berndt, R., Solid-State Physics
Betten, D., Mathematics
Bilger, W., Ecology
Bischof, K., Marine Biology
Blaschek, W., Pharmaceutical Biology
Bodendiek, R., Mathematics
Böning, C., Theoretical Oceanography
Bonitz, M., Theoretical Physics
Bork, H.-R., Ecology System Research
Bosch, T., General Zoology
Brendelberger, H., Zoology and Limnology
Cemič, L., Mineralogy and Petrology
Clement, B., Pharmaceutical Chemistry
Colijn, F., Coastal Ecology
Corves, C., Geography
Dahmke, A., Applied Geology
Demuth, R., Teaching of Chemistry
Depmeier, W., Mineralogy and Crystallography
Devey, C., Geology
Dierssen, K., Botany
Dommenget, D., Meteorology
Dullo, W. C., Palaeo-Oceanography
Duttmann, R., Geography
Eisenhauer, A., Marine Ecogeology
Euler, M., Teaching of Physics
Frank, M., Geology
Götze, H.-J., Geophysics
Grootes, P., Experimental Physics, Isotope Research
Grotemeyer, J., Physical Chemistry
Hackney, R., Geophysics
Hammann, M., Teaching Methods of Biology
Hanel, R., Fishery Biology
Hänsel, W., Pharmaceutical Chemistry
Hartke, B., Theoretical Chemistry
Hartl, G. B., Zoology
Hassenpflug, W., Geography
Heber, J., Mathematics
Helbig, V., Physics
Herges, R., Organic Chemistry
Herzig, P., Marine Science
Hoernle, K., Vulcanology, Magmatic Petrology
Hoppe, H. G., Microbiology
Imhoff, J., Marine Microbiology
Irle, A., Probability Theory and Mathematical Statistics
Kempken, F., Botany
Kipp, L., Experimental Physics
Koester, D., Astronomy and Astrophysics, Theoretical Physics
König, H., Mathematics
Körtzinger, A., Organic Marine Chemistry
Krupinska, K., Cell Biology
Kuhnt, W., Geology and Palaeontology
Kunze, T., Pharmaceutical Chemistry
Latif, M., Meterology
Leippe, M., Zoology
Lindhorst, T., Organic Chemistry
Lochte, K., Plankton
Lüning, U., Organic Chemistry
Macke, A., Meteorology
Mäder, H., Physical Chemistry
Magnussen, O. M., Experimental Physics
Mayerle, R., Applied Coastal Geology
Mikelskis-Seifert, S., Teaching Methods of Physics
Müller, B., Pharmaceutical Technology
Müller, D., Mathematics
Müller, M., Physics
Nelle, O. A., Ecology
Nerdel, C., Teaching Methods of Chemistry
Newig, J., Geography
Pehlke, E., Theoretical Physics
Piel, A., Experimental Physics
Prechtl, H., Teaching Methods of Biology
Rabbel, W., Geophysics
Reise, K., Biological Oceanography
Reston, T. J., Marine Geophysics
Revilla Diez, J., Economy of Geography
Riebesell, U., Marine Biology
Roeder, T., Zoology
Rösler, U., Stochastics
Ruprecht, E., Meteorology
Sauter, M., Botany
Schäfer, P., Geology
Schanze, S., Teaching Methods of Chemistry
Schenk, V., Petrology and Mineralogy
Schmidt, R., Mathematics
Schmitz-Streit, R. A., Microbiology
Schnack, D., Ichthyology
Schneider, R., Geology
Schönheit, P., Microbiology
Schrempp, B., Theoretical Physics
Schulz-Friedrich, R., Botany
Schuster, H. G., Theoretical Physics
Send, U., Physical Oceanography
Sommer, U., Sea-Floor Ecology
Spengler, U., Teaching Methods of Mathematics
Spinas, O., Logic
Spindler, M., Polar Ecology
Stattegger, K., Geology and Palaeontology
Stellmacher, B., Mathematics
Sterr, H., Physical Geography
Stock, N., Inorganic Chemistry
Stoffers, P., Geology
Suess, E., Marine Environmental Geology
Temps, F., Physical Chemistry
Tuczek, F., Inorganic Chemistry
Uhlarz, H., Botany
Visbeck, M., Physical Oceanography
von Klitzing, R., Physical Chemistry
von Rohr, G., Geography
Wahl, M., Marine Biology and Zoology
Wallace, D., Marine Chemistry
Walther, G., Teaching of Mathematics
Willebrand, J., Oceanography
Wimmer-Schweingruber, R., Experimental Physics

Faculty of Medicine (Christian-Albrechts-Platz 4, 24098 Kiel; tel. (431) 8802126; e-mail dekanat@med.uni-kiel.de; internet www.uni-kiel.de/fak/med/med.html):

Albers, H.-K., Dentistry
Aldenhoff, J., Psychiatry, Psychotherapy
Alzheimer, C., Psychology
Ambrosch, P., Otorhinolaryngology
Baron, R., Neurology
Bleich, M., Physiology
Cremer, J., Surgery
Deuschl, G., Neurology and Neurophysiology
Fickenscher, H., Medical Microbiology
Fischer-Brandies, H., Dentistry
Fölsch, U. R., Internal Medicine
Gerber, W.-D., Clinical Psychology
Gieseler, F., Internal Medicine
Glüer, C., Medicinal Physics
Grote, W., Human Genetics
Hassenpflug, J., Orthopaedics
Heller, M., Radiological Diagnosis
Henze, E., Nuclear Medicine
Herdegen, T., Physiology, Molecular Pharmacology
Illert, M., Physiology
Jansen, O., Neuroradiology
Jonat, W., Gynaecology and Obstetrics
Jünemann, K.-P., Urology
Just, U., Biochemistry
Kaatsch, H.-J., Legal Medicine
Kabelitz, D., Medical Microbiology and Immunology
Kalthoff, H., Immunology and Cell Biochemistry
Kern, M., Dentistry
Kimmig, B. N., Clinical Radiology
Klöppel, G., Pathology and Pathological Anatomy
Kneba, M., Internal Medicine
Kovacs, G., Clinical Radiology
Kramer, H.-H., Child Medicine, Child Cardiology
Krawczak, M., Human Genetics
Kremer, B., Surgery
Kunzendorf, U., Internal Medicine, Nephrology
Lucius, R., Anatomy
Lüllmann-Rauch, R., Anatomy
Maser, E., Toxicology
Mehdorn, H., Neurosurgery
Mettler, L., Gynaecology
Oehmichen, M., Legal Medicine
Parwaresch, R., Haematopathology
Plagmann, H.-Ch., Dentistry
Proksch, E., Dermatology and Venereology
Roider, J., Opthalmology
Rose-John, S., Biochemistry
Saftig, P., Biochemistry
Schöcklmann, H., Nephrology, Internal Medicine
Scholz, J., Anaesthesiology
Schrappe, M., Paediatrics
Schreiber, S., Internal Medicine and Gastroenterology
Schröder, J. M., Experimental Dermatology
Schünke, M., Anatomy
Schütze, G., Child Psychiatry
Schwartz, T., Dermatology
Sievers, J., Anatomy
Simon, R., Cardiology
Stephani, U., Paediatrics, Neuropaediatrics
Stick, C., Physiology
Tonner, P., Anaesthesiology
Weiler, N., Anaesthesiology
Wiltfang, J., Dental Surgery

Faculty of Philosophy (Christian-Albrechts-Pl. 4, 24098 Kiel; tel. (431) 8803055; e-mail dekan@philfak.uni-kiel.de; internet www.uni-kiel.de/fakultas/philosophie):

Biller, K.-H., Pedagogics
Bliesener, T., Medieval and Modern History
Brinkhaus, H., Indology
Brinkmann, W., Pedagogics
Conzelmann, A., Sports Psychology
Cornelissen, C., Modern and Contemporary History
Dormeier, H., Medieval and Modern History
Engel, A., Slavic Philology
Ferstl, R., Clinical Psychology
Fleischmann, B., English Philology
Fouquet, G., Economic and Social History
Gómez-Montero, J., Romance Philology
Göttsch-Elten, S., Folklore
Gross, K., English Philology

HAAS, R., English Language and Literature
HAMEYER, U., Pedagogics
HANISCH, M., Teaching of History
HARRINGTON, J., Phonetics
HELDMANN, K., Classical Philology
HOEKSTRA, J., Friesian Philology
HOINKES, U., Romance Philology
HORATSCHEK, A. M., English Philology
JAWORSKI, R., East European History
JOBST, C., Art History
JONGEBLOED, H. C., Pedagogics
KAPP, V., Romance Philology
KÄPPEL, L., Classical Philology
KERSTING, W., Philosophy
KLEIN, D., Old German Literature
KÖHNKEN, G., Diagnostic and Differential Psychology
KONERSMANN, R., Teaching of Philosophy
KONRADT, U., Industrial, Marketing and Organizational Psychology
KROPE, P., Pedagogics
KUDER, U., Art History
KÜHNE, U., Ancient History, Medieval Linguistics
LINCK, G., Sinology
MAROLD, E., Old Norse Philology
MAUSFELD, R., Psychology
MEIER, A., History of Modern German Literature
MEYER, M., English Philology
MIETHLING, W.-D., Sports Pedagogics
MOERKE, O., Early Modern and Modern History
MÖLLER, J., Psychology
MOSEL, U., Linguistics
MÜLLER, J., Prehistory and Early History
MÜLLER, W.-U., Prehistory and Early History
NÜBLER, N., Slavic Philology
OECHSLE, S., Music
PALLASCH, W., Pedagogics
PETERSEN, J., Pedagogics
PISTOR-HATAM, A., Oriental Philology
POHL, K.-H., Teaching of History
PRAHL, H.-W., Pedagogics
PRENZEL, M., Pedagogics
RADICKE, J., Classical Philology
REBAS, H., Northern History
RIIS, T., History of Schleswig-Holstein
RÜHLING, L., Modern Scandinavian Literature
SCHMALTZ, B., Classical Archaeology
SCHMIDT, A., Folklore
SIELERT, U., Pedagogics
SIMON, B., Psychology
SOMMER, M., Philosophy
SPONHEUER, B., Music
STEINDORFF, L., East European History
THUN, H., Romance Philology
TUCHOLSKI-DÄKE, B.-C., Art
ULRICH, W., German Philology, Teaching of German Language
VON CARNAP-BORNHEIM, C., Prehistory and Early History
WEISS, P., Ancient History
WEISSER, B., Sports Medicine
WIESEHÖFER, J., Ancient History
WULFF, H. J., Theatre and Film Studies
WÜNSCH, M., History of Modern German Literature

Faculty of Theology (Leibnitzstr. 4, 24118 Kiel; tel. (431) 8802124; e-mail dekanattheo@email.uni-kiel.de; internet www.uni-kiel.de/fak/theol):

BARTELMUS, R., Old Testament Studies, Biblical and Middle Eastern Languages
BOBERT, S., Practical Theology
HÜBNER, U., Old Testament Studies and Biblical Archaeology
MECKENSTOCK, G., Systematic Theology
PREUL, R., Practical Theology
ROSENAU, H., Systematic Theology
SÄNGER, D., New Testament Studies
SCHILLING, J., Church History
VON BENDEMANN, R., New Testament Studies

ATTACHED INSTITUTES

Institut für Sicherheitspolitik an der Christian-Albrechts-Universität zu Kiel (ISPK) (Institute for Security Policy at Kiel University (ISPK)): Westring 400, 24118 Kiel; tel. (431) 880-2697; e-mail shansen@politik.uni-kiel.de; internet www.ispk.org; CEO STEFAN HANSEN; Dir Prof. Dr J. KRAUSE; publ. *Analysen zur Sicherheitspolitik/German Strategic Studies, Kieler Analysen zur Sicherheitspolitik*.

Institut für Weltwirtschaft an der Universität Kiel (Institute for World Economics at Kiel University): Düsternbrooker Weg 120, 24105 Kiel; e-mail webservices@ifw-kiel.de; Pres. Prof. D. SNOWER.

Leibniz-Institut für Meereswissenschaften (IFM-GEOMAR) (Leibniz Institute of Marine Sciences): Wischhofstr. 1–3, 24148 Kiel; e-mail info@geomar.de; Dir Prof. Dr P. HERZIG.

Leibniz-Institut für die Pädagogik der Naturwissenschaften und Mathematik an der Universität Kiel (Leibniz Institute for Science and Mathematics Education at Kiel University): Olshausenstr. 62, 24098 Kiel; tel. (431) 880-5084; e-mail csec@ipn.uni-kiel.de; internet www.ipn.uni-kiel.de; Scientific Dir Prof. Dr OLAF KÖLLER; Admin. Dir BENT HINRICHSEN.

Lorenz-von-Stein-Institut für Verwaltungswissenschaften an der Universität Kiel (Lorenz von Stein Institute for Management Sciences at Kiel University): Olshausenstr. 40, 24098 Kiel; e-mail institut@lvstein.uni-kiel.de; Dir Prof. Dr JOACHIM JICKELI.

Schleswig-Holsteinisches Institut für Friedenswissenschaften (Schleswig Holstein Institute for Peace Studies): Kaiserstr. 2, 24143 Kiel; Dir Prof. Dr K. POTTHOFF

DEUTSCHE HOCHSCHULE FÜR VERWALTUNGSWISSENSCHAFTEN SPEYER

Freiherr-vom-Stein-Str. 2, 67346 Speyer
Telephone: (6232) 6540
E-mail: dhv@dhv-speyer.de
Internet: www.dhv-speyer.de
Founded 1947
State control
Languages of instruction: German, English
Academic year: May to January
Rector: Prof. Dr STEFAN FISCH
Vice-Rector: Prof. Dr JOACHIM WIELAND
Admin. Officer: CHRISTIANE MÜLLER
Librarian: (vacant)
Library of 302,000 vols
Number of teachers: 90 (incl. 72 part-time)
Number of students: 500

PROFESSORS

BOHNE, E., Public Administration
FÄRBER, G., Public Finance and Economics
FISCH, R., Empirical Social Sciences
FISCH, S., Modern History
HILL, H., Public Administration, Public Law
JANSEN, D., Sociology of Organizations
KNORR, A., International Economics
KÖNIG, T., Political Science
MAGIERA, S., Public Law, European Law and Public International Law
MERTEN, D., Public Law, Social Law
MÜHLENKEMP, H., Public Finance
PITSCHAS, R., Public Administration, Development Policy and Public Law
REINERMANN, H., Public Administration, Information Technology
SIEDENTOPF, H., Public Administration, Public Law
SOMMERMANN, K.-P., Public Law, Constitutional Law, Comparative Law
WIRTZ, B., Information and Communication Management
ZIEKOW, J., Public Law and Administrative Law

ATTACHED INSTITUTE

Forschungsinstitut für Öffentliche Verwaltung (Research Institute for Public Administration): e-mail foev@foev-speyer.de; Dir Prof. Dr JAN ZIEKOW

DEUTSCHE SPORTHOCHSCHULE KÖLN
(German Sport University Cologne)

Am Sportpark Müngersdorf 6, 50933 Cologne
Telephone: (221) 49820
Internet: www.dshs-koeln.de
Founded 1920 in Berlin, reopened in Cologne 1947
State control
Academic year: October to September (2 terms)
Rector: Prof. Dr WALTER TOKARSKI
Chancellor: Dr JOHANNES HORST
Vice-Rector: Prof. Dr HEIKO STRÜDER
Vice-Rector: Prof. Dr STEPHAN WASSONG
Librarian: Dr JÜRGEN SCHIFFER
Number of teachers: 230
Number of students: 5,381
Publications: *Impulse* (2 a year), *Kurier*

EBERHARD-KARLS-UNIVERSITÄT TÜBINGEN

Geschwister-Scholl-Pl., 72074 Tübingen
Telephone: (7071) 290
E-mail: info@uni-tuebingen.de
Internet: www.uni-tuebingen.de
Founded 1477
Academic year: October to September
Rector: Prof. Dr BERND ENGLER
Pro-Rector for Research: Prof. Dr HERBERT MÜTHER
Pro-Rector for Structure and Int. Affairs: Prof. Dr HEINZ-DIETER ASSMANN
Pro-Rector for Students, Teaching and Learning: Prof. Dr STEFANIE GROPPER
Chancellor: Dr ANDREAS ROTHFUß
Librarian: Dr MARIANNE DÖRR
Number of teachers: 2,000
Number of students: 24,400
Publications: *attempto! Forum der Universität Tübingen* (2 a year), *Jahresbericht des Rektors* (1 a year), *Uni Tübingen aktuell* (8 a year)

DEANS

Faculty of Biology: Prof. Dr VOLKER DREHSEN
Faculty of Catholic Theology: Prof. Dr ALBERT BIESINGER
Faculty of Chemistry and Pharmacy: Prof. Dr BARBARA REMMERT
Faculty of Cultural Sciences: Prof. Dr INGO B. AUTENRIETH
Faculty of Economics: Prof. Dr JÜRGEN LEONHARDT
Faculty of Geosciences: Prof. Dr JOSEF SCHMID
Faculty of Information Science and Computer Science: Prof. Dr WOLFGANG ROSENSTIEL
Faculty of Law: Prof. Dr HERMANN REICHOLD
Faculty of Mathematics and Physics: Prof. Dr WOLFGANG KNAPP
Faculty of Medicine: Prof. Dr INGO B. AUTENRIETH
Faculty of Modern Languages: Prof. Dr JOHANNES KABATEK

Faculty of Philosophy and History: Prof. Dr GEORG SCHILD
Faculty of Protestant Theology: Prof. Dr FRIEDRICH SCHWEITZER

PROFESSORS

Faculty of Biology (Auf der Morgenstelle 28, 72076 Tübingen; tel. (7071) 2976853; e-mail dek-bi@uni-tuebingen.de; internet www.mikrobio.uni-tuebingen.de):

BRAUN, V., Microbiology
ENGELS, E.-M., Development Physiology
GÖTZ, F., Microbiological Genetics
HAMPP, R., Botany
HARTER, K., Plant Physiology
JÜRGENS, G., Development Genetics
MAIER, W., Zoology
MALLOT, H., Cognitive Neurosciences
MICHIELS, N., Evolution Ecology of Animals
NORDHEIM, A., Molecular Biology
OBERWINKLER, F., Botany
SCHNITZLER, H.-U., Zoophysiology
SCHÖFFL, F., Genetics
WOHLLEBEN, W., Microbiology, Biotechnology

Faculty of Catholic Theology (Liebermeisterstr. 18, 72076 Tübingen; tel. (7071) 2972544; e-mail u02-info@uni-tuebingen.de; internet www.uni-tuebingen.de/kath-theologie):

BIESINGER, A., Educational Religion
ECKERT, M., Fundamental Theology
FREYER, T., Dogmatic Theology
FUCHS, O., Practical Theology
GROSS, W., Old Testament
HILBERATH, B. J., Systematics
HOLZEM, A., Medieval and Modern Church History
MIETH, D., Moral Theology and Social Sciences
PUZA, R., Church Law
SEELIGER, H.-R., Ancient Church History, Patrology, Christian Archaeology
THEOBALD, M., New Testament

Faculty of Chemistry and Pharmacy (Auf der Morgenstelle 8, 72076 Tübingen; tel. (7071) 2972920; e-mail dekanat-chem-pharm@uni-tuebingen.de; internet www.uni-tuebingen.de/chemie):

HAMPRECHT, B., Biochemistry
HEIDE, L., Pharmacology
LAUFER, S., Pharmacology
MAIER, M., Organic Chemistry
MEIXNER, A., Physical Chemistry
NÜRNBERGER, T., Organic Biochemistry
OBERHAMMER, H., Physical Chemistry
RUTH, P., Pharmacology
STEHLE, T., Biochemistry
STRÄHLE, J., Inorganic Chemistry
WESEMANN, L., Inorganic Chemistry
ZIEGLER, T., Organic Chemistry

Faculty of Cultural Sciences (Hölderlinstr. 19, 72074 Tübingen; tel. (7071) 2976858; e-mail a11-info@uni-tuebingen.de; internet www.uni-tuebingen.de/kultur-dekanatl):

ANTONI, K., Japanology
BUTZENBERGER, K., Indology, Comparative Religion
EGGERT, M., Pre- and Ancient History
GERÖ, ST., Oriental Christian Philology and Culture
HOFMANN, H., Classical Philology
KLEIN, P., Art History
LEITZ, C., Egyptology
LEONHARDT, J., Latin Philology
PERNICKA, E., Archaeometry, Archaeometallurgy
RICHTER-BERNBURG, L., Oriental Studies
SCHAEFER, T., Classical Archaeology
SCHMID, M. H., Music
SCHUBERT, G., Sinology
STELLRECHT, I., Ethnography
SZLEZÁK, TH., Greek Philology
VOGEL, H.-U., Sinology
VOLK, K., Oriental History

Faculty of Economics (Nauklerstr. 47, 72074 Tübingen; tel. (7071) 2972563; e-mail w04.dekanat@uni-tuebingen.de; internet www.uni-tuebingen.de/uni/w04):

BATEN, J., Economic History
BERNDT, R., Commerce
BUCH, C.-M., Economics
CANSIER, D., Economics
GRAMMIG, J., Economics and Statistics
HECKER, R., Commerce
HOFMANN, C., Commerce
JAHNKE, B., Commerce
KOHLER, W., Economics
NEUS, W., Commerce
PULL, K., Commerce
SCHAICH, E., Economics and Statistics
SCHÖBEL, R., Commerce
STADLER, M., Economics
STARBATTY, J., Economics
WAGNER, F. W., Commerce

Faculty of Geosciences (Sigwartstr. 17, 72076 Tübingen; tel. (7071) 2976861; e-mail e16-info@uni-tuebingen.de; internet www.uni-tuebingen.de/geo):

CONARD, N., Palaeohistory and Protohistory
EBERLE, D., Geography
FÖRSTER, H., Geography
FRISCH, W., Geology
HADERLEIN, S., Environmental Mineralogy
KUCERA, M., Micropalaeontology
MOSBRUGGER, V., Palaeontology
SATIR, M., Geological Chemistry

Faculty of Information Science and Computer Science (Sand 13, 72076 Tübingen; tel. (7071) 2977046; e-mail dekanat@informatik.uni-tuebingen.de; internet www.informatik.uni-tuebingen.de):

CARLE, G., Computer Science
DIEHL, M., Psychology
HAUCK, P., Computer Science
HAUTZINGER, M., Psychology
HESSE, F., Psychology
HUSON, D., Computer Science
KLAEREN, H., Computer Science
KOHLBACHER, O., Computer Science
LANGE, K.-J., Computer Science
ROSENSTIEL, W., Computer Science
SCHWAN, S., Psychology
STAPF, K.-H., Psychology
STRASSER, W., Computer Science
ULRICH, R., Psychology
ZELL, A., Computer Science

Faculty of Law (tel. (7071) 2972545; e-mail dekanat@jura.uni-tuebingen.de; internet www.jura.uni-tuebingen.de):

ASSMANN, H.-D., Civil Law, Trade and Commercial Law
GÜNTHER, H.-L., Penal Law
HAFT, F., Penal Law and Procedural Law
KÄSTNER, K.-H., Civil Law, State Church Law
KERNER, H.-J., Criminology
KIRCHHOF, F., Public Law
KÜHL, K., Penal Law and Procedural Law
MAROTZKE, W., Civil Law and Procedural Law
MÖSCHEL, W., Civil, Trade and Commercial Law
NETTESHEIM, M., Public Law, European Law, Civil Law
PICKER, E., Civil Law, Labour and Trade Law
REICHOLD, H., Public Law, Trade and Commercial Law, Labour Law
REMMERT, B., Public Law, European Law and Constitution History
RONELLENFITSCH, M., Public Law
SCHIEMANN, G., Civil Law
SCHRÖDER, J., Penal and Private Law, History of German Law
VITZTHUM, W. G., Public Law
VOGEL, J., Penal Law, Procedural Law
WEBER, U., Penal Law, Procedural Law
WESTERMANN, H. P., Civil, Trade and Commercial Law

Faculty of Mathematics and Physics (Auf der Morgenstelle 4, 72076 Tübingen; tel. (7071) 2972567; e-mail dekanat.physik@uni-tuebingen.de; internet www.physik.uni-tuebingen.de/dekanat):

BATYREV, V., Algebra
FÄSSLER, A., Theoretical Physics
HERING, C., Geometry
JOCHUM, J., Experimental Physics
KAUP, W., Complex Analysis
KERN, D., Basic Physical Computer Science
KLEY, W., Computational Physics
LUBICH, C., Numerical Analysis
PLIES, E., Applied Physics
REINHARDT, H., Theoretical Physics
RUDER, H., Theoretical Astrophysics
SANTANGELO, A., Astronomy, Astrophysics
SCHÄTZLE, R., Analysis
SCHOPOHL, N., Theoretical Physics
SCHREIBER, F., Biophysical Structures
TEUFEL, S., Mathematical Methods in Natural Sciences
WERNER, K., Astronomy and Astrophysics
YSERENTANT, H., Numerical Analysis
ZERNER, M., Stochastics
ZIMMERMANN, C., Experimental Physics

Faculty of Medicine (Geissweg 5, 72076 Tübingen; tel. (7071) 2972566; e-mail judith.jovanovic@med.uni-tuebingen.de; internet www.medizin.uni-tuebingen.de/pages/med_-fakultaet):

AUTENRIETH, I. B., Medical Microbiology
BAMBERG, M., Radiography
BARES, R., Nuclear Medicine
BARTZ-SCHMIDT, K.-U., Ophthalmology
BECKER, H. D., Surgery
BIRBAUMER, N., Psychology
BUCHKREMER, G., Psychiatry
BÜLTMANN, B., Pathology
CLAUSSEN, C., Radiography
DICHGANS, H., Neurology
DIETZ, K., Medical Biometrics
DREWS, U., Anatomy
FUCHS, J., Child Surgery
GAWAZ, M., Internal Medicine
GOSSER, T., Neurology
GÖZ, G., Dentistry
GREGOR, M., Internal Medicine
HÄRING, H.-U., Internal Medicine
HOFBECK, M., Paediatrics
JAHN, G., Medical Virology
JUCKER, M., Neurology
KANDOLF, R., Molecular Pathology
KANZ, L., Internal Medicine
KLOSINSKI, G., Child and Youth Psychiatry
KNOBLOCH, J., Tropical Medicine
KÖNIGSRAINER, A., Surgery
KRÄGELOH-MANN, J., Paediatrics
LANG, F., Physiology
LÖST, C., Dentistry
MEYERMANN, R., Neuropathology
NIESS, A., Sports Medicine
OSSWALD, H., Pharmacology
POETS, C. F., Paediatrics
RAMMENSEE, H.-G., Immunology
REINERT, S., Maxillofacial Surgery
RIESS, O., Clinical Genetics
RÖCKEN, M., Dermatology
SCHALLER, H.-E., Plastic, Hand and Burns Surgery
SCHWEIZER, P., Child Surgery
SELBMANN, H.-K., Medical Statistics and Data Processing
STENZL, A., Urology
TATAGIBA, M., Neurosurgery
THIER, H. P., Neurology
UNERTL, K., Anaesthesiology
VOIGT, K., Neuroradiology
WAGNER, H.-J., Anatomy
WALLWIENER, D., Gynaecology
WEBER, H., Dentistry
WEHNER, H.-D., Forensic Medicine

WEISE, K., Traumatology
WIESING, U., Medical Ethics
WULKER, N., Orthopaedics
ZENNER, H.-P., Otorhinolaryngology
ZIEMER, G., Thoracic and Cardiovascular Surgery
ZIPFEL, S., Psychosomatic Medicine, Psychotherapy
ZRENNER, E., Ophthalmology

Faculty of Modern Languages (Wilhelmstr. 50, 72074 Tübingen; tel. (7071) 2972952; e-mail dek-nphil@uni-tuebingen.de; internet www.uni-tuebingen.de/neuphil-dekanat):

BAUER, M., English Philology
BERGER, T., Slavonic Philology
BRAUNGART, G., German Philology
ENGLER, B., English Philology
FICHTE, J., English Philology
HINRICHS, E., Computing Science of Linguistics
HOTZ-DAVIES, I., English Philology
HUBER, CH., Medieval German Literature
KEMPER, H.-G., German Philology
KILCHER, A., German Philology
KLUGE, R.-D., Slavonic Philology
KOBATEK, J., Romance Philology
KOCH, P., German Philology
KOHN, K., English Philology
MATZAT, W., Romance Philology
MOOG-GRÜNEWALD, M., Romance Philology
REINFANDT, C., English Philology
REIS, M., German Philology
RIDDER, K., Medieval German Literature
SCHAHADAT, S., Slavonic Philology
UEDING, G., Rhetorics
VON STECHOW, A., Theoretical Linguistics
WERTHEIMER, J., German Philology

Faculty of Philosophy and History (*Philosophy Section,* Bursagasse 1, 72070 Tübingen; tel. (7071) 2976852; e-mail dekanat@philosophie.uni-tuebingen.de; internet www.uni-tuebingen.de/philosophie*History Section*, Sigwartstr. 17, 72076 Tübingen; tel. (7071) 2972568; e-mail stefan.zaunder@uni-tuebingen.de; internet www.uni-tuebingen.de/dekanat-geschichte):

BEYRAU, D., East European History
DOERING-MANTEUFFEL, A., Modern and Contemporary History
FRANK, M., Philosophy
HARTMANN, W., Medieval and Modern History
HEIDELBERGER, M., Philosophy
HÖFFE, O., Philosophy
KOCH, A. F., Philosophy
KOLB, F., Ancient History
LANGEWIESCHE, D., Medieval and Modern History
LORENZ, S., Medieval and Modern History
SCHINDLING, A., Medieval and Modern History

Faculty of Protestant Theology (Liebermeisterstr. 12, 72076 Tübingen; tel. (7071) 2972538; e-mail ev.theologie@uni-tuebingen.de; internet www.uni-tuebingen.de/ev-theologie):

BAYER, O., Systematic Theology
BLUM, E., Old Testament
DRECOLL, V., Church History
DREHSEN, V., Practical Theology
ECKSTEIN, H.-J., New Testament
HENNIG, G., Practical Theology
HERMS, E., Systematic Theology
HOFIUS, O., New Testament
JANOWSKI, B., Old Testament
KÖPF, U., Church History
LICHTENBERGER, H., New Testament and Ancient Jewish Culture
SCHWEITZER, F., Practical Theology
SCHWÖBEL, C., Systematic Theology

Faculty of Social and Behavioural Sciences and Pedagogics (Wächterstr. 67, 72074 Tübingen; tel. (7071) 2976857; e-mail s08info@uni-tuebingen.de; internet www.uni-tuebingen.de/faksozver):

BOECKH, A., Political Studies
DEUTSCHMANN, CH., Sociology
DIGEL, H., Theory of Physical Education
GILDEMEISTER, R., Sociology
HORN, K.-P., Pedagogics
HRBEK, R., Political Studies
HUBER, G., Pedagogics
JOHLER, R., Cultural Studies
MÜLLER, S., Social Pedagogics
RITTBERGER, V., Political Studies
SCHRADER, J., Pedagogics
THIEL, A., Theory of Physical Education
TREPTOW, R., Pedagogics
WANK, V., Theory of Physical Education

ATTACHED INSTITUTES

Goethe-Wörterbuch: Frischlinstr. 7, 72074 Tübingen; Dir of Commission Prof. Dr W. KÜHLMANN.

Institut für Wissensmedien (Media Institute): Konrad-Adenauer-Str. 40, 72072 Tübingen; Dir Prof. Dr FRIEDRICH W. HESSE

EBS UNIVERSITÄT FÜR WIRTSCHAFT UND RECHT

Gustav-Stresemann-Ring 3, 65189 Wiesbaden
Telephone: (611) 710200
E-mail: info@ebs.edu
Internet: www.ebs.edu
Founded 1971 as European Business School, present name and status 2010
Private control
Languages of instruction: English, German
Academic year: October to September
Pres. and CEO: Prof. ROLF CREMER
Provost: Dr GEORG NIKOLAUS GARLICHS
Vice-Pres.: Prof. Dr GERRICK FREIHERR V. HOYNINGEN-HUENE
Vice-Pres.: Prof. Dr ROLF TILMES
Head Librarian: SILVA SCHELLHAS
Library of 32,000 vols
Number of teachers: 85
Number of students: 1,600

DEANS

Business School: Prof. Dr ROLF TILMES
Law School: Prof. Dr GERRICK FREIHERR HOYNINGEN-HUENE

ERNST-MORITZ-ARNDT-UNIVERSITÄT GREIFSWALD

Domstr. 11, 17487 Greifswald
Telephone: (3834) 860
E-mail: rektor@uni-greifswald.de
Internet: www.uni-greifswald.de
Founded 1456
Academic year: October to September
Chancellor: Dr WOLFGANG FLIEGER
Rector: Prof. Dr RAINER WESTERMANN
Pro-Rector: Prof. Dr MICHAEL HERBST
Pro-Rector: Prof. Dr FRIEDER DÜNKEL
Number of teachers: 235
Number of students: 12,000
Publications: *Greifswalder Universitätsreden* (irregular), *Wissenschaftliche Beiträge* (irregular)

DEANS

Faculty of Law and Economics: Prof. Dr WALTER RIED
Faculty of Mathematics and Natural Sciences: Prof. Dr KLAUS FESSER
Faculty of Medicine: Prof. Dr HEYO K. KROEMER
Faculty of Philosophy: Prof. Dr ALEXANDER WÖLL
Faculty of Theology: Prof. Dr HEINRICH ASSEL

EUROPA-UNIVERSITÄT VIADRINA (Viadrina European University)

Grosse Scharrnstr. 59, 15230 Frankfurt an der Oder
Telephone: (335) 55340
E-mail: study@euv-frankfurt-o.de
Internet: www.euv-ffo.de
Founded 1991
Languages of instruction: German, English, Polish
Academic year: October to July
Pres.: Dr GUNTER PLEUGER
Chancellor: CHRISTIAN ZENS
Registrar: BEATRIX ECKERT
Int. Office: PETRA WEBER
Librarian: Dr HANS-GERD HAPPEL
Library of 525,000 vols
Number of teachers: 190
Number of students: 6,200

DEANS

Faculty of Cultural and Social Studies: Prof. Dr KONSTANZE JUNGBLUTH
Faculty of Economics: Prof. Dr SVEN HUSMANN
Faculty of Law: Prof. Dr MATTIAS PECHSTEIN

ATTACHED COLLEGE

Collegium Polonicum: e-mail colpol@europa-uni.de; (situated in Slubice in Poland, and managed jointly by the Europa-Universität Viadrina and the Adam Mickiewicz University in Poznań, Poland)

FERNUNIVERSITÄT IN HAGEN (Distance-Learning University in Hagen)

58084 Hagen
Universitätsstr. 11, 58097 Hagen
Telephone: (2331) 9872444
E-mail: info@fernuni-hagen.de
Internet: www.fernuni-hagen.de
Founded 1974
State control
Language of instruction: German
Academic year: October to September
54 Study centres within Germany, Austria, Switzerland, Hungary and Russia
Rector: Prof. Dr Ing. HELMUT HOYER
Vice-Rector: Prof. Dr RAINER OLBRICH
Vice-Rector: Prof. Dr RAINER OLBRICH
CEO and Chancellor: REGINA ZDEBEL
Librarian: KARIN MICHALKE (acting)
Library of 800,000 vols, 2,000 print journals, 36,000 ejournals
Number of teachers: 942
Number of students: 74,223
Publications: *Anleitung zur Belegung, FernUni Perspektive* (newspaper of the univ.), *Forschungsbericht, Informationen zum Studium, Schriftenreihen* (scientific publ.)

DEANS

Faculty of Business Administration and Economics: Prof. Dr Hab. THOMAS HERING
Faculty of Culture and Social Sciences: Prof. Dr THEO BASTIAENS
Faculty of Law: Prof. Dr ANDREAS HARATSCH
Faculty of Mathematics and Computer Science: Prof. Dr RUTGER VERBEEK

FREIE UNIVERSITÄT BERLIN

Kaiserswerther Str. 16–18, 14195 Berlin
Telephone: (30) 8381
E-mail: praesident@fu-berlin.de
Internet: www.fu-berlin.de
Founded 1948
Academic year: October to July
Pres.: Prof. Dr PETER-ANDRÉ ALT

Exec. Vice-Pres.: Prof. Dr MONIKA SCHÄFER-KORTING
Vice-Pres.: Prof. Dr WERNER VÄTH
Vice-Pres.: Prof. Dr MICHAEL BONGARDT
Vice-Pres.: Prof. Dr Ing. BRIGITTA SCHÜTT
Dir for Admin. and Finance: PETER LANGE
Librarian: Prof. Dr ULRICH NAUMANN

Library: see under Libraries and Archives
Number of teachers: 2,800
Number of students: 32,000

DEANS

Dept of Biology, Chemistry and Pharmacy: Prof. Dr HARTMUT H. HILGER
Dept of Earth Sciences: Prof. Dr ULRICH CUBASCH
Dept of Economics: Prof. Dr RONNIE SCHÖB
Dept of Education and Psychology: Prof. Dr HARM KUPER
Dept of History and Cultural Studies: Prof. Dr VERENA BLECHINGER-TALCOTT
Dept of Law: Prof. Dr MARTIN SCHWAB
Dept of Mathematics and Computer Science: Prof. Dr RUPERT KLEIN
Dept of Philosophy and Humanities: Prof. Dr JOACHIM KÜPPER
Dept of Physics: ROBERT BITTL
Dept of Political and Social Sciences: Prof. Dr KLAUS BECK
Dept of Veterinary Medicine: Prof. Dr LEO BRUNNBERG
Medical School—Charité: Prof. Dr ANNETTE GRÜTERS-KIESLICH

CENTRAL ATTACHED INSTITUTES

John F. Kennedy-Institut für Nordamerikastudien (J. F. K. Institute of North American Studies): Lanstr. 7, 14195 Berlin; tel. (30) 83852703; e-mail jfki@zedat.fu-berlin.de; internet web.fu-berlin.de/jfki; Chair. DETLEF BROSE.

Lateinamerika-Institut (Institute of Latin American Studies): Rüdesheimer Str. 54–56, 14197 Berlin; tel. (30) 83853073; e-mail ai@zedat.fu-berlin.de; internet web.fu-berlin.de/lai; Chair. Prof. Dr MARIANNE BRAIG.

Osteuropa-Institut (Institute of East European Studies): Garystr. 55, 14195 Berlin; tel. (30) 83853380; e-mail oei@zedat.fu-berlin.de; internet www.oei.fu-berlin.de; Chair. DETLEF BROSE

FRIEDRICH-ALEXANDER-UNIVERSITÄT ERLANGEN-NÜRNBERG

POB 35 20, 91023 Erlangen
Schlosspl. 4, 91054 Erlangen
Telephone: (9131) 850
E-mail: praesident@uni-erlangen.de
Internet: www.uni-erlangen.de
Founded 1743, merged with Univ. Altdorf 1809
State control
Pres.: Prof. Dr KARL-DIETER GRÜSKE
Vice-Pres.: Prof. Dr CHRISTOPH KORBMACHER
Vice-Pres.: Prof. Dr HANS-PETER STEINRÜCK
Vice-Pres.: Prof. JOHANNA HABERER
Chancellor: THOMAS A. H. SCHÖCK
Librarian: Dr KONSTANZE SÖLLNER
Library: see under Libraries and Archives
Number of teachers: 590
Number of students: 28,677
Publications: *Erlanger Bausteine zur fränkischen Heimatforschung, Erlanger Forschungen, Geologische Blätter für Nordost-Bayern und angrenzende Gebiete, Jahresbericht, Jahresbibliographie und Forschungsbericht, Unikurier, Unikurier aktuell*

DEANS

Faculty of Engineering: Prof. Dr GÜNTER ILGENFRITZ
Faculty of Humanities, Social Sciences and Theology: Prof. Dr HEIDRUN STEIN-KECKS
Faculty of Law, Business and Economics: Prof. Dr MICHAEL AMBERG
Faculty of Medicine: Prof. Dr JÜRGEN SCHÜTTLER
Faculty of Sciences: Prof. Dr FRANK DUZAAR

FRIEDRICH-SCHILLER-UNIVERSITÄT JENA
(Friedrich Schiller University of Jena)

07737 Jena
Telephone: (3641) 931040
E-mail: rektor@uni-jena.de
Internet: www.uni-jena.de
Founded 1558
Academic year: October to September
State control
Chancellor: Dr KLAUS BARTHOLMÉ
Rector: Prof. Dr KLAUS DICKE
Vice-Rector for Graduate Academy: Prof. Dr ERIKA KOTHE
Vice-Rector for Research: Prof. THORSTEN HEINZEL
Vice-Rector for Teaching and Structure: Prof. Dr JENS HAUSTEIN
Library: see under Libraries and Archives
Number of teachers: 6,979
Number of students: 20,000
Publication: *Uni-Journal Jena* (online, www.uni-jena.de/journal)

DEANS

Faculty of Biology and Pharmacy: Prof. Dr FRANK HELLWIG
Faculty of Chemical and Earth Sciences: Prof. Dr REINHARD GAUPP
Faculty of Economics and Business Administration: Prof. Dr ANDREAS FREYTAG
Faculty of Law: Prof. Dr GÜNTER JEROUSCHEK
Faculty of Mathematics and Computer Science: Prof. Dr HANS-JÜRGEN SCHMEIßER
Faculty of Medicine: Prof. Dr KLAUS BENNDORF
Faculty of Philosophy: Prof. Dr HERMANN FUNK
Faculty of Physics and Astronomy: Prof. Dr BERND BRÜGMANN
Faculty of Social and Behavioural Sciences: Prof. Dr STEPHAN LESSENICH
Faculty of Theology: Prof. Dr MICHAEL WERMKE

GEORG-AUGUST-UNIVERSITÄT GÖTTINGEN

Wilhelmspl. 1, 37073 Göttingen
Telephone: (551) 390
E-mail: poststelle@uni-goettingen.de
Internet: www.uni-goettingen.de
Founded 1737
Academic year: October to July
Pres.: Prof. Dr ULRIKE BEISIEGEL
Vice-Pres.: Prof. Dr HILTRAUD CASPER-HEHNE
Vice-Pres.: Prof. Dr JOACHIM MÜNCH
Vice-Pres.: Dipl. MARKUS HOPPE
Vice-Pres.: Prof. Dr WOLFGANG LÜCKE
Librarian: Dr NORBERT LOSSAU
Number of teachers: 800
Number of students: 24,380
Publications: *Georgia-Augusta* (2 a year), *Jahresforschungsbericht* (every 2 years), *Spektrum* (4 a year)

DEANS

Faculty of Agricultural Sciences: Prof. Dr ACHIM SPILLER
Faculty of Biology: Prof. Dr RALF FICNER
Faculty of Chemistry: Prof. Dr CLAUDIA STEINEM
Faculty of Economic Sciences: Prof. Dr OLAF KORN
Faculty of Forest Sciences and Forest Ecology: Prof. Dr CHRISTOPH KLEINN
Faculty of Geoscience and Geography: Prof. Dr SHARON WEBB
Faculty of Humanities: Prof. Dr UDO FRIEDRICH
Faculty of Law: Prof. Dr ANDREAS SPICKHOFF
Faculty of Mathematics and Computer Science: Prof. Dr DIETER HOGREFE
Faculty of Medicine: Prof. Dr CORNELIUS FRÖMMEL
Faculty of Physics: Prof. Dr HANS CHRISTIAN HOFSÄSS
Faculty of Social Sciences: Prof. Dr GABRIELE ROSENTHAL
Faculty of Theology: Prof. Dr CHRISTINE AXT-PISCALAR

GOETHE-UNIVERSITÄT FRANKFURT AM MAIN

POB 11 19 32, 60054 Frankfurt am Main
Senckenberganlage 31, 60325 Frankfurt am Main
Telephone: (69) 7980
E-mail: presse@uni-frankfurt.de
Internet: www.goethe-universitaet.de
Founded 1914
Academic year: October to September (2 semesters)
Pres.: Prof. Dr WERNER MÜLLER-ESTERL
Vice-Pres.: Prof. Dr MANFRED SCHUBERT-ZSILAVECZ
Vice-Pres.: Prof. Dr MARIA ROSER VALENTI
Vice-Pres.: Prof. Dr MATTHIAS LUTZ-BACHMANN
Vice-Pres.: Prof. Dr RAINER KLUMP
Chancellor: HANS GEORG MOCKEL
Library Dir: BERNDT DUGALL
Number of teachers: 2,656
Number of students: 36,625
Publications: *Forschung Frankfurt* (4 a year), *Forschungsbericht* (1 a year), *Uni-Report* (6 or 7 a year)

DEANS

Department of Biochemistry, Chemistry and Pharmaceutical Sciences: Prof. Dr DIETER STEINHILBER
Department of Biological Sciences: Prof. Dr A. STARZINSKI-POWITZ
Department of Computer Science and Mathematics: Prof. Dr TOBIAS WETH
Department of Economics and Business Administration: Prof. Dr ALFONS WEICHENRIEDER
Department of Educational Sciences: Prof. Dr BARBARA FRIEBERTSHÄUSER
Department of Geosciences and Geography: Prof. Dr ROBERT PÜTZ
Department of Law: Prof. Dr MANFRED WANDT
Department of Linguistic, Cultural and Civilization Studies, Art Studies: Prof. Dr RÜDIGER KRAUSE
Department of Medical Science: Prof. Dr JOSEF M. PFEILSCHIFTER
Department of Modern Languages: Prof. Dr SUSANNE OPFERMANN
Department of Philosophy and History: Prof. Dr ANDRÉ FUHRMANN
Department of Physics: Prof. Dr MICHAEL HUTH
Department of Protestant Theology: Prof. Dr HANS-GÜNTER HEIMBROCK
Department of Psychology and Sports Sciences: Prof. Dr HELFRIED MOOSBRUGGER
Department of Roman Catholic Theology: Prof. Dr THOMAS SCHMELLER
Department of Social Sciences: Prof. Dr UTA RUPPERT

PROFESSORS

Department of Biochemistry, Chemistry and Pharmaceutical Sciences (Max-von-Laue-Str. 9, 60438 Frankfurt am Main; tel. (69) 79829545; e-mail dekanatfb14@uni-frankfurt.de):

AUNER, N., Inorganic Chemistry
BADER, H.-J., Chemistry Teaching
BAMBERG, E., Biophysical Chemistry
BRUTSCHY, B., Physical Chemistry
DINGERMANN, TH., Pharmaceutical Biology
DRESSMAN, J. B., Pharmaceutical Technology
EGERT, E., Organic Chemistry
ENGELS, J., Organic Chemistry
GÖBEL, M., Organic Chemistry
KARAS, M., Analytical Chemistry
KOLBESEN, B., Inorganic Chemistry
KREUTER, J., Pharmaceutical Technology
LAMBRECHT, G., Pharmacology for Natural Scientists
LUDWIG, B., Biochemistry
MARSCHALEK, R., Pharmaceutical Biology
MOSANDL, A., Food Chemistry
MÜLLER, W. E., Pharmacology and Toxicology
PRISNER, TH. F., Physical Chemistry
REHM, D., Physical and Organic Chemistry
RÜTERJANS, H., Physical Biochemistry
SCHUBERT-ZSILAVECZ, M., Pharmaceutical Chemistry
STARK, H., Pharmaceutical Chemistry
STEINHILBER, D., Pharmaceutical Chemistry
STOCK, G., Theoretical Chemistry
WACHTVEITL, J., Physical Chemistry
WAGNER, M., Inorganic Chemistry

Department of Biological Sciences (Max-von-Laue-Str. 9, 60438 Frankfurt am Main; tel. (69) 79846471; e-mail dekanat15@bio.uni-frankfurt.de):

BEREITER-HAHN, J., Cell Research
BRÄNDLE, K., Zoology
BRENDEL, M., Biology for Doctors
BRÜGGEMANN, W., Botany
DROBNIK, O., Architecture and Business Systems
ENTIAN, K.-D., Microbiology
FEIERABEND, F., Botany
FLEISSNER, G., Zoology
GEIHS, K., Practical Informatics
GNATZY, W., Zoology
HAGERUP, T., Theoretical Informatics
KAHL, G., Botany
KEMP, R., Applied Informatics
KOENIGER, N., Apiculture
KROEGER, A., Microbiology
KRÖMKER, D., Graphical Data Processing
KUNZ, W., Drafting Methods
LANGE-BERTALOT, H., Botany
MASCHWITZ, U., Zoology
NOVER, L., Botany
OSIEWACZ, H., Botany
PONS, F., Microbiology
PRINZINGER, R., Zoology
PROTSCH VON ZIETEN, R., Anthropology
SANDMANN, G., Botany
SCHMIDT-SCHAUSS, M., Artificial Intelligence
SCHNITGER, G., Theoretical Informatics
STARZINSKI-POWITZ, A., Human Genetics
STEIGER, H., Microbiology
STREIT, B., Zoology
TROMMER, G., Biology Teaching
WALDSCHMIDT, K., Applied Informatics
WILTSCHKO, W., Zoology
WITTIG, R., Botany
WOTSCHKE, D., Computer Languages
ZICARI, R., Databases
ZIMMERMANN, H., Zoology
ZIZKA, G., Botany

Department of Computer Science and Mathematics (Robert-Mayer-Str. 10, 60054 Frankfurt am Main; tel. (69) 79824602; e-mail dekan@fb12.uni-frankfurt.de):

BAUMEISTER, J. B., Optimum and Convex Functions
BEHR, H., Pure Mathematics
BIERI, R., Pure Mathematics
BLIEDTNER, J., Pure Mathematics
CONSTANTINESCU, F., Mathematics
DE GROOTE, H., Applied Mathematics
DINGES, H., Probability Theory and Statistics
FÜHRER, L., Mathematics Teaching
KERSTING, G., Stochastics
KLOEDEN, P. E., Applied Mathematics
KRUMMHEUER, G., Mathematics Teaching
LUCKHARDT, H., Fundamental Mathematics
METZLER, W., Mathematics
MÜLLER, K. H., Applied Mathematics
REICHERT-HAHN, M., Mathematics
SCHNORR, C., Applied Mathematics
SCHWARZ, W., Mathematics
SIEVEKING, M., Applied Mathematics
WAKOLBINGER, A., Probability Theory
WEIDMANN, J., Mathematics
WOLFART, J., Mathematics

Department of Economics and Business Administration (Grüneburgpl. 1, 60323 Frankfurt am Main; tel. (69) 79834601; e-mail dekanat02@wiwi.uni-frankfurt.de):

BARTELS, H. G., Business Administration, Operational Research
BAUER, T., Economic Systems and Transition
BINDER, M., Macroeconomics
BLONSKI, M., Microeconomics
BÖCKING, H.-J., Corporate Governance
EWERT, R., Controlling and Auditing
FITZENBERGER, B., Labour Economics
GEBHARDT, G., Economic Management
GOMBER, P., e-Finance
HALIASSOS, M., Macroeconomics and Financial Markets
HASSLER, U., Statistics
HOLTEN, R., Business Information Systems
HOMMEL, M., Auditing and Invoicing
HORLEBEIN, M., Economic Pedagogics
HUJER, R., Statistics and Econometrics
ISERMANN, H., Business Administration
KAAS, K. P., Industrial Economics
KLAPPER, D., Marketing
KLUMP, R., Business Development
KÖNIG, W., Economic Management
KRAHNEN, J. P., Financial Management
KRÜGER, D., Macroeconomy
LAUX, H., Theory of Organization
MATHES, H. D., Production Planning
MAURER, R., Investment
MELLWIG, W., Industrial Economics
NATTER, M., Trade
NAUTZ, D., Empirical Macroeconomy
RANNENBERG, K., Business Computing
ROMMELFANGER, H., Mathematics for Economists
SCHEFOLD, B., Political Economics
SCHLAG, CH., Financial Economics
SCHMIDT, R., Economic Management
SKIERA, B., Electronic Commerce
VELTHUIS, L., Organization and Management
WAHRENBURG, M., Business Administration (Banking)
WALZ, U., Industry Economics
WEICHENRIEDER, A., Financial Economics
WIELAND, V., Money Theory and Policy

Department of Educational Sciences (POB 109, Senckenberganlage 15, 60054 Frankfurt am Main; tel. (69) 79828729; e-mail dekanatfb4@em.uni-frankfurt.de):

BRAKEMEIER-LISOP, I., Economic Pedagogics
BRUMLIK, M., Pedagogics
CREMER-SCHÄFER, H., Pedagogics and Social Pedagogics
DEPPE-WOLFINGER, H., Special Education
DUDEK, P., Pedagogics
FAUST-SIEHL, G., Primary Education
GRUSCHKA, A., Teacher Training
HESS, H., Social Pedagogics
HOFMANN-MÜLLER, C. H., Pedagogics
JACOBS, K., Special and Remedial Education
KADE, J., Theory and Practice of Adult Education
KALLERT, H., Social Pedagogics
KAMINSKI, W., Pedagogics
KATZENBACH, D., Pedagogics
MARKERT, W., Economic Pedagogics
MEIER, R., Primary Teacher Training
NITTEL, D., Social Pedagogics and Adult Education
NYSSEN, F., Teacher Training
OVERBECK, A., Special Education
RADTKE, F.-O., Pedagogics
RANG, B., History and Pedagogics of Women's Studies
SCHLÖMERKEMPER, J., Pedagogics
SCHOLZ, G., Primary Education
ZANDER, H., Social Pedagogics
ZENZ, G., Social Pedagogics

Department of Geosciences and Geography (Altenhöferallee 1, 60438 Frankfurt am Main; tel. (69) 79840208; e-mail dekanat-geowiss@em.uni-frankfurt.de):

ALBRECHT, V., Teaching of Geography
ANDRES, W., Physical Geography
BATHELT, H., Economic Geography
BREY, G., Mineralogy
BRINKMANN, W. L. F., Hydrology
HASSE, J., Teaching of Geography
HERBERT, F., Theoretical Meteorology
HUESSNER, H., Geology and Palaeontology
JUNGE, A., Geophysics
KLEINSCHMIDT, G., Geology
KOWALCZYK, G., Regional Geology
MÜLLER, G., Mathematical Geophysics
OSCHMANN, W., Palaeontology
PÜTTMANN, W., Environmental Analysis
RUNGE, J., Physical Geography
SCHAMP, E., Economic Geography
SCHICKHOFF, I., Human Geography
SCHMELING, H., Solid Earth Physics
SCHMIDT, U., Atmospheric Physics
SCHÖNWIESE, C., Meteorological Environmental Research
SCHROEDER, R., Palaeontology
STEIN, N., Physical Geography
STEININGER, F. F., Palaeontology and Historical Geology
THARUN, E., Cultural Geography
THIEMAYER, H., Hydrology
WOLF, K., Cultural Geography

Department of Law (Grüneburgpl. 1, 60323 Frankfurt am Main; tel. (69) 79834206; e-mail ddekanatfb1@rz.uni-frankfurt.de):

ALBRECHT, P., Criminology and Criminal Law
BAUMS, TH., Business Law (Banking and Media)
CAHN, A., Law and Finance
CORDES, A., European History of Law
EBSEN, I., Constitutional, Administrative and Social Law
FABRICIUS, D., Criminal Law, Criminology and Psychology of Law
FRANKENBERG, G., Public Law
GILLES, P., Legal Procedure, Civil and Comparative Law
GÜNTHER, K., Theory of Law, Penal Law and Law of Criminal Procedure
HAAR, B., Civil Law
HASSEMER, W., Theory of Law, Social and Criminal Law
HERMES, G., Public Law
HOFMANN, R., Civil Law
KADELBACH, S., Public Law, European Law

KARGL, W., Theory of Law, Philosophy of Law and Criminal Law
KOHL, H., Civil Law
NEUMANN, U., Social, Criminal, and Criminal Adjective Law and Philosophy of Law
OGOREK, R., Roman Law, Civil Law
OSTERLOH, L., Public Law, Tax Law
PRITTWITZ, C., Criminal Law
REHBINDER, E., Business, Environmental and Comparative Law
RÜCKERT, J., History of Law
SACKSOFSKY, U., Public Law and Comparative Law
SIEKMANN, H., Money and Bank Law
SIRKS, B., History of Law and Civil Law
STOLLEIS, M., Public Law, History of Law
TEUBNER, G., Civic Rights, Commercial Law
VESTING, T., Public Law, Media Law
WANDT, M., German and International Civil Law, Commercial and Insurance Law
WEISS, M., Labour Law and Civic Rights
WELLENHOFER, M., Civil and Process Law
WIELAND, J., Public Law, Financial Law and Tax Law
ZEKOLL, J., Civil Law

Department of Linguistic, Cultural and Civilization Studies, Art Studies (Mertonstr. 17–21, 60054 Frankfurt am Main; tel. (69) 79825023; e-mail dekanat-fb09@em.uni-frankfurt.de):

BASTIAN, H. G., Teaching of Music
BÜCHSEL, M., History of European Art
DAIBER, Oriental Studies
ERDAL, M., Turkish Studies
FASSLER, M., European Ethnology
FISCHER, J., Art Teaching
FREIDHOF, G., Slavonic Studies
GIPPERT, J., Comparative Linguistics
HERDING, K., Art History
LANGER, G., Slavonic Studies
MEYER, J.-W., Archaeology
NEU, T., Art Teaching
NEUMEISTER, C., Classical Philology
NOTHOFER, B., Southeast Asian Studies
NOVA, A., Art History
NOWAK, A., Musicology
RAECK, W., Classical Archaeology
RICHARD, B., Art Teaching
SCHLÜTER, M., Jewish Studies
SCHMITZ, TH., Greek Philology
SIEVERT, A., Art Teaching
VOSSEN, R., African Languages
WELZ, G., European Ethnology

Department of Medical Science (Theodor-Stern-Kai 7, 60590 Frankfurt am Main; tel. (69) 63016010; e-mail dekan@kgu.de):

AUBURGER, G., Applied Neurology
BITTER, K., Maxillofacial Surgery
BÖHLES, H. J., Paediatrics
BÖTTCHER, H. D., Radiation Therapy
BRAAK, H., Anatomy
BRADE, V., Hygiene, Microbiology
BRANDT, U., Biochemistry
BRATZKE, H., Forensic Medicine
BRETTEL, H.-F., Forensic Medicine
BUSSE, R., Physiology
CASPARY, W., Internal Medicine and Gastroenterology
CHANDRA, P., Therapeutic Biochemistry
DELLER, T., Anatomy
DEPPE, H.-U., Medical Sociology
DOERR, H. W., Medical Virology
DUDZIAK, R., Anaesthesiology
ELSNER, G., Industrial Medicine
ENCKE, A., General and Abdominal Surgery
FELLBAUM, CH., Pathology and Pathological Anatomy
FIEGUTH, H.-B., Thoracic Surgery
FÖRSTER, H., Applied Biochemistry
GALL, V., Child Audiology
GEIGER, H., Internal Medicine
GEISSLINGER, G., Clinical Pharmacology
GIERE, W., Documentation and Data Processing
GRONER, B., Molecular Infection and Tumour Biology
GROSS, W., Physiological Chemistry
GRÜNWALD, F., Nuclear Medicine
GSTÖTTNER, W., Ear, Nose and Throat Surgery
HANSMANN, M.-L., Pathology
HEIDEMANN, D., Dental and Maxillofacial Medicine
HELLER, K., Surgery
HOELZER, D., Haematology
HOFMANN, D., Child Health
HOFSTETTER, R., Child Cardiology
HOHMANN, W., Materials in Dentistry
JONAS, D., Urology
JORK, K., General Medicine
KAUERT, G., Forensic Toxicology
KAUFMANN, M., Gynaecology
KAUFMANN, R., Dermatology and Venereology
KERSCHBAUMER, F., Orthopaedics and Orthopaedic Surgery
KLINGEBIEL, T., Child Health
KLINKE, R., Physiology
KOCH, F.-H., Ophthalmology
KORF, H.-W., Anatomy
KUHL, H., Experimental Endocrinology
LANGENBECK, U., Human Genetics
LAUER, H.-CHR., Dentistry
LEUSCHNER, U., Gastroenterology
MAURER, K., Psychiatry
MELCHNER VON DYDIOWA, H., Clinical Molecular Biology
MOELLER, M., Medical Psychology
MORITZ, A., Thoracic, Heart and Vessel Surgery
MÜLLER-ESTERL, W., Biological Chemistry
MÜLSCH, A., Physiology
NENTWIG, G.-H., Dental and Maxillofacial Medicine
NÜRNBERGER, F., Anatomy, Neurobiology
OHRLOFF, CH., Ophthalmology and Experimental Ophthalmology
OVERBECK, G., Psychosomatics
PFEILSCHIFTER, J. M., Pharmacology and Toxicology
PFLUG, B., Psychiatry
POUSTKA, F., Child and Adolescent Psychiatry
RÄTZKE, P., Dental and Maxillofacial Medicine
SCHMIDT, H., Paediatric Radiology
SCHMITZ-RIXEN, TH., Vascular Surgery
SCHOPF, P., Maxillofacial Surgery
SCHUBERT, R., Hygiene
SEIFERT, V., Neurosurgery
SIEFERT, H., History of Medicine
SIGUSCH, V., Sexology
STEIN, J., Gastroenterology and Clinical Nutrition
STEINMETZ, H., Neurology
STÜRZEBECHER, E., Medical Acoustics
USADEL, K.-H., Internal Medicine
VOGL, TH., Radiological Diagnosis
VON JAGOW, G., Psychological Chemistry
VON LOEWENICH, V., Child Health
WAGNER, TH., Internal Medicine and Allergistics
WINCKLER, J., Anatomy
ZANELLA, F., Neuroradiology
ZEIHER, A. M., Internal Medicine
ZICHNER, L., Orthopaedics

Department of Modern Languages (Grüneburgpl. 1, 60629 Frankfurt am Main; tel. (69) 79832742; e-mail dekanat10@lingua.uni-frankfurt.de):

BOHN, V., Modern German Philology
BROGGINI, G., German Philology
BUSCHENDORF, C., American Studies
ERFURT, J., Romance Philology
EWERS, H., German Philology and Literature (Children's Literature)
FREY, W., German
GARSCHA, K., Romance Philology
GREWENDORF, G., German Linguistics
HAMACHER, W., Modern German Philology
HANSEN, O., American Studies
HELLINGER, M., English Studies
HERRMANN, W., Teaching of German Language and Literature
KELLER, U., English
KLEIN, H. G., Romance Philology
KÜHNEL, W., English and American Studies
LAUERBACH, G., English Studies
LEHMANN, H.-T., Theatre Studies
LEUNINGER, H., German Linguistics
LINDNER, B., German Language and Literature Teaching
LOBSIEN, E., English
METZNER, E., German
MITTENZWEI, I., Modern German
OPFERMANN, S., American Studies
OSSNER, J., Language Science of Modern German
QUETZ, J., English Teaching
RAITZ, W., History of German Literature
REICHERT, K., English/American Language
ROSEBROCK, C., Teaching of Literary Appreciation
RÜTTEN, R., French Language and Literature
SCHARLAU, B., Romance Philology
SCHEIBLE, H., German Language and Literature
SCHLOSSER, H. D., German
SCHLÜPMANN, H., Film Science
SCHNEIDER, G., Romance Philology
SCHRADER, H., Teaching of French
SEITZ, D., German
SOLMECKE, G., Teaching of English Language
STEGMANN, T., Romance Languages and Literature
WEISE, W.-D., English Teaching
WIETHÖLTER, W., Modern German Literature
WOLFZETTEL, F., Romance Philology
ZIMMERMANN, TH., Semantics

Department of Philosophy and History (Grüneburgpl. 1, 60323 Frankfurt am Main; tel. (69) 79832758; e-mail dekanat08@em.uni-frankfurt.de):

BREUNIG, P., Archaeology
CLAUSS, M., Ancient History
DETEL, W., Philosophy
ESSLER, W. K., Philosophy, Logic and Educational Theory
FEEST, CHR., Ethnology
FRIED, J., Ancient History
GALL, L., Medieval and Modern History
GREFE, E.-H., Teaching of History
HENNING, J., Prehistory
HONNETH, A., Social Philosophy
KOHL, K.-H., Ethnology
KULENKAMPFF, A., Philosophy
LENTZ, C., Ethnology
LÜNING, J., Prehistory
LUTZ-BACHMANN, M., Medieval Philosophy
MERKER, B., Philosophy
MUHLACK, U., General History
MÜLLER, H., Medieval Philosophy
PLUMPE, W., Economic and Social History
RECKER, M.-L., Recent History
SCHORN-SCHÜTTE, L., The Renaissance
VON KAENEL, H. M., Greek and Roman History

Department of Physics (Max-von-Laue-Str.1, 60438 Frankfurt am Main; tel. (69) 79847202; e-mail dekanat@physik.uni-frankfurt.de):

ASSMUS, W., Experimental Physics
BECKER, R., Applied Physics
DREIZLER, R., Theoretical Physics
ELZE, T., Nuclear Physics
GÖRNITZ, T., Physics Teaching
GREINER, W., Theoretical Physics

HAUG, H., Theoretical Physics
HENNING, W., Experimental Nuclear Physics
JELITTO, R., Theoretical Physics
KEGEL, W., Theoretical Physics
KING, D. A., History of Natural Sciences
KOPIETZ, P., Theoretical Solid State Physics
LACROIX, A., Applied Physics
LANG, M., Experimental Physics
LYNEN, U., Nuclear Physics
MÄNTELE, W., Biophysics
MARUHN, J., Theoretical Physics
MESTER, R., Applied Physics
MOHLER, E., Applied Physics
RATZINGER, U., Applied Physics
RISCHKE, D.-H., Theoretical Heavy Ion Physics
ROSKOS, H., Experimental Physics
SALTZER, W., History of Science
SCHMIDT-BÖCKING, H., Experimental Atomic Physics
SCHUBERT, D., Physics for Doctors
SIEMSEN, F., Physics Teaching
STOCK, R., Experimental Nuclear Physics
STÖCKER, H., Theoretical Physics
STRÖBELE, H., Experimental Nuclear Physics

Department of Protestant Theology (Grüneburgpl. 1, 60629 Frankfurt am Main; tel. (69) 79833344; e-mail dekanat.evtheol@em.uni-frankfurt.de):

DEUSER, H., Protestant Theology
FAILING, W.-E., Protestant Theology
HEIMBROCK, H. G., Protestant Theology
WEBER, E., Protestant Theology

Department of Psychology and Sports Science (Kettenhofweg 128, 60054 Frankfurt am Main; tel. (69) 79823267; e-mail dekanat@psych.uni-frankfurt.de):

BALLREICH, A., Training Science
BANZER, W., Prevention and Rehabilitation
BAUER, W., General Psychology
DEGENHARDT-EWERT, A., Diagnostic Psychology
ECKENSBERGER, L. H., Psychology
EMRICH, E., Sport Science
GIESEN, H., Educational Psychology
GOLD, A., Pedagogical Psychology
HAASE, H., Psychology and Sociology of Sport
HODAPP, V., Diagnostic Psychology
KNOPF, M., Psychology
LANGFELDT, H.-P., Pedagogical Psychology
LAUTERBACH, W., Clinical Psychology
MOOSBRUGGER, H., Psychological Methodology, Statistics
PREISER, S., Educational Psychology
PROHL, R., Sports
ROHDE-DACHSER, CH., Psychoanalysis
SARRIS, V., Psychology
SCHMIDTBLEICHER, D., Training Science
SCHWANENBERG, E., Social Psychology
SIRETEANU, R., Physiological Psychology
ZAPF, D., Psychology

Department of Roman Catholic Theology (Grüneburgplatz 1, 60323 Frankfurt am Main; tel. (69) 79833346; e-mail dekanat07@uni-frankfurt.de):

DENINGER-POLZER, G., Catholic Theology
HAINZ, J., Exegesis of the New Testament
HOFFMANN, J., Moral Theology, Social Ethics
KESSLER, H., Systematic Theology
RASKE, M., Practical Theology
SCHREIJÄCK, T., Catholic Theology
WIEDENHOFER, S., Systematic Theology

Department of Social Sciences (Robert-Mayer-Str. 5, 60054 Frankfurt am Main; tel. (69) 79822521; e-mail dekanat.fb03@soz.uni-frankfurt.de):

ALLERBECK, K., Sociology
ALLERT, T., Sociology and Social Psychology
APITZSCH, U., Sociology
BOSSE, H., Theory of Socialization
BROCK, L., International Politics
CLEMENZ, M., Sociology of Education
ESSER, J., Study of Politics, Sociology
GERHARD, U., Sociology
GLATZER, W., Social Structures
GRESS, F., Political Science
HELLMANN, G., Foreign Policy
HIRSCH, J., Political Science
HOFMANN, G., Methods of Social Research, Statistics
HONDRICH, K. O., Sociology
KAHSNITZ, D., Polytechnic and Technical Instruction Course
KELLNER, H.-F., Sociology
KRELL, G., Political Science
MANS, D., Methods of Social Research
MAUS, I., History of Political Ideas
MÜLLER, H., Political Science
NEUMANN-BRAUN, K., Sociology
NONNENMACHER, F., Teaching of Social Sciences
OEVERMANN, U., Sociology, Social Psychology
PROKOP, D., Mass Communications Research
PUHLE, H.-J., Political Science
RODENSTEIN, M., Sociology
ROPOHL, G., Polytechnic and Technical Instruction Course
ROTTLEUTHNER-LUTTER, M., Methodology
SCHMID, A., Polytechnic and Technical Instruction Course
SCHUMM, W., Sociology
SIEGEL, T., Sociology of Industrialized Societies
STEINERT, H., Sociology
TATUR, M., Political Science and Political Sociology

HAFENCITY UNIVERSITÄT/ UNIVERSITÄT FÜR BAUKUNST UND METROPOLENENTWICKLUNG (HafenCity University Hamburg—University of the Built Environment and Metropolitan Development)

Großer Grasbrook 9, 20457 Hamburg
Telephone: (40) 428272730
E-mail: kommunikation@hcu-hamburg.de
Internet: www.hcu-hamburg.de

Founded 2006
State control
Languages of instruction: English, German

Pres.: Dr Ing. WALTER PELKA
Vice-Pres. for Research: Prof. Dr GESA ZIEMER
Vice-Pres. for Teaching and Studies: Prof. Dr HARALD STERNBERG

DEANS

Architecture (Bachelors): Prof. REINHOLD JOHRENDT
Architecture (Masters): Prof. Dr WOLFGANG WILLKOMM
Civil Engineering (Bachelors): Prof. Dr HOLGER HAMFLER
Civil Engineering (Masters): Prof. Dr MANUEL KRAHWINKEL
Geomatics (Bachelors): Prof. Dr THOMAS SCHRAMM
Geomatics and Hydrography (Masters): Prof. Dr THOMAS SCHRAMM
Metropolitan Culture (Bachelors): Prof. Dr ALEXA FÄRBER
Resource Efficiency in Architecture and Planning (Masters): Prof. Dr WOLFGANG DICKHAUT
Urban Design: Prof. Dr BERND KNIESS
Urban Planning (Bachelors): Prof. Dr MICHAEL KOCH
Urban Planning (Masters): Prof. Dr GERNOT GRABHER

HEINRICH-HEINE-UNIVERSITÄT DÜSSELDORF

Universitätsstrasse 1, 40225 Düsseldorf
Telephone: (211) 8100
E-mail: planung@zuv.uni-duesseldorf.de
Internet: www.uni-duesseldorf.de

Founded 1965; fmrly Medizinische Akademie, f. 1907
State control
Language of instruction: German
Academic year: October to September

Rector: Prof. Dr MICHAEL PIPER
Chancellor: ULF PALLME KÖNIG
Vice-Rector for Excellence in Teaching: Prof. Dr ULRICH VON ALEMANN
Vice-Rector for Research and Innovation: Prof. Dr LUTZ SCHMITT
Vice-Rector for Structural Devt: Prof. Dr KLAUS PFEFFER
Vice-Rector for Univ. Management and Internationalization: Prof. Dr AXEL BUCHNER
Librarian: Dr IRMGARD SIEBERT

Library: see under Libraries and Archives
Number of teachers: 2,016
Number of students: 17,000

DEANS

Faculty of Arts: Prof. Dr HANS T. SIEPE
Faculty of Business Administration and Economics: Prof. Dr BERND GÜNTER
Faculty of Law: Prof. Dr JAN BUSCHE
Faculty of Mathematics and Natural Sciences: Prof. Dr ULRICH RUETHER
Faculty of Medicine: Prof. Dr JOACHIM WINDOLF
Faculty of Philosophy: Prof. Dr BRUNO BLECKMANN

PROFESSORS

Faculty of Business Administration and Economics (Universitätsstr. 1, Bldg 24.31, 40225 Düsseldorf; tel. (211) 8113620; e-mail wiwi.fakultaet@uni-duesseldorf.de; internet www.wiwi.uni-duesseldorf.de):

BORNER, C., Business Administration and Finance
DEGEN, H., Statistics and Econometrics
FRANZ, K. P., Control and Taxation
GÜNTER, B., Business Administration and Marketing
HAMEL, W., Management and Business Administration
SCHIRMEISTER, R., Business Administration and Finance
SMEETS, H.-D., Economics
THIEME, H. J., Economics
WAGNER, G. R., Business Administration, Production Management and Environmental Economics

Faculty of Law (Universitätsstr. 1, Gebäude 24.91 U1 R65, 40225 Düsseldorf; tel. (211) 8111414; e-mail dekanat.jura@uni-duesseldorf.de; internet www.jura.uni-duesseldorf.de):

ALTENHAIN, K., Criminal Law
BUSCHE, J., Civil Law
DIETLEIN, J., Public Law
FEUERBORN, A., Civil Law, Industrial Law and International Civil Law
FRISTER, H., Criminal Law and Law of Criminal Procedure
HEY, J., Entrepreneurial Tax Law
JANSEN, N., German and International Private Law
LOOSSCHELDERS, D., Civil Law and International Law
LORZ, R. A., German and International Public Law
MICHAEL, L., Public Law
MORFOCK, M., Public Law, Sociology of Law and Economic Law
NOACK, U., Civil Law and Commercial Law

OLZEN, D., Civil Law and Law of Civil Procedure
POHLMAN, P., Civil Law and International Commercial Law
PREUSS, N., Civil Law, International Economic Law, Commercial Law
SCHLEHOFER, H., Criminal Law and Law of Criminal Procedure

Faculty of Mathematics and Natural Sciences (Universitätsstr. 1, Bldg 25.32, 40225 Düsseldorf; tel. (211) 8112193; e-mail schmitzu@mail.math-nat-fak.uni-duesseldorf.de; internet www.math-nat-fak.uni-duesseldorf.de):

ALFERMANN, A.-W., Botany
AURICH, V., Informatics
BOTT, M., Biochemistry
BRAUN, M., Organic Chemistry
BUCHNER, A., Psychology
BUELDT, G., Biological Structural Research
CONRAD, S., Informatics
DHONT, J.-K., Physics
EGGER, R., Theoretical Physics
ERNST, J. F., Microbiology
FISCHER, G., Mathematics
FRANK, W., Inorganic and Structural Chemistry
GANTER, CH., Inorganic and Structural Chemistry
GETZLAFF, M., Applied Physics
GÖRLITZ, A., Physics
GREVEN, H., Zoology
GRIESHABER, M., Zoophysiology
GRUNEWALD, F., Mathematics
HEGEMANN, J., Microbiology
HEHL, F.-J., Psychology
HEIL, M., Psychology
HEINZEL, T., Experimental Physics
HOCHBRUCK, M., Applied Mathematics
HOLLENBERG, C., Microbiology
HÖLTJE, H.-D., Pharmacy
HUSTON, J. P., Psychology
JAEGER, K.-E., Molecular Enzyme Technology
JAHNS, H. M., Botany
JANSSEN, A., Statistics and Documentation
JANSSEN, K., Mathematics
JARRE, F., Mathematics
JORDAN, E., Physical Geography
KERNER, O., Mathematics
KIRSCHBAUM, C., Psychology
KISKER, E., Applied Physics
KLÄUI, W., Inorganic Chemistry
KLEINEBUDDE, P., Pharmaceutical Technology
KLEINERMANNS, K., Physical Chemistry
KLÜNERS, J., Mathematics
KNUST, E., Genetics
KÖHLER, K., Mathematics
KÖHNEN, W., Teaching of Mathematics
KORNYSHEV, A., Physics
KOWALLIK, K. V., Botany
KRAUTH, J., Psychology
KUCKLÄNDER, U., Pharmaceutical Chemistry
KUNZ, W., Genetics
LÄER, S., Clinical Pharmacy
LEUSCHEL, M., Informatics
LI, S.-M., Pharmaceutical Biology and Biotechnology
LIKOS, CH., Theoretical Physics
LÖSCH, R., Botany
LÖWEN, H., Theoretical Physics
LUNAU, K., Neurobiology
MARIAN, CH., Theoretical Chemistry
MARTIN, W., Botany
MAURE, M., Informatics
MEHLHORN, H., Zoology
MEISE, R., Mathematics
MEWIS, A., Inorganic and Structural Chemistry
MÜLLER, T., Organic Chemistry
MUSCH, J., Psychology
NÄGELE, G., Physics
OLBRICH, S., Informatics
PAUSE, B., Psychology
PIETROWSKY, R., Psychology
PIETRUSZKA, J., Bio-organic Chemistry
PRETZLER, G., Experimental Physics
PROKSCH, P., Pharmaceutical Biology
PUKHOV, A., Theoretical Physics
RATSCHEK, H., Mathematics
REITER, D., Laser and Plasma Physics
RIESNER, D., Physical Biology
RITTER, H., Organic Chemistry
ROSE, C. R., Neurobiology
ROTHE, J., Informatics
RUETHER, U., Zoophysiology
SAHM, H., Biotechnology
SAMM, U., Plasma Physics
SCHIERBAUM, K., Raw Materials Science
SCHILLER, S., Experimental Physics
SCHLUE, W.-R., Neurobiology
SCHMITT, L., Biochemistry
SCHÖTTNER, M., Informatics
SCHRÖER, S., Mathematics
SCHURR, U., Botany
SEIDEL, C., Physical Chemistry
SIMON, R., Genetics
SINGHOF, W., Mathematics
SPATSCHEK, K.-H., Theoretical Physics
STANDT-BICKEL, C., Organic Chemistry
STAUDT, C., Organic Chemistry
STEFFEN, K., Mathematics
STOERIG, P., Psychology
STREHBLOW, H.-H., Physical Chemistry
VOLLMER, G., Teaching of Chemistry
VON HAESELER, A., Bioinformatics
WAGNER, R., Physical Biology
WANKE, E., Informatics
WEBER, H., Pharmacy
WEIN, N., Teaching Geography
WEINKAUF, R., Physical Chemistry
WEISS, H., Biochemistry
WENZENS, G., Geography
WESTHOFF, P., Botany
WILLBOLD, D., Physical Biology
WILLI, O., Experimental Physics
WISBAUER, R., Mathematics
WITSCH, K., Mathematics
WUNDERLICH, F., Parasitology

Faculty of Medicine (Universitätsstr. 1, Bldg 11.72, Moorenstr. 5, 40225 Düsseldorf; tel. (211) 8104602; e-mail med.dekanat@uni-duesseldorf.de; internet medfak.uniklinikum-duesseldorf.de):

ABHOLZ, H.-H., General Medicine
ACKERMANN, R., Urology
ALBERTI, L., Psychosocial Disturbances
ANGERSTEIN, W., Phoniatry and Audiology
BARZ, J., Forensic Medicine
BAYER, R., Physiology
BECKER, J., Dentistry
BENDER, H. G., Obstetrics and Gynaecology
BÖCKING, A., General Pathology and Pathological Anatomy
BOEGE, F., Clinical Chemistry and Laboratory Diagnostics
BOJAR, H., Physiological Chemistry
BORNSTEIN, ST., Internal Medicine
BORSCH-GALETKE, E., Industrial Medicine
BUDACH, W., Radiology
DALDRUP, T., Forensic Toxicology
DALL, P., Obstetrics and Gynaecology
DRESCHER, D., Dentistry
FISCHER, J. H., Pharmacology and Toxicology
FÖRSTER, I., Molecular Immunology
FRANZ, M., Psychiatry, Clinical Psychology
FRITZEMEIER, C. U., Dentistry
FÜRST, G., Radiology
GABBERT, H. E., Pathology
GAEBEL, W., Psychiatry
GAMS, E., Cardiological Surgery
GANZER, U., Otorhinolaryngology
GERAEDTS, M., Health Sciences and Social Medicine
GERHARZ, C.-D., Pathology
GIANI, G., Diabetes Research, Biometry
GÖBEL, U., Paediatrics
GÖDECKER, A., Physiology
GOTTMAN, K., Neurophysiology
GRABENSEE, B., Internal Medicine
HAAS, H., Neurophysiology
HAAS, R., Internal Medicine
HARTUNG, H.-P., Neurology
HARTWIG, H.-G., Anatomy
HÄUSSINGER, D., Internal Medicine
HEINZ, H.-P., Medical Microbiology
HENGEL, H., Virology
HERFORTH, A., Dentistry
HERING, P., Laser Medicine
HERNER, B., Neurology
HEUCK, C. C., Clinical Chemistry and Biochemistry
HEUGGE, U., Dermatology
HOHLFELD, T., Experimental Pharmacology
HOMEY, B., Dermatology
IDEL, H., Hygiene
JANSSEN, A., Opthalmology
KAHL, R., Toxicology
KELM, M., Internal Medicine
KNOEFEL, W., Internal Surgery
KRAUSPE, R., Orthopaedics
KRUTMANN, J., Dermatology and Venereology
KÜBLER, N., Dentistry and Plastic Surgery
LABISCH, A., History of Medicine
LINS, E. J. F., Neuroradiology
LUDWIG, S., Molecular Medicine
MAI, J. K., Neuroanatomy
MANNHOLD, R., Investigation of Molecular Active Substances
MAU, J., Statistics and Biomathematics in Medicine
MAYATEPEK, E., General Paediatrics
MEYER, U., Dentistry
MÖDDER, U., Clinical Radiology
MORGENSTERN, J., Applied Biomedicine
MSCHEN, M., Immunology
MUELLER, H. W., Neurobiology
MUELLER, H. W., Nuclear Medicine
MÜLLER-WIELAND, D., Clinical Biochemistry
NANENBERG, H., Paediatrics
NOVOTNY, G. E. K., Anatomy
NÜRNBERG, B., Physiological Chemistry
PFEFFER, K. D., Medical Microbiology
POREMBA, C., Pathology
RAAB, W., Dentistry
REHKAEMPER, G., Brain Research
REIFFENBERGER, G., Neuropathology
RITZ-TIMME, S., Forensic Medicine
ROSS, H.-G., Physiology
ROYER-POKORA, B., Human Genetics
RUZICKA, T., Dermatology and Venereology
SANDMANN, W., Surgery
SCHARF, R., Haematology
SCHERBAUM, W. A., Internal Medicine
SCHMIDT, K. G., Paediatrics
SCHMITT, G., Radio-oncology
SCHNEIDER, F., Psychiatry
SCHNEIDER, M., Internal Medicine
SCHNITZLER, A., Neurology
SCHRADER, J., Physiology
SCHRÖR, K., Pharmacology and Toxicology
SCHULZE-OSTHOFF, K., Molecular Medicine
SEITZ, R., Neurology
SIEGRIST, J., Medical Sociology
SIES, H., Physiological Chemistry
STAHL, W. J., Physiological Chemistry
STEIGER, H.-J., Neurology
STEINGRÜBER, H.-J., Medical Psychology
STRAUER, B.-E., Internal Medicine
STÜTTGEN, U., Dentistry
SUNDMACHER, R., Ophthalmology
TARNOW, J., Anaesthesiology
THÄMER, V., Physiology
TRESS, W., Psychiatry
VOM DAHL, ST., Industrial Medicine
WEHLING, P., Molecular Orthopaedics
WENDEL, U., Paediatrics
WINDOLF, J., Internal Surgery
WINTERER, G., Neurology, Psychiatry
ZILLES, K., Anatomy

Faculty of Philosophy (Universitätsstr. 1, Bldg 23.21 Ebene 00 Raum 63—Dekanats büro, 40225 Düsseldorf; tel. (211) 8112936; e-mail dobbeler@phil-fak.uni-duesseldorf.de; internet www.phil-fak.uni-duesseldorf.de):

APTROOT, M., Yiddish Culture, Language and Literature
BARZ, H., Education
BAURMANN, M., Sociology
BEEH, V., Germanic Philology
BIRNBACHER, D., Philosophy
BLECKMANN, B., Ancient History
BÖHME-DÜRR, K., Media Sciences
BÖRNER-KLEIN, D., Yiddish Studies
BORSÒ, V., Romance Languages and Literature
BRANDES, D., Culture and History of Germans in Eastern Europe
BROCKE, M., Yiddish Studies
BÜHLER, A., Philosophy
BUSSE, D., Germanic Philosophy
BUSSE, W., English
DIETZ, S., Philosophy
FRIEDL, H., English
GEISLER, H., Romance Languages and Literature
GLOGER-TIPPELT, G., Developmental and Educational Psychology
GOMILLE, M., English
GÖRLING, R., Media and Cultural Sciences
GÖTZ VON OLENHUSEN, I., Modern History
HARTMANN, P., Sociology
HECKER, H., East European History
HERWIG, H., Germanic Philology
HÜLSEN-ESCH, A., Art History
HUMMEL, H., Politics
KANN, C., Philosophy
KELLER, R., Germanic Philology
KILBURY, J., Computer Linguistics
KÖRNER, H., Art History
KOUTEVA, T., English
KROPP, S., Politics
KRUMEICH, G., Modern History
KÜPPERS, J., Classical Philology
LABISCH, A., History of Medicine
LAHIRI, A., Linguistics
LAUDAGE, J., Medieval History
LEINEN, F., Romance Philology
MAE, M., Modern Japan
MATUSSEK, P., Modern German
MILLER-KIPP, G., Education
MOLITOR, H., Modern History
NOUN, CH., Modern History
POTT, H.-G., Modern German
REICHEL, M., Classical Philology
RETTIG, W., Romance Philology
REUBAND, K. H., Sociology
ROHRBACHER, S., Yiddish Studies
SCHAFROTH, E., Romance Languages and Literature
SCHURZ, G., Philosophy
SCHWARZER, C., Education
SEIDEL, T., English
SHIMADA, S., Modern Japan
SIEPE, H., Romance Philology
STEIN, D., English
STEIN, M., Classical Philology/Latin Sciences
STIERSTORFER, K., English
STOCK, W. G., English
TIEGEL, G., Sport
VON ALEMANN, U., Politics
VOWE, G., Communication and Media Sciences
WEBER, CH., Modern History
WEISS, R., Communication and Media Sciences
WITTE, B., Modern German
WUNDERLI, P., Romance Philology

ATTACHED INSTITUTES

Arbeitsgemeinschaft Elektrochemischer Forschungsinstitutionen AGEF eV: Universitatsstr. 1, 40225 Düsseldorf; e-mail arckel@mpie.de; Chair. Prof. Dr J. W. SCHULTZE.

Deutsches Diabetes-Forschungsinstitut an der Heinrich-Heine-Universität Düsseldorf: Auf'm Hennekamp 65, 40225 Düsseldorf; e-mail kontakt@ddz.uni-duesseldorf.de; Dir Prof. Dr D. MÜLLER-WIELAND.

Deutsches Krankenhausinstitut: Tersteegenstr. 3, 40474 Düsseldorf; e-mail info@dki.de; Dir UDO MÜLLER.

Düsseldorfer Institut für Dienstleistungs-Management: Dir Prof. Dr W. HAMEL.

Eichendorff-Institut—Literaturwissenschaftliches Institut der Stiftung Haus Oberschlesien: 6-Hösel, Bahnhofstr. 71, 40883 Ratingen; Dir Prof. Dr B. WITTE.

Institut für Biologische Informationsverarbeitung, Forschungszentrum Jülich GmbH: Dir Prof. Dr G. BÜLDT.

Institut für Biotechnologie, Forschungszentrum Jülich GmbH: 52428 Jülich; Dir Prof. Dr H. SAHM.

Institut für Chemie und Dynamik der Geosphäre: 52428 Jülich; e-mail info@fz-juelich.de; Dir Prof. Dr U. SCHURR.

Institut für die Kultur und Geschichte der Deutschen im ostlichen Europa: Dir Prof. Dr DETLEF BRANDES.

Institut für Internationale Kommunikation: Hildebrandtstr. 4, 40215 Düsseldorf; e-mail info@iik-duesseldorf.de; Man. Dir Dr M. JUNG.

Institut für Medizin, Forschungszentrum Jülich GmbH: 52428 Jülich; Dir Prof. Dr K. ZILLES.

Institut für Umweltmedizinische Forschung an der Heinrich-Heine-Universität Düsseldorf: see under Research Institutes.

Institut 'Moderne im Rheinland': e-mail info@moderne-im-rheinland.com; Dir Prof. Dr CEPL-KAUFMANN.

Neurologisches Therapiezentrum (NTC) an der Heinrich-Heine-Universität Düsseldorf: Hohensandweg 37, 40591 Düsseldorf; Dir Prof. Dr V. HÖMBERG.

Ostasien-Institut: Dir Prof. Dr MICHIKO MAE.

Technische Akademie Wuppertal eV: Postfach 100409, 42004 Wuppertal; Man. Dir Dipl. ERICH GIESE

HELMUT SCHMIDT UNIVERSITÄT/ UNIVERSITÄT DER BUNDESWEHR HAMBURG
(University of the Federal Armed Forces, Hamburg)

POB 70 08 22, 22008 Hamburg
Holstenhofweg 85, 22043 Hamburg
Telephone: (40) 65411
Internet: www.hsu-hh.de
Founded 1972
State control
Languages of instruction: English, German
Academic year: October to September
Chancellor: VOLKER STEMPEL
Pres.: Prof. Dr WILFRIED SEIDEL
Vice-Pres.: Prof. Dr KLAUS BECKMANN
Vice-Pres.: Prof. Dr Ing. JENS WULFSBERG
Library of 800,000 vols
Number of teachers: 100
Number of students: 2,800
Publications: *Uniforschung* (1 a year), *Uniforum* (1 a year)

DEANS

Dept of Economics and Social Sciences: Prof. Dr MICHAEL STAACK
Dept of Educational Science: Prof. Dr CHRISTINE ZEUNER
Dept of Electrical Engineering: Prof. Dr Ing. JOACHIM HORN
Dept of Mechanical Engineering: Prof. Dr Ing. ALEXANDER FAY

HOCHSCHULE FÜR FILM UND FERNSEHEN 'KONRAD WOLF' POTSDAM-BABELSBERG
(University of Film and Television 'Konrad Wolf')

Marlene-Dietrich-Allee 11, 14482 Potsdam
Telephone: (331) 62020
E-mail: info@hff-potsdam.de
Internet: www.hff-potsdam.de
Founded 1954
State control
Language of instruction: German
Pres.: Prof. Dr DIETER WIEDEMANN
Vice-Pres.: Prof. MARTIN STEYER
Head of Library: LYDIA WIEHRING VON WENDRIN
Library of 100,000 vols
Number of teachers: 100
Number of students: 500
Publication: *BFF (Beiträge zur Film- und Fernsehwissenschaft)* (irregular)

DEANS

Faculty I: Prof. INGOLF COLLMAR
Faculty II: Prof. INGO KOCK
Faculty III: Prof. Dr CLAUDIA WEGENER

HOCHSCHULE WISMAR

Philipp-Müller-Str., POB 1210, 23952 Wismar
Telephone: (3841) 7530
E-mail: postmaster@hs-wismar.de
Internet: www.hs-wismar.de
Founded 1908 as Ingenieurhochschule Wismar, renamed 1939, 1969, 1988; current name adopted 1992
State control
Language of instruction: German
Academic year: September to August
Rector: Prof. Dr BODO WIEGAND-HOFFMEISTER
Vice-Rector for Education: Prof. Dr MICHAEL SCHLEICHER
Vice-Rector for Research: Prof. Dr Hab. MARION WIENECKE
Head of Admin.: Dr MEIKE QUAAS
Librarian: UTE KINDLER
Library of 65,000 vols
Number of teachers: 250
Number of students: 8,000

DEANS

Architecture and Design: Prof. HANKA POLKEHN
Business: Prof. Dr JOACHIM WINKLER
Engineering: Prof. Dr Ing. INGO MÜLLER

HUMBOLDT-UNIVERSITÄT ZU BERLIN

Unter den Linden 6, 10099 Berlin
Telephone: (30) 20932946
E-mail: pr@hu-berlin.de
Internet: www.hu-berlin.de
Founded 1810
State control
Academic year: October to September
Pres.: Prof. Dr JAN-HENDRIK OLBERTZ
Vice-Pres. for Academic and Int. Affairs: Prof. Dr MICHAEL KÄMPER-VAN DEN BOOGAART
Vice-Pres. for Finance/Personnel and Technical Matters: Dr FRANK EVESLAGE
Vice-Pres. for Research: Prof. Dr PETER A. FRENSCH

Librarian: Dr M. BULATY
Library: see under Libraries and Archives
Number of teachers: 2,167 (incl. 411 professorships, no FTEs)
Number of students: 36,636
Publications: *Humboldt-Spektrum* (4 a year), *Humboldt-Zeitung* (12 a year during each semester)

DEANS

Charité—Berlin University Medicine: Prof. Dr KARL MAX EINHÄUPL (Chair. of Exec. Board)
Faculty of Agriculture and Horticulture: Prof. Dr FRANK ELLMER
Faculty of Arts and Humanities I: Prof. MICHAEL SEADLE
Faculty of Arts and Humanities II: Prof. Dr HELGA SCHWALM
Faculty of Arts and Humanities III: Prof. Dr BERND WEGENER
Faculty of Arts and Humanities IV: Prof. Dr ERNST VON KARDOFF
Faculty of Law: Prof. Dr BERND HEINRICH
Faculty of Mathematics and Natural Sciences I: Prof. Dr ANDREAS HERRMANN
Faculty of Mathematics and Natural Sciences II: Prof. Dr ELMAR KULKE
Faculty of Theology: Prof. Dr DOROTHEA WENDEBOURG
School of Business and Economics: Prof. Dr OLIVER GÜNTHER

INTERNATIONAL SCHOOL OF MANAGEMENT

Otto-Hahn-Str. 19, 44227 Dortmund
Telephone: (231) 9751390
E-mail: ism.dortmund@ism.de
Internet: www.ism.de
Founded 1990 as IDB-Wirtschaftsakademie, present name 1992
Private control
Pres.: Prof. Dr BERT RÜRUP
Vice-Pres.: Prof. Dr INGO BÖCKENHOLT
Man. Dir: WOLFGANG DITTMANN
Number of students: 800

JACOBS UNIVERSITY BREMEN GMBH

Campus Ring 1, 28759 Bremen
Telephone: (421) 20040
E-mail: info@jacobs-university.de
Internet: www.jacobs-university.de
Founded 1999
Private control
Language of instruction: English
Academic year: September to May
Pres.: Prof. Dr JOACHIM TREUSCH
Chair.: Prof. Dr KARIN LOCHTE
Dir for Academic Affairs: ANTONIA GOHR
Dir for Admissions: JON IKRAM
Dir for Campus Activities and College Coordination: MARITA HARTNACK
Dir for Corporate Communications and Media Relations: PETER WIEGAND
Dir for Information Resources and Multimedia (IRC): HANS ROES
Dir for Resource Devt: ULF HANSEN
Dir for Student Marketing: CHRISTINE SOUDERS
Dir for Studies: MANDY BOEHNKE
Vice-Pres. for Science Park and Business Devt: Dr ALEXANDER ZIEGLER-JOENS
Librarian: HANS ROES
Library of 45,000 vols, 14,500 ebooks, 100 journals, 35,000 ejournals
Number of teachers: 385
Number of students: 1,245

DEANS

Jacobs Centre for Lifelong Learning and Institutional Development: Prof. Dr URSULA M. STAUDINGER
School of Engineering and Science: Prof. Dr BERNHARD KRAMER
School of Humanities and Social Sciences: Prof. Dr HENDRIK BIRUS

JOHANNES GUTENBERG UNIVERSITY MAINZ

55099 Mainz
Saarstr. 21, 55122 Mainz
Telephone: (6131) 390
E-mail: presse@uni-mainz.de
Internet: www.uni-mainz.de
Founded 1477, closed 1816, reopened 1946
State control
Pres.: Prof. Dr GEORG KRAUSCH
Chancellor: GOETZ SCHOLZ
Vice-Pres. for Learning and Teaching: Prof. Dr MECHTHILD DREYER
Vice-Pres. for Research: Prof. Dr WOLFGANG HOFMEISTER
Librarian: Dr ANDREAS BRANDTNER
Library: see under Libraries and Archives
Number of teachers: 4,150
Number of students: 36,500
Publications: *Forschungsbericht*, *Forschungsmagazin*, *JGU Magazin* (online, www.uni-mainz.de/magazin)

DEANS

Faculty of Biology: Prof. Dr HANS ZISCHLER
Faculty of Catholic and Protestant Theology: Prof. Dr ULRICH VOLP
Faculty of Chemistry, Pharmaceutical Sciences and Geosciences: Prof. Dr HOLGER FREY
Faculty of History and Cultural Studies: Prof. Dr DORIS PRECHEL
Faculty of Law, Management and Economics: Prof. Dr ANDREAS ROTH
Faculty of Philosophy and Philology: Prof. Dr STEPHAN JOLIE
Faculty of Physics, Mathematics and Computer Science: Prof. Dr PETER G. J. VAN DONGER
Faculty of Translation Studies, Linguistics and Cultural Studies: Prof. Dr ANDREAS GIPPER
Mainz Academy of Arts: Prof. WINFRIED VIRNICH
Mainz School of Music: Prof. Dr LUDWIG STRIEGEL
University Medical Centre: Prof. Dr NORBERT PFEIFFER

PROFESSORS

Faculty of Biology (Gresemundweg 2, 55128 Mainz; tel. (6131) 3922548; internet www.uni-mainz.de/fb/biologie/biologie.html):

ALT, K. W.
BÖHNING-GAESE, K.
CLAßEN-BOCKHOFF, R.
DECKER, H.
EISENBEIS, G.
HANKELN, T.
HENKE, W.
KADEREIT, J. W.
KAMP, G.
KÖNIG, H.
MARKL, J.
MARTENS, J.
NEUMEYER, C.
PAULSEN, H.
PFLUGFELDER, G.
ROTHE, G.
SCHMIDT, E. R.
SEITZ, A.
STÖCKER, W.
TECHNAU, G.
TROTTER, J.
UNDEN, G.
WEGENER, G.
WERNICKE, W.
WOLFRUM, U.
ZISCHLER, H.

Faculty of Catholic and Protestant Theology (Forum 6, 55099 Mainz; tel. (6131) 3922215; e-mail kath-dekanat@uni-mainz.de; internet www.theologie.uni-mainz.de):

BAUMEISTER, T.
DIETZ, W.
DINGEL, I.
FECHTNER, K.
FRANZ, A.
HELL, L.
HORN, F. W.
LANDMESSER, C.
LEHNARDT, A.
MEIER, J.
REISER, M.
REITER, J.
RIEDEL-SPANGENBERGER, I.
SIEVERNICH, M.
SIMON, W.
SLENCZKA, N
WEYER-MENKHOFF, S.
WIßMANN, H.
ZWICKEL, W.

Faculty of Chemistry, Pharmaceutical Sciences and Geosciences (Becherweg 14, 55128 Mainz; tel. (6131) 3922273; e-mail dekan19@uni-mainz.de; internet www.uni-mainz.de/fb/chemie/fbhome):

BANHART, F.
BASCHÉ, T.
DANNHARDT, G.
DOMRÖS, M.
EPE, B.
ESCHER, A.
FAHRENHOLZ, F.
FELSER, C.
FOLEY, S. F.
FREY, H.
GAUß, J.
GRUNERT, J.
HOFFMANN, T.
JANSHOFF, A.
KERSTEN, M.
KLINKHAMMER, K.
KOCH-BRANDT, C.
KRATZ, J. V.
KRÖNER, A.
KUNZ, H.
LANGGUTH, P.
LÖWE, H.
MEIER, H.
MEYER, G.
NUBBEMEYER, U.
PASSCHIER, C. W.
PINDUR, U.
PREUß, J.
RATTER, B. M. W.
REGENAUER-LIEB, K.
REICH, T.
RENTSCHLER, E.
RÖSCH, F.
SCHENK, D.
SCHMIDT, M.
SIROCKO, F.
STÖCKIGT, J.
TREMEL, W.
WILCKE, W.
WILKEN, R.
WITULSKI, B.
ZENTEL, R.

Faculty of History and Cultural Studies (Jakob-Welder-Weg 18, 55128 Mainz; tel. (6131) 3923346):

ALTHOFF, J.
BEER, A.
BIERSCHENK, T.
BLÜMER, WI.
BRAUN, E. A.
FELTEN, F. J.

GAUDZINSKI-WINDHEUSER, S.
KASTENHOLZ, R.
KIẞENER, M.
KREIKENBOM, D.
KUSBER, J.
LENTZ, C.
MATHEUS, M.
MÜLLER, M.
OY-MARRA, E.
PARE, C. F. E.
PESCHLOW, U.
PRECHEL, D.
PRINZING, G.
RÖDDER, A.
SCHUMACHER, L.
VERHOEVEN-VAN ELSBERGEN, U.
WALDE, C.
WIESEND, R.

Faculty of Law, Management and Economics (Jakob-Welder-Weg 9, 55128 Mainz; tel. (6131) 3922225; e-mail dekanat-fb03@uni-mainz.de; internet www.uni-mainz.de/fachbereiche/1754.php):

BECK, K.
BELLMANN, K.
BOCK, M.
BREUER, K.
BRONNER, R.
DÖRR, D.
DREHER, M.
ERB, V.
EULER, R.
FINK, U.
FRIEDL, G.
GOERKE, L.
GRÖSCHLER, P.
GURLIT, E.
HAAS, U.
HABERSACK, M.
HAIN, K.-E.
HEIL, O. P.
HENTSCHEL, V.
HEPTING, R.
HERGENRÖDER, C. W.
HETTINGER, M.
HUBER, F.
HUBER, P.
HUFEN, F.
KAISER, D.
KOLMAR, M.
KUBE, H.
LEISEN, D.
MÜLBERT, P. O.
OECHSLER, J.
PEFFEKOVEN, R.
RAMMERT, S.
ROTH, A.
RUTHIG, J.
SAUERNHEIMER, K
SCHULZE, P. M.
TRAUTMANN, S.
VOLKMANN, U.
WEDER, B.
ZOPFS, J.

Faculty of Philosophy and Philology (Jakob-Welder-Weg 18, 55128 Mainz; tel. (6131) 3920005; e-mail fsb05@uni-mainz.de):

BISANG, W.
BOESCHOTEN, H.
BRENDEL, E.
BREUER, U.
DREYER, M.
ECKEL, W.
EICHLER, K.-D.
ERLEBACH, P.
FISCHER, E.
FÜSSEL, S.
GEISLER, E.
GIRKE, W.
GÖBLER, F.
GRÄTZEL, S.
HORNUNG, A.
KREUDER, F.
KROPP, M.
LAMPING, D.
LEY, K.
MARTIN, A.
MEIBAUER, J.
MEISIG, K.
METZINGER, T.
MÜLLER-WOOD, A.
NÜBLING, D.
PORRA, V.
REITZ, B.
SARHIMAA, A.
SCHEIDING, O.
SCHULTZE, B.
SEELBACH, D.
SIMON, M.
SOLBACH, A.
SPIES, B.
STAIB, B.
STÖRMER-CAYSA, U.
VEITH, W. H.
VON HOFF, D.
WEHR, B.

Faculty of Physics, Mathematics and Computer Science (Staudingerweg 9, 55128 Mainz; tel. (6131) 3922267; e-mail info@phmi.uni-mainz.de; internet www.phmi.uni-mainz.de):

ADRIAN, H.
ARENDS, H.-J.
BACH, V.
BINDER, K.
BLOCH, I.
BORRMANN, S.
BROCKMANN, R.
DE JONG, T.
DOLL, T.
ELMERS, H.-J.
GÖTTLER, H.
GRAMSCH, B.
HANKE-BOURGEOIS, M.
HEIL, W.
HÖPFNER, R.
HUBER, G.
JAENICKE, R.
JÜNGEL, A.
KLEINKNECHT, K.
KLENKE, A.
KÖPKE, L.
LEHN, M.
MÜLLER-STACH, S.
OSTRICK, M.
PALBERG, T.
PAPADOPOULOS, N.
PERL, J.
POCHODZALLA, J.
REUTER, M.
ROWE, D. E.
SANDER, H.-G.
SCHILCHER, K.
SCHILLING, R.
SCHLEINKOFER, G.
SCHÖMER, E.
SCHÖNHENSE, G.
SCHUH, H.-J.
TAPPROGGE, S
VAN DONGEN, P. J.
VAN STRATEN, D.
VON HARRACH, D.
WALZ, J.
WERNLI, H.
WIRTH, V.
WITTIG, H.
ZUO, K.

Faculty of Social Sciences, Media and Sports (Colonel-Kleinmann-Weg 2, 55128 Mainz; tel. (6131) 3922247; e-mail fritsche@mail.uni-mainz.de):

AUFENANGER, S.
AUGUSTIN, D.
BÜRMANN, J.
DITTGEN, H.
DORMANN, C.
DRUWE, U.
FALTER, J. W.
GARZ, D.
GROB, N.
HAMBURGER, F.
HECHT, H.
HEINEMANN, E.
HILLER, W.
HRADIL, S.
HUFNAGEL, E.
JUNG, K.
KEPPLINGER, H. M.
KOEBNER, T.
KOLBE, F.-U.
KROHNE, H. W.
KUNCZIK, M.
KUNZ, V.
MEINHARDT, G.
MESSING, M.
MÜLLER, N.
NIENSTEDT, H.-W.
OCHSMANN, R.
PREISENDÖRFER, P.
RENNER, K.N.
RICKER, R.
ROLLER, E.
SCHELLE, C.
SCHNEIDER, N. F.
SCHWEPPE, C.
SEIFFGE-KRENKE, I.
VON FELDEN, H.
WILKE, J.
WOLFF, V.
ZIMMERLING, R.

Faculty of Translation Studies, Linguistics and Cultural Studies (An der Hochschule 2, 76711 Germersheim; tel. (7274) 5080; e-mail dekan06@uni-mainz.de; internet www.fask.uni-mainz.de):

FORSTNER, M.
GIPPER, A.
HUBER, D.
KELLETAT, A.
KLENGEL, S.
KUPFER, P.
LOENHOFF, J.
MENZEL, B.
MÜLLER, K. P.
PERL, M.
SCHREIBER, M.
STOLL, K.-H.
VON BARDELEBEN, R.
WORBS, E.

Mainz School of Music (Binger Str. 26, 55122 Mainz; tel. (6131) 3935538; e-mail wenkel@mail.uni-mainz.de; internet www.musik.uni-mainz.de):

BERNING, A., Academy of Art
BLUME, J., Theory of Music
DAUS, J., College of Music
DELNON, G., Stage Theory
DEUTSCH, N., Oboe
DEWALD, T., Singing
DOBNER, M., Double Bass
DREYER, L., Music Theory
EDER, C., Singing
FRANK, B., Piano
GAVRIC, D., Chamber Music
GERMER, K., Piano
GMEINDER, J., Clarinet
GNANN, G., Church Music
HAHN, G., Academy of Art
HELLMANN, U., Academy of Art
KAISER, H.-J., Church Music
KIEFER, P., Modern Music
KIESSLING, D., Academy of Art
KNOCHE-WENDEL, E., Academy of Art
MARX, K., Chamber Music
REICHERT, M., Modern Music
SHIH, A., Violin
SPACEK, V., Academy of Art
STRIEGEL, L., Music Theory
VETRE, O., Piano
VIRNICH, W., Academy of Art
VOGELGESANG, K., Academy of Art
WALLFISCH, R., Violoncello
ZARBOCK, H., Piano
ZIMMERMANN, J., Academy of Art

University Medical Centre (Obere Zahlbacher Str. 63, 55131 Mainz; tel. (6131) 39-33180; internet dekanat.medizin.uni-mainz.de):

BARTENSTEIN, P.
BEHL, C.
BEHNEKE, N.
BEUTEL, M. E.
BHAKDI, S.
BIRKLEIN, F.
BLETTNER, M.
BORK, K.
BRISENO, B.
BROCKERHOFF, P.
BUHL, R.
D'HOEDT, B.
DICK, B.
DIETERICH, M.
DÜBER, C.
DUSCHNER, H.
FISCHER, T.
FÖRSTERMANN, U.
GALLE, P. R.
HAAF, T.
HEINE, J.
HEINEMANN, M.
HEINRICHS, W.
HIEMKE, C.
HOMMEL, G.
HUBER, C.
JAGE, J.
JANSEN, B.
JUNGINGER, T.
KAINA, B.
KEMPSKI, O.
KIRKPATRICK, C. J.
KLEINERT, H.
KNOP, J.
KÖLBL, H.
KONERDING, M. A.
KRAFT, J.
KÜMMEL, W. F.
LACKNER, K. J.
LETZEL, S.
LEUBE, R.
LOOS, M.
LÜDDENS, H.
LUHMANN, H.
LUTZ, B.
MAEURER, M.
MANN, W.
MICHAELIS, J.
MÜLLER, W. E. G.
MÜLLER-KLIESER, W.
MÜNTEFERING, H.
MÜNZEL, T.
MUSHOLT, T.
NEURATH, M.
NIX, W.
OESCH, F.
OTTO, G.
PAUL, N. W.
PERNECZKY, A.
PFEIFFER, N.
PIETRZIK, C.
PLACHTER, B.
POHLENZ, J.
POLLOW, K.
POMMERENING, K.
REDDEHASE, M. J.
REITTER, B.
RESKE-KUNZ, A. B.
ROMMENS, P. M.
SAHIN, U.
SCHELLER, H.
SCHIER, F.
SCHILD, H.
SCHMIDBERGER, H.
SCHMITT, H. J.
SCHRECKENBERGER, M.
SCHREIBER, W.
SCHULTE, E.
SCHUMACHER, R.
SOMMER, C.
STOETER, P.
STOFFT, E.
STOPFKUCHEN, H.
STREECK, R. E.
THEOBALD, M.
THÜROFF, J. W.
TREEDE, R.-D.
VAUPEL, P.
VON BAUMGARTEN, R.
WAGNER, W.
WEBER, M. M.
WEHRBEIN, H.
WEILEMANN, L. S.
WERNER, C.
WILLERSHAUSEN, B.
WOJNOWSKI, L.
WÖLFEL, T.
ZABEL, B.
ZANDER, R.
ZEPP, F.
ZÖLLNER, E. J.

ATTACHED INSTITUTES

Forschungsinstitut Lesen und Medien (Institute for Media Research): Fischtorpl. 23, 55116 Mainz; Dir Prof. Dr STEPHAN FÜSSEL.

Institut für Europäische Geschichte (Institute for European History): e-mail ieg2@ieg-mainz.de; see under Research Institutes.

Institut für Geschichtliche Landeskunde (Institute for Historical Regional Studies of Rhineland-Palatinate): Universität, Johann-Friedrich-von-Pfeiffer-Weg 3, 55099 Mainz; e-mail igl@uni-mainz.de; Dirs Prof. Dr A. HAVERKAMP, Prof. Dr W. KLEIBER, Prof. Dr M. MATHEUS.

Institut für Internationales Recht des Spar-, Giro- und Kreditwesens (Institute for International Law of Banking): Universität, Saarstrasse 21, Haus Recht und Wirtschaft, 55122 Mainz; e-mail info@institut-kreditrecht.de; Dirs Prof. Dr W. HADDING, Prof. Dr U. H. SCHNEIDER.

Institut für Mikrotechnik GmbH (Institute for Microtechnology): Postfach 421364, 55071 Mainz;Carl-Zeiss-Str. 18–20, 55129 Mainz; e-mail info@imm-mainz.de; Dir Prof. Dr W. EHRFELD.

Tumorzentrum Rheinland-Pfalz eV (Tumour Centre Rhineland-Palatinate): Am Pulverturm 13, 55101 Mainz; e-mail lenz@mail.uni-mainz.de; Dir Prof. Dr C. HUBER

JULIUS-MAXIMILIANS-UNIVERSITÄT WÜRZBURG

Sanderring 2, 97070 Würzburg
Telephone: (931) 310
E-mail: universitaet@zv.uni-wuerzburg.de
Internet: www.uni-wuerzburg.de
Founded 1582
State control
Academic year: October to September

Pres.: Prof. Dr A. FORCHEL
Vice-Pres.: Prof. Dr E. PACHE
Vice-Pres.: Prof. Dr M. GOTZ
Vice-Pres.: Prof. Dr M. LOHSE
Vice-Pres.: Prof. Dr W. RIEDEL
Dir for Finance and Admin.: E. KRUSE
Chief Librarian: Dr KARL SÜDEKUM

Library: 3m. vols
Number of teachers: 900
Number of students: 22,500
Publications: *RückBlick* (2 a year), *UniZeit*

DEANS

Faculty of Biology: Prof. Dr THOMAS DANDEKAR
Faculty of Catholic Theology: Prof. Dr ERICH GARHAMMER
Faculty of Chemistry and Pharmacy: Prof. Dr ULRIKE HOLZGRABE
Faculty of Economics: Prof. Dr CHRISTIAN GRUND
Faculty of Law: Prof. Dr ERIC HILGENDORF
Faculty of Mathematics and Computer Science: Prof. Dr UWE HELMKE
Faculty of Medicine: Prof. Dr MATTHIAS FROSCH
Faculty of Philosophy I (Historical, Philological, Culture and Geographical Sciences): Prof. Dr ULRICH KONRAD
Faculty of Philosophy II (Philosophy, Education Sciences and Social Sciences): Prof. Dr WOLFGANG SCHNEIDER
Faculty of Physics and Astronomy: Prof. Dr THOMAS TREFZGER

PROFESSORS

Faculty of Biology (Am Hubland, Biozentrum, 97074 Würzburg; tel. (931) 3184440; e-mail i-tbi@biozentrum.uni-wuerzburg.de):

DANDEKAR, TH., Bioinformatics
GOEBEL, W., Microbiology
HEDRICH, R., Botany
HEISENBERG, M., Genetics
LINSENMAIR, K. E., Zoology
MÜLLER, M., Pharmaceutical Biology
RIEDERER, M., Botany
SCHEER, U., Zoology
ZIMMERMANN, U., Biotechnology

Faculty of Catholic Theology (Sanderring 2, 97070 Würzburg; tel. (931) 3182252; e-mail thde001@mail.uni-wuerzburg.de):

DROESSER, G., Christian Sociology
DÜNZL, F., Church History
ERNST, S., Moral Theology
GARHAMMER, E., Pastoral Theology
HALLERMANN, H., Theological Law
HEININGER, B., New Testament Exegesis
KLAUSNITZER, W., Basic Theology and Comparative Religion
MEUFFELS, O., Dogmatics
SEIDL, TH., Old Testament Exegesis and Biblical Oriental Languages
WEISS, W., History of the Frankish Church
ZIEBERTZ, H.-G., Religious Instruction

Faculty of Chemistry and Pharmacy (Am Hubland, 97074 Würzburg; tel. (931) 8885364; e-mail hopf.dekanat@uni-wuerzburg.de):

BRAUNSCHWEIG, H., Inorganic Chemistry
BRINGMANN, G., Organic Chemistry
FISCHER, U., Biochemistry
HOLZGRABE, U., Pharmaceutical Chemistry
TACKE, R., Inorganic Chemistry
WÜRTHNER, F., Organic Chemistry
ZIMMERMANN, I., Pharmaceutical Technology

Faculty of Economics (Sanderring 2, 97070 Würzburg; tel. (931) 312901; e-mail f-wifak@wifak.uni-wuerzburg.de):

BERTHOLD, N., Political Economy
BOFINGER, P., Political Economy
BOGASCHEWSKY, R., Industrial Management
FEHR, J., Economics
FREERICKS, W., Business Management Taxation
KUKUK, M., Econometrics
LENZ, H., Accounting and Consultancy
MEYER, M., Marketing
SCHULZ, N., Political Economy
THOME, R., Economics and Computer Science
WÄLDE, K., Political Economy
WENGER, E., Banking

Faculty of Law (Domerschulstr. 16, 97070 Würzburg; tel. (931) 3182389; e-mail dekanat@jura.uni-wuerzburg.de):

DREIER, H., Philosophy of Law, Political and Administrative Law
HARKE, J., Civil Law, Roman Law and Historical Comparative Law

Hilgendorf, E., Criminal Law, Criminal Procedural Law
Kieninger, E.-M., German and European Civil Law, International Civil Law
Laubenthal, K., Criminology and Penal Law
Pache, E., State Law, International Law, International Economic Law, Economic Administrative Law
Remien, O., Civil Law and European Economic Law
Scherer, I., Civil Law
Schulze-Fielitz, H., Public Law, Environmental Law and Administrative Science
Sosnitza, O., Civil Law
Suerbaum, J., Public and Administrative Law
Weber, C., Civil Law and Labour Law
Weitzel, J., Civil Law, History of European Law and Procedural Law
Zieschang, F., Criminal Law, Criminal Procedural Law

Faculty of Mathematics and Computer Science (Am Hubland, 97074 Würzburg; tel. (931) 8885021; e-mail dekan@mathinfo.uni-wuerzburg.de):

Albert, J., Computer Science
Dobrowolski, M., Applied Mathematics
Falk, M., Mathematical Statistics
Grundhöfer, Th., Mathematics
Helmke, U., Mathematics
Kanzow, Ch., Applied Mathematics
Kolla, R., Computer Science
Müller, P., Mathematics and Algebra
Noltemeier, H., Computer Science
Puppe, F., Computer Science
Ruscheweyh, S., Mathematics
Schilling, K., Technical Computer Science
Tran-Gia, P., Computer Science
Wagner, K. W., Computer Science
Weigand, H.-G., Teaching of Mathematics

Faculty of Medicine (Josef-Schneider-Str. 2, Klinikum (Haus D7), 97080 Würzburg; tel. (931) 20155458; e-mail f-medizin@uni-wuerzburg.de):

Beckmann, H., Psychiatry
Bröcker, E.-B., Dermatology, Venerology and Allergology
Dietl, J., Obstetrics and Gynaecology
Drenckhahn, D., Anatomy
Einsele, H., Internal Medicine
Elert, O., Thoracic and Cardiovascular Surgery
Ertl, G., Internal Medicine
Eulert, J., Orthopaedics
Flentje, M., Radiology
Frosch, M., Hygiene and Microbiology
Grehn, F., Ophthalmology
Hacker, J., Molecular Biology of Infections
Hagen, R., Molecular Biology of Infections
Hahn, D., Radiodiagnostics
Helms, J., Otorhinolaryngology
Höhn, H., Human Genetics
Hünig, T., Virology
Karschin, A., Neurophysiology
Klaiber, B., Dentistry
Koepsell, H., Anatomy
Kuhn, M., Physiology
Lohse, M., Pharmacology
Lutz, W., Toxicology
Müller-Hermelink, H. K., Pathology
Patzelt, D., Forensic and Social Medicine
Rapp, U., Medical Radiology
Reiners, Ch., Medical Radiology
Rethwilm, A., Virology
Reuther, J., Dentistry, Maxillofacial Surgery
Richter, E.-J., Dental and Facial Medicine
Riedmiller, H., Urology
Roewer, N., Anaesthesiology
Roosen, K., Neurosurgery
Schartl, M., Physiological Chemistry
Sebald, W., Physiological Chemistry
Sendtner, M., Clinical Neurobiology
Speer, C., Paediatrics
Stellzig-Eisenhauer, A., Dental and Facial Orthopaedics
Stolberg, M., History of Medicine
Toyka, K. V., Neurology
Walter, U., Clinical Biochemistry and Pathobiochemistry
Warnke, A., Child Psychiatry

Faculty of Philosophy I and Institute of Geosciences (Residenzpl. 2, 97070 Würzburg; tel. (931) 312879; e-mail f-philfak1@uni-wuerzburg.de):

Brückner, H., Indology
Brusniak, F., Music Education, Teaching of Music
Erler, M., Classical Philology
Hannick, Ch., Slavic Philology
Hettrich, H., Comparative Linguistics
Konrad, U., Musicology
Kuhn, D., Oriental Philology
Schier, W., Prehistoric Archaeology
Scholz, U. W., Classical Philology
Schönbein, M., Japanology
Sinn, U., Classical Archaeology
Wilhelm, G., Oriental Philology

Faculty of Philosophy II (Am Hubland, 97074 Würzburg; tel. (931) 8885221; e-mail f-philfak2@mail.uni-wuerzburg.de):

Achilles, J., American Studies
Alt, P.-A., History of Modern German Literature
Altgeld, W., Modern and Contemporary History
Brunner, H., German Philology
Burgschmidt, E., English Linguistics
Daxelmüller, C., European Ethnology
Dietz, K., Early History
Flachenecker, H., Frankish History
Fuchs, F., Medieval History
Kohl, St. M., English Literature and British Cultural Studies
Kummer, S., History of Art
Neugebauer, W., Modern History
Penzkofer, G., Romance Philology
Pfotenhauer, H., History of Modern German Literature
Pötters, W., Romance Philology
Wolf, N. R., German Linguistics

Faculty of Physics and Astronomy (Am Hubland, 97074 Würzburg; tel. (931) 8885720; e-mail f-physik@physik.uni-wuerzburg.de):

Claessen, R., Experimental Physics
Dyakonov, V., Experimental Physics, Energy Research
Forchel, A., Semiconductor Technology and Physics
Gerber, G., Experimental Physics
Hanke, W., Theoretical Physics
Heuer, D., Physics Teaching
Jakob, P., Biophysics
Kinzel, W., Computational Physics
Mannheim, K., Astronomy
Molenkamp, L., Experimental Physics
Rückl, R., Theoretical Physics
Umbach, E., Experimental Physics

JUSTUS-LIEBIG-UNIVERSITÄT GIESSEN

Ludwigstr. 23, 35390 Giessen
Telephone: (641) 990
Internet: www.uni-giessen.de

Founded 1607
public control
Languages of instruction: English, German
Academic year: October to September (2 terms)

Pres.: Prof. Dr Joybrato Mukherjee
Vice-Pres: Prof. Dr Eva Burwitz-Melzer
Vice-Pres: Prof. Dr Katja Becker
Head of Admin.: Dr Michael Breitbach
Librarian: Dr Peter Reuter

Library: 3.6m. vols, 5,500 periodicals, 21,000 electronic periodicals
Number of teachers: 1,700 incl. 300 Profs
Number of students: 24,000

Publication: *Spiegel der Forschung* (1 a year)

DEANS

Department of Agrarian Sciences, Nutritional Sciences, Environmental Management: Prof. Dr Ute Leonhäuser
Department of Biology, Chemistry and Geosciences: Prof. Dr Volkmar Wolters
Department of Economics: Prof. Dr Jürgen Meckl
Department of History and Cultural Studies: Prof. Dr Peter von Möllendorff
Department of Human Medicine: Prof. Dr Trinad Chakraborty
Department of Language, Literature and Culture: Prof. Dr Cora Dietl
Department of Law: Prof. Dr Jens Adolphsen
Department of Mathematics and Information Studies, Physics, Geography: Prof. Christian Diller
Department of Psychology and Sport: Prof. Dr Markus Knauff
Department of Social and Cultural Studies: Prof. Dr Jutta Ecarius
Department of Veterinary Medicine: Prof. Dr Martin Kramer

PROFESSORS

Department of Agrarian Sciences, Nutritional Sciences, Environmental Management (Bismarckstr. 24, 35390 Giessen; tel. (641) 9937001):

Bauer, S., Project and Regional Planning
Becker-Brandenburg, K., Nutritional Biochemistry
Boland, H., Agricultural Extension and Communication
Bräunig, D., Management of Services for Persons
Brückner, H.-O., Food Science
Dzapo, V., Genetics, Breeding and Husbandry of Pigs and Small Animals
Erhardt, G., Animal Breeding and Genetics
Evers, A., Comparative Health and Social Policy
Felix-Henningsen, P., Soil Science and Soil Conservation
Frede, H.-G., Resources Management
Friedt, W., Plant Breeding
Gäth, S., Waste Management and Environmental Research
Herrmann, R., Agricultural and Food Market Analysis
Hoffmann, I., Nutritional Ecology
Honermeier, B., Crop Science
Hoy, S., Farm Animal Housing and Biology
Hummel, H. E., Biological and Biotechnical Plant Protection
Kämpfer, P., Recycling Microbiology
Kogel, K.-H., Molecular Plant Pathology
Köhler, W., Biometry and Population Genetics
Krawinkel, M., Human Nutrition, International Nutrition
Kühl, R. W., Food Economics and Marketing Management
Kuhlmann, F., Farm Management
Kunz, C., Human Nutrition, Evaluation of Food
Leithold, G., Organic Farming
Leonhäuser, I.-U., Nutrition Education and Consumer Behaviour
Meier, U., Economics of Private Households and Family Sciences
Mühling, K.-H., Biochemical Aspects of Plant Nutrition
Neuhäuser-Berthold, M., Human Nutrition
Nuppenau, E. A., Agricultural and Environmental Policy

OPITZ VON BOBERFELD, W., Grassland Management and Forage Growing
OTTE, A., Landscape Ecology and Landscape Planning
PALLAUF, J., Animal Nutrition
SCHLICH, E., Home Engineering
SCHMITZ, P. M., Agricultural and Development Economics and Policy Analysis
SCHNELL, S., General and Soil Microbiology
SCHNIEDER, B., Housing and Human Ecology
SCHUBERT, S., Plant Nutrition
SEUFERT, H., Agricultural Engineering
VILCINSKAS, A., Applied Entomology

Department of Biology, Chemistry and Geosciences (Heinrich-Buff-Ring 58, 35392 Giessen; tel. (641) 9935001):

ASKANI, R., Organic Chemistry
BINDEREIF, A., Biochemistry
CLAUß, W., Animal Physiology
DORRESTEIJN, A. W. CH., Zoology
EHRENHOFER-MURRAY, A. E., Cosmetics
EMMERMANN, R., Mineralogy
ESSER, G., Plant Ecology
FORCHHAMMER, K., Microbiology
FRANKE, W., Geology
FRÖBA, M., Inorganic Chemistry
GEBELEIN, H., Chemistry Teaching
HAACK, U., Mineralogy
HUGHES, J., Plant Physiology
IPAKTSCHI, J., Organic Chemistry
JÄGER, H.-J., Experimental Plant Ecology
JANEK, J., Physical Chemistry
KLEE, R., Biology Teaching
KLUG, G., Microbiology
KUNTER, M., Anthropology
KUNZE, C., Botany
LAKES-HARLAN, R., Sensory Physiology
MARTIN, M., Immunology
MAYER, J., Teaching of Biology
OVER, H., Physical Chemistry
PINGOUD, A., Biochemistry
RENKAWITZ, R., Genetics
SCHINDLER, S., Inorganic Chemistry
SCHREINER, P., Organic Chemistry
SCHULTE, E., Zoology
SPENGLER, B., Analytical Chemistry
TRENCZEK, M., Zoology
VAN BEL, A. J. E., Organic Botany
VOLAND, E., Philosophy
WAGNER, G., Botany
WIEKE, T., Zoology and Biodiversity
WOLTERS, V., Animal Ecology

Department of Economics (Licher Str. 74, 35394 Giessen; tel. (641) 9922001; e-mail dekanat@wirtschaft.uni-giessen.de):

ABERLE, G., General Economics, Price Theory, Industrial Organization and Competition Policy, Transport Economics
ALEXANDER, V., General Economics, Money, Credit and Currency
BESSLER, W., General Business Administration, Finance and Banking
ESCH, F.-R., General Business Administration, Marketing
GLAUM, M., Business Administration, International Management, Accounting and Auditing
HEMMER, H.-R., General Economics, Development Economics
KABST, R., General Business Administration, Human Resource Management
KRÜGER, W., General Business Management, Organization, Leadership
MECKL, H., General Economics, International Economics
MORLOCK, M., General Business Management, Risk Management and Insurance
MÜLLER, H., General Economics, Economics for Subsidiary Students, Environmental Economics
RINNE, H., Statistics and Econometrics
SCHERF, W., General Economics, Public Finance
SCHWICKERT, A., General Business Administration, Computer Science in Business
SPENGEL, C., General Business Administration, Company Taxation
WEIßENBERGER, B., Business Administration, Management of Industrial Corporations, Controlling

Department of History and Cultural Studies (Otto-Behaghel-Str. 10, Haus G, 35394 Giessen; tel. (641) 9928000; e-mail dekanat@fb04.uni-giessen.de):

BÄUMER, F.-J., Religious Education Studies and Teaching of Religion
BAUMGARTNER, M., History of Art
CARL, H., Medieval and Modern History
EISEN, U., Bible Studies, Old Testament and New Testament
GOSEPATH, S., Practical Philosophy
GRÄB-SCHMIDT, E., Systematic Theology
HARTMANN, A., Islamic Studies
HAUSER, L., Systematic Theology
KIRCHNER, M., Turcology
KRASSER, H., Classical Philology
KURZ, W., Religion Lessons
LENGER, F., Medieval and Modern History
LEXUTT, A., History of the Church
MARTINI, W., Classical Archaeology
OSWALT, V., History Teaching
PROSTMEIER, F., Bible Studies, New Testament
QUANDT, S., History Teaching
REINELE, C., German Regional History
REULECKE, J., Modern History
RÖSENER, W., Medieval and Modern History
SPEITKAMP, W., Modern History
SPICKERNAGEL, E., History of Art
TAMMEN, S., History of Art
VON MÖLLENDORFF, P., Greek Philology

Department of Human Medicine (Rudolf-Buchheim-Str. 6, 35392 Giessen; tel. (641) 9948001):

ALZEN, G., Paediatric Radiology
BAUER, R., Nuclear Medicine
BAUMGART-VOGT, E., Anatomy and Cellular Biology
BECK, E., Molecular Biology
BECKMANN, D., Medical Psychology
BEIN, G., Clinical Immunology and Transfusion Medicine
BOHLE, R., Pathology
BÖKER, D.-K., Neurosurgery
BRETZEL, R., Internal Medicine
CHAKRABORTY, T., Medical Microbiology
DREYER, F., Pharmacology and Toxicology
EIKMANN, T., Hygiene
ENGELHART-CABILLIC, R., Radiology
FERGER, D., Dentistry
FLEISCHER, G., Auditory Research
FRIEDRICH, R., Molecular Genetics and Virology
GALLHOFER, B., Psychiatry
GERLICH, W., Medical Virology
GEYER, R., Biochemistry
GIELER, U., Psychosomatics and Psychotherapy
GLANZ, H., Otorhinolaryngology
GRIMMINGER, F., Internal Medicine, Pneumology
HEMPELMANN, G., Anaesthesiology and Operative Intensive Medicine
HOWALDT, H.-P., Surgery of the Mouth, Jaws and Face
KAPS, M., Neurology
KATZ, N., Clinical Chemistry
KAUFMANN, H., Ophthalmology
KIESSLING, J., Audiology
KLIMEK, J., Dentistry
KOCKAPAN, C., Endodontics
KRAWINKEL, M., Paediatrics, Nutritional Science
KREUDER, J., Paediatrics
KUMMER, W., Anatomy and Cellular Biology
LINDEMANN, H., Paediatrics
LOHMEYER, J., Internal Medicine
MEINHARDT, A., Anatomy and Cellular Biology
MERSCH-SUNDERMANN, V., Indoor-Air Toxicology and Environmental Toxicology
MEYLE, J., Paradontology
MIDDENDORFF, R., Anatomy and Cellular Biology
MÜLLER, U., Human Genetics
NEUBAUER, B., Paediatrics
PADBERG, W., Visceral, Thoracic and Transplantation Surgery
PANCHERZ, H. J., Dental Orthopaedics
PIPER, H. M., Physiology
PRALLE, H., Internal Medicine
PREISSNER, K., Biochemistry
RAU, W. S., Radiological Diagnostics
REIMER, C., Clinical Psychosomatics and Psychotherapy
REITER, A., Paediatric Haematology and Oncology
ROELCKE, V., History of Medicine
SAUER, H., Physiology
SCHACHENMAYR, W., Neuropathology
SCHÄFFER, R., Cytopathology
SCHILL, W.-B., Dermatology and Andrology
SCHLÜTER, K.-D., Physiology
SCHNETTLER, R., Accident Surgery
SCHRANZ, D., Paediatric Cardiology
SCHULZ, A., Pathology
SEEGER, W., Internal Medicine, Pneumology
SKRANDIES, W., Physiology
STÜRZ, H., Orthopaedics
TILLMANNS, H., Internal Medicine, Cardiology
TINNEBERG, H.-R., Gynaecology
TRAUPE, H., Neuroradiology
VOGT, P., Cardiology, Vascular Surgery
WEIDNER, W., Urology
WEILER, G., Forensic Medicine
WETZEL, W.-E., Paediatric Dentistry
WÖSTMANN, B., Gerodontology and Clinical Aspects of Dental Materials

Department of Language, Literature and Culture (Otto-Behaghel-Str. 10, Haus G, 35394 Giessen; tel. (641) 9931001):

BERSCHIN, H., Romance Linguistics
BORGMEIER, R., Modern English and American Literature
EHLER, S., Teaching of German Language and Literature
EHRISMANN, O., German Language, Historical Linguistics
FEIEKE, H., German Linguistics and Teaching of German Language
FINTER, H., Applied Theatre Studies
FLOECK, W., Spanish Literature
FRITZ, G., German Philology
GANSEL, C., Teaching of German Language and Literature
GAST, W., Teaching of German Language and Literature
GOEBBELS, H., Applied Theatre Studies
GRAF, A., Slavonic Literatures
HORSTMANN, U., Modern English and American Literature
KURZ, G., History of Modern German Literature
LEGUTKE, M., Teaching of English Language
LEIBFRIED, E., General Literature and History of Literature
LOBIN, H., Applied Linguistics and Computer Linguistics
MEISSNER, F.-J., Teaching of Romance Languages and Literature
MUKHERJEE, J., English Language
NÜNNING, A., English and American Literature and Cultural Studies
OESTERLE, G., Modern German Literature
PRINZ, M., Teaching of Romance Languages and Literature
RAMGE, H., German Linguistics
RIEGER, D., Romance Literature

RÖSLER, D., German as a Foreign Language
SEEL, M., Philosophy
STENZEL, H., Romance Literature and Cultural Studies
WINGENDER, M., Slavonic Linguistics
WINKELMANN, O., Romance Linguistics

Department of Law (Licher Str. 72, 35394 Giessen; tel. (641) 9921000; e-mail dekanat@fb01.uni-giessen.de):

BEHNICKE, C., Civil Law, Commercial Law, Comparative Law, International Civil Law
BRITZ, G., Public Law, European Law
BRYDE, B.-O., Public Law
EKKENGA, J., Civil Law, Commercial Law
GIESEN, R., Civil Law, Labour and Social Law
GROPP, W., Criminal Law, Criminal Procedural Law
GROSS, T., Public Law, Administrative Science
HAMMEN, H., Civil Law, Commercial Law
HECKER, B., Criminal Law, Criminal Procedural Law
KREUZER, A., Criminology, Juvenile Criminal Law
LANGE, K., Public Law, Administration Teaching
LIPP, M., German Legal History and Civil Law
MARAUHN, T., Public Law, International Public Law, European Law
SCHAPP, J., Civil Law and Philosophy of Law
WALKER, W.-D., Civil Law, Labour Law, Civil Procedural Law
WOLFSLAST, G., Criminal Law, Criminal Procedural Law

Department of Mathematics and Information Studies, Physics, Geography (Heinrich-Buff-Ring 16, 35392 Giessen; tel. (641) 9933000):

BARTSCH, T., Analysis
BAUMANN, B., Mathematics, Algebra
BEUTELSPACHER, A., Mathematics, Geometry
BUHMANN, M., Numerical Mathematics
BUNDE, A., Theoretical Physics
CASSING, W., Theoretical Physics
DÜREN, M., Experimental Physics
FELIX-HENNINGSEN, P., Soil Science, Land Conservation
FENSKE, C., Mathematics
FRANKE, M., Teaching of Mathematics
GIESE, E., Economic Geography
HÄUSLER, E. K., Stochastics
HAVERSATH, J. B., Teaching of Geography
HERMANN, G., Experimental Physics
KANITSCHEIDER, B., Philosophy of Natural Sciences
KING, L., Geography
KOHL, C.-D., Applied Physics
KÜHN, W., Experimental Physics
METAG, V., Experimental Physics
METSCH, K., Mathematics, Geometry
MEYER, B., Experimental Physics
MOSEL, U., Theoretical Physics
MÜLLER, A., Experimental Physics
OVERBECK, L., Mathematics
PROFKE, L., Didactics of Mathematics
SALZBORN, E., Nuclear Physics
SAUER, T., Numerical Mathematics
SCHEID, W., Theoretical Physics
SCHLETTWEIN, D., Applied Physics
SCHOLZ, U., Geography
SCHWARZ, G., Teaching of Physics
SEIFERT, V., Geography
STUTE, W., Mathematical Statistics
TIMMESFELD, F. G., Mathematics, Algebra
WALTHER, H.-O., Mathematics, Analysis
WERLE, O., Didactics of Geography

Department of Psychology and Sport (Otto-Behaghel-Str. 10, Haus F1, 35394 Giessen; tel. (641) 9926000; e-mail dekanat@fb06.uni-giessen.de):

BORG, I., Applied Psychological Methods
BRUNNSTEIN, J., Educational Psychology
ENNEMOSER, M., Special Educational Psychology
FRESE, M., Work and Organizational Psychology
GEGENFURTNER, K., General and Experimental Psychology
GLOWALLA, U., Educational Psychology
HALDER-SINN, P., Psychological Diagnosis
HENNIG, J., Differential Psychology
MUNZERT, J., Sports Psychology
NEUMANN, H., Sport and Training
PROBST, H., Special Educational Psychology
SCHUSTER, C., Psychological Methodology
SCHWARZER, G., Developmental Psychology
SCHWIER, J., Sport and Teaching of Sport
SPORER, S., Social Psychology
STIENSMEIER-PELSTER, J., Educational Psychology

Department of Social and Cultural Studies (Karl-Glöckner-Str. 21, Haus E/B, 35394 Giessen; tel. (641) 9923001; e-mail dekan@fb03.uni-giessen.de; internet www.uni-giessen.de/fb03):

BIRCKENBACH-WELLMANN, H.-M., Political Science, European Studies
BULLERJAHN, C., Political Science, European Studies
CLAUS-BACHMANN, M., Music
DUBIEL, H., Sociology
DUNCKER, L., Educational Science
EBERS, A., Comparative Health and Social Policy
ECARIUS, J., Educational Science
FORNECK, H., Educational Science
FRITZSCHE, K., Political Science
GRONEMEYER, R., Sociology
HOFMANN, C., Educational Science
HOLLAND-CUNZ, B., Political Science, Gender Studies
KREBS, D., Empirical Research in Social Sciences
LEGGEWIE, C., Political Science
LIPPITZ, W., Philosophy of Education, Comparative Studies of Education
MOSER, V., Educational Science
NECKEL, S., Sociology
NITSCHE, P., Music
PHLEPS, T., Music
REIMANN, B., Sociology
RICHTER-REICHENBACH, K.-S., Teaching of Art
SANDER, W., Teaching of Social Sciences
SCHMIDT, P., Empirical Social Research
SCHWANDER, M., Educational Science
SEIDELMANN, R., Political Science, International Relations
SPICKERNAGEL, E., History of Art
STACHOWIAK, F., Educational Science
STANICZEK, J., Art Practice
STÖPPLER, R., Educational Science
WILLEMS, H., Microsociology and Qualitative Methods
WISSINGER, J., Educational Science

Department of Veterinary Medicine (Frankfurter Str. 74, 35392 Giessen; tel. (641) 9938001; e-mail dekanat@vetmed.uni-giessen.de):

BALJER, G., Infectious Diseases and Hygiene
BAUERFEIND, R., Control of Epidemics
BERGMANN, M., Veterinary Anatomy, Histology and Embryology
BOSTEDT, H., Physiology and Pathology of Reproduction
BÜLTE, M., Veterinary Nutrition
CLAUß, W., Animal Physiology
DIENER, M., Veterinary Physiology
DOLL, K., Diseases of Ruminants
EISGRUBER, H., Hygiene of Food of Animal Origin and Consumer Protection
ERHARDT, G., Animal Breeding and Genetics of Domestic Animals
GERSTBERGER, R., Veterinary Physiology
HOFFMANN, B., Physiology and Pathology of Reproduction
KALETA, E., Diseases and Hygiene of Poultry
KÖLLE, S., Veterinary Anatomy, Histology and Embryology
KRAMER, M., Small Animal Surgery
KRESSIN, M., Veterinary Anatomy, Histology and Embryology
LEISER, R., Veterinary Anatomy, Histology and Embryology
LITZKE, L.-F., Equine Surgery
MORITZ, A., Internal Medicine
NEIGER, R., Small Animal Internal Medicine
PETZINGER, E. D., Pharmacology and Toxicology
REINACHER, M., Pathology
REINER, G., Department of Swine Diseases (Internal Medicine and Surgery)
RÜMENAPF, T., Clinical Virology
THIEL, H.-J., Virology
USLEBER, E., Milk Science
WENGLER, G., Virology and Cellular Biology
WÜRBEL, H., Animal Welfare and Ethology
ZAHNER, H., Parasitology

KARLSRUHER INSTITUTS FÜR TECHNOLOGIE

Kaiserstr. 12, 76131 Karlsruhe
Telephone: (721) 6080
E-mail: info@kit.edu
Internet: www.kit.edu

Founded 2009 by merger of Forschungszentrum Karlsruhe and Universität Karlsruhe (f. 1825)
State control
Academic year: October to September
Pres.: Prof. Dr HORST HIPPLER
Pres.: Prof. Dr EBERHARD UMBACH
Vice-Pres. for Finance and Business Affairs: Dr ALEXANDER KURZ
Vice-Pres. for Human Resources and Law: ELKE-LUISE BARNSTEDT
Vice-Pres. for Research and Information: Prof. Dr DETLEF LÖHE
Vice-Pres. for Research and Innovation: Dr PETER FRITZ
Chief Admin. Officer: (vacant)
Librarian: Dipl. Ing. CHRISTOPH-HUBERT SCHÜTTE

Library of 2,040,000 vols, 71,500 print and electronic periodicals
Number of teachers: 1,200
Number of students: 21,000

Publications: *ClicKIT* (online), *Fridericiana* (2 a year), *LooKIT* (online)

DEANS

Faculty of Architecture: Prof. Dipl. Ing. MARKUS NEPPL
Faculty of Chemical and Process Engineering: Prof. Dr Ing. HERRMANN NIRSCHL
Faculty of Chemistry and Biosciences: Prof. Dr STEFAN BRÄSE
Faculty of Civil, Geo- and Environmental Sciences: Prof. Dr Ing. BERNHARD HECK
Faculty of Computer Science: Prof. Dr HEINZ WÖRN
Faculty of Economics and Business Engineering: Prof. Dr CLEMENS PUPPE
Faculty of Electrical Engineering and Information Technology: Prof. Dr GERT F. TROMMER
Faculty of Humanities and Social Sciences: Prof. Dr KLAUS BÖS

Faculty of Mathematics: Prof. Dr FRANK HERRLICH
Faculty of Mechanical Engineering: Prof. Dr Ing. MARTIN GABI
Faculty of Physics: Prof. Dr HEINZ KALT

PROFESSORS

Faculty of Architecture:
BAVA, H.
BÖKER, H. J.
CRAIG, S.
GOTHE, K.
JANSON, A.
NÄGELI, W.
NEPPL, M.
PFEIFFER, M.
RICHTER, P.
SCHNEIDER, N.
SCHULZE, U.
SEWING, W.
VON BOTH, P.
WAGNER, A.
WALL, A.

Faculty of Chemical and Process Engineering:
BOCKHORN, H.
FRIMMEL, F. H.
HUBBUCH, I.
KASPER, G.
KIND, M.
KOLB, T.
KRAUSHAAR-CZERNETSKI, B.
NIRSCHL, H.
OELLRICH, L.
OLIVEROS, E.
POSTEN, C.
REIMERT, R.
SCHABEL, W.
SCHABER, K.
SCHAUB, G.
SCHUCHMANN, H.
SYLDATK, C.
WETZEL, T.
WILLENBACHER, N.
ZARZALIS, N.

Faculty of Chemistry and Biosciences:
AHLRICHS, R.
BARNER-KOWOLLIK, C.
BASTMEYER, M.
BOCKHORN, H.
BRÄSE, S.
DEUTSCHMANN, O.
FELDMANN, C.
FISCHER, R.
GECKEIS, H.
HIPPLER, H.
KÄMPER, J.
KAPPES, M.
KLOPPER, W.
LAMPARTER, T.
MARKO, D.
METZLER, M.
NICK, P.
OLZMANN, M.
PODLECH, J.
POWELL, A.
PUCHTA, H.
RICHERT, C.
ROESKY, P.
SCHUSTER, R.
SCHWARZ, U.
TARASCHEWSKI, H.
ULRICH, A.
WEDLICH, D.
WILHELM, M.

Faculty of Civil, Geo- and Environmental Sciences:
BLAß, H. J.
BURGER, D.
GEHBAUER, F.
GENTES, S.
GREILING, R.
HECK, B.
HENNES, M.
HINZ, S.
HOHNECKER, E.
JIRKA, G.
KRAMER, C.
LENNERTS, K.
MEURER, M.
MÜLLER, H.
NESTMANN, F.
ROOS, R.
RUCK, B.
SCHILLING, F.
SCHMITT, G.
SCHWEIZERHOF, K.
STEMPNIEWSKI, L.
STOSCH, H.-G.
STÜBERN, D.
TRIANTAFYLLIDIS, T.
UHLMANN, M.
UMMENHAFER, T.
VOGT, J.
WAGNER, W.
WINTER, J.
ZUMKELLER, D.

Faculty of Electrical Engineering and Information Technology:
BECKER, J.
BOLZ, A.
BRAUN, M.
DÖSSEL, O.
DOSTERT, K.
FREUDE, W.
IVERS-TIFFÉE, E.
JONDRAL, F.
KREBS, V.
LEIBFRIED, T.
LEMMER, U.
LEUTHOLD, J.
MOREIRA, A.
MÜLLER-GLASER, K.-D.
NOE, M.
PUENTE, F.
SIEGEL, M.
TROMMER, G.
TUUMM, M.
ZWICK, T.

Faculty of Humanities and Social Sciences:
BÖHN, A.
BÖS, K.
FISCHER, M.
FRIES, S.
GIDION, G.
GLEITSMANN-TOPP, R.-J.
GRUNWALD, A.
GUTMANN, M.
JAPP, U.
NOLLMANN, G.
PFADENHAUER, M.
REKUS, J.
SCHÜTT, H.-P.
SCHWAMEDER, H.

Faculty of Mathematics:
ALEFELD, G.
AUMANN, G.
BÄUERLE, N.
DÖRFLER, W.
HENZE, N.
HERRLICH, F.
HEUVELINE, V.
JANNHE, T.
KAUCHER, E.
KIRSCH, A.
LAST, G.
LEUZINGER, E.
PLUM, M.
REICHEL, W.
RIEDER, A.
SCHMIDT, C.-G.
VERAANT, L.
WEIL, W.
WEIß, J.-P.
WEIS, L.
WIENERS, N.

Faculty of Mechanical Engineering:
ALBERS, A.
BAUER, H.-J.
BÖHLKE, T.
BRETTHAUER, G.
CACCUCI, D.
ELSHER, P.
FLEISCHER, J.
FURMANS, K.
GABI, M.
GAUTERIN, F.
GEIMER, M.
GRATZFELD, P.
GUMBSCH, P.
HENNING, F.
HOFFMANN, M. J.
KRAFT, O.
LANZA, G.
LÖHE, D.
MAAS, U.
OERTEL, H.
OVTCHAROVA, J.
PROPPE, C.
SAILE, V.
SEEMANN, W.
SPICHER, U.
STILLER, C.
WANNER, A.
ZÜLCH, G.
ZUM GAHR, K.-H.

Faculty of Physics:
BAUMBACH, T.
BEHENG, K. D.
BLÜMER, H.
BUSCH, K.
DE BOER, W.
DREXLIN, G.
FEINDT, M.
GERTHSEN, D.
GUAST, G.
JONES, S.
KALT, H.
KLINGSHIRN, C.
KOHMEIER, C.
KÜHN, J.
MÜLLER, TH.
NIERSTE, U.
SCHIMMERL, T.
SCHÖN, G.
SHNIRMAN, A.
STEINHAUSER, M.
USTINOV, A.
VON LÖHNEYSEN, H.
WEGENER, M.
WEIß, G.
WENZEL, F.
WÖLFLE, P.
WULFHEKEL, W.
ZEPPENFELD, D.

KATHOLISCHE UNIVERSITÄT EICHSTÄTT-INGOLSTADT

Ostenstrasse 26–28, 85072 Eichstätt
Telephone: (8421) 932-3300
E-mail: info@ku.de
Internet: www.ku.de
Founded 1980, reviving a foundation of 1564
Academic year: April to February
Vice-Pres.: Prof. Dr MANFRED BROCKER
Vice-Pres.: Prof. Dr ULRICH KÜSTERS
CEO: THOMAS KLEINERT
Librarian: Dr MARIA LÖFFLER
Library of 1,600,000 vols
Number of teachers: 460
Number of students: 4,500
Publications: *Agora* (2 a year), *Eichstätter Beiträge* (2 a year), *Eichstätter Materialen* (2 a year), *Eichstätter Studien* (3 a year)

DEANS

Faculty of Economic Sciences: Prof. Dr MAX RINGLSTETTER
Faculty of History and Social Sciences: Prof. Dr THOMAS FISCHER LUKS

Faculty of Languages and Literature: Prof. Dr KLAUS-DIETER ALTMEPPEN
Faculty of Mathematics and Geography: Prof. Dr HARALD PECHLANER
Faculty of Philosophy and Education: Prof. Dr FRANZ-MICHAEL KONRAD
Faculty of Religious Education: Prof. Dr MARKUS EHAM
Faculty of Social Studies: Prof. Dr RENATE OXENKNECHT-WITZSCH
Faculty of Theology: Prof. Dr BURKARD ZAPFF

PROFESSORS

Faculty of Economic Sciences (Auf den Schanz 49, 85049 Eichstätt; tel. (8421) 9371801; e-mail elisabeth.batz@ku-eichstaett.de; internet www.ku-eichstaett.de/fakultaeten/wwf):

BURGER, A., General Business Management
BÜSCHKEN, J., Business Administration and Marketing
DJANANI, C., General Business Management
FISCHER, H., Economics
FISCHER, T. M., General Business Management Controlling
FUCHS, M., Law for Economists
GENOSKO, J., Economic and Social Policy
KUHN, H., Business Administration, Production and Operations Management
KÜSTERS, U., Statistics
KUTSCHKER, M., General Business Management, International Management
LUTTERMANN, C., Law for Economists
RINGLSTETTER, M., General Business Management
SCHNEIDER, J., Economics
STAUSS, B., Business Administration and Services Management
WILDE, K., General Business Management and Economic Information Technology
WILKENS, M., General Business Management, Financing

Faculty of History and Social Sciences (Universitätsallee 1, 85072 Eichstätt; tel. (8421) 931286; e-mail gertraud.reinwald@ku-eichstaett.de; internet www.ku-eichstaett.de/fakultaeten/ggf):

DETJEN, J., Political Science
DICKERHOF, H., Medieval History
GRECA, R., Sociology
KÖNIG, H.-J., Latin American History
LAMNEK, S., Sociology
LUKS, L., Contemporary Eastern European History
MALITZ, J., Ancient History
MÜLLER, R. A., Early Modern History
RUPPERT, K., Modern and Contemporary History
SCHREIBER, W., Theory and Teaching of History
SCHUBERT, K., Political Science
SCHWINN, T., Sociology
TREIBER, A., Folklore
ZSCHALER, F., History of Economics and Social Development

Faculty of Languages and Literature (Universitätsallee 1, 85072 Eichstätt; tel. (8421) 931517; e-mail monika.bittl@ku-eichstaett.de; internet www.ku-eichstaett.de/fakultaeten/slf):

BAMMESBERGER, A., English Linguistics
DICKE, G., German Literature
GSELL, O., Romance Linguistics
HÖMBERG, W., Journalism
KLÖDEN, H., Romance Linguistics
KRAFFT, P., Classical Philology
MARTIN, F.-P., Teaching of French Language
MUELLER, K., German as a Foreign Language
NATE, R., English Literature
NEUMANN, M., Modern German Literature
PITTROF, T., New German Literature
RENK, H. E., Teaching of German Language and Literature
RONNEBERGER-SIBOLD, E., Historic German Linguistics
SCHNACKERTZ, H.-J., American Literature
TONNEMACHER, J., Journalism
TSCHIEDEL, H.-J., Classical Philology
WEHLE, W., Romance Literature
WEIGAND, R. U., Medieval German Literature
ZIMMER, G., Classical Archaeology

Faculty of Mathematics and Geography (Ostenstr. 28, 85072 Eichstätt; tel. (8421) 931456; e-mail claudia.banzer@ku-eichstaett.de; internet www.ku-eichstaett.de/fakultaeten/mgf):

BECHT, M., Physical Geography
BISCHOFF, W., Mathematics
BLATT, H.-P., Mathematics
DESEL, J., Informatics
DIEHL, S., Informatics
FELIX, R., Mathematics
FISCHER, H., Mathematics
HEMMER, I., Teaching of Geography
HOPFINGER, H., Geography
KUTSCH, H., Physical Geography
PECHLANER, H., Tourism
RESSEL, P., Mathematics
RICKER, W., Mathematics
ROHLFS, J., Mathematics
SOMMER, M., Mathematics
STEINBACH, J., Geography

Faculty of Philosophy and Education (Ostenstr. 26, 85072 Eichstätt; tel. (8421) 931298; e-mail dekanat.ppf@ku-eichstaett.de; internet www.ku-eichstaett.de/fakultaeten/ppf):

BRÜNGER, P., Music Education
FELL, M., Adult Education
FETZ, R., Philosophy
GEISER, G., Pedagogics of Work
GRABOWSKI, F., Psychology
HABISCH, A., Central Institute for Marriage and Family in Society
HELLBRÜCK, J., Psychology
JENDROWIAK, H.-W., General Pedagogics
KALS, E., Psychology
KERKHOFF, G., Psychology
KÖCK, M., Pedagogics of Work
KONRAD, F.-M., Historical and Comparative Pedagogy
KÖPPEL, G., Art
LÄMMERMANN, G., Protestant Theology
LOVEN, C., Musicology
LUTTER, K., Sports
SCHMIDT, H.-L., Social Pedagogics
SCHÖNIG, W., Pedagogics of School
SCHULTHEIS, K., Elementary Education
THOMAS, F., Psychology
ZIMMERMANN, M., Art History

Faculty of Religious Education (vocational courses) (Pater-Philipp-Jeningen-Platz 6, 85072 Eichstätt; tel. (8421) 931275; e-mail dekanat.rpf@ku-eichstaett.de; internet www.ku-eichstaett.de/fakultaeten/rpf):

EHAM, M., Music and Voice Training
KURTEN, P., Dogmatics
MEIER, U., Religious Education
OBERRÖDER, W., Theory and Practice of Church Work
SCHUSTER, B., Psychology
SILL, B., Moral Theology and Social Ethics
STAUCHIGL, B., Pedagogics
TAGLIACARNE, P., Old Testament
TRAUTMANN, M., New Testament
WILLERS, U., Fundamental Theology and Philosophy

Faculty of Social Studies (vocational courses) (Ostenstr. 26, 85072 Eichstätt; tel. (8421) 931246; e-mail dekanat.fsw@ku-eichstaett.de; internet www.ku-eichstaett.de/fakultaeten/swf):

BARTOSCH, U., Pedagogics
BECK, C., Social Work
ERATH, P., Social Work
GÖPPNER, H.-J., Psychology
KLUG, W., Social Work
OXENKNECHT-WITZSCH, R., Law
SCHIEREN, S., Political Science

Faculty of Theology (P.-Philipp-Jeningen-Platz 6, 8507 Eichstätt; tel. (8421) 931437; e-mail karin.lepschy@ku-eichstaett.de; internet www.ku-eichstaett.de/fakultaeten/thf):

BÄRSCH, F., Liturgy
BÖTTIGHEIMER, C., Fundamental Theology
FISCHER, N., Philosophy and Basic Questions of Theology
GERWING, M., Dogmatics
GROSS, E., Religious Teaching and Teaching of Catholic Religion
HOFMANN, J., Old Church History and Patrology
MAIER, K., Middle and New Church History
MAYER, B., New Testament
MÖDE, E., Homiletics
MÜLLER, S. E., Moral Theology
SCHIFFERLE, A., Pastoral Theology
WEIß, A., Canon Law/History of Church Law
ZAPFF, B., Old Testament

KLU WISSENSCHAFTLICHE HOCHSCHULE FÜR LOGISTIK UND UNTERNEHMENSFÜHRUNG
(Kühne Logistics University)

Grosser Grasbrook 17, 20457 Hamburg
Telephone: (40) 328707110
E-mail: info@the-klu.org
Internet: www.the-klu.org
Private control
Academic year: September to August
Teaching and research in the fields of logistics, management and economics
Pres. and Man. Dir: Prof. Dr THOMAS STROTHOTTE
Man. Dir: Prof. Dr MARC GOTTSCHALD
Dean of Programmes: Prof. Dr ALAN C. MCKINNON
Dean of Research: Prof. Dr SÖNKE ALBERS

LEIBNIZ UNIVERSITÄT HANNOVER

POB 6009, 30060 Hanover
Welfengarten 1, 30167 Hanover
Telephone: (511) 7620
E-mail: info@pressestelle.uni-hannover.de
Internet: www.uni-hannover.de
Founded 1831
Pres.: Prof. Dr Ing. ERICH BARKE
Vice-Pres. for Finance and Admin.: GÜNTER SCHOLZ
Vice-Pres. for Research: Prof. Dr KLAUS HULEK
Vice-Pres. for Teaching, Academic Programmes and Continuing Education: Prof. Dr GABRIELE DIEWALD
Library Dir: UWE ROSEMANN
Library: see under Libraries and Archives
Number of teachers: 1,272
Number of students: 35,000

DEANS

Faculty of Architecture and Landscape: Prof. MARGITTA BUCHERT
Faculty of Civil Engineering and Geodetic Science: Prof. CHRISTIAN HEIPKE
Faculty of Economics and Management: Prof. ANDREAS WAGENER
Faculty of Electrical Engineering and Computer Science: Prof. BERNARDO WAGNER
Faculty of Humanities: Prof. ROLF WERNING
Faculty of Law: Prof. HENNING RADTKE
Faculty of Mathematics and Physics: Prof. ROLF HAUG

Faculty of Mechanical Engineering: Prof. JÖRG SEUME
Faculty of Natural Sciences: Prof. MARKUS KALESSE
Quest Leibniz Research School: Prof. Dr WOLFGANG ERTMER

PROFESSORS

Faculty of Architecture and Landscape (Schlosswender Str. 1, 30159 Hanover; tel. (511) 7624276; e-mail hobert@dek-arch.uni-hannover.de):

BARTH, H. G., Regional Planning
BRAUM, M., Town Planning
BUCHERT, M., History of Art and Construction
DWORSKY, A., Rural Design
ECKERLE, E., Fine Arts
EHRMANN, W., Work Methods and Processing of Wood and Artificial Materials
FRIEDRICH, J., Design and Building Construction
FURCHE, A., Structural Design and Research
FÜRST, D., Regional Planning
GABRIEL, I., Construction and Design
GANZERT, J., History of Art and Construction
GENENGER, H.-G., Architecture
GERKEN, H., Planning Technology
HAAREN, CHR. V., Conservation
HACKER, E., Conservation
KAPPELER, D., Painting and Graphic Arts
KAUP, P., Construction and Design
KENNEDY, M., Resource-Saving in Building
LÉON, H., Building Typology and Design Section
LITTMAN, K., Work Methods and Processing of Wood and Artificial Materials
LÖSKEN, G., Open Space Planning and Garden Architecture
OPPERMANN, B., Open Space Planning
PARAVICINI, U., Theory of Architecture
POHL, W.-H., Building Materials Technology
REICH, M., Plant Ecology
SCHMID-KIRSCH, A., Drawing and Computer-Assisted Design
SCHOMERS, M., Design
SCHULTE, K., Industrial Design
SLAWIK, H., Construction and Design
TESSIN, W., Planning-Related Sociology
TROJAN, K., Town Planning
TURKALI, Z., Construction and Design
VON SEGGERN, H., Open Space Planning
WEILACHER, U., Landscape Architecture
WÖBSE, H. H., Landscape Aesthetics and Design
WOLSCHKE-BULMAHN, J., Open Space Planning and Garden Architecture
ZIBELL, B., Theory of Architecture

Faculty of Civil Engineering and Geodetic Science (Callinstr. 34, Hanover; tel. (511) 7622447; e-mail dekanat@fb-bauing.uni-hannover.de; internet www.fb-bauing.uni-hannover.de):

ACHMUS, M., Foundations, Dams
BILLIB, M., Hydrology
BLÜMEL, W., Foundations, Dams
DAMRATH, R., Applied Informatics
DOEDENS, H., Water Supply
FRIEDRICH, B., Traffic Economics, Highway System, Town Planning
GRÜNBERG, J., Concrete Construction
HOFFMANN, B., Hydrology
HOTHAN, J., Traffic Economics, Highway Systems, Town Planning
IWAN, G., Construction Management
KONECNY, G., Photogrammetry and Engineering Surveying
KUNST, S., Water Supply
LECHER, K., Hydrology
LIERSE, J., Building Construction
LOHAUS, L., Building Materials Science
MARKOFSKY, M., Flow Mechanics
MULL, R., Hydrology
MÜLLER, U., Graduate Centre for Environmentally Relevant Fluxes in Water and Soil
MÜLLER-KIRCHENBAUER, H., Foundations, Dams
NACKENHORST, U., Mechanics and Computational Mechanics
PELZER, H., General Surveying
ROKAHR, R., Statics and Geomechanics
ROSEMEIER, G., Flow Mechanics
ROSENWINKEL, K.-H., Water Supply
ROTHERT, H., Statics
SCHAUMANN, P., Steel Construction
SCHELLING, W., Building Technology
SEEBER, G., Geodesy
SESTER, M., Cartography
SIEFERT, T., Railways and Roads
SIEKER, F., Hydrology
VERWORN, H.-R., Hydrology
WRIGGERS, P., Mechanics and Computational Mechanics
ZIELKE, W., Flow Mechanics
ZIMMERMANN, C., Hydroengineering

Faculty of Economics and Management (Königsworther Platz 1, 30167 Hanover; tel. (511) 7625350; e-mail heer@mbox.vul.uni-hannover.de; internet www.wiwi.uni-hannover.de):

BREITNER, M. H., Computer Science
FÖRSTER, G., Business Taxation
GEIGANT, F., Money, Credit, Currency
GERLACH, K., Political Economy and Labour Economics
HANSEN, U., Marketing
HASLINGER, F., Economics
HEINEMANN, H.-J., International Economic Relations
HOFMANN, CH., Controlling
HOMBURG, S., Public Economics
HÜBL, L., Economic Policy
HÜBLER, O., Econometrics
JÖHNK, M.-D., Econometrics and Statistics
KIRSCH, H.-J., Economics
LÖFFLER, A., Economics
MENKHOFF, L., Money, Credit, Currency
MEYER, W., Economic Policy
MÜLLER, U., Economic Systems, Anti-Trust Policy and Stabilization
RIDDER, H.-G., Personnel Management
SCHMIDT, U., Economics
SCHULENBURG, J.-M. GRAF VON DER, Insurance
SCHWARZE, J., Computer Science
STEINLE, C., Management Economics
WAIBEL, H., Horticultural Economics
WIEDMANN, K.-P., Marketing

Faculty of Electrical Engineering and Computer Science (Appelstr. 9A, 30167 Hanover; tel. (511) 76219645; e-mail fbbuero@et.uni-hannover.de; internet www.et.uni-hannover.de):

BARKE, E., Microelectronic Systems
EUL, H., High Frequency Technology
GARBE, H., Basic Electrical Engineering
GERTH, W., Control Technology
GOCKENBACH, E., High Voltage
GRABINSKI, H., Theoretical Electrical Engineering
GRAUL, J., Semiconductor Technology and Materials of Electrical Engineering
HAASE, H., Electrical Engineering
HOFMANN, K., Semiconductor Technology and Materials of Electrical Engineering
JOBMANN, K., General Communications Technology
KUCHENBECKER, H.-P., General Communications Technology
LIEDTKE, C.-E., Theoretical Communications Technology
MARQUARDT, J., High Frequency Technology
MATHIS, W., Theoretical Electrical Engineering
MUCHA, J., Theoretical Electrical Engineering
MÜLLER-SCHLOER, C., Computing Sciences
MUSMANN, H.-G., Theoretical Communications Technology
NACKE, B., Electrical Process Technology
NEJDL, W., Knowledge-Based Systems
NESTLER, J., Power Electronics
OSTEN, J., Technology and Materials of Electrical Engineering
OSWALD, B. R., Electricity Supply
PIRSCH, P., Microelectronical Engineering
PONICK, B., Electrical Machines and Drives
SEINSCH, H. O., Electrical Machines and Drives
STÖLTING, H.-D., Electrical Machines and Drives
WAGNER, B., Electrical Systems and Teaching of Electrical Engineering

Faculty of Law (Königsworther Platz 1, 30167 Hanover; tel. (511) 7628104; e-mail dekanat@jura.rw.uni-hannover.de; internet www.jura.uni-hannover.de):

ABELTSHAUSER, T., Civil Law
BUCK, P., Civil Law
BUTZER, H., Public Law
CALLIESS, R.-P., Criminal Law
DORNDORF, E., Civil Law
EPPING, V., Public Law
FABER, H., Public Law
FENGE, H., Civil Law
FOLZ, H.-E., Public Law
FORGÓ, N., Civil Law
FRANK, J., Economics
HESSE, H. A., Teaching of Law, Sociology of Law
KILIAN, W., Civil Law
KÜHNE, J.-D., Public Law
MAGOULAS, G., Economics
MASSING, O., Politics
MEDER, S., Civil Law, History of Law
MEIER, B.-D., Criminal Law
NAHAMOWITZ, P., Theory of Organization and Planning
NOCKE, M., Teaching of Law
OPPERMANN, B., Civil Law
PFEIFFER, C., Criminology
RÜPING, H., Criminal Law
SALJE, P., Civil Law
SCHNEIDER, H.-P., Public Law
SCHWARZE, R., Civil Law
SCHWERDTFEGER, G., Public Law
TREIBER, H., Theory of Organization and Planning
WAECHTER, K., Public Law
WALTHER, M., Teaching of Law and Philosophy
WENDELING-SCHRÖDER, U., Civil Law
WOLF, CH., Civil Law
ZIELINSKI, D., Criminal Law

Faculty of Mathematics and Physics (tel. (511) 7624466; e-mail dekanat@math.uni-hannover.de):

BARINGHAUS, L., Mathematical Stochastics
BARKE, E., Microelectronic Systems
BÄUERLE, N., Mathematical Stochastics
BESSENRODT, CH., Mathematics
BOTHMER, H.-CH. V., Mathematics
BREHM, B., Atomic Processes
DANZMANN, K., Experimental Physics
DEMMIG, F., Plasma Physics
DRAGON, N., Theoretical Physics
EBELING, W., Mathematics
ERNÉ, M., Mathematics
ERTMER, W., Experimental Physics
ESCHER, J., Applied Mathematics
ETLING, D., Theoretical Meteorology
EVERTS, H.-U., Theoretical Physics
FORSTER, P., Applied Mathematics
GROSS, G., Meteorology
GROSSER, J., Atomic Processes
GRÜBEL, R., Probability Theory and Statistics
HAUF, T., Meteorology
HAUG, R., Experimental Physics

HEINE, J., Applied Mathematics
HENZLER, M., Experimental Physics
HOTJE, H., Mathematics
HULEK, K., Mathematics
KOCK, M., Plasma Physics
LECHTENFELD, O., Theoretical Physics
LEWENSTEIN, M., Theoretical Physics
LIPECK, U., Computer Science
MIKESKA, H. J., Theoretical Physics
MÜHLBACH, G., Approximation Theory and Numerical Analysis
MÜLLER, D., Computer Science
NEJDL, W., Computer Science
OESTREICH, M., Experimental Physics
PARCHMANN, R., Computer Science
PFNÜR, H., Experimental Physics
PIRSCH, P., Microelectronic Systems
PRALLE, H., Head of Regional Computer Centre, Lower Saxony
REINEKE, J., Mathematics
SAUER, P. U., Theoretical Physics
SCHMIDT-WESTPHAL, U., Mathematics
SCHNOEGE, K. J., Applied Mathematics
SCHULZ, E., Plasma Physics
SCHULZ, H., Theoretical Physics
SECKMEYER, G., Meteorology
STARKE, G., Applied Mathematics
STEFFENS, K., Mathematics
STEPHAN, E., Applied Mathematics
SZCZERBICKA, H., Systems Engineering
TIEMANN, E., Experimental Physics
VOLLMER, H., Computer Science
WAGNER, B., Systems Engineering
WELLEGEHAUSEN, B., Applied Physics
WOLTER, F.-E., Applied Systems
ZAWISCHA, D., Theoretical Physics

Faculty of Mechanical Engineering (Im Moore 11B, 30167 Hanover; tel. (511) 7622779; e-mail dekan@maschinenbau.uni-hannover.de; internet www.maschinenbau.uni-hannover.de):

BACH, F.-W., Materials
BESDO, D., Mechanics
BRAUNE, R., Mechanisms and Machine Elements
DEKENA, B., Production Engineering and Machine Tools
DOEGE, E., Metal Forming and Machines
GATZEN, H.-H., Microtechnology
GERTH, W., Machine Dynamics
GIETZELT, M., Steam and Fuel Engineering
HAFERKAMP, H. D., Materials
HALLENSLEBEN, M. L., Macromolecular Chemistry
HEIMANN, B., Machine Dynamics
KABELAC, S., Thermodynamics
LOUIS, H., Material Testing
MEIER, G. E. A., Fluid Mechanics
MERKER, G. P., Internal Combustion Engine
MEWES, D., Chemical Engineering
NYHUIS, P., Factory Building and Logistics
OVERMEYER, L., Conveying Technology and Mining Machinery
POLL, G., Construction Science
POPP, K., Mechanics
RAUTENBERG, M., Radial Compressors
REDEKER, G., Factory Building
REHFELDT, D., Welding Technology
REITHMEIER, E., Measurement and Control Technology
RIESS, W., Turbo Machinery
ROSEMANN, H., Construction Science
SCHULZE, L., Department Planning, Control of Warehouse and Transport Systems
SCHWERES, M., Labour Science, Ergonomics
SENME, J., Turbo Machinery
STEGEMANN, D., Nuclear Technology
VOSS, G., Railway Machines
WIENDAHL, H.-P., Plant Engineering and Production Control

Faculty of Natural Sciences (Schneiderberg 50, 30167 Hanover; tel. (511) 7623318; internet www.unics.uni-hannover.de/geo/index.html):

ANDERS, A., Biophysics
ARNOLD, A., Human Geography
AULING, G., Microbiology
BECKER, J. A., Physical Chemistry
BEHRENS, P., Inorganic Chemistry
BELLGARDT, K.-H., Technical Chemistry
BERGER, R. G., Applied Chemistry
BINNEWIES, M., Inorganic Chemistry
BÖTTCHER, J., Soil Science
BRAKHAGE, A., Microbiology
BUCHHOLZ, H. J., Human Geography
BUHL, J.-CH., Mineralogy
BUTENSCHÖN, H., Organic Chemistry
CARO, J., Physical Chemistry
DUDDECK, H., Organic Chemistry
FENDRIK, I., Biophysics
FISCHER, R., Palaeontology
FISCHER, W. R., Soil Science
HAHN, A., Domestic Technology
HALLENSLEBEN, M. L., Macromolecular Chemistry
HAU, B., Phytopathology
HEITJANS, P., Physical Chemistry
HESSE, D., Technical Chemistry
HITZMANN, B., Technical Chemistry
HOFFMANN, H. M. R., Organic Chemistry
HOLTZ, F., Mineralogy
HÖRMANN, D., Gardening Management
HORST, W., Plant Nutrition
HOTHORN, L., Biology Informatics
HUCHZERMEYER, B., Botany
HÜPPE, J., Palaeoecology
IMBIHL, R., Physical Chemistry
JACOBSEN, H.-J., Molecular Biology
JUG, K., Theoretical Chemistry
KIRSHNING, A., Organic Chemistry
KLOPPSTECH, K., Botany
KOLB, A., Biophysics
KRETZMER, G., Technical Chemistry
KUHLMANN, H., Plant Nutrition
KUHNT, G., Physical Geography
KUSTER, H., Palaeoecology
LIEFNER, I., Economic Geography
MAISS, E., Phytopathology
MARTEN, I., Biophysics
MEYER, H. H., Organic Chemistry
MOSIMANN, T., Physical Geography
NAUMANN, I., Domestic Technology
NIEMEYER, R., Botany
POTT, R., Botany
RATH, T., Horticulture
ROTZOLL, G., Technical Chemistry
SCHÄTZL, L., Economic Geography
SCHENK, E.-W., Gardening Management and Accountancy
SCHENK, M., Plant Nutrition
SCHEPER, T., Technical Chemistry
SCHERER, G., Crop Physiology
SCHMIDT, A., Botany
SCHMIDT, E., Horticultural Economics
SCHMITZ, U. K., Applied Genetics
SCHÖNHERR, J., Fruit Science
SCHÜLKE, I., Geology
SCHÜNGERL, K., Technical Chemistry
SEREK, M., Gardening Management and Accountancy
SPETHMANN, W., Nursery Gardening
STÜTZEL, Vegetable Science
TANTAU, H.-J., Horticultural Engineering
TATLIOGLU, T., Applied Genetics
URLAND, W., Inorganic Chemistry
VAN DER PLOEG, R., Soil Science
VOGT, C., Inorganic Chemistry
VON BLANCKENBURG, F., Mineralogy
WAIBEL, H., Horticultural Economics
WATKINSON, B. M., Food Science
WINSEMANN, J., Geology
WINTERFELDT, E., Organic Chemistry
WÜNSCH, G., Inorganic Chemistry
ZIMMER, K., Ornamental Plants

Faculty of Philosophy (Königsworther Platz 1, 30167 Hanover; tel. (511) 7624556; e-mail dekanat@fbls.uni-hannover.de; internet www.fbls.uni-hannover.de):

ACHINGER, G., Sociology
AHLERS, I., Human Geography
ANTES, P., Study of Religions
ASCHOFF, H.-G., Modern History and Ecclesiastical History
AVERKORN, R., Medieval History
BARMEYER-HARTLIEB, H., Modern History
BAUSENHART, G., Roman Catholic Religious Education
BAYER, K., German
BECKER-SCHMIDT, R., Psychology
BERG, D., Medieval History
BEUTLER, K., Education
BEZZEL, CH., German Language
BICKES, H., German Language
BILLMANN-MAHECHA, H., Psychology
BINDEL, W.-R., Special Education
BIRKNER, G., English Philology
BLANKE, B., Political Science
BLELL, G., Teaching of English
BLEY, H., Modern History
BOLSCHO, D., Pedagogy
BÖNSCH, M., School Pedagogy
BRODTMANN, D., Sports
BROKMEIER, P., Political Science
BRÜGGEMANN, H., Modern German Literature
BUCKMILLER, M., Political Science
BULTHAUP, P., Philosophy
CALLIES, H., Ancient History
CLAUSSEN, D., Sociology
DAIBER, K.-F., Study of Religions
DIEWALD, G., Modern German Literature
DISCHNER-VOGEL, G., Modern German Literature
DITTRICH, J.-H., Technology of Clothing and Textiles
DORDEL, H. J., Sports
DUDEN, B., Sociology
EBINGHAUS, H., Physics
EGGERT, D., Psychology
EGGS, E., Romance Philology and Language
EHRHARDT, J., Education
EHRHARDT, M. L., German
FELDMANN, K., Sociology
FISCHER, H., German Literature
FRACKMANN, M., Social Education
FRANZKE, R., Social Education
FÜLLBERG-STOLLBERG, O., Modern History
GHOLAMASAD, D., Sociology
GIPSER, D., Special Education
GLAGE, L., English Literature
GLITHO, S., Modern German Literature
GÖRTZ, H.-J., Roman Catholic Religious Education
HAENSCH, D., Political Science
HASEMANN, K., Mathematics
HAUPTMEYER, C.-H., Early Medieval History
HEINEMANN, M., Education
HERWIG, J., Music
HIEBER, L., Sociology
HOECKER, B., Political Science
HOEGES, D., Romance Philology and Literature
HÖLKER, K., Romance Philology and Literature
HORSTER, D., Education
ILIEN, A., Education
JANSSEN, B., School Pedagogy
JETTER, K., Therapy
JOHANNSEN, F., Evangelical Religious Education
JUNGK, D., Vocational Education
KENTLER, H., Social Education
KIESELBACH, T., Psychology
KNAPP, G.-A., Psychology
KOETHEN, E., Art and Visual Media, Teaching of Art and Visual Media
KÖPCKE, K. M., German
KORFF, F.-W., Philosophy
KREUTZER, L., Modern German Literature

KRIWET, I., Education of Mentally Handicapped People
KROVOZA, A., Psychology
KRUIP, G., Roman Catholic Religious Education
KÜHNE, A., Psychology
KUNTZ, K. M., Education
KUPETZ, R., Teaching of English, Applied Linguistics
LAGA, G., Sociology
LEMKE, C., Political Science
LENK, E., German Literature
LOHRER-PAPE, Arts
LUDWIG, O., German Language
MANZ, W., Vocational Education
MAYER, R., English Literature
MENSCHING, G., Philosophy
MESCHKAT, K., Sociology
MICKLER, O., Sociology
MÜHLHAUSEN, K., Education
MÜLLER, R.-W., Political Science
NARR, R., School Pedagogy
NAUMANN, G., Home Technology
NAUMANN, H., German
NEGT, O., Sociology
NOLL, A.-H., Social Studies
NOLTE, H.-H., Medieval History
NOORMANN, J., Teaching of Evangelical Relations
OELSCHLÄGER, H., Educational Planning and Reform
PAEFGEN, E., German
PEIFFER, L., Sports
PERELS, J., Political Science
PETERS, J., Modern German Literature
RAUFUSS, D., Education
RECTOR, M., Modern German Literature
REHKÄMPER, K., Modern German Literature
REISER, H., Special Education
REUMANN, R.-D., Technology of Clothing and Textiles
RIEDEL, M., Modern History
RIEMEN, F., Music
RIES, W., Philosophy
ROHLOFF, H., English Philosophy
RUNTE, A., Modern German Literature
RUST, H., Sociology
RÜTTERS, K., Vocational Education
SANDERS, H., Romance Philology and Literature
SAUER, W., German Language
SCHAEFFNER, L., Adult Education
SCHÄFER, G., Political Science
SCHLOBINSKI, P., German Language
SCHMAUDERER, E., Food Science
SCHMID, H.-D., History and History Teaching
SCHMIDT, M., Adult Education
SCHMITZ, K., Education
SCHÖNBERGER, F., Special Education
SCHREIBER, G., Technology of Clothing and Textile
SCHUCHARDT, E., Education
SCHULZE, R., English Language and Linguistics
SCHWARZ, B., Medieval History
SIEBERT, H., Adult Education
STIMPFLE, A., Roman Catholic Religious Education
SWIENTEK, CH., Special Education
TIEDEMANN, J., Psychology
TILCH, H., Social Education
TREBELS, A. H., Sports
TROCHOLEPCZY, B., Roman Catholic Religious Education
URBAN, A., Psychology
VASSEN, F., Modern German Literature
VESTER, M., Political Science
VON SALDERN, A., Modern History
WACKER, A., Psychology
WAGNER-HASEL, B., Ancient History
WATKINSON, B. M., Food Science
WEBER, H., English Philology
WELLENDORF, F., Psychology
WELZER, H., Psychology
WENZEL, F., Scientific and Technical Russian
WERNER, W., Roman Catholic Religious Education
WERNING, R., Education of Mentally Handicapped People
WILHARM, I., History and History Teaching
WILKEN, E., Special Education
WIPPERMANN, H., Mathematics
WÜNDERICH, V., Latin American History
WÜNDERICH, V., Sociology
ZIEHE, T., Education

LEUPHANA UNIVERSITÄT LÜNEBURG

Scharnhorststr. 1, 21335 Lüneburg
Telephone: (4131) 6770
E-mail: praesidium@leuphana.de
Internet: www.leuphana.de

Founded 1946
State control

Pres.: Prof. Dr SASCHA SPOUN
Vice-Pres.: Prof. Dr BURKHARDT FUNK
Vice-Pres.: Prof. Dr FERDINAND MÜLLER-ROMMEL
Vice-Pres.: HOLM KELLER
Vice-Pres.: Prof. Dr NILS OLE OERMANN
Librarian: TORSTEN AHRENS

Library of 664,000 vols, 1,255 print journals, 23,296 ejournals
Number of teachers: 443
Number of students: 7,541
Publication: *Forschungsberichte* (every 3 years)

DEANS

Faculty of Business and Economics: Prof. Dr THOMAS WEIN
Faculty of Education: Prof. Dr SILKE RUWISCH
Faculty of Humanities and Social Sciences: Prof. Dr PETER PEZ
Faculty of Sustainability: Prof. Dr Ing. WOLFGANG K. L. RUCK

LUDWIG-MAXIMILIANS-UNIVERSITÄT MÜNCHEN

Geschwister-Scholl-Pl. 1, 80539 Munich
Telephone: (89) 21800
E-mail: praesidium@lmu.de
Internet: www.lmu.de

Founded 1472
Academic year: October to July

Pres.: Prof. Dr BERND HUBER
Vice-Pres.: Prof. Dr BEATE KELLNER
Vice-Pres.: Prof. Dr CHRISTOPH MÜLKE
Vice-Pres.: Prof. Dr MARTIN WIRSING
Vice-Pres.: Dr SIGMUND STIUTZING
Vice-Pres.: Prof. Dr ULRICH POHL
Dir of Library: Dr KLAUS-RAINER BRINTZINGER

Library: see under Libraries and Archives
Number of teachers: 3,576
Number of students: 46,723
Publications: *'Einsichten'* (1 a year), *LMU at a glance* (every 2 years), *MUM* (4 a year), *Veranstaltungskalender* (12 a year), *Vorlesungsverzeichnis* (2 a year)

DEANS

Faculty of Biology: Prof. Dr BENEDIKT GROTHE
Faculty of Business Administration: Prof. Dr THOMAS HESS
Faculty of Catholic Theology: Prof. Dr KONRAD HILPERT
Faculty of Chemistry and Pharmacy: Prof. Dr MARTIN BEIL
Faculty of Cultural Studies: Prof. Dr KLAUS VOLLMER
Faculty of Economics: Prof. Dr ANDREAS HAUFLER
Faculty of Geosciences: Prof. Dr WOLFRAM MAUSER
Faculty of History and the Arts: Prof. Dr MARIE-JANINE CALIC
Faculty of Languages and Literatures: Prof. Dr ULRICH SCHWEIER
Faculty of Law: Prof. Dr ALFONS BÜRGE
Faculty of Mathematics, Computer Science and Statistics: Prof. Dr HEINRICH HUSSMANN
Faculty of Medicine: Prof. Dr MAXMILIAN REISER
Faculty of Philosophy, Philosophy of Science and the Study of Religion: Prof. Dr JULIAN NIDA-RUEMELIN
Faculty of Physics: Prof. Dr AXEL SCHENZLE
Faculty of Protestant Theology: Prof. Dr CHRISTOPH LEVIN
Faculty of Psychology and Educational Sciences: Prof. Dr JOACHIM KAHLERT
Faculty of Social Sciences: Prof. Dr HANS-BERND BROSIUS
Faculty of Veterinary Medicine: Prof. Dr JOACHIM BRAUN

MARTIN LUTHER-UNIVERSITÄT HALLE-WITTENBERG

06099 Halle (Saale)
Universitätspl. 10, 06108 Halle
Telephone: (345) 5520
E-mail: rektor@uni-halle.de
Internet: www.uni-halle.de

Founded 1502 (Wittenberg), 1694 (Halle), 1817 (Halle-Wittenberg)
Academic year: October to September

Rector: Prof. Dr UDO STRÄTER
Vice-Rector: Prof. Dr CHRISTOPH WEISER
Vice-Rector: Prof. BIRGIT DRÄGER
Vice-Rector: Prof. Dr GESINE FOLJANTY-JOST
Chancellor: Dr MARTIN HECHT

Number of teachers: 340
Number of students: 17,500
Publication: *Scientia halensis* (4 a year)

DEANS

Faculty of Law, Economics and Business: Prof. Dr CHRISTIAN TIETJE
Faculty of Medicine: Prof. Dr MICHAEL GEKLE
Faculty of Natural Sciences I: Prof. Dr REINHARD NEUBERT
Faculty of Natural Sciences II: Prof. Dr WOLF WIDDRA
Faculty of Natural Sciences III: Prof. Dr PETER WYCISK
Faculty of Philosophy I: Prof. Dr BURKHARD SCHNEPEL
Faculty of Philosophy II: Prof. Dr GERD ANTOS
Faculty of Philosophy III: Prof. Dr HARALD SCHWILLUS
Faculty of Theology: Prof. Dr MICHAEL DOMSGEN

MEDIZINISCHE HOCHSCHULE HANNOVER
(Hanover Medical School)

Carl-Neuberg-Str. 1, 30625 Hanover
Telephone: (511) 5320
E-mail: pressestelle@mh-hannover.de
Internet: www.mh-hannover.de

Founded 1965

Pres.: Prof. Dr DIETER BITTER-SUERMANN
Vice-Pres.: Dr ANDREAS TECKLENBURG
Vice-Pres.: HOLGER BAUMANN
Librarian: Dr ANNAMARIE FELSCH-KLOTZ

Library of 280,000 vols
Number of teachers: 614
Number of students: 3,197

DEANS

Biology: Prof. Dr G. GROS
Dentistry: Prof. Dr H. TSCHERNITSCHEK

Medicine: Prof. Dr HERMANN HALLER

PROFESSORS

Anatomy:

GROTE, C., Neuroanatomy
GRUBE, D., Microscopic Anatomy
PABST, R., Functional and Applied Anatomy
UNGEWICKELL, E., Anatomy

Biochemistry:

GAESTEL, M., Physiological Chemistry
GERARDY-SCHAHN, R., Cellular Chemistry
LENZEN, S., Biochemistry
MANSTEIN, D., Biophysical Chemistry

Laboratory Medicine:

BLASCZYK, R., Transfusion Medicine
FÖRSTER, R., Immunology
GOSSLER, A., Molecular Biology
HEDRICH, H.-J., Animal Research
SCHULZ, T., Laboratory Medicine
SUERBAUM, S., Microbiology and Hospital Hygiene

Medical Technologies:

HECKER, H., Biometry
MATTHIES, H., Medical Computing

Pathology, Genetics and Forensic Medicine:

KREIPE, H.-H., Pathology
SCHLEGELBERGER, B., Pathology, Genetics and Forensic Medicine
SCHMIDTKE, J., Human Genetics
TRÖGER, H.-D., Medical Law

Pharmacology and Toxicology:

JUST, I., Toxicology
RESCH, K., Pharmacology
STICHTENOTH, O., Clinical Pharmacology
WRBITZKY, R., Occupational Medicine

Physiology:

BRENNER, B., Molecular and Cell Physiology
FAHLKE, C., Neurophysiology
GROS, G., Vegetative Physiology
MAASEEN, N., Sports Physiology/Sports Medicine

Public Health Care:

GEYER, S., Medical Sociology
HUMMERS-PRADIER, E., General Medicine
LANGE, K., Medical Psychology
LOHFF, B., History, Ethics and Philosophy of Medicine
SCHWARTZ, F. W., Epidemiology, Social Medicine and Health Systems Research

OTTO-FRIEDRICH-UNIVERSITÄT BAMBERG

Kapuzinerstr. 16, 96045 Bamberg
Telephone: (951) 8630
E-mail: post@uni-bamberg.de
Internet: www.uni-bamberg.de

Founded 1647
State control
Academic year: October to September (2 semesters)

Pres.: Prof. Dr Hab. GODEHARD RUPPERT
Vice-Pres. for Research: Prof. Dr ANNA STEINWEG
Vice-Pres. for Teaching: Prof. Dr SEBASTIAN KEMPGEN
Chancellor: Dr DAGMAR STEUER-FLIESER
Librarian: Dr FABIAN FRANKE

Library: see under Libraries and Archives
Number of teachers: 138
Number of students: 10,409

Publications: *Bamberger Beiträge zur Englischen Sprachwissenschaft* (1 a year), *Bamberger Editionen. Hg. v. H. Unger und H. Wentzlaff-Eggebert*, *Bamberger Geographische Schriften* (1–2 a year), *Bamberger Universitätszeitung "uni.doc"* (7 a year), *Bericht des Rektors*, *Gratia: Bamberger Schriften zur Renaissanceforschung* (2 a year), *Forschungsforum* (1 a year), *Informationen* (irregular), *Personal- und Vorlesungsverzeichnis* (1 a term), *Pressemitteilungen*, *Uni.kat*, *uni.-vers* (2 a year)

DEANS

Faculty of Human Sciences and Education: Prof. Dr SIBYLLE RAHM
Faculty of Humanities: Prof. Dr KLAUS VAN EICKELS
Faculty of Information Systems and Applied Computer Science: Prof. Dr CHRISTOPH SCHLIEDER
Faculty of Social Sciences, Economics and Business Administration: Prof. Dr THOMAS GEHRING

PROFESSORS

Faculty of Human Sciences and Education:

ARTELT, C., Educational Research
BEDFORD-STROHM, H., Protestant Theology/Systematic Theology and Contemporary Theological Issues
BENDER, W., Andragogy
CARBON, C., General Psychology and Methodology
CARSTENSEN, C., Psychology (Empirical Educational Research)
FAUST, G., Primary School Education
HERAN-DÖRR, E., Primary School Education (Science Education)
HOCK, M., Educational Psychology
HÖRMANN, G., Pedagogics
HÖRMANN, S., Music Pedagogy and Music Didactics
LAUTENBACHER, S., Physiological Psychology
LAUX, L., Psychology
RAHM, S., School Education
REINECKER, H., Clinical Psychology and Psychotherapy
RITTER, W., Protestant Theology/Religious Pedagogy and Didactics
ROßBACH, H., Early Childhood Education
RÜSSELER, J., General Psychology
SCHAAL, S., Science Education
SCHÄFER, CH., Philosophy I
SCHRÖDTER, M., Social Pedagogy
STEINWEG, A., Mathematics Education and Computer Science Education
WEINERT, S., Developmental Psychology
WOLSTEIN, J., Pathopsychology

Faculty of Humanities:

ABRAHAM, U., German Language and Literature Instruction
ALBRECHT, S., Art History (Medieval Art History)
ALZHEIMER, H., European Ethnology
BARTL, A., Modern German Literature
BECKER, T., German Linguistics
BEHMER, M., Media Studies (Journalism Research)
BEHZADI, L., Arabic Studies
BENNEWITZ, I., Medieval German Philology
BIEBERSTEIN, K., Old Testament
BRANDT, H., Ancient History
BRASSAT, W., History of Art (Early Modern and Modern Art)
BREITLING, S., Building Research
BRUNS, P., Church History and Patrology
DE RENTIIS, D., Romance Philology
DIX, A., Historical Geography
DORNHEIM, A., Modern and Contemporary History
DREWELLO, R., Building Preservation Sciences
ECKER, H., Diffusion Processes of Literature
ENZENSBERGER, H., History (Diplomatics and Palaeography)
ERICSSON, I., Medieval and Post Medieval Archaeology
FÖLLINGER, S., Greek Studies
FRANKE, P., Islamic Studies
FREYBERGER, B., History Instruction
GIER, A., Romance Literature
GLÜCK, H., German Linguistics and German as a Foreign Language
GÖLER, D., Human Geography I (Social and Population Geography)
HAASE, M., Romance Philology
HÄBERLEIN, M., Early Modern History
HEIMBACH-STEINS, M., Christian Social Theory
HERZOG, C., Turkish Studies
HOFFMANN, B., Iranian Studies
HOUSWITSCHKA, C., English Literature
HUBEL, A., Monument Preservation and Restoration
ILLIES, C., Philosophy II
ILYASOV, D., Islamic Art and Archaeology
JANSOHN, C., British Culture
JÜNKE, C., Spanish and Latin American Literature
KEMPGEN, S., Slavic Linguistics
KONRAD, M., Archaeology of the Roman Provinces
KORN, L., Islamic Art and Archaeology
KRUG, M., English Linguistics
KÜGLER, J., New Testament Sciences
MARX, F., Modern German Literature
MÜLLER, M., English and American Studies (American Literatures)
NOEL, P., German Linguistics
RAEV, A., Slavic Art and Cultural History
RAHNER, J., Systematic Theology
SAALFELD, T., Comparative Politics
SCHÄFER, A., Prehistoric Archaelogy
SCHAMBECK, M., Religious Education
SCHELLMANN, G., Geography II (Physical Geography and Landscape History)
SCHINDLER, A., Medieval German Philology
SCHÖTTLER, H., Pastoral Theology
STÖBER, R., Communication Studies
TALABARDON, S., Jewish Studies
THEIS-BERGLMAIR, A., Communication Theory and Journalism
ULRICH, M., Romance Linguistics
VAN EICKELS, K., Medieval History incl. Regional History of the Middle Ages
VON ERDMANN, E., Slavic Literatures
WAGNER-BRAUN, M., Economic and Innovation History

Faculty of Information Systems and Applied Computer Science:

FERSTL, O., Information Systems (Industrial Application Systems)
HEINRICH, A., Media Informatics
KRIEGER, U., Computer Networks Group
LÜTTGEN, G., Software Engineering and Programming Languages
MENDLER, M., Foundation of Computer Science
SCHLIEDER, C., Computing in the Cultural Sciences
SCHMID, U., Applied Informatics (Cognitive Systems)
SINZ, E. J., Information Systems (Systems Engineering)
WEITZEL, T., Information Systems and Services
WIRTZ, G., Practical Computer Science, Distributed and Mobile Systems

Faculty of Social Sciences, Economics and Business Administration (Feldkirchenstr. 21, 96052 Bamberg; tel. (951) 8632501; e-mail dekanat@sowi.uni-bamberg.de; internet www.uni-bamberg.de/sowi):

ANDRESEN, M., Human Resource Management
BECKER, W., Business Administration
BIRK, U.-A., Social Security
BLIEN, U., Sociology (Labour Market and Area Studies)
BLOSSFELD, H., Sociology
BRÜCKER, H., Economics (European Markets)
DERLIEN, H., Public Administration
ECKEL, C., International Economics

EGNER, T., Business Administration and Taxation
EIERLE, B., International Accounting and Auditing
ENGELHARD, J., Business Administration (International Management)
ENGELHARDT-WÖLFLER, H., Population Studies
GEHRING, T., International Policy
IVENS, B., Marketing
MUCK, M., Financial Control
MÜNCH, R., Sociology
OEHLER, A., Finance, Management, and Business Administration
PIEPER, R., Town and Social Planning
RÄSSLER, S., Statistics and Econometrics
RIEGER, E., Sociology of Transnational and Global Processes
SCHNEIDER, T., Sociology (Educational Inequality in the Life-Course)
SCHOEN, H., Political Sociology
SCHWARZE, J., Social Policy
SEMBILL, D., Business and Human Resource Education
STOCKÉ, V., Sociology (Longitudinal Educational Research)
STRUCK, O., Ergonomics and Sociology of Work
SUCKY, E., Operations Management and Business Logistics
WALZL, M., Economics (Industrial Economics)
WENZEL, H., Public Economics
WESTERHOFF, F., Economics (Economic Policy)
ZINTL, R., Political Science
ZOHLNHÖFER, R., Comparative Public Policy

OTTO-VON-GUERICKE-UNIVERSITÄT MAGDEBURG

POB 4120, 39016 Magdeburg
Universitätspl. 2, 39106 Magdeburg
Telephone: (391) 6701
E-mail: rektor@ovgu.de
Internet: www.ovgu.de

Founded 1953, present status 1993
State control
Academic year: October to September (2 semesters)
Chancellor: VOLKER ZEHLE (acting)
Rector: Prof. Dr JENS STRACKELJAN
Vice-Rector for Planning and Devt: Prof. Dr JÜRGEN CHRISTEN
Vice-Rector for Research: Prof. Dr VOLKER LEHMANN
Vice-Rector for Study: Prof. Dr FRANTISKA SCHEFFLER
Librarian: Dr Ing. ECKHARD BLUME
Library of 1,220,336 vols, 2,223 journals, 22,736 ejournals
Number of teachers: 1,743
Number of students: 13,891
Publications: *Research-Report* (1 a year), *Science Journal* (2 a year), *Uni-Report* (12 a year)

DEANS

Faculty of Computer Sciences: Prof. Dr GUNTER SAAKE
Faculty of Economics and Management: Prof. Dr KARL-HEINZ PAQUÉ
Faculty of Electrical Engineering and Information Technology: Prof. Dr ANDREAS LINDEMANN
Faculty of Humanities: Prof. Dr BARBARA DIPPELHOFER-STIEM
Faculty of Mathematics: Prof. Dr ALEXANDER POTT
Faculty of Mechanical Engineering: Prof. Dr KARL-HEINRICH GROTE
Faculty of Medicine: Prof. Dr HERRMANN-JOSEF ROTHKOETTER
Faculty of Natural Sciences: Prof. Dr ANNA KATHARINA BRAUN
Faculty of Process and Systems Engineering: Prof. Dr HELMUT WEISS

PROFESSORS

Faculty of Computer Sciences (Universitätspl. 2, Bldg 29, 39106 Magdeburg; tel. (391) 67-58532):
ARNDT, H.-K., Management Informations Systems
DITTMANN, J., Advanced Multimedia and Security
GROSCH, T., Computational Visualistics
HORTON, G., Simulation and Graphics
KAISER, J., Operating and Distributed Systems
KRUSE, R., Neural and Fuzzy Systems
LINDEMANN, A., Data and Knowledge Engineering
NETT, E., Real-time Systems and Communications
PREIM, B., Computer Graphics
RÖSNER, D., Knowledge and Language Engineering
SAAKE, G., Technical and Business Information Systems
SCHIRRA, S., Algorithmics
SCHULZE, T., Enterprise Modelling and Simulation
SPILIPOULOU, M., Knowledge Management and Discovery
THEISEL, H., Visual Computing
TÖNNIES, K., Computer Graphics
TUROWSKI, K., Business Informatics

Faculty of Economics and Management (Universitätspl. 2, Bldg 22, 39106 Magdeburg; tel. (391) 6718583):
BETHMANN, D., Macroeconomics
BURGARD, U., Civil Rights, Commercial and Economic Law
CHWOLKA, A., Accounting
GISCHER, H., Monetary Economics and Public Finance Economic
INDERFURTH, K., Production and Logistics
KIRSTEIN, R., Economics of Business and Law
KNABE, A., Financial Science
LAUDIEN, S., Int. Management
LUKAS, E., Innovation and Financial Management
MÜLLER, H., Consumer Behaviour
PAQUE, K., Int. Economics
RAITH, M., Entrepreneurship
REICHLING, P., Banks and Finance
SADRIEH, A., e-Business
SARSTEDT, M., Marketing
SCHANZ, S., Taxation
SCHLÄGEL, C., International Business
SCHOENDUBE-PIRCHEGGER, B., Corporate Accounting and Controlling
SPENGLER, T., Corporate Management and Organization
VOGT, B., Empirical Research in Economics
VOIGT, G., Operations Management
WÄSCHER, G., Management Science
WEIMANN, J., Economic Policy

Faculty of Electrical Engineering and Information Technology (Universitätspl. 2, Bldg 10, 39106 Magdeburg; tel. (391) 6718641):
AL-HAMADI, A., Neuroinformation Technology
BURTE, E., Semiconducted Technology
DIEDRICH, C., Integrated Automation
FINDEISEN, R., Systems Theory and Automatic Control
HAUPTMANN, P., Sensors and Measurement Technology
KIENLE, A., Modelling
LEIDHOLD, R., Electric Drive Systems
LEONE, M., Electromagnetic Theory
LINDEMANN, A., Power Electronics
MICHAELIS, B., Technical Computer Science
OMAR, A., RF and Communications Technology
ROSE, G., Medical Telematics
SCHMIDT, B., Microsystems
SEIFFERT, U., Neural Systems
STYCZYNSKI, Z., Power Networks and Renewable Energy Source
VICK, R., Electromagnetic Compatibility
WENDEMUTH, A., Cognitive Systems

Faculty of Humanities (Universitätspl. 2, Bldg 40, 39104 Magdeburg; tel. (391) 6756356):
BELENTSCHIKOW, R., Slavic Studies
BERGIEN, A., English Linguistics
BRUCHHÄUSER, H., Didactics of Business and Admin.
BÜNNING, F., Technical Education and Didactics
BURKHARDT, A., German Linguistics
CHRISTOPHE, B., Int. Relations
DICK, M., Business Education
DIPPELHOFER-STIEM, B, Methods of Empirical Social Research
DÖRNER, O., Adult and Continuing Education
DREHER, M., Ancient History
EDELMANN-NUSSER, J., Sport and Technology
FORNDARN, E., Int. Relations and Political Theory
FREUND, S., Medieval History
FRITZSCHE, P., Human Rights Education
FROMMBERGER, D., Vocational Education
FROMME, J., Educational Science Media Research
FUHRER, U., Developmental and Educational Psychology
GIRMES, R., General Education and Theory of School
GREVE, J., Macro Sociology
JENEWEIN, K., Didactics Technical Subjects
JOBST, S., Int. and Intercultural Education
KAISER, F., Personality and Social Psychology
KERSTEN, H., American Studies
LABOUVIE, E., Modern History/Gender Studies
LOHMANN, G., Practical Philosophy
LYRE, H., Theoretical Philosophy
MAROTZKI, W., General Education
MATTHIES, E., Environmental Psychology
PETERS, S., English Culture and Literature
RAAB, J., Micro Sociology
RENZSCH, W., European Studies
SATJUKOW, S., Modern History
SCHEGA, L., Training and Health
SCHILLING, M., Older Literature
SCHMICKER, S., Organizational Psychology
SCHÜRRMANN, E., Cultural Philosophy, Philosophical Anthropology and Philosophy of Technology
SÜSS, H., Methology, Psychodiagnostic and Evaluation Research
TRAPPMANN, V., European Society
UNGER, T., Modern Literature

Faculty of Mathematics (Universitätspl. 2, Bldg 02, 39106 Magdeburg; tel. (391) 6718663):
AVERKOV, G., Geometry of Optimization
BURKSCHAT, M., Mathematical Stochastic
CHRISTOPH, G., Mathematical Stochastic
DECKELMICK, K., Analysis and Numerics
GAFFKE, N., Mathematical Stochastic
GRUNAU, H., Analysis and Numerics
HENK, M., Algebra and Geometry
HENNING, H., Algebra and Geometry
KAIBEL, V., Discrete Optimization
KLOPSCH, B., Algebra and Geometry
POTT, A., Algebra and Geometry
SAGER, S., Algorithmic Optimization
SCHWABE, R., Mathematical Stochastic
SIMON, M., Analysis and Numerics
TOBISKA, L., Analysis and Numerics
WARNECKE, G., Analysis and Numerics
WILLEMS, W., Algebra and Geometry

Faculty of Mechanical Engineering (Universitätspl. 2, Bldg 10, 39106 Magdeburg; tel. (391) 6718520):

ALTENBACH, H., Technical Mechanics
BERTRAM, A., Strength of Materials
DETERS, L., Mechanical Components and Tribology
GABBERT, U., Numerical Mechanics
GROTE, K., Engineering Design
HALLE, T., Metallic Materials
JÜTTNER, S., Joining Technology
KALTERFELD, A., Material Handling Systems
KARPUSCHEWSKI, B., Machining
KÜHNLE, H., Factory Operations and Manufacturing Systems
MÖHRING, H., Manufacturing Units
MOLITOR, M., Metrology and Quality Management
RICHTER, K., Material Handling Systems
SCHEFFLER, M., Non-metallic Materials
SCHENK, M., Logistical Systems
STRACKELJAN, J., Technical Dynamics
VAJNA, S., Information Technologies in Mechanical Engineering
WITTEN, P., International Distribution Logistics
ZADEK, H., Logistics

Faculty of Medicine (Leipzigerstr. 44, 39120 Magdeburg; tel. (391) 6715762):

BERNARDING, J., Biometrics and Medical Computer Science
BODE-BOEGER, S., Clinical Pharmacology
BÖCKELMANN, I., Occupational Medicine
BRINKSCHULTE, E., History, Ethics and Theory of Medicine
DIETRICH, D., Pharmacology and Toxicology
DÜZEL, E., Cognitive Neurology and Dementia Research
FISCHER, K., Biochemistry and Cell Biology
GARDEMANN, A., Pathobiochemistry
HEIM, M., Transfusion Medicine and Immunohaematology
HERRMANN, M., General Medicine
HOFFMANN, W., Molecular Biology and Medical Chemistry
ISERMANN, B., Clinical Chemistry
LESSIG, R., Forensic Medicine
MAWRIN, C., Neuropathology
NAUMANN, M., Experimental Internal Medicine
REISER, G., Neurobiochemistry
ROBRA, B., Social Medicine and Health Economics
ROESSNER, A., Pathology
ROTHKÖTTER, H., Anatomy
SABEL, B., Medical Psychology
SCHLÜTER, D., Medical Microbiology
SCHRAVEN, B., Molecular and Clinical Immunology
SKALEY, M., Neuroradiology
ZENKER, M., Human Genetics

Faculty of Natural Sciences (Universitätspl. 2, Bldg 16, 39106 Magdeburg; tel. (391) 6718676):

BOCK, J., Structural Plasticity
BRAUN, A., Zoology/Developmental Neurobiology
BRAUN, J., Cognitive Biology
CHRISTEN, J., Solid State Physics
GOLDHAHN, R., Experimental Physics/Materials Physics
HAUSER, M., Biophysics
KASSNER, K., Computational Theoretical Physics
KORZ, V., Neuronal and Behavioural Plasticity
KROST, A., Semiconductor Epitaxy
MARWAN, W., Regulatory Biology
MERTENS, S., Statistical Physics and Nonlinear Dynamics
MÜLLER, S., Structure Formation
NOESSELT, T., Biological Psychology
OHL, F., Neuroprostheses
POLLMANN, S., Experimental Psychology
RICHTER, J., Theory of Condensed Matter II
SCHAPER, F., Systems Biology
SPECK, O., Biomedical Magnetic Resonance
STANNARIUS, R., Non-linear Phenomena
STORCK, O., Genetics and Molecular Neurobiology
ULLSPERGER, M., Neuropsychology
WIERSIG, J., Theory of Condensed Matter I

Faculty of Process and Systems Engineering (Universitätspl. 2, Bldg 10, 39106 Magdeburg; tel. (391) 6718442):

EDELMANN, F., Inorganic Chemistry
HAAK, E., Organic Chemistry
KÖSER, H., Environmental Engineering
KRAUSE, U., Engineering and Plant Safety
MÖRL, L., Chemical Apparatus Construction
REICHL, U., Bioprocess Engineering
SCHEFFLER, F., Technical Chemistry
SCHIRZER, D., Organic Chemistry
SCHMIDT, J., Technical Thermodynamics
SEIDEL-MORGENSTERN, A., Chemical Process Engineering
SPECHT, E., Thermodynamics and Combustion
SUNDMACHER, K., Process Systems Engineering
THÈVENIN, D., Fluid Mechanics and Flow Technology
THOMAS, J., Mechanical Process Engineering
TSOTSAS, E., Thermal Process Engineering
WEISS, H., Physical Chemistry

PÄDAGOGISCHE HOCHSCHULE FREIBURG
(Freiburg University of Education)

Kunzenweg 21, 79117 Freiburg
Telephone: (761) 6820
E-mail: epp@ph-freiburg.de
Internet: www.ph-freiburg.de

Founded 1962
State control

Rector: Prof. Dr ULRICH DRUWE
Vice-Rector for Academic Affairs: Prof. Dr HANS-WERNER HUNEKE
Vice-Rector for Research: Prof. Dr TIMO LEUDERS
Chancellor: HENDRIK BÜGGELN
Number of students: 4,432

DEANS

Faculty of Cultural Studies and Social Sciences: Prof. Dr MECHTILD FUCHS
Faculty of Education: Prof. Dr ELMAR STAHL
Faculty of Mathematics, Science and Technology: Prof. Dr ULRIKE SPÖRHASE

PÄDAGOGISCHE HOCHSCHULE HEIDELBERG
(Heidelberg University of Education)

Keplerstr. 87, 69120 Heidelberg
Telephone: (6221) 4770
E-mail: info@ph-heidelberg.de
Internet: www.ph-heidelberg.de
public control

Rector: Prof. Dr ANNELIESE WELLENSIEK
Pro-Rector: Prof. Dr GERHARD HÄRLE
Pro-Rector: Prof. Dr ANNE SLIWKA
Chancellor: CHRISTOPH GLASER

Number of teachers: 180
Number of students: 4,200

DEANS

Faculty of Cultural Studies and Humanities: Prof. Dr GEORG ZENKERT
Faculty of Education and Social Sciences: Prof. Dr KLAUS SARIMSKI
Faculty of Natural, Human and Social Sciences: Prof. Dr BETTINA ALAVI

PÄDAGOGISCHE HOCHSCHULE KARLSRUHE
(Karlsruhe University of Education)

POB 11 10 62, 76060 Karlsruhe
Bismarckstr. 10, 76133 Karlsruhe
Telephone: (721) 9253
E-mail: studium@ph-karlsruhe.de
Internet: www.ph-karlsruhe.de

Founded 1962
State control

Rector: Prof. Dr LIESEL HERMES
Vice-Rector for Academic Affairs: Prof. Dr SABINE LIEBIG
Vice-Rector for Research and Professional Devt: Prof. Dr GABRIELE WEIGAND
Chancellor: Dr WOLFGANG TZSCHASCHEL

Number of teachers: 180
Number of students: 3,000

DEANS

Faculty I: Prof. Dr KLAUS PETER RIPPE
Faculty II: Prof. Dr HEIDI RÖSCH
Faculty III: Prof. Dr WALTRAUD RUSCH

PÄDAGOGISCHE HOCHSCHULE LUDWIGSBURG
(Ludwigsburg University of Education)

POB 220, 71602 Ludwigsburg
Reuteallee 46, 71634 Ludwigsburg
Telephone: (7141) 1400
E-mail: rektorat@ph-ludwigsburg.de
Internet: www.ph-ludwigsburg.de

Founded 1962
State control

Rector: Prof. Dr MARTIN FIX
Vice-Rector for Academic and Int. Affairs: Prof. Dr JÖRG-U. KEßLER
Vice-Rector for Research and Professional Devt: Prof. Dr CHRISTINE BESCHERER
Chancellor: VERA BRÜGGEMANN

Number of teachers: 380
Number of students: 5,300

DEANS

Faculty of Cultural Studies and Science: Prof. Dr ROBERT LANG
Faculty of Education and Social Science: Prof. Dr PETER KIRCHNER
Faculty of Special Education: Prof. Dr MARTINA HIELSCHER-FASTABEND

PÄDAGOGISCHE HOCHSCHULE SCHWÄBISCH GMÜND
(Schwäbisch Gmünd University of Education)

Oberbettringer Str. 200, 73525 Schwäbisch Gmünd
Telephone: (7171) 9830
E-mail: info@ph-gmuend.de
Internet: www.ph-gmuend.de

Founded 1825
State control

Rector: Prof. Dr ASTRID BECKMANN
Vice-Rector for Academic Affairs: Prof. Dr. HELMAR SCHÖNE
Vice-Rector for Research, Devt and Int. Relations: Prof. Dr HANS-MARTIN HAASE
Chancellor: EDGAR BUHL

Library of 300,000 vols, 670 current periodicals
Number of students: 2,700

DEANS

Faculty I: Prof. Dr MARITA KAMPSHOFF
Faculty II: Prof. Dr ERIKA BRINKMANN

PÄDAGOGISCHE HOCHSCHULE WEINGARTEN
(Weingarten University of Education)

Kirch Pl. 2, 88250 Weingarten
Telephone: (751) 5010
E-mail: poststelle@ph-weingarten.de
Internet: www.ph-weingarten.de
Founded 1947
State control
Rector: Dr MARGRET RUEP
Vice-Rector for Academic Affairs: Prof. Dr WERNER KNAPP
Vice-Rector for Research and Devt: Prof. Dr Hab. JOACHIM ROTTMANN
Chancellor: ULRICH KLEINER
Library of 290,000 vols
Number of teachers: 140
Number of students: 2,400

DEANS

Faculty I: Dr Hab. URSULA PFEIFFER
Faculty II: Dr PETRA BURMEISTER

PHILIPPS-UNIVERSITÄT MARBURG

Biegenstr. 10–12, 35032 Marburg
Telephone: (6421) 2820
E-mail: pressestelle@verwaltung.uni-marburg.de
Internet: www.uni-marburg.de
Founded 1527
State control
Academic year: October to July (2 terms)
Pres.: Prof. Dr KATHARINA KRAUSE
Vice-Pres.: Prof. Dr FRANK BREMMER
Vice-Pres.: Prof. Dr HARALD LACHNIT
Vice-Pres.: Prof. Dr JOACHIM SCHACHTNER
Chancellor: Dr FRIEDHELM NONNE
Library Dir: Dr H. NEUHAUSEN
Library: see under Libraries and Archives
Number of teachers: 2,144
Number of students: 21,000
Publication: *Journal* (2 a year)

DEANS

Faculty of Biology: Prof. Dr PAUL GALLAND
Faculty of Business Administration and Economics: Prof. Dr PAUL ALPAR
Faculty of Chemistry: Prof. Dr STEFANIE DEHNEN
Faculty of Education: Prof. Dr WOLFGANG SEITTER
Faculty of Foreign Languages and Cultures: Prof. Dr SONJA FIELITZ
Faculty of Geography: Prof. Dr MARKUS HASSLER
Faculty of German Studies and History of the Arts: Prof. Dr JOACHIM HERRGEN
Faculty of History and Cultural Studies: Prof. Dr VERENA POSTEL
Faculty of Law: Prof. Dr GILBERT GORNIG
Faculty of Mathematics and Computer Science: Prof. Dr MANFRED SOMMER
Faculty of Medicine: Prof. Dr MATTHIAS ROTHMUND
Faculty of Pharmacy: Prof. Dr MICHAEL KEUSGEN
Faculty of Physics: Prof. Dr WOLFRAM HEIMBRODT
Faculty of Protestant Theology: Prof. Dr WOLF-FRIEDRICH SCHÄUFELE
Faculty of Psychology: Prof. Dr RAINER K. SCHWARTING
Faculty of Social Sciences and Philosophy: Prof. Dr CHRISTOPH DEMMERLING

PROFESSORS

Faculty of Biology (Karl-von-Frisch-Str., 35032 Marburg; tel. (6421) 2822047; e-mail pega@mailer.uni-marburg.de):

BATSCHAUER, A., Plant Physiology, Photobiology
BÖLKER, M., Genetics
BRANDL, R., Animal Ecology
BREMER, E., Microbiology
BUCKEL, W., Microbiology
GALLAND, P., Plant Physiology, Photobiology
HASSEL, M., Morphology
HELDMAIER, G., Zoology
HOMBERG, U., Animal Physiology
KAHMANN, R., Genetics
KIRCHNER, C., Zoology
KLEIN, A., Molecular Genetics
KOST, G., Botany, Mycology
LINGELBACH, U., Zoology, Parasitology
MAIER, U., Cell Biology and Botany
MATTHIES, D., Plant Ecology
PLACHTER, H., Nature Conservancy Studies
RENKAWITZ-POHL, R., Molecular Genetics
THAUER, R., Microbiology
WEBER, H. C., Botany
ZIEGENHAGEN, B., Nature Conservancy Biology

Faculty of Business Administration and Economics (Universitätsstr. 25, 35032 Marburg; tel. (6421) 2821722; e-mail dekanat@wiwi.uni-marburg.de):

ALPAR, P., Economics, Computer Science
FEHL, U., Economic Theory
FELD, L., Financial Science
FLEISCHER, K., Statistics
GERUM, E., Commerce
GÖPFERT, I., Commerce, Logistics
HASENKAMP, U., Business Management and Economic Information Studies
KERBER, W., Political Economy
KIRK, M., Development Policy, Agricultural Economics and Cooperative Science
KRAG, J., Commerce
LINGENFELDER, M., Marketing
PRIEWASSER, E., Banking
RÖPKE, J., Economic Theory
SCHIMENZ, B., Business Economics
SCHÜLLER, A., Economic Theory
STORZ, C., Japanese Economics
WEHRHEIM, M., Commerce

Faculty of Chemistry (Hans-Meerwin-Str., 35032 Marburg; tel. (6421) 2825543; e-mail dekanat@chemie.uni-marburg.de):

BRÖRING, M., Inorganic Chemistry
ELSCHENBROICH, CHR., Inorganic Chemistry
ENSINGER, W., Analytical and Nuclear Chemistry
ESSEN, L.-O., Biochemistry
FRENKING, G., Chemistry-Related Computer Studies
GERMANO, G., Physical Chemistry
GREINER, A., Macromolecular Chemistry
HAMPP, N., Physical Chemistry
HARBRECHT, B., Inorganic Chemistry
HILT, G., Organic Chemistry
KOERT, W., Organic Chemistry
MARAHIEL, M., Biochemistry
MÜLLER, U., Inorganic Chemistry
SCHRADER, T., Organic Chemistry
SEUBERT, A., Analytical Chemistry
STUDER, A., Organic Chemistry
SUNDERMEYER, J., Metal-Organic Chemistry
UHL, W., Inorganic Chemistry
WEITZEL, K.-M., Physical Chemistry
WENDORFF, J., Physical Chemistry

Faculty of Education (Wilhelm-Röpke-Str. 6B, 35032 Marburg; tel. (6421) 2824770; e-mail dekan21@mailer.uni-marburg.de):

ACKERMANN, H., General Teaching
BECKER, P., Sociology of Sports
BÜCHNER, P., Sociology of Education
HAFENEGER, B., Extracurricular Education
KÖNIGS, F., General Teaching, Applied Linguistics
KUCKARTZ, U., Education
LAGING, R., Sports Science
LERSCH, R., School Education
NUISSL VON REIN, E., Adult Education
PROKOP, U., Socialization Theory
ROHR, E., Education
ROHRMANN, E., Education
SCHNOOR, H., Pedagogics
SEEWALD, J., Educational Kinesiology
SEITTER, W., Education
SOMMER, H.-M., Sports Medicine

Faculty of Foreign Languages and Cultures (Wilhelm-Röpke-Str. 6D, 35032 Marburg; tel. (6421) 2824764; e-mail kissling@mailer.uni-marburg.de):

BISCHOFF, V., American Literature
HAHN, M., Indology
HANDKE, J., English Linguistics
HOFER, H., Romance Philology
IBLER, R., Slavic Philology
KÖNSGEN, E., Latin Philology of the Middle and Modern Ages
KUESTER, M., English Studies
LEONHARDT, J., Classic Philology
POPPE, E., General Language and Celtology
RIEKEN, E., Comparative Language
SCHALLER, H., Slavic Philology
SCHMITT, A., Classic Philology
SOMMERFELD, W., Ancient Oriental Studies
STILLERS, R., Romance Philology
UHLIG, C., English and American Philology
WENINGER, S., Semitistics
ZIMMERMANN, R., English Linguistics
ZOLLNA, J., Romance Philology

Faculty of Geography (Deutschhausstr. 10, 35032 Marburg; tel. (6421) 2825916; e-mail jansen@mailer.uni-marburg.de):

BARTHELT, H., Cultural Geography
BENDIX, J., Climatic Geography and Geoecology
BRÜCKNER, H., Morphology and Geoecology
MIEHE, G., Geography of Asia and East Africa
OPP, CH., Physical Geography
PAAL, M., Cultural Geography
PLETSCH, A., Cultural Geography and Geography of North America
STRAMBACH, S., Cultural Geography

Faculty of German Studies and History of the Arts (Wilhelm-Röpke-Str. 6A, 35032 Marburg; tel. (6421) 2824542; e-mail dekan09@mailer.uni-marburg.de):

ALBERT, R., German Language
ANZ, TH., Modern German Literature
BERTELSMEIER-KIERST, C., German Philology
DEDNER, B., Modern German Literature
DOHM, B., Modern German Literature
HEINZLE, J., German Philology
HELLER, H.-B., Modern German Literature
HENZE-DÖHRING, G., Music
HERKLOTZ, I., History of Art
HERRGEN, J., German Linguistics
HEUSINGER, L., Informatics in History of Art
KRAUSE, K., History of Art
KREMERS, E., Graphics and Painting
KÜNZEL, H., Phonetics
MIX, Y.-G., Modern German Literature
OSINSKI, J., Modern German Literature
PRÜMM, K., Media Teaching
SCHLESEWSKY, M., Neurolinguistics
SCHMIDT, J., Dialect and Linguistics
SCHÜTTE, W., History of Art
WIESE, R., German Linguistics

Faculty of History and Cultural Studies (Wilhelm-Röpke-Str. 6C, 35032 Marburg; tel. (6421) 2824518; e-mail dekan06@mailer.uni-marburg.de):

BÖHME, H. W., Prehistory
BORSCHEID, P., Social and Economic History
CONZE, E., Modern History
DREXHAGE, H.-J., Ancient History
ERRINGTON, R. M., Ancient History
FRONING, H., Classical Archaeology
HARDACH, G., Social and Economic History
KAMPMANN, C., Modern History

KRIEGER, W., Modern History
LAUTER, H., Classical Archaeology
MEYER, A., Medieval History
MÜLLER-KARPE, A., Prehistory
PAUER, E., Japanese Studies
PLAGGENBORG, S., East European History
POSTEL, V., Medieval History
ÜBELHÖR, M., Sinology
WINTERHAGER, W. E., Modern History

Faculty of Law (Universitätsstr. 6, 35032 Marburg; tel. (6421) 2823101; e-mail dekanat01@mailer.uni-marburg.de):

BACKHAUS, R., Roman and Civil Law
BÖHM, M., Public Law
BUCHHOLZ, ST., German Legal History and Civil Law
DETTERBECK, S., Public Law
FREUND, G., Criminal and Procedural Law, Philosophy of Law
FROTSCHER, W., Public Law
GORNIG, G.-H., Public Law
GOUNALAKIS, G., Civil and Comparative Law
HORN, H.-D., Public Law
LANGENBÜCHER, K., Civil Law
LANGER, W., Criminal and Procedural Law
MENKHAUS, H., Japanese Law
MUMMENHOFF, W., Civil and Labour Law
RADTKE, H., Criminal Law, Procedural Law
RÖSSNER, D., Criminal Law, Procedural Law
RUPPRECHT, H.-A., Papyrology
SCHANZE, E., Civil Law
VOIT, W., Civil Law
WERTENBRUCH, J., Civil Law

Faculty of Mathematics and Computer Science (Hans-Meerwein-Str., 35032 Marburg; tel. (6421) 2825463; e-mail dekan@mathematik.uni-marburg.de):

BAUER, T., Geometrical Algebra
DAHLKE, S., Numerics
FREISLEBEN, B., Practical Informatics
GROMES, W., Analysis
GUMM, H.-P., Theoretical Informatics
HESSE, W., Software Engineering
HÜLLERMEIER, E., Informatics
KNÖLLER, F. W., Topology and Geometry
LOOGEN, R., Functional Programmes
MAMMITZSCH, V., Probability Theory and Mathematical Statistics
PORTENIER, C., Analysis
SCHLICKEWEI, H. P., Algebra
SCHUMACHER, G., Topology and Geometry
SCHWENTICK, T., Theoretical Informatics
SEEGER, B., Databases
SOMMER, M., Practical Informatics
ULTSCH, A., Neuroinformatics
UPMEIER, H., Analysis
WELKER, V., Combinatorics

Faculty of Medicine (Baldingerstr., 35032 Marburg; tel. (6421) 2866201; e-mail dekanat@post.med.uni-marburg.de):

ARNOLD, R., Internal Medicine
AUMÜLLER, G., Anatomy
AUSTERMANN, K.-H., Maxillofacial Surgery
BACK, T., Neurology
BASLER, H.-D., Psychology
BAUER, W., Molecular Biology
BAUM, E., General Medicine
BEHR, T., Nuclear Medicine
BERGER, R., Otorhinolaryngology
BERTALANFFY, H., Neurosurgery
BESEDOVSKY, H., Physiology
BIEN, S., Neurosurgery
CETIN, Y., Anatomy
CZUBAYKO, F., Pharmacology
DAUT, J., Physiology
DIBBETS, J., Dentistry
DONNER-BANZHOFF, N., General Medicine
EILERS, M., Molecular Biology
ENGENHART-CABILLIC, R., Radiotherapy
FEHRENBACH, H.-G., Pneumology
FLORES DE JACOBY, L., Paradontology
GARTEN, W., Virology
GÖKE, R., Internal Medicine
GOTZEN, L., Surgery
GRISS, P., Orthopaedics
GRZESCHIK, K.-H., Human Genetics
GUDERMANN, T., Pharmacology and Toxicology
HAPPLE, R., Dermatology
HASILIK, A., Physiological Chemistry
HEBEBRAND, J., Child Psychiatry
HEEG, K., Microbiology
HOFMANN, R., Urology
JONES, D., Orthopaedics
KANN, P., Internal Medicine
KLENK, H.-D., Virology
KLINGMÜLLER, V., Nuclear Diagnosis
KLOSE, K., Radiology
KRAUSE, W., Andrology
KRETSCHMER, V., Transfusion Medicine
KRIEG, J. C., Psychology
KROLL, P., Ophthalmology
KUHN, K., Medical Informatics
LANG, R. E., Experimental Nuclear Medicine
LILL, R., Cytobiology
LISS, B., Physiology
LOHOFF, M., Microbiology
LOTZMANN, K.-U., Dentistry
MAIER, R., Neonatology
MAISCH, B., Cardiology
MAX, M., Anaesthesiology and Intensive Therapy
MOLL, R., Pathology
MOOSDORF, R., Cardiac Surgery
MUELLER, U., Medical Sociology
MÜLLER, R., Molecular Biology
NEUBAUER, A., Internal Medicine
OERTEL, W., Neurology
PIEPER, K., Dentistry for Children
RADSAK, K., General Medicine
REMSCHMIDT, H., Child Psychology
RENZ, H., Interdisciplinary Medical Centre
RÖPER, J., Physiology
ROSENOW, F., Neurology
ROTHMUND, M., Surgery
RUPP, H., Cardiology
SCHÄFER, H., Medical Biometry
SCHMIDT, S., Obstetrics
SCHWARZ, R., Parasitology
SEITZ, J., Anatomy
SEYBERTH, H. W., Child Medicine, Clinical and Theoretical Pharmacology
SOMMER, N., Neurology (Neuroimmunology)
STACHNISS, V., Dentistry
STEINIGER, B., Anatomy
STREMPEL, J., Ophthalmology
VOGELMEIER, C., Pneumology
VOIGT, K.-H., Physiology
WAGNER, H.-J., Radiology
WAGNER, W., Obstetrics
WEIHE, E., Anatomy
WERNER, J., Otolaryngology, Head and Neck Surgery
WULF, H., Anaesthesiology and Intensive Therapy

Faculty of Pharmacy (Wilhelm-Roser-Str. 2, 35032 Marburg; tel. (6421) 2825890; e-mail dekanat.pharmazie@mailer.uni-marburg.de):

FRIEDRICH, C., History of Pharmacy
HANEFELD, W., Pharmaceutical Chemistry
HARTMANN, R., Pharmaceutical Chemistry
KEUSGEN, M., Pharmaceutical Chemistry
KISSEL, T., Pharmaceutical Technology and Biopharmacy
KLEBE, G., Pharmaceutical Chemistry
KRIEGLSTEIN, J., Pharmacology and Toxicology
KUSCHINSKY, K., Pharmacology and Toxicology
LINK, A., Pharmaceutical Chemistry
MATERN, U., Pharmaceutical Biology
MATUSCH, R., Pharmaceutical Chemistry
PETERSEN, M., Pharmaceutical Biology

Faculty of Physics (Renthof 6, 35032 Marburg; tel. (6421) 2821314; e-mail dekanat@physik.uni-marburg.de):

BREMMER, F., Applied Physics
ECKHARDT, B., Theoretical Physics
ECKHORN, R., Applied Physics
GEBHARD, F., Theoretical Physics
HEIMBRODT, W., Experimental Physics
HÖFER, U., Experimental Physics
JAKOB, P., Experimental Physics
KIRA, M., Theoretical Physics
KOCH, S., Theoretical Physics
LENZ, P., Theoretical Physics
NEUMANN, H., Theoretical Physics
PÜHLHOFER, F., Experimental Physics
RIES, H., Experimental Physics
RÜHLE, W., Experimental Physics
STÖCKMANN, H.-J., Experimental Physics
THOMAS, P., Theoretical Physics
WEISER, G., Experimental Physics

Faculty of Protestant Theology (Alte Universität, Lahntor 3, 35032 Marburg; tel. (6421) 2822441; e-mail dekan05@mailer.uni-marburg.de):

AVEMARIE, F., New Testament
BARTH, H.-M., Systematic Theology
BIENERT, W., Church History
DABROCK, P., Social Ethics
DRESSLER, B., Practical Theology
ELSAS, C., Religious History
JEREMIAS, J., Old Testament
KAISER, J.-C., Church History
KESSLER, R., Old Testament
KOCH, G., Christian Archaeology
KORSCH, D., Systematic Theology
MARTIN, G. M., Practical Theology
NETHÖFEL, W., Social Ethics
PINGGERA, K., Church History
SCHNEIDER, H., Church History
SCHWEBEL, H., Religious Communication
STANDHARTINGER, A., New Testament
WAGNER-RAU, H., Practical Theology

Faculty of Psychology (Gutenbergstr. 18, 35032 Marburg; tel. (6421) 2823674; e-mail dekanpsy@mailer.uni-marburg.de):

LACHNIT, H., General Psychology
LIEBHART, E., Educational Psychology
LOHAUS, A., Developmental Psychology
RIEF, W., Clinical Psychology
RÖHRLE, B., Clinical Psychology
RÖSLER, F., Cognitive Psychology, Neuroscience
ROST, D., Educational Psychology
SCHEIBLECHNER, H., Psychological Methodology
SCHMIDT-ATZERT, L., Psychological Diagnostics
SCHULZE, H.-H., Psychological Methodology
SCHWARTING, R., General and Physiological Psychology
SOMMER, G., Clinical Psychology
STELZL, I., Psychological Methodology and Diagnostics
STEMMLER, G., Psychological Diagnostics
WAGNER, U., Social Psychology

Faculty of Social Sciences and Philosophy (Wilhelm-Röpke-Str. 6B, 35032 Marburg; tel. (6421) 2824726; e-mail ciok@mailer.uni-marburg.de):

BERG-SCHLOSSER, D., Political Science
BIELING, H.-J., Political Science
BORIS, H.-D., Sociology
BRANN, K., European Ethnology
DEPPE, F., Political Science
FÜLBERTH-SPERLING, G., Political Science
FUNDER, M., Sociology
GUTMANN, M., Philosophy
JANICH, P., Philosophy
KÄSLER, D., Sociology
KISSLER, L., Sociology
KURZ-SCHERF, I., Political Science
LÜDTKE, H., Sociology
MERKEL, I., Ethnology

MÜNZEL, M., Ethnology
NOETZEL, T., Political Science
PYE, M., General Religious Science
RUPP, H.-K., Political Science
SCHILLER, TH., Political Science
VON BREDOW, W., Political Science
ZIMMERMANN, H.-P., European Ethnology

PHILOSOPHISCH-THEOLOGISCHE HOCHSCHULE—THEOLOGISCHE FAKULTÄT SVD ST AUGUSTIN (Philosophical-Theological College—Faculty of Theology SVD St Augustin)

Arnold-Janssen-Str. 30, 53757 St Augustin
Telephone: (2241) 237222
E-mail: pth.rektor@steyler.de
Internet: www.pth-augustin.eu

Founded 1932
Private control
Language of instruction: German
Academic year: October to July

Chancellor: Dr HEINZ KULÜKE
Vice-Chancellor: Dr RALF HUNING
Rector: Prof. Dr BERND WERLE
Vice-Rector: Prof. Dr PETER RAMERS
Librarian: GUIDO HACKELBUSCH

Library of 500,000 vols
Number of teachers: 32
Number of students: 170

Publications: *International Journal of Cultural and Religious Studies from China, International Journal of Cultural Anthropology, Science of Religion and Linguistics, International Journal of Missiological Studies*

PHILOSOPHISCH-THEOLOGISCHE HOCHSCHULE DER SALESIANER DON BOSCOS BENEDIKTBEUERN

Don-Bosco-Str. 1, 83671 Benediktbeuern
Telephone: (57) 88201
E-mail: info@pth-bb.de
Internet: www.pth-bb.de

Founded 1931
Private control

Chancellor: Dr PASCUAL CHÁVEZ
Rector: Prof. Dr LOTHAR BILY
Vice-Rector: Prof. Dr NORBERT WOLFF
Head Librarian: Dr PHILIPP GAHN
Number of students: 600

PHILOSOPHISCH-THEOLOGISCHE HOCHSCHULE VALLENDAR GMBH

Pallottistr. 3, 56179 Vallendar
Telephone: (261) 64020
E-mail: sfein@thv.de
Internet: www.pthv.de

Founded 1896
Private control

Chancellor: JACOB NAMPUDAKAM
Rector: Prof. Dr PAUL RHEINBAY
Vice-Rector: Prof. Dr FRANK WEIDNER
Vice-Rector: Prof. Dr JOACHIM SCHMIEDL

Library of 135,000 vols, 228 current periodicals, 18 incunabula

DEANS

Faculty of Nursing Science: Prof. Dr FRANK WEIDNER
Faculty of Theology: Prof. Dr JOACHIM SCHMIEDL

RHEINISCH-WESTFÄLISCHE TECHNISCHE HOCHSCHULE AACHEN

Templergraben 55, 52056 Aachen
Telephone: (241) 801
E-mail: international@zhv.rwth-aachen.de
Internet: www.rwth-aachen.de

Founded 1870 as Polytechnikum, attained univ. status 1880
Academic year: October to September

Rector: Prof. Dr Ing. ERNST M. SCHMACHTENBERG
Vice-Rector for Education: Prof. Dr rer.nat. ALOYS KRIEG
Vice-Rector for Human Resources: Prof. HEATHER HOFMEISTER
Vice-Rector for Industry and Business Relations: Prof. Dr Ing. Dipl.-Wirt. Ing. GÜNTHER SCHUH
Vice-Rector for Research: Prof. Dr med. ROLF ROSSAINT
Chancellor: MANFRED NETTEKOVEN
Head of Int. Office: Dr HEIDE NADERER
Head of Public Relations Office: TONI WIMMER
Head of Technology Transfer and Research Funding: Dr REGINA OERTEL
Librarian: Dr ULRIKE EICH

Library: see under Libraries and Archives
Number of teachers: 4,248
Number of students: 33,000

DEANS

Faculty of Architecture: Prof. PETER J. RUSSELL
Faculty of Arts and Humanities: Prof. Dr PAUL HILL
Faculty of Civil Engineering: Prof. Dr EKKEHARD WENDLER
Faculty of Business and Economics: Prof. Dr MICHAEL BASTIAN
Faculty of Electrical Engineering and Information Technology: Prof. Dr MICHAEL VORLÄNDER
Faculty of Georesources and Materials Engineering: Prof. Dr KARL BERNHARD FRIEDRICH
Faculty of Mathematics, Computer Science and Natural Sciences: Prof. Dr SIMON
Faculty of Mechanical Engineering: Prof. Dr KLAUS HENNING
Faculty of Medicine: Prof. Dr JOHANNES NOTH

PROFESSORS

Faculty of Architecture (Schinkelstr. 1, 52056 Aachen; tel. (241) 8095000809; e-mail dekan@architektur.rwth-aachen.de; internet arch.rwth-aachen.de):

BAUM, M., Design Construction
BRUCHHAUS, G., District Planning and Design
COERSMEIER, U., Interior Design
HOFFMANN, H., Visual Form
HUMBLÉ, F., Building Planning and Design
JANSEN, M., History of Urban Devt
KADA, K., Building Design and Function
KRAUSE, C., Landscape Ecology and Landscape Design
LAUENSTEIN, H., Open Space and Landscape Planning
MARKSCHIES, A., History of Art
NICOLIC, V., Building Construction and Design
PIEPER, J., History of Architecture and Conservation
RUOFF, J., Environment, Services and Design
RUSSELL, P., Computer-Aided Design
SCHMIDT, H., Conservation
SCHNEIDER, H. N., Building Construction and Design
SCHULZE, M., Sculpture
SELLE, K., Planning Theory and Town Planning
TRAUTZ, M., Building Construction (Structural Design)
VAN DEN BERGH, W., Housing and Residential Devt
VINKEN, G., Theory of Architecture
WACHTEN, K., Urban Design and Country Planning

Faculty of Arts and Humanities (Kármánstr. 17–19, 52056 Aachen; tel. (241) 8096002; e-mail adrian.leipold@fb7.rwth-aachen.de; internet www.rwth-aachen.de/fb7):

BEIER, R., Applied Linguistics
BEIN, T., Medieval German Language and Literature
DERINGER, L., English and American Language and Literature
ERTLER, K., Romance Languages and Literatures
ESSER, A., Philosophy
FICK, M., German Literature
GELLHAUS, A., German Literature
GILLMAYR-BUCHER, S., Biblical Studies
HAMMERICH, K., Sociology
HEINEN, A., Modern and Contemporary History
HILL, P. B., Sociology
HORCH, H.-O., German and Jewish Literature
HÖRNING, K.-H., Sociology
HORNKE, L., Psychology
JÄGER, L., Linguistics and Media Theory
JAKOBS, E.-M., Communication Science
KEIL, G., Theoretical Philosophy
KELLERWESSEL, W., Philosophy
KERNER, M., Medieval and Modern History
KÖNIG, H., Political Science
LEWATER, D., Education Science
LIEDTKE, F., German Language
LUEKE, U., Theology
MEY, H., Sociology
MEYER, G., Theology
MEYER, P. G., English Linguistics (Synchronic)
MICHELSEN, U. A., Education
MOESSNER, L., English Linguistics and Medieval Studies
MÜSSELER, J., Work Psychology and Cognition
NEUSCHAEFER, A., Romance Languages and Literatures
NIEHR, T., German Language
PANGRITZ, A., Theology
RICHTER, E., Political Science
ROTTE, R., Political Science
SCHERBERICH, K., History
SCHMITZ, S., German Language
SPIJKERS, W., Psychology
STETTER, C., Germanic Linguistics
VON HAEHLING, R., History
WENZEL, P., English Literature

Faculty of Civil Engineering (Mies-van-der-Rohe-Str. 1, 52074 Aachen; tel. (241) 8025075; e-mail dekanat@fb3.rwth-aachen.de; internet www.rwth-aachen.de/fb3):

BECKMANN, K. J., Urban and Transport Planning
BENNING, W., Geodesy
BRAMERSHUBER, W., Building Materials Research
BRUNK, M. F., Construction Management and Building Services
DOETSCH, P., Waste Management
FELDMANN, M., Steel and Light-Metal Construction
GÜLDENPFENNING, J., Mechanics and Building Construction
HEGGER, J., Structural Concrete
KÖNGETER, J., Hydraulic Engineering and Water Resources Management
MESKOURIS, K., Structural Statistics and Dynamics
NACKEN, H., Engineering Hydrology
OSEBOLD, R., Construction Management—Project Management
PINNEKAMP, J., Sanitary and Waste Engineering
RAUPACH, M., Building Materials Research
REICHMUTH, J., Airport and Air-Transportation Research
STEINAUER, B., Road Engineering, Earth Works and Tunnelling

WENDLER, E., Transport Economics, Railway Engineering and Railway Operations
ZIEGLER, M., Geotechnics in Civil Engineering

Faculty of Business and Economics (Kármánstr. 17–19, 52056 Aachen; tel. (241) 8096000; e-mail dekanat-fb8@rwth-aachen.de; internet www.wiwi.rwth-aachen.de):

BASTIAN, M., Business Information Systems and Operations
BRETTEL, M., Business Admin. and Sciences for Engineers and Scientists (Centre for Entrepreneurship)
BREUER, W., Business Administration (Finance)
DYCKHOFF, H., Business Theory, Environmental Management and Industrial Controlling
FEESS, E., Economics (Microeconomics)
HARMS, P., Macroeconomics
HÖMBURG, R., Business Taxation and Auditing
HUBER, C., Civil Law, Business and Labour Law
LORZ, O., Int. Economics
MÖLLER, H. P., Business Admin., Accounting and Finance
REIMERS, K., Business Information Systems (Electronic Business)
SCHRÖDER, H.-H., Technology and Innovation Management
SEBASTIAN, H.-J., Optimization of Distribution Networks
STEFFENHAGEN, H., Corporate Policy and Marketing
THOMES, P., Economic and Social History
VON NITZSCH, R., Business Management
WOYWODE, M., Int. Management

Faculty of Electrical Engineering and Information Technology (Muffeter Weg 3, 52074 Aachen; tel. (241) 8027572; e-mail dekanat@fb6.rwth-aachen.de; internet www.fb6.rwth-aachen.de):

AACH, T., Image Processing
ASCHEID, G., Integrated Signal Processing Systems
BEMMERL, T., Operation Systems and Scalable Computing
DE DONCKER, R., Power Electronic and Electrical Drives
HAMEYER, K., Electrical Mechanics
HAUBRICH, H.-J., Power Systems and Power Economics
HEINEN, S., Integrated Analogue Circuits
JANSEN, R., Electromagnetic Theory
KAISER, W., History of Engineering and Technology
KRAISS, K.-F., Technical Informatics and Computer Science
KURZ, H., Semiconductor Technology
LEONHARDT, K. S., Medical Information Technology
LEUPERS, R., Software for Systems on Silicon
MAEHOENEN, P. H., Wireless Networks
MATHAR, R., Information Theory
MEYR, H., Integrated Signal Processing Systems
MOKWA, W., Materials in Electrical Engineering
NOLL, T. G., Electrical Engineering and Computer Systems
OHM, J.-R., Communications Engineering
SAUER, U., Electrochemical Energy Conversion
SCHNETTLER, A., High Voltage Technology
VARY, P., Communication Systems and Data Processing
VESCAN, A., GaN Device Technology
VORLÄNDER, M., Technical Acoustics
WALKE, B., Communications Networks
WASER, R., Materials in Electrical Materials

Faculty of Georesources and Materials Engineering (Intzestr. 1, 52056 Aachen; tel. (241) 8095665; e-mail dekanat-fb5@rwth-aachen.de; internet www.rwth-aachen.de):

Section of Geoscience:

AZZAM, R., Engineering Geology and Hydrogeology
BREUER, H., Geography, Economic and Applied Geography
CLAUSER, C., Applied Geophysics
FLAJS, G., Geology and Palaeontology
GRÄF, P., Geography, Physical Geography and Climatology
HAVLIK, G., Geography, Physical Geography and Climatology
HEGER, G., Crystallography
KRAMM, U., Mineralogy and Geochemistry
KUKLA, P., Geology and Palaeontology
LEHMKUHL, F., Geography, Physical Geography and Geoecology
LITTKE, R., Geology and Geochemistry of Petroleum and Coal
MEYER, M., Mineralogy and Economic Geology
ROTH, G., Applied Crystallography and Mineralogy
STANJEK, H., Clay Mineralogy
URAI, J. L., Structural Geology, Tectonics and Geomechanics

Section of Metallurgy and Materials Technology:

BLECK, W., Materials Science of Steels
BUERIG-POLACZ, A., Foundry Technology
CONRADT, R., Glass and Ceramic Composites
EMMERICH, H., Computational Materials Engineering
EPPLE, U., Process Control Engineering
FRIEDRICH, B., Process Metallurgy and Metal Recycling
GOTTSTEIN, G., Physical Metallurgy and Metal Physics
KAYSSER, W. A., Materials Science of Nonferrous Metals
KÖHNE, H., Heat and Mass Transfer
KOPP, R., Metal Forming
ODOJ, R., Materials Chemistry
PFEIFER, H., High Temperature Engineering
SCHNEIDER, J., Materials Chemistry
SENK, D. G., Metallurgy of Iron and Steel
TELLE, R., Ceramics and Refractories

Section of Mining Engineering:

FRENZ, W., Mining and Environment
HEIL, J., Coking, Briquetting and Thermal Waste Treatment
MARTENS, P. N., Mining Engineering
NIEHAUS, K., Excavation and Mining Equipment
NIEMANN-DELIUS, C., Surface Mining and Drilling
PRETZ, T., Processing and Recycling of Solid Waste Materials
PREUSSE, A., Mine Surveying, Mining Subsidence Engineering and Geophysics in Mining
SEELIGER, A., Mining and Metallurgical Machine Engineering
WOTRUBA, H., Mineral Processing

Faculty of Mathematics, Computer Science and Natural Sciences (Templergraben 64, 52064 Aachen; tel. (241) 8094500; e-mail dekan@fb1.rwth-aachen.de; internet www.fb1.rwth-aachen.de):

ALBRECHT, M., Organic Chemistry
BALLMANN, J., Mechanics
BAUMANN, H., Chemistry
BEGINN, U., Macromolecular and Supramolecular Chemistry
BEMELMANS, V., Mathematics
BENEKE, M., Theoretical Physics
BERGER, C., Experimental Physics
BERLAGE, T., Computer Science (Life Science Informatics)
BERNREUTNER, W., Theoretical Physics
BISCHOF, C., Computer Science (Scientific Computing)
BLUEMICH, B., Macromolecular Chemistry/NMR
BLÜGEL, S., Theoretical Physics
BOCK, H. H., Applied Statistics
BOEHM, A., Experimental Physics
BOHRMANN, J., Zoology and Human Biology
BOLM, C., Chemistry
BORCHERS, J., Computer Science (Media Computing)
BRAEUNIG, P.-M., Developmental Biology and Morphology of Animals
BRUECKEL, T., Experimental Physics
CAPELLMANN, H., Theoretical Physics
CONRATH, U., Plant Biochemistry
CRAMER, E., Applied Statistics
DAHMEN, W., Mathematics
DEDERICHS, P. H., Theoretical Physics
DOHM, V., Theoretical Physics
DRONSKOWSKI, R., Theoretical and Synthetic Solid-State Chemistry
ELLING, L., Biomaterial Sciences
ENDERS, D., Organic Chemistry
ENGLERT, U., Inorganic Chemistry
ENSS, V., Mathematics
ESSER, K.-H., Applied Mathematics
FELD, L., Experimental Physics
FISCHER, R., Molecular Biotechnology
FLEISCHHAUER, J., Theoretical Chemistry
FLÜGGE, G., Experimental Physics
FRENTZEN, M., Botany
GAIS, H.-J., Organic Chemistry
GÄRTNER, F., Computer Science (Dependable Systems)
GIESL, J., Computer Science
GRAEDEL, E., Mathematical Foundations of Computer Science
GÜNTHERODT, G., Experimental Physics
HARTMEIER, W., Biotechnology
HEINKE, H., Experimental Physics
HERMANN, P., Mathematics
HISS, G., Mathematics
HÖLDERICH, W., Fuel Chemistry
HROMKOVIC, J., Computer Science (Algorithms and Complexity)
IBACH, H., Experimental Physics
INDERMARK, K., Computer Science (Programming Languages)
JANK, G., Engineering Mathematics
JARKE, M., Computer Science (Information Systems)
JONGEN, H. TH., Mathematics
KAMPS, U., Statistics
KLEE, D., Biomaterials
KLEMRADT, U., Experimental Physics
KLINNER, U., Applied Microbiology
KOBBELT, L., Computer Science (Computer Graphics and Multimedia)
KÖLLE, U., Organometallic and Coordination Chemistry of the Transition Metals
KOWALEWSKI, S., Computer Science (Embedded Systems)
KREIBIG, U., Experimental Physics
KREUZALER, F., Botany/Molecular Genetics
KRIEG, A., Mathematics
KULL, H.-J., Theoretical Physics
LAKEMEYER, G., Computer Science (Knowledge-Based Systems)
LEITNER, W., Technical Chemistry and Petrochemistry
LENGELER, B., Experimental Physics
LIAUW, M., Technical Chemistry and Reaction Engineering
LICHTER, H., Computer Science (Software Construction)
LÜCHOW, A., Theoretical and Computational Chemistry
LUEKEN, H., Inorganic Chemistry
LUKSCH, P., Computer Science
LÜTH, H., Experimental Physics
MAIER-PAAPE, S., Mathematics

MARTIN, M., Physical Chemistry
MERKE, I., Physical Chemistry
MÖLLER, M., Macromolecular Chemistry
MÜLLER-KRUMBHAAR, H., Theoretical Physics
NAGEL, M., Computer Science (Software Engineering)
NEY, H., Computer Science (Pattern Recognition)
NOELLE, S., Mathematics
OKUDA, J., Organometallic Chemistry
PAHLINGS, H., Mathematics
PLESKEN GEN. WIGGER, W., Mathematics
PRIEFER, U., Biology (Soil Ecology)
PRINZ, W., Computer Science (Cooperation Systems)
RAABE, G., Theoretical Chemistry
RAUHUT, B., Statistics and Mathematics of Economics
RICHTERING, W., Physical Chemistry
ROSSMANITH, P., Computer Science (Theoretical Computer Science)
SALZER, A., Organometallic Chemistry
SCHAEL, S., Experimental Physics
SCHÄFFER, A., Environmental Biology and Chemodynamics
SCHMITZ, D., Experimental Physics
SCHOELLER, H., Theoretical Physics
SCHOLLWOECK, U., Theoretical Physics
SCHROEDER, U., Computer Science (Computer-Based Learning)
SCHUPHAN, I., Biology (Ecology, Ecotoxicology, Ecochemistry)
SCHWEIGERT, CH., Theoretical Physics
SEIDEL, T., Computer Science (Data Mining)
SELKE, W., Theoretical Physics
SIELING, D., Physics
SIMON, U., Inorganic Chemistry and Nanomaterials
SLUSARENKO, A., Plant Physiology
SPANIOL, O., Computer Science (Communication Systems)
STAHL, W., Physical Chemistry
STAPF, S., Macromolecular Chemistry
THOMAS, W., Computer Science (Logic and Discrete Systems)
TRIESCH, E., Mathematics
URBAN, K., Experimental Physics
VON DER MOSEL, H., Mathematics
VON PLESSEN, G., Experimental Physics
WAGNER, H., Biology
WALCHER, S., Mathematics
WEINHOLD, E., Bio-Organic Chemistry
WENZL, H., Experimental Physics
WIEGNER, M., Mathematics
WOLF, K., Microbiology
WUTTIG, M., Experimental Physics
ZEIDLER, M., Physical Chemistry

Faculty of Mechanical Engineering (Eilfschornsteinstr. 18, 52062 Aachen; tel. (241) 8095305; e-mail dekanat-fb4@rwth-aachen.de; internet www.fb4.rwth-aachen.de):

ABEL, D., Automatic Control
ALLES, W., Flight Dynamics
BEHR, M. A., Computational Analysis of Technical Systems
BEISS, P., Materials Technology
BOBZIN, K., Surface Technology, Materials Science
BOHN, D., Steam and Gas Turbines
BRECHER, C., Machine Tools
BÜCHS, Z., Bioprocess Engineering
CORVES, B., Mechanism Theory and Dynamics of Machines
DELLMANN, T., Rail Vehicles and Materials-Handling Technology
DILTHEY, U., Welding Technology
EL-MAGD, E. A., Engineering Materials
FELDHUSEN, J., Engineering Design
GOLD, P. W., Machine Elements and Design
GRIES, T., Textile Engineering
GRUENEFELD, G., Laser Technology
HABERSTROH, E., Synthetic Rubber Technology
HENNING, K., Methods of Cybernetics in Engineering Sciences
ITSKOV, M., Continuum Machines
KLOCKE, F., Manufacturing Technology
KNEER, R., Heat and Mass Transfer
KUGELER, K., Reactor Safety and Reactor Technology
LOOSEN, P., Technology of Optical Systems
LUCAS, K., Technical Thermodynamics
MAIER, H.-R., Ceramic Components in Mechanical Engineering
MARQUARDT, W., Process Systems Engineering
MELIN, T., Chemical Engineering
MICHAELI, W., Plastics Processing
MODIGELL, M., Mechanical Unit Operations
MURRENHOFF, H., Fluid Power Drives and Control
NIEHUIS, R., Jet Propulsion and Turbo Machinery
OLIVIER, H., High-Temperature Gas Dynamics
PETERS, N., Technical Mechanics
PFENNING, A., Thermal Unit Operations
PISCHINGER, S., Internal Combustion Engines
PITZ-PAAL, R., Solar Technology
POPRAWE, R., Laser Technology
REIMERDES, H.-G., Aerospace and Lightweight Structures
SCHLICK, C., Industrial Engineering and Ergonomics
SCHMACHTENBERG, E., Plastics Materials Technology
SCHMITT, R., Metrology and Quality Management
SCHOMBURG, W. K., Construction and Devt of Microsystems
SCHROEDER, W., Fluid Dynamics
SCHUH, G., Production Engineering
SCHULZ, W., Laser Production Processes
SINGHEISER, L., Materials for Energy Technology
STOLTEN, D., Fuel Cells
WALLENTOWITZ, H., Automotive Engineering
WEICHERT, D., General Mechanics

Faculty of Medicine (Pauwelstr. 30, 52074 Aachen; tel. (241) 8089167; e-mail dekanat@ukaachen.de; internet www.ukaachen.de):

AMUNTS, K., Structural-Functional Brain Mapping
AUTSCHBACH, R., Thoracic and Cardiovascular Surgery
BEIER, H., Anatomy and Reproductive Biology
BERNHAGEN, J., Biochemistry
BÜLL, U., Nuclear Medicine
CONRADS, G., Medical Microbiology
DIEDRICH, P., Orthodontics
DOTT, W., Hygienics and Environmental Medicine
EBLE, M. J., Radiotherapy
ELLING, I., Biomaterial Science
ELLRICH, J., Neurosurgery
FAHLKE, C., Physiology
FINK, G., Cognitive Neurology
FLOEGE, J., Internal Medicine
GAUGGEL, G., Medical Psychology and Medical Sociology
GERZER, R., Aerospace Medicine
GILSBACH, J., Neurosurgery
GRESSNER, A. M., Clinical Chemistry and Pathobiochemistry
GREVEN, J., Pharmacology and Toxicology
GRÜNDER, G., Experimental Neuropsychiatry
GÜNTHER, R., Diagnostic Radiology
HANRATH, P., Internal Medicine
HEIMANN, G., Paediatrics
HEINRICH, P., Biochemistry
HERPERTZ-DAHLMANN, B., Child and Adolescent Psychiatry and Psychotherapy
HILGERS, R.-D., Medical Statistics
HÖRNCHEN, H., Paediatrics
HUBER, W., Neurolinguistics
JAHNEN-DECHENT, W., Cell and Molecular Biology at Interfaces
JAKSE, G., Urology
KAUFMANN, P., Anatomy
KNÜCHEL-CLARKE, C., Pathology
KORR, H., Anatomy
KRAUS, T., Occupational Medicine
KUHLEN, H., Anaesthesiology
KÜPPER, W., Laboratory Animal Science
LAMPERT, F., Conservative Dentistry, Periodontics and Preventive Dentistry
LENDLEIN, A., Technology and Devt of Medical Products
LEONHARDT, S., Medical Informatics Technology
LUECKHOFF, A., Physiology
LUESCHER, B., Biochemistry and Molecular Biology
LUETTICKEN, R., Medical Microbiology
MARX, R., Dental Materials
MATERN, H., Internal Medicine
MATHIAK, K., Behavioural Psychobiology
MERK, H. F., Dermatology
MURKEN, A. H., History of Medicine and Hospitals
NEULEN, J., Gynaecological Endocrinology and Reproductive Medicine
NEUSCHAEFER-RUBE, C., Phoniatrics and Pedaudiology
NIENDORF, T., Experimental MR-Imaging
NIETHARD, F. U., Orthopaedics
NOTH, J., Neurology
OSIEKA, R., Internal Medicine
PAAR, O., Surgery
PALLUA, N., Plastic Surgery, Hand and Reconstructive Surgery
RATH, W., Gynaecology
RIEDIGER, D., Oral, Maxillofacial and Plastic Facial Surgery
RINK, L., Immunology
RITTER, K., Virology
ROSSAINT, R., Anaesthesiology
SCHMALZIG, G., Pharmacology and Toxicology
SCHMITZ-RODE, T., Diagnostic Radiology
SCHNEIDER, F., Psychiatrics and Psychotherapy
SCHUMPELICK, V., Surgery
SEGHAYE, M.-C., Paediatric Cardiology
SPIEKERMANN, H., Prosthodontics
SPITZER, K., Medical Informatics
THRON, A., Neuroradiology
VÁSQUEZ-JIMÉNEZ, J., Paediatric Heart Surgery
WALTER, P., Opthalmology
WEBER, C., Cardiovascular Molecular Biology
WEIS, J., Neuropathology
WELLMANN, A., Pathology (Cytology)
WESTHOFEN, M., Otorhinolaryngology
WILLMES-VON HINCKELDEY, K., Neuropsychology
ZENKE, M., Biomedical Engineering and Cell Biology
ZERRES, K., Human Genetics

AFFILIATED INSTITUTIONS

Aachen Global Academy GmbH: Kármánstr. 17, 52056 Aachen; Dir Dr CHRISTOPH K. HEINEN.

Aachener Demonstrationslabor für integrierte Produktionstechnik GmbH: Seilbachstr. 25, 52062 Aachen; Dir Dr WERNER FISCHER.

ACCES eV—Materials + Processes: Intzestr. 5, 52072 Aachen; e-mail welcome@access-technology.de; Dir ROBERT GUNTLIN.

Deutsches Wollforschungsinstitut eV (German Wool Research Institute): Veltmanplatz 8, 52062 Aachen; Dir Prof. Dr MARTIN MÖLLER.

Forschungsinstitut für Rationalisierung (Institute for Research in Rationalization): Pontdriesch 14–16, 52062 Aachen; tel. (241) 477050; e-mail info@fir.rwth-aachen.de; internet www.fir.rwth-aachen.de; CEO Prof. Dr Ing. VOLKER STICH.

Forschungsinstitut für Wasser- und Abfallwirtschaft (Research Institute for Water and Waste Management): Mies-van-der-Rohe-Str. 17, 52062 Aachen; e-mail fiw@fiw.rwth-aachen.de; Dir FRIEDRICH-WILHELM BOLLE.

Forschungsstelle Technisch-Wirtschaftliche Unternehmensstrukturen der Stahlindustrie (Research Department for Technical and Economic Corporate Structures in the Steel Industry): Intzestr. 1, 52072 Aachen; Dir Prof. Dr WINFRIED DAHL.

Fraunhofer-Institut für Produktionstechnologie (Fraunhofer Institute for Production Technology): Steinbachstr. 17, 52074 Aachen; e-mail info@ipt.fraunhofer.de; Dir Prof. Dr G. SCHUH.

Freunde und Förderer der RWTH Aachen: Wüllnerstr. 9, 52062 Aachen; em. Prof. ROLAND WALTER.

Institut für Kunststoffverarbeitung in Industrie und Handwerk (Institute for Plastics Technology): Ponstr. 49–55, 52062 Aachen; e-mail zentrale@ikv.rwth-aachen.de; Dir Prof. Dr WALTER MICHAELI.

Institut für Prozess- und Anwendungstechnik Keramik (Institute for Process and Application Technology in Ceramics): e-mail webmaster@ipak.rwth-aachen.de; Dir Prof. Dr HORST R. MAIER.

Prüf- und Entwicklungsinstitut für Abwassertechik: Mies-van-der-Rohe-Str. 1, 52074 Aachen; e-mail info@pia.rwth-aachen.de; Dir Dr ELMAR DORGELOH.

Technische Akademie, Wuppertal eV: Hubertusallee 18, 42117 Wuppertal; e-mail taw-wuppertal@taw.de; Dir Dr MARTIN STACHOWSKE.

WZLfoum an der RWTH Aachen: Steinbachstr. 53, 52074 Wuppertal; e-mail info@wzlforum.rwth-aachen.de; Dir Dr TORSTEN KURR

RHEINISCHE FRIEDRICH-WILHELMS-UNIVERSITÄT BONN

53012 Bonn
Regina-Pacis-Weg 3, 53113 Bonn
Telephone: (228) 2870
E-mail: presse@uni-bonn.de
Internet: www3.uni-bonn.de

Founded 1786, refounded 1818
State control
Academic year: October to September

Rector: Prof. Dr JÜRGEN FOHRMANN
Chancellor: Dr REINHARDT LUTZ
Deputy Rector for Finances: Prof. Dr ARMIN B. CREMERS
Deputy Rector for Public and Int. Relations: Prof. Dr CHRISTA E. MÜLLER
Deputy Rector for Research and Academic Staff Devt: Prof. Dr JÜRGEN VON HAGEN
Deputy Rector for Teaching, Studies, and Studies Reform: Prof. Dr VOLKMAR GIESELMANN
Library Dir: Dr RENATE VOGT
Library: see under Libraries and Archives
Number of teachers: 4,030
Number of students: 31,200
Publications: *Academica Bonnensia*, *Alma Mater*, *Bonner Akademische Reden*, *Bonner Universitäts-Nachrichten "Forsch"* (4 a year), *Bonn University News International* (in English, 1 a year), *Politeia*, *Studium Universale*

DEANS

Faculty of Agriculture: Prof. Dr PETER STEHLE
Faculty of Arts: Prof. Dr PAUL GEYER
Faculty of Catholic Theology: Prof. Dr CLAUDE OZANKOM
Faculty of Law and Economics: Prof. Dr KLAUS SANDMANN
Faculty of Mathematics and Natural Sciences: Prof. Dr ULF-G. MEIßNER
Faculty of Medicine: Prof. Dr MAX P. BUAR
Faculty of Protestant Theology: Prof. Dr UDO RÜTERSWÖRDEN

PROFESSORS

Faculty of Agriculture (Meckenheimer Allee 174, 59115 Bonn; tel. (228) 732866; e-mail landwirtschaftliche.fakultaet@uni-bonn.de; internet www.lwf.uni-bonn.de):

BERG, E., Agricultural Economics
DEHNE, H., Phytopathology
FÖRSTNER, W., Photogrammetry
GALENSA, R., Food Science and Food Chemistry
GOLDBACH, H., Plant Nutrition
HELFRICH, H.-P., Practical Mathematics
ILK, K. H., Satellite-Assisted Physical Geodesy
KÖPKE, U., Ecological Agriculture
KÜHBAUCH, W., Plant Breeding
KUNZ, B., Food Technology and Food Biotechnology
KUTSCH, TH., Agricultural and Domestic Sociology
LÉON, J., Plant Production and Breeding
NOGA, G., Fruit and Vegetable Production
SCHELLANDER, K., Animal Breeding
SCHIEFER, G., Agricultural Economy
SCHNABL, H., Botany
STEHLE, P., Nutrition
WEIß, E., House and Town Planning
WITTMANN, D., Agricultural Zoology and Ecology

Faculty of Arts (Am Hof 1, 53113 Bonn; tel. (228) 737295; internet www.philfak.uni-bonn.de):

BONNET, A.-M., History of Art
BREDENKAMP, J., Psychology
BRÜGGEN, E., Germanic Studies
COX, H. L., Folklore
DAHLMANN, D., East European History
DUMKE, D., Psychology
EHLERS, E., Social and Economic Geography
ESSER, J., English Philology
FEHN, K., Historical Geography
FISCHER, E., Musicology
FOHRMANN, J., Germanic Studies
GALSTERER, H., Ancient History
GROTZ, R., Geography
HESS, W., Communication and Phonetics
HILDEBRAND, K., Medieval and Modern History
HILGENHEGER, N., Education
HIRDT, W., Romance Philology
HOGREBE, W., Philosophy
HONNEFELDER, L., Philosophy
HÖNNIGHAUSEN, L., English Philology
KAISER, K., Political Science
KARSTEN, D., Political Science
KEIPERT, H., Slavonic Studies
KELZ, H., Phonetics
KLAUER, K. C., Psychology
KLEIN, TH., Germanic Studies
KLIMKEIT, H.-J., Comparative Religion
KOHRT, M., Germanic Studies
KÖLZER, T., Medieval and Modern History, Archival Science
KREINER, J., Japanology
KUBIN, W., Sinology
KUHN, A., History
KÜHNHARDT, L., Political Science
LADENTHIN, V., Education
LANGE, W. D., Romance Philology
LAUREYS, M., Philology
MECHLING, H., Sports
MIELSCH, H., Archaeology
NEUBAUER, W., Psychology
OEHLER, D., Comparative Science of Literature
PANTZER, P., Japanology
POHL, H., Constitutional History, Economics, Social History
POTTHOFF, W., Slavonic Studies
PREM, H. J., Ethnology
REICHL, K., English Philology
RÖßLER, U., Egyptology
ROSEN, K., Ancient History
SCHALLER, H.-J., Sports
SCHMITT, C., Roman Philology
SCHNEIDER, H., Germanic Studies
SCHOLZ, O. B., Psychology
SCHWARZ, H.-P., Political Science
SIMEK, R., Germanic Studies
STUHLMANN-LAEISZ, R., Logic and Foundations
WEEDE, E., Sociology
WILD, S., Semitic Philology
WINIGER, M., Geography
WOLF, H. J., Romance Philology
ZIMMER, ST., Linguistics
ZWIERLEIN, O., Classical Philology

Faculty of Catholic Theology (An der Schlosskirche 2–4, Bonn; tel. (228) 737344):

FABRY, H. J., Old Testament
FINDEIS, H.-J., New Testament
FÜRST, W., Pastoral Theology
GERHARDS, A., Liturgy
HOPPE, R., New Testament Science
HOSSFELD, F.-L., Old Testament Science
HÖVER, G., Moral Theology
LÜDECKE, N., Canon Law
MENKE, K.-H., Dogmatics, Theological Propaedeutics
MUSCHIOL, G., Church History
SCHÖLLGEN, G., Ancient Church History and Patrology
SCHULZ, M., Dogmatics
SONNEMANS, H., Fundamental Theology

Faculty of Law and Economics (Adenauerallee 24–42, 53113 Bonn; tel. (228) 739101; e-mail dekanat@jura.uni-bonn.de; internet www.jura.uni-bonn.de):

BÖSE, D., Political Economy
BREITUNG, J., Economics
BREUER, R., Public Law
DI FABIO, U., Public Law
DOLZER, R., German and International Public Law
FLEISCHER, H., Civil Law
HERDEGEN, M., Public Law
HILLGRUBER, CHR., Public Law
KINDHÄUSER, U., Criminal Law
KNÜTEL, R., Roman and Civil Law
KÖNDGEN, J., Civil Law
KORTE, B., Operational Research
KRÄKEL, M., Business Administration
LÖWER, W., Public Law
MOLDOVANU, B., Economic Theory, Mathematical Theory of Economics
NEUMANN, M., Economic Policy
PAEFFGEN, H.-U., Criminal Law
PIETZCKER, J., Public Law
ROTH, W.-H., Civil Law, International Private Law, and Comparative Law
SANDMANN, K., Economic Policy
SCHILKEN, E., Civil Law
SCHMIDT-PREUß, M., Public Law
SCHWEIZER, U., Economic Policy
SHAKED, A., Economic Policy
THEISSEN, E., Business Administration
VERREL, T., Criminology
VON HAGEN, J., Economics
WAGNER, G., Civil Law
WALTERMANN, R., Civil Law
ZACZYK, R., Criminal Law, Philosophy of Law
ZIMMER, D., Commercial Law
ZIMMERMANN, K., Economic Policy

Faculty of Mathematics and Natural Sciences (Wegelerstr. 10, 53113 Bonn; tel. (228) 732233; e-mail dekan@iam.uni-bonn.de; internet www.math-nat-fakultaet.uni-bonn.de):

ALBEVERIO, S., Mathematics
ALT, H. W., Mathematics
AUMANN, D., Chemistry
BALLMANN, W., Mathematics
BARGON, J., Physical Chemistry
BARTHLOTT, W., Botanics
BLECKMANN, H., Zoology
BRIESKORN, E., Mathematics
CREMERS, A. B., Informatics
DE BOER, K., Astronomy
DIETZ, K., Theoretical Physics
DIKAU, R., Geography
DÖTZ, K. H., Organic Chemistry
ECKMILLER, R., Informatics
EHLERS, E., Social and Economic Geography
FREHSE, J., Applied Mathematics
GLOMBITZA, K.-W., Pharmaceutical Biology
GRIEBEL, M., Scientific Computing
GROTZ, R., Geography
HAMENSTÄDT, U., Mathematics
HARDER, G., Mathematics
HERZOG, V., Cell Biology
HILDEBRANDT, S., Mathematics
HILGER, E., Experimental Physics
HUBER, M. G., Theoretical Atomic Physics
KARPINSKI, M., Informatics
KELLER, R., Zoology
KILIAN, K., Experimental Atomic Physics
KIRFEL, A., Mineralogy
KLEIN, F., Experimental Physics
KLEMPT, E., Experimental Physics
LEISTNER, E., Pharmaceutical Biology
LIEB, I., Mathematics
MADER, W., Inorganic Chemistry
MAIER, K., Experimental Physics
MASCHUW, R., Atomic Physics
MEBOLD, U., Radio Astronomy
MENZ, G., Geography
MENZEL, D., Botany
MESCHEDE, D., Experimental Physics
MONIEN, H., Theoretical Physics
MÜLLER, W., Mathematics
NAHM, W., Mathematical Physics
NEUGEBAUER, H., Geophysics
NICKEL, P., Pharmaceutical Chemistry
NIECKE, E., Inorganic and Analytical Chemistry
NILLES, H. P., Theoretical Physics
PEYERIMHOFF, S., Theoretical Chemistry
RAITH, M., Geology and Petrology
SANDHAS, W., Theoretical Physics
SANDHOFF, K., Biochemistry
SAUER, K. P., Zoology and Ecological Studies
SCHOCH, B., Physics
SCHÖNHAGE, A., Informatics
SIMMER, C., Meteorology
SPETH, J., Theoretical Physics
STEFFENS, K. J., Pharmaceutical Technology
THEIN, J., Geology
TRÜPER, H. G., Microbiology
VÖGTLE, F., Chemistry
VON KOENIGSWALD, W., Palaeontology
WANDELT, K., Physical Chemistry
WANDREY, CH., Biotechnology
WERMES, N., Experimental Physics
WILLECKE, K., Genetics
WINIGER, M., Geography

Faculty of Medicine (Sigmund-Freud-Str. 25, Haus 23, 53105 Bonn-Venusberg; tel. (228) 28719200; e-mail med-deha@ukb.uni-bonn.de; internet www.med.uni-bonn.de):

BAUR, M. P., Medical Statistics
BIDLINGMAIER, F., Clinical Biochemistry
BIEBER, TH., Dermatology and Venereology
BIERSACK, H.-J., Nuclear Medicine
ELGER, C. E., Epileptology
EXNER, M., Hygiene
FRANZ, TH., Anatomy
GÖTHERT, M., Pharmacology, Toxicology
GROTE, J., Physiology
HANFLAND, P., Experimental Haematology
HANSIS, M. L., Clinical Quality Management
HERBERHOLD, C., Otorhinolaryngology
HIRNER, A., Surgery
HOEFT, A., Anaesthesiology
JÄGER, A., Dentistry
KOECK, B., Dentistry
LENTZE, M. J., Paediatrics
LIEDTKE, R., Psychosomatic Medicine and Psychotherapy
LÜDERITZ, B., Internal Medicine, Cardiology
MADEA, B., Forensic Medicine
MAIER, W., Psychiatry
MÜLLER, ST., Urology
NOLDEN, R., Dentistry
PFEIFER, U., Pathology, Pathological Anatomy
PROPPING, P., Human Genetics
REICH, R., Oral and Maxillofacial Surgery
SAUERBRUCH, T., Internal Medicine
SCHAAL, K. P., Medical Microbiology
SCHILD, H. H., Radiology
SCHILLING, K., Anatomy
SCHMITT, O., Orthopaedics
SCHOTT, H., History of Medicine
SCHRAMM, J., Neurosurgery
SEITZ, H. M., Medical Parasitology
SPITZNAS, M., Ophthalmology
VETTER, H., Internal Medicine
WAHL, G., Oral Surgery
WIESTLER, O., Neuropathology

Faculty of Protestant Theology (Am Hof 1, 53113 Bonn; tel. (228) 737366):

BADER, G., Systematic Theology
HAUSCHILDT, E., Practical Theology
KINZIG, W., Church History
KREß, H., Systematic Theology, Social Ethics
MEYER-BLANCK, M., Theology Education
PANGRITZ, A., Systematic Theology
RÖHSER, G., New Testament
RÜTERSWÖRDEN, U., Old Testament
SCHMIDT-ROST, R., Practical Theology
STOCK, K., Systematic Theology
WOLTER, M., New Testament

RUHR-UNIVERSITÄT BOCHUM

Universitätsstr. 150, 44801 Bochum
Telephone: (234) 32201
E-mail: international@ruhr-uni-bochum.de
Internet: www.ruhr-uni-bochum.de

Founded 1965
State control
Languages of instruction: English, German
Academic year: October to July

Rector: Prof. Dr ELMAR W. WEILER
Chancellor: GERHARD MÖLLER
Vice-Rector for Planning, Structure and Finance: Prof. Dr W. LÖWENSTEIN
Vice-Rector for Research and Early Career Researchers: Prof. Dr J. WINTER
Vice-Rector for Teaching, Continuing Education and Media: Prof. Dr UTA WILKENS
Librarian: Dr ERDMUTE LAPP

Library of 2,000,000 vols
Number of teachers: 3,150
Number of students: 39,000

DEANS

Faculty of Biology and Biotechnology: Prof. Dr A. FAISSNER
Faculty of Catholic Theology: Prof. Dr C. FREVEL
Faculty of Chemistry and Biochemistry: Prof. Dr W. SANDER
Faculty of Civil and Environmental Engineering: Prof. Dr Ing. M. RADENBERG
Faculty of East Asian Studies: Prof. Dr J. PLASSEN
Faculty of Economics: Prof. Dr H. KARL
Faculty of Electrical Engineering and Information Technology: Prof. Dr P. AWAKOWICZ
Faculty of Geosciences: Prof. Dr J. RENNER
Faculty of History: Prof. Dr G. LUBICH
Faculty of Law: Prof. Dr ADELHEID WOLTERS
Faculty of Mathematics: Prof. Dr H. DEHLING
Faculty of Mechanical Engineering: Prof. Dr Ing. WERNER THEISEN
Faculty of Medicine: Prof. Dr K. ÜBERLA
Faculty of Philology: Prof. Dr R. KLABUNDE
Faculty of Philosophy and Education: Prof. Dr J. WIRTH
Faculty of Physics and Astronomy: Prof. Dr R. J. DETTMAR
Faculty of Protestant Theology: Prof. Dr P. WICK
Faculty of Psychology: Prof. Dr O. WOLF
Faculty of Social Sciences: Prof. Dr J. STRAUB
Faculty of Sports Science: Prof. Dr A. NEUMAIER

PROFESSORS

Faculty of Biology and Biotechnology (tel. (234) 3224573; internet www.biologie.ruhr-uni-bochum.de):

BENNERT, W., Plant Taxonomy
DENHARDT, G., General Zoology and Neurobiology
DISTLER, C., General Zoology and Neurobiology
FAISSNER, A., Cell Morphology and Molecular Neurobiology
GERWERT, K., Biophysics
HAEUPLER, H., Geobotany
HAPPE, T., Plant Biochemistry, Photobiotechnology
HATT, H., Cell Physiology
HOFFMANN, K.-P., General Zoology and Neurobiology
HOFMANN, E., Protein Crystallography, Biophysics
JANCKE, D., Cognitive Neurobiology, General Zoology and Neurobiology
KIRCHNER, W. H., Behavioural Biology and Teaching of Biology
KÜCK, U., General and Molecular Botany
LINK, G., Plant Cell Physiology and Molecular Biology, Plant Physiology
LÜBBEN, M., Biophysics
LÜBBERT, H., Animal Physiology
NARBERHAUS, F., Biology of Micro-Organisms
NECKER, R., Animal Physiology
NICKELSEN, J., Biology of Micro-Organisms
ÖTTMAYER, W., Plant Biochemistry
PÖGGELER, S., General and Molecular Botany
RAETHER, W., Special Zoology
RÖGNER, M., Plant Biochemistry
SCHAUB, G., Animal Taxonomy, Parasitology
SCHLITTER, J., Biophysics
SCHMIDT, M., General Zoology and Neurobiology
SCHÜNEMANN, O., General and Molecular Botany
SCHWENN, J.-D., Plant Biochemistry
STÖRTKUHL, K., Cell Physiology, Sensory Physiology
STÜTZEL, T., Plant Taxonomy, Spermatophytes
WAHLE, P., Developmental Neurobiology, General Zoology and Neurobiology
WEILER, E., Plant Physiology
WETZEL, C., Cell Physiology

Faculty of Catholic Theology (tel. (234) 3222619; e-mail kath-theol-fak@ruhr-uni-bochum.de):

DAMBERG, W., Medieval and Modern Church History
DSCHULNIGG, P., New Testament

FREVEL, C., Old Testament Exegesis and Theology
GEERLINGS, W., Church History, Patrology
GÖLLNER, R., Practical Theology
KNAPP, M., Fundamental Theology
KNOCH, W., Dogmatics
REINHARDT, H. J. F., Canon Law
WIEMEYER, J., Christian Social Ethics
ZELINKA, U., Moral Theology

Faculty of Chemistry and Biochemistry (tel. (234) 3224732; e-mail chemie-dekanat@ruhr-uni-bochum.de; internet www.ruhr-uni-bochum.de/chemie):

BENNECKE, G., Receptor Biochemistry
DYKER, G., Organic Chemistry
FEIGEL, M., Organic Chemistry
FISCHER, R., Inorganic Chemistry
GRÜNERT, W., Technical Chemistry
HAVENITH-NEWEN, M., Physical Chemistry
HERMANN, C., Physical Chemistry
HEUMANN, R., Molecular Neurobiochemistry
HOLLMANN, M., Receptor Biochemistry
HOVEMANN, B., Molecular Cell Biochemistry
MARX, D., Theoretical Chemistry
MUHLER, M., Technical Chemistry
MÜLLER, S., Organic Chemistry
SANDER, W., Organic Chemistry
SCHUHMANN, W., Analytical Chemistry
SHELDRICK, W. S., Analytical Chemistry
SOMMER, K., Didactics of Chemistry
STAEMMLER, V., Theoretical Chemistry
VON KIEDROWSKI, G., Organic Chemistry
WEINGÄRTNER, H., Physical Chemistry
WÖLL, C., Physical Chemistry

Faculty of Civil and Environmental Engineering (tel. (234) 3226124; e-mail dekanat-bi@ruhr-uni-bochum.de; internet www.ruhr-uni-bochum.de/fbi):

BREITENBÜCHER, R., Building Materials
BRILON, W., Traffic Engineering
BRUHNS, O. T., Mechanics
HACKL, K., Mechanics
HARTMANN, D., Applied Computer Science
HÖFFER, R., Aerodynamics and Fluid Mechanics
KINDMANN, R., Steel and Composite Constructions
MESCHKE, G., Structural Mechanics
ORTH, H., Environmental Engineering
REESE, S., Computational Mechanics and Simulation
SCHERER, M., Surveying and Geodesy
SCHMID, G., Structural Mechanics and Computer Simulation
SCHUMANN, A., Hydrology, Water Resources Management and Environmental Engineering
STANGENBERG, F., Reinforced and Prestressed Concrete Structures
STOLPE, H., Environmental Technology and Ecology
TRIANTAFYLLIDIS, TH., Soil Mechanics
WILLEMS, W., Structural Design and Building Physics

Faculty of East Asian Studies (tel. (234) 3226189; e-mail anne.mueller@ruhr-uni-bochum.de; internet www.ruhr-uni-bochum.de/oaw):

EGGERT, M., Korean Studies
FINDEISEN, R., Chinese Language and Literature
GU, X., East Asian Politics
KLENNER, W., East Asian Economics
MATHIAS, R., Japanese History
RICKMEYER, J., Japanese Language and Literature
ROETZ, H., Chinese History and Philosophy

Faculty of Economics (tel. (234) 32-22884; e-mail wiwi-dekanat@ruhr-uni-bochum.de; internet www.wiwi.ruhr-uni-bochum.de):

BAUER, T., Empirical Economics
BENDER, D., International Economic Relations
DIRRIGL, H., Controlling
FOLKERS, C., Public Finance
GABRIEL, R., Business Informatics
HAMMANN, P., Management and Marketing
HAUCUP, J., Economic Policy
KARL, H., Economic Policy
KÖSTERS, W., Monetary Economics
LÖSCH, M., Statistics and Econometrics
MAG, W., Theoretical Industrial Economics
MANN, T., Law Concerning the Economy
NIENHAUS, V., Economic Policy
PAUL, S., Banking and Finance
PELLENS, B., International Accounting
SCHIMMELPFENNIG, J., Theoretical and Applied Microeconomics
SMOLNY, W., Applied Economics
STEVEN, M., Production and Operations
STREIM, H., Financial Accounting and Auditing
VOIGT, S., Economic Policy
WERNERS, B., Operations Research and Accounting

Faculty of Electrical Engineering and Information Technology (tel. (234) 3225666; e-mail dekanat-ei@ruhr-uni-bochum.de; internet www.et.ruhr-uni-bochum.de):

AWAKOWICZ, P., General Electrical Engineering/Plasma Technology
BALZERT, H., Software Engineering
BRINKMANN, R. P., Theoretical Electrical Engineering/Plasma Technology
ERMERT, H., High-Frequency Engineering
FISCHER, H. D., Communications Engineering
GÖCKLER, H., Digital Signal Processing
HAUSNER, J., Integrated Systems
HOFMANN, M., Optoelectronic Devices and Materials
HUDDE, H., Sound and Vibration
KUNZE, U., Electronic Materials and Nanoelectronics
LANGMANN, U., Integrated Circuits
LUNZE, J., Automation
MARTIN, R., Information Technology and Communication Acoustics
MELBERT, J., Electronic Circuits and Measurement Techniques
OEHM, J., Circuit Design
PAAR, CH., Communication Security
SADIGHI, A.-R., Applied Data Security
SCHMILZ, G., Medical Engineering
SCHWENK, J., Network and Data Security
SOURKOUNIS, C., Power System Technology
STEIMEL, A., Power Engineering
TÜCHELMANN, Y., Integrated Information Systems

Faculty of Geosciences (tel. (234) 3223505; e-mail geodekanat@ruhr-uni-bochum.de; internet www.ruhr-uni-bochum.de/exogeol/geowiss.html):

ALBER, M., Engineering Geology
BUTZIN, B., Geography
CHAKRABORTY, S., Mineralogy and Petrology
FLEER, H., Climatology and Hydrogeology
FRIEDRICH, W., Geophysics
GIES, H., Mineralogy and Crystallography
HOHN, U., Economic and Social Geography
JÜRGENS, C., Geo-Remote Sensing
LÖTSCHER, L., Geography and Cultural Geography
MARESCH, W. V., Mineralogy
MÜLLER, J.-C., Cartography
MUTTERLOSE, J., Palaeontology and Geology
OTTO, K.-H., Didactics of Geography
RENNER, J., Seismology
SCHMITT, TH., Geography
STÖCKHERT, B., Geology
WOHNLICH, ST., Applied Geology
ZEPP, H., Physical Geography

Faculty of History (tel. (234) 3222525; e-mail dekan-gw@ruhr-uni-bochum.de; internet www.ruhr-uni-bochum.de/geschichtswissenschaft):

BERGER, S., Social History and Social Movements
BERNS, C., Archaeology
BORUTTA, M., History of Mediterranean Culture
BRAUCH, N., Didactics of History
EBEL-ZEPEZAUER, W., Pre- and Proto-History
GOSCHLER, C., Contemporary History
GÜNTHER, L.-M., Ancient History
HÖLSCHER, L., Theory of History
HOPPE-SAILER, R., History of Modern Art
JÖCHNER, C., History of Early Modern Art
KOLLER, M., History of the Ottoman Empire and Turkish History
LEMMES, F., European History
LICHTENBERGER, A., Archaeology
LINKE, B., Ancient History
LUBICH, G., History of the Middle Ages with a focus on the Early and High Middle Ages and Auxilliary Sciences
MAIER, H., History of Technology and Environmental History
MATHIAS, R., East Asian Studies
MORSTADT, B., Archaeology of the Phenician Diaspora
PLAGGENBORG, S., Eastern European History
REHM, U., History of Medieval Art
SCHULTE, R., Modern History, Gender Studies
STÖLLNER, T., Pre- and Proto-history
URBAN, A., History of Modern Art with a focus on New Media
VON ROSEN, V., History of Art
VON RÜDEN, V., Pre- and Proto-history
WALA, M., History of North America
ZIEGLER, D., Economic and Business History
ZWIERLEIN, C., History of the Environment

Faculty of Law (tel. (234) 3226566; e-mail denise.sablotny@jura.ruhr-uni-bochum.de; internet www.ruhr-uni-bochum.de/jura):

BERNSMANN, K., Criminal Law, Criminal Procedural Law
BORGES, G., Civil Law, Media Law and Law of Information Technology
BURGI, M., Public Law
FELTES, TH., Criminology
GREMER, W., Public Law, European Law
HÖRNLE, T., Criminal Law, Criminal Procedural Law
HUSTER, S., Public Law
KINDLER, P., Civil Law, Commercial Law, International Civil Law and Comparative Law
KRAMPE, CHR., Civil Law, Ancient Law and Roman Law
MUSCHELER, K., History of German Law, Civil Law, Church Law
POSCHER, R., Public Law, Sociology of Law
PUTTLER, A., Public Law
SCHILDT, B., History of Law, Civil Law
SCHREIBER, K., Procedural Law, Civil and Labour Law
SEER, R., Tax Law and Administrative Law
SIEKMANN, H., Public Law
THIELBOERGER, P., Public Law and International Law
WANK, R., Civil Law, Commercial and Labour Law
WINDEL, A., Procedural Law, Civil Law
WOLF, J., Public Law
WOLTERS, G., Criminal Law, Criminal Procedural Law

Faculty of Mathematics (tel. (234) 3223476; e-mail ffm@ruhr-uni-bochum.de; internet www.ruhr-uni-bochum.de/ffm):

ABRESCH, U., Mathematics
AVANZI, R., Mathematics

BARTENWERFER, W., Mathematics
BERTSCH, E., Computer Science
DEHLING, H., Mathematics
DETTE, H., Mathematics
DOBBERTIN, H., Mathematics, Cryptology
EICHELSBACHER, P., Mathematics
FLENNER, H., Mathematics
GERRITZEN, L., Mathematics
HEINZNER, P., Mathematics
HUCKLEBERRY, A. T., Mathematics
KIRSCH, W., Mathematical Physics
KNIEPER, G., Mathematics
KRIECHERBAUER, T., Mathematics
LAURES, G., Mathematics
MATTHIES, G., Mathematics
SIMON, H., Mathematics, Computer Science
STORCH, U., Mathematics
VERFÜRTH, R., Mathematics
WASSERMANN, G., Differential Topology

Faculty of Mechanical Engineering (tel. (234) 3226191; e-mail dekanmb@itm.ruhr-uni-bochum.de; internet www.ruhr-uni-bochum.de/maschinenbau):

ABRAMOVICI, M., Computer Science
EGGELER, G., Materials Science
MEIER, Production Systems
PAPENFUSS, H.-D., Applied Fluid Mechanics
POHL, M., Materials Testing
PREDKI, W., Mechanical Components—Industrial and Automotive Power Transmission
REINIG, G., Control Systems Engineering
ROGG, B., Fluid Mechanics
RÖHM, H.-J., Chemical and Environmental Engineering
SCHERER, V., Energy Plant Technology
SCHWEIGER, G., Applied Laser Technology and Measuring Systems
STOFF, H., Fluid Flow Machines
STÖVER, D. H. H., Materials Processing
STRATMANN, M., Materials Surfaces and Interfaces
SVEJDA, P., Thermodynamics of Mixtures
THEISEN, W., Materials Technology
WAGNER, G., Mechanical Components and Materials Handling
WAGNER, H.-J., Energy Systems and Energy Economics
WAGNER, W., Thermodynamics
WEIDNER, E., Process Engineering
WELP, E. G., Mechanical Components and Methodical Design

Faculty of Medicine (tel. (234) 3224960; e-mail medizin@rub.de; internet www.ruhr-uni-bochum.de/medizin):

ADAMIETZ, J. A., Radiology
ALTMEYER, P., Dermatology and Venereology
BRÜNING, TH., Industrial Medicine
BUFE, A., Paediatrics
BURCHERT, W., Radiology
DAZERT, S., Otorhinolaryngology
DERMIETZEL, R., Anatomy
ENGERT, J., Paediatric Surgery
EPPLEN, J., Genetics
ERDMANN, R., Biochemistry
EYSEL, U., Physiology
GATERMANN, S., Medical Microbiology
GOODY, R., Physiological Chemistry
GRONEMEYER, U., Ophthalmology
GUZMAN Y ROTAECHE, J., Pathology
HARDERS, A. G., Neurosurgery
HASENBRING, M., Medical Psychology
HERPERTZ, S., Psychosomatic Medicine and Psychotherapy
HEUSER, L., Radiology
HOHLBACH, G.-R., Surgery
HORSTKOTTE, D., Internal Medicine
INOUE, K., Anaesthesiology
JENSEN, A. W. O., Gynaecology and Obstetrics
KLEESIEK, K., Clinical Chemistry and Pathobiochemistry
KLEIN, H. H., Internal Medicine
KOESLING, D., Pharmacology and Toxicology
KÖRFER, R., Thoracic and Cardiovascular Surgery
KÖSTER, O., Radiology
KRÄMER, J., Orthopaedics
KRIEG, M., Clinical Chemistry
LACZKOVICS, A., Surgery, Thoracic and Cardiovascular Surgery
LAUBENTHAL, H., Anaesthesiology
LIERMANN, D., Radiology
MALIN, J.-P., Neurology
MANNHERZ, H. G., Anatomy and Cell Biology
MAYER, H., Paediatric Cardiology
MELLER, K., Experimental Cytology
MORGENROTH, K., Pathology
MÜGGE, A., Internal Medicine
MUHR, G., Surgery
MÜLLER, I., History of Medicine
MÜLLER, K.-M., Pathology
NICOLAS, V., Radiology
NOLDUS, J., Urology
PESKAR, B., Clinical Experimental Medicine
PIENTKA, L., Geriatrics
POTT, L., Cellular Physiology
PRZUNTEK, H., Neurology
PUCHSTEIN, CH., Anaesthesiology
REUSCH, P., Pharmacology and Toxicology
RIEGER, CH., Paediatrics
RUMP, L. C., Nephrology
RUSCHE, H. H., General Medicine
SCHLEGEL, U., Neurology
SCHMIDT, W. E. W., Internal Medicine
SCHMIEGEL, W.-H., Internal Medicine
SCHULTZE-WERNINGHAUS, G., Internal Medicine
STEINAU, H.-U., Surgery
TRAMPISCH, H. J., Medical Informatics and Biomathematics
TRAPPE, H.-J., Internal Medicine
TSCHÖPE, D., Internal Medicine
ÜBERLA, K. T., Virology
UHE, W., Surgery
VIEBAHN, R., Surgery
VON DÜRING, M., Anatomy
WERNER, J., Biomedical Engineering
WILHELM, M., Hygiene
WOLFF, K.-D., Maxillofacial Surgery
ZENZ, M., Anaesthesiology

Faculty of Philology (tel. (234) 3222623; internet www.dekphil.ruhr-uni-bochum.de):

BASTERT, B., German Philology
BAUSCH, K.-R., Romance Philology
BEHRENS, R., Romance Philology
BEILENHOFF, W., Cinematography and Television Studies
BERNHARD, G., Romance Philology
BEYER, M., English Philology
BOETTCHER, W., Teaching of German Language and Literature
BOLLACHER, M., Modern German Literature
DEUBER-MANKOWSKI, A., Media Studies
EBEL, E., Scandinavian Studies
EFFE, B., Classical Philology
EIKELMANN, M., German Philology
ENDRESS, G., Arabic and Islamic Studies
FLUCK, H.-R., German Linguistics
FREITAG, K., American Studies
GLEI, R., Classical Philology/Latin
HASS, U., Theatre Studies
HEDIGER, V., Media Studies
HIMMELMANN, N., General Linguistics
HISS, G., Theatre Studies
HOUWEN, L., English Philology
KISS, T., General Linguistics
KLABUNDE, R., General Linguistics
KLODT, C., Classical Philology/Latin
KNAUTH, K. A., Romance Philology
KRENN, H., Romance Philology
LEBSANFT, F., Romance Philology
MENGE, H., German Linguistics
NIEDERHOFF, B., English
PITTNER, K., German Linguistics
PLUMPE, G., Modern German Literature
REICHMUTH, S., Islamic Studies
RUPP, G., Didactics of German Philology
SAPPOK, C., Slavonic Studies
SCHMID, U., Slavonic Studies
SCHMITZ-EMANS, M., General and Comparative Literature
SCHNEIDER, M., Modern German Literature
SCHÖNEFELD, D., English Philology
SIMONIS, L., General and Comparative Literature
SPANGENBERG, P., Media Sciences
STEINBRÜGGE, L., Romance Philology
THOMAS, B., Media Studies
TIETZ, M., Romance Philology
UHLENBRUCH, B., Russian and Soviet Culture
WARTH, E.-M., Cinematography and Television Studies
WEBER, I., English Philology
WEGERA, K.-P., History of German Language
WIEHL, P., Germanic Philology
ZELLE, C., Modern German Literature

Faculty of Philosophy and Education (tel. (234) 3222712; e-mail reinhild.topp@ruhr-uni-bochum.de):

ADICK, C., Comparative Education
BELLENBERG, G., Educational Research Focus on Schools
DRIESCHNER, M., Natural Philosophy
HAARDT, A., Philosophy
HARNEY, K., Vocational Education and Lifelong Learning, Methods of Educational Research
HERZIG, B., Learning and Teaching Research
JAESCHKE, W., Classic German Philosophy
KEINER, E., History of Education
LESSING, H.-U., Philosophical Anthropology and Theory of the Humanities
MEYER-DRAWE, K., General Education
MOJSISCH, B., History of Philosophy
PARDEY, Logic and Philosophy of Language
PULTE, H., History and Philosophy of Science
ROSEMANN, B., Educational Psychology
SCHMIDT, K., Classic German Philosophy, Symbolic and Mathematical Logic
SCHOLTZ, G., History and Theory of the Humanities
SCHWEIDLER, Practical Philosophy
STEIGLEDER, K., Ethics in Medicine and Biosciences
WITTPOTH, J., Adult Education

Faculty of Physics and Astronomy (tel. (234) 3223445; e-mail dekanat@physik.ruhr-uni-bochum.de; internet physik.ruhr-uni-bochum.de):

CHINI, R., Astrophysics
CZARNETZKI, U., Experimental Physics
DETTMAR, R.-J., Astronomy
DRAUTZ, R., Theoretical Physics
EFETOV, K., Theoretical Physics
EPELBAUM, E., Theoretical Physics
EREMIN, I., Theoretical Physics
GERWERT, K., Biophysics
GRAUER, R., Theoretical Physics
HÄGELE, D., Experimental Physics
HAVENITH-NEWEN, M., Physical Chemistry
KÖHLER, U., Experimental Physics
LINSMEIER, C., Experimental Physics
MEYER, A., Experimental Physics
MEYER, W., Experimental Physics
POLYAKOV, U., Theoretical Physics
RITMAN, J., Experimental Physics
ROLDAN CUENYA, B., Experimental Physics
SCHLICKEISER, R., Theoretical Physics
SCHÖNER, G., Neuroinformatics
SOLTWISCH, H., Experimental Physics
STEINBACH, I., Theoretical Physics
TJUS, J., Experimental Physics
UNTERBERG, B., Experimental Physics

von Keudell, A., Experimental Physics
Wieck, A., Experimental Physics
Wiedner, U., Experimental Physics
Wiskott, L., Neuroinformatics

Faculty of Protestant Theology (tel. (234) 322250; e-mail ulrike.burgner@ruhr-uni-bochum.de; internet www.ruhr-uni-bochum.de/ev-theol):

Beyer, F.-H., Practical Theology
Ebach, J., Old Testament
Geldbach, E., Ecumenical and Denominational Studies
Jähnichen, T., Christian Social Science
Karle, J., Practical Theology
Krech, V., Religious Science
Strohm, C., Church History (Reformation and Modern)
Thiel, W., Old Testament
Thomas, G., Systematic Theology
Wengst, K., New Testament Exegesis and Theology
Wick, P., New Testament
Wyrwa, D., Church History

Faculty of Psychology (tel. (234) 3224606; e-mail psy-dekanat@ruhr-uni-bochum.de; internet www.ruhr-uni-bochum.de/psy-dekanat):

Bierhoff, H.-W., Social Psychology
Bock, M., Psychology of Language and Communication
Daum, I., Neuropsychology
Güntürkün, O., Biopsychology
Guski, R., Cognitive and Environmental Psychology
Hasenbring, M., Medical Psychology
Reulecke, W., Sport Psychology
Rosemann, B., Educational Psychology
Schölmerich, A., Development Psychology
Schulte, D., Clinical Psychology and Psychiatry
Wottawa, H., Methodology, Diagnostic and Evaluation
Zimolong, B., Industrial and Organizational Psychology

Faculty of Social Sciences (tel. (234) 32222967; e-mail christel.maleszka@ruhr-uni-bochum.de; internet www.ruhr-uni-bochum.de/sowi):

Althammer, J., Social Politics
Andersen, U., Political Science
Bleek, W., Political Science
Heinze, R. G., Sociology
Lehner, F., Political Science
Lenz, I., Sociology
Minssen, H., Labour Organization
Nolte, H., Social Psychology
Ott, N., Social Politics
Petzina, D., Social and Economic History
Pries, L., Participation and Organization
Rohwer, G., Methodology of Social Science and Social Statistics
Schmidt, G., Political Science
Strohmeier, K. P., Sociology
Tiede, M., Mathematical and Empirical Procedure in Social Sciences
Voss, W., Mathematical and Empirical Procedure in Social Sciences
Widmaier, Political Science
Wolff, J., Sociology of Developing Countries

Faculty of Sport Science (Gebäude UHW, Stiepelerstr. 129, 44801 Bochum; tel. (234) 3227793; e-mail sportwiss-dekanat@ruhr-uni-bochum.de; internet www.ruhr-uni-bochum.de/spowiss):

Beckers, E., Pedagogy of Sport
Ferranti, A., Applied Training Science
Heck, H. J., Medicine in Sport
Kellmann, M., Sports Psychology
Klein, M. L., Sociology of Sport, Sports Management
Neumaier, A., Theory of Movement, Biomechanics

Centre for Further Education (Geb. LOTA, 44780 Bochum; tel. (234) 322-6466; e-mail wbz@ruhr-uni-bochum.de; internet www.ruhr-uni-bochum.de/wbz):

Muhler, M.

Institute for Development Research and Development Policy (tel. (234) 3222418; e-mail ieeoffice@ruhr-uni-bochum.de; internet www.ruhr-uni-bochum.de/iee):

Andersen, U., Society, Politics, Public Admin.
Bender, D., International Economic Relations
Dürr, H., Social and Economic Geography
Nienhaus, V., Economic Policy
Voss, W., Statistics and Econometrics
Wolf, J., International Law
Wolff, J. H., Society, Politics, Public Admin.

Institute for Energy and Natural Resources Law (tel. (234) 3227333; e-mail tbe@ruhr-uni-bochum.de; internet www.ruhr-uni-bochum.de/ibe):

Dresen, L., Seismology
Hüffer, U., Civil Law, Commercial Law
Ipsen, K., Public Law
Stein, D., Pipe Construction and Maintenance
Tettinger, P. J., Public Law
Unger, H., Nuclear and Modern Energy Systems
von Danwitz, T., Public Law, European Law

Institute for German Cultural Studies (tel. (234) 3227863; e-mail idf@ruhr-uni-bochum.de; internet www.ruhr-uni-bochum.de/deutschlandforschung):

Andersen, U., Political Science
Anweiler, D., Educational Research, Comparative Educational Research
Bleek, W., Political Science
Faulenbach, B., Modern History
Klussmann, P. G., Modern German Literature
Kross, E., Didactics of Geography
Voss, W., Mathematical and Empirical Procedure in Social Sciences

Institute for Industrial Engineering (tel. (234) 3227730; internet www.iaw.ruhr-uni-bochum.de/iaw):

Minnssen, H. (Dir)

Institute for Industrial Science (tel. (234) 3223293; internet www.iaw.ruhr-uni-bochum.de):

Kailer, N., Personnel and Qualifications
Minssen, H., Organization of Work
Schnauber, H., Working Systems Design
Staudt, E., Economics of Work

Institute for International Law of Peace and Human Rights (tel. (234) 3227366; internet www.ruhr-uni-bochum.de/ifhv):

Anersen, U., Political Science (Dir)

Institute for Neuro-Computing (tel. (234) 3227965; e-mail institut@neuroinformatik.ruhr-uni-bochum.de; internet www.neuroinformatik.ruhr-uni-bochum.de):

Schöner, G., Theoretical Biology
von der Malsburg, Ch., Systems Biophysics

Institute for Social Movements (44789 Bochum, Clemensstr. 17–19; tel. (234) 3224687; internet www.ruhr-uni-bochum.de/isb):

Tenfelde, K., Social History and Social Movements

Institute for Teacher Training (tel. (234) 3211942; e-mail zfl-kontakt@ruhr-uni-bochum.de; internet www.ruhr-uni-bochum.de/zfl):

Bausch, K. R., Romance Philology
Bellenberg, G., Educational Science
Kammertöns, A., Didactics of Social Sciences
Ott, N., Social Politics
Tietz, M., Romance Philology
Wieck, A., Experimental Physics

STEINBEIS-HOCHSCHULE BERLIN
(Steinbeis University Berlin)

Gürtelstr. 29a/30, 10247 Berlin
Telephone: (30) 2933090
E-mail: shb@stw.de
Internet: www.steinbeis-hochschule.de
Founded 1998
Private control
Pres. and Man. Dir: Prof. Dr Johann Löhn
Number of students: 4,000

STIFTUNG TIERÄRZTLICHE HOCHSCHULE HANNOVER
(University of Veterinary Medicine Hanover, Foundation)

POB 71 11 80, 30559 Hanover
Bünteweg 2, 30559 Hanover
Telephone: (511) 95360
E-mail: info@tiho-hannover.de
Internet: www.tiho-hannover.de
Founded 1778
Pres.: Dr Gerhard Greif
Vice-Pres. for Academic Affairs: Prof. Dr Andrea Tipold
Vice-Pres. for Research: Prof. Dr Burkhard Meinecke
Number of teachers: 58
Number of students: 2,360

TECHNISCHE UNIVERSITÄT BERGAKADEMIE FREIBERG

Akademiestr. 6, 09599 Freiberg
Telephone: (3731) 390
E-mail: rektorat@zuv.tu-freiberg.de
Internet: tu-freiberg.de
Founded 1765
State control
Academic year: October to August
Rector: Prof. Dr Bernd Meyer
Vice-Rector for Education: Prof. Dr Silvia Rogler
Vice-Rector for Research: Prof. Dr Broder Merkel
Chancellor: Dr Andreas Handschuh
Number of teachers: 383
Number of students: 5,458
Publications: *Fakultät Mathematik und Informatik Preprints, Freiberger Forschungshefte, Wissenschaftliche Mitteilungen des Instituts für Geologie*

DEANS

Faculty of Chemistry and Physics: Prof. Dr Michael Schlömann
Faculty of Economics and Business Administration: Prof. Dr Carsten Felden
Faculty of Geosciences, Geoengineering and Mining: Prof. Dr Carsten Drebenstedt
Faculty of Materials Science and Technology: Prof. Dr Hab. Horst Biermann
Faculty of Mathematics and Computer Science: Prof. Dr Hab. Bernhard Jung
Faculty of Mechanical, Process and Energy Engineering: Prof. Dr Hab. Alfons Ams

TECHNISCHE UNIVERSITÄT BERLIN

Str. des 17 Juni 135, 10623 Berlin
Telephone: (30) 3140
E-mail: pressestelle@tu-berlin.de
Internet: www.tu-berlin.de
Founded 1879 by merger of The Bauakademie (Building Academy) of Berlin (f. 1799)

and the Gewerbeakademie (f. 1821); current name adopted 1946
Pres.: Prof. Dr Ing. JÖRG STEINBACH
Vice-Pres.: Prof. Dr GABRIELE WENDORF
Vice-Pres.: Prof. Dr ULRIKE WOGGON
Vice-Pres.: Prof. Dr Ing. WOLFGANG HUHNT
Chancellor: Dr ULRIKE GUTHEIL
Librarian: Dr WOLFGANG ZICK
Library: see under Libraries and Archives
Number of teachers: 3,184
Number of students: 29,510
Publications: *Mitteilungsblatt der TUB* (26 a year), *TU intern* (9 a year), *TU International* (4 a year), *Universitätsführer* (every two years), *Vorlesungsverzeichnis* (2 a year)

DEANS
Economics and Management: Prof. Dr JÜRGEN ENSTHALER
Electrical Engineering and Computer Sciences: Prof. ANJA FELDMANN
Humanities: Prof. Dr ADRIAN VON BUTTLAR
Mathematics and Natural Sciences: Prof. Dr CHRISTIAN THOMSEN
Mechanical Engineering and Transport Systems: Prof. Dr Ing. UTZ VON WAGNER
Planning, Building, Environment: Prof. Dr JOHANN KÖPPEL
Process Sciences: Prof. Dr LOTHAR KROH

TECHNISCHE UNIVERSITÄT CAROLO WILHELMINA ZU BRAUNSCHWEIG

Pockelsstr. 14, 38106 Braunschweig
Telephone: (531) 3910
E-mail: president@tu-bs.de
Internet: www.tu-braunschweig.de
Founded 1745 as Collegium Carolinum; became Herzogliche Polytechnische Schule 1862 and Technische Hochschule 1877; present name 1968
State control
Academic year: October to September (2 terms)
Pres.: Prof. Dr Ing. JÜRGEN HESSELBACH
Vice-Pres.: Prof. Dr HEIKE FASSBENDER
Vice-Pres.: Prof. Dr MARTIN KORTE
Vice-Pres.: DIETMAR SMYREK
Vice-Pres.: Prof. Dr THOMAS SPENGLER
Head of Int. Office: Dr ASTRID SEBASTIAN
Library Dir: Prof. Dr Hab. DIETMAR BRANDES
Library: see under Libraries and Archives
Number of teachers: 230 full-time professors
Number of students: 13,500
Publications: *Forschungsbericht* (every 5 years), *Mitteilungen der Carolo-Wilhelmina* (1 or 2 a year), *Personal- und Vorlesungsverzeichnis* (2 a year), *TU-aktuell* (6 a year), *Veröffentlichung der Technischen Universität Braunschweig* (1 a year)

DEANS
Carl-Friedrich-Gauß Faculty: Prof. Dr DIRK C. MATTFELD
Faculty of Architecture, Civil Engineering and Environmental Sciences: Prof. Dr OTTO RICHTER
Faculty of Electrical Engineering, Information Technology, Physics: Prof. Dr JOCHEN LITTERST
Faculty of Humanities and Pedagogics: Prof. Dr GOTTFRIED ORTH
Faculty of Life Sciences: Prof. Dr DIETER JAHN
Faculty of Mechanical Engineering: Prof. Dr Ing. PETER HECKER

TECHNISCHE UNIVERSITÄT CHEMNITZ
(Chemnitz University of Technology)

09107 Chemnitz
Telephone: (371) 5310
E-mail: pressestelle@tu-chemnitz.de
Internet: www.tu-chemnitz.de
Founded 1836 as Königliche Gewerbschule Chemnitz, present status 1986, present name 1997
State control
Academic year: October to September
Rector: Prof. Dr ARNOLD VAN ZYL
Vice-Rector for Knowledge and Technology Transfer: Prof. Dr ANDREAS SCHUBERT
Vice-Rector for Research and Young Scientists: Prof. Dr HEINRICH LANG
Vice-Rector for Teaching and Learning: Prof. Dr CHRISTOPH FASBENDER
Chancellor: Dr EBERHARD ALLES
Library Dir: ANGELA MALZ
Library: see under Libraries and Archives
Number of teachers: 156
Number of students: 10,850
Publication: *TU-Spektrum* (3 a year)

DEANS
Department of Behavioural and Social Sciences: Prof. Dr UDO RUDOLPH
Department of Computer Science: Prof. Dr WOLFRAM HARDT
Department of Economics and Business Administration: Prof. Dr PETER GLUCHOWSKI
Department of Electrical Engineering and Information Technology: Prof. Dr MADHUKAR CHANDRA
Department of Humanities: Prof. Dr STEFAN PFEIFFER
Department of Natural Sciences: Prof. Dr KARL HEINZ HOFFMANN
Faculty of Mathematics: Prof. Dr DIETER HAPPEL
Faculty of Mechanical Engineering: Prof. Dr KLAUS NENDEL

TECHNISCHE UNIVERSITÄT CLAUSTHAL

Adolph-Roemer-Str. 2A, 38678 Clausthal-Zellerfeld
Telephone: (5323) 720
E-mail: info@tu-clausthal.de
Internet: www.tu-clausthal.de
Founded 1775 as Bergakademie Clausthal, attained univ. status 1968
State control
Academic year: April to March
Pres.: Prof. Dr THOMAS HANSCHKE
Vice-Pres.: Dr Ing. INES SCHWARZ
Vice-Pres. for Information Management and Infrastructure: Prof. Dr ANDREAS RAUSCH
Vice-Pres. for Research and Technology Transfer: Prof. Dr Ing. VOLKER WESLING
Vice-Pres. for Teaching and Academic Programmes: Prof. Dr Ing. OLIVER LANGEFELD
Librarian: Dr HELMUT CYNTHA
Number of teachers: 180 (incl. 90 ordinary Profs)
Number of students: 3,569
Publications: *Lösestunde*, *Mitteilungsblatt*, *Vorlesungsverzeichnis* (1 a year)

DEANS
Faculty of Energy and Environment: Prof. Dr Ing. NORBERT MEYER
Faculty of Mathematics/Computing and Engineering: Prof. Dr JÜRGEN DIX
Faculty of Natural and Material Sciences: Prof. Dr ALBRECHT WOLTER

TECHNISCHE UNIVERSITÄT DARMSTADT

64277 Darmstadt
Karolinenpl. 5, 64289 Darmstadt
Telephone: (6151) 1601
E-mail: praesident@pvw.tu-darmstadt.de
Internet: www.tu-darmstadt.de
Founded 1836 as Höhere Gewerbeschule, acquired univ. status in 1877
State control
Pres.: Prof. Dr HANS JÜRGEN PRÖMEL
Chancellor: Dr MANFRED EFINGER
Vice-Pres.: Prof. Dr Ing. CHRISTOPH MOTZKO
Vice-Pres.: Prof. Dr Ing. MARTIN HEILMAIER
Vice-Pres.: Prof. Dr PETRA GEHRING
Vice-Pres.: Prof. Dr REINER ANDERL
Library: see under Libraries and Archives
Number of teachers: 270
Number of students: 23,100
Publications: *Forschen—the science magazine* (2 a year), *Hoch[3]* (7 a year)

DEANS
Architecture: Dipl. Ing. MARKUS GASSER
Biology: Prof. FELICITAS PFEIFER
Chemistry: Prof. Dr GERD BUNTKOWSKY
Civil Engineering and Geodesy: Prof. Dr Ing. HANS-JOACHIM LINKE
Computational Engineering: Prof. Dr Ing. UWE RÜPPEL
Computer Science: Prof. Dr OSKAR VON STRYK
Electrical Engineering and Information Technology: Prof. Dr Ing. HELMUT F. SCHLAAK
History and Social Sciences: Prof. Dr MICHÈLE KNODT
Humanities: Prof. Dr WOLFGANG ELLERMEIER
Law and Economics: Prof. Dr DIRK SCHIERECK
Material and Earth Sciences: Prof. Dr Hab. RALF RIEDEL
Mathematics: Prof. Dr JAN HENDRIK BRUINIER
Mechanical Engineering: Prof. Dr Ing. UWE KLINGAUF
Mechanics: Prof. Dr Ing. MARTIN OBERLACK
Physics: Prof. Dr BARBARA DROSSEL

PROFESSORS
ABELE, E., Mechanical Engineering
ABROMEIT, H., History and Social Sciences
ADAMY, J. H., Electrical Engineering and Information Technology
ALBE, K., Material Sciences and Geoscience
ALBER, G., Physics
ALBER, H. D., Mathematics
ALBERT, B., Chemistry
ALEXA, M., Computing
ALFF, L., Material Sciences and Geoscience
ANDERL, R., Mechanical Engineering
ARICH-GERZ, B., History and Social Sciences
ARSLAN, U., Construction Engineering and Geodesy
BÄCHMANN, K., Chemistry
BALD, S., Construction Engineering and Geodesy
BALZER, G., Electrical Engineering and Information Technology
BARENS, I., Law and Economic Science
BAYREUTHER, F., Law and Economic Science
BECKER, M., Construction Engineering and Geodesy
BECKER, W., Mathematics
BERGER, C., Mechanical Engineering
BERGES, J., Physics
BERKING, H., History and Social Sciences
BETSCH, O., Law and Economic Science
BETTE, K. H., Human Sciences: Developmental Sciences, Psychology and Sport Science
BIBEL, W., Computing
BINDER, A., Electrical Engineering and Information Technology
BIRKHOFER, H., Mechanical Engineering
BIRKL, G., Physics
BÖHM, H. R., Construction Engineering and Geodesy

BOKOWSKI, J., Mathematics
BOLTZE, M., Construction Engineering and Geodesy
BORCHERDING, K., Human Sciences: Developmental Sciences, Psychology and Sport Science
BRAUN-MUNZINGER, P., Physics
BREUER, B. J., Mechanical Engineering
BRICKMANN, J., Chemistry
BRUDER, R., Mathematics
BRUDER, R., Mechanical Engineering
BUCHLER, J. W., Chemistry
BUCHMANN, A., Computing
BUCHMANN, J., Computing
BURMEISTER, P., Mathematics
BUSCH, M., Chemistry
BUSCHINGER, A., Biology
BUXMANN, P., Law and Economic Science
CASPARI, V., Law and Economic Science
CLAUS, P., Chemistry
CORNEL, P., Construction Engineering and Geodesy
CREUTZIG, J., Mathematics
DENCHER, N., Chemistry
DENINGER-POLZER, G., History and Social Sciences
DINSE, K. P., Chemistry
DIPPER, C., History and Social Sciences
DOMSCHKE, W., Law and Economic Science
DÖRSAM, E., Mechanical Engineering
DROSSEL, B., Physics
DÜR, M., Mathematics
ECKERT, C., Computing
ECKERT, J., Material Sciences and Geoscience
EGLOFF, G., History and Social Sciences
ELLERMEIER, W., Mathematics
ELSÄßER, W., Physics
ENCARNACAO, J., Computing
ENDERS, J., Physics
ENSINGER, W., Material Sciences and Geoscience
ENTORF, H., Law and Economic Science
EPPLE, B., Mechanical Engineering
EULER, P., Human Sciences: Developmental Sciences, Psychology and Sport Science
EVEKING, H., Electrical Engineering and Information Technology
EXNER, H. E., Material Sciences and Geoscience
FARWIG, R., Mathematics
FÄSSLER, T. F., Chemistry
FEILE, R., Physics
FERREIRO MÄHLMANN, R., Material Sciences and Geoscience
FESSNER, W.-D., Chemistry
FRIEDL, P., Chemistry
FRYDE-STROMER V. REICHENBACH, N., History and Social Sciences
FUEß, H., Material Sciences and Geoscience
FUJARA, F., Physics
FÜRNKRANZ, J., Computing
GALUSKE, R., Biology
GAMM, G., History and Social Sciences
GATERMANN, D., Architecture
GEHRING, P., History and Social Sciences
GERSHMAN, A., Electrical Engineering and Information Technology
GERSTENECKER, C., Construction Engineering and Geodesy
GIERSCH, C., Biology
GIVSAN, H., History and Social Sciences
GLESNER, M., Electrical Engineering and Information Technology
GÖPFERT, W., Construction Engineering and Geodesy
GÖRINGER, U., Biology
GÖTTSCHING, L., Mechanical Engineering
GRAUBNER, C.-A., Construction Engineering and Geodesy
GREWE, N., Physics
GRIEM, J., History and Social Sciences
GROCHE, P., Mechanical Engineering
GROSS, D., Mathematics
GROSSE-BRAUCKMANN, K., Mathematics
GRUBER, E., Chemistry
GRÜBL, P., Construction Engineering and Geodesy
GRUTTMANN, F., Construction Engineering and Geodesy
HAASE, W., Chemistry
HAGEDORN, P., Mathematics
HAHN, H., Material Sciences and Geoscience
HAMPE, M., Mechanical Engineering
HÄNSEL, F., Human Sciences: Developmental Sciences, Psychology and Sport Science
HANSELKA, H., Mechanical Engineering
HÄNSLER, E., Electrical Engineering and Information Technology
HARD, M., History and Social Sciences
HARTKOPF, T., Electrical Engineering and Information Technology
HARTMANN, E., Mathematics
HARTMANN, H., Human Sciences: Developmental Sciences, Psychology and Sport Science
HARTMANN, M. L., History and Social Sciences
HARTNAGEL, H. L., Electrical Engineering and Information Technology
HASSLER, U., Law and Economic Science
HAUSCHILD, M., Architecture
HEGGER, M., Architecture
HEIDER, J., Biology
HEIL, E., Mathematics
HEINELT, H., History and Social Sciences
HELM, C., Law and Economic Science
HERRMANN, C., Mathematics
HIEBER, M., Mathematics
HIMSTEDT, W., Biology
HINDERER, M., Material Sciences and Geoscience
HINRICHSEN, V., Electrical Engineering and Information Technology
HOFFMANN, D. H. H., Physics
HOFFMANN, H. J., Computing
HOFFMANN, R., Computing
HOFMANN, K. H., Mathematics
HOFMANN, T., Computing
HOHENBERG, G., Mechanical Engineering
HOLSTEIN, T. W., Biology
HOPPE, A., Material Sciences and Geoscience
HUSS, S., Computing
HÜTT, M.-T., Biology
IHRINGER, T., Mathematics
ISERMANN, R., Electrical Engineering and Information Technology
JAEGERMANN, W., Material Sciences and Geoscience
JAGER, J., Construction Engineering and Geodesy
JAKOBY, R., Electrical Engineering and Information Technology
JANICH, N., History and Social Sciences
JANICKA, J., Mechanical Engineering
JANNIDIS, F., History and Social Sciences
JOSWIG, M., Mathematics
KAISER, F., Physics
KAISER, W., Biology
KALDENHOFF, R., Biology
KAMMERER, P., Computing
KANGASHARJU, J., Computing
KANKELEIT, E., Physics
KAST, W., Mechanical Engineering
KATZENBACH, R. H., Construction Engineering and Geodesy
KEIMEL, K., Mathematics
KEMPE, S., Material Sciences and Geoscience
KIEHL, M., Mathematics
KINDLER, J., Mathematics
KLEEBE, H.-J., Material Sciences and Geoscience
KLEIN, A., Electrical Engineering and Information Technology
KLEIN, H.-F., Chemistry
KLINGAUF, U., Mechanical Engineering
KNODT, M., History and Social Sciences
KOCH, A., Computing
KOHLENBACH, U., Mathematics
KOLMAR, H., Chemistry
KÖNIG, H. D., Electrical Engineering and Information Technology
KONIGORSKI, U., Electrical Engineering and Information Technology
KOOB, M., Architecture
KÖRDING, A., Physics
KOSTKA, A., Electrical Engineering and Information Technology
KRAIS, B., History and Social Sciences
KRAMER, L., Mathematics
KÜBLER, J., Physics
KÜHNE, T., Computing
KÜMMERER, B., Mathematics
LANDAU, K., Mechanical Engineering
LANG, J., Mathematics
LANGANKE, K., Physics
LANGE, J., Construction Engineering and Geodesy
LANGHEINRICH, W., Electrical Engineering and Information Technology
LANGNER, G., Biology
LAYER, PAUL G., Biology
LEHN, J., Mathematics
LEICHNER, R., Human Sciences: Developmental Sciences, Psychology and Sport Science
LICHTENTHALER, F., Chemistry
LIEBENWEIN, W., Architecture
LINKE, H.-J., Construction Engineering and Geodesy
LORCH, W., Architecture
LOTH, R., Mechanical Engineering
LÖW, M., History and Social Sciences
LUFT, G., Chemistry
LUSERKE, M., History and Social Sciences
LÜTTGE, U., Biology
MARKERT, R., Mathematics
MARLY, J., Law and Economic Science
MARTIN, A., Mathematics
MATHÉY, G. K., Architecture
MÄURER, H., Mathematics
MAY, A., Mathematics
MAY, H. D., Material Sciences and Geoscience
MEIßNER, P., Electrical Engineering and Information Technology
MEZINI, M., Computing
MOLEK, H., Material Sciences and Geoscience
MOTZKO, C., Construction Engineering and Geodesy
MÜHLHÄUSER, M. E., Computing
MÜLLER, R., Mathematics
MÜLLER, W. F., Material Sciences and Geoscience
MÜLLER-PLATHE, F., Chemistry
MULSER, P., Physics
MÜNK, H. D., Human Sciences: Developmental Sciences, Psychology and Sport Science
MUTSCHLER, P., Electrical Engineering and Information Technology
NEEB, K.-H., Mathematics
NESTLE, N., Physics
NEUHOLD, E., Computing
NEUNHOEFFER, H., Chemistry
NICKEL, E., Law and Economic Science
NOLTE, W., Mathematics
NORDMANN, A., History and Social Sciences
NORDMANN, R., Mechanical Engineering
OBERLACK, M., Mathematics
ORTNER, E., Law and Economic Science
ORTNER, H., Material Sciences and Geoscience
OSTERMANN, K., Computing
OSTROWSKI, M., Construction Engineering and Geodesy
OTTO, M., Mathematics
PAHL, G., Mechanical Engineering
PAULINYI, A., History and Social Sciences
PAUL-KOHLHOFF, A., Human Sciences: Developmental Sciences, Psychology and Sport Science
PAVLIDIS, D., Electrical Engineering and Information Technology
PETZINKA, K.-H., Architecture
PFEIFER, F., Biology
PFEIFER, G., Architecture
PFEIFFER, W., Electrical Engineering and Information Technology
PFLÜGER, M., Law and Economic Science

PFNÜR, A., Law and Economic Science
PFOHL, H.-C., Law and Economic Science
PINNAU, R., Mathematics
PLENIO, H. H., Chemistry
PONGRATZ, L., Human Sciences: Developmental Sciences, Psychology and Sport Science
PORTO, M., Physics
PUHANI, P., Law and Economic Science
QUICK, R., Law and Economic Science
RAUH, H., Material Sciences and Geoscience
REGGELIN, M., Chemistry
REHAHN, M., Chemistry
REIF, U., Mathematics
REISTER, D., Construction Engineering and Geodesy
RETZKO, H. G., Construction Engineering and Geodesy
RICHTER, A., Physics
RIEDEL, R., Material Sciences and Geoscience
RITTER, K., Mathematics
RÖDEL, J., Material Sciences and Geoscience
ROESNER, K., Mathematics
ROSE, H., Physics
ROTH, R., Physics
RÜPPEL, U., Construction Engineering and Geodesy
RÜRUP, H.-A., Law and Economic Science
RÜTZEL, J., Human Sciences: Developmental Sciences, Psychology and Sport Science
SASS, I., Material Sciences and Geoscience
SCHABEL, S., Mechanical Engineering
SCHÄFER, M., Mechanical Engineering
SCHÄFER, R., Chemistry
SCHÄFER, S. M., Construction Engineering and Geodesy
SCHAPPACHER, N., Mathematics
SCHEBEK, L., Construction Engineering and Geodesy
SCHEFFOLD, E., Mathematics
SCHEU, S., Biology
SCHIELE, B., Computing
SCHIFFER, H.-P., Mechanical Engineering
SCHLAAK, H., Electrical Engineering and Information Technology
SCHLEMMER, H., Construction Engineering and Geodesy
SCHMALZ-BRUNS, R., History and Social Sciences
SCHMID, V., Law and Economic Science
SCHMIDT, B., Chemistry
SCHMIDT, R., Human Sciences: Developmental Sciences, Psychology and Sport Science
SCHMIDT-CLAUSEN, H.-J., Electrical Engineering and Information Technology
SCHMIEDE, R., History and Social Sciences
SCHMITZ, B., Human Sciences: Developmental Sciences, Psychology and Sport Science
SCHNEIDER, J., Chemistry
SCHNEIDER, U. H., Law and Economic Science
SCHNEIDER, W. C., History and Social Sciences
SCHNELLENBACH-HELD, M., Construction Engineering and Geodesy
SCHOTT, D., History and Social Sciences
SCHUBERT, E., Construction Engineering and Geodesy
SCHULZ, H., Mechanical Engineering
SCHÜRMANN, H., Mechanical Engineering
SCHÜRR, A., Electrical Engineering and Information Technology
SCHUSTER, R., Chemistry
SCHÜTH, C., Material Sciences and Geoscience
SCHWABE-KRATOCHWIL, A., Biology
SCHWALKE, U., Electrical Engineering and Information Technology
SEELIG, W., Physics
SEILER, T. B., Human Sciences: Developmental Sciences, Psychology and Sport Science
SESINK, W., Human Sciences: Developmental Sciences, Psychology and Sport Science
SESSELMEIER, W., Law and Economic Science
SESSLER, G., Electrical Engineering and Information Technology
SIEKER, S., Law and Economic Science
SORGATZ, H., Human Sciences: Developmental Sciences, Psychology and Sport Science
SPECHT, G., Law and Economic Science
SPELLUCCI, P., Mathematics
STADTLER, H., Law and Economic Science
STAHL, M., History and Social Sciences
STEINMETZ, R., Electrical Engineering and Information Technology
STENZEL, J., Electrical Engineering and Information Technology
STEPHAN, P. C., Mechanical Engineering
STOFFEL, B., Mechanical Engineering
STREICHER, T., Mathematics
STÜHN, B., Physics
SURI, N., Computing
TEICH, E., History and Social Sciences
THIEL, G., Biology
TREBELS, W., Mathematics
TROPEA, C., Mechanical Engineering
TSAKMAKIS, C., Mathematics
TSCHUDI, T., Physics
ULLRICH-EBERIUS, C., Biology
URBAN, W., Construction Engineering and Geodesy
VIADA, E., Mathematics
VOGEL, H., Chemistry
VOGT, M., History and Social Sciences
VON NEUMANN-COSEL, P., Physics
VON SEGGERN, H., Material Sciences and Geoscience
VON STRYK, O., Computing
VORMWALD, M., Construction Engineering and Geodesy
VOß, H.-G., Human Sciences: Developmental Sciences, Psychology and Sport Science
WALDSCHMIDT, H., Computing
WALTER, H., Computing
WALTHER, C., Computing
WALTHER, T., Physics
WAMBACH, J., Physics
WEGMANN, H., Mathematics
WEIHE, K., Computing
WEILAND, T., Electrical Engineering and Information Technology
WEINBRUCH, S., Material Sciences and Geoscience
WEISCHEDE, D., Architecture
WEIßMANTEL, H., Electrical Engineering and Information Technology
WÉKÉL, J., Architecture
WERTHSCHÜTZKY, R., Electrical Engineering and Information Technology
WIEMEYER, J., Human Sciences: Developmental Sciences, Psychology and Sport Science
WILHELM, M., Mechanical Engineering
WILLE, R., Mathematics
WINNER, H., Mechanical Engineering
WIPF, H., Physics
WIRTH, A. E. H., Law and Economic Science
WOLF, K.-D., History and Social Sciences
WÖLFEL, H., Mechanical Engineering
WOLLENWEBER, E., Biology
WROBEL, B., Construction Engineering and Geodesy
WURL, H.-J., Law and Economic Science
ZANKE, U., Construction Engineering and Geodesy
ZILGES, A., Physics
ZOUBIR, A. M. D. E., Electrical Engineering and Information Technology

TECHNISCHE UNIVERSITÄT DORTMUND

44221 Dortmund
August-Schmidt-Str. 4, 44227 Dortmund
Telephone: (231) 75511
E-mail: huesing@verwaltung.tu-dortmund.de
Internet: www.tu-dortmund.de

Founded 1968
State control
Languages of instruction: German, English
Academic year: April to February

Rector: Prof. Dr URSULA GATHER
Vice-Rector for Academic Affairs: Prof. Dr METIN TOLAN
Vice-Rector for Diversity Management: Prof. Dr BARBARA WELZEL
Vice-Rector for Finance: Prof. Dr UWE SCHWIEGELSHOHN
Vice-Rector for Research: Prof. Dr ANDREJ GÓRAK
Chancellor: ALBRECHT EHLERS
Library: see under Libraries and Archives
Number of students: 24,000
Publications: *Mundo* (2 a year), *Unizet* (10 a year)

DEANS

Architecture and Civil Engineering: Prof. Ing. WALTER A. NOEBEL
Art and Sport: Prof. Dr GÜNTHER RÖTTER
Biochemical and Chemical Engineering: Prof. Dr Ing. SEBASTIAN ENGELL
Chemistry: Prof. Dr HEINZ REHAGE
Computer Science: Ing. GABRIELE KERN-ISBERNER
Culture Studies: Prof. Dr HORST PÖTTKER
Economics and Social Sciences: Prof. Dr WOLFGANG B. SCHÜNEMANN
Education and Sociology: Prof. Dr THOMAS GOLL
Electrical Engineering and Information Technology: Prof. Dr Ing. CHRISTIAN WIETFELD
Human Sciences and Theology: Prof. Dr ERNSTPETER MAURER
Mathematics: Prof. Dr STEFAN TUREK
Mechanical Engineering: Prof. Dr Ing. DIRK BIERMANN
Physics: Prof. Dr BERNHARD SPAAN
Rehabilitation Sciences: Prof. Dr ELISABETH WACKER
Spatial Planning: Prof. CHRISTA REICHER
Statistics: Prof. Dr CLAUS WEIHS

PROFESSORS

Architecture and Civil Engineering (tel. (231) 7552074; e-mail dekanat@busch.bauwesen.tu-dortmund.de; internet www.bauwesen.tu-dortmund.de):

BARTHOLD, F.-J., Numerical Methods and Information Processing
BLECKEN, U., Construction Management and Machines
BOFINGER, H., Design and Building Theory
HASSLER, U., Conservation and Building Research
HETTLER, A., Soil Mechanics and Foundation Engineering
MÄCKLER, C., Urban Design
MAURER, R., Concrete Engineering
MÜLLER, H., Environmental Architecture
NALBACH, G., Design, Spatial Design and the Fundamentals of Presentation
NEISECKE, J., Building Materials
NOEBEL, W., Design and Industrial Building
OBRECHT, H., Structural and Computational Mechanics
ÖTES, A., Structural Design
SCHIFFERS, K.-H., Organization of Building Planning and Site Management (OPS)
STANDKE, G. R., Design and Building Construction
UNGERMANN, D., Steel Construction

Art and Sport (tel. (231) 7554153; e-mail dek16ri@pop.tu-dortmund.de; internet www.tu-dortmund.de/fb16):

Institute of Art and Education:

BERTRAM-MÖBIUS, U.
BUSSE, K.-P.
VAN HAAREN, B.
WELZEL, B.

Institute of Geography and Education:

NUTZ, M.
SCHMIDT-KALLERT, E.

Institute of Music and Education:

ABEGG, W.
HOUBEN, E.
RÖTTER, G.
STEGEMANN, M.
VON SCHOENEBECK, M.

Institute of Sport and Education:

BRÄUTIGAM, M.
STARISCHKA, S.
THIELE, J.

Institute of Textile Design and Education/ Comparative Textile Sciences:

MENTGES, G.

Biochemical and Chemical Engineering (tel. (231) 7552362; e-mail dekanat@ct.tu-dortmund.de; internet www.chemietechnik.tu-dortmund.de):

AGAR, D., Technical Chemistry
BEHR, A., Technical Chemistry
ENGELL, S., Plant Control Technology
FAHLENKAMP, H., Environmental Technology
FRIEDRICH, C., Technical Microbiology
GÓRAK, A., Fluid Separation Processes
KÖSTER, U., Materials Science
SADOWSKI, G., Thermodynamics
SCHMID, A., Chemical Biotechnology
SCHMIDT-TRAUB, H., Plant Technology
STRAUß, K., Energy Processing and Fluid Mechanics
WALZEL, P., Mechanical Process Engineering
WEIß, E., Chemical Plant Technology
WICHMANN, R., Biological Engineering

Chemistry (tel. (231) 7553720; e-mail dekan-chemie@chemie.tu-dortmund.de; internet www.chemie.tu-dortmund.de):

EILBRACHT, P., Organic Chemistry
GEIGER, A., Physical Chemistry
GRAF, D., Biology
HAAG, R., Organic Chemistry
JURKSCHAT, K., Inorganic Chemistry
KELLER, H.-L., Inorganic Chemistry
KRAUSE, N., Organic Chemistry
LIPPERT, B., Inorganic Chemistry
MELLE, I., Chemistry Teaching
MINKWITZ, R., Inorganic Chemistry
MITCHELL, T. N., Organic Chemistry
NIEMEYER, C. M., Biological and Chemical Microstructure Technology
REHAGE, H., Physical Chemistry
SANDMANN, A., Biology
SCHMUTZLER, R.-W., Physical Chemistry
VERBEEK, B., Biology
WALDMANN, H., Organic Chemistry
WINTER, R., Physical Chemistry

Computer Science (tel. (231) 7552121; e-mail kossmann@dekanat.cs.tu-dortmund.de; internet www.informatik.tu-dortmund.de):

BISKUP, J., Information Systems
BUCHHOLZ, P., Modelling and Simulation
DITTRICH, G., Automata and Systems Theory
DOBERKAT, E.-E., Software Technology
KERN-ISBERNER, G., Information Engineering
KRUMM, H., Computer Networks and Distributed Systems
LINDEMANN, C., Computing Systems and Performance Analysis
MARWEDEL, P., Technical Computer Science, Embedded Systems
MORIK, K., Artificial Intelligence
MÜLLER, H., Computer Graphics
MÜTZEL, P., Algorithm Engineering
PADAWITZ, P., Compiler Construction
REUSCH, B., Automata and Sequential Logic Systems Theory
SCHWEFEL, H.-P., Systems Analysis
STEFFEN, B., Programming Systems
WEDDE, H., Operating Systems/Computer Architecture
WEGENER, I., Efficient Algorithms and Complexity Theory

Cultural Studies (tel. (231) 7552919; e-mail zimmerma@mail.fb15.tu-dortmund.de; internet www.fb15.tu-dortmund.de):

Institute of English and American Studies:

BIMBERG, C.
GRÜNZWEIG, W.
KRAMER, J.
NOLD, G.
PETERS, H.

Institute of German Language and Literature:

BRÜNNER, G.
CONRADY, P.
DENNELER, I.
GERHARD, U.
HOFFMANN, L.
KÜHN, R.
LINK, J.
PARR, R.
QUASTHOFF, U.
RIEMENSCHNEIDER, H.
RISHOLM, E.
STORRER, A.

Institute of History:

HÖMIG, H.
SOLLBACH, G.
ZETTLER, A.

Institute of Journalism:

BOHRMANN, H.
BRANAHL, U.
EURICH, C.
HEINRICH, J.
KOPPER, G.
MACHILL, M.
PÄTZOLD, U.
PÖTTKER, H.
RAGER, G.

Economics and Social Sciences (tel. (231) 7553182; e-mail elke.klika@wiso.tu-dortmund.de; internet www.wiso.tu-dortmund.de):

HIRSCH-KREINSEN, H., Technology and Society
HOLLÄNDER, H., Macroeconomic Theory
HOLZMÜLLER, H., Marketing
JEHLE, E., Operations Management and Logistics
KRAFT, K., Economics (Economic Policy)
LACKES, R., Business Information and Management Information Systems
LEININGER, W., Microeconomic Theory
LIENING, A., Teaching of Economics
NEUENDORFF, H., Sociology
RECHT, P., Operations Research and Economic Informatics
REICHMANN, T., Management Accounting
RICHTER, W., Public Economics
SCHÜNEMANN, W., Private Law
TEICHMANN, U., Money and Credit
WAHL, J., Investments and Finance
WELGE, M., Management
WEYER, J., Sociology

Education and Sociology (tel. (231) 7552194; e-mail dekanat@fb12.tu-dortmund.de; internet www.fb12.tu-dortmund.de):

Institute of General and Vocational Education:

PÄTZOLD, G.
VOGEL, P.
WIGGER, L.

Institute of School Development Research:

BOS, W.
HOLTAPPELS, H.
SCHULZ-ZANDER, R.

Institute of Social and Elementary Education:

BIERFLEITER, C.
FRIED, L.
NOLDA, S.
UHLENDORFF, U.

Institute of Teaching Science:

BEUTEL, S.-I.
KOCH-PRIEWE, B.
WIEDERHOLD, K.-A.
WILDT, J.

Sociology:

BÜHRMANN, A. D.
GOLL, T.
HITZLER, R.
HORNBOSTEL, S.
KALBITZ, R.
NAEGELE, G.
REICHERT, M.
STALLBERG, E.

Electrical Engineering and Information Technology (tel. (231) 7552123; e-mail info@dekanat.e-technik.tu-dortmund.de; internet www.e-technik.tu-dortmund.de):

FIEDLER, H., Integrated Systems
GÖTZE, J., Information Processing
HANDSCHIN, E., Electric Power Supply
KAYS, R., Communication Technology
KULIG, S., Electric Machines, Drive and Power Electronics
NEYER, A., Microstructure Technology
PEIER, D., High Voltage Engineering
SCHEHRER, R., Electronic Systems and Switching
SCHRÖDER, H., Circuits and Systems
SCHUMACHER, K., Microelectronics
SCHWIEGELSHOHN, U., Computer Engineering
VOGES, E., High Frequency Technology

Human Sciences and Theology (tel. (231) 7552886; e-mail leschner@fb14.tu-dortmund.de; internet www.fb14.tu-dortmund.de):

Catholic Theology:

DORMEYER, D.
METTE, N.
MÖLLE, H.
RUSTER, T.

Home Economics:

EISSING, G.

Organizational Psychology:

KASTNER, M.
KLEINBECK, U.

Philosophy:

FALKENBERG, B.
POST, W.
WINGERT, L.

Politics:

MEYER, T.

Protestant Theology:

BÜTTNER, G.
GREWEL, H.
MAURER, E.
MUNZEL, F.
POLA, T.
RIESNER, R.

Psychology:

GASCH, B.
KASTNER, M.
KLEINBECK, U.
LASOGGA, F.
METZ-GÖCKEL, H.
NEUMANN, R.
ROEDER, B.
ZIMMERMANN, P.

Mathematics (tel. (231) 7553051; e-mail dekan@mathematik.tu-dortmund.de; internet www.mathematik.tu-dortmund.de):

ACHTZIGER, W., Applied Mathematics
BECKER, E., Algebra
BLUM, H., Applied Mathematics
HAZOD, W., Analysis and Stochastics
HENN, H.-W., Mathematics Teaching
KABALLO, W., Analysis
KOCH, H., Analysis
KREUZER, M., Algebra

KUZMIN, D., Applied Mathematics and Numerics
MENKE, K., Function Theory
MÖLLER, M., Approximation Theory
MÜLLER, G., Mathematics Teaching
ROSENBERGER, G., Algebra
SCHARLAU, R., Geometry and Algebra
SCHWACHTHÖFER, L., Differential Geometry
SELTER, C., Mathematics Teaching
SIBURG, F., Function Theory
SKUTELLA, M., Discrete Optimization
STEINMETZ, N., Function Theory
STÖCKLER, J., Approximation Theory
TUREK, S., Applied Mathematics and Numerics
VOIT, M., Analysis and Stochastics
ZAMFIRESCU, T., Geometry and Algebra

Mechanical Engineering (tel. (231) 7552723; e-mail dekan@mb.tu-dortmund.de; internet www.mb.tu-dortmund.de):

CLAUSEN, U., Transport Systems and Logistics
CROSTACK, H.-A., Quality Control
DEUSE, J., Work and Production Systems
HOMPELTEN, M., Transportation and Storage
JANSEN, R., Logistics
KAUDER, K., Fluid Energy Machines
KLEINER, M., Forming Technology and Lightweight Construction
KREIS, W., Machine Elements, Design and Handling Techniques
KUHN, A., Plant Organization
KÜNNE, B., Machine Elements
OTT, B., Technical Didactics
SVENDSEN, B., Mechanics
THERMANN, K., Machine Dynamics
TILLMANN, W., Materials Technology
UHLE, M., Measurement Technology
WEINERT, K., Machining Technology

Physics (tel. (231) 7553503; e-mail dekanat@physik.tu-dortmund.de; internet www.physik.tu-dortmund.de):

BAACKE, J., Theoretical Physics
BAYER, M., Experimental Physics
BÖHMER, R., Experimental Physics
GERLACH, B., Theoretical Physics
GÖBLING, C., Experimental Physics
KEITER, H., Theoretical Physics
NIEMAX, K., Plasma and Laser Spectrochemistry
PASCHOS, E., Theoretical Physics
PFLUG, A., Physics Teaching
REYA, E., Theoretical Physics
RHODE, W., Experimental Physics
SPAAN, B., Experimental Physics
SUTER, D., Experimental Physics
TOLAN, M., Experimental Physics
WEBER, W., Theoretical Physics
WEISS, T., Acceleration Physics
WESTPHAL, C., Experimental Physics
WILLE, K., Accelerator Physics
WOGGON, U., Experimental Teaching

Rehabilitation Sciences (Emil-Figge-Str. 50, 44227 Dortmund; tel. (231) 7554541; e-mail dekanat.fb13@tu-dortmund.de; internet www.tu-dortmund.de/fb13):

Adapted Physical Activity and Movement Therapy:

HÖLTER, G.

Art Education and Art Therapy:

JÁDI, F.

Education for Individuals with Mental Disabilities:

DÖNHOFF, K.
HAVEMAN, M.
MEYER, H.

Gender Research in Special Needs Education:

SCHILDMANN, U.

Music Education and Music Therapy:

MERKT, I.

Rehabilitation for Individuals with Blindness and Visual Impairments:

CSOCSÁN, E.
WALTHES, R.

Rehabilitation for Individuals with Communication Disorders:

DUPUIS, G.
KATZ-BERNSTEIN, N.

Rehabilitation and Education for Individuals with Disabilities:

DEDERICH, M.

Rehabilitation for Individuals with Emotional and Behavioural Disorders:

PETERMANN, U.

Rehabilitation for Individuals with Learning Difficulties:

SCHMETZ, D.
WEMBER, F.

Rehabilitation for Individuals with Physical Disabilities:

LEYENDECKER, C.

Rehabilitation Psychology:

FRANKE, A.
FRÖSTER, H.

Rehabilitation Technology:

BÜHLER, C.

Sociology in Rehabilitation:

WACKER, E.

Vocational Education and Training:

BIERMANN, H.

Spatial Planning (August-Schmidt-Str. 10, 44221 Dortmund; tel. (231) 7552284; e-mail dekanat.rp@tu-dortmund.de; internet www.raumplanung.tu-dortmund.de):

BADE, F.-J., Regional Economics
BAUMGART, S., Urban and Regional Planning
BECKER, R., Women's Studies and Housing in Spatial Planning
BLOTEVOGEL, H.-H., Regional and Federal Planning
DAVID, C.-H., Law and Spatial Planning
DAVY, B., Land Policy and Management
FINKE, L., Ecology and Landscape Planning
HENNINGS, G., Industrial and Commercial Development Planning
HOLZ-RAU, C., Transport Planning
KRAUSE, K.-J., Urban and Landscape Design
KREIBICH, V., Spring Centre, Urban and Regional Geography
KROES, G., Spring Centre, Urban and Regional Geography
KUNZMANN, K., Spatial Planning in Europe
REICHER, C., Urban Design and Land Use Planning
RÖDDING, W., Systems Theory and Systems Engineering
SCHMALS, K. M., Sociology and Spatial Planning
TIETZ, H.-P., Supply and Disposal Systems in Spatial Planning
VELSINGER, P., Political Economics, Regional Economics

Statistics (Vogelpothsweg 87, 44227 Dortmund; tel. (231) 7553113; e-mail dekanat@statistik.tu-dortmund.de; internet www.statistik.tu-dortmund.de):

GATHER, U., Mathematical Statistics and Industrial Application
HARTUNG, J., Statistics Applied in Engineering
ICKSTADT, K., Statistics in Biosciences
KRÄMER, W., Economic and Social Statistics
KUNERT, J., Mathematical Statistics and Scientific Application
TRENKLER, G., Statistics and Econometrics
URFER, W., Statistical Methods in Genetics and Ecology
WEIHS, K., Computer-Aided Statistics

TECHNISCHE UNIVERSITÄT DRESDEN

Mommsenstr. 9, 01062 Dresden
Telephone: (351) 4630
E-mail: infostelle@tu-dresden.de
Internet: www.tu-dresden.de
Founded 1828, univ. status 1961
State control
Academic year: October to September
Rector: Prof. Dr Ing. Hab. HANS MÜLLER-STEINHAGEN
Vice-Rector for Academic and Int. Affairs: Prof. Dr Hab. URSULA SCHAEFER
Vice-Rector for Research: Prof. Dr Hab. GERHARD ROEDEL
Vice-Rector for Structure and Devt: Prof. Dr Hab. KARL LENZ
Chancellor: WOLF-ECKHARD WORMSER
Library: see under Libraries and Archives
Number of teachers: 419
Number of students: 36,066 (not incl. Faculty of Medicine)
Publication: *Wissenschaftliche Zeitschrift* (6 a year)

DEANS

'Carl Gustav Carus' Faculty of Medicine: Prof. Dr HEINZ REICHMANN
Faculty of Architecture: Prof. Dr Ing. Hab. HANS-GEORG LIPPERT
Faculty of Arts, Humanities and Social Science: Prof. Dr BRUNO KLEIN
Faculty of Business and Economics: Prof. Dr Hab. ALEXANDER KARMANN
Faculty of Civil Engineering: Prof. Dr Ing. RAINER SCHACH
Faculty of Computer Science: Prof. Dr STEFAN GUMHOLD
Faculty of Education: Prof. Dr Hab. GISELA WIESNER
Faculty of Electrical Engineering and Information Technology: Prof. Dr KLAUS JANSCHEK
Faculty of Forestry, Geosciences and Hydrosciences: Prof. Dr Hab. HANS-GERD MAAS
Faculty of Law: Prof. Dr HORST-PETER GÖTTING
Faculty of Linguistics, Literature and Cultural Studies: Prof. Dr Hab. KARLHEINZ JAKOB
Faculty of Mathematics and Natural Sciences: Prof. Dr BERNHARD GANTER
Faculty of Mechanical Engineering: Prof. Dr Ing. Hab. ECKHARD BEYER
'Friedrich List' Faculty of Transportation and Traffic Sciences: Prof. Dr Ing. CHRISTIAN LIPPOLD

TECHNISCHE UNIVERSITÄT HAMBURG-HARBURG
(Hamburg University of Technology)

Schwarzenbergstr. 93, 21071, Hamburg
Telephone: (40) 428780
E-mail: pressestelle@tuhh.de
Internet: www.tuhh.de
Founded 1978
Languages of instruction: English, German
Academic year: October to September
Pres.: Prof. Dr GARABED ANTRANIKIAN
Vice-Pres. for Education: Prof. Dr SÖNKE KNUTZEN
Vice-Pres. for Research: Prof. Dr JÜRGEN GRABE
Vice-Pres. for Univ. Devt: Prof. Dr VIKTOR SIGRIST
Chancellor: KLAUS-JOACHIM SCHEUNERT
Librarian: INKEN FELDSIEN-SUDHAUS

Library of 480,000 vols, 700 print journals, 6,000 ejournals
Number of teachers: 710
Number of students: 6,000

DEANS
Civil Engineering: Prof. Dr Ing. GÜNTER ROMBACH
Electrical Engineering and Information Technology: Prof. Dr Ing. ARNE JACOB
Management Sciences and Technology: Prof. Dr CHRISTIAN LÜTHJE
Mechanical Engineering: Prof. Dr NORBERT HOFFMANN
Process and Chemical Engineering: Prof. Dr Ing. STEFAN HEINRICH
Vocational Subject Education: Prof. Dr Ing. CLAUS EMMELMANN

TECHNISCHE UNIVERSITÄT ILMENAU

POB 10 05 65, 98684 Ilmenau
Ehrenbergstr. 29, 98693 Ilmenau
Telephone: (3677) 690
E-mail: rektor@tu-ilmenau.de
Internet: www.tu-ilmenau.de
Founded 1953 as Hochschule für Elektrotechnik, present name and status 1992
State control
Academic year: October to September
Rector: Prof. Dr Hab. PETER SCHARFF
Vice-Rector for Science: Prof. Dr Ing. KLAUS AUGSBURG
Vice-Rector for Teaching: Prof. Dr Ing. JÜRGEN PETZOLDT
Chancellor: Dr MARGOT BOCK
Librarian: GERHARD VOGT
Number of teachers: 714
Number of students: 8,010
Publications: *'Information/Dokumentation'* (proceedings, every 2 years), *Tagungsberichte des Internationalen Kolloquiums* (1 a year), *Wissenschaftliches Magazin*

DEANS
Faculty of Computer Science and Automation: Prof. Dr Ing. Hab. JENS HAUEISEN
Faculty of Economics: Prof. Dr Hab. RAINER SOUREN
Faculty of Electrical Engineering and Information Technology: Prof. Dr Ing. Hab. FRANK BERGER
Faculty of Mathematics and Natural Sciences: Prof. Dr Hab. NICOLA DÖRING
Faculty of Mechanical Engineering: Prof. Dr Ing. Hab. PETER KURTZ

TECHNISCHE UNIVERSITÄT KAISERSLAUTERN

POB 3049, 67653 Kaiserslautern
Gottlieb-Daimler-Str., 67663 Kaiserslautern
Telephone: (631) 2050
E-mail: internationales@uni-kl.de
Internet: www.uni-kl.de
Founded 1970 as Universität Trier Kaiserslautern, separated 1975
State control
Languages of instruction: English, German
Academic year: October to September
Pres.: Prof. Dr HELMUT J. SCHMIDT
Vice-Pres. for Research and Technology: Prof. Dr BURKARD HILLEBRANDS
Vice-Pres. for Student and Academic Affairs: Prof. Dr Ing. LOTHAR LITZ
Chancellor: STEFAN LORENZ
Head Librarian: JOAN FERSCHINGER
Library of 435,000 vols
Number of teachers: 767
Number of students: 12,510

DEANS
Faculty of Architecture: Prof. BERND MEYERSPEER
Faculty of Biology: Prof. Dr JOHANNES HERRMANN
Faculty of Business Studies and Economics: Prof. Dr STEFAN ROTH
Faculty of Chemistry: Prof. Dr JENS HARTUNG
Faculty of Civil Engineering: Prof. Dr Ing. WOLFGANG KURZ
Faculty of Computer Science: Prof. Dr ARND POETZSCH-HEFFTER
Faculty of Electrical and Computer Engineering: Prof. Dr Ing. NORBERT WEHN
Faculty of Mathematics: Prof. Dr RENE PINNAU
Faculty of Mechanical and Process Engineering: Prof. Dr Ing. BERND SAUER
Faculty of Physics: Prof. Dr MICHAEL FLEISCHHAUER
Faculty of Regional Planning: Prof. Dr Ing. GERHARD STEINEBACH
Faculty of Social Sciences: Prof. Dr THOMAS SCHMIDT

PROFESSORS
Faculty of Architecture, Regional Planning and Civil Engineering:
BAYER, D., Digital and Methodical Modelling
BECKMANN, R., Ecological Planning and Environmental Compatibility
BÖHM, W., Theory of Buildings and Design
CASTORPH, M., Component-Orientated Planning Processes
DENNHARDT, H., Regional Planning
FILIBECK, R., Construction Management
GÖPFERT, N., Statics of Rising Structures
GOTZ, M., Urban Construction and Planning
HEINRICH, B., Building Physics and Equipment
HOFRICHTER, H., Architecture, History of Town Planning
KAHLFED, P., Industrial Construction III and Design
KLEINE-KRANEBURG, H., Industrial Construction II and Design
KLOPF, H., Load-bearing Structure Design
KOEHLER, G., Civil Engineering
MECHTCHERINE, V., Construction Material Technology
MEDINA-WARMBURG, H., Construction History
MERX, L., Representation and Composition
MEYERSPEER, B., Industrial Construction I and Design
NADLER, M., Building Development
SCHMITT, T. G., Water Management in Residential Areas
SCHNELL, J., Concrete and Building Construction
SEITZ, E., Room Design
SPANNOWSKY, W., Public Law
SPELLENBERG, A., Urban Sociology
STEITZBACH, G., Urban Planning
STREICH, B., Computer-Assisted Design and Construction
TOBIAS, K., Ecological Planning and Environmental Compatibility
TOPP, H. H., Traffic Management
TROEGER-WEIß, A., Regional Development and Planning
TRUMPKE, K., Surveying
VRETTOS, C., Soil Mechanics and Foundation Engineering
WASSERMANN, K., Civil Engineering
WITTEK, U., Civil Engineering
WÜST, H.-S., Landscaping

Faculty of Biology:
ANKER, T., Biotechnology
BRÜNE, A., Cell Biology
BÜDEL, D., Systematic Botany
CULLUM, J. A., Genetics
DEITMER, J. W., Zoology
FRIAUF, A., Animal Physiology
HAHN, A., Phytopathology
HAKENBECK, R., Microbiology
LAKATOS, A., Ecology
LEITZ, A., Animal Development
NEUHAUS, A., Physiology of Plants
SCHMIDT, H., Physiological Ecology
ZANKL, H., Human Biology and Genetics

Faculty of Chemistry:
EISENBRAND, G., Food Chemistry and Toxicology
ERNST, S., Technical Chemistry
HARTMANN, M., Chemical Technology
HARTUNG, J., Organic Chemistry
HIMBERT, G., Organic Chemistry
KIETZTMANN, T., Biochemistry
KREITER, C., Inorganic Chemistry
KRÜGER, H. J., Inorganic Chemistry
KUBALL, H.-G., Physical Chemistry
KUBIK, S., Organic Chemistry
MARKO, D., Food Chemistry and Toxicology
MEMMER, R., Physical and Theoretical Chemistry
MEYER, W., Physical and Theoretical Chemistry
NIEDER-SCHATTEBURG, A., Physical and Theoretical Chemistry
REGITZ, M., Organic Chemistry
SCHERER, O. J., Inorganic Chemistry
SCHRENK, D., Food Chemistry and Toxicology
SITZMANN, H., Inorganic Chemistry
THIEL, W., Inorganic Chemistry
TROMMER, W., Organic Chemistry, Biochemistry

Faculty of Computer Science:
BERNS, K., Robotic Systems
BREUEL, T., Pattern Recognition
DENGEL, A., Knowledge-Based Systems
DEßLOCK, S., Heterogenous Information Systems
EBERT, A., Visualization
GOTZHEIN, R., Networked Systems
HAGEN, H., Graphic Data Processing, Computer Geometry
HÄRDNER, T., Data Management Systems
HEINRICH, S., Numerical Algorithms in Computer Science
LIGGESMEYER, P., Software Engineering Dependability
MADLENER, K., Principles of Computer Science
MAYER, O., Principles of Programming and Computer Languages
MER, P., Shared Algorithms
MÜLLER, P., Integrated Communication Systems
NEHMER, J., Software Technology
POETZSCH-HEFFTER, A., Software Technology
RAUSCH, A., Software Technology
ROMBACH, D., Software Engineering
SCHMITT, J., Shared Systems (DISCO)
SCHNEIDER, K., Reactive Systems
SCHÜRMANN, B., Modelling of Embedded Systems
UMLAUF, G., Algorithms
WIEHAGEN, R., Algorithmic Learning (Theory)

Faculty of Electrical Engineering:
BAIER, P. W., Radio Frequency Communication
BEISTER, J., Circuits
FREY, A., Agent-Based Automation
HAUCK, A., Power Electronics (Teaching)
HUTH, H., Mechatronics and Electrical Drives
KOENIG, A., Integrated Sensor Systems
KUNZ, A., Electronic Design Automation
LITZ, L., Automatic Control
LIU, A., Control Systems
POTCHINKOV, M., Digital Signal Processing
TIELERT, R., Principles of Microelectronics

TUTTAS, A., Power Systems Transmission and Power Plants (Teaching)
URBANSKY, R., Public Telecommunications Engineering
WEHN, N., Microelectronics
WEISS, P., High-Voltage Engineering, Principles of Electrical Engineering
ZENGERLE, R., Theory of Electrical and Electronic Engineering, Optical Communications

Faculty of Mathematics:

BECKER, H., Mathematics
BRAKHAGE, H., Applied Mathematics
DEMPWOLFF, U., Mathematics
FRANKE, J., Stochastics
FREEDEN, W., Mathematics
GREUEL, G.-M., Topology
HAMACHER, H., Econometrics
LÜNEBURG, H., Mathematics
NEUNZERT, H., Mathematics
PFISTER, G., Computer Algebra
PRÄTZEL-WOLTERS, D., Mathematics
RADBRUCH, K., Mathematics, Teaching of Mathematics
SCHOCK, E., Applied Mathematics
SCHWEIGERT, D., Mathematics
TRAUTMANN, G., Pure Mathematics
VON WEIZÄCKER, H., Analysis

Faculty of Mechanical Engineering:

AURICH, J. C., Institute of Manufacturing Engineering and Production Management
BART, H.-J., Chemical Engineering
EIFLER, D., Materials Science
EIGNER, M., Product Development
FLIERL, R., Workgroup for Combustion Engines
HABERLAND, R., Precision Engineering
HELLMANN, D., Fluid Mechanics
MAURER, G., Thermodynamics
RENZ, R., Recyclability in Product Design and Disassembly
RIPPERGER, S., Institute for Particle Technology
SAUER, B., Machine Components
SCHINDLER, C., Institute of Design Engineering
ZÜLKE, D., Production Automation

Faculty of Physics:

AESCHLIMANN, M., Experimental Physics
BEIGANG, R., Experimental Physics
BERGMANN, K., Experimental Physics
DILL, R., Experimental Physics
EGGERT, S., Theoretical Physics
FLEISCHHAUER, M., Theoretical Physics
FOUCKHARDT, H., Experimental Physics
HILLEBRANDS, B., Experimental Physics
HOTOP, H., Experimental Physics
HÜBNER, W., Theoretical Physics
JODL, H.-G., Teaching of Physics, Experimental Physics
KORSCH, J., Theoretical Physics
KRÜGER, H., Theoretical Physics
KUPSCH, J., Theoretical Physics
OESTERSCHULZE, E., Experimental Physics
SCHMORANZER, H., Experimental and Applied Physics
SCHNEIDER, H. C., Theoretical Physics
SCHÜNEMANN, V., Experimental Physics
URBASSEK, H. M., Applied Physics
ZIEGELER, C., Technical Physics

Faculty of Social and Economic Sciences:

ARNOLD, R., Education
BLIEMEL, F., Marketing
CORSTEN, H., Production Management
DUTKE, S., Psychology
ENSTHALER, J., Civil and Economic Law
FESER, H.-D., Economics and Economic Policy I
GESMANN-NUISSL, D., Business Law
HÖLSCHER, R., Finance and Investment
JAINTER, T., Sports
LINGNAU, H.V., Management Accounting and Management Control Systems
NEUSER, W., Philosophy
PÄTZOLD, H., Education
RITTBERGER, B., Politics
VON HAUFF, M., Economics and Economic Policy
WENDT, O., Information Systems and Operations Research
WILZEWSKI, J., Politics
ZINK, K. J., Business Management

AFFILIATED INSTITUTES

Deutsches Forschungszentrum für Künstliche Intelligenz GmbH (DFKI) (Research Centre for Artificial Intelligence): Erwin-Schrödinger-Str. (Gebäude 57), Postfach 2080, 67663 Kaiserslautern; e-mail info@dfki.de; Dir (vacant).

Institut für Oberflächen- und Schichtanalytik GmbH (Institute for Surface and Coating Analysis): Trippstadter Str. 120, 67763 Kaiserslautern; Dir Prof. Dr MICHAEL KOPNARSKI.

Institut für Verbundwerkstoffe GmbH (IVW) (Institute for Composite Materials): Erwin-Schrödinger-Str., 67663 Kaiserslautern; Dir Prof. Dr Ing. MANFRED NEITZEL

TECHNISCHE UNIVERSITÄT MÜNCHEN

Arcisstr. 21, 80333 Munich
Telephone: (89) 28901
E-mail: praesident@tu-muenchen.de
Internet: www.tum.de

Founded 1868
State control
Academic year: October to September

Pres.: Prof. Dr WOLFGANG A. HERRMANN
Vice-Pres.: Dr Ing. KAI WÜLBERN
Vice-Pres.: Prof. Dr Ing. MENG LIQIU
Vice-Pres.: Prof. Dr PETER GRITZMANN
Vice-Pres.: Prof. Dr THOMAS HOFMANN
Chancellor: ALBERT BERGER
Librarian: Dr REINER KALLENBORN

Library: see under Libraries and Archives
Number of teachers: 6,025
Number of students: 26,302

DEANS

Centre of Life and Food Sciences Weihenstephan: Prof. Dr ALFONS GIERL
Faculty of Architecture: Prof. Dipl. Ing. REGINE KELLER
Faculty of Chemistry: Prof. Dr ULRICH HEIZ
Faculty of Civil Engineering and Geodesy: Prof. Dr Ing. GERHARD MÜLLER
Faculty of Electrical Engineering and Information Technology: Prof. Dr Ing. ULF SCHLICHTMANN
Faculty of Informatics: Prof. Dr HELMUT KRCMAR
Faculty of Mathematics: Prof. Dr GREGOR KEMPER
Faculty of Mechanical Engineering: Prof. Dr Ing. HANS-PETER KAU
Faculty of Medicine: Prof. PETER HENNINGSEN
Faculty of Physics: Prof. Dr MARTIN STUTZMANN
Faculty of Sports: Prof. Dr JÜRGEN BECKMANN
School of Education: Prof. Dr MANFRED PRENZEL
School of Management: Prof. GUNTHER FRIEDL

PROFESSORS

Centre of Life and Food Sciences Weihenstephan (Alte Akademie 8, 85354 Freising; tel. (8161) 713258; e-mail dekanat@wzw.tum.de; internet www.wzw.tu-muenchen.de):

AUERNHAMMER, H., Agricultural Engineering
BACK, W., Brewing Technology I
BAUER, J., Animal Hygiene
DANIEL, H., Physiology of Nutrition
DELGADO, A., Fluid Mechanics and Process Automation
ENGEL, K.-H., Food and Nutrition
FAULSTICH, M., Technology of Biogenic Products
FORKMANN, G., Floriculture
FRIEDRICH, J., Physics
FRIES, H.-R., Animal Breeding
GIERL, A., Genetics
GRILL, E., Botany
HABE, W., Landscape Ecology
HAUNER, H., Nutritional Medicine
HOCK, B., Cell Biology
HRABÉ DE ANGELIS, M., Experimental Genetics
KETTRUP, A., Ecological Chemistry and Environmental Analytics
KÖGEL-KNABNER, I., Soil Science
KULOZIK, U., Food Process Engineering
LANGOSCH, D., Biopolymer Chemistry
LANGOWSKI, H.-C., Brewery Installations and Food Packaging Technology
LATZ, P., Landscape Architecture and Planning
MANLEY, G. A., Zoology
MATYSSEK, R., Ecophysiology of Plants
MENZEL, A., Ecoclimatology
MEWES, H.-W., Genome-Orientated Bioinformatics
MEYER, H., Physiology
MEYER-PITTROFF, R., Energy and Environmental Technologies of the Food Industry
MOOG, M., Forestry
MOSANDL, R., Silviculture and Forest Planning
PARLAR, H., Chemical-Technical Analysis and Chemical Food Technology
PFADENHAUER, J., Vegetation Ecology
PRETZSCH, H., Forest Yield Science
QUEDNAU, H.-D., Work Science and Applied Computer Science
RECHKEMMER, G., Biofunctionality of Food
ROTHENBURGER, W., Horticultural Economics
SCHEMANN, M., Human Biology
SCHLEIFER, K.-H., Microbiology
SCHMIDHALTER, U., Plant Nutrition
SCHNITZLER, W. H., Vegetable Science
SCHNYDER, H., Grassland
SCHÖN, J., Land Engineering
SCHOPF, R., Animal Ecology
SKERRA, A., Biological Chemistry
SOMMER, K., Machinery and Apparatus
SUDA, M., Politics and History of Forestry
VALENTIEN, C., Landscape Architecture and Design
VOGEL, R., Industrial Microbiology
WARKOTSCH, W., Forest Industry and Applied Computer Science
WEGENER, G., Wood Science and Wood Engineering
WEISSER, H., Brewery Construction and Food Packaging Technology
WENZEL, G., Plant Cultivation
WOLF, P. F. J., Phytopathology
WOLFRAM, G., Human Nutrition
WURST, W., Developmental Genetics
ZANDER, J., Land Use Planning and Nature Conservation

Faculty of Architecture (tel. (89) 28922351; e-mail marga.cervinka@lrz.tu-muenchen.de; internet www.arch.tu-muenchen.de):

BARTHEL, R., Structural Engineering
BOCK, T., Building Implementation and Information Technology
COTELO LÓPEZ, V., Design and the Conservation of Historical Buildings
DEUBZER, H., Design, Spatial Art and Lighting Design
EBNER, P., Housing and Housing Economics
EMMERLING, E., Restoration, Art Technology and Conservation
FINK, D., Integrated Construction

HAUSLADEN, G., Indoor Climate and Mechanical Services
HERZOG, T., Building Technology
HORDEN, R., Architecture and Product Development
HUGUES, T., Building Construction and Materials
HUSE, N., History of Art
KIESSLER, U., Integrated Buildings
KOENIGS, W., History of Building and Building Research
KRAU, I., Town Planning and Urban Development
LATZ, P., Landscape Architecture and Planning
MUSSO, F., Design, Building Construction and Materials Science
OSTERTAG, D., House Technology
REICHENBACH-KLINKE, M., Planning and Construction in Rural Areas
STRACKE, F., Urban Development and Regional Planning
THIERSTEIN, A., Territorial and Spatial Development
WIENANDS, R., Principles of Design and Representation
WITTENBORN, R., Visual Design
WOLFRUM, S., Urban and Regional Planning
ZBINDEN, U., Building Construction and Design Methodology

Faculty of Chemistry (Lichtenbergstr. 4, 85748 Garching; tel. (89) 2893001; e-mail dekanat@ch.tum.de; internet www.chemie.tu-muenchen.de):

BACH, T., Organic Chemistry I
BACHER, A., Organic Chemistry and Biochemistry
BONDYBEY, V. E., Physical Chemistry
BUCHNER, J., Biotechnology
DOMCKE, W., Theoretical Chemistry
FÄSSLER, T., Inorganic Chemistry
HEIZ, U., Physical Chemistry I
HERRMANN, W., Inorganic Chemistry
HINRICHSEN, O., Chemical Technology I
KESSLER, H., Organic Chemistry II
KETTRUP, A., Ecological Chemistry and Environmental Analytics
LANGOSCH, D., Bipolymer Chemistry
LERCHER, J., Chemical Technology II
LIMBERG, C., Inorganic Chemistry
NEUMEIER, D., Clinical Chemistry and Pathobiochemistry
NIEßNER, R., Hydrogeology, Hydrochemistry and Environmental Analytical Chemistry
NITSCH, W., Chemical Engineering
NUYKEN, O., Macromolecular Substances
PLANK, J., Construction Chemistry
SCHIEBERLE, P., Food Chemistry
SCHIEMANN, O., Physical Chemistry II
SCHMIDBAUR, H., Inorganic and Analytical Chemistry
SKERRA, A., Biological Chemistry
TÜRLER, A., Radiochemistry
VEPREK, S., Chemistry of Inorganic Materials

Faculty of Civil Engineering and Geodesy (tel. (89) 28922400; e-mail dekanat@bv.tum.de; internet www.bv.tum.de):

ALBRECHT, G., Steel-Girder Construction
BLETZINGER, K., Structural Analysis
BÖSCH, H.-J., Tunnel Construction, Building Management
BUSCH, F., Traffic Engineering and Control
EBNER, H., Photogrammetry
FAULSTICH, M., Water Quality Control and Waste Management
GRUNDMANN, H., Building Mechanics
HAUSER, G., Building Physics
KIRCHHOFF, P., Transport and Town Planning
LEYKAUF, G., Road, Railway and Airfield Construction
MAGEL, H., Ground Preparation and Land Development
MENG, L., Cartography
MÜLLER, G., Building Mechanics
RANK, E., Building Informatics
RUMMEL, R., Astronomical and Physical Geodesy
SCHIESS, R., Building Materials and Materials Testing
SCHIESSL, P., Building Materials and Materials Testing
SCHIKORA, K., Analysis of Civil Engineering Structures
SCHUNCK, E., Building Construction
SPAUN, G., Geology
STROBL, TH., Hydraulic and Water Resources Engineering
THURO, K., Geology
VALENTIN, F., Hydraulics and Hydrography
VOGT, N., Foundations, Soil Mechanics and Rock Mechanics
WILDERER, P., Water Quality and Waste Management
WINTER, S., Building Construction
WUNDERLICH, T., Geodesy
ZILCH, K., Concrete Structures
ZIMMERMANN, J., Building Process Management

Faculty of Economics and Social Sciences (tel. (89) 28925066; e-mail dekanat@wi.tum.de; internet www.wi.tu-muenchen.de):

ACHLEITNER, A., KfW Entrepreneurial Finance
ANN, C., Corporate Law and Intellectual Property
BÄUMLER, G., Physical Education (Psychology)
BELZ, F., Brewing and Food Industry
BLÜMELHUBER, C., Marketing and Distribution
BÜSSING, A., Psychology
ENNEKING, U., Agribusiness and Food Industry
GRANDE, E., Political Science
GROSSER, M., Science of Movement and Training
HACKER, W., Psychology
HEINRITZ, G., Geography
HEISSENHUBER, A., Agricultural Economics and Farm Management
HENKEL, J., Technology and Innovation Management
HOFMANN, W., Political Science
HOLZHEU, F., Economics
KARG, G., Consumer Economics
KASERER, C., Financial Management and Capital Markets
KOLISCH, R., Technical Services and Operational Management
LEIST, K.-H., Physical Education Teaching
LÜCK, W., Business Management, Accounting, Auditing and Consulting
MOOG, M., Forest Management
REICHWALD, R., Information, Organization and Management
SALHOFER, K., Environmental Economics and Agricultural Policy
SCHELTEN, A., Pedagogics
STEINMÜLLER, H., Social Policy and Insurance
SUDA, M., Forest Policy and Forest History
TRINCZEK, R., Sociology
VON WEIZSÄCKER, R. FRHR., Economics
WEINDLMAIER, J., Dairy and Food Industry Management
WENGENROTH, U., History of Engineering
WILDEMANN, H., Management, Logistics and Production
WITT, D., Service Management
ZACHMANN, K., History of Technology

Faculty of Electrical Engineering and Information Technology (tel. (89) 28928378; e-mail dekanat@ei.tum.de; internet www.e-technik.tu-muenchen.de):

AMANN, M., Semiconductor Technology
ANTREICH, K., Computer-Aided Design
BIRKHOFER, A., Reactor Dynamics and Reactor Safety
BOECK, W., High Voltage Engineering and Power Plants
BUSS, M., Automatic Control Engineering
DIEPOLD, K., Data Processing
EBERSPÄCHER, J., Communication Networks
FÄRBER, G., Real-Time Computer Systems
GÜNTHER, C., Communication and Navigation
HAGENAUER, J., Communications Engineering
HEKERSDORF, A., Integrated Systems
KINDERSBERGER, J., High Voltage Engineering and Electric Power Transmission
KOCH, A., Measurement Systems and Sensor Technology
LANG, M., Man–Machine Communication
LUGLI, P., Nanoelectronics
NOSSEK, J., Circuit Theory and Signal Processing
RIGOLL, G., Man–Machine Communication
RUGE, I., Integrated Circuits
RUSSER, P., High Frequency Engineering
SCHLICHTMANN, U., Electronic Design Automation
SCHMIDT, G., Control Engineering
SCHMITT-LANDSIEDEL, D., Technical Electronics
SCHRÖDER, D., Electrical Drives
SWOBODA, J., Data Processing
WACHUTKA, G., Physics of Electrotechnology
WAGNER, U., Energy Economy and Application Technology
WOLF, B., Medical Electronics

Faculty of Informatics (Boltzmannstr. 3, 85748 Garching; tel. (89) 28917590; e-mail gemkow@in.tum.de; internet www.informatik.tu-muenchen.de):

BAYER, R., Computer Science
BICHLER, M., Internet-Based Information Systems
BODE, A., Computer Organization, Parallel Computer Architecture
BRAUER, W., Theoretical Computer Science and Foundations of Artificial Intelligence
BROY, M., Software and Systems Engineering
BRÜGGE, B., Applied Software Engineering
BUNGARTZ, H.-J., Computer Science in Engineering, Numerical Programming
EICKEL, J., Computer Science
FELDMANN, A., Network Architecture
GRUST, T., Database Systems
HEGERING, H.-G., Technical Informatics—Computer Networks
HUBWIESER, P., Didactics of Informatics
JESSEN, E., Computer Science
KNOLL, A., Robotics and Embedded Systems
KRAMER, S., Bioinformatics
KRCMAR, H., Information Systems
MATTHES, F., Software Engineering for Business Applications
MAYR, E. W., Efficient Algorithms
NAVAB, N., Computer-Aided Medical Procedures
RADIG, B., Image Understanding and Knowledge-Based Systems
SCHLICHTER, J., Applied Informatics/Collaborative Systems
SEIDL, H., Formal Languages, Compiler Construction, Software Construction
SPIES, P., System Architecture
WESTERMANN, R., Computer Graphics and Visualization
ZENGER, C., Computer Science

Faculty of Mathematics (Boltzmannstr. 3, 85747 Garching; tel. (89) 28916806; e-mail dekanat@ma.tum.de; internet www.ma.tum.de):

BORNEMANN, F., Scientific Computing
BROKATE, M., Mathematical Modelling
BULIRSCH, R., Numerical Analysis
FRIESEKE, G., Global Analysis
GRITZMANN, P., Combinatorial Geometry
HOFFMAN, K.-H., Mathematical Modelling
KEMPER, G., Algorithmic Algebra
KLÜPPELBERG, C., Statistics
LASSER, R., Biomathematics
LOSS, M., Global Analysis
RENTROP, P., Numerical Analysis
RICHTER-GEBERT, J., Geometry and Visualization
RITTER, K., Optimization
SCHEURLE, J., Dynamic Systems
SPOHN, H., Mathematical Physics
ZAGST, R., Mathematical Finance

Faculty of Mechanical Engineering (Boltzmannstr. 15, 85748 Garching; tel. (89) 2895020; e-mail wagner@mw.tum.de; internet www.mw.tu-muenchen.de):

ADAMS, N., Aerodynamics
BAIER, H., Lightweight Structures
BENDER, K., Information Technology
BUBB, H., Ergonomics and Human Factors
GREGORY, J. K., Materials
GÜNTHER, A., Material Flow and Logistics
GÜNTHNER, W., Production Technology
HEIN, D., Thermal Power Plants
HEINZL, J., Precision Mechanics and Microengineering
HEISSING, B., Automotive Engineering
HOFFMANN, H., Metal Forming and Casting
HÖHN, R., Machine Elements
KAU, H. P., Flight Propulsion
LASCHKA, B., Fluid Mechanics
LINDEMANN, U., Product Development
LOHMANN, B., Automatic Control
PEUKERT, W., Chemical Process Engineering
PEUKERT, W., Solid Fuel Process Engineering
REINHART, G., Assembly Systems and Factories
RENIUS, K. T., Agricultural Machinery
SACHS, G., Flight Mechanics and Control
SATTELMAYER, T., Thermodynamics
SCHILLING, R., Fluid Mechanics
SCHMITT, D., Aeronautical Engineering
STICHLMAIR, J., Process Engineering
STROHMEIER, K., Apparatus and Plant Construction
ULBRICH, H., Applied Mechanics
WACHTMEISTER, G., Internal Combustion Engines
WALL, W., Computational Mechanics
WALTER, U., Astronautics
WERNER, E., Materials Science and Mechanics
WEUSTER-BOTZ, D., Biochemical Engineering
WINTERMANTEL, E., Medical Engineering
ZÄH, M., Machine Tools and Industrial Management

Faculty of Medicine (Ismaninger Str. 48, 81675 Munich; tel. (89) 41402121; e-mail huebener@nt1.chir.med.tu-muenchen.de; internet www.med.tu-muenchen.de):

ARNOLD, W., Otorhinolaryngology
BURDACH, S., Paediatrics
CLASSEN, M., Internal Medicine
CONRAD, B., Neurology
EISENMENGER, W., Forensic Medicine
EMMRICH, P., Paediatrics
ERFLE, V., Virology
FÖRSTL, H., Psychiatry and Psychotherapy
GÄNSBACHER, B., Experimental Oncology and Therapy Research
GÖTTLICHER, M., Clinic for Industrial and Environmental Medicine
GRADINGER, R., Orthopaedics and Sport Orthopaedics
GREIM, H., Toxicology and Environmental Hygiene
HALLE, M., Preventive and Rehabilitative Sports Medicine
HARTUNG, R., Urology
HAUNER, H., Nutritional Medicine
HESS, J., Paediatric Cardiology
HÖFLER, H., General Pathology and Pathological Anatomy
HOFMANN, F., Molecular Medicine
HOFMANN, F., Pharmacology and Toxicology
HORCH, H.-H., Dentistry
JESCHKE, D., Preventive and Rehabilitative Sports Medicine
KIECHLE, M., Gynaecology
KOCHS, E. F., Anaesthesiology
KUHN, K. A., Medical Statistics and Epidemiology
LANGE, R., Cardiac Surgery
LANZL, I. M., Ophthalmology
MEITINGER, T., Genetics
MERTZ, M., Ophthalmology
MOLLS, M., Radiotherapy and Radiological Oncology
NEISS, A., Medical Statistics and Epidemiology
NEUMEIER, D., Clinical Chemistry and Pathobiochemistry
NOWAK, D., Clinic for Industrial and Environmental Medicine
PESCHEL, C., Internal Medicine III
RING, J., Dermatology and Allergology
RUMMENY, E. J., X-Ray Diagnostics
SCHMID, R., Internal Medicine II
SCHÖMIG, A.-W., Internal Medicine I
SCHWAIGER, M., Nuclear Medicine
SIEWERT, J.-R., Surgery
SPEICHER, M., Genetics
TRAPPE, A. E., Neurosurgery
VON RAD, M., Clinical Psychology and Psychotherapy
WAGNER, H., Clinical Microbiology, Immunology and Hygiene
WILMANNS, J. C., Medical History and Ethics

Faculty of Physics (James Franck Str., 85748 Garching; tel. (89) 28912492; e-mail dekanat@physik.tu-muenchen.de; internet www.physik.tu-muenchen.de):

ABSTREITER, G., Experimental Semiconductor Physics I
BÖNI, P., Experimental Physics
BURAS, A. J., Theoretical Physics IV
DIETRICH, K., Theoretical Physics I
FEULNER, P., Physics
FISCHER, S., Theoretical Physics II
FRIEDRICH, H., Theoretical Physics
FRIEDRICH, J., Physics
GROSS, R., Technical Physics
GROß, A., Theoretical Physics
KINDER, H., Experimental Physics
KLEBER, M., Theoretical Physics
KOCH, F., Physics
KRÜCKEN, R., Physics
LAUBEREAU, A., Experimental Physics
LINDNER, M., Theoretical Particle and Astro-Particle Physics
NETZ, R., Theoretical Physics II
PARAK, F. G., Physics and Biophysics
PAUL, S., Physics I
PETRY, W., Experimental Physics
RIEF, M., Physics
RING, P., Theoretical Physics
STIMMING, U., Physics
STUTZMANN, M., Experimental Semiconductor Physics II
VOGL, P., Theoretical Physics III
VAN HEMMEN, J. L., Theoretical Physics
VON FEILITZSCH, F., Experimental Physics and Astro-Particle Physics
WEISE, W., Theoretical Physics
ZWERGER, W., Theoretical Physics V

Faculty of Sports (Connollystr. 32, 80809 Munich; tel. (89) 28924601; e-mail dekanat.sport@sp.tum.de; internet www.sport.tu-muenchen.de):

HACKFORTH, J., Sport, Media and Communication
KELLER, J. A., Sport Psychology
LEIST, K.-H., Sport Pedagogy
MICHNA, H., Sport and Health Promotion
TUSKER, F., Human Movement Science and Training

TIERÄRZTLICHE HOCHSCHULE HANNOVER
(University of Veterinary Medicine Hanover)

POB 71 11 80, 30545 Hanover
Bünteweg 2, 30559 Hanover
Telephone: (511) 95360
E-mail: info@tiho-hannover.de
Internet: www.tiho-hannover.de

Founded 1778 as Königliche Rossarzneischule, attained univ. status 1887
State control
Academic year: October to September

Pres.: Dr GERHARD GREIF
Vice-Pres. for Research: Prof. Dr ULRICH NEUMANN
Vice-Pres. for Teaching: Prof. Dr ANDREA TIPOLD

Library of 230,000 vols, 1,000 print journals, 3,000 ejournals
Number of teachers: 122
Number of students: 2,360

Publications: *TiHo-Anzeiger* (8 a year), *TiHo Forschung fürs Leben* (1 a year)

HEADS

Centre for Food Toxicology: Prof. Dr HEINZ NAU
Clinic for Cattle: Prof. Dr HEINRICH BOLLWEIN
Clinic for Horses: Prof. Dr KARSTEN FEIGE
Clinic for Pigs, Small Ruminants, Forensic Medicine and Ambulatory Service: Prof. Dr K.-H. WALDMANN
Clinic for Poultry: Prof. Dr SILKE RAUTENSCHLEIN
Clinic for Small Domestic Animals: Prof. Dr INGO NOLTE
Department of Analytical Chemistry and Endocrinology: Prof. Dr H.-O. HOPPEN
Department of Biometry, Epidemiology and Data Processing: Prof. Dr L. KREIENBROCK
Department of Fish Pathology and Fish Farming: Prof. Dr WOLFGANG KÖRTING
Department of General Radiology and Medical Physics: Prof. Dr HERMANN SEIFERT
Department of History of Veterinary Medicine and Domestic Animals: Prof. Dr JOHANN SCHÄFFER
Department of Immunology: Prof. Dr WOLFGANG LEIBOLD
Institute of Anatomy: Prof. Dr CHRISTIANE PFARRER
Institute for Animal Behaviour and Protection: Prof. Dr HANSJOACHIM HACKBARTH
Institute of Animal Breeding and Genetics: Prof. Dr OTTMAR DISTL
Institute for Animal Ecology and Cell Biology: Prof. Dr BERND SCHIERWATER
Institute for Animal Hygiene and Protection: Prof. Dr JÖRG HARTUNG
Institute for Animal Nutrition: Prof. Dr J. KAMPHUES
Institute of Epidemics: Prof. Dr THOMAS BLAHA
Institute for Food Quality and Safety: Prof. Dr G. KLEIN
Institute for Microbiology: Prof. Dr PETER VALENTIN-WEIGAND
Institute for Parasitology: Prof. Dr THOMAS SCHNEIDER
Institute for Pathology: Prof. Dr WOLFGANG BAUMGÄRTNER
Institute for Physiology: Prof. Dr GERHARD BREVES

Institute for Physiological Chemistry: Prof. Dr HASSAN Y. NAIM
Institute for Reproductive Medicine: Prof. Dr EDDA TÖPFER-PETERSEN
Institute for Virology: Prof. Dr VOLKER MOENNIG
Institute for Wildlife Research: Prof. Dr BURKHARD MEINECKE
Institute for Zoology: Prof. Dr ELKE ZIMMERMANN

UKRAINISCHE FREIE UNIVERSITÄT
(Ukrainian Free University)

Barellistr. 9A, 80638 Munich
Telephone: (89) 99738830
E-mail: sekretariat@ufu-muenchen.de
Internet: www.ufu-muenchen.de

Founded 1921
private, state-approved
Languages of instruction: Ukrainian, English, German
Academic year: October to August (incl. Summer Courses July–August)

Rector: Prof. Dr YAROSLAVA MELNYK
Chancellor/Registrar: Mag. ANDRIY DOVGANYUK
Librarian: IWANNA REBET

Number of teachers: 56
Number of students: 110

Publications: *Naukovi Zapysky UVU* (1 a year), *Naukovi Zbirnyky UVU*, *Specimina dialectorum ucrainorum*, *Studien zu deutsch–ukrainischen Beziehungen*

DEANS

Faculty of Law and Economics: Prof. Dr MARIA PRYSHLAK
Faculty of Philosophy: Prof. Dr MARK VON HAGEN
Faculty of Ukrainian Studies: Prof. Dr TAMARA HUNDOROVA

PROFESSORS

Faculty of Law and Economics (tel. (89) 99738842):

FUTEY, B., Law
ISAJIW, V., Sociology
KOSTYCKY, M., Law
MYHUL, I., Political Economics
NAGY, L., Geography
PYNZENYK, V., Political Economics
SUBTELNY, O., History of Political Ideas
SZAFOWAL, N., Political Science

Faculty of Philosophy:

ANDRIEWSKY, O., History
DACKO, I., Theology
GUDZIAK, B., Church History
JERABEK, B., Education
KIPA, A., Comparative Literature
KOSYK, W., History
KYSILEWSKA-TKACH, A., Education
LABUNKA, M., Ukrainian History
MAKSYMTSCHUK, W., Comparative Literature
PIETSCH, R., Philosophy
RUDNYTZKY, L., Comparative Literature
STEPOWYK, D., Cultural History
SYSYN, F., History
ZLEPKO, D., History of Eastern Europe
ŽUK, L., Ukrainian Music
ŽUK, R., History of Architecture

Faculty of Ukrainian Studies:

AVVAKUMOV,, G., Church Slavonic
KOPTILOV, V., Ukrainian Language and Literature
KOZAK, S., Slavonic Literature
MELNYK, Y., Ukrainian Literature
MUSHINKA, M., Ukrainian Ethnology
POHRIBNYJ, A., Ukrainian Language and Literature
PRYSJAZNIJ, M., Journalism
SALYHA, T., History of Ukrainian Literature

UNIVERSITÄT AUGSBURG

Universitätsstr. 2, 86159 Augsburg
Telephone: (821) 5980
E-mail: info@aaa.uni-augsburg.de
Internet: www.uni-augsburg.de

Founded 1970
State control
Language of instruction: German
Academic year: October to July

Pres.: Prof. Dr ALOIS LOIDL (acting)
Vice-Pres.: Prof. Dr ALOIS LOIDL
Vice-Pres.: Prof. Dr ALEX TUMA
Vice-Pres.: Prof. Dr WERNER WIATER
Chancellor: ALOIS ZIMMERMAN
Librarian: Dr ULRICH HOHOFF

Library: see under Libraries and Archives
Number of teachers: 458
Number of students: 16,606

Publication: *Mitteilungen Institut fur Europaeische Kulturgeschichte*

DEANS

Faculty of Applied Computer Science: Prof. Dr WOLFGANG REIF
Faculty of Catholic Theology: Prof. Dr GREGOR WURST
Faculty of Economics: Prof. Dr KLAUS TUROWSKI
Faculty of History and Philology: Prof. Dr SABINE DOERING-MANTEUFFEL
Faculty of Law: Prof. Dr ULRICH M. GASSNER
Faculty of Mathematics and Natural Sciences: Prof. Dr ACHIM WIXFORTH
Faculty of Philosophy and Social Sciences: Prof. Dr WERNER SCHNEIDER

PROFESSORS

Faculty of Applied Computer Science (86135 Augsburg; tel. (821) 5982174; e-mail reif@informatik.uni-augsburg.de; internet www.uni-augsburg.de/fakultaeten/fai):

ANDRÉ, E., Multimedia Concepts and Applications
BAUER, B., Software and Programming Languages
FRIEDMANN, A., Physical Geography
HAGERUP, T., Theoretical Computing
HILLENBRAND, H., Didactics
HILPERT, M., Human Geography
JACOBEIT, J., Physical Geography
KIESSLING, W., Databases and Information Systems
LIENHART, R., Multimedia Computing
MÖLLER, B., Databases and Information Systems
PEYKE, G., Human Geography
POSCHWATTA, W., Human Geography
REIF, W., Software and Programming Languages
SCHNEIDER, T., Didactics
THIEME, K., Human Geography
UNGERER, T., Information and Communication Systems
VOGLER, W., Software and Programming Languages
WIECZOREK, U., Didactics

Faculty of Catholic Theology (Universitätsstr. 10, 86159 Augsburg; tel. (821) 5985820; e-mail dekanat@kthf.uni-augsburg.de; internet www.kthf.uni-augsburg.de):

ARNTZ, K., Moral Theology
BALMER, H. P., Philosophy
GÜTHOFF, E., Church Law
HAUSMANNINGER, TH., Christian Ethics
KIENZLER, K., Basic Theology
KÜPPERS, K., Liturgy Science
RIEDL, GERDA, New Testament Exegesis
SCHEULE, R. (acting), Christian Ethics
SEDLMEIER, F. (acting), Old Testament Exegesis
WURST, F., Church History

Faculty of Economics (Universitätsstr. 16, 86159 Augsburg; tel. (821) 5984015; e-mail dekanat@wiwi.uni-augsburg.de; internet www.wiwi.uni-augsburg.de):

BAMBERG, G., Statistics
BOEHLE, F., Socio-Economics
BUHL, H. U., Business Administration
COENENBERG, A., Business Administration
FLEISCHMANN, B., Business Administration
GIEGLER, H., Sociology
GIERL, H., Business Administration
HANUSCH, H., Economics
HEINHOLD, M., Business Administration
KIFMANN, M., Sociology
KLEIN, R., Sociology
LAU, C., Sociology
LEHMANN, E., Business Management
MAUSSNER, A., Economics
MEIER, M., Economics
MICHAELIS, D., Economics
NEUBERGER, O., Psychology
PFAFF, A., Economics
SCHITTKO, U., Econometrics
STEINER, M., Business Administration
STENGEL, M., Psychology
TUMA, A., Business Administration
TUROWSKI, K., Business Informatics and Systems Engineering
WELZEL, P., Economics

Faculty of History and Philology (Universitätsstr. 10, 86159 Augsburg; tel. (821) 5982764; e-mail dekan.phil2@phil.uni-augsburg.de; internet www.philhist.uni-augsburg.de):

BICKENDORF, G., Art History
BUBLITZ, W., English Linguistics
BURKHARDT, J., History of Early Modern Times
DOERING-MANTEUFFEL, S., Folklore
ELSPASS, S., German Language
FÄCKE, C., French Didactics
GEPPERT, H. V., German and Comparative Literature
GÖTZ, D., Applied Linguistics
HERINGER, H.-J., German as a Foreign Language, German Philology
JACOB, J., Modern German
KAUFHOLD, M., Medieval History
KIESSLING, R., Bavarian and Swabian History
KOCKEL, V., Classical Archaeology
KRAUSS, H., Romance Literature
LAUSBERG, M., Classical Philology
LÖSER, F., German Language and Medieval History
MAYER, M., English Literature
MIDDEKE, M., English Literature
SCHEERER, T. M., Hispanic Studies
SCHRÖDER, K., Didactics of English
SCHWARZE, S., Romance Languages
TSCHOPP, S. S., History of European Culture
WEBER, G., Ancient History
WERNER, R., Applied Linguistics
WILLIAMS, W., German Language and Medieval Literature
WIRSCHING, A., Modern and Contemporary History
ZAPF, H., American Studies

Faculty of Law (Universitätsstr. 24, 86159 Augsburg; tel. (821) 5984500; e-mail dekan@jura.uni-augsburg.de; internet www.jura.uni-augsburg.de):

ALBERS, M., Civil Law
APPEL, I. (acting), Constitutional Law
BECKER, C., Civil Law, History of European Law
BEHR, V., Civil Law
BOTTKE, W., Penal Law
BUCHNER, H., Civil Law
GASSNER, U. M., Public Law
GSELL, B., Civil Law
JAKOB, W., Public Law

KORT, M., Civil Law
LEISTNER, M., Civil Law, Trade and Labour Law
MASING, J. (acting), Constitutional and Administrative Law
MÖLLERS, TH., Civil Law, Economic Law, European Law
NEUNER, J., Civil Law, Labour and Trade Law
ROSENAU, H., International Penal Law
ROTSCH, T., Penal Law
VEDDER, CH. (acting), Public Law

Faculty of Mathematics and Natural Sciences (Universitätsstr. 14, 86159 Augsburg; tel. (821) 5982250; e-mail dekan@mnf.uni-augsburg.de; internet www.uni-augsburg.de/einrichtungen/mnf):

BEHRINGER, K., Experimental Plasma Physics
BRÜTTING, W., Experimental Physics
CLAESSEN, R., Experimental Physics
COLONIUS, F., Applied Mathematics
DORFMEISTER, J., Analysis and Geometry
ECKERN, U. (acting), Theoretical Physics
ESCHENBURG, J., Differential Geometry
GIESL, P., Nonlinear Analysis
HAIDER, F., Experimental Physics
HÄNGGI, P., Theoretical Physics
HARTMANN, L., Chemistry, Physics and Material Sciences
HEINRICH, L., Applied Mathematics
HEINTZE, E., Pure Mathematics
HILSCHER, H., Didactics of Physics
HÖCK, K. H., Theoretical Physics
HOPPE, R. H. W., Applied Mathematics
HORN, S., Experimental Physics
INGOLD, G.-L., Theoretical Physics
JUNGNICKEL, D., Applied Mathematics, Discrete Mathematics, Optimization, Operations Research
KAMPF, A., Theoretical Physics
KIELHÖFER, H.-J., Applied Analysis
KOPP, T., Physics
LOIDL, A., Experimental Physics
MANNHART, J., Experimental Physics
PUKELSHEIM, F., Applied Mathematics
RELLER, A., Solid State Chemistry
RITTER, J., Pure Mathematics
SCHERER, W., Chemistry, Physics and Material Sciences
SCHERTZ, R., Mathematics
SCHNEIDER, E., Didactics
SIEBERT, K. (acting), Applied Analytical Mathematics
STRITZKER, B., Experimental Physics
UNWIN, A., Computer-Oriented Statistics and Data Analysis
VOLLHARDT, D., Theoretical Physics
WIXFORTH, A., Experimental Physics
ZIEGLER, K., Theoretical Physics
ZIMMERMAN, R., Chemistry

Faculty of Philosophy and Social Sciences (Universitätsstr. 10, 86159 Augsburg; tel. (821) 5982605; e-mail dekan.phil1@phil.uni-augsburg.de; internet www.philso.uni-augsburg.de):

ALTENBERGER, H., Sports Education
ASBACH, O., Protestant Philosophy
ASCHENBRÜCKER, K., Didactics
BOEHLE, F., Sociology
BRUNOLD, A., Social Studies
EILDERS, C., Communications
GIEGLER, H., Sociology and Empirical Social Research
HERWARTZ-EMDEN, L., Pedagogics
HOYER, J., Music
KIRCHNER, C. (acting), Art Education
KRAEMER, R. D., Musical Training
LAEMMERMANN, G., Protestant Theology with Didactics of Religion
LAMES, M., Movement and Training
LAU, C., Sociology
MACHA, H., Pedagogics
MAINZER, K., Philosophy
MATTHES, E., Pedagogics
MÜHLEISEN, H.-O., Political Science
OBENDORFER, B., Protestant Theology
REINMANN, G., Media Education
SCHNEIDER, W., Sociology
SCHRÖER, C., Philosophy
SCHULTZE, R.-O., Political Science
STENGEL, M., Psychology
ULICH, D., Psychology
VON GEMÜNDEN, P., Protestant Theology
WIATER, W., Pedagogics
WÜSTNER, K., Psychology

UNIVERSITÄT BAYREUTH

95440 Bayreuth
Telephone: (921) 550
E-mail: kanzler@uvw.uni-bayreuth.de
Internet: www.uni-bayreuth.de

Founded 1972
Academic year: October to September

Pres.: Prof. Dr RÜDIGER BORMANN (acting)
Vice-Pres.: Prof. Dr HANS-WARNER SCHMIDT
Vice-Pres.: Prof. Dr STEFAN JABLONSKI
Vice-Pres.: Prof. Dr STEFAN LEIBLE
Chancellor: Dr MARKUS ZANNER
Librarian: RALF BRUGBAUER

Library: see under Libraries and Archives
Number of teachers: 186
Number of students: 9,530

DEANS

Faculty of Applied Natural Sciences: Prof. Dr Ing. DIETER BRÜGGEMANN
Faculty of Biology, Chemistry and Geosciences: Prof. Dr STEPHAN CLEMENS
Faculty of Cultural Studies: Prof. Dr LUDGER KÖRNTGEN
Faculty of Language and Literature: Prof. Dr RAINER OßWALD
Faculty of Law and Economics: Prof. Dr MARKUS MÖSTL
Faculty of Mathematics, Physics and Computer Science: Prof. Dr HANS F. BRAUN

PROFESSORS

Faculty of Applied Natural Sciences (tel. (921) 557101):

AKSEL, N., Applied Mechanics and Fluid Dynamics
ALTSTÄDT, V., Polymerics
BRÜGGEMANN, D., Technical Thermodynamics, Transport Processes
FISCHERAUER, G., Measurement Technology and Control Engineering
FREITAG, R., Bioprocess Technology
GLATZEL, U., Metallic Materials
JESS, A., Chemical Engineering
KRENKEL, W., Ceramic Materials
MOOS, R., Working Materials
RIEG, F., Engineering Design and CAD
STEINHILPER, R., Environmentally Compatible Production Technology
WILLERT-PORADA, M., Materials Processing

Faculty of Biology, Chemistry and Geosciences (tel. (921) 552229):

BACH, L., Urban and Regional Planning
BALLAUFF, M., Physical Chemistry I
BECK, E., Plant Physiology
BEIERKUHNLEIN, C., Biogeography
BITZER, K., Geology
BOGNER, F. X., Didactics of Biology
BREU, J., Inorganic Chemistry I
DETTNER, K., Animal Ecology II
DRAKE, H. L., Soil Microbiology
FOKEN, T., Micrometeorology
FRANK, H., Environmental Pollution
HAUHS, M., Ecological Modelling
HOFFMANN, K. H., Animal Ecology I
HÜSER, K., Geomorphology
HUWE, B., Soil Science
KEMPE, R., Inorganic Chemistry II
KEPPLER, H., Experimental Geophysics
KOMOR, E., Plant Physiology
KRAUSCH, G., Physical Chemistry II
KRAUSS, G., Biochemistry
LEHNER, C., Genetics
LIEDE-SCHUMANN, S., Plant Systematics
LOHNERT, B., Geographical Development Research
MAIER, J., Economic Geography
MATZNER, E., Soil Sciences
MEYER, O., Microbiology
MONHEIM, R., Cultural Geography
MORYS, P., Inorganic Chemistry
MÜLLER, A., Macromolecular Chemistry II
MÜLLER-MAHN, D., Population and Social Geography
OBERMAIER, G., Didactics of Geography
PEIFFER, ST., Hydrology
PLATZ, G., Physical Chemistry I
POPP, H., Urban and Rural Geography
RAMBOLD, G., Plant Systematics
RÖSCH, P., Structure and Chemistry of Biopolymers
RUBIE, D., Structure and Dynamics of Earth Materials
SCHMID, F. X., Biochemistry
SCHMIDT, H.-W., Macromolecular Chemistry I
SCHOBERT, R., Organic Chemistry
SCHUMANN, W., Genetics
SEIFERT, F., Experimental Geosciences
SEIFERT, K., Organic Chemistry I/II
SENKER, J., Organic Chemistry I
SPRINZL, M., Biochemistry
STEUDLE, E., Plant Ecology
TENHUNEN, J., Plant Ecology
ULLMANN, M., Biocomputer Science
UNVERZAGT, C., Bio-Organic Chemistry
VON HOLST, D., Animal Physiology
WESTERMANN, B., Cell Biology
WRACKMEYER, B., Inorganic Chemistry II
ZECH, W., Soil Science and Soil Geography
ZÖLLER, L., Geomorphology

Faculty of Cultural Studies (tel. (921) 554101):

BARGATZKY, T., Ethnology
BERNER, U., Religious Studies I
BETZWIESER, T., Musicology
BOCHINGER, CH., Religious Studies II
BORMANN, L., Evangelical Theory III
BOSBACH, F., History
BREHM, W., Sport Science and Physical Education
EBNER, R., Catholic Religious Teaching II
HAAG, L., School Education
HEGSELMANN, R., Philosophy I
HIERY, H., History
KLUTE, G., Ethnology (Africa)
KOCH, L., Education
KÜGLER, J., Catholic Theology I
LANGE, D., History (Africa)
LINDGREN, U., History of Science
NEUBERT, D., Developmental Sociology
PUTZ-OSTERLOH, W., Psychology
RITTER, W., Protestant Theology II
SCHEIT, H., Social Philosophy
SCHMIDT, W., Sports Medicine
SCHOBERTH, W., Evangelical Theology I
SCHORCH, G., Elementary School Education
SCHÜSSLER, R., Philosophy II
SPITTLER, G., Ethnology
UNGERER-RÖHRICH, U., Sports
WEISS, D., Bavarian Regional Geology
ZIESCHANG, K., Sport Science and Physical Education
ZINGERLE, A., Sociology
ZÖLLER, M., Sociology II

Faculty of Language and Literature (tel. (921) 553625):

BEGEMANN, C., New German Literature
BENESCH, K., English Literature
BERGER, G., Romance Linguistics
DRESCHER, M., Roman and General Linguistics
HAUSENDORF, H., German Linguistics
IBISZIMOW, D., African Studies II
KHAMIS, S., Literatures in African Languages

KLOTZ, P., German Language and Literature
MIEHE, G., African Linguistics I
MÜLLER, J., Media Studies
MÜLLER-JACQUIER, B., Intercultural German Language and Literature
OSSWALD, R., Islamic Studies
OWENS, J., Arabic Studies
SCHMID, H.-J., English Linguistics
STEPPAT, M., English Literature
VILL, S., Theatre Studies
WOLF, G., Early German Philology

Faculty of Law and Economics (tel. (921) 552894):
BERG, W., Public Law
BÖHLER, H., Economics III
BREHM, W., Civil Law
DANNECKER, G., Criminal Law
EMMERICH, V., Civil Law
EYMANN, T., Economics VIII
GÖRGENS, E., Economics II
GUNDEL, J., Public Law
HEERMANN, P., Civil Law
HERZ, B., Economics I
KAHL, W., Public Law
KLIPPEL, D., Civil Law, History of Law
KÜHLMANN, T., Economics IV
LEPSIUS, O., Public Law
LESCHKE, M., Economics V
LORITZ, K.-G., Civil Law II
MECKL, R., Economics IX
MICHALSKI, L., Civil Law
MÖSTL, M., Public Law and Constitutional History
NAGEL, E., Health Service Management and Health Sciences
OBERENDER, P., Economics IV
OHLY, A., Civil Law
REMER, A., Economics VI
SCHLÜCHTERMANN, J., Economics V
SCHMITZ, R., Criminal Law
SIGLOCH, J., Economics II
SPELLENBERG, U., Civil Law
ULRICH, V., Economics III
WORATSCHEK, H., Economics VIII

Faculty of Mathematics, Physics and Computer Science (tel. (921) 553196):
BAPTIST, P., Mathematics and Didactics
BRAND, H., Theoretical Physics III
BRAUN, H., Experimental Physics V
BÜTTNER, H., Theoretical Physics I
CATANESE, F., Mathematics VIII
ESKA, G., Experimental Physics V
GRÜNE, L., Applied Mathematics
HENRICH, D., Applied Computer Science III
KERBER, A., Mathematics
KÖHLER, J., Experimental Physics IV
KÖHLER, W., Experimental Physics IV
KRAMER, L., Theoretical Physics II
KRÄMER, M., Mathematics
KÜPPERS, J., Experimental Physics III
LAUE, R., Computer Science
LEMPIO, F., Applied Mathematics
MERTENS, F.-G., Theoretical Physics I
MÜLLER, W., Mathematics
OTT, A., Experimental Physics I
PASCHER, H., Experimental Physics I
PESCH, H. J., Engineering Mathematics
PETERNELL, T., Mathematics
RAUBER, T., Applied Computer Science II
REHBERG, I., Experimental Physics V
REIN, G., Applied Mathematics
RIEDER, H., Applied Mathematics
ROESSLER, E., Experimental Physics II
SCHAMEL, H., Theoretical Physics
SCHITTKOWSKI, K., Computer Science
SCHWOERER, M., Experimental Physics II
SEILMEIER, A., Experimental Physics III
SIMADER, C. G., Mathematics
VAN SMAALEN, S., Crystallography
VON WAHL, W., Applied Mathematics
WESTFECHTEL, B., Applied Computer Science
ZIMMERMANN, W., Applied Computer Science

ATTACHED INSTITUTES

Afrikazentrum (IWALENA-Haus) (Africa Centre): Dir Dr T. WENDL.

Bayerisches Forschungsinstitut für Experimentelle Geochemie und Geophysik (Bayerisches Geoinstitut, IBGI) (Bavarian Research Institute for Experimental Geochemistry and Geophysics): e-mail bayerisches.geoinstitut@uni-bayreuth.de; Dir Prof. Dr D. RUBIE.

Bayreuther Institut für Europäisches Recht und Rechts Kultur, insbesondere Rechtsvergleichung und Wirtschaftsrecht (Bayreuth Institute for European Law and Legal Culture, Comparative Law and Economic Law): Dir Prof. Dr P. HÄBERLE.

Bayreuther Institut für Makromolekülforschung (BIMF) (Bayreuth Institute for Macromolecular Research): ; Dir Prof. Dr H.-W. SCHMIDT.

Bayreuther Institut für Terrestrische Ökosystemforschung (BITÖK) (Bayreuth Institute for Terrestrial Ecology Research): Dir Prof. Dr E. MATZNER.

Bayreuther Zentrum für Kolloide und Grenzflächen (BZKG) (Bayreuth Centre for Colloids and Interfaces): Dir Prof. Dr M. BALLAUFF.

Bayreuther Zentrum für Molekulare Biowissenschaften (BZMB) (Bayreuth Centre for Molecular Biosciences): Dir Prof. Dr O. MEYER.

Bayreuther Zentrum für Ökologie und Umweltforschung (Bayreuth Centre for Ecology and Environmental Research): Dir Prof. Dr E. MATZNER.

Forschungsinstitut für Musiktheater (FIMT) (Research Institute for Music Theatre): e-mail fimt.thurnau@uni-bayreuth.de; Dir (vacant).

Institut für Afrikastudien (IAS) (Institute for African Studies): Dir Prof. Dr H. POPP.

Institut für Materialforschung (Institute for Materials Research): e-mail info@bam.de; Dir Prof. Dr G. ZIEGLER.

Zentrum zur Förderung des Mathematisch- Naturwissenschaftlichen Unterrichts (Centre for Mathematical and Scientific Instruction): Dir Prof. Dr F. X. BOGNER

UNIVERSITÄT BIELEFELD

POB 10 01 31, 33501 Bielefeld
Universitätsstr. 25, 33615 Bielefeld
Telephone: (521) 10600
E-mail: post@uni-bielefeld.de
Internet: www.uni-bielefeld.de

Founded 1969
State control
Academic year: April to March

Rector: Prof. Dr Ing. GERHARD SAGERER
Vice-Rector for Financial Affairs and Resources: Prof. Dr ROLF KÖNIG
Vice-Rector for Int. Relations and Communications: Prof. Dr SABINE ANDRESEN
Vice-Rector for Quality Devt: Prof. Dr JOHANNES HELLERMANN
Vice-Rector for Research, Young Researchers and Transfer: Prof. Dr MARTIN EGELHAAF
Chancellor: HANS-JÜRGEN SIMM
Librarian: Dr MICHAEL HÖPPNER

Library of 2,200,000 vols
Number of teachers: 4,567
Number of students: 18,935

Publications: *Bielefelder Universitätsgespräche* (irregular), *Bielefelder Universitätszeitung* (4 a year), *Forschungsbericht* (online), *Forschungsmagazin* (2 a year), *Jahresbericht des Rektors und Statistisches Jahrbuch* (1 a year), *Personalverzeichnis/Lehrveranstaltungen* (2 a year), *Pressedienst Forschung* (irregular)

DEANS

Faculty of Biology: Prof. Dr BERND WEISSHAAR
Faculty of Chemistry: Prof. Dr NORBERT SEWALD
Faculty of Economics: Prof. Dr HERBERT DAWID
Faculty of Educational Science: Prof. Dr SUSANNE MILLER
Faculty of Health Sciences: Prof. Dr CLAUDIA HORNBERG
Faculty of History, Philosophy and Theology: Prof. Dr UWE WALTER
Faculty of Law: Prof. Dr MICHAEL KOTULLA
Faculty of Linguistics and Literature: Prof. Dr KAI KAUFFMANN
Faculty of Mathematics: Prof. Dr MICHAEL RÖCKNER
Faculty of Physics: Prof. Dr DOMINIK SCHWARZ
Faculty of Psychology and Sports Science: Prof. Dr FRANK NEUNER
Faculty of Sociology: Prof. Dr VERONIKA TACKE
Faculty of Technology: Prof. Dr JENS STOYE

UNIVERSITÄT BREMEN

POB 33 04 40, 28334 Bremen
Bibliothekstr., 28359 Bremen
Telephone: (421) 2181
E-mail: presse@uni-bremen.de
Internet: www.uni-bremen.de

Founded 1971
State control
Academic year: October to September (2 terms)

Rector: Prof. Dr WILFRIED MÜLLER
Chancellor: GERD-RÜDIGER KÜCK
Pro-Rector: Prof. Dr HEIDE SCHWELHOWE
Pro-Rector: Prof. Dr ROLF DRECHSLER
Pro-Rector: Prof. Dr YASEMIN KARAKAŞOĞLU
Librarian: MARIA ELISABETH MÜLLER

Number of teachers: 366
Number of students: 18,000

Publications: *Bremer Uni Schlüssel* (5 a year), *Highlights* (Research Report, 2 a year), *Impulse aus der Forschung* (2 a year)

DEANS

Biology and Chemistry: Prof. Dr SÖRGE KELM
Business Studies and Economics: Prof. Dr JOCHEN ZIMMERMANN
Cultural Studies: Prof. Dr JÜRGEN LOTT
Geosciences: Prof. Dr GERHARD BOHRMANN
Human and Health Sciences: Prof. Dr BIRGIT VOLMERG
Law: Prof. Dr GRALF-PETER CALLIES
Linguistics and Literary Studies: Prof. Dr MATTHIS KEPSER
Mathematics and Computer Science: Prof. Dr JAN PELESKA
Physics and Electrical Engineering: Prof. Dr JENS FALTA
Pedagogy and Education Sciences: Prof. Dr NORBERT RICKEN
Production Engineering, Mechanical Engineering and Process Engineering: Prof. Dr ARNIM VON GLEICH
Social Sciences: Prof. Dr TASSILO SCHMITT

PROFESSORS

Department 1 (Electrical Engineering; Physics)

Electrical Engineering:
ANHEIER, W., Microelectronics, Digital Systems
ARNDT, F., High Frequency Technology
BENECKE, W., Silicon-Micromechanics, Sensors and Actuators

BINDER, J., Micro- and Sensor-Systems, and Space Technology
GRÄSER, A., Automation Engineering
GRONWOLD, D., Electrical Technology
KAMMEYER, K.-D., Communications
LAUR, R., Electronics and Microelectronics
LOHMANN, B., Automatic Control
MARTE, G., Electronics
MEINERZHAGEN, B., Field Theory
MÜLLER, W., Analysis of the Engineering Professions
ORLIK, B., Electrical Drives and Power Electronics
RAUNER, F., Electrical Technology
SILBER, D. H., Power Electronics and Devices

Physics:

AUGSTEIN, E., Meteorology and Physics of the Oceans
BLECK-NEUHAUS, J., Experimental and Environmental Physics
BOSECK, S., Experimental Physics
BURROWS, P., Environmental Physics
CZYCHOLL, G., Theoretical Physics
DIEHL, H., Biophysics
DREYBRODT, W., Experimental Physics, Molecular Spectroscopy
FALTA, J., Surface Science of Semiconductors
GUTOWSKI, J., Semiconductor Optics
HOMMEL, D., Epitaxy of Semiconductors
JÜPTNER, W., Laser Application
KÜNZI, K., Environmental Physics
LANGE, H., Sociology of Labour
NIEDDERER, H., Teaching of Physics
NOACK, C. C., Theoretical Physics
OLBERS, D., Theoretical Physics
PAWELZIK, K., Theoretical Biology
RICHTER, P., Theoretical Physics
ROETHER, W., Physical Oceanography in the Polar Regions
RYDER, P., Physics of Metals
SCHMITZ-FEUERHAKE, I., Experimental Physics
SCHWEDES, H., Teaching of Science
SCHWEGLER, H., Theoretical Physics, Theoretical Biophysics
STAUDE, W., Experimental Physics
VON AUFSCHNAITER, S., Teaching of Physics

Department 2 (Biology; Chemistry)

Biology:

ARNTZ, W., Ocean Ecology
BLOHM, D., Biotechology
ENTRICH, H., Theory and Practice of Education in the Natural Sciences
FAHLE, M., Neurobiology and Human Biology
FISCHER, H., Marine Microbiology
FLOHR, H., Biology
GRIMME, L. H., Biology, Biochemistry
HAGEN, W., Marine Zoology
HEYSER, W., Botany
HILDEBRANDT, A., Biology
KIRST, G.-O., Marine Botany
KOENIG, F., Botany
KREITER, A., Neurobiology
MOSSAKOWSKI, D., Evolutionary Biology
POERTNER, H.-O., Marine Biology
REINHOLD-HUREK, B., Microbiology
ROTH, G., Neurobiology
SAINT-PAUL, U., Marine Ecology
SCHLOOT, W., Genetics, Human Genetics
SMETACEK, V., Marine Biology
VALLBRACHT, A., Virology
WITTE, H., Zoology
WOLFF, M., Marine Ecology

Chemistry:

BALZER, W., Marine Chemistry
BEYERSMANN, D., Biochemistry
BREUNIG, H.-J., Inorganic Chemistry
GABEL, D., Organic Chemistry, Biochemistry
JAEGER, N., Physical Chemistry
JASTORFF, B., Organic Chemistry
JUST, E., Teaching of Chemistry
LEIBFRITZ, D., Organic Chemistry
MEWS, R., Inorganic Chemistry
MONTFORTS, F., Organic Chemistry
PLATH, P., Chemistry
RIEKENS, R., Teaching of Chemistry
RÖSCHENTHALER, G., Inorganic Chemistry
SCHREMS, O., Physical Chemistry
SCHROER, W., Physical Chemistry
SCHULZ-EKLOFF, G., Physical Chemistry
STOHRER, W.-D., Chemistry
THIEMANN, W., Physical Chemistry
WANCZEK, K., Inorganic Chemistry
WÖHRLE, D., Chemistry

Department 3 (Computer Science; Mathematics)

Computer Science:

BORMANN, U., Computer Networks
BRUNS, F.-W., Technology Design
FRIEDRICH, J., Computing and Society
GOGOLLA, M., Database Systems
HAEFNER, K., Education Technologies, Social Impacts and Transport Implications
HERZOG, O., Expert Systems and Foundations of Artificial Intelligence
KREOWSKI, H.-J., Theoretical Computer Science
KRIEG-BRÜCKNER, B., Programming Languages, Compilers and Software Engineering
KUBICEK, H., Information Management and Telecommunications
MAASS, S., Women's Studies and Technology
NAKE, F., Graphic Data Processing and Interactive Systems
PELESKA, J., Operating Systems, Distributed Systems
RÖDIGER, K.-H., Software Engineering and Ergonomics
SZCZERBICKA, H., Computer Architecture and Modelling

Mathematics:

ARNOLD, L., Random Dynamic Systems
BAENSCH, E., Numerical Methods for Partial Differential Equations
BECKER, G., Teacher Education
BOEHM, M., Modelling and Partial Differential Equations
BUNSE-GERSTNER, A., Numerical Linear Algebra
DENNEBERG, D., Non-Additive Integration, Risk, Uncertainty and Insurance
DEUTSCH, M., Logic and Foundations of Mathematics
DOMBROWSKI, H.-D., Mathematical Foundations of Physics
FISCHER, H. W., Complex Analysis
GAMST, J., Algorithmic Algebra and Number Theory
HERRLICH, H., Topology, Category Theory
HINRICHSEN, D., Systems and Control Theory
HOFFMANN, R.-E., Topology, Categories and Lattices
HORNEFFER, K., Differential Geometry, Mathematical Foundations of Physics
HUPPERTZ, H., Teacher Education
KRAUSE, U., Positive Dynamic Systems
LINDENAU, V., Teacher Education
MAASS, P., Inverse Problems and Wavelets
MÜNZNER, H.-F., Differential Geometry, Dynamic Systems
OELJEKLAUS, E., Complex Algebraic Geometry
OSIUS, G., Statistics, Biometry
PEITGEN, H.-O., Complex Systems, Computer-Aided Radiology
PORST, H.-E., Categorical Algebra
SCHÄFER, R., Numerical Hydrogeology
WISCHNEWSKY, M., Modelling, Neural Networks, Fuzzy Systems

Department 4 (Commercial and Technical Science; Economics for Engineering; Production Engineering):

BAUCKHAGE, K., Chemical and Process Engineering
BRINKSMEIER, E., Manufacturing Technology
GENTHNER, K., Technical Thermodynamics, Heat and Mass Transfer
GOCH, G., Metrology, Automation and Quality Science
GRATHWOHL, G., Ceramic Materials and Components
HARIG, H., Material Technology and Composites
HEEG, F.-J., Work Science
HENNEMANN, O. D., Bonding Technology and Polymers
HIRSCH, B. E., Production Resources, Logistics, Telematics
HOPPE, M., Vocational Teaching of Metal Engineering
KIENZLER, R., Applied Mechanics and Structural Mechanics
KUNZE, H.-D., Near Net Shape Production Technologies
MAYR, P., Material Science
MÜLLER, D. H., Engineering Design, CAE, CAD
RÄBIGER, N., Environmental Process Engineering
RATH, H. J., Technical Mechanics and Fluid Mechanics
SEPOLD, G., Laser and Plasma Technologies for Materials Processing
VISSER, A., Production Facilities
WITTKOWSKY, A., Design and Development of Technology

Department 5 (Geosciences):

BLEIL, U., Marine Geophysics
BROCKAMP, O., Mineralogy, Petrography, Clay Mineralogy
DEVEY, C., Petrology of the Ocean Crust
FISCHER, R. X., Crystallography
FÜTTERER, D., Geology
HENRICH, R., Sedimentology, Palaeo-Oceanography
HERTERICH, K., Palaeo-Oceanographic Modelling
JÖRGENSEN, B. B., Biogeochemistry
KUSS, H. J., Geology, Stratigraphy, Sedimentology
MILLER, H., Geophysics
OLESCH, M., Geology of the Polar Regions, Petrology
SCHULZ, H., Geochemistry, Hydrogeology
SPIESS, V., Marine Technology, Marine Environmental Geophysics
VILLINGER, H., Marine Technology, Geophysical Sensor Development
WEFER, G., Geology
WILLEMS, H., Historical Geology and Palaeontology

Department 6 (Law):

BÖLLINGER, L., Criminal Law
BRÜGGEMEIER, G., Civil and Economic Law
DAMM, R., Civil Law, Economic Law
DÄUBLER, B., Labour, Commercial and Economic Law
DERLEDER, P., Civil and Banking Law
DUBISCHAR, R., Civil Law
FEEST, J., Criminal Law and Criminology
FRANCKE, R., Legal Didactics
GESSNER, V., Comparative Law and Legal Sociology
HART, D., Economic Law
HINZ, M., Public Law and Political and Legal Sociology
HOFFMANN, R., Public Law, Labour Law and Political Science
JOERGES, C., Civil and Comparative Law
KNIEPER, R., Civil and Economic Law
LICHTENBERG, H., Labour and European Law

REICH, N., Civil and European Law
RINKEN, A., Public Law
RUEHE, U., Public Law
RUST, U., Gender Law
SCHEFOLD, D., Public Law
SCHMIDT, E., Civil Law and Procedure
SCHMINCK-GUSTAVUS, C., History of Law
SCHUMANN, K. F., Criminology
STUBY, G., Public Law and Political Science
THOSS, P., Criminal Law
WASHNER, R., Labour Law
WESSLAU, E., Criminal Law and Procedure
WINTER, G., Public and Environmental Law

Department 7 (Economics):

BAUER, E., Marketing of Research and Management
BIESECKER, A., Economic Theory
BRITSCH, K., Economic Statistics
DWORATSCHEK, S., Project Management
ECKSTEIN, W., Economics of Logistic Systems
ELSNER, W., Economic, Industrial and Regional Policy, Institutional Evolutionary Economics
FRANCKE, R., Economic Theory
GERSTENBERGER, H., Theory of State and Society
GRENZDÖRFFER, K., Economic Statistics, Labour Economics
HAASIS, H.-D., Production Management and Industrial Organization
HEIDE, H., Town and Country Planning
HICKEL, R., Public Finance
HUFFSCHMID, J., Political Economy, Economic Policy
KALMBACH, P., Economics
KOPFER, H., Economics of Logistics Systems
LEITHÄUSER, G., Economic Policy
LEMPER, A., Foreign Trade Theory and Politics
LIONVILLE, J., International Economics
MARX, F. J., Financial Accounting and Business Taxation
PODDIG, TH., Finance
SCHAEFER, H., Theory, Forecasting and Control
SCHMÄHL, W., Economics and Social Policy
SCHWIERING, D., Economics
SELL, A., International Economics
STEIGER, O., General Economic Theory and Monetary Economics
STUCHTEY, R. W., Economics of Marine Transport
VON DER VRING, TH., Political Economy
WOHLMUTH, K., Comparative Economic Systems
ZACHCIAL, M., Transport Science and Transport Planning

Department 8 (Social Sciences)

Cultural History of Eastern Europe:

EICHWEDE, W., History and Politics of Socialist Countries
KRASNODEBSKY, Z., Polish Social and Cultural History
STÄDTKE, K., Cultural History of Eastern Europe

Geography:

BAHRENBERG, G., Social and Economic Geography
SCHRAMKE, W., Geography, Teaching of Geography
TAUBMANN, W., Cultural Geography
TIPPKÖTTER, R., Geography of Soils
VENZKE, J.-F., Physical Geography

History:

BARROW, L., Social and Political History of England
EICHWEDE, W., History and Politics of Socialist Countries
HACHTMANN, R., History of the 19th and 20th Centuries
HÄGERMANN, D., Medieval History
HAHN, M., History of Business, Political Theories
HOEDER, D., Social History of the USA
KLOFT, H., Ancient History
KOPITZSCH, F., History
KRAUSS, M., History of 19th- and 20th-Century Social Economics
RECH, M., Prehistoric and Medieval History
SCHMIDT, J., Curricula in Economic and Social Studies
WAGNER, W., Politics, History of Political Education

Politics:

ALBERS, D., Labour Relations
EICHWEDE, W., History and Politics of Socialist Countries
KOOPMANN, K., Didactics of Social Science Education
LIEBERT, U., Comparative Politics, European Integration
LOTHAR, R., Politics, and Federal and Constitutional Law
PETERS, B., Political Theory and History of Ideas
SCHMIDT, M., Politics, Comparative Social Policies
WAGNER, W., Politics, History of Political Education
WIRTH, M., Parliamentary System of Federal Germany
ZOLL, R., History and Theory of Trade Unions
ZÜRN, M., Politics

Postgraduate Programme Development Policy with Focus on Non-Governmental Organizations:

VON FREYHOLD, M., Development Policy and Sociology of Development

Sociology:

KRÄMER-BADONI, T., Town and Regional Planning
KRAUSE, D., Educational Planning
KRÜGER, M., Social Analysis
LAUTMANN, R., General Sociology and Sociology of Law
LUEDEMANN, CHR., Statistics and Empirical Research
PETER, L., Labour and Industrial Sociology
QUENSEL, S., Resocialization and Rehabilitation
REICHELT, H., Theory of Science and Society
SENGHAAS, D., Peace and Conflict Studies
VON FREYHOLD, M., Social Science
WEYMANN, A., Social Theory, Educational Research

Department 9 (Cultural Sciences)

Art:

BUDDEMEIER, H., Communication, Mass Media
MÜLLER, M., Art History and Cultural Studies
PETERS, M., Art Education
SCHADE-THOLEN, S., Art History, Aesthetics

Cultural Science:

DRÖGE, F., Mass Communication Research
DUERR, H. P., Ethnology and Cultural History
NADIG, M., European Ethnology and Cultural Anthropology
RICHARD, J., Teaching of Drama
RICHTER, D., German Literature

Music:

BRECKOFF, W., Teaching of Music
KLEINEN, G., Teaching of Music, Musicology
RIEGER, E., Musicology

Philosophy:

MOHR, G., Practical Philosophy
SANDKÜHLER, H. J., Theoretical Philosophy
STÖCKLER, M., Philosophy of Natural Sciences

Religious Science:

KIPPENBERG, H.-G., Theory and History of Religions
LOTT, J., Religious Education
SCHULZ, H., Comparative Religion

Sport:

ARTUS, H. G., Teaching of Physical Education
BRAUN, H., History of Sport
FIKUS, M., Psychomotor Behaviour
SCHEELE, K., Sports Medicine

Department 10 (Literature and Language Studies)

Communication:

BACH, G., Teaching of English
BARROW, L., Social and Political History of England
BATEMANN, J. A., Applied Functional Linguistics, Natural Language Processing and Translation Science
DAHLE, W., German Language and Literature
EMMERICH, W., German Literature
FRANZBACH, M., Literature and Social History of Spain and Latin America
GALLAS, H., German Literature
JÄGER, H.-W., History of German Literature
KOCH, H. A., German and Comparative Literature
LIEBE-HARKORT, K., German as a Foreign Language
LIENERT, E., German Literature of the Middle Ages and the Early Modern Period
MENK, A.-K., Linguistics
PASTERNACK, G., Theory of Literature
PAUL, L., Applied Linguistics
SAUTERMEISTER, G., History of German Literature
STOLZ, TH., Linguistics
WAGNER, K.-H., Linguistics
WILDGEN, W., Linguistics
ZIMMERMANN, K., Spanish and Portuguese Linguistics

Department 11 (Health and Human Studies)

Psychology:

BAUMGÄRTL, F., Psychological Diagnosis
BERNDT, J., Physiology
GNIECH, G., Psychology
HEINZ, W.-R., Sociology and Social Psychology
HENNING, H.-J., Psychology
KIESELBACH, TH., Psychology
LEITHÄUSER, T., Developmental Psychology
PETERMANN, F., Clinical Psychology
REINKE, E., Clinical Psychology
STADLER, M., Psychology
VETTER, G., Theory of Learning
VOGT, R., Psychology
VOLMERG, B., Psychology

Public Health:

FRENTZEL-BEYME, R., Occupational and Environmental Epidemiology
GREISER, E., Occupational Health and Social Medicine
MÜLLER, R., Health Policy, Occupational Health and Social Medicine

Social Education:

AMENDT, G., Sub-Cultures
BAUER, R., Social Pedagogy
BLANDOW, J., Social Education
BROCKMANN, A.-D., Town and Regional Planning
HEINSON, G., Social Pedagogy
KEIL, A., General Education
LEIBFRIED, S., Social Planning
MERKEL, J., Pre-School Education

Teacher Training:

GOERRES, ST., Social Gerontology

HYAMS-PETER, H.-U., Social Education
KRÜGER-MÜLLER, H., Sociology
LITTEK, W., Education and Economics
ORTMANN, H., Educational Sciences
VAN MAANEN, H., Nursing Sciences

Work Study:

MÜLLER, R., Health Policy, Occupational Health and Social Medicine
SENGHASS-KNOBLOCH, E., Humanization of Work
SPITZLEY, H., Technology and Society

Department 12 (Social and Educational Sciences)

Education Diploma:

DIETZE, L., Public Law
ROTH, L., Theory of Teaching
SCHÖNWÄLDER, H. G., Educational Planning and Economics
STRAKA, G., Extracurricular Education
ZIECHMANN, J., Psychology of Learning

Educational Science:

BECK, J., Educational Social Sciences
BOEHM, U., Structure and Development of Education
DRECHSEL, R., Education
DRECHSEL, W., Educational Social History
HUISKEN, F., Educational Political Economy
POLZIN, M., Aesthetic Education
PREUSS, O., Sociology of Education
UBBELOHDE, R., Educational Science
VINNAI, G., Analytical Social Psychology
VOIGT, B., Teacher Training

Further Education:

GERL, H., Adult Education
GÖRS, D., Distance Education
HOLZAPPFEL, G., Curricular Planning
KUHLENKAMP, D., Educational Planning
MADER, W., Adult Education
SCHLUTZ, E., Adult Education
WOLLENBERG, J., Adult Education in Political Science

Primary Education:

MILHOFFER, P., Sociology and Political Education
SCHMITT, R., Developmental Psychology
SPITTA, G., Beginning of German Language

Teaching the Handicapped:

DÖHNER, O., Medicine of Mental Illness
FEUSER, G., Education of Mentally Disturbed Children
HOMBURG, G., Educating People with Speech Defects
JANTZEN, W., History of Educating the Handicapped
KRETSCHMANN, R., Training of the Educationally Handicapped
PIXA-KETTNER, U., Educating People with Speech Defects
REINCKE, W., Education for the Mentally Disturbed

Work Experience:

FISCHER, W. C., Consumer Economics
FRÖLEKE, H., Nutrition
HUISKEN, F., Educational Science
SCHRÖDER, A., Textile Technology

UNIVERSITÄT DER BUNDESWEHR MÜNCHEN

Werner-Heisenberg-Weg 39, 85577 Neubiberg
Telephone: (89) 60040
E-mail: info@unibw.de
Internet: www.unibw.de

Founded 1973
Academic year: October to September (3 semesters)

Pres.: Prof. Dr MERITH NIEHUSS
Vice-Pres. for Academics: Prof. Dr UWE M. BORGHOFF
Vice-Pres. for College of Applied Sciences: Prof. Dr Ing. MATTHIAS HEINITZ
Vice-Pres. for Research: Prof. Dr MICHAEL EẞIG
Chancellor: SIEGFRIED RAPP
Library Dir: Dr MARIA MANN-KALLENBORN

Library: 1.1m. vols
Number of teachers: 200
Number of students: 3,700

Publications: *'Der Hochschulkurier'* (3 a year), *Forschungsbericht*

DEANS

Faculty of Aeronautics and Astronautics: Prof. Dr Ing. CHRISTIAN MUNDT
Faculty of Civil Engineering and Surveying: Prof. Dr Ing. MANFRED KEUSER
Faculty of Economics and Organizational Sciences: Prof. Dr STEFAN KOOS
Faculty of Education: Prof. Dr Hab. MANUELA PIETRAẞ
Faculty of Electrical Engineering and Information Technology: Prof. Dr Ing. K. HOFFMANN
Faculty of Informatics: Prof. Dr MARK MINAS
Faculty of Political and Social Sciences: Prof. Dr Hab. URSULA MÜNCH

UNIVERSITÄT DER KÜNSTE BERLIN
(Berlin University of the Arts)

POB 12 05 44, 10595 Berlin
Einsteinufer 43–53, 10587 Berlin
Telephone: (30) 31850
E-mail: beratung@udk-berlin.de
Internet: www.udk-berlin.de

Founded 1975 by amalgamation of the Staatliche Hochschule für Bildende Künste (f. 1696) and the Staatliche Hochschule für Musik und Darstellende Kunst (f. 1869)

Pres.: Prof. MARTIN RENNERT
First Vice-Pres.: Prof. Dr Ing. CHRISTOPH GENGNAGEL
Vice-Pres.: Prof. GUNDEL MATTENKLOTT
Chancellor: WOLFGANG ABRAMOWSKI
Library Dir: ANDREA ZEYNS

Library of 650,000 vols
Number of students: 4,300

DEANS

College of Architecture, Media and Design: Prof. Dr MICHAEL BOLLÉ
College of Fine Arts: Prof. Dr TANJA MICHALSKY
College of Music: Prof. Dr WOLFGANG DINGLINGER
College of Performing Arts: Prof. Dr KARL-LUDWIG OTTO

UNIVERSITÄT DES SAARLANDES

POB 15 11 50, 66041 Saarbrücken
Telephone: (681) 3020
E-mail: praesident@uni-saarland.de
Internet: www.uni-saarland.de

Founded 1948
Academic year: October to July

Pres.: Prof. Dr VOLKER LINNEWEBER
Vice-Pres. for Admin. and Finance: MARTINA PETERMANN
Vice-Pres. for Education: Prof. Dr MANFRED J. SCHMITT
Vice-Pres. for European and Cultural Affairs: Prof. Dr PATRICIA OSTER-STIERLE
Vice-Pres. for Planning and Strategy: Prof. Dr ALEXANDER BAUMEISTER
Librarian: Dr BERND HAGENAU

Library: see under Libraries and Archives
Number of teachers: 1,570
Number of students: 16,929

Publications: *Annales Universitatis Saraviensis* (4 a year), *Campus* (irregular), *Forschungsbericht* (1 a year), *Jahresbibliographie* (1 a year), *Vorlesungsverzeichnis* (2 a year, online)

DEANS

Faculty of Humanities I: Prof. Dr PETER RIEMER
Faculty of Humanities II: Prof. Dr ROLAND MARTI
Faculty of Humanities III: Prof. Dr JOCHEN KUBINIOK
Faculty of Law and Economics: Prof. Dr CHRISTIAN SCHOLZ
Faculty of Medicine: Prof. MICHAEL MENGER
Faculty of Natural Sciences and Technology I: Prof. MARK GROVES
Faculty of Natural Sciences and Technology II: Prof. HELMUT SEIDEL
Faculty of Natural Sciences and Technology III: Prof. Dr WILHELM F. MAIER

PROFESSORS

Faculty of Humanities I: History and Cultural Sciences (tel. (681) 3022300; e-mail u.weisgerber@pfdek.uni-sb.de):

BEHRINGER, W., Early Times
BRANDOLINI, A., Art Education
DE JONG, R., Art Education
DETZLER, B., Art Education
GIRARDET, K. M., Ancient History
GOERTZ, S., Practical Theology and Social Ethics
GRABAS, M., Economic and Social History
GÜTHLEIN, K., History of Art
HAUSIG, D., Art Education
HECKMANN, H., Philosophy
HINSCH, W., Philosophy
HUDEMANN, R., Modern and Contemporary History
HULLMANN, H., Art Education
HÜTTENHOFF, M., Protestant Theology
KASTEN, B., Medieval History
KRAUS, W., New Testament
KUBISCH, C., Art Education
LICHTENSTERN, C., History of Art
MAKSIMOVIC, I., Art Education
NESTLER, W., Art Education
NORTMANN, U., Philosophy
OHLIG, K.-H., Theology
POPP, H., Art Education
REINSBERG, C., Classical Archaeology
RIEMER, P., Classical Philology
ROMPZA, S., Art Education
ROSENBACH, U., Art Education
SACHSSE, R., Art Education
SCHERZBERG, L., Systematic Theology
SCHMITT, R., Comparative Indo-Germanic Languages
SCHNEIDER, H., Medieval History
SCHRÖDER, B., Religious Education
WALICZKY, M., Art Education
WINZEN, A., Art Education
ZIMMERMANN, C., Cultural History and Media History

Faculty of Humanities II: Language, Literature and Cultural Studies (tel. (681) 3023360; e-mail g.braun@pfdek.uni-sb.de):

ALBERT, M., Romance Philology
BARRY, W. J., Phonetics, Phonology
BÉHAR, P., German for Francophones
BEM, J., Romance Philology
CROCKER, M., Psycholinguistics
DEMSKE, U., German Linguistics
ENGEL, M., German Language and Literature
GERZYMISCH-ARBOGAST, H., English Translation
GHOSH-SCHELLHORN, M., English Philology
GIL ARROYO, A., Translation Studies, Romance Languages
GÖTZE, L., German as a Foreign Language
HALLER, J., Mechanical Transmission
HAUBRICHS, W., Medieval German Literature
KLEINERT, S., Romance Philology

LOHMEIER, A.-M., Modern German Philology and Literature
LÜSEBRINK, H.-J., Romance Civilization, Intercultural Communication
MARTENS, K., English Philology, American Literature
MARTI, R., Slavonic Philology
NORRICK, N., English Philology, Linguistics
OSTER-STIERLE, P., French Literature
PINKAL, M., Computer Languages
SAUDER, G., Modern German Philology and Literature
SCHMELING, M., General and Comparative Literature
SCHWEICKARD, W., Romance Philology
SPRAUL, H., Russian
STEINER, E., English Linguistics and Translation
USZKOREIT, H., Computer Linguistics

Faculty of Humanities III: Empirical Humanities (tel. (681) 3023700; e-mail s.mersdorf@pfdek.uni-sb.de; internet www.uni-saarland.de/fak5):

ASCHERSLEBEN, G., Developmental Psychology
BRÜCHER, W., Geography
BRÜNKEN, R., Education Science
EMRICH, E., Kinesiology and Exercise Science
HERZMANN, P., Education Science
KERKOFF, G., Clinical Neuropsychology
KRAUSE, R., Psychology
KUBINIOK, J., Physical Geography
LÖFFLER, E. W., Physical Geography
MAXEINER, J., Education
SPINATH, F., Differential Psychology and Diagnostics
STARK, R., Personal Development and Education
STOCKMANN, R., Sociology
WASSMUND, H., Political Science
WENTURA, D., General Psychology and Methodology
WINTERHOFF-SPURK, P., Psychology
WINTERMANTEL, M., Social Psychology
WYDRA, G., Sports Education
ZIMMERMANN, H. H., Information Science

Faculty of Law and Economics (tel. (681) 3022003; e-mail dekanat@rewi.uni-sb.de; internet www.rewi.uni-sb.de):

ALBERT, M., Economics
AUTEXIER, C., French Public Law
BECKMANN, R., Civil, Commercial, Economic and Labour Law
BIEG, H., Business Economics
CHIUSI, T., Civil Law, Roman Law
FRIEDMANN, R., Statistics
GLASER, H., Business Economics
GRÖPL, C., State and Management Law
GRÖPPEL-KLEIN, A., Business Economics
HERBERGER, M., Civil Law, Theory of Law, Computer Applications in Jurisprudence
JUNG, H., Penal and Procedural Law, Criminal Law, Law of Criminal Procedure, Criminology and Comparative Criminal Jurisprudence
KORIATH, H., Criminal Law, Criminal Procedural Law, Philosophy of Law, Sociology of Law
KUẞMAUL, H., Business Economics
KÜTING, K., Business Economics
LOOS, P., Business Economics
MARTINEK, M., Civil, Commercial and Economic Law, International Private Law and Comparative Jurisprudence
MATUSCHE-BECKMANN, A., Civil, Commercial and Economic Law and Labour Law
MENG, W., Public Law, International Law, European Community Law
MOMSEN, C., Penal and Procedural Law
NICKEL, S., Business Economics
PIERZIOCH, C., Economics
RANIERI, F., European Civil Law
RÜSSMANN, H., Civil and Procedural Law, Philosophy of Law
SCHMIDT, G., Business Economics
SCHMIDTCHEN, D., Economics
SCHOLZ, C., Business Economics
STEIN, T., European Law, European Public Law, International Law
STROHMEIER, S., Business Economics
WADLE, E., History of German Law, Civil Law
WASCHBUSCH, G., Business Economics
WENDT, R., Constitutional and Administrative Law, Revenue and Tax Law
WETH, S., German and European Procedural and Industrial Law
WITZ, C., French Public Law
ZENTES, J., Business Economics

Faculty of Medicine (Medizinische Fakultät, Universitätskliniken des Saarlandes, 66421 Homburg; tel. (6841) 1624737; e-mail mfdekan@med-rz.uni-sb.de):

ABDUL-KHALIQ, H., Paediatrics
BOCK, R., Anatomy
BOHLE, R., Pathology
BÖHM, M., Internal Medicine
BRUNS, D., Physiology
BUCHTER, A., Occupational Medicine
CAVALIÉ, A., Pharmacology and Toxicology
FALKAI, P., Psychiatry and Psychotherapy
FASSBENDER, K., Psychiatry and Psychotherapy
FEIDEN, W., Neuropathology
FLOCKERZI, V., Pharmacology and Toxicology
FREICHEL, M., Pharmacology and Toxicology
FUHR, G., Medical Technology
GORTNER, L., Paediatrics
GRAF, N., Paediatrics
HANNIG, M., Oral and Maxillofacial Medicine
HERRMANN, E., Mathematical Modelling in Molecular Medicine
HERRMANN, M., Microbiology
HERRMANN, W., Clinical Chemistry
HOTH, M., Physiology
HÜTTERMANN, J., Biophysics
KIENECKER, E.-W., Anatomy
KINDERMANN, W., Sports Medicine
KIRSCH, C.-M., Nuclear Medicine
KÖHLER, H., Internal Medicine
KOHN, D., Orthopaedics
LARSEN, R., Anaesthesiology
LIPP, P., Molecular Cell Biology
LISSON, J., Oral and Maxillofacial Medicine
LÖBRICH, M., Biophysics and Physical Basis of Medicine
MAURER, H. H., Pharmacology and Toxicology
MEESE, E., Human Genetics and Molecular Biology
MENGER, M., Institute for Clinical and Experimental Surgery
MESTRES-VENTURA, P., Anatomy
MEYERHANS, A., Virology
MONTENARH, M., Medical Biochemistry
MÜLLER-LANTZSCH, N., Virology
PFREUNDSCHUH, M., Internal Medicine
POHLEMANN, T., Casualty Surgery
POSPIECH, P., Oral and Maxillofacial Medicine
REITH, W., Diagnostic Radiology
RETTIG, J., Physiology
RÖSLER, M., Psychiatry, Neurology
RÜBE, CH., Radiotherapy
SCHÄFERS, H.-J., Surgery
SCHEIDIG, A., Structural Biology
SCHILLING, M., Surgery
SCHMIDT, W., Gynaecology and Obstetrics
SCHMITZ, F., Neuroanatomy
SCHULZ, I., Physiology
SEITZ, B., Occular Medicine
SPITZER, W. C., Maxillofacial Surgery
STAHL, H., Medical Biochemistry
STEUDEL, W.-I., Neurosurgery
STÖCKLE, M., Urology
SYBRECHT, G. W., Internal Medicine
THIEL, G., Medical Biochemistry
TILGEN, W., Dermatology and Venereology
VON GONTARD, A., Child Psychiatry
WALLDORF, U., Developmental Biology
WANKE, K., Neurology, Psychiatry
WILSKE, J., Forensic Medicine
ZEUZEM, S., Internal Medicine
ZIMMERMANN, R., Physiological Chemistry

Faculty of Natural Sciences and Technology I: Mathematics and Computer Science (tel. (681) 3025070; e-mail sekr.fakultaet@mx.uni-saarland.de; internet www.uni-saarland.de/fak6):

ALBRECHT, E., Mathematics
BACKES, M., Computer Science
BLÄSER, M., Computer Science
BROSAMLER, G.-A., Mathematics
DECKER, W., Mathematics
ESCHMEIER, J., Mathematics
FUCHS, M., Mathematics
GEKELER, E.-U., Mathematics
HERFET, T., Computer Science
HERMANNS, H., Computer Science
HISCHER, H., Teaching of Mathematics
JOHN, V., Mathematics
KOCH, C., Computer Science
KOHLER, M., Mathematics
LENHOFF, H., Bioinformatics
LOUIS, A. K., Mathematics
PAUL, W., Information Science
RJASANOW, S., Mathematics
SCHEIDIG, H., Informatics
SCHREYER, F.-O., Mathematics
SCHULZE-PILLOT, R., Mathematics
SEIDEL, R., Theoretical Informatics
SIEKMANN, J., Informatics
SLUSALLEK, P., Informatics
SMOLKA, G., Information Science
WAHLSTER, W., Informatics
WEICKERT, J., Mathematics
ZELLER, A., Software Engineering

Faculty of Natural Sciences and Technology II: Physics and Electrical Engineering (tel. (681) 3024943; e-mail dekan.fak7@mx.uni-saarland.de; internet www.uni-saarland.de/fak7):

BECHER, C., Physical Engineering
BIRRINGER, R., Physical Engineering
DYCZIJ-EDLINGER, R., Electrical Theory
HARTMANN, U., Experimental Physics
JAKOBS, K., Experimental Physics
JANOCHA, H., Process Automation
KLAKOW, D., Speech Processing
KLIEM, H., Electrical Engineering Physics
KNORR, K., Physical Engineering
KÖNIG, K., Microsensor Technology
KRÜGER, J. K., Experimental Physics
KUGI, A., Systems Theory and Control Engineering
LÜCKE, M., Theoretical Physics
MÖLLER, M., Electronics and Circuits
NICOLAY, T., High Frequency Engineering
PELSTER, R. (acting), Experimental Physics
RIEGER, H., Theoretical Physics
SANTEN, L., Theoretical Physics
SCHÜTZE, A., Measurement
SEIDEL, H., Micromechanics
WAGNER, C., Experimental Physics
WICHERT, T., Physical Engineering
XU, C., Microelectronics

Faculty of Natural Sciences and Technology III: Chemistry, Pharmacy, Materials Science (tel. (681) 3022400; e-mail dekan.fak8@mx.uni-saarland.de; internet www.uni-saarland.de/fak8):

BAUER, P., Botany
BECK, H. P., Inorganic and Analytical Chemistry, Radiochemistry
BERNHARDT, I., Biophysics
BERNHARDT, R., Biochemistry
BLEY, H., Production Engineering
BUSCH, R., Metallic Materials
CLASEN, R., Materials Science
DIEBELS, S., Applied Mechanics

GIFFHORN, F., Microbiology
HARTMANN, R. W., Pharmaceutical Chemistry
HEGETSCHWEILER, K., Inorganic Chemistry
HEINZLE, E., Technical Bioengineering
HELMS, V., Computational Biology
HUBER, C., Analytical Chemistry
JAUCH, J., Organic Chemistry
KAZMAIER, U., Organic Chemistry
KIEMER, A. K., Pharmaceutical Biology
KRÖNING, M., Non-Destructive Materials Testing
LEHR, C.-M., Pharmaceutical Technology
MAIER, W., Technical Chemistry
MÜCKLICH, F., Work Materials
MÜLLER, R., Pharmaceutical Biotechnology
MÜLLER, U., Zoology and Physiology
POSSART, W., Polymers and Surfaces
SCHMIDT, H., New Materials
SCHMITT, M., Microbiology
SPRINGBORG, M., Physical Chemistry
VEHOFF, H., Materials Science, Methodology
VEITH, M., Inorganic Chemistry
WALTER, J., Genetics
WEBER, C., Construction Engineering
WENZ, G., Macromolecular Chemistry

UNIVERSITÄT DUISBURG-ESSEN

Campus Duisburg, Forsthausweg 2, 47057 Duisburg
Telephone: (203) 3790
Campus Essen, Universitätsstr. 2, 45141 Essen
Telephone: (201) 1831
Internet: www.uni-due.de
Founded 2003 by merger of Gerhard-Mercator-Universität Duisburg (f. 1972) and Universität-Gesamthochschule-Essen (f. 1972)
Academic year: October to September (2 semesters)
Rector: Prof. Dr ULRICH RADTKE
Vice-Rector for Diversity Management: Prof. Dr UTE KLAMMER
Vice-Rector for Research, Junior Academic Staff and Knowledge Transfer: Prof. Dr JÖRG SCHROEDER
Vice-Rector for Resource Planning: Dr INGRID LOTZ-AHRENS
Vice-Rector for Teaching and Learning: Prof. Dr FRANZ BOSBACH
Chancellor: Dr RAINER AMBROSY
Librarian: ALBERT BILO (Essen)
Librarian: SIGURD PRAETORIUS (Duisburg)
Library: 2.5m. vols, 4,000 print journals, 17,500 ejournals
Number of teachers: 3,579
Number of students: 31,806
Publications: *Essener Unikate* (2 a year), *Forschungsbericht* (every 2 years), *Forum Forschung* (1 a year), *Results of Mathematics* (4 a year)

DEANS

Faculty of Biology: Prof. Dr BERND SURES
Faculty of Chemistry: Prof. Dr MATTHIAS EPPLE
Faculty of Economics and Business Administration: Prof. Dr MICHAEL GOEDICKE
Faculty of Educational Sciences: Prof. Dr HORST BOSSONG
Faculty of Engineering: Prof. Dr Ing. DIETER SCHRAMM
Faculty of Humanities: Prof. Dr DIRK HARTMANN
Faculty of Mathematics: Prof. Dr WERNER HAUßMANN
Faculty of Medicine: Prof. Dr MICHAEL FORSTING
Faculty of Physics: Prof. Dr MICHAEL SCHRECKENBERG
Faculty of Social Sciences: Prof. Dr GERHARD BÄCKER
Mercator School of Management: Prof. Dr ALF KIMMS

ATTACHED RESEARCH INSTITUTES

Deutsches Textilforschungszentrum Nord-West eV: e-mail jochen.gutmann@dtnw.de; internet www.dtnw.de; Dir Prof. Dr JOCHEN GUTMANN.

Deutsch-Französisches Institut für Automation und Robotik (IAR): Speaker Prof. Dr Ing. STEVEN X. DING.

Entwicklungszentrum für Schiffstechnik und Transportsysteme eV: e-mail dst@dst-org.de; Dir Prof. Dr P. ENGELKAMP.

Essener Kolleg für Geschlechterforschung: e-mail geschlechterkolleg@uni-due.de; internet www.uni-due.de/ekfg; Exec. Dir Dr MAREN A. JOCHIMSEN.

Forschungsinstitut für wirtschaftliche Entwicklungen im Pazifikraum eV (FIP): Dir Prof. Dr GÜNTER HEIDUK.

Foundation Centre of Turkish Studies: e-mail zft@zft-online.de; internet www.tamvakfi.de/index.html; Dir Prof. Dr HACI HALIL USLUCAN.

Institut für Energie- und Umwelttechnik eV (IUTA): e-mail info@iuta.de; internet www.iuta.de; Dir Prof. Dr K. G. SCHMIDT.

Institut für Experimentelle Mathematik (IEM): e-mail direktor@iem.uni-due.de; internet www.exp-math.uni-essen.de; Dir Prof. Dr H. VINCK.

Institut für Mobil- und Satellitenfunktechnik GmbH (IMST GmbH): internet www.imst.de; Dirs Prof. Dr Ing. INGO WOLFF, Dr Ing. PETER WALDOW.

Instituts für Niederrheinische Kulturgeschichte und Regionalenwicklung: Dir Prof. Dr DIETER GEUENICH.

Institut für Prävention und Gesundheitsförderung: e-mail eat@teamgesundheit.de; internet www.ipg-uni-essen.de; Dir Dr ALFONS SCHRÖER.

IWW Rheinisch-Westfälisches Institut für Wasserforschung gemeinnützige GmbH: e-mail rektor@uni-duisburg-essen.de; internet www.iww-online.de; Dirs Dr Ing. WOLF MERKEL, KLAUS-DIETER NEUMANN.

Rhein-Ruhr-Institut für Sozialforschung und Politikberatung eV (RISP): e-mail risp@uni-due.de; internet www.risp-duisburg.de; applied regional socio-economic research; promotes communication and co-operation between the academic world and public and private sector institutions in the Ruhrgebiet; Dir Prof Dr HERIBERT SCHATZ.

Salomon Ludwig Steinheim Institut für Deutsch-Jüdische Geschichte eV (StI): e-mail steinheim@steinheim-institut.org; internet sti1.uni-duisburg.de; research and adult education on Jewish history in Germany from the Renaissance to the present; Dir Prof. Dr MICHAEL BROCKE

UNIVERSITÄT ERFURT
(University of Erfurt)

POB 90 02 22, 99105 Erfurt
Nordhäuser Str. 63, 99089 Erfurt
Telephone: (361) 7370
E-mail: praesidiumsbuero@uni-erfurt.de
Internet: www.uni-erfurt.de
Founded 1392, refounded 1994
State control
Pres.: Prof. Dr KAI BRODERSEN
Vice-Pres. for Academic Affairs: Prof. Dr ANDREA SCHULTE
Vice-Pres. for Int. Affairs: Prof. Dr MYRIAM WIJLENS
Vice-Pres. for Research and Young Academics: Prof. Dr BETTINA ROCKENBACH
Chancellor: Dr MICHAEL HINZ
Library Dir: CHRISTIANE SCHMIEDEKNECHT
Number of teachers: 108
Number of students: 5,483

DEANS

Faculty of Catholic Theology: Prof. Dr JOSEF FREITAG
Faculty of Education: Prof. Dr MANFRED ECKERT
Faculty of Philosophy: Prof. Dr PATRICK RÖSSLER
Faculty of Political Science: Prof. Dr MANFRED KÖNIGSTEIN
Max Weber College for Cultural and Social Sciences: (vacant)

UNIVERSITÄT FLENSBURG
(University of Flensburg)

Auf dem Campus 1, 24943 Flensburg
Telephone: (461) 80502
E-mail: praesidium@uni-flensburg.de
Internet: www.uni-flensburg.de
Founded 1994
Pres.: Prof. Dr WALTRAUD WENDE
Vice-Pres. for Academic Affairs: Prof. Dr MATTHIAS BAUER
Vice-Pres. for Research and Int. Affairs: Prof. Dr STEPHAN PANTHER
Chancellor: FRANK KUPFER
Head Librarian: Dr ECKHARD EICHLER
Library of 265,000 vols
Number of students: 4,200

UNIVERSITÄT HAMBURG

Edmund-Siemers-Allee 1, 20146 Hamburg
Telephone: (40) 428380
E-mail: praesident@uni-hamburg.de
Internet: www.uni-hamburg.de
Founded 1919
State control
Academic year: October to July
Pres.: Dr Dr DIETER LENZEN
Vice-Pres.: Prof. Dr HOLGER FISCHER
Vice-Pres.: Prof. Dr ROSEMARIE MIELKE
Vice-Pres.: Prof. Dr HANS SIEGFRIED STIEHL
Chancellor: Dr KATRIN VERNAU
State and Univ. Librarian: Prof. Dr GABRIELE BEGER
Library: see under Libraries and Archives
Number of teachers: 3,172
Number of students: 40,996

DEANS

Faculty of Education, Psychology and Human Movement: Prof. Dr EVA ARNOLD
Faculty of Humanities: Prof. Dr OLIVER HUCK
Faculty of Law: Prof. Dr TILMAN REPGEN
Faculty of Mathematics, Informatics and Natural Sciences: Prof. Dr HEINRICH GRAENER
Faculty of Medicine: Prof. Dr UWE KOCH-GROMUS
School of Business, Economics and Social Sciences: Prof. Dr GABRIELE LÖSCHPER

PROFESSORS

Department of Biology (Allende-Pl. 2, 20146 Hamburg; tel. (40) 428380):
ABRAHAM, R., Entomology
ADAM, G., Phytopathology
BAUCH, J., Timber Biology
BEUSMANN, V., Biotechnics, Society and Environment
BOCK, E., General Microbiology
BÖTTGER, M., General Botany
BRANDT, A., Zoology
BRETTING, H., Zoology
BUCHHOLZ, F.

CHOPRA, V., Anthropology
DREYLING, G., Applied Botany
ECKSTEIN, D., Timber Biology
FLEISCHER, A., Work Science
FORTNAGEL, P., Botany
FRÜHWALD, A., Mechanical Processing of Timber
GANZHORN, J., Zoology
GEWECKE, M., Zoology, Animal Physiology
GIERE, O., Zoology
GRIMM, R., Zoology
HAHN, H., Zoology, Ecology
HARTMANN, H., Systematic Botany
HEINZ, E., Botany
HEUVELDOP, J., International Forest Management
JÜRGENS, N., Biological Systems, Plant Evolution
KAUSCH, H., Hydrobiology
KIES, L., General Botany
KRISTEN, U., General Botany
LIEBEREI, R., Phytopathology
LÖRZ, H., Applied Plant Molecular Biology
MANTAU, U., Economics of Forestry
MERGENHAGEN, D., Cell Biology
MÜHLBACH, H.-P., Molecular Genetics
PARZEFALL, J., Zoology
PATT, R., Chemical Timber Technology
PRATJE, E., General Botany
REISE, K., Heligoland Biological Institute
RENWRANTZ, L., Zoology
RESSEL, J., Wood Physics
RODEWALD, A., Anthropology and Human Genetics
SCHÄFER, W., Biology
SCHURIG, V.
STAHL-BISKUP, E., Pharmaceutical Biology
TEMMING, A., Fisheries Sciences
WEBER, A., General Botany
WIENAND, U., General Botany
WIESE, K., Neurophysiology
WILKENS, H., Zoology
ZEISKE, E., Zoology

Department of Chemistry (Martin-Luther-King-Pl. 6, 20146 Hamburg; tel. (40) 428380):

BASLER, W. D.
BEIER, U., Home Economics
BENNDORF, C., Physical Chemistry
BISPING, B., Food Microbiology and Hygiene
BREDEHORST, R., Biochemistry
DEPPERT, W., Molecular Biochemistry
DUCHSTEIN, H.-J., Pharmaceutical Chemistry
FÖRSTER, S., Physical and Macromolecular Chemistry
FRANCKE, W., Organic Chemistry
GEFFKEN, D., Pharmaceutical Chemistry
HECK, J., Inorganic Chemistry
HEISIG, P., Pharmaceutical Biology, Microbiology
KAMINSKY, W., Inorganic Chemistry
KERSCHER, M., Personal Hygiene
KÖNIG, W., Organic Chemistry
KRAMOLOWSKY, R., Inorganic Chemistry
KRICHELDORF, H., Applied Chemistry
KULICKE, W., Technical Chemistry
LECHERT, H., Physical Chemistry
MARGARETHA, P., Organic Chemistry
MEIER, C., Organic Chemistry
MEYER, B., Organic Chemistry
MIELCK, J., Pharmaceutical Technology
MORITZ, H.-U., Technical and Macromolecular Chemistry
MÜHLHAUSER, I., Health
REHDER, D., Inorganic Chemistry
STAHL-BISKUP, E., Pharmaceutical Biology
STEINHART, J., Food Chemistry
THIEM, J., Organic Chemistry
THORN, E., Technical and Macromolecular Chemistry
WELLER, H., Electrochemistry

Department of Computer Science (Vogt-Kölln-Straße 30, 22527 Hamburg; tel. (40) 428830):

BRUNNSTEIN, K., Computer Applications
DRESCHLER-FISCHER, L., Cognitive Systems
FLOYD, C., Software Technics
FREKSA, C.
HABEL, C., Information and Documentation
JANTZEN, M., Computer Theory
KAISER, K., Computer Applications
KUDLEK, M., Computer Theory
LAMERSDORF, W., Technical Basics of Computer Science
MENZEL, W.
MERTSCHING, B.
MÖLLER, D.
NEUMANN, B., Cognitive Systems
OBERQUELLE, H., Computer Theory
PAGE, B., Computer Applications
ROLF, A., Computer Theory
SCHEFE, P., Computer Applications
STIEHL, H.-S., Cognitive Systems
VALK, R., Computer Theory
VON DER HEIDE, K., Technical Basics of Computer Science
VON HAHN, W., Natural Language Systems
WOLFINGER, B., Computer Organization
ZÜLLIGHOVEN, H.

Department of Cultural History and Cultural Science (Rothenbaumchaussee 67–69, 20148 Hamburg; tel. (40) 428384051):

ALTENMÜLLER, H., Egyptology
DÖMLING, W., Music
FEHR, B., Classical Archaeology
GREEVE, B., Music
HENGAUTNER, T., Folklore
HIPP, H., History of Art
KEMP, W., Art History
KOKOT, W., Ethnology
KURTH, D., Egyptology
LANG, H., Ethnology
LEHMANN, A., German Archaeology and Folklore
MISCHUNG, B., Ethnology
NIELSEN, I., Classical Archaeology
PETERSEN, P., Musicology
REUDENBACH, B., Art History
ROLLE, R., Prehistory of Europe
RÖSING, H., Systematic Music
SCHNEIDER, A., Systematic Music
SMAILUS, O., Ancient American Languages and Culture
WAGNER, M., Art History
WARNKE, M., History of Art

Department of Earth Sciences (Bundestraße 55, 20146 Hamburg; tel. (40) 428385230):

BACKHAUS, J., Oceanography
BANDEL, K., Palaeontology and Historical Geology
BETZLER, C., Geology
BISMAYER, U., Mineralogy, Crystallography
BRÜMMER, B., Meteorology
DAHM, T.
FRAEDRICH, K., Meteorology
GAJEWSKI, D., Geophysics
GRASSL, H., Meteorology
GRIMMEL, E., Geography
GUSE, W., Mineralogy
HILLMER, G., Geology and Palaeontology
JASCHKE, D., Geography
LAFRENZ, J., Geography
LEUPOLT, B., Geography
MAKRIS, J., Geophysics
MEINCKE, J., Regional Oceanography
MICHAELIS, W., Organic Geochemistry
MIEHLICH, G., Soil Science
NAGEL, F. N., Geography
OSSENBRÜGGE, J., Geography
POHL, D., Mineralogy
RASCHKE, E., Meteorology
REUTHER, C.-D., Geology
ROSSMANITH, E., Mineralogy
SCHATZMANN, M., Meteorology
SCHLEICHER, H., Mineralogy, Petrography
SCHWARZ, R., Geography
SPAETH, CH., Geology and Palaeontology
SPIELMANN, H.-O., Geography
SÜNDERMANN, J., Oceanography
TARKIAN, M., Mineralogy
THANNHEISER, D., Geography
TIETZ, G. F., Sedimentary Petrography
TOL, R. S., Sustaining the Environment
VINX, R., Mineralogy
WONG, H. K., Geology
ZAHEL, W., Oceanography

Department of Economic Sciences (Von-Melle-Park 5, 20146 Hamburg; tel. (40) 428380):

ADAMS, M., Economic Law
ALTROGGE, G., Business Administration
ARNOLD, B., National Economy
CZERANOWSKY, G., Business Administration
ENGELHARDT, G., National Economy
FREIDANK, C.-C., Business Administration, Auditing Taxation
FUNKE, M., National Economy
GROTHERR, S., Business Administration
HANSEN, K., Business Administration
HANSMANN, K.-W., Business Administration
HASENKAMP, G., National Economy
HAUTAU, H., National Economy
HESBERG, D.
HOFMANN, H., National Economy
HOLLER, M., National Economy
HUMMELTENBERG, W., Business Administration
KRAUSE-JUNG, G., International Finance
KÜPPER, W., Business Administration
LAYER, M., Business Administration
LORENZEN, G., National Economy
LUCKE, B., National Economy
MAENNIG, W., National Economy
NELL, M., Insurance
PFÄHLER, W., National Economy
PRESSMAR, D., Business Administration
REITSPERGER, W. D., Business Administration
RIETER, H., National Economy
RINGLE, G., Business Administration
SATTLER, H., Business Administration
SCHÄFER, H.-B., National Economy
SCHEER, C., Finance
SCHLITTGEN, R., National Economy, Statistics
SCHMIDT, H., Business Administration
SEELBACH, H., Business Administration
STAHLECKER, H.-P., National Economy, Statistics
STOBER, R., Economic Law
STRAUBHAAR, T.
STREITFERDT, L., Business Administration
TIMMERMANN, V., National Economy
TOL, R. (Endowed Chair, Sustaining the Environment)
VON OEHSEN, J. H., Finance
WEGSCHEIDER, K., National Economy, Statistics

Department of Education (Von-Melle-Park 8, 20146 Hamburg; tel. (40) 428380):

AUFENANGER, S.
BASTIAN, J.
BECK, I.
BOLLMANN, H.
BOS, W.
BRAND, W.
BRUSCH, W.
BÜRGER, W.
BUTH, M.
CLAUßEN, B.
COMBE, A.
DECKE-CORNILL, H.
DEGENHART, S.
DEHN, M.
DUISMANN, G.
EHNI, H. W.
FAULSTICH, P.
FAULSTICH-WIELAND, H.
FIEDLER, U.
FILIPP, K.
GEBHARD, U.

GOGOLIN, I.
GRAMMES, T.
GRENZ, D.
GUDJONS, H.
GÜNTHER, K.-R.
HARTER-MEYER, R.
HARTMANN, W.
HEMMER, K.
HOFSÄSS, T.
JUNG, H. W.
KAISER, G.
KAISER, H.-J.
KIPP, M.
KLEIN, P.
KOKEMOHR, R.
KOLLER, H.-C.
KRAUTHAUSEN, G.
KRETSCHMER, J.
KÜNNE, W.
LECKE, B.
LEGLER, W.
LOHMANN, I.
MARTENS, E.
MAYER, C.
MEYER, H.
MEYER, M.
MIELKE, R.
MITCHELL, G.
NEUMANN, U.
NEVERS, P.
NOLTE, M.
OPASCHOWSKI, H.
PAZZINI, K.-J.
PETERSEN, J.
RAUER, W.
RENZELBERG, G.
RICHTER, H.
ROTHWEILER, M.
SCARBATH, H.
SCHÄFER, H.-P.
SCHENK, B.
SCHERLER, K.
SCHREIER, H.
SCHUCK, K. D.
SEYD, W.
SPRETH, G.
STRUCK, P.
STRUVE, K.
STÜTZ, G.
TENFELDE, W.
TRAMM, T.
VOLLMER, T.
VON BORRIES, B.
WAGNER, A.
WALLRABENSTEIN, W.
WARZECHA, B.
WEICHERT, W.
WEISSE, W.
WELLING, A.
WILLENBERG, H.
WIMMER, K.-M.
WOCKEN, H.
WUDTKE, H.
ZIMPEL, A.

Department of History and Philosophy (Rothenbaumchaussee 67–69, 20148 Hamburg; tel. (40) 428384049):

ANGERMANN, N., Medieval and Modern History
BARTUSCHAT, W., Philosophy
CLEMENS, G., Modern European History (Western European Integration)
DEININGER, J., Ancient History
DIEDERICH, W., Philosophy
DINGEL, J., Classical Philology
EIDENEIER, H., Byzantine and Modern Greek Philology
FINZSCH, N., Modern and North American History
FREDE, D., Philosophy
GÄHDE, U., Philosophy
GALL, D., Classical Philology
GOETZ, H.-W., Medieval and Modern History
GOLCZEWSKI, F., Eastern European History
HALFMANN, H., Ancient History
HARLFINGER, D., Classical Philology
HERGEMÖLLER, B.-U., Medieval History
HERZIG, A., Modern History
KÜNNE, W., Philosophy
MEJCHER, H., Modern History
MOLTHAGEN, J., Ancient History
PIETSCHMANN, H., Modern History
RECKI, B., Philosophy
SARNOWSKY, V., Medieval History
STEINVORTH, U., Philosophy
VOGEL, B., Modern History

Department of Language, Literature and Media Studies (Rothenbaumchaussee 67–69, 20148 Hamburg; tel. (40) 428380):

BERG, T., English Linguistics
BLESSIN, S., German Literature, German as a Foreign Language
BÖRNER, W., Linguistics
BRAUNMÜLLER, K., Germanic Philology
BRINKER, K., German Linguistics
BUNGARTEN, T., German Linguistics
CORTHALS, J., Comparative Language Studies
DAMMANN, G., German Literature
DIEWALD, G., German Linguistics
EDMONDSON, W., Language Instruction Research
FISCHER, L., German Literature
FISCHER, R., German Sign Language
FREYTAG, H., German Philology
FREYTAG, W., German Literature
FRIEDL, B., American Studies
GREINER, N., English Literature
GUTJAHR, O., Modern German Literature
GUTKNECHT, C., English Language
HABEL, C., Language Processing
HARTENSTEIN, K., Russian
HASEBRINK, E., Empirical Communications Science
HELIMEKI, E., Finno-Ugric Philology
HENKEL, N., German Philology
HENNIG, J., German Linguistics
HICKETHIER, K., German Literature
HILL, P., Slavonic Philology
HODEL, R., Slavonic Philology
HOTTENROTH, P.-M., French and Italian Linguistics
HOUSE, J., Language Instruction Research
HÜHN, P., English Philology
IBANEZ, R., Hispanic Linguistics
KÖSTER, U., German Literature
LATOUR, B., German as a Foreign Language
LEHMANN, V., Language Instruction Research
LLEO, C., Hispanic Linguistics
MEIER, J., German Linguistics
MEISEL, J. M., Romance Philology
MEYER, W., Romance Philology
MEYER-ALTHOFF, M.
MEYER-MINNEMANN, K., Romance Philology
MÜLLER, H.-H., German Literature
NEUMANN, M., Romance Philology
PANTHER, K.-U., English Linguistics
PÉTURSSON, M., General Applied Phonetics
PRESCH, G., German Linguistics
PRILLWITZ, S., German Linguistics
REHBEIN, J., German Linguistics, German as a Foreign Language
REICHARDT, D., Romance Philology
REINITZER, H., German Literature
RODENBURG, H.-P., American Studies
SAGER, S., German Linguistics
SCHLUMBOHM, D., Romance Philology
SCHMID, W., Slavonic Literature
SCHMIDT, J., English Philology
SCHMIDT-KNÄBEL, S., German Linguistics
SCHÖBERL, J., German Literature
SCHÖNERT, J., German Literature
SCHÖPP, J. K., American Studies
SCHULLER, M., German Literature
SCHULMEISTER, R., Higher School Didactics
SCHULTZE, B., English Philology
SEGEBERG, H., German Literature
SETTEKORN, W., French
TERNES, E., Phonetics
TRAPP, F., Modern German Literature
VINKEN, B., Romance Philology
VOIGT, B., Spanish
VON HAHN, W., Natural Language Systems
WERGIN, U., Modern German Literature
WINTER, H.-G., German Literature
WITTSCHIER, H. W., Romance Philology

Department of Law (Rothenbaumchaussee 41, 20148 Hamburg; tel. (40) 428380):

BEHRENS, P., Civil, Commercial and International Private Law
BORK, R., Civil, Commercial, Economic and International Private Law
BRUHA, T., Public, European and International Law
BULL, H. P., Constitutional and Administrative Law
FELIX, D., Public and Social Law
FEZER, G., Criminal Law
FROTSCHER, G., International Financial and Taxation Law
GIEHRING, H., Criminal Law
HAAG, F., Sociology
HANSEN, U., Criminal Law
HILF, M., Public, European and International Law
HIRTE, H., Public, Commercial and Business Law
HOFFMAN-RIEM, W., Public, Administrative, Revenue and Tax, and Economic Law
JACHMANN, M., Public, Financial and Taxation Law
JOOST, D., Civil and Labour Law
KARPEN, U., Public Law
KELLER, R., Criminal Law
KOCH, H.-J., Public Law, Philosophy of Law
KÖHLER, M., Criminal Law, Philosophy of Law
KRIECHBAUM, M., Roman Law
LADEUR, K.-H., Public Law
LAGONI, R., Public, Maritime, International and Constitutional Law
LUCHTERHANDT, O., Public and Eastern Law
LÜDICKE, J., International Financial and Taxation Law
MAGNUS, U., Civil Law
MANKOWSKI, P., Civil, Comparative and International Private and Procedural Law
MARTENS, K. P., Civil, Labour and Commercial Law
MERKEL, R., Criminal Law, Philosophy of Law
MORITZ, K., Civil and Labour Law, Sociology of Law
OETER, S., Public, International and European Law
OTT, C., Sociology of Law, Civil, Commercial and Company, and Economic Law
PASCHKE, M., Civil, Commercial and Economic Law
PFARR, H., Civil and Labour Law
RAMSAUER, U., Public Law
RANDZIO, R., Civil Law
RITTSTIEG, H., Public Law
SCHÄFER, H.-B., National Economy
SCHEERER, S., Criminology
SCHWABE, J., Public Law
SESSAR, K., Criminology and Juvenile Criminal Law
SONNEN, B.-R., Criminal Law
STOBER, R., Economic Law
STRUCK, G., Civil Law
VILLMOW, B., Criminology
WALZ, R., Commercial, Economic, Civil and Tax Law
WERBER, M., Civil and Insurance Law

Department of Mathematics (Bundesstr. 55, 20146 Hamburg; tel. (40) 428384106):

ANDREAE, T.

BANDELT, H.-J.
BÄR, C.
BERNDT, R.
BRÜCKNER, H.
DADUNA, H.
DIESTEL, R.
ECKHARDT, U.
GEIGER, C.
HASS, R.
HOFMANN, W. D.
HÜBNER, G.
HÜNEMÖRDER, C.
KRÄMER, H.
KREMER, E.
KREUZER, A.
LAUTERBACH
MICHALICEK, J.
MÜLLER, H.
NEUHAUS, G.
OBERLE, H. J.
ORTLIEB, C.
REICH, K.
RIEMENSCHNEIDER, O.
SCHRÖDER, E.
SEIER, W.
STRADE, H.
STRUCKMEIER, J.
TAUBERT, K.
WERNER, B.
WOLFSCHMIDT, G.

Department of Medicine (Universitätsklinikum Hamburg-Eppendorf, Martinistr. 52, 20246 Hamburg; tel. (40) 428030):

ADAM, G., X-ray Diagnosis
AGARWAL, D., Human Genetics
ALBERTI, W., Radiotherapy
BAISCH, H., Biophysics
BAUR, X., Industrial Medicine
BECK, H., Anaesthesiology
BEIL, F. U., Internal Medicine
BEISIEGEL, U., Biochemistry
BENTELE, K., Paediatrics
BERGER, J., Mathematics and Computer Applications of Medicine
BERGER, M., Child Psychology
BERNER, W., Psychiatry
BÖGER, R., Clinical Pharmacology
BOHUSLAVIZKI, H., Nuclear Medicine
BRAENDLE, L.-W., Gynaecology and Obstetrics
BRAULKE, T., Pathophysiology and Molecular Biological Genetic Health
BRAUMANN, K.-M., Internal-Physiological Sports Medicine
BROMM, B., Physiology
BULLINGER, M., Medical Psychology
BURDELSKI, M., Paediatrics
CLAUSEN, M., Nuclear Medicine
DALLEK, M., Surgery, Accident Surgery
DAVIDOFF, M., Anatomy
DELLING, G., General Pathology and Pathological Anatomy
DENEKE, F.-W., Psychosomatic Medicine
DÖRING, V., Surgery
DRIESCH, P., Dermatology and Venereology
EHMKE, H., Physiology
EIERMANN, T., Transfusion Medicine
ENGELMANN, K., Ophthalmology
FEUCHT, H.-H., Medical Microbiology and Immunology
FIEDLER, W., Internal Medicine
FLEISCHER, B., Immunology, Virology
GAL, A., Medical Genetics
GÖTZE, P., Psychiatry
GRETEN, H., Internal Medicine
HALATA, Z., Anatomy
HAND, I., Psychiatry
HEGEWISCHE-BECKER, S., Internal Medicine
HELLWEGE, H., Paediatrics
HELMCHEN, U., Pathology
HESS, M., Otorhinolaryngology
HÖHNE, K.-H., Information and Data Processing in Medicine
HÖLTJE, W.-J., Maxillary Surgery
HORSTMANN, R., Internal Medicine
HOSSFELD, D., Internal Medicine
HÜBENER, K.-H., Radiology
HULAND, H., Urology
HUNEKE, A., Gynaecology and Obstetrics
IZBICKI, J., Surgery
JÄNICKE, F. K.-H., Gynaecology and Obstetrics
JANKE-SCHAUB, G., Paediatrics
JENTSCH, T., Cell Biology
JÜDE, H. D., Dental Medicine
JUNG, H., Biophysics and Radiobiology
KAHL-NIEKE, B., Orthodontics
KAULFERS, P.-M., Medical Microbiology
KAUPEN-HAAS, H., Medical Sociology
KOCH, U., Otorhinolaryngology
KOCH-GROMUS, U., Medical Psychology
KOHLSCHÜTTER, A., Paediatrics
KOLLEK, R., Biotechnology
KORTH, M., Pharmacology
KRAUSZ, M., Psychiatry
KREYMANN, K. G., Internal Medicine
KRUPPA, J., Physiological Chemistry
KRUSE, H.-P., Internal Medicine
KÜHNL, P., Transfusions, Immuno-Haematology
LAMBRECHT, W., Surgery
LAUFS, R., Medical Microbiology and Immunology
LEICHTWEISS, H.-P., Physiology
LEUWER, R., Otorhinolaryngology
LOCKEMANN, U., Legal Medicine
LÖNING, T., General Pathology, Pathological Anatomy
MACK, D., Medical Microbiology, Infection Epidemiology and Hospital Hygiene
MANGOLD, U., Anatomy
MARQUARDT, H., General Toxicology
MAYR, G. W., Physiological Chemistry
MEINERTZ, T., Cardiology
MESTER, J., Nuclear Medicine
MOLL, I., Dermatology, Venereology
MÜHLHAUSER, I., Health
MÜLLER, D., Neurosurgery
MÜLLER-WIEFEL, D. E., Internal Medicine
MUNZEL, T., Internal Medicine
NABER, D., Psychiatry
NEUBER, K., Dermatology and Venereology
NEUMAIER, M., Clinical Chemistry
NOLDUS, J., Neurology
PANTEL, K., Molecular Genetics in Gynaecological Ontomology
PAUS, R., Dermatology and Venereology
PFEIFFER, E., Hygiene
PFEIFFER, G., Neurology
PFORTE, A., Internal Medicine
PLATZER, U., Dentistry
PONGS, O., Neurology
PÜSCHEL, U., Forensic Medicine
RICHARD, G., Ophthalmology
RICHTER, D., Physiological Chemistry
RICHTER, R., Medical Psychology, Psychosomatics
RIEDESSER, P., Paediatric Psychology
ROGIERS, X., Surgery
ROTHER, U., Radiological Diagnostics in Dental Medicine
RUDAT, T., Radiotherapy
RUEGER, J. M., Accident Surgery
RUMBERGER, E., Physiology
RUTHER, K., Ophthalmology
RUTHER, W., Orthopaedics
SCHACHNER CAMARTIN, M., Neurobiology
SCHÄFER, H., General Pathology and Pathological Anatomy
SCHALLER, C., Neurobiology
SCHIFFNER, U., Dental Medicine
SCHMALE, H., Biochemistry
SCHMELZLE, R., Dental Medicine
SCHMIDT, G., Sexology
SCHMOLDT, A., Forensic Medicine
SCHNEPPENHEIM, R., Paediatric Haematology and Oncology
SCHOLZ, H., Pharmacology and Toxicology
SCHRÖDER, H. J., Physiology
SCHULTE AM ESCH, J., Anaesthesiology
SCHULTE-MARKWORT, M., Child and Youth Psychiatry
SCHULZE, C., Anatomy
SCHULZE, W., Anatomy
SCHUMACHER, U., Anatomy
SCHWARZ, J., Physiology
SCHWORM, H. D., Ophthalmology
SEITZ, H.-J., Physiological Chemistry
SOEHENDRA, N., Surgery
STAHL, R., Internal Medicine
STANDL, T., Anaesthesiology
STAVROU, D., Neuropathology
STEINER, P., Radiology
STRÄTLING, W., Physiological Chemistry
TANNICH, E., Molecular Parasitology
THAISS, F., Internal Medicine
TROJAN, A., Social Medicine
ULLRICH, K. H. O., Paediatrics
UßMULLER, J., Otorhinolaryngology
VAN DEN BUSSCHE, H., Didactics
VONDERLAGE, M., Physiology
WAGENER, C., Clinical Chemistry
WEIL, J., Paediatric Cardiology
WEILLER, C., Neurology
WESTENDORF, J., Toxicology, Pharmacology
WIEDEMANN, K. B., Biological Psychiatry
WIELAND, T., Pharmacology
WILL, H. K., Microbiology
WILLIG, R. P., Paediatrics
WINDLER, E., Internal Medicine
WINTERPACHT, A., Human Genetics
ZANDER, A., Bone Marrow Transplantation
ZEUMER, H., Neuroradiology
ZYWIETE, F., Biophysics, Radiobiology

Department of Oriental Studies and Asia–Africa Institute (Rothenbaumchaussee 67/69, 20148 Hamburg; tel. (40) 428384054; e-mail aai@uni-hamburg.de):

CARLE, R., Indonesian and South Seas Languages
CONRAD, L., Islamic Sciences
EBERSTEIN, B., Sinology
EMMERICK, R., Iranian Studies
FRIEDRICH, M., Sinology
GERHARDT, L., African Languages and Cultures
JACKSON, D., Tibetology
KAPPERT, P., Turkish Studies
ORANSKAIA, T., Indic Studies
POHL, M., Japanese Politics
REH, M., African Languages and Cultures
ROTTER, G., Islamic Studies
SASSE, W., Chinese
SCHMITHAUSEN, L., Indology
SCHNEIDER, R., Japanese
STUMPFELDT, H., Sinology
TERWIEL, B., Thai Language and Culture
UHLIG, S., African Languages and Cultures
WEZLER, A., Indology

Department of Physical Education (Mollerstr. 10, 20148 Hanburg; tel. (40) 428382474):

BRAUMANN, K.-M.
EICHLER, G.
FUNKE-WIENEKE, J.
LANGE-AMELSBERG, J.
NIEDLICH, H.-D.
STRIPP, K.
TIEDEMANN, C.
TIWALD, H.
WEINBERG, P.

Department of Physics (Dammtorstr. 12, 2 stock, 20354 Hamburg; tel. (40) 428384056):

BARTELS, J., Theoretical Physics
BLOBEL, V., Experimental Physics
BÜSSER, F.-W., Experimental Physics
FAY, D., Theoretical Physics
FREDENHAGEN, K., Theoretical Physics
GERAMB, H. V. VON, Theoretical Physics
HANSEN, W., Experimental Physics
HEINZELMANN, G., Experimental Physics
HEITMANN, D., Applied Physics
HEMMERICH, A., Experimental Physics
HEUER, R.-D., Elementary Particle Physics

HEYSZENAU, H., Theoretical Physics
HUBER, G., Experimental Physics
JOHNSON, R., Experimental Physics
KLANNER, R., Experimental Physics
KÖTZLER, J., Applied Physics
KRAMER, B., Theoretical Physics
MACK, G., Theoretical Physics
MERKT, U., Experimental Physics
NAROSKA, B., Experimental Physics
NEUHAUSER, W., Experimental Physics
OEPEN, H. P., Experimental Physics
PFANNKUCHE, D., Theoretical Physics
REIMERS, D., Astronomy
SCHARNBERG, K., Theoretical Physics
SCHMIDT-PARZEFALL, W., Experimental Physics
SCHMITT, J., Astronomy
SCHMÜSER, P., Experimental Physics
SCOBEL, W., Experimental Physics
SENGSTOCK, K., Experimantal Physics
SONNTAG, B., Experimental Physics
SPITZER, H., Fundamental Physics
WAGNER, A., Elementary Particle Physics
WENDKER, H., Astronomy
WICK, K., Experimental Physics
WIESENDANGER, R., Experimental Physics
WURTH, W., Experimental Physics
ZIMMERER, G., Experimental Physics

Department of Protestant Theology (Sedanstr. 19, 20146 Hamburg; tel. (40) 428380):

AHRENS, T., Missions
DIERKEN, J., Systematic Theology
GRÜNBERG, W., Practical Theology
GUTMANN, H.-M., Practical Theology
KOCH, T., Systematic Theology
LINDNER, W. V., Practical Theology
LOHR, W., Church and Dogmatic History
MAGER, I., Church History and Dogma
MOXTER, M., Systematic Theology
SCHRAMM, T., New Testament
SCHRÖTER, J., New Testament
SCHUMANN, O., Religious and Missionary Science
SELLIN, G., New Testament
STEIGER, J. A., Church and Dogmatic History
TIMM, S., Old Testament
WILLI-PLEIN, I., Old Testament

Department of Psychology (Von-Melle-Park 5, 20146 Hamburg; tel. (40) 428385460):

BAMBERG, E.
BERBALK, H.
BURISCH, M.
BUSE, L.
DAHME, B.
ECKERT, J.
HEINZE, B.
LANGER, I.
OETTINGEN, G
ORTH, B.
PAWLIK, K.
PROBST, P.
RHENIUS, D.
SCHMIDTCHEN, S.
SCHULZ VON THUN, F.
SCHWAB, R.
TONNIES, S.
VAGT, G.
WITT, H.
WITTE, E.

Department of Social Sciences (Allende-Pl. 1, 20146 Hamburg; tel. (40) 42838-0):

EICHNER, K., Sociology
GOERTZ, H.-J., Social and Economic History
GREVEN, M., Political Science
HEINEMANN, K., Sociology
JAKOBEIT, C., Political Science
KAUPEN-HAAS, H.
KLEINSTEUBER, H. J., Political Science
LANDFRIED, C., Political Science
LÜDE, R. VON, Sociology
MILLER, M., Sociology
NEVERLA, I., Journalism, Communications
PIEPER, M., Sociology
RASCHKE, P., Political Science
RENN, H., Sociology
RUNDE, P., Sociology
SCHEERER, S., Criminology
SEßAR, K., Criminology
TETZLAFF, R., Political Science
TROITZSCH, U., Social Sciences
VILLMOW, B., Criminology
WEISCHENBERG, S., Communications Science, Journalism

UNIVERSITÄT HEIDELBERG

POB 10 57 60, 69047 Heidelberg
Grabengasse 1, 69117 Heidelberg
Telephone: (6221) 540
E-mail: rektor@rektorat.uni-heidelberg.de
Internet: www.uni-heidelberg.de

Founded 1386
Academic year: October to September

Rector: Prof. Dr BERNHARD EITEL
Vice-Rector for Education: Prof. Dr FRIEDERIKE NÜSSEL
Vice-Rector for Int. Affairs: Prof. Dr THOMAS PFEIFFER
Vice-Rector for Quality Devt: Prof. Dr KARLHEINZ SONNTAG
Vice-Rector for Research and Structure: Prof. Dr THOMAS RAUSCH
Chancellor: Dr MARINA FROST
Librarian: Dr VEIT PROBST

Library: see under Libraries and Archives
Number of teachers: 4,259
Number of students: 28,266

Publications: *Alumni Revue* (2 a year), *Personalia* (12 a year), *Ruperto Carola* (3 a year), *Unispiegel* (5 a year)

DEANS

Faculty of Behavioural and Cultural Studies: Prof. Dr ANDREAS KRUSE
Faculty of Biosciences: Prof. Dr THOMAS HOLSTEIN
Faculty of Chemistry and Earth Sciences: Prof. Dr A. STEPHEN K. HASHMI
Faculty of Economics and Social Sciences: Prof. Dr JÜRGEN EICHBERGER
Faculty of Law: Prof. Dr HERBERT KRONKE
Faculty of Mathematics and Computer Sciences: Prof. Dr R. RANNACHER
Faculty of Medicine (Heidelberg): Prof. Dr CLAUS R. BARTRAM
Faculty of Medicine (Mannheim): Prof. Dr KLAUS VAN ACKERN
Faculty of Modern Languages: Prof. Dr CHRISTIANE VON STUTTERHEIM
Faculty of Philosophy: Prof. Dr HEINZ-DIETRICH LÖWE
Faculty of Physics and Astronomy: Prof. Dr MANFRED SALMHOFER
Faculty of Theology: Prof. Dr WINRICH LÖHR

PROFESSORS

Faculty of Behavioural and Cultural Studies (Voßstr. 2, Gebäude 37, I. OG, 69115 Heidelberg; tel. (6221) 542894; e-mail dekanat@verkult.uni-heidelberg.de):

BOENICKE, R., Education
HAGEMANN, D., Psychology
KRUSE, A., Ethnology
KRUSE, A., Gerontology
ROTH, K., Sports

Faculty of Biosciences (Im Neuenheimer Feld 234, 69120 Heidelberg; tel. (6221) 545648; e-mail dekanat-bio@urz.uni-heidelberg.de):

BADING, H., Neurobiology
HELL, R., Heidelberg Plant and Fungal Biology Graduate School
HOLSTEIN, T., Zoology
JÄSCHKE, A., Pharmacy and Molecular Biotechnology

Faculty of Chemistry and Earth Sciences (Im Neuenheimer Feld 234, 69120 Heidelberg; tel. (6221) 544844; e-mail dcg@urz.uni-heidelberg.de):

BUBENZER, O., Geography
CEDERBAUM, L., Physical Chemistry
HASHMI, S., Organic Chemistry
HIMMEL, H.-J., Inorganic Chemistry
SCHÖLER, F., Earth Sciences

Faculty of Economics and Social Sciences (Bergheimer Str. 58, 69115 Heidelberg; tel. (6221) 543445; e-mail wiso-dekanat@urz.uni-heidelberg.de):

CROISSANT, A., Political Science
GOESCHL, T., Interdisciplinary Institute for Environmental Economics
IRMEN, A., Economics
SCHWINN, T., Sociology

Faculty of Law (Friedrich-Ebert-Anlage 6–10, 69117 Heidelberg; tel. (6221) 547631; e-mail dekanat@jurs.uni-heidelberg.de):

BALDUS, C., Historical Law
DÖLLING, D., Criminal Law
EBKE, W., German and European Company and Business Law
HESS, B., Foreign and International Private and Business Law
KIRCHHOF, P., Fiscal and Tax Law
MÜLLER-GRAFF, P., Civil, Commercial, Corporate and Commercial Law, European Law and Comparative Law
VON HOYNINGEN-HUENE, G., Civil Law, Labour Law and Insolvency

Faculty of Mathematics and Computer Sciences (Im Neuenheimer Feld 288, 69120 Heidelberg; tel. (6221) 545758; e-mail dekanat@mathi.uni-heidelberg.de):

DAHLHAUS, R., Applied Mathematics
GERTZ, M., Computer Sciences
WINGBERG, K., Mathematics

Faculty of Medicine (Heidelberg) (Im Neuenheimer Feld 672, 69120 Heidelberg; e-mail dekanat@med.uni-heidelberg.de):

AUFFARTH, G., Ophthalmology
BARTRAM, C., Human Genetics
BÜCHLER, M., Surgery
ECKART, W., History of Medicine
ENK, A., Dermatology
EWERBECK, V., Orthopaedics
GERNER, H., Orthopaedics
HACKE, W., Neurology
HECKER, M., Physiology and Pathophysiology
HERZOG, W., Internal Medicine
HOFFMANN, G., Paediatrics
HOHENFELLNER, M., Urology
KAUCZOR, H., Radiology
KIESER, M., Medical Biometrics and Computer Science in Medicine
KIRSCH, J., Anatomy
KRÄUSSLICH, H., Hygiene
MARTIN, E., Anaesthesiology
MATTERN, R., Forensic Medicine
MEUER, S., Immunology
MÜHLING, J., Dentistry
MUNDT, C., Psychiatry
PLINKERT, P., Oto–Rhino–Laryngology
SCHIRMACHER, P., Pathology
SOHN, C., Women's Hospital
TRIEBIG, G., Social and Industrial Medicine
UNTERBERG, A., Neurosurgery

Faculty of Medicine (Mannheim) (Theodor-Kutzer-Ufer 1-3, 68167 Mannheim; tel. (621) 3839770; e-mail dekan@medma.uni-heidelberg.de):

FISCHER, J., Public Health
GOERDT, S., Dermatology and Venereal Disease
GRODEN, C., Neuroradiology
HOF, H., Medicine Microbiology and Hygiene
HÖRMANN, K., Oto–Rhino–Laryngology
JONAS, J., Ophthalmology

KLÜTER, H., Transfusions Medicine and Immunology
MARX, A., Pathology
MEYER-LINDENBERG, A., Mental Health
MICHEL, M., Urology
NEUMAIER, M., Clinical Chemistry
POST, S., Surgery
SCHAD, L., Computer-Assisted Clinical Medicine
SCHARF, H., Orthopaedics
SCHMIEDER, K., Neurological Surgery
SCHÖNBERG, S., Clinical Radiology
SCHROTEN, A., Paediatrics
SÜTTERLIN, M., Women's Hospital
VAN ACKERN, K., Anaesthesiology
WEIß, C., Medical Statistics, Biomathematics and Information
WENZ, F., Experimental Radiation Oncology
WESSEL, L., Children's Surgery
WIELAND, T., Pharmacology and Toxicology

Faculty of Modern Languages (Voßstr. 2, Gebäude 37, 69115 Heidelberg; tel. (6221) 542891; e-mail neuphil-fak@uni-hd.de):

FRANK, A., Computer Linguistics
GLAUSER, B., English Philology
GVOZDANOVIC, J., Slavic Philology
HUBER, C., Translating and Interpreting
LICHT, T., Philology of the Middle Ages
RIECKE, J., German Philology
RIECKE, J., Language Laboratory
ROESCH, G., German as a Foreign Language Philology
WEIAND, C., Romance Philology

Faculty of Philosophy (Voßstr. 2, Bldg 4370, 69115 Heidelberg; tel. (6221) 542329; e-mail philosophische-fakultaet@uni-hd.de):

AHN, G., Religious Studies
ENDERWITZ, S., Languages and Cultures of the Near East
HERREN-OESCH, M., History
HESSE, M., European Art History
JÖRDENS, A., Papyrology
KLOSS, G., Classical Studies
LEDDEROSE, L., East Asian Art History
LEOPOLD, S., Musicology
LÖWE, H., History of Eastern Europe
MCLAUGHLIN, P., Philosophy
MARAN, J., Prehistory and Protohistory and Middle Eastern Archaeology
MITTLER, B., Sinology
PANAGIOTOPOULOS, D., Classical Archaeology
QUACK, J., Egyptology
SCHNEIDMÜLLER, B., History of Franconia and the Palatinate
SEIFERT, W., Japanese Studies
STEPHAN-KAISSIS, C., Byzantine Archaeology and Art History
TRAMPEDACH, K., Ancient History and Epigraphics
WEINFURTER, S., History of Franconia and the Palatinate

Faculty of Physics and Astronomy (Albert-Ueberle-Str. 3–5 2OG Ost, 69120 Heidelberg; tel. (6221) 549298; e-mail dekanat@physik.uni-heidelberg.de):

GREBEL, E., Astronomical Computing Institute
KLESSEN, R., Theoretical Astrophysics
MEIER, K., Kirchhoff-Institute for Physics
PLATT, U., Environmental Physics
QUIRRENBACH, A., National Observatory King Chair
WAMBSGANß, J., Astronomical Computing Institute
WEIDEMÜLLER, M., Physics
WETTERICH, C., Theoretical Physics

Faculty of Theology (Hauptstr. 231, 1 OG, 69117 Heidelberg; tel. (6221) 543334; e-mail dekanat@theologie.uni-heidelberg.de):

EURICH, J., Study of Christian Social Service
LIENHARD, F., Practical-Theological Seminary
LÖHR, W., Scientific-Theological Seminary
NÜSSEL, F., Ecumenical Institute

ATTACHED INSTITUTES

Biochemie-Zentrum Heidelberg (Heidelberg University Biochemistry Centre): Im Neuenheimer Feld 328, 69129 Heidelberg; Dir Prof. Dr M. BRUNNER.

BioQuant: Im Neuenheimer Feld 267, Raum 741, 69120 Heidelberg; e-mail www-info@bioquant.uni-heidelberg.de; Dir Prof. Dr HANS-GEORG KRÄUSSLICH; Dir Prof. Dr JÜRGEN WOLFRUM; Dir Prof. Dr ROLAND EILS.

Forschungszentrum für Internationale und Interdisziplinäre Theologie (Research Centre for International and Interdisciplinary Theology): Hauptstr. 240, 69117 Heidelberg; e-mail kontakt.fiit@uni-hd.de; Dir Prof. Dr ANDREAS KRUSE; Dir Prof. MICHAEL WELKER; Dir Prof. Dr PETER LAMPE.

Heidelberg Center for American Studies (HCA): Curt und Heidemarie Engelhorn Palais, Hauptstr. 120, 69117 Heidelberg; e-mail hca@uni-hd.de; internet www.hca.uni-hd.de; Dir Prof. Dr DETLEF JUNKER.

Institut für Technische Informatik als zentrale Einrichtung der Universität Heidelberg: B6, 26, Bauteil B, 8131 Mannheim; Dir Prof. Dr K.-H. BRENNER.

Interdisziplinäres Zentrum für Neurowissenschaften (Interdisciplinary Centre for Neuroscience): Im Neuenheimer Feld 307, 69120 Heidelberg; Dir Prof. Dr HILMAR BADING.

Interdisziplinäres Zentrum für Wissenschaftliches Rechnen (Interdisciplinary Centre for Scientific Computing): Im Neuenheimer Feld 368, 69120 Heidelberg; e-mail wissrech@iwr.uni-heidelberg.de; Dir Prof. Dr HANS GEORG BOCK.

Südasien-Institut (South Asia Institute): Im Neuenheimer Feld 330, 69120 Heidelberg; tel. (6221) 548900; e-mail info@sai.uni-heidelberg.de; internet www.sai.uni-heidelberg.de; Dir Prof. Dr HANS HARDER.

Zentrum für Astronomie (Centre for Astronomy of Heidelberg University): Mönchhofstr. 12–14, 69120 Heidelberg; Dir Prof. Dr JOACHIM WAMBSGANß.

Zentrum für Molekulare Biologie der Universität Heidelberg (Centre for Molecular Biology of Heidelberg University): Im Neuenheimer Feld 282, 69120 Heidelberg; Dir Prof. Dr BERND BUKAU.

Zentrum für Soziale Investitionen und Innovationen (Centre for Social Investment): Adenauerpl. 1, 69115 Heidelberg; e-mail csi@csi.uni-heidelberg.de; Dir Prof. Dr HELMUT K. ANHEIER

UNIVERSITÄT HILDESHEIM

Marienburger Pl. 22, 31141 Hildesheim
Telephone: (5121) 8830
E-mail: studyinfo@uni-hildesheim.de
Internet: www.uni-hildesheim.de
Founded 1978
State control
Academic year: October to September
Pres.: Prof. Dr WOLFGANG-UWE FRIEDRICH
Vice-Pres.: Dr CHRISTOPH STRUTZ
Vice-Pres. for Academic Affairs: Prof. Dr TONI THOLEN
Vice-Pres. for Continuing Education: Dr MARGITTA RUDOLPH
Vice-Pres. for Research: Prof. Dr STEPHAN POROMBKA
Library Dir: Dr EWALD BRAHMS
Library of 500,000 vols
Number of teachers: 85
Number of students: 5,325
Publication: *Uni Hildesheim. Das Magazin* (2 a year)

DEANS

Faculty I (Education and Sociology): Prof. Dr MARTIN SCHREINER
Faculty II (Cultural Education): Prof. Dr TILMAN BORSCHE
Faculty III (Information and Communication): Prof. Dr FRIEDRICH LENZ
Faculty IV (Mathematics, Natural Sciences, Economics and Computer Science): Prof. Dr KLAUS AMBROSI

PROFESSORS

Faculty I (Education and Sociology) (tel. (5121) 883401):

BORSCHE, T., Philosophy
BRÄNDLE, W., Protestant Theology
CLOER, E., General Pedagogy
EBERLE, H.-J., Social Pedagogy
FRIEDRICH, W., Political Science
HELFRICH-HÖLTER, W., Psychology
HOPF, CH., Sociology
JAUMANN-GRAUMANN, O., Education
KECK, R., Education
KÖHNLEIN, W., General Science
KUNERT, H., General Education Studies
MEIER-HILBERT, G., Geography
MÜLLER, B., Social Pedagogy
NICKEL, U., Sport
OVERESCH, M., History
SCHREINER, M., Protestant Theology
SIEBERG, H., Sociology
STRANG, H., Social Education Studies
WALLRAVEN, K., Sociology
WERNER, W., Catholic Theology
WOLFF, ST., Social Education Studies

Faculty II (Cultural Education) (tel. (5121) 883601):

BERG, J., Media Education
FRÜHSORGE, G., Fine Arts
GIFFHORN, H., Media Education
GORNIK, H., German Literature and Linguistics
GROMES, H., Theatre
GÜNZEL, R., Fine Arts and Visual Communication
HÜGEL, H.-O., Popular Culture
KURZENBERGER, H.-J., Theatre
LÖFFLER, W., Music and Aural Communication
MENZEL, W., German Language and Linguistics
NOLTE, J., Fine Arts and Visual Communication
SCHNEIDER, W., Cultural Politics
TESKE, U., Fine Arts
VIETTA, J., Literature
WEBER, R., Music and Aural Communication

Faculty III (Information and Communication) (tel. (5121) 883801):

ARNTZ, R., Romance Languages and Linguistics
BENEKE, J., English, Linguistics and Intercultural Communication
DIRKS, U., English Studies
HAUENSCHILD, CH., Computational Linguistics
SABBAN, A., Romance Languages and Linguistics
WOMSER-HACKER, CH., Information Science

Faculty IV (Mathematics, Natural Sciences, Economics and Computer Science):

AMBROSI, K., Computer Science
BENTZ, H.-J., Mathematics
FLECHSIG, E., Chemistry
FRANZBECKER, W., Technical Studies
KAHLE, D., Mathematics
KIERDORF, H., Biology

KOLB, G., General Economics
KREUTZKAMP, TH., Mathematics
SCHWARZER, E., Physics
STURM, H., Biology
WEGNER, N., Technology

UNIVERSITÄT HOHENHEIM

70593 Stuttgart
Telephone: (711) 4590
E-mail: post@uni-hohenheim.de
Internet: www.uni-hohenheim.de
Founded 1818
Academic year: October to September
Rector: Prof. Dr STEPHAN DABBERT
Pro-Rector: Prof. Dr MICHAEL KRUSE
Pro-Rector: Prof. Dr ANDREAS PYKA
Pro-Rector: Prof. Dr JOCHEN WEISS
Registrar: JULIA HENKE
Univ. Librarian: K.-W. HORSTMANN
Number of teachers: 690
Number of students: 9,220

DEANS

Faculty of Agricultural Sciences: Prof. Dr JOACHIM SAUERBORN
Faculty of Business, Economics and Social Sciences: Prof. Dr DIRK HACHMEISTER
Faculty of Natural Sciences: Prof. Dr HEINZ BREER

PROFESSORS

Faculty of Agricultural Sciences:
AMSELGRUBER, W., Anatomy and Physiology of Domestic Animals
ASCH, F., Management of Crop Water Stress in the Tropics and Subtropics
BAHRS, E., Farm Management
BECKER, T., Rural Markets and Rural Marketing
BELLOWS, A. C., Gender and Nutrition
BENNEWITZ, J., Farm Animal Genetics and Breeding
BERGER, T., Land Use Economics in the Tropics and Subtropics
BESSEI, W., Animal Breeding
BIRNER, R., Social and Institutional Change in Agricultural Development
BOTTINGER, S., Fundamentals of Agricultural Engineering
BROCKMEIER, M., International Agricultural Trade and World Food Security
CADISCH, G., Agronomy in the Tropics and Subtropics
CLAUPEIN, W., Plant Production
DABBERT, S., Production Theory in Agriculture
DOLUSCHITZ, R., Farm Management
FANGMEIER, A., Plant Ecology and Ecotoxicology
GERHADS, R., Weed Science
GRETHE, H., Agricultural and Food Policy
GRIEPENTROG, H., Measurement and Testing Technology
HOELZLE, L., Environmental and Animal Health
HOFFMANN, V., Agricultural Communication
JUNGBLUTH, T., Agricultural Technology
KANDELER, E., Soil Biology
KÖLLER, K., Agricultural Technology in Developing Countries
KRUSE, A., Conversion Technology and Life Cycle Assessment of Renewable Resources
KRUSE, M., Seed Technology
LEWANDOWSKI, I., Biobased Products and Energy Crops
LUDEWIG, U., Nutritional Crop Physiology
MELCHINGER, A., Genetics and Plant Breeding
MOSENTHIN, R., Animal Nutrition
MUELLER, J., Agricultural Engineering in the Tropics and Subtropics
MUELLER, T., Fertilization and Soil Matter Dynamics
PIEPHO, H.-P., Bioinformatics
RODEHUTSCORD, M., Animal Nutrition
SAUERBORN, J., Ecology of Tropical and Subtropical Areas
SCHMID, K., Crop Biodiversity and Breeding Informatics
STAHR, K., Soil Sciences
STEFANSKI, V., Behavioural Physiology of Farm Animals
STRECK, T., Biogeophysics
VALLE ZÁRATE, A., Stockbreeding in Tropical and Subtropical Areas
VOEGELE, R., Phytopathology
WEBER, G., Special Plant Breeding
WUENSCHE, J., Crop Physiology of Speciality Crops
ZEBITZ, C., Plant Protection
ZELLER, K., Rural Development Economics and Policy

Faculty of Business, Economics and Social Sciences:
AHLHEIM, M., Environmental Economics
BACKES-HAASE, A., Vocational Training
BAREIS, P., Taxation and Management
BELKE, A., International Economics
BUSS, E., Sociology
CAESAR, R., Financing
DITTMAN, A., Law
ESCHER-WEINGART, C., Law
GERYBADZE, A., International Management
HABENICHT, W., Industrial Economics
HACHMEISTER, B., Accounting and Finance
HAGEMANN, H., Economic Theory
HERDZINA, K., Economics
JUNGKUNZ, D., Vocational Teaching
KIRN, C., Informatics
KUHNLE, H., Business Administration
MACHARZINA, K., Management and Organizational Research
MAST, C., Journalism
MELL, U., Theology and Didactics
MÜHLENKAMP, H., Economics of Social Sciences
MÜLLER, C., Entrepreneurship
PFETSCH, B., Communication Policy
SCHENK, M., Communication and Social Research
SCHRAMM, M, Theology and Didactics
SCHULER, H., Psychology
SCHULZ, W., Environmental Management
SCHWALBE, U., Industrial Economics
SEEL, B., Household Management
SPAHN, P., Economics
STREB, D., Social and Economic History
TROSSMANN, E., Controlling
VOETH, M., Marketing
WAGENHALS, G., Statistics and Econometry

Faculty of Natural Sciences:
BEIFUSS, U., Bioorganic Chemistry
BIESALSKI, H. K., Biochemistry and Nutritional Science
BISCHOFF, S. C., Nutritional Medicine/Prevention
BLUM, M., Zoology
BOSY-WESTPHAL, A., Applied Nutritional Science/Dietetics
BREER, H., Physiology
CARLE, R., Plant Foodstuff Technology
FISCHER, L., Biotechnology
FRITZ-STEUBER, J., Cellular Microbiology
GRAEVE, L., Biochemistry and Nutrition
HANKE, W. R. L., Membran Physiology
HAUSMANN, R., Bioprocess Engineering
HINRICHS, J., Animal Foodstuff Technology
HITZMANN, B., Process Analysis and Cereal Technology
HUBER, A., Biosensoric
JETTER, K., Applied Mathematics
KOLLING-PATERNOGA, R., Food Process Engineering
KOHLUS, R., Food Process Engineering
KUHN, A., Microbiology
KÜPPERS, M., Botany
MACKENSTEDT, U., Zoology
MENZEL, P., Chemistry and Ecology
PFITZNER, A., General Virology
PREISS, A., General Genetics
SCHALLER, J., Plant Physiology
SCHMIDT, H., Food Microbiology
SCHWACK, W., Food Chemistry and Analytical Chemistry
SPRING, O., Biodiversity and Plant Interaction
STEIDLE, J., Animal Ecology
STRASDEIT, H., Bioinorganic Chemistry
STROBELE, N., Molecular and Applied Diet Psychology
VETTER, W., Food Chemistry
WEISS, J., Food Structure and Functionality Laboratories
WULFMEYER, V., Physics and Meteorology

UNIVERSITÄT KASSEL

Präsidialverwaltung, Mönchebergstr. 19, 34109 Kassel
Telephone: (561) 8040
E-mail: presse@uni-kassel.de
Internet: www.uni-kassel.de
Founded 1971
State control
Language of instruction: German
Academic year: October to July
Pres.: Prof. Dr ROLF-DIETER POSTLEP
Vice-Pres.: Prof. Dr ANDREAS HÄNLEIN
Vice-Pres.: Prof. Dr CLAUDIA BRINKER-VON DER HEYDE
Vice-Pres.: Prof. Dr MARTIN LAWERENZ
Chancellor: Dr ROBERT KUHN
Librarian: Dr AXEL HALLE
Library: see under Libraries and Archives
Number of teachers: 1,212
Number of students: 20,643

DEANS

Architecture, Urban Planning, Landscape Planning: Prof. Dr Ing. STEFAN KÖRNER
Business and Economics: Prof. Dr GEORG VON WANGENHEIM
Civil and Environmental Engineering: Prof. Dr Ing. VOLKHARD FRANZ
Educational Science, Humanities and Music: Prof. Dr PAUL-GERHARD KLUMBIES
Electrical Engineering, Computer Science: Prof. Dr Ing. JOSEF BÖRCSÖK
Languages and Literature: Prof. Dr ANDREAS GARDT
Mathematics and Natural Science: Prof. Dr FRIEDRICH W. HERBERG
Mechanical Engineering: Prof. Dr Ing. OLAF WÜNSCH
Social Work, Psychology: Prof. Dr STEPHAN RIXEN
Social Sciences: Prof. Dr BERND OVERWIEN

ATTACHED RESEARCH INSTITUTES

Centre for Environmental Systems Research (CESR): internet www.usf.uni-kassel.de/cesr; Dir Prof. Dr ANDREAS ERNST.

Centre for Nanostructure Science and Technology (CINSaT): e-mail info@cinsat.uni-kassel.de; Dir Prof. Dr KLAUS MASSELI.

Competence Centre for Climate Change Mitigation and Adaptation (CLIMA): e-mail clima@uni-kassel.de; Dir Dr MICHAELA SCHALLER.

International Centre for Development and Decent Work (ICDD): e-mail icdd@uni-kassel.de; Exec. Dir Prof. Dr CHRISTOPH SCHERRER.

International Centre for Higher Education Research (INCHER-Kassel): Moenchebergstr. 17, 34109 Kassel; tel. (561) 8042415; e-mail mahe@uni-kassel.de; internet www.incher.uni-kassel.de; Dir Prof. Dr BARBARA KEHM

UNIVERSITÄT KOBLENZ-LANDAU

Campus Koblenz, POB 20 16 02, 56016 Koblenz
Universitätsstr. 1, 56070 Koblenz
Telephone: (261) 2870
Campus Landau, Fortstr. 7, 76829 Landau
Telephone: (6341) 2800
E-mail: service@uni-koblenz-landau.de
Internet: www.uni-koblenz-landau.de

Founded 1990
State control
Pres.: Prof. Dr ROMAN HEILIGENTHAL
Vice-Pres. for Academic Affairs: Prof. Dr PETER ULLRICH
Vice-Pres. for Research: Prof. Dr ULRICH SARCINELLI
Chancellor: SIMONE MERTEL-SCHERER

Number of teachers: 500
Number of students: 13,000

UNIVERSITÄT KONSTANZ (University of Konstanz)

78457 Konstanz
Universitätsstr. 10, 78464 Konstanz
Telephone: (7531) 880
E-mail: posteingang@uni-konstanz.de
Internet: www.uni-konstanz.de

Founded 1966
Academic year: October to September
Rector: Prof. Dr ULRICH RÜDIGER
Vice-Rector for Int. Affairs: Prof. Dr KATHARINA HOLZINGER
Vice-Rector for Research: Prof. Dr ANDREAS MARX
Vice-Rector for Study Programmes: Prof. Dr CARSTEN EULITZ
Chancellor: JENS APITZ
Librarian: PETRA HÄTSCHER

Library: see under Libraries and Archives
Number of teachers: 177
Number of students: 10,081
Publication: *Uni'kon*

DEANS

Faculty of Humanities: Prof. Dr THOMAS HINZ
Faculty of Law, Economics and Politics: Prof. Dr FRIEDRICH BREYER
Faculty of Sciences: Prof. Dr MARTIN SCHEFFNER

PROFESSORS

Faculty of Humanities

Department of History and Sociology:

GEORG, W., Sociology
GIESEN, B., Sociology
GOTTER, U., History
GÖTZ, T., Empirical Educational Research
HAUSER, S., History
HINZ, T., Sociology
KIRSCH, T., Sociology
KLEEBERG, B., History
KNORR, C., Sociology
OSTERHAMMEL, J., History
PIETROW-ENNKER, B., History
RECKWITZ, A., Sociology
REICHHARDT, S., History
RIEHLE, H., Sports Science
SCHLÖGL, K., History
SIGNORI, G., History
WELTECKE, D., History
WISCHERMANN, C., History
WOLL, A., Sport Science

Department of Linguistics:

BAYER, J.
BRAUN, B.
BREU, W.
BUTT, M.
DEHÉ, N.
EULITZ, C.
GRIJZENHOUT, J.
KABAK, B.
KAISER, G.
PLANKE, F.
REMBERGER, E.-M.
ROMERO, M.

Department of Literature:

ASSMANN, A.
BAUDY, G.
FEICHTINGER, B.
JOAN I TOUS, P.
KOSCHORKE, A.
KÜMMEL-SCHNUR, A.
MATALA DE MAZZA, E.
MERGENTAL, S.
MURASOV, J.
NISCHIK, R.
OCHSNER, B.
OTTO, I.
POLASCHEGG, A.
QUAST, B.
SPRENGER, U.
STIEGLER, B.
THÜRLEMANN, F.
VOGEL, J.
WEITIN, T.
ZIMMERMANN, T.

Department of Philosophy:

ROSEFELDT, T.
SEEBASS, G.
SPOHN, W.
STEMMER, P.
WEBER, M.

Faculty of Law, Economics and Politics

Department of Economics:

ALÓS-FERRER, C.
BREYER, F.
BRÜGGEMANN, R.
BRUTTEL, L.
DEISSINGER, T.
FISCHBACHER, U.
FRANKE, G.
FRIEHE, T.
GENSER, B.
GLASER, M.
GRIEBEN, W.
HERTWECK, M.
HOCHHOLDINGER, S.
JACKWERTH, J.
KAAS, L.
LUKAS, C.
POHLMEIER, W.
SANDER, H.
SCHOLL, A.
SEIFRID, J.
STEFANI, U.
URSPRUNG, H.

Department of Politics and Management:

BEHNKE, N.
BOERNER, S.
FREITAG, M.
HOLZINGER, K.
KELLER, B.
KNILL, C.
SCHNEIDER, G.
SCHNEIDER, V.
SEIBEL, W.
SELB, P.

School of Law:

ALTHAMMER, C.
ARMGARDT, M.
BOECKEN, W.
EISELE, J.
ENNUSCHAT, J.
FEZER, K.
GLÖCKNER, J.
HAILBRONNER, K.
IBLER, M.
KOCH, J.
RENGIER, R.
RÖHL, H.
SCHÖNBERGER, C.
STADLER, A.
THEILE, H.

Faculty of Sciences

Department of Biology:

ADAMSKA, J.
APELL, H.
BÜRKLE, A.
COOK, A.
DEUERLING, E.
DIEDRICHS, K.
DIETRICH, D.
ECKMANN, R.
GALIZIA, G.
GRÖTTRUP, M.
HAUCK, C.
KROTH, P.
KÜPPER, H.
LEIST, M.
MAY, E.
MAYER, T.
MENDGEN, K.
MEYER, A.
OHLSCHLÄGER, P.
PEETERS, F.
ROTHAUPT, K.
SCHEFFNER, M.
SCHINK, B.
STÜRMER, C.
WELTE, W.
WIKELSKI, M.

Department of Chemistry:

EXNER, T.
GROTH, U.
HARTIG, J.
HAUSER, K.
MARX, A.
MECKING, S.
MÖLLER, H.
MÜLLER, G.
POLARZ, S.
PRZYBYLSKI, M.
WITTMANN, V.
ZUMBUSCH, A.

Department of Computer and Information Science:

BERTHOLD, M.
BRANDES, U.
DEUSSEN, O.
KEIM, D.
KOCH, M.
KUHLEN, R.
LEUE, S.
MERHOF, D.
REITERER, H.
SAUPE, D.
SCHOLL, M.
WALDVOGEL, M.

Department of Mathematics and Statistics:

BARTHEL, G.
BERAN, J.
DENK, R.
DREHER, H.
FREISTÜHLER, H.
HOFFMANN, D.
JUNK, M.
KOHLMANN, M.
RACKE, R.
SCHEIDERER, C.
SCHNÜRER, O.
SCHROPP, J.
SCHWEIGHOFER, M.

Department of Physics:

BELZIG, W.
BURKARD, G.
DEKORSY, T.
FUCHS, M.
GANTEFÖR, G.
HAHN, G.
LEIDERER, P.
LEITENSTORFER, A.
MARET, G.
NIELABA, P.
NOWAK, U.
RÜDIGER, U.
SCHEER, E.

Department of Psychology:
ELBERT, T.
GOLLWITZER, P.
HÜBNER, R.
KEMPF, W.
KIBLER, J.
KÜTTNER, C.
RENNER, B.
ROCKSTROH, B.
SCHUPP, H.
SONNENTAG, S.

UNIVERSITÄT LEIPZIG

POB 10 09 20, 04009 Leipzig
Ritterstr. 26, 04109 Leipzig
Telephone: (341) 97108
E-mail: karin.hermann@uni-leipzig.de
Internet: www.uni-leipzig.de
Founded 1409
State control
Academic year: October to September (2 semesters)
Rector: Prof. Dr BEATE A. SCHÜCKING
Vice-Rector for Devt and Transfer: Prof. Dr THOMAS LENK
Vice-Rector for Education and Int. Affairs: Prof. Dr CLAUS ALTMAYER
Vice-Rector for Research and Young Academics: Prof. Dr MATTHIAS SCHWARZ
Chancellor: Dr FRANK NOLDEN
Library Dir: Prof. Dr ULRICH JOHANNES SCHNEIDER
Library: see under Libraries and Archives
Number of students: 35,000

DEANS

Faculty of Biosciences, Pharmacy and Psychology: Prof. Dr MATTHIAS MÜLLER
Faculty of Chemistry and Mineralogy: Prof. Dr CHRISTOPH SCHNEIDER
Faculty of Economics and Management: Prof. Dr Ing. JOHANNES RINGEL
Faculty of Education: Prof. Dr THOMAS HOFSÄSS
Faculty of History, Art and Oriental Studies: Prof. Dr FRANK ZÖLLNER
Faculty of Law: Prof. Dr CHRISTIAN BERGER
Faculty of Mathematics and Computer Science: Prof. Dr MATTHIAS SCHWARZ
Faculty of Medicine: Prof. Dr JOACHIM THIERY
Faculty of Philology: Prof. Dr WOFGANG LÖRSCHER
Faculty of Physics and Earth Sciences: Prof. Dr JÜRGEN HAASE
Faculty of Social Sciences and Philosophy: Prof. Dr GÜNTER BENTELE
Faculty of Sport Science: Prof. Dr MARTIN BUSSE
Faculty of Theology: Prof. Dr KLAUS FITSCHEN
Faculty of Veterinary Medicine: Prof. Dr UWE TRUYEN

PROFESSORS

Faculty of Biosciences, Pharmacy and Psychology (Brüderstr. 35, 04103 Leipzig; tel. (341) 9736700; e-mail dekanat.bio@uni-leipzig.de):
BECK-SICKINGER, A. G., Biochemistry
BUSOT, F., Terrestrial Ecology
EGER, K., Pharmaceutical Chemistry
HARMS, H., Environmental Microbiology
HAUSCHILDT, S., Immunobiology
HOFMANN, H.-J., Biophysical Chemistry
JESCHENIAK, D., Cognitive Psychology
MOHR, G., Industrial and Organizational Psychology
MORAWETZ, W., Special Botany
MÖRL, M., Biochemistry and Molecular Biology
MÜLLER, M., Experimental Psychology and Cognitive Neuroscience
NIEBER, K., Pharmacology
PETERMANN, H., Psychology of Personality and Psychological Intervention
POEGGEL, G., Human Biology
RAUWALD, J.-W., Pharmaceutical Biology
REISSER, W., General and Applied Botany
ROBITZKI, A., Molecular Biological-Biochemical Processing Technology
RÜBSAMEN, R., Neurobiology
SASS, H., Genetics
SCHILDBERGER, K.-M., General Zoology and Animal Behaviour Physiology
SCHLEGEL, M., Molecular Evolution and Systematics of Animals
SCHRÖDER, H., Clinical Psychology
SCHRÖGER, E., Cognitive Psychology and Biological Psychology
VON COLLANI, G., Cognitive Social Psychology
WILHELM, CHR., Plant Physiology
WITRUK, E., Educational Rehabilitation Psychology

Faculty of Chemistry and Mineralogy (Johannisallee 29, 04103 Leipzig; tel. (341) 9736000; e-mail dekanat@chemie.uni-leipzig.de; internet www.uni-leipzig.de/chemie):
BENTE, K., Mineralogy, Crystallography
BERGER, ST., Analytical Chemistry
BREDE, O., Physical Chemistry
GIANNIS, A., Organic Chemistry
HEY-HAWKINS, E., Inorganic Chemistry
HOFFMANN, R., Bioanalytics
KRAUTSCHEID, H., Inorganic Chemistry
MORGNER, H., Physical Chemistry
PAPP, H., Technological Chemistry
REINHOLD, J., Theoretical Chemistry
SCHNEIDER, C., Organic Chemistry
STRÄTER, N., Structural Analysis of Biopolymers

Faculty of Economics and Management (Marschnerstr. 31, 04109 Leipzig; tel. (341) 9733500; e-mail dekanat@wifa.uni-leipzig.de; internet www.uni-leipzig.de/wifa):
BRUHNKE, K.-H., Industrial Engineering and Structural Engineering: Technical and Infrastructural Management
DIEDRICH, R., Business Management: Controlling and Management Accounting
EISENECKER, U., Manager Information Systems: Software Development, Business and Administration
FÖHR, S., Business Management: Personnel Management
FRANCZYK, B., Manager Information Systems: Information Management
GRAW, K.-U., Industrial Engineering and Structural Engineering: Laying of Foundations/Hydraulic Engineering
HASSE, R., Economics: Economic Policy
HEILEMANN, U., Empirical Economics and Econometrics
HOLLÄNDER, R., Environmental Management in Small and Medium Enterprises
KALISKE, M., Industrial Engineering and Structural Engineering: Statics and Dynamics of Structures
LANG, S., Economics, Statistics
LENK, T., Economics: Public Finance Theory
LÖBLER, H., Business Management: Marketing
PAHL, B., Industrial Engineering and Structural Engineering: Drafting/Construction Design
PARASKEWOPOULOS, S., Economics: Macroeconomics
PELZL, W., Business Management: Real Estate Management
POSSELT, T., Business Management: Service Management
RAUTENBERG, H.-G., Business Management: Management Accounting and Corporate Taxation
RINGEL, J., Urban Management
SCHMIDT, H., Business Management: Accounting and Auditing
SCHUHMACHER, F., Business Management: Corporate Finance
SINGER, H. J., Business Management: Banking
TUE, V., Industrial Engineering and Structural Engineering: Solid Construction/Building Material Technology
VOLLMER, U., Economics and Currency
WAGNER, F., Business Management: Insurance Company Management
WANZEK, T., Industrial Engineering and Structural Engineering: Steel-Girder Construction
WIESE, H., Economics: Microeconomics

Faculty of Education (Karl-Heine-Str. 22B, 04229 Leipzig; tel. (341) 9731400; e-mail dekanat.fakerz@uni-leipzig.de; internet www.uni-leipzig.de/~erzwiss):
DOBSLAFF, O., Special Education, Language and Speech Pathology
HOFSÄSS, T., Special Education, Learning Disabilities
HOPPE-GRAFF, S., Educational Psychology
HÖRNER, W., Comparative Education
KLAUSER, F., Economics, Business Education and Management Training
KNOLL, J., Adult Education
MARX, H., Psychology in School and Instruction
MELZER, M., School Education
MUTZECK, W., Behaviour Problems and Therapy in Special Education
SCHULZ, D., School Education
TOEPELL, M., Teaching Primary School Mathematics
VON WOLFFERSDORFF-EHLERT, C., Social Education
WOLLERSHEIM, H. W., General Education

Faculty of History, Art and Oriental Studies (Burgstr. 21, 04109 Leipzig; tel. (341) 9737000; e-mail dekgko@rz.uni-leipzig.de; internet www.uni-leipzig.de/fak/gesch.htm):
BAUMBACH, G., Drama
BAXMANN, J., Drama (Dance)
BÜNZ, E., History of Saxony
CAIN, H.-U., Classical Archaeology
DENZEL, M. A., Social and Economic History
DINER, D., Jewish History and Culture
EBERHARD, W., East and Middle European History
EBERT, H.-G., Islamic Law
FEURICH, H.-J., Teaching of Music
FISCHER-ELFERT, H.-W., Egyptology
FRANCO, E., Indology
GERTEL, J., Economy and Social Geography of the Middle East
GIRSHAUSEN, TH., Drama
HEEG, G., Drama
HEYDEMANN, G., Modern History
HÖPKEN, W., East and South-East European History
JONES, A., African History
KAPPEL, R., African Politics and Economy
KLOTZ, S., Systematic Musical Science
LANGE, B., History of Art
LOOS, H., Historical Music Science
MAREK, M., History of Art
MORITZ, R., Classical Sinology
PREISSLER, H., History of Middle Eastern Religions
RICHTER, S., Japanology
RIECKHOFF-HESSE, S., Prehistory and Early History
RIEKENBERG, M., Comparative History and Ibero-American History
RUDERSDORF, M., History of the Early Modern Era
SCHUBERT, CH., Classical History
SCHULZ, E., Arabic Linguistic and Translation Science
SCHULZ, F., Teaching of Art
SEIWERT, H., General and Comparative Religion
SÖRENSEN, P. K., Central Asian Studies
STRECK, B., Ethnology
STRECK, M., Ancient Near East

TOPFSTEDT, TH., History of Art
VON FRANZ, R., Modern Sinology
VON HEHL, U., Modern History
WOLFF, E., African Studies
ZÖLLNER, F., History of Art

Faculty of Law (Burgstr. 27, 04109 Leipzig; tel. (341) 9735100; e-mail simue@rz.uni-leipzig.de; internet www.uni-leipzig.de/~jura):

BECKER-EBERHARD, E., Civil Law and Civil Action Law
BERGER, CHR., Civil and Civil Trial Law, Copyright
BOEMKE, B., Civil and Industrial Law, Social Legislation
DEGENHART, C., Commercial, Environmental and Planning Law
DOLEZALEK, G., Civil Law
DRYGALA, T., Civil Law, Commercial, Social and Business Law
ENDERS, CHR., Public Law
GOERLICH, H., Public, Constitutional and Administrative Law
HÄUSER, F., Civil, Industrial and Banking Law
KAHLO, M., Criminal and Criminal Trial Law, Legal Philosophy
KERN, B.-R., Civil and Medical Law, History of Law
KLESCZEWSKI, D., Criminal Trial Law and European Criminal Law
KÖCK, W., Environmental Law
OLDIGES, M., Public Law
RAUSCHER, TH., Private International Law, Comparative and Civil Law
SCHUMANN, H., Criminal and Commercial Law
STADIE, M.-H., Tax Law and Public Law
WELTER, R., Civil Law, German and International Economic Law

Faculty of Mathematics and Computer Science (Augustuspl. 10–11, 04109 Leipzig; tel. (341) 9732100; e-mail matinf@mathematik.uni-leipzig.de; internet www.uni-leipzig.de/matinf):

BEYER, K., Applied Mathematics
BORNELEIT, P., Teaching of Mathematics
BREWKA, G., Intelligent Systems
FREY, R., Discrete Mathematics
FRITZSCHE, B., Probability Theory
GIRLICH, H.-J., Stochastics
GRUHN, V., Applied Telematics
GÜNTHER, M., Partial Differential Equations
HERRE, H., Formal Concepts of Computer Science
HERZOG, B., Principles of Mathematics, Logic, Theory of Numbers
HEYER, G., Natural Language Processing
HUBER-KLAWITTER, A., Theoretical Mathematics
IRMSCHER, K., Computer Networks and Split Systems
KEBSCHULL, U., Technical Information Technology
KIRSTEIN, B., Mathematical Statistics
KUNKEL, P., Numerical Mathematics and Scientific Computing
KÜRSTEN, K.-D., Operator Algebra
LUCKHAUS, ST., Mathematical Optimization
MIERSEMANN, E., Calculus of Variations
RADEMACHER, H.-B., Differential Geometry
RAHM, E., Databases
SCHMÜDGEN, K., Functional Analysis
SCHUMANN, R., Analysis
SCHWARZ, M., Mathematics in Science
STADLER, P., Bioinformatics
STÜCKRAD, J., Algebra
WOLLENBERG, M., Mathematical Physics

Faculty of Medicine (Liebigstr. 27, 04103 Leipzig; tel. (341) 9715930; e-mail teichh@medizin.uni-leipzig.de):

ADAM, H., Anaesthesiology and Intensive Therapy
ALEXANDER, H., Obstetrics and Gynaecology
ALLGAIER, C., Pharmacology and Toxicology
ANGERMEYER, M., Psychiatry
ARENDT, T., Neuroanatomy
ARNOLD, K., Medical Physics and Biophysics
ASMUSSEN, G., Physiology
BADER, A., Cell Biology
BAERWALD, C., Internal Medicine, Rheumatology
BAIER, D., Obstetrics and Gynaecology
BLATZ, R., Medical Microbiology
BÖHME, H.-J., Biochemistry
BRÄHLER, E., Medical Psychology
BÜHRDEL, P., Paediatrics
DANNHAUER, K.-H., Orthodontics
DECKERT, F., Diagnostic Radiology
DIETZ, A., Otorhinolaryngology
DONATH, E., Medical Physics and Biophysics
EICHFELD, U., Thorax Surgery
EILERS, J., Physiology
EMMRICH, P., Pathology
ENGELE, J., Anatomy, Embryology
ENGELMANN, L., Internal Medicine, Intensive Medicine
ESCHRICH, K., Biochemistry
ETTRICH, C., Child and Adolescent Psychiatry, Psychotherapy
FROSTER, U., Genetics
GEBHARDT, R., Biochemistry
GERTZ, H.-J., Psychiatry
GEYER, M., Psychosomatic Medicine and Psychotherapy
GLANDER, H.-J., Andrology
GRÄFE, H.-G., Paediatric Surgery
GRÜNDER, W., Medical Physics and Biophysics
GUMMERT, J. F., Cardiac Surgery
HÄNTZSCHEL, H., Internal Medicine, Rheumatology
HAUSS, J. P., Abdominal, Transplantation and Vascular Surgery
HEMPRICH, A., Maxillofacial Surgery
HENGSTLER, J., Molecular Toxicology
HERBARTH, O., Environmental Medicine
HIRSCH, W., Diagnostic Radiology
HÖCKEL, M., Obstetrics and Gynaecology
HORN, F., Molecular Immunology
HUMMELSHEIM, H., Neurology
ILLES, P., Pharmacology and Toxicology
JAKSTAT, H., Dental Prosthetics and Materials
JANOUSEK, J., Paediatric Cardiology
JASSOY, C., Molecular Virology
JENTSCH, H., Parodontology
JOSTEN, CH., Traumatology
KAHN, TH., Diagnostic Radiology
KÄSTNER, I., History of Medicine
KELLER, E., Paediatrics
KIESS, W., Paediatrics
KLEEMANN, W. J., Forensic Medicine
KLÖTZER, B., Surgery
KÖNIG, F., Anaesthesiology and Intensive Therapy
KÖNIG, H.-H., Health Economy
KÖRHOLZ, D., Paediatrics, Haematology and Oncology
KORTMANN, R.-D., Radiotherapy
KOSTELKA, M., Paediatrics, Cardiac Surgery
LIEBERT, U. G., Virology
LÖFFLER, M., Medical Informatics, Statistics and Epidemiology
MEIXENSBERGER, J., Neurosurgery
MERKENSCHLAGER, A., Paediatrics
MERTE, K., Restorative Dentistry
METZNER, G., Clinical Immunology, Allergology
MOHR, F.-W., Cardiac Surgery
MÖSSNER, J., Internal Medicine, Gastroenterology
MOTHES, TH., Clinical Chemistry
NIEDERWIESER, D., Internal Medicine, Haematology
NÖRENBERG, W., Pharmacology and Toxicology
OLTHOFF, D., Anaesthesiology and Intensive Therapy
PASCHKE, R., Internal Medicine, Endocrinology
PFÄFFLE, R., Paediatrics, Endocrinology, Gastroenterology
PFEIFFER, D., Internal Medicine, Cardiology
PLÖTTNER, G., Psychosomatic Medicine and Psychotherapy
PREISS, R., Clinical Pharmacology
REIBER, TH., Dental Prosthetics and Materials
REICHENBACH, A., Neurophysiology
RICHTER, V., Clinical Chemistry, Metabolic Disorders
RIEDEL-HELLER, S., Public Health
RIHA, O., History of Medicine
RODLOFF, A., Medical Microbiology
SABRI, O., Nuclear Medicine
SANDHOLZER, H., Internal Medicine
SCHELLENBERGER, W., Biochemistry
SCHMIDT, F., Diagnostic Radiology
SCHOBER, R., Neuropathology
SCHÖNEBERG, T., Biochemistry, Molecular Endocrinology
SCHREINICKE, G., Industrial Medicine
SCHUBERT, ST., Internal Medicine
SCHULER, G., Internal Medicine, Cardiology
SCHUSTER, V., Paediatrics
SCHWARZ, J., Neurology
SCHWARZ, R., Social Medicine
SCHWOKOWSKI, CH., Surgical Oncology
SEIBEL, P., Molecular Cell Therapy
SIMON, J.-C., Dermatology
SPANEL-BOROWSKI, K., Anatomy
STICHERLING, M., Dermatology
STUMWOLL, M., Internal Medicine, Gastroenterology, Hepatology
TANNAPFEL, A., Pathology
THIERY, J., Laboratory Medicine
TILLMANN, H.-L., Internal Medicine, Gastroenterology and Hepatology
TREIDE, A., Child Dentistry
VON CRAMON, Y., Cognitive Neurology
VON SALIS-SOGLIO, G., Orthopaedics
WAGNER, A., Neurology
WIEDEMANN, P., Ophthalmology
WILD, H. A., Paediatric Orthopaedics
WINTER, A., Medical Informatics
WIRTZ, H., Internal Medicine, Pulmology
WITTEKIND, C., Pathology, Immunopathology
ZIMMER, H.-G., Physiology

Faculty of Philology (Beethovenstr. 15, 04107 Leipzig; tel. (341) 9737300; e-mail dekphilo@uni-leipzig.de; internet www.uni-leipzig.de/~philol):

BARZ, I., Contemporary German Linguistics and Lexicology
BAUMANN, K., Applied Linguistics/LSP Communication (English, Russian, German)
BICKEL, B., Linguistic Typology and Diversity
DE TORO, A., Romance Literature
DEUFERT, M., Classical Philology and Latin Literature
EILERT, H., Modern German Literature
FELTEN, U., French and Italian Literature
FIX, U., Contemporary German Linguistics
GÄRTNER, E., Romance Linguistics
GOTTZMANN, C., Old German Literature
HARRESS, B., Slavic Literature and Cultural History
HINRICHS, U., Southern Slavic Linguistics and Translation Science
HOFFMANN-MAXIS, A., General and Comparative Literature and Literary Theory

KEIL, H., North American Cultural History
KOENEN, A., American Literature
LÖRSCHER, W., English Linguistics
MEIER, B., Teaching of German
MÜLLER, G., General Linguistics
NASSEN, U., Children's Literature and Juvenile Literature
ÖHLSCHLÄGER, G., German Linguistics
PECHMANN, TH., Psycholinguistics
POLLNER, C., English Linguistics
RITZER, M., Modern German Literature
RYTEL-KUC, D., West Slavic Linguistics
SCHENKEL, E., English Literature
SCHMITT, A. P., Linguistics and Translation Studies (English)
SCHWARZ, W., Literature and Cultural History of the Western Slavs
SCHWEND, J., Cultural Studies (Great Britain)
SIER, K., Classical Philology and Greek Literature
STOCKINGER, L., Modern German Literature
TSCHIRNER, E., German as a Foreign Language
UDOLPH, J., Onomastic Science
WERNER, E., Serbian Studies
WIESE, I., Contemporary German Linguistics
WOTJAK, B., German as a Foreign Language, Lexicology of Contemporary German Linguistics
WOTJAK, G., Romance Linguistics and Translation Science (Spanish and French)
ZYBATOW, G., Slavic Linguistics

Faculty of Physics and Earth Sciences (Linnéstr. 5, 04103 Leipzig; tel. (341) 9732400; e-mail dekan@physik.uni-leipzig.de):

BUTZ, T., Experimental Physics
EHRMANN, W., Geology
ESQUINAZI, P. D., Experimental Physics
FREUDE, D., Chemical Physics
GLÄSSER, W., Geology, Hydrogeology
GRILL, W., Experimental Physics
GRUNDMANN, M., Experimental Physics
HEINRICH, J., Physical Geography and Landscape-based Environmental Research
HEINTZENBERG, J., Atmospheric Physics
HERRMANN, H., Chemistry of the Atmosphere
IHLE, D., Theoretical Physics
JACOBI, CHR., Meteorology
JACOBS, F., Geophysics
JANKE, W., Theoretical Physics
KÄRGER, J., Experimental Physics
KÄS, J., Experimental Physics
KIRSTEIN, W., Geography and Geoinformatics
KORN, M., Theoretical Geophysics
KREMER, F., Experimental Physics
KROY, K.-D., Theoretical Physics
LENTZ, S., Regional Geography
LÖSCHE, M., Experimental Physics
MELLES, M., Geology
METZ, W., Theoretical Meteorology
OEHME, W., Teaching of Physics
RAUSCHENBACH, B., Applied Physics
RENNER, E., Modelling of Atmospheric Processes
RUDOLPH, G., Theoretical Physics
SALMHOFER, M., Theoretical Physics
SIBOLD, K., Theoretical Physics
TETZLAFF, G., Meteorology
WEILAND, U., Urban Ecology
WIESSNER, R., Anthropogeography, Economic Geography and the Labour Market

Faculty of Social Sciences and Philosophy (Burgstr. 21, 04109 Leipzig; tel. (341) 9735600; e-mail foerster@rz.uni-leipzig.de):

BARTELBORTH, TH., Philosophy of Science
BENTELE, G., Public Relations
ELSENHANS, H., Political Science and International Politics
FACH, W., Political Theory
FENNER, C., Comparative Politics
FLAM, H., Sociology
FRÜH, W., Empirical Communications and Media Research
GIESEN, K.-G., International Politics
GOTTWALD, S., Logic
HALLER, M., Journalism and Media Science
HUBER, M., International Politics
KALTER, F., Sociology
KÖHNKE, K., Theory and Philosophy of Culture
KUTSCH, A., Historical and Systematic Communication Studies
LÜBBE, W., Philosophy
MACHILL, M., Journalism and Media Science
MEGGLE, G., Philosophy
MEUSCHEL, S., Political Systems
MÜHLER, K., Sociology
SCHORB, B., Teaching of Media Studies, Further Education
SIEGRIST, H., Comparative History of Modern Europe
STEINMETZ, R., Media and Media Culture
STEKELER-WEITHOFER, P., Philosophy
STIEHLER, H.-J., Empirical Communications and Media Research
VOBRUBA, G., Sociology
VOSS, T., Sociology

Faculty of Sports Science (Jahnallee 59, 04109 Leipzig; tel. (341) 9731600; e-mail spodekan@rz.uni-leipzig.de; internet www.uni-leipzig.de/~sportfak):

ALFERMANN, D., Psychology of Sport
BUSSE, M., Sports Medicine
INNENMOSER, J., Sports Therapy, Sport for Handicapped People
KRUG, J., General Movement and Training Science

Faculty of Theology (Otto-Schill-Str. 2, 04109 Leipzig; tel. (341) 9735400; e-mail dekanat@theologie.uni-leipzig.de; internet www.uni-leipzig.de/~theolweb):

BERLEJUNG, A., Old Testament
FITSCHEN, K., Church History
HANISCH, H., Religious Education
HERZER, J., New Testament
LUX, R., Old Testament
PETZOLDT, M., Principles of Theology, Hermeneutics
PETZOLDT, M., Systematic Theology
RATZMANN, W., Practical Theology
SCHNEIDER, G., Systematic Theology
SCHRÖTER, J., New Testament
WARTENBERG, G., Church History
WOHLRAB-SAHR, M., Religious and Church Sociology

Faculty of Veterinary Medicine (An den Tierkliniken 19, 04103 Leipzig; tel. (341) 9738000; e-mail dekanat@vetmed.uni-leipzig.de):

ALBER, G., Immunology
BLESSING, M., Molecular Pathogenesis
BRAUN, R., Milk Hygiene
DAUGSCHIES, A., Parasitology
EDINGER, J., Orthopaedics
EINSPANIER, A., Endocrinology
FEHLHABER, K., Food Hygiene and Consumer Protection
FERGUSON, J., Large-Animal Surgery
FUHRMANN, H., Physiological Chemistry
GÄBEL, G., Physiology
GREVEL, V., Small-Animal Surgery
KRAUTWALD-JUNGHANNS, M.-E., Bird Diseases
KRÜGER, M., Bacteriology and Mycology
LÜCKER, E., Meat Hygiene
MÜLLER, H., Virology
OECHTERING, G., Small-Animal Medicine
SALOMON, F.-V., Anatomy
SCHOON, H.-A., Histopathology and Clinical Pathology
SCHUSSER, G., Large-Animal Medicine
SEEGER, J., Histology and Embryology
SOBIRAJ, A., Obstetrics and Gynaecology
TRUYEN, U., Epidemiology
UNGEMACH, F. R., Pharmacology and Pharmacy

ATTACHED RESEARCH INSTITUTE

Institute of German Literature: Wächterstr. 34, 04107 Leipzig; tel. (341) 9730300; e-mail kahl@uni-leipzig.de; internet www.uni-leipzig.de/dll

PROFESSORS

HASLINGER, J., Literary Aesthetics
TREICHEL, H.-U., German Literature

UNIVERSITÄT MANNHEIM
(University of Mannheim)

Schloss, 68131 Mannheim
Telephone: (621) 1812222
E-mail: info@uni-mannheim.de
Internet: www.uni-mannheim.de

Founded 1907 as Städtische Handelshochschule, attached to Heidelberg Univ. 1933, reopened as Wirtschaftshochschule 1946, univ. status 1967
Languages of instruction: German, English
Academic year: April to February

Rector: Prof. Dr ERNST-LUDWIG VON THADDEN
Pro-Rector: Prof. Dr EVA ECKKRAMMER
Pro-Rector: Prof. Dr THORSTEN MEISER
Pro-Rector: Prof. Dr THOMAS PUHL
Chancellor: Dr SUSANN-ANNETTE STORM
Librarian: CHRISTIAN BENZ

Library: see under Libraries and Archives
Number of teachers: 140
Number of students: 11,500

DEANS

Business School: Dr JÜRGEN M. SCHNEIDER
School of Humanities: Prof. Dr ANNETTE KEHNEL
School of Law and Economics: Prof. Dr GEORG BITTER
School of Mathematics and Information Sciences: Prof. Dr HEINZ JÜRGEN MÜLLER
School of Social Sciences: Prof. Dr MICHAEL DIEHL

UNIVERSITÄT OSNABRÜCK

POB 44 69, 49069 Osnabrück
Neuer Graben/Schloss, 49074 Osnabrueck
Telephone: (541) 9690
E-mail: pressestelle@uni-osnabrueck.de
Internet: www.uni-osnabrueck.de

Founded 1973
Languages of instruction: German, English
Academic year: October to September

Pres.: Prof. Dr WOLFGANG LUECKE
Vice-Pres. for Budget and Human Resources: Prof. Dr WILFRIED HÖTKER
Vice-Pres. for Research and Graduate Student Devt: Prof. Dr MAY-BRITT KALLENRODE
Vice-Pres. for Study and Teaching: Prof. Dr JOACHIM HAERTLING
Registrar: Dr UWE SIELEMAN
Librarian: FELICITAS HUNDHAUSEN

Number of teachers: 500
Number of students: 11,500

Publication: *Universitätszeitung* (6 a year)

DEANS

Faculty of Biology and Chemistry: Prof. Dr ROLAND BRANDT
Faculty of Culture and Geography: Prof. Dr HELEN KORIATH
Faculty of Economics: Prof. Dr THOMAS GAUBE

Faculty of Education and Cultural Studies: Prof. Dr Dietrich Helms
Faculty of Human Sciences: Prof. Dr Kai-Uwe Kühnberger
Faculty of Language and Literature: Prof. Dr Peter Schneck
Faculty of Law: Prof. Dr Arndt Sinn
Faculty of Mathematics and Information Science: Norbert de Lange
Faculty of Physics: Prof. Dr Philipp Maass
Faculty of Social Sciences: Prof. Dr Ulrich Schneckener

UNIVERSITÄT PADERBORN

Warburger Str. 100, 33098 Paderborn
Telephone: (5251) 600
E-mail: pressestelle@zv.uni-paderborn.de
Internet: www.uni-paderborn.de

Founded 1972
State control
Language of instruction: German
Academic year: October to July

Pres.: Prof. Dr Nikolaus Risch
Vice-Pres.: Prof. Dr Bernd Frick
Vice-Pres.: Prof. Dr Dorothee M. Meister
Vice-Pres.: Prof. Dr Wilhelm Schäfer
Chancellor: Dr Jürgen Plato
Library Dir: Dr Dietmar Haubfleisch

Library of 1,700,000 vols, 1,500 periodicals
Number of teachers: 1,350
Number of students: 14,769

Publications: *Forschungsforum* (1 a year), *Paderborner Universitätsreden* (irregular), *Paderborner Universitätszeitung* (2 a year)

DEANS

Faculty of Arts and Humanities: Prof. Dr Volker Peckhaus
Faculty of Business Administration and Economics: Prof. Dr Peter F. E. Sloane
Faculty of Computer Science, Electrical Engineering and Mathematics: Prof. Dr Franz Josef Rammig
Faculty of Cultural Studies: Prof. Dr Franz Göttmann
Faculty of Mechanical Engineering: Prof. Dr Detmar Zimmer
Faculty of Science: Prof. Dr Hans-Joachim Warnecke

PROFESSORS

Faculty of Arts and Humanities:

Allkemper, A.
Arnold, R.
Autsch, S.
Bauer, G.
Beder, J.
Brauerhoch, A.
Bublitz, H.
Burrichter, R.
Cortiel, J.
Ecker, G.
Eckhardt, J.
Ehland, C.
Eke, N.
Englisch, B.
Feldbusch, E.
Freitag, C.
Gembris, H.
Göttmann, F.
Grotjahn, R.
Hagengruber, R.
Herzig, B.
Hofmann, M.
Hornák, S.
Jacke, C.
Kamp, H.
Keil, W.
Klenke, D.
Koelle, L.
Kolhoff-Kahl, I.
Krettenauer, T.
Kuhlmann, H.
Kürtz, A.
Lang, B.
Langenbacher-Liebgott, J.
Laubenthal, A.
Lemke, I.
Leutzsch, M.
Marx, N.
Meister, D.
Müller, S.
Müller-Lietzkow, J.
Öhlschläger, C.
Peckhaus, V.
Pienemann, M.
Rendtorff, B.
Ribbat, C.
Schaper, N.
Scharlau, I.
Schmitz, S.
Schroeter-Wittke, H.
Schuster, B.
Seng, E.
Söll, F.
Steinecke, A.
Ströter-Bender, J.
Strotmann, A.
Strube, M.
Süßmann, J.
Tönnies, M.
Tophinke, D.
von Stosch, K.
Wilk, N.
Winkler, H.
Zielke, G.

Faculty of Business Administration and Economics:

Barton, D.
Betz, S.
Beutner, M.
Dangelmaier, W.
Diller, M.
Eggert, A.
Eggert, W.
Fahr, R.
Feng, Y.
Fischer, J.
Frick, B.
Gilroy, B.
Gries, T.
Haake, C.
Hogreve, J.
Iseke, A.
Kliewer, N.
Koberstein, A.
Kremer, H.
Krieger, T.
Krimphove, D.
Kundisch, D.
Löffler, A.
Müller, J.
Rosenthal, K.
Schiller, B.
Schneider, G.
Schneider, M.
Sloane, P.
Suhl, L.
Sureth, C.
Werner, T.

Faculty of Computer Science, Electrical Engineering and Mathematics:

Belli, F.
Bender, P.
Blömer, J.
Böttcher, S.
Brinkmann, A.
Bruns, M.
Bürgisser, P.
Dellnitz, M.
Dietz, H.
Domik-Kienegger, B.
Engels, G.
Gausch, F.
Häb-Umbach, R.
Hansen, S.
Hauenschild, W.
Henning, B.
Hilleringmann, U.
Kastens, U.
Keil, R.
Kleine, B.
Köckler, N.
Magenheim, J.
Meyer, F.
Noé, R.
Rammig, F.
Rinkens, H.

Faculty of Mechanical Engineering:

Gausemeier, J.
Homberg, W.
Kenig, E.
Koch, R.
Mahnken, R.
Maier, H.
Moritzer, E.
Richard, H.
Schmid, H.
Schöppner, V.
Sextro, W.
Trächtler, A.
Tröster, T.
Vrabec, J.
Zimmer, D.

Faculty of Science:

Becker, H.
Brandl-Bredenbeck, H.
Bremser, W.
Fels, G.
Grundmeier, G.
Henkel, G.
Heseker, H.
Huber, K.
Kitzerow, H.
Kuckling, D.
Lindner, J.
Lischka, K.
Meier, C.
Meier, T.
Olivier, N.
Reinhold, P.
Risch, N.
Schindlmayr, A.
Schlegel-Matthies, K.
Schmidt, C.
Schmidt, W.
Schubert, V.
Sohler, W.
Warnecke, H.
Weiß, M.
Zrenner, A.

UNIVERSITÄT PASSAU

Innstr. 41, 94032 Passau
Telephone: (851) 5090
E-mail: info@uni-passau.de
Internet: www.uni-passau.de

Founded 1973
State control
Languages of instruction: English, German
Academic year: October to September

Pres.: Prof. Dr Burkhard Freitag
Vice-Pres. for Int. Relations: Prof. Ursula Reutner
Vice-Pres. for Research: Prof. Harry Haupt
Vice-Pres. for Teaching and Study: Prof. Dr Rainer Wernsmann
Head of Admin.: Dr Andrea Bör
Dir for Library Services: Dr Steffen Wawra

Library: see under Libraries and Archives
Number of teachers: 820
Number of students: 11,316

DEANS

Faculty of Arts and Humanities: Prof. Dr Daniela Wawra
Faculty of Business Administration and Economics: Prof. Dr Carola Jungwirth
Faculty of Computer Science and Mathematics: Prof. Dr Ilia Polian
Faculty of Law: Prof. Dr Dennis Solomon

PROFESSORS

Department of Catholic Theology (94030 Passau; tel. (851) 5092001; internet www.ktf.uni-passau.de):

FONK, P., Theological Ethics
LANDERSDORFER, A., Ecclesiastical History
MENDL, J., Religious Education
SCHWANKL, O., Exegesis and Biblical Theology
STINGLHAMMER, H., Dogmatics and Fundamental Theology

Faculty of Arts and Humanities (94030 Passau; tel. (851) 5092601; e-mail dekanat.phil@uni-passau.de; internet www.phil.uni-passau.de):

ANHUF, D., Physical Geography
BACH, M., Sociology
BARBATO, M., International Politics
BARMEYER, C., Intercultural Communication
BERNERT, W., Didadactics of Teaching Social Studies
BRANDL, M., Mathematics Didactics
DECKER, J.-O., Modern German Literature and Media Semiotics
ERKENS, F., Medieval History
FITZ, K., American Studies
GAMERITH, W., Regional Geography
GELLNER, W., Political Science
GLAS, A., Art and Aesthetic Education
GÖLER, D., Jean Monnet Chair for European Politics
GRÖTECKE, I. E., Art History and Visual Culture Studies
HAHN, O., Journalism
HARNISCH, R., German Philology
HARTWIG, S., Romanic Literature and Culture
HEINRICH, H., Methods of Empirical Social Research
HESSE, B., English Cultural and Media Studies
HINZ, M., Romance Area and Literary Studies with a Focus on Italy
HOHLFELD, R., Communication Studies
KAMM, J., English Literature and Culture
KNIEPER, T., Computer-Mediated Communication
KORFF, R., Southeast Asian Studies
KRAH, H., German Literature and Film
KRAUS, H.-CH., Modern and Contemporary History
LISKE, M.-TH., Philosophy
MÄGDEFRAU, J., Secondary Education (Realschule)
MICHLER, A., History Didactics
MOGEL, H., Psychology
MÜLLER, K., German Literature and Language Education
NARCISS, S., Psychology II
NOLTE, T., Medieval German Literature
PADMANABHAN, M., Comparative Development and Cultural Studies with a focus on Southeast Asia
PISSAREK, M., German Literature and Language Education
POLLAK, G., General Pedagogy
REHBEIN, M., Digital Humanities
REUTNER, U., Romance Languages and Cultures
SCHELLBERG, G., Music Education II
SCHENZ, C., Education/Primary and Pre-Primary Education
SEIBERT, N., School Pedagogy
STAHL, B., International Politics
STAMPFL, I., Music Education I
STOLL, O., Ancient History
STRUCK, E., Human Geography
THIES, C., Philosophy
UFFELMANN, D., Slavic Literature and Cultures
VAN GISTEREN, L., Developmental Psychology
URHAHNE, D., Educational Psychology
WALTER, K., Romance Area and Literary Studies with a focus on France
WAWRA, D., English Language and Culture
WÜNSCH, T., Modern History of Eastern Europe and its Cultures
ZEHNPFENNING, B., Political Theory and History of Ideas

Faculty of Business Administration and Economics (94030 Passau; tel. (851) 5092401; e-mail dekanat@wiwi.uni-passau.de; internet www.wiwi.uni-passau.de):

BAUERNSCHUSTER, S., Economic Policy
DILLER, M., Tax Management
ENTROP, O., Banking and Finance
FIEDLER, M., Management, People and Information
GRIMM, M., Development Economics
HÄUSSLER, C., Organization, Technology Management and Entrepreneurship
HAUPT, H., Statistics
JUNGWIRTH, C., International Management
KLEINSCHMIDT, P., Information Systems I
KÖNIG, A., Technology, Innovation and Entrepreneurship
KRÄMER, J., Internet Business
KRAUTHEIM, S., International Economics
LAMBSDORFF, J. G., Economic Policy
LEHNER, F., Information Systems II
MÖLLER, M., Accountancy and Auditing
OBERMAIER, R., Accounting and Control
SCHOLZ, M., Information Systems with a focus on Electronic Commerce
SCHUMANN, J. H., Marketing and Innovation
TOTZEK, D., Marketing and Services
WAGNER, N., Finance and Control
ZIEGLER, H., Production and Logistics

Faculty of Computer Science and Mathematics (94030 Passau; tel. (851) 5093001; e-mail dekanat@fim.uni-passau.de; internet www.fim.uni-passau.de):

AMFT, O., Sensor Technology
APEL, S., Software Product Lines
BEYER, D., Software Systems
BRANDENBURG, F.-J., Theoretical Computer Science
DE MEER, H., Computer Networks and Computer Communications
FORSTER-HEINLEIN, B., Applied Mathematics
GRANITZER, M., Media Computer Science
KAISER, T., Mathematics
KOSCH, H., Distributed Information Systems
KRANZ, M., Embedded Systems
KREUZER, M., Symbolic Computation
LENGAUER, CH., Programming
MOOSMÜLLER, G., Statistics Teaching Unit
MÜLLER-GRONBACH, T., Stochastics and its Applications
POLIAN, I., Computer Engineering
POSEGGA, J., IT Security
REISER, H., Assistant Security in Information Systems
RÜFFER, B., Dynamic Systems
SAUER, T., Digital Image Processing
SCHENKEL, R., Information Management
SCHWARTZ, N., Algebraic Geometry
WIRTH, F., Dynamic Systems

Faculty of Law (94030 Passau; tel. (851) 5092201; e-mail dekanat.jura@uni-passau.de; internet www.jura.uni-passau.de):

ALTMEPPEN, H., Civil Law, Commercial and Business Law
BAYREUTHER, F., Civil Law and Labour Law
BUNG, J., Criminal Law and Procedure, Criminology and Philosophy of Law
DEDERER, H.-G., Constitutional and Administrative Law, Public International Law, European and International Economic Law
ENGLÄNDER, A., Criminal Law and Criminal Procedure
ESSER, R., German, European and International Criminal Law, Criminal Procedure and White-Collar Crime
FEDTKE, J. M., Common Law
HAU, W., Civil Law, Civil Procedure, Private International Law
HECKMANN, D., Public Law, Security Law and Internet Law
HERRMANN, C., Constitutional and Administrative, European Law, European and International Economic Law
HORNUNG, G., Public Law, IT Law and Legal Informatics
KRAMER, U., Public Law
KUHN, T., Civil Law
MÜSSIG, U., Civil Law, German and European Legal History
POELZIG, M., Civil Law, German and International Business Law
PUTZKE, H., Penal Law
RIEHM, T., Civil Law and Procedure
SCHLINKER, S., Civil Law, German and European Legal History
SOLOMON, D., Civil Law, Private International Law and Comparative Law
VON LEWINSKI, K., Public Law, IT Law and Legal Informatics
WERNSMANN, R., Constitutional, Administrative, Public Finance and Tax Law

UNIVERSITÄT POTSDAM

POB 60 15 53, 14415 Potsdam
Am Neuen Palais 10, 14469 Potsdam
Telephone: (331) 9770
E-mail: presse@uni-potsdam.de
Internet: www.uni-potsdam.de

Founded 1991
Languages of instruction: German, English
Academic year: October to September

Pres.: Dr THOMAS GRÜNEWALD (acting)
Vice-Rector for Int. Affairs and Strategic Devt: Prof. Dr RIA DE BLESER
Vice-Rector for Research and Young Academics: Prof. Dr BERND WALZ
Vice-Rector for Scientific and Technology Transfer and Innovation: Prof. Dr DIETER WAGNER
Vice-Rector for Teaching and Study: Dr THOMAS GRÜNEWALD
Dir for Library: Dr ULRIKE MICHALOWSKY

Library: 1.3m. vols, 2,850 print journals, 8,000 ejournals
Number of teachers: 226 professors, 923 other academic staff
Number of students: 20,000

DEANS

Faculty of Economic and Social Sciences: Prof. Dr KLAUS H. GOETZ
Faculty of Human Sciences: Prof. Dr RIA DE BLESER
Faculty of Law: Prof. Dr HARTMUT BAUER
Faculty of Mathematics and Natural Sciences: Prof. Dr REIMUND GERHARD
Faculty of Philosophy: Prof. Dr JOHANN EV. HAFNER

UNIVERSITÄT REGENSBURG

93040 Regensburg
Universitätsstr. 31, 93053 Regensburg
Telephone: (941) 94301
E-mail: kontakt@ur.de
Internet: www.uni-regensburg.de

Founded 1962
State control
Languages of instruction: English, German
Academic year: October to September

Pres.: Prof. Dr UDO HEBEL
Vice-Pres.: Prof. Dr NIKOLAUS KORBER
Vice-Pres.: Prof. Dr CHRISTOPH WAGNER
Vice-Pres.: Prof. Dr BERNHARD WEBER
Head of Admin.: Dr CHRISTIAN BLOMEYER

Dir of Univ. Library: Dr RAFAEL BALL
Library: see under Libraries and Archives
Number of teachers: 2,637
Number of students: 21,174
Publications: *Anwendungsorientierte Forschung, Blick in die Wissenschaft* (online), *Research Report*

DEANS

Faculty of Biology and Pre-Clinical Medicine: Prof. Dr ERNST TAMM
Faculty of Business, Economics and Management Information Systems: Prof. Dr MICHAEL DOWLING
Faculty of Catholic Theology: Prof. Dr HARALD BUCHINGER
Faculty of Chemistry and Pharmacy: Prof. Dr BURKHARD KÖNIG
Faculty of Languages, Literature and Cultural Studies: Prof. Dr JOCHEN MECKE
Faculty of Law: Prof. Dr TONIO WALTER
Faculty of Mathematics: Prof. Dr ULRICH BUNKE
Faculty of Medicine: Prof. Dr TORSTEN REICHERT
Faculty of Philosophy, Fine Arts, History and Humanities: Prof. Dr CHRISTIAN KUNZE
Faculty of Physics: Prof. Dr ANDREAS SCHÄFER
Faculty of Psychology, Educational Sciences and Physical Education: Prof. Dr PETER FISCHER

UNIVERSITÄT ROSTOCK

18051 Rostock
Ulmenstr. 69, Bldg 3, 18057 Rostock
Telephone: (381) 4980
E-mail: rektor@uni-rostock.de
Internet: www.uni-rostock.de
Founded 1419
State control
Academic year: October to September
Rector: Prof. Dr WOLFGANG SCHARECK
Vice-Rector for Research and Research Education: Prof. Dr URSULA VAN RIENEN
Vice-Rector for Student Affairs: HEIKO MARSKI
Vice-Rector for Study, Education and Evaluation: Prof. Dr STEFAN GÖBEL
Chancellor: Dr MATHIAS NEUKIRCHEN
Library Dir: RENATE BÄHKER
Library: see under Libraries and Archives
Number of teachers: 1,364
Number of students: 15,138
Publications: *Archiv der Freunde der Naturgeschichte in Mecklenburg, Erziehungswissenschaftliche Beiträge, Forschungsbericht der Universität Rostock, Pädagogisches Handeln, Rostocker Agrar- und Umweltwissenschaftliche Beiträge, Rostocker Arbeitspapiere zu Rechnungswesen und Controlling, Rostocker Arbeitspapiere zu Wirtschaftsentwicklung und Human Resource Development, Rostocker Beiträge zur Deutschen und Europäischen Geschichte, Rostocker Beiträge zur Regional- und Strukturforschung, Rostocker Beiträge zur Sprachwissenschaft, Rostocker Beitrage zur Verkehrswissenschaft und Logistik, Rostocker Forum Theologie, Rostocker Informatik-Berichte, Rostocker Informationen zu Politik und Verwaltung, Rostocker Materialen für Landschaftsplanung und Raumentwicklung, Rostocker Mathematisches Kolloquium, Rostocker Medizinische Beiträge, Rostocker Meeresbiologische Beiträge, Rostocker Philosophische Manuskripte, Rostocker Schriften zur Bank und Finanzmarktforschung, Rostocker Schriften zum Bankrecht, Rostocker Studien zur Kulturwissenschaft, Schiffbauforschung, Thunen-Reihe Angewandter Volkswirtschftstheorie*, and various faculty publs

DEANS

Faculty of Agricultural and Environmental Science: Prof. Dr ELMAR MOHR
Faculty of Computer Science and Electrical Engineering: Prof. Dr Ing. Hab. BERNHARD LAMPE
Faculty of Economic and Social Sciences: Prof. Dr SUSANNE HOMÖLLE
Faculty of Law: Prof. Dr JÖRG BENEDICT
Faculty of Mathematics and Natural Sciences: Prof. Dr CHRISTOPH SCHICK
Faculty of Mechanical Engineering and Marine Technology: Prof. Dr Ing. Hab. EGON HASSEL
Faculty of Medicine: Prof. Dr EMIL CHRISTIAN REISINGER
Faculty of Philosophy: Prof. Dr HANS-JÜRGEN VON WENSIERSKI
Faculty of Theology: Prof. Dr MARTINA KUMLEHN

UNIVERSITÄT SIEGEN
(University of Siegen)

57068 Siegen
Herrengarten 3, 57068 Siegen
Telephone: (271) 7400
E-mail: rektor@uni-siegen.de
Internet: www.uni-siegen.de
Founded 1972
State control
Academic year: October to July (2 semesters)
Rector: Prof. Dr HOLGER BURCKHART
Vice-Rector: Prof. Dr FRANZ-JOSEF KLEIN
Vice-Rector: Prof. Dr HANNA SCHRAMM-KLEIN
Vice-Rector: Prof. Dr PETER HARING BOLIVAR
Vice-Rector: Prof. Dr THOMAS MANNEL
Chancellor: ULF RICHTER
Librarian: WERNER REINHARDT
Library of 1,234,833 vols
Number of teachers: 882
Number of students: 14,036
Publications: *Diagonal, LiLi—Zeitschrift für Literaturwissenschaft und Linguistik, MuK—Massenmedien und Kommunikation, Navigationen, Reihe Medienwissenschaften, Reihe Siegen*, Research Report, *Siegen: Sozial* (2 a year), *Siegener Hochschulzeitung, Siegener Pädagogische Studien, SPIEL* (2 a year)

DEANS

Faculty of Arts: Prof. Dr PETRA M. VOGEL
Faculty of Business Economics, Business IT and Commercial Law: Prof. Dr VOLKER WULF
Faculty of Education, Architecture, Arts: Prof. Dr Ing. HILDEGARD SCHRÖTELER-VON BRANDT
Faculty of Science and Technology: Prof. Dr ULLRICH PIETSCH

UNIVERSITÄT STUTTGART
(University of Stuttgart)

POB 10 60 37, 70049 Stuttgart
Telephone: (711) 6850
E-mail: poststelle@uni-stuttgart.de
Internet: www.uni-stuttgart.de
Founded 1829 as Gewerbeschule, univ. status 1967
State control
Language of instruction: English
Academic year: October to September
Rector: Prof. Dr-Ing. WOLFRAM RESSEL
Vice-Rector for Org.: Prof. Dr-Ing. MANFRED BERROTH
Vice-Rector for Academic Affairs and Continuing Education: Prof. Dr FRANK GIEßELMANN
Vice-Rector for Research and Technology: Prof. Dr SABINE LASCHAT
Registrar: BETTINA BUHLMANN
Chief Librarian: W. STEPHAN
Library: see under Libraries and Archives
Number of teachers: 2,750
Number of students: 20,000
Publications: *alumniNews, Mediendienst Forschung, Themenheft Forschung, Uni-Kurier* (2 a year)

DEANS

Aerospace Engineering and Geodesy: Prof. Dr Ing. ALFRED KLEUSBERG
Architecture and Urban Planning: Prof. Ing. ARNO LEDERER
Chemistry: Prof. Dr HANS-JOACHIM WERNER
Civil and Environmental Engineering: Prof. Dr Ing. ULLRICH MARTIN
Computer Science, Electrical Engineering and Information Technology: Prof. Dr Ing. JOACHIM SPEIDEL
Energy Technology, Process Engineering and Biological Engineering: Prof. Dr Ing. MICHAEL SCHMIDT
Engineering Design, Production Engineering and Automotive Engineering: Prof. Dr Ing. OLIVER SAWODNY
Humanities: Prof. Dr PETER SCHOLZ
Management, Economics and Social Sciences: Prof. Dr FRANK C. ENGLMANN
Mathematics and Physics: Prof. Dr RICHARD DIPPER

PROFESSORS

Aerospace Engineering and Geodesy (Universitätsbereich Vaihingen, Pfaffenwaldring 27, Zi.02, Stuttgart; tel. (711) 6852400; e-mail dekanat@f06.uni-stuttgart.de; internet www.f06.uni-stuttgart.de):

AUWETER-KURTZ, M., Space Transportation Technology
DRECHSLER, K., Aircraft Construction
FRITSCH, D., Photogrammetry and Land Surveying
GRAFAREND, E. W., Geodetic Science
KELLER, W., Physical Geodetic Science
KLEUSBERG, A., Navigation
KRÄMER, E., Aerodynamics
KRÖPLIN, B.-H., Statics and Dynamics of Aerospace Structures
KÜHN, M., Aerodynamics
MÖHLENBRINK, W., Aviation Telemetry
MUNZ, C.-D., Air and Gas Dynamics
REICHEL, R., Aviation Systems
RÖSER, H.-P., Space Systems
STAUDACHER, S., Turbojet Engines
VOIT-NITSCHMANN, R., Aircraft Construction
VON WOLFERSDORF, J., Aerospace Thermodynamics
WAGNER, S., Air and Gas Dynamics
WEIGAND, B., Aerospace Thermodynamics
WELL, K. H., Guidance and Control of Aerospace Vehicles
WOLF, D., Theory and Modelling of Geodetic Systems

Architecture and Urban Planning (Universitätsbereich Stadtmitte, Keplerstr. 11, 70714 Stuttgart; tel. (711) 1213223; e-mail dekanat@f01.uni-stuttgart.de; internet www.architektur.uni-stuttgart.de):

ADAM, J., Design and Construction
BEHLING, S., Building Construction and Design
BOTT, H., City Planning and Urban Design
CHERET, P., Building Construction and Design
DE BRUYN, G., Theory of Architecture and Design
EISENBIEGLER, G., Structures and Constructional Design
ERTEL, H., Building Materials, Building Physics, Mechanical Equipment

HARLANDER, T., Housing and Design
HERRMANN, D., Building Materials, Building Physics, Mechanical Equipment
HÜBNER, P., Building Construction and Design
JESSEN, J., City and Regional Planning
JOCHER, T., Housing and Design
KAULE, G., Landscape Planning and Ecology
KIMPEL, D., History of Architecture
KNIPPERS, J., Structures and Constructional Design
KNOLL, W., Drawing, Drafting and Modelling
MORO, J. L., Planning and Construction of High-Rise Buildings
PESCH, F., City Planning and Urban Design
PODREKA, B., Interior Design and Architectural Design
RIBBECK, E., Planning and Building Development
SCHÖNWANDT, W., Foundations of Planning
SCHÜRMANN, P., Building Materials, Building Physics, Mechanical Equipment
SOBEK, W., Lightweight Structures and Conceptual Design
TRAUB, H., Drawing, Drafting and Modelling
ULLMANN, F., Interior Design and Architectural Design

Biological and Geosciences (Universitätsbereich Vaihingen, Herdweg 51, 70174 Stuttgart; tel. (711) 1211334; e-mail dekanat@g04.uni-stuttgart.de; internet www.uni-stuttgart.de/geowissenschaft):

BLÜMEL, W. D., Geography
GAEBE, W., Cultural Geography
GHOSH, R., Bioenergetics
GOERTZ, H. D., Zoology
HEYER, A., Botany
JESKE, H., Molecular Biology and Virology of Plants
KELLER, P., Mineralogy and Crystal Chemistry
MASSONNE, H.-J., Mineralogy and Crystal Chemistry
MATTES, R., Industrial Genetics
MUTTI, M., Geology and Palaeontology
NUßBERGER, S., Biophysics
PFIZENMAIER, K., Cell Biology and Immunology
SCHEURICH, P., Molecular Immunology
SCHNEIDER, G., Geophysics
SEUFERT, W., Industrial Genetics
SEYFRIED, H., Geology and Palaeontology
SPRENGER, G., Microbiology
WIELANDT, E., Geophysics
WOLF, D. H., Biochemistry
WOLLNIK, F., Animal Physiology

Chemistry (Universitätsbereich Vaihingen, Pfaffenwaldring 55, 7.OG, Stuttgart; tel. (711) 6854584; e-mail dekanat@f03.uni-stuttgart.de; internet www.uni-stuttgart.de/chemie):

ALDINGER, F., Non-Metallic Inorganic Materials
ARZT, E., Metallurgy
BECKER, G., Inorganic Chemistry
BERTAGNOLLI, H., Physical Chemistry
CHRISTOFFERS, J., Organic Chemistry
EISENBACH, C., Chemical Engineering
GIESSELMANN, F., Physical Chemistry
GUDAT, D., Inorganic Chemistry
HASHMI, S., Organic Chemistry
JÄGER, V., Organic Chemistry
KAIM, W., Inorganic Chemistry
LASCHAT, S., Organic Chemistry
MITTELMEIJER, E., Metallurgy
RODUNER, E., Physical Chemistry
SCHLEID, T., Inorganic Chemistry
SCHMID, R., Technical Biochemistry
WEITKAMP, J., Chemical Engineering
WERNER, H.-J., Theoretical Chemistry
WOLF, D., Biochemistry
ZABEL, F., Physical Chemistry

Civil and Environmental Engineering (Universitätsbereich Vaihingen, Pfaffenwaldring 7, 2.OG, Stuttgart; tel. (711) 6856234; e-mail dekanat@fak2.uni-stuttgart.de; internet www.uni-stuttgart.de/bauingenieur):

BÁRDOSSY, A., Water Management
BERNER, F., Construction Industry
EHLERS, W., Engineering Mechanics
ELIGEHAUSEN, R., Materials Science in Structural Engineering
ENGESSER, K.-H., Biological Cleaning of Used Air
FRIEDRICH, M., Transport Planning and Traffic Control
GERTIS, K., Building Physics
HELMIG, R., Hydromechanics and Hydrosystems Modelling
KRANERT, M., Sanitary Engineering, Wastewater and Solid Waste Management
KUHLMANN, U., Design and Construction
MARTIN, U., Railway and Transportation Engineering
METZGER, J., Hydrochemistry and Hydrobiology, Sanitary Engineering, Wastewater and Solid Waste Management
MIEHE, C., Engineering Mechanics
MÖHLENBRINK, W., Applied Geodesy
MORO, J. L., Planning and Construction of High-Rise Buildings
NOVÁK, B., Large-Scale Construction
PINNEKAMP, J., Wastewater Engineering
RAMM, E., Structural Engineering
REINHARDT, H.-W., Materials Science in Structural Engineering
RESSEL, W., Road and Transport Planning and Engineering
ROTT, U., Water Quality Management, Sanitary Engineering
SEDLBAUER, K., Constructional Physics
SOBEK, W., Interdisciplinary Research, Architecture and Civil Engineering
TREUNER, P., Regional Development Planning
VERMEER, P. A., Geotechnology
WIEPRECHT, S., Water Engineering

Computer Science, Electrical Engineering and Information Technology (Universitätsbereich Vaihingen, Pfaffenwaldring 47, Zi. 4.116, Stuttgart; tel. (711) 6857234; e-mail dekanat@f-iei.uni-stuttgart.de; internet www.f-iei.uni-stuttgart.de):

BERROTH, M., Communications Engineering
BUNGARTZ, H.-J., Simulation of Large Systems
CLAUS, V., Formal Concepts of Computer Science
DIEKERT, V., Theoretical Computer Science
EGGENBERGER, O., Operating Systems
ERTL, T., Dialogue Systems
ESPARZA, J., Secure and Reliable Software Systems
FRÜHAUF, N., Display Technology
GÖHNER, P., Control Engineering and Process Automation
KASPER, E., Semiconductor Engineering
KÜHN, P. J., Communications Switching and Data Techniques
LAGALLY, K., Operating Systems
LANDSTORFER, F., Radio Frequency Technology
LEHMANN, E., Export Systems
LEVI, P., Computer Vision
LUDEWIG, J., Software Engineering
MITSCHANG, B., User Software
PLÖDEREDER, E., Programming Languages
ROLLER, D., Computer Science Fundamentals
ROTH-STIELOW, J., Power Electronics and Control Engineering
ROTHERMEL, K., Distributed Systems
RUCKER, W., Theory of Electrical Engineering
SCHÄFER, Energy Conversion
SPEIDEL, J., Telecommunications
TENBOHLEN, S., High-Voltage Technology
WERNER, J. H., Physical Electronics
WUNDERLICH, H.-J., Computer Architecture
YANG, B., Network and Systems Theory

Mathematics and Physics (Universitätsbereich Vaihingen, Pfaffenwaldring 57, 70550 Stuttgart; tel. (711) 6852400; e-mail dekanat@f08.uni-stuttgart.de; internet www.uni-stuttgart.de/mathephysik):

BECHINGER, C., Experimental Physics
BLIND, G., Mathematics
BRÜDERN, J., Mathematics
DENNINGER, G., Physics
DIETRICH, S., Theoretical Physics
DIPPER, R., Mathematics
DOSCH, H., Experimental Physics
DRESSEL, M., Experimental Physics
GEKELER, E., Mathematics
HÄHL, H., Mathematics
HERRMANN, H., Theoretical Physics
HESSE, C., Mathematics
HÖLLIG, K., Mathematics
KÜHNEL, W., Mathematics
LUNK, A., Plasma Research
MAHLER, G., Theoretical Physics
MICHLER, P., Experimental Physics
MIELKE, A., Mathematics
MURAMATSU, A., Theoretical Physics
PFAU, T., Institute of Physics
PÖSCHEL, J., Mathematics
SANTOS, L., Theoretical Physics
SCHWEITZER, D., Experimental Physics
SEIFERT, U., Theoretical Physics
STRAUSS, W., Mathematics
TREBIN, H.-R., Theoretical and Applied Physics
WALK, H., Mathematics
WEIDL, T., Mathematics
WEISS, U., Theoretical Physics
WOHLMUTH, B., Mathematics
WRACHTRUP, J., Experimental Physics
WUNNER, G., Theoretical Physics

Mechanical Engineering (Universitätsbereich Vaihingen, Pfaffenwaldring 9, 5.OG, 70569 Stuttgart; tel. (711) 6856470; e-mail dekanat@f07.uni-stuttgart.de; internet www.f07.uni-stuttgart.de):

ALLGÖWER, F., Systems Theory in Engineering
BARGENDE, M., Combustion Engines
BERTSCHE, B., Machine Elements (Gear Design, Cab Sealing Technology)
BINZ, H., Machine and Gearing Design
BRUNNER, H., Interface Chemistry
BULLINGER, H.-J., Industrial Science and Technology Management
BUSSE, G., Non-Destructive Testing
CASEY, M., Thermal Turbo-Engines
EBERHARD, P., Mechanics
EIGENBERGER, G., Chemical Process Engineering
EYERER, P., Polymer Testing and Polymer Science
FRIEDRICH, H., Vehicle Concepts
FRITZ, H. G., Polymer Processing
GADOW, R., Manufacturing Technologies of Ceramic Compounds and Composites
GAUL, L., Mechanics
GILLES, E. D., System Dynamics and Control Systems
GÖDE, E., Fluid Machines and Hydraulic Pumps
GRAF, T., Network Engineering
HAASE, H., Technical Thermodynamics
HEIN, K. R. G., Process Engineering and Steam Boiler Technology
HEISEL, U., Machine Tools
KISTNER, A., Engineering Mechanics
KLEMM, P., Control Engineering
KÜCK, H., Time Measuring, Precision Engineering and Microengineering
LAURIEN, E., Nuclear Engineering
LOHNERT, G., Nuclear Engineering and Energy Systems
MAIER, T., Technical Design

MERTEN, C., Chemical Engineering
MÜLLER-STEINHAGEN, H., Thermodynamics and Heat Engineering
NAGEL, J., Biomedical Technology
OSTEN, W., Technical Optics
PIESCHE, M., Mechanical Production Engineering
PLANCK, H., Textile Technology and Process Engineering
PRITSCHOW, G., Control Technology of Machine Tools and Production Systems
REUSS, H.-C., Automobile Mechatronics
REUSS, M., Biochemical Engineering
ROOS, E., Materials Testing, Materials Science and Strength of Materials
SANDMAIER, H., Time Measuring, Precision Engineering and Microengineering
SCHINKÖTHE, W., Design and Production in Precision Engineering
SCHMAUDER, S., Process Development
SCHMIDT, M., Heating and Air-Conditioning Engineering
SEIFERT, H., Thermal Waste Utilization
SIEGERT, K., Metal Forming
SPATH, D., Technology Management
VOSS, A., Energy Economics
WEHKING, K.-H., Conveyer and Transmission Technology, Gear Technology
WEHLAN, H., Process Control Engineering
WESTKÄMPER, E., Industrial Production and Plant
WIEDEMANN, J., Motor Vehicle Engineering
ZEITZ, M., System Dynamics Control

Philosophy and History (Universitätsbereich Stadtmitte, Keplerstr. 17, KII, 3.OG, 70174 Stuttgart; tel. (711) 1213089; e-mail dekanat@f09.uni-stuttgart.de; internet www.f09.uni-stuttgart.de):

ALEXIADOU, M., Linguistics and English
BAHLKE, J., Early Modern History
BARK, J., Modern German Literature
CZERWINSKI, P., German Philology
DOGIL, G., Computational Linguistics
GÖBEL, W., American Studies and Modern English Literature
HUBIG, C., Theory of Science and Technical Philosophy
KAMP, H., Formal Logic and Philosophy of Language
KRÜGER, R., Roman Studies
MAAG, G., Italian Studies
OLSHAUSEN, E., Ancient History
PAFEL, J., Linguistics and German
PYTA, W., Modern History
QUARTHAL, F., Regional History of Baden-Württemberg
REICHERT, F., History
ROHRER, CH., Computational Linguistics
SEEBER, H. U., Modern English Literature
STEIN, A., Linguistics/Roman Studies
STEINER, R., History of Arts
STÜRNER, W., History
THOMÉ, H., Modern German Literature
VON HEUSINGER, K., Linguistics and German
WYSS, B., History of Arts

Management, Economics and Social Sciences (Universitätsbereich Stadtmitte, Keplerstr. 17, KII, 10 OG, 70174 Stuttgart; tel. (711) 1213046; e-mail dekanat@wiso.uni-stuttgart.de; internet www.uni-stuttgart.de/wiso):

ACKERMANN, K.-F., Economics
ALT, W., Sports
ARNOLD, U., Economics
BRINKHOFF, K.-P., Sports
ENGLMANN, F., Economics
FRANKE, S. F., Economic Policy and Public Law
FROMM, M., Educational Theory
FUCHS, D., Political Science
GABRIEL, O. W., Political Science
HERZWURM, G., Economics
HORVÁTH, P., Economics
KEMPER, H.-G., Economics
MAJER, H., Economics
NICKOLAUS, R., Vocational and Economic Education
REISS, M., Economics
RENN, O., Sociology of Environment and Technology
SCHÄFER, H., Economics
SCHLICHT, W., Sports
URBAN, D., Sociology
WOECKENER, B., Economics
ZAHN, E., Economics

UNIVERSITÄT TRIER

54286 Trier
Universitätsring 15, 54296 Trier
Telephone: (651) 2010
E-mail: presse@uni-trier.de
Internet: www.uni-trier.de

Founded 1473, reopened 1970
Academic year: October to September

Pres.: Prof. Dr PETER SCHWENKMEZGER
Vice-Pres.: Prof. Dr JOACHIM HILL
Vice-Pres.: Prof. Dr THOMAS RAAB
Chancellor: Dr KLAUS HEMBACH (acting)
Librarian: Dr HILDEGARD MÜLLER

Library: see under Libraries and Archives
Number of teachers: 600
Number of students: 14,600

Publications: *Trierer Beiträge* (1 a year), *UNI-Journal* (4 a year)

DEANS

Faculty I: Pedagogy, Philosophy and Psychology: Prof. Dr CONNY H. ANTONI
Faculty II: Language and Literature: Prof. Dr ULRICH PORT
Faculty III: History, Political Science, Classical Archaeology, Egyptology, Art History, Papyrology: Prof. Dr UWE JUN
Faculty IV: Management Economics, Sociology, Political Economy, Applied Mathematics, Computer Science and Ethnology: Prof. Dr RALF MÜNNICH
Faculty V: Law: Prof. Dr JAN VON HEIN
Faculty VI: Geography and Geosciences: Prof. Dr INGO EBERLE
Faculty VII: Theology: Prof. Dr JOACHIM THEIS

PROFESSORS

Faculty I: Pedagogy, Philosophy and Psychology (Fachbereich I, 54286 Trier; tel. (651) 2012015; e-mail kohrg@uni-trier.de; internet www.psychologie.uni-trier.de/fbi):

ANTON, F., Psychobiology
BECKER, P., Psychology
BRANDTSTÄDTER, J., Psychology
CONNY, A., Psychology
DÖRFLINGER, B., Philosophy
FILIPP, S.-H., Psychology
HELLHAMMER, D., Psychology
HOMFELDT, H.-C., Pedagogy
HONIG, M. S., Pedagogy
KRAMPEN, G., Psychology
MEYER, J., Psychobiology
MULLER, C., Psychobiology
MÜLLER-FOHRBRODT, G., Pedagogy
PRECKEL, F., Psychology
RUSTEMEYER, D., Pedagogy
SCHÄCHINGER, H., Psychobiology
SCHELLER, R., Psychology
SCHWENKMEZGER, P., Psychology
WALTHER, E., Psychology
WENDER, K. F., Psychology

Faculty II: Language and Literature (Fachbereich II, 54286 Trier; tel. (651) 2012210; e-mail dienhart@uni-trier.de; internet www.uni-trier.de/uni/fb2/dekanat):

ALTHAUS, H. P., German Linguistics, Yiddish Language
BENDER, K.-H., Romance Literature
BREUER, H., English Literature
BUCHER, H.-J., Media Studies
CHIAO, W., Sinology
EIGLER, U., Classical Philology
GÄRTNER, K., German Philology
GELHAUS, H., German Linguistics
GÖSSMANN, H., Japanese Studies
HASLER, J., English and American Literature
HÖLZ, K., Romance Literature
HURM, G., English Literature
KLOOSS, W., English Philology
KÖHLER, H., Romance Literature
KÖHLER, R., Linguistic Data Processing
KÖSTER, J.-P., Applied Linguistics, Phonetics
KRAMER, J., Romance Philology
KREMER, D., Romance Philology
KRÖNER, H. O., Classical Philology
KÜHLWEIN, W., English Philology
KÜHN, P., German as a Foreign Language
LIANG, Y., Sinology
LOIPERDINGER, M., Media Studies
MOULIN, C., Old German Philology
NEUBERG, S., Yiddish Studies
NIEDEREHE, H.-J., Romance Philology
PIKULIK, L., Modern German Literature
PLATZ, N., English Literature
POHL, K. H., Chinese Studies
REINHARDT, H., Modern German Literature
RESSEL, G., Slavistics
RIEGER, B., Linguistic Data Processing, Computer Languages
RÖLL, W., German Philology, Yiddish Language
SCHOLZ-CIONCA, S., Japanese Studies
SCHÖẞLER, F., New German Literature
STAHL, H., Slavic Literature
STRAUSS, J., English Philology
STUBBS, M., English Linguistics
THORAU, H.-E., Portuguese Philology
TIMM, E., Yiddish Language
UERLINGS, H., Modern German Literature
WIMMER, R., German Linguistics
WÖHRLE, G., Classical Philology
ZIRKER, H., English Literature

Faculty III: History, Political Science, Classical Archaeology, Egyptology, Art History, Papyrology (Fachbereich III, 54286 Trier; tel. (651) 2012144; e-mail merz@uni-trier.de; internet www.uni-trier.de/uni/fb3/dekanat/fb3.html):

ANTON, H. H., Medieval History
CLEMENS, L., History
DORN, F., History
EBELING, D., History
FRANZ, G., History
GERHARDT, C., History
GESTRICH, A., Modern History
HAVERKAMP, A., Medieval History
HEINEN, H., Ancient History
HERRMAN-OTTO, E., Ancient History
HOLTMANN, W., History
IRSIGLER, F., Cultural History
KETTENHOFEN, E., History
KÖNIG, I., History
KRAMER, B., Papyrology
MOLT, P., Political Science
RAPHAEL, L., Modern and Recent History
SCHMID, W., History
SCHNABEL-SCHÜLE, H., Modern History
TACKE, A., Art History
VEEN, H. J., Political Science
VLEEMING, S. P., Egyptology
VOLTMER, E., History
WEBER, W., History
WIELING, H., History
WÖHRLE, G., Greek Philology

Faculty IV: Management Economics, Sociology, Political Economy, Applied Mathematics, Computer Science and Ethnology (Fachbereich IV, 54286 Trier; tel. (651) 2012640; e-mail dekanfb4@uni-trier.de; internet www.uni-trier.de/uni/fb4/dekanat/index.htm):

AMBROSI, C. M., Political Economy
ANTWEILER, C., Ethnology
BAUM, D., Computer Science

BERGMANN, R., Computer Science
BRAUN, H., Sociology
CZAP, H., Computer Science
DICKERTMANN, D., Political Economy
DIEHL, S., Computer Science
ECKERT, R., Sociology
EL-SHAGI, E. S., Political Economy
FILC, W., Political Economy
FEHR, H. J., Accounting
FERNAU, H., Computer Science
GAWRONSKI, W., Mathematics
HAHN, A., Sociology
HAMM, B., Sociology
HARDES, H.-D., Political Economy
HECHELTJEN, P., Political Economy
JÄCKEL, M., Sociology
KLÄS, F., Accounting
KNAPPE, E., Political Economy
LEHMANN, M., Management Economics
LIEBIG, M., Sociology
MILDE, H., Management Economics
MÜNNICH, R., Economics
NÄHER, S., Computer Science
OFFERMANN-CLAS, CH., European Community
RÜCKLE, D., Management Economics
SACHS, E., Mathematics
SADOWSKI, D., Management Economics
SCHERTLER, W., Strategic Management
SCHMIDT, A., Economics
SPEHL, H., Political Economy
STURM, P., Computer Science
SWOBODA, B., Management Economics
WÄCHTER, H., Management Economics
WALTER, B., Computer Science
WEIBER, R., Management Economics

Faculty V: Law (Fachbereich V—Rechtswissenschaft, 54286 Trier; tel. (651) 2012524; e-mail dekanatfb5@uni-trier.de; internet www.uni-trier.de/uni/fb5/fachbereich/dekanat.htm):

AXER, P., Public Law
BACHMANN, G., Civil Law, Commercial Law
BIRK, R., Private Law, Labour Law, Conflict of Laws
BURMESTER, G., National and International Finance and Tax Law
DORN, F., Private Law, Legal History, Comparative Law
ECKHARDT, D., Civil Law
HENDLER, R., Constitutional and Administrative Law
JÄGER, C., Criminal Law
KREY, V., Criminal Law, Criminal Procedure, Legal Methods
KÜHNE, H.-H., Criminal Law, Criminology, Criminal Procedure
RAAB, T., Public Law, Commercial Law, Labour Law
REIFF, P., Private Law, Commercial Law, Corporation Law, Insurance Law
REINHARDT, M., Constitutional and Administrative Law
ROBBERS, G., Public Law, Ecclesiastical Law, Philosophy of Law
RÜFNER, T., Public Law, German and International Civil Law
SCHRÖDER, M., Public, International and EU Law
VON HOFFMANN, B., Private Law, Conflict of Laws, Comparative Law

Faculty VI: Geography and Geosciences (Fachbereich VI, 54286 Trier; tel. (651) 2014530; e-mail dekanatfb6@uni-trier.de; internet dekanatfb6.uni-trier.de):

ALEXANDER, J., Physical Geography
BECKER, CHR., Applied Geography and Geography of Tourism
BLÖMEKE, B., Ecotoxicology
BOLLMANN, J., Cartography
CALTEUX, G., Geography of Tourism
DIESTER-HAAß, L., Biogeography
EBERLE, I., Economic and Social Geography
FISCHER, K., Inorganic and Analytical Chemistry
HEINEMANN, G., Climatology
HILL, J., Remote Sensing
HOFFMANN, R., Geography and its Teaching
MONHEIM, H., Applied Geography, Urban and Regional Planning and Development
RIES, J. B., Physical Geography
SAILER, U., Cultural and Regional Geography
SYMADER, W., Hydrology
THOMAS, F., Geobotany
VOGEL, H., Communal Science
WAGNER, J.-F., Geology

Faculty VII: Theology (Universitätsring 19, 54296 Trier; tel. (651) 2013520; e-mail theofak@uni-trier.de; internet www.uni-trier.de/uni/theo):

BOHLEN, Biblical Studies
BRANDSCHEIDT, Old Testament
ECKERT, New Testament
EULER, Fundamental Theology
FIEDROWICZ, Medieval Church History and Christian Archaeology
GÖBEL, Moral Philosophy
HEINZ, Liturgical Studies
KRÄMER, Church Law
KRIEGER, Philosophy I
OCKENFELS, Medieval Church History
SCHNEIDER, Church History
SCHÜßLER, Philosophy II
THEIS, Religious Instruction
VODERHOLZER, Dogma and History of Dogma
WAHL, Pastoral Theology

UNIVERSITÄT ULM

89069 Ulm
Telephone: (731) 5010
E-mail: praesident@uni-ulm.de
Internet: www.uni-ulm.de
Founded 1967 as Medizinische-Naturwissenschaftliche Hochschule, univ. charter 1967
State control
Language of instruction: German
Academic year: October to September
Pres.: Prof. Dr KARL JOACHIM EBELING
Vice-Pres. for Academic Affairs: Prof. Dr ULRICH STADTMÜLLER
Vice-Pres. for Medicine: Prof. Dr KLAUS-MICHAEL DEBATIN
Vice-Pres. for Research: Prof. Dr PETER BÄUERLE
Chancellor: DIETER KAUFMANN
Chief Librarian: SIEGFRIED FRANKE
Number of teachers: 480
Number of students: 8,300
Publication: *Uni Ulm Intern* (8 a year)

DEANS

Faculty of Engineering and Computer Science: Prof. Dr Ing. MICHAEL WEBER
Faculty of Mathematics and Economics: Prof. Dr WERNER KRATZ
Faculty of Medicine: Prof. Dr KLAUS-MICHAEL DEBATIN
Faculty of Natural Sciences: Prof. Dr AXEL GROß

UNIVERSITÄT VECHTA
(University of Vechta)

POB 15 53, 49364 Vechta
Driverstr. 22, 49377 Vechta
Telephone: (4441) 150
E-mail: info@uni-vechta.de
Internet: www.uni-vechta.de
Founded 1830, present status 1995, current name adopted 2010
State control
Pres.: Prof. Dr MARIANNE ASSENMACHER
Vice-Pres. for Research and Young Researchers: Prof. Dr MARTIN WINTER
Vice-Pres. for Teaching and Academic Programmes: Dr MARION RIEKEN
Head Librarian: Dr GUNTER GEDULDIG
Library of 508,000 vols
Number of teachers: 204
Number of students: 3,132

UNIVERSITÄT WITTEN/HERDECKE
(Witten/Herdecke University)

Alfred-Herrhausen-Str. 50, 58448 Witten
Telephone: (2302) 9260
E-mail: public@uni-wh.de
Internet: www.uni-wh.de
Founded 1982
Private control
Languages of instruction: German, English
Academic year: October to September
Chancellor: MICHAEL ANDERS
Librarian: IRIS KOCH
Library of 150,000 vols, 500 periodicals
Number of teachers: 295
Number of students: 1,437

DEANS

Faculty of Health: Prof. Dr STEFAN WIRTH
Faculty of Humanities and Arts: Prof. Dr HANS-JÜRGEN LANGE
Faculty of Management and Economics: Prof. Dr DIRK SAUERLAND

UNIVERSITÄT ZU KÖLN

Albertus-Magnus-Pl., 50923 Cologne
Telephone: (221) 4700
E-mail: aaa@verw.uni-koeln.de
Internet: www.uni-koeln.de
Founded 1388
State control
Languages of instruction: English, German
Academic year: October to July
Rector: Prof. Dr AXEL FREIMUTH
First Pro-Rector and Pro-Rector for Research and Junior Scholars: Prof. Dr THOMAS LANGER
Pro-Rector for Academic Careers, Diversity and Int. Affairs: Prof. Dr MICHAEL BOLLIG
Pro-Rector for Planning, Finances and Gender: Prof. Dr ANJA STEINBECK
Pro-Rector for Teaching and Studies: Prof. Dr STEFAN HERZIG
Chancellor: Dr MICHAEL STÜCKRADT
Librarian: Prof. Dr W. SCHMITZ
Library: see under Libraries and Archives
Number of teachers: 5,500
Number of students: 47,000
Publications: *Forschung_365* (in English and German), *Kölner Universitätszeitung* (in German)

DEANS

Faculty of Human Sciences: Prof. Dr HANS JOACHIM ROTH
Faculty of Humanities and Arts: Prof. Dr STEFAN GROHÉ
Faculty of Law: Prof. Dr MARTIN HENSSLER
Faculty of Management, Economics and Social Sciences: Prof. Dr WERNER MELLES
Faculty of Mathematics and Natural Sciences: Prof. Dr ANSGAR BÜSCHGES
Faculty of Medicine: Prof. Dr med. THOMAS KRIEG

PROFESSORS

Faculty of Economics, Business Administration and Social Sciences (tel. (221) 4705607; e-mail dekanat@wiso.uni-koeln.de; internet www.wiso.uni-koeln.de):

ANDEREGG, R. G., Political Economy
BAUM, H., Economics
BEUERMANN, G., Business Administration
DELFMANN, W., Business Administration

DERIGS, U., Information Systems, Operations Research
DONGES, J., Economics
EEKHOFF, J., Economics
EISENFÜHR, F., Business Administration
FELDERER, B., Economics
FELDSIEPER, M., Economics
FISCHER, L., Business Psychology
FRESE, E., Business Administration
FRIEDRICHS, J., Sociology
FUNK, P., Economics
GLÄSSER, E., Economic Geography
HARTMANN-WENDELS, T., Business Administration
HERZIG, N., Business Administration, Taxation
JÄGER, T., Political Science
JAGODZINSKI, W., Sociology
KEMPF, A., Business Administration, Finance
KITTERER, W., Economics
KÖHLER, R., Marketing
KOPPELMANN, U., Business Administration
KUHNER, C., Business Administration
LEIDHOLD, W., Political Science
LINDNER-BRAUN, C., Sociology
LÖBBECKE, C., Electronic Commerce
MELLIS, W., Business Informatics
MEULEMANN, H., Sociology
MOSLER, K., Statistics, Econometrics
MÜLLER-HAGEDORN, L., Business Administration
PIERENKEMPER, T., Economic History
RETTIG, R., Economics
RÖSNER, H. J., Social Politics
SCHELLHAASS, H. M., Economics
SCHMID, F., Statistics
SCHRADIN, H. R., Business Administration, Insurance
SCHULZ-NIESWANDT, F., Social Policy
SEIBT, D., Information Science, Business Administration
STERNBERG, R., Economic Geography
TEMPELMEIER, H., Business Administration
VON WEIZSÄCKER, C. C., Economics
WAGNER, M., Sociology
WESSELS, W., Political Science
WIED-NEBBELING, S., Economics
WISWEDE, G., Business Psychology
ZERCHE, J., Social Policy

Faculty of Education (tel. (221) 4705777; e-mail dekanat@ew.uni-koeln.de; internet www.uni-koeln.de/ew-fak):

ADOLPHI, K., Biology
ANACKER, U., General Education
AUERNHEIMER, G., Intercultural Education
BANNWARTH, H., Biology
BARTELS, G., Geography
BECKER-MROTZEK, M., German
BOMBEK, M., Textile Design
BREULL, W.-R., Biology and Human Biology
BROSSEDER, J., Catholic Theology
BUKOW, W.-D., Sociology
BURSCHEID, H. J., Mathematics
BUTTERWEGGE, C., Political Science
DONNERSTAG, J., English
GLÜCK, G., General Education and School Education
GRÜNEWALD, B., Philosophy
GÜNTHER, HARTMUT, German Language and Literature
GÜNTHER, HENNING, General Education and School Education
HAIDER-HASEBRINK, H., Psychology
HURRELMANN, B., German Language and Literature
KLEIN, K., Biology
KOCH-PRIEWE, B., General Education and School Education
KOENEN, K., Protestant Theology
KÜNZEL, H., Adult Education
LAMM, H., Psychology
LLARYORA, R., Sociology
MESSELKEN, H., German Language and Literature
MINSEL, W.-R., Psychology
OTT, T., Music
RECH, P., Art
REICH, K., General Education
REINERS, C., Chemistry
SCHÄFER, G., General Education
SCHMIDT, S., Mathematics
SCHNEIDER, R., Music
SCHOLTEN, C., Roman Catholic Theology
SCHÖN, E., German Language and Literature
SCHRÖDER, J., History
SEIBEL, H. D., Sociology
STOCK, A., Theology
STRUVE, H., Mathematics
THIEMANN, F., General Education
THIEME, G., Geography
TIMM, U., Biology
TÖNNIS, G., Art
VOLKENBORN, A., Mathematics
WEGENER-SPÖHRING, G., General Education
WEISER, W., Mathematics
WICHARD, W., Biology
WICKERT, J., Psychology
WIEGERSHAUSEN, H.-W., Art
WILKENDING, G., German Language and Literature
ZILLESSEN, D., Protestant Theology

Faculty of Law (tel. (221) 4702218; e-mail jura-dekanat@uni-koeln.de; internet www.dekanat.de):

BAUR, J. F., Civil Law, Commercial Law, European Law
BÖCKSTIEGEL, K.-H., International and Constitutional Law, German and International Commercial Law
DAUNER-LIEB, B., Civil Law, Commercial Law, Industrial Law
DEPENHEUER, O., Public Law, Philosophy of Law
GRUNEWALD, B., Civil Law, Commercial Law
HENSSLER, M., Civil Law, Commercial Law, Industrial Law
HOBE, S., Public Law, International Law, European Law
HÖFLING, W., Constitutional Law, Administrative Law, Financial Law
HORN, N., Civil Law, German and International Commercial and Banking Law, Philosophy of Law
HÜBNER, U., Insurance Law, Civil Law, Commercial Law, Foreign and International Private Law
LANG, J., Tax Law, Public Law
MANSEL, H.-P., Civil Law, International Private Law, Comparative Law
MITTENZWEI, I., Civil Law, Civil Process Law, Philosophy of Law
MUCKEL, S., Public Law, Canon Law
NESTLER, C., Criminal Law, Criminal Case Law
PRÜTTING, H., Civil Law, Industrial Law
SCHIEDERMAIR, H., Public Law, International Law, Philosophy of Law
SCHMITT-KAMMLER, A., Constitutional and Administrative Law
SEIER, J., Criminal Law, Criminal Case Law
TETTINGER, P. J., Constitutional and Administrative Law
WALTER, M., Criminology, Criminal Law
WALTHER, S., Criminal Law, Criminal Procedural Law, Comparative Law
WEIGEND, T., Criminal Law, Criminal Procedural Law, Comparative Criminal Law, Criminology

Faculty of Mathematics and Natural Sciences (tel. (221) 4705643; e-mail math-nat-fakultaet@uni-koeln.de; internet www.uni-koeln.de/math-nat-fak):

ARMBRUST, M., Mathematics
ARNDT, H., Zoology
BACHEM, A., Applied Mathematics and Informatics
BELOW, R., Micropalaeontology and Palaeoecology
BERKESSEL, A., Organic Chemistry
BERKING, S., Zoology
BESLER, H., Geography
BOHATÝ, L., Crystallography
BOTHE, H., Botany
BRUNOTTE, E., Geography
BUNDSCHUH, P., Mathematics
BÜSCHGES, A., Zoology
CAMPOS-ORTEGA, J. A., Developmental Physiology
COENEN, H. H., Nuclear Chemistry
DEITERS, U., Physical Chemistry
DOHMEN, J., Genetics
DOST, M., Physics
ECKART, A., Experimental Physics
EILENBERGER, G., Theoretical Physics
ERMER, O., Organic Chemistry
FAIGLE, U., Applied Mathematics
FLÜGGE, U.-I., Botany
FREIMUTH, A., Experimental Solid State Physics
GOMPPER, G., Theoretical Physics
GRIESBECK, A. G., Organic Chemistry
HAUSEN, K., Zoology
HEHL, F. W., Theoretical Physics
HENKE, W., Mathematics
HERBIG, H.-G., Palaeontology and Historical Geography
HOHLNEICHER, G., Physical Chemistry
HOWARD, J. C., Genetics
HÜLSKAMP, M., Botany
ILGENFRITZ, G., Physical Chemistry
JOLIE, J., Experimental Physics
JÜNGER, M., Informatics
KAUPP, U. B., Biophysical Chemistry
KAWOHL, B., Mathematics
KEMPER, B., Genetics and Genetic Engineering
KERSCHGENS, M., Meteorology
KLEIN, H. W., Biochemistry
KORSCHING, S., Genetics
KRAAS, F., Anthropogeography
KRAMER, R., Biochemistry
KRUMSIEK, K., Geology
KÜPPER, T., Mathematics
LAMOTKE, K., Mathematics
LANGE, H., Mathematics
LANGER, T., Genetics
LEPTIN, M., Genetics
LESCH, M., Mathematics
LEYTHAEUSER, D., Geology
MELKONIAN, M., Botany
MEYER, G., Inorganic Chemistry
MICKLITZ, H., Experimental Physics
MÜHLBERG, M., Crystallography
MÜLLER-HARTMANN, E., Theoretical Physics
NATTERMANN, T., Theoretical Physics
NAUMANN, D., Inorganic and Analytical Chemistry
NEUBAUER, F. M., Geophysics and Meteorology
NEUMANN, M., Applied Mathematics
NEUWIRTH, W., Physics
NIMTZ, G., Physics
NIPPER, J., Geography
PAETZ GEN. SCHIECK, H., Physics
PALME, H., Mineralogy
PLICKERT, G., Zoology
POHLEY, H.-J., Developmental Biology
RADTKE, U., Geography
RAJEWSKY, K., Molecular Genetics
RAMMENSEE, W., Mineralogy
RAPOPORT, M., Mathematics
RECKZIEGEL, H., Mathematics
RICKEN, W., Geology
ROTH, S., Developmental Biology
RUSCHEWITZ, U., Inorganic Chemistry
SCHIEDER, R., Experimental Physics
SCHIERENBERG, E., Zoology
SCHLICHTER, D., Zoology
SCHMALZ, H.-G., Organic Chemistry

SCHMITZ, K., Botany
SCHNEIDER-POETSCH, HJ., Botany
SCHNETZ, K., Genetics
SCHOMBURG, D., Biochemistry
SCHRADER, R., Informatics
SEIDEL, E., Geochemistry
SEYDEL, R., Mathematics
SOYEZ, D., Anthropogeography
SPECKENMEYER, E., Informatics
SPETH, P., Geophysics and Meteorology
STAUFFER, D., Theoretical Physics
STERNER, R., Biochemistry
STREY, R., Physical Chemistry
STRÖHER, H., Experimental Nuclear Physics
STUTZKI, J., Physics
TAUTZ, D., Genetics
TEZKAN, B., Geophysics
THORBERGSSON, G., Mathematics
TIEKE, B., Physical Chemistry
TOPP, W., Zoology
TROTTENBERG, U., Applied Mathematics
WALKOWIAK, W., Zoology
WEISSENBÖCK, G., Botany
WERR, W., Developmental Biology
WESEMANN, L., Inorganic Chemistry
ZIRNBAUER, M., Theoretical Physics
ZITTARTZ, J., Theoretical Physics

Faculty of Medicine (tel. (221) 4780; e-mail med-dekanat@medizin.uni-koeln.de; internet www.medizin.uni-koeln.de):

ABKEN, H., Onco-Genetics, Cell Biology
ADDICKS, K., Anatomy
BALDAMUS, C., Internal Medicine
BAUMANN, M. A., Dentistry
BERGDOLT, K., History of Medicine, Medical Ethics
BERTHOLD, F., Paediatrics
BÖRNER, U., Anaesthesiology
BRUNKWALL, J. S., Surgery
BUZELLO, W., Anaesthesiology
DECKERT-SCHLÜTER, M., Neuropathology
DE VIVIE, E. R., Thorax- and Cardio-Surgery
DIEHL, V., Internal Medicine
DIENES, H. P., Pathology and Pathological Anatomy
DÖPFNER, M., Psychopathology
ENGELMANN, U., Urology
ERDMANN, E., Internal Medicine
FRICKE, U., Pharmacology and Toxicology
FUHR, U., Pharmacology
GOESER, T., Internal Medicine
HACKENBROCH, M. H., Orthopaedics
HAUPT, G., Urology
HEISS, W.-D., Neurology and Psychiatry
HERHOLZ, K., Neurology
HERZIG, S., Pharmacology and Toxicology
HESCHELER, J., Physiology
HÖLSCHER, A. H., Surgery
HÖPP, H.-W., Internal Medicine
KERSCHBAUM, T., Dentistry
KLAUS, W., Pharmacology and Toxicology
KLOSTERKÖTTER, J., Psychiatry
KLUG, N., Neurosurgery
KOEBKE, J., Anatomy
KÖHLE, K., Psychosomatic Medicine and Psychotherapy
KONEN, W., Ophthalmology
KRIEG, T., Dermatology and Venereology
KRIEGLSTEIN, G. K., Ophthalmology
KRONE, W., Internal Medicine
KRÖNKE, M., Hygiene and Microbiology
LACKNER, K., Clinical Radiology
LAUTERBACH, K. W., Health Economics
LECHLER, E., Internal Medicine
LEHMACHER, W., Medical Statistics, Informatics and Epidemiology
LEHMANN, K., Anaesthesiology
LEHMKUHL, G., Child and Adolescent Psychiatry
MAHRLE, G., Dermatology
MALLMANN, P., Gynaecology and Obstetrics
MICHALK, D., Paediatrics
MÖSGES, R., Medical Informatics
MÜLLER, R.-P., Radiology
MÜLLER-WIELAND, D., Internal Medicine
NEISS, W. F., Anatomy
NIEDERMEIER, W., Dental Prosthetics
NOACK, M. J., Dentistry
NOEGEL, A. A., Biochemistry
PAULSSON, M., Biochemistry
PFAFF, H., Medical Sociology
PFEIFFER, P., Dentistry
PFISTER, H., Virology
PFITZER, G., Physiology
PIEKARSKI, C., Industrial Medicine
REHM, K. E., Surgery and Accident Surgery
ROTH, B., Paediatrics
RÜSSMANN, W., Ophthalmology
SCHEFFNER, M., Biochemistry
SCHICHA, H., Nuclear Medicine
SCHIRMACHER, P., Pathology
SCHRÖDER, H., Anatomy
STENNERT, E., Otorhinolaryngology
STURM, V., Neurosurgery
THIELE, J., Pathology
TROIDL, H., Surgery
TSCHUSCHKE, V., Medical Psychology
WIELCKENS, K., Clinical Chemistry
WIESNER, R. J., Physiology
ZÖLLER, J. E., Dental Surgery

Faculty of Philosophy (tel. (221) 4702212; e-mail dekan.philfak@uni-koeln.de; internet www.uni-koeln.de/phil-fak):

AERTSEN, J., Philosophy
ALEXANDER, M., Modern History
ALLEMANN-GHIONDA, C., Intercultural Education
ANTOR, H., English Philology
ARMBRUSTER, C., Romance Philology
AX, W., Classical Philology
BALD, W.-D., Applied Linguistics
BEHREND-ENGELHARDT, H., African Studies
BENTE, G. M., Psychology
BERRESSEM, H., American Studies
BIEG, L., Modern Chinese Literature
BLAMBERGER, G., Modern German Literature
BLATTMANN, M., Medieval History
BLUMENTHAL, P., Romance Philology
BOLLIG, M., Cultural Anthropology
BOS, G., Jewish Studies
BOSCHUNG, D., Classical Archaeology
BOSINSKI, G., Prehistory and Early History
BRENNER, P. J., Modern German Literature
BUCK, E., Theatre, Film and Television Studies
CASIMIR, M., Cultural Anthropology
CLAESGES, U., Philosophy
DÄMMER, H.-W., Prehistory and Early History
DANN, O., Modern History
DIEM, W., Islamic Studies
DIMMENDAAL, G. J., African Studies
DRUX, R., Modern German Literature
DÜLFFER, J., Modern History
DÜSING, K., Philosophy
ECK, W., Ancient History
EHMCKE, F., Japanese Studies
ELEY, L., Philosophy
ENGELS, O., Medieval and Modern History
ERICKSON, J., Applied Linguistics
FISCHER, G., Psychology
FISCHER, T., Classical Archaeology
FRISCH, P., Classical Philology
FROST, U., Education
GARCÍA-RAMÓN, J. L., Linguistics
GAUS, J., History of Art
GEYER, P., Romance Philology
GÖRLACH, M., English Philology
GREIVE, A., Romance Philology
GROEBEN, N., Psychology
GRONEWALD, M., Classical Philology
GÜNTHER, R., Musicology
HEINE, B., African Studies
HEUSER, R., Chinese Law
HÖHN, H.-J., Catholic Theology
HOLKESKAMP, K.-J., Early History
HUSSY, W., Psychology
ISENMANN, E., Medieval History
JÄRVENTAUSTA, M., Finnish Studies
JENAL, G., Medieval History
KABLITZ, A., Romance Philology
KAEHLER, K., Philosophy
KÄMPER, D., Musicology
KAPP, D. B., Indology and Tamil Studies
KINDERMANN, U., Medieval Latin
KLEINSCHMIDT, E., Modern German Literature
KREUTZER, G., Nordic Philology
KUNISCH, J., Medieval and Modern History
KWASMAN, T., Jewish Studies
LEBEK, W. D., Classical Philology
LENERZ, J., German Philology
LIEBRAND, C., Modern German Literature and Gender Studies
MANUWALD, B., Classical Philology
MERTENS, G., Education
NEUHAUS, V., Modern German and Comparative Literature
NEUMEIER, B., English Philology
NITSCH, W., Romance Philology
NUSSBAUM, N., Art History and Urban Conservation
OBST, U., Slavonic Philology
OST, H., Art History
PAPE, W., Modern German Philology
PETERS, U., Medieval German Literature
PLÖGER, W., Education
POTTHAST, B., Latin American History
PRIMUS, B., German Linguistics
ROLSHOVEN, J., Philological and Linguistic Computing
RÜPPELL, H., Education
SALBER, W., Psychology
SASSE, H.-J., Comparative Linguistics
SCHARPING, T., Sinology
SCHMIDT, C., East European History
SCHMIDT-DENTER, U., Psychology
SCHNEIDER, I., Theatre, Film and Television Studies
SCHNEIDER, W., Education
SCHUMACHER, R., Musicology
SEIFERT, U., Musicology
STEPHAN, E., Psychology
STRUVE, T., Medieval History
TAUCHMANN, K., Ethnology
THALLER, M., Informatics in Historical and Cultural Studies
THISSEN, H. J., Egyptology
ULLMANN, H.-P., Modern History
VON BLUMRÖDER, C., Musicology
VON GRAEVENITZ, A., Art History
VON HESBERG, H., Classical Archaeology
VON WEIHER, E., Ancient Oriental Philology
WIENBRUCH, U., Philosophy
ZAHRNT, M., Early History
ZELINSKY, B., Slavonic Philology
ZEUSKE, M., Iberian and Latin American History
ZICK, G., Art History
ZIEGELER, H. J., Medieval German Literature
ZIMMERMANN, A., Prehistory and Early History

Faculty of Special Education (tel. (221) 4704640; internet www.uni-koeln.de/hp-fak):

BUCHKREMER, H., General Therapy and Social Education
CONINX, F., Education of the Deaf and Hard of Hearing
DREHER, W., Education of the Mentally Handicapped
FENGLER, J., Psychology
FISCHER, K., Physical Education
FORNEFELD, B., Education of the Mentally Handicapped
KIRFEL, B., Sociology of the Handicapped
LAUTH, G., Psychology and Psychotherapy
LIST, G., Psychology
MASENDORF, F., Special Education and Rehabilitation of the Educationally Subnormal

OSKAMP, U., Education of the Physically Handicapped
PIEL, W., Music Therapy
SCHLEIFFER, R., Psychiatry and Psychotherapy
SEIFERT, R., Education of the Physically Handicapped
TSCHERNER, K. W. H., Teaching of the Educationally Subnormal
WEINWURM-KRAUSE, E.-M., Psychology and Psychiatry
WICHELHAUS, B., Art Therapy
WILLAND, H., Special Education and Rehabilitation of the Educationally Subnormal
WISOTZKI, K. H., Education of the Deaf and Hard of Hearing
WÖRNER, G., Arts and Crafts

UNIVERSITÄT ZU LÜBECK (University of Lübeck)

Ratzeburger Allee 160, 23538 Lübeck
Telephone: (451) 5000
E-mail: presse@uni-luebeck.de
Internet: www.uni-luebeck.de

Founded 1973 as Medizinische Universität zu Lübeck, present name and status 2002
State control
Rector: Prof. Dr PETER DOMINIAK
Vice-Pres.: Prof. Dr ENNO HARTMANN
Vice-Pres.: Prof. Dr GABRIELE GILLESSEN-KAESBACH
Vice-Pres.: Prof. Dr THOMAS MARTINETZ
Chancellor: Dr OLIVER GRUNDEI
Librarian: RENA GIESE
Number of teachers: 232
Number of students: 2,500
Publications: *Focus MUL* (4 a year), *Forschungsbericht*

PROFESSORS

Faculty of Medicine:

ARNOLD, H., Neurosurgery
BRUCH, H.-P., Surgery
DIEDRICH, K., Gynaecology and Obstetrics
DOMARUS, H., Maxillary and Facial Surgery
DOMINIAK, P., Pharmacology, Toxicology and Clinical Pharmacology
FEHM, H. L., Internal Medicine
FELLER, A. C., Pathology
GROSS, W. L., Rheumatology
HALSBAND, H., Paediatric Surgery
HOHAGEN, F., Psychiatry
JELKMANN, W., Physiology
JOCHAM, D., Urology
KATUS, H. A., Internal Medicine
KESSEL, R., Industrial Medicine
KIRCHNER, H., Immunology and Transfusional Medicine
KNÖLKER, U., Child and Adolescent Psychiatry
KÖMPF, D., Neurology
KRUSE, K., Paediatrics
LAQUA, H., Ophthalmology
LÖHR, J., Orthopaedics
OEHMICHEN, M., Forensic Medicine
RASPE, H.-H., Social Medicine
RICHTER, E., Radiotherapy and Nuclear Medicine
SCHMIELAU, F., Medical Psychology
SCHMUCKER, P., Anaesthesiology
SCHWINGER, E., Human Genetics
SCZAKIEL, G., Molecular Medicine
SEYFARTH, M., Clinical Chemistry
SIEVERS, H. H., Cardiac Surgery
SOLBACH, W., Medical Microbiology and Hygiene
WEERDA, H., Otolaryngology
WEISS, H.-D., Radiology
WESTERMANN, J., Anatomy
WOLFF, H. H., Dermatology and Venereology

Faculty of Science and Technology:

AACH, T., Signal Processing and Process Control
DOSCH, W., Software Engineering
DÜMBGEN, L., Mathematics
ENGELHARDT, D., History of Medicine and Science
FISCHER, B., Mathematics
HARTMANN, E., Biology
HERCZEG, M., Multimedia and Interactive Systems
HOGREFE, D., Telematics
KONECNY, E., Medical Technology
LINNEMANN, V., Practical Informatics
MAEHLE, E., Computer Engineering
MARTINETZ, TH., Neuro- and Bioinformatics
MÜLLER, K.-P., Medical Molecular Biology
PETERS, TH., Chemistry
PÖPPL, S., Medical Informatics and Statistics
PRESTIN, J., Mathematics
REISCHUK, K. R., Theoretical Computer Science
RIETSCHEL, E.-TH., Immunochemistry and Biochemical Microbiology
ROELCKE, V., History of Medicine and Science
SCHÄFER, G., Biochemistry
TRAUTWEIN, A., Physics
VOSWINCKEL, P., History of Medicine and Science
ZEUGMANN, TH., Theoretical Computer Science

WESTFÄLISCHE WILHELMS-UNIVERSITÄT MÜNSTER

Schlosspl. 2, 48149 Münster
Telephone: (251) 830
E-mail: verwaltung@uni-muenster.de
Internet: www.uni-muenster.de

Founded 1780, became Acad. in 1818, present status 1902
State control
Academic year: October to July (2 terms)
Rector: Prof. Dr URSULA NELLES
Vice-Rector for Int. Affairs and Young Researchers: Prof. Dr CORNELIA DENZ
Vice-Rector for Research: Prof. Dr STEPHAN LUDWIG
Vice-Rector for Strategic Planning and Quality Assurance: Prof. Dr JÖRG BECKER
Vice-Rector for Teaching, and Student Affairs: Dr MARIANNE RAVENSTEIN
Chancellor: MATTHIAS SCHWARTE
Library: see under Libraries and Archives
Number of teachers: 551
Number of students: 39,000

DEANS

Faculty of Biology: Prof. Dr DIRK PRÜFER
Faculty of Business, Economics and Information Systems: Prof. Dr THOMAS APOLTE
Faculty of Chemistry and Pharmacy: Prof. Dr BART JAN RAVOO
Faculty of Economics: Prof. Dr THOMAS APOLTE
Faculty of Education and Social Studies: Prof. Dr VOLKER GEHRAU
Faculty of Geosciences: Prof. Dr HANS KERP
Faculty of History/Philosophy: Prof. Dr JÜRGEN HEIDRICH
Faculty of Law: Prof. Dr THOMAS HOEREN
Faculty of Mathematics and Computer Sciences: Prof. Dr MATTHIAS LÖWE
Faculty of Medicine: Prof. Dr WILHELM SCHMITZ
Faculty of Philologies: Prof. Dr CHRISTOPH STROSETZKI
Faculty of Physics: Prof. Dr TILMANN KUHN
Faculty of Protestant Theology: Prof. Dr KONRAD HAMMANN
Faculty of Psychology and Sport and Exercise Sciences: Prof. Dr MARKUS LAPPE
Faculty of Roman Catholic Theology: Prof. Dr KLAUS MÜLLER
Music Department: Prof. MICHAEL KELLER

WHU—OTTO BEISHEIM SCHOOL OF MANAGEMENT

Burgpl. 2, 56179 Vallendar
Telephone: (261) 65090
E-mail: whu@whu.edu
Internet: www.whu.edu

Founded 1984
Private control
Languages of instruction: German, English
Academic year: September to August
Rector: Prof. Dr MICHAEL FRENKEL
Pro-Rector: Prof. Dr MARKUS RUDOLF
Chancellor: Dr PETER STOMBERG
Librarian: HANNELORE PÖTHIG
Library of 40,300 vols, 250 journals
Number of teachers: 125
Number of students: 757

PROFESSORS

BAEDORF, K.
BREXENDORF, T. O.
CZERNY, A.
EHRGOTT, M
EINST, H.
FASSNACHT, M., Marketing and Commerce
FENDEL, R., Monetary Economics
FISCHER, T.
FRENKEL, M., Macroeconomics and Int. Economics
GRICHNIK, D., Entrepreneurship
HACK, A.
HÖFFLER, F., Regulatory Economics
HÖGL, M., Leadership and Human Resource Management
HOZOG, W.
HÜSCHELRATH, K.
HUCHZERMEIER, A., Production Management
HUTZSCHENREUTER, T., Corporate Strategy and Electronic Media Management
JENSEN, O., Business-to-Business Marketing
JOHANNING, L., Empirical Capital Market Research
JOST, P.-J., Organization Theory
KAUFMANN, L., Int. Business and Supply Management
KLEIN, S.
KLEINDIENST, I., Strategy Processes
LAMMERS, C., Corporate Finance
LICHTENTHALER, U.
MAHLENDORF, M.
NÖLDEKE, M., Finance
REHM, S.-V., Business Information Science and Information Management
REIMANN, F.
RUDOLF, F., Organization Theory
RÜLKE, J.-C.
SCHÄFFER, U., Management Accounting and Control
SCHAUZ, D.
SCHUBERT, S.
SCHWEIZER, D.
SELLHORN, T.
SPINLER, S.
WEBER, J., Controlling and Telecommunications
WEIGAND, J., Microeconomics and Industrial Organization

Colleges

GENERAL

ESCP Europe Wirtschaftshochschule Berlin (ESCP Europe Business School Berlin): Heubnerweg 6, 14059 Berlin; tel. (30) 320070; e-mail info.de@escpeurope.eu; internet www.escpeurope.eu; f. 1985; campuses in France, UK, Germany, Italy, and

Spain; masters and doctoral programmes in business admin. and management; 125 teachers; Rector Prof. Dr AYAD AL-ANI; Pro-Rector Prof. Dr ULRICH PAPE; Library Dir REGINA GOLLNICK.

Frankfurt School of Finance and Management: Sonnemannstr. 9–11, 60314 Frankfurt am Main; tel. (69) 1540080; e-mail info@frankfurt-school.de; internet www.frankfurt-school.de; f. 1957; bachelors, masters and doctoral programmes in finance and management; 1,800 teachers; 7,800 students; Pres. Prof. Dr UDO STEFFENS; Vice-Pres. and Man. Dir INGOLF JUNGMANN; Vice-Pres. for Research Prof. Dr HARTMUT KLIEMT; Vice-Pres. for Teaching Prof. Dr MICHAEL H. GROTE.

Handelshochschule Leipzig (HHL) (Leipzig Graduate School of Management): Jahnallee 59, 04109 Leipzig; tel. (341) 985160; e-mail info@hhl.de; internet www.hhl.de; f. 1898; full-time, part-time masters and doctoral programmes in business and management; Rector Prof. Dr ANDREAS PINKWART; Chancellor Dr AXEL BAISCH; Head Librarian ANDREA LIEB.

Internationales Hochschulinstitut Zittau (IHI) (International Graduate School Zittau): Markt 23, 02763 Zittau; tel. (83) 612700; e-mail info@ihi-zittau.de; internet www.ihi-zittau.de; f. 1993; interdisciplinary and int. masters and doctoral programmes; library: 170,306 vols; 200 students; Rector Prof. Dr Hab. ALBERT LÖHR; Pro-Rector for Research Prof. Dr Hab. MARTIN HOFRICHTER; Chancellor KARIN HOLLSTEIN (acting).

Schiller International University – Germany: Bergstr. 106, 69121 Heidelberg; tel. (6221) 45810; e-mail campus@siu-heidelberg.de; internet www.siu-heidelberg.de; f. 1964 as independent int. univ.; language of instruction: English (all campuses); campuses in France, Germany, Spain, Switzerland, UK and USA (for which see respective chapters); depts of commercial art, computer studies, engineering management, int. business, int. tourism and hospitality management, int. relations and diplomacy, literature, para-legal studies, pre-medicine; degrees at Florida (USA) campus conferred under charter granted by State of Florida; degrees at all other campuses conferred under charter granted by State of Delaware (USA); library: 10,000 vols (total for all campuses); 25 teachers (Heidelberg campus only); 1,519 students (total for all campuses, of which 210 at Heidelberg campus); Dir THOMAS LEIBRECHT.

Wissenschaftskolleg zu Berlin (Institute for Advanced Study): Wallotstr. 19, 14193 Berlin; tel. (30) 890010; e-mail wiko@wiko-berlin.de; internet www.wiko-berlin.de; f. 1980; private instn for int. and interdisciplinary post-doctoral research; 40 Fellows; library mainly reference colln; Rector Prof. Dr LUCA GIULIANI; Sec. Dr JOACHIM NETTELBECK; Head Librarian Dr SONJA GRUND; publ. *Köpfe und Ideen* (1 a year).

ART, ARCHITECTURE

Akademie der Bildenden Künste (Academy of Fine Arts): Akademiestr. 2–4, 80799 Munich; tel. (89) 38520; e-mail post@adbk.mhn.de; internet www.adbk.de; f. 1770 (Charter conferred 1808 and 1953); languages of instruction: German, English; library: 122,000 vols, 100 current periodicals; 35 professors; 700 students; Chancellor (vacant); Vice-Chancellor PETER SACHER; Librarian INGE SICKLINGER-SEUß; Librarian SABINE MUSKE.

Akademie der Bildenden Künste in Nürnberg (Academy of Fine Arts in Nuremberg): Bingstr. 60, 90480 Nuremberg; tel. (911) 94040; e-mail info@adbk-nuernberg.de; internet www.adbk-nuernberg.de; f. 1662; master and postgraduate courses; arts, sculpture, visual arts, painting, artistic concepts, art education, gold- and silversmithing, graphic design, art history; library: 26,200 vols; 27 teachers; 350 students; Pres. Prof. OTTMAR HÖRL; Vice-Pres. Prof. Dr CHRISTIAN DEMAND; Vice-Pres. Prof. HOLGER FELTEN; Chancellor PETER OCHS; Vice-Chancellor UTE GRÖTSCH; Librarian MARTINA KEMMSIES.

Bauhaus Kolleg: see entry for Bauhaus Dessau Foundation.

Deutsche Film- und Fernsehakademie Berlin GmbH (German Film and Television Academy, Berlin GmbH): Potsdamer Str. 2, 10785 Berlin; tel. (30) 257590; e-mail info@dffb.de; internet www.dffb.de; f. 1966; 40 teachers; 250 students; library: 80,000 vols; Dir Prof. JAN SCHÜTTE.

Hochschule für Bildende Künste Braunschweig (Braunschweig University of Art): Johannes-Selenka-Pl. 1, 38118 Brunswick; tel. (531) 3919122; e-mail hbk@hbk-bs.de; internet www.hbk-bs.de; f. 1963; depts of art (painting, graphics, sculpture, film, video, performing arts and photography), design (industrial and graphic), art teaching, art history; institute for media and film studies, institute for art history and visual research; languages of instruction: German, English; Pres. Prof. Dr HUBERTUS VON AMELUNXEN; Vice-Pres. GERHARD BALLER; Vice-Pres. RAIMUND KUMMER; Vice-Pres. ULI PLANK; Vice-Pres. ULRIKE BERGERMANN; library: 120,000 vols; 1,200 students; publs *Schriftenreihe* (3–5 a year), *Vorlesungsverzeichnis/Studienführer* (2 a year).

Hochschule für Bildende Künste Dresden: POB 16 01 53, 01287 Dresden; Güntzstr. 34, 01307 Dresden; tel. (351) 492670; e-mail rektorat@serv1.hfbk-dresden.de; internet www.hfbk-dresden.de; f. 1764; stage and theatre design, costume design, painting, sculpture, graphics, restoration, art therapy; languages of instruction: German, English; library: 55,000 vols, 112 periodicals; 31 teachers; 650 students; Rector Prof. CHRISTIAN SERY; Pro-Rector Prof. ELKE HOPFE; Pro-Rector Prof. JENS BÜTTNER; Chancellor HANS-JÜRGEN SCHÖNEMANN; Head Librarian KARIN HUß; Librarian CHRISTINE POSSEGGA.

Hochschule für Bildende Künste Hamburg: Lerchenfeld 2, 22081 Hamburg; tel. (428) 989264; e-mail presse@hfbk.hamburg.de; internet www.hfbk-hamburg.de; f. 1767, present name and status 1955; depts of design, film, graphic art, typography, photography, painting, drawing, sculpture, stage design, theory and history of art, time-based media; Pres. MARTIN KÖTTERING; Vice-Pres. Dr HANNE LORECK; Vice-Pres. RAIMUND BAUER; Chancellor HORST-VOLKERT THIEL; Head Librarian INES RABE.

Hochschule für Grafik und Buchkunst Leipzig (Academy of Visual Arts, Leipzig): Wächterstr. 11, 04107 Leipzig; tel. (341) 21350; e-mail hgb@hgb-leipzig.de; internet www.hgb-leipzig.de; f. 1764 as Zeichnungs-, Mahlerey und Architectur-Akademie, present name 1950; painting, graphic arts, book art, graphic design, photography, media art; 48 teachers; 600 students; library: 40,000 vols, 100 current periodicals; Rector Prof. JOACHIM BROHM; Chancellor MARIA-CORNELIA ZIESCH; Librarian CLAUDIA-MARIA DARMER.

Hochschule für Künste Bremen (University of the Arts Bremen): Am Speicher XI 8, 28217 Bremen; tel. (421) 95951000; e-mail studsek@hfk-bremen.de; internet www.hfk-bremen.de; f. 1988; library: 40,000 vols; 265 teachers; 900 students; Rector Prof. Dr MANFRED CORDES; Chancellor REGINE OKORO.

Kunstakademie Düsseldorf (Academy of Fine Art, Düsseldorf): Eiskellerstr. 1, 40213 Düsseldorf; tel. (211) 13960; e-mail postmaster@kunstakademie-duesseldorf.de; internet www.kunstakademie-duesseldorf.de; f. 1773; 50 teachers; 700 students; library: 110,000 vols; Rector Prof. ANTHONY CRAGG; Pro-Rector Prof. Dr SIEGFRIED GOHR; Pro-Rector Prof. GEORG HEROLD; Chancellor DIETRICH KOSKA.

Kunsthochschule Berlin-Weissensee, Hochschule für Gestaltung (Berlin Weissensee School of Art): Bühringstr. 20, 13086 Berlin; tel. (30) 477050; e-mail rektor@kh-berlin.de; internet www.kh-berlin.de; f. 1946; fine arts, industrial design, ceramics, fashion design, textile design, communication design, architecture, stage design, sculpture; 550 students; 39 teachers; library: 20,000 vols; Rector LEONIE BAUMANN; Pro-Rector Prof. ELSE GABRIEL; Pro-Rector Prof. CAROLA ZWICK; Chancellor SILVIA DURIN.

Staatliche Akademie der Bildenden Künste (National Academy of Fine Arts): POB 6267, 76042 Karlsruhe; Reinhold-Frank-Str. 67, 76133 Karlsruhe; tel. (721) 9265210; e-mail rektorat@kunstakademie-karlsruhe.de; internet www.kunstakademie-karlsruhe.de; f. 1854; art education, fine arts, drawing, painting, sculpture; library: 40,000 vols; 300 students; Rector Prof. ERWIN GROSS; Chancellor RÜDIGER WEIS; Librarian RENATE WINKLER-WILDE.

Staatliche Akademie der Bildenden Künste (Stuttgart State Academy of Art and Design): Am Weissenhof 1, 70191 Stuttgart; tel. (711) 284400; e-mail info@abk-stuttgart.de; internet www.abk-stuttgart.de; f. 1761; art, graphics, sculpture, architecture, design, conservation, ceramics, textiles and industrial design; 850 students; Rector PETRA VON OLSCHOWSKI; Pro-Rector Prof. Dr NILS BÜTTNER; Pro-Rector Prof. TOBIAS WALLISSER; Pro-Rector Prof. VOLKER LEHNERT; Chancellor Dr MATTHIAS KNAPP.

Staatliche Hochschule für Bildende Künste–Städelschule (State College for Arts-Städelschule): Dürerstr. 10, 60596 Frankfurt; tel. (69) 6050080; e-mail rektor@staedelschule.de; internet www.staedelschule.de; f. 1817; art, architecture, film, sculpture, painting, drawing, architecture (conceptual design); 9 profs; 150 students; library: 16,000 vols; Pres. Prof. Dr FELIX SEMMELROTH; Rector Prof. Dr NIKOLAUS HIRSCH; Dir for Admin. ANDREAS LENK; Librarian KAREN LA MACCHIA.

ECONOMICS, POLITICAL AND SOCIAL SCIENCES, PUBLIC ADMINISTRATION

Hochschule für Politik München: Ludwigstr. 8, 80539 Munich; tel. (89) 285018; e-mail hfp-muenchen@hfp.mhn.de; internet www.hfp.mhn.de; f. 1950, present status 1981; theory of politics, law, economics, int. politics and contemporary history; library: 45,000 vols; 150 teachers; 950 students; Rector Prof. Dr RUPERT STETTNER; Pro-Rector Dr HORST MAHR; Librarian Dr BERND MAYERHOFER; publs *Junge Wissenschaft* (irregular), *Schriftenreihe* (irregular), *Zeitschrift für Politik* (4 a year).

Hochschule für Rechtswissenschaft (Bucerius Law School): POB 30 10 30, 20304 Hamburg; Jungiusstr. 6, 20355 Hamburg; tel. (40) 307060; e-mail info@law-school.de; internet www.law-school.de; f. 2000; doctoral and post-doctoral courses in law; library: 90,000 vols; 23 teachers; 561 students; Pres. Prof. Dr KARSTEN SCHMIDT; Vice-Pres. Prof. Dr FLORIAN FAUST; CEO Dr

HARIOLF WENZLER; Library Dir MARTIN VORBERG.

Stuttgart Institute of Management and Technology: Filderhauptstr. 142, 70599 Stuttgart; tel. (711) 4510010; e-mail information@uni-simt.de; internet www.uni-simt.de; f. 1998; MBA in int. management, finance and investment, management information systems, technology and innovation management; int. exec. MBA; part-time programmes; 68 teachers (8 full-time, 60 part-time); 150 students; CEO Prof. Dr JOHANN LÖHN.

LANGUAGES

Akademie für Fremdsprachen GmbH—Private Fachschule (Academy of Foreign Languages—Private School): POB 15 01 04, 10663 Berlin; Lietzenburger Str. 102, 10707 Berlin; tel. (30) 88663393; e-mail post@akafremd.de; internet www.akafremd.de; f. 1971; translators' and interpreters' courses in German, English, French, Spanish, Italian, Russian, and courses in German as a foreign language; 1,600 students; Man. Dir NORBERT ZÄNKER.

MEDICINE

Medizinische Akademie Erfurt (Medical Academy Erfurt): Nordhäuser Str. 74, PSF 595, 99089 Erfurt; tel. (361) 790; f. 1954; 121 teachers; 750 students; library: 140,000 vols; Rector Prof. Dr W. KÜNZEL; Pro-Rector Prof. Dr G. ENDERT; Medical Dir Prof. Dr W. KRAFFT; Librarian Dr B. ADLUNG.

MUSIC AND DRAMA

Filmakademie Baden-Württemberg (Baden-Württemberg Film Academy): Akademiehof 10, 71638 Ludwigsburg; tel. (7141) 9690; e-mail info@filmakademie.de; internet www.filmakademie.de; f. 1991; full-time programmes in film and media, production, sound design; 300 teachers; Dir Prof. THOMAS SCHADT.

Hochschule für Musik (University of Music): 79095 Freiburg im Breisgau; Schwarzwaldstr. 141, 79102 Freiburg im Breisgau; tel. (761) 319150; e-mail info@mh-freiburg.de; internet www.mh-freiburg.de; f. 1946; bachelor, postgraduate and doctoral courses in music; 160 teachers; 540 students; Chair. Dr OTMAR ZWIEBELHOFER; Rector Dr RÜDIGER NOLTE; Vice-Rector Prof. HELMUT LÖRSCHER; Vice-Rector Prof. SCOTT SANDMEIER.

Hochschule für Musik (University of Music Wuerzburg): Hofstallstr. 6–8, 97070 Würzburg; tel. (931) 321870; e-mail hochschule@hfm-wuerzburg.de; internet www.hfm-wuerzburg.de; f. 1804; bachelor, postgraduate, doctorate, pre-college programmes in music; library: 14,200 vols, 45,400 music scores, 47 current periodicals; 220 teachers; 597 students; library: 14,300 vols; Pres. Prof. HELMUT ERB; Vice-Pres. Prof. Dr THOMAS MÜNCH; Vice-Pres. THEODOR NÜßLEIN; Chancellor Dr EVA STUMPF-WIRTHS; Librarian BARBARA KONRAD.

Hochschule für Musik 'Carl Maria von Weber' Dresden (University for Music 'Carl Maria von Weber' Dresden): POB 12 00 39, 01001 Dresden; Wettiner Pl. 13, 01067 Dresden; tel. (351) 4923600; e-mail rektorat@hfmdd.de; internet www.hfmdd.de; f. 1856; attached institute for musicology (in co-operation with the Heinrich-Schütz Archive), institute for music medicine, studio for voice research, studio for electronic music; library: 80,000 vols, 7,000 records and CDs, contains Heinrich-Schütz archive; 80 teachers; 631 students; Rector EKKEHARD KLEMM; Pro-Rector for Artistic Practice Prof. ANDREAS BAUMANN; Pro-Rector for Education and Studies Prof. ELISABETH HOLMER; publ. *Schriftenreihe der Hochschule für Musik* (irregular).

Hochschule für Musik Detmold (University of Music Detmold): Neustadt 22, 32756 Detmold; tel. (5231) 9755; e-mail info@hfm-detmold.de; internet www.hfm-detmold.de; f. 1946; library: 157,800 vols; 120 teachers; 580 students; Rector Prof. MARTIN CHRISTIAN VOGEL; Vice-Rector Prof. ANDRÉ STÄRK; Vice-Rector Prof. NORBERT STERTZ; Chancellor HANS BERTELS.

Hochschule für Musik 'Franz Liszt' Weimar (Franz Liszt School of Music Weimar): POB 2552, 99406 Weimar; Pl. der Demokratie 2/3, 99423 Weimar; tel. (3643) 5550; e-mail study@hfm-weimar.de; internet www.hfm-weimar.de; f. 1872, current name adopted 1956; instruction in: keyboard, string and wind instruments, accordion, guitar, jazz/pop instruments and vocal, composition, conducting, singing and music teaching, church music and musicology; 132 teachers; 950 students; library: 65,000 vols and 45,000 tapes; Pres. Prof. Dr CHRISTOPH STÖLZL; Vice-Pres. for Teaching Prof. Dr HELMUT WELL; Vice-Pres. for Performance Studies Prof. ELMAR FULDA; Chancellor CHRISTINE GURK (acting).

Hochschule für Musik 'Hanns Eisler' (University for Music 'Hanns Eisler'): Charlottenstr. 55, 10117 Berlin; tel. (30) 90269700; e-mail rektorat@hfm.in-berlin.de; internet www.hfm-berlin.de; f. 1950 as German Acad. of Music, present name 1964; depts of voice, music, stage and theatre direction; strings, harp and guitar; brass, woodwind, percussion and conducting; and piano, accordion and composition/harmony; 433 teachers (113 full-time, 320 part-time); 702 students; Rector Prof. JÖRG-PETER WEIGLE; Pro-Rector Prof. JÖRG MAINKA; Pro-Rector GERT MÜLLER; Chancellor HANS-JOACHIM VÖLZ; Librarian HILDEGARD KLEEBAUM.

Hochschule für Musik Karlsruhe (University of Music Karlsruhe): POB 6040, 76040 Karlsruhe; Am Schloss Gottesaue 7, 76131 Karlsruhe; tel. (721) 66290; internet www.hfm-karlsruhe.de; f. 1884; library: 115,000 vols; 200 teachers; 560 students; Rector Prof. HARTMUT HÖLL; Pro-Rector Prof. ANDREA RAABE; Pro-Rector Prof. Dr JOHANNES M. WALTER; Pro-Rector Prof. MICHAEL UHDE; Chancellor WOLFRAM SCHERER; Library Dir MARC WEISSER (acting).

Hochschule für Musik Nürnberg (College for Music Nurnberg): Veilhofstr. 34, 90489 Nuremberg; tel. (911) 2318443; e-mail hfm-praesidium@hfm-nuernberg.de; internet www.hfm-n-a.de; f. 1873 as Leopold Mozart Konservatorium; current name adopted 1999; int. college of higher education; concerts, productions, International Leopold Mozart Competition for Young Violinists, Studio for Old and New Music; library: 9,000 vols; 98 teachers; 400 students; Pres. Prof. MARTIN ULLRICH; Vice-Pres. Prof. Dr RENATE ULLRICH; Vice-Pres. ALFONS BRANDL; Chancellor HANS-WERNER ITTMANN.

Hochschule für Musik Saar (University of Music Saar): Bismarckstr. 1, 66111 Saarbrücken; tel. (681) 967310; e-mail presse@hfm.saarland.de; internet www.hfm.saarland.de; f. 1947; 120 teachers; 400 students; library: 82,000 vols; Rector Prof. THOMAS DUIS; Pro-Rector Prof. JÖRG NONNWEILER; Chancellor WOLFGANG BOGLER; Librarian EDGAR COUDRAY.

Hochschule für Musik, Theater und Medien Hannover (University of Music, Drama and Media Hanover): Emmichpl. 1, 30175 Hanover; tel. (511) 31001; e-mail hmt@hmtm-hannover.de; internet www.hmt-hannover.de; f. 1961; courses of training for musicians, actors, music teachers, musicologists and media scientists; 350 teachers; 1,400 students; library: 203,000 vols; Pres. Prof. Dr SUSANNE RODE-BREYMANN; Vice-Pres. Prof. Dr BEATE SCHNEIDER; Vice-Pres. Prof. GUDRUN SCHRÖFEL; Vice-Pres. JANN BRUNS; Vice-Pres. Prof. MARKUS BECKER; Vice-Pres. Prof. VOLKER JACOBSEN.

Hochschule für Musik und Darstellende Kunst Frankfurt am Main (Frankfurt University of Music and Performing Arts (HfMDK)): Eschersheimer Landstr. 29–39, 60322 Frankfurt am Main; tel. (69) 1540070; e-mail praesident@hfmdk-frankfurt.de; internet www.hfmdk-frankfurt.info; f. 1878 as Konservatorium, Hochschule since 1938; music, dance, drama; library: 100,000 vols; 385 teachers; 900 students; Pres. Prof. THOMAS RIETSCHEL; Chancellor ANGELIKA GARTNER; Librarian Dr ANDREAS ODENKIRCHEN.

Hochschule für Musik und Darstellende Kunst Mannheim (University of Music and Performing Arts Mannheim): N 7, 18, 68161 Mannheim; tel. (621) 2923503; e-mail praesidium@muho-mannheim.de; internet www.muho-mannheim.de; f. 1899; orchestral instruments, keyboard instruments, voice concert and opera, conducting orchestra and choir; 200 teachers; 550 students; Pres. Prof. RUDOLF MEISTER; Vice-Pres. Prof. EHRHARD WETZ; Chancellor THILO FISCHER; Librarian KATHRIN WINTER.

Hochschule für Musik und Tanz Köln: Unter Krahnenbäumen 87, 50668 Cologne; tel. (221) 9128180; e-mail kristin.homeier@hfmt-koeln.de; internet www.mhs-koeln.de; f. 1925, reorganized 2009; centres in Cologne, Aachen and Wuppertal; instrumental music and musicology, dance studies; 330 teachers; 1,800 students; library: 136,000 vols, 8,600 records, 400 films; Pres. Prof. REINER SCHUHENN; Vice-Pres. Prof. Dr HEINZ GEUEN; Vice-Pres. Prof. JOACHIM ULLRICH; Chancellor URSULA WIRTZ-KNAPSTEIN; publ. *Journal* (2 a year).

Hochschule für Musik und Theater (Hamburg University of Music and Theatre): Harvestehuder Weg 12, 20148 Hamburg; tel. (40) 42848201; e-mail info@hfmt.hamburg.de; internet www.hfmt-hamburg.de; f. 1950; music education, music therapy, musicology, cultural and media management, opera, theatre; library: 20,000 vols; 250 teachers; 750 students; Pres. Prof. ELMAR LAMPSON; Vice-Pres. Prof. Dr MICHAEL VON TROSCHKE; Chancellor BERNHARD LANGE; Librarian MAIKE ARNEMANN; Librarian SILKE BROSE.

Hochschule für Musik und Theater 'Felix Mendelssohn Bartholdy' Leipzig (University of Music and Theatre 'Felix Mendelssohn Bartholdy' Leipzig): POB 10 08 09, 04008 Leipzig; Grassistr. 8, 04107 Leipzig; tel. (341) 214455; e-mail rektor@hmt-leipzig.de; internet www.hmt-leipzig.de; f. 1843; library: 50,000 vols, 150 current periodicals; 900 students; Rector Prof. ROBERT EHRLICH; Vice-Rector Prof. HANNS-MARTIN SCHREIBER; Vice-Rector Prof. MARTIN KÜRSCHNER; Chancellor OLIVER GRIMM.

Hochschule für Musik und Theater München (College for Music and Theatre Munchen): Arcisstr. 12, 80333 Munich; tel. (89) 28903; e-mail verwaltung@musikhochschule-muenchen.de; internet website.musikhochschule-muenchen.de; f. 1846; 300 teachers; 900 students; Pres. Prof. Dr SIEGFRIED MAUSER; Chancellor Dr ALEXANDER KRAUSE.

Internationales Musikinstitut Darmstadt (IMD) (International Music Institute

Darmstadt (IMD)): Nieder-Ramstäder Str. 190, 64285 Darmstadt; tel. (6151) 132416; e-mail imd@darmstadt.de; internet www.internationales-musikinstitut.de; f. 1946; int. holiday courses on contemporary music (composition, interpretation); int. music lending library (works since beginning of 20th century) of 35,000 scores, 5,000 vols, 4,000 tapes, 1,500 records; Dir THOMAS SCHÄFER; Assoc. Dir JÜRGEN KREBBER.

Musikhochschule Lübeck (University of Music Lübeck): Grosse Petersgrube 21, 23552 Lübeck; tel. (451) 15050; e-mail info@mh-luebeck.de; internet www.mh-luebeck.de; f. 1933; musical training on all instruments, opera singing and performing, training of music teachers, sacred music (Protestant and Catholic), preparatory training of professional musicians and music teachers; library: 110,000 vols; 130 teachers; 500 students; Rector Prof. INGE-SUSANN RÖMHILD; Vice-Rector Prof. JÖRG LINOWITZKI; Chancellor JÜRGEN R. CLAUßEN; Librarian TORSTEN SENKBEIL.

Robert-Schumann-Hochschule Düsseldorf (Robert Schumann School of Music and Media): Fischerstr. 110, 40476 Düsseldorf; tel. (211) 49180; e-mail kontakt@rsh-duesseldorf.de; internet www.rsh-duesseldorf.de; f. 1935; audio and video engineering, media, music, music promotion; library: 120,000 vols; 195 teachers; 900 students; Rector Prof. RAIMUND WIPPERMANN; Pro-Rector Prof. Dr VOLKER KALISCH; Pro-Rector Prof. THOMAS LEANDER; Chancellor Dr CATHRIN MÜLLER-BROSCH.

Staatliche Hochschule für Musik und Darstellende Kunst (University of Music and Performing Arts Stuttgart): Urbanstr. 25, 70182 Stuttgart; tel. (711) 2124631; e-mail rektor@mh-stuttgart.de; internet www.mh-stuttgart.de; f. 1857; 200 teachers; 800 students; library: 127,000 vols; Rector Prof. Dr WERNER HEINRICHS; Pro-Rector Prof. MATTHIAS HERMANN; Pro-Rector Prof. SHOSHANA RUDIAKOV; Chancellor ALBRECHT LANG.

PHILOSOPHY, THEOLOGY

Augustana Hochschule: Waldstr. 11, 91564 Neuendettelsau; tel. (9874) 5090; e-mail hochschule@augustana.de; internet www.augustana.de; f. 1947; library: 150,000 vols, 350 periodicals; 30 teachers; 200 students; Rector Prof. Dr MARKUS BUNTFUß; Librarian ARMIN STEPHAN.

Hochschule für Jüdische Studien Heidelberg (HfJS): Landfriedstr. 12, 69117 Heidelberg; tel. (21) 5419200; e-mail info@hfjs.eu; internet www.hfjs.eu; f. 1979; Jewish studies; library: 50,000 vols, 500 periodicals; 8 profs; First Vice-Rector Prof. Dr JOHANNES HEIL; Library Dir MARGARETHA BOOCKMANN; publs *Mussaf*, *Trumah*.

Hochschule für Philosophie (Munich School of Philosophy): Kaulbachstr. 31A, 80539 Munich; tel. (89) 23862300; e-mail info@hfph.mwn.de; internet www.hfph.mwn.de; f. 1925; library: 199,000 vols; 20 teachers; 500 students; Pres. Prof. Dr MICHAEL BORDT; Chancellor Dr DINA BRANDT; Librarian Dr JOHANNES BAAR; publ. *Theologie und Philosophie* (4 a year).

Kirchliche Hochschule Wuppertal/Bethel: Missionstr. 9A/B, 42285 Wuppertal; tel. (202) 2820100; e-mail info@kiho-wuppertal-bethel.de; internet www.kiho-wuppertal-bethel.de; f. 2007 by merger of Kirchlichen Hochschule Bethel (f. 1905) and Kirchlichen Hochschule Wuppertal (f. 1935); Protestant; library: 100,000 vols; 15 teachers; 200 students; Rector Prof. Dr SIEGFRIED KREUZER; Pro-Rector Prof. Dr HENNING WROGEMANN.

Lutherische Theologische Hochschule Oberursel (Lutheran Theological University Oberursel): Altkönigstrasse 150, 61440 Oberursel; tel. (6171) 91270; e-mail verwaltung@lthh-oberursel.de; internet www.lthh-oberursel.de; f. 1947; library: 40,000 vols, 100 periodicals; 8 teachers; 30 students; Rector Prof. Dr ACHIM BEHRENS; Librarian Prof. Dr GILBERTO DA SILVA; publ. *Lutherische Theologie und Kirche* (4 a year).

Philosophisch-Theologische Hochschule Sankt Georgen (St George Graduate School of Philosophy and Theology): Offenbacher Landstr. 224, 60599 Frankfurt am Main; tel. (69) 60610; e-mail rektorat@sankt-georgen.de; internet www.sankt-georgen.de; f. 1926 (since 1950 combined with Jesuit Theological Faculty, f. 1863); biblical studies, classical and modern languages, historical theology, philosophy, practical theology, systematic theology; library: 421,552 vols, 633 current periodicals, 11,497 e-journals; 23 teachers; 460 students; Chancellor Prof. Dr ADOLFO NICOLÁS; Vice-Chancellor Dr STEFAN KIECHLE; Rector Prof. Dr HEINRICH WATZKA; Pro-Rector Prof. Dr KLAUS KIEßLING; publs *Frankfurter Theologische Studien* (2–3 a year), *Sankt Georgener Hochschulschriften* (1 a year), *Theologie und Philosophie* (4 a year).

Theologische Fakultät Fulda (Staatlich anerkannte Wissenschaftliche Hochschule) (Fulda Theology Faculty): Eduard-Schick-Pl. 2, 36037 Fulda; tel. (661) 87220; e-mail rektorat@thf-fulda.de; internet www.thf-fulda.de; f. 1748; library: 200,000 vols, 200 print journals; 20 teachers; 44 students; Rector Prof. Dr Hab. CHRISTOPH GREGOR MÜLLER; Library Dir Dr BERTHOLD JÄGER; publs *Fuldaer Hochschulschriften*, *Fuldaer Studien*.

Theologische Fakultät Paderborn (Faculty of Theology in Paderborn): Kamp 6, 33098 Paderborn; tel. (5251) 1216; e-mail rektorat@theol-fakultaet-pb.de; internet www.theol-fakultaet-pb.de; f. 1615; library: 260,000 vols, 810 incunabula; 26 teachers; 390 students; Rector Prof. Dr BERTHOLD WALD; Pro-Rector Prof. Dr PETER SCHALLENBERG; publ. *Theologie und Glaube* (4 a year).

Theologische Fakultät Trier: Universitätsring 19, 54296 Trier; tel. (651) 2013520; e-mail theofak@uni-trier.de; internet www.theo.uni-trier.de; f. 1950; library: 400,000 vols; 315 students; Chancellor Dr REINHARD MARX (Bishop of Trier); Rector Prof. Dr KLAUS PETER DANNECKER; publ. *Trierer Theologische Zeitschrift* (4 a year).

TECHNOLOGY

Burg Giebichenstein Kunsthochschule Halle (Burg Giebichenstein University of Art and Design Halle): POB 20 02 52, 06003 Halle; Neuwerk 7, 06108 Halle; tel. (345) 775150; e-mail burgpost@halle.de; internet www.burg-halle.de; f. 1915; library: 82,000 vols, 140 journals; 90 teachers; 980 students; Rector Prof. AXEL MÜLLER-SCHÖLL; Vice-Rector Prof. ANDREA TINNES; Vice-Rector Prof. KARIN SCHMIDT-RUHLAND; Vice-Rector Prof. Dr NIKE BÄTZNER; Chancellor WOLFGANG STOCKERT.

Attached Research Institutes:

Institut Computer Art & Design: tel. (345) 7751900; e-mail ca&d@burg-halle.de; internet cad.burg-halle.de; Dir BERND HANISCH.

Institut für Software Consulting und Entwicklung: tel. (345) 7751701; e-mail isce@burg-halle.de; internet www.burg-halle.de/~isce; Dir Prof. JOSEF WALCH.

Institut idea (Interior Design, Environment and Architecture): tel. (345) 7751868; e-mail idea@burg-halle.de; internet www.burg-halle.de/~idea.

Hochschule Anhalt (FH) (Anhalt University of Applied Sciences): Bernburger Str. 55, 06366 Köthen; tel. (3496) 671000; e-mail c.knothstk@hs-anhalt.de; internet www.hs-anhalt.de; f. 1891, present status 1992; Köthen: biotechnology and food processing, chemical and environmental engineering, computer science, electrical engineering, mechanical engineering (plant construction); Bernburg: agriculture, business economics, food and health management, landscape architecture and planning; Dessau: architecture, civil engineering, design, surveying; 7,700 students; Pres. Prof. Dr Hab. DIETER ORZESSEK; Vice-Pres. for Information Technology Prof. EINAR KRETZLER; Vice-Pres. for Academic Studies and Teaching Prof. Dr CAROLA GRIEHL; Vice-Pres. for Research and Foreign Relations Prof. Dr RUDOLF LÜCKMANN; Head Librarian BETTINA ELZE.

Hochschule für Technik, Wirtschaft und Kultur Leipzig (Leipzig College of Applied Sciences): POB 30 11 66, 04251 Leipzig; Karl-Liebknecht-Str. 132, 04277 Leipzig; tel. (341) 30760; e-mail poststelle@htwk-leipzig.de; internet www.htwk-leipzig.de; f. 1992; architecture, book trade/publishing, business administration, business mathematics, civil engineering, computer science, electrical engineering, engineering with management (electrical engineering, energy engineering, mechanical engineering, civil engineering), library and information science, mechanical engineering, multimedia technology, museology, printing technology, publishing, social work, international management; library: 320,000 vols; 180 teachers; 7,000 students; Rector Prof. Dr RENATE LIECKFELDT; Vice-Rector for Education Prof. Dr Hab. SIBYLLE SEYFFERT; Vice-Rector for Scientific Devt and Research Prof. Dr Ing. MICHAEL KUBESSA; Chancellor ULRICH ZIEGLER.

Hochschule Mittweida—University of Applied Sciences (Mittweida College—University of Applied Sciences): POB 14 57, 09644 Mittweida; Technikumpl 17, 09648 Mittweida; tel. (3727) 580; e-mail kontakt@hs-mittweida.de; internet www.hs-mittweida.de; f. 1867; building engineering, computer sciences, economic sciences, electrical engineering, electronics, environmental engineering, mathematics, mechanical engineering, media management, media technology, microelectronics, microsystems engineering, physical engineering, physics, precision engineering, social sciences, steel and metal construction; library: 140,000 vols; 298 teachers; 5,300 students; Rector Prof. Dr Ing. LOTHAR OTTO; Vice-Rector Prof. Dr Ing. Hab. GERHARD THIEM; Vice-Rector Prof. Dr MONIKA HÄUßLER-SCZEPAN; Vice-Rector Prof. Dr Ing. MICHAEL HÖSEL; Chancellor SYLVIA BÄßLER.

Hochschule Zittau/Görlitz—University of Applied Sciences (Zittau/Görlitz College—University of Applied Sciences): POB 1454, 02754 Zittau; Theodor-Koerner-Allee 16, 02763 Zittau; tel. (3583) 611400; e-mail info@hs-zigr.de; internet wwwcms.hs-zigr.de; f. 1992; architecture, business management, business mathematics, business studies, chemistry, civil engineering, communications psychology, computer science, ecology and environmental protection, electrical and electronic engineering, electrical engineering, industrial engineering, marketing, mechanical engineering, mechatronics, power and environmental engineering, process engineering, real estate and housing management, social education, social work, special needs education, tourism, translating English and Czech; library: 179,254 vols; 130 teachers; 3,800 students; Rector Prof. Dr F. ALBRECHT; Vice-Rector for Research Prof. Dr Ing. ROLAND GIESE; Vice-Rector for Education Prof. Dr TOBIAS ZSCHUNKE; Chancellor KARIN HOLLSTEIN.

Westsächsische Hochschule Zwickau – University of Applied Sciences (West Saxon College Zwickau–University of Applied Sciences): Dr-Friedrichs-Ring 2A, 08056 Zwickau; tel. (375) 5360; e-mail rektorat@fh-zwickau.de; internet www.fh-zwickau.de; f. 1992; schools of applied arts, applied economics, architecture, electrical engineering, health and healthcare management, languages, mechanical and automotive engineering, physical and computer sciences, textile and leather production engineering; library: 198,000 vols; 191 teachers; 4,700 students; Rector Prof. Dr Hab. GUNTER KRAUTHEIM; Vice-Rector Prof. Dr GUNDOLF BAIER; Vice-Rector Prof. Dr Ing. MATTHIAS RICHTER; Vice-Rector Prof. Dr UTE ROSENBAUM; Chancellor Prof. Dr JOACHIM KÖRNER; publs *Campus*[3], *Hochschulforschungsbericht* (1 a year), *Hochschulführer* (1 a year).

GHANA

The Higher Education System

In 1957 the former British dependencies of Togoland and Gold Coast declared the independent state of Ghana, which subsequently became a republic in 1960. The first institution of higher education, Achimota College, was founded in 1924, and the first university-level institution, University College of the Gold Coast, was founded in 1948 in conjunction with the University of London (United Kingdom), and achieved full university status in 1961; it is now known as University of Ghana, and is based in the capital, Accra. Some 82,346 students were enrolled in higher education in 1996/97, with 23,126 students attending the country's five universities. In 2006/07 some 140,000 students were enrolled in tertiary education, and by 2010/11 this figure had risen to 285,900. In recent years the number of private higher education institutions has increased substantially as demand for places has risen. By 2012, according to Ministry of Education figures, there were 44 private tertiary institutions offering degree programmes and nine public universities.

Higher education is administered by the Ministry of Education. The National Council for Tertiary Education is the body that advises the Government on higher education policy. The National Accreditation Board (NAB), which was established in 1993, classifies institutions of higher education as universities, university colleges, polytechnics, colleges, schools, institutes, academies or tutorial colleges. The NAB is responsible for accrediting private and public institutions of higher education, approving programmes of study, ensuring quality assurance, and determining degree equivalency. Institutions of higher education usually have two-tier systems of governance, consisting of a Council, which oversees administrative issues such as finance and personnel, and either a Senate or Academic Board, which deals with academic issues. The Chancellor is the head of the University. In 1988/89 tuition fees were introduced in tertiary education. The Government currently provides around 70% of funding for public universities and the remaining 30% is raised from fees and donations. Private institutions are primarily funded by student fees.

Admission to university is based on suitable scores in either six subjects at SSSCE (Senior Secondary School Certificate Examinations) level or three subjects at A-level. In some cases, prospective students also have to take an entrance examination. The main undergraduate degree is the three- to four-year Bachelors, although both University of Ghana and Kwame Nkrumah University of Science and Technology offer two-year undergraduate Diploma programmes in a wide range of vocational disciplines, the University of Cape Coast offers two-year and three-year undergraduate Diploma programmes and the University of Education, Winneba offers undergraduate Diploma programmes in educational subjects. The Bachelors degree is based on the US-style credit and semester scheme, and students are required to accrue a specified number of credits in major and minor subjects in order to graduate. A substantial number of privately run universities and university colleges have recently been established in Ghana. These new institutions also offer four-year Bachelors degree programmes. However, until the quality of these degrees can be properly assessed, each private institution is affiliated to one of the public universities, which is responsible for awarding the final qualifications. Only the nine state-controlled universities offer postgraduate degrees, which include one- to two-year Masters and Postgraduate Diploma programmes, and Doctorate programmes (entrance to which is currently based on the holding of a Masters) lasting a minimum of three years and requiring the presentation of a thesis.

The National Coordinating Committee for Technical and Vocational Education and Training is the government body responsible for technical and vocational education. The leading institutions for technical and vocational education are the polytechnics, which were elevated to higher education-level status in 1993. The polytechnics, of which there are currently 10 in Ghana, offer four main qualifications: Vocational Craft Certificate, Advanced Craft Certificate, Diploma and Higher National Diploma.

Regulatory and Representative Bodies

GOVERNMENT

Ministry of Chieftaincy and Traditional Affairs: POB 1627, State House, Accra; tel. (30) 2685012; e-mail chieftancycultur@yahoo.com; Minister HENRY SEIDU DAANAA.

Ministry of Education: POB M45, Accra; tel. (30) 2662772; Minister JANE OPOKU-AGYEMAN.

ACCREDITATION

National Accreditation Board: IPS-Trinity Rd, POB CT 3256, Cantonments, Accra; tel. (30) 2518570; e-mail nabsec@nab.gov.gh; internet www.nab.gov.gh; f. 1993; attached to Min. of Education; accredits public and private tertiary instns with respect to the content and standard of their programmes; determines the equivalences of diplomas, certificates and other qualifications awarded by instns in Ghana or elsewhere; 15 mems; Chair. Prof. D. A. AKYEAMPONG; Exec. Sec. KWAME DATTEY.

NATIONAL BODY

National Council for Tertiary Education: POB M28, Accra; tel. (30) 2770198; e-mail info@ncteghana.org; f. 1993; attached to Min. of Education; advises the Min. on the devt of tertiary education instns in Ghana and on their financial needs; recommends nat. standards on staff, costs, accommodation and time utilization, and monitors the implementation of any approved nat. standards by the instns; Exec. Sec. PAUL EFFAH.

Learned Societies

GENERAL

Centre for National Culture: POB 2738, Accra; tel. (30) 2664099; f. 1958; incl. a research section; Chair. NII AYITEY AGBOFU II; Dir M. K. AMOATEY; publ. *DAWURO*.

Ghana Academy of Arts and Sciences: POB M.32, Accra; tel. (30) 2772002; e-mail gaas@ug.edu.gh; internet www.gaas-gh.org; f. 1959; Pres. Dr S. K. B. ASANTE; Hon. Sec. Prof. KWESI YANKAH; publ. *Proceedings* (1 a year).

UNESCO Accra Cluster Office: POB CT 4949, Accra; 8 Mankralo St, East Cantonments, Accra; tel. (30) 2740840; e-mail accra@unesco.org; designated Cluster Office for Benin, Côte d'Ivoire, Ghana, Nigeria, Sierra Leone and Togo; Dir ELIZABEH MOUNDO.

ARCHITECTURE AND TOWN PLANNING

Ghana Institute of Architects: Architecture House No 3, Ninth Rd East Ridge, POB MB 272, Accra; e-mail info@gia.org.gh; internet www.gia.org.gh; f. 1962; 300 mems; Pres. Arq. ARDOTEI BROWN; Hon. Sec. JOSEPH E. HAYFORD; publs *Ghana Architect*, *PATO*.

BIBLIOGRAPHY, LIBRARY SCIENCE AND MUSEOLOGY

Ghana Library Association: POB 4105, Accra; tel. (30) 2763523; e-mail info@gla-net.org; internet www.gla-net.org; f. 1962; 300 mems; Pres. Dr PERPETUA DADZIE; Sec. COMFORT ASARE; publ. *Ghana Library Journal* (1 a year).

ECONOMICS, LAW AND POLITICS

Ghana Bar Association: POB 4150, Accra; tel. (30) 2226748; e-mail info@ghanabar.org;

2,500 mems; Nat. Pres. PAUL ADU-GYAMFI; Nat. Sec. BENSON NUTSUKPUI.

EDUCATION

West African Examinations Council: Examination Loop, POB GP 125, Accra; tel. (30) 2248967; e-mail waechqrs@africaonline.com.gh; internet www.waecheadquartersgh.org; f. 1952 by the 4 W African Commonwealth countries; nat. offices in Lagos, Nigeria; Accra, Ghana; Freetown, Sierra Leone; Banjul, The Gambia; Monrovia, Liberia; conducts the W African Sr School Certificate Examination (WASSCE) for The Gambia, Sierra Leone, Nigeria and Ghana; Basic Education Certificate Examination for The Gambia, Ghana and Sierra Leone; and 9th and 12th grade examinations for Liberia; also selection examinations for entry into secondary schools and similar instns and the public services; entrance and final examinations for teacher-training colleges, commercial and technical examinations at the request of the various Ministries of Education; holds examinations on behalf of Educational Testing Service, Princeton, NJ, USA and examining authorities in the UK and W Africa; 5 mem. countries; Chair. Prof. PIUS AUGUSTINE IKE OBANYA; Registrar/Chief Exec. Dr IYI UWADIAE; publs *Research Reports* (abstracts and findings of research projects conducted by the Ccl), *West African Journal of Educational and Vocational Measurement*.

HISTORY, GEOGRAPHY AND ARCHAEOLOGY

Ghana Geographical Association: PMB, Kumasi; e-mail uro@knust.edu.gh; f. 1955; attached to Kwame Nkrumah Univ. of Science and Technology; Pres. Dr EVA TAGOE-DARKO; Sec.-Gen. Dr PRINCE OSEI-WUSU; publ. *Ghana Geographical Journal*.

Historical Society of Ghana: POB 12, Legon, Accra; e-mail info@historicalsocietygh.com; internet www.historicalsocietygh.com; f. 1952; fmrly Gold Coast and Togoland Historical Soc.; sponsors research, organizes an annual conf open to general public; publishes journals, books, theses and documentaries; 1,200 mems; Pres. Prof. IRENE K. ODOTEI; Sec. Prof. ROBERT ADDO-FENNING; publ. *Transactions* (1 a year).

LANGUAGE AND LITERATURE

Alliance Française: Liberation Link, Airport Residential Area, POB CT 4904, Accra; tel. (30) 2760278; e-mail info@alliancefrancaiseghana.org; internet www.alliancefrancaiseghana.org; offers courses and examinations in French language and culture, and promotes cultural exchange with France; attached teaching centres in Cape Coast, Kumasi, Takoradi and Tema.

British Council: Liberia Rd, POB GP 771, Accra; tel. (30) 2683068; e-mail infoaccra@gh.britishcouncil.org; internet www.britishcouncil.org/ghana; f. 1943; conducts British examinations, supports personal and professional development through physical and electronic resources; projects include school and higher education partnership, leadership training; attached centre in Kumasi; library of 4,000 vols, more than 50 periodicals; 1,500 video cassettes and DVDs, electronic resources; Dir MOSES ANIBABA.

Ghana Association of Writers: PAWA house, Roman Ridge, POB LG 375, Legon, Accra; tel. (30) 2946369; e-mail admin@ghanawriters.org; internet www.ghanawriters.org; f. 1957; literary evenings, annual congress; Pres. KWASI GYAN-APENTENG; Sec.-Gen. Dr CAMYNTA BAEZIE; publ. *Angla* (1 a year).

Goethe-Institut: 30 Kakramadu Rd, Cantonments, Accra; tel. (30) 2776764; e-mail info@accra.goethe.org; internet www.goethe.de/af/acc/deindex.htm; f. 1961; offers courses and examinations in German language and culture and promotes cultural exchange with Germany; library of 2,603 vols; Dir ELEONORE SYLLA.

MEDICINE

Pharmaceutical Society of Ghana: POB 2133, Accra; tel. (30) 2228341; f. 1935; 8 regional brs; library of 250 vols; 1,200 mems; Pres. ALEXANDER NII OTO DODDO; Exec. Sec. DENNIS SENA AWITTY; publ. *The Ghana Pharmaceutical Journal* (4 a year).

NATURAL SCIENCES

General

Ghana Science Association: POB 7, Legon; tel. (30) 2732605; e-mail gsa@ug.edu.gh; f. 1959; Nat. Pres. Prof. DANIEL OBENG-OFORI; Nat. Sec. I. J. KWAME ABOH; publ. *The Ghana Journal of Science*.

RELIGION, SOCIOLOGY AND ANTHROPOLOGY

Ghana Sociological Association: c/o Dept of Sociology, Univ. of Ghana, Legon; f. 1961; financial aid from the universities and the Academy of Arts and Sciences; academic activities, conferences; 215 mems; Pres. Pres. DAN-BRIGHT DZORGBO; Sec. Dr AJHASSAN SULEMANA ANAMZOYA; publ. *Ghana Journal of Sociology*.

TECHNOLOGY

Ghana Institution of Engineers: 13 Continental Rd, Roman Ridge, POB 7042, Accra-North, Accra; tel. (30) 2760867; e-mail secretariat@ghie.org.gh; internet www.ghie.org.gh; f. 1968; 1,000 mems; Pres. Ing. BEN R. ANIAGYEI; Exec. Sec. Ing. Dr DESMOND ARYEE-BOI; publ. *The Ghana Engineer* (4 a year).

Research Institutes

GENERAL

Council for Scientific and Industrial Research (CSIR): POB M.32, Accra; tel. (30) 2777651; internet www.csir.org.gh; f. 1958; functions incl. advice to the Govt, encouragement of scientific and industrial research relevant to nat. devt and commercialization of research results; coordination of research in all its aspects in Ghana, and collation, publ. and dissemination of research results; library: Institute for Scientific and Technological Information: see under Libraries and Archives; Dir-Gen. Prof. E. OWUSU-BENNOAH; Sec. E. ODARTEI-LARYEA; publs *CSIR Handbook*, *Ghana Journal of Agricultural Science*, *Ghana Journal of Science*.

Attached Research Institutes:

Animal Research Institute: POB AH20, Achimota; tel. (21) 401846; e-mail e-mailari@africaonline.com.gh; f. 1957; Dir Dr K. G. ANING.

Building and Road Research Institute: Univ. POB 40, Knust, Kumasi; tel. (51) 60064; internet www.brri.org; f. 1952; research into bldg and road problems, traffic and transportation, geosciences, material sciences; library of 15,244 vols; Dir EUGENE ATIEMO; publs *Construction Cost Indices* (4 a year), *Journal of Building and Road Research* (2 a year).

CSIR-Crops Research Institute: POB 3785, Kwadaso, Kumasi; tel. (3220) 60389; e-mail cridirector@cropsresearch.org; internet www.cropsresearch.org; Dir Rev. Dr HANS ADU DAPAAH; Librarian LAWRENCIA DONKOR ACHEAMPONG.

Food Research Institute: POB M.20, Accra; tel. (30) 2519091; e-mail director@fri.csir.org.gh; internet www.fri.csir.org.gh; f. 1964; food processing, preservation, storage, analysis, marketing; library of 4,500 vols; Dir Dr NANAM TAY DZIEDZOAVE; Librarian RAPHAEL K. KAVI; publ. *Bulletin*.

Forestry Research Institute of Ghana: POB 63, Knust, Kumasi; tel. (3220) 60123; e-mail director@csir-forig.org.gh; Dir Dr VICTOR K. AGYEMAN; publ. *Ghana Journal of Forestry* (every 2 years).

CSIR-Oil Palm Research Institute: POB 74, Kade; tel. (3420) 610257; e-mail kusi@opri.csir.org.gh; internet www.csir.org.gh; f. 1964; Dir Dr S. K. DERY (acting).

CSIR-Plant Genetic Resources Research Institute: POB 7, Bunso; tel. (28)9525118; e-mail info@pgrri.csir.org.gh; internet www.csir.org.gh; f. 1964; Dir Dr LAWRENCE MISA ABOAGYE.

CSIR-Savanna Agricultural Research Institute: POB TL 52, Tamale; tel. (3720) 91205; e-mail rokowusu@yahoo.com; internet www.csir.org.gh; f. 1947, fmrly known as Nyankpala Agricultural Experimental Station; present status 1996; research in food and fibre crops in 3 northern regions of Ghana; plant breeding, agronomy, plant protection, soil fertility improvement, post-harvest, agricultural economics and rural sociology; library of 5,000 vols; Dir Dr STEPHEN NUTSUGAH.

Science and Technology Policy Research Institute: POB CT 519, Cantonments, Accra; tel. (30) 2773856; e-mail director@stepri.csir.org.gh; Dir Dr J. O. GOGO.

Soil Research Institute: Academy PO, Kwadaso, Kumasi; tel. (51) 50353; e-mail soil@aol.com.gh; f. 1951; Dir Dr R. D. ASIAMAH.

Water Research Institute: POB AH.38, Achimota; tel. (30) 2775357; e-mail wri@ghana.com; Dir Dr C. A. BINEY.

AGRICULTURE, FISHERIES AND VETERINARY SCIENCE

Cocoa Research Institute of Ghana: POB 8, New Tafo-Akim; tel. (27) 7609900; e-mail crig@crig.org; internet www.crig.org; f. 1938; research on cocoa, cola, coffee, shea nuts and cashews; 3 substations; 3 cocoa plantations for research and devt of cocoa by-products; library of 17,700 vols, 8,222 pamphlets, 2,054 journals; Exec. Dir Dr F. M. AMOAH; publ. *Technical Bulletin*.

NATURAL SCIENCES

Physical Sciences

Geological Survey Department: POB M 80, Accra; The Ministries, Kinbu Rd, Accra; tel. (30) 2679236; e-mail info@gsd.ghanamining.org; internet www.ghana-mining.org/ghanaims/institutions/geologicalsurveydepartmentgsd/tabid/156/default.aspx; f. 1913; geological mapping and geophysical surveying; research and evaluation of mineral resources; library of 30,000 vols; Dir CHARLES EDWARD ODURO.

Ghana Meteorological Agency: POB LG 87, Legon; tel. (30) 27012520; e-mail meteo@africaonline.com.gh; internet www.meteo.gov.gh; f. 1937 as Ghana Meteorological Services Dept; present name 2004; provision of meteorological information, advice and warnings for the benefit of agriculture, civil and military aviation, surface and marine transport, operational hydrology and management of energy and water resources to mitigate the effects of natural disasters such as floods, storms, and drought on socio-economic devts and projects; Dir ZINEDEME MINIA.

Libraries and Archives

Accra

Accra Central Library: Thorpe Rd, POB 2362, Accra; tel. (30) 2665083; f. 1950; central reference library; central lending library; central children's library; mobile library unit; union catalogues; Regional Librarian GUY AMARTEFIO.

Council for Scientific and Industrial Research-Institute for Scientific and Technological Information (INSTI): POB M.32, Accra; tel. (30) 2778808; e-mail insti@csir.org.gh; internet www.csir.org.gh; f. 1964; attached to Ccl for Scientific and Industrial Research; collects, processes, stores and disseminates indigenous, scientific and technological information; 23,473 vols, 60 current periodicals; Dir JOEL SAM; Librarian GRACE OBENG-KORANTENG; publs *Gains News* (4 a year), *Ghana Journal of Agricultural Science* (2 a year), *Ghana Journal of Science* (2 a year), *Ghana Science Abstracts* (1 a year), *Union List of Agricultural Serials in Ghana*, *Union List of Scientific and Technological Journals in Ghana*.

George Padmore Research Library on African Affairs: POB 2970, Accra; tel. (30) 2247768; e-mail padmoreresearch@ghanalibraryboard.com; internet www.ghanalibraryboard.org; f. 1961; Nat. Bibliographic Agency and Legal Deposit Library; collection, processing and dissemination of recorded literature related to history, culture, anthropology, economics, law and public administration of all Africa; incl. Ghana National Collection; manages the ISBN/ISSN/ISMN Ghana Agency; 640,000 vols, 80 periodicals; Librarian OMARI MENSAH TENKORANG; publs *Ghana National Bibliography* (6 a year and 1 a year), *special subject bibliographies* (irregular).

Ghana Library Authority: Thorpe Rd, POB 663, Accra; tel. (30) 2662795; e-mail info@ghla.org.gh; internet www.ghla.org.gh; f. 1950; comprises Accra Central Library, regional libraries at Bolgatanga, Cape Coast, Ho, Koforidua, Kumasi, Sekondi, Sunyani, Tamale, Wa; George Padmore Research Library on African Affairs (*q.v.*); 37 br. libraries, mobile libraries, children's libraries; 1,383,712 vols; research library 35,029 vols, adults' libraries 1,167,653 vols; Dir of Library Services DAVID CORNELIUS.

Public Records and Archives Administration Department: POB GP. 3056, Accra; tel. (30) 2221234; e-mail praad@4u.com.gh; internet www.praad.gov.gh; f. 1946 as Nat. Archives of Ghana (legal recognition 1955); preserves Ghana's historical records; regional offices in Kumasi, Cape Coast, Sekondi, Tamale, Sunyani, Koforidua and Ho; provision of Record Centre services for the keeping of semi-current records of Mins, Municipalities, Depts and Agencies of the Govt of Ghana and some other private instns; setting of standards in record management practices for governmental instns; provides search services to the public; certification of archival documents; conservation of archival documents of Ghana; 2,000 documents to provide supplementary services to the searchroom; Dir FELIX NYARKO AMPONG (acting); publs *Brochure*, *Class Lists of the Holdings of PRAAD*.

Kumasi

Ashanti Regional Library: Bantama Rd, POB 824, Kumasi; tel. (51) 2784; f. 1954; lending, reference and extension services for adults, students and school children; 20,000 vols, incl. local colln on Ghana of 450 vols; Librarian KOFI S. ANTIRI.

Kwame Nkrumah University of Science and Technology Library: University PO, Kumasi; tel. (3220) 60133; e-mail library@knust.edu.gh; internet www.knust.edu.gh; f. 1951; 202,810 vols, 340 periodicals, 9,000 ejournals; Univ. Librarian Dr HELENA R. ASAMOAH-HASSAN.

Legon

University of Ghana Library (Balme Library): POB 24, Legon; tel. (302) 512407; e-mail balme@ug.edu.gh; f. 1948; comprises Arabic, UN, World Bank, Africana, Braille, Volta Basin Research Project collns and Students' Reference libraries; 384,936 vols; Librarian Prof. EDWIN ELLIS BADU.

Sekondi

Western Regional Library: Old Axim Rd, POB 174, Sekondi; tel. (31) 46816; f. 1955; 41,480 vols; Librarian S. Y. KWANSA.

Museums and Art Galleries

Accra

Ghana National Museum: POB GP 3343, Accra; 2 Barnes Rd, Adabraka, Accra; tel. (30) 2221633; e-mail gmmb-acc@africaonline.com.gh; internet www.ghanamuseums.org/national-museum.php; f. 1957; controlled by the Ghana Museums and Monuments Board; archaeological and ethnological findings from all over Ghana and West Africa; modern works by Ghanaian artists; preservation and conservation of ancient forts and castles and traditional buildings; Exec. Dir Dr ZAGBA NARH OYORTEY (acting); Deputy Dir for Museums RAYMOND AGBO.

Museum of Science and Technology: POB 3343, Accra; tel. (30) 2223963; f. 1965; temporary exhibition hall with an open-air cinema is used for the display of working models, charts, films and other exhibits on science and technology; collection of exhibits for permanent galleries has begun; temporary exhibitions are taken to the regions, films shown to colleges and schools, and regional and nat. Science Fairs are organized; Asst Dir K. A. ADDISON.

Cape Coast

Cape Coast Castle Museum: POB 281, Cape Coast; tel. (42) 32701; e-mail ghct@ghana.com; f. 1971; cultural history of Ghana's Central region; Sr Curator ALBERT WUDDAH-MARTEY.

Universities

KWAME NKRUMAH UNIVERSITY OF SCIENCE AND TECHNOLOGY

University PO, Kumasi
Telephone: (233) 3220-60331
E-mail: vc@knust.edu.gh
Internet: www.knust.edu.gh
Founded 1951 as College of Technology, present status 1961
State control
Language of instruction: English
Academic year: August to May (2 semesters)
Chancellor: HM ASANTEHENE OTOMFUO OSEI TUTU II
Vice-Chancellor: Prof. WILLIAM O. ELLIS
Pro-Vice-Chancellor: Prof. S. N. ODAI
Dean of Students: Dr K. OWUSU-DAAKU
Registrar: KOBBY YEBO OKRAH
Librarian: Dr HELENA R. ASAMOAH-HASSAN
Library of 130,975 vols, 5,300 print journal titles, 30,000 ejournals
Number of teachers: 801
Number of students: 34,438
Publication: *Journal of the University of Science and Technology*

DEANS

Dental School: Dr FRANCIS ADU-ABABIO
Faculty of Agriculture: Prof. R. AKROMAH
Faculty of Allied Health Sciences: Prof. J. APPIAH-POKU
Faculty of Art: Prof. K. OPOKU-AMANKWA
Faculty of Law: Prof. S. OFFEH
Faculty of Pharmacy and Pharmaceutical Sciences: Prof. T. C. FLEISCHER
Faculty of Renewable Natural Resources: Prof. W. ODURO
Faculty of Social Sciences: Prof. K. O. AKUOKO
Institute of Distance Learning: Prof. I. K. DONTWI
School of Business: J. M. FRIMPONG
School of Graduate Studies: Prof. C. K. KANKAM
School of Veterinary Medicine: Dr RAPHAEL D. FOLITSE

PROFESSORS

College of Agriculture and Natural Resources:
ABAIDOO, R. C.
AKROMAH, R., Agriculture
AMISAH, S., Fisheries and Watershed Management
ATUAHENE, C., Animal Science
AWUAH, R. T., Crop and Soil Science
BOATENG, P. Y., Horticulture
BONSU, M., Crop and Soil Science
DONKOR, A., Animal Science
ODURO, W., Wildlife and Range Management
ODURO, W., Renewable Natural Resources
OKAI, D. B., Animal Science
OPPONG, S. K., Wildlife and Range Management
OSAFO, E. L. K., Animal Science
OSEI, S. A., Animal Science
QUANSAH, C., Crop and Soil Science
SAFO, E. Y., Crop and Soil Science

College of Architecture and Planning:
AFRANE, S. K., Planning
ADARKWA, K. K., Planning
ASIAMA, S. O., Land Economy
AYARKWA, J., Building Technology
BADU, E., Architecture
DINYE, R. D., Land Economy
INTSIFUL, G. W. K., Architecture
KASANGA, R. K., Land Economy

College of Art and Social Sciences:
ABE, G. O., Religious Studies
ACKAM, R. T., Painting and Sculpture
DELAQUIS, H. B. A., Painting and Sculpture
FRIMPONG, J. M., School of Business
OFFEI, S., Law
OHENE ADU, D. A., Fine Art
OHENE-MANU, J., Social Sciences
OKLEME, S. K., English
OPOKU-AGYEMANG, K., Languages
OWUSU-SARPONG, A., Languages

College of Engineering:
AGODZO, S. K., Agricultural
AMPADU, S. I. K., Civil
AWUAH, E., Civil

Bart-Plange, A., Agricultural
Boadu, F. K., Geological
Duker, A. A., Geomatic
Dzisi, K. A., Agricultural
Forson, F. K., Mechanical
Glakpe, E. K., Mechanical
Kwofie, S., Materials
Kyei-Baffour, N., Agricultural
Mensah, E., Agricultural
Momade, F. W. Y., Materials
Odai, S. N., Civil
Salifu, M., Civil

College of Health Sciences:

Abantanga, F. A., Surgery
Acheampong, J. W., Medicine
Addy, E. A., Community Health
Adosraku, R. K., Pharmaceutical Chemistry
Adu-Sarkodie, Y., Clinical Microbiology
Agbelusi, G. A., Dentistry
Agbenyega, E. T., Physiology
Akinwande, J. A., Dentistry
Amedofu, G. K., Ear, Eye, Nose and Throat
Ankrah, T. C., Medicine
Appiah-Poku, J., Behavioural Sciences
Ayim, J. S. K., Pharmaceutical Chemistry
Bedu-Addo, G., Medicine
Brobby, G. W., Ear, Eye, Nose and Throat
Danso, K. A., Obstetrics and Gynaecology
Duwiejua, M., Clinical and Social Pharmacy
Eghan, jr, B. A., Medicine
Fleischer, T. C., Pharmacy
Frempong, E. H., Clinical Microbiology
Frimpong, M. T., Molecular Medicine
Khalil, D., Nursing
Kwakye, J. K., Pharmaceutical Chemistry
Mensah, A. Y., Pharmacognosy
Mensah, M. L. K., Herbal Medicine
Ofori-Kwakye, K., Pharmaceutics
Ohene-Yeboah, M., Surgery
Okine, N. N. A., Pharmaceutical Chemistry
Opare-Sem, O. K., Medicine
Oyeremi, M. O., Veterinary
Sarpong, K., Pharmacognosy

College of Science:

Adimado, A. A., Chemistry
Amponsah, S. K., Mathematics
Boateng, N. B., Chemistry
Danuor, S. K., Physics
Dontwi, I. K., Mathematics
Duca, K., Biochemistry and Biotechnology
Dzogbefia, V. P., Biochemistry and Biotechnology
Menyeh, A., Physics
Nkum, R. K.
Obiri Danso, K., Theoretical and Applied Biology
Oduro, I., Biochemistry and Biotechnology
Oldham, J. H., Biochemistry and Biotechnology
Yeboah-Gyan, K., Theoretical and Applied Biology

UNIVERSITY FOR DEVELOPMENT STUDIES

POB 1350, Tamale
Telephone: (71) 22078
E-mail: prs@uds.edu.gh
Internet: new.uds.edu.gh

Founded 1992
State control
Academic year: September to July (3 semesters)
Language of instruction: English
Accredited by Nat. Accreditation Bd, Ghana Medical and Dental Council, Nurses and Midwives Council of Ghana

Vice-Chancellor: Prof. Kaku Sagary Nokoe (acting)
Pro-Vice-Chancellor: Prof. David Millar
Registrar: S. M. Kuuire (acting)
Librarian: I. K. Antwi

Library of 31,906 vols
Number of teachers: 271
Number of students: 10,587

Publications: *Academic Calendar* (every 5 years), *Faculties and Departments at a Glance* (every 2 years), *Ghana Journal of Development Studies* (every 2 years), *Strategic Plan* (every 5 years)

DEANS

Faculty of Agriculture: Dr Gabriel Teye
Faculty of Applied Sciences: Dr Kenneth Pelig-Ba
Faculty of Integrated Development Studies: Rev. Prof. Abraham Berinyuu
Faculty of Planning and Land Management: Dr Francis Bacho
Faculty of Renewable Natural Resources: Dr Thomas Bayorbor
Graduate School: Prof. David Millar
School of Medicine and Health Sciences: Dr Ebenezer N. Gyader (acting)

UNIVERSITY OF CAPE COAST

University PO, Cape Coast
Telephone: (42) 32480
E-mail: vcucc@yahoo.com
Internet: www.ucc.edu.gh

Founded 1962
Language of instruction: English
State control
Academic year: August to June (2 semesters)

Chancellor: Dr Sam Esson Jonah
Pro-Chancellor: Dr Charles Mensa
Vice-Chancellor: Prof. E. A. Obeng
Pro-Vice-Chancellor: Prof. K. Yankson
Registrar: S. Kofi Ohene
Librarian: Alfred K. Martey

Number of teachers: 300
Number of students: 11,637

Publications: *ASEMKA* (Faculty of Arts, 2 a year), *Journal of Educational Management* (IEPA, 2 a year), *Journal of Social Sciences* (Faculty of Social Sciences, 2 a year), *Journal of the Institute of Education* (IEPA, 2 a year), *Oguaa Educator* (Faculty of Education, 2 a year), *Primary Teacher* (Dept of Primary Education, 2 a year)

DEANS

Faculty of Arts: Prof. D. D. Kuupole
Faculty of Education: Dr J. A. Opare (acting)
Faculty of Science: Prof. V. P. Y. Gadzekpo
Faculty of Social Sciences: Prof. K. Awusabo-Asare
Graduate Studies: Prof. Jane Naana Opoku Agyemang
School of Agriculture: Prof. P. K. Turkson

UNIVERSITY OF EDUCATION, WINNEBA

POB 25, Winneba
Telephone: (432) 22269
E-mail: info@uew.edu.gh
Internet: www.uew.edu.gh

Founded 1992 as Univ. College of Education of Winneba by merger of 7 colleges: present name and status 2004; attached to Nat. Council for Tertiary Education
State control
Academic year: August to May (2 semesters)

Vice-Chancellor: Prof. Akwasi Asabere-Ameyaw
Pro-Vice-Chancellor: Prof. Mawutor Avoke
Registrar: Christopher Y. Akwaa-Mensah
Finance Officer: Benjamin K. Kpodo
Librarian: Valentina Bannerman

Library of 121,913 vols, 2,798 periodicals, 23,100 online journals, 38 online databases and over 138 CD-ROMs
Number of teachers: 398
Number of students: 45,663

Publications: *African Journal of Special Needs Education*, *Ghana Educational Media and Technology Association Journal*, *Ghana Journal of Higher Education Management*, *The Social Educator*

DEANS

Faculty of Agriculture Education, Mampong: Dr J. K. Kagya-Agyemang
Faculty of Business Education, Kumasi: Francis Donkor
Faculty of Educational Studies, Winneba: Prof. Anthony Afful-Broni
Faculty of Languages Education, Winneba: Prof. J. Y. Sekyi-Baidoo
Faculty of Science Education, Winneba: Prof. M. K. Amedeker
Faculty of Social Sciences Education, Winneba: Prof. A. Y. Quarshiga
Faculty of Vocational and Technical Education, Kumasi: Dr Martin Amoah
School of Creative Arts, Winneba: Prof. M. P. Dzansi-McPalm
School of Research and Graduate Studies, Winneba: Prof. Mawutor Avoke

ATTACHED RESEARCH INSTITUTES

Centre for Educational Policy Studies: Winneba; tel. (432) 20337; e-mail aabroni@uew.edu.gh; Dir Rev. Dr Fr Anthony Afful-Broni.

Centre for Hearing and Speech Services: Winneba; tel. (246) 782776; e-mail ynyaduoffei@yahoo.com; Coordinator Yaw Nyadu Offei.

Centre for School and Community Science and Technology Studies: Winneba; tel. (432) 22268; e-mail jophusam@gmail.com; Dir Prof. Jophus Anamuah-Mensah (acting).

Institute for Educational Development and Extension: Winneba; tel. (432) 22497; e-mail aboagye@yahoo.com; Dir Prof. Joseph K. Aboagye (acting).

National Centre for Research into Basic Education: Winneba; tel. (432) 20415; e-mail rofori@gmail.com; Dir Dr Richard Ofori

UNIVERSITY OF GHANA

POB LG 25, Legon-Accra
Telephone: (21) 500381
E-mail: academic@ug.edu.gh
Internet: www.ug.edu.gh

Founded 1948 as Univ. College of Gold Coast, present status 1961
State control
Language of instruction: English
Academic year: August to May
Campuses at Accra City, Korle-Bu-Accra

Chancellor: HE Kofi Annan
Vice-Chancellor: Prof. Ernest Aryeetey (acting)
Pro-Vice-Chancellor for Academic and Student Affairs: Prof. E. Kweku Osam
Pro-Vice-Chancellor for Research, Innovation and Devt: Prof. John O. Gyapong
Dir for Finance: J. E. Minlah
Registrar: J. M. Budu
Librarian: Prof. Edwin E. Badu

Number of teachers: 897
Number of students: 38,376

Publications: *Campus Update*, *Legon Journal of Science and Technology*, *Legon Journal of the Humanities*, *Newsfile*, *Universitas*

DEANS

Business School: Prof. Kwame Ameyaw Domfeh

Dental School: Prof. GRACE PARKINS (acting)
Faculty of Arts: Rev. Prof. CEPHAS N. OMENYO
Faculty of Engineering Sciences: Prof. RICHARD JINKS BANI
Faculty of Law: Prof. E. K. QUASHIGAH
Faculty of Science: Prof. DANIEL K. ASIEDU
Faculty of Social Sciences: Prof. SAMUEL AGYEI-MENSAH
International Programmes: Prof. NAA AYIKAILEY ADAMAFIO
Medical School: Prof. YAO TETTEY (acting)
School of Agriculture: Prof. JOHN OFOSU-ANIM
School of Allied Health Sciences: Dr PATRICK AYEH-KUMI
School of Graduate Studies: Prof. KWADWO OFORI
School of Nursing: Dr ERNESTINA SARFOA DONKOR
School of Pharmacy: Prof. ARTHUR COMMEY SACKEYFIO
School of Public Health: Prof. RICHARD ADANU
School of Veterinary Science: Prof. KWAME GEORGE ANING

PROFESSORS

ABEKOE, M. K., Dept of Soil Science
ABOAGYE, G. S., Dept of Animal Science
ABOR, J., Business School
ADAMAFIO, N. A., Dept of Biochemistry, Cell and Molecular Biology
ADANU, R., School of Public Health
ADDAE-MENSAH, I., Dept of Chemistry
ADDAI, F., Medical School
ADDO, H., Medical School
ADIKU, S., Dept of Soil Science
ADINKU, W., School of Performing Arts
ADOO-ADEKU, K., Institute of Continuing and Distance Education
ADZAKU, F., Medical School
AFARI, E., School of Public Health
AFFRAM, R., Medical School
AFOAKWA, E., Dept of Nutrition and Food Science
AFREH-NUAMAH, K., Agriculture Research Centre, Kade
AGYEI-MENSAH, S., Dept of Geography and Resource Development
AGYEKUM, K., Dept of Linguistics
AHIADEKE, C., Institute of Statistical, Social and Economic Research
AHUNU, B., Dept of Animal Science
AKABZAA, T., Dept of Earth Science
AKPABLI, C., Dept of Chemistry
AKUSSAH, H., Dept of Information Studies
AL-HASSAN, R., Agricultural Economics
AMANOR, K., Institute of African Studies
AMEKA, G., Dept of Botany
AMFO, N., Dept of Linguistics
AMOAH, E., Dept of Study of Religions
AMPOFO, J., Institute of African Studies
AMUZU, J., Dept of Physics
ANARFI, J., Regional Institute for Population Studies
ANIM, J., Medical School
ANING, K., School of Veterinary Medicine
ANKRAH, N., Noguchi Memorial Institute for Medical Research
ANKRAH-BADU, G., Medical School
ANTWI, D., Dept for the Study of Religions
ANYIDOHO, K., Dept of English
ARMAH, G., Noguchi Memorial Institute for Medical Research
ARMAR-KLEMESU, M., Noguchi Memorial Institute for Medical Research
ARYEETEY, E., Institute of Statistical, Social and Economic Research
ASANTE, F., Institute of Statistical, Social and Economic Research
ASANTE, I., Dept of Botany
ASANTE-POKU, S., Medical School
ASIBEY-BERKO, E., Dept of Nutrition and Food Science
ASIEDU, D., Dept of Earth Science
ASOMANING, W., Dept of Chemistry
ATTA-PETERS, D., Dept of Earth Science
ATTUQUAYEFIO, D., Dept of Animal Biology and Conservation Sciences
AWUMBILA, B., School of Veterinary Medicine
AWUMBILA, M., Dept of Geography and Resource Development
AYERNOR, G., Dept of Nutrition and Food Science
AYERTEY, J., Dept of Crop Science
AYETTEY, A., Medical School
BADU, E., Information Studies
BANI, R., Engineering Sciences
BANOENG-YAKUBU, B., Dept of Earth Science
BARYEH, E., Agricultural Engineering
BENING, R., Dept of Geography and Resource Development
BINKA, F., School of Public Health
BIRITWUM, R., Medical School
BLAY, E., Dept of Crop Science
BOACHIE-ANSAH, J., Dept of Archaeology and Heritage Studies
BOAFO-ARTHUR, K., Dept of Political Science
BOAKYE, D., Noguchi Memorial Institute for Medical Research
BOLEKA, J., Dept of Modern Languages
BOSOMPEM, K., Noguchi Memorial Institute for Medical Research
BOSU, W., School of Veterinary Medicine
CARBOO, D., Dept of Chemistry
CLEGG-LAMPTEY, J., Medical School
CODJOE, S., Regional Institute for Population Studies
COLLINS, E., Dept of Music
DAKO, K., Dept of English
DANQUAH, E., Dept of Crop Science
DANSO, S., Dept of Soil Science
DARKO, R., Medical School
DODOO, F., Regional Institute for Population Studies
DODOO, J., Dept of Modern Languages
DOMFEH, K., Business School
DOVLO, E., Dept for the Study of Religions
DOWUONA, G., Dept of Soil Science
EDOH, D., Dept of Zoology
ENU-KWESI, L., Dept of Botany
FAYORSEY, C., Dept of Sociology
FIANU, D., Dept of Family and Consumer Sciences
GADZEKPO, A., School of Communication Studies
GOKA, B., Medical School
GORDON, C., Dept of Animal Biology and Conservation Sciences
GYAPONG, J., School of Public Health
GYASI, E., Dept of Geography and Resource Development
GYASI, R., Medical School
HESSE, A., Medical School
HEVI-YIBOE, L., Dept of Home Science
HINSON, R., Business School
KANSU-KYEREMEH, K., School of Communication Studies
KINGSFORD-ADABOH, R., Dept of Chemistry
KLUFIO, G., Medical School
KORAM, K., Noguchi Memorial Institute for Medical Research
KOTEY, E., Faculty of Law
KUMADO, C., Faculty of Law
KUMAGA, F., Dept of Crop Science
KWAPONG, O., Institute of Continuing and Distance Education
KWAWUKUME, E., Medical School
LARTEY, A., Dept of Nutrition and Food Science
LARTEY, M., Medical School
LAUER, H., Dept of Philosophy
MATE-KOLE, C., Dept of Psychology
MATE-KOLE, M., Medical School
MENSA-BONSU, H., Faculty of Law
NAAEDER, S., Medical School
NARTEY, V., Dept of Chemistry
NEEQUAYE, A., Medical School
NEEQUAYE, J., Medical School
NEWMAN, M., Medical School
NII-YARTEY, F., School of Performing Arts
NKYEKYER, K., Medical School
NTI, C., Dept of Family and Consumer Sciences
NTIAMOA-BAIDU, Y., Dept of Animal Biology and Conservation Sciences
NYAKO, E., Basic Dental Science
OBED, S., Medical School
OBENG-OFORI, D., Dept of Crop Science
ODAMTTEN, Dept of Botany
ODOTEI, I., Institute of African Studies
ODURO, K., Dept of Crop Science
OFFEI, S., Dept of Crop Science
OFORI, K., Dept of Crop Science
OFORI-DANSO, K., Marine and Fisheries Sciences Dept
OFOSU-ANIM, J., Dept of Crop Science
OHENEBA-SAKYI, Y., Institute of Continuing and Distance Education
OKINE, L., Dept of Biochemistry, Cell and Molecular Biology
OMENYO, C., Dept of Study of Religions
OPARE-OBISAW, C., Dept of Home Science
OPOKU, J., Dept of Psychology
OSAM, E., Linguistics
OWUSU, E., Dept of Animal Biology and Conservation Science
OWUSU, M., School of Performing Arts
OWUSU-BENNOAH, E., Dept of Soil Science
PARKINS, G., Basic Dental Science
PHILLIPS, W., Dept of Chemistry
QUAKYI, I., School of Public Health
QUARTEY, Q., Institute for Statistical, Social and Economic Research
QUASHIGAH, E., Faculty of Law
RODRIGUES, O., Medical School
SAAH, K., Dept of Linguistics
SACKEY, B., Centre for Social Policy Studies
SACKEY, S., Dept of Biochemistry
SAKYI-DAWSON, E., Dept of Nutrition and Food Science
SARPONG, D., Agricultural Economics
SEFA-DEDEH, S., Nutrition and Food Science
SEFFAH, J., Medical School
SEINI, A., Agricultural Economics
SENAH, K., Dept of Sociology
SONGSORE, J., Dept of Geography and Resource Development
STEINER-ASIEDU, M., Dept of Nutrition and Food Science
SUTHERLAND-ADDY, E., Institute of African Studies
TAGOE, C., Medical School
TANO-DEBRAH, K., Dept of Nutrition and Food Science
TETTEY, Y., Medical School
TONAH, S., Dept of Sociology
TSIKATA, D., Institute of Statistical, Social and Economic Research
TWUM-DANSO, K., Medical School
WELBECK, J., Medical School
WELLINGTON, H., Dept of Archaeology and Heritage Studies
WILSON, M., Noguchi Memorial Institute for Medical Research
WIREDU, E., School of Allied Health Sciences
WIREDU, J., Dept of English
YANGYUORU, M., Agriculture Research Centre, Kpong
YANKAH, K., Dept of Linguistics
YANKSON, P., Dept of Geography and Resource Development

ATTACHED INSTITUTES

Centre for Gender Studies and Advocacy: Dir Prof. DZODZI TSIKATA.

Centre for Migration Studies: Dir Prof. MARIAMA AWUMBILA.

Centre for Social Policy Studies: Dir Dr ELLEN BORTEI DOKU-ARYEETEY.

Centre for Tropical Clinical Pharmacology and Therapeutics: Dir Dr ALEXANDER NII OTO DODOO.

Ecology Laboratory Centre: Dir Prof. P. K. OFORI-DANSON.

Institute for Environment and Sanitation Studies: Legon, Accra; tel. (30) 2512819; e-mail dadarko@ug.edu.gh; State control; Dir Prof. CHRISTOPHER GORDON.

Institute of Adult Education: POB 31, Legon, Accra; Dir R. A. AGGOR.

Institute of African Studies: POB 73, Legon, Accra; e-mail iasgen@ug.edu.gh; Dir Prof. AKOSUA ADOMAKO AMPOFO.

Institute of Agricultural Research: e-mail diar@ug.edu.gh; Dir Prof. KWAME AFREH-NUAMAH.

Institute of Continuing and Distance Education: Dir Prof. YAW OHENEBA-SAKYI.

Institute of Statistical, Social and Economic Research: POB 74, Legon, Accra; e-mail info@isser.edu.gh; Dir Prof. CLEMENT AHIADEKE.

Language Centre: Dir Dr GORDON S.K. ADIKA.

Legon Centre for International Affairs and Diplomacy: Legon, Accra; Dir Dr VLADIMIR ANTWI-DANSO (acting).

Noguchi Memorial Institute for Medical Research: POB 25, Legon, Accra; e-mail oboateng@noguchi.ug.edu.gh; f. 1979; international centre for basic and applied research; Dir Prof. A. K. NYARKO; Provost Rev. Prof. A. S. AYETTEY (acting).

Regional Institute for Population Studies: POB 96, Legon, Accra; e-mail rips@ug .edu.gh; f. 1972 with UN aid; Dir Dr FRANCIS DODOO (acting).

Regional Training Centre for Archivists: POB 60, Legon, Accra; Head C. O. KISIEDU.

School of Communication Studies: POB 53, Legon, Accra; e-mail scs@ug.edu.gh; Dir Dr MARGARET IVY AMOAKOHENE.

School of Performing Arts: POB LG19, Legon, Accra; tel. (30) 2500308; e-mail sparts@ug.edu.gh; internet spa.ug.edu.gh; library of 12,174 vols; Dir Dr AWO MANA ASIEDU (acting); Asst Registrar BERNARDINE BEDIAKO-POKU.

School of Public Health: POB LG13, Legon, Accra; e-mail sph@ug.edu.gh; library of 2,000 vols; 42 teachers; 617 students; Dean Prof. R. K. ADANU.

United Nations University Institute for Natural Resources in Africa: PMB, Kotoka International Airport, Accra; e-mail inra@unu.edu; Dir Dr ELIAS TAKOR AYUK.

AGRICULTURAL RESEARCH STATIONS

Agricultural Research Station, Accra: POB 38, Legon, Accra; Officer-in-Charge Dr E. A. CANACOO.

Agricultural Research Station, Kade: POB 43, Kade; Officer-in-Charge Dr J. K. OSEI.

Agricultural Research Station, Kpong: POB 9, Kpong; Officer-in-Charge Dr E. O. DARKWA

Colleges

Accra Polytechnic: POB GP 561, Accra; tel. (30) 2662263; f. 1949; technical and vocational education with practical research programmes in manufacturing, commerce, science and technology; from technician to HND level; library: 15,800 vols; 340 teachers; 6,400 students; Prin. Prof. RALPH K. ASABERE.

Accra Technical Training Centre: POB M.177, Accra; f. 1966 to train tradesmen for industry and civil service; attached to Min. of Education; library: 10,500 vols; 350 students; Prin. T. K. ADZEI.

Ghana Institute of Management and Public Administration: Greenhill, POB 50, Achimota; tel. (21) 405805; f. 1961; research, consultancy, human resource development, strategic studies and policy analysis and postgraduate studies, diploma, certificate and Masters degree programmes; library: 50,000 vols; 30 teachers; Dir-Gen. Dr STEPHEN ADEI; publs *Administrators' Digest*, *Ghana Economic Outlook* (2 a year), *GIMPA News* (4 a year), *Greenhill Case Studies Book*, *Greenhill Journal of Administration* (2 a year).

Ho Polytechnic: POB 217, Ho, Volta Region; tel. (91) 26456; e-mail gafeti@africaonline.com.gh; f. 1968; training of middle-level management personnel and technicians to HND standard; library: 13,000 vols; 100 teachers; 2,500 students; Prin. Dr G. M. AFETI; Registrar F. K. DZINEKU.

Koforidua Technical Institute: POB 323, Koforidua; f. 1960; library: 2,000 vols; 9 teachers; 206 students; Prin. P. C. NOI.

Kpandu Technical Institute: Technical Div., POB 76, Kpandu, Volta Region; f. 1956; library: 4,000 vols; 70 teachers; 689 students; Prin. J. Y. VODZI.

National Film and Television Institute (NAFTI): PMB, GPO, Accra; tel. (30) 2777610; e-mail nafti@ghana.com; f. 1978; 4-year Bachelors of Fine Arts degree courses in film and television production with spec. emphasis on the production of educational programmes, and feature, informative, animation, documentary and industrial films; mem. of CILECT, Int. Asscn of Film and Television Schools; receives financial help from public funds and technical assistance from NGOs and UNESCO; 2-year diploma courses in film and television production; exchange programmes; library: specialized library of 51,000 vols; 68 students; Dir MARTIN LOH; publ. *NAFTI Concept*.

Sunyani Polytechnic: POB 206, Sunyani; tel. (61) 23278; e-mail spolytec@ghana.com .gh; f. 1967 as Technical Institute; present name and status 1997; technical and business education, electrical and electronic engineering, hotel, catering and institutional management, secretaryship and management studies; accredited by Int. Professional Managers' Asscn (IPMA—UK) and Chartered Institute of Marketing (UK); library: 11,020 vols; 180 teachers; 4,528 students; Prin. Dr KWASI NSIAH-GYABAA; Sec. S. A. OBOUR.

Takoradi Polytechnic: POB 256, Takoradi; tel. (31) 22918; f. 1955; library: 10,250 vols, 48 periodicals; 130 teachers; 4,500 students; Prin. Dr SAMUEL OBENG APORI; Sec. KOFI MANUKURE-HENAKU.

West Africa Computer Science Institute: POB 1643, Mamprobi, Accra; tel. (30) 2229927; e-mail wacsi@internetghana.com; f. 1988; ind. college providing training in computers, accounting and related fields; 10 teachers; 300 students; Pres. AIKINS BRIGHT KUMI; Prin. LAWRENCE NYARKO.

GREECE

The Higher Education System

The country's first universities were established shortly after Greece secured its independence from Ottoman Turkish rule in 1830. Ethniko Metsovio Polytechneio (National Technical University of Athens) was founded in 1836, and both Anotati Scholi Kalon Technon (Athens School of Fine Arts) and Ethnikon Kai Kapodistriakon Panepistimion Athinon (National and Kapodistrian University of Athens) were founded in 1837. Institutions of higher education are separated into two categories, Anotera Ekpedeftika Idrimata (AEI) and Technologika Ekpedeftika Idrimata (TEI). AEIs are university-level institutions and TEIs are technological higher education institutions, which were officially upgraded to university status in 2001 but are still regarded as distinct from AEIs. In 2012 there were 24 AEIs and 16 TEIs accredited by the State. There were also 11 Academies and Schools, which offer four-year courses that are equivalent to university courses, and the Akadimies Emborikou Naftikou (Merchant Marine Academies), which award degrees equivalent to those awarded by TEIs. Overall responsibility for higher education lies with the Ministry of Education and Religious Affairs, and the Constitution stipulates that only public institutions may provide higher education. AEIs and TEIs are autonomous institutions. Although Greek public institutions of higher education do not charge tuition fees, no grants and few scholarships are provided.

Admission to higher education is on the basis of the Apolyterio, the leading secondary school certificate, and Vevaiosi Provasis, a certificate of access to higher education, which is calculated according to scores in the Apolyterio. Although Greece is a signatory to the Bologna Process, the proposed changes to the education system met with widespread protest and the required reforms have yet to be implemented; however, the traditional degree system does theoretically consist of three stages (although most students complete their studies at the end of the first stage, which lasts between four and six years). Some first-stage degrees are compatible with the Bologna system, while others—such as medicine, engineering and architecture—are not. In both AEIs and TEIs, the main degree is the Ptychio, which is a four-year programme of study in most subjects, but in some subjects lasts five years (engineering, agriculture, veterinary studies, dentistry and architecture) and in medicine lasts six years. To take postgraduate degrees, which are only offered at AEIs, students holding the Ptychio must undergo a selection process or sit examinations. The first postgraduate degree is the Metaptychiakon Spoudon, which lasts two years and is broadly equivalent to the Masters. Finally, the Didaktor is a doctoral-level degree awarded following a period of research and submission of a thesis.

According to the Greek Constitution, the establishment of private institutions of higher education is forbidden, and qualifications offered by private institutions are not regarded as equivalent to qualifications from public institutions. However, private institutions may operate as Ergastiria Eleutheron Spoudon (Laboratories of Liberal Studies), purely with a view to providing education related to the arts and professional studies. These institutions, which charge substantial fees, are often franchises of foreign universities (many of them British and American), and sometimes non-profit accredited institutions, which advertise themselves as private universities or as centres from public universities abroad. Degrees issued by these institutions, which come under the jurisdiction of the Ministry of Development, are not recognized by the Greek State. Proposals put forward in 2009 to afford official recognition to the Ergastiria Eleutheron Spoudon as private universities met with widespread opposition and were subsequently abandoned. Private institutions are also permitted in the technical/vocational education sector (see below). Following legislative amendments carried out in 2008 and 2010, private organizations are now authorized to offer foreign undergraduate and postgraduate programmes under the monitoring of the Greek Ministry of Education and Religious Affairs.

Technical and vocational education is overseen by different government bodies, notably the Ministry of Education and Religious Affairs, the Organization of Vocational Education and the Ministry of Labour and Social Protection. The Organization of Vocational Education runs Instituta Epangelmatikis Katartisis (IEKs, Institutes of Vocational Training), which offer courses of study lasting between two and four years and leading to the award of diplomas. There are currently around 120 IEKs in the public sector and 60 in the private sector. The Employment and Manpower Organization has a National Council for Vocational Training, which oversees apprenticeships and on-the-job training. The apprenticeships, entrance to which is based on the Apolyterio, last for three years and lead to the award of diplomas.

Figures given for 2005/06 showed that 170,629 students were enrolled in universities (this excludes data from the Medical School of Athens), while 142,114 were enrolled in technical, vocational and ecclesiastical institutions.

With Greece beset by a multitude of economic woes, controversial legislation regarding a new educational framework was approved by Parliament in August 2011. The main provisions of the bill were: the abolishment of the status of universities as sanctuaries; the establishment of a 15-member board of trustees (including six external appointees) in each higher education institution; the opening of the selection process to appoint new university rectors and presidents to international competition; a tightening up of permitted completion times for degrees (three years for undergraduates, a single year for postgraduate degrees and two years for a doctoral degree); five-yearly external assessments of teaching staff; more stringent controls on the funding of individual institutions with incentives for good performance; the merger, renaming or complete abolishment of a number of universities; the supplementary funding of higher education institutions by private finance and a reduction in the States's financial commitment; and the assumption by private companies of the responsibility to connect universities to the marketplace. The reforms met with widespread opposition (including strikes and the occupation of university buildings) among both students and staff.

Regulatory and Representative Bodies

GOVERNMENT

Ministry of Culture and Sports: Bouboulinas 20–22, 106 82 Athens; tel. 213-1322100; e-mail grplk@culture.gr; internet www.yppo .gr; Minister PANOS PANAGIOTOPOULOS.

Ministry of Education and Religious Affairs: 37, Andrea Papandreou, 151 80 Marousi; tel. (210) 3442508; internet www .minedu.gov.gr; Minister KONSTANTINOS ARVANITOPOULOS.

ACCREDITATION

Hellenic NARIC: 54, Ag. Konstantinou St, 104 37 Athens; tel. (210) 5281000; e-mail information_dep@doatap.gr; internet www .doatap.gr; f. 2005; supervised by the Min. of Education and Religious Affairs; responsible for recognition of univ. or technological degrees awarded by foreign HEIs; provides information about educational systems and accreditation of HEIs in Greece and abroad; Head of Dept of Information BESSY ATHANASOPOULOU.

NATIONAL BODIES

National Organization for the Certifica-

tion of Qualifications and Vocational Guidance: 41, National Resistance Ave, 142 34 Attica; tel. (210) 2709000; internet www.eoppep.gr; f. 2011 by merger of Nat. Accreditation Centre for Continuing Vocational Training (EKEPIS), the Nat. Centre for Vocational Orientation (EKEP) and the Nat. Org. for the Certification of Qualifications (EOPP); operates under the supervision of the Min. of Education and Religious Affairs; ensures provision of high quality services in education, training and counselling that will lead to acknowledged and certified qualifications; Chair CONSTANTINE KALTSAS; Vice-Pres. Dr NICHOLAS GEORGIADIS PANAGIOTIS.

Synodos Prytaneon Ellinikon Panepistimion (Hellenic Universities Rectors' Synod): 30, Panepistimiou St, 106 79 Athens; tel. (210) 3689719; internet www.synodos-aei.gr; f. 1987; non-legislative organ; admin. and coordination of Greek univs; represents Greece in the Conf. of Rectors and Pres of European Univs; 23 univs; Sec. LILIANA NIKOLETOPOULOU.

Learned Societies

GENERAL

Akadimia Athinon (Academy of Athens): 28, Panepistimiou Ave, 106 79 Athens; tel. (210) 3664700; e-mail info@academyofathens.gr; internet www.academyofathens.gr; f. 1926; ind.; promotes the sciences, humanities and arts; supervised by Min. of Education and Religious Affairs; conducts scientific research; attached research institutes: see under Research Institutes; 217 mems (43 ordinary, 19 foreign, 149 corresp., 6 hon.); library: see under Libraries and Archives; Pres. GEORGE CONTOPOULOS; Sec.-Gen. VASSILIOS CH. PETRAKOS; publ. *Praktika* (Proceedings, 3 a year).

Stavros Niarchos Foundation: 86A, Vasilissis Sofias Ave, 115 28 Athens; tel. (210) 8778300; e-mail info@snf.org; internet www.snf.org; f. 1996; makes grants to non-profit org. around the world, in areas of arts and culture, education, health and medicine and social welfare; Chief Legal Counsel GEORGE AGOURIDIS.

Syndesmos Hellinidon Epistimonon (SEE) (Hellenic Association of University Women): 44A, Voulis St, 105 57 Athens; tel. (210) 3234268; e-mail info@see1924.gr; internet www.see1924.gr; f. 1924; non-governmental, non-profit org.; supports women scientists with regard to their professional advancement and devt; promotes visibility and participation of women of Greece in social and public life; 500 mems; library of 1,258 vols; Pres. Dr PARASKEVI BATRA; First Vice-Pres. DESPINA DIDIKA-LOGIADOU.

BIBLIOGRAPHY, LIBRARY SCIENCE AND MUSEOLOGY

Enosi Ellinon Vivliothikonomon kai Epistimon Pliroforisis (EEBEP) (Association of Greek Librarians and Information Scientists): Akadimias 84, 106 72 Athens; tel. (210) 3302128; e-mail info@eebep.gr; internet eebep.gr; f. 1968; recognizes and promotes science of librarianship and recognition of the role of librarians in society; encourages application of professional ethics; promotes library education issues at all levels; 500 mems; Pres. GEORGIOS GLOSSIOTIS; Vice-Pres. DIMITRIOS POLITIS; Gen. Sec. EIRINA THOMOPOUOU HOREMI; publ. *Bibliothikes kai Pliroforisi (Libraries and Information)*.

EDUCATION

Association of Educational Technologists: POB 45015, St Anargyroi, 135 10 Attica; tel. (697) 3275324; e-mail ete@ete.gr; internet www.ete.gr; scientific assn; conducts research; addresses issues related to vocational education and training in Greece; focuses on social recognition of the role of the teacher; 4,000 teachers; Pres. GEORGE MOUSTAKAS; Vice-Pres. TRIVELLAS SERAPHEIM; Gen. Sec. VASAGIORGIS NIKOLAOS; publ. *Education Technology Update* (4 a year).

Hellenic Adult Education Association: 12, Ikonomou str. Exarheia, 106 83 Athens; tel. (210) 6012297; e-mail adulteduc@adulteduc.gr; internet www.adulteduc.gr; f. 2004; scientific non-profit asscn; promotes philosophy and principles of adult education; scientific research; consultation services; tutoring and training programmes; 900 mems; Pres. ALEXIS GRAIN; publ. *Adult Education*.

Syllogos pros Diadosin ton Hellenikon Grammaton (Society for the Promotion of Greek Education): Odos Pindarou 15 (136), Athens; f. 1869; 9 mems; Pres. PHILIP DRAGOUMIS; Sec.-Gen. ALEXANDRATOS PANAYIOTIS.

FINE AND PERFORMING ARTS

Enosis Hellinon Mousourgon (Greek Composers' Union): c/o V. Sofias Ave and Kokkali St, Athens' Concert Hall, 115 21 Athens; tel. (210) 7256607; e-mail gcu@otenet.gr; internet www.gcu.org.gr; f. 1931; protects and promotes the work of Greek composers in Greece and beyond; 208 mems; Pres. THEODORE ANTONIOU; Gen. Sec IOSSIF PAPADATOS; publs *Antifono*, *Polytonon* (6 a year).

Epimelitirion Ikastikon Technon Ellados (Chamber of Fine Arts of Greece): 42, Valtetsiou St, 106 81 Athens; tel. (210) 3300016; e-mail chafartg@otenet.gr; internet www.eete.gr; f. 1944; attached to Min. of Culture and Sports and the Nat. Cttee of the Int. Asscn of Art/Asscn Internationale des Arts Plastiques (AIAP/UNESCO); promotes fine arts; supports artists; organizes exhibitions and confs in Greece and abroad; 4,600 mems; library of 2,000 vols; Pres. ASPASIA PAPADOPERAKI; Vice-Pres. DIONISSIS VALASSIS; Sec.-Gen. URANIA VOLONAKI.

HISTORY, GEOGRAPHY AND ARCHAEOLOGY

Archaeologiki Hetairia (The Archaeological Society at Athens): 22, Panepistimiou, 106 72 Athens; tel. (210) 3609689; e-mail archet@otenet.gr; internet www.archetai.gr; f. 1837; assists the State in its work of protecting, improving and studying Greek antiquities; 401 mems; library of 118,500 vols; Pres. EPAMINONDAS SPILIOTOPOULOS; Vice-Pres. ANNA BENAKI-PSAROUDA; publs *Archaiologike Ephemeris* (1 a year), *Ergon tes Archaiologikes* (The Work of the Archaeological Society, 1 a year), *Mentor* (4 a year), *Praktika tes Archaiologikes Hetairias* (Proceedings of the Archaeological Society, 1 a year).

Hellenic Geographical Society: 11, Voucourestiou St, 106 71 Athens; tel. (210) 3631112; f. 1919; 148 mems; Pres. DIMITRIOS DIMITRIADIS; Gen. Sec. GEORGE IVANTCHOS.

Historical and Ethnological Society of Greece: Nat. Historical Museum, 13, Stadiou St, Old Parliament Bldg, 105 61 Athens; tel. (210) 3237617; e-mail info@nhmuseum.gr; internet www.nhmuseum.gr; f. 1882; attached to Directorate of Modern Cultural Heritage, Min. of Education and Religious Affairs, Culture and Sports; collects material that contributes to the study of middle and modern Greek history and literature and the life and language of Greek people; operates the Nat. Historical Museum; 200 mems; library of 15,000 vols; Pres. DIONYSIOS-ANGELOS MINOTOS; Sec.-Gen. IOANNIS MAZARAKIS-AINIAN; Dir EFTHYMIA PAPASPYROU.

LANGUAGE AND LITERATURE

British Council: 17, Kolonaki Sq., 106 73 Athens; tel. (210) 3692333; e-mail customerservices@britishcouncil.gr; internet www.britishcouncil.org/greece.htm; f. 1939; teaching centre; offers courses and exams in English language and British culture; promotes cultural exchange with the UK; attached office in Thessaloniki; f. 1939; Dir DESMOND LAUDER.

Etairia Ellinon Logotechnon (Hellenic Literary Society): 8, College and Gennadi St, 106 78 Athens; tel. (210) 3834559; e-mail eel@otenet.gr; internet www.eel.org.gr; f. 1934; 700 mems; Pres. ELEFTHERIA ANAGNOSTAKI-TZAVARA.

Etairia Ellinon Theatricon Syngrapheon (Society of Greek Playwrights): 24, Psaromiligou, 105 53 Athens; tel. (210) 3232472; e-mail info@eeths.gr; internet www.eeths.gr; f. 1894; 120 mems; Pres. HENRY BELIES; Gen. Sec. GIORGOS CHRISTOFILAKIS.

Goethe Institut: 14-16, Omirou, POB 30383, 100 33 Athens; tel. (210) 3661000; e-mail info@athen.goethe.org; internet www.goethe.de/athen; f. 1952; offers courses and exams in German language and culture; promotes cultural exchange with Germany; attached centre in Thessaloniki; library of 16,000 vols; Deputy Dir ULRIKE NTRISNER.

Instituto Cervantes: 23, Metropolis, 105 57 Athens; tel. (210) 3634117; e-mail cenate@cervantes.es; internet atenas.cervantes.es; f. 1976 as Spanish Cultural Institute 'Queen Sophia', current name adopted 1992; offers courses and exams in Spanish language and culture; promotes cultural exchange with Spain and Spanish-speaking Latin and Central America; library of 26,000 vols; Dir VICTOR ANDRESCO PERALTA.

NATURAL SCIENCES

Mathematical Sciences

Elliniki Mathimatiki Eteria (Greek Mathematical Society): 34, Panepistimiou, 106 79 Athens; tel. (210) 3617784; e-mail info@hms.gr; internet www.hms.gr; f. 1918; 34 regional brs; seminars, lectures, summer schools, educational policy; 15,000 mems; library of 2,000 vols; Pres. KALOGEROPOULOS GREGORY; Gen. Sec. EMMANUEL KRITIKOS; publs *Astrolavos* (Informatics Review, 2 a year), *Deltion* (Bulletin, 1 a year), *Euclides* (4 a year), *International Journal for Mathematics in Education*, *Mathimatiki Epitheorissi* (Review, 2 a year).

Physical Sciences

Enosis Ellinon Chimikon (Association of Greek Chemists): 27, Odos Kanningos, 106 82 Athens; tel. (210) 3821524; e-mail info@eex.gr; internet www.eex.gr; f. 1924; official adviser to the State on matters relating to chemistry; promotes chemical science in industry, education and research; protects the benefits and the professional rights of chemists; 14,000 mems; library of 5,000 vols, 100 periodicals; Pres. GEORGE ARVANITIS; Gen. Sec. FOTIS MAKRIPOULIA; publs *ChemBioChem*, *Chemistry: A European Journal*, *ChemPhysChem*, *European Journal of Inorganic Chemistry*, *European Journal of Organic Chemistry*.

Geological Society for Greece: 50, Konstantilieri St, POB 71539, 162 31 Byron; tel. (210) 7644677; e-mail geosocie@geosociety.gr; internet www.geosociety.gr; f. 1951; non-profit org.; promotes knowledge of all topics of Greece's geology; cttees of economic geology, geological heritage, geomorphology and environment, geoscience teaching, mineralogy and geochemistry, engineering geology, hydrogeology, palaeontology-stratigraphy, structural geology and tectonics; 600 mems; Pres. EFTHIMIOS LEKKAS; Sec.-Gen. DIMITRIS GALANAKIS.

Panhellenic Association of Life Sciences: 83, Ebro, 115 27 Ambelokipi; tel. (210) 5224632; e-mail grammateia@gmail.com; internet www.pev.gr; f. 1973 as Panhellenic Asscn of Biologists, current name adopted 2004; professional org. of Greek scientists; 2,300 mems; Pres. MANOS PAPADAKIS; Gen. Sec. S. PLATANISTIOTI.

RELIGION, SOCIOLOGY AND ANTHROPOLOGY

Greek Society for Ethnology: 43, Eressou St, 106 81 Athens; tel. (210) 3819465; e-mail societyforethnology@yahoo.com; internet www.societyforethnology.gr; promotes anthropological thinking and research in Greece; anthropological folklore, cultural ecology and physical anthropology, ethnohistory, ethnolinguistics, historical anthropology, history of mentalities, with an emphasis on sociobiology and human classification; Pres. Dr ANDROMAHI OIKONOMOU; publ. *Ethnologhia*.

TECHNOLOGY

Elliniki Epitropi Atomikis Energhias (Greek Atomic Energy Commission): Patriarxou Grigoriou and Neapoleos, POB 60092, 153 10 Agia Paraskevi, Athens; tel. (210) 6506700; e-mail info@eeae.gr; internet www.eeae.gr; f. 1954, present status 1987; attached to Gen. Secretariat of Research and Technology, Min. of Education and Religious Affairs; ind.; responsible for nuclear power and technology issues and for the protection of the population, workers and environment from ionization and artificially produced non-ionizing radiation; Pres. Dr CHRISTOS HOUSIADAS; Vice-Pres. SIMOS SIMOPOULOS.

Research Institutes

GENERAL

Ethniko Idryma Erevnon (National Hellenic Research Foundation (NHRF)): 48, Vassileos Constantinou Ave, 116 35 Athens; tel. (210) 7273700; e-mail eie@eie.gr; internet www.eie.gr; f. 1958; attached to Gen. Secretariat for Research and Technology, Min. of Education and Religious Affairs; carries out basic and applied research in its own institutes (humanities and natural sciences); library of 2,000 periodicals, Euronet facilities, specialized libraries attached to the humanities institutes, Nat. Documentation Centre: see under Libraries and Archives; Dir Dr EFSTRATIOS I. KAMITSOS.

Attached Research Institutes:

Institute of Biology, Medicinal Chemistry and Biotechnology: 48, Vassileos Constantinou Ave, 116 35 Athens; tel. (210) 7273753; internet www.eie.gr/nhrf/institutes/ibmcb/index-en_ibmcb.html; f. 2012 by merger of Institute of Biological Research and Biotechnology with Institute of Organic and Pharmaceutical Chemistry of the NHRF; acts as a focal point for innovation at the interface of chemistry and biology through a modern interdisciplinary approach to the solution of state-of-the-art issues in the areas of health, drug research and biotechnology; Dir Dr ALEXANDER PINTZAS.

Institute of Historical Research: 48, Vassileos Constantinou Ave, 116 35 Athens; tel. (210) 7273619; e-mail iie@eie.gr; internet www.eie.gr/nhrf/institutes/ihr/index-en_ihr.html; f. 2012; research of the political, economic, social and cultural history of the Hellenic area and the regions where Hellenism has been active, from prehistoric antiquity to the modern era; depts of Byzantine research, Greek and Roman antiquity and Neo-Hellenic research; library of 40,000 vols, 1,100 periodicals; Dir CHRYSOCHOIDES KRITON; publs *Historical Review* (1 a year), *Symmeikta* (1 a year).

Institute of Theoretical and Physical Chemistry: 48, Vassileos Constantinou Ave, 116 35 Athens; tel. (210) 7273792; internet www.eie.gr/nhrf/institutes/tpci/index-en.html; f. 1979; advancement of scientific research in the fields of theoretical and computational chemistry and physics, and experimental physical chemistry—chemical physics; Dir EFSTRATIOS I. KAMITSOS.

AGRICULTURE, FISHERIES AND VETERINARY SCIENCE

Benaki Phytopathological Institute: 8, Stefanou Delta St, 145 61 Kifissia, Athens; tel. (210) 8180206; internet www.bpi.gr; f. 1929; attached to Min. of Rural Devt and Food; phytopathology, entomology, agricultural zoology, pesticides; 13 laboratories; museum of zoological and entomological specimens, incl. 22,000 species, and culture collns; library of 11,423 vols, 30,000 reprints, 1,400 current periodicals; Dir Dr KYRIAKOULA MACHERA; publ. *Hellenic Plant Protection Journal* (2 a year, in English).

Hellenic Centre for Marine Research: POB 712, 190 13 Anavissos, Attica; tel. (229) 1076462; internet www.hcmr.gr; f. 2003 by merger of Nat. Centre for Marine Research (NCMR; f. 1985) with Institute of Marine Biology of Crete (IMBC; f. 1987); attached to Gen. Secretariat of Research and Technology; marine and freshwater fisheries and biology, marine chemistry, geology and geophysics; operational oceanography, aquaculture, inland waters, marine biology and genetics; operates 2 research vessels, a hydrobiological research station (with aquarium and museum) of Rhodes, and the Thalassocosmos aquarium in Crete; library of 17,000 vols, 180 journals; Pres. COSTAS EMMANUEL SYNOLAKIS; publ. *Mediterranean Marine Science Journal* (2 a year).

Attached Research Institutes:

Institute of Aquaculture: POB 2214, Gournes Pediados, 710 03, Heraklion, Crete; tel. (2810) 337766; e-mail msimbc@her.hcmr.gr; internet innovator.ath.hcmr.gr/newhcmr1/secondpage.php?id=39; carries out basic and applied research on the devt of technology transfer, on developing know-how and provision, as well as, on providing specialized services in the fisheries management field; Dir Dr PASCAL DIVANACH.

Institute of Inland Waters: POB 712, 190 13 Anavissos, Attica; tel. (229) 1076458; internet www.hcmr.gr/inlandwaters; f. 1994; develops and applies tools and methodologies for the conservation, management and rational exploitation of aquatic resources; Dir Dr DIAPOULIS ARISTEIDIS.

Institute of Marine Biological Resources: POB 712, 190 13 Anavissos, Attica; tel. (210) 9821354; internet innovator.ath.hcmr.gr/newhcmr1/secondpage.php?id=38; f. 1985; research and devt in fisheries and coastal zone management; Dir Dr CONSTANTINOS PAPACONSTANTINOU.

Institute of Marine Biology and Genetics: POB 2214, 710 03 Heraklion, Crete; Hellenic Centre for Marine Research Bldg, Gournes (former American base) 715 00, Heraklion, Crete; tel. (2810) 337801; internet innovator.ath.hcmr.gr/newhcmr1/secondpage.php?id=40; f. 2003; studies of the population structure of natural and cultivated stocks, function of the ecosystems, changes induced by natural or anthropogenic factors, bio-conservation, etc.; Dir Dr ANTONIS MAGOULAS.

Institute of Oceanography: POB 712, 190 13 Anavissos, Attica; tel. (229) 1076452; internet innovator.ath.hcmr.gr/newhcmr1/secondpage.php?id=37; f. 1985; multidisciplinary, physical, chemical, biological and geological, marine and coastal research; Deputy Dir Dr EVANGELOS PAPATHANASSIOU.

ECONOMICS, LAW AND POLITICS

Centre of International and European Economic Law: POB 14, 551 02 Thessaloniki; tel. (2310) 486900; e-mail kdeod@cieel.gr; internet www.cieel.gr; f. 1978; nat. documentation and research centre, specializing in European Union law, protection of human rights in Europe, int. economic law; European Documentation Centre by decision of the EEC (now EU); library of 55,000 vols, 192 periodicals; Pres. Prof. VASSILIOS SKOURIS; Dir Prof. VASSILIOS CHRISTIANOS; publs *Hellenic Review of European Law* (4 a year in Greek, 1 a year in English), *Public Procurement—State Aid and Market* (3 a year).

Centre of Planning and Economic Research: 11, Amerikis, 106 72 Athens; tel. (210) 3676400; e-mail kepe@kepe.gr; internet www.kepe.gr; f. 1959 as Centre of Economic Research; attached to Min. of Regional Devt and Competitiveness; scientific study of the economic problems of Greece (devt policies and sectors, fiscal and monetary policy, human resources and social policies and macroeconomic analysis and projections); cooperates with other Greek research institutes; library of 30,200 vols, 850 periodical titles, 315 series of statistical bulletins; Chair. Prof. ELIAS TZAVALIS (acting); Scientific Dir Prof. PANAGIOTIS G. KORLIRAS; publs *Economic Perspectives* (3 a year), *Greek Economic Outlook* (4 a year).

Hellenic Centre for European Studies (EKEM): 4, Xenofontos St, 105 57 Athens; tel. (210) 3215549; e-mail info@ekem.gr; internet www.ekem.gr; f. 1988; attached to Min. of Foreign Affairs; non-profit-making ind. org.; advises the Govt, academic bodies and private companies on matters of European policy and integration; organizes conferences and seminars; library: maintains Depository Library of the EU, with 7,000 vols; Pres. and Dir-Gen. PANAGIOTIS KOUTSOUMPELIS.

Hellenic Institute of International & Foreign Law: 73, Solonos, 106 79 Athens; tel. (210) 3615646; e-mail hiifl@hiifl.gr; internet www.hiifl.gr; f. 1939; attached to Min. of Justice, Transparency and Human Rights and the Min. of Foreign Affairs; promotes legal research; supplies legal information on foreign, community, int. and Greek laws; library of 50,000 vols; Dir Dr SPYRIDON VI VRELLIS; publ. *Revue hellénique de droit international* (Hellenic Review of

International Law, 2 a year, in English and French).

Institute of International Public Law and International Relations: 12, Vass. Herakliou St, 546 25 Thessaloniki; tel. (2310) 552295; e-mail ipilir@otenet.gr; internet www.institut-iplir.gr; f. 1966; attached to Min. of Justice, Transparency and Human Rights; research, documentation and education centre; promotes knowledge in all subjects of int. studies; organizes confs, seminars, round table discussions and lectures on int. law and int. relations; library: World Bank and UN depository library; Dir Prof. Dr KALLIOPI KOUFA; publ. *Thesaurus Acroasium* (1 a year).

Kentron Ereunes Historias Hellenikou Dikaiou (Research Centre for the History of Greek Law): 14, Anagnostopoulou, 106 73 Athens; tel. (210) 3664627; e-mail keied@academyofathens.gr; internet www.academyofathens.gr; f. 1929; attached to Acad. of Athens; conducts research on legal instns from antiquity, Byzantine and post-Byzantine times; library of 12,000 vols; Pres. Prof. APOSTOLOS GEORGIADIS; Dir Dr LYDIA PAPARRIGA-ARTEMIADI; publs *Epetiris* (1 a year), *Parartima tes Epetiridos* (supplement to *Epetiris*, 1 a year), *Pragmateiai tes Akademias Athenon* (Academy of Athens).

FINE AND PERFORMING ARTS

Kentro Erevnas Byzantinis kai Metabyzantinis Technis (Research Centre for Byzantine and Post-Byzantine Art): 14, Odos Anagnostopoulou, 106 73 Athens; tel. (210) 3664613; e-mail kevmt@academyofathens.gr; internet academyofathens.gr; f. 1994; attached to Akadimia Athinon (Acad. of Athens); research on Byzantine archaeology and wall-paintings in Balkans, Turkey and Cyprus; library of 10,000 vols; Supervisor Acad. PANAYOTIS L. VOCOTOPOULOS; Dir IOANNA BITHA (acting).

HISTORY, GEOGRAPHY AND ARCHAEOLOGY

Centre for Asia Minor Studies: 11-13, Kydathineon, 105 58 Athens; tel. (210) 3239225; e-mail kms@otenet.gr; internet users.otenet.gr/~kms; f. 1933 as Folklore Archive of Asia Minor, current name adopted 1949; ind., private, non-profit, research org.; history and civilization of Greek communities in Asia Minor before 1922; library of 15,000 vols, 501 MSS; oral history archive of 150,000 MS pages; photographic archive of 5,000 photographs; folk music archive of 1,000 records, 700 cassettes; spec. collns: Karamanli books, and Greek books, newspapers and periodicals printed in Turkey, maps, MSS; Pres. Prof. M. B. SAKELLARIOU; Dir Dr S. TH. ANESTIDIS (acting); publ. *Deltio K. M. S.* (1 a year).

Deutsches Archäologisches Institut, Abteilung Athen (German Archaeological Institute at Athens): 1, Feidiou St, 106 78 Athens; tel. (210) 3307400; e-mail sekretariat.athen@dainst.de; internet www.dainst.org; f. 1874; research in archaeology and in related fields incl. excavations, expeditions and other projects; library of 80,000 vols; Dir Prof. Dr KATJA SPORN; Academic Dir Dr REINHARD SENFF; publ. *Mitteilungen des Deutschen Archäologischen Instituts, Athenische Abteilung* (1 a year).

Foundation of the Hellenic World: 38, Poulopoulou St, 118 51 Athens; tel. (212) 2545000; e-mail info@fhw.gr; internet www.fhw.gr; f. 1993; not-for-profit; historical and archaeological research; organizes confs, seminars, film projections, printed publs, visual and sound recordings; Cultural Centre: Hellenic Cosmos located at 254 Pireos St, 177 78 Athens; library of 10,000 vols, 200 journals; Pres. LAZAROS D. EFRAIMOGLOU; Man. Dir DIMITRIS EFRAIMOGLOU; publ. *IMEROS* (1 a year).

Institute for Balkan Studies: 31A, Meg. Alexandrou Ave, POB 50932, 540 14 Thessaloniki; tel. (2310) 832143; e-mail imxa@imxa.gr; internet www.imxa.gr; f. 1953; attached to Min. of Education and Religious Affairs; research into the history, archaeology, culture, int. relations, economics and other aspects of the Balkan Peninsula; organizes confs and other academic meetings; teaching the Balkan languages, Russian and Polish; runs Greek summer courses; library of 25,000 vols, 700 periodicals; Pres. Prof. IOANNIS TSEKOURAS; publs *Balkan Studies* (1 a year), *Valkanika Symmeikta* (1 a year, in Greek).

International Centre for Classical Research/Hellenic Society for Humanistic Studies: 47, Alopekis St, 140 Athens; f. 1959; study of and research into ancient Greek culture, scientific research and promotion of popular education through confs and publs; 700 mems; library of 20,000 vols; Pres. Prof. ARISTOXENOS D. SKIADAS; Sec.-Gen. GEORGE BABINIOTIS; publs *Antiquity and Contemporary Problems, Studies and Research*.

Kentron Erevnis Archaiotitos (Research Centre for Antiquity): 14, Odos Anagnostopoulou St, 106 73 Athens; tel. (210) 3664648; e-mail kea@academyofathens.gr; internet www.academyofathens.gr; f. 1977; attached to Acad. of Athens; research and publs on ancient Greek and Roman art, culture and history; Dir Dr VASILIKI MACHAIRA; Supervisor Prof. MICHAEL TIVERIOS.

Kentron Erevnis Messeonikou kai Neou Ellinismou (Research Centre for Medieval and Modern Hellenism): 14, Anagnostopoulou St, 106 73 Athens; tel. (210) 3664611; e-mail kemne@academyofathens.gr; internet www.kemne-academyofathens.gr; f. 1930; attached to Acad. of Athens; research and publs on medieval and modern Hellenism; library of 24,000 vols; Dir RODIE-ANGELIKI STAMOULI (acting); publ. *Mesaionika kai Nea Ellinika* (Medieval and Modern Greek Studies, 1 a year).

Kentron Erevnis Neoterou Ellinismou (Research Centre for the Study of Modern Greek History): 14, Anagnostopoulou St, 106 73 Athens; tel. (210) 3664602; e-mail keine@academyofathens.gr; internet www.keine-academyofathens.gr; f. 1945 as Historical Archive of Modern Hellenism, current name adopted 1966; attached to Acad. of Athens; collects, studies and publishes sources related to the metropolitan, peripheral and emigrant history of the Hellenic world since 19th century; library of 10,000 vols, 12,000 microfilms; Pres. MICHAEL SAKELLARIOU; Dir HELEN GARDIKAS-KATSIADAKIS (acting); publ. *Neoellinika Istorika*.

Svenska Institutet i Athen (Swedish Institute at Athens): 9, Mitseon St, 117 42 Athens; tel. (210) 9232102; e-mail swedinst@sia.gr; internet www.sia.gr; f. 1948; researches into Greek antiquity and archaeology; cultural exchange between Sweden and Greece; library of 40,000 vols; Dir Dr ARTO PENTTINEN; publs *Annual of the Swedish Institute in Athens and Rome, Opuscula*.

LANGUAGE AND LITERATURE

Kentron Ereunes Hellenikes kai Latinikes Grammateias (Research Centre for Greek and Latin Literature): 14, Anagnostopoulou St, 106 73 Athens; tel. (210) 3664630; e-mail keelg@academyofathens.gr; internet www.academyofathens.gr; f. 1955, current name adopted 2003; attached to Acad. of Athens; undertakes scholarly research aiming at critical edns and commentaries of works of Greek and Latin literature; Pres. NICOLAOS CONOMIS; Dir KONSTANTINOS OIKONOMAKOS.

Research Centre for Modern Greek Dialects: 22, Alexandrou Soutsou, 106 71 Athens; tel. (211) 2111000; e-mail ksilneg@academyofathens.gr; internet www.academyofathens.gr/ilne; f. 1914; attached to Acad. of Athens; compiles *Historical Dictionary of Modern Greek Dialects*; maintains modern Greek dialectal archives; linguistic research, especially on modern Greek dialects; research on modern Greek onomastics (incl. relevant archives of place names, proper names, etc.); library of 9,300 vols; Pres. Prof. Dr MICHAIL SAKELLARIOU; Dir CHRISTINA BASSEA-BEZANTAKOU.

Research Centre for Scientific Terms and Neologisms: 17, Smolensky St, 114 73 Athens; tel. (210) 3664732; e-mail geon@academyofathens.gr; internet www.academyofathens.gr; f. 1966 as Bureau for Scientific Terms and Neologisms, current name adopted 2003; attached to Acad. of Athens; research studies on Greek neologisms and terminology; library of 1,000 vols; Pres. THANASSIS VALTINOS; Dir Dr ANASTASIA CHRISTOFIDOU.

MEDICINE

Institute of Molecular Biology and Biotechnology: 100, Nikolaou Plastira St, 700 13 Heraklion; tel. (2810) 391100; e-mail central@admin.forth.gr; internet www.imbb.forth.gr; f. 1983; attached to Foundation for Research and Technology—Hellas; basic and applied research in emerging areas of biomedical science; collaborates with Univ. of Crete in postgraduate studies; Dir VASSILIS PACHNIS.

Hellenic Pasteur Institute: 127, Vasilissis Sofias Ave, 115 21 Athens; tel. (210) 6478800; internet www.pasteur.gr; f. 1920; attached to Min. of Education and Religious Affairs and the Min. of Health and Social Solidarity; private, non-profit org.; research of bacteriology, biotechnology, immunology, immunobiotechnology, microbiology, molecular biology, molecular genetics, molecular parasitology, neurobiology, oncology, virology; library of 3,500 vols and 155 periodicals; Dir-Gen. and Chair. Prof. ANTONIOS ANTONIADIS (acting).

NATURAL SCIENCES

Physical Sciences

Institouton Geologikon kai Metalleutikon Ereunon (Institute of Geology & Mineral Exploration): 1, Spirou Louis St, Olympic Village, Acharnae, 136 77 Athens; tel. (213) 1337000; e-mail dirgen@igme.gr; internet www.igme.gr; f. 1976; attached to Min. of the Environment, Energy and Climate Change; consultant to the govt on geoscientific matters and on mine legislation; surveys and evaluates all mineral raw materials, except hydrocarbons, and groundwater resources; library of 10,000 vols, 40,000 journals, 4,500 maps, 5,000 reprints and 10,000 reports; Dir-Gen. Prof. CONSTANTINE PAPAVASILIOU; publs *Geological and Geophysical Research, Special Research*.

Institute of Applied and Computational Mathematics: 100, Nikolaou Plastira, 700 13 Heraklion; tel. (2810) 391802; e-mail central@admin.forth.gr; internet www.iacm.forth.gr; f. 1985, present status 1987; attached to Foundation for Research and Technology—Hellas; participates in interdisciplinary research projects, mainly by developing and applying mathematical methods and tools for modelling and solving complex problems in the sciences and technology; Dir Prof. VASSILIOS A. DOUGALIS.

Institute of Environmental Research and Sustainable Development: POB 20048, 118 10 Athens; tel. (210) 3490116; internet www.meteo.noa.gr; f. 1858, fmrly Institute of Meteorology and Physics of the Atmospheric Environment, current name adopted 1998; attached to Nat. Observatory of Athens; laboratories of atmospheric chemistry, atmospheric pollution, calibration of meteorological instrumentation, radiation measurement; Dir Dr KAMBEZIDIS HARRY (acting).

Institute of Geodynamics: c/o Nat. Observatory of Athens, POB 20048, 118 10 Athens; tel. (210) 3490195; internet www.gein.noa.gr; f. 1842; attached to Nat. Observatory of Athens; areas of research incl. geophysics, neotectonics and seismotectonics, physics of the earth's interior, plate tectonics, seismology, volcanology and geothermy; collects and processes various seismological–geophysical parameters; elaborates research projects and relevant studies; trains and provides services to third bodies; Dir Prof. K. MACROPOULOS.

Kentron Erevnis Phissikistis Atmospheras kai Climatologias (Research Centre for Atmospheric Physics and Climatology): 24, Omirou, 106 72 Athens; tel. (210) 8832048; e-mail kefak@academyofathens.gr; internet www.academyofathens.gr; f. 1977; attached to Acad. of Athens; studies climate fluctuations in any period and observations related to the upper layers of the atmosphere; collects and processes observations related to air pollution; Pres. PANOS LIGOMENIDIS; Dir GEORGE TSELIOUDIS.

National Observatory of Athens: POB 20048, 118 10 Athens; tel. (210) 3490000; internet www.noa.gr; f. 1842; operates institutes of astronomy, astrophysics, space applications and remote sensing, astroparticle physics, environmental research and sustainable devt, geodynamics; provides training in collaboration with Greek and foreign univs for graduate students; library of 60,000 vols; Dir Dr KANARIS TSINGANOS; publs *Annals of the National Observatory of Athens*, *Memoirs of the National Observatory of Athens*.

NESTOR Institute for Astroparticle Physics: 111, Anagnostara, 240 01 Pylos; tel. (27230) 23300; e-mail info@nestor.org.gr; internet www.nestor.org.gr; f. 2003; attached to Nat. Observatory of Athens; under authority of the Gen. Secretariat for Research and Technology of the Min. of Devt; Dir LEONIDAS K. RESVANIS.

Research Centre for Astronomy and Applied Mathematics: c/o Acad. of Athens, 4, Soranou Efesiou, 115 27 Athens; tel. (210) 6597602; e-mail keaem@academyofathens.gr; internet astro.academyofathens.gr; f. 1959 as Office for Research and Calculations, current name adopted 1966; attached to Acad. of Athens; compares theoretical results with observational data from ground-based as well as from space observatories; areas of research incl. cosmology and gravitation, galactic dynamics and galactic morphology, magnetohydrodynamics, nonlinear dynamics and chaos theory, solar physics, magnetohydrodynamics; organizes seminars and confs; library of 1,051 vols, 500 vols of conf. proceedings, 13 series of journals; Dir PANOS A. PATSIS (acting).

Research Centre of Pure and Applied Mathematics: c/o Medical and Biological Research Foundation (IIBEAA), 4, Soranou Efesiou St, 115 27 Athens; tel. (210) 3597159; e-mail kethem@academyofathens.gr; internet www.academyofathens.gr; f. 1992, fmrly Research Office of Pure Mathematics; attached to Acad. of Athens; scientific cooperation with appropriate nat. and int. scientific establishments; implements scientific talks or seminars; Pres. GEORGE CONTOPOULOS; Dir GEORGE KASTIS (acting); Supervisor ATHANASIOS S. FOKAS.

PHILOSOPHY AND PSYCHOLOGY

Kentron Erevnis Ellinikis Philosophias (Research Centre for Greek Philosophy): 14, Anagnostopoulou St, 106 73 Athens; tel. (210) 3664625; e-mail keef@academyofathens.gr; internet www.academyofathens.gr; f. 1966; attached to Acad. of Athens; studies ancient Greek philosophical sources and texts; confs and monthly seminars on Greek philosophy; compiles and evaluates modern bibliography on Greek philosophy; library of 10,000 vols; Pres. Prof. KONSTANTINOS DESPOTOPOULOS; Dir Dr MARIA PROTOPAPAS-MARNELI; Supervisor Prof. EVANGHELOS MOUTSOPOULOS (acting); publ. *Philosophia* (1 a year).

RELIGION, SOCIOLOGY AND ANTHROPOLOGY

Athens Center of Ekistics: 23, Strat. Syndesmou St, 106 73 Athens; tel. (210) 3623216; e-mail ekistics@otenet.gr; internet www.ekistics.org; f. 1963; research, education, collaboration and documentation in the devt of human settlements; secretariat of World Soc. for Ekistics; library of 1,000 vols, 100 periodical titles (historic colln of 20,000 vols largely transferred in 2003 to School of Architecture, Nat. Technical Univ. of Athens, *q.v.*); Pres. PANAYIS PSOMOPOULOS; publ. *Ekistics* (6 a year).

Hellenic Folklore Research Centre: 3, Ipitou St, 105 57 Athens; tel. (210) 3318042; e-mail keel@academyofathens.gr; internet www.kentrolaografias.gr; f. 1918, present status 1926; attached to Acad. of Athens; collects and publishes folklore material; compiles bibliographies; preserves collns of folklore texts; incl. scholarly publs in form of books, maps, records, DVDs, etc.; library of 40,000 vols; Pres. PANOS LIGOMENIDES; Dir AIKATERINI POLYMEROU-KAMILAKI; publ. *Annual of the Research Centre for Hellenic Folklore* (1 a year, in Greek).

Institute for Mediterranean Studies: 130, Melissinou and Nikiforou Foka, POB 119, 741 00 Rethymnon; tel. (28310) 25146; e-mail info@ims.forth.gr; internet www.ims.forth.gr; f. 1985; attached to Foundation for Research and Technology—Hellas; research in human and social sciences and promotes application of advanced technologies in this field; collaborates with Univ. of Crete in postgraduate studies in Turkology; library of 5,000 vols; Dir Prof. CHRISTOS HADZIIOSSIF; publ. *Halcyon Days in Crete*.

Kentron Erevnis Ellinikis Koinonias (Research Centre for Greek Society): 8, Milioni St, 106 80 Athens; tel. (210) 3609990; e-mail keek@academyofathens.gr; internet www.academyofathens.gr; f. 1978; attached to Acad. of Athens; social research into Greek soc., esp. historical devt of the Greek family and the social and economic consequences of migration; rural reform and consequent sociopathy in rural areas; publ. of essays; library of 6,000 vols; Pres. CONSTANTINOS DESPOTOPOULOS; Dir Prof. M. G. LILY STYLIANOUDI; publ. *Elliniki Koinonia* (1 a year).

National Centre for Social Research (EKKE): 9 Kratinou and Athinas St, 105 52 Athens; tel. (210) 7491678; e-mail president@ekke.gr; internet www.ekke.gr; f. 1959 as Centre of Social Studies; attached to Min. of Education and Religious Affairs; promotes the devt of theoretically informed social research; promotes int. cooperation; research fields: cultural and social trends, political sociology, social anthropology, social policy, urban and rural sociology, urban studies; library of 35,000 vols, 350 journal subscriptions, 10,000 ejournals; Pres. and Dir Prof. NICOLAS DEMERTZIS; publ. *Epitheorissi Koinonikon Erevnon* (The Greek Review of Social Research, 3 a year, print and online, www.grsr.gr).

Patriarchal Institute for Patristic Studies: 64, Eptapirgiou St, Moni Vlatadon, 546 34 Thessaloniki; tel. (2310) 203620; e-mail director@pipm.gr; internet www.pipm.gr; f. 1965; promotes study and research of Christian literature in gen., patristic theology, patrology and their neighbouring theological disciplines; library of 50,000 vols, 500 vols of periodicals; Dir GEORGE MARTZELOS; publ. *Kleronomia* (Inheritance, 2 a year).

TECHNOLOGY

Chemical Process and Energy Resources Institute: 6th km, Harilaou—Thermi, 570 01 Thessaloniki; tel. (2310) 498112; e-mail cperi@cperi.certh.gr; internet www.cperi.certh.gr; f. 2012 by merger of Chemical Process Engineering Research Institute (f. 1985) with the Institute for Solid Fuels Technology and Applications (f. 1987); research and technological devt; laboratories of aerosol and particle technology, environmental and energy processes, environmental fuels and hydrocarbons, inorganic materials, natural resources and renewable energies utilization, polymer reaction engineering, process systems design and implementation; scientific seminars, confs and workshops; Dir Dr ATHANASIOS G. KONSTANDOPOULOS.

Foundation for Research and Technology—Hellas: POB 1385, 711 10 Heraklion; 100, Nikolaou Plastira St, 700 13 Heraklion; tel. (2810) 391500; e-mail central@admin.forth.gr; internet www.forth.gr; f. 1983; reports to the Gen. Secretariat for Research and Technology of the Min. of Education and Religious Affairs, Culture and Sports; institutes of applied and computational mathematics (Heraklion), chemical engineering sciences (Patras), computer science (Heraklion), electronic structure and laser (Heraklion), mediterranean studies (Rethymnon), molecular biology and biotechnology (Heraklion); div. of biomedical research of the institute of molecular biology and biotechnology (Ioannina); Dir Prof. COSTAS FOTAKIS.

Institute for Astronomy, Astrophysics, Space Applications & Remote Sensing: c/o Nat. Observatory of Athens, Lofos Nymfon, Thiseio, POB 20048, 118 10 Athens; tel. (210) 8109172; e-mail sec_astrospace@noa.gr; internet www.astro.noa.gr; f. 2012 by merger of Institute of Astronomy and Astrophysics with Institute for Space Applications and Remote Sensing; attached to Nat. Observatory of Athens; research of the sun, stars, stellar systems, interstellar medium, extragalactic astronomy, cosmology; Dir Dr I. A. DAGLIS.

Institute of Chemical Engineering Sciences: c/o Foundation for Research and Technology—Hellas, Stadiou St, POB 1414, 265 04 Patras; tel. (2610) 965300; e-mail info@iceht.forth.gr; internet www.iceht.forth.gr; f. 1984, present status 1987; attached to Foundation for Research and Technology—Hellas; fundamental and technological research; biosciences/biotechnology, energy/environment, nanotechnology/new materials; provides technical services such as instrumental analysis of chemical composition and physicochemical properties, quality assessment, machine and electronics shops, etc.; library of 1,500 vols, 50 journals; Dir Prof. COSTAS GALIOTIS.

Institute of Computer Science: c/o Foundation for Research and Technology—Hellas, 100, Nikolaou Plastira St, 700 13 Heraklion; tel. (2810) 391600; e-mail ics@ics.forth.gr; internet www.ics.forth.gr; f. 1983; attached to Foundation for Research and Technology—Hellas; basic and applied research in information and communication technologies; laboratories of bio-informatics, computational medicine, computer architecture and VLSI systems, computational vision and robotics, distributed computing systems, human-computer interaction, information systems, signal processing, telecommunications; Dir Prof. CONSTANTINE STEPHANIDIS; publ. *Universal Access in the Information Society*.

Institute of Electronic Structure and Laser: c/o Foundation for Research and Technology—Hellas, 100, Nikolaou Plastira, POB 1527, 711 10 Heraklion; tel. (2810) 391300; e-mail central@admin.forth.gr; internet www.iesl.forth.gr; f. 1983; attached to Foundation for Research and Technology—Hellas; divs of laser interactions and photonics, materials and devices; Dir Prof. COSTAS FOTAKIS (acting).

National Centre for Scientific Research 'Demokritos': Agia Paraskevi, POB 60228, 153 10 Athens; tel. (210) 6503000; e-mail president@central.demokritos.gr; internet www.demokritos.gr; f. as Nuclear Research Centre 'Demokritos', current name adopted 1985; promotes technological innovation and education; research carried out by div. of applied technologies and institutes of biology, informatics telecommunications, materials science, microelectronics, nuclear physics, nuclear technology and radiation protection, physical chemistry, radioisotopes and radiodiagnostic products; library of 20,000 vols, 300,000 technical reports, 1,500 periodicals; Dir and Pres. of the Board Dr DIMITRIS NIARCHOS; Librarian Dr VASSILIOS GEORGIOU; publ. *DEMO Reports*.

Telecommunication Systems Institute: Technical Univ. of Crete, Kounoupidiana, 731 00 Chania; tel. (28210) 37260; e-mail info@tsi.gr; internet www.tsi.gr; f. 1995; attached to Technical Univ. of Crete; govt-sponsored and ind.; promotes graduate education, research and devt in automated services over communication networks, broadband networks, communication and computer networks, digital communication systems, signal processing for physical layer communications, speech and language processing, wireless communication networks; Dir Prof. VASSILIS DIGALAKIS.

Libraries and Archives

Athens

Academy of Athens Library: 28, Panepistimiou Ave, 106 79 Athens; tel. (210) 3664790; e-mail library@academyofathens.gr; internet www.academyofathens.gr; f. 1926; collects and publishes Greek historical legal documents, incl. those of the Byzantine and post-Byzantine periods; 140,000 vols; Pres. VASILIOS CH. PETRAKOS; Head Librarian EIRINI TSOURI.

Athens University of Economics and Business Library: 76, Patission St, 104 34 Athens; tel. (210) 8221456; e-mail library@aueb.gr; internet www.lib.aueb.gr; f. 1928; 3 documentation centres: European Documentation Centre (EDC; f. 1992), Depository Library of OECD (f. 1997), and Depository Library of WTO (f. 2004); 100,000 vols, 1,000 journals, 1,000 ejournals, 150 CD-ROMs, 404 serial titles; Dir MARIA FOUNTA; Head Prof. MICHALIS VAZIRGIANNIS.

Benaki Museum Library: 1, Koumbari St and Vas. Sofias Ave, 106 74 Athens; tel. (210) 3671027; e-mail library@benaki.gr; internet www.benaki.gr; f. 1931; Greek and art history, folklore, intellectual life and religion, during Turkish rule and modern times; Islamic and Far Eastern Art; not a lending library; 150,000 vols; Head Librarian PANOREA GAITANOU.

Eugenides Foundation Library: 387, Syggrou Ave, 175 64 Athens; tel. (210) 9469631; e-mail lib@eugenfound.edu.gr; internet www.eugenfound.edu.gr; f. 1966; 60,000 vols, 400 periodicals, 400 CD-ROMs and DVDs, 260 video cassettes; Head Librarian HARA BRINDESI.

Gennadius Library: 61, Souidias St, 106 76 Athens; tel. (210) 7210536; e-mail gen_recep@ascsa.edu.gr; internet www.ascsa.edu.gr/index.php/gennadius; f. 1926; attached to American School of Classical Studies at Athens; books, MSS, archives, and works of art documenting the heritage of Hellenism; research and educational programmes; 120,000 vols; Dir Dr MARIA GEORGOPOULOU; Sr Librarian IRINI SOLOMONIDI; publ. *The New Griffon* (1 a year).

Hellenic Parliament Library: Parliament Bldg, 100 21 Athens; tel. (210) 3707227; e-mail reference@parliament.gr; internet www.hellenicparliament.gr; f. 1844; supports parliamentary work; organizes exhibitions; collns of archives, books, maps, MSS, modern and contemporary Greek art, newspapers and journals, nat. historic treasures; information on the parliamentary activities and the legislative procedure, on current legislation and records of parliamentary debates; 725,000 vols; Head of Library EVANGELOS DRAKOPOULOS.

Library and Information Centre, Panteion University: 136, Sygrou Ave, 176 71 Athens; tel. (210) 9201001; e-mail libp@panteion.gr; internet www.library.panteion.gr; f. 1991; promotes educational and research activities of Panteion Univ.; primarily for mems of the univ. community, but aimed at a wider audience with research interests; 80,000 vols, 780 periodicals, 13,500 electronic journals, 260 CDs, 600 video cassettes and DVDs; Dir NTINA KAKALI.

Music Library of Greece 'Lilian Voudouri': Vasilissis Sofias and Kokkali, 115 21 Athens; tel. (210) 7282778; e-mail library@megaron.gr; internet www.mmb.org.gr; f. 1994; attached to Friends of Music Soc.; holds the Greek Music Archives—Western music, Greek art music from antiquity and the Byzantine period to the present, Greek folk music, traditional music from all parts of the world and jazz; research and educational programmes; 132,000 vols, 22,000 vols of microforms, 400 periodicals, 10,000 recordings; Head of Library STEFANIA MERAKOS.

National Documentation Centre: 48, Vassileos Constantinou Ave, 116 35 Athens; tel. (210) 7273900; e-mail ekt@ekt.gr; internet www.ekt.gr; f. 1980; attached to Nat. Hellenic Research Foundation; documentation, information and support on science research and technology issues; supervised by the Gen. Secretariat for Research and Technology of the Min. of Devt; Dir Dr EVI SACHINI; publ. *Innovation, Research and Technology* (4 a year).

National Library of Greece: 32, Odos Panepistimiou St, 106 79 Athens; tel. (210) 3382601; e-mail director@nlg.gr; internet www.nlg.gr; f. 1832 as Public Library, merged with Athens Univ. library 1842; organizes and disseminates works on Greek science and culture; operates as nat. bibliographic centre; 2.5m. vols; 4,500 MSS; serves as the national bibliographical centre and as the nat. centre for ISBN and ISSN; Gen. Dir ANTONIA ARACHOVA.

National Technical University of Athens Central Library: 9, Odos Heroon Polytechniou, Zografou Campus, 157 73 Athens; tel. (210) 7723878; e-mail library@central.ntua.gr; internet www.lib.ntua.gr; f. 1836; supports undergraduate and graduate studies and applied research; 215,000 vols, 100,000 periodicals; Librarian MARIA KALAMPALIKI.

Nordic Library at Athens: 7, Kavalotti, 117 42 Athens; tel. (210) 9249210; e-mail library@norlib.gr; internet www.norlib.gr; f. 1995; jt venture by archaeological institutes of Denmark, Finland, Norway and Sweden; Greek archaeology and ancient Greek religion and history; 40,000 vols, 450 periodicals; Head Librarian EVI CHARITOUDI.

Technical Chamber of Greece—Documentation and Information Unit: 23–25, Lekka St, 105 62 Athens; tel. (210) 3291701; e-mail tee_lib@tee.gr; internet library.tee.gr; f. 1927; 60,000 vols, 1,400 periodicals, 2,200 scientific works; Head of Unit KATERINA TORAKI.

Chania

Technical University of Crete Library: Univ. Campus, Kounoupidiana, 731 00 Chania; tel. (28210) 37273; e-mail info@library.tuc.gr; internet www.library.tuc.gr; f. 1984; 64,408 vols, 38,151 journals, 182 periodicals, maps and dissertations; Dir MARIA NTAOUNTAKI.

Chios

Koraes Central Public and Historical Library of Chios: 2, Koraes St, 821 00 Chios; tel. (227) 1044246; e-mail bibkor@aegean.gr; internet www.koraeslibrary.gr; f. 1792; colln of rare and unique Homeric edns; exhibitions; educational programmes; 200,000 vols; Pres. CHRISTOS BELLES; Chief Officer ANASTASIOS SARRIS.

Patras

Library & Information Service—University of Patras: University Campus, Rio, 265 04 Patras; tel. (10) 969621; e-mail info@lis.upatras.gr; internet www.lis.upatras.gr; f. 1964 in Athens, present location 1966, present bldg 2003; research and devt projects; collns of gen. informative material, monographs and journals; access to databases, both text and multimedia; open access particularly to students, employees, teaching and admin. staff; external users required to pay fees; 200,000 vols, 3,400 journals, 1,166 ebooks; Pres. Prof. PAVLOS KORDOPATIS; Deputy Dir GIANNIS TSAKONAS.

Piraeus

University of Piraeus Library: Univ. of Piraeus Sub-Level 2, 80, Dimitriou and Karaoli Sts, 185 34 Piraeus; tel. (210) 4142022; e-mail library@unipi.gr; internet www.lib.unipi.gr; f. 1930; banking, business administration, digital studies, economics, European and int. finance, industrial management, informatics, maritime studies, statistics and actuarius; 65,000 vols; Dir ANTHI KATSIRIKOU.

Rethymnon

Library & Information Centre—University of Crete: Gallos Campus, 741 00 Rethymnon; tel. (283) 1077810; e-mail libr_@_lib.uoc.gr; internet www.lib.uoc.gr; f. 1978; education, humanities, social science and political science; 4 brs at Heraklion; Dir ELENI DIAMANTAKI.

Thessaloniki

Aristotle University of Thessaloniki Library: Central Library, 541 24 Thessaloniki; tel. (2310) 995354; e-mail grammateia@lib.auth.gr; internet www.lib.auth.gr; f. 1927, present bldg 1974; attached to Aristotle Univ. of Thessaloniki; rare books from the 18th and 19th centuries; 1,000,000 vols, 5,500 printed journals, 25,000 ejournals, 7,055 dissertations; Pres. CHRIS BABAJIMOPOULOS; Head of Library CATHERINE NASTA.

University of Macedonia Library & Information Centre: Central Library, 156, Egnatias St, POB 1591, 540 06 Thessaloniki; tel. (2310) 891752; e-mail maclib@uom.gr; internet www.lib.uom.gr; f. 1962, present location 1990; offers educational and reference work; supports research; training seminars on information literacy; 68,000 vols, 2,000 audio CDs and records; Dir ANNA FRAGKOU.

Veria

Veria Central Public Library: 8, Ellis St, POB 236, 591 00 Veria; tel. (233) 1024494; e-mail info@libver.gr; internet www.libver.gr; f. 1952; attached to Min. of Education and Religious Affairs; education, information and entertainment; 2 mobile libraries; 100,000 vols.

Volos

Library of the Three Hierarchs: Demetriados-Ogl, 382 21 Volos; tel. (242) 1025641; f. 1907; history, literature, philosophy, physical sciences, religion; 23,000 vols; Asst Dir ACHILLES K. GLAVATOS.

University of Thessaly Library & Information Centre: 2, Metamorforseos St, 383 33 Volos; tel. (242) 1006338; e-mail libinfo@lib.uth.gr; internet www.lib.uth.gr; f. 1988; offers services to both the Univ. of Thessaly's academic community members and to the gen. public; constituted by the Central Library and its brs incl. depts of biochemistry–biotechnology, medicine, physical education and sport science, veterinary science, the Kitsos Makris Folklore Centre, School of Agricultural Sciences; 112,000 vols, 75,000 books and 37,000 journals; Dir Dr IOANNIS CLAPSOPOULOS.

Museums and Art Galleries

Athens

Acropolis Museum: 15, Dionysiou Areopagitou, 117 42 Athens; tel. (210) 9000900; e-mail info@theacropolismuseum.gr; internet www.theacropolismuseum.gr; f. 1865; contains the sculptures discovered on the Acropolis; illustrates the origins of Attic art, pedimental compositions, archaic horsemen, Korai, sculptures of the Parthenon, Temple of Niké, Erechtheion; Pres. Prof. DIMITRIOS PANDERMALIS.

B&M Theocharakis Foundation for the Fine Arts & Music: 9, Vassilissis Sofias Ave and 1, Merlin St, 106 71 Athens; tel. (210) 3611206; e-mail info@theocharakis-foundation.gr; internet www.thf.gr; f. 2004; stages periodical exhibitions, concerts, lectures, seminars and other activities; focuses on modern music and fine arts and its continued devt over the 20th and 21st century; promotes the work of Greek artists abroad; sponsors educational and academic research.

Benaki Museum: 1, Koumbari St and Vas. Sofias Ave, 106 74 Athens; tel. (210) 3671000; e-mail benaki@benaki.gr; internet www.benaki.gr; f. 1930; 40,000 items; Greek art from Neolithic to late Roman period; Byzantine and post-Byzantine; Greek folk art and costumes; historic memorabilia from the War of Independence in 1821 to 1936; 18th and 19th century paintings, engravings and drawings; works of art by N. Hadjikyriakos-Ghikas; Coptic and Islamic art; textiles and embroidery from Far East and W Europe; Neolithic to modern Chinese porcelain; children's toys and games from antiquity to the mid-20th century; historical and photographic archives (Documentation Centre for Neo-Hellenic Architecture); library: see under Libraries and Archives; Dir Prof. Dr ANGELOS DELIVORRIAS; publ. *Mouseio Benaki* (Benaki Museum, 1 a year).

Byzantine and Christian Museum: 22, Vas. Sophias Ave, 106 75 Athens; tel. (213) 2139572; e-mail info@byzantinemuseum.gr; internet www.byzantinemuseum.gr; f. 1914; attached to Min. of Education and Religious Affairs; more than 25,000 objects since 3rd century to 20th century AD, incl. sculptures, icons, wall paintings, ceramics, textiles, drawings, engravings, copies of wall paintings and mosaics of the Byzantine and post-Byzantine eras; religious artefacts of the Early Christian, Byzantine, Medieval, post-Byzantine and later periods; library of 10,800 vols, 280 journals; Dir Dr EUGENIA HALKIA; publ. *ILISSIA* (2 a year, in English and Greek).

National Archaeological Museum: 44, Patission St, 106 82 Athens; tel. (213) 2144800; e-mail eam@culture.gr; internet www.namuseum.gr; f. 1893; 11,000 exhibits covering Greek civilization from the beginnings of prehistory to late antiquity; collns incl. original Greek sculptures and Roman copies of Greek originals; sculptures of the Archaic, Classical, Hellenistic and Roman periods; Neolithic objects from Thessaly; Bronze Age relics from the mainland and the Aegean Islands; Mycenaean treasures; frescoes and pottery from Thera; rich collns of Greek vases and terracottas; collns of jewels and bronzes; Egyptian antiquities; library of 20,000 vols; Dir Dr GEORGE KAKAVAS.

National Gallery—Alexandros Soutzos Museum: 1, Michalakopoulou St, 116 01 Athens; 50, Vassileos Konstantinou, 115 28 Athens; tel. (210) 7235937; e-mail secretary@nationalgallery.gr; internet www.nationalgallery.gr; f. 1900 as Nat. Gallery, merged with Alexandros Soutzos Estate 1954, current name adopted 1954; 16,000 works of drawings, painting, sculpture, engraving and other forms of art from the post-Byzantine period to date; W European paintings; library of 23,000 vols; Dir Prof. MARINA LAMBRAKI-PLAKA.

National Historical Museum: Old Parliament Bldg, 13, Stadiou St, 105 61 Athens; tel. (210) 3237617; e-mail info@nhmuseum.gr; internet www.nhmuseum.gr; f. 1960; attached to Historical and Ethnological Soc. of Greece; modern Greek history from 1453 to 1940; paintings, engravings and prints, architectural drawings, sculptures, flags, arms and armoury, personal and commemorative objects, coins and seals, costumes and jewellery, home and professional equipment; Pres. DIONYSIOS-ANGELOS MINOTOS; Dir EFTHYMIA PAPASPYROU.

National Museum of Contemporary Art: Vas. Georgiou B 17–19 and Rigilis St, 106 75 Athens; tel. (210) 9242111; e-mail protocol@emst.gr; internet www.emst.gr; f. 2000; paintings, installations, photography, video, new media, 'experimental' architecture and industrial design; Dir ANNA KAFETSI.

Paul and Alexandra Canellopoulos Museum: 12, Theorias, 105 55 Athens; tel. (210) 3212313; e-mail info@canellopoulosmuseum.gr; internet www.pakanellopoulosfoundation.org; f. 1976; attached to Paul & Alexandra Canellopoulos Foundation; 6,000 items and works of art from prehistoric to modern times; ancient and Byzantine art; Chair. NELLOS CANELLOPOULOS.

Stoa of Attalos: 24, Adrianou, 105 55 Athens; tel. (210) 3210185; f. 1956; colls incl. all material found in the excavations of the Athenian Agora, illustrating 5,000 years of Athenian history; Dir P. KALLIGAS.

Zoological Museum of the University of Athens: Dept of Biology, Panepistimioupolis, 157 84 Athens; tel. (210) 7274609; e-mail zoolmuse@biol.uoa.gr; internet www.biol.uoa.gr/zoolmuseum; f. 1858; attached to Nat. Natural History Museum; permanent and temporary exhibitions on Greek and world fauna incl. birds, mammals, shells, insects, marine vertibrates and invertebrates, amphibians and reptiles; research in biogeography, conservation biology, ecology, palaeoanthropology, palaeopathology, systematics; Curator Dr CHLOE-ANN ADAMOPOULOU.

Chania

Archaeological Museum of Chania: 28, Halidon, 731 31 Chania; tel. (282) 1090334; e-mail keepka@culture.gr; internet www.culture.gr; f. 1963; housed in the katholikon of the Venetian monastery of St Francis; artefacts from the late Neolithic and Bronze Age (Minoan times), Iron Age; jewellery, sculptures, inscriptions, columns, mosaics, pottery, stone carvings, seals; Dir ANASTASIA TZIGOUNAKI.

Maritime Museum of Crete: Akti Kountourioti, 731 36 Chania; tel. (282) 1091875; e-mail mar-mus@otenet.gr; internet www.mar-mus-crete.gr; f. 1973; 2,500 exhibits of models of ships, naval instruments and devices, paintings, heirlooms, gleanings from the sea bottom, shells, photographs, etc. from Bronze Age, Byzantine period, Independence Struggle, Balkan Wars, World War II, Post-War period; permanent maritime colln and reconstructed Minoan ship; Pres. MANOLIS PETRAKIS.

Corfu

Archaeological Museum of Corfu: 1, Vrela Armeni, 491 00 Corfu; tel. (266) 1030680; e-mail hepka@culture.gr; internet www.culture.gr; f. 1967; covers history of Corfu from prehistoric, historic to Roman times; Menekratis lion, clay pottery, terracotta statuettes from shrines of Corfu; Gorgon-Medusa pediment from the great temple of Artemis, constructed in 585BC; closed for renovation till 2015; Dir DIAMADO RIGAKOU.

Museum of Asiatic Art: St Michael and St George's Palace, 491 00 Corfu; tel. (266) 1030443; e-mail matk@culture.gr; internet www.culture.gr; f. 1926 as Museum of Chinese and Japanese Art, current name adopted 1974; 11,000 exhibits from 11th century BC to 20th century AD from Cambodia, China, India, Japan, Korea, Nepal, Pakistan, Tibet, Thailand and Cambodia; pottery, wood-carvings, paintings, prints, weapons, sculptures AD; Dir ZERNIOTI DESPINA.

Corinth

Archaeological Museum of Ancient Corinth: 200 07 Ancient Corinth; tel. (274) 1031207; e-mail lzepka@culture.gr; internet www.culture.gr; f. 1932; archaic, Asclepieion, classical, Hellenistic, prehistoric, Roman collns; sculptures and inscriptions; Dir KISSAS KONSTANTINOS.

Delphi

Archaeological Museum: 330 54 Delphi; tel. (226) 5082313; e-mail iepka@culture.gr; internet www.culture.gr; f. 1903; history of the Delphic sanctuary from 8th century BC to its decline in Late Antiquity; colins of architectural sculptures, statues and minor objects that were donated; library of 5,200 vols; Dir ATHANASIA PSALTI.

Heraklion

Heraklion Archaeological Museum: Xanthoudidou and Xatzidaki St, 712 02 Heraklion, Crete; tel. (281) 0279000; e-mail amh@culture.gr; internet www.culture.gr; f. 1935; a special regional dept of the Min. of Culture and Sports; colln of Minoan art (pottery, carved stone objects, seals, small sculptures, metal objects, wall-paintings); traces the devt of Cretan cultural heritage up to the Late Roman period; Dir RETHEMIOTAKIS GEORGIOS.

Nafplion

Komboloi Museum: 25, Staikopoulou St, 211 00 Nafplion; tel. (275) 2021618; e-mail komuseum@otenet.gr; internet www.komboloi.gr; f. 1998; supervised by Min. of Culture and Sports; 1000 komboloi (prayer beads) from 1750–1950; komboloi belonging to Buddhists, Catholics, Greeks, Hindus, Muslims and Orthodox monks; Man. ELENI EVANGELINOU; Man. RALLOU GROMITSARI.

Peloponnesian Folklore Foundation: 1, Vas. Alexandrou, 211 00 Nafplion; tel. (275) 2028947; e-mail pff@otenet.gr; internet www.pli.gr; f. 1974; research, presentation, study and preservation of the material culture of the Peloponnese and the whole of Greece (costume, music and dance); operates Childhood Museum 'Stathmos'; colln of 30,000 artefacts; library of 11,900 vols; Pres. and Dir IOANNA PAPANTONIOU; publs *Endymatologica*, *Ethnographica*.

Naxos

Petalouda Art Gallery: Chora Naxos, 843 00 Naxos; tel. (228) 5024531; e-mail info@petalouda-art.com; internet www.petalouda-art.com; f. 1998; modern and contemporary paintings, sculptures and photos; Dir GUY POUZOL.

Olympia

Archaeological Museum of Olympia: Ancient Olympia, 270 65 Olympia; tel. (262) 4022529; e-mail zepka@culture.gr; internet www.culture.gr; f. 1970, present status 2004; Greek Geometric and Archaic bronzes; 2 pediments from Temple of Zeus, Hermes of Praxiteles, Victory of Paionios; finds from Sanctuary of Olympia and Pheidias' workshop; Roman sculpture; stores and conserves terracottas, bronze, stone, mosaics and minor objects; Dir GEORGIA XATZI-SPILIOPOULOU.

Paiania

Vorres Museum: 1, Parodos Diadochou Constantinou, 190 02 Paiania, Attica; tel. (210) 6642520; e-mail mvorres@otenet.gr; internet www.vorresmuseum.gr; f. 1983; covers 2,000 years of Greek history; contemporary Greek paintings and sculptures (second half of the 20th century); Pyrgi folk art colln of peasant artefacts, Greek carpets, ceramics, icons, rare furniture and antiquities; Pres. IAN VORRES.

Rethymnon

Archaeological Museum of Rethymno: Fortetza, 741 00 Rethymnon; tel. (283) 1054668; e-mail protocol@keepka.culture.gr; internet www.culture.gr; f. 1991; artefacts from the late Neolithic period, early to late Minoan periods, Geometric and Archaic periods, Hellenistic and Roman periods; Dir ANASTASIA TZIGOUNAKI.

Historical and Folklore Museum of Rethymno: 28-30 M. Vernardou St, 741 00 Rethymnon; tel. (283) 1023398; internet www.culture.gr; f. 1974; 5,000 items of folk art; textiles, embroideries, costumes, baskets, ceramics, metalwork objects, agricultural implements and tools of traditional occupations, coins, historical documents, photographs, maps, flags, weapons; Pres. FALY G. VOYATZAKIS.

Rhodes

Archaeological Museum of Rhodes: Megalou Alexandrou Sq., 85 100 Rhodes; tel. (224) 1075674; e-mail protocol@kbepka.culture.gr; internet www.culture.gr; f. 1440; Italian occupation, Rhodes and other Dodecanese excavations; Mycenaean jewellery, vases and small objects from Ialysos and Kamiros tombs; from the Geometric to the Classical period (9th–4th century BC); Classical and Hellenistic sculptures and coins; library of 38,480 vols; Dir MARIA MIHAILIDOU.

Rhodes Jewish Museum: Dossiadou and Simiou Sts, 851 00 Rhodes; tel. (224) 1022364; e-mail jcrhodes@otenet.gr; internet www.rhodesjewishmuseum.org; f. 1997; attached to Rhodes Jewish Historical Foundation; exhibits photographic materials, utensils, prayer bags, documents, MSS, costumes; housed in fmr women's prayer rooms at 16th century Kahal Shalom synagogue; closed during the winter season starting November; Pres. BELLA ANGEL RESTIS; Admin. Dir CARMEN COHEN.

Thessaloniki

Archaeological Museum of Thessaloniki: 6, Manoli Andronikou St, POB 50619, 540 13 Thessaloniki; tel. (231) 0830538; e-mail info.amth@culture.gr; internet www.amth.gr; f. 1962, fmrly Yeni Cami (f. 1925); exhibitions on prehistoric Macedonia, the birth of Macedonian cities, Macedonia from the 7th century BC to Late Antiquity, and Thessaloniki; educational activities for children and adults; archaeological and historical lectures; modern theatrical productions of ancient drama; library of 9,000 vols; Dir Dr POLYXENA ADAM-VELENI; publs *Archeologiko Ergo ste Makedonia kai Thrace* (1 a year), *Crater* (1 a year), *Thessaloniki Philippou Vassilissan*.

Macedonian Museum of Contemporary Art: 154, Egnatia St, 546 36 Thessaloniki; tel. (231) 0240002; e-mail mmcart@mmca.org.gr; internet www.mmca.org.gr; f. 1979; 2,000 works by Greek and foreign artists; educational programmes for children; library of 3,000 vols; Pres. XANTHIPPE SKARPIA-HEUPEL.

Science Centre and Technology Museum 'NOESIS': 6th km Thessaloniki, Thermi Rd, 570 01, Thessaloniki; tel. (231) 0483000; e-mail info@noesis.edu.gr; internet www.noesis.edu.gr; f. 1978, fmrly Technical Museum of Thessaloniki, reorg. 2001; temporary exhibition hall; digital planetarium; cosmotheatre; exhibition related to science and technology; Dir CHRIS G. PAPADAKIS.

State Museum of Contemporary Art: 21, Kolokotroni, Moni Lazariston, 564 30 Thessaloniki; tel. (231) 0589140; e-mail info@greekstatemuseum.com; internet www.greekstatemuseum.com; f. 1997; Costakis colln of 1,275 works of Russian avant-garde art; 200 paintings and sculptures; houses Centre of Contemporary Art; educational activities and scientific confs; library of 4,000 vols; Dir MARIA TSANTSANOGLOU.

Thessaloniki Museum of Photography: c/o Thessaloniki Central Post Office, 38, Vas. Irakliou St, 541 01 Thessaloniki; 3, Navarchou Votsi St, Warehouse A, Port of Thessaloniki, 546 24 Thessaloniki; tel. (231) 0566716; e-mail data.thmp@culture.gr; internet www.thmphoto.gr; f. 1997; historical and contemporary Greek and int. photography; collects, preserves and promotes photographic heritage; collns and archives incl. 100,000 photographic objects; library of 17,000 vols; Dir VANGELIS IOAKIMIDIS.

Thessaloniki Olympic Museum: 3, Ag. Dimitriou and September St, 546 36 Thessaloniki; tel. (231) 0968531; e-mail director@olympicmuseum.org.gr; internet www.olympicmuseum-thessaloniki.org; f. 1998, fmrly Sports Museum of Thessaloniki, current name adopted 2008; history of athletics; objects related to the Olympic Games, such as suits, equipment, Olympic medals, memorabilia and publs from the Olympic orgs; Dir KYRIAKI OUDATZI.

Universities

ANOTATI SCHOLI KALON TECHNON (Athens School of Fine Arts)

42, Patision St, 106 82, Athens
Telephone: (210) 3897121
E-mail: rector@asfa.gr
Internet: www.asfa.gr
Founded 1837 as School for the Arts, present name and status 1930
State control
Languages of instruction: English, Greek
Academic year: October to to June

Rector: Prof. GEORGE CHARVALIAS
Vice-Rector: Assoc. Prof. MANOLIS BABOUSSIS
Library of 57,000 vols
Number of teachers: 40
Number of students: 1,221

PROFESSORS

ARFARAS, M., Printmaking
BOTSOGLOU, C., Painting
CHRISTAKIS, T., Painting
HOULIARAS, G., Sculpture
LAPPAS, G., Sculpture
LOUIZIDI, N., Theoretical Courses
PANSELINOU, N., Theoretical Courses
PAPAGIANNIS, THEODOROS, Sculpture
PATRASKIDIS, T.
PSYCHOPEDIS, J., Painting
SAKELLION, D., Painting
VALAVANIDIS, Y., Painting
ZIAKAS, G., Painting

ARISTOTELEIO PANEPISTIMIO THESSALONIKIS (Aristotle University of Thessaloniki)

Aristotle University of Thessaloniki Campus, 541 24 Thessaloniki
Telephone: (2310) 996000
E-mail: pr@auth.gr
Internet: www.auth.gr
Founded 1925
State control
Language of instruction: Greek
Academic year: September to August

Rector: JOHN A. MYLOPOULOS
Vice-Rector for Academic Affairs and Personnel: Dr A. LIALIOU DESPO
Vice-Rector for Finance and Devt: Dr JOHN D. PANTIS
Vice-Rector and Pres. of the Special Account for Research Grants: SOPHIA A. KOUIDOU-ANDREOU
Head of Int. Relations: HELEN KOTSAKI
Librarian: Prof. CHRISTOS BABATZIMOPOULOS

Library: see under Libraries and Archives
Number of teachers: 2,150
Number of students: 81,500
Publications: *Panepistimioupoli* (4 a year), catalogue, scientific annals and faculty periodicals

DEANS

Faculty of Education: Prof. DIMITRA KOGKIDOU
Faculty of Engineering: Prof. KONSTANTINOS-VASILIOS KATSABALOS
Faculty of Fine Arts: Prof. NAZIRIS DIMITRIOS
Faculty of Law, Economics and Political Sciences: Prof. NICHOLAS PARASKEVOPOULOS
Faculty of Philosophy: Prof. MILTIADIS PAPANIKOLAOU
Faculty of Science: Prof. SPYROS PAVLIDES
Faculty of Theology: Prof. MICHAIL TRITOS

DIMOKRITEIO PANEPISTIMIO THRAKIS
(Democritus University of Thrace)

Admin. Bldg, University Campus, 691 00, Komotini
Telephone: (253) 1039000
E-mail: intrela@duth.gr
Internet: www.duth.gr
Founded 1973
State control
Language of instruction: Greek
Academic year: September to August
Rector: Prof. KONSTANTINOS REMELIS
Vice-Rector for Academic Affairs and Staff: Prof. ALEXANDER KORTSARIS
Vice-Rector for Student and External Affairs: Prof. GEORGE KOSTAS
Library of 274,209 vols, 4,040 journals
Number of teachers: 584
Number of students: 24,884

DEANS

Department of Agricultural Development: ZAFEIRIS ABAS
Department of Civil Engineering: CHRIS G. KARAYANNIS
Department of Electrical Engineering and Computer Engineering: A. SAFIGIANNI
Department of Environmental Engineering: K. OUZOUNIS
Department of Forestry and Management of the Environment and Natural Resources: KONSTANTINOS SOUTSAS
Department of Greek Literature: C. IOANNIDOU
Department of History and Ethnology: K. CHATZOPOULOS
Department of International Economic Relations and Development: I. MOURMOURIS
Department of Languages, Literature and Culture of the Black Sea Countries: KONSTANTINOS BOTSARIS
Department of Molecular Biology and Genetics: RAPHAEL SANDALTZOPOULOS
Department of Pre-school Education Sciences: L. GOGOU
Department of Production and Management Engineering: S. SPARTALIS
Department of Social Administration: G. KATROUGALOS
Faculty of Educational Sciences: TH. VOUGIOUKLIS
Faculty of Engineering: I. DIAMANTIS
Faculty of Law: A. CHARALAMPAKIS
Faculty of Medicine: K. SIMOPOULOS
Faculty of the Science of Physical Education and Sport: MARIA MICHALOPOULOU
Pedagogical Department of Primary Education: E. TARATORI

PROFESSORS

BELLOS, K., Open Channel Hydraulics
BEZIRTZOGLOU, E., Microbiology with Emphasis in Microbial Ecology
BOUROS, D., Pneumonology
CHARALAMPAKIS, A., Criminal Law
DALAKOURAS, T., Criminal Procedural Law
DEMETRIOU, D., Civil Procedural Law
DIAMANTIS, I., Engineering Geology with Emphasis on Groundwaters
DIMITRIOU, T., Anatomy
DIMOPOULOS, C., Criminology
GALANOPOULOS, K., Agricultural Economics
GDOUTOS, E., Applied Mechanics
GKODOLIAS, G., Sports Medicine Focused on Musculoskeletal Injuries and Diseases
GOGOU-KRITIKOU, L., Sociology of Education
HRISSANTHOU, V., River Engineering
ILIADIS, L., Forest Informatics
KAGALOU, I., Ecology
KALAVROS, K., Civil Procedural Law and Law of Arbitration
KARABINIS, A., Reinforced Concrete Structures
KARAFYLLIDIS, I., Design, Modelling and Simulation of Microelectronic and Nanoelectronic Devices, Circuits and Systems.
KARAYANNIS, C., Reinforced Concrete Structures. Numerical Methods, Analysis and Design
KONSTANTINIDIS, A., Criminal Procedure Law
KONTOGIANNI, V., Modern Greek Literature
KOSTA, G., Sports Recreation
KOTSIOU, S., Internal Medicine
KOUTROUBAS, S., Agronomy
KOUTROUMANIDIS, T., Applied Economic Statistics
KOZOBOLIS, V., Ophthalmology
KYRIACOU, G., Microwaves
LAIOS, A., Special Training Theory on Basketball Coaching
LAPARIDIS, K., Special Training Theory on Basketball Coaching
LAZARIDES, M., Vascular Surgery
LYGOURAS, J., Electronic Systems
MANIOTIS, D., Civil Procedural Law
MARIA, K., Mechanical Behaviour and Durability of Materials-Fracture Mechanics-Corrosion of Steel in Concrete
MAROULAKOU, I., Genetics
MATSOUKIS, P., Coastal Hydraulics and Engineering
MAVROMARA, P., Biochemistry
MAVROMMATIS, G., Data Analysis in Physical Education and Sport Biomechanics
MICHALOPOULOU, M., Skill Acquisition in Physical Activity and Sports
PANOSKALTSIS, V., Civil Engineering
PANTAZOPOULOU, S., Analysis and Design of Reinforced Concrete Structures
PANTELIDOU, K., Civil Law
PANTOKRATORAS, A., Fluid Mechanics
PAPADOPOULOS, B., General Topology with Emphasis on Topologies on Function Spaces
PAPADOPOULOS, N., Histology-Embryology
PAPAMARKOS, N., Electric Circuits, Digital Filters, Digital Image Processing
PASSADAKIS, P., Nephrology
PAVLOU, S., Criminal Law
PNEUMATIKOS, I., Intensive Care Medicine
POULIS, G., Ecclesiastical Law
PRASSOPOULOS, P., Radiology-Gastrointestinal Radiology
PROFILLIDIS, V., Railway Engineering-Transportation Management
RADOGLOU, K., Forest Ecophysiology
RIGAS, A., Processing of Electromagnetic Stochastic Signals
SOULIS, J., Computational and Experimental Hydraulics/Fluid Mechanics
SOUTSAS, K., Environmental and Regional Policy-Forest Resources and Quantitative Methods
STAMATOPOULOS, S., Civil Procedural Law
THODIS, E., Nephrology
TOKATLIDIS, I., Genetics and Plant Breeding
TOKMAKIDIS, S., Exercise Physiology
TOULOUPIDIS, S., Urology
TSATALAS, K., Haematology
TZIATZI, M., Byzantine Philology
VAOS, G., Paediatric Surgery
VARGEMEZIS, V., Nephrology
VASILIOU, G., Pesticides and Ecotoxicology
YOUNI, M., Legal History
ZACHAROPOULOS, D., Mechanics of Materials and Fracture Mechanics

ELLINIKO ANOIKTO PANEPISTIMIO
(Hellenic Open University)

18, Parodos Aristotelous St, 263 35 Patras
Telephone: (261) 0367300
E-mail: info@eap.gr
Internet: www.eap.gr
Founded 1992
State control
Pres.: Prof. HARALAMBOS COCCOSSIS
Vice-Pres.: PANAGIOTIS GIANNOPOULOS
Sec.-Gen.: CHARALAMBOS RODOPOULOS
Number of teachers: 1,565
Number of students: 26,240 (15,541 undergraduate, 10,699 postgraduate)

DEANS

School of Applied Arts: (vacant)
School of Humanities: ALEXIOS KOKKOS
School of Science and Technology: SKODRAS ATHANASSIOS
School of Social Sciences: DIMITRIOS A. GIANNIAS

ETHNIKO METSOVIO POLYTECHNEIO
(National Technical University of Athens)

28, Oktovriou (Patision) 42, 106 82 Athens
Telephone: (210) 7722017
E-mail: webmaster@ntua.gr
Internet: www.ntua.gr
Founded 1836
State control
Language of instruction: Greek
Academic year: October to July (2 semesters)
Schools of applied mathematical and physical science, architecture, chemical engineering, civil engineering, electrical and computer engineering, mechanical engineering, mining engineering and metallurgy, naval architecture and marine engineering, rural and surveying engineering
Rector: SIMOS E. SIMOPOULOS
Vice-Rector: IOANNIS AVARITSIOTIS
Vice-Rector: ANTONIA MOROPOULOU
Librarian: MARIA KALAMPALIKI
Library: see under Libraries and Archives
Number of teachers: 700
Number of students: 11,500 (8,500 undergraduate, 1,500 graduate, 1,500 doctoral)
Publications: *Pyrphoros* (24 a year), *Scientific Papers*

PROFESSORS

AFRATI, F., Electrical and Computer Engineering
ANAGNOSTOU, M., Electrical and Computer Engineering
ANASTASSOPOULOU, I., Materials Science and Engineering
ANDREOPOULOS, A., Synthesis and Development of Industrial Processing
ANDROUTSOPOULOS, G., Process Analysis and Plant Design
ANTONOPOULOS, K., Mechanical Engineering
ASSIMAKOPOULO, D., Process Analysis and Plant Design
ASSIMAKOPOULOS, V., Electrical and Computer Engineering
ATHANASOULIS, G., Naval Architecture and Marine Engineering

AVARITSIOTIS, J., Electrical and Computer Engineering
BAFA, G., Process Analysis and Plant Design
BATIS, G., Materials Science and Engineering
BOUDOUVIS, A., Process Analysis and Plant Design
BOURKAS, P., Electrical and Computer Engineering
CAPROS, P., Electrical and Computer Engineering
CAPSALIS, C., Electrical and Computer Engineering
CARAYANNIS, G., Electrical and Computer Engineering
CHRYSSOULAKIS, J., Materials Science and Engineering
CONSTANTINOU, F., Electrical and Computer Engineering
COTTIS, P., Electrical and Computer Engineering
DERVOS, K., Electrical and Computer Engineering
DIALINAS, E., Electrical and Computer Engineering
FRANGOPOULOS, CH., Naval Architecture and Marine Engineering
FRANGOS, P., Electrical and Computer Engineering
FTICOS, CHR., Synthesis and Development of Industrial Processing
GLYTSIS, E., Electrical and Computer Engineering
HATZIARGYRIOU, N., Electrical and Computer Engineering
HIZANIDIS, K., Electrical and Computer Engineering
KAKATSIOS, X., Mechanical Engineering
KAKLIS, P., Naval Architecture and Marine Engineering
KANELLOPOULOS, J., Electrical and Computer Engineering
KASELOURI-RIGOPOULOU, V., Chemical Sciences
KAYAFAS, E., Electrical and Computer Engineering
KOLISIS, FR., Synthesis and Development of Industrial Processing
KOLLIAS, S., Electrical and Computer Engineering
KOUKIOS, E., Synthesis and Development of Industrial Processing
KOULOUMBI, N., Materials Science and Engineering
KOUMANTAKIS, I., Geological Sciences
KOUSSIOURIS, T., Electrical and Computer Engineering
KOUTSOURIS, D., Electrical and Computer Engineering
KRIKELIS, N., Mechanical Engineering
KYRTATOS, N., Naval Architecture and Marine Engineering
LIVADITI, K., Geological Sciences
LOIS, E., Synthesis and Development of Industrial Processing
LOIZIDOU-MALAMIS, M., Chemical Sciences
LOUKAKIS, TH., Naval Architecture and Marine Engineering
MACHIAS, A., Electrical and Computer Engineering
MAGLARIS, V., Electrical and Computer Engineering
MAMALIS, A., Mechanical Engineering
MANIAS, S., Electrical and Computer Engineering
MARAGOS, P., Electrical and Computer Engineering
MARATOS, N., Electrical and Computer Engineering
MARINOS-KOURI, D., Process Analysis and Plant Design
MARKATO, N., Process Analysis and Plant Design
MARKOPOULOU-IGGLESI, O., Chemical Sciences
MAROULI, Z., Process Analysis and Plant Design
MATHIOUDAKIS, K., Mechanical Engineering
MAVRAKOS, S., Naval Architecture and Marine Engineering
MITROU, N., Electrical and Computer Engineering
MOROPOULOU, A., Materials Science and Engineering
MPERGELES, G., Mechanical Engineering
MPOSKOS, E., Geological Sciences
NEOU-SYNGOUNA, P., Metallurgy and Materials Technology
OCHSENKUEHN-PETROPOULOU, M., Chemical Sciences
PANAGIOTOU, G. N., Mining Engineering
PANAGOPOULOS, C., Metallurgy and Materials Technology
PANAGOPOULOS, K. J., Mining Engineering
PAPADIMITRIOU, G., Metallurgy and Materials Technology
PAPAILIOU, K., Mechanical Engineering
PAPAKONSTANTINOU, G., Electrical and Computer Engineering
PAPANIKOLAOU, A., Naval Architecture and Marine Engineering
PAPANTONIS, D., Mechanical Engineering
PAPASPYRIDES, C. D., Synthesis and Development of Industrial Processing
PAPAVASILOPOULOS, G., Electrical and Computer Engineering
PAPAYANNAKI, L., Process Analysis and Plant Design
PAPAYANNAKOS, N., Process Analysis and Plant Design
PAPAZOGLOU, V., Naval Architecture and Marine Engineering
PARASKEVOPOULOS, P., Electrical and Computer Engineering
PASPALIARIS, I., Metallurgy and Materials Technology
PEKMESTZI, K., Electrical and Computer Engineering
PHILIPPOPOULOS, K., Process Analysis and Plant Design
PROTONOTARIOS, E., Electrical and Computer Engineering
PSARAFTIS, CH., Naval Architecture and Marine Engineering
RAKOPOULOS, K., Mechanical Engineering
ROGDAKIS, E., Mechanical Engineering
ROUBANI-KALANZOPOULOU, F., Materials Science and Engineering
ROUMELIOTIS, J., Electrical and Computer Engineering
SAMOUILIDIS, E., Electrical and Computer Engineering
SELLIS, T., Electrical and Computer Engineering
SFANTSIKOPOULOS, M., Mechanical Engineering
SIMITZIS, J., Materials Science and Engineering
SIMOPOULOS, S., Mechanical Engineering
SKORDALAKIS, E., Electrical and Computer Engineering
SPENTZAS, K., Mechanical Engineering
SPYRELLIS, N., Chemical Sciences
STAFYLOPATIS, A. G., Electrical and Computer Engineering
STAMATAKI, S., Mining Engineering
STASSINOPOULOS, G., Electrical and Computer Engineering
STATHOPULOS, I. A., Electrical and Computer Engineering
STOURNAS, S., Synthesis and Development of Industrial Processing
SYKAS, E., Electrical and Computer Engineering
TATSIOPOULOS, I., Mechanical Engineering
THEODOROU, N., Electrical and Computer Engineering
THEODOROU, TH., Materials Science and Engineering
THEOLOGOU, M., Electrical and Computer Engineering
TRIANTAFYLLOU, G., Naval Architecture and Marine Engineering
TSALAMENGAS, J., Electrical and Computer Engineering
TSANAKAS, P., Electrical and Computer Engineering
TSANGARIS, G., Materials Science and Engineering
TSANGARIS, S., Mechanical Engineering
TSEZOS, M., Metallurgy and Materials Technology
TSIMAS, S., Chemical Sciences
TZABIRAS, G., Naval Architecture and Marine Engineering
TZAFESTAS, S., Electrical and Computer Engineering
UZUNOGLOU, N., Electrical and Computer Engineering
VASSILIOU, P., Materials Science and Engineering
VASSILIOU, Y., Electrical and Computer Engineering
VGENOPOULOS, A., Geological Sciences
VLYSSIDIS, A., Synthesis and Development of Industrial Processing
VOMVORIDIS, J., Electrical and Computer Engineering
VOURNAS, C., Electrical and Computer Engineering
XANTHAKIS, J., Electrical and Computer Engineering
YOVA, D., Electrical and Computer Engineering
ZACHOS, S., Electrical and Computer Engineering
ZEVGOLIS, E. N., Metallurgy and Materials Technology

ETHNIKON KAI KAPODISTRIAKON PANEPISTIMION ATHINON
(National and Kapodistrian University of Athens)

30, Odos Panepistimiou, 106 79 Athens
Telephone: (210) 3689770
E-mail: rector@uoa.gr
Internet: www.uoa.gr
Founded 1837 as Othonian Univ., current name adopted 1932
State control
Language of instruction: Greek
Academic year: October to June (2 semesters)
Rector: Prof. T. PELEGRINIS
Vice-Rector for Academic Affairs and Personnel: Prof. A. DOUKOUDAKIS
Vice-Rector for Financial Affairs and Devt: Prof. TH. SFIKOPOULOS
Vice-Rector for Student Care and Int. Relations: Prof. THEODORE D. LIAKAKOS
Number of teachers: 2,200
Number of students: 122,000 (110,000 undergraduate, 12,000 postgraduate)

DEANS

School of Health Sciences: KONSTANTINOS DIMOPOULOS
School of Law, Economics and Political Sciences: CHRISTOS ROZAKIS
School of Philosophy: (vacant)
School of Science: Prof. HARALAMBOS PAPAGEORGIOU
School of Theology: Prof. MARIOS P. BEGZOS

GEOPONIKO PANEPISTIMIO ATHINON
(Agricultural University of Athens)

75, Iera Odos, 118 55 Athens
Telephone: (210) 5294802
E-mail: r@aua.gr
Internet: www.aua.gr
Founded 1920 as the Highest College of Agriculture, current name adopted 1989
State control
Depts of agricultural biotechnology, animal science, crop science, food science and tech-

nology, natural resources management and agricultural engineering, rural economics and development, science

Rector: CONSTANTINOS FEGGEROS

Vice-Rector for Academic Affairs and Personnel: EPAMINONDAS PAPLOMATAS

Vice-Rector for Financial Affairs and Devt: GEORGIOS PAPADAKIS

Library Dir: MARIA KANINI

Library of 800 vols, 16,000 ejournals

Number of teachers: 177

Number of students: 3,500

HAROKOPIO PANEPISTIMION (Harokopio University)

70, El. Venizelou St, 176 71 Athens

Telephone: (210) 9549100

E-mail: rector@hua.gr

Internet: www.hua.gr

Founded 1929, present status 1990

State control

Academic year: September to June (2 semesters)

Depts of dietics and nutritional science, geography, home economics and ecology, informatics and telematics

Rector: Prof. DIMOSTHENIS ANAGNOSTOPOULOS

Vice-Rector for Academic Affairs and Personnel: Assoc. Prof. EVAGELIA GEORGITSOYIANNI

Vice-Rector for Financial Affairs and Devt: Assoc. Prof. APOSTOLOS PAPADOPOULOS

Librarian: IFIGENIA VARDAKOSTA

Library of 22,000 vols, 431 journals

Number of teachers: 65

Number of students: 430

HELLENIC AIR FORCE ACADEMY

Dekelia Air Base, Tatoi

Telephone: (210) 8193399

E-mail: cmdr.hafa@haf.gr

Internet: www.haf.gr/en/career/academies/si

Founded 1931 as Air Force School, present status 1964; attached to Hellenic Air Force

State control

Academic year: September to August (2 semesters)

Depts of aerodynamics-flight engineering, aeronautical engineering, technical engineering, construction tests-infrastructure works, automatic control, aerospace technology, defence systems and operations, electronics, electric power, telecommunications, informatics and computers, leadership-command, human sciences and physiology, mathematics-natural sciences, mechanical engineering, material technology, production organization, thermodynamics, propulsive and energy systems; conducts scientific research in aviation technology

Cmdr: Major Gen. ATHANASIOS TSALIKIS

Publication: *EVELPIS*

HELLENIC MILITARY ACADEMY

166 73 Vari

Telephone: (210) 8904000

Internet: www.sse.gr

Founded 1828

State control

Academic year: September to August (2 semesters)

Courses in applied sciences, chemistry, engineering, history, humanities and social studies, psychology

Cmdr: Major Gen. ILIAS LEONTARIS

Number of students: 235

Publication: *EVELPIS*

HELLENIC NAVAL ACADEMY

Hadjikyriakou Ave, 185 39 Piraeus

Telephone: (210) 4581301

E-mail: gensec@snd.edu.gr

Internet: www.hna.gr

Founded 1845

State control

Academic year: September to June (2 semesters)

Cmdr: A. THEODOSSIOU

Lt Gov.: K. KARAGEORGIS

Pres. for Academic Affairs: MICHAEL FAFALIOS

Publication: *Nafsivios Country*

IKONOMIKON PANEPISTIMION ATHINON (Athens University of Economics and Business)

76, Patission St, 104 34 Athens

Telephone: (210) 8203911

E-mail: webmaster@aueb.gr

Internet: www.aueb.gr

Founded 1920 as Athens School of Commercial Studies, current name adopted 1989

State control

Academic year: September to August (2 semesters)

Depts of accounting and finance, business administration, economics, informatics, international and European economic studies, management science and technology, marketing and communication, statistics

Rector: Prof. KONSTANTINE GATSIOS

Vice-Rector for Academic Affairs: Prof. EMMANOUIL GIAKOUMAKIS

Vice-Rector for Economic Affairs: Prof. GEORGE GIAGLIS

Library: see under Libraries and Archives

Number of teachers: 272

Number of students: 11,313

DEANS

School of Business: Prof. GEORGE SIOMKOS

School of Economic Sciences: Prof. ANASTASIOS XEPAPADEAS

School of Information Sciences and Technology: Prof. PANOS CONSTANTOPOULOS

PROFESSORS

ALOGOSKOUFIS, G., Economics
APOSTOLOPOULOS, T., Informatics
AVLONITIS, G., Marketing and Communication
BALTAS, G., Marketing and Communication
BALTAS, N., Economics
BOURANTAS, D., Management Science and Technology
CHATZIPANAGIOTOU, P., International and European Economic Studies
CHRISTODOULAKIS, N., International and European Economic Studies
CONSTANTOPOULOS, P., Informatics
COURCOUBETIS, K., Informatics
DELLAPORTAS, P., Statistics
DIAMANDIS, P., Business Administration
DIMELI, S., Informatics
DOUKIDIS, G., Management Science and Technology
FRANGOS, N., Statistics
GATSIOS, K., Economics
GEORGOUTSOS, D., Accounting and Finance
GHICAS, D., Accounting and Finance
GIAGLIS, G., Management Science and Technology
GIAKOUMAKIS, E., Informatics
GRITZALIS, D., Informatics
HALIKIAS, I., Marketing and Communication
IOANNOU, G., Management Science and Technology
KALAMBOUKIS, T., Informatics
KALYVITIS, S., International and European Economic Studies
KATERINIS, P., Informatics
KATSOULACOS, I., Economics
KAVUSSANOS, M., Accounting and Finance
KOLLINTZAS, T., Economics
KONTOYIANNIS, I., Informatics
KORLIRAS, P., Economics
KOURETAS, G., Business Administration
KYRIAZIDOU, A., Economics
LIOUKAS, S., Management Science and Technology
LOISIDES, I., International and European Economic Studies
LOURI, E., Economics
MAGIROU, E., Informatics
MILIS, I., Informatics
MOUTOS, T., International and European Economic Studies
NIKOLOPOULOS, A., Business Administration
PAGOULATOS, G., International and European Economic Studies
PANARETOS, I., Statistics
PANAS, E., Statistics
PANIGYRAKIS, G., Business Administration
PAPADAKIS, V., Business Administration
PATSOURATIS, V., Marketing and Communication
PHILIPPOPOULOS, A., Economics
POLYZOS, G., Informatics
PRASTACOS, G., Management Science and Technology
REFENES, A., Management Science and Technology
SAKELLARIS, P., Economics
SIOMKOS, G., Business Administration
SPINELLIS, D., Management Science and Technology
STAMOULIS, G., Informatics
TSAKLOGLOU, P., International and European Economic Studies
TSIONAS, E., Economics
TZAVALIS, I., Economics
VASILAKIS, S., International and European Economic Studies
VENIERIS, G., Accounting and Finance
VETTAS, N., Economics
XEKALAKI, E., Statistics
XEPAPADEAS, A., International and European Economic Studies
YANNACOPOULOS, A., Statistics
YANNAKOUDAKIS, E., Informatics
ZANIAS, G., International and European Economic Studies
ZAZANIS, M., Statistics
ZOGRAFOS, K., Management Science and Technology

INTERNATIONAL HELLENIC UNIVERSITY

14th km Thessaloniki-Moudania, 570 01 Thermi

Telephone: (231) 0474560

E-mail: info@ihu.edu.gr

Internet: www.ihu.edu.gr

Founded 2005

State control

Language of instruction: English

Chair.: Prof. COSTAS TH. GRAMMENOS

Deputy Chair.: Prof. NICOLAS MOUSSIOPOULOS

Chief Librarian: GEORGIA ROIDOULI

Library of 8,000 vols

DEANS

School of Economics and Business Administration: NICOLAS MOUSSIOPOULOS (acting)

School of Humanities: Prof. BASIL C. GOUNARIS

School of Science and Technology: Prof. IOANNIS VLAHAVAS

IONIO PANEPISTIMIO
(Ionian University)

POB 663, 72, Ioannou Theotoki St, 491 00 Corfu
Telephone: (266) 1087625
E-mail: int_rel@ionio.gr
Internet: www.ionio.gr
Founded 1824, fmrly Ionian Acad.
State control
Academic year: October to July
Depts of archives and library science, Asian studies, audio and visual arts, foreign languages, translation and interpreting, history, informatics, music studies
Rector: Prof. ANASTASIA SALI-PAPASALI
Vice-Rector for Academic Affairs and Human Resources: Assoc. Prof. CHRYSSOULA MIRANDA KALDI
Vice-Rector for Financial Management and Devt: Assoc. Prof. STAVROS KATSIOS
Library of 80,000 vols, 700 magazines, 3,500 audiovisual CDs, cassettes, vinyl records, microfilms

PANEPISTIMION AEGAEOU
(University of the Aegean)

Admin. Bldg, University Hill, 811 00 Mytilene
Telephone: (225) 1036000
E-mail: rector@aegean.gr
Internet: www.aegean.gr
Founded 1984
Schools of business, environment, humanities, sciences, social sciences; campuses: Chios, Karlovasi, Lesvos, Mytilene, Rhodes
Rector: Prof. PARIS TSARTAS
Vice-Rector for Academic Affairs and Student Welfare: Assoc. Prof. Dr NIKOS SOULAKELLIS
Vice-Rector for Finance and Devt: Assoc. Prof. Dr IOANNIS KALLAS
Vice-Rector for Research and Strategic Management: Prof. ANGELIQUE DIMITRACOPOULOU
Librarian: ELLI VLACHOU
Library of 86,674 vols
Number of teachers: 276
Number of students: 11,959 (9,688 undergraduate, 2,271 postgraduate)

PANEPISTIMION IOANNINON
(University of Ioannina)

POB 1186, 451 10 Ioannina
Telephone: (265) 1007105
E-mail: piro@cc.uoi.gr
Internet: www.uoi.gr
Founded 1964, present status 1970
State control
Language of instruction: Greek
Academic year: September to June (2 semesters)
Rector: Prof. TRIANTAFYLLOS A. D. ALBANIS
Vice-Rector: Prof. GEORGIOS D. KAPSALIS
Vice-Rector: Prof. ISAAC E. LAGARIS
Vice-Rector: Prof. VENETSANOS G. MAVREAS
Registrar: L.-N. PAPALOUKAS
Library Dir: Dr GEORGIOS ZACHOS (acting)
Library of 310,000 vols
Number of teachers: 549
Number of students: 17,040 (13,523 undergraduate, 1,300 postgraduate, 2,217 doctoral)
Publications: *Eperitis 'Dodoni I'* (history and archaeology, 1 a year), *Eperitis 'Dodoni II'* (philology, 1 a year), *Eperitis 'Dodoni III'* (philosophy, education and psychology, 1 a year)

DEANS
School of Education: Prof. POLYXENI PANGE
School of Medicine: Prof. MARGARITA TZAFLIDOU
School of Natural Resources and Enterprises Management (Agrinio): (vacant)
School of Philosophy: Assoc. Prof. ATHANASIOS AGELLOU
School of Sciences: Prof. CHRISTOS BAIKOUSIS
School of Sciences and Technology: (vacant)

PROFESSORS
School of Education (tel. (265) 1097454):
DIMOU, G., Pedagogics and Psychology of Learning Disabilities
KANAVAKIS, M., Pedagogics
KAPSALIS, G.
KARAFYLIS, G., Society Philosophy
KARPOZILOU, M.
KONSTANTINOU, C., School Pedagogics
STAVROU, L., Psychology of Pre-school Education
TZOULIS, CH., Modern Greek Literature
ZAHARIS, D., Evolutionary Psychology in Education

School of Medicine (tel. (265) 1097201):
AGNADI-GIRA, N. J., Pathological Anatomy
ANDRONIKOU, S., Neo-natology
ASIMAKOPOULOS, C., Otorhinolaryngology
BERIS, A., Orthopaedics
BOURANTAS, C., Pathology, Haematology
DROSOS, A., Pathology-rheumatology
EFRAIMIDIS, S., Radiology
EVANGELOU, A., Physiology
FOTSIS, TH., Biological Chemistry
GEORGATOS, S., Biology
GEROULANOS, ST., History of Medicine
GLAROS, D., Medical Physics
HATZIS, I., Dermatology
IOANNIDIS, I., Hygiene
KALEF-EZRA, J., Medical Physics
KANAVAROS, P., Anatomy-Histology
KAPPAS, A., Surgery
KIRITSIS, A., Neurology
KONSTANTOPOULOS, S., Pathology and Pneumonology
LOLIS, D., Obstetrics and Gynaecology
MALAMOU-MITSI, V., Pathology
MARSELOS, M.-A., Medical Pharmacology
MAVREAS, V., Psychiatry
PAPADOPOULOS, G., Anaesthiology
PARASKEVAIDIS, C., Organic Peptide Chemistry
PAVLIDIS, N., Oncology
PSILAS, C., Ophthalmology
SEFERIADIS, C., Biological Chemistry
SIAMOPOULOS, K., Pathology and Nephrology
SIAMOPOULOU-MAVRIDOU, A., Paediatrics
SKEVAS, A., Otorhinolaryngology
SOFIKITIS, N., Urology
SOUCACOS, P., Orthopaedics
TSIANOS, E., Oncology
TZAFLIDOU, M., Medical Physics
XENAKIS, T., Orthopaedics

School of Natural Resources and Enterprises Management (Agrinio):
FOTOPOULOS, CH., Administration of Agricultural Enterprises
MATTHOPOULOS, D., Administration of Environment and Natural Resources

School of Philosophy (tel. (265) 1097176):
APOSTOLOPOULOU, G., History, Interpretation and Practice of Philosophy
ATHANASIOU, L., Language Teaching and Evaluation
CHADJIDAKI-BAHARA, T., Byzantine Archaeology
GOTOVOS, A., Pedagogics
HADJIDAKI-BACHARA, T., Byzantine Archaeology
KAPSOMENOS, E., Modern Greek Literature and Literary Theory
KARPOZILOS, A.-D., Medieval Greek Literature
KATSOURIS, A., Ancient Greek Philology
KONDORINI, B., History and Archaeology
KONSTANDINIDIS, C., Ancient and Medieval Greek Literature
KORDOSIS, M., Ancient and Medieval Greek Literature
MARAGOU, E., Classical Archaeology
MAVROMATIS, J., Byzantine Philology and Post-Byzantine Philology
MAVROYIORGOS, Y., Pedagogic Educational Policy
NOUTSOS, CH., History of Education
NOUTSOS, P., Philosophy
PALIOURAS, A., Byzantine Archaeology
PAPACONSTANDINOU, P., Pedagogics
PAPADIMITRIOU, E., Philosophy
PAPADOPOULOS, A., Prehistoric Archaeology
PAPAGEORGIOU, G., Modern History
PAPAPOSTOLOU, J., Classical Archaeology
PERISSINAKIS, J., Ancient Greek Literature
PLOUMIDIS, G., Venetian History and Historical Geography
RAIOS, D., Ancient Greek and Latin Philology
SIOROKAS, G., Modern European History
STASINOS, D., Psychology
SYNODINOU, A., Ancient Greek Philology
TRIANTI, A., Archaeology
TSANGALAS, K., Folklore

School of Sciences (tel. (265) 1097190):
AKRIVIS, G., Computer Science
ALBANIS, T., Environmental Protection
ALISSANDRAKIS, C., Physics of the Sun and Space
ASSIMAKOPOULOS, P., Nuclear Physics and Radio Ecology
BAIKOUSIS, CH., Differential Geometry
BATAKIS, N., Physics
BOLIS, TH., Combinatorial Group Theory
BOLOVINOS, AG., Atomic and Molecular Physics
DOUGIAS, S., Mathematical Analysis
DRAINAS, C., Chemistry
EVANGELOU, SP., Physics, Theory of Condensed Matter
EVMIRIDIS, N., Inorganic Chemistry
FERENTINOS, K., Statistics
FILOS, C., Mathematical Analysis
GALATSANOS, N., Computer Science
GEROTHANASIS, I., Organic Chemistry
GRAMMATIKOPOULOS, M., Differential Equations
HADJILIADIS, N., Inorganic and General Chemistry
HASANIS, T., Differential Geometry
KAMARATOS, E., Physical Chemistry
KAMBANOS, T., Inorganic Chemistry
KARAKOSTAS, G., Mathematical Analysis and Applications
KATSARAS, A., Functional Analysis
KATSOULIS, V., Meteorology and Climatology
KONDOMINAS, M., Chemistry
KOSMAS, M., Chemistry
KOSTARAKIS, P., Physics
KOUFOGIORGOS, TH., Differential Geometry
KOVALA-DEMERTZI, D., Inorganic Chemistry
LAGARIS, I., Computer Science
LEONDARIS, G., Physics, Elemental Multiplets
LOUKAS, S., Statistics
MANESIS, E., Physics, High Energy Theory
MARMARIDIS, N., Algebra
MASSALAS, CH., Continuum Physics and Mechanics
PANTIS, G., Theory of Nuclear Physics
PHILOS, C., Differential Equations
POMONIS, F., Industrial Chemistry
SAKARELLO DAITSO, M., Biochemistry
SAKARELLOS, C., Organic Peptide Chemistry
SDOUKOS, A., Industrial Chemistry
SFIKAS, Y. G., Differential Equations
STAVROULAKIS, I., Differential Equations
TAMVAKIS, K., Elementary Particle Theory and Cosmology

TRIANTIS, F., High-Energy Physics and Related Technological Applications
TSAMATOS, P., Mathematical Analysis
TSANGARIS, J., Inorganic and General Chemistry
VAGIONAKIS, C., Physics
VERGADOS, J., Theoretical Physics

School of Sciences and Technology:

CHARALAMBOPOULOS, A., Material Science
DRAINAS, C., Chemistry
KAXIRAS, E., Material Science
MASSALAS, CH., Continuum Physics and Mechanics
PSARROPOULOU, A., Animal Physiology

Independent Department of Economics:

PALYVOS, TH., Economics

PANEPISTIMIO KRITIS (University of Crete)

Gallos Univ. Campus, 741 00 Rethymnon
Telephone: (283) 1077900
E-mail: secretary@rector.uoc.gr
Internet: www.uoc.gr

Founded 1973
State control
Language of instruction: Greek
Academic year: September to August (2 semesters)

Rector: Prof. EURIPEDES STEPHANOU
Vice-Rector for Academic Affairs and Personnel: Prof. CONSTANTINE TZANAKIS
Vice-Rector for Financial Planning and Devt and for Infrastructure and Student Affairs: Prof. GEORGE TZIRITAS
Library Dir: ELENI DIAMANTAKI

Library: see under Libraries and Archives
Number of teachers: 506
Number of students: 16,900 (14,400 undergraduate, 2,500 postgraduate)

Publication: *Ariadne* (1 a year)

DEANS

School of Education: Prof. ANTONIS HURDAKIS
School of Medicine: Prof. Dr ANDREAS MAGIORIS
School of Philosophy: Prof. KATERINA KOPAKA
School of Sciences and Engineering: Prof. NIKOS KYLAFIS
School of Social Sciences: Prof. SKEVOS PAPAIOANNOU

PANEPISTIMION MAKEDONIAS (University of Macedonia)

156, Egnatia St, POB 1591, 540 06 Thessaloniki
Telephone: (231) 0844825
E-mail: pubrel@uom.gr
Internet: www.uom.gr

Founded 1957 as Graduate Industrial School of Thessaloniki
State control
Academic year: September to August (2 semesters)

Depts of accounting and finance, applied informatics, Balkan, Slavic and Oriental studies, business administration, economics, educational and social policy, international and European studies, marketing and operations management, music science and art, technology management

Rector: Prof. YANNIS A. HAJIDIMITRIOU
Vice-Rector: Prof. CHRISTOS CONSTANTATOS
Vice-Rector for Economic Planning and Devt: Assoc. Prof. ACHILLEAS ZAPRANIS
Library Dir: ANNA FRAGKOU

Library: see under Libraries and Archives
Number of teachers: 108
Number of students: 8,000

PROFESSORS

ALYGIZAKIS, A., Music Science and Art
BARALEXIS, S., Accounting and Finance
CHARALAMPOUS, D., Educational and Social Studies
GEORGANTA, Z., Applied Informatics
IOANNIDIS, D., Economics
KAPSALIS, A., Educational and Social Studies
KARAGIANNI, S., Economics
KARFAKIS, C., Economics
KATOS, A., Applied Informatics
KATRANIDIS, S., Economics
KONSTANTOPOULOU, C., Applied Informatics
KOUSKOUVELIS, I., International, European, Economic and Political Studies
LABRIANIDIS, L., Economics
LAZARIDIS, J., Accounting and Finance
LAZOS, B., Business Administration
MARGARITIS, K., Applied Informatics
MOURMOURAS, I., Economics
NOULAS, A., Accounting and Finance
PALIVOS, T., Economics
PAPADIMITRIOU, J., Applied Informatics
PAPADOPOULOS, D., Accounting and Finance
PAPAMATTHEOU MATSCHKE, H.-U., Music Science and Art
PAPARRIZOS, K., Applied Informatics
PAULIDIS, G., Educational and Social Studies
PEKOS, G., Applied Informatics
PIPEROPOULOS, G., Business Administration
SKALIDIS, E., Accounting and Finance
TARABANIS, K., Business Administration
THEMELI, C., Accounting and Finance
THEODOSIOU, I., Economics
TRIARHOU, L., Educational and Social Studies
TSIOTRAS, G., Business Administration
TSOPELA, V., Music Science and Art
VELENTZAS, K., Economics
XIARHOS, S., Economics
XIROTIRI-KOUFIDOU, S., Business Administration
XOURIS, D., Business Administration

PANEPISTIMION PATRON (University of Patras)

Univ. Campus, 265 04 Patras
Telephone: (261) 0991822
E-mail: rectorate@upatras.gr
Internet: www.upatras.gr

Founded 1964
State control
Languages of instruction: English, Greek
Academic year: September to May (2 semesters)

Rector: Prof. GEORGE PANAYIOTAKIS
Deputy Rector for Academic Affairs and Personnel: Prof. PANTELIS KYPRIANOS
Deputy Rector for Financial Planning and Devt: Prof. IOANNA NTAOULI-NTEMOUSI
Deputy Rector for Strategic Research, Planning and Devt: Prof. NIKOLAOS AVOURIS
Sec.-Gen.: CHRISTINA KOLOKITHA

Library: see under Libraries and Archives
Number of teachers: 744
Number of students: 29,235 (25,228 undergraduate, 4,007 postgraduate)

DEANS

School of Engineering: Prof. NICKOLAOS ANIFANTIS
School of Health Sciences: Prof. VENETSANA KYRIAZOPOULOU
School of Humanities and Social Sciences: Prof. CHRISTOS TEREZIS
School of Natural Sciences: Prof. CHRISTOS KORDULIS

PROFESSORS

School of Engineering

Department of Architecture:

POLYDORIDES, N.

Department of Chemical Engineering:

DASSIOS, G.
KENNOU, ST.
KOUTSOUKOS, P.
KRAVARIS, K.
LADAS, S.
LYBERATOS, G.
NIKOLOPOULOS, P.
PANDIS, S.
PAVLOU, S.
PAYATAKES, A.
RAPAKOULIAS, D.
TSAHALIS, D.
TSAMOPOULOS, J.
TSITSILIANIS, K.
VAYENAS, C.
VERYKIOS, X.

Department of Civil Engineering:

ANAGNOSTOPOULOS, S.
ATHANASOPOULOS, G.
ATMATZIDIS, D.
BESKOS, D.
CHRYSIKOPOULOS, K.
DEMETRACOPOULOS, A.
DRITSOS, ST.
FARDIS, M.
KALERIS, V.
KARABALIS, D.
MAKRIS, N.
PAPAGEORGIOU, A.
STEFANIDIS, G.
THEODORAKOPOULOS, D.
TRIANTAFYLLOU, A.

Department of Computer Engineering and Informatics:

ALEXIOU, G.
BERBERIDIS, K.
BOURAS, CH.
CHRISTODOULAKIS, D.
GALLOPOULOS, E.
KAKLAMANIS, CH.
KIROUSSIS, E.
KOSMADAKIS, S.
LIKOTHANASSIS, S.
NIKOLOS, D.
PAPATHEODOROU, TH.
SPIRAKIS, P.
TRIANTAPHILLOU, P.
TSAKALIDIS, A.
VARVARIGOS, E.
ZAROLIAGKIS, CH.

Department of Electrical and Computer Engineering:

ALEXANDRIDIS, A.
ANTONAKOPOULOS, TH.
AVOURIS, N.
BIRBAS, A.
BITSORIS, G.
FAKOTAKIS, N.
GALATSANOS, N.
GIANNAKOPOULOS, G.
GOUTIS, C.
GROUMPOS, P.
HOUSSOS, E.
KOTSOPOULOS, ST.
KOUBIAS, S.
KOUFOPAVLOU, O.
KOUSSOULAS, N.
MOURTZOPOULOS, I.
MOUSTAKIDES, G.
PIMENIDIS, T.
SAFACAS, A.
SERPANOS, D.
SPYROU, N.
STOURAITIS, A.
TZES, A.
VOVOS, N.

Department of Engineering Sciences:

HATZIKONSTANTINOU, P.
IOAKIMIDIS, N.
KOUTROUVELIS, I.
LIANOS, P.
MARKELLOS, V.

PAPADAKIS, K.
PERDIOS, E.
POLITIS, C.
SFETSOS, K.
VELGAKIS, M.

Department of Mechanical Engineering and Aeronautics:

AIKATERINARIS, I.
ANIFANTIS, N.
ASPRAGATHOS, N.
CHRYSSOLOURIS, G.
FASSOISS, S.
KALLINTERIS, I.
KARAKAPILIDIS, N.
KOSTOPOULOS, V.
MISSIRLIS, I.
PANTELAKIS, S.
PAPANICOLAOU, G.
POLYZOS, D.
SARAVANOS, D.

School of Health Sciences

Faculty of Medicine:

ALEXANDRIDIS, TH.
ALEXOPOULOS, D.
ANASTASIOU, E.
ANDONOPOULOS, A.
ATHANASIADOU-GIKA, A.
BASSIARIS, H.
BERATI, S.
DIMAKOPOULOS, P.
DIMOPOULOS, J.
DOUGENIS, D.
DRAINAS, D.
FLORDELLIS, CH.
GARTAGANIS, S.
GOGOS, C.
GOUMAS, P.
KALFARENTZOS, F.
KALOFONOS, CH.
KALPAKSIS, D.
KARAVIAS, D.
KOSTOPOULOS, G.
KYRIAZOPOULOU, V.
MANTAGOS, S.
MARAZIOTIS, TH.
MOSXONAS, N.
MOUZAKI, A.
NIKIFORIDIS, G.
NIKOLOPOULOU, V.
PALIOGIANNI, PH.
PALLIKARAKIS, N.
PANAGIOTAKIS, G.
PANAGIOTOPOULOS, I.
PAPANASTASIOU, D.
PAPATHANASOPOULOS, P.
PERIMENIS, P.
SIABLIS, D.
SKOPA, CH.
SPYROPOULOS, K.
SYNETOS, D.
TSAMBAOS, D.
TYLLIANAKIS, M.
TZORAKOELETHERAKIS, E.
VASILAKOS, P.
VLACHOJANNIS, J.
ZOUMBOS, N.

Department of Pharmacy:

CORDOPATIS, P.
TZARTOS, S.

School of Humanities and Social Sciences

Department of Educational Sciences and Early Childhood Education:

RAVANIS, K.
XIROMERITI, A.
ZOGZA, V.

Department of Philology:

RALLI, A.

Department of Philosophy:

PATELI, I.
TEREZIS, CH.

Department of Primary Education:

BOUZAKIS, J.
DELLIS, I.
GEORGOGIANNIS, P.
KATSILLIS, I.
KOLEZA, E.
KRIVAS, S.
LAMPROPOULOU, V.
PORPODAS, C.
VERGIDIS, D.

Department of Theatre Studies:

STEFANOPOULOS, TH.
XAAS, D.

School of Natural Sciences

Department of Biology:

ALAHIOTIS, ST.
CHRSISTODOULAKIS, D.
DEMOPOULOS, N.
DIMITRIADIS, G.
GEORGIADIS, TH.
GEORGIOU, CH.
ILIOPOULOU, I.
KAMARI-FITOU, G.
KOUTSIKOPOULOS, C.
MANETAS, I.
PSARAS, G.
STEPHANOU, G.
TZANOUDAKIS, D.
YANNOPOULOS, G.
ZACHAROPOULOU, A.
ZAGRIS, N.

Department of Chemistry:

BARLOS, K.
CHRISTOPOULOS, TH.
GLAVAS, S.
IOANNOU, P.
KALLITSIS, I.
KANELLAKI, M.
KARAISKAKIS, G.
KARAMANOS, N.
KLOURAS, N.
KORDOULIS, CH.
KOUTINAS, A.
LYCOURGHIOTIS, A.
MANESI, E.
MAROULIS, G.
MATSOUKAS, J.
MIKROYIANNIDIS, J.
NTALAS, E.
PAPAIOANNOU, D.
PERLEPES, S.
POULOS, C.
TSEGENIDIS, TH.
VYNIOS, D.
ZAFIROPOULOS, TH.

Department of Geology:

CHRISTANIS, K.
CONTOPOULOS, N.
FERENTINOS, G.
FRYDAS, D.
HATZIPANAGIOTOU, K.
KALLERGIS, G.
KATAGAS, C.
KOUKIS, G.
LABRAKIS, N.
PAPAMARINOPOULOS, S.
TSELENTIS, G.
TSOLIS-KATAGAS, P.
VARNAVAS, S.
ZELILIDIS, A.

Department of Material Science:

GALIOTIS, C.
PHOTINOS, D.

Department of Mathematics:

BOUNTIS, A.
COTSIOLIS, A.
DROSSOS, C.
FILIPPOU, A.
KAFOUSSIAS, N.
KONTOLATOU, A.
KOTSIOLIS, A.
KOUROUKLIS, S.
METAKIDES, G.
PAPANTONIOU, V.
PHILIPPOU, A.
PINTELAS, P.
PNEVMATIKOS, S.
SAMARIS, N.
SIAFARIKAS, P.
TSOUBELIS, D.
TZANNES, V.
VRAHATIS, M.
ZAGOURAS, CH.

Department of Physics:

ANASTASOPOULOS, V.
BAKAS, I.
FOTOPOULOS, S.
GEORGAS, A.
GEROGIANNIS, V.
GIANNOULIS, P.
GOUDIS, CHR.
HARITANTIS, I.
KARAHALIOS, G.
KOURIS, ST.
MYTILINEOU, E.
PERSEFONIS, P.
PIZANIAS, M.
SAKKOPOULOS, S.
TOPRAKTSIOGLOU, CH.
YIANOULIS, P.
ZDETSIS, A.
ZIOUTAS, K.

PANEPISTIMIO PELOPONNESOU
(University of the Peloponnese)

28, Erithrou Stayrou and Kariotaki St, 221 00 Tripolis
Telephone: (271) 0230000
E-mail: secr-rector@uop.gr
Internet: www.uop.gr
Founded 2000
State control
Academic year: September to August
Faculties of economics, history, archaeology and cultural resources management, informatics and telecommunications, nursing, philology, political science and international relations, social and education policy, sport management
Rector: Prof. KONSTANTINOS MASSELOS
Number of students: 6,000

PROFESSORS

Department of Social and Education Policy (Damaskinou and Kolokotroni Sts, 201 00 Korinth; tel. (274) 1074991; e-mail sep-secr@uop.gr):

KLADIS, D., Education Policy
KOULAIDIS, V., Design of Educational Programmes
KOULOURI, C., History of Modern Greek Education and Society

Department of Telecommunications Science and Technology (End of Karaiskaki St, 221 00 Tripolis; tel. (271) 0372163; e-mail ntalagan@uop.gr):

BOUCOUVALAS, A. C.
MARAS, A.

PANEPISTIMION PIREOS
(University of Piraeus)

80, Karaoli and Dimitriou St, 185 34 Piraeus
Telephone: (210) 4142000
E-mail: publ@unipi.gr
Internet: www.unipi.gr
Founded 1938 as School for Industrial Studies, current name adopted 1989
State control
Academic year: September to August (2 semesters)
Depts of business administration, digital systems, economics, statistics and insurance science, financial management and banking, industrial management, informatics, mari-

time studies, and international and European studies
Rector: Prof. GEORGIOS OIKONOMOU
Vice-Rector for Academic Affairs: Prof. GEORGE VASSILACOPOULOS
Vice-Rector for Economic Planning and Devt: Prof. LAMBROS LAIOS
Library: see under Libraries and Archives
Number of teachers: 90
Number of students: 11,400
Publication: *Spoudai* (4 a year)

PANEPISTIMIO THESALIAS
(University of Thessaly)

Argonafton and Filellinon, 382 21 Volos
Telephone: (242) 1074000
E-mail: info@uth.gr
Internet: www.uth.gr
Founded 1984
State control
Academic year: September to June (2 semesters)
Schools of agricultural sciences, engineering, health sciences, humanities
Rector: Prof. KONSTANTINOS GOURGOULIANIS
Vice-Rector for Academic Affairs and Personnel: Prof. IOANNIS THEODORAKIS
Vice-Rector for Economic and Student Affairs, Public and Int. Relations: Prof. MICHALIS ZOUBOULAKIS
Vice-Rector for Research and Devt: Prof. VASSILIS BONTOZOGLOU
Library Dir: Dr IOANNIS CLAPSOPOULOS
Library: see under Library and Archives
Number of teachers: 560
Number of students: 12,266 (9,647 undergraduate, 1,471 postgraduate, 1,148 doctoral)

PANTEION PANEPESTIMION IKONOMIKON KAI POLITCON EPISTIMON
(Panteion University of Social and Political Sciences)

136, Sygrou Ave, 176 71 Athens
Telephone: (210) 9201013
E-mail: rector@panteion.gr
Internet: www.panteion.gr
Founded 1927
State control
Academic year: October to June (2 semesters)
Graduate and postgraduate studies; depts of communication, media and culture, economic and regional development, foreign languages, international and European studies, law, political science and history, psychology, public administration, social anthropology, social policy, sociology
Rector: Prof. GREGORY J. TSALTAS
Vice-Rector for Academic Affairs and Personnel: Prof. ISMENE KRIARI-KATRANI
Vice-Rector for Finance and Devt: Prof. EVANGELOS PRONTZAS
Library: see under Libraries and Archives
Number of students: 7,500

POLYTECHNION KRITIS
(Technical University of Crete)

Agiou Markou St, 731 32 Chania
Telephone: (282) 1037001
E-mail: rector@central.tuc.gr
Internet: www.tuc.gr
Founded 1977
State control
Language of instruction: Greek
Academic year: September to August (2 semesters)
Depts of architectural engineering, electronic and computer engineering, environmental engineering, mineral resources engineering, production engineering and management, sciences; research and devt projects; operates Telecommunication Systems Institute
Rector: Prof. YANNIS A. PHILLIS
Vice-Rector for Academic Affairs and Personnel: Prof. THEODOROS MARKOPOULOS
Vice-Rector for Finance, Planning and Devt: Prof. YANNIS SARIDAKIS
Head Librarian: MARIA DAOUNTAKI
Library: see under Libraries and Archives
Number of teachers: 175
Number of students: 3,994 (3,515 undergraduate, 479 postgraduate and doctoral)

PROFESSORS

AGIOUTANIS, Z.
ALEVIZOS, G.
AVDELAS, G.
BALAS, K.
BILALIS, N.
CHRISTIDIS, G.
CHRISTODOULAKIS, S.
CHRISTODOULOU, M.
CHRISTOPOULOS, D.
DARRAS, T.
DELLIS, A.
DIAMADOPOULOS, E.
DIGALAKIS, V.
DOLLAS, A.
DOUMPOS, M.
ECONOMOPOULOS, A.
ELLINAS, D.
EXADAKTYLOS, G.
FOSCOLOS, A.
FRAGOMIHELAKIS, M.
GALETAKIS, M.
GEKAS, V.
GEORGILAKIS, P.
GIDARAKOS, E.
GRIGOROUDIS, E.
GRYSPOLAKIS, J.
KALAITZAKIS, K.
KALLITHRAKAS, K. N.
KALOGERAKIS, N.
KANDYLAKIS, D.
KARAKASSIS, I.
KARATZAS, G.
KATSANOS, A.
KAVOURIDIS, K.
KELESIDIS, V.
KOMNITSAS, K.
KONTOGIANNIS, T.
KOSMATOPOULOS, E.
KOSTAKIS, G.
KOUBARAKIS, E.
KOUIKOGLOU, V.
LAZARIDIS, M.
LIODAKIS, G.
MANOUTSOGLOU, E.
MANTZAVINOS, D.
MARIA, E.
MARKOPOULOS, T.
MATHIOUDAKIS, M.
MATSATSINIS, N.
MERTIKAS, S.
MIGDALAS, A.
MONOPOLIS, D.
MOUSTAIZIS, S.
MOUSTAKIS, V.
NIKOLAIDIS, N.
NIKOLOS, I.
PANTINAKIS, A.
PAPADOPOULOU, E.
PAPAGEORGIOU, M.
PASADAKIS, N.
PATELIS, D.
PATERAKIS, M.
PERDIKATSIS, V.
PETRAKIS, E.
PETRAKIS, M.
PHILLIS, Y.
PNEVMATIKATOS, D.
POTAMIANOS, A.
POULIEZOS, A.
PROVIDAKIS, K.
SAMELIS, A.
SAMOLADAS, V.
SARIDAKIS, Y.
SIDIROPOULOS, N.
SINOLAKIS, K.
SKIADAS, C.
STAMPOLIADIS, E.
STAVRAKAKIS, G.
STAVROULAKIS, P.
SYNOLAKIS, C.
TRAFALIS, T.
TSANIS, I.
TSETSEKOU, A.
TSOMPANAKIS, I.
TSOURVELOUDIS, N.
VAFIDIS, A.
VAMVOUKA, D.
VAROTSIS, N.
YENTEKAKIS, Y.
ZERVAKIS, M.
ZOPOUNIDIS, K.

UNIVERSITY OF CENTRAL GREECE

2-4, Papasiopoulou, 351 00 Lamia
Telephone: (223) 1066730
Internet: www.ucg.gr
Founded 2003
State control
Academic year: October to June (2 semesters)
Depts of informatics with applications in biomedicine, regional economic devt
Chair.: Prof. DIMITRIOS LOUKOPOULOS
Head Librarian for Dept of Computer Science and Biomedical Informatics: ARIETTA PAPAIOANNOU
Library Man. for Dept of Economic Regional Development: ADRIANNA KATSANTONI

UNIVERSITY OF WESTERN MACEDONIA

Parko Agiou Dimitriou, 501 00 Kozani
Telephone: (246) 1056200
E-mail: info@uowm.gr
Internet: www.uowm.gr
Founded 2003
State control
Academic year: September to May (2 semesters)
Faculties of education, engineering; ind. depts of applied and visual arts (Florina), and Balkan studies (Florina)
Pres.: IOANNIS MANOLOPOULOS
Chair.: THEODORE CHATZIPANTELIS
Dir for Admin. and Financial Management: THOMAS BELO
Library of 15,000 vols
Number of teachers: 91
Number of students: 4,000

Colleges

ARCHAEOLOGY, GREEK STUDIES

American School of Classical Studies at Athens: 54, Souidias St, 106 76 Athens; tel. (213) 0002400; e-mail ascsa_info@ascsa.edu.gr; internet www.ascsa.edu.gr; f. 1881; research institute and postgraduate school for students of classical and post-classical literature, history and archaeology; library: 220,000 vols (Gennadius and Blegen libraries); 13 teachers; 350 students; Dir JAMES WRIGHT; publ. *Hesperia* (4 a year).

British School at Athens: 52, Souedias, 106 76 Athens; tel. (211) 1022800; e-mail admin@bsa.ac.uk; internet www.bsa.ac.uk; f. 1886; archaeology and Hellenic studies; Fitch Laboratory for research and analysis; library: over 70,000 vols, 1,300 journals;

Chair. Prof. Lord COLIN RENFREW; Dir Prof CATHERINE MORGAN; London Sec. PHILIPPA WALLER; publ. *The Annual* (1 a year).

École Française d'Athènes (French School of Athens): 6, Didotou, 106 80 Athens; tel. (210) 3679900; e-mail efa@efa.gr; internet www.efa.gr; f. 1846; library: 1,781,631 vols; Dir ALEXANDER FARNOUX.

Scuola Archeologica Italiana di Atene (Italian School of Archaeology at Athens): 14, Odos Parthenonos, 117 42 Athens; tel. (210) 9239163; e-mail segretario@scuoladiatene.it; internet www.scuoladiatene.it; f. 1909; post-graduate studies in Aegean prehistory and early history, archaeology, epigraphy and antiquities, ancient architecture; research and excavations in Greece; library: 54,000 vols; Dir Prof. EMANUELE A. GRECO; Library Dir Dr STEFANO GARBIN; publs *Annuario della Scuola Archeologica di Atene e delle Missioni Italiane in Oriente* (1 a year), *Monografie della Scuola Archeologica di Atene e delle Missoni Italiane in Oriente* (irregular), *Notiziario* (2 a year), *Tripodes* (irregular).

ARTS, DRAMA, MUSIC

American College of Greece: 6, Gravias St, Aghia Paraskevi, 153 42 Athens; tel. (210) 6009800; e-mail admissions@acg.edu; internet www.acg.edu; f. 1875; accredited by the New England Asscn of Schools and Colleges; comprises Deree College (BA courses in art history, dance, economics, English, history, music, philosophy, psychology, sociology, BSc course in business administration, MBA), ALBA Graduate Business School and Pierce College (high school); library: 129,000 vols, 19,000 periodicals, 3,200 DVDs, CDs, video cassettes, multimedia CD-ROMs; 250 teachers; 3,822 students (excluding ALBA Graduate Business School); Pres. Dr DAVID G. HORNER.

Kratiko Odeio Thessaloniki (State Conservatory of Thessaloniki): 15, Fragon St, 546 25 Thessaloniki; tel. (231) 0510551; e-mail odiokrat@otenet.gr; internet www.odiokrat.gr; f. 1914; studies in strings, winds and percussion instruments, advanced theory; schools of Byzantine music, melodrama, monody, orchestra conducting; library: 13,500 vols, magazines, scores, recordings, archives; 60 teachers; 630 students; Chair. ANTONIOS GIFTOPOULOS; Dir GEORGIOS KONSTANTINIDIS.

National Theatre of Greece Drama School: 35, Pireos, 105 53 Athens; tel. (210) 5225634; e-mail dramaschool@n-t.gr; internet www.n-t.gr; f. 1930; trains and provides guidance to young people intending to become professional actors; costume and make-up design, dance and expressive movement, Greek dancing, history of theatre, history of cinema, modern Greek literature, musical speech training, stage combat, technical dance and gymnastics, theatrical song and set, theory dramatology; Head of Studies VICTOR ARDITTIS.

Odeion Athinon (Conservatory of Athens): 17-19, Rigillis Vas. Georgiou and B, 106 75 Athens; tel. (210) 7244260; e-mail info@odeionathinon.gr; internet www.odeionathinon.gr; f. 1871; instrumental, theoretical and vocal studies; operates Drama School; Pres. ARIS GAROUFALIS; Dir NICK TSOUCHLOS.

Odeion Ethnikon (National Conservatory): 8, Maizonos and 18, Mayer Sts, 104 38 Athens; tel. (210) 5233175; e-mail ethnodio@otenet.gr; f. 1926; sections for music and opera; 200 teachers; 5,000 students; Dir PERIKLES KOUKOS; publ. *Deltio* (1 a year).

Technological Educational Institutes

Kavala Institute of Technology: St. Loucas, 654 04 Kavala; tel. (2510) 462177; e-mail tei@teikav.edu.gr; internet www.teikav.edu.gr; f. 1976 as Education Centre for Vocational Studies, present status 2007; schools of agricultural technology, management and economics, technological applications; 11 attached depts and 1 ind. dept of nursing; library: 32,000 vols, 550 journals; Pres. ATHANASIOS MITROPOULOS.

Technological Educational Institute of Athens: Ag. Spiridonos, 112 10 Athens; tel. (210) 5385100; internet www.teiath.gr; f. 1983; 4-year courses; faculties of technological applications, management and economics, health and caring professions, food technology and nutrition, and fine arts and design; library: 60,000 vols, 700 journals; 35,000 students; Pres. Dr DIMITRIS K. NINOS.

Technological Educational Institute of Chalkida: Evia Psachna, 344 00 Chalkida; tel. (222) 8099500; e-mail tei@teihal.gr; internet www.teihal.gr; f. 1983; schools of business and economics, engineering, technological applications; ind. depts of foreign languages, physical education; Pres. Dr JOHN STATHARAS.

Technological Educational Institute of Crete: Estavromenos, POB 1939, 710 04 Heraklion; tel. (281) 0250752; e-mail info@staff.teicrete.gr; internet www.teicrete.gr; f. 1983; schools of agricultural technology, applied technology (also in Chania and Rethymnon), health and welfare services, management and economics (also in Agio Nikolao and Ierapetra); depts of general sciences, foreign languages and physical education; 200 teachers; 10,000 students; Pres. Prof. EVANGELOS KAPETANAKIS.

Technological Educational Institute of Epirus: Gefira Arachthou, POB 110, 471 00 Arta; tel. (268) 1050001; e-mail info@entiposis.gr; internet www.teiep.gr; f. 1994; schools of agricultural technology, health and welfare professions, management and economics, music technology; brs at Arta, Athens, Preveza and Igoumenitsa; library: 37,680 vols, 170 journals; Pres. Dr GRIGORIOS GKIKAS.

Technological Educational Institute of Ionian Islands: Iosif Momferatou and Ilia Miniati, 281 00 Argostoli; tel. (267) 1025820; e-mail dioikisi@teiion.gr; internet www.teiion.gr; f. 2003; depts of applications of information technology in administration and economy (Lefkada), business administration (Cephalonia), environmental technology and ecology (Zante), information technology and telecommunications (Lefkada), organic farming and food technology (Cephalonia), protection and conservation of cultural heritage (Zante), public relations and communication (Cephalonia), sound and musical instruments technology (Cephalonia); Pres. Prof. NAPOLEAN MARAVEGIAS; publs *Review of Mediterranean Cultural Heritage*, *Ta Nea tou T.E.I Ionian Islands* (The News of T.E.I Ionian Islands).

Technological Educational Institute of Kalamata: Antikalamos, 241 00 Kalamata; tel. (272) 1045100; e-mail lib@teikal.gr; internet www.teikal.gr; f. 1988; schools of agricultural technology, health and welfare professions, management and economic; Chair. Prof. ANDREAS KANAKIS; publs *International Journal of Economic Sciences and Applied Research*, *Journal of Engineering Science and Technology*.

Technological Educational Institute of Kastoria: Fourka Area, POB 30, 521 00 Kastoria; tel. (246) 7087060; internet kastoria.teikoz.gr; f. 1996; attached to Technological Educational Institution of W Macedonia; depts of information and computer technology, international trade, public affairs and communications; library: 23,000 vols; Dir GIANNIS BAPTIST.

Technological Educational Institute of Lamia: 3rd km, Old Nat. Rd, 351 00 Athens; e-mail pubintrel@teilam.gr; internet www.teilam.gr; f. 1994; faculties of health and medical care professions, technological applications; 5 depts and 2 ind. depts of business and advertising (Amfissa), forestry and natural environment management (Karpenisi); Pres. Prof. STAVROS KARKANIS.

Technological Educational Institute of Larissa: 411 10 Larissa; tel. (241) 0684200; e-mail pr@teilar.gr; internet www.teilar.gr; f. 1983, present status 2001; schools of agricultural technology, business and economics, health and welfare professions, technological applications; Centre of Foreign Languages and Physical Education; brs in Karditsa and Trikala; library: 60,000 vols; Pres. Dr IOANNIS KOKORAS; publs *iMentor—Information Excellence*, *MIBES Transactions* (1 a year, in English), *PRIME* (1 a year, in Greek).

Technological Educational Institute of Messolonghi: Nea Ktiria, 302 00 Messolonghi; tel. (263) 1058200; e-mail prsdnt@teimes.gr; internet www.teimes.gr; f. 1983; faculties of agricultural technology, and management and economics; library: 19,264 vols; Pres. Assoc. Prof. Dr VANGELIS POLITIS-STERGIOU.

Technological Educational Institute of Patras: 1, Megalou Alexandrou, 263 34 Patras; tel. (261) 0369104; internet www.teipat.gr; f. 1970 as Centre of Professional Technological Education (K.A.T.E), present status 1983; schools of management and economy, sciences of health and care, technological applications; library: 25,000 vols, 200 periodicals; Pres. Prof. Dr SOCRATES N. KAPLANIS.

Technological Educational Institute of Piraeus: 250, Peter Ralli Thivon, 122 44 Egaleo; tel. (210) 5381100; internet www.teipir.gr; f. 1983; school of applied technology; faculty of management and economics; depts of chemistry and materials technology, and mathematics; foreign language centre and physical education; library: 26,000 vols, 160 periodicals; 1,000 teachers; 20,000 students; Pres. VRYZIDIS LAZARUS.

Technological Educational Institute of Serres: Terma Magnisias, 621 24 Serres; tel. (232) 1049101; e-mail pr@teiser.gr; internet www.teiser.gr; f. 1983, present location 1993; faculties of administration and economics, applied technology, and fine arts and design; library: 20,000 vols; 400 teachers; 12,000 students; Pres. DIMIRIOS PASCHALOUDIS.

Technological Educational Institute of Thessaloniki: POB 141, 574 00 Thessaloniki; tel. (231) 0791100; e-mail pubrel@admin.teithe.gr; internet www.teithe.gr; f. 1983; schools of agricultural technology, applied technology, health professions; faculty of food technology and nutrition; library: 35,000 vols, 326 journals; 18,000 students; publ. *Periscope* (3 a year).

Technological Educational Institute of Western Macedonia: Kila Kozani, 501 00 Kozani; tel. (246) 1040161; internet www.teikoz.gr; f. 1983; schools of agricultural technology, applied technology, business and economics; library: 12,000 vols; Pres. Dr GEORGE CHARALAMBIDES.

GRENADA

The Higher Education System

Before 1968 higher education in Grenada was limited to the provision of sponsorship for study abroad. In that year Grenada acquired the Extra-Mural Department of the University of the West Indies (UWI) and the Grenada Teacher-Training College was founded, its two-year programme being monitored and certified by the UWI. In 1974 the Government established a number of other colleges relevant to the country's social and economic needs. St George's University, which is an independent international university in the island's capital offering undergraduate and graduate degrees in medicine, veterinary medicine, public health, the health sciences, nursing, arts and sciences, and business was established (as a School of Medicine) in 1976. During 1979–83 the new People's Revolutionary Government enhanced existing teacher-training programmes and increased scholarships offered for university and technical education abroad. The Institute for Further Education in Grenada, which approximated the idea of a university, was also established during this period. In 1988 the restored, post-colonial Government amalgamated eight institutions (the Grenada Teachers' College, the Grenada Technical and Vocational Institute, the Institute for Further Education, the National Institute of Handicraft, the Mirabeau Agricultural Training School, the Domestic Arts Institute, the Continuing Education Programme and the School of Pharmacy) to form the Grenada National College, which was renamed the T. A. Marryshow Community College (TAMCC) in 1996. In the same year the UWI and St George's University expanded their activities. In 2004 there were 91 Grenadian students registered at the UWI, in 2006 there were 2,710 full-time, enrolled students at the TAMCC and in 2012 St George's University had a total enrolment of 5,880 students (the majority of whom were from the USA). Technical Centres have been established in St Patrick's, St David's and St John's. In 2011 plans to open a teaching hospital in Grenada were announced.

The Government is responsible for higher education, although both St George's University and the UWI enjoy a greater degree of autonomy than does the TAMCC. The TAMCC, which offers courses leading to the award of Certificates, Associate Degrees and Baccalaureate Degrees, is required by law to report directly to the Ministry of Education and Human Resource Development, primarily for financial purposes and for powers of jurisdiction. Higher education is governed by the Grenada Education Act, and the St George's University (School of Medicine) Act, 1976. The Ministry of Education and Human Resource Development is the main source of funding for the TAMCC. It also provides some support for the UWI, although this is largely funded through the collective contributions of the Caribbean countries to the UWI as a whole. St George's University is funded mainly by student fees. From 2011 the Australian Agency for International Development was to provide opportunities through the Australian Leadership Awards Scholarship for Grenadian students to undertake Masters or Doctorate degrees at Australian universities.

Regulatory Bodies

GOVERNMENT

Ministry of Education and Human Resource Development: Botanical Gardens, Tanteen, St George; tel. 440-2737; internet moe.gov.gd; Minister ANTHONY BOATSWAIN.

Ministry of Tourism, Civil Aviation and Culture: Ministerial Complex, Botanical Gardens, Tanteen, St George's; tel. 440-0366; e-mail tourism@gov.gd; Minister Dr ALEXANDRA OTWAY-NOEL.

Learned Society

HISTORY, GEOGRAPHY AND ARCHAEOLOGY

Grenada National Trust: Grenada Nat. Museum, Young St, St George's; tel. 440-3725; e-mail contact@grenadanationaltrust.gd; f. 1967; preserves evidence of the history and growth of the island, and supports the Grenada National Museum; 240 mems; Pres. GORDON DE LA MOTHE; Sec. KAY SIMON.

Libraries and Archives

St George's

Founders Library, St George's University: POB 7, St George's; tel. 444-1573; e-mail library@sgu.edu; internet www.sgu.edu; f. 1979; 13,000 vols, 350 periodicals; Dir JOHN MCGUIRK.

Grenada Public Library/Sheila Buckmire Memorial Library: Carenage, St George's; tel. 440-2506; e-mail fedon2000@yahoo.com; f. 1853; attached to Min. of Education and Human Resource Devt; 60,000 vols; Dir for Libraries S. LILLIAN SYLVESTER; Librarian DEON DAVID.

Museum

St George's

Grenada National Museum: Young St, St George's; tel. 440-3725; f. 1976; Dir JEANNE FISHER; Curator HUGH THOMAS; publs *Art 'y' Facts* (2 a year), *Relics*.

Universities and Colleges

ST GEORGE'S UNIVERSITY

Univ. Centre, POB 7, St George's

Telephone: 444-4175

E-mail: sguinfo@sgu.edu

Internet: www.sgu.edu

Founded 1977

Private control

Language of instruction: English

Academic year: August to June

Chancellor: CHARLES R. MODICA

Registrar: MARGARET LAMBERT

Library Dir: JOHN MCGUIRK

Library: see under Libraries and Archives

Number of teachers: 820 (120 full-time, 700 part-time)

Number of students: 5,000

DEANS

Arts and Sciences: T. HOLLIS

Basic Sciences: A. PENSICK

Clinical Studies: STEPHEN WEITZMAN

Veterinary Medicine: (vacant)

T. A. Marryshow Community College (TAMCC): Tanteen, St George's; tel. 440-1389; e-mail tamcc@caribsurf.com; internet www.tamcc.edu.gd; f. 1988 by merger of the Grenada Teachers' College, the Grenada Technical and Vocational Institute, the Institute for Further Education, the National Institute of Handicraft, the Mirabeau Agricultural Training School, the Domestic Arts Institute, the Continuing Education Programme and the School of Pharmacy; present name and status 1996; Prin. Dr JEFFERY BRITTON (acting); Registrar C. NIGEL GRAVESANDE; Dean of Applied Arts and Technology DESMOND LA TOUCHE; Dean of Arts, Sciences and Professional Studies Dr DUNBAR STEELE.

University of the West Indies School of Continuing Studies: Marryshow House, H. A. Blaize St, POB 439, St George's; tel. 440-2451; e-mail rtscsuwi@caribsurf.com; internet www.uwichill.edu.bb/bnccde/grenada; f. 1956; library: 10,000 vols; folk theatre, telecommunications distance-teaching centre; 27 teachers; 150 students; Resident Tutor BEVERLEY A. STEELE.

GUATEMALA

The Higher Education System

Under Spanish colonial rule, Guatemala was part of the Viceroyalty of New Spain. Independence was obtained from Spain in 1821, from Mexico in 1824 and from the Federation of Central American States in 1838. The oldest university is the Universidad de San Carlos de Guatemala (USAC), which was founded by King Carlos II of Spain in 1676. USAC currently includes 10 faculties, eight schools and maintains 18 regional campuses throughout the country. In 2010 there were 146,741 students enrolled in USAC. In total, there are 14 universities, of which 12 are privately run. The most recent university, Universidad Da Vinci de Guatemala, opened its doors in 2012. Figures for 2006/07 showed that some 233,885 students were enrolled in further and higher education.

The main requirement for admission to university is the Bachiller or Bachillerato, the secondary-school qualification. The Licenciado is the undergraduate degree and is awarded after four to five years, although some subjects (such as medicine, which requires six years' study) require longer periods of study. The Licenciado usually entails submission of a thesis. In professional fields of study, a professional title is awarded. Following the Licenciado, the first postgraduate degree is the Maestría, which is awarded after two years of study. However, the Doctorado can also be awarded following two years of study after the Licenciado, although some doctoral programmes require a Maestría. Both the Maestría and the Doctorado entail the submission of a thesis.

Technical and vocational education is offered by the universities and specialized post-secondary institutions (including the National School of Agricultural Sciences, the National Institute of Fine Arts, the National School of Agriculture and the Central American Forestry School). The main vocational qualifications are the Diplomado or Técnico, awarded after two or three-and-a-half years of study. The Instituto Técnico de Capitación y Productividad provides apprenticeships and courses.

The responsibility for higher education in Guatemala, by constitutional mandate, is shared by USAC, which is exclusively in charge of state-owned higher and professional university education, and by the private universities. The former is an autonomous institution, with legal status, which regulates and governs itself, while the latter are authorized and controlled by the Consejo de la Enseñanza Privada Superior (CEPS—Council of Private Higher Education), which is made up of two representatives each of USAC and of the private universities and one representative of the professional colleges. CEPS is responsible for setting up the Sistema Nacional de Acreditación de la Educación Superior (National System of Accreditation for Private Higher Education). In 2005 Guatemala joined the Consejo Centroamericano de Acreditación de la Educación Superior (Central American Accreditation Council for Higher Education) whose remit is to harmonize and improve the quality of higher education in the region. USAC is also a member of the Consejo Superior Universitario Centroamericano, the regional organization for public universities.

Regulatory and Representative Bodies

GOVERNMENT

Ministry of Culture and Sports: 6 Calle y 6 Avda, Zona 1, Guatemala City; tel. 22395000; e-mail info@mcd.gob.gt; internet www.mcd.gob.gt; Minister Lic. CARLOS BATZÍN CHOJOJ.

Ministry of Education: 6A Calle 1-87, Zona 10, 01010 Guatemala City; tel. 24119595; e-mail info@mineduc.gob.gt; internet www.mineduc.gob.gt; Minister Lic. CYNTHIA DEL ÁGUILA.

NATIONAL BODIES

Consejo de la Enseñanza Privada Superior (Council of Private Higher Education): Edif. Colegios Profesionales, Segundo Nivel, 0 Calle 15-46 Zona 15, Col. El Maestro, Guatemala City; tel. 23696344; internet www.ceps.edu.gt; f. 1966.

Learned Societies

GENERAL

Academia de Ciencias Médicas, Físicas y Naturales de Guatemala (Academy of Medical, Physical and Natural Sciences of Guatemala): 13 Calle 1-25, Zona 1, 01901 Guatemala City; tel. 24769745; e-mail carmensamayoa@gmail.com; f. 1945; 80 mems; library of 4,000 vols; Pres. Dr ENRIQUE ACEVEDO; Sec.-Gen. Prof. MARÍA DEL CARMEN SAMAYOA.

FINE AND PERFORMING ARTS

Sociedad Pro-Arte Musical (Musical Society): 12 Calle 2-09, Zona 3, Apdo 980, Guatemala City; f. 1945; 200 mems; Pres. LULÚ C. DE HERRARTE; Exec. Sec. DORA G. DE MENDIZÁBAL.

HISTORY, GEOGRAPHY AND ARCHAEOLOGY

Academia de Geografía e Historia de Guatemala (Geographical and Historical Academy of Guatemala): 3 Avda 8-35, Zona 1, 01001 Guatemala City; tel. 22323544; e-mail acgeohis@gmail.com; internet www.academiageohist.org.gt; f. 1923; 45 mems; library of 30,000 vols; Pres. BARBARA KNOKE DE ARATHOON; Sec. GUILLERMO DÍAZ ROMEU; publs *Anales* (1 a year), *Biblioteca Goathemala*, *Viajeros*.

LANGUAGE AND LITERATURE

Academia Guatemalteca de la Lengua (Guatemala Academy of Letters): 12 Calle 6-40, Zona 9, Of. 403-404, Edif. Plazuela, Guatemala City; tel. 23322824; e-mail aglesp@yahoo.com; f. 1887; corresp. of the Real Academia Española (Madrid, Spain); library of 5,000 vols; Dir MARIO ANTONIO SANDOVAL SAMAYOA; Sec.-Gen. FRANCISCO MORALES SANTOS.

Alliance Française: 5A Calle 10-55, Zona 13, Finca la Aurora, Guatemala City; tel. 22075757; e-mail comunicaciones@alianzafrancesa.org.gt; internet www.alianzafrancesa.org.gt; offers courses and exams in French language and culture, and promotes cultural exchange with France; attached teaching offices in La Antigua and Quetzaltenango; Dir-Gen. ARNAUD CARRÈRE.

NATURAL SCIENCES

Biological Sciences

Asociación Guatemalteca de Historia Natural (Guatemalan Association of Natural History): Jardín Botánico, Universidad de San Carlos, Mariscal Cruz 1–56, Zona 10, Guatemala City; f. 1960; 86 mems; Pres. Dr MARIO DARY RIVERA.

TECHNOLOGY

Colegio de Ingenieros de Guatemala (Guatemala Engineers Association): 7A Avda 39-60, Zona 8, 01008 Guatemala City; tel. 24717544; e-mail juntadirectiva@cig.org.gt; internet www.colegiodeingenierosguatemala.org; f. 1947; 1,965 mems; Pres. FERNANDO MENDEZ CASTEJON; Sec. MANUEL DE JESUS CASTELLANOS DUBON; publ. *Revista Ingeniería* (4 a year).

Research Institutes

ECONOMICS, LAW AND POLITICS

Centro de Investigaciones Económicas Nacionales (Centre for National Economic Studies): 10 Calle 3-17, Zona 10, Edif. Aseguradora General, Nivel 5, Guatemala City; tel. 23311564; e-mail cien@cien.org.gt; internet www.cien.org.gt; f. 1981; study of economic and social problems; Pres. MARIO ADOLFO CUEVAS MÉNDEZ; Sec. Lic. VERÓNICA SPROSS DE RIVERA; publ. *Carta Económica* (12 a year).

Instituto Nacional de Estadística (National Statistical Institute): 8A Calle 9-55, Zona 1, Guatemala City; tel. 22322808; e-mail comunicacion@ine.gob.gt; internet www.ine.gob.gt; f. 1879 as Sección de Estadística, current name adopted 1985; compiles and publishes nat. statistics; Man. Lic. RUBEN NARCISO CRUZ; publs *Censo Nacional Agropecuario* (National Agricultural Census, online), *Censo Nacional de Población y de Habitación* (National Population and Dwellings Census, online), *Indice de Precios al Consumidor* (Retail Price Index, 12 a year, online).

HISTORY, GEOGRAPHY AND ARCHAEOLOGY

Instituto de Antropología e Historia (Institute of Anthropology and History): 12 Avda 11-65, Zona 1, 01001 Guatemala City; tel. 22325956; e-mail guatepazidaeh@yahoo.com; f. 1946; attached to Min. of Culture and Sports; research on Middle-American history, Mayan archaeology, ethnology, philology and Spanish colonial history; supervises archaeological sites, monuments and museums; library of 12,000 vols; Dir-Gen. Arq. ARTURO PAZ; publ. *Revista Anual de Antropología e Historia de Guatemala* (1 a year).

Instituto Geográfico Nacional 'Ing. Alfredo Obiols Gómez' (National Geographic Institute 'Ing. Alfredo Obiols Gómez'): Avda Las Américas 5-76, Zona 13, Guatemala City; tel. 22488100; e-mail ign@ign.gob.gt; internet www.ign.gob.gt; f. 1932; promotes, coordinates and supports scientific research; forms, manages and updates the National Information System; Dir Gen. GUILLERMO SANTOS MANSILLA.

MEDICINE

Instituto de Nutrición de Centro América y Panamá (INCAP) (Institute of Nutrition of Central America and Panama): Calzada Roosevelt 6–25, Zona 11, Apdo Postal 1188, Guatemala City; tel. 23157900; e-mail e-mail@incap.int; internet www.incap.int; f. 1949; mem. countries: Belize, Costa Rica, El Salvador, Guatemala, Honduras, Nicaragua, Panama; administered by Pan American Health Bureau Organization (PAHO)/World Health Organization (WHO); library of 12,000 vols; Dir CAROLINA SIU BERMUDEZ.

NATURAL SCIENCES

Biological Sciences

Centro de Estudios Conservacionistas (Centre for Conservation Studies): Avda La Reforma 0–63, Zona 10, 01010 Guatemala City; tel. 23310904; e-mail cecon@usac.edu.gt; internet www.usac.edu.gt/cecon; f. 1981; management and admin. of protected areas; investigation and studies of biodiversity and sustainable management of natural resources; management of nat. botanical garden and nat. biodiversity database; Dir FRANCISCO CASTAÑEDA MOYA.

Physical Sciences

Instituto Nacional de Sismología, Vulcanología, Meteorología e Hidrología (National Institute of Seismology, Vulcanology, Meteorology and Hydrology): 7A Avda 14-57, Zona 13, Guatemala City; tel. 22613238; e-mail direccion@insivumeh.gob.gt; internet www.insivumeh.gob.gt; f. 1976; Dir EDDY HARDIE SÁNCHEZ; publs *Mareas Oceánicas* (Tidal Forecast, 12 a year, electronic), *Normales Climáticas* (Climate Statistics, electronic), *Pronóstico de 1 a 3 Dias* (electronic), *Pronóstico de Fin de Semana* (52 a year, electronic), *Tiempo Presente* (Current Forecast, electronic).

TECHNOLOGY

Dirección General de Energía Nuclear (Nuclear Energy Directorate): 24 Calle 21-12, Zona 12, Apdo Postal 1421, Guatemala City; tel. 24770746; f. 1978; work concerns peaceful application of nuclear energy in medicine, industry, agriculture, etc.; library of 1,200 vols; Dir Ing. RAÚL EDUARDO PINEDA GONZÁLEZ.

Libraries and Archives

Guatemala City

Archivo General de Centro América (General Archives of Central America): 4 Avda 7-41, Zona 1, 01001 Guatemala City; tel. 22516695; e-mail agcasecretaria@yahoo.com; internet www.archivogeneraldecentroamerica.com; f. 1968; comprises 2 sections: La Colonia, archive with 8,427 files of 99,157 documents relating to Guatemala, Chiapas, El Salvador, Honduras, Nicaragua and Costa Rica; library contains ancient and modern historical vols; periodicals pertaining to the colonial epoch and the period of independence; microfilm and photocopying service for researchers; Dir ARTURO VALDÉS OLIVA.

Biblioteca Central de la Universidad de San Carlos de Guatemala (Central Library of the University of San Carlos of Guatemala): Ciudad Universitaria, Zona 12, Guatemala City; tel. 24187880; e-mail jefaturabibliotecacentral@usac.edu.gt; internet biblioteca.usac.edu.gt; f. 1967; economics, humanities and multidisciplinary collns; thesis colln; newspaper and magazine colln; Guatemalan colln, Carlos Mérida colln; 82,881 vols, 756 periodical titles; Dir Licda LIDEY MAGALY PORTILLO (acting).

Biblioteca del Banco de Guatemala (Guatemala Bank Library): 7A Avda 22-01, Zona 1, Apdo 365, Guatemala City; tel. 24296000; internet www.banguat.gob.gt/biblio; f. 1955; 38,000 vols; Librarian JULIO C. MARISCAL.

Biblioteca del Organismo Judicial (Judiciary Library): 21 Calle 7-70, Zona 1, Guatemala City; tel. 22487000; e-mail biblioteca@oj.gob.gt; f. 1881; 10,000 vols; Dir DORA CRISTINA GODOY LÓPEZ; publs *Informador Bibliotecario* (52 a year, electronic), *Informador Bibliotecario Mensual* (12 a year, electronic).

Biblioteca Nacional de Guatemala (National Library of Guatemala): 5A Avda 7-26, Zona 1, Guatemala City; tel. 22322443; e-mail binaguat@gmail.com; f. 1879; 350,000 vols; Dir Lic. ILONKA MATUTE.

Quetzaltenango

Biblioteca Pública de Quetzaltenango (Public Library of Quetzaltenango): a/c Casa Cultura Occidente 7A, Calle 11-35, Zona 1, Quetzaltenango; 25,000 vols; Dir JULIO CÉSAR ALVAREZ.

Museums and Art Galleries

Chichicastenango

Museo Regional de Chichicastenango (Chichicastenango Regional Museum): 5A Avda 4-47, Zona 1, Chichicastenango; tel. 54192869; f. 1950; articles of the Maya-Quiché culture; Dir RAÚL PÉREZ MALDONADO.

Guatemala City

Museo Nacional de Arqueología y Etnología de Guatemala (National Museum of Archaeology and Ethnology of Guatemala): 6A Calle 7A Avda, Salón No 5, Finca La Aurora, Zona 13, Guatemala City; tel. 24754399; e-mail info@munae.gob.gt; internet www.munae.gob.gt; f. 1866; colln of some 3,000 archaeological pieces, mainly Mayan art, and 1,000 ethnological exhibits; Dir Licda DANIEL AQUINO LARA; publ. *Revista* (2 a year).

Museo Nacional de Arte Moderno 'Carlos Mérida' (National Museum of Modern Art 'Carlos Mérida'): Edif. No 6, Finca La Aurora, Zona 13, Guatemala City; tel. 24720467; f. 1975; paintings, sculpture, engravings, drawings, etc.; Dir Arq. JOSÉ MARIO O. MAZA PONCE.

Museo Nacional de Historia (National Museum of History): 9A Calle 9–70, Zona 1, Guatemala City; tel. 22536149; f. 1975; 19th- and 20th-century paintings, sculpture, documents, furniture and tools, all from Guatemala; Dir ITALO MORALES HIDALGO.

Museo Nacional de Historia Natural 'Jorge A. Ibarra' (National Museum of Natural History 'Jorge A. Ibarra'): 6A Calle 7-30, Zona 13, Complejo de Museos Nacionales, Guatemala City; tel. 24720468; e-mail mnhn.jorgeibarra@gmail.com; f. 1950; geological, botanical and zoological specimens; conservation projects of 2 endemic species of reptiles; library of 2,625 vols; Curator LESTER SAMUEL MELÉNDEZ GARCÍA.

Universities

UNIVERSIDAD DA VINCI DE GUATEMALA
(Da Vinci University of Guatemala)

Vía 6, 3-42, Zona 4, Guatemala City
Telephone: 23283333
E-mail: info@udv.edu.gt
Internet: www.udv.edu.gt

Founded 2012
Private control

Rector: Dr JOSÉ CYRANO RUIZ CABARRÚS
Vice-Rector: Dr LUIS MANUEL ÁLVAREZ ÁLVAREZ
Sec.-Gen.: Lic. ROSSA MARIA MORALES DE RÍOS

DEANS

Faculty of Educational Sciences: Lic. ANÍBAL ARIZMENDY MARTÍNEZ ESCOBEDO
Faculty of Engineering: Ing. JUAN LUIS FUENTES FUMAGALLI
Faculty of Management and Business: Ing. JUAN LUIS FUENTES FUMAGALLI

UNIVERSIDAD DE OCCIDENTE
(West University)

Avda Las Américas 10A, Calle 9-84, Zona 9, Quetzaltenango
Telephone: 77630983
E-mail: info@udeo.edu.gt
Internet: www.udeo.edu.gt

Founded 2010
Private control

Rector: Ing. Agr. EMILIO CONDE GOICOLEA
Vice-Rector: Dr Lic. JORGE ROLANDO BARRIENTOS PELLECER
Vice-Rector for Int. Relations: Lic. MOISÉS MOYA
Sec.: Lic. FRANCISCO BARRIOS ROSALES

DEANS

Faculty of Economic Sciences: Lic. DENNIS IVÁN RODAS ANZUETO

Faculty of Engineering: Ing. CARLOS EDUARDO MORALES LAM
Faculty of Law: Lic. PEDRO GUZMÁN

UNIVERSIDAD DE SAN CARLOS DE GUATEMALA
(University of San Carlos of Guatemala)

Ciudad Universitaria, Zona 12, 01012 Guatemala City
Telephone: 24439672
E-mail: webmaster@usac.edu.gt
Internet: www.usac.edu.gt
Founded 1676 by King Carlos II, est. in its present form 1927, autonomous status 1944
State control
Language of instruction: Spanish
Academic year: January to November
Rector: Lic. ESTUARDO GÁLVEZ BARRIOS
Sec.-Gen.: Dr CARLOS ALVARADO CEREZO
Registrar: Ing. ROLANDO GRAJEDA
Librarian: Licda MERCEDES DE BEECK
Library: see under Libraries and Archives
Number of teachers: 2,600
Number of students: 146,741
Publications: *Revista de la Universidad de San Carlos de Guatemala* (4 a year), *Universidad* (12 a year), *USAC al Día* (26 a year)

DEANS

Faculty of Agronomy: Dr LAURIANO FIGUEROA QUIÑÓNEZ
Faculty of Architecture: Arq. CARLOS ENRIQUE VALLADARES CEREZO
Faculty of Chemistry and Pharmacy: Lic. OSCAR MANUEL COBAR PINTO
Faculty of Dentistry: Dr MANUEL ANIBAL MIRANDA RAMIREZ
Faculty of Economics: Lic. JOSE ROLANDO SECAIDA MORALES
Faculty of Engineering: Ing. MURPHY OLIMPO PAIZ RECINOS
Faculty of Humanities: Lic. WALTER RAMIRO MAZARIEGOS BIOLIS
Faculty of Law and Social Sciences: Lic. AVIDÁN ORTIZ ORELLANA
Faculty of Medicine: Dr JESÙS ARNULFO OLIVA LEAL
Faculty of Veterinary Medicine: Dr LEONIDAS AVILA PALMA

UNIVERSIDAD DEL ISTMO
(Central University)

7A Avda 3-67 Zona 13, Guatemala City
Telephone: 24291400
Internet: www.unis.edu.gt
Founded 1998
Private control
Rector: Ing. MANUEL ÁNGEL PÉREZ LARA
Vice-Rector: Lic. MARCO ANTONIO GARCÍA KIHN
Vice-Rector for Academic Affairs: Lic. LINDA YOLANDA PAZ QUEZADA
Sec.: Lic. MARIO ROBERTO ESPAÑA
Library of 23,000 vols

DEANS

Faculty of Architecture and Design: Arq. ANA MARÍA GARCÍA
Faculty of Communication: Lic. CAROLINA DE ASTURIAS
Faculty of Economics and Business: Lic. EDIN VELÁSQUEZ
Faculty of Education: MIRNA DE GONZÁLEZ
Faculty of Engineering: Ing. OTTO CASTILLO
Faculty of Law: Dra JARY MÉNDEZ MADDALENO

UNIVERSIDAD DEL VALLE DE GUATEMALA

18 Avda 11-95 Zona 15, Vista Hermosa III, 01015 Guatemala City
Telephone: 23640336
E-mail: info@uvg.edu.gt
Internet: www.uvg.edu.gt
Founded 1966
Private control
Language of instruction: Spanish
Academic year: January to November
Rector: Lic. ROBERTO MORENO GODOY
Vice-Rector for Academic Affairs: MARÍA LUISA DURANDO DE BOEHM
Vice-Rector for Admin.: Ing. LUIS FERNANDO ANDRADE
Sec.: Lda. VICTORIA EUGENIA ROSALES
Librarian: Dra MARÍA EMILIA LÓPEZ
Library of 96,600 vols, 120 current periodicals
Number of teachers: 420
Number of students: 3,650
Publication: *Revista UVG* (1 a year)

DEANS

Faculty of Education: GABRIELA CASTRO DE BÚRBANO
Faculty of Engineering: FERNANDO PAIZ MENDOZA
Faculty of Science and Humanities: Dr ADRIÁN FRANCISCO GIL MÉNDEZ
Faculty of Social Sciences: Dr ANDRÉS ALVAREZ CASTAÑEDA
Research Institute: Dra MÓNICA STEIN
University College: Lic. MARICRUZ ÁLVAREZ MURY

UNIVERSIDAD FRANCISCO MARROQUIN
(Francisco Marroquin University)

Calle Manuel F. Ayau (6 Calle Final), Zona 10, 01010 Guatemala City
Telephone: 23387700
E-mail: inf@ufm.edu
Internet: www.ufm.edu
Founded 1971
Private control
Language of instruction: Spanish
Academic year: January to December
Rector: Ing. GIANCARLO IBÁRGÜEN S.
Sec.-Gen.: Lic. RICARDO CASTILLO
Librarian: Lic. JAQUELINE DE LEÓN
Library of 58,000 vols, 3,000 ebooks, 850 DVDs
Number of teachers: 450
Number of students: 2,408
Publications: *Areté*, *Laissez-Faire* (2 a year), *Revista de la Facultad de Derecho* (2 a year)

DEANS

Faculty of Architecture: Arq. ROBERTO QUEVEDO
Faculty of Dentistry: Dr RAMIRO ALFARO ARELLANO
Faculty of Economics: Dr FRITZ THOMAS
Faculty of Education: Licda SIANG AGUADO DE SEIDNER (Dir)
Faculty of Law: Dr MILTON ESTUARDO ARGUETA PINTO
Faculty of Medicine: Dr FEDERICO GUILLERMO ALFARO ARELLANO
Graduate School of Social Sciences: Dr ARMANDO DE LA TORRE (Dir)
School of Nutrition: Dr JORGE TULIO RODRÍGUEZ (Dir)
School of Psychology: Dr YETILÚ DE BAESSA (Dir)

UNIVERSIDAD GALILEO
(Galileo University)

7A Avda, Calle Dr Eduardo Suger Cofiño, Zona 10, 01010 Guatemala City
Telephone: 24238000
E-mail: info@galileo.edu
Internet: www.galileo.edu
Founded 2000
Private control
Rector: Dr JOSÉ EDUARDO SUGER COFIÑO
Vice-Rector: Dra MAYRA ROLDÁN DE RAMÍREZ
Vice-Rector for Admin.: Lic. JEAN PAUL SUGER
Sec.-Gen.: Lic. JORGE FRANCISCO RETOLAZA

DEANS

Faculty of Biology, Chemistry and Pharmacy: Dr ANA LUCIA VALLE
Faculty of Communication: Lic. LEIZER KACHLER
Faculty of Computer Systems Engineering and Computer Science: Ing. JOSÉ EDUARDO SUGER CASTILLO
Faculty of Construction Engineering: MARIO RODOLFO GANDARA SPILLARI
Faculty of Education: Dr BERNARDO RENÉ MORALES FIGUEROA
Faculty of Health Sciences: Dra VILMA JUDITH CHÁVEZ DE POP
Faculty of Science and Sport Technology: SERGIO ARNOLDO CAMARGO MURALLES
Faculty of Science, Technology and Industry: Ing. JORGE IVÁN ECHEVERRÍA PERMOUT
School of Management: Dra MARCELA PORTA

UNIVERSIDAD INTERNACIONES
(InterNaciones University)

Blvd San Isidro y 12 Calle, Zona 16, Guatemala City
Telephone: 23798171
E-mail: info@uni.edu.gt
Internet: www.uni.edu.gt
Founded 2009
Private control
Rector: Lic. MARCEL ARNOLD REICHENBACH COLOMA
Vice-Rector for Acad. Affairs: Lic. MARÍA EUGENIA RAMÍREZ MOTTA
Vice-Rector for Admin.: Dra GILDA MARINA CASTELLANOS BAIZA DE ILLESCAS
Sec. Gen.: Ing. JORGE ENRIQUE VARGAS MANTILLA

DEANS

Faculty of Economics and Business: Ing. JORGE ENRIQUE VARGAS MANTILLA
Faculty of Humanities: Lic. MARÍA EUGENIA RAMÍREZ MOTTA
Faculty of Science and Technology: Dr RICARDO CORDON ENGEL

UNIVERSIDAD MARIANO GÁLVEZ
(Mariano Gálvez University)

3A Avda 9-00 Zona 2, Interior Finca El Zapote, Guatemala City
Telephone: 24111800
E-mail: info@umg.edu.gt
Internet: www.umg.edu.gt
Founded 1966
Private control
Language of instruction: Spanish
Academic year: February to November
Rector: Lic. ALVARO ROLANDO TORRES MOSS
Vice-Rector: Lic. HUGO CÉSAR MORALES Y MORALES
Vice-Rector: Dr ALFREDO SAN JOSÉ
Sec.-Gen.: Dra RUBY SANTIZO DE HERNÁNDEZ
Registrar: Lic. JOSÉ CLODOVEO TORRES MOSS
Librarian: GLORIA MARINA ARROYO
Library of 9,000 vols
Number of teachers: 400
Number of students: 10,000

Publication: *Boletín Mensual* (12 a year)

UNIVERSIDAD MESOAMERICANA
(Mesoamerican University)

40 Calle 10-01, Zona 8, Guatemala City
Telephone: 24138000
E-mail: info@umes.edu.gt
Internet: www.umes.edu.gt
Founded 1999
Private control
Faculties of humanities and social sciences, economics, law and social sciences, social communication
Rector: Dr FÉLIX JAVIER SERRANO URSÚA
Vice-Rector: Lic. JORGE RUBÉN CALDERÓN GONZÁLEZ
Sec.: Lic. CARLOS ENRIQUE CHIAN RODRÍGUEZ

UNIVERSIDAD PANAMERICANA
(Pan American University)

Diagonal 34, 31-43 Zona 16, Guatemala City
Telephone: 23901200
E-mail: info@upana.edu.gt
Internet: www.upana.edu.gt
Founded 1993, present status 1999
Private control
Rector: Mag. MYNOR AUGUSTO HERRERA LEMUS
Vice-Rector for Academic Affairs: ALBA ARACELY RODRÍGUEZ DE GONZALEZ
Vice-Rector for Admin.: CÉSAR CUSTODIO
Library of 10,000 vols

DEANS
Faculty of Applied Sciences: Ing. RUTH DINORAH MORALES COMPARINI (Coordinator)
Faculty of Communication Sciences: Lic. ALFRED KALTSHMITT LUJÁN
Faculty of Economics: CÉSAR CUSTODIO
Faculty of Educational Sciences: Lic. DINNO MARCELO ZAGHI GARCIA
Faculty of Law and Justice: Lic. OTTO GONZÁLEZ
Faculty of Medical and Health Sciences: Dr ROBERTO OROZCO
Faculty of Social Sciences:
Faculty of Theology: Dr SAMUEL BERBERIAN
School of Psychological Sciences: Lic. ELIZABETH HERRERA DE TAN

UNIVERSIDAD RAFAEL LANDÍVAR
(Rafael Landívar University)

Vista Hermosa III, Zona 16, Guatemala City
Telephone: 24262626
E-mail: info@url.edu.gt
Internet: www.url.edu.gt
Founded 1961
Private control
Language of instruction: Spanish
Academic year: January to November
Rector: ROLANDO ALVARADO
Vice-Rector for Academic Affairs: Dra LUCRECIA MÉNDEZ DE PENEDO
Vice-Rector for Admin.: Lic. ARIEL RIVERA IRÍAS
Gen. Sec.: LUIS QUAN
Librarian: REGINA ROMERO DE LA VEGA
Library of 206,073 vols
Number of teachers: 1,042
Number of students: 11,146
Publications: *Aprapalabra*, *Cultura de Guatemala* (3 a year), *Estudios Sociales* (4 a year), *Revista de Literatura*, *Vida Universitaria* (12 a year)

DEANS
Faculty of Agricultural and Environmental Sciences: Dr ADOLFO OTTONIE MONTERROSO RIVAS
Faculty of Architecture and Design: OVIDIO MORALES CALDERÓN
Faculty of Economics and Business: LIGIA GARCÍA
Faculty of Engineering: Ing. CARLOS RICARDO GARCÍA BICKFORD
Faculty of Health Sciences: Dr CLAUDIO A. RAMÍREZ
Faculty of Humanities: HILDA CABALLEROS DE MAZRIEGOS
Faculty of Law and Social Sciences: Dr ROLANDO ESCOBAR MENALDO
Faculty of Political and Social Sciences: VICTOR GALVEZ BORRELL
Faculty of Theology: RODOLFO ALBERTO MARÍN ANGULO

UNIVERSIDAD RURAL DE GUATEMALA
(Rural University of Guatemala)

7A Calle 6-49, Zona 2, Guatemala City
Telephone: 22546211
E-mail: soportevirtual@urural.edu.gt
Internet: www.urural.edu.gt
Founded 1995
Private control
Rector: Dr FIDEL REYES LEE
Sec.: Lic. LESBIA TEVALÁN CASTELLANOS

DEANS
Faculty of Economics: Lic. CARLOS HUMBERTO ECHEVERRÍA GUZMÁN
Faculty of Education: Lic. GEORGINA MARISOL RODRÍGUEZ
Faculty of Law and Social Sciences: Dra JISELA YADEL REYNOSO TRUJILLO
Faculty of Natural Sciences and Environment: Ing. BRAUDIO LEONIDES MORAN BURGOS

UNIVERSIDAD SAN PABLO DE GUATEMALA
(San Pablo University of Guatemala)

4A Calle 23-03, Zona 14, 01014 Guatemala City
Telephone: 23265174
E-mail: info@uspg.edu.gt
Internet: www.uspg.edu.gt
Founded 2006
Private control
Rector: Dr RICARDO FRANCISCO ANTILLON MORALES
Vice-Rector for Acad. Affairs: MARCO TULIO MÉRIDA CIFUENTES
Sec.-Gen.: LUIS FELIPE CABRERA FRANCO

DEANS
Faculty of Architecture and Arts: MAGDA BEATRIZ ZAPATA ESPINOZA
Faculty of Education: IMELDA JANETH CORONADO DE CAMARGO
Faculty of Engineering and Applied Sciences: Ing. LUIS JACINTO QUAN CHU
Faculty of Health Sciences: Ing. JAVIER ARTURO BOLAÑOS BENDFELT
Faculty of Law and Justice: WILLY ALBERTO GOMEZ TIRADO
Faculty of Theology: MARIO RENE ARCHILA CRUZ

Schools of Art and Music

Conservatorio Nacional de Música 'Germán Alcántara' (National Academy of Music 'Germán Alcántara'): 3A Avda 4-61, Zona 1, 01001 Guatemala City; tel. 22328726; internet www.conservatorionacional.gob.gt; f. 1875; 40 teachers; 900 students; Dir LUIS A. LIMA Y LIMA.

Escuela Nacional de Artes Plásticas 'Rafael Rodríguez Padilla' (National School of Plastic Arts 'Rafael Rodríguez Padilla'): 6 Avda 22-00, Zona 1, Guatemala City; f. 1920; library: 2,500 vols; Dir ZIPACNÁ DE LEÓN; publ. *Revista de la Escuela Nacional de Artes Plásticas 'Rafael Rodríguez Padilla'*.

GUINEA

The Higher Education System

Guinea (formerly French Guinea) was part of French West Africa until it gained its independence in 1958, and the education system is still based on the French system. There are two state-controlled universities, Université Gamal Abdel Nasser de Conakry (founded in 1962) and Université Julius Nyéréré de Kankan (founded in 1963, current name and status since 1987). The privately controlled Université Kofi Annan de Guinée, which comprises five faculties and one institution, was established in Conakry in 1999. Additional institutions of higher education include professional schools and institutes attached to the universities, such as the École Nationale de la Santé, which is classed as a professional school, or the École Normale Supérieure d'Enseignement Technique, which is considered a university institute. Since 2007 the Ministère de l'Enseignement Supérieur et de la Recherche Scientifique (Ministry of Higher Education and Scientific Research) is the main controlling body; however, higher education institutions enjoy significant autonomy. Higher education is wholly financed by the Government (except for private institutions). In 2007/08 80,200 students were enrolled in further and higher education.

Students must hold the secondary school qualification, Baccalauréat Deuxième Partie, and sit a competitive entrance examination in order to be admitted to university. As in many other Francophone countries in Africa, the three-tier, Bologna-style higher education degree system (Licence/Maîtrise/Doctorat) was adopted in 2001. The undergraduate degree is the Licence/Licence Professionnelle, which is awarded after four years. Undergraduates may also receive a professional diploma (Diplôme), depending on the subject. Students studying towards the Diplôme d'État de Docteur en Pharmacie or the Diplôme d'État de Docteur en Médecine study for five or six years, respectively. After the Licence, the Maîtrise is the first postgraduate qualification, which is awarded after one year of study. Finally, the third stage of university-level qualifications is the Doctorat, which is a research-based, two-year course leading to the submission of a thesis.

Post-secondary technical/vocational education in Guinea is provided by university faculties. Upon the successful completion of a three-year training course, students are awarded the Brevet de Technicien Supérieur.

Regulatory Bodies

GOVERNMENT

Ministry of Culture, Arts and Heritage: Villa 46, Cité des Nations, Conakry; tel. 60-21-26-69; Minister AHMED TIDIANE CISSÉ.

Ministry of Employment, Technical Education and Vocational Training: Villa 46, Cité des Nations, Conakry; internet www.guinee.gov.gn; Minister DAMANTAN ALBERT CAMARA.

Ministry of Higher Education and Scientific Research: face à la Cathédrale Sainte-Marie, BP 964, Conakry; tel. 30-45-12-17; Minister TÉLIWEL BAILO DIALLO.

Ministry of Pre-University Education and Literacy: Boulbinet, BP 2201, Conakry; tel. 30-45-19-17; Minister Dr IBRAHIMA KOUROUMA.

Learned Society

LANGUAGE AND LITERATURE

PEN Centre de Guinée: BP 107, Labé; tel. 30-44-14-75; e-mail centrepenguinee@gmail.com; f. 1989; 32 mems; library of 92 vols; Sec. ZEINAB KOUMANTHIO DIALLO; publ. *Pour Mémoire*.

Research Institutes

GENERAL

Direction Nationale de la Recherche Scientifique et Technique: Conakry, BP 561; f. 1958; Dir Dr FODE SOUMAH.

AGRICULTURE, FISHERIES AND VETERINARY SCIENCE

Centre de Recherche Agronomique de Foulaya: BP 156, Kindia; tel. 30-61-01-48; e-mail iragdq@irag.org.gn; f. 1946; Dir Dr MAHMOUD CAMARA.

Institut de Recherche Agronomique de Guinée: Blvd du Commerce, BP 1523, Conakry; tel. 30-21-19-57; e-mail iragdg@biasy.net.gn.

Libraries and Archives

Conakry

Archives Nationales: BP 1005, Conakry; tel. 30-44-42-97; f. 1960; Dir ALMANY STELL CONTE.

Bibliothèque Nationale: BP 561, Conakry; tel. 30-46-10-10; f. 1958; 40,000 vols, also spec. colln on slavery (500 books, pamphlets and MSS); Dir LANSANA SYLLA.

Museum

Conakry

Musée National: BP 139, Conakry; tel. 30-45-10-66; f. 1960; Dir SORY KABA.

Universities

UNIVERSITÉ GAMAL ABDEL NASSER DE CONAKRY

BP 1147, Conakry
Telephone: 30-46-46-89
E-mail: uganc@mirinet.net.gn
Founded 1962
State control
Rector: OUSMANE SYLLA
Vice-Rector for Academics: JEAN-MARIE TOURÉ
Vice-Rector for Research: Dr M. KODJOUGOU DIALLO
Sec.-Gen.: GALEMA GUILAVOGUI
Dir for Library: MANSA KANTÉ
Library of 4,000 vols
Number of teachers: 824
Number of students: 5,000
Publications: *Guinée Médicale*, *Horizons*

DEANS

Faculty of Arts and Humanities: GOUDOUSSY DIALLO
Faculty of Law, Economics and Management: HAWA FOFANA
Faculty of Medicine and Pharmacy: (vacant)
Faculty of Science: Dr DJELIMANDJAN CONDÉ
Polytechnic Institute: Prof. NANAMOUDOU MAGASSOUBA (Dir-Gen.)

UNIVERSITÉ JULIUS NYÉRÉRÉ DE KANKAN

Ministère de l'Enseignement Supérieur et de la Recherche Scientifique, Conakry
Telephone: 30-71-20-93
Founded 1963; univ. status 1987
State control
Academic year: October to June
Rector: Dr TAMBA TAGBINO
Vice-Rector for Academics: Dr MAWIATOU BAH
Vice-Rector for Research: Dr MAMADOU SAMBA BARRY
Sec.-Gen.: KABA SIDIBE
Dir for Financial Affairs: IBRAHIM KALIL TOUNKARA
Dir for Int. Relations and Cooperation: MARTIN KOIVOGUI
Dir for Univ. Publs: ELHADJ NAMANDIAN DOUMBOUYA
Library Dir: KARIM KOUROUMA
Library of 12,160 vols
Number of teachers: 95
Number of students: 3,012
Publication: *Revue Scientifique de l'Université de Kankan* (2 a year)

DEANS

École Supérieure des Sciences de l'Information: SIBA BILIVOGUI

Faculty of Economics and Management: Dr BILLY FADOUA CONDE
Faculty of Language and Literature: Dr MORI SAÏDOU FOFANA
Faculty of Natural Sciences: Dr ABDOULAYE MOUCTAR DIALLO
Faculty of Social Sciences: Dr ADRIEN KOFFA KAMANO

Colleges

École Nationale de la Santé: Conakry; tel. 30-29-52-49; Dir BARRY YAYA.

Institut Supérieur Agronomique et Vétérinaire 'Valéry Giscard d'Estaing' de Faranah: BP 131, Faranah; tel. 30-81-02-15; e-mail isav1@mirinet.net.gn; f. 1978; faculties of agriculture, agricultural engineering, rural economics, stockbreeding and veterinary medicine, waters and forestry; common core syllabus; library: 3,629 vols, 207 periodicals; 110 teachers; 2,515 students; Dir-Gen. Dr YAZORA SOROPOGUI.

GUINEA-BISSAU

The Higher Education System

Guinea-Bissau was formerly Portuguese Guinea (Guiné), during which time education as a whole was geared to serve a narrow élite, consisting mainly of the colonial rulers' children. The country gained its independence in 1974 following a military coup in Portugal. The first institution of higher education, a school of law (which gained higher status as the Faculdade de Direito de Bissau with Portuguese funding and cooperation in 1990), was established in 1979, followed by centres for medicine, education, nursing and sports. In 1999 a government decree placed all these institutions under the authority of the then Ministry of National and Higher Education (formerly Ministry of Education), with a view to establishing a university at the National Institute of Studies and Research. In 2010 the Ministry of National Education, Youth, Culture and Sport launched a three-year plan (2011–13), among the objectives of which were to increase the number of students (especially female) studying at higher eduction level, to improve the system of learning, to promote scientific research, and to increase the role of the private sector.

In 2000/2001 only 473 students were enrolled in tertiary education. Some 200 students completed their studies in Havana, Cuba, in 2002, while a further 186 had scholarships to study in Paris, France, and Dakar, Senegal. To counter this trend, in 2003 the Universidade Amílcar Cabral, Guinea-Bissau's first university, was founded. In the same year a private university, the Universidade Colinas de Boé, also opened. In 2004, after three years of a feasibility study, the Universidade Lusófona de Humanidades e Tecnologias based in Lisbon, Portugal, opened its own subsidiary, the Universidade Lusófona de Guiné. In 2005/06 3,689 students were enrolled in tertiary education; 3,000 in public institutions and 689 in private institutions. By the end of 2008 internal financial problems had caused Amílcar Cabral University to lose its autonomous status and it was subsumed into the Universidade Lusófona de Guiné. In September 2011 a new private university, the Universidade Jean Piaget Guiné-Bissau (an extension of the Portuguese Instituto Jean Piaget), was opened.

Technical and vocational education is available at two public institutions, the Centre of Administrative Training and the Centre of Experimental Training, as well as at privately controlled institutions. In 2006 there were 303 students following technical and vocational studies at public institutions and 251 at private institutions.

Regulatory Bodies

GOVERNMENT

Ministry of National Education, Youth, Culture and Sport: Rua Areolino Cruz, Bissau; tel. 3202244; Minister ALFREDO GOMES.

Research Institutes

GENERAL

Centro de Estudos da Guiné-Bissau (Study Centre of Guinea-Bissau): CP 37, Bissau; f. 1945.

Instituto Nacional de Estudos e Pesquisa (INEP) (National Institute of Studies and Research): CP 112, Bairro Cobornel, Bissau; Complexo Escolar 14 de Novembro, Bissau; tel. 3251867; e-mail inep.dg.bissau@gmail.com; internet www.inep-bissau.org; f. 1987, damaged during conflict between govt forces and rebels in 1999, restoration, with the support of int. scholars, began in 2000; library of 40,000 vols, incl. archives and museum; also holds periodicals, photographs, plays, press cuttings; fees for using facility and for exhibitions.

Libraries and Archives

Bissau

Biblioteca Nacional da Guiné-Bissau (National Library of Guinea-Bissau): Praça do Impéro, CP 37, Bissau; f. 1970.

Museums and Galleries

Bissau

Museu da Guiné-Bissau (Museum of Guinea Bissau): Praca do Impéro, CP 37, Bissau; f. 1945; library of 14,000 vols; collns of economics, ethnography, history, natural science.

Museu Etnografico Nacional (National Ethnographical Museum): Complexo Escolar 14 de Novembro, CP 338, Bissau; tel. 3215600; photographic archive depicting former colln of African masks and statues (largely destroyed during military conflict in 1998).

University and Colleges

UNIVERSIDADE AMÍLCAR CABRAL

Endereço Bairro da Ajuda, 2a Fase, CP 659, Bissau

Telephone: 3255970
E-mail: geral@uac.com

Founded 2003
State control

Faculties of agricultural and veterinary science, economics, letters and communications, science, technology; school of physical education and sport

Rector: Prof. Dr TCHERNO DJALÓ

Faculdade de Direito da Guiné-Bissau: Complexo Escolar 14 de Novembro, CP 595, Bissau Codex; tel. 3252770; e-mail geral@fdbissau.com; internet www.fdbissau.com; f. 1990; Dir FODÉ ADULAI MANÉ.

Instituto Nacional para o Desenvolvimento da Educação (INDE): Rua Dr Herman Gmeiner, Bairro 7, 2A Fase, CP 132, Bissau; tel. 3204534; e-mail indebissau@hotmail.com; Pres. ALFREDO GOMES; Dir-Gen. AUGUSTO PEREIRA.

GUYANA

The Higher Education System

Guyana, formerly British Guiana, achieved independence from the United Kingdom in 1966. The Free Education Act of 1976 guaranteed the right to free education at all levels from pre-school to higher education. The Ministry of Education is the supreme body for higher education. The University of Guyana (founded in 1963) is the only state-controlled university, but higher education is also available at professional schools, technical institutes and colleges. The University of Guyana, which comprises five faculties, three schools and one institute, offers a range of undergraduate courses including Certificates (two-year programmes in education and humanities), Diplomas (two-year programmes in applied subjects including forestry, accountancy and computer science), Associate degrees (two-three year programmes in health science, including pharmacy, environmental health and medical technology) and Bachelors degrees (lasting four years, or five years for medicine and dentistry). Graduate Diplomas and Masters degrees (requiring one or two years of further study after a Bachelors degree) are offered at postgraduate level. In 2005 the privately controlled GreenHeart Medical University was opened in the capital, Georgetown, offering professional degree programmes in medicine, nursing and pharmacy. In 2010/11 an estimated 6,546 students were enrolled at the University of Guyana. In the same academic year 4,779 students were enrolled at technical and vocational institutes, and 2,001 were studying at teacher-training colleges. Students who are unable to afford university tuition fees may be offered a student loan from the state-run student loans agency.

The Caribbean Examinations Council Secondary Education Certificate is the standard requirement for admission to Bachelors degree programmes at the University of Guyana, although British GCE O- and A-Levels are also accepted. In addition, law, medicine and dentistry courses require applicants to have passed the Caribbean Advanced Proficiency Examination. Students who do not meet the standard entry requirements may nevertheless secure a place by passing the University of Guyana entrance examination.

Technical and vocational education is provided at various institutions and at different levels. The Council for Technical and Vocational Education was established in 2004 to draw up a national system of performance testing and certification. The University of Guyana has an Institute of Distance and Continuing Education, which runs extramural courses and has been used by the Government to increase literacy rates in the country; the Adult Education Association offers similar programmes. Other institutions offering technical/vocational courses include: the Cyril Potter College of Education (founded in 1928) which provides training for pre-primary, primary and secondary teachers, the Government Technical Institute (which provides programmes leading to the award of qualifications such as the Craft Certificate, Technician Certificate and Technician Diploma), the Guyana Industrial Training Centre (which offers short courses in six basic trade areas), the Guyana School of Agriculture (founded 1963), the Carnegie School of Home Economics and the School of Nursing (which offers three-year Diploma courses leading to registered nurse status). A five-year National Development Plan for technical and vocational education and training was introduced in 2009 to restructure and expand the sector according to employment possibilities and national economic needs.

The National Accreditation Council, which was created in 2005, maintains a register of accredited programmes at tertiary level. Programme registration is voluntary.

Regulatory Bodies

GOVERNMENT

Ministry of Culture, Youth and Sport: 71 Main St, N Cummingsburg, Georgetown; tel. 227-7860; e-mail mincys@guyana.net.gy; internet www.mcys.gov.gy; Minister Dr FRANK ANTHONY.

Ministry of Education: 21 Brickdam, Georgetown; tel. 223-7900; internet www.education.gov.gy; Minister PRIYA DEVI MANICKCHAND.

ACCREDITATION

National Accreditation Council: 68 Brickdam, Stabroek, Georgetown; tel. 225-9526; e-mail info@nac.gov.gy; internet www.nac.gov.gy; f. 2005; attached to Min. of Education; aims to establish quality assurance system for education and training in Guyana; Head of Secretariat NATASHA SINGH-LEWIS.

Learned Societies

GENERAL

Bureau of Statistics: 57 High St, Kingston, POB 1070, Georgetown; tel. 227-1155; e-mail info@statisticsguyana.gov.gy; internet www.statisticsguyana.gov.gy; f. 1957; conducts censuses; Chair. Dr ASHNI KUMAR SINGH; Vice-Chair. LENNOX BENJAMIN.

Guyana Marine Turtle Conservation Society: Lot 8, Vergenoegen, East Bank Essequibo; tel. 260-2613; e-mail coordinator@gmtcs.org; internet www.gmtcs.org; f. 2000; education and awareness; scientific research; Patron. SAMUEL HINDS; Chair. Dr RAQUEL THOMAS.

ECONOMICS, LAW AND POLITICS

Institute of Chartered Accountants of Guyana: 216 Lance Gibbs St, Queenstown, POB 10-1055, Georgetown; tel. 223-7547; e-mail admin@icag.org.gy; internet www.icag.org.gy; f. 1966, current name adopted 1974; Pres. RONALD ALLI; Sec. PRAMILA PERSAUD.

EDUCATION

Adult Education Association of Guyana Inc. M.S.: 88 Carmichael St, POB 10-1111, Georgetown; tel. 225-0758; e-mail aea@guyana.net.gy; f. 1957; 1,000 mems; aims to provide opportunities for Guyanese to improve their skills, raise the level of awareness of their culture, acquire a critical understanding of major contemporary issues; programmes: academic, technical, scientific, creative art, commercial and professional devt; operates remedial school for people who have dropped out of school and slow learners; runs adult literacy classes; Exec. Dir PATRICIA DAVID.

LANGUAGE AND LITERATURE

Alliance Française: 276 Peter Rose St, Georgetown; tel. 226-0854; e-mail archerdus@yahoo.com; f. 1950; offers courses and exams in French language and culture and promotes cultural exchange with France.

Research Institutes

AGRICULTURE, FISHERIES AND VETERINARY SCIENCE

Inter-American Institute for Cooperation on Agriculture (IICA): Lot 18, Brickdam, Stabroek, POB 10-1089, Georgetown; tel. 226-8347; e-mail iica.gy@iica.int; internet www.iica.int; f. 1974; Guyana br. of the specialized agency of the OAS for the agricultural sector; promotes food safety and the prosperity of the rural sector in the Americas; provides innovative technical cooperation to the mem. states; library of 1,560 vols, 25 periodicals; Rep. WILMOT GARNETT (acting); publ. *COMUNIICA* (4 a year).

MEDICINE

Pan American Health Organization/World Health Organization, Guyana: Lot 8, Brickdam, Stabroek, POB 10-969, Georgetown; tel. 225-3000; e-mail e-mail@guy.paho.org; internet www.paho.org/guy; f. 1902; technical cooperation in: family and community health, incl. maternal and child health; non-communicable diseases; communicable diseases; environmental health; disaster risk reduction, preparedness and response; health systems and services, incl. human resources for health; social determinants of health; and programme planning and management for nat. health devt; Rep. Dr ADRIANUS VLUGMAN.

NATURAL SCIENCES

Guyana Geology and Mines Commission: Upper Brickdam, Georgetown; tel. 226-5591; internet www.ggmc.gov.gy; f. 1979; research in exploration, mining, and use of minerals and mineral products; library of 15,195 vols, 11 periodicals, 24,200 maps, 56 microfiches, 27 microfilms.

Hydrometerological Service of Guyana: 18 Brickdam, Stabroek, Georgetown; tel. 225-9303; internet www.hydromet.gov.gy; f. 1965; attached to Ministry of Agriculture; research in advancement of hydrological, oceanographic and meteorological sciences.

Libraries and Archives

Georgetown

Documentation Centre, Caribbean Community Secretariat: Turkeyen, Greater Georgetown, POB 10827, Georgetown; tel. 222-0001; e-mail doccentre@caricom.org; internet www.caricom.org; f. 1980; provides information support for the programmes, projects and activities of the Caribbean Community; 38,579 vols, 18,312 books and pamphlets, 20,267 official documents, 16,954 monographic titles, 5,039 microfiches, 240 CD-ROMs, 73 journals, 3 newspapers; collns (documents): CARICOM; Project Officer SANDRA BARKER.

National Library of Guyana: 76/77 Church and Main Sts, POB 10-240, Georgetown; tel. 227-4053; internet www.nationallibraryofguyana.com; f. 1909; combines the functions of a nat. library and public library; legal depository for material printed in Guyana; 397,893 vols; spec. collns: Caribbeana, library science, papers of A. J. Seymour and Ian McDonald, UNESCO deposit; Chief Librarian GILLIAN MERLE THOMPSON (acting); publ. *Guyanese National Bibliography* (4 a year).

University of Guyana Library: Turkeyen Campus, POB 10-1110, Georgetown; tel. 222-5401; e-mail ugbclibrary@uog.edu.gy; internet www.ugbclibrary.uog.edu.gy; f. 1963; 200,000 vols, 3,000 periodicals; spec. collns: UN deposit colln, Caribbean Research Library, Law Colln; Librarian GWYNETH GEORGE; publs *Additions in Science and Technology* (6 a year), *Additions in the Humanities* (6 a year), *Caribbean Additions* (6 a year).

Museums and Art Galleries

Georgetown

Dutch Heritage Museum: 94 Carmichael St, Cummingsburg, Georgetown; tel. 656-2496; f. 2007; attached to Nat. Trust of Guyana; colln incl. bottles, crockery, antique prints, maps, flags, seals.

Guyana National Museum: Company Path, North St, Georgetown; tel. 225-7191; e-mail guyananationalmuseum@yahoo.com; f. 1853 by the Royal Agricultural and Commercial Society; subjects covered incl. industry, art, history, anthropology, zoology; serves as national repositories; Administrator NADIA MADHO; publ. *Journal* (1 a year).

Incorporates:

Guyana Zoological Park, National Parks Commission: Regent and Vlissengen Rds, Georgetown; tel. 225-8016; e-mail gm_npc@yahoo.com; f. 1952; specializes in the display, care and management of S American fauna; library of 50 vols; Gen. Man. YOLANDA VASCONCELLOS.

Museum of African Heritage: Lot 13, Barima Ave, Bel Air Park, Georgetown; tel. 226-5519; f. 1985, current name adopted 2001; colln incl. African art, musical instruments, games, clothing; library: library incl. W African and African Guyanese colln; Admin. JENNY DALY.

Walter Roth Museum of Anthropology: 61, Main St, N Cummingsburg, Georgetown; tel. 226-8486; e-mail walterrothmuseum@gmail.com; f. 1974; offers training in cultural anthropology and archaeology; publ. *Archaeology and Anthropology* (1 a year, online).

University

UNIVERSITY OF GUYANA

POB 101110, Turkeyen, Greater Georgetown
Telephone: 222-5423
E-mail: publicrelations@uog.edu.gy
Internet: www.uog.edu.gy

Founded 1963
State control
Language of instruction: English
Academic year: 2 terms, beginning September and January

Campuses in Turkeyen and Berbice

Pro-Chancellor: Dr PREM MISIR
Vice-Chancellor and Prin.: Prof. JACOB OPADEYI
Deputy Vice-Chancellor: PHILIP DA SILVA
Registrar: VINCENT ALEXANDER
Librarian: GWYNETH GEORGE

Library: see under Libraries and Archives
Number of teachers: 248
Number of students: 6,549
Publication: *University of Guyana Bulletin* (1 a year)

DEANS

Faculty of Agriculture and Forestry: OWEN BOVELL
Faculty of Health Sciences: Dr ANTHONY DE FREITAS
Faculty of Natural Sciences: Dr ADIL ANSARI
Faculty of Social Sciences: Dr PALOMA MOHAMMED
Faculty of Technology: ELENA TRIM
School of Earth and Environmental Sciences: Dr PAULETTE BYNOE
School of Education and Humanities: CLAUDETTE AUSTIN

PROFESSORS

BISHOP, A., Law
BRITTON, P., Law
EVERSELY, C., Law
LONCKE, J., French, Literature and Music
MASSIAH, K., Law
PERSICO, A., Spanish
SAMAD, D., English
TEWARI, B. B., Chemistry
THOMAS, C. Y., Economics and Business Administration
VERMA, V. N., Chemistry

College

American International School of Medicine: 89 Middleton and Sandy Babb Sts, Georgetown; tel. 225-2242; e-mail info@aism.edu; internet www.aism.edu; f. 1999; 21 teachers, 19 permanent, 2 visiting; Pres. Dr COLIN A. WILKINSON.

HAITI

The Higher Education System

Haiti (formerly Saint-Domingue) was under French sovereignty until 1804, when it gained its independence, but later came under US supervision from 1915 until 1934. The traditional education system has strong French influences, though some private institutions follow the American system. French and Creole are the official languages of instruction. The Ministère de l'Education Nationale de la Formation Professionnelle (MENFP—Ministry of Education and Professional Training) has responsibility for education. There are three universities, the state-controlled Université d'Etat d'Haiti (UEH, founded in 1920) and the private Université Quisqueya (founded in 1988) and Université Roi Henri Christophe (founded in 1980). Before the January 2010 earthquake, the Haitian system of higher education comprised at least 159 institutions, divided into disparate public and private sectors. The former consisted of a small network of 14 public, government-run institutions of higher education (Instituts d'Enseignement Superieur, IESs), including the UEH. The 13 other IESs were either affiliated with or independent of the UEH. In contrast, the private higher education sector consisted of a vast array of 145 institutions of varying quality. Of the 145 private establishments, only 10 provided high-quality, accredited education; of the remaining 135 (often religious-based institutions), 97 did not have permission to operate from the governmental Agency of Higher Education and Scientific Research. In 2007 the Ministry of Education and Professional Training reported that higher education enrolment in Haiti was approximately 40,000 students. Of these, 28,000 were in public institutions and 12,000 in private ones.

The main secondary school qualification, the Baccalauréat II, is the leading requirement for admission to higher education. There are, in addition, entrance examinations for certain courses. Undergraduates study for three to four years for the Diplôme d'Etudes Supérieures, Certificat d'Etudes Supérieures, or a professional title. However, the course leading to the award of the Diplôme de Docteur en Médecine lasts for seven years. The first postgraduate degree is the Maîtrise, received after one year of study following the undergraduate degree. The second postgraduate degree is the Doctorat, but is only available in the fields of ethnology and development sciences.

Many buildings in Port-au-Prince and its surrounding areas were destroyed in the earthquake of January 2010. At least 28 of the country's major universities were completely destroyed and the rest seriously damaged, and hundreds of students perished. Following the disaster, which killed around 316,000 people, a massive international reconstruction and rehabilitation campaign was launched. In May 2010 the Agence Universitaire de la Francophonie (AUF) hosted a meeting of more than 100 representatives in Montréal, Canada, to discuss an action plan for the reconstruction of Haiti's universities. During 2010–11, as students awaited the physical reconstruction of their colleges and universities, numerous distance education courses were offered by various foreign universities. In addition, an operational plan was put into place by the MENFP for the years 2010–15 to rebuild the Haitian education system. In early 2012 the new Université Roi Henri Christophe was inaugurated in Limonade near the northern city of Cap-Haïtien at a cost of some US $30m., jointly financed by the Haitian Government and Dominican Republic business community. Its first intake of some 1,500 students was in October 2012.

Regulatory Bodies

GOVERNMENT

Ministry of Culture: angle rues de la République et Geffrard 509, Port-au-Prince; tel. 22213238; e-mail dg1@haiticulture.org; Minister JOSETTE DARGUSTE.

Ministry of National Education and Vocational Training: 5 rue Dr Audain, Port-au-Prince; tel. 22221036; e-mail menfp_info@eduhaiti.gouv.ht; internet www.eduhaiti.gouv.ht; Minister VANNEUR PIERRE.

Learned Societies

GENERAL

UNESCO Office Port-au-Prince: 19, Delmas 60, Musseau par Bourdon, Petion Ville, Port-au-Prince; tel. 25110460; e-mail portauprince@unesco.org; Dir BECHIR LAMINE.

BIBLIOGRAPHY, LIBRARY SCIENCE AND MUSEOLOGY

Le Bibliophile: Cap-Haïtien; f. 1923; promotes knowledge and readership of world literature; 28 mems; Pres. SILVIO FASCHI; Sec. LOUIS TOUSSAINT; publs *La Citadelle* (52 a year), *Stella* (12 a year).

LANGUAGE AND LITERATURE

Alliance Française: 99 rue Lamartinière, BP 131, Port-au-Prince; tel. 22440016; e-mail dgalliancefr_haiti@yahoo.fr; offers courses and examinations in French language and culture and promotes cultural exchange with France; attached offices in Cap-Haïtien, Gonaïves, Jacmel, Jeremies, Les Cayes, Port-de-Paix.

NATURAL SCIENCES

General

Conseil National des Recherches Scientifiques (National Council for Scientific Research): Département de la Santé Publique et de la Population, Port-au-Prince; f. 1963; coordinates scientific devt and research, particularly in the field of public health; Pres. Prof. VICTOR NOËL; Sec. M. DOUYON.

Research Institute

RELIGION, SOCIOLOGY AND ANTHROPOLOGY

Bureau National d'Ethnologie: angle rue St Honoré ave Magloire Ambroise, Place des Héros de l'Indépendance, POB 915, Port-au-Prince; tel. 22225232; f. 1941; depts of African and Haitian ethnography, pre-Columbian archaeology; Dir-Gen. Dr EROL JOSUÉ.

Libraries and Archives

Port-au-Prince

Archives Nationales d'Haiti: 22 angle rues Geffrard et Borgella, POB 1299, Port-au-Prince; tel. 38639649; internet www.archivesnationales.gouv.ht; f. 1860; Dir-Gen. JEAN WILFRID BERTRAND.

Bibliothèque Haitienne des F. I. C.: 180 rue du Centre, POB 1758, Port-au-Prince; tel. 22232148; f. 1912, opened in 1920; Haitian literature, newspapers since the 19th century, history of St Domingue and Haiti, Haitian legislation; 15,000 vols; Dir ERNEST EVEN.

Bibliothèque Nationale d'Haiti: 193 rue du Centre, Port-au-Prince; tel. 22221198; f. 1940; 23,000 vols, 419 periodicals; Dir FRANÇOISE BEAULIEU THYBULLE.

Museums and Art Galleries

Port-au-Prince

Centre d'Art: 58 rue Roy, Port-au-Prince; tel. 22222018; f. 1944; arranges representative exhibitions of Haitian art in the Americas and Western Europe; Dir FRANCINE MURAT.

Musée du Panthéon National Haitien: place des Héros de l'Indépendance, Champ de Mars, Port-au-Prince Ouest; tel.

22223167; e-mail mupanah@yahoo.fr; f. 1983; Dir-Gen. MARIE-LUCIE VENDRYES.

Universities

UNIVERSITÉ D'ÉTAT D'HAITI

21 ruelle Rivière, HT6112 Port-au-Prince
Telephone: 22442943
E-mail: recteur@ueh.edu.ht
Internet: www.ueh.edu.ht

Founded 1820
State control
Language of instruction: French
Academic year: October to July

Rector: JEAN VERNET HENRY
Vice-Rector for Academic Affairs: JEAN POINCY
Vice-Rector for Research: FRITZ DESHOMMES
Sec.-Gen.: WILSON DORLUS

Library of 10,000 vols
Number of teachers: 2,500
Number of students: 25,000

DEANS

Faculty of Agronomy and Veterinary Medicine: Dr JOCELYN LOUISSAINT
Faculty of Applied Linguistics: ROGÉDA DORCÉ DORCIL
Faculty of Ethnology: Dr JACQUES JOVIN
Faculty of Humanities: JEAN RENOL ELIE
Faculty of Law and Economic Sciences: JOVIS W. BELLOT
Faculty of Law, Economic Sciences and Management (Cap-Haïtien): JUSNERD NELSON
Faculty of Medicine and Pharmacy: Dr JEAN CLAUDE CADET
Faculty of Odontology: Dr SAMUEL PROPHETE
Faculty of Science: HÉRISSÉ GUIRAND

UNIVERSITÉ QUISQUEYA

218 ave Jean-Paul II, Haut de Turgeau, Port-au-Prince
Telephone: 22214516
E-mail: universitequisqueya@uniq.edu.ht
Internet: www.uniq.edu

Founded 1988
Private control
Language of instruction: French
Academic year: September to July

Rector: Dr JACKY LUMARQUE
Vice-Rector for Academic Affairs: Dr MARIE-GISELE PIERRE
Vice-Rector for Research and Univ. Extension: EVENS EMMANUEL
Sec.-Gen.: DARLINE ALEXIS
Librarian: JOSIANE FOUREAU

Library of 7,000 vols, incl. 4,000 books
Number of teachers: 258
Number of students: 2,529
Publication: *Revue Juridique de l'UniQ* (4 a year)

DEANS

Faculty of Agriculture and Environment Sciences: EDMOND MAGNY
Faculty of Economics and Administrative Sciences: Dr RAULIN LINCIFORT CADET
Faculty of Education Sciences: LOUIS DELIMA CHERY
Faculty of Health Sciences: Dr GENEVIEVE POITEVIEN
Faculty of Law and Political Sciences: BERNARD GOUSSE
Faculty of Science, Engineering and Architecture: Prof. Dr EVENSON CALIXTE

UNIVERSITÉ ROI HENRI CHRISTOPHE

45, rue 18 H&1, POB 98, HT110 Cap-Haïtien
Telephone: 28161926
E-mail: contact@urhc.edu.ht
Internet: www.urhc.edu.ht

Founded 1980
Private control

Pres.: Dr LOUIS J. NOISIN
Vice-Pres.: Ing. GÉDÉON JOSEPH
Vice-Pres. for Academics: Dr ARTEVEL PIERRE JÉROME
Vice-Pres. for Admin.: Dr HERNS MONROSE
Vice-Pres. for Devt: CARMEL M. TOUSSAINT
Vice-Pres. for External Affairs: JEAN GERVAIS SAINT LOT
Vice-Pres. for Finance: CHANTAL N. STAPLE
Sec.-Gen.: RONEL NEMORIN
Number of students: 100

DEANS

Faculty of Administrative Sciences: CARLO JOSEPH
Faculty of Agricultural Sciences: ERVÉ ULYSSE
Faculty of Applied Sciences: Ing. GÉDÉON JOSEPH
Faculty of Nursing: G. ROMÉLUS

Colleges

Ecole Nationale des Arts et Métiers: Blvd J. J. Desalines, POB 1542, Port-au-Prince; tel. 4468300; f. 1983; Dir EMERANTE DE PRADINES MORSE.

Ecole Nationale de Technologie Médicale: Faculty of Medicine and Pharmacy, Université d'Etat d'Haiti, 89 rue Oswald Durand, POB 2599, 6110 Port-au-Prince; tel. 22220487; e-mail fmp@ueh.edu.ht; Dir PAULETTE ALEXANDRE CHAMPAGNE.

Institut International d'Etudes Universitaires: c/o Fondation Haitienne de Développement, 106 ave Christophe, Port-au-Prince; Dir Y. ARMAND.

HONDURAS

The Higher Education System

The oldest institution of higher education is the Universidad Nacional Autónoma de Honduras (UNAH), which was founded in 1847 and has numerous campuses throughout the country. There are two other state universities and seven private ones, but the UNAH is currently the largest in the country in terms of student enrolment. The Ministry of Education is responsible for the provision of higher education in the public sector. In 2009/10 169,878 students were enrolled in tertiary education.

The secondary school qualification Bachillerato (Académico) or equivalent is the main requirement for admission to higher education. The primary undergraduate degrees are the Licenciado or professional title, awarded after four years of study (although some courses last longer), and the Bachillerato Universitario, a technological qualification awarded after three to four years. Following the Licenciado, the postgraduate Maestría degree is awarded after two to three years of study. In fields where a Licenciado is not available, holders of a Bachillerato Universitario may also gain admission to postgraduate studies.

Higher technical and vocational education is offered by professional colleges and schools. The leading sub-degree level qualification is the Técnico or Técnico Universitario, which requires one-and-a-half years of study.

The Reglamento de la Ley de Educación Superior of 1989 established the Consejo de Educación Superior (Council of Higher Education) to oversee and regulate the country's higher education sector. The responsibilities of the Council, which is headed by the President of the UNAH, include setting and enforcing higher education policy and approving the creation of public and private universities. The three public universities are all members of the Consejo Superior Universitario Centroamericano (Central American Higher Education Council), the regional organization for public universities; two of them (UNAH and Universidad Pedagógica Nacional 'Francisco Morazán') and the private Universidad Católica de Honduras also adhere to the Consejo Centroamericano de Acreditación de la Educación Superior (Central American Accreditation Council for Higher Education), whose remit is to harmonize and improve the quality of higher education in the region.

Regulatory Bodies

GOVERNMENT

Ministry of Culture, Art and Sports: Col. Palmira, Edif. Castillo y Poujol, Tegucigalpa; tel. 2235-4700; e-mail binah@sdnhon.org.hn; internet www.scad.gob.hn; Minister TULIO MARIANO GONZÁLEZ.

Ministry of Education: 1a Avda Entre 2a y 3a Calle, Comayagüela, Tegucigalpa; tel. 2238-4325; e-mail info@se.gob.hn; internet www.se.gob.hn; Minister Dr MARLON OTONIEL ESCOTO VALERIO.

Learned Societies

ARCHITECTURE AND TOWN PLANNING

Colegio de Arquitectos de Honduras (College of Honduran Architects): Apdo 1974, Tegucigalpa; Col. Lomas del Guijarro Sur, contiguo al Instituto Salesiano San Miguel, Tegucigalpa; tel. 2235-8828; internet www.arquitectoshonduras.org; f. 1979; library; 727 mems; Pres. Arq. JACOBO EDMUNDO BERTRAND; Sec. Arq. GLENDA XIOMARA LAGOS; publ. *Arquitectura y Contexto* (4 a year).

LANGUAGE AND LITERATURE

Alliance Française: Apdo Postal 3445, Tegucigalpa; Col. Lomas del Guijarro, 100 m antes del Instituto Sagrado Corazón, Tegucigalpa; tel. 2221-1692; e-mail información@aftegucigalpa.com; internet www.aftegucigalpa.com; f. 1959; offers courses and examinations in French language and culture and promotes cultural exchange with France; attached teaching office in San Pedro Sula; Dir-Gen. JUAN FRANSCISCO BONIL.

Research Institutes

GENERAL

Instituto Hondureño de Cultura Interamericana (IHCI) (Honduran Institute of Inter-American Culture): Apdo 201, Tegucigalpa; 2da Avda Calle Real Entre 5ta y 6ta Calle, Comayagüela; tel. 2237-9480; e-mail info@ihcihn.com; internet www.ihcihn.com; f. 1939; courses in English, bilingual secretarial studies; art gallery; library of 8,000 vols; Dir ROSARIO ELENA CÓRDOVA.

AGRICULTURE, FISHERIES AND VETERINARY SCIENCE

Fundación Hondureña de Investigación Agrícola (FHIA) (Honduran Foundation for Agricultural Research): Apdo Postal 2067, San Pedro Sula; tel. 2668-2827; e-mail fhia@fhia-hn.org; internet www.fhia.org.hn; f. 1984; library of 30,000 vols, 600 journals; Dir-Gen. Dr ADOLFO MARTINEZ.

Instituto Hondureño del Café (Honduran Coffee Institute): Apdo Postal 3147, Tegucigalpa; Tres Caminos, Calle Principal, Tegucigalpa; tel. 2235-8070; e-mail webmaster@ihcafe.hn; internet www.ihcafe.hn; f. 1970; Gen. Man. Lic. VÍCTOR HUGO MOLINA.

Instituto Nacional Agrario (National Agrarian Institute): Col. La Alameda, 4ta Avda entre 10ma y 11va calles, No 1009, Tegucigalpa; tel. 2239-8401; e-mail transparencia@ina.hn; internet www.ina.hn; f. 1961; Exec. Dir FÉLIX NECTALY MEDINA AGURCIA; Sec. Gen. SARA RUTH AMADOR.

HISTORY, GEOGRAPHY AND ARCHAEOLOGY

Instituto Hondureño de Antropología e Historia (Honduran Institute of Anthropology and History): Apdo 1518, Tegucigalpa; Villa Roy, Barrio Buenos Aires, Tegucigalpa; tel. 2220-6954; internet www.ihah.hn; f. 1952; library of 12,000 vols; research and conservation of cultural property, archaeology, history, ethnography, linguistics, museology; Dir VIRGILIO PAREDES TRAPERO; Sec.-Gen. HECTOR PORTILLO MACHUCA; publ. *Yaxkin* (1 a year).

Libraries and Archives

San Pedro Sula

Biblioteca Publica Benjamín Franklin (Benjamin Franklin Public Library): 3 Calle, 3 y 4 Avdas, No 20, Barrio El Centro, San Pedro Sula; tel. 2557-2084; e-mail biblioteca@centrocultural-sps.com; f. 1973.

Tegucigalpa

Archivo Nacional de Honduras (National Archives of Honduras): Barrio El Centro, Avda Cristóbal Colón, Calle Salvador Mendieta 1117, Tegucigalpa; e-mail archivonacional@yahoo.com; f. 1880; 700 linear m of documents; 2,700 vols and 100 periodicals; Dir CARLOS WILFREDO MALDONADO.

Biblioteca Nacional de Honduras 'Juan Ramón Molina' (Juan Ramón Molina National Library of Honduras): Apdo Postal 4563, Tegucigalpa; Avda Cervantes, Tegucigalpa; tel. 2222-8577; e-mail binah@sdnhon.org.hn; f. 1880; coordinates national and international exchange; shares legal deposit with other centres; 70,000 vols; Dir EDUARDO BÄHR; publ. *Anuario Bibliográfico*.

Biblioteca Roberto Ramírez (Roberto Ramírez Library): Banco Central de Honduras, Edif. Anexo 5 y 6 Avda Entre 11 y 12 Calle, Comayaguela, Tegucigalpa; tel. 2237-7979; e-mail usbi@bch.hn; internet biblioteca.bch.hn; f. 1950; attached to Banco Central de Honduras.

Biblioteca 'Wilson Popenoe' ('Wilson Popenoe' Library): Apdo 93, Tegucigalpa; Escuela Agrícola Panamericana, Tegucigalpa; tel. 2287-2000; internet www.zamorano.edu/biblioteca; f. 1946; attached to Escuela Agrícola Panamericana Zamorano; tropical agriculture; 22,721 vols, 950 periodicals, 1,200 DVDs; Librarian WILLIAM JOVANNY PEDRAZA; publ. *CEIBA*.

Sistema Bibliotecario Universidad Nacional Autónoma de Honduras (Library System National Autonomous University of Honduras): Edif. de Biblioteca, 3°, Carretera a Suyapa, Ciudad Universitaria, Tegucigalpa; tel. 2235-3361; e-mail biblioteca@unah.edu.hn; internet www.unah.edu.hn/?cat=1538; f. 1970; attached to Universidad Nacional Autónoma de Honduras; 200,000 vols; Dir PATRICIA HERNÀNDEZ CAÑADAS.

Museums and Art Galleries

Comayagua

Museo de Comayagua (Museum of Comayagua): Barrio San Francisco, Cuadra al Norte de la Plaza Central, Comayagua; tel. 2772-0386; f. 1946; attached to Instituto Hondureño de Antropología e Historia; studies the evolutionary history and heritage of the Valley of Comayagua from the paleozoic era, pre-historic, colonial and republican periods; library of 1,203 vols; Dir MIRIAM FLORENCIA ZAPATA MEJIA.

Copán

Museo Regional de Arqueología Maya (Regional Museum of Mayan Archaeology): Ciudad de Copán; f. 1939; objects relate exclusively to Maya culture; Dir Prof. OSMIN RIVERA.

Cortés

Museo de la Fortaleza de San Fernando de Omoa (Museum Fort San Fernando de Omoa): Bario San Fernando de Omoa, Cortés; tel. 2658-9167; attached to Instituto Hondureño de Antropología e Historia; f. 1959; colonial and historical items; Dir GERARDO JOHNSON.

Tegucigalpa

Fundación Museo del Aire de Honduras (Air Museum Foundation of Honduras): Atrás del Club de Oficiales de la FAH, Toncontín, Tegucigalpa; tel. 9992-4543; e-mail museo_del_aire@live.com; display of historic aircraft; Dir ANTHONY ERIS STEVENSON.

Fundación para el Museo del Hombre Hondureño (Foundation for the Museum of the Honduran Man): Apdo 852, Tegucigalpa; Avda Miguel de Cervantes, Casa Ramón Rosa, frente a Librería Guaymuras, Tegucigalpa; tel. 2220-1678; e-mail asistente@museodelhombre.com; internet www.museodelhombre.com; f. 1989; colln of paintings by Honduran artists; art gallery; library of 4,000 vols on art and culture; Pres. ARMIDA DE LÓPEZ CONTRERAS; Sec. IOVANNA RAVELO.

Museo de Historia Natural (Museum of Natural History): Edif. de Ciencias Biológicas, J1, Blvd Suyapa Ciudad Universitaria, Tegucigalpa; tel. 2275-8553; attached to Universidad Nacional Autónoma de Honduras; colln of fossils of prehistoric animals.

Trujillo

Museo de la Fortaleza de Santa Bárbara (Museum of the Fortress of Santa Barbara): Barrio el Centro Esq. Opuesta del Banco Atlántida, Trujillo; tel. 2434-4535; e-mail fortalezatrujillo@yahoo.com; attached to Instituto Hondureño de Antropología e Historia.

Universities

UNIVERSIDAD CATÓLICA DE HONDURAS 'NUESTRA SEÑORA REINA DE LA PAZ'
(Catholic University of Honduras 'Our Lady Queen of Peace')

Campus Corporativo San José, Tegucigalpa
Telephone: 2238-6794
E-mail: contactosj@unicah.edu
Internet: www.unicah.edu
Founded 1992
Private control
Language of instruction: Spanish
Academic year: February to November
Faculties of administrative studies, engineering, health sciences, religious studies, social sciences
Rector: Dr ELIO DAVID ALVARENGA AMADOR

UNIVERSIDAD CRISTIANA EVANGÉLICA NUEVO MILENIO
(New Millennium Evangelical Christian University)

Barrio las Acacias, 14 y 15 Calle, 3era Avda, Sector N.O., San Pedro Sula
Telephone: 2557-0732
Internet: www.ucenm.net
Founded 2001
Private control
Language of instruction: Spanish
Academic year: February to November
Rector: MARÍA ANTONIA FERNÁNDEZ DE SUAZO
Dir Academic: Lic. WALDINA ERAZO
Dir Admin.: Ing. ROLDAN SUAZO
Dir Distance Education: CRISTIAN MOLINA
Dir Research and Curriculum Design: ADOLFO BOCALLETI
Sec.-Gen.: NELSON BAUDILIO LÓPEZ

UNIVERSIDAD DE SAN PEDRO SULA
(University of San Pedro Sula)

Avda Circunvalación, San Pedro Sula, Cortés
Telephone: 2561-8777
E-mail: info@usps.edu
Internet: www.usap.edu
Founded 1978
Private control
Language of instruction: Spanish
Academic year: February to November
Pres.: Abog. CARLOS ENRIQUE BUESO
Rector: Lic. ROBERTO MARTINEZ ARIAS
Vice-Rector: SENÉN VILLANEUVA HENDERSON
Sec.-Gen.: Lic. OSVALDO VALLADARES

DEANS

Faculty of Economics and Administrative Sciences: JUAN CARLOS GAMERO
Faculty of Technical Sciences: Dra BEATRIZ BRITO

UNIVERSIDAD JOSÉ CECILIO DEL VALLE
(José Cecilio del Valle University)

Apdo Postal 917, Tegucigalpa
Col. Humuya, Avda Altiplano, Calle Poseidón, Tegucigalpa
Telephone: 2280-8528
E-mail: info@ujcv.edu.hn
Internet: www.ujcv.edu.hn
Founded 1978
Private control
Language of instruction: Spanish
Academic year: February to November
Campus in Comayagua
Rector: FRANCISCO JOSÉ ROSA
Vice-Rector for Academic Affairs: MARTHA MELIDA MORALES GUTIÉRREZ
Vice-Rector for Innovation and Research: MARIO LANZA SANTAMARÍA
Sec.-Gen.: SAYRA VARGAS

UNIVERSIDAD METROPOLITANA DE HONDURAS
(Metropolitan University of Honduras)

Edif. No 1 Plaza COLPROSUMAH, Cruce del Blvd Centro América y Suyapa, Contiguo a casa presidencial, lado posterior, Tegucigalpa
Telephone: 2280-1111
E-mail: mercadeo@unimetro.edu.hn
Internet: www.unimetro.edu.hn
Founded 2002
Private control
Language of instruction: Spanish
Academic year: February to November
Rector: ERNESTO ARMANDO ENAMORADO BLANCO

UNIVERSIDAD NACIONAL AUTÓNOMA DE HONDURAS
(National Autonomous University of Honduras)

Apdo Postal 3560, Tegucigalpa
Blvd Suyapa, Ciudad Universitaria, Tegucigalpa
Telephone: 2232-2110
E-mail: die@unah.edu.hn
Internet: www.unah.edu.hn
Founded 1847
autonomous control
Language of instruction: Spanish
Academic year: February to December
Rector: JULIETA CASTELLANOS
Vice-Rector for Academics: Dr RUTILIA CALDERÓN
Admin. Sec.: RAÚL FLORES
Gen. Sec.: AFREDO HAWIT
Librarian: ORFYLIA PINEL
Library: see under Libraries and Archives
Publications: *Catálogo de Estudios*, *Memoria Anual*, *Presencia Universitaria*, *Revista de la Universidad*

DEANS

Faculty of Chemistry and Pharmacy: GODOFREDO CRUZ
Faculty of Dentistry: Dra LOURDES MURCIA
Faculty of Economics: BELINDA FLORES DE MENDOZA
Faculty of Engineering: ADOLFO RACHEL QUAN
Faculty of Law and Social Sciences: JORGE ROBERTO MARADIAGA MARADIAGA
Faculty of Medicine and Nursing: RENATO VALENZUELA
Faculty of Space Science: MARÍA CRISTINA PINEDA DE CARÍAS

UNIVERSIDAD NACIONAL DE AGRICULTURA
(National University of Agriculture)

Km 9, carretera que conduce a Dulce Nombre de Culmi, Suborb Catacamas, Catacamas
Telephone: 2799-4905
E-mail: informacion@unag.edu.hn
Internet: www.unag.edu.hn
Founded 1950
public control
Language of instruction: Spanish
Academic year: February to November
Depts of agricultural economics, agricultural engineering, animal production, general studies, nature and environment, plant production, research and extension
Rector: OSCAR OVIDIO REDONDO FLORES
Vice-Rector for Academic Affairs: Dr MARLON ONIEL ESCOTO

Vice-Rector for Admin.: VICTOR JAVIER GONZALES
Sec.-Gen.: CARLOS MANUEL ULLOA
Library of 10,000 vols
Publication: *AGROENA*

UNIVERSIDAD PEDAGÓGICA NACIONAL 'FRANCISCO MORAZÁN'
(Francisco Morazán National Pedagogical University)

Apdo Postal 3394, Tegucigalpa
Col. el Dorado, Frente a Plaza Miraflores, Tegucigalpa
Telephone: 2239-8842
E-mail: info@upnfm.edu.hn
Internet: www.upnfm.edu.hn
Founded 1956 as Escuela Superior del Profesorado, in cooperation with UNESCO, current name and status 1989
public control
Academic year: February to November (two semesters)
Rector: DAVID ORLANDO MARÍN
Vice-Rector for Academic Affairs: HERMES ALDUVIN DÍAZ LUNA
Vice-Rector for Admin.: RAFAEL BARAHONA
Vice-Rector for Research and Graduate Studies: YENNY AMINDA EGUIGURE
Vice-Rector for Univ. Centre for Distance Learning: GUSTAVO ADOLFO CERRATO
Sec.-Gen.: CELFA IDALISIS BUESO
Library of 105,000 vols
Number of students: 30,000
Publications: *Codice* (12 a year), *Revista Paradigma* (4 a year)

DEANS
Faculty of Humanities: JOSÉ DARIO CRUZ
Faculty of Science and Technology: JOSÉ GERARDO FUENTES

UNIVERSIDAD TECNOLÓGICA CENTROAMERICANA
(Central American Technological University)

Campus Tegucigalpa, Tegucigalpa
Telephone: 2268-1000
E-mail: admisionteg@unitec.edu
Internet: www.unitec.edu
Founded 1987
Private control
Language of instruction: Spanish
Academic year: February to November
Rector: LUIS ZELAYA MEDRANO

UNIVERSIDAD TECNOLÓGICA DE HONDURAS
(Technological University of Honduras)

Carretera a Armenta, Frente a Rio Blanco, San Pedro Sula
Telephone: 2551-8900
Internet: www.uth.hn
Founded 1986 as Instituto Superior Tecnológico; current name and status 1996
Private control
Language of instruction: Spanish
Academic year: February to November
Campuses in El Progreso, Islas de la Bahia, La Ceiba, Puerto Cortés, Santa Bárbara, Siguatepeque, Tegucigalpa
Pres.: Lic. ROGER D. VALLADARES
Rector: RICARDO ANTILLÓN
Vice-Rector: JAVIER MEJÍA
Sec.-Gen.: ROMELL GALO
Academic Dir-Gen.: JOSÉ JESÚS MORA

Colleges

Centro de Diseño, Arquitectura y Construcción/Universidad del Diseño (Centre of Design, Architecture and Construction): Col. Tepeyac, Avda Gracias a Dios, Calle Ocotepeque, Casa 1323, Tegucigalpa; tel. 2232-4874; e-mail rector@cedac.edu.hn; internet www.cedac.edu.hn; f. 1996; campuses in Tegucigalpa, Valle de Sula; Rector Arq. MARIO E. MARTIN.

Escuela Agrícola Panamericana Zamorano (Zamorano Pan-American Agricultural School): Apdo Postal 93, Tegucigalpa; tel. 2287-2000; e-mail zamorano@zamorano.edu; internet www.zamorano.edu; f. 1942; private, non-profit pan-American instn of higher education; library: 22,721 vols; Rector Dr ROBERTO CUEVAS GARCÍA; Dean for Academics Dr RAÚL HERNÁN ZELAYA; publ. *CEIBA*.

Escuela Nacional de Ciencias Forestales (ESNACIFOR) (National School of Forest Sciences): Apdo Postal No 2, Siguatepeque; Carretera del Norte, Col. Las Américas, Siguatepeque, Comoyagua; tel. 2773-0011; e-mail relacionesexternas@esnacifor.edu; internet www.esnacifor.hn; f. 1969; Exec. Dir MIGUEL CONRADO VALDEZ CASTRO; Sec.-Gen. Abog. GERARDO TOMÉ; publ. *Revista Técnica Científica TATASCAN*.

HUNGARY

The Higher Education System

Higher education in Hungary dates back to the 14th century, with the establishment in 1367 of Pécsi Tudományegyetem (University of Pécs). Other long-established universities include Debreceni Egyetem (University of Debrecen; founded in 1912), Debreceni Református Hittudományi Egyetem (University of Reformed Theology of Debrecen; founded in 1538) and Evangélikus Hittudományi Egyetem (Evangelical–Lutheran Theological University; founded in 1557). In 1999–2000 the system of higher education underwent a major reorganization, as a result of which from 1 January 2000 there were 30 state-run universities and colleges, 26 church universities and colleges, and six colleges run by foundations. In 2005 a new Act on Higher Education legislated the creation of a new system of university degrees (see below), and introduced financial and managerial reforms. By 2012 there were 19 public universities, seven private universities, and nine and 32 public and private colleges, respectively. In 2010/11 the figure for student enrolment in further and higher education (both full- and part-time) was estimated at 361,347.

The Ministry of National Resources (through the State Secretariat for Education) is responsible for establishing and recognizing institutions of higher education, which must gain accreditation from the Hungarian Accreditation Committee and Higher Education and Scientific Council. The Act on Higher Education (2005) established an Economic Council to take responsibility for all decisions regarding the financing and management of the higher education sector. Universities and colleges are autonomous institutions and set their own curricula and courses.

Since 2004 admission to higher education has been based purely on results in the Erettsegi or Matura, the main secondary school qualifications (with the exception of foreign language courses, which require advanced level examinations). Previously, admission had been based on a combination of the Erettsegi/Matura and competitive entrance examinations. In September 2006 a Bachelors-Masters-Doctorate university degree system was introduced, based on the principles of the Bologna Process. The new courses are based on a 'credit semester' system, with students accruing a specified number of European Credit Transfer and Accumulation System (ECTS) credits each semester in order to graduate. The main undergraduate degree is the Bachelors, which lasts six to eight semesters (three to four years) for which students must accumulate 180–240 ECTS credits. Following the Bachelors, the Masters is the first postgraduate degree, lasting two to four semesters (one to two years), during which students must accrue 60–120 ECTS credits (teacher training lasts five semesters or two-and-a-half years and requires 150 ECTS credits). In total, combined Bachelors and Masters studies must not last less than 10 nor more than 12 semesters. A single one-tier Masters programme, entailing five to six years of study and the accumulation of 300–360 ECTS, is offered in religious education, a number of arts subjects, veterinary medicine, architecture, dentistry, pharmaceutics, law and medicine. Finally, the Doctoral degree (PhD or Doctor of Liberal Arts) is a six-semester programme (three years) requiring 180 ECTS credits.

Courses leading to the Főiskola Oklevel (College Diploma) are offered by the főiskola (colleges of higher education), which constitute the predominant section of higher education in Hungary. The college programmes, which are more practically orientated than their university counterparts, last three to four years and include the preparation of a thesis. Unless officially accredited, colleges are not authorized to award university degrees. However, from 2008 the Főiskola Oklevel was being phased out to allow full transition to the Bologna Process system of awards.

Technical and vocational education, which is overseen by the Ministry for National Economy, has been integrated into the mainstream public education system and the old system of apprenticeships has been phased out. Courses are offered by post-secondary vocational schools, colleges and universities and last two to three years. Students are awarded the Technikusi Oklevel qualification and the title of Technikus (Technician). All vocational qualifications issued by the state authorities have been registered on the National Register of Vocational Qualifications. This register imposes a set of requirements that all vocational qualifications have to meet, such as curriculum and qualification standards.

In 2011 a new National Higher Education Act provoked protests by students against a clause requiring those who receive government funding for their studies to remain working in the country for seven to 15 years after their graduation. There were also other controversial measures on which the national union of Hungarian students claimed it had not been consulted, including the introduction of quotas for entrance to certain fields of study. The Act also brought into existence the Hungarian Accreditation Committee, a national body of experts tasked with the control, assurance and evaluation of the scientific quality of education, scientific research and artistic activity at higher education institutions.

Regulatory and Representative Bodies

GOVERNMENT

Ministry of Human Resources: Budapest, Arany János utca 6-8, 1051; Budapest, Szalay u. 10–14, 1055; tel. (1) 795-1200; e-mail info@nefmi.gov.hu; internet www.kormany.hu/en/ministry-of-human-resources; Minister ZOLTÁN BALOG.

ACCREDITATION

ENIC/NARIC Hungary: Educational Authority, Hungarian Equivalence and Information Centre, Budapest, Szalay u. 10–14, 1055; tel. (1) 374-2212; e-mail ekvivalencia@oh.gov.hu; internet www.naric.hu; Head GÁBOR MÉSZÁROS.

Magyar Felsőoktatási Akkreditációs Bizottság (Hungarian Accreditation Committee): Budapest, Krisztina krt. 39/B, 1013; tel. (1) 344-0314; e-mail titkarsag@mab.hu; internet www.mab.hu; f. 1993; ind. body accrediting higher education instns and study programmes in disciplinary groups, in 5-year cycles; evaluates applications to set up new higher education instns and new study programmes (framework requirements on nat. and programme applications on institutional level); 23 mems; Pres. Prof. Dr ERVIN BALÁZS; Sec.-Gen. TIBOR SZÁNTÓ.

NATIONAL BODIES

Felsőoktatási Konferenciák Szövetsége (Confederation of Hungarian Conferences on Higher Education): Budapest, Ajtósi Dürer sor 19-21, 1146; tel. (1) 344-0310; e-mail bilik@fksz.huninet.hu; Sec.-Gen. Dr ISTVÁN BILIK.

Magyar Rektori Konferencia (Hungarian Rectors' Conference): Benczúr, u. 43, IV/3, 1068; tel. (70) 932-4203; e-mail mrk@mail.mrk.hu; internet www.mrk.hu; f. 2006; represents higher education instns and works to protect their interests; 72 heads of higher education mem. instns; Pres. Prof. Dr BARNA MEZEY; Co-Pres. Dr ÉVA KRISZT.

Learned Societies

GENERAL

Magyar Tudományos Akadémia (Hungarian Academy of Sciences): Budapest, Széchenyi István sq. 9, 1051; tel. (1) 411-6100; e-mail info@titkarsag.mta.hu; internet www.mta.hu; f. 1831; supports and represents scientific fields and disseminates scientific results; sections of agricultural sciences, biological sciences, chemical sciences, earth sciences, economics and law, engineering sciences, linguistics and literary scholarship, mathematics, medical sciences, philosophy and historical sciences, physical sciences; attached research institutes: see under Research Institutes; 707 mems (incl. 203 hon., 250 ordinary, 92 corresp., 162 external); library: see under Libraries and Archives; Pres. Dr JÓZSEF PÁLINKÁS; Gen. Sec. Dr TAMÁS NÉMETH; publs *Across Languages and Cultures* (2 a year, print and online), *Acta Agronomica Hungarica* (4 a year, print and online), *Acta Alimentaria* (4 a year, print and online), *Acta Antiqua* (4 a year, print and online), *Acta Archaeologica* (2 a year, print and online), *Acta Biologica Hungarica* (4 a year, print and online), *Acta Botanica Hungarica* (4 a year, print and online), *Acta Chromatographica* (4 a year, print and online), *Acta Ethnographica Hungarica* (2 a year, print and online), *Acta Geodaetica et Geophysica Hungarica* (4 a year, print and online), *Acta Historiae Artium* (4 a year, print and online), *Acta Juridica Hungarica* (4 a year, print and online), *Acta Linguistica Hungarica* (4 a year, print and online), *Acta Microbiologica et Immunologica Hungarica* (4 a year, print and online), *Acta Oeconomica* (4 a year, print and online), *Acta Orientalia* (4 a year, print and online), *Acta Physiologica Hungarica* (4 a year, print and online), *Acta Phytopathologica et Entomologica Hungarica* (2 a year, print and online), *Acta Veterinaria* (4 a year, print and online), *Central European Geology* (4 a year, print and online), *Cereal Research Communications* (4 a year, print and online), *Clinical and Experimental Medical Journal* (4 a year, print and online), *Community Ecology* (2 a year, print and online), *European Journal of Microbiology and Immunology* (2 a year, print and online), *Hungarian Studies* (2 a year, print and online), *International Review of Applied Sciences and Engineering* (2 a year, print and online), *Interventional Medicine & Applied Science* (4 a year, print and online), *Journal of Behavioral Addictions* (4 a year, print and online), *Journal Evolutionary Psychology* (4 a year, print and online), *Journal of Flow Chemistry* (irregular, print and online), *Journal of Planar Chromatography-Modern TLC* (6 a year, print and online), *Learning & Perception* (irregular, print and online), *Nanopages* (irregular, print and online), *Pollack Periodica* (3 a year, print and online), *Progress in Agricultural Engineering Sciences* (1 a year, print and online), *Society and Economy* (irregular, print and online), *Studia Musicologica* (4 a year, print and online), *Studia Scientiarium Mathematicarum Hungarica* (4 a year, print and online), *Studia Slavica* (2 a year, print and online).

Műszaki és Természettudományi Egyesületek Szövetsége (Federation of Technical and Scientific Societies): Budapest, Kossuth Lajos tér 6–8, 1055; tel. (1) 474-7908; e-mail mtesz@mtesz.hu; internet www.mtesz.hu; f. 1948; coordinates, collaborates work of the founder 14 professional socs of that time and protects their interests; 40 mem. socs; Pres. Prof. Dr GÁBOR VERESS; Dir-Gen. ILONA SZŰCSNÉ POSZTOVICS.

Széchenyi Irodalmi és Művészeti Akadémia (Széchenyi Academy of Letters and Arts): Budapest, Széchenyi István tér 9, 1051; tel. (1) 331-4117; e-mail szima@titkarsag.mta.hu; internet mta.hu/cikkek/szechenyi-irodalmi-es-muveszeti-akademia-104911; f. 1825 as an ind. section of Hungarian Acad. of Sciences, ind. 1992; sections of fine arts, letters, music, theatre and film, architecture; 90 mems, 80 full mems, 10 hon. mems; Pres. KÁROLY MAKK; Exec. Pres. FERENCZ GYŐZŐ; Exec. Sec. MAGDA FERCH.

AGRICULTURE, FISHERIES AND VETERINARY SCIENCE

Magyar Agrártudományi Egyesület (Hungarian Association of Agricultural Sciences): Budapest, Kossuth Lajos tér 6–8, 1055; tel. (1) 353-1950; e-mail mail.mae@mtesz.hu; internet maekerteszet.terasz.hu; f. 1951; 17 affiliated socs; 8,500 mems; Pres. Dr ÁKOS MÁTHÉ; Sec. Dr OSZKÁR KÖCK; publ. *Magyar Mezőgazdaság* (Hungarian Agriculture, 12 a year).

Magyar Élelmezésipari Tudományos Egyesület (METE) (Hungarian Scientific Society for Food Industry): Budapest, Dombóvári út 6–8, 1117; tel. (1) 214-6692; e-mail mail.mete@mtesz.hu; f. 1949; attached to Fed. of Technical and Scientific Socs; poultry breeding and processing, viticulture, sugar industry, confectionery, grain processing, meat industry, cold storage, canning, paprika, tobacco, oil, soap, cosmetics, brewery, bakery, distillery; 3,800 mems; Pres. Dr SZABÓ GÁBOR; Sec.-Gen. Dr VÉHA ANTAL; publs *A Hús* (Meat, 4 a year), *Ásványvíz-Üdítőital-Gyümölcslé* (Mineral Water-Soft-drink-Juice, 4 a year), *Cukoripar* (Sugar Industry, 4 a year), *Édesipar* (Confectionery Industry, 4 a year), *Élelmezési Ipar* (Food Industry, 12 a year), *Hűtőipar* (Frozen Food Industry, 4 a year), *Molnárok Lapja* (Millers' Journal, 6 a year), *Olaj, Szappan, Kozmetika* (Oil, Soap, Cosmetics, 6 a year), *Sütőipar* (Baking Industry, 4 a year), *Szeszipar* (Distilling Industry, 4 a year), *Tejgazdaság* (Dairy Industry, 2 a year).

Országos Erdészeti Egyesület (Hungarian Forestry Association): Budapest, Budakeszi u. 91, 1021; tel. (1) 201-6293; e-mail titkarsag@oee.hu; internet www.oee.hu; f. 1866; forestry, forest industries, environment protection; 5,000 mems; library of 22,000 vols; Pres. PÉTER ZAMBÓ; Sec.-Gen. GERGELY LOMNICZI.

ARCHITECTURE AND TOWN PLANNING

Építéstudományi Egyesület (Scientific Society for Building): Budapest, Fő u. 68, 1027; tel. (1) 201-8416; e-mail info@eptud.org; internet www.eptud.org; f. 1949, current name adopted 1990; 3,500 mems; Pres. Dr GÁBOR SÉNYI; Sec.-Gen. FERENC SEMMELWEIS; publs *Magyar Építőipar* (Hungarian Building Industry, 6 a year, print and online, www.eptud.org/node/19), *Magyar Épületgépészet* (Hungarian Sanitary and Installation Engineering, 10 a year, print and online, www.eptud.org/node/20).

BIBLIOGRAPHY, LIBRARY SCIENCE AND MUSEOLOGY

Magyar Könyvtárosok Egyesülete (Association of Hungarian Librarians): Budapest, Budavári Palota F épület 439 szoba, 1827; tel. (1) 311-8634; e-mail mke@oszk.hu; internet mke.info.hu; f. 1935; decision-making, library education and training; promotes librarianship and information sharing between libraries and librarians; 2,200 mems (incl. institutional mems); Pres. KLÁRA BAKOS; Sec.-Gen. MIKLÓS FEHÉR; publ. *Könyvtárvilág* (online, www.mke.info.hu/konyvtarvilag).

Magyar Levéltárosok Egyesülete (Association of Hungarian Archivists): Budapest, POB 233, 1364; Budapest, Teve u. 3–5, 1139; tel. (1) 298-7616; e-mail mle.titkarsag@gmail.com; internet www.leveltaros.hu; f. 1986; 850 mems; Pres. ÁRPÁD TYEKVICSKA.

EDUCATION

Nemzeti Közművelődési és Közgyűjteményi Intézet (National Institute for Community Culture and Public Collection): Budapest, Corvin tér 8, 1011; tel. (1) 225-6000; e-mail mmi@mmi.hu; internet www.mmi.hu; f. 1951; analyzes social effect of cultural values, changes in content and organization of community education and activities of cultural communities; organizes training for professionals in community education; centre for life-long education, folk art, minority cultures, amateur artistic and leisure pursuits, community devt, arts and crafts; spec. colln on past and present Hungarian folk high schools; 80 mems; library of 60,000 vols; Dir-Gen. MAGDOLNA ZÁVOGYÁN; publ. *SZIN* (6 a year, print and online).

FINE AND PERFORMING ARTS

Magyar Zenei Tanács (Hungarian Music Council): Budapest, Pálya u. 4–6, 1012; tel. (1) 318-4243; e-mail info@hunmusic.hu; internet www.hunmusic.hu; f. 1990; promotes and protects Hungarian music culture and values by social means; fosters devt of social basis of music through the education system and ind. musical activities; 62 mems (incl. 38 civil mem. orgs, 14 associated mem. instns, 10 individual mems); library of 7,400 vols, 13,600 scores, 1,700 CDs, 5,600 records, 800 tapes with 1,400 Hungarian compositions; Pres. ZSÓFIA ZIMÁNYI; Exec. Sec. AGNES PÁLDY; publs *Magyar Zene* (Hungarian Music, 4 a year), *Polifónia* (irregular).

Magyar Zeneművészeti Társaság (Hungarian Music Society): Budapest, Bertalan u. 15, 1111; tel. (30) 351-8383; e-mail emzete@gmail.com; internet www.mzt2008.hu; f. 1987; fosters cultivation of Hungarian music, promotes interests of musical artists, educates young people's musical taste, preserves Hungarian music past and present, performs only Hungarian contemporary pieces in concerts of the Mini-Festival, held in the last weekend of every January; 60 mems; Pres. KLÁRA KÖRMENDI; Sec. ESZTER AGGHÁZY.

Országos Színháztörténeti Múzeum és Intézet (Hungarian Theatre Museum and Institute): Budapest, Krisztina krt. 57, 1013; tel. (1) 375-1184; e-mail oszmi@szinhaziintezet.hu; internet szinhaziintezet.hu; f. 1952, current name adopted 1991; research into theatre history and theory, information on Hungarian drama and theatre for abroad and on world drama and theatre for Hungarian professionals; controls theatrical memorial places and Bajor Gizi Actors' Museum; 38 mems; library of 65,000 vols; Dir Dr PIROSKA ÁCS; publs *Színháztudományi szemle* (1 a year), *Világszínház* (6 a year).

HISTORY, GEOGRAPHY AND ARCHAEOLOGY

Magyar Földmérési, Térképészeti és Távérzékelési Társaság (Hungarian Society for Surveying, Mapping and Remote Sensing): Budapest, Bosnyák tér 5, 1149; tel. (1) 222-5117; e-mail info@mfttt.hu; internet www.mfttt.hu; f. 1956; 1,000 mems; Pres. Dr JÓZSEF ÁDÁM; Sec.-Gen. TIBOR DOBAI; publ. *Geodézia és Kartográfia* (Geodesy and Cartography).

Magyar Irodalomtörténeti Társaság (Society of Hungarian Literary History): Budapest, Piarista köz 1, 1052; tel. (1) 337-7819; e-mail irodalomtortenet@folyoirat.elte.hu; f. 1912; Pres. SÁNDOR IVÁN KOVÁCS; Gen. Sec. MIHÁLY PRAZNOVSZKY; publ. *Irodalomtörténet* (Literary History, 4 a year, print and online, www.irodalomtortenet.hu).

Magyar Történelmi Társulat (Hungarian Historical Society): Budapest, Uri u. 53, 1014; tel. (1) 224-6700; e-mail info@tortenelmitarsulat.hu; internet www.tortenelmitarsulat.hu; f. 1867; Pres. ISTVÁN OROSZ; Gen. Sec. ATTILA PÓK; publ. *Századok* (Centuries, 6 a year, print and online, www.szazadok.hu).

LANGUAGE AND LITERATURE

Alliance Française: Szeged, Dugonics tér 2, 6720; tel. (62) 420-427; e-mail szeged@af.org.hu; internet www.af.org.hu; offers courses and examinations in French language and culture; promotes cultural exchange with France; attached offices in Debrecen, Gyor, Miskolc and Pécs; Pres. Dr CSERNUS SÁNDOR; Dir ERIC BLIN.

British Council: Budapest, Madách Imre u. 13–14, Bldg B, Fl. 4, 1075; tel. (1) 483-2020; e-mail information@britishcouncil.hu; internet www.britishcouncil.hu; teaching centre; offers courses and examinations in English language and British culture; promotes cultural exchange with the UK; Dir JIM MCGRATH; Teaching Centre and Examinations Man. JOHN PARE.

Goethe-Institut: Budapest, Ráday u. 58, Ungarn, 1092; tel. (1) 374-4070; e-mail info@budapest.goethe.org; internet www.goethe.de/budapest; offers courses and examinations in German language and culture; promotes cultural exchange with Germany; library of 13,000 vols; Dir JUTTA GEHRIG.

Hungarian PEN Centre: Budapest, Károlyi Mihály u. 16, 1053; tel. (1) 411-0270; e-mail hungary@penclub.t-online.hu; internet www.pen-international.org/centres/hungarian-centre; f. 1926; 325 mems; Pres. GÉZA SZŐCS; Sec.-Gen. FERENC TOLVAJ.

Instituto Cervantes: Budapest, Vörösmarty u. 32, 1064; tel. (1) 354-3670; e-mail instituto@cervantes.hu; internet budapest.cervantes.es; offers courses and exams in Spanish language and culture and promotes cultural exchange with Spain and Spanish-speaking Latin and Central America; CEO ROSA MARÍA SÁNCHEZ-CASCADO NOGALES.

Magyar Írószövetség (Hungarian Writers' Association): Budapest, POB 546, 1397; Budapest, Bajza u. 18, 1062; tel. (1) 322-8840; e-mail titkarsag@iroszovetseg.hu; internet www.iroszovetseg.hu; f. 1945; 1,100 mems; library of 180,000 vols; Pres. JÁNOS SZENTMÁRTONI; Sec. KINGA ERŐS.

Magyar Nyelvtudományi Társaság (Society of Hungarian Linguistic): Budapest, Múzeum krt. 4/a, 1088; tel. (1) 137-6819; e-mail tarsasag@mnyt.hu; internet www.mnyt.hu; f. 1904; 660 mems; Pres. JENŐ KISS; Gen. Sec. DEZSŐ JUHÁSZ; publ. *Magyar Nyelv* (The Hungarian Language, 4 a year, print and online).

Magyar Ujságirók Országos Szövetsége (Association of Hungarian Journalists): Budapest, Vörösmarty u. 47/a, 1064; tel. (1) 478-9040; e-mail recepcio@muosz.hu; internet www.muosz.hu; f. 1896; 5,000 mems; Pres. KARÓLY TÓTH; Sec. GABRIELLA FEJÉR.

MEDICINE

Magyar Gyógyszerészeti Társaság (Hungarian Society for Pharmaceutical Sciences): Budapest, Gyulai Pál u. 16, 1085; tel. (1) 266-9395; e-mail titkarsag@mgyt.hu; internet www.mgyt.hu; f. 1924; 1,200 mems; Pres. Prof. Dr ÉVA SZÖKŐ; Sec. Dr LÁSZLÓ KÁROLYHÁZY; publs *Acta Pharmaceutica Hungarica* (4 a year, print and online), *Gyógyszerészet* (12 a year, print and online).

Magyar Orvostársaságok és Egyesületek Szövetsége (MOTESZ) (Association of Hungarian Medical Society): Budapest, POB 200, 1364; Budapest, Szigony u. 43, 1083; tel. (1) 312-3807; e-mail info@motesz.hu; internet www.motesz.hu; f. 1966; encourages devt of Hungarian healthcare; promotes interests of mem. socs; 30,000 mems, 127 mem. socs; Pres. Prof. Dr TIBOR ERTL; Dir-Gen. Dr BÉLA SZALMA; publ. *MOTESZ Magazine* (4 a year, print and online).

NATURAL SCIENCES

General

Tudományos Ismeretterjesztő Társulat (Society for the Dissemination of Scientific Knowledge): Budapest, Bródy Sándor u. 16, 1088; tel. (1) 327-8900; e-mail titnet@webinform.hu; internet www.titnet.hu; f. 1841; 17,000 mems; library of 20,000 vols; Dir ESZTER PIRÓTH (acting); publs *Élet és Tudomány* (Life and Science, 52 a year), *Természet Világa* (World of Nature, 12 a year), *Valóság* (Reality, 12 a year).

Biological Sciences

Magyar Biofizikai Társaság (Hungarian Biophysical Society): Budapest, POB 433, 1675; tel. (1) 202-1216; e-mail mbfttitkarsag@gmail.com; internet www.mbft.hu; f. 1961; manages and develops research projects and supports education in the fields of biophysics and in related disciplines; 450 mems; Pres. Dr PÉTER ZÁVODSZKY; Sec.-Gen. Dr GYŐZŐ GARAB; publ. *Magyar Biofizikai Társaság Értesítője* (every 3 years).

Magyar Biokémiai Egyesület (Hungarian Biochemical Society): Debrecen, POB 6, 4012; Debrecen, Nagyerdei krt. 98, 4032; tel. (52) 416-432; e-mail mbke@med.unideb.hu; internet www.mbkegy.hu; f. 1949; 954 mems; Pres. Prof. LÁSZLÓ FÉSÜS; Sec.-Gen. Prof. BEÁTA G. VÉRTESSY; publ. *Biokémia* (4 a year, print and online).

Magyar Biológiai Társaság (Hungarian Biological Society): Budapest, Bródy Sandor u. 16, 1088; tel. (1) 225-3273; e-mail mbt@mail.tvnet.hu; internet www.mbt.mtesz.hu; f. 1952; 1,500 mems; Pres. Dr DESI SURÁNYI; Sec.-Gen. Dr CHARLES PENKSZA; publs *Állattani Közlemények* (1 a year, print and online, www.mbt-ak.mtesz.hu), *Antropológiai Közlemények* (1 a year, print and online, www.mbt.mtesz.hu/034anthropologia_kozlemenyek/index.html), *Botanikai Közlemények* (1 a year, print and online, www.mbt-bk.mtesz.hu), *Természetvédelmi Közlemények* (1 a year, print and online, www.mbtktv.mtesz.hu/kiadvanyok.html).

Magyar Biomassza Társaság (Hungarian Biomass Association): Sopron, Ady Endre u. 5, 9400; tel. (99) 357-480; e-mail mbmt@asys.hu; f. 1991; Pres. Prof. Dr JENŐ KOVÁCS; Gen. Sec. Prof. Dr BÉLA MAROSVÖLGYI.

Magyar Rovartani Társaság (Hungarian Entomological Society): Budapest, Baross u. 13, 1088; tel. (1) 267-7100; e-mail magyarrovartanitarsasag@gmail.com; internet www.magyarrovartanitarsasag.hu; f. 1910; 408 mems; Pres. Dr KÁROLY VIG; Sec. GELLÉRT PUSKÁS; publ. *Folia Entomologica Hungarica / Rovartani Közlemények* (1 a year).

Mathematical Sciences

Bolyai János Matematikai Társulat (János Bolyai Mathematical Society): Budapest, Falk Miksa u. 12.I/4, H-1055; tel. (1) 225-8410; e-mail bolyai.tarsulat@renyi.mta.hu; internet www.bolyai.hu; f. 1891; 2,000 mems; Pres. GYULA KATONA; Gen. Sec. ANDRÁS RECSKI; publs *Abacus* (9 a year), *Alkalmazott Matematikai Lapok* (Gazette for Applied Mathematics, 2 a year), *Combinatorica* (6 a year), *Középiskolai Matematikai Lapok* (Mathematical Gazette for Secondary Schools, 9 a year), *Matematikai Lapok* (Mathematical Gazette, 2 a year), *Periodica Mathematica Hungarica* (2 a year).

Physical Sciences

Eötvös Loránd Fizikai Társulat (Roland Eötvös Physical Society): Budapest, POB 49, 1525; Budapest, Konkoly Thege M. u. 29–33, 1121; tel. (1) 201-8682; e-mail elft@elft.hu; internet www.elft.hu; f. 1891; supports and facilitates studies and research in physics and astronomy; 1,800 mems; Pres. NORBERT KROÓ; Gen.-Sec. JENŐ KÜRTI; publ. *Fizikai Szemle* (Physics Review, 12 a year).

Hungarian Association for Geo-Information (HUNAGI): Budapest, Pethényi ú. 11B, 1122; tel. (30) 415-8276; e-mail hunagi@hunagi.hu; internet www.hunagi.hu; f. 1994; facilitates availability, accessibility and useability of GI; strengthens visibility of Hungarian achievements in the field of Earth Observation and Spatial Data Infrastructures; maintains institutional links with European and Global orgs (EUROGI, GSDI and ISDE); serves as SDIC in the context of European Directive implementations (INSPIRE, PSI); organizes thematic confs, project workshops; 64 govt agencies, non-governmental orgs, academic instns and private sector mems; library of 200 vols, archived domestic and int. publs and leaflets circulated since early 1990s in the subjects GIS, Remote Sensing; Pres. and Chair. ZSOLT BARKÓCZI; Sec.-Gen. Dr GÁBOR REMETEY-FÜLÖPP; Sec. ZOLTÁN MITNYAN; publs *Geodézia és Kartográfia*, *Geomatika*.

Magyar Asztronautikai Társaság (Hungarian Astronautical Society): Budapest, Ipari park u. 10, 1044; tel. (30) 585-0867; e-mail mant@mant.hu; internet www.mant.hu; f. 1956; raises public awareness about space exploration and uses; organizes lectures, confs, youth forums, summer space camps, issues periodicals, releases media material; 300 mems; Pres. JÁNOS SOLYMOSI; Gen. Sec. Dr LÁSZLÓ BACSÁRDI; publ. *Űrtan Évkönyv* (1 a year, in Hungarian).

Magyar Geofizikusok Egyesülete (Association of Hungarian Geophysicists): Budapest, Kolumbusz u. 17–23, 1145; tel. (1) 201-9815; e-mail mageof@mageof.hu; internet www.mageof.hu; f. 1954; monitors and assists training of experts and maintains contacts with univ. depts; organizes presentations, seminars, confs, symposia and discussions; 650 mems; Pres. Dr ISTVÁN KÉSMÁRKY; Sec. ATTILA CSABA KOVÁCS; publ. *Magyar Geofizika* (Hungarian Geophysics, 4 a year).

Magyar Hidrológiai Társaság (Hungarian Hydrological Society): Budapest, Üllői ú. 25, Fl. 4, Room 433–437, 1091; tel. (1) 201-7655; e-mail titkarsag@hidrologia.hu; internet www.hidrologia.hu; f. 1917; promotes and enables advanced knowledge and experience in the field of water science and technology among professionals; 5,000 mems; Pres. Dr LAJOS SZLÁVIK; Sec.-Gen. ZOLTÁN KLING; publs *Hidrológiai Közlöny* (Hydrological Journal, 6 a year), *Hidrológiai Tájékoztató* (Circular on Hydrology, 1 a year).

Magyarhoni Földtani Társulat (Hungarian Geological Society): Budapest, POB 61, 1255; Budapest, Csalogány u. 12. I/1, 1051; tel. (1) 201-9129; e-mail mft@mft.t-online.hu; internet www.foldtan.hu; f. 1848; formation and training of geoscientists; organizes meetings, workshops, confs, study tours, itinerary meetings and congresses; regional brs in Budapest, Central and N Transdanubia, Great Hungarian Plain, N Hungary, S Transdanubia; 1,040 mems; Pres. Dr CSABA BAKSA; Sec.-Gen. Dr TIBOR CSERNY.

Magyar Karszt-és Barlangkutató Társulat (Hungarian Speleological Society): Budapest, Pusztaszeri u. 35, 1025; tel. (1) 346-0495; e-mail mkbt@t-online.hu; internet www.barlang.hu; f. 1910; promotes discovery, registration and documentation of the karstfields and caves; 1,000 mems; library of 5,000 vols; Pres. Dr SZABOLCS LEÉL-ÖSSY; Sec.-Gen. ATTILA KISS; publ. *Karszt és Barlang* (with summaries in English, 1 a year, print and online, www.barlang.hu/pages/p/kbindex.htm).

Magyar Kémikusok Egyesülete (Hungarian Chemical Society): Budapest, 1 Kerulet, Hattyú u, 16, Fl. 8, 1015; tel. (1) 201-6883; e-mail mail@mke.org.hu; internet www.mke.org.hu; f. 1907; 2,000 mems; Pres. Dr LIVIA SARKADI; Sec.-Gen. Dr ATTILA KOVÁCS; publs *Középiskolai Kémiai Lapok* (Secondary School Chemical Papers, 5 a year, print and online (www.kokel.mke.org.hu)), *Magyar Kémiai Folyóirat* (Hungarian Journal of Chemistry, 12 a year, print and online (www.mkf.mke.org.hu)), *Magyar Kémikusok Lapja* (Hungarian Chemical Journal, 12 a year, print and online (www.mkl.mke.org.hu)), *Membrántechnika és Ipari Biotechnológia* (Membrane Technology and Industrial Biotechnology, irregular).

Magyar Meteorológiai Társaság (Hungarian Meteorological Society): Budapest, Kitaibel P. u. 1, 1024; tel. (1) 346-4780; e-mail titkarsag@mettars.hu; internet www.mettars.hu; f. 1925; 480 mems; Pres. Dr ZOLTÁN DUNKEL; Gen. Sec. Dr ÁKOS NÉMETH; publ. *Légkör* (4 a year, print and online, www.mettars.hu/legkor).

Optikai, Akusztikai Film-és Színháztechnikai Tudományos Egyesület (Scientific Society for Optics, Acoustics, Motion Pictures and Theatre Technology): Budapest, Bartók Béla út 15A, Fl. 15, 1114; tel. (1) 783-4781; e-mail info@opakfi.hu; internet www.opakfi.hu; f. 1933; optics, acoustics, noise reduction, fine mechanics, theatre and motion pictures technology, scientific programmes, education, research and devt managment; keeps int. connections; organizing nat. and int. scientific congresses, seminars; cooperation with Hungarian Acad. of Science, different Hungarian univs, industrial research and devt instns; 1,500 mems; Pres. Dr GÁBOR LUPKOVICS; Gen. Sec. Dr FERENC KVOJKA; publs *Akusztikai Szemle* (Acoustics Journal, 4 a year), *Elektrónikai Technológia-Mikrotechnika* (Electronic Technology-Microtechnics), *Kép és Hangtechnika* (Picture and Audio Techniques).

PHILOSOPHY AND PSYCHOLOGY

Magyar Filozófiai Társaság (Hungarian Philosophical Association): Szeged, Petőfi Sándor sgt. 30–34, 6722; tel. (62) 546-652; e-mail laczkos@bibl.u-szeged.hu; internet www.mft-hps.hu; f. 1901, reorganized 1989; cultivates and promotes Hungarian philosophical traditions; popularizes philosophical culture; 400 mems; Pres. BÉLA BACSO; Hon. Sec. SÁNDOR LASCKÓ.

Magyar Pszichológiai Társaság (Hungarian Psychological Association): Budapest, POB 50, 1241; Budapest, Izabella u. 46, 1064; tel. (1) 461 4521; e-mail mpt@ppk.elte.hu; internet www.mpt.hu; f. 1928; 1,293 mems; Pres. ATTILA OLÁH; Sec.-Gen. ANDRÁS VARGHA; publ. *Magyar Pszichológiai Szemle* (Hungarian Psychological Review).

RELIGION, SOCIOLOGY AND ANTHROPOLOGY

Magyar Néprajzi Társaság (Hungarian Ethnographical Society): Budapest, Kossuth Lajos tér 12, 1055; tel. (1) 269-1272; e-mail neprajzitarsasag@gmail.com; internet www.neprajzitarsasag.hu; f. 1889; 1,340 mems; Pres. SÁNDOR BODÓ; Sec.-Gen. LAJOS KEMECSI; publ. *Etnographia* (Ethnography, 4 a year, print and online).

Magyar Szociológiai Társaság (Hungarian Sociological Association): Budapest, Országház u. 30, 1014; tel. (1) 624-7718; e-mail mszt@szociologia.hu; internet www.szociologia.hu; f. 1978; confs, debates, discussions for domestic and int. researchers in order to facilitate and maintain int. sociological partnerships; follows nat. and int. sociological research and its results; cooperates with the instns of science and education to discuss training of sociologists; 628 mems; Pres. Prof. GYÖRGY CSEPELI; Sec.-Gen. VERONIKA PAKSI; publs *Review of Sociology* (2 a year, print and online), *Szociológiai Szemle* (3 a year, print and online, www.szociologia.hu/page.php?item=1390).

TECHNOLOGY

Bőr-, Cipő-, és Bőrfeldolgozóipari Tudományos Egyesület (Scientific Society of the Leather, Shoe and Allied Industries): Budapest, Baross u. 39, 1047; tel. (1) 272-0011; e-mail bimeo@bimeo.hu; f. 1930; Pres. Dr FERENC SCHMÉL; publ. *Bőr és Cipőtechnika* (Leather and Shoe News, 6 a year).

Energiagazdálkodási Tudományos Egyesület (Scientific Society of Energy Economics): Budapest, POB 451, 1372; Budapest, Üllői u. 25. IV/421, 1091; tel. (1) 353-2751; e-mail titkarsag@ete-net.hu; internet www.ete-net.hu; f. 1949; 3,000 mems; Pres. Dr ISTVÁN BAKÁCS; Sec.-Gen. Dr LÁSZLÓ MOLNÁR; publ. *Energiagazdálkodás* (Energetics, 12 a year, print and online, www.ete-net.hu).

Faipari Tudományos Egyesület (Scientific Society of the Timber Industry): Budapest, Fő u. 68, 1027; tel. (1) 201-9929; e-mail fate.bp@freemail.hu; f. 1950; 1,800 mems; Pres. Dr TIBOR HORVÁTH; publ. *Faipar* (Timber Industry).

Gépipari Tudományos Egyesület (GTE) (Scientific Society for Mechanical Engineers): Budapest, POB 433, 1371; Budapest, Fő u. 68, 1027; tel. (1) 202-0656; e-mail mail@gteportal.eu; internet www.gteportal.eu; f. 1949; sciences of mechanical engineering, dissemination of technical culture, assisting technical and economic devt of Hungary; 4,800 mems; library of 1,500 vols; Pres. Prof. Dr JÁNOS TAKÁCS; Sec.-Gen. Dr LAJOS BORBÁS; publs *Gép* (Machine, 12 a year), *Gépgyártás* (Production Engineering, 12 a year), *Gépipar* (Machinery, 12 a year), *Járművek* (Vehicles, 12 a year), *Műanyag és Gumi* (Plastics and Rubber, 12 a year).

Hírközlési és Informatikai Tudományos Egyesület (Scientific Association for Infocommunication): Budapest, Kossuth Lajos tér 6–8, 1055; tel. (1) 353-1027; e-mail info@hte.hu; internet www.hte.hu; f. 1949; organizes confs, discussions, seminars, technical exhibitions; postgraduate courses; recommendations for official organs, public discussion and criticism of technical, economic, scientific and educational matters; engineering activities; 2,500 mems; Pres. Prof. Dr GÁBOR HUSZTY; Sec.-Gen. ISTVÁN BARTOLITS; publ. *Híradástechnika* (Infocommunications Journal, 4 a year, in English and Hungarian, print and online, www.hiradastechnika.hu).

Közlekedéstudományi Egyesület (Hungarian Scientific Association for Transport): Budapest, Kossuth Lajos tér 6–8, 1055; tel. (1) 353-2005; e-mail info@ktenet.hu; internet www.ktenet.hu; f. 1949; 7,200 mems (incl. 7,000 individual mems, 200 mem. orgs); Pres. Dr JÁNOS FÓNAGY; Sec.-Gen. Dr JÁNOS TÓTH; publs *Közlekedéstudományi Szemle* (Transportation Science Review), *Közúti és Mélyépitési Szemle* (Civil Engineering Review), *Városi Közlekedés* (Urban Transport).

Magyar Elektrotechnikai Egyesület (Hungarian Electrotechnical Association): Budapest, Madách Imre u. 5. Fl. 3, 1075; tel. (1) 353-0117; e-mail mee@mee.hu; internet www.mee.hu; f. 1900; promotes academic, educational and practical fields of electrotechnics; 6,206 mems (6,000 mems, 150 supporting mems, 56 regional and co orgs); Pres. Dr PÉTER GÖRGEY; Sec. MIKLÓS DANYEK; publ. *Electrotechnika* (Electrical Engineering, 12 a year).

Magyar Iparjogvédelmi és Szerzői Jogi Egyesület (Hungarian Association for the Protection of Industrial Property and Copyright): Budapest, Kossuth Lajos tér 6–8, 1055; tel. (1) 153-1661; e-mail mie@t-online.hu; internet www.mie.org.hu; f. 1962; organizes confs, lectures, seminars in areas of legal protection of technical and intellectual works; disseminates information about intellectual property rights through its mems in secondary and high schools; 2,250 mems; Pres. Dr VILMOS BACHER; Sec.-Gen. Dr ISTVÁN GÖDÖLLE.

Méréstechnikai és Automatizálási Tudományos Egyesület (Scientific Society for Measurement, Automation and Informatics): Budapest, Kossuth Lajos tér 6–8, III/318, 1055; tel. (1) 332-9571; e-mail mate@mate-net.hu; internet www.mate-net.hu; f. 1952; organizes int. confs, symposia, training courses and workshops; 1,075 mems, 65 affiliated orgs; Pres. Dr LÁSZLÓ LUDVIG; Sec.-Gen. BALÁZS BODNÁR; publ. *Mérés és Automatika* (Measurement and Automation).

Neumann János Számitógép-tudományi Társaság (John von Neumann Computer Society): Budapest, Báthori u. 16, 1054; tel. (1) 472-2730; e-mail titkarsag@njszt.hu; internet www.njszt.hu; f. 1968; promotes study, devt and application of computer sciences; 2,400 mems (incl. 2, 300 individual mems, 100 corporate mems); library of 3,000 vols; Pres. Dr FERENC FRIEDLER; Man. Dir ISTVÁN ALFÖLDI.

Országos Magyar Bányászati és Kohászati Egyesület (Hungarian Mining and Metallurgical Society): Budapest, Október 6 u. 7, 1051; tel. (1) 201-7337; e-mail ombke@ombkenet.hu; internet www.ombkenet.hu; f. 1892; promotes scientific, technical, economic devt of mining and metallurgy; 4,000 mems; library of 1,500 vols; Pres. Dr LAJOS NAGY; Sec.-Gen. Dr KÁROLY LENGYEL; publs *Bányászat* (Mining, 6 a year, print and online (www.ombkenet.hu/bkl/banyaszat.htm)), *Kohászat* (Metallurgy, 6 a year, print and online (www.ombkenet.hu/bkl/kohaszat.htm)), *Kőolaj és Földgáz* (Oil and Gas, irregular, print and online (www.ombkenet.hu/bkl/koolaj.htm)).

Papír- és Nyomdaipari Műszaki Egyesület (Technical Association of the Hungarian Paper and Printing Industry): Budapest, Fő u. 68, 1027; Budapest, Tahi u. 53–59, 1134; tel. (1) 783-0347; e-mail pnyme@pnyme.hu; internet www.pnyme.hu; f. 1948; 1,800 individual mems, 130 corporate mems; Pres. Dr ENDRE FÁBIÁN; Dir SÁNDOR PESTI; publs *Magyar Grafika* (Hungarian Printers and Graphic Designers, 6 a year, print and online (www.mgonline.hu)), *Papíripar* (Paper Industry, 6 a year, print and online).

Szervezési és Vezetési Tudományos Társaság (Society for Organization and Management Science): Budapest, Orbánhegyi u. 14, 1126; tel. (1) 202-1083; e-mail szvt@szvt.hu; internet www.szvt.hu; f. 1970; 5,000 mems; Pres. Dr PÉTER SVÁB; publ. *Ipar-Gazdaság* (Industrial Economy, 12 a year).

Szilikátipari Tudományos Egyesület (Scientific Society of the Silicate Industry): Budapest, Bécsi u. 122–124, 1034; tel. (1) 201-9360; e-mail info@szte.org.hu; internet www.szte.org.hu; f. 1949; promotes technical, scientific and economic progress of the silicate industry; supports professional devt and public activity of the technical and economic experts; organizes scientific confs; 7 divs: concrete, cement, fine ceramics, stone and gravel, insulating materials, brick and tile, glass; 2,300 mems; library of 2,500 vols; Pres. Dr János Szépvölgyi; Sec.-Gen. István Asztalos; publ. *Építőanyag* (Building Materials, 4 a year, print and online).

Textilipari Műszaki és Tudományos Egyesület (Hungarian Society of Textile Technology and Science): Budapest, Thököly u. 58–60, 1146; tel. (1) 201-8782; e-mail info@tmte.hu; internet www.tmte.hu; f. 1948; 1,300 mems; Pres. Dr Pál Pataki; Gen. Man. Dr Katalin Lakatosné Győri; publ. *Magyar Textiltechnika* (Hungarian Textile Engineering, 6 a year).

Research Institutes

AGRICULTURE, FISHERIES AND VETERINARY SCIENCE

Állattenyésztési és Takarmányozási Kutatóintézet (Research Institute for Animal Breeding and Nutrition): Herceghalom, Gesztenyés u. 1, 2053; tel. (23) 319-133; e-mail atk@atk.hu; internet www.atk.hu; f. 1896 as Állatélettani és Takarmányozási Kísérleti Állomást, reorganized and current name adopted 1991; basic and applied research into genetics, large animal breeding, microbiology, nutrition, nutrition biology and reproductive biology; library of 4,800 vols; Dir-Gen. Prof. Dr József Rátky; publ. *Állattenyésztés és Takarmányozás* (Animal Production, 6 a year, with English summaries).

Gabonakutató Nonprofit Közhasznú Kft. (Cereal Research Non-Profit Ltd.): Szeged, POB 391, 6701; Szeged, Alsó kikötő sor 9, 6726; tel. (62) 435-235; e-mail info@gabonakutato.hu; internet www.gabonakutato.hu; f. 1924; research into cultivation of wheat, barley, oats, maize, triticale, sunflower, linseed, winter rapeseed, red clover, soybean, sorghum, Sudan grass, millet; breeding, agronomy, seed trading, dietetic food; library of 12,000 vols; Dir László Szilágyi; Librarian Lajosné Buza; publ. *Cereal Research Communications* (4 a year).

Magyar Tejgazdasági Kisérleti Intézet (Hungarian Dairy Research Institute): Mosonmagyaróvár, Lucsony u. 24, 9200; tel. (96) 215-711; e-mail mtki@mtki.hu; internet www.mtki.hu; f. 1903; brs in Budapest and Pécs; scientific research into raw materials, technology, engineering, chemistry, microbiology, economics; library of 5,700 vols; Dir Dr András Unger.

Magyar Tudományos Akadémia, Agrártudományi Kutatóközpont, Állatorvostudományi Intézet (Institute for Veterinary Medical Research, Centre for Agricultural Research, Hungarian Academy of Sciences): Budapest, POB 18, 1581; Budapest, Hungária krt. 21, 1143; tel. (1) 252-2455; e-mail titkarsag@vmri.hu; internet www.vmri.hu; f. 1949; research in infectious and parasitic diseases of domestic and wild animals (virology, bacteriology, fish parasitology); library of 6,750 vols; Dir Dr Tibor Magyar (acting); publ. *Acta Veterinaria Hungarica* (4 a year, print and online, www.vmri.hu/~acta).

Magyar Tudományos Akadémia Agrártudományi Kutatóközpont Mezőgazdasági Intézet (Agricultural Institute, Centre for Agricultural Research, Hungarian Academy of Sciences): Martonvásár. Brunszvik u. 2, 2462; tel. (22) 569-500; e-mail atk@agrar.mta.hu; internet www.mgki.hu; f. 1949; research into plant breeding, genetics, physiology and planting of maize and wheat; library of 16,000 vols; Dir Zoltán Bedő; publs *Acta Agronomica Hungarica* (4 a year), *Martonvásár* (2 a year).

Magyar Tudományos Akadémia Agrártudományi Kutatóközpont Növényvédelmi Intézet (Plant Protection Institute, Hungarian Academy of Sciences): Budapest II, Herman Ottó u. 15, POB 102, 1525; tel. (1) 487-7500; e-mail bbar@nki.hu; internet www.nki.hu; f. 1880 as State Phylloxera Research Station, reorganized 1950; research into plant diseases, insect pests, pesticide chemistry and plant biochemistry, biotechnology, virology; 100 mems; library of 20,000 vols; Dir Dr Levente Kiss.

Magyar Tudományos Akadémia Agrártudományi Kutatóközpont Talajtani és Agrokémiai Intézet (Institute for Soil Sciences and Agricultural Chemistry, Centre for Agricultural Research, Hungarian Academy of Sciences): Budapest, POB 102, 1525; Budapest, Herman Ottó u. 15, 1022; tel. (1) 212-2265; e-mail lehoczky@rissac.hu; internet www.mta-taki.hu; f. 1949; research into soil physics, chemistry, geography and cartography, reclamation of salt-affected and sandy soils, irrigation, conservation, fertilization, soil mineralogy, soil microbiology, soil ecology, recultivation; library of 27,000 vols; Dir Prof. Dr Éva Lehoczky; publ. *Agrokémia és Talajtan* (Agrochemistry and Soil Science, 2 a year).

Szőlészeti és Borászati Kutató Intézet, Kecskemét (Research Institute for Viticulture and Oenology): Kecskemét-Miklóstelep, Úrihegy 5/A, POB 25, 6000; tel. (76) 494-888; e-mail titkarsag@szbkik.hu; f. 1898; viticulture, oenology, economy; library of 7,200 vols; Dir Dr Ernő Péter Botos; publ. *Bor és Piac* (12 a year).

Takarmánytermesztési Kutató Intézet (Feed Crops Research Institute): Iregszemcse, Napraforgo u. 1, 7095; tel. (74) 481-127; internet www.ke.hu/menu/370/369; f. 1936; attached to Kaposvár Univ.; research in breeding, maintaining and devt of production of sunflower and leguminous plants; develops gene banks and conducts resistance testing experiments; Dir Sándor Baranyai.

VITUKI Környezetvédelmi és Vízgazdálkodási Kutató Intézet Non-Profit Kft (VITUKI Environmental and Water Management Research Institute Non-Profit Ltd): Budapest, POB 27, 1453; Budapest, Kvassay Jenő u. 1, 1095; tel. (1) 215-6140; e-mail vituki@vituki.hu; internet www.vituki.hu; f. 1952; basic and applied research associated with hydrological data collection, processing, storage, information; hydrology of groundwater, karst water, regional soil moisture control; hydromechanics of hydraulic structures; pollution and quality control of water; hydrological and hydraulic problems in agricultural water management (drainage, irrigation); air pollution control; odour and noise control; remediation; waste management; library of 13,000 vols; Man. Dir Anita Csúzy; publs *Hydrological Yearbook of Hungary* (1 a year), *VITUKI Proceedings* (1 a year).

BIBLIOGRAPHY, LIBRARY SCIENCE AND MUSEOLOGY

Könyvtári Intézet (Hungarian Library Institute): Budapest, Budavári Palota F-épület, 1827; tel. (1) 224-3788; e-mail kint@oszk.hu; internet ki.oszk.hu; f. 2000, fmrly Centre for Library Science and Methodology (f. 1959); attached to Nat. Széchényi Library; research and devt, promotion of inter-library cooperation, reading devt, public relations, training and library documentation services; library science; library of 110,000 vols; Dir Katalin Bánkeszi; publs *A Magyar Könyvtári Szakirodalom Bibliográfiája* (Bibliography of Hungarian Library Literature, 2 a year), *Humántudományi Tanulmányok és Cikkek Adatbzisa (HUMANUS)* (online database of nat. and int. articles on literature, linguistics and history, www.oszk.hu/humanus), *Könyv Könyvtár Könyvtáros* (Books Library Librarian, 12 a year, print and online, ki.oszk.hu/3k), *Könyvtári Figyelő* (Library Review, in Hungarian with summaries in English, 4 a year, print and online, ki.oszk.hu/kf).

ECONOMICS, LAW AND POLITICS

Magyar Tudományos Akadémia Közgazdaság-és Regionális Tudományi Kutatóközpont Közgazdaság-tudományi Intézet (Institute of Economics, Research Centre for Economic and Regional Studies, Hungarian Academy of Sciences): Budapest, Budaörsi u. 45, 1112; tel. (1) 309-2652; e-mail titkarsag@econ.core.hu; internet econ.core.hu; f. 1954; research into macroeconomics, growth and economic policy, labour economics and human resources, public and institutional economics, microeconomics and sectoral economics, int. economics, mathematical economics, history of economic thought, agricultural economics and rural devt, economics of technological change; empirical industrial org.; globalization, EU-integration and convergence; public economics and public policies; economics of education; library of 45,000 vols, 124 periodicals; Dir-Gen. Prof. Károly Fazekas; publs *Budapesti Munkagazdaságtani Füzetek* (Budapest Working Papers on the Labour Market, in English and Hungarian, 9 or 10 a year), *Műhelytanulmányok* (Discussion Papers, in English and Hungarian, 9 or 10 a year), *Munkaerőpiaci tükör* (Labour Market Yearbook, with chapters in English), *Munkatudományi Kutatások* (Labour Research Volumes, 1 a year), *Verseny és Szabályozás* (Competition and Regulation, in Hungarian, 12 a year).

Magyar Tudományos Akadémia Közgazdaság- és Regionális Tudományi Kutatóközpont Világgazdasági Intézet (Institute for World Economics, Research Centre for Economic and Regional Studies of the Hungarian Academy of Sciences): Budapest, Budaörsi u. 45, 1112; tel. (1) 309-2643; e-mail vki@krtk.mta.hu; internet www.vki.hu; f. 1973; research into world economics; library of 102,000 vols; Dir Dr Károly Fazekas; publs *Kihívások* (Challenges, irregular), *Műhelytanulmányok* (Workshop Studies, irregular), *Working Papers* (in English, irregular).

Magyar Tudományos Akadémia Társadalomtudományi Kutatóközpont Jogtudományi Intézete (Institute for Legal Studies of the Hungarian Academy of Sciences): Budapest, Országház u. 30, 1014; tel. (1) 355-7384; e-mail argyelan@jog.mta.hu; internet www.mta-jti.hu; f. 1949; depts of legal theory, int. law, constitutional and admin. law, civil law, criminal law, comparative law, human rights; library of 52,000 vols, 70 periodicals; Dir Prof. Dr Vanda Lamm; publs *Acta Juridica Hungarica* (2 a year), *Állam- és Jogtudomány* (2 a year), *Jogtudományi Közlöny* (11 a year), *Föld-rész*.

Magyar Tudományos Akadémia Társadalomtudományi Kutatóközpont Politikai Tudományok Intézet (Institute for Political Science, Centre for Social Sciences, Hungarian Academy of Sciences): Budapest, Országház u. 30, 1014; tel. (1) 224-6700; e-mail titkarsag@tk.mta.hu; internet www.mtapti.hu; f. 1991; study of political systems, party politics, nat. and local govt, political culture, elections, problems of integration with the EU, migration, security policy and NATO; library of 43,000 vols; Dir Prof. Dr ANDRÁS KÖRÖSÉNYI; publ. *Politikatudományi Szemle* (Review of Political Science, 4 a year, in Hungarian, print and online).

Teleki László Alapítvány (László Teleki Foundation): Budapest, POB 615, 1539; tel. (1) 224-3832; e-mail telekialapitvany@gmail.com; internet www.telekialapitvany.hu; f. 1999; prepares analytical material and information for foreign policy instns; research on theoretical issues of int. relations; organizes round-table confs, seminars, lectures; reference library; Dir Prof. GYÖRGY GRANASZTÓI; publs *Külügyi Szemec* (4 a year in Hungarian, 2 a year in English), *Reyio* (4 a year in Hungarian, 1 a year in English).

EDUCATION

Felsóoktatási Kutatóintézet (Hungarian Institute for Higher Educational Research): Budapest, Ajtósi Dürer sor 19–21, 1146; tel. (1) 221-0365; e-mail oktataskutato@ella.hu; internet www.hier.iif.hu; f. 1981, current name adopted 2004; applied social research and postgraduate training in school education, higher education and vocational education; library of 23,000 vols; Dir Dr ILONA LISKO; publs *Educatio* (4 a year, print and online, www.hier.iif.hu/hu/educatio.php), *Kutatás Közben* (Research Papers, 6 a year).

FINE AND PERFORMING ARTS

Bartók Béla Zeneművészeti Intézete (Bela Bartók Music Institute): Miskolc-Egyetemváros, POB 1, 3515; tel. (46) 343-800; e-mail zennoemi@uni-miskolc.hu; internet www.uni-miskolc.hu/~bbziweb; f. 1901; attached to Univ. of Miskolc; pedagogical institute, trains teachers of orchestral music; Dir Prof. Dr ZOLTÁN SÁNDOR.

Magyar Tudományos Akadémia Bölcsészettudományi Kutatóközpont Művészettörténeti Intézet (Institute for Art History, Research Centre for the Humanities, Hungarian Academy of Sciences): Budapest, POB 9, 1250; Budapest, Országház u. 30, 1014; tel. (1) 224-6700; e-mail arthist@arthist.mta.hu; internet www.arthist.mta.hu; f. 1969; research on Hungarian art since 10th century; library of 47,000 vols; Dir Dr JÓZSEF SISA; publ. *Ars Hungarica* (4 a year).

Magyar Tudományos Akadémia Bölcsészettudományi Kutatóközpont Zenetudományi Intézet (Institute for Musicology, Research Centre for the Humanities, Hungarian Academy of Sciences): Budapest, POB 28, 1250; Budapest, Táncsics Mihály u. 7, 1014; tel. (1) 356-6858; e-mail zti@btk.mta.hu; internet www.zti.hu; f. 1961; incorporates Bartók Archives, Museum of Music History, and depts of Folk Dances, Folk Music, History of Early Music, History of Hungarian Music; 100,000 recorded melodies; library of 150,000 vols; Dir Dr PÁL RICHTER; Sec. PÉTER HALÁSZ; publ. *Studia Musicologica* (4 a year).

HISTORY, GEOGRAPHY AND ARCHAEOLOGY

Magyar Tudományos Akadémia Bölcsészettudományi Kutatóközpont Régészeti Intézete (Research Centre for the Humanities, Hungarian Academy of Sciences, Institute of Archaeology): Budapest, Úri u. 49, 1014; tel. (1) 356-4567; e-mail konyvtar@archeo.mta.hu; internet www.archeo.mta.hu; f. 1958; research in archaeology and associated sciences; 58 mems; library of 73,911 vols; Dir Prof. CSANÁD BÁLINT; publs *Antaeus* (yearbook, in German and English), *Magyarország Régészeti Topográfiája* (Archaeological Topography of Hungary), *Varia Archaeologica Hungarica* (in foreign languages, irregular).

Magyar Tudományos Akadémia Bölcsészettudományi Kutatóközpont Történettudományi Intézete (Institute of Historical Science, Research Centre for Humanities of the Hungarian Academy of Sciences): Budapest, POB 9, 1250; Budapest, Úri u. 53, 1014; tel. (1) 224-6755; e-mail titkarsag@tti.hu; internet www.tti.hu; f. 1949; 6 depts of Hungarian history and comparative European history, one dept of documentation and bibliography; library of 100,000 vols; Dir PÁL FODOR; publs *Történelmi Szemle* (The Historical Review, 4 a year), *Világtörténet* (World History, 4 a year).

Magyar Tudományos Akadémia Csillagászati és Földtudományi Kutatóközpont Földrajztudományi Intézet (Geographical Institute, Research Centre for Astronomy and Earth Sciences of the Hungarian Academy of Sciences): 1112 Budapest, Budaörsi u. 45; tel. (1) 309-2600; e-mail kocsisk@mtafki.hu; internet www.mtafki.hu; f. 1950; research in physical and human geography; library of 71,967 vols; Dir Dr KÁROLY KOCSIS; publs *Földrajzi Tanulmányok, Geographical Abstracts from Hungary, Studies in Geography in Hungary*.

Magyar Tudományos Akadémia Közgazdaság és Regionális Tudományi Kutatóközpont Regionális Kutatások Intézete (Institute of Regional Studies, Research Centre for Economic and Regional Studies, Hungarian Academy of Sciences): Pécs, POB 199, 7601; Pécs, Papnövelde u. 22, 7621; tel. (72) 523-800; e-mail rkk@rkk.hu; internet www.rkk.hu; f. 1943; research into economics, ethnography, geography, govt, history, regional planning and, sociology; 60 mems; library of 44,700 vols; Dir Prof. Dr LÁSZLÓ FARAGÓ; Scientific Sec. SZILÁRD RÁCZ; publs *Alföldi Tanulmányok* (irregular), *Tér és Társadalom* (4 a year).

LANGUAGE AND LITERATURE

Magyar Tudományos Akadémia Bölcsészettudományi Kutatóközpont Irodalomtudományi Intézet (Institute for Literary Studies of the Hungarian Academy of Sciences): Budapest, Ménesi u. 11–13, 1118; tel. (1) 279-2760; e-mail iti@iti.mta.hu; internet www.iti.mta.hu; f. 1956; research in Hungarian and world literature; library of 170,000 vols; Dir Dr GÁBOR KECSKEMÉTI; publs *Helikon* (4 a year), *Irodalomtörténeti Füzetek* (studies, irregular), *Irodalomtörténeti Közlemények* (6 a year, print and online, itk.iti.mta.hu), *Literatura* (4 a year, print and online, www.iti.mta.hu/literatura.html), *Magyar Könyvszemle*, *Neohelicon* (2 a year).

Magyar Tudományos Akadémia Nyelvtudományi Intézet (Research Institute for Linguistics of the Hungarian Academy of Sciences): Budapest, POB 360, 1394; Budapest IV, Benczúr u. 33, 1068; tel. (1) 321-4830; e-mail linginst@nytud.mta.hu; internet www.nytud.hu; f. 1949; research in corpus linguistics, historical linguistics, lexicography, neuro- and sociolinguistics, phonetics, theoretical linguistics; library of 45,000 vols; Dir Prof. Dr ISTVÁN KENESEI; publs *Acta Linguistica Hungarica* (4 a year), *Magyar Fonetikai Füzetek* (Hungarian Papers in Phonetics, 2 a year), *Nyelvtudományi Közlemények* (Linguistic Publications, 2 a year).

MEDICINE

Magyar Tudományos Akadémia Kísérleti Orvostudományi Kutatóintézet (Institute of Experimental Medicine of the Hungarian Academy of Sciences): Budapest, POB 67, 1450; Budapest, Szigony u. 43, 1083; tel. (1) 210-9400; e-mail info@koki.hu; internet www.koki.hu; f. 1952; basic biomedical research in neuroscience, incl. studies on neurotransmission, learning and memory, behaviour, ischaemic and epileptic brain damage, central and peripheral control of hormone secretion; library of 18,500 vols; Dir Prof. Dr TAMAS F. FREUND.

Mozgássérültek Pető András Nevelőképző és Nevelőintézete (András Pető Institute of Conductive Education and Conductor Training College): Budapest, Kútvölgyi u. 6, 1125; tel. (1) 224-1500; e-mail info@peto.hu; internet www.peto.hu; f. 1945; conductive education for 1,200 children and adults with motor disorders of neurological origin; undergraduate conductor training; conductor-helper postgraduate specialist training; higher-level vocational training in youth protection; library of 35,000 vols; Dir Dr FRANZ SCHAFFHAUSER; publ. *Conductive Education: Occasional Papers* (2 a year).

Országos Epidemiológiai Központ (National Centre for Epidemiology): Budapest IX, Gyáli u. 2–6, 1097; tel. (1) 476-1100; e-mail oekfoigazgatosag@oek.antsz.hu; internet www.oek.hu; f. 1927 as Hungarian Royal Nat. Institute of Public Health, present name and status 1998; research in bacteriology, epidemiology, microbiology, mycology, parasitology, vaccines and virology; library of 30,000 vols; Dir-Gen. Dr MÁRTA MELLES; publs *EPINFO* (52 a year), *Mikrobiológiai Körlevél* (Microbiological Circular, 4 a year).

Országos Epidemiológiai Központ Mikrobiológiai Kutatócsoport (Microbiological Research Group of the National Centre for Epidemiology): Budapest, Pihenő u. 1, 1529; tel. (1) 394-5044; e-mail oek.mkcs@gmail.com; f. 1963; research into DNA methylation, HIV/AIDS, interferon, oncogenic viruses, virus tumours; library of 2,000 vols; Dir Dr JÁNOS MINÁROVITS.

Országos 'Fréderic Joliot-Curie' Sugárbiológiai és Sugáregészségügyi Kutató Intézet (Frédéric Joliot-Curie National Research Institute for Radiobiology and Radiohygiene): Budapest, POB 101, 1775; Budapest XXII, Anna u. 5, 1221; tel. (1) 482-2001; e-mail radbiol@osski.hu; internet www.osski.hu; f. 1957, current name adopted 1959; attached to Min. of Health; radiohygiene, incl. protection of workers from radiation; radiobiology research on effects of external ionizing radiation and inc. radioisotopes; radiation and radioisotope applications; medical preparedness for response to radio-nuclear emergencies; teaching within the Semmelweis Medical School, Budapest; library of 7,000 vols; Dir-Gen. Dr GÉZA SÁFRÁNY.

Országos Haematológiai és Immunológiai Intézet (National Institute of Haematology and Immunology): Budapest, POB 424, 1519; Budapest, Daróczi u. 24, 1113; tel. (1) 466-5877; f. 1948; research and clinical activities in haematology and immunology, incl. bone-marrow transplantation; library of 10,000 vols, 91 periodicals; Dir Prof. Dr GYŐZŐ PETRÁNYI; publs *Haematologia* (4 a year, in English), *Transzfúzió* (4 a year, in Hungarian).

Országos Onkológiai Intézet (National Institute of Oncology): Budapest, POB 21, 1525; Budapest, Ráth György u. 7–9, 1122; tel. (1) 224-8600; internet www.oncol.hu; f. 1952; attached to Min. of Health; experimental and clinical activities in epidemiology and oncology research and treatment; depts of chemotherapy, diagnostic imaging, histopathology, nuclear medicine and radiotherapy; library of 15,973 vols, 164 periodicals; Dir Dr Milkós Kásler; publ. *Magyar Onkológia* (4 a year, print and online).

NATURAL SCIENCES

Biological Sciences

Magyar Tudományos Akademia Dunakutató Intézet (Danube Research Institute of the Hungarian Academy of Sciences): Tihany, Klebelsberg Kuno. u. 3, 8237; tel. (27) 345-023; e-mail guti.g@mta-dki.hu; internet www.mta-dki.hu; f. 2011; research in biodiversity, climatology, hydrobiology, landscape ecology, restoration ecology, wildlife; Dir Dr Gábor Guti.

Magyar Tudományos Akadémia Ökológiai Kutatóközpont Balatoni Limnológiai Intézete (Balaton Limnological Institute, Centre for Ecological Research, Hungarian Academy of Sciences): Tihany, POB 35, 8237; Tihany, Klebelsberg Kuno u. 3, 8237; tel. (87) 448-244; e-mail intezet@tres.blki.hu; internet www.blki.hu; f. 1927; research particularly in hydrobiology, experimental zoology; library of 16,000 vols; Dir Prof. Dr Péter Bíró; Sec. Krisztina Komár-omi.

Magyar Tudományos Akadémia Ökológiai Kutatóközpont Ökológiai és Botanikai Intézete (Institute of Ecology and Botany, Centre for Ecological Research, Hungarian Academy of Sciences): Vácrátót, Alkotmány u. 2–4, 2163; tel. (28) 360-122; e-mail obki@botanika.hu; internet www.obki.hu; f. 1952; theoretical and experimental research in botany, flora, plant, taxonomy, dendrology, aquatic ecology, plant ecology, vegetation and community ecology, functional ecology, forest ecology, landscape ecology, grassland ecology, nature conservation, conservation biology, vegetation mapping, climate change, lichenology, land-use history, botanical gardens, gardening, river restoration, shallow lakes; library of 10,000 vols; Dir Dr András Báldi.

Magyar Tudományos Akadémia Szegedi Biológiai Kutatóközpont (Biological Research Centre of the Hungarian Academy of Sciences): Szeged, POB 521, 6701; Szeged, Temesvári krt. 62, 6726; tel. (62) 599-769; e-mail foigazgatoi.titkarsag@brc.mta.hu; internet www.brc.hu; f. 1971; library of 30,000 vols; Dir-Gen. Prof. Pál Ormos; Sec. Zsuzsa Keczan.

Attached Institutes:

Biofizikai Intézet (Institute of Biophysics): Szeged, POB 521, 6701; Szeged, Temesvári krt. 62, 6726; tel. (62) 599-614; e-mail biofizika.titkarsag@brc.mta.hu; internet www.brc.hu/biophysics.php; f. 1971; research in biological energy transduction, optical properties of chromoproteins, plasticity of nervous system and structure-function relationships of biological material; Dir Dr Pal Ormos; Sec. Zsófia Melczer.

Biokémiai Intézet (Institute of Biochemistry): Szeged, POB 521, 6701; Szeged, Temesvári krt. 62, 6726; tel. (62) 599-654; e-mail biokemia.titkarsag@brc.mta.hu; internet www.brc.hu/biochemistry.php; f. 1971; research in gene/cell regulation, microbial genomics, molecular stress and neurobiological/receptor studies; Dir Dr György Pósfai; Sec. Olga Miklós.

Genetikai Intézet (Institute of Genetics): Szeged, POB 521, 6701; Szeged, Temesvári krt. 62, 6726; tel. (62) 599-657; e-mail genetika.titkarsag@brc.mta.hu; internet www.brc.hu/genetics.php; f. 1971; research in chromosome structure and function studies, genetic regulation of devt, immunity and symbiosis and investigation of DNA repair processes; Dir Dr Miklós Erdélyi; Sec. Csilla Soltész.

Növénybiológiai Intézet MTA Biológiai Kutatóközpont (Institute of Plant Biology, Biological Research Centre, Hungarian Academy of Sciences): Szeged, POB 521, 6701; Szeged, Temesvári krt. 62, 6726; tel. (62) 599-714; e-mail novenybiologia.titkarsag@brc.mta.hu; internet www.brc.mta.hu/plant_biology.php; f. 1971; research on molecular background of light perception, photosynthetic energy conversion and utilization by plants; stress responses and stress tolerance of agronomically important plant species; embriogenesis; cell-cycle regulation; devt of biotechnological approaches for the production of plants with improved stress resistance; Dir Dr Imre Vass; Sec. Mariann Karolyi.

Természetvédelmi Hivatal, Madártani Intézet (Authority for Nature Conservation, Institute for Ornithology): Budapest, Költő u. 21, 1121; tel. (1) 795-2474; e-mail ktha@vm.gov.hu; internet www.termeszetvedelem.hu; f. 1893; library of 8,000 vols, 1,000 periodicals; Librarian József Büki; publ. *Aquila* (1 a year).

Mathematical Sciences

Magyar Tudományos Akadémia Rényi Alfréd Matematikai Kutatóintézet (Alfréd Rényi Institute of Mathematics, Hungarian Academy of Sciences): Budapest, POB 127, 1364; Budapest, Reáltanoda u. 13–15, 1053; tel. (1) 483-8300; e-mail math@renyi.hu; internet www.renyi.hu; f. 1950; research into pure and applied mathematics; library of 60,000 vols; Dir Péter P. Pálfy; Scientific Sec. Ágnes Szilárd; publ. *Studia Scientiarum Mathematicarum Hungarica*.

Physical Sciences

Magyar Földtani és Geofizikai Intézet (Hungarian Geological and Geophysical Institute): Budapest, POB 106, 1442; Budapest XIV, Stefánia u. 14, 1143; tel. (1) 251-0999; e-mail mfgi@mfgi.hu; internet www.mfgi.hu; f. 2012 by merger of Magyar Állami Földtani Intézet (f. 1869) and Eötvös Loránd Geofizikai Intézet (f. 1907); depts of data management, earth physics, geological and geophysical collns; library of 30,000 vols; Dir Dr Tamás Fancsik; publ. *Geophysical Transactions* (4 a year).

Magyar Tudományos Akadémia Atommagkutató Intézet (Institute for Nuclear Research, Hungarian Academy of Sciences): Debrecen, Bem tér 18/c, 4026; tel. (52) 509-200; e-mail director@atomki.mta.hu; internet www.atomki.mta.hu; f. 1954; atomic physics, biological and medical research, devt of methods and instruments, earth and cosmic sciences, environmental research, materials science and analysis, nuclear physics, particle physics; library of 55,000 vols; Dir Dr Zsolt Fülöp; Scientific Sec. Zoltán Máté.

Magyar Tudományos Akadémia Csillagászati és Földtudományi Kutatóközpont Konkoly Thege Miklós Csillagászati Intézete, Asztrofizikai Obszervatórium (Konkoly Observatory of the Hungarian Academy of Sciences): Budapest, POB 67, 1525; Budapest, Konkoly Thege Miklós u. 15–17, 1121; tel. (1) 391-9322; internet www.konkoly.hu; f. 1899; Piszkéstető, Galyatető (f. 1962) mountain station, with Schmidt telescope, Cassegrain-reflector and 100 cm Ritchey-Chretien telescope; library of 40,000 vols (incl. 20,000 books and 20,000 journals and publs); Dir Péter Ábrahám; publs *Information Bulletin on Variable Stars of Commission 27 and 42 of the IAU* (print and online, www.konkoly.hu/IBVS/IBVS.html), *Mitteilungen der Sternwarte der Ungarischen Akademie der Wissenschaften* (Communications from the Konkoly Observatory of the Hungarian Academy of Sciences).

Magyar Tudományos Akadémia Csillagászati és Földtudományi Kutatóközpont Csillagászati Intézetének Napfizikai Obszervatóriuma (Heliophysical Observatory of the Hungarian Academy of Sciences): Debrecen, POB 30, 4010; Debrecen, Egyetem tér 1, 4010; tel. (52) 311-015; internet fenyi.sci.klte.hu; f. 1958; studies of solar activity: sunspots, solar flares, prominences; library of 10,000 vols, 20 periodicals, 5,500 sunspot drawings (1872–1919), 100,000 full-disc solar photographs; Head András Ludmány.

Magyar Tudományos Akadémia Energiatudományi Kutatóközpont (Centre for Energy Research of the Hungarian Academy of Sciences): Budapest, POB 49, 1525; Budapest, Konkoly Thege Milkós u. 29–33, 1121; tel. (1) 392-2222; internet www.energia.mta.hu; f. 2012 by merger of Institute of Isotopes (f. 1959) and KFKI Atomic Energy Research Institute (f. 1992); research in fields of adsorption, catalysis, fuel behaviour studies, health physics, molecular spectroscopy, nuclear safety, nuclear spectroscopy, photochemistry, radioactive tracer technique, radiation chemistry, reactor physics, surface chemistry, thermal hydraulics; library of 14,000 vols; Dir-Gen. Dr János Gadó.

Magyar Tudományos Akadémia Geodéziai és Geofizikai Kutató Intézete (Geodetical and Geophysical Research Institute of the Hungarian Academy of Sciences): Sopron, Csatkai Endre u. 6–8, 9400; tel. (99) 508-340; e-mail konyvtar@ggki.hu; internet www.ggki.hu; f. 1955 as 2 separate laboratories, merged as 1 institute 1972; research in advanced problems of geodesy and geophysics including seismology; library of 34,000 vols; Dir Péter Ábrahám; publs *Acta Geodaetica et Geophysica Hungarica* (4 a year), *Geomatikai Közlemények* (Publications in Geomatics, 1 a year).

Magyar Tudományos Akadémia Természettudományi Kutatóközpont (Research Centre for Natural Sciences, Hungarian Academy of Sciences): Budapest, POB 17, 1525; Budapest, Pusztaszeri u. 59–67, 1025; tel. (1) 438-1100; e-mail ttk@ttk.mta.hu; internet www.ttk.mta.hu; f. 1954; 6 research centres: Institute of Materials and Environmental Chemistry, Institute of Enzymology, Institute of Cognitive Neuroscience and Psychology, Institute of Molecular Pharmacology, Institute of Technical Physics and Materials Science, Institute of Organic Chemistry; library of 60,000 vols; Dir-Gen. György Miklós Keserű.

Magyar Tudományos Akadémia Természettudományi Kutatóközpont Műszaki Fizikai és Anyagtudományi Intézet (Institute for Technical Physics and Materials Science, Research Centre for Natural Sciences, Hungarian Academy of Sciences): Budapest, POB 49, 1525; Budapest, Konkoly Thege Miklós u. 29–33, 1121; tel. (1) 392-2224; e-mail info@mfa.kfki.hu; internet www.mfa.kfki.hu; f. 1992; depts of thin film physics, nanostructures, microtechnology, ceramics and nanocomposites, photonics, complex systems; library of 120,000 vols; Dir Prof. ISTVÁN BÁRSONY.

Pannon Egyetem Műszaki Kémiai Kutatóintézet (Research Institute of Chemical and Process Engineering, University of Pannonia): Veszprem, POB 125, 8200; Veszprém, Egyetem u. 10, 8200; tel. (88) 624-040; e-mail mizsey@mukki.richem.hu; internet www.richem.hu; f. 1960; fundamental and applied research in traditional chemical engineering, bioengineering and systems engineering; library of 8,500 vols; Dir Dr PÉTER MIZSEY; publ. *Hungarian Journal of Industrial Chemistry* (print and online).

Uránia Csillagvizsgáló (Urania Public Observatory): Budapest, Sánc u. 3B, 1016; tel. (1) 386-9233; e-mail urania@t-online.hu; internet www.urania-budapest.hu/new_page4.html; f. 1947; centre of the Hungarian amateur astronomy movement; 8-inch Heyde refractor, 6-inch Zeiss reflector; library of 1,700 vols; Dir OTTO ZOMBORI; publ. *Uránia Füzetek* (Urania Letters, 1 a year).

PHILOSOPHY AND PSYCHOLOGY

Magyar Tudományos Akadémia Bölcsészettudományi Kutatóközpont Filozófiai Intézete (Institute of Philosophy, Research Centre for the Humanities of the Hungarian Academy of Sciences): Budapest, POB 9, 1250; Budapest, Úri u. 53, 1014; tel. (1) 224-6784; e-mail office@webmail.phil-inst.hu; internet www.phil-inst.hu; f. 1957; research into history of philosophical thought, methodological problems of social sciences, philosophy of politics, religion and science, problems of epistemology; library of 26,000 vols; Dir JÁNOS BOROS; Sec. LÁSZLÓNÉ TRINGER.

Magyar Tudományos Akadémia Természettudományi Kutatóközpont Kognitív Idegtudományi és Pszichológiai Intézet (Institute of Cognitive Neuroscience and Psychology, Research Centre for Natural Sciences of Hungarian Academy of Sciences): Budapest, POB 398, 1394; Budapest, Victor Hugo u. 18–22, 1132; tel. (1) 354-2290; e-mail info@mtapi.hu; internet www.mtapi.hu; f. 1902; basic research in cognitive psychophysiology and neuropsychology, developmental psychology, social psychology and personality, research on educational psychology, psychology of decision-making, cross-cultural psychology; library of 20,000 vols, 350 periodicals; Dir Dr ISTVÁN CZIGLER; publ. *Pszichológia* (4 a year).

RELIGION, SOCIOLOGY AND ANTHROPOLOGY

Magyar Tudományos Akadémia Bölcsészettudományi Kutatóközpont Néprajztudományi Intézet (Institute of Ethnology of the Hungarian Academy of Sciences): Budapest, POB 29, 1250; Budapest, Országház u. 30, 1014; tel. (1) 224-6700; e-mail etnologia@etnologia.mta.hu; internet www.etnologia.mta.hu; f. 1967; research in ethnology of the Hungarian people, gen. anthropology, folklore and traditions, study of gypsies; library of 68,000 vols; Dir Dr BALÁZS BALOGH; Scientific Sec. LANDGRAF ILDIKÓ; publs *Documentatio Ethnographica*, *Életmód és Tradició*, *Folklór Archivum*, *Folklór és Tradició*, *Magyar Néprajz*, *Népi Kultura—Népi Társadalom*, *Néprajzi tanulmányok*.

Magyar Tudományos Akadémia Társadalomtudományi Kutatóközpont Szociológiai Intézet (Institute for Sociology, Centre for Social Sciences, Hungarian Academy of Sciences): Budapest, POB 20, 1250; Budapest, Országház u. 30, 1014; tel. (1) 224-0790; e-mail info@socio.mta.hu; internet www.socio.mta.hu; f. 1963; scientific research in sociology, power and social stratification, social inequality and conflict, local govt and power relations, civil soc. and environmental movements; library of 8,000 vols; Dir BÉLA JANKY; Scientific Sec. TAMÁS P. TÓTH; publs *INFO—Társadalomtudomány* (INFO—Social Science, 4 a year), *Kultúra és Közösség* (Culture and Community), *socio.hu* (online, www.socio.hu), *Szociológiai Tanulmányok* (Studies in Sociology), *Társadalomkutatás* (Research in the Social Sciences, 4 a year).

TECHNOLOGY

Magyar Tudományos Akadémia Számítástechnikai és Automatizálási Kutatóintézete (Institute for Computer Science and Control of the Hungarian Academy of Sciences): Budapest, POB 63, 1518; Budapest, Kende u. 13–17, 1111; tel. (1) 279-6000; e-mail pr@sztaki.mta.hu; internet www.sztaki.hu; f. 1964; conducts research in intelligent computing, control and information systems, new computation structures and computer applications for engineering, production and admin. systems; library of 45,600 vols, 200 periodicals; Dir Dr PÉTER INZELT; publ. *Transactions* (irregular).

Szilikátipari Központi Kutató és Tervező Intézet (Central Research and Design Institute for the Silicate Industry): Budapest, Bécsi u. 122–124, 1034; tel. (1) 188-2360; f. 1953; research and technological design in the silicate sciences and building materials industry; library of 25,000 vols, 7,000 periodicals; Dir CSABA ÁRPÁD RÉTI; publs *Transactions* (irregular, in English, French, German, Russian), *Tudományos Közlemények* (irregular, summaries in English, French, German, Russian).

Villamosenergiaipari Kutató Intézet (Institute for Electric Power Research): Budapest, POB 80, 1251; Budapest, Gellérthegy u. 17, 1016; tel. (1) 457-8273; e-mail i.kromer@veiki.hu; f. 1949; research and devt on safety assessment of nuclear power plants, combustion technology and environmental management, mechanical and power engineering technology, equipment of the electricity networks, high-voltage and high-power laboratory testing, systems of control engineering and telemechanics; library of 25,000 vols; Gen. Man. Dr ISTVÁN KRÓMER; publ. *VEIKI Publications* (1 a year, in Hungarian, with abstracts in English).

Libraries and Archives

Budapest

Budapest Főváros Levéltára (Budapest City Archives): Budapest, Teve u. 3–5, 1139; tel. (1) 298-7500; e-mail bfl@bparchiv.hu; internet bfl.archivportal.hu; f. 1901; 23,000 m of bookshelves; Dir Dr LÁSZLÓ A. VARGA; publ. *Budapesti Negyed* (4 a year).

Budapesti Corvinus Egyetem Entz Ferenc Könyvtár és Levéltár (Corvinus University of Budapest, Entz Ferenc Library and Archives): Budapest, Villányi u. 29–43, 1118; tel. (1) 482-6300; internet efkl.uni-corvinus.hu; f. 1860; horticulture, floriculture, nursery, medicinal plants, fruit-growing, landscape and garden architecture, urban planning, environmental protection; food industry, canning technology, food fermentation, processing of animal products, processing of cereals and industrial plants, oenology, brewing; 320,000 vols, 365 current periodicals; Dir Dr ANDREA VIOLA; publ. *'Lippay János' Tudományos Ülésszak Előadásai* (every 2 years).

Budapesti Corvinus Egyetem Központi Könyvtár (Corvinus University of Budapest Central Library): Budapest, Közraktar u. 4–6, 1093; tel. (1) 482-7019; e-mail konyvtar@uni-corvinus.hu; internet www.lib.uni-corvinus.hu; f. 1850; agriculture, business and finance, economic sciences, environmental protection, management sciences, political science, public admin., social sciences, sociology, world economy; 471,466 vols; Dir-Gen. ZSUZSANNA NAGY.

Budapesti Műszaki és Gazdaságtudományi Egyetem Országos Műszaki Információs Központ és Könyvtár (BME OMIKK) (Budapest University of Technology and Economics National Technical Information Centre and Library): Budapest, POB 91, 1518; Budapest, Budafoki u. 4–6, 1111; tel. (1) 463-3534; e-mail info@omikk.bme.hu; internet www.omikk.bme.hu; f. 1848; 2,084,352 vols, 340,000 periodicals; spec. colln of rare books published before 1800; Dir-Gen. BÉLA LISZKAY; publ. *Tudományos és Műszaki Tajekoztatas* (Scientific and Technical Information, 12 a year, print and online, tmt.omikk.bme.hu).

Eötvös Loránd Tudományegyetem Egyetemi Könyvtár (Library of Eötvös Loránd University): Budapest, Ferenciek tere 6, 1052; tel. (1) 411-6738; e-mail titkarsag@lib.elte.hu; internet www.konyvtar.elte.hu; f. 1635; central library of the Univ. and scientific library for philosophy, psychology, medieval history, religion and history of Christianity; 1,500,000 vols, 1,339 periodicals, 60,000 MSS, 185 codices, 1,150 incunabula, 2,600 old Hungarian printed works (to 1711), 9,600 old and rare books; Dir Dr LÁSZLÓ SZÖGI; publ. *Visszhang az Egyetemi Könyvtár Évkönyvei* (University Library Annals, irregular).

Fővárosi Szabó Ervin Könyvtár (Metropolitan Ervin Szabó Library): Budapest, Szabó Ervin tér 1, 1088; tel. (1) 411-5052; e-mail info@fszek.hu; internet www.fszek.hu; f. 1904; sociology, humanities, literature, history of Budapest; 51 brs across Budapest; 3,217,759 vols (incl. 2,372,540 vols of books and bound periodicals, 6,437 cartographic documents, 53,389 printed music documents, 147,861 audio documents, 63,602 picture documents, 20,015 electronic documents, 553,915 other types of document), 1,145 current periodicals; Dir-Gen. Dr PÉTER FODOR.

Gyógyszerészeti és Egészségügyi, Minőség- és Szervezetfejlesztési Intézet Egészségpolitikai Szakkönyvtár (National Institute for Quality- and Organizational Development in Healthcare and Medicines Health Policy Library): Budapest, Hold u. 1, 1054; tel. (1) 354-5377; e-mail konyvtar@gyemszi.hu; internet www.eski.hu; f. 1949; library for Min. of Health staff, health policy makers, health professionals, healthcare managers, health workers; colln incl. Hungarian publs on health policy and related fields, statistics, social and family affairs; selected publs from foreign literature; deposit library of the European regional office of the WHO; 40,000 vols; Dir-Gen. Dr GYÖRGY SURJÁN; Head of Library Dr MÁRIA PALOTAI; publs *Magyar Orvosi Bibliográfia* (Hungarian Medical Bibliography, 4 a year, online), *Nővér* (A Hungarian Journal of Nursing Theory and Practice, 6 a year, print and online, www.eski.hu/new3/kiadv/nover/novinden.htm).

Hadtörténeti Könyvtár és Térképtár (Library of Military History and Cartographic Collection): Budapest, POB 7, 1250; Budapest, Kapisztrán tér 2–4, 1014; tel. (1)

325-1672; e-mail him.konyvtar@hm-him.hu; internet www.hadtorteneti.net; f. 1920; 61,563 records in the catalogue; 190,000 vols, 500,000 maps; Dir LÁSZLÓ VESZPRÉMY; publs *Bibliography* (1 a year), *Hadtörténelmi Közlemények* (Review of Military History, 4 a year).

Iparművészeti Múzeum Könyvtára (Library of the Museum of Applied Arts): Budapest, Üllői u. 33–37, 1091; tel. (1) 456-5177; e-mail konyvtar@imm.hu; internet www.imm.hu; f. 1874; scientific research library for the decorative arts; 80,000 vols, 20,000 periodicals; Dir Dr ÁGNES PRÉKOPA; publ. *Ars Decorativa* (1 a year).

Keve András Madártani és Természetvédelmi Szakkönyvtár (Andras Keve Library for Ornithology and Nature Conservation): Budapest, Költő u. 21, 1121; tel. (1) 202-2530; e-mail bartlb@dinpi.hu; internet www.termeszetvedelem.hu/konyvtar; f. 1893; 9,000 vols, 20,000 periodicals, 1,500 scientific reports; Librarian BOGLÁRKA SIPOS-BARTL; publ. *Aquila* (1 a year).

Központi Statisztikai Hivatal Könyvtár (Hungarian Central Statistical Office Library): Budapest, Keleti Károly u. 5, 1024; tel. (1) 345-6105; e-mail konyvtar@ksh.hu; internet konyvtar.ksh.hu; f. 1867; nat. and research library of statistics and demography; 850,000 vols, books, periodicals, maps and electronic documents; Dir-Gen. ÁGNES FÜLÖP; publ. *Magyarország Történeti Helységnévtára* (Historical Gazetteer of Hungary).

Liszt Ferenc Zeneművészeti Egyetem Könyvtára (Library of the Ferenc Liszt Academy of Music): Budapest, Liszt Ferenc tér 8, POB 206, 1391; tel. (1) 462-4673; internet www.zeneakademia.hu; f. 1875; research library for Hungarian music history; 70,000 vols, 100 journals; 500,000 musical scores plus 90,000 vols and periodicals, 150,000 records; Dir GÉZA KOCSIS.

Magyar Nemzeti Galéria Könyvtára (Library of the Hungarian National Gallery): Budapest, POB 31, 1250; Budapest, Szent György tér 2, 1014; tel. (2) 439-7455; e-mail library@mng.hu; internet www.mng.hu; f. 1957; books on art from all over the world, specializing in Hungarian sculpture, wood carvings, panel paintings, Baroque art, art since the 12th century; 80,000 vols, 27,000 catalogues, 8,800 periodicals, 15,000 slides; Head of Library ANELIA TŰŰ.

Magyar Nemzeti Múzeum Központi Könyvtára (Central Library of the Hungarian National Museum): Budapest, Múzeum körút 14–16, 1088; tel. (1) 327-7727; e-mail konyvtar@hnm.hu; internet www.hnm.hu; f. 1952; 270,000 vols of books and periodicals; Dir-Gen. Dr LÁSZLÓ CSORBA; Sec. IBOLYA PAP Ó. KOVÁCS; publs *Bibliotheca Humanitatis Historica*, *Catalogi Musei Nationalis Hungariae*, *Communicationes Archaeologicae Hungaria*, *Folia Archaeologica* (1 a year), *Folia Historica* (1 a year), *Inventaria Praehistorica Hungariae*, *Monumenta Avarorum Archaeologica*.

Magyar Nemzeti Levéltár (National Archives of Hungary): Budapest, POB 3, 1250; Budapest, Bécsi kapu tér 2–4, 1014; tel. (1) 225-2800; e-mail info@mnl.gov.hu; internet www.mnl.gov.hu; f. 1756; 83,000 m of shelving; records since the 12th century; Dir-Gen. Dr ZSUZSANNA MIKÓ; publs *Archivenet*, *Levéltári Közlemények*, *Levéltári Szemle* (journal).

Magyar Tudományos Akadémia Földrajztudományi Kutató Intézet Könyvtára (Scientific Library of the Geographical Research Institute of the Hungarian Academy of Sciences): Budapest, Budaörsi u. 45, 1112; tel. (1) 309-2600; e-mail magyar@sparc.core.hu; internet www.mtafki.hu; f. 1952; 73,244 vols (incl. 38,451 books, 8,232 journals, 8,378 MSS, 18,081 maps, 102 CDs and DVDs); Librarian ÁRPÁD MAGYAR; publs *Elmélet-módszer-gyakorlat* (Theory-Methods-Practice), *Földrajzi Értesítő*, *Studies in Geography in Hungary*.

Magyar Tudományos Akadémia Könyvtára és Információs Központ (Library and Information Centre of the Hungarian Academy of Sciences): Budapest, POB 1002, 1245; Budapest V, Arany János u. 1, 1051; tel. (1) 411-6100; e-mail titkarsag@konyvtar.mta.hu; internet konyvtar.mta.hu; f. 1826; colln incl. oriental MSS, old prints and incunabula; depository library for Academy's dissertations; Academy's archives; 1,587,921 vols, 364,817 periodicals, 718,450 MSS, 32,591 microfilms, 811 electronic documents, 69 audiovisual titles; Dir-Gen. Prof. GÁBOR NÁRAY-SZABÓ.

Magyar Zsidó Levéltár (Hungarian Jewish Archives): Budapest, Síp u. 12, 1075; tel. (1) 413-5551; e-mail info@milev.hu; internet www.milev.hu; f. 1916; Jewish pieces of archaeology and art history, religious objects; family tree research centre, picture gallery of Hungarian Jewish heritage; Dir and Head Archivist ZSUZSANNA TORONYI; publ. *Makor*.

Országgyűlési Könyvtár (Library of the Hungarian Parliament): Budapest, Kossuth Lajos tér 1–3, 1055; tel. (1) 441-4468; e-mail info@ogyk.hu; internet www.ogyk.hu; f. 1870; EU depository library, UN depository library; 908,674 vols; parliamentary papers (Hungarian and foreign), contemporary history, admin. and legal sciences, economics, politics, sociology and statistics; spec. collns: Foreign Parliamentary Colln, EU Depository Library, Hungarian Parliamentary Colln, UN Depository Library; Head of Library SZILÁRD MARKÓJA; publs *HUNDOK* (bibliographical descriptions and abstracts of foreign analytical articles about Hungary, print and online), *PRESSDOK* (review on CD-ROM of Hungarian newspapers and periodicals, print and online), *Világpolitikai Információk Adatbázisa* (Database of Information on World Politics, print and online).

Országos Idegennyelvü Könyvtár és Zenei Gyűjtemény (National Library of Foreign Literature and Music Collection): Budapest, POB 469, 1462; Budapest, Molnár u. 11, 1056; tel. (1) 318-3688; e-mail tajekoztato@oik.hu; internet www.oik.hu; f. 1956 as Gorkij State Library; specializing in foreign literature, theory of literature, linguistics, language teaching materials, musicology, music scores and records, literature concerning nat. minorities and ethnicities; 370,000 vols; Dir-Gen. TIBORNÉ MENDER; publs *Műfordítás Adatbázis* (Literary Translations Database), *Nemzeti és Etnikai Kisebbségi Adatbázis* (Database of Minorities-related Articles).

Országos Mezőgazdasági Könyvtár és Dokumentációs Központ (National Agricultural Library and Documentation Centre): Budapest, Attila u. 93, 1012; tel. (1) 489-4900; e-mail omgkref@omgk.hu; internet www.omgk.hu; f. 1951; 309,476 vols, 300 periodicals; Gen. Dir GABRIELLA LŰKŐ-ÖRSI; Sec. PETRONELLA VINCZE; publs *Agrárkönyvtári Hírvilág* (Agricultural Library News, 4 a year, online), *Magyar Mezőgazdasági Bibliográfia* (Hungarian Agricultural Bibliography, 4 a year).

Országos Pedagógiai Könyvtár és Múzeum (National Educational Library and Museum): Budapest, Könyves Kálmán u. 40, 1089; tel. (1) 323-5508; e-mail titkarsag@opkm.hu; internet www.opkm.hu; f. 1877, reorganized 1958; methodological library for education; pedagogical museum; 550,000 vols; Dir Dr KATALIN VARGA; publs *Könyv és Nevelés* (Books and Education, 4 a year, online, olvasas.opkm.hu/portal/felso_menusor/konyv_es_neveles2), *Külföldi Pedagógiai Információ* (International Educational Information, on CD-ROM), *Magyar Pedagógiai Irodalom* (Hungarian Educational Literature, on CD-ROM).

Országos Rabbiképző—Zsidó Egyetem Könyvtára (Library of the Jewish Theological Seminary–University of Jewish Studies): Budapest, POB 21, 1428; Budapest, Bérkocsis u. 2, 1085; tel. (1) 267-5415; e-mail kocsis@or-zse.hu; internet www.rabbi.hu/konyvtar.htm; f. 1877; 100,000 vols; Dir BERTA BIRÓ BÉRI.

Országos Széchényi Könyvtár (National Széchényi Library): Budapest, Budavári Palota F-épület, 1827; tel. (1) 224-3700; e-mail inform@oszk.hu; internet www.oszk.hu; f. 1802; 7m. vols (incl. 2m. books, 330,000 vols of serial publs, 76,000 printed music records, 1m. units of MSS, 200,000 maps, 310,000 engravings, 24,000 sound records, 3m. posters and small prints, 270,000 microfilm copies); Dir-Gen. Dr ANDREA SAJÓ; publs *A Kárpát-medence koraújkori könyvtárai* (Libraries of the Early Modern Age in the Carpathian Basin, irregular), *Bibliotheca Sciantiae et Artis* (1 a year), *Időszaki kiadványok bibliográfiája–Új Periodikumok* (Hungarian National Bibliography, 4 a year), *Kartográfiai Dokumentumok* (Cartographic Documents, 2 a year), *Libri de Libris* (irregular), *Magyar Könyvszemle* (Hungarian Book Review, 4 a year), *Magyar Nemzeti Bibliográfia, Margarithe Bibliothecae Nationalis Hungariae* (irregular), *Nemzeti Téka* (National Thecae, irregular), *Zeneművek* (Music and Musicology Documents, 2 a year).

Pázmány Péter Katolikus Egyetem, Hittudományi Kar Könyvtára (Library of the Péter Pázmány Catholic University's Faculty of Theology): Budapest, Veres Pálné u. 24, 1053; tel. (1) 484-3054; internet www.htk.ppke.hu; f. 1635; history, theology and linguistics; 70,000 vols, 9,800 periodicals; spec. collns: books from c. 1880, Colln of the Brothers of St Paul (f. 1775, 12,000 vols, incunabula and MSS from the 15th and 16th centuries), the Library of the Central Catholic Seminary (f. 1805, 17,300 vols); Library Dir MÁRIA TARJÁN.

Politikatörténeti Intézet Könyvtára (Library of the Institute of Political History): Budapest, Alkotmány u. 2, 1054; tel. (1) 301-2024; e-mail konyvtar@phistory.hu; internet www.polhist.hu; f. 1948; 156,000 vols, 45 current periodicals; Librarian DÓRA VARGA.

Semmelweis Egyetem Egészségtudományi Kar Könyvtár (Semmelweis University Faculty of Health Sciences Library): Budapest, POB 229, 1428; Budapest, Vas u. 17, 1088; tel. (1) 486-5955; e-mail lib@se-etk.hu; internet www.se-etk.hu; f. 1975; 50,000 vols; Head IMOLA JEHODA.

Semmelweis Egyetem Központi Könyvtára (Central Library of Semmelweis University): Budapest, Mikszáth tér. 5, 1088; tel. (1) 317-0948; e-mail info@lib.sote.hu; internet www.lib.sote.hu; f. 1828; 293,000 vols; Dir Dr LÍVIA VASAS.

Semmelweis Egyetem Testnevelési és Sporttudományi Kar Könyvtára (Library of the Faculty of Physical Education and Sport Sciences, Semmelweis University): Budapest, POB 69, 1525; Budapest, Alkotás u. 44, 1123; tel. (1) 487-9235; e-mail linda@tf.hu; internet tf.hu/oktatas/konyvtar; f. 1925; colln covers physical education, sport, human kinesiology, management, mental health, recreation and allied domains; literature by Hungarian and foreign authors; 100,000 vols,

77 domestic and 4 foreign trade papers, 100 periodicals; Dir Dr MELINDA LÉCES.

Szent István Egyetem Állatorvos-tudományi Könyvtár, Levéltár és Múzeum (Veterinary Science Library, Archives and Museum—Szent István University): Budapest, István u. 2, 1078; tel. (1) 478-4226; e-mail library.univet@aotk.szie.hu; internet library.univet.hu; f. 1787; 85,000 vols, 120 current periodicals; spec. collns: ancient veterinary literature, historical archives; museum of veterinary history; distance education for veterinarians; Dir ÉVA ORBÁN; publ. *Bibliography of Hungarian Veterinary Literature* (online).

Debrecen

Debreceni Egyetem Egyetemi és Nemzeti Könyvtár (University and National Library—University of Debrecen): Debrecen, POB 39, 4010; Debrecen, Egyetem tér 1, 4032; tel. (52) 410-443; e-mail info@lib.unideb.hu; internet www.lib.unideb.hu; f. 1918, present name and status 2001; 2,700,000 vols and periodicals, 25,000 MSS, 26,000 cassettes, CDs and DVDs; Dir-Gen. Dr MÁRTA VIRÁGOS; publ. *Könyv és Könyvtár* (1 a year, print and online, konyveskonyvtar.lib.unideb.hu/index.php).

Debreceni Egyetem Egyetemi és Nemzeti Könyvtár Kenézy Élettudományi Könyvtára (University of Debrecen, University and National Library, Kenezy Life Sciences Library): Debrecen, Egyetem tér 1, 4032; tel. (52) 518-610; e-mail kenezy@lib.unideb.hu; internet kenezy.lib.unideb.hu; f. 1947; 300,000 vols; spec. collns: history of medicine and bibliographies on life sciences published in 1910s and 1920s, publs of Medical and Health Science Centre and the Biology and Chemistry Institutes of the Univ. of Debrecen; Librarian GYÖNGYI KARÁCSONY.

Tiszántúli Református Egyházkerületi és Kollégiumi Nagykönyvtár (College Library of the Transtibiscan Church District and Library of Theology): Debrecen, Kálvin tér 16, 4044; tel. (52) 516-856; e-mail theca@silver.drk.hu; internet silver.drk.hu; f. 1538; 560,000 vols, 1,600 old books (published before 1711), 146 incunabula; spec. collns: incunabula. maps, Bibles, small prints and posters, obituaries, school reports, MSS, Early Hungarian Printed Books; Dir Dr BOTOND GÁBORJÁNI SZABÓ.

Esztergom

Főszékesegyházi Könyvtár (Library of Esztergom Cathedral): Esztergom, Pázmány Péter u. 2, 2500; tel. (33) 510-130; e-mail bibliotheca@invitel.hu; internet www.bibliothecaesztergom.hu; f. 11th century; 250,000 vols incl. Fugger, Batthyany and Mayer collns; spec. collns: incunabula, small prints and posters, maps, engravings and drawings; Dir BÉLA CZÉKLI.

Gödöllő

Szent István Egyetem Kosáry Domokos Könyvtár és Levéltár (Szent István University Library and Archives): Gödöllő, Páter Károly u. 1, 2100; tel. (28) 410-804; e-mail konyvtar@lib.szie.hu; internet lib.szie.hu; f. 1945 frmly Szent István Egyetem Gödöllői Tudományos Könyvtár, current name adopted 2008; 370,000 vols, 535 current periodicals; Dir Dr ERZSÉBET KOÓSNÉ TÖRÖK; publ. *Bibliográfia* (every 2 or 3 years).

Keszthely

Pannon Egyetem, Georgikon Kar, Kari Könyvtár és Levéltár (University of Pannonia, Georgikon Faculty, Faculty Library and Archives): Keszthely, Deák Ferenc u. 16, POB 66, 8360; tel. (83) 545-117; e-mail hpcs@georgikon.hu; internet www.georgikon.hu/lib; f. 1797, reorganized 1954; 150,000 vols; Dir CSILLA PÓR; publ. *Georgikon for Agriculture* (2 a year).

Miskolc

Miskolci Egyetem Könyvtár, Levéltár, Múzeum (University of Miskolc Library, Archives, Museum): Miskolc-Egyetemváros, 3515; tel. (46) 565-324; e-mail konyvtar@uni-miskolc.hu; internet www.lib.uni-miskolc.hu; f. 1735; 1m. vols, 113,000 periodicals; Gen. Dir ERZSÉBET BURMEISTER.

Pannonhalma

Főapátsági Könyvtár Pannonhalma (Benedictine Abbey Library): Pannonhalma, Vár 1, 9090; tel. (96) 570-142; e-mail fokonyvtar@osb.hu; internet bences.hu/cikk/fokonyvtar.html; f. 1802; colln of early records, MSS, codices, source material for the Hungarian language; 350,000 vols; Dir KONRÁD DEJCSICS.

Pécs

Pécsi Tudományegyetem Egyetemi Könyvtára (University Library of Pécs): Pécs, POB 227, 7601; Pécs, Universitas u. 2/A, 7622; tel. (72) 501-650; internet www.lib.pte.hu; f. 1774; 1,165,000 vols; Gen. Dir Prof. Dr ÁGNES FISCHERNÉ-DÁRDAI.

Pécsi Tudományegyetem Pekár Mihály Orvosi és Élettudományi Szakkönyvtár (University of Pécs Mihály Pekár Medical and Life Sciences Library): Pécs, Szigeti u. 12, 7624; tel. (72) 536-000; e-mail kolcsonzo@aok.pte.hu; internet www.aok.pte.hu; f. 1926; colln covers medicine, health sciences, chemistry, physics and biology; 472,413 vols; Dir Dr TÜNDE GRACZA.

Sárospatak

Sárospataki Református Kollégium Tudományos Gyűjteményei Nagykönyvtára (Scholarly Collection of the Reformed College of Sárospatak): Sárospatak, Rákóczi u. 1, 3950; tel. (47) 311-057; e-mail reftud@iif.hu; internet www.patakarchiv.hu; f. 1531; 404,974 vols; Dir DÉNES DIENES; publ. *Egyháztörténeti Szemle* (4 a year, online, www.egyhtortszemle.hu).

Sopron

Nyugat-Magyarországi Egyetem Központi Könyvtár és Levéltár (Central Library and Archives of the University of West Hungary): Sopron, POB 132, 9401; Sopron, Bajcsy-Zsilinszky u. 4, 9400; tel. (99) 518-223; e-mail library@nyme.hu; internet ilex.efe.hu; f. 1735; 5 mem. libraries serving different faculties of the Univ. of West Hungary located in Győr, Mosonmagyaróvár, Sopron, Székesfehérvár and Szombathely; 315,286 vols; Head SÁNDOR SARKADY.

Szeged

Somogyi Károly Városi és Megyei Könyvtár (Károly Somogyi City and County Library): Szeged, Dóm tér 1–4, 6720; tel. (62) 425-525; e-mail library@sk-szeged.hu; internet www.sk-szeged.hu; f. 1881; 820,000 vols; Dir ZSUZSANNA SEBŐK PALÁNKAI; publs *Csongrád Megyei Könyvtáros* (Librarian of Csongrád County), *Szegedi Műhely* (Workshop of Szeged).

Szegedi Tudományegyetem Klebelsberg Kuno Könyvtára (University of Szeged, Klebelsberg Library): Szeged. POB 393, 6701; Szeged, Ady tér 10, 6722; tel. (62) 546-633; e-mail ref@bibl.u-szeged.hu; internet www.bibl.u-szeged.hu; f. 1921; 1.5m. vols; spec. collns: military history, war crimes and the Holocaust; Chinese, Mongolian, Tibetan and Turkish language and history; European Documentation Centre; Oriental Colln; Social theory, Contemporary history Colln; Dir Dr KEVEHÁZI KATALIN; publs *Acta Bibliothecaria*, *Dissertationes ex Bibliotheca Universitatis de Attila József Nominatae*.

Veszprém

Pannon Egyetem, Egyetemi Könyvtár és Levéltár (University of Pannonia, Library and Archive): Veszprém, Egyetem str. 10, 8200; Veszprém, Wartha Vince u. 1, 8200; tel. (88) 624-336; e-mail hazitibo@almos.uni-pannon.hu; internet konyvtar.uni-pannon.hu; f. 1949; 255,516 vols; Gen. Dir Dr GÁBOR TÓTH; publs *Hungarian Journal of Industrial Chemistry* (4 a year), *Studia Germanica Universitatis Vesprimensis* (4 a year).

Zirc

Reguly Antal Műemlékkönyvtár (Antal Reguly Historical Library): Zirc, Rákóczi tér 1, 8420; tel. (88) 593-800; e-mail info.reguly@oszk.hu; internet www.oszk.hu/reguly_antal_muemlekkonyvtar; f. 1720; attached to Nat. Széchényi Library; 68,618 vols; religious library; contains books esp. on theology and history; Librarian KATALIN URBÁN.

Museums and Art Galleries

Badacsony

Egry József Emlékmúzeum (József Egry Memorial Museum): Badacsony, Egry József Sétány 12, 8261; tel. (87) 431-044; e-mail vmk@badacsonyiprogramok.hu; f. 1973; memorial and art gallery of works by Lake Balaton landscape painter József Egry.

Baja

Türr István Múzeum: Baja, Deák Ferenc u. 1, POB 55, 6501; tel. (79) 324-173; e-mail bajaimuzeum@gmail.com; internet www.bajaimuzeum.hu; f. 1937; archaeological and ethnographic collns, modern Hungarian painters, local history; library of 14,000 vols; Dir ZITA KOVÁCS; publs *Bajai Dolgozatok*, *Türr István Múzeum Kiadványai*.

Balassagyarmat

Palóc Múzeum: Balassagyarmat, Palóc liget 1, 2660; tel. (35) 300-168; e-mail info@palocmuzeum.hu; internet palocmuzeum.hu; f. 1891, present name and status 1950; ethnography, local folk art and shepherds' art; collns of Nógrád costumes, embroidery, folk religion and folk instruments; local history, literary history (Imre Madách and Kálmán Mikszáth relics); library of 13,000 vols; Dir Dr ÁGNES LENGYEL.

Békéscsaba

Munkácsy Mihály Múzeum: Békéscsaba, Széchenyi u. 9, 5600; tel. (66) 328-040; e-mail mmm@bmmi.hu; internet www.munkacsy.hu; f. 1899; archaeological, historical and regional ethnographic collns, modern Hungarian paintings, ornithology, natural science; paintings and legacies of the painter Mihály Munkácsy (1844–1900); library of 16,000 vols, 3,800 periodicals; Dir Dr IMRE SZATMÁRI.

Budapest

Bartók Béla Emlékház (Béla Bartók Memorial House): Budapest II, Csalán u. 29, 1025; tel. (1) 394-2100; e-mail bartok-1981@t-online.hu; internet www.bartokmuseum.hu; f. 1981; organizes musical programmes and concerts; Dir JÁNOS SZIRÁNYI.

Bélyegmúzeum (Stamp Museum): Budapest, Hársfa u. 47, 1074; tel. (1) 342-3757; e-mail iroda@belyegmuzeum.hu; internet www.belyegmuzeum.hu; f. 1930; colln of 13m. Hungarian and foreign stamps; philatelic history; exhibitions locally and abroad; library of 5,000 vols; Dir GABRIELLA NIKODÉM; publ. *Yearbook*.

Budapesti Történeti Múzeum (Budapest History Museum): Budapest, Szent György tér 2, 1014; tel. (1) 487-8800; e-mail btm@mail.btm.hu; internet www.btm.hu; f. 1887; medieval antiquities, medieval royal castle, Gothic statues; library of 45,700 vols; Dir-Gen. Dr SÁNDOR BODÓ; publs *Budapest Régiségei* (Antiquities of Budapest), *Monumenta Historica Budapestinensia* (irregular), *Tanulmányok Budapest Múltjából* (Studies on the History of Budapest).

Attached Museums:

Aquincum Múzeum: Budapest, Szentendrei u. 135, 1031; tel. (1) 430-1081; e-mail aquincum@aquincum.hu; internet www.aquincum.hu; f. 1894; prehistory and Roman history of Budapest; Dir Dr PAULA ZSIDI; publ. *Aquincumi Füzetek* (excavations and rescue work at the Aquincum Museum).

Fővárosi Képtár—Kiscelli Múzeum (Museum Kiscell—Municipal Picture Gallery): Budapest, Kiscelli u. 108, 1037; tel. (1) 388-7817; e-mail fovarosi_keptar@mail.btm.hu; internet www.btmfk.iif.hu; f. 1889; colln of 19th–20th century Hungarian fine art incl. paintings, sculptures, drawings, 18th–20th century prints, contemporary fine art, coins, medals; Dir PÉTER FITZ.

Budavári Mátyás-templom Egyházművészeti Gyüjteménye (Matthias Church of Buda Castle Ecclesiastical Art Collection): Budapest, Szentháromság tér 2, 1014; tel. (1) 488-7716; e-mail muzeum@matyas-templom.hu; internet www.matyas-templom.hu; f. 1964; permanent colln of Roman Catholic religious objects in the gallery of Matthias Church; organizes concerts; Dir MÁTÉFFY BALÁZS.

Hadtörténeti Múzeum (Military History Museum): Budapest, Kapisztrán tér 2–4, 1014; tel. (1) 325-1600; internet www.militaria.hu; f. 1918; Hungarian and Hungarian-related militaria incl. arms, medals, flags, uniforms, art, books, documents, photographs, posters, prints, maps; library of 300,025 vols; Dir Col. Dr JÓZSEF LUGOSI; publs *A Hadtörténeti Múzeum Értesítője / Acta Musei Militaris in Hungaria* (Yearbook of the Hungarian Military Museum, 1 a year, with summaries in English and German), *Hadtörténelmi Közlemények* (Quarterly of Military History).

Holokauszt Emlékközpont (Holocaust Memorial Centre): Budapest, Páva u. 39, 1094; tel. (1) 455-3333; e-mail info@hdke.hu; internet www.hdke.hu; f. 2004; permanent exhibition on history of the Jewish and Roma Holocaust with original documents and objects; organizes museum pedagogical programmes and cultural performances; Dir Prof. Dr SZABOLCS SZITA (acting).

Iparművészeti Múzeum (Museum of Applied Arts): Budapest, Üllői u. 33–37, 1091; tel. (1) 456-5107; e-mail info@imm.hu; internet www.imm.hu; f. 1872; European and Hungarian decorative arts; library: see under Libraries and Archives; Gen. Dir (vacant); Sec. MAGDOLNA POICH; publ. *Ars Decorativa* (1 a year, print and online, www.imm.hu/hu/contents/71,Ars+Decorativa).

Component Museums:

Hopp Ferenc Kelet-Ázsiai Művészeti Múzeum (Ferenc Hopp Museum of Eastern Asiatic Arts): Budapest, Andrássy u. 103, 1062; tel. (1) 456-5110; e-mail hopp.budapest@museum.hu; internet www.hoppmuzeum.hu; f. 1919; collns of Asiatic arts; permanent and periodic exhibitions; research; museum education; publishing; archives; museum library; library of 29,000 vols; Dir Dr GYÖRGYI FAJCSÁK.

Nagytétényi Kastélymúzeum (Castle Museum Nagytétény): Budapest, Kastélypark u. 9–11, 1225; tel. (1) 207-0005; e-mail info@nagytetenyi.hu; internet www.nagytetenyi.hu; f. 1948; European furniture of the 15th to the 19th centuries; Dir ANDREA FODOR (acting).

Ráth György Múzeum: Budapest, Városligeti fasor 12, 1068; tel. (1) 342-3916; f. 1906; permanent exhibitions of art of Chinese ceramics, colln of Japanese woodcuts, Oriental art colln in Hungary; Chief Curator Dr GYÖRGYI FAJCSÁK.

Katasztrófavédelem Központi Múzeuma: Budapest, Martinovics tér 12, 1105; tel. (1) 261-3586; e-mail kok.muzeum@katved.gov.hu; internet muzeum.katasztrofavedelem.hu; f. 1955, current name adopted 2012; incl. old fire-fighting equipment, carts, pumps and hoses; universal and Hungarian history of fire protection, its means and organization; 120,000 photographs and negatives; library of 15,000 vols; Curator IMRE BERKI; publ. *Tűzoltó Múzeum Évkönyve* (Yearbook).

Közlekedési Múzeum (Transport Museum): Budapest, Városligeti krt 11, 1146; tel. (1) 273-3840; e-mail info@mmkm.hu; internet www.mmkm.hu/index.php/hu/kozlekedesimuzeum; f. 1896; models of railway locomotives and rolling stock, old vehicles, railway, nautical, aeronautical, road and urban transport collns, road- and bridge-building; 4 br. museums incl. aviation and railway exhibitions with open-air displays; library of 95,000 vols; Dir Dr MIHÁLY KRÁMLI; publ. *A Közlekedési Múzeum Évkönyve*.

Liszt Ferenc Emlékmúzeum és Kutatóközpont (Ferenc Liszt Memorial Museum and Research Centre): Budapest VI, Vörösmarty u. 35, 1064; tel. (1) 413-0440; e-mail info@lisztmuseum.hu; internet www.lisztmuseum.hu; f. 1986; reconstruction of composer Franz Liszt's (1811–1886) residence in the bldg of the Old Acad. of Music, with his instruments, furniture, library and other memorabilia; permanent and temporary exhibitions; colln of Liszt's music MSS, letters and other documentation, in collaboration with the Research Library for Music History; Dir Dr ZSUZSANNA DOMOKOS.

MMKM Elektrotechnikai Múzeuma (Museum of Electrical Engineering): Budapest, Kazinczy u. 21, 1075; tel. (1) 342-5750; e-mail info@emuzeum.hu; internet elektromuzeum.hu; f. 1970; attached to Hungarian Museum of Science, Technology and Transport; historic colln of electrical engineering; library of 12,000 vols; Dir Dr ILDIKÓ ANTAL.

Magyar Építészeti Múzeum (Hungarian Museum of Architecture): Budapest, Mókus u. 20, 1036; tel. (1) 388-6170; internet www.archimus.hu; f. 1968; architecture and history of architecture; library of 7,000 vols; Dir KÁROLY BUGAR-MÉSZÁROS; publ. *Pavilon* (1 a year).

Magyar Kereskedelmi és Vendéglátóipari Múzeum (Hungarian Museum of Trade and Tourism): Budapest, Korona tér 1, 1036; tel. (1) 375-6249; e-mail mkvm@iif.hu; internet www.mkvm.hu; f. 1966; documentation colln and database on trade history; commercial poster colln; trade history photo colln; numismatic colln; documentation colln, database, poster and photo colln of history of catering industry; fine art colln; library of 45,700 vols; Dir IMRE KISS; Sec. JÁGER ANIKÓ VASVÁRI.

Magyar Mezőgazdasági Múzeum (Museum of Hungarian Agriculture): Budapest, POB 129, 1367; Budapest, Városliget, Vajdahunyadvár, 1146; tel. (1) 363-1117; e-mail info@mmgm.hu; internet www.mmgm.hu; f. 1896; colln, preservation and presentation of objects and documents related to the history of agriculture and agro-industries in Hungary; confs; provincial brs; library of 100,000 vols; Dir-Gen. Dr GYÖRGY FEHÉR; publs *Agrártörténeti Szemle* (Agricultural History Review, 2 a year), *Bibliographia Historiae Rerum Rusticarum Internationalis* (International Bibliography of Agrarian History, every 4 years), *Magyar Mezőgazdasági Múzeum Közleményei* (Proceedings, every 2 years).

Magyar Műszaki és Közlekedési Múzeum (Hungarian Museum of Science, Technology and Transport): Budapest, POB 37, 1426; Budapest, Városligeti krt 11, 1146; tel. (1) 273-3840; e-mail info@mmkm.hu; internet www.mmkm.hu; f. 2009 by merger of Transport Museum (f. 1896) and Nat. Museum for Science and Technology (f. 1973); colln covers inventions and prototypes with reference to natural science and technology, historic exhibits from the early days of industry and its devt to the present; colln of locomotives and wagons on a 1:5 scale; railway technology; history of road traffic, history of sailing and history of flight and space flight; library of 150,000 vols, 2,889 m of written material; Dir Dr MIHÁLY KRÁMLI; publs *A Közlekedési Múzeum Évkönyve* (Yearbook of the Transport Museum), *Technikatörténeti Szemle* (Review of History of Technology).

Magyar Nemzeti Galéria (Hungarian National Gallery): Budapest, POB 31, 1250; Budapest, Szent György tér 2, 1014; tel. (1) 201-9082; e-mail info@mng.hu; internet www.mng.hu; f. 1957; collns incl. Hungarian art since the 11th century, paintings, sculptures, drawings, engravings, medals; photograph archive of 60,000 black and white negatives and 1,000 slides; library of 76,000 vols; Dir Dr LÓRÁND BERECZKY; publ. *A Magyar Nemzeti Galéria Évkönyve* (Annals).

Magyar Nemzeti Múzeum (Hungarian National Museum): Budapest, Múzeum krt 14–16, 1088; tel. (1) 327-7700; e-mail hnm@hnm.hu; internet www.hnm.hu; f. 1802; colln of archaeology, numismatics, historical photographs, historical repository; library: see under Libraries and Archives; Dir Dr LÁSZLÓ CSORBA; publs *Bibliotheca Humanitatis Historica*, *Communicationes Archaeologicae Hungariae* (1 a year), *Folia Archaeologica* (1 a year), *Folia Historica* (1 a year), *Inventaria Praehistorica Hungariae*, *Múzeumi Műtárgyvédelem* (Protection of Museum Art Objects, 1 a year), *Régészeti Füzetek* (Fasciculi Archaeologici).

Magyar Sportmúzeum (Hungarian Museum of Sport): Budapest, Istvánmezei u. 3–5, 1146; tel. (1) 252-1696; e-mail info@sportmuzeum.hu; internet www.sportmuzeum.hu; f. 1967; documents and photos of history of sport in Hungary and abroad; 7,000 books, 35,000 plaques and medals, 4,000 trophies, 500,000 photographs, films; Dir Dr LAJOS SZABÓ.

Magyar Természettudományi Múzeum (Hungarian Natural History Museum): Budapest, Baross u. 13, 1088; Budapest, Ludovika tér 2–6, 1083; tel. (1) 210-1085; e-mail mtminfo@mttm.hu; internet www.nhmus.hu; f. 1802; depts of mineralogy and petrography, geology and palaeontology, botany, zoology, anthropology; library of 300,000 vols, 1,720 periodicals; Dir-Gen. Dr ISTVÁN MATSKÁSI; publs *Acta Zoologica Academiae Scientiarum Hungaricae* (4 a year), *Annales Historico-Naturales Musei Nationalis Hungarici* (1 a year), *Folia Entomologica Hungarica* (1 a year), *Fragmenta Palaeontologica Hungarica* (1 a year), *Studia Botanica Hungarica* (1 a year).

Néprajzi Múzeum (Museum of Ethnography): Budapest, Kossuth Lajos tér 12, 1055; tel. (1) 473-2400; e-mail info@neprajz.hu; internet www.neprajz.hu; f. 1872; collns and research activities cover peasant and tribal folk cultures; ethnographic archive with 28,000 MSS and 318,000 photographs, 252 films; folk music archive with 62,000 entries; library of 169,000 vols; Dir Dr LAJOS KEMECSI; publs *Fontes Musei Ethnographiae*, *Hungarian Folklore Bibliography* (1 a year), *MaDok-füzetek*, *Magyar Néprajzi Bibliográfia* (Bibliography of Hungarian Ethnography, 1 a year), *Néprajzi Értesítő* (Yearbook), *Tabula* (2 a year).

Öntödei Múzeum (Foundry Museum): Budapest, Bem József u. 20, 1027; tel. (1) 201-4370; e-mail ontode@mmkm.hu; internet mmkm.hu/index.php/hu/ontodeimuzeum; f. 1969; attached to Hungarian Museum of Science and Technology; used by Ábrahám Ganz and others until 1964; original foundry equipment; history of technological devt of foundry trade, old mouldings; library of 1,483 vols; Man. GABOR KEPES.

Petőfi Irodalmi Múzeum (Petőfi Literary Museum): Budapest, POB 71, 1364; Budapest, Károlyi Mihály u. 16, 1053; tel. (1) 317-3611; e-mail muzeuminf@pim.hu; internet www.pim.hu; f. 1954; literature since the 19th century; 30,000 photographs, 4,900 sound recordings; art colln of 20,000 items; 3 provincial brs: Kassák Museum, Endre Ady Memorial Museum, Jókai Memorial Room; library of 400,000 vols, 950,000 MSS; Dir Dr CSILLA E. CSORBA; Scientific Sec Dr GÁBOR PALKÓ.

Postamúzeum (Postal Museum): Budapest, Benczúr u. 27, 1068; tel. (1) 269-6838; e-mail info@postamuzeum.hu; internet www.postamuzeum.hu; f. 1955; permanent exhibition of the history of post and telecommunications; library of 11,000 vols; Dir JÚLIA KISFALUDI; publs *Hírközlési Múzeumi Alapítvány*, *Postai és Távközlési Múzeumi Alapítvany Évkönyve* (1 a year).

Semmelweis Orvostörténeti Múzeum, Könyvtár és Levéltár (Semmelweis Museum, Library and Archives of the History of Medicine): Budapest, Apród. u. 1–3, 1013; tel. (1) 375-3533; e-mail semmelweis@museum.hu; internet www.semmelweis.museum.hu; f. 1965; collects and exhibits items on history of medicine; organizes extracurricula courses for univ. and college students on history of medicine, intellectual history and history of learning; library of 122,000 vols, 20,000 periodicals; Gen. Dir BENEDEK VARGA; publ. *Orvostörténeti Közlemények / Communicationes de Historia Artis Medicinae* (1 a year).

Szépművészeti Múzeum (Museum of Fine Arts): Budapest, POB 463, 1396; Budapest, Dózsa György u. 41, 1146; tel. (1) 469-7100; e-mail info@szepmuveszeti.hu; internet www.szepmuveszeti.hu; f. 1896, opened 1906; collns and galleries incl. Egyptian and Greco-Roman antiquities, foreign paintings, sculptures, drawings and engravings; library of 150,000 vols; Dir-Gen. Dr LÁSZLÓ BAÁN; publ. *MúzeumCafé* (24 a year).

Attached Museum:

Vasarely Múzeum: Budapest, Szentlélek tér 6, 1033; tel. (1) 388-7551; e-mail vasarely.budapest@museum.hr; internet www.vasarely.hu; f. 1987; Dir LILLA SZABÓ.

Textil és Textilruházati Ipartörténeti Múzeum (Museum of the Textile and Clothing Industry): Budapest III, Lajos u. 138, 1036; tel. (1) 430-1387; e-mail textilmuzeum@t-online.hu; f. 1972; exhibits from Hungary and Central Europe; library of 3,690 vols; Dir NOÉMI NÉPESSY; publ. *Évkönyv* (Year Book).

Zenetörténeti Múzeum (Museum of Music History): Budapest, Táncsics Mihály u. 7, 1014; tel. (1) 214-6770; e-mail museum@zti.hu; internet www.zti.hu/museum; f. 1969; attached to Institute of Musicology of the Hungarian Acad. of Sciences; colln of instruments, MSS, personal objects used by great musicians; library of 1,200 vols; Dir ANNA BARANYI.

Cegléd

Kossuth Múzeum: Cegléd, Muzeum u. 5, 2700; tel. (53) 310-637; e-mail kossuthmuzeum@kossuthmuzeum.com; internet www.kossuthmuzeum.com; f. 1917; relics of Lajos Kossuth; ethnography, archaeology, arts, numismatics collns; library of 14,000 vols; Dir ERZSÉBET REZNÁK; publ. *Ceglédi Füzetek* (1 a year).

Debrecen

Déri Múzeum: Debrecen, Déri tér 1, 4026; tel. (52) 417-560; e-mail deri@derimuzeum.hu; internet www.derimuz.hu; f. 1920; archaeological, ethnographic, fine and applied art, natural history, literary and local history collns and exhibitions; library of 50,000 vols, photographic archive of 100,500 negatives and slides; Dir Dr JÁNOS ANGI; Sec. KRISZTINA MÓZSI; publs *A Déri Múzeum Évkönyve* (Yearbook), *Múzeumi Kurir* (Review).

Dunaújváros

Fejér Megyei Múzeumok Igazgatósága—Intercisa Múzeum: Dunaújváros, Városháza tér 4, 2400; tel. (25) 408-970; e-mail intercisamuz@gmail.com; f. 1951; prehistoric, Roman and medieval collns; regional history, archaeology and ethnography; library of 5,900 vols; Curator Dr MÁRTA MATUSSNÉ LENDVAI.

Eger

Dobó István Vármúzeum (István Dobó Castle Museum): Eger, Vár 1, 3300; tel. (36) 312-744; e-mail varmuzeum@egrivar.hu; internet www.egrivar.hu; f. 1872; originally archiepiscopal picture gallery and museum; enlarged by Fort Eger excavation material 1949; local remains of archaeology, ethnography, history of literature and of arts; relics of the Turkish occupation; library of 30,000 vols; Dir Dr TIVADAR PETERCSÁK; publs *Agria* (Yearbook), *Studia Agriensia*.

Esztergom

Balassa Bálint Múzeum: Esztergom, Mindszenty tér 5, 2501; tel. (33) 500-175; e-mail balassamuzeum@balassamuzeum.hu; internet www.balassamuzeum.hu; f. 1894; history, archaeology, numismatics, applied arts; library of 12,000 vols; Dir Dr EDIT TARI.

Keresztény Múzeum (Christian Museum): Esztergom, Mindszenty tér 2, 2500; tel. (33) 413-880; e-mail keresztenymuzeum@vnet.hu; internet www.christianmuseum.hu; f. 1875; Hungarian, Italian, Dutch, Austrian and German late medieval and Renaissance paintings and sculpture; collns of baroque and modern art, decorative arts, prints and drawings; library of 11,000 vols; Dir PÁL CSÉFALVAY.

Magyar Környezetvédelmi és Vízügyi Múzeum/Duna Múzeum (Hungarian Environmental and Water Management Museum): Esztergom, Kölcsey u. 2, 2500; tel. (33) 500-250; e-mail info@dunamuzeum.hu; internet www.dunamuzeum.hu; f. 1973; history of water management; library of 9,700 vols; Curator TIMEA SZALKAI; publ. *Vizgazdálkodás* (Water Management).

Magyar Nemzeti Múzeum Vármúzeuma: Esztergom, Szent István tér 1, 2500; tel. (33) 415-986; e-mail varmegom@invitel.hu; internet www.mnmvarmuzeuma.hu; f. 1967; excavated and reconstructed royal palace from the times of the Hungarian House of the Árpáds; municipal history of Esztergom as royal seat in the Middle Ages; Dir GÁBOR REZI KATÓ; Sec. ZOLTÁN VIGH.

Fertőd

Esterházy-kastély Fertőd (Esterházy Castle Museum—Fertőd): Fertőd, Joseph Haydn u. 2, 9431; tel. (99) 537-640; e-mail eszterhaza@t-online.hu; internet www.esterhazy-kastely.com; f. 1959; historic castle of Esterházy family; local documents, furnishings, applied art, memorabilia of composer Franz Joseph Haydn; Dir JOLÁN BAK.

Gyöngyös

Mátra Múzeum: Gyöngyös, Kossuth u. 40, 3200; tel. (37) 505-530; e-mail matramuzeum@ace.hu; internet www.matramuzeum.hu; f. 1957; natural history: palaeontology, zoology and botany of Hungary and Europe; history of hunting; local history; aquariums; library of 12,000 vols; Chief Curator Dr EDIT GÁL; publ. *Folia Historico-naturalia Musei Matraensis* (1 a year).

Győr

Xántus János Múzeum: Győr, POB 1633, 9001; Győr, Széchenyi tér 5, 9022; tel. (96) 310-588; e-mail xantus@gymsmuzeum.hu; internet xantus.gymsmuzeum.hu; f. 1854; archaeological colln containing relics of the ancient town of Arrabona (now Győr); history, art, anthropology, Roman lapidarium; picture gallery; library of 20,000 vols; Dir GYULA PERGER; publ. *Arrabona* (1 a year).

Gyula

Erkel Ferenc Múzeum (Ferenc Erkel Museum): Gyula, Kossuth u. 17, 5700; tel. (66) 361-236; e-mail info@erkelmuzeumbaratai.hu; internet www.erkelmuzeumbaratai.hu; f. 1868; archaeology, art, local history, musicological and ethnographic collns; library of 9,052 vols; Dir EMÍLIA MARTYIN NAGYNÉ.

Hajdúböszörmény

Hajdúsági Múzeum: Hajdúböszörmény, Kossuth Lajos u. 1, 4220; tel. (52) 229-038; e-mail hajdusagi.hajduboszormeny@museum.hu; internet www.hajdusagimuzeum.hu; f. 1924; sections of archaeology, ethnography, history and fine arts; library of 15,000 vols; Dir GYULA SZEKERES; publs *Évkönyv* (every 2 years, in German and Hungarian), *Közlemények* (1 a year, in English, German, Hungarian, Russian).

Herend

Herendi Porcelánművészeti Múzeum (Herend Porcelain Museum): Herend, Kossuth u. 140, 8440; tel. (88) 523-197; e-mail cassa.muzeum@herend.com; internet herend.com/en/visiting-herend/muzeum; f. 1964; exhibits from the famous china factory, est. 1826; library of 4,500 vols; Dir MAGDOLNA SIMON.

Hódmezővásárhely

Tornyai János Múzeum és Közművelődési Központ (Janos Tornyai Museum and Cultural Centre): Hódmezővásárhely, Dr

Rapcsák András u. 16–18, 6800; tel. (62) 242-224; e-mail tjm@tjm.hu; internet tornyaimuzeum.hu; f. 1905; archaeological, ethnographic and folk-art collns, Tornyai paintings and Medgyessy sculptures; pottery and farm museum; library of 6,000 vols; Dir Dr IMRE NAGY.

Jászberény

Jász Múzeum: Jászberény, Táncsics- u. 5, 5100; tel. (57) 412-753; e-mail jaszmuzeum@invitel.hu; internet www.djm.hu/jasz-muzeum.html; f. 1873; collns from the late Stone, Copper, Bronze and Iron Ages; ethnography, local history; fine art and natural history collns; library of 6,593 vols; Dir Dr BATHÓ EDIT HORTINÉ; publ. *Jászsági Füzetek Sorozat* (1 a year).

Kalocsa

Viski Károly Múzeum: Kalocsa, Szent István Király u. 25, 6300; tel. (78) 462-351; e-mail info@viskikarolymuzeum.hu; internet www.viskikarolymuzeum.hu; f. 1932; collns of ethnography, archaeology, historical, fine art, minerals, medals; library of 9,000 vols; Dir IMRE ROMSICS.

Kaposvár

Rippl-Rónai Megyei Hatókörű Városi Múzeum: Kaposvár, Fő u. 10, 7400; tel. (82) 314-011; e-mail titkarsag@smmi.hu; internet www.smmi.hu; f. 1909; archaeological and ethnographic collns, contemporary history, fine arts, natural history; library of 13,000 vols; Dir and Chief Curator Dr LEVENTE ÁBRAHÁM; publs *Múzeumi Tájékoztató*, *Somogyi Múzeumok Füzetei*, *Somogyi Múzeumok Közleményei*.

Karcag

Györffy István Nagykun Múzeum: Karcag, Kálvin u. 4, 5300; tel. (59) 312-087; e-mail karcagimuzeum@gmail.hu; internet www.djm.hu/gyorffy-istvan-nagykun-muzeum.html; f. 1906; regional museum, ethnography; library of 8,000 vols; Curator Dr MIKLÓS NAGY MOLNÁR.

Kecskemét

Bozsó Gyűjtemény (Bozsó Collection): Kecskemét, Klapka u. 34, 6000; tel. (76) 324-625; e-mail bozsoal@mail.datanet.hu; internet www.bozso.net; f. 1993; preserves and displays the work of Hungarian artist János Bozsó; Dir KLÁRA LÓRÁND.

Katona József Emlékház (József Katona Memorial House): Kecskemét, Katona József u. 5, 6000; tel. (76) 328-420; e-mail klio.ilona@t-online.hu; internet nepiiparmuveszet.hu/kje.html; f. 1971; life and work of 18th century writer József Katona; organizes lectures and lessons on history of Hungarian literature and cultural history of the town of Kecskemét; library of 16,600 vols; Dir MÁRIA DÁVID KRISKÓNÉ; Chief Curator ILONA KŐRÖSI SZÉKELY.

Magyar Naiv Művészek Múzeuma (Museum of Hungarian Naive Art): Kecskemét, Gáspár András u. 11, 6000; tel. (76) 324-767; e-mail kecskem1@t-online.hu; f. 1976; exhibitions of works of Hungarian primitive painters and sculptors; Dir Dr JÁNOS BÁRTH; publ. *Magyar Naiv Művészek Múzeuma*.

Szórakaténusz Játékmúzeum és Műhely (Toy Museum and Workshop): Kecskemét, Gáspár András u. 11, 6000; tel. (76) 481-469; e-mail muzeumesmuhely@szorakatenusz.hu; internet www.szorakatenusz.hu; f. 1981; colln of 25,000 artefacts; library of 3,000 vols; Dir ÁGNES KALMÁR; publ. *Studies of the History of Toys*.

Keszthely

Balatoni Múzeum: Keszthely, Múzeum u. 2, 8360; tel. (83) 312-351; e-mail info@balatonimuzeum.hu; internet www.balatonimuzeum.hu; f. 1898; 380,000 artefacts; prehistoric, historic and ethnographic collns relating to Lake Balaton; 23 paintings of János Halápy; aquarium; library of 29,000 vols; Dir Dr BÁLINT HAVASI.

Helikon Kastélymúzeum (Helikon Castle Museum): Keszthely, Kastély u. 1, 8360; tel. (83) 314-194; e-mail titkarsag@helikonkastely.hu; internet helikonkastely.hu; f. 1974; 18th century castle built by the Festetics family; exhibitions: aristocratic lifestyle, arts of the Islamic world, Helikon library; coach museum, hunting museum and historical model railway exhibit; library of 94,000 vols; Dir Dr LÁSZLÓ CZOMA; Sec. ANNAMARIA BERNATH.

Kiskőrös

Petőfi Szülőház és Emlékmúzeum (Petőfi Birthplace and Memorial Museum): Kiskőrös, Petőfi Sq. 5, POB 71, 6200; tel. (78) 312-566; e-mail petofimuzeum@koroskabel.hu; internet petofimuzeum.hu; f. 1985; preserves Hungarian poet Sándor Petőfi's birthplace, furniture and private papers and documents; displays art colln related to the life and works of the poet; Dir Dr LUCZA ILONA KISPÁLNÉ.

Kiskunfélegyháza

Bács-Kiskun Megyei Múzeumi Szervezet Kiskun Múzeum: Kiskunfélegyháza, Dr Holló Lajos u. 9, 6100; tel. (76) 461-468; e-mail kiskun.kiskunfelegyhaza@museum.hu; internet www.kiskunmuzeum.hu; f. 1902; collns of archaeology, numismatic, historical, ethnography, fine and applied art; library of 20,000 vols; Dir MÁRTA MÉSZÁROS.

Kiskunhalas

Thorma János Múzeum: Kiskunhalas, Köztársaság u. 2, 6400; tel. (77) 422-864; e-mail muzeum@halas.hu; internet www.muzeum.halas.hu; f. 1874; 88,000 artefacts of ethnography, archaeology, local history, fine and applied arts, numismatics; library of 7,000 vols; Dir AURÉL SZAKÁL.

Kőszeg

Városi Múzeum (Municipal Museum): Kőszeg, Jurisics tér 6, 9730; tel. (94) 360-240; e-mail kozmuvelodes@savariamuseum.hu; f. 1932; colln of castle and town history; library of 9,300 vols; Dir JÓZSEF RÉVÉSZ.

Mátészalka

Szatmári Múzeum: Mátészalka, Kossuth u. 5, 4700; tel. (44) 502-646; e-mail szatmuz@keletnet.hu; internet www.szatmarimuzeum.hu; f. 1975; colln of carriages, wagons and equipages; local history and ethnographic collns; Dir Dr LÁSZLÓ CSERVENYÁK.

Miskolc

Herman Ottó Múzeum: Miskolc, Görgey Artúr u. 28, 3529; tel. (46) 560-170; e-mail latogato@hermuz.hu; internet www.hermuz.hu; f. 1899, current name adopted 1953; collns of archaeology, regional ethnography, fine arts and applied arts, natural science, minerals of Hungary, local history, literary history, history of photography; library of 44,000 vols; Dir Dr TAMÁS PUSZTAI; Sec. Dr LÁSZLÓ SIMON; publs *A Herman Ottó Múzeum Évkönyve* (Yearbook), *A Miskolci Herman Ottó Múzeum Közleményei* (Communications), *Documentatio Borsodiensis*, *Natura Borsodiensis*, *Néprajzi Kiadványok* (Ethnographical Studies), *Officina Musei*.

Kohászati Múzeum (Museum of Metallurgy): Miskolc-Felsőhámor, Palota u. 22, 3517; tel. (46) 379-375; e-mail kohmuz@kohmuz.t-online.hu; internet www.kohmuz.t-online.hu; f. 1949; history of the foundry, science and technology; archaeological foundry of the 9th to 12th centuries; technical monument from the 18th century, the Fazola foundry; Dir ISTVÁN GULYA.

Mohács

Kanizsan Dorottya Múzeum: Mohács, Városház u. 1, 7700; tel. (69) 311-536; e-mail kdm@jpm.hu; internet mohacs.jpm.hu; f. 1923; ethnography of the Serbs, Croats and Slavs; library of 2,300 vols; Curator JAKAB FERKOV.

Mosonmagyaróvár

Hansági Múzeum: Mosonmagyaróvár, Fő u. 19, 9200; tel. (96) 212-094; e-mail hansagi@hansagimuzeum.hu; internet hansagi.gymsmuseum.hu; f. 1882; regional museum; archaeology, ethnography, lapidarium, local history, paintings by János Szale, Gyurkovits colln; library of 7,216 vols; Dir ZOLTÁN SZÉKELY.

Nagycenk

Széchenyi István Emlékmúzeum (Széchenyi István Memorial Museum): Nagycenk, Kiscenki u. 3, 9485; tel. (99) 360-023; e-mail soproni@gymsmuseum.hu; internet www.muzeum.sopron.hu; f. 1973; history of the Széchenyi family and life (iconography, bibliography) of 19th century statesman Count István Széchenyi; library of 5,000 vols; Dir Dr IMRE TÓTH; Librarian BEATA KOLLERITS.

Nagykanizsa

Thury György Múzeum: Nagykanizsa, Fő u 5, 8800; tel. (93) 317-233; e-mail tgym@zmmi.hu; internet www.zmmi.hu/thury; f. 1919, current name adopted 1951; archaeological and ethnographical collns, local history displays, numismatics; library of 5,000 vols; Curator CSILLA SZÁRAZ.

Nagykőrös

Arany János Múzeum: Nagykőrös, Ceglédi u. 19, 2751; tel. (53) 350-810; e-mail pmiajm@matavnet.hu; internet www.c3.hu/~pmiajm; f. 1928; regional museum; archaeology, ethnography, local history, literary documents of poet J. Arany; library of 20,019 vols; Dir Dr NOVÁK LÁSZLÓ; publs *Acta Musei*, *Archivum Musei*.

Nyirbátor

Báthori István Múzeum Nyirbátor: Nyirbátor, Károlyi Mihály u. 15, 4300; tel. (42) 281-760; e-mail bathori.nyirbator@museum.hu; internet www.nyirbim.hu; f. 1955; colln on archaeology, local history and art; library of 2,900 vols; Dir Dr SAROLTA SZABÓ.

Nyiregyháza

Jósa András Múzeum: Nyíregyháza, Benczúr tér 21, POB 57, 4401; tel. (42) 315-722; e-mail jam@jam.nyirbone.hu; f. 1868; collns of archaeology, ethnography and local history; fine and applied arts, numismatics; library of 35,000 vols; Dir Dr JÁNOS BENE; publ. *A nyíregyházi Jósa András Múzeum Évkönyve* (1 a year).

Pannonhalma

Pannonhalmi Főapátság Gyűjteménye (Abbey of Pannonhalma Collection): Pannonhalma, Vár 1, 9090; tel. (96) 570-191; e-mail foapatsag.pannonhalma@museum.hu; f. 1802; paintings, sculptures, applied arts in an ancient Benedictine Abbey.

Pápa

Gróf Esterházy Károly Kastély- és Tájmúzeum (Count Charles Esterházy Castle and Regional Museum): Pápa, POB 208, 8501; Pápa, Fő tér 1, Várkastély, 8500; tel. (89) 313-584; e-mail esterhazykastely@papa.hu; internet esterhazykastely.papa.hu; f. 1960; ethnographical, archaeological and industrial collns from the town and environment; library of 10,000 vols; Dir Dr ISTVÁN NAGY; publ. *Acta Musei Papensis* (1 a year).

Pécs

Csontváry Múzeum: Pécs, Janus Pannonius u. 11, 7621; tel. (72) 310-544; e-mail jpm@jpm.hu; internet www.pecsimuzeumok.hu; f. 1973; attached to Directorate of Baranya Co Museums; art gallery comprising selected works by the Expressionist painter Tivadar Csontváry Kosztka; Man. GÁBOR TILLAI.

Janus Pannonius Múzeum: Pécs, Káptalan u. 5, 7621; tel. (72) 514-040; e-mail jpm@jpm.hu; internet www.pecsimuzeumok.hu; f. 1904; colln on natural sciences, archaeology, ethnography, modern Hungarian art, local history; library of 25,000 vols; Dir Dr JULIA FABÉNYI; publ. *Dunántuli Dolgozatok* (Trans-Danubian Studies).

Képző- és Iparművészeti Gyűjtemények (Fine and Applied Arts Collections): Pécs, Káptalan u. 4, 7621; tel. (72) 514-040; e-mail art@jpm.hu; f. 1957; attached to Directorate of Baranya County Museums; examples of the Nagybánya school (Hollósy, Ferenczy), pre-war art (Rippl-Rónai, Gulácsy), the Eight (Pór, Kernstok, Berény, Tihanyi), Activism (Nemes Lampért, Uitz, Mattis-Teutsch), the Avant-garde (Breuer, Molnár, Moholy-Nagy), artists with social sensitivity (Dési Huber, Derkovits, Goldman, Bokros Birman), the school of Rome and artists of Szentendre (Vajda, Ámos, Barcsay, Czóbel, Kmetty), the European school (Korniss, Gyarmathy, Anna Margit); Curator JÓZSEF SÁRKÁNY.

Modern Magyar Képtár (Gallery of Modern Hungarian Art): Pécs, Papnövelde u. 5, 7621; tel. (72) 891-328; f. 1957; attached to Directorate of Baranya County Museums; permanent exhibition of 20th-century Hungarian art.

Vasarely Múzeum: Pécs, Káptalan u. 3, 7621; tel. (71) 676-2446; e-mail jpm@jpm.hu; f. 1976; attached to Directorate of Baranya County Museums; art gallery comprising works by Hungarian-born French artist Victor Vasarely; Man. GÁBOR TILLAI.

Rudabánya

Alapítvány Érc- és Ásványbányászati Múzeum (Museum of Mining of Metals and Minerals): Rudabánya, Petőfi u. 24, 3733; tel. (48) 353-151; e-mail eabmuz@axelero.hu; f. 1956; history of the industry, exhibitions; Curator BÉLA SZUROMI.

Salgótarján

Nógrádi Történeti Múzeum (Nógrád Historical Museum): Salgótarján, POB 3, 3101; Salgótarján, Múzeum tér 2, 3100; tel. (32) 520-700; e-mail nogradimuzeum@nogradi-muzeumok.hu; internet www.nogradi-muzeumok.hu; f. 1959; social history since the 19th century, history of art, literary history, numismatics, industrial history, esp. mining; library of 16,000 vols; Dir Dr ÉVA SZIRÁCSIK; publ. *Yearbook of the Museums of Nógrád County*.

Sárospatak

Magyar Nemezeti Múzeum, Rákóczi Múzeum: 3950 Sárospatak, Szent Erzsébet u. 19; tel. (47) 311-083; e-mail info@rakoczimuzeum.hu; internet www.rakoczimuzeum.hu; f. 1950; housed in the Castle of Sárospatak; historical, ethnographic, archaeological, applied art collns; library of 20,000 vols; Dir Dr EDIT TAMÁS.

Sárvár

Nádasdy Ferenc Múzeum: Sárvár, Várkerület 1, 9600; tel. (95) 320-158; e-mail info@nadasdymuzeum.hu; internet www.nadasdymuzeum.hu; f. 1951; late Renaissance and Baroque Hungarian milieu reconstructed in state rooms of 16th century castle; historical documentary colln; library of 3,900 vols; Dir ZOLTÁN TAKÁCS.

Sopron

Győr-Moson-Sopron Megyei Múzeumok Igazgatósága Soproni Múzeum: Sopron, Fő tér 8, 9400; tel. (99) 311-327; e-mail soproni@gymsmuzeum.hu; internet www.muzeum.sopron.hu; f. 1867; archaeology, folk art, pharmacy, medieval synagogue, local Baroque art and Storno Collns in 11 exhibition halls; exhibits early modern and contemporary history of Sopron and its surroundings from the 17th to 20th century; library of 30,000 vols; Dir Dr IMRE TÓTH; Librarian BEATA KOLLERITS.

Központi Bányászati Múzeum (Central Mining Museum): Sopron, Templom u. 2, 9400; tel. (99) 312-667; e-mail info@kbm.hu; internet www.kbm.hu; f. 1957; science and technology; history of mining in the Carpathian basin since prehistoric age; Dir Dr ERZSÉBET BIRCHER KOVÁCSNÉ.

Szarvas

Tessedik Sámuel Múzeum: Szarvas, Vajda Péter u. 1, 5540; tel. (66) 216-608; e-mail szarvasimuzeum@gmail.com; internet www.szarazmalom.hu; f. 1951, present status 2009; archaeology, ethnography and local history collns; Dir Dr ZOLTÁN ROSZIK.

Szécsény

Kubinyi Ferenc Múzeum: Szécsény, Ady Endre-u. 7, 3170; tel. (32) 370-143; e-mail kubinyi.f@freemail.hu; f. 1973; archaeology and local history; library of 8,400 vols; Curator Dr JUDIT TORONYI GUSZTINÉ.

Szeged

Móra Ferenc Múzeum: Szeged, Roosevelt tér 1–3, 6720; tel. (62) 549-040; e-mail info@mfm.u-szeged.hu; internet www.mfm.u-szeged.hu; f. 1883; archaeological, ethnographic and biological collns, history of arts and regional collns; library of 50,000 vols, spec. collns: Sándor Bálint bequest of 5,500 vols on archaic religions and beliefs, old books of prayers and liturgies, Győző Csongor Bequest of 5,500 vols on local history; Dir Dr OTTÓ FOGAS; publs *Monographia Archaeologica* (1 a year), *Studia Archaeologica* (1 a year), *Studia Ethnographica* (1 a year), *Studia Historiae Literarum et Artium* (1 a year), *Studia Historica* (1 a year), *Studia Naturalia* (1 a year).

Székesfehérvár

Szent István Király Múzeum (King Saint Stephen Museum): Székesfehérvár, Fő u. 6, 8000; tel. (22) 315-583; e-mail szikm@iif.hu; internet www.szikm.hu; f. 1873; prehistoric, Roman and medieval collns, anthropological, musical and numismatic colln, regional ethnography, art gallery, stones of the Basilica of King St Stephen; library of 90,000 vols; Dir ZSÓFIA DEMETER; Librarian MÁRIA BRAILA; publ. *Alba Regia* (Scientific Almanac).

Szekszárd

Wosinsky Mór Megyei Múzeum: Szekszárd, Szent István tér 26, 7100; tel. (74) 316-222; e-mail wmmm@terrasoft.hu; internet wmmm.hu/aktualitasok; f. 1896; collns of folk art, archaeology, history, fine arts and applied arts, literature; library of 26,393 vols, 25 current periodicals; Dir Dr JÁNOS GÁBOR ÓDOR; publ. *Yearbook*.

Szentendre

Pest Megyei Múzeumok Igazgatósága Ferenczy Múzeum Szentendre: Szentendre, Fő tér 6, 2000; tel. (26) 310-244; e-mail info@pmmi.hu; internet www.pmmi.hu; f. 1951; paintings, drawings, sculptures and Gobelin tapestries; centre for 30 museums in Pest County; library of 24,000 vols, 210 periodicals; Dir Dr LÁSZLÓ SIMON; publ. *Studia Comitatensia* (yearbook of papers published by the Museums of Pest County).

Szabadtéri Néprajzi Múzeum (Hungarian Open Air Museum): Szentendre, Sztaravodai u., POB 63, 2000; tel. (26) 502-500; e-mail sznm@sznm.hu; internet www.skanzen.hu; f. 1967; vernacular architecture and furniture; archive of 110,000 photographs; 20,000 ethnographical, historical, architectural documents, films, maps, drawings; library of 50,000 vols; Dir Dr MIKLÓS CSERI; Scientific Sec. Dr ZSOLT SÁRI; publs *Ház és Ember* (1 a year), *Téka* (4 a year).

Szentes

Koszta József Múzeum: Szentes, Kossuth tér 1, 6600; tel. (63) 313-352; e-mail muzeum@szentesinfo.hu; internet www.muzeum.gportal.hu; f. 1894; archaeological and ethnographical colln and paintings by Koszta; Dir Dr MÁRIA BÉRES.

Szigetvár

Zrínyi Miklós Vármúzeum: Szigetvár, Vár u. 1, 7900; tel. (73) 311-442; f. 1917; local history colln, relating particularly to the period of Turkish occupation (16th to 17th centuries).

Szolnok

Damjanich János Múzeum: Szolnok, Kossuth tér 4. POB 128, 5001; tel. (56) 510-150; e-mail info@djm.hu; internet www.djm.hu/damjanich-janos-muzeum.html; f. 1933; archaeology, ethnography, palaeontology, fine arts, applied art and local history collns; library of 50,000 vols; Dir Dr RÓBERT KERTÉSZ; publ. *Tisicum* (1 a year).

Szombathely

Savaria Múzeum: Szombathely, Kisfaludy Sándor u. 9, 9700; tel. (94) 500-720; e-mail info@savariamuseum.hu; internet www.savariamuseum.hu; f. 1872; natural history, archaeology, local cultural history, ethnography; library of 32,000 vols; Dir Dr ZOLTÁN NAGY; publs *Praenorica—Folia Historico-Naturalia* (irregular), *Savaria* (Journal, 1 a year).

Tác

Gorsium Régészeti Park (Gorsium Archaeological Park): Tác, Fövenypuszta Ady E. u. 56, 8121; tel. (22) 362-443; e-mail lak5706@mail.iif.hu; f. 1963; excavations of a Roman city, the ruins showing the original shape; Dir Prof. Dr JENŐ FITZ.

Tata

Komárom-Esztergom Megyei Múzeumok Igazgatósága Kuny Domokos Megyei Múzeum: Tata, Alkotmány u. 1, 2890; tel. (34) 487-888; e-mail titkarsag@kunymuzeum.hu; internet www.kunymuzeum.hu; f. 1954; history, archaeology, ethnology, art, palaeobotany collns; library of 27,000 vols; Dir RICHÁRD SCHMIDTMAYER; publ. *Komárom-Esztergom Megyei Múzeumok Közleményei* (in Hungarian with English and German summaries).

Vác

Tragor Ignác Múzeum: Vác, Zrínyi u. 41/a, 2600; tel. (27) 500-750; e-mail tragormuzeum@pmmi.hu; internet www

.pmmi.hu/en/museum/17/intro; f. 1895; archaeology, ethnography, local history and fine arts exhibits; library of 10,565 vols, 4,760 periodicals and newsletters; Dir KLÁRA KŐVÁRI; publ. *Váci Könyvek* (Bulletin).

Várpalota

Magyar Vegyészeti Múzeum (Hungarian Chemistry Museum): Várpalota, POB 39, 8101; Várpalota, Thury-vár, 8100; tel. (88) 575-670; e-mail info@vegyeszetimuzeum.hu; internet www.vegyeszetimuzeum.hu; f. 1963; searches, collects, conserves, evaluates and presents technical relics incl. objects, written documents of Hungarian chemical science, education and industry; 8,800 museum objects; 43,500 industrial historical documents; library of 18,400 vols; Dir VARGÁNÉ NYÁRI KATALIN.

Vértesszőllős

Magyar Nemzeti Múzeum Vértesszőllősi Bemutatóhelye (Archaeological Exhibition Hall of the Hungarian National Museum): Vértesszőllős, Előembertelep, Kőbánya, 2837; tel. (34) 710-350; e-mail hnm@hnm.hu; internet www.hnm.hu; f. 1975; permanent open-air exhibition; dwelling-place and remains of early man; part of Archaeology Dept of Nat. Museum; Curator Dr VIOLA DOBOSI.

Veszprém

Laczkó Dezső Múzeum: Veszprém, Erzsébet sétány 1, 8200; tel. (88) 426-081; e-mail titkar@vmmuzeum.hu; internet www.c3.hu/~vmmuzeum; f. 1903; ethnographic, archaeological, historical, fine and industrial arts, history of literature, numismatic exhibits from Veszprém Co; library of 36,000 vols; Dir Dr ZSUZSA FODOR; publs *Publicationes Museorum Comitatus Vesprimiensis* (Communications of the Museums of Veszprém County), *Veszprém Megyei Múzeumok Közleményei*.

Visegrád

Magyar Nemzeti Múzeum Mátyás Király Múzeum Visegrád (King Matthias Museum): Visegrád, Fő u. 23, 2025; tel. (26) 597-010; e-mail info@visegradmuzeum.hu; internet visegradmuzeum.hu; f. 1933; 13th-century upper and lower castle with Roman and medieval archaeological remains; partially restored 15th-century royal palace; library of 10,000 vols; Dir MÁTYÁS SZŐKE.

Zalaegerszeg

Göcseji Múzeum: Zalaegerszeg, Batthyány u. 2, POB 176, 8900; tel. (92) 314-537; e-mail muzeum@zmmi.hu; internet www.zmmi.hu/gocsej; f. 1950; collns of arts, regional history, archaeology and ethnography; library of 20,658 vols; Dir IMRE KAJÁN; publ. *Zalai Múzeum* (1 a year).

Magyar Olaj- és Gázipari Múzeum (Hungarian Oil and Gas Museum): Zalaegerszeg, Wlassics Gyula. u. 13, 8900; tel. (92) 313-632; e-mail moim@olajmuzeum.hu; internet www.olajmuzeum.hu; f. 1969; exhibitions of the history of professional and technical devt of the oil industry; colln of equipment, documents, photographs; library of 9,000 vols; Dir JÁNOS TÓTH.

Zirc

Bakonyi Természettudományi Múzeum (Bakony Mountains Natural History Museum): Zirc, Rákóczi tér 3–5, 8420; tel. (88) 575-300; e-mail btmz@bakonymuseum.koznet.hu; internet www.bakonymuseum.koznet.hu; f. 1972; natural history exhibits from Bakony Mountains, minerals from the Carpathian Basin; library of 25,000 vols, incl. 17,000 journals; Dir ÁGOTA KASPER; publs *A Bakony természettudományi kutatásának eredményei* (Results of Research into the Natural History of Bakony, 1 a year), *Folia Musei Historico-naturalis Bakonyiensis* (A Bakonyi Természettudományi Múzeum Közleményei, Communications of the Bakony Mountains Natural History Museum, 1 a year).

State Universities

BUDAPESTI CORVINUS EGYETEM
(Corvinus University of Budapest)

Budapest, Fővám tér 8, 1093
Telephone: (1) 482-5000
E-mail: rektor@uni-corvinus.hu
Internet: www.uni-corvinus.hu

Founded 1853, current name adopted 2004
State control
Languages of instruction: English, Hungarian
Academic year: September to June

Rector: Prof. Dr ZSOLT ROSTOVÁNYI
Vice-Rector for Devt: Prof. Dr MIHÁLY GÖRÖG
Vice-Rector for Education: Prof. Dr ZOLTÁN SZÁNTÓ
Vice-Rector for Research: Prof. Dr LÁSZLÓ PALKOVICS
Dir-Gen. for Central Library: ZSUZSANNA NAGY

Library of 500,000
Number of teachers: 821
Number of students: 13,000

Publications: *Applied Ecology and Environmental Research* (2 a year), *Társadalom és Gazdaság* (Society and Economy, 2 a year in Hungarian; 3 a year in English)

DEANS

Faculty of Business Administration: Prof. ÁGNES HOFMEISTER
Faculty of Economics: Dr LÁSZLÓ TRAUTMANN
Faculty of Food Science: Prof. Dr GYULA VATAI
Faculty of Horticultural Science: Prof. KÁROLY HROTKÓ
Faculty of Landscape Architecture: Prof. Dr KINGA SZILÁGYI
Faculty of Social Sciences: Dr LÁSZLÓ CSICSMANN

PROFESSORS

ÁBAFFY, J., Computer Science
ÁBEL, I., Macroeconomics
ÁGH, A., Politics
ANGYAL, Á., Management and Organization
BALATON, K., Management and Organization
BALÁZS, P., World Economics
BÁNFI, T., Finance
BARICZ, R., Accountancy
BEKKER, Z., Economic Theory
BERÁCS, J., Marketing
BERNÁTH, J., Herb and Aroma Products
BIACS, P., Microbiology
BLAHO, A., World Economics
BOD, P., Economic Policy
BRADEAN, N., International Relations
CHIKÁN, A., Logistics
CSABA, L., Comparative Economics
CSÁKI, C., Agricultural Economics
CSEMEZ, A., Landscape Planning and Development
CSER, L., Computer Science
CSIMA, P., Landscape Protection
CSIZMADIA, S., Political Science
DEÁK, D., Economic Law
DEÁK, I., Computer Science
DOBÁK, M., Management and Organization
EGEDY, G., Social Theory
FELFÖLDI, J., Physics and Control
FERTŐ, I., Agricultural Economics
FODOR, P., Applied Chemistry
FORGÓ, F., Operations Research
FÜSTÖS, L., Environmental Economics
GÁBOR, I., Human Resources
GÁL, P., World Economics
GALASI, P., Human Resources
GÁLIK, M., Media Economics
GEDEON, P., Comparative Economics
GÖRÖG, M., Strategy and Project Management
HADAS, M., Sociology
HAJDU, I., Food Economy
HÁMORI, B., Comparative Economics
HOFMEISTER, Á., Marketing
HORÁNYI, Ö., Communication
HROTKÓ, K., Pomology
ILONSZKI, G., Political Science
IVÁNYI, A., Strategy and Project Management
JÁMBOR, I., Landscape Technology and Garden Techniques
JÁMBORNÉ BENCZÚR, E., Floriculture and Dendrology
JENEI, G., Public Administration
KÁLLAY, M., Oenology
KARDOSNÉ KAPONYI, E., International Relations
KEREKES, S., Environmental Management
KISS, L., International Relations
KONCZ, K., Human Resources
KOSÁRY, J., Applied Chemistry
KOVÁCS, E., Operations Research
KUCZI, T., Sociology
LADÁNYI, J., Sociology
LÁNCZI, A., Political Science
LÁNG, Z., Technology
LENGYEL, G., Sociology
LŐRINC, A., International Relations
LUKÁCS, N., Plant Physiology
MARÁZ, A., Microbiology
MÁTHÉ, G., Jurisprudence
MÉSZÁROS, T., Strategy and Project Management
MEZŐSNÉ SZILÁGYI, K., Garden and Open Space Design
MISZLIVETZ, F., Global and European Integration
MÓCZÁR, J., Mathematical Economics
MOKSONY, F., Sociology
NOVÁKY, E., Future Studies
PALKOVICS, L., Plant Pathology
PEDRYC, A., Genetics and Plant Breeding
RÁCZ, L., Jurisprudence
RADICS, L., Ecology and Sustainable Economic Systems
RIMÓCZI, I., Botanics
ROSTOVÁNYI, Z., International Relations
SÁRKÖZY, T., Business Law
SCHMIDT, G., Floriculture and Dendrology
SCHNELLER, I., Urban Planning
STEFANOVITSNÉ BÁNYAI, É., Applied Chemistry
SURÁNYI, S., Finance
SZABÓ, K., Comparative Economics
SZABÓ, S. A., Food Chemistry
SZÁNTÓ, Z., Sociology
SZÁVAI, F., International Relations
SZÁZ, J., Investment and Corporate Finance
TAKÁCS, P., Jurisprudence
TALLÓS, P., Mathematics
TAMÁS, A., Jurisprudence
TARI, E., Management and Strategy
TEMESI, J., Operations Research
TERBE, I., Vegetable and Mushroom Growing
TÖRÖK, G., Private Law
TÓTH, M., Pomology
ÚJVÁRI, M., Sociology
VASTAG, G., Computer Science
VATAI, G., Food Engineering
VECSENYI, J., Development of Enterprises
VÉGVÁRI, G., Pomology
VIRÁG, M., Corporate Finance
VITA, L., Statistics
ZALAI, E., Econometrics
ZÁMBORINÉ NÉMETH, É., Medicinal and Aromatic Plants
ZSOLNAI, L., Business Ethics

BUDAPESTI MŰSZAKI ÉS GAZDASÁGTUDOMÁNYI EGYETEM (Budapest University of Technology and Economics)

Budapest, Műegyetem rkp. 3, 1111
Telephone: (1) 463-1111
E-mail: rektor@mail.bme.hu
Internet: www.bme.hu

Founded 1782 as Institutum Geometricum Hydrotechnicum and reorganized as Hungarian Palatine Joseph Technical Univ. in 1871, current name adopted 2000
State control
Languages of instruction: English, French, German, Hungarian, Russian
Academic year: September to June

Rector: Prof. Dr GÁBOR PÉCELI
Vice-Rector for Education: Prof. Dr ÁKOS JOBBÁGY
Vice-Rector for Gen. Affairs: Dr GYÖRGY ANDOR
Librarian: BÉLA LISZKAY

Number of teachers: 1,190
Number of students: 22,567

Publication: *A Budapesti Műszaki Egyetem Évkönyve* (1 a year)

DEANS

Faculty of Architecture: Dr GÁBOR BECKER
Faculty of Chemical Technology and Biotechnology: Dr FERENC FAIGL
Faculty of Civil Engineering: Dr LÁSZLÓ DUNAI
Faculty of Economic and Social Sciences: Dr JÁNOS KÖVESI
Faculty of Electrical Engineering and Informatics: Dr LÁSZLÓ VAJTA
Faculty of Mechanical Engineering: Dr TIBOR CZIGÁNY
Faculty of Natural Sciences: Dr JÁNOS PIPEK
Faculty of Transportation Engineering and Vehicle Engineering: Dr ISTVÁN VARGA

PROFESSORS

Centre for Learning Innovation and Adult Learning (Budapest, Egry J. u. 1, 1111; tel. (1) 463-3866; e-mail info@edu-inno.bme.hu; internet www.edu-inno.bme.hu):

SZŰCS, A.

Faculty of Architecture (tel. (1) 463-3521; e-mail dekanihivatal@epitesz.bme.hu; internet www.epitesz.bme.hu):

BALÁZS, M., Architectural Culture and Design
BALOGH, B., Design
BECKER, G., Building Constructions
CSÁGOLY, F., Architectural Culture and Design
DOMOKOS, G., Computational (Non-linear) Mechanics
KOLLÁR, L., Composite Materials and Load-bearing Structures
KONTRA, J., Mechanical Engineering
MEZŐS, T., Architectural Design
PÁLFY, S., Architectural and Urban Design
WAGNER, P., Architectural Design

Faculty of Chemical Technology and Biotechnology (tel. (1) 463-3571; e-mail vbk-dekan@mail.bme.hu; internet www.ch.bme.hu):

BORSA, J., Plastics and Rubber Industries
CSONKA, G., Inorganic Chemistry
FAIGL, F., Organic Chemical Technology
FEKETE, J., Analytical Chemistry
HORVAI, G., Analytical Chemistry
HÓRVÖLGYI, Z., Physical Chemistry
HUSZTHY, P., Organic Chemistry
KEGLEVICH, G., Organic Chemical Technology
KUBINYI, M., Physical Chemistry
LÁSZLÓ, K., Physical Chemistry
MAROSI, G., Organic Chemical Technology
MIZSEY, P., Chemical Unit
NYULÁSZI, L., Inorganic Chemistry
POKOL, G., Analytical Chemistry
POPPE, L., Organic Chemistry
PUKÁNSZKY, B., Plastics and Rubber Industries
SALGÓ, A., Biochemistry and Food Technology
SIMÁNDI, B., Chemical Unit
VÉRTESSY, B., Enzymology
VESZPRÉMI, T., Inorganic Chemistry

Faculty of Civil Engineering (tel. (1) 463-3531; e-mail fonad.ildiko@epito.bme.hu; internet www.epito.bme.hu):

ÁDÁM, J., Geodesy and Surveying
BAGI, K., Structural Mechanics
BARSI, Á., Photogrammetry and Geoinformatics
BOJTÁR, I., Structural Mechanics
DUNAI, L., Structural Engineering
FARKAS, G., Structural Engineering
FI, I., Highway and Railway Engineering
JÓZSA, J., Hydraulic and Water Resources Engineering
KONCSOS, L., Sanitary and Environmental Engineering
PATONAI, D., Architectural Engineering
SZILÁGYI, J., Hydraulic and Water Resources Engineering
TÖRÖK, Á., Construction Materials and Engineering Geology
VÖLGYESI, L., Geodesy and Surveying

Faculty of Economic and Social Sciences (tel. (1) 463-3591; e-mail gtk-dekani@gtdh.bme.hu; internet www.gtk.bme.hu):

ANTALOVITS, M., Ergonomics and Psychology
BENEDEK, A., Pedagogy and Technical Education
FORRAI, G., Philosophy and History of Science
IZSÓ, L., Ergonomics and Psychology
KOLTAI, T., Business and Management
KÖVESI, J., Business and Management
LOSONCZ, M., Economics
MAJOR, I., Economics
MARGITAY, T., Philosophy and History of Science
MEYER, D., Economics
NAGY, K. S., Sociology
PERECZ, L., Philosophy and History of Science
TARAFÁS, I., Finance
TÖRÖK, Á., Economics
VERESS, J., Economics and Business Policy

Faculty of Electrical Engineering and Informatics (Budapest, Egry F. u. 18, 1111; tel. (1) 463-3581; e-mail titkarsag@vik-dh.bme.hu; internet www.vik.bme.hu):

BARANYI, P., Telecommunication and Telematics
BERTA, I., High-Voltage Engineering
BIRÓ, J., Telecommunication and Telematics
GYŐRFI, L., Mathematics
HARSÁNYI, G., Electronic Technology
IMRE, S., Telecommunications
JEREB, L., Telecommunications
JOBBÁGY, Á., Measurement and Instrument Engineering
KERECSEN, I., Electronic Devices
KEVICZKY, L., Automation
KÓCZY, L., Telecommunication and Telematics
KOLLÁR, I., Measurement and Instrument Engineering
LEVENDOVSZKY, J., Telecommunications
MIZSEI, J., Electronic Devices
OLASZY, G., Telecommunication and Telematics
PATARICZA, A., Measurement and Instrument Engineering
PÁVÓ, J., Microwave Telecommunications
PÉCELI, G., Measurement and Instrument Engineering
RECSKI, A., Mathematics
SALLAI, G., Telecommunication and Telematics
SIMONYI, G., Mathematics
SZABÓ, C., Telecommunications
SZIRMAY-KALOS, L., Process Control
TELEK, M., Telecommunications
TIEN, V. DO, Telecommunications
VAJDA, I., Electrical Machines
VAJDA, I., Telecommunications
VAJK, I., Automation
VESZPRÉMI, K., Electrical Machines

Faculty of Mechanical Engineering (tel. (1) 463-3541; e-mail gepeszd@mail.bme.hu; internet www.gpk.bme.hu):

ÁBRAHÁM, G., Optical Engineering
CZIGÁNY, T., Polymer Engineering
KARGER-KOCSIS, J., Polymer Engineering
KORONDI, P., Mechatronical Engineering
LÁNG, P., Process Engineering
MONOSTORI, L., Production Engineering
STÉPÁN, G., Applied Mechanics
SZABÓ, L., Applied Mechanics
VÁRADI, K., Machine and Product Design

Faculty of Natural Sciences (tel. (1) 463-3561; e-mail ttk-dekani@ttdh.bme.hu; internet www.ttk.bme.hu):

ASZÓDI, A., Nuclear Energy and Nuclear Safety
HORVÁTH, M., Analysis (differential equations)
JÁNOSSY, A., Experimental Solid State Physics
KÁROLYI, G., Nuclear Technology
KERTÉSZ, J., Statistical and Computational Physics
KOVÁCS, G., Cognitive Neuroscience
KROÓ, A., Analysis (approximation theory)
MIHÁLY, G., Experimental Solid State Physics
PETZ, D., Analysis (matrix analysis)
RÉVÉSZ, S., Geometry
RICHTER, P., Optics and Applied Physics
RÓNYAI, L., Algebra
SIMON, F., Experimental Solid State Physics
SIMON, K., Stochastics
SIMONOVITS, A., Differential Equations
SZÁNTAI, T., Differential Equations
SZUNYOGH, L., Solid State Physics (Theory)
TÓTH, B., Stochastics
VIDNYÁNSZKY, Z., Cognitive Neuroscience
VIROSZTEK, A., Solid State Physics
ZARÁND, G., Theoretical Physics

Faculty of Transportation Engineering and Vehicle Engineering (Budapest, Bertalan L. u. 2, 1111; tel. (1) 463-3551; e-mail kozld@mail.bme.hu; internet www.kozlekedes.bme.hu):

BÉDA, P., Chassis and Lightweight Structures
BOKOR, J., Transport Automatics
ELEŐD, A., Vehicle Parts
GÁSPÁR, P., Control for Transportation and Vehicle Systems
PALKOVICS, L., Motor Vehicles
ROHÁCS, J., Aircraft and Ships
SZIRÁNYI, T., Material Handling and Logistics Systems
TAKÁCS, J., Machine Production Technology
TÁNCZOS, L., Transport Economics
TARNAI, G., Transport Automatics
VÁRLAKI, P., Transport Automatics
ZOBORY, I., Railway Vehicles

Institute of Continuing Engineering Education (Budapest, Egry J. u. 1, 1111; tel. (1) 463-2471; e-mail info@mti.bme.hu; internet www.mti.bme.hu):

BENEDEK, A.

International Education Centre (Budapest, Műegyetem rkp. 7–9, 1111; tel. (1) 463-3981; e-mail balogh.valeria@kth.bme.hu; internet www.icepe.bme.hu):

TÓTHNÉ VARGA, Á.

DEBRECENI EGYETEM
(University of Debrecen)

Debrecen, Egyetem tér 1, 4032
Telephone: (52) 512-900
E-mail: info@unideb.hu
Internet: www.unideb.hu

Founded 1538 as Reformed College of Debrecen, current name adopted 2000
State control
Languages of instruction: English, Hungarian
Academic year: September to June

Rector: Prof. Dr ISTVÁN FÁBIÁN
Vice-Rector for Education: Prof. Dr ANDRÁS JÁVOR
Vice-Rector for Scientific Affairs: Prof. Dr ZSOLT PÁLES
Vice-Rector for Strategic Affairs: Prof. Dr ZOLTAN SZILVASSY
Registrar: Dr JUDIT BALOGH
Dir of the Univ. and Nat. Library: Dr MÁRTA VIRÁGOS

Library of 2,700,000 vols
Number of teachers: 1,430
Number of students: 30,400

Publications: *Acta Andragogiae* (1 a year), *Acta Classica* (1 a year), *Acta Debrecina* (1 a year), *Acta Geographica Ac Geologica et Meteorologica Debrecina* (1 a year), *Acta Neerlandica* (1 a year), *Acta pericemonologica rerum ambientum Debrecina* (irregular), *Acta Physica et Chimica* (1 a year), *A Debreceni Egyetem évkönyve* (1 a year), *A Debreceni Egyetem Magyar Nyelvtudományi Intézetének kiadványai* (1 a year), *Agrártudományi közlemények* (irregular), *Collectio iuridica Universitatis Debreceniensis* (irregular), *Competitio* (4 a year), *Debreceni szemle* (4 a year), *Ethnica* (irregular), *Ethnographica Folcloristica Carpatica* (1 a year), *Folia Uralica Debreceniensia* (1 a year), *Gond* (4 a year), *Hungarian Journal of English and American Studies* (2 a year), *Italianistica Debreceniensis* (1 a year), *Journal of Agricultural Sciences* (irregular), *Kitaibelia* (2 a year), *Könyv és Könyvtár* (1 a year), *Magyar Nyelvjárások* (1 a year), *Módszerek és eljárások* (1 a year), *Ökortudományi Értesítő* (1 a year), *Posztbizánci Közlemények* (every 2 years), *Publ. Mathematicae* (2 a year), *Sprachteorie und Germanistiche Linguistik* (2 a year), *Studia Litteraria* (1 a year), *Studia Romanica* (linguistics, 1 a year), *Studies in Linguistics* (1 a year), *Teaching Mathematics and Computer Science* (2 a year), *Történeti Tanulmányok* (irregular)

DEANS

Faculty of Agriculture and Food Sciences and Environmental Sciences: Prof. Dr Hab. ISTVÁN KOMLÓSI
Faculty of Applied Economics and Rural Development: Prof. Dr ANDRÁS NÁBRÁDI
Faculty of Arts and Humanities: Dr KLÁRA PAPP
Faculty of Child and Adult Education: Dr ÉVA KOVÁCS-BAKOSI
Faculty of Dentistry: Dr CSABA HEGEDÜS
Faculty of Economics and Business Administration: Dr JUDIT KAPÁS
Faculty of Engineering: Dr EDIT SZŰCS
Faculty of Health: Dr GERGELY FÁBIÁN
Faculty of Informatics: Dr GYÖRGY TERDIK
Faculty of Law: Dr JÓZSEF SZABADFALVI
Faculty of Medicine: Dr LÁSZLÓ CSERNOCH
Faculty of Music: Dr MIHÁLY DUFFEK
Faculty of Pharmacy: Dr MIKLÓS VECSERNYÉS
Faculty of Public Health: Dr MARGIT BALÁZS
Faculty of Science and Technology: Dr KORNÉL SAILER

PROFESSORS

Faculty of Agriculture and Food Sciences and Environmental Sciences (Debrecen, POB 36, 4015; tel. (52) 508-412; e-mail mtkdekan@agr.unideb.hu; internet portal.agr.unideb.hu):

BARDÓCZ, Z.
BLASKÓ, L.
CSAPÓ, J.
FÁRI, M.
GONDA, I.
GYŐRI, Z., Food Processing and Quality Control
JÁVOR, A.
KÁTAI, J., Soil Science and Microbiology
KOVÁCS, A.
MIHÓK, S., Animal Husbandry, Breeding and Nutrition
NAGY, J., Land Cultivation
PEPÓ, PÁL, Genetics and Plant Breeding
PEPÓ, PÉTER, Crop Production and Applied Ecology
SINÓROS SZABÓ, B., Land Cultivation
TAMÁS, J.

Faculty of Applied Economics and Rural Development (Debrecen, POB 36, 4015; tel. (52) 508-444; e-mail dekan@gvk.unideb.hu; internet portal.agr.unideb.hu):

ERTSEY, I., Economic Analysis and Statistics
LAZÁNYI, J., Rural Development
NÁBRÁDI, A., Farm Business Management
NAGY, G., Rural Development
NEMESSÁLYI, ZS., Farm Business Management
REKE, B.
SZABÓ, G., Agricultural and General Economics
SZABÓ, Z.

Faculty of Arts and Humanities (Debrecen, POB 38, 4010; tel. (52) 512-900; e-mail pappk@dragon.unideb.hu; internet btk.unideb.hu):

ABÁDI-NAGY, Z., North American Studies
AGYAGÁSI, K.
BARTA, J., Medieval and Early Modern World History
BARTHA, E., Ethnography
BITSKEY, I., Old Hungarian Literature
CZIEGLER, I., General Psychology
DEBRECZENI, A.
DOBOS, I.
GÖRÖMBEI, A., Modern Hungarian Language
HAJNÁDY, Z.
HUNYADI, L., Applied Linguistics
IMRE, L., 19th-century Hungarian Literature
IMRE, M.
KERTÉSZ, A., German Linguistics
KLEIN, S., Psychology
NÉMETH, GY., Ancient History
NOVÁK RÓZSA, E., History of Philosophy
PAPP, I.
SOLYMOSI, L., History
SZABÓ, L., Ethnography
VARGA, P.
VIRÁGOS, ZS., North American Studies

Faculty of Child and Adult Education (Hajdúböszörmény, Désány István u. 1–9, 4220; tel. (52) 229-433; e-mail titkarsag@ped.unideb.hu; internet www.degyfk.hu):

BÁLINT, P.
KOVÁCSNÉ, E. B.
VARGA, G.

Faculty of Dentistry (Debrecen, POB 13, 4012; tel. (52) 255-308; e-mail info@edu.unideb.hu; internet dental.deoec.hu):

MAJOR, P.
PAP, G.
PETH, A.
STOYAN, G.
SZTRIK, J.
TERDIK, G.
VÉGH, J.
VERTSE, T.

Faculty of Economics and Business Administration (Debrecen, Kassai u. 26, 4028; tel. (52) 416-580; e-mail mura@tigris.klte.hu; internet econ.unideb.hu):

CSABA, L., Economics
KORMOS, J.
LOSONCZI, L.
MAKÓ, C.
POLÓNYI, I., Management and Marketing

Faculty of Engineering (Debrecen, Ótemető u. 2–4, 4028; tel. (52) 415-155; e-mail info@mfk.unideb.hu; internet www.mfk.unideb.hu):

CSANÁDY, G.
FERNEZELYI, S.
GULYÁS, L.
HAJDU, M.
HALÁSZ, G.
HORVÁTH, R., Chemical Engineering
JOLÁNKAI, G.
KALMÁR, F.
KOCSIS, I.
KŐSZEGHY, A., Settlement Engineering
KOVÁCS, I.
KULCSÁR, A., Construction Industry
MAJOR, J.
POKRÁDI, L., General Machinery
TELEKES, G.
TIBA, ZS., General Machinery
TÓTH, L.
VARGA, S. E.

Faculty of Health (Nyíregyháza, Sóstói u. 2–4, 4400; tel. (42) 404-411; e-mail info@de-efk.hu; internet www.de-efk.hu):

CSERI, J.
FÁBIÁN, G.
GÓTH, L., Labour Analysis and Clinical Diagnostics
HAJNAL, B.
KALAPOS, I., Preventive Medicine for District Nurses
LUKÁCSKÓ, ZS., Social Work
PUNYICZKI, M.

Faculty of Informatics (Debrecen, POB 12, 4010; tel. (52) 512-985; e-mail admin@inf.unideb.hu; internet www.inf.unideb.hu):

DÖMÖSI, P., Computer Science
PAP, G., Applied Mathematics and Probability Theory
SZTRIK, J., Informatics Systems and Networks
TERDIK, G., Information Technology

Faculty of Law (Debrecen, POB 81, 4010; tel. (52) 512-701; e-mail info@law.unideb.hu; internet jog.unideb.hu):

DÉNES, I. Z., Social Sciences
FARKAS, A.
HORVÁTH, M. T.
SZABADFALVI, J., Philosophy and Sociology of Law
SZABÓ, B., History of Law
VÁRNAY, E.

Faculty of Medicine (Debrecen, POB 69, 4012; tel. (52) 258-085; e-mail kjuhasz@med.unideb.hu; internet aok.unideb.hu):

ANTAL, M., Anatomy, Histology and Embryology
BAKÓ, GY., Internal Medicine
BALLA, GY., Neonatology
BALLA, J.
BERTA, A., Ophthalmology
BODA, Z., Internal Medicine
BODOLAY, E.
BOGNÁR, L.
BORSOS, A., Obstetrics and Gynaecology
CSERNOCH, L.
CSIBA, L., Neurology

DAMJANOVICH, S., Biophysics and Cell Biology
DOMBRÁDI, V., Medical Chemistry
ÉDES, I., Cardiology
ERDŐDI, F.
FEKETE, I.
FEKETE, K.
FÉSÜS, L., Biochemistry and Molecular Biology
FÜLESDI, B.
GALUSKA, L.
GÁSPÁR, R., Biophysics and Cell Biology
GERGELY, L., Medical Microbiology
GERGELY, P., Medical Chemistry
GÓTH, J.-P.
HERNÁDI, Z., Obstetrics and Gynaecology
HUNYADI, J., Dermatology and Venereology
KAPPELMAYER, J.
KISS, A.
KISS, C.
KOVÁCS, L., Physiology
KOVÁCS, P.
LUKÁCS, G., Surgery
MARÓDI, L., Paediatrics
MATESZ, K., Anatomy, Histology and Embryology
MÁTYUS, L.
MIKÓ, I.
MOLNÁR, P.
MUSZBEK, L., Clinical Biochemistry and Molecular Pathology
NAGY, E.
NAGY, L.
NÁNÁSI, P., Physiology
NEMES, Z., Pathology
OLÁH, E., Paediatrics
PARAGH, GY., Internal Medicine
RAJNAVÖLGYI, S., Immunology
REMENYIK, E.
SÁPY, P., Surgery
SIPKA, S., Internal Medicine
SZABÓ, B.
SZABÓ, G., Biophysics and Cell Biology
SZÁNTÓ, J.
SZEKANECZ, Z.
SZIKLAI, I., Otolaryngology
SZILVÁSSY, Z., Pharmacology
SZÖLLŐSI, J., Biophysics and Cell Biology
SZONDY, Z.
SZŰCS, G., Physiology
TÓTH, CS., Urology
TÓTH, Z., Obstetrics and Gynaecology
TŐZSÉR, J.
TRÓN, L., Positron Emission Tomography Centre
UDVARDY, M., Internal Medicine
VARGA, S., Central Service Laboratory
VIRÁG, L.
ZEHER, M., Internal Medicine

Faculty of Music (Debrecen, Egyetem tér 2, 4032; tel. (52) 419-366; e-mail music@music.unideb.hu; internet www.zene.unideb.hu):

DUFFEK, M.
KAMMERER, A.
KARASSZON, D.
MATUZ, I.
MOHAY, M.
MOHOS NAGY, E.
NEMES, F.
SZABÓ, J.

Faculty of Pharmacy (Debrecen, Nagyerdei krt. 98, 4012; tel. (52) 512-900; internet www.pharmacol.dote.hu/pharmacy):

BLASKÓ, G.
GUNDA, T.
HALMOS, G.
HERCZEGH, P.
TÓSAKI, Á., Pharmacological Effects

Faculty of Public Health (Debrecen, POB 9, 4012; tel. (52) 417-267; internet www.nk.unideb.hu):

ÁDÁNY, R., Hygiene and Epidemiology
BALÁZS, M.
ILYÉS, I.
MOLNÁR, P.

Faculty of Science and Technology (Debrecen, POB 18, 4010; tel. (52) 512-900; e-mail dettkto@science.unideb.hu; internet ttk.unideb.hu):

ANTUS, S.
BÁNYAI, I.
BATTA, B.
BAZSA, G.
BEKE, D.
ERDŐDINÉ, K.
FÁBIÁN, I.
FARKAS, E.
GAÁL, I.
GÁSPÁR, V.
GYŐRY, K.
JOÓ, F.
JOÓ, P.
KERÉNYI, A.
LÓKI, J.
MAKSA, G.
MOLNÁR, L.
NAGY, A.
NAGY, P.
PÁLES, Z.
PÁLINKÁS, J.
PATONAY, T.
POSTA, J.
RÁBAI, G.
SAILER, K.
SIPICZKI, M.
SOMSÁK, L.
SÓVÁGÓ, I.
SÜLI-ZAKAR, I.
SZÉKELYHIDI, L.
TÓTH, I.
TÓTHMÉRÉSZ, B.
TRÓCSÁNYI, Z.
VARGA, Z.
VIBÓK, A.
ZSUGA, M.

Conservatory (Debrecen, Egyetem tér 2, 4032; tel. (52) 411-226; e-mail adamk@dragon.klte.hu):

ÁDÁM, K., Stringed Instruments
KAMMERER, A., Brass and Percussion
KEDVES, T., Stringed Instruments
KISS, V. P., Stringed Instruments
KÖKÉNYESSY, M., Stringed Instruments
MATÚZ, I., Woodwind
SZESZTAY, ZS., Music Theory, Choir Conducting

Farm and Regional Research Institute (Debrecen, Böszörményi u. 138, 4032; tel. (52) 508-334; e-mail csapone@helios.date.hu):

KONCZ, T., Dir

Hajdúböszörményi College Faculty of Education (Hajdúböszörmény, Désány I u. 1–9, 4220; tel. (52) 229-433; e-mail tit8003@helka.iif.hu):

BAKOSI, É., Children's Education
FRÁTER, K., Children's Education
KÖVÉR, I., Children's Education
VARGA, GY., Social Studies

Institute of Information Technology:

GISPERT, S.
MAJOR, P.
PAP, G.
PETHŐ, A.

EÖTVÖS LORÁND TUDOMÁNYEGYETEM
(Eötvös Loránd University)

Budapest, POB 109, 1056
Budapest, Egyetem tér 1–3, 1053
Telephone: (1) 411-6500
E-mail: rektor@elte.hu
Internet: www.elte.hu

Founded 1635, current name adopted 1950
State control
Academic year: September to June (2 terms)

Rector: Prof. Dr BARNA MEZEY
Vice-Rector for Education: Dr CSABA BORSODI
Vice-Rector for Science, Research and Innovation: Prof. Dr ERNŐ KESZEI
Vice-Rector for Strategic Affairs: Prof. Dr ANDRÁS KARÁCSONY
Dir-Gen.: Dr KATALIN JUHÁSZNÉ HUSZTY
Sec.-Gen.: Dr ZOLTÁN RÓNAY

Library: see under Libraries and Archives
Number of teachers: 1,420
Number of students: 30,800

Publications: *Acta Facultatis Politico-iuridicae Universitatis Scientiarum Budapestinensis*, *Annales* (geological, juridical and geological series, 1 a year)

DEANS

Bárczi Gusztáv Faculty of Special Education: Dr PÉTER ZÁSZKALICZKY
Faculty of Education and Psychology: Prof. Dr ATTILA OLÁH
Faculty of Humanities: Dr TAMÁS DEZSŐ
Faculty of Informatics: Dr ZOLTÁN HORVÁTH
Faculty of Law and Political Science: Dr MIKLÓS KIRÁLY
Faculty of Primary and Pre-School Education: Prof. Dr GYÖRGY MIKONYA
Faculty of Science: Dr PÉTER SURJÁN
Faculty of Social Sciences: Dr KATALIN TAUSZ

PROFESSORS

Faculty of Humanities (Budapest, Múzeum krt 4/A, 1088; tel. (1) 485-5251; e-mail dekan@btk.elte.hu; internet www.btk.elte.hu):

ADAMIK, T., Latin Language and Literature
BALÁZS, G., Linguistics
BALOGH, A., Modern World History
BANCZEROWSKI, J., Polish Language and Literature
BÁRDOSI, V., Romance Studies
BENCE, GY., Ethics and Social Philosophy
BERTÉNYI, I., Medieval and Early Modern Hungarian History
BÍRÓ, F., 18th- and 19th-century Hungarian Literature
DÁVID, G., Oriental Studies
DOMOKOS, P., Finno-Ugric Linguistics
ERDÉLYI, Á., Philosophy
FODOR, S., Semitic Philology and Arabic Studies
GAÁL, E., Egyptology
GÉHER, I., English
GERGELY, A., History
GERGELY, J., Modern and Contemporary Hungarian History
GERŐ, A., Economic and Social History
GIAMPAOLO, S., Romance Studies
GLATZ, F., Historical Auxiliary Sciences
GÓSY, M., Linguistics
GRANASZTÓI, G., Romance Studies
GYIVICSÁN, A., Slavonic Studies
HESSKY, P., German Linguistics
HORVÁTH, I., Old Hungarian Literature
JEREMIÁS, E., Oriental Studies
KARA, GY., Central Asian Studies
KARDOS, J., History
KARDOS, J., Historical Auxiliary Sciences
KELEMEN, J., Ethics and Social Philosophy
KÉLÉNYI, G., History of Art
KENYERES, Z., Modern Hungarian Literature
KESZLER, B., Contemporary Hungarian Linguistics
KISS, J., Hungarian Historical Linguistics and Dialectology
KLAUDY, K., Linguistics
KNIPF, E., German
KOMORÓCZY, G., Assyriology and Hebrew Studies
KÓSA, L., Cultural History
KOVÁCS, A., Slavonic Studies
KOVÁCS, S. I., Old Hungarian Literature
KÖVECSES, Z., English
KRAUSZ, T., History

KULCSÁR SZABÓ, E., Comparative Literature
LUDASSY, M., Ethics and Social Philosophy
LUFT, U., Egyptology
MANHERZ, K., Germanic Linguistics
MAROSI, E., Art History
MASÁT, A., Scandinavian Languages and Literature
MEDGYES, P., English Teacher Training
MISKOLCZY, A., Romance Studies
NÉMETH, G., History
NYOMÁRKAY, I., Slavic Philology
OROSZ, M., German
PALÁDI-KOVÁCS, A., Ethnography
PALOTÁS, E., East European History
PASSUTH, K., Art History
PÉTER, M., Eastern Slavonic and Baltic Philology
PROKOPP, M., History of Art
PUSKÁS, I., History
RACZKY, P., Archaeology
RADNÓTI, S., Aesthetics
ROMSICS, I., Modern and Contemporary Hungarian History
RÓNAY, L., Modern Hungarian Literature
SIPOS, L., Literary History
SOLYMOSI, L., History
STEIGER, K., Philosophy
SZABICS, I., French Language and Literature
SZABÓ, K., Medieval World History
SZABÓ, M., Classical Archaeology
SZÁVAI, J., Comparative and World Literature
SZEGEDY-MASZÁK, M., Comparative Literature
SZÉKELY, G., History
SZVÁK, G., History
TOLCSVAI, N. G., Linguistics
TÓTH, B., Romance Studies
TVERDOTA, G., Literary History
VARGA, L., English
VARGYAI, GY., Historical Auxiliary Sciences
VÁSÁRI, I., Turkish Studies
VOIGT, V., Folklore
VÖRÖS, I., French Language and Literature

Faculty of Law and Political Science (Budapest, Egyetem tér 1–3, 1053; tel. (1) 411-6516; e-mail ajtkdekan@ludens.elte.hu; internet www.ajk.elte.hu):

BIHARI, M., Political Science
BÖHM, A., Political Science
BURJÁN, L., International Law
ERDEI, Á., Criminal Procedural Law
FICZERE, L., Public Administration Law
FÖLDESI, T., Philosophy
FÖLDI, A., Roman Law
GÖNCZÖL, K., Criminology
HAMZA, G., Roman Law
HARMATHY, A., Civil Law
HORVÁTH, P., Universal Legal and Political History
KARÁCSONY, A., Philosophy
KÖRÖSNYI, A., Political Science
KUKORELLI, I., Constitutional Law
LENKOVITS, B., Civil Law
LÉVAY, M., Criminology
LÓRINCZ, L., Public Administration Law
MEZEI, B., Universal Legal and Political History
PACSOLAY, P., Political Science
PÁNDI, G., Public Administration Law
POKOL, B., Political Science
SÁJO, A., Civil Law
SÁRI, J., Constitutional Law
SCHLETT, I., Political Science
STUMPF, I., Political Science
SZABÓ, MÁRTON, Political Science
SZABÓ, MÁTÉ, Political Science
SZILÁGYI, P., Theory of Law
TAMÁS, A., Theory of Law
VALKI, L., International Law
VÉKÁS, L., Civil Law

Faculty of Science (Budapest, Pázmány Péter sétány 1/A, 1117; tel. (1) 372-2545; internet science.elte.hu):

BERCZIK, Á., Systematic Zoology and Ecology
BÖDDI, B., Biology
BODZSÁR, É., Biology
CSÁNYI, V., Behaviour Genetics
CSIKOR, F., Theoretical Physics
DEMETROVICS, J., Information Systems
DÉTÁRI, L., Biology
DÓZSA-FARKAS, K., Biology
ERDEI, A., Immunology
FARSANG, GY., Inorganic and Analytical Chemistry
FODOR, Z., Theoretical Physics
FRANK, A., Operational Research
GALÁCZ, A., Palaeontology
GERE, G., Biology
GESZTI, T., Physics of Complex Systems
GRÁF, L., Biochemistry
GYENIS, G., Biology
GYURJÁN, I., Plant Anatomy
HEGYI, G., Biology
HORVÁTH, Z., Theoretical Physics
KISS, Á., Atomic Physics
KISS, E., Mathematics
KOMJÁTH, P., Computer Science
KONDOR, I., Physics of Complex Systems
KOVÁCS, J., Biology
KÜRTI, J., Physics
LACZKOVICH, M., Analysis
LÁNG, F., Biology
LENDVAI, J., General Physics
LOVÁSZ, L., Computer Science
NAGY, D. L., Atomic Physics
ORMOS, P., Physics
OROSZ, L., Biology
PÁLFY, P., Algebra and Number Theory
PALLA, L., Theoretical Physics
PATKÓS, A., Atomic Physics
PODANI, J., Biology
POLONYI, J., Atomic Physics
SÁRMAY, G., Immunology
SASS, M., General Zoology
SZABÓ, K., Physical Chemistry
SZALAY, S., Atomic Physics
SZATHMÁRI, E., Plant Taxonomy and Ecology
SZIGETI, Z., Biology
TÉL, T., Theoretical Physics
TICHY, G., Solid State Physics
UNGÁR, T., General Physics
VESZTERGOMBI, G., Physics
VICSEK, T., Biological Physics
VINCZE, I., Physics
ZÁVODSZKÝ, P., Biological Physics

Institute and Postgraduate Centre for Sociology and Social Policy (Budapest, Pollack Mihály tér 10, 1088):

ANGELUSZ, R., Sociology
CSEPELI, GY., Social Psychology
FERGE, ZS., Social Policy
HUSZÁR, T., Historical Sociology
NÉMEDI, D., Social Theory
PATAKI, F., Social Psychology
SOMLAI, P., Social Theory

Teacher-Training Faculty (Budapest, Kazinczy u. 23–27, 1075):

CS. VARGA, I., Hungarian Language and Literature
DEMETER, J., Hungarian Language and Literature
DRUZSIN, F., Hungarian Language and Literature
DUKKON, Á., Hungarian Language and Literature
ESTÓK, J., History
FRIED, I., Italian Language and Literature
GAIZER, F., Chemistry
GÖDÉNY, E., Hungarian Language and Literature
GRÉTSY, L., Hungarian Linguistics
HAJDU, P., Social Theory
HEGYVÁRI, N., Mathematics
HELTAI, P., English
HORVÁTH, G., Geography
JÁSZÓ, A., Hungarian Linguistics
MADARÁSZ, I., Hungarian Linguistics
MILKOVITS, I., Biology
NÉMETH, A., Educational Science
SALAMON, K., History
SAPSZON, F., Music
SIPOSNÉ-JÁGER, K., Biology
UZONYI, P., German
ZÁVODSKY, G., History
ZIRKULI, P., French Language and Literature

KAPOSVÁRI EGYETEM
(Kaposvár University)

Kaposvár, POB 16, 7400
Kaposvár, Guba Sándor u. 40, 7400
Telephone: (82) 505-800
E-mail: rektor@ke.hu
Internet: www.ke.hu

Founded 2000 from Faculty of Animal Husbandry of Pannon Agrártudományi Egyetem (Pannon Univ. of Agricultural Sciences) and Csokonai Vitéz Mihály Teacher-Training College
State control
Language of instruction: Hungarian
Academic year: September to June

Rector: Prof. Dr FERENC SZÁVAI
Vice-Rector for Education: Dr ZOLTÁN KOVÁCS
Vice-Rector for Gen. and Scientific Affairs: Prof. Dr IMRE REPA

Number of teachers: 250
Number of students: 4,800

Publication: *Acta Agraria Kaposváriensis* (4 a year)

DEANS

Faculty of Animal Science: Prof. Dr ISTVÁN HOLLÓ
Faculty of Arts: Dr ERZSÉBET LIEBER (acting)
Faculty of Economic Science: Dr LÁSZLÓ BALOGH
Faculty of Pedagogy: Dr ZOLTÁN KOVÁCS

PROFESSORS

Faculty of Animal Science:

BABINSZKY, L., Animal Nutrition
BOGENFÜRST, F., Poultry Breeding
CSAPÓ, J., Biochemistry
DÉR, F., Plant Production
GYENIS, J., Process Engineering
HECKER, W., Academy of Horse Riding
HORN, P., Pig Production
HORVÁTH, GY., Social Sciences
KOVÁCS, M., Physiology and Animal Hygiene
PAÁL, J., Mathematics and Computer Science
REPA, I., Digital Imaging, Radiology
SARUDI, J., Chemistry and Biochemistry
STEFLER, J., Cattle Production
SZAKÁLY, S., Food Science
SZÉLES, GY., Farm Economics
SZENDRŐ, ZS., Animal Breeding
TAKÁTSY, T., Agricultural Engineering

LISZT FERENC ZENEMŰVÉSZETI EGYETEM
(Liszt Academy of Music)

Budapest, Liszt Ferenc tér 8, 1061
Telephone: (1) 462-4600
Internet: www.lfze.hu

Founded 1875
State control
Academic year: September to June

Depts of chamber music, church music, composition, conducting, folk music, jazz, keyboard and harp, musicology and music theory, strings, vocal and opera studies, woodwind and brass

Pres.: Dr ANDRÁS BATTA
Vice-Pres.: ANDRASEA VIGH
Vice-Pres. for Education: CSABA KUTNYÁNYSZKY
Sec.: Dr SÁNDOR BANKÓ
Chief Librarian: GÉZA KOCSIS
Library of 187,000 vols
Number of teachers: 160
Number of students: 770.

ATTACHED INSTITUTES

Bartók Béla Zeneművészeti Szakközépiskola és Gimnázium (Béla Bartók Conservatory of Music and Secondary School): Budapest, Nagymező u. 1, 1065; tel. (1) 321-7514; e-mail bbzsz@lisztakademia.hu; internet konzi.hu; f. 1840; 118 teachers; 385 students; Dir Dr SZABOLCS BENKŐ; Sec. ÁGOTA KNIPPEL; Librarian ANDREA KAMILLA DARVASSI; publ. *Bóbita Magazin, Müpa Magazin*

MAGYAR KÉPZŐMŰVÉSZETI EGYETEM
(Hungarian University of Fine Arts)

Budapest, POB 761, 1384
Budapest, Andrássy u. 69–71, 1062
Telephone: (1) 342-1738
E-mail: info@mke.hu
Internet: www.mke.hu
Founded 1871
State control
Rector: Dr Hab. FRIGYES KŐNIG
Vice-Rector: Dr Hab. ZOLTÁN SZEGEDY-MASZÁK
Vice-Rector for Education: ESZTER RADÁK
Registrar: ISTVÁNNÉ PONGÓ
Library Dir: KATALIN MAJKÓ
Library of 60,000 vols, 90 periodicals
Number of teachers: 130
Number of students: 550

PROFESSORS

FARKAS, Á., Sculpture
KOCSIS, I., Graphic Art
MENRÁTH, P., Restoration
MOLNÁR, K., Applied Graphic Art
NAGY, G., Painting
PETERNÁK, M., Multimedia Studies
SZABADI, J., Art History
SZÉKELY, L., Stage and Costume Design
TÖLG-MOLNÁR, Z., Painting

MISKOLCI EGYETEM
(University of Miskolc)

Miskolc-Egyetemváros, 3515
Telephone: (46) 565-111
E-mail: rektor@uni-miskolc.hu
Internet: www.uni-miskolc.hu
Founded 1735 as School of Mining and Metallurgy, current name adopted 1990
State control
Languages of instruction: English, Hungarian
Academic year: September to June
Rector: Prof. Dr ANDRÁS TORMA
Vice-Rector for Academic Affairs: Dr ZSUZSANNA BALAJTI OVÁRI
Vice-Rector for Gen. Affairs: Dr ZITA HORVÁTH
Vice-Rector for Research and Int. Affairs: TAMÁS KÉKESI
Vice-Rector for Strategy and Devt: KÁROLY JÁRMAI
Sec.-Gen.: Dr DEZSŐ SZAKÁLY
Dir for Library and Archives: Dr ERZSÉBET BURMEISTER
Library of 602,000 vols, 161,000 periodicals
Number of teachers: 750
Number of students: 11,000

Publications: *Miskolc Journal of International Law, Miskolci Egyetem Közlemények* (irregular, in Hungarian), *Publications of the University of Miskolc* (irregular, in English, German and Russian)

DEANS

Faculty of Arts: Dr MÁRIA KOVÁCS-ILLÉS
Faculty of Earth Science and Engineering: Prof. Dr PÉTER SZŰCS
Faculty of Economics: Prof. Dr GYÖRGY KOCZISZKY
Faculty of Healthcare: Dr EMŐKE KISSTÓTH
Faculty of Law: Prof. Dr ÁKOS FARKAS
Faculty of Materials Science and Engineering: Prof. ZOLTÁN GÁCSI
Faculty of Mechanical Engineering and Informatics: Prof. Dr EDGÁR BERTÓTI

PROFESSORS

Faculty of Arts (tel. (46) 565-111; e-mail boltcsop@uni-miskolc.hu; internet bolcsesz.uni-miskolc.hu):

A. MOLNÁR, F., Hungarian Linguistics, History of Hungarian Linguistics
ANDRIK-HELL, J., Philosophy
B. GERGELY, P., Hungarian Linguistics
BONA, G., Military History
CSEPELI, GY., Social Psychology
FERENCZI, L., Literature of the Enlightenment, Romanticism and Regional History
FORRAI, G., History of Philosophy
GÁNGÓ, G., Literary History, Philosophy
GYULAI, É., Cultural History and Museology
HELTAI, J., Old Hungarian Literature
ILLÉS-KOVÁCS, M., Hungarian Linguistics
KABDEBÓ, L., Contemporary Hungarian Literature
KECSKEMÉTI, G., Literary History, Old Hungarian Literature
KEMÉNY, G., Hungarian Linguistics, Stylistics
KNAUSZ, I., Science of Education
KOTICS, J., Cultural and Visual Anthropology
KULCSÁR, P., Medieval History
LENDVAI, F., Social Philosophy
SCHWENDTNER, T., History of Philosophy, Science of Philosophy
SIMIGNÉ FENYŐ, S., Applied Linguistics
SZABÓ, M., Political Science, Political Discourse
SZABÓ-TÓTH, K., Family Sociology
SZIGETI, J., Central European Literature and Culture
SZILI, J., Literary History
VIGA, GY., Ethnography

Faculty of Earth Science and Engineering (tel. (46) 565-051; e-mail rekbdhiv@uni-miskolc.hu; internet www.mfk.uni-miskolc.hu):

BARTHA, G., Geodesy and Mine Surveying
BÉRCZI, I., Geology and Mineral Resources
BÓDI, T., Reservoir Engineering
BŐHM, J., Process Engineering
BOKÁNYI, L, Process Engineering
CSŐKE, B., Process Engineering
DEBRECZENI, A., Mining and Geotechnology
DOBOS, E., Geography and Environmental Science
DOBRÓKA, M., Geophysics
ELEKES, T., Geography and Environmental Sciences
FAITLI, J., Process Engineering
FEDERER, I., Petroleum Engineering
FÖLDESSY, J., Geology and Mineral Resources
GYULAI, Á., Geophysics
HARTAI, É., Geology and Mineral Resource
HAVASI, I., Geodesy and Mine Surveying
HEVESI, A., Geography and Environmental Sciences
KOCSIS, K., Human Geography
KOVÁCS, B., Hydrogeology and Engineering Geology
LADÁNYI, G., Equipment for Geotechnology
LAKATOS, I., Mining Chemistry
LÉNÁRT, L., Hydrogeology and Engineering Geology
LESS, GY., Geology and Mineral Resources
MÁDAI, F., Geology and Mineral Resources
MADARÁST, T., Hydrogeology and Engineering Geology
MOLNÁR, J., Mining and Geotechnology
MOLNÁR, J., Geography and Environmental Sciences
ORMOS, T., Geophysics
SISKA-SZILASI, B., Human Geography
SOMOSVÁRI, ZS., Mining and Geotechnology
SZABÓ, I., Hydrogeology and Engineering Geology
SZAKÁLL, S., Mineralogy
SZŰCS, P., Hydrogeology and Engineering Geology
TAKÁCS, G., Petroleum Engineering
TIHANYI, L., Natural Gas Engineering
TOTH, A., Natural Gas Engineering
TURAI, E., Geophysics
TURZO, Z., Petroleum Engineering

Faculty of Economics (tel. (46) 565-111; e-mail gtkinfo@uni-miskolc.hu; internet gtk.uni-miskolc.hu):

BENEDEK, J., Regional Policy
BESENYEI, L., Business Statistics and Forecasting
BOZSIK, S., Finance
CZABÁN, J., Business Economics
DANKÓ, L., International Marketing
FEKETE, E., Rural Policy
ILLÉS, M., Business Economics
KOCZISZKY, GY., Regional Economics
KUNOS, I., Human Resources
NAGY, A., Economic Theory
NAGY, Z., World Economy and Comparative Economics
PÁL, T., Accounting
PELCZ-GÁLL, I., Entrepreneurship
PISKÓTI, I., Marketing Strategy and Communication
SZAKÁLY, D., Innovation and Technology Management
SZINTAY, I., Management
SZITA, K., Environment
VERES-SOMOSI, M., Organizational Behaviour

Faculty of Healthcare (tel. (46) 366-560; e-mail rekefk@uni-miskolc.hu; internet www.uni-miskolc.hu/~wwweti):

BARKAI, L., Paediatrics, Paediatric Pulmonology, Diabetology
BERKŐ, P., Gynaecology, Obstetrics
DÓZSA, C., Health Insurance, Health Management
FODOR, B., Nanobiotechnology, Nanomedicine
FORNET, B., Conventional Radiology, Ions Diagnostics
HARKÁNYI, Z., Radiology
KISS-TÓH, E., Sociology, Social Policy
LÁZÁR, I., Radiology
LOMBAY, B., Paediatrics, Radiology
MARTOS, J., Radiology, Neuroradiology
PAPP, M., Orthopedics
PEJA, M., Rehabilitation
RÁCZ, O., Physiology, Pathophysiology, Clinical Chemistry
SÁGODI, L., Paediatrics, Gynaecology, Paediatric Gynaecology
SZABÓ, L., Paediatrics, Nephrology
SZABÓ, Z., Surgery, Hand Surgery, Traumatology
SZAKOLCZAI-SÁNDOR, N., Marketing, Business Studies
SZÁNTÓ, A., Marketing, Business Studies
SZEBENI, J., Nanobiotechnology, Nanomedicine

ÚJSZÁSZY, L., Internal Medicine, Gastroenterology
VALIKOVICS, A., Neurology, Psychiatry
VELKEY, I., Paediatrics, Neurology, Paediatric Neurology
WINKLER, G., Internal Medicine, Endocrinology, Diabetology

Faculty of Law (tel. (46) 565-171; e-mail jogdhiv@uni-miskolc.hu; internet jogikar.uni-miskolc.hu):

BARTA, J., Business Law
BIRÓ, GY., Civil Law
BRAGYOVA, A., Constitutional Law
CSÁK, CS., Labour Law and Agricultural Law
ERDŐS, É., Financial Law
FARKAS, Á., Criminal Procedural Law and Law Enforcement
GÖRGÉNYI, I., Criminal Law and Criminology
JÁMBOR-RÓTH, E., Criminal Procedural Law and Law Enforcement
LÉVAY, M., Criminal Law and Criminology
LÉVAY-FAZEKAS, J., European and International Private Law
MAJTÉNYI, L., Information and Media Law
NYITRAI, P., Administrative Law
PAULOVICS, A., Constitutional Law
PRUGBERGER, T., Labour Law and Agricultural Law
SÁRY, P., Roman Law
STIPTA, I., Legal History
SZABÓ, M., Legal Theory and Legal Sociology
TORMA, A., Administrative Law
WOPERA, ZS., Civil Procedural Law

Faculty of Materials Science and Engineering (tel. (46) 565-091; e-mail makdekani@uni-miskolc.hu; internet www.mak.uni-miskolc.hu):

GÁCSI, Z., Materials Science
GÖMZE, A. L., Ceramics and Silicate Engineering
KAPTAY, GY., Chemistry
KÉKESI, T., Metallurgy
MAROSSY, K., Polymer Technology
PALOTÁS, Á. B., Combustion Technology and Thermal Energy
ROÓSZ, A., Materials Science, Physical Metallurgy
SZŰCS, I., Combustion Technology, Energy
TÖRÖK, T., Metallurgy

Faculty of Mechanical Engineering and Informatics (tel. (46) 565-130; e-mail gkdh5@uni-miskolc.hu; internet www.gepesz.uni-miskolc.hu):

BARANYI, L., Heat and Fluid Engineering
BERTÓTI, E., Mechanics
CZIBERE, T., Heat and Fluid Engineering
DÖBRÖCZÖNI, Á., Machine Elements
DUDÁS, I., Production Engineering
ECSEDI, I., Mechanics
FARKAS, J., Materials Handling and Logistics
HORVÁTHNÉ VARGA, A., Mechanics
ILLÉS, B., Materials Handling and Logistics
JÁRMAI, K., Materials Handling and Logistics
JUHÁSZ, I., Descriptive Geometry
KACSUK, P., Automation
KOZÁK, I., Mechanics
KUNDRÁK, J., Production Engineering
LÉVAI, I., Materials Handling and Logistics
LUKÁCS, J., Mechanical Technology
MANG, B., Materials Handling and Logistics
NYÍRI, A., Heat and Fluid Engineering
PÁCZELT, I., Mechanics
PARIPÁS, B., Physics
PATKÓ, GY., Machine Tools
RONTÓ, M., Mathematical Analysis
SZABÓ, SZ., Heat and Fluid Engineering
SZALADNYA, S., Materials Handling and Logistics
SZARKA, T., Electrotechnology and Electronics
SZEIDL, GY., Mechanics
SZENTIRMAI, L., Electrotechnology and Electronics
SZIGETI, J., Mathematical Analysis
TAJNAFŐI, J., Machine Tools
TISZA, M., Mechanical Technology
TÓTH, L., Mechanical Technology
TÓTH, T., Information Engineering

MOHOLY-NAGY MŰVÉSZETI EGYETEM
(Moholy-Nagy University of Art and Design Budapest)

Budapest, Zugligeti ú. 9–25, 1121
Telephone: (1) 392-1180
E-mail: kommunikacio@mome.hu
Internet: www.mome.hu

Founded 1880, fmrly Magyar Iparművészeti Egyetem, present status 1971, current name adopted 2006
State control
Languages of instruction: English, Hungarian
Academic year: September to June

Institutes of architecture, design, media, theoretical studies

Rector: Prof. GÁBOR KOPEK
Vice-Rector: Prof. LÁSZLÓ ZSÓTÉR
Chancellor: Dr ZSOMBOR NAGY
Dir of Finance: ÁGNES BALOGH
Dir of Int. and Public Relations: ZSOLT PETRI
Librarian: KLÁRA LÉVAI

Library of 42,000 vols
Number of teachers: 100
Number of students: 570

Publications: *Diploma* (1 a year), *Kék Ég* (4 a year), *Made in MOME* (1 a year)

NEMZETI KÖZSZOLGÁLATI EGYETEM
(National University of Public Service)

Budapest, POB 15, 1581
Budapest X, Hungária krt. 9–11, 1101
Telephone: (1) 432-9000
E-mail: nke@uni-nke.hu
Internet: www.uni-nke.hu

Founded 2012 by merger of Zrínyi Miklós Univ. of Nat. Defence, Police College, Faculty of Public Admin. of Corvinus Univ. of Budapest
State control

Rector: Prof. Dr ANDRÁS PATYI
Vice-Rector for Continuing Education and Int. Affairs: Dr NORBERT KIS
Vice-Rector for Education: Dr GÁBOR KOVÁCS
Vice-Rector for Strategic and Institutional Devt: Prof. Dr JÓZSEF PADÁNYI
Gen. Sec.: Dr JÓZSEF HORVÁTH
Library Dir-Gen.: KLÁRA BAKOS

Number of teachers: 600
Number of students: 8,000

DEANS

Faculty of Law Enforcement: Prof. Dr PÉTER RUZSONYI
Faculty of Military Sciences and Officer Training: Dr GÁBOR BOLDIZSÁR
Faculty of Public Administration: Dr ÁKOS CSERNY

NYUGAT-MAGYARORSZÁGI EGYETEM
(University of West Hungary)

Sopron, POB 132, 9401
Sopron, Bajcsy-Zsilinszky u. 4, 9400
Telephone: (99) 518-100
E-mail: rectoro@nyme.hu
Internet: www.nyme.hu

Founded 2000 by merger of Univ. of Sopron (f. 1762), Mosonmagyaróvár Faculty of Agriculture (f. 1818) of Pannon Univ. of Agricultural Sciences, Apáczai Csere János Teacher-Training College (f. 1778), Benedek Elek College of Education (f. 1959)
State control
Language of instruction: Hungarian
Academic year: September to June

Rector: Prof. Dr SÁNDOR FARAGÓ
Vice-Rector: Prof. Dr ANDRÁS NÁHLIK
Vice-Rector: Prof. Dr LÁSZLÓ VARGA
Vice-Rector: Dr SÁNDOR CSEH
Sec.-Gen.: Dr MÁRIA MERÉNYI
Head of Library: SÁNDOR SARKADY, JR

Library of 745,000 vols
Number of teachers: 580
Number of students: 10,500

Publications: *Acta Agronomica Ovariensis* (2 a year, in English, Hungarian), *Acta Facultatis Forestalis* (in English, German), *Acta Facultatis Ligniensis* (in English, German), *Acta Silvatica & Lignaria Hungarica* (1 a year), *Apáczai Csere János Tanítóképző Főiskolai Kar Tanulmánykötet* (1 a year, in Hungarian), *Apáczai tanulmánykötetek* (1 a year, in Hungarian), *Benedek könyvek* (irregular, in Hungarian), *Bibliotheca Slavica Savariensis* (irregular, in Croatian, English, Hungarian, Russian, Slovenian), *Faipar* (Wood Science, 4 a year, in Hungarian with English summary), *Flora Pannonica* (Journal of Phytogeography and Taxonomy), *Folia Anthropologica* (1 a year, in Hungarian), *Gazdaság & Társadalom* (English abstracts, 4 a year, in English, German, Hungarian), *Kanitzia* (1 a year, in Hungarian), *Karst Development* (1 a year, in English), *Karsztfejlődés* (1 a year, in Hungarian), *Magyar Vízivad Közlemények* (Hungarian Waterfowl Publ., 1 or 2 a year, in English, Hungarian), *Tilia* (Journal of Botany, 1 or 2 a year, in Hungarian), *Studia Slavica Savariensia* (Journal of Linguistics and Literary Sciences, 1 a year, in English, German, Hungarian, Russian, Serbo-Croatian), *Tudomány Napja* (1 a year, in Hungarian)

DEANS

Apáczai Csere János Faculty: Dr PÉTER SZABÓ
Benedek Elek Faculty of Pedagogy: Dr GYÖRGY KATONA
Faculty of Agricultural and Food Sciences: Prof. Dr REZSŐ SCHMIDT
Faculty of Arts: Dr KATALIN MOLNÁR-HORVÁTH
Faculty of Economics: Prof. Dr CSABA SZÉKELY
Faculty of Forestry: Prof. Dr FERENC LAKATOS
Faculty of Geoinformatics: Dr GÁBOR MÉLYKÚTI
Faculty of Natural Sciences: Prof. Dr JÓZSEF GYURÁCZ
Faculty of Visual Arts and Music, Education and Sport: Dr TIBOR POLGÁR
Faculty of Wood Sciences: Prof. Dr LÁSZLÓ JEREB

ÓBUDAI EGYETEM
(Óbuda University)

Budapest, Bécsi u. 96/b, 1034
Telephone: (1) 666-5603
Internet: uni-obuda.hu

Founded 2010
State control

Rector: Prof. Dr JÁNOS FODOR
Vice-Rector: Prof. Dr JANÓS FODOR
Vice-Rector for Information Technology and Institutional Devt: Dr JÓZSEF TICK

Vice-Rector for Research: Prof. Dr MIHÁLY RÉGER
Chancellor: Dr JÓZSEF GÁTI
Dir of Finance: ANDRÁS BOROS
Library Dir: MIHÁLYNÉ STRASSZER
Number of students: 13,000
Publication: *Acta Polytechnica Hungarica* (5 a year, print and online, uni-obuda.hu/journal)

DEANS

Donát Bánki Faculty of Mechanical and Safety Engineering: Dr SÁNDOR HORVÁTH
John von Neumann Faculty of Informatics: Dr LÁSZLÓ NÁDAI
Kandó Kálmán Faculty of Electrical Engineering: Dr PÉTER TURMEZEI
Károly Keleti Faculty of Economics: Dr ANDRÁS MEDVE
Keleti Faculty of Business and Management: Dr ANDRÁS MEDVE
Sándor Rejtő Faculty of Light Industry and Environmental Protection Engineering: Dr ISTVÁN PATKÓ

PANNON EGYETEM
(University of Pannonia)

Veszprém, Egyetem u. 10, POB 158, 8200
Telephone: (88) 624-000
E-mail: pr@uni-pannon.hu
Internet: www.uni-pannon.hu
Founded 1949
State control
Languages of instruction: English, Hungarian
Academic year: September to June
Rector: Prof. Dr FERENC FRIEDLER
Chancellor: Dr ANDRÁS KATONA
Rector's Commr for Economic Affairs: Prof. Dr ANDRÁS GELENCSÉR
Rector's Commr for Education Affairs: Prof. Dr FERENC HARTUNG
Rector's Commr for Regional Devt: Prof. Dr ZOLTÁN GAÁL
Gen. Dir for Economic Affairs: MÁRIA ZSIBORÁCS PETRÓ
Head of Office of External Affairs: Dr ILDIKÓ HORTOBÁGYI
Head of Quality Control Office: Dr CSIZMADIA TIBOR
Head of Rector's Office: ANGÉLA BOGNÁR SABJANICS
Gen. Dir for Library and Archives: GÁBOR TÓTH
Library: see under Libraries and Archives
Number of teachers: 333
Number of students: 6,247 (4,576 full-time, 1,671 part-time)
Publication: *Hungarian Journal of Industrial Chemistry* (4 a year)

DEANS

Faculty of Economics: Dr LAJOS SZABÓ
Faculty of Engineering: Dr ISTVÁN SZALAI
Faculty of Information Technology: Dr ROZÁLIA PIGLER-LAKNER
Faculty of Modern Philology and Social Sciences: Dr GÉZA HORVÁTH
Georgikon Faculty: Dr PÉTER J. POLGÁR

PROFESSORS

Faculty of Economics:
- GAÁL, Z., Management and Economy
- HALMAI, P., Economics
- KOVÁCS, Z., Management of Maintenance
- MIHÁLYI, P., Economics
- TELCS, A., Management
- TÖRÖK, A., Management and Economy
- VERES, Z., Economics
- VINCZE, L., Economics

Faculty of Engineering:
- ABONYI, J., Chemical and Process Engineering
- BÉLAFI BAKÓ, K., Bioengineering, Membrane Technology
- GELENCSÉR, A., Environmenatal Sciences
- GUBICZA, L., Bioengineering, Membrane Technology
- HANCSÓK, J., Chemical and Process Engineering
- HORVÁTH, O., Chemistry
- KAIZER, J., Chemistry
- KRISTÓF, J., Environmental Engineering
- KRISTÓF HORVÁTH, E., Environmental Engineering
- LENDVAY, GY., Chemistry
- LIKER, A., Environmental Sciences
- MECSI, J., Mechanical Engineering
- PADISÁK, J., Bioengineering
- PÓSFAI, M., Environmental Sciences
- RÉDEY, A., Environmental Engineering
- SKODA-FÖLDES, R., Chemistry
- TIMÁR, I., Mechanical Engineering

Faculty of Information Technology:
- BEZDEK, K., Mathematics
- FRIEDLER, F., Computer Sciences
- HANGOS, K., Electrical Engineering and Information Systems
- HARTUNG, F.
- KLEMES, J., Chemical and Process Engineering
- MIZSEY, P., Chemical and Process Engineering
- NAGY, E., Chemical and Process Engineering
- PITUK, M., Mathematics
- SZÉPVÖLGYI, J., Chemical and Process Engineering
- TERLAKY, T., Computer Sciences
- TUZA, ZS., Computer Sciences
- VONDERVISZT, F., Biophysics and Nanotechnology

Faculty of Modern Philology and Social Sciences:
- FÖLDES, CS., German Language, Literature and Culutre
- KOCZISZKI, E., German Language, Literature and Culture
- KOVÁCS, A., Hungarian Literature and Culture
- SINGLETON, D., Hungarian and Applied Linguistics

Georgikon Faculty of Agriculture:
- ANDA, A., Meteorology and Water Management
- BERCSÉNYI, M., Aqua Culture
- BIZÓ SÁRDI, K., Crop Production and Soil Science
- DUBLECZ, K., Animal Nutrition and Feed Safety
- GALIBA, G., Crop Prodruction and Soil Science
- HOFFMANN, S., Crop Production and Soil Science
- HUSVÉTH, F., Animal Sciences and Animal Husbandry
- KOCSIS, L., Horticulture and Viticulture
- KOCSONDI, J., Economics
- PUPOS, T., Corporate Economics and Rural Development

PÉCSI TUDOMÁNYEGYETEM
(University of Pécs)

Pécs, Vasvári Pál u. 4, 7622
Telephone: (72) 501-500
E-mail: info@pte.hu
Internet: www.pte.hu
Founded 2000 by merger of Janus Pannonius Univ., Medical Univ. of Pécs, Illyés Gyula Teacher Training College of Szekszárd
State control
Academic year: September to May (2 terms)
Rector: Prof. Dr JÓZSEF BÓDIS
Sr Vice-Rector for Academic Affairs, Int. Relations and Communications: Dr LÁSZLÓ I. KOMLÓSI
Vice-Rector for Financial and Strategic Affairs: Dr GYULA ZELLER
Vice-Rector for Science and Innovation: Dr GÁBOR L. KOVÁCS
Chief Admin.Officer: Dr KATALIN URBÁN
Chief Librarian: Dr ÁGNES DÁRDAI
Number of teachers: 2,000
Number of students: 33,200
Publications: *Pécsi Orvostudományi Egyetem Évkönyve* (1 a year), *Specimina Fennica* (irregular), *Specimina Geographica* (irregular), *Specimina Nova Dissertationum ex Institutio Historico* (irregular), *Specimina Sibirica* (irregular), *Studia Iuridica Auctoritatae Universitatis Pécs Publicata* (4 a year), *Studia Oeconomica Auctoritatae Universitatis Pécs Publicata* (4 a year), *Studia Paedagogica Auctoritate Universitatis Pécs Publicata* (irregular), *Studia Philosophica et Sociologica Auctoritatae Universitatis Pécs Publicata* (4 a year), *Szép Literatúrai Ajándék* (4 a year), *Tudományos Dialóg* (6 a year), *Univ Pécs* (every 2 weeks)

DEANS

Faculty of Adult Education and Human Resources Development: Dr ZSOLT NEMESKÉRI
Faculty of Business and Economics: Dr JÓZSEF ULBERT
Faculty of Health Sciences: Prof. JÓZSEF BETLEHEM
Faculty of Humanities: Dr FERENC FISCHER
Faculty of Law: Dr GYULA BERKE
Faculty of Music and Visual Arts: Prof. COLIN FOSTER
Faculty of Sciences: Prof. ISTVÁN GERESDI
Illyés Gyula Faculty of Education: Dr BÉLA HORVÁTH
Medical School: Prof. ATTILA MISETA
Mihály Pollack Faculty of Engineering and Information Technology: Dr BÁLINT BACHMANN

PROFESSORS

Faculty of Business and Economics (Pécs, Rákóczi u. 80, 7622; tel. (72) 501-599; e-mail kapcsolat@ktk.pte.hu; internet www.ktk.pte.hu):
- BARAKONYI, K., Strategic Management
- BÉLYÁCZ, I., Corporate Finance and Accounting
- BUDAY-SÁNTHA, A., Agricultural, Environmental and Regional Economics
- DOBAY, P., Business Informatics
- FARKAS, F., Management
- KOMLÓSI, S., Decision-making
- LÁSZLÓ, GY., Corporate Finance and Accounting
- OROSZI, S., Economics
- REKETTYE, G., Marketing
- SIPOS, B., Strategic Management
- TAKÁCS, B., Marketing
- TÖRŐCSIK, M., Marketing
- TÓTH, T., Economic History
- VARGA, J., Decision-making
- VÖRÖS, J., Decision-making

Faculty of Health Sciences (Pécs, Vörösmarty u. 4, 7621; tel. (72) 513-671; e-mail info@etk.pte.hu; internet www.etk.pte.hu):
- BÓDIS, J., Obstetrics and Gynaecology
- BUDA, J., Public Health
- CHOLNOKY, P., Paediatrics
- CSERE, T., Radiology
- FARKAS, M., Nuclear Medicine
- FIGLER, M., Gastroenterology
- GYÓDI, GY., Paediatrics
- HARTMANN, G., Physiology
- HORVÁTH, B., Obstetrics and Gynaecology

ILLEI, GY., Obstetrics and Gynaecology
JEGES, S., Biostatistics
KELEMEN, J., Chemistry
KISS, T., Biology
KOMÁROMY, L., Biology
KOPA, J., Neurosurgery
KOVÁCS, L. G., Neuroendocrinology
KRÁNITZ, J., Orthopaedics
LAKY, R., Traumatology
ROZSOS, I., Surgery
SULYOK, E., Paediatrics
TAHIN, T., Medical Sociology
TÁRNOK, F., Gastroenterology

Faculty of Humanities (Pécs, Ifjúság u. 6, 7624; tel. (72) 503-600; e-mail btkinfo@pte.hu; internet www.btk.pte.hu):

ANDRÁSFALVY, B., Ethnography
BÓKAY, A., Literature and Culture of the English-Speaking People
BOROS, J., History of Philosophy
ERÖS, F., Psychology
FISHER, F., Modern History
FONT, M., Medieval and Early Modern History
FORRAY, R. K., Linguistics
HETESI, I., Classical Literary History and Comparative Literature
KÁLMÁN, C. GY., Modern Literary History and Theory of Literature
KARSAI, GY., Classical Philology
KASSAI, I., Linguistics
KÉZDI, B., Personality, Development and Clinical Psychology
KISBÁN, E., Ethnography
KOMLÓSI, L., English Linguistics
KUPA, L., Sociology and Social Policy
LÁSZLÓ, J., Psychology
NAGY, E., Sociology and Social Policy
NAGY, I., Classical Literary History and Comparative Literature
ORMOS, M., Modern History
PÓCS, É., Ethnography
ROHONYI, Z., Classical Literary History and Comparative Literature
SZÉPE, GY., Linguistics
TASSONI, L., Italian Studies
THOMKA, B., Modern Literary History and Theory of Literature
VARGYAS, P., Ancient History and Archaeology
VISY, ZS., Ancient History and Archaeology
WEISS, J., History of Philosophy
WILD, K., German Linguistics

Faculty of Law (Pécs, 48-as tér 1, 7622; tel. (72) 501-599; internet ajk.pte.hu):

ANDRÁSSY, GY., Political Science and Social Theory
BRUHÁCS, J., International and European Law
KAJTÁR, I., History of Law and Roman Law
KECSKÉS, L., Civil Law
KENGYEL, M., Civil Procedural Law and Sociology of Law
KISS, GY., Labour Law and Social Welfare Law
KISS, L., Administrative Law
KORINEK, L., Criminal Law
TÓTH, M., Criminal Law
TREMMEL, F., Criminal Procedural Law
VISEGRÁDY, A., Philosophy of Law and State

Faculty of Music and Visual Arts (Pécs, Damjanich u. 30, 7624; tel. (72) 501-540; e-mail mail@art.pte.hu; internet www.art.pte.hu):

BENCSIK, I., Sculpture
JOBBÁGY, V., Music
KESERŰ, I., Painting
KIRCS, L., Music
PINCZEHELYI, S., Painting
RÉTFALVI, S., Sculpture
TILLAI, A., Music
VIDOVSZKY, L., Theory of Art

Faculty of Sciences (Pécs, Ifjúság u. 6, 7624; tel. (72) 503-600; e-mail kapcsolat@gamma.ttk.pte.hu; internet www.ttk.pte.hu):

AGÁRDI, P., Cultural Studies
BERGOU, J., Theoretical Physics
BORHIDI, A., Botany
CSOKNYA, M., Zoology and Neurobiology
ERDŐSI, F., Institute of Geography
FISCHER, E., Zoology and Neurobiology
HÁMORI, J., Zoology and Neurobiology
KLEIN, S., Human Resource Development
KOLLÁR, L., Inorganic Chemistry and Technology
KORPA, CS., Theoretical Physics
KŐSZEGFALVI, GY., Institute of Geography
KOZMA, L., Adult Education
LOVÁSZ, GY., Institute of Geography
MAJER, J., General and Applied Ecology
NAGY, G., General Physics and Chemistry
PESTI, M., General and Environmental Microbiology
SZABÓ, L., Botany
SZEIDL, L., Mathematics
TOMCSÁNYI, T., Genetics and Molecular Biology
TÓTH, J., Institute of Geography
UHRIN, B., Mathematics
VUICS, T., Institute of Geography

Illyés Gyula Faculty of Education (Szekszárd, Rákóczi u. 1, 7100; tel. (74) 528-300; e-mail info@igyk.pte.hu; internet www.igyfk.pte.hu):

ANDRÁSSY, GY., Philosophy
BAJNER, M., Foreign Languages
BORBÉLY, S., Hungarian Language and Literature
BÚS, I., Education
FUSZ, GY., Visual Education
HORVÁTH, B., Hungarian Language and Literature
KURUCZ, R., Education and Psychology
NAGY, J. T., Philosophy of Law
TOLNAI, GY., Social Policy
TOTHNÉ LITOVKINA, A., Foreign Languages
VÁRADY, Z., History of Science

Medical School (Pécs, Szigeti u. 12, 7624; tel. (72) 536-200; e-mail dekani.hivatal@aok.pte.hu; internet www.aok.pte.hu):

ÁNGYÁN, L., Physiology
BAJNÓCZKY, I., Forensic Medicine
BARTHÓ, L., Pharmacology
BARTHÓNÉ SZEKERES, J., Medical Microbiology and Immunology
BELÁGYI, J., Central Research Laboratory
BELLYEI, Á., Orthopaedics
BOGÁR, L., Anaesthesiology and Intensive Therapy
CZIRJÁK, L., Internal Medicine
CZOPF, J., Neurology
DÓCZI, T., Neurosurgery
EMBER, I., Public Health
EMŐDY, L., Microbiology
ERTL, T., Obstetrics and Gynaecology
FEKETE, M., Paediatrics
FISCHER, E., Pharmacology
GALLYAS, F., Neurosurgery
GÖTZ, F., Urology
GREGUS, Z., Pharmacology
HIDEG, K., Central Research Laboratory
HORVÁTH, L., Radiology
HORVÁTH ÖRS, P., Surgery
KAJTÁR, P., Paediatrics
KARÁTSON, A., Internal Medicine
KELÉNYI, G., Pathology
KELLERMAYER, M., Clinical Biochemistry
KETT, K., Surgery
KILÁR, F., Central Research Laboratory
KOLLÁR, L., Surgery
KOSZTOLÁNYI, GY., Paediatrics
KOVÁCS, B., Ophthalmology
KOVÁCS, S., Pathophysiology
KRÁNICZ, J., Orthopaedics
KROMMER, K., Obstetrics and Gynaecology
LÁZÁR, GY., Anatomy
LÉNÁRD, L., Physiology
LUDÁNY, A., Clinical Chemistry
MÉHES, K., Paediatrics
MEZŐNÉ FARKAS, B., Dermatology
MOLNÁR, D., Paediatrics
MÓZSIK, GY., Internal Medicine
NAGY, L., Family Medicine
NÉMETH, P., Immunology and Biotechnology
NYÁRÁDY, J., Traumatology
PAJOR, L., Pathology
PAPP, L., Cardiology
PÁR, L., Internal Medicine
PINTÉR, A., Paediatrics
PYTEL, J., Otorhinolaryngology
SÁNDOR, A., Biochemistry
SCHNEIDER, I., Dermatology
SÉTÁLÓ, GY., Anatomy
SOLTÉSZ, GY., Paediatrics
SOMOGYI, B., Biophysics
SÜMEGI, B., Biochemistry
SZABÓ, GY., Oral Medicine
SZABÓ, I., Behavioural Science
SZABÓ, I., Obstetrics and Gynaecology
SZEBERÉNYI, J., Biology
SZÉKELY, M., Pathophysiology
SZELÉNYI, Z., Pathophysiology
SZOLCSÁNYI, J., Pharmacology
TEKERES, M., Intensive Therapy and Anaesthesia
TÉNYI, J., Public Health
THAN, G., Obstetrics and Gynaecology
TÓTH, GY., Chemistry
TRIXLER, M., Psychiatry and Medical Psychology
VERECZKEI, L., Behavioural Science
VÉRTES, M., Physiology

Mihály Pollack Faculty of Engineering and Information Technology (Pécs, Boszorkány u. 2, 7624; tel. (72) 503-650; e-mail titkar@pmmik.pte.hu; internet pmmk.pte.hu):

ARADI, L., Public Utilities, Geodesy and Environmental Protection
ÁSVÁNYI, J., Automation
BACHMAN, Z., Design and Architecture
BÁRSONY, J., Statics and Supporting Structures
BUDAY, L., Education
CSÉBFALVI, GY., Statics and Supporting Structures
FÜLÖP, L., Building Structures
HÜBNER, M., Urban Development
JÓZSA, L., Electric Networks
KISS, E., Education
KISTELEGDI, I., Building Structures
KLINCSIK, M., Mathematics
LENKEI, P., Statics and Supporting Structures
ORBAN, F., Mechanical Engineering
ORBÁN, J., Materials, Geotechnics and Transport Engineering
TÓTH, Z., Urban Development
VAJDA, J., Building Construction
VARGA, L., Education
VÍG MIKLÓSNE, L. A., Mathematics

SEMMELWEIS EGYETEM
(Semmelweis University)

Budapest, Üllői ut. 26, 1085
Telephone: (1) 459-1500
E-mail: titkarsag.rektor@semmelweis-univ.hu
Internet: www.semmelweis-univ.hu
Founded 1769 as Medical Faculty of the Univ. of Nagyszombat, present status 1951, present name 2000 upon integration with Imre Haynal Univ. of Health Sciences and Hungarian Univ. of Physical Education
State control
Languages of instruction: English, German, Hungarian
Academic year: September to June

Rector: Prof. Dr ÁGOSTON SZÉL
Vice-Rector for Gen. and Clinical Affairs: Prof. Dr JÁNOS GÁL
Vice-Rector for Educational Affairs: Prof. Dr JÓZSEF TÍMÁR
Vice-Rector for Scientific Affairs: Prof. Dr MÁRIA JUDIT MOLNÁR
Dir for Int. Relations: Dr MARCEL POP
Gen. Dir for Central Library: Dr LIVIA VASAS

Library of 623,030 vols
Number of teachers: 1,171
Number of students: 12,785

Publications: *Kalokagathia* (4 a year), *Orvosi Könyvtárak* (4 a year), *Orvosképzés* (4 a year), *Pathology Oncology Research* (4 a year), *Studia Physiologica*

DEANS

Faculty of Dentistry: Prof. Dr PÉTER HERMANN
Faculty of Health and Public Services: Dr PÉTER GAÁL
Faculty of Health Sciences: Prof. Dr ZOLTÁN ZSOLT NAGY
Faculty of Medicine: Prof. Dr LÁSZLÓ HUNYADY
Faculty of Pharmacy: Prof. Dr ROMÁNA ZELKÓ
Faculty of Physical Education and Sport Sciences: Prof. Dr ZSOLT RADÁK
School of Doctoral Studies: Prof. Dr KÁROLY RÁCZ

PROFESSORS

Faculty of Dentistry (Budapest, Üllői út 26., 1085; tel. (1) 266-0453; e-mail kobor@fok.usn.hu):

BÁNÓCZY, J., Oral Biology
BARABAS, J., Maxillofacial Surgery
DIVINYI, T., Maxillofacial Surgery
DOBÓ NAGY, CS., Oral Diagnostics
FÁBIÁN, T., Prosthodontics
FAZEKAS, Á., Conservative Dentistry
FEJÉRDY, P., Prosthodontics
GERA, I., Periodontics
HERMANN, P., Prosthodontics
NAGY, G., Oral Diagnostics
NYÁRASDY, I., Conservative Dentistry
SIMON, GY., Oralbiology
SZABÓ, GY., Maxillofacial Surgery
TARJÁN, I., Pedodontics and Orthodontics
VARGA, G., Oral Biology
WINDISCH, P., Periodontics
ZELLES, T., Oral Biology

Faculty of Health and Pubic Services (Budapest, Kútvölgyi út 2., 1125; tel. (1) 488-7600; e-mail dekani@ekk.sote.hu):

NAGY, E., Mental Health
TOMCSÁNYI, T., Mental Health

Faculty of Health Sciences (Budapest, Vas u. 17, 1088; tel. (1) 486-5910; e-mail kakuk.m@se-etk.hu):

LÉVAY, GY., Morphology and Physiology
RÁCZ, J., Addictology
SZABOLCS, J., Dietetics

Faculty of Medicine (Budapest, Üllői út 26., 1085; tel. (1) 317-9057; e-mail vegh.anna@med.semmelweis-univ.hu):

ACSÁDY, GY., Vascular Surgery
ÁDÁM, E., Medical Microbiology
ÁDÁM, V., Medical Biochemistry
ALFÖLDY, F., Transplantation and Surgery
ANDERLIK, P., Medical Microbiology
ARATO, A., Paediatrics
BANCZEROWSKI, P., Neurosurgery
BANHEGYI, G., Molecular Biology and Pathobiochemistry
BÁNHIDY, F., Obstetrics and Gynaecology
BENDER, GY., Orthopedics
BENYÓ, Z., Clinical Experimental Research
BÉRCZI, V., Radiology and Oncotherapy
BERECZKI, D., Neurology
BITTER, J., Psychiatry and Psychotherapy
BROOSER, G., Ophthalmology
BUZÁS, E., Genetics
CSABA, GY., Genetics
CSANDA, E., Neurology
CSEH, K., Public Health
CSERMELY, P., Molecular Biology and Pathobiochemistry
CSILLAG, A., Anatomy
DARVAS, K. I., Surgery
DE CHÂTEL, R., Internal Medicine
DEMETER, J., Internal Medicine
DONÁTH, T., Anatomy
ENTZ, L., Vascular Surgery
ENYEDI, P., Physiology
FALLER, J., Surgery
FALUDI, G., Mental Health
FALUS, A., Genetics
FARKAS, H., Internal Medicine-Research Laboratory
FEHÉR, E., Anatomy
FEKETE, B., Internal Medicine
FEKETE, GY., Paediatrics
FERDINÁNDY, P., Pharmacology and Pharmacotherapy
FIDY, J., Biophysics
FLAUTNER, L., Surgery
FONYÓ, A., Physiology
FÜRST, ZS., Pharmacology and Pharmacotherapy
GÁL, J., Anaesthesiology and Intensive Therapy
GÉHER, P., Rheumatology and Physiotherapy
GERGELY, P., Immunology
GERŐ, L., Internal Medicine
GLÁZ, E., Internal Medicine
GÖMÖR, B., Rheumatology and Physiotherapy
GYIRES, K., Pharmacology and Pharmacotherapy
HAJDÚ, J., Obstetrics and Gynaecology
HALÁSZ, B., Human Morphology
HOLLÓ, G., Ophthalmology
HORKAY, F., Cardiac Surgery
HORVÁTH, A., Dermatology and Venereology
HORVÁTH, I., Pulmonology
HUNYADY, L., Physiology
HUTÁS, I., Pulmonology
HÜTTL, K., Cardiology
JÁRAY, J., Transplantation and Surgery
JENEY, A., Pathology and Experimental Cancer Research
KÁDÁR, A., Pathology
KALABAY, L., Family Medicine
KÁLMÁN, M., Anatomy
KAMONDI, A., Neurology
KARÁDI, I., Internal Medicine
KÁRPÁTI, S., Dermatology and Venereology
KECSKEMÉTI, V., Pharmacology and Pharmacotherapy
KELLER, E., Forensic Medecine
KELLERMAYER, M., Biophysics
KELTAI, M., Cardiology
KEMPLER, P., Internal Medicine
KÉRI, GY., Molecular Biology and Pathobiochemistry
KERPEL-FRONIUS, S., Pharmacology and Pharmacotherapy
KISS, I., Geriatrics
KNOLL, J., Pharmacology and Pharmacotherapy
KÓBORI, L., Transplantation and Surgery
KOLLAI, M., Clinical Experimental Research
KOLLER, Á., Pathophysiology
KOPPER, L., Pathology and Experimental Cancer Research
KOVÁCS, J., Behavioural Sciences
KOVALSZKY, I., Pathology and Experimental Cancer Research
KÖVES, K., Human Morphology
KULKA, J., Pathology
KUPCSULIK, P., Surgery
LAKATOS, P., Internal Medicine
LANGER, R., Transplantation and Surgery
LAPIS, K., Pathology and Experimental Cancer Research
LIGETI, E., Physiology
LOSONCZY, GY., Pulmonology
LOZSÁDI, K., Cardiology
LUDWIG, E., Infectology
MACHOVICH, R., Medical Biochemistry
MAJOROSSY, K., Anatomy
MANDL, J., Molecular Biology and Pathobiochemistry
MARSCHALKÓ, M., Dermatology and Venerology
MASSZI, T., Internal Medicine
MATOLCSY, A., Pathology and Experimental Cancer Research
MERKELY, B., Cardiology
MILTÉNYI, M., Paediatrics
MOLNÁR, M. J., Genomic Medicine
MONOS, E., Clinical Experimental Research
NAGY, GY., Human Morphology
NAGY, K., Medical Microbiology
NAGY, P., Pathology
NAGY, Z., Cardiovascular Surgery
NAGY, Z. ZS, Ophthalmology
NÁSZ, I., Medical Microbiology
NEMES, A., Cardiovascular Surgery
NÉMETH, J., Ophthalmology
NYÁRY, I., Neurosurgery
NYIRÁDY, P., Urology
OLÁH, I., Human Morphology
ONDREJKA, P., Surgery
PAJOR, A., Obstetrics and Gynaecology
PALKOVITS, M., Anatomy
PAPP, J., Internal Medicine
PAPP, M., Neurology
PÁSZTOR, E., Neurosurgery
PAULIN, F., Obstetrics and Gynaeology
PÉNZES, I., Anaesthesiology and Intensive Therapy
PERNER, F., Transplantology and Surgery
POÓR, GY., Rheumatology and Physiology
PRÉDA, I., Cardiology
PROHÁSZKA, Z., Internal Medicine-Research Laboratory
RÁCZ, K., Internal Medicine
RÉPÁSSY, G., Internal Medicine
RÉTHELYI, M., Anatomy
REUSZ, GY., Paediatrics
RIBÁRI, O., Otorhynolaryngology
RIGÓ, J., Obstetrics and Gynaecology
RÖHLICH, P., Human Morphology
ROMICS, I., Urology
RONTO, GY., Biophysics
ROSIVALL, L., Pathophysiology
ROZGONYI, F., Dermatology and Venerology
SANDOR, J., Surgery
SARKADI, B., Biophysics
SÁPI, Z., Pathology
SASVÁRI, M., Molecular Biology and Pathobiochemistry
SCHAFF, ZS., Pathology
SCHULER, D., Paediatrics
SCHULTHEISZ, E., Public Health
SIMON, T., Public Health
SMELLER, L., Biophysics
SOMOGYI, A., Internal Medicine
SÓTONYI, P., Forensic Medicine
SPÄT, A., Physiology
SPERLÁGH, B., Pharmacology and Pharmacotherapy
SRÉTER, L., Internal Medicine
SÜVEGES, I., Ophthalmology
SZABO, A., Paediatrics
SZABÓ, A., Laboratory Medicine
SZABÓ, Z., Cardiovascular Surgery
SZALAY, F., Internal Medicine
SZATHMÁRI, M., Internal Medicine
SZÉKÁCS, B., Geriatrics
SZÉL, Á., Human Morphology and Developmental Biology
SZENDE, B., Pathology and Experimental Cancer Research
SZENDRŐI, M., Orthopaedics
SZERI, I., Medical Microbiology
SZILVÁSI, I., Nuclear Medicine

SZIRMAI, I., Neurology
SZŐKE, GY., Orthopedics
TEMESVÁRI, E., Dermatology and Venerology
TIHANYI, T., Surgery
TÍMÁR, J., Pathology
TIMÁR, L., Paediatrics, Infectious Diseases
TÖMBÖL, T., Anatomy
TOMPA, A., Public Health
TRETTER, L., Medical Biochemistry
TRINGER, L., Psychiatry and Psychotherapy
TULASSAY, T., Paediatrics
TULASSAY, ZS., Internal Medicine
TÚRY, F., Behavioural Sciences
URBANCSEK, J., Obstetrics and Gynaecology
VARGA, M., Ophthalmology
VÁSÁRHELYI, B., Laboratory Medicine
VASTAG, E., Pulmonology
VEREBÉLY, T., Paediatrics
VIGH, B., Human Morphology
VIZI, E. SZ., Pharmacology and Pharmacotherapy
VIZKELETY, T., Orthopedics
WÉBER, GY., Experimental and Clinical Surgery
WENGER, T., Human Morphology and Developmental Biology
ZRÍNYI, M., Biophysics

Faculty of Pharmacy (Budapest, Üllői út 26., 1085; tel. (1) 266-0449; e-mail dredan.judit@pharma.semmelweis-univ.hu):

BAGDY, GY., Pharmacodynamics
KLEBOVICH, J., Pharmaceutics
LEDNICZKY, L., Pharmacology
MAGYAR, K., Pharmacodynamics
MARTON, S., Pharmaceutics
MÁTYUS, P., Organic Chemistry
NOSZÁL, B., Pharmaceutical Chemistry
NOVÁK, K., Pharmaceutical Chemistry
PAÁL, T., Drug Monitoring
SZÁSZ, GY., Pharmaceutical Chemistry
SZŐKE, É., Pharmacognosy
SZÖKŐ, E., Pharmacodynamics
TEKES, K., Pharmacodynamics
TÖRÖK, T., Pharmacodynamics
VINCZE, Z., University Pharmacy, Pharmacy Administration
ZELKO, R., Pharmacy Administration

Faculty of Physical Education and Sport Sciences (Budapest, Alkotás u. 44, 1123; tel. (1) 356-7327; e-mail vegh@tf.hu):

BERKES, I., Health Sciences and Sport Medicine
GOMBOCZ, J., Theory and Teaching of Physical Education
HAMAR, P., R.G., Dance, Aerobics
ISTVÁNFI, CS., Physical Education Theory and Pedagogy
NAGY, E., Physical Education Theory and Pedagogy
NYAKAS, CS., Sport Sciences Research
RADÁK, ZS., Sport Sciences Research
SIPOS, K., Psychology
SZABO, K., Psychology
SZÉCSÉNYI, J., Athletics
TAKÁCS, F., Social Sciences
TIHANYI, J., Biomechanics
TOTH, M., Health Sciences and Sport Medicine

SZÉCHENYI ISTVÁN EGYETEM
(Széchenyi István University)

Győr, Egyetem tér 1, 9026
Telephone: (96) 503-400
E-mail: information@sze.hu
Internet: uni.sze.hu

Founded 1968 as Transportation and Telecommunications Faculty of Technical Sciences, present name and status 2002
State control
Languages of instruction: English, German, Hungarian
Academic year: September to June

Rector: Dr PÉTER FÖLDESI
Gen. Vice-Rector: Dr GÁBOR KOVÁCS
Sec.-Gen.: Dr ZSOLT KOVÁCS
Dir for Library: ANIKÓ FIGULA

Library of 240,000 vols, 1,000 periodicals
Number of teachers: 360
Number of students: 10,600 (6,800 undergraduate, 1,200 postgraduate, 2,600 distant learning)

Publications: *Acta Technica Jaurinensis* (3 a year, print and online, journal.sze.hu), *Hungarian Electronic Journal of Sciences* (online, hej.sze.hu), *Jog-Állam-Politika* (4 a year), *Tudományos Füzetek*

DEANS

Deák Ferenc Faculty of Law and Political Sciences: Dr JUDIT CSC LÉVAYNÉ DR. FAZEKAS
Faculty of Engineering Sciences: Prof. Dr JÁNOS ÉGERT
Kautz Gyula Faculty of Economics: Dr ILONA PAPP
Petz Lajos Institute of Health and Social Studies: Dr SÁNDOR NAGY (Dir)
Varga Tibor Institute of Musical Art: Dr ISTVÁN RUPPERT

SZEGEDI TUDOMÁNYEGYETEM
(University of Szeged)

Szeged, Dugonics tér 13, 6720
Telephone: (62) 544-000
E-mail: rektor@rekt.u-szeged.hu
Internet: www.u-szeged.hu

Founded 1872, refounded 1921, present name and status 2000
State control
Language of instruction: Hungarian
Academic year: September to June

Rector: Prof. Dr GÁBOR SZABÓ
Vice-Rector for Education: Prof. Dr MÁRIA HOMOKI-NAGY
Vice-Rector for Foreign Affairs and Public Relations: Prof. JÓZSEF PAL
Vice-Rector for Gen. Affairs: Prof. Dr BÉLA RÁCZ
Vice-Rector for Science, Research Devt and Innovation: Prof. Dr ANDRÁS VARRÓ
Sec.-Gen.: Dr MATÉ DÖMÖTÖR
Librarian: PALOTÁSNÉ RÓZA PÁNTI

Library: see under Libraries and Archives
Number of teachers: 2,180
Number of students: 25,300

Publications: *Acta Academiae Paedagogicae Szegediensis: series linguistica, litteraria et aesthetica, Acta Antiqua et Archaeologica, Acta Biologica Szegediensis* (2 a year, print and online), *Acta Climatologica et Chorologica, Acta conventus de iure civili, Acta Cybernetica* (2 a year, print and online), *Acta Hispanica, Acta Historiae Litterarum Hungaricarum, Acta Historica, Acta juridica et politica, Acta Mineralogica-Petrographica, Acta Romanica, Acta Sana, Acta Scientarum Mathematicarum, Acta Universitatis Szegediensis: sectio linguistica, Agrár-és vidékfejlesztési szemle, Alkalmazott nyelvészeti mesterfüzetek, Journal of environmental geography, Nyelvészeti füzetek*

DEANS

Faculty of Agriculture: Prof. Dr Hab. KÁROLY BODNÁR
Faculty of Arts: Prof. Dr Hab. SÁNDOR CSERNUS
Faculty of Dentistry: Prof. Dr KATALIN NAGY
Faculty of Economics and Business Administration: Dr MÁRTON VILMÁNYI
Faculty of Engineering: Prof. Dr ANTAL VÉHA
Faculty of Health Sciences and Social Studies: Dr MÁRIA BARNAI
Faculty of Law and Political Sciences: Prof. Dr IMRE SZABÓ
Faculty of Medicine: Prof. Dr LÁSZLÓ VÉCSEI
Faculty of Music: Prof. Dr FERENC KEREK
Faculty of Pharmacy: Prof. Dr Hab. HOHMANN JUDIT
Faculty of Science and Informatics: Prof. Dr KLÁRA HERNÁDI
Juhász Gyula Teacher Training Faculty: Prof. Dr GÁBOR GALAMBOS

PROFESSORS

Faculty of Agriculture (Hódmezővásárhely, Andrássy u. 15, 6800; tel. (62) 532-990; e-mail bodnar@mgk.u-szeged.hu; internet www.mgk.u-szeged.hu):

PÉTER, J., Nutrition
TANÁCS, L., Plant Protection

Faculty of Arts (Szeged, Egyetem u. 2, 6722; tel. (62) 544-360; e-mail dekan@primus.arts.u-szeged.hu; internet www.arts.u-szeged.hu):

ANDERLE, Á., Hispanic Studies
A. SAJTI, E., History
BAKRÓ-NAGY, M., Finno-Ugrian Linguistics
BALÁZS, M., Early Hungarian Literature
BARNA, G., Ethnology
BASSOLA, P., German Linguistics
CSABAI, M., Psychology
CSAPÓ, B., Education
CSEJTEI, D., Philosophy
CSÚRI, K., Languages
GYENGE, Z., Philosophy
IVANICS, M., Languages
J. NAGY, L., Modern World History and Mediterranean Studies
KARSAI, L., Modern World History
KENESEI, I., English and American Studies
KONTRA, M., Applied Linguistics
KOCSIS, M., Languages
LEPAHIN, V., Russian Language and Literature
MAKK, F., Auxiliary Sciences of History
MÁTÉ-TÓTH, A., Study of Religions
NAGY, J., Education
ODORICS, F., Literature
PÁL, J., Italian Language and Literature
PENKE, O., French Language and Literature
RÓNA-TAS, A., Altaic Studies
SZAJBÉLY, M., Classic Hungarian Literature
SZŐNYI, G., English and American Studies
SZÖRÉNYI, L., Comparative Literature
TOMKA, B., History
VIDÁKOVICH, T., Education
VÍGH, É., Italian Language and Literature
WINKLER, I., Psychology
WOJTILLA, G., Ancient History

Faculty of Dentistry (Szeged, Tisza L. krt. 64, 6720; tel. (62) 545-299; e-mail stoma@stoma.szote.u-szeged.hu; internet www.stoma.u-szeged.hu):

GORZÓ, I., Operative Dentistry and Endodontology
NAGY, K., Dentistry, Oral Surgery
PIFFKÓ, J., Dentistry
RAKONCZAY, Z., Prosthodontics and Oral Biology

Faculty of Economics and Business Administration (Szeged, Kálvária sgt. 1, 6722; tel. (62) 544-360; e-mail dekan@primus.arts.u-szeged.hu; internet www.eco.u-szeged.hu):

BENET, I., World Economics and European Economic Integration
BOTOS, K., Finance
DINYA, L., Marketing and Management
KOVÁCS, A., Finance
LENGYEL, I., Economics and Economic Development
REKETTYE, G., Marketing and Management
VOSZKA, E., Economics and Business Studies

Faculty of Engineering:
HODÚR, C., Unit Operation and Environmental Techniques
MATUZ, J., Engineering
MOLNÁR, P., Agricultural Economics and Rural Development
RAJKÓ, R., Unit Operation and Environmental Techniques
SZABÓ, G., Unit Operation and Environmental Techniques
VÉHA, A., Food Technology

Faculty of Health Sciences and Social Studies (Szeged, Temesvári krt. 31, 6726; tel. (62) 544-947; e-mail poma@efk.u-szeged.hu; internet www.efk.u-szeged.hu):
BÁRÁNY, F., Social Work and Social Policy
BODA, M., Applied Medicine

Faculty of Law (Szeged, Tisza L. krt. 54, 6720; tel. (62) 544-197; e-mail ajtk.dekani@juris.u-szeged.hu; internet www.juris.u-szeged.hu):
BADÓ, A., Philosophy and Sociology of Law
BALOGH, E., Legal History
BLAZOVICH, L., Legal History
BLUTMAN, L., International Law
BODNÁR, L., International Law
CZÚCZ, O., Social and Labour Law
HAJDÚ, J., Social and Labour Law
HOMOKI-NAGY, M., Legal History
JAKAB, É., Roman Law
KATONA, T., Statistics and Demography
MARTONYI, J., International Private Law
NAGY, F., Criminal Law and Criminal Procedure
NAGY, L., Economics
PACZOLAY, P., Political Sciences
POKOL, B., Philosophy and Sociology of Law
STIPTA, I., Legal History
SZABÓ, I., Civil Law and Civil Procedure
TRÓCSÁNYI, L., Constitutional Law

Faculty of Medicine (Szeged, Tisza L. krt. 109, 6725; tel. (62) 545-015; e-mail office.aokdh@med.u-szeged.hu; internet www.szote.u-szeged.hu):
ÁBRAHÁM, G., Internal Medicine
BARI, F., Medical Physics and Informatics
BÁRTFAI, G., Tocology and Gynaecology
BARZÓ, P., Neurological Surgery
BATA, Z., Medicine
BENDER, T., Orthopaedics
BENEDEK, G., Physiology
BOLDOGKŐI, Z., Medical Biology
BORBÉNYI, Z., Internal Medicine and Cardiology
BOROS, M., Experimental Surgery
CSERNI, G., Medicine
DEÁK, J., Medicine
DÉKÁNY, I., Medicine
DUDA, E., Medical Microbiology
DUX, L., Biochemistry
ENGELHARDT, J., Neurology
FACSKÓ, A., Medicine
FERDINANDY, P., Biochemistry
FORSTER, T., Internal Medicine and Cardiology
GRÓSZ, A., Anaesthesiology and Intensive Therapy
GULYA, K., Toxicology and Immunology
HAJNAL, F., Family Medicine
HANTOS, Z., Medical Physics and Informatics
HEGYI, P., Medicine
HORVÁTH, G., Medicine
IVÁNYI, B., Pathology
JANÁKY, M., Ophthalmology
JANCSÓ, G., Physiology
JANKA, Z., Neurology and Psychiatry
JÁRDÁNHÁZY, T., Neurology
JÓRI, J., Otorhinolaryngology and Head and Neck Surgery
KAHÁN, Z., Oncotherapy
KÁLMÁN, J., Neurology and Psychiatry
KATONA, M., Paediatrics
KEMÉNY, L., Dermatology and Allergology
KÉRI, S., Physiology
KISS HŐGYE, M., Internal Medicine and Cardiology
KOLOZSVÁRI, L., Ophthalmology
LÁZÁR, G., Pathophysiology
LEPRÁN, I., Pharmacology and Pharmacotherapy
MÉRAY, J., Medicine
MIHÁLY, A., Anatomy, Histology and Embryology
MOLNÁR, J., Anatomy, Histology and Embryology
MOLNÁR, Z., Anaesthesiology and Intensive Therapy
NAGY, E., Clinical Microbiology
NAGY, F., Internal Medicine
NAGYMAJTÉNYI, L., Public Health
ORVOS, H., Medicine
PAJOR, L., Urology
PÁL, A., Tocology and Gynaecology
PALKÓ, A., Radiology
PÁVICS, L., Nuclear Medicine
PETRI, A., Surgery
PIFFKÓ, J., Oral And Maxillofacial Surgery
PRÁGAI, B., Medical Microbiology and Immunology
ROVÓ, L., Medicine
RUDAS, L., Anaesthesiology and Intensive Therapy
SIMONKA, J., Traumatology
SOMFAY, A., Pulmonology
SZABAD, J., Medical Biology
SZABÓ, G., Pathophysiology
SZABÓ, J., Medical Genetics
SZTRIHA, L., Paediatrics
TAKÁCS, T., Internal Medicine
THURZÓ, L., Oncotherapy
TÓTH, G., Medical Chemistry
TÓTH, K., Orthopaedics
TÚRI, S., Paediatrics
URBÁN, E., Medicine
VARGA, A., Traumatology
VARGA, E., Forensic Medicine
VARRÓ, A., Pharmacology and Pharmacotherapy
VAS, Á., Internal Medicine
VÉCSEI, L., Neurology
VÉGH, Á., Pharmacology and Pharmacotherapy
WITTMANN, T., Internal Medicine
ZARÁNDI, M., Medical Chemistry

Faculty of Music (Szeged, Tisza L. krt. 79–81, 6722; tel. (62) 544-605; e-mail kerek@music.u-szeged.hu; internet www.music.u-szeged.hu):
KEREK, F., Piano
SZECSŐDI, F., Strings
TEMESI, M., Solo Singing

Faculty of Pharmacy (Szeged, Zrinyi u. 9, 6720; tel. (62) 545-022; e-mail office@pharm.u-szeged.hu; internet www.pharm.u-szeged.hu):
CSÓKA, I., Pharmacy
DOMBI, G., Pharmaceutical Analysis
FALKAY, G., Pharmacodynamics
FÜLÖP, F., Pharmaceutical Chemistry
HÓDI, K., Pharmaceutical Technology
HOHMANN, J., Pharmacognosy
PAÁL, T., Drug Regulatory Affairs
RÉVÉSZ, P., Pharmaceutical Technology

Faculty of Science and Informatics (Szeged, Aradi vértanúk tere 1, 6720; tel. (62) 544-681; e-mail annuse@sci.u-szeged.hu; internet www.sci.u-szeged.hu):
BENEDICT, M., Theoretical Physics
BOR, Z., Optics and Quantum Electronics
BOROS, I., Genetic and Molecular Biology
CSENDES, T., Computational Optimization
CSIRIK, J., Computer Science
CZÉDLI, G., Mathematics
DOMBI, A., Mechanic and Material Science
DOMBI, J., Informatics
ERDEI, L., Plant Biology
ERDŐHELYI, A., Physical Chemistry and Material Science
ÉSIK, Z., Principles of Computer Science
FEHÉR, L., Theoretical Physics
FEKETE, É., Comparative Physiology
FÜLÖP, Z., Principles of Computer Science
GAJDA, T., Inorganic and Analytical Chemistry
GULYA, K., Zoology and Cell Biology
GYIMÓTHY, T., Software Engineering
HANNUS, I., Applied and Environmental Chemistry
HERNÁDI, K., Applied and Environmental Chemistry
HETÉNYI, M., Mineralogy, Geochemistry and Petrography
IGLÓI, F., Theoretical Physics
KÉRCHY, L., Analysis
KISS, T., Inorganic and Analytical Chemistry
KÓNYA, Z., Chemistry
KOVÁCS, K., Biotechnology
KOVÁCS, Z., Economic Geography
KRÁMLI, A., Applications of Analysis
KRISZTIN, T., Applied Numerical Mathematics
MAJOR, P., Applications of Analysis
MARÓTI, P., Medical Physics and Biophysics
MARÓY, P., Genetic and Molecular Biology
MEZŐSI, G., Physical Geography and Geoinformatics
NEMCSÓK, J., Biochemistry
PAP, G., Applications of Analysis
PÉTER, A., Inorganic and Analytical Chemistry
RÁCZ, B., Optics and Quantum Electronics
SCHNEIDER, G., Chemistry
SOLYMOSI, F., Chemistry
SZABÓ, G., Optics and Quantum Electronics
SZATMÁRI, S., Experimental Physics
SZENDREI, Á., Algebra and Numeric Theory
SZENDREI, M. B., Algebra and Numeric Theory
SZENTE, M., Comparative Physiology
TAMÁS, G., Comparative Physiology
TOLDI, J., Comparative Physiology
TOMBÁCZ, E., Physical Chemistry and Material Science
TÓTH, T. M., Geography
TOTIK, V., Set Theory and Mathematical Logic
VÁGVÖLGYI, C., Microbiology
WÖLFLING, J., Chemistry
ZÁDORI, L., Mathematics

Juhász Gyula Teacher Training Faculty (Szeged, Boldogasszony sgt. 6, 6722; tel. (62) 546-050; e-mail galambos@jgytf.u-szeged.hu; internet www.jgytf.u-szeged.hu):
GALAMBOS, G., Computer Science
NAGY, J., Hungarian Language
NÁNAI, L., Physics
PUKÁNSZKY, B., Education
RÁCZ, L., Applied Humanities
SZABÓ, T., Applied Humanities

SZENT ISTVÁN EGYETEM
(Szent István University)

Gödöllő, Páter Károly u. 1, 2100
Telephone: (28) 522-000
E-mail: info@szie.hu
Internet: szie.hu
Founded 1945 as Gödöllő Univ. of Agricultural Sciences, present status 2000
State control
Languages of instruction: English, German, Hungarian
Academic year: September to June
Rector: Dr LÁSZLÓ SOLTI
Vice-Rector for Education: Dr JÁNOS BEKE

Vice-Rector for Int. Relations: Dr ERIKA MICHÉLI
Vice-Rector for Research: Dr LÁSZLÓ HORNOK
Gen-Sec.: TIBOR MEZEI
Library Dir: ERZSÉBET TÖRÖK KOÓSNÉ
Library: see attached libraries and archives in Gödöllő, Budapest, Jászberény, Szarvas, Gyula, Békéscsaba
Number of teachers: 670
Number of students: 17,000

DEANS

Faculty of Agricultural and Environmental Sciences: Dr CSABA GYURICZA
Faculty of Applied Arts and Pedagogy: Dr IMRE LIPCSEI
Faculty of Economics, Agriculture and Health Studies: Dr JÁNOS PUSKÁS
Faculty of Economics and Social Sciences: Dr LÁSZLÓ VILLÁNYI
Faculty of Mechanical Engineering: Dr ISTVÁN SZABÓ
Faculty of Veterinary Science: Prof. Dr PÉTER SÓTONYI
Ybl Miklós Faculty of Architecture and Civil Engineering (Budapest): Dr FERENC MAKOVÉNYI

PROFESSORS

Faculty of Agricultural and Environmental Sciences:

ANDRÁS, D.
ERIKA, M.
ERZSÉBET, K.
FERENC, G.
FERENC, L.
FERENC, S.
FERENC, V.
GÁBOR, B.
GYÖRGY, F.
GYÖRGY, H.
GYÖRGY, V.
JÁNOS, K.
JÁNOS, T.
JÓZSEF, K.
JUDIT, D.
LAJOS, H.
LÁSZLÓ, B.
LÁSZLÓ, HESZKY
LÁSZLÓ, HORNOK
LÁSZLÓ, HORVÁTH
MÁRTA, B.
MÁRTON, J.
MIHÁLY, W.
MIKLÓS, M.
PÉTER GERGELY, P.
SÁNDOR, C.
ZOLTÁN, M.
ZOLTÁN, T.

Faculty of Economics and Social Sciences:

ANDRÁS, N.
BÁLINT CSABA, I.
CSABA, M.
CSABA, S.
GYÖRGY IVÁN, C.
IMRE, L.
ISTVÁN, F.
ISTVÁN, S.
JÓZSEF, L.
JÓZSEF, M.
JÓZSEF, V.
LAJOS, S.
LÁSZLÓ, H.
LÁSZLÓ, K.
LÁSZLÓ, V.
MAGDOLNA, C.
PÉTER, H.
TAMÁS, S.
TAMÁS, T.
TOMAY TAMÁS, S.
ZOLTÁN, S.

Faculty of Mechanical Engineering:

ATTILA, V.
CSIZMADIA BÉLA, M.
DEZSŐ, F.
GÁBOR, K.
ISTVÁN, B.
ISTVÁN, F.
ISTVÁN, H.
JÁNOS, B.
LAJOS, L.
LÁSZLÓ, F.
LÁSZLÓ, T.
PÉTER, S.
ZOLTÁN, V.
ZSOLT, S.

Faculty of Veterinary Science:

ENDRE, B.
GÁBOR, S.
JÁNOS, F.
JÁNOS, V.
JÁNOS LÁSZLÓ, V.
JÓZSEF ZSIGMOND, S.
LÁSZLÓ, F.
LÁSZLÓ, Z.
KÁROLY, V.
KATALIN, H.
MIKLÓS, R.
OTTÓ, S.
PÁL, R.
PÁL, S.
PÉTER, G.
PÉTER, L.
PÉTER, N.
PÉTER, S.
RÓBERT, F.
SÁNDOR, C.
SÁNDOR GYÖRGY, F.
TIBOR, G.
VILMOS LÁSZLÓ, F.

Ybl Miklós Faculty of Architecture and Civil Engineering:

GÁBOR, T.
KÁROLY, Z.
RUDOLF, K.

PROFESSORS FROM THE FORMER UNIVERSITY OF HORTICULTURE AND FOOD TECHNOLOGY

BALÁZS, S., Vegetable Production
BALOGH, S., Food Industry Economics
BÉKÁSSY-MOLNÁR, E., Food Technology
BERNÁTH, J., Medicinal Plants
BOROSS, L., Chemistry and Biochemistry
CSEMEZ, A., Landscape Architecture
CSEPREGI, P., Viticulture
DALÁNYI, L., Landscape Architecture
DEÁK, T., Microbiology
DIMÉNY, I., Agricultural Economics
DINYA, L., Economics and Marketing
EPERJESI, I., Oenology
ERDÉLYI, E., Food Technology
FARKAS, J., Food Preservation
FEKETE, A., Food Physics
FODOR, P., Chemistry and Biochemistry
GLITS, M., Plant Pathology
HARNOS, ZS., Mathematics
HORVÁTH, G., Plant Physiology
HOSCHKE, A., Brewing and Distillation
JÁMBOR, I., Landscape Architecture
KISS, I., Food Preservation
KÖRMENDY, I., Food Preservation
KOSÁRY, J., Chemistry and Biochemistry
LÁNG, Z., Technical Department
MÉSZÁROS, Z., Entomology
MŐCSÉNYI, M., Landscape Architecture
PAIS, I., Chemistry
PAPP, J., Fruit Growing
RIMÓCZI, I., Botany
SÁRAI, T., Food Technology
SÁRKÖZY, P., Agricultural Economics
SASS, P., Fruit Growing
SCHMIDT, G., Floriculture and Dendrology
SZABÓ, S. A., Food Chemistry
VARSÁNYI, I., Food Preservation
VELICH, I., Plant Genetics and Selection
VERMES, L., Agrometeorology and Water Management

SZINHÁZ- ÉS FILMMŰVÉSZETI EGYETEM
(University of Theatre and Film Arts)

Budapest, Vas u. 2C, 1088
Telephone: (1) 318-8111
E-mail: rektorihivatal@szfe.hu
Internet: www.filmacademy.hu
Founded 1865, present name and status 2000
State control
BA in motion picture directing, editing, sound and television production; MA in production design, directing documentary and feature films; doctoral degree
Rector: TAMÁS ASCHER
Vice-Rector for Film and Television: ANDRÁS BÁRDOS
Vice-Rector for Theatre: GÉZA D. HEGEDŰS (acting)
Sec.-Gen.: L. TISZEKER
Library Dir: KNORRNÉ CSÁNYI ZSUZSA
Number of teachers: 110
Number of students: 270

Private Universities

ANDRÁSSY GYULA BUDAPESTI NÉMET NYELVŰ EGYETEM/ ANDRÁSSY UNIVERSITÄT BUDAPEST
(Andrássy University Budapest)

Budapest, POB 1422, 1464
Budapest, Pollack Mihály tér 3, 1088
Telephone: (1) 266-3101
E-mail: uni@andrassyuni.hu
Internet: www.andrassyuni.hu
Founded 2001
Private control
Language of instruction: German
Academic year: September to August
Rector: Prof. Dr ANDRÁS MASÁT
Pro-Rector: Prof. Dr STEFAN OKRUCH
Chancellor: ÁKOS DOMAHIDI
Library Dir: ESZTER BOGNÁR
Library of 15,000 vols, 15 periodicals

DEANS

Faculty of Central European Studies: Prof. Dr Hab. GEORG KASTNER
Faculty of Comparative Law and Governance: Dr HENDRIK HANSEN
Faculty of International Relations: Dr DIETRICH F. R. POHL

DEBRECENI REFORMÁTUS HITTUDOMÁNYI EGYETEM
(Debrecen Reformed Theological University)

Debrecen, Kálvin tér 16, 4026
Telephone: (52) 516-820
E-mail: info@drhe.hu
Internet: www.drhe.hu
Founded 1538, current name adopted 1993
Private control
Depts of Biblical theology and church history, dogmatic, New Testament, Old Testament, practical theology, religious education, sociology of the church
Rector: Prof. Dr KÁROLY FEKETE
Vice-Rector for Education: Dr ILDIKÓ PALÁSTHY
Vice-Rector for Gen. Affairs: Dr ZOLTÁN KUSTÁR
Univ. Sec.: Dr ILONA MECSEI
Library Dir: Dr JÁNOS MOLNÁR
Library of 600,000 vols
Number of teachers: 35
Number of students: 300

EVANGÉLIKUS HITTUDOMÁNYI EGYETEM
(Evangelical-Lutheran Theological University)

Budapest, Rózsavölgyi köz 3, 1141
Telephone: (1) 469-1050
E-mail: teologia@lutheran.hu
Internet: teol.lutheran.hu
Founded 1557
Private control
Depts of church history, church music, New Testament theology, Old Testament theology, practical theology, religion and social sciences, systematic theology
Rector: Dr LAJOS SZABÓ
Sec.-Gen.: SZŰCSNÉ PRŐHLE LÍVIA
Library Man.: Dr KÁROLY BÁCSKAI
Library of 59,000 vols, 119 periodicals
Number of teachers: 15
Number of students: 160

KÁROLI GÁSPÁR REFORMÁTUS EGYETEM
(Gáspár Károli University of the Reformed Church in Hungary)

Budapest, Kálvin tér 9, 1091
Telephone: (1) 455-9060
E-mail: international@kre.hu
Internet: www.kre.hu
Founded 1855 as Reformed Theological Academy of Budapest, present status 1900
Private control
Rector: Prof. Dr PÉTER BALLA
Vice-Rector: Prof. Dr MISKOLCZI BODNÁR PÉTER
Vice-Rector for Gen. Affairs: Dr KÁROLY BOZSONYI
Sec.-Gen.: Dr BARNABÁS
Library: 2m. vols
Number of teachers: 20
Number of students: 190

DEANS

Faculty of Humanities: Dr ENIKŐ SEPSI
Faculty of Law: Dr PÉTER ANTALÓCZY
Faculty of Teacher Training: Dr ÁRPÁD SZENCZI
Faculty of Theology: Dr JÓZSEF ZSENGELLÉR

KÖZÉP—EURÓPAI EGYETEM
(Central European University)

Budapest, Nádor u. 9, 1051
Telephone: (1) 327-3000
E-mail: public@ceu.hu
Internet: www.ceu.hu
Founded 1991
Private control
Language of instruction: English
Academic year: September to June
Depts of cognitive science, economics, environmental sciences and policy, gender studies, history, international relations and European studies, legal studies, mathematics and its applications, medieval studies, philosophy, political science, public policy, sociology and social anthropology; schools of business, historical and interdisciplinary studies, political science, public policy
Pres. and Rector: Prof. JOHN SHATTUCK
Sr Vice-Pres.: Prof. Dr LIVIU MATEI
Provost and Academic Pro-Rector: Dr KATALIN FARKAS
Pro-Rector for Hungarian and EU Affairs: Dr LÁSZLÓ KONTLER
Vice-Pres. for External Relations: ILDIKO MORAN
Vice-Pres. for Student Services: PETER JOHNSON
Library of 168,000 vols of books, 1,500 periodicals
Number of teachers: 300
Number of students: 1,540

DEANS

Business School: Prof. MEL HORWITCH
School of Public Policy: Prof. WOLFGANG H. REINICKE

ORSZÁGOS RABBIKÉPZŐ–ZSIDÓ EGYETEM
(Jewish Theological Seminary–University of Jewish Studies)

Budapest, POB 21, 1428
Budapest, Bérkocsis u. 2, 1084
Telephone: (1) 318-7049
E-mail: kocsis@or-zse.hu
Internet: www.or-zse.hu
Founded 1877
Private control
Depts of educational sciences and social work, history and philosophy of religion, Jewish cultural history, language, liturgy, scripture
Rector: Dr Y. A. SCHÖNER
Library of 110,000 vols
Number of teachers: 90
Number of students: 270

PÁZMÁNY PÉTER KATOLIKUS EGYETEM
(Pázmány Péter Catholic University)

Budapest, Szentkirályi u. 28, 1088
Telephone: (1) 429-7200
E-mail: rekthiv@ppke.hu
Internet: www.ppke.hu
Founded 1635
Private control
Academic year: September to June
Rector: Rev. Dr SZABOLCS ANZELM SZUROMI
Library of 400,000 vols
Number of teachers: 650
Number of students: 8,500
Publications: *Folia Canonica* (review of Eastern and Western Canon Law in 5 languages, 1 a year), *Folia Theologica* (1 a year), *Kánonjog* (Canon Law, 2 a year, in Hungarian), *Teológia* (4 a year, in Hungarian)

DEANS

Faculty of Humanities and Social Sciences: Dr MÁTÉ BOTOS
Faculty of Information Technology and Bionics: Dr PÉTER SZOLGAY
Faculty of Law and Political Science: Dr ZS. ANDRÁS VARGA
Faculty of Theology: Dr GÉZA KUMINETZ

Colleges

Adventista Teológiai Főiskola (Adventist Theological College): Pécel, Ráday u. 12, 2119; tel. (28) 547-295; e-mail atf@adventista.hu; internet atf.adventista.hu; BSc in theology; depts of Old Testament theology, New Testament theology, church history; Rector Dr JÓZSEF SZILVÁSI; Vice-Rector Dr TIBOR TONHAIZER.

Altalános Vállalkozási Főiskola (Budapest College of Management): Budapest, Villányi u. 11–13, 1114; tel. (1) 381-8100; e-mail informatika@avf.hu; internet www.avf.hu; f. 1996; depts of applied behavioural sciences, business management, economics, economic law, finance and accounting, foreign languages, international relations, marketing and communication, methodology, social sciences; library: 40,000 vols; Rector Dr PÁL VASTAGH; Dir-Gen. JÁNOS ANTAL; Library Dir ANNA JANECSKÓ; publ. *Ikszikszí* (irregular, print and online, www.avf.hu/xxi).

Apor Vilmos Katolikus Főiskola (Apor Vilmos Catholic University College): Vác, Konstantin tér 1–5, 2600; tel. (27) 511-150; e-mail avkf@avkf.hu; internet www.avkf.hu; f. 1992; 3,500 students; Rector Dr MÁRIA ERDŐ; Vice-Rector for Academic Affairs Dr ERZSÉBET KOVÁCS; Vice-Rector for Scientific Affairs Dr MARCEL PILECKY; Library Dir KATALIN ENDRÉSZ.

A Tan Kapuja Buddhista Főiskola (Dharma Gate Buddhist College): Budapest, Börzsöny u. 11, 1098; tel. (1) 280-6712; e-mail tankapu@tkbf.hu; internet www.tkbf.hu; f. 1991; accredited BA and MA degrees in Buddhist theology; Rector JÁNOS JELEN.

Baptista Teológiai Akadémia (Baptist Theological Academy): Budapest VI, Benczúr u. 31, 1068; tel. (1) 342-7534; e-mail bta@bta.hu; internet www.bta.hu; BA in theology and church music; MA in theology; 500 students; Rector Prof. Dr TIBOR ALMÁSI.

Bhaktivedanta Hittudományi Főiskola (Bhaktivedanta College for Religious Science): Budapest, Attila u. 8, 1039; tel. (1) 321-7787; e-mail info@bhf.hu; internet www.bhf.hu; f. 2001; offers bachelors in Vaishnava theology; library: 11,000 vols, 2,000 journals, 3,500 vols of spec. colln, 1,400 digital files; Rector Dr MAGDOLNA BANYÁR; Vice-Rector Dr LÁSZLÓ TÓTH-SOMA; Dir for Library RÁTKAI GERGŐ; publ. *TATTVA* (online, tattva.hu).

Budapesti Gazdasági Főiskola (Budapest Business School): Budapest, Buzogány u. 11–13, 1149; tel. (1) 383-4799; e-mail international@bgf.hu; internet www.bgf.hu; f. 2000; 17,800 students; Rector Dr EVA SANDORNÉ-KRISZT; Vice-Rector Dr BALÁZS FERKELT; Vice-Rector for Education and Service Dr KATALIN SZABAD; Vice-Rector for Scientific Affairs Dr ANDRÁS VIGVÁRI; Sec.-Gen. Dr SZILVIA ÁCS; Head of Library SZILVIA KOROM.

Budapesti Kommunikációs és Üzleti Főiskola (Budapest College of Communication and Business): Budapest, Nagy Lajos király u. 1–9, 1148; tel. (1) 273-3090; e-mail international@bkf.hu; internet www.bkf.hu; f. 2000; 7,000 students; Rector Dr Hab. LÁSZLÓ VASS; Vice-Rector for Education Dr EMESE PUPEK; Vice-Rector for Int. Relations Dr JOLÁN RÓKA; Vice-Rector for Research Dr FERENC KISS; Sec.-Gen. Dr GÁBOR BATHÓ; Head of Library KORNÉLIA BÁNHEGYI KOLLÁR.

Dunaújvárosi Főiskola (College of Dunaújváros): Dunaújváros, POB 152, 2401; Dunaújváros Táncsics Mihály u. 1/A, 2401; tel. (25) 551-100; e-mail duf@mail.duf.hu; internet www.duf.hu; f. 1969, present status 2000; 110 teachers; 3,500 students; Rector Dr LÁSZLÓ BOGNÁR; Vice-Rector for Research and Gen. Affairs Dr LÁSZLÓ KADOCSA; Vice-Rector for Communications Dr ISTVÁN ANDRÁS; Vice-Rector for Education Dr JENŐ SZÁNTÓ.

Egri Hittudományi Főiskola: Eger, POB 53, 3301; Eger, Foglár Gy. u. 6, 3301; tel. (36) 312-916; e-mail rektor@eghf.hu; internet www.eghf.hu; f. 1700; BA and MA in theology; library: 45,000 vols; Rector Dr LAJOS DOLHAI; Dir for Library JÁNOS HUGYECZ.

Eötvös József Főiskola (Eötvös József College): Baja, Szegedi u. 2, 6500; tel. (79) 524-624; e-mail info@ejf.hu; internet www.ejf.hu; f. 1870, present status 2002; Rector Dr MELICZ ZOLTÁN; Vice-Rector Prof. Dr MIHÁLY SÁRI; Vice-Rector Dr TIBOR DRÁVAVÖLGYI; Sec.-Gen. Dr PÁLITY IBOLYA VUITYNÉ; Dir for Library ILONA MAJORNÉ BODOR.

Esztergomi Hittudományi Főiskola (Theological College of Esztergom): Esztergom, Szent István tér 10, 2500; tel. (33) 541-971; internet www.eszhf.hu; undergraduate and postgraduate degrees in theology; Rector Dr János Székely; Chief Librarian Katalin Szalai.

Eszterházy Károly Főiskola (Eszterházy Károly College): Eger, Eszterházy tér 1, 3300; tel. (36) 520-400; e-mail dir@ektf.hu; internet www.ektf.hu; f. 1948; Rector Dr Zoltán Hauser; Vice-Rector for Devt Dr Lajos Kis-Tóth; Vice-Rector for Education Dr Katalin Thiel Lőrinczné; Vice-Rector for Science and Int. Relations Dr Ferenc Mátyás; Sec.-Gen. Dr Ferenc Koncsos; Dir for Library Központi Könyvtár.

Gábor Dénes Főiskola (Dennis Gabor College): Budapest, POB 146, 1518; Budapest, Mérnök u. 39, 1119; tel. (1) 203-0283; e-mail info@gdf.hu; internet www.gdf.hu; f. 1992; study programmes in art and design, business and management, computer engineering, financial administration, web programming; Rector Dr Sarolta Zárda; Vice-Rector Dr István Ákos Vári-Kakas; Sec.-Gen. Zsuzsánna Lengyel; publ. *Informatika* (2 a year).

Gál Ferenc Főiskola Szeged (Theological College of Szeged): Szeged, POB 692, 6701; Szeged, Dóm tér 6, 6720; tel. (62) 425-738; e-mail gfhf@gfhf.hu; internet www.gfhf.hu; f. 1995, current name adopted 2008; Rector Dr Gábor Kozma; Vice-Rector Dr Attila Thorday; Head of Library Ildikó Kövécs.

Györi Hittudománti Főiskola (Theological College of Györ): Györ, Káptalandomb 7, 9021; tel. (96) 313-055; internet www.gyhf.hu; f. 1627; depts of Bible studies, dogmatics, philosophy, theological ethics; Rector Dr Zoltán Lukácsi.

Károly Róbert Főiskola (Károly Róbert College): Gyöngyös, Mátrai u. 36, 3200; tel. (37) 518-300; e-mail titkarsag@karolyrobert.hu; internet www.karolyrobert.hu; f. 2003, frmly College of Economics and Agriculture of Szent István Egyetem in Gödöllő; library: 30,000 vols; Rector Dr Sándor Magda; Gen. Vice-Rector Prof. Dr István Wachtler; Vice-Rector for Education Dr Helgertné Szabó Ilona; Vice-Rector for Sciences Prof. Dr László Dinya; Sec.-Gen. Dr Márta Ferenczi; Library Coordinator Ágnes Göröcsné Orsó.

Kecskeméti Főiskola (Kecskemét College): Budapest, POB 700, 6001; Kecskemét, Izsáki u. 10, 6000; tel. (76) 501-960; e-mail rh@kefo.hu; internet www.kefo.hu; f. 2000 by merger of College of Mechanical Engineering and Automation, Teacher Training College and Univ. of Horticulture and Food-Processing, Horticultural Faculty Kecskemét; 105 teachers; 6,000 students; Rector Dr József Danyi; Gen. Vice-Rector Dr Róbert Rigó; Scientific Vice-Rector Prof. Dr Árpád Ferencz; Dir for Library Némethné Falusi Erzsébet.

Kodolányi János Főiskola (Kodolányi János University of Applied Sciences): Székesfehérvár, Fürdő u. 1, 8000; tel. (22) 543-310; e-mail international@kjf.hu; internet www.kodolanyi.hu; f. 1992; library: 17,000 vols; 350 teachers; 10,000 students; depts of andragogy and cultural studies, applied pedagogy, applied social studies, communication and media studies, economics and management, English studies, German studies, jazz performance and singing, methodology, social studies and humanities, tourism; Rector Dr Péter Szabó; Vice-Rector for Devt and Quality Management Dr Hab. Gyöngyvér Hervai Szabó; Vice-Rector for Education Dr Vizi László; Vice-Rector for Gen. Affairs Berta Ákos; Vice-Rector for Int. Adult Education Dr Hoffmann Orsolya; Sec.-Gen. Dr László Vizi; Library Dir Péterné Beniczky.

Nemzetközi Üzleti Főiskola (International Business School Budapest): Budapest, Tárogató u. 2–4, 1021; tel. (1) 391-2500; e-mail info@ibs-b.hu; internet www.ibs-b.hu; f. 1991, present status 1997; depts of arts management, economics, finance and accounting, foreign languages, international studies, quantitative methodology and IT, management skills, management studies, marketing, social sciences, tourism; library: 15,000 vols of books, 3,000 dissertations, 30 journal titles; 3,300 students; Rector Dr László Láng; Head of Library Tamás Nusser.

Nyíregyházi Főiskola (College of Nyíregyháza): Nyíregyháza, Sóstói u. 31/b, 4400; tel. (42) 599-400; internet www.nyf.hu; f. 2000 by merger of György Bessenyei Teachers Training College (f. 1962) and Nyíregyháza Agricultural College Faculty of the Agricultural Univ. of Gödöllő (f. 1961); Rector Prof. Dr Zoltán Jánosi; Deputy Rector for Strategic and Scientific Affairs Prof. Dr György Gát; Deputy Rector for Training Dr Zoltán Kovács; Sec.-Gen. Dr Tünde Mezei.

Pápai Református Teológiai Akadémia (Pápa Reformed Theological Seminary): Pápa, Március 15 tér 13–14, POB 141, 8500; tel. (89) 312-331; e-mail rektori@prta.hu; internet www.prta.hu; f. 1992; undergraduate and postgraduate degrees in theology; library: 65,000 vols; Rector Dr Gábor Vladár; Vice-Rector Dr Gergely Hanula.

Pécsi Hittudományi Főiskola (Episcopal Theological College of Pécs): Pécs, Papnövelde u. 1–3, 7621; tel. (72) 513-060; e-mail rektor@pphf.hu; internet www.pphf.hu; f. 1742; depts of applied theology, Bible studies, catechetical pedagogy, church history, philosophy and social sciences, systematic theology; Rector Dr Zsolt Cziglányi; Library Dir Dr Miklósné Boda.

Pünkösdi Teológiai Főiskola (Pentecostal Theological College): Budapest, Gyömrői u. 89, 1183; tel. (1) 297-0413; e-mail ptf@ptf.hu; internet www.ptf.hu; f. 1991; offers Bachelors degrees in catechist training, pastoral studies; Rector Paul Gracza; Vice-Rector Csaba Ungvári.

Sapientia Szerzetesi Hittudományi Főiskola (Sapientia College of Theology of Religious Orders, Budapest): Budapest, Piarista köz 1, 1052; tel. (1) 486-4411; e-mail rektor@sapientia.hu; internet www.sapientia.hu; f. 2000; offers BA with specialization in catechism and pastoral assistance; MA with specialization in theology, teaching of religious education, teaching of ethics, teaching of family and child protection, pastoral counselling and organizational development; library: 63,000 vols, 17,000 periodicals; 375 students; Rector Dr Sándor Jakab Várnai; Vice-Rector Dr Györgyi Szatmári; Sec.-Gen. Dr Réka Borókay; Head of Library Beáta Török; publ. *Sapientiana* (2 a year).

Sárospataki Református Teológiai Akadémia (Sárospatak Reformed Theological Academy): Sárospatak, Rákóczi u. 1, 3950; tel. (47) 312-947; e-mail dekania@srta.hu; internet www.srta.hu; f. 16th century, re-established with present status 1991; offers bachelors in catechist-pastoral assistant, reformed church community's organizer and masters in divinity, theological studies; Rector Prof. Dr Sándor Enghy; Vice-Rector Prof. Dr Dénes Dienes; publ. *Sárospataki Füzetek* (Sárospatak Papers, 2 a year, print and online, www.srta.hu/letoltes/lista/sarospataki-fuzetek).

Sola Scriptura Teológiai Főiskola (Sola Scriptura Ministers Training and Theological College): Budapest, POB 253, 1536; Budapest, Remete u. 16/A, 1121; tel. (1) 391-0180; e-mail sola@sola.hu; internet www.sola.hu; f. 1992; depts of church history, New Testament, Old Testament, practical theology, systematic theology; library: 15,000 vols; Rector Dr Zsuzsanna Vankó; Sec.-Gen. Dr Nándor Neparáczki; Head of Library Laura Lilik.

Szent Atanáz Görög Katolikus Hittudományi Főiskola (Szent Atanáz Greek-Catholic Theological College): Nyíregyháza, POB 303, 4401; Nyíregyháza, Bethlen G. u. 13–19, 4400; tel. (42) 597-600; e-mail atanaz@atanaz.hu; internet www.atanaz.hu; f. 1995; Bachelors degrees in catechism and pastoral assistance; masters in theology and religious education; library: 38,000 vols, 787 periodicals; Rector Dr Tamás Véghseő; Vice-Rector Prof. Dr István Seszták; Vice-Rector Prof. Dr Péter Szabó; publs *Athanasiana*, *Folia Athanasiana*, *Folia Canonica*, *Studia Biblica Athanasiana*.

Szent Pál Akadémia (Szent Pál Academy): Budapest, Gyömrői u. 69, 1103; tel. (1) 432-2720; e-mail titkarsag@szpa.hu; internet www.szpa.hu; f. 2005; offers MSc in theology; Rector Prof. Judit Németh; Vice-Rector Dr István László Mészáros; Sec.-Gen. András Horváth.

Szolnoki Főiskola (College of Szolnok): Szolnok, Tiszaligeti sétány 14, 5000; tel. (56) 510-300; e-mail szolf@szolf.hu; internet www.szolfportal.hu; f. 1993, current name adopted 2000; offers Bachelors courses in agribusiness and rural development engineering, agricultural engineering and technical management, commerce and marketing, finance and accounting, international business, mechanical engineering in the agriculture and food industry, tourism and catering; 115 teachers; 3,000 students; Rector Dr Imre Túróczi; Head Librarian Julianna Kincses.

Tomori Pál Főiskola (Tomori Pál College): Kalocsa, Szent István király u. 2–4, 6300; tel. (78) 564-600; e-mail info@tpfk.hu; internet www.tpfk.hu; f. 2004; undergraduate and postgraduate degrees in business management, finance and accounting, international studies and liberal arts; library: 130,236 vols, 5,444 audiovisual documents; Rector Dr Rózsa Meszlényi; Vice-Rector for Education Zoltán Domboróczky; Vice-Rector for Science Dr Tompa Jánosné Daubner Katalin.

Veszprémi Érseki Hittudományi Főiskola (Archiepiscopal Theological College of Veszprém): Veszprém, Jutasi u. 18/2, 8200; tel. (88) 426-116; internet www.vhf.hu; Rector Dr István Varga; Librarian Péter Baranya.

Wesley János Lelkészképző Főiskola (John Wesley Theological College): Budapest, POB 200, 1410; Budapest, Dankó u. 11, 1086; tel. (1) 577-0500; e-mail fotitkar@wjlf.hu; internet www.wesley.hu; f. 1991; faculties of ecology, pedagogy, social work, theology; undergraduate programmes in environmental science, faith teaching, pedagogical science, social work, theology and clerical study, theology and ministerial collaboration; postgraduate programmes in complex art therapy, drama pedagogy, family consultance and family therapy, field street social work, forest and agricultural environment; Rector Dr Gábor Iványi; Sec.-Gen. István Barna; Library Dir Tamás Majsai.

Zsigmond Király Főiskola (King Sigismund College): Budapest, POB 16, 1312; Budapest, Kelta u. 2, 1039; tel. (1) 454-7600; e-mail mail@zskf.hu; internet www.zskf.hu; f. 2000; BA in andragogy, business and management, communication and media studies, economic, information technology, finance and accounting, humanities studies, human resource management, international business, international studies, political science, sociology; MA in andragogy, communication and media studies, international economy and business, international studies, political science, religious studies; Rector Prof. Dr József Bayer.

Schools of Art and Music

Budapesti Kortárstánc Főiskola (Budapest Contemporary Dance Academy): Budapest, Perc u. 2, 1036; tel. (1) 250-3046; e-mail budapest@tanc.org.hu; internet www.tanc.org.hu; f. 2004; BA and MA courses with specialization in contemporary dance; Rector Dr Iván Angelus; Sec.-Gen. Kamilla Reidl.

Magyar Táncművészeti Főiskola Budapest (Hungarian Dance Academy Budapest): Budapest, POB 439, 1592; Budapest, Columbus u. 87–89, 1145; tel. (1) 273-3434; e-mail info@mtf.hu; internet www.mtf.hu; f. 1950 as State Ballet Institute, present status 1983, current name adopted 1990; undergraduate degrees in choreography, dance art, dance coaching; postgraduate degrees in classical ballet, folk dance; Rector György Szakály; Gen.-Sec. Dr Tünde Hobaj (acting).

ICELAND

The Higher Education System

The Icelandic higher education system dates back to the foundation of the University of Iceland in 1911, uniting three former schools: Prestaskólinn, Læknaskólinn and Lagaskólinn, which taught theology, medicine and law, respectively. The University of Iceland remains the principal institution of higher learning in Iceland, but since the 1970s new institutions of higher education have emerged with a more specialized focus, providing greater diversity at that level. The Ministry of Education, Science and Culture is responsible for formal education at all levels. In state-controlled institutions students only pay modest registration fees, while private institutions are also permitted to charge tuition fees. All students are eligible for some financial support from the Icelandic Student Loan Fund; the exact amount depends on each individual's financial and personal situation. Furthermore, grants are available for postgraduate students in research universities. In 2012 there were 27 tertiary-level education institutions in Iceland with a combined enrolment of 18,001 students.

Legislation on higher education institutions (the Universities Act, No. 136/1997) enacted in 1997 establishes the general framework for the activities of these institutions. In this Act, the term 'háskóli' is used to refer both to traditional universities and institutions that do not carry out research. Separate legislation for each public higher education institution, and the charters of privately controlled universities, define their engagement in research, internal organization, etc. Iceland is a signatory of the Bologna Declaration and the Higher Education Act of July 2006 fully implemented the Bologna Process. All legislative reforms and regulations are handled by a national Bologna follow-up group based in the Ministry of Education, Science and Culture. A two-cycle degree system that conforms to the Bologna regulations is well established for most courses, with the exception of medical-related subjects.

According to the Act on Public Higher Education Institutions (2008, amended in 2010), the University of Iceland and the University of Akureyri are granted autonomy and the administration of each is entrusted to a University Council and a Rector. The Rector appoints a Dean for each of the university's constituent schools. Each public university is allocated an independent budget from the state treasury; it may also generate income by other means. The State draws up performance-related contracts with all higher education institutions, defining how the institution intends to achieve its objectives and what the Government's financial contribution shall be.

Entry to undergraduate courses is based on the Stúdentspróf (matriculation examination). Many institutions have restricted admission based on the average mark obtained or marks in subjects that are deemed relevant. Mature students are not always required to hold the Stúdentspróf if they have specific work experience. Courses are assessed in terms of credits. Short courses resulting in a certificate or diploma are available in a limited number of subjects. The Baccalaureatus (Bachelors degree), usually in arts, science or education, is three to four years in length (90–180 European Credit Transfer and Accumulation System—ECTS—credits). A number of institutions provide one- to two-year programmes following the Baccalaureatus, leading to postgraduate certificates in various subjects. The University of Iceland awards the Meistarapróf (Masters degree) after a two-year course for holders of the Baccalaureatus. In some cases, a first-class Baccalaureatus is required. The Magister Paedagogiae degree in education is only offered in Icelandic studies. All courses require completion of a major thesis or research project. There are two types of Doktorspróf (Doctorate degree) available at the University of Iceland. The Doctor Philosophiae is three or four years in length and follows the Meistarapróf. The Doctor Scientiarum and the Doctor Medicinae degree courses are based on the Kandidatspróf or the Meistarapróf degrees. In exceptional circumstances, a holder of a good Baccalaureatus may be allowed to undertake a Doctorate degree; however, studies would have to last for four years. Doctoral courses have traditionally been completely research-based; however, in recent years the courses, which each comprise 180–240 ECTS credits, have become more structured (involving taught courses and independent research).

Specialized vocational schools (Sérskóli) and industrial vocational schools (Ionskóli) offer courses for specialized employment in a skilled trade. Since the 1990s many Sérskóli have been upgraded to higher education level. Students in the certified trades are required to take 25 unit-credits in general academic subjects to complement their technical training. The majority of courses take four years and the training programme is usually a study contract with a master craftsman or industrial firm. The programmes are administered and maintained by a trade or organizational council. Apprentices completing their studies take the Sveinspróf (Journeyman's Examination) to practise their chosen trade. Students may progress to become a Meistarabréf (Master Craftsman) after a period of work experience and advanced study at a vocational school. Alternatively, students may progress to university after a specified period of additional studies. The Meistarabréf gives the holder the right to train apprentices, operate a business or manage an enterprise.

Icelandic students have a long tradition of studying abroad for their higher education. More than 10% of Icelandic students in higher education study abroad, most of them in postgraduate studies.

Regulatory and Representative Bodies

GOVERNMENT

Ministry of Education, Science and Culture: Sölvhólsgötu 4, 150 Reykjavík; tel. 545-9500; e-mail postur@mrn.is; internet www.menntamalaraduneyti.is; Minister ILLUGI GUNNARSSON.

ACCREDITATION

ENIC/NARIC Iceland: Office for Academic Affairs, Univ. of Iceland, Sudurgotu, 101 Reykjavík; tel. 525-4360; e-mail thordkri@hi.is; Dir for Academic Affairs ÞÓRÐUR KRISTINSSON.

NATIONAL BODIES

Samstarfsnefnd háskólastigsins (Standing Committee of the Rectors of Icelandic Higher Education Institutions): Univ. of Iceland, Aðalbygging A-139, Sæmundargötu 2, 101 Reykjavík; tel. 525-5242; e-mail solveign@hi.is; internet www.hi.is/adalvefur/samstarfsnefnd_haskolastigsins; f. 1987; 8 mems; Chair. KRISTÍN INGÓLFSDÓTTIR; Sec. ÞÓRÐUR KRISTINSSON.

Learned Societies

AGRICULTURE, FISHERIES AND VETERINARY SCIENCE

Bændasamtök Íslands (Farmers' Association of Iceland): Baendahöllinni við Hagatorg, 107 Reykjavík; tel. 563-0300; e-mail bondi@bondi.is; internet www.bondi.is; f. 1995; 3,500 farmer mems in 15 district asscns and 13 sector orgs; library of 10,000 vols; Chair. HARALDUR BENEDIKTSSON; Dir EIRÍKUR BLÖNDA; publ. *Freyr* (12 a year).

BIBLIOGRAPHY, LIBRARY SCIENCE AND MUSEOLOGY

Upplýsing—Félag bókasafns- og upplýsingafræða (Information—Icelandic Library and Information Science Association): Lyngási 18, 210 Garðabæ; tel. 864-6220; e-mail upplysing@upplysing.is; internet www.upplysing.is; f. 2000 by merger of Bókavardafélag Islands, Félag bókasafnsfraedinga, Félag bókavarda í rannsóknarbókasöfnum, Félag um almenningsbókasöfn og skólasöfn; strengthens, encourages and works for the recognition of the importance of the services of libraries and information centres; 600 mems; Pres. MARGRÉT SIGURGEIRSDÓTTIR; Sec. INGIBJÖRG ÖSP ÓTTARSDÓTTIR; publ. *Bókasafnið* (1 a year).

FINE AND PERFORMING ARTS

Bandalag Íslenzkra Listamanna (Federation of Icelandic Artists): POB 637, 121 Reykjavík; tel. 862-4808; e-mail bil@bil.is; internet www.bil.is; f. 1928; promotes the role of artists and performers in the cultural and artistic devt of soc.; 3,500 mems; Pres. KOLBRÚN HALLDÓRSDÓTTIR.

Constituent Organizations:

Arkítektafélag Íslands (Icelandic Architects' Association): Engjateigur 9, 105 Reykjavík; tel. 551-1465; e-mail ai@ai.is; internet www.ai.is; f. 1936, present name 1956; 250 mems; Pres. LOGI MÁR EINARSSON; Sec. HRÓLFUR KARL CELA.

Félag Íslenzkra Leikara (Icelandic Actors' Association): Lindargötu 6, 101 Reykjavík; tel. 552-6040; e-mail fil@fil.is; internet www.fil.is; professional org. of actors, dancers, singers, set and costume designers and authors; 400 mems; Chair. RANDVER ÞORLÁKSSON; Sec. SNORRI FREYR HILMARSSON.

Félag Íslenzkra Listdansara (Icelandic Association of Professional Dancers): Lindargötu 6, 101 Reykjavík; tel. 699-6903; e-mail dance@dance.is; internet www.dance.is; f. 1947; provides a link between asscn, dancers, teachers, schools and choreographers; 111 mems; Chair. GUÐMUNDUR HELGASON.

Félag Íslenzkra Tónlistarmanna (Icelandic Musicians' Association): Rauðagerði 27, 108 Reykjavík; e-mail fiston@fih.is; internet www.fiston.is; f. 1940; professional asscn of Icelandic musicians, soloists and directors; 160 mems; Chair. KRISTIN MJÖLL JAKOBSDÓTTIR; Sec. HALLVEIG RÚNARSDÓTTIR.

Félag Kvikmyndagerðarmanna (Icelandic Film Makers' Association): Hverfisgata 54, 101 Reykjavík; e-mail formadur@filmmakers.is; internet www.filmmakers.is; f. 1966; 150 mems; Chair. HRAFNHILDUR GUNNARSDÓTTIR; Sec. ANNA THORA STEINÞÓRSDÓTTIR.

Félag Leikstjóra á Íslandi (Icelandic Association of Directors): Lindargötu 6, 101 Reykjavík; tel. 562-1025; e-mail leikstjorar@leikstjorar.is; internet www.leikstjorar.is; f. 1972; guards interests of its mems regarding copyright, artistic and social interests; 81 mems; Chair. JÓN PÁLL EYJÓLFSSON.

Rithöfundasamband Íslands (Writers Union of Iceland): Gunnarshúsi, Dyngjuvegi 8, 104 Reykjavík; tel. 568-3190; e-mail rsi@rsi.is; internet www.rsi.is; f. 1974; safeguards interests and rights of authors according to int. standards; works to defend freedom and honour of literature; 350 mems; Chair. KRISTÍN STEINSDÓTTIR; Dir RAGNHEIÐUR TRYGGVADÓTTIR.

Samband Íslenzkra Myndlistarmanna (Association of Icelandic Visual Artists): POB 1115, 121 Reykjavík; Hafnarstræti 16, 101 Reykjavík; tel. 551-1346; e-mail sim@sim.is; internet www.sim.is; f. 2002; 700 mems; Chair. SIGURÐARDÓTTIR HRAFNHILDUR.

Samtök Kvikmundaleikstjóra (Film Directors Guild of Iceland): Sudurgötu 14, 101 Reykjavík; e-mail skl-filmdirectors@gmail.com; internet skl-filmdirectors.net; 53 mems; Chair. RAGNAR BRAGASON.

Tónskáldafélag Íslands (Society of Icelandic Composers): Laufásvegi 40, 101 Reykjavík; tel. 552-4972; internet www.listir.is; f. 1946; 130 mems; Chair. KJARTAN ÓLAFSSON.

Tónlistarfélagið (Music Society): Bjarmaland 19, 108 Reykjavík; f. 1930; operates a College of Music; affiliated socs in major towns; Chair. BALDVIN TRYGGVASON; Man. RUT MAGNÚSSON.

HISTORY, GEOGRAPHY AND ARCHAEOLOGY

Fornleifastofnun Íslands (Institute of Archaeology, Iceland): Bárugötu 3, 101 Reykjavík; tel. 551-1033; e-mail fsi@instarch.is; internet www.instarch.is; f. 1989; promotes research and publication in archaeology and related fields; provides educational grants; Pres. ADOLF FRIÐRIKSSON; publ. *Archaeologia Islandica*.

Sögufélag (Historical Society of Iceland): Skeifunni 3B, 108 Reykjavík; tel. 588-9060; e-mail sogufelag@sogufelag.is; internet www.sogufelag.is; f. 1902; publ. of historical research and primary documents; 800 mems; Pres. Prof. GUÐNI JÓHANNESSON; Sec. SÚSANNA MARGRÉT GESTSDÓTTIR; publ. *SAGA* (2 a year).

LANGUAGE AND LITERATURE

Hið Íslenzka bókmenntafélag (Icelandic Literary Society): Skeifan 3B, Reykjavík; tel. 588-9060; e-mail hib@islandia.is; internet www.hib.is; f. 1816; research work and publishing; 2,200 mems; Pres. Dr SIGURÐUR LÍNDAL; Sec. REYNIR AXELSSON; publ. *Skírnir* (2 a year).

NATURAL SCIENCES

General

Vísindafélag Íslendinga (Icelandic Academy of Sciences): Bárugötu 3, 101 Reykjavík; e-mail visfel@hi.is; internet www.visindafelag.is; f. 1918; 144 mems; Pres. THÓRARINN GUÐJÓNSSON; Sec. THÓRUNN RAFNAR; publs *Ráðstefnurit* (irregular), *Rit*.

Physical Sciences

Jöklarannsóknafélag Íslands (Iceland Glaciological Society): POB 5128, 125 Reykjavík; e-mail jorfi@jorfi.is; internet www.jorfi.is; f. 1950; 500 mems; Pres. MAGNÚS TUMI GUDMUNDSSON; Sec. THORSTEIN THORSTEINSSON; publ. *Jökull* (1 a year).

TECHNOLOGY

Verkfræðingafélag Íslands (Association of Chartered Engineers in Iceland): Engjateigi 9, 105 Reykjavík; tel. 535-9300; e-mail skrifstofa@verktaekni.is; internet www.vfi.is; f. 1912; promotes engineering and scientific expertise; 2,200 mems; Chair. KRISTINN ANDERSEN; Gen. Man. ÁRNI BJÖRN BJÖRNSSON; publ. *Árbók* (Yearbook).

Research Institutes

GENERAL

Rannsókna- og Þróunarmiðstöð (University of Akureyri Research Centre): Borgum v/ Norðurslóð, 600 Akureyri; tel. 460-8900; e-mail rha@unak.is; internet www.rha.is; f. 1992; attached to Univ. of Akureyri; multidisciplinary research into a wide array of fields, incl. aquaculture, economic devt, geography, management and sociology; Dir HJALTI JÓHANNESSON (acting).

ECONOMICS, LAW AND POLITICS

Alþjóðamálastofnun (Institute of International Affairs): Gimli við Sturlugötu, 101 Reykjavík; tel. 525-5262; e-mail ams@hi.is; internet stofnanir.hi.is/ams/is; f. 1990; attached to Univ. of Iceland; encourages cooperation and discussions between scholars and other parties interested in Icelandic foreign affairs and int. politics; serves as forum for academic relations and interdisciplinary research projects; Dir PIA HANSSON.

Hagfræðistofnun (Institute of Economic Studies): Oddi v/Sturlugötu, 101 Reykjavík; tel. 525-4535; e-mail ioes@hi.is; internet hhi.hi.is; f. 1989; attached to Univ. of Iceland; works to create a research environment competent in the economic analysis of int. issues; emphasis on policy analysis for small and open economies; Chair. Prof. RAGNAR ÁRNASON.

Hagstofa Íslands (Statistics Iceland): Borgartúni 21A, 150 Reykjavík; tel. 528-1000; e-mail information@statice.is; internet www.statice.is; f. 1914; collects, processes and disseminates data on the economy and soc.; divs of economic statistics, social statistics, business statistics, resources and services; Dir-Gen. ÓLAFUR HJÁLMARSSON; publs *Hagskinna—Historical Statistics*, *Hagskýrslur Íslands* (Statistics of Iceland), *Hagtíðindi* (Statistics Monthly), *Landshagir* (Statistical Yearbook of Iceland).

Lagastofnun Háskóla Íslands (Institute of Law, University of Iceland): Lögbergi, 101 Reykjavík; tel. 525-5203; e-mail lagastofnun@hi.is; internet www.lagastofnun.hi.is; f. 1974; attached to Univ. of Iceland; conducts research and devt in the field of law; Chair. Prof. MARIA ELVIRA MENDEZ PINEDO; Dir MARÍA THEJLL.

HISTORY, GEOGRAPHY AND ARCHAEOLOGY

Stofnun Árna Magnússonar í Íslenskum Fræðum (Árni Magnússon Institute for Icelandic Studies): Árnagarði v/Suðurgötu, 101 Reykjavík; tel. 525-4010; e-mail arnastofnun@hi.is; internet www.arnastofnun.is; f. 1972 as Árni Magnússon Institute in Iceland, present name adopted 2006 following merger with Icelandic Language Institute, Univ. of Iceland Institute of Lexicography, Sigurður Nordal Institute and Place-Name Institute of Iceland; attached to Univ. of Iceland; practical and theoretical research pertaining to Icelandic culture, history, language and literature; library of 40,000 vols, 156 journals; Chair. LÁRA MAGNÚSARDÓTTIR; Dir Prof. GUÐRÚN NORDAL.

MEDICINE

Tilraunastöð Háskóla Íslands i meinafræði að Keldum (Institute for Experimental Pathology, University of Iceland): v/ Vesturlandsveg, 112 Reykjavík; tel. 585-5100; e-mail postur@keldur.is; internet www.keldur.is; f. 1948; attached to Univ. of Iceland; basic research in biology and medicine of animals and humans; applied veterinary research, health control, diagnostic services and expert advice on animal diseases; provides continuing education and information for veterinarians; library of 4,000 vols; Dir SIGURÐUR INGVARSSON; publ. *Icelandic Agricultural Sciences* (irregular).

NATURAL SCIENCES

General

Rannsoknamidstod Íslands (Icelandic Centre for Research): Laugavegur 13, 101 Reykjavík; tel. 515-5800; e-mail rannis@rannis.is; internet www.rannis.is; f. 1994; attached to Min. of Education, Science and Culture; advises the Govt and Parliament on all aspects of science, technology and innovation; promotes int. cooperation in science and technology; Gen. Dir Dr HALLGRÍMUR JÓNASSON; Head of Admin. HERDÍS THORGRÍMSDÓTTIR.

Attached Research Institutes:

Hafrannsóknastofnunin (Marine Research Institute): Skúlagötu 4, 121 Reykjavík; tel. 575-2000; e-mail hafro@hafro.is; internet www.hafro.is; f. 1965; attached to Min. of Fisheries; research into marine biological and oceanographic sciences; spec. divs for pelagic fish, demersal fish, flatfish, technology and fishing gear, hydrography, phytoplankton, zooplankton and benthos; library of 6,500 vols, 400 periodicals; Dir-Gen. JÓHANN SIGURJÓNSSON; Sec. EYDÍS O. L. CARTWRIGHT.

Icelandic Building Research Institute (IBRI): Keldnaholt, 112 Reykjavík; tel. 570-7300; e-mail helpdesk@rabygg.is; internet www.rabygg.is/rheocenter/ibri.html; f. 1965; attached to Min. of Industry and Commerce; scientific research and services for the construction and bldg industries; Dir HÁKON ÓLAFSSON; Man. Dr OLAFUR H. WALLEVIK.

Idntæknistofnun Íslands (IceTec Technological Institute of Iceland): Keldnaholt, 112 Reykjavík; tel. 570-7100; internet www.randburg.com/is/iti; attached to Min. of Industry; research on raw materials, machinery and end products to improve quality and competitiveness of Icelandic industrial production; spec. divs for training and information, industrial devt, technical services and for research; Chair. MAGNÚS FRIÐGEIRSSON; Dir HALLGRÍMUR JÓNASSON.

Rannsóknastofnun landbúnadarins (Agricultural Research Institute): Keldnaholt, 112 Reykjavík; tel. 577-1010; e-mail rala@rala.is; internet landbunadur.rala.is/landbunadur/wgrala.nsf/key2/english.html; f. 1965; attached to Min. of Agriculture; govt-financed research and experimental devt in agriculture; spec. divs for animal-breeding, ecology and cultivation and farming technology; Chair. SIGURÐUR ÞRÁINSSON; Dir JON ERIC.

Surtseyjarfélagið (Surtsey Research Society): POB 352, 121 Reykjavík; e-mail surtsey@ni.is; internet www.surtsey.is; f. 1965; promotes and coordinates scientific work in geo- and biological sciences on the island of Surtsey; Chair. HALLGRÍMUR JÓNASSON; Sec. KARL GUNNARSSON; publ. *Surtsey Research*.

Biological Sciences

Náttúrufræðistofnun Íslands (Icelandic Institute of Natural History): Urriðaholtsstræti 6–8, POB 125, 212 Garðabær Sími; tel. 590-0500; e-mail ni@ni.is; internet www.ni.is; f. 1889, current name adopted 1947; attached to Min. for the Environment and Natural Resources; participates in environmental consultant work on sustainable use of natural resources and land devt; assesses the conservation status of species, habitats and ecosystems; library of 12,000 vols, 450 periodicals; Dir-Gen. JÓN GUNNAR OTTÓSSON; Sec. ELÍNBORG ÞORGRÍMSDÓTTIR; publs *Acta Botanica Islandica* (irregular), *Bliki* (irregular), *Fjölrit Náttúrufræðistofnunar* (irregular).

Physical Sciences

Vedurstofa Íslands (Icelandic Meteorological Office): Bústaðavegi 7–9, IS 108 Reykjavík; tel. 522-6000; e-mail office@vedur.is; internet www.vedur.is; f. 1920; attached to Min. for the Environment and Natural Resources; weather forecasts, climatology, aerology, sea ice, volcanology, seismology, hydrology, avalanches and landslides; library of 10,000 vols; Dir-Gen. ÁRNI SNORRASON; publ. *Skýrsla* (irregular).

PHILOSOPHY AND PSYCHOLOGY

Heimspekistofnun Háskóla Íslands (Institute of Philosophy): Hugvísindastofnun, Sæmundargötu 2, 101 Reykjavík; tel. 525-4000; e-mail sjon@hi.is; internet heimspekistofnun.hi.is; supports philosophical research and publs; organizes confs and lectures; Dir Prof. ROBERT H. HARALDSSON.

RELIGION, SOCIOLOGY AND ANTHROPOLOGY

ASÍS—Icelandic Centre for Asian Studies: c/o Faculty of Foreign Languages, Literature and Linguistics Main Bldg, 3rd Floor, 101 Reykjavík; tel. 525-4400; e-mail hug@hi.is; f. 2005; attached to Univ. of Iceland; Dir Dr GEIR SIGURÐSSON.

Educational Research Institute (School of Education, University of Iceland): Gimli, Herbergi 242, Stakkahlid, 105 Reykjavík; tel. 525-4165; e-mail krishar@hi.is; internet stofnanir.hi.is/menntavisindastofnun/en/english; f. 2010; conducts research and provides advice and services with the aim of strengthening research in the field of education and related fields; Chair. Prof. JON TORFI JÓNASSON; Dir KRISTÍN ERLA HARÐARDÓTTIR.

Libraries and Archives

Akureyri

Amtsbókasafnið á Akureyri (Municipal Library of Akureyri): Brekkugötu 17, 600 Akureyri; tel. 460-1250; e-mail bokasafn@akureyri.is; internet www.akureyri.is/amtsbokasafn; f. 1827; 191,568 vols; Chief Librarian HÓLMKELL HREINSSON.

Hafnarfjörður

Bókasafn Hafnarfjarðar (Hafnarfjörður Public Library): Strandgötu 1, 220 Hafnarfjörður; tel. 585-5690; e-mail bokasafn@hafnarfjordur.is; internet www2.hafnarfjordur.is/bokasafn; f. 1922; Head Librarian AÐALBJÖRG SIGÞÓRSDÓTTIR.

Ísafjörður

Bókasafn Ísafjarðar (Ísafjarðar Public Library): Gamlasjúkrahúsið, POB 138, 400 Ísafjörður; tel. 450-8220; e-mail bokasafn@isafjordur.is; internet www.isafjordur.is/bokasafn; f. 1889; 120,000 vols; Library Dir JÓNA SÍMONÍA BJARNADÓTTIR.

Reykjavík

Borgarbókasafn Reykjavíkur (Reykjavík City Library): Tryggvagötu 15, 101 Reykjavík; tel. 411-6100; e-mail borgarbokasafn@borgarbokasafn.is; internet www.borgarbokasafn.is; f. 1923; 5 brs and bookmobile; 500,000 vols; City Librarian PÁLÍNA MAGNÚSDÓTTIR.

Landsbókasafn Íslands-Háskólabókasafn (National and University Library of Iceland): Arngrímsgötu 3, 107 Reykjavík; tel. 525-5600; e-mail upplys@landsbokasafn.is; internet www.landsbokasafn.is; f. 1994 by merger of the Nat. Library of Iceland (f. 1818) and the Univ. Library (f. 1940); 1m. vols of books, journals and other materials, 16,000 MSS; Nat. Librarian INGIBJÖRG STEINUNN SVERRISDÓTTIR.

Þjóðskjalasafn Íslands (National Archives of Iceland): Laugavegur 162–164, 105 Reykjavík; tel. 590-3300; e-mail upplysingar@skjalasafn.is; internet www.archives.is; f. 1882; colln of historical documents since 12th century; Nat. Archivist EIRÍKUR G. GUÐMUNDSSON; Chair. MAR JONSSON.

Museums and Art Galleries

Húsavík

Hvalasafnið á Húsavík (Húsavík Whale Museum): Hafnarstétt 1, 640 Húsavík; tel. 414-2800; e-mail info@whalemuseum.is; internet www.whalemuseum.is; f. 1997; provides information and education on the whale's biology, ecology and habitat, and the history of whaling in Iceland; Man. EINAR GÍSLASON.

Hvolsvöllur

Skogar Folk Museum: Rd 1, 861 Hvolsvöllur; tel. 487-8845; e-mail skogasafn@skogasafn.is; f. 1949; open-air museum depicting old village life; Sod farm, Skal farm, Grof farm, magistrate's house, museum church, old schoolhouse, the smithy, communications museum and transportation museum.

Reykjavík

Listasafn Einars Jónssonar (Einar Jónsson Museum): Eiríksgötu, POB 1051, 121 Reykjavík; tel. 551-3797; e-mail lej@lej.is; internet www.lej.is; f. 1923; houses 300 sculptures and paintings by Einar Jónsson (1874–1954); Dir JÚLLIANA GOTTSKÁLKSDÓTTIR.

Listasafn Íslands (National Gallery of Iceland): Fríkirkjuvegi 7, 101 Reykjavík; tel. 515-9600; e-mail list@listasafn.is; internet www.listasafn.is; f. 1884; houses collns of art of 19th and 20th century Icelandic and int. art; holds 10,000 works; books on and about 20th century art in the Nordic countries; collns of photography, media criticism and commentary concerning Icelandic art, exhibition catalogues, booklets and other printed material; Dir Dr HALLDOR BJORN RUNÓLFSSON.

Listasafn Reykjavíkur (Reykjavík Art Museum): Reykjavík; tel. 590-1200; e-mail listasafn@reykjavik.is; internet www.artmuseum.is; f. 1973; visual arts collns and exhibitions; highlights major trends and currents in contemporary art; 3 collns of works by Asmundur Sveinsson, Johannes S. Kjarval, Erró; outdoor sculptures; architecture colln; Dir HAFTHOR YNGVASON.

Nýlistasafnið (Living Art Museum (Nýló)): Skúlagata 28, 101 Reykjavík; tel. 551-4350; e-mail nylo@nylo.is; internet nylo.is; f. 1978; holds approx. 2,000 works; Dir GUNNHILDUR HAUKSDÓTTIR.

Þjóðminjasafn Íslands (National Museum of Iceland): Suðurgata 41, 101 Reykjavík; tel. 530-2200; e-mail thjodminjasafn@thjodminjasafn.is; internet www.thjodminjasafn.is; f. 1863; houses 2,000 objects, dating from the Settlement Age to the present; 1,000 photographs since beginning of 20th century; library of 20,000 vols and 300 magazines; Dir MARGRÉT HALLGRÍMSDÓTTIR.

Vopnafjordur

Bustarfell Museum: Hofsárdalur, 690 Vopnafjordur; tel. 471-2211; e-mail bustarfell@simnet.is; internet www.bustarfell.is; f. 1982; depicts the history of Icelandic farming and lifestyle changes from 18th century to mid-20th century; Chair. BJÖRG EINARSDÓTTIR; Man. BERGHILDUR FANNEY HAUKSDÓTTIR.

Universities

HÁSKÓLI ÍSLANDS (University of Iceland)

Sæmundargötu 2, 101 Reykjavík
Telephone: 525-4000
E-mail: hi@hi.is
Internet: www.hi.is

Founded 1911, merged with Kennaraháskóli Íslands (Iceland Univ. of Education) 2008; attached to Min. of Education, Science and Culture
State control
Languages of instruction: English, Icelandic
Academic year: September to June

Rector: Prof. KRISTÍN INGÓLFSDÓTTIR
Pro-Rector for Academic Affairs: JÓN ATLI BENEDIKTSSON
Dir for Academic Affairs: ÞÓRÐUR KRISTINSSON
Dir for Finance: JENNÝ BÁRA JENSDÓTTIR
Dir for Human Resources: GUÐRÚN JÓHANNA GUÐMUNDSDÓTTIR
Dir for Marketing and Public Relations: JÓN ÖRN GUÐBJARTSSON
Dir for Operations and Resources: GUÐMUNDUR R. JÓNSSON
Dir for Science, Innovation and Research: HALLDÓR JÓNSSON

Library: see under Libraries and Archives
Number of teachers: 3,050
Number of students: 14,000

Publications: *Árbók Háskóla Íslands* (1 a year), *Ritaskrá Háskóla Íslands* (1 a year), *Tímarit Háskóla Íslands* (1 a year)

DEANS

School of Education: Prof. JÓHANNA EINARSDÓTTIR
School of Engineering and Natural Sciences: HILMAR BRAGI JANUSSON
School of Health Sciences: Prof. INGA ÞÓRSDÓTTIR
School of Humanities: ÁSTRÁÐUR EYSTEINSSON
School of Social Sciences: DAÐI MÁR KRISTÓFERSSON

HÁSKÓLINN Á AKUREYRI (University of Akureyri)

Sólborg, Norðurslóð 2, 600 Akureyri
Telephone: 460-8000
E-mail: unak@unak.is
Internet: www.unak.is

Founded 1987
State control
Languages of instruction: English, Icelandic
Academic year: August to June

Rector: Dr STEFÁN B. SIGURÐSSON
Man. Dir: OLAFUR HALLDORSSON
Dir for Academic Admin.: STEINUNN AÐALBJARNARDÓTTIR
Dir for Information Services: ASTRID MARGRÉT MAGNÚSDÓTTIR
Number of teachers: 100
Number of students: 2,000

DEANS

School of Business and Science: Dr ÖGMUNDUR KNÚTSSON
School of Health Sciences: Dr ÁRÚN KRISTÍN SIGURÐARDÓTTIR
School of Humanities and Social Sciences: Dr SIGURDUR KRISTINSSON

HÁSKÓLINN Á BIFRÖST (Bifröst University)

311 Borgarnes
Telephone: 433-3000
E-mail: bifrost@bifrost.is
Internet: www.bifrost.is

Founded 1918 as Cooperative College, present status 1988, present name 2006
Private control
Languages of instruction: English, Icelandic
Academic year: September to August

Rector: BRYNDÍS HLÖÐVERSDÓTTIR
Vice-Rector: Prof. Dr JON OLAFSSON
Library Dir: ANDREA JÓHANNSDÓTTIR

Library of 10,000 vols
Number of teachers: 60
Number of students: 1,300

Publication: *Bifröst Journal of Social Science* (online (bjss.bifrost.is))

DEANS

Faculty of Business: SIGURBJÖRN EINARSSON
Faculty of Law: HELGA KRISTÍN AUÐUNSDÓTTIR
Faculty of Social Sciences: JÓN ÓLAFSSON

PROFESSORS

BJARNASON, A., Business
BLÖNDAL, E., Law
EINARSSON, A., Business
LINDAL, S., Law
ÓLAFSSON, J., Social Sciences
PAPANASTASSIOU, M., Business

HÁSKÓLINN Á HÓLUM (Hólar University College)

Hólar i Hjaltadal, 551 Sauðárkrókur
Telephone: 455-6300
E-mail: holaskoli@holar.is
Internet: www.holar.is

Founded 1882 as Búnadarskólinn á Hólum i Hjaltadal (Hólar Agricultural School), present name and status 2003
State control

Depts of fish biology and aquaculture, equine science, rural tourism

Rector: Dr ERLA BJÖRK ÖRNÓLFSDÓTTIR
Dir: SIGURBJÖRG B. OLAFSDOTTIR

Library of 6,000 vols
Number of teachers: 42
Number of students: 50

HÁSKÓLINN Í REYKJAVÍK (Reykjavík University)

Menntavegi 1, 101 Reykjavík
Telephone: 599-6200
E-mail: ru@ru.is
Internet: www.ru.is

Founded 1998, absorbed Tækniskóli Íslands (Icelandic College of Engineering and Technology) 2005
Private control
Languages of instruction: English, Icelandic
Academic year: August to June

Rector: Dr ARI KRISTINN JÓNSSON
Provost: JOHN B. VANDER SANDE
Library Dir: GUÐRÚN TRYGGVADÓTTIR
Number of teachers: 143
Number of students: 3,000

DEANS

School of Business: Dr FRIÐRIK MÁR BALDURSSON
School of Computer Science: Dr BJÖRN ÞÓR JÓNSSON
School of Law: GUÐMUNDUR SIGURÐSSON
School of Science and Engineering: Dr GUÐRÚN ARNBJÖRG SÆVARSDÓTTIR

LANDBUNAÐARHÁSKÓLI ÍSLANDS (Agricultural University of Iceland)

Hvanneyri, 311 Borgarnes
Telephone: 433-5000
E-mail: lbhi@lbhi.is
Internet: www.lbhi.is

Founded 2005; attached to Min. of Agriculture

Rector: Dr ÁGÚST SIGURÐSSON
Pro-Rector for Education: BJÖRN ÞORSTEINSSON
Pro-Rector for Research: ÁSLAUG HELGADÓTTIR

Library of 20,000 vols
Number of teachers: 30
Number of students: 250

Publication: *Fjölrit Bændaskólans* (1 a year)

DEANS

Faculty of Animal and Land Resources: ÁSLAUG HELGADÓTTIR
Faculty of Environmental Sciences: ÓLAFUR ARNALDS
Faculty of Vocational and Continuing Education: GUÐRÍÐUR HELGADÓTTIR (Head)

LISTAHÁSKÓLI ÍSLANDS (Iceland Academy of the Arts)

Þverholti 11, 105 Reykjavík
Telephone: 552-4000
E-mail: lhi@lhi.is
Internet: www.lhi.is

Founded 1998 by merger of Reykjavik College of Music, Icelandic College of Arts and Crafts, and Icelandic Drama School
Private control
Academic year: August to May

Rector: HJÁLMAR H. RAGNARSSON
Man. Dir: MAGNÚS LOFTSSON
Dir for Academic Affairs: BJÖRG JÓNA BIRGISDÓTTIR
Dir for Research Services: ÓLÖF GERÐUR SIGFÚSDÓTTIR
Library Dir: SARA STEF. HILDARDÓTTIR

Library of 42,000 vols
Number of teachers: 40 full-time, 200 part-time
Number of students: 452

DEANS

Dept of Art Education: KRISTÍN VALSDÓTTIR
Dept of Design and Architecture: SIGRÚN BIRGISDÓTTIR
Dept of Fine Arts: KRISTJÁN STEINGRÍMUR JÓNSSON
Dept of Music: MIST ÞORKELSDÓTTIR
Dept of Theatre and Dance: STEINUNN KNÚTSDÓTTIR

SÖNGSKÓLINN Í REYKJAVÍK (Reykjavík Academy of Singing and Vocal Arts)

Snorrabraut 54, POB 2005, 125 Reykjavík
Telephone: 552-7366
E-mail: songskolinn@songskolinn.is
Internet: www.songskolinn.is

Founded 1973

Private control

Prin. and Artistic Dir: GARÐAR CORTES

Asst Prin. and Financial Dir: ÁSRÚN DAVÍÐSDÓTTIR

Head for Theory Teaching: JÓN KRISTINN CORTEZ

Head for Vocal Training: ÓLÖF KOLBRÚN HARÐARDÓTTIR

Number of teachers: 31

Number of students: 200

TÓNLISTARSKÓLINN Í REYKJAVÍK
(Reykjavík College of Music)

Skipholti 33, 105 Reykjavík

Telephone: 553-0625

E-mail: tono@tono.is

Internet: www.tono.is

Founded 1930

private control

Language of instruction: Icelandic

Academic year: August to June

Depts of bass, piano, string instruments, theoretical studies

Chair.: ANDRI ARNASON

Prin.: KJARTAN OSKARSSON

Vice-Prin.: ÞÓRUNN GUDMUNDSDOTTIR

Number of teachers: 55

INDIA

The Higher Education System

The modern higher education system was established while India was under British rule. Among the oldest institutions are Presidency University (founded in 1817—formerly entitled Presidency College, the institution was upgraded to the status of a full university in 2010), Deccan College Postgraduate and Research Institute (founded in 1821) and Sanskrit College (founded in 1824). In 1857 major universities were founded at Mumbai (formerly Bombay), Madras and Kolkata (formerly Calcutta). The main representative body of Indian universities, the Association of Indian Universities, was founded in 1925 and re-established as a statutory body in 1947, when India gained its independence. In 1953 the University Grants Commission (UGC) was created to act between the central Government and the states as the coordinating body on higher education. In 2005/06 India had a total of 337 universities and institutions with university status, and some 13,413 university and affiliated colleges. By 2011 these figures had risen to 634 universities and 33,023 colleges, with a total enrolment of about 1.7m. students.

Universities are autonomous institutions, mostly funded by the states' governments, except for the 42 'central' universities, which are funded by the central Government. Universities are classified as either 'unitary' or 'affiliating'. Unitary universities conduct all undergraduate and postgraduate teaching, while in affiliating universities the teaching of undergraduates is conducted by affiliated colleges. There are also two other types of universities, 'deemed' and 'institutions of national importance'. Deemed universities are single-discipline institutions that have been granted university status by the UGC, and the institutions of national importance (including the globally acclaimed Indian Institutes of Technology) are funded directly by the Government but are distinct from central universities. The states account for 90% of university funding, with the rest coming from central Government. Student fees account for a small percentage of universities' income. In 2012 there were 145 private universities in India judged competent by the UGC to award degrees. The autonomous National Assessment and Accreditation Council (founded in 1994) is the national body responsible for accreditation and quality assurance.

Universities have broadly the same administrative structure. The Vice-Chancellor is both the administrative and the academic head of the university. The Senate or Court, Syndicate and Executive Council or Board of Management are the primary administrative bodies, responsible for institutional budgets and management. The Academic Council oversees all academic aspects of the institution, including teaching and research. Faculties are the most important academic divisions, and are headed by Deans. Boards of Study determine programmes of study.

Admission to higher education is on the basis of one of the different Higher Secondary School Certificates. Standard undergraduate Bachelors degrees last three years, although some programmes in professional fields of study last four years (engineering, veterinary medicine, agriculture, dentistry and pharmacy) or five to five-and-a half years (architecture and medicine, respectively). The Bachelors of Law is either a five-year first degree or a two- to three-year second degree. The first postgraduate degree is the Masters. Admission to the Masters may vary depending on the institution; a Bachelors is the most common requirement, but institutions may also set an entrance examination, while applicants for Masters programmes in the fields of architecture, engineering, pharmacy and technology must sit the Graduate Aptitude Test in Engineering. Masters programmes are two to three years in length. Following the Masters, there is a pre-doctoral programme called the Master of Philosophy (MPhil), a one-and-a-half year course. Finally, the Doctorate (PhD) is awarded three years after the Masters and at least two years after the MPhil. PhD students are required to write a substantial thesis based on original research and to undergo an oral examination.

Technical and vocational education is overseen by several different bodies: the Central Apprenticeship Council, the National Council for Training in Vocational Trades, the National Council for Educational Research and Training, the Joint Council for Vocationalization of Education, the AICTE and State Boards of Technical Education. The Joint Council for Vocationalization of Education was founded in 1990 and is the body tasked with implementing and maintaining the national standard of vocational education. Universities, polytechnics and colleges offer one- to four-year Diploma courses in most subjects.

In 2011 the Government stated that it proposed to raise the proportion of young people attending university from the existing 12% to 30% by 2025. With a view to meeting the aspirations of a rapidly growing middle class and to catering for the demands of the burgeoning economy, public expenditure on higher education was greatly increased in the 12th Five-Year Plan (2012–17), compared with the previous plan, and there were proposals to establish hundreds of new institutions throughout India.

Regulatory and Representative Bodies

GOVERNMENT

Department of Higher Education: Shastri Bhawan, New Delhi 110001; tel. (11) 23383936; e-mail dhe-mhrd@nic.in; internet mhrd.gov.in/higher_education; attached to Min. of Human Resource Devt; Minister of Human Resource Devt Dr M. M. PALLAM RAJU; Sec. for Dept of Higher Education ASHOK THAKUR; Spec. Secretary for Technical Education AMITA SHARMA.

Ministry of Culture: Room 501, 'C' Wing, Shastri Bhawan, New Delhi 110115; tel. (11) 23386765; e-mail officemoc@gmail.com; internet indiaculture.nic.in; Minister CHANDRESH KUMARI KATOCH.

Ministry of Human Resource Development: Shastri Bhawan, New Delhi 110001; tel. (11) 23782698; e-mail hrm@nic.in; internet mhrd.gov.in; Min. M. MANGAPATI PALLAM RAJU.

Ministry of Science and Technology: Technology Bhavan, New Mehrauli Rd, New Delhi 110016; tel. (11) 26567373; e-mail dstinfo@nic.in; internet dst.gov.in; Minister SUDINI JAIPAL REDDY.

ACCREDITATION

National Assessment and Accreditation Council (NAAC): POB 1075, Nagarbhavi, Bengaluru 560072, Karnataka; tel. (80) 23005100; e-mail director.naac@gmail.com; internet www.naac.gov.in; f. 1994; assesses and accredits instns of higher education in India; Chair. Dr DINESH SINGH; Dir Prof. H. A. RANGANATH.

FUNDING

University Grants Commission (UGC): Bahadur Shah Zafar Marg, New Delhi 110002; tel. (11) 23232701; e-mail webmaster@ugc.ac.in; internet www.ugc.ac.in; f. 1953, present status 1956; attached to Dept of Higher Education, Min. of Human Resource Devt; provides funds to instns of higher education; coordinates, determines and maintains standards in instns of higher education; library of 41,850 vols; Chair. Prof. VED PRAKASH (acting); Sec. VIBHA PURI DAS; publ. *Higher Education in India*.

NATIONAL BODIES

All India Council for Technical Education (AICTE): 7th Fl., Chanderlok Bldg, Janpath, New Delhi 110001; tel. (11) 23724151; e-mail admin@aicte.ernet.in; internet www.aicte-india.org; f. 1945; promotes quality in technical education; plans, coordinates devt of technical education system; regulates, maintains norms and standards; Chair. of Ccl Prof. S. S. MANTHA (acting); Vice-Chair. of Ccl Prof. S. S. MANTHA; publ. *Technical Education in Independent India 1999 (Compendium)*.

Association of Indian Universities: AIU House, 16 Comrade Indrajit Gupta Marg (Kotla Marg), New Delhi 110002; tel. (11) 23230059; e-mail info@aiuweb.org; internet www.aiuweb.org; f. 1925 as Inter-University Board, present status 1967, present name 1973; serves as an inter-university org.; acts as representative of univs of India; library of 20,000 vols, 150 periodicals, annual reports, calendars, handbooks and Acts of the various univs and Supreme Court of India judgments in the field of education; Pres. Dr P. T. CHANDE; Vice-Pres. Dr S. N. PURI; Sec.-Gen. Prof. A. D. N. BAJPAI; Sec.-Gen. Prof. BEENA SHAH; publs *Equivalence of Foreign Degrees* (irregular), *Handbook of Computer Education* (1 a year), *Handbook of Library and Information Science* (1 a year), *Handbook of Management Education* (1 a year), *Handbook of Medical Education* (1 a year), *Handbook on Distance Education* (1 a year), *Handbook on Engineering Education* (1 a year), *Handbook on Health Sciences Education* (1 a year), *Scholarships for Study Abroad and at Home* (1 a year), *Tryst with Health Science Education*, *Universities Handbook* (every 2 years).

Indian Adult Education Association (IAEA): 17B Indraprastha Estate, New Delhi 110002; tel. (11) 23379282; e-mail iaeaindia@yahoo.com; internet www.iaea-india.org; f. 1939 under the Indian Socs Registration Act 1860; promotes adult, non-formal, lifelong education in India; holds community devt conferences, seminars, workshops; vocational education; 2,500 mems; library: Amarnath Jha Library (f. 1957) 23,500 books, 110 periodicals; Pres. Prof. K. C. CHOUDHARY; Gen. Sec. Dr MADAN SINGH; publs *Indian Journal of Adult Education* (4 a year), *Indian Journal of Population Education* (4 a year), *Jago Aur Jagao* (12 a year, in Hindi), *Proudh Shiksha* (12 a year, in Hindi).

National Council of Educational Research and Training (NCERT): Sri Aurobindo Marg, New Delhi 110016; tel. (11) 26560620; e-mail proncert@hotmail.com; internet www.ncert.nic.in; f. 1961; academic adviser to the Min. of Human Resource Devt; coordinates research and devt in all brs of education; organizes pre- and in-service training; publishes school textbooks, instructional material for teachers and educational surveys; 8 major constituent units: Nat. Institute of Education, and Central Institute of Educational Technology in New Delhi, Central Institute of Vocational Education in Bhopal and 5 regional Institutes of Education at Ajmer, Bhopal, Bhubaneswar, Mysore and Shillong; Pres. KAPIL SIBAL; Dir Prof. G. RAVINDRA; publs *Indian Educational Abstracts*, *Indian Educational Review* (2 a year), *Journal of Indian Education*, *Journal of Value Education*, *School Science* (4 a year), *The Primary Teacher*.

Learned Societies

GENERAL

India International Centre: 40 Max Mueller Marg, New Delhi 110003; tel. (11) 24619431; e-mail director.iic@nic.in; internet www.iicdelhi.nic.in; f. 1958; int. cultural org. for promotion of amity and understanding between the different communities in the world; programme of lectures, discussions, film evenings, etc.; 6,600 mems; library of 37,000 vols, 160 periodicals, also houses the India Collection of 3,000 rare documents on British India, the Himalayan Club Library of 9,500 vols, Bilgrami Colln of 700 vols; Pres. Prof. M. G. K. MENON; Dir Dr KAVITA A. SHARMA; Sec. RAVINDER DATTA; publs *IIC Diary* (6 a year), *IIC Quarterly*, *Mid-Year Review of the Indian Economy*, *Occasional Publication*.

Indian Council for Cultural Relations (ICCR): Azad Bhavan, Indraprastha Estate, New Delhi 110002; tel. (11) 23379309; e-mail president@iccrindia.net; internet www.iccrindia.net; f. 1950; establishes and strengthens cultural relations between India and other countries; br. offices in Bengaluru, Chandigarh, Chennai, Cuttack, Goa, Guwahati, Hyderabad, Jaipur, Kolkata, Lucknow, Mumbai, Pune, Shillong, Thiruvananthapuram, Varanasi; cultural centres in Abu Dhabi (United Arab Emirates), Astana (Kazakhstan), Bali (Indonesia), Bangkok (Thailand), Berlin (Germany), Cairo (Egypt), Colombo (Sri Lanka), Dhaka (Bangladesh), Durban (S Africa), Dushanbe (Tajikistan), Georgetown (Guyana), Jakarta (Indonesia), Johannesburg (S Africa), Kabul (Afghanistan), Kathmandu (Nepal), Kuala Lumpur (Malaysia), Lautoka (Fiji), London (United Kingdom), Moscow (Russia), Paramaribo (Suriname), Phoenix (Mauritius), Port of Spain (Trinidad and Tobago), São Paulo (Brazil), Suva (Fiji), Tashkent (Uzbekistan), Thimpu (Bhutan), Tokyo (Japan); activities incl. exchange visits between scholars, artists and people of eminence in the field of art and culture; exchange of exhibitions; int. confs and seminars, lectures by renowned scholars incl. Azad Memorial Lectures; establishment of chairs and centres of Indian studies abroad and welfare of overseas students in India; admin. of Jawaharlal Nehru Award for Int. Understanding; presentation of books and Indian art objects to univs, libraries and museums in other countries; library: over 56,000 vols on India and other countries; 197 rare MSS; Pres. Dr KARAN SINGH; Dir-Gen. SURESH K. GOEL; Vice-Pres. Prof. BHARATI RAY; Vice-Pres. Prof. SYED SHAHID MAHDI; publs interpretations of Indian art and culture and translations of Indian works into foreign languages, *African Quarterly* (4 a year, in English), *Gagananchal* (4 a year, in Hindi), *Indian Horizons*, *Papeles de la India* (4 a year, in Spanish), *Rencontre avec l'Inde* (4 a year, in French), *Thaqafat-ul-Hind* (4 a year, in Arabic).

Indian Institute of World Culture: No 6 Shri B. P. Wadia Rd, Basavangudi, Bengaluru 560004, Karnataka; tel. (80) 26678581; e-mail iiwc@vsnl.net; internet www.iiwcindia.org; f. 1945; sister instn of United Lodge of Theosophists; provides opportunities for cultural and intellectual devt; promotes exchange of thought between India and other countries; raises the consideration of nat. and world problems to the plane of moral and spiritual values; fosters a sense of universal brotherhood; 3,100 mems; library of 40,000 vols, 400 periodicals; Pres. Justice M. N. VENKATACHALIAH; Vice-Pres. R. N. NAGARAJ; Hon. Sec. Y. M. BALAKRISHNA; publ. *Transactions*.

Jammu and Kashmir Academy of Art, Culture and Language: Lal Mandi, Srinagar 190001, Jammu and Kashmir; tel. (194) 2311521; internet jkculture.com; f. 1958; promotes arts, culture and languages of the State; collns of gramophone records, cassettes, paintings, jewellery, calligraphy, costumes, contemporary paintings, sculpture; library of 20,000 vols, 650 rare MSS, 250 laminated photographs, 90 opera and folk song recordings; Patron HE The GOVERNOR OF JAMMU AND KASHMIR; Pres. Gen. OMAR ABDULLAH; Sec. ZAFAR IQBAL MANHAS; publs *Encyclopaedia Kashmirana*, *Hamara Adab* (1 a year anthology in Urdu, Kashmiri, Gojri, Pahari, Dogri, Punjabi, Hindi, Ladakhi), *Sheeraza* (12 a year in Urdu, 6 a year in Kashmiri, Dogri, Punjabi and Hindi, 4 a year in Ladakhi, Pahari, Gojri and 1 a year in English and Balti).

AGRICULTURE, FISHERIES AND VETERINARY SCIENCE

Agri-Horticultural Society of India: 1 Alipore Rd, Kolkata 700027, West Bengal; tel. (33) 24791713; e-mail ahsi@vsnl.net; internet www.agrihorticultureindia.com; f. 1820; 2,579 mems; library of 400 vols; Pres. SHARAD KHAITAN; Sr Vice-Pres. S. B. GANGULY; Vice-Pres. Dr SHYAMAL KUMAR BASU; Sec. NIRUPOM SEN; publs *Encyclopedia of Himalayan Medicinal Flora*, *Horticultural Journal* (1 a year).

Agri-Horticultural Society of Madras: New-134 Cathedral Rd, Gopalapuram, Chennai 600086, Tamil Nadu; tel. (44) 28116816; f. 1835; 3,410 mems; Patron HE The GOV. OF TAMIL NADU; Chair. R. SADASIVAM; Hon. Sec. Prof. J. RAMCHANDRAN.

Crop Improvement Society of India: Dept of Plant Breeding and Genetics, Punjab Agricultural Univ., Ludhiana 141004, Punjab; tel. (161) 2401960; e-mail registrar@pau.edu; f. 1974; disseminates knowledge on crop improvement through lectures, symposia, publs; arranges excursions and explorations; cooperates with nat. and int. orgs; 200 mems; Pres. Dr G. S. SIDHU; Sec. Dr G. S. CHAHAL; publ. *Crop Improvement* (3 a year).

Indian Dairy Association: IDA House, Sector IV, R. K. Puram, New Delhi 110022; tel. (11) 26170781; e-mail idahq@rediffmail.com; internet www.indairyasso.org; f. 1948; apex body of dairy industry in India; provides a common forum for dairy fraternity; advancement of dairy science and industry, farming, animal husbandry, animal sciences; brs incl. dairy farming and research on breeding, management of dairy livestock; 3,000 mems; library: Mansingh Bhai Patel Library of 700 vols, 100 periodicals; Pres. Dr N. R. BHASIN; Vice-Pres A. K. KHOSLA; Vice-Pres ARUN NARKA; publs *Indian Dairyman* (12 a year), *Indian Journal of Dairy Science* (6 a year).

Indian Society of Agricultural Economics: C-104 First Fl., Sadguru Complex–1, Near Vagheshwari, Gen. A. K. Vaidya Marg, Goregaon (E), Mumbai 400063, Maharashtra; tel. (22) 28493723; e-mail isae@bom7.vsnl.net.in; internet www.isaeindia.org; f. 1939; promotes the study of social and economic problems of agriculture and rural areas, and technical competence for teaching and research in agricultural economics and allied subjects; 1,644 mems and subscribers; library of 22,349 vols; Pres. Dr C. RAMASAMY; Vice-Pres. Dr R. VISHWANATHAN; Vice-Pres. Dr S. M. MUNDINAMANI; Vice-Pres. Dr ANJANI KUMAR; Vice-Pres. Dr R. S. SIDHU; Vice-Pres. Dr RAKESH SINGH; Hon. Sec. and Treas. Dr C. L. DADHICH; Hon. Jt Sec. VIJAYA VENKATESH; publs *Comparative Experience of Agricultural Development in Developing Countries of Asia and the South-East Since World War II (1972)*, *Evaluation of Land Reforms (with special reference to the Western Region of India)*, *The Indian Journal of Agricultural Economics* (4 a year).

Indian Society of Soil Science: Nat. Socs Block, First Fl., Nat. Agricultural Science Centre Complex, Dev Prakash Shastri Marg, Pusa, New Delhi 110012; tel. (11) 25841991; e-mail isss1934@gmail.com; internet www.isss-india.org; f. 1934; cultivates and promotes soil science and its allied disciplines;

disseminates knowledge of soil science and its applications; cooperation with Int. Soc. of Soil Science and similar orgs; organizes seminars, symposia, confs, meetings, etc.; 2,350 mems; Pres. Prof. Dr R. K. RATTAN; Vice-Pres. Dr JAGDISH PRASAD; Vice-Pres. Prof. Dr G. S. DASOG; Sec. Dr D. R. BISWAS; publ. *Journal of Indian Society of Soil Science* (4 a year).

ARCHITECTURE AND TOWN PLANNING

Indian Institute of Architects: Prospect Chambers Annexe, Dr D. N. Rd, Fort, Mumbai 400001, Maharashtra; tel. (22) 22046972; e-mail iiaho@mtnl.net.in; internet www.iia-india.org; f. 1917 as Architectural Students Association, present name and status 1929; promotes aesthetic, scientific and practical efficiency of the architectural profession; sponsors architectural education; sets qualifying standards for the profession; provides a forum for discussing related subjects; 15,000 mems; library of 3,000 vols; Pres. PRAFULLA KARKHANIS; Vice-Pres. JIT KUMAR GUPTA; Jt Hon. Sec. PARESH KAPADIA; Jt Hon. Sec. DEBABRATA GHOSH; publ. *Journal of Indian Institute of Architects* (12 a year).

BIBLIOGRAPHY, LIBRARY SCIENCE AND MUSEOLOGY

Indian Association of Special Libraries and Information Centres (IASLIC): P. 291, CIT Scheme No. 6M, Kankurgachi, Kolkata 700054, West Bengal; tel. (33) 23629651; e-mail iaslic@vsnl.net; internet www.iaslic1955.org.in; f. 1955; promotes study and research into spec. librarianship and information science; conducts short-term training courses on the subject, holds confs and coordinates activities among special libraries and spec. interest groups; publishes seminar and conf. papers and books on information and library science; translation and reprographic services; 2,900 mems; library of 4,060 vols, 50 current periodicals; Hon. Pres. Dr JATINDRANATH SATPATHI; Vice-Pres. Prof. ARJUN DASGUPTA; Hon. Gen. Sec. Prof. PIJUSHKANTI PANIGRAHI; publs *Conference Proceedings*, *Indian Library Science Abstracts (ILSA)* (1 a year), *Journal of IASLIC (JIASLIC)* (4 a year), *Seminar Proceedings*.

Indian Library Association: A–40/41, Flat 201, Ansal Bldg, Mukherjee Nagar, Delhi 110009; tel. (22) 27651743; e-mail ask@ilaindia.net; internet www.ilaindia.net; f. 1933; 7,000 mems; library of 2,000 vols; Pres. Prof. ASHU SHOKEEN; Sr Vice-Pres. Dr O. N. CHAUBEY; Gen. Sec. Dr PARDEEP RAI; publ. *Journal of Indian Library Association* (2 a year).

Museums Association of India: c/o Nat. Museum Institute, Nat. Museum, Janpath, New Delhi 110011; tel. (11) 23792249; e-mail pradumman@hotmail.com; internet www.museumsai.com; f. 1944; professional discussions, seminars, confs, exhibitions, courses in museology; 558 life mems, 15 institutional mems; library of 25,000 books, 5,000 research journals; Pres. Dr P. K. SHARMA (acting); Sec. Dr ANAND BURDHAN; publ. *MAI Journal*.

National Book Trust, India: 5 Nehru Bhawan, Institutional Area, Vasant Kunj, New Delhi 110070; tel. (11) 26707700; e-mail nbtindia@ndb.vsnl.net.in; internet www.nbtindia.org.in; f. 1957; publishes moderately priced books for general readers in 12 Indian languages and English, gives assistance to authors, illustrators and publishers to produce books for children, neo-literates and the higher education sector; organizes book fairs, exhibitions, seminars and workshops; promotes Indian books abroad; Chair. Prof. BIPAN CHANDRA; Dir M. A. SIKANDAR.

ECONOMICS, LAW AND POLITICS

All India Bar Association: DS-423/424, New Rajinder Nagar, New Delhi 110060; tel. (11) 28743284; e-mail allindiabar@gmail.com; internet www.allindiabar.org; f. 1959; Chair. ADISH C. AGGARWALA.

Indian Council of World Affairs: Sapru House, Barakhamba Rd, New Delhi 110001; tel. (11) 23317246; e-mail dg@icwa.in; internet www.icwa.in; f. 1943; non-governmental instn for study of Indian and int. relations and world affairs; 1,500 mems; library of 128,000 vols, 376 periodicals, UN and EU depository; Pres. M. H. ANSARI; Dir-Gen. S. T. DEVARE; Deputy Dir-Gen. SARVAJIT CHAKRAVARTI; Dir MANIKA JAIN; publs *Foreign Affairs* (12 a year), *India Quarterly*.

Indian Economic Association: Dept of Economics, Arts Block–III, Panjab Univ., Chandigarh 160014, Punjab; tel. (172) 22779140; e-mail iea@pu.ac.in; internet iea.puchd.ac.in; f. 1917; provides forum for economists of India; 3,500 mems; Patron and Chair. Prof. R. C. SOBTI; Pres. Prof. SUKHADEO THORAT; Vice-Pres. Prof. L. K. MOHANA RAO; Hon. Sec. Dr ANIL KUMAR THAKUR; publ. *Indian Economic Journal* (4 a year).

Institute of Chartered Accountants of India: POB 7100, New Delhi 110002; ICAI Bhawan, Indraprastha Marg, New Delhi 110002; tel. (11) 39893989; e-mail icaiho@icai.org; internet www.icai.org; f. 1949; a statutory body est. under an Act of Parliament for the regulation of the profession of chartered accountants in India; contributes in the fields of education, professional devt, maintenance of high accounting, auditing and ethical standards; 161,859 mems; library: Central Ccl Library 62,000 vols; Pres. G. RAMASWAMY; Vice-Pres. JAYDEEP N. SHAH; Sec. T. KARTHIKEYAN; publs *Gateway to International Trade-E Communiqué of the Committee on Trade Laws & WTO*, *ICAI Patrika*, *Management Accounting and Business Finance*, *The Chartered Accountant* (12 a year).

EDUCATION

All India Association for Educational Research: N1/55 IRC Village, Bhubaneswar 751015, Orrisa; tel. (674) 2550611; e-mail aiaer@rediffmail.com; internet www.aiaer.net; f. 1987; develops and promotes educational research; holds annual and periodical confs on various themes; 3,228 mems; Patron Prof. B. K. PASSI; Pres. Prof. SURAJ PRAKASH MALHOTRA; Gen. Sec. and Editor Prof. SUNIL BEHARI MOHANTY; Treas. DHRUBA CHARAN MISHRA; publ. *Journal of All India Association for Educational Research* (2 a year).

Hyderabad Educational Conference: 19 Bachelors' Quarters, Jawaharlal Nehru Rd, Hyderabad, 500001, Andhra Pradesh; f. 1913; promotes academic research, assists needy students; library of 9,500 vols; Pres. SYED MASOOD ALI; Sec. GHOUSE MOHIUDDIN; publs *Educational Annual* (in Urdu), *Proceedings of Public Sessions* (in Urdu), *Ruh-e-Tarraqui* (in Urdu).

Jamsetjee Nesserwanjee Petit Institute: 312 Dr Dadabhoy Naoroji Rd, Fort, Mumbai 400001, Maharashtra; tel. (22) 22048463; e-mail petitheritage_01@yahoo.co.in; f. 1856; organizes lectures and makes accessible literary, scientific and philosophic works; 4,210 mems; library: see under Libraries and Archives; Pres. Sir DINSHAW M. PETIT; Hon. Sec N. M. PATEL; Hon. Sec RODA ANKALESARIA.

National Bal Bhavan: Kotla Rd, New Delhi 110002; tel. (11) 23232672; e-mail infoprogsection@gmail.com; internet www.nationalbalbhavan.nic.in; f. 1956; autonomous instn est. by Min. of Human Resource Devt; provides planned environment and creative activities based on Arts and Science to children between the ages of 5 and 16; provides leadership and guidance to teachers towards fostering a creative approach in teaching of art and science, organizes orientation courses for teachers and parents; runs a repertory theatre for children, the Nat. Children's Museum and a nat. training resource centre; library: children's library of 43,347 vols, reference library of 11,584 vols; Chair. ANSHU VAISH; Vice-Chair. BRAJESH PRASAD; publ. *Akkar Bakkar and Akkar Bakkar Times* (booklet entirely produced by the children).

FINE AND PERFORMING ARTS

All India Fine Arts and Crafts Society: 1 Rafi Marg, New Delhi 110001; tel. (11) 23711315; e-mail aifacsarts@yahoo.co.in; internet www.aifacs.org.in; f. 1928; holds art exhibitions incl. the All India Annual Art Exhibition of painting, photography, sculpture, graphics, traditional art and water colours and drawings, exhibitions of Indian art abroad and exhibitions of arts and crafts from foreign countries in India, talks and film shows on art; 550 mems; library of 5,300 vols; Pres. RAM V. SUTAR; Chair. Prof. PARAMJEET SINGH (acting); publs *Arts News* (12 a year), *Roopa Lekha* (1 a year).

Art Society of India: Sandhurst House, 524 S.V.P. Rd, Opera House, Mumbai 400004, Maharashtra; tel. (22) 23888550; e-mail theartsocietyofindia@gmail.com; internet www.artsocietyofindia.org; f. 1918; promotes art and artists all over India; colln of rare art books; 1,000 mems; library of 2,000 vols; Pres. PRAFULLA DAHANUKAR; Vice-Pres. KANU NAYAK; Chair. VASUDEO KAMATH; Hon. Sec. Dr GOPAL NENE; Hon. Jt Sec. VIJAYRAJ BODHANKAR.

Bombay Art Society: Jehangir Art Gallery, Mahatma Gandhi Rd, Mumbai 400023, Maharashtra; tel. (22) 22044058; e-mail contactus@bombayartsociety.org; internet www.bombayartsociety.org; f. 1888; holds all-India annual art exhibition; 450 life mems, 150 ordinary mems, 200 student mems; Pres. PRAFULLA DAHANUKAR; Chair. UTTAM PACHARANE; Sec Prof. NARENDRA VICHARE; publ. *Art Journal*.

India International Photographic Council: First Fl., 21 Bharti Artists Colony, Vikas Marg, New Delhi 110092; tel. (11) 65751099; e-mail info@iipconline.org; internet www.iipconline.org; f. 1983; 6,000 mems; Pres. ASHOK TALWAR; Gen. Sec. Dr O. P. SHARMA; publ. *IIPC Photographic Journal* (12 a year).

Indian Society of Oriental Art (Calcutta): 15 Park St, Kolkata 700016, West Bengal; tel. (33) 22174805; f. 1907; promotes and researches all aspects of ancient and contemporary Indian, Oriental art; 320 mems; library of 3,500 vols; Sec. INDIRA NAG CHAUDHURI; publ. *Journal* (1 a year).

Lalit Kala Akademi (National Academy of Art): Rabindra Bhavan, 35 Ferozshah Rd, New Delhi 110001; tel. (11) 23009200; e-mail lka@lalitkala.gov.in; internet lalitkala.gov.in; f. 1954; autonomous, govt-financed; sponsors nat. and int. exhibitions, such as the Nat. Exhibition of Art (annual) and Triennale-India; arranges seminars, lectures, films, etc.; regional centres in Bhubaneswar, Chennai, Garhi, Kolkata, Lucknow, Shimla; library of 8,000 vols; Chair. ASHOK VAJPAYI; Vice-Chair. K. R. SUBBANNA; publs *Lalit Kala Ancient* (2 a year), *Lalit Kala Contemporary*

(4 a year), *Samkaleen Kala* (4 a year, in Hindi).

Sangeet Natak Akademi (National Academy of Music, Dance and Drama): Rabindra Bhavan, Feroze Shah Rd, New Delhi 110001; tel. (11) 23387246; e-mail mail@sangeetnatak.gov.in; internet www.sangeetnatak.org; f. 1952; preserves and develops the performing arts of India; documents the performing arts through films, tapes and photographs; maintains a museum of musical instruments, costumes, masks and puppets; offers financial assistance to music, dance and theatre institutions; administers the Jawaharlal Nehru Manipur Dance Academy (Imphal), Kathak Kendra (New Delhi), and Rabindra Rangashala (New Delhi); conducts festivals, seminars; gives awards and fellowships for outstanding work; 66 mems; library of 20,000 vols and audiovisual library of tapes and discs; Chair. LEELA SAMSON; Vice-Chair. SHANTA SERBJEET SINGH; Sec. JAYANT KASTUAR; publ. *Sangeet Natak Akademi Journal* (4 a year).

HISTORY, GEOGRAPHY AND ARCHAEOLOGY

Bharata Itihasa Samshodhaka Mandala: 1321 Sadashiva Peth, Pune 411030, Maharashtra; tel. (20) 24472581; f. 1910; collects, conserves and publishes historical materials; colln of 3,500 coins; 33,000 Persian, Sanskrit and Marathi MSS; 1.6m. documents, about 1,200 old Indian paintings; 1,000 copperplates, sculptures and other antiquarian objects, museum of paintings; 675 mems; library of 40,000 vols; Pres. (vacant); Chair. Dr S. GOKHALE; Sec. Dr S. M. BHAVE; publs *Journal* (4 a year), *Puraskrita Granthamala*, *Sviya Granthamala Series*.

Geographical Society of India: c/o Dept of Geography, Univ. of Calcutta, 35 Ballygunge Circular Rd, Kolkata 700019, West Bengal; tel. (33) 65500698; e-mail geosocietyindia@gmail.com; internet geographicalsocietyofindia.org; f. 1933, fmrly Calcutta Geographical Society, present name and status 1951; geographical lectures, seminars, excursions and exhibitions; encouragement of geographical research and training; 750 mems; library of 14,200 vols, 5,709 journals; Pres. Dr PRITHVISH NAG; Vice-Pres. Prof. MANATOSH KR. BANDYOPADHYAY; Vice-Pres. Prof. PIJUSH KANTI SAHA; Vice-Pres. SUPROVA RAY; Vice-Pres. Dr SUBHASH CH. DATTA; Vice-Pres. (vacant); Hon. Sec. Prof. RANJAN BASU; publ. *Geographical Review of India* (4 a year).

LANGUAGE AND LITERATURE

Academy of Sanskrit Research: Melkote, Mandya Dist. 571431, Karnataka; tel. (8236) 209178; e-mail asrbng@vsnl.com; internet www.sanskritacademy.org; f. 1976, present name and status 1978; promotion and propagation of Sanskrit language, publication of studies and expositions of Sanskrit works, organization of oratorical and recitation competitions, regular lectures and seminars in Sanskrit and Tamil on well-known Sanskrit poets and philosophers by eminent scholars, occasional production of Sanskrit drama; library of 28,000 vols on philosophy, literature, culture, Vedanta, aesthetics, agriculture, etc.; 200 mems; Dir and Jt Sec. Prof. BHASHYAM SWAMY; Registrar S. KUMAR; publ. *Tattvadipah* (2 a year).

Alliance Française in India: 72 Lodi Estate, New Delhi 110003; tel. (11) 43500200; e-mail dgaf@afindia.org; internet www.afindia.org; offers courses and examinations in French language and culture and promotes cultural exchange with France; attached teaching centres in Ahmedabad, Bengaluru, Bhopal, Chandigarh, Chennai, Coimbatore, Hyderabad, Indore, Jaipur, Karikal, Kochi, Kolkata, Madurai, Mahe, Mumbai, Panjim, Pondichery, Pune, Rajkot, Secunderabad, Trivandrum; Coordinator ALAIN RECHNER.

British Council: British High Commission, 17 Kasturba Gandhi Marg, New Delhi 110001; tel. (11) 23711401; e-mail delhi.enquiry@in.britishcouncil.org; internet www.britishcouncil.org/india; teaching centre; offers courses and exams in English language and British culture and promotes cultural exchange with the UK; attached offices in Ahmedabad, Bengaluru, Chandigarh, Chennai, Hyderabad, Kolkata, Mumbai, Pune; library of 30,000 vols; Dir ROB LYNES.

Goethe-Institut Max Müller Bhavan: 3 Kasturba Gandhi Marg, New Delhi 110001; tel. (11) 23329506; e-mail info@delhi.goethe.org; internet www.goethe.de/newdelhi; the 6 brs of the Goethe-Institut in India are named after the German Indologist Max Müller (1823–1900); offers courses and examinations in German language and culture; promotes cultural exchange with Germany; attached centres in Bengaluru, Chennai, Mumbai, Kolkata and Pune; Dir for S Asia Region HEIKO SIEVERS.

Kendriya Hindi Nideshalaya (Central Hindi Directorate): Min. of Human Resource Devt, Dept of Education, West Block 7, R. K. Puram, New Delhi 110066; tel. (11) 26178454; e-mail aro-chd.edu@nic.in; internet www.hindinideshalaya.nic.in; f. 1960; preparation and publ. of bilingual and trilingual dictionaries of Indian and foreign languages; teaching of Hindi by correspondence courses to Indians and foreigners; extension courses; c. 300 mems; library of 80,000 vols; Dir Prof. Dr K. VIJAY KUMAR; publs *Bhasha* (6 a year), *Sahityamala*, *Varshiki* (1 a year).

Linguistic Society of India: c/o Dept of Linguistics, Deccan College, Pune 411006, Maharashtra; tel. (20) 26698744; e-mail secretaryil@gmail.com; f. 1928; promotes scientific study of language; 700 mems; library of 6,000 vols; Pres. P. BHASKARARAO; Vice-Pres. A. G. NATARAJAN; Sec. K. S. NAGARAJA; publ. *Indian Linguistics* (1 a year).

Madras Literary Society: College Rd, Chennai 600006, Tamil Nadu; tel. (44) 28279666; f. 1812, became Auxiliary of the Royal Asiatic Soc. of Great Britain and Ireland 1830; library of 150,000 vols, incl. 30,000 19th-century edns; Pres. M. GOPALAKRISHNAN; Hon. Sec. U. RAMESH RAO; publs *Madras Journal of Literature and Science*, *Transactions of the Literary Society of Madras*.

Mythic Society: 14/1 Nrupatunga Rd, Bengaluru 560001, Karnataka; tel. (80) 22215034; e-mail themythicsociety@gmail.com; internet mythicsociety.org; f. 1909; promotes study of anthropology, archaeology, art and architecture, culture, epigraphy, folklore, ethnology, history, indology, Karnataka history, literature and allied subjects, mythology, traditions; 400 mems; library of 40,000 vols, incl. spec. collns of Mysore history; Pres. Prof M. K. L. N. SASTRY; Vice-Pres. Dr M. SIVAKUMARASWAMY; Hon. Sec. Dr M. G. NAGARAJ; publ. *Quarterly Journal of the Mythic Society*.

PEN All-India Centre: Theosophy Hall, 40 New Marine Lines, Mumbai 400020, Maharashtra; tel. (22) 22032175; e-mail india.pen@gmail.com; f. 1933; offers platform for readers, writers, people interested in literary arts and culture in general; Pres. Dr DAUJI GUPTA; Sec. RANJIT HOSKOTE (acting); publ. *The Indian PEN* (4 a year).

Sahitya Akademi (National Academy of Letters): Rabindra Bhavan, 35 Ferozeshah Rd, New Delhi 110001; tel. (11) 23386626; e-mail secy@ndb.vsnl.net.in; internet sahitya-akademi.gov.in; f. 1954; devt of Indian literature, coordination of literary activities in the Indian languages and research in Indian languages and literature; publ. of literary works; promotion of cultural exchanges with other countries; awards annual prizes for original works and translations; organizes seminars, symposia and workshops on literary subjects; Gen. Ccl consists of 8 eminent persons in the field of letters elected in their personal capacity, nominees of the Central and State Govts, 20 reps of the univs and 1 rep. of each of the 24 languages of India recognized by the Akademi, and 1 rep. each of the Lalit Kala Akademi, the Sangeet Natak Akademi, the Indian Ccl for Cultural Relations, the Raja Rammohun Roy Library Foundation and the Indian Publishers' Asscns; library of 125,000 vols; Pres. Prof. SUNIL GANGOPADHYAY; Vice-Pres. Dr VISHWANATH PRASAD TIWARI; publs *Indian Literature* (6 a year, in English), *Samakaleena Bharatiya Sahitya* (6 a year, in Hindi), *Sanskrita Pratibha* (2 a year, in Sanskrit).

MEDICINE

All India Ophthalmological Society: Room 111, First Fl., OPD Block, R. P. Centre, All India Institute of Medical Sciences, Ansari Nagar, New Delhi 110029; tel. (11) 26588327; e-mail aiosoffice@yahoo.com; internet www.aios.org; f. 1930; cultivates and promotes the study and practice of ophthalmic sciences; develops social contacts among ophthalmologists; 13,000 mems; Pres. Dr ASHOK GROVER; Pres.-Elect Dr N. S. D. RAJU; Vice-Pres. Dr ANITA PANDA; Hon. Gen. Sec. Dr LALIT VERMA; publ. *Indian Journal of Ophthalmology* (6 a year).

Association of Medical Physicists of India: c/o Radiological Physics and Advisory Div., Bhabha Atomic Research Centre, CT and CRS Bldg, Anushaktinagar, Mumbai 400094, Maharashtra; tel. (22) 24447077; e-mail sdsbarc@gmail.com; internet www.ampi.org.in; f. 1976; promotes application of physics to medical and biological sciences; organizes annual conf., workshops, lectures, awards, research grants, travel fellowships within India; provides forum for medical physicists, radiation oncologists and others interested in this field; 1,607 mems; Pres. Dr KANTA CHHOKRA; Vice-Pres. Dr K. THAYALAN; Sec. Dr SUNIL DUTT SHARMA; publ. *Journal of Medical Physics* (4 a year).

Association of Surgeons of India: 21 Swamy Sivananda Salai, Chepauk, Chennai 600005, Tamil Nadu; tel. (44) 25383459; e-mail asi@md5.vsnl.net.in; internet www.asiindia.org; f. 1938; promotes practice of the art and science of surgery; organizes scientific conferences, workshops etc.; 14,200 mems; library: approx. 12,000 vols; Pres. Dr RAMA KANT; Hon. Sec. Dr R. K. KARWASRA; publ. *Indian Journal of Surgery* (6 a year).

Bombay Medical Union: Blavatsky Lodge Bldg, Grant Rd, Mumbai 400007; tel. (22) 23612880; f. 1883; 250 mems; Pres. Dr U. N. BASTODKAR; Sec. Dr M. K. THACKER.

Federation of Obstetric and Gynaecological Societies of India: Model Residency CHS, Ground Fl., 605 Bapurao Jagtap Marg, Jacob Circle, Mahalaxmi E, Mumbai 400011, Maharashtra; tel. (22) 23021648; e-mail fogsi2007@gmail.com; internet www.fogsi.org; f. 1950; organizes annual congress for exchange of views in various aspects of the subject; organizes workshops on family planning, etc.; medical education programme;

holds periodic int. seminars; 25,000 individual mems, 209 mem. socs; Pres. Dr P. C. MAHAPATRA; Sec.-Gen. and Pres.-Elect Dr P. K. SHAH; publ. *Journal of Obstetrics & Gynaecology of India* (6 a year).

Helminthological Society of India: c/o Prof. Nirupama Agrawal, Dept of Zoology, Lucknow Univ., Lucknow, Uttar Pradesh; e-mail info@helminthologicalsocietyofindia.com; internet www.helminthologicalsocietyofindia.com; Pres. Prof. NIRUPAMA AGARWAL; Treas. Prof. K.C. PANDEY; publ. *Indian Journal of Helminthology* (2 a year).

Indian Cancer Society: 74 Jerbai Wadia Rd, Bhoiwada, Parel, Mumbai 400012, Maharashtra; tel. (22) 24125238; e-mail ics_mumbai@yahoo.com; internet www.indiancancersociety.org; f. 1951; supports cancer research; aids sufferers from cancer, improves facilities for diagnosis, treatment and rehabilitation; educates the public and the medical profession; organizes nat. confs; spreads awareness; brs in Bihar, Delhi, Karnataka, Kolkata, Nagpur, Uttar Pradesh; Chair. Dr NIHAL KAVIRATNE; Vice-Chair. KEWAL NOHRIA; Hon. Sec. and Man. Trustee Dr ARUN P. KURKURE; publ. *Indian Journal of Cancer* (4 a year).

Indian Medical Association: I. M. A. House, Indraprastha Marg, New Delhi 110002; tel. (11) 23370009; e-mail inmedici@vsnl.com; internet www.ima-india.org; f. 1928; promotes and advances medical and allied sciences; represents doctors of modern scientific system of medicine; 178,000 mems; Pres. Dr VINAY AGGARWAL; Pres.-Elect Dr G. K. RAMACHANDRAPPA; Hon. Sec.-Gen. Dr D. R. RAI; publs *Apka Swasthya* (12 a year), *Family Medicine India* (4 a year), *I. M. A. News* (12 a year), *Journal of the Indian Medical Association* (12 a year), *Your Health* (12 a year).

Indian Pharmaceutical Association: Kalina, Santacruz (E), Mumbai 400098, Maharashtra; tel. (22) 26671072; e-mail ipacentre@ipapharma.org; internet www.ipapharma.org; f. 1939; represents fields of the pharmaceutical profession namely industry, regulatory, community pharmacy, hospital pharmacy and education; advises govt on matters of professional importance; organizes training programmes; 10,000 mems; Pres. Dr C. GOPALAKRISHNA MURTY; Chair. for Community Pharmacy Div. and Vice-Pres. RAJ VAIDYA; Chair. for Education Div. and Vice-Pres. T. V. NARAYANA; Chair. for Hospital Pharmacy Div. and Vice-Pres. Dr R. N. GUPTA; Chair. for Industrial Pharmacy Div. and Vice-Pres. KAUSHIK DESAI; Chair. for Regulatory Affairs Div. and Vice-Pres. RAM BANARASE; Hon. Gen. Sec. S. D. JOAG; publs *Indian Journal of Pharmaceutical Sciences* (6 a year), *Pharma Times* (12 a year).

Indian Public Health Association: 110 Chittaranjan Ave, Kolkata 700073, West Bengal; tel. (33) 22573373; e-mail office@iphaonline.org; internet www.iphaonline.org; f. 1956; promotion of public health and allied sciences; 22 state and local brs; holds annual convention, meetings, confs, etc.; organizes training programme on various areas of interest of public health; 6,215 mems; Pres. Dr J. RAVI KUMAR; Sec.-Gen. Dr DIPIKA SUR; Treas. Dr SUBHRA S. BASU; publ. *Indian Journal of Public Health* (4 a year).

Indian Society for Medical Statistics: National Institute of Medical Statistics, Indian Council of Medical Research, Dept of Health Research, Min. of Health and Family Welfare, Govt of India, Ansari Nagar, New Delhi 110029; tel. (11) 26588636; e-mail generalsecretary@isms-india.com; internet www.isms-india.com; f. 1983; contributes to the devt of medical statistics and strengthens the application of statistics in medicine, health and related disciplines; organizes annual confs, refresher courses, symposia; 480 mems; Pres. Prof. T. KRISHNAN; Pres.-Elect Prof. D. K. SUBBAKRISHNA; Gen. Sec. Dr R. J. YADAV.

Indian Society of Anaesthesiologists: 67–8 Shanti Nagar, Kakinada 533003, Andhra Pradesh; e-mail isanhq@gmail.com; internet www.isaweb.in; f. 1947; professional society of anaesthesiologist–physicians of India; conducts programmes, workshops and conference at regional and nat. levels, publishes literature supplements, clinical protocols, patient information brochures; 14,853 mems; Pres. Dr DEEPAK MALVIYA; Vice-Pres. Dr A. S. KAMESWARA RAO; Sec. Dr S. S. C. CHAKRA RAO; publ. *Indian Journal of Anaesthesia* (6 a year).

Medical Council of India: Pocket 14, Sector 8, Dwarka Phase 1, New Delhi 110077; tel. (11) 25367033; e-mail mci@bol.net.in; internet www.mciindia.org; f. 1934; maintenance of uniform standards of medical education; reciprocity in mutual recognition of medical qualifications with other countries; maintenance of Indian Medical Register; Chair. Dr K. K. TALWAR; Sec. Dr SANGEETA SHARMA; publ. *Indian Medical Register*.

National Academy of Medical Sciences: NAMS House, Ansari Nagar, Mahatma Gandhi Marg, New Delhi 110029; tel. (11) 26589289; e-mail nams_aca@yahoo.com; internet www.nams-india.org; f. 1961 as Indian Academy of Medical Sciences, present name 1976; promotes knowledge of medical sciences in India; maintains coordination between medical and other scientific acads, socs, asscns, instns, govt medical and scientific depts and services; 5,780 mems (830 fellows, 4,950 ordinary mems); Pres. Dr K. K. TALWAR; Vice-Pres. Dr C. SRINIVASULU BHASKARAN; Hon. Sec. Dr SANJAY WADHWA; publ. *ANAMS* (1 a year).

Pharmacy Council of India: POB 7020, New Delhi 110002; Combined Councils' Bldg, Kotla Rd, Aiwan-E-Ghalib Marg, New Delhi 110002; tel. (11) 23239184; e-mail pci@ndb.vsnl.net.in; internet pci.nic.in; f. 1949; attached to Min. of Health and Family Welfare; statutory body; sets and maintains educational standards for qualification and registration in pharmacy and coordinates the practice; Pres. Prof. B. SURESH; Vice-Pres. D. CHAKRABORTY; Registrar and Sec. ARCHNA MUDGAL.

NATURAL SCIENCES

General

Indian Academy of Sciences: POB 8005, Bengaluru 560080, Karnataka; C. V. Raman Ave, Sadashivanagar, Bengaluru 560080, Karnataka; tel. (80) 22661200; e-mail office@ias.ernet.in; internet www.ias.ac.in; f. 1934; promotes science in its pure and applied forms; activities incl. publ. of scientific journals and spec. vols, organizing meetings of the fellowship and discussions on important topics, recognizing scientific talent, improvement of science education and supporting issues of concern to the scientific community; 1,115 full individual mems (1010 fellows, 52 hon. fellows, 53 assoc. mems); library of 1,000 vols; Pres. Prof. DIPANKAR CHATTERJI; Sec. Prof. UDAY MAITRA; Sec. Prof. RAGHAVAN VARADARAJAN; Treas. Prof. J. SRINIVASAN; Exec. Sec. G. CHANDRAMOHAN; publs *Bulletin of Materials Science* (6 a year), *Current Science* (24 a year), *Journal of Astrophysics and Astronomy* (4 a year), *Journal of Biosciences* (4 a year), *Journal of Chemical Sciences* (6 a year), *Journal of Earth System Science* (6 a year), *Journal of Genetics* (3 a year), *Pramana–Journal of Physics* (12 a year), *Proceedings–Mathematical Sciences* (4 a year), *Resonance: Journal of Science Education* (12 a year), *Sadhana–Academy Proceedings in Engineering Sciences* (6 a year).

Indian National Science Academy: Bahadur Shah Zafar Marg, New Delhi 110002; tel. (11) 23221931; e-mail esoffice@insa.nic.in; internet www.insaindia.org; f. 1935 as National Institute of Sciences of India, current name adopted 1970; promotes scientific knowledge, coordination between scientific bodies, and safeguards the interests of scientists in India; adhering org. of ICSU; 780 mems (676 fellows, 104 foreign fellows); library of 21,000 vols; Pres. Dr KRISHAN LAL; Vice-Pres. Prof. ALOK BHATTACHARYA; Vice-Pres. Prof. M. L. MUNJAL; Vice-Pres. Prof. N. SATHYAMURTHY; Vice-Pres. Prof. R. RAJARAMAN; Vice-Pres. Prof. S. K. SAIDAPUR; Vice-Pres. Prof. S. S. AGARWAL; publs *Indian Journal of History of Science* (4 a year), *Indian Journal of Pure and Applied Mathematics* (6 a year), *Proceedings of the Indian National Science Academy* (4 a year), *Progress of Science in India*.

Indian Science Congress Association: 14 Dr Biresh Guha St, Kolkata 700017, West Bengal; tel. (33) 22874530; e-mail iscacal@vsnl.net; internet sciencecongress.nic.in; f. 1914; advances and promotes science in India; holds annual congress; 12,000 mems; library of 8,000 vols, 60 periodicals; Gen. Pres. Dr GEETHA BALI; Gen. Pres.-Elect Dr MANMOHAN SINGH; Exec. Sec. Dr AMIT KRISHNA DE; Gen. Sec. for Membership Affairs Dr MANOJ KUMAR CHAKRABARTI; Gen. Sec. for Scientific Activities Dr VIJAY LAXMI SAXENA; publs *Everyman's Science* (4 a year), *Proceedings* (1 a year, in 4 parts).

National Academy of Sciences, India: 5 Lajpatrai Rd, Allahabad 211002, Uttar Pradesh; tel. (532) 2640224; e-mail allahabad.nasi@gmail.com; internet www.nasi.nic.in; f. 1930; promotes research in all brs of science; 4,644 mems (incl. 1,436 fellows, 29 honorary fellows, 84 foreign fellows); Pres. Prof. A. K. SHARMA; Gen. Sec Prof. KRISHNA MISRA; Gen. Sec Prof. JITENDRA PAUL KHURANA; Exec. Sec., CPIO and Vigilance Officer Dr NIRAJ KUMAR; publs *Annual Number* (1 a year), *National Academy of Sciences Letters* (6 a year), *Proceedings* in two sections— *Section A: Physical Sciences, Section B: Biological Sciences* (8 a year).

Biological Sciences

Association of Microbiologists of India: c/o Prof. D. K. Singh, Dept of Zoology, Univ. of Delhi, S Campus, New Delhi 110007; tel. (11) 27667191; e-mail dileepksingh@gmail.com; f. 1938; provides common platform for academicians, researchers, scientists and persons working in different areas of basic and applied microbiology; 2,900 mems (incl. 400 corporate mems); library of 3,000 vols; Pres. Prof. R. C. KUHAD; Pres.-Elect Prof. L. VENKATESWARA RAO; Gen. Sec. Dr T. K. ADHYA; Treas. Dr D. K. SINGH; publ. *Indian Journal of Microbiology* (4 a year).

Bombay Natural History Society (BNHS): Hornbill House, Salim Ali Chowk, Shahid Bhagat Singh Rd, Mumbai 400001, Maharashtra; tel. (22) 22821811; e-mail info@bnhs.org; internet www.bnhs.org; f. 1883; studies natural history, ecology and conservation in Indian sub-continent; research programmes in field zoology; 5,000 mems; library of 22,000 vols, 5,000 journals; Pres. B. G. DESHMUKH; Hon. Sec. Dr ASHOK KOTHARI; Dir Dr ASAD R. RAHMANI; Librarian NIRMALA REDDY; publs *Hornbill* (4 a year), *Journal of Bombay Natural History Society*.

Indian Biophysical Society: c/o Sec., IBS Dept of Chemical Sciences, Tata Institute of Fundamental Research, Homi Bhabha Rd, Colaba, Mumbai 400005, Maharashtra; tel. (22) 22782278; e-mail ibs@tifr.res.in; internet www.tifr.res.in/~ibs; f. 1961; holds seminars, symposia, etc.; 773 mems; Pres. Prof. N. R. JAGANNATHAN; Vice-Pres. Prof. B. JAYARAM; Vice-Pres. Prof. D. CHATTERJI; Vice-Pres. Prof. M. MAITI; Sec. Prof. K. V. R CHARY; publ. *Proceedings* (1 a year).

Indian Botanical Society: c/o Prof. V. P. Singh, Dept of Plant Science, M. J. P Rohil Khund Univ., Bareilly, Uttar Pradesh; internet indianbotsoc.org; f. 1920; Pres. Prof. S. V. S. CHAUHAN; Vice-Pres. Prof. S. R. YADAV; Sec. Prof. V. P. SINGH; publ. *Journal of Indian Botanical Society*.

Indian Phytopathological Society: Div. of Plant Pathology, Indian Agricultural Research Institute, New Delhi 110012; tel. (11) 25848418; e-mail ipsdis@yahoo.com; internet www.ipsdis.org; f. 1947; professional forum for promoting science of phytopathology; focuses on bacteriology, fungal pathology, mycology, nematology, phytoplasmology, virology; holds seminars, symposia, etc.; 2,000 mems; Sec. Dr PRATIBHA SHARMA; publ. *Indian Phytopathology* (4 a year).

Indian Society of Genetics and Plant Breeding: POB 11312, New Delhi 110012; A Block, F–2, First Fl., NASC Complex, D. P. S. Marg, New Delhi 110012; tel. (11) 25843437; e-mail isgpb1941@gmail.com; internet www.isgpb.co.in; f. 1941; 1,850 mems (incl. 900 life mems, 45 foreign mems, 14 hon. fellows); Pres. Dr B. S. DHILLON; Sec. Dr G. P. SINGH; publ. *Indian Journal of Genetics and Plant Breeding* (4 a year).

Marine Biological Association of India: POB 1604, CMFRI Campus, Kochi 682018, Kerala; tel. (484) 2394867; e-mail mail@mbai.org.in; internet www.mbai.org.in; f. 1958; promotes research on marine sciences in the Asia-Pacific region; organizes lectures, symposia and seminars on specific subjects; offers requisite information to research workers and students undertaking research in marine biological sciences; 1,000 mems; Pres. Dr A. GOPALAKRISHNAN; Sec. Dr K. SUNILKUMAR MOHAMED; publs *Journal of the Marine Biological Association of India* (2 a year), *Memoirs* (irregular), *Proceedings* (irregular).

Society of Biological Chemists (India): Indian Institute of Science, Bengaluru 560012, Karnataka; tel. (80) 23601412; e-mail sbcihq@gmail.com; internet www.iisc.ernet.in/sbci; f. 1930; coordinates work of biological chemists in India; organizes symposia and annual meetings; sponsors symposia, seminar and workshops for nat. and int. scientists; 2,500 mems; Pres. Dr V. NAGARAJA; Vice-Pres. Dr UMESH VARSHNEY; Vice-Pres. Dr DHURBAJYOTHI CHATTOPADHYAY; Vice-Pres. Dr SUDHA BHATTACHARYA; publs *Biochemical Reviews* (1 a year), *Indian Journal of Biochemistry and Biophysics*, *Proceedings and Abstracts* (1 a year).

Mathematical Sciences

Allahabad Mathematical Society: 10 C. S. P. Singh Marg, Allahabad 211001, Uttar Pradesh; tel. (532) 2623553; e-mail ams10marg@gmail.com; internet www.amsallahabad.org; f. 1958; furthers the cause of advanced study and research in various brs of mathematics, incl. theoretical physics and mathematical statistics; organizes conferences, lectures, symposia; 100 mems; library of 5,000 vols; Pres. Prof. DHARMA P. GUPTA; publ. *Indian Journal of Mathematics* (2 a year).

Bharata Ganita Parisad: Dept of Mathematics and Astronomy, Univ. of Lucknow, Lucknow 226007, Uttar Pradesh; tel. (522) 2740019; f. 1950, fmrly Banaras Mathematical Society; 475 mems; library of 16,000 vols; Pres. Prof. J. B. SHUKLA; Gen. Sec. Prof. A. NIGAM; publ. *Ganita* (2 a year).

Calcutta Mathematical Society: Asutosh Bhavan, AE–374, Sector I, Salt Lake City, Kolkata 700064, West Bengal; tel. (33) 23378882; e-mail cms@cal2.vsnl.net.in; internet www.calmathsoc.org; f. 1908; lectures, seminars, symposia, workshops in mathematical sciences; research projects sponsored by various funding agencies; 1,050 mems; library of 17,215 vols; Pres. Prof. Dr RAJKUMAR ROYCHOWDHURY; Sec. Prof. Dr SANJOY SEN; publs *Bulletin of the Calcutta Mathematical Society* (6 a year), *Journal of the Calcutta Mathematical Society* (1 a year), *Review Bulletin of the Calcutta Mathematical Society* (2 a year).

Indian Mathematical Society: Dept of Mathematics, Univ. of Pune, Pune 411007, Maharashtra; e-mail sknimbhorkar@gmail.com; internet www.indianmathsociety.org.in; f. 1907 as Analytic Club, present name 1910; promotes mathematical study and research; 1,600 mems; library of 4,000 vols; Pres. Prof. GEETHA SRINIVASA RAO; Gen. Sec. Prof. N. K. THAKARE; Treas. Prof. S. K. NIMBHORKAR; publs *Journal of the Indian Mathematical Society* (4 a year), *Mathematics Student* (4 a year).

Physical Sciences

Astronautical Society of India: ISRO Satellite Centre, Airport Rd, Bengaluru 560017, Karnataka; tel. (80) 25265628; e-mail pati@iiap.ernet.in; internet www.asindia.org; f. 1990; recognizes talented Indian individuals who have made significant contributions in fostering astronautics in India; conducts technical meetings to disseminate technical and other information related to astronautics; 750 mems; Pres. G. MADHAVAN NAIR; Vice-Pres. AVINASH CHANDER; Exec. Sec. V. KOTESWARA RAO; publ. *Memoirs* (irregular).

Electrochemical Society of India: Indian Institute of Science Campus, Bengaluru 560012, Karnataka; tel. (80) 23600977; e-mail ecsocind@gmail.com; internet www.ecsi.in; f. 1964; promotes the science and technology of electrochemistry, electrodeposition and plating, corrosion incl. high-temperature oxidation, electrometallurgy and metal finishing, semi-conductors and electronics, batteries, solid electrolytes, solid state electrochemistry, and protection of metals and materials against environmental attack; 670 mems; library of 4,000 vols; Pres. M. RAVINDRANATH; Sec. Dr G. ANANDA RAO; publ. *Journal* (4 a year).

Indian Chemical Society: 92 Acharya Prafulla Chandra Rd, Kolkata 700009, West Bengal; tel. (33) 23609497; e-mail indi3478@dataone.in; internet indianchemsoc.org; f. 1924; nat. forum for chemists and mems of allied disciplines; 2,000 mems; library of 10,500 vols; Pres. Prof. M. C. CHATTOPADHYAYA; Hon. Sec. Prof. P. L. MAJUMDER; publ. *Journal of Indian Chemical Society* (12 a year).

Optical Society of India: Dept of Applied Optics and Photonics, Applied Physics Bldg, Calcutta Univ., 92 Acharya Prafulla Chandra Rd, Kolkata 700009, West Bengal; tel. (33) 23522411; e-mail info@osiindia.org; internet www.osiindia.org; f. 1965; promotes and diffuses knowledge of all brs of pure and applied optics; organizes seminars, workshops and confs; 700 mems; library of 400 vols; Pres. Prof. B. P. PAL; Vice-Pres. Prof. ANURAG SHARMA; Gen. Sec. Dr KALLOL BHATTACHARYA; publ. *Journal of Optics* (4 a year).

RELIGION, SOCIOLOGY AND ANTHROPOLOGY

Asiatic Society: 1 Park St, Kolkata 700016, West Bengal; tel. (33) 22290779; e-mail asiaticsociety@gmail.com; internet www.asiaticsocietycal.com; f. 1784, fmrly Royal Asiatic Society of Bengal; studies humanities and sciences in India; research on Indology and Oriental studies; public museum exhibiting Asokan Rock Edict, copper plates, sculptures, archival records, 24,000 old coins, 75 oil paintings; 1,292 mems, 64 research fellows; library of 149,000 vols, 47,000 MSS in 26 languages, 80,000 journals; Pres. Prof. BISWANATH BANERJI; Sec. Prof. MIHIR KUMAR CHAKRABARTY; publs *Journal of the Asiatic Society* (4 a year), *Memoirs of the Asiatic Society*.

Asiatic Society of Mumbai: Town Hall, Shahid Bhagat Singh Rd, Mumbai 400001, Maharashtra; tel. (22) 22660956; e-mail asiaticsociety1804@gmail.com; internet www.asiaticsocietymumbai.org; f. 1804 as Bombay Literary Soc., present name 2005; promotes and publishes research in culture, art and literature of Asia and India; investigates and encourages sciences, arts and literature in relation to Asia and India; offers scholarships and fellowships; holds seminars and lectures on current, historical and cultural subjects; 3,365 mems; library of 253,334 vols, 2,847 MSS, 293 printed *pothis*, 11,830 old coins; Chief Patron HE THE GOVERNOR OF MAHARASHTRA; Pres. Dr AROON TIKEKAR; Hon. Sec. V. V. GANPULE; publ. *Journal of Asiatic Society of Mumbai*.

Indian Anthropological Association: Dept of Anthropology, Univ. of Delhi, Delhi 110007; tel. (11) 27667329; e-mail iaadelhi@rediffmail.com; internet www.indiananthropology.org; f. 1964; provides a platform to anthropologists and those working on allied disciplines; promotes study, research and publ. in anthropology; holds seminars, confs; 400 mems; Pres. Prof. Dr S. M. PATNAIK; Gen. Sec. S. K. CHAUDHURY; publs *Directory of Anthropologists in India* (every 4–5 years), *Indian Anthropologist* (2 a year).

Indian Society for Afro-Asian Studies: 297 Sarswati Kunj, Indraprastha Extension, New Delhi 110092; tel. (11) 22722801; f. 1980; analyzes political, economic, social and cultural situation of Afro-Asian countries; 621 mems; Pres. LALIT BHASIN; Sec. Dr DHARAMPAL.

Theosophical Society: Int. HQ, Adyar, Chennai 600020, Tamil Nadu; tel. (44) 24912474; e-mail intl.hq@ts-adyar.org; internet www.ts-adyar.org; f. 1875 in New York, USA, present location 1882; forms a nucleus of universal brotherhood of humanity without distinction of race, creed, sex, caste or colour; encourages the study of comparative religion, philosophy and science; investigates unexplained laws of nature and the powers latent in man; 41,779 mems throughout the world; library: see under Libraries and Archives; Pres. RADHA BURNIER; Vice-Pres. LINDA OLIVEIRA; Sec. KUSUM SATAPATHY; publs *Theosophical Digest* (4 a year), *The Theosophist* (12 a year), *Wake Up India* (4 a year).

TECHNOLOGY

Aeronautical Society of India: 13B, Indraprastha Estate, New Delhi 110002; tel. (11) 23370516; e-mail aerosoc@bol.net.in; internet www.aerosocietyindia.in; f. 1948; promotion and diffusion of knowledge of aeronautical sciences and aircraft engineering; advancement of aeronautical profession; 6,500 mems, 53 corporate mems; library of 4,000 vols; Chief Patron Hon. PRIME MIN. OF INDIA; Pres. Dr VIJAY MALLYA; Pres.-Elect G. M. RAO; Hon. Sec.-Gen. ASHOK BHUSHAN; Sec. YATINDRA KUMAR; publ. *Journal of Aerospace Sciences and Technologies* (4 a year).

Geological, Mining and Metallurgical Society of India: c/o Geology Dept, Univ. of Calcutta, 35 Ballygunge Circular Rd, Kolkata 700019, West Bengal; tel. (33) 24753681; e-mail boses_in@yahoo.com; f. 1924; 315 mems; Pres. Prof. A. K. GHOSH; Jt Sec. SANTANU BOSE; Jt Sec. P. SIKDAR; publ. *Indian Journal of Geology* (4 a year).

India Society of Engineers: 12B Netaji Subhas Rd, Kolkata 700001, West Bengal; tel. (33) 22300105; e-mail contact@indiasocietyofengineers.org; internet www.indiasocietyofengineers.org; f. 1934; 8,000 mems; library of 20,000 vols; Pres. A. C. SINHA; Gen. Sec. D. B. CHOWDHURY; publ. *Science and Engineering* (12 a year, in English).

Indian Ceramic Society: c/o CSIR-Central Glass and Ceramic Research Institute, 196 Raja S. C. Mullick Rd, Jadavpur, Kolkata 700032, West Bengal; tel. (33) 24138878; e-mail incers@cgcri.res.in; internet www.incers.org; f. 1928; promotes advancement of ceramic science, arts and technologies; holds annual sessions, meetings, discussions, symposia, exhibitions; 2,000 mems; Pres. Dr A. K. CHATTOPADHYAY; Vice-Pres. A. K. DE; Hon. Sec. ATANU RANJAN PAL; Hon. Jt Sec. Dr C. D. MADHUSOODANA; Hon. Treas. B. S. GANGULI; publ. *Transactions of the Indian Ceramic Society* (4 a year).

Indian Institute of Metals: Metal House, Plot 13/4, Block AQ, Sector V, Salt Lake City, Kolkata 700091, West Bengal; tel. (33) 23679768; e-mail jcmarwah@yahoo.com; internet www.iim-india.net; f. 1947; chapters based in Ambarnath, Angul, Baroda, Bengaluru, Bhadravati, Bhilai, Bhopal, Bhubaneswar, Bokaro, Burnpur, Chandigarh, Chennai, Chittorgarh, Coimbatore, Delhi, Duburi, Durgapur, Ghatsila, Hazira, Hisar, Howrah, Hyderabad, Ichapur, Jaipur, Jamshedpur, Kalpakkam, Kanpur, Katni, Keonjhar, Kharagpur, Khetrinagar, Kolar Gold Field, Kolkata, Korba, Mumbai, Nagpur, Paloncha, Pune, Raigarh, Ranchi, Roorkee, Rourkela, Salem, Sunabeda, Surathkal, Trichy, Trivandrum, Udaipur, Varanasi, Vijaynagar, Visakhapatnam; 10,000 mems; Pres. M. NARAYANA RAO; Jt Hon. Sec. Dr AMOL A. GOKHALE; Jt Hon. Sec. Dr D DE SARKAR; Sec.-Gen. J. C. MARWAH; publs *IIM Metal News* (6 a year), *Journal of Phase Eqilibria* (6 a year), *Transactions of the Indian Institute of Metals* (6 a year).

Indian National Academy of Engineering (INAE): Sixth Fl., Vishwakarma Bhawan, Shaheed Jeet Singh Marg, New Delhi 110016; tel. (11) 26582635; e-mail inaehq@inae.org; internet www.inae.org; f. 1987; promotes gen. advancement of engineering and technology and related sciences and disciplines; awards professorships, fellowships and scholarships; 666 fellows, 52 foreign fellows; Pres. Dr BALDEV RAJ; Vice-Pres. for Academic, Professional and International Affairs Dr K. V. RAGHAVAN; Vice-Pres. for Fellowships, Awards and Corporate Communication Prof. PREM KRISHNA; Vice-Pres. for Finance and Establishment Dr M. J. ZARABI.

Indian Society of Mechanical Engineers (ISME): Engineering Today Corporate Bldg, Professional Service Centre, Plot No 23-B, Meera Road, Devaraj Nagar, Selaiyur, Chennai 600073, Tamil Nadu; tel. (11) 26311259; e-mail info@ismeindia.com; internet www.ismeindia.com; f. 1975; 480 mems; Pres. Prof. G. S. SEKHON; Sec. Dr S. G. DESHMUKH; publs *Journal of Engineering Design* (4 a year), *Journal of Engineering Production* (4 a year), *Journal of Thermal Engineering* (4 a year).

Institution of Electronics and Telecommunication Engineers (IETE): 2 Institutional Area, Lodhi Rd, New Delhi 110003; tel. (11) 43538821; e-mail sec.gen@iete.org; internet www.iete.org; f. 1953; promotes advancement of science and technology of electronics, telecommunication, information technology; 69,000 mems; Pres. Dr SURENDRA PAL; Vice-Pres. M. L. GUPTA; Vice-Pres. V. APPAKUTTY; Vice-Pres. Prof. Dr M. BASAVARAJ; Sec.-Gen. S. R. AGGARWAL; publs *IETE Journal of Education* (4 a year), *IETE Journal of Research* (6 a year), *IETE Technical Review* (6 a year).

Institution of Engineers (India): 8 Gokhale Rd, Kolkata 700020, West Bengal; tel. (33) 22238230; e-mail sdg@ieindia.org; internet www.ieindia.org; f. 1920; engineering professional soc. in India imparting non-formal engineering education; inc. by Royal Charter 1935; 94 centres; 60 libraries; over 500,000 mems; Pres. G. PRABHAKAR; Sec. and Dir-Gen. R. K. SANAN; publs *Divisional Journals* (12 a year, 15 engineering journals), *IEI News* (12 a year), *Inter-Disciplinary* (2 a year), *Technorama* (3 a year).

Mineralogical Society of India: Dept of Geology, Univ. of Mysore, Manasa Gangothri, Mysore 570006, Karnataka; tel. (821) 2514144; e-mail msimys@googlemail.com; f. 1959; advances knowledge of crystallography, mineralogy, petrology, etc., by means of research and by holding confs, meetings, discussions; 400 mems; library of 1,500 vols; Chair. C. NAGANNA; Sec. C. SRIKANTAPPA; publ. *The Indian Mineralogist*.

Systems Society of India: IT Centre, Dayalbagh Educational Institute, New Delhi Campus, Model School, Soami Nagar, New Delhi 110017; e-mail deivishalsahni@rediffmail.com; internet www.sysi.org; f. 1981; nat. professional org. for systems science and engineering; numerous chapters incl. Agra, Aligarh, Bengaluru, Chandigarh, Chennai, Hyderabad, Jaipur, Kanpur, Kharagpur, Kozhikkode, Lucknow, Ludhiana, Manipal, New Delhi, Secunderabad, Sikkim, Thiruvananthapuram, Vellore, Visakhapatnam; 1,800 mems; Pres. Prof. PREM KUMAR KALRA; Vice-Pres. Prof. D. ANAND RAO; Vice-Pres. Prof. SIDDHARTHA MUKHOPADHYAY; Sec. Dr VISHAL SAHNI; publ. *Journal of Systems Science and Engineering* (2 a year).

Research Institutes

GENERAL

Council of Scientific and Industrial Research: Anusandhan Bhawan, 2 Rafi Marg, New Delhi 110001; tel. (11) 23711251; e-mail itweb@csir.res.in; internet www.csir.res.in; f. 1942; attached to Min. of Science and Technology; provides scientific, industrial research and devt; library of 20,000 vols; Pres. PRIME MIN. OF INDIA; Vice-Pres. VILASRAO DESHMUKH; Dir-Gen. Prof. SAMIR K. BRAHMACHARI; publ. *Technical Manpower Bulletin* (12 a year).

Attached Research Institutes:

Advance Material and Process Research Institute: Near Habibganj Naka, Hoshangabad Rd, Bhopal 462024; tel. (755) 2457105; e-mail ampriinfo@ampri.res.in; internet www.ampri.res.in; f. 1981 as Regional Research Laboratory, present name 2007; research and devt on minerals and materials with particular focus on aluminium; activities categorized under lightweight materials, nanostructured materials, smart and functional materials, waste to wealth; Dir Prof. Dr B. K. MISHRA.

Central Building Research Institute: Roorkee 247667, Uttarakhand; tel. (1332) 272243; e-mail director@cbri.res.in; internet www.cbri.res.in; f. 1947; research and devt in all aspects of building science and technology; work divided into 4 areas: shelter planning, building materials, structural and foundations engineering, disaster mitigation incl. fire engineering; library of 44,778 vols; Dir Dr S. K. BHATTACHARYYA; publ. *Bhavanika* (4 a year, in Hindi).

Central Drug Research Institute: Chattar Manzil Palace, M. G. Marg, Lucknow 226001, Uttar Pradesh; tel. (522) 2612411; e-mail director@cdri.res.in; internet www.cdriindia.org; f. 1951; biochemical, molecular biological, pharmacological, chemical, microbiological, endocrinological, biophysical, parasitological and biomedical research; drug discovery and devt; library of 21,300 vols; Dir Dr TUSHAR KANTI CHAKRABORTY; publs *Drugs and Pharmaceuticals Industry Highlights* (12 a year), *Drugs and Pharmaceuticals Current R & D Highlights* (4 a year), *Ocean Drugs Alert* (4 a year).

Central Electrochemical Research Institute: Karaikudi 630006, Tamil Nadu; tel. (4565) 227550; e-mail director.cecri@gmail.com; internet www.cecri.res.in; f. 1948; electrochemical and allied research; regional centres in Chennai, Mandapam, Tuticorin; library of 31,755 vols; Dir Dr VIJAYAMOHANAN K. PILLAI (acting).

Central Electronics Engineering Research Institute: Pilani, 333031, Rajasthan; tel. (1596) 242111; e-mail chandra@ceeri.ernet.in; internet www.ceeri.res.in; f. 1953; design and construction of electronic equipment, components and test equipment; research in electronic devices and systems; major research and devt programmes incl. areas such as microwave tubes, semiconductor devices; electronics systems; Dir Dr CHANDRA SHEKHAR; publ. *CEERI News* (4 a year).

Central Food Technological Research Institute: Mysore 570020, Karnataka; tel. (821) 2515910; e-mail iandp@cftri.res.in; internet cftri.com; f. 1950; generates, applies knowledge of food science and food technology for optimal conservation and utilisation of food resources; promotes devt of food industry; library of 36,300 vols; Dir Dr G. VENKATESWARA RAO (acting); publs *Food Digest* (4 a year), *Food Patents* (4 a year), *Food Technology Abstracts* (12 a year).

Central Glass and Ceramic Research Institute: 196 Raja S. C. Mullick Rd, Kolkata 700032, West Bengal; tel. (33) 24735829; e-mail director@cgcri.res.in; internet www.cgcri.res.in; f. 1950; fundamental and applied research on special kinds of glass, ceramics, sol-gel, refractories, ceramic coatings, composites and allied areas; library of 25,000 vols; Dir Prof. INDRANIL MANNA.

Central Institute of Medicinal and Aromatic Plants: PO–CIMAP, Lucknow 226015, Uttar Pradesh; tel. (522) 2359623; e-mail director@cimap.res.in; internet www.cimap.res.in; f. 1959 as Central Indian Medicinal Plants Organisation; coordination of activities in the devt of cultivation and use of medicinal and aromatic plants on organized basis; research in biological and chemical sciences;

research centres at Bengaluru, Hyderabad, Pantnagar, Purara; library of 2,688 vols; Dir Dr CHANDRA SHEKHAR NAUTIYAL; publs *Farm Bulletin* (irregular), *Journal of Medicinal and Aromatic Plant Sciences (JMAPS)* (4 a year), *Yatharth* (4 a year).

Central Institute of Mining and Fuel Research: Barwa Rd, Dhanbad 826001, Jharkhand; tel. (326) 2296023; e-mail dcmrips@yahoo.co.in; internet www.cimfr.nic.in; f. by merger of Central Fuel Research Institute (f. 1946) and Central Mining Research Institute (f. 1956); research on coal, lignite, allied subjects and other sources of fuel; environmental management and waste utilization; library of 35,000 vols; Dir Dr AMALENDU SINHA; publ. *Fuel Science and Technology* (4 a year).

Central Leather Research Institute: Adyar, Chennai 600020, Tamil Nadu; tel. (44) 24915238; e-mail clrim@vsnl.com; internet www.clri.org; f. 1948; activities incl. education, research, training, testing, designing, forecasting, planning, social empowerment in science and technology relating to leather; leather processing, creative designing of leather products; library of 46,000 vols, 150 periodicals; Dir Prof. ASIT BARAN MANDAL; publ. *Leather Science Abstract Services* (12 a year).

Central Mechanical Engineering Research Institute: Mahatma Gandhi Ave, Durgapur 713209, West Bengal; tel. (343) 2546818; e-mail director@cmeri.res.in; internet www.cmeri.org; f. 1958; research and devt areas incl. energy and processing plants, farm machinery and post-harvesting technology, life enhancement studies, mechanical design and manufacturing technology, rapid prototyping and tooling, robotics and mechatronics; library of 60,000 vols; Dir Dr S. N. MAITY.

Central Road Research Institute: PO CRRI, Delhi–Mathura Rd, New Delhi 110025; tel. (11) 26848917; e-mail director.crri@nic.in; internet www.crridom.gov.in; f. 1952; research and devt in bridges and instrumentation engineering, geotechnical engineering, pavement engineering and materials, planning and management, road devt, traffic engineering and road safety, transportation planning and environment; library of 55,017 vols, 150 periodicals, 655 microforms, 688 maps; Dir Dr S. GANGOPADHYAY; publs *CRRI Road Abstracts* (4 a year), *Highway Documentation* (12 a year).

Central Salt and Marine Chemicals Research Institute: Gijubhai Badheka Marg, Bhavnagar 364021, Gujarat; tel. (278) 2567760; e-mail salt@csmcri.org; internet www.csmcri.org; f. 1954 as Central Salt Research Institute; preparation of salt, magnesium compounds, bromine and bromides; cultivation and use of marine algae; desalination of water by solar stills, electrodialysis and reverse osmosis, waste water treatment using membrane processes, wasteland research; library of 48,000 vols; Dir Dr P. K. GHOSH.

Central Scientific Instruments Organization: Sector 30, Chandigarh 160030; tel. (172) 2657190; e-mail drpawankapur@yahoo.com; internet www.csio.res.in; f. 1959; research, design, devt, repair and maintenance of scientific and industrial instruments; technical training and diploma courses in instrument technology; library of 38,700 vols, 180 periodicals; Dir Dr PAWAN KAPUR (acting); publ. *Communications in Instrumentation* (4 a year).

Centre for Cellular and Molecular Biology: Habsiguda, Uppal Rd, Hyderabad 500007, Andhra Pradesh; tel. (40) 27160222; e-mail director@ccmb.res.in; internet ccmb.res.in; f. 1977; research in frontier areas and multi-disciplinary areas of modern biology; devt of biochemical and biotechnology in India; Dir Dr CH. MOHAN RAO; publ. *CCMB Highlights*.

Indian Institute of Chemical Biology: 4 Raja S. C. Mullick Rd, Kolkata 700032, West Bengal; tel. (33) 24730492; e-mail director@iicb.res.in; internet www.iicb.res.in; f. 1935 as Indian Institute of Medical Research, present name 1956; solution of medical problems through fundamental and applied research in the basic biological sciences, with emphasis on projects bearing directly on the country's current biological and medical needs; library of 46,355 vols, 190 journals; Dir Prof. SIDDHARTHA ROY (acting).

Indian Institute of Chemical Technology: Uppal Rd, Hyderabad 500607, Andhra Pradesh; tel. (40) 27193030; e-mail yadav@iict.res.in; internet www.iictindia.org; f. 1944 as Central Laboratories for Scientific and Industrial Research, present status 1956, present name 1989; agrochemicals, biotechnology, chemical engineering, coal, gas and energy, drugs and intermediates, inorganic chemicals and materials, natural products chemistry, organic coatings and polymers, design engineering of chemical plant, fluoroorganics, inorganic and physical chemistry (catalysis and material science), lipid sciences and technology, oils and fats, speciality and fine chemicals; library of 40,000 vols, 500 periodicals; Dir Dr J. S. YADAV.

Indian Institute of Integrative Medicine: POB 3, Canal Rd, Jammu 180001, Jammu and Kashmir; tel. (191) 2569111; e-mail director@iiim.res.in; internet iiim.res.in; f. 1941 as Drug Research Laboratory, present name and status 2005; research and devt on Bioprospecting of plant and microbial resources for genes and natural molecules for drug devt; natural product chemistry; chemical biology; fermentation and enzyme technology, molecular biology and gene cloning; metabolic pathway engineering; cultivation and utilization of drugs and essential oil bearing plants; chemical engineering and design backup for packaging of technologies; library of 43,873 vols; Dir Dr RAM A. VISHWAKARMA.

Indian Institute of Petroleum: PO IIP, Mohkampur, Dehradun 248005, Uttarakhand; tel. (135) 2660113; e-mail info@iip.res.in; f. 1960; research and devt in the field of petroleum, natural gas, petrochemicals and use of petroleum products; trains technical personnel; assists Bureau of Indian Standards in framing standards for petroleum products; patents inspection centre of the Indian Patents Office and is open to the public for studying patent specifications; library of 15,000 vols, 14,000 periodicals; Dir Dr M. O. GARG; publ. *Vikalp* (4 a year).

Indian Institute of Toxicology Research: POB 80, Mahatma Gandhi Marg, Lucknow 226001, Uttar Pradesh; tel. (522) 2613357; e-mail director@iitrindia.org; internet www.iitrindia.org; f. 1965, fmrly Industrial Toxicology Research Centre; studies the effects of industrial pollution; research groups incl. environmental toxicology, food, drug and chemical toxicology, nanomaterial toxicology, regulatory toxicology, systems toxicology and health risk assessment; library of 8,342 vols, 13,842 periodicals; Dir Dr K. C. GUPTA; publ. *Vishvigyan Sandesh*.

Institute of Himalayan Bioresource Technology: POB 6, Palampur, 176061, Himachal Pradesh; tel. (1894) 230411; e-mail director@ihbt.res.in; internet ihbt.res.in; f. 1983; biodiversity conservation, tea husbandry and manufacture, agrotechnology, processing and post-harvest technologies for floriculture, aromatic and herbal plants; Dir Dr P. S. AHUJA.

Institute of Microbial Technology: Sector 39A, Chandigarh 160036; tel. (172) 2690785; e-mail director@imtech.res.in; internet imtech.res.in; f. 1984; research and devt in biosensors and nanotechnology, bio-computing and mathematical modeling, biochemical engineering, cell biology and immunology, genetic engineering and microbiology, protein science and engineering, immunology and fermentation technology, microbial biodiversity; library of 15,809 vols; Dir Dr GIRISH SAHNI.

Institute of Minerals and Materials Technology: Bhubaneshwar, 751013, Orissa; tel. (674) 2581126; e-mail bkm@immt.res.in; internet www.immt.res.in; f. 1964 fmrly Regional Research Laboratory, Bhubaneswar; research in problems relating to minerals and materials resources and technology; conducts oriented programmes in mining and mineral/bio-mineral processing, metal extraction and materials characterization, process engineering, industrial waste management, pollution monitoring and control, marine and forest products devt, utilization of medicinal and aromatic plants and appropriate technologies for society devt; library of 13,265 vols, 16,232 vols of bound journals; Dir Prof. B. K. MISHRA.

National Aerospace Laboratories: PB 1779, Bengaluru 560017, Karnataka; tel. (80) 25273351; e-mail mns@nal.res.in; internet www.nal.res.in; f. 1959 as National Aeronautical Laboratory in New Delhi, present location 1960, present name 1993; research and devt in aircraft design, testing and operation; supports nat. aerospace programmes; library of 110,000 vols; Dir Dr A. R. UPADHYA.

National Botanical Research Institute: Rana Pratap Marg, Lucknow 226001, Uttar Pradesh; tel. (522) 2297800; e-mail director@nbri.res.in; f. 1953; research into economic botany; colln, introduction, propagation and improvement of ornamental and economic plants; 520 mems; library of 53,414 vols; Dir Dr C. S. NAUTIYAL; publ. *Applied Botany Abstracts* (4 a year).

National Chemical Laboratory: Dr Homi Bhabha Rd, Pune 411008, Maharashtra; tel. (20) 25902000; e-mail director@ncl.res.in; internet www.ncl-india.org; f. 1950; research areas incl. biochemical sciences, catalysis, chemical engineering, materials chemistry, organic chemistry, polymer science, process devt; library of 138,452 vols; Dir Dr SOURAV PAL.

National Environmental Engineering Research Institute: Nehru Marg, Nagpur 440020, Maharashtra; tel. (712) 2249885; e-mail director@neeri.res.in; internet www.neeri.res.in; f. 1958 as Central Public Health Engineering Research Institute, present name 1974; research and devt in environmental monitoring, environmental biotechnology, solid and hazardous waste management, environmental systems design, modelling and optimization, air and water pollution control, sewage and industrial wastewater treatment, instrumentation and environmental impact studies; library of 46,500 vols, journals, reports, conference proceedings, CDs and audiovisual films; 200 int. and nat. peer-reviewed current periodicals; online access to 3,000 scientific and technical journals; Dir Dr SATISH R. WATE; publs *Journal of Environmental Science and Engineering* (4 a year), *Paryavaran Patrika* (2 a year, in Hindi).

National Geophysical Research Institute: Uppal Rd, Hyderabad 500606, Andhra Pradesh; tel. (40) 23434700; e-mail information@ngri.res.in; internet www.ngri.org.in; f. 1961; basic and applied research into mineral exploration and investigation of the Earth's interior through seismic, geomagnetic, electric, geochemical and paleogeophysical studies; library of 19,173 vols, 13,895 bound vols of journals, 120 subscribed journals; Dir Dr Y. J. BHASKAR RAO.

National Institute for Interdisciplinary Science and Technology: Thiruvananthapuram 695019, Kerala; tel. (471) 2515220; e-mail director@niist.res.in; internet www.niist.res.in; f. 1975, fmrly Regional Research Laboratory, present name 2007; research areas incl. agroprocessing, biotechnology, chemical sciences, environmental technology, materials and minerals, process engineering; Dir Dr SURESH DAS.

National Institute of Oceanography: Dona Paula, 403004, Goa; tel. (832) 2450275; e-mail ocean@nio.org; internet www.nio.org; f. 1966; investigates marine instrumentation and archaeology and physical, chemical, geological and biological oceanography; functions as the Nat. Oceanographic Data Centre; research on marine geophysics and instrumentation; maintenance of data pertaining to the Indian Ocean at Planning and Data Div.; regional centres in Kochi, Mumbai, Visakhapatnam; library of 35,000 vols, 20,000 vols of journals; Dir Dr S. R. SHETYE.

National Institute of Science, Technology and Development Studies: Pusa Gate, K. S. Krishnan Marg, New Delhi 110012; tel. (11) 25846064; e-mail director@nistads.res.in; internet www.nistads.res.in; f. 1980, present name 1981; research on technological and social change, resource planning and use for regional devt; library of 20,138 vols, 250 periodicals, 2,000 social science journals; Dir Dr P. BANERJEE (acting); publ. *CLOSS* (4 a year).

National Metallurgical Laboratory: Jamshedpur 831007, Jharkhand; tel. (657) 2345000; e-mail director@nmlindia.org; internet www.nmlindia.org; f. 1950; research and devt areas incl. applied and analytical chemistry, energy and environment, extractive metallurgy, materials engineering, materials evaluation, mineral processing, surface engineering; library of 43,875 vols; Dir Dr S. SRIKANTH; publ. *Journal of Metallurgy and Materials Science*.

National Physical Laboratory: Dr K. S. Krishnan Marg, New Delhi 110012; tel. (11) 45609212; e-mail root@nplindia.org; internet www.nplindia.org; f. 1950; fundamental and applied research in physics; maintenance of standards; testing and calibration of equipment; library of 109,000 vols; Dir Prof. R. C. BUDHANI; publs *Ionospheric Data* (4 a year), *Sameeksha* (4 a year).

North-East Institute of Science and Technology: Jorhat 785006, Assam; tel. (376) 2370121; e-mail director@rrljorhat.res.in; internet www.neist.res.in; f. 1961; research into coal, petroleum, pulp and paper, natural product chemistry, cement, drugs and pharmaceuticals, synthetic organic chemistry, essential oils and medicinal plants, general and earthquake engineering, biochemistry, biotechnology, material science, building materials, soil engineering, testing and analysis; library of 24,500 books, 22,000 back vols and standards, patents, reports and theses; Dir Dr P. G. RAO; publs *Infowatch* (52 a year), *Bioinformation up to date* (12 a year), *NEIST Highlights* (1 a year), *NEIST Jorhat Technologies* (irregular), *NEIST News* (6 a year).

Structural Engineering Research Centre: CSIR Campus, Taramani, Chennai 600113, Tamil Nadu; tel. (44) 22549124; e-mail director@sercm.org; internet www.serc.res.in; f. 1965; wind engineering and experimentation and earthquake engineering; structural health monitoring and evaluation; forensic analysis; metal structure behaviour, transmission line towers and analysis design and testing; computational structural mechanics; sustainable materials and composites and structural engineering construction and technology; library of 13,500 vols, 146 periodicals; Dir Dr NAGESH R. IYER; publ. *Journal of Structural Engineering* (6 a year).

Structural Engineering Research Centre: Central Govt Enclave, POB 10, Ghaziabad 201002, Uttar Pradesh; tel. (575) 2712967; e-mail root@cssercg.ren.nic.in; f. 1965; research into various aspects of structural engineering, incl. problems connected with bridges and long-span structures and high-rise bldgs, natural disaster mitigations and materials science; library of 8,500 vols; Dir V. K. GHANEKAR; publ. *Journal* (4 a year).

Iqbal Institute: Hazratbal, Srinagar 190006, Jammu and Kashmir; tel. (194) 2410201; f. 1977; attached to Univ. of Kashmir; Dir Prof. BASHIR AHMAD NAHVI.

Motilal Nehru Institute of Research & Business Administration (MONIRBA): Chatham Lines Campus, Allahabad, Uttar Pradesh; tel. (532) 2250840; e-mail info@monirba.com; internet www.monirba.com; f. 1965; attached to Univ. of Allahabad; research in management education; offers postgraduate course in management; library of 13,000 vols; Dir Prof. ALOK SRIVASTAV.

AGRICULTURE, FISHERIES AND VETERINARY SCIENCE

Agro-Economic Research Centre: Visva-Bharati Univ., PO Santiniketan 731235, West Bengal; tel. (3463) 252751; e-mail debashis.sarkar@visva-bharati.ac.in; f. 1954, present status 1995; conducts research in agricultural economics; library of 6,000 vols; Dir DEBASHIS SARKAR.

Central Arid Zone Research Institute: Jodhpur 342003, Rajasthan; tel. (291) 2786788; e-mail director@cazri.res.in; internet www.cazri.res.in; f. 1952 as Desert Afforestation Station, present name and status 1959; divs of agricultural engineering for arid production systems, integrated land use management and farming systems, livestock production systems and range management, natural resources and environment, plant improvement, propagation and pest management, training and production economics, transfer of technology; regional research stations in Pali, Bikaner, Jaisalmer, Bhuj; library of 21,716 vols, 56,500 journals, 2,141 reprints; Dir Dr M. M. ROY; publs *Annals of Arid Zone* (4 a year), *DEN News* (4 a year).

Central Inland Fisheries Research Institute: Monirampur (Post), Barrackpore, Kolkata 700120, West Bengal; tel. (33) 25921190; e-mail cifri@vsnl.com; internet www.cifri.ernet.in; f. 1947 as Central Inland Fisheries Research Station, present status 1967; researches into ecology of rivers, production functions of inland water bodies in the country, reservoirs, flood plain wetlands, estuaries and lakes; appraisal of inland fisheries resources, fisheries management of selected rivers, reservoirs, ox-bow lakes and estuaries; pen culture of carp and prawns; biology of fish and prawns; water pollution studies, conservation and environmental modelling; fish diseases and their control; also conducts information and training programmes; regional offices in Allahabad, Bengaluru, Cochin, Guwahati, Kolkata, Vadodara; library of 9,050 vols, 5,277 vols of bound journals, 4,256 reprints; Dir Prof. Dr ANIL PRAKASH SHARMA; publ. *Indian Fisheries Abstracts* (2 a year).

Central Rice Research Institute: Cuttack, 753006, Orissa; tel. (671) 2367757; e-mail crrictc@ori.nic.in; internet crri.nic.in; f. 1946; attached to Indian Council of Agricultural Research; research on basic and applied aspects of all disciplines of rice culture; library of 12,000 vols, 77,000 periodicals; Dir Dr T. K. ADHYA; publs *Oryza* (4 a year), *Rice Research News* (4 a year).

Central Tobacco Research Institute: Rajahmundry 533105, Andhra Pradesh; tel. (883) 2448995; e-mail ctri@sify.com; internet www.ctri.org.in; f. 1947; attached to Indian Council of Agricultural Research; under the Indian Council of Agric. Research (Ministry of Agriculture and Rural Reconstruction, Govt of India); applied and fundamental research on all types of tobacco grown in India; regional stations at Guntur, Kalavacherla, Vedasandur, Hunsur, Dinhata, Jeelugumilli and Kandukuru; library of 22,000 vols, 159 periodicals; Dir Dr V. KRISHNAMURTHY.

Indian Agricultural Statistics Research Institute: Library Ave, Pusa, New Delhi 110012; tel. (11) 25847121; e-mail director@iasri.res.in; internet www.iasri.res.in; f. 1930, present status 1970, current name adopted 1978; attached to Indian Council of Agricultural Research; research in experimental designs, sample surveys, statistical genetics, statistical genomics, forecasting techniques, econometric techniques; statistical computing; computer applications and bioinformatics; conducts postgraduate courses; in-service training and sponsored nat. and int. training in agricultural statistics, computer application and bioinformatics; provides advisory service to agricultural scientists; provides consultancy service in data processing; develops computer software and information systems; library of 26,486 vols, 8,735 journals, 38 online journals, 9,482 reports, 967 theses; Dir Dr V. K. BHATIA; publs *Agricultural Research Data Book* (1 a year), *Sankhyiki Vimarsh* (1 a year).

Indian Council of Agricultural Research (ICAR): Krishi Bhavan, Dr Rajendra Prasad Rd, New Delhi 110114; tel. (11) 23382629; e-mail dg.icar@nic.in; internet www.icar.org.in; f. 1929, fmrly Imperial Council of Agricultural Research; attached to Min. of Agriculture; promotes agricultural and animal husbandry research in conjunction with state govts, central and state research instns; provides consultancy and information on agriculture, horticulture, resource management, animal sciences, agricultural engineering, fisheries, agricultural extension, agricultural education, home science and agricultural communication; coordinates agricultural research and devt programmes and develops links at nat. and int. level with related orgs to enhance the quality of life of the farming community; research centres; human resource devt in the field of agricultural sciences; oversees numerous agricultural univs nationally; establishes Krishi Vigyan Kendras (farm training centres) responsible for training, research and demonstration of the latest agricultural technology; library of 62,665 vols, 62,080 titles; Dir-Gen. Dr S. AYYAPPAN; Sec. RAJIV MEHRISHI; publs *Fishery Technology*, *Indian Farming* (12 a year), *Indian Horticulture* (6 a year), *Indian Journal of Agricultural Sciences* (12 a year), *Indian Journal of Animal Sciences* (12 a year), *Indian Journal of Fisheries* (4 a year), *Indian Phytopathology* (4 a year), *Journal of Horticultural Sciences*, *Kheti* (12 a year), *Krishi Chayanika* (4 a year), *Phal-Phool* (4 a year).

Indian Council of Forestry Research and Education: PO New Forest, Dehradun 248006, Uttarakhand; tel. (135) 2224537; e-mail sec@icfre.org; internet www.icfre.gov.in; f. 1906; promotes, conducts, coordinates research, education and extension covering all aspects of forestry; regional research institutes and centres at Aizawl, Allahabad, Bengaluru, Coimbatore, Chhindwara, Dehradun, Hyderabad, Jabalpur, Jodhpur, Jorhat, Ranchi, Shimla; library of 160,000 vols, 600 periodicals; Pres. JAYANTHI NATARAJAN; Dir-Gen. Dr V. K. BAHUGUNA; Sec. Dr SUDHANSHU GUPTA; publ. *Indian Forester*.

Indian Plywood Industries Research and Training Institute: POB 2273, Tumkur Rd, Yeshwanthpur PO, Bengaluru 560022, Karnataka; tel. (80) 28394231; e-mail contactus@ipirti.gov.in; internet www.ipirti.gov.in; f. 1962, current name adopted 1992; attached to Min. of Environment and Forests; researches on saw-milling, plywood-manufacturing techniques, preservative treatment of wood and wood-based panels, devt of synthetic and natural adhesives; testing of panel products; training in mechanical wood-processing technology; specialized short-term courses; library of 8,500 vols, 2,618 journals; Chair. VIJAI SHARMA; Dir Dr C. N. PANDEY; Jt Dir Dr S. K. NATH.

Indian Veterinary Research Deemed Institute: Izatnagar 243122, Uttar Pradesh; tel. (581) 2300096; e-mail dirivri@ivri.up.nic.in; internet www.ivri.nic.in; f. 1889, deemed univ. status 1983; campuses at Bengaluru, Bhopal, Izatnagar, Kolkata, Mukteswar, Palampur and Srinagar; research divs of animal biochemistry, animal biotechnology, animal genetics and breeding, animal nutrition, animal physiology, avian diseases, biostatistics, livestock production and management, livestock products technology, poultry science, veterinary bacteriology, veterinary epidemiology, veterinary extension education, veterinary gynaecology and obstetrics, veterinary immunology, veterinary medicine, veterinary parasitology, veterinary pathology, veterinary pharmacology, veterinary public health, veterinary surgery, veterinary virology; library of 250,000 vols, 228 periodicals; Dir and Vice-Chancellor Prof. MAHESH CHANDRA SHARMA (acting); Dir for Academic Affairs Dr V. P. SINGH; Registrar PANKAJ KUMAR (acting).

National Sugar Institute: PO NSI Kalyanpur, Kanpur 208017, Uttar Pradesh; tel. (512) 2570730; e-mail nsikanpur@nic.in; internet nsi.gov.in; f. 1936, current name adopted 1957; attached to Min. of Consumer Affairs, Food and Public Distribution (Dept of Food and Public Distribution); undertakes research, teaching and consultancy activities in all aspects of sugar technology and allied industries; library of 7,858 vols; Dir Prof. DEEPANKAR MUKHERJEE; publs *N.S.I. News*, *Sharkara*.

Rubber Research Institute of India: Rubber Board PO, Kottayam 686009, Kerala; tel. (481) 2353311; e-mail info@rubberboard.org.in; internet www.rubberboard.org.in; f. 1955; promotes devt of the industry; scientific, technological and economic research in improved methods of planting, cultivation, processing and consumption of natural rubber; library of 55,000 vols; Chair. SHEELA THOMAS; Dir for Research Dr JAMES JACOB; publs *Indian Rubber Statistics* (1 a year), *Natural Rubber Research* (2 a year), *Rubber* (12 a year, in Malayalam), *Rubber Growers' Companion* (4 a year), *Rubber Statistical News* (12 a year).

Vasantdada Sugar Institute: Manjari (Bk.), Tal. Haveli, Dist. Pune 412307, Maharashtra; tel. (20) 26902100; e-mail vsilib@vsnl.com; internet www.vsisugar.com; f. 1975, fmrly Deccan Sugar Institute, current name adopted 1989; agronomy, agricultural economics, agricultural engineering, agricultural microbiology, alcohol technology, electronics and computers, entomology, molecular biology and genetic engineering, plant pathology, plant physiology, environmental sciences, sugar instrumentation, sugarcane breeding, sugar engineering, sugar technology, sugar chemistry, soil science, tissue culture; library of 18,200 vols, 115 periodicals; Pres. SHARADCHANDRAJI PAWAR; Dir-Gen. SHIVAJIRAO C. DESHMUKH; Librarian N. S. PATHAN.

BIBLIOGRAPHY, LIBRARY SCIENCE AND MUSEOLOGY

Documentation Research and Training Centre/Indian Statistical Institute: 8th Mile, Mysore Rd, R. V. College PO, Bengaluru 560059, Karnataka; tel. (80) 28483002; e-mail drtc@isibang.ac.in; internet drtc.isibang.ac.in; f. 1962; conducts research in the fields of library science, documentation and information science; trains documentalists; provides an advisory service to industry, academic and research instns; library of 20,000 vols; Head Prof. A. R. D. PRASAD; publ. *DRTC Annual Seminar*.

ECONOMICS, LAW AND POLITICS

Centre for the Study of Law and Governance: New Mehrauli Rd, New Delhi 110067; tel. (11) 26704021; e-mail chair_cslg@jnu.ac.in; internet www.jnu.ac.in/cslg; f. 2001; attached to Jawaharlal Nehru Univ.; multidisciplinary research and teaching on law and governance; library of 3,500 vols; Chair. Prof. AMIT PRAKASH.

Indian Institute of Public Administration: Indraprastha Estate, Ring Rd, New Delhi 110002; tel. (11) 23702400; e-mail contact-us@iipa.org.in; internet www.iipa.org.in; f. 1954; promotes the study of public admin.; dissemination of knowledge, research, training, advisory, consultancy; library: 2m. vols, 350 periodicals; Pres. MOHAMMAD HAMID ANSARI; Chair. T. N. CHATURVEDI; Dir Dr RAKESH HOOJA; Registrar Dr NARESH KUMAR; publs *Documentation in Public Administration* (4 a year), *Indian Journal of Public Administration* (4 a year), *Nagarlok* (4 a year).

Institute for Defence Studies and Analyses: 1 Development Enclave, Near USI, Rao Tula Ram Marg, New Delhi 110010; tel. (11) 26717983; e-mail idsa_delhi@hotmail.com; internet www.idsa.in; f. 1965; researches on nat. security, undertakes study on methods of warfare, strategy, disarmament and int. relations; library of 56,000 vols, 15,000 journals, 1,500 maps; Pres. A. K. ANTONY; Dir-Gen. ARVIND GUPTA; publs *CBW Magazine*, *Journal of Defence Studies* (4 a year), *Strategic Analysis* (6 a year), *Strategic Digest* (12 a year).

Institute for Social and Economic Change: Nagarabhavi, Bengaluru 560072, Karnataka; tel. (80) 23217010; e-mail director@isec.ac.in; internet www.isec.ac.in; f. 1972; social and economic devt in India; library of 121,000 vols of books, reports and bound periodicals, 300 periodicals; Pres. THE GOV. OF KARNATAKA; Dir Dr R. S. DESHPANDE; Registrar R. NARAYANAN; publ. *Journal of Social and Economic Development* (2 a year).

Madras Institute of Development Studies: 79 Second Main Rd, Gandhinagar, Adyar, Chennai 600020, Tamil Nadu; tel. (44) 24412589; e-mail office@mids.ac.in; internet www.mids.ac.in; f. 1971; contributes to economic and social devt of Tamil Nadu State and India; undertakes studies and research in micro-devt problems; aims at upgrading economic research in S Indian univs through research methodology courses and studies; fosters inter-univ. cooperation of S states and promotes inter-disciplinary research; recognized by Univ. of Madras for PhD courses; library of 56,500 vols; Chair. Prof. R. RADHAKRISHNA; Dir Prof. R MARIA SALETH; publ. *Review of Development and Change* (2 a year).

National Council of Applied Economic Research: Parisila Bhavan, 11 Indraprastha Estate, New Delhi 110002; tel. (11) 23379861; e-mail infor@ncaer.org; internet www.ncaer.org; f. 1956; autonomous research org.; studies economic problems for govt, int. orgs and private business; library of 87,000 vols, 400 periodicals, microfiche colln of census of India 1872–1951, CD databases; Pres. NANDAN M. NILEKANI; Vice-Pres. M. S. VERMA; Sec. Dr JATINDER S. BEDI; Dir-Gen. Dr SHEKHAR SHAH; publs *Artha Suchi* (4 a year), *Macrotrack* (12 a year), *Margin—The Journal of Applied Economic Research* (4 a year).

National Productivity Council: Utpadakta Bhavan, 5–6 Institutional Area, Lodhi Rd, New Delhi 110003; tel. (11) 24690331; e-mail info@npcindia.org; internet www.npcindia.org; f. 1958; promotes productivity culture in India; helps to increase productivity in every sector of the nat. economy; regional offices at Bengaluru, Bhubaneshwar, Bhopal, Chandigarh, Chennai, Gandhi Nagar, Guwahati, Hyderabad, Jaipur, Kanpur, Kolkata, Mumbai, Patna; library of 30,000 vols, 80 journals; Chair. R. P. SINGH; Dir-Gen. N. C. VASUDEVAN; publs *Productivity* (4 a year), *Productivity News* (6 a year), *Utpadakta* (12 a year, in Hindi).

Socio-Economic Research Institute: C–19 and C–39 College St Market, Kolkata 700007, West Bengal; tel. (33) 22410775; economics and economic history, sociology and social history, demography focusing on the historical demography of India; Dir Prof. DURGAPRASAD BHATTACHARYA.

EDUCATION

Educational Multimedia Research Centre: Hazratbal, Srinagar 190006, Jammu and Kashmir; tel. (194) 2420610; e-mail office@emmrckashmir.com; internet www.emmrckashmir.com; f. 1992; attached to Univ. of Kashmir; creates educational documentaries; Dir SHAHID RASOOL.

Indian Institute of Advanced Study: Rastrapati Niwas, Shimla 171005, Himachal Pradesh; tel. (177) 2832930; e-mail directoriias@gmail.com; internet www.iias.org; f. 1964; undertakes postdoctoral research, esp. in the humanities and social sciences; functions as Inter-Univ. Centre for Humanities and Social Sciences on behalf of the Univ. Grants Commission of India; library of 190,000 vols, 335 journals; Chair. Prof. BHALCHANDRA MUNGEKAR; Dir Prof. PETER RONALD DE SOUZA; Sec. S. P. THAKUR; publs *Studies in Humanities and Social Sciences* (2 a year), *Summerhill: IIAS Review* (2 a year).

Indian Psychometric and Educational Research Association: Dept of Education, Patna Training College Campus, Patna 800004, Bihar; tel. (612) 50985; f. 1969; promotes, develops, undertakes the study of, and research into psychology, education, statistics, etc.; library of 3,700 vols; Pres. Dr A. K. P. SINHA; Gen. Sec. Dr R. P. SINGH; publ. *Indian Journal of Psychometry and Education*.

FINE AND PERFORMING ARTS

National Institute of Design: Paldi, Ahmedabad 380007, Gujarat; tel. (79) 26623692; e-mail info@nid.edu; internet www.nid.edu; f. 1961; est. by the govt of India as a research, training and service org. in industrial and communication design; library of 23,000 vols, 130 current periodicals, 75,000 slides, 2,044 tapes and records, 1,545 other audiovisual aids and 600 well-designed objects for reference; Chair. SALMAN HAIDAR; Dir PRADYUMNA VYAS; publs *Design and Environment: An Introductory Manual, Design Samvad, Design the Indian Context*.

National Research Laboratory for Conservation of Cultural Property: Sector E/3, Aliganj, Lucknow 226024, Uttar Pradesh; tel. (522) 2335359; e-mail kharbade@yahoo.com; internet www.nrlc.gov.in; f. 1976; develops conservation of cultural property; conducts research into conservation techniques of objects of art and provides technical assistance to museums and related instns; training in conservation for Asian countries sponsored by UNESCO; regional laboratory in Mysore; library of 12,000 vols, 130 periodical subscriptions; Dir Dr B. V. KHARBADE.

HISTORY, GEOGRAPHY AND ARCHAEOLOGY

Archaeological Survey of India: Janpath, New Delhi 110011; tel. (11) 23013574; e-mail directorgeneralasi@gmail.com; internet www.asi.nic.in; f. 1902; attached to Min. of Culture; excavating, preservation, surveying and maintenance of archaeological sites; advanced archaeological training; library of 80,000 vols containing rare material; Dir-Gen. Dr GAUTAM SENGUPTA; publs *Indian Archaeology—A Review* (1 a year), *Memoirs of the Archaeological Survey of India*.

Research Institutes:

Institute of Archaeology: Red Fort, Delhi 110006; tel. (11) 23277107; e-mail dirins.asi@gmail.com; f. 1959 as School of Archaeology, present name and status 1985; research and training in multidisciplinary field of archaeology, antiquarian law, conservation, epigraphy, numismatics, museology; Dir P. B. S. SENGAR.

Indian Council of Historical Research: 35 Ferozeshah Rd, New Delhi 110001; tel. (11) 23382321; e-mail ms_ichr@rediffmail.com; internet www.ichrindia.org; f. 1972; gives grants for doctoral theses, research projects, historical journals, and for bibliographical and documentation works; organizes and supports seminars, workshops and conferences for promotion of historical research; library of 70,000 vols; Chair. Prof. BASUDEV CHATTERJI; publs *Indian Historical Review* (2 a year), *Itihas* (2 a year).

Kashi Prasad Jayaswal Research Institute: Museum Bldg, Patna 800001, Bihar; f. 1904; promotes historical research; library of 31,650 vols; Dir Dr JATA SHANKAR JHA; publ. *Prajna-Bharati*.

Kamarupa Anusandhana Samiti (Assam Research Society): Dighlipukhuri, Guwahati 781001 Assam; tel. (361) 2605267; f. 1912; historical and archaeological research; Pres. Dr BISWANARAYAN SHASTRI; Jt Sec. ATULANANDA GOSWAMI; publ. *Journal of the Assam Research Society* (1 a year).

Karnatak Historical Research Society: Diwan Bahadur Rodda Rd, Dharwad 1, Karnataka; f. 1914; promotes historical research in Karnataka; popularizes the study of history and culture by lectures, slides, exhibitions, celebrations of historical events, excursions, etc.; sections for research in language, culture and Vedic literature, socio-economic problems; library of 3,000 vols; Pres. RAJA S. G. ACHARYA; Chair. Dr P. R. PANCHAMUKHI; Sec A. R. PANCHAMUKHI; Sec G. G. NADGIR; publ. *Karnatak Historical Review* (2 a year, in English and Kannada).

National Atlas and Thematic Mapping Organisation: C. G. O. Complex, 7th Fl., DF–Block, Bidhan Nagar, Kolkata 700064, West Bengal; tel. (33) 22343699; e-mail natmo@vsnl.net; internet www.natmo.gov.in; f. 1956 as National Atlas Organization, present name 1978; cartographical research and preparation of nat. atlas of India; library of 19,000 vols, 500 journals, 78,000 maps, 350 atlases; Dir ASHOK KUMAR MALIK; Jt Dir Dr ASHIM KUMAR DASGUPTA; publs *Agricultural Resources Atlas of India* (in English), *Atlas of Forest Resources* (in English), *Atlas of Kolkata, Atlas of Water Resources, Irrigation Atlas of India* (in English), *National Atlas of India* (English and Hindi edns), *Satellite Atlas of India, Tourist Atlas of India* (in English).

Population Research Centre: Dept of Economics, Univ. of Kashmir, Hazratbal, Srinagar 190006, Jammu and Kashmir; tel. (194) 2427541; e-mail prcsrinagar@rediffmail.com; f. 1985; attached to Univ. of Kashmir; Hon. Dir Prof. A. S. BHAT.

Survey of India: Hathibarkala Estate, Dehradun 248001, Uttarakhand; tel. (135) 2747051; e-mail helpdesk.soi@gov.in; internet www.surveyofindia.gov.in; f. 1767; attached to Dept of Science and Technology; engaged in topographical, geographical and geodetic preparation of large-scale devt project maps; acts as adviser to the govt of India on all survey matters; Surveyor-Gen. Dr SWARNA SUBBA RAO; Additional Surveyor-Gen. Major Gen. ANIL KUMAR.

LANGUAGE AND LITERATURE

Abul Kalam Azad Oriental Research Institute: Public Gardens, Hyderabad 500004, Andhra Pradesh; tel. (40) 23230805; e-mail akaori@gmail.com; internet akaori.tk; f. 1959; research in history, philosophy, culture, Islamic studies and languages; library of 14,000 vols, 133 MSS; Pres. MAHMOOD BIN MUHAMMAD; Vice-Pres. for Academic Board Prof. SYED SIRAJUDDIN; Vice-Pres. for Administration Prof. AFZAL MUHAMMAD; Hon. Sec. and Dir MIR KAMALUDDIN ALI KHAN.

Academy of Sanskrit Research: Mandya Dist., Melkote 571431, Karnataka; tel. (8236) 209178; e-mail asrbng@vsnl.com; internet www.sanskritacademy.org; f. 1976; affiliated to Univ. of Mysore, and Kannada Univ., Hampi; affiliated to Rashtriya Sanskrit Sansthan, New Delhi, for undergraduate, postgraduate and doctoral courses; research and study of Vedas, Agamas and comparative philosophy, with primary focus on Visistadvaita; researches Sanskrit speech synthesis, natural language processing, machine translation, Sanskrit teaching through computer media; collects scientific information available in Sanskrit texts; library of 28,000 vols, 10,500 palm-leaf and paper MSS; Pres. C. N. SEETHARAM; Dir Prof. Dr BHASHYAM SWAMY; Registrar S. KUMAR; Librarian M. S. CHANDRASHEKAR; publ. *Tattva Dipah* (1 a year).

Advanced Centre for Technical Development of Punjabi Language, Literature and Culture: Punjabi Univ., Patiala 147002, Punjab; tel. (175) 3046171; e-mail sangam2005@gmail.com; internet www.learnpunjabi.org; f. 2004; attached to Punjabi Univ.; conducts research and devt in linguistic and computational aspects of Punjabi language and culture; Dir Dr GURPREET SINGH LEHAL.

Anjuman-i-Islam Urdu Research Institute: 92 Dr Dadabhoy Nowroji Rd, Mumbai 400001, Maharashtra; tel. (22) 22651354; e-mail anjuman_uri@rediffmail.com; f. 1948; research in Urdu; PhD in Arabic, Persian, Urdu and Islamic Studies; library of 20,200 vols; Pres. Dr ZAHIR I. KAZI; Dir Dr ABDUS SATTAR DALVI; Librarian SAYED MOHAMMED TAHER; publ. *Nawa-e-Adab* (4 a year).

Bhandarkar Oriental Research Institute: 812 Shivajinagar, Law College Rd, Pune 411004, Maharashtra; tel. (20) 25656932; e-mail bori@dataone.in; internet www.bori.ac.in; f. 1917; Sanskrit, Indological and Oriental studies; library of 135,000 vols, 28,000 MSS; Hon. Sec. Dr MAITREYEE DESHPANDE; publ. *Annals of BORI* (1 a year).

Gujarat Research Society: Dr Madhuri Shah Campus, Ramkrishna Mission Marg, Khar (W), Mumbai 400052, Maharashtra; tel. (22) 26462691; f. 1936; organizes and coordinates research in social and cultural activities; teacher-training; library of 10,000 vols; Pres. K. P. HAZARAT; publ. *Journal* (4 a year).

International Academy of Indian Culture: J 22 Hauz Khas Enclave, New Delhi 110016; tel. (11) 26515800; f. 1935; studies India's artistic, literary and historic relations with other Asian countries; library of 200,000 vols, 40,000 MSS; Dir Prof. LOKESH CHANDRA; publ. *Satapitaka Series*.

K. R. Cama Oriental Institute: 136 Mumbai Samachar Marg, Opposite Lion Gate, Fort, Mumbai 400023, Maharashtra; tel. (22) 22843893; e-mail krcamaoi@hotmail.com; internet www.krcamaorientalinstitute.org; f. 1916; promotes study and research in religions, history and culture of the East; library of 29,372 vols, 2,000 MSS, 219 journals; Pres. MUNCHERJI N. M. CAMA; Jt Hon. Sec. HOMAI N. MODI; Jt Hon. Sec. Dr NAWAZ B. MODY; publ. *Journal of the K. R. Cama Oriental Institute* (1 a year).

Kuppuswami Sastri Research Institute: 84 Thiru V. Kalayanasundaranar Rd, Mylapore, Chennai 600004, Tamil Nadu; tel. (44) 24985320; e-mail ksrinst@gmail.com; internet www.ksri.in; f. 1944; attached to Univ. of Madras; promotion of Oriental learning esp. Indology; lectures, seminars, workshops; library of 60,000 vols, incl. 1,500 palm-leaf MSS; Dir Dr V. KAMESWARI; Sec. B. MADHAVAN; publ. *Journal of Oriental Research* (1 a year).

Mumbai Marathi Granth Sangrahalaya: 172 Mumbai Marathi Granth Sangrahalaya Marg, Naigaon, Dadar, Mumbai 400014, Maharashtra; tel. (22) 24134211; f. 1898; research in Marathi language and literature; library of 185,020 vols; Pres. S. K. PATIL.

Oriental Institute of Indian Languages: Univ. of Mysore, Kautilya Circle, Mysore 570005, Karnataka; tel. (821) 2423136; promotes inter-regional and inter-continental understanding through the study of languages; Dir Dr H. P. DEVAKI.

Oriental Research Institute: Univ. of Mysore, Kautilya Circle, Mysore, 570005, Karnataka; tel. (81) 2420331; e-mail mrcmys@yahoo.com; f. 1891; attached to Univ. of Mysore; colln of 35,000 palm leaf bundles and paper MSS; library of 28,300 vols and 50 periodicals; Dir K. RAJAGOPALACHAR; publ. *Mysore Orientalist* (1 a year).

Sri Venkateswara University Oriental Research Institute: Tirupati 517502, Andhra Pradesh; tel. (877) 2289414; internet www.svuniversity.in; f. 1939; attached to Sri Venkateswara Univ.; given by T. T. DEVASTHANAMS to the Univ. in 1956; researches in language and literature, philosophy and religion, art and archaeology, ancient Indian history and culture; library of 42,000 vols, 16,948 palm-leaf and paper MSS; publs *Sri Venkateswara Oriental Series*, *SVU Oriental Journal*.

Vishveshvaranand Vedic Research Institute: Sadhu Ashram, Hoshiarpur 146021, Punjab; tel. (1882) 223582; e-mail vvrinstitute@yahoo.co.in; f. 1903; academic and cultural studies on Indian literatures and religion; Vedic researches and Sanskrit education; teaching, research and study in Indology; Pres. PUNAM SURI; Dir Prof. I. D. UNIYAL; publs *Research Bulletin* (1 a year, in English), *Vishva Jyoti* (12 a year, in Hindi), *Vishva Sankritam* (cultural research, 4 a year, in Sanskrit).

MEDICINE

Advanced Centre for Treatment, Research and Education in Cancer (ACTREC): Tata Memorial Centre, Kharghar, Navi Mumbai 410210, Maharashtra; tel. (22) 27405000; e-mail mail@actrec.gov.in; internet www.actrec.gov.in; f. 1952 as Cancer Research Centre; basic and clinical research and devt on cancers prevalent in India; library of 5,481 books, 9,642 bound vols of journals, 51 current periodicals; Dir Dr R. SARIN; publ. *Scientific Report* (1 a year).

B. M. Institute of Mental Health: Ashram Rd, near Nehru Bridge, Maninagar, Ahmedabad 380009, Gujarat; tel. (79) 26578256; f. 1951; comprehensive mental health services, teaching, and research; psychiatric clinic for the emotionally disturbed; clinic for children with learning difficulties; occupational therapy and rehabilitation services; speech clinic; postgraduate training in psychodiagnostics and counselling; offers diploma in working with the developmentally handicapped; library of 6,484 vols; Dir Prof. G. T. SWAMY; publ. *Mental Health Review* (1 a year).

Central Leprosy Teaching and Research Institute: Min. of Health and Family Welfare, Govt of India, Chengalpattu 603001, Tamil Nadu; tel. (44) 27426274; e-mail dircltri@dataone.in; f. 1955; WHO regional training centre; basic and applied research in Leprosy; library of 13,000 vols, 33 periodicals; Dir Dr P. K. OOMMEN.

Central Research Institute: Kasauli, Solan 173204, Himachal Pradesh; f. 1905; attached to Min. of Health and Family Welfare; medical research, graduate and postgraduate training, manufacture of biological products; Institute of the Govt of India; library of 30,000 vols; Dir Dr J. SOKHEY.

Haffkine Institute for Training, Research and Testing: Acharya Donde Marg, Parel, Mumbai 400012, Maharashtra; tel. (22) 24160947; e-mail haffkineinstitute@gmail.com; internet www.haffkineinstitute.org; f. 1896 as Plague Research Laboratory, present name 1925; prin. centre of research in infectious diseases, biomedical and allied sciences in India; devt of biologicals, such as vaccines, sera; library of 26,500 back vols of scientific journals, more than 10,500 books, 4,000 microfiches and a CD-ROM colln; Dir Dr ABHAY CHOWDHARY; Asst Dir Dr S. P. VAIDYA.

Indian Brain Research Association: Dept of Biochemistry, Univ. of Calcutta, 35 Ballygunge Circular Rd, Kolkata 700019, West Bengal; f. 1964; library of 2,000 vols; Pres. Prof. J. J. GHOSH; publ. *Brain News* (2 a year).

Indian Council of Medical Research: POB 4911, Ansari Nagar, New Delhi 110029; tel. (11) 26588895; e-mail headquarters@icmr.org.in; internet www.icmr.nic.in; f. 1911 as Indian Research Fund Association, present name 1949; formulates, promotes, coordinates and funds medical research; maintains the National Institute of Nutrition (Hyderabad), National Institute of Virology (Pune), Tuberculosis Research Centre (Chennai), National Institute of Cholera and Enteric Diseases (Kolkata), Institute of Pathology (New Delhi), National Institute of Occupational Health (Ahmedabad), Institute of Immunohaematology (Mumbai), National Institute for Research in Reproductive Health (Mumbai), Entero Virus Research Centre (Mumbai), Vector Control Research Centre (Pondicherry), Central Jalma Institute for Leprosy (Agra), Malaria Research Centre (Delhi), Institute for Research in Medical Statistics (New Delhi), National Institute of Epidemiology (Chennai), Institute of Cytology and Preventive Oncology (New Delhi), Rajendra Memorial Research Institute of Medical Sciences (Patna), National AIDS Research Institute (Pune), National Centre for Laboratory Animal Sciences (Hyderabad), Food and Drug Toxicology Research Centre (both Hyderabad), Centre for Research in Medical Entomology (Madurai), ICMR Genetic Research Centre (Mumbai), and six Regional Medical Research Centres (Bhubaneswar, Dibrugarh, Jabalpur, Jodhpur, Port Blair, Belgaum); library of 20,000 vols; Dir-Gen. Dr VISHWA MOHAN KATOCH; publs *ICMR Patrika* (in Hindi, 12 a year), *Indian Journal of Malariology* (4 a year), *Indian Journal of Medical Research* (12 a year, with supplements).

Institute of Child Health: 11 Dr Biresh Guha St, Kolkata 700017, West Bengal; tel. (33) 22893526; e-mail ichcal@yahoo.com; internet www.ichcalcutta.org; f. 1956; affiliated to College for Child Health, Univ. of Calcutta; depts of biochemistry, clinical paediatrics, dermatology, ophthalmology and otorhinolaryngology, paediatric surgery, pathology, physiotherapy, preventive paediatrics, psychiatry, radiology; Pres. KRISHNA BOSE; Dir Prof. Dr APURBA GHOSH; publ. *Annals of the Institute of Child Health*.

King Institute of Preventive Medicine: Guindy, Chennai 600032, Tamil Nadu; tel. (44) 22501520; e-mail kipmguindy@yahoo.com; internet www.tnhealth.org/meking.htm; f. 1899; postgraduate training in microbiology; library of 25,026 vols of books and journals; Dir Dr K. V. MURTHY; Deputy Dir P. GUNASEKHARAN.

National Centre for Disease Control: Directorate Gen. of Health Services, 22 Sham Nath Marg, New Delhi 110054; tel. (11) 23913148; e-mail dirnicd@nic.in; internet nicd.nic.in; f. 1909 as Central Malaria Bureau, Malaria Institute of India 1938, named National Institute of Communicable Diseases 1963; research and training centre in field of communicable and vector-borne diseases; brs at Alwar (Rajasthan), Coonoor (Tamil Nadu) and Jagdalpur (Madhya Pradesh) (all for research and training in epidemiology), Jagdalpur (Chhattisgarh), Rajahmundry (Andhra Pradesh) and Varanasi (Uttar Pradesh) (all for research and training on helminthology), Patna (medical entomology and vector control), Bengaluru (zoonosis); library of 36,579 vols of books and journals, 251 maps, 89 photocopies and 1,400 annual reports from various orgs; Dir Dr L. S. CHAUHAN; publs *CD Alert* (12 a year), *Health News Clipping* (12 a year).

National Institute of Nutrition: Indian Council of Medical Research, Jamai-Osmania, Tarnaka, Hyderabad, 500007, Andhra Pradesh; tel. (40) 27197200; e-mail nin@ap.nic.in; internet www.ninindia.org; f. 1918 as Beri-Beri Enquiry Unit, Deficiency Disease Enquiry 1925, Nutrition Research Laboratories 1928; prin. research and training centre for South and South-East Asia; incl. centres for Food and Drug Toxicology Research, Nat. Centre for Laboratory Animal Sciences and Nat. Nutrition Monitoring Bureau; library of 64,265 vols, 33,725 periodicals, 12,916 reports, 17,624 books; Dir Dr B. SESIKERAN; publs *Nutrition* (4 a year), *Nutrition News* (6 a year).

National Jalma Institute for Leprosy and other Mycobacterial Diseases: POB 101, Dr M. Miyazaki Marg, Tajganj, Agra 282001, Uttar Pradesh; tel. (562) 2331751; e-mail jalma@sancharnet.in; f. 1966 as India Centre of JALMA; centre officially handed over to the Govt of India and the Indian Ccl of Medical Research, named the Central JALMA Institute for Leprosy in 1976, present status and name in 2005; part of Indian Ccl of Medical Research; treatment, research and training on leprosy, tuberculosis and HIV/AIDS; library of 2,496 books, 40 journals; Dir Dr KIRAN KATOCH.

National Tuberculosis Institute: Govt of India, 'Avalon' 8, Bellary Rd, Bengaluru 560003, Karnataka; tel. (80) 23441192; e-mail ntiindia@blr.vsnl.net.in; internet ntiindia.kar.nic.in; f. 1959; research in epidemiology, applied tuberculosis bacteriology, sociological aspects and systems research with regard to tuberculosis control; training and control programme; information centre on tuberculosis; digital library of institute papers published in periodicals and publs; library of 14,000 vols, 55 periodicals, 120 audiovisual; Dir Dr PRAHLAD KUMAR.

Pasteur Institute: Health Complex, Red Hills, Laitumkhrah, Shillong, Meghalaya 793003; internet meghealth.nic.in/dhs_res/pasteur_inst.html; f. 1915; library of 7,311 vols; Dir N. G. BANERJEE.

Pasteur Institute of India: Coonoor 643103 (Nilgiris), Tamil Nadu; tel. (423) 2231350; e-mail directorpiic@dataone.in; internet www.pasteurinstituteindia.com; f. 1907 as Pasteur Institute of Southern India, present name and status 1977; production of DTP group of vaccines and tissue culture anti-rabies vaccine; rabies diagnosis (RFFIT); library of 20,000 vols; Dir Dr B. SEKAR; Asst Dir Dr K. N. VENKATARAMANA.

Vallabhbhai Patel Chest Institute: POB 2101, Univ. of Delhi, Delhi 110007; tel. (11) 27402400; e-mail admin@vpci.org.in; internet www.vpci.org.in; f. 1949; attached to Univ. of Delhi; postgraduate teaching and research in respiratory diseases and allied biomedical sciences; library of 30,000 vols; Chair. Prof. P. N. TANDON; Dir Prof. RAJENDRA PRASAD; publ. *Indian Journal of Chest Diseases and Allied Sciences* (4 a year).

Vector Control Research Centre: Medical Complex, Indira Nagar, Puducherry 605006; tel. (413) 2272396; e-mail vcrc@vsnl.com; internet vcrc.res.in; f. 1975; attached to Indian Ccl of Medical Research; affiliated with Pondicherry Univ.; develops epidemiological surveillance tools and strategies for prevention and control of vector-borne diseases, incl. malaria, filariasis and dengue fever; research and postgraduate training; library of 15,367 vols; Dir Dr PURUSOTHAMAN JAMBULINGAM.

NATURAL SCIENCES

General

Bose Institute: 93/1 Acharya Prafulla Chandra Rd, Kolkata 700009, West Bengal; tel. (33) 23502402; e-mail director@bic.boseinst.ernet.in; internet www.boseinst.ernet.in; f. 1917; advances the science and diffusion of knowledge; research undertaken by depts of biochemistry, biophysics, botany, chemistry, microbiology, physics; experimental stations at Falta, Shamnagar, Madhyamgram and Darjeeling; library of 24,883 vols; Dir Prof. SIBAJI RAHA; Registrar TUSHAR K. GHORUI; publ. *Transactions*.

Indian Association for the Cultivation of Science (IACS): 2A–2B Raja S C Mullick Rd, Kolkata 700032; tel. (33) 24734971; e-mail helpdesk@iacs.res.in; internet www.iacs.res.in; f. 1876; researches in theoretical physics, spectroscopy, material science, solid state physics, physical chemistry, biological chemistry, energy research unit, polymer science unit, organic and inorganic chemistry; library of 63,205 vols; Pres. Prof. S. K. JOSHI; Dir Prof. K. BHATTACHARYYA; publ. *Indian Journal of Physics*.

UNESCO Office in New Delhi: B-5/29 Safdarjung Enclave, New Delhi 110029; tel. (11) 26713000; e-mail newdelhi@unesco.org; internet www.unesco.org/newdelhi; f. 1948; UNESCO's first decentralized office in Asia; acts as designated cluster office for four countries in S Asia (Bhutan, India, Maldives and Sri Lanka); science and technology programmes in 11 South and Central Asian countries and including communication, education and culture programmes; library: documentation and information centre, 30,000 UNESCO documents, reports, etc.; spec. collns: science and technology, education, social sciences, culture and communication; films library, posters, CD-ROMs, CDs; Dir ISKRA PANVESKA.

Biological Sciences

Birbal Sahni Institute of Palaeobotany: 53 University Rd, Lucknow 226007, Uttar Pradesh; tel. (522) 2740008; e-mail director@bsip.res.in; internet www.bsip.res.in; f. 1946 as Institute of Palaeobotany; aims to develop palaeobotany in all its botanical and geological aspects; scientific research on the fundamental and applied aspects of fossil plants and their bearing on the origins of life; evolutionary linkages; biostratigraphy; fossil fuel exploration; phytogeography; repository of fossil plants; library of 5,664 vols, 15,995 current periodicals, 14,826 journals, 40,097 reprints, 300 microfilms; Dir Prof. Dr NARESH CHANDRA MEHROTRA; publ. *The Palaeobotanist* (3 a year).

Botanical Survey of India: CGO Complex, Third MSO Bldg, Block F (5th and 6th Fl.), DF Block, Sector I, Salt Lake City, Kolkata 700064, West Bengal; tel. (33) 23344963; e-mail bulletinbsi@gmail.com; internet bsi.gov.in; f. 1890; botanical surveys and research; HQ: Central Nat. Herbarium and Indian Botanic Garden at Howrah; Industrial Section, Indian Museum at Kolkata; regional circles at Allahabad, Pune, Coimbatore, Jodhpur, Port Blair, Shillong, Dehradun, Itanagar and Gangtok; library of 250,000 vols; Dir Dr PARAMJIT SINGH; publs *Indian Floras, Flora of Protected Areas, Nelumbo, Parijat, Vanaspati Vani* (in Hindi).

Jawaharlal Nehru Tropical Botanic Garden and Research Institute: Palode, Thiruvananthapuram 695562, Kerala; tel. (472) 2869246; e-mail director_tbgri@rediffmail.com; internet www.jntbgri.in; f. 1979; botanical garden, an arboretum, a medicinal plant garden and laboratories for botanical, horticultural, plant biotechnical, ethnomedicinal, ethnopharmacological and phytochemical research; conservation of rare and endangered tropical plant species; promotion of research and devt studies of plants of medicinal and economic importance; herbarium of 23,650 mounted specimens and 35,000 duplicates of vascular plants; museum; library of 9,100 vols, 102 journals; Dir Dr P. G. LATHA (acting); publ. *Index Seminum*.

Zoological Survey of India: Prani Vigyan Bhawan, M Block, New Alipore, Kolkata 700053, West Bengal; tel. (33) 24006892; internet zsi.gov.in; f. 1916; activities incl. maintenance of Nat. Zoological collns, faunistic surveys and research on systematic zoology, wildlife, environmental conservation, etc.; regional stations at Calicut, Canning, Chennai, Dehradun, Digha, Ganjam, Hyderabad, Itanagar, Jabalpur, Jodhpur, Patna, Port Blair, Pune, Shillong, Solan; library of 90,000 vols, 800 zoological journals; Dir Dr K. VENKATARAMAN; publs *Bibliography of Indian Zoology, Conservation Area Series, Fauna of India, Handbooks, Journal of Indian Zoology* (1 a year), *Memoirs of the Zoological Survey of India, Prani Jagat* (in Hindi), *Records* (4 a year), *State Fauna Series*.

Mathematical Sciences

Institute of Mathematical Sciences: IV Cross Rd, CIT Campus, Taramani, Chennai 600113, Tamil Nadu; tel. (44) 22543100; e-mail director@imsc.res.in; internet www.imsc.res.in; f. 1962; research in pure and applied mathematics, theoretical physics, theoretical computer science; library of 67,000 vols, 260 periodicals; Dir Prof. R. BALASUBRAMANIAN; publ. *I. M. Sc. Reports*.

Physical Sciences

Astronomical Observatory of St Xavier's College: 30 Mother Teresa Sarani, Kolkata 700016, West Bengal; tel. (33) 22551264; e-mail shiva@sxccal.edu; f. 1875; Dir Dr JOHN FELIX RAJ.

Bhabha Atomic Research Centre: Trombay, Mumbai 400085, Maharashtra; tel. (22) 25505050; e-mail director@barc.gov.in; internet www.barc.gov.in; f. 1944; nat. centre for research in and devt of atomic energy for non-military purposes; facilities incl. 3 research reactors; Van de Graaff accelerator; laboratories at Srinagar, Gulmarg and Gauribidanur; isotope production unit; central workshops; pilot plants for production of heavy water, zirconium, titanium; uranium metal plant; food irradiation and processing laboratory; reactor engineering laboratory and test facilities; library of 200,000 vols, 1,200 technical journals, 450,000 technical reports; Dir Dr R. K. SINHA.

Geodetic and Research Branch, Survey of India: 17 E. C. Rd, POB 77, Dehradun 248001, Uttarakhand; tel. (135) 2654528; e-mail dgrb.soi@nic.in; f. 1800; geodetic and allied geophysical activities, incl. devt and research of instrumentation; library of 55,000 vols; Dir Dr M. G. ARUR.

Geological Survey of India: 27 Jawahar Lal Nehru Rd, Kolkata 700016, West Bengal; tel. (33) 22861676; e-mail dg-gsi@gsi.gov.in; internet www.portal.gsi.gov.in; f. 1851; activities incl. surveying and mapping, mineral exploration, specialized investigations, other exploration, research and devt, information dissemination, human resource devt, project modernization and replacement; library: 5m. vols; Dir-Gen. A. SUNDARAMOORTHY (acting); publs *Catalogue Series* (irregular), *Indian Minerals* (4 a year), *Manual Series* (irregular), *Memoirs of the Geological Survey of India* (irregular), *Miscellaneous Publications* (irregular), *Palaeontologica Indica* (irregular), *Records of the Geological Survey of India. Part I–VIII* (1 a year).

India Meteorological Department: Mausam Bhawan, Lodi Rd, New Delhi 110003; tel. (11) 43824201; internet www.imd.gov.in; f. 1875; attached to Min. of Earth Sciences; nat. meteorological service of India; 6 regional offices at New Delhi, Mumbai, Kolkata, Madras, Nagpur and Guwahati; 11 meteorological centres at Thiruvananthapuram, Bangalore, Hyderabad, Bhubaneshwar, Lucknow, Jaipur, Srinagar, Ahmedabad, Patna, Chandigarh and Bhopal; 10 cyclone detection radars; Positional Astronomy Centre at Kolkata; provides weather service; scientific activities cover research in all brs of meteorology, incl. agricultural and hydrometeorology, radiometeorology, satellite and environmental meteorology, atmospheric electricity, seismology; New Delhi is Regional Telecommunication Hub and Regional Meteorological Centre under WMO World Weather Watch; Regional Specialised Meteorological Centre for Tropical Cyclones; also Regional Area Forecast Centre under ICAO; Dir-Gen. Dr AJIT TYAGI (acting); publs *Indian Astronomical Ephemeris* (1 a year), *Indian Weather Review, MAUSAM* (4 a year).

Indian Bureau of Mines: Second Fl., 'Indira Bhavan', Civil Lines, Nagpur 440102, Maharashtra; tel. (712) 2560041; e-mail cg@ibm.gov.in; internet ibm.nic.in; f. 1948; govt dept responsible for the conservation and devt of mineral resources and protection of mining environment; aid in mine and mineral devt; technical consultancy in mining and mineral-processing, colln and dissemination of mineral statistics and information, preparation of feasibility reports of mining projects, incl. benefication plants, and preparation of environmental management plans; conducts market surveys on minerals and mineral commodities; regional offices at Ajmer, Bengaluru, Bhubaneswar, Chennai, Dehradun, Goa, Guwahati, Hyderabad, Jabalpur, Kolkata, Nagpur, Nellore, Ranchi, Udaipur; pilot plants and ore dressing laboratories at Ajmer, Bengaluru, Nagpur; library of 50,000 vols, 10,000 periodicals; Controller-Gen. C. S. GUNDEWAR; publ. *Indian Minerals Yearbook*.

Indian Institute of Astrophysics: Second Block, Koramangala, Bengaluru 560034, Karnataka; tel. (80) 25530583; e-mail diriia@iiap.res.in; internet www.iiap.res.in; f. 1786 as private observatory in Madras; study of solar physics, stellar physics, solar system objects, theoretical astrophysics incl. ionosphere, cosmology, solar-terrestrial relationship and instrumentation; field stations at Gauribidanur, Hanle, Kavalur and Kodaikanal, and a research unit at Hosakote; library of 19,000 vols; Dir Prof. S. S. HASAN; publ. *Reprints*.

Indian Institute of Geomagnetism: Plot 5, Sector 18, Near Kalamboli Highway, New Panvel (W), Navi Mumbai 410218, Maharashtra; tel. (22) 27480000; e-mail postmast@iigs.iigm.res.in; internet www.iigm.res.in; f. 1861 as Colaba observatory, present status 1971; observatories in Alibag, Jaipur, Nagpur, Gulmarg, Shillong, Pondicherry, Rajkot, Silchar, Tirunelveli, Vishakapatnam, Port Blair; World Data Centre WDC-C2 for geomagnetism; operates geomagnetic observatory over Antarctica; basic research in upper atmospheric physics, solid earth geophysics and allied fields, environmental magnetism; research centres at Tirunelveli, Tamil Nadu

(Equatorial Geophysical Research Laboratory) and at Allahabad, Uttar Pradesh (K. S. Krishnan Geomagnetic Research Laboratory); library of 23,000 vols; Dir Prof. Mita Rajaram (acting); publs *Griha-Patrika Spandan*, *Indian Magnetic Data* (1 a year).

Indian Space Research Organization (ISRO): Antariksh Bhavan, New BEL Rd, Bengaluru 560094, Karnataka; tel. (80) 23415275; e-mail satish@isro.gov.in; internet www.isro.gov.in; f. 1972; devt of satellites, launch vehicles and ground stations for satellite-based communications, resources survey and meteorological services; operates Vikram Sarabhai Space Centre, Space Applications Centre at Ahmedabad, ISRO Satellite Centre at Bangalore, SHAR Centre at Sriharikota Island, Liquid Propulsion System Unit at Trivandrum and Bangalore, Devt and Educational Communications Unit at Ahmedabad, ISRO Telemetry Tracking and Command Network at Bangalore, ISRO Inertial Systems Unit, Trivandrum, INSAT Master Control Facility, Hassan; Nat. Remote Sensing Agency at Hyderabad, Physical Research Laboratory at Ahmedabad and Nat. Mesosphere-Stratosphere-Troposphere Radar Facility at Gadanki; Chair. Dr K. Radhakrishnan; publs *Journal of Spacecraft Technology* (2 a year), *Space India* (4 a year).

Indira Gandhi Centre for Atomic Research: Dept of Atomic Energy, Kalpakkam 603102, Tamil Nadu; tel. (44) 27480267; e-mail dir@igcar.gov.in; internet www.igcar.gov.in; f. 1971; attached to Dept of Atomic Energy, Govt of India; conducts research in fast reactor technology and related disciplines; library of 65,000 vols, 820 journals, 200,000 research reports; Dir S. C. Chetal.

Institute for Plasma Research: Bhat, Gandhinagar 382428, Gujarat; tel. (79) 23962001; e-mail kaw@ipr.res.in; internet www.ipr.res.in; f. 1986; research in theoretical plasma physics; library of 21,260 vols, 11,096 technical reports, 2,568 reprints, 105 periodicals; Dir Prof. P. K. Kaw; publ. *Plasma Processing Update* (4 a year).

Inter-University Centre for Astronomy and Astrophysics: POB 4, Ganeshkhind, Pune Univ. Campus, Pune 411007, Maharashtra; tel. (20) 25604100; e-mail aocp@iucaa.ernet.in; internet www.iucaa.ernet.in; f. 1988; fundamental research and training in all aspects of astronomy and astrophysics; MSc and PhD, refresher courses, research workshops, etc.; Dir Prof. Ajit K. Kembhavi; publs *Khagol* (4 a year), *Lecture Notes*.

Mining, Geological and Metallurgical Institute of India: GN-38/4, Sector V, Salt Lake City, Kolkata 700091, West Bengal; tel. (33) 23573987; e-mail mgmi@cal2.vsnl.net.in; f. 1906; library of 3,500 vols; Pres. R. K. Saha; Vice-Pres. T. K. Lahiry; Hon. Sec. Dr D. Sarkar; Hon. Jt Sec. P. Roy; publ. *Transactions* (1 a year).

National Centre of Experimental Mineralogy and Petrology: Univ. of Allahabad, 14 Chathum Lines, Bank Rd, Allahabad 211002, Uttar Pradesh; tel. (532) 2250840; e-mail info@ncemp.org; internet www.ncemp.org; f. 1996; attached to Univ. of Allahabad; research fields incl. high pressure and high temperature physics and chemistry of the earth; Dir Prof. S. D. Dixit; Coordinator Dr Mrigank Mauli Dwivedi.

National Institute of Rock Mechanics: Champion Reefs PO, Kolar Gold Fields 563117, Karnataka; tel. (8153) 275004; e-mail nirm@nirm.in; internet www.nirm.in; f. 1988; research in applied and basic rock mechanics; library of 1,400 vols; Dir Dr P. C. Nawani; Registrar A. N. Nagarajan.

Nizamiah and Japal-Rangapur Observatories and Centre of Advanced Study in Astronomy: Dept of Astronomy, Osmania Univ., Hyderabad 500007, Andhra Pradesh; tel. (40) 27017306; e-mail pies@ouastr.ernet.in; f. 1908,current name adopted 1919; attached to Osmania Univ.; library of 15,000 vols, 4,000 periodicals; Dir Prof. P. V. Subrahmanyam; publ. *Astronomical*.

Physical Research Laboratory: Navrangpura, Ahmedabad 380009, Gujarat; tel. (79) 26314000; e-mail info@prl.res.in; internet www.prl.res.in; f. 1947; research fields incl. astronomy and astrophysics, earth sciences, gravitation and cosmology, non-linear dynamics, nuclear, atomic and molecular physics, particle physics, planetary sciences and exploration, quantum optics and quantum information, solar physics, space and atmospheric sciences; library of 55,000 vols, 150 journals, 1,200 maps; Chair. Prof. U. R. Rao; Dir Prof. Jitendra Nath Goswami.

Raman Research Institute: C. V. Raman Ave, Sadashivanagar, Bengaluru 560080, Karnataka; tel. (80) 23610122; e-mail office@rri.res.in; internet www.rri.res.in; f. 1948; astronomy and astrophysics, light and matter physics, soft condensed matter and theoretical physics; library of 65,800 vols; Dir Prof. Ravi Subrahmanayan; Librarian B. M. Meera.

Saha Institute of Nuclear Physics: 1/AF, Bidhannagar, Kolkata 700064, West Bengal; tel. (33) 23375345; e-mail director.sinp@saha.ac.in; internet www.saha.ac.in/cs/www; f. 1950 as Institute of Nuclear Physics, present name 1956; conducts advanced research and teaching in nuclear science (radioactive ion beams, high-energy physics, quark gluon plasma); research in physics (atomic physics, condensed matter physics, high-energy physics, microelectronics, nuclear physics, plasmic physics, surface and general mathematical physics) and biophysical sciences (cell biology genetic toxicology, macromolecular crystallography, membrane biophysics, molecular genetics, nuclear and radiochemistry, photochemistry, radiation chemistry and biology, structural biology and biomolecular spectroscopy, ultrastructural research); library of 34,972 books, 50,279 journals, 25,000 reports, 944 CD-ROMs; Dir Prof. Milan K. Sanyal; Registrar V. V. Mallikarjuna Rao.

PHILOSOPHY AND PSYCHOLOGY

Centre of Behavioural and Cognitive Sciences: Senate Hall Campus, Univ. of Allahabad, Allahabad 211002, Uttar Pradesh; tel. (532) 2460738; e-mail office@cbcs.ac.in; internet www.cbcs.ac.in; f. 2002; attached to Univ. of Allahabad; research areas incl. perception, attention, emotions, consciousness, creativity, decision making, social cognition, language processing, learning disabilities, cognitive devt; Head Narayanan Srinivasan.

Pratap P. G. Research Centre of Philosophy: POB 80, Umavi Nagar, Jalgaon, Jalgaon 425001, Maharashtra; tel. (257) 2258428; e-mail info@nmu.ac.in; f. 1916 as Indian Inst. of Philosophy, present name and status 1993; attached to North Maharashtra Univ.; comparative study of Indian and European philosophy; offers master's degree in philosophy; library of 5,705 vols; Head Dr Archana Degaonkar; publs *The Philosophical Quarterly* (4 a year), *Tattvajnana Mandir* (in Marathi).

Yoga Institute: Shri Yogendra Marg, Prabhat Colony, Santa Cruz (E), Mumbai 400055, Maharashtra; tel. (22) 26122185; e-mail info@theyogainstitute.org; internet www.theyogainstitute.org; f. 1918; promotes self-education, physical, mental, moral and psychic, aided by science of Yoga; conducts academic and scientific research in Yoga culture and technique; runs teacher training Inst. of Yoga and a Psychosomatic Clinic based on Yoga; library of 4,500 vols; Pres. Dr Jayadeva Yogendra; Dir Hansaji Jayadeva Yogendra; publs *Cyclopaedia Yoga*, *Yoga and Total Health* (12 a year), *Yoga Studies*.

RELIGION, SOCIOLOGY AND ANTHROPOLOGY

Anjuman-i-Islam Urdu Research Association: 92 Dadabhoy Nawroji Rd, Mumbai 400001, Maharashtra; library of 5,000 vols; Pres. Dr Zaheer Kazi.

A. N. Sinha Institute of Social Studies: Patna 800001, Bihar; tel. (612) 2221395; e-mail root@ssaansi.ren.nic.in; f. 1958; undertakes teaching and research in social sciences, esp. economics, sociology, social psychology, political science; library of 58,206 vols; Dir Navin Verma; Sec. Jitendra Pandey; publ. *Journal of Social and Economic Studies* (4 a year).

Anthropological Survey of India: 27 Jawaharlal Nehru Rd, Kolkata 700016, West Bengal; tel. (33) 22861796; e-mail director@ansi.gov.in; internet www.ansi.gov.in; f. 1945; attached to Min. of Culture; research in cultural and physical anthropology, human ecology, linguistics, psychology, folklore, biochemistry and radiology; library of 40,935 vols; Dir Prof. K. K. Misra.

Applied Interdisciplinary Development Research Institute, Youth Entrepreneurship Development Organization (YEDO): 119-B Gill Nagar Extension, First Fl., Choolaimedu, Chennai 600094, Tamil Nadu; tel. (44) 65317697; e-mail peteryedo@hotmail.com; f. 1985; interdisciplinary devt education, training, research, consultancy, information dissemination in fields of sustainable agricultural devt, youth empowerment, empowerment of street children, women's empowerment, indigenous knowledge and local resources devt, environmental education, employability skill, business entrepreneurship skills, social entrepreneurship skills, network marketing entrepreneurship skills; library of 2,000 vols; Exec. Dir Dr A. Peter; publ. *Employability & Entrepreneurship Soft Skills Digest*.

Centre of Central Asian Studies: Hazratbal, Srinagar 190006, Jammu and Kashmir; tel. (194) 2415553; e-mail ccas_ku@yahoo.com; internet ccas.uok.edu.in; f. 1978; attached to Univ. of Kashmir; interdisciplinary research on South and Central Asia; organizes confs, seminars and workshops; awards research degrees; library of 20,000 vols; Dir Prof. Aijaz Bandey Bandey; publ. *Journal of Central Asian Studies* (1 a year).

Ethnographic and Folk Culture Society: C-24, K Rd, Mahanagar Extn, Lucknow 226006, Uttar Pradesh; tel. (522) 2372362; e-mail efcs@sancharnet.in; internet www.efcsindia.com; f. 1945; research into anthropological sciences; museum of Folk Life and Culture; library; Pres. Prof. T. N. Madan; Hon. Gen. Sec. Dr Sukant K. Chaudhary; publs *Indian Journal of Physical Anthropology and Human Genetics* (2 a year), *Manav* (2 a year, in Hindi), *The Eastern Anthropologist* (4 a year).

Indian Council of Social Science Research (ICSSR): JNU Institutional Area, Aruna Asaf Ali Marg, New Delhi 110067; tel. (11) 26741849; e-mail info@icssr.org; internet www.icssr.org; f. 1969; sponsors and coordinates research in social sciences, provides financial assistance for research programmes, awards fellowships and grants; sponsors confs, seminars, training programmes and publs; provides partial support to 28 social science research institutes; collaborates with int. bodies in research programmes; Nat. Social Science Documentation Centre (NASSDOC: see under Libraries and Archives); Data Archives; regional centres in Mumbai, Kolkata, Chandigarh, Delhi, Hyderabad, and Shillong; library of 35,000 books, 150,000 periodicals; Chair. Prof SUKHADEO THORAT; Dir of Research Institute and Regional Centre Dr S. N. M. KOPPARTY; Dir of Research Project Dr K. L. KHERA; Dir of Research Survey, Publications and Sales Dr G. S. SAUN; Dir of NASSDOC SAVITRI DEVI; publs *ICSSR Journal of Abstracts and Reviews: Economics* (2 a year), *ICSSR Journal of Abstracts and Reviews: Geography* (2 a year), *ICSSR Journal of Abstracts and Reviews: Political Science* (2 a year), *ICSSR Journal of Abstracts and Reviews: Sociology and Social Anthropology* (2 a year), *Indian Psychological Abstracts and Reviews* (2 a year), *Indian Social Science Review*.

Institute of Applied Manpower Research: Sector A-7, Plot 25, Institutional Area, Narela, Delhi 110040; tel. (11) 27787214; e-mail iamrindia@nic.in; internet www.iamrindia.gov.in; f. 1962; autonomous body under Planning Comm.; studies and disseminates information on the nature, characteristics and utilization of human resources in India; develops methodologies for forecasting supply and demand; compiles information on technical manpower; organizes seminars, confs, study courses and training programmes in techniques of manpower planning at nat. and int. levels and provides consultancy services; conducts degree and diploma courses in Human Resource Planning and Devt for int. participants in collaboration with Commonwealth Secretariat, London, UK; library of 26,500 vols, 150 journals; Pres. for Gen. Ccl MONTEK SINGH AHLUWALIA; Dir-Gen. Dr SANTOSH MEHROTRA; Librarian AJIT KUMAR; publs *Manpower Documentation* (12 a year), *Manpower Journal* (4 a year), *Manpower Profile India* (1 a year), *Technical Manpower Profile* (every 5 years).

Institute of Economic Growth: Univ. of Delhi Enclave, N Campus, Delhi 110007; tel. (11) 27667101; e-mail system@iegindia.org; internet www.iegindia.org; f. 1958; PhD supervision in the fields of economic and social devt; research in agriculture and rural devt, environment and resource economics, globalization and trade, industry, labour and welfare, macro-economic policy and modelling, population and devt, health policy, social change and social structure; specialized library and documentation service; Chair. NITIN DESAI; Dir Prof. BINA AGARWAL; publs *Contributions to Indian Sociology: New Series* (2 a year), *Monthly Monitor*, *Institute of Economic Growth Studies in Asian Social Development* (irregular), *Studies in Economic Development and Planning*.

Namgyal Institute of Tibetology: Deorali, Gangtok 737101, Sikkim; tel. (3592) 281525; e-mail tibetologyinfo@gmail.com; internet www.tibetology.net; f. 1958, fmrly Sikkim Research Institute of Tibetology; promotes research on religion, history, language, art and culture of the people of Tibetan cultural area incl. Sikkim; library of 60,000 vols of Tibetan literature (canonical of all sects and secular) in MSS and xylographs; Pres. BALMIKI PRASAD SINGH; Dir TASHI DENSAPA; publ. *Bulletin of Tibetology* (2 a year).

National Institute of Rural Development: Rajendranagar, Hyderabad 500030, Andhra Pradesh; tel. (40) 24008526; e-mail cit@nird.gov.in; internet www.nird.org.in; f. 1958; autonomous servicing and consultancy agency for central and state govts; training for govt and non-govt officials; a Centre on Rural Documentation (CORD) provides computerized library services; devt research into all facets of rural life; offers consultancy service to nat. and int. orgs; repackages govt and other literature on rural devt for wider dissemination; library of 95,000 vols; Dir-Gen. Dr M. V. RAO (acting); publs *CORD Abstracts* (6 a year), *CORD Alerts* (26 a year), *CORD Index* (12 a year), *Handbook of Rural Development Statistics* (1 a year), *Journal of Rural Development* (4 a year), *Recommendations of Seminars and Workshops* (1 a year), *Research Highlights* (1 a year).

Rural Development Organization: Lamsang Bazar, PO Lamsang, 795146 Manipur; tel. (85) 310961; f. 1975; research, socio-economic devt programme for the rural poor, skill training programme; Library and Documentation Centre, AIDS Prevention and Control Programme, Community Health Centre, Micro-credit scheme, rural bank; library of 10,000 vols; Gen. Sec. W. BRAJABIDHU SINGH; publ. *Loyalam* (12 a year).

V. V. Giri National Labour Institute: Sector 24, Gautam Budh Nagar, Noida 201301, Uttar Pradesh; tel. (120) 2411472; e-mail vvgnli@vsnl.com; internet www.vvgnli.org; f. 1974, present name 1995; research, training and consultancy; library of 57,293 vols; Dir-Gen. V. P. YAJURVEDI; publs *Award Digest: Journal of Labour Legislation* (6 a year), *Labour and Development* (2 a year), *Shram Vidhan* (6 a year, in Hindi).

TECHNOLOGY

Ahmedabad Textile Industry's Research Association: PO Ambavadi Vistar, Ahmedabad 380015, Gujarat; tel. (79) 26307921; e-mail director@atira.in; internet www.atira.in; f. 1949; textile consultation, training and research, information and testing services; library of 41,000 vols; Chair. SANJAY LALBHAI; Dir Dr A. K. SHARMA; publs *ACT (ATIRA Communications on Textiles)* (4 a year), *TEXINCON* (4 a year).

Automotive Research Association of India: POB 832 Pune 411004, Maharashtra; Survey No. 102, Vetal Hill, Off Paud Rd, Kothrud, Pune 411038, Maharashtra; tel. (20) 30231111; e-mail director@araiindia.com; internet www.araiindia.com; f. 1966; research instn of the Automotive Industry with the Min. of Industry; provides facilities for research and devt; product design; evaluation of equipment and standardization; certification for the Indian automotive and component industry; compilation and dissemination of technical information to the automotive and engineering industry; testing laboratories; library of 13,000 vols, 34 periodicals; Dir SHRIKANT R. MARATHE; publs *Automotive Abstracts* (12 a year), *ARAI Update* (4 a year, online).

Bioinformatics Centre: Hazratbal, Srinagar 190006, Jammu and Kashmir; tel. (194) 2421353; e-mail andrabik@kashmiruniversity.net; f. 2000; attached to Univ. of Kashmir; Dir Prof. Dr KHURSHID IQBAL ANDRABI.

Birla Research Institute for Applied Sciences: Birlagram 456331, Nagda, Madhya Pradesh; tel. (7366) 246760; e-mail info@birlainstitute.co.in; internet www.birlainstitute.co.in; f. 1965; registered soc.; helps nat. industrial growth; research in pulp, cellulose fibre and pollution abatement; Pres. K. K. MAHESHWARI; Dir-Gen. ADITYA N. SHRIVASTAVA.

Bombay Textile Research Association: Lal Bahadur Shastri Marg, Ghatkopar (W), Mumbai 400086, Maharashtra; tel. (22) 25003651; e-mail btra@vsnl.com; internet www.btraindia.com; f. 1954; research on process and product devts with emphasis on cleaner processing technologies; textile testing services; technical consultancy services in textile manufacturing; certification and training services; recognized for postgraduate studies by Univ. of Mumbai; library of 22,400 vols; Dir Dr ASHOK N. DESAI; publ. *BTRA Scan* (4 a year).

Bureau of Indian Standards (BIS): Manak Bhavan, 9 Bahadur Shah Zafar Marg, New Delhi 110002; tel. (11) 23230131; e-mail info@bis.org.in; internet www.bis.org.in; f. 1947; library of 740,000 standards and technical publs, 416 periodicals; Dir-Gen. SHARAD GUPTA; Dir for Library Services ROMA ROY; publs *Current Published Information on Standardization*, *Standards India*, *Standards Worldover—Monthly Additions to Library*.

Central Institute for Research on Cotton Technology: DARE, Govt of India, Adenwala Rd, Matunga, Mumbai 400019, Maharashtra; tel. (22) 24127273; e-mail circot@vsnl.com; internet www.circot.res.in; f. 1924; attached to Indian Council of Agricultural Research; research and devt in post-harvest technologies in cotton, extraction and usage of other natural fibres; library of 7,161 vols; Dir Dr SAJAL KUMAR CHATTOPADHYAY.

Central Water and Power Research Station: Khadakwasla, Pune 411024, Maharashtra; tel. (20) 24103200; e-mail wapis@cwprs.gov.in; internet www.cwprs.gov.in; f. 1916, present status 1936; basic and applied research in hydraulic engineering and allied subjects; activities in fields of hydrology and water resources analysis, river engineering, reservoir and appurtenant structures, coastal and offshore engineering, ship hydrodynamics, hydraulic machinery, foundations and structures, mathematical modelling, instrumentation and control, applied earth sciences; library of 70,779 vols, 200 periodicals; Dir Dr ISHWER DATT GUPTA.

Centre of Biomedical Magnetic Resonance: Sanjay Gandhi Postgraduate Institute of Medical Sciences Campus, Raebareli Rd, Lucknow 226014, Uttar Pradesh; tel. (522) 2668700; e-mail cbmrlko@gmail.com; internet cbmr.res.in; attached to Univ. of Allahabad; f. 2002; attached to Univ. of Allahabad; medicine, NMR spectroscopy, biochemistry, electronics, computer science, mathematics and psychology; Dir Prof. C. L. KHETRAPAL.

Indian Institute of Natural Resins & Gums: Namkum, Ranchi 834010, Jharkhand; tel. (651) 2260117; e-mail iinrg@ilri.ernet.in; internet ilri.ernet.in/~iinrg; f. 1924, fmrly Indian Lac Research Institute, present name 2007; research and devt on all aspects of lac and other natural gums and resins (excluding production) such as harvesting, tapping, processing, product devt, training, information repository, technology dissemination, nat. and int. cooperation; library of 28,742 vols of books and journals; Dir Dr RANGANATHAN RAMANI IYER.

Indian Rubber Manufacturers Research Association: Plot No. 254/1B, Rd 16V, Wagle Industrial Estate, Thane (W) 400604, Maharahstra; tel. (22) 25811348; e-mail info@irmra.org; internet www.irmra.org; f. 1959; attached to Min. of Commerce and Industry; research and devt relating to rubber and allied industries; library of 5,000 vols; Dir Dr P. THAVAMANI (acting).

Institute of Hydraulics and Hydrology: Poondi, (Via) Trivellore, Chingleput 602023, Tamil Nadu; f. 1945; library of 8,000 vols and 5,870 journals; Dir K. SUBRAMANIAM.

Institute of Technology: Varanasi 221005, Uttar Pradesh; tel. (542) 2368106; e-mail director@itbhu.ac.in; internet www.itbhu.ac

.in; f. 1971 by merger of Banaras Engineering College (f. 1919), College of Mining and Metallurgy (f. 1923) and College of Technology; attached to Banaras Hindu Univ.; applied science and engineering; library of 93,016 vols, 17,706 periodicals; Dir Prof. K. P. SINGH.

Irrigation and Power Research Institute: Amritsar; e-mail psip2010@gmail.com; research in irrigation and hydraulic engineering; Dir J. NATH.

National Council for Cement and Building Materials: 34 Km-Stone, Delhi-Mathura Rd, Ballabgarh 121004, Haryana; tel. (129) 4192222; e-mail info@ncbindia.com; internet www.ncbindia.com; f. 1966 as Cement Research Institute of India, present name and status 1985; provides intensive and planned research and devt support to cement, concrete and allied industries in the fields of new materials, technology devt and transfer, continuing education and industrial services; library of 46,220 vols, 100 periodicals; Dir-Gen. A. PAHUJA; publs *Cement Standards of the World*, *NCB Current Contents* (documentation list, 6 a year).

National Institute of Hydrology: Jalvigyan Bhawan, Roorkee 247667, Uttarakhand; tel. (1332) 272106; e-mail nihmail@nih.ernet.in; internet www.nih.ernet.in; f. 1978; attached to Min. of Water Resources; research in all aspects of water resources; library of 7,000 vols, 3,000 technical reports, 87 periodicals, etc.; Dir R. D SINGH; publs *Jal Vigyan Sameeksha*, *Research Reports*.

Pulp and Paper Research Institute: Jaykaypur, Rayagada 765017, Orissa; tel. (6856) 234077; e-mail contactpapri@gmail.com; f. 1971; researches in pulp and paper technology, forestry, environment and pigment; library of 6,340 vols, periodicals; Deputy Dir Dr JAGDISH CHANDRA PANIGRAHI; Librarian RABINDRA KUMAR SAHOO.

Research Designs & Standards Organization: Manaknagar, Lucknow 226011, Uttar Pradesh; tel. (522) 2451221; e-mail dg@rdso.railnet.gov.in; internet www.rdso.indianrailways.gov.in; f. 1957 by merger of Central Standards Office (f. 1930) and Railway Testing and Research Centre (f. 1952); attached to Min. of Railways; conducts studies on the design and standardization of all railway infrastructure and equipment; tests and trials of new railway stock and other assets; researches into the economic and effective maintenance of operating practices; library of 170,000 vols, 130 periodicals; Dir-Gen. V. RAMACHANDRAN; Additional Dir-Gen. V. K. JAIN.

Synthetic & Art Silk Mills' Research Association: Sasmira Marg, Worli, Mumbai 400030, Maharashtra; tel. (22) 24935351; e-mail sasmira@vsnl.com; internet www.sasmira.org; f. 1950; research and devt in man-made textiles; technical textiles; technical education (postgraduate and diploma courses) in the field of man-made fibres, textile technology, textile chemistry, knitting technology and retail, marketing and management; library of 30,555 vols; Pres. MAGANLAL H. DOSHI; Vice-Pres. MIHIR R. MEHTA; Exec. Dir U. K. GANGOPADHYAY; publ. *Man-Made Textiles in India* (12 a year).

Libraries and Archives

Andhra Pradesh

British Council Library: 5–9–22 Sarovar Centre, Secretariat Rd, Hyderabad 500063, Andhra Pradesh; tel. (40) 23483333; e-mail bl.hyderabad@in.britishcouncil.org; f. 1979; library services; seminars; workshops; film screening on climate change and low carbon; 25,000 vols, 2,500 DVDs; information on higher education in the UK; Man. AJAY MERCHANT; Asst Man. EASWARAN NAMPOOTHIRI.

Sri Gowthami Regional Library/ Gowthami Grandhalayam: Rajahmundry 533104, Andhra Pradesh; tel. (883) 2476908; f. 1898; research library; spec. colln of rare 19th century periodicals in English and Telugu, rare colln of old Telugu books; 82,000 vols, 428 palm-leaf MSS; Librarian JAMMI RAMA RAO.

State Central Library: Afzalgunj, Hyderabad 500012, Andhra Pradesh; tel. (40) 24615621; f. 1891, present status 1955; 438,283 vols; Librarian T. V. VEDAMRUTHAM.

Bihar

Bihar Secretariat Library: Patna 800015, Bihar; f. 1885; 106,300 vols; Chief Librarian P. N. SINHA DOSHI.

Khuda Bakhsh Oriental Public Library: Ashok Rajpath, Patna 800004, Bihar; tel. (612) 2300209; e-mail pat_khopl@dataone.in; internet www.kblibrary.bih.nic.in; f. 1891; attached to Min. of Culture; 278,187 vols, 39,395 bound periodicals, 1,980 audio and 1,030 video cassettes, 182 slides, 2,195 microfilms of MSS; Mughal, Iranian, Central Asian and Rajput paintings; Dir Dr IMTIAZ AHMAD; Admin. Officer NAZIRUL HASNAIN; publ. *Khuda Bakhsh Library Journal* (4 a year).

Shrimati Radhika Sinha Institute and Sachchidananda Sinha Library/State Central Library, Bihar: GPO, Sinha Library Rd., Patna 800001, Bihar; tel. (612) 2221674; f. 1924; 180,000 vols, 600 periodicals; Librarian Dr R. S. P. SINGH.

Chandigarh

British Council Library: SCO 183–187, Sector 9C, Madhya Marg, Chandigarh 160009; tel. (172) 2745195; e-mail bl.chandigarh@in.britishcouncil.org; f. 2000; 20,000 vols, 300 audio cassettes, 600 CD-ROMs, 2,500 children's books, 3,000 DVDs, 1,500 IT books; Man. BIPIN KUMAR.

Delhi

Central Archaeological Library: Nat. Archives Annexe, 2nd Fl., Janpath, New Delhi 110001; tel. (11) 23387475; e-mail asilibrary2011@gmail.com; internet www.asi.nic.in; f. 1902; attached to Archaeological Survey of India; colln on history, archaeology, anthropology, architecture, art, epigraphy and numismatics, Indology, literature, geology, etc; 103,480 vols, 5,776 maps, 85 current periodicals; A. L. I. Officer Dr JAG RAM YADAV.

Central Secretariat Library: G Wing, Shastri Bhavan, New Delhi 110001; tel. (11) 23389684; e-mail directcsl@gmail.com; internet www.csl.nic.in; f. 1890; attached to Min. of Culture; lending, reference, reprographic divs, background material on selected topics and biographies; spec. collns: area study, Indian official documents, foreign official documents, Hindi and Indian regional languages publs; 550,000 vols, 730 periodicals; Dir Dr P. R. GOSWAMI.

Delhi Public Library: S.P. Mukherjee Marg, Delhi 110006; tel. (11) 23946239; e-mail dpl@dpl.gov.in; internet www.dpl.gov.in; f. 1951 in asscn with UNESCO; attached to Min. of Culture; est. as a model for public library devt in SE Asia; central library, 1 zonal library, 3 br. libraries, Braille section, 70 mobile libraries, 39 sub-br. and community libraries, 29 deposit stations; 1.6m. vols, 1,000 periodicals; Dir-Gen. Dr M. C. RAGHAVAN.

Indian Council of World Affairs Library: Sapru House, Barakhamba Rd, New Delhi 110001; tel. (11) 23359159; e-mail librarian@icwa.in; internet www.icwa.in; f. 1943; research collns on social sciences with spec. reference to int. relations, int. law and int. economics; Press library; maps, microfilms and microfiches; UN and EU documents; 140,000 vols, 376 periodicals, 2.45m. press clippings; Librarian G. C. K. RAI; publ. *India Quarterly* (in-house journal).

Indira Gandhi National Centre for the Arts: 1 Central Vista Mess, Janpath, New Delhi 110001; tel. (11) 23388445; e-mail pjha@ignca.nic.in; internet ignca.nic.in; f. 1987; resource centre with reference material relating to Indian arts and culture; Dir of Cultural Informatics PRATAPANAND JHA.

National Archives of India: Janpath, New Delhi 110001; tel. (11) 23383436; e-mail archives@nic.in; internet nationalarchives.nic.in; f. 1891 in Kolkata as the Imperial Record Dept, transferred to New Delhi in 1911 and to present site in 1926; valuable collns of public records, maps, private papers and microfilm covering 40 km of shelf space; 200,000 vols incl. 1,78,000 books and reports, 3,299 proscribed publications, 400 selections from vernacular native newspapers, 4,225 selections from Govt of India and State Govt records, 4,590 vols of Indian parliamentary papers, 1,285 vols of Fort William College colln, 3,560 journals and periodicals, 1,778 gazettes, 2,960 publs in foreign languages; Dir-Gen. Prof. MUSHIRUL HASAN; publ. *Indian Archives* (2 a year).

National Institute of Science Communication and Information Resources: *Pusa Campus*: Dr K. S. Krishnan Marg, New Delhi 110012; tel. (11) 25846301; *Satsang Vihar Marg Campus*: 14 Satsang Vihar Marg, Spec. Institutional Area, New Delhi 110067; tel. (11) 26560141; e-mail gp@niscair.res.in; internet www.niscair.res.in; f. 2002 by merger of Nat. Institute of Science Communication and Indian Nat. Scientific Documentation Centre; attached to Ccl of Scientific and Industrial Research; nat. science library; disseminates scientific and technological information to the scientific community and the gen. public; provides networking services and network-based online services; bibliographical information retrieval from national and international online and CD-ROM databases; 240,000 vols; Dir Dr GANGAN PRATHAP; publs *Annals of Library and Information Studies* (4 a year), *Bharatiya Vaigyanic evam Audyogic Anusandhan Patrika* (2 a year, in Hindi), *Indian Journal of Biochemistry and Biophysics* (6 a year), *Indian Journal of Biotechnology* (4 a year), *Indian Journal of Chemical Technology* (6 a year), *Indian Journal of Chemistry, Sec A* (12 a year), *Indian Journal of Chemistry, Sec B* (12 a year), *Indian Journal of Engineering and Materials Sciences* (6 a year), *Indian Journal of Experimental Biology* (12 a year), *Indian Journal of Fibre and Textile Research* (4 a year), *Indian Journal of Marine Sciences* (4 a year), *Indian Journal of Pure and Applied Physics* (12 a year), *Indian Journal of Radio and Space Physics* (6 a year), *Indian Journal of Traditional Knowledge* (4 a year), *Indian Science Abstracts* (26 a year), *Journal of Intellectual Property Rights* (6 a year), *Journal of Scientific and Industrial Research* (12 a year), *Medicinal and Aromatic Plants Abstracts* (6 a year), *Natural Product Radiance* (6 a year).

National Social Science Documentation Centre: 35 Ferozshah Rd, New Delhi 110001; tel. (11) 23074393; e-mail nassdoc@icssr.org; internet www.icssr.org/doc_main.htm; f. 1969; attached to Indian Ccl of Social Science Research; provides information and documentation service for social scientists, policy-makers and others working in the academic and govt sectors, business and industry; provides library and reference services, document delivery and reprographic services, consultancy service, select bibliography service, training courses; 15,000 vols, 11,000 bound vols of periodicals, 565 current periodicals, 150,000 serial vols, 5,000 PhD theses, 3,000 research projects and reports, conf. papers, working papers; Dir Dr P. R. GOSWAMI; Deputy Dir SAVITRI DEVI; Deputy Dir INDRA KAUL; publs *Annotated Index of Indian Social Science Journals* (2 a year), *Bibliographic Reprints* (irregular), *Conference Alert* (4 a year).

Nehru Memorial Museum & Library: Teen Murti House, New Delhi 110011; tel. (11) 23794407; e-mail radheyshyam58@yahoo.com; internet www.nehrumemorial.nic.in; f. 1964; attached to Min. of Culture; archival collns on modern Indian history with emphasis on Indian nationalism; research centre for interdisciplinary studies in modern Indian history and society; large colln of newspapers, microfilms, private papers, institutional records, photographs and oral history recordings; 27,000 vols, 18,500 microfilm rolls, 465 journals; Chair. KARAN SINGH; Dir Prof. Dr MAHESH RANGARAJAN.

Gujarat

British Council Library: Bhaikaka Bhavan, Law Garden Rd, Ahmedabad 380006, Gujarat; tel. (79) 26464693; e-mail bl.ahmedabad@in.britishcouncil.org; f. 1979; adult lending, junior colln, English language colln, British home DVDs colln, colln of magazines on contemporary Britain; 25,000 vols; Man. MOUMITA BHATTACHARYA.

Central Library: Nr Mandvi Gate, Vadodara 390006, Gujarat; tel. (265) 2415713; f. 1910; 301,000 vols; State Librarian KAUSHIK SHAH; publ. *Granth Deep* (4 a year).

Gujarat Vidyapeeth Granthalaya (Gujarat Vidyapeeth Library): Ashram Rd, Ahmedabad 380014, Gujarat; tel. (79) 40016260; e-mail libhod@gujaratvidyapith.org; internet www.gujaratvidyapith.org/centrallibrary.htm; f. 1920; Univ., State Central and Public Library combined; depository colln; 594,497 vols, 400 journals, 691 MSS, 209 microfilms; Librarian Dr RAXA A. PATEL (acting).

Seth Maneklal Jethabhai Pustakalay (M. J. Library): Ellisbridge, Near Town Hall, Ahmedabad 380006, Gujarat; tel. (79) 26578513; internet www.amcmjlibrary.com; f. 1933; UNESCO programmes for children's libraries; 178,317 vols; Chair. ASITBHAI RAVINDRAPRASAD VORA; Librarian Dr BIPENCHANDRA J. MODI (acting).

Himachal Pradesh

Library of Tibetan Works & Archives: Gangchen Kyishong, Dharamsala 176215, Himachal Pradesh; tel. (1892) 222467; e-mail info@ltwa.net; internet www.ltwa.net; f. 1970; repository for Tibetan artefacts, statues, MSS, Thangkas (traditional scroll paintings), photographs, other resources attributing to Tibetan culture; 113,000 vols incl. MSS, books, xylographs, documents, illuminated scriptures; Dir Ven. Geshe LHAKDOR; Gen. Sec. NGAWANG YESHI; publ. *The Tibet Journal* (4 a year).

Karnataka

British Council Library: Prestige Takt, 23 Kasturba Rd Cross, Opposite Visweswaraya Industrial and Technological Museum, Bengaluru 560001, Karnataka; tel. (80) 22489220; e-mail bl.bangalore@in.britishcouncil.org; f. 1960; 28,000 vols; Man. CHARU SAPRA.

Karnataka Government Secretariat Library: Room No 11, Ground Fl., Vidhana Soudha, Dr Ambedkar Veedhi, Bengaluru 560001, Karnataka; tel. (80) 22033462; e-mail s_library@rediffmail.com; internet vslib.kar.nic.in; f. c. 1919; colln of govt reports, compendiums; 129,100 vols, 20 newspapers, 70 periodicals; Chief Librarian ANANTH N. KASKAR.

State Central Library: Cubbon Park, Bengaluru 560001, Karnataka; tel. (80) 22212128; f. 1914; 140,000 vols; State Librarian and Head of Public Libraries N. D. BAGERI.

Kerala

Kerala State Central Library: Palayam, Vikas Bhavan PO, Thiruvananthapuram, Kerala; tel. (471) 2322895; e-mail aascl@statelibrary.kerala.gov.in; internet www.statelibrary.kerala.gov.in; f. 1829 as Trivandrum People's Library, present name 1958, present status 1992; colln incl. documents in different languages such as English, Malayalam, Hindi, Tamil, Sanskrit, in various disciplines; 367,243 vols, 215 journals; State Librarian P. SUPRABHA; Deputy State Librarian P. K. SOBHANA.

Maharashtra

Jamsetjee Nesserwanjee Petit Institute Library: 312 Dr Dadabhoy Naoroji Rd, Fort, Mumbai 400001, Maharashtra; tel. (22) 22048463; e-mail petitheritage_01@yahoo.co.in; f. 1856 as 'Fort Improvement Library'; attached to Jamsetjee Nesserwanjee Petit Institute; 160,000 vols; Admin. J. R. MODY.

Punjab

Panjab University Extension Library: Panjab Univ. Regional Centre, Civil Lines, Ludhiana 141001, Punjab; tel. (161) 2443830; e-mail dkapur@pu.ac.in; internet puel.puchd.ac.in; f. 1960; attached to Panjab Univ.; serves educational instns within a radius of 60 km; 167,000 vols; Dir DEEPAK KAPUR (acting).

Tamil Nadu

Adyar Library and Research Centre: Theosophical Soc., Adyar, Chennai 600020, Tamil Nadu; tel. (44) 24913528; e-mail alrc.hq@ts-adyar.org; internet www.ts-adyar.org/content/adyar-library-and-research-centre; f. 1886; attached to Theosophical Soc.; colln incl. Chinese Tripitakas, Tibetan Kanjur and Tanjur, rare works in Latin and other western languages, research journals; 250,000 vols, 20,000 palm-leaf MSS, 225 int. journals; Dir Dr S. SANKARANARAYANAN; Librarian Prof. C. A. SHINDE (acting); publ. *Brahmavidya* (1 a year).

Connemara Public Library: Pantheon Rd, Egmore, Chennai 600008, Tamil Nadu; tel. (44) 28193751; e-mail librarian@connemarapubliclibrarychennai.com; internet www.connemarapubliclibrarychennai.com; f. 1896; deposit library from 1954 for all Indian publs; information centre for UN and allied agencies and for Asian Devt Bank; 722,000 vols, 3,500 periodicals; Librarian Dr KANNAPPAN THANGAMARI (acting); publ. *Tamil Nadu State Bibliography* (12 a year, in Tamil).

Government Oriental Manuscripts Library and Research Centre: Univ. Library Bldg, Chepauk, Chennai 600005, Tamil Nadu; tel. (44) 25365130; internet www.telupu.com/goml.html; f. 1869; acquisition, preservation and publn of rare and important colln of MSS in Sanskrit, Islamic and S Indian languages; 25,373 vols, 72,314 MSS; Curator M. SESHAGIRI SASTRI.

Indian Institute of Technology Madras Central Library: Chennai 600036, Tamil Nadu; tel. (44) 22574951; e-mail hchandra@iitm.ac.in; internet www.cenlib.iitm.ac.in; f. 1959; colln of technical and scientific books (German and English); partial archive of scientific films; user education programmes; 242,720 vols, 1,384 current periodicals, 448 films, 1,600 microfilms and microfiches; Chief Librarian Dr HARISH CHANDRA.

Madras Literary Society Library: College Rd, Nungambakkam, Chennai 600006, Tamil Nadu; tel. (44) 28279666; f. 1812; 80,000 vols; Librarian UMA MAHESHWARI; Hon. Sec. MOHAN RAMAN.

Uttar Pradesh

Acharya Narendra Dev Pustakalaya (Acharya Narendra Dev Library): 10 Ashoka Marg, Lucknow; f. 1959; public library; spec. emphasis on social sciences; 125,000 vols, 150 periodicals; Sr Librarian NARESH SINGH.

Allahabad Government Public Library: Chandra Shekher Azad Park (Alfred Park), Allahabad 211002, Uttar Pradesh; tel. (532) 2460197; e-mail info@allahabadpublib.org; internet www.allahabadpublib.org; f. 1864; old govt publs, gazettes, parliamentary papers and blue books of the 19th century, old newspapers, journals and magazines; reference and research service; 110,000 vols; Librarian GOPAL MOHAN SHUKLA.

West Bengal

Centre for Asian Documentation: K-15, CIT Bldgs, Christopher Rd, POB 11215, Kolkata 700014, West Bengal; provides reference services; Dir S. CHAUDHURI; publs *Index Asia Series in Humanities* (irregular), *Index Indo-Asiasticus* (4 a year), *Index Internationalis Indicus* (1 in 3 years), *Indian Biography* (1 a year), *Indian Science index* (1 in 2 years).

National Library: Belvedere, Kolkata 700027, West Bengal; tel. (33) 24791381; e-mail nldirector@rediffmail.com; internet www.nationallibrary.gov.in; f. 1903 by merger of the Calcutta Public Library (f. 1836) and Imperial Library (f. 1891); depository and research library; 4,145 microfilms, 94,500 microfiches, 17,650 periodicals; incl. Central Reference Library, at the same address, compiles *Indian National Bibliography*, but does not hold a book colln; 2.18m. vols, 84,952 maps, 3,127 MSS; Dir-Gen. Prof. SWAPAN CHAKRAVORTY; Librarian H. P. GEDAM; Librarian Dr R. RAMACHANDRAN; publs *Bibliographical Control in India*, *Bibliographies*, *Conservation of Library Materials*, *General Collection Author and Subject Catalogues*, *India's National Library—Systematization and Modernization*, *Indological Studies and South Asia Bibliography*, *Rabindra Grantha Suchi* (vol 1 part 1), *The National Library and Public Libraries in India*.

Museums and Art Galleries

Andhra Pradesh

Andhra Pradesh State Museum: Hyderabad 500034, Andhra Pradesh; f. 1930, fmrly Hyderabad Museum, current name adopted 1968; sculpture, epigraphy, arms and weapons, bidriware, bronze objects, miniatures and paintings, MSS, numismatics, European paintings (prints), decorative and modern arts, textiles; excavations at Yeleswaram Pochampal, Peddabankur; Dir Dr V. V. KRISHNA SASTRY.

Archaeological Museum: Amaravati, Guntur 522439, Andhra Pradesh; tel. (8645) 255225; e-mail asamnkonda@gmail.com; f. 1966; prehistoric and historical antiquities, mainly sculptures belonging to Buddhism (3rd–4th centuries AD) and Hinduism (15th–16th centuries AD); Asst Superintending Archaeologist BABUJI RAO CHERUKURI.

Salar Jung Museum: Hyderabad 500002, Andhra Pradesh; tel. (40) 24576443; e-mail salarjungmuseum@gmail.com; internet www.salarjungmuseum.in; f. 1951; paintings, textiles, porcelain, jade, carpets, MSS, antiques, ivory, glass, silver- and bronze-ware; children's section; library of 62,772 vols, incl. Persian, Arabic and Urdu MSS; Dir Dr A. NAGENDER REDDY; publ. *SJM Bi-Annual Research Journal*.

Assam

Assam State Museum: Gopinath Bordoloi Rd, Mawhati, Ambari, Guwahati 781001, Assam; tel. (361) 2550245; f. 1940; indological and archaeological studies; library of 5,850 vols; Dir Dr R. D. CHOUDHURY.

Bihar

Archaeological Museum: Bodh Gaya, Gaya, Bihar; tel. (631) 2200739; f. 1956; bronze and stone sculptures of Buddhist and Brahmanical faith of Pala period, scenes related to Buddhist pantheon, Surya, Zodiac signs on railings of Sunga age, etc.; Asst Superintending Archaeologist S. K. SINHA.

Archaeological Museum: Archaeological Survey of India, Nalanda, Bihar; tel. (6112) 281824; f. 1917; collns of antiquities belonging to 5th–12th century AD, sculptures made of stone, bronze, stucco, terracotta, basalt stone; Asst Superintending Archaeologist K. C. SRIVASTAVA.

Patna Museum: Patna-Gaya Rd, Buddha Marg, Patna 800001; tel. (612) 2235731; f. 1917; archaeology, bronzes, ethnology, geology, arms and armour, natural history, art, coins, plaster casts, Tibetan paintings; Dr Rajendra Prasad's colln (first Pres. of India); Buddha Relic casket, sculpture park, shatabdi smarak etc.; publishes research on art, archaeology and ethnology; seminars and lectures; Dir J. P. N. SINGH; Curator ARVIND MAHAJAN.

Delhi

Archaeological Museum Red Fort, Delhi: Mumtaz Mahal, Red Fort, Delhi 110006; tel. (11) 23267961; f. 1909; historical collns of the Mughal period; old arms, seals and signets, letters, MSS, coins, miniatures, Mughal dresses and relics of India's War of Independence; library of 420 vols; Asst Superintending Archaeologist V. D. JADHAV.

National Gallery of Modern Art: Jaipur House, India Gate, New Delhi 110003; tel. (11) 23386111; e-mail info@ngmaindia.gov.in; internet ngmaindia.gov.in; f. 1954; attached to Min. of Culture; contemporary art (paintings, sculpture, drawings, graphics, architecture, industrial design, photography, prints and minor arts); Dir Prof. RAJEEV LOCHAN.

National Gandhi Museum/Gandhi Memorial Museum: Rajghat, New Delhi 110002; tel. (11) 23310168; e-mail gandhimuseumdelhi@gmail.com; internet www.gandhimuseum.org; f. 1953; collects and displays Gandhi's records and mementos and promotes the study of his life and work; library of 45,000 vols, 25,000 documents, 80 periodicals, films and recordings, 9,000 photographs, large picture galleries; Chair. Prof. BIMAL PRASAD; Dir Dr SANGITA MALLIK; Head of Library S. K. BHATNAGAR.

National Handicrafts & Handlooms Museum/Crafts Museum: Pragati Maidan, Bhairon Marg, New Delhi 110001; tel. (11) 23371641; e-mail craftsmuseumindia@gmail.com; internet www.nationalcraftsmuseum.nic.in; f. 1956; attached to Min. of Textiles; Indian traditional crafts and tribal arts; 22,000 objects incl. bronze images, lamps and incense burners, ritual accessories, utensils and other items of everyday use, wood and stone carving, papier mache, ivories, dolls, toys, puppets and masks, jewellery, decorative metalware incl. bidri work, paintings, terracotta, cane and bamboo work; library of 12,000 vols; Chair. Dr RUCHIRA GHOSE.

National Museum of India: 1 Janpath, New Delhi 110011; tel. (11) 23019272; internet www.nationalmuseumindia.gov.in; f. 1949; attached to Min. of Culture; depts of art, archaeology, anthropology, modelling, presentation, preservation, publication, library and photography; displays 2,00,000 works of exquisite art incl. Indian prehistoric tools, protohistoric remains from Harappa, Mohenjodaro, etc., representative collns of sculptures, terracottas, stuccos and bronzes from 2nd century BC to 18th century AD; illustrated MSS and miniatures; Stein Colln of Central Asian murals and other antiquities; decorative arts; textiles, coins and illuminated epigraphical charts; armour; copperplate etchings; woodwork; library of 43,400 vols; Dir-Gen. R. C. MISHRA; Dir of Collection and Administration U. DAS.

National Museum of Natural History: Tansen Marg, Mandi House, New Delhi 110001; tel. (11) 23314849; e-mail dirnmnh@gmail.com; internet nmnh.nic.in; f. 1978; attached to Min. of Environment and Forests; galleries on natural history, ecology; conservation cell; educational programmes for children and other groups, school loan service, mobile museum for rural extension service; controls regional museums of natural history in Mysore, Bhopal, Bhubaneswar, Sawai Madhopur; library of 35,000 vols; Dir Dr BHARGAVIAMMA VENUGOPAL.

National Rail Museum: Chanakyapuri, New Delhi 110021; tel. (11) 26881816; e-mail mail.contactnrm@yahoo.in; internet www.nrm.indianrailways.gov.in; f. 1977; displays exhibits, working and dummy models, coats of arms, records, historical documents, photographs, charts depicting the devt and growth of railways in India; exhibits a model of the Patiala State Monorail Trainways (in operation from 1907 to 1927), the Fairy Queen (built in 1855), the Prince of Wales Saloon (built in 1875); library of 6,000 vols, 1,100 MSS; Dir UDAY SINGH MEENA.

Rabindra Bhavan Art Gallery: 35 Ferozeshah Rd, New Delhi; tel. (11) 23387241; e-mail lka@bol.net.in; f. 1955; permanent gallery of the Lalit Kala Akademi (Nat. Academy of Art), and venue of the Nat. Exhibition of Art and Triennale-India (international art); Chair. Dr SARAYU V. DOSHI; publs *Lalit Kala Ancient* (2 a year), *Lalit Kala Contemporary* (4 a year), *Samkaleen Kala* (4 a year, in Hindi).

Shankar's International Dolls Museum: Nehru House, 4 Bahadur Shah Zafar Marg, New Delhi 110002; tel. (11) 23316970; e-mail cbtnd@cbtnd.com; internet www.childrensbooktrust.com/dm.htm; f. 1965; 6,700 exhibits from all over the world; Dir SHANTA SRINIVASAN.

Gujarat

Baroda Museum and Picture Gallery: Sayaji Bagh, Vadodra 390018, Gujarat; tel. (265) 2793801; f. 1887, museum completed in 1894 and picture gallery in 1920; Indian archaeology; prehistoric and historic; Indian art: ancient, medieval and modern; numismatic collns; modern Indian paintings; industrial art; Asiatic and Egyptian collns; Greek, Roman, European civilizations and art; European paintings; ethnology, zoology, geology, economic botany; library of 19,000 vols; Dir R. D. PARMAR; Curator V. M. PATEL; publ. *Museums in Gujarat*.

Sarabhai Foundation—Calico Museum of Textiles: Sarabhai Foundation, Shahibag, Ahmedabad 380004, Gujarat; tel. (79) 22868172; e-mail calicomuseum@gmail.com; internet www.calicomuseum.com; f. 1948; colln of 17th- and 18th-century Indian textiles and costumes, shawls, large tents, carpets, religious textiles and artefacts, Indian miniature paintings, Indian bronzes and reconstructed carved wooden façades from 17th to 19th centuries; Man. Trustee GIRA SARABHAI; Dir D. S. MEHTA; publ. *Historical Textiles of India at Calico Museum*.

Jammu and Kashmir

Shri Pratap Singh Museum: Lalmandi, Srinagar 190008, Jammu and Kashmir; internet spsmuseum.org; f. 1898; colln incl. numismatics and MSS, miniature paintings, weapons and utensils, musical instruments, furniture and decorative items, textiles and carpets, items of leather, grass and willow work, sculptures, tiles and other artefacts excavated in various parts of Kashmir, history, stuffed birds and animals; library of 1,300 vols about cultural subjects; Curator M. S. ZAHID.

Karnataka

Government Museum: Kasturba Gandhi Rd, Bengaluru 560001, Karnataka; tel. (080) 22864483; f. 1866; art, archaeology, industrial art and natural history; houses prehistoric artefacts belonging to the Neolithic period; library of 2,000 vols; Curator (vacant).

Visvesvaraya Industrial and Technological Museum: Kasturba Rd, PMB 5216, Bengaluru 560001, Karnataka; tel. (80) 22866200; e-mail vitm@vsnl.com; internet www.vismuseum.org.in; f. 1962; attached to Nat. Ccl of Science Museums; promotes interest in science and technology, and to explain the application of technology in industry and human welfare; artefacts related to engines, transportation, telecommunication, aviation, rockets, computational devices etc.; library of 10,230 vols, also audiovisual materials; Dir K. V. BHATTA.

Maharashtra

Central Museum: Civil Lines, Nagpur 440001, Maharashtra; tel. (712) 2546314; f. 1863; objects relating to archaeology, art, tribal art and culture, natural history, sculpture, weapons and metal objects; Curator S. M. GURAV (acting).

Chhatrapati Shivaji Maharaj Vastu Sangrahalay (Chhatrapati Shivaji Maharaj Museum): 159–161 Mahatma Gandhi Rd, Fort, Mumbai 400023, Maharashtra; tel. (22) 22844484; e-mail csmvsmumbai@gmail.com; internet www.themuseummumbai.com; f. 1905, fmrly Prince of Wales Museum of Western India; archaeology, Chinese and Japanese colln, Indian decorative art, Indian miniature paintings, natural history; library of 30,000 vols; Dir SABYASACHI MUKHERJEE.

Dr Bhau Daji Lad Mumbai City Museum: 19/A Rani Baug, Veer Mata Jijbai Bhonsle Udyan, Dr Baba Saheb Ambedkar Rd, Byculla E, Mumbai 400027, Maharashtra; tel. (22) 23731234; e-mail bdlmuseum@gmail.com; internet www.bdlmuseum.org; f. 1872; reference library on Indian and foreign art, archaeology, ethnology, geology, history, numismatics and museology; exhibits of agriculture and village life, armoury, cottage industries, ethnology, fine arts, crafts, fossils, Indian coins, minerals, misc. colln, Old Mumbai colln; oldest museum in Mumbai; Man. Trustee and Hon. Dir TASNEEM ZAKARIA MEHTA; Sr Asst Curator PREEMA JOHN.

Manipur

Manipur State Museum: Polo-ground, Imphal, Manipur; colln of portraits of Manipur's former rulers.

Orissa

Orissa State Museum: BJB Nagar, Lewis Rd, Bhubaneswar 751006, Orissa; tel. (674) 2431597; internet orissamuseum.nic.in; f. 1932; archaeology, epigraphy, numismatics, armoury, arts and crafts, contemporary art, anthropology, palm-leaf MSS, natural history; library of 22,000 vols, 2,000 periodicals; Superintendent MANJUSHREE SAMANTARAI (acting); publ. *Orissa Historical Research Journal* (4 a year).

Rajasthan

Government Museum: Bikaner 334001, Rajasthan; tel. (151) 2528894; f. 1937; colln of terracottas, sculptures, bronzes, coins, inscriptions, Rajasthani paintings, documents, arms and costumes, specimens of folk-culture; colln incl. 71 stone sculptures, 10 inscriptions, 92 miniature paintings, 124 terracottas, 27 metallic objects, 574 arms, 22,241 coins, 1,108 objects of local art, craft and textiles; Curator K. N. VYAS.

Maharaja Sawai Man Singh II Museum: City Palace, Jaipur 302002, Rajasthan; tel. (141) 2615681; e-mail info@msmsmuseum .com; f. 1959; textiles and costumes, armoury, Mughal and Rajasthani miniature paintings, Persian and Mughal carpets, transport accessories, regalia, historical documents, maps and plans, MSS library of 10,000 Sanskrit, Persian, Hindi and Rajasthani MSS; Dir B. M. S. PARMAR.

Rajputana Museum: Ajmer 305001, Rajasthan; f. 1908; archaeology; rare sculptures, architectural carvings, old coins, epigraphs, Rajput paintings, arms and armour of Rajasthan; Curator R. D. SHARMA.

Tamil Nadu

Fort Museum: Archaeological Survey of India, Fort St George, Chennai 600009, Tamil Nadu; tel. (44) 25671127; f. 1948; exhibits belong mainly to the days of the East India Co; Asst Superintending Archaeologist P. S. SRIRAMAN.

Government Museum: Pantheon Rd, Egmore, Chennai 600008, Tamil Nadu; tel. (44) 28193238; e-mail govtmuse@tn.gov.in; internet www.chennaimuseum.org; f. 1851; archaeology, ancient and modern Indian art, S Indian bronzes, Buddhist sculptures, numismatics, philately, anthropology, botany, zoology, geology, chemical conservation education, contemporary art, design and display; Dir M. A. SIDDIQUE; publ. *Madras Museum Bulletins*.

Uttar Pradesh

Archaeological Museum: Varanasi 221007, Uttar Pradesh; tel. (542) 2595095; e-mail museumsrnthasi@gmail.com; f. 1910; archaeological site museum; Buddhist and Hindu colln from 3rd century BC to 12th century AD; Deputy Superintending Archaeologist S. K. GHOSAL.

Bharat Kala Bhavan: Banaras Hindu Univ., Varanasi 221005, Uttar Pradesh; tel. (542) 316337; e-mail bharatkalabhavan@sify .com; internet www.bhu.ac.in/kala/ index_bkb.htm; f. 1920, present status 1950; attached to Banaras Hindu Univ.; 100,000 holdings incl. archaeological materials, paintings, textiles and costumes, decorative art, personalia collns; Indian philately and literary collns; archival materials; library: approx. 14,000 vols and periodicals, 26,511 MSS; Dir Prof. DEV PRAKASH MISHRA; publs *Chhavi*, *Kala Nidhi*.

Government Museum: Dampier Nagar, Mathura 281001, Uttar Pradesh; f. 1874; 40,000 items, dominated by sculptures, terracottas of Mathura School to Kushana and Gupta period; coins, paintings; library: reference library of 20,000 vols.

Uttar Pradesh State Museum: Banarasibagh, Lucknow, Uttar Pradesh; tel. (522) 2206158; f. 1863; collns of sculptures, terracottas, copper plates, numismatics, paintings, MSS, textiles and natural history specimens; anthropological colln; library of 15,000 vols; Dir R. C. TIWARI.

West Bengal

Asutosh Museum of Indian Art: Centenary Bldg, Univ. of Calcutta, Kolkata 700073, West Bengal; f. 1937; exhibits 25,000 items consisting of sculptures, paintings, folk-art objects, textiles, terracottas, etc.; library of 2,000 vols and periodicals; Curator Dr NIRANJAN GOSWAMI.

Birla Industrial and Technological Museum: Nat. Ccl of Science Museums, Govt. of India, 19A Gurusaday Rd, Kolkata 700019, West Bengal; tel. (33) 22802815; e-mail bitm@cal2.vsnl.net.in; internet www .bitmcal.org; f. 1959; attached to Nat. Ccl of Science Museums; portrays the history and devt of science and technology; 8 satellite centres and 8 mobile science exhibition buses in rural areas; educational programmes for students and teachers and the gen. public; film and CD library; archives; spec. collns on history and devt of science and technology, arts, painting, museology, etc.; library of 14,000 vols incl. periodicals; Dir SK. EMDADUL ISLAM; publ. *Popscience* (2 a year).

Indian Museum: 27 Jawaharlal Nehru Rd, Kolkata 700016, West Bengal; tel. (33) 22861679; e-mail imbot@cal2.vsnl.net.in; internet www.indianmuseumkolkata.org; f. 1814; collns of archaeology, art, coins, anthropology, geology, botany, zoology; herbarium; library of 45,000 vols; Dir Dr SAKTI KALI BASU; Librarian Dr PATRA CHITTARANJAN.

Rabindra Bhavana: Santiniketan, Birbhum 731235, West Bengal; tel. (3463) 262751; e-mail registrar@visva-bharati.ac .in; f. 1942; colln of MSS, letters, books, newspaper clippings, gramophone records, photographs, cine-film, paintings by Tagore and tape recordings of his voice; library of 40,000 books and over 12,000 bound journals; publ. *Rabindra–Viksa* (2 a year).

Victoria Memorial Hall: 1 Queens Way, Kolkata 700071, West Bengal; tel. (33) 22231890; e-mail victomem@cal2.vsnl.net .in; internet www.victoriamemorial-cal.org; f. 1921; museum of medieval Indian history and culture, and British Indian history of the late 18th and early 19th centuries; wide colln of oilpaintings and watercolours by European artists of 18th and 19th centuries; sketches, miniatures, engravings, photographs, sculptures, maps, MSS, furniture, stamps, coins, medals, textiles, arms and armour; library of 13,030 vols; Chair. GOVERNOR OF WEST BENGAL; Sec. and Curator Prof. CHITTARANJAN PANDA.

Universities

There are three types of university in India: Affiliating and Teaching (most teaching done in colleges affiliated to the university, but some teaching, mostly postgraduate, undertaken by the university); Unitary (all teaching done on one campus); and Central (universities established by Acts of Parliament). It is not possible, for reasons of space, to give details of affiliated colleges.

ACHARYA N. G. RANGA AGRICULTURAL UNIVERSITY

Rajendranagar, Hyderabad 500030, Andhra Pradesh
Telephone: (40) 24015011
E-mail: angrau@ap.nic.in
Internet: www.angrau.net

Founded 1964 as Andhra Pradesh Agricultural Univ., current name adopted 1996
State control
Languages of instruction: English, Telugu
Academic year: July to June

Chancellor: HE GOV. OF ANDHRA PRADESH
Vice-Chancellor: V. NAGI REDDY (acting)
Registrar: Dr K. V. S. MEENA KUMARI (acting)
Dir for Extension: Dr P. GIDDA REDDY
Dir for Research: Dr R. SUDHAKAR RAO
Dean of Student Affairs: Dr D. RAJARAM REDDY (acting)
Librarian: Dr K. VEERANJANEYULU

Library of 200,000 vols, 500 periodicals
Number of teachers: 1,035
Number of students: 3,853

Publication: *Journal of Research ANGRAU* (4 a year)

DEANS

Faculty of Agriculture: Dr T. YELLMANDA REDDY
Faculty of Agricultural Engineering and Technology: Dr T. V. SATYANARAYANA
Faculty of Home Science: Dr A. SHARADA DEVI
Postgraduate Studies: Dr V. B. BHANU MURTHY

ACHARYA NAGARJUNA UNIVERSITY

Nagarjuna Nagar 522510, Andhra Pradesh
Telephone: (863) 2346182
E-mail: isc@anu.ac.in
Internet: www.nagarjunauniversity.ac.in

Founded 1976 as Nagarjuna University, present name 1994
State control
Language of instruction: English
Academic year: July to April

Chancellor: HE GOV. OF ANDHRA PRADESH
Vice-Chancellor: Prof. K. VIYYANNA RAO (acting)
Registrar: Prof. M. V. N. SARMA
Librarian: Dr K. VENKATA RAO

Library of 123,200 vols, 302 periodicals
Number of teachers: 148
Number of students: 1,700

DEANS

Faculty of Commerce and Management: Prof. G. PRASAD
Faculty of Education: Dr J. PRASANTH KUMAR
Faculty of Engineering: Dr A. SUDHAKAR
Faculty of Humanities: Prof. R. SARASWATHI
Faculty of Law: Prof. L. JAYASREE
Faculty of Natural Sciences: Prof. Z. VISHNUVARDHAN
Faculty of Pharmacy: Prof. N. RAMA RAO
Faculty of Physical Sciences: Prof. B. SYAMA SUNDAR
Faculty of Social Sciences: Prof. M. V. N. SARMA

PROFESSORS

Faculty of Commerce:

BRAHMANANDAM, G. N., Commerce
DAKSHINA MURTHY, D., Commerce
GANJU, M. K., Commerce
HANUMANTHA RAO, K., Commerce
NARASIMHAM, V. V. L., Commerce
PRASAD, G., Commerce
UMAMAHESWARA RAO, T., Commerce
VIYYANNA RAO, K., Commerce

Faculty of Engineering:

THRIMURTY, P., Computer Science and Engineering

Faculty of Humanities:

BALAGANGADHARA RAO, Y., Telugu and Languages
BHASKARA MURTHY, D., Ancient History and Archaeology
KRUPACHARY, G., Telugu and Languages
KUMARASWAMY, Y., Ancient History and Archaeology
NIRMALA, T., Telugu and Oriental Languages
PUNNA RAO, A., Telugu and Oriental Languages
RAMA SASTRY, N. A., Telugu and Languages
RAMALAKSHMI, P., Ancient History and Archaeology
SARASWATHI, R., English
SUBRAHMANYAM, B. R., Ancient History and Archaeology

Faculty of Law:

HARAGOPAL REDDY, Y. R.
RANGAIAH, N., Law
VIJAYANARAYANA REDDY, D.

Faculty of Natural Sciences:

BALAPARAMESWARA RAO, M., Aquaculture
DURGA PRASAD, M. K., Zoology
GOPALAKRISHNA REDDY, T., Zoology
LAKSHMI, N., Botany
MALLAIAH, K. V., Botany
NARASIMHA RAO, P., Botany
NIRAMALA MARY, T., Botany
RAMAMOHANA RAO, P., Botany
RAMAMURTHY NAIDU, K., Botany
RANGA RAO, V., Geology
SANTHA KUMARI, D., Botany
SHARMA, S. V., Zoology

Faculty of Physical Sciences:

ANJANEYULU, Y., Chemistry
GOPALA KRISHNA MURTHY, P. V., Physics
HARANADH, C., Physics
KOTESWARA RAO, G., Mathematics
NARASIMHAM, V. L., Statistics
NARAYANA MURTHY, P., Physics
PRAKASA RAO, L., Mathematics
PRAKASA RAO, N. S., Chemistry
RAMA BADRA SARMA, I., Mathematics
RAMAKOTAIAH, D., Mathematics
RANGACHARYULU, H., Physics
SATYANANDAM, G., Physics
SATYANARAYANA, P. V. V., Chemistry
SHYAM SUNDAR, B., Chemistry
SIVA RAMA SARMA, B., Chemistry
VENKATACHARYULU, P., Physics
VENKATESWARA REDDY, Y., Mathematics

Faculty of Social Sciences:

ASHEERVADH, N., Political Science
BAPUJI, M., Political Science
BHAVANI, V., Political Science
NARAYANA RAO, C., Political Science
RAGHAVULU, C. V., Political Science and Public Administration
RAJA BABU, K., Economics
RAJU, C. S. N., Economics
SUDHAKARA RAO, N., Economics

ALAGAPPA UNIVERSITY

Alagappa Nagar, Karaikudi 630003, Tamil Nadu
Telephone: (4565) 228080
E-mail: registraralagappauniv@gmail.com
Internet: www.alagappauniversity.ac.in

Founded 1985
State control
Academic year: July to April (2 terms)

Chancellor: HE GOV. OF TAMIL NADU
Pro-Chancellor: P. PALANIAPPAN
Vice-Chancellor: Dr S. SUDALAIMUTHU
Registrar: Dr K. MANIMEKALAI (acting)
Controller of Examinations: Dr V. MANICKAVASAGAM
Dean of College Devt Ccl: Dr T. R. GURUMOORTHY
Dean of Student Welfare: Dr S. KALIAMOORTHY
Librarian: Dr A. THIRUNAVUKKARASU

Faculties of arts, education, management, science

Library of 64,000 vols, 121 periodicals
Number of teachers: 150
Number of students: 1,545.

ATTACHED CENTRES

Centre for Gandhian Studies: Dir Dr V. S. S. KANNAN.

Centre for Nehru Studies: Dir Dr B. DHARMALINGAM.

Centre for Rural Development: tel. (4565) 225842; Dir Dr A. NARAYANAMOORTHY

ALIGARH MUSLIM UNIVERSITY

Aligarh 202002, Uttar Pradesh
Telephone: (571) 2700220
E-mail: amucontrollerexams@gmail.com
Internet: www.amu.ac.in

Founded 1875 as Anglo-Mohamedan Oriental College, univ. status 1920
State control
Language of instruction: English
Academic year: July to May

Chancellor: (vacant)
Pro-Chancellor: MD. RAHMATULLAH KHAN SHERWANI
Vice-Chancellor: ZAMEER UDDIN SHAH
Registrar: Prof. Dr V. K. ABDUL JALEEL
Controller of Examinations: Prof. PERVEZ MUSTAJAB
Proctor: Prof. MUJAHID BAIG
Dean of Students' Welfare: Prof. AINUL HAQUE KHAN
Librarian: Prof. SHABAHAT HESSIAN

Library: 1.15m. vols; MSS in Arabic, Persian, Urdu and Hindi
Number of teachers: 1,400
Number of students: 30,000

Publication: *Aligarh Muslim University Gazette* (12 a year)

DEANS

Faculty of Agricultural Sciences: Prof. FARZANA ALIM
Faculty of Arts: Prof. QAZI AFZAL HUSAIN
Faculty of Commerce: Prof. SIBGHATULLAH FAROOQUI
Faculty of Engineering and Technology: Prof. S. MAHDI ABBAS RIZVI
Faculty of Law: Prof. MOHAMMAD SHABBIR
Faculty of Life Sciences: Prof. MASOOD AHMAD
Faculty of Management Studies and Research: Prof. JAVAID AKHTAR
Faculty of Medicine: Prof. A. K. VERMA
Faculty of Science: Prof. ABHA LAKSHMI SINGH
Faculty of Social Sciences: Prof. C. P. S. CHAUHAN
Faculty of Theology: Prof. SYED ALI MOHAMMAD NAQVI
Faculty of Unani Medicine: Prof. TAJUDDIN

ANDHRA UNIVERSITY

Visakhapatnam 530003, Andhra Pradesh
Telephone: (891) 2844444
E-mail: registrar@andhrauniversity.info
Internet: www.andhrauniversity.info

Founded 1926
State control
Languages of instruction: English, Telugu
Academic year: July to March

Colleges of arts and commerce, engineering, engineering for women, law, pharmacy, science and technology

Chancellor: HE GOV. OF ANDHRA PRADESH
Vice-Chancellor: Dr D. SAMBASIVA RAO
Rector: Prof. PRASAD REDDY
Registrar: Dr K. SAMRAJYA LAKSHMI (acting)
Dean of Academic Affairs: Prof. G. GNANAMANI
Dean of College Devt Ccl: Prof. S. K. V. SURYANARAYANA RAJU
Dean of Postgraduate Examinations: Prof. K. VISWESWARA RAO
Dean of Student Affairs: Prof. NIMMA VENKATA RAO
Dean of Undergraduate Examinations: Prof. L. D. SUDHAKARA BABU
Librarian: Prof. K. SOMASEKHARA RAO

Library of 431,800 vols
Number of teachers: 883
Number of students: 150,000

ANNA UNIVERSITY

Sardar Patel Rd, Guindy, Chennai 600025, Tamil Nadu
Telephone: (44) 22353445
E-mail: vc@annauniv.edu
Internet: www.annauniv.edu

Founded 1978 as Perarignar Anna Univ. of Technology, current name adopted 1982
State control
Language of instruction: English
Academic year: July to May

Vice-Chancellor: Prof. Dr P. KALIRAJ JAWAHAR
Registrar: Dr S. SIVANESAN
Controller of Examinations: Dr M. VENKATESAN
Dir for Admissions: Dr S. NAGARAJAN
Dir for Research: Dr USHA NATESAN
Dir for Student Affairs: Dr S. GANESAN
Dir for Univ. Library: Dr T. THYAGARAJAN (acting)

Library of 200,000 vols, 500 periodicals, 20,000 ejournals
Number of teachers: 800
Number of students: 19,000

DEANS

Alagappa College of Technology: Dr K. SANKARAN
College of Engineering: Dr M. SEKAR
Madras Institute of Technology: Dr S. THAMARAISELVI
School of Architecture and Planning: Dr RANEE MARIA VEDAMUTHU

ANNAMALAI UNIVERSITY

Annamalai Nagar 608002, Tamil Nadu
Telephone: (4144) 238248
E-mail: info@annamalaiuniversity.ac.in
Internet: www.annamalaiuniversity.ac.in

Founded 1929
State control
Languages of instruction: English, Tamil
Academic year: July to June

Chancellor: HE GOV. OF TAMIL NADU
Pro-Chancellor: Dr M. A. M. RAMASWAMY
Vice-Chancellor: Dr M. RAMANATHAN
Registrar: Dr M. RATHINASABAPATHI

Controller of Examinations: Dr R. MEENAKSHISUNDARAM
Librarian: Dr M. SURIYA

Library of 463,000 vols, 340 periodicals, palm-leaf MSS in Tamil and Sanskrit, gramophone records
Number of teachers: 2,945
Number of students: 33,011
Publication: *Annamalai University Research Journal*

DEANS
Faculty of Agriculture: Dr RM KATHIRESAN
Faculty of Arts: Dr D. SELVARAJU
Faculty of Dentistry: Dr RAVI DAVID AUSTIN
Faculty of Education: Dr G. VISVANATHAN
Faculty of Engineering and Technology: Prof. B. PALANIAPPAN
Faculty of Fine Arts: Prof. A. K. PALANIVEL
Faculty of Indian Languages: Dr P. L. MUTHUVEERAPPAN
Faculty of Marine Sciences: Dr T. BALASUBRAMAIAN
Faculty of Medicine: Dr N. CHIDAMBARAM
Faculty of Science: Dr AN. KANNAPPAN

ASSAM AGRICULTURAL UNIVERSITY

Jorhat 785013
Telephone: (376) 2340008
E-mail: vc@aau.ren.nic.in
Internet: www.aau.ac.in
Founded 1969
State control
Language of instruction: English
Academic year: August to July
Vice-Chancellor: Dr K. M. BUJARBARUAH
Registrar: Dr KRISHNA GOHAIN
Jt Academic Registrar: Dr ANUP K. DAS
Chief Librarian: Dr P. K. TALUKDAR

Library of 137,159 vols
Number of teachers: 480
Number of students: 1,686
Publications: *Ghare-Pathare* (12 a year, in Assamese), *Journal of Research*, *Krishibikshan* (4 a year, in Assamese), *Package of Practices for Kharif Crops* (2 a year, in English), *Package of Practices for Rabi Crops* (2 a year, in English)

DEANS
Faculty of Agriculture: Dr DIPTI KR. BORAH
Faculty of Home Science: Dr SATVINDER KAUR
Faculty of Veterinary Science: Dr R. N. GOSWAMI

ASSAM UNIVERSITY

Silchar 788011, Assam
Telephone: (3842) 270801
E-mail: auliba@sancharnet.in
Internet: www.aus.ac.in
Founded 1994
State control
Academic year: July to June
Chief Rector: HE GOV. OF ASSAM
Chancellor: Dr M. S. SWAMINATHAN
Vice-Chancellor: Prof. TAPODHIR BHATTACHARJEE
Pro Vice-Chancellor for Diphu Campus: Prof. B. MATE
Pro Vice-Chancellor for Silchar Campus: Prof. G. D. SHARMA
Finance Officer: Dr A. SEN (acting)
Controller of Examinations: Dr P. DEBNATH
Proctor: Dr M. DUTTA CHOUDHRY
Dir, CDC: Dr B. R. CHOUDHURY
Registrar: S. SENGUPTA
Librarian: V. D. SHRIVASTAVA

Library of 52,557 vols, 186 periodicals
Number of teachers: 140
Number of students: 1,446
Publications: *Journal of Assam University*, *Science in society: proceedings of regional symposium, Silchar: Problems of urban development of a growing city*

DEANS
School of Environmental Sciences: Prof. A. GUPTA
School of Humanities: Dr N. B. BISWAS
School of Information Sciences: Prof. G. P. PANDEY
School of Languages: Prof. S. DEVI
School of Life Sciences: Prof. G. D. SHARMA
School of Management Studies: Dr N. B. DEY
School of Physical Sciences: Prof. K. HEMACHANDRAN
School of Social Sciences: Prof. GOPALJI MISHRA
School of Technology: Prof. A. K. SEN

AWADHESH PRATAP SINGH UNIVERSITY

Rewa 486003, Madhya Pradesh
Telephone: (7662) 230050
E-mail: ccapsu@gmail.com
Internet: www.apsurewa.ac.in
Founded 1968
State control
Languages of instruction: Hindi, English
Academic year: July to June
Chancellor: HE GOV.OF MADHYA PRADESH
Vice-Chancellor: Prof. A. D. N. BAJPAI
Registrar: Dr R. S. PANDEY
Librarian: G. K. SINGH

Library of 31,000 vols
Number of teachers: 841 (42 at univ., 799 at affiliated colleges)
Number of students: 47,254 (incl. affiliated colleges)
Publication: *Vindhya Bharati* (4 a year)

DEANS
Faculty of Arts: R. R. MATHUR
Faculty of Ayurveda: Dr R. V. SOHGUNRA
Faculty of Commerce: Prof. I. P. TRIPATHI
Faculty of Education: Dr RASHAMI SHUKLA
Faculty of Home Science: Dr A. K. SHRIVASTAVA
Faculty of Law: R. R. MATHUR
Faculty of Life Science: Dr R. N. SHUKLA
Faculty of Medicine: Dr M. K. RATHORE
Faculty of Prachya Sanskrit: Dr BHASHKARACHARYA TRIPATHI
Faculty of Science: Dr S. K. NIGAM
Faculty of Social Science: Dr A. K. SHRIVASTAVA

BABA FARID UNIVERSITY OF HEALTH SCIENCES

Sadiq Rd, Faridkot 151203, Punjab
Telephone: (1639) 256232
E-mail: generalinfo@bfuhs.ac.in
Internet: www.bfuhs.ac.in
Founded 1998
State control
Language of instruction: English
Academic year: July to June
Chancellor: HE GOV. OF PUNJAB
Vice-Chancellor: Prof. Dr SHIVINDER SINGH GILL
Registrar: Dr DARSHAN SINGH SIDHU
Controller of Examination: Dr RAVINDER KAUR
Dean of College Devt: Prof. Dr P. S. SANDHU
Deputy Librarian and Head: Dr RAJEEV MANHAS

Library of 30,000 vols
Number of students: 24,000
Publications: *Baba Farid University Dental Journal*, *Baba Farid University Nursing Journal*

DEANS
Faculty of Ayurveda: Dr RAVINDER KAUR SHUKLA
Faculty of Dental Sciences: Dr VIMAL SIKRI
Faculty of Homeopathy: Dr TEJINDER PAL SINGH
Faculty of Medical Sciences: Dr SUDHIR KHICHI
Faculty of Nursing Sciences: Dr JASBIR KAUR
Faculty of Physiotherapy: Dr H. HARIHARA PRAKASH

BABASAHEB BHIMRAO AMBEDKAR UNIVERSITY

Vidya Vihar, Rai Bareilly Rd, Lucknow 226025, Uttar Pradesh
Telephone: (522) 2440822
E-mail: info@bbauindia.org
Internet: www.bbauindia.org
Founded 1996
State control
Academic year: July to June (2 terms)
Chancellor: Prof. U. R. RAO
Vice-Chancellor: Prof. B. HANUMAIAH
Registrar: Prof. SANJEEV KUMAR SINGH
Controller of Examination: MITHAI LAL KANAUJIA
Dean of Student Welfare: Prof. S. VICTOR BABU
Proctor: Prof. R. B. RAM
Librarian: K. L. MAHAWAR (acting)

Library of 9,000 vols, 40 current periodicals

DEANS
School of Ambedkar Studies: Prof. KAMESHWAR CHOUDHARY
School for Biosciences and Biotechnology: Prof. R. B. RAM
School for Environmental Sciences: Prof. R. P. SINGH
School for Home Sciences: Dr SUNITA MISHRA
School for Information Science and Technology: Prof. N. R. SATYANARAYANA
School for Management Studies: Prof. KAMESHWAR CHOUDHARY
School of Legal Studies: Prof. AJAY KUMAR
School of Physical Sciences: Dr R. G. SONKAWADE

BANARAS HINDU UNIVERSITY

Varanasi 221005, Uttar Pradesh
Telephone: (542) 2368938
E-mail: vcbhu1@gmail.com
Internet: www.bhu.ac.in
Founded 1916
State control
Languages of instruction: English, Hindi
Academic year: July to April (three terms)
Vice-Chancellor: Dr LALJI SINGH
Registrar: Prof. V. K. KUMRA
Controller of Examination: Dr K. P. UAPDHYAY
Dean of Students: Prof. A. R TRIPATHI
Chief Proctor: Prof. H. C. S. RATHOR
Librarian: Dr A. K. SRIVASTAVA

Library: 1.3m. vols
Number of teachers: 1,700
Number of students: 20,000
Publications: *BHU Journal*, *Prajna*

DEANS
Faculty of Agriculture: Prof. SUBEDAR SINGH
Faculty of Arts: Prof. KAMAL SHEEL
Faculty of Ayurveda: Prof. C. B. JHA
Faculty of Commerce: Prof. V. S. SINGH
Faculty of Dental Science: Prof. T. P. CHATURVEDI
Faculty of Education: Prof. P. N. SINGH
Faculty of Information Technology: Prof. G. N. AGRAWAL
Faculty of Law: Dr D. P. VERMA

Faculty of Management Studies: Prof. S. K. Singh
Faculty of Medicine: Prof. B. D. Bhatia
Faculty of Performing Arts: Prof. Sharda Velanker
Faculty of Sanskrit Vidya Dharma Vijnan Sankaya: Prof. R. C. Pandey
Faculty of Science: Prof. B. K. Ratha
Faculty of Social Science: Prof. A. K. Jain
Faculty of Visual Arts: Prof. B. Agrawal

BANGALORE UNIVERSITY

Jnanabharathi Campus, Jnana Bharathi Post Bengaluru 560056, Karnataka
Telephone: (80) 23213023
E-mail: buvicechancellor@bub.ernet.in
Internet: www.bub.ernet.in
Founded 1964
State control
Languages of instruction: English, Kannada
Academic year: June to March
Chancellor: HE Gov. of Karnataka
Vice-Chancellor: Prof. N. Prabhu Dev
Pro-Chancellor: Dr V. S. Acharya
Dir for College Devt Ccl: Prof. Mohamad Farooq Ahmed
Dir for Planning, Monitoring and Evaluation: Prof. G. Mohan Kumar
Dir for Physical Education: Dr Munireddy
Dir for Student Welfare: Dr Nandini
Registrar: Prof. R. M. Ranganath
Librarian: Dr P. V. Konnur
Library of 350,000 vols, 450 periodicals, 50,000 journals
Number of teachers: 456
Number of students: 300,000
Publications: *Bash Bharathi* (2 a year), *Janapriya Vignana* (12 a year), *Sadhane* (Kannada, 4 a year), *Vidya Bharathi*, *Vignana Bharathi*

DEANS

Faculty of Arts: N. Rangaswamy
Faculty of Commerce and Management: K. Janardhnam
Faculty of Education: M. B. Swamy Keerthinarayana
Faculty of Engineering: B. R. Niranjan
Faculty of Law: K. N. Hanumantharayappa
Faculty of Science: K. Puttaraju

BARKATULLAH VISHWAVIDYALAYA (Barkatullah University)

Hoshangabad Rd, Bhopal 462026, Madhya Pradesh
Telephone: (755) 2491800
E-mail: buregistrar@yahoo.co.in
Internet: www.bubhopal.nic.in
Founded 1970 as Bhopal Univ., current name adopted 1988
State control
Languages of instruction: English, Hindi
Chancellor: HE Gov. of Madhya Pradesh
Vice-Chancellor: Prof. Nisha Dube
Rector: Prof. D. C. Gupta
Registrar: Dr Sanjay P. Tiwari
Proctor: Prof. Neerja Sharma
Dir for College Devt Council: H. S. Yadav
Dean for Student Welfare: Dr Vivek Sharma
Controller of Examination: Dr S. V. S. Rajput
Librarian: Dr Arvind Chouhan
Library of 75,000 vols
Number of teachers: 1,100
Number of students: 40,000 (incl. affiliated colleges)

DEANS

Faculty of Arts: Prof. H. Khan
Faculty of Commerce: Dr D. P. Sharma
Faculty of Education: Dr Neerja Sharma
Faculty of Engineering: Dr A. S. Mehta
Faculty of Law: H. L. Jain
Faculty of Life Sciences: Dr N. C. Sharma
Faculty of Management: Dr N. R. Bhandari
Faculty of Science: Dr K. K. Rao
Faculty of Social Sciences: Dr H. S. Yadav

BENGAL ENGINEERING AND SCIENCE UNIVERSITY

PO Botanic Garden, Howrah 711103, West Bengal
Telephone: (33) 26684561
E-mail: vc@becs.ac.in
Internet: www.becs.ac.in
Founded 1856 as Civil Engineering College, Calcutta, 1992 deemed univ. status as Bengal Engineering College, current name and univ. status 2004
State control
Chancellor: HE Gov. of West Bengal
Vice-Chancellor: Dr Ajoy Kumar Ray
Dean of Research: Dr B. N. Datta
Dean of Students: A. K. Ghosh
Registrar: Dr Biman Bandyopadhyay
Finance Officer: Manindra Nath Sarkar
Controller of Examinations: Dr Bhaswati Mitra
Librarian: Dr Hari Prasad Sharma
Library of 200,000 vols, 300 periodicals
Number of students: 2,500

DEANS

Faculty of Basic and Applied Sciences: Prof. Bichitra Kumar Guha
Faculty of Engineering and Technology: Prof. Amit Kumar Das
Faculty of Social and Management Sciences: Prof. Manas Kumar Sanyal

CONSTITUENT SCHOOLS

Purabi Das School of Information Technology: Shibpur, Howrah, West Bengal; tel. (33) 26689312; e-mail office@pdsit.becdu.ac.in; internet pdsit.becs.ac.in; Dir Prof. Arindam Biswas.

School of Community Science and Technology (SOCSAT): f. 2004; offers MSc course on food and nutrition science; Dir Dr Bhaswati Mitra.

School of Disaster Mitigation Engineering: f. 2007; interdisciplinary research to facilitate and develop different mitigation processes against natural hazards; Dir Prof. Dr Ambarish Ghosh.

School of Ecology Infrastructure and Human Settlement Management: tel. (33) 26684561; Dir Prof. Sudip Kumar Roy.

School of Management Science (SOMS): f. 1999 as B. E. College School of Management Sciences, present name and status 2004; marketing, finance, operations, human resources, information technology; offers MBA and doctorate programme; Dir Prof. S. C. Saha.

School of Material Science and Engineering (SMSE): internet matsc.becs.ac.in; f. 2001; offers postgraduate courses in materials research; Dir Dr Nilratan Bandyopadhyay.

School of Mechatronics & Robotics: tel. (33) 26684561; e-mail pabitrakroy@hotmail.com; offeres postgraduate programme on mechatronics; Dir Prof. Pabitra Kumar Ray.

School of Safety and Occupational Health Engineering: offers postgraduate courses; Dir Prof. Bidyut Kumar Bhattacharya.

School of VLSI Technology: tel. (33) 26684561; internet vlsi.becs.ac.in; f. 2006; offers postgraduate and doctorate programmes; Dir Prof. Hafizur Rahman

BERHAMPUR UNIVERSITY

Berhampur 760007, Orissa
Telephone: (680) 2343234
E-mail: vcbuorissa@gmail.com
Internet: bamu.nic.in
Founded 1967
State control
Language of instruction: English
Academic year: June to May
Chancellor: HE Gov. of Orissa
Vice-Chancellor: Prof. J. K. Mohapatra
Comptroller: C. R. Satapathy
Controller of Examinations: Prof. M. Padhy
Chair. of Postgraduate Ccl: Prof. N. K. Tripathy
Dir of College Devt Ccl: Prof. B. C. Choudhury
Dir of Distance Education Ccl: Prof. B. K. Biswasroy
Registrar: B. P. Rath
Librarian: J. M. Panigrahy (acting)
Library of 96,997 vols, 33,000 back vols of journals
Number of teachers: 168
Number of students: 31,550
Publication: *Research Journal* (1 a year)

PROFESSORS

Acharya, S., Oriya
Baral, J. K., Political Science
Das, D., Oriya
Das, G. N., Linguistics
Das, H. H., Political Science
Das, N. C., Physics
Khan, P. A., Botany
Majhi, J., Electronics
Mishra, S. K., English
Misra, B. N., Botany
Misra, P. M., Marine Science
Mohanty, S. P., Physics
Mohapatra, N. C., Physics
Padhisharma, R., Economics
Panda, C. S., Chemistry
Panda, G. P., Law
Panda, G. S., Business Administration
Panda, J., Commerce
Panda, P., Economics
Panigrahy, G. P., Chemistry
Parhi, N., Mathematics
Pati, S. C., Chemistry
Patnaik, B. K., Zoology
Patra, G. C., Industrial Relations and Labour Welfare
Prasad, R., Zoology
Rao, E. R., English
Rath, D., Mathematics
Sahu, P. K., Commerce
Samal, J. K., History
Verma, G. P., Zoology

BHARATHIAR UNIVERSITY

Coimbatore 641046, Tamil Nadu
Telephone: (422) 2428100
E-mail: regr@buc.edu.in
Internet: www.b-u.ac.in
Founded 1982
State control
Academic year: July to April
Chancellor: HE Gov. of Tamil Nadu
Pro-Chancellor: Hon. Min. for Higher Education, Govt of Tamil Nadu
Vice-Chancellor: Dr C. Swaminathan
Registrar: Dr P. Thirumalvalavan
Controller of Examinations: Dr K. G. Senthil Vasan
Dir for School of Distance Education: Dr N. Balasubramanian
Public Relations Officer: N. J. Murali Mohan
Dir for Research: Dr S. Manian
Dean of College Devt Ccl: Dr P. K. Manoharan
Librarian: Dr P. Vinayakamoorthy

Library of 120,000 vols, 150 periodicals, 7,000 ejournals
Number of teachers: 130
Number of students: 2,300
Founded 1982

DEANS
Arts: Dr S. M. RAVICHANDRAN
Commerce: Dr G. GANESAN
Curriculum Development: Dr K. SWAMINATHAN
Education: Dr M. JAYAKUMAR
Research: Dr S. MANIAN
Science: Dr C. NAMASIVAYAM
Social Sciences: Dr R. VENKATAPATHY

BHARATHIDASAN UNIVERSITY

Palkalaiperur, Tiruchirappalli 620024, Tamil Nadu
Telephone: (431) 2407072
E-mail: office@bdu.ac.in
Internet: www.bdu.ac.in
Founded 1982
State control
Languages of instruction: English, Tamil
Academic year: June to April
Chancellor: HE GOV. OF TAMIL NADU
Pro-Chancellor: Hon. MIN. FOR HIGHER EDUCATION, GOVT OF TAMIL NADU
Vice-Chancellor: Dr K. MEENA
Registrar: Dr T. RAMASWAMY (acting)
Controller of Examinations: Dr S. SRIDHARAN
Librarian: Dr S. SRINIVASA RAGAVAN (acting)
Library of 95,000 vols, 204 periodicals
Number of teachers: 195
Number of students: 2,372

DEANS
Faculty of Arts: Dr N. RAJENDRAN
Faculty of Indian and Other Languages: Dr B. MATHIVANAN
Faculty of Science, Engineering and Technology: Dr M. DANIEL

BHAVNAGAR UNIVERSITY

Gaurishanker Lake Rd, Bhavnagar 364002, Gujarat
Telephone: (278) 2430002
E-mail: registrarbu@emailplus.org
Internet: www.bhavuni.edu
Founded 1979
State control
Language of instruction: Gujarati
Academic year: June to March (2 terms)
Chancellor: HE GOV. OF GUJARAT
Vice-Chancellor: Dr D. R. KORAT
Registrar: A. M. YUSUFZAI
Controller of Examinations: K. L. BHATT
Dir for External Studies: B. N. DESAI
Librarian: Dr B. M. GOHEL
Library of 107,137 vols, 175 journals
Number of teachers: 400
Number of students: 20,959

DEANS
Faculty of Arts: Prof. H. N. VAGHELA
Faculty of Commerce: Dr M. K. PATEL (acting)
Faculty of Education: Prof. J. P. MAIYANI
Faculty of Engineering: Prof. S. R. OZA
Faculty of Law: Dr J. A. PANDYA
Faculty of Management: Dr J. P. MAJMUDAR
Faculty of Medicine: Dr C. B. TRIPATHI
Faculty of Rural Studies: MOHANBHAI KOTADIYA
Faculty of Science: Prof. BHARTIBEN P. DAVE

BHUPENDRA NARAYAN MANDAL UNIVERSITY

Laloo Nagar, Madhepura 852113, Bihar
Telephone: (6476) 222059
E-mail: vcbnmu_2007@rediffmail.com
Internet: bnmu.bih.nic.in
Founded 1992
State control
27 Constituent colleges, 24 affiliated colleges, 2 postgraduate centres
Vice-Chancellor: Prof. QAMAR AHSAN
Pro-Vice-Chancellor: Dr NAND KISHORE SINGH
Dean for Students Welfare: MD. NAZIR UDDIN
Proctor: Dr SHIV NARAYAN YADAV
Registrar: BADRI P. YADAV
Controller of Examinations: Dr R. K. P. RAMAN

BIDHAN CHANDRA KRISHI VISWAVIDYALAYA (Bidhan Chandra Agricultural University)

PO Krishi Viswavidyalaya, Mohanpur, Nadia 741252, West Bengal
Telephone: (3473) 222666
E-mail: bckvvc@gmail.com
Internet: www.bckv.edu.in
Founded 1974
State control
Language of instruction: English
Academic year: July to June
Chancellor: HE GOV. OF WEST BENGAL
Vice-Chancellor: Dr RANAJIT KUMAR SAMANTA
Registrar: ASOK BANERJEE
Dir for Farms: Dr T. K. KUMAR
Dir for Research: Prof. A. MITRA
Dean of Student Welfare: Dr J. K. DAS
Asst Librarian: M. NEOGI
Library of 69,430 vols, 208 periodicals
Number of teachers: 263
Number of students: 1,466
Publication: *Prayas* (1 a year)

DEANS
Faculty of Agricultural Engineering: Prof. R. K. BISWAS
Faculty of Agriculture: Prof. AFTAB UZ ZAMAN
Faculty of Horticulture: Prof. SATYA NARAYAN GHOSH
Postgraduate Studies: Prof. R. K. BISWAS

BIHAR AGRICULTURAL UNIVERSITY

Sabour, Bhagalpur 813210, Bihar
Telephone: (641) 2452606
E-mail: vcbausabour@gmail.com
Internet: www.bausabour.ac.in
Founded 2010
State control
Languages of instruction: English, Hindi
Vice-Chancellor: Dr M. L. CHOUDHARY
Dir for Admin.: ADITYA PRASAD
Dir for Extension Education: Dr R. K. SOHANE
Dir for Planning: Dr ARUN KUMAR
Dir for Research: Dr RAVI GOPAL SINGH
Dir for Student Welfare: Dr ASHOK KUMAR
Registrar: Dr C. L. MAURYA
Comptroller: N. P. SINHA
Assoc. Librarian: Dr RAJESH KUMAR
Library of 42,203 vols, 72 titles of periodicals, 2,768 full text ejournals, 650 ebooks, 558 theses; spec. colln of old prints published in the 17th century, 500 photographs of Mahatma Gandhi
Number of teachers: 456
Publication: *BAU Kisan Samachar* (4 a year, in Hindi)

DEANS
Bhola Paswan Shastri Agricultural College: Dr RAJESH KUMAR
Bihar Agricultural College: Dr M. KUMAR
Bihar Veterinary College: Dr M. K. CHOUDHARY
College of Agriculture: Dr D. P. S. DIWAKAR
College of Horticulture: Dr PANCHAM K. SINGH
Mandan Bharti Agricultural College: Dr UMESH SINGH

BIRSA AGRICULTURAL UNIVERSITY

Kanke, Ranchi 834006, Jharkhand
Telephone: (651) 2450832
E-mail: bausupport@gmail.com
Internet: www.baujharkhand.org
Founded 1981
State control
Languages of instruction: English, Hindi
Academic year: July to June
Chancellor: HE GOV. OF JHARKHAND
Vice-Chancellor: Dr M. P. PANDEY
Dir for Admin.: Dr L. B. SINGH
Dir for Extension Education: Dr R. P. SINGH
Dir for Research: Dr M. P. PANDEY
Dir for Student Welfare: Dr N. K. ROY
Registrar: Dr N. KUDADA
Comptroller: R. R. PRASAD
Librarian: RAMJEE PRASAD
Library of 73,078 vols
Number of teachers: 200
Number of students: 700
Publication: *Journal of Research*

DEANS
Faculty of Agriculture: Dr A. K. SARKAR
Faculty of Forestry: Dr A. K. SARKAR
Faculty of Veterinary Science and Animal Husbandry: Dr S. K. SINGH
Postgraduate Studies: Dr Z. A. HAIDER

BUNDELKHAND UNIVERSITY

Jhansi 284003, Uttar Pradesh
Telephone: (510) 2320496
E-mail: registrar@bujhansi.org
Internet: www.bujhansi.org
Founded 1975
State control
Chancellor: HE GOV. OF UTTAR PRADESH
Vice-Chancellor: Prof. S. V. S. RANA
Pro-Vice-Chancellor: Prof. PANKAJ ATRI
Registrar: UDAY VIR SINGH YADAV
Dean of Student Welfare: Dr SUNIL KABIA
Librarian: Dr S. C. SROTIA
Library of 10,000 vols
Number of teachers: 434
Number of students: 38,000

DEANS
Faculty of Agriculture: Dr M. D. PRAJAPATI
Faculty of Arts: Dr M. L. MAURYA
Faculty of Commerce: Prof. PANKAJ ATRI
Faculty of Education: Dr ANJANA RATHORE
Faculty of Engineering: Dr DHEER SINGH
Faculty of Law: Prof. L. C. SAHU
Faculty of Medicine: Dr GANESH KUMAR
Faculty of Science: Prof. S. P. SINGH

UNIVERSITY CENTRE
Veerangana Jhalkaribai Centre for Women Studies and Development: tel. (510) 2321103; e-mail wsc_bu@rediffmail.com; Dir Dr APARNA RAJ; publ. *International Journal for Women and Gender Research* (2 a year)

CENTRAL AGRICULTURAL UNIVERSITY

POB 23, Iroisemba, Imphal 795004, Manipur
Telephone: (385) 2415933
E-mail: vcofficecau@yahoo.in
Internet: www.cau.org.in

Founded 1993
State control
Language of instruction: English
Academic year: July to June (2 semesters)

Chancellor: Dr H. K. JAIN
Vice-Chancellor: Prof. Dr S. N. PURI
Registrar: Dr P. M. PILLAI
Dir for Research: Dr M. ROHINI KUMAR SINGH

Library of 57,483 vols, 315 periodicals
Number of teachers: 211
Number of students: 1,176

DEANS

College of Agricultural Engineering and Post-Harvest Technology: Dr P. K. SRIVASTAVA
College of Agriculture: Prof. Dr N. IBOTON SINGH
College of Fisheries: Dr J. R. DHANZE
College of Home Science: Dr KRISHNA SHEELA
College of Horticulture and Forestry: Prof. B. N. HAZARIKA
College of Post Graduate Studies: Dr V. K. KHANNA
College of Veterinary Science and Animal Husbandry: Dr L. HMAR

PROFESSORS

BHATTACHARYA, D., Soil Science and Agricultural Chemistry
LAISHRAM, J. M., Plant Breeding and Genetics
MEITEI, W. I., Horticulture
NANDEESHA, M. C., Aquaculture
RAGHUVANSHI, R. S., Food and Nutrition
RATHORE, D. S., Pomology
SINGH, M. D., Animal Husbandry and Dairying
SINGH, M. P., Agricultural Entomology
SINGH, M. R. K., Plant Breeding and Genetics
SINGH, N. I., Plant Pathology
SINGH, N. R., Agricultural Economics
SINGH, R. K. K., Soil Science and Agricultural Chemistry
SINGH, Y. J., Agricultural Engineering

CHANDRA SHEKHAR AZAD UNIVERSITY OF AGRICULTURE & TECHNOLOGY

Nawabganj, Kanpur 208002, Uttar Pradesh
Telephone: (512) 2534156
E-mail: info@csauk.ac.in
Internet: www.csauk.ac.in

Founded 1975 by merger of Govt Agriculture College (f. 1906) and U. P. College of Veterinary Science and Animal Husbandry
State control
Languages of instruction: English, Hindi
Academic year: July to June

Chancellor: HE GOV. OF UTTAR PRADESH
Vice-Chancellor: Prof. Dr P. K. SHARMA
Comptroller: Y. P. SINGH
Dean of Students' Welfare: Dr SAMIR PAL
Dir for Agricultural Experiment Station: Dr L. P. TEWARI
Dir for Extension: Dr M. P. YADAV
Registrar: Dr RAJENDRA SINGH KANAUJIA
Librarian: Dr R. A. YADAV

Library of 64,300 vols, 4,481 periodicals
Number of teachers: 318
Number of students: 1,187

DEANS

Faculty of Agricultural Engineering and Technology: Dr J. P. YADAV
Faculty of Agriculture: Dr M. P. YADAV
Faculty of Home Science: Dr POONAM SINGH

CHATRAPATI SHAHU JI MAHARAJ UNIVERSITY, KANPUR

Kalyanpur, Kanpur 208024, Uttar Pradesh
Telephone: (512) 2570450
E-mail: helpline@kanpuruniversity.org
Internet: www.kanpuruniversity.org

Founded 1966 as Kanpur Univ., present name 1997
State control
Languages of instruction: English, Hindi
Academic year: July to June

Chancellor: HE GOV. OF UTTAR PRADESH
Vice-Chancellor: Prof. ASHOK KUMAR
Registrar: SYED WAQAR HUSSAIN
Dean of Students Welfare: Prof. R. C. KATIYAR
Proctor: Dr K. K. BEHAL
Librarian: Dr S. P. SINGH

Library of 47,000 vols
Number of students: 275,000

DEANS

Faculty of Agriculture: Dr A. K. SRIVASTAVA
Faculty of Arts: GOPAL JI SRIVASTAVA
Faculty of Ayurved and Unani: Dr RAVI DUTT TRIPATHI
Faculty of Commerce: Dr P. C. CHATURVEDI
Faculty of Education: Dr SHANTA SAXENA
Faculty of Engineering: Dr RENU JAIN
Faculty of Law: SRILEKHA VIDYARTHI
Faculty of Life Sciences: Prof. NANDLAL
Faculty of Management: Prof. S. K. SRIVASTAVA
Faculty of Medicine: Dr S. K. KATIYAR
Faculty of Science: Dr P. K. MATHUR

CHAUDHARY CHARAN SINGH HARYANA AGRICULTURAL UNIVERSITY

Hissar 125004, Haryana
Telephone: (1662) 237720
E-mail: vc@hau.ernet.in
Internet: hau.ernet.in

Founded 1970
State control
Language of instruction: English
Academic year: July to June

Chancellor: HE GOV. OF HARYANA
Vice-Chancellor: Dr KRISHAN SINGH KHOKHAR
Registrar: Dr S. S. DAHIYA
Dir for Extension: Dr J. S. DHANKHAR
Dir for Research: Dr R. P. NARWAL
Controller of Examinations: Dr V. K. KALRA
Librarian: Dr R. S. WALDIA

Library of 340,740 vols (239,437 books, 101,303 vols of periodicals)
Number of teachers: 602
Number of students: 1,748

Publications: *Haryana Kheti* (12 a year), *HAU Journal of Research* (2 a year)

DEANS

College of Agricultural Engineering and Technology: Dr M. K. GARG
College of Agriculture: Dr SUCHETA KHOKHAR
College of Basic Sciences and Humanities: Dr SANTOSH DHILLON
College of Home Science: Dr SAROJ S. JEET SINGH
Postgraduate Studies: Dr R. P. NARWAL

CHAUDHARY CHARAN SINGH UNIVERSITY

Meerut 200005, Uttar Pradesh
Telephone: (121) 2763539
E-mail: registrar@ccsuniversity.ac.in
Internet: www.ccsuniversity.ac.in

Founded 1965 as Meerut Univ.
State control
Languages of instruction: English, Hindi

Chancellor: HE GOV. OF UTTAR PRADESH
Vice-Chancellor: Dr VIPIN GARG
Registrar: OM PRAKASH
Dean of Students Welfare: Prof. H. S. BALYAN
Proctor: Prof. YOGENDRA SINGH
Deputy Librarian: Dr JAMAL AHMED SIDDIQUI

Library of 131,525 vols, 26,262 journals, 150 periodicals
Number of students: 125,365

Publications: *Indian Journal of Political Science, Journal of Political and Public Administration*

DEANS

Faculty of Agriculture: Prof. B. RAMESH
Faculty of Arts: Prof. R. S. AGRAWAL
Faculty of Commerce and Management: Dr M. L. GUPTA
Faculty of Education: (vacant)
Faculty of Engineering Technology: Prof. RAKESH KUMAR
Faculty of Law: Dr HARIOM PANWAR
Faculty of Medicine: Dr K. K. GUPTA
Faculty of Science: Prof. ASHOK KUMAR

CHAUDHARY DEVI LAL UNIVERSITY

Barnala Rd, Sirsa 125055, Haryana
Telephone: (1666) 239819
Internet: www.cdlu.in

Founded 2003
State control
Language of instruction: English
Academic year: July to May (3 terms)

Chancellor: HE GOV. OF HARYANA
Vice-Chancellor: Dr K. C. BHARDWAJ
Registrar: Dr MANOJ SIWACH
Dean of Students Welfare: Prof. S. K. GAHLAWAT
Proctor: Prof. SHAMSHER SINGH
Controller of Examinations: Prof. PRAVEEN AGHAMKAR
Librarian: Dr D. P. WARNE

Library of 25,767 vols

DEANS

Faculty of Commerce and Management: Prof. SULTAN SINGH
Faculty of Education: Prof. SHAMSHER SINGH JANG BAHADUR
Faculty of Engineering and Technology: Prof. VIKRAM SINGH
Faculty of Humanities: Prof. ANU SHUKLA
Faculty of Law: Prof. HARBANSH
Faculty of Life Sciences: Prof. SURESH KUMAR GAHLAWAT
Faculty of Physical Sciences: Prof. PARVEEN AGHAMKAR
Faculty of Social Sciences: Dr RAJBIR SINGH DALAL

CHAUDHARY SARWAN KUMAR HIMACHAL PRADESH KRISHI VISHVAVIDYALAYA
(Chaudhary Sarwan Kumar Himachal Pradesh Agricultural University)

Palampur, Kangra 176062, Himachal Pradesh
Telephone: (1894) 230521
E-mail: vc@hillagric.ac.in
Internet: www.hillagric.ac.in

Founded 1978, fmrly Faculty of Agriculture of Himachal Pradesh Univ.
State control
Language of instruction: English
Academic year: July to June

Chancellor: HE GOV. OF HIMACHAL PRADESH
Vice-Chancellor: Dr SHYAM KUMAR SHARMA
Comptroller: JITENDER MOHAN AWASTHI (acting)

Dir for Extension Education: Dr DESH RAJ
Dir for Research: Dr S. P. SHARMA
Registrar: RUPALI THAKUR
Librarian: Dr K. K. KATOCH (acting)

Library of 82,003 vols
Number of teachers: 315
Number of students: 1,156

Publications: *Himachal Journal of Agricultural Research* (2 a year), *Parvatiya Khetibari* (4 a year)

DEANS

College of Agriculture: Dr PRADEEP K. SHARMA (acting)
College of Basic Sciences: Dr R. G. SUD (acting)
College of Home Science: Dr SUMATI REKHA MALHOTRA (acting)
College of Veterinary and Animal Sciences: Dr A. C. VARSHNEY (acting)
Postgraduate Studies: Dr R. K. SHARMA

COCHIN UNIVERSITY OF SCIENCE & TECHNOLOGY

Cochin 682022, Kerala
Telephone: (484) 2577290
E-mail: registrar@cusat.ac.in
Internet: www.cusat.ac.in

Founded 1971 as Univ. of Cochin, current name and status 1986
State control
Language of instruction: English
Academic year: July to April

Chancellor: HE GOV. OF KERALA
Pro-Chancellor: Hon. MIN. FOR EDUCATION, GOVT. OF KERALA
Vice-Chancellor: Dr RAMACHANDRAN THEKKEDATH
Pro-Vice-Chancellor: Dr POULOSE JACOB
Registrar: Dr A. RAMACHANDRAN
Controller of Examinations: V. K. RAMACHANDRAN NAIR
Librarian: Dr S. DEVI ANTHERJANAN

Library of 70,000 vols, 280 current journals
Number of teachers: 197
Number of students: 2,100

Publications: *Indian Manager*, *Law Review*, *Statistical Methods*

DEANS

Faculty of Engineering: Prof. PHILIP KURIAN
Faculty of Environmental Studies: Prof. K. MOHANKUMAR
Faculty of Humanities: Prof. R. SASIDHARAN
Faculty of Law: Dr A. M. VARKEY
Faculty of Marine Science: Dr H. S. RAM MOHAN
Faculty of Medical Science and Technology: Dr P. G. R. PILLAI
Faculty of Science: Prof. R.MURALEEDHARAN NAIR
Faculty of Social Sciences: Prof. M. BHASI
Faculty of Technology: Dr K. VASUDEVAN

PROFESSORS

ALIYAR, S., Hindi
ARAVINDAKSHNAN, A., Hindi
BABU, T. J., Civil Engineering
BABU SUNDAR, S., Computer Application
BALACHAND, A. N., Physical Oceanography
BALAKRISHNAN, K. G., Electronics
CHACKO, J., Chemical Oceanography
CHANDRASEKHARAN, M., Biotechnology
CHANDRASEKHARAN, N. S., Legal Studies
CHANDRASEKHARAN PILLAI, K. N., Legal Studies
DAMODARAN, K. T., Marine Sciences
DAMODARAN, R., Marine Sciences
EASWARI, M., Hindi
FRANCIS, C. A., Management Studies
GEORGE, K. E., Polymer Science and Rubber Technology
GEORGE, K. K., Management Studies
GEORGE VARGHESE, K., Management Studies
GIRIJAVALLABHAN, C. P., Physics
GOPALAKRISHNA KURUP, P., Marine Sciences
HRIDAYANATHAN, C., Industrial Fisheries
JACOB, P. K., Computer Science
JATHAVEDAN, M., Mathematics
JOSEPH, R., Polymer Science and Rubber Technology
KORAKANDY, R., Industrial Fisheries
KRISHNAMURTHY, A., Mathematical Sciences
KRISHNANKUTTY, P., Ship Technology
KURIAKOSE, A. P., Polymer Science and Rubber Technology
KURIAKOSE, V. L., Physics
MADHUROADANA KENUP, B., Industrial Fisheries
MARY JOSEPH, T., Management Studies
MATHAI, E., Physics
MATHEW, K. T., Electronics
MATHEW, S., Industrial Fisheries
MATHEWS ABRAHAM, B., Civil Engineering
MOHAMMED YUSSUF, K., Applied Chemistry
MOHAN KUMAR, K., Atmospheric Science
MOHANAN, N., Hindi
MOHANAN, P., Electronics
MOHANDAS, A., Environmental Studies
MURALEEDHARAN NAIR, K. R., Statistics
MURUGESAN REDDIAR, K., German
NANDAKUMARAN, V. M., Photonics
NARAYANAN NAMPOOTHIRI, V. P., Photonics
PAVITHRAN, K. B., Management Studies
PHILIP, B., Marine Biology, Microbiology and Biochemistry
PHILIP, J., Instrumentation
PILLAI, P. R. S., Electronics
POULOSE JACOB, K., Computer Science
RADHAKRISHNAN, P., Photonics
RAJAN, C. K., Atmospheric Science
RAJAPPAN NAIR, K. P., Physics
RAJASENAN, D., Applied Economics
RAMACHANDRAN, A., Industrial Fisheries
RAMACHANDRAN NAIR, V. K., Statistics
RAM MOHAN, H. S., Marine Sciences
RAVINDRA-NATHA MENON, N. R., Marine Sciences
SABIR, M., Physics
SADASIVAN NAIR, G., Legal Studies
SAJAN, K., Marine Sciences
SALIH, M., Marine Biology, Microbiology and Biochemistry
SASIDHARAN, R., Hindi
SEBASTIAN, K. L., Applied Chemistry
SERALATHAN, P., Marine Geology and Geophysics
SHANMUGHAN, M., Hindi
SIVASANKARA PILLAI, V. N., Environmental Studies
SOMASEKHARAN NAIR, E. M., Ship Technology
SUDARSHANAN PILLAI, P., Management Studies
SUGUNAN, S., Applied Chemistry
SUKUMARAN NAIR, H. K., Applied Economics
SUKUMARAN NAIR, M. K., Applied Chemistry
SUNEETHA BAI, L., Hindi
THRIVIKRAMAN, T., Mathematical Sciences
UNNIKRISHNAN NAIR, N., Statistics
VALLABHAN, G., Photonics
VASUDEVAN, K., Electronics
VIJAYAKUMAR, K. P., Physics
WILSON, P. R., Management Studies
YUSUFF, M., Applied Chemistry

DEEN DAYAL UPADHYAY GORAKHPUR UNIVERSITY

Civil Lines, Gorakhpur 273009, Uttar Pradesh
Telephone: (551) 2201577
E-mail: registrar@ddugu.edu.in
Internet: www.ddugu.edu.in

Founded 1957 as Gorakhpur Univ., current name adopted 1997
State control
Languages of instruction: English, Hindi
Academic year: July to April (2 terms)

Chancellor: HE GOV. OF UTTAR PRADESH
Vice-Chancellor: Prof. Dr PRAVIN CHANDRA TRIVEDI
Registrar: BYAS NARAYAN SINGH
Controller of Examinations: Prof. N. N. TRIPATHI
Dean of Students Welfare: H. S. BAJPAI
Proctor: Dr O. P. PANDEY
Librarian: J. L. UPADHYAY

Library of 387,100 vols, 800 periodicals
Number of teachers: 300
Number of students: 115,000

DEANS

Faculty of Agriculture: Prof. V. K. SHUKLA
Faculty of Arts: Prof. M. M. TRIVEDI
Faculty of Commerce: Prof. A. K. SRIVASTAVA
Faculty of Education: Prof. P. C. SHUKLA
Faculty of Law: Prof. ARVIND KUMAR MISHRA
Faculty of Science: Prof. RAJENDRA PRASAD

DEV SANSKRITI VISHWAVIDYALAYA (Dev Sanskriti University)

Shantikunj–Gayatrikunj, Haridwar 249411, Uttarakhand
Telephone: (1334) 261367
E-mail: registrar@dsvv.ac.in
Internet: www.dsvv.ac.in

Founded 2002
Private control
Languages of instruction: English, Hindi
Academic year: July to June

Chancellor: Dr PRANAV PANDYA
Vice-Chancellor: Dr SUKH DEV SHARMA
Pro-Vice-Chancellor and Controller of Examination: Dr CHINMAY PANDYA
Registrar: SANDEEP KUMAR
Librarian: Dr KALPANA GAYAKWAD

Library of 11,000 vols, 1,000 ejournals
Number of teachers: 125
Number of students: 1,800 (800 full-time, 1,000 part-time)

Publications: *Alternative and Complementary Therapies*, *Clinical Biochemistry*, *Indian Journal of Traditional Knowledge*, *Journal of Biological Systems*, *Journal of New Approaches to Medicine and Health*, *Life Sciences*, *Tumor Biology*

DEANS

School of Yog and Health: Dr CHINMAY PANDYA

DEVI AHILYA VISHWAVIDYALAYA (Devi Ahilya University)

c/o Registrar, R. N. T. Marg, Indore 452001, Madhya Pradesh
Telephone: (731) 2527532
E-mail: registrar.davv@dauniv.ac.in
Internet: www.dauniv.ac.in

Founded 1964 as Univ. of Indore, current name adopted 1988
Languages of instruction: English, Hindi
State control
Academic year: July to May (3 terms)

Chancellor: HE GOV. OF MADHYA PRADESH
Vice-Chancellor: Dr D. P. SINGH
Rector: Dr RAJ KAMAL
Registrar: Dr R. D. MUSALGOANKAR
Dean of Student Welfare: Dr RAJIV DIXIT
Librarian: Dr G. H. S. NAIDU

Library of 215,260 vols, 204 journals
Number of teachers: 324 (240 full-time)
Number of students: 9,000 on campus; 160,000 in affiliated colleges

DEANS

Faculty of Arts: Dr C. DEOTALE
Faculty of Ayurveda: Dr P. P. AGRAWAL
Faculty of Commerce: Dr D. D. MUNDRA
Faculty of Dentistry: Dr H. C. NEEMA

Faculty of Education: Dr S. VAIDYA
Faculty of Electronics: Dr RAJKAMAL
Faculty of Engineering: (vacant)
Faculty of Engineering Sciences: (vacant)
Faculty of Life and Home Sciences: Dr R. BHARADWAJ
Faculty of Management Studies: Dr R. D. PATHAK
Faculty of Medicine: Dr K. BHAGAWAT
Faculty of Pharmacy: Dr S. C. CHATURVEDI
Faculty of Physical Education: (vacant)
Faculty of Science: Dr K. K. PANDEY
Faculty of Social Sciences and Law: Dr B. Y. LALITHAMA

DHARMSINH DESAI UNIVERSITY

College Rd, Nadiad 387001, Gujarat
Telephone: (268) 2520502
E-mail: vc@ddu.ac.in
Internet: www.ddu.ac.in

Founded 1968 as Dharmsinh Desai Institute of Technology; deemed univ. status 2000; state univ. status 2005
State control
Pres.: Dr N. D. DESAI
Vice-Chancellor: Dr H. M. DESAI
Controller of Examinations and Acting Registrar: Prof. M. R. BHAVSAR
Dean of Students Welfare: Prof. K. N. SHETH
Library of 46,176 vols, 181 journals

DEANS

Faculty of Business Administration: Prof. G. S. SHAH
Faculty of Commerce: Prof. M. K. TRIVEDI
Faculty of Dental Science: Dr B. S. JATHAL
Faculty of Pharmacy: Dr S. P. ADESHARA
Faculty of Technology: Dr D. G. PANCHAL

DIBRUGARH UNIVERSITY

c/o Registrar, Dibrugarh Univ., Dibrugarh 786004, Assam
Telephone: (373) 2370231
E-mail: info@dibru.ac.in
Internet: www.dibru.ac.in
Founded 1965
State control
Languages of instruction: Assamese, English
Academic year: January to December
Depts of anthropology, applied geology, Assamese, chemistry, commerce, economics, education, English, history, life science, mathematics, petroleum technology, pharmaceutical sciences, physics, political science, sociology, statistics; 121 affiliated colleges
Chancellor: HE GOV. OF ASSAM
Vice-Chancellor: Prof. Dr K. K. DEKA
Registrar: Prof. M. N. DUTTA
Librarian: (vacant)
Library of 164,677 vols, 5,200 periodicals
Number of teachers: 227 (univ. depts)
Number of students: 58,850 (incl. affiliated colleges)
Publications: *Assam Economic Journal*, *Assam Statistical Review*, *Dibrugarh University Journal of Education*, *Dibrugarh University Journal of English Studies*, *Journal of Historical Research*, *Mathematical Forum*, *Padartha Vigyan Patrika* (physics, 1 a year, in Assamese), *Pharmray*

DRAVIDIAN UNIVERSITY

Srinivasa Vanam, Kuppam, Chitoor 517425, Andhra Pradesh
Telephone: (8570) 278220
Internet: www.dravidianuniversity.ac.in
Founded 1997
State control
Academic year: July to June
Depts of comparative Dravidian literature and philosophy, computers and allied sciences, Dravidian and computational linguistics, education and human resource development, English and communication, folklore and tribal studies, history, archaeology and culture, Kannada language and translation studies, Tamil language and translation studies, Telugu language and translation studies
Chancellor: HE GOV. OF ANDHRA PRADESH
Vice-Chancellor: Prof. N. PRABHAKARA RAO
Registrar: Dr N. HEMAKSHI ACHARI (acting)
Dean for Academic Affairs: Prof. D. ANANDA NAIDU
Library of 55,000 vols
Number of students: 165

DR BABASAHEB AMBEDKAR MARATHWADA UNIVERSITY

Univ. Campus, Aurangabad 431004, Maharashtra
Telephone: (240) 2400431
E-mail: registrar@bamu.net
Internet: www.bamu.net
Founded 1958 as Marathwada Univ., current name adopted 1994
State control
Languages of instruction: English, Marathi
Academic year: June to April (2 terms)
Chancellor: HE GOV. OF MAHARASHTRA
Vice-Chancellor: Dr V. M. PANDHARIPANDE
Registrar: Dr S. T. SANGLE
Dir for Board of College and Univ. Devt: Dr A. G. KHAN
Controller of Examinations: Dr ASHOK MANGESH CHAVAN
Librarian: Dr D. K. VEER
Library of 326,450 vols
Number of teachers: 3,275 (incl. affiliated colleges)
Number of students: 130,534

DEANS

Faculty of Arts: Dr HANDIBAG BHARAT SOPANRAO
Faculty of Commerce: Dr LAGHANE KALYAN BHAUSAHEB
Faculty of Education: Dr SHOBHANA VISHWANATH JOSHI
Faculty of Engineering and Technology: Dr SHINDE ULHAS BHANUDASRAO
Faculty of Fine Arts: Dr MOHEKAR ASHOK
Faculty of Law: Dr BHIMANENI HANUMAIAH CHOUDARY
Faculty of Management Science: Dr LAGHANE KALYAN BHAUSAHEB
Faculty of Physical Education: Dr SHAIKH SHAFIODDIN SHARIFODDIN
Faculty of Science: Dr MOHEKAR ASHOK DNYANDEORAO
Faculty of Social Sciences: Dr KHANDARE VILAS BHIKAJI

DR BABASAHEB AMBEDKAR OPEN UNIVERSITY

R. C. Technical Compound, Sarkhej-Gandhinagar Highway, Sola, Ahmedabad 380060, Gujarat
Telephone: (79) 27663747
E-mail: baouvc@yahoo.com
Internet: www.baou.org
Founded 1994
State control
Academic year: August to July
Schools of commerce and management, computer science, distance education and education technology, humanities and social sciences; 507 study centres
Chancellor: HE GOV.OF GUJARAT
Vice-Chancellor: Dr MANOJ SONI
Registrar: PIYUSHBHAI R. SHAH (acting)
Dir for Academic Affairs: Dr DHAVAL PANDYA (acting)
Librarian: C. N. SHAH
Number of students: 100,000

DR BABASAHEB AMBEDKAR TECHNOLOGICAL UNIVERSITY

Vidyavihar, Lonere, Raigad 402103, Maharashtra
Telephone: (2140) 275333
E-mail: registrar@dbatu.ac.in
Internet: www.dbatu.ac.in
Founded 1989
State control
Depts of chemical engineering, civil engineering, computer engineering, electronics and telecommunication engineering, electrical engineering, information technology, mechanical engineering, petrochemical engineering
Chancellor: HE GOV. OF MAHARASHTRA
Vice-Chancellor: Dr RAJU B. MANKAR
Registrar: Dr GIRISH M. DESHMUKH (acting)
Dean of Research and Devt: Dr P. K. BRAHMANKAR
Librarian: SHRIKANT P. VAIDYA
Library of 72,000 vols, 87 periodicals

DR BALASAHEB SAWANT KONKAN KRISHI VIDYAPEETH (Dr Balasaheb Sawant Konkan Agricultural University)

Ratnagiri, Dapoli 415712, Maharashtra
Telephone: (2358) 282411
E-mail: root@kkv.ren.nic.in
Internet: www.dbskkv.org
Founded 1972
State control
Academic year: July to May
Language of instruction: English
Chancellor: HE GOV. OF MAHARASHTRA
Vice-Chancellor: Dr V. MEHATA
Registrar: R. N. KULKARNI
Librarian: S. M. RODGE
Library of 32,384 vols, 128 periodicals

DEANS

Faculty of Agricultural Engineering: Dr A. G. PAWAR
Faculty of Agriculture: Dr V. B. MEHTA
Faculty of Fisheries: Dr P. C. RAJE

CONSTITUENT AND AFFILIATED COLLEGES

College of Agricultural Engineering and Technology: Manki-Palvan, Tal-Chiplun, Ratnagiri 415641; tel. (2355) 233181; e-mail caetmp@yahoo.co.in; f. 2003; Dir V. N. GAWANDE.

College of Agriculture: Saralgaon, Tal-Murbad, Thane 421401; tel. (2524) 240770; f. 2001.

College of Fisheries: Ratnagiri 415629, Maharashtra; tel. (2352) 232987; e-mail rtg_fishcoll@sancharnet.in; f. 1981.

College of Horticulture: Kharawate-Dahiwali, Ratnagiri 415606, Maharashtra; tel. (2355) 264017; f. 2001.

Govindraoji Nikam College of Agriculture: Mandki-Palvan. Tal-Chiplun, Ratnagiri 415629, Maharashtra; tel. (2355) 233181; e-mail gncamp@redifmail.com; f. 2001; Dir Dr T. L. CHORAGE

DR B. R. AMBEDKAR OPEN UNIVERSITY

Prof. G. Ram Reddy Marg, Rd 46, Jubilee Hills, Hyderabad 500033, Andhra Pradesh
Telephone: (40) 23680333

E-mail: registrar@braou.ac.in
Internet: www.braou.ac.in

Founded 1982, fmrly Andhra Pradesh Open Univ.
Academic year: July to June

Chancellor: HE Gov. of Andhra Pradesh
Vice-Chancellor: Dr P. Prakash
Registrar: Prof. C. Sunder Venkataiah
Dir for Academic Affairs: Prof. V. Venkaiah
Controller of Examinations: Prof. N. Venkatanarayana
Public Relations Officer: P. Mohan Rao
Librarian: Dr G. Sujatha

Library of 137,793 vols, 173 journals
Number of teachers: 63
Number of students: 173,827

DEANS

Faculty of Arts: Prof. M. S. Hayat
Faculty of Commerce: Prof. K. Swamy
Faculty of Sciences: Prof. Girija Neti
Faculty of Social Sciences: Prof. E. Sudha Rani

PROFESSORS

Chandrasekhara Rao, V., Library Science
Damayanthi Devi, I., Zoology
Gnanaprasuna, K., Physics
Hayat, S., Urdu
Jadhao, Y., Hindi
Kiranmayi, Y. S., Business Management
Koteswara Rao, K., Commerce
Kuppuswamy Rao, K., Mathematics
Nethi, G., Zoology
Prasad, V. S., Public Administration
Pushpa Ramakrishna, C., English
Rajashekar Reddy, S. V., Geology
Ramachandraiah, G., Chemistry
Ramachandraiah, M., Botany
Ramaiah, P., Economics
Srinivasacharyulu, G., Evaluation
Sundara Rao, B., Economics
Umapathi Varma, Y. V., Educational Technology
Vasunadan, R., Telugu
Venkaiah, V., Business Management
Vidyavathi, A., Sociology

DR B. R. AMBEDKAR UNIVERSITY

Paliwal Park, Agra 282003, Uttar Pradesh
Telephone: (562) 2820051
E-mail: info@dbrau.ac.in
Internet: www.dbrau.ac.in

Founded 1927 as Agra Univ.; current name adopted 1996
Languages of instruction: English, Hindi
Academic year: July to May

Chancellor: HE Gov. of Uttar Pradesh
Vice-Chancellor: Dr D. N. Jauhar
Registrar: A. K. Arvind
Dean of Students Welfare: Prof. Rajendra Sharma
Dean of Research: Prof. Rajesh Dhakery
Hon. Librarian: Dr U. C. Sharma

Library of 166,087 vols, 150 journals
Number of students: 123,000

DEANS

Faculty of Arts: Prof. A. K. Singh
Faculty of Commerce: Dr Murari Lal
Faculty of Education: (vacant)
Faculty of Engineering: (vacant)
Faculty of Home Science: Dr Bharti Singh
Faculty of Law: Dr J. C. Kulshreshtha
Faculty of Management: Dr Luv Kush Mishra
Faculty of Medical Science: Prof. K. K. Gupta
Faculty of Science: Prof. Diwaker Kahre

DR HARISINGH GOUR VISHWAVIDYALAYA
(Dr Harisingh Gour University)

Gour Nagar, Univ. Campus, Sagar 470003, Madhya Pradesh
Telephone: (7582) 222574
E-mail: sagaruniversity@mp.nic.in
Internet: www.dhsgsu.ac.in

Founded 1946 as Univ. of Saugor, current name adopted 1983
Languages of instruction: Hindi, English
Academic year: July to April (2 terms)

Chancellor: HE Gov. of Madhya Pradesh
Vice-Chancellor: Prof. N. S. Gajbhiye
Rector: Prof. Dr K. S. Pitre
Registrar: Prof. N. K. Jain
Controller of Examination: Prof. Ram Prasad
Dean of Academic Affairs: Prof. M. S. Tiwari
Dean of Faculty Affairs: Prof. K. S. Pitre
Dir for Research and Devt: R. N. Yadava
Dean of Students Affairs: Prof. Uma Shankar Gupta
Librarian: Mukesh Kumar Sahu (acting)

Library of 310,000 vols
Number of teachers: 300
Number of students: 80,000

Publication: *Madhya Bharti—Research Journal* (1 a year, Hindi and English)

DEANS

School of Applied Sciences: Prof. S. K. Shukla
School of Arts, Education and Information Sciences: Prof. K. C. Sahoo
School of Biological and Chemical Sciences: Prof. O. P. Shrivastava
School of Commerce and Management: Prof. J. K. Jain
School of Engineering and Technology: Prof. A. K. Singhai
School of Humanities and Social Sciences: Prof. K. C. Jain
School of Languages: Prof. Virendra Mohan
School of Law: Prof. Virendra Mohan
School of Mathematical and Physical Sciences: Prof. Ram Prasad

DR N. T. R. UNIVERSITY OF HEALTH SCIENCES, ANDHRA PRADESH

Vijayawada 520008, Andhra Pradesh
Telephone: (866) 2451206
E-mail: ntruhs@hotmail.com
Internet: ntruhs.ap.nic.in

Founded 1986
State control
Language of instruction: English
Academic year: July to June

Faculties of dental sciences, Indian systems of medicine, medical laboratory technology, modern medicine, nursing, nutrition and physiotherapy; 316 affiliated colleges

Chancellor: HE Gov. of Andhra Pradesh
Vice-Chancellor: Prof. A. V. Krishnam Raju
Registrar: Prof. T. Venugopal Rao
Librarian: R. Nalini (acting)

Number of teachers: 3,000
Number of students: 9,000 undergraduate, 3,000 postgraduate

DR PANJABRAO DESHMUKH KRISHI VIDYAPEETH
(Dr Panjabrao Deshmukh Agricultural University)

PO Krishi Nagar, Akola 444104, Maharashtra
Telephone: (724) 2258372
E-mail: vc@pdkv.ac.in
Internet: www.pdkv.ac.in

Founded 1969
State control
Languages of instruction: English, Marathi
Academic year: July to June

Chancellor: HE Gov. of Maharashtra
Pro-Chancellor: Min. for Agriculture, Govt of Maharashtra
Vice-Chancellor: Dr V. M. Myande
Registrar: Dr V. M. Bhale
Dir of Extension Education: Dr V. K Mahorkar
Dir of Research: Dr S. V. Sarode

Library of 140,500 vols
Number of teachers: 650
Number of students: 3,650

Publications: *Krishi Patrika* (in Marathi, 12 a year), *PKV Research Journal* (2 a year), *Post Graduate Institute Research Journal* (1 a year)

DEANS

Faculty of Agricultural Engineering: Dr D. S. Kharche
Faculty of Agriculture: Dr V. K. Mahorkar

CONSTITUENT COLLEGES

College of Agricultural Engineering and Technology: PO Krishi Nagar, Akola 444104, Maharashtra; tel. (724) 2258405; f. 1970; offers undergraduate course in agricultural engineering; Assoc. Dean Dr P. M. Nimkar.

College of Agriculture: PO Krishi Nagar, Akola 444104, Maharashtra; tel. (724) 2259117; f. 1955; offers BSc in agriculture; Assoc. Dean V. D. Patil.

College of Agriculture: Nagpur 440001, Maharashtra; tel. (712) 2522621; e-mail adac_ngp@yahoo.com; f. 1906; offers BSc and MSc in agriculture; library of 59,185 vols; Assoc. Dean Dr C. S. Choudhari.

College of Forestry: PO Krishi Nagar, Akola 444104, Maharashtra; tel. (724) 2258889; e-mail adfcakola@gmail.com; f. 1985; offers BSc in forestry; Assoc. Dean Dr J. S. Zope.

College of Horticulture: PO Krishi Nagar, Akola, 444104, Maharashtra; f. 1984; offers BSc in horticulture; Dean Dr V. K. Mahorkar.

Postgraduate Institute: PO Krishi Nagar, Akola, 444104, Maharashtra; tel. (724) 2258826; f. 1970; offers postgraduate courses in agriculture, agricultural engineering; Assoc. Dean Dr R. B. Somani

DR RAM MANOHAR LOHIA AVADH UNIVERSITY

Hawai Patti, Allahabad Rd, Faizabad 224001, Uttar Pradesh
Telephone: (5278) 246223
E-mail: vc@rmlau.ac.in
Internet: www.rmlau.ac.in

Founded 1975 as Avadh Univ.
Languages of instruction: English, Hindi
Academic year: July to June

Chancellor: HE Gov. of Uttar Pradesh
Vice-Chancellor: Prof. R. C. Saraswat (acting)
Registrar: S. K. Shukla
Finance Officer: A. Srivastava
Librarian: S. K. Singh

Number of teachers: 19 (univ.), 2,006 (affiliated colleges)
Number of students: 45,220 (univ. and affiliated colleges)

DEANS

Faculty of Arts: Prof. A. K. Mishra
Faculty of Commerce and Management: Dr H. P. Pandey
Faculty of Education: (vacant)
Faculty of Law: Dr Y. Singh
Faculty of Science: Prof. N. S. Dhramwal

DR SARVEPALLI RADHAKRISHNAN RAJASTHAN AYURVEDA UNIVERSITY

Kadwad, Jodhpur–Nagaur Highway Rd, Jodhpur 342037, Rajasthan
Telephone: (291) 5153702
E-mail: rau_jodhpur@yahoo.co.in
Internet: www.raujodhpur.org
Founded 2003
State control
Academic year: July to June
Languages of instruction: Sanskrit, Hindi, English
Vice-Chancellor: Prof. RADHEY SHYAM SHARMA
Registrar: SOHAN LAL SHARMA
Controller of Examinations: SHASHI SHEKHAR JOSHI
Librarian: Dr RAKESH KUMAR SHARMA
Library of 11,500 vols, 30 journals
Number of teachers: 40
Number of students: 7,000

DEANS

Faculty of Ayurved: Prof. AJAY KUMAR SHARMA
Faculty of Homeopathy: Prof. ATUL KUMAR
Faculty of Unani: Prof. MOHD. SHOEB AZMI

DR YASHWANT SINGH PARMAR UNIVERSITY OF HORTICULTURE & FORESTRY

Nauni, Solan 173230, Himachal Pradesh
Telephone: (1792) 252363
E-mail: vcuhf@yahoo.com
Internet: www.yspuniversity.ac.in
Founded 1962 as Himachal Agricultural College and Research Institute, current name and status 1985
State control
Academic year: August to July
Chancellor: HE GOV. OF HIMACHAL PRADESH
Vice-Chancellor: Dr K. R. DHIMAN
Registrar: B. R. KAMAL
Comptroller: GIAN RAITA
Librarian: Dr M. S. PATHANIA
Dir for Extension Education: Dr A. K. SHARMA
Dir for Research: Dr K. R. DHIMAN
Library of 63,000 vols, 90 periodicals
Number of teachers: 222
Number of students: 755

DEANS

College of Forestry: Dr R. C. SHARMA
College of Horticulture: Dr S. D. KASHYAP

PROFESSORS

AGNIHOTRI, R. P., Regional Horticultural Research Station, Jachh
BARWAL, V. S., Post-harvest Technology
BAWA, R., Regional Centre, NAEB
BAWEJA, H. S., Directorate of Extension Education
BHALLA, R., Regional Horticultural Research Station, Mashobra
BHARDWAJ, M. L., Krishi Vigyan Kendra, Chamba
BHARDWAJ, S., Regional Horticultural Research Station, Mashobra
BHARDWAJ, S. S., Regional Horticultural Research Station, Bajarua
BHARDWAJ, S. V., Biotechnology
BHATIA, H. S., Regional Horticultural Research Station, Bajarua
BHATIA, R., Regional Horticultural Research Station, Jachh
CHAND, R., Forest Products
CHANDEL, J. S., Fruit Science
CHANDEL, R. P. S., Entomology and Apiculture
CHAUHAN, N. S., Forest Products
CHAUHAN, P. S., Regional Horticultural Research Station, Mashobra
CHAUHAN, U., Entomology and Apiculture
DORHOO, N. P., Directorate of Research
DUBEY, J. K., Directorate of Extension Education
GARG, R. C., Mycology and Plant Pathology
GUPTA, A. K., Mycology and Plant Pathology
GUPTA, B., Silviculture and Forestry
GUPTA, D., Entomology and Apiculture
GUPTA, J. K., Entomology and Apiculture
GUPTA, N. K., Silviculture and Forestry
GUPTA, P. R., Entomology and Apiculture
GUPTA, R., Directorate of Extension Education
GUPTA, S. K., Mycology and Plant Pathology
GUPTA, Y. C., Floriculture and Landscaping
JOSHI, A. K., Horticultural Research Station, Dhaulakuan
JOSHI, V. K., Post-harvest Technology
KANBID, B. R., Directorate of Extension Education
KANWAR, H. S., Seed technology and Production Centre
KANWAR, K., Biotechnology
KASHYAP, S. D., Silviculture and Forestry
KAUR, M., Basic Sciences
KAUR NATH, A., Biotechnology
KAUSHAL, P., Regional Centre (NAEB)
KHAJURIA, D. R., Regional Horticultural Research Station, Bajarua
KHAN, M. L., Entomology and Apiculture
KHANNA, A. S., Entomology and Apiculture
KHURANA, D. K., Tree Improvement and Genetic Resources
KORLA, B. N., Vegetable Science
KUMAR, J., Regional Horticultural Research Station, Bajarua
KUMAR, K., Fruit Breeding and Genetic Resources
KUMAR, P., Basic Sciences
KUMAR, R., Entomology and Apiculture
KUMARI, A., Directorate of Extension Education
MAHAJAN, S., Computer and Instrumentation Centre
MANKOTA, M. S., Regional Horticultural Research Station, Mashobra
MEHTA, K., Fruit Science
NARANG, M. L., Forest Protection Unit
NEGI, Y. S., Business Management
PRASHAR, R. S., Litchi and Mango Research Station, Nagrota Bagwan
RAI, K., Forest Products
RAINA, J. N., Soil Science and Water Management
RAINA, R., Forest Products
RAM, V., Mycology and Plant Pathology
RANA, B. S., Entomology and Apiculture
RANA, S. S., Regional Horticultural Research Station, Jachh
RANDEV, A. K., Regional Horticultural Research Station, Mashobra
REHALIA, A. S., Pomology
SHAMET, G. S., Silviculture and Forestry
SHARMA, A. K., Regional Horticultural Research Station, Jachh
SHARMA, A. K., Basic Sciences
SHARMA, D. D., Fruit Science
SHARMA, D. D., Social Sciences
SHARMA, D. K., Regional Horticultural Research Station, Jachh
SHARMA, G. C., Horticultural Research Station, Kandaghat, Solan
SHARMA, G. K., Directorate of Extension Education
SHARMA, G. K., Fruit Breeding and Genetic Resources
SHARMA, H. R., Horticultural Research Station, Kandaghat, Solan
SHARMA, I. D., Entomology and Apiculture
SHARMA, I. M., Mycology and Plant Pathology
SHARMA, I. P., Soil Science and Water Management
SHARMA, J. N., Mycology and Plant Pathology
SHARMA, K. C., Temperate Horticultural Research Station, Kotkhai
SHARMA, K. D., Post-harvest Technology
SHARMA, L. R., Social Sciences
SHARMA, N., Fruit Science
SHARMA, O. P., Directorate of Extension Education
SHARMA, P. C., Post-harvest Technology
SHARMA, R., Social Sciences
SHARMA, R. C., Forest Protection Unit
SHARMA, R. L., Mycology and Plant Pathology
SHARMA, S. K., Biotechnology
SHARMA, S. K., Mycology and Plant Pathology
SHARMA, S. S., Basic Sciences
SHARMA, V., Basic Sciences
SHIRKOT, C. K., Basic Sciences
SHUKLA, Y. R., Vegetable Science
SINGH, N. B., Tree Improvement and Genetic Resources
SINGH THAKUR, A., Basic Sciences
SRIVASTAVA, D. K., Biotechnology
SUD, A., Regional Horticultural Research Station, Mashobra
SUMAN, B. C., Mycology and Plant Pathology
THAKUR, B. S., Krishi Vigyan Kendra, Kandaghat, Solan
THAKUR, K. S., Post-harvest Technology
THAKUR, M. C., Vegetable Science
THAKUR, P. D., Mycology and Plant Pathology
THAKUR, P. S., Silviculture and Forestry
THAKUR, S., Regional Horticultural Research Station, Jachh
THAKUR, V., Environmental Science
THAKUR, V. S., Regional Horticultural Research Station, Mashobra
THAPA, C. D., Mycology and Plant Pathology
TOMER, C. S., Fruit Science
TRIPATHI, D., Soil Science and Water Management
VERMA, K. S., Environmental Science

EFL UNIVERSITY (ENGLISH AND FOREIGN LANGUAGES UNIVERSITY)

Hyderabad 500605, Andhra Pradesh
Telephone: (402) 27098131
E-mail: ciefors@ciefl.ac.in
Internet: www.efluniversity.ac.in
Founded 1958 as Central Institute of English, deemed univ. status 1973, current name and central univ. status 2007
State control
Academic year: June to May
Vice-Chancellor: Prof. MOHAMMAD MIYAN (acting)
Registrar: LATA MALLIKARJUNA (acting)
Controller of Examinations: U. J. SURESH
Dean of Students Welfare: Dr V. SUDHAKAR
Librarian: N. SATISH (acting)
Library of 143,000 vols, 150 journals
Number of teachers: 98
Number of students: 2,276
Publications: *Contextures* (2 a year), *ESSAIS* (2 a year), *Journal of English and Foreign Languages* (2 a year), *Occasional Papers in Linguistics*, *Russian Philology* (1 a year)

DEANS

School of Asian Studies: Dr MAYA PANDIT NARKAR
School of Communication Studies: Dr G. NAGA MALLIKA
School of Distance Education: Dr TAPAS SHANKAR RAY
School of English Language Education: Dr G. RAJAGOPAL
School of English Literary Studies: Dr D. VENKAT RAO
School of Germanic Studies: Dr MEENAKSHI REDDY
School of Inter-Disciplinary Studies: Dr M. MADHAVA PRASAD
School of Language Sciences: Dr K. G. VIJAYKRISHNAN

School of Middle-East and African Studies: Dr MOHSIN USMANI
School of Romance Studies: Dr NIRUPAMA RASTOGI
School of Russian Studies: Dr RAMDAS AKELLA

FAKIR MOHAN UNIVERSITY

Balasore 756019, Orissa
Telephone: (6782) 275768
E-mail: fmuniversity@rediffmail.com
Internet: www.fmuniversity.nic.in
Founded 1999
State control
Academic year: July to May
Depts of applied physics and ballistics, biotechnology, business management, environment science, information and communication technology, population studies, social sciences
Chancellor: HE GOV. OF ORISSA
Vice-Chancellor: Dr KUMAR B. DAS
Chair. of Postgraduate Council: Prof. BHAGABAN DAS
Controller of Examination and Acting Registrar: Dr PARSHURAM BISWAL
Library of 15,431 vols
Number of students: 23,542
Publication: *Anveṣā*

GAUHATI UNIVERSITY

Main Campus, Gauhati 781014, Assam
Telephone: (3661) 2570415
Kokrajhar Campus, PO Rangalikhata (Debargaon) Kokrajhar 783370, Assam
Telephone: (3661) 277183
E-mail: vc@gauhati.ac.in
Internet: www.gauhati.ac.in
Founded 1948
State control
Language of instruction: English
Academic year: July to May (3 terms)
Chancellor: HE GOV. OF ASSAM
Vice-Chancellor: Prof. O. K. MEDHI
Registrar: Dr UTTAM CHANDRA DAS
Controller of Examinations: Dr PRAFULLA K. DEKA
Treas.: HEM CHANDRA GAUTAM
Librarian: B. C. GOSWAMI
Library of 517,000 vols
Number of teachers: 281
Number of students: 118,213

DEANS
Faculty of Arts: Prof. UMESH DEKA
Faculty of Commerce: Prof. NAYAN BARUAH
Faculty of Engineering: Prof. D. BHATTACHARJEE
Faculty of Law: Prof. B. CHAKRAVERTY
Faculty of Medicine: Dr P. D. BORA
Faculty of Science: Prof. S. K. SARMA

CONSTITUENT COLLEGE
University Law College: Gauhati; Prin. Dr B. K. CHAKRABORTY

GOA UNIVERSITY

Taleigao Plateau, 403206, Goa
Telephone: (832) 6519048
E-mail: registrar@unigoa.ac.in
Internet: www.unigoa.ac.in
Founded 1985
State control
Academic year: June to April
Chancellor: HE GOV. OF GOA
Vice-Chancellor: Prof. Dr DILEEP N. DEOBAGKAR
Registrar: Prof. Dr VIJAYENDRA P. KAMAT
Controller of Examinations: LEO V. MACEDO
Librarian: V. GOPAKUMAR
Library of 140,363 vols, 432 journals
Number of students: 1,179

DEANS
Faculty of Commerce: Dr Y. V. REDDY
Faculty of Design: Prof. DILEEP N. DEOBAGKAR
Faculty of Education: Prof. DILEEP N. DEOBAGKAR
Faculty of Engineering: Prof. RAJESH B. LOHANI
Faculty of Languages and Literature: Prof. RAVINDRANATH S. MISHRA
Faculty of Law: Dr MARIAN PINHEIRO
Faculty of Life Science and Environment: Prof. Dr G. N. NAYAK
Faculty of Management Studies: NANDKUMAR MEKOTH
Faculty of Medicine: Prof. Dr MAHESH G. SARDESSAI
Faculty of Natural Sciences: Prof. J. A. E. DESA
Faculty of Performing, Fine Art and Music: M. V. VENGURLEKAR
Faculty of Social Sciences: Prof. Dr A. V. AFONSO

GOVIND BALLABH PANT UNIVERSITY OF AGRICULTURE AND TECHNOLOGY

Udham Singh Nagar, Pantnagar 263145, Uttarakhand
Telephone: (5944) 233350
E-mail: vcgbpuat@gmail.com
Internet: www.gbpuat.ac.in
Founded 1960
State control
Languages of instruction: English, Hindi
Academic year: July to June (2 terms)
Chancellor: HE GOV.OF UTTARAKHAND
Vice-Chancellor: Dr SUBHASH KUMAR
Dean for Student Welfare: D. S. MURTY
Registrar: Dr J. P. PANDEY
Librarian: Dr S. P. JAIN
Library of 400,000 vols, 3,400 periodical titles
Number of teachers: 546
Number of students: 4,847
Publications: *Indian Farmers Digest* (12 a year, in English), *Kisan BHARTI* (12 a year, in Hindi), *Pantnagar Journal of Research* (2 a year)

DEANS
College of Agribusiness Management: Dr DEVANDRA KUMAR
College of Agriculture: Dr J. KUMAR
College of Basic Sciences and Humanities: Dr UMA MALKANIA
College of Fishery Sciences: Dr I. J. SINGH
College of Home Science: Dr RITA SINGH RAGHUVANSHI
College of Technology: Dr H. C. SHARMA
College of Veterinary and Animal Sciences: Dr G. K. SINGH
Postgraduate Studies: Dr N. S. MURTY

GUJARAT AYURVED UNIVERSITY

Chanakya Bhavan, Jamnagar 361008, Gujarat
Telephone: (288) 2552014
E-mail: directoripgt@ayurveduniversity.com
Internet: www.ayurveduniversity.edu.in
Founded 1967
State control
Languages of instruction: English, Gujarati, Hindi, Sanskrit
Academic year: June to April (2 terms)
Chancellor: HE GOV. OF GUJARAT
Vice-Chancellor: Dr MEDHAVI LAL SHARMA
Registrar: R. M. JHALA (acting)
Dir of Institute of Postgraduate Training and Research in Ayurveda: Prof. M. S. BAGHEL
Dir for Pharmacy: Dr P. K. PRAJAPATI (acting)
Librarian: S. M. JANI
Library of 32,701 vols
Number of teachers: 369
Number of students: 2,456
Publications: *Ayu* (research at the Univ., 4 a year), *Traditional Medicine International* (4 a year).

CONSTITUENT COLLEGE
Shree Gulabkunverba Ayurved Mahavidyalaya: tel. (288) 2676864; e-mail gacollege@ayurveduniversity.com; Prin. Dr G. L. ATARA

GUJARAT UNIVERSITY

POB 4010, Navrangpura, Ahmedabad 380009, Gujarat
Navrangpura, Ahmedabad 380009, Gujarat
Telephone: (79) 26301341
E-mail: registrar@gujaratuniversity.ac.in
Internet: www.gujaratuniversity.ac.in
Founded 1949
State control
Languages of instruction: English, Gujarati, Hindi
Academic year: June to April (2 terms)
Chancellor: HE GOV. OF GUJARAT
Vice-Chancellor: Dr MUKUL SHAH (acting)
Pro-Vice-Chancellor: Dr MUKUL SHAH
Registrar: MINESH S. SHAH (acting)
Librarian: ASHVIN BHAVSAR
Library of 335,000 vols
Number of teachers: 4,610
Number of students: 279,764 (230,875 undergraduate, 48,889 postgraduate)

DEANS
Faculty of Arts: M. D. CHAVDA
Faculty of Commerce: Dr N. D. SHAH
Faculty of Education: Dr A. G. KACHHIYA
Faculty of Law: L. S. PATHAK
Faculty of Medicine: Dr KALPESH A. SHAH
Faculty of Science: Prof. B. V. PATEL

GULBARGA UNIVERSITY

Jnana Ganga, Gulbarga 585106, Karnataka
Telephone: (8472) 263202
E-mail: reggug@rediffmail.com
Internet: www.gulbargauniversity.kar.nic.in
Founded 1980
State control
Languages of instruction: English, Kannada
Academic year: June to March
Chancellor: HE GOV. OF KARNATAKA
Pro-Chancellor: MIN. FOR HIGHER EDUCATION, GOVT OF KARNATAKA
Vice-Chancellor: Prof. E. T. PUTTAIAH
Registrar: Prof. S. L. HIREMATH
Librarian: Dr R. B. GADDAGIMATH
Library of 320,000 vols, 410 journals, 9,500 ejournals
Number of teachers: 160
Number of students: 68,450

DEANS
Faculty of Arts: Prof. MOHD ABDUL HAMEED
Faculty of Commerce: Prof. B. M. KANAHALLI
Faculty of Education: Prof. SYEDA AKTHAR
Faculty of Law: Prof. S. S. PATIL
Faculty of Science and Technology: Prof. Y. M. JAYARAJ
Faculty of Social Science: Prof. B. S. MAHESHWARAPPA

GURU GHASIDAS VISHWAVIDYALAYA (Guru Ghasidas University)

Koni, Bilaspur 495009, Chhattisgarh
Telephone: (7752) 260209
E-mail: centraluniv@ggu.ac.in
Internet: www.ggu.ac.in
Founded 1983
Vice-Chancellor: (vacant)
Dir of College Devt Council and Acting Registrar: M. S. K. KHOKHAR
Controller of Examinations: Prof. A. S. RANDIVE
Dean of Student Welfare: Dr S. V. S. CHOUHAN
Librarian: Dr U. N. SINGH
Library of 104,000 vols

DEANS
Faculty of Arts: Dr B. B. SHUKLA
Faculty of Education: A. KUJUR
Faculty of Engineering: Prof. S. M. SAHA
Faculty of Home Science: Dr J. SHARMA
Faculty of Law: Dr A. B. SONI
Faculty of Life Science: Prof. B. M. MUKHERJEE
Faculty of Management and Commerce: Prof. L. M. MALVIYA
Faculty of Medical Science: Dr V. D. TIWARI
Faculty of Natural Resources: Prof. S. S. SINGH
Faculty of Physical Education: Prof. S. S. SINGH
Faculty of Science: Prof. A. K. SAXENA
Faculty of Social Science: Dr J. P. SHARMA

GURU GOBIND SINGH INDRAPRASTHA UNIVERSITY

Sector-16C, Dwarka, Delhi 110075
Telephone: (11) 25302170
E-mail: mail@ipu.edu
Internet: ipu.ac.in
Founded 1998
State control
Academic year: August to July
Chancellor: VIJAI KAPOOR
Vice-Chancellor: Prof. DILIP K. BANDYOPADHYAY
Registrar: Dr B. P. JOSHI
Proctor: Prof. SUMAN GUPTA
Controller of Examinations: Dr PRAVIN CHANDRA
Dir for Academic Affairs: Prof. AVINASH C. SHARMA
Dir for Students Welfare: Prof. A. S. BENIWAL
Librarian: SUBHASH DESHMUKH
Library of 15,690 vols
Number of students: 40,000

DEANS
University School of Architecture and Planning: Prof. B. V. R. REDDY
University School of Basic and Applied Sciences: Prof. VINOD KUMAR
University School of Biotechnology: Prof. R. K. GUPTA
University School of Chemical Technology: Prof. S. S. SAMBI
University School of Education: Prof. SAROJ SHARMA
University School of Engineering and Technology: Prof. NUPUR PRAKASH
University School of Environmental Management: Prof. PRODYUT BHATTACHARYA
University School of Humanities and Social Sciences: Prof. ANUP BENIWAL
University School of Information Technology: Prof. NAVIN RAJPAL
University School of Law and Legal Studies: Prof. SUMAN GUPTA
University School of Management Studies: Prof. ANU S. LATHER
University School of Mass Communication: Prof. ANUP BENIWAL
University School of Medicine and Para-Medical Health Sciences: Prof. H. K. KAR

GURU JAMBESHWAR UNIVERSITY OF SCIENCE & TECHNOLOGY

Delhi Rd, Hisar 125001, Haryana
Telephone: (1662) 263101
E-mail: gju_tech@yahoo.com
Internet: www.gjust.ac.in
Founded 1995
Academic year: July to May (2 semesters)
Chancellor: HE GOV. OF HARYANA
Vice-Chancellor: Dr M. L. RANGA
Registrar: Prof. R. S. JAGLAN
Proctor: Prof. RAJESH MALHOTRA
Dean of Academic Affairs: Prof. M. S. TURAN
Dean of Student Welfare: Prof. KULDIP BANSAL
Dean of Colleges: Prof. DHARMINDER KUMAR
Controller of Examinations: Prof. R. S. JAGLAN
Proctor: Prof. RAJESH MALHOTRA
Librarian: Prof. J. K. SHARMA
Library of 73,732 vols, 184 periodicals

DEANS
Faculty of Engineering and Technology: Prof. DHARMINDER KUMAR
Faculty of Environmental and Bio Sciences Technology: Prof. C. P. KAUSHIK
Faculty of Management Studies: Prof. S. C. KUNDU
Faculty of Media Studies: Prof. MANOJ DAYAL
Faculty of Medical Sciences: Prof. S. K. SHARMA
Faculty of Non-Conventional Sources of Energy and Environmental Science: Prof. N. RAM
Faculty of Pharmaceutical Sciences: Prof. D. N. MISHRA
Faculty of Physical Sciences: Prof. RAJESH MALHOTRA
Faculty of Religious Studies: Prof. C. P. KAUSHIK
Faculty of Science and Technology Interface: Prof. K. BANSAL
Haryana School of Business: Prof. B. K. PUNIA

GURU NANAK DEV UNIVERSITY

G. T. Rd, Amritsar 143005, Punjab
Telephone: (183) 2258802
E-mail: reg_gndu@yahoo.com
Founded 1969
State control
Languages of instruction: English, Hindi, Punjabi
Academic year: July to June
Chancellor: HE GOV. OF PUNJAB
Vice-Chancellor: Prof. Dr AJAIB SINGH BRAR
Registrar: Dr INDERJIT SINGH
Library of 436,000 vols
Number of teachers: 311 (in univ. campus)
Number of students: 9,063
Publications: *Amritsar Law Journal* (1 a year), *Guru Nanak Journal of Sociology* (2 a year), *Indian Journal of Quantitative Economics* (2 a year), *Journal of Management Studies* (1 a year), *Journal of Regional History* (1 a year), *Journal of Sikh Studies* (2 a year, in English), *Journal of Sports Traumatology and Allied Sports Science* (1 a year), *Khoj Darpan* (2 a year, in Punjabi), *Personality Study and Group Behaviour* (1 a year), *Pradhikrit* (1 a year, in Hindi), *PSE Economic Analyst* (2 a year, in English), *Punjab Journal of English Studies* (1 a year), *Punjab Journal of Politics* (2 a year), *University Samachar* (4 a year)

DEANS
Faculty of Agriculture and Forestry: Dr J. S. BAL
Faculty of Applied Sciences: Dr NARPINDER SINGH
Faculty of Arts and Social Sciences: Dr RADHA SHARMA
Faculty of Economics and Business: Dr VIKRAM CHADHA
Faculty of Education: Dr SURINDERPAL KAUR DHILLON
Faculty of Engineering and Technology: Dr K. S. KAHLON
Faculty of Humanities and Religious Studies: Dr SHASHI BALA
Faculty of Languages: Dr BARKAT ALI
Faculty of Law: Dr RAJNIDERJIT KAUR PAWAR
Faculty of Life Sciences: Prof. Dr A. J. S. BHANWER
Faculty of Physical Education: Dr SUKHDEV SINGH
Faculty of Physical Planning and Architecture: Eng. PARAMJIT SINGH MAHOORA
Faculty of Sciences: Dr RAKESH MAHAJAN
Faculty of Sport Medicine and Physiotherapy: Dr JASPAL SINGH SANDHU
Faculty of Visual Arts and Performing Arts: Dr RAJINDERJIT KAUR PAWAR

HEMCHANDRACHARYA NORTH GUJARAT UNIVERSITY

University Rd, POB 21, Patan 384265, Gujarat
Telephone: (2766) 230456
E-mail: vc@ngu.ac.in
Internet: www.ngu.ac.in
Founded 1986
State control
Language of instruction: Gujarati
Academic year: June to April
Chancellor: HE GOV. OF GUJARAT
Vice-Chancellor: Dr HEMIXABEN RAO
Pro-Vice-Chancellor: (vacant)
Registrar: Dr D. M. PATEL (acting)
Controller of Examinations: Dr K. N. PATEL (acting)
Dir for Physical Education and Youth Activities: Dr J. D. DAMOR (acting)
Librarian: M. G. PATEL (acting)
Library of 55,900 vols, 123 periodicals
Number of teachers: 1,829
Number of students: 43,080
Publications: *Anart* (1 a year), *Udichya* (26 a year)

DEANS
Faculty of Arts: Dr JAYESHBHAI N. BAROT
Faculty of Commerce: Prof. B. D. PATEL
Faculty of Education: Prof. Dr BHARATBHAI D. DAVE
Faculty of Engineering Technology: KISHORSINH G. MARADIYA
Faculty of Law: Prin.: Dr JAGDEEP U. NANAVATI
Faculty of Management Studies: Dr B. A. PRAJAPATI
Faculty of Medicine: Dr PINAKIN N. TRIVEDI
Faculty of Pharmacy: Dr C. N. PATEL
Faculty of Rural Studies: Prof. AMRUTBHAI B. PATEL
Faculty of Science: Prof. Dr B. L. PUJANI

HEMWATI NANDAN BAHUGUNA GARHWAL UNIVERSITY

Srinagar Pauri Garhwal 246174, Uttarakhand
Telephone: (1346) 252143
E-mail: registrar.hnbgu@gmail.com
Internet: hnbgu.ac.in
Founded 1973, fmrly Garhwal Univ., current name adopted 1989
State control

Languages of instruction: English, Hindi
Academic year: July to May
Chancellor: HE Gov. of Uttar Pradesh
Vice-Chancellor: Prof. S. K. Singh (acting)
Registrar: Dr U. S. Rawat
Hon. Librarian: Prof. M. S. M. Rawat
Library of 138,144 vols, 100 journals
Number of teachers: 251
Number of students: 150,000 (incl. colleges)

DEANS
Faculty of Agriculture: Prof. N. D. Todariya
Faculty of Arts: Prof. B. M. Khanduri
Faculty of Ayurveda: Dr Puja Bardwaj
Faculty of Commerce: Prof. Alok Saklani
Faculty of Education: Prof. K. B. Budhori
Faculty of Engineering: Dr M. L. Dewal
Faculty of Law: Dr S. K. Mittal
Faculty of Medicine: Dr A. N. Mehrotra
Faculty of Non-formal Education: Prof. A. Misra
Faculty of Science: Prof. R. D. Gaur

HIDAYATULLAH NATIONAL LAW UNIVERSITY

Uparwara Post, Abhanpur New Raipur 493661, Chhattisgarh
Telephone: (771) 3057603
E-mail: registrar@hnlu.ac.in
Internet: www.hnlu.ac.in
Founded 2003
State control
Schools of administration of justice, continuing and clinical legal education (SAJCCLE), business and global trade laws devy (SBGTLD), constitutional and administrative governance (SCAG), int. legal studies (SILS), juridical and social sciences (SJSS), science, technology and sustainable devt (SSTSD); regional centre in Bilaspur
Chancellor: Hon. Rajeev Gupta
Vice-Chancellor: Prof. Dr Sukh Pal Singh
Registrar: B. C. Biswas
Controller of Examination: Prof. Anand Pawar
Librarian: Shiva Parihar

HIMACHAL PRADESH UNIVERSITY

Summer Hill, Shimla 171005, Himachal Pradesh
Telephone: (177) 2830273
E-mail: gad.hpu@gmail.com
Internet: www.hpuniv.nic.in
Founded 1970
State control
Languages of instruction: English, Hindi
Academic year: July to May
Chancellor: HE Gov. of Himachal Pradesh
Vice-Chancellor: Prof. A. D. N. Bajpai
Registrar: C. P. Verma
Controller of Examinations: Prof. Narendra Avasthi
Dean of Students Welfare: Prof. T. C. Bhalla
Dean of Studies: Prof. H. S. Banyal
Librarian: (vacant)
Library of 200,000 vols
Number of teachers: 260
Number of students: 6,461

DEANS
Faculty of Ayurveda: Dr Y. K. Sharma
Faculty of Commerce and Management Studies: Prof. Maneet Mahajan
Faculty of Dental Sciences: Dr Ashu Gupta
Faculty of Education: Prof. Harbans Singh
Faculty of Engineering and Technology: Dr Niraj Sharma
Faculty of Languages: Prof. Vidya Sharda
Faculty of Law: Prof. Suresh Kapoor
Faculty of Life Sciences: Prof. H. S. Banyal
Faculty of Performing and Visual Arts: Dr C. L. Verma
Faculty of Physical Science: Prof. M. L. Parmar
Faculty of Social Sciences: Dr B. S. Marh

INDIRA GANDHI KRISHI VISHWAVIDYALAYA
(Indira Gandhi Agricultural University)

Krishak Nagar, Raipur 492006, Chattisgarh
Telephone: (771) 2443166
E-mail: matappandey@yahoo.in
Internet: igau.edu.in/igkv
Founded 1987
State control
Chancellor: HE Gov. of Chhattisgarh
Vice-Chancellor: Prof. M. P. Pandey
Registrar: S. R. Ratre
Librarian: Dr Madhav Pandey
Library of 35,000 vols, 310 journals

DEANS
College of Agriculture and Research Station, Kawardha: Dr M. P. Thakur
College of Agriculture, Raipur: Dr O. P. Kashyap
College of Dairy Technology: Dr U. K. Mishra
College of Fisheries Science: Dr H. K. Vardia
College of Veterinary and Animal Husbandry: Dr K. C. P. Singh
Faculty of Agricultural Engineering: Dr R. K. Sahu
B. R. S. M. College of Agricultural Engineering and Technology: Dr Vinay Kumar Pandey
R. M. D. College of Agriculture and Research Station, Ambikapur: Dr S. S. Shaw
S. G. College of Agriculture: Dr S. S. Rao
T. C. B. College of Agriculture and Research Station, Bilaspur: Dr C. R. Gupta

INDIRA GANDHI NATIONAL OPEN UNIVERSITY

Maidan Garhi, New Delhi 110068
Telephone: (11) 29571000
E-mail: vc@ignou.ac.in
Internet: www.ignou.ac.in
Founded 1985
State control
Languages of instruction: English, Hindi
Academic year: January to December
Schools of agriculture, communication, computer and information science, continuing education, education, engineering technology, extension and development studies, foreign languages, gender and development studies, health sciences, humanities, interdisciplinary and trans-disciplinary studies, journalism and new media studies, law, management studies, sciences, social sciences social work, tourism and hospitality service sectorial management, translation studies and training, vocational education and training; 3,000 study centres
Vice-Chancellor: Prof. M. Aslam (acting)
Pro-Vice-Chancellor: (vacant): Prof. Mahendra P. Lama
Registrar: Dr Pankaj Khare
Librarian: Sudhir K. Arora
Library of 119,338 vols, 472 journals
Number of teachers: 255
Number of students: 280,000
Publication: *Indian Journal of Open Learning* (2 a year)

INDIRA KALA SANGIT VISHWAVIDYALAYA
(Indira Kala Sangeet University)

Khairagarh, Rajnandgaon 491881, Chhattisgarh
Telephone: (7820) 234232
E-mail: reg@iksvv.com
Internet: www.iksvv.com
Founded 1956
State control
Languages of instruction: English, Hindi
Academic year: July to June (2 terms)
Chancellor: HE Gov. of Chhattisgarh
Vice-Chancellor: Prof. Dr Mandavi Singh
Registrar: P. S. Dhruv
Deputy Librarian: Ramesh Patel
Library of 44,047 vols, 41 periodicals, 97 MSS
Number of teachers: 586
Number of students: 9,680
Publications: *Bharat Bhashyam*, *Bhatkhande Smriti Granth*, *Kala Sourabh*, *Ki Sangit Yatra*, *Meri Dakshin Bharat*, *Sangit Suryodaya*, *Shiv Mangalam*

DEANS
Faculty of Arts: Prof. Dr I. D. Tiwari
Faculty of Dance: Prof. Jyoti Buxi
Faculty of Folk Music and Arts: Dr Bharat Patel
Faculty of Music: Prof. Dr Anil Bihari Beohar
Faculty of Visual Arts: Prof. Dr M. C. Sharma

JADAVPUR UNIVERSITY

Main Campus: 188 Raja S. C. Mullick Rd, Jadavpur, Kolkata 700032, West Bengal
Telephone: (33) 24146666
Salt Lake Campus: Plot 8, Block LB, Sector 3, Salt Lake City, Kolkata 700098, West Bengal
Telephone: (33) 23355215
E-mail: registrar@admin.jdvu.ac.in
Internet: www.jadavpur.edu
Founded 1955
State control
Language of instruction: English
Academic year: July to June (2 terms)
Chancellor: HE Gov. of West Bengal
Vice-Chancellor: Prof. Abhijit Chakraborty
Pro-Vice-Chancellor: Prof. Siddhartha Datta
Dean for Students: Dr Rajat Ray
Registrar: Dr Pradip Kumar Ghosh
Controller of Examinations: Dr Satyaki Bhattacharyya
Chief Librarian: Manilal Murmu (acting)
Library of 598,594 vols, 1,391 journals
Number of teachers: 662
Number of students: 9,441
Publications: *Essays and Studies* (2 a year), *Journal of Comparative Literature* (1 a year), *Journal of History* (1 a year), *Journal of International Relations* (1 a year), *Journal of Philosophy* (2 a year), *Journal of the Department of Bengali* (1 a year)

DEANS
Faculty of Arts: Prof. Nilanjana Gupta
Faculty of Engineering and Technology: Prof. Niladri Chakraborty
Faculty of Science: Prof. Dr Subhash Chandra Bhattacharya

CENTRES FOR ADVANCED STUDIES
Centre for Ambedkar Studies: tel. (33) 24146008; Coordinator Prof. B. Chatterjee.
Centre for European Studies: tel. (33) 24839962; e-mail europa_1997@rediffmail.com; f. 1997; Coordinator Dr Kousik Roy; Coordinator Dr Suchetana Chattopadhyay.
Centre for Human Settlement Planning: tel. (33) 24146852; e-mail monideep@cal.vsnl

.net.in; f. 1996; Coordinator Prof. TAPAS BHATTACHARYA.

Centre of Indology: tel. (33) 24146115; Coordinator Prof. DEBARCHANA SARKAR.

Centre for Knowledge Based Systems: tel. (33) 24146723; e-mail ckbsjuin@vsnl.com; f. 1987; Coordinator Dr SMITA SADHU.

Centre for Marxian Studies: tel. (33) 24146008; Coordinator Prof. B. CHATTERJEE.

Centre for Microprocessor Application for Training, Education and Research: tel. (33) 24146766; internet www.cmaterju.org; f. 1983; Coordinator Prof. MITA NASIPURI.

Centre for Mobile Computing and Communication: tel. (33) 23356122; e-mail pkdas@ieee.org; internet www.cmccju.org; f. 2003; Coordinator Prof. PRADIP K. DAS.

Centre for Plasma Studies: tel. (33) 24137902; e-mail mk@jufs.ernet.in; f. 1993; Coordinator Prof. S. C. BHATTACHARYYA.

Centre for Quality Management System: tel. (33) 24146207; internet www.cqmsju.org; f. 1994; Coordinator Prof. S. K. GHOSH.

Centre for Refugee Studies: tel. (33) 24146019; e-mail opmcrs@cal2.vsnl.net.in; f. 1997; Coordinator Prof. SANJUKTA BHATTACHARYA.

Centre for Surface Science: tel. (33) 24146411; e-mail cssju@yahoo.co.uk; f. 1992; Coordinator Prof. SUBHASH CHANDRA BHATTACHARYA.

Condensed Matter Physics Research Centre: tel. (33) 24138917; e-mail sujata@phys.jdvu.ac.in; f. 1990; Coordinator Prof. SUJATA TARAFDAR.

IC Design and Fabrication Centre: tel. (33) 24146833; e-mail juicc@vsnl.com; f. 1986; Coordinator Prof. CHANDAN KUMAR SARKAR.

Nuclear and Particle Physics Research Centre: tel. (33) 2414666; f. 2000; Coordinator Prof. D. C. GHOSH.

Relativity and Cosmology Research Centre: tel. (33) 24138917; e-mail asitb@cal3.vsnl.net.in; f. 1994; Coordinator Prof. SHEKHAR BHUSHAN DUTTA.

Sir C. V. Raman Centre for Physics and Music: Coordinator Prof. S. DATTA

JAGADGURU RAMANANDACHARYA RAJASTHAN SANSKRIT UNIVERSITY

Village Madau, Post Bhankhrota, Jaipur 302026, Rajasthan
Telephone: (141) 5132021
E-mail: jrrsu@yahoo.com
Internet: www.jrrsanskrituniversity.ac.in
Founded 2001
State control
Languages of instruction: Hindi, Sanskrit
Academic year: July to May
Chancellor: HE GOV. OF RAJASTHAN
Vice-Chancellor: Prof. R. DEVNATHAN
Registrar: SUNIL SHARMA
Controller of Examinations: SUBHASH SHARMA (acting)
Dir for Academic Affairs: Prof. VINOD SHARMA
Dir for Research and Publs: Prof. TARASHANKAR SHARMA (acting)
Library of 32,215 vols, 80 periodicals
Number of teachers: 27
Number of students: 800
Publications: *Vayam*, *Vyakhyanmanimala*

JAGADGURU RAMBHADRACHARYA HANDICAPPED UNIVERSITY

Chitrakoot, Karwi, 210204 Uttar Pradesh
Telephone: (5198) 224481
E-mail: jrhuniversity@yahoo.com
Internet: www.jrhu.com
Founded 2001
Private control
Chancellor: JAGADGURU RAMANANDACHARYA SWAMI RAMBHADRACHARYA JI
Vice-Chancellor: Prof. B. PANDEY
Registrar: Dr KAMLESH KUMAR
Publication: *Samanubhuti*

DEANS

Faculty of Computer and Information Sciences, Commerce and Management, Fine Art: Dr A. C. MISHRA
Faculty of Humanities, Music, Education: Prof. YOGESH CHANDRA DUBEY
Faculty of Social Sciences: Prof. YOGESH CHANDRA DUBEY

JAI NARAIN VYAS UNIVERSITY

Bhagat ki Kothi, Pali Rd, Jodhpur 342001, Rajasthan
Telephone: (291) 2649733
E-mail: info@jnvu.edu.in
Internet: www.jnvu.edu.in
Founded 1962, fmrly Jodhpur Univ.
State control
Languages of instruction: English, Hindi
Academic year: July to April
Chancellor: HE GOV OF RAJASTHAN
Vice-Chancellor: Dr B. S. RAJPUROHIT
Registrar: NIRMLA MEENA
Librarian: Dr K. L. SHARMA
Library of 277,229 vols
Number of teachers: 336
Number of students: 24,063
Publications: *The Beacons* (Engineering), *Annals of Economics*, *International Journal of Finance and Economic Studies* (1 a year), *Journal of Accounting and Control* (1 a year)

DEANS

Faculty of Arts, Social Sciences and Education: Dr A. MATHUR
Faculty of Commerce and Management Studies: Dr R. C. S. RAJPUROHIT
Faculty of Engineering and Architecture: Dr ARVIND RAI
Faculty of Law: Dr R. N. SHARMA
Faculty of Science: Dr A. K. MALIK

PROFESSORS

BANERJI, K. K., Chemistry
BHANDARI, S., Mining Engineering
DHARIWAL, S. R., Physics
GUPTA, V. P., Civil Engineering
LALWANI, S. J., Commerce
MALI, S. L., Electrical Engineering
OHRI, M. L., Civil Engineering
SETRIA, M. R., Structural Engineering
SHARMA, D., Civil Engineering
SHARMA, U. S., Civil Engineering
SHEKHANAT, K. S., Rajasthani
SHRIVASTAVA, R. S., Sociology
SURANA, D. M., Mining Engineering
SURANA, P., Sociology
SURANA, S. L., Electrical Engineering
TIWARI, R. P., Mechanical Engineering

JAI PRAKASH VISHWAVIDYALAYA (Jai Prakash University)

Rahul Sankrityan Nagar, Chapra 841301, Bihar
Telephone: (6152) 243898
Internet: jpv.bih.nic.in
Founded 1990
State control
Languages of instruction: English, Hindi
Academic year: July to June
Vice-Chancellor: Prof. Dr RAM VINOD SINHA
Pro Vice-Chancellor: Dr DINESH PRASAD SINHA
Dean of Student Welfare: Dr RAMANAND RAM
Proctor: Dr L. P. YADAV
Registrar: Prof. BIJAY PRATAP KUMAR
Controller of Examinations: Dr DIVANSHU KUMAR

DEANS

Faculty of Commerce: (vacant)
Faculty of Humanities: Prof. Dr BIRENDRA NARAYN YADAV
Faculty of Science: Prof. Dr RAJESHWAR PD. SINGH
Faculty of Social Sciences: Prof. Dr RAMA SHANKAR SINGH

JAMIA MILLIA ISLAMIA

Maulana Mohammad Ali Johar Marg, Jamia Nagar, New Delhi 110025
Telephone: (11) 26981717
E-mail: dir.cit@jmi.ac.in
Internet: jmi.ac.in
Founded 1920, present status 1988
State control
Languages of instruction: Urdu, Hindi, English
Academic year: July to June
Chancellor: FAKHRUDDIN T. KHORAKIWALA
Vice-Chancellor: NAJEEB JUNG
Pro-Vice-Chancellor: Prof. SYED MOHAMMAD RASHID
Registrar: Prof. Dr S. M. SAJID
Dean of Student Welfare: Dr TASNEEM MEENAI
Librarian: Dr GAYAS MAKHDUMI
Library of 324,870 vols, 3,000 periodicals, 448 MSS
Number of teachers: 933
Number of students: 14,264
Publications: *Islam and the Modern Age* (4 a year, in English), *Islam Aur Asr-e-Jadeed* (4 a year, in Urdu), *Jamia Risala* (4 a year, in Urdu), *Tadrees Nama* (4 a year, in Urdu), *Third Frame* (4 a year, in English)

DEANS

Faculty of Architecture and Ekistics: Prof. S. M. AKHTAR
Faculty of Dentistry: Prof. RAGINI
Faculty of Education: Prof. AEJAZ MASIH
Faculty of Engineering and Technology: Prof. KHALID MOIN
Faculty of Fine Arts: Prof. Z. A. ZARGAR
Faculty of Humanities and Languages: Prof. S. M. AZIZUDDIN HUSAIN
Faculty of Law: Prof. ROSE VARGHESE
Faculty of Natural Sciences: Prof. KHALIL AHMAD
Faculty of Social Sciences: Prof. KHAN MASOOD AHMAD

ATTACHED INSTITUTES

AJK Mass Communication Research Centre: tel. (11) 26986810; e-mail contact@ajkmcrc.org; internet ajkmcrc.org; f. 1982; Dir Prof. OBAID SIDDIQUI.

Centre for Culture Media and Governance: tel. (11) 26933810; e-mail ccmgjmi@gmail.com; f. 2004; Dir Prof. BISWAJIT DAS.

Centre for European and Latin American Studies: tel. (11) 26981717; f. 2004; Dir Prof. SONYA SURABHI GUPTA.

Centre for Gandhian Studies: tel. (11) 26985473; e-mail gandhiancentre.jamia@gmail.com; f. 2004; Dir Dr A. P. SEN.

Centre for Interdisciplinary Research in Basic Sciences: tel. (11) 26983409; e-mail faizan_ahmad@yahoo.com; f. 2004; Dir Prof. PANKAJ SARAN.

Centre for Jawaharlal Nehru Studies: tel. (11) 26981717; e-mail dir.cjns@jmi.ac.in; f. 2004; Dir Prof. SHAHID AHMAD.

Centre for Management Studies: tel. (11) 26985519; e-mail dir.cms@jmi.ac.in; f. 2004; Dir Prof. U. M. AMIN.

Centre for Physiotherapy and Rehabilitation Sciences: tel. (11) 26980544; f. 2004; Dir Prof. Dr M. EJAZ HUSSAIN.

Centre for the Study of Comparative Religions and Civilizations: tel. (11) 29535399; e-mail religions.jmi@gmail.com; f. 2004; Dir Dr AMIYA P. SEN.

Centre for Theoretical Physics: tel. (11) 26984830; e-mail office@ctp-jamia.res.in; internet www.ctp-jamia.res.in; f. 2006; Dir Prof. M. SAMI.

Centre for West Asian Studies: tel. (11) 26983328; e-mail dir.cwas@jmi.ac.in; f. 2004; Dir Dr ANWAR ALAM.

Dr K. R. Narayanan Centre for Dalit and Minorities Studies: tel. (11) 26981717; f. 2005; Dir Prof. AZRA RAZZACK.

Dr Zakir Husain Institute of Islamic Studies: tel. (11) 26841202; f. 1971; Dir Prof. AKHTARUL WASEY.

Maulana Mohamed Ali 'Jauhar' Academy of International Studies: tel. (11) 26987582; f. 1988; library of 12,000 vols, 5,000 periodicals; Dir T. C. A. RANGACHARI.

Nelson Mandela Centre for Peace and Conflict Resolution: tel. (11) 26981717; e-mail centreforpeace@rediffmail.com; f. 2004; Dir Prof. TASLEEM MEENAI.

Sarojini Naidu Centre for Women Studies: tel. (11) 26981270; e-mail sncwsjmi@yahoo.co.in; f. 2000; library of 528 vols; Dir Prof. BULBUL DHAR JAMES

JAWAHARLAL NEHRU KRISHI VISHWAVIDYALAYA, JABALPUR (Jawaharlal Nehru Agricultural University, Jabalpur)

PB 80, Krishnagar, Jabalpur 482004, Madhya Pradesh
Telephone: (761) 2681778
E-mail: registrarjnkvv@yahoo.co.in
Internet: www.jnkvv.nic.in

Founded 1964
State control
Languages of instruction: Hindi, English
Academic year: July to June

Chancellor: HE GOV. OF MADHYA PRADESH
Vice-Chancellor: Prof. Dr GAUTAM KALLOO
Registrar: B. B. MISHRA
Comptroller: G. S. KURVETI
Dean of Student Welfare: Dr P. K. BISEN (acting)

Library of 84,000 vols, incl. periodicals
Number of students: 2,282

Publication: *JNKVV Research Journal* (4 a year)

DEANS

Faculty of Agricultural Engineering: Dr D. K. MISHRA (acting)
Faculty of Agriculture: Dr V. S. TOMAR
Faculty of Veterinary Science and Animal Husbandry: Dr K. S. JOHAR

CONSTITUENT COLLEGES

College of Agricultural Engineering, Jabalpur: Dean Dr TARUN KUMAR BHATTACHARYA.

College of Agriculture, Ganjbasoda: Dean Dr R. V. SINGH.

College of Agriculture, Jabalpur: Dean Dr D. K. MISHRA (acting).

College of Agriculture, Rewa: Dean Dr S. K. RAO (acting).

College of Agriculture, Tikamgarh: Dean Dr P. K. MISHRA

JAWAHARLAL NEHRU TECHNOLOGICAL UNIVERSITY

Kukatpally, Hyderabad 500085, Andhra Pradesh
Telephone: (40) 23158661
E-mail: vcjntu@yahoo.com
Internet: www.jntu.ac.in

Founded 1972
State control
Academic year: July to April

192 Affiliated engineering colleges, 12 pharmacy colleges, 3 architectural colleges

Chancellor: HE GOV. OF ANDHRA PRADESH
Vice-Chancellor: Prof. RAMESHWAR RAO
Rector: Dr M. CHANDRA SHEKAR
Registrar: Dr M. CHANDRA SHEKAR
Dir for Academics and Planning: Dr G. K. VISWANADH
Dir for Admissions: Dr A. VINAY BABU (acting)
Controller of Examinations: Dr RAM MOHAN REDDY
Librarian: Prof. N. RUPSINGH NAIK (acting)

Library of 48,000 books, 128 periodicals
Number of teachers: 457
Number of students: 34,000 (incl. affiliated colleges).

CONSTITUENT COLLEGE

JNTUH College of Engineering, Hyderabad: Nachupally (Kondagattu), Kodimyal mandal, Karimnagar 505501, Andhra Pradesh; tel. (8724) 2290000; e-mail cejjntuh@gmail.com; internet jntuhcej.ac.in; f. 1965; library of 14,100 vols, 20 journals; Prin. Dr B. SUDHEER PREM KUMAR (acting)

JAWAHARLAL NEHRU UNIVERSITY

New Mehrauli Rd, New Delhi 110067
Telephone: (11) 26742650
E-mail: registrar@mail.jnu.ac.in
Internet: www.jnu.ac.in

Founded 1969
State control
Language of instruction: English
Academic year: July to May

Chancellor: Prof. K. KASTURIRANGAN
Vice-Chancellor: Prof. S. K. SOPORY
Rector: Prof. SUDHA PAI
Registrar: Dr SANDEEP CHATTERJEE
Chief Proctor: Prof. P. C. RATH
Dean for Student Welfare: Prof. ABDUL NAFEY
Librarian: Dr RAMESH C. GAUR

Library of 500,000 vols, 723 periodicals
Number of teachers: 525
Number of students: 8,500

Publications: *Hispanic Horizon* (2 a year), *International Studies* (4 a year), *Journal of School of Languages* (2 a year), *Studies in History* (2 a year)

DEANS

School of Arts and Aesthetics: Prof. IRA BHASKAR
School of Biotechnology: Prof. RAKESH BHATNAGAR
School of Computational and Integrative Sciences: Prof. R. N. K. BAMEZAI
School of Computer and Systems Sciences: Prof. C. P. KATTI
School of Environmental Sciences: Prof. A. K. ATTRI
School of International Studies: Prof. K. WARIKOO
School of Language, Literature and Culture Studies: Prof. M. A. ISLAHI
School of Life Sciences: Prof. B. N. MALLICK
School of Physical Sciences: Prof. S. GHOSH
School of Social Sciences: Prof. M. MUKHERJEE

JAYPEE UNIVERSITY OF INFORMATION TECHNOLOGY

Waknaghat, PO Waknaghat, Kandaghat, Solan 173234, Himachal Pradesh
Telephone: (1792) 257999
E-mail: yaj.medury@jiit.ac.in
Internet: www.juit.ac.in

Founded 2002
Private control
Language of instruction: English
Academic year: July to June

Depts of bioinformatics and biotechnology, civil engineering, computer science and engineering, electronics and communication engineering, humanities and social sciences, information and communication technology, mathematics, pharmacy, physics and material sciences

Chancellor: HE GOV. OF HIMACHAL PRADESH
Pro-Chancellor: Dr MANOJ GAUR
Vice-Chancellor: Prof. S. K. KAK
Registrar and Dir for Admin. and Students Welfare: Brig. (retd) BALBIR SINGH
Dean for Academics and Research: Prof. T. S. LAMBA
Dean for Biotechnology: Prof. R. S. CHAUHAN
Controller of Examination: Prof. SUNIL KUMAR KHAH
Librarian: SHRI RAM

Library of 32,881 vols
Number of teachers: 135
Number of students: 2,118

PROFESSORS

BARMAN, P. B., Physics & Material Sciences
BHOOSHAN, S. V., Electronics and Communication Engineering
CHAUHAN, R. S., Biotechnology and Bioinformatics
DAHIYA, D., Computer Science & Engineering
GALI, V. S., Civil Engineering
GHRERA, S. P., Computer Science and Information Technology
GUPTA, A. K., Biotechnology and Bioinformatics
KHAH, S. K., Physics & Material Sciences
KULSHRESHTHA, D. C., Electronics and Communication Engineering
LAMBA, T. S., Electronics & Communication Engineering
SINGH, G., Electronics & Communication Engineering
SINGH, H., Mathematics
SINGH, K., Mathematics
TANDON, C., Biotechnology & Bioinformatics

JIWAJI UNIVERSITY

Vidya Vihar, Gwalior 474011, Madhya Pradesh
Telephone: (751) 2442712
E-mail: info@idejug.org
Internet: www.jiwaji.edu

Founded 1964
Languages of instruction: English, Hindi
Academic year: July to April

Chancellor: HE GOV. OF MADHYA PRADESH
Vice-Chancellor: Prof. M. KIDWAI
Rector: Prof. J. N. GAUTAM
Registrar: Dr ANAND MISHRA
Dean of Students Welfare: Dr D. S. CHANDEL
Librarian: R. G. GARG

Library of 140,000 vols, 142 journals
Number of students: 47,358

Publications: *Humanities* (2 a year), *Science* (2 a year)

DEANS

Faculty of Arts: Dr H. C. GUPTA
Faculty of Commerce and Management: Dr D. C. SHARMA
Faculty of Life Science: (vacant)
Faculty of Physical Education: (vacant)
Faculty of Science: (vacant)
Faculty of Social Sciences: Dr P. L. SABLOOK

JUNAGADH AGRICULTURAL UNIVERSITY

Motibaug, Junagadh 362001, Gujarat
Telephone: (285) 2672080
E-mail: vc@jau.in
Internet: www.jau.in

Founded 1972, fmrly Gujarat Agricultural Univ., present name and status 2003
State control
Language of instruction: English
Academic year: July to March

Chancellor: HE GOV. OF GUJARAT
Vice-Chancellor: Dr N. C. PATEL
Registrar: Dr K. B. JADEJA
Dir for Extension: Dr A. M. PARAKHIA
Dir for Research and Dean for Postgraduate Studies: Dr C. J. DANGARIA
Dir for Student Welfare: Dr P. V. PATEL (acting)
Librarian: PUFFY DAVE (acting)

Library of 25,000 vols, 300 periodicals
Number of teachers: 400
Number of students: 1,000

DEANS

Faculty of Agricultural Engineering and Technology: Dr N. K. GONTIA
Faculty of Agriculture: Dr J. V. BARAD
Faculty of Basic Science and Humanities: (vacant)
Faculty of Fisheries Science: Dr A. Y. DESAI
Faculty of Horticulture: (vacant)
Faculty of Veterinary Science and Animal Husbandry: Dr P. H. TANK (acting)
Postgraduate Faculty of Agri-Business Management: Dr K. A. KHUNT

CONSTITUENT COLLEGES

Aspee College of Home Science: Sardar Krushinagar; Prin. Dr M. M. PATEL (acting).

Aspee College of Horticulture and Forestry: Navsari; Prin. Dr B. M. PATEL (acting).

B. A. College of Agriculture: Anand; Prin. Dr D. J. PATEL.

College of Agricultural Engineering and Technology: Junagadh; Prin. Dr S. C. B. SIRIPURAPU.

College of Agriculture, Junagadh: e-mail agricol@jau.in; Prin. Dr D. D. MALAVIA.

College of Agriculture, Sardar Krushinagar: e-mail agricol@jau.in; Prin. Dr S. R. S. DANGE (acting).

College of Fisheries Science: Veraval; tel. (2876) 242052; e-mail cofvrl@yahoo.co.in; internet www.jau.in; library of 5,250 vols; 18 teachers; 250 students; Prin. and Dean Dr A. Y. DESAI.

College of Veterinary Science and Animal Husbandry, Anand: Prin. Dr M. B. PANDE (acting).

College of Veterinary Science and Animal Husbandry, Sardar Krushinagar: Prin. Dr M. C. DESAI.

Mansukhlal Chhaganlal College of Dairy Science: Anand; Prin. Dr R. S. SHARMA.

N. M. College of Agriculture: Navsari; Prin. Dr H. N. VYAS

KAKATIYA UNIVERSITY

Vidyaranyapuri, Warangal 506009, Andhra Pradesh
Telephone: (8712) 2438866
E-mail: registrar@kakatiya.ac.in
Internet: www.kuwarangal.com

Founded 1967 as postgraduate centre of Osmania Univ., current name and status 1976
State control
Languages of instruction: English, Telugu, Urdu

Chancellor: HE GOV. OF ANDHRA PRADESH
Vice-Chancellor: Prof. B. VENKAT RAMAN
Registrar: Prof. K. SAYULU
Controller of Examinations: Prof. K. DAVID
Dean of College Devt Council: Prof. S. JAGANNATHA SWAMY
Deputy Librarian: K. RAMANAIAH

Library of 135,919 vols, 337 journals
Number of teachers: 248
Number of students: 96,500

Publication: *Kakatiya Journal of English Studies and Vimarshini*

DEANS

Faculty of Arts: Prof. M. RAJESHWAR
Faculty of Commerce and Business Management: Prof. OMPRAKASH
Faculty of Education: Prof. N. RAMNATH KISHAN
Faculty of Engineering: Prof. SESHA SRINIVAS
Faculty of Law: L. NARASIMHA REDDY
Faculty of Pharmaceutical Sciences: Prof. V. KISHAN
Faculty of Science: Prof. T. BHASKAR RAO
Faculty of Social Sciences: Prof. T. JYOTHI RANI

CONSTITUENT COLLEGES

Institute of Advanced Studies in Education: Prin. Prof. C. SAMMAIAH.

School of Distance Learning and Continuing Education: tel. (870) 2438899; e-mail info@sdlceku.co.in; internet www.sdlceku.co.in; Dir Prof. K. VENKATANARAYANA.

University Arts and Science College, Warangal: Prin. Prof. M. RAJAGOPALA CHARY.

University College of Engineering: Prin. Prof. SHOWRY.

University College, Warangal: Prin. Prof. M. RAMASWAMY.

University College of Law, Warangal: Prin. Dr VIMALA DEVI.

University College of Pharmaceutical Sciences, Warangal: Prin. Prof. C. VERESHAM.

University Postgraduate College, Godavarikhani: Prin. Dr LAXMAN NAIK.

University Postgraduate College, Khammam: Prin. Dr VARALAXMI.

University Postgraduate College, Nirmal: Prin. Dr SWARNALATHA.

University Postgraduate College, Warangal: Prin. Prof. G. RAJAIAH

KAMESHWAR SINGH DARBHANGA SANSKRIT UNIVERSITY

Kameshwar Nagar, Darbhanga 846008, Bihar
Telephone: (6272) 222178
E-mail: info@ksdsu.edu.in

Founded 1961
State control
Languages of instruction: Hindi, Sanskrit
Academic year: July to June

Chancellor: HE GOV. OF BIHAR
Vice-Chancellor: Dr KULAND JHA
Registrar: KANHALYA JEE CHOUBEY
Librarian: J. MAHTO

Library of 100,000 vols, 15,000 periodicals, 10,000 MSS
Number of students: 515,000

Publication: *Vishwa Maneesha* (4 a year)

DEANS

Faculty of Darshan: R. S. JHA
Faculty of Jyotish: R. C. JHA
Faculty of Puran: (vacant)
Faculty of Samaj Shstra: K. MISHRA
Faculty of Veda: S. MISHRA
Faculty of Vyakaran: V. MISHRA

KANNADA UNIVERSITY, HAMPI

Vidyaranya, Hospet 583276, Karnataka
Telephone: (8394) 241337
E-mail: mail@kannadauniversity.org
Internet: www.kannadauniversity.org

Founded 1991
State control
Languages of instruction: English, Kannada
Academic year: June to April

Chancellor: HE GOV. OF KARNATAKA
Pro-Chancellor: Dr V. S. ACHARYA
Vice-Chancellor: Dr H. C. BORALINGAIAH
Registrar: Dr MANJUNATHA BEVINAKATTI

Library of 52,000 vols, 68 jounals
Number of teachers: 70
Number of students: 1,200

Publications: *Budakattu Karnataka* (Tribal Karnataka), *Janapada Karnataka* (Folklore of Karnataka), *Journal of Karnataka Studies* (2 a year, in English), *Kannada Adhyayana,* (Kannada Studies), *Karnataka Adhyayana,* (Karnataka Studies), *Mahila Adhyayana* (Women Studies), *Namma Kannada* (Our Kannada)

DEANS

Fine Arts: Prof. S. C. PATIL
Languages: Prof. PANDURANGA BABU
Social Sciences: Dr T. P. VIJAY

KANNUR UNIVERSITY

Mangattuparamba, Kannur Univ. Campus, Kannur 670567, Kerala
Telephone: (497) 2782351
E-mail: registrar@kannuruniversity.ac.in
Internet: www.kannuruniversity.ac.in

Founded 1996
State control

Chancellor: HE GOV. OF KERALA
Pro-Chancellor: Hon. MIN. FOR EDUCATION, GOVT OF KERALA
Vice-Chancellor: Dr P. K. MICHAEL THARAKAN
Pro-Vice-Chancellor: Dr A. P. KUTTYKRISHNAN
Registrar: Dr A. ASHOKAN
Controller of Examinations: Dr S. PRADEEP KUMAR
Public Relations Officer: ACHUTHANANDAN KUNIYIL

Library of 26,980 vols, 151 periodicals

DEANS

Faculty of Ayurveda: Dr V. P. SADHANANDAN
Faculty of Commerce and Management: Dr M. BHASI
Faculty of Communication: Dr SUJETHA NAIR
Faculty of Education: Dr M. S. LALITHAMMA
Faculty of Engineering: Dr V. GOPAKUMAR
Faculty of Humanities: Dr K. V. KUNHIKRISHNAN
Faculty of Languages and Literature: Dr T. B. VENUGOPALA PANICKER
Faculty of Law: Dr D. RAJEEV
Faculty of Modern Medicine: Dr K. BHASKARAN
Faculty of Science: Dr P. K. VIJAYAN

Faculty of Social Science: Prof. DAMODARAN NAMBOOTHIRI

KARNATAK UNIVERSITY

Pavate Nagar, Dharwad 580003, Karnataka
Telephone: (836) 2215252
E-mail: registrar@kud.ac.in
Internet: www.kud.ac.in
Founded 1949
State control
Language of instruction: English
Academic year: June to April
Chancellor: HE GOV. OF KARNATAKA
Pro-Chancellor: Hon. MIN. FOR HIGHER EDUCATION, GOVT OF KARNATAKA
Vice-Chancellor: Prof. H. B. WALIKAR
Registrar: Dr S. B. HINCHIGERI
Librarian: Dr S. B. PATIL
Library of 342,031 vols
Number of teachers: 222 postgraduate, 5,556 in colleges
Number of students: 5,000
Publications: *Bharati Vidyarthi* (4 a year), *Humanities, Journal of the Karnataka University—Science, Social Sciences; Karnataka Bharati* (4 a year)

DEANS
Faculty of Arts: Prof. Dr H. M. MAHESHWARAIAH
Faculty of Commerce: Prof. Dr S. G. HUNDEKAR
Faculty of Education: Prof. Dr H. M. KASHINATH
Faculty of Law: Prof. Dr C. RAJSHEKHAR
Faculty of Management: Prof. Dr M. S. SUBHAS
Faculty of Science and Technology: Prof. Dr S. C. PURANIK
Faculty of Social Sciences: Prof. Dr C. G. HUSSAIN KHAN

CONSTITUENT COLLEGES
Karnatak Arts College: Dharwad; f. 1917; Prin. Dr S. S. HERLEKAR.
Karnatak Science College: Dharwad 580001; f. 1919; Prin. Dr B. G. NADAKATTI.
University College of Education: f. 1962; Prin. Dr R. T. JANTALI.
University College of Law: f. 1962; Prin. C. S. PATIL.
University College of Music and Fine Arts: f. 1975; Prin. H. A. KHAN

KARNATAKA STATE OPEN UNIVERSITY

Manasagangotri, Mysore 570006, Karnataka
Telephone: (821) 2519941
E-mail: registrarksou@gmail.com
Internet: ksoumysore.edu.in
Founded 1969 as Institute of Correspondence Course and Continuing Education, current name and status 1996
State control
Academic year: August to June
Chancellor: HE GOV. OF KARNATAKA
Pro-Chancellor: Hon. MIN. OF HIGHER EDUCATION, GOVT OF KARNATAKA
Vice-Chancellor: Dr K. S. RANGAPPA
Registrar: K. R. JAYAPRAKASH RAO
Dean of Academic Affairs: Dr JAGADEESH
Dean of Study Centres: Dr M. SUSHEELA URS
Deputy Librarian: M. GOPALSWAMY
Library of 80,000 vols
Number of teachers: 60
Number of students: 100,000

CHAIRS OF DEPARTMENTS
Commerce and Management: Prof. JAGADEESHA
Economics: S. SHIVANNA
Education: Dr N. LAKSHMI
English: Y. ALIJAZ AHMED
Hindi: B. G. CHANDRALEKHA
History: Dr G. RAMANATHAN
Kannada: D. T. BASAVARAJ
Management: Dr JAGADEESH
Political Science and Public Administration: S. M. SEETHAMMA
Sanskrit: Dr N. RADHAKRISHNA BHAT
Sociology: N. DODDASIDIAH
Tamil: M. TAMILMARAN
Telugu: Dr A. RAMANATHAM NAIDU
Urdu: BALQUEES BANU

KARNATAKA STATE WOMEN'S UNIVERSITY

Dr Ambedkar Circle, Station Rd, Bijapur 586101, Karnataka
Telephone: (8352) 240030
E-mail: wu_bij@kar.nic.in
Internet: www.kswu.ac.in
Founded 2003
State control
Languages of instruction: English, Kannada
Academic year: July to June
Chancellor: HE GOV. OF KARNATAKA
Pro-Chancellor: Hon. MIN. FOR HIGHER EDUCATION, GOVT OF KARNATAKA
Vice-Chancellor: Prof. GEETHA BALI
Registrar: Dr G. R. NAIK
Librarian: P. G. TADASAD (acting)
Library of 56,746 vols, 240 periodicals
Number of teachers: 46
Number of students: 16,027

DEANS
Faculty of Commerce and Management: Dr S. B. KAMASHETTY
Faculty of Education: Prof. R. S. YELI
Faculty of Languages: Prof. VIJAYASHREE SABARAD
Faculty of Science and Technology: Dr S. V. HALSE
Faculty of Social Sciences: Prof. Dr S. A. KAZI

KARUNYA UNIVERSITY

Karunya Nagar, Coimbatore 641114, Tamil Nadu
Telephone: (422) 2614496
E-mail: info@karunya.edu
Internet: www.karunya.edu
Founded 1986 as Karunya Institute of Technology, current name and deemed univ. status 2004, univ. status 2006
State control
Language of instruction: English
Schools of biotechnology and health sciences, civil engineering, computer science and technology, electrical sciences, food sciences and technology, management, mechanical sciences, science and humanities; depts of physical education, value education
Vice-Chancellor: Dr PAUL P. APPASAMY
Registrar: Dr ANNE MARY FERNANDEZ
Librarian: Dr J. DOMINIC
Dean of Academic Affairs: Dr C. JOSEPH KENNADY
Dean for Devt and Collaborations: Dr ANNE MARY FERNANDEZ
Dean for Postgraduates: Dr T. MICHAEL N. KUMAR
Dir for Placement and Training: ANDRE AROUME
Dir for Projects and Training: Dr C. T. DEVADAS
Dir for Students: Dr NINAN P. JOHN
Library of 71,407 vols, 41,214 periodical titles, 254 journals
Number of teachers: 461
Number of students: 7,217
Publication: *Karunya Journal of Research*

KAVIKULGURU KALIDAS SANSKRIT VISHWAVIDYALAYA (Kavikulguru Kalidas Sanskrit University)

Mauda Rd, Ramtek, Nagpur 441106, Maharashtra
Telephone: (7114) 255549
E-mail: admin@sanskrituni.net
Internet: sanskrituni.net
Founded 1997
State control
Academic year: July to May
Chancellor: HE GOV. OF MAHARASHTRA
Vice-Chancellor: Dr PANKAJ T. CHANDE
Librarian and Acting Registrar: Dr HARSHDA DAVE
Dean of Faculty: Dr N. J. PURI
Number of teachers: 22
Number of students: 1,148

KERALA AGRICULTURAL UNIVERSITY

Vellanikkara, Thrissur 680656, Kerala
Telephone: (487) 2370432
E-mail: registrar@kau.in
Internet: www.kau.edu
Founded 1972
State control
Language of instruction: English
Academic year: June to March
Chancellor: HE GOV. OF KERALA
Vice-Chancellor: K. R. VISWAMBHARAN
Registrar: Dr P. B. PUSHPALATHA (acting)
Comptroller: PRASADA RAO (acting)
Dir of Academic and Postgraduate Studies: Dr P. K. ASHOKAN (acting)
Dir of Extension: Dr P. V. BALACHANDRAN
Dir of Research: Dr T. R. GOPALAKRISHNAN
Dir of Student Welfare: Dr JOSE J. CHUNGATH
Librarian: K. P. SATHIAN (acting)
Library of 115,000 vols
Number of teachers: 823
Number of students: 2,445
Publications: *Journal of Tropical Agriculture* (2 a year), *Journal of Veterinary and Animal Science* (2 a year)

DEANS
Faculty of Agricultural Engineering: Dr SVERUP JOHN
Faculty of Agriculture: Dr M. SIVASWAMY
Faculty of Fisheries: Dr MOHANA KUMARAN NAIR
Faculty of Veterinary and Animal Sciences: Dr E. NANU

CONSTITUENT COLLEGES
College of Agriculture, Padannakkad: Kasaragod 671328, Kerala; tel. (467) 2280616; internet www.kau.edu/coapadnnakkad.htm; f. 1994.
College of Agriculture, Vellayani: Thiruvananthapuram 695522, Kerala; tel. (471) 2381002; e-mail deanagri@kau.in; internet www.kau.edu/coavellayani.htm; f. 1955; (fmrly affiliated to Univ. of Kerala).
College of Cooperation, Banking and Management: Thrissur 680656, Kerala; tel. (487) 2370367; e-mail ccbm@kau.in; internet www.kau.edu/cbm.htm; f. 1981.
College of Forestry: Thrissur 680656, Kerala; tel. (487) 2370050; e-mail adforestry@kau.in; internet forestry.kau.edu; Head Dr K. VIDYASAGAR; publ. *Journal of Tropical Agriculture* (2 a year).
College of Horticulture: Thrissur 680656, Kerala; tel. (487) 2438301; e-mail adhort@kau.in; internet www.kauhort.in; f. 1972; library of 29,600 vols; 120 teachers; 600 students; Assoc. Dean Dr P. K. VALSALAKUMARI; Librarian Dr A. T. FRANCIS.

Kelappaji College of Agricultural Engineering and Technology: Tavanur, Malappuram 679573, Kerala; tel. (494) 2686009; e-mail kcaet@kau.in; internet www.kau.edu/kcaettavanur.htm; f. 1963 as Rural Institute, present name and status 1985

KRANTIGURU SHYAMJI KRISHNA VERMA KACHCHH UNIVERSITY

Mundra Rd, Bhuj, Kachchh 370001, Gujarat
Telephone: (2832) 235001
E-mail: info@kskvkachchhuniversity.org
Internet: kskvku.digitaluniversity.ac
Founded 2003
State control
Faculties of arts, commerce, education, law, science, technology; 39 affiliated colleges
Vice-Chancellor: Dr K. V. GOR
Registrar: A. H. GOR
Controller of Examinations: A. P. MEJTA
Number of teachers: 200
Number of students: 15,000

KUMAUN UNIVERSITY

Nainital 263001, Uttar Pradesh
Telephone: (5942) 235563
Internet: www.kuntl.in
Founded 1973
Private control
Languages of instruction: English, Hindi
Academic year: July to June (2 terms)
Chancellor: HE GOV. OF UTTARAKHAND
Vice-Chancellor: Prof. V. P. S. ARORA
Registrar: Dr KAMAL K. PANDE
Librarian: Prof. R. K. PANDE
Library of 90,000 vols
Number of teachers: 573
Number of students: 75,000

DEANS

Faculty of Arts: Prof. D. S. POKHARIA
Faculty of Commerce and Management: Prof. P. C. KAVIDYAL
Faculty of Education: Prof. A. BHARTI
Faculty of Law: Dr P. C. JOSHI
Faculty of Medical Education: Dr N. S. JYALA
Faculty of Science: Prof. C. C. PANT
Faculty of Technology: Prof. GANGA BISHT

PROFESSORS

Faculty of Arts:
BISHT, H. S., Geography
BISHT, L. S., Economics
BISHT, L. S., Hindi
DUBE, M. P., Political Science
GUPTA, R. K., Hindi
PANDE, G. C., Economics
PANDEY, D. C., Economics
PATHAK, S., History
POKHARIA, D. S., Hindi
RAWAT, A. S., History
RUWALI, K. D., Hindi
SAH, N. K., Economics
SAHAI, V., History
SINGH, O. P., Geography
TRIPATHI, D. R., Sanskrit

Faculty of Commerce and Management:
BISHT, N. S., Business Administration
RANA, N. S., Commerce
TIWARI, J. C., Commerce

Faculty of Education:
DURGAPAL, S.
JOSHI, J. K.
JUYAL, P. D.
SHUKLA, S. C.

Faculty of Science:
BHATT, S. D., Zoology
BISHT, C. S., Mathematics
BISHT, G., Chemistry
BISHT, M., Zoology
CHANDRA, M., Chemistry
CHANDRA, S., Botany
DHAMI, H. S., Mathematics
JOSHI, G. C., Botany
JOSHI, L., Chemistry
KAUSHAL, B. R., Zoology
KHAMI, K. S., Chemistry
KHETWAL, K. S., Chemistry
KUMAR, S., Geology
KUMAR, S., Zoology
LOHANI, A. B., Mathematics
MATHELA, C. S., Chemistry
MATHPAL, K. N., Chemistry
MEHROTRA, R. M., Chemistry
MEHTA, S. P. S., Chemistry
MELKANI, K. B., Chemistry
MISHRA, V. N., Chemistry
PANDEY, K., Physics
PANDEY, K. N., Botany
PANDEY, S. B., Mathematics
PANGETI, Y. P. S., Botany
PANT, C. C., Geology
PANT, D. N., Mathematics
PANT, M. C., Physics
PANT, R. P., Mathematics
PANT, T. C., Physics
SHAH, L., Zoology
SINGH, R. P., Forestry
SINGH, S. P., Botany
VARMA, K. R., Botany

KURUKSHETRA UNIVERSITY

Kurukshetra 136119, Haryana
Telephone: (1744) 238039
E-mail: kulib@kuk.ernet.in
Internet: www.kuk.ac.in
Founded 1956
State control
Languages of instruction: English, Hindi
Academic year: July to June
Chancellor: HE GOV. OF HARYANA
Vice-Chancellor: Dr D. D. S. SANDHU
Registrar: Dr SURINDER DESWAL
Dean of Academic Affairs: Prof. Dr GIRISH CHOPRA
Dean of Colleges: Prof. Dr D. D. ARORA
Dean of Students Welfare: Prof. Dr NAFA SINGH
Dir of Public Relations: Dr BRIJESH SAWHNEY
Proctor: Prof. MOHINDER SINGH
Librarian: Dr M. S. JAGLAN
Library of 354,549 vols, 350 periodicals and online journals
Number of teachers: 390
Number of students: 5,584
Publications: *Jeevanti* (in Hindi), *Journal of Haryana Studies* (in English), *Kalanidhi* (magazine, in Hindi), *Kuru Jyoti* (in English, Sanskrit and Hindi), *Kurukshetra Law Journal* (in English), *Praci Jyoti* (in English), *Research Journal for Arts and Humanities* (in English and Hindi), *Sambhawana* (in Hindi)

DEANS

Faculty of Arts and Languages: Dr MADHU BALA
Faculty of Commerce and Management: Dr D. D. ARORA
Faculty of Education: Dr O. P. GAHLAWAT
Faculty of Engineering and Technology: Dr P. K. SURI
Faculty of Indic Studies: Dr BHIM SINGH
Faculty of Law: Dr VARSHA RAZDAN
Faculty of Life Sciences: Dr SHARDA RANI
Faculty of Sciences: Prof. ANIL VOHRA
Faculty of Social Sciences: Dr R. TANWAR

PROFESSORS

Faculty of Arts and Languages (tel. (1744) 234374):
GUPTA, L. C., Hindi
KAANG, A. S., Punjabi
SHARMA, S. D., English

Faculty of Commerce and Management:
BANSAL, M. L., Commerce
BHARDWAJ, D. S., Tourism
DWIVEDI, R. S., Management
GUPTA, S. L., Management
HOODA, R. P., Commerce
JAIN, M. K., Management
MITTAL, R. K., Commerce
SHARMA, V. D., Management

Faculty of Education:
MALHOTRA, S. P.
MAVI, N. S.
YADAV, D. S.

Faculty of Indic Studies (tel. (1744) 238347):
KUSHWAHA, S. K., Fine Arts
SAXENA, MADU BALA, Music
SHARMA, INDU BALA, ISIS
SINGH, A., Sanskrit

Faculty of Law:
AGGARWAL, V. K.
KUMARI, D.
VARANDANI, G.

Faculty of Science (tel. (1744) 239235):
ANEJA, K. R., Microbiology
ARYA, S. P., Chemistry
ASTHANA, V. K., Geography
CHATURVEDI, D. K., Physics
CHOPRA, G., Zoology
GEORGE, P. J., Electronics Science
GUPTA, S. C., Chemistry
KAKKAR, L. R., Chemistry
KUMARI, S., Statistics
LUNKAD, S. K., Geology
MATTA, N. K., Botany
MEHTA, J. R., Chemistry
MITTAL, I. C., Zoology
MUKHERJEE, D., Botany
NAND, LAL, Earth Sciences
RANI, S., Botany
ROHTASH, C., Zoology
SHARMA, N. D., Physics
SHARMA, V. K., Geography
SINGH, H., Biochemistry
SURI, P. K., Computer Science
TREHAN, K., Botany
VINOD KUMAR, Mathematics

Faculty of Social Sciences:
KUNDU, T. R., Economics
KHURANA, G., History
PATHANIA, S., History
SHARMA, P. D., Political Science
SHARMA, R. K., History
SINGH, H., Public Administration
TANWAR, R., History
TUTEJA, K. L., History
UPADHYAYA, R. K., Social Work
VASHIST, B. K., Economics

KUVEMPU UNIVERSITY

Jnana Sahyadri, Shankaraghatta, Shimoga 577451, Karnataka
Telephone: (8282) 256221
E-mail: reg_admn@kuvempu.ac.in
Internet: www.kuvempu.ac.in
Founded 1987
State control
Academic year: August to April
Chancellor: HE GOV. OF KARNATAKA
Pro-Chancellor: Hon. MIN. FOR HIGHER EDUCATION, GOVT OF KARNATAKA
Vice-Chancellor: Prof. S. A. BARI
Registrar: Prof. T. R. MANJUNATH
Dir for College Devt Ccl: Dr B GANESH
Dir for Student Welfare: Dr C. SHIVAKUMARSWAMY
Librarian: Dr K. C. RAMAKRISHNEGOWDA
Library of 70,000 vols, 4,124 vols of periodicals
Number of teachers: 93
Number of students: 950 (postgraduate)

DEANS

Faculty of Arts: Dr A. RAMEGOWDA
Faculty of Commerce: Dr R. HIREMANI NAIK
Faculty of Education: Dr S. S. PATIL
Faculty of Engineering: Prof. D. ABDUL BUDAN
Faculty of Law: Prof. EASHWAR BHAT
Faculty of Medicine: Dr C. M. RAMESH
Faculty of Science and Technology: Dr P. V. VAIDYA

LALIT NARAYAN MITHILA VISHVIDYALAYA (Lalit Narayan Mithila University)

Kameshwarnagar, POB 13, Darbhanga 846004, Bihar
Telephone: (6272) 222463
E-mail: vclnmu@indiatimes.com
Internet: lnmu.bih.nic.in

Founded 1972 as Mithila Univ., current name adopted 1975
State control
Languages of instruction: English, Hindi
Academic year: June to May

Chancellor: HE GOV. OF BIHAR
Vice-Chancellor: Dr RAJ MANI PRASAD SINHA
Pro-Vice-Chancellor: Dr GOPAL PRASAD SINGH
Registrar: Dr KUMARESH PRASAD SINGH
Librarian: (vacant)

Library of 186,859 vols, 54 journals
Number of teachers: 1,251
Number of students: 110,355

DEANS

Faculty of Commerce: Dr N. C. PRASAD
Faculty of Education: Dr N. K. SINGH
Faculty of Humanities: Dr K. D. JHA
Faculty of Law: (vacant)
Faculty of Medicine: Dr CHITTRANJAN ROY
Faculty of Science: Prof. JAIKER JHA
Faculty of Social Science: Dr N. K. SINGH

PROFESSORS

JHA, B. N., Mathematics
JHA, S. M., Maithili
LALL, G., Commerce
PANDEY, S., Zoology
PATHAK, R. K., Hindi
PRASAD, A. B., Botany
RAHMAN, M., Urdu
ROY, B. K., History
THAKUR, B., Economics
THAKUR, R. N., Political Science
THAKUR, Y., Chemistry

MADHYA PRADESH BHOJ (OPEN) UNIVERSITY

Kolar Rd, Raja Bhoj Marg, Bhopal 462016, Madhya Pradesh
Telephone: (755) 2492090
E-mail: vc.sks.mpbou@gmail.com
Internet: www.bhojvirtualuniversity.com

Founded 1991
Academic year: July to June

Vice-Chancellor: Prof. Dr S. K. SINGH
Registrar: Dr ANAND KAMBLE
Librarian: J. P. SONI

Library of 7,000 vols
Number of students: 150,000

DIRECTORS OF REGIONAL CENTRES

Bhopal: (vacant)
Gwalior: Dr A. P. S. CHOUHAN
Indore: Dr DINESH VARSHNEY
Jabalpur: Dr K. K. TIWARI
Rewa: Dr S. S. PARIHAR
Sagar: Dr R. S. KASANA
Satna: Dr RAJIV TIWARI
Ujjain: Dr NAGESH SHINDE

PROFESSORS

DHAKAD, S. K.
DUBEY, S. K.
GARDE, V. D.
GOEL, R. M.
GREWAL, J. S.
MISRA, R. D.
SAXENA, M. C.
SESHADRI, C. S.
TOMAR, S. K.

MADURAI KAMARAJ UNIVERSITY

Palkalai Nagar, Madurai 625021, Tamil Nadu
Telephone: (452) 2459455
E-mail: mkuregistrar@rediffmail.com
Internet: www.mkuniversity.org

Founded 1966
State control
Languages of instruction: English, Tamil
Academic year: June to April

Chancellor: HE GOV. OF TAMIL NADU
Vice-Chancellor: Dr KALYANI MATHIVANAN
Controller of Examinations and Acting Registrar: Dr M. RAJIAKODI
Dean of College Devt Ccl: Dr S. DAVID AMIRTHA RAJAN
Dean of Curriculum Devt: Dr G. SUBRAMANIAN
Dean of Endowment and Devt: Dr P. M. AJMALKHAN
Dean of Research and Devt: Dr K. VELUTHAMBI
Academic Dean: Dr K. IYAKUTTI
Librarian: A. SRIMURUGAN

Library of 300,000 vols, 500 periodicals
Number of teachers: 377 (excluding affiliated colleges)
Number of students: 133,100 (including affiliated colleges)

Publication: *Journal of Biology Education* (4 a year)

PROFESSORS

School of Biological Sciences (tel. (452) 2458471 ext. 369):

GUNASEKARAN, P., Genetics
KANDULA, S., Immunology
MARIMUTHU, G., Animal Behaviour and Physiology
MUNAVAR, H., Molecular Biology
PALIWAL, K., Plant Morphology and Algology
SELVAM, G. S., Biochemistry
SHANMUGASUNDARAM, S., Microbial Technology
SUDHAKARSAMY, P., Plant Sciences

School of Biotechnology (tel. (452) 2458471 ext. 384):

DHARMALINGAM, K., Genetic Engineering
KRISHNASWAMY, S., Bioinformatics
PALANIVELU, P., Molecular Microbiology
VELUTHAMBI, K., Plant Biotechnology

School of Business Studies (tel. (452) 2458471 ext. 359):

ALAGAPPAN, V., Commerce
CHANDRAN, C., Management Studies
CHINNIAH, V., Management Studies
PANDIAN, P., Commerce
RAMAMOORTHY, K., Commerce
RAVICHANDRAN, K., Management Studies
SEKAR, P. C., Management Studies
SURYA RAO, U., Management Studies

School of Chemistry (tel. (452) 2458471 ext. 347):

ATHAPPAN, P. R., Inorganic Chemistry
GANDHIDASAN, R., Natural Products Chemistry
MURUGESAN, R., Physical Chemistry
MUTHUSUBRAMANIAN, S., Organic Chemistry
PERUMAL, S., Organic Chemistry
PITCHUMANI, K., Natural Products Chemistry
RAJAGOPAL, S., Physical Chemistry
RAMACHANDRAN, M. S., Physical Chemistry
RAMARAJ, R., Physical Chemistry
RAMESH, P., Natural Products Chemistry
RAMU, A., Inorganic Chemistry
SIVAKOLUNTHU, S., Inorganic Chemistry
VAIDYANATHAN, S., Physical Chemistry

School of Earth and Atmospheric Sciences (tel. (452) 2458471 ext. 245):

ILANGOVAN, P., Environmental Remote Sensing and Cartography
KRISHNAN, N., Environmental Remote Sensing and Cartography
LAKSHMI, K., Geography
PARTHASARATHY, G. R., Geography
SANTHAKUMARI, A., Geography
SHANMUGANANDAN, S., Geography

School of Economics (tel. (452) 2458471 ext. 353):

DEIVAMANI, K., Human Resources Devt Economics
DHULASI BIRUNDHA, V., Agricultural Economics
HARIDOSS, R., Mathematical Economics
HARIHARAN, S. V., Mathematical Economics
MANONMONEY, N., Industrial Economics
MUTHULAKSHMI, R., Rural Devt Economics
SARASWATHI, N., Rural Devt Economics
VIJAYALAKSHMI, S., Econometrics

School of Education (tel. (452) 2458471 ext. 356):

KRISHNAN, K., Education

School of Energy Environment and Natural Resources (tel. (452) 2458471 ext. 365):

KUMARAGURU, A. K., Environment Studies
MAHADEVAN, A., Futures Studies
PAULRAJ, S., Solar Energy
SUNDARAM, A., Futures Studies

School of English and Foreign Languages (tel. (452) 2458471 ext. 361):

CHELLIAH, S., English and Comparative Literature
PARAMESWARI, D., English and Comparative Literature
SANKARAKUMAR, A., English and Comparative Literature

School of Historical Studies (tel. (452) 2458471 ext. 354):

CHANDRA BABU, B. S., Medieval History
DANIEL, D., Modern History
GOPALKRISHNAN, P. B., Modern History
JAYARAJ, K. V., Modern History
RAMASWAMY, T., Ancient History

School of Indian Languages (tel. (452) 2458471 ext. 362):

GIRIPRAKASH, T. S., Telugu and Comparative Literature
HARIKRISHNA BHAT, B., Kannada

School of Information and Communication Sciences (tel. (452) 2458471 ext. 364):

MANONMANI, T., Communication
SANTHA, A., Journalism and Science Communication

School of Mathematics (tel. (452) 2458471 ext. 339):

ARIVARIGNAN, G., Applied Mathematics and Statistics
BASKARAN, R., Mathematics
KARUNAKARAN, V., Mathematics

School of Performing Arts (tel. (452) 2458471 ext. 248):

AYYANAR, V., Art History, Aesthetics and Fine Arts
MUTHIAH, I., Folklore
SETHURAMAN, G., Art History, Aesthetics and Fine Arts

School of Physics (tel. (452) 2458471 ext. 352):

ARUMUGAM, G, Computer Science

IYAKUTTI, K., Microprocessor and Computer
NATARAJAN, S., Computer Science
NAVANEETHAKRISHNAN, K., Theoretical Physics
RAMACHANDRAN, K., Theoretical Physics
RAMAKRISHNAN, V., Microprocessor and Computer
UMAPATHY, S., Theoretical Physics

School of Religions, Philosophy and Humanist Thought (tel. (452) 2458471 ext. 342):
AJMALKHAN, P. M., Islam and Islamic Tamil Studies
ANDIAPPAN, S., Gandhian Studies and Ramalinga Philosophy
JEYAPRAGASAM, S., Gandhian Studies and Ramalinga Philosophy
MUTHUMOHAN, N., Gurunanak Studies

School of Social Sciences (tel. (452) 2458471 ext. 360):
KANNAN, R., Sociology
MADHANAGOPAL, R., Political Science
NALINI, B., Sociology
PERIAKARUPPAN, P., Political Science
SINGARAM, I., Sociology
THARA BHAI, L., Sociology

School of Tamil Studies (tel. (452) 2458471 ext. 347):
ATHITHAN, A., Linguistics
MANIVEL, M., Manuscriptology, Tamilology
MOHAN, N. R., Comparative Literature
SARADHAMBAL, C., Comparative Literature
SASIREHA, S., Literary Criticism
THIRUMALAI, M., Literary Criticism
VENKATARAMAN, S., Modern Literature

MAGADH UNIVERSITY

Bodh-Gaya 824234, Bihar
Telephone: (631) 2200572
E-mail: info@magadhuniversity.org
Internet: magadhuniversity.org

Founded 1962
State control
Languages of instruction: English, Hindi
Academic year: June to May

Chancellor: HE GOV. OF BIHAR
Vice-Chancellor: Dr ARVIND KUMAR
Pro-Vice-Chancellor: Prof. Dr B. P. SHASTREE
Registrar: Dr D. K. YADAV (acting)
Proctor: Dr S. H. SHARMA
Dean of Student Welfare: Dr K. B. SHARMA
Controller of Examinations: Dr SHUSHIL KUMAR SINGH
Librarian: Prof. NALIN SHASHTRI

Library of 162,161 vols, 1,381 MSS
Number of teachers: 2,000
Number of students: 200,000

DEANS

Faculty of Commerce: Dr V. K. SINGH
Faculty of Engineering: Dr K. P. SINGH
Faculty of Humanities: Dr I. K. MASIH
Faculty of Law: Dr D. N. MISHRA
Faculty of Management: Dr M. MURARI
Faculty of Medicine: Dr M. S. KUMAR
Faculty of Science: Dr R. L. PRASAD
Faculty of Social Science and Education: Dr B. SINGH

PROFESSORS

AGRAWAL, B. N., Political Science
AGRAWAL, N. C., Commerce
AMBASHTHA, A. V., Commerce
GUPTA, L. N., Commerce
JHA, B. K., Political Science
LAL, B. K., Philosophy
MISHRA, C. N., Sanskrit
NATH, B., Philosophy
PRASAD, B. K., Philosophy
PRASAD, B. N., Mathematics
PRASAD, N., English
ROY, L. M., Economics
ROY, P., Hindi
SAHAI, S., Ancient Indian and Asian Studies
SHRIVASTAVA, J. P., Chemistry
SINGH, A. N., Physics
SINGH, B. K., Psychology
SINGH, B. P., Political Science
SINGH, G. P., Physics
SINGH, H. G., Economics
SINGH, J. P., English
SINGH, R. C. P., Ancient Indian and Asian Studies
SINGH, S., Mathematics
SINGH, S. B., Zoology
SINHA, D. P., Zoology
SINHA, H. P., Philosophy
SINHA, N. C. P., Psychology
SINHA, S. P., Economics
SINHA, V. N., Philosophy
THAKUR, U., Ancient Indian and Asian Studies
TIWARY, P., Mathematics
VERMA, B. B., Commerce
VISHESHWARAM, S., Mathematics

MAHARAJA GANGA SINGH UNIVERSITY

N. H. 15, Jaisalmer Rd, Bikaner 334004, Rajasthan
Telephone: (151) 2212041
E-mail: info@mgsubikaner.ac.in
Internet: www.mgsubikaner.ac.in

Founded 2003 as Bikaner Univ., current name adopted 2008
State control

Faculties of arts, commerce, education, law, science, social science; 297 affiliated colleges in Bikaner, Churu, Hanumangarh, Sriganganagar

Vice-Chancellor: Dr GANGA RAM JAKHER
Registrar: RAJENDRA SINGH KAVIA
Comptroller: ARVIND SINGH SHEKHAWAT
Controller of Examinations: Dr K. K. KOCHAR (acting)
Number of students: 190,000

MAHARAJA SAYAJIRAO UNIVERSITY OF BARODA

Vadodara 390002, Gujarat
Telephone: (265) 2795521
E-mail: registrar@msubaroda.ac.in
Internet: www.msubaroda.ac.in

Founded 1949
State control
Language of instruction: English
Academic year: June to April (2 terms)

Chancellor: Dr MRUNALINI DEVI PUAR
Vice-Chancellor: Prof. YOGESH SINGH
Pro-Vice-Chancellor: (vacant)
Registrar: M. M. BEEDKAR (acting)
Librarian: Dr MAYANK J. TRIVEDI

Library of 456,033 vols
Number of teachers: 1,230
Number of students: 35,000

Publications: *Journal of Animal Morphology and Physiology*, *Journal of Education and Psychology*, *Journal of Oriental Institute*, *Journal of Technology and Engineering* (1 a year), *Pavo*, *Swadhyaya*

DEANS

Faculty of Arts: Prof. NITIN J. VYAS
Faculty of Commerce: Dr PARIMAL H. VYAS
Faculty of Education and Psychology: Prof. RAMESHCHANDRA G. KOTHARI
Faculty of Family and Community Sciences: Prof. UMA JOSHI
Faculty of Fine Arts: (vacant)
Faculty of Journalism and Communication: (vacant)
Faculty of Law: (vacant)
Faculty of Management Studies: Prof. G. C. MAHESHWARI
Faculty of Medicine: Dr A. T. LEUVA
Faculty of Performing Arts: (vacant)
Faculty of Science: (vacant)
Faculty of Social Work: Prof. M. N. PARMAR
Faculty of Technology and Engineering: Prof. AMBIKANANDAN. MISHRA

PROFESSORS

Faculty of Arts:
CHOODAWAT, P. S., Sociology
JUNEJA, O. P., English
KAR, P., English
MEHTA, S. Y., Gujarati
MOHITE, D. H., Political Science
PANDYA, N. M., Economics
PANTHAM, T., Political Science
PAREKH, V. S., Archaeology
PATEL, K. H., Environmental Archaeology
PATEL, P. J., Sociology
REDE, L. A., Economics
SHAH, M. N., Economics
SIDDIQI, M. H., Persian
SONAWANE, V. H., Archaeology

Faculty of Commerce:
BHATT, A. S., Commerce and Business Administration
MOHITE, M. D., Cooperation
PANCHOLI, P. R., Business Economics
PATEL, B. S., Commerce and Business Administration
SANDHE, A. G., Commerce and Business Administration
SHAH, K. R., Economics
SINGH, S. K., Business Economics
SYAN, J. K., Banking and Business Finance
VYAS, I. P., Commerce and Business Administration

Faculty of Education and Psychology:
GOEL, D., Education
JOSHI, S. M., Educational Administration
YADAV, M. S., Education

Faculty of Fine Arts:
PANCHAL, R. R., Sculpture
PATEL, V. S., Graphic Arts

Faculty of Home Science:
BALKRISHNAIH, B., Clothing and Textiles
MANI, U. V., Foods and Nutrition
SARASWATI, T. S., Human Development and Family Studies
SHAH, A., Home Science Extension and Communication

Faculty of Law:
PARIKH, S. N., Law
RATHOD, J. C., Law

Faculty of Management Studies:
DADI, M. M., Management
DHOLAKIA, M. N., Management
JOSHI, K. M., Management
MAHESHWARI, G. C., Management

Faculty of Medicine:
BHOTI, S. J., Ophthalmology
BONDRE, K. V., Anatomy
BUCH, V. P., Radiology
CHANDWANI, S., Physiology
CHAUHAN, L. M., Obstetrics and Gynaecology
DESAI, M. R., Obstetrics and Gynaecology
GHOSH, S., Biochemistry
HATHI, G., Physiology
HEMAVATI, K. G., Pharmacology
JHALA, D. R., Paediatrics
JOSHI, G. D., Preventative and Social Medicine
KARELIA, L. S., Pathology
MAZUMDAR, U., Dentistry
MEHTA, J. P., Surgery
MEHTA, N. C., Medicine
PATHAK, K., Medicine
PATRA, B. S., Surgery
PATRA, S. B., Pathology
RAWAL, H. H., Anaesthesia
SAINATH, M., Ophthalmology

SANGHVI, N. G., Medicine
SAXENA, S. B., Microbiology
SHAH, A. U., Preventative and Social Medicine
SHAH, D. N., Preventative and Social Medicine
SHAK, K. D., Surgery
SHARMA, S. N., Plastic Surgery
SHETH, R. T., Ophthalmology
SHUKLA, G. N., Surgery
TIWARI, R. S., Ear, Nose and Throat
VAISHNAVI, A. J., Orthopaedics
VANKAR, G. K., Psychiatry
VOHRA, P. A., Radiology
VYAS, D. C., Anatomy

Faculty of Performing Arts:
BHONSLE, D. K., Vocal Music
SHAH, P., Dance

Faculty of Science:
AMBADKAR, P. M., Zoology
BHATTACHARYA, P. K., Chemistry
CHATTOO, B., Microbiology
CHHATPAR, H. S., Microbiology
DESAI, N. D., Geology
DESAI, S. J., Geology
DEVI, S. G., Chemistry
GOYAL, O. P., Mathematics
KATYARE, S. S., Biochemistry
MEHTA, T., Biochemistry
PADH, H., Biochemistry
PAREKH, L. J., Biochemistry
PATEL, H. C., Statistics
PATEL, M. P., Geology
PATEL, N. V., Mathematics
PILO, B., Zoology
RAKSHIT, A. K., Chemistry
RAMCHANDRAN, A. V., Zoology
RANGASWAMY, V. C., Geography
RAO, K. K., Microbiology
SHAH, A. C., Chemistry
SHREEHARI, M., Statistics
SOMAYAJULU, D. R. S., Physics
TELANG, S. D., Biochemistry

Faculty of Social Work:
ANJARIA, V. N., Social Work
NAVALE, A. S., Social Work
SAXENA, S. B., Social Work

Faculty of Technology and Engineering:
AGRAWAL, S. K., Metallurgical Engineering
AGRAWAL, S. R., Applied Mathematics
BALARAMAN, R., Pharmacy
BANGLORE, V. A., Textile Engineering
BASA, D. K., Metallurgical Engineering
BHAGIA, R. M., Applied Mechanics
BHATT, G. D., Mechanical Engineering
BHATT, R. D., Civil Engineering
BHAVNANI, H. V., Civil Engineering
BHAVSAR, N., Electrical Engineering
BIYANI, K. R., Applied Mechanics
CHUDASAMA, U. V., Applied Chemistry
DE, D. K., Textile Engineering
DESAI, P. B., Mechanical Engineering
DESHPANDE, S. V., Architecture
DIVEKAR, M. H., Chemical Engineering
ETHIRAJULU, K., Chemical Engineering
GADGEEL, V. I., Metallurgical Engineering
GOROOR, S. P., Water Management
GUHA, S., Textile Chemistry
GUPTE, S. G., Electrical Engineering
JOSHI, S. M., Electrical Engineering
JOSHI, T. R., Applied Physics
KANITKAR, S. A., Electrical Engineering
KAPADIA, V. H., Textile Engineering
LOIWAL, A. S., Mechanical Engineering
MISHRA, A. N. R., Pharmacy
MISHRA, S. H., Pharmacy
MODI, P. M., Water Management
MOINUDDIN, S., Chemical Engineering
MORTHY, R. S. R., Pharmacy
NANAVATI, J. I., Mechanical Engineering
PAI, K. B., Metallurgical Engineering
PAREKH, B. S., Computer Science
PARMAR, N. B., Civil Engineering
PATEL, A. A., Mechanical Engineering
PATEL, B. A., Electrical Engineering
PATEL, H. J., Computer Science
PATEL, N. M., Applied Mechanics
PATHAK, V. D., Applied Mathematics
PATODI, S. C., Applied Mechanics
POTBHARE, V. N., Applied Physics
PRAJAPATI, J. J., Civil Engineering
PURANIK, S. A., Chemical Engineering
PUTHANPURAYIL, P., Mechanical Engineering
RAJPUT, H. G., Training and Placement
SAVANI, A. K., Civil Engineering
SHAH, A. N., Civil Engineering
SHAH, D. L., Applied Mechanics
SHAH, S. G., Electrical Engineering
SHROFF, A. V., Applied Mechanics
SUBRAMANYAM, N., Chemical Engineering
SUKLA, H. J., Mechanical Engineering
SUNDAR MORTI, N. S., Metallurgical Engineering
SUTARIA, P. N., Civil Engineering
THAKUR, S. A., Electrical Engineering
TRIVEDI, A. I., Electrical Engineering
VASDEV, S., Chemical Engineering
VORA, R. A., Applied Chemistry
VYAS, J. K., Applied Mechanics
YADAV, R., Pharmacy

Centre for Continuing and Adult Education and Community Services:
PARALIKAR, K. R.

Oriental Institute:
NANAVATI, R. I.
WADEKAR, M. L.

CONSTITUENT COLLEGES

Baroda Sanskrit Mahavidyalaya: Vadodara; internet www.msubaroda.ac.in/sanskrit; f. 1915; Prin. YOGESH B. OAZ.

Manibhai Kashibai Amin Arts and Science College and College of Commerce: Padra; f. 1965; Prin. W. V. AHIRE (acting).

Oriental Institute: tel. (265) 2425121; e-mail mlwadekar@hotmail.com; Dir Prof. Dr M. L. WADEKAR.

Polytechnic: Vadodara; f. 1957; Prin. DILIP M. PATEL

MAHARANA PRATAP UNIVERSITY OF AGRICULTURE AND TECHNOLOGY

Udaipur 313001, Rajasthan
Telephone: (294) 2471101
E-mail: vc@mpuat.ac.in
Internet: www.mpuat.ac.in

Founded 1999 as Agricultural Univ.
State control

Chancellor: HE GOV. OF RAJASTHAN
Vice-Chancellor: Dr SARABJIT SINGH CHAHAL
Registrar: L. N. MANTRI
Dir for Extension Education: Dr P. L. MALIWAL
Dir for Research: Dr S. R. MALOO
Controller of Examinations: Dr VIRENDRA NEPALIA
Librarian: Dr R. SWAMINATHAN

Library of 150,710 vols, 128 journals

DEANS

Faculty of Agriculture: Dr S. L. GODAWAT (acting)
Faculty of Dairy and Food Technology: Dr MAYA CHOUDHARY (acting)
Faculty of Engineering: Dr N. S. RATHORE
Faculty of Fisheries: Dr VIMAL SHARMA
Faculty of Home Science: Dr AARTI SANKHLA
Faculty of Horticulture and Forestry: Dr L. K. DASHORA

MAHARASHTRA ANIMAL AND FISHERY SCIENCES UNIVERSITY

Futala Rd, Telangkhedi, Nagpur 440001, Maharashtra
Telephone: (712) 2511784
E-mail: mafsudet@yahoo.co.in
Internet: www.mafsu.in

Founded 2000
State control
Language of instruction: English
Academic year: June to May

Chancellor: HE GOV. OF MAHARASHTRA
Pro-Chancellor: MIN. FOR ANIMAL HUSBANDRY, DAIRY DEVT, FISHERIES, GOVT OF MAHARASHTRA
Vice-Chancellor: Dr A. K. MISRA
Registrar: S. K. KHILARI
Dean for Students Welfare: Dr J. P. KORDE
Dir for Extension and Training: Dr N. N. ZADE
Dir for Instructions: Dr S. A. BAKSHI
Dir of Research: Dr L. B. SARKATE
Controller of Examination: Dr S. V. UPADHYAY
Univ. Librarian: S. N. GAWANDE

DEANS

Faculty of Dairy Technology: Dr A. B. KADU
Faculty of Fishery Science: Dr D. R. KALOREY
Faculty of Veterinary Science: Dr S. A. BAKSHI
Lower Education: Dr N. N. ZADE

CONSTITUENT COLLEGES

Bombay Veterinary College: Parel, Mumbai 400012, Maharashtra; tel. (22) 24130162; e-mail bvcdean@mafsu.in; f. 1886; Dean Dr A. SAMAD.

College of Dairy Technology: Warud (Pusat), Dist. Yavatmal 445204, Maharashtra; tel. (7233) 247269; e-mail dtc@mafsu.in; f. 1992; Dean Dr D. N. BAJAD.

College of Fishery Science: Nagpur 440006, Maharashtra; tel. (712) 2567192; e-mail dewanandkalorey@rediffmail.com; f. 2007; Dean Dr D. R. KALORE.

College of Fishery Science: Udgir, Dist. Latur 413517, Maharashtra; tel. (2385) 256672; e-mail adfish.udgir@gmail.com; f. 2006; Dean Dr B. R. KHARATMOL.

College of Veterinary and Animal Sciences, Parbhani: Parbhani 431402, Maharashtra; tel. (2452) 220044; e-mail bhosle_ns@rediffmail.com; f. 1972; Dean Dr N. S. BHONSLE.

College of Veterinary and Animal Sciences, Udgir: Udgir, Dist. Latur 413517, Maharashtra; tel. (2385) 257448; e-mail udgirvet@yahoo.com; f. 1987; Dean Dr R. C. TAKARKHEDE.

Krantisinh Nana Patil College of Veterinary Science: Satara Dist., Shirval 412801, Maharashtra; tel. (2169) 244227; e-mail deanknpvet@yahoo.co.in; f. 1988; Assoc. Dean Dr HEMANT BIRADE.

Nagpur Veterinary College: Seminary Hills, Nagpur 440006, Maharashtra; tel. (712) 2511259; e-mail nvc@mafsu.in; f. 1958; Dean Dr C. R. JANGDE.

Postgraduate Institute of Veterinary and Animal Sciences, Akola: Murtizapur Rd, Akola 444104, Maharashtra; tel. (724) 2258643; e-mail pgivas@mafsu.in; f. 1970; Dean Dr V. H. KALBANDE

MAHARASHTRA UNIVERSITY OF HEALTH SCIENCES

Vani Rd, Mhasrul, Nashik 422004, Maharashtra
Telephone: (253) 2539292
E-mail: registrar@muhsnashik.com

Internet: www.muhsnashik.com
Founded 1998
Academic year: June to May
Chancellor: HE GOV. OF MAHARASHTRA
Vice-Chancellor: Dr ARUN JAMKAR (acting)
Registrar: Dr ADINATH N. SURYAKAR
Controller of Examinations: Dr UDAYSINGH RAORANE (acting)

DEANS

Faculty of Allied Health Sciences: Dr RESHMA DESAI
Faculty of Ayurveda: Dr S. G. DESHMUKH
Faculty of Dental Science: Dr M. G. PAWAR
Faculty of Homeopathy: Dr A. N. BHASME
Faculty of Medical: Dr S. D. DALVI

MAHARISHI MAHESH YOGI VEDIC VISHWAVIDYALAYA
(Maharishi Mahesh Yogi Vedic University)

Karaundi, Sihora, Paan Umariya, Katni 483332, Madhya Pradesh
Telephone: (7625) 2400986
E-mail: mmyvv@mahaemail.com
Internet: www.mmyvv.com
Founded 1995
State control
Academic year: July to June
Vedic science and technology; distance education dept in Jabalpur; campuses in Bhopal, Indore, Jabalpur
Vice-Chancellor: Prof. BHUVNESH SHARMA
Pro-Vice-Chancellor: B. S. MEHTA
Registrar: ARVIND SINGH RAJPUT
Number of teachers: 6,000
Number of students: 250,000

MAHARSHI DAYANAND SARASWATI UNIVERSITY

Pushkar Bye Pass, Ghooghara, Ajmer 305009, Rajasthan
Telephone: (145) 2787056
Internet: www.mdsuajmer.ac.in
Founded 1987 as Univ. of Ajmer; present name 1992
State control
Chancellor: HE GOV. OF RAJASTHAN
Vice-Chancellor: ATUL SHARMA
Controller of Examination and Registrar: BALWANT SINGH (acting)
Dean of Colleges and Students Welfare: Prof. S. PALRIA
Dean of Postgraduate Studies: Prof. K. K. SHARMA
Library of 43,000 vols, 176 periodicals
Number of students: 135,000

DEANS

Faculty of Commerce: Prof. B. P. SARASWAT
Faculty of Education: Prof. L. GOYAL
Faculty of Law: MADAN LAL PITALYA
Faculty of Management Studies: Prof. MANOJ KUMAR
Faculty of Sciences: Dr G. K. KOHLI
Faculty of Social Sciences: Dr LAXMI THAKUR

PROFESSORS

BHARDWAJ, T. N., Botany
DUBE, S. N., Mathematics
JOSHI, R. P., Political Science
VASHISHTHA, V. K., History

MAHARSHI DAYANAND UNIVERSITY, ROHTAK

Rohtak 124001, Haryana
Telephone: (1262) 274327
E-mail: mduniversity@yahoomail.com
Internet: www.mdurohtak.com
Founded 1976 as Rohtak Univ., present status 1977
State control
Languages of instruction: English, Hindi
Academic year: July to June
Chancellor: HE GOV. OF HARYANA
Vice-Chancellor: Prof. R. P. HOODA
Registrar: Dr S. P. VATS
Dean of Academic Affairs: Prof. R. VINAYEK
Dean of College Devt Ccl: Prof. DALEEP SINGH
Dean of Student Welfare: Prof. RAJBIR SINGH
Dir for Distance Education: Prof. NARENDER KUMAR
Librarian: Dr PREM SINGH
Library of 325,292 vols, 400 periodicals
Number of teachers: 350
Number of students: 223,585
Publication: *Maharishi Dayanand University Rohtak Research Journal (Arts)* (2 a year)

DEANS

Faculty of Commerce: Prof. Dr M. S. MALIK
Faculty of Education: Prof. Dr INDIRA GHULL
Faculty of Engineering and Technology: Prof. S. P. KHATKAR
Faculty of Humanities: Prof. B. S. MEHRA
Faculty of Law: Dr PROMILA CHUGH
Faculty of Life Sciences: Prof. Dr S. N. MISHRA
Faculty of Management Sciences: Prof. H. S. GHOSH ROY
Faculty of Performing and Visual Arts: Prof. Dr BHARTI SHARMA
Faculty of Pharmaceutical Sciences: Prof. ARUN NANDA
Faculty of Physical Sciences: Prof. N. R. GARG
Faculty of Social Sciences: Prof. Dr K. S. SANGWAN

MAINTAINED INSTITUTE

Institute of Law and Management Studies, Gurgaon: Sector 40, Gurgaon Haryana; tel. (124) 2383443; e-mail ilmsmdu@gmail.com; f. 2002; Dir Prof. PREET SINGH

MAHATAMA GANDHI ANTARRASHTRIYA HINDI VISHWAVIDYALAYA
(Mahatma Gandhi International Hindi University)

Post Manas Mandir, Gandhi Hills, Wardha 442001, Maharashtra
Telephone: (7152) 230907
E-mail: vc@hindivishwa.org
Internet: www.hindivishwa.org
Founded 1997
State control
Academic year: July to May
Vice-Chancellor: Prof. VIBHUTI NARAIN RAI
Pro-Vice-Chancellor: Prof. A. ARAVINDAKSHAN
Registrar: Dr K. G. KHAMARE
Publications: *Bahuvachan* (4 a year, in Hindi), *Hindi: Language, Discourse, Writing* (4 a year, in English), *Hindi Vishwa Samachar* (house journal, in Hindi), *Pustak Varta* (24 a year, in Hindi)

DEANS

School of Culture: Prof. MANOJ KUMAR
School of Language: Prof. UMASHANKAR UPADHYAY
School of Literature: Prof. SURAJ PALIWAL
School of Translation and Interpretation: Prof. A. P. SRIVASTAVA

CENTRES

Adult Continuing Education Extension and Field Outreach Centre: tel. (7151) 242812; e-mail klvp_k@yahoo.com; Dir Prof. K. VASWANI (acting).
Distance Education Centre: Dir Prof. NADEEM HASNAIN.
Dr Babasaheb Ambedkar Dalit and Tribal Studies Centre: Dir Prof. L. KARUNYAKARA.
Dr Bhadant Anand Kausalyayan, Buddhist Studies Centre: Dir M. L. KASARE.
Indian and Foreign Language Advanced Studies Centre.
Mahatma Gandhi Fuiji Guru Ji Peace Studies Centre: Dir Dr MANOJ KUMAR.
Technology Studies Centre: e-mail mahendra@hindivishwa.org; Dean Prof. MAHENDRA KUMAR PANDEY

MAHATMA GANDHI CHITRAKOOT GRAMODAYA VISHWAVIDYALAYA
(Mahatma Gandhi Chitrakoot Gramodaya University)

Dist. Satna, Chitrakoot 485331, Madhya Pradesh
Telephone: (7670) 265413
E-mail: mgcgv@rediffmail.com
Internet: www.ruraluniversity-chitrakoot.org
Founded 1991
State control
Academic year: July to June
Vice-Chancellor: Prof. G. SINGH
Registrar: Dr R. S. TRIPATHI
Librarian: Dr R. P. BAJPAI
Library of 32,644 vols, 54 journals

DEANS

Faculty of Agriculture and Animal Sciences: Dr A. K. GUPTA
Faculty of Ayurveda: E. A. UPADHYAY
Faculty of Commerce: Dr Y. UPADHYAY
Faculty of Education: Dr S. R. S. SENGAR
Faculty of Fine Arts: Prof. K. D. MISHRA
Faculty of Humanities and Social Sciences: Dr A. VERMA
Faculty of Rural Reconstruction: Dr R. C. SINGH
Faculty of Science: Dr R. C. TRIPATHI

MAHATMA GANDHI KASHI VIDYAPITH
(Mahatma Gandhi Kashi University)

Varanasi 221002, Uttar Pradesh
Telephone: (542) 2222689
E-mail: support@mgkvp.ac.in
Internet: www.mgkvp.ac.in
Founded 1921
State control
Chancellor: HE GOV. OF UTTAR PRADESH
Vice-Chancellor: Dr PRITHVISH NAG
Registrar: SAHAB LAL MAURYA
Controller of Examinations: Prof. NAND LAL
Dean of Student Welfare: Prof. MUNNI LAL
Librarian: SHIV RAM VERMA
Library of 234,701 vols

DEANS

Faculty of Commerce and Management: Prof. MATA BADAL SHUKLA
Faculty of Education: Prof. MANVENDRA KISHOR DAS
Faculty of Humanities: Prof. AJIJ HAIDAR
Faculty of Law: Dr SUBHASH CHANDRA SINGH
Faculty of Science and Technology: Prof. SATYA SINGH
Faculty of Social Sciences: Prof. RATHINDRA PRASAD SEN
Faculty of Social Work: Prof. MANIBHUSHAN PANDEY
Madan Mohan Malviya Institute of Hindi Journalism: Prof. RAM MOHAN PATHAK

MAHATMA GANDHI UNIVERSITY

Priyadarshini Hills PO, Kottayam 686560, Kerala
Telephone: (481) 2731001
E-mail: vc@mgu.ac.in
Internet: mgu.ac.in
Founded 1983 as Gandhiji Univ.
State control
Language of instruction: English
Academic year: June to March
Chancellor: HE Gov. of Kerala
Vice-Chancellor: Prof. Dr Rajan Gurukkal
Pro-Vice-Chancellor: Prof. Dr Rajan Varughese
Registrar and Acting Librarian: Prof. M. R. Unni
Controller of Examinations: Dr Thomas John Mampra
Dir for College Devt Ccl: Dr P. P. Raveendran
Public Relations Officer: G. Sreekumar
Library of 4,000 online nat. and int. journals
Number of teachers: 5,000
Number of students: 150,000

DEANS

Faculty of Behavioural Science: Dr Razeena Padmam
Faculty of Commerce: Dr K. B. Pavithran
Faculty of Education: Dr A. Sudharma
Faculty of Engineering and Technology: Dr Sunil K. Narayanankutty
Faculty of Environmental Sciences: Dr C. T. Aravindakumar
Faculty of Language and Literature: Dr Upot Sherin
Faculty of Law: Prof. Dr K. Vikraman Nair
Faculty of Management Studies: Prof. Dr K. Sreeranganadhan
Faculty of Science: Dr Chandu Venugopal
Faculty of Social Science: Dr K. M. Seethi
Faculty of Technology and Applied Sciences: Dr Sabu Thomas

MAHATMA JYOTIBA PHULE ROHILKHAND UNIVERSITY

Pilibhit Bye Pass Rd, Bareilly 243006, Uttar Pradesh
Telephone: (581) 2527263
E-mail: info@mjpru.ac.in
Internet: www.mjpru.ac.in
Founded 1975 as Rohilkhand Univ., present status 1985, current name adopted 1997
State control
Languages of instruction: English, Hindi
Academic year: July to June
Chancellor: HE Gov. of Uttar Pradesh
Vice-Chancellor: Prof. Satya P. Gautam
Registrar: B. K. Pandey
Dean of Students Welfare: Prof. Neelima Gupta
Librarian: Prof. A. K. Sinha
Library of 450,000 vols
Number of teachers: 1,062
Number of students: 65,000

DEANS

Faculty of Advanced Social Sciences: Prof. R. P. Yadav
Faculty of Agriculture: Dr P. Veer
Faculty of Applied Sciences: Prof. V. P. Singh
Faculty of Arts: Dr S. Sharma
Faculty of Commerce: Dr B. N. Chaurasia
Faculty of Dental Sciences: (vacant)
Faculty of Education and Allied Sciences: Prof. N. P. Singh
Faculty of Engineering and Technology: Prof. Ashvini K. Gupta
Faculty of Law: Prof. Reena
Faculty of Management Studies: Prof. Pradeep Kumar Yadav
Faculty of Sciences: Prof. Y. K. Gupta

MAHATMA PHULE KRISHI VIDYAPEETH (Mahatma Phule Agricultural University)

Rahuri, Ahmednagar 413722, Maharashtra
Telephone: (2426) 243861
E-mail: registrar.mpkv@nic.in
Internet: mpkv.mah.nic.in
Founded 1968
State control
Academic year: July to May
Chancellor: HE Gov. of Maharashtra
Pro-Chancellor: Min. for Agriculture
Vice-Chancellor: Dr Tukaram Annapa More
Registrar: B. H. Palwe
Dir for Extension Education: Dr S. M. Pokharkar
Dir for Research: Dr H. G. More
Librarian: P. A. Shinde
Library of 87,825 vols
Number of students: 2,200
Publications: *Journal of Maharashtra Agricultural University* (3 a year, in English), *Shi Suga* (3 a year, in Marathi)

DEANS

Faculty of Agricultural Engineering: Prof. R. K. Parkale
Faculty of Agriculture: Dr S. S. Kadam

CONSTITUENT COLLEGES

College of Agricultural Engineering, Rahuri: f. 1969; Assoc. Dean Prof. G. B. Bangal.

College of Agriculture, Dhule: f. 1960; Assoc. Dean Dr Y. M. Shinde.

College of Agriculture, Kolhapur: f. 1963; Assoc. Dean Prof. S. T. Kanjale.

College of Agriculture, Pune: f. 1906; library of 37,838 vols, 50 periodicals; Assoc. Dean Dr V. M. Pawar.

Postgraduate Agricultural Institute, Rahuri: f. 1972; library of 80,000 vols; Assoc. Dean Dr S. S. Kadam

MAKHANLAL CHATURVEDI RASHTRIYA PATRAKARITA EVAM SANCHAR VISHWAVIDYALAYA (Makhanlal Chaturvedi National University of Journalism and Communication)

POB RSN/560, Trilochan Singh Nagar, Shahpura, Bhopal 462016, Madhya Pradesh
B-38 Vikas Bhawan, Press Complex, Zone-1, M. P. Nagar, Bhopal 462011, Madhya Pradesh
Telephone: (755) 2725307
E-mail: mcu.pravesh@gmail.com
Internet: www.mcu.ac.in
Founded 1991
State control
Academic year: August to July
Depts of computer science and applications, electronic media, journalism, management, mass communication, new media technology, public relations and advertising studies, publications, research, short-term training programmes, textbook writing
Vice-Chancellor: Prof. B. K. Kuthiala
Rector: Prof. C. P. Agrawal
Registrar: Dr Chander Sonane
Controller of Examinations: Rajesh Pathak
Registrar: Anil Choubey
Librarian: G. N. Vyas
Library of 15,000 vols
Publication: *Media Mimansa* (4 a year)

MANGALORE UNIVERSITY

Mangalagangotri, Konaje Mangalore 574199, Karnataka
Telephone: (824) 2287276
E-mail: info@mangaloreuniversity.ac.in
Internet: www.mangaloreuniversity.ac.in
Founded 1980
State control
Languages of instruction: English, Kannada
Academic year: June to April
Chancellor: HE Gov. of Karnataka
Pro-Chancellor: Hon. Min. of Higher Education, Govt of Karnataka
Vice-Chancellor: Prof. T. C. Shivashankara Murthy
Registrar: Prof. K. Chinnappa Gowda
Dir for College Devt Ccl: Dr T. N. Shreedhara (acting)
Dir for Physical Education: Dr H. Nagalingappa
Dir for Students Welfare: Prof. A. M. A. Khader
Librarian: Dr M. K. Bhandi
Library of 192,598 vols, 316 journals
Number of teachers: 140
Number of students: 1,303 (univ.), 41,579 (affiliated colleges)

DEANS

Faculty of Arts: Prof. K. Abhaya Kumar
Faculty of Commerce: Prof. A. Raghurama
Faculty of Education: Dr H. Nagalingappa
Faculty of Law: Dr K. Vinoda Rai
Faculty of Science: K. Krishna Bhat

MANIPUR UNIVERSITY

Canchipur, Imphal 795003, Manipur
Telephone: (385) 2435276
E-mail: vcoffice@manipuruniv.ac.in
Internet: manipuruniv.ac.in
Founded 1980, present status 2005
State control
Language of instruction: English
Academic year: July to June
Chief Rector: HE Gov. of Manipur
Chancellor: Prof. Dilip Nachane
Vice-Chancellor: Prof. H. Nandakumar Sarma
Registrar: Prof. N. Lokendra Singh
Controller of Examinatons: Prof. N. Ibotombi Singh
Dean of Student Welfare: Prof. R. K. Hemakumar Singh
Dir for College Devt Ccl: Dr R. K. Ranjan Singh
Librarian: Dr Th. Khomdon Singh
Library of 162,035 vols, 205 nat. and 38 int. journals
Number of teachers: 163 (postgraduate depts only)
Number of students: 1,792 (postgraduate depts only)

DEANS

School of Humanities: Prof. P. Nabachandra Singh
School of Human and Environmental Science: Prof. N. Deva Singh
School of Life Sciences: Prof. N. Irabanta Singh
School of Mathematical and Physical Sciences: Prof. M. Dhaneshwar Singh
School of Medical Sciences: Prof. T. Yumjao Babu Singh
School of Social Sciences: Prof. E. Bijoykumar Singh

CONSTITUENT COLLEGE

Manipur Institute of Technology (MIT): Takyelpat, Imphal, Manipur; tel. (385) 2445422; e-mail mitimphal1998@gmail.com;

internet mitimphal.in; f. 1998, present status 2005; Prin. Dr TH. KULLACHANDRA SINGH

MANONMANIAM SUNDARANAR UNIVERSITY

Abishekapatti, Tirunelveli 627012, Tamil Nadu
Telephone: (462) 2333741
E-mail: info@msuniv.ac.in
Internet: www.msuniv.ac.in
Founded 1990
State control
Chancellor: HE GOV. OF TAMIL NADU
Pro-Chancellor: Hon. MIN. FOR HIGHER EDUCATION, GOVT OF TAMIL NADU
Vice-Chancellor: Dr R. T. SABAPATHY MOHAN
Registrar: Dr S. MANICKAM
Controller of Examinations: K. S. P. DURAIRAJ
Dean of College Devt Ccl: Dr C. KANNAN
Librarian: Dr A. THIRUMAGAL
Library of 94,021 vols
Number of students: 65,000

DEANS
Faculty of Arts: Dr P. GOVINDARAJU
Faculty of Languages: Dr A. BHAWAANI
Faculty of Science: Dr D. PATHINETTAM PADIYAN

MARATHWADA KRISHI VIDYAPEETH (Marathwada Agricultural University)

Krishinagar, Parbhani, 431402, Maharashtra
Telephone: (2452) 223801
E-mail: vc@mkv.ac.in
Internet: www.mkv.ac.in
Founded 1972
State control
Language of instruction: English
Academic year: June to May
Chancellor: HE GOV. OF MAHARASHTRA
Pro-Chancellor: Hon. MIN. FOR AGRICULTURE AND MARKETING, GOVT OF MAHARASHTRA
Vice-Chancellor: Dr K. P. GORE
Registrar: Dr B. B. BHOSALE
Dir for Extension Education: Dr N. D. PAWAR
Dir for Instruction: Dr V. S. SHINDE
Dir for Research: Dr G. R. MORE
Librarian: Dr B. T. MUNDHE
Library of 104,379 vols
Number of teachers: 282
Number of students: 2,017
Publication: *Sheti Bhati* (12 a year, in Marathi)

PROFESSORS
Faculty of Agricultural Technology:
KULKARNI, D. N., Food Science and Cereal Technology
WANKHEDE, D. B., Biochemistry
Faculty of Agriculture:
CHAVAN, B. N., Agronomy
DHAVAN, A. S., Agricultural Chemistry and Soil Science
GORE, K. P., Agricultural Engineering
JANDHALE, S. G., Agricultural Extension
KULKARNI, U. G., Plant Physiology
NADRE, K. R., Agricultural Extension
NARWADKAR, P. R., Horticulture
PAWAR, N. D., Agricultural Economics and Statistics
SHELKE, D. K., Agronomy
SONTAKKE, M. B., Horticulture
Faculty of Home Science:
MURALI, D., Home Management
PATANAM, V., Child Devt and Family Relations
ROHINDEVI, P., Food and Nutrition

CONSTITUENT COLLEGES
College of Agricultural Engineering: Parbhani; Assoc. Dean Dr S. B. SONI.
College of Agricultural Technology: Parbhani; Assoc. Dean Dr V. S. SHINDE.
College of Agriculture, Ambajogai: Ambajogai; Assoc. Dean Dr P. R. ABEGAONKAR.
College of Agriculture: Badnapur; Assoc. Dean Dr G. B. KHANDAGALE.
College of Agriculture: Latur; Assoc. Dean Dr D. P. WASKAR.
College of Agriculture: Osmanabad; Assoc. Dean Dr A. S. DHAWAN.
College of Agriculture: Parbhani; Assoc. Dean Dr N. D. PAWAR.
College of Home Science: Parbhani; Assoc. Dean Prof. D. MURLI

MAULANA AZAD NATIONAL URDU UNIVERSITY

Gochibowli, Hyderabad 500032, Andhra Pradesh
Telephone: (40) 23008402
E-mail: manuu@indiainfo.com
Internet: www.manuu.ac.in
Founded 1998
State control
Language of instruction: Urdu
Chancellor: Dr SYEDA SAIYIDAIN HAMEED
Vice-Chancellor: Prof. MOHAMMAD MIYAN
Registrar: Prof. H KHATIJA BEGUM (acting)
Controller of Examinations: Prof. S. A. WAHAB (acting)
Librarian: Dr ABBAS KHAN (acting)
Library of 14,500 vols, 54 periodicals
Number of students: 56,000

DEANS
School of Arts and Social Sciences: Prof. S. M. RAHMATULLAH
School of Education and Training: Prof. H. KHATIJA BEGUM
School of Languages, Linguistics and Indology: Prof. AMINA KISHORE
School of Management and Commerce: Prof. MOHD. SAEED
School of Mass Communications: Prof. T. V. KATTIMANI
School of Political Science and Public Administration: Prof. S. M. RAHMATULLAH
School of Sciences: Prof. K. R. IQBAL AHMED

REGIONAL CENTRES
Bangalore Regional Centre—MANUU: Al-Ameen Commercial Complex, POB 27058, 2nd Fl., Hosur Rd, Bengaluru 560027, Karnataka; tel. (80) 22228329; Dir Dr KHAZI ZIAULLAH.
Bhopal Regional Centre—MANUU: 12 Ahmedabad Palace, Koh-e-Fiza, Bhopal, Madhya Pradesh; tel. (755) 2736930; Dir Dr MOHD AHSAN.
Darbhanga Regional Centre—MANUU: Super Market, Moula Ganj, Darbhanga 846004, Bihar; tel. (6272) 258755; Dir Dr S. E. H. IMAM AZAM.
Delhi Regional Centre—MANUU: B-1/275, Ground Fl., Zaidi Apts, T. I. T. Rd Okhla, Jamia Nagar, New Delhi, 110025; tel. (11) 26934762; Dir Dr SHAHID PERVEZ.
Kolkata Regional Centre—MANUU: Flat 5, 2nd Fl., 9A Lower Range, Kolkata 700017, West Bengal; tel. (33) 22894568; Dir SAHAB SINGH (acting).
New Mumbai Regional Centre—MANUU: A-1, CHS Ltd, F-1/6, 2nd Fl., Dev Hotel, Sector 5, Vahsi, New Mumbai 400703, Maharashtra; tel. 22-27820515; Dir Dr MD. ARSHAD EKBAL.
Patna Regional Centre—MANUU: 2nd Fl., Bihar State Co-operative Bank Bldg, Ashok Rajpath, Patna 800004, Bihar; tel. (612) 2300413; Dir Dr HASNUDDIN HAIDER.
Srinagar Regional Centre—MANUU: 18B Jawahar Nagar, Srinagar 190001, Jammu and Kashmir; tel. (914) 2310221; Regional Dir Dr M. AIJAZ ASHRAF

MAULANA MAZHARUL HAQUE ARABIC AND PERSIAN UNIVERSITY

5 Bailey Rd, Patna 800001, Bihar
Telephone: (612) 6456010
E-mail: mmhapupatna@yahoo.in
Internet: mmhapu.bih.nic.in
Founded 1998
State control
Chancellor: HE GOV. OF BIHAR
Vice Chancellor: Dr MD. SHAMSUZZOHA
Pro-Vice-Chancellor: Dr S. K. JABEEN
Registrar: Dr M. G. MUSTAFA
Controller of Examinations: Dr S. M. KARIM

MIZORAM UNIVERSITY

POB 190, Aizawl 796004, Mizoram
Tanhril, Aizawl, Mizoram
Telephone: (389) 2330654
E-mail: registrar@mzu.edu.in
Internet: www.mzu.edu.in
Founded 2001
State control
Academic year: July to June
Language of instruction: English
Vice-Chancellor: Prof. R. LALTHANTLUANGA
Registrar: Prof. THANGCHUNNUNGA (acting)
Controller of Examinations: Prof. R. L. THANMAWIA (acting)
Dean of Students Welfare: Dr LALNUNTLUANGA
Dir for College Devt Ccl: S. K. GHOSH
Librarian: Dr LALREMSIAMI
Library of 78,311 vols, 247 journals
Number of teachers: 272
Number of students: 3,305

DEANS
School of Earth Sciences and Natural Resource Management: Prof. P. RINAWMA
School of Economics, Management and Information Sciences: Prof. THANGCHUNGNUNGA
School of Education and Humanities: Prof. B. B. MISHRA
School of Engineering and Technology: Prof. R. P. TIWARI (acting)
School of Fine Arts, Architecture and Fashion Technology: Prof. R. P. TIWARI (acting)
School of Life Sciences: Prof. GANESH CHANDRA JAGETIA
School of Physical Sciences: Prof. R. K. THAPA
School of Social Science: Prof. J. V. JEYA SINGH

CONSTITUENT COLLEGE
Pachhunga University College: College Veng, Aizawl 796001, Mizoram; tel. (389) 2322257; e-mail tawnenga5@yahoo.com; internet pucollege.in; f. 1958 as Aijal College; present name 1979; 2002 became constituent college; 84 teachers; 1,290 students; Prin. Dr TAWNENGA (acting)

MOHAN LAL SUKHADIA UNIVERSITY

Pratap Nagar, Udaipur 313039, Rajasthan
Telephone: (294) 2471035
E-mail: registrar@mlsu.ac.in
Internet: www.mlsu.ac.in
Founded 1962 as Udaipur Univ., current name adopted 1982
State control
Languages of instruction: English, Hindi

Academic year: July to June
Chancellor: HE Gov. of Rajasthan
Vice-Chancellor: Prof. I. V. Trivedi
Registrar: Mohan Lal Sharma
Dean of Postgraduate Studies: Prof. K. Venugopalan
Dean of Student Welfare: Prof. S. R. Vyas
Librarian: Prof. A. K. Goswami

Library of 287,000 vols
Number of teachers: 264
Number of students: 110,000

DEANS

Univ. College of Commerce and Management Studies: Prof. D. S. Chundawat
Univ. College of Law: Prof. Farida Shah
Univ. College of Science: Prof. Maheep Bhatnagar
Univ. College of Social Sciences and Humanities: Prof. Sharad Srivastava

MOTHER TERESA WOMEN'S UNIVERSITY

Kodaikanal 624102, Tamil Nadu
Telephone: (4542) 241122
E-mail: registrar@motherteresawomenuniv.ac.in
Internet: www.motherteresawomenuniv.ac.in
Founded 1984
State control
Languages of instruction: English, Tamil
Academic year: June to May

Depts of biotechnology, computer science, economics, education, English, family life management, historical studies and tourism management, management, music, physics, sociology, Tamil, visual communication

Chancellor: HE Gov. of Tamil Nadu
Pro-Chancellor: Hon. Min. for Higher Education, Govt of Tamil Nadu
Vice-Chancellor: Prof. Dr Aruna Sivakami Ananthakrishnan
Registrar: Dr P. N. Premalatha (acting)
Controller of Examinations: Dr S. Sundari

Library of 87,000 vols
Number of teachers: 34
Number of students: 1,000

PROFESSORS

Aravanan, T., Tamil
Phil, M., Education

CONSTITUENT COLLEGES

Government Arts College for Women: Nilakottai 624208, Tamil Nadu; tel. (4543) 233196.

Mother Teresa Women's University College: Attuvampatti Campus, Kodaikanal, Tamil Nadu; f. 1985.

M. V. Muthiah Pillai Arts College for Women: Thadikombu Rd, Angunagar, Dindigul 624008; tel. (451) 2422011

NAGALAND UNIVERSITY

Lumami, Zunheboto 798627, Nagaland
Telephone: (369) 2268270
E-mail: nuregistrar@yahoo.in
Internet: www.nagauniv.org.in
Founded 1994
State control
Language of instruction: English
Academic year: September to August
Chief Rector: HE Gov. of Nagaland
Chancellor: Prof. Yoginder K. Alagh
Vice-Chancellor: Prof. Bolin Kumar Konwar
Registrar: Dr P. H. Naik
Dean of Student Welfare: Dr John Seam
Dir for College Devt Ccl: Dr Tongpang Ao
Controller of Examinations: (vacant)
Asst Librarian: Lucy Bendang

Library of 32,916 vols, 75 periodicals
Number of teachers: 112
Number of students: 19,151 (18,349 undergraduate, 802 postgraduate)

DEANS

School of Agricultural Sciences and Rural Devt: Prof. R. C. Nayak
School of Engineering and Technology: (vacant)
School of Humanities and Education: Prof. Imtisungba (acting)
School of Management: (vacant)
School of Sciences: Prof. N. S. Jamir
School of Social Sciences: Prof. A. Lanunungsang Ao

NALANDA OPEN UNIVERSITY

Biscomaun Bhawan, Gandhi Maidan, Patna 800001, Bihar
Telephone: (612) 2201013
E-mail: nalopuni@sancharnet.in
Internet: www.nalandaopenuniversity.com
Founded 1987
State control
Academic year: June to May
Chancellor: HE Gov. of Bihar
Vice-Chancellor: Prof. Jitendra Singh
Pro-Vice-Chancellor: Dr Kaushlendra Kumar Singh
Registrar: Dr Sidheshwar Prasad Sinha

Library of 50,000 vols

NALANDA UNIVERSITY

53, Lodi Estate, Council for Social Development Bldg, 2nd Fl., New Delhi, 110003
Rajgir Nalanda 803116, Bihar
Telephone: (611) 2255330
Internet: www.nalandauniv.edu.in
Founded 2014 originally est. in AD 5
State control

Schools of ecology and environment studies, historical studies

Chancellor: Prof. Amartya Sen
Vice-Chancellor: Dr Gopa Sabharwal

NALSAR UNIVERSITY OF LAW

3-5-874/18 Hyderguda, Hyderabad 500029, Andhra Pradesh
Justice City, Shameerpet, Rangareddy Dist., Hyderabad 500078, Andhra Pradesh
Telephone: (40) 23498200
E-mail: admissions@nalsar.ac.in
Internet: www.nalsar.ac.in
Founded 1998
Sstate control
Academic year: July to June
Vice-Chancellor: Prof. Dr Faizan Mustafa
Registrar: Prof. Madabhushi Sridhar

Library of 17,000 vols

Publications: *Environmenal Law & Practice Review*, *Media Law Review* (1 a year), *NALSAR Law Review* (2 a year), *The Indian Journal Law & Economics*

NARENDRA DEVA UNIVERSITY OF AGRICULTURE & TECHNOLOGY

Narendranagar, Kumarganj, Faizabad 224229, Uttar Pradesh
Telephone: (5270) 262161
E-mail: nduat@up.nic.in
Internet: www.nduat.co.nr
Founded 1974
State control
Languages of instruction: Hindi, English
Chancellor: HE Gov. of Uttar Pradesh
Vice-Chancellor: Dr R. S. Kureel
Registrar: Dr Padmaker Tripathi
Dir of Extension Education: Dr Kanti Prasad
Dir of Research: Dr H. P. Tripathi

Library of 42,000 vols
Number of teachers: 67
Number of students: 432

DEANS

College of Agriculture: Dr J. P. Mishra
College of Agriculture Engineering: Eng. R. D. Singh
College of Fisheries: Dr J. P. Mishra
College of Home Science: Dr Suman Bhanot
College of Horticulture: Dr J. P. Mishra
College of Veterinary Science and Animal Husbandry: Dr H. N. Singh

CONSTITUENT COLLEGE

Mahamaya College of Agricultural Engineering & Technology: Faizabad Ambedkar Nagar, Uttar Pradesh; f. 2002 as Engineering faculty of NDUAT

NATIONAL LAW INSTITUTE UNIVERSITY

Bhopal Bhadbhada Rd, Barkheri Kalan, POB 369, Bhopal 462003, Madhya Pradesh
Telephone: (755) 2696965
E-mail: nliu@nliu.ac.in
Internet: www.nliu.ac.in
Founded 1998
State control
Academic year: July to April
Dir: Prof. Dr S. S. Singh
Registrar: Chandrakanta M. Garg
Deputy Librarian: Dr Shivpal Singh Kushwaha

NATIONAL LAW UNIVERSITY, JODHPUR

NH-65, Nagour Rd, Mandore, Jodhpur 342304, Rajasthan
Telephone: (291) 2577530
E-mail: nlu-jod-rj@nic.in
Internet: www.nlujodhpur.ac.in
Founded 2001
State control
Language of instruction: English
Chancellor: Hon. Chief Justice of Rajasthan
Vice-Chancellor: Justice N. N. Mathur
Registrar: Ratan Lahoti
Librarian: Vinod D.

Library of 11,508 books, 108 journals, 1,400 electronic journals
Number of teachers: 46
Number of students: 548

Publications: *Journal of Governance* (2 a year), *Scholasticus* (2 a year), *Trade Law and Development* (2 a year)

DEANS

Faculty of Law: Prof. Dr I. P. Massey
Faculty of Management: Prof. Dr U. R. Daga
Faculty of Policy Science: Dr Alok Kumar Gupta (acting)
Faculty of Science: Prof. Dr K. K. Banerjee

NETAJI SUBHAS OPEN UNIVERSITY

1 Woodburn Park, Kolkata 700020, West Bengal
Telephone: (33) 22835157
E-mail: admin@wbnsou.ac.in
Internet: www.wbnsou.ac.in
Founded 1997
State control
Language of instruction: Bengali

Undergraduate and postgraduate degree programmes in accountancy, Bengali, botany, chemistry, commerce, computer science, economics, education, English, environmental science, geography, history, management, mathematics, physics, political science, public admin., sociology, zoology; 6 campuses in Kolkata; 191 study centres

Chancellor: HE GOV. OF WEST BENGAL
Vice-Chancellor: Prof. SUBHA SHANKAR SARKAR
Registrar: Prof. BIKAS GHOSH (acting)
Dir for Humanities and Social Sciences: Prof. DEBNARAYAN MODAK
Dir for Science: Prof. KAJAL DE
Dir for Study Centre: Dr ASHIT BARAN AICH
Controller of Examinations: A. DAS
Number of students: 100,000

NIRMA UNIVERSITY OF SCIENCE AND TECHNOLOGY

Sarkhej Gandhinagar Highway, Chandlodia, Gota, Ahmedabad 382481, Gujarat
Telephone: (2717) 241911
E-mail: asst_registrar@nirmauni.ac.in
Internet: www.nirmauni.ac.in

Founded 1994; current name and status 2003
Private control

Pres.: Dr KARSANBHAI K. PATEL
Vice-Pres.: AMBUBHAI PATEL
Vice-Chancellor: Dr N. V. VASANI
Exec. Registrar: D. P. CHHAYA

Library of 79,000 vols, 787 periodicals

DEANS

Faculty of Law: Dr PURVI POKHARIYAL
Faculty of Management: Dr C. GOPALKRISHNAN
Faculty of Pharmacy: Dr MANJUNATH GHATE (acting)
Faculty of Science: Dr G. NARESHKUMAR (acting)
Faculty of Technology and Engineering: Prof. K. KOTECHA

NIZAM'S INSTITUTE OF MEDICAL SCIENCES

Punjagutta, Hyderabad 500082, Andhra Pradesh
Telephone: (40) 23489000
E-mail: nims@ap.nic.in
Internet: nims.ap.nic.in

Founded 1964 as Nizam's Orthopaedic Hospital; current name and status 1989
State control

Depts of anaesthesiology and intensive care, biochemistry, cardio-thoracic surgery, cardiology, chest clinic, clinical pharmacology and therapeutics, dental, dermatology, endocrinology and metabolism, gastroenterology, general medicine, gynaecology, medical oncology, microbiology, nephrology, neurology, neurosurgery, nuclear medicine, orthopaedics, paediatrics, pathology, physiotherapy, plastic surgery, radiation oncology, radiology and imageology, rheumatology, surgical gastroenterology, surgical oncology, transfusion medicine, urology, vascular surgery

Dir: Dr A. DHARMA RAKSHAK
Dean: Dr V. R. SRINIVASAN
Medical Superintendent: Dr N. SATYANARAYANA
Exec. Registrar: J. BHASKARA RAO (acting)

Number of teachers: 139

NORTH EASTERN HILL UNIVERSITY

PO NEHU Campus, Shillong 793022, Meghalaya
Umshing Mawkynroh, Shillong 793022, Meghalaya
Telephone: (364) 2550101
Internet: www.nehu.ac.in

Founded 1973
State control
Language of instruction: English
Academic year: August to July

Chief Rector: HE GOV. OF MEGHALAYA
Chancellor: Prof. M. G. K. MENON
Vice-Chancellor: Prof. A. N. RAI
Pro Vice-Chancellor: Prof. M. MYRBOH
Registrar: DEBOBRATA DEB
Controller of Examinations: Dr L. CAJEE
Dean of Student Welfare: Prof. R. N. SHARAN
Dir for College Devt Ccl: Dr C. R. DIENGDOH
Librarian: Dr I. MAJAW

Library of 267,000 vols
Number of teachers: 342
Number of students: 32,000

Publication: *NEHU Journal of Social Sciences and Humanities* (2 a year)

DEANS

School of Education: Prof. P. K. GUPTA
School of Economics, Management and Information Science: Prof. N. M. PANDA
School of Human and Environmental Sciences: Prof. B. S. MIPUN
School of Humanities: Prof. J. WAR
School of Life Sciences: Prof. A. K. MISRA
School of Physical Sciences: Prof. H. K. MUKHERJEE
School of Social Sciences: Prof. L. S. GASSAH
School of Technology: Prof. S. CHOUDHURY

NORTH MAHARASHTRA UNIVERSITY

POB 80, Jalgaon 425002, Maharashtra
Telephone: (257) 2258405
E-mail: registrar@nmu.ac.in
Internet: www.nmu.ac.in

Founded 1990
State control
Languages of instruction: English, Hindi, Marathi
Academic year: June to May

Chancellor: HE GOV. OF MAHARASHTRA
Vice-Chancellor: Prof. Dr SUDHIR U. MESHRAM
Registrar: Dr ASHOK MAHAJAN
Dir for Public Relations: Prof. DILIP HUNDIWALE
Controller of Examinations: Dr BORSE AMULRAO UTTAMRAO (acting)
Librarian: Dr T. R. BORSE

Library of 28,728 vols, 85 periodicals
Number of teachers: 3,174
Number of students: 47,974

DEANS

Faculty of Arts and Fine Arts: Prof. NERKAR NARAYAN MAHADU
Faculty of Commerce and Management: Prof. Dr CHAUDHARI PRAMOD RAMBHAU
Faculty of Education: Dr PATIL NALINI PITAMBAR
Faculty of Engineering and Technology: Prof. PATIL JAYANTRAO BHAURAO
Faculty of Law: Prof. B. YUVAKUMAR REDDY
Faculty of Medicine and Pharmacy: Prof. PATIL VIJAY RAGHUNATH
Faculty of Mental, Moral and Social Sciences: Dr PAITHANE ASARAM SAKHARAM
Faculty of Science: Prof. Dr BHAUSAHEB PAWAR

NORTH ORISSA UNIVERSITY

Sriram Chandra Vihar, Takatpur, Baripada, Mayurbhanj 757003, Orissa
Telephone: (6792) 255127
Internet: www.nou.nic.in

Founded 1998
State control
Academic year: June to May

Depts of anthropology and tribal studies, bioinformatics, biotechnology, botany, business admin., chemistry, computer science and application, economics, finance and control, law, library and information science, mathematics and computing, physics, remote sensing and geographic systems, wildlife, zoology; 80 affiliated colleges

Chancellor: HE GOV. OF ORISSA
Vice-Chancellor: Prof. SANGHAMITRA MOHANTY
Registrar: Dr MADHUSUDAN SAHOO
Controller of Examinations: Dr L. D. NAYAK
Librarian: Prof. N. N. DASH (acting)

Library of 2,647 vols
Number of students: 10,320

ORISSA UNIVERSITY OF AGRICULTURE AND TECHNOLOGY

Dist. Khurda, Bhubaneswar 751003, Orissa
Telephone: (674) 2397769
E-mail: ouatmain@hotmail.com
Internet: ouat.ac.in

Founded 1962
State control
Language of instruction: English
Academic year: July to July

Chancellor: HE GOV. OF ORISSA
Vice-Chancellor: Prof. D. P. RAY
Registrar: SANGRAM KESHARI RAY
Dean of Extension Education: Dr S. S. NANDA
Dean of Research: Dr MADAN MOHAN PANDA
Dean of Students Welfare: Dr B. D. MISHRA
Controller of Examinations: Dr BIRANCHI NARAYAN ROUTRAY
Librarian: Dr R. K. MAHAPATRA

Library of 900,000 vols, 133 periodicals
Number of teachers: 512
Number of students: 3,082

DEANS

College of Agricultural Engineering and Technology: Dr M. K. KHAN
College of Agriculture: Dr D. NAIK
College of Veterinary Science and Animal Husbandry: Dr P. K. DEHURI

OSMANIA UNIVERSITY

Hyderabad 500007, Andhra Pradesh
Telephone: (40) 27098043
E-mail: registrar@osmania.ac.in
Internet: www.osmania.ac.in

Founded 1918
State control
Languages of instruction: English, Hindi, Telugu, Urdu, Marathi
Academic year: June to April (two terms)

Chancellor: HE GOV. OF ANDHRA PRADESH
Vice-Chancellor: Prof. S. SATYANARAYANA
Registrar: Prof. V. KISHAN RAO
Dean of College Devt Ccl: Prof. P. YADAGIRI SWAMY
Dean of Devt: Prof. A. RAVINDRANATH
Dean of Student Affairs: Prof. B. LAXMAIAH
Public Relations Officer: Prof. B. S. RAO
Librarian: V. REVATHI (acting)

Library of 521,259 vols, 6,825 MSS
Number of teachers: 5,000
Number of students: 300,000

Publication: *Osmania Journal of English Studies*

DEANS

Faculty of Arts: Prof. P. L. VISHWESHWAR RAO
Faculty of Business Management: Prof. A. VIDYADHAR REDDY
Faculty of Commerce: Prof. K. V. ACHALAPATHI
Faculty of Education: Prof. K. S. SUDHEER REDDY
Faculty of Engineering: Prof. R. RAMESH REDDY
Faculty of Informatics: Prof. LAXMI RAJAMANI

Faculty of Law: Prof. T. VIDYA KUMARI
Faculty of Oriental Languages: Dr M. A. JAMEEL KHAN
Faculty of Science: Prof. U. V. SUBHA RAO
Faculty of Social Sciences: Prof. S. BHUPATHI RAV
Faculty of Technology: Prof. J. S. N. MURTHY

UNIVERSITY COLLEGES

Institute of Advanced Study in Education: f. 1918; Prin. Prof. P. AYODHYA.

University College of Arts and Social Sciences: tel. (40) 27098298; e-mail info@ouartscollege.com; f. 1918; Prin. Prof. T. KESHAVNARAYANA.

University College of Commerce and Business Management: f. 1975; Prin. Prof. VEDULLA SHEKHAR.

University College of Engineering: tel. (40) 27098254; e-mail webmaster@uceou.edu; internet www.uceou.edu; f. 1929; library of 76,300 vols; Prin. Prof. A. VENUGOPAL REDDY.

University College of Law: tel. (40) 27098254; internet www.osmanialawcollege.org; f. 1960; Prin. Dr G. B. REDDY.

University College of Physical Education: tel. (40) 27090711; f. 1928; Prin. Prof. SYED IBRAHIM.

University College of Science: f. 1918; 200 teachers; 1,000 students; Prin. Prof. MADDY SATYANARAYANA REDDY.

University College of Technology: tel. (40) 27682291; e-mail principal@ouct.org; internet www.uctou.ac.in; f. 1969; Prin. Prof. T. SANKARSHANA.

CONSTITUENT COLLEGES

Nizam College: Basheerbagh, Hyderabad 500001, Andhra Pradesh; tel. (40) 23234231; e-mail principal@nizamcollege.ac.in; internet www.nizamcollege.ac.in; f. 1887; Prin. Prof. ASHOK NAIDU.

Postgraduate College of Law, Hyderabad: Basheerbagh, Hyderabad 500001, Andhra Pradesh; tel. (40) 23231092; e-mail pgclou@yahoo.com; internet www.osmania.ac.in/pgcl; f. 1899; Prin. Dr A. NARSING RAO.

Postgraduate College of Science: Saifabad, Hyderabad 500004, Andhra Pradesh; tel. (40) 23393530; e-mail oupgcss@gmail.com; internet www.oupgcollege.ac.in; f. 1951; Prin. Prof. T. PARTHASARATHY.

Postgraduate College, Secunderabad: Sadar Patel Rd, Secunderabad 500003, Andhra Pradesh; tel. (40) 27902169; e-mail principal@oupgcs.ac.in; internet www.oupgcs.ac.in; f. 1947; 65 teachers; 1,400 students; Prin. Prof. K. POCHANNA.

University College for Women: Hyderabad, Andhra Pradesh; tel. (40) 24657813; e-mail oucwkoti@rediffmail.com; internet www.oucwkoti.ac.in; f. 1924; Prin. Prof. AMARJIT KAUR.

District Postgraduate Colleges:

Postgraduate College, Biknoor: f. 1976; Prin. Dr U. UMESH KUMAR.

Postgraduate Centre, Mahaboobnagar: f. 1987; Head Dr N. ASHOK.

Postgraduate Centre, Mirzapur: f. 1980; Prin. Dr B. MANOHAR.

Postgraduate Centre, Nalgonda: f. 1987; Prin. Dr S. ANJAIAH.

PANDIT RAVISHANKAR SHUKLA UNIVERSITY, RAIPUR

Amanaka G. E. Rd, Raipur 492010, Chhattisgarh
Telephone: (771) 2262540
E-mail: vc_raipur@prsu.org.in
Internet: www.prsu.ac.in

Founded 1964
Languages of instruction: Hindi, English
Private control
Academic year: July to June (2 terms)

Chancellor: HE GOV. OF CHHATTISGARH
Vice-Chancellor: Prof. SHIV KUMAR PANDEY
Registrar: INDU ANANT
Librarian: M. I. AHMED

Library of 160,000 vols
Number of students: 125,000

DEANS

Faculty of Arts: Dr CHITTARANJAN KAR
Faculty of Ayurved: Dr D. K. KATARIA
Faculty of Commerce: AMIR CHAND JAIN
Faculty of Education: Dr B. K. MEHTA
Faculty of Engineering: Dr H. KUMAR
Faculty of Home Science: Dr V. RAJ
Faculty of Law: Dr A. A. KHAN
Faculty of Management: Dr R. P. DAS
Faculty of Science: Dr G. L. MUNDHRA
Faculty of Social Sciences: Dr M. A. KHAN
Faculty of Technology: Dr SHAILENDRA SARAF

CONSTITUENT SCHOOLS

Centre for Regional Studies and Research: f. 1993; Dir Prof. O. P. VERMA.

Centre for Women Studies: f. 2001.

Institute of Management: f. 1993; Dir Dr R. P. DAS.

Institute of Pharmacy: tel. (771) 2262832; e-mail info@iopraipur.ac.in; internet www.iopraipur.ac.in; f. 2001; Dir Dr S. SARAF.

Institute of Teachers Education: .

Institute of Tourism and Hotel Management: f. 2002; Dir Dr L. S. NIGAM.

School of Studies in Adult, Continuing Education and Extension: f. 1985; Dir Dr BINA PATHAK.

School of Studies in Ancient Indian History, Culture and Archaeology: f. 1971; Dir Prof. L. S. NIGAM.

School of Studies in Anthropology: f. 1965; Dir Dr MANJULA GUHA.

School of Studies in Biotechnology: f. 2003; Dir Dr K. L. TIWARI.

School of Studies in Chemistry: f. 1972; Dir Dr RAMA PANDE.

School of Studies in Comparative Religion and Philosophy: f. 1985; Dir Dr BHAGWANT SINGH.

School of Studies in Computer Science: e-mail dropvyas@gmail.com; internet www.prsu.ac.in/soscs.html; f. 1992; Dir Prof. O. P. VYAS.

School of Studies in Economics: f. 1971; Dir Dr USHA DUBEY.

School of Studies in Electronics: f. 1994; Dir Dr KAVITA THAKUR.

School of Studies in Geography: f. 1965; Dir Dr M. P. GUPTA.

School of Studies in Geology and Water Resource Management: f. 1984; Dir Dr M. W. Y. KHAN.

School of Studies in History: f. 1971; Dir Dr M. A. KHAN.

School of Studies in Law: f. 1982; Dir Dr A. ALIM KHAN.

School of Studies in Library and Information Science: f. 1971; Dir Dr A. K. VERMA.

School of Studies in Life Sciences: f. 1977; Dir Dr VIBHUTI RAI.

School of Studies in Literature and Languages: Dir Dr K. L. VERMA.

School of Studies in Mathematics: f. 1991; Dir Dr B. K. SHARMA.

School of Studies in Physical Education: f. 1972; Dir Dr RITA VENU GOPAL.

School of Studies in Physics: f. 1972; Dir Dr S. BHUSHAN.

School of Studies in Psychology: f. 1965; Dir Dr P. SINGH.

School of Studies in Sociology: f. 1965; Dir Dr P. K. SHARMA.

School of Studies in Statistics: f. 1977; Dir Dr GAURI SHANKAR

PANJAB UNIVERSITY

Sector 14, Chandigarh 160014
Telephone: (172) 2534867
E-mail: regr@pu.ac.in
Internet: www.puchd.ac.in

Founded 1947
State control
Languages of instruction: English, Hindi, Punjabi, Urdu
Academic year: July to April

Chancellor: VICE-PRES. OF INDIA
Vice-Chancellor: Prof. ARUN KUMAR GROVER
Registrar: Prof. A. K. BHANDARI
Librarian: RAJ KUMAR

Library of 720,000 vols
Number of teachers: 698
Number of students: 17,000

Publications: *Indian Journal of Distance Education*, *Panjab University Management Review*, *Parakh*, *Parishodh*, *P. U. Research Journal* (Science), *P. U. Research Journal* (Social Sciences), *P. U. Research Journal* (Journal of University Institute of Legal Studies)

DEANS

Faculty of Arts: Dr MADAN MOHAN PURI
Faculty of Business Management and Commerce: Prof. S. P. SINGH
Faculty of Design and Fine Arts: JOGINDER SINGH
Faculty of Education: NIRMAL KAUR
Faculty of Engineering and Technology: Prof. D. K. VOHRA
Faculty of Languages: Dr ANIRUDH JOSHI
Faculty of Law: GOPAL KRISHAN CHATRATH
Faculty of Medical Sciences: Dr K. S. CHUGH
Faculty of Pharmaceutical Sciences: Prof. V. K. KAPOOR
Faculty of Science: Prof. R. K. PATHAK

PATNA UNIVERSITY

Ashok Raj Path, Patna 800005, Bihar
Telephone: (612) 2670531
E-mail: registrar-pu-bih@nic.in
Internet: www.patnauniversity.ac.in

Founded 1917, present status 1952
State control
Languages of instruction: Hindi, English
Academic year: June to May (3 terms)

Chancellor: HE GOV. OF BIHAR
Vice-Chancellor: Prof. Dr SHAMBU NATH SINGH
Pro-Vice-Chancellor: Prof. Dr J. P. SINGH
Registrar: Dr VIBHASH KUMAR YADAV
Dean of Student Welfare: Dr P. K. PODDAR
Controller of Examination: Dr BINAY SOREN
Librarian: Dr JAIDEV MISHRA

Library of 400,000 vols, 87 periodicals
Number of teachers: 448
Number of students: 18,741

Publication: *University of Patna Journal*

DEANS

Faculty of Commerce: Dr UMESH MISHRA
Faculty of Education: ASHUTOSH KUMAR
Faculty of Humanities: S. M. ASHOK
Faculty of Law: Dr RAKESH VERMA
Faculty of Science: Dr U. K. SINHA

Faculty of Social Science: Dr BHARTI S. KUMAR

PROFESSORS

ADHIKARI, S., Geography
AHMAD, S. U., Sociology
AKHTAR, M. M., Physics
ALAM, M. S., Persian
ALAM, P. A., Urdu
ARSHAD, E. A., Urdu
ARYA, R. S., Philosophy
ASHOK, S. M., English
AZAD, A., Urdu
AZAD, R., Chemistry
BANERJEE, N. N., Botany
BANERJEE, S., Political Science
BEGAM, S., Urdu
BHAKTA, C., Chemistry
BHATT, P., Zoology
BLAKTA, S., Mathematics
CHOUDHARY, A. K., Physics
CHOUDHARY, M. N., Hindi
CHOUDHARY, N. K., Economics
CHOUDHARY, R., Philosophy
CHOUDHARY, R. B., Sanskrit
CHOUDHARY, S., Political Science
DAS, R. N., Mathematics
DUBEY, G. R., Education
DUBEY, S., Psychology
DUBEY, V. S., Geology
DUTTA, P., History
DUTTA, S. A., English
GHOSH, A. K., Chemistry
GHOSH, P., History
GUHA, S. N., Physics
GUPTA, A. D., Sociology
GUPTA, A. K., Botany
GUPTA, F., Sanskrit
HASANARAN, S. J., Mechanical Engineering
JAISWAL, R., Mathematics
JHA, B., Maithili
JHA, H., Sociology
JHA, I., Education
JHA, K., Psychology
JHA, N. N., Physics
JHA, R., Ancient Indian History and Archaeology
JHA, R., English
JHA, S. M., Mathematics
JHA, U., Chemistry
KALIM, Z., English
KARAN, V., Maithili
KATHURIA, S., Botany
KHAN, S. A., Statistics
KUMAR, A., English
KUMAR, A., Sanskrit
KUMAR, B., Chemistry
KUMAR, B., Statistics
KUMAR, B. S., History
KUMAR, N., Mechanical Engineering
KUMAR, R. V., History
KUMAR, S., Civil Engineering
KUMAR, S., Sociology
KUMARI, A., Statistics
KUMARI, R., Sociology
KUMARI, S., Hindi
LAL, S., Chemistry
MAHTO, K., Geography
MAHTO, R. U., Commerce
MALTIYAR, K. K., Geography
MATHUR, K. N. L., Physics
MIRZA, K., Political Science
MISHRA, A., Statistics
MISHRA, B. K., Geology
MISHRA, H., English
MISHRA, J. S., History
MISHRA, N. M., Physics
MISHRA, R. G., Sanskrit
MISHRA, R. N., Statistics
MISHRA, R. S., Statistics
MISHRA, U., Commerce
MITRA, K. A., Physics
MOHAN, M., Zoology
MUKHERJEE, D., Physics
MUKHERJEE, I., Botany
MURARI, R., Economics
NATH, A., Zoology
NILIMA, N., Hindi
OJHA, G. P., Political Science
PADAMDEO, S. R., Botany
PANDEY, B. N., Commerce
PANDEY, M. K., Sanskrit
PANDEY, N. M., English
PANDEY, N. N., Physics
PASWAN, B., Hindi
PASWAN, K. N., Geography
PODAR, P. K., History
PRAJAPATI, G. K., Education
PRAKASH, D., Chemistry
PRASAD, A., Chemistry
PRASAD, A., Statistics
PRASAD, B., Mathematics
PRASAD, D., Mathematics
PRASAD, D., Sociology
PRASAD, K., Geology
PRASAD, K., History
PRASAD, R. D., Hindi
PRASAD, R. K., Chemistry
PRASAD, R. N., Philosophy
PRASAD, R. P., Chemistry
PRASAD, S. A. K., Mathematics
PRASAD, S. L., Geography
QUADRI, E. A., Civil Engineering
RAJGARHIA, C., Mathematics
RANI, P., Zoology
ROHATAGI, A. K., Geology
ROY, D. N., Bengali
ROY, R., English
ROY, R. B. R., Hindi
ROY, S., Chemistry
ROY, V. R., Psychology
RUDRA, S., Economics
SAHAY, R. R., Philosophy
SHARDENDU, Hindi
SHARMA, B., Mathematics
SHARMA, D. K., Mathematics
SHARMA, D. K., Physics
SHARMA, J. P., Education
SHARMA, M. D., Bengali
SHARMA, N. K., Hindi
SHARMA, P. L., History
SHARMA, R. N., Sociology
SHARMA, S., Psychology
SHARMA, S. N., Botany
SHARMA, S. N., Physics
SHARMA, S. N., Political Science
SHAW, G., Home Science
SHEKHAR, J., Commerce
SHREE, V., Philosophy
SHUKLA, H., Political Science
SHUKLA, K. N., Zoology
SHUKLA, P., Psychology
SHUKLA, R., Geology
SIDDIQUI, F. K., Arabic
SIDDIQUI, M. G., Persian
SIDDIQUI, M. O., Botany
SINGH, A., Economics
SINGH, A. K., Ancient Indian History and Archaeology
SINGH, A. K., History
SINGH, A. K., Psychology
SINGH, A. K. S., Hindi
SINGH, A. N., History
SINGH, B. P., Economics
SINGH, C., Commerce
SINGH, D. P., Hindi
SINGH, G., Hindi
SINGH, J., Physics
SINGH, J. M. P., Hindi
SINGH, J. P., Sociology
SINGH, K. N., Mechanical Engineering
SINGH, K. P., English
SINGH, K. S. P., Civil Engineering
SINGH, L. K. P., Geography
SINGH, N. K., Geology
SINGH, N. K. P., History
SINGH, N. N. P., History
SINGH, P., Philosophy
SINGH, P. D., Chemistry
SINGH, R. B. P., Geography
SINGH, R. P., Chemistry
SINGH, S., Botany
SINGH, S., Home Science
SINGH, S. C., History
SINGH, S. D. N., Sociology
SINGH, S. K., Mechanical Engineering
SINGH, S. K., Statistics
SINGH, S. K. P., Economics
SINGH, S. K. P., History
SINGH, S. N., Chemistry
SINGH, S. N., Economics
SINGH, S. P. Y., Hindi
SINGH, S. S., Ancient Indian History and Archaeology
SINHA, A. K., Civil Engineering
SINHA, A. K., Statistics
SINHA, A. P., Economics
SINHA, B. K., Mathematics
SINHA, G., Psychology
SINHA, H. B. P., Mathematics
SINHA, K., Economics
SINHA, K. S., Mathematics
SINHA, L., Political Science
SINHA, M., Psychology
SINHA, M., Sanskrit
SINHA, M. N., Geology
SINHA, M. P., Zoology
SINHA, M. R., English
SINHA, N., Geology
SINHA, P., Psychology
SINHA, P. K., Mathematics
SINHA, P. K., Mechanical Engineering
SINHA, R. C., Philosophy
SINHA, R. J., Chemistry
SINHA, R. K., Zoology
SINHA, R. M. P., Physics
SINHA, S., English
SINHA, S., Philosophy
SINHA, S. K., Civil Engineering
SINHA, S. S., Education
SINHA, U. K., Botany
SINHA, V., Psychology
SINHA, V. K., Zoology
SINHA, V. N. P., Geography
SIRKAR, J., Economics
SRINIVASAN, P., Physics
SRIVASTAVA, S. K., Zoology
SRIVASTAVA, U. K., Civil Engineering
SUKLA, B., Sociology
TAHAN, K., Persian
THAKUR, B. K., Geology
THAKUR, J., Physics
THAKUR, S. J., English
THAKUR, V. K., History
TIWARI, B., Hindi
TIWARY, N. P., Philosophy
TIWARY, P. N., History
TRIPATHY, A. N., Sanskrit
TULSIYAN, S. S., Economics
VARMA, M., Philosophy
VERMA, C., Zoology
VERMA, J., Psychology
VERMA, M., Economics
VERMA, P. C., Economics
VERMA, R. K., Mathematics
VERMA, S. P., Physics
VERMA, U., Geography
YADAV, A., Physics
YADAV, A. K. P., Physics
YASIN, S., Zoology

CONSTITUENT COLLEGES

Bihar College of Engineering: Mahendru, Patna; f. 1924; 4-year course; 46 teachers; 450 students; Prin. Dr A. K. SINHA.

Bihar National College: Bankipur, Patna 4; tel. (612) 2300619; e-mail principalbnc@puccmail.ac.in; f. 1917; 84 teachers; 1,263 students; Prin. Dr K. K. MALTIAR.

College of Arts and Crafts: Patna 800001; tel. (612) 2235348; e-mail princpalcac@puccmail.ac.in; f. 1938; 5 teachers; 150 students; Prin. Dr ATUL ADITYA PANDEY (acting).

Directorate of Distance Education: tel. (612) 2672941; e-mail contact@ddepu.org; internet www.ddepu.org; 16,000 students; Dir Prof. Dr PRASANT DUTTA.

Institute of Library and Information Science: tel. (612) 2672381; e-mail lib@puccmail.ac.in; Prin. Dr JAIDEVA MISHRA.

Institute of Psychological Research and Service: tel. (612) 2370096; Prin. Dr VEENA SINHA.

Institute of Public Administration: tel. (612) 2670284; e-mail pgpubadmn@puccmail.ac.in; Dir Dr HARIDWAR SHUKLA.

Magadh Mahila College: tel. (612) 2223454; e-mail info@magadhmahilacollege.org; internet www.magadhmahilacollege.org; f. 1946; 30 teachers; 918 students; Prin. Prof. Dr DOLLY SINHA.

National Institute of Technology: tel. (612) 2670631; Prin. Dr U. C. RAY.

Patna College: tel. (612) 2671589; e-mail princpalpc@puccmail.ac.in; f. 1863; parent instn of 3 other colleges; 48 teachers; 2,363 students; Prin. Dr L. K. PRASAD SINGH.

Patna Dental College: tel. (612) 2665130; Prin. Dr D. K. SINGH.

Patna Law College: tel. (612) 2670510; e-mail princpallc@puccmail.ac.in; f. 1906; 20 teachers; 868 students; Prin. Dr RAKESH VERMA.

Patna Medical College: tel. (612) 2300343; internet patnamedicalcollege.com; f. 1925; under admin. control of the Govt of Bihar; 60 teachers; 900 students; Prin. Dr R. K. P. SINGH.

Patna Science College: tel. (612) 6453576; e-mail princpalpsc@puccmail.ac.in; f. 1927; 56 teachers; 1,002 students; Prin. Dr KASHI NATH.

Patna Training College: tel. (612) 2302037; e-mail princpalptc@puccmail.ac.in; f. 1908; 10 teachers; 126 students; Prin. Dr KHAGENDRA KUMAR.

Patna Women's College: tel. (612) 2531186; e-mail princpalpwc@puccmail.ac.in; internet www.patnawomenscollege.in; f. 1940; 44 teachers; 2,309 students; Prin. Dr SIS. DORIS D'SOUZA.

Vanijya Mahavidyalaya: tel. (612) 2670782; e-mail princpalvmv@puccmail.ac.in; f. 1953; 12 teachers; 704 students; Prin. Dr UMESH MISHRA.

Women's Training College: tel. (612) 2218809; e-mail princpalwtc@puccmail.ac.in; f. 1951; 11 teachers; 244 students; Prin. Dr JESSIE GEORGE

PERIYAR UNIVERSITY

Bangalore Main Rd, Salem 636011, Tamil Nadu

Telephone: (427) 2345766
E-mail: info@periyaruniversity.ac.in
Internet: periyaruniversity.ac.in

Founded 1997
State control
Academic year: July to June
Languages of instruction: English, Tamil

Faculties of arts, commerce, education, engineering, languages and science; 66 affiliated colleges

Chancellor: HE GOV. OF TAMIL NADU
Pro-Chancellor: Hon. MIN. FOR EDUCATION, GOVT OF TAMIL NADU
Vice-Chancellor: Dr K. MUTHUCHELIAN
Registrar: Dr P. MATHAIYAN (acting)
Controller of Examinations: Dr A. JAYAKUMAR
Univ. Librarian: Dr N. SUBRAMANIAN

Library of 48,000 vols, 168 periodicals
Number of teachers: 108
Number of students: 1,100

PONDICHERRY UNIVERSITY

R. Venkataraman Nagar, Kalapet, Puducherry 605014

Telephone: (413) 2655179
E-mail: registrar_office@yahoo.com
Internet: www.pondiuni.edu.in

Founded 1985
State control
Languages of instruction: English, Hindi, Tamil
Academic year: July to June

Chancellor: HE VICE-PRES. OF INDIA
Chief Rector: HE GOV. OF PUDUCHERRY
Vice-Chancellor: Prof. J. A. K. TAREEN
Registrar: S. LOGANATHAN
Public Relations Officer: N. ARUNAGIRI
Controller of Examinations: Dr J. SAMPATH
Librarian: Dr R. SAMYUKTHA

Library of 190,954 vols, 377 journals, 31,414 ebooks
Number of teachers: 460 (3,892 in affiliated colleges)
Number of students: 6,000 (Univ.), 44,680 (affiliated colleges and institutes)

Publications: *Indian Journal of Philosophy, Religion & Culture, International Journal of Economics and Management Science, International Journal of Micro-Finance (SOMFER), International Journal of South Asian Studies, International Research Journal of Social Sciences, Journal of Social Sciences and Humanities, Viswabharathi—Sanskrit, Yatra*

DEANS

Madanjeet School of Green Energy Technologies: Prof. J. A. K. TAREEN
Ramanujam School of Mathematics and Computer Sciences: Dr A. M. S. RAMASAMY
School of Education: Prof. M. S. LALITHAMMA
School of Engineering and Technology: Dr V. PRITHIVIRAJ (acting)
School of Humanities: Prof. R. VENGUATTARAMANE
School of Life Sciences: Prof. Dr P. P. MATHUR
School of Management: Prof. M. RAMADASS
School of Mathematical Sciences: Prof. A. M. S. RAMASAMY
School of Media and Communication: Prof. M. S. PANDIAN
School of Medical Sciences: Dr S. MAHADEVAN (acting)
School of Performing Arts: Dr K. A. GUNASEKARAN
School of Physical, Chemical and Applied Sciences: Prof. H. SURYA PRAKASH RAO
School of Social Sciences and Int. Studies: Prof. N. K. JHA
Subramania Bharathi School of Tamil Language and Literature: Prof. Dr R. NALANGILLI

ATTACHED INSTITUTES

Bioinformatics Centre: tel. (413) 2655211; e-mail bicpu2001@yahoo.co.in; internet www.bicpu.edu.in; Dir Dr P. P. MATHUR.

Centre for Human Rights: f. 1999; Dir Dr T. S. N. SASTRY.

Centre for Nehru Studies: Dir Dr B. KRISHNAMURTHY.

Centre for Pollution Control and Energy Technology: Dir Dr S. A. ABBASI.

Centre for Women's Studies: f. 1999; Dir Dr V. T. USHA.

Centre for Yoga Studies: f. 2000; Dir Dr D. SAKTHIGNANAVEL

POTTI SREERAMULU TELUGU UNIVERSITY

Lalitha Kala Kshetram, Public Gardens, Nampally, Hyderabad 500004, Andhra Pradesh

Telephone: (40) 23230435
E-mail: info@teluguuniversity.ac.in
Internet: teluguuniversity.ac.in

Founded 1985
State control

Chancellor: HE GOV. OF ANDHRA PRADESH
Vice-Chancellor: Prof. ANUMAANDLA BHOOMAIAH
Registrar: Prof. BATTU RAMESH
Librarian: L. PANDURANGAIAH

Library of 100,000 vols (55,000 Telugu, 43,000 English), 150 periodicals

DEANS

School of Comparative Studies: Prof. C. MRUNALINI
School of Fine Arts: Prof. C. KRISHNA REDDY
School of Folk and Tribal Lore: Prof. ANUMAANDLA BHOOMAIAH
School of History, Culture and Archaeology: Prof. R. CHANDRA SEKHAR REDDY
School of Language Development: Dr A. USHA DEVI
School of Social and Other Sciences: C. V. B. SUBRAHMANYAM
School of Telugu Literature: Prof. Y. SUDHAKARA RAO

PRESIDENCY UNIVERSITY KOLKATA

86/1 College St, Kolkata 700073, West Bengal

Telephone: (33) 22412738
E-mail: registrar@presiuniv.ac.in
Internet: www.presiuniv.ac.in

Founded 1817 as Hindoo College, Presidency College of Bengal 1885, present name and status 2010
State control
Academic year: July to May (2 semesters)

Depts of Bengali, biological sciences, chemistry, economics, English, geography, geology, Hindi, history, mathematics, philosophy, physics, political science, sociology, statistics

Vice-Chancellor: Prof. MALABIKA SARKAR
Registrar: PRABIR DASGUPTA

Library of 373,422 vols, 152,425 periodicals and multimedia resources
Number of teachers: 199
Number of students: 2,198

Publication: *Prasangiki* (1 a year)

DEANS

Humanities and Social Sciences: Prof. SHANTA DUTTA
Science: SOMAK RAYCHAUDHURY

PUNJAB AGRICULTURAL UNIVERSITY

Ludhiana 141004, Punjab

Telephone: (161) 2401960
E-mail: registrar@pau.edu
Internet: www.pau.edu

Founded 1962
State control
Languages of instruction: English, Punjabi
Academic year: August to July (2 terms)

Chancellor: HE GOV. OF PUNJAB
Vice-Chancellor: Dr BALDEV SINGH DHILLON
Registrar: Dr RAJ KUMAR MAHEY
Controller of Examinations: Dr B. S. SOHAL
Dir for Extension Education: Dr MUKHTAR SINGH GILL
Dir for Research: Dr S. S. GOSAL
Dir for Student Welfare: Dr DEVINDER SINGH CHEEMA

Dean for Postgraduate Studies: Dr GURSHARAN SINGH
Librarian: Dr JASVINDER KAUR SANGHA
Library of 257,724 vols, 6,849 journals, 36,043 theses, 101,311 periodicals, 22 ebooks
Number of teachers: 1,182
Number of students: 2,067
Publications: *Changi Kheti* (12 a year, in Punjabi), *Journal of Research* (4 a year, in English), *Package of Practices for Crops of the Punjab* (2 a year), *Progressive Farming* (12 a year, in English), *Punjab Agricultural Handbook* (1 a year)

DEANS

College of Agricultural Engineering and Technology: Dr PRIT PAL SINGH LUBANA
College of Agriculture: Dr DEVINDER SINGH CHEEMA
College of Basic Science and Humanities: Dr RAJINDER SINGH SIDHU
College of Home Science: Dr NEELAM GREWAL

PUNJAB TECHNICAL UNIVERSITY

Jalandhar–Kapurthala Highway, Kapurthala 144601, Punjab
Telephone: (1822) 662521
E-mail: deanacad@ptu.ac.in
Internet: www.ptu.ac.in
Founded 1997
State control
Courses in biotechnology, engineering, pharmacy, hotel management and airlines, natural sciences, technology; 300 affiliated colleges, 1,500 learning centres
Chancellor: HE GOV. OF PUNJAB
Vice-Chancellor: Dr RAJNEESH ARORA
Registrar: SAROJINI GAUTAM SHARDA
Library of 2,000 vols

PUNJABI UNIVERSITY

Patiala 147002, Punjab
Telephone: (175) 3046366
E-mail: regpup@pbi.ac.in
Internet: www.punjabiuniversity.ac.in
Founded 1962, present status 1969
State control
Languages of instruction: English, Punjabi
Academic year: July to May (3 terms)
Chancellor: HE GOV. OF PUNJAB
Vice-Chancellor: Dr JASPAL SINGH
Registrar: Dr A. S. CHAWLA
Dean for Academic Affairs: Dr S. S. TIWANA
Dean for College Devt Ccl: Dr J. A. KHAN
Dean for Research: Dr JASWINDER SINGH
Dean for Students Welfare: Dr KULBIR SINGH DHILLON
Dir for Public Relations: Dr GURMEET SINGH MAAN
Librarian: Dr SAROJ BALA
Library of 500,000 books, 600 journals
Number of teachers: 500
Number of students: 9,000
Publication: *Journal of Religious Studies* (4 a year)

DEANS

Faculty of Arts and Culture: Dr GURNAM SINGH
Faculty of Business Studies: Dr J. S. PASRICHA
Faculty of Education and Information Science: Dr KIRANDEEP KAUR
Faculty of Engineering and Technology: Dr S. S. TIWANA
Faculty of Languages: Dr TEJINDER KAUR
Faculty of Law: Dr HARPAL KAUR KHEHRA
Faculty of Life Sciences: Dr ARUNA BHATIA
Faculty of Medicine: Dr NARINDER KAUR MULTANI
Faculty of Physical Sciences: Dr H. S. BHATTI
Faculty of Social Sciences: Dr S. S. TIWANA

RABINDRA BHARATI UNIVERSITY

Emerald Bower Campus: 56A Barrackpore Trunk Rd, Kolkata 700050, West Bengal
Jorasanko Campus: 6/4, Dwarkanath Tagore Lane, Kolkata 700007, West Bengal
Telephone: (33) 25568019
E-mail: registrar@rbu.ac.in
Internet: www.rbu.ac.in
Founded 1962
State control
Languages of instruction: English, Bengali
Academic year: June to May (3 terms)
Chancellor: HE GOV. OF WEST BENGAL
Vice-Chancellor: Prof. KARUNA SINDHU DAS
Registrar: Dr TAPATI MUKHERJEE
Dean for Students Welfare: Dr AVIK LAHIRI
Public Relations Officer: SURANJANA BHATTACHARYA
Librarian: SATYABRATA GHOSAL
Library of 92,500 vols, 258 periodicals
Number of teachers: 165
Number of students: 6,759
Publications: departmental journals (1 a year: Bengali, Sanskrit, English, Education, Economics, Library and Information Science, Vedic Studies, Study and Research on Tagore, Rabindra Sangeet), *Rabindra Bharati Journal* (1 a year, in English), *Rabindra Bharati University Patrika* (1 a year, in Bengali)

DEANS

Faculty of Arts: Prof. SANAT KUMAR GHOSH
Faculty of Fine Arts: Dr SOMNATH SINHA
Faculty of Visual Arts: PARAG RAY

RAJENDRA AGRICULTURAL UNIVERSITY

Pusa, Samastipur 848125, Bihar
Telephone: (6274) 240226
E-mail: info@pusavarsity.org.in
Internet: www.pusavarsity.org.in
Founded 1970
State control
Languages of instruction: English, Hindi
Academic year: July to June (2 terms)
Chancellor: HE GOV. OF BIHAR
Vice-Chancellor: Dr V. P. SINGH
Registrar: Dr R. C. RAI
Dir for Admin.: DEBASHISH DUTTA
Dir for Extension Education: Dr J. P. UPADHYAY
Dir for Research: Dr V. P. SINGH
Dir of Students Welfare: Dr S. K. CHANDRA
Librarian: Dr B. N. MISHRA
Library of 54,000 vols and 2,000 MSS
Number of teachers: 400
Number of students: 1,200
Publications: *Adhunik Kisan* (12 a year), *Research Journal* (4 a year)

DEANS

Faculty of Agricultural Engineering: Dr A. K. P. SINGH
Faculty of Agriculture: Dr MADAN SINGH
Faculty of Basic Science and Humanities: Dr V. K. SHAHI
Faculty of Home Science: Dr ARTI SINHA
Faculty of Veterinary Science: Dr J. N. SINGH
Postgraduate Studies: Dr V. K. CHOUDHARY

PROFESSORS

Faculty of Agricultural Engineering:
- KUMAR, A., Soil Conservation
- RAM, R. B., Farm Machinery

Faculty of Agriculture:
- CHOUDHARY, L. B., Plant Breeding
- MISHRA, S. S., Agronomy
- OJHA, K. L., Plant Pathology
- PRASAD, B., Soil Science
- SAKAL, R., Soil Science
- SHARMA, R. P. ROY, Agronomy
- SINGH, B. K., Agronomy
- SINGH, R. K., Seed Technology
- THAKUR, R., Plant Breeding
- YAZDANI, S. S., Entomology and Agricultural Zoology

Faculty of Veterinary Science:
- MOHAN, M., Animal Breeding and Genetics
- PRASAD, C. B., Veterinary Microbiology
- SINGH, M. K., Veterinary Pharmacology
- SINHA, R. R. P., Animal Nutrition
- SRIVASTAVA, P. S., Veterinary Parasitology

ATTACHED COLLEGES

College of Agricultural Engineering: f. 1983; depts of farm machinery, farm power and renewable energy, irrigation and drainage engineering, post-harvest technology and agricultural structures, soil and water conservation engineering; Dean Dr A. P. MISHRA.

College of Basic Sciences and Humanities: f. 1981; depts of biochemistry and chemistry, botany and plant physiology, genetics and molecular biology, language, mathematics and computer application, microbiology, physics, statistics; Dean Dr V. K. SHAHI.

College of Fisheries: Dholi; f. 1984; Prin. Dr S. C. RAI.

College of Home Science: Pusa; f. 1982; depts of child devt, clothing and textiles, family resource management, foods and nutrition; Dean Dr MEERA SINGH.

Tirhut College of Agriculture: Dholi, Muzaffarpur; f. 1960; Prin. Dr U. K. MISHRA

RAJIV GANDHI PROUDYOGIKI VISHWAVIDYALAYA/STATE TECHNOLOGICAL UNIVERSITY OF MADHYA PRADESH
(Rajiv Gandhi Technical University)

Airport By-pass, Gandhi Nagar, Bhopal 462036, Madhya Pradesh
Telephone: (755) 2678899
E-mail: vc@rgtu.net
Internet: www.rgtu.net
Founded 1998
State control
Vice-Chancellor: Prof. PIYUSH TRIVEDI
Rector: Prof. V. K. SETHI
Registrar: Dr A. K. S. BHADORIA
Controller of Examinations: Dr A. K. SINGH
Library of 24,720 vols
Number of students: 130,000

DEANS

Faculty of Applied Sciences: Prof. ANIL GOYAL
Faculty of Computer and Information Technology: Prof. SANJAY SILAKARI
Faculty of Electrical and Electronics: Prof. S. C. CHOUBEY
Faculty of Industrial Technology: Prof. MUKESH PANDEY
Faculty of Pharmacy: Prof. T. R. SAINI

RAJIV GANDHI UNIVERSITY

Rono Hills, Doimukh 791112, Arunachal Pradesh
Telephone: (360) 2277253
E-mail: registrar@rgu.ac.in
Internet: www.rgu.ac.in
Founded 1984, as Arunachal Univ.; current name adopted 2006
State control
Language of instruction: English
Academic year: June to May
Chancellor: Prof. MRINAL MIRI

Vice-Chancellor: Prof. TAMO MIBANG
Registrar: AMITAVA MITRA
Asst Librarian: D. K. PANDEY

Library of 100,000 vols, 200 periodicals
Number of teachers: 100
Number of students: 500

DEANS

Faculty of Education: Prof. K. C. KAPOOR
Faculty of Environmental Sciences: Prof. R. S. YADAVA
Faculty of Languages: Prof. N. NAGARAJU
Faculty of Management: Prof. R. C. PARIDA
Faculty of Social Sciences: Prof. N. C. ROY

RAJIV GANDHI UNIVERSITY OF HEALTH SCIENCES, KARNATAKA

Fourth 'T' Block, Jayanagar, Bengaluru 560041, Karnataka
Telephone: (80) 26961926
E-mail: drpsp@rguhs.ac.in
Internet: www.rguhs.ac.in

Founded 1996
State control
Courses in anaesthesia, ayurveda, cardiology, dentistry, homeopathy, hospital management, medical laboratory technology, medicine, naturopathy and yogic sciences, nursing, perfusion technology, pharmacy, physiotherapy, psycho-social rehabilitation, radiography, renal dialysis technology, respiratory technology, surgery, unani medicine
Chancellor: HE GOV. OF KARNATAKA
Vice-Chancellor: Dr K. S. SRIPRAKASH
Registrar: Dr D. PREM KUMAR
Librarian: Dr R. RAMA RAJ URS

RANCHI UNIVERSITY

Shaheed Chowk, Ranchi 834001, Jharkhand
Telephone: (651) 2208553
E-mail: admin@ranchiuniversity.org.in
Internet: ranchiuniversity.org.in

Founded 1960
State control
Chancellor: HE GOV. OF JHARKHAND
Vice-Chancellor: Prof. Dr A. A. KHAN
Pro-Vice-Chancellor: Dr V. P. SHARAN
Registrar: Dr JYOTI KUMAR
Controller of Examinations: Dr A. K. MAHTO
Dean of Student Welfare: Dr C. S. P. LUGUN

Library of 100,000 vols
Number of teachers: *c.* 2,000
Number of students: 67,500

Publications: *Journal of Agricultural Science*, *Journal of Historical Research*, *Journal of Social Research*, *Political Scientist*, *Research Journal of Philosophy*, *The Geographical Outlook*, *The University Journal*

DEANS

Faculty of Commerce: Dr S. N. L. DAS
Faculty of Education: Dr APARAJITA JHA
Faculty of Engineering: Dr A. K. MISHRA
Faculty of Humanities: Dr BIMLA KUMARI
Faculty of Law: RAJ KUMAR WALIA
Faculty of Medicine: Prof. Dr S. N. CHOUDHARY
Faculty of Science: Dr M. M. P. SINGH
Faculty of Social Sciences: Prof. J. P. SINGH

RANI DURGAVATI VISHWAVIDYALAYA, JABALPUR
(Rani Durgavati University, Jabalpur)

Saraswati Vihar, Pachpedi, Jabalpur 482001, Madhya Pradesh
Telephone: (761) 2600567
E-mail: rdvvcc1@rediffmail.com
Internet: www.rdunijbpin.org

Founded 1957 as Jabalpur Univ., current name adopted 1983
State control
Languages of instruction: English, Hindi
Academic year: July to April (4 terms)

Chancellor: HE GOV. OF MADHYA PRADESH
Vice-Chancellor: Prof. J. M. KELLER
Dir for College Devt Ccl: Prof. P. L. AHIRWAR
Dean of Student Welfare: Prof. SURENDRA SINGH
Registrar: Dr U. N. SHUKLA
Librarian: Y. L. CHOPRA

Library of 183,000 vols
Number of teachers: 1,053
Number of students: 95,000

DEANS

Faculty of Arts: Prof. T. N. SHUKLA
Faculty of Ayurveda: Prof. G. L. TITONI
Faculty of Commerce: Dr S. P. GUPTA
Faculty of Education: (vacant)
Faculty of Homeopathic Medicine and Surgery: (vacant)
Faculty of Home Science: (vacant)
Faculty of Law: (vacant)
Faculty of Life Sciences: Prof. ANJANA SHARMA
Faculty of Management: (vacant)
Faculty of Mathematical Science: (vacant)
Faculty of Medicine: (vacant)
Faculty of Science: Prof. J. M. KELLER
Faculty of Social Sciences: (vacant)

RASHTRASANT TUKADOJI MAHARAJ NAGPUR UNIVERSITY

Chhatrapati Shivaji Maharaj Admin. Premises, Rabindranath Tagore Marg, Nagpur 440001, Maharashtra
Telephone: (712) 2522456
E-mail: info@nagpuruniversity.org
Internet: www.nagpuruniversity.org

Founded 1923, fmrly Nagpur Univ.
State control
Languages of instruction: English, Hindi, Marathi
Academic year: June to March (2 terms)

Chancellor: HE GOV. OF MAHARASHTRA
Vice-Chancellor: Dr VILAS SHRIDHAR SAPKAL
Registrar: Dr MAHESHKUMAR YENKIE
Controller of Examinations: Dr KANE
Librarian: Dr P. S. G. KUMAR

Library of 365,833 vols, 14,313 MSS
Number of teachers: 4,074
Number of students: 95,664

DEANS

Faculty of Arts: A. K. DEY
Faculty of Ayurvedic Medicine: S. SHARMA
Faculty of Commerce: N. H. KHATRI
Faculty of Education: R. S. DAGAR
Faculty of Engineering and Technology: H. THAKARE
Faculty of Home Science: Dr A. G. MOHARIL
Faculty of Law: SUNDARAM
Faculty of Medicine: Dr W. B. TAYADE
Faculty of Science: Dr T. M. KARDE
Faculty of Social Sciences: V. H. GHORPADE

CONSTITUENT COLLEGES

Bar. S. K. Wankhede College of Education: Nagpur; tel. (712) 2520775; e-mail bskw@rediffmail.com; f. 1945; 16 teachers; 320 students; Prin. Dr VANDANA DIWAKAR MANAPURE.

Dr B. R. Ambedkar College of Law: f. 1925; 10 teachers; 2,571 students; Prin. Dr J. L. APARAJIT.

Laxminarayan Institute of Technology: tel. (712) 2561107; e-mail yenkiemskm@rediffmail.com; internet www.nagpuruniversity.org/litnagpur; f. 1942; 50 teachers; 510 students; Dir Dr MAHESHKUMAR YENKIE

SAMBALPUR UNIVERSITY

Jyoti Vihar, Burla, Sambalpur 768019, Orissa
Telephone: (663) 2430157
E-mail: registrar@suniv.ac.in
Internet: www.suniv.ac.in

Founded 1967
State control
Language of instruction: English
Academic year: June to May

Chancellor: GOV. OF ORISSA
Vice-Chancellor: Prof. BISHNU C. BARIK
Registrar: SUDHANSHU SEKHAR RATH
Dir for College Devt Ccl: Prof. KUMUD RANJAN PANIGRAHI
Controller of Examination: Dr MANAS RANJAN PUJARI
Librarian: RAJENDRA KUMAR THATY

Library of 122,523 vols, 15,000 periodicals
Number of teachers: 1,653
Number of students: 36,225

Publications: *Journal* (Science, 1 a year), *Journal of Humanities* (1 a year), *Saptarshi* (4 a year)

DEANS

Faculty of Arts: Prof. S. NANDA
Faculty of Commerce: Prof. D. P. NAYAK
Faculty of Education: (vacant)
Faculty of Engineering: Dr R. K. MISHRA
Faculty of Law: Prof. G. K. RATH
Faculty of Medicine: Prof. A. K. SARANGI
Faculty of Science: Dr M. K. BEHERA

SAMPURNANAND SANSKRIT VISHVAVIDYALAYA
(Sampurnanand Sanskrit University)

Varanasi 221002, Uttar Pradesh
Telephone: (542) 2204089; (542) 2206617
E-mail: info@ssvv.ac.in
Internet: www.ssvv.ac.in

Founded 1958
State control
Academic year: August to June

Chancellor: HE GOV. OF UTTAR PRADESH
Vice-Chancellor: Prof. BINDA PRASAD MISHRA
Registrar: Dr RAJNEESH KUMAR SHUKLA
Dean of Students Welfare: Prof. RAMESH KUMAR DWIVEDI
Proctor: Dr KEDARNATH TRIPATHI
Dir of Research: Dr RAJA RAM SHUKLA
Librarian: Dr SURYAKANT

Library of 262,000 vols, 1m. MSS of Sanskrit text
Number of students: 35,000

DEANS

Adhunika Gyan Vijyana Faculty: Dr VISHVAMBHAR NATH
Faculty of Philosophy: Prof. RAM KISHORE TRIPATHI
Sahitya Sanskriti Faculty: Prof. GANGADHAR PANDA
Sramana Vidya Faculty: Prof. YADUNATH DUBEY
Veda-Vedanga Faculty: Prof. SADANAND SHUKLA

SARDAR PATEL UNIVERSITY

University Rd, Vallabh Vidyanagar, Anand 388120, Gujarat
Telephone: (2692) 226812
E-mail: vcspu@yahoo.co.in
Internet: www.spuvvn.edu

Founded 1955
State control
Languages of instruction: English, Gujarati, Hindi
Academic year: June to April (2 terms)
Chancellor: HE GOV. OF GUJARAT

Vice-Chancellor: Prof. HARISH PADH
Registrar: TUSHAR MAJMUDAR (acting)
Librarian: (vacant)

Library of 231,000 vols
Number of teachers: 162
Number of students: 45,634

Publications: *Artha-Vikas* (Economics Journal), *Journal of Education and Psychology*, *Mimamsa* (Journal of English Literature), *Prajna* (Journal of Basic Sciences), *Prajna* (Journal of Social Sciences and Business Studies), *Sheel Shrutam* (12 a year)

DEANS

Faculty of Arts: Dr H. P. TRIVEDI
Faculty of Business Studies: Dr KETKI SHETH
Faculty of Education: Dr V. T. BHAMWARI
Faculty of Engineering and Technology: Prin.: Dr L. M. MANOCHA
Faculty of Home Science: Dr REKHA EMANUEL
Faculty of Homoeopathy: Dr LEENA DIGHE
Faculty of Law: APRURVA C. PATHAK
Faculty of Management: Dr R. P. PATEL
Faculty of Medicine: Dr SHIRISH H. SHRIVASTAVA
Faculty of Pharmaceutical Science: Dr D. K. RAVAL
Faculty of Science: Dr D. S. RAJ

SARDAR VALLABH BHAI PATEL UNIVERSITY OF AGRICULTURE AND TECHNOLOGY

Modipuram, Meerut 250110, Uttar Pradesh
Telephone: (121) 2888502
E-mail: university@svbpuniversitymerrut.org
Internet: www.svbpmeerut.ac.in

Founded 2000
State control

Chancellor: HE GOV. OF UTTAR PRADESH
Vice-Chancellor: Prof. A. K. BAKHSHI
Registrar: Dr C. S. PRASAD
Dean of Postgraduate Studies: Dr DEVI SINGH
Dean of Student Welfare: Dr J. YADAV
Dir for Experiment Station: Dr S. A. KARKHI
Dir for Extension: Dr BABU RAM

Library of 6,623 vols, 242 periodicals

DEANS

College of Agriculture: Dr RAGHUVIR SINGH
College of Biotechnology: Dr ANIL SIROHI (acting)

SAURASHTRA UNIVERSITY

Univ. Campus, University Rd, Rajkot 360005, Gujarat
Telephone: (281) 2576347
E-mail: registrar@sauuni.ernet.in
Internet: www.saurashtrauniversity.edu

Founded 1967
State control
Languages of instruction: English, Gujarati, Hindi
Academic year: June to March (2 terms)

Chancellor: HE GOV. OF GUJARAT STATE
Vice-Chancellor: Dr MAHENDRABHAI K PADALIA
Pro-Vice-Chancellor: (vacant)
Registrar: R. G. PARMAR
Controller of Examinations: JAGDISH M. MAMTORA
Librarian: NILESH N. SONI

Library of 171,577 vols, 230 periodicals
Number of teachers: 3,614 (incl. affiliated colleges)
Number of students: 140,234 (incl. affiliated colleges)

DEANS

Faculty of Architecture: (vacant)
Faculty of Arts: S. J. JHALA (acting)
Faculty of Business Management: Dr P. L. CHAUHAN
Faculty of Commerce: R. M. TALVANIA
Faculty of Education: B. R. RAMANUJ
Faculty of Engineering: S. PARIKH
Faculty of Home Science: V. CHHICHHIYA
Faculty of Homeopathy: Dr B. M. PANDA (acting)
Faculty of Law: N. C. SHUKLA (acting)
Faculty of Medicine: Dr D. K. SHAH
Faculty of Rural Studies: D. R. MARTHAK
Faculty of Science: Dr G. BHIMANI

SHER-E-KASHMIR UNIVERSITY OF AGRICULTURAL SCIENCES AND TECHNOLOGY OF JAMMU

Main Campus Chatha, Jammu 180009, Jammu and Kashmir
Telephone: (191) 2263714
E-mail: vc@skuast.org
Internet: www.skuast.org

Founded 1999
State control
Language of instruction: English
Academic year: August to July

Chancellor: HE GOV. OF JAMMU AND KASHMIR
Vice-Chancellor: Dr B. MISHRA
Registrar: B. B. GUPTA
Librarian: Dr V. SREENIVASULU

Library of 24,603 vols, 163 periodical titles
Number of teachers: 169
Number of students: 660

DEANS

Faculty of Agriculture: Dr AJAY KOUL
Faculty of Veterinary Sciences and Animal Husbandry: Dr A. R. NAZKI

SHER-E-KASHMIR UNIVERSITY OF AGRICULTURAL SCIENCES AND TECHNOLOGY OF KASHMIR

Shalimar Campus, Srinagar 191121, Jammu and Kashmir
Telephone: (194) 2461271
E-mail: vcskuastk@jk.nic.in
Internet: www.skuastkashmir.ac.in

Founded 1982
State control
Languages of instruction: English, Urdu
Academic year: August to July

Chancellor: HE GOV. OF JAMMU AND KASHMIR
Vice-Chancellor: Dr TEJ PARTAP
Registrar: Dr F. A. ZAKI
Dir for Extension Education: Dr AFIFA S. KAMILI
Dir for Research: Dr SHAFIQ A. WANI
Univ. Librarian: BASHIR AHMAD

Library of 66,243 vols, 110 periodicals
Number of teachers: 420
Number of students: 928

Publication: *SKUAST-K Journal of Research*

DEANS

Faculty of Agriculture: Dr MUSHTAQ AHMAD
Faculty of Fisheries: Dr MASOOD-UL-HASAN BALKHI
Faculty of Forestry: Dr M. Y. ZARGAR
Faculty of Postgraduate Studies: Dr BADRUL HASAN
Faculty of Veterinary Science and Animal Husbandry: Dr SHABIR AHMAD

SHIVAJI UNIVERSITY, KOLHAPUR

Vidyanagar, Kolhapur 416004, Maharashtra
Telephone: (231) 2609000
E-mail: registrar@unishivaji.ac.in
Internet: www.unishivaji.ac.in

Founded 1962
State control
Languages of instruction: English, Marathi
Academic year: June to April (2 terms)

Chancellor: HE GOV. OF MAHARASHTRA
Vice-Chancellor: Dr N. J. PAWAR
Pro-Vice-Chancellor: (vacant)
Registrar: Dr D. V. MULEY
Controller of Examinations: Dr B. M. HIRDEKAR
Librarian: R. K. KAMAT (acting)

Library of 248,502 vols, 6,923 MSS, 298 periodicals
Number of teachers: 3,483
Number of students: 200,000

Publication: *University Journal* (Humanities and Social Sciences sections)

DEANS

Faculty of Arts and Fine Arts: Dr ANIL PANDURANG GAVALI
Faculty of Ayurvedic and Homeopathic Medicine: (vacant)
Faculty of Commerce: Dr RAMCHANDRA GANPAT PHADATARE
Faculty of Education: MEGHA VISHRAM GULAVANI
Faculty of Engineering and Technology: SURESH MARUTI SAWANT
Faculty of Law: (vacant)
Faculty of Medicine: Dr RAMKRISHNA AYCHIT
Faculty of Science: Dr CHANDRAKANT JAGANNATH KHILARE
Faculty of Social Sciences: Dr JAGANNATH SHAMRAO PATIL

CONSTITUENT CENTRES

Centre for Community Development: tel. (231) 2690571; f. 2000; Dir MANJUSHA DESHPANDE.

Centre of Gandhian Studies: f. 2000; Dir Dr R. B. PATIL.

Centre for Women's Studies: f. 2000; Dir Dr MEDHA NANIVADEKAR.

Shahu Research Centre: f. 1970; Dir Dr M. P. PATIL

SHREEMATI NATHIBAI DAMODAR THACKERSEY WOMEN'S UNIVERSITY

1 Nathibai Thackersey Rd, New Marine Lines, Mumbai 400020, Maharashtra
Telephone: (22) 22031879
E-mail: vc@sndt.ac.in
Internet: www.sndt.ac.in

Founded 1916
State control
Languages of instruction: English, Gujarati, Marathi, Hindi
Academic year: June to March (2 terms)

Chancellor: HE GOV. OF MAHARASHTRA
Vice-Chancellor: Dr VASUDHA KAMAT
Pro-Vice-Chancellor: Dr VANDANA CHAKRAVATI
Registrar: Dr MADHU MADAN
Controller of Examinations: Dr MANDHARE
Librarian: Dr SUSHAMA POWDWAL

Library of 335,000 vols
Number of teachers: 744 full-time, 238 part-time
Number of students: 50,000

DEANS

Faculty of Arts: Dr SHASHI KASHYAP
Faculty of Commerce: Dr KALYANI VENKATESHWARAN
Faculty of Education: Dr LEENA DESHPANDE
Faculty of Fine Arts: AVIRAJ TAYADE
Faculty of Home Sciences: Dr SHOBHA UDIPI
Faculty of Library Science: PARUL ZAVERI
Faculty of Nursing: NANCY FERNANDES
Faculty of Social Sciences: Dr MANGALA JUNGALE

CONSTITUENT COLLEGES

C. U. Shah College of Pharmacy: Sir Vithaldas Vidyavihar Juhu Rd, Mumbai 400049; tel. (22) 26608551; e-mail cuscp@yahoo.co.in; f. 1980; Prin. Dr S. Y. GABHE.

Janakidevi Bajaj Institute of Management Studies: Sir Vithaldas Thackersey Vidya Vihar, Juhu Rd, Mumbai 400049, Maharshtra; tel. (22) 26606626; e-mail jdbims@gmail.com; internet www.jdbims.net; f. 1997; Dir Prof. Dr GULNAR H. SHARMA.

Leelabai Thackersey College of Nursing: 1 Nathibai Thackersey Rd, Mumbai 400020, Maharashtra; tel. (22) 22087422; e-mail ltcn@rediffmail.com; internet ltcnsndt.org; f. 1952; Prin. ALKA KALAMBI.

Premcoonverbai Vithaldas Damodar Thackersey College of Education for Women: tel. (22) 22063267; e-mail pvdtce@sndt.ac.in; f. 1959; Prin. Dr HARSHA MANCHANT.

Premlila Vithaldas Polytechnic: Sir Vithaldas Vidyavihar Juhu Rd, Santacruz (W), Mumbai 400049; tel. (22) 26608676; e-mail pvp@pvpsndt.org; internet www.pvpsndt.org; f. 1976; Prin. VARSHA JAIN (acting).

Shree Hansraj Pragji Thackersey School of Library Science: e-mail shptsndt@gmail.com; f. 1961; Prin. Prof. SUSHAMA POWDWAL.

Shreemati Nathibai Damodar Thackersey College of Arts, and Shreemati Champaben Bhogilal College of Commerce and Economics for Women: tel. (22) 22093789; e-mail bbpsndt@gmail.com; f. 1931; Prin. Dr B. B. PRADHAN.

Shreemati Nathibai Damodar Thackersey College of Arts and Commerce for Women: Karve Rd, Maharshi Karve Vidyavihar, Pune 411038; f. 1916; Prin. (vacant).

Shreemati Nathibai Damodar Thackersey College of Education for Women: Karve Rd, Maharshi Karve Vidyarihar, Pune 411038; tel. (22) 25433416; e-mail sndt_education_pune@yahoo.co.in; f. 1964; Prin. Dr LEENA DESHPANDE.

Shreemati Nathibai Damodar Thackersey College of Home Science: Karve Rd, Pune 411038, Maharashtra; tel. (22) 25432097; e-mail principal@sndthsc.com; internet www.sndthsc.com; f. 1968; Prin. VEENA SANT.

Sir Vithaldas Thackersey College of Home Science: Juhu Tara Rd, Santacruz (W), Mumbai 400049, Maharashtra; tel. (22) 26602504; e-mail svtcollegehomescience@yahoo.co.in; internet www.svt.edu.in; f. 1959; Prin. Dr JAGMEET MADAN (acting).

Usha Mittal Institute of Technology: Juhu–Tara Rd, Sir Vithaldas Vidyavihar Juhu Rd, Santacruz (W), Mumbai 400049, Maharashtra; tel. (22) 26606040; e-mail principal@umit.ac.in; internet www.umit.ac.in; Dir Dr SANJAY S. PAWAR

SHRI JAGANNATH SANSKRIT VISHWAVIDYALAYA
(Shri Jagannath Sanskrit University)

Shri Vihar, Puri 752003, Orissa

Telephone: (6752) 251669
E-mail: sanskrit.university@yahoo.co.in
Internet: sjsv.nic.in

Founded 1981
State control

Depts of advaita vedanta, computer application, dharmashastra, jyotirvigyan, nyaya, physical education, sahitya, sarvadarshan, veda, vedanta, vyakarana

Chancellor: HE GOV. OF ORRISA
Vice-Chancellor: Prof. ALEKHA CHANDRA SARANGI
Registrar: Dr NILAKANTHA PATI
Registrar: Dr R. C. DASH
Controller of Examinations: DEBI PRASANNA RATH
Librarian: Prof. JAYA KRUSHNA MISHRA (acting)

Library of 35,000 vols, 500 journals, 200 MSS

Publication: *Jagannath Jyotih* (irregular)

SHRI MATA VAISHNO DEVI UNIVERSITY

Sub-Post Office Kakryal, Katra 182320, Jammu and Kashmir

Telephone: (1991) 285535
E-mail: info@smvdu.ac.in
Internet: smvdu.net.in

Founded 2004
State control

Chancellor: HE GOV. OF JAMMU AND KASHMIR
Vice-Chancellor: Prof. R. N. K. BAMEZAI
Registrar: ROOP AVTAR KAUR
Dean of Students: Prof. R. S. MISRA
Librarian: SUBRATA DEB

Library: approx. 25,000 vols, 1250 online periodicals and 87 print periodicals, e-resources: 500 CDs/DVDs, databases: ABI Inform Global, MathSciNet, EIS Statistical, Memberships: INDEST-AICTE CONSORTIUM, DELNET

DEANS

College of Engineering: Prof. M. L. GARG
College of Management: Prof. D. MUKHOPADHYAY
College of Philosophy, Culture and Languages: Prof. R. S. MISRA
College of Sciences: Prof. VIJESHWAR VERMA

SIDO KANHU MURMU UNIVERSITY

S. P. College Rd, Dumka 814101, Jharkhand

Telephone: (6434) 223006
E-mail: info.skmu@gmail.com
Internet: skmu.edu.in

Founded 1992 as Siddhu Kanhu Univ., current name adopted 2000
State control
Academic year: June to May

Vice-Chancellor: Dr VICTOR TIGGA
Pro-Vice-Chancellor: Dr ARVIND KUMAR
Dean for Student Welfare: Dr MANOJ KUMAR SINHA
Registrar: Dr A. N. PATHAK (acting)
Librarian: Dr AJIT KUMAR SINGH

SIKKIM MANIPAL UNIVERSITY OF HEALTH, MEDICAL AND TECHNOLOGICAL SCIENCES

Fifth Mile, Tadong, Gangtok 737102, Sikkim

Telephone: (3592) 270294
E-mail: study@smu.edu.in
Internet: www.smu.edu.in

Founded 1995
State control
Academic year: August to July

Depts of applied sciences, engineering, management, medical science, nursing, philosophy, physiotherapy

Chancellor: HE GOV. OF SIKKIM
Pro-Chancellor: Dr RAMDAS PAI
Vice-Chancellor: Dr SOMNATH MISHRA
Registrar: NAMRATA THAPA.

CONSTITUENT INSTITUTIONS

School of Basic and Applied Sciences: Majitar, Rangpo 737132, East Sikkim; internet sbas.smu.edu.in.

Sikkim Manipal College of Nursing: Fifth Mile, Tadong, Gangtok 737102, Sikkim; internet smcon.smu.edu.in; f. 2001; Prin. MRIDULA DAS.

Sikkim Manipal College of Physiotherapy: Fifth Mile, Tadong, Gangtok 737102, Sikkim; internet smcpt.smu.edu.in; f. 2001; Prin. Dr NIKITA JOSHI.

Sikkim Manipal Institute of Medical Science: Fifth Mile, Tadong, Gangtok 737102, Sikkim; e-mail smims_dean@yahoo.com; internet smims.smu.edu.in; Dean Dr RAVINDER NATH SALHAN.

Sikkim Manipal Institute of Technology: Majitar Rangpo 737132, East Sikkim; tel. (3592) 246353; internet smit.smu.edu.in; f. 1997; Dir Dr SOMNATH MISHRA; Dean Prof. Dr ACHINTYA CHOUDHURY

SREE SANKARACHARYA UNIVERSITY OF SANSKRIT

Sree Sankarapuram, Ernakulam, Kalady 683574, Kerala

Telephone: (484) 2463380
E-mail: sureg@sancharnet.in
Internet: www.ssus.ac.in

Founded 1993
State control
Academic year: June to April

Faculties of arts, education, Sanskrit studies and social sciences; courses in Mohiniyattom, Bharatanatyam, mural painting, Vedic studies, Sanskrit (core); regional centres in Ettumanoor, Kalady, Koyilandy, Panmana, Payyannur, Thiruvananthapuram, Thrissur, Thuravoor, Tirur

Chancellor: HE GOV. OF KERALA
Pro-Chancellor: Hon. MIN. FOR EDUCATION AND CULTURE
Vice-Chancellor: Dr J. PRASAD
Pro-Vice-Chancellor: Dr S. RAJASEKHARAN
Registrar: Dr K. RAMACHANDRAN
Prin. and Dean for Studies: Dr N. K. SANKARAN

Library of 53,000 vols, 125 periodicals, 350 MSS

SRI KRISHNADEVARAYA UNIVERSITY

Sri Venkateswarapuram PO, Anantapur 515003, Andhra Pradesh

Telephone: (8554) 255700
E-mail: registrar@skuniversity.org
Internet: www.skuniversity.org

Founded 1968, univ. status 1981
Language of instruction: English
Academic year: December to October

Chancellor: HE GOV. OF ANDHRA PRADESH
Vice-Chancellor: Prof. K. RAMAKRISHNA REDDY
Registrar: Dr N. RAVINDRANATH
Dean of College Devt Ccl: Prof. P. INDIRA
Controller of Examinations: P. SAMUEL
Dir for Centre for Distance Education: Prof. B PANEESWARA RAJU
Librarian: Dr P. KAMAIAK

Library of 114,000 vols, 190 periodicals
Number of teachers: 154
Number of students: 1,500

DEANS

Faculty of Engineering: (vacant)
Faculty of Languages and Literature: Prof. H. S. BRAHMANADA
Faculty of Law: Prof. S. SESHAIAH
Faculty of Life Sciences: Prof. K. RADHAKRISHNAIAH
Faculty of Management: Prof. C. R. REDDY RAO
Faculty of Physical Sciences: Prof. D. R. V. PRASAD RAO

Faculty of Social Sciences: Prof. C. U. MOHAN

PROFESSORS

ANKI REDDY, K. C., Mathematics
BASHA MOHIDEEN, M., Zoology
BRAHMAJI RAO, S., Chemistry
ENOCK, K., Telugu
GHOUSE, M., Law
GOPAL, B. R., History
KAMESWARA RAO, A.
KANTHA RAO, M. L., Economics
KOTESWARA RAO, T., Telugu
KRISHNA, D. V., Mathematics
MANOHARA MURTHY, N., Physics
NAIDU, V. T., Rural Development
NARAYANA, N., Economics
PRAKASHA RAO, C. G., Botany
RAGHUNATHA SARMA, S., Telugu
RAMA MURTHY, V., Physics
RAMAKRISHNA RAO, A., English
RAMAKRISHNA RAO, P., Biochemistry
RAMAKRISHNA RAO, T. V., Physics
RAMAVATHARAM, S. I., Law
SEETHARAMASWAMY, R., Mathematics
SHARMA, D. P., Commerce
SUBBA RAO, C., English
SUBBARAMAIAH, S., Economics
SUBBI REDDY, T., Commerce
SUBRAHMANYAM, S. V., Physics
SUDARSHAN RAO, T. P., Law
SWAMINATHAN, E., Geography
TIRUPATHI NAIDU, V., Rural Development
VENKATA REDDY, C., Economics
VENKATA REDDY, D., Chemistry
VENKATA REDDY, K., English
VENKATA REDDY, K., Rural Development
VENKATASIVA MURTHY, K. N., Mathematics

POSTGRADUATE CENTRE

SKU, Kurnool: f. 1977; library of 25,000 vols, 30 periodicals; courses in area planning and regional devt in economics, microprocessors in physics, MSc. computer science and management studies, natural products in chemistry, operations research and statistical quality control, Telugu; Dir Prof. C. UMASANKAR

SRI PADMAVATHI MAHILA VISVAVIDYALAYAM/WOMEN'S UNIVERSITY
(Sri Padmavathi Women's University)

Tirupati 517502, Andhra Pradesh
Telephone: (877) 2248417
E-mail: vcspmvv@yahoo.co.in
Internet: www.spmvv.ac.in
Founded 1983
State control
Academic year: July to June
Chancellor: HE GOV. OF ANDHRA PRADESH
Vice-Chancellor: Prof. N. PRABHAKARA RAO (acting)
Registrar: Dr E. MANJU VANI
Controller of Examinations: Dr C. L. PRABHAVATI
Dean of Academic Affairs: Prof. K. BHARATHI
Dean of Examinations: Prof. T. KALYANI DEVI
Dean of Students Affairs: Prof. M. V. RAMANAMMA
Deputy Librarian: Dr D. RAJESWARI
Library of 72,850 books, 8,500 vols of periodicals, 217 journals
Number of students: 1,032

DEANS

School of Sciences: Prof. D. BHARATHI
School of Social Sciences, Humanities and Management: Prof. M. VIJAYA LAKSHMI

SRI VENKATESWARA UNIVERSITY

Tirupati 517502, Andhra Pradesh
Telephone: (877) 2289414
E-mail: registrarsvu@gmail.com
Internet: svuniversity.ac.in
Founded 1954, present status 1956
State control
Languages of instruction: English, Telugu
Academic year: June to April (2 terms)
Chancellor: HE GOV. OF ANDHRA PRADESH
Vice-Chancellor: M. G. GOPAL (acting)
Registrar: Prof. J. PRATAP REDDY
Controller of Examinations: M. RAMASWAMY
Dean of College Devt Council: Prof. MV. SRIKANTH REDDY
Dir of Research: Prof. S. BUDDHUDU
Librarian: Dr M. R. CHANDRAN
Library: Libraries of 278,974 vols
Number of teachers: 400
Number of students: 5,000

DEANS

College of Arts: Prof. C. P. KASAIAH
College of Biological and Earth Sciences: Prof. P. SREENIVASULU
College of Commerce, Management and Information Sciences: Prof. S. BALARAMI REDDY
College of Education and Extension Studies: Prof. D. USHA RANI
College of Engineering: Prof. M. M. NAIDU
College of Humanities: Prof. S. G. D. CHANDRASEKHAR
College of Int. Studies: Prof. D. K. KRANTH CHOWDARY
College of Mathematical and Physical Sciences: Prof. C. SUBBARAMI REDDY

POSTGRADUATE CENTRES

Postgraduate Centre, Kadapa: f. 1977; library of 20,000 vols, 40 periodicals; Dir Prof. G. SIVA REDDY.

Postgraduate Centre, Kavali: f. 1929; library of 17,500 vols, 40 periodicals; Dir Prof. B. D. RAMI REDDY

SWAMI KESHWANAND RAJASTHAN AGRICULTURAL UNIVERSITY, BIKANER

Bikaner 334006, Rajasthan
Telephone: (151) 2250025
E-mail: reg@raubikaner.org
Internet: www.raubikaner.org
Founded 1987
Vice-Chancellor: Dr A. K. DAHAMA
Registrar: RAJENDRA PRASAD MISHRA
Dean of Postgraduate Studies: Dr B. L. POONIA
Controller of Examinations: Dr N. K. KHATRI
Dir or Distance Education: Dr A. K. PUROHIT
Dir for Extension Education: Dr P. N. KALLA
Dir for Student Welfare: Dr P. R. KOTHARI
Dir for Research: Dr R. P. JANGIR
Controller of Examinations: Dr N. K. KHATRI
Librarian: CHETAN P. RAJPUROHIT
Library of 10,000 vols
Number of teachers: 425
Number of students: 2,250

DEANS

College of Agriculture (Bikaner): Dr M. P. SAHU
College of Agriculture (Lalsot): Dr A. K. GUPTA
College of Home Science: Dr ARCHANA RAJ SINGH
College of Veterinary and Animal Science: A. K. GAHLOT
S. K. N. College of Agriculture: Dr G. L. KESHWA

CONSTITUENT COLLEGES

College of Agriculture: tel. (151) 2250292; e-mail coa@agricolbikaner.org; f. 1988; Dean Dr M. P. SAHU.

College of Home Science: tel. (151) 2250692; e-mail chsc_bkn@hotmail.com; Dean Dr ARCHANA RAJ SINGH.

College of Veterinary and Animal Science: tel. (151) 2543419; publ. *Journal of Camel Practice and Research, Journal of Canine Development and Research, Veterinary Practitioner*.

Institute of Agribusiness Management (IABM): tel. (151) 2252981; e-mail director@iabmbikaner.org; internet www.iabmbikaner.org; f. 2000; Dir Dr RAJESH SHARMA.

SKN College of Agriculture: Jobner; tel. (1425) 254022; Dean Dr G. L. KESHWA

SWAMI RAMANAND TEERTH MARATHWADA UNIVERSITY

Vishnupuri, Nanded 431606, Maharashtra
Telephone: (2462) 229243
E-mail: registrar@srtmun.ac.in
Internet: www.srtmun.ac.in
Founded 1994
State control
Academic year: June to April
Chancellor: HE GOV. OF MAHARASHTRA
Vice-Chancellor: Dr PANDIT BHALCHANDRA VIDYASAGAR
Pro-Vice-Chancellor: Prof. Dr DILIP UKEY
Registrar: Dr VILAS N. SHINDE
Dir for Student Welfare: GANESH VITHALRAO SHINDE
Controller of Examinations: Dr V. K. BHOSALE
Librarian: Dr J. N. KULKARNI
Library of 43,586 vols, 119 nat. and 32 int. periodicals
Number of teachers: 87
Publication: *New Vision*

DEANS

Faculty of Arts: Dr B. S. JADHAV
Faculty of Commerce: Dr K. S. BADADE
Faculty of Education: Dr B. M. GORE
Faculty of Physical Sciences: P. N. DESHMUKH
Faculty of Science: Dr G. D. BAGADE
Faculty of Social Sciences: Dr U. D. SAWANT

TAMIL NADU AGRICULTURAL UNIVERSITY

Coimbatore 641003, Tamil Nadu
Telephone: (422) 6611200
E-mail: registrar@tnau.ac.in
Internet: www.tnau.ac.in
Founded 1971
State control
Language of instruction: English
Academic year: July to June (2 semesters)
Chancellor: HE GOV. OF TAMIL NADU
Pro-Chancellor: Hon. MIN. OF AGRICULTURE, GOVT OF TAMIL NADU
Vice-Chancellor: Dr P. MURUGESA BOOPATHI
Registrar: Dr S. D. SUNDAR SINGH
Controller of Admissions: Dr B. SANTHANAKRISHNAN
Deputy Librarian: K. PERUMALSAMY
Library of 161,146 vols, 380 periodicals
Number of teachers: 955
Number of students: 2,791
Publications: *Journal of Agriculture Resource Management* (2 a year, in English), *Journal of External Education* (4 a year, in English), *Madras Agricultural Journal* (12 a year, in English), *South Indian Horticulture* (4 a year, in English)

DEANS

Agricultural College and Research Institute, Coimbatore: Dr R. KRISHNASAMY
Agricultural College and Research Institute, Killikulam: Dr T. M. THIAGARAJAN

Agricultural College and Research Institute, Madurai: Dr N. KEMPUCHETTY
Agricultural Engineering College and Research Institute, Coimbatore: Dr R. MANIAN
Agricultural Engineering College and Research Institute, Kumulur: Dr C. T. DEVADAS
Anbil Dharmalingham Agricultural College and Research Institute, Tiruchirappalli: Dr S. ANTHONI RAJ
Forest College and Research Institute, Mettupalayam: Prof. K. S. NEELAKANDAN
Home Science College and Research Institute, Madurai: Dr K. SHEELA
Horticultural College and Research Institute, Coimbatore: Dr E. VADIVEL
Horticultural College and Research Institute, Periyakulam: Dr S. ANBU
School of Postgraduate Studies, Coimbatore: Dr S. KOMBAIRAJU

CONSTITUENT COLLEGES

Agricultural College and Research Institute, Coimbatore: tel. (422) 6611210; e-mail deanagri@tnau.ac.in; internet www.tnau.ac.in/agcbe.

Agricultural College and Research Institute, Killikulam: Vallanadu 628252, Tamil Nadu; tel. (4630) 2461226; e-mail deanagrikkm@tnau.ac.in; internet www.tnau.ac.in/kkm/b.html; f. 1984; library of 500 vols; 65 teachers; 450 students; Dean Dr V. SUBRAMANIAN.

Agricultural College and Research Institute, Madurai: Madurai 625104; tel. (452) 2422956; e-mail deanagrimdu@tnau.ac.in; internet www.tnau.ac.in/agrimdu.html; ean Dr N. KEMBUCHETTY.

Agricultural Engineering College and Research Institute, Coimbatore: tel. (422) 5511255; e-mail deancaecbe@tnau.ac.in; internet www.tnau.ac.in/aecricbe; Dean Dr A. SAMPATHRAJAN.

Agricultural Engineering College and Research Institute, Kumulur: Tiruchirappalli 621712, Tamil Nadu; tel. (431) 2541218; e-mail deancaekum@tnau.ac.in; f. 1972; Dean Dr C. T. DEVADAS.

Anbil Dharmalingam Agricultural College and Research Institute: Tiruchirappalli 620009, Tamil Nadu; f. 1992; Dean Dr A. ANTHONI RAJ.

Forest College and Research Institute: Mettupalayam 641301, Tamil Nadu.

Home Science College and Research Institute, Madurai: Madurai 625104; e-mail manimegalaigobalasamy@yahoo.co.in; f. 1980; Dean Dr G. MANIMEGALAI.

Horticultural College and Research Institute, Coimbatore: tel. (422) 5511371; e-mail deanhortcbe@tnau.ac.in; internet www.tnau.ac.in/horcbe; Dean Dr D. VEERARAGAVATHATHAM.

Horticultural College and Research Institute, Periyakulam: Periyakulam 625604, Tamil Nadu; tel. (4546) 234661; e-mail deanhortpkm@tnau.ac.in; internet www.tnau.ac.in/pkm; f. 1957 as Fruit Research Station, present name and status 1990; Dean V. PONNUSWAMI; publ. *Agricultural Economics Research Review*, *Agricultural Marketing*, *Agricultural Situation in India*.

School of Postgraduate Studies, Coimbatore: e-mail deanspgs@tnau.ac.in; internet www.tnau.ac.in/pg; f. 1971

TAMIL NADU DR AMBEDKAR LAW UNIVERSITY

5 Dr D. G. S. Dinakaran Salai, Chennai 600028, Tamil Nadu
Telephone: (44) 24610813
E-mail: vc@tndalu.org
Internet: www.tndalu.ac.in
Founded 1997
State control
Depts of business law, constitutional law and human rights, criminal law and criminal justice administration, environmental law and legal order, international law and organization, intellectual property rights
Chancellor: HE GOV. OF TAMIL NADU
Vice-Chancellor: Dr V. VIJAYKUMAR
Registrar: Dr D. GOPAL (acting)
Controller of Examinations: Prof. J. VINCENT COMRAJ
Public Relations Officer: A. SHAJJATH HUSSAIN
Dean of College Devt Ccl: Prof. Dr P. VANANGAMUDI
Dean of Postgraduate Studies: Prof. A. RAGHUNATHA REDDY
Dean of Student Affairs and Examinations: Prof. Dr D. GOPAL
Deputy Librarian: Dr S. K. ASOK KUMAR
Library of 18,803 vols
Number of students: 7,300
Publication: *Law Journal* (1 a year).

CONSTITUENT SCHOOLS

School of Excellence in Law: f. 2002; Dir Dr M. S. SOUNDARAPANDIAN.

Tamil Nadu Dr Ambedkar Law University Law College, Chengalpattu: f. 2003

TAMIL NADU DR M. G. R. MEDICAL UNIVERSITY

69 Anna Salai, Guindy, Chennai 600032, Tamil Nadu
Telephone: (44) 22301760
E-mail: mail@tnmgrmu.ac.in
Internet: www.tnmgrmu.ac.in
Founded 1988
State control
Chancellor: HE GOV. OF TAMIL NADU
Pro-Chancellor: Hon. MIN. FOR HEALTH, GOVT OF TAMIL NADU
Vice-Chancellor: Dr MAYIL VAHANAN NATARAJAN
Registrar: Dr R. SRILAKSHMI
Controller of Examinations: Dr K. SIVASANGEETHA
Librarian: Dr N. C. JAYAMANI

PROFESSORS

Faculty of Ayurveda:
SESHADHRI, V.
Faculty of Basic Medical Sciences:
BANUMATHY, S. P., Anatomy
MANICKAVASAGAM, S.
NALINI, A., Pharmacology
RAJESWARI, C., Microbiology
SHERIFF, Biochemistry
VADIVELU, Forensic Medicine
Faculty of Biomedical Sciences:
SAMUEL, N. M.
Faculty of Community Health, Social Sciences and History of Medicine:
PRITHVI, A.
Faculty of Dentistry:
JAGANNATHAN, J., Conservative Dentistry
SWAMINATHAN, T. N., Prosthodontics
Faculty of Medicine and Medical Specialities:
BHIRMANANDHAM, C. V., Cardiology
JAGANNATHAN, K., Thoracic Medicine
JAYANTHI, Gastroenterology
PALANIAPPAN, V., Psychiatry
PANCHAPAKESA RAJENDRAN, C., Rheumatology
RAJAN, S. K., General Medicine
RAVIKANNAN, Medical Oncology
SENTHAMIL SELVI, G., Dermatology
USMAN, N., Venerology
Faculty of Nursing:
SAHU, G.
Faculty of Obstetrics and Gynaecology and Related Specialities:
ANUSUYA, P., Obstetrics and Gynaecology
MATHAI, M., Obstetrics and Gynaecology
RAMACHANDRAN, M., Obstetrics and Gynaecology
SAMBANDAN, S., Obstetrics and Gynaecology
SOUNDARAM, K., Obstetrics and Gynaecology
TAMILMANI, D., Obstetrics and Gynaecology
Faculty of Paediatrics and Paediatric Specialities:
CHANDRASEKARAN, K., Paediatrics
CHERIAN, T., Paediatrics
SARKUNAM, C. S. R., Paediatrics
TAMILARASU, P. T., Paediatrics
TAMILVANAN, S., Paediatrics
Faculty of Pharmacy:
PRAKASH, M. S.
RAJENDRAN, A.
RAO, G. S.
SRIDHARAN, A.
Faculty of Siddha:
GANAPATHY, G.
IQBAL, P. I.
PATRAYAN, A.
RAJESWARI, A.
SAKUNTHALA, P. R.
Faculty of Surgery and Surgical Specialities:
CHANDRASEKARAN, M., Surgical Endocrinology
DAMODARAN, S., Surgical Gastroenterology
JESUDASON, B., Surgery
PUSHPARAJ, K., Neurosurgery
RATHINAM, T., Ears, Nose and Throat

TAMIL NADU VETERINARY AND ANIMAL SCIENCES UNIVERSITY

Madhavaram Milk Colony, Chennai 600051, Tamil Nadu
Telephone: (44) 25551586
E-mail: tanuvas@vsnl.com
Internet: www.tanuvas.tn.nic.in
Founded 1989
State control
Academic year: July to June
Chancellor: HE GOV. OF TAMIL NADU
Vice-Chancellor: Dr P. THANGARAJU
Registrar: Dr C. BALACHANDRAN
Controller of Examinations: Dr S. R. SRINIVASAN (acting)
Dir for Extension Education: Dr D. KATHIRESAN
Dir for Research: Dr D. THYAGARAJAN
Number of teachers: 466
Number of students: 1,457
Publications: *Kaalnadai Kathir* (6 a year), *Meenvala Madal* (12 a year), *Tamilnadu Journal of Veterinary and Animal Sciences* (6 a year)

DEANS

Faculty of Basic Sciences: Dr S. A. ASOKAN
Faculty of Fisheries Science: Dr M. C. NANDEESHA
Faculty of Food Sciences: Dr D. THYAGARAJAN
Faculty of Veterinary and Animal Sciences: Dr C. CHANDRAHASAN
Madras Veterinary College: Dr B. MURALI MANOHAR

CONSTITUENT INSTITUTIONS

Centre for Animal Health Studies: Dir Dr V. PURUSHOTHAMAN.

Centre for Animal Production Studies: Dir Dr M. BABU.

Fisheries College and Research Institute: Thoothukudi 628008, Tamil Nadu; Dir Dr V. K. VENKATARAMANI.

Institute of Animal Nutrition: LRS Campus, Kattankolathur PO, Kattupakkam 603203, Tamil Nadu; Dir Dr M. MURUGAN.

Institute of Food and Dairy Technology: Koduvalli, Chennai 600052, Tamil Nadu; Dir Dr ROBINSON J. J. ABRAHAM

TAMIL UNIVERSITY

Administrative Bldg, Trichy Rd, Thanjavur 613005, Tamil Nadu
Telephone: (4362) 226720
E-mail: contact@tamiluniversity.ac.in
Internet: www.tamiluniversity.ac.in

Founded 1981
State control
Languages of instruction: English, Tamil
Academic year: July to April

Chancellor: HE GOV. OF TAMIL NADU
Vice-Chancellor: T. CHANDRAKUJMAR (acting)
Registrar: S. PARIMALA
Public Relations Officer: Dr THIRU G. PANNEER SELVAM
Controller of Examinations: Prof. Dr M. JEGADESAN
Library Dir: Dr B. SUNDARESAN

Library of 136,324 vols, 393 periodicals
Number of teachers: 74
Number of students: 265

DEANS

Faculty of Arts: Dr T. CHANDRA KUMAR
Faculty of Developing Tamil: Dr H. CHITHIRAPUTHIRAPILLAI
Faculty of Languages: Dr A. RAMANATHAN
Faculty of Manuscriptology: V. R. MADHAVAN
Faculty of Science: Dr N. ADHIYAMAN

TEZPUR UNIVERSITY

Napaam, Sonitpur, Tezpur 784028, Assam
Telephone: (3712) 267007
E-mail: administration@tezu.ernet.in
Internet: www.tezu.ernet.in

Founded 1994
State control
Academic year: July to June

Vice-Chancellor: Prof. MIHIR KANTI CHAUDHURI
Pro-Vice-Chancellor: Prof. AMARJYOTI CHOUDHURY
Registrar: Dr ALAK KUMAR BURAGOHAIN
Controller of Examinations: Dr BHUBANESWAR SAHARIA
Dean of Research and Devt: Prof. N. S. ISLAM
Dean of Student Welfare: Prof. DHANAPATI DEKA
Deputy Librarian: Dr MUKESH SAIKIA

Library of 50,082 vols, 1,011 journals
Number of teachers: 100
Number of students: 700

DEANS

School of Engineering: Prof. M. BHUYAN
School of Humanities and Social Sciences: Prof. SUNIL K. DUTTA
School of Management Sciences: Prof. MRINMOY KUMAR SHARMA
School of Science and Technology: Prof. N. DEKA BARUAH

THIRUVALLUVAR UNIVERSITY

Serkkadu, Vellore 632106, Tamil Nadu
Telephone: (416) 2274755
Internet: thiruvalluvaruniversity.ac.in

Founded 2002

Depts of biotechnology, chemistry, economics, English, mathematics, zoology; 96 affiliated colleges in dists of Cuddalore, Thiruvannamalai, Vellore, Villupuram

Chancellor: HE GOV. OF TAMIL NADU
Pro-Chancellor: Hon. MIN. FOR HIGHER EDUCATION, GOVT OF TAMIL NADU
Vice-Chancellor: Dr A. JOTHI MURUGAN
Registrar and Acting Controller of Examination: Dr B. KRISHNAMURTHY
Librarian: Dr P. VINAYAGAMOORTHY

TILKA MANJHI BHAGALPUR UNIVERSITY

Bhagalpur 812007, Bihar
Telephone: (641) 2620100
E-mail: vc.drkndubey@gmail.com
Internet: www.tmbu.org

Founded 1960 as Bhagalpur Univ., current name adopted 1991
State control
Academic year: June to May

Chancellor: HE GOV. OF BIHAR
Vice-Chancellor: Dr K. N. DUBEY
Pro-Vice-Chancellor: Prof. KUMARESH PRASAD SINGH
Registrar: Prof. CHANDRA MOHAN DAS
Controller of Examinations: Dr MADHUSUDAN JHA
Dean of Student Welfare: Dr JYOTINDRA CHAUDHARY
Librarian: MD. ANWARUL HUSSAIN

Library of 140,000 vols, 125 periodicals
Number of teachers: 1,220
Number of students: 60,827

DEANS

Faculty of Commerce: Dr R. K. SINHA
Faculty of Education: HARENDRA P. SINGH
Faculty of Engineering: Dr C. R. PRATAP
Faculty of Humanities: Dr G. N. JHA
Faculty of Medicine: Dr ANIL KUMAR VERMA
Faculty of Science: Dr R. P. SAHAI
Faculty of Social Science: Dr R. D. SHARMA

TRIPURA UNIVERSITY

Suryamaninagar, Tripura (W) 799022, Tripura
Telephone: (381) 2374801
E-mail: tripurauniversity@rediffmail.com
Internet: tripurauniv.in

Founded 1987, present status 2007
State control
Languages of instruction: Bengali, English
Academic year: June to May

Rector: HE GOV. OF TRIPURA
Chancellor: Prof. AMIYA KUMAR BAGCHI
Vice-Chancellor: Prof. ARUNODAY SAHA
Pro-Vice-Chancellor: Prof. B. K. AGARWALA
Registrar: Dr KALYAN BIJOY JAMATIA
Controller of Examinations: B. C. SINHA
Dir for College Devt Ccl: S. DEBBARMA
Deputy Librarian: G. P. CHAKRABORTY

Library of 97,500 vols, 141 journals
Number of teachers: 120
Number of students: 19,000 (incl. affiliated colleges)

DEANS

Faculty of Arts and Commerce: Prof. P. K. HALDAR
Faculty of Science: Prof. B. K. DE

PROFESSORS

AGGARWAL, B. K., Life Science
BHOWMIK, R. N., Mathematics
CHAUDHURIU, M., Bengali
CHAUDHURY, D. K., History
DEBNATH, P., Commerce
DEY, A., Mathematics
DEY, B. K., Physics
DEY, S. N., Sanskrit
DINDA, B., Chemistry
GHOSH, D., Life Science
HALDAR, P. K., Commerce
ROY, A. D., Life Science
SAHA, A., Economics
SRIVASTAVA, R. C., Life Science

UNIVERSITY OF AGRICULTURAL SCIENCES

Gandi Krishni Vignan Kendra, Bengaluru 560065, Karnataka
Telephone: (80) 23330984
E-mail: registrar@uasbangalore.edu.in
Internet: www.uasbangalore.edu.in

Founded 1964
State control
Languages of instruction: English, Kannada
Academic year: September to August (2 terms)

Chancellor: HE GOV. OF KARNATAKA
Pro-Chancellor: MIN. OF AGRICULTURE, KARNATAKA
Vice-Chancellor: Dr K. NARAYANA GOWDA
Dir for Extension: Dr R. S. KULKARNI
Dir for Research: Dr H. SHIVANNA
Dir for Student Welfare: Dr K. P. RAMA PRASANNA
Registrar: Dr CHIKKADEVAIAH
Librarian: Dr K. K. MANJUNATHA

Library of 191,192 vols
Number of teachers: 1,082
Number of students: 2,500 undergraduates and 1,000 graduates

Publications: *Mysore Journal of Agricultural Sciences* (4 a year), 10 series (UAS Research, UAS Extension, UAS Education, etc.)

DEANS

College of Agriculture: Dr B. MALLIK

PROFESSORS

ABDUL RAHMAN, S., Parasitology
ANANTHANARAYANA, R., Chemistry and Soils
ANILKUMAR, T. B., Plant Pathology
ASHOK, T. H., Horticulture
AVADHANI, K. K., Genetics and Plant Breeding
BHAT, G. S., Dairy Chemistry
CHALLAIAH, Agricultural Extension
CHANDRAKANTH, M. G., Agricultural Economics
CHANDRAMOULI, K. N., Anatomy
CHANDRAPPA, H. M., Plant Breeding
CHANDRASHEKAR GUPTA, T. R., Fishery Oceanography
CHANNAPPA, T. C., Agricultural Engineering
CHENGAPPA, P. G., Agricultural Marketing
CHIKKADEVAIAH, Seed Processing Engineering
CHOWDEGOWDA, M., Agricultural Engineering
DAS, T. K., Animal Nutrition
DEVEGOWDA, G., Poultry
ESHWARAPPA, G., Agricultural Extension
FAROOQ MOHAMMED, Veterinary Physiology
FAROOQI, A. A., Medicinal and Aromatic Plants
GANGADHAR, K. S., Gynaecology and Obstetrics
GEETHA RAMACHANDRA, Biochemistry
GIRIJA, P. R., Psychology
GOPALA GOWDA, H. S., Agricultural Microbiology
GOPALAKRISHNA HEBBAR, Agricultural Economics
GOPALAKRISHNA RAO, Agricultural Extension

GOVINDAIAH, M. G., Animal Genetics and Breeding
GOVINDAN, R., Entomology
GOWDA, H., Pharmacology
GUNDURAO, D. S., Mathematics
GURUMURTHY, Statistics
GURURAJ HUNSIGI, Agronomy
HEGDE, S. V., Microbiology
HONNEGOWDA, Pharmacology
HUDDAR, A. G., Horticulture
JAGADISH, A., Entomology
JAGADISH KUMAR, Pharmacology
JAGANNATH, M. S., Parasitology
JANARDHANA, K. V., Crop Physiology
JAVAREGOWDA, S., Agricultural Engineering
JAYADEVAPPA, S. M., Surgery
JAYARAMAIAH, M., Sericulture
JOSEPH BHAGYARAJ, D., Agricultural Microbiology
JOSHI SHAMASUNDAR, Botany
KAILAS, M. M., Dairy Production
KARUNASAGAR, I., Fishery Microbiology
KATTEPPA, Y., Agricultural Extension
KESHAVAMURTHY, K. V., Plant Pathology
KESHAVANATH, P., Aquaculture
KHAN, M. M., Horticulture
KRISHNA, K. S., Agricultural Extension
KRISHNAPPA, A. M., Soil Science
KRISHNAPRASAD, Agricultural Entomology
KRISHNAPRASAD, P. R., Pathology
KRISHNEGOWDA, K. T., Agronomy
KULAKARNI, R. S., Agricultural Botany
KUMARASWAMY, A. S., Water Management and Plant Breeding
LAKKUNDI, N. H., Agricultural Entomology
LOKANATH, G. R., Poultry for Meat
MALLIK, B., Acarology
MALLIKARJUNAIAH, R. R., Microbiology
MANJUNATH, A., Plant Breeding
MELANTA, R., Horticulture
MOHAN JOSEPH, Fishery Biology
MUNI LAL DUBEY, B., Gynaecology and Obstetrics
MUNIYAPPA, T. V., Agricultural Extension
MUNIYAPPA, V., Plant Pathology
MUSHTARI BEGUM, J., Home Science
NAGARAJA SETTY, M. V., Plant Breeding
NAGARAJU, Animal Sciences
NANJEGOWDA, D., Nematology
NARASIMHAMURTHY, S., Mathematics
NARAYANA, K., Pharmacology
NARAYANA GOWDA, K., Agricultural Extension
NARAYANAGOWDA, J. V., Horticulture
NARENDRANATH, R., Physiology
PANCHAKSHARAIAH, S., Agronomy
PARAMASHIVAIAH, B. M., Animal Science
PARAMESWAR, N. S., Plant Breeding
PARASHIVAMURTHY, A. S., Soil Science
PARVATHAMMA, S., Mathematics
PARVATHAPPA, H. C., Soil Science and Agricultural Chemistry
PRABHAKAR HEGDE, B., Dairy Production
PRABHAKAR SETTY, T. K., Agronomy
PRABHUSWAMY, H. P., Agricultural Entomology
PRASAD, T. G., Crop Physiology
PRATAP KUMAR, K. S., Poultry Science
PUTTASWAMY, Entomology
RAGHAVAN, R., Veterinary Microbiology
RAJ, J., Microbiology
RAJAGOPAL, D., Apiculture
RAMACHANDRAPRASAD, T. V., Agronomy
RAMANJANEYULU, G., Dairy Technology
RAMAPRASANNA, K. P., Seed Technology
RANGANATHAIAH, K. G., Plant Pathology
RAVI, P. C., Agricultural Marketing
SAMIULLA, R., Horticulture
SATHYAN, B. A., Plant Breeding
SATHYANARAYANA RAO, G. P., Agricultural Extension
SESHADRI, V. S., Agricultural Extension
SHANBHOGUE, S. L., Fishery Biology
SHANKAR, P. A., Dairy Microbiology
SHANKAREGOWDA, B. T., Plant Sciences
SHANTHA JOSEPH, Fishery Economics
SHANTHA R. HIREMATH, Plant Breeding
SHANTHAMALLAIAH, N. R., Crop Production
SHARIEF, R. A., Plant Science
SHESHAPPA, D. S., Fishery Engineering
SHIVAPPA SHETTY, K., Microbiology
SHIVANNA, H., Plant Breeding and Genetics
SHIVARAJ, B., Agronomy
SHIVASHANKAR, K., Agronomy
SIDDARAMAIAH, A. L., Plant Pathology
SIDDARAMAIAH, B. S., Agricultural Extension
SIDDARAMAPPA, R., Soil Science
SIDDARAMEGOWDA, T. K., Biotechnology
SINGLACHAR, M. A., Agronomy
SOMASHEKARAPPA, G., Agricultural Extension
SRIDHARA, S., Zoology
SRIHARI, K., Zoology
SRIKAR, L. N., Biochemistry
SRINIVASA GOWDA, M. V., Economics
SRINIVASA GOWDA, R. N., Poultry Pathology
SURYA PRAKASH, S., Agricultural Economics
SUSHEELA DEVI, L., Soil Science and Agricultural Chemistry
THIMME GOWDA, S., Agronomy
UDAYAKUMAR, M., Crop Physiology
UPADHYA, A. S., Veterinary Microbiology
UTTAIAH, B. C., Horticulture
VAIDEHI, M. P., Home Science
VAJRANABAIAH, S. N., Crop Physiology
VASUDEVAPPA, Inland Fisheries
VEERABHADRAIAH, V., Agricultural Extension
VENKATASUBBAIAH, K., Botany
VENKATESH REDDY, T., Post-Harvest Technology
VENUGOPAL, Agricultural Extension
VENUGOPAL, N., Agricultural Meteorology
VIDYACHANDRA, B., Plant Breeding
VIJAYASARATHI, S. K., Veterinary Microbiology
VIRAKTHAMATH, C. A., Agricultural Entomology
VISHWANATH, D. P., Soil Science
VISWANATH, S., Virology
VISWANATHA, S. R., Plant Breeding
VISWANATHA REDDY, V. N., Gynaecology and Obstetrics
VISWANATHA SASTRY, K. M., Veterinary Medicine
YADAHALLI, Y. H., Agronomy

CONSTITUENT COLLEGES

College of Agriculture—Hassan: POB 39, Karekere, Hassan 573201, Karnataka; tel. (8172) 290517; e-mail dihassan@uasbangalore.edu.in; f. 1996; offers undergraduate courses in agriculture, agricultural biotechnology, food science; library of 5,000 vols; Dir Dr M. A. SHANKAR.

College of Agriculture—Mandya: Mandya-Melkote Rd, Mandya, Kamataka; tel. (8232) 277211; e-mail sanvt1654@rediffmail.com; f. 1991; offers undergraduate course in agriculture; 219 students; Dean Dr V. T. SANNAVEERAPPANAVAR.

College of Agriculture—Shimoga: Savalanga Rd, Navile, Shimoga, Karnataka; tel. (8182) 270705; f. 1990; offers undergraduate and postgraduate courses, research in agriculture; depts of crop improvement, crop production, crop protection, social science; Dean Dr M. S. GANESHBABU.

College of Forestry: Kunda Rd, Ponnampet Kodagu, Karnataka; tel. (8274) 49365; e-mail diforestry@uasbangalore.edu.in; f. 1995; offers undergraduate, postgraduate courses in forestry; Dean Dr N. A. PRAKASH.

College of Sericulture: Chintamani–Kolar Rd, Chintamani 563125, Karnataka; tel. (58154) 290546; e-mail disericulture@gmail.com; f. 1995; offers undergraduate courses in agriculture, sericulture; Dir Prof. Dr N. NAGARAJA

UNIVERSITY OF ALLAHABAD

Allahabad 211002, Uttar Pradesh
Telephone: (532) 2461089
E-mail: mkc@allduniv.ac.in
Internet: www.allduniv.ac.in
Founded 1887
State control
Languages of instruction: English, Hindi
Academic year: July to April
Chief Rector: HE GOV. OF UTTAR PRADESH
Chancellor: Dr VERGHESE KURIEN
Vice-Chancellor: Prof. A. K. SINGH
Registrar: J. N. MISHRA
Controller of Examinations: Prof. H. S. UPADHYAYA
Dean of College Devt: Prof. L. R. SINGH
Dean of Research and Devt: Prof. N. R. FAROOQI
Dean of College Devt: Prof. R. K. SINGH
Librarian: Dr A. P. GAKHAR
Library of 630,490 vols, 418 journals
Number of teachers: 385
Number of students: 37,694

DEANS

Faculty of Arts: Prof. M. P. DUBEY
Faculty of Commerce: Prof. S. A. ANSARI
Faculty of Law: Prof. L. M. SINGH
Faculty of Science: Prof. S. D. DIXIT

UNIVERSITY OF BURDWAN

Rajbati, Bardhaman 713104, West Bengal
Telephone: (342) 2634975
E-mail: pio@buruniv.ac.in
Internet: www.buruniv.ac.in
Founded 1960
State control
Languages of instruction: Bengali, English
Academic year: June to May
Chancellor: HE GOV. OF WEST BENGAL
Vice-Chancellor: Prof. Dr SUBRATA PAL
Pro-Vice-Chancellor for Admin. and Academic: Dr SHOROSIMOHAN DAN
Jt Registrar: Dr DEBIDAS MONDAL
Controller of Examinations: Dr SUKUMAR MUKHOPADHYAY
Deputy Librarian: Dr KANCHAN KAMILA
Library of 195,926 vols, 24,812 journals, 300 periodicals
Number of teachers: 205
Number of students: 3,293
Publications: *Bangla Bibhagiya Patika*, *Bengali Journal*, *English Journal*, *History Journal*, *Journal of Mass Communication*, *Law Review*, *Philosophy Journal*, *Political Science Journal*, *Sanskrit Journal*, *Science Journal*, *Socio-Political Journal*

PROFESSORS

BAGCHI, S., Chemistry
BAGCHI, S. B., Statistics
BANDOPADHYAY, D. N., English
BANDYOPADHYAY, M. K., Sanskrit
BANDYOPADHYAY, T. C., Zoology
BANERJEE, A. K., Economics
BANERJEE, C., Mathematics
BANERJEE, G., Mathematics
BANERJEE, K., Geography
BANERJEE, M., Chemistry
BASU, D. K., Philosophy
BASU, P. S., Botany
BASU, S., Bengali
BASU, S., Chemistry
BHATTACHARYYA, A., Philosophy
BHATTACHARYYA, A., Sanskrit
BHATTACHARYYA, A. K., Music
BHATTACHARYYA, A. K., Physics
BHATTACHARYYA, G. N., Sanskrit
BHATTACHARAYYA, K., Chemistry
BHATTACHARAYYA, K., Mathematics
BHATTACHARAYYA, P. K., Botany
BHATTACHARYYA, R. P., Sanskrit

BISWAS, S. C., Library and Information Science
BISWAS, S. K., Commerce
CHAKRABARTI, T., Sanskrit
CHAKRABORTY, B., Bengali
CHAKRABORTY, C. S., Zoology
CHAKRABORTY, K., Bengali
CHAKRABORTY, N. D., Mathematics
CHAKRABORTY, P., Economics
CHAKRABORTY, P., Zoology
CHAKRABORTY, P. C., English
CHAKRABORTY, P. K., Economics
CHAKRABORTY, S., Bengali
CHAKRABORTY, S., Zoology
CHAKRABORTY, S. K., Mathematics
CHATTERJEE, K. K., English
CHATTERJEE, S. K., Institute of Science Education
CHATTOPADHYAY, A., Statistics
CHATTOPADHYAY, K. C., Mathematics
CHATTOPADHYAY, N. C., Botany
CHATTOPADHYAY, R. R., Bengali
CHAUDHURY, M. K., Bengali
CHAUDHURY, P. K., Zoology
DAS, A. K., Chemistry
DAS, P., Commerce
DAS, T. K., Physics
DASGUPTA, S. S., Physics
DE, A. K., Bengali
DE, G. S., Chemistry
DE, N. K., Geography
DUTTA, D. M., Business Administration
GHOSH, B., Sociology
GUPTA, K., Botany
GUPTA, L. N., Bengali
HOQUE, A., Philosophy
HUI, A. K., English
KHAN, G. C., Philosophy
KUNDU, R. K., English
KUSHARI, D. P., Botany
MAHARATNA, A., Economics
MAJUMDAR, G., Zoology
MALLIK, A. K., Commerce
MALLIK, P., Physics
MALLIK, U. K., Commerce
MITRA, A., Sociology
MITRA, C., Geography
MONDAL, K. K., Mathematics
MONDAL, P. K., Philosophy
MUKHERJEE, A., Botany
MUKHERJEE, B., Sanskrit
MUKHERJEE, R. N., Mathematics
MUKHOPADHYAY, A. K., Botany
MUKHOPADHYAY, A. K., Chemistry
MUKHOPADHYAY, A. K., Political Science
MUKHOPADHYAY, R. N., Botany
MUKHOPADHYAY, S., Computer Science
NANDI, A. P., Zoology
NANDI, B., Botany
PRAMANIK, N. C., Political Science
PRASAD, N., Geography
RAY, A. B., Political Science
RAY, M. K., English
ROY, A., History
ROY, D., Business Administration
ROY, R. K., Physics
ROY, S., Zoology
ROY, S. K., Physics
ROY, S. K., Political Science
ROY CHOUDHURY, S. K., Mathematics
SAMAD, A., Mathematics
SAMANTA, B. C., Physics
SAMANTA, L. K., Physics
SARKAR, A. K., Zoology
SARKAR, B. C., Physics
SARKHEL, J., Commerce
SARMA, P., Botany
SENGUPTA, S. K., Business Administration
SIDDHANTA, U. K., Instrumentation Centre
SINGH, S. S., Law
SINHA, B. C., Hindi
THAKUR, S., Chemistry

UNIVERSITY OF CALCUTTA

Senate House, 87/1, College St, Kolkata 700073, West Bengal
Telephone: (33) 22410071
E-mail: admin@caluniv.ac.in
Internet: www.caluniv.ac.in

Founded 1857

Teaching and Affiliating
Language of instruction: English
Academic year: July to June

Chancellor: GOVERNOR OF WEST BENGAL
Vice-Chancellor: Prof. ASIS KUMAR BANERJEE
Pro-Vice-Chancellor for Academic Affairs: Prof. SURANJAN DAS
Pro-Vice-Chancellor for Business and Finance: Prof. TAPAN KUMAR MUKHERJEE
Registrar: Dr BASAB CHAUDHURI
Librarian: Dr SOUMITRA SARKAR

Library of 795,000 vols
Number of teachers: 667
Number of students: 91,741

Publications: *Calcutta Review* (4 a year), *UNICAL* (4 a year)

DEANS

Faculty of Agriculture and Veterinary Science: Prof. R. K. SARKAR
Faculty of Arts: Prof. A. K. BANDYOPADHYAY
Faculty of Commerce, Social Welfare and Business Management: Prof. R. CHAKRABORTY
Faculty of Education, Journalism and Library Information Science: Prof. T. BASU
Faculty of Engineering and Technology: Prof. S. SEN
Faculty of Fine Arts, Music and Home Science: Prof. S. BANDYOPADHYAY
Faculty of Law: Prof. I. G. AHMED
Faculty of Science: Prof. D. CHATTOPADHYAY

PROFESSORS

University College of Agriculture (5 Ballygunge Circular Rd, Kolkata 700019):

BASU, R. N.
BHATTACHARYYA, B.
GHOSH, K.
GUPTA, S. K.
MAJUMDAR, B. C.
MAJUMDAR, M. K.
SADHU, M. K.

University College of Arts (1 Reformatory St, Kolkata 700027; tel. (33) 22410071):

ACHARYA, S. N., Sanskrit
ALQUADRI, S. M. S., Ancient Indian History and Culture
BANDYOPADHYAY, A., History
BANDYOPADHYAY, B. N., Sociology
BANDYOPADHYAY, S., Ancient Indian History and Culture
BANERJEE, A. K., Economics
BANERJEE, H., History
BANERJEE, H. K., Economics
BANERJEE, M., Philosophy
BANERJEE, S., Economics
BANERJEE, S., English
BASU, R., Sanskrit
BHATTACHARYA, A., Ancient Indian History and Culture
BHATTACHARYA, A., Philosophy
BHATTACHARYA, B., Pali
BHATTACHARYA, K., Linguistics
BHATTACHARYYA, S. K., Sociology
BHAUMIK, A. C., Museology
BURKE, I. K., Ancient Indian History and Culture
CHAKRABARTI, B., Library and Information Science
CHAKRABARTI, D., English
CHAKRABARTI, R., Ancient Indian History and Culture
CHAKRABARTI, R., Philosophy
CHAKRABARTI, S., English
CHATTERJEE, R., Islamic History and Culture
CHATTERJEE, R., Political Science
CHATTOPADHYAY, S.
CHATURVEDI, J., Hindi
CHAUDHURI, A., Economics
CHAUDHURI, B., South and South-East Asian Studies
CHOUDHURI, S., Islamic History and Culture
DAS, S., History
DASGUPTA, A., Economics
DASGUPTA, A., Library and Information Science
DE, B. B., Ancient
DUTTA, P. K., Political Science
DUTTA GUPTA, S., Political Science
GANGULY, M. K., Sanskrit
GANGULY, S. S., Bengali
GHOSH, D., Sanskrit
GHOSH, J., Bengali Language and Literature
GHOSH, P., South and South-East Asian Studies
GOSWAMI, K. R., Philosophy
GUPTA, C., Archaeology
GUPTA, D., Philosophy
KHAN, M., Bengali Language and Literature
MAHAPATRA, R., Tamil
MAITRA, J., Ancient Indian History and Culture
MAJUMDAR, M., Bengali Language and Literature
MALLIK, A., Economics
MUKHERJEE, B., Political Science
MUKHERJEE, B. K., Bengali Language and Literature
MUKHERJEE, S. K., Museology
MUKHOPADHYAY, B. K., Bengali Language and Literature
MUKHOPADHYAY, S. K., Political Science
NATH, M. K., Linguistics
PANDEY, C., Hindi
PARAMANIK, S. K., Sociology
RAY, A., Islamic History and Culture
RAY, J. K., History
ROY, A. K., South and South-East Asian Studies
ROY, D. K., Museology
ROY, S., English
SANYAL, J., English
SANYAL, K., Economics
SEN, K., Philosophy
SEN, P. K., Philosophy
SEN, R., Philosophy
SEN, S. K., Linguistics
SENGUPTA, S., Sanskrit
SHARMA, A., Hindi
SHAW, S., Hindi
SIKDAR, S. N., Economics
TAQI, Y. R., Urdu
VASUDEVAN, H. S., History

University College of Commerce, Social Welfare and Business Management (87/1 College St, Kolkata 700073; tel. (33) 22410071):

BANERJEE, B.
BANERJEE, S.
SINHA, G. C.

University College of Law (51/1 Hazra Rd, Kolkata 700019; tel. (33) 24755801):

AHMED, I. G.

University College of Management (1 Reformatory St, Kolkata 700027; tel. (33) 2479-1645):

CHAKRABARTI, R.
DHAR, S., Business Management
KHASNABIS, R., Business Management

University College of Science (35 Ballygunge Circular Rd, Kolkata 700019):

ACHARYA, S. K., Pure Mathematics
ADHIKARY, M. R., Pure Mathematics
BAGCHI, B., Applied Mathematics
BANDHYOPADHYAY, M. K., Geography

BANERJEE, A., Chemistry
BANERJEE, A. B., Biochemistry
BANERJEE, D., Physics
BANERJEE, J., Chemistry
BANERJEE, M., Botany
BANERJEE, S. B., Zoology
BASU, A., Statistics
BASU, S. R., Geography
BHATTACHARYYA, A., Zoology
BHATTACHARYYA, A., Marine Science
BHATTACHARYYA, A. K., Biochemistry
BHATTACHARYYA, C., Geology
BHATTACHARYYA, D. K., Pure Mathematics
BHATTACHARYYA, M., Anthropology
BHATTACHARYYA, P. K., Physics
CHAKRABARTI, B. C., Pure Mathematics
CHAKRABARTI, C. G., Applied Mathematics
CHATTERJEE, A., Botany
CHATTERJEE, N. B., Zoology
CHATTERJEE, P. K., Psychology
CHATTERJEE, S. P., Physiology
CHATTOPADHYAY, D., Biochemistry
CHOUDHURI, P. K., Applied Mathematics
CHOWDHURY, B., Anthropology
CHOWDHURY, U., Biophysics
DAS, J., Pure Mathematics
DAS, J. N., Applied Mathematics
DAS, K. C., Physics
DAS, K. P., Applied Mathematics
DAS, T. K., Physics
DASCHOWDHURY, A. B., Anthropology
DASGUPTA, C. K., Biophysics
DASGUPTA, U., Biophysics
DATTA GUPTA, A. K., Zoology
DE, S. S., Applied Mathematics
GANGULY, S., Pure Mathematics
GHATAK, K. P., Electronics Science
GHOSH, C. K., Biochemistry
GHOSH, P. N., Physics
GHOSH, S., Botany
LAHIRI, P., Zoology
MAITY, B. R., Zoology
MALLICK, R., Botany
MANNA, B., Zoology
MONDAL, A., Biochemistry
MUKHERJEE, D., Geology
MUKHERJEE, M., Biochemistry
MUKHERJEE, P., Botany
MUKHERJEE, S., Botany
MUKHERJEE, S., Geology
MUKHOPADHYAY, A. S., Zoology
MUKHOPADHYAY, S. C., Geography
NANDA, D. K., Zoology
PAL, S. G., Zoology
PAN, N. R., Physics
PRAMANIK, A. K., Applied Mathematics
PURAKAYASTHA, R., Botany
RAY, S., Botany
ROY, R., Anthropology
ROYCHAUDHURY, P., Applied Mathematics
ROYCHOUDHURY, D., Electronics Science
ROYCHOWDHURY, A., Physics
ROYCHOWDHURY, P., Physics
ROYCHOWDHURY, R., Botany
SAHA, G. B., Psychology
SAHA, P. K., Geography
SAMAJPATI, N., Botany
SAMANTA, B. K., Geology
SANYAL, A. B., Biophysics
SARKAR, S. K., Physics
SEN, R. N., Applied Mathematics
SEN, S., Botany
SENGUPTA, A., Geology
SENGUPTA, D., Biochemistry
SIRCAR, P. K., Botany
THAKUR, A. R., Biophysics

University College of Technology:

BANDHYOPADHYAY, S., Computer Science
BANIK, A. K., Chemical Engineering
BASU, A. K., Chemical Technology
BASU, D. K., Applied Physics
BASU, P. K., Radiophysics and Electronics
BHATTACHARJEE, A. K., Computer Science
BHATTACHARYYA, D. K., Chemical Technology
BHATTACHARYYA, S., Chemical Engineering
BHATTACHARYYA, T. K., Chemical Technology
CHAKRABORTY, A. K., Applied Physics
CHAKRABORTY, A. N., Radiophysics and Electronics
CHATTERJEE, N. K., Chemical Technology
CHATTOPADHYAY, D., Radiophysics and Electronics
DAS, V., Polymer Science and Technology
DASGUPTA, A. K., Radiophysics and Electronics
DAS PODDAR, P. K., Chemical Technology
DATTA, A. K., Applied Physics
DATTA, A. N., Radiophysics and Electronics
DATTA, B. K., Chemical Engineering
GHOSH, P., Polymer Science and Technology
GUPTA, S. N., Polymer Science and Technology
LAHIRI, C. R., Chemical Technology
MAJUMDER, R. N., Chemical Technology
MITRA, N. K., Chemical Technology
MITRA, T. K., Applied Physics
MUKHOPADHYAY, A. K., Applied Physics
NATH, N. G., Radiophysics and Electronics
PARIA, B. B., Chemical Engineering
PARIA, H., Radiophysics and Electronics
PURKAIT, N. N., Radiophysics and Electronics
RAKSHIT, P. C., Radiophysics and Electronics
ROY, P., Chemical Engineering
ROY, S. K., Radiophysics and Electronics
SAHA, P. K., Radiophysics and Electronics
SEN, A. K., Radiophysics and Electronics
SENGUPTA, P. K., Polymer Science and Technology

CONSTITUENT COLLEGES

All India Institute of Hygiene and Public Health: e-mail aiihph@cal.vsnl.net.in; internet www.aiihph.gov.in; Dir Dr B. N. GHOSH; see under Colleges.

Institute of Postgraduate Medical Education and Research: 244 Acharyya J. C. Bose Rd, Kolkata 700020; e-mail director@ipgmer.gov.in; internet www.ipgmer.gov.in; Dir Prof. D. SEN.

Presidency College: 86/1 College St, Kolkata; f. 1817; Prin. (vacant).

Sanskrit College: Bankim Chatterjee St, Kolkata; e-mail admin@sanskritcollege.co.in; internet www.sanskritcollege.co.in; f. 1824; Prin. B. P. BHATTACHARYYA.

School of Tropical Medicine: Kolkata; Dir Dr B. D. CHATTERJEE.

There are also 37 professional colleges and 207 affiliated colleges

UNIVERSITY OF CALICUT

PO Calicut Univ., Malappuram 673635, Kerala
Telephone: (494) 2401144
E-mail: reg@unical.ac.in
Internet: www.universityofcalicut.info
Founded 1968
State control
Languages of instruction: English, Malayalam
Academic year: June to March
Chancellor: HE GOV. OF KERALA
Vice-Chancellor: Dr M. ABDUL SALAM
Pro-Vice Chancellor: Prof. K. RAVEENDRANATH
Registrar: Dr M. V. JOSEPH
Controller of Examinations: Dr C. D. SEBASTIAN
Dean of Students Welfare: P. V. VALSARAJAN
Dir for Public Relations: T. P. RAJEEVAN (acting)
Dir for School of Distance Education: Dr K. KRISHNANKUTTY
Registrar: Dr T. K. NARAYANAN
Librarian: Dr ABDUL AZIZ T. A. (acting)
Library of 150,000 vols
Number of teachers: 166 (Univ. Depts), 5,920 (Affiliated Colleges)
Number of students: 305,000 (Univ. Depts and Affiliated Colleges)
Publications: *Calicut University Research Journal* (2 a year), *Interventions*, *Journal of South Indian History*, *Malyala Vimarsam*, *Ruchi*, *The Malabar*

DEANS

Faculty of Ayurveda: Dr P. K. WARRIER
Faculty of Commerce and Management Studies: Dr E. P. SAINUL ABIDEEN
Faculty of Dentistry: Dr M. HARINDRANATH
Faculty of Education: Dr K. P. MANOJ
Faculty of Engineering: Dr M. P. CHANDRA SEKHARAN
Faculty of Fine Arts: Dr VAYALA VASUDEVAN PILLAI
Faculty of Health Science: T. SANKARAN NAIR
Faculty of Homeopathy: Dr M. P. PRAKASAN
Faculty of Humanities: Dr D. P. NAIR
Faculty of Journalism: Dr SYED AMJAD AMAMED
Faculty of Languages and Literature: Dr IQBAL AHAMMAD
Faculty of Law: Prof. K. V. NARAYANIKUTTY
Faculty of Medicine: Dr R. VELAYUDHAN NAIR
Faculty of Science: Dr P. RAMESAN

UNIVERSITY OF DELHI

Delhi 110007
Telephone: (11) 27667011
E-mail: vc@du.ac.in
Internet: www.du.ac.in
Founded 1922
State control
Languages of instruction: English, Hindi
Academic year: July to April (3 terms)
Chancellor: VICE-PRES. OF INDIA
Pro-Chancellor: CHIEF JUSTICE OF INDIA
Vice-Chancellor: Prof. DINESH SINGH
Pro-Vice-Chancellor: Prof. VIVEK SUNEJA
Registrar: R. K. SINHA
Dir of South Campus: Prof. UMESH RAI
Dir of Campus of Open Learning: Dr SAVITA DATTA
Dean of Colleges: Prof. SUDISH PACHAURI
Dean of Examinations: Prof. R. C. SHARMA
Dean of Int. Relations for Science and Technology: Prof. K. SREENIVAS
Dean of Int. Relations for Social Sciences and Humanities: Prof. ANAND PRAKASH
Dean of Research: Prof. AJAY KUMAR
Dean of Students Welfare: Prof. J. M. KHURANA
Proctor: Prof. H. P. SINGH
Librarian: R. N. VASHISTA
Library: 1.45m. vols, 1,290 journals, 700 MSS
Number of teachers: 270
Number of students: 150,000

DEANS

Faculty of Applied Social Sciences and Humanities: Prof. V. K. KAUL
Faculty of Arts: Prof. H. S. PRASAD
Faculty of Ayurvedic and Unani Medicine: Dr RAJNI SUSHMA
Faculty of Commerce and Business Studies: Prof. I. M. PANDEY
Faculty of Education: Prof. ANITA RAMPAL
Faculty of Interdisciplinary and Applied Sciences: Prof. AVINASHI KAPOOR
Faculty of Law: Prof. GURDIP SINGH
Faculty of Management Studies: Prof. RAJ S. DHANKAR
Faculty of Mathematical Sciences: Prof. BAL KISHAN DASS

Faculty of Medical Sciences: Prof. JOLLY ROHATGI
Faculty of Music and Fine Arts: Prof. ANUPAM MAHAJAN
Faculty of Open Learning: Dr SAVITA DATTA
Faculty of Science: Prof. S. C. BHATIA
Faculty of Social Sciences: Prof. NANDINI SUNDAR
Faculty of Technology: Prof. RAJ SENANI

CONSTITUENT COLLEGES

Acharya Narendra Dev College: Govindpuri, Kalkaji, New Delhi 110019; tel. (11) 26294542; e-mail principalandc@gmail.com; internet andcollege.du.ac.in; f. 1991; depts of biomedical sciences, botany, chemistry, commerce, computer science, electronics, English, mathematics, physics, zoology; foreign language centre; 1,450 students; Prin. Dr SAVITHRI SINGH; Vice-Prin. Dr SUNITA HOODA.

Aditi Mahavidyalaya: Delhi Auchandi Rd, Bawana, Delhi 110039; tel. (11) 2752741; e-mail info@amv94.org; internet www.amv94.org; f. 1994; library of 20,000 vols; 62 teachers; 1,348 students; Chair. Prof. MATADIN; Prin. Dr KALPANA BHRARA.

Atma Ram Sanatan Dharam College: Dhaula Kuan, New Delhi 110021; tel. (11) 24113436; e-mail principal.arsd@gmail.com; internet www.arsdcollege.net; f. 1959, fmrly Sanatan Dharma College; library of 100,000 vols; Chair. CHANDER MOHAN; Prin. Dr SANDEEP KUMAR SHARMA.

Ayurvedic & Unani Tibbia College & Hospital: Ajmal Khan Rd, Karol Bagh, New Delhi 110005; tel. (11) 23524180; e-mail pmstibbiacollege@rediffmail.com; library of 30,000 vols; 55 teachers; 500 students; Prin. Dr AHMAD YASIN; Nodal Officer Prof. Dr MOHAMMAD IDRIS.

Bhagini Nivedita College: Kair, Near Najafgarh, New Delhi 110043; tel. (11) 28017485; e-mail bnc.kair@gmail.com; internet www.bhagininiveditacollege.in; f. 1993; library of 17,800 vols, 54 periodicals and journals; 48 teachers; 800 students; Chair. Prof. VIBHA CHATURVEDI; Prin. Dr PURABI SAIKIA.

Bharati College: C–4 Janak Puri, New Delhi 110058; tel. (11) 43273000; e-mail administrator@bharaticollege.com; internet www.bharaticollege.com; f. 1971 as Bharati Mahila College; 1,500 students; Prin. Dr PROMODINI VARMA.

Daulat Ram College: 4 Patel Marg, Maurice Nagar, Delhi 110007; tel. (11) 27667863; e-mail daulatramcollegedu@gmail.com; internet www.daulatramcollege.in; f. 1960 as Pramila College, present name 1964; library of 80,000 vols; 163 teachers; 3,200 students; Prin. Dr SUSHMA TANDON (acting).

Gargi College: Siri Fort Rd, Delhi 110049; tel. (11) 26494544; e-mail gargicollege@sify.com; internet www.gargicollege.in; f. 1967; library of 60,469 vols; Prin. Dr MEERA RAMACHANDRAN.

Hans Raj College: Mahatma Hans Raj Marg, Malka Ganj, Delhi 110007; tel. (11) 27667747; e-mail contact@hansrajcollege.co.in; internet hansrajcollege.co.in; f. 1948; 3,700 students; Dir Dr V. K. KAWATRA.

Hindu College: University Enclave, Delhi 110007; tel. (11) 27667184; e-mail hinducol@del3.vsnl.net.in; internet www.hinducollege.org; f. 1899; library of 116,688 vols; 120 teachers; 2,000 students; Prin. Dr VINAY KUMAR SRIVASTAVA; Vice-Prin. Dr PRADUMN KUMAR.

Indraprastha College for Women: 31 Sham Nath Marg, Delhi 110054; tel. (11) 23954085; e-mail principalipc@yahoo.in; internet www.ipcollege.org; f. 1924; library of 112,464 vols; 2,200 students; Prin. Dr BABLI MOITRA SARAF.

Institute of Home Economics: F–4 Hauz Khas Enclave, New Delhi 110016; tel. (11) 26532402; e-mail queries@ihedu.com; internet www.ihe-du.co.in; f. 1961, present status 1969; library of 22,000 vols; 800 students; offers bachelors and masters degree in biochemistry, home science, fabric and apparel science, food and nutrition; Chair. Prof. I. P. SINGH; Dir Dr KUMUD KHANNA.

Janki Devi Memorial College: Sir Ganga Ram Hospital Marg, New Delhi 110060; tel. (11) 25787754; e-mail jdmcollege@hotmail.com; internet jdm.du.ac.in; f. 1959; depts of commerce, economics, English, family and child welfare, Hindi, history, mathematics, music, philosophy, physical education, political science, Sanskrit, sociology; library of 100,000 vols, 82 journals; 2,000 students; 100 teachers; Prin. Dr INDU ANAND.

Jesus and Mary College: Chankayapuri, New Delhi 110021; tel. (11) 26110041; e-mail info@jmc.ac.in; internet www.jmc.ac.in; f. 1968; library of 50,000 vols; 2,500 students; Prin. Dr Sis. MARINA JOHN.

Kalindi College: E Patel Nagar, New Delhi 110008; tel. (11) 25787604; e-mail kalindisampark.du@gmail.com; internet www.kalindicollege.org; f. 1967; depts of chemistry, computer science, commerce, economics, English, geography, Hindi, journalism, mathematics, music, political science, physical education, physics, Sanskrit, zoology and botany; library of 69,739 vols; 100 teachers; 2,000 students; Chair. SANJAY K. JHA; Prin. Dr ANULA MAURYA.

Kamla Nehru College: August Kranti Marg, New Delhi 110049; tel. (11) 26494881; e-mail kamla.nehru_du@hotmail.com; internet kamalanehrucollege.org/knc; f. 1964 as Govt College for Women, present name 1972; depts of commerce, economics, English, geography, Hindi, history, journalism, mathematics, philosophy, physical education, Punjabi, political science, psychology, Sanskrit, sociology; Prin. Dr MINOTI CHATTERJEE.

Lady Irwin College: New Delhi; e-mail ladyirwincrc@yahoo.in; internet www.ladyirwin.edu.in; f. 1950.

Lady Shri Ram College for Women: New Delhi; e-mail lsrc@lsr.edu.in; internet lsr.edu.in; f. 1956.

Lakshmibai College: Delhi; e-mail lakshmibaicollege@yahoo.co.in; internet lbc.du.ac.in; f. 1965.

Maitreyi College: New Delhi; e-mail maitreyi1967@yahoo.co.in; internet www.maitreyi.ac.in; f. 1967.

Mata Sundri College: New Delhi; e-mail matasundricollege@hotmail.com; internet ms.du.ac.in; f. 1967.

Moti Lal Nehru College: New Delhi; e-mail motilalnehru64@gmail.com; internet mlncdu.ac.in; f. 1964.

P.G.D.A.V. College: New Delhi; internet pgdavcollege.edu.in; f. 1957.

Rajdhani College: New Delhi; e-mail info@rajdhani.du.ac.in; internet rajdhani.du.ac.in; f. 1964.

Ramjas College: Delhi; e-mail principalramjascollege@gmail.com; internet www.ramjascollege.edu; f. 1917.

Sri Guru Gobind Singh College of Commerce: Pitampura, Delhi 110088; tel. (11) 27321109; e-mail sggscc@rediffmail.com; internet www.sggscc.ac.in; f. 1984; library of 29,000 vols, 50 journals; 65 teachers; 1,800 students; Chair. S. JOGINDER SINGH WALIA; Prin. Dr JATINDER BIR SINGH; publ. *Amrit, Annual Research Journal, Journal of Business Thought*.

St Stephen's College: Delhi; e-mail info@ststephens.edu; internet www.ststephens.edu; f. 1881.

Satyawati Co-educational College: Delhi; e-mail principal@satyawati.du.ac.in; internet satyawati.du.ac.in; f. 1972.

Shaheed Bhagat Singh College: New Delhi; e-mail sbscprincipal@gmail.com; internet www.sbsc.in; f. 1967.

Shivaji College: New Delhi; e-mail shivajicollege.ac@gmail.com; internet www.shivajicollege.ac.in; f. 1961.

Shri Aurobindo College: New Delhi; e-mail info@aurobindocollege.in; internet aurobindocollege.in; f. 1972.

Shri Guru Teg Bahadur Khalsa College: Delhi; internet www.sgtbkhalsadu.ac.in; f. 1951.

Shri Ram College of Commerce: Delhi; internet www.srcc.edu; f. 1926.

Shyam Lal College: Delhi; e-mail principal@shyamlal.du.ac.in; internet www.shyamlal.du.ac.in; f. 1964.

Shyama Prasad Mukherjee College: New Delhi; e-mail syamaprasad@vsnl.net; internet www.syamaprasadcollege.ac.in; f. 1969.

Sri Venkateswara College: New Delhi; e-mail principal@svc.ac.in; internet www.svc.ac.in; f. 1961.

Swami Shardhanand College: Delhi; e-mail info@ssncollege.com; internet www.ssncollege.com; f. 1967.

Vivekanand Mahila College: Delhi; e-mail principal@vivekanandacollege.edu.in; internet www.vivekanandacollege.edu.in; f. 1970.

Zakir Hussain College: Delhi; e-mail zakirhusaindelhicollege@gmail.com; internet www.zakirhusaindelhicollege.in; f. 1948.

UNIVERSITY MAINTAINED COLLEGES

College of Vocational Studies: New Delhi; e-mail principal@cvsdu.com; internet www.cvsdu.com; f. 1972.

Deshbandhu College: Kalkaji, New Delhi; e-mail dbcollege.du@gmail.com; internet www.deshbandhucollege.ac.in; f. 1952.

Dyal Singh College: New Delhi; e-mail principal@dsc.du.ac.in; internet dsc.du.ac.in; f. 1959.

Kirori Mal College: Delhi; e-mail info@kmcollege.ac.in; internet www.kmcollege.ac.in; f. 1954.

Miranda House for Women: Delhi; e-mail mhouse@ndf.vsnl.net.in; internet www.mirandahouse.ac.in; f. 1948.

School of Correspondence Courses and Continuing Education: Delhi; internet sol.du.ac.in; f. 1962.

University College of Medical Sciences: Delhi; tel. (11) 22582106; e-mail principal@ucms.ac.in; internet www.ucms.ac.in; f. 1971.

Vallabhbhai Patel Chest Institute: see under Research Institutes.

GOVERNMENT MAINTAINED COLLEGES

Ayurvedic and Unani Tabbia College: New Delhi; e-mail pmstibbiacollege@rediff.com; f. 1974.

College of Art: 20-22, Tilak Marg, New Delhi 110001; e-mail proca.delhi@nic.in; internet www.colart.delhigovt.nic.in; f. 1972.

College of Pharmacy: New Delhi; f. 1971.

Delhi College of Engineering: Kashmeri Gate, Delhi 6; f. 1959.

Delhi Institute of Technology: Delhi; f. 1983.

Lady Hardinge Medical College: New Delhi; e-mail dean_medical@du.ac.in; f. 1949.

Maulana Azad Medical College: New Delhi; e-mail mamcregistrar@gmail.com; internet www.mamc.ac.in; f. 1958.

Rajkumari Amrit Kaur College of Nursing: Lajpat Nagar, Part 4, New Delhi 110024; e-mail principal@rakcon.com; internet rakcon.com; f. 1946.

ATTACHED RESEARCH CENTRES

Agricultural Economics Research Centre: tel. (11) 27667588; Dir P. S. VASHISHTHA.

Centre for Environmental Management of Degraded Ecosystem: tel. (11) 27662402; Dir Prof. INDERJIT.

Centre for Interdisciplinary Studies of Mountain and Hill Environment (CISMHE): e-mail info@cismhe.org; f. 1990; Dir Dr V. KUMAR.

Developing Countries Research Centre (DCRC): tel. (11) 27666281; e-mail dcrc@dcrcdu.org; internet www.dcrcdu.org; f. 1993; Dir Prof. M. MOHANTY.

Dr B. R. Ambedkar Centre for Biomedical Research (ACBR): tel. (11) 27667151; Dir Prof. V. BRAHMACHARI.

Women's Study Development Centre: tel. (11) 27667151; e-mail office@wsdc.du.ac.in; f. 1987; Dir Prof. V. CHATURVEDI

UNIVERSITY OF HYDERABAD

Central University PO, Hyderabad 500046, Andhra Pradesh
Telephone: (40) 23132102
E-mail: yakkala@uohyd.ernet.in
Internet: www.uohyd.ac.in

Founded 1974
State control
Language of instruction: English
Academic year: July to April

Chief Rector: HE GOV. OF ANDHRA PRADESH
Chancellor: R. CHIDAMBARAM
Vice-Chancellor: Prof. S. E. HASNAIN
Pro-Vice-Chancellor: Prof. V. KANNAN
Registrar: Dr PRAKASH SARANGI
Public Relations Officer: A. J. THOMAS
Controller of Examinations: Dr V. RAO
Librarian: Dr M. K. RAO

Library of 257,000 vols
Number of teachers: 200
Number of students: 2,000

DEANS

School of Chemistry: Prof. M. PERIASAMY
School of Engineering Sciences and Technology: Prof. A. T. BHATNAGAR
School of Humanities: M. G. RAMANAN
School of Life Sciences: Prof. A. S. RAGHAVENDRA
School of Management Studies: Prof. V. V. RAMANA
School of Mathematics and Computer and Information Sciences: Prof. T. AMARANATH
School of Medical Sciences: Prof. M. RAMANADHAM
School of Performing Arts, Fine Arts and Communication: Prof. V. PAVARALA
School of Physics: Prof. V. SRIVASTAVA
School of Social Sciences: Prof. E. HARIBABU

UNIVERSITY OF JAMMU

Baba Sahib Ambedkar Rd, Jammu (Tawi) 180006, Jammu and Kashmir
Telephone: (191) 2431365
E-mail: nodalpoint@jammuuniversity.in
Internet: www.jammuuniversity.in

Founded 1969
State control
Language of instruction: Dogri, English, Hindi, Punjabi, Sanskrit, Urdu
Academic year: July to March

Chancellor: HE GOV. OF JAMMU AND KASHMIR
Vice-Chancellor: Prof. VARUN SAHNI
Registrar: Dr P. S. PATHANIA
Librarian: Prof. VERINDER GUPTA (acting)

Library of 350,000 vols, 250 periodicals
Number of teachers: 259
Number of students: 33,453

Publications: *Distance Education Journal*, *Social Sciences and Arts Journal*

DEANS

Faculty of Arts: Prof. ARCHANA KESAR
Faculty of Business Studies: Prof. R. D. SHARMA
Faculty of Education: Prof. LOKESH VERMA
Faculty of Law: Prof. V. P. MANGOTRA
Faculty of Life Sciences: Prof. ANIMA LANGER
Faculty of Mathematical Science: Prof. SOM DUTT
Faculty of Research Studies: Prof. RAJIVE GUPTA
Faculty of Sciences: Prof. RAJIVE GUPTA
Faculty of Social Sciences: Prof. JIGAR MOHD.

PROFESSORS

AIMA, A., Management Studies
ANAND, V. K., Botany
BADYAL, S. K., Physics and Electronics
BANDHU, D., Distance Education
BHAT, B. L., Economics
CHARAK, P., English
CHOUDHARY, R., Political Science
DHAR, B. L., Geology
DHOTRA, J. R., Management Studies
DUTTA, S. P., Environmental Science
GANAI, N. A., Law
GOHIL, R. N., Botany
GUPTA, N., Hindi
GUPTA, R., Chemistry
GUPTA, R., Economics
GUPTA, S. C., Zoology
GUPTA, S. P., Commerce
GUPTA, V., Dogri
GUPTA, V. K., Physics and Electronics
HAMAL, I. A., Botany
JYOTI, M. K., Zoology
KAHN, S. R., Psychology
KALSOTRA, B. L., Chemistry
KAUR, K., Political Science
KESAR, A., Dogri Studies
KHOSA, S. K., Physics and Electronics
KOMAL, B. S., Mathematics
KOUL, G. L., Computer Science
KUMAR, R., Hindi
LANGER, A., Botany
MAGOTRA, L. K., Physics and Electronics
MAGOTRA, V. P., Law
MALHAN, I. V., Library Science
MANDOKA, R., English
MASOODI, G. S., Law
MOHD, J., History
OM, H., History
PANDA, J. R., Sociology
PARIHAR, L., Law
PRASAD, G. V. R., Geology
RANA, M. R., Management Studies
RAZDAN, K. B., English
SEHGAL, B. P. S., Law
SHARMA, I. B., Chemistry
SHARMA, K., Management Studies
SHARMA, N. R., Education
SHARMA, O. P., Economics
SHARMA, R. D., Commerce
SHARMA, R. L., Chemistry
SHARMA, S. K., Law
SIDDIQUI, K. H., Urdu
SINGH, A. P., Mathematics
SINGH, G., Computer Science
SINGH, G., Geography
SINGH, S., Law
SUDAN, C. S., Geology
SUMBLI, K., Education
SURI, S. P., Education
TIWARI, R. J., Statistics
VERMA, L., Education
WADAN, D. S., Punjabi
WAKHLU, A. K., Botany
WANGOO, C. L., Mathematics

UNIVERSITY OF KALYANI

Kalyani, Nadia 741235, West Bengal
Telephone: (33) 25828220
E-mail: vckalyani@klyuniv.ac.in
Internet: www.klyuniv.ac.in

Founded 1960
State control
Language of instruction: English
Academic year: June to May

Chancellor: HE GOV. OF WEST BENGAL
Vice-Chancellor: Prof. ALOK KUMAR BANERJEE
Registrar: UTPAL BATTACHARYYA
Controller of Examinations: Dr BIMALENDU BISWAS (acting)
Dean of Student Welfare: Dr ASIT KUMAR DAS
Deputy Librarian: Dr ASITAVA DAS

Library of 154,973 vols, 102 journals
Number of teachers: 217
Number of students: 4,000

DEANS

Faculty of Arts and Commerce: Prof. ASHOK SEN GUPTA
Faculty of Education: Dr SUBHALAKSHMI NANDI
Faculty of Engineering, Technology and Management: Dr JYOTSNA KUMAR MANDAL
Faculty of Science: Prof. SHITAL KUMAR CHATTOPADHYAY

PROFESSORS

Bengali (tel. (33) 25828750 ext. 278):
BANERJEE, R.
CHOUDHURI, D.
GHATAK, K.
GHATAK, K. S.
SHAW, R.

Biochemistry and Biophysics (tel. (33) 25828750 ext. 293):
BHATTACHARYYA, D. K.
ROY, P. K.

Botany (tel. (33) 25828378 ext. 317):
BHATTACHARYYA, S.
BISWAS, A. K.
CHAUDHURI, S.
GHOSH, P. D.
SEN, T.

Chemistry (tel. (33) 25828750 ext. 305):
DEY, K.
GUHA, A.
LAHIRI, S. C.
MAJUMDER, K. C.
MAJUMDER, M. N.
MUKHERJEE, J.
SARKAR, A. R.

Commerce (tel. (33) 25828750 ext. 286):
BHATTACHARYYA, P. K.
KONAR, D. N.
MAJHI, M. M.

Ecology:
SANTRA, S. C.

Economics (tel. (33) 25828750 ext. 288):
BHATTACHARYYA, R. N.
DUTTA, M.
GHOSH, B.
PAL, D. P.

Education (tel. (33) 25828348):
BASU, M. K.

English (tel. (33) 25828750 ext. 276):
BHATTACHARYYA, D. P.
CHAKRABORTY, B.
DAS, N.

DEB, P. K.

Folklore (tel. (33) 25828750 ext. 271):

CHAKRABORTY, B. K.

Mathematics (tel. (33) 25828750 ext. 310):

BASU, M.
CHAKRABORTY, H.
DAS, A. G.
DEY, U. C.
KONAR, A.
MUKHERJEE, S.
SANYAL, D. C.
SENGUPTA, P. R.

Physical Education (tel. (33) 25820184 ext. 273):

BANERJEE, A. K.
BHOWMICK, S.
GHOSH, S. R.

Physics (tel. (33) 25820184):

BHATTACHARYYA, A. B.
BISWAS, S.
CHAUDHURI, S.
DASGUPTA, P.
DEB, S. K.
ROY, A. C.
ROY, S.
RUDRA, P.

Political Science (tel. (33) 25828750 ext. 284):

MUKHOPADHYAY, A.

Sociology (tel. (33) 25828750 ext. 279):

DASGUPTA, H.
DASGUPTA, S. K.
MANNA, S.

Statistics (tel. (33) 25828750 ext. 295):

DAS, P.
MITRA, T. K.
PANDA, R. N.

Zoology (tel. (33) 25828750 ext. 315):

BHATTACHARYYA, D. K.
CHAKRABORTY, S.
DEY, N. C.
HALDER, D. P.
JANA, B. B.
KHUDA BAX, A. R.
KONAR, S. K.
KUNDU, S.
MANNA, C. K.
MUKHERJEE, D. K.
SAHU, C. R.

UNIVERSITY OF KASHMIR

Hazratbal, Srinagar 190006, Jammu and Kashmir
Telephone: (194) 2420078
E-mail: info@kashmiruniversity.ac.in
Internet: www.kashmiruniversity.ac.in

Founded 1948, present status 1969
State control
Academic year: March to December

Chancellor: HE GOV. OF JAMMU AND KASHMIR
Vice-Chancellor: Prof. Dr TALAT AHMAD
Registrar: Prof. S. FAYAZ AHMAD
Controller of Examinations: Prof. A. S. BHAT
Dean of Academic Affairs: Prof. ALI MOHAMMAD SHAH
Dean of College Devt Ccl: Prof. MUSHTAQ AHMAD KAW
Dean of Student Welfare: Prof. NELOFAR KHAN
Librarian: REYAZ RUFAI

Library of 631,217 vols, 297 journals, 363 MSS
Number of teachers: 280
Number of students: 30,000 (incl. affiliated colleges)

Publication: *Journal of Himalayan Ecology and Sustainable Development*

DEANS

Faculty of Applied Sciences and Technology: Prof. NISAR AHMAD SHAH
Faculty of Arts: Prof. N. A. MALIK
Faculty of Biological Sciences: Dr G. M. SHAH
Faculty of Commerce and Management Studies: Prof. SHABIR AHMAD BHAT
Faculty of Dentistry: Prof. RIYAZ FAROOQ
Faculty of Education: Prof. M. A. KHAN
Faculty of Engineering: Prof. N. A. SHAH
Faculty of Law: Prof. LATEEF AHMAD WANI
Faculty of Medicine: Prof. QAZI MASOOD
Faculty of Music and Fine Arts: Prof. A. AZIZ UL AUZEEM (acting)
Faculty of Oriental Learning: Prof. MANZOOR AHMAD KHAN
Faculty of Physical and Material Sciences: Prof. S. JAVEID
Faculty of Social Sciences: Prof. M. ASHRAF WANI

PROFESSORS

ABDUL AZIZ, Mathematics
ALVI, W. A., Library and Information Science
AZURDAH, M. Z., Urdu
BABA, N. A., Political Science
BHAT, A. S., Law
BHAT, G. M., Economics
BHAT, M. I., Geology
BHAT, R. C., Zoology
CHANNA, A., Zoology
CHESTI, M. Z., Zoology
DABLA, B. A., Sociology
DHAR, R. L., Zoology
DHAR, T. N., English
DOST, M., Economics
FAROOQ, A., Physics
JAMWAL, K. S., Physics
JAVAID, A. Q., Urdu
KAW, M. A., Central Asian Studies
KHAN, A. H., Distance Education
KHAN, A. M., Central Asian Studies
KHAN, A. R., Zoology
KHAN, B. A., Economics
KHAN, M. I., History
KURSHID, A., Management Studies
LONE, M. S., Kashmiri
MALIK, G. M., Education
MALIK, G. R., English
MALIK, N. A., Urdu
MASOODI, M. M., Persian
MATTOO, A. M., Central Asian Studies
MATTOO, A. R., Management Studies
MIR, A. A., Law
MIR, G. Q., Law
MIR, M., Law
MIR, M. A., Law
MUNSHI, A. H., Botany
MUZAMER, A. M., Urdu
NADEEM, N. A., Education
NIAZMAND, M. S., Persian
NISAR, A., Economics
PEER, M. A., Computer Science
PUNJABI, R., Distance Education
QUADRI, S. M. A., Law
QURESHI, A. W., Economics
QURESHI, M. A., Chemistry
RAFIQUI, A. Q., History
RAIS, A., Geography
RATHER, A. R., Education
SAPRU, B. L., Botany
SHAH, A. M., Environmental Services
SHAH, A. M., Management Studies
SHAH, G. M., Zoology
SHAH, N. A., Electronics
SIKANDAR, F., Botany
SOFI, M. A., Mathematics
SYED, F. A., Commerce
TAK, A. H., English
TANTRAY, G. N., Centre of Adult Continuing Education and Extension
WAFAI, B. A., Botany
WANI, M. A., History

UNIVERSITY OF KERALA

Thiruvananthapuram 695034, Kerala
Telephone: (471) 2305738
E-mail: ku.release@gmail.com
Internet: www.keralauniversity.ac.in

Founded 1937
State control
Language of instruction: English
Academic year: June to May

Chancellor: HE GOV. OF KERALA
Pro-Chancellor: Hon. MIN. FOR EDUCATION AND CULTURE, GOVT OF KERALA
Vice-Chancellor: Dr A. JAYAKRISHNAN
Pro-Vice-Chancellor: Dr J. PRABHASH
Registrar: P. RAGHAVAN (acting)
Controller of Examinations: Dr M. JAYAPRAKAS (acting)
Dir of College Devt Ccl: Dr M. JAYAPRAKASH
Dir of Planning and Devt: Dr J. RAJAN (acting)
Public Relations Officer: S. D. PRINS
Librarian: J. USHA

Library of 280,804 vols
Number of teachers: 5,799
Number of students: 123,310

Publications: *International Journal of Kerala Studies, Journal of Indian History*

DEANS

Faculty of Applied Sciences: Prof. Dr V. P. MAHADEVAN PILLAI
Faculty of Arts: Prof. Dr MAYA DUTT
Faculty of Ayurveda: Dr A. NALINAKSHAN
Faculty of Commerce: Dr K. SASI. KUMAR
Faculty of Dentistry: Dr N. O. VARGHESE
Faculty of Education: Dr M. S. GEETHA
Faculty of Engineering and Technology: Dr B. ANIL
Faculty of Fine Arts: Dr P. VENUGOPALAN
Faculty of Homoeopathy: Dr V. M. JANAKIKKUTTY
Faculty of Law: Dr K. C. SUNNY
Faculty of Management Studies: Dr J. RAJAN
Faculty of Medicine: Dr K. S. CHANDRASEKHAR
Faculty of Oriental Studies: Dr C. R. PRASAD
Faculty of Physical Education: Dr USHA SUJITH NAIR
Faculty of Science: Dr ASHALATHA S. NAIR
Faculty of Social Sciences: Dr G. GOPAKUMAR

UNIVERSITY CENTRES

Centre for Adult Continuing Education and Extension (CACEE): tel. (471) 2302523; e-mail cacee@keralauniversity.edu; Dir Prof. B. VIJAYAKUMAR.

Centre for Bioinformatics: tel. (471) 2308759; e-mail sankar.achuth@gmail.com; internet www.cbi.keralauniversity.edu; f. 2005; library of 1,800 vols; Dir Dr ACHUTHSANKAR S. NAIR.

Centre for Canadian Studies: tel. (471) 2306422; e-mail ccskerala@gmail.com; internet www.canadastukeralauniv.edu.in; f. 1991; Dir Dr JAMEELA BEGUM.

Centre for Convergence Media Studies: tel. (471) 2301045; Dir M. VIJAYAKUMAR.

Centre for Gandhian Studies: f. 1970; Dir Dr J. M. RAHIM.

Centre for Marine Diversity: tel. (471) 2412434; e-mail k.padmakumar@vsnl.com; Dir Dr K. PADMAKUMAR.

Centre for Vedanta Studies: f. 1984; Dir Dr K. MAHESWARAN NAIR.

Centre for Women's Studies: tel. (471) 2441515; f. 1986; Dir Dr G. S. JAYASREE.

International Centre for Kerala Studies: tel. (471) 2412168; f. 1988; library of 10,000 vols; Dir Dr N. SAM.

Population Research Centre: tel. (471) 418796; e-mail prc.kerala@nic.in; f. 1983; Dir Dr K. KRISHNAKUMARI.

Sree Narayana Study Centre for Social Change: tel. (471) 2418421; f. 1996; Dir Dr K. VIJAYAN.

Survey Research Centre: f. 1979; Dir C. P. SURESH.

University Observatory: tel. (471) 2322732; f. 1837; Dir Dr V. K. VAIDYAN.

V. K. Krishna Menon Study Centre for International Relations: tel. (471) 2418307; Dir Dr G. GOPAKUMAR

UNIVERSITY OF LUCKNOW

Badshah Bagh, Lucknow 2740086, Uttar Pradesh
Telephone: (522) 2740086
E-mail: info@lkouniv.ac.in
Internet: www.lkouniv.ac.in
Founded 1921
State control
Languages of instruction: English, Hindi
Academic year: July to April
Chancellor: HE GOV. OF UTTAR PRADESH
Vice-Chancellor: Prof. MANOJ K. MISHRA
Pro-Vice-Chancellor: Prof. U. N. DWIVEDI
Registrar: Dr G. P. TRIPATHI
Controller of Examinations: Prof. Y. TYAGI
Dean of Student Welfare: Prof. RAKESH CHANDRA
Hon. Librarian: Prof. NIRUPAMA AGARWAL
Library of 550,000 vols, 60,000 vols, 2,000 MSS
Number of teachers: 661
Number of students: 48,625

DEANS

Faculty of Architecture: NEHRU LAL
Faculty of Arts: Prof. A. K. SENGUPTA
Faculty of Commerce: Prof. VAISHAMPAYAN
Faculty of Education: SUBODH KUMAR
Faculty of Fine Arts: Dr RAJIV NAYAN
Faculty of Law: O. N. MISHRA
Faculty of Science: Prof. U. N. DWIVEDI

UNIVERSITY OF MADRAS

Chepauk, Chennai 600005, Tamil Nadu
Telephone: (44) 25399422
E-mail: vcoffice@unom.ac.in
Internet: www.unom.ac.in
Founded 1857
State control
Languages of instruction: English, Tamil
Academic year: July to April
Chancellor: HE GOV. OF TAMIL NADU
Pro-Chancellor: Hon. MIN. FOR EDUCATION
Vice-Chancellor: Prof. Dr G. THIRUVASAGAM
Registrar: Dr T. LEO ALEXANDER (acting)
Dean of Academic Affairs: Dr G. RAVINDRAN
Dean of College Devt Ccl: Dr M. R. SRINIVASAN (acting)
Dean of Research: Dr G. KOTESWARA PRASAD
Dean of Students Affairs: Dr P. T. KALAICHELVAN
Librarian: Dr R. VENGAN (acting)
Library of 506,295 vols
Number of students: 107,518
Publication: *Annals of Oriental Research*

DEANS

Faculty of Arts: Dr R. THANDAVAN
Faculty of Fine Arts: Dr N. RAMANATHAN
Faculty of Indian and Other Languages: Dr V. JAYADEVAN
Faculty of Law: Dr N. BALU
Faculty of Science: Dr D. LALITHA KUMARI
Faculty of Teaching: Dr D. RAJA GANESAN

UNIVERSITY OF MUMBAI

M. G. Rd, Fort, Mumbai 400032, Maharashtra
Telephone: (22) 22708700
E-mail: vc@fort.mu.ac.in
Internet: www.mu.ac.in
Founded 1857 as Univ. of Bombay, current name adopted 1996
State control
Language of instruction: English
Academic year: June to April (2 terms)
Chancellor: HE GOV. OF MAHARASHTRA
Vice-Chancellor: Dr RAJAN M. WELUKAR
Pro-Vice-Chancellor: (vacant)
Registrar: Dr M. S. KURHADE (acting)
Controller of Examinations: DINESH BHONDE
Librarian: Prof. VIJAYA RAJHAMA
Library of 699,321 vols, 12,000 periodicals, 15,000 MSS
Number of students: 262,350
Publications: *Journal of the University of Bombay, Prakrit and Pali, Sanskrit, University of Bombay Studies, University Economics Series, University Series in Monetary and International Economics, University Sociology Series*

DEANS

Faculty of Arts: Dr PRALHAD G. JOGDAND
Faculty of Commerce: Principal: Dr T. P. MADHU NAIR
Faculty of Fine Arts: (vacant)
Faculty of Law: (vacant)
Faculty of Science: Dr MADHURI KIRAN
Faculty of Technology: Dr SURESH KISANRAO UKARANDE

PROFESSORS

Faculty of Arts:
ABHEDI, R. S. A., Urdu
ANNAKUTY, V. K., German Literature and Russian
BANDIVADEKAR, C. M., Comparative Literature
BHARADWAJ, M. A., Econometrics
BHARUCHA, N., Post-Colonial Literature
BHAT NAYAK, V., Mathematics
BHONGLE, N., 20th-Century Indian Literature in English
BOKIT, S. V., Industrial Policy and Development Banking
BHOWMIK, S. K., Sociology
CHAWATHE, P. D., Graphs Theory
CORREA, R., Economics
DALVI, A. M. I., Urdu
DESHPANDE, J. V., Mathematics
DOSSAL, M., History
GIRI, R. D., Mathematics
GUHA, S. B., Geography
GUMMADI, N., General Economics
JADHAV, A. S., Geography
JANWA, H. L., Algebra
JOGDAND, P. G., Sociology
JOSHI, S. A., Philosophy
JOSHI, S. M., Statistical Inference
KAMATH, P. M., American Studies
KHOKLE, V. S., Socio-linguistics
KUMARESAN, S., Mathematics
LIMAYE, N. B., Mathematics
LUKMANI, V. M., English
MODY, N. B., Civics and Politics
MOHANTY, S. P., Social Demography
MOMIN, A. R., Cultural Anthropology
MUNGEKAR, B. I., Economics
NABAR, S. P., Statistics
NABAR, V., Indo-English Literature
NACHANE, D. N., Quantitative Economics
NADKARNI, M. G., Mathematics
NEMADE, B. V., Comparative Literature
PETHE, A. M., Economics
PHADKE, V. S., Geography
RAJHANSA, V. P., Reference Service
RAO, M. J. M., General Economics
SABNIS, R. S., Monetary and Industrial Economics
SANDESARA, J. C., Industrial Economics
SANE, S. S., Mathematics
SAWANT, S. D., Agricultural Economics
SEETA PRABHU, K., Economics
SEN, M., Experimental Psychology
SIRDESHPANDE, M. R., French
SRIRAMAN, S., Transport Economics
TIKEKAR, A. C., Library Science
TIWARI, R., Hindi
VAIDYA, S. S., Marathi
VANAJA, N., Algebra
VASANT KARNIK, A., Economics
VASANTKUMAR, T., Kannada Literature
VYAS, V. S., Music

Faculty of Commerce:
ANAGOL, M., Banking
GHOSH, P. K., Personnel Management
IYER, V. R., Management
MANERIKAR, V. V., Research Methodology
MURTHY, G. N., Finance and Accounts
SANTANAM, H., Operational Research

Faculty of Law:
KHODIE, N., Mercantile Law
RAO, M., Law
WARKE, P. C., Law

Faculty of Science:
BAGADE, U. S., Life Sciences
FULEKAR, M. H., Life Sciences
GAJBHIYE, N. S., Physics
GOGAVALE, S. V., Experimental Electronic and Plasma Physics
HOSANGADI, B. D., Organic Chemistry
JOSHI, V. N., Computer Science
KULKARNI, A. R., Plant Sciences
NARAYANAN, P., Life Sciences
NARSALE, A. M., Physics
PATEL, S. B., Experimental Nuclear Physics
PRATAP, R., Electronics
RANGWALA, A. A., Theoretical Physics
SHETHNA, Y. I., Life Sciences
SIVAKAMI, S., Life Sciences
VASANTHAKUMAR, T., Kannada

Faculty of Technology:
AKAMANCHI, K. G., Pharmaceutical Chemistry
ATHAWALE, V. D., Chemistry
BHAT, N. V., Physics
CHANDALIA, S. B., Chemical Engineering
DIXIT, S. G., Physics
JOSHI, J. B., Chemical Engineering
KALE, D. D., Polymer Technology
KULKARNI, P. R., Food Science and Technology
KULKARNI, V. M., Medicinal Chemistry
LOKHANDE, H. T., Fibre Science
MALSHE, V. C., Paint Technology
MASHRAQUI, S. H., Chemistry
MHASKAR, R. D., Chemical Engineering
NYAYADHISH, V. B., Mathematics
PAI, J. S., Biochemical Engineering
PANGARKAR, V. G., Chemical Engineering
RAJADYAKSHA, R. A., Physical Chemistry
RAO, H. M., Engineering
SESHADRI, S., Dyestuffs Technology
SHARMA, M. M., Chemical Engineering
SHENAY, V. A., Textile Chemistry
SUBRAMANIAN, V. V. R., Oil Technology
TELI, M. D., Fibre Science
TIWARI, K. K., Chemical Engineering
TUNGARE, S. A., Architecture
VARADARAJAN, T. S., Applied Physics
VENKATESEN, T. K., Oil Chemistry
YADAV, G. D., Chemical Engineering

UNIVERSITY OF MYSORE

Crawford Hall, Mysore 570006, Karnataka
Telephone: (821) 2419361
E-mail: registrar@uni-mysore.ac.in
Internet: www.uni-mysore.ac.in
Founded 1916
State control
Languages of instruction: English, Kannada
Academic year: June to March (2 terms)
Chancellor: HE GOV. OF KARNATAKA

Vice-Chancellor: Prof. Dr V. G. TALAWAR (acting)
Registrar: Prof. P. S. NAIK
Dir of College Devt Ccl: Prof. K. SRIHARI
Dir of Students Welfare: D. K. SRINIVASA
Librarian: Dr C. P. RAMSESH

Library of 800,000 vols, 2,400 journals
Number of students: 56,500

DEANS

Faculty of Arts: Prof. S. MASOOD SIRAJ
Faculty of Commerce: Prof. B. R. ANANTHAN
Faculty of Education: Prof. K. YESHODHARA
Faculty of Engineering: Prof. CHENNA VENKATESH
Faculty of Law: Dr H. K. NAGARAJA
Faculty of Medicine: Dr KAMALA
Faculty of Science and Technology: Prof. MEWA SINGH

UNIVERSITY COLLEGES

College of Fine Arts for Women: Prin. Dr C. BHATT.

Maharaja's College: e-mail info@mcm.ac.in; Prin. Dr C. SIDDARAJU.

University College of Physical Education: Prin. Dr M. CHANDRAKUMAR.

University Evening College: Prin. SARVAMANGALA BAI.

Yuvaraja's College: Prin. SUMINTHRA BAI

UNIVERSITY OF NORTH BENGAL

PO North Bengal Univ., Raja Rammohunpur, Darjeeling 734430, West Bengal
Telephone: (353) 2582099
E-mail: regnbu@sancharnet.in
Internet: www.nbu.ac.in

Founded 1962
State control
Academic year: July to June

Chancellor: HE GOV. OF WEST BENGAL
Vice-Chancellor: Prof. ARUNABHA BASUMAJUMDAR
Registrar: Dr DILIP K. SARKAR
Librarian: M. MANDAL

Library of 234,835 vols, 700 periodicals
Number of teachers: 154
Number of students: 100,602

DEANS

Faculty of Arts, Commerce and Law: Prof. R. GHOSH
Faculty of Science: Prof. B. N. CHAKRABARTY

PROFESSORS

Arts, Commerce and Law:
BHADRA, R. K., Sociology
BHATTA, A., Bengali
BHATTACHARJEE, C., Philosophy
CHAKRABORTY, B. B., Philosophy
CHAKRABORTY, U., English
GHOSH, R., Philosophy
MONDAL, SK. R., Centre for Himalayan Studies
MUKHOPADHYAY, C., Economics
MUKHOPADHYAY, R. S., Sociology
ROY MOULIK, S. K., English
SAHU, R., Centre for Himalayan Studies
SENGUPTA, P. K., Political Science
SENGUPTA, P. R., Commerce
UPADHYAY, B. K., Nepali

Science:
BOSE, M. K., Mathematics
DAS, A. P., Botany
DASGUPTA, D., Physics
HAZRA, D. K., Chemistry
KARANJAI, S. B., Mathematics
MANNA, N. R., Computer Science and Applications
MUKHOPADHYAY, A., Zoology
NANDI, K. K., Mathematics
ROY, A., Chemistry
ROY, P. S., Chemistry
SAHA, S. K., Chemistry
SARKAR, P. K., Botany

UNIVERSITY OF PETROLEUM AND ENERGY STUDIES

PO Bidholi, Via-Prem Nagar, Dehradun 284007, Uttaranchal
Telephone: (135) 2776201
E-mail: info@upesindia.org
Internet: upes.ac.in

Founded 2003
Private control

Chancellor: Dr S. J. CHOPRA
Pres.: SANJAY KAUL
Vice-Chancellor: Dr PARAG DIWAN
Pro-Vice-Chancellor: Prof. G. C. TIWARI
Registrar: SANDEEP MEHTA

Number of teachers: 222
Number of students: 5,000

Publication: *UPES Journal*

DEANS

College of Engineering Studies: Dr SHRIHARI
College of Legal Studies: Dr R. H. GORANE
College of Management and Economic Studies: Dr ANIRBAN SENGUPTA

UNIVERSITY OF PUNE

Ganeshkhind Rd, Pune 411007, Maharashtra
Telephone: (20) 25696061
E-mail: regis@unipune.ac.in
Internet: www.unipune.ac.in

Founded 1948
State control
Languages of instruction: English (optional), Marathi
Academic year: June to March (2 terms)

Chancellor: HE GOV. OF MAHARASHTRA
Vice-Chancellor: Dr SANJAY CHAHANDE
Registrar: Dr MANIK LAXMANRAO JADHAV
Controller of Examination: Dr S. M. AHIRE
Librarian: Dr NEELA J. DESHPANDE

Library of 436,866 vols, 4,439 MSS
Number of teachers: 293
Number of students: 6,648 (univ.), 397,395 in affiliated colleges

DEANS

Faculty of Arts: Prof. SUDHAKER PANDEY
Faculty of Commerce: Dr J. S. UDHAV RAO
Faculty of Education: Prof. S. S. ARJUN RAO
Faculty of Engineering: Prof. K. G. KASHIRAM
Faculty of Law: Dr SHIEKH RASHEED
Faculty of Medicine: Dr C. P. DIGAMBAR
Faculty of Mental, Moral and Social Science: Dr B. G. LAKSHMAN
Faculty of Science: Dr M. K. CHANDRAKANT

ATTACHED INSTITUTES

Inter-University Centre for Astronomy and Astrophysics: tel. (20) 25604100; e-mail nkd@iucaa.ernet.in; internet www.iucaa.ernet.in; Dir AJIT K. KEMBHAVI.

National Centre for Cell Science: tel. (20) 25708000; Dir Dr SHEKHAR C. MANDE

UNIVERSITY OF RAJASTHAN

JLN Marg, Jaipur 302004, Rajasthan
Telephone: (141) 2708824
E-mail: info@uniraj.ernet.in
Internet: www.uniraj.ac.in

Founded 1947 as Univ. of Rajputana, present name 1956
State control
Languages of instruction: English, Hindi
Academic year: July to May (2 terms)

Chancellor: HE GOV. OF RAJASTHAN
Vice-Chancellor: Prof. B. L. SHARMA
Pro-Vice-Chancellor: (vacant)
Registrar: NISHKAM DIVAKAR
Controller of Examinations: P. L. RAIGAR
Librarian: Prof. PRADEEP BHATNAGAR

Library of 371,500 vols, 65,000 bound periodicals
Number of teachers: 575
Number of students: 175,000

DEANS

Faculty of Arts: Prof. SUDHA RAI
Faculty of Commerce: Prof. SOM DEO
Faculty of Education: Dr B. S. RATHORE
Faculty of Engineering and Technology: S. G. MODANI
Faculty of Fine Arts: Prof. SUMAN YADAV
Faculty of Law: Prof. MRIDUL SRIVASTAVA
Faculty of Management Studies: (vacant)
Faculty of Science: Prof. B. K. SHRIVASTAV
Faculty of Social Sciences: Prof. ASHA KAUSHIK

UNIVERSITY COLLEGES

Commerce College: e-mail commerce@uniraj.ernet.in; f. 1956.

Evening Law College: e-mail law2@uniraj.ernet.in.

Law College: e-mail law@uniraj.ernet.in.

Maharaja's College: e-mail maharaja@uniraj.ernet.in; f. 1944.

Maharani's College: e-mail info@maharanicollege.org; f. 1944.

Rajasthan College: e-mail rajasthan@uniraj.ernet.in; f. 1956

U. P. RAJARSHI TANDON OPEN UNIVERSITY

Shantipuram, Phaphamau, Allahabad 211013, Uttar Pradesh
Telephone: (532) 2447035
E-mail: uprtou@yahoo.co.in
Internet: www.uprtou.ac.in

Founded 1999

Schools of agriculture sciences, computer and information sciences, education, health sciences, humanities, management, science, social sciences; 5 regional centres, 400 study centres

Chancellor: HE GOV. OF UTTAR PRADESH
Vice-Chancellor: Prof. A. K. BAKHSHI
Registrar: Dr A. K. SINGH
Controller of Examination: Dr R. P. S. YADAV
Librarian: Dr T. N. DUBEY

Library of 14,069 vols

UTKAL UNIVERSITY

PO Vani Vihar, Bhubaneswar 751004, Orissa
Telephone: (674) 2581387
E-mail: admission@utkaluniversity.ac.in
Internet: www.utkaluniversity.ac.in

Founded 1943
State control
Languages of instruction: English, Oriya
Academic year: July to June

Chancellor: HE GOV. OF ORISSA
Vice-Chancellor: Prof. PRASANT KUMAR SAHOO
Registrar: Prof. D. N. JENA
Dir of Students Welfare: Prof. BRAHMANANDA PADHI
Controller of Examinations: Dr S. K. DAS
Chief Librarian: Dr P. K. MOHANTY (acting)

Library of 237,695 vols, 236 periodicals
Number of teachers: 8,521
Number of students: 200,000

DEANS

Faculty of Arts: Prof. K. M. PATRA
Faculty of Commerce: Dr GUNANIDHI SAHOO
Faculty of Education: M. DAS

Faculty of Engineering: Dr NILAKANTHA PATTANAIK
Faculty of Law: INDRAJIT RAY
Faculty of Medicine: Dr R. N. DASH
Faculty of Science: Dr P. K. JESTHI

CONSTITUENT COLLEGES

Madhusudan Law College: Cuttack; e-mail mslawcollege@rediffmail.com; internet mslawcollege.org; f. 1949; Prin. Dr D. P. KAR.

University Law College: Vani Vihar, Bhubaneswar 751004; e-mail univlawcollege@rediffmail.com; internet ulcbbsr.org; f. 1975; Prin. Dr P. K. PADHI

UTKAL UNIVERSITY OF CULTURE

Sardar Patel Hall Complex, Unit-II, Bhubaneshwar 751009, Orrisa
Telephone: (674) 2535484
E-mail: mail@uuc.ac.in
Internet: www.uuc.ac.in
Founded 1999
State control
Academic year: July to June
Schools of architecture and archaeology, culture studies, language and literature, occupational studies, Orissan studies, performing arts, visual arts; 38 affiliated colleges (2 govt, 36 private)
Chancellor: HE GOV. OF ORISSA
Vice-Chancellor: Prof. AMIYA KUMAR PATTANAYAK
Registrar and Acting Controller of Examinations: Dr SACHINDRA RAUL
Library of 3,000 vols

VARDHAMAN MAHAVEER OPEN UNIVERSITY

Rawatbatha Rd, Akhelgarh, Kota 324010, Rajasthan
Telephone: (744) 2471254
E-mail: reg@vmou.ac.in
Internet: vmou.ac.in
Founded 1987 as Kota Open Univ., current name adopted 2002
Depts of botany, commerce, computer science, economics, education, English, Hindi, history, Indian tradition and culture, journalism, law, library and information science, management, political science; regional centres in Ajmer, Bikaner, Jaipur, Jodhpur, Kota, Udaipur; 6 regional centres, 87 study centres
Chancellor: HE GOV. OF RAJASTHAN
Vice-Chancellor: Prof. NARESH DADHICH
Registrar: B. L. KOTHARI
Library: over 100,000 vols, 200 periodicals
Number of students: 35,000

VEER BAHADUR SINGH PURVANCHAL UNIVERSITY

Devkali Jasopur, Saraykhaja, Jaunpur 222001, Uttar Pradesh
Telephone: (5452) 252244
E-mail: registrar.vbspu@gmail.com
Internet: vbspu.ac.in
Founded 1987, fmrly Purvanchal Univ.
State control
Chancellor: HE GOV. OF UTTAR PRADESH
Vice-Chancellor: Prof. SUNDER LAL
Registrar: Dr B. L. ARYA
Dean of Students Welfare: Prof. RAMJEE LAL
Controller of Examinations: R. S. YADAV
Librarian: Prof. M. P. SINGH
Library of 95,000 vols, 350 journals
Number of students: 380,000 (incl. affiliated colleges)

DEANS

Faculty of Applied Social Science: Dr AJAI PRATAP SINGH
Faculty of Management Studeies: Dr MANAS PANDEY
Faculty of Science: Prof. D. D. DUBEY
U. N. S. Institute of Engineering: Dr ASHOK SRIVASTAVA

VEER KUNWAR SINGH UNIVERSITY

Ara 802301, Bihar
Telephone: (6182) 223559
E-mail: registrar@vksu-ara.org
Internet: www.vksu-ara.org
Founded 1992
State control
Academic year: June to May
Chancellor: HE GOV. OF BIHAR
Vice-Chancellor: Dr I. C. KUMAR
Registrar: Dr QAMAR AHSAN
Librarian: Dr J. P. SINGH

DEANS

Faculty of Commerce: Dr D. K. TIWARI
Faculty of Humanities: Dr R. P. RAI
Faculty of Science: Dr R. P. PANDEY
Faculty of Social Science: Dr GANDHIJEE RAI

VEER NARMAD SOUTH GUJARAT UNIVERSITY

Udhna–Magdalla Rd, Surat 395007, Gujarat
Telephone: (261) 2227141
E-mail: sgu@sgu.ernet.in
Internet: www.vnsgu.ac.in
Founded 1967 as South Gujarat Univ., current name adopted 2004
State control
Language of instruction: Gujarati
Academic year: June to March (2 terms)
Chancellor: HE GOV. OF GUJARAT
Vice-Chancellor: Dr DAKSHESH RASHIKLAL THAKAR
Pro-Vice-Chancellor: (vacant)
Registrar: J. R. MEHTA
Librarian: (vacant)
Library of 178,160 vols, 243 periodicals
Number of teachers: 105 (univ. postgraduate dept)
Number of students: 3,794 (univ. postgraduate dept)

DEANS

Faculty of Arts: G. P. SANADHYA
Faculty of Commerce: J. M. NAIK
Faculty of Education: Dr K. V. DESAI
Faculty of Law: Dr V. B. DESAI
Faculty of Management: Dr S. K. VAJPEYEE
Faculty of Medicine: Dr S. KUMAR
Faculty of Rural Studies: Dr V. J. SOMANI
Faculty of Science: N. B. MAHIDA

VIDYASAGAR UNIVERSITY

PO Vidyasagar Univ., Midnapore 721102, West Bengal
Telephone: (32) 22275297
E-mail: registrar@vidyasagar.ac.in
Internet: www.vidyasagar.ac.in
Founded 1981
State control
Languages of instruction: English, Bengali, Hindi
Academic year: July to June
Chancellor: HE GOV. OF WEST BENGAL
Vice-Chancellor: Prof. RANJAN CHAKRABARTI
Registrar: Dr RANAJIT DHAR
Controller of Examinations: Dr NIRANJAN KUMAR MANDAL
Dean of Students Welfare: (vacant)
Librarian: AMIYA SARKAR (acting)
Library of 103,000 vols, 135 periodicals, 140 ebooks, 6,000 ejournals
Number of teachers: 135
Number of students: 38,500 (incl. affiliated colleges)
Publications: *Journal of Biological Sciences* (1 a year), *Journal of Commerce* (1 a year), *Journal of Library and Information Science* (1 a year), *Journal of Philosophy and the Life World* (1 a year), *Journal of Physical Sciences* (1 a year), *Politics and Society* (1 a year)

DEANS

Faculty of Arts and Commerce: (vacant)
Faculty of Science: (vacant)

PROFESSORS

BANERJEE, T. K., Political Science with Rural Administration
BATTACHARYA, T., Zoology
KHAN, L. A., Bengali
MAHAPATRA, P. K., Physics
MAITI, M., Applied Mathematics
MISRA, P. K., Philosophy and Life-World
MUKHOPADHAYA, S., Computer Science and Electronics
PATI, B. R., Microbiology
RANJAN DE, B., Chemistry and Chemical Technology
SAHA, S. C., Electronics

VIKRAM UNIVERSITY, UJJAIN

University Rd, Ujjain 456010, Madhya Pradesh
Telephone: (734) 2514270
E-mail: vcvikramujn@gmail.com
Internet: www.vikramuniv.net
Founded 1957
State control
Languages of instruction: English, Hindi
Academic year: July to June
Chancellor: HE GOV. OF MADHYA PRADESH
Vice-Chancellor: Dr T. R. THAPAK
Registrar: Dr B. L. BUNKAR
Dean of Students Welfare: Dr RAKESH DHAND
Dir for College Devt Ccl: Dr GOPAL UPADHYAY
Librarian: Dr KAUSHIK BOSE (acting)
Library of 160,856 vols, 4,800 vols of periodicals
Number of students: 31,472

DEANS

Faculty of Arts: Dr N. OBEROI
Faculty of Commerce: Dr R. SONI
Faculty of Education: Dr N. SHINDE
Faculty of Information Technology: Dr S. K. GHOSH
Faculty of Life Science: Dr S. K. BILLORE
Faculty of Management: Dr N. RAO
Faculty of Physical Science: Prof. V. W. BHAGWAT
Faculty of Social Science: Dr S. PANDE

VINOBA BHAVE UNIVERSITY

Hazaribag 825301, Jharkhand
Telephone: (6546) 294003
E-mail: info@vbuhazaribag.org
Internet: vbu.co.in
Founded 1992
State control
Academic year: July to May
Chancellor: HE GOV. OF JHARKHAND
Vice-Chancellor: Dr RAVINDRA NATH BHAGAT
Pro-Vice-Chancellor: Prof. Dr ANJANI KUMAR SRIVASTAVA
Registrar: Dr ENAM NABI SIDDIQUI
Dean of Students Wefare: Dr MARGARET LAKRA
Controller of Examinations: Dr A. M. SIDDIQUI
Deputy Librarian: P. K. SINGH

DEANS

Faculty of Ayurveda: Dr H. P. PANDEY
Faculty of Commerce: Dr S. N. SINGH
Faculty of Education: Dr K. SINGH
Faculty of Engineering: Dr S. K. SINGH
Faculty of Homeopathy: Dr K. SINGH
Faculty of Humanities: Dr GYANESHWAR KUMAR
Faculty of Law: Dr D. K. SHARMA
Faculty of Medicine: Dr S. N. BAIROLIYA
Faculty of Science: Dr S. B. CHOWDHARY
Faculty of Social Sciences: Dr C. P. SHARMA

VISVA—BHARATI

Santiniketan, Birbhum 731235, West Bengal
Telephone: (3463) 261531
E-mail: registrar@visva-bharati.ac.in
Internet: www.visva-bharati.ac.in

Founded 1951
State control
Languages of instruction: Bengali, English
Academic year: July to April (3 terms)

Institutes of agricultural science, dance, drama and music, education, fine arts, humanities and social sciences, rural reconstruction, science, Tagore studies and research; 15 centres

Chancellor: Hon. PRIME MIN. OF INDIA
Rector: HE GOV. OF WEST BENGAL
Vice-Chancellor: Prof. SUSHANTA DATTAGUPTA
Pro-Vice-Chancellor: Prof. UDAYA NARAYANA SINGH
Registrar: Dr MANI MUKUT MITRA
Librarian: Prof. P. JASH (acting)

Library of 750,000 vols
Number of teachers: 516
Number of students: 6,500

Publications: *Journal of Philosophy*, *Visva-Bharati Patrika* (4 a year)

VISVESVARAYA TECHNOLOGICAL UNIVERSITY

Santhibastawad Rd, Machhe, Belgaum 590018, Karnataka
Telephone: (831) 2498100
E-mail: registrar@vtu.ac.in
Internet: www.vtu.ac.in

Founded 1994
State control
Academic year: August to January, February to July (2 semesters)

Courses in chemical engineering, civil engineering, computer science engineering, electrical engineering, electronics engineering, industrial production engineering, mechanical engineering, textile engineering; 175 affiliated colleges and regional centres in Bangalore, Belgaum, Gulbarga and Mysore

Chancellor: HE GOV OF KARNATAKA
Pro-Chancellor: MIN. FOR HIGHER EDUCATION, GOVT OF KARNATAKA
Vice-Chancellor: Dr H. MAHESHAPPA
Registrar: Prof. S. A. KORI
Number of students: 79,766.

ATTACHED CENTRES

Bosch Rexroth Centre: GSSS Institute of Eng. and Tech., Metagalli Industrial Area, Kasaba Hobli, K. R. S. Rd, Mysore, Karnataka; e-mail vtubosch@vtu.ac.in.

E-Learning Centre: SJCE STEP SEED Bldg, SJCE Campus, Mysore, 570006; e-mail elearning@vtu.ac.in; internet elearning.vtu.ac.in

WB NATIONAL UNIVERSITY OF JURIDICAL SCIENCES

Dr Ambedkar Bhavan, 12 LB Block, Sector III, Salt Lake City, Kolkata 700098, West Bengal
Telephone: (33) 23357379
E-mail: nujs@vsnl.com
Internet: www.nujs.edu

Founded 1999
State control

Schools of criminal justice and administration, economic and business laws, legal practice and development, private laws and comparative jurisprudence, public law and governance, social sciences, technology, law and development; centres for consumer protection and welfare, human rights and citizenship studies, studies in World Trade Organization laws, studies for women and law

Chancellor: CHIEF JUSTICE OF INDIA
Vice-Chancellor: Prof. Dr MAHENDRA P. SINGH
Registrar: Dr SURAJIT C. MUKHOPADHYAY
Librarian: Dr V. K. THOMAS

Library of 100,000 vols, 124 journals

Publications: *Journal of Indian Law and Society* (2 a year), *NUJS Law Review* (4 a year)

WEST BENGAL UNIVERSITY OF ANIMAL AND FISHERY SCIENCES

37 and 68 Kshudiram Bose Sarani, Kolkata 700037, West Bengal
Telephone: (33) 25563450
Internet: wbuafscl.ac.in

Founded 1995
State control
Academic year: July to June

Chancellor: HE GOV. OF WEST BENGAL
Vice-Chancellor: Prof. C. S. CHAKRABARTI
Registrar: Dr DIPAL KUMAR DE (acting)
Controller of Examination: Prof. NISHITH RANJAN PRASHAN (acting)
Librarian: C. GUPTA (acting)

Library of 17,000 vols, 80 journals

DEANS

Faculty of Dairy Technology: Prof. MALOY SANYAL (acting)
Faculty of Fishery Sciences: Prof. KUSHAN CH. DORA (acting)
Faculty of Veterinary and Animal Sciences: Prof. DIPAK KUMAR DE

WEST BENGAL UNIVERSITY OF TECHNOLOGY

BF 142, Sector II, Salt Lake City, Kolkata, 700064, West Bengal
Telephone: (33) 23210731
E-mail: registrar@wbut.ac.in
Internet: www.wbut.ac.in

Founded 2001
State control
Academic year: July to June
Language of instruction: English

Chancellor: HE GOV. OF WEST BENGAL
Vice-Chancellor: Prof. SABYASACHI SENGUPTA
Pro Vice-Chancellor: P. K. MAHAPATRA
Registrar: Dr SYED RAFIKUL ISLAM
Controller of Examinations: Prof. A. K. GUHA

Library of 30,000 vols, 60 periodicals, 8 e-journals
Number of teachers: 37
Number of students: 235

YASHWANTRAO CHAVAN MAHARASHTRA OPEN UNIVERSITY

Dnyangangotri, Near Gangapur Dam, Nashik 422222, Maharashtra
Telephone: (253) 2231714
E-mail: vc.ycmou@gmail.com
Internet: ycmou.digitaluniversity.ac

Founded 1989
State control
Languages of instruction: English, Hindi, Marathi
Academic year: July to June

Schools of agricultural sciences, architecture, commerce and management, computer science, continuing education, education, health sciences, humanities and social sciences, science and technology; 226 academic programmes, 1,500 study centres

Chancellor: HE GOV. OF MAHARASHTRA
Vice-Chancellor: Dr R. KRISHNAKUMAR
Registrar: (vacant)
Deputy Librarian: Dr MADHUKAR SHEWALE

Library of 44,235 vols, 106 journals, 3,322 CD-ROMs
Number of teachers: 4,300
Number of students: 2,400,000

Publications: *Dnyangangotri* (4 a year), *Mukta Vidya* (2 a year), *Wamvad* (12 a year)

Institutes of National Importance

Institutes of National Importance are established, or so designated, through Acts of Parliament and are thereby granted degree-awarding powers.

ALL-INDIA INSTITUTE OF MEDICAL SCIENCES

Ansari Nagar, New Delhi 110029
Telephone: (11) 26588500
E-mail: director@aiims.ac.in
Internet: www.aiims.edu

Founded 1956
State control

Depts of anaesthesiology, anatomy, biochemistry, biomedical engineering, biophysics, biostatistics, biotechnology, blood bank, cardiac anaesthesiology, cardiac biochemistry, cardiac pathology, cardiac radiology, cardiology, cardiothoracic and vascular surgery, dental surgery, dermatology and venereology, emergency medicine, endocrinology and metabolism, forensic medicine, gastroenterology and human nutrition, gastrointestinal surgery, haematology, histocompatibility and immunogenetics, hospital administration, laboratory medicine, microbiology, nephrology, neuro-anaesthesiology, neurology, neuropathology, neuro-radiology, neurosurgery, nuclear magnetic resonance, nuclear medicine, obstetrics and gynaecology, orthopaedics, otorhinolaryngology, paediatric surgery, paediatrics, pathology, pharmacology, physical medicine and rehabilitation, physiology, radio diagnosis, reproductive biology, surgical disciplines, urology

Dir: Prof. Dr R. C. DEKA (acting)
Dean: Dr RANI KUMAR
Registrar: V. P. GUPTA
Chief Librarian: Dr K. P. SINGH

Library of 138,669 vols, 957 periodicals
Number of teachers: 543
Number of students: 1,442

Publication: *The National Medical Journal of India* (6 a year)

PROFESSORS

Anaesthesiology:
- ARORA, M. K.
- BATRA, R. K.
- CHANDERLEKHA
- DUREJA, G. P.
- JAYALAKSHMI, T. S.
- PAWAR, D. K.
- SAXENA, R.

Anatomy:
- AJMANI, M. L.
- KUCHERIA, K.
- KUMAR, R.
- MEHRA, R. D.
- SABHERWAL, U.
- WADHWA, S.

Biochemistry:
- RAO, D. N.
- SINGH, N.
- SINHA, S.

Biomedical Engineering:
- ANAND, S.
- RAY, A. R.
- SINGH, H.
- TANDON, S. N.

Biophysics:
- MISHRA, R. K.
- RAO, G. S.
- SINGH, T. P.

Biostatistics:
- SUNDARAM, K. R.

Biotechnology:
- PRASAD, H. K.
- SHARMA, Y. D.
- TYAGI, J. S.

Cardiology:
- BAHL, V. K.
- KOTHARI, S. S.
- REDDY, K. S.
- SAXENA, A.

Centre of Community Medicine:
- KAPOOR, S. K.
- PANDAV, C. S.
- REDDAIAH, V. P.

Dental Surgery:
- PARKASH, H.
- SHAH, N.

Dermatology and Venereology:
- KHANNA, N.
- SHARMA, V. K.
- VERMA, K. K.

Endocrinology and Metabolism:
- AMMINI, A. C.

Forensic Medicine:
- DOGRA, T. D.

Gastroenterology and Human Nutrition:
- ACHARYA, S. K.
- JOSHI, Y. K.
- KAPIL, U.

Gastrointestinal Surgery:
- CHATTOPADHYAY, T. K.

Haematology:
- CHOUDHRY, V. P.
- KUMAR, R.
- SAXENA, R.

Hospital Administration:
- CHAUBEY, P. C.
- SHARMA, R. K.

Laboratory Medicine:
- JAILKHANI, B. L.
- MUKHOPADHYAY, A. K.

Medicine:
- GULERIA, R.
- KUMAR, A.
- MISRA, A.
- SHARMA, S. K.
- SOOD, R.

Microbiology:
- BANERJEE, U.
- BROOR, S.
- SAMANTARAY, J. C.
- SETH, P.

Nephrology:
- DASH, S. C.
- TIWARI, S. C.

Nuclear Magnetic Resonance Imaging:
- JAGANNATHAN, N. R.

Nuclear Medicine:
- BANDOPADHYAYA, G. P.
- MALHOTRA, A.
- PANT, G. S.

Obstetrics and Gynaecology:
- KRIPLANI, A.
- KUMAR, S.
- MITTAL, S.

Orthopaedics:
- BHAN, S.
- JAYASWAL, A.
- KOTWAL, P. P.
- RASTOGI, S.

Otorhinolaryngology:
- BAHADUR, S.
- DEKA, R. C.
- SHARMA, S. C.

Paediatric Surgery:
- GUPTA, D. K.
- MITRA, D. K.

Paediatrics:
- ARORA, N. K.
- ARYA, L. S.
- BHAN, M. K.
- KALRA, V.
- PAUL, V. K.

Pathology:
- CHOPRA, P.
- DAWAR, S.
- KAPILA, K.
- PANDA, S. K.
- SARKAR, C.
- SINGH, M. K.
- VERMA, K.
- VIJAYARAGHAVAN, M.

Pharmacology:
- GROVER, J. K.
- GUPTA, Y. K.

Physical Medicine and Rehabilitation:
- SINGH, U.

Physiology:
- BIJLANI, R. L.
- KUMAR, V. M.
- SENGUPTA, J.

Psychiatry and De-addiction Centre:
- KHANDELWAL, S. K.
- MEHTA, M.
- RAY, R.
- TRIPATHI, B. M.

Radio Diagnosis:
- GUPTA, A. K.
- MUKHOPADHYAY, S.
- VASHIST, S.

Reproductive Biology:
- KUMAR, A.
- SARKAR, N. N.

Surgical Disciplines:
- KUMAR, A.
- MEHTA, S. N.
- MISRA, M. C.
- SRIVASTAVA, A.

Transplant Immunology and Immunogenetics:
- MEHRA, N. K.

Urology:
- GUPTA, N. P.
- HERNAL, A. K.

ATTACHED CENTRES

Cardiothoracic Sciences Centre: f. 1982; Prin. Prof. BALRAM AIRAN.

Centre for Dental Education and Research: f. 2003; Prin. Prof. Dr NASEEM SHAH.

College of Nursing: e-mail mvatsa@aiims.ac.in; Prin. M. VATSA.

Dr R. P. Centre for Ophthalmic Sciences: tel. (11) 26589695; e-mail pschiefrpc@yahoo.com; f. 1967; Prin. Prof. R. V. AZAD.

Jai Prakash Narayan Apex Trauma Centre: e-mail cc@jpnatc.com.

National Drug Dependence Treatment Centre: Sector 19, Kamla Nehru Nagar, Ghaziabad, Uttar Pradesh; tel. (120) 2788974; e-mail nddtc.aiims@qmail.com; f. 1988; Prin. Dr RAJAT RAY.

Neurosciences Centre: f. 2003; Prin. Prof. H. H. DASH

DAKSHINA BHARAT HINDI PRACHAR SABHA

35–B Tennur High Rd, Tiruchirapalli 620017, Tamil Nadu

Telephone: (431) 2791399
E-mail: exam@hindisabhatrichy.com
Internet: www.hindisabhatrichy.com

Founded 1928, present name and status 1964
State control
Language of instruction: Hindi
Academic year: July to June

Chancellor: R. VENKATARAMAN
Vice-Chancellor: B. D. JATTI
Pro-Vice-Chancellor: V. A. SHARMA
Registrar: R. F. NEERLAKATTI
Registrar: Dr P. H. SETHUMADHAVA RAO

Library of 100,000 vols (within Nat. Hindi Research Library)

INDIAN INSTITUTE OF TECHNOLOGY, BOMBAY

Powai, Mumbai 400076, Maharashtra

Telephone: (22) 25722545
E-mail: director@iitb.ac.in
Internet: www.iitb.ac.in

Founded 1958
State control
Language of instruction: English
Academic year: July to April

Depts of aerospace engineering, bioscience and bioengineering, chemical engineering, chemistry, civil engineering, computer science and engineering, earth sciences, electrical engineering, energy science and engineering, humanities and social sciences, industrial design centre, mathematics, mechanical engineering, materials and metallurgical engineering, physics

Dir: Prof. DEVANG V. KHAKHAR
Registrar: B. S. PUNALKAR
Dean for Academic Programme: Prof. V. M. GADRE
Dean for Faculty Affairs: Prof. A. K. SURESH
Dean for Int. Relations: Prof. SUBHASIS CHAUDHURI
Dean for Research and Devt: Prof. RANGAN BANERJEE
Dean for Student Affairs: Prof. U. A. YAJNIK
Librarian: Dr DAULAT JOTHWANI

Library of 414,475 vols, 1,442 periodicals
Number of teachers: 495
Number of students: 5,865.

ATTACHED RESEARCH CENTRES

Advanced Centre for Research in Electronics: tel. (22) 25767690; e-mail head.acre@iit.ac.in; Head Prof. RAMAN S. SRINIVASA.

Centre for Aerospace Systems Design and Engineering: tel. (22) 25767840; e-mail head.casde@iit.ac.in; Head Prof. P. M. MUJUMDAR.

Centre for Environmental Science and Engineering: tel. (22) 25767853; e-mail head.cese@iit.ac.in; Head Prof. S. R. ASOLEKAR.

Centre for Formal Design and Verification of Software: tel. (22) 25768700; e-mail head.cfdvs@iit.ac.in; Head Prof. G. SIVAKUMAR.

Centre for Studies in Resources Engineering: tel. (22) 25767263; e-mail head.csre@iit.ac.in; Head Prof. H. S. PANDALAI.

Centre for Technology Alternatives in Rural Areas: tel. (22) 25767500; e-mail head.ctara@iit.ac.in; Head Prof. A. W. DATE.

Computer Aided Design Centre: tel. (22) 25767796; e-mail head.cad@iit.ac.in; Head Prof. R. K. MALIK.

Industrial Design Centre: tel. (22) 25767819; e-mail head.idc@iit.ac.in; Head Prof. R. POOVAIAH.

Sophisticated Analytical Instrumentation Facility: tel. (22) 25767691; e-mail head.saif@iit.ac.in; Head Prof. A. R. KULKARNI.

ATTACHED SCHOOLS

Kanwal Rekhi School of Information Technology: tel. (22) 25767900; e-mail head.kresit@iit.ac.in; Head Prof. A. RANADE.

School of Biosciences and Bioengineering: tel. (22) 25767207; e-mail head.bio@iit.ac.in; Head Prof. K. K. RAO.

Shailesh J. Mehta School of Management: tel. (22) 25767781; e-mail head.som@iit.ac.in; Head Prof. KARUNA JAIN

INDIAN INSTITUTE OF TECHNOLOGY, DELHI

Hauz Khas, New Delhi 110016
Telephone: (11) 26582222
E-mail: director@admin.iitd.ac.in
Internet: www.iitd.ac.in

Founded 1961, present status 1963
State control
Academic year: July to May

Dir: Prof. R. K. SHEVGAONKAR
Registrar: Dr RAKESH KUMAR (acting)
Dean for Alumni Affairs and Int. Programmes: Prof. ASHOK GUPTA
Dean for Industrial Research and Devt: Prof. S. N. SINGH
Dean for Postgraduate Studies and Research: Prof. K. GUPTA
Dean for Students: Prof. SHASHI MATHUR
Dean for Undergraduate Studies: Prof. SANTANU CHAUDHURY
Librarian: Dr JAGDISH ARORA

Library of 307,832 vols
Number of teachers: 421
Number of students: 4,931.

ATTACHED SCHOOLS

Amar Nath and Shashi Khosla School of Information Technology: tel. (11) 26596056; internet www.it.iitd.ac.in; Coordinator Prof. SANJIVA PRASAD.

Bharti School of Telecommunication Technology and Management: tel. (11) 6596200; internet bsttm.iitd.ac.in; f. 2000; Coordinator Dr RANJAN BOSE

INDIAN INSTITUTE OF TECHNOLOGY, GUWAHATI

N Guwahati, Guwahati 781039, Assam
Telephone: (361) 2690401
E-mail: director@iitg.ernet.in
Internet: www.iitg.ernet.in

Founded 1994
State control
Language of instruction: English
Academic year: July to April

Depts of biotechnology, chemical engineering, chemistry, civil engineering, computer science and engineering, design, electronics and electrical engineering, humanities and social sciences, mathematics, mechanical engineering, physics

Dir: (vacant)
Deputy Dir: Prof. SUKUMAR NANDI
Registrar: Dr BRAJENDRA NATH RAYCHOUDHURY
Dean for Academic Affairs: Prof. ALIKA KHARE
Dean for Faculty Affairs: Prof. ANANT SRINIVASAN
Dean for Research and Devt: Prof. DEBABRAT CHAKRABORTY
Dean for Student Affairs: Prof. BHISHMA PATEL

Library of 150,000 vols
Number of teachers: 330
Number of students: 4,500.

ATTACHED CENTRES

Centre for Educational Technology: tel. (361) 2583001; e-mail cet@iitg.ernet.in; internet www.iitg.ernet.in/cet; Head Prof. S. TALUKDAR.

Centre for Energy: tel. (361) 2583150; e-mail energyoff@iitg.ernet.in; internet www.iitg.ernet.in/ceer; f. 2004; Head Prof. ALOKE KUMAR GHOSHAL.

Centre for the Environment: tel. (361) 2583050; e-mail evc_off@iitg.ernet.in; f. 2004; Head Dr GOPAL DAS.

Centre for Mass Media Communication: tel. (361) 2582454; e-mail dasak@iitg.ernet.in; internet www.iitg.ernet.in/mmc; f. 2004; Dir Prof. AMARENDRA KUMAR DAS.

Centre for Nanotechnology: tel. (361) 2583075; e-mail nano_off@iitg.ernet.in; internet www.iitg.ernet.in/nano; f. 2004; Dir Dr SIDDHARTHA SANKAR GHOSH

INDIAN INSTITUTE OF TECHNOLOGY, KANPUR

IIT PO, Kanpur 208016, Uttar Pradesh
Telephone: (512) 2590151
E-mail: registrar@iitk.ac.in
Internet: www.iitk.ac.in

Founded 1959
State control
Language of instruction: English

Depts of engineering, humanities and science

Dir: Prof. SANJAY G. DHANDE
Deputy Dir: Prof. SURESH CHANDRA SRIVASTAVA
Dean for Academic Affairs: Prof. SANJAY MITTAL
Dean for Faculty Affairs: Prof. V. CHANDRASEKHAR
Dean for Research and Devt: Prof. A. K. CHATURVEDI
Dean for Resource Planning and Generation: Prof. MANINDRA AGGARWAL
Dean for Student Affairs: Prof. A. K. GHOSH
Registrar: SANJEEV S. KASHALKAR
Librarian: R. MISHRA

Library of 390,000 vols and 900 periodicals
Number of teachers: 309
Number of students: 3,731.

ATTACHED RESEARCH CENTRES

Advanced Centre for Materials Science: internet www.iitk.ac.in/acms; f. 1978; Head SANDEEP SANGAL.

Centre for Laser Technology: tel. (512) 2597341; e-mail panig@iitk.ac.in; internet www.iitk.ac.in/celt; Head Prof. P. K. PANIGRAHI.

Centre for Mechatronics: tel. (512) 2597995; internet www.iitk.ac.in/robotics; Coordinator Prof. N. VYAS.

Computer Aided Design Laboratory: tel. (512) 2597170; e-mail achat@iitk.ac.in; internet www.iitk.ac.in/cad; Coordinator Dr A. CHATTERJEE.

National Information Centre of Earthquake Engineering: tel. (512) 2597866; e-mail nicee@iitk.ac.in; internet www.nicee.org; Coordinator Prof. DURGESH C. RAI.

National Wind Tunnel Facility: tel. (512) 2597843; e-mail kamal@iitk.ac.in; internet www.iitk.ac.in/nwtf; f. 1999; Head Dr KAMAL PODDAR.

Samtel Centre for Display Technologies: tel. (512) 2597353; e-mail saboo@iitk.ac.in; internet www.iitk.ac.in/scdt; f. 2000; Head Dr DEEPAK GUPTA.

SIDBI Innovation and Incubation Centre: tel. (512) 2596646; e-mail siic@iitk.ac.in; internet www.iitk.ac.in/siic; Coordinator Dr B. V. PHANI

INDIAN INSTITUTE OF TECHNOLOGY, KHARAGPUR

Kharagpur 721302, West Bengal
Telephone: (3222) 255221
E-mail: director@iitkgp.ernet.in
Internet: www.iitkgp.ac.in

Founded 1950
State control
Academic year: July to April

Depts of aerospace engineering, agricultural and food engineering, architecture and regional planning, biotechnology, chemical engineering, chemistry, civil engineering, computer science and engineering, cryogenic engineering, electrical engineering, electronics and electrical communication engineering, geology and geophysics, humanities and social sciences, industrial engineering and management, information technology, materials science, mathematics, mechanical engineering, metallurgical and materials engineering, medical science and technology, mining engineering, ocean engineering and naval architecture, physics and meteorology

Dir: Prof. DAMODAR ACHARYA
Deputy Dir: A. K. MAJUMDAR
Registrar: Dr T. K. GHOSAL (acting)
Academic Dean: AMIT PATRA
Dean for Continuing Education: S. SENGUPTA
Dean for Faculty and Planning: A. BASAK
Dean for Postgraduates and Research: P. K. J. MOHAPATRA
Dean for Student Affairs: S. BHATTACHARYYA
Chair. of Central Library: Prof. N. R. MANDAL

Library of 300,000 vols, 1,130 periodicals
Number of teachers: 500
Number of students: 5,000

INDIAN INSTITUTE OF TECHNOLOGY, MADRAS

IIT PO, Chennai 600036, Tamil Nadu
Telephone: (44) 22578100
E-mail: registrar@iitm.ac.in
Internet: www.iitm.ac.in

Founded 1959
State control
Language of instruction: English
Academic year: July to April

Depts of aerospace engineering, applied mechanics, biotechnology, chemical engineering, chemistry, civil engineering, computer science and engineering, electrical engineering, engineering design, humanities and social sciences, management studies, mathematics, mechanical engineering, metallurgical and materials engineering, ocean engineering, physics

Dir: Prof. BHASKAR RAMAMURTHI
Dean for Academic Courses: Prof. K. RAMAMURTHY
Dean for Academic Research: Prof. K. KRISHNAIAH
Dean for Admin.: P. SRIRAM
Dean for Industrial Consultancy and Sponsored Research: Prof. JOB KURIEN
Dean for Planning: Prof. DAVID KOILPILLAI
Dean for Students: Prof. L. S. GANESH
Registrar: A. THIRUNAVUKKARASU
Librarian: Dr HARISH CHANDRA

Library: see under Libraries and Archives
Number of teachers: 477
Number of students: 5,232

Publications: *Journal of Mathematical and Physical Science* (6 a year), *Research Consultancy, Expertise and Facilities* (1 a year)

INDIAN INSTITUTE OF TECHNOLOGY, ROORKEE

Roorkee 247667, Uttaranchal
Telephone: (1332) 285311
E-mail: regis@iitr.ernet.in
Internet: www.iitr.ac.in

Founded 1847, fmrly Univ. of Roorkee
State control

Depts of alternative hydro energy, architecture, biotechnology, chemical engineering, chemistry, civil engineering, earth sciences, earthquake engineering, electrical engineering, electronic and computer engineering, humanities, hydrology, management studies, mathematics, mechanical and industrial engineering, metallurgical engineering, paper technology engineering, physics, water resources

Dir: Prof. PRADIPTA BANERJI
Deputy Dir: Prof. D. K. PAUL
Dean for Academic Research: Prof. SURENDRA KUMAR
Dean for Admin.: Prof. G. S. SRIVASTAVA
Dean for Alumni Affairs: Prof. S. P. GUPTA
Dean for Faculty Affairs: Prof. H. O. GUPTA
Dean of Saharanpur Campus: Prof. I. M. MISHRA
Dean for Sponsored Research and Industrial Consultancy: Prof. J. D. SHARMA
Dean for Student Welfare: Prof. N. K. GOEL
Registrar: A. K. SRIVASTAVA
Librarian: YOGENDRA SINGH

Library of 320,000 vols

INDIAN STATISTICAL INSTITUTE

203 Barrackpore Trunk Rd, Kolkata 700108, West Bengal
Telephone: (33) 25752001
E-mail: postmaster@isical.ac.in
Internet: www.isical.ac.in

Founded 1931
State control
Academic year: July to June

Regional centres located in Bangalore, Chennai, Coimbatore, Delhi, Giridih, Hyderabad, Mumbai, Pune, Vadodara

Dir: Prof. BIMAL K. ROY
Dean of Studies: Prof. G. M. SAHA
Chief Librarian: Prof. D. DASGUPTA (acting)

Library of 215,000 vols

Publication: *Sankhya: The Indian Journal of Statistics*

PROFESSORS

BAGCHI, B.
BAGCHI, D. K.
BAGCHI, S.
BAGCHI, S. C.
BANDYOPADHAY, S.
BHAT, B. V. R.
BHATIA, R.
BHATT, A. G.
BHATTACHARYA, B.
BHATTACHARYA, B. B.
BHATTACHARYA, S.
BHIMASANKARAM, P.
BOSE, A.
BOSE, M.
CHAKRAVARTY, S. R.
CHANDA, B.
CHANDA, S.
CHANDRA, T. K.
CHATTOPADHYAY, M.
CHAUDHURI, P.
CHOWDHURI, B. B.
COONDOO, D.
DANDAPAT, B. S.
DAS, A.
DAS, J.
DAS, N.
DAS, S.
DAS, S. P.
DASGUPTA, A. K.
DASGUPTA, D.
DASGUPTA, R.
DELAMPADY, M.
DEWANJI, A.
DEY, A.
DUTTA GUPTA, J.
GHOSE, M.
GOSWAMI, A.
GUPTA, M. R.
GUPTA, R.
JEGANATHAN, P.
KARANDIKAR, R. L.
KUNDU, M. K.
MAITI, P.
MAJUMDER, A.
MAJUMDER, H. P.
MAJUMDER, P. K.
MAJUMDER, P. P.
MAZUMDER, B. S.
MITRA, S.
MONDAL, B. N.
MUKHERJEA, K. K.
MURTHY, C. A.
MUTHURAMALINGAM, P. L.
NARAYANA, N. S. S.
PAL, N. R.
PARUI, S. K.
PAUL, M.
RAHA, A. B.
RAJEEV, B.
RAMACHANDRAN, V. K.
RAMAMURTHY, K.
RAMASUBRAMANIAM, S.
RAMASWAMY, B.
RAO, A. R.
RAO, I. K.
RAO, S. B.
RAO, T. J.
RAO, T. S. S. R. K.
RAY, K. S.
REDDY, B. M.
ROY, B. K.
ROY, P.
ROY, R.
ROY, S.
ROY CHOWDHURY, P.
SAHA, D.
SAHA, G. M.
SAMANTA, T.
SARBADHIKARI, H.
SARKAR, A.
SARKAR, N.
SASTRY, N. S. N.
SEN, A.
SENGUPTA, A.
SENGUPTA, D.
SIKDAR, K.
SINHA, B. P.
SINHA, K. B.
SITARAM, A.
SRIVASTAVA, S. M.
SWAMINATHAN, M.
THANGAVALU, S.
TRIPATHI, T. P.
VIJAYAN, K. S.

ATTACHED CENTRE

International Statistical Education Centre (ISEC): tel. (33) 25752521; e-mail isec@isical.ac.in; internet www.isical.ac.in/~isecweb; f. 1950; Prin. Prof. M. PAL

NATIONAL INSTITUTE OF PHARMACEUTICAL EDUCATION AND RESEARCH

Sector 67, SAS Nagar, Mohali 160062, Punjab
Telephone: (172) 2214682
E-mail: registrar@niper.ac.in
Internet: www.niper.nic.in

Founded 1991
State control
Academic year: July to June

Depts of biotechnology, medicinal chemistry, natural products, pharmaceutical analysis, pharmaceutical management, pharmaceutical technology, pharmaceutics, pharmacology and toxicology, pharmacy practice

Dir: Prof. K. K. BHUTANI (acting)
Dean: Prof. U. C. BANERJEE
Registrar: P. J. P. SINGH WARAICH (acting)

Library of 5,715 vols, 17,528 bound vols of journals

Publication: *Current Research & Information on Pharmaceutical Sciences (CRIPS)* (4 a year)

PROFESSORS

BANERJEE, U. C., Pharmaceutical Technology
BANSAL, A. K., Pharmaceutics
BHUTANI, K. K., Natural Products
CHAKRABORTI, A. K., Medicinal Chemistry
DEY, C. S., Biotechnology
RAO, P. R., Pharmacology and Toxicology
SINGH, S., Pharmaceutical Analysis
TIWARI, P., Pharmacy Practice

POSTGRADUATE INSTITUTE OF MEDICAL EDUCATION AND RESEARCH

Sector 12, Chandigarh 160012, Punjab
Telephone: (172) 2747585
E-mail: pgimer-chd@nic.in
Internet: www.pgimer.nic.in

Founded 1962
State control
Academic year: January to December orJuly to June

Dir: Dr YOGESH CHAWLA
Dean: Prof. AMOD GUPTA
Deputy Dir for Admin.: Prof. SURJIT SINGH
Registrar: NARESH VIRDI
Librarian: Dr HARJEET SINGH

Library of 99,399 vols, 530 periodicals

PROFESSORS

BHANSALI, A., Endocrinology
CHAWLA, H. S., Oral Health Sciences
CHAWLA, Y. K., Hepatology
DHALIWAL, L. K., Obstetrics and Gynaecology
GILL, S. S., Orthopaedics
GUPTA, A., Ophthalmology
GUPTA, A. K., Hospital Administration
GUPTA, M., Anatomy
JINDAL, S. K., Pulmonary Medicine
JINDAL, S. K., Telemedicine

JOSHI, K., Histopathology
KANWAR, A. J., Dermatology, Venereology and Leprosy
KHANDELWAL, N., Radio Diagnosis and Imaging
KHANDUJA, K. L., Biophysics
KHOSLA, V. K., Neurosurgery
KOHLI, K. K., Biochemistry
KULHARA, P., Psychiatry
KUMAR, R., School of Public Health
MALLA, N., Parasitology
MANDAL, A. K., Urology
MARWAHA, N., Blood Transfusion
MINZ, M., Renal Transplant Surgery
NARANG, A., Paediatrics
PANDA, N. K., Otolaryngology
PANDHI, P., Pharmacology
PRABHAKAR, S., Experimental Medicine and Biotechnology
PRABHAKAR, S., Neurology
RAJWANSHI, A., Cytology and Gynaecological Pathology
RAO, K. L. N., Paediatric Surgery
RATHO, R. K., Virology
SAKHUJA, V., Nephrology
SHARMA, M., Medical Microbiology
SHARMA, R. K., Plastic Surgery
SHARMA, S. C., Radiotherapy
SINGH, D., Forensic Medicine
SINGH, K., Gastroenterology
TALWAR, K. K., Cardiology
VASISHTA, R. K., Immunopathology
VERMA, S., Internal Medicine
WADHWA, S., Physical and Rehabilitation Medicine
WIG, J., Anaesthesia
WIG, J. D., General Surgery

SANJAY GANDHI POSTGRADUATE INSTITUTE OF MEDICAL SCIENCES

Raebareli Rd, Lucknow 226014, Uttar Pradesh

Telephone: (33) 25752004
Internet: www.sgpgi.ac.in

Founded 1983
State control

Depts of anaesthesiology, biostatistics, cardiology, cardiovascular and thoracic surgery, critical care medicine, endocrine surgery, endocrinology, gastroenterology, haematology, immunology, medical genetics, microbiology, nephrology, neurology, neurosurgery, nuclear medicine, pathology, radiodiagnosis, radiotherapy, surgical gastroenterology, transfusion medicine, urology

Dir: Prof. R. K. SHARMA

SREE CHITRA TIRUNAL INSTITUTE FOR MEDICAL SCIENCES AND TECHNOLOGY

Thiruvananthapuram 695011, Kerala

Telephone: (471) 443152
E-mail: director@sctimst.ac.in
Internet: www.sctimst.ac.in

Founded 1973, present status 1980
State control
Academic year: January to December

Depts and divs of anesthesiology, biochemistry, blood transfusion services, cardiology, cardiovascular and thoracic surgery, cellular and molecular cardiology, health science studies, microbiology, neurology, neurosurgery, pathology, radiology

Pres.: Dr R. CHIDAMBARAM
Dir: Dr K. RADHAKRISHNAN
Deputy Dir: P. B. SOURABHAN
Dean for Academic Affairs: Dr JAGAN MOHAN THARAKAN
Registrar: Dr A. V. GEORGE
Librarian: S. JAYACHANDRA DAS

Library of 25,170 vols, 164 journals

SRI VENKATESWARA INSTITUTE OF MEDICAL SCIENCES

Alipiri Rd, Tirupati 517507, Andhra Pradesh

Telephone: (877) 2287152
E-mail: svimshosp@yahoo.com
Internet: svimstpt.ap.nic.in

Founded 1993, present status 1995

Depts of anaesthesiology, biochemistry, cardiology, cardiothoracic surgery, casuality, dietetics, endocrinolgy, gastroenterology, general medicine, genito-urinary surgery, nephrology, nuclear medicine, neurology, neurosurgery, oncology, microbiology, pathology, physiotherapy radiology, transfusion medicine

Library of 5,662 vols, 138 journals

Dir: Dr B. VENGAMMA
Dean: Dr D. RAJASEKHAR
Librarian: Dr B. VIJAYA KUMAR

Deemed Universities

Deemed Universities (also known as Deemed-to-be Universities) are institutions that have been conferred the status of a university by virtue of their long tradition of teaching, or specialization and excellence in a particular field of study.

Amrita Vishwa Vidyapeetham (Amrita University): Amritanagar, Coimbatore 641112, Tamil Nadu; tel. (422) 2685000; e-mail univhq@amrita.edu; internet www.amrita.edu; f. 1994, deemed univ. status 2003; campuses at Amritapuri, Bengaluru, Kochi, Mysore; schools of arts and sciences, ayurveda, biotechnology, business, dentistry, communication, education, engineering, hospital management, journalism, medicine, microbiology, nursing, pharmacy, visual media studies; 1,500 teachers; 15,000 students; Vice-Chancellor Dr P. VENKAT RANGAN; Dean of Admin. Dr S. KRISHNAMOORTHY; Dean of Corporate Relations Prof. C. PARAMESHWARAN.

Atal Bihari Vajpayee Indian Institute of Information Technology and Management: Morena Link Rd, Gwalior 474010, Madhya Pradesh; tel. (751) 2449702; e-mail director@iiitm.ac.in; f. 2001; depts of computer science, electronics, finance, human resources, information technology, marketing and networking; Dir Prof. S. G. DESHMUKH.

Avinashilingam Deemed University for Women: Mettupalayam Rd, Coimbatore 641043, Tamil Nadu; tel. (422) 2440241; e-mail registrar@avinuty.ac.in; internet www.avinuty.ac.in; f. 1957, deemed univ. status 1988, current name adopted 2008; faculties of business admin., education, engineering, community education and entrepreneurship devt, home science, humanities, science; library: 135,330 vols, 510 periodicals; 4,436 students; Chancellor Dr T. S. K. MEENAKSHI SUNDARAM; Vice-Chancellor Dr SHEELA RAMACHANDRAN; Registrar Dr GOWRI RAMAKRISHNAN; Controller of Examinations Dr G. P. JEYANTHI; publ. *Indian Journal of Nutrition and Dietetics* (4 a year).

Attached Centres:

Centre for Women's Studies: Avinashilingam University for Women, Coimbatore 641043, Tamil Nadu; tel. (422) 2433408; e-mail cws_adu@yahoo.com; internet www.cws-adu.org; f. 2000; Dir K. C. LEELAVATHY.

Gandhian Studies Centre: Avinashilingam University for Women, Coimbatore 641043, Tamil Nadu; tel. (422) 2440241; e-mail gsc@avinuty.ac.in; f. 2005; Coordinator Dr K. THANGAMANI.

Banasthali Vidyapith (Banasthali University): *Banasthali Campus*: Banasthali 304022, Rajasthan; tel. (1438) 228341; *Jaipur Campus*: C-62, Sarojini Marg, C Scheme, Jaipur 302001, Rajasthan; tel. (141) 5118721; e-mail info@banasthali.ac.in; internet www.banasthali.org; f. 1935 as Shri Shantabai Shiksha Kutir, current name adopted 1943, deemed univ. status 1983; faculties of education, fine arts, home science, humanities, management, science, social sciences; library: 178,000 vols, 600 periodicals; 210 teachers; 4,182 students; Pres. Prof. CHITRA PUROHIT; Vice-Pres. Prof. USHA THAKKAR; Vice-Chancellor Prof. ADITYA SHASTRI; Librarian Dr S. D. VYAS.

Bharath University: 173 Agharam Rd, Selaiyur, Chennai 600073, Tamil Nadu; tel. (44) 22290742; e-mail vc@bharathuniv.ac.in; internet www.bharathuniv.com; f. 1984; deemed univ. status 2003; schools of architecture, automotive technology, bio sciences, computer sciences, dental sciences, electronics engineering, electrical engineering, infrastructure engineering, information sciences, management studies, mechanical sciences, medical sciences, paramedical sciences, science and humanities; library: 100,000 vols, 80 periodicals; Chancellor Eng. J. SUNDEEP AANAND; Vice-Chancellor Dr K. P. THOOYAMANI; Registrar Prof. Dr S. M. RAJENDRAN.

Bharati Vidyapeeth Deemed University: Lal Bahadur Shastri Rd, 13 Sadashiv Peth, Pune 411030, Maharashtra; tel. (20) 24407273; e-mail bharati@vsnl.com; internet www.bharatividyapeeth.edu; f. 1964, deemed univ. status 1996; composed of 32 constituent instns incl. Medical College, Dental College and Hospital, College of Ayurved, Homoeopathic Medical College, College of Nursing, Yashwantrao Mohite College of Arts, Science and Commerce, New Law College, Yashwantrao Chavan Institute of Social Science Studies and Research, Social Science Centre, Research and Development Centre in Pharmaceutical Sciences and Applied Chemistry, Institute of Environment Education and Research, Pune College of Pharmacy, Institute of Management and Entrepreneurship Development, College of Engineering, College of Physical Education, Rajiv Gandhi Institute of Biotechnology and Information Technology, Interactive Research School for Health Affairs; library: 300,000 vols, 1,645 journals; 8,386 students; Chancellor Dr PATANGRAO KADAM; Vice-Chancellor Prof. Dr SHIVAJIRAO KADAM; Registrar G. JAYAKUMAR.

Bhatkhande Music Institute Deemed University: 1 Kaiserbagh, Lucknow 226001, Uttar Pradesh; tel. (522) 2210318; e-mail info@bhatkhandemusic.edu.in; internet www.bhatkhandemusic.edu.in; f. 1926, deemed univ. status 2000; faculties of applied music, dance, instrumental music, musicology and research, percussion instruments, training and vocal music; Vice-Chancellor Prof. SHRUTI SADOLIKAR KATKAR; Registrar Dr NEELAM AHLAWAT.

Birla Institute of Technology, Ranchi: Mesra, Ranchi 835215, Jharkhand; tel. (651) 2275444; e-mail registrar@bitmesra.ac.in; internet www.bitmesra.ac.in; f. 1955, deemed univ. status 1986; extension centres in Allahabad, Chennai, Jaipur, Kolkata, Lalpur, Noida and Patna; int. centres in Bahrain, Muscat and Ras Al Khaimah (UAE); depts of applied sciences, architecture, biotechnology, engineering and technology, hotel management and catering technology, management, pharmaceutical sciences; library: 125,506 vols, 124 periodicals; 149 teachers; 10,000 students; Vice-Chancellor Dr AJAY CHAKRABARTY; Registrar Dr R. K. VERMA (acting); Librarian Dr USHA JHA (acting); publs *Journal of Hospitality Application & Research* (1 a year), *Journal of Manufacturing Technology and Research* (4 a year), *PHARMBIT* (2 a year).

Birla Institute of Technology and Science: Vidhya Vihar Campus, Pilani 333031, Rajasthan; tel. (1596) 245073; e-mail mmsanand@bits-pilani.ac.in; internet www.bits-pilani.ac.in; f. 1964; campuses in Goa, Dubai and Hyderabad; library: 230,091 vols, 559 periodicals; 535 teachers; 17,898 students; Chancellor Dr K. K. BIRLA; Vice-Chancellor Prof. BIJENDRA NATH JAIN; Registrar Prof. M. M. S. ANAND; Librarian Dr M. ISHWARA BHAT; publ. *Journal of Cooperation among University, Research and Industrial Enterprises* (4 a year).

Central Institute of Fisheries Education: Seven Bungalows, University Rd, Anderi, Mumbai 400061, Maharashtra; tel. (22) 26361446; e-mail contact@cife.edu.in; f. 1961; deemed univ. status 1989; centres in Kolkata, Kakinada, Rohtak and Powerkheda; library: 27,326 vols; Dir Dr D. KUMAR; Registrar C. LAL.

Central Institute of Higher Tibetan Studies: Sarnath, Varanasi 221007, Uttar Pradesh; tel. (542) 2585148; e-mail ngawang_samten@yahoo.com; f. 1977, deemed univ. status 1988; faculties of language and literature, philosophy, social science, Tibetan fine arts, Tibetan medicine and astrology; library: 56,000 vols on Buddhist, Tibetan, Indian and Himalayan Studies in Tibetan, Hindi, Sanskrit and other languages; Dir NGAWANG SAMTEN; Registrar R. D. AGARWAL; publs *Dhih-A Rare Buddhist Texts Research Journal, 8 series of research vols.*

Christ University: Hosur Rd, Bengaluru 560029, Karnataka; tel. (80) 40129100; e-mail mail@christuniversity.in; internet www.christuniversity.in; f. 1969 as Christ College, current name and deemed univ. status 2008; library: 111,125 vols, 298 periodicals; Chancellor Dr THOMAS AYKARA; Vice-Chancellor Dr THOMAS C. MATHEW; Pro-Vice-Chancellor Dr Fr ABRAHAM; Registrar Prof. J. SUBRAMANIAM; Controller of Examinations Prof. BABY MATHEW.

Datta Meghe Institute of Medical Sciences: Atrey Layout, Pratap Nagar, Nagpur 440022, Maharashtra; tel. (712) 3295207; e-mail info@dmims.org; internet www.dmimsu.edu.in; f. deemed univ. status 2005; constituent colleges: Jawaharlal Nehru Medical College, Mahatma Gandhi Ayurved College, Ravi Nair Physiotherapy College, Sharad Pawar Dental College, Smt. Radhikabai Meghe Memorial College of Nursing; Chancellor Hon. DATTAJI MEGHE; Pro-Chancellor Dr VEDPRAKASH ISHRA; Vice-Chancellor ANIL MADHAV PATWARDHAN; Registrar Prof. R. M. BORLE.

Dayalbagh Educational Institute: Dayalbagh, Agra 282005, Uttar Pradesh; tel. (562) 2801545; e-mail admin@dei.ac.in; internet www.dei.ac.in; f. 1981; faculties of arts, commerce, education, engineering, science and social sciences and technical college; library: 150,000 vols, 180 journals; 180 teachers; 2,493 students; Dir Prof. V. G. DAS; Registrar Prof. ANAND MOHAN; Librarian Dr MANGE RAM (acting); publ. *Journal of Science and Engineering Research* (1 a year).

Deccan College Postgraduate and Research Institute: Deccan College Rd, Yerwada, Pune 411006, Maharashtra; tel. (20) 26513204; e-mail info@deccancollegepune.ac.in; internet www.deccancollegepune.ac.in; f. 1821, deemed univ. status 1990; depts of archaeology, linguistics, Sanskrit and lexicography; library: 128,764 books, 31,647 vols of bound periodicals, 150 journals; 127 students; Pres. Dr G. B. DEGLURKAR; Dir Prof. V. P. BHATTA; Dir Prof. V. S. SHINDE; Registrar N. S. GAWARE; Librarian TRUPTI MORE.

Defence Institute of Advanced Technology: Girinagar, Pune 411025, Maharashtra; tel. (20) 24304021; e-mail registrar@diat.ac.in; internet www.diat.ac.in; f. 1952 as Institute of Armament Studies, current name adopted 1967, deemed univ. status 2000; postgraduate courses in aerospace engineering, computer science and engineering, electronics engineering, energetic materials and polymers, laser and electro optics, mechanical engineering, modelling and simulation; library: 90,000 vols; Vice-Chancellor Dr PRAHLADA; Dean of Academic Affairs Dr P. K. KHANNA; Registrar Dr R. PREMKUMAR.

Dr B. R. Ambedkar National Institute of Technology: Jalandhar 144004, Punjab; tel. (181) 2690301; e-mail admin@nitj.ac.in; f. 1987, deemed univ. status 2002; depts of applied chemistry, applied mathematics, applied physics, chemical and biological engineering, civil engineering, computer science, electronics and communication engineering, humanities, industrial engineering, instrumentation and control engineering, leather technology engineering, management, mechanical engineering, textile technology eng.; Dir Prof. MOIN UDDIN; Registrar Dr A. L. SANGAL.

Dr M. G. R. University: Periyar E. V. R. High Rd, (NH4 Highway), Maduravoyal, Chennai 600095, Tamil Nadu; tel. (44) 23782176; e-mail contact@drmgrdu.ac.in; internet www.drmgrdu.ac.in; f. 1988, deemed univ. status 2003; faculties of dental surgery, engineering and technology, humanities and sciences, nursing, physiotherapy; library: 100,000 vols, 302 periodicals; Pres. Eng. A. C. S. ARUNKUMAR; Vice-Chancellor Dr P. ARAVINDAN (acting); Registrar Prof. C. B. PALANIVELU; publ. *Advance Computing Science International Journal of Computational Intelligence (ACS-IJCI)* (4 a year).

Forest Research Institute University: PO New Forest, Dehradun, Uttaranchal; tel. (135) 2755277; e-mail aimark@icfre.org; internet fri.icfre.gov.in; f. 1906 as Imperial Forest Research Institute, deemed univ. status 1991; MSc degree courses in environment management, forestry, wood science and technology; also offers postgraduate diploma courses and doctorate degree courses; library: 150,000 vols, 300 journals; 82 students; Dean of Academic Affairs Dr RAMESH K. AIMA; Dir Dr S. S. NEGI; Registrar Dr A. K. TRIPATHI.

Gandhigram Rural Institute: Dindigul Dist., Gandhigram 624302, Tamil Nadu; tel. (451) 2452371; e-mail grucc@ruraluniv.ac.in; internet www.ruraluniv.ac.in; f. 1956, deemed univ. status 1976; library: 137,250 vols, 210 periodicals; 118 teachers; 2,024 students; Vice-Chancellor Dr S. M. RAMASAMY; Registrar Dr N. NARAYANASAMY; Librarian Dr J. ABRAHAM; library: 103,300 vols, 285 periodicals; publ. *Journal of Extension and Research* (2 a year).

Gokhale Institute of Politics and Economics: BMCC Rd, Deccan Gymkhana, Pune 411004, Maharashtra; tel. (20) 25650287; e-mail gokhaleinstitute@gipe.ac.in; internet www.gipe.ac.in; f. 1930, deemed univ. status 1993; library: 261,537 vols, 440 periodicals; Dir Prof. RAJAS PARCHURE; publ. *Artha Vijanana* (4 a year, in English).

Gujarat Vidyapith (Gujarat University): Ashram Rd, Ahmedabad 380014, Gujarat; tel. (79) 27540746; e-mail registrar@gujaratvidyapith.org; internet www.gujaratvidyapith.org; f. 1920 as Rashtriya Vidyapith, deemed univ. status 1963; languages of instruction: Hindi, Gujarati; campuses at Ahmedabad, Anand, Gandhinagar, Kheda, Valsad; Chancellor NARAYANBHAI DESAI; Vice-Chancellor SUDARSHAN IYENGAR; Registrar Dr RAJENDRA KHIMANI (acting); Librarian BHARTIBEN DESAI (acting); library: 534,987 vols, 600 journals, 691 MSS; 105 teachers; 1,774 students; publ. *Vidyapith* (4 a year).

Gurukul Kangri Vishwavidyalaya (Gurukul Kangri University): PO Gurukul Kangri, Haridwar 249404, Uttar Pradesh; tel. (1334) 249013; e-mail registrargkv@yahoo.co.in; internet www.gkvharidwar.org; f. 1902, deemed univ. status 1962; faculties of ayurved and medical science, distance education, engineering, humanities, life science, management studies, science, technology; library: 133,667 vols; 103 teachers; 1,558 students; Chancellor SUDERSHAN KUMAR SHARMA; Vice-Chancellor Prof. SWATANTRA KUMAR; Pro-Vice-Chancellor Prof. MAHAVIR AGARWAL; Registrar Prof. A. K. CHOPRA; Librarian Dr J. P. VIDYALANKAR; library: 135,000 vols; publs *Arya Bhatt* (4 a year), *Gurukula Patrika* (12 a year), *Gurukil Business Review, Journal of Natural & Physical Sciences, Gurukul Shodh Bharati, Prahlad* (4 a year), *Vedic Path* (4 a year).

Indian Agricultural Research Institute: Pusa Campus, New Delhi 110012; tel. (11) 25843375; e-mail director@iari.res.in; internet www.iari.res.in; f. 1905, deemed univ. status 1958; schools of basic sciences, crop improvements, crop protection, resource management and social sciences; library: 600,000 vols; 360 teachers; 600 students; Dir Dr H. S. GUPTA; Jt Dir for Education and Dean Dr H. S. GAUR; Jt Dir for Extension Dr K. VIJAYARAGAVAN; Jt Dir for Research Dr MALAVIKA DADLANI; Registrar and Jt Dir for Admin. B. N. RAO; Librarian USHA KHEMCHANDANI.

Indian Institute of Foreign Trade: IIFT Bhawan, B–21, Qutab Institutional Area, New Delhi 110016; tel. (11) 26965124; e-mail iift@iift.ac.in; internet www.iift.edu; f. 1963, deemed univ. status 2002; library: 84,000 vols and 800 journals; Dir K. T. CHACKO; Registrar L. D. MAGO; Head of Kolkata Centre Dr K. RANGARAJAN; publs *Focus WTO, Foreign Trade Review*.

Indian Institute of Information Technology: Deoghat, Jhalwa, Allahabad 211011, Uttar Pradesh; tel. (532) 2922000; e-mail director@iiita.ac.in; internet www.iiita.ac.in; f. 1999, deemed univ. status 2000; Dir Dr M. D. TIWARI; Dean of Academic Affairs Prof. S. SANYAL; Dean of Research and Devt Prof. G. C. NANDI; Dean of Student Affairs Prof. R. C. TRIPATHI.

Indian Institute of Science: Bengaluru 560012, Karnataka; tel. (80) 23600757; e-mail regr@admin.iisc.ernet.in; internet www.iisc.ernet.in; f. 1909; faculties of engineering and science; library: 411,676 vols; 434 teachers; 1,794 students; Dir Prof. P. BALARAM; Assoc. Dir Prof. N. BALAKRISHNAN; Registrar R. MOHAN DAS; Public Relations Officer V. THILAGAM; Librarian R. KRISHNA MURTHY.

Indian Law Institute: Bhagwan Dass Rd, New Delhi 110001; tel. (11) 23386321; e-mail ili@ili.ac.in; internet ili.ac.in; f. 1956, deemed univ. status 2004; courses in admin. law, alternative dispute resolution, corporate laws and management, cyber law, environmental law, human rights law, intellectual property rights law, int. trade law, labour law, securities and banking law, tax law;

library: 75,000 vols, 270 periodicals; Dir Prof. S. SIVAKUMAR (acting); Registrar DALIP KUMAR; publs *Annual Survey of Indian Law*, *Journal of the Indian Law Institute* (4 a year).

Indian School of Mines University: Dhanbad 826004, Jharkhand; tel. (326) 2296559; e-mail dt@ismdhanbad.ac.in; internet www.ismdhanbad.ac.in; f. 1926, deemed univ. status 1967; depts of applied chemistry, applied geology, applied geophysics, applied mathematics, applied physics, computer science and engineering, electrical engineering, electronics engineering, fuel and mineral engineering, humanities and social science, management studies, mechanical engineering and mining machinery engineering, petroleum engineering; language of instruction: English; academic year July to June; library: 80,000 books, 35,000 bound vols of journals; 105 teachers; 1,035 students; Dir Prof. D. C. PANIGRAHI; Dean of Academics Prof. R. VENUGOPAL; Dean of Faculty and Planning Prof. A. CHATTOPADHYAY; Dean of Research and Devt Prof. R. VENUGOPAL; Dean of Student Welfare Prof. S. LAIK; Registrar M. K. SINGH; Librarian Dr PARTHA DE.

Indian Veterinary Research Deemed Institute: Izatnagar 243122, Uttar Pradesh; tel. (581) 2300096; e-mail dirivri@ivri.up.nic.in; internet www.ivri.nic.in; f. 1889, deemed univ. status 1983; campuses at Bengaluru, Bhopal, Izatnagar, Kolkata, Mukteswar, Palampur and Srinagar; research divs of animal biochemistry, animal biotechnology, animal genetics and breeding, animal nutrition, animal physiology, avian diseases, biostatistics, livestock production and management, livestock products technology, poultry science, veterinary bacteriology, veterinary epidemiology, veterinary extension education, veterinary gynaecology and obstetrics, veterinary immunology, veterinary medicine, veterinary parasitology, veterinary pathology, veterinary pharmacology, veterinary public health, veterinary surgery, veterinary virology; library: 250,000 vols, 228 periodicals; Dir and Vice-Chancellor Prof. MAHESH CHANDRA SHARMA (acting); Dir for Academic Affairs Dr V. P. SINGH; Registrar PANKAJ KUMAR (acting).

Indira Gandhi Institute of Development Research: Gen. A. K.Vaidya Marg, Goregaon (E), Mumbai 400065, Maharashtra; tel. (22) 28400919; e-mail dean@igidr.ac.in; internet www.igidr.ac.in; f. 1987, deemed univ. status 1995; library: 40,000 vols, 460 periodicals; 26 teachers; 90 students; Dir and Vice-Chancellor Prof. S. MAHENDRA DEV; Registrar JAI MOHAN PANDIT; Librarian G. K. MANJUNATH.

Institute of Advanced Studies in Education Deemed University: Gandhi Vidya Mandir, Sardarshahr 331401, Rajasthan; tel. (1564) 223054; e-mail info@iaseuniversity.org.in; internet www.iaseuniversity.org.in; f. 1950, deemed univ. status 2002; faculties of education, information technology, management, medicine; campuses at Bhubaneswar and Bikaner; library: 95,000 vols; 10,000 students; Chancellor Dr L. M. SINGHVI; Dir MILAP DUGAR; Registrar R. S. SUROLIA.

International Institute for Population Sciences: Govandi Station Rd, Deonar, Mumbai 400088, Maharashtra; tel. (22) 25563254; e-mail director@iips.net; internet www.iipsindia.org; f. 1956 as Demographic Training and Research Centre, present name and deemed univ. status 1985; depts of devt studies, extramural studies and distance education, fertility studies, mathematical demography and statistics, migration and urban studies, population policies and programmes, public health and mortality studies; library: 78,732 vols, 13,794 bound periodicals, 305 journals, 170 CD-ROMs; 30 teachers; 120 students; Dir Dr FAUJDAR RAM; Registrar Dr M. K. KULKARNI; Librarian D. D. MESTRI.

International Institute of Information Technology: Gachibowli, Hyderabad 500032, Andhra Pradesh; tel. (40) 66531000; e-mail query@iiit.net; f. 1998; undergraduate and postgraduate courses in various disciplines of information technology; research centres in bioinformatics, building science, communications, earthquake engineering, education, data engineering, open software, technology consultancy, visual embedded systems technology, visual information technology; library: 6,000 vols; Dir Prof. RAJEEV SANGAL; Librarian V. PRABHAKAR SARMA.

Jain Vishva Bharati Institute: Dist. Nagaur, Ladnun 341306, Rajasthan; tel. (1581) 222110; e-mail registrar@jvbi.ac.in; internet jvbi.ac.in; f. 1991; depts of Acharya Kalu Kanya Mahavidhyalaya, computer applications, education, jainology and comparative religion and philosophy, non-violence and peace, Prakrit and Jain agama, science of living, preksha meditation and yoga, social work; library: 46,260 books, 116 periodicals, 6,000 MSS; Vice-Chancellor Dr SAMANI CHARITRA PRAJNA; Dir for Research Prof. Dr BACHH R. DUGAR; Registrar Prof. J. P. N. MISHRA; Librarian H. C. R. SIDDAPPA.

Jamia Hamdard: Hamdard Nagar, New Delhi 110062; tel. (11) 26059688; e-mail inquiry@jamiahamdard.edu; internet www.jamiahamdard.edu; f. 1963, deemed univ. status 1989; faculties of allied health sciences, Islamic studies and social science, management studies and information technology, medicine, nursing, pharmacy and science; library: 175,000 vols, 124 periodicals, 5,000 MSS; 2,100 students; Chancellor SAIYID HAMID; Vice-Chancellor Dr G. N. QAZI; Registrar Dr FIRDOUS AHMAD WANI; Dean of Student Welfare Prof. S. H. ANSARI; Provost Dr MOHD. AMIR; Proctor Prof. R. K. KHAR; Librarian Dr AJAY KUMAR SINGH (acting).

Janardan Rai Nagar Rajasthan Vidyapeeth University: 93 Parshwanath Colony, Ajmer Rd, Jaipur, Rajasthan; tel. (141) 2811581; e-mail info@jrnrvpu.org; internet www.jnrvuniversity.com; f. 1937 as Rajasthan Vidyapeeth, deemed univ. status 1987; faculties of arts and commerce, computer science, management, medical science, science; 12 constituent instns; library: 244,000 books, 140 periodicals, 5,300 students; Vice-Chancellor Prof. DIVYA PRABHA NAGAR; Registrar Dr VIJAY SINGH PANWAR; Dir for Distance Education Dr C. P. AGARWAL; Librarian K. L. VAISHNAV.

Constituent Colleges:

Homeopathic Medical College and Hospital: Udaipur; e-mail homoeopathic@jrnrvpu.org.

Institute of Management Studies: Udaipur; tel. (294) 2490632; e-mail imsjrnrvu_director@yahoo.co.in; Dir Prof. RAJEEV JAIN.

Institute of Rajasthan Studies: Udaipur; e-mail rajasthanstudies@jrnrvpu.org.

Lokmanya Tilak Teachers Training College: Dabok, Udaipur 313022, Rajasthan; tel. (294) 2655327; e-mail info@lokmanyatilakcollege.org; internet www.lokmanyatilakcollege.org; faculty of education; Dean and Prin. Prof. DIVYA PRABHA NAGAR.

M. V. Shramjeevi College: Town Hall Link Rd, Udaipur; e-mail shramjeevi@jrnrvpu.org; faculties of commerce, humanities and social sciences; Prin. Prof. N. K. PANDYA.

Udaipur School of Social Work: Dabok, Udaipur; e-mail social@jrnrvpu.org; Prin. (vacant).

Jawaharlal Nehru Centre for Advanced Scientific Research: Jakkur, Bengaluru 560064, Karnataka; tel. (80) 22082750; e-mail academic@jncasr.ac.in; internet www.jncasr.ac.in; f. 1989; deemed univ. status 2002; research in chemistry and physics of materials, educational technology and geodynamics, engineering mechanics, evolutionary and organismal biology, molecular biology and genetics, theoretical sciences; library: 10,000 vols, 71 periodicals; 40 teachers; 200 students; Pres. M. R. S. RAO; Librarian NABONITA GUHA; publs *Chemistry and Physics of Materials*, *Engineering Mechanics*, *Evolutionary and Organismal Biology*, *Geodynamics*, *Molecular Biology and Genetics*, *Theoretical Science*.

Kalinga Institute of Industrial Technology: Bhubaneshwar 751024, Orissa; tel. (674) 2725113; e-mail kiit@kiit.ac.in; internet www.kiit.ac.in; f. 1992, deemed univ. status 2004; schools of applied sciences, biotechnology, civil engineering, computer application, economics, electrical engineering, electronics engineering, fashion technology, film and media sciences, humanities and social sciences, languages, law, management, mechanical engineering, rural management, sculpture, technology, yoga and spiritualism; constituent instns: Kalinga Institute of Medical Sciences, Kalinga Institute of Social Sciences, KIIT Int. School, KIIT Science College, Kalinga Polytechnic; library: 200,000 vols; 800 teachers; 17,000 students; Chancellor Prof. R. P. KAUSHIK; Vice-Chancellor Prof. Dr ASHOK S. KOLASKAR; Rector Prof. SATYENDRA PATNAIK; Registrar and Dir for Admissions Dr SASMITA SAMANTA.

Lakshmibai National University of Physical Education, Gwalior: Mela Rd, Shakti Nagar, Gwalior 474002, Madhya Pradesh; tel. (751) 4000902; e-mail registrarlnupe@gmail.com; internet www.lnipe.gov.in; f. 1957, fmrly Lakshmibai National College of Physical Education, deemed univ. status 1995; depts of coaching, fitness and dance, computer science and applied statistics, health sciences and yoga therapy, research, devt and advanced studies, sports management and journalism, teacher education, youth affairs and sports; library: 52,000 vols; Vice-Chancellor S. S. PAWAR; Registrar Dr L. N. SARKAR; publ. *Indian Journal of Physical Education, Sports Medicine and Exercise Science* (2 a year).

Malaviya National Institute of Technology, Jaipur: Jawahar Lal Nehru Marg, Jaipur 302017, Rajasthan; tel. (141) 2529078; e-mail director@mnit.ac.in; internet mnit.ac.in; f. 1963, deemed univ. status 2002; depts of architecture, chemical engineering, chemistry, civil engineering, computer engineering, electrical engineering, electronics and communication engineering, humanities, mathematics, management studies, mechanical engineering, metallurgical and materials engineering, physics, structural engineering; library: 133,600 vols; 150 teachers; 1,700 students; Dir Prof. I. K. BHAT; Dean of Academic Affairs ROHIT GOYAL; Dean of Admin. ALOK RANJAN; Dean of Faculty Affairs ASHOK SHARMA; Dean of Research and Devt A. B. GUPTA; Dean of Student Affairs MANOJ SINGH GAUR.

Manipal University: University Bldg, Madhav Nagar, Manipal 576104, Karnataka; tel. (820) 2571978; e-mail admissions@manipal

.edu; internet www.manipal.edu; f. 1953, deemed univ. status 1993; library: 62,000 vols, 600 periodicals; 2,400 teachers; 20,000 students; Chancellor Dr RAMDAS M. PAI; Pro-Chancellor Dr H. S. BALLAL; Vice-Chancellor Dr K. RAMNARAYAN; Pro-Vice-Chancellor Dr H. VINOD BHAT; Registrar Dr G. K. PRABHU.

Maulana Azad National Institute of Technology: Bhopal 462051, Madhya Pradesh; tel. (755) 5206006; e-mail info@manit.ac.in; internet www.manit.ac.in; f. 1960, deemed univ. status 2002; depts of architecture and planning, computer application, energy centre, eng., humanities, management, physical education, remote sensing and GIS, science; library: 114,694 vols, 100 journals; 200 teachers; 4,000 students; Dir Dr K. K. APPU KUTTAN; Dean of Academic Affairs Dr A. M. SHANDILYA; Dean of Faculty Welfare Dr D. M. D. DESHPANDE; Dean of Research and Consultancy Dr G. DIXIT; Dean of Student Affairs Dr V. K. KHARE; Registrar Dr SAVITA RAJE; Librarian Prof. AJAY PANDEY.

Meenakshi Academy of Higher Education and Research/Meenakshi University: 12 Vembuli Amman Koil St, West K. K. Nagar, Chennai, 600078, Tamil Nadu; tel. (44) 23643955; e-mail info@maher.ac.in; internet www.maher.ac.in; f. 2004; constituent colleges: Ammal Dental College and Hospital, College of Nursing, College of Physiotherapy, Dept of Eng. and Technology, Medical College and Research Institute; Chancellor A. N. RADHAKRISHNAN; Vice-Chancellor Dr P. JAYAKUMAR (acting); Registrar A. N. SANTHANAM.

Constituent Colleges:

Arulmigu Meenakshi Amman College of Nursing: Enathur, Kancheepuram Tamil Nadu.

Meenakshi Ammal Dental College and Hospital: Chennai 600095, Tamil Nadu.

Meenakshi College of Nursing: Chennai 600095, Tamil Nadu.

Meenakshi College of Occupational Therapy: Chennai 600095, Tamil Nadu.

Meenakshi College of Physiotherapy: West K. K. Nagar, Chennai 600078, Tamil Nadu.

Meenakshi Medical College and Research Institute: Enathur, Kancheepuram, Tamil Nadu.

Mody Institute of Technology & Science: Dist. Sikar, Lakshmangarh 332311, Rajasthan; tel. (1573) 225001; e-mail registrar@mitsuniversity.ac.in; internet www.mitsuniversity.ac.in; f. 1998, deemed univ. status 2004; faculties of arts, science, commerce, engineering and technology, law, management studies; library: 48,169 vols, 247 journals; 74 teachers; 1,250 students; Chancellor R. P. MODY; Vice-Chancellor Prof. Dr N. V. SUBBA REDDY; Registrar Prof. AMAL KUMAR.

Motilal Nehru National Institute of Technology: Allahabad 211004, Uttar Pradesh; tel. (532) 2271101; e-mail director@mnnit.ac.in; internet www.mnnit.ac.in; f. 1961; depts of applied mechanics, chemistry, civil engineering, computer science and engineering, electrical engineering, electronics and communications engineering, humanities and social science, management studies, mathematics, mechanical engineering, physics; library: 104,382 vols, 290 journals; Dir Prof. P. CHAKRABARTI; Dean of Academic Affairs Dr S. K. DUGGAL; Dean of Faculty Welfare Dr A. K. MISRA; Dean of Student Affairs Dr VINOD YADAV; Registrar SARVESH K. TIWARI (acting); Librarian SURYA KANT TIWARI (acting).

Narsee Monjee Institute of Management Studies (NMIMS): V. L. Mehta Rd, Vile Parle (W), Mumbai 400056, Maharashtra; tel. (22) 26134577; e-mail enquiry@nmims.edu; internet www.nmims.edu; f. 1981, deemed univ. status 2003; schools of architecture, business management, commerce, distance learning, pharmacy, science, technology management and engineering; library: 42,000 books, 308 periodicals; 200 teachers; 9,000 students; Chancellor AMRISH PATEL; Vice-Chancellor Prof. Dr RAJAN SAXENA (acting); Pro-Vice-Chancellor Dr M. N. WELLING; Registrar VARSHA PARAB (acting); Librarian VRUSHALI RANE; publs *MOSAIC*, *NMIMS Management Review* (2 a year).

National Brain Research Centre: NH 8, Manesar 122050, Haryana; tel. (124) 2845200; e-mail info@nbrc.ac.in; internet www.nbrc.ac.in; f. 2003; main research areas incl. computational neuroscience, molecular and cellular neuroscience, systems neuroscience; Dir Prof. SUBRATA SINHA; Registrar K. V. S. KAMESWARA RAO.

National Dairy Research Institute: Karnal 132001, Haryana; tel. (184) 2252800; e-mail dir@ndri.res.in; internet www.ndri.res.in; f. 1923, deemed univ. status 1989; research divs in animal biochemistry, animal biotechnology, dairy cattle breeding, dairy cattle nutrition, dairy cattle physiology, dairy chemistry, dairy economics, statistics and management, dairy engineering, dairy extension, dairy microbiology, dairy technology; library: 90,000 vols and 250 periodicals; Dir Dr A. K. SRIVASTAVA; Jt Dir for Academic Affairs Dr G. R. PATIL; Jt Dir for Research Dr S. L. GOSWAMI; Jt Dir for Admin. and Registrar J. KEWALRAMANI; Dir for Library Services Dr B. R. YADAV; publ. *Dairy Samachar* (4 a year).

National Institute of Educational Planning and Administration: 17–B Sri Aurobindo Marg, New Delhi 110016; tel. (11) 26863562; e-mail nuepa@nuepa.org; internet www.nuepa.org; f. 1962, deemed univ. status 2006; State control; depts of educational admin., educational finance, educational planning, educational policy, foundations of education, school and non-formal education, higher and professional education, comparative education and int. cooperation, inclusive education, educational management information system; library: 53,500 vols, 350 current journals; Vice-Chancellor Prof. R. GOVINDA; Registrar Dr B. K. SINGH; Librarian DEEPAK MAKOL; publs *Journal of Educational Planning and Administration* (4 a year), *Paripreksha* (3 a year, in Hindi).

National Institute of Mental Health and Neurosciences: POB 2900, Hosur Rd, Bengaluru 560029, Karnataka; tel. (80) 26995005; e-mail regt@nimhans.kar.nic.in; internet www.nimhans.kar.nic.in; f. 1974, deemed univ. status 1994; depts of biophysics, biostatistics, epidemiology, human genetics, mental health education, mental health and social psychology, neuroanaesthesia, neurochemistry, neuroimaging and interventional radiology, neurology, neuromicrobiology, neuropathology, neurophysiology, neurosurgery, neurovirology, nursing, psychiatric and neurological rehabilitation, psychiatric social work, psychiatry, psychopharmacology, speech pathology and audiology; library: 75,000 vols, 315 periodicals; Vice-Chancellor Dr P. SATISHCHANDRA; Registrar Dr V. RAVI; Library and Information Officer Dr H. S. SIDDAMALLAIAH; publs *DEADDICTION* (4 a year), *NIMHANS Journal* (4 a year).

National Institute of Technology, Agartala: Jirania, Agartala 799055, Tripura; tel. (381) 2346630; e-mail nitaedc@gmail.com; internet www.nitagartala.in; f. 1965, fmrly Tripura Engineering College, deemed univ. status 2006; depts of civil engineering, computer science and engineering, electrical engineering, electrical and electronics engineering, mechanical engineering, production engineering, transportation engineering; library: 34,000 vols, 200 journals; Dir Prof. Dr PROBIR KUMAR BOSE; Vice-Prin. P. C. DAS; Dean of Academic Affairs Dr RICHI PRASAD SHARMA; Dean of Faculty Welfare Dr P. CHAKRABORTY; Dean of Student Welfare Dr RAJSEKHAR PANUA; Registrar Dr NABIN KUMAR KOLE; Librarian RAHUL BANERJEE.

National Institute of Technology, Calicut: Calicut 673601, Kerala; tel. (495) 2286800; e-mail director@nitc.ac.in; internet www.nitc.ac.in; f. 1961, deemed univ. status 2002; depts of architecture and civil engineering, chemical engineering, computer science and engineering, electrical engineering, electronics engineering, humanities, mathematics, mechanical engineering, science; library: 121,001 vols, 328 journals; Dir Dr M. N. BANDYOPADHYAY; Dean of Academic Affairs Dr V. K. GOVINDAN; Dean of Faculty Welfare Dr JOSE MATHEW; Dean of Students' Welfare Dr C. MURALEEDHARAN; Registrar P. K. SATHEESH KUMAR RAJA; Librarian Dr SWEETY MATHEW (acting).

National Institute of Technology, Durgapur: Durgapur 713209, West Bengal; tel. (343) 2546397; e-mail director@admin.nitdgp.ac.in; internet www.nitdgp.ac.in; f. 1960, fmrly Regional Engineering College, deemed univ. status 2002; depts of applied mechanics and drawing, biotechnology, chemical engineering, chemistry, civil engineering, computer science and engineering, electrical engineering, electronics and communication engineering, geology, humanities, information technology, management studies, mathematics, mechanical engineering, metallurgical and materials engineering, physics; library: 120,000 vols, 180 journals; 162 teachers; 1,800 students; Chair. Dr BIKASH SINHA; Dir Prof. Dr TARKESHWAR KUMAR; Dean of Academic Affairs Prof. S. B. DAS; Dean of Admin. Prof. P. P. SENGUPTA; Dean of Faculty Affairs Prof. S. K. MITRA; Dean of Students Welfare Prof. G. SANYAL; Registrar Dr A. GANGOPADHYAY (acting); Librarian Dr MANIK MANDAL.

National Institute of Technology, Hamirpur: Hamirpur 177005, Himachal Pradesh; tel. (1972) 222258; e-mail director@nitham.ac.in; internet www.nith.ac.in; f. 1986, deemed univ. status 2002; depts of architecture, chemistry, computer science and engineering, civil engineering, electrical engineering, electronics and communications engineering, humanities and social sciences, mathematics, mechanical engineering, physics; library: 72,359 vols, 382 CD-ROMs; 68 teachers; 900 students; Dir Prof. RAJNISH SHRIVASTAVA; Dean of Academic Affairs Dr SUSHIL CHAUHAN; Dean of Faculty Devt Dr RAKESH SEHGAL; Dean of Student Welfare Dr RAMAN PARTI; Registrar A. S. SINGHA; Librarian (vacant).

National Institute of Technology, Jamshedpur: Jamshedpur 831014, Jharkhand; tel. (657) 2373392; e-mail director@nitjsr.ac.in; f. 1960; depts of applied mechanics, chemistry, civil engineering, computer science and engineering, electrical engineering, electronics engineering, mathematics and humanities, mechanical engineering, metallurgical engineering and materials science, physics, production engineering and science; Dir Dr A. MISHRA; Dean of Academic Affairs Dr R. J. SINGH; Dean of Admin. Dr S. N. SINHA; Dean of Student Affairs N. K. NARAIN; Registrar Dr M. K. BANERJEE; Librarian Dr N. BHARTI.

National Institute of Technology, Karnataka: Surathkal, Srinivasnagar PO, Mangalore 575025, Karnataka; tel. (824) 2474000; e-mail registrar@nitk.ac.in; internet www.nitk.ac.in; f. 1960, deemed univ. status 2002; depts of applied mechanics, chemical engineering, chemistry, civil engineering, computer engineering, electronics and communication, humanities, social sciences and management, information technology, mathematical and computational sciences, metallurgical and materials engineering, mining engineering, physics; library: 100,000 vols; 195 teachers; Dir Prof. G. UMESH (acting); Dean of Academic Affairs Prof. SUMAM DAVID; Dean of Students Welfare Prof. GOPAL MUGERAYA; Registrar Dr M. GOVINDARAJ; Librarian ANASUYA C. CHAKARI.

National Institute of Technology, Kurukshetra: Kurukshetra 136119, Haryana; tel. (1744) 238122; e-mail registrarnitk@rediffmail.com; internet www.nitkkr.ac.in; f. 1963, deemed univ. status 2002; depts of business admin., chemistry, civil engineering, computer application, computer engineering, electrical engineering, electronics and communication engineering, humanities and social sciences, mathematics, mechanical engineering, physics; library: 160,177 vols; Dir Prof. ANAND MOHAN; Dean of Academic Affairs Dr A. K. GUPTA; Dean of Faculty Welfare Dr V. K. SEHGAL; Dean of Student Welfare Dr V. K. ARORA; Registrar G. R. SAMANTRAY; Librarian Dr KRISHAN GOPAL.

National Institute of Technology, Patna: Patna 799055, Bihar; tel. (381) 2371715; internet www.nitp.ac.in; f. 1886 as Pleaders Survey Training School, Bihar College of Engineering 1924, present status 2004; depts of civil engineering, computer science and engineering, electrical engineering, electronics and communications engineering, information technology, mechanical engineering; library: 55,000 vols; Dir Dr U. C. RAY; Registrar Prof. Dr VIDYA SAGAR; Dean of Academic Affairs Dr U. S. TRAIR; Dean of Students Welfare Dr S. M. JHA.

National Institute of Technology, Raipur: G. E. Rd, Raipur 492010, Chhattisgarh; tel. (771) 2254200; internet www.nitrr.ac.in; f. 1963, fmrly Govt Engineering College, Raipur, present status 2005; depts of applied geology, applied mechanics, architecture, biomedical engineering, bio-technology, chemical engineering, chemistry, civil engineering, computer science and engineering, electrical engineering, electronics and telecommunication engineering, English, information technology, mathematics, mechanical engineering, mining engineering, metallurgical engineering, physics; Chair. VIJAY R. KIRLOSKAR; Dir Dr S. K. PANDEY; Dean of Academic Affairs Dr A. M. RAWANI; Dean of Faculty Welfare Dr A. B. SONI; Dean of Student Welfare Dr A. P. RAJIMWALE.

National Institute of Technology, Rourkela: Rourkela 769008, Orissa; tel. (661) 2476773; e-mail info@nitrkl.ac.in; internet www.nitrkl.ac.in; f. 1955, fmrly Regional Engineering College, deemed univ. status 2002; depts of applied mathematics, biotechnolgy and medical engineering, ceramic engineering, chemical engineering, chemistry, civil engineering, computer science and engineering, electrical engineering, electronics and communication engineering, humanities and social sciences, mechanical engineering, metallurgical and materials engineering, mining engineering, physics; library: 150,000 vols; Dir Prof. SUNIL KUMAR SARANGI; Dean of Academic Affairs Prof. SANTANU BHATTACHARYA; Dean of Faculty Welfare Prof. P. C. PANDA; Dean of Research and Consultancy Prof. MAHABIR PANDA; Dean of Student Affairs Prof. KARTIK CHANDRA BISWAL; Registrar Eng. S. K. UPADHYAY; Librarian Y. S. RAO.

National Institute of Technology, Silchar: Cachar, Silchar 788010, Assam; tel. (3842) 224879; e-mail director@nits.ac.in; internet www.nits.ac.in; f. 1967 as Regional Engineering College, deemed univ. status 2002; depts of chemistry, civil engineering, electrical engineering, electronics and communication engineering, humanities and social sciences, mathematics, mechanical engineering, physics; library: 62,050 vols, 2,024 CD–ROMs, 114 journals; 880 students; Dir Prof. N. V. DESHPANDE; Dean of Academic Affairs Prof. A. K. SIL; Dean of Planning and Devt Prof. SATYABRATA CHOUDHURY; Dean of Research Prof. R. GUPTA; Dean of Student Affairs Prof. A. K. SINHA; Registrar P. K. PAUL.

National Institute of Technology, Srinagar: Hazratbal 190006, Jammu and Kashmir; tel. (194) 2421347; e-mail director@nitsri.net; internet www.nitsri.net; f. 1960, deemed univ. status 2003; depts of chemical engineering, chemistry, civil engineering, computer science engineering, electrical engineering, electronics and communication engineering, humanities, information technology, mathematics, mechanical engineering, metallurgical engineering, physics; library: 78,000 vols, 6,000 bound vols of journals; Dir Prof. RAJAT GUPTA; Dean of Academic Affairs Prof. AJAZ HUSSAIN MIR; Dean of Faculty Affairs Prof. SIRAJ AHMAD; Dean of Students Affair Prof. RAJINDER AMBARDAR; Registrar M. ASHRAF QURASHI (acting); Librarian A. R. DAR.

National Institute of Technology, Tiruchirapalli: Tanjore Main Rd, Nat. Highway 67, Tiruchirappalli 620015, Tamil Nadu; tel. (431) 2503000; e-mail deanac@nitt.edu; internet www.nitt.edu; f. 1964, deemed univ. status 2003; depts of architecture, chemical engineering, chemistry, civil engineering, computer applications, computer science and engineering, electrical and electronics engineering, electronics and communication engineering, English, humanities, instrumentation and control engineering, management studies, mathematics, mechanical engineering, metallurgical engineering, physics, production engineering; Centre for Energy and Environmental Science and Technology; library: 100,000 books, 15,943 bound periodicals, 179 current periodicals, 4,500 online journals; 192 teachers; 2,190 undergraduates, 1,025 postgraduates; Dir Dr SRINIVASAN SUNDARRAJAN; Dean for Academic Programme Dr N. ANANTHARAMAN; Dean for Faculty Welfare Prof. V. RAMPRASAD; Dean for Students Welfare Dr K. SANKARANARAYANASAMY; Registrar Dr A. K. BANERJEE (acting).

National Institute of Technology, Warangal: Warangal 506004, Andhra Pradesh; tel. (870) 2459191; e-mail director@nitw.ac.in; internet www.nitw.ac.in; f. 1959 as Regional Engineering College, current name and deemed univ. status 2002; depts of biotechnology, centre for management studies, chemical engineering, chemistry, civil engineering, computer science and engineering, electrical engineering, electronics and communication engineering, mathematics and humanities, mechanical engineering, metallurgical and materials engineering, physical education, physics; library: 143,254 vols, 210 periodicals; 200 teachers; 3,000 students; Dir Prof. T. SRINIVASA RAO; Dean of Academic Affairs Prof. T. RAMESH; Dean of Faculty Affairs Prof. R. C. SASTRY; Dean of Student Affairs Prof. G. RADHAKRISHNAMACHARYA; Registrar Prof. P. ANAND RAJ; Librarian R. SAMMI REDDY.

National Law School of India University: POB 7201, Nagarbhavi, Bengaluru 560072, Karnataka; tel. (80) 23213160; e-mail registrar@nls.ac.in; internet www.nls.ac.in; f. 1987, present status 1991; library: 40,000 books, 15,000 bound periodicals, 140 journals; 30 teachers; 400 students; Vice-Chancellor Prof. Dr R. VENKATA RAO; Registrar Prof. V. NAGARAJ; publs *Indian Journal of Law and Technology* (1 a year), *National Law School of India Review* (2 a year), *Socio-Legal Review* (1 a year).

Attached Research Institutes:

Centre for Child and the Law: NLSIU, PO 7201, Nagarbhavi, Bengaluru 560072; tel. (80) 23160528; e-mail ccl@nls.ac.in; internet www.nls.ac.in/ccl; f. 1996; Coordinator Dr NEETHU SHARMA.

Centre for Environmental Education, Research and Advocacy: tel. (80) 23160527; e-mail ceera@nls.ac.in; internet www.nlsenlaw.org; f. 1997; Coordinator Dr OMPRAKASH V. NANDIMATH.

Centre for Intellectual Property Research and Advocacy: tel. (80) 23160532; e-mail cipra@nls.ac.in; internet www.iprlawindia.org; Coordinator Dr T. RAMAKRISHNA.

Centre for Study of Social Exclusion and Inclusive Policy: tel. (80) 23160533; f. 2008; Coordinator Prof. Dr S. JAPHET.

Centre for Women and the Law: tel. (80) 23160532; e-mail cwl@nls.ac.in; Coordinator Dr V.S. ELIZABETH.

Institute of Law and Ethics in Medicine: tel. (80) 23160529; e-mail tilem@nls.ac.in; Coordinator Dr V. NAGARAJ.

National Institute for Alternate Disputes Resolution: tel. (80) 23160533; Coordinator Dr V. NAGARAJ.

National Institute of Human Rights: tel. (80) 23160533; e-mail nihr@nls.ac.in; f. 1998; Coordinator ANURADHA SAIBABA.

National Museum Institute: Janpath, New Delhi 110011; tel. (11) 23011901; e-mail dgnationalmuseum@gmail.com; internet nmi.gov.in; f. 1983, deemed univ. status 1989; postgraduate courses in conservation and restoration of works of arts, history of art, museology; library: 2,500 books, 60,000 slides; Vice-Chancellor Dr C. V. ANANDA BOSE; Dean Prof. ANUPA PANDE; Registrar K. K. KULSHRESHTHA; Librarian Dr B. N. SINGH.

National University of Educational Planning and Administration: 17–B Sri Aurobindo Marg, New Delhi 110016; tel. (11) 26863562; e-mail nuepa@nuepa.org; internet www.nuepa.org; f. 1962 as Asian Regional Centre for Educational Planners and Administrators, current name adopted 1965, deemed univ. status 2006; offers courses for education personnel of developing countries and district education officers; other in-service training courses; research in various aspects of educational planning and management; consultancy service for developing countries, State govts and other orgs; collaboration with UNESCO and other foreign agencies; library: 53,500 vols, 250 current journals; Vice-Chancellor Prof. R. GOVINDA; Registrar Dr B. K. SINGH; Librarian DEEPAK MAKOL; publs *Journal of Educational Planning and Administration* (4 a year), *Pariprakshya* (in Hindi).

Nava Nalanda Mahavihara: Nalanda, Nalanda 803111, Bihar; tel. (611) 2281672; e-mail nnmdirector@sify.com; internet navanalandamahavihara.org; f. 1951, deemed univ. status 2006; administered by Dept of Culture, Min. of Human Resources Devt; studies and research in Pali, Buddhism, philosophy, ancient Indian and Asian studies; diploma in languages: Chinese, Japanese, Tibetan, Hindi, Sanskrit and Pali; library: 52,500 vols; Dir Prof. Dr Ravindra Panth; Registrar Dr S. P. Sinha; Librarian Dr K. K. Pandey; publs *Atthakatha*, *Pali Tipitaki*.

Padmashree Dr D. Y. Patil Vidyapeeth (Padmashree Dr D. Y. Patil University): Sector 15, CBD Belapur, Navi Mumbai 400614, Maharashtra; tel. (22) 39285999; e-mail dypuniversity@gmail.com; internet www.dypatil.in; f. 2002; Chancellor Dr D. Y. Patil; Pro-Chancellor Dr Ajeenkya D. Patil; Vice-Chancellor Prof. James Thomas; Registrar Dr F. A. Fernandes; Controller of Examinations Radha Ramamurthy.

Constituent Colleges:

Dr D. Y. Patil Dental College and Hospital: Dental Hospital Bldg, Dr D. Y. Patil Vidyanagar, Sector 7, Nerul, Navi Mumbai 400706, Maharashtra; tel. (22) 30965899; e-mail dentistry@dypatil.edu.

Dr D. Y. Patil Medical College: New Medical College Bldg, Dr D. Y. Patil Vidyanagar, Sector 5, Nerul, Navi Mumbai 400706, Maharashtra; tel. (22) 27709218; e-mail medicine@dypatil.edu.

PEC University of Technology: Sector 12, Chandigarh 160012; tel. (172) 2753064; e-mail admissions@pec.ac.in; internet www.pec.ac.in; f. 1947, deemed univ. status 2004; depts of aeronautical engineering, civil engineering, computer science engineering, electrical engineering, electronics and electrical communication engineering, mechanical engineering, metallurgical engineering, production engineering; library: 108,028 vols, 90 journals; Dir Dr Manoj K. Arora; Deputy Dir Dr A. M. Kalra; Dean for Academic Affairs Dr Sanjeev Sofat; Dean for Research, Planning and Devt Dr Uma Batra; Dean for Student Welfare Dr Praveen Kalra; Registrar Dr Ashwani Prashar (acting); Head Librarian P. S. Kang.

Rashtriya Sanskrit Sansthan: 56–57 Institutional Area, Janakpuri, New Delhi 110058; tel. (11) 28524993; e-mail rsks@nda.vsnl.net.in; internet www.sanskrit.nic.in; f. 1970, deemed univ. status 2002; campuses in Allahabad, Bhopal, Guruvayoor, Jaipur, Jammu, Lucknow, Mumbai, Puri, Sringeri and Vedvyas; library: 213,581 vols, 51,133 MSS; Pres. Hon. Min. for Human Resource Devt, Govt of India; Vice-Chancellor Prof. Radhavallabh Tripathi; Registrar Prof. K. B. Subbarayudu; publ. *Sanskrit Vimarsh* (1 a year).

Rashtriya Sanskrit Vidyapeetha: Tirupati 517507, Andhra Pradesh; tel. (8574) 2286799; e-mail registrar_rsvp@yahoo.com; f. 1961; library: 60,000 vols and 5,000 MSS; Vice-Chancellor Prof. Harekrishna Satapathy; Registrar A. Gurumurthi; Dean of Academic Affairs Prof. K. E. Govindan.

Sam Higginbottom Institute of Agriculture, Technology & Sciences: Post Agriculture Institute, Allahabad 211007, Uttar Pradesh; tel. (532) 2684281; e-mail registrar@shiats.edu.in; internet www.shiats.edu.in; f. 1910, fmrly Allahabad Agricultural Institute, deemed univ. status 2000, current name adopted 2009; faculties of agriculture, arts and culture, basic sciences, biotechnology, business studies, engineering and technology, health and medical sciences, humanities and social sciences, management studies, pharmacy and health science, science, social sciences, theology, veterinary science and animal husbandry; library: 85,000 vols; Chancellor Dr Mani Jacob; Pro-Chancellor Dr J. A. Oliver; Vice-Chancellor Prof. Dr Rajendra B. Lal; Pro-Vice-Chancellor Prof. Dr S. B. Lal; Registrar Prof. Dr A. K. A. Lawrence; Dir for Extension Prof. Dr Nahar Singh; Dir for Research Prof. Dr Arif A. Broadway; Librarian S. P. Mallick.

Sardar Vallabhbhai National Institute of Technology: Ichhchhanath, Surat 395007, Gujarat; tel. (261) 2259571; e-mail director@svnit.ac.in; internet www.svnit.ac.in; f. 1961; depts of applied mechanics, applied science and humanities, chemical engineering, civil engineering, computer engineering, electrical engineering, electronics engineering, mechanical engineering, production engineering; library: 100,000 vols; Dir Dr P. D. Porey; Dean of Academic Affairs Dr N. J. Mistry; Dean of Faculty Welfare Dr H. J. Nagasheth; Dean of Students Welfare Dr R. A. Christian; Registrar H. A. Parmar; Librarian Dr J. Banerjee.

Sathyabama University: Jeppiaar Nagar, Rajiv Gandhi Rd, Chennai 600119, Tamil Nadu; tel. (44) 24503150; e-mail registrar@sathyabamauniversity.ac.in; internet www.sathyabamauniversity.ac.in; f. 1987 as Sathyabama Engineering College, deemed univ. status 2001; depts of architecture, bioinformatics, biomedical engineering, biotechnology, chemical engineering, civil engineering, computer application, computer science and engineering, electrical and electronics engineering, electronics and communication engineering, electronics and control engineering, electronics and instrumentation engineering, electronics and telecommunication engineering, information technology, management sciences, mechanical engineering, production engineering, science and visual communication; library: 60,000 vols, 334 journals; Chancellor Dr Jeppiaar; Dir Mariazeena Johnson; Dir Marie Johnson; Vice-Chancellor Dr B. Sheela Rani; Registrar Dr S. S. Rau; Controller of Examinations Prof. K. V. Narayanan; Dean of Academic Research Dr P. E. Sankaranarayanan; Dean of Postgraduate Studies Dr N. Manoharan; publs *International Journal on Applied Bio Engineering*, *International Journal on Design and Manufacturing Technology*, *International Journal on Information Sciences and Computing*, *International Journal on Intelligent Electronic System*, *National Journal on Advances in Building and Mechanics*, *National Journal on Advances in Computing and Management*, *National Journal on Chembio*, *National Journal on Electronic Sciences and Systems*.

School of Planning and Architecture: 4 Block B, Indraprastha Estate, New Delhi 110002; tel. (11) 23702375; e-mail info@spa.ac.in; internet www.spa.ac.in; f. 1941, current name adopted 1959, deemed univ. status 1979; depts of architectural conservation, architecture, building engineering and management, environmental planning, housing, industrial design, landscape architecture, physical planning, regional planning, transport planning, urban design, urban planning; library: 74,759 vols; 62 teachers; 694 students; Dir Prof. A. K. Sharma; Dean of Studies Prof. Dr Neelima Risbud; Registrar Dr D. R. Bains; Controller of Examination Prof. Dr Vinay Maitri; Librarian Najma Rizvi; publ. *SPACE* (4 a year).

Shanmugha Arts, Science, Technology & Research Academy (SASTRA) University: Tirumalaisamaduram, Thanjavur 613401, Tamil Nadu; tel. (4362) 264101; e-mail admissions@sastra.edu; internet www.sastra.edu; f. 1984 as Shanmugha College of Engineering, deemed univ. status 2001; schools of chemical engineering and biotechnology, civil engineering, computing, electrical and electronics engineering, humanities and sciences, management, mechanical engineering; library: 78,000 vols, 300 journals; 700 teachers; 9,000 students; Vice-Chancellor Prof. R. Sethuraman; Registrar S. N. Srivastava; Dean of Student Affairs Prof. M. Narayanan; Dean of Research Dr K. Thiyagarajan.

Attached Centres:

Centre for Advanced Research in Indian System of Medicine: internet www.sastra.edu/carism; Dean Dr G. Victor Rajamanickam.

Centre for Nanotechnology and Advanced Biomaterials: tel. (4362) 304000; e-mail swami@sastra.edu; internet www.sastra.edu/centab; Dir Dr S. Swaminathan.

Shri Lal Bahadur Shastri Rashtriya Sanskrit Vidyapeetha: Qutub Institional Area, New Delhi 110016; tel. (11) 46060606; e-mail info@slbsrsv.ac.in; internet www.slbsrsv.ac.in; f. 1962; deemed univ. status 1987; faculties of adhunik gyan vigyan, darshan sankay, sahitya sanskriti, ved vedang; library: 63,926 vols, 17 periodicals; Chancellor P. N. Bhagwati; Vice-Chancellor Prof. Shashi Prabha Jain (acting); Registrar Dr B. K. Mohapatra.

Sri Chandrasekharenda Saraswathi Viswa Mahavidyalaya (SCSVMV University): Sri Jayendra Saraswathi St, Enathur 631561, Tamil Nadu; tel. (44) 27264301; e-mail registrar@kanchiuniv.ac.in; internet www.kanchiuniv.ac.in; f. 1993; depts of ayurvedic medicine, Sanskrit and Indian culture, science and humanities, electrical engineering, mechanical engineering, computer science and engineering, electronics and communications, management studies; library: 200,000 vols; Chancellor Dr P. V. Vaidyanathan; Vice-Chancellor Dr C. V. Vaidyanathan; Registrar Prof. Dr V. S. Vishnu Potty (acting); Controller of Examinations Dr G. Srinivasu; Librarian R. Murali (acting).

Sri Ramachandra University: Porur, Chennai 600116, Tamil Nadu; tel. (44) 24765512; e-mail registrarsru@gmail.com; internet www.srmc.edu; f. 1985, deemed univ. status 1994; depts of anaesthesiology, cardiac care, chest and tuberculosis, dermatology, emergency, trauma and critical care, endocrinology, ears, nose and throat, general medicine, general surgery, medical gastroenterology, nephrology, neurology, neurosurgery, obstetrics and gynaecology, ophthalmology, orthopaedics, paediatric medicine, paediatric surgery, paediatric urology, plastic and reconstructive surgery, psychiatry, radiology and imaging sciences, surgical gastroenterology and urology; library: 29,158 vols, 451 periodicals; 4,500 students; Chancellor V. R. Venkataachalam; Pro-Chancellor Dr S. P. Thyagarajan; Pro-Chancellor Dr T. K. Partha Sarathy; Vice-Chancellor Dr S. Rangaswami; Dean of Faculties Dr K. V. Somasundaram; Registrar N. Natarajan; Controller of Examinations Dr Vijayalakshmi Thanasekaraan.

Sri Sathya Sai Institute of Higher Learning: Vidyagiri, Prasanthi Nilayam, Anantapur 515134, Andhra Pradesh; tel. (8555) 287235; e-mail registrar@sssu.edu.in; internet sssihl.edu.in; f. 1981; depts of accounting and finance, biosciences, chemistry, commerce, economics, education, English language and literature, history and Indian culture, home sciences, management, mathematics and computer science, philosophy, physics, political science, Telugu language and literature; campuses at Anantapur, Bengaluru; library: 150,000 vols, 150 periodicals; 115 teachers; 1,100 students; Vice-Chancellor Prof. J. Shashidhara Prasad; Registrar Dr Naren Ramji; Controller of Examinations Prof. G. Srinivas Srirangar-

AJAN; Dir for Prasanthi Nilayam Campus Prof. A. SUDHIR BHASKAR; Dir for Anantapur Campus Dr DWARAKA RANI RAO; Dir for Brindavan Campus SANJAY SAHNI; publs *International Journal of Modern Physics* (4 a year), *Journal of Applied Mathematics and Stochastic Analysis* (4 a year), *Third Concept: An International Journal of Ideas* (6 a year).

SRM University: *Head Office*: 3 Veerasamy St, W Mambalam, Chennai; 600033, Tamil Nadu; tel. (44) 24742836 *Kattankulathur Campus*: SRM Nagar, Kattankulathur, Kancheepuram; 603203, Tamil Nadu; tel. (44) 27452270; *Modi Nagar Campus*: Delhi-Meerut Rd, Sikrikalan Modi Nagar, Ghaziabad 201204, Uttar Pradesh; tel. (1232) 234301; *Ramapuram Campus*: Bharathi Salai, Ramapuram, Chennai 600089, Tamil Nadu; tel. (44) 43923042; *Trichy Campus*: Irangalur Post, Mannachanallur Taluk, Tiruchirapalli 621105, Tamil Nadu; tel. (431) 2910599; e-mail registrar@srmuniv.ac.in; internet www.srmuniv.ac.in; f. 1985 as S. R. M. Engineering College, deemed univ. status 2002, current name adopted 2006; faculties of engineering, management, medicine, science and humanities; library: 179,212 vols, 774 periodicals; 2,600 teachers; 38,000 students; Chancellor T. R. PACHAMUTHU; Vice-Chancellor Dr M. PONNAVAIKKO; Pro-Vice-Chancellor Dr P. THANGARAJ; Registrar Dr N. SETHURAMAN; Librarian Dr P. RAJENDRAN.

Swami Vivekananda Yoga Anusandhana Samsthana/S-VYASA: 19 Eknath Bhavan, Gavipuram Circle, K. G. Nagar, Bengaluru 560019, Karnataka; tel. (80) 26608645; e-mail info@svyasa.org; internet www.svyasa.org; divs of yoga and humanities, yoga and life sciences, yoga and management studies, yoga and physical sciences, yoga and spirituality; Vice-Chancellor Prof. H. R. NAGENDRA; Sec. T. MOHAN.

Symbiosis International University: Senapati Bapat Rd, Pune 411004, Maharashtra; tel. (20) 25652444; e-mail infocentre@symbiosis.ac.in; internet www.symbiosis.ac.in; f. 1979; deemed univ. status 2002; constituent institutes: Centre for Information Technology, Centre for Management and Human Resource Development, Centre for Management Studies, College of Nursing, English Language Teaching Institute, Institute of Business Management, Institute of Computer Studies and Research, Institute of Design, Institute of Foreign and Indian Languages, Institute of Geo-informatics, Institute of Health Sciences, Institute of International Business, Institute of Management Studies, Institute of Mass Communication, Institute of Operations Management, Institute of Telecom Management, Law College; 217 teachers (43 full-time, 7 part-time, 167 visiting); 45,000 students; Pres. Dr S. B. MAJUMDAR; Vice-Chancellor Dr BHUSHAN PATWARDHAN; Prin. Dir Dr VIDYA YERAVDEKAR; Registrar V. S. POL.

Tata Institute of Fundamental Research: Homi Bhabha Rd, Mumbai 400005, Maharashtra; tel. (22) 22782000; e-mail webmaster@tifr.res.in; internet www.tifr.res.in; f. 1945, deemed univ. status 2003; attached research centres: National Centre for Biological Sciences (Bengaluru), National Centre for Radio Astrophysics (Pune), Homi Bhabha Centre for Science Education (Mumbai); attached field stations: Balloon Facility (Hyderabad), High Energy Gamma Ray Observatory (Panchmarhi), Radio Astronomy Centre (Ooty), TIFR Centre Maths (Bengaluru), TIFR Gravitation Laboratory (Gauribidanur); schools of mathematics, natural sciences, technology and computer science; Dir Prof. MUSTANSIR BARMA.

Tata Institute of Social Sciences: POB 8313, Deonar, Mumbai 400088, Maharashtra; tel. (22) 25525000; e-mail sparasuraman@tiss.edu; internet www.tiss.edu; f. 1936, deemed univ. status 1964; schools of health systems studies, management and labour studies, rural devt, social sciences, social work; independent centres for lifelong learning, media and cultural studies, research methodology, Jamsetji Tata Centre for Disaster Management; library: 105,000 vols; 106 students; Dir Prof. S. PARASURAMAN; Deputy Dir Prof. LEENA KASHYAP; Registrar Prof. NEELA DABIR; Librarian Dr M. M. KOGANURAMATH; publ. *The Indian Journal of Social Work*.

TERI University: India Habitat Centre, Lodi Rd, New Delhi 110003; Plot No 10, Institutional Area, Vasant Kunj, New Delhi 110070; tel. (11) 26122222; e-mail registrar@teri.res.in; internet www.teriuniversity.ac.in; f. 1998, deemed univ. status 1999, current name adopted 2006; Chancellor Dr R. K. PACHAURI; Vice-Chancellor Prof. BHAVIK R. BAKSHI (acting); Registrar RAJIV SETH; Librarian Dr BHARATI PALIWAL; publ. *Journal of Resources, Energy, and Development* (2 a year).

Thapar University: POB 32, Patiala 147004, Punjab; tel. (175) 2393021; e-mail registrar@thapar.edu; internet www.thapar.edu; f. 1956, deemed univ. status 1985; schools of chemistry and biotechnology, management and social sciences, mathematics and computer applications, physics and material science; library: 55,000 vols; 102 teachers; 1,340 students; Dir Dr ABHIJIT MUKHERJEE; Deputy Dir Dr K. K. RAINA; Registrar J. E. SAMUEL RATNAKUMAR; Dean of Academic Affairs Dr S. K. MOHAPATRA; Dean of Research and Sponsored Projects Dr P. K. BAJPAI; Dean of Student Affairs Dr SEEMA BAWA.

Tilak Maharashtra Vidyapeeth: Vidyapeeth Bhavan, Gultekdi, Pune 411037, Maharashtra; 1242 Sadashiv Peth, Pune 411030, Maharashtra; tel. (20) 24261856; e-mail tmvadmin@tmv.edu.in; internet www.tmv.edu.in; f. 1921, deemed univ. status 1987; campuses at Aurangabad, Delhi, Mumbai; library: 77,674 vols, 2,000 MSS; 35 teachers; 5,508 students; Chancellor VISHWANATH GOPAL PALSHIKAR; Vice-Chancellor Dr DEEPAK JAYANT TILAK; Registrar Dr UMESH KESKAR; Controller of Examinations JAGDISH SALVE; Librarian REVATI DESHMUKH.

Vinayaka Missions University: NH–47 Sankari Main Rd, Ariyanoor, Salem 636308, Tamil Nadu; tel. (427) 3987000; e-mail vmu@vinayakamission.com; internet www.vinayakamission.com; f. 2001; 13 constituent colleges in Chennai, Karaikal, Pondicherry, Salem; Chancellor Dr A. SHANMUGASUNDARAM; Vice-Chancellor Prof. Dr V. R. RAJENDRAN; Registrar Prof. Y. ABRAHAM; Controller of Examinations Dr A. BALASUNDARAM.

Visvesvaraya National Institute of Technology: South Ambazari Rd, Nagpur 440010, Maharashtra; tel. (712) 2222828; e-mail registrar@vnit.ac.in; internet www.vnit.ac.in; f. 1960 as Visvesvaraya Regional College of Engineering, deemed univ. status 2002; depts of applied chemistry, applied mechanics, applied physics, architecture, civil engineering, electrical engineering, electronics and computer science, humanities, mathematics, mechanical engineering, metallurgical engineering, mining engineering; library: 103,249 vols, 9,096 periodicals; 1,500 undergraduates, 200 postgraduates; Dir Dr S. S. GOKHALE; Registrar Dr B. M. GANVEER; Dean of Academic Affairs Dr RAJENDRA PATRIKAR; Dean of Faculty Welfare Dr R. K. INGLE; Dean of Students Welfare Dr A. P. PATIL; Librarian Dr H. T. THORAT.

Colleges

BUSINESS

Administrative Staff College of India: Bella Vista, Raj Bhavan Rd, Khairabad, Hyderabad 500082; tel. (40) 66533000; f. 1956; conducts post-experience management devt programmes for officials in govt, execs and mans in industry and non-govt orgs; undertakes research and consultancy assignments for nat. and int. orgs; library: 74,000 vols, 500 periodicals, online databases; Dir-Gen. Dr S. K. RAO; Dean of Research and Consultancy Prof. M. CHANDRASEKHAR; Dean of Training and Confs Dr PARAMITA DAGUPTA; Registrar and Sec. Col (Retd) TEJINDER SINGH; Librarian Dr N. G. SATISH; publ. *ASCI Journal of Management* (2 a year).

Indian Institute of Management, Ahmedabad: Vastrapur, Ahmedabad 380015; tel. (79) 66323456; e-mail director@iimahd.ernet.in; internet www.iimahd.ernet.in; f. 1962; 2-year postgraduate, 4-year doctoral programme in management; gen. and functional management programmes for practising managers, and special programmes for govt officials, univ. teachers and sectors such as agriculture, public systems; undertakes project research and consulting in the field of management; library: 174,497 vols, 527 journals; 80 teachers; 400 postgraduate programme students; 50 PhD-level students; Chair. Dr VIJAYPAT SINGHANIA; Dir Prof. SAMIR K. BARUA; publ. *Vikalpa* (4 a year).

Indian Institute of Management, Bangalore: Bannerghatta Rd, Bengaluru 560076, Karnataka; tel. (80) 26582450; e-mail info@iimb.ernet.in; internet www.iimb.ernet.in/iimb; f. 1973; library: 220,000 vols, 34 online databases, 695 print journals, 850 electronic journals; 80 teachers; 425 students; Chair. MUKESH AMBANI; Dir Prof. PANKAJ CHANDRA; publ. *IIMB Management Review* (2 a year).

Indian Institute of Management, Calcutta: Diamond Harbour Rd, Joka, Kolkata 700104, West Bengal; tel. (33) 24678310; e-mail director@iimcal.ac.in; internet www.iimcal.ac.in; f. 1961; 2-year MBA course in computer-aided management, 3-year part-time MBA in business management; doctoral and extension courses; centres for studies in human values, devt and environment policy, rural devt and environment management; executive devt; faculty devt through research and consulting services; library: 160,000 vols, 500 journals; 77 teachers; 669 students; Chair. AJIT BALAKRISHNAN; Dir Prof. Dr SHEKHAR CHAUDHURI; publs *Decision* (2 a year), *Journal of Human Values* (2 a year).

Indian Institute of Management, Indore: Prabandh Shikhar, Rau–Pithampur Rd, Indore 453331, Madhya Pradesh; tel. (731) 2439666; e-mail webman@iimidr.ac.in; internet www.iimidr.ac.in; f. 1996; library: 24,139 vols and 425 periodicals; 53 teachers; Chair. L. N. JHUNJHUNWALA; Dir Prof. Dr N. RAVICHANDRAN; publ. *International Journal of Management Practices and Contemporary Thought (IMPACT)*.

Indian Institute of Management, Kozhikode: IIMK Campus PO, Kozhikode 673570, Kerala; tel. (495) 2803001; e-mail director@iimk.ac.in; internet www.iimk.ac.in; f. 1997; library: 30,000 vols, 1,120 periodicals; 319 students; Dir Dr DEBASHIS CHATERJEE; Librarian Dr M. G. SREEKUMAR.

Indian Institute of Management, Lucknow: Prabandh Nagar, Off Sitapur Rd,

Lucknow 226013, Uttar Pradesh; tel. (522) 2734101; e-mail diroffice@iiml.ac.in; internet www.iiml.ac.in; f. 1984; 2-year postgraduate programme in agri-business management, exec. devt programmes; undertakes research and consulting projects in the field of management; main areas: agriculture, health, education, rural development, state public enterprises, corporate management, information technology and systems, entrepreneurship, corporate communication and media relations, leadership and human values; centre for entrepreneur devt and new venture management, agricultural management centre; library: 60,000 vols; 66 teachers; 480 postgraduate students; Chair. Dr JAMSHED J. IRANI; Dir Dr DEVI SINGH; Dean of Academic Affairs Prof. MANOJ ANAND; Dean of Noida Campus Prof. ARCHANA SHUKLA; Dean of Planning and Devt Prof. R. L. RAINA; publ. *Metamorphosis* (2 a year).

GENERAL

Fergusson College: Pune 411004; tel. (20) 25654212; e-mail principal@fergusson.edu; internet www.fergusson.edu; f. 1885; affiliated to Univ. of Pune; undergraduate and postgraduate courses in computer, electronics, humanities and social sciences, information technology, natural sciences; library: 300,000 vols; 5,500 students; Prin. Dr RAVINDRASINH G. PARDESHI; Vice-Prin. Prof. A. B. BHIDE; Vice-Prin. Dr N. M. KULKARNI; Vice-Prin. Prof. P. M. PAWAR; Vice-Prin. REKHA PALSHIKAR; Vice-Prin. Dr SHOBANA ABHYANKAR.

Hans Raj College: Mahatma Hans Raj Marg, Malka Ganj, Delhi 110007; tel. (11) 27667747; e-mail contact@hansrajcollege.co.in; internet hansrajcollege.co.in; f. 1948; attached to Univ. of Delhi; BA in economics, English, Hindi, history, mathematics, Sanskrit; BSc in botany, chemistry, computer science, physics, zoology; 3,700 students; Prin. Dr V. K. KAWATRA (acting).

Institute of Diploma Studies: f. 1997; attached to Nirma Univ. of Science and Technology; depts of chemical engineering, computer engineering, electrical engineering, electronics and communication engineering, information technology, mechanical engineering, plastic engineering; library: 60,000 vols, 400 print periodicals, 8,000 e-journals; Prin. Prof. V. R. IYER.

Institute of Management: Sarkhej–Gandhinagar Highway, Ahmedabad 382481, Gujarat; e-mail grnair@imnu.ac.in; tel. (2717) 241900; internet www.imnu.ac.in; f. 1996; attached to Nirma Univ. of Science and Technology; library: 27,000 vols, 7,000 journals; Dir Dr C. GOPALKRISHAN; Librarian MONITA K. SHASTRI.

Lady Shri Ram College for Women: Lajpat Nagar–IV, New Delhi 110024; tel. (11) 26434459; e-mail lsrc@lsr.edu.in; internet www.lsr.edu.in; f. 1956; depts of commerce, economics, education, English, Hindi, history, journalism, mathematics, philosophy, physical education, political science, psychology, Sanskrit, sociology, statistics; constituent college of Delhi Univ.; library: 100,000 vols, 150 journals; 150 teachers; 2,000 students; Prin. Dr MEENAKSHI GOPINATH; Librarian A. P. YADAV.

Loyola College: Nungambakkam, Chennai 600034, Tamil Nadu; tel. (44) 28178200; e-mail helpdesk@loyolacollege.edu; internet www.loyolacollege.edu; f. 1925, present status 1978; depts of advanced zoology and biotechnology, chemistry, commerce, computer science, economics, English, foreign languages, history and applied history, mathematics, oriental languages, philosophy, physical education, physics, plant biology and biotechnology, social work, sociology, statistics, Tamil, visual communication; Institutes of Dialogue with Cultures and Religions, Entomology Research, Frontier Energy, Industrial and Social Science Research, People Studies, Vocational Education; library: 109,000 vols, 236 journals; 116 teachers; 7,021 students; Rector K. AMAL; Prin. Dr B. JEYARAJ; Sec. Dr JOE ARUN.

Madras Christian College: Tambaram, Chennai 600059, Tamil Nadu; tel. (44) 22390675; e-mail principal@mcc.edu.in; internet www.mcc.edu.in; f. 1837; depts of chemistry, commerce, economics, English, history, languages, mathematics, philosophy, physics, public admin., social work, statistics, Tamil; 5,000 students; Prin. R.W. ALEXANDER JESUDASAN.

Presidency College, Chennai: Chennai, Tamil Nadu; tel. (44) 28544894; e-mail info@presidencychennai.com; internet www.presidencychennai.com; f. 1840; depts of arts and commerce, languages, science; library: 150,000 vols, 95 journals; Prin. Prof. M. DHANUSHKODI; Librarian K. V. RAMALINGAM.

St Joseph's College: POB 27094, 36 Lalbagh Rd, Bengaluru 560027, Tamil Nadu; tel. (80) 22211429; e-mail principal@sjc.ac.in; internet www.sjc.ac.in; f. 1882; Prin. Dr DANIEL FERNANDES.

St Stephen's College: University Enclave, Delhi 110007; tel. (11) 27667271; e-mail info@ststephens.edu; internet www.ststephens.edu; f. 1881; attached to Univ. of Delhi; depts of chemistry, computer science, economics, English, history and political science, mathematics, Persian, philosophy, physics, Sanskrit and Hindi, Urdu; library: 12,000 vols; Prin. Dr VALSON THAMPU; Vice-Prin. Dr R. CLEMENT RAJKUMAR; Dean NANDITA NARAIN; Dean of Academic Affairs Dr S. V. ESWARAN.

St Xavier's College, Ahmedabad: Navarangpura, Ahmedabad, Gujarat; internet www.stxavierscollege.net; f. 1955; depts of biochemistry, biology, chemistry, computer science, economics, electronics, English, Gujarati and Hindi, mathematics, physics, psychology, Sanskrit, statistics; library: 69,241 vols, 25 journals; Pres. WILLIAM K. ABRANCHES; Vice-Pres. AMALRAJ SEBASTIAN; Librarian HARBHAM JADEJA.

St Xavier's College, Kolkata: 30 Park St, Kolkata 700016, West Bengal; tel. (33) 22551101; e-mail principal@sxccal.edu; internet www.sxccal.edu; f. 1860; faculties of arts, business admin., commerce, education, science; library: 18,800 vols; Rector GEORGE PONODATH; Prin. Dr J. FELIX RAJ; Librarian Fr FELIX RAJ.

St Xavier's College, Mumbai: 5 Mahapalika Marg, Mumbai 400001, Maharashtra; tel. (22) 22620661; e-mail webadmin@xaviers.edu; internet www.xaviers.edu; f. 1860; affiliated to Univ. of Mumbai; faculties of arts, business management, commerce, mass media, science; institutes of communication, counselling, management and research, social research and action; library: 120,000 vols, 90 periodicals; Rector Dr ARUN DE SOUZA; Prin. Dr FRAZER MASCARENHAS; Librarian MEDHA TASKAR.

Symbiosis College of Arts and Commerce: Senapati Bapat Rd, Pune 411004, Maharashtra; tel. (20) 25653903; e-mail contact@symbiosiscollege.edu.in; internet www.symbiosiscollege.edu.in; f. 1983; affiliated to Symbiosis Int. Univ.; liberal arts college; Prin. Dr HRISHIKESH SOMAN.

LANGUAGES

Central Institute of Indian Languages: Dept of Higher Education, Language Bureau, Min. of Human Resource Devt, Govt of India, Manasagangothri, Hunsur Rd, Mysore 570006, Karnataka; tel. (821) 2515820; e-mail bhasha@sancharnet.in; internet www.ciil.org; f. 1969; assisting and coordinating the devt of Indian languages; preparation of grammars and dictionaries of tribal and border languages; inter-disciplinary research; preparation of materials for teaching and learning; 290 academic and technical staff; 7 Regional Language Centres in Mysore (languages: Kannada, Telugu, Malayalam, Tamil), Bhubaneswar (languages: Assamese, Bengali, Oriya), Pune (languages: Marathi, Gujarati, Sindhi), Patiala (languages: Urdu, Punjabi, Kashmiri), Solan (Urdu), Lucknow (Urdu) and Guwahati (NE languages); centres for creative writing and lexicography, educational technology and media studies, excellence in classical languages, human resource devt, information on language sciences, language planning, language technology, linguistic and cultural documentation, materials production, speech sciences, testing and evaluation, tribal and endangered languages; library: 63,500 vols and 250 periodicals; Dir Prof. RAJESH SACHDEVA.

LAW

Amity Law School: F–1 Block, Sector 125, Amity Univ. Campus, Noida 201303, Uttar Pradesh; tel. (120) 4392681; e-mail director@als.amity.edu; internet www.amity.edu/als; affiliated to Guru Gobind Singh Indraprastha Univ.; f. 2000; library: 150,000 vols, 80 periodicals; Pres. Dr ASHOK K. CHAUHAN; Dir Prof. M. K. BALACHANDRAN.

Government Law College: A Rd, Churchgate, Mumbai 400020, Maharastra; tel. (22) 22041707; e-mail glcstudentscouncil@gmail.com; internet www.glcmumbai.com; f. 1855 as Govt Law School, present name 1925; library: 36,000 vols, 38 journals; Prin. Dr MANJUSHA S. MOLWANE (acting); publs *Journal of Law and Society*, *Law Review*.

ILS Law College: Law College Rd, Pune 411004, Maharashtra; tel. (20) 25656775; e-mail ilslaw@vsnl.com; internet www.ilslaw.edu; f. 1924; 3-year and 5-year LLB degree; masters in labour laws, labour welfare; diploma in taxation laws; library: 45,000 vols, 100 periodicals; 1,600 students; Prin. VAIJAYANTI JOSHI.

Indian Academy of International Law and Diplomacy: 9 Bhagwan Dass Rd, New Delhi 110001; tel. (11) 23384458; e-mail isil@giasdl01.vsnl.net.in; internet www.isil-aca.org/indian-academy-intl-law.htm; f. 1964; incls research institute and library; offers courses in int. law and diplomacy, human rights, int. humanitarian and refugee laws, int. trade and business law, law of air transport and aviation liability, int. law and law of int. instns; library: 25,000 vols; Pres. RAM NIWAS MIRDHA; publ. *Indian Journal of International Law* (4 a year).

Institute of Law: f. 2007; attached to Nirma Univ. of Science and Technology; Dir Prof. PURVI POKHRIYAL (acting).

Symbiosis Law School: Senapati Bapat Rd, Pune 411004, Maharashtra; tel. (20) 25655114; e-mail info@symlaw.ac.in; internet www.symlaw.ac.in; f. 1977; constituent of Symbiosis Int. Univ.; Chancellor Dr S. B. MUJUMDAR; Vice-Chancellor Dr BHUSHAN PATWARDHAN; Prin. Dir Dr VIDYA YERAVDEKAR; Dir Dr SHASHIKALA GURPUR; Librarian KALPANA JADHAV.

MEDICINE

All India Institute of Hygiene and Public Health: 110 Chittaranjan Ave, Kolkata 700073, West Bengal; tel. (33) 315286; f. 1932; depts of behavioural sciences, biochemistry and nutrition, epidemiology and health education, maternal and child health, microbiology, occupational health, public health administration, public health nursing, sanitary engineering, social and preventive medicine, statistics and demography, veterinary public health; library: 85,000 vols, 250 current periodicals; 112 teachers (incl. 14 professors); 300 students; Dir Prof. K. J. NATH.

Armed Forces Medical College: Wanowrie, Pune 411040, Maharashtra; tel. (20) 26026001; internet afmc.nic.in; f. 1948; library: 20,000 bound journals; depts of anaesthesiology, anatomy, biochemistry, nursing, community, dental surgery, dermatology, forensic medicine, hospital admin., internal medicine, microbiology, obstetrics and gynaecology, opthalmology, orthopaedics, otorhinolaryngology, pathology, paediatrics, pharmacology, physiology, psychiatry, radiodiagnosis and imaging, surgery, transfusion medicine; Dir and Commandant G. S. JONEJA; Dean MANOJ LUTHRA; publ. *Medical Journal Armed Forces of India (MJAFI)*.

Christian Medical College, Vellore: Vellore 632004, Tamil Nadu; tel. (416) 2282010; e-mail directorate@cmcvellore.ac.in; internet www.cmch-vellore.edu; f. 1948; graduate courses in laboratory technology, medical records science, medicine, occupational therapy, physiotherapy; 11 postgraduate medical diploma courses; 23 postgraduate degree courses; 11 higher speciality courses; variety of allied health sciences diploma programmes; Dir Dr SURANJAN BHATTACHARJI; Dean, College of Nursing BHARATHI JACOB.

Institute of Pharmacy: Nirma Univ., Sarkhej-Gandhinagar Highway, Ahmedabad 382481, Gujarat; e-mail rp.ip@nirmauni.ac.in; f. 2004; attached to Nirma Univ. of Science and Technology; library: 6,792 vols, 114 periodicals; Dir and Prin. Dr MANJUNATH GHATE (acting).

Jawaharlal Institute of Postgraduate Medical Education and Research: Dhanvantri Nagar, Puducherry 605006; tel. (413) 2272380; e-mail director@jipmer.edu.in; internet www.jipmer.edu; f. 1823 as Ecole de Medicine de Pondicherry, present name 1964; affiliated to Pondicherry Univ.; depts of anaesthesiology, anatomy, biochemistry, cardiology, cardiothoracic and vascular surgery, dermatology, dentistry, ear, nose and throat, emergency medical services, forensic medicine and toxicology, medicine, medical education, microbiology, neurology, obstetrics and gynaecology, ophthalmology, orthopaedics, paediatrics, pathology, plastic surgery, pharmacology, physiology, preventive and social medicine, psychiatry, radiodiagnosis, radiotherapy, sexually transmitted diseases, surgery, TB and chest diseases, urology; library: 36,713 vols; Dir Dr K. S. V. K. SUBBA RAO; Dean Dr K. S. REDDY.

Kasturba Medical College, Manipal: Manipal Univ., Manipal 576104, Karnataka; tel. (820) 2922367; e-mail dean.kmc@manipal.edu; f. 1953; attached to Manipal Univ.; depts of anatomy, ayurvedic medicine, biochemistry, biotechnology, community medicine, dermatology, ear, nose and throat, forensic medicine, hospital administration, laser spectroscopy, medical education, nephrology, obstetrics and gynaecology, ophthalmology, orthopaedics, paediatric surgery, pathology, plastic surgery, psychiatry, radiodiagnosis and imaging, surgery, TB and respiratory diseases, urology, yoga; Dean Dr P. SRIPATHI RAO.

Lady Hardinge Medical College: C–604 Shivaji Stadium Bus Terminal Co. Place, Shaheed Bhagat Singh Marg, New Delhi 110001; tel. (11) 23363728; e-mail info@lhmc.in; internet www.lhmc.in; f. 1914; library: 27,000 vols, 24,000 bound and 160 current periodicals; affiliated to Univ. of Delhi; depts of anaesthesiology, anatomy, biochemistry, ear, nose and throat, forensic medicine, microbiology, obstetrics and gynaecology, ophthalmology, orthosurgery, paediatrics, pathology, pharmacology, physiology, psychiatry, radiology, radiotherapy, skin, surgery, venereal diseases; Prin. Prof. Dr G. K. SHARMA; Vice-Prin. Prof. A. K. DUTTA.

Maulana Azad Medical College: Bahadur Shah Zafar Marg, New Delhi 110002; tel. (11) 23239271; e-mail info@mamc.ac.in; internet www.mamc.ac.in; f. 1959; depts of anaesthesia, anatomy, biochemistry, community medicine, dentistry, dermatology and sexually transmitted diseases, ear, nose and throat, forensic medicine, microbiology, obstetrics and gynaecology, orthopaedics, paediatrics, pathology, pharmacology, physiology, radiodiagnosis, radiotherapy, surgery; Dean Dr A. K. AGARWAL; Registrar for Academics S. M. HAIDER.

National Institute of Health and Family Welfare (NIHFW): Baba Gang Nath Marg, Munirka, New Delhi 110067; tel. (11) 26165959; e-mail info.nihfw@nic.in; internet www.nihfw.org; f. 1977; in-service training, MD course in community health admin., biomedical research, research and consultancy; regional centre for health management; documentation and reprographic services; library: 41,000 vols and 308 periodicals; Dir Prof. MADHULEKHA BHATTACHARYA (acting); publ. *NIHFW Journal* (4 a year).

SCIENCE AND TECHNOLOGY

See Institutes of National Importance for details of Indian Institutes of Technology.

Government College of Engineering and Ceramic Technology: 73 Abinash Chandra Banerjee Lane, Kolkata 700010, West Bengal; tel. (33) 23701263; e-mail gcect.kolkata@gmail.com; internet www.gcect.ac.in; f. 1941 as Bengal Ceramic Institute, Calcutta, renamed College of Ceramic Technology 1962, present status 2001; library: 13,000 vols, 65 journals; Prin. Dr P. G. PAL; Librarian P. B. PATRA.

Government College of Engineering and Textile Technology: 12 William Carey Rd, Serampore, Hooghly, West Bengal; tel. (33) 26621058; internet www.gcetts.org; f. 1908; library: 12,000 vols (incl. books, journals, reports, proceedings, pamphlets and lab manuals); Registrar KAUSHIK ROY; Librarian ANANDA MAJUMDER.

Institute of Radiophysics and Electronics: 92 Acharya Prafulla Chandra Rd, Kolkata 700009, West Bengal; tel. (33) 23509115; e-mail subal.kar@fulbrightmail.org; internet www.irpel.org; f. 1949; attached to Univ. of Calcutta; houses postgraduate teaching and research dept of Univ. of Calcutta, Faculty of Technology; 3-year post-BSc integrated course leading to BTech. degree, and two-year post-BTech./BE course leading to MTech. degrees in radiophysics and electronics and in information technology; conducts training programmes; research facilities in ionosphere, radio wave propagation, radio astronomy, solid state and microwave electronics, millimetre wave technology, solid state devices, plasma and quantum electronics, optoelectronics, control systems and micro-computers, communication theory and systems, microelectronics and VLSI technology; maintains ionosphere field station at Haringhata and radio astronomy field station at Kalyani; recognized as a Centre of Advanced Study by the University Grants Commission; library: 18,000 vols, 5,000 journals; 36 teachers; 240 students; Head Prof. SUBAL KAR.

Institute of Science: Nirma University Sarkhej-Gandhinagar Highway, Ahmedabad 382481, Gujarat; e-mail ap_os@nirmauni.ac.in; f. 2004; attached to Nirma Univ. of Science and Technology; library: 22,000 vols; Dir Prof. G. NARESH KUMAR.

Institute of Technology: Nirma Univ., Sarkhej-Gandhinagar Highway, Ahmedabad 382481, Gujarat; e-mail director.it@nirmauni.ac.in; f. 1995; attached to Nirma Univ. of Science and Technology; depts of chemical engineering, civil engineering, electrical engineering, humanities, information technology and computer engineering, mathematics, mechanical engineering; library: 22,000 vols; Dir Dr KETAN KOTECHA.

National Institute of Fashion Technology: Hauz Khas, Near Gulmohar Park, New Delhi 110016; tel. (11) 26542000; e-mail director.ho@nift.ac.in; internet www.nift.ac.in; f. 1986; undergraduate and postgraduate diploma courses relevant to the textiles and clothing industries; library of 17,000 books and docs; campuses in New Delhi, Bhopal, Bengaluru, Bhubaneswar, Mumbai, Kolkata, Gandhinagar, Hyderabad, Chennai, Patna, Kannur, Kangra, Shillong, Jodhpur, Raebareli; Dir ARCHANA SHARMA AWASTHI; publ. *Fashion and Beyond* (4 a year).

Schools of Art and Music

Academy of Architecture: 278 Shankar Ghanekar Marg, Prabhadevi, Mumbai 400025, Maharashtra; tel. (22) 24301024; e-mail contact@aoamumbai.in; internet www.aoamumbai.in; f. 1955; offers Bachelors degree course in architecture; library: 5,600 vols and 2,000 slides; Chair. Prof. SUMANT H. WANDREKAR.

Bharatiya Vidya Bhavan: Munshi Sadan, Bhartiya Vidya Bhavan Chowk, Kulapati K. M. Munshi Marg, Mumbai 400007, Maharashtra; tel. (22) 23631261; e-mail bhavan@bhavans.info; internet www.bhavans.info; f. 1938; colleges of arts, science, commerce and engineering; runs schools, Academy of Foreign Languages, College of Sanskrit; dept of Ancient Insights and Modern Discoveries; Ayurveda Research Centre; Institute of Communication and Management; Institute of Management and Research; schools of music, dancing, dramatic art; library: 76,688 vols and 1,404 MSS; Pres. SURENDRALAL G. MEHTA; Vice-Pres. B. N. SRIKRISHNA; Vice-Pres. MURLI S. DEORA; Dir-Gen. and Exec. Sec. H. N. DASTUR; publs *Astrological Journal* (1 a year, in English and Gujarati), *Bharatiya Vidya* (4 a year, in Sanskrit), *Bhavan's Dimdima* (children's magazine, 12 a year, in English), *Bhavan's Journal* (26 a year), *Navneet* (12 a year, in Hindi), *Navneet-Samarpan* (12 a year, in Gujarati), *Samvid* (4 a year, in Sanskrit), 11 vols of the *History and Culture of the Indian People*, and various series.

Attached College:

Bhartiya Vidya Bhavan's Sardar Patel College of Engineering: Bhavan's Campus, Munshi Nagar, Andheri (W), Mumbai 400058, Maharashtra; tel. (22) 26289777; e-mail spce01@bom2.vsnl.net.in; internet www.spce.ac.in; f. 1962; depts of civil, electrical, mechanical and structural engineering; library of 45,000 vols, 70 journals; Exec. Chair and Dean Dr M. L. SHRIKANT; Prin. Dr P. H. SAWANT; Librarian SANJAY JAYARAM SAWANT.

Kalakshetra Foundation: Thiruvanmiyur, Chennai 600041, Tamil Nadu; tel. (44) 24524057; e-mail director@kalakshetra.in; internet www.kalakshetra.in; f. 1936; centre for education in classical music, dancing, theatrical art, painting and handicrafts; maintains a weaving centre for the production of silk and cotton costumes in traditional design and a Kalamkari Unit for dyeing and hand-block printing with vegetable dyes; Dr U. V. Swaminatha Aiyar library noted for classical MSS and literature in Tamil; library: 10,000 books on dance, music, painting, literature and religion; Dir PRIYADARSINI GOVIND; Deputy Dir KARUNAKER K. MENON.

Music Academy: 168 T. T. K. Rd, Royapettah, Chennai 600014, Tamil Nadu; tel. (44) 28112231; e-mail music@musicacademymadras.com; internet www.musicacademymadras.in; f. 1927; research and study of Indian music; directs Teachers' College of Music; library: 5,300 vols; Pres. N. MURALI; Vice-Pres. C. V. KARTHIK NARAYANAN; Vice-Pres. HABIBULLAH BADSHA; Vice-Pres. N. GOPALASWAMI; Vice-Pres. R. SESHSAYEE; Vice-Pres. R. SRINIVASAN; publ. *Journal*.

National School of Drama: Bahawalpur House, 1 Bhagwandas Rd, New Delhi 110001; tel. (11) 23382821; e-mail nationalschoolofdrama@gmail.com; internet nsd.gov.in; f. 1959; 3-year diploma course, short-term theatre training workshops; Theatre-in-Education Company working with and performing for children; library: 28,000 vols, 2,500 slides, records, etc.; 16 teachers; 60 students; Dir Dr ANURADHA KAPUR; Registrar BHANWAR SINGH; publs *Rang Prasang* (2 a year, in Hindi), *Theatre India* (2 a year, in English).

Sri Varalakshmi Academies of Fine Arts: Ramavilas, Kashipathy Agarahar, Chamaraja Double Rd, Mysore 570004, Karnataka; f. 1945; educational and cultural research instn; gives advanced courses of study in Karnataka music; library: 5,000 vols; Prin. C. V. SRIVATSA; Head Research Dept Prof. R. SATHYANARAYANA.

INDONESIA

The Higher Education System

The oldest institution of higher education is the Institut Teknologi Bandung (Bandung Institute of Technology), which was founded in 1920 when Indonesia was part of the Dutch East Indies. In 1949 Indonesia gained independence from the Netherlands. The Portuguese colony of Timor-Leste (formerly East Timor) was annexed in 1975 and administered as a province of Indonesia until 1999, when it was transferred to a UN transitional administration before achieving sovereign independence in 2002. Higher education facilities consist of different types of institutions, which include public and private universities (universitas), higher colleges (sekolah tinggi), teacher training institutes (institut keguruan dan ilmu pendidikan), Islamic universities (universitas Islam), Christian universities (universitas Kristen), academies (akademi) and polytechnics (politeknik). Universities (including technical institutes) offer a full range of undergraduate and postgraduate degrees; teacher training institutes and Islamic universities have full degree-awarding powers; academies are specialized institutions of higher education related to a particular profession; and polytechnics are technical and vocational institutions offering diploma-level education. In 2009/10 there were 3,011 tertiary institutions (the vast majority of which were in the private sector) with a total enrolment of 4,337,039 students. The Directorate-General of Higher Education is the government body responsible for overall control of higher education, but the Directorate of Islamic Higher Education is responsible for the Islamic universities.

Admission to public universities is on the basis of the Entrance Examination to State Universities (Ujian Masuk Perguruan Tinggi Negeri), while admission to polytechnics requires the applicant to complete secondary education and sit an entrance examination (Ujian Masuk Politeknik). The Entrance Examination to State Universities is divided into two streams: social sciences and natural sciences. Institutions may also make an offer of admission based on Interest and Ability Tracing (Penelusuran Minat dan Kemampuan), a system for monitoring secondary school students.

Indonesia operates a US-style 'credit semester' system (officially introduced in 1979) for awarding undergraduate and postgraduate degrees, divided into three stages (sarjana). The first stage is the undergraduate degree (Sarjana Satu), the course for which lasts a minimum of eight semesters (four years) and requires 144–160 credits. Degrees in professional fields, such as medicine, dentistry, veterinary science and engineering, may last for an additional one to three years. The second stage (and first postgraduate degree) is the Magister, a course of study requiring 36–50 credits and lasting at least four semesters (two years). The third and last stage is the Doktor, also lasting at least four semesters (two years) and requiring a further 40–60 credits.

Post-secondary technical and vocational education is offered by polytechnics and academies. Students are awarded one of four diplomas (D1–D4) depending on length of course (one to four years) or area of specialization. The diploma D4 is regarded as equivalent to the Sarjana Satu. Vocational education is also offered at postgraduate level through 'specialist' courses, which are offered in a narrow range of subjects, including medicine, pharmacy, law and accountancy. The first specialist vocational qualification, Ijazah Spesialis (SP1), is awarded after two years of study and requires 26–50 credits, and the second, Ijazah Spesialis (SP2), is awarded after 40–50 credits having been accrued following SP1.

The National Accreditation Board for Higher Education (Badan Akreditasi Nasional Perguruan Tinggi) was founded in 1994 as part of the Directorate-General of Higher Education and is the body responsible for accrediting both public and private institutions of higher education. Courses are ranked on a scale A–D, with A being 'very good' and D 'unsatisfactory'. C is the minimum requirement for accreditation.

Regulatory and Representative Bodies

GOVERNMENT

Directorate-General of Higher Education: Gedung D, Jl. Raya Jend Sudirman Pintu I, Jakarta; tel. (21) 57946105; e-mail dikti@dikti.go.id; internet www.dikti.go.id; Dir-Gen. Prof. Dr Ir DJOKO SANTOSO.

Ministry of Education and Culture: Jl Jenderal Sudirman, Senayan, Jakarta 12070; tel. (21) 5703303; e-mail pengaduan@kemdikbud.go.id; internet www.kemdiknas.go.id; Minister MOHAMMAD NUH.

ACCREDITATION

Badan Akreditasi Nasional Perguruan Tinggi (National Accreditation Board for Higher Education): Komplek Ditjen Jend. Mandikdasmen, Depdiknas RI, Gd D, Lantai 1, Jl. RS. Fatmawati Cipete, Jakarta 12410; tel. (21) 7668690; e-mail sekretariat.banpt@gmail.com; internet ban-pt.depdiknas.go.id; f. 1994; Chair. Prof. KAMANTO SUNARTO.

Learned Societies

BIBLIOGRAPHY, LIBRARY SCIENCE AND MUSEOLOGY

Asosiasi Museum Indonesia (Indonesian Museum Association): c/o Museum Nasional, Jl. Merdeka Barat 12, Jakarta 10110; tel. (21) 3868172; e-mail asosiasi_museum_indonesia@yahoo.com; internet www.asosiasimuseumindonesia.or.id; f. 2004; Chair. Drs SOETRISNO.

Ikatan Pustakawan Indonesia (Indonesian Library Association): Jl. Salemba Raya 28A, Jakarta 10430; tel. (21) 7872353; e-mail supriatno@pnri.go.id; f. 1954; Pres. DADY P. RACHIMANANTA; Sec.-Gen. H. ZULFIKAR ZEN.

EDUCATION

UNESCO Office Jakarta and Regional Science Bureau for Asia and the Pacific: Jl. Galuh (II) 5, Kebayoran Baru, POB 1273/JKT, Jakarta 12110; tel. (21) 7399818; e-mail jakarta@unesco.org; internet www.unesco.or.id; represents Brunei, Indonesia, Malaysia, Philippines and Timor-Leste; Dir Dr HUBERT GIJZEN.

LANGUAGE AND LITERATURE

Alliance Française: Jl. Raya Puputan I, 13A, Denpasar 80235; tel. (361) 234143; e-mail info@afdenpasar.org; internet www.afdenpasar.org; offers courses and examinations in French language and culture and promotes cultural exchange with France; centres in Balikpapan, Bandung, Denpasar, Lampung, Manado, Medan, Padang and Semarang; Dir AUDREY LAMOU; Librarian FEYBE I. MOKOGINTA.

British Council: S. Widjojo Centre, Jl. Jenderal Sudirman Kav 71, Jakarta 12190; tel. (21) 2524115; e-mail information@britishcouncil.or.id; internet www.britishcouncil.org/indonesia; teaching centre; offers courses and examinations in English language and British culture and promotes cultural exchange with the UK; attached office in Surabaya; library of 18,000 vols; Dir Dr PATRICK BRAZIER; Man., English Language Services SIMON COLLEDGE.

Goethe-Institut: Jl. Sam Ratulangi 9–15, POB 3640, Jakarta 10350; tel. (21) 23550208; e-mail info@jakarta.goethe.org; internet www.goethe.de/jakarta; f. 1961; offers courses and examinations in German language and culture and promotes cultural exchange with Germany; attached centre in Bandung; library of 10,000 vols, 1,600 audiovisual items, 40 periodicals; Dir HEINRICH BLOEMEKE.

MEDICINE

Ikatan Dokter Indonesia (Indonesian Medical Association): Jl. Dr Sam Ratulangi

29, Menteng, Jakarta 10350; tel. (21) 3150679; e-mail pbidi@idionline.org; internet www.idionline.org; f. 1950; 45,131 mems; Chair. Prof. Dr FACHMI IDRIS; Sec.-Gen. Dr SLAMET BUDIARTO; publs *BIDI* (26 a year), *Majalah Kedokteran Indonesia* (12 a year).

NATURAL SCIENCES

Physical Sciences

Astronomical Association of Indonesia: Jakarta Planetarium, Cikini Raya 73, Jakarta 10330; tel. (21) 2305146; f. 1920; promotes advancement of astronomical science; Chair. Prof. Dr BAMBANG HIDAYAT; Sec. Drs S. DARSA; Treas. Dr WINARDI SUTANTYO.

TECHNOLOGY

Persatuan Insinyur Indonesia (Indonesian Institute of Engineers): Jl. Halimun 39, Jakarta 12980; tel. (21) 8352180; e-mail info@pii.or.id; internet www.pii.or.id; 27,000 mems; Pres. ABURIZAL BAKRIE; Sec.-Gen. I. SUCIPTO UMAR.

Research Institutes

GENERAL

Lembaga Ilmu Pengetahuan Indonesia (Indonesian Institute of Sciences): Jl. Jendral Gatot Subroto 10, Jakarta 12710; tel. (21) 5251542; e-mail kepala@lipi.go.id; internet www.lipi.go.id; f. 1967; govt agency; promotes the devt of science and technology; serves as the nat. centre for regional and int. scientific cooperation; organizes nat. research centres; library of 150,000 titles; Head Prof. Dr UMAR ANGGARA JENIE; publs *Annales Bogorienses* (2 a year), *Berita Biologi* (4 a year), *Berita Iptek* (4 a year), *IPT Technical Journal* (4 a year), *Jurnal Kimia Terapan Indonesia* (3 a year), *Journal of Tropical Ethnobiology* (2 a year), *Jurnal Ekonomi dan Pembangunan* (2 a year), *Jurnal Elektronika dan Pembangunan* (6 a year), *Jurnal Masyarakat dan Budaya* (2 a year), *Jurnal Penduduk dan Pembangunan* (2 a year), *Jurnal Teknologi Informasi* (3 a year), *Korosi: Majalah Ilmu dan Teknologi* (2 a year), *Limnotek* (2 a year), *Majalah Perencanaan LIPI* (2 a year), *Majalah Widyariset* (12 a year), *Masyarakat Indonesia: Majalah Ilmu-ilmu Sosial Indonesia* (2 a year), *Oseanologi dan Limnologi di Indonesia* (6 a year), *Prosea Newsletter* (4 a year), *Reinwardtia: A Journal on Taxonomic Botany, Plant Sociology and Ecology* (irregular), *Riset Geologi dan Pertambangan*, *Telaah: Berkala Ilmu Pengetahuan dan Teknologi* (2 a year), *Treubia: Journal on Zoology of the Indo-Australian Archipelago* (irregular), *Warta Biotek* (4 a year), *Warta KIM* (12 a year), *Warta Kimia Analitik* (2 a year), *Warta Oseanografi* (4 a year).

AGRICULTURE, FISHERIES AND VETERINARY SCIENCE

Badan Penelitian dan Pengembangan Kehutanan (Forestry Research and Development Agency): Manggala Wanabakti Bldg, Blk 1, 11 Fl., Jl. Jend. Gatot Subroto, Jakarta 10270; tel. (21) 5730392; e-mail datinfo@forda-mof.org; internet www.forda-mof.org; f. 1983; attached to Kementerian Kehutanan (Min. of Forestry); 503 research scientists; library of 36,679 vols, 16,552 journals, 3,032 vols in reference colln, 7,235 textbooks; Dir-Gen. Dr IMAN SANTOSO; Sec. WISNU PRASTOWO; publs *Breeding Tree Improvement Journal* (3 a year), *Dipterocarpaceae Journal* (2 a year), *Forest Product Bulletin* (2 a year), *Forestry Socio Economic Journal* (4 a year), *Info Hutan* (4 or 6 a year), *Info Sosial Ekonomi Kehutanan* (magazine, 4 a year), *Journal of Forest and Nature Conservation Research* (5 or 6 a year), *Journal of Forest Products Research* (4 a year), *Journal of Forestry Policy Analysis* (series, 3 a year), *Journal of Forestry Research* (2 a year), *Mitra Hutan Tanaman* (3 a year), *Plantation Forest Research Journal* (3 a year), *Silva Sains* (1 a year), *Tekno Hutan Tanaman* (3 a year).

Balai Besar Industri Agro (Centre for Agro-Based Industry): Jl. Ir H. Juanda 11, Bogor 16122; tel. (251) 8324068; e-mail cabi@bbia.go.id; internet www.bbia.go.id; f. 1909; attached to Min. of Industry; provides services for agriculture-based industry through training, consultancy, chemical and microbiological testing, research and devt, certification, environmental management, technical inspection, design engineering on food processing and calibration; Dir YANG YANG SETIAWAN; publ. *Warta IHP* (Journal of Agro-Based Industry, 2 a year).

Balai Besar Penelitian Veteriner Bogor (Indonesian Research Centre for Veterinary Science (IRCVS), Indonesian Agency for Agricultural Research and Development (IAARD), Ministry of Agriculture): Jl. R. E. Martadinata 30, POB 151, Bogor 16164; tel. (251) 8331048; e-mail balivet@indo.net.id; internet bbalitvet.litbang.deptan.go.id; f. 1908; depts of bacteriology, toxicology and mycology, parasitology, pathology, virology, balitvet culture colln (BCC), BSL-3 Modular Laboratory; library of 12,627 vols, 92 e-books and 1,119 journals; Head Dr HARDIMAN.

Balai Penelitian Bioteknologi Perkebunan Indonesia (Indonesian Biotechnology Research Institute for Estate Crops): Jl. Salak 1A, Bogor 16151; tel. (251) 8333382; e-mail ipardboo@indo.net.id; internet www.ipard.com; f. 1933; supportive research in plant molecular biology and immunology, microbes and bioprocessing; library of 13,493 vols, 1,597 periodicals, 3,109 reprints, 70 theses; Head of Unit Dr Ir DARMONO TANIWIRYONO; publ. *Menara Perkebunan* (2 a year, in English and Indonesian).

Pusat Penelitian dan Pengembangan Hortikultura (Indonesian Centre for Horticulture Research and Development—ICHORD): Jl. Raya Ragunan 29A, Pasarminggu, Jakarta 12520; tel. (21) 7805768; e-mail puslitbanghorti@litbang.deptan.go.id; internet hortikultura.litbang.deptan.go.id; research and devt of horticultural crops; Dir Dr YUSDAR HILMAN; publs *IPTEK* (1 a year), *Jurnal Hortikultura* (4 a year), *Katalog* (1 a year).

Attached Institutes:

Balai Penelitian Tanaman Buah Tropika (Indonesian Tropical Fruit Research Institute): Jl. Raya Solok-Aripan Km 8; tel. (755) 20137; e-mail balitbu@gmail.com; internet balitbu.litbang.deptan.go.id.

Pusat Penelitian dan Pengembangan Peternakan (Central Research Institute for Animal Sciences Research and Development): Jl. Raya Pajajaran, Kav E-59, Bogor, West Java 16151; tel. (251) 322185; e-mail criansci@indo.net.id; internet peternakan.litbang.deptan.go.id; f. 1950; researches into farm animals and animal parasites and diseases; library of 14,000 vols, 1,199 periodicals; Dir Dr BESS TIASNAMURTI; publs *Ilmu Peternakan dan Veteriner* (4 a year), *Indonesian Journal of Animal and Veterinary Sciences*, *Proceedings of the National Seminar* (1 a year), *Wartazoa* (4 a year).

Pusat Penelitian dan Pengembangan Tanaman Pangan (Centre for Food Crops Research and Development): Jl. Merdeka 147, Bogor 16111; tel. (251) 334089; internet www.puslittan.bogor.net; f. 1961; food crops research and devt; library of 3,000 vols; Dir Dr ACHMAD M. FAGI; publ. *Contributions of CRIFC* (4–6 a year).

Attached Institutes:

Balai Penelitian Bioteknologi Tanaman Pangan (Research Institute for Biotechnology of Food Crops): Jl. Tentara Pelajar 3A, Bogor 16111; tel. (251) 337975; Dir Dr DJOKO S. DAMARDJATI; publs *Buletin Penelitian* (Research Bulletin, 2–4 a year), *Penelitian Pertanian* (Agricultural Research, 3–4 a year, in Indonesian and English).

Balai Penelitian Tanaman Jagung dan Serealia Lain (Research Institute for Maize and Other Cereals): Jl. Ratulangi, Kotak Pos 173, Maros 90511, Ujung Pandang, Sulawesi Selatan Telp; tel. (411) 371016; Dir Dr MARSUM DAHLAN; publ. *Agrikam: Buletin Penelitian Pertanian* (Agricultural Research Bulletin, 2–4 a year, with English summary).

Balai Penelitian Tanaman Kacang-kacangan dan Umbi-umbian Malang (Research Institute for Legumes and Root Crops): Jl. Raya Kendal Payak, Kotak Pos 66, Malang, Jawa Timur 65101; tel. (341) 81468; Dir Dr SUYAMTO; publ. *Penelitian Palawija* (Palawija Research, 2 a year, in Indonesian, and abstract in English).

Balai Penelitian Tanaman Padi (Research Institute for Rice): Jl. Raya 9, Sukamandi—Tromol Pos 11, Cikampek Subang, Jawa Barat 41255; tel. (264) 520157; Dir Dr ANDI HASANUDDIN; publ. *Media Sukamandi* (Research at Sukamandi, 2–4 a year, with English summary).

Balai Penelitian Tanaman Pangan Lahan Rawa (Research Institute for Food Crops on Swampy Areas): Jl. Kebun Karet, Lok Tabat, Kotak Pos 31, Kalimantan, Selatan Banjarbaru 70712; tel. (511) 4772534; Dir ACHMADI; publ. *Pemberitaan Penelitian* (2–4 a year, in Indonesian and English).

Pusat Penelitian Kelapa Sawit (Indonesian Oil Palm Research Institute): Jl. Brigjen Katamso 51, Medan 20158; tel. (61) 7862477; e-mail admin@iopri.org; internet www.iopri.org; f. 1916; promotes agricultural improvement on the member estates; library of 11,000 vols, 20,000 periodicals; Dir Dr Ir WITJKSANA; publs *Berita* (in Indonesian), *Oil Palm Statistics* (in Indonesian), *Rainfall Records* (in Indonesian).

Pusat Penelitian Perkebunan Gula Indonesia (Indonesian Sugar Research Institute): Jl. Pahlawan 25, Pasuruan 67126; tel. (343) 421086; e-mail puslitgula@ipard.com; f. 1887; library of 15,000 vols; Dir Dr MIRZAWAN PDN; publs *Berita* (Communications), *Majalah Penelitian Gula* (Sugar Journal, 4 a year).

Balai Penelitian Tanah (Soil Research Institute): Jl. Ir H. Juanda 98, Bogor 16123; tel. (251) 8323012; e-mail balittanah@litbang.deptan.go.id; internet www.balittanah.litbang.deptan.go.id; f. 1905; library of 4,000 vols; agrobiology, soil conservation and soil fertility; Head Dr Ir ALI JAMIL.

ARCHITECTURE AND TOWN PLANNING

Research Institute for Human Settlements: Jl. Panyawungan, Cileunyi Wetan, Bandung 40393; tel. (22) 798393; e-mail info@puskim.pu.go.id; internet puskim.pu.go.id; f. 1953, current name adopted 2005; library of 27,000 vols; Dir Prof. Dr ANITA FIRMANTI; publs *Journal of Human Settlements* (3 a year, in English), *Jurnal Permukiman* (2 a year, in Bahasa Indonesia),

Masalah Bangunan (1 a year, in Bahasa Indonesia).

ECONOMICS, LAW AND POLITICS

Badan Pusat Statistik (BPS Statistics Indonesia): Jl. Dr Sutomo 6–8, Jakarta 10710; tel. (21) 3841195; e-mail bpshq@bps.go.id; internet www.bps.go.id; f. 1960; library of 60,000 vols, 1,100 periodicals; Dir Dr SOEDARTI SURBAKTI.

Centre for Strategic and International Studies: Jl. Tanah Abang III/23–27, Jakarta 10160; tel. (21) 3865532; e-mail csis@csis.or.id; f. 1971; policy-oriented studies in int. and nat. affairs in collaboration with industry, commerce, and the political, legal and journalistic communities; library of 50,000 vols, 377 journals and 20 newspapers; Exec. Dir Dr RIZAL SUKMA; publs *Analisis CSIS* (4 a year), *The Indonesian Quarterly* (in English).

Indonesian Institute of World Affairs: c/o Univ. of Indonesia, Kampus UI, Depok 16424; Chair. Prof. SUPOMO; Sec. SUDJATMOKO.

Lembaga Administrasi Negara (National Institute of Public Administration): Jl. Veteran 10, Jakarta 10110; tel. (21) 3868201; e-mail humas@lan.go.id; internet www.lan.go.id; f. 1957; conducts research and studies on public admin.; fosters and organizes training for govt officials; provides consultancies on human resource management, regional autonomy, devt, public policy, public service management; library of 16,712 vols; Chair. Dr ASMAWI REWANSYAH; publs *Jurnal Administrasi Publik*, *Jurnal Administrator Borneo*, *Jurnal Diklat Aparatur*, *Jurnal Ilmu Administrasi*, *Jurnal Kapita Selekta Administrasi Negara*, *Manajemen Pembangunan*, *Transformasi Administrasi*.

Balai Pengkajian dan Pengembangan Komunikasi dan Informatika/BPPKI Yogyakarta (Assessment and Development Centre for Communication and Information): Daya Jl Imogiri Barat km 5 Dusun Wejo Kel. Bangun Harjo, Sewun Bantul, Yogyakarta 55187; internet balitbang.kominfo.go.id/balitbang/bppki-yogyakarta; f. 1953 as Lembaga Pers dan Pendapat Umum; current name adopted 2008; attached to Min. of Communication and Informatics; centres in Bandung, Banjarmasin, Jakarta, Makassar, Manado, Medan and Surabaya; library of 4,500 vols; Head Dr EKA HANDAYANI; publ. *Jurnal IPTEK-KOM* (2 a year).

HISTORY, GEOGRAPHY AND ARCHAEOLOGY

Pusat Penelitian Arkeologi (Research Centre of Archaeology): Jl. Raya Condet Pejaten 4, Pasar Minggu, Jakarta 12510; tel. (21) 7988131; e-mail arkenas@bit.net.id; brs in Yogyakarta, Denpasar, Palembang, Bandung, Banjarmasin, Makassar, Manado, Ambon and Jayapura; library of 15,000 vols; Dir Dr HARIS SUKENDAR; publs *Aspects*, *Amerta*, *Kalpataru*.

LANGUAGE AND LITERATURE

Pusat Bahasa. Departemen Pendidikan Nasional (Language Centre of the Ministry of National Education): POB 6259, Jl. Daksinapati Barat IV, Rawamangun, Jakarta 13220; tel. (21) 4706678; e-mail masterfbs@bahasa-sastra.web.id; f. 1975; language-planning policies, research in linguistics and vernaculars, compiling of dictionaries, coordinating and supervising language devt and cultivation, applied research in language education; library of 20,000 vols; Dir DENDY SUGONO; publs *Bahasa dan Sastra* (6 a year), *Informasi Pustaka Kebahasaan* (4 a year), *Lembar Komunikasi* (6 a year).

MEDICINE

Badan Pengawas Obat dan Makanan (National Agency of Drug and Food Control): Jl. Percetakan Negara 23, Jakarta 10560; tel. (21) 42883309; e-mail informasi@pom.go.id; internet www.pom.go.id; f. 2000; legislation, regulation and standardization of drug and food industries; licensing and certification of pharmaceutical industry; evaluation of products; sampling and laboratory testing of products; inspection of production and distribution facilities; investigation and law enforcement; auditing of product advertising and promotion; research on drug and food policy implementation; public communication, information and education; Head Dra LUCKY S. SLAMET; Sec. Dr M. HAYATIE AMAL.

Eijkman Institute: Jl. Diponegoro 69, Jakarta 10430; tel. (21) 3917131; internet www.eijkman.go.id; f. 1888 as Research Laboratory for Pathology and Bacteriology, current name adopted 1938, closed in 1960s, reopened 1993; carries out fundamental research of strategic biomedical importance; Dir Prof. Dr SANGKOT MARZUKI.

Laboratorium Kesehatan Daerah (Pathological Laboratory, Ministry of Health): Jl. Rawasari Slt 2, Jakarta 10510; tel. (21) 4247408; f. 1906; investigation and control of contagious and endemic diseases in Sumatra; library of 3,000 vols; Dir Dr ISKAK KOIMAN.

Perusahaan Negara Bio-Farma (Pasteur Institute): Jl. Pasteur 9, POB 47, Bandung 40161; Dir M. S. NASUTION.

Pusat Penelitian dan Pengembangan Pelayanan dan Technologi Kesehatan (Health Services and Technology Research and Development Centre): Jl. Indrapura 17, Surabaya 60176; tel. (31) 3528748; internet www.litbang.depkes.go.id/p4tk; f. 1975; library of 14,500 books, 750 magazine titles; Dir Dr H. SUWANDI MAKMUR; publs *Bulletin of Health System Research* (2 a year), *Warta JIP* (4 a year).

NATURAL SCIENCES

General

Institut de Recherche pour le Développement (IRD): Wisma Anugraha, Jl. Taman Kemang 32B, Jakarta 12730; tel. (21) 71792114; e-mail ird-indo@rad.net.id; internet www.id.ird.fr; f. 1944; agroforestry, agronomy, anthropology, aquaculture, archaeology, ethno-ecology, fisheries, geography; see main entry under France; Dir Dr PATRICE LEVANG.

Biological Sciences

Pusat Penelitian Biologi (Research Centre for Biology): Jl. Raya Jakarta, Bogor Km 46, Cibinong, Bogor 16911; tel. (21) 8797612; e-mail biologi@mail.lipi.go.id; internet biologi.lipi.go.id; f. 1817; 424 mems; library of 49,180 vols, 4,393 bound periodicals, c. 600 current periodicals, 24,587 reprints, 4,377 unpublished reports, 7,155 newspaper clippings, 2,463 maps; Dir Dr SITI NURAMALIATI PRIJONO; publs *Berita Biologi*, *Reinwardtia*, *Treubia*, *Laporan Tahunan*, *Laporan Teknik* (1 a year), *Laporan Kemajuan* (4 a year), *Warta Kita* (6 a year), *pamphlets*.

Attached Institutes:

Balai Penelitian dan Pengembangan Botani (Research and Development Institute for Botany): Jl. Raya Juanda 22, Bogor; f. 1884; Head Dr JOHANIS PALAR MOGEA.

Balai Penelitian dan Pengembangan Mikrobiologi (Research and Development Institute for Microbiology): c/o Kebun Raya Indonesia; f. 1884; Head Dr SUBADRI ABDULKADIR.

Balai Penelitian dan Pengembangan Zoologi (Research and Development Institute for Zoology): Jl. Raya Juanda 3, Bogor; Head Drs MOHAMAD AMIR.

UPT Balai Pengembangan Kebun Raya (Bogor Botanical Gardens): f. 1817; Head Dr SUHIRMAN; publs *Alphabetical List of Plant Species*, *Index Seminum* (1 a year), *Warta Kebun Raya* (irregular).

Physical Sciences

Badan Meteorologi Klimatologi dan Geofisika (Meteorology, Climatology and Geophysics Agency): Jl. Angkasa 1, No. 2, Kemayoran, POB 3540, Jakarta 10720; tel. (21) 4246321; internet www.bmkg.go.id; drafting nat. policies relating to meteorology, climatology and geophysics; data and information services; research and devt; Dir-Gen. Dr WORO B. HARIJONO.

Badan Tenaga Nuklir Nasional (National Atomic Energy Agency): Jl. Kuningan Barat, Mampang Prapatan, POB 4390, Jakarta 12710; tel. (21) 5251109; e-mail humas@batan.go.id; internet www.batan.go.id; Dir-Gen. DJALI AHIMSA.

Dinas Geodesi, Jawatan Topografi TNI-AD (Geodetic Section, Army Topographic Service): Jl. Bangka 1, Bandung; f. 1855; library of 2,000 vols, 2,500 periodicals; Dir MOH TAWIL.

Observatorium Bosscha (Bosscha Observatory): Jl. Peneropongan Bintang, Lembang, Java; tel. (22) 2786001; e-mail kunjungan@as.itb.ac.id; internet bosscha.itb.ac.id; f. 1925; since 1951 the observatory has been part of the Dept of Astronomy, Bandung Institute of Technology, Bandung; Dir Dr BAMBANG HIDAYAT; publs *Annals* (irregular), *Contributions* (irregular).

Pusat Penelitian Oseanografi (Research Centre for Oceanography): Jl. Pasir Putih 1, Ancol Timur, POB 4801/JKTF, Jakarta 14430; tel. (21) 64713850; e-mail p30.lipi@jakarta.wasantara.net.id; internet www.oseanologi.lipi.go.id; f. 1905; library of 2,000 vols, 250 periodical titles; Dir Dr Ir KURNAN SUMADHIHARYA; publs *Marine Research in Indonesia* (irregular), *Oseana* (4 a year), *Oseanologi di Indonesia* (irregular).

Pusat Survei Geologi (Centre for Geological Survey): Jl. Diponegoro 57, Bandung 40122; tel. (22) 7218482; e-mail contact@grdc.esdm.go.id; internet www.grdc.esdm.go.id; f. 1979; geological and geophysical research and systematic mapping; Dir Dr A. DJUMARMA WIRAKUSUMAH; publs *Geofisika dan Tematik*, *Journal of Geology and Mineral Resources*, *Peta Geologi*, *Publikasi Khusus* (spec. publs), *Publikasi Teknik* (Technical Papers: Geophysics, Palaeontology Series).

TECHNOLOGY

Akademi Teknologi Kulit (Academy of Leather Technology): Jl. Rongroad Selatan, Glugo, Panggungharjo, Sewon, Bantul, Yogyakarta 55188; tel. (274) 383727; e-mail info@atk.ac.id; internet www.atk.ac.id; f. 1958; provides 3 year diploma in the field of leather, footwear, and leather products technology; Dir Ir ELIS NURBALIA.

Bagian Fotogrametri, Dittopad (Institute of Photogrammetry): Jl. Kalibaru Timur V 47, Jakarta; tel. (21) 4256087; e-mail untungdhimas@gmail.com; f. 1937; attached to Indonesian Nat. Military; researches on problems relating to photogrammetry, aerotriangulization, topographical maps, etc.; library of 1,500 vols (incl. books and periodicals); Head UNTUNG DOMINIC.

Balai Besar Kerajinan dan Batik (Batik and Handicraft Research Institute): Jl. Kusumanegara 7, Yogyakarta; tel. (274) 546111; internet www.batik.go.id; f. 1951; research, testing and training courses; 108 mems; library of 1,792 vols; Dir SOEPARMAN S. TEKS.

Balai Besar Kulit, Karet dan Plastik (BBKKP) (Centre for Leather, Rubber and Plastic—CLRP): Jl. Sokonandi 9, Yogyakarta 55166; tel. (274) 563939; e-mail bbkkp@bbkkp.go.id; internet www.bbkkp.go.id; f. 1927; library of 4,000 vols; Dir RAMELAN SUBAGYO.

Dinas Hidro-Oseanografi (Naval Hydro-Oceanographic Office): Jl. Pantai Kuta V1, Jakarta 14430; tel. (21) 64714810; e-mail infohid@dishidros.go.id; internet dishidros.go.id; f. 1951; hydrographical survey of Indonesia; publishes tide tables; Head Drs DEDE YULIADI.

Direktorat Metrologi (Directorate of Metrology): Jl. Pasteur 27, Bandung 40171; tel. (22) 4203597; e-mail ditmet@bdg.centrin.net.id; f. 1923; Dir for Metrology AMIR SAHARUDDIN SJABRIAL.

Lembaga Research dan Pengujian Materiil Angkatan Darat (Military Laboratory for Research and Testing Material, Ministry of Defence): Jl. Ternate 6–8, Bandung; f. 1865; library of 1,500 vols; Dir Brig.-Gen. N. A. KUSOMO.

Pusat Penelitian dan Pengembangan Sumber Daga Air (Research Institute for Water Resources): Jl. Ir H. Juanda 193, POB 841, Bandung 40135; tel. (22) 2504053; e-mail pusair@bdg.centrin.net.id; internet www.pusair.domainvalet.com; f. 1966; attached to Agency for Research and Devt, Min. of Settlement and Regional Infrastructure; surveys, investigates and researches in the field of water resources devt; comprises experimental stations for hydrology, water resources, the environment, hydraulic structures and geotechnics, irrigation, swamps and coastal regions, rivers and sabo; library of 6,000 vols, 3,000 reports, 9,000 periodicals; Dir DYAH RAHAYU PANGESTI; publs *Bulletin Pusair* (2 a year), *Jurnal Penelitian dan Pengembangan Pengairan* (2 a year), *Technical and Research Report* (1 a year).

Sekolah Tinggi Teknologi Tekstil (Institute of Textile Technology): Jl. Jakarta 31, Bandung 40272; tel. (22) 7272580; e-mail gunazka@yahoo.co.id; internet www.stttekstil.ac.id; f. 1922 as Textiel Inrichting en Batik Proefstation (TIB); research and higher education in field of textile engineering, textile chemistry, technology and business, garments, fashion design; Rector Dr NOERATI; Head of Textile Engineering Dept GUNAWAN.

Libraries and Archives

Jakarta

Arsip Nasional Republik Indonesia (National Archives of Republic of Indonesia): Jl. Ampera Raya 7, S Jakarta 12560; tel. (21) 7805851; e-mail info@anri.go.id; internet www.anri.go.id; f. 1892; preserves documents as a nat. heritage and nat. account of the planning, execution and performance of the nat. life; provides records for govt and public activities; supervises the management of current operational records and the colln, storage, preservation, safe-keeping and use of historical archives; c. 25 km archives; 55,869 films, 9,932 negative microfilms, 4,732 positive microfilms, 7,200 microfisches, 43,276 sound recordings, 871 reel to reel sounds, 27,350 video cassettes, 1,663,000 photographs, 2,120 optical discs; Dir-Gen. GINA MASUDAH HUSNI (acting); publs *Jurnal Kearsipan* (2 a year), *Majalah Arsip* (3 a year), *Naskah Sumber Arsip* (irregular), *Penerbitan Sumber Sejarah Lisan* (irregular).

Perpustakaan Dewan Perwakilan Rakyat Republik Indonesia (Library of Indonesian Parliament): Jl. Jenderal Gatot Subroto, Jakarta 10270; tel. (21) 5715876; f. 1946; 200,000 vols; Librarian ROEMNINGSIH.

Perpustakaan Nasional (National Library of Indonesia): Jl. Salemba Raya 28A, POB 3624, Jakarta 10002; Jl. Merdeka Selatan 11, Pusat, Jakarta 10002; tel. (21) 3922669; internet www.pnri.go.id; f. 1980, by a merger of four libraries; depository library of Indonesia; spec. collns: Indonesian newspapers since 1810, Indonesian periodicals since 1779, Indonesian maps since 17th century, Indonesian dissertations, Indonesian monographs since 17th century; 750,000 vols; Dir MASTINI HARDJO PRAKOSO; publs *Bibliografi Nasional Indonesia* (4 a year), *Indexs artikel suratkabar* (Press Index, 4 a year), catalogues, subject bibliographies.

Perpustakaan Sejarah Politik dan Sosial (Library of Political and Social History): Medan Merdeka Seletan 11, Jakarta; f. 1952; incl. the Nat. Bibliographic Centre (Kantor Bibliografi Nasional) deposit library; 65,000 vols; Librarian Drs SOEKARMAN; publs *Checklist of Serials in the Libraries of Indonesia*, *Publications—Indonesia*, *Regional Bibliography of Social Sciences*.

Pusat Dokumentasi dan Informasi Ilmiah—Lembaga Ilmu Pengetahuan Indonesia (PDII-LIPI) (Indonesian Scientific Knowledge Centre): Jl. Jendral Gatot Subroto 10, POB 4298, Jakarta 12042; tel. (21) 5733465; e-mail admin@pdii.lipi.go.id; internet www.pdii.lipi.go.id; f. 1965; 58,552 books, 4,783 periodicals, 14,022 theses and dissertations, 75,000 microforms, 40,000 research reports, 11,679 patents; Head Dra JUSNI DJATIN; publs *Abstract of Research and Survey Reports* (irregular), *Baca* (Read, 3 a year), *Daftar Terbitan Berkala Indonesia yang Telah Mempunyai ISSN* (Indonesian Serials with ISSN, irregular), *Directory of Special Libraries and Information Sources in Indonesia* (irregular), *FOKUS* (issues covering 17 subjects, 6 a year), *Index of Indonesian Learned Periodicals*, *Index to Papers Submitted to Seminars* (irregular), *Union Catalog of Serials* (irregular).

South Sulawesi

Perpustakaan Umum Makassar (Makassar Public Library): Jl. Madukelleng 3, POB 16, Ujung Pandang 90112; f. 1969; organizes lending library services in brs throughout S Sulawesi Province; film and music programmes; foreign-language courses; children's library services; exhibitions and talks; 42,000 vols; Dir (vacant).

UPT Perpustakaan Universitas Hasanuddin (Hasanuddin University Library): Kampus UNHAS Tamalanrea, Jl. Perintis Kemerdekaan km 10, Ujung Pandang 90245; tel. (411) 587027; e-mail library@unhas.ac.id; internet www.unhas.ac.id/perpustakaan; f. 1956; 122,000 vols, 3,821 periodicals, 23,421 dissertations and theses; Head Dra NOER JIHAD SALEH; publs *Iaporan Tahunan*, *Info Pustaka*, *Warta Perpustakan*.

West Java

Perpustakaan Pusat Institut Teknologi Bandung (Central Library, Bandung Institute of Technology): Jl. Ganesha 10, Bandung 40132; tel. (22) 2500089; e-mail info@lib.itb.ac.id; internet www.lib.itb.ac.id; f. 1920; colln of rare books, pamphlets and reports on Indonesia; colln on science, technology, fine arts and business; 245,161 vols, 791 current periodicals, 40,000 bound vols; Dir Dr MAHMUDIN MAHMUDIN; Head of Library Services ENA SUKMANA; publ. *ITB Journal* (published in four series: Engineering Science, Information and Communication Technology, Science, Visual Art and Design; print and online (proceedings.itb.ac.id)).

Perpustakaan Pusat Penelitian dan Pengembangan Geologi (Library of Geological Research and Development Centre): Jl. Diponegoro 57, Bandung 40122; tel. (22) 772601; e-mail p3gl@mgi.esdm.go.id; internet www.mgi.esdm.go.id; 11,000 vols, 904 periodicals, 4,609 maps, 11,021 reports, 9,034 reprints, 400 microfiches; Chief Librarian RINI H. MARINO.

Perpustakaan (Pusat) Universitas Indonesia: Kampus UI, Depok 16424; tel. (21) 7864134; e-mail libserv@ui.edu; internet www.lib.ui.ac.id; Head of Library Dra LUKI WIJAYANTI.

Pusat Perpustakaan Angkatan Darat (Central Military Library): Jl. Kalimantan 6, Bandung; 36,000 vols in Central Library, and about 20,000 vols in departmental, territorial and college and office libraries; Dir Brig.-Gen. SOESATYO.

Pusat Perpustakaan Pertanian dan Komunikasi Penelitian (Indonesian Centre for Agricultural Library and Technology Dissemination): Jl. Ir Haji Juanda 20, Bogor 16122; tel. (251) 8321746; e-mail pustaka@pustaka-deptan.go.id; internet www.pustaka-deptan.go.id; f. 1842; 400,000 vols; Dir Ir FARID HASAN BAKTIR; publs *Abstrak Hasil Penelitian Pertanian Indonesia* (Indonesian Agricultural Research Abstract, 2 a year), *Indek Biologi dan Pertanian Indonesia* (Indonesian Biology and Agricultural Index, 3 a year), *Indonesian Journal of Agriculture* (2 a year), *Indonesian Journal of Agricultural Science* (2 a year), *Jurnal Bioteknologi Pertanian* (Indonesian Journal of Agricultural Biotechnology, 2 a year), *Jurnal Penelitian dan Pengembangan Pertanian* (Indonesian Journal of Agricultural Research and Development, 2 a year).

UPT Perpustakaan Institut Pertanian Bogor (Bogor Agricultural University Library): Kampus Darmaga, POB 199, Bogor 16680; tel. (251) 8621073; e-mail perpustakaan@bima.ipb.ac.id; internet perpustakaan.ipb.ac.id; f. 1963; 159,000 vols, 3,500 periodicals; Head Librarian TOHA NURSALAM; publs *Forum Pasca Sarjana*, *Indonesian Journal of Tropical Agriculture*.

Yogyakarta

Perpustakaan Islam (Islamic Library): c/o Min. of Religious Affairs, Jl. Lapangan Banteng Barat 3–4, Jakarta 10710; Jl. P. Mangkubumi 38, Yogyakarta; internet www.perpustakaan-islam.com; f. 1942; attached to Min. of Religious Affairs; 70,000 vols; MSS and periodicals; Dir Drs H. ASYHURI DAHLAN; Librarian MOH. AMIEN MANSOER.

Perpustakaan Jajasan Hatta (Hatta Foundation Library): Malioboro 85, Yogyakarta; 43,000 vols; Librarian R. SOEDJATMIKO.

Badan Perpustakaan dan Arsip Daerah Yogyakarta (Regional Library and Archives of Yogyakarta): Jl Tentara Rakyat Mataram No 29, Yogyakarta 55231; tel. (274) 513969; f. 1949; 120,000 vols; Head BUDI WIBOWO; Sec. Drs ALIP SUDARDJO.

Museums and Art Galleries

Aceh

Museum Nanggroe Aceh Darussalam: Jl. Sultan Alaidin Mahmudsyah 12, Baiturrahman, Banda Aceh 23241; tel. (651) 23144; f. 1915, as the House of Aceh, present name and status 2002; weaponry, household furnishings, ceremonial costumes, gold jewellery and calligraphy.

Museum Nangguor Pidie: Jl. Teuku Cik Ditiro, Sigli, Pidie Regency.

Museum Perjuangan Iskandar Muda: Jl. Kelurahan Penniti, Kecamatan Baiturrahman, Banda Aceh.

Bali

Blanco Renaissance Museum: POB 80571, Ubud, Bali; tel. (361) 975502; e-mail a-blanco@indo.net.id; internet www.blancomuseum.com; f. 1998, fmr studio of artist Antonio Blanco; collns of paintings.

Museum Bali: Jl. Mayor Wisnu 1, Denpasar, Bali; tel. (361) 222680; e-mail upt.museumbali@yahoo.co.id; f. 1932; exhibits of Bali culture; library of 1,970 vols, 1,605 magazines, 1,023 transcriptions of lontars (palm leaves); Dir Drs IDA BAGUS NYOMAN BAWA; publs *Karya Widia tak berkala*, *Majalah Saraswati*.

Museum Gedong Kirtya: Jl. Veteran 20, Singaraja; tel. (362) 22645; f. 1928; collns incl. ancient Balinese letters, chronicles and *kakawin* (Balinese poetry) written on palm leaves.

Museum Puri Lukisan: Jl. Raya Ubud, Ubud, Bali; tel. (361) 971-159; e-mail info@museumpurilukisan.com; internet www.mpl-ubud.com; f. 1956, administered by Yayasan Ratna Wartha foundation (f. 1953); colln incl. Balinese paintings and woodcarvings.

Museum Seni Agung Rai (Agung Rai Museum of Art): Jl. Pengosekan, Ubud, Gianyar 80571; tel. (361) 975742; e-mail info@armamuseum.com; internet www.armamuseum.com; f. 1996; colln of paintings; special temporary exhibitions; theatre performances; dance, music, and painting classes; bookshop, library and reading room; cultural workshops; seminars and training programmes; centre for visual and performing arts; Chair. AGUNG RAI.

Neka Art Museum: Jl. Raya Campuhan, Kedewatan Village, Ubud, Gianyar 80571; tel. (361) 975074; e-mail info@museumneka.com; internet www.museumneka.com; f. 1982; Dir SUTEJA NEKA.

Rudana Museum: Jl. Cok Rai Pudak 44 Peliatan, Ubud, Bali 80571; tel. (361) 975779; e-mail info@museumrudana.com; internet www.museumrudana.com; f. 1995; Man. Dir PUTU SUPADMA RUDANA.

Central Java

Museum Jawa Tengah Ranggawarsita: Jl. Abdulrahman Saleh 1, Semarang; tel. (6224) 760238; e-mail museumronggowarsito@yahoo.com; internet www.museumranggawarsita.com; f. 1989; collns in art, ethnography, biology, geology, ceramics and technology; Head STEVEN TIMISELA.

Museum Masjid Agung Demak: Jl. Sultan Fatah 57, Demak; tel. (291) 685532; f. 1975.

Museum Soesilo Soedarman: Gentasari-Kroya, Cilacap; tel. (282) 494400; f. 2000; collns of rifles, pistols and machine-guns.

Museum Tosan Aji Purworejo: Jl. Mayjend Sutoyo 10, Purworejo; collns of prehistoric artefacts in stone mortar, Hindu religious statues, yonis, statues of Shiva-Parvati.

Jakarta

Fine Art and Ceramic Museum: Jl. Pos Kota 2, West Jakarta; tel. (21) 6907062; f. built 1870, f. as Fine Arts Gallery 1976; colln of 400 items: sculpture, graphics, wood totems and batik paintings; spec. collns incl. masterpieces of Indonesian artists Hendra Gunawan, Raden Saleh; collns of ceramics from various regions.

Jakarta History Museum: Jl. Taman Fatahillah 1, West Jakarta 11110; tel. (21) 6929101; exhibits from prehistoric Jakarta; establishment of Jayakarta in 1527; 16th-century Dutch colonization to independence of Indonesia.

Museum Listrik dan Energi Baru (Electricity and Renewable Energy Museum): Jl. Raya Taman Mini, Jakarta 13560; tel. (21) 8413451; e-mail museumlistrik@yahoo.com; internet www.museumlistrik.com; history, outdoor exhibits of electric technology; Dir Drs SOETRISNO.

Museum Nasional (National Museum): Jl. Merdeka Barat 12, Pusat Jakarta; tel. 360796; e-mail museumnasional@indo.com; internet www.museumnasional.org; f. 1778, fmrly Museum Pusat; library of 360,000 vols (now part of Nat. Library); depts of ceramics, ethnography, prehistory, classical archaeology, anthropology, MSS and education; publs subject catalogues; Dir Dr ENDANG SRI HARDIATI.

Museum Wayang (Puppet Museum): Jl. Pintu Besar Utara 27, Tamansari, West Jakarta 11110; tel. (21) 6929560; e-mail info@museumwayang.com; displays leather and wood puppets; colln of 4,000 puppets.

Textile Museum: Jl. Aipda K. S. Tubun 4, Central Jakarta; tel. (21) 5606613; f. 1975; displays traditional *kain* (skirt worn by Indonesian men and women).

North Sumatra

Museum Deli Serdang: Kompleks Perkantoran Pemkab Deli Serdang, Desa Jati Sari, Kecamatan Lubuk Pakam, Lubuk Pakam; tel. (61) 7951994; internet pariwisatadeliserdang.info; f. 2003; attached to Min. of Culture and Tourism.

Museum Karo Lingga: Desa Lingga Kabupaten Karo, Kelurahan Desa Lingga, Kecamatan Simpang Empat, Karo; f. 1977.

Museum Negeri Provinsi Sumatra Utara (State Museum of North Sumatra): Jl. H. M. Joni 51, Medan 20217; tel. (61) 7366792; e-mail hartini.museumsumut@yahoo.co.id; f. 1982; Museum Head Dra SRI HARTINI.

Museum Simalungun: Jl. Sudirman 20 Pematang Siantar, Kelurahan Proklamasi, Kecamatan Siantar Barat, Siantar; tel. (622) 21954; f. 1940.

Papua

Museum Loka Budaya: Jl. Raya Abeoura-Setani, Kelurahan Hedam, Kecamatan Abepura, Kabupaten Jayapura; f. 1970; colln of 2,000 ethnographic objects of tribes in Papua.

Museum Negeri Provinsi Papua (Papua State Museum): Jl. Raya Sentani Km 17, 8 Waena-Jayapura Kelurahan Waena, Kecamatan Abepura, Kabupaten Jayapura; f. 1981; colln of 3,447 items: geology, biology, ethnography, archaeology, history, numismatics, physiology, ceramics, fine arts, human profiles, maps and dioramas.

Riau

Museum Daerah Riau Sang Nila Utama (Riau Regional Museum of Nila Utama): Jl. Jend. Sudirman 194; tel. (761) 33466; historical relics of the Riau Province.

Museum Sultan Syarif Kasim: Jl. Jend. Sudirman, Bengkalis; collns incl. royal jewellery, hand-woven embroidery, batik fabrics.

South Sumatra

Monumen Perjuangan Rakyat (MONPERA) Sumatera Bagian Selatan (People's Struggle Monument of South Sumatera): Jl. Merdeka, Palembang 30132; tel. (711) 358450; f. 1988; library of 356 titles; Guide and Admin. Staff LIDYA ELIZA.

Museum Negeri Propinsi Sumatera Selatan (State Museum of South Sumatra): Jl. Srijaya 288, km 5.5, Kecamatan Sukarami, Palembang 30139; tel. (711) 411382; e-mail trissedabalaputradewa@gmail.com; f. 1984; Information Officer TRISSEDA ANGRAINI.

Museum Pahlawan Nasional Dr A. K. Gani (Museum of National Hero Dr A. K. Gani): Jl. MP Mangkunegara 1/RT01, Sukamaju Sako, Palembang 30168; tel. (711) 824046; e-mail museum_akgani@yahoo.com; f. 2006, govt undertaking 2008; exhibits related to life of Adenan Kapau Gani, leader of nat. freedom movement; Sec. SURAWIJAYA GANI.

Museum Sultan Mahmud Badaruddin II: Jl. Sultan Mahmud Badaruddin II 2; tel. (711) 358450; f. 1823, present status 2004; collns incl. numismatics, ceramics and fine arts.

West Sumatra

Museum Kereta Api Sawahlunto: Jl. Kampung Teleng, Kelurahan Pasar, Kecamatan Lembah Segar, Sawahlunto; tel. (754) 61023; collns of cars, steam locomotives, communication devices; photo documentation.

Museum Mande Rubiah: Kampung Lubuk Sitepung, Nagari Lunang, Kecamatan Lunang Silaut, Kabupaten Pesisir Selatan; collns of MSS, coins, weapons, kitchen utensils, ceremonial tools, traditional wear, porcelain dishes, lamps and canes.

Museum Perjuangan Tridaya Eka Dharma: Jl. Panorama 24 Kelurahan Kayu Kubu, Kecamatan Guguk Panjang, Kecamatan Bukittinggi; collns incl. traditional tools and weapons.

Museum Rumah Kelahiran Bung Hatta: Jl. Soekarno, Hatta 37, Bukit Tinggi; tel. (752) 23503; birth home of Mohammad Hatta.

Yogyakarta

Museum Dewantara Kirti Griya: Jl. Tamansiswa 31, Yogyakarta; tel. (274) 389208; f. 1970.

Museum Geoteknologi Mineral UPN 'Veteran' Yogyakarta: Jl. Babarsari 2, Tambakbayan, Yogyakarta; tel. (274) 486991; e-mail museummgmt@upnyk.ac.id; internet museum.upnyk.ac.id; f. 1988.

Museum Monumen Pergerakan Wanita Indonesia (Museum of the Women's Movement): Jl. Laksda Adisucipto 88, Yogyakarta; tel. (274) 587818; displays household appliances and kitchen equipment.

Museum Pusat AD 'Dharma Wiratama' (Central Army Museum): Jl. Jend. Sudirman 47, Yogyakarta; tel. (274) 561417; f. 1956, present location 1982; collns of weapons, inventory, optical and communications equipment; spec. travelling exhibitions; lectures and workshops.

Museum Rumah Jawa Tembi Bantul: Jl. Parang Tritis, Km 8.4 Tembi, Timbulharjo, Sewon, Bantul, Yogyakarta; tel. (274) 368004; f. 1999.

Museum Wayang Kekayon Yogyakarta (Kekayon Puppet Museum Yogyakarta): Jl. Yogya Wonosari, Km 7 no 277, Yogyakarta; tel. (274) 513218; puppet masks and clothing.

Ullèn Sentalu (Javanese Culture and Art Museum): Jl. Boyong Kaliurang, Sleman, Yogyakarta; tel. (274) 880158; internet www.ullensentalu.com; f. 1994; art heritage wealth, culture and history from the Javanese civilization.

State Universities

INSTITUT PERTANIAN BOGOR
(Bogor Agricultural University)

Jl. Lingkar Akademik, Kampus IPB Darmaga, Bogor 16680
Telephone: (251) 622642
E-mail: humas@ipb.ac.id
Internet: www.ipb.ac.id

Founded 1963
State control
Languages of instruction: Indonesian, English(for foreign visiting professors)
Academic year: September to June (2 semesters)

Rector: Dr Ir Henry Suhardiyanto
Vice-Rector for Academic Affairs and Student Affairs: Prof. Dr Ir H. Yonny Kusmaryono
Vice-Rector for Business and Communication: Dr Ir H. Arif Iman Suroso
Vice-Rector for Resources and Devt: Prof. Dr Ir Hermanto Siregar
Vice-Rector for Research and Collaboration: Dr Ir H. Miftah Anas Fauzi
Registrar: Dr Setyo Pertiwi
Administrator: Ir Udin M. Wahjudin
Librarian: Ir Toha Nursalam

Number of teachers: 1,327
Number of students: 19,440

Publications: *Buletin Hama dan Penyakit Tumbuhan, Buletin Ilmu Tanah, Communication Agriculture, Feed and Nutrition Journal, Forum Pasca Sarjana, Gema Penelitian, Indonesian Journal of Tropical Agriculture, Jurnal Ilmu Pertanian Indonesian, Jurnal Primatologi, Media Konservasi, Media Peternakan, Media Veteriner, Teknologi*

DEANS

Faculty of Agriculture: Prof. Dr M. Chosin
Faculty of Agricultural Technology: Prof. Dr M. Bambang Pramudya Noorachmat
Faculty of Animal Science: Prof. Dr H. Soedarmadi
Faculty of Economics and Management: Prof. Dr Bunasor Sanim
Faculty of Fisheries and Marine Science: Dr E. Haris
Faculty of Forestry: Prof. Dr Yusuf Sudohadi
Faculty of Mathematics and Natural Sciences: Dr Siswadi
Faculty of Veterinary Medicine: Dr F. H. Pasaribu

INSTITUT SENI INDONESIA SURAKARTA
(Indonesia Institute of the Arts Surakarta)

Jl. ki Hajar Dewantara 19, Kentingan, Jebres, Surakarta 57126
Telephone: (271) 647658
E-mail: direct@isi-ska.ac.id
Internet: www.isi-ska.ac.id

Founded 1965 as Akademi Seni Karawitan Indonesia (ASKI), merged with Akademi Seni Tari Indonesia (ASTI) to form Sekolah Tinggi Seni Indonesia Surakarta 1983, present status 2006
public control

Rector: Prof. Dr T. Slamet Suparno

Library of 36,588 vols
Number of teachers: 203
Number of students: 852

INSTITUT SENI INDONESIA YOGYAKARTA
(Indonesia Institute of the Arts Yogyakarta)

Jl. Parangtritis Km 6.5, POB 1210, Yogyakarta 55188
Telephone: (274) 373659
E-mail: arts@isi.ac.id
Internet: www.isi.ac.id

Founded 1984, fmrly known as Institut Seni Indonesia Yogyakarta
Language of instruction: Indonesian
Academic year: September to June

Rector: Drs Soeprapto Soedjono
Vice-Rector for Academic Affairs: Prof. Dr A. M. Hermin Kusmayati
Vice-Rector for Admin. and Financial Affairs: Drs Siswadi
Vice-Rector for Students Affairs: Drs Syafruddin
Registrar: G. Budi Priyatmo
Librarian: Dra Herlin Noviar Subaryanti

Library of 44,368 vols
Number of teachers: 329
Number of students: 1,922

Publications: *ARS, Visual Arts Journal, EKSPRESI, Research Journal, FENOMEN, Research Journal, RESITAL, Performing Arts Journal, REKAM, Recorded Media Arts Journal, SENI, Journal for the Arts* (4 a year), *SURYA SENI, Postgraduate Journal*

DEANS

Faculty of Performing Arts: Drs Triyono Bramantyo Pamudjo Santoso
Faculty of Recorded Media Arts: Drs Alex Andri Luthfi R.
Faculty of Visual Arts: Dr M. Agus Burhan

INSTITUT TEKNOLOGI BANDUNG
(Bandung Institute of Technology)

Jl. Tamansari 64, Bandung 40116
Jl. Ganesha 10, Bandung 40132
Telephone: (22) 2500935
E-mail: webmaster@itb.ac.id
Internet: www.itb.ac.id

Founded 1920, present form 1959 as a merger of the faculties of mathematics, natural sciences and engineering of the Univ. of Indonesia
State control
Language of instruction: Indonesian
Academic year: August to July

Rector: Prof. Dr Ir Djoko Santoso
Vice-Rector for Academic Affairs: Dr Ir Adang Surahman
Vice-Rector for Gen. Admin.: Prof. Dr Ir Djoko Santoso
Vice-Rector for Devt, Planning, Admin. and Information Systems: Dr Ir Rizal Zainuddin Tamin
Librarian: Dr Ir Robert Manurung

Number of teachers: 1,263
Number of students: 15,031

Publications: *Akta Farmasetika Indonesia* (12 a year), *Buletin Geologi* (3 a year), *Geodesi dan Surveying* (2 a year), *Journal of Mathematics and Science* (2 a year), *Journal Pusat Pengembangan Perencanaan Wilayah Kota* (1 a year), *Jurnal Atap* (1 a year), *Jurnal Teknik dan Manajemen Industri* (3 a year), *Jurnal Teknik Lingkungan* (2 a year), *Jurnal Teknik Sipil* (4 a year), *Jurnal Teknologi Mineral* (3 a year), *Kontribusi Fisika* (4 a year), *Maalah Ilmiah Himpunan Matematika Indonesia* (2 a year), *Majalah Ilmiah Teknik Electro* (3 a year), *Majalah Mesin* (3 a year)

DEANS

Faculty of Civil Engineering and Planning: Prof. Dr Ir Tommy Firman
Faculty of Fine Arts and Design: Drs Setiawan Sabana
Faculty of Industrial Technology: Prof. Dr Ir Djoko Sujarto
Faculty of Mathematics and Natural Sciences: Dr Ing. Cynthia Linaya Radiman
Faculty of Mineral Technology: Prof. Dr Ir Made Emmy Relawat
Graduate Programme: Prof. Dr Ir Soelarso (Dir)
School of Business and Management: Prof. Dr Surna Tjahja Djajadiningrat

PROFESSORS

Achmad, S. A., Chemistry
Agoes, G., Pharmacy
Algamar, K., Environmental Engineering
Ansjar, M., Mathematics
Arifin, A., Mathematics
Arismunandar, W., Mechanical Engineering
Asikin, S., Geology
Bagiasna, K., Mechanical Engineering
Barmawi, M., Physics
Bintoro, S. B., City Planning
Brodjonegro, S. S., Mechanical Engineering
Brotosiswojo, B. S., Physics
Chatib, B., Environmental Engineering
Dhanutirto, H., Pharmacy
Diran, O., Mechanical Engineering
Djajadiningrat, A. H., Environmental Engineering
Djajadiningrat, S. T., Industrial Engineering
Djajaputra, A. A., Civil Engineering
Djajasugita, F. A., Electrical Engineering
Djalari, Y. A., Design
Djauhari, M. A., Mathematics
Djojodihardjo, H., Mechanical Engineering
Firman, K., Pharmacy
Firman, T., City Planning
Gani, A. Z., Industrial Engineering
Gde Raka, I. D., Industrial Engineering
Handojo, A., Engineering Physics
Harahap, F., Mechanical Engineering
Harjosuparto, S., Chemical Engineering
Harlandja, B., Civil Engineering
Haroen, Y., Electrical Engineering
Harsokoesoemo, D., Mechanical Engineering
Hendradjaya, L., Physics
Hidayat, B., Astronomy
Jenjie, S. D., Mechanical Engineering
Kahar, J., Geodesy
Kamil, S., Mechanical Engineering
Kana, J. C., Petroleum Engineering
Karsa, K., Electrical Engineering
Koesoemadinata, R. P., Geology
Kusbiantoro, City Planning
Liang, O. B., Chemistry
Liong, T. H., Physics
Mangunwijaya, A., Mining Engineering
Mardihartanto, F. X., Industrial Engineering
Mardisewojo, P., Petroleum Engineering
Martodjojo, S., Geology
Martojo, W., Mining Engineering
Merati, I. G. W., Civil Engineering
Mira, S., Geodesy
Nabanan, S. M., Mathematics
On, T. M., Physics
Padmawinata, K., Pharmacy
Pirous, A. D., Design
Pringgoprawiro, H., Geology
Pringgoprawiro, M., Physics
Prodjosoemarto, P., Mining Engineering
Pulunggono, A., Geology
Rahayu, S. I., Chemistry

RAIS, J., Geodesy
RELAWATYI, S. E., Geology
RIDWAN, A. S., Civil Engineering
SAMADIKUN, S., Electrical Engineering
SAMPURNO, Geology
SANTOSO, D., Geophysics
SAPIIE, S., Electrical Engineering
SASMOJO, S., Chemical Engineering
SASTRAMIHARDJA, I., Chemical Engineering
SASTRODIHARDJO, S., Biology
SATIADARMA, K., Pharmacy
SEMBIRING, R. K., Mathematics
SILABAN, P., Physics
SIRAIT, K. T., Electrical Engineering
SIREGAR, C., Pharmacy
SIREGAR, H. P. S., Petroleum Engineering
SISWOSUWARNO, M., Mechanical Engineering
SJAFRUDDIN, A., Civil Engineering
SJUIB, F., Pharmacy
SLAMET, J. S., Environmental Engineering
SOEDIRO, I., Pharmacy
SOEDJITO, B. B., City Planning
SOEGIJANTO, R. M., Engineering Physics
SOEGIJOKO, S., Electrical Engineering
SOELARSO, Mechanical Engineering
SOEMARTO, S., Environmental Engineering
SOEMINTAPOERA, K., Electrical Engineering
SOEMODINOTO, W., Mining Engineering
SOENARKO, B., Engineering Physics
SOEPANGKAT, H. P., Physics
SOERIA-ATMADJA, R., Geology
SOERIAATMADJA, R. E., Biology
SUDARWATI, S., Biology
SUDIRMAN, I., Industrial Engineering
SUDRADJAT, I., Architecture
SUHARTO, D., Mechanical Engineering
SUHUD, R., Civil Engineering
SUJARTO, D., City Planning
SUKARMADIJAYA, H., Environmental Engineering
SULE, D., Mining Engineering
SUMAWIGANDA, S., Civil Engineering
SURAATMADJA, D., Civil Engineering
SURDIA, N. M., Chemistry
SURDIA, T., Metallurgical Engineering
SUTJIATMO, B., Mechanical Engineering
SUWONO, A., Mechanical Engineering
TABRANI, P., Design
TAROEPRATJEKA, H., Industrial Engineering
TJAHJATI, S. B., City Planning
TOHA, I. S., Industrial Engineering
TUAH, H., Civil Engineering
UMAR, F., Mining Engineering
WANGSADINATA, W., Civil Engineering
WARDIMAN, A., Engineering Physics
WAWOROENTOE, W. J., City Planning
WIDAGDO, Design
WIDODO, R. J., Electrical Engineering
WIRASONJAYA, S., Architecture
WIRJOMARTONO, S. H., Mechanical Engineering
WIRJOSUMARTO, H., Mechanical Engineering
WISJNUPRAPTO, Environmental Engineering
ZAINUDDIN, I. M., Design
ZEN, M. T., Geology

INSTITUT TEKNOLOGI SEPULUH NOPEMBER
(Technology Institute of Sepuluh Nopember)

POB 900/SB, Surabaya 60008
Located at: Kampus ITS, Sukolilo, Surabaya 60111, East Java
Telephone: (31) 5923411
E-mail: int_off@its.ac.id
Internet: www.its.ac.id

Founded 1960
State control
Language of instruction: Indonesian
Academic year: September to June

Rector: Dr Ir PRIYO SUPROBO
Vice-Rector for Academic Affairs: Prof. Ir NOOR ENDAH B. MOCTAR
Vice-Rector for Admin.: Ir R. SYARIF WIDJAYA
Vice-Rector for Student Affairs: Dr Ir ACHMAD JAZIDIE
Head of the Academic Admin. and Student Affairs Bureau: Drs HARRY SANTOSO
Head of the Admin. Planning and Information System Bureau: Ir ARIE KISMANTO
Head of the Gen. Admin. and Finance Bureau: NURIJATI HAMID
Librarian: Drs ACHMAD

Library of 45,994 vols
Number of teachers: 1,043
Number of students: 17,384
Publications: *Berita ITS*, *Iptek*, *various faculty bulletins*

DEANS

Faculty of Civil Engineering and Planning: Prof. Dr Ir PRIYO SUPROBO
Faculty of Industrial Technology: Dr Ir TRIYOGI YUWONO
Faculty of Information Technology: Prof. Ir ARIEF DJUNAIDI
Faculty of Mathematics and Sciences: Prof. Dr SUASMORO
Faculty of Ocean Engineering: Ir ASJHAR IMRON

DIRECTORS

Polytechnic of Electronics: Dr Ir TITON DUTONO
Polytechnic of Ship Building: Ir SUWARNO TAHID
Research and Public Service Institute: Prof. Ir I. NYOMAN SUTANTRA

PROFESSORS

ALTWAY, A., Chemical Engineering
ANWAR, N., Civil Engineering
BAKTIR, A., Chemical Engineering
DJANALI, S., Informatics Engineering
DJUNAIDY, A., Information System Engineering
ERSAM, T., Chemical Engineering
HADI, W., Environmental Engineering
KOESTALAM, P., Civil Engineering
LINUWIH, S., Statistics
MOCHTAR, I. B., Civil Engineering
MOCHTAR, N. E., Civil Engineering
NUH, M., Electrical Engineering
NURSUHUD, D., Mechanical Engineering
PENANGSANG, H. O., Electrical Engineering
PRATIKTO, W. A., Ocean Engineering
PURNOMO, M. H., Electrical Engineering
PURWONO, R., Structural Engineering
PUTU RAKA, I. G., Civil Engineering
RACHIMOELLAH, M., Chemistry
RAMELAN, R., Mechanical Engineering
RENANTO, Chemical Engineering
SANTOSA, M., Architecture
SANTOSO, H. R., Architecture
SARNO, R., Informatics Engineering
SILAS, J., Architecture
SOEBAGIO, Electrical Engineering
SOEGIONO, Ocean Engineering
SUASMORO, H., Physics
SUKARDJONO, S., Electrical Engineering
SUPROBO, P., Civil Engineering
SUTANTRA, N., Mechanical Engineering
SUTRISNO, H., Electrical Engineering
SUWARNO, J., Chemical Engineering
SUWARNO, N., Chemical Engineering
TJANDRASA, H., Informatics Engineering
WAHYUDI, H., Civil Engineering

UNIVERSITAS AIRLANGGA
(Universitas Airlangga)

Jl. Mulyorejo, Kampus C, Surabaya 60115
Telephone: (31) 5966864
E-mail: international@unair.ac.id
Internet: unair.ac.id

Founded 1954
Languages of instruction: English, Indonesian
Academic year: September to August

Rector: Prof. Dr H. FASICH
Vice-Rector for Academic and Learning, Research and Public Service: Prof. Dr ACHMAD SYAHRANI
Vice-Rector for Gen. Admin.: Dr MOHAMMAD NASIH
Vice-Rector for Planning, Devt, Partnership and Information Systems: Prof. SOETJIPTO SETYAWAN
Chief, Bureau for Gen. Academic Admin. and Student Affairs: Dr ZAINAL ARIFIN
Chief, Bureau for Gen. Admin.: Dra Hj. SUNARTI
Chief, Bureau for Planning Admin. and Information Systems: ROSMELYANI
Librarian: RR. RATNANINGSIH

Number of teachers: 1,642
Number of students: 27,000
Publications: *Buletin Toraks Kardiovaskular Indonesia* (4 a year), *Folia Medika Indonesiana* (4 a year), *Majalah Kedokteran Gigi* (4 a year), *Majalah Kedokteran Surabaya* (4 a year), *Majalah Kedokteran Tropis Indonesia* (4 a year), *Majalah Kesehatan Masyarakat* (4 a year), *Majalah Masyarakat Kebudayaan Politik* (4 a year), *Surabaya Journal of Surgery* (4 a year), *Yuridika* (4 a year)

DEANS

Faculty of Dentistry: Prof. Dr R. M. COEN PRAMONO
Faculty of Economics and Business: Prof. Dr MUSLICH ANSORI
Faculty of Fisheries and Marine: Prof. Dr SRI SUBEKTI
Faculty of Humanities: Prof. ARIBOWO SIAHAAN
Faculty of Law: MUHAMMAD ZAIDUN
Faculty of Medicine: Prof. Dr AGUNG PRANOTO
Faculty of Nursing: Prof. PURWANINGSIH SUPRIYADI
Faculty of Pharmacy: Dr UMI ATHIJAH
Faculty of Psychology: Dr SEGER HANDOYO
Faculty of Public Health: Prof. Dr TRI MARTIANA
Faculty of Sciences and Technology: Prof. Dr WIN DARMANTO
Faculty of Social and Political Sciences: Drs I. BASIS SUSILO
Faculty of Veterinary Medicine: Dr Drh. ROMZIAH SIDIK

UNIVERSITAS ANDALAS

Kampus Limau Manis, Padang 25163
Telephone: (751) 71181
E-mail: rektor@unand.ac.id
Internet: www.unand.ac.id

Founded 1956
Language of instruction: Indonesian
Academic year: September to June

Rector: MARLIS RAHMAN
Vice-Rector for Academic Affairs: AMIRMUSLIM MALIK
Vice-Rector for Admin. and Finance: DJASWIR ZEIN
Vice-Rector for Student Affairs: FIRMAN HASAN
Head Librarian: MARAMIS

Number of teachers: 1,396
Number of students: 13,009
Publications: *Andalas Medical Journal*, *Jurnal Antropologi*, *Jurnal Ekonomi Manajemen*, *Jurnal Matematika dan Ilmu Pengetahuan Alam*, *Jurnal Pembangunan dan Perubahan Sosial Budaya*, *Jurnal Penelitian Andalas*, *Jurnal Peternakan dan Lingkungan*, *Jurnal Teknologi Pertanian* (Journal of Agricultural Technology), *Justisia*, *Lingua: Jurnal Bahasa dan Sastra*, *Potetika*, *Teknika*, *Warta Pengabdian Andalas*

DEANS

Faculty of Agriculture: BUJANG RUSMAN
Faculty of Animal Husbandry: AZINAR KAMARUDDIN
Faculty of Arts: SYAFRUDDIN SULAIMAN
Faculty of Economics: SJAFRIZAL
Faculty of Engineering: DAHNIL ZAINUDDIN
Faculty of Law and Social Science: AZHAR RAUF
Faculty of Mathematics and Natural Sciences: HAZLI NURDIN
Faculty of Medicine: RUSDAN DJAMIL
Faculty of Political and Social Sciences: DAHRUL DAHLAN
Polytechnic of Agriculture: MASRUL JALAL
Polytechnic of Engineering: ALIZAR HASAN

UNIVERSITAS BENGKULU (University of Bengkulu)

Jl. Raya Kandang Limun, Bengkulu 38371
Telephone: (736) 21170
E-mail: rektorat@unib.ac.id
Internet: www.unib.ac.id

Founded 1982

Rector: Prof. Dr Ir ZAINAL MUKTAMAR
Chief Admin. Officer (BATIK): Dr FACHRUR-ROZI AZIZ
Librarian: Ir BAMBANG GONGGO M.

Library of 20,600 vols
Number of teachers: 726
Number of students: 10,477

DEANS

Faculty of Agriculture: DWINARDI APRIYANTO
Faculty of Economics: Dr RIDWAN NURAZI
Faculty of Education: Prof. Drs SAFNIL
Faculty of Law: M. ABDI
Faculty of Social Sciences: Drs PANJI SUMINAR
Faculty of Technology: KHAIRUL AMRI

UNIVERSITAS BRAWIJAYA

Jl. Veteran, Malang, 65145
Telephone: (341) 575777
E-mail: rektorat@ub.ac.id
Internet: www.ub.ac.id

Founded 1963
State control
Language of instruction: Indonesian
Academic year: September to August

Rector: Prof. Dr Ir YOGI SUGITO
Vice-Rector: Prof. Dr Ir BAMBANG SUHARTO
Vice-Rector: WARKUM SUMITRO
Vice-Rector: Ir H. R. B. AINURRASYID
Head of Academic Admin. and Cooperation Bureau: RISTIKA HARDJITO
Head of Financial Admin. and Planning Bureau: Dra ERNANI KUSDIANTINA
Head of Student Admin. Bureau: Dra Haja IMAM SAFI'I
Librarian: Dra WELMIN SUNYI ARININGSIH

Library of 298,708 vols
Number of teachers: 1,785
Number of students: 43,650

Publications: *Agrivita, Journal of Agricultural Science* (3 a year, online, agrivita.ub.ac.id), *EDUCAFL: E-Journal of Education of English as a Foreign Language* (2 a year, online, educafl.ub.ac.id), *Habitat* (2 a year, online, habitat.ub.ac.id), *Humanitas* (2 a year), *Indonesian Journal of Human Nutrition* (2 a year, online, ijhn.ub.ac.id), *Journal Arena Hukum* (2 a year, online, arenahukum.ub.ac.id), *Journal of Indonesian Applied Economics* (2 a year, online, jiae.ub.ac.id), *Journal of Tropical Life Science* (1 a year, online, jtrolis.ub.ac.id), *Journal of Tropical Plant Protection* (2 a year, online, jtpp.ub.ac.id), *Jurnal Akuntansi Multiparadigma* (3 a year, online, jamal.ub.ac.id), *Jurnal Aplikasi Manajemen* (3 a year, online, jurnaljam.ub.ac.id), *Jurnal Ilmu Administrasi Publik* (2 a year, online, journalfia.ub.ac.id/index.php/jiap), *Jurnal Ilmu dan Teknologi Hasil Ternak* (2 a year, online, jitek.ub.ac.id), *Jurnal Ilmu-ilmu Peternakan* (2 a year, online, jiip.ub.ac.id), *Jurnal LP3* (2 a year, online, erudio.ub.ac.id), *Jurnal Manajemen Sumberdaya Perairan* (2 a year, online, jurnalmsp.ub.ac.id), *Jurnal Pembangunan Alam Lestari* (2 a year, online, jpmi.ub.ac.id), *Jurnal Pengabdian Masyarakat Indonesia* (2 a year), *Jurnal Tata Kota dan Daerah* (2 a year, online, tatakota.ub.ac.id), *Jurnal Teknologi Pertanian* (3 a year, online, jtp.ub.ac.id), *Jurnal Ternak Tropika* (2 a year, online, ternaktropika.ub.ac.id), *Natural-B* (2 a year), *Natural Jurnal* (2 a year, online, natural-b.ub.ac.id), *Pointer* (2 a year, online, jurnalpointer.ub.ac.id), *Prasetya* (48 a year), *Profit* (1 a year, online, ejournalfia.ub.ac.id/index.php/profit), *Rekayasa Mesin* (2 a year, online, rekayasamesin.ub.ac.id), *Rekayasa Sipil* (2 a year, online, rekayasasipil.ub.ac.id), *Solid* (2 a year), *Stratejik* (2 a year, online, ejournalfia.ub.ac.id/index.php/stratejik), *Techno* (2 a year), *The Journal of Experimental Life Science* (2 a year, online, jels.ub.ac.id), *Wacana* (3 a year, online, wacana.ub.ac.id), *Wartamina* (6 a year)

DEANS

Faculty of Administrative Science: Prof. Dr SUMARTONO WIDJANARKO
Faculty of Agricultural Technology: Dr Ir BAMBANG SUSILO
Faculty of Agriculture: Prof. Ir SUMERU ASHARI
Faculty of Animal Husbandry: Prof. Dr Ir KUSMARTONO SUBROTO
Faculty of Cultural Science: Prof. Dr FRANCIEN HERLEN TOMASOWA
Faculty of Economics and Business: Dr GUGUS IRIANTO
Faculty of Engineering: Prof. Ir HARNEN SULISTIO
Faculty of Fisheries and Marine Science: Prof. Dr Ir EDDY SUPRAYITNO
Faculty of Law: Dr S. H SIHABUDIN
Faculty of Medicine: Dr KARYONO MINTAROEM
Faculty of Natural Science and Mathematics: Prof. Dr MARJONO
Faculty of Social and Political Science: Prof. Dr Ir DARSONO WISADIRANA
Programme of Information Technology and Computer Science: Ir SUTRISNO
Programme of Veterinary Science: Prof. Dr PRATIWI TRISUNUWATI

PROFESSORS

ACHMAD, H., Medicine
ACHMADY, Z. A., Administration
ACHMANU, Animal Husbandry
ALHABSJI, T., Administration
ALI, M. M., Medicine
ARIFFIN, Aeroclimatology
ASHARI, M. S., Agriculture
ASTUTI, M. S., Law
BAISOENI, H., Mathematics
CHUZAEMI, S., Animal Husbandry
FADJAR, A. M., Law
FANANI, Z., Animal Husbandry
FAUZI, A., Administration
GINTING, E., Animal Husbandry
GURITNO, B., Agriculture
HADIASTONO, T., Agriculture
HAIRIAH, K., Agriculture
HAKIM, L., Animal Husbandry
HANDAYANTO, E., Agriculture
HARIJONO, Agricultural Technology
HARSONO, O. S. H., Economics
HIDAYAT, A., Medicine
HIDAYAT, M., Medicine
ICHSAN, M., Administration
IDRUS, M. S., Economics
ISLAMY, M. I., Administration
ISMANI, Administration
KALIM, H., Medicine
KIPTIYAH, S. M., Economics
KOENTJOKO, Animal Husbandry
KUMALANINGSIH, S., Agricultural Technology
LOEKITO, R. M., Medicine
LUTH, T., Law
MARTAWIJAYA, S., Economic Development
MIMBAR, S. M., Agriculture
MISMAIL, B., Electrical Engineering
MOELJADI, H., Economics
MOENANDIR, J., Agriculture
MUNIR, M., Agriculture
MUNIR, M., Law
MUSTADJAB, M. M., Agriculture
NIMRAN, U., Administration
NUGROHO, W. H., Mathematics
PURNOMO, H., Animal Husbandry
RASYID, Y., Agriculture
RUBAI, M., Law
SALEH, M., Economics
SARGOWO, D., Medicine
SASTRAHIDAYAT, I. R., Agriculture
SEMAOEN, M. I., Agriculture
SITOMPUL, S. M., Agriculture
SJAMSUDDIN, S., Administration
SODIKI, A., Law
SOEBAKTININGSIH, Medicine
SOEBARINOTO, Animal Husbandry
SOEHONO, L. A., Mathematics
SOEKARTAWI, Agriculture
SOEMARNO, Agriculture
SOEPARMAN, S., Engineering
SOEPRAPTO, R., Administration
SOETANTO, H., Animal Husbandry
SOEWARTO, S., Medicine
SUBROTO, B., Accounting
SUDARMA, M. S., Accounting
SUGIJANTO, Agriculture
SUGITO, Y., Agriculture
SUHARDJONO, Research Methodology
SUHARTO, B., Agricultural Technology
SUKESI, K., Agriculture
SULISTYOWATI, L., Agriculture
SUMITRO, S. B., Agricultural Technology
SUNUHARYO, B. S., Administration
SUPRIYANTO, E., Fisheries
SUSANTO, M. H., Economics
SUSANTO, T., Agricultural Technology
SYAFRADJI, M. S., Economics
SYAMSIDI, S. R. C., Agriculture
SYAMSULBAHRI, Agriculture
SYEKHFANI, Agriculture
THANTAWI, Economics
TRIADJI, B., Economics
TRISUNUWATI, P., Epidemiology
TROENA, E. A., Economics
UTOMO, W. H., Agriculture
WAHAB, S. A., Administration
WARDANA, N. G., Engineering
WARDIYATI, T., Agriculture
WIDJANARKO, S. B., Agricultural Technology
WIDODO, M. A., Medicine
ZAIN, D., Economics

UNIVERSITAS CENDERAWASIH

Jl. Kamp Wolker, Kampus UNCEN Waena, Jayapura, 99358
Telephone: (967) 572108
E-mail: uncen@uncen.ac.id
Internet: www.uncen.ac.id

Founded 1962
Language of instruction: Indonesian
Academic year: September to July

Faculties of economics, education and teacher training, engineering, law, mathematics, medicine, natural sciences, public health, social and political sciences

Rector: Prof. Dr BALTHASAR KAMBUAYA
Vice-Rector: Drs FESTUS SIMBIAK
Vice-Rector: Drs YOHANIS RANTE
Vice-Rector: Drs PAULUS LOUIS HOMERS

Vice-Rector: Drs NAFFI SANGGENAFA
Gen. Admin. Officer: Ir H. SUMANTO
Academic and Student Admin. Officer: Drs M. HATTU
Librarian: Drs A. C. SUNGKANA HADI

Library of 56,000 vols
Number of teachers: 520
Number of students: 6,800

Publications: *Bulletin of Irian Jaya Development*, *Tifa Agro*

UNIVERSITAS DIPONEGORO
(Diponegoro University)

Jl. Prof. Sudarto, Tembalang, Semarang 50275
Telephone: (24) 7460014
E-mail: io@undip.ac.id
Internet: www.undip.ac.id

Founded 1956
Academic year: September to August

Rector: Prof. Ir EKO BUDIHARDJ
Vice-Rector for Academic Affairs: Prof. Dr S. P. HADI
Vice-Rector for Admin. and Finance: Prof. Dr Ir Y. S. DARMANTO
Vice-Rector for Devt and Collaboration: Dr Dr SUSILO WIBOWO
Vice-Rector for Student Affairs: Dr Ir BAMBANG TRIONO BASUKI
Head of Admin. and Academic Bureau: Drs PRIYO SANTOSO
Head of Gen. Admin. Bureau: Dra KUSRINI
Head of Planning Admin. and Information Systems Bureau: Dra ISMARTINI
Head of Student Admin. Bureau: Dra PRANTIKASIH
University Librarian: Dra ARI WIDJAYANTI

Library of 191,224 vols
Number of teachers: 1,618
Number of students: 38,522

Publications: *Berita Penelitian*, *Berita UNDIP*, *Bhakti*, *Buletin Fekom*, *Bulletin Dharma Wanita*, *Bulletin Fakultas Peternakan & Perikanan*, *Cakrawala*, *Edent*, *Forum*, *Gallery*, *Gema*, *Gema Keadilan*, *Gema Teknologi*, *Hayam Wuruk*, *Ilmiah Politeknik*, *Info*, *Kinetika*, *Konsolidasi*, *Lembaran Imu Sastra*, *Mahaprika*, *Majalah*, *Majalah Kedokteran*, *Manunggal*, *Masalah-Masalah Hukum*, *Masalah Teknik*, *Media*, *Media Ekonomi & Bisnis*, *Nuansa*, *Opini*, *Prasasti*, *Publica*, *Pulsa*, *Respect*, *Teknis*, *Transient*, *Warta Perpustakaan*, *Zigma*

DEANS

Faculty of Animal Husbandry: Dr Ir BAMBANG SRIGANDONO
Faculty of Economics: Dr H. M. CHABACHIB
Faculty of Engineering: Prof. Ir EKO WAHYUNI
Faculty of Fisheries and Marine Science: Prof. Dr Ir YOHANES HUTALIRAT
Faculty of Law: ACHMAD BUSRO
Faculty of Letters: Prof. Dr RAHAYU PRIHATMI
Faculty of Mathematics and Natural Sciences: Dr Drs WALIYU SETIA RUDI
Faculty of Medicine: Prof. Dr KABULRACHMAN
Faculty of Public Health: Dr LUDFI SANTOSO
Faculty of Social and Political Sciences: Drs WARSITO

DIRECTORS

Community Service Institute: Drs SUWARSO
Education Development Institute: Drs YUSMILARSO
Research Institute: Prof. Dr Dr I. RIWANTO

PROFESSORS

ANGGORO, S., Aquatic Biology
ATMOMARSONO, U., Animal Science
BUDIHARDJO, E., Architecture
BUDI PRAYITNO, S., Aquaculture
DARMANTO, Y. S., Fisheries Resources
DARMONO, S., Nutrition
DJOKO MOELJANTO, S., Internal Medicine
DJULIATI SUROYO, A. M., Social and Economic History
FAIK HEYDER, A., Surgery
FATIMA MUIS, S., Nutrition
GHOZALI, I., Methodology
HADIHARDAJA, J., Steel Construction
HADISAPUTRO, S., Public Health
HARRY KISTANO, N., Letters
HARTONO, B., Neurology
HARTONO, S. R., Commercial Law
HUTABARAT, S., Oceanography
HUTABARAT, Y., Aquatic Culture
KABULRACHMAN, Dermatovenerology
KARYANA, S., Traditional Javanese Culture
KELIB, A., Islamic Law
KRISTIANTI, L., Paediatrics
MANGUNWIHARDJO, S., Financial Management
MIYASTO, Economics
MULADI, H., Criminal Law
MUSTAFID, Mathematics
NASUTION, I., Pharmacology and Theraputics
NAWAWI ARIEF, B., Criminal Law
NOTOATMOJO, H., Paediatrics
PARSUDI ABDULROCHIM, I., Internal Medicine
P. HADI, S., Environmental Studies
PRAMONO, N., Obstetrics and Gynaecology
PRAPTOHARDJO, U., Gynaecology and Obstetrics
PRIHATMI, M. S. R., Literature
RACHMATULLAH, P., Physiology
RAHAYU PRIHATMI, S., Literature
REDJEKI, H. S., Law
RIWANTO, Surgery
SARJADI, H., Anatomy, Pathology
SATOTO, Nutrition
SERIKAT PUTRAJAYA, N., Criminal Law
SOEBOWO, Anatomy, Pathology
SOEDARSONO, Animal Production
SOEDJARWO, Indonesian Literature
SOEDJATI, Linguistics
SOEJOENOES, A., Obstetrics and Gynaecology
SOEMANTRI, A., Paediatrics, Haematology
SOENARTO, S., Internal Medicine
SOETOMO, I., Linguistics
SOETOMO, S., Planology
S. TRASTOTENOJO, M., Paediatrics
SUDARYONO, Linguistics
SUDIGBIA, Paediatrics
SUGANGGA, Proscriptive Law
SULTANA, A., Histology
SUNARJO, S., Anaesthiology
SUNARTI, D., Animal Production
SUPRIHARYONO, A., Fisheries
SURYANTO, B., Agribusiness Management
SUSANTO, I. S., Criminal Law
SUTRISNO, I., Animal Husbandry
SYA'RANI, L., Fisheries
WARASIH, E., Law and Society
WARELLA, Y., Sociology and Politics
WIBOWO, S., Andrology
WILARDJO, S., Ophthalmology

UNIVERSITAS GADJAH MADA

Bulaksumur, Yogyakarta 55281
Telephone: (274) 588688
E-mail: rektor@ugm.ac.id
Internet: www.ugm.ac.id

Founded 1949
State control
Languages of instruction: English, Indonesian
Academic year: September to June

Rector: Prof. Dr PRATIKNO
Sr Vice-Rector for Academic, Research, and Community Service: Prof. Dr SUNARMININGSIH RETNO
Sr Vice-Rector for Admin., Research and Devt and Human Resources Devt: Ir ADAM PAMUDJI RAHARDJO
Vice-Rector for Information System and Finance: Dr DIDI ACHJARI
Vice-Rector for Students, Alumni and Business Devt: Prof. TONY ATYANTO DHAROKO
Exec. Sec.: Drs DJOKO MOERDIYANTO

Number of teachers: 2,520
Number of students: 54,000

Publications: *Agritech* (4 a year, agricultural technology), *Berita Kedokteran Masyarakat* (4 a year, medicine), *Berkala Ilmiah MIPA* (2 a year, mathematics and natural sciences), *Biologi* (2 a year, biology), *Buletin Peternakan* (4 a year, animal husbandry), *Dentistry* (3 a year), *Fiat Justicia* (2 a year, law), *Gadjah Mada International Journal of Business* (2 a year, economics and business), *Humaniora* (4 a year, humanities), *Indonesian Journal of Geography* (2 a year), *Journal of Indonesian Economy and Business*, *Journal of The Medical Science* (4 a year, medicine), *Jurnal Fisika Indonesia* (4 a year, mathematics and natural sciences), *Jurnal Ilmu Kehutanan* (2 a year, forestry), *Majalah Farmasi Indonesia* (4 a year, pharmacy), *Majalah Geografi Indonesia* (2 a year, geography), *Majalah Ilmiah Forum Fakultas Teknik*, *Manusia dan Lingkungan* (3 a year), *Media Teknik* (4 a year, engineering), *Medicine* (4 a year), *Mimbar Hukum* (3 a year, law), *The Indonesian Journal of Dental Research* (3 a year, dentistry), *Warta Pengabdian* (3 a year, community service)

DEANS

Faculty of Agricultural Technology: Dr Ir DJAGAL WISESO MARSENO
Faculty of Agriculture: Prof. Ir TRIWIBOWO YUWONO
Faculty of Animal Science: Prof. Dr Ir TRI YUWANTA
Faculty of Biology: Dr RETNO PENI SANCAYANINGSIH
Faculty of Cultural Sciences: Dr IDA ROCHANI ADI
Faculty of Dentistry: Drg. SOEHARDONO
Faculty of Economics: Prof. MARWAN ASRI
Faculty of Engineering: Ir TUMIRAN
Faculty of Forestry: Prof. Dr Ir MOCHAMMAD NA'IEM
Faculty of Geography: Prof. Dr SURATMAN
Faculty of Law: Prof. Dr MARSUDI TRIATMODJO
Faculty of Mathematics and Natural Sciences: Dr CHAIRIL ANWAR
Faculty of Medicine: Dr TITI SAVITRI PRIHATININGSIH
Faculty of Pharmacy: Prof. Dr MARCHABAN
Faculty of Philosophy: Dr M. MUKHTASAR SYAMSUDDIN
Faculty of Psychology: Prof. Dr FATUROCHMAN
Faculty of Social and Political Sciences: Dr HERMIN INDAH WAHYUNI
Faculty of Veterinary Medicine: Prof. Dr Drh. BAMBANG SUMIARTO MOECHAROM
Graduate School: Prof. Dr HARTONO
Vocational School: MUHAMMAD ARROFIQ

UNIVERSITAS HALUOLEO

Kampus Hijau Bumi Tridharma Anduonohu, Kendari 93132
Telephone: (401) 3190105
E-mail: info@unhalu.ac.id
Internet: www.uho.ac.id

Founded 1981
State control
Academic year: September to June

Rector: Prof. Dr Ir USMAN RIANSE
Vice-Rector: Drs SULEMAN
Vice-Rector: Drs H. AHMAD BAKKARENG
Vice-Rector: Drs LA ODE MUH. ARSYAD TENO

Vice-Rector: Drs H. ALIBAS YUSUF
Librarian: Drs L. HAISU

Library of 43,000 vols
Number of teachers: 450
Number of students: 9,000

Publications: *Agri Plus* (6 a year), *Gema Pendidikan* (6 a year), *Journal Haluoleo* (4 a year), *Majalah Ekonomi* (6 a year), *Sosial Politik* (6 a year)

DEANS

Faculty of Agriculture: Dr Ir H. GUSTI RAY SADIMANTARA
Faculty of Animal Husbandry: Dr Ir TAKDIR SAILI
Faculty of Economics: HASAN AEDY
Faculty of Education: Drs H. MUHAMMAD GAZALI
Faculty of Fisheries and Marine Sciences: Prof. LA ODE MUH. ASLAN
Faculty of Pharmacy: Prof. Dr SAHIDIN
Faculty of Science: Dr PASRUN ADAM
Faculty of Social and Political Sciences: Drs H. M. NUR RAKHMAN

UNIVERSITAS HASANUDDIN

Jl. Perintis Kemerdekaan, Kampus Unhas Tamalanrea, Makassar 90245
Telephone: (411) 584002
E-mail: cio@unhas.ac.id
Internet: www.unhas.ac.id

Founded 1956
State control
Language of instruction: Bahasa Indonesia
Academic year: September to February

Rector: Prof. Dr Dr IDRUS A. PATURUSI
Vice-Rector for Academic Affairs: Prof. Dr DADANG A. SURIAMIHARJA
Vice-Rector for Admin. and Financial Affairs: Dr A. WARDIHAN SINRANG
Vice-Rector for Student and Alumni Affairs: Ir NASARUDDIN SALAM
Deputy Rector for Cooperative and Devt Affairs: Prof. Dr DWIA ARIES TINA P
Registrar: Dra BETTY E. DUMA
Librarian: Prof. Dr MUH. NADJIB (acting)

Number of teachers: 2,027
Number of students: 28,149

Publications: *Identitas UNHAS* (12 a year), *Interaski/LPPM* (3 a year), *Jupiter/Perpustakaan* (2 a year)

DEANS

Faculty of Agriculture: Prof. Dr Ir YUNUS MUSA
Faculty of Animal Sciences: Prof. Dr Ir SYAMSUDDIN HASAN
Faculty of Dentistry: Prof. MASJUR NASIR
Faculty of Economics: Prof. Dr MUHAMMAD ALI
Faculty of Engineering: Dr Ir WAHYU H. PIARAH
Faculty of Law: Prof. Dr ASWANTO
Faculty of Letters: Prof. BURHANUDDIN ARAFAH
Faculty of Marine Sciences and Fisheries: Prof. Dr Ir ANDI NIARTININGSIH
Faculty of Mathematics and Natural Sciences: Prof. Dr ABDUL WAHID WAHAB
Faculty of Medicine: Prof. Dr IRAWAN YUSUF
Faculty of Public Health: Prof. Dr H. M. ALIMIN MAIDIN
Faculty of Social and Political Sciences: Prof. Dr HAMKAH NAPING

UNIVERSITAS INDONESIA

Main Campus Kampus UI Depok, Jakarta 16424
Jl. Salemba Raya no. 4, Jakarta 10430
Telephone: (21) 7867222
E-mail: io-ui@ui.ac.id
Internet: www.ui.ac.id

Founded 1849 as School for Javanese Doctors
State control
Languages of instruction: Indonesian, English
Academic year: August to June (2 semesters)

Pres.: Prof. Dr GUMILAR RUSLIWA SOMANTRI
Vice-Pres. for Academic Affairs and Student Affairs: Prof. Dr Ir MUHAMMAD ANIS
Vice-Pres. for Human Resources, Finance, and Gen. Admin. Affairs: TAFSIR NURCHAMID
Vice-Pres. for Research, Devt and Industrial Cooperation: SUNARDJI
Univ. Sec.: Prof. Dr I. KETUT SURAJAYA
Head of Academic Quality Assurance Body: Prof. Dr HANNA BACHTIAR ISKANDAR
Librarian: Prof. Dr Ir RIRI FITRI SARI

Library: 5m. vols
Number of teachers: 6,694
Number of students: 49,183

Publications: *Antropologi Indonesia, Asean Marketing Journal, CIVIC, Journal for Civil Society Empowerment, EBAR (Economic Business Accounting Review), Ekonomi dan Keuangan Indonesia (Economics and Finance in Indonesia), EKSIS: Jurnal Ekonomi Keuangan dan Bisnis Islami, Gifted Review, Jurnal Keberbakatan dan Kreativitas, Glasnost, Jurnal Kajian Slavia - Rusia, GLOBAL, Jurnal Politik Internasional, Indonesian Capital Market Review, Indonesian Journal of Dentistry, JAKASTRA: Jurnal Aplikasi Kajian Strategik, Jurnal Akutansi dan Keuangan Indonesia, Jurnal Bisnis & Birokrasi, Jurnal Ekonomi dan Pembangunan Indonesia, Jurnal Hukum Internasional (Indonesian Journal of International Law), Jurnal Ilmu Komputer dan Teknologi Informasi (ICIS), Jurnal Kajian Timur Tengah dan Islam, Jurnal Kajian Wilayah Eropa, Jurnal Kajian Pengembangan Perkotaan, Jurnal Keperawatan Indonesia, Jurnal Kriminologi Indonesia, Jurnal Lingkungan dan Pembangunan (Environment & Development), Jurnal MTI (Magister Teknologi Informasi), Jurnal Polisi Indonesia, Journal of Population* (2 a year), *Jurnal Psikologi Sosial, Jurnal Sains Indonesia, Jurnal Studi Amerika, Jurnal TEKNOLOGI: Journal of Technology, KESMAS, Jurnal Kesehatan Masyarakat Nasional, KILAS, Majalah Ilmu Kefarmasian, Makara* (Health Sciences edn) (2 a year), *Makara* (Science edn) (2 a year), *Makara* (Social Sciences and Humanities edn) (2 a year), *Makara* (Technology edn) (2 a year), and various faculty bulletins, *MASYARAKAT: Jurnal Sosiologi, Medical Journal of Indonesia, The South East Asian Journal of Management, Thesis, Jurnal Penelitian Ilmu Komunikasi, Wacana, Jurnal Ilmu Pengetahuan Budaya*

DEANS

Faculty of Computer Sciences: Dr Prof. T. BASARUDIN
Faculty of Dentistry: Prof. BAMBANG IRAWAN
Faculty of Economics: Prof. FIRMANZAH
Faculty of Engineering: Dr Ir BAMBANG SUGIARTO
Faculty of Humanities: Dr BAMBANG WIBAWARTA
Faculty of Law: Prof. SAFRI NUGRAHA
Faculty of Mathematics and Sciences: Dr Prof. ADI BASUKRIADI
Faculty of Medicine: Dr RATNA SITOMPUL
Faculty of Nursing: Prof. Dra DEWI IRAWATI
Faculty of Psychology: Dr WILMAN DAHLAN MANSOER
Faculty of Public Health: Prof. Dr BAMBANG WISPRIYONO
Faculty of Social and Political Sciences: Dr BAMBANG SHERGI LAKSMONO
Graduate Studies: Prof. CHANDRA WIJAYA (Dir)

UNIVERSITAS ISLAM NEGERI SYARIF HIDAYATULLAH JAKARTA (Syarif Hidayatullah State Islamic University (UIN) Jakarta)

Jl. Ir H. Juanda, 95 Ciputat, Banten 15412
Telephone: (21) 7401925
E-mail: info@uinjkt.ac.id
Internet: www.uinjkt.ac.id

Founded 1960, as the State Academy of Islamic Studies, renamed the Syarif Hidayatullah State Institute of Islamic Studies 1998, univ. status 2002
State control

Rector: Prof. Dr KOMARUDDIN HIDAYAT
Vice-Rector for Academic Affairs: Dr JAMHARI
Vice-Rector for Gen. Admin.: Prof. Dr AMSAL BACHTIAR
Vice-Rector for Institutional Development: Dr SUDARNOTO ABDUL HAKIM
Vice-Rector for Students Affairs: Prof. Dr THIB RATA

DEANS

Faculty of Adab and Humanities: Dr H. ABDUL CHOIR
Faculty of Da'wa and Communication: Dr ARIEF SUBHAN
Faculty of Dirasat Islamiya: Prof. Dr ABUDDIN NATA
Faculty of Economics and Social Science: ABDUL HAMID
Faculty of Medicine and Health Sciences: Prof. Dr M. K. TAJUDIN
Faculty of Psychology: Dr YAHYA UMAR
Faculty of Shari'a and Law: Prof. Dr M. AMIN SUMA
Faculty of Science and Technology: Dr Ir SYOPIANSYAH JAYA PUTRA
Faculty of Tarbiya and Teaching Sciences: Prof. Dr DEDE ROSYADA
Faculty of Usul-al Din and Philosophy: Dr AMIN NURDIN

UNIVERSITAS JAMBI

Kampus Universita Jambi, Jl. Raya Jambi, Muara Bulian, Km 15 Mendalo, Jambi 36361
Telephone: (741) 583377
E-mail: unja@unja.ac.id
Internet: www.unja.ac.id

Founded 1963
Language of instruction: Indonesian
Academic year: September to August

Rector: H. KEMAS ARSYAD SOMAD
Vice-Rector for Academic Affairs: Drs H. ARDINAL
Vice-Rector for Admin.: Dr Ir A. RAHMAN
Vice-Rector for External and Internal Affairs: Dr AULIA TASMAN
Vice-Rector for Student Affairs: Dr Drs MAIZAR KARIM
Head of Bureau of Academic Admin., Student Affairs, Planning and Information Systems: Drs IBRAHIM
Head of Bureau of Gen. Admin. and Finance: Drs H. A. GANI
Librarian: SYAFRI SYAM

Library of 140,000 vols
Number of teachers: 696
Number of students: 13,563

Publication: *Berita UNJA* (12 a year)

DEANS

Faculty of Agriculture: Dr Ir ZILKIFLI
Faculty of Animal Husbandry: Ir AFZALANI
Faculty of Economics: Dr AFRIZAL
Faculty of Education: Drs AFFAN MALIK
Faculty of Law: TAUFIK YAHYA
Postgraduate Programmes: Dr SURATNO

UNIVERSITAS JEMBER

Jl. Kalimantan 37, Jember 68121

Telephone: (331) 331042

E-mail: humas@unej.ac.id

Internet: www.unej.ac.id

Founded 1964

State control

Languages of instruction: Indonesian, English, French

Academic year: July to June

Rector: Prof. Dr H. KABUL SANTOSO

Vice-Rector for Academic Affairs: Dr Ir IDHA HARIYANTO

Vice-Rector for Admin. and Finance: Prof. Drs KADIMAN

Vice-Rector for Student Affairs: PURNOMO

Registrar: Drs MADE PEDUNGAN SARDHA

Dir of Agricultural Polytechnic: Ir H. SUHARJO WIDODO

Dir of Univ. Research Institute: Drs LIAKIP

Librarian: Drs MAHFUD A.

Library of 117,441 vols

Number of teachers: 783

Number of students: 12,933

Publications: *Argopuro, Dian Wanita, Gema Universitas*

DEANS

Faculty of Agricultural Technology: Ir WAGITO

Faculty of Agriculture: Ir Hj. SITI HARTANTI

Faculty of Dentistry: Drg. BOB SOEBIJANTORO

Faculty of Economics: Drs H. SUKUSNI

Faculty of Law: SAMSI KUSAIRI

Faculty of Letters: Drs SUDJADI

Faculty of Social and Political Sciences: Prof. Drs H. BARIMAN

Faculty of Teacher Training & Educational Sciences: Drs SUKARDJO

UNIVERSITAS JENDERAL SOEDIRMAN

Jl. H. R. Boenyamin 708, Purwokerto, Central Java

Telephone: (281) 635292

E-mail: info@unsoed.ac.id

Internet: www.unsoed.ac.id

Founded 1963

Language of instruction: Indonesian

Academic year: September to August (two semesters)

Rector: Prof. RUBIJANTO MISMAN

Vice-Rector for Academic Affairs: Dr SUDJARWO

Vice-Rector for Admin. Affairs: Prof. Dr H. KAMIO

Vice-Rector for Student Affairs: KOMARI

Chief Registrar: Ir BAMBANG PURNOMO

Librarian: Drs CHAMDI

Number of teachers: 750

Number of students: 13,000

Publications: *Journal of Rural Development* (4 a year), *Majalah Ilmiah Unsoed* (biological scientific journal, 4 a year)

DEANS

Faculty of Agriculture: Ir SUMIRAT BRONTO WALUYO

Faculty of Animal Husbandry: Prof. Dr Ir SWANDIARINI

Faculty of Biology: Prof. Dr Haji TRIANI HARDIYATI

Faculty of Economics: Drs GATOT SUPRIHANTO

Faculty of Law: ABDUL AZIS NASIHUDIN

Faculty of Social Sciences and Politics: Drs SUHARI

UNIVERSITAS LAMBUNG MANGKURAT

Kampus UNLAM, Jl. Brigjen H. Hasan Basry, POB 279, Banjarmasin 70123

Telephone: (511) 54177

E-mail: pr4@unlam.ac.id

Internet: www.unlam.ac.id

Founded 1958 as private univ., state control 1960

public control

Language of instruction: Indonesian

Academic year: September to August

Rector: Prof. Dr I H. MUHAMMAD RUSLAN

Vice-Rector for Academic Affairs: Prof. Dr H. MUHAMMAD HADIN MUHJAD

Vice-Rector for Admin. Affairs: Prof. Dr H. AKHMAD GAZALI

Vice-Rector for Student Affairs: Prof. Dr Ir H. IDIANNOR MAHYUDDIN

Vice-Rector for Planning and Cooperation Affairs: Prof. Dr H. SUTARTO HADI

Head of Planning Admin. and Information Systems: Drs H. ARY ACHDYANI

Head of General Admin., Financial and Employee Affairs: HERRY SUPRIYANTO

Head of Admin., Academic and Students Affairs: Dra H. FITRIYANI A. KUSASI

Number of teachers: 1,042

Number of students: 17,144

Publications: *Kalimantan Agriculture* (4 a year), *Kalimantan Scientiae* (2 a year), *Orientasi* (4 a year), *Vidya Karya* (2 a year)

DEANS

Faculty of Agriculture: Ir H. RODINAH

Faculty of Economics: Drs H. FAHMI RIZANI

Faculty of Engineering: Ir H. NORMAN RUSLAN

Faculty of Fisheries: Ir RISWANDI BANDUNG

Faculty of Forestry: Ir SUNARDI

Faculty of Law: HELMI

Faculty of Medicine: Dr H. HASYIM FACHIR

Faculty of Social and Political Sciences: Drs SALADDIN GHALIB

Faculty of Teacher-Training and Education: Drs H. AHMAD SOFYAN

UNIVERSITAS LAMPUNG (University of Lampung)

Jl Prof. Dr Soemantri Brojonegoro 1, Bandar Lampung 35145

Telephone: (721) 709611

E-mail: info@unila.ac.id

Internet: www.unila.ac.id

Founded 1965

State control

Languages of instruction: Indonesian, English

Academic year: August to June (2 terms)

Rector: Prof. Dr Ir SUGENG P. HARIANTO

Vice-Rector I for Academic Affairs: Prof. Dr Ir HASRIADI MAT AKIN

Vice-Rector II for Admin. and Finance Affairs: Ir SULASTRI RAMLI

Vice-Rector III for Student Affairs: Dr D. M. SUNARTO

Vice-Rector IV for Cooperation, Planning and Information Affairs: Dr SATRIA BANGSAWAN

Admin. Gen. and Finance Bureau Leader: HARSONO SUCIPTO

Admin. Planning, Management Information System and Cooperation Bureau Leader: Drs MARDI SYAHPERI

Research Centre Leader: Prof. JOHN HENDRI

Public Service Leader: Dr BUDI KOESTORO

Man. Dir: Prof. Dr Ir ABDUL KADIR SALAM

Library Dir: Drs SUGIANTA

Number of teachers: 1,173

Number of students: 25,944

Publications: *Buletin Penelitian, Warta Pengabdian pada Masyarakat*

DEANS

Faculty of Agriculture: Prof. WAN ABBAS ZAKARIA

Faculty of Economics: TOTO GUNARTO

Faculty of Education and Teacher Training: Prof. Dr SUDJARWO

Faculty of Engineering: Dr LUSMELIA

Faculty of Law: ADIUS SEMENGUK

Faculty of Mathematics and Natural Science: Dr SUTYARSO

Faculty of Social and Political Sciences: Drs AGUS HADIAWAN

DIRECTORS

Bureau of Legal Consultation and Aid: M. PULUNG

Centre of Languages: Drs DEDI SUPRIYADI

Centre of Public Services: Drs KANTAN ABDULLAH

Institute of Demography: MUCHSIN BADAR

Institute of Environmental Studies: Prof. Dr K. E. S. MANIK

Institute of Management: SUDANAR

Lampungnese Culture Studies: Dr VIVIT BARTOVEN

Research Centre: Dr FADDEL DJAUHAR

UNIVERSITAS MALIKUSSALEH

Jl. Tgk Chik Ditiro, 26 Lancang Garam Lhokseumawe, Aceh

Telephone: (645) 41373

E-mail: info@unimal.ac.id

Internet: www.unimal.ac.id

Founded 1969

State control

Rector: APRIDAR

Vice-Rector I: FERY

Vice-Rector II: MARBAWI

Vice-Rector III: DAHLAN

Vice-Rector IV: ISKANDAR

Number of teachers: 600

Number of students: 10,000

DEANS

Agriculture: JAMIDI

Economics: WAHYUDDIN

Engineering: SYAMSUL BAHRI

Law: SUMIADI

Politics: FAUZI

UNIVERSITAS MATARAM

Jl. Majapahit 62, Mataram 83125

Telephone: (370) 633007

E-mail: rektorat@unram.org

Internet: www.unram.ac.id

Founded 1962

public control

Language of instruction: Bahasa

Academic year: September to August

Rector: Dr SUNARPI

Vice-Rector for Academic Affairs: Dr L. SAPTA KARYADI

Vice-Rector for Admin. Affairs: Dr HAILUDIN

Vice-Rector for External Cooperation: SUWARDJI

Vice-Rector for Student Affairs: Dr NASRUDIN

Registrar: MUHIBAH NASRUDIN

Admin. Officer: SYAMSUDIN

Librarian: LALU BUDIMAN

Library of 87,557 vols

Number of teachers: 1,018

Number of students: 17,457

Publications: *Agroteksos* (4 a year), *Komunitas* (2 a year), *Research Institution Journal* (3 a year)

DEANS

Faculty of Agriculture: Prof. Dr M. SARJAN

Faculty of Animal Science: Prof. Dr YUSUF A. SUTARYONO

Faculty of Economics: Prof. Dr THATOK ASMUNY
Faculty of Education and Teaching: Prof. Dr MAHSUN
Faculty of Engineering: FATURACHMAN
Faculty of Law: Prof. Dr GALANG ASMARA
Faculty of Medicine: Prof. Dr MULYANTO

UNIVERSITAS MULAWARMAN

Kampus Gunung. Kelua, Samarinda 75119
Telephone: (541) 741118
E-mail: rektorat@unmul.ac.id
Internet: www.unmul.ac.id

Founded 1962 as Mulawarman School of Higher Learning, present status 1963
state Control
Languages of instruction: Bahasa Indonesia, English
Academic year: September to August

Rector: Prof. Dr ARIFFIEN BRATAWINATA
Vice-Rector for Academic Affairs: Prof. Dr MAMAN SUTISNA
Vice-Rector for Admin. and Finance: SUYATNO WIJOYO
Vice-Rector for Devt and Cooperation: Prof. Dra Hj. RUSMILAWATI
Vice-Rector for Student Affairs: Prof. Drs EDDY SUBANDRIJO
Head of Gen. Admin. and Finance Bureau: MASRIANI
Library Dir: SUBIANTORO

Library of 89,090 vols
Number of teachers: 988
Number of students: 40,932 (37,816 undergraduate, 3,116 graduate)
Publications: *Frontir* (2 a year), *Natural Life*, *Socio-Humanities*

DEANS

Faculty of Agriculture: Ir GUSTI HAFIZIANSYAH
Faculty of Cultural Science: Dr SURYA SILI
Faculty of Economics: Dr ANIS RACHMA UTARI
Faculty of Education and Teacher Training: Drs ICHRAR ASBAR
Faculty of Engineering: Ir H. DHARMA WIDADA
Faculty of Fisheries and Marine Science: Ir SULISTYAWATI
Faculty of Forestry: Dr CHANDRA DEWANA BOER
Faculty of Information Technology and Communication: Prof. Dr JAMALUDDIN
Faculty of Law: Dr LA SINA
Faculty of Mathematics and Natural Sciences: Dr SUDRAJAT
Faculty of Medicine: Dr EMIL BACHTIAR MOERAD
Faculty of Pharmacy: Dr LAODE RIJAI
Faculty of Public Health: Dra SITI BADRAH
Faculty of Social and Political Sciences: D. B. PARANOAN

UNIVERSITAS NEGERI GORONTALO

Jl. Jend. Sudirman, 6 Kota, Gorontalo
Telephone: (435) 821125
Internet: www.ung.ac.id

Founded 1963
State control

Rector: Prof. Dr Ir H. NELSON POMALINGO
Vice-Rector I: Dr SYAMSU QAMAR BADU
Vice-Rector II: Drs NAWIR SUNE
Vice-Rector III: Drs HAMZAH UNO
Vice-Rector IV: Dr MAHLUDIN BARUADI

DEANS

Faculty of Agriculture: Ir ZULZAIN ILAHUDE
Faculty of Education: Drs SAMATOWA USMAN
Faculty of Engineering: Drs NAWIR SUNE
Faculty of Health Sciences and Sports: Dra RAMA P. HIOLA
Faculty of Literature and Culture: Dra HJ. MALABAR SAYAMA
Faculty of Mathematics and Natural Sciences: Dr RAMLI UTINA
Faculty of Social Sciences: Drs MOONTI USMAN

UNIVERSITAS NEGERI JAKARTA
(State University of Jakarta)

Jl. Rawamangun Muka, Jakarta 13220
Telephone: (21) 4890046
E-mail: administrator@unj.ac.id
Internet: www.unj.ac.id

Founded 1957
State control

Faculties of economy, engineering, languages and arts, mathematics and natural sciences, science and education, social sciences, sports

Rector: Dr BEDJO SUJANTO
Vice-Rector I: Dr ZAINAL RAFLI
Vice-Rector II: Dr SYARIFUDIN
Vice-Rector III: Drs FACHRUDDIN ARBAH
Vice-Rector IV: Dr SOEPRIJANTO

UNIVERSITAS NEGERI MAKASSAR
(State University of Makassar)

Jl. A. P. Pettarani, Makassar 90222
Telephone: (411) 869854
E-mail: international.office@unm.ac.id
Internet: www.unm.ac.id

Founded 1961
State control

Faculties of arts and design, economics, education, engineering, languages and literature, mathematics and natural sciences, psychology, sports science

Rector: Prof. Dr H. ARISMUNANDAR
Vice-Rector I: Prof. Dr SOFYAN SALAM
Vice-Rector II: Prof. Dr ANDI ICHSAN
Vice-Rector III: Prof. Dr HAMSU ABDUL GANI
Vice-Rector IV: Dr NURDIN NONI

UNIVERSITAS NEGERI MALANG
(State University of Malang)

Jl. Semarang 5, Malang 65145
Telephone: (341) 551312
E-mail: info@um.ac.id
Internet: um.ac.id

Founded 1954
State control
Languages of instruction: English, Indonesian
Academic year: July to June

Rector: Prof. Dr H. SUPARNO (acting)
Vice-Rector I: Dr H. KUSMINTARDJO
Vice-Rector II: Prof. Dr H. AH. ROFI'UDDIN
Vice-Rector III: Drs H. KADIM MASJKUR
Vice-Rector IV: Drs H. ISNANDAR

Library of 56,251 vols
Number of teachers: 929
Number of students: 25,100
Publications: *Jurnal Bahasa dan Seni*, *Jurnal Ilmu Pendidikan*, *Jurnal Pendidikan dan Pembelajaran*, *Jurnal Sekolah Dasar*, *TEFLIN*

DEANS

Faculty of Economy: Dr ERY TRI DJATMIKA RUDIANTO WAHJU WARDHANA
Faculty of Education: Prof. Dr H. HENDYAT SUTOPO
Faculty of Engineering: Prof Dr Ir H.DJOKO KUSTONO
Faculty of Letters: Prof. Dr H. DAWUD
Faculty of Science and Mathematics: Dr H. ISTAMAR SYAMSURI
Faculty of Social Sciences: Prof. Dr HARIYONO
Faculty of Sports Science: Dr ROESDIYANTO
Programme of Postdoctoral Studies: Prof. Dr MARTHEN PALI

UNIVERSITAS NEGERI MANADO
(State University of Manado)

Tondano, Manado
E-mail: info@mail.unima.ac.id
Internet: www.unima.ac.id

Founded 1955
State control

Rector: Prof. Dr PHILOTEUS E. A. TUERAH

UNIVERSITAS NEGERI MEDAN
(State University of Medan)

Jl. Willem Iskandar Pasar V, Medan 20221
Telephone: (61) 6613365
E-mail: sekretariat@unimed.ac.id
Internet: www.unimed.ac.id

Founded 1956
State control

Rector: SYAWAL GULTOM

UNIVERSITAS NEGERI PAPUA
(Papua State University)

Manokwari
Internet: www.unipa.ac.id

Founded 2000
State control

Faculties of agriculture and agricultural technology, animal husbandry, economics, fisheries and marine science, forestry, mathematics and natural sciences

Rector: Prof. Dr Ir FRANS WANGGAI

UNIVERSITAS NEGERI SEMARANG
(State University of Semarang)

Semarang
E-mail: io@unnes.ac.id
Internet: www.unnes.ac.id

Founded 1961
State control

Faculty of economics and law, education, engineering, languages and arts, mathematics and natural sciences, social sciences, sports

Rector: Prof. Dr H. SUDIJONNO SASTROATMODJO
Vice-Rector for Academic Affairs: Prof. Dr SUPRIADI RUSTAD
Vice-Rector for Gen. Admin.: Drs WAHYONO
Vice-Rector for Devt and Cooperation: Prof. Dr FATHUR ROKHMAN
Vice-Rector for Student Affairs: Dr MASRUKHI

UNIVERSITAS NEGERI SURABAYA
(State University of Surabaya)

Jl. Ketintang, Surabaya
Telephone: (31) 828009
E-mail: rektor@um.ac.id
Internet: www.unesa.ac.id

Founded 1960
State control

Rector: Prof. Dr H. SUPARNO

UNIVERSITAS NEGERI YOGYAKARTA

Karangmalang, Yogyakarta 55281
Telephone: (274) 586168
E-mail: humas@uny.ac.id
Internet: www.uny.ac.id

Founded 1964
State control

Rector: Prof. SUGENG MARDIYONO

UNIVERSITAS NUSA CENDANA
(Nusa Cendana University)

Jl. Adisucipto, Penfui, Kupang 85001
Telephone: (380) 881580
E-mail: puskomundana@undana.ac.id

Internet: www.undana.ac.id
Founded 1962
State control
Languages of instruction: English, Indonesian
Academic year: July to June
Rector: Prof. Ir FRANS UMBU DATTA
Vice-Rector for Academic Affairs: Drs DAVID PANDIE
Vice-Rector for Admin. Affairs: Drs DOPPY ROY NENDISSA
Vice-Rector for Cooperation Affairs: Ir FABIAN HARRY LAWALU
Vice-Rector for Student Affairs: Ir MAXIMILIAN KAPA
Chief Admin. Officer for Academic, Students and Information Systems: Drs DAUD U. Z. KAMURI
Chief Admin. Officer for Finance and Facilities: Drs JOSEPH WULAGENING
Librarian: Drs GORIS SABON
Number of teachers: 900
Number of students: 15,000
Publications: *Liguminesa Journal* (4 a year), *Media Eksakta Journal* (4 a year), *Nusa Cendana Journal* (4 a year), *Sinergia* (12 a year), *Warta Undana* (12 a year)

DEANS
Faculty of Agriculture: Dr MARTHEN PELOKILLA
Faculty of Animal Husbandry: Ir AGUS KONDA MALIK
Faculty of Law: Dr SUKARDAN ALOVSIUS
Faculty of Medicine: Dr HERU TJAHYONO
Faculty of Public Health: Ir GUSTAF OEMATAN
Faculty of Science and Engineering: Dr MANGGADAS LUMBAN GAOL
Faculty of Social and Political Sciences: Prof. Dr ALOYSIUS LILIWERI
Faculty of Teacher Training and Education: Drs LUKAS BILI BORA

UNIVERSITAS PADJADJARAN

Jl. Dipati Ukur 35, Bandung 40132
Telephone: (22) 2503271
E-mail: info@unpad.ac.id
Internet: www.unpad.ac.id
Founded 1957
State control
Languages of instruction: Indonesian, English
Academic year: August to July (two semesters)
Rector: Prof. Dr H. A. HIMENDRA WARGAHADIBRATA
Vice-Rector for Academic Affairs: Prof. Dr H. PONPON S. IDJRADINATA
Vice-Rector for Admin.: M. WAHYUDIN ZARKASYI
Vice-Rector for Cooperation: Prof. Dr H. USMAN HARDI
Vice-Rector for Planning, Information Systems and Supervision: Prof. T. SUGANDA
Vice-Rector for Student Affairs: SYARIF A. BARMAWI
Librarian: Prof. Dr I. NURPILIHAN
Library of 178,441 vols
Number of teachers: 1,868
Number of students: 40,482
Publications: *Agrikulture* (Agriculture, 3 a year), *Bionatura* (Sciences, 3 a year), *Jurnal Ekonomi* (Economics, 2 a year), *Jurnal Kedokteran Bandung* (Medicine, 3 a year), *Jurnal Keperawatan* (Nursing, 2 a year), *Puslitbangkum* (Law, 2 a year), *Sosiohumaniora* (Social Sciences, 3 a year)

DEANS
Faculty of Agriculture: Prof. Dr SADELI NATASASMITA
Faculty of Animal Husbandry: Prof. Dr NASIPAN USRI
Faculty of Communication Science: Drs SOLEH SOEMIRAT
Faculty of Dentistry: Dr SETIAWAN NATASAMITA
Faculty of Economics: Prof. Dr H. SURIPTO SAMID
Faculty of Law: Prof. Dr MAN SUPARMAN SASTRAWIDJAJA
Faculty of Letters: Prof. Dr H. EDI SUHARDI EKADJATI
Faculty of Mathematics and Natural Sciences: Prof. Dr SUPRIATNA
Faculty of Medicine: Dr FIRMAN FUAD WIRAKUSUMAH
Faculty of Psychology: Dr H. SURYANA SUMANTRI
Faculty of Social and Political Science: Drs TACHJAN

UNIVERSITAS PALANGKARAYA

Jl. Yos Sudarso, Kotak Pos 2, Palangka Raya, 73112
Telephone: (536) 26878
E-mail: info@universitaspalangkaraya.ac.id
Internet: www.upr.ac.id
Founded 1963
Language of instruction: Indonesian
Academic year: July to June
Rector: Drs NAPA J. AWAT
Vice-Rector I: Drs HERIYANTO M. GARANG
Vice-Rector II: Drs DADANG LORIDA
Vice-Rector III: H. M. DAMIRI
Vice-Rector IV: Prof. Dr H. AHMADI ISA
Academic and Students' Admin. Officer: Drs LEUNHARD BAN YEN
Librarian: Dra ISTIRAHAYU
Number of teachers: 501
Number of students: 5,265
Publications: *Garantung* (12 a year), *Optimal* (12 a year), *Suara Tunjung Nyaho* (12 a year), *Wahana* (12 a year)

DEANS
Faculty of Agriculture: Ir SINTO R. NOEHAN
Faculty of Economics: Drs EFENDY D. TIMBANG
Faculty of Education and Teacher Training: Drs HENRY SINGARASA

UNIVERSITAS PATTIMURA AMBON

POB 95, Jl. Ir M. Putuhena Poka, Ambon 97233
Telephone: (911) 322626
E-mail: sisdiksat@unpatti.ac.id
Internet: www.unpatti.ac.id
Founded 1956, present status 1962
Language of instruction: Indonesian
Academic year: August to July
Rector: Dr Ir J. L. NANERE
Vice-Rector for Academic Affairs: Prof. P. J. SIWABESSY
Vice-Rector for Admin. and Finance: J. LEIWAKABESSY
Vice-Rector for Student Affairs: Ir J. J. TUHUMURY
Registrar: Drs E. LEUWOL
Librarian: ALI ZAWAWI
Number of teachers: 636
Number of students: 7,516
Publication: *Media Unpatti* (12 a year)

DEANS
Faculty of Agriculture: Ir J. PUTINELLA
Faculty of Economics: Drs L. A. RASJID
Faculty of Fisheries: Ir J. M. NANLOHY
Faculty of Law: C. M. PATTIRUHU
Faculty of Social and Political Sciences: Drs M. RENUR
Faculty of Teacher Training and Education: Drs T. J. A. UNEPUTTY
Faculty of Technology: Ir J. ASTHENU

DIRECTORS
Institute of Community Service: Dr MUS. HULISELAN
Institute of Research: Dr Ir P. SITIAPESSY

UNIVERSITAS PENDIDIKAN GANESHA SINGARAJA

Bali
Telephone: (362) 22570
E-mail: humas@undiksha.ac.id
Internet: www.undiksha.ac.id
State control
Faculties of education, languages and arts, mathematics and natural sciences, social education, sports and health, technical and vocational education
Rector: Dr I NYOMAN SUDIANA
Vice-Rector I: Dr I GUSTI PUTU SUHARTA
Vice-Rector II: Dr I NYOMAN JAMPEL
Vice-Rector III: Drs I PUTU SUHARTA
Vice-Rector IV: Dr I KETUT SEKEN
Library of 37,818 vols, 4,275 titles

UNIVERSITAS PENDIDIKAN INDONESIA

Jl. Dr Setiabudhi 229, Bandung 40154
Telephone: (22) 2013161
Internet: www.upi.edu
Founded 1954 as Perguruan Tinggi Pendidikan Guru (Teacher's Education College), reformed as Bandung Institute of Teaching and Educational Sciences 1964, present status 1999
State control
Faculties of educational sciences, language and art, science, social studies, sports and health, technology
Rector: Prof. SUNARYO KARTADINATA
Number of teachers: 1,302
Number of students: 22,700

UNIVERSITAS RIAU

Kampus Bina Widya Km 12.5, Pekanbaru 28293
Telephone: (761) 63266
E-mail: administrator@unri.ac.id
Internet: www.unri.ac.id
Founded 1962
State control
Language of instruction: Indonesian
Academic year: September to July
Rector: Prof. Dr ASHALUDDIN JALIL
Vice-Rector for Academic Affairs: Prof. Dr ARAS MULYADI
Vice-Rector for Admin.: Dr YANUAR HAMZAH
Vice-Rector for Planning and Cooperation: Dr ADHY PRAYITNO
Vice-Rector for Student Affairs: Drs RAHMAD
Librarian: AGUS SUTIKNO
Library of 25,000 vols
Number of teachers: 1,251
Number of students: 24,643
Publications: *Dawat* (journal of Malay language and culture, 4 a year), *Jurnal Agritek* (agricultural technology, 2 a year), *Jurnal Ekonomi* (economics, 4 a year), *Jurnal Ilmu Sosial dan Politik* (social and political sciences, 4 a year), *Jurnal Natur Indonesia* (2 a year), *Jurnal Penelitian* (general scientific research, 4 a year), *Jurnal Perikanan dan Ilmu Kelautan* (fisheries and marine science, 2 a year), *Terubuk* (fisheries bulletin, 4 a year)

DEANS

Faculty of Agriculture: Prof. Dr USMAN PATO
Faculty of Economics: Drs KENNEDY
Faculty of Engineering: Dr BAHRI
Faculty of Fisheries: Prof. Dr BUSTARI
Faculty of Law: Prof. Dr SUNARMI
Faculty of Medicine: Dr TASWIN YACOB
Faculty of Natural Sciences and Mathematics: Prof. Dr ADEL ZAMRI
Faculty of Politics and Social Science: Drs ALI YUSRI
Faculty of Teacher Training and Education: Prof. Dr M. NUR

PROFESSORS

ADAM, D., Government and Law
AHMAD, M., Marine Sciences and Fisheries
DAHRIL, T., Planktonology and Water Quality
DIAH, M., Education
HASAN, K., Education
IMRAN, A., Islamology
ISKANDAR, D., Physics
KASMY, M. F., Physics
KASRY, A., Aquatic Resources Management
MAHMUD, S., Education
MARZUKI, S., History Education
RAB, T., Enzymology
RAHMAN, M., Mathematics
RASYAD, A., Agriculture
SAAD, M., Rural Sociology
SAMAD, R., Education
SUWARDI, History
UMAR, S. M., Education
USMAN, F., Agriculture

UNIVERSITAS SAM RATULANGI

Kampus UNSRAT Bahu, Manado 95115
Telephone: (431) 863886
E-mail: rektorat@unsrat.ac.id
Internet: www.unsrat.ac.id
Founded 1961
State control
Language of instruction: Indonesian
Academic year: starts September
Rector: Prof. Dr DONALD A. RUMOKOY
Vice-Rector: Prof. Dr J. SH POLIL MANDANG
Vice-Rector: Prof. Dr PAULUS KINDANGEN
Vice-Rector: Prof. Dr B. H. R. KALRUPAN
Vice-Rector: Prof. Dr DAVID A. KALIGIS
Vice-Rector: Prof. Dr Ir JEFREY I KINDANGEN
Vice-Rector: Prof. Drs MAJID ABDULLAH
Head of Bureau for Academic and Student Admin.: H. J. MEWENGKANG
Head of Central Library: D. SILANGEN
Number of teachers: 1,496
Number of students: 12,526
Publication: *Palakat-Inovasi*

DEANS

Faculty of Agriculture: Dr Ir D. T. SEMBEL
Faculty of Animal Husbandry: Prof. Dr D. A. KALIGIS
Faculty of Economics: Prof. NY. I. NAJOEN
Faculty of Engineering: R. J. M. MANDAGI
Faculty of Fisheries and Maritime Sciences: Prof. Dr S. BERHIMPON
Faculty of Law: Prof. ADOLF DAPU
Faculty of Letters: Drs ROBERT TANDI
Faculty of Mathematics and Natural Science: Dr S. RONDONUWU
Faculty of Medicine: Dr J. W. SIAGIAN
Faculty of Public Health: Prof. Dr JOOTJE M.L. UMBOH
Faculty of Social Sciences and Politics: Drs J. J. LONTAAN

PROFESSORS

ALAMSJAH, Soil Physics
BUDIARSO, Technology
DUNDU, B., Microbiology
JAN, H., Statistics
KAKAUHE, R. P. L., Management Accounting
KAPOJOS-MONGULA, I. C. R., Civil Law
KARINDA, D. S., English and Dutch
KASINEM-S., Commercial Law
KORAH, M. W., Marketing Management Science
MANDANG, J. H. A., Ahli Mata
MUNIR, M., Paediatrics
MUSA, A., Modern Indonesian History
MUSA KARIM, Indonesian Literature
PALAR, W. T., Agrarian Studies
PALENEWEN, J. L., Ecology
PANDA, H. O., Surgery
PUNUH-GO, S., Civil Law
ROGI, M., Economic Development
SALEH, M., Indonesian Government System
SINOLUNGAN, J. M., Medical Psychology
SOEPENO, Customary Law
SUPIT, J. T., Sociology
TANGKUDUNG, R. S., Civil Administration
TIMBOELENG, K. W., Physics and Research Methodology
TUSACH, N. A., Civil Law
WANTASEN, D., Soil Physics
WAWOROENTOE, S. A., Physics
WAWOROENTOE, W. J., Urban and Regional Planning
WILAR, A. F., Veterinary Science
WOKAS, F. H. M., Plant Protection
WOWOR, G. E., Gynaecology
WUMU, J., History of Economics

UNIVERSITAS SEBELAS MARET SURAKARTA
(Sebelas Maret University Surakarta)

Jl. Ir Sutami 36A, Surakarta 57126
Telephone: (271) 646994
E-mail: io@uns.ac.id
Internet: www.uns.ac.id
Founded 1976
State control
Language of instruction: Indonesian
Academic year: August to July
Rector: Prof. Dr H. MOHAMMED SYAMSULHADI
Vice-Rector for Academic Affairs: Prof. Dr RAVIK KARSIDI
Vice-Rector for Admin. Affairs: Prof. Dr Ir SHOLAHUDDIN
Vice-Rector for Cooperation Affairs: Prof. Dr ADI SULISTYONO
Vice-Rector for Student Affairs: Drs DWI TIYANTO
Librarian: Drs HARMAWAN
Library of 380,938 vols
Number of teachers: 1,568
Number of students: 35,468
Publications: *Issues In Social and Environmental Accounting* (journal), *Mediator* (student magazine, 12 a year)

DEANS

Faculty of Agriculture: Prof. Dr BAMBANG PUJIASMANTO
Faculty of Economics: Dr WISNU UNTORO
Faculty of Engineering: Prof. Dr KUNCORO DIHARJO
Faculty of Law: Prof. Dr HARTIWININGSIH
Faculty of Letters and Arts: Dr RIYADI SANTOSA
Faculty of Mathematics and Natural Sciences: Prof. Dr ARI HANDONO RAMELAN
Faculty of Medicine: Prof. Dr ZAINAL ARIFIN ADNAN
Faculty of Social and Political Science: Prof. Dr PAWITO
Faculty of Teacher Training and Education: Prof. Dr FURQON HIDAYATULLAH
Postgraduate Programme: Prof. Dr Ir AHMAD YUNUS

UNIVERSITAS SRIWIJAYA

Jl. Jaksa Agung R. Suprapto, Palembang, South Sumatra
Telephone: (711) 26004
E-mail: yadiutama@ilkom.unsri.ac.id
Internet: www.unsri.ac.id
Founded 1960
State control
Language of instruction: Indonesian
Academic year: July to June
Rector: Prof. Dr BADIA PERIZADE
Vice-Rector I: Dr ZULFIKARI DAHLAN
Vice-Rector II: KENCANA DEWI
Vice-Rector III: H. ANIS SAGAF
Vice-Rector IV: Dr ABDUL HAMID RASYID
Admin. Bureau: Drs HERMAN MURSAL
Librarian: Dra CHUZAIMAH DIEM
Number of teachers: 540 full-time, 617 part-time
Number of students: 8,427
Publications: *Majalah Universitas Sriwijaya* (3 a year), and faculty bulletins

DEANS

Faculty of Agriculture: ZULJATI SYAHRUL
Faculty of Dentistry: Prof. Dr ARSUAD
Faculty of Economics: BADIA PERIZADE
Faculty of Education: Dr ZULKIFLI DAHLAN (acting)
Faculty of Engineering: Dr HASAN BASRI
Faculty of Law: SOFYAN HASAN
Faculty of Teacher Training: Prof. Dr DJAHIR BASIR

PROFESSORS

HALIM, A., Linguistics
HARDJOWIJONO, G., Paediatrics
MUKTI, H. D., Advanced Management
MUSLIMIN, A., Administrative Law
SOELAIMAN, M., Adat Law

UNIVERSITAS SUMATERA UTARA
(University of North Sumatra)

Jl. Dr. T. Mansur 9, Kampus USU, Medan 20155
Telephone: (61) 8216575
E-mail: usu@karet.usu.ac.id
Internet: www.usu.ac.id
Founded 1952
State control
Languages of instruction: Indonesian, English
Academic year: August to July
Rector: Prof. CHAIRUDDIN P. LUBIS
Vice-Rector for Academic Affairs: Prof. Dr SUMONO
Vice-Rector for Admin. Affairs: Dr SUBHILHAR
Vice-Rector for Asset Management: Ir ISMAN NURIADI
Vice-Rector for Planning, Cooperation and Foreign Affairs: Prof. Dr SUKARIA SINULINGGA
Vice-Rector for Student Affairs: Dr LINDA MAAS
Head of Library and Information System: Drs A. RIDWAN SIREGAR
Library of 500,000 vols
Number of teachers: 1,750
Number of students: 28,000

DEANS

Faculty of Agriculture: Dr ZULKIFLI NASUTION
Faculty of Dentistry: Prof. ISMET D. NASUTION
Faculty of Economics: Drs JHON T. RITONGA
Faculty of Engineering: Dr NAWAWY LOEBIS
Faculty of Law: Prof. Dr RUNTUNG
Faculty of Letters: Prof. BAHREN UMAR SIREGAR
Faculty of Mathematics and Sciences: Prof. EDDY MARLIANTO
Faculty of Medicine: Dr T. BAHRI ANWAR
Faculty of Political and Social Science: Drs M. ARIF NASUTION
Faculty of Public Health: (vacant)
School of Postgraduate Studies: Dr T. CHAIRUN NISA

UNIVERSITAS SYIAH KUALA

Jl. Darussalam, Kopelma Darussalam, Banda Aceh 23111
Telephone: (651) 7410250
E-mail: rektor@unsyiah.ac.id
Internet: www.unsyiah.ac.id

Founded 1961
State control
Language of instruction: Indonesian
Academic year: August to June

Rector: DARNI
Vice-Rector I: Dr SAMSUL RIZAL
Vice-Rector II: Dr EDDY NUR ILYAS
Vice-Rector III: Drs RUSLI YUSUF
Vice-Rector IV: DARUSMAN
Chief Academic Admin. Officer: Drs BACHTIAR EFENDI
Chief Admin. Officer: Drs MUSTAFA USMAN
Librarian: Drs SANUSI

Number of teachers: 1,278
Number of students: 16,715

Publications: *Agripet* (2 a year), *Agrista, Ekobis, Jurnal Kedokteran Syiah Kuala, Jurnal Teknik Sipil* (3 a year), *Kanun Fakultas Hukum, Managemen dan Bisnis, Medica Veterinaria, Mekanikal Komputasi & Numerical, Mon Mata* (4 a year), *Natural, Rekayasa Elektrika, Rekayasa Kimia & Lingkungan, Teknorama, Telaah dan Riset, Wacana Pendidikan* (4 a year), *Warta Unsyiah*

DEANS

Faculty of Agriculture: Ir ISMAYANI
Faculty of Economics: Prof. Dr SAID MUHAMMAD
Faculty of Engineering: Prof. Dr Ir HUSAINI
Faculty of Law: MAWARDI ISMAIL
Faculty of Mathematical and Natural Sciences: Dr MUSTANIR
Faculty of Medicine: Dr SYAHRUL
Faculty of Teacher Training and Education: Dr M. YUSUF AZIZ
Faculty of Veterinary Science: Dr MAHDI ABRAR

UNIVERSITAS TADULAKO

Kampus Bumi, Tadulako Tondo, Sulawesi, Palu 94118
Telephone: (451) 422611
E-mail: lemlit@untad.ac.id
Internet: www.untad.ac.id

Founded 1981

Rector: Drs MOHAMMAD RASYID
Vice-Rector: T. A. M. TILAAR
Vice-Rector: ARIFUDDIN BIDIN
Vice-Rector: SAHABUDDIN MUSTAPA
Vice-Rector: Dr MAIN LABASO
Head of General Admin. Bureau: RAFIGA PONULELE
Librarian: Drs MUH. ASRI HENTE

Library of 30,042 vols
Number of teachers: 660
Number of students: 6,500

DEANS

Faculty of Agricultural Sciences: Ir MASRIL BUSTAMI
Faculty of Economics: ARSYAD MAARDANIN
Faculty of Law: ISMAIL KASIM
Faculty of Social and Political Sciences: Drs ZAINUDDIN BOLONG
Faculty of Teacher Training: Drs H. TJATJO THAHA
Diploma Programme for Technical Sciences: Ir GALIB ISHAK

UNIVERSITAS TANJUNGPURA

Jl. Ahmad Yani Pontianak, Kalbar, Pontianak 78124
Telephone: (561) 739636
E-mail: untan@untan.ac.id
Internet: www.untan.ac.id

Founded 1959
Language of instruction: Indonesian
Academic year: begins September

Rector: Prof. Hj. ASNIAR ISMAIL
First Vice-Chancellor: Prof. Dr HENDRO S. SUDAGUNG
Registrar: RADJALI HADIMASPUTRA
Head of Gen. Admin. Bureau: MAYARANA RANITA
Librarian: SUTARMIN

Number of teachers: 734
Number of students: 9,305

DEANS

Faculty of Agriculture: Prof. Ir ALAMSYAH
Faculty of Economics: ASNIAR SUBAGYO
Faculty of Engineering: Ir Haji PONY SEDYANINGSIH
Faculty of Law: Prof. ANWAR SALEH
Faculty of Social and Political Sciences: Prof. Dr Sy. IBRAHIM ALKADRIE
Faculty of Teaching and Education: Prof. Drs JAWADI HASID

UNIVERSITAS TERBUKA
(Indonesian Open Learning University)

Jl. Cabe Raya, Pondok Cabe, Pamulang Tangerang Selatan-Banten 15418
Telephone: (21) 7490941
E-mail: humas@ut.ac.id
Internet: www.ut.ac.id

Founded 1984
State control
Language of instruction: Indonesian

Rector: Prof. Dr Ir TIAN BELAWAT
Vice-Rector: Dr YUNI TRI HEWINDATI
Vice-Rector: Ir NADIA SRI DAMAJANTI
Vice-Rector: HASMONEL
Vice-Rector: Drs MAXIMUS GORKY SEMBIRING
Registrar: Drs ACHMAD RAZAD
Librarian: Dr EFFENDI WAHYONO

Library of 42,311 vols
Number of teachers: 791
Number of students: 639,049

Publications: *Journal of Open and Distance Learning* (5 a year), *Journal of Education* (5 a year), *Journal of Indonesian Studies* (2 a year), *Journal of Mathematics, Science and Technology* (5 a year), *Journal of Management Organization* (5 a year), *Komunika* (4 a year), *Suara Terbuka* (4 a year)

DEANS

Faculty of Economics: Dr YUN ISWANTO
Faculty of Education and Teacher Training: Dr RUSTAM
Faculty of Mathematics and Natural Science: Dr NURAINI SOLEIMAN
Faculty of Social and Political Science: Dr DARYONO

PROFESSORS

BELAWATI, T., Economics
SUPARMAN, M. A., Elementary Education
WINATAPUTRA, U. S., Citizenship

UNIVERSITAS TRUNOJOYO MADURA

Bangkalan, East Java
Telephone: (31) 3014091
E-mail: humas@trunojoyo.ac.id
Internet: www.trunojoyo.ac.id

Founded 2001
State control

Rector: Prof. Dr Ir H. ARIFFIN
Vice-Rector I: Drs BAMBANG SABARIMAN
Vice-Rector II: Dr Ir SLAMET SUBARI
Vice-Rector III: H. BOED MUSTIKO

DEANS

Faculty of Agriculture: Ir MOH. FAKHRY
Faculty of Economics: Prof. IWAN TRIYUNWONO
Faculty of Engineering: Ir SOEPRAPTO
Faculty of Law: H. MOH. AMIR HAMZAH

UNIVERSITAS UDAYANA
(Udayana University)

Bukit Jimbaran Campus, Badung 80361
Telephone: (361) 701954
E-mail: info@unud.ac.id
Internet: www.unud.ac.id

Founded 1962
State control
Academic year: August to December
Language of instruction: Indonesian

Rector: Prof. Dr I MADE BAKTA
Deputy Rector for Academic Affairs: Prof. Dr I. KOMANG GDE BENDESA
Deputy Rector for Finance and Gen. Affairs: Dr I NYOMAN ARCANA
Deputy Rector for Cooperation and Information Affairs: Prof. Drs Dr I MADE SUASTRA
Deputy Rector for Student Affairs: Prof. Dr Ir I GEDE PUTU WIRAWAN

Library of 21,390 vols
Number of teachers: 1,644
Number of students: 20,125

Publications: *Berita Udayana* (12 a year), *Majalah Ilmiah Universitas Udayana* (4 a year), *Majalah Kedokteran Unud* (4 a year)

DEANS

Faculty of Agriculture: Dr I NYOMAN RAI
Faculty of Agricultural Technology: Prof. Dr GANDA PUTRA
Faculty of Animal Husbandry: Dr BAGUS GAGA PARTAMA
Faculty of Economics: Prof.Dr WIKSUANA
Faculty of Engineering: Dr I WAYAN REDANA
Faculty of Law: Prof. Dr I GUSTI NGURAH WAIROCANA
Faculty of Letters: Prof.Dr I WAYAN CIKA
Faculty of Mathematics and Natural Sciences: Prof. Dr A. A. GDE RAKA DALEM
Faculty of Medicine and Health Sciences: Prof. Dr KETUT SUASTIKA
Faculty of Social Sciences and Political Sciences: Prof. Dr Drs I WAYAN SUANDI
Faculty of Tourism: Drs I PUTU ANOM
Faculty of Veterinary Science: Prof. Dr I MADE DAMRIYASA

PROFESSORS

ADIPUTRA, N., Occupational Health
ARDANA, G. G., History
ARDIKA, W., Archaeology
ARGA, Agricultural Economics
ARHYA, N., Biochemistry
ARKA, B., Veterinary Science
ARYANTA, W. R., Food Microbiology
ASTININGSIH, K., Poultry Production
ASTITI, T. I. P., Custom Law
ATMAJA, D. G., Law
BAGUS, G. N., Indonesian Language
BAGUS, G. N., Social Anthropology
BAKTA, M., Internal Medicine
BAWA, W., Indonesian Language
BHINAWA, N., Animal Production
BUDHA, K., Surgery
BUNGAYA, G., Management
DJAGRA, I. B., Animal Production
KALAM, A. A. R., Arts and Design
LANA, K., Animal Nutrition
LANANG, O., Genetics
MANIK, G., Animal Husbandry
MANUABA, I. B. A., Human Physiology
MARDANI, N. K., Biology (Environmental Studies)
MASTIKA, M., Animal Nutrition
MATRAM, R. B., Veterinary Physiology
NALA, G. N., Human Physiology

NEHEN, K., Economic Devt
NETRA SUBADIYASA, N., Soil Science
NITIS, M., Animal Nutrition
OKA, I. B., Pharmacology
PANGKAHILA, J. A., Sexology
PUTHERA, G. A. G., Human Histology
PUTRA, D. K. H., Animal Physiology
RATA, I. B., Archaeology
RIKA, K., Forage Science
SAIDI, H. S., Islamology
SIRTA, N., Custom Law
SOEWIGIONO, S., Gastroenterology
SUARNA, I. M., Forage Science
SUATA, I. K., Microbiology
SUDHARTA, T. R., Sanskrit Language
SUDJATHA, W., Food and Technology
SUKARDI, E., Human Anatomy
SUKARDIKA, K., Microbiology
SURAATMAJA, S., Paediatrics
SURYADHI, N. T., Public Health
SUTAWAN, N., Social and Agricultural Economics
SUTER, K., Food Technology
SUTHA, G. K., Law
SUTJIPTA, N., Social and Agricultural Economics
SUWETA, G. P., Veterinary Science
SUYATNA, G., Social Economics
TJITARSA, I. B., Public Health
WIDNYANA, M., Law
WINAYA, P. D., Soil Fertility
WIRAWAN, D. N., Public Health
WITA, W., Cardiology

Private Universities

MAHASARASWATI DENPASAR UNIVERSITY

Jl. Kamboja 11A, Denpasar, Bali
Telephone: (361) 227019
E-mail: info@unmas.ac.id
Internet: www.unmas.ac.id
Founded 1962
Private control
Languages of instruction: English, Indonesian
Academic year: September to June
Vice-Rector: Dr Ir N UTARI VIPRIYANTI
Number of teachers: 165
Number of students: 5,760
Publications: *Ekonomi Pembangunan*, *Santiaji Pendidikan*

DEANS

Faculty of Agriculture: PUTU SUJANA
Faculty of Dentistry: MAHENDRI KUSUMAWATI
Faculty of Technology: NGURAH SUNATHA

PETRA CHRISTIAN UNIVERSITY

Jl. Siwalankerto 121–131, Surabaya 60236
Telephone: (31) 8439040
E-mail: info@peter.petra.ac.id
Internet: www.petra.ac.id
Founded 1961
Private control
Languages of instruction: Indonesian, English
Academic year: August to July (2 semesters)
Rector: Prof. Ir Dr ROLLY INTAN
Vice-Rector for Academic Affairs: Dr Ir HANNY HOSIANA TUMBELAKA
Vice-Rector for Finance and Admin.: Dra JULIANA ANGGONO
Vice-Rector for Student Affairs: Drs FREDERICK JONES SYARANAMUAL
Registrar: Dra WIDIARTI SUPRAPTO
Librarian: LIAUW TOONG TJIEK
Library: 141,806 books, 11,866 audiovisual items
Number of teachers: 642
Number of students: 6,960
Publications: *Accounting and Finance Journal* (2 a year), *Architecture Dimension* (2 a year), *Civil Engineering Dimension* (2 a year), *Electrical Journal* (2 a year), *Industrial Engineering Journal* (industrial engineering dept, 2 a year), *Informatic Journal* (2 a year), *K@TA* (language and literature, 2 a year), *Management and Entrepreneur Journal* (2 a year), *Mechanical Engineering Journal* (2 a year), *Nirmana* (visual communication design dept, 2 a year)

DEANS

Faculty of Art and Design: ANDRIAN DEKTISA HAGIJANTO
Faculty of Civil Engineering and Planning: Ir HANDOKO SUGIHARTO
Faculty of Communication Science: Drs FELICIA GOENAWAN
Faculty of Economics: Drs DIAH DHARMAYANTI
Faculty of Industrial Technology: Ir DJONI HARYADI SETIABUDI
Faculty of Letters: Drs RIBUT BASUKI

UNDIKNAS UNIVERSITY

Jl. Bedugul 39 Sidakarya, Denpasar 80225
Telephone: (361) 723868
E-mail: info@undiknas.ac.id
Internet: www.undiknas.ac.id
Founded 1969
Private control
Rector: Prof. Dr GEDE SRI DAMA

DEANS

Faculty of Administrative Science and Communication: Dr I NYOMAN SUBANDA
Faculty of Economics and Business: Prof. Dr IDA BAGUS RAKA SUARDANA
Faculty of Information and Engineering: I WAYAN SUTAMA
Faculty of Law: Prof. Dr I NYOMAN BUDIANA
Faculty of Social Science and Political Science: Dr I NYOMAN SUBANDA

UNIVERSITAS 17 AGUSTUS 1945, JAKARTA (17 August 1945 University, Jakarta)

Jl. Sunter Permai Raya Sunter Agung, Podomoro, Jakarta Utara 14350
Telephone: (21) 6410287
E-mail: untag@untag-jkt.org
Internet: www.untag-jkt.org
Founded 1945
Private control
Faculties of administration, economics, engineering, law, pharmacy, social and political science
Rector: Dr THOMAS NOACH PEEA

UNIVERSITAS 17 AGUSTUS 1945, SURABAYA (17 August 1945 University, Surabaya)

Telephone: (31) 5931800
E-mail: info@untag.ac.id
Internet: www.untag-sby.ac.id
Founded 1958
Language of instruction: Indonesian
Academic year: September to August
Faculties of agricultural science, economics, law, letters, psychology, social and political sciences

UNIVERSITAS AL-AZHAR

Complex of Al-Azhar Mosque, Jakarta 12110
Telephone: (211) 7279275
E-mail: info@uai.ac.id
Internet: www.uai.ac.id
Founded 2000
Private control
Rector: Prof. Dr Ir ZUHAL
Vice-Rector for Corporate Devt: DJOKOSANTOSO MOELJONO
Vice-Rector for Public Admin. and Human Resources: Drs MUHSIN LUBIS
Vice-Rector for Student Affairs and Academic Div.: Dr Ir AHMAD H. LUBIS

DEANS

Faculty of Economics: Prof. Dr SAYUTI HASIBUAN
Faculty of Engineering: Prof. Dr Ir SARDY
Faculty of Islamic Religion: Dr NURHAYATI DJAMAS
Faculty of Law: Prof. Dr ERMAN RAJAGUKGUK
Faculty of Mathematics and Science: Dr Ir WITONO BASUKI
Faculty of Psychology: Prof. HARSONO WIRYOSUMARTO
Faculty of Social and Political Sciences: Prof. Dr YAHYA A. MUHAIMIN

UNIVERSITAS ATMA JAYA YOGYAKARTA

Campus Bldg II, Thomas Aquinas Rd, Babarsari 44, Yogyakarta 55281
Telephone: (274) 487711
E-mail: kkp@uajy.ac.id
Internet: www.uajy.ac.id
Founded 1965
Private control
Rector: Dr R. MARYATMO
Vice-Rector for Academic Affairs: Ir IGNATIUS PRAMANA YUDA
Vice-Rector for Admin., Finance and Human Resources: Dr THERESIA ANITA CHRISTIAN
Vice-Rector for Student Affairs and Alumni: Dr MARIO ANTONIUS BIROWO

UNIVERSITAS BAITURRAHMAH

Jl. Raya by-pass Km 15, Aie Pacah, Padang
Telephone: (751) 463069
Internet: www.unbrah.ac.id
Founded 1979
Private control

DEANS

Faculty of Dentistry: R. RAMA PUTRANTO
Faculty of Economics: Dr H. YANDI SUKRI
Faculty of Medicine: Prof. H. AMIRMUSLIM MALIK
Faculty of Public Health: Dr WINARDI

UNIVERSITAS BALIKPAPAN

Jl. Pupuk Raya, Gn. Bahagia, Balikpapan
Telephone: (542) 765442
E-mail: info@uniba-bpn.ac.id
Internet: www.uniba-bpn.ac.id
Private control
Rector: Prof. Dr ELLYANO S. LASAM

DEANS

Faculty of Economics: Drs HAIRUL ANAM
Faculty of Law: Drs MUHAMAD MUHDAR
Faculty of Sastras: Dra SITI HAFSAH
Faculty of Technology: Ir POEGOEH

UNIVERSITAS BATANGHARI JAMBI

Jl. Slamet Riyadi Broni, Jambi
Telephone: (741) 60673
E-mail: rektorat@unbari.ac.id
Internet: www.unbari.ac.id
Private control
Language of instruction: Indonesian
Academic year: September to February

Chair.: H. FACHRUDDIN RAZI
Library of 11,000 vols and 7,000 titles
Number of teachers: 224
Number of students: 6,045
Publications: *Economics Faculty* (online (eksis.unbari.ac.id)), *Journal of University* (online (e-journal.unbari.ac.id))

DEANS
Faculty of Agriculture: Ir M. SUGIHARTONO
Faculty of Economics: OSRITA HAPSARA
Faculty of Law: M. ZEN ABDULLAH
Faculty of Science Education: Dr FARIDA HARYANI
Faculty of Technology: Ir AZWARMAN

UNIVERSITAS BINA DARMA

Jl. Jend. Ahmad Yani, Palembang
E-mail: universitas@mail.binadarma.ac.id
Internet: www.binadarma.ac.id
Founded 1993
Private control
Faculties of communication, computer science, economy, engineering, language and literature, psychology
Pres.: Prof. Ir BUCHORI RACHMAN

UNIVERSITAS BINA NUSANTARA (Bina Nusantara University)

Kampus Anggrek, Jl. Kebon Jeruk Raya 27, Kebon Jeruk, Jakarta Barat 11530
Telephone: (21) 53696969
E-mail: publicrelations@binus.edu
Internet: www.binus.ac.id
Founded 1974
Private control
Rector: Prof. Dr Ir HARJANTO PRABOWO
Vice-Rector for Academic Devt: IMAN HERWIDIANA KARTOWISASTRO
Vice-Rector for Collaboration and Institutional Devt: WAYAH S. WIROTO
Vice-Rector for Operation and Resources: S. KOM. NELLY
Vice-Rector for Student Affairs and Community: Drs ANDREAS CHANG

UNIVERSITAS BORNEO TARAKAN (Borneo University)

Jl. Amal Lama 1, POB 170, Tarakan 77123
Telephone: (551) 5507023
E-mail: ubt@borneo.ac.id
Internet: www.borneo.ac.id
Founded 1999
Private control
Faculties of agriculture, economics, fisheries, law, technology
Rector: ABDUL JABARSYAH

UNIVERSITAS BUNG HATTA

Jl Sumatra Ulak Karang, Padang, 25133
Telephone: (751) 7051678
E-mail: rektorat@bung-hatta.ac.id
Internet: www.bunghatta.ac.id
Founded 1981
Private control
Rector: Prof. Dr NIKI LUKVIARMAN
Librarian: AMA ISNAYETI
Number of teachers: 285
Number of students: 7,497

DEANS
Faculty of Civil Engineering: Ir HENDRI WARMAN
Faculty of Economics: Dr NELMIDA
Faculty of Fisheries: Ir H. YEMPITA EFENDI
Faculty of Humanities: Dr PUSPAWATI
Faculty of Industrial Technology: Dr MULYANEF
Faculty of Law: ASTUTI PALUPI
Teacher Training Education and Science Faculty: Dr MARSIS

UNIVERSITAS DWIJENDRA

Jl. Kamboja 17, Denpasar, Bali
Telephone: (361) 224383
E-mail: info@undwi.ac.id
Internet: www.undwi.ac.id
Founded 1982
Private control
Rector: Dr I KETUT WIRAWAN
Vice-Rector I: Dr Ir PUTU GDE ERY SUARDANA
Vice-Rector II: Dra NI MADE SUARNINGSIH
Vice-Rector III: Drs IDA BAGUS RAI

DEANS
Faculty of Agriculture: Ir GEDE SEDANA
Faculty of Engineering: Ir IDA BAGUS GDE MANUABA
Faculty of Law: Dr PUTU DYATMIKAWATI
Faculty of Science Communication: Dra IDA AYU RATNA WESNAWATI
Faculty of Teaching and Science Education: Drs I MADE SILA

UNIVERSITAS EKASAKTI

Jl. Veteran Dalam, 26B, Padang, 25131
Telephone: (2751) 28859
E-mail: agussikki@yahoo.com
Internet: www.univ-ekasakti-pdg.ac.id
Founded 1973
Private control
Rector: Prof. Dr ANDI MUSTARI
Vice-Rector I: Dr AGUSSALIM MANGULUANG
Vice-Rector II: Prof. Dr NASRUN
Vice-Rector III: NURFAN AGUS
Librarian: Dra SAUFNI CHALID
Library of 8,648 titles

DEANS
Faculty of Agriculture: I KETUT BUDARAGA
Faculty of Computer Management Information: JUSMITA WERIZA
Faculty of Economics: TETI CHANDRAYANTI
Faculty of Engineering: Ir ABU RIZAL
Faculty of Law: Dr OTONG ROSADI
Faculty of Sastras: RAFLIS
Faculty of Social Science and Political Science: SUMARTONO
Faculty of Teacher Training: FEBY MEUTHIA YUSUF

UNIVERSITAS HKBP NOMMENSEN (Huria Kristen Batak Protestan Nommensen University)

Jl. Sutomo 4A, POB 1133, Medan
Telephone: (61) 4522922
E-mail: uhn@nommensen.org
Internet: www.nommensen.org
Founded 1954
Private control: Batak Christian Protestant Church
Language of instruction: Indonesian
Academic year: September to July
Rector: Ir B. RICSON SIMARMATA
Vice-Rector for Academic Affairs: Drs RAFLES D. TAMPUBOLON
Vice-Rector for Financial Affairs: Drs PANTAS SILABAN
Vice-Rector for Student Affairs: Ir HOTMAN MANURUNG
Dir for Community Service: Ir B. T. SIMANJORANG
Dir for Research: Dr Ir JONGKER TAMPUBOLON
Number of teachers: 310
Number of students: 7,549
Publication: *VISI* (scientific magazine)

DEANS
Faculty of Agriculture: Ir P. PARLIN LUMBANRAJA
Faculty of Animal Husbandry: Ir HERLINA SARAGI
Faculty of Arts: Drs BEN M. PASARIBU
Faculty of Economics: Drs ADANAN SILABAN
Faculty of Education: Dr TAGOR PANGARIBUAN
Faculty of Engineering: Ir SINDAK HUTAURUK
Faculty of Law: TULUS SIAMBATON
Faculty of Public and Business Admin.: Drs MONANG SITORUS

UNIVERSITAS IBNU CHALDUN JAKARTA

Jl. Pemuda I, Kav. 97, POB 1224, Rawamangun, Jakarta 13220
Telephone: (21) 4722059
E-mail: humas@ibnuchaldun.com
Internet: www.ibnuchaldun.com
Founded 1956
State control
Languages of instruction: Indonesian, English, Arabic
Academic year: September to June
Rector: Prof. Dr QOMARI ANWAR
Vice-Rector: Dr HARTINI SALAMAH
Vice-Rector: ANAS YANUN
Vice-Rector: ANTHONY HILMAN
Registrar: Dra ERWINA
Librarian: Ir M. FERYZAL
Number of teachers: 115
Number of students: 10,000
Publications: *Muqaddimah* (Learning about Islam), *Editorial Campus*

DEANS
Faculty of Agriculture: Ir SAPRI
Faculty of Communication: Drs NARSO
Faculty of Economics: Drs URHEN LUKMAN
Faculty of Islamic Religion: SUHARDIN
Faculty of Law: NURLELY DARWIS
Faculty of Social and Political Science: Drs AIDIL FITRI
Institute of Social Research: Dr ASDIH CHANIAGO

UNIVERSITAS IBN KHALDUN BOGOR

Jl. K. H. Sholeh Iskandar Km 2, POB 172, Bogor 16162
Telephone: (251) 356884
E-mail: rector@mail.uika-bogor.ac.id
Internet: www.uika-bogor.ac.id
Founded 1961
Private control
Language of instruction: Indonesian
Chancellor: Prof. Dr Ir H. AFFENDI ANWAR
Rector: Dr Ir SUNSUN SAEFULHAKIM
Head of Academic Admin.: Dra HERAWATI
Head of Gen. Admin.: Hj. TITING SUHARTI
Librarian: Dra TATI TARSITI
Number of teachers: 300
Number of students: 4,293
Publication: *Islamic Journal of Technology, Institutional and Humanity Development* (2 a year)

DEANS
Faculty of Economics: H. AHMAD MUBAROK
Faculty of Education: Drs YUSUF SHOBIRI
Faculty of Engineering: Dr Ir PRAWOTO
Faculty of Islamic Studies: Drs H. E. BAHRUDDIN
Faculty of Law: BARLY
Graduate School of Islamic Studies: Dr K. H. DIDIN HAFIDHUDDIN

UNIVERSITAS ISLAM INDONESIA
(Islamic University of Indonesia)

Gedung Rektorat, Jl. Kaliurang Km 14.5, Yogyakarta 55584
Telephone: (274) 898444
E-mail: rektorat@uii.ac.id
Internet: www.uii.ac.id
Founded 1945
Private control
Language of instruction: Indonesian
Academic year: July to June

Rector: Dr Luthfi Hasan
Vice-Rector for Academic Affairs: Dr S. F. Marbun
Vice-Rector for Admin. and Financial Affairs: Dr H. Muqodim
Vice-Rector for Collaborative Affairs: Dr A. Akhyar Adnan
Vice-Rector for Student Affairs: Ir H. Bachnas
Chief Admin. Officer: Drs H. Syafaruddin Alwi
Librarian: Dra Muryanti

Library of 73,000 vols
Number of teachers: 365
Number of students: 18,375

Publication: *UII News* (12 a year)

DEANS

Faculty of Civil Engineering and Planning: Prof. Dr Ir Widodo
Faculty of Economics: Drs Suwarsono
Faculty of Industrial Technology: Ir H. Bachrun Sutrisno
Faculty of Islamic Science: Drs H. Mudhofar Akhwan
Faculty of Law: Dr Jawahir Thontowi
Faculty of Mathematics and Science: Jaka Nugraha
Faculty of Medical Science: Prof. Dr Dr Rusdi Lamsuddin
Faculty of Psychology: Dr Sukarti

PROFESSORS

Ahmad Antono, Concrete Structures
Asymuni, H., Islamic Court
Atmadja, M. K., International Law
Baharuddin Lopa, Criminal Law
Bernadib, S. I., Methods of Educational Evaluation, Educational Philosophy
Chotib, H. A., Ushl al-Fiqh
Dahlan, H. Z., Principles of Islamic Law
Fatkhurrahman, History of Islam and Islamic Law
Haditono, S. R., Individual Psychology
Hardjoso, R., Irrigation
Hasan Poerbohadiwidjaja, Environmental Planning
Koesnoe, H. M., Private Procedural Law
Kusnadi Hardjosumantri, Environment Law
Mochtar Yahya, H., General Philosophy
Muh Zein, Method and Evaluation of Islamic Education
Muladi, Politics of Law
Parlindungan, A. P., Agrarian Law
Partadiredja, H. A., Indonesian Economy
Pragnyono, R., Fluid Mechanics
Purnomo, B., Criminal Law
Riyanto, B., Development Economy
Satjipto Rahardjo, Sociology of Law
Siti Rahayu, Psychology
Soedikno Mertokoesoemo, Civil Law, Jurisprudence
Soedirdjo, Educational Counselling, Curriculum Advancement
Soekanto, Business Policy
Soelistyo, International Economy
Soeparno, Analytical Geometry
Sri Sumantri, Constitutional Law
Sunardjo, R., Irrigation Technology
Suyuti, H. Z., Statistics
Syachran Basah, Administrative Law
Syafti Ma'arif, A., Islamic Cultural History
Tugiman, N., Indonesian Language
Umar, H. M., Modern Islamic Ideology
Umar Assasuddin, English
Warsito, Polymer Chemistry
Yusuf, H. H., Hadiths I, II, III

UNIVERSITAS ISLAM JAKARTA

Jl Balai Takyat, Utan Kayu, Kecamatan Matraman, Jakarta 13120
Telephone: (21) 8566451
E-mail: informasi@uid.ac.id
Internet: www.uid.ac.id
Founded 1951
Also faculty of Arabic studies

Pres.: Prof. Dr Soemedi
Rector: Prof. Dr Razali Usman
Registrar: Rasjidi Oesman
Librarian: Zainal Abidin

Number of teachers: 30
Number of students: 310

DEANS

Faculty of Economic Management: Drs H. Burhanuddin
Faculty of Industrial Engineering: Ir Achmad Sutrisna
Faculty of Islamic Studies: Prof. Dr H. Aziz Fachrurrozi
Faculty of Law: Dra Farhana

UNIVERSITAS ISLAM NUSANTARA

Jl. Soekarno-Hatta 530, POB 1579, Bandung 40286
Telephone: (22) 7509656
E-mail: info@uninus.ac.id
Internet: www.uninus.ac.id
Founded 1959 as Universitas Nahdlatul Ulama, present name 1976
Private control
Languages of instruction: English, Indonesian
Academic year: September to August

Chancellor: Mayjen H. Achmad Rustandi
Rector: Dr Didin Wahidin
Deputy Rector: Dr Suhendra Yusuf
Deputy Rector: Dr Gatot Yusuf Effendi
Deputy Rector: Dr Husen Saeful Insan
Registrar: Drs Salim Noor
Librarian: Drs Undang Sudarsana

Number of teachers: 456
Number of students: 8,463

Publications: *Literat* (4 a year), *Nusantara Educational Review* (3 a year), *Suara UNINUS* (4 a year)

DEANS

Faculty of Agriculture: Ir Okke Rosmaladewi
Faculty of Communication Sciences: Drs Yoyo Kartoyo
Faculty of Economics: Drs Wahdi Suardi
Faculty of Education and Teachers Training: Dr Hendi Suhendraya
Faculty of Engineering and Technology: Ir Asep Wasid
Faculty of Islamology: Drs Arifin Sanusi
Faculty of Law: Drs Chandra Iswara
Graduate School of Educational Management (Doctoral Programme): Prof. Dedi Mulyasana
Graduate School of Educational Management (Masters Programme): Prof. Dr E. Mulyasa
Graduate School of Islamic Education (Masters Programme): Prof. Dr Nurachman
Graduate School of Law (Masters Programme): Prof. Dr Dedi Ismatullah

PROFESSORS

Faculty of Agriculture:
Aisyah, H., Pedology
Sadeli, H.

Faculty of Communication Sciences:
Husein, S. I., Communications Sciences

Faculty of Economics:
Surachman, H., Management Economics

Faculty of Education and Literature:
Effendy, E. R., Mathematics
Emuh, Arabic
Faisal, Y. A., Indonesian Literature
Rusyana, Y., Indonesian Literature
Slamet, H. A., Indonesian Language
Soeharto, B., Non-Formal Education
Syamsuddin, Curriculum Development and Methodology

Faculty of Engineering:
Handali, D., Mathematics
Sumarno, Mathematics

Faculty of Islamology:
Djatnika, H. R., Islamology
Helmy, H., Islamology
Salimuddin, Islamology

Faculty of Law:
Basyah, S., Public Administration Law
Rasyidi, L., Family Law
Sanusi, H. A., Law, Public Administration and Education

UNIVERSITAS ISLAM RIAU
(Islamic University of Riau)

Jl. Kaharuddin Nasution 113, Perhentian, Marpoyan, Pekanbaru, Riau 28284
Telephone: (761) 674834
E-mail: nataugm@yahoo.com
Internet: uir.ac.id
Founded 1962
Academic year: July to June

Rector: Prof. Dr Muchtar Ahmad
Vice-Rector I: Prof. Dr Dadang Iskandar
Vice-Rector II: Amir Hasan
Vice-Rector III: Ariffien Mansyoer
Vice-Rector IV: Drs Suardi Loekman
Librarian: Firdaus

Library of 5,150 vols
Number of teachers: 660 (160 full-time, 500 part-time)
Number of students: 7,391

Publications: *Alam* (4 a year), *Dinamika Pertanian* (4 a year), *Presfektif* (2 a year), *Saintis* (2 a year), *Siasat* (2 a year)

DEANS

Faculty of Agriculture: Ir T. Iskandar Johan
Faculty of Economics: Drs Shahdanur
Faculty of Education: Drs Nazirun
Faculty of Engineering: Ali Musnal
Faculty of Islamic Theology: Ali Nur
Faculty of Law: Arifin Boer
Faculty of Political and Sociological Sciences: Zaini Ali

UNIVERSITAS ISLAM SUMATERA UTARA
(Islamic University of North Sumatra)

Jl Karya Bakti No 34, Pangkalan Masyhur, Medan 20217
Telephone: (61) 7866932
E-mail: infokom@uisu.ac.id
Internet: www.uisu.ac.id
Founded 1952
Private control
Language of instruction: Indonesian
Academic year: July to June

Chancellor: Brig.-Gen. (retd) H. A. Manaf Lubis
Rector: Dr Ir Mhd Asaad
Vice-Rector: Syofyan
Vice-Rector: Drs Yanhar Jamaluddin
Vice-Rector: Dra Asnawati Matondang
Vice-Rector: Drs H. Syarifuddin El Hayat
Registrar: Drs Abdul Hakim Siregar

Librarian: Drs SUDIAR SUDARGO
Number of teachers: 800
Number of students: 10,000
Publications: *Al Jamiah-UISU* (3 a year), *Jurnal Tijarah Edisi* (2 a year, online, fe.uisu.ac.id/ejournal)

DEANS

Faculty of Agriculture: Ir MHD NUH
Faculty of Economics: Drs AHMAD GHAZALI
Faculty of Education and Teaching: Drs LIESNA ANDRIANY
Faculty of Engineering: Ir H. M. ICHWAN NASUTION
Faculty of English Literature: Drs MISRAN SUDIONO
Faculty of Islamic Studies: Drs BURHANUDDIN SITOMPUL
Faculty of Law: ANAITULLAH
Faculty of Medicine: Dr H. ASWIN SOEFI LUBIS
Faculty of Political Science: Drs DANAN JAYA

UNIVERSITAS JAYABAYA

Campus A Jl. Pulomas Selatan kav 23, Jakarta Timur 13210
Telephone: (21) 4700877
Campus C Jl. Raya Bogor km 28, Cimanggis, Jakarta Timur 13210
Telephone: (21) 8719958
E-mail: info@jayabaya.ac.id
Internet: www.jayabaya.ac.id
Founded 1958
Chancellor: Dr H. MOESLIM TAHER
Rector: Prof. H. AMIR SANTOSO
Vice-Rector I: Hj. POPON SJARIF ARIFIN
Vice-Rector II: Drs H. SYAHID SUHANDI AZIS
Vice-Rector III: MANSYUR KARDI
Number of teachers: 782
Number of students: 15,000

DEANS

Faculty of Communication Science: DARMA SETIAWAN
Faculty of Economics: Prof. Dr Hj. MIRRIAM
Faculty of Law: Prof. Dr H. YUDHA BHAKTI
Faculty of Law and Management: H. INDARTONO RIVAI
Faculty of Political and Social Sciences: H. AMIR SANTOSO
Faculty of Technology: DARMA SETIAWAN

UNIVERSITAS KADER BANGSA PALEMBANG

Campus A Jl. Mayjend. H. M. Ryacudu 88, Palembang
Telephone: (711) 510173
Internet: www.ukb.ac.id
Founded 2000
Private control
Programmes in engineering, health studies, legal studies, midwifery, pharmacy
Rector: H. T. WATHAN
Vice-Rector I: FERRY PRESCA
Vice-Rector II: Dr Hj. IRZANITA
Vice-Rector III: AHMAD DINAR

UNIVERSITAS KATOLIK INDONESIA ATMA JAYA

Semanggi Campus Jl. Jend. Sudirman 51, Jakarta 12930
Telephone: (21) 5703306
Pluit Campus Jl. Pluit Raya 2, Jakarta 14440
Telephone: (21) 6691944
E-mail: rek@atmajaya.ac.id
Internet: www.atmajaya.ac.id
Founded 1960
Languages of instruction: Indonesian, English
Academic year: July to June
Chair. of Board: Drs R. DJOKOPRANOTO
Rector: Prof. Dr BERNADETTE N. SETIADI
Vice-Rector: Ir ST. NUGROHO KRISTONO
Vice-Rector: Dr MARCELLINUS MARCELLINO
Vice-Rector: Drs PETRUS PIUS SALAMIN
Vice-Rector: Dr LILIANA SUGIHARTO
Librarian: Dr DIAO AI LIEN
Library of 70,260 vols
Number of teachers: 1,071
Number of students: 13,452
Publications: *Atma nan Jaya* (science, 3 a year), *Gloria Juris* (law and human rights, 2 a year), *Jurnal Administrasi dan Bisnis* (administration and business, 4 a year), *Jurnal Ekonomi dan Bisnis* (economics and business, 2 a year), *Majalah Kedokteran* (medical science, 3 a year), *Metris* (science and technology, 4 a year), *Respons* (social ethics, 2 a year)

DEANS

Faculty of Business Administration: Dr POL A. Y. AGUNG NUGROHO
Faculty of Economics: Drs SOFIAN SUGIOKO
Faculty of Engineering: Dr M. M. LANNY W. PANDJAITAN
Faculty of Law: ANTONIUS P. S. WIBOWO
Faculty of Medicine: Dr SATYA JOEWANA
Faculty of Psychology: Dr ENGELINA TANZIL BONANG
Faculty of Teacher Training and Education: Dr LAURA F. N. SUDARNOTO
Faculty of Technobiology: Prof. Dr ANTONIUS SUWANTO
Graduate School: Dr ALOISIUS AGUS NUGROHO

UNIVERSITAS KATOLIK PARAHYANGAN (Parahyangan Catholic University)

Ciumbuleuit 94, Bandung 40141
Telephone: (22) 2032655
E-mail: humas@unpar.ac.id
Internet: www.unpar.ac.id
Founded 1955
Private control
Languages of instruction: Indonesian, English
Academic year: August to June
Chair. for Board of Trustees: Prof. Dr Ir B. S. KUSBIANTORO
Rector: Prof. ROBERTUS WAHYUDI TRIWEKO
Vice-Rector for Academic Affairs: Dr PIUS SUGENG PRASETYO
Vice-Rector for Resources Affairs: Dra J. DHARMA LESMONO
Vice-Rector for Students and Alumni Affairs: Dr LAURENTIUS TARPIN
Librarian: Dra SISKA TAMPUBOLON
Library of 123,937 vols, 2,733 CD-ROMS
Number of teachers: 543 (387 full-time, 156 part-time)
Number of students: 9,516
Publications: *Bina Ekonomi* (4 a year), *Jurnal CEBIS* (2 a year), *Melintas* (4 a year), *Profil* (4 a year), *Pro Justitia* (4 a year), *Potensia* (4 a year), *Rekasaya* (4 a year), *Research Journal* (2 a year), *Transportasi* (3 a year)

DEANS

Faculty of Economics: Dr ELIZABETH TIUR MANURUNG
Faculty of Engineering: Dr ANASTASIA CAROLINE SUTANDI
Faculty of Industrial Technology: Dr PAULUS SUKAPTO HEATUBUN
Faculty of Information Technology and Science: Dr PAULUS CAHYONO TJIANG
Faculty of Law: Prof. Dr SENTOSA SEMBIRING
Faculty of Philosophy: Dr HARIMANTO SURYANUGRAHA
Faculty of Social and Political Sciences: Dr MANGADAR SITUMORANG
Graduate and Postgraduate Programmes: Prof. Dr BAMBANG SUGIHARTO

PROFESSORS

BROTOSISWOJO, B. S., Computer Physics
DIRJOSISWORO, S., Law
DJAJAPUTERA, A., Civil Engineering
NIMPOENO, J. S., Psychology
RAHARDJO, P. P., Geotechnology
SIDHARTA, B. A., Law
SIREGAR, S., Architecture
SJAFRUDDIN, A., Law
SOELARNOSIDJI, D., Geotechnology in Civil Engineering
SUHARTO, IGN., Chemical Engineering
SUNDJAJA, R. S., Management
SURJOATMONO, B., Civil Engineering
WINARDI, Economics

UNIVERSITAS KLABAT

Airmadidi, Manado 95371
Telephone: (431) 891035
E-mail: email@unklab.ac.id
Internet: www.unklab.ac.id
Founded 1965
Private control
Language of instruction: Indonesian
Academic year: August to June
Rector: Dr AMELIUS TOMMY MAMBU
Publications: *Computer Journal*, *JIBE*, *JIU*

DEANS

School of Agronomy: MAX SAHETAPY
School of Computer Science: EDSON YAHUDA PUTRA
School of Economics: Dr BENNY LULE
School of Education: BILL WULLUR
School of Secretarial Science: ANTJE BERTHA DIMPUDUS
School of Theology: Dr MAX HART WAURAN

UNIVERSITAS KRISNADWIPAJANA

Jl. Raya Jati Waringin, Pondok Gede, Jakarta 13077
Telephone: (21) 8462229
E-mail: humas@unkris.ac.id
Founded 1952
Language of instruction: Indonesian
Academic year: February to December
Rector: Dr LODEWIJK GULTOM
Vice-Rector I: PUGUH SANTOSO
Vice-Rector II: Hj. LINDA ISMAIL
Vice-Rector III: Drs EDWARD DOLOKSARIBU
Dir for Postgraduate Programmes: Prof. Dr RUSLI RAMLI
Sec.: WAYAN SUGIYANA
Librarian: Dr DASPAN
Number of teachers: 128
Number of students: 2,000

DEANS

Faculty of Economics: Drs MUHADI RIYANTO
Faculty of Law: Dr LODEWIJK GULTOM
Faculty of Science Administration: Drs JACK R. SIDABUTAR
Faculty of Technology: RUSJDI HADJERAT

UNIVERSITAS KRISTEN INDONESIA (Christian University of Indonesia)

Jl. Mayjen Sutoyo 2, Cawang, Jakarta 13630
Telephone: (21) 8092425
E-mail: humas-uki@uki.ac.id
Internet: www.uki.ac.id
Founded 1953
Rector: Prof. Dr K. TUNGGUL SIRAIT
Vice-Rector for Academic Affairs: Dr A. S. L. RAMPEN
Vice-Rector for Admin. Planning and Devt: E. GUNAWAN
Vice-Rector for Student Affairs: A. SIREGAR

Number of teachers: 739
Number of students: 8,000
Publications: *Dialektika, Dinamika Pendidikan, Emas, Honeste Vivere, Jurnal Ekonomi, Logos, UKI Bulletin*

DEANS
Faculty of Economics: Drs A. ZABUA
Faculty of Education: TOGAP LINANJUNTAK
Faculty of English Language and Literature: Dr L. S. BANGUN
Faculty of Law: Dr BERNARD HUTABARAK
Faculty of Medicine: Dr S. M. L. TORUAN
Faculty of Social and Political Science: Prof. Dr PAYUNG BANGUN
Faculty of Technology: Dr A. SOEBAGIO

UNIVERSITAS KRISTEN MARANATHA
(Maranatha Christian University)

Jl. Prof. Suria Sumantri 65, Bandung 40164
Telephone: (22) 2012186
E-mail: humas@maranatha.edu
Internet: www.marantha.edu
Founded 1965
Language of instruction: Indonesian
Academic year: September to August
Rector: Prof. Dr Ir H. P. SEPTORATNO SIREGAR
Vice-Rector I: Ir RUDY WAWOLUMAJA
Vice-Rector II: Ir NOEK SULANDARI
Vice-Rector III: Pdt. FERLY DAVID
Vice-Rector IV: Dr FELIX KASIM
Number of teachers: 500
Number of students: 12,000
Publications: *Journal Kedoktoran* (Medicine Journal, 1 a year), *Majalah Ilmiah Maranatha* (Maranatha Scientific Magazine, 4 a year), *Media Komunikasi Maranatha* (Maranatha Communication Media, 3 a year)

DEANS
Faculty of Art and Design (Undergraduate Programme): Dr GAI SUHARJA
Faculty of Economics (Undergraduate Programme): TEDY WAHYUSAPUTRA
Faculty of Engineering, (Undergraduate Programme): Prof. Dr Ir BENJAMIN SOENARKO
Faculty of Information Technology (Undergraduate Programme): RADIANT VICTOR IMBAR
Faculty of Letters (Undergraduate Programme): Drs EDWARD ALDRICH LUKMAN
Faculty of Medicine (Undergraduate Programme): Dr SURJA TANURAHARDJA
Faculty of Psychology (Undergraduate Programme): Drs R. SANOESI SUSANTO
Master of Accounting (Postgraduate Programme): RIKI MARTUSA
Master of Management (Postgraduate Programme): Dra IKA GUNAWAN
Master of Psychology (Postgraduate Programme): Dr PARWATI SUPANGAT

UNIVERSITAS KRISTEN SATYA WACANA
(Satya Wacana Christian University)

Jl. Diponegoro 52–60, Salatiga 50711
Telephone: (298) 321212
E-mail: humas@adm.uksw.edu
Internet: www.uksw.edu
Founded 1956
Languages of instruction: Indonesian, English(for special programmes only)
Academic year: August to July
Rector: Prof. Rev. JOHN A. TITALEY
Deputy Rector I: Prof. Ir Dr DANNY MANONGGA
Deputy Rector II: (vacant)
Deputy Rector III: YAFET Y. W. RISSY
Deputy Rector IV: MARTHA NANDARI
Deputy Rector V: Dr FERDY S. RONDONUWU
Registrar: SUHARYADI
Librarian: EVALIEN SURYATI
Number of teachers: 285 (full-time)
Number of students: 10,975
Publications: *Agric* (2 a year), *Cakrawala* (2 a year), *Ekonomi dan Bisnis* (2 a year), *English.edu* (2 a year), *Musik* (2 a year), *Prosiding Seminar Nasional Sains dan Pendidikan Sains* (1 a year), *Satya Widya* (2 a year), *Techne* (2 a year)

DEANS
Faculty of Agriculture and Business: Prof. Dr Ir SONNY HERU PRIYANTO
Faculty of Biology: Dr RULLY ADI NUGROHO
Faculty of Communication and Social Sciences: Dr PAMERDI GIRI WILOSO
Faculty of Economics and Business: Dr HARI SUNARTO
Faculty of Education and Teacher Training: Dr BAMBANG S. SULASMONO
Faculty of Health Science: Dr FERRY F. KARWUR
Faculty of Information Technology: ANDEKA ROCKY TANAAMAH
Faculty of Language and Literature: HENDRO SETIAWAN HUSADA
Faculty of Law: M. HARYANTO
Faculty of Performing Arts: PAULUS DWI HANANTO
Faculty of Psychology: BERTA ESTI ARI PRASETYA
Faculty of Science and Mathematics: LUSIAWATI DEWI
Faculty of Theology: Dr Rev. RENOWATI
Faculty of Engineering and Computer Science: HANDOKO
Postgraduate Programmes: Prof. Dr KUTUT SUWONDO

UNIVERSITAS MAHAPUTRA MUHAMMAD YAMIN SOLOK

Jl. Raya Koto Baru 7, Solok 27361
Telephone: (755) 20128
E-mail: info@ummy.ac.id
Private control
Programmes in accounting, agribusiness, agrotechnology, biology, economic development, legal studies, livestock, management and mathematics

UNIVERSITAS MEDAN AREA

Campus 1 Jl. Kolam 1, Medan 20223
Telephone: (61) 7366878
Campus 2 Jl. Jend Gatot Subroto 395, Medan 20118
Telephone: (61) 4567330
Campus 3 Jl. Sei Serayu 70A, Medan 20118
Telephone: (61) 8214875
E-mail: uma001@indosat.net.id
Internet: www.universitasmedanarea.com
Founded 1983
Private control
Faculties of agriculture, engineering, law, social and political sciences and psychology

UNIVERSITAS METHODIST INDONESIA

Campus 1 Jl. Hang Tuah 8, Medan 20152
Telephone: (61) 4536735
Campus 2 Jl. Setia Budi Pasar II, Tg. Sari
E-mail: info@umi-mdn.ac.id
Internet: umi-medan.info
Founded 1969
Private control
Rector: Dr THOMSON P. NADAPDAP
Vice-Rector I: Prof. Dr J. NAIBAHO
Vice-Rector II: Dr P. SIMANJUNTAK
Vice-Rector III: Drs OCTAVIAN RAGNAR SITORUS

DEANS
Faculty of Agriculture: Ir BERTON E. LUMBANTOBING
Faculty of Computer Science: Drs LISTON SIHITE
Faculty of Economics: Drs RAFIDIN HUTAPEA
Faculty of Literature: Drs P. SIMANJUNTAK
Faculty of Medicine: Dr HOPHOPTUA SIAHAAN

UNIVERSITAS MUHAMMADIYAH ACEH

Jl. Muhammadiyah 91, Desa Bathoh Lueng Bata, Banda Aceh 23245
Telephone: (651) 31583
E-mail: info@unmuha.ac.id
Founded 1969
Private control
Library of 1,300 titles

UNIVERSITAS MUHAMMADIYAH JAKARTA

Campus A Jl. K. H. Ahmad Dahlan, Cirendeu Ciputat, Jakarta Selatan
Telephone: (21) 7401894
Campus B Jl. Cempaka Putih Tengah 27, Jakarta Pusat
Telephone: (21) 4256024
E-mail: info@umj.ac.id
Internet: www.umj.ac.id
Faculties of agriculture, economics, law, medicine, religion, social and political sciences, technology
Rector: AGUS SUNARTO

UNIVERSITAS MUHAMMADIYAH KUPANG

Jl. K. H. Ahmad Dahlan 17, Kota Kupang, Kupang, Nusa Tengarra Timur
Telephone: (380) 833693
E-mail: info@unmuh-kupang.ac.id
Internet: www.unmuh-kupang.ac.id
Founded 1987
Private control
Rector: Prof. Dr SANDI MARYANTO
Library of 5,282 vols, 15,882 periodicals

DEANS
Fishery Faculty: RUSYDI

UNIVERSITAS MUHAMMADIYAH MALANG
(Muhammadiyah University of Malang)

Jl. Raya Tlogomas 246, Malang 65144
Telephone: (341) 464318
E-mail: webmaster@unix.umm.ac.id
Internet: www.umm.ac.id
Founded 1966
Languages of instruction: Indonesian, English
Academic year: September to June
Rector: Drs H. MUHADJIR EFFENDY
Vice-Rector for Academic Affairs: Ir H. MUH. HAMZAH
Vice-Rector for Financial Affairs: Drs H. WAKIDI
Vice-Rector for Student Affairs: Ir H. ALI SAIFULLAH
Chief of Academic Admin.: Ir DAMAT
Chief of Public Admin.: Drs H. FAUZAN
Librarian: WAHJOE DWI PRIJONO
Number of teachers: 816
Number of students: 20,274
Publications: *Bestari Journal* (4 a year), *Bestari Tabloid* (12 a year)

DEANS
Faculty of Agriculture: Ir MISBAH RUHIYAT

Faculty of Animal Husbandry: Ir ABDUL MALIK
Faculty of Economics: Drs WAHYU HIDAYAT RIYANTO
Faculty of Engineering: Ir SUNARTO
Faculty of Islamic Education: Drs MOH. NURHAKIM
Faculty of Law: MOKH. HAJIH
Faculty of Medicine: Ir H. MUH. HAMZAH (acting)
Faculty of Psychology: Drs LATIPUN
Faculty of Social and Political Science: Dra VINA SALVIANA
Faculty for Teacher Training and Education: Drs AHSANUL IN'AM

UNIVERSITAS MUHAMMADIYAH MATARAM

Jl. K. H. A. Dahlan 1, Pegesangan, Mataram
Telephone: (370) 633723
E-mail: contact@ummat.ac.id

Founded 1980
Private control

Rector: Ir H. SUHARTO TJITROHADJONO

Library of 8,500 titles
Number of teachers: 80
Number of students: 1,930

UNIVERSITAS MUHAMMADIYAH SUMATERA UTARA

Jl. Kapt. Mukhtar Basri 3, Medan 20238
Telephone: (61) 6619056
Internet: www.umsu.ac.id

Founded 1957
Private control

Rector: H. BAHDIN NUR TANJUNG
Vice-Rector I: Drs H. ARMANSYAH
Vice-Rector II: H. SUHARWADI K. LUBIS
Vice-Rector III: Drs AGUSSANI

DEANS

Faculty of Agriculture: Ir ALRIDIWIRSAH
Faculty of Economics: PASARIBU ZULASPAN TUPTI
Faculty of Engineering: RAHMATULLAH
Faculty of Islamic Religion: AKRIM
Faculty of Law: FARID WAJDI
Faculty of Medicine: TAUFIQ
Faculty of Social and Political Sciences: R. KUSNADI
Faculty of Teacher Training and Education: Hj. NUR'AIN LUBIS

UNIVERSITAS MUHAMMADIYAH TAPANULI SELATAN DI PADANG SIDEMPUAN

Jl. Sutan Moch. Arief 32, Padang Sidempuan, Tapanuli Selatan 22716
Telephone: (634) 21696

Founded 1983
Private control

Rector: H. MARAGINDA HARAHAP

UNIVERSITAS MUSLIM NUSANTARA AL-WASHLIYAH

Medan
E-mail: admin@umnaw.com
Internet: www.umnaw.com
Private control

Rector: Prof. Hj. Sri SULISTYAWATI

DEANS

Faculty of Agriculture: Ir ERNITA
Faculty of Economics: ARBY BACHTIAR
Faculty of Law: PURBA NELVITIA
Faculty of Mathematics and Natural Sciences: PANDAPOTAN NASUTION
Faculty of Sastras: S. S. SUFATMI
Faculty of Teacher Training and Education: Drs ULIAN BARUS

UNIVERSITAS NAHDLATUL WATHAN MATARAM

Jl. Kaktus 1–3, Mataram 82137
Telephone: (370) 641275
E-mail: mataram.unw@gmail.com
Internet: unwmataram.ac.id
Private control

UNIVERSITAS NASIONAL

Jl. Sawo Manila, Pasar Minggu, Jakarta 12520
Telephone: (21) 7806700
E-mail: info@unas.ac.id
Internet: www.unas.ac.id

Founded 1949
Private control
Language of instruction: Indonesian
Academic year: October to August

Rector: Drs EL AMRY BERMAWI PUTERA
Vice-Rector for Academic Affairs: Dr MOCH. RUM ALIM
Vice-Rector for Research and Devt Community Services: Drs ERNAWATI SINAGA
Vice-Rector for Financial and Gen. Admin. Affairs: Drs EKO SUGIYANTO
Vice-Rector for Int. Cooperation and Students Affairs: Drs FALDY RASYIDIE
Univ. Librarian: Drs FATHUDDIN

Library of 32,181 vols, 20,206 books, 205 magazines and journals, 12 bulletins, 11,695 theses
Number of teachers: 683
Number of students: 7,000

Publications: *Ilmu Dan Budaya* (social science, 12 a year), *Jurnal Poelitik* (political science), *Jurrnal Sawo Manila* (literature)

DEANS

Faculty of Agriculture: Ir TRI WALUYO
Faculty of Biology: Drs IMRAN S. L. TOBING
Faculty of Economics: SURYONO EFENDI
Faculty of Engineering and Science: Ir AJAT SUDRAJAT
Faculty of Health Science: Dr ROSMAWATY LUBIS
Faculty of Informatics, Communications and Technology: Dr ISKANDAR FITRI
Faculty of Law: SURAJIMAN
Faculty of Literature and Languages: Drs WAHYU WIBOWO
Faculty of Social and Political Science: Prof. Drs H. B. TAMAM ACHDA

UNIVERSITAS NGURAH RAI DENPASAR

Jl. Padma Penatih, Denpasar, Timur
Telephone: (361) 468349
E-mail: fisip@unr.ac.id
Internet: www.unr.ac.id

Founded 1981
Private control

UNIVERSITAS PAKUAN

Jl. Pakuan, POB 452, Bogor 16143
Telephone: (251) 8312206
E-mail: info@unpak.ac.id
Internet: www.unpak.ac.id

Founded 1961

Chancellor: Dr H. MASHUDI
Rector: ACHMAD SUBROTO
Sec.: R. H. NATANEGARA

Number of teachers: 60
Number of students: 350

DEANS

Faculty of Economics: Drs USMAN ZAKARIA
Faculty of Law: BINTATAR SINAGA
Faculty of Mathematics and Natural Science: Ir SOEDARSONO
Faculty of Technology: DJAUHARI NOOR

UNIVERSITAS PANCASILA

Srengseng Sawah, Jagakarsa, Pasar Minggu, Jakarta Selatan 12640
Telephone: (21) 7270086
E-mail: info@univpancasila.ac.id
Internet: www.univpancasila.ac.id

Founded 1966
Language of instruction: Indonesian
Academic year: September to August

Chair.: Dr Ir SISWONO YUDOHUSODO
Rector: Dr EDIE TOET HENDRATNO
Vice-Rector for Academic Affairs: Ir SUHARSO
Vice-Rector for Finance and Admin.: Dra DEWI TRIRAHAYU
Vice-Rector for Student Affairs: Dr MUHAMMAD IBRAHIM
Vice-Rector for Cooperation and Venture: Drs SUROTO

Library of 30,906 vols
Number of teachers: 472
Number of students: 8,000

Publications: *Jurnal Farmasi*, *Jurnal Teknik*, *Media Humas*, *Retorika*, *Suara Ekonomi*

DEANS

Faculty of Communication: Prof. Dr ANDI MUHAMMAD
Faculty of Economy: Dr TRI WIDYASTUTI
Faculty of Engineering: Ir FAUZRI FAHIMUDDIN
Faculty of Law: Dr INDAH HARLINA
Faculty of Pharmacy: Drs I. WAYAN REDJA
Faculty of Tourism: Dr RIADIKE MASTRA

UNIVERSITAS PEMBANGUNAN PANCABUDI

Jl. Jend. Gatot Subroto, Km 4, 5 Simpang Sei Sikambing, Medan, 20122
Telephone: (61) 8455571
E-mail: unpab@pancabudi.ac.id
Internet: www.pancabudi.ac.id

Founded 1961
Private control
Academic year: July to June

Rector: Mag. H. MUHAMMAD ISA INDRAWAN
Vice-Rector for Academic Affairs: Mag. SAMRIN
Vice-Rector for Admin. and Finance: Mag. SAIMARA SEBAYANG
Vice-Rector for Student Affairs: Mag. RIADIONO
Vice-Rector for Cooperation and Business: Mag. INDRAJAYA LUBIS

Number of teachers: 191
Number of students: 6,000

DEANS

Faculty of Agriculture: Mag. MARAHADI SIREGAR
Faculty of Economic Studies: Mag. MUHAMAD TOYIB DAULAY
Faculty of Islamic Studies: Mag. MUHAMMAD JAMIL
Faculty of Law: Mag. RIADIONO
Faculty of Metaphysics: Mag. M. JAMIL
Faculty of Technology: Mag. LENI MARLINA

UNIVERSITAS PGRI KUPANG

Jl. Anggur 10 Naikoten I, Kupang 85118
Telephone: (380) 821824
E-mail: pgrintt@yahoo.com

UNIVERSITAS SAMAWA

Jl. Raya Sering, Sumbawa, Besar
Telephone: (371) 625848
E-mail: unsasumbawa@yahoomail.com
Private control

UNIVERSITAS SERAMBI MEKKAH

Jl. Tengku Imum Lueng Bata Desa Bathoh, Banda Aceh 23249
Telephone: (651) 26160
Internet: serambimekkah.ac.id
Founded 1985
Private control
Rector: Prof. Dr M. ISA SULAIMAN

UNIVERSITAS SISINGAMANGARAJA XII TAPANULI UTARA DI SIBORONG-BORONG

Tapanuli Utara, Siborongborong
Telephone: (633) 41017
Founded 1987
Private control
Rector: Ir ADRIANI SIAHAAN
Vice-Rector: Ir ARVITA SIHALOHO
Vice-Rector: Ir T. B. PAKPAHAN
Vice-Rector: Drs MAULIATE SIMORANGKIR

DEANS

Faculty of Agriculture: ELSERIA SIBURIAN
Faculty of Economics: Dr AGUSNI PASARIBU
Faculty of Engineering: Ir M. SIAHAAN
Faculty of Law: TUNGGUL SIMORANGKIR
Faculty of Teacher Training and Education: Drs DONVER PANGGABEAN

UNIVERSITAS SULTAN AGENG TIRTAYASA

Jl Raya Jakarta KM 4, Pakupatan, Serang, Banten
Telephone: (254) 280330
E-mail: info@untirta.ac.id
Internet: www.untirta.ac.id
Founded 2001
Private control
Faculties of economics, engineering
Rector: Ir RAHMAN ABDULLAH

UNIVERSITAS TABANAN

Jl. Wagimin 8, Kediri, Tabanan, Bali
Telephone: (361) 811605
Founded 1981
Private control
Rector: Ir IDA BAGUS GDE WIRAKUSUMA
Library of 1,901 vols, 2,356 periodicals

UNIVERSITAS TRIKARYA

Jl. Gaperta Ujung 58, Perladangan Helvetia, Medan Helvetia, Medan 20124
Telephone: (61) 8450419
E-mail: univ_trikarya@plasa.com
Founded 2002
Private control

UNIVERSITAS TRISAKTI

Jl. Kyai Tapa 1, Grogol, Jakarta 11440
Telephone: (21) 5663232
E-mail: sekun@trisakti.ac.id
Internet: www.trisakti.ac.id
Founded 1965
Language of instruction: Indonesian
Academic year: September to August
Rector: Prof. Dr THOBY MUTIS
Vice-Rector for Academic Affairs: Prof. Dr H.YUSWAR Z BASRI,
Vice-Rector for Cooperation and Human Resources: Ir ASRI NUGRAHANTI
Vice-Rector for Personnel, Admin. and Finance: Prof. Dr ITJANG D. GUNAWAN
Vice-Rector for Student Affairs: H. I. KOMANG SUKA'ARSANA
Secretariat: H. SOFAN
Head of Library: Dra FARIDA SALIM
Number of teachers: 2,681 (1,691 full-time, 701 part-time)
Number of students: 30,754
Publication: *Masyarakat Kampus* (24 a year)

DEANS

Faculty of Art and Design: Prof. Drs YUSUF AFFENDI DJALARI
Faculty of Civil Engineering and Planning: Dr Ir EKA SEDIADI RASYAD
Faculty of Dentistry: Dr BAMBANG S. TRENGGONO
Faculty of Earth and Energy Technology: Ir H. MOH THAMRIN
Faculty of Economics: Prof. Dr FARIDA JASFAR
Faculty of Industrial Technology: Ir DOCKY SARASWATI
Faculty of Landscape Architecture and Environmental Technology: Ir IDA BAGUS RABINDRA
Faculty of Law: ENDAR PULUNGAN
Faculty of Medicine: Prof. JULIUS E. SURYAWIDJAJA

UNIVERSITAS VETERAN REPUBLIK INDONESIA

Jl. Baruga Raya Kampus II, Ujung Pandang
Telephone: (411) 491203
Internet: www.uvri.ac.id
Faculties of education, history, law

UNIVERSITAS WARMADEWA (Warmadewa University)

Jalan Terompong No 24, Tanjung Bungkak, Denpasar, Bali
Telephone: (361) 223858
E-mail: info@warmadewa.ac.id
Internet: www.warmadewa.ac.id
Founded 1984
Private control
Academic year: September to August
Rector: Prof. Dr I. MADE SUKARSA
Vice-Rector I: Drs I. NYOMAN KARDANA
Vice-Rector II: IDA BAGUS UDAYANA PUTRA
Vice-Rector III: Ir A. A. NGURAH MAYUN WIRAJAYA
Library of 10,323 vols
Number of teachers: 362
Number of students: 4,996
Publications: *Gema Agro*, *Kertha Wicaksana*, *KRISNA*, *Sadhana Sastra*, *Sarathi*, *Singhadwala*, *Sintesa*, *UNDAGI*, *VISI Ekonomika*, *Wacana Ekonomi*, *Wicaksana*

DEANS

Faculty of Agriculture: I. NYOMAN KACA
Faculty of Economics: I. GUSTI NGURAH SANJAYA
Faculty of Engineering: I. WAYAN PARWATA
Faculty of Law: NI LUH MADE MAHENDRAWATI
Faculty of Literature: Drs NYOMAN SUJAYA
Faculty of Medical and Health Sciences: Prof. Dr D. P. WIDJANA
Faculty of Social and Political Sciences: Drs I. WAYAN SUDEMEN
Faculty of Post Graduate: Prof. Dr GEDE SURANAYA PANDIT

PROFESSORS

ARTYA, I. N., Medicine and Health Sciences
JENDRA, I. W.
PANDIT, I. G. S., Agriculture
RUNA, I. W., Engineering
SUKARSA, I. M., Economics
SUTRISINA, P., Medicine and Health Sciences
WIDJANA, D. P., Medicine and Health Sciences

Institutes

ABFI Institute Perbanas: Jl. Perbanas, Karet Kuningan, Setiabudi, Jakarta 12940; tel. (21) 5252533; e-mail info@perbanasinstitute.ac.id; internet www.perbanasinstitute.ac.id; f. 2007, by merger of Sekolah Tinggi Ilmu Ekonomi (College of Economics, f. 1969) and Sekolah Tinggi Manajemen Informatika dan Komputer (College of Information Management and Computers, f. 1993); offers programmes in banking, general management and risk management; Rector Dr Ir FATCHUDIN; Vice-Rector for Academic Affairs Dr STEPH SUBANIDJA; Vice-Rector for Graduate Programmes Prof. Dr ADLER HAYMANS MANURUNG; Vice-Rector for Human Resource Devt Dr WILSON R. LUMBANTOBING; Vice-Rector for Student and Alumni Affairs Dr DAVID SITUMORANG.

Balai Pengkajian Teknologi Pertanian Jawa Barat (West Java Research Institute for Agricultural Technology): Jl. Kayuambon 80, Lembang, Bandung 40391; tel. (22) 2786238; e-mail bptp-jabar@litbang.deptan.go.id; internet jabar.litbang.deptan.go.id; f. 1994.

Institut Filsafat Theologi dan Kepemimpinan Jaffray (IFTK Jaffray Jakarta) (Institute for Theological and Leadership Philosophy Jaffray): Jl. Jatinegara Timur II 35, Jakarta 13350; tel. (21) 8570986; e-mail iftkj@centrin.net.id; internet www.iftk-jaffray.com; f. 1932, present name and status 1991; Rector Dr Drs JERRY RUMAHLATU; Vice-Rector for Academic Affairs NASOKHILI GIAWA; Vice-Rector for Admin. and Finance Dr MAGDALENA TOMATALA; Vice-Rector for Student Affairs PHILEMON INDAKRAY.

Institut Ilmu Sosial dan Ilmu Politik Jakarta (Institute of Social and Political Sciences): Jl. Raya Lenteng Agung 32, Jakarta Selatan 12610; tel. (21) 7806223; e-mail admin@iisip.ac.id; internet www.iisip.ac.id; f. 1953; faculties of administration, communication, social and political sciences; Rector MASLINA W. HUTASUHUT.

Institut Pertanian STIPER Yogyakarta: Jl. Nangka II, Maguwoharjo, Depok, Sleman, Yogyakarta 55282; tel. (247) 885479; e-mail info@instiper.ac.id; internet www.instiper.ac.id; f. 1958; faculties of agricultural technology, agriculture, forestry; library: 789 reference titles, 327 journals; Rector Dr Ir PURWADI; Vice-Rector Dr Ir HARSAWARDANA; Vice-Rector I Dr Ir A. SIH AYIEK SAYEKTI.

Institut Sains dan Teknologi AKPRIND Yogyakarta: Jl. Kalisahak 28, Komplek, Balapan 55222; tel. (274) 563029; e-mail ista@indo.net.id; internet www.akprind.ac.id; faculties of applied science, industrial technology and mineral technology.

Institut Sains dan Teknologi TD Pardede: Jl. Dr TD Pardede 8, Kecamatan, Medan 20153; tel. (61) 4569877; e-mail mail@istp.ac.id; internet www.istp.ac.id; f. 1987; faculties of civil engineering and planning, mineral technology and industrial technology; Rector Ir RUDOLF SITORUS; Vice-Rector I Drs L. SIHOMBING; Vice-Rector II Ir OMNY PARNGARIBUAN; Vice-Rector III Ir SIBARANI.

Institut Teknologi Adhi Tama Surabaya: Jl. Arief Rachman Hakim 100, Surabaya; tel. (31) 5945043; internet www.itats.ac.id; library: 19,165 book titles; Rector HADI SETIYAWAN; Vice-Rector I ARIEF RACHMAN;

Vice-Rector II KUNTO EKO SUSILO; Vice-Rector III BAMBANG SETYONO.

Institut Teknologi Indonesia: Jl. Raya Puspiptek Serpong, Tangerang, Banten 15320; tel. (21) 7561102; internet www.iti.ac.id.

Institut Teknologi Medan: Jl. Gedung Arca 52, Medan 20217; tel. (61) 7363771; e-mail itm@itm.ac.id; internet www.itm.ac.id; f. as Akademi Teknik Dwiwarna, name changed to Institut Teknologi Sumatera 1963, Sekolah Tinggi Teknik Medan 1976, present name and status 1984; Rector Ir MAHRIZAL MASRI; Vice-Rector I Ir ILMI ABDULLAH; Vice-Rector II MUNAJAT; Vice-Rector III MAHYUZAR MASRI.

Institut Teknologi Nasional (National Institute of Technology): Mustafa 23, Bandung 40124; tel. (22) 7272215; internet www.itenas.ac.id; f. 1972 as Akademi Teknologi Nasional, present name and status 1984; Rector Prof. Dr Ir HARSONO TAROEPRATJEKA; Vice-Rector for Academic and Student Affairs Ir SYAHRIL SAYUTI; Vice-Rector for Finance and Gen. Admin. Ir YANTI HELIANTY; Vice-Rector for Planning and Cooperation Dr IMAM ASCHURI.

Higher Colleges

Sekolah Tinggi Bahasa Asing (STBA) Yapari-ABA Bandung: Jl. Cihampelas 194, Bandung 40131; tel. (22) 2035426; e-mail info@stbayapariaba.ac.id; internet stbayapariaba.ac.id; Private control.

Sekolah Tinggi Filsafat Driyarkara (School of Philosophy Driyarkara): Jl. Cempaka Putih Indah 100A, Jembatan Serong Rawasari, Jakarta 10520; tel. (21) 4247129; e-mail stfd@dnet.net.id; internet www.driyarkara.ac.id; f. 1969; offers programmes in philosophy and science theology; 316 students; Chair. Prof. Dr A. EDDY KRISTIYANTO; publ. *Driyarkara* (4 a year).

Sekolah Tinggi Ilmu Ekonomi Malangkuçeçwara (Malangkuçeçwara School of Economics): Jl. Terusan Candi Kalasan, Blimbing, Malang 65142; tel. (341) 491813; e-mail info@stie-mce.ac.id; internet www.stie-mce.ac.id; f. 1971; depts of accounting and finance; Pres. NEVI DANILA; Vice-Pres. Drs BUNYAMIN; Vice-Pres. Drs TACHJUDDIN; Vice-Pres. Drs KADARUSMAN.

Sekolah Tinggi Ilmu Ekonomi Pasundan (Higher College for Economics Pasundan): Jl. Usman Ambon 4, Kacang Pedang, Pangkalpinang 33125; tel. (717) 438735; e-mail info@stie-ibek.ac.id; internet stiepas.ac.id; f. 2000; offers programmes in accounting and management; Chair. YOLANDA PUSPASARI.

Sekolah Tinggi Ilmu Ekonomi Solusi Bisnis Indonesia (Higher College for Economics and Business Solutions Indonesia): Jl. Ring Rd Utara 17, Condong Catur, Yogyakarta 55283; tel. (274) 887984; internet stie-sbi.ac.id; programmes in accounting and management; Chair. LUCIA IKA FITRIASTUTI.

Sekolah Tinggi Ilmu Sosial dan Ilmu Politik Kebangsaan–Masohi (College of Social and Political Science): Jl. Christina Martha Tiahahu 15, Masohi; tel. (914) 22057; internet www.stisipkebangsaanmasohi.com; f. 1999; administered by Yayasan Perguruan Tinggi Kebangsaan (Nat. Higher Education Foundation) Masohi; Chair. Drs J. KAPRESSY.

Sekolah Tinggi Manajemen Informatika dan Teknik Komputer (STIKOM) Surabaya (Higher College of Information Management and Computer Engineering Surabaya): Jl. Kedung Baruk 98, Surabaya; tel. (31) 8721731; e-mail info@stikom.edu; internet www.stikom.edu; f. 1983.

Sekolah Tinggi Teknik Poliprofesi Medan: Jl. Sei Batanghari 3–4, Medan; tel. (61) 8446729; e-mail layanan@sttp-poliprofesi.ac.id; internet sttp-poliprofesi.ac.id; f. 2002; Dir AKMAN DAULAY.

Sekolah Tinggi Teknologi Jakarta: Jl. Jatiwaringin Raya 278, Pondok Gede, Jakarta; tel. (21) 8462316; e-mail sttj@cbn.net.id; internet www.sttj.ac.id; f. 1972; Chair. ROSSI SETIADJI.

Sekolah Tinggi Teknologi Nuklir–BATAN (Higher College for Nuclear Technology): Jl. Babarsari POB 6101 YKBB, Yogyakarta 55281; tel. (247) 484085; internet www.sttn-batan.ac.id; f. 1982.

School of Art and Music

Akademi Seni Karawitan Indonesia Padang Panjang (Academy for Traditional Music and Dance): Jl. Puti Bungsu 35, Padang Panjang, Sumatera Barat; tel. (752) 82077; f. 1966; offers diploma courses in ballet, dance, music and music performance; library: 6,196 vols; 62 teachers; 428 students; Dir Prof. MARDJANI MARTAMIN; Registrar BAHRUL PADEK; Librarian Drs ANNAS HAMIR.

IRAN

The Higher Education System

The first modern institution of higher education was the Dar al-Fanun, a technical institute founded in 1851. In 1928 two more technical institutes were founded, now known as Iran University of Science and Technology and K. N. Toosi University of Technology. In 1934 Dar al-Fanun was incorporated into the newly established University of Tehran, the first multi-disciplinary institution of higher education. Universities were closed following the Islamic revolution in 1979 but were gradually reopened from 1983. In accordance with the political doctrine of Vilayat-e Faqih (the Guardianship of the Jurists) which was established following the 1979 revolution, all levels of education are overseen by the High Council of the Cultural Revolution, which was set up to ensure that Iranian education was appropriate to the aims of the revolution and reflected its Islamic principles. The duties of the Council, which is composed of 33 members, including the President of Iran and noted religious and non-religious scholars, include approving the establishment of institutions of higher education, appointing professors and lecturers, determining curriculum content and the content of textbooks and educational materials. Public universities and colleges are administered by the Ministry of Science, Research and Technology, and medical universities (which are classified separately) are controlled by the Ministry of Health and Medical Education. These state-run establishments do not charge tuition fees. In 1982 an 'open' university, Islamic Azad University, was founded, which now has more than 400 branches in cities and towns throughout the country (and a further three in Afghanistan, Dubai and Lebanon). It is not funded by central government, it administers its own entrance examination and charges tuition fees. Payame Noor University was founded in 1987 and offers correspondence courses and continuing adult education; although a state-owned institution, the Payame Noor University charges tuition fees. There are more than 50 state-operated universities, and by 2010/11 there was a total of almost 4.1m. students enrolled in higher education establishments in Iran, with 1.54m. of these at the Islamic Azad University. Other higher education institutions include general and professional colleges, technological institutes and vocational establishments.

To enter degree programmes at universities and institutes of higher education, students must hold a High School Diploma and a Pre-university Certificate and must sit the competitive University Entrance Examination (Kunkur). (Islamic Azad University administers its own entrance examination.) Iranian higher education is based on a 'credit semester' system; one credit is gained following 17 hours of taught classes, 34 hours of laboratory work or 51 hours of practical ('workshop') experience. The first undergraduate qualification is the Associate degree (Kardani), awarded after four semesters (two years) and requiring at least 72 credits. An Associate degree can be a terminal qualification (qualifying the holder in professions such as teaching, nursing and engineering) or it can serve as the first stage of a Bachelors degree. The Bachelors (Karshenasi) is the second (and main) undergraduate degree, lasting eight semesters (four years) and requiring a minimum of 135 credits. First degrees offering professional titles are available in pharmacy, medicine, dentistry and veterinary science; these last for 11 semesters (six years) and require at least 200 credits. A student with the Bachelors may progress to postgraduate education, which consists of the Masters (Karshenasi-Arshad) and Doctorate. The Masters is a course lasting four semesters (two years) and requiring at least 32 credits (of which the thesis accounts for 10 units). The final university degree is the Doctorate, which consists of two stages: first, the student must complete 60 credits of classroom-based learning; second, a period of original research leading to submission of a thesis is required. The Doctorate course, entrance to which requires a Masters degree in a related discipline and a successful performance in an entrance examination, lasts a total of four to five years.

University courses must be accredited by either the Ministry of Science, Research and Technology Directorate of Development or the Ministry of Health and Medical Education.

Technical and vocational education, which is offered at thousands of institutions throughout the country, is administered by the Technical and Vocational Training Organization, under the auspices of the Ministry of Co-operatives, Labour and Social Welfare. Non-formal training is also offered by employers.

In 2012 there were reports that individual universities had applied quota systems to certain subjects in order to restrict access by female students. For example, Qom University had not allowed female students to enrol on economics, commerce and industrial engineering programmes, and the University of Tehran had accepted only male students on a number of its engineering, mining, forestry and mathematics courses.

Regulatory Bodies

GOVERNMENT

Ministry of Culture and Islamic Guidance: POB 1515-11365, Baharestan Sq., Tehran 11365; tel. (21) 33966050; e-mail info@farhang.gov.ir; internet www.farhang.gov.ir; Minister ALI JANNATI.

Ministry of Education: Si-e-Tir St, Emam Khomeini Sq., Tehran; tel. (21) 32421; e-mail negah@medu.ir; internet www.medu.ir; Minister ALI ASGHAR FANI.

Ministry of Health and Medical Education: POB 310, Jomhouri Islami Ave, Hafez Crossing, Tehran 11344; tel. (21) 88363560; e-mail pr@behdasht.gov.ir; internet www.behdasht.gov.ir; Minister HASSAN QAZIZADEH HASHEMI.

Ministry of Science, Research and Technology: POB 15875-4375, Central Bldg, Ostad Nejatollahi Ave, Tehran; tel. (21) 82231000; e-mail info@msrt.ir; internet www.msrt.ir; Minister JAFAR TOFIGHI DARIAN.

Learned Societies

GENERAL

UNESCO Office Tehran: Bahman Bldg, Sa'ad Abad Palace Complex, Tehran 19894; tel. (21) 22751315; e-mail tehran@unesco.org; internet www.unesco.org/tehran; designated Cluster Office for Afghanistan, Iran, Pakistan and Turkmenistan; Dir QUNLI HAN.

ECONOMICS, LAW AND POLITICS

Iran Management Association: POB 15855-359, Tehran; Karimkhan Blvd 1 cnr of Asjodi St, Tehran; tel. (21) 8827878; e-mail info@iranmanagement.org; internet www.iranmanagement.org; f. 1960; promotes sound management principles and techniques for the improvement of management in Iran, and to create understanding and cooperation among managers in Iran and other countries; 200 individual and 300 institutional mems; library of 8,000 vols; Sec.-Gen. PARVIZ BAYAT; publs *Management Magazine* (12 a year, in Persian, with summary in English), *Modiriat* (Management, 6 a year).

HISTORY, GEOGRAPHY AND ARCHAEOLOGY

British Institute of Persian Studies: c/o British Acad., 10 Carlton House Terrace, London, SW1Y 5AH, United Kingdom; tel. (20) 7969-5203; e-mail bips@britac.ac.uk *Tehran:* 1553, Khiaban-e Dr Ali Shariati, Qolhak, Tehran 19396–13661; tel. (21) 22601937; e-mail bips@parsonline.net; internet www.bips.ac.uk; f. 1961; cultural institute, with special emphasis on history, archaeology and all aspects of Iranian studies; 400 mems; library of 10,000 books and MSS; Hon. Sec. (London Office) PETER DAVIES; Librarian (Tehran Office) FARIBA RAYHANPOUR; publ. *Iran* (1 a year).

LANGUAGE AND LITERATURE

British Council: North Entrance, British Embassy Compound, Shariati St, Qholhak, Tehran 19396-13661; tel. (21) 2001222; e-mail info@ir.britishcouncil.org; internet www.britishcouncil.org/iran; offers courses and exams in English language and British culture and promotes cultural exchange with the UK; Dir ANDREW MURRAY.

MEDICINE

Iranian Society of Microbiology: Department of Microbiology and Immunology, Faculty of Medicine, Univ. of Tehran, Tehran; tel. (21) 88955810; e-mail ijmicrobiology@gmail.com; internet www.ism.ir; f. 1940; 185 mems; Gen. Sec. G. H. NAZARI; publ. *Iranian Journal of Microbiology*.

NATURAL SCIENCES

Mathematical Sciences

Iranian Mathematical Society: POB 13145-418, Tehran; tel. (21) 8808855; e-mail iranmath@ims.ir; internet www.ims.ir; f. 1971; 2,750 mems; Pres. E. S. MAHMOODIAN; publs *Bulletin* (2 a year), *Farhang va Andishaye Riyazi* (2 a year).

Research Institutes

GENERAL

Institute for Humanities and Cultural Studies (IHCS): 64 St, Seyyed Jamal-eddin Ave, Tehran 14374; tel. (21) 88048037; e-mail info@ihcs.ac.ir; internet www.ihcs.ac.ir; f. 1981; research faculties: cultural studies, literature, history, history and philosophy of science, religious studies, linguistics, social sciences; library of 120,000 vols; Dir Dr HAMID REZA AYATOLLAHI; publs *Afaq al-Hizarah al-Islamiyyah* (2 a year), *Journal of Humanities* (4 a year), *Philosophy of Science* (2 a year), *Science and Religion Bulletin* (2 a year), *The Farhang* (4 a year), *Women Research* (2 a year).

AGRICULTURE, FISHERIES AND VETERINARY SCIENCE

Agricultural Biotechnology Research Institute of Iran (ABRII): POB 4119, Mardabad Ave, Karaj 31585; tel. (261) 2708282; e-mail khayam@abrii.ac.ir; internet www.abrii.ac.ir; f. 1983 as the Plant Biotechnology Department of Seed and Plant Improvement Institute; depts of cellular and molecular biology, genetics, genomics, microorganisms and biosafety, physiology and proteomics, technical services and research support and tissue culture and gene transformation; Dir-Gen. Dr MOJTABA KHAYYAM NEKOUEI.

Iran Animal Science Research Institute: POB 31585-1483, Alborz, Tehran; tel. (263) 4430010; e-mail info@asri.ir; internet www.asri.ir; f. 1933; research on cattle, water buffalo, sheep, goats, poultry and honeybees; library of 6,500 vols, 176 periodicals; Gen. Dir Dr HORMOZ MANSOURY; publ. *Animal Husbandry Research Institute*.

Plant Pests and Diseases Research Institute: POB 19395-1454, Evin/Tabnak St, Tehran; tel. (21) 2403012; e-mail info@ppdri.ac.ir; internet www.ppdri.ac.ir; f. 1943; research on pests and diseases of agricultural crops, botany, entomology, biological control, pesticides and agricultural zoology; library of 55,000 vols (English and Persian), 480 periodicals (English and Persian); Dir Dr G. A. ABDOLLAHI; publs *Applied Entomology and Phytopathology* (1 a year, in Persian and English), *Iranian Journal of Plant Pathology* (1 a year, in Persian and English), *Journal of the Entomological Society of Iran* (1 a year, in Persian and English), *Rostaniha—Botanical Journal of Iran* (1 a year, in Persian and English).

Razi Vaccine and Serum Research Institute: POB 31975–148, Karaj 31976-19751; tel. (261) 4570038; e-mail admin@rvsri.com; internet www.rvsri.com; f. 1930; epizootological and ecological studies of animal diseases and human and animal biology; research and preparation of all veterinary vaccines, some human vaccines and therapeutic sera; postgraduate courses in virology and microbiology; languages of instruction: Persian, English; library of 13,000 books, 800 periodicals; Gen. Dir Prof. ABDOLHOSSEIN DALIMI; publ. *Archives of the Razi Institute* (1 a year, in English).

ECONOMICS, LAW AND POLITICS

Institute for Political and International Studies (IPIS): Shahid Bahonar Ave, Shahid Aghaee St, POB 19395-1793, Tehran; tel. (21) 22802671; e-mail cominfo@ipis.ir; internet www.ipis.ir; f. 1983; acts as a research and information centre on int. relations, law, economics and Islamic studies, with emphasis on the Middle East, the Persian Gulf and Central Asia; holds conferences and seminars on contemporary int. issues; library of 200,000 vols; Pres. ALI AHANI; Dir-Gen. Dr SEYED R. MOSAVI; publs *Amyu Darya* (in English and Russian), *Central Asia and Caucasus Review Quarterly* (in Persian), *Foreign Policy Quarterly* (in Persian), *Iranian Journal of International Affairs Quarterly* (in English), *Islam and International Relations* (in Persian), *Journal of Alalaghat Aliranieh* (in Arabic).

Institute for Trade Studies and Research: 240 N Kargar St, POB 14185-671, Tehran 14187; tel. (21) 6622378; e-mail info@itsr.ir; internet www.itsr.ir; f. 1980; library of 70,000 vols; Pres. MAHMOOD DODANGEH; publs *Commercial Surveys* (6 a year), *Iranian Journal of Trade Studies (IJTC)* (4 a year).

HISTORY, GEOGRAPHY AND ARCHAEOLOGY

Institut Français de Recherche en Iran: Ave Shahid Nazari, 52 rue Adib, POB 15815-3495, Tehran 94371; tel. (21) 66401192; e-mail ifri@ifriran.org; internet www.ifriran.org; f. 1897, present name 1983; research into Iranian civilization, contact between French and Iranian scholars; library of 42,000 vols; Dir PHILLIPPE ROCHARD; publs *Abstracta Iranica* (1 a year), *Cahiers de la DAFI, Bibliothèque Iranienne*.

National Cartographic Centre: POB 13185-1684, Azadi Sq., Meraj Ave, Tehran; tel. (21) 6000031; internet www.ncc.org.ir; f. 1953; library of 4,000 vols, 2,500 reports; Dir Dr M. MADAD; publ. *Naghshebardari* (Journal of Surveying, 4 a year).

MEDICINE

Institut Pasteur: 69 Pasteur Ave, Tehran; tel. (21) 66953311; e-mail office@pasteur.ac.ir; internet www.pasteur.ac.ir; f. 1921; vaccines, research in microbiology, biochemistry, biopharmaceuticals, biotechnology and human genetics, molecular biology, parasitology and mycology, physiology and pharmacology; teaching and postgraduate training; Dir-Gen. Dr ABDOLHOSSEIN ROUHOL AMINI NAJAFABADI; publ. *Iranian Biomedical Journal*.

NATURAL SCIENCES

Institute for Research in Fundamental Sciences: POB 19395-5746, Niavaran Bldg, Niavaran Sq., Tehran; tel. (21) 22287013; e-mail ipminfo@ipm.ir; internet www.ipm.ir; f. 1989; schools of astronomy, cognitive sciences, computer science, mathematics, nanoscience, particles and accelerators, philosophy, physics; Dir M. J. A. LARIJANI; publ. *Akhbar* (4 a year).

RELIGION, SOCIOLOGY AND ANTHROPOLOGY

Anthropological Research Institute: Azadi Ave, Zanjan Int., POB 13445-719, Tehran; tel. (21) 6016367; f. 1937; attached to Iranian Cultural Heritage Organization; Dir MOHAMMAD MIRSHOKRAEE.

Islamic Research Foundation, Astan Quds Razavi: POB 91735-366, Mashhad; tel. (511) 2232501; e-mail intrelation@islamic-rf.ir; internet www.islamic-rf.ir; f. 1984; research into Islamic subjects: the Koran, the Hadith, jurisprudence, scholastic theology, Islamic history, Islamic text editing, translating Islamic books and encyclopedias, study of Islamic arts, production of Islamic CDs; nat. and int. seminars; library of 98,000 vols; Man. Dir Prof. ALI AKBAR ELAHI KHURASANI; publ. *Mishkat* (4 a year).

TECHNOLOGY

Electric Power Research Centre: POB 15745-448, Shahrak Ghods, Pounak Bakhtari Blvd, Tehran; tel. (21) 8079401; f. 1983; attached to Min. of Energy; library of 12,000 vols, 151 periodicals; Pres. S. M. TABATABAEE; publ. *Journal of Electrical Science and Technology* (4 a year).

Libraries and Archives

Isfahan

Municipal Library: Shahied Nikbakht St, POB 81638, Isfahan; tel. (31) 621200; f. 1991; 60,000 vols.

University of Isfahan Library: Isfahan; e-mail lib@ui.ac.ir; internet book.ui.ac.ir/cgi-bin/lib; 112,150 vols, half in Persian and Arabic, the remainder in European languages; Persian MSS and incunabula; Dir Dr HOSSEIN HARSIJ.

Mashhad

Ferdowsi University of Mashhad Information Centre and Central Library: POB 331-91735, Mashhad; tel. (511) 8789263; e-mail cent-lib@um.ac.ir; internet c-library.um.ac.ir; f. 1971; 539,609 vols; Dir of Information Centre and Central Library Prof. Dr MEHRDAD MOHRI.

Organizations of Libraries, Museums and Documents Center of Astan-e Quds-e Razavi: POB 91735-177, Mashhad; tel. (511) 2219553; e-mail info@aqlibrary.org; internet www.aqlibrary.org; f. 1457; general library and assistance for researchers; 52 constituent libraries; document centre; 12 specialized museums; 3,500,000 vols, 2,900,000 digitized books, 84,000 rare MSS incl. 16,057 MSS of the Holy Koran, 44,000 old lithographic books, MSS microfilms, 36,671 CDs of MSS and 9,300 hand-written materials; 8,000,000 pieces of deed, 10,000 titles of periodicals, 12,000 issues of journals, 1,268,000 copies of journals and magazines; Gen. Dir Dr ALI MUHAMMAD BARADRAN RAFIEI; publ. *The Library and Information Science* (4 a year).

Tabriz

Tabriz Public Library (Ketabkhaneh Melli Tabriz): Tabriz; 12,816 vols; Dir SEYYED MASOUD NAQIB.

Tarbiat Library: Daneshsara Sq., Tabriz; tel. (41) 5222190; f. 1921; 29,750 vols; Dir HOSSEIN ASADI.

University of Tabriz Central Library and Documentation Centre: Tabriz; tel. (411) 3392941; e-mail c-library@tabrizu.ac.ir; internet www.tabrizu.ac.ir; f. 1967; 110,877 vols, 6,231 microfiches, 4,300 maps, 6,231 microfilms, 1,643 periodicals, 647 audiovisual cassettes; Librarian T. NAJJARY.

Tehran

Central Library and Documentation Centre of Shahid Beheshti University: Evin, Tehran 19834; tel. (21) 293155; f. 1960; 315,529 vols, 3,190 periodicals; Librarian Dr ZAHRA GOOYA; publs *Sourat Ketabkhaye Fehrest Shodeh, Tazebaye Ketabkhaneh*.

Central Library and Documentation Centre of University of Tehran: Enghelab Ave, Tehran; tel. (21) 61112362; internet library.ut.ac.ir; f. 1949, re-housed 1970; Central Library of 850,000 vols, faculty libraries of 950,000 vols; Librarian Dr A. A. ENAYATI.

Centre for Socio-Economic Documentation and Publications: Baharestan Sq., Tehran 11365; tel. 33271; internet www.spac.ir; f. 1962, reorganized 1982; attached to Planning and Budget Org.; brs in 6 divs: technical services, information services and network affairs, libraries (Central Library, Archive for Devt Maps and Projects and 25 regional libraries), editing, graphics and production, distribution; libraries: 300,000 vols, 576 periodicals, 1,627 titles microforms, 16,000 titles devt projects, 18,000 maps and plans, databases of selected articles; Dir MOHAMMAD REZA SAEEDI; publ. *Periodical Index to Socio-Economic Articles* (4 a year).

Institute for Political and International Studies Library and Documentation Centre: POB 19395-1793, Tajrish, Tehran; tel. (21) 2571010; e-mail cominfo@ipis.ir; internet www.ipis.ir; f. 1983; attached to the Foreign Ministry; spec. library and assistance for researchers; 20,000 vols on Islamic science, history, politics, economics, law, geography, diplomacy, military studies; 400 periodicals; Dir-Gen. Dr S. M. K. SAJJADPOUR; publs *African Studies Journal* (2 a year), *Al-Alaaghaat* (4 a year), *Amu Darya* (4 a year), *Asiyaje Miyaneh va Ghofghaaz* (4 a year), *Iranian Journal of International Affairs* (4 a year), *Siyasat-e-Khare* (Journal of Foreign Policy, 4 a year).

Iran Bastan Museum Library: Khiaban-e Imam Khomeini, Khiaban-e Sium-e Tir, Tehran 11365; f. 1964; 17,000 vols; Dir M. R. RIYAZI KESHE.

Iran University of Medical Sciences and Health Services Central Library and Documentation Centre: POB 14155-6439, Tehran; tel. (21) 8058644; e-mail centrlib@iums.ac.ir; internet www.iums.ac.ir; f. 1975; 35,000 books, 1,323 current periodicals, 9,355 theses, 3,000 audiovisual titles; Dir SUSSAN ERTEJAEI.

Iranian Cultural Heritage Organization Documentation Centre: POB 13445-1594, Tehran; tel. (21) 6003126; e-mail info@ichodoc.ir; internet www.ichodoc.ir; f. 1994; 36,000 vols, 237 periodicals, 15,667 research reports, 2,030 films, 22,180 maps, 70,000 photographs, 155,560 slides, 125,000 negatives, 122 video cassettes, 204 audio cassettes, 771 CDs, 923 posters, 4,000 microfiches; Dir FARIBA FARZAM.

Iranian Information and Documentation Centre (IRANDOC): 1090 Englab St, POB 13185-1371, Tehran; tel. (21) 66494980; e-mail info@irandoc.ac.ir; internet www.irandoc.ac.ir; f. 1968; attached to Min. of Higher Education; research; training; information and knowledge management services; work in the fields of basic sciences, agriculture, medical sciences, humanities and technology; advises and assists in the establishment of specialized information centres and acts as the nat. reference centre; organizes, processes and disseminates scientific and technological documents; key role in nat. and ministerial orgs; 24,000 vols, 210 current periodicals, 70,000 student dissertations; Dir SEYYED OMID FATEMI; publs *Abstracts of Scientific/Technical Papers* (4 a year), *Current Research in Iranian Universities and Research Centres* (4 a year), *Directory of Scientific Meetings held in Iran* (4 a year), *Dissertation Abstracts of Iranian Graduates Abroad* (4 a year), *Ettela s Resani* (Technical Bulletin, 4 a year), *Information Science & Technology Journal, Iranian Dissertation Abstracts* (4 a year), *Iranian Government Reports* (4 a year), *Iranian Scholars and Experts* (1 a year), *Science Thesauri*.

Library of the Bank Markazi Jomhouri Islami Iran (Central Bank of the Islamic Republic of Iran): Pegah St, Mirdamad Blvd, POB 11365-8531, Tehran; tel. (21) 29953263; e-mail libinfoservices@cbi.ir; internet lib.cbi.ir/libcbi; f. 1960; 110,000 books and reports; Dir MAHROKH LOTFI.

Malek National Library and Museum: Melal-e Mottahed (UN) St, Bagh-e Melli (National Garden), Imam Khomeini Ave, POB 111555/547, Tehran; tel. (21) 66743744; e-mail library@malekmuseum.org; internet www.malekdlib.org; f. 1937; attached to Malek Nat. Museum; 70,000 vols 19,000 recorded titles of MSS, 80,000 printed books in Persian-Arabic, 650 periodicals and 9,000 vols of printed books in other languages; Dir and Man. SEYED MOJTABA HOSSEINI; publ. *Dariche*.

National Library and Archives of Iran: National Library Blvd, Haqani Expressway (West–East), POB 15875-3693, Tehran 1537614111; tel. (21) 88644080; e-mail pria@nlai.ir; internet www.nlai.ir; f. 1937; 684,465 books (510,479 in Persian and Arabic, 173,986 in other languages), 1m. periodicals, 172,000 MSS documents and patchworks, 14,729 Arabic and Persian MSS, 67,280 pamphlets and sheets, 9,848 lithographic prints, 320,093 non-book items; Dir KAZEM MOOSAVI BOJNOURDI; publ. *Iranian National Bibliography* (1 a year, online and CD-ROM).

Parliament Library (1): Ketabkhane-ye Majles-e Shora-ye Eslami 1, Baharestan Sq., POB 11365-866, Tehran; tel. (21) 33126092; internet www.majlislib.com; f. 1912; 272,000 books, 28,000 bound vols of 5,000 Persian, Arabic and Latin periodicals, 24,000 MSS vols, 12m. nat. and historical documents, 10,000 photographs, 460 magnetic tapes, 90 old maps, 17,500 MSS on microfilm, 3,000 CDs of MSS, 27 vols of theses and dissertations, 12,000 govt reports, 300 microfilms and 250 CDs of old Iranian periodicals; UN depository; museum (see under Museums and Art Galleries); Dir SEYYED MOHAMMAD ALI AHMADI ABHARI; publs *Name-ye Baharestan* (2 a year), *Payam-e Baharestan* (12 a year).

Attached Library:

Parliament Library (2): Ketabkhaneh Majles-e Shora-ye Eslami 2, Emam Khomeini Ave, Tehran 13174; tel. (21) 6135335; f. 1959; spec. colln on Iranian, Islamic and Oriental studies: 49,554 printed books, 5,166 bound vols of 395 Persian, Arabic and Latin periodicals; Dir SEYYED MOHAMMAD ALI AHMADI ABHARI.

Museums and Art Galleries

Isfahan

Armenian Museum of All Saviour's Cathedral: POB 81735-115, Julfa, Isfahan; tel. (311) 6243471; e-mail sourbv@yahoo.com; internet www.newjulfa.org; f. 1930, rehoused 1971 with additions; under the supervision of the Diocesan Council of the Armenians in Isfahan; 750 ancient MSS, 570 paintings, miniatures and antique church vestments, tomb portraits; library of 25,000 vols.

Chehel Sotun Museum: Isfahan; Dir KARIM NIKZAD.

Mashhad

Astan-e Qudse Razavi Museums: Sahn-e-Kausar, Mashhad 91348-43388; tel. (511) 2241105; e-mail info@aqlibrary.org; internet www.aqm.ir; f. 1937, inaugurated 1945; Anthropology Museum, Central Museum, Weapons Museum, Koran Museum, Stamp Museum, Astronomical Instruments and Clocks Museum, Natural Objects and Shells Museum, Crystal and Porcelain Museum, Coins and Medals Museum, Carpet Museum, colln of Holy Koran and precious objects presented by HE Ayatollah Khamenei, History of Mashhad Museum and Paintings Museum; Dir MOHSEN AMIRY NIA.

Qom

Qom Museum: Eram St, Qom; tel. (25) 7741491; f. 1936; under the supervision of the Archaeological Service; Dir B. YOSEFZADEH.

Shiraz

Pars Museum: Shiraz; tel. (11) 24151; f. 1938; exhibits incl. MSS, earthenware, ancient coins; Dir MOHAMMAD HOSSEIN ESTAKHR; Curator HASRAT ZADEH SORUDE.

Tehran

Golestan Palace Museum: POB 11365-4595, Tehran 11149; tel. (21) 3113335; e-mail info@golestanpalace.org; internet www.golestanpalace.ir; f. 1894; Dir PARVIN SADR SEGHT-OL-ESLAMI.

Iran Bastan Museum: Khiaban-e Imam Khomeini, Khiaban-e Sium-e Tir, Tehran 11364; tel. (21) 6672061; f. 1946; archaeological and cultural research; conservation, repair and exhibition of cultural material; 4 depts; library of 15,924 vols; Dir J. GOLSHAN.

Malek Museum: Melale Mottahed Ave, Tehran; tel. (21) 66726613; e-mail khoddari@yahoo.com; internet www.aqmlm.ir; f. 1937, opened new bldg in 1997; various objects of historical interest: coins, paintings, metalwork and woodwork, royal decrees, carpets, philatelic colln; library: see under Libraries and Archives; Museum Dir and Head of Research Dept Dr SAID KHODDARI NAINI.

Mardom Shenassi Museum (Ethnological Museum): Maidan Panzdah Khordad, POB 11365-9595, Tehran 11149; tel. (21) 3110653; f. 1888; Dir ALIREZA ANISI.

Parliament Museum: Muze-ye Majles-e Shora-ye Eslami, POB 11365-866, Baharestan Sq., Tehran; tel. (21) 3130919; internet www.majlislib.com; f. 1999; 294 old Iranian paintings, 714 artistic and traditional handicrafts and gifts presented to the speakers of the Islamic Consultative Assembly by foreign dignitaries, 150 rolls of old carpets, 70 chairs and tables, small colln of antiques; Dir SEYYED MOHAMMAD ALI AHMADI ABHARI.

Tehran Museum of Contemporary Art: N Karegar Ave, Laleh Park, Tehran; tel. (21) 88951324; e-mail info@tmoca.com; internet www.tmoca.com; f. 1977; library of 26,000 vols in formation; Dir MAHMOOD SHALOOEI.

Universities

AHWAZ JONDISHAPOUR UNIVERSITY OF MEDICAL SCIENCES

Golestan-bol, University City Central Bldg, Ahwaz 61357-15794
Telephone: (611) 3339092
E-mail: info@ajums.ac.ir
Internet: www.ajums.ac.ir
Founded 1988, fmrly part of Shahid Chamran Univ.
Academic year: September to June
Pres.: Dr HAYAT MOMBEINI
Registrar: Dr M. E. MOTLAQ
Librarian: B. DASHTBOZORGI
Number of teachers: 410
Number of students: 5,300
Publications: *Jondishapour Journal of Pharmaceutical Sciences* (2 a year), *Scientific Medical Journal* (4 a year)

DEANS
College of Dentistry: Dr M. SHOKRI
College of Health: M. LATIFI
College of Nursing: Z. ABBASPOUR
College of Pharmacology: Dr A. HEMATI
College of Physiotherapy: Dr M. J. SHATERZADEH
Medical College: Dr M. FEGHHI
Paramedicine College: Dr M. KARANDISH

PROFESSORS
ASHNAGHAR, A.
BEHROOZ, M.
KALANTARI, H.
MAKVANDI, M.
MARAGHI, S.
MOGHADAM, A. Z.
PEDRAM, M.
ZANDIAN, K.

ALLAMEH TABATABA'I UNIVERSITY

POB 15815-3487, Tehran
Telephone: (21) 8901521
Internet: www.atu.ac.ir
Founded 1984, following merger of Univ. Complex for Literature and Humanities and Univ. Centre for Public and Business Administration
State control
Languages of instruction: English, Persian
Academic year: September to June
Pres.: Dr SEYED SADRODDIN SHARIATI
Vice-Chancellor for Academic Affairs: Prof. Dr AHMAD TAMIMDARI
Vice-Chancellor for Admin. and Finance: Prof. Dr JAFAR BABAJANI
Vice-Chancellor for Research and Int. Relations: Prof. Dr HOSSEIN RAHMANSERESHT
Vice-Chancellor for Student Affairs: Prof. Dr HOSSEIN SALIMI
Registrar: Ms SEPEHRI
Chief Librarian: Dr ZAHRA SEIFKASHANI
Number of teachers: 360 (full-time)
Number of students: 12,200
Publication: Each faculty publishes its own journal.

DEANS
Faculty of Economics: Prof. Dr HAMID SHORAKA
Faculty of Law and Politics: Asst Prof. Dr GHOLAM-ALI CHEGENIZADE
Faculty of Management and Accounting: Asst Prof. Dr ABULFAZL KAZZAI
Faculty of Persian Literature and Foreign Languages: Prof. Dr SAEED VAEZ
Faculty of Psychology and Education: MORTEZA AMINFAR
Faculty of Social Sciences: Asst Prof. Dr MAHAMMAD ZAHEDIASL

ATTACHED RESEARCH INSTITUTES
Center for Studies on Iranian Economy (CSIE): Dean Asst Prof. Dr SAEED MOSHIRI.
International Centre for Insurance Education and Research (ICIER): Dean Asst Prof. Dr MOHAMMAD-GHOLI YOSEFI

AL-ZAHRA UNIVERSITY

Vanak, Tehran 19938-91176
Telephone: (21) 88035187
E-mail: office@alzahra.ac.ir
Internet: www.alzahra.ac.ir
Founded 1965, name changed 1981
State control
Language of instruction: Persian
Academic year: September to June
Chancellor: Dr MAHBOUBEH MIBASHERI
Vice-Chancellor for Academic Affairs: Dr YADOLLAH ORDUKHANI
Vice-Chancellor for Admin. and Finance: Dr MAHNAZ MOLLANAZARI
Vice-Chancellor for Research: Dr SIMIN HOSSEINIAN
Vice-Chancellor for Student Affairs: SHAHIN GHAHREMAN IZADI
Dir of Int. Relations: Dr AZAM SAZVAR
Librarian: Dr QODSI ZIARANI MOHAMMADI
Library of 121,569 vols
Number of teachers: 600
Number of students: 7,940
Publications: *Journal of Art 'Jelveye Honar'*, *Journal of Hadith and Qu'ran Studies*, *Journal of Humanities*, *Journal of Science*, *Journal of Women Studies*

DEANS
Faculty of Engineering: Dr JAFAR BAGHERI NEJAD
Faculty of Fine and Applied Arts: Dr ABULQASEM DADVAR
Faculty of Literature, Foreign Languages and History: Dr ENSIEH KHAZALI
Faculty of Physical Education and Sports Science: Dr PARVANEH NAZAR ALI
Faculty of Psychology and Education: Dr MOJDEH VAZIRI
Faculty of Sciences: Dr REZA SABET DARIYANI
Faculty of Social Sciences and Economics: Dr SUSAN BASTANI
Faculty of Theology: Dr ZAHRA RABBANI

ATTACHED RESEARCH CENTRE
Women's Research Centre: tel. (21) 8049809; e-mail golkhoo@alzahra.ac.ir; Dir Dr SHEKOOFEH GOLKHOO

AMIRKABIR UNIVERSITY OF TECHNOLOGY

424 Hafez Ave, Tehran 15875-4413
Telephone: (21) 64543400
E-mail: aghdam@aut.ac.ir
Internet: www.aut.ac.ir
Founded 1958 as Tehran Polytechnic
State control
Academic year: September to June
Depts of aerospace engineering, chemical engineering, civil and environmental engineering, computer and information technology, electrical engineering, industrial engineering, maritime engineering, mathematics and computer science, medical engineering, mining and metallurgical engineering, physics, polymer engineering, textile engineering
Pres.: Prof. ALIREZA RAHAI
Vice-Pres. for Academic Affairs: Prof. MOHAMMAD HASAN SEBT
Vice-Pres. for Admin. and Finance Affairs: Dr ALI MOHAMMAD KIMIAGARI
Vice-Pres. for Research and Technology: Dr MAHDI IRANNEJAD
Vice-Pres. for Student Affairs: Dr BEHROOZ AREZOO
Dir for Int. Affairs: Dr M. SAFAVI
Librarian: Prof. NAJJARIAN
Library of 100,000 vols (15 departmental libraries)
Number of teachers: 475
Number of students: 12,000
Publication: *Amirkabir Journal of Science and Technology* (4 a year).

ATTACHED RESEARCH INSTITUTES
Advanced Textiles Materials and Technology Research Institute: internet atmt.aut.ac.ir.
Concrete Technology and Durability Research Centre: tel. (21) 64543074; e-mail concrete@aut.ac.ir; internet www.aut.ac.ir/ctdr; Dir Prof. ALI AKBAR RAMEZANIANPOUR.
Energy Research Centre: tel. (21) 64542611; e-mail erc@aut.ac.ir; internet www.aut.ac.ir/research/erc/home.htm; Dir Prof. BAHRAM DABIR.
Synthetic Fibres and Textile Research Centre: Dir Dr MOHAMMAD REZA BABAEI

BU-ALI SINA UNIVERSITY

Shariati Ave, University Sq., Hamadan 65174
Telephone: (811) 8273952
Internet: www.basu.ac.ir
Founded 1973
State control
Academic year: September to June
Pres.: Dr M. GHOLAMI
Vice-Pres. for Admin. and Finance: Dr A. KAREGAR BIDEH
Vice-Pres. for Devt: M. R. TAHMASEBI
Vice-Pres. for Education: Dr G. R. KHANLARI
Vice-Pres. for Research: Dr S. J. SABOUNCHI
Vice-Pres. for Student Affairs: Dr M. SHARIFIAN
Librarian: Dr M. S. GHAEMIZADEH
Number of teachers: 280
Number of students: 7,500
Publication: *Agricultural Research* (2 a year)

DEANS
Faculty of Agriculture: Dr M. J. SOLEIMANI
Faculty of Engineering: Dr M. NILI
Faculty of Letters and Humanities: Dr F. MIRZAII
Faculty of Science: Prof. H. ILUKHANI
Faculty of Teacher Training (Malayer): Dr M. JALALI
Faculty of the Veterinary College: Dr H. SHOKRIAN

FERDOWSI UNIVERSITY OF MASHHAD

Azadi Sq., Ferdowsi Univ. Campus, Mashhad 91779-48974
Telephone: (511) 8836037
E-mail: intr@um.ac.ir
Internet: www.um.ac.ir
Founded 1949
State control
Language of instruction: Persian
Academic year: September to June (2 semesters)

Chancellor: Prof. ALI REZA ASHOURI
Vice-Chancellor for Academic Affairs: Dr MAHDI. KHAJAVI
Registrar: Dr MAHMOOD REZAI ROKN ABAD
Dir for the Int. Relations Office: Dr ABEDIN VAHEDIAN
Librarian: Dr BEHROOZ MAHRAM

Library of 536,312 vols
Number of teachers: 660
Number of students: 19,600

Publications: *Ferdowsi Review: An Iranian Journal of English Language* (in English), *Iranian Journal of Animal Biosystematics* (in English), *Iranian Journal of Animal Science Studies*, *Iranian Journal of Health and Physical Activity* (in English), *Iranian Journal of Veterinary Science and Technology* (4 a year), *Journal of Agricultural Machinery Engineering (JAME)*, *Journal of Agroecology*, *Journal of Applied Sciences in Mechanics*, *Journal of Arabic Language and Literature* (in Arabic), *Journal of Cell and Molecular Research*, *Journal of Civil Engineering* (in Persian), *Journal of Economics and Agricultural Development* (in Persian), *Journal of Educational and Psychological Studies* (in Persian), *Journal of Evolution Management*, *Journal of Historical Research and Studies*, *Journal of History and Culture*, *Journal of Horticulture Science*, *Journal of Iranian Field Crop Research*, *Journal of Iranian Grain Research*, *Journal of Islamic Philosophy and Thoughts*, *Journal of Jurisprudence (Fiqh) and Islamic Foundations*, *Journal of Knowledge and Development*, *Journal of Knowledge and Technology*, *Journal of Language and Translation*, *Journal of Linguistics and Khorasani Dialects*, *Journal of Metallurgical and Material Engineering*, *Journal of Plant Protection*, *Journal of Qur'anic Sciences and Hadith*, *Journal of Separation and Transport Phenomena*, *Journal of Social Sciences*, *Journal of the School of Economics and Business Administration* (4 a year), *Journal of Water and Soil*, *Mashhad Research Journal of Mathematical Sciences* (in English)

DEANS

Faculty of Administration and Economics: Dr M. SALIMI FAR
Faculty of Agriculture: Dr REZA VALIZADEH
Faculty of Architecture and Urban Engineering: Dr A. SHOOSHTARI
Faculty of Education and Psychology: Dr M. SAEEDI REZVANI
Faculty of Engineering: Dr HOSSAIN NOEEI BAGHBAN
Faculty of Letters and Humanities: Dr A. TALEBZADEH SHOOSHTARI
Faculty of Mathematical Sciences: Dr A. ERFANIAN MOSHIRI NEZHAD
Faculty of Natural Resources and Environment: Dr SH. DANESH
Faculty of Physical Education: A. HASHEMI JAVAHERI
Faculty of Sciences: Dr M. RAHIMI ZADEH
Faculty of Theology: Dr H. NAGHI ZADEH
Faculty of Veterinary Science: Dr M. MALEKI
Nishabour School of Fine Arts: Dr G. HASANI DARAMIAN
Shirvan School of Agriculture: Dr A. KHOSHNOUD YAZDI

IRAN UNIVERSITY OF SCIENCE AND TECHNOLOGY

Narmak, Tehran 16846-13114
Telephone: (21) 77240303
E-mail: interiust@iust.ac.ir
Internet: www.iust.ac.ir

Founded 1928
State control
Language of instruction: Persian
Academic year: September to June (2 semesters)

Chancellor: Dr MOHAMMAD SAEED JABALAMELI
Vice-Chancellor for Admin. and Finance: Dr BIJAN GHAFFARI
Vice-Chancellor for Education: Dr MOHAMMAD FATHIAN
Vice-Chancellor for Research and Technology: Dr MOHAMMAD HASSAN BAZIAR
Vice-Chancellor for Student Affairs: Dr ROUHOLLAH TALEBI
Vice-Chancellor for Students' Cultural Affairs: Dr MOHAMMAD KHALAJ AMIR HOSSEINI
Dir for Int. and Scientific Cooperation Office: Dr HADI KHORAMISHAD
Head of Graduate Studies: Dr MOHAMMAD REZA MOGHBELI
Registrar: Dr SEYED HOSSEIN RAZAVI
Librarian: Dr SEYED MAHDI ALAVI AMLASHI

Library of 42,804 vols (incl. 12,862 Persian books, 25,732 foreign books, 805 Persian reference books, 3,405 foreign reference books), 1,054 journals, more than 1,400 subscriptions to academic magazines, more than 23,000 titles of thesis, 1,000 ebooks
Number of teachers: 370 (full-time)
Number of students: 12,200

Publications: *International Journal of Architecture and Urban Planning* (2 a year, in English), *International Journal of Civil Engineering* (4 a year, in English), *International Journal of Industrial Engineering and Production Management* (4 a year, in Persian), *International Journal of Industrial Engineering and Production Research* (4 a year, in English), *International Journal of Optimization in Civil Engineering* (4 a year, in English), *Iranian Journal of Electrical and Electronic Engineering* (4 a year, in English), *Iranian Journal of Materials Science and Engineering* (4 a year, in English)

DEANS

Behshahr Branch-Iran University of Science and Technology: Dr MOHAMMAD MOHAMMADPOUR OMRAN
Dept of Chemistry: Dr RAHMATOLLAH RAHIMI
Dept of Foreign Languages: Dr ESMAEEL ABDOLLAHZADEH
School of Architecture and Environmental Design: Eng. ABDOLHAMID NOGHREH KAR
School of Automotive Engineering: Dr MOHAMMAD HASSAN SHOJAEE FARD
School of Chemical Engineering: Dr MOHAMMAD TAGHI SADEGHI
School of Civil Engineering: Dr HOSSEIN SALEHZADEH
School of Computer Engineering: Dr NASER MOZAYANI
School of Electrical Engineering: Dr AHMAD CHELDAVI
School of Industrial Engineering: Dr ALIREZA MOINI
School of Management and Progress Engineering: Dr ALIREZA MOINI
School of Mathematics: Dr GHOLAMHOSSEIN YARI
School of Mechanical Engineering: Dr REZA TAGHAVI
School of Metallurgy and Materials Engineering: Dr SEYED MOHAMMAD-ALI BOUTORABI
School of Physics: Dr SEYED ROUHOLLAH AGHDAEE
School of Railway Engineering: Dr DAVOOD YOUNESIAN

PROFESSORS

ABOUTALEBI, M.-R., School of Metallurgy and Materials Engineering
AFSHAR, A., School of Civil Engineering
AHMADIAN, H., School of Mechanical Engineering
AMINI, F., School of Civil Engineering
ARABI, H., School of Metallurgy and Materials Engineering
ARYANEZHAD, M.-B.-Q., School of Industrial Engineering
AYATOLLAHI, M. R., School of Mechanical Engineering
BAZIAR, M. H., School of Civil Engineering
BEHBAHANI, H., School of Civil Engineering
BEITOLLAHI, A., School of Metallurgy and Materials Engineering
BOUTORABI, S. M.-A., School of Metallurgy and Materials Engineering
CHELDAVI, AHMAD, School of Electrical Engineering
DANESHJOU, K., School of Mechanical Engineering
ESRAFILIAN, E., School of Mathematics
FALLAHI, M., Department of Foreign Languages
FARMAN, H., School of Physics
GHASEMZADEH, R., School of Metallurgy and Materials Engineering
GHODRATI AMIRI, G., School of Civil Engineering
GOLESTANI-FARD, F., School of Metallurgy and Materials Engineering
HABIBNEJAD KORAYEM, M., School of Mechanical Engineering
HASHEMINEJAD, S. M., School of Mechanical Engineering
HEDJAZI, J., School of Metallurgy and Materials Engineering
HODJAT KASHANI, F., School of Electrical Engineering
JASBI, A., School of Industrial Engineering
JAVADPOUR, J., School of Metallurgy and Materials Engineering
KAVEH, A., School of Civil Engineering
KHARRAZI, Y., School of Metallurgy and Materials Engineering
MAJIDI, H., School of Physics
MALEK NEJAD, K., School of Mathematics
MARGHUSSAIN, V., School of Metallurgy and Materials Engineering
MIRDAMADI, S., School of Metallurgy and Materials Engineering
MOHAMMAD MORADI, A., School of Architecture and Environmental Design
MOHAMMAD NEJAD, S., School of Electrical Engineering
MOHAMMADI, K., School of Electrical Engineering
MOHAMMADI, T., School of Chemical Engineering
NOOROSSANA, R., School of Industrial Engineering
ORAIZI, H., School of Electrical Engineering
RAZAVIZADEH, H., School of Metallurgy and Materials Engineering
REZAIE, H., School of Metallurgy and Materials Engineering
ROEENTAN, G., School of Electrical Engineering
SADJADI, S. J., School of Industrial Engineering
SAIDI MEHRABAD, M., School of Industrial Engineering
SANAEI, E., School of Civil Engineering
SEYED-HOSSEINI, S. M., School of Industrial Engineering
SEYED SADJADI, S., Dept of Chemistry
SHABESTARI, S. G., School of Metallurgy and Materials Engineering
SHAYANFAR, H., School of Electrical Engineering
SHAYGANMANESH, A., School of Mathematics
SHIDFAR, A., School of Mathematics
SHOJAEEFARD, M. H., School of Automotive Engineering
SHOKRIEH, M. M., School of Mechanical Engineering
SHOULAIE, A., School of Electrical Engineering

SOLEIMANI, M., School of Electrical Engineering

TAEB, A., School of Chemical Engineering

ATTACHED RESEARCH INSTITUTES

Asphalt Concrete Mixture and Bitumen Research Centre: tel. (21) 77240281; e-mail abrc@iust.ac.ir; Dir Dr HASSAN ZIARI.

Automotive Engineering Research Centre: tel. (21) 77491224; Dir Dr MOHAMMAD HASSAN SHOJAEEFARD.

Cement Research Centre: tel. (21) 77240475; e-mail crc@iust.ac.ir; Dir Dr ALI ALLAHVERDI.

Centre of Excellence for Advanced Materials and Processing: tel. (21) 77240291; e-mail ceamp@iust.ac.ir; Dir Dr FARHAD GOLESTANI FARD.

Centre of Excellence for Fundamental Studies in Structural Engineering: tel. (21) 77240399; Dir Dr ALI KAYEH.

Centre of Excellence for Power Systems Automation and Operation: tel. (21) 77240585; e-mail info@power-excellence.ir; Dir Dr SHAHRAM JADID.

Electronic Research Centre: tel. (21) 77240487; e-mail erc@iust.ac.ir; Dir Dr SATTAR MIRZAKUCHAKI.

Green Research Centre: tel. (21) 77491223; e-mail jadid@iust.ac.ir; Dir Dr SHAHRAM JADID.

Information Technology Research Centre: tel. (21) 77491192; e-mail akbari@iust.ac.ir; Dir Dr AHMAD AKBARI.

Iran Aluminium Research Centre: tel. (21) 77240599; Dir Dr MOHAMMAD-TAGHI SALEHI.

Iran Composites Institute: tel. (21) 77491206; e-mail shokrieh@iust.ac.ir; internet www.irancomposits.org; Dir Dr MAHMOOD MEHRDAD SHOKRIEH.

Technology Incubator of IUST: tel. (21) 77497788; e-mail incubator@iust.ac.ir; Dir Dr MOHAMMAD REZA JAHED MOTLAGH.

Transportation Research Centre: tel. (21) 77240399; Dir Dr AFSHIN SHARIAT

ISFAHAN UNIVERSITY OF MEDICAL SCIENCES AND HEALTH SERVICES

Hezar-Jerib Ave, Isfahan
Telephone: (311) 7923077
E-mail: international@mui.ac.ir
Internet: www.mui.ac.ir

Founded 1950
State control
Language of instruction: Persian
Academic year: September to June

Chancellor: Dr GHOLAMREZA ASGHARI
Vice-Chancellor for Academic Affairs: Dr TAHEREH CHANGIZ
Vice-Chancellor for Finance and Admin. Affairs: Dr ALI REZA YOUSEFI
Vice-Chancellor for Food and Pharmaceutical Affairs: Dr ABBAS ALI JAFARIAN DEHKORDI
Vice- Chancellor for Health Affairs: Dr ABBAS ALI JAVADI
Vice-Chancellor for Research and Technology Affairs: Dr PEYMAN ADIBI
Vice-Chancellor for Student Affairs: Dr ZABIHOLLAH SHAHMORADI
Vice-Chancellor for Treatment Affairs: Dr HEIDAR ALI DAVARI
Head of Libraries: Dr ROYA KELISHADI

Library of 84,517 vols (incl. 42,315 Persian books, 35,286 English books), 1,716 Persian journals, 5,200 English journals
Number of teachers: 704
Number of students: 9,058

Publications: *ARYA Atherosclerosis* (6 a year), *Dental Research Journal* (6 a year), *International Journal of Preventive Medicine* (12 a year), *Iranian Journal of Nursing and Midwifery Research* (6 a year), *Journal of Medical Signal and Sensors* (4 a year), *Journal of Research in Medical Sciences* (12 a year), *Journal of Research in Pharmaceutical Sciences* (4 a year)

DEANS

Faculty of Dentistry: Dr ABBAS ALI KHADEMI
Faculty of Health: Dr MOHAMMAD MEHDI AMIN
Faculty of Management and Information Services: Dr MAHMOOD KEYVANARA
Faculty of Medicine: Dr MOHAMMAD REZA SABRI
Faculty of New Technology: Dr SHAGHAYEGH HAGHJOO
Faculty of Nursing and Midwifery: Dr FARIBA TALEGHANI
Faculty of Nutrition: Dr AHMAD ESMAEELZADEH
Faculty of Pharmacy and Pharmaceutical Sciences: Dr MOHSEN MINAEEYAN
Faculty of Rehabilitation Sciences: Dr JAVID MOSTMAND

ISFAHAN UNIVERSITY OF TECHNOLOGY

Isfahan 84156-83111
Telephone: (311) 3912505
E-mail: isco@cc.iut.ac.ir
Internet: www.iut.ac.ir

Founded 1977
State control
Language of instruction: Persian
Academic year: September to July

Pres.: Dr G. R. GHORBANI
Vice-Pres. for Academic Affairs: Dr MOJTABA AZHARI
Vice-Pres. for Finance and Admin.: Dr MOHAMMAD HASSAN ABBASI
Vice-Pres. for Research: Dr SEYED HASAN GHAZIASKAR
Vice-Pres. for Student Affairs: Dr ALI AKBAR ALEM RAJABI
Registrar: Dr SOROUSH ALIMORADI
Library Dir: Dr MOSTAFA KARIMAIAN EGHBAL

Library of 88,000 vols, 2,500 periodicals
Number of teachers: 440
Number of students: 9,000

Publications: *Esteghlal* (Journal of Engineering, 2 a year), *Iranian Journal of Physics Research*, *Journal of Sciences and Technology of Agriculture and Natural Resources*

DEANS

College of Agriculture: Dr MORTEZA ZAHEDI
Faculty of Chemical Engineering: Dr GH. ETEMAD
Faculty of Chemistry: Dr S. H. GHAZIASKAR
Faculty of Civil Engineering: Dr M. M. SAADATPOUR
Faculty of Electrical and Computer Engineering: Dr M. A. MONTAZERI
Faculty of Industrial Engineering: Dr GH. A. RAISSI ARDALI
Faculty of Materials Engineering: Dr M. A. GOLOZAR
Faculty of Mathematics: Dr H. R. ZOHOURI-ZANGENAH
Faculty of Mechanical Engineering: Dr A. SABONCHI
Faculty of Mining Engineering: Dr J. TAJADOD
Faculty of Natural Resources: Dr A. JALALIAN
Faculty of Physics: Dr H. AKBARZADEH
Faculty of Textile Technology: Dr S. H. AMIRSHAHI

PROFESSORS

AKBARZADEH, H., Physics
AMINI, S. M., Computational Physics
AMINZADEH, A., Chemistry
BASSIR, H., Mining Engineering
HAGHANY, A., Pure Mathematics
HAJRASOOLIHA, SH., Soil Science
KALBASI, M., Soil Science
MALLAKPOUR, S. E., Chemistry
MOLKI, M., Mechanical Engineering
MOUSAVI, S. F., Agriculture
PARSAFAR, GH., Chemistry
PARSIAN, A., Statistics
REZAEI, A., Plant Breeding, Cytogenetics
ROSTAMI, A. A., Mechanical Engineering
SAADATPOUR, M. M., Civil Engineering
TAHANI, V., Electronic Engineering

ISLAMIC AZAD UNIVERSITY

159 7th Boostan St, Pasdaran Ave, Tehran 16666-37611
Telephone: (21) 22565149
E-mail: info@intl.iau.ir
Internet: www.intl.iau.ir

Founded 1982
Private control
Language of instruction: Persian
Academic year: September to September

Colleges of agricultural engineering, arts, civil engineering, humanities, medicine and basic sciences; each of the University's 350 brs, which are located throughout Iran, offers a selection of the courses run by the univ.

Pres.: Dr FARHAD DANESHJOO
Vice-Pres. for Academic Affairs: Dr BOLANDI
Vice-Pres. for Construction and Devt: A. SHAHRAKI
Vice-Pres. for Coordination Affairs: M. S. KALHOR
Vice-Pres. for Cultural Affairs: M. PIRAYANDEH
Vice-Pres. for Financial and Admin. Affairs: KHOJASTEH
Vice-Pres. for Int. Affairs: Dr HOSEIN SADEGHI SHOJA
Vice-Pres. for Medical Affairs: Dr H. YAHYAVI
Vice-Pres. for Non-Profit Schools: M. MIRSHAMSI
Vice-Pres. for Parliamentary Affairs: Dr F. FARMAND
Vice-Pres. for Research Affairs: Dr AFSHAR
Vice-Pres. for Student Affairs: Dr J. AZIZIAN
Librarian: P. MAHASTI SHOTORBANI

Library: 8.2m. vols
Number of teachers: 37,900
Number of students: 2,000,000

Publications: *Armane-e-Pazhouhesh*, *Bassirat* (Vision, 4 a year), *Daneshnameh* (4 a year), *Danesh va Pezhouhesh* (4 a year), *Economics and Management* (4 a year), *Ensan Va Andishe* (Man and Thought, 4 a year), *Geographic Space* (4 a year), *Jelvegahe-do-payam* (4 a year), *Journal of Agricultural Sciences* (4 a year), *Journal of Medical Sciences* (4 a year), *Journal of Sciences* (4 a year), *Koushk* (4 a year), *Mobin* (4 a year), *Namaye Pazhoohosh* (4 a year), *Nedaye-Daneshgah* (4 a year), *Nedaye Golestan* (4 a year), *Nourolelm* (4 a year), *Omran* (4 a year), *Pazhoheshnameh I* (4 a year), *Pazhuhesh–DINI* (4 a year), *Peyke Dime* (4 a year), *Pooyesh* (4 a year), *Pouya* (4 a year), *Rah-avar*, *Rahavard* (4 a year), *Rouyesh* (4 a year), *Scientific-Cultural Letter of Research* (4 a year), *Scientific Research Journal* (4 a year), *Scientific Research Periodical* (4 a year), *Scientific Research Quarterly*, *Sedaye Didar* (4 a year), *Selselat-Al-Zahab* (4 a year), *Sokhane Ashna* (4 a year), *Tazeha* (4 a year), *Tolu-e-Andishe* (4 a year), *Yeganeh* (4 a year), *Zakaria Razi* (4 a year)

KERMANSHAH UNIVERSITY OF MEDICAL SCIENCES

Shahid Beheshti Blvd, Kermanshah
Telephone: (831) 8354434
E-mail: info@kums.ac.ir
Internet: www.kums.ac.ir

Founded 1986, fmrly part of Razi Univ.
State control
Academic year: September to July

Chancellor: Dr SAMAD NORIZAD
Vice-Chancellor for Admin. and Financial Affairs: Dr EBRAHIM SHAKIBA
Vice-Chancellor for Education and Research: Dr HAMIDREZA OMRANI
Vice-Chancellor for Food and Drugs: Dr REZA TAHVILIAN
Vice-Chancellor for Health: Dr HAHAB MOINI MOSTOFI
Vice-Chancellor for Research: Dr FARID NAJAFI
Vice-Chancellor for Treatment: Dr TUORAJ AHMADI JUOYBARI
Librarian: SAYED JALAL KAZEMI OSKUEE

Library of 96,000 vols
Number of teachers: 230
Number of students: 3,100

Publications: *Behbood* (4 a year, scientific quarterly), *Journal of Injury and Violence Research*

DEANS

Faculty of Dentistry: Dr HAMID REZA MOZAFARI
Faculty of Health: Dr YAHYA SAFARI
Faculty of Medicine: Dr SAYED HAMID MADANI
Faculty of Nursing: Dr ALIREZA KHATONI
Faculty of Pharmacy: Dr BABAK GHOLAMIN
Faculty of Paramedics: FATEME DARABI

K. N. TOOSI UNIVERSITY OF TECHNOLOGY

POB 15875-4416, 470 Mirdamad Ave W, 19697-64499 Tehran
Telephone: (21) 88881003
E-mail: oisc@kntu.ac.ir
Internet: www.kntu.ac.ir

Founded 1928, present name 1987
State control
Languages of instruction: Persian, English
Academic year: September to June

Pres.: Dr SEYED MOHAMMAD TAGHI BATHAEE
Vice-Pres. for Admin. and Finance: Dr FARID NAJAFEE
Vice-Pres. for Education: Dr A. SHAHANI
Vice-Pres. for Research: Dr HAMID ABRISHAMI MOGHADAM
Vice-Pres. for Student Affairs: Dr HASSAM KARIMI MAZRAE
Librarian: Dr M. VARSHOSAZ

Library of 44,506 vols
Number of teachers: 240
Number of students: 5,600

Publications: *Abangan Magazine* (4 a year), *Journal of Robotics*, *Olum-o-Mohandesi'ye Nasir* (2 a year)

DEANS

Faculty of Aerospace Engineering: Dr M. MOSAVI NAIENIAN
Faculty of Civil Engineering: Dr MOGHADAS TAFRESHI
Faculty of Electrical and Computer Engineering: Dr AHMADIAN
Faculty of Geodesy and Geomatics Engineering: Dr VOSOOGHI
Faculty of Industrial Engineering: Dr KHOSHALHAN
Faculty of Mechanical Engineering: Dr Z. BASHAR HAGH
Faculty of Science: Dr SALEH KOOTAHI

MASHHAD UNIVERSITY OF MEDICAL SCIENCES

Daneshghah Ave, POB 91375-345, Mashhad
Telephone: (511) 8022022
E-mail: info.en@mums.ac.ir
Internet: www.mums.ac.ir

Founded 1945
Academic year: October to July

Pres.: Dr MOSTAFA MEHRABI BAHAR
Vice-Pres. for Education: Dr MOHAMMAD REZA DARABI MAHBOUB
Vice-Pres. for Food and Drug Affairs: Dr MOHAMMAD REZA SABERI
Vice-Pres. for Health: Dr REZA SAEEDI
Vice-Pres. for Management and Resources Devt: Dr SEYYED MOHAMMAD HOSSEIN BAHREYNI
Vice-Pres. for Research: Dr MOHSEN TAFAGHODI
Vice-Pres. for Student Affairs: Dr MAHDI EBRAHIMI
Vice-Pres. for Treatment Affairs: Dr MAHMOUD AZARPAZHOOH
Librarian: P. MODIRAMANI
Librarian: Z. JANGI

Library of 100,000 vols
Number of teachers: 560
Number of students: 5,700

Publications: *Asia Oceania Journal of Nuclear Medicine & Biology* (4 a year), *Asia Pacific Journal of Medical Toxicology* (4 a year), *Avicenna Journal of Phytomedicine* (4 a year), *Evidence Based Care* (4 a year), *Future of Medical Education Journal* (4 a year), *International Journal of Pediatrics* (4 a year), *Iranian Journal of Basic Medical Sciences* (4 a year), *Iranian Journal of Medical Physics* (4 a year), *Iranian Journal of Neonatology* (4 a year), *Iranian Journal of Obstetrics, Gynaecology and Infertility* (52 a year), *Iranian Journal of Otorhinolaryngology* (4 a year), *Journal of Dental Material and Techniques* (4 a year), *Journal of Fasting and Health* (4 a year), *Journal of Fundamentals of Mental Health* (4 a year), *Journal of Mashhad Dental School* (4 a year), *Journal of Midwifery and Reproductive Health* (4 a year), *Journal of Paramedical Sciences & Rehabilitation* (4 a year), *Journal of Patient Safety & Quality Improvement* (4 a year), *Medical Journal of Mashhad University of Medical Sciences* (4 a year), *Nanomedicine Journal* (4 a year), *Reviews in Clinical Medicine* (4 a year)

DEANS

Faculty of Dentistry: Dr HASAN HOSEINPOUR JAJARM
Faculty of Health: Dr ALI TAGHIPOUR
Faculty of Health and Paramedical Sciences: Dr ABBAS AZIMI
Faculty of Medicine: Dr ALIREZA KHOOIE
Faculty of Nursing and Midwifery: Dr ABBASS HEIDARY
Faculty of Pharmacy: Dr MOHSEN IMEN SHAHIDI

MAZANDARAN UNIVERSITY

POB 416, Pasdaran St, Babolsar 47415
Telephone: (11252) 32095
E-mail: um@umz.ac.ir
Internet: www.umz.ac.ir

Founded 1975 as Reza Shah Kabir Univ., name changed 1980
State control
Language of instruction: Persian
Academic year: September to June

Pres.: Dr GHASEM ALIZADEH AFROUZI
Vice-Pres. for Academic Affairs: Dr SAEED MIRZANEJAD
Vice-Pres. for Admin. and Finance: Dr BAHRAM SADEGHPOUR
Vice-Pres. for Research: Dr AHMAS JAFARI SAMIMI
Vice-Pres. for Student Affairs: Dr MORTEZA ALAVIAN
Registrar: Dr ALI BAGHERI KHALILI
Librarian: Dr REZA NOORZAD

Number of teachers: 320
Number of students: 11,300

DEANS

Faculty of Art and Architecture: Dr GHOLAMREZA MALEKSHAHI
Faculty of Basic Sciences: Dr YAHYA TALEBI
Faculty of Economics and Admin. Sciences: Dr ALIREZA POURFARAJ
Faculty of Humanities and Social Sciences: Dr GHOLAMREZA PIROUZ
Faculty of Law and Political Science: Dr KIOMARS KALANTARI
Faculty of Physical Sciences: Dr SHADMEHR MIRDAR

PAYAME NOOR UNIVERSITY

POB 19395-4697, Lashkarak Rd, Tehran 19569
Telephone: (21) 22442042
E-mail: int@pnu.ac.ir
Internet: www.pnu.ac.ir

Founded 1987
State control
Languages of instruction: Persian, English
Academic year: September to July (2 semesters)

Pres.: Prof. ABOLFAZL FARAHANI
Vice-Pres. for Admin., Finance and Devt: Dr SEYED MOHAMMAD SADRI
Vice-Pres. for Education and Continuing Education: Dr ALIREZA DELAFKAR
Vice-Pres. for Planning, Devt and Provincial Affairs: REZA RASOULI
Vice-Pres. for Social and Cultural Affairs: Dr ALIREZA AZHDAR
Vice-Pres. for Technology and Research: Dr AHMAD AKHOUND
Dir of the Int. Office: Dr HAMID REZA ZIAEI
Librarian: Dr HOSSEIN ZARE

Library: 1.4m. vols (total for all centres)
Number of teachers: 3,500

Publications: *Journal of Basic Sciences* (4 a year), *Journal of Humanities* (4 a year), *Peyke Noor Journal* (6 a year)

DEANS

Department of Agricultural Sciences: Dr BAKHSHI KHANIKI
Department of Art and Architecture: Dr JAHAN BAKHSH
Department of Educational Sciences and Psychology: Dr LOGHMAN KESHAVARZ
Department of Management, Economics and Accountancy: Dr MOHAMMAD TAGHI AMINI
Faculty of Basic Sciences: Prof. SEYED AHMAD MIRSHOKRAIE
Faculty of Engineering: Dr GHAZI ZADEH
Faculty of Foreign Languages and Literature: Dr FATEMEH KOUPA
Faculty of Social Sciences: Dr HOOSHANG KHOSROWBEIGI
Faculty of Theology and Islamic Sciences: Dr SEYED ALI ALAMOLHODA

PETROLEUM UNIVERSITY OF TECHNOLOGY

569 Hafez Ave, Tehran 15996-45313
Telephone: (21) 8804272
E-mail: info@put.ac.ir
Internet: www.put.ac.ir

Founded 1939 as Abadan Institute of Technology
State control, under Min. of Petroleum

Languages of instruction: English, Persian
Academic year: September to June

Chancellor: Dr D. H. PANJESHAHI
Vice-Chancellor for Academic Affairs: Dr M. R. SHISHESAZ
Vice-Chancellor for Finance and Admin.: A. ALIMORADY
Vice-Chancellor for Research Affairs: Dr B. ROUZBEHANI
Vice-Chancellor for Research and Postgraduate Studies: Dr A. EMAMZADEH
Vice-Chancellor for Student Affairs: Dr N. NABHANI
Registrar: Dr M. FARZAM
Number of teachers: 100
Number of students: 1,500

DEANS

Faculty of Accounting and Finance (Tehran): Dr A. EMAMZADEH
Faculty of Chemical and Petrochemical Engineering (Abadan): Dr T. JADIDI
Faculty of Petroleum Engineering (Ahwaz): Dr K. SALAHSHOOR

ATTACHED INSTITUTE

Mahmood-Abad Institute for Marine Sciences: POB 161, Mahmood-Abad; Dir H. RAZAEE

RAZI UNIVERSITY

Bagh-e-Abrisham, Kermanshah
Telephone: (831) 4274501
E-mail: info@razi.ac.ir
Internet: www.razi.ac.ir

Founded 1974
State control
Languages of instruction: English, Persian
Academic year: January to September

Chancellor: Prof. MOHAMMAD MEHDI KHODAEI
Vice-Chancellor for Academic Affairs: Dr ALI BIDMESHKIPOUR
Vice-Chancellor for Research Affairs: Dr SAEED JALALI HONARMAND
Vice-Chancellor for Student Affairs: Dr ABDOLALI CHALE-CHALE
Number of teachers: 380
Number of students: 15,000

DEANS

School of Agriculture: Dr FARDIN HOJABRI
School of Engineering: Dr NAJAF BIGLARI
School of Literature and Humanities: Dr VAHID SABZIANPOUR
School of Physical Education: Dr VAHID TADIBI
School of Science: Dr REZA HASHEMI
School of Social Science: Dr KHODAMORAD MOMENI
School of Veterinary Medicine: Dr ALI GHASHGHAII

SEMNAN UNIVERSITY OF MEDICAL SCIENCES

POB 35195-163, Molavi Blvd, Semnan
Telephone: (231) 3320112
E-mail: info@sem-ums.ac.ir
Internet: www.sem-ums.ac.ir

Founded 1988 as Semnan College of Medical Sciences; present name and status 1990
Academic year: September to June (2 semesters)
Works in collaboration with seven hospitals in the Semnan province

Chancellor: Dr ALI RASHIDI-POUR
Vice-Chancellor for Academic and Research Affairs: Dr VAHID SEMNANI
Vice-Chancellor for Drugs and Food: Dr SIAMAK YAGHMAIAN
Vice-Chancellor for Financial and Admin. Affairs: Dr BEHPOUR YOUSEFI
Vice-Chancellor for Health Affairs: Dr JAFAR JANDAGHI
Vice-Chancellor for Student Affairs: Dr MOHAMMAD AMOUZADEH KHALILI
Vice-Chancellor for Treatment: Dr MOHAMMAD BAGHER SABERI ZAFARGHANDI
Head Librarian: Dr GHOLAMREZA IRAJIAN
Library of 41,863 vols, 125 current periodicals, 417 theses
Number of teachers: 120
Number of students: 1,420
Publications: *Avay-e-Elm* (medical research, 2 or 3 a year, in Persian), *Health communicators, focus on Health* (2 a year, in Persian), *Health magazine* (2 a year, in Persian), *Koomesh Medical Journal* (4 a year, in Persian)

DEANS

Faculty of Health: MOHAMMAD BAGHER DELKHOSH
Faculty of Medicine: Dr MOHAMMAD E. AMINBEIDOKHTI
Faculty of Nursing and Paramedical Sciences: SAEED HAJIAGHAJANI
Faculty of Rehabilitation: Dr AMIR H. BAKHTIARI

SHAHED UNIVERSITY

POB 15875-5794, 115 N Kargar Ave, Tehran
Telephone: (21) 6413734
E-mail: publicrelation@shahed.ac.ir
Internet: www.shahed.ac.ir

Founded 1989
State control
Academic year: September to June

Chancellor: Dr MAHMOOD NOORISAFA
Vice-Chancellor for Academic Affairs: Dr SEIYED KAZEM FOROOTAN
Vice-Chancellor for Admin. and Financial Affairs, and Devt: Dr MOSTAFA KIAIE
Vice-Chancellor for Cultural Affairs: Dr ALI AZAM KHOSRARI
Vice-Chancellor for Research: Dr SOGHRAT FAGHIHZADEH
Vice-Chancellor for Student Affairs: Dr KAMRAR SAGHAFI
Librarian: ABFOLREZA NOROOZI CHACOLI
Library of 215,000 vols, 240 periodicals
Number of teachers: 220
Number of students: 3,000
Publication: *Daneshvar* (4 a year)

DEANS

Faculty of Agriculture: Dr MASOOD ISFAHANI
Faculty of Art: ALI ASGAR SHIRAZI
Faculty of Basic Sciences: Dr IRAJ RASOOLI
Faculty of Dentistry: Dr SEIYED SHOJAEDDIN SHAYEGH
Faculty of Engineering: Dr JALAL NAZARZADEH
Faculty of Humanities and Literature: Dr MOHAMMAD REZA IMAM
Faculty of Medical Sciences: Dr SEIYED SAEID SEIYED MORTAZ

SHAHID BAHONAR UNIVERSITY OF KERMAN

POB 76169-133, Kerman
Telephone: (341) 3220041
E-mail: sbuk@mail.uk.ac.ir
Internet: www.uk.ac.ir

Founded 1974, teaching commenced 1975
State control
Languages of instruction: Persian, English
Academic year: September to June
Colleges of agriculture, art, basic sciences, engineering, literature and human sciences, management and economics, mathematics and computer science, physical education and sports science, veterinary sciences; faculties of agriculture (Jiroft), higher education (Bam), mining (Zarand), technology (Sirjan)

Pres.: AHMAD AMIRI KHORASANI
Vice-Pres. for Admin. and Finance: AKBAR HOSSEINI POUR
Vice-Pres. for Education: HOSSEIN MOHEBI
Vice-Pres. for Research: MOHAMMAD RANJBAR HAMGHAVANDI
Vice-Pres. for Student Affairs: MANSOUR SAHEBZAMANI
Registrar: Dr M. A. VALI
Librarian: M. SHAFIIE
Library of 150,000 vols
Number of teachers: 400
Number of students: 12,500

SHAHID BEHESHTI UNIVERSITY

Evin, 19834 Tehran 19839-63113
Telephone: (21) 29901
E-mail: info@sbu.ac.ir
Internet: www.sbu.ac.ir

Founded 1960 as Nat. Univ. of Iran; present name 1983
State control
Language of instruction: Farsi
Academic year: September to June

Pres.: Prof. AHMAD SHAABANI
Vice-Pres. for Admin. and Finance: Dr BEHROOZ DORI
Vice-Pres. for Education and Graduate Studies: Dr BAHMAN HONARI
Vice-Pres. for Information and Communication Technology: Dr FEREIDOON SHAMS
Vice-Pres. for Research and Technology: Dr PEYMAN SALEHI
Vice-Pres. for Student and Cultural Affairs: Dr MORTEZA SAMNOON MAHDAVI
Dir for Collegiate Relations and Int. Scientific Cooperation: Dr HOSSEIN POUR AHMADI
Dir for Public Relations: HADI SALEHI ZADEH
Registrar: Dr MASOOD SHARIFI
Library: see under Libraries and Archives
Number of teachers: 500
Number of students: 13,600
Publications: *Ayeneh Isar*, *Ayeneh Ma'refat* (Research Journal of Philosophy and Discourse), *Daneshnameh*, *Journal of Earth Sciences*, *Journal of Family Research*, *Journal of Human Sciences*, *Management Excellence*, *Management Perspective*, *Rahyaft* (Political and International Approaches, 4 a year), *Quarterly Applied Psychology*, *Revue de Recherche Juridique*, *Soffeh* (architecture)

DEANS

Faculty of Architecture and Urban Planning: Dr AKBAR HAJ EBRAHIM ZARGAR
Faculty of Biological Sciences: Dr MASSOD SHEIDAI
Faculty of Earth Sciences: Dr HASSAN LASHKARI
Faculty of Economics and Political Sciences: Dr MOHAMMAD NASER SHERAFAT JAHROMI
Faculty of Education and Psychology: HAMID REZA POURETAMAD
Faculty of Electrical and Computer Engineering: Dr SEYED EBRAHIM AFJEII
Faculty of Law: Dr GOODARZ EFTEKHAR JAHROMI
Faculty of Letters and Human Sciences: Dr AKBAR MAJDODINE
Faculty of Management and Accounting: Dr MOHAMMAD ESMAEIL FADAEI
Faculty of Mathematical Sciences: Dr MOHAMMAD ZOKAEI
Faculty of New Technologies and Energy Engineering: Dr ABAS SAIDI
Faculty of Physical Education and Sports Sciences: Dr KHOSRO EBRAHIM
Faculty of Sciences: Dr MEHRDAD FARHOUDI
Faculty of Theology and Religions: Dr HASSAN SAEEDI

PROFESSORS

ABASSI, A., Literature and Human Sciences
ABBAS ZADEGAN, S. M., Education and Psychology
ABBASPOUR, M., Electrical and Computer Engineering
ABDI DANESHPOUR, Z., Architecture and Urban Planning
ABDOLAHI, M., Environmental Sciences Research Institute
ABDOLI, A., Environmental Sciences Research Institute
ABDOLI, B., Physical Education and Sports Sciences
ABEDIN, A., Education and Psychology
ABEDIN, A., Family Research Institute
ABOLGHASEMI, M., Education and Psychology
ABOLGHASEMI, S. M., Literature and Human Sciences
ADABI, M. H., Earth Sciences
ADIB RAD, N., Education and Psychology
ADIBZADEH, B., Architecture and Urban Planning
AFJEI, S. E., Electrical and Computer Engineering
AGHDAEE, M., Physical Education and Sports Sciences
AHARI, Z., Architecture and Urban Planning
AHMAD ZADEH, F., Environmental Sciences Research Institute
AHMADI, F., Architecture and Urban Planning
AHMADI, S. H., Literature and Human Sciences
AHMADZADEH, S., Literature and Human Sciences
AKBARI, M. A., Literature and Human Sciences
AKBARI GHAMSARI, A., Literature and Human Sciences
AKBARIAN, M., Management and Accounting
ALAEI, A., Architecture and Urban Planning
ALAMOL HODA, J., Education and Psychology
ALASKARI, Z., Literature and Human Sciences
ALAVI, S. A., Earth Sciences
ALAVINIA, S., Literature and Human Sciences
ALBORZ, M., Mathematical Sciences
ALEM TABRIZ, A., Management and Accounting
ALIREZAEI, S., Earth Sciences
ALSHAHIR BIFARHANG MAJDODDIN, A., Literature and Human Sciences
AMINI, M., Law
AMINI HOURA, M., Architecture and Urban Planning
AMIR ARJOMAND, A., Law
ANSARINIA, S., Architecture and Urban Planning
ARAB MAZAR, A., Economic and Political Sciences
ARABMAZAR YAZDI, M., Management and Accounting
ARBABI, M., Law
ARBABIAN, A., Management and Accounting
ARDEBILI, M. A., Law
ARDEBILI, M. H., Management and Accounting
AREFI, M., Education and Psychology
ASADI, G., Management and Accounting
ASGHARI, A. H., Mathematical Sciences
ASGHARIAN JEDDI, A., Architecture and Urban Planning
ASHTIANI, M., Education and Psychology
ASLANKHANI, M., Physical Education and Sports Sciences
ASSADI, B., Economic and Political Sciences
AVANI, G., Literature and Human Sciences
AYATOLLAHZADEH SHIRAZI, M. M., Mathematical Sciences
AZADEH, A. A., Mathematical Sciences
AZARI, H., Mathematical Sciences
AZGHANDI, A., Economic and Political Sciences
BA EZAT, F., Education and Psychology
BABAPOOR, M. M., Department of Islamic Teachings
BADIEI, M., Architecture and Urban Planning
BAGHERIAN, F., Education and Psychology
BAHADORI BARCHELOEI, M., Electrical and Computer Engineering
BAHADORIFAR, M., Earth Sciences
BAHAR NEJAD, Z., Department of Islamic Teachings
BAHARI ARDESHIRI, A. A., Literature and Human Sciences
BAHER, G., Management and Accounting
BANA RAZAVI, M., Economic and Political Sciences
BARGH JELVE, S., Environmental Sciences Research Institute
BEHESHTI AVAL, S. B., Architecture and Urban Planning
BEHZAD, M., Mathematical Sciences
BEHZADI SHIRKALA, M., Earth Sciences
BEIGZADEH, E., Law
BERANJEH TORABI, D. M., Literature and Human Sciences
BLACK, J. E., Environmental Sciences Research Institute
BOZORGAN NIA, M. A., Literature and Human Sciences
CHALABI, M., Literature and Human Sciences
CHENARI, A. A., Literature and Human Sciences
CHIME, N., Family Research Institute
DADASHI, M. S., Physical Education and Sport Sciences
DADGAR, U., Law
DADKAN, M. H., Physical Education and Sport Sciences
DANESH, E., Education and Psychology
DANESHPOUR PARVAR, F., Literature and Human Sciences
DARABKOLAIE, E., Department of Islamic Teachings
DARABPOUR, M., Law
DARGAHI, A., Electrical and Computer Engineering
DARGAHI, H., Economic and Political Sciences
DARIUSH HAMEDANI, H., Mathematical Sciences
DARKOOSH, S. A., Economic and Political Sciences
DAVOODI, P., Economic and Political Sciences
DEHGAN, A., Department of Islamic Teachings
DEHGHAN, M., Family Research Institute
DEHZAD, B., Earth Sciences
DELSHAD, S., Literature and Human Sciences
DEYHIMFARD, R., Environmental Sciences Research Institute
DEZFOULIAN, K., Literature and Human Sciences
DIDARI, R., Literature and Human Sciences
DORRI, B., Management and Accounting
EBRAHIM, K., Physical Education and Sport Sciences
EBRAHIMI, M. M., Mathematical Sciences
EBRAHIMI VARKIANI, M., Department of Islamic Teachings
EFTEKHAR JAHROMI, G., Law
EJTEHADI, M., Literature and Human Sciences
EMADZADEH, G., Literature and Human Sciences
ESHGHI, M., Electrical and Computer Engineering
ESLAHCHI, C., Mathematical Sciences
ESLAMI, R., Law
ESMAEILI, J., Electrical and Computer Engineering
ESMAILPOUR MOTLAGH, A., Literature and Human Sciences
ESPANDAR, R., Earth Sciences
ESTARAMI, E., Literature and Human Sciences
ETEZADI, L., Architecture and Urban Planning
FADAEI NEJAD, M. E., Management and Accounting
FAGHIHI, M. R., Mathematical Sciences
FAKHARI, A. H., Law
FAKHARI TEHRANI, F., Architecture and Urban Planning
FALLAHI, A., Architecture and Urban Planning
FALSAFI, H., Law
FANNI, Z., Earth Sciences
FARDANESH, M. A., Economic and Political Sciences
FARSIJANI, H., Management and Accounting
FARZAD, F., Management and Accounting
FATEMI JAHROMI, S. A., Literature and Human Sciences
FATHI VAJAR GAH, K., Education and Psychology
FATTAH, A., Electrical and Computer Engineering
FERDOSI, S., Education and Psychology
FEYZOLLAHZADEH, A., Literature and Human Sciences
FOROOZESH, N., Mathematical Sciences
FOYOZAT, E., Literature and Human Sciences
GADAK, A., Law
GANJALI, M., Mathematical Sciences
GHADIMI, H., Architecture and Urban Planning
GHADIRI, F., Family Research Institute
GHAEM, G., Architecture and Urban Planning
GHAFFARI, A., Architecture and Urban Planning
GHAFOORI, M., Economic and Political Sciences
GHAHREMANI, M., Education and Psychology
GHANAATSHOAR, M., Laser and Plasma Research Institute
GHANBARI, M. J., Law
GHANBARI MAMAN, H., Economic and Political Sciences
GHAREHCHEH, M., Management and Accounting
GHARI SEYED FATEMI, M., Law
GHASEMI HAMED, A., Law
GHASEMPOUR, A., Environmental Sciences Research Institute
GHASEMZADEH, A., Management and Accounting
GHAVAM, A., Economic and Political Sciences
GHAVAMI ZADEH, R., Electrical and Computer Engineering
GHAVIMI, M., Literature and Human Sciences
GHOAMREZAEI, M., Literature and Human Sciences
GHORBANI, M., Earth Sciences
GHOUCHANI, F., Management and Accounting
GOLDOOST JOUYBARI, R., Law
GOLKAR, K., Architecture and Urban Planning
GOOYA, Z., Mathematical Sciences
HADDADI, S. M., Literature and Human Sciences
HADIZADEH, A., Management and Accounting
HAGHIGHAT, R., Earth Sciences
HAGHIGHI, M., Management and Accounting
HAJ EBRAHIM ZARGAR, A., Architecture and Urban Planning
HAJ JABBARI, S., Mathematical Sciences
HAJI GHASEMI, K., Architecture and Urban Planning
HAJI KARIMI, A., Management and Accounting
HAJI MIR ARAB, M., Economic and Political Sciences
HAJIABOLHASAN, H., Mathematical Sciences
HAJI-YOUSEFI, A. M., Economic and Political Sciences
HAMIDIZADEH, M. R., Management and Accounting
HAMIDREZA, G., Laser and Plasma Research Institute
HANAEI KASHANI, M. S., Literature and Human Sciences
HANJANI, S. A., Law
HASAN ZADE KIABI, B., Environmental Sciences Research Institute

HASHEMI, S. A., Economic and Political Sciences
HASHEMI, S. H., Environmental Sciences Research Institute
HASHEMI, S. M., Law
HASHEMIPOUR, O., Electrical and Computer Engineering
HASSANI, A., Literature and Human Sciences
HASSANI, M., Earth Sciences
HEKMAT, N., Literature and Human Sciences
HERAVI, I., Management and Accounting
HERAVI, M., Architecture and Urban Planning
HESHMATZADEH, M. B., Economic and Political Sciences
HEYDARI, M., Education and Psychology
HEYDARI, M., Family Research Institute
HEYDARIAN., M. T., Literature and Human Sciences
HOJJAT, M., Department of Islamic Teachings
HONARI, B., Mathematical Sciences
HOSHI, A., Management and Accounting
HOSSEINABADI, A., Law
HOSSEINALIPOUR, S., Architecture and Urban Planning
HOSSEINI, S. M., Management and Accounting
HOSSEINI BARMAEI, S. F., Law
HOSSEINI BARZI, M., Earth Sciences
HOSSEINPOUR KAZEMI, M., Economic and Political Sciences
HOSSEINZADEH, M., Management and Accounting
HOVANLO, F., Physical Education and Sport Sciences
HOZHABR KIANI, K., Economic and Political Sciences
ILKHANI, M., Literature and Human Sciences
ILKHANI, S. C., Literature and Human Sciences
JABERIPOUR, G., Electrical and Computer Engineering
JAFARI ROHANI, B., Mathematical Sciences
JAHANKHANI, A., Management and Accounting
JALALI, A., Electrical and Computer Engineering
JALALI, M., Architecture and Urban Planning
JAVIDRUZI, M., Architecture and Urban Planning
JOUDAT, M. R., Architecture and Urban Planning
KAFAIE, S. M. A., Economic and Political Sciences
KANANI, M. R., Environmental Sciences Research Institute
KARIMIAN, F., Literature and Human Sciences
KASSAEE, M., Management and Accounting
KHAKZAD, A., Earth Sciences
KHALATBARI, A., Literature and Human Sciences
KHALEDI, S., Earth Sciences
KHALFEH SHOUSHTARI, M. E., Literature and Human Sciences
KHALIGHI, A., Literature and Human Sciences
KHANSARI MOUSAVI, S., Literature and Human Sciences
KHATAMI, A., Literature and Human Sciences
KHATAMI, M. J., Architecture and Urban Planning
KHATTAT, N. K., Literature and Human Sciences
KHEYRANDISH, A., Environmental Sciences Research Institute
KHLLAT, F., Mathematical Sciences
KHODA PANAHI, M. K., Education and Psychology
KHODADADI, A., Mathematical Sciences
KHODAI KALATEBAI, N., Literature and Human Sciences
KHODAIAN, S., Earth Sciences
KHOMAMIZADEH, F., Law
KHORASANI ZADEH, M., Architecture and Urban Planning
KHORSAND, H., Electrical and Computer Engineering
KHORSHIDI, G., Management and Accounting
KHOSH KONESH, A., Education and Psychology
KHOSHBAKHT, K., Environmental Sciences Research Institute
KOOSHA, J., Law
KOUCHAKZADE, M., Environmental Sciences Research Institute
LAJEVARDI, M., Earth Sciences
LAJEVARDI, S. J., Management and Accounting
LARI, A., Physical Education and Sport Sciences
LASHKARI, H., Earth Sciences
LATIFI, H., Laser and Plasma Research Institute
LESSAN PEZESHKI, H., Literature and Human Sciences
LIAGHATI, H., Environmental Sciences Research Institute
LOTF ABADI, H., Education and Psychology
LOTFALIKANI, A., Earth Sciences
MAHDAVI, M. S., Literature and Human Sciences
MAHDAVI DAMGHANI, A. M., Environmental Sciences Research Institute
MAHDAVI HERSINI, S. E., Education and Psychology
MAHMOUDI, H., Environmental Sciences Research Institute
MAHMOUDI, M., Mathematical Sciences
MAJIDI KHAMENEH, B., Earth Sciences
MAKHZAN MOUSAVI, S. A., Literature and Human Sciences
MANAVI TEHRAN, A., Economic and Political Sciences
MANI, M. A., Economic and Political Sciences
MANSOORBAKHT, G., Literature and Human Sciences
MANSOUR, L., Education and Psychology
MARANDI, M. R., Department of Islamic Teachings
MASHAYEKH FARIDANI, S., Architecture and Urban Planning
MASOUDI, R., Laser and Plasma Research Institute
MASOUMZADEH KIAEI, M. A., Economic and Political Sciences
MAZAHERI TEHRANI, M. A., Education and Psychology
MAZAHERI TEHRANI, M. A., Family Research Institute
MAZLOOMNEZHAD, B., Electrical and Computer Engineering
MEHRA, N., Law
MEHRDAD, S. M., Environmental Sciences Research Institute
MEHRPOUR MOHAMMADABADI, H., Law
MEHRSHAHI, E., Electrical and Computer Engineering
MEMARIAN, A., Architecture and Urban Planning
MESGARI, A. A., Literature and Human Sciences
MESHKANI, M. R., Mathematical Sciences
MILANI, V., Mathematical Sciences
MINA KARI, M., Education and Psychology
MINOUEI, S., Environmental Sciences Research Institute
MIR JALILI, M. H., Environmental Sciences Research Institute
MIR RIAHI, S., Architecture and Urban Planning
MIR SHAMS SHAHSHAHANI, S., Literature and Human Sciences
MIRI, S., Architecture and Urban Planning
MIRMOHAMMAD SADEGHI, H., Law
MOEINI, M., Physical Education and Sport Sciences
MOGHIM ESLAM, G., Laser and Plasma Research Institute
MOGHISEH, H., Department of Islamic Teachings
MOHAGHEGH AHMADABADI (DAMAD), S. M., Law
MOHAJERANI, A., Laser and Plasma Research Institute
MOHAMMADI, H. R., Earth Sciences
MOHAMMADZADEH, H., Earth Sciences
MOHSENI ARMAKI, S. M., Laser and Plasma Research Institute
MOMAYEZ, A., Architecture and Urban Planning
MOMENI, I., Earth Sciences
MOMENI, M., Earth Sciences
MOMTAZ, F., Literature and Human Sciences
MONIRI, M., Mathematical Sciences
MONSHIZADEH, R., Earth Sciences
MORTAZAVI, S., Education and Psychology
MOSADEGH RASHTI, A. A., Literature and Human Sciences
MOSHARAFOLMOLK, M., Literature and Human Sciences
MOSHIRI, F., Architecture and Urban Planning
MOSTAFAVI, H., Environmental Sciences Research Institute
MOSTAFAVI KASHANI, S. M., Law
MOSTAFAVI NIA, S. M. K., Department of Islamic Teachings
MOTTAGHI, H., Management and Accounting
MOUSA POUR, N., Education and Psychology
MOUSAVI, M. R., Earth Sciences
MOUTABI, F., Family Research Institute
NADIMI, H., Architecture and Urban Planning
NADIMI, H., Literature and Human Sciences
NAHREYNI, F., Law
NAJAFI ABRANDABADI, H., Law
NAJAFIAN, B., Earth Sciences
NAMAZI, H., Economic and Political Sciences
NAMAZIAN, A., Architecture and Urban Planning
NAMAZIZADEH, M., Physical Education and Sport Sciences
NAMVAR GHAREH SHIRAN, E., Electrical and Computer Engineering
NASSERY, H. R., Earth Sciences
NAVAEI, K., Architecture and Urban Planning
NAVI, K., Electrical and Computer Engineering
NAZARI, A., Architecture and Urban Planning
NAZEMI, E., Electrical and Computer Engineering
NEJAD EBRAHIMI, S., Environmental Sciences Research Institute
NEMATOLLAHI, V., Literature and Human Sciences
NIKBAKHT, H. R., Law
NIKNAM, A., Laser and Plasma Research Institute
NIKPEY, A., Law
NILI, M. Y., Architecture and Urban Planning
NOBAHAR, R., Law
NOFARASTI, M., Economic and Political Sciences
NOJOUMIAN, A. A., Literature and Human Sciences
NOOR BALOOCHI, S., Mathematical Sciences
NOORI NAEINI, S., Economic and Political Sciences
NOURANI POUR, R., Education and Psychology
NOURBAHA, R., Law
NOURI ROUDSARI, O., Environmental Sciences Research Institute
NOURSHAHI, M., Physical Education and Sport Sciences
ORKAMANI AZAR, F., Electrical and Computer Engineering
OSSEINION, S. A., Mathematical Sciences
PADIDAR, M., Architecture and Urban Planning
PAKDAMAN, S., Education and Psychology
PAKZAD, J., Architecture and Urban Planning
PALIZBAN, F., Literature and Human Sciences
PANAGHI, L., Family Research Institute
PARCHAMI, D., Literature and Human Sciences
PARDAKHTCHI, M., Education and Psychology

PARSA, M. A., Architecture and Urban Planning
PARVIN JAHROMI, K., Mathematical Sciences
PAZUKI, A., Architecture and Urban Planning
POOR KAZEMI, M. H., Economic and Political Sciences
POORBARAT, M., Mathematical Sciences
POORSINA, M., Department of Islamic Teachings
POUR AHMADI MIEBODI, H., Economic and Political Sciences
POUR ETEMAD, H. R., Education and Psychology
POUR KERAMATI, V., Architecture and Urban Planning
POUR KERMANI, M., Earth Sciences
POUR MOAFI, S. M., Earth Sciences
POURETEMAD, H., Family Research Institute
POURKIANI, M., Physical Education and Sport Sciences
RAFATI, H., Environmental Sciences Research Institute
RAFIPOOR, F., Literature and Human Sciences
RAHGOSHAI, M., Earth Sciences
RAHMANI, B., Earth Sciences
RAHMANI FAZLI, A., Earth Sciences
RASA, I., Earth Sciences
RASEKH, M., Law
RASHIDIAN, A., Literature and Human Sciences
RASI, M., Literature and Human Sciences
RASOULI NARAGHI, G., Architecture and Urban Planning
RASTKAR, A. R., Laser and Plasma Research Institute
RAZAVI ZADEH, G., Electrical and Computer Engineering
RAZAVIAN, M. T., Earth Sciences
RAZJOUYAN, M., Architecture and Urban Planning
RAZMGAH, F., Architecture and Urban Planning
REZA, M. T., Environmental Sciences Research Institute
REZAEIAN, A., Management and Accounting
REZAZADE VALUJERDI, A., Electrical and Computer Engineering
ROHANI RANKOUHI, M. T., Electrical and Computer Engineering
ROOZBEHAN, M., Economic and Political Sciences
ROSHAN, M., Family Research Institute
ROSOULI, H., Literature and Human Sciences
ROUSTA, A., Management and Accounting
SABAHI, H., Environmental Sciences Research Institute
SABBAGHIAN, Z., Education and Psychology
SADAT KYAIE, M., Department of Islamic Teachings
SADEGHI, A., Earth Sciences
SADEGHI, A., Law
SADEGHI PEY, N., Architecture and Urban Planning
SADJADI, S. A. M., Literature and Human Sciences
SADOOGH VANINI, H., Earth Sciences
SADR, S. K., Economic and Political Sciences
SADRIA, A., Architecture and Urban Planning
SAEIDI, A., Earth Sciences
SAFFAR, M. J., Law
SAFFARI, A., Law
SAHBA YAGHMAEI, M., Laser and Plasma Research Institute
SAIDI, H., Department of Islamic Teachings
SAJADI, J., Earth Sciences
SALAHI MALEK, Y., Economic and Political Sciences
SALEHI, P., Environmental Sciences Research Institute
SALEHI ZADEH, H., Department of Islamic Teachings
SALEHPOUR, Y., Family Research Institute
SALEMI, A., Environmental Sciences Research Institute
SAMNON, M., Department of Islamic Teachings
SAMSAMI, H., Economic and Political Sciences
SANEI DAREHBIDI, M., Literature and Human Sciences
SANIEI, N., Electrical and Computer Engineering
SARAFI, M., Earth Sciences
SARIOLGHALAM, M., Economic and Political Sciences
SARTIPI POUR, M., Architecture and Urban Planning
SAVARAEI, P., Law
SAVOJI, M. H., Electrical and Computer Engineering
SEIFI, S. J., Law
SEIFI, Z., Law
SERVAT, M. M., Literature and Human Sciences
SERVATI, M. R., Earth Sciences
SEYED HASHEMI, S. E., Department of Islamic Teachings
SEYED MIRZAEI, S. M., Literature and Human Sciences
SHABANI, N., Environmental Sciences Research Institute
SHABANI, R., Literature and Human Sciences
SHAEGHI, A. A., Environmental Sciences Research Institute
SHAFIE HOLIHI, K., Mathematical Sciences
SHAH HOSSEINI, H., Electrical and Computer Engineering
SHAHBAZI, E., Environmental Sciences Research Institute
SHAHIDA, M. R., Earth Sciences
SHAHIDI, S., Education and Psychology
SHAHLAEE, A., Mathematical Sciences
SHAHNI KARAMAZADEH, N., Mathematical Sciences
SHAHRIARI, S., Earth Sciences
SHAHSHAHANI, S., Literature and Human Sciences
SHAHVARANI, A., Mathematical Sciences
SHAMLOO, B., Law
SHAMS, A., Law
SHAMSFARD, M., Electrical and Computer Engineering
SHARIF TEHRANI, S. R., Architecture and Urban Planning
SHARIFI, M., Education and Psychology
SHARIFI, M., Family Research Institute
SHARIFI, M. J., Electrical and Computer Engineering
SHEIKH, M. A., Literature and Human Sciences
SHEIKHHASSANI, G. H., Earth Sciences
SHEMIRANI, A., Earth Sciences
SHERAFAT, M. N., Economic and Political Sciences
SHOEIBI, A., Architecture and Urban Planning
SHOKRI, B., Laser and Plasma Research Institute
SIMBAR, F., Economic and Political Sciences
SOHEIL, K., Literature and Human Sciences
SOKHANVAR, J., Literature and Human Sciences
SOLEIMANI, D., Literature and Human Sciences
SONBOLI, A., Environmental Sciences Research Institute
TABARSA, G., Management and Accounting
TABATABEI, S., Electrical and Computer Engineering
TAFAZOLI, F., Economic and Political Sciences
TAGHI, Z., Architecture and Urban Planning
TAHBAZ, M., Architecture and Urban Planning
TAHMASBIAN, K., Family Research Institute
TAJIK, M. R., Economic and Political Sciences
TALEB ZADEH, M., Education and Psychology
TALEBI, D., Management and Accounting
TAVAKKOLI, M., Department of Islamic Teachings
TAVAKOLI, A., Economic and Political Sciences
TAVAKOLINIA, J., Earth Sciences
TAVASOLI, S. H., Laser and Plasma Research Institute
TAVASSOLIZADEH, N., Law
TEHRANCHI, M. M., Laser and Plasma Research Institute
THOMAS ZADEH, R., Literature and Human Sciences
TOUSI ARDEKANI, M., Mathematical Sciences
VAEZ IRAVANI, F., Electrical and Computer Engineering
VAEZI, A., Literature and Human Sciences
VAHDANI MOGHADAM, M., Laser and Plasma Research Institute
VAHID DOSTJERDI, F., Literature and Human Sciences
VAHIDI, T., Architecture and Urban Planning
VAHIDI ASL, M. Q., Mathematical Sciences
VATANKHAH, M., Economic and Political Sciences
VAZIRI FARAHANI, B., Architecture and Urban Planning
VAZIRI FARAHANI, P., Architecture and Urban Planning
VIZEH FAYAZ, O., Literature and Human Sciences
VOSOOGHI ABEDINI, M., Earth Sciences
YAMANI DOUZI SORKHABI, M., Education and Psychology
YAVARI, M. E., Economic and Political Sciences
YAZDI, M., Earth Sciences
YOSOFI, S. A., Mathematical Sciences
ZADE MOHAMMADI, A., Family Research Institute
ZAKER ALHOSSEINI, A., Electrical and Computer Engineering
ZAKERZADEH, A., Literature and Human Sciences
ZAND, E., Environmental Sciences Research Institute
ZAREI, M. H., Law
ZEKAVAT, K., Architecture and Urban Planning
ZIATAVANA, M. H., Earth Sciences
ZOKAEI, M., Mathematical Sciences

SHAHID BEHESHTI UNIVERSITY OF MEDICAL SCIENCES AND HEALTH SERVICES

POB 4139-19395, Shahid Chamran Highway, Evin, Tehran
Telephone: (21) 2401022
E-mail: icrd@sbmu.ac.ir
Internet: www.sbmu.ac.ir
Founded 1961 as Melli University; present name 1986
State control
Language of instruction: Farsi
Academic year: September to June
Chancellor: Dr HABIBOLLA PEYRAVI
Vice-Chancellor for Academic Affairs: Dr D. YADEGARI
Vice-Chancellor for Admin. and Finance: Dr R. ABOUFAZELI
Vice-Chancellor for Curative and Pharmaceutical Affairs: Dr S. S. RAZAVI
Vice-Chancellor for Health: Dr A. RAMEZANKHANI
Vice-Chancellor for Research: Dr M. JORJANI
Vice-Chancellor for Student and Cultural Affairs: Dr M. HOSSEINI KHAMENE
Dir for Int. Relations and Congress Management: Dr F. OKHOVATIAN
Librarian: A. MOHADES RAAD
Library of 5,458 vols, 3,000 current journals, 60 e-books
Number of teachers: 1,040
Number of students: 6,000
Publications: *Bina* (Journal of Ophthalmology, 4 a year), *Digestive Disease Digest* (12 a year), *International Journal of Endocrinology and Metabolism* (4 a year), *Iranian Journal of Infectious Disease and Tropical*

Medicine (4 a year), *Iranian Journal of Plastic and Reconstructive Surgery* (4 a year), *Iranian Journal of Urology* (4 a year), *Journal of Dentistry* (4 a year), *Journal of Medical Education* (4 a year), *Journal of the Pharmaceutical Research Centre* (4 a year), *Pejouhandeh* (4 a year), *Research in Medical Subjects* (4 a year, in Persian), *Tanaffos* (Respiration, 4 a year)

DEANS

Faculty of Allied Medicine: Dr S. H. MOGHADAM-NIA
Faculty of Dentistry
Faculty of Medicine: Dr M. MARDANI
Faculty of Nutrition and Industrial Food Sciences: Dr N. KALANTARI
School of Nursing and Midwifery: Dr M. YAZDJERDI
Faculty of Pharmacy: Dr M. MOSADEGH
School of Public Health: Dr H. KHATAMI
Faculty of Rehabilitation: Dr M. GHASSEMY BOROMAND

SHAHID CHAMRAN UNIVERSITY

Ahvaz, Khouzestan
Telephone: (611) 3330022
E-mail: webmaster@cua.ac.ir
Internet: www.scu.ac.ir

Founded 1955 as Jundi Shapur Univ., present name 1983
State control
Language of instruction: Farsi
Academic year: September to June

Chancellor: Dr MORTEZA ZARGAR SHOOSHTARI NOURI
Vice-Chancellor for Academic Affairs: Dr M. A. FIROOZI
Vice-Chancellor for Admin. and Finance: Dr GHOMESHI
Vice-Chancellor for Research and Technology: Dr H. R. GHAFOURI
Vice-Chancellor for Student Affairs: M. MOGHBELAL-HOSSEIN
Dir for Int. Affairs: Mr SADROS-SADAT
Registrar: M. JANNEJAD
Librarian: Dr A. FARAJPAHLOU

Number of teachers: 520
Number of students: 13,310

Publications: *Journal of Education and Psychology* (4 a year, in Persian), *Journal of Engineering* (1 a year, in Persian), *Journal of Literature and Islamic Studies* (1 a year, in Persian), *Journal of Veterinary Medicine* (1 a year, in FPersian), *Scientific Journal of Agriculture* (4 a year, in Persian), *University Journal of Science* (1 a year, in Persian)

DEANS

Faculty of Agriculture: Dr NABIPOUR
Faculty of Arts: M. KOLLAHKAJ
Faculty of Economic and Social Science: Dr NABAVI
Faculty of Education and Psychology: Dr M. KOUKABI
Faculty of Engineering: Dr M. JOORABIAN
Faculty of Geology and GIS: G. RANGZAN
Faculty of Literature and Humanities: Dr MOVAHED
Faculty of Mathematics and Computer Science: H. HARIZAVI
Faculty of Physical Education: Dr A. H. HABIBI
Faculty of Science: Dr M. CHITSAZAN
Faculty of Theology and Islamic Studies: Dr A. MATOORI
Faculty of Veterinary Science: Dr M. GHORBANPOUR
Faculty of Water Science Engineering: Dr S. M. KASHEFIPOUR

SHAHID SADOUGHI UNIVERSITY OF MEDICAL SCIENCES

POB 89195-734, 2 Bouali Ave, Yazd
Telephone: (351) 82470171
E-mail: ib@ssu.ac.ir
Internet: www.ssu.ac.ir

Founded 1983
State control
Language of instruction: Persian
Academic year: September to June

Chancellor: Dr AHMAD HAERIAN
Vice-Chancellor for Academic Affairs: Dr MR. MANSORIAN
Vice-Chancellor for Admin. and Financial Affairs: Dr MH. EHRAMPOUSH
Vice-Chancellor for Health: Dr M. KARIMI
Vice-Chancellor for Research Affairs: Dr S. M. YASSINI
Vice-Chancellor for Student Services: Dr HOSSEINI
Dir of Int. Affairs: Dr SM. KALANTAR
Registrar: A. M. ALI HEIDARI

Library of 40,000 vols, 278 journals
Number of teachers: 240
Number of students: 1,800

DEANS

Faculty of Dentistry: Dr TALEBI
Faculty of Medicine: Dr RAFIEAN
Faculty of Nursing and Midwifery: Dr SEYED HASSANI
Faculty of Paramedicine: Dr KHALILI
Faculty of Public Health: Dr EHRAMPOUSH

SHAHREKORD UNIVERSITY OF MEDICAL SCIENCES

POB 88184, Kashany Ave, Shahrekord
Telephone: (381) 34590
Internet: www.skums.ac.ir

Founded 1986
State control
Language of instruction: Persian

Pres.: Dr M. HASHEMZADEH
Vice-Chancellor for Admin. and Financial Affairs: F. SHARAFATI
Vice-Chancellor for Curative, Drug and Food Affairs: Dr E. NOORIAN
Vice-Chancellor for Education and Research: Dr M. R. SAMIEY NASAB
Vice-Chancellor for Student and Cultural Affairs: Dr H. DAVOODPOUR
Librarian: Dr A. AMINI

Library of 33,000 vols
Number of teachers: 130
Number of students: 1,400

DEANS

Faculty of Medicine: Dr M. ROGHANY
Faculty of Nursing and Midwifery: M. RAHIMY
Broujen Faculty of Nursing: S. BANAEYAN

SHARIF UNIVERSITY OF TECHNOLOGY

POB 11365-8639, Tehran
Telephone: (21) 66005419
E-mail: scientia@sharif.edu
Internet: www.sharif.edu

Founded 1965 as Aryamehr Univ., present name 1979
State control
Languages of instruction: Persian, English
Academic year: September to May

Depts of aerospace engineering, chemical engineering and petroleum, chemistry, civil engineering, computer engineering, electrical engineering, industrial engineering, management and economics, materials science and engineering, mathematical sciences, mechanical engineering, philosophy of science, physics

Pres.: Prof. SAEED SOHRABPOUR
Vice-Pres. for Admin. and Finance: Prof. SEYED ALI AKBAR EKRAMI
Vice-Pres. for Education and Graduate Studies: Prof. ALI MEGHDARI
Vice-Pres. for Planning and Budget: ALI ASGHAR ESKANDAR BAYATI
Vice-Pres. for Research: Dr REZA ROOSTA AZAD
Vice-Pres. for Student Affairs: Dr BIJAN VOSOOGHI VAHDAT
Chair. of Office of Int. and Scientific Cooperation (OISC): Prof. ABOLHASSAN VAFAI
Dean of Assessment: ALI KARIMI TAHERI
Dean of Education: ABOL GHASEM DOLATI
Dean of Extra Curriculum: MOHAMMAD MIRZAI
Dean of Financial Affairs: MOHAMMAD FOROOTAN
Dean of Graduate Studies: AMIR DANESHGAR
Dean of Human Resources: HAMID REZA MADAAH HOSSEINI
Dean of Industrial Cooperation: SEYYED JAMALEDIN HASHEMIAN
Dean of Research Affairs: MASOUD TAJRISHI
Dean of Student Affairs: SEYED REZA NAGHINASAB
Librarian: Prof. HAMID MEHDIGHOLI

Library of 242,000 vols (130,000 in English, 12,000 in Persian), 100,000 periodicals
Number of teachers: 300
Number of students: 8,000

Publications: *Scientia Iranica* (6 a year, in English), *Sharif* (scientific and research, 4 a year, in Persian).

ATTACHED RESEARCH CENTRES

Advanced Communications Research Institute: tel. (21) 6165910; e-mail acri@sharif.edu; internet acri.sharif.ir.

Advanced Information and Communication Technology Centre: e-mail info@aictc.ir; internet www.aictc.com; Dir Dr HAMID REZA RABIEE.

Advanced Manufacturing Research Centre (AMRC): e-mail amrc@sharif.edu; internet sina.sharif.edu/~amrc; Dir MOJTABA TAHMOURES.

Centre of Excellence in Earthquake Engineering: Dir Prof. M. T. KAZEMI.

Centre of Excellence in Energy Conversion: Azadi St, Tehran; tel. (21) 66165549; e-mail ceec@mech.sharif.edu; internet mech.sharif.edu/~ceec2; languages of instruction: Farsi, English; Dir Dr S. K. HANNANI.

Electronics Research Centre: tel. (21) 66005517; e-mail erc@sina.sharif.edu; internet www.sharif-erc.com; Dir Prof. MAHMOUD TABIANI.

Institute for Nanoscience and Nanotechnology: tel. (21) 66164123; e-mail inst@sharif.edu; internet nano.sharif.ir; Dir Prof. AZAM IRAJI ZAD.

Institute for Transportation Studies and Research: Dir Dr HOSSEIN POURZAHEDI.

Sharif Applied Physics Research Centre: tel. (21) 616-4542; e-mail appliedphysics@mehr.sharif.edu; internet physics.sharif.edu/~appliedphysics; Dir Dr AHMAD AMJADI.

Sharif Energy Research Institute: Dir Dr YADDOLLAH SABOUHI.

Water Energy Research Centre: tel. (21) 66005118; e-mail torkian@sina.sharif.ac.ir; internet sharif.ir/~werc; Dir Dr AYOOB TORKIAN

SHIRAZ UNIVERSITY

Jam-e-Jam Ave, Shiraz 71946-84636
Telephone: (71) 6286416
E-mail: sadeghi@shirazu.ac.ir
Internet: www.shirazu.ac.ir

Founded 1946 as Pahlavi Univ., present name 1979
State control
Languages of instruction: Persian, English
Academic year: October to July (2 semesters)
Chancellor: Dr MOHAMMAD HADI SADEGHI
Vice-Chancellor for Academic Affairs: Dr ABDOLHOSAIN JAHANMIRI
Vice-Chancellor for Admin. and Financial Affairs: Dr EBRAHIM HADIAN
Vice-Chancellor for Research Affairs: Dr GHOLAMHOSEIN ZAMANI
Vice-Chancellor for Student and Cultural Affairs: Dr MOHAMMAD MOAZZENI
Dir of Public Relations: MOJTABA TOOBAEI
Librarian: Dr ZAHIR HAYATI
Number of teachers: 580
Number of students: 12,500
Publications: *Journal of Social Sciences and Humanities, Iran Agricultural Research, Iranian Journal of Science and Technology*

DEANS

Junior Agricultural College, Darab: SAMAD ERFANIFAR
School of Agriculture: Dr YAHYA EMAM
School of Arts and Architecture: Dr MAHYAR ARDSHIRI
School of Education and Psychology: Dr MOHSEN KHADEMI
School of Engineering: Dr SEYYED SHAHABEDIN AYATOLAHI
School of Law: Dr PARVIZ AMERI
School of Literature and Human Sciences: Dr ABDULMAHDI RIAZI
School of Science: Dr NOZAR SAMANI
School of Veterinary Medicine: Dr SEYYED SHAHRAM SHEKARFOROUSH
Teacher Training College, Kazeroon: SEYYED MOHTASHAM MOHAMMADI

TABRIZ UNIVERSITY OF MEDICAL SCIENCES

Golgasht Ave, Tabriz
Telephone: (411) 3347345
E-mail: iro@tbzmed.ac.ir
Internet: www.tbzmed.ac.ir
Founded 1985, fmrly part of Univ. of Tabriz
State control
Languages of instruction: Persian, English
Academic year: October to July
Chancellor: Dr A. R. JODATI
Vice-Chancellor for Admin. and Finance: Dr A. JAVAD ZADEH
Vice-Chancellor for Education: Dr J. HANAEE
Vice-Chancellor for Food and Medicines: Dr A. GARJANI
Vice-Chancellor for Health Services: Dr A. R. NIKNIAZ
Vice-Chancellor for Research: Dr RASHIDI
Vice-Chancellor for Student Affairs: Dr A. A. TAHER AGDAM
Vice-Chancellor for Treatment: Dr M. KHOSHBATEN
Registrar: Dr M. VARSCHOCHI
Librarian: Mrs MASOOMI
Number of teachers: 500
Number of students: 4,700
Publications: *Journal of Basic Science in Medicine, Journal of Nursing and Obstetrics, Medical Journal, Pharmaceutical Science, Research Journal*

DEANS

Faculty of Dentistry: Dr J. YAZDANI
Faculty of Medical Rehabilitation Science: Dr R. KHANDAGI
Faculty of Medicine: Dr M. BARZEGAR
Faculty of Nursing and Obstetrics: Dr Z. MAYABI
Faculty of Paramedical Sciences: Dr A. RAFI
Faculty of Pharmacy: Dr M. H. ZARRINTAN
Faculty of Public Health and Nutrition: Dr M. R. SIYAHI

ATTACHED RESEARCH CENTRES

Biotechnology Research Center: tel. (411) 3364038; e-mail brc.info@tbzmed.ac.ir; internet www.tbzmed.ac.ir/biotechnology; Dir Prof. SIAVOUSH DASTMALCHI.

Haematology Oncology Research Center: tel. (411) 3343811; e-mail irajkermani@hotmail.com; internet horc.tbzmed.ac.ir; Dir Dr IRAJ ASVADI KERMANI.

Research Centre for Pharmaceutical Nanotechnology: tel. (411) 3367914; e-mail yomidi@tbzmed.ac.ir; internet nano.tbzmed.ac.ir; Dir Dr YADOLLAH OMIDI.

Tuberculosis and Lung Disease Center: tel. (411) 3364901; e-mail ansarink@tbzmed.ac.ir; internet www.tbzmed.ac.ir/tlrc; Dir Dr KHALIL ANSARIN

TARBIAT MODARRES UNIVERSITY

POB 14155-4838, Intersection of Chamran and Ale-Ahmad Highways, Tehran
Telephone: (21) 8011001
E-mail: intl@modares.ac.ir
Internet: www.modares.ac.ir
Founded 1982
Academic year: September to June
Pres.: Dr FARHAD DANESHJOO
Vice-Pres. for Academic Affairs: Dr M. T. AHMADY
Vice-Pres. for Admin. and Financial Affairs: Dr H. BAHRAMI
Vice-Pres. for Research: Dr M. F. MOUSAVI
Vice-Pres. for Student Affairs: Dr A. MALEKI MOGHADDAM
Librarian: Dr AHMAD ZAVARAN HOSEINI
Library of 80,000 vols, 2,552 periodicals
Number of teachers: 440
Number of students: 3,600

DEANS

Faculty of Agriculture: Dr T. TAVAKOLI
Faculty of Arts: Dr M. R. POORJAAFAR
Faculty of Basic Medical Sciences: Dr M. RASAEE
Faculty of Basic Sciences: Dr H. NADERIMANESH
Faculty of Engineering: Dr SHOJAOSSADATI
Faculty of Humanities: Dr S. AYEENEVAND
Faculty of Natural Resources and Marine Sciences: Dr SAHARI

TEHRAN UNIVERSITY OF MEDICAL SCIENCES (TUMS)

21 Dameshgh St, Vali-e-Asr Ave, POB 14155-5799, Tehran 141675-3955
Telephone: (21) 88896696
E-mail: int-gsia@tums.ac.ir
Internet: www.tums.ac.ir
Founded 1851, present status 2010
State control
Language of instruction: Persian
Academic year: September to June
Chancellor: Prof. ALI JAFARIAN
Vice-Chancellor for Global Strategies and Int. Affairs: Dr ALI ARABKHERADMAND
Vice-Chancellor for Cultural Affairs: Dr MOHSEN PARVIZ
Vice-Chancellor for Student Affairs: Dr MOSTAFA MOHAGHEGH
Vice-Chancellor for Education: Dr MOHAMMAD JALILI
Vice-Chancellor for Food and Medicine: Dr MOHAMMAD REZA SHAMS ARDEKANI
Vice-Chancellor for Health Services: Dr ARASH RASHIDIAN
Vice-Chancellor for Research: Dr AKBAR FOTOUHI
Library of 45,244 vols, 3,681 journals, 14,623 theses, 202 research projects
Number of teachers: 2,063
Number of students: 15,675
Publications: *Acta Medica Iranica, Anesthesiology and Pain, Asian Journal of Sports Medicine, Audiology, Basic & Clinical Cancer Research, DARU Journal of Pharmaceutical Sciences, Dermatology and Cosmetic, HAYAT, Hospital, International Journal of Hematology-Oncology and Stem Cell Research, Iranian Journal of Arthropod-Borne Diseases, Iranian Journal of Diabetes and Lipid Disorders, Iranian Journal of Environmental Health Science & Engineering, Iranian Journal of Epidemiology, Iranian Journal of Health and Environment, Iranian Journal of Medical Ethics and History of Medicine, Iranian Journal of Medical Hypotheses and Ideas, Iranian Journal of Microbiology, Iranian Journal of Neurology, Iran Journal of Nursing, Iranian Journal of Parasitology, Iranian Journal of Pediatrics, Iranian Journal of Pharmacology & Therapeutics, Iranian Journal of Psychiatry, Iranian Journal of Psychiatry and Clinical Psychology, Iranian Journal of Public Health, Iranian Journal of Radiology, Iran Occupational Health, Journal of Dental Medicine, Journal of Dentistry of Tehran University of Medical Sciences, Journal of Family and Reproductive Health, Journal of Health Administration, Journal of Health and Safety at Work, Journal of Medical Ethics and History of Medicine, Journal of School of Public Health and Institute of Public Health Research, Medical Journal of the Islamic Republic of Iran, Modern Rehabilitation, Payavard Salamat, Teb va Tazkiyeh, Tehran University Medical Journal (TUMJ), The Journal of Tehran University Heart Center*

DEANS

International Campus: Dr ALI ARAB KHERADMAND
School of Advanced Technologies in Medicine: Dr ALIREZA AHMADIAN
School of Allied Medical Sciences: Dr REZA SAFDARI
School of Dentistry: Dr MUHAMMAD BAYAT
School of Medicine: Dr SYYED AMIRHOSSEIN EMAMI
School of Nursing and Midwifery: Dr MOHAMMAD ALI CHERAGHI
School of Pharmacy: Dr MOHAMMAD SHARIFZADEH
School of Public Health: Dr ALI AKBARI SARI
School of Rehabilitation Sciences: Dr MOHAMMAD AKBARI
School of Traditional Medicine: Dr MOHAMMAD REZA SHAMS ARDAKANI

PROFESSORS

AGHAKHANI, K., Forensic Medicine
AKBARIAN-NIA, M., Neurology
ARAB MOHAMMAD HOSSEONI, A., Paediatrics
AZAR, M., Neurosurgery
BIDARI, A., Emergency Medicine
BOLOURI, B., Biophysics
DANESHI, A., Otorhinolaryngology
FIROUZRAY, M., Biochemistry
GHAFFARPOUR, G., Dermatology
GHALEHBANDI, M., Psychiatry
HADIZADEH, H., Radiology
HASHEMI, F., Pathology
HASHEMI, M., Ophthalmology
HEYDARI, M., Surgery
HOMAYOUNFAR, H., Physiology
IMANI, F., Anaesthesiology
JAFARI, D., Orthopaedics
JAVAD MOUSSAVI, S. A., Internal Medicine
JOGHATAEI, M. T., Anatomy

KASHANIAN, M., Obstetrics and Gynaecology
KAZAMI, A., Reconstructive Surgery
MAHMOUDIAN, M., Pharmacology
MAJIDPOUR, A., Infectious Diseases
MOLAVI NOJOUMI, M., Social Medicine
MOVAHHED, M., Nuclear Medicine
OURMAZDI, H., Parasitology
RASTEGAR LARI, A., Microbiology
SALEKMOGHADDAM, A., Immunology
SHAHROKH, H., Urology
YEKKEH YAZDANDOUST, R., Clinical Psychology

UNIVERSITY OF ART

POB 11155-655, Tehran
58 Sarhang Sakhai St, Hafez Ave., Tehran 11368-13518
Telephone: (21) 66734001
E-mail: art-university@art.ac.ir
Internet: www.art.ac.ir
Founded 1980, by merger with Conservatory of Music, College of Decorative Arts, College of Dramatic Arts, College of Nat. Music and Farabi Univ., present name 1991; attached to Min. of Science, Research & Technology
State control
Language of instruction: Persian
Academic year: October to September
Pres.: Dr SAEED KASAN FALLAH
Vice-Pres. for Admin. and Finance: AHMAD RAHBARI
Vice-Pres. for Instruction: Dr MAJID SALEHI
Vice-Pres. for Research: Dr MOHAMMADREZA HOSNAI
Vice-Pres. for Student Affairs: Dr SAEED MAJIDI
Library of 50,000 vols
Number of teachers: 400 (100 full-time, 300 part-time)
Number of students: 3,500
Publications: *Dastavard* (4 a year), *Honarnameh* (4 a year)

DEANS

Architecture and Urban Planning: Dr MOSTAFA KIANI
Cinema and Theatre: Dr SHAHAB ADEL
Faculty of Applied Arts: Dr AHMAD TONDI
Music: Dr MOHAMMADREZA AZADEHFAR
Visual and Applied Arts: Dr JAVAD SALIMI

UNIVERSITY OF GILAN

POB 1841, Mellat St, Rasht
Telephone: (131) 3221999
E-mail: khazar@cd.gu.ac.ir
Internet: www.gu.ac.ir
Founded 1977
State control
Language of instruction: Persian
Academic year: September to June (2 semesters)
Chancellor: Dr DAWOUD AHMADI DASTJERDI
Vice-Chancellor for Academic Affairs: Dr REZA FOTOUHI GHAZVINI
Vice-Chancellor for Finance and Admin.: ESMAEIL MAGHSODI
Vice-Chancellor for Research Affairs: Dr ABOLFAZL DARVIZEH
Vice-Chancellor for Student Affairs: Dr MALEK-MOHAMMAD RANJBAR
Office of Int. and Scientific Relations: Dr MASOUD VAHABI MOGHADDAM
Office of Public Relations: Dr HASSAN TAJIK
Librarian: Dr REYHANEH SARIRI
Number of teachers: 310
Number of students: 6,710
Publication: *Mahnameh* (12 a year, in Persian)

DEANS

Faculty of Agriculture: Dr AHAD SAHRAGARD
Faculty of Engineering: Dr HOSSEIN HAFTHCHENARI
Faculty of Fine Arts and Architecture: HAMZEH GHOLAM-ALI-ZADEH
Faculty of Fishery and Aquatic Animals: Dr MSOUD SATTARI
Faculty of Humanities: Dr MOHAMMAD KAZEM YOUSEFPOUR
Faculty of Natural Resources: Dr ZYAEDDIN MIRHOSSEINI
Faculty of Physical Education: Dr ARSALAN DAMIRCHI
Faculty of Sciences: Dr ESMAEIL ANSARI

UNIVERSITY OF ISFAHAN

Hezar Jerib St, Isfahan 81746-73441
Telephone: (311) 7932128
E-mail: int-office@ui.ac.ir
Internet: www.ui.ac.ir
Founded 1946, present status 1958
State control
Language of instruction: Persian
Academic year: September to July
Chancellor: Dr HOOSHANG TALEBI
Vice-Chancellor for Academic Affairs and Graduate Studies: Dr IBRAHIM MIRSHAH JAFARI
Vice-Chancellor for Finance and Admin.: Dr VALIOLLAH MIRKHANI
Vice-Chancellor for Research and Technology: Dr MOHAMMAD RABANI
Vice-Chancellor for Student and Cultural Affairs: Dr ALI AKBAR KAJBAF
Dir for Int. Relations: Dr ARASH SHAHIN
Librarian: Dr AMIR GHAMARANI
Library of 484,863 vols
Number of teachers: 546
Number of students: 15,000
Publications: *Comparative Theology* (2 a year), *Geography and Environmental Planning* (4 a year), *Geography Researches* (4 a year), *Historical Researches* (4 a year), *International Economics* (2 a year), *Iranian Journal of Petrology* (4 a year), *Iranian Journal of Plant Biology* (2 a year), *Journal of Financial Accounting Research* (2 a year), *Journal of Persian Language and Literature (GOHARE GOYA)* (4 a year), *Journal of Regional and Urban Planning* (4 a year), *Journal of Researches in Linguistics* (4 a year), *Literature Arts* (4 a year), *Metaphysic* (4 a year), *Practical Sociology* (4 a year), *Researches in Sedimentary and Cryptology* (4 a year), *Researches on Persian Language Literature* (4 a year), *Taxonomy and Biosystematics* (2 a year)

DEANS

Faculty of Administrative Sciences and Economics: Dr SEYYED JAVAD EMAM JOMEH ZADEH
Faculty of Educational Sciences and Psychology: Dr HAMID NESHATDOST
Faculty of Engineering and Technology: Dr MOHAMMAD SADEGH HATAMIPOOR
Faculty of Foreign Languages: Dr MAHMOUD REZA GASHMARDI
Faculty of Literature and Humanities: Dr MOHAMMAD BIDHENDI
Faculty of Mathematics and Computer Studies, Khansar: Dr MAHDI ELYASI
Faculty of Physical Education and Sports Sciences: Dr SEYYED MOHAMMAD MARANDI
Faculty of Pure Sciences: MAJID ASADI
Faculty of Sciences and New Technology: Dr MOHAMADREZA ABDI

UNIVERSITY OF SISTAN AND BALUCHISTAN

POB 98135-987, Zahedan
Telephone: (541) 2445981
Internet: www.usb.ac.ir
Founded 1974
State control
Language of instruction: Persian
Academic year: September to July (2 semesters)
Chancellor: Dr A. AKBARI
Vice-Chancellor for Academic Affairs: M. H. SANGTARASH
Vice-Chancellor for Admin. and Finance: Dr AMIN REZA KAMALYAN
Vice-Chancellor for Research: Dr RAHBAR RAHIMI
Vice-Chancellor for Student Affairs: Dr A. A. MORYDI FARIMANI
Registrar: Dr ABDOLLAH WASIGH ABBASI
Dir of Central Library: Dr RAHMATOLLAH LASHKARIPOUR
Number of teachers: 300
Number of students: 12,000
Publications: *Applied Engineering* (2 a year, in Persian), *Divine and Law* (2 a year, in Persian), *Geography & Development* (2 a year, in Persian), *History and Archaeology* (2 a year, in Persian), *Iranian Journal of Fuzzy System* (2 a year), *Journal of Engineering and Science* (2 a year, in Persian), *Journal of Humanities* (4 a year, in Persian), *Persian Language and Literature* (2 a year, in Persian)

DEANS

College of Humanities (Iranshar): Eng. AZARAG
College of Humanities (Zahedan): Dr A. A. AHANGAR
Engineering College: Dr S. FARAHAT
Fine Arts College: Dr M. MEHRAN
Science College: Dr A. A. MIRZAIE

PROFESSORS

AKBARI, A., Agricultural Economics
ATASHI, H., Chemical Engineering
AZIMI, P., Mathematics
ESHGI, H., Chemistry
KHOSHNOODI, M., Chemical Engineering
LASHKARIPOUR, G. R., Geology
MANSORI-TORSHIZI, H. M., Chemistry
NOORA, A. A., Mathematics
RAHIMI, R., Chemical Engineering
REZVANI, A. R., Chemistry
SARDASHTI, A. R., Chemistry
SHARIATI, H., Mathematics
TORMANZAHI, A., Agriculture
VALIZADEH, J., Agriculture
YAZDANI, B.-O., Humanities

UNIVERSITY OF TABRIZ

29th Bahman Blvd, Tabriz 51666-14766
Telephone: (411) 3355994
E-mail: international@tabrizu.ac.ir
Internet: www.tabrizu.ac.ir
Founded 1946, fmrly Univ. of Azarabadegan
State control
Language of instruction: Persian
Academic year: September to June (2 semesters)
Chancellor: Prof. PARVIZ AJIDEH
Vice-Chancellor for Academic and Post-Graduate Studies: Dr M. T. ALAMI
Vice-Chancellor for Finance and Admin. Affairs: Dr RASOOL MOHAMMADREZAEI
Vice-Chancellor for Cultural Affairs: Dr M. R. HOSSEINZADEH
Vice-Chancellor for Research Affairs: Prof. A. ROSTAMI
Vice-Chancellor for Student Affairs: Dr H. NAVID
Registrar: Dr M. ABBASZADEH
Dir for Int. Academic Collaboration: Dr H. SABOURI
Librarian: Dr T. NAJJARI
Library of 112,154 vols

Number of teachers: 640
Number of students: 185,000
Publications: *Journal of Agricultural Sciences* (4 a year), *Journal of English Language Teaching and Learning* (2 a year), *Journal of the Faculty of Engineering* (4 a year), *Journal of the Faculty of Humanities and Social Sciences* (4 a year), *Pazhoohesh* (Record of University Research Activities, 2 a year)

DEANS

Ahar College of Agriculture: Dr F. SHAHBAZI
Faculty of Agriculture: Dr ALI HOSSEINZADEH DALIR
Faculty of Chemistry: Dr M. GH. HOSSEINI
Faculty of Civil Engineering: Prof A. HADIDI
Faculty of Economics, Management, and Business: Prof. M. MOTAFAKKER AZAD
Faculty of Education and Psychology: Dr M BEYRAMI
Faculty of Electrical and Computer Engineering: Dr Z. DAEI KOOZEHKONANI
Faculty of Geography: Prof. M. H. REZAEI MOGHADDAM
Faculty of Law and Social Sciences: Dr R. IZADI
Faculty of Mathematical Sciences: Dr G. R. HOJJATI
Faculty of Mechanical Engineering: Dr M. T. SHERVANI-TABAR
Faculty of Natural Sciences: Dr M. MOAYYED
Faculty of Persian Literature and Foreign Languages: Dr F. FARROKHI
Faculty of Physics: Dr S. ASHRAFI
Faculty of Theology and Islamic Sciences: Dr N. FOROUHI
Faculty of Veterinary Medicine: Dr R. ASADPOUR
Marand Faculty of Engineering: Dr R. JOMEIRI
Research Institute for Applied Physics and Astronomy: Dr M. SAHRAI BARENJI
Research Institute for Fundamental Sciences: Dr M. MOAZZEN
School of Engineering Emerging Technologies: Prof. A. ROSTAMI

PROFESSORS

Faculty of Agriculture (tel. (411) 3341316; e-mail agri-dean@tabrizu.ac.ir):
MASSIHA, S., Horticulture
MOGHADDAM-VAHED, M., Plant Breeding
PEYGHAMIE, E., Plant Pathology
RAHIMZADEH KHOEI, F., Agronomy
VALIZADEH, M., Genetics and Breeding

Faculty of Chemistry (tel. (411) 3355998; e-mail chemfac@tabrizu.ac.ir):
BLOURCHIAN, S. M., Organosilicon Chemistry
DJOZAN, D. J., Analytical Chemistry
ENTEZAMI, A. A., Polymer Chemistry
GOLABI, S. M., Electroanalytical Chemistry
MANZOORI, J., Analytical Chemistry, Spectroscopy
POURNAGHI AZAR, M. H., Electroanalytical Chemistry
SOROURADDIN ABADI, M. H., Analytical Chemistry
ZAFARANI-MOATTAR, M. T., Physical Chemistry

Faculty of Education and Psychology (tel. (411) 3341133):
HOSSEINI-NASAB, D., Training Psychology

Faculty of Engineering (tel. (411) 3356022; e-mail joeng@tabrizu.ac.ir):
BEHRAVESH, A., Structural Engineering
DILMAGHANI, S., Civil Engineering
HASANZADEH, Y., Heat and Fluid Transfer Engineering
HOSSEINI, S. H., Power Electronics
KEYANVASH, A., Metallurgy
KHANMOHAMMADI, S., Automatic Engineering
KHOSHRAVAN-AZAR, M. E., Heat Transfer Engineering
PIROUZ-PANAH, V., Internal Combustion Engines

Faculty of Humanities and Social Sciences (tel. (411) 3344286):
BANIFATEMEH, H., Social Sciences
ESFAHANIYAN, D., History
HARIRI-AKBARI, M., Political Sociology
RAJAEI ASL, A. H., Physical Geography

Faculty of Mathematics (tel. (411) 3356032):
MEHRVARZ, A. A., Algebra
N-DEHGAN, Y., Mathematical Analysis
SHAHABI, M. A., Mathematics
TOOMANIAN, A., Differential Geometry

Faculty of Natural Sciences (tel. (411) 3356027):
HOSSEINPOUR FEIZI, M. A., Radiobiology

Faculty of Persian Literature and Foreign Languages (tel. (411) 3341150):
BAGHERI, M., Culture and Ancient Languages
EJLALI, A. P., Persian Language and Literature
IRANDOOST, R., French Language and Literature
LOTFIPOUR SAEDI, K., Applied Linguistics
NAVALI, M., Philosophy
SARKARATI, B., Ancient Iranian Languages

Faculty of Physics (tel. (411) 3356030):
BIDADI, H., Solid-state Physics
JAFARIZADEH, M., Physics of Elementary Particles
KALAFI, M., Solid-state Physics
MOHAMMAD-ZADEH JASSUR, D., Atomic Physics
SOBHANIAN, S., Atomic Physics, Plasma
TAJALLI SAIFI, H., Atomic Physics, Lasers

ATTACHED COLLEGES

College of Engineering (Bonab Campus): Dir M. R. A. PARSA.

College of Engineering (Marand Campus): Dir S. HOSSEINI.

College of Veterinary Medicine: Dir Dr H. KARIMIE

UNIVERSITY OF TEHRAN

Enghelab Ave, Tehran 14174
Telephone: (21) 66469807
E-mail: international@ut.ac.ir
Internet: www.ut.ac.ir
Founded 1934
Language of instruction: Persian
Academic year: September to July (2 semesters)
Pres.: Dr FARHAD RAHBAR
Vice-Pres. for Academic Affairs: Dr S. M. GHAMSARI
Vice-Pres. for Admin.: Dr S. M. MOGHIMI
Vice-Pres. for Int. Affairs: Dr S. MOHAMMAD ALI MOUSAVI
Vice-Pres. for Planning: Dr S. R. AMELI
Vice-Pres. for Research and Technology: Prof. GHASEM AMOOABEDINY
Vice-Pres. for Student and Cultural Affairs: Prof. A. SEIF
Univ. Librarian: Dr F. FAHIMNIA
Library: see under Libraries and Archives
Number of teachers: 2,360
Number of students: 38,500

DEANS

College of Agriculture and Natural Resources: Dr M. HOSSEIN OMID
College of Engineering: Dr MAHMOOD KAMAREIEE
College of Fine Arts: Dr M. AZIZI
Faculty of Economics: Dr MANSOOR KHALILI ARAGHI
Faculty of Geography: Dr POOR AHMAD
Faculty of Law and Political Science: Dr S. FAZELLOLLAH MOOSAVI
Faculty of Literature and Foreign Languages: Dr S. FARIDE ALAVI
Faculty of Literature and Humanities: Dr KARIMI DOOSTAN
Faculty of Management and Business Administration: Dr S. REZA S. JAVADIN
Faculty of New Sciences and Technologies: Prof. HASAN JALILI
Faculty of Physical Education: Dr GOODARZI
Faculty of Psychology and Educational Science: Dr G. ALI AFROOZ
Faculty of Science: Dr ALI MAGHARI
Faculty of Social Sciences: Dr G. REZA GAMSHIDIHA
Faculty of Theology and Islamic Studies: Dr S. M. REZA EMAM
Faculty of Veterinary Medicine: Dr PARVIZ TAJIK
Graduate Faculty of Environment: Dr G. REZA NABI BIDHENDI

URMIA UNIVERSITY

POB 165, Urmia 57153
Telephone: (441) 3448131
E-mail: chancellor@urmia.ac.ir
Internet: www.urmia.ac.ir
Founded 1965
Academic year: September to July
Chancellor: Dr GOUDARZ SADEGHI-HASHJIN
Vice-Chancellor for Devt: Dr ESFANDYAR MARDANI
Vice-Chancellor for Education: Dr ESMAIL AYAN
Vice-Chancellor for Personnel and Finance: GHOLAMREZA MANSOORFAR
Vice-Chancellor for Research: Dr MOHAMMAD MEHDI BARADARANI
Vice-Chancellor for Student Affairs: Dr MAHMOOD RAZAZADEH
Registrar: Dr ALIREZA MOZAFFARI
Librarians: Dr FARHAD FARROKHI ARDEBILI, MOHAMMADREZA FARHADPOOR
Library of 58,000 vols
Number of teachers: 290
Number of students: 8,500
Publications: *Neda* (12 a year), *Pajooheshgaran* (4 a year)

DEANS

Faculty of Agriculture: Dr ASGHAR KHOSROWSHAHI
Faculty of Engineering: Dr IRAJ MIRZAEE
Faculty of Literature and Humanities: Dr ABDOLLAH TOLOEE-AZAR
Faculty of Science: Prof. M. NOJAVAN ASHGARI
Faculty of Veterinary Medicine: Dr B. DALIR NAGHADEH

YAZD UNIVERSITY

Safaeiah, POB 89195-741, Yazd
Telephone: (351) 8123376
E-mail: lib-head@yazduni.ac.ir
Internet: www.yazduni.ac.ir
Founded 1988
State control
Languages of instruction: English, Persian
Academic year: September to June
Pres.: Dr SEYYED ALI MOHAMMAD MIRMOHAMMADI MEYBODI
Vice-Pres. for Education: Dr FATEMAH GHADERI
Vice-Pres. for Finance and Admin.: Dr MOHAMMAD HOSEIN HAKIMI
Vice-Pres. for Research: Dr AHMAD MIRZAEI
Vice-Pres. for Student Affairs: Dr SEYED HEIDAR MIRFAKHRADINI
Registrar: Dr ALI AKBAR DEHGHAN
Librarian: MOHAMMAD TAHMASEBI
Library of 201,470 vols (incl. Persian and Latin vols)

Number of teachers: 390
Number of students: 11,300
Publication: *Kavoshnameh* (2 a year)

DEANS

Faculty of Art and Architecture: Dr NOGHSAN MOHAMMADI
Faculty of Engineering: Dr SEFID
Faculty of Humanities: Dr ABUEI
Faculty of Natural Resources and Desert Studies: Dr DASTOORANI
Faculty of Science: Dr NOORBALA

RESEARCH CENTRES

Desert and Dryland Research Institute: tel. (351) 8211670; e-mail ddri@yazduni.ac.ir; f. 1998.

Engineering and Applied Science Research Center: tel. (351) 8211670; e-mail easr@yazduni.ac.ir

Colleges

Iran Banking Institute: POB 19395-4814, 207 Pasdaran Ave, Tehran; tel. (21) 2848000; internet www.ibi.ac.ir; f. 1963; 4-year BA degree courses in banking, accounting and computer science, and MA degree courses in banking, accounting and law; library: 24,000 vols; 2,500 students; Chancellor Dr MEHDI EMRANI.

IRAQ

The Higher Education System

The University of Baghdad (founded 1957) is the oldest university in Iraq. As a result of increasing petroleum revenues in the 1970s, the higher education sector expanded significantly, and in addition to the universities a large number of technical institutes were established. However, during the 1980s and 1990s higher education was affected by economic privations caused by war with Iran (1980–88) and sanctions imposed by the international community following Iraq's invasion of Kuwait in 1990 and defeat by a US-led coalition in 1991. In March–April 2003 another US-led coalition invaded Iraq, captured Baghdad and toppled the Baathist regime of Saddam Hussain. Since 2003 higher education has been subject to comprehensive reform, including the establishment of new universities and technical colleges (the latter offering Bachelors, Higher Diplomas and Masters) and the upgrading of a number of technical institutes to technical colleges; however, many academics have been killed, moved abroad or taken permanent leave of absence, student numbers have fallen, and in some areas Islamist groups have imposed segregated classes or forced female students to adopt Islamic forms of dress. The Ministry of Higher Education and Scientific Research oversees the administration of the 19 public universities and other colleges and technical institutes. In 2012 there were also 28 private universities and colleges. Higher education institutions in the Kurdish Autonomous Region (KAR) are overseen by the Kurdish Ministry of Higher Education and Scientific Research, but are still required to seek official recognition from the central Ministry in Baghdad. The language of instruction is generally Arabic (although Kurdish and English are used in the KAR and English is used in medicine and dentistry). In 2002/03 there were approximately 240,000 undergraduates attending 65 institutions of higher education. Although UNESCO estimated that 424,908 students were enrolled in tertiary education in 2005, it was reported in 2006 that a growing number of students were failing to attend school or university as a result of the worsening security situation in many parts of the country. Since the US-led invasion of Iraq in 2003 thousands of Iraqi students have fled north to the relatively stable KAR. During the past five years or so, at least 10 new universities have opened in the Kurdish area, bringing the region's total to 19, and the construction of another five universities is planned (including one in al Hamdaniya).

Students must complete upper secondary education to be admitted to undergraduate studies at public universities. Each year the Ministry of Higher Education and Scientific Research determines entry requirements, which vary from programme to programme (as well as from year to year). The main undergraduate degree is the Bachelors, which lasts four years, although longer periods of study are required for pharmacy, architecture, dentistry, veterinary medicine (all five years) and medicine (six years). The first postgraduate degree is the Masters, lasting two to three years and incorporating both taught and research elements; the degree culminates in the submission of a thesis. The final university degree is the Doctor of Philosophy (PhD), which takes at least a further three years of study beyond the Masters and which also includes both taught and research elements, with students required to pass examinations based on classroom-based work before proceeding to the research/thesis element. At some universities a specialist entrance examination must be passed in order to commence the PhD programme. The overall number of PhD students has declined substantially over the last two decades or so.

Technical and vocational education is dominated by technical colleges and institutes, of which there is currently a combined total of more than 60. The Foundation for Technical Education (as the Foundation of Technical Institutes was renamed in 2002) is the government body responsible for administering these institutions and technical degrees and diplomas. The Technician Diploma is a two-year course offered by technical institutes, of which there were 37 in 2004. (Some technical institutes are directly affiliated to government ministries, depending on the area of specialization.) Holders of the Technician Diploma can gain direct entry to the second year of the four-year Bachelor of Technology programme, offered by technical colleges. The majority of these courses are in the fields of engineering and medicine. Following the Bachelor of Technology, technical colleges offer a two-year Higher Diploma of Technology, mainly in engineering disciplines. The Master of Technology is similar to the Higher Diploma of Technology, but contains a greater element of research.

The Ministry of Higher Education and Scientific Research is the body responsible for recognizing universities and other higher education institutions (although, since most universities and technical institutions are relatively autonomous, central planning by the Ministry does not always have much affect on educational establishments). Despite the fact that the Government has made various attempts, with the aid of international organizations such as UNESCO, to develop a coherent and independent quality assurance agency, such a body has yet to materialize.

In July 2009 the Iraqi Government launched a five-year, US$1,000m. higher education plan to boost the country's science and technology workforce while promoting knowledge-based sustainable development. The plan, which would primarily be funded by Iraq's petroleum revenues, was to be carried out in two phases: first, as part of a large-scale scholarship initiative, up to 10,000 Iraqi students would be sent abroad to undertake technical/scientific degrees at universities in Australia, Canada, the United Kingdom and the USA (incentives would be offered for the students to return to work in their home country); and the second phase would involve a massive overhaul of the entire Iraqi higher education infrastructure, including the construction of new laboratories and the establishment of internet connections.

Regulatory Bodies

GOVERNMENT

Ministry of Culture: POB 624, Qaba bin Nafi Sq., Sadoun St, Baghdad; tel. (1) 5383171; internet www.mocul.gov.iq; Minister SAADOUN AL-DULAIMI.

Ministry of Education: Saad State Enterprises Bldg, Near Convention Centre, Baghdad; tel. (1) 8832571; e-mail general@moedu.gov.iq; internet www.moedu.gov.iq; Minister Dr MUHAMMAD ALI TAMIM.

Ministry of Higher Education and Scientific Research: 52 Rusafa St, Baghdad; tel. (1) 2806315; e-mail info@mohesr.gov.iq; internet www.mohesr.gov.iq; Minister ALI MOHAMMAD HUSSEIN ALI AL-ADEEB.

Ministry of Science and Technology: Baghdad; e-mail inprb@most.gov.iq; internet www.most.gov.iq; Minister ABD AL-KARIM YASSIN AL-SAMARRAI.

Learned Societies

EDUCATION

Arab Literacy and Adult Education Organization (ARLO): POB 3217, 113 Abu Nawas St, Baghdad; tel. (1) 7186246; f. 1966 by ALECSO to promote co-operation in all aspects of literacy and adult education between the Arab states; all Arab states are mems; library of 14,700 vols; Dir HASHIM ABU ZEID EL-SAFI (acting); publ. *The Education of the Masses* (2 a year).

LANGUAGE AND LITERATURE

British Council: 10 Spring Gardens, London, SW1A 2BN, UK; tel. (161) 957-7755; e-mail iraq@britishcouncil.org; internet www.britishcouncil.org/iraq; f. 1940; offers courses and exams in English language and promotes cultural exchange with the UK; based in London until further notice; Chief Exec. MARTIN DAVIDSON.

Iraqi Academy of Science: Waziriya, Baghdad; tel. (1) 4224202; e-mail iraqacademy@yahoo.com; internet www.iraqacademy.iq; f. 1947; promotes the Arabic language and heritage, supports research in Arabic and Muslim history, history of Iraq and Arabic language and heritage, and maintaining Kurdish and Assyrian languages; 37 mems; Pres. Prof. Dr AHMED MATLOUB; publ. *Majallat al-Mejmah al-Ilmi* (literary, 4 a year).

MEDICINE

International Iraqi Medical Association: e-mail adilmahd@emirates.net.ae; internet www.iimaonline.net; NGO supporting Iraqi physicians at home and abroad; annual conf.; Pres. Dr ALI HARJAN; Dir of Public Relations Dr ADIL AL-MANSOURI; publ. *Journal*.

Iraqi Medical Association: Maari St, al-Mansoor, Baghdad; tel. (1) 5374209; e-mail nfo@ima-iq.org; internet www.ima-iq.org; f. 1920; Pres. Prof. Dr NADHIM A. KASIM; publ. *Iraqi Medical Journal* (2 a year, in Arabic and English).

NATURAL SCIENCES

General

Federation of Arab Scientific Research Councils: POB 13027, Baghdad; tel. (1) 8881709; f. 1976; strengthens collaboration among scientific research ccls, instns, centres and univs in all Arab states; plans jt research projects among Arab states, esp. those related to Arab devt plans; 15 mem. states; library of 800 vols, 600 periodicals, 1.1m. patent documents from USA, EPO, WIPO; Sec.-Gen. Prof. Dr TAHA T. AL-NAIMI; publs *Federation News*, *Journal of Computer Research*.

Research Institutes

EDUCATION

Centre for Educational and Psychological Research: Univ. of Baghdad, 9 Waziriya, Baghdad; e-mail master@esprc.uobaghdad.edu.iq; internet www.esprc.uobaghdad.edu.iq; f. 1966; educational and psychological research studies to make education an effective power for the acceleration of economic and social devt; library of 6,000 vols; Dir Dr MOHAMMED ALI KHALAF; publ. *Journal of Educational Psychological Research* (2 a year).

HISTORY, GEOGRAPHY AND ARCHAEOLOGY

British Institute for the Study of Iraq: 10 Carlton House Terrace, London, SW1Y 5AH, UK; tel. (20) 7969-5274; e-mail bisi@britac.ac.uk; internet www.bisi.ac.uk; f. 1932 as the British School of Archaeology; present name 2007; promotes, supports and undertakes research in Iraq and neighbouring countries; covers the subjects of archaeology, history, anthropology, geography, language and other related domains from earliest times to the present; grants are available for research; 800 mems; library: the library is currently housed by the British embassy in Baghdad, the number of vols is unknown; Chair. Prof. ROGER MATTHEWS; Vice-Chair. Dr HARRIET CRAWFORD; publs *Iraq* (1 a year), *The International Journal of Contemporary Iraqi Studies* (3 a year).

PHILOSOPHY AND PSYCHOLOGY

Psychological Research Centre: Univ. of Baghdad Complex, Jaderiyah, Baghdad; tel. (1) 7786678; e-mail psychocenter@hotmail.com; internet www.psychocenteriraq.com; psychological and parapsychological research and training; library of 3,070 vols (1,992 Arabic, 1,078 English); publs *Journal of Psyche and Life* (6 a year, incl. section in English), *Journal of Psychological Sciences* (4 a year, in Arabic and English), *Psychological Health* (4 a year, in Arabic).

TECHNOLOGY

Nuclear Research Centre: Tuwaitha, Baghdad; f. 1967; fmr main establishment of Iraq Atomic Energy Commission, now under control of International Atomic Energy Agency; administrative responsibility assumed by the Iraqi Ministry of Science and Technology.

Libraries and Archives

Arbil

University of Salahaddin Central Library: Kirkuk St, Arbil; tel. (66) 2260089; e-mail library@usalah.org; f. 1968; 263,705 vols, 530 current periodicals; Dir Dr MOHAMMAD MUSTAFA.

Baghdad

Al-Awqaf Central Library (Ministry of Endowments and Religious Affairs Central Library): POB 14146, Baghdad; tel. (1) 4169362; f. 1928; 30,000 vols; Contact HASAN FREIH; publ. *Al-Rissala-al-Islamiya*.

Al-Mustansiriya University Library: POB 14022, Waziriya, Baghdad; e-mail library@uomustansiriyah.edu.iq; f. 1963; 311,800 vols, 30,000 vols of periodicals, 330 rolls of film, 280 current periodicals; also 11 college libraries with 33,000 vols, 850 periodicals; part of the colln was looted 2003; Dir FAISAL ANWAN AL-TAEE.

Arab Gulf States Information and Documentation Center: POB 5063, Baghdad; tel. (1) 5433914; f. 1981; affiliated to the Board of Ministers of Information of the Arab Gulf States; aims to gather information from many sources, and to systematize, analyse and exchange it; supports the basic structure of existing information services; 7 mem. states; provides a consultancy service; databases, microfilms; specialized library of 8,000 vols; Dir-Gen. HAYFA A. JAJAWI.

Educational Documentation Library: Ministry of Education, Educational Campus, Baghdad; tel. (1) 8860000-2178; f. 1921; 37,000 vols, 73 periodicals; Librarian Dr KADHIM G. AL-KHAZRAJI.

Iraqi Academy Library: Waziriya, Baghdad; f. 1947; 60,000 vols, 32 original MSS, 1,600 copied MSS, 1,500 microfilms; Librarian SABAH NOAH.

Iraqi Museum Library: Salhiya Quarter, Baghdad West; tel. (1) 8840876; f. 1934; archaeology, history of civilization, art, architecture, cultural heritage; evacuation of colln undertaken before the US-led military intervention of 2003, currently in storage; 229,000 vols, 34,000 MSS; Dir ZAINAT AL-SAMAKRI; publ. *Al-Maskukat*.

Iraqi National Library and Archives: POB 594, Baghdad; tel. (1) 4141303; e-mail iraqnla@googlemail.com; internet www.iraqnla-iq.com; f. 1961; 500,000 vols destroyed in 2003 fire; some holdings are frozen to prevent deterioration; legal deposit centre and national bibliographic centre; Dir-Gen. SAAD ESKANDER.

Scientific Documentation Centre: Abu Nuas Rd, POB 2441, Baghdad; tel. (1) 7760023; f. 1972; scientific information services to researchers at the institutes/centres of the Scientific Research Council (*q.v.*), and to others working in Iraqi laboratories, incl. UNDP experts; 7 libraries are being developed, each attached to a research centre of the Council, incl. the Central Science Library; in-service training for students of Library Science and Documentation and librarians; 20 staff mems; Dir Dr FAIK ABDUL S. RAZZAQ.

University of Baghdad Central Library: POB 47303, Jadiriya, Baghdad; e-mail maktaba.unive@yahoo.com; f. 1959; section in Al-Waziriya looted and some stock stolen April 2003; major reconstruction under way; govt and UN depository library; acts as Exchange and governmental Bibliographical Centre; publ. *Current Contents of Iraqi Universities' Journals* (temporarily ceased publication).

Basrah

University of Basrah Central Library: Basrah; f. 1964; 1m. vols; Librarian Dr TARIK AL-MANASSIR.

Mosul

University of Mosul Central Library: Mosul; tel. 810162; f. 1967; looted April 2003, although its collns were left intact; 24 br. libraries; 140,000 vols, 3,500 periodicals, depository of UN and Iraqi govt publs; Dir MAHMUD JIRJIS; publs *Adab Al-Rafidain* (irregular), *Al-Rafidain Engineering* (irregular), *Annals of the College of Medicine-Mosul* (irregular), *Catalogue* (1 a year), *Iraqi Journal of Veterinary Sciences* (irregular), *Journal of Education and Science* (irregular), *Journal of Rafidain Development* (irregular), *Mesopotamia Journal of Agriculture* (irregular), *Research Work of University Faculty Members* (1 a year).

Museums and Art Galleries

Arbil

Arbil Museum: Arbil; tel. (66) 522273; objects from Iraqi history up to Arabic-Islamic period.

Baghdad

Abbasid Palace Museum: Baghdad; tel. (1) 4164950; a restored palace dating back to the late Caliphs of the Abbasid dynasty (13th century AD); an exhibition of Arab antiquities and scale models of important Islamic monumental buildings in Iraq. Opened as a Museum in 1935.

Baghdad Museum: Sahat al Risafi, Baghdad; tel. (1) 4165317; f. 1970; museum of folklore and costumes, natural history; photographic exhibition on history of Baghdad; Memorial Exhibition, containing the royal relics of King Faisal I; picture gallery; Dir ALAE AL-SHIBLI.

Iraq Military Museum: A'dhamiya, Baghdad; f. 1974 by merger of Arms Museum (f. 1940) and Museum of War (f. 1966); contains old Arabian weapons, Othmanic firearms and contemporary Iraqi weapons.

Iraq National Museum: Salhiya Quarter, Baghdad West; internet www

.theiraqmuseum.org; f. 1923; looted April 2003, resulting in theft or destruction of approx. 15,000 items; closed until Feb. 2009 when it was re-opened to select groups; colln incl. antiquities dating from the early Stone Age to the beginning of the 18th century AD, incl. large colln of Islamic objects; Al-Sarraf gallery contains Islamic coins; library: see under Libraries and Archives; Dir AMIRA EIDAN; publs *Al-Maskukat* (2 a year), *Sumer* (1 a year).

Iraq Natural History Research Centre and Museum: Bab al Muadham, Baghdad; tel. (1) 4165790; f. 1946; attached to the University of Baghdad; incl. sections on zoology, botany and geology; research work in natural history; exhibitions of animals, plants, rocks and minerals pertaining to Iraq; organizes cultural, educational and scientific training programmes; library of 31,000 vols, 850 periodicals; Dir H.-A. ALI; publs *Bulletin of the Iraq Natural History Research Centre*, *Iraq Natural History Research Centre Publications* (series of scientific papers, in English (with Arabic summaries), dealing with the natural history of Iraq and neighbouring countries).

National Museum of Modern Art: Al-Nafoura Square, Bal Al-Sharqi, Baghdad; f. 1962; Supervisor AMER AL UBAIDI.

Mosul

Mosul Museum: Dawassa, Mosul; tel. (60) 2430; f. 1951; collns of Assyrian antiquities of the 9th and 8th centuries BC found at Nimrud, objects uncovered in the ruins of Hatra dating from the 2nd century BC to the 2nd century AD, agricultural tools and pottery vessels from 5000–4000 BC, photographs of excavated buildings at Tepe Gawra, maps of the Assyrian Empire, Nimrud and Hatra; Prehistoric and Islamic exhibits; assists in discovery and maintenance of several archaeological sites; library: c. 2,000 vols; Dir HAZIM A. AL HAMEED.

Nasiriya

Nasiriya Museum: Nasiriya; tel. (42) 233851; Sumerian and other archaeological objects found in Ur, Al-Abeed and Aridu; Dir ABDUL AMIR HAMDANI.

Samarra

Samarra Museum: Samarra; tel. (21) 722114; f. 1936; it is housed in one of the old city gates, and contains objects excavated in the ruins of ancient Samarra; also historic maps, writings, pictures.

Universities

AL-IRAQIA UNIVERSITY

Adhmai, Habiet Khatoun, Baghdad
Telephone: (1) 4254257
E-mail: info@aliraqia.edu.iq
Internet: aliraqia.edu.iq
Founded 1989
State control
Language of instruction: Arabic
Academic year: September to August
Pres.: Prof. Dr ZIYAD M. RASHEED AL ANI (acting)
Vice-Pres. for Admin. Affairs: Dr ANMMAR AHMED MOHAMED
Vice-Pres. for Scientific Affairs: Prof. Dr IBRAHEEM ABID SAIL
Librarian: Dr KAIS ABDULLATIF AHMED
Library of 57,760 vols, 3,826 periodical titles
Number of teachers: 647
Number of students: 13,070 (12,724 undergraduate, 346 postgraduate)
Publications: *Aldananeer*, *Al-khaber*, *Journal of Educational and Scientific Studies*, *Midad al-adab*, *Voice of The Iraqia University* (12 a year)

DEANS
College of Arts: Dr ABDULLAH HASAN AL-HADITHI
College of Economics and Administration: Dr HIKMET FARIS TA'AAN
College of Education: Dr ADNAN ALI AL-FRAJI
College of Education for Girls: Dr OMER MAJEED ABID
College of Law: Dr ZIYAD HAMED AL-SUMAYDAAI
College of Mass Media: Dr NAHIDH FADHIL ZIDAN
College of Medicine: Dr HUSSAM DAOOD SAEID
College of Religions' Fundamentals: Prof. Dr SUBHI FANDI AL-KUBEISI
College of Shari'a: Dr ABDULMUNAEM KHALIL AL-HITI

AL MUSTANSIRIYA UNIVERSITY

POB 14022, Waziriya, Baghdad
Telephone: (1) 4168501
E-mail: mustuni@uruklink.net
Founded 1963
State control
Languages of instruction: Arabic, English
Academic year: September to June
Pres.: Dr IHSAN K. AL KURSHY (acting)
Vice-Pres. for Admin.: ADEL H. AL BAGHDADI (acting)
Vice-Pres. for Scientific Affairs: Dr KANAN A. ABDUL RAZAK (acting)
Librarian: MAISOON A. AL OBIADY
Library: see under Libraries and Archives
Number of teachers: 1,555
Number of students: 23,748
Publications: *Al Mustansiriya Journal of Science*, *Al Mustansiriya Literary Review*, *Journal of Administration and Economics*, *Journal of the College of Education*, *Journal of the College of Teachers*, *Journal of Dialah Education*, *Journal of Engineering and Pollution*, *Journal of the Founding Leader for National and Socialist Studies*, *Journal of Medical Research*, *Journal of Middle Eastern Studies*

DEANS
College of Administration and Economics: Dr ALI J. AL OBIADY
College of Arts: Dr MUHAMED O. AL SHEMARY
College of Dental Studies: Dr RAAD M. JADOA
College of Education: Dr SABAH A. ATTY
College of Engineering: Dr ALI M. AL ATHARY
College of Medicine: Dr MUHAMED H. AL WAN
College of Science: Asst Prof. KADUM H. AL MOSSAWI
College of Sports: Asst Prof. Dr SAMEER M. ALAWE

AL NAHRAIN UNIVERSITY

POB 64074, Jadiriyah, Baghdad
Telephone: (1) 7767810
E-mail: saduni@uruklink.net
Internet: www.alnahrain-university.org
Founded 1993 as Saddam Univ.; present name 2003
Pres.: MAHMOOD H. HAMMASH (acting)
Vice-Pres. for Admin.: FAYEK J. AL AZZAWI
Librarian: ZAINAB H. RASHID
Library of 65,963 vols
Number of teachers: 285
Number of students: 1,180

DEANS
College of Engineering: Dr MAZIN A. KADHIM
College of Law: Dr BASIM M. SALEH
College of Medicine: Dr MAHMOOD H. HAMASH
College of Political Sciences: Dr MAZIN I. AL RAMADANI
College of Science: Dr FALAH A. ATTAWI

UNIVERSITY OF AL-QADISIYA

POB 88, Diwaniya, al Qadisiya governorate
Telephone: (36) 628066
E-mail: info@qadissuni.edu.iq
Internet: www.qadissuni.edu.iq
Founded 1987
State control
Colleges of agriculture, education, law, nursing, pharmacy, veterinary medicine; faculties of admin. and economics, arts, computer science and mathematics, dentistry, engineering, medicine, physical education, science
Pres.: Dr EHSAN SHARIF KAZEM AL-QURESHI (acting)
Vice-Pres. for Admin.: ABDUL KARIM HIKMAT (acting)
Library of 2,000 vols
Number of teachers: 407

UNIVERSITY OF AL TA'AMEEM

Baghdad Rd, Kirkuk, al Ta'ameem governorate
Telephone: 418531
E-mail: fqislam@uruklink.net
Founded 2003
State control
Pres.: KAMAK OTHMAN OMEAR (acting)
Vice-Pres. for Admin.: ABRAHIM ATEA SALIH (acting)
Vice-Pres. for Scientific Affairs: NAJAT QADIR OMEAR (acting)
Number of teachers: 60

UNIVERSITY OF ANBAR

Ramadi, al Anbar governorate
Telephone: (1) 8864814
E-mail: anbar_university@yahoo.com
Internet: www.uoanbar.edu.iq
Founded 1987
State control
Languages of instruction: Arabic, English
Pres.: Prof. Dr KHALIL IBRAHIM AL-DULEIMI (acting)
Vice-Pres. for Admin. Affairs: Dr SAADI MAJEED ASHOUR
Vice-Pres. for Scientific Affairs: Prof. Dr ESSAM KHUDHEIR AL-HADITHY (acting)
Number of teachers: 464
Number of students: 10,776

DEANS
College of Agriculture: Dr IBRAHIM HAMMAD ALSAAD
College of Arts: Dr HABEEB MOHAMMED FARHAN
College of Computer Science: Dr MURTADHA MOHAMMED HAMAD
College of Dentistry: Prof. Dr RAFAEL HAMEED RASHEED
College of Economics and Administration (Falluja): Dr KHALIL KHALAF JASIM
College of Economics and Administration (Ramadi): Dr AWADH KHALAF DALAF AL-ESSAWI
College of Education (Qaim): Prof. Dr HAMMAD NAWAF FARHAN
College of Education for Humanities Science: Prof. Dr ZEYDAN KHALAF OMER AL-ASSAFI
College of Education for Pure Sciences: Dr AZMI TAWFIQ HUSSEIN
College of Engineering: Dr ADEL ENHEIR
College of Female Education: Prof. Dr WALEED FARAJ HUMADI
College of Islamic Sciences (Falluja): Dr OMER ALI MOHAMMED

College of Islamic Sciences (Ramadi): Prof. Dr BASHIR MEHDI ALTEIF AL-KUBEISY
College of Law (Falluja): Dr ASA'AD UBEID AZIZ AL-JUMEILY
College of Law (Ramadi): Prof. Dr HAMDI SALIH MAJEED
College of Medicine: Dr SALAH NOURI AL-ANI
College of Physical Education: Prof. Dr JUMAA MOHAMMED AWADH
College of Sciences: Prof. Dr EMMAD ABDUL RAHMAN MOHAMMED SALIH
College of Veterinary Medicine: Dr MEHDI SALIH SHALAL

UNIVERSITY OF BABYLON

POB 4, Al Hilla, Babylon
Telephone: (30) 246562
E-mail: uniheadoffice@uobabylon.edu.iq
Internet: www.uobabylon.edu.iq
Founded 1991
State control
Languages of instruction: Arabic, English
Chancellor: Prof. Dr ADEL HADI HUSSEIN AL-BAGHDADI
Vice-Chancellor for Admin. Affairs: Prof. Dr AHMED KHALEEL AL-HUSSEINI
Vice-Pres. for Scientific Affairs: QAHTAN HADI AL-JEBORI (acting)
Int. Relations Officer: Dr ASAM ALJEBORY
Library of 54,512 vols, 7,781 periodicals
Number of teachers: 1,798
Number of students: 20,136
Publications: *Detective Magazine*, *Iraqi Journal of Engineering Mechanics and Materials Engineering*, *Journal of Babylon*, *Journal of College of Basic Education for Educational Sciences and Humanities*, *Journal of Human Sciences*, *Journal of Napo*, *Journal of the Faculty of Management and Economics Center for Economic Studies*, *Journal of the Iraqi National*, *Journal of the Science of Physical Education*, *Journal of the University of Babylon*, *Medical Journal of Babylon*

DEANS
College of Administration and Economics: Prof. Dr AHMED KHALEEL AL-HUSSEINI
College of Arts: Dr MOAH ARRAQ AL-ZIGGIBI
College of Basic Education: Dr MOHAMED SHAKER AL-RUBAIEEY
College of Dentistry: Dr MAHDY YAQUB
College of Engineering: Dr ADEL ABAS AL-MOSAWY
College of Fine Art: Dr ALI ALRUBAIEY
College of Human Science: Dr FAHEEM HUSSEIN AL-TURAYHI
College of Information Technology: Dr TAWFIQ A. ABAS AL-ASSADI
College of Law: Dr ALI ASSAL ALKHAFAJI
College of Materials Engineering: Dr KADHEM FINTTEL AL-SULTANY
College of Medicine: Dr MUSHTAQ ABDUL ATHEM AL-WETWET
College of Nursing: Dr AMMEN AGEEL AL-YASERY
College of Pharmacology: Dr SABAH NEEMA AL-THAMEER
College of Physical Education: Dr AMAL ALI SELOMY
College of Pure Science: Dr HABEB THAMER
College of Quranic Studies: Dr ALI ABDUL FATAH
College of Science: Dr HAYDER KAMEL AL-SAADY
College of Science College for Girls: Dr ENNAS AL-RUBAIEY
Musayyib College of Engineering and Technology: Dr ALI ABDUL AMEER AL-ZUBAIDY

UNIVERSITY OF BAGHDAD

POB 17635, Jadiriya, Baghdad
Telephone: (1) 7787819
E-mail: info@univofbaghdad.com
Internet: www.univofbaghdad.org
Founded 1957
State control
Languages of instruction: Arabic, English
Academic year: September to June
Pres.: MOSA JAWAD AZIZ AL MOSAWE
Vice-Pres. for Admin.: Dr NIHAD M. ABDUL RAHMAN
Vice-Pres. for Scientific Affairs: Dr RIYADH AZIZ HADI
Registrar: Dr HUSEIN KUDHAIR ABDUL-HUSEIN
Librarian: Dr MAJID ABDUL-KAREEM
Library: see under Libraries and Archives
Number of teachers: 3,517
Number of students: 85,000
Publications: *Ibn al Haitham Journal for Pure and Applied Sciences* (2 a year), *Iraqi Journal of Pharmaceutical Sciences* (4 a year), *Iraqi Journal of Science* (4 a year), *Iraqi Journal of Veterinary Medicine* (2 a year), *Iraqi Natural History Museum Bulletin* (4 a year), *Journal of Agricultural Sciences* (2 a year), *Journal of Engineering* (irregular), *Journal of Legal Sciences* (4 a year), *Journal of Political Science* (4 a year), *Journal of Sports Education* (irregular), *Journal of the College of Administration and Economics* (4 a year), *Journal of the College of Dentistry* (irregular), *Journal of the College of Education for Women* (2 a year), *Journal of the College of Languages* (1 a year), *Journal of the College of Shari'a* (2 a year), *Journal of the Faculty of Medicine* (4 a year), *Statistical Bulletin* (1 a year), *The Academic* (4 a year), *The Professor* (4 a year)

DEANS
College of Administration and Economics: Dr MUHAMMAD AL-MA'AMOORI
College of Agriculture: Dr HAMZA AL-ZUBAIDI
College of Arts: Dr FLAIH AL-RIKABI
College of Dentistry: Dr ALI AL-KAFAJI
College of Education (Ibn al Haitham): Dr ABDUL-JABBAR ABDUL-QADIR MUKHLIS
College of Education (Ibn Rushd): Dr OHOOD ABDUL-WAHID ABDUL-SAMAD
College of Education for Women: Dr AMIR MUHAMMAD ALI
College of Engineering: Dr QASSIM MUHAMMAD DOS
College of Fine Arts: Dr AQEEL MAHDI
College of Islamic Sciences: Dr MUHAMMAD SALIH
College of Languages: Dr TALIB AL-QURAISHI
College of Law: Dr ALI AL-RUFAE
College of Medicine: Dr FADHIL AL-JANABI
College of Nursing: MOHAMMAD FADHIL KHALIFA
College of Pharmacy: Dr ALAA ABDUL-HUSSEIN
College of Political Science: Dr AMIR JABBAR FAYADH
College of Science: Dr SALIH MOHAMMAD ALI
College of Sports Education: Dr RIYADH KHALIL KHAMAS
College of Veterinary Medicine: Dr FAREED AL-TAHAN

AFFILIATED CENTRES
Astronomical Research Unit: attached to College of Science; Dir Dr HAMEED MIJWIL AL NIAIMI.
Centre for International Studies: internet cis.uobaghdad.edu.iq; attached to College of Political Science; Dir Dr ABDUL GHAFOUR KARIM ALI.
Centre for Palestinian Studies: internet www.cps.uobaghdad.edu.iq; attached to College of Political Science; Dir Asst Prof. Dr ALI AL-JIBOURI.
Centre for the Revival of Arab Scientific Heritage: internet www.rashc.uobaghdad.edu.iq; Dir NABILA ABDUL MUNIM.
Centre for Urban and Regional Planning (Postgraduate studies): internet www.iurp.uobaghdad.edu.iq; Dir Dr WADHAH SAID YAHYA.
Educational and Psychological Research Centre: e-mail perc@perc.uobaghdad.edu.iq; internet www.perc.uobaghdad.edu.iq; attached to College of Education, Ibn Rushd; Dir MAHDI AL SAMARRAE

UNIVERSITY OF BASRAH

POB 49, Basrah
Telephone: (1) 8868520
E-mail: basrauniversity@satline.net
Internet: www.uobasrah.edu.iq
Founded 1964
State control
Languages of instruction: Arabic, English
Academic year: September to June
Pres.: Prof. Dr THAMER AHMAD HAMDAN
Vice-Pres. for Academic Affairs and Higher Studies: Dr SHAKER ABDUL SALEM NI'MA
Vice-Pres. for Admin. Affairs: Dr SAGED SAAD HASSAN
Librarian: Dr AMER ABID MUHSIN AL SAAD
Library: see under Libraries and Archives
Number of teachers: 1,033
Number of students: 99,751
Publications: *Arab Gulf Journal*, *Basrah Journal of Agricultural Sciences*, *Basrah Journal of Sciences*, *Basrah Journal of Surgery*, *Economic Studies*, *Gulf Economics Journal*, *Iraqi Journal of Polymers*, *Journal of Arts*, *Journal of Basrah Research*, *Journal of Physical Education*, *Marina Mesopotamica*, *Medical Journal of Basrah University*

DEANS
Faculty of Administration and Economics: Dr YOUSIF ALI AL-ASADY
Faculty of Agriculture: Dr SHAKER HANTOOSH ADAY
Faculty of Arts: Dr ABDULLAH SALEM A. AL-MALIKI (acting)
Faculty of Dentistry: Dr ALI ABBAS HABEEB
Faculty of Education for Humanities: Dr HUSSAIN AODA HASHIM AL-EDANY
Faculty of Education (Qurna): Dr WALEED ABDUL RIDHA JBAIL AL DAKHIL
Faculty of Engineering: Dr NABEEL ABDULRAZZAQ JASIM (acting)
Faculty of Fine Arts: ABDUL KAREEM ABOOD AODA AL-KAN'ANY (acting)
Faculty of Medicine: Prof. Dr THAMER AHMED HAMDAN
Faculty of Nursing: Dr NA'EL HUSSAIN ALI AL-NAZZAL (acting)
Faculty of Pharmacy: Dr SHAKER ABDUL SALEM NA'MA
Faculty of Physical Education: Dr MONTATHER MAJEED ALI MOHAMMED (acting)
Faculty of Science: Prof. FALHI ABDUL HASSAN ALI AL-QATRANI
Faculty of Veterinary Science: Dr BASIL ABDUL ZAHRA ABBAS

UNIVERSITY OF DIYALA

POB 2, Baquba Post Office, Baquba, Diyala governorate, Al-Muradia, Old Baquba-Baghdad Way
Telephone: (790) 1978420
E-mail: diyala_university@yahoo.com
Internet: www.uodiyala.edu.iq
Founded 1999

Languages of instruction: Arabic, English
Academic year: September to July
State control
Pres.: Prof. Dr MAHMOUD SHAKER RASHEED (acting)
Vice-Pres. for Admin. Affairs: Dr AMER M. IBRAHIM
Vice-Pres. for Scientific Affairs: Dr AMER M. IBRAHIM (acting)
Number of teachers: 867
Number of students: 14,782
Publication: *Al Afaak Al Jadida* (in Arabic)

DEANS

College of Administration and Economics: Dr HAITHAM YAQUB YOSEF
College of Agriculture: Dr ADEL NORI GOMA'A
College of Basic Education: Dr ABBAS FADIL GAWAD
College of Education (Al-Razi): Dr ABBAS ABOOD FARHAN
College of Education (Al-Asmaee): Dr MAHMOUD FAIAD HUMMADI
College of Engineering: Dr ADEL KHALEEL MAHMOUD
College of Fine Arts: Prof. Dr ALAA SHAKEER M.
College of Islamic Sciences: AHMED ABID AL SATTAR GASIM
College of Law: Dr ABID AL-AZIZ SHAABAN KHALID
College of Medicine: Dr KHUDHAIR KH. IBRAHIM
College of Science: Dr DHAHIR ABID AL-HADI
College of Sport Education: Dr MAHIR ABID AL-LATEEF
College of Veterinary Medicine: Dr ABID AL RAZZAQ SHAFEEQ

UNIVERSITY OF DUHOK

Zakho Rd 38, Kurdistan Region, Dohuk governorate
Telephone: (62) 7227060
E-mail: relations@uod.ac
Internet: www.uod.ac
Founded 1992; attached to Min. of Higher Education and Scientific Research
State control
Languages of instruction: Arabic, English, Kurdish
Academic year: September to August
Pres.: Dr ASMAT MOHAMMED KHALID (acting)
Vice-Pres. for Admin. Affairs: Dr SALEEM H. HAJI (acting)
Vice-Pres. for Int. Relations: Dr DAWOOD S. ATRUSHI
Vice-Pres. for Scientific Affairs: Dr HASAN AMEEN MOHAMMED (acting)
Library of 11,770 vols
Number of teachers: 791
Number of students: 9,100
Publication: *Govara Zankoya*

DEANS

College of Law and Politics: Dr NADHIM YOUNS OTHMAN
College of Medicine: Dr FARHAD KHURSHEED MOHAMMED
College of Nursing: Dr AHMED MOHAMMED SALIH
College of Physical Education: Dr ODEAT ODISHO
College of Science: Dr AHMED MOHAMMED SALIH
College of Veterinary Medicine: Dr NADHIM SULAIMAN A. AZIZ
Faculty of Agriculture: Dr MOAFAQ SULAIMAN
Faculty of Education: Prof. AUDIATE ODISHO
Faculty of Engineering and Applied Science: Prof. NAZAR M. S. NUMAN
Faculty of Evening Studies: Prof. ELIAS KHALAF
Faculty of Humanities: Dr MOSA
Faculty of Medicine: Dr ARIF YOUNIS BALATI
Higher Institute of Learning: Dr ASMAT MOHAMMED KHALID (Head)
Scientific Research Centre: JALADET JUBREAL (Head)

UNIVERSITY OF KARBALA

Al Dhbbat district, Karbala, Karbala governorate
Telephone: (32) 321364
E-mail: info@uokerbala.edu.iq
Internet: www.uokerbala.edu.iq
Founded 2002
State control
Academic year: September to July
Colleges of administration and economics, agriculture, education, engineering, law, medicine, pharmacy, science
Pres.: A. H. ALWAN (acting)
Library of 25,000 vols
Number of teachers: 222
Number of students: 5,000

UNIVERSITY OF KUFA

Kufa, POB 21, Najaf, al Najaf governorate
Telephone: (33) 346094
E-mail: info@kuiraq.com
Internet: www.kuiraq.com
Founded 1987; attached to Min. of Higher Education and Scientific Research
Public control
Languages of instruction: Arabic, English
Academic year: September to June
Pres.: Prof. RAZAK AL-ESSA (acting)
Vice-Pres. for Admin.: Asst Prof. ABDUL-SAHIB AL-BAGHDADY
Vice-Pres. for Scientific Affairs: Prof. MUHSIN AL-DHALEMI
Library of 23,500 vols
Number of teachers: 1,425
Number of students: 18,519
Publications: *Al-Ghary Journal for Economical and Administrative Researches*, *Al-Kufa Journal for Agricultural Sciences*, *Al-Kufa Journal for Legal and Political Sciences*, *Al-Kufa Journal for Medical and Veterinary Sciences*, *Al-Kufa Journal for Nursing Science*, *Arabic Language and Its Arts*, *Biology Journal*, *Chemical Sciences Journal*, *College of Education Journal for Human Sciences*, *College of Jurisprudence Journal*, *Geographic Researches Journal*, *Kufa Engineering Journal*, *Kufa Journal of Arts*, *Kufa Medical Journal*, *Kufa Studies Center Journal*, *Mathematics and Computers Journal*, *Physics Journal*

DEANS

College of Agriculture: Prof. SADOON SADOON
College of Athletic Education: Asst Prof. QASEM HASSAN
College of Basic Education: Asst Prof. IBTISAM AL-MADANY
College of Dentistry: Asst Prof. ABBAS AL-HWEIZY
College of Economy and Administration: Prof. MAZIN ESSA
College of Education: Asst Prof. BASEM BAQER
College of Education for Girls: Asst Prof. SAAD AZIZ
College of Engineering: Asst Prof. ALAA MAHDI
College of Jurisprudence: Prof. SABAH UNOUZ
College of Law and Political Sciences: Asst Prof. ALI AL-SHUKRI
College of Mathematics and Computer Sciences: Asst Prof. YAHYA AL-MAYALI
College of Medicine: Prof. MUHAMMED SAEED
College of Nursing: Asst Prof. ABDUL-KAREEM ABDULLAH
College of Pharmacy: Asst Prof. RAHEEM AL-SAEDI
College of Sciences: Prof. ABDUL-MAJEED AL-SAADI
College of Veterinary Medicine: Prof. AHMED AL-AZZAM

PROFESSORS

ABAS ALSAED SALMAN, J., Agriculture Sciences
ABDUL-AMEER AL-DALEMY, M., Abdominal Medicine
ABDUL-HAMSA AL-SHAMARY, P., Micro Alive
ABDUL-RASSWL AL-GHAKANEI, N., Economy
ABOUD AL-KAFAF, A., Geography
ABU HAMD AL-ALI, R., Economy
ABU RAHEAL AL-FATLAWEI, A., Geography
ADEA EASSA AL-MHANA, J., Medicine and Surgery
AKAB AL-WAIALY, T., Modern History
ALEASA, A., Biochemistry
AL-HASSENI, H., Mathematics
AL-HASSNWEI, S., Pharmacy
ALI AL-FEDAWEE, A., Paediatrics
ALI AL-SAKEAR, M., Arabic Language
ALI ALHAKEMI, H., History
ALI SAMEA AL-ALI, M., Geography
AL-JUMAILI, S., Biology
AL-KHALIDI, A., Turkish
AL-KUTUBI, S., Mathematics
ALMOUSA AL-ASADI, K., Geography Natural
AL-SAEEDI, A., Biology
AL-SHARMANY, M., Agriculture Sciences
ALWAN AL-FATLAWI, A., Arabic Language
ASER MOSSA AL-GORATEI, H., Arabic Literature
HAFAD AL-KAFAGEI, A., Arabic Literature
HAMOD AL-SHAMA, Y., Physiology
HASSAN AL-SNEAD, A., Physics
HASSAN AL-ENASSI, T., History
HUSSEIN AL-KUFEE, A., Diseases Medicine
HUSSEIN AL-ZAMALY, N., Medicines
JALEEL ABDUL-HASSAN AL-GHALEBEI, A., Economy
KADEM THEDAN AL-FATLAWEI, K., Economy
MERZA AL-HUMAIRI, T., Biology
MHASSEN ALBU-AREBI, N., Philosophy
MOHAMED AL-ATHAREI, A., Economy
MOHAMED AL-JANABI, H., Abdominal Medicine
MUHSIN AL-YASIRI, A., Arabic Language
RADEE ABUOD NASAR, M., Islamic Sciences
RAKBAN AL-KAFAGEI, A., Law
RESHED JABBER AL-ABEADI, H., Nutriments Sciences
RWAH ALI AL-MUOSWEAI, S., Administration
SADAK ALSHIKE RADEA, M., Economy
SADDON AJEAL AL-AJEALI, S., Agriculture Sciences
TALAB AL-MUOSWEA, A., Geography
TARASH ZAOARI AL-JANABI, H., Micro Alive

UNIVERSITY OF MOSUL

Al Majmoa Al Thaqafia, Mosul
Telephone: (60) 810733
E-mail: president@uomosul.edu.iq
Internet: www.uomosul.edu.iq
Founded 1967 as a separate univ., fmrly part of the Univ. of Baghdad
State control
Languages of instruction: Arabic, English
Academic year: September to June (2 terms)
Pres.: OBAY S. AL DEWACHI (acting)
Vice-Pres. for Admin.: Dr ADNAN ALSAFAWI (acting)
Vice-Pres. for Scientific Affairs: Dr NAZAR MAJEED QIBI (acting)
Librarian: Dr NASSER ABDUL RAAZAQ MULLA JASSIM
Library: see under Libraries and Archives
Number of teachers: 4,343
Number of students: 35,766

Publications: *Adab al Rafidain* (4 a year), *Al Rafidain Engineering Sciences* (4 a year), *Al Rafidain Dental Journal* (4 a year), *Al Rafidain Journal of Computer Science* (4 a year), *Al Rafidain Journal of Earth Science* (4 a year), *Al Rafidain Journal of Law* (4 a year), *Al Rafidain Journal of Science* (4 a year), *Al Rafidain Journal of Statistical Science* (4 a year), *Al Rafidain Sports Science Journal* (4 a year), *Annals of The Medical College* (4 a year), *College of Basic Education Research Journal* (4 a year), *Iraq Journal of Agricultural Science* (4 a year), *Iraqi Journal of Pharmacy* (4 a year), *Iraqi Journal of Veterinary Medicine* (4 a year), *Journal of Education and Science* (4 a year), *Regional Studies* (4 a year), *Studies Mosulia* (4 a year), *Tanmiat al Rafidain* (4 a year)

DEANS

College of Administration: Dr FAWAZ GARALLA AL DOLUMY
College of Agriculture: Prof. Dr NAHIL MOHAMMED ALI
College of Archeology: Prof. Dr ALI YASIN ALJUBURI
College of Arts: MUHAMMAD BASIL AL AZZAWI
College of Basic Education: Dr FADHIL KHALIL IBRAHIM
College of Dentistry: Dr TAHANI A. A. AL SANDOOK
College of Education: Dr ABDL WAHID DH. TAHA
College of Education for Girls: Prof. Dr KHAWLA AHMED AL-FLAEH
College of Electronic Engineering: Dr BASIL SH. MAHMOOD
College of Engineering: Dr FAROOQ KHALIL AMOORI
College of Environmental Science and Technology: Prof. Dr MOAATH HAMID MUSTAFA
College of Fine Arts: Dr ADEL SAEED AL SAFAR
College of Islamic Sciences: Prof. Dr ABDULLA FATHI AL DHAHIR
College of Law: Prof. Dr AKRAM MAHMOOD HUSSEIN
College of Mathematics and Computer Science: Dr THAFER RAMATHAN MUTTAR
College of Medicine: Dr MUZAHIM FATAH AL CHETACHI
College of Medicine (Nineveh): Prof. Dr FARIS BAKIR AL SAWAF
College of Nursing: Dr SUBHE HUSEIN AL GUBORE
College of Pharmacy: Prof. Dr BASIL MOHAMMED AL KHAYAT
College of Physical Education: Dr YASSIN TAHA MOHAMMAD ALI
College of Political Science: Dr MUFEED TH. YOUNIS
College of Science: Dr IHSAN A. MUSTAFA AL ABDULLAH
College of Veterinary Medicine: Dr FOUAD KASIM MOHAMMAD

UNIVERSITY OF SALAHADDIN

Karkuk St, Runaki 235–323, Arbil, Kurdistan region
Telephone: (66) 2230409
E-mail: design@suh-edu.com
Internet: www.suh-edu.com
Founded 1968 in Sulaimaniya as Univ. of Sulaimaniya; present name and location 1981
State control
Languages of instruction: Arabic, English, Kurdish
Academic year: September to June (two terms)
Pres.: Dr MOHAMMAD S. MOHAMMAD
Vice-Pres. for Scientific Affairs: Dr AHMAD ANWAR AMIN DEZAYE
Librarian: Dr MOHAMMAD MUSTAFA
Library: see under Libraries and Archives
Number of teachers: 800
Number of students: 10,965 (10,597 undergraduate, 368 postgraduate)
Publications: *Statistical Abstract* (1 a year), *University News* (12 a year, in Arabic), *Zanco* (scientific journal, in Arabic and English)

DEANS

College of Administration and Economics: Asst Prof. Dr DLER ISMAIL HAQI
College of Agriculture: Asst Prof. Dr FARHAD HASSAN AZEEZ
College of Arts: Prof. Dr AZAD MUHAMMAD AMEEN NAQISHBANDI
College of Dentistry: Dr DASHTI BAIZ DZAYI
College of Education: Prof. Dr KAREEM SALIH ABDUL
College of Engineering: Dr FARAYDOON HADI MAROUF
College of Law: NAJDAT SABRI AQRAWI
College of Medicine: Asst Prof. Dr HAMA NAJIM JAFF
College of Nursing: Dr FARHAD JALEEL KHAYAT
College of Pharmacy: Dr TAFUR JALAL KHLEL
College of Physical Education: IIDREES MUHAMMAD TAHIR
College of Political Science: Dr AHMED MUSTAFA SULAIMAN
College of Science: Asst Prof. ROSTEM KAREEM SAED
College of Teacher Training: Asst Prof. Dr AZAD JALAL SHAREEF

UNIVERSITY OF SULAIMANIYA

2/3/205 Kani-Askan, Sulaimaniya
Telephone: (53) 2127453
E-mail: info@univsul.com
Internet: www.univsul.org
Founded 1968
State control
Languages of instruction: Arabic, English, Kurdish
Colleges of administration and economics, agriculture, dentistry and commerce, education, engineering, fine arts, humanities, languages, nursing, physical education, law, medicine, science, veterinary medicine
Pres.: KAMAL KHOSHNAW (acting)
Vice-Pres. for Admin.: SHAWNM ABDUL QADIR (acting)
Vice-Pres. for Scientific Affairs and Postgraduate Research: NAZAR M. MUHAMMAD AMIN (acting)
Library of 24,689 vols
Number of teachers: 489
Number of students: 8,000

UNIVERSITY OF TECHNOLOGY

Al Sinah St, Baghdad
Telephone: (1) 7746532
E-mail: shekhly@uruklink.net
Internet: www.uotiq.org
Founded 1975; fmrly the College of Engineering Technology of the University of Baghdad
State control
Languages of instruction: Arabic, English
Academic year: October to July
Pres.: Dr WAIL NOORALDEN AL RIFAIE (acting)
Vice-Pres. for Admin. and Scientific Affairs: KRIKOR SIROB (acting)
Registrar: Dr ABDU AL HUSAIN SAKHI
Librarian: AYAD J. SHAMIS ELDEN
Library of 25,000 vols
Number of teachers: 961 (668 full-time, 293 part-time)
Number of students: 7,752

PROFESSORS

AL HADEETHI, A., Structural Engineering
AL HAIDARY, J. T., Production Engineering and Metallurgy
AL MUTALIB IBRAHIM, A., Applied Sciences
AL SAMAAUI, A., Structural Engineering
AL SAMRAAI, J. M. A., Electrical Engineering
AL TOORNAJI, M., Production Engineering and Metallurgy
HAMMUDI, W. KH., Applied Sciences
KHAIRI, W., Computer and Control Engineering
KHORSEED, N., Structural Engineering
MAJEED, J., Mechanical Engineering
TAWFICK, H., Mechanical Engineering

UNIVERSITY OF THI-QAR

Nasiriya, Thi-Qar governorate
Internet: www.unidhiqar.com
Founded 2002
State control
Pres.: ISMAIL OBEID ALSNAVI (acting)
Vice-Pres. for Admin.: QASIM MOHAMMAD (acting)
Vice-Pres. for Scientific Affairs: ABBAS HUSSEIN (acting)
Number of teachers: 155
Number of students: 5,639

DEANS

College of Arts: FADEL KAZEM SADIK
College of Education: MOHAMED JASSIM MOHAMMED
College of Engineering: HAIDAR SAAD REFINERY
College of Medicine: NAJI MAJID
College of Sciences: NAJAH RASSOL AL JABBRAI

UNIVERSITY OF TIKRIT

POB 42, Salah al Din, Tikrit
Telephone: (21) 825743
E-mail: tikrituniversity@hotmail.com
Founded 1987
State control
Languages of instruction: Arabic, English
Academic year: September to June
Pres.: Prof. Dr MAHER S. AL JUBORI (acting)
Librarian: SABAH S. KHALEFE
Number of teachers: 701
Number of students: 6,824
Publications: *Iraqi Journal of Educational and Psychological Sciences and Sociology* (4 a year), *Surra Min Raa Journal* (4 a year), *Tikrit Journal of Agricultural Sciences* (4 a year), *Tikrit Journal of Economic Sciences* (4 a year), *Tikrit Journal of Engineering Sciences* (4 a year), *Tikrit Journal of Humanities* (4 a year), *Tikrit Journal of Pharmaceutical Sciences* (4 a year), *Tikrit Journal of Pure Sciences* (4 a year), *Tikrit Medical Journal* (4 a year)

DEANS

College of Administration and Economics: Asst Prof. Dr SABAH F. MAHMOOD
College of Agriculture: Prof. Dr ABDULLAH AHMED AL SAMARRAIE
College of Dentistry: Prof. Dr ADNAN H. MOHAMMED
College of Education: Asst Prof. Dr ALI SALIH HUSSEIN
College of Education (Samarra): Asst Prof. Dr MUHAMMAD IBRAHIM HUSSEIN
College of Education for Women: Asst Prof. Dr JAID Z. MUKHLIF
College of Engineering: Asst Prof. Dr HAYDAR SAAD YASEEN AL JUBAIR
College of Law: Asst Prof. Dr DHAMIN HUSSEIN
College of Medicine: Asst Prof. Dr ABID AHMAD SALMAN

College of Pharmacy: Prof. Dr ALI ISMAIL UBEID
College of Science: Asst Prof. Dr SUBHI ATIA MAHMOOD

PROFESSORS

ABDOON, H. F., Islamic Jurisprudence
ABDULLAH, A. A.-M., Veterinary Science
ALAAH, M. M., Microbiology
AL AZIZ, M. A., Veterinary Science
AL BAYDHANI, I. S., Modern History
AL HUSSEIN, S. A., Biology
ALI, A. A.-G. M., Medicine
ALI, K. I., Politics
ALI, N. H., Physical Education
AL JUBURI, A. H. M., Arabic Language
AL-JUBURI, M. S. A., Arabic Language
AL JUMAILI, S. H. A., Arabic Language
AL-KUTUBI, S. H., Mathematics
AL NAJAFEE, H. M., Civil Engineering
AL OMER, A. K., Arabic Language
ALRAHMAN, Y. A. A., Medicine
AL SAMARRAIE, A. A.-K. M., Physical Education
AL SAMARRAIE, A. A.-M. H., Chemistry
AL SHIQARCHI, S. T., Chemistry
AL TAAI, A. A. H., Arabic Language
AUBED, A. I., Pharmacology and Toxicology
AZIZ, A. A., Chemistry
DAWOOD, A. S., Plant Protection
DAWOOD, I. S., Biology
DEKRAAN, S. B., Chemistry
GHANIM, Y. M.-A., Medicine
HAMAD, G. Q., Arabic Language
HANTOSH, F. G., Chemistry
HUSEIN, M. H., Civil Engineering
KAMEL, A. A.-M., Modern History
KAMEL, F. M., Food Technologies
LATEEF, R. A., Crops
MAHMOUD, S. A., Chemistry
MOHAMMED, A. H., Dentistry
MOHAMMED, A. H., Economics
MOHAMMED, M. M., Medicine
MUKHIF, J. Z., Arabic Language
MUSA, M. M., Veterinary Science
RASEED, A. A-M., Economics
SAIED, J. M., Animal Production
SHIHAB, A. F., Biology
WADY, A. A.-R. A., History

UNIVERSITY OF WASSIT

Kut, Wassit governorate
Telephone: (23) 313861
E-mail: info@uowasit.edu.iq
Internet: www.uowasit.edu.iq

Founded 2003
State control

Pres.: Dr JABBAR YASSER AL MAYAH
Number of teachers: 109

College

Foundation of Technical Education: Baghdad; internet www.fte.edu.iq; f. 1972; attached to Min. of Higher Education and Scientific Research; groups all the institutes of technology; Pres. ALKADEM JAAFAR ALYASIRI.

IRELAND

The Higher Education System

Higher education in Ireland dates from the foundation of the University of Dublin Trinity College in 1592; the next oldest institutions are the Royal College of Physicians of Ireland (founded 1654) and the National University of Ireland, Maynooth (formerly St Patrick's College, founded 1795). Until 1920 the 32 counties of Ireland were part of the United Kingdom; however, in that year Ireland was partitioned: the six north-eastern counties remained part of the United Kingdom, and the 26 southern counties sought independence. In 1922 the southern counties achieved dominion status, under the British Crown, as the Irish Free State. Ireland achieved full sovereignty within the Commonwealth in 1937, and the Republic of Ireland was declared in 1949. There are four universities—the University of Dublin (Trinity College), the National University of Ireland (a federal university system of constituent universities comprising the University College of Cork, the University College of Dublin, the National University of Ireland, Galway, and the National University of Ireland, Maynooth), Dublin City University and the University of Limerick—as well as other institutions of higher education including colleges, institutes of technology, schools of art and music, and professional establishments. Under the Universities Act (1997) and the Qualifications Act (1999), Ireland participates in the Bologna Process. The State pays tuition fees, but students are required to pay a registration fee on commencing higher education. In 2010/11 89,273 full-time students were enrolled in the university sector, and 62,885 students were enrolled at technology colleges; there was a total overall enrolment at tertiary level of 161,840 students.

Admission to higher education is generally administered by the Central Applications Office and requires the Leaving Certificate examination. In accordance with the Bologna Process, the university awards system consists of Bachelors, Masters and Doctorate degrees. The Bachelors (Ordinary or Honours) is the main undergraduate degree and lasts for three to four years (180–240 European Credit Transfer and Accumulation System—ECTS—credit units). However, degrees in some disciplines, such as dentistry, veterinary medicine, architecture (all five years) and medicine (six years), may last longer. Following the Bachelors, a student may take the Masters, the first postgraduate degree. The Masters is a one- to two-year programme of study (60–120 ECTS credit units), and may be either a taught or a research degree. The second postgraduate degree (and final university-level award) is the doctorate, which is normally a research-based Doctor of Philosophy (PhD) course lasting three to four years and requiring the presentation of a thesis. Other doctoral programmes also now exist, including professional and performance/practice-based courses. In addition to the universities, higher education is offered by other types of institution, including Institutes of Technology and so-called 'Designated' Institutions. Until 2012 awards from these establishments were assured by the Higher Education and Training Awards Council (HETAC, founded 2001). Quality assurance of universities was organized through the independent Irish Universities Quality Board (IUQB, established in 2002), however the devolved statutory responsibility was with the universities themselves. The Higher Education Authority also had a statutory right to review the quality assurance procedures in the universities, having consulted with the universities and the National Qualifications Authority of Ireland (NQAI). On 6 November 2012 Quality and Qualifications Ireland (QQI) was established as a new integrated agency under the Qualifications and Quality Assurance (Education and Training) Act 2011, replacing HETAC, NQAI and incorporating the functions of IUQB. The constituent bodies will continue to exist until full transfer of responsibility to QQI has been completed. The QQI will be responsible for promoting, maintaining, developing and implementing the National Framework of Qualifications.

Technical and vocational education is offered by colleges, the Dublin Institute of Technology and Industrial Training Authority centres. Until 2012 the Further Education and Training Awards Council was the statutory body overseeing all continuing and adult education and administering a wide range of certificated courses. It also has been amalgamated into the QQI. The most prominent vocational award is the National Vocational Certificate (Levels 1–6).

In 2011 the National Strategy for Higher Education to 2030 was launched to implement wide-ranging reforms of the higher education sector.

Regulatory and Representative Bodies

GOVERNMENT

Department of Arts, Heritage and the Gaeltacht: 23 Kildare St, Dublin 2; tel. (1) 6313800; e-mail press.office@ahg.gov.ie; internet www.ahg.gov.ie; Minister JIMMY DEENIHAN.

Department of Education and Skills: Marlborough St, Dublin 1; tel. (1) 8892304; e-mail info@education.gov.ie; internet www.education.ie; Minister RUAIRÍ QUINN.

ACCREDITATION

Accreditation Commission on Colleges of Medicine (ACCM): 131 Belmont, Southern Cross Rd, Bray, Co Wicklow; tel. (87) 2388502; e-mail office@accredmed.org; internet www.accredmed.org; f. 1995; accreditation of medical colleges on behalf of govts in Sint Maarten, Island Territory of Saba, Cayman Islands and Nevis Island; 12 mems; Chair. Prof. RAYMOND FITZGERALD; Hon. Sec. and Treas. Dr ANTHONY PEACOCK.

ENIC/NARIC Ireland: 26/27 Denzille Lane, Dublin 2; tel. (1) 9058100; e-mail info@qualrec.ie; internet www.qualrec.ie; Man. of Qualifications Recognition NIAMH LENEHAN.

Quality and Qualifications Ireland (QQI): 26/27 Denzille Lane, Dublin 2; tel. (1) 9058100; e-mail consultation@qqi.ie; internet www.qqi.ie; f. 2012 by merging Further Education and Training Awards Council, Higher Education and Training Awards Council, Nat. Qualifications Authority of Ireland and Irish Univs Quality Board; maintains, develops and reviews the Nat. Framework of Qualifications; Chair. GORDON CLARK; Chief Exec. Dr PADRAIG WALSH.

State Examinations Commission: Cornamaddy, Athlone, Co Westmeath; tel. (90) 6442700; e-mail sec.pressoffice@examinations.ie; internet www.examinations.ie; f. 2003; responsible for the provision and quality of the Irish State Examinations; aims to deliver an efficient, fair and accessible examination and assessment system in conjunction with school authorities and education providers; Chair. RICHARD LANGFORD; CEO AIDAN FARRELL.

FUNDING

Higher Education Authority: Brooklawn House, Crampton Ave, Shelbourne Rd, Ballsbridge, Dublin 4; tel. (1) 2317100; e-mail info@hea.ie; internet www.hea.ie; statutory planning and devt body for higher education and research in Ireland; has wide advisory powers throughout the whole of the tertiary education sector; funding authority for univs and a number of designated higher education instns; Chair. JOHN HENNESSY; Chief Exec. TOM BOLAND.

Science Foundation Ireland: Wilton Park House, Wilton Pl., Dublin 2; tel. (1) 6073200; e-mail info@sfi.ie; internet www.sfi.ie; f. 2000; nat. funding body for research in the fields of science and engineering; 3 key areas of interest: biotechnology, information and communications technology, and sustainable energy and energy-efficient technologies;

Dir-Gen. Prof. MARK FERGUSON; Sec. and COO DONAL KEANE.

NATIONAL BODIES

Central Applications Office: Tower House, Eglinton St, Galway; tel. (91) 509800; internet www.cao.ie; f. 1976; processes applications for first-year undergraduate courses offered by the higher-education instns in Ireland; Chair. PAUL GILLER; CEO IVOR GLEESON.

Irish Universities Association: 48 Merrion Sq., Dublin 2; tel. (1) 6764948; e-mail marguerita.lardner@iua.ie; internet www.iua.ie; rep. body of the heads of the 7 Irish univs; seeks to advance univ. education and research through the formulation and pursuit of collective policies and actions on behalf of the Irish univs thereby contributing to Ireland's social, cultural and economic wellbeing; Pres. Prof. PATRICK PRENDERGAST; CEO NED COSTELLO; publ. *IUA Review* (irregular).

National Council for Special Education: 1–2 Mill St, Trim, Co Meath; tel. (46) 9486400; e-mail press@ncse.ie; internet www.ncse.ie; f. 2003; formally est. 2005; plans and coordinates provision of education and support services to persons (particularly children) with spec. educational needs; Chair. EAMON STACK; CEO TERESA GRIFFIN.

Learned Societies

GENERAL

Royal Dublin Society: Anglesea Rd, Ballsbridge, Dublin 4; tel. (1) 6680866; e-mail info@rds.ie; internet www.rds.ie; f. 1731; advancement of agriculture, industry, science and the arts; 6,000 mems; library: see under Libraries and Archives; Pres. MATTHEW DEMPSEY; Registrar EILEEN BYRNE; publ. *Minerva* (3 a year).

Royal Irish Academy: Academy House, 19 Dawson St, Dublin 2; tel. (1) 6762570; e-mail info@ria.ie; internet www.ria.ie; f. 1785; acad. for the sciences, humanities and social sciences in Ireland; promotes excellence in scholarship, recognizes achievements in learning and undertakes research projects; advises on and contributes to public debate and public policy formation in science, technology and culture; maintains a library; 550 mems (474 ordinary, 76 hon.); library of 35,000 vols, 31,000 pamphlets, 1,800 sets of current periodicals, 2,500 MSS; Pres. Prof. MARY E. DALY; Sec. Prof. VANI BOROOAH; publs *Biology and Environment* (3 a year), *Eriu* (1 a year), *Irish Journal of Earth Sciences* (1 a year), *Irish Studies in International Affairs* (1 a year), *Mathematical Proceedings* (2 a year), *Proceedings Section C* (Archaeology, Celtic Studies, History, Linguistics, Literature, 1 a year).

AGRICULTURE, FISHERIES AND VETERINARY SCIENCE

Royal Horticultural Society of Ireland: Cabinteely House, The Park, Cabinteely, Dublin 18; tel. (1) 2353912; e-mail info@rhsi.ie; internet www.rhsi.ie; f. 1816; 1,000 mems; Pres. ROBERT S. MYERSCOUGH; Sec. CORA KENNEDY; publ. *The Journal* (3 a year).

Society of Irish Foresters: Glenealy, Co Wicklow; tel. (404) 44204; e-mail sif@eircom.net; internet www.societyofirishforesters.ie; f. 1942; advances and spreads the knowledge of forestry in all its aspects; promotes professional standards in forestry and the regulation of the forestry profession in Ireland; annual study tour, field days, annual symposium, lectures; continuing professional development programme; 700 mems; Pres. PACELLI BREATHNACH; publ. *Irish Forestry* (2 a year).

Veterinary Council of Ireland: 53 Lansdowne Rd, Ballsbridge, Dublin 4; tel. (1) 6684402; e-mail info@vci.ie; internet www.vci.ie; f. 2006; 2,370 registered mems; Registrar VALERIE BEATTY.

ARCHITECTURE AND TOWN PLANNING

Architectural Association of Ireland: 26 North Great George's St, Dublin 1; tel. (1) 6761703; e-mail contact@architecturalassociation.ie; internet www.architecturalassociation.ie; f. 1896; 450 mems; Pres. FERGUS NAUGHTON; Sec. RONAN MCCANN; publ. *Building Material* (6 a year).

Royal Institute of the Architects of Ireland: 8 Merrion Sq., Dublin 2; tel. (1) 6761703; e-mail info@riai.ie; internet www.riai.ie; f. 1839; 3,300 mems; Pres. ROBIN MANDAL; Dir JOHN GRABY; publs *Architecture Ireland* (6 a year), *House* (2 a year).

Society of Chartered Surveyors Ireland: 38 Merrion Sq., Dublin 2; tel. (1) 6445500; e-mail info@scsi.ie; internet www.scsi.ie; f. 2011 by merger of Society of Chartered Surveyors and the Irish Auctioneers and Valuers Institute; constituent body of the Royal Instn of Chartered Surveyors; Pres. MICHEÁL O'CONNOR; Dir-Gen. CIARA MURPHY.

BIBLIOGRAPHY, LIBRARY SCIENCE AND MUSEOLOGY

Library Association of Ireland: 138–144 Pearse St, Dublin 2; tel. (53) 051849716; e-mail president@libraryassociation.ie; internet www.libraryassociation.ie; f. 1928; courses: continuing professional devt, Assoc. of the Library Asscn of Ireland (ALAI), Fellow of the Library Asscn of Ireland (FLAI); holds confs; lobbies govt; 400 mems; Pres. JANE CANTWELL; Hon. Sec. BETTY CODD; publ. *An Leabharlann: The Irish Library* (2 a year, online).

ECONOMICS, LAW AND POLITICS

Chartered Accountants Ireland: Belfast Office: 32–38 Linenhall St, Belfast, BT2 8BG, UK; Chartered Accountants House, 47 Pearse St, Dublin 2; tel. (1) 6377200; e-mail ca@icai.ie; internet www.charteredaccountants.ie; f. 1888 by Royal Charter; 23,000 mems; library of 20,000 vols; Pres. BRENDAN LENIHAN; Vice-Pres. TONY NICHOLL; publ. *Accountancy Ireland* (6 a year).

Honorable Society of King's Inns: Henrietta St, Dublin 1; tel. (1) 8744840; e-mail info@kingsinns.ie; internet www.kingsinns.ie; f. 1541; provides training course to enable students to be admitted to the degree of barrister-at-law; 4,000 mems; library of 100,000 vols; Dean of School of Law MARY FAULKNER; Registrar MARCELLA HIGGINS; publ. *Irish Student Law Review* (1 a year).

Statistical and Social Inquiry Society of Ireland: c/o Economic and Social Research Institute, Whitaker Sq., Sir John Rogerson's Quay, Dublin 2; tel. (1) 8632019; e-mail secretary@ssisi.ie; internet www.ssisi.ie; f. 1847; 500 mems; Pres. Prof. J. FITZGERALD; Hon. Sec. SEÁN LYONS; publ. *Journal* (1 a year).

EDUCATION

Church Education Society: c/o Church of Ireland House, Church Ave, Rathmines, Dublin 6; tel. (1) 4978422; e-mail ces@ireland.anglican.org; f. 1839; Asst Sec. and Treas. JENNIFER BYRNE.

FINE AND PERFORMING ARTS

Aosdána: 70 Merrion Sq., Dublin 2; tel. (1) 6180200; e-mail aosdana@artscouncil.ie; internet aosdana.artscouncil.ie; f. 1981; attached to Arts Council; an affiliation of artists engaged in architecture, choreography, literature, music and visual arts; membership ltd. to 250 mems; Registrar LIZ POWELL.

Arts Council: 70 Merrion Sq., Dublin 2; tel. (1) 6180200; e-mail info@artscouncil.ie; internet www.artscouncil.ie; f. 1951; Irish Govt agency; gives grant-aid to many organizations incl. the theatre, opera, arts centres, arts festivals, exhibitions and publishers; also awards bursaries and scholarships to individual artists; offers advice and information on arts to Govt, individuals and orgs; Chair. Dr OLIVE BRAIDEN.

Irish Recorded Music Association: IRMA House, 1 Corrig Ave, Dun Laoghaire Co Dublin; tel. (1) 2806571; e-mail irma_info@irma.ie; internet www.irma.ie; f. 1948; 55 mems; Chair. WILLIE KAVANAGH; Dir-Gen. DICK DOYLE; publs *Music Events Diary*, *Policy Statement of Music Education*.

Royal Hibernian Academy: 15 Ely Pl., Dublin 2; tel. (1) 6612558; e-mail info@rhagallery.ie; internet www.rhagallery.ie; f. 1823; painting, sculpture, installation and mixed media; 5 galleries; 66 mems (13 hon., 44 acads, 9 assoc.); Pres. DES MCMAHON; Sec. ABIGAIL O'BRIEN.

HISTORY, GEOGRAPHY AND ARCHAEOLOGY

Cork Historical and Archaeological Society: c/o Hon. Treasurer, 13 Lislee Rd, Maryborough, Douglas, Cork; tel. (21) 541076; e-mail griffinjosephmurray@gmail.com; internet www.corkhist.ie; f. 1891; 400 mems; Pres. Prof. WILLIAM O'BRIEN; Hon. Sec. ANN EGAN; publ. *Journal* (1 a year).

Folklore of Ireland Society: c/o Nat. Folklore Colln, Newman Bldg, University College Dublin, Belfield, Dublin 4; tel. (1) 7168216; e-mail cumann.bealoideasa@gmail.com; internet www.bealoideas.ie; f. 1927; public lectures on folk traditions; 650 mems; Pres. ANRAÍ Ó BRAONÁIN; Sec. LIAM Ó CONCHUBHAIR; publ. *Béaloideas* (1 a year).

Geographical Society of Ireland: c/o GSI Secretary, Dept of Geography, NUI Maynooth, Maynooth 4; tel. (1) 7168179; e-mail rory.hearne@nuim.ie; internet www.geographicalsocietyireland.ie; f. 1934; 200 mems; Pres. Dr FRANCES FAHY; Sec. Dr JOANNE ROURKE; publ. *Irish Geography* (3 a year).

Military History Society of Ireland: Newman House, 86 St Stephen's Green, Dublin 2; tel. (1) 2985617; e-mail alanoif@indigo.ie; internet www.mhsi.ie; f. 1949; 1,000 mems; Pres. Dr HARMAN MURTAGH; Hon. Sec. for Correspondence Dr PATRICK MCCARTHY; publ. *The Irish Sword* (2 a year).

Old Dublin Society: 138–144 Pearse St, Dublin 2; tel. (1) 8734222; e-mail olddublinsociety@dublin.ie; internet www.olddublinsociety.ie; f. 1934; promotes study of history and antiquities of Dublin; 275 mems; library of 1,300 vols; Pres. Rev. BERNARDINE RUDDY; Hon. Sec. for Programme BRYAN MACMAHON; publ. *Dublin Historical Record* (2 a year).

Royal Society of Antiquaries of Ireland: Society House, 63 Merrion Sq., Dublin 2; tel. (1) 6761749; e-mail rsai@rsai.ie; internet www.rsai.ie; f. 1849; preserves, examines and illustrates all ancient monuments and memorials of the arts, manners and customs of the past, as connected with the antiquities, language, literature and history of Ireland;

1,100 mems; library of 13,000 vols; Pres. Dr RACHEL MOSS; Dir NIAMH MCCABE; publ. *Journal* (1 a year).

LANGUAGE AND LITERATURE

Alliance Française Dublin: 1 Kildare St, Dublin 2; tel. (1) 6761732; e-mail info@alliance-francaise.ie; internet www.alliance-francaise.ie; f. 1960; offers courses in general French, French conversation, specialized French, French for primary schools; also offers diploma courses and corporate courses; promotes French culture; attached offices in Galway, Kilkenny, Limerick, Waterford and Wexford; Dir PHILIPPE MILLOUX; Sec.-Gen. GERRY NYHAN.

British Council: Newmount House, 22/24 Lower Mount St, Dublin 2; tel. (1) 6764088; e-mail info@ie.britishcouncil.org; internet www.britishcouncil.ie; offers courses and examinations in English language and British culture and promotes cultural exchange with the UK; promotes creative and knowledge economy of the UK; Dir MICHAEL WHITE.

Conradh na Gaeilge (Gaelic League): 6 Harcourt St, Dublin 2; tel. (1) 4757401; e-mail eolas@cnag.ie; internet www.cnag.ie; f. 1893; 200 brs; promotes Irish language; Pres. CÓILÍN Ó CEARBHAILL; Gen. Sec. ARD-RÚNAÍ JULIAN DE SPÁINN; publs *An tUltach* (12 a year), *Feasta* (12 a year).

Goethe-Institut: 62 Fitzwilliam Sq., Dublin 2; tel. (1) 6801110; e-mail info@dublin.goethe.org; internet www.goethe.de/dublin; offers courses and examinations in German language and culture and promotes cultural exchange with Germany; library of 9,000 vols; Dir MECHTILD MANUS.

Instituto Cervantes: Lincoln House, Lincoln Pl., Dublin 2; tel. (1) 6311500; e-mail cendub@cervantes.es; internet dublin.cervantes.es; f. 1991; offers courses and examinations in Spanish language and culture and promotes cultural exchange with Spain and Spanish-speaking Latin and Central America; library of 11,000 vols; Dir ROSA LEÓN CONDE.

Irish PEN: c/o The United Arts Club, 3 Upper Fitzwilliam St, Dublin 12; tel. (87) 2835382; e-mail info@irishpen.com; internet www.irishpen.com; f. 1921; 62 mems; Chair. KAY BOLAND; Treas. TIMMY CONWAY.

Irish Texts Society: c/o Hon. Secretary, 69A Balfour St, London, SE17 1PL, UK; e-mail hon.treasurer@irishtextssociety.org; internet www.irishtextssociety.org; f. 1898; advances public education by promoting the study of Irish literature; publishes texts in the Irish language, with translations, notes, etc.; archives of Soc. have been placed in the Univ. College Cork Library; 640 mems; Pres. Prof. MÁIRE HERBERT; Hon. Sec. SEÁN HUTTON.

MEDICINE

Apothecaries' Hall: 95 Merrion Sq., Dublin 2; tel. (1) 6762147; Gov. Dr MALACHY POWELL; Registrar Dr BRENDAN POWELL.

Dental Council: 57 Merrion Sq., Dublin 2; tel. (1) 6762069; e-mail info@dentalcouncil.ie; internet www.dentalcouncil.ie; f. 1928 as the Dental Board, superseded by the Dental Council in 1985; Pres. Dr EAMON CROKE; Chief Officer and Registrar DAVID O'FLYNN.

Irish Medical Organisation: 10 Fitzwilliam Pl., Dublin 2; tel. (1) 6767273; e-mail imo@imo.ie; internet www.imo.ie; f. 1984 by merger of the Irish Medical Association and the Irish Medical Union; 6,000 mems; Pres. Dr MATTHEW SADLIER; CEO SUSAN CLYNE; publ. *Irish Medical Journal* (10 a year).

Medical Council: Kingram House, Kingram Pl., Dublin 2; tel. (1) 4983100; e-mail info@mcirl.ie; internet www.medicalcouncil.ie; f. 1978; 18,000 mems; Pres. Prof. FREDDIE WOOD; CEO CAROLINE SPILLANE.

Pharmaceutical Society of Ireland (PSI)/The Pharmacy Regulator: PSI House, 15–19 Fenian St, Dublin 2; tel. (1) 2184000; e-mail info@thepsi.ie; internet www.thepsi.ie; f. 1875; reorganized 2007; Pres. EOGHAN HANLY; Registrar and CEO MARITA KINSELLA.

Royal Academy of Medicine in Ireland: Frederick House, Fourth Fl., 19 South Frederick St, Dublin 2; tel. (1) 6334820; e-mail helenmoore@rcpi.ie; internet www.rami.ie; f. 1882; 1,200 mems; Pres. Dr PATRICK O'SULLIVAN; Gen. Sec. and Treas. Prof. KEN O'HALLORAN; publ. *Irish Journal of Medical Science* (4 a year).

NATURAL SCIENCES

Biological Sciences

Dublin University Biological Association: POB 14, Regent House, Trinity College, Dublin 2; e-mail biosoc@csc.tcd.ie; internet biosoc.wordpress.com; f. 1874; hosts lectures and discussion groups on medical topics and arranges book sales and social events; 550 mems; library of 200 vols; Pres. Prof. PAUL RIDGWAY; Sec. MARY JOYCE; publ. *Trinity Student Medical Journal* (online, www.tcd.ie/tsmj).

Dublin Zoo: Phoenix Park, Dublin 8; tel. (1) 4748900; e-mail info@dublinzoo.ie; internet www.dublinzoo.ie; f. 1830; 9,000 mems; Dir LEO OOSTERWEGHEL; Sec. SUSAN O'BRIEN (acting).

Physical Sciences

Institute of Chemistry of Ireland: POB 9322, Cardiff Lane, Dublin 2; e-mail info@instituteofchemistry.org; internet www.chemistryireland.org; f. 1950; 800 mems; Pres. PATRICK T. HOBBS; Hon. Sec. Dr JAMES P. RYAN; publ. *Irish Chemical News* (2 a year).

Institute of Physics in Ireland: c/o School of Physics, University College Dublin, Belfield, Dublin 4; tel. (1) 7162216; e-mail ireland@iop.org; internet www.iopireland.org; f. 1964 as the Irish Br. of the Institute of Physics; 2,000 mems; Chair. Dr PETER VAN DER BURGT; Sec. Dr FRANCIS PEDRESCHI; publ. *Physics World* (12 a year).

Irish Astronomical Society: c/o 146 Santry Close, Santry, Dublin 9; tel. (87) 6398143; e-mail irishastrosoc@gmail.com; internet www.irishastrosoc.org; f. 1937; 150 mems; Pres. DEREK STACEY; Sec. PHILIP O'REILLY; publs *Orbit* (6 a year), *Sky High* (1 a year).

PHILOSOPHY AND PSYCHOLOGY

Psychological Society of Ireland: 2nd Fl., Grantham House, Grantham St, Dublin 2; tel. (1) 4720105; e-mail info@psihq.ie; internet www.psihq.ie; f. 1970; advances psychological knowledge, maintains standards of professional training and practice, seeks devt of psychological services; 2,500 mems; Pres. Dr MARGARET O'ROURKE; Hon. Sec. Dr CATHERINE DARKER; publs *The Irish Journal of Psychology*, *The Irish Psychologist*.

Theosophical Society in Ireland: 31 Pembroke Rd, Dublin 4; tel. (1) 6602517; e-mail marieharkness@yahoo.co.uk; internet www.theosophyireland.com; f. 1919; encourages the study of comparative religion, philosophy and science; Pres. JOHN DOHERTY; Sec. MARIE HARKNESS.

University Philosophical Society: Graduate Memorial Bldg, Trinity College, Dublin 2; tel. (87) 2108423; e-mail president@tcdphil.com; internet www.tcdphil.com; f. 1684, refounded 1854; composition, reading and discussion of papers on literary, political, philosophical and scientific subjects; 8,000 mems; Pres. SARAH MORTELL; Sec. CLARE NI CHEALLAIGH; publs *Laws*, *Philander* (1 a year).

TECHNOLOGY

Biomedical and Clinical Engineering Association of Ireland: 8 Priory Hall, Stillorgan, Dublin; tel. (21) 45843116; e-mail treasurer@beai.ie; internet www.beai.ie; f. 1992; Chair. MEABH SMITH; Sec. BRIAN KEARNEY; publ. *BEAI Spectrum* (4 a year).

Engineers Ireland: 22 Clyde Rd, Ballsbridge, Dublin 4; tel. (1) 6651300; e-mail info@engineersireland.ie; internet www.engineersireland.ie; f. 1835 as Civil Engineers Society of Ireland, current name adopted 2005; promotes knowledge and advancement of the engineering profession, conducts examinations and confers the designations 'Chartered Engineer', 'Associate Engineer' and 'Engineering Technician'; 24,000 mems; Pres. Dr JOHN O'DEA; Dir-Gen. JOHN POWER; publ. *Engineers Journal* (6 a year).

Institution of Civil Engineers (Republic of Ireland Division): 8 Ardglas, Dundrum, Dublin 16; tel. (1) 2224260; e-mail secretariat@ice.org.uk; internet www.ice.org.uk/nearyou/europe/rep-of-ireland; f. 1818; 881 mems; library of 130,000 vols; Chair. DON N. MCENTEE; publs *Municipal Engineer* (4 a year), *New Civil Engineer* (52 a year).

The Institution of Engineering and Technology: ESB National Grid, Lower Fitzwilliam St, Dublin 2; e-mail jrutherford@theiet.org; internet mycommunity.theiet.org/communities/home/213; f. 2006 following merger of the Institution of Electrical Engineers and the Institution of Incorporated Engineers; 90 mems; Chair. Dr JOHN GING; Sec. JOHN RUTHERFORD.

Research Institutes

GENERAL

National Centre for Sensor Research: Research and Engineering Bldg, Dublin City University, Glasnevin, Dublin 9; tel. (1) 7008821; e-mail ncsr@dcu.ie; internet www.ncsr.ie; f. 1999; attached to Dublin City University; multi-disciplinary facility that aims to develop future sensory technologies for economic and societal benefit for application in, *inter alia*, health monitoring and diagnostics, environmental monitoring and nanomedicine; Dir Prof. DERMOT DIAMOND; Sec. MARY FALLON.

Science Policy Research Centre: Graduate Business School, Univ. College Dublin, Carysfort, Blackrock, Dublin 4; tel. (1) 7068263; e-mail joe.cogan@ucd.ie; f. 1969; small private library; carries out research and undertakes commissioned studies in areas related to technology and innovation policy; Dir Prof. D. J. COGAN.

AGRICULTURE, FISHERIES AND VETERINARY SCIENCE

Teagasc (Agriculture and Food Development Authority): Oak Park, Carlow; tel. (59) 9170200; e-mail info@teagasc.ie; internet www.teagasc.ie; f. 1988; nat. body providing advisory, research, education and training services to the agriculture and food industry; activities are integrated and managed through 6 divs; Chair. Dr NOEL CAWLEY; Dir Prof. GERRY BOYLE; publs *Irish Journal of Agricultural and Food Research* (2 a year), *Today's Farm* (6 a year), *TResearch* (4 a year).

Divisions:

Ashtown Food Research Centre: Ashtown, Dublin 15; tel. (1) 8059500; e-mail declan.troy@teagasc.ie; internet www.teagasc.ie/ashtown; centre providing research, devt and consultancy services for all aspects of food production (except dairy products), food safety and nutrition, and market studies; Head Dr DECLAN TROY.

Kildalton College: Piltown, Co Kilkenny; tel. (51) 644400; e-mail kildalton.college@teagasc.ie; internet www.teagasc.ie/training/colleges/kildalton; nat. crops div. and headquarters for advisory and training services in Teagasc S; Prin. FRANK MURPHY.

Kinsealy Research Centre: Malahide Rd, Dublin, 17; tel. (1) 8460644; e-mail bfarrell@grange.teagasc.ie; nat. beef div.; HQ for advisory and training services in Teagasc N; Dir DONAL CAREY.

Moorepark-Animal and Grassland Research and Innovation Centre: Fermoy, Co Cork; tel. (25) 42222; e-mail moorepark_dairy@teagasc.ie; internet www.agresearch.teagasc.ie/moorepark; nat. centre for research in dairying and pig production; Head of Animal and Grassland Research and Innovation Programme Dr PATRICK DILLON; Head FRENCH PADRAIG.

National Dairy Products Research Centre: Moorepark, Fermoy, Co Cork; tel. (25) 42222; e-mail ldonnelly@moorepark.teagasc.ie; nat. centre providing research, devt and consultancy services; Dir Dr PATRICK DILLON.

Rural Economy Research Centre: Athenry, Co Galway; tel. (91) 845200; e-mail pseery@athenry.teagasc.ie; internet www.agresearch.teagasc.ie/rerc; nat. centre for rural devt; Dir PETER SEERY.

BIBLIOGRAPHY, LIBRARY SCIENCE AND MUSEOLOGY

Irish Manuscripts Commission: 45 Merrion Sq., Dublin 2; tel. (1) 6761610; e-mail support@irishmanuscripts.ie; internet www.irishmanuscripts.ie; f. 1928; publishes primary MSS sources for Irish history located in public and private archives in Ireland and abroad; Chair. Prof. JAMES MCGUIRE; publ. *Analecta Hibernica* (irregular).

ECONOMICS, LAW AND POLITICS

Economic and Social Research Institute: Whitaker Sq., Sir John Rogerson's Quay, Dublin 2; tel. (1) 8632000; e-mail admin@esri.ie; internet www.esri.ie; f. 1960; library of 40,000 vols; Dir Prof. FRANCES RUANE; Librarian SARAH BURNS; publs *Medium Term Review* (every 2 years), *The Economic and Social Review* (4 a year).

UCD Geary Institute: Geary Bldg, Belfield, Dublin 4; tel. (1) 7164615; e-mail geary@ucd.ie; internet www.ucd.ie/geary; f. 1999; attached to Univ. College Dublin; supports frontier methods of investigation and provides objective analysis and solutions that address the economic and social challenges facing policy makers; Dir Prof. PHILIP O'CONNELL.

MEDICINE

Health Research Board: 73 Lower Baggot St, Dublin 2; tel. (1) 2345000; e-mail hrb@hrb.ie; internet www.hrb.ie; f. 1986 by merger of the Medico-Social Research Board and the Medical Research Council of Ireland; funds health research; synthesizes evidence to inform health policy formulation; Chair. Dr DECLAN BEDFORD; Chief Exec. Dr GRAHAM LOVE.

Molecular Medicine Ireland: Newman House, 85A St Stephen's Green, Dublin 2; tel. (1) 4779820; e-mail info@molecularmedicineireland.ie; internet www.molecularmedicineireland.ie; f. 2002 as the Dublin Molecular Medicine Centre; current name adopted 2008; collaboration between National Univ. of Ireland Galway, Royal College of Surgeons in Ireland, Trinity College Dublin, Univ. College Cork and Univ. College Dublin; aims to accelerate the translation of biomedical research into improved health care diagnostics and therapies; Chair. TOM LYNCH; Chief Exec. Dr GRAHAM LOVE.

NATURAL SCIENCES

Physical Sciences

Marine Institute: Rinville, Oranmore, Co Galway; tel. (91) 387200; e-mail institute.mail@marine.ie; internet www.marine.ie; f. 1991; promotes the sustainable devt of marine industry through strategic funding programmes and essential scientific services, and safeguards the marine environment through research and environmental monitoring; Chair. Dr JOHN KILLEEN; CEO Dr PETER HEFFERNAN.

National Institute for Bioprocessing Research and Training: Fosters Ave, Mount Merrion, Blackrock, Dublin 4; tel. (1) 2158100; e-mail info@nibrt.ie; internet www.nibrt.ie; f. 2006; Chair. JOE HARFORD; CEO Dr REG SHAW.

National Institute for Cellular Biotechnology: Dublin City Univ., Ballymun Rd and Collins Ave, Dublin 9; tel. (1) 7005700; e-mail nicb@dcu.ie; internet www.nicb.dcu.ie; f. 2001; attached to Dublin City Univ.; collaboration between Dublin City Univ., Institute of Technology Tallaght and National Univ. of Ireland, Maynooth; Dir Prof. MARTIN CLYNES.

Libraries and Archives

Cork

Cork City Libraries: 57–61 Grand Parade, Cork; tel. (21) 4924900; e-mail libraries@corkcity.ie; internet www.corkcitylibraries.ie; f. 1892; central library, 6 local libraries and 1 mobile library; 420,017 vols, incl. extensive local studies and reference collns in books, newspapers and journals; large music colln in Rory Gallagher Music Library; City Librarian LIAM RONAYNE.

Cork County Library and Arts Service: County Library Bldg, Carrigrohane Rd, Cork; tel. (21) 4546499; e-mail corkcountylibrary@corkcoco.ie; internet www.corkcoco.ie/library; 1,080,000 vols, 90 periodicals; 28 brs, 5 mobile libraries; Librarian (vacant).

Cork Institute of Technology Bishopstown Library: Rossa Ave, Bishopstown, Cork; tel. (21) 4335106; e-mail library.info@cit.ie; internet library.cit.ie; f. 1994; brs at Cork School of Music, Crawford College of Art and Design and National Maritime College of Ireland; 65,000 vols; Librarian DERRY DELANEY; Deputy Librarian MICHAEL COSTELLO.

UCC Library: Boole Library, Univ. College Cork, College Rd, Cork; tel. (21) 4902794; e-mail library@ucc.ie; internet booleweb.ucc.ie; f. 1849; Boole Library (main campus), Boston Scientific Health Sciences Library; operates a jt library service with Cork University Hospital Library; 735,000 vols, incl. Irish MSS colln (microfilm), Senft (philosophy), Torna (Irish), Cooke (travel), John E. Cummings Memorial Colln (humour), Langlands Colln (Africa); 2,194 serials and 81,000 ejournals; Dir for Library Services COLETTE MCKENNA.

Dublin

Central Catholic Library: 74 Merrion Sq., Dublin 2; tel. (1) 6761264; e-mail catholiclibrary@imagine.ie; internet www.catholiclibrary.ie; f. 1922; controlled by the Central Catholic Library Asscn; lending and reference depts containing material on every aspect of Catholicism, on other Christian denominations and other religions, Irish history and culture, philosophy; 100,000 vols, incl. large journal colln, spec. colln of 2,000 vols on Christian art, Ireland Colln; Librarian Dr TERESA WHITINGTON; Hon. Librarian PETER COSTELLO.

Chester Beatty Library: Dublin Castle, Dublin 2; tel. (1) 4070750; e-mail info@cbl.ie; internet www.cbl.ie; f. 1953; donated to the Irish nation by Sir Alfred Chester Beatty in 1968; collns of Islamic and E Asian art, Western and Biblical MSS and miniatures; incunabula and other printed books; Dir FIONNUALA CROKE.

Dublin City Public Libraries and Archive: 138–144 Pearse St, Dublin 2; tel. (1) 6744800; e-mail dublinpubliclibraries@dublincity.ie; internet www.dublincitypubliclibraries.ie; f. 1884; spec. collns incl. early Dublin printing and fine binding, incunabula, political pamphlets and cartoons, Dublin periodicals and 18th-century plays, Abbey Theatre material, Swift and Yeats material; local history colln in books, newspapers and pictures; rep. holdings of modern Dublin presses; spec. music library; language learning centre; 2.4m. vols; City Librarian MARGARET HAYES.

Houses of the Oireachtas (Parliament) Library and Research Service: Leinster House, Kildare St, Dublin 2; tel. (1) 6184701; e-mail library.and.research@oireachtas.ie; internet www.oireachtas.ie/parliament/about/libraryresearchservice; f. 1922; information and research services to support the work of both Houses of the Oireachtas (Parliament), cttees and individual mems of Parliament; Head of Library and Research Service MADELAINE DENNISON; publ. *Spotlight Series* (12 a year).

Irish Theatre Archive: c/o Dublin City Libraries and Archive, 138–144 Pearse St, Dublin 2; tel. (1) 6744800; e-mail cityarchives@dublincity.ie; internet www.dublincity.ie; f. 1981; collects and preserves Ireland's theatre heritage; colln incl. programmes, posters, play-scripts, promptbooks, etc.; organizes lecture series, exhibitions; Hon. Archivist Dr MARY CLARK.

Law Library of Ireland: Four Courts, Dublin 7; tel. (1) 8175000; e-mail barcouncil@lawlibrary.ie; internet www.lawlibrary.ie; controlled by the Bar Council of Ireland; open to mems of the Irish Bar only; 100,000 vols; Chair., Professional Services Cttee DAVID NOLAN S. C.; publ. *The Bar Review* (irregular).

Library Council: 53–54 Upper Mount St, Dublin 2; tel. (1) 6761167; e-mail info@librarycouncil.ie; internet www.librarycouncil.ie; f. 1947 by Public Libraries Act; advises local authorities and the Min. for the Environment, Heritage and Local Govt on the devt of public library services; provides an information service on libraries and librarianship; operates the inter-library lending system for Ireland, and provides the Secretariat for the Cttee on Library Cooperation in Ireland; operates Public Lending Remuneration Office est. by the Copyright and Related Rights (Amendment) Act 2007; Dir NORMA MCDERMOTT; publ. *Irish Library News* (11 a year).

Marsh's Library: St Patrick's Close, Dublin 8; tel. (1) 4543511; e-mail keeper@marshlibrary.ie; internet www.marshlibrary.ie; f. 1701; 25,000 vols and 300 MSS; Keeper Dr JASON MCELLIGOTT.

National Archives of Ireland: Bishop St, Dublin 8; tel. (1) 4072300; e-mail mail@nationalarchives.ie; internet www.nationalarchives.ie; f. 1988 by merger of Public Record Office (f. 1867) and State Paper Office (f. 1702); preserves and makes accessible the records of Depts of State, courts, other public service orgs and private donors; 50,000 linear m of archives; Dir FRANCES MCGEE (acting).

National Library of Ireland: Kildare St, Dublin 2; tel. (1) 6030213; e-mail info@nli.ie; internet www.nli.ie; f. 1877; collects, preserves, promotes and makes accessible documentary and intellectual record of life of Ireland; 8m. vols incl. Irish printing colln, pamphlets, periodicals, newspapers, 1m. MSS, incl. 1,200 Gaelic MSS, 630,000 photographic negatives, 90,000 prints and drawings, ephemera and music; Dir CATHERINE FAHY (acting); Keeper of Collns and Chief Herald COLETTE O'FLAHERTY; publ. *NLI News & Events* (3 a year).

RCSI Library: Mercer St Lower, Dublin 2; tel. (1) 4022407; e-mail library@rcsi.ie; internet www.rcsi.ie/library; f. 1784; 75,000 vols; also at Beaumont Hospital; spec. collns: archives of RCSI and Dublin hospitals, 10,000 rare books, medical pamphlets from 17th century; Chief Librarian KATE KELLY.

RDS Library and Archives: Merrion Rd, Ballsbridge, Dublin 4; tel. (1) 2407254; e-mail librarydesk@rds.ie; internet www.rds.ie/library; f. 1731; 100,000 vols, incl. more than 4,000 relating to Ireland; 6,000 works and pamphlets on all brs of agricultural science up to 1920, incl. 1,500 works of equestrian interest; reference colln of more than 2,000 vols, Fitzgerald letters; Dublin horse show archives; papers of Dr Horace H. Poole, Richard M. Barrington and John Edmund Carew; the records of the Radium Institute and the Maymes Ansell Archive of Equestrian Photographs; Dir JOANNA QUINN; Librarian GERARD WHELAN.

Representative Church Body Library: Braemor Park, Churchtown, Dublin 14; tel. (1) 4923979; e-mail library@ireland.anglican.org; internet www.library.ireland.anglican.org; f. 1931; 40,000 vols, mainly theology, history, ethics and education; Church of Ireland archives; parish registers, diocesan papers and MSS colln, mainly ecclesiastical; Librarian and Archivist Dr RAYMOND REFAUSSÉ; Asst Librarian and Archivist Dr SUSAN HOOD.

Trinity College Library: College St, Dublin 2; tel. (1) 8961652; e-mail dutylibrarian@tcd.ie; internet www.tcd.ie/library; f. 1592; Univ. and British/Irish legal deposit library; 6m. printed vols, 80,000 ejournals and 350,000 ebooks, 6,000 MSS, incl. the Book of Kells and other medieval MSS; collns of 17th- and 18th-century French printed materials and caricatures; extensive colln of music scores and maps; Librarian and College Archivist HELEN SHELTON (acting); publ. *Long Room* (1 a year).

University College Dublin Library: Belfield, Dublin 4; tel. (1) 7167583; e-mail library@ucd.ie; internet www.ucd.ie/library; f. 1908; 5 brs; 1.2m. vols, 8,000 periodicals; spec. collns incl. pre-1850 imprints, Baron Palles (Law) Library of 2,500 vols, Zimmer (Celtic) Library of 2,000 vols, C. P. Curran (Irish literature), John McCormack (music), Colm Ó Lochlainn (Irish printing), F. J. O'Kelley (Irish printing) and John L. Sweeney (Literature) collns; MSS colln; literary archives and papers incl. those of Sean O'Riordain, Patrick Kavanagh, Mary Lavin, Maeve Binchy and Frank McGuinness; Univ. Librarian Dr JOHN BROOKS HOWARD.

Galway

Galway City Centre Library: St Augustine St, Galway; tel. (91) 561666; e-mail info@galwaylibrary.ie; internet www.galwaylibrary.ie/en/services/library/; f. 1927; Ballybane, City Centre and Westside Library; Librarian PATRICK MCMAHON.

Galway County Libraries: Island House, Cathedral Sq., Galway; tel. (91) 562471; e-mail info@galwaylibrary.ie; internet www.galwaylibrary.ie; f. 1927; 10 full-time and 19 part-time brs; 1 mobile library; 550,000 vols; Co Librarian PATRICK MCMAHON.

James Hardiman Library: National Univ. of Ireland, University Rd, Galway; tel. (91) 493399; e-mail library@nuigalway.ie; internet www.library.nuigalway.ie; f. 1849; attached to Nat. Univ. of Ireland; 463,000 vols; 350 archival collns in areas of theatre, literature, politics and history; Univ. Librarian JOHN COX.

Limerick

Limerick City Public Library: The Granary, Michael St, Limerick; tel. (61) 407510; e-mail citylib@limerickcity.ie; internet www.limerickcity.ie/library; f. 2010; 4 br. libraries; Sr Exec. Librarian DAMIEN BRADY.

Maynooth

Library, National University of Ireland, Maynooth: Maynooth, Co Kildare; tel. (1) 7083884; e-mail library.information@nuim.ie; internet library.nuim.ie; f. 1795; 460,000 vols and 42,000 ejournals; spec. collns: Ken Saro-Wiwa's private prison letters and correspondence with Irish nun Sis. Majella McCarron; Librarian CATHAL MCCAULEY.

Waterford

Waterford City Council Central Library: Lady Lane, Waterford; tel. (51) 849975; e-mail library@waterfordcity.ie; internet www.waterfordcity.ie/library; 3 brs; audio-listening and language-learning facilities; Librarian JANE CANTWELL.

Waterford County Library Headquarters: Ballyanchor Rd, Lismore, Co Waterford; tel. (58) 21370; e-mail libraryhq@waterfordcoco.ie; internet www.waterfordcountylibrary.ie; 8 brs; County Librarian EDDIE BYRNE (acting); Exec. Librarian GER CROUGHAN.

Museums and Art Galleries

Cork

Cork Public Museum: Fitzgeralds Park, The Mardyke, Cork; tel. (21) 4270679; e-mail museum@corkcity.ie; internet www.corkcity.ie/services/corporateandexternalaffairs/museum; f. 1910; sections devoted to Irish history and archaeology, also municipal, social and economic history, Cork glass, silver and lace; items of spec. interest incl. the Cork helmet horns, the Garryduff gold bird, the Roche silver collar, civic maces, municipal oar, freedom boxes and Grace Cup of Cork Corporation; Curator STELLA CHERRY.

Dublin

Dublin City Gallery The Hugh Lane: Charlemont House, Parnell Sq. N, Dublin 1; tel. (1) 2225550; e-mail info.hughlane@dublincity.ie; internet www.hughlane.ie; f. 1908; works of Irish, English and European schools of painting, and pictures from the Sir Hugh Lane colln; sculptures; Francis Bacon's studio; contemporary art; Dir Dr BARBARA DAWSON.

Dublin Writers Museum: 18 Parnell Sq., Dublin 1; tel. (1) 8722077; e-mail writers@dublintourism.ie; internet www.writersmuseum.com; f. 1991; history of Irish literature; library; Operations Man. NYRÉE LANDRY; Curator ROBERT NICHOLSON.

Irish Museum of Modern Art: Royal Hospital, Military Rd, Kilmainham, Dublin 8; tel. (1) 6129900; e-mail info@imma.ie; internet www.imma.ie; f. 1991; works by Irish and non-Irish artists since the beginning of the 20th century; Chair. EOIN MCGONIGAL; Dir SARAH GLENNIE (acting).

James Joyce Tower and Museum: Sandycove Point, Sandycove, Co Dublin; tel. (1) 2809265; e-mail joycetower@failteireland.ie; internet www.jamesjoycetower.com; f. 1962; papers and personal effects of the writer (1882–1941) and critical works about him; library of 550 vols; Curator ROBERT NICHOLSON.

National Botanic Gardens Glasnevin: Glasnevin, Dublin 9; tel. (1) 8040300; e-mail botanicgardens@opw.ie; internet www.botanicgardens.ie; f. 1795; incl. Irish National Herbarium; visitor centre combines a lecture hall, restaurant and display area with exhibits relating to the history and purpose of the gardens; library of 40,000 vols, incl. collns of illustrated botanical works, periodicals and rare books; Dir Dr MATTHEW JEBB; publ. *Glasra—Contributions from the National Botanic Gardens, Glasnevin* (1 a year).

National Gallery of Ireland: Merrion Sq. West, Dublin 2; tel. (1) 6615133; e-mail info@ngi.ie; internet www.nationalgallery.ie; f. 1864; nat., historical and portrait galleries; continental European, British and Irish masters since the 14th century; 15,000 paintings, sculptures, works on paper and objets d'art; library of 70,000 vols; research services comprise the Fine Art Library (50,000 vols), NGI Archive, Diageo Print Room, ESB Centre for the Study of Irish Art and the Yeats Archive; Dir SEAN RAINBIRD.

National Museum of Ireland: Kildare St, Dublin 2; tel. (1) 6777444; e-mail marketing@museum.ie; internet www.museum.ie; f. 1877 as Museum of Science and Art, current name adopted 1908; colln of 4m. objects and specimens incl. art and industry, antiquities, folklife and natural history; Dir RAGHNALL Ó FLOINN.

Galway

Galway Arts Centre: 47 Dominick St, Galway; tel. (91) 565886; e-mail info@galwayartscentre.ie; internet www.galwayartscentre.ie; f. 1982; Nun Island Theatre; houses nat. and int. contemporary art works; also provides classes in art, writing and photography; Man. Dir PARAIC BREATHNACH.

Galway City Museum: Spanish Parade, Galway; tel. (91) 532460; e-mail museum@galwaycity.ie; internet www.galwaycitymuseum.ie; f. 2006; 1,000 objects of Galway cultural heritage; permanent and touring exhibitions dealing with archaeology, art and craft, local history; Dir and Curator EITHNE VERLING.

Limerick

Limerick City Gallery of Art: Carnegie Bldg, Pery Sq., Limerick; tel. (61) 310633; e-mail artgallery@limerickcity.ie; internet gallery.limerick.ie; f. 1948 as the Limerick Free Art Gallery; contemporary art works of nat. and int. artists, selected exhibit of works from the permanent colln of Irish art from 18th–20th centuries; also holds the Nat. Colln of Contemporary Drawing and the Michael O'Connor Int. Poster Colln; Dir and Curator HELEN CAREY.

Maynooth

National Science Museum: Maynooth Campus, Maynooth, Co Kildare; e-mail niall .mckeith@may.ie; internet www.nuim.ie/ museum; f. 1934; attached to St Patrick's College Maynooth; houses ecclesiastical and scientific artefacts; Curator Dr NIALL MCKEITH.

Strokestown

Strokestown Park—The Irish National Famine Museum: Strokestown Park, Strokestown, Co Roscommon; tel. (71) 9633013; e-mail info@strokestownpark.ie; internet www.strokestownpark.ie/museum.html; f. 1994; collns related to the history of the Great Irish Famine of the 1840s; Gen. Man. JOHN O'DRISCOLL.

Waterford

Waterford County Museum: St Augustine St, Dungarvan, Co Waterford; tel. (58) 45960; e-mail info@waterfordmuseum.ie; internet www.waterfordmuseum.ie; artefacts pertaining to the history of Dungarvan and the western Waterford area from medieval times through to the 20th century; collns incl. militaria, coins, 5,500 photographs and video footage; Curator WILLIAM FRAHER.

Universities

DUBLIN CITY UNIVERSITY

Ballymun Rd and Collins Ave, Glasnevin, Dublin 9
Telephone: (1) 7005000
E-mail: public.affairs@dcu.ie
Internet: www.dcu.ie
Founded 1980 as Nat. Institute for Higher Education, Dublin; univ. status 1989
State control
Academic year: September to May
Chancellor: Dr MARTIN MCALEESE
Pres.: Prof. BRIAN MACCRAITH
Deputy-Pres.: JIM DOWLING
Chief Operations Officer: Dr DECLAN RAFTERY
Vice-Pres. for Research and Innovation: Prof. ALAN HARVEY
Vice-Pres. for Academic Affairs and Registrar: Prof. EITHNE GUILFOYLE
Dir for Library Services: PAUL SHEEHAN
Library of 250,000 vols
Number of teachers: 1,762
Number of students: 11,126 (8,782 full-time, 1,564 part-time, 780 distance learning)

DEANS

Dublin City University Business School: Dr ANNE SINNOTT
Faculty of Engineering and Computing: Prof. BARRY MCMULLIN
Faculty of Humanities and Social Sciences: Prof. JOHN DOYLE
Faculty of Science and Health: Prof. JOHN COSTELLO
Graduate Studies: Dr LISA LOONEY

ATTACHED INSTITUTE

Oscail-DCU Online Education: Bea Orpen Bldg, Glasnevin, Dublin 9; tel. (1) 7005481; e-mail oscail@dcu.ie; internet www .dcu.ie/oscail/index.shtml; f. 1982; exec. arm of the Nat. Distance Education Ccl; Academic Dir SEAMUS FOX

NATIONAL UNIVERSITY OF IRELAND (NUI)

49 Merrion Sq., Dublin 2
Telephone: (1) 4392424
E-mail: registrar@nui.ie
Internet: www.nui.ie
Founded 1908
Chancellor: Dr MAURICE A. MANNING
Vice-Chancellor: Prof. PHILIP NOLAN
Pro Vice-Chancellor: Prof. ANDREW J. DEEKS
Pro Vice-Chancellor: Dr MICHAEL B. MURPHY
Pro Vice-Chancellor: Dr JAMES J. BROWNE
Registrar: Dr ATTRACTA HALPIN
Publication: *Éigse: A Journal of Irish Studies* (irregular)

CONSTITUENT COLLEGES

National University of Ireland, Galway

University Rd, Galway
Telephone: (91) 524411
E-mail: info@nuigalway.ie
Internet: www.nuigalway.ie
Founded 1845 as Queen's College, Galway; became Univ. College, Galway in 1908; current name adopted 1997
Languages of instruction: English, Irish
Academic year: September to June
Pres.: Dr JAMES J. BROWNE
Deputy Pres. and Registrar: Prof. PÓL Ó DOCHARTAIGH (acting)
Vice-Pres. for Capital Projects: KEITH WARNOCK
Vice-Pres. for Innovation and Performance: Prof. CHRIS CURTIN
Vice-Pres. for Research: Prof. LOKESH JOSHI
Vice-Pres. for the Student Experience: Dr PAT MORGAN
Sec.: Dr GEARÓID Ó CONLUAIN
Bursar: Dr MARY DOOLEY
Library: see under Libraries and Archives
Number of teachers: 550
Number of students: 17,000

DEANS

College of Arts, Social Sciences and Celtic Studies: Dr EDWARD HERRING
College of Business, Public Policy and Law: Dr KIERAN CONBOY
College of Engineering and Informatics: Prof. GERRY LYONS
College of Medicine, Nursing and Health Sciences: Prof. B. G. LOFTUS
College of Science: Prof. TOM SHERRY
Postgraduate Studies: Dr LUCY BYRNES

PROFESSORS

Faculties of Arts, Social Sciences and Celtic Studies:
- BARRY, K., English
- BRADLEY, D., Spanish
- CANNY, N. P., History
- CURTIN, C. A., Political Science and Sociology
- ERSKINE, A. W., Classics
- JAMES, J., Psychology
- MAC CRAITH, M., Modern Irish
- NÍ DHONNCHADHA, M., Old and Middle Irish and Celtic Philology
- O'BRIEN, C., Italian
- Ó GORMAILE, P., French
- RICHARDSON, W., German
- RICHARDSON, W., Spanish
- SCHMIDT-HANISSA, H., German
- STROHMAYER, U., Geography
- WADDELL, J., Archaeology
- WORNER, M. H., Philosophy

Faculty of Commerce:
- COLLINS, J. F., Accountancy and Finance
- CUDDY, M. P., Economics
- GREEN, R. H., Management
- WARD, J. J., Marketing

Faculty of Engineering:
- CUNNANE, C., Hydrology
- LYONS, G. J., Information Technology
- MCNAMARA, J. F., Mechanical Engineering
- O'DONOGHUE, P. E., Civil Engineering
- WILCOX, D., Electronic Engineering

Faculty of Law:
- O'MALLEY, W. A., Business Law
- QUINN, G., Law
- SCHABAS, W., Human Rights Law

Faculty of Science:
- BUTLER, R., Chemistry
- COLLERAN, E., Microbiology
- GUIRY, M. D. R., Botany
- HINDE, J. P., Statistics
- HURLEY, T. C., Mathematics
- KANE, M. T., Physiology
- LOWNES, N., Biochemistry
- RYAN, P. A., Geology
- SMITH, T. J., Biomedical Engineering and Science
- WALTON, P. W., Applied Physics

School of Medicine:
- CALLAGY, G., Pathology
- CANTILLON, P., General Practice
- CORMICAN, M., Bacteriology
- DOCKERY, P., Anatomy
- EGAN, L., Pharmacology and Therapeutics
- KERIN, M., Surgery
- LAFFEY, J., Anaesthesia
- LOFTUS, B. G., Paediatrics
- MCCARTHY, P. A., Radiology
- MCDONALD, C., Psychiatry
- MORRISON, J., Obstetrics and Gynaecology
- O'BRIEN, T., Medicine
- WHEATLEY, A., Physiology

National University of Ireland, Maynooth

Maynooth, Co Kildare
Telephone: (1) 7086000
E-mail: communications@nuim.ie
Internet: www.nuim.ie
Founded 1795 as St Patrick's College, Maynooth, which divided in 1997 into Nat. Univ. of Ireland, Maynooth, and a continuing St Patrick's College, Maynooth
State control
Languages of instruction: English, Irish
Academic year: September to June
Pres.: Prof. PHILIP NOLAN
Vice-Pres. for Academic Affairs, Registrar and Deputy-Pres.: Prof. AIDAN MULKEEN
Vice-Pres. for Innovation: Prof. RAY O'NEILL
Vice-Pres. for Research: Prof. BERNARD MAHON
Vice-Pres. for Strategy and Quality: Prof. JIM WALSH
Bursar: Dr MIKE O'MALLEY
Librarian: CATHAL MCCAULEY
Library: see under Libraries and Archives
Number of teachers: 466
Number of students: 9,000
Publications: *ReSearch Magazine*, *The Bridge Alumni Magazine*

DEANS

Faculty of Arts, Celtic Studies and Philosophy: Dr THOMAS O'CONNOR
Faculty of Science and Engineering: Dr FIONA LYDDY
Faculty of Social Sciences: Dr ROWENA PECHENINO
International and Graduate Studies: Prof. RONAN REILLY

University College Cork

Western Rd, Cork
Telephone: (21) 4903000
E-mail: registrar@ucc.ie
Internet: www.ucc.ie

Founded 1845 as Queen's College, Cork; current name adopted 1908
Academic year: October to September
Pres.: Dr MICHAEL MURPHY
Sr Vice-Pres. for Academic Affairs and Registrar: Prof. PAUL GILLER
Vice-Pres. for External Relations: TREVOR HOLMES
Vice-Pres. for Research and Innovation: Prof. ANITA R. MAGUIRE
Vice-Pres. for Student Experience: CORNELIUS O'BRIEN
Vice-Pres. for Teaching and Learning: Prof. BETTIE HIGGS
Corporate Sec.: MICHAEL FARRELL
Chief Financial Officer and Bursar: DIARMUID COLLINS
Librarian and Head of Information Services: JOHN A. FITZGERALD
Number of teachers: 2,280 (539 full-time, 1,741 part-time)
Number of students: 20,000 full-time
Publication: *Chimera* (1 a year)

DEANS

College of Arts, Celtic Studies and Social Sciences: Prof. CAROLINE FENNELL
College of Business and Law: Prof. URSULA KILKELLY
College of Medicine and Health: Prof. JOHN HIGGINS (acting)
College of Science, Engineering and Food Science: Prof. PAUL MCSWEENEY

University College Dublin

Belfield, Dublin 4
Telephone: (1) 7167777
E-mail: communications@ucd.ie
Internet: www.ucd.ie
Languages of instruction: English, Irish
Founded 1854
Academic year: September to May
Pres.: Prof. ANDREW J. DEEKS
Registrar and Deputy Pres.: Prof. MARK ROGERS
Vice-Pres. for Finance and Bursar: GERRY O'BRIEN
Vice-Pres. for Research, Innovation and Impact: Prof. ORLA FEELY
Librarian: Dr JOHN B. HOWARD
Library: see under Libraries and Archives
Number of teachers: 1,047 f.t.e.
Number of students: 24,000
Publication: *Irish University Review* (2 a year)

PRINCIPALS

College of Agriculture, Food Science and Veterinary Medicine: Prof. MICHAEL MONAGHAN
College of Arts and Celtic Studies: Prof. MAEVE CONRICK
College of Business and Law: Prof. CIARAN O'HOGARTAIGH
College of Engineering and Architecture: Prof. GERALD BYRNE
College of Health Sciences: Prof. DESMOND FITZGERALD
College of Human Sciences: Prof. BRIAN NOLAN
College of Sciences: Prof. JOE CARTHY

PROFESSORS

(Many professors are members of more than one faculty; entry here is shown under one faculty only)

College of Arts and Celtic Studies (Newman Bldg, Belfield, Dublin 4; tel. (1) 7168101; e-mail artsceltic@ucd.ie):

BARNES, J. C., Italian
BARTLETT, T., Modern Irish History
BREATNACH, P. A., Classical Irish
CALDICOTT, C. E. J., French
CLAYTON, M., Old and Middle English
CRUICKSHANK, D. W., Spanish
FANNING, J. R., Modern History
KIBERD, D., Anglo-Irish Literature and Drama
MCCARTHY, M. J., History of Art
MAYS, J. C. C., Modern English and American Literature
MEIKLE, J. L., American Studies
NÍ CATHÁIN, M. P., Early (incl. Medieval) Irish Language and Literature
Ó CATHÁIN, S., Irish Folklore
RAFTERY, B., Celtic Archaeology
RIDLEY, H. M., German
SMITH, A., Classics
WATSON, S., Modern Irish Language and Literature
WHITE, H., Music

College of Business and Law (Carysfort Ave, Blackrock, Dublin 4; tel. (1) 7168852):

BOURKE, P., Banking and Finance
BRADLEY, M. F., International Marketing
BRENNAN, N., Management
CASEY, J. P., Law
DEEGAN, A., Management Information Systems
HOURIHAN, A. P., Management of Financial Institutions
KELLY, W. A., Business Administration
LAMBKIN, M. V., Marketing
O'BRIEN, F. J., Accountancy
OSBOROUGH, W. N., Jurisprudence and Legal History
ROCHE, W. K., Industrial Relations and Human Resources
WALSH, E., Accounting

College of Engineering, Mathematical and Physical Sciences (UCD Engineering and Materials Science Centre, Belfield, Dublin 4; tel. (1) 7161864; e-mail engscience@ucd.ie):

BOLAND, P.
BRAZIL, T.
BYRNE, G., Mechanical Engineering
DINEEN, S.
GARDINER, S. J.
GRUNEWALD, M.
IVANKOVIC, A.
KEALY, L., Architecture
LYNCH, P.
MACELROY, J. M. D.
O'BRIEN, E. J., Civil Engineering
OTTEWILL, A.
SHANNON, P. M.
SMYTH, B.

College of Human Sciences (Newman Bldg (Room G210), Belfield, Dublin 4; tel. (1) 7168619; e-mail mary.buckley@ucd.ie):

BENSON, C., Psychology
BOLAND, P. J., Statistics
BURKE, M., Library and Information Studies
BUTTIMER, A., Geography
DINEEN, S., Mathematics
DRUDY, S., Education
GARVIN, T. C., Politics
LAFFAN, B., European Politics
LAFFEY, T. J., Mathematics
MENNELL, S., Sociology
MORAN, D., Philosophy
NEARY, J. P., Political Economy
OUHALLA, J., Linguistics
WALSH, B. M., National Economics of Ireland and Applied Economics

College of Life Sciences (Belfield, Dublin 4; tel. (1) 7162684; e-mail life-sciences@ucd.ie):

BAIRD, A., Veterinary Physiology and Biochemistry
BANNIGAN, J. G., Anatomy
BELLENGER, C. R., Veterinary Surgery
BOLAND, M. P., Animal Husbandry
BRADY, H. R., Medicine and Therapeutics
BRESNIHAN, B., Rheumatology
BURY, G., General Practice
CARRINGTON, S., Veterinary Anatomy
CASEY, P. R., Clinical Psychiatry
COLLINS, J. D., Farm Animal Clinical Studies
CURRY, J., Agricultural Zoology
CUSACK, D. A., Legal Medicine
DAWSON, K. A., Physical Chemistry
DERVAN, P. A., Pathology
DRUMM, B., Paediatrics
DUKE, E., Zoology
ENGEL, P. C., Biochemistry
ENNIS, J. T., Radiology
FITZGERALD, M. X., Medicine
FITZPATRICK, C., Child and Adolescent Psychiatry
FITZPATRICK, J. M., Surgery
GARDINER, J. J., Forestry
GREEN, A., Medical Genetics
HALL, W. W., Medical Microbiology
HEGARTY, A. F., Organic Chemistry
HENNERTY, M. J., Horticulture
JONES, B. R., Small Animal Clinical Studies
KEANE, M., Computer Science
KENNEDY, M. J., Geology
MACERLEAN, D. P., Radiology
MCKENNA, B., Food Science
MCKENNA, T. J., Investigative Endocrinology
MCNICHOLAS, F., Child and Adolescent Psychiatry
MORIARTY, D. C., Anaesthesiology
O'BRIEN, C., Ophthalmology
O'CALLAGHAN, E., Mental Health Research
O'HERLIHY, C., Obstetrics and Gynaecology
O'HIGGINS, N. J., Surgery
POWELL, D., Investigative Endocrinology
QUINN, P. J., Veterinary Microbiology and Parasitology
ROCHE, J. F., Animal Husbandry and Production
RYAN, M. P., Pharmacology
SHEAHAN, B., Veterinary Pathology
STEER, M., Botany
TREACY, M. M., Nursing
WALSH, E., Crop Science

ATTACHED SCHOOL

Michael Smurfit Graduate Business School: Carysfort Ave, Blackrock, Co. Dublin; tel. (1) 7168934; e-mail smurfitschool@ucd.ie; internet www.smurfitschool.ie; Dean Prof. CIARÁN Ó HÓGARTAIGH

TRINITY COLLEGE DUBLIN, THE UNIVERSITY OF DUBLIN

College Green, Dublin 2
Telephone: (1) 8961000
E-mail: communications@tcd.ie
Internet: www.tcd.ie
Founded 1592
Academic year: August to June
Chancellor: MARY TERESE WINIFRED ROBINSON
Pro-Chancellor: Prof. DERMONT FLANNAN MCALEESE
Pro-Chancellor: Dr MARY ELIZABETH FRANCES HENRY
Pro-Chancellor: Dr EDWARD MCPARLAND
Pro-Chancellor: Dame JOCELYN BELL BURNELL
Pro-Chancellor: Hon. Sir DONNELL DEENY
Pro-Chancellor: Prof. VINCENT JOHN SCATTERGOOD
Provost and Pres.: Dr PATRICK JOHN PRENDERGAST
Vice-Provost and Chief Academic Officer and Deputy Pres.: Prof. LINDA HOGAN
Registrar: SHANE PATRICIA ANN ALLWRIGHT
Chief Operating Officer: GERALDINE RUANE
Dean and Vice-Pres. for Research: VINNY CAHILL
Vice-Pres. for Global Relations: Prof. JANE OHLMEYER

Dean of Students: KEVIN O'KELLY
Library: see under Libraries and Archives
Number of teachers: 1,440 (incl. academic research staff)
Number of students: 16,646 (14,871 full-time, 1,775 part-time incl. postgraduate)
Publication: *Hermathena* (2 a year)

DEANS

Faculty of Arts, Humanities and Social Sciences: Prof. JAMES JOHN RUFUS WICKHAM
Faculty of Engineering, Mathematics and Science: Prof. DAVID CLIVE WILLIAMS
Faculty of Health Sciences: Prof. MARY MCCARRON
Graduate Studies: AIDEEN LONG

PROFESSORS

AHMAD, K., Computer Science
ANWYL, R., Neurophysiology
BACIK, I., Criminal Law, Criminology and Penology
BARNES, L., Dermatology
BARRY, F., International Business and Development
BARRY, J., Population Health Medicine
BEGLEY, C., Nursing and Midwifery
BENOIT, K., Quantitative Social Sciences
BERGIN, C., Infectious Diseases
BLAU, W., Physics of Advanced Materials
BOLAND, F., Engineering Science
BOLAND, J., Chemistry Research
BRADLEY, D., Population Genetics
BYRNE, R., Cognitive Science
CAFFREY, M., Membrane Structural and Functional Biology
CAHILL, V., Computer Science
CAMPBELL, N., Phonetics and Speech Sciences
CARSON, R., Cognitive Neuroscience of Ageing (Neurobehavioural Enhancement)
CASSIDY, L., Ophthalmology
CHAHOUD, A., Latin
COFFEY, W., Electrical Engineering
COLEMAN, D., Oral and Applied Microbiology
COLEMAN, J., Chemical Physics
CONLON, K., Surgery
CONNON, S., Synthetic Chemistry
CUNNANE, G., Rheumatology
CUNNINGHAM, E., Animal Genetics
DALY, S., Obstetrics and Gynaecology
DASILVA, L., Telecommunications
DORMAN, C., Microbiology
DRURY, L., Astronomy
DYER, M., Construction Innovation
FALLON, P., Translational Immunology
FEARON, P., Psychiatry
FITZPATRICK, D., Modern History
FITZPATRICK, J., Mechanical Engineering
FLINT, S., Oral Medicine
FOSTER, T., Molecular Microbiology
FRODL, T., Integrated Neuroimaging
GALLAGHER, L., Child and Adolescent Psychiatry
GALLAGHER, M., Comparative Politics
GILL, M., Psychiatry
GILLIGAN, R., Social Work and Social Policy
GRATTON, J., French
GRENE, N., English Literature
GRENFELL, M., Education
GRIMSON, J., Health Informatics
GUNNLAUGSSON, T., Chemistry
HARDIMAN, O., Neurology
HASLETT, J., Statistics
HEGNER, M., Physics
HENNESSY, M., Computer Science Research
HINTON, J., Microbial Pathogenesis
HOGAN, L., Ecumenics
HOLLYWOOD, D., Clinical Oncology
HORNE, J., Modern European History
HUMPHRIES, P., Medical Molecular Genetics
KAMBER, B., Geology and Mineralogy
KANE, D., Rheumatology
KENNEDY, H., Forensic Psychiatry
KENNY, R., Geriatric Medicine
KEOGAN, M., Radiology
KRAMER, A., European History
LANE, P., Political Economy
LANE, S., Respiratory Medicine
LAWLOR, B., Old Age Psychiatry
LITTLE, M., Nephrology
LUCEY, J., Psychiatry
LYNCH, M., Cellular Neuroscience
LYNCH, T., Urological Surgery
MARSH, M., Comparative Political Behaviour
MARTIN, S., Medical Genetics
MCCONNELL, D., Genetics
MCELWAIN, J., Orthopaedic Surgery
MCGILP, J., Surface and Interface Optics
MCGING, B., Greek
MCGOVERN, E., Cardiothoracic Surgery
MCGOWAN, M., Germanic Studies
MCLOUGHLIN, D., Psychiatry
MCMANUS, D., Early Irish
MEANEY, J., Radiology
MILLS, K., Experimental Immunology
MURPHY, D., Obstetrics
MURPHY, P., Clinical Microbiology
NORMAND, C., Health Policy and Management
NUNN, J., Special Care Dentistry
O'BYRNE, K., Oncology
O'CONNELL, B., Restorative Dentistry
O'CONNOR, H., Gastroenterology
O'DONNELL, J., Haematology
O'DOWD, T., General Practice
O'FARRELLY, C., Comparative Immunology
O'HAGAN, J., Economics
O'HALPIN, E., Contemporary Irish History
OHLMEYER, J., Modern History
O'KELLY, F., General Practice
O'LEARY, J., Pathology
O'MAHONY, M., Civil Engineering
O'MARA, S., Psychology
O'NEILL, L., Biochemistry
O'SULLIVAN, C., Visual Computing
O'SULLIVAN, M., Pathology
PARNELL, J., Systematic Botany
PETHICA, J., Physics Research
PLUNKETT, P., Emergency Medicine
RADOMSKI, M., Pharmacology
RAMASWAMI, M., Neurogenetics
REILLY, R., Neural Engineering
REYNOLDS, J., Surgery
ROBERTSON, I., Psychology
ROBINSON, I., History
ROGERS, T., Clinical Microbiology
ROWAN, M., Neuropharmacology
SCOTT, D., French (Textual and Visual Studies)
SENGE, M., Organic Chemistry
SHATASHVILI, S., Natural Philosophy
SHVETS, I., Applied Physics
SIMONS, P., Moral Philosophy
SINGLETON, B., Drama and Theatre Studies
SMITH, O., Haematology
STASSEN, L., Oral and Maxillofacial Surgery
SWANWICK, G., Psychiatry
TAYLOR, D., Materials Engineering
TIMON, C., Otolaryngology
TREACY, E., Paediatrics
WALSH, J., Clinical Medicine
WOLFE, K., Genome Evolution

RECOGNIZED COLLEGES

Irish School of Ecumenics (Confederal School of Religions, Theology and Ecumenics, Trinity College Dublin): Irish School of Ecumenics and Loyola Institute Bldg, Main Campus, Trinity College Dublin, College Green, Dublin 2; tel. (1) 8964770; e-mail isedir@tcd.ie; internet www.tcd.ie/ise; academic year September to April; Head of Discipline Prof. GILLIAN WYLIE

UNIVERSITY OF LIMERICK

Limerick
Telephone: (61) 202700
E-mail: vpa@ul.ie
Internet: www.ul.ie

Founded 1972 as Nat. Institute for Higher Education, Limerick, present status 1989
State control
Language of instruction: English
Academic year: September to May
Pres. and Vice-Chancellor: Prof. DON BARRY
Vice-Pres. for Academics and Registrar: Prof. PAUL MCCUTCHEON
Vice-Pres. for Research: Dr MARY SHIRE
Dir for Finance: JOHN FIELD
Dir for Human Resources: TOMMY FOY
Dir for Library: GOBNAIT O'RIORDAN
Library of 872,000 vols
Number of teachers: 791
Number of students: 12,100
Publications: *PESS e-Zine*, *Research Works*, *UL Links*

DEANS

Faculty of Arts, Humanities and Social Sciences: Prof. TOM LODGE
Faculty of Education and Health Sciences: Prof. MARY O'SULLIVAN
Faculty of Science and Engineering: Prof. EDMOND MAGNER
Graduate School: Dr HUW LEWIS
Kemmy Business School: Dr PHILIP O'REGAN

Institutes of Technology

Athlone Institute of Technology: Dublin Rd, Athlone, Co Westmeath; tel. (90) 6468000; e-mail info@ait.ie; internet www.ait.ie; f. 1970; schools of business, engineering, humanities, science, and dept of lifelong learning; library: 29,000 vols and 260 print journals; 300 teachers; 4,000 students; Pres. Prof. CIARÁN Ó CATHÁIN; Sec. JOHN MCKENNA.

Cork Institute of Technology: Rossa Ave, Bishopstown, Cork; tel. (21) 4326100; e-mail info@cit.ie; internet www.cit.ie; f. 1912; faculties of business and humanities, engineering and science; library: 92,000 vols, 80,000 ebooks, 25,000 journals, 12,000 periodicals; 824 teachers (455 full-time, 369 part-time); 12,000 students (6,000 full-time, 6,000 part-time); Pres. Dr BRENDAN J. MURPHY; Vice-Pres. for Academic Affairs and Registrar Dr BARRY O'CONNOR; Vice-Pres. for Devt MICHAEL DELANEY; Vice-Pres. for Finance and Admin. PAUL GALLAGHER.

Attached Centres:

Centre for Advanced Manufacturing and Management Systems: Dir PAUL KEANE.

Centre for Surface and Interface Analysis: Dirs E. M. CASHELL, L. MCDONNELL.

Clean Technology Centre: Dir D. CUNNINGHAM.

Constituent Schools:

Cork School of Music: Union Quay, Cork; tel. (21) 4807310; e-mail geoffrey.spratt@cit.ie; internet www.cit.ie/aboutcit/facultiesandcolleges/citcorkschoolofmusic; f. 1878; Dir Dr GEOFFREY SPRATT.

Crawford College of Art and Design: Sharman Crawford St, Cork; tel. (21) 4335200; e-mail orla.flynn@cit.ie; internet www.cit.ie/aboutcit/facultiesandcolleges/citcrawfordcollegeofartanddesi1; f. 1884; Head ORLA FLYNN (acting).

National Maritime College: Ringaskiddy, Co Cork; tel. (21) 4335600; e-mail reception@nmci.ie; internet www.nmci.ie; Head Capt. CONOR MOWLDS.

Dublin Institute of Technology: 143–149 Rathmines Rd, Dublin 6; tel. (1) 4023000; e-mail directory@dit.ie; internet www.dit.ie;

f. 1978 by bringing together 6 established colleges; formally established 1993; colleges of arts and tourism, business, engineering and built environment, sciences and health; library: 350,000 vols and 35,000 journals; 1,500 teachers, (incl. part-time); 25,000 students, (incl. part-time); Pres. Prof. BRIAN NORTON; Dir for Academic Affairs Dr MICHAEL MULVEY; Dir for Finance and Physical Resources PAUL FLYNN; Dir for Human Resources DAVID CAGNEY; Dir for Research and Enterprise Dr ELLEN HAZELKORN; Registrar BRIAN FORBES; publs *Arrow@DIT*, *Eureka* (online, www.dit.ie/researchandenterprise/eurekaezine), *Irish Communications Review* (irregular, print and online, www.icr-online.ie/icr), *International Journal of Engineering Education* (print and online, www.ijee.dit.ie), *Level3* (1 a year, print and online, level3.dit.ie).

Dundalk Institute of Technology: Dublin Rd, Dundalk, Co Louth; tel. (42) 9370200; e-mail info@dkit.ie; internet www.dkit.ie; f. 1970; schools of business and humanities, engineering, health and science, and informatics and creative arts; library: 30,000 vols; Pres. DENIS CUMMINS; Registrar ANN CAMPBELL; publ. *the link* (2 a year).

Dun Laoghaire Institute of Art, Design and Technology: Carraiglea Park, Kill Ave, Dun Laoghaire, Co Dublin; tel. 2394000; e-mail info@iadt.ie; internet www.iadt.ie; f. 1997; faculties of enterprise and humanities, film, art and creative technologies; 2,000 students; Chair. RÓNÁN Ó MUIRTHILE; Pres. Dr ANNIE DOONA; Registrar Dr MARIAN O'SULLIVAN; Sec. BERNARD MULLARKEY.

Galway-Mayo Institute of Technology: Dublin Rd, Galway; tel. (91) 753161; e-mail info@gmit.ie; internet www.gmit.ie; f. 1972; br. in Mayo; centre for creative arts and media, college of tourism and arts, school of business, school of engineering and school of science; library: 130,000 vols, 186 audio books, 1,306 DVDs, 80,000 ebooks, 500 print journals, access to 30,000 online journal articles; 375 teachers; 9,000 students (5,000 full-time, 4,000 part-time incl. postgraduate); Chair. DES MAHON; Pres. MICHAEL CARMODY; Registrar MICHAEL HANNON; Librarian MARGARET WALDRON.

Institute of Technology Blanchardstown: Blanchardstown Rd North, Dublin 15; tel. (1) 8851000; e-mail info@itb.ie; internet www.itb.ie; f. 1999; schools of business and humanities, informatics and engineering; 67 teachers; 1,060 students (626 full-time, 356 part-time, 78 apprentices); Pres. Dr MARY MEANEY; Registrar RICHARD GALLERY; Librarian AIDIN O'SULLIVAN; publ. *Journal* (2 a year).

Institute of Technology Carlow: Kilkenny Rd, Carlow; tel. (59) 9175000; e-mail info@itcarlow.ie; internet www.itcarlow.ie; f. 1970; campuses in Wexford and Wicklow County; schools of business and humanities, engineering, science; library: 25,000 vols; 200 teachers; 4,000 students; Pres. Dr PATRICIA MULCAHY; Registrar DAVID DENIEFFE; publ. *RADIUS*.

Institute of Technology Sligo: Ash Lane, Sligo; tel. (71) 9155222; e-mail info@itsligo.ie; internet www.itsligo.ie; f. 1970; library: 23,000 vols; 495 full-time teachers; 4,300 full-time students; 250 apprentices; Pres. Prof. TERRI SCOTT; Registrar BRENDAN MC CORMACK; Sec. and Financial Controller JOHN COSGROVE.

Institute of Technology Tallaght: Tallaght, Dublin 24; tel. (1) 4042000; e-mail info@ittdublin.ie; internet www.it-tallaght.ie; f. 1992; schools of business and humanities, engineering, science and computing; 3,700 students; Pres. PAT MACLAUGHLIN (acting); Registrar JOHN VICKERY; Sec. THOMAS STONE.

Institute of Technology Tralee: Clash, Tralee, Co Kerry; tel. (66) 7145600; e-mail info@ittralee.ie; internet www.ittralee.ie; f. 1977; schools of business, computing and humanities, health and social sciences, and science, technology, engineering and mathematics; library: 40,000 vols and 150 journals; 250 teachers; 3,500 students (incl. part-time); Pres. Dr OLIVER MURPHY; Sec. and Financial Controller DONAL FITZGIBBON; Registrar Dr MICHAEL HALL.

Letterkenny Institute of Technology: Port Rd, Letterkenny, Co Donegal; tel. (74) 9186000; e-mail reception@lyit.ie; internet www.lyit.ie; f. 1971; schools of business, engineering, science, and tourism; library: 30,000 vols; 200 teachers; 2,500 students; Pres. PAUL HANNIGAN; Registrar BILLY BENNETT; Sec. and Financial Controller JUSTIN WALSH.

Limerick Institute of Technology: Moylish Park, Limerick; tel. (61) 293000; e-mail information@lit.ie; internet www.lit.ie; f. 1852; faculty of applied science, engineering and technology; schools of art and design, business and humanities and LIT Tipperary; 500 teachers; 6,000 students; Pres. Dr MARIA HINEFELAAR; Vice-Pres. for Academic Affairs and Registrar TERRY TWOMEY (acting); Vice-Pres. for Research Devt and Enterprise Dr FERGAL BARRY.

Waterford Institute of Technology: Cork Rd, Waterford; tel. (51) 302000; e-mail info@wit.ie; internet www.wit.ie; f. 1970; schools of business, engineering, lifelong learning and education, health sciences, humanities, and science; library: 215,000 vols, 400 periodicals, 400 journals; 715 full-time teachers; 10,061 students (7,581 full-time, 2,480 part-time); Pres. Dr RUAIDHRÍ NEAVYN; Registrar Dr DEREK O'BYRNE; Sec. and Financial Controller TONY MCFEELY.

Colleges of Education

Church of Ireland College of Education: 96 Upper Rathmines Rd, Dublin 6; tel. (1) 4970033; e-mail info@cice.ie; internet www.cice.ie; f. 1811; attached to Trinity College Dublin, The Univ. of Dublin; library: 30,000 vols; Prin. Dr ANNE LODGE; Head of Library Services SUE MILLER.

Marino Institute of Education: Griffith Ave, Dublin 9; tel. (1) 8057700; e-mail info@mie.ie; internet www.mie.ie; f. 1874; attached to Trinity College Dublin, The Univ. of Dublin; Pres. Dr ANNE O'GARA.

Mary Immaculate College: South Circular Rd, Limerick; tel. (61) 204300; e-mail president@mic.ul.ie; internet www.mic.ul.ie; f. 1898; attached to Univ. of Limerick; faculties of arts and education; 3,000 students; Pres. Prof. MICHAEL A. HAYES; Vice-Pres. for Academic Affairs and Registrar Dr EUGENE WALL.

Mater Dei Institute of Education: Clonliffe Rd, Dublin 3; tel. (1) 8086500; e-mail info@materdei.dcu.ie; internet www.materdei.ie; f. 1966; attached to Dublin City Univ.; schools of education, humanities and theology; library: 160,000 vols; 50 teachers; 545 students; Dir ANDREW G. MCGRADY; Admin. Sec. BELINDA GRIFFIN.

St Angela's College: Lough Gill, Sligo; tel. (71) 9143580; e-mail admin@stangelas.nuigalway.ie; internet www.stangelas.nuigalway.ie; f. 1952; attached to Nat. Univ. of Ireland, Galway; academic depts of nursing, health sciences and disability studies; education; home economics; library: 22,000 vols; 900 students; Pres. Dr ANNE TAHENY.

St Patrick's College, Drumcondra: Drumcondra, Dublin 9; tel. (1) 8842000; e-mail presidents.office@spd.dcu.ie; internet www.spd.dcu.ie; f. 1993; attached to Dublin City Univ.; faculties of education and humanities; library: 160,000 vols and 550 journals; 58 teachers; 2,500 students; Pres. DAIRE KEOGH; Registrar Dr PÁDRAIG Ó DUIBHIR; publs *Studia Hibernica* (1 a year), *The Irish Journal of Education* (irregular).

St Patrick's College, Thurles: Cathedral St, Thurles, Co Tipperary; tel. (50) 421201; e-mail office@stpats.ie; internet www.stpats.ie; f. 1837; Pres. Fr TOM FOGARTY; Registrar PAULA HOURIGAN.

Other Higher Education Providers

All Hallows College: Gracepark Rd, Drumcondra, Dublin 9; tel. (1) 8520700; e-mail info@allhallows.ie; internet www.allhallows.ie; f. 1842; attached to Dublin City Univ.; library: 25,000 vols; Pres. Dr PATRICK J. MCDEVITT; Dir DORRIE BALFE; Librarian HELEN BRADLEY.

American College Dublin: 2 Merrion Sq., Dublin 2; tel. (1) 6768941; e-mail info@amcd.ie; internet www.amcd.ie; f. 1993; Pres. and CEO Dr DONALD E. ROSS; Registrar DAVID WEBB.

Burren College of Art: Newton Castle, Ballyvaughan, Co Clare; tel. (65) 7077200; e-mail anna@burrencollege.ie; internet www.burrencollege.ie; f. 1993; Pres. MARY HAWKES-GREEN; Dean Prof. CONOR MCGRADY; Librarian ROBERT ELLIS.

Carlow College: College St, Carlow; tel. (59) 9153200; e-mail infocc@carlowcollege.ie; internet www.carlowcollege.ie; f. 1782; Pres. Mgr CAOIMHÍN Ó NÉILL; Head Librarian DAVID MURPHY.

College of Computer Training: 30–34 Westmoreland St, Dublin 2; tel. (1) 6333444; e-mail info@cct.ie; internet www.cct.ie; f. 2006; faculties of business, engineering, and ICT and computing; Dir NEIL GALLAGHER.

Dorset College: 66 Dorset St Lower, Dublin 1; tel. (1) 8611111; e-mail info@dorset-college.ie; internet www.dorset-college.ie; f. 1983; Registrar ELAINE COHALAN.

Dublin Business School: 13/14 Aungier St, Dublin 2; tel. (1) 4177500; e-mail admissions@dbs.ie; internet www.dbs.ie; f. 1975; schools of arts, and business and law; Pres. SEAMUS PUIRSEIL; CEO GERRY MULDOWNEY.

Dublin Institute for Advanced Studies: 10 Burlington Rd, Dublin 4; tel. (1) 6140100; e-mail hod@cp.dias.ie; internet www.dias.ie; f. 1940; schools of celtic studies, cosmic physics and theoretical physics; Chair. of Ccl V. CUNNANE; Registrar CECIL KEAVENEY.

Garda College: Templemore, Co Tipperary; tel. (50) 435400; e-mail college_admin@garda.ie; internet www.garda.ie; f. 1964; attached to An Garda Síochána; programmes in police leadership; Commissioner NOIRÍN O'SULLIVAN.

Grafton College of Management Sciences: 7 Gardiner Row, Dublin 1; tel. (1) 8726597; e-mail info@graftoncollege.ie; internet www.graftoncollege.ie; f. 2003.

Griffith College: South Circular Rd, Dublin 8; tel. (1) 4150400; e-mail international@gcd.ie; internet www.gcd.ie; f. 1974; campuses in

Cork and Limerick; 7,000 students; Pres. DIARMUID HEGARTY; Dir LEO O'BRIEN.

Hibernia College Dublin: 2 Clare St, Dublin 2; tel. (1) 6610168; e-mail info@hiberniacollege.net; internet www.hiberniacollege.com; f. 2000; offers online degree programmes; Pres. Dr SEAN M. ROWLAND; Chair. DON THORNHILL; Registrar NAOMI JACKSON.

Honorable Society of Kings Inn: Henrietta St, Dublin 1; tel. (1) 8744840; e-mail info@kingsinns.ie; internet www.kingsinns.ie; f. 1940; school of law; library: 100,000 vols; Treas. SEÁN AYLWARD.

IBAT College Dublin: 16–19 Wellington Quay, Dublin 2; tel. (1) 2461509; e-mail enquiry@ibat.ie; internet www.ibat.ie; f. 2004; also in Swords; Dir SHANE ORMSBY.

ICD Business School: Wicklow House, 84–88 S Great George's St, Dublin 2; tel. (1) 6333222; e-mail admin@icd.ie; internet www.icd.ie; f. 2001; Dir VINCENT BARRY; Registrar JOYCE ZHAO.

Institute of Public Administration: 57–61 Lansdowne Rd, Ballsbridge, Dublin 4; tel. (1) 2403600; e-mail information@ipa.ie; internet www.ipa.ie; f. 1957; attached to Nat. Univ. of Ireland; library: 40,000 vols, 300 periodicals; 1,400 students; Dir-Gen. BRIAN CAWLEY; publ. *Administration* (4 a year).

Irish Management Institute: Sandyford Rd, Dublin 16; tel. (1) 2078513; e-mail programmeadvisors@imi.ie; internet www.imi.ie; f. 1952; Chair. SEAN DORGAN.

Kimmage Development Studies Centre: Kimmage Manor, Whitehall Rd, Dublin 12; tel. (1) 4064380; e-mail info@kimmagedsc.ie; internet www.kimmagedsc.ie; f. 1974; Chair. FINTAN FARRELLY; Dir Dr ROB KEVLIHAN.

Law Society of Ireland: Blackhall Pl., Dublin 7; tel. (1) 6724800; e-mail general@lawsociety.ie; internet www.lawsociety.ie; f. 1852; 12,000 mems; library: 14,000 vols; Pres. JOHN P. SHAW; Dir-Gen. KEN MURPHY; publs *Gazette* (12 a year), *Law Directory* (1 a year).

LIT Tipperary: Nenagh Rd, Thurles, Co Tipperary; tel. (504) 28000; e-mail tippadmissions@lit.ie; internet www.lit.ie/tipperary/default.aspx; f. 1998; current name adopted 2010; attached to Limerick Institute of Technology; campuses in Thurles and Clonmel; library: 17,479 vols, 330 periodicals; 600 students; Head COLIN MCLEAN (acting).

Military College: The Curragh Camp, Co Kildare; tel. (45) 4450003; e-mail press@military.ie; internet www.military.ie/education-hq/military-college; f. 1930; attached to Defence Forces Ireland; 4 constituent schools: the command and staff school, the infantry school, the cadet school and the United Nations Training School Ireland.

Milltown Institute: Milltown Park, Sandford Rd, Ranelagh, Dublin 6; tel. (1) 2776300; e-mail info@milltown-institute.ie; internet www.milltown-institute.ie; f. 1968; faculty of theology and spirituality; library: 139,000 vols; Rector Prof. FINBARR CLANCY; Registrar Dr THOMAS WHELAN (acting).

National College of Art and Design: 100 Thomas St, Dublin 8; tel. (1) 6364200; e-mail fios@ncad.ie; internet www.ncad.ie; f. 1746; faculties of design, education, fine art, and visual culture; 75 teachers; 1,500 students (incl. part-time); Dir DECLAN MCGONAGLE; Sec. and Registrar DAMIAN DOWNES.

National College of Ireland: Mayor St, Dublin 1; tel. (1) 4498514; e-mail info@ncirl.ie; internet www.ncirl.ie; f. 1951 as Catholic Workers College; current name adopted 2000; schools of business and computing; library: 45,000 vols, 255 periodicals and 64,400 journals; 350 teachers (130 full-time, 220 part-time); 5,000 students; Pres. Dr PHILLIP MATTHEWS.

National Media College: 13 Harcourt St, Dublin 2; tel. (1) 4780905; e-mail info@nationalmediacollege.ie; internet www.nationalmediacollege.ie; f. 2000; Dir Dr KELLY MCERLEAN.

Newpark Music Centre: Newtownpark Ave, Blackrock, Co Dublin; tel. (1) 2883740; e-mail enquiries@newparkmusic.ie; internet www.newparkmusic.ie; f. 1979; br. in Glasthule; Dir NIALL O'BRIEN.

Royal College of Surgeons in Ireland (RCSI): 123 St Stephen's Green, Dublin 2; tel. (1) 4022100; e-mail info@rcsi.ie; internet www.rcsi.ie; f. 1784; attached to Nat. Univ. of Ireland; faculties of dentistry, nursing and midwifery, radiology, sports and exercise medicine; schools of medicine, nursing, pharmacy, physiotherapy, postgraduate studies; 859 teachers; 3,909 students; Pres. PATRICK J. BROE; CEO and Registrar Prof. CATHAL KELLY; publ. *Journal* (4 a year).

Royal Irish Academy of Music: 36–38 Westland Row, Dublin 2; tel. (1) 6764412; e-mail info@riam.ie; internet www.riam.ie; f. 1848, inc. 1889; 75 teachers; 1,000 students; Chair. Dr BRIAN AYLWARD; Dir DEBORAH KELLEHER; Sec. and Finance Officer KEVIN KELLEHER.

St Nicholas Montessori College Ireland: 16 Adelaide St, Dun Laoghaire, Dublin; tel. (1) 2806064; e-mail info@snmci.ie; internet www.snmci.ie; f. 1980; campuses in Cork and Limerick; Dir IAN MCKENNA; Dir for Academic Affairs KAY O'SULLIVAN; Librarian MARK TICHER.

St Patrick's College, Maynooth: Maynooth, Co Kildare; tel. (1) 7083600; e-mail president@spcm.ie; internet www.maynoothcollege.ie; f. 1795; comprises National Seminary and Pontifical University; library: 65,000 vols; 8,000 students (incl. part-time); Pres. Right Rev. Mgr HUGH G. CONNOLLY; Sec. Rev. DONAL O'NEILL.

Shannon College of Hotel Management: Shannon Int. Airport, Shannon, Co Clare; tel. (61) 712210; e-mail info@shannoncollege.com; internet www.shannoncollege.com; f. 1951; attached to Nat. Univ. of Ireland; library: 10,000 vols; 27 teachers; 400 students; Dir PHILLIP J. SMYTH; Deputy Dir and Registrar KATE O'CONNELL; Librarian AILISH LARKIN.

ISRAEL

The Higher Education System

The earliest institutions of higher education were founded when Palestine was a province of the Ottoman Turkish Empire, and tended to be religious, technical or arts schools. The oldest specialist institution is the Etz Hayim, General Talmud, Torah and Grand Teshivah (founded 1847), and the oldest university-level institution is the Technion—Israel Institute of Technology (founded in Haifa in 1912; inaugurated 1924). Following the First World War (1914–18), Palestine became a League of Nations mandate under British administration and increased Jewish immigration led to the expansion of the higher education sector: the Hebrew University of Jerusalem was founded in 1918 and inaugurated in 1925. The Arab and Jewish communities began to develop parallel forms of communal government, including separate education systems. In May 1948 the United Kingdom terminated its Palestinian mandate, and an independent Jewish State of Israel was declared. Several university-level institutions were established shortly thereafter, including the Weizmann Institute of Science (founded in Rehovot in 1949), Bar-Ilan University (founded 1953; inaugurated 1955) and Tel-Aviv University (founded 1953; inaugurated 1956). In addition to the eight public universities, other institutions of higher education include colleges and higher institutes. All of Israel's public universities and a number of the colleges are subsidized by the State; students pay only a small part of the actual cost of their higher education in the form of tuition fees. The Council for Higher Education Law (1958) established the Council for Higher Education to oversee Israeli higher education, including accreditation of institutions and quality assurance. There is a three-stage process of accreditation. First, the institution is allowed to advertise programmes of study, invite applications from students and start teaching courses; however, the institution is not allowed to award degrees or other qualifications. Secondly, an institution is permitted to be opened and maintained as a provisional institution of higher education but without accreditation and without awarding the relevant qualifications. Thirdly, and finally, the institution is accredited as an institution of higher education and authorized to award degrees.

In 2010/11 there were 245,719 students in institutions of higher education, compared with 76,056 in 1989/90. In addition, there were 42,840 students in the Open University, compared with 13,007 in 1989/90. In 2010/11 there were 38,340 students studying for a Masters degree at university level and a further 12,425 in colleges and teacher training seminars. Programmes for the Doctoral degree are offered only in the research universities. The number of doctoral students increased steadily from 3,910 in 1990 to 10,590 in 2010/11.

The school leavers' certificate or bagrut (matriculation) is the main criterion for admission to higher education. Applicants may also be required to undergo psychometric testing and attend a personal interview, depending on the institution. The Bachelors degree is the standard university-level undergraduate qualification, and the course usually lasts three years. However, some disciplines require longer periods of study, such as nursing (four years) and medicine (six years). Bachelors degrees from non-university institutions, usually colleges and higher institutes, tend to be awarded in conjunction with a professional title or indicate the area of specialization. The first postgraduate-level degree is the Masters, a one- to two-year programme of study that may or may not include a thesis component. A Masters with a thesis component (Type A) allows admission to doctoral studies; a Masters without a thesis (Type B) generally does not. The second (and highest) postgraduate qualification is the Doctorate (most commonly a PhD), which lasts two years.

Technical and vocational education at the post-secondary level is offered by technical colleges, regional colleges and non-university institutions of higher education. The first qualification at this level is the Technai (Qualified Technician), which lasts one year full-time or two years part-time. The other main qualification is the Handassai (Practical Engineer), which is divided into two tracks, Type A and Type B. Handassai (Type A) is a one-year programme of study, while Handassai (Type B) lasts two years. Admission to Technai and Handassai courses requires a bagrut or completion of 12 years of education.

The proportion of ultra-Orthodox adults outside the labour force increased steadily during the late 20th and early 21st centuries. In 2010 the Council for Higher Education formulated a plan to encourage these ultra-Orthodox adults into higher education in order to improve their employability. This measure formed part of a five-year plan covering the whole higher education system. In early 2010, in an attempt to halt the 'brain drain' of Israel's leading scientists who were increasingly leaving the country to conduct research abroad, the Government approved the establishment of 30 academic centres of excellence—Israeli Centres for Research Excellence (I-CORE)—over the next five years.

Regulatory and Representative Bodies

GOVERNMENT

Ministry of Culture and Sport: Kiryat Hamemshala, Hamizrachit, Bldg 3, POB 49100, 91490 Jerusalem; tel. (3) 6367223; e-mail ministerts@most.gov.il; internet www.mcs.gov.il; Minister LIMOR LIVNAT.

Ministry of Education: 34 Shivtei Israel St, POB 292, 91911 Jerusalem; tel. (2) 5602222; e-mail info@education.gov.il; internet www.education.gov.il; Minister SHAI PIRON.

Ministry of Science, Technology and Space: Govt Offices, Bldg 3, Hakirya Hamizrahit, POB 49100, 91490 Jerusalem; tel. (2) 5411101; e-mail minister@most.gov.il; internet www.most.gov.il; Minister YAAKOV PERRY.

ACCREDITATION

Council for Higher Education: POB 4037, 91040 Jerusalem; tel. (2) 5679911; e-mail meida@che.org.il; internet www.che.org.il; f. 1958; recommends to the Govt the granting of licences to higher education institutes, and accreditation, and authorizes awarding of degrees; 24 mems; Chair. THE MINISTER OF EDUCATION; Dir-Gen. STEVEN G. STAV.

ENIC/NARIC Israel: Dept for Evaluation of Foreign Academic Degrees, Ministry of Education, 2 Devora Haneviah St, 91911 Jerusalem; tel. (2) 5603702; e-mail diplomot@education.gov.il; Dir TZIPY WEINBERG.

Quality Assessment Division (QAD)—Israeli Council for Higher Education (CHE): 21 Balfour St, Second Fl., Jerusalem; tel. (2) 5094444; e-mail michal@che.org.il; internet www.che.org.il; f. 2004; periodical assessment of study programmes; improves quality of higher education; increases awareness of the quality assessment process; develops systems in HEIs for the continual evaluation of academic quality; Head of Div. and Deputy Dir-Gen. MICHAL NEUMANN.

Learned Societies

GENERAL

Israel Academy of Sciences and Humanities: POB 4040, 91040 Jerusalem; tel. (2) 5676222; e-mail academy@academy.ac.il; internet www.academy.ac.il; f. 1959; sections of Humanities and Natural Sciences; academic centre in Cairo, Egypt; 87 mems; Pres. Prof. MENAHEM YAARI; Vice-Pres. Prof. RUTH ARNON; Exec. Dir Dr MEIR ZADOK; Chair. of Humanities Prof. YOHANAN FRIEDMANN; Chair. of Natural Sciences Prof. RAPHAEL MECHOULAM.

BIBLIOGRAPHY, LIBRARY SCIENCE AND MUSEOLOGY

Israel Society of Libraries and Information Professionals (ASMI): 8 Blum St, 44253 Kefar Saba; tel. (77) 2151800; e-mail asmi@asmi.org.il; internet www.asmi.org.il; f. 1966; promotes the utilization of recorded knowledge by disseminating information in the fields of science, technology and the humanities, and facilitates written and oral communication; 400 mems; Chair. Dr SHAHAF HAGAFNI; publs *Igeret* (irregular), *Information and Librarianship* (1 a year).

Israeli Center for Libraries: Baruch Hirsh 22, POB 801, 51103 Benei Berak; tel. (3) 6180151; e-mail icl@icl.org.il; internet www.hasifria.org.il/icl/heb/main; f. 1965; provides centralized processing and other services for libraries; organizes non-academic librarianship courses; Chair. JACOB AGMON; Dir ORLY ONN; publs *Basifriyot* (12 a year), *Yad Lakore* (1 a year).

Museums Association of Israel: POB 7, 75100 Rishon Le-Zion; tel. (3) 9565977; e-mail secretariat@icom.org.il; internet www.icom.org.il; f. 1964 to foster public interest in museums and cooperation among asscn members; affiliated to International Council of Museums (ICOM); 55 mems; Chair. ITZHAK BRENNER.

ECONOMICS, LAW AND POLITICS

International Association of Jewish Lawyers and Jurists: 10 Daniel Frish St, 64731 Tel-Aviv; tel. (3) 6910673; e-mail iajj@goldmail.net.il; internet www.intjewishlawyers.org; f. 1969; contributes towards establishing int. order based on law and promotion of human rights; examines legal problems related to Jewish communities; holds int. congresses and seminars; 10 centres (in Israel and abroad); affiliated with the World Jewish Congress (WJC); Pres. ALEX HERTMAN; Exec. Dir RONIT GIDRON-ZEMACH; publ. *Justice* (4 a year).

Israel Bar: 10 Daniel Frish St, 64731 Tel-Aviv; tel. (3) 6362200; e-mail vaadmerkazi@israelbar.org.il; internet www.israelbar.org.il; f. 1961; autonomous statutory body to incorporate and represent lawyers in Israel; 16,000 mems; Pres. YORI GEIRON; Gen. Dir LINDA SHAFIR; Chair., Nat. Ccl AMOS VAN EMDEN; publs *Hapraklit* (12 a year), *Orech Hadin* (2 a year).

Attached Organizations:

David Rotlevi National Mediation Institute of the Israel Bar: tel. (3) 6362221; Jt Chairs SHAY SEGAL, MOSHE TCHETCHIK.

Institute for Continuing Legal Studies: 82 Menachem Begin Rd, 67138 Tel-Aviv; tel. (3) 5616550; e-mail machon@israelbar.org.il; Jt Chairs Dr YORAM DANZIGER, Prof. AHARON NAMDAR.

Israel Political Science Association: c/o Dept of Political Studies, Bar-Ilan University, 52900 Ramat-Gan; tel. (3) 5318578; e-mail ispsa.mail@gmail.com; internet www.ispsa.org; 100 mems; Chair. Prof. SAM LEHMAN WILZIG.

FINE AND PERFORMING ARTS

ACUM (Society of Authors, Composers and Music Publishers in Israel): ACUM House, 9 Tuval St, POB 1704, 52117 Ramat-Gan; tel. (3) 6113400; e-mail acum@acum.org.il; internet www.acum.org.il; f. 1936; copyright; promotion of music and literature; 4,000 mems; Chief Exec. Officer YORIK BEN-DAVID.

Israel Music Institute: 55 Menachem Begin Rd, POB 51197, 6713813 Tel-Aviv; tel. (3) 6247095; e-mail imi.org.il@gmail.com; internet www.imi.org.il; f. 1961; publishes and promotes Israeli music and musicological works throughout the world; produces CDs on Israeli music celebration festival; Israel Music Information Centre; Central Library of Israeli Music; mem. of the Int. Asscn of Music Information Centres and Int. Fed. of Serious Music Publishers; library: 2,500 scores, 2,000 audio recordings; Chair. AVI HANANI; Dir YORAM YOUNGERMAN.

Israel Painters and Sculptors Association: 9 Alharizi St, 64244 Tel-Aviv; tel. (3) 5246685; e-mail artassoc@netvision.net.il; f. 1934 to advance plastic arts in Israel and protect artists' interests; affiliated to the International Association of Art; organizes group exhibitions and symposia; provides assistance to immigrant artists; maintains a gallery for members' exhibitions; graphic arts workshop and materials supply store; 3 brs; 2,000 mems; Chair. RACHEL SHAVIT.

HISTORY, GEOGRAPHY AND ARCHAEOLOGY

Historical Society of Israel: 2 Betar St, POB 4179, 91041 Jerusalem; tel. (2) 5650444; e-mail info@shazar.org.il; internet www.shazar.org.il; f. 1926; promotes the study of general and Jewish history; 1,000 mems; library: Library of Jewish History, Judaica, 25,000 vols; Chair. Prof. MICHAEL HEYD; Sec.-Gen. ZVI YEKUTIEL; publs *Historia* (general history, 2 a year, in Hebrew, with summary in English), *Zion* (Jewish history, 4 a year, in Hebrew with summary in English).

Israel Antiquities Authority: POB 586, 91004 Jerusalem; tel. (2) 6204622; internet www.antiquities.org.il; f. 1948; govt authority; engages in archaeological excavations and surveys, inspection and preservation of antiquities and ancient sites, scientific publs; custodianship of all antiquities; Dir of Antiquities SHUKA DORFMAN; Sec. H. MENAHEM; publs *Archaeological Survey of Israel* (irregular), *Atiqot* (irregular), *Excavations and Surveys in Israel* (2 a year).

Israel Geographical Association: c/o Dept of Geography, Bar-Ilan University, 52900 Ramat-Gan; internet www.geography.org.il; f. 1961; 650 mems; Pres. YEHUDA CRADUS; Sec. Dr GABI LIPSHITZ; publ. *Ofakim*.

Israel Prehistoric Society: POB 1502, Jerusalem; e-mail kobivardi@gmail.com; internet www.prehistory.org.il; f. 1958; 100 mems; incl. the 'M. Stekelis' Museum of Prehistory; Chair Dr JACOB VARDI; Treas. NIRA ALPERSON; publ. *Mitekufat Haeven* (1 a year, in Hebrew and English).

Jerusalemer Institut der Görres-Gesellschaft (Jerusalem Institute of the Görres Society): Notre Dame of Jerusalem Center, POB 4595, 91044 Jerusalem; tel. (2) 6271170; f. 1908; fmrly Orientalisches Institut der Görres-Gesellschaft; art, history, archaeology, biblical studies, Christian iconography; library, photo archive, computerized index of Christian monuments in the Holy Land; Pres. Prof. WOLFGANG BERGSDORF.

LANGUAGE AND LITERATURE

Academy of the Hebrew Language: Givat Ram Campus, 91904 Jerusalem; tel. (2) 6493555; e-mail acad2u@huji.ac.il; internet hebrew-academy.huji.ac.il; f. 1953; studies the vocabulary, structure and history of the Hebrew language and is the official authority for its devt; is compiling a historical dictionary of the Hebrew language; library specializing in Hebrew and Semitic languages; 38 mems (23 full, 15 advisory); Pres. Prof. M. BAR-ASHER; Chief Scientific Sec. R. GADISH; publs *Leshonenu* (4 a year), *Leshonenu La'am* (4 a year), *Zikhronot*.

British Council: Crystal House, 12 Hahilazon St, Ramat-Gan, 52136 Tel-Aviv; tel. (3) 6113600; e-mail info@britishcouncil.org.il; internet www.britishcouncil.org/israel; promotes cultural relations between the UK and other countries by offering opportunities for inter-cultural dialogue and knowledge sharing in science, education, English language, sports and arts; offers preparation and testing for International English Language Testing System (IELTS) and administers various British professional and academic exams; attached offices in Nazareth and W Jerusalem; Dir JIM BUTTERY; Head of English Language Testing HELEN SYKES.

Goethe-Institut: 15 Sokolov St, 92144 Jerusalem; tel. (2) 5610627; e-mail info@jerusalem.goethe.org; internet www.goethe.de/jerusalem; offers courses and exams in German language and culture and promotes cultural exchange with Germany; attached centre in Tel-Aviv; Dir Dr FRIEDRICH DAHLHAUS.

Hebrew Writers Association in Israel: Writers' House, 6 Kaplan St, Tel-Aviv; tel. (3) 6953257; internet www.hebrew-writers.org; f. 1921; 450 mems; publ. *Moznayim* (12 a year).

Instituto Cervantes: Shulamit 7, 64371 Tel-Aviv; tel. (3) 5279992; e-mail centel@cervantes.es; internet telaviv.cervantes.es; offers courses and exams in Spanish language and culture and promotes cultural exchange with Spain and Spanish-speaking Latin and Central America; library of 19,000 vols; Dir VICTOR ANDRESCO.

Palestinian PEN Centre: Wadi al-Juz, Al-Khaldi St 4, Jerusalem; tel. (2) 6262970; f. 1992; 50 mems; Pres. HANAN AWWAD.

MEDICINE

Israel Gerontological Society: POB 2371, 55000 Kiryat Ono; tel. (3) 5357161; e-mail igs@netvision.net.il; internet www.gerontology.org.il; f. 1956; 600 mems; Chair. Prof. JACOB LOMRANZ; Vice-Chair. Dr YITSHAL BERNER; publ. *Gerontology* (4 a year).

Israel Medical Association: POB 3604, 52136 Ramat-Gan; 35 Jabotinsky St, 2 Twin Towers, Level 11, 52136 Ramat-Gan; tel. (3) 6100444; e-mail tguvot@ima.org.il; internet www.ima.org.il; f. 1912; Pres. Dr YORAM BLACHAR; publs *Harefuah* (26 a year, in Hebrew, abstracts in English), *Israel Medical Association Journal* (12 a year).

Israel Society for Neuroscience: POB 666, 75106 Rishon Le Zion; tel. (3) 9694126; e-mail michal.gilady@isfn.org.il; internet www.isfn.org.il; Pres. ILIANA GOZES.

Israel Society of Internal Medicine: Dept of Internal Medicine, Meir Medical Centre, 44281 Kfar Sava; tel. (9) 7472534; e-mail rozado@clalit.org.il; internet www.isim.org.il; f. 1958; 4 regional centres; a division of the Israel Medical Association (IMA), and affiliated to the International Society of Internal Medicine (ISIM); organizes scientific meetings and congresses; participates in the planning of postgraduate education in internal medicine and improving conditions of internal medicine practitioners; 750 mems; Chair. Prof. MORDECHAI RAVID; Sec. Dr MEIR LAHAV.

Society for Medicine and Law in Israel: 30 Arlozerov St, Petach-Tikva; tel. (3) 9231047; e-mail acarmi@research.haifa.ac.il; f. 1972; 3 brs; affiliated to the World Asscn for Medical Law (WAML); examines and recommends amendments to medical laws; organizes int. conferences; 1,600 mems; Pres.

A. CARMI; publ. *Refuah U'Mishpat* (Medicine & Law, 4 a year, in Hebrew).

NATURAL SCIENCES

General

Association for the Advancement of Science in Israel: c/o Prof. M. Jammer, Dept of Physics, Bar-Ilan University, 52100 Ramat-Gan; tel. (3) 5318433; f. 1953; 5,200 mems; Pres. Prof. M. JAMMER; publ. *Proceedings of Congress of Scientific Societies.*

Biological Sciences

Entomological Society of Israel: POB 6, 50250 Bet-Dagan; tel. (3) 9683729; e-mail vtada@volcani.agri.gov.il; internet entomology.org.il; f. 1962; promotes, improves and disseminates the science of entomology (incl. acarology) in Israel; holds 1 full-day meeting per year; 224 mems; Pres. Prof. ADA RAFAELI; Sec. Dr VICTORIA SOROKER; publ. *Israel Journal of Entomology.*

Israel Society of Plant Sciences: c/o Hebrew University of Jerusalem, 76100 Rehovot; tel. (4) 9489443; e-mail ispb@post.tau.ac.il; internet www.tau.ac.il/lifesci/ispb; f. 1936; aims to promote the advancement of the fundamental and applied brs of botanical science; conducts research, organizes lectures and field work; over 300 mems; Pres. Dr SHAHAL ABBP; publ. *Israel Journal of Plant Sciences.*

Israel Society of Biochemistry and Molecular Biology: POB 9095, 52190 Ramat-Efal; tel. (3) 6355038; e-mail isbmb1@gmail.com; internet www.tau.ac.il/lifesci/isbmb; 350 mems; Pres. Prof. MICHAEL EISENBACH; Sec. Prof. ORNA ELROY-STEIN.

Society for the Protection of Nature in Israel: 4 Hashfela St, 66183 Tel-Aviv; tel. (3) 5375063; e-mail teleteva@spni.org.il; internet www.teva.org.il; f. 1953; promotes nature conservation and quality of the environment; operates 24 local brs, 26 field-study centres, 7 biological information centres; research centres on birds, mammals, reptiles, insects, plants and caves; maintains close cooperation with the Nature Reserves Authority, the Environmental Protection Service and the Council for Beautiful Israel; organizes int. seminars on nature conservation education; 100,000 mems; Chair. YOAV SAGI; Exec. Dir EITAN GEDALIZON; publs *Eretz Magazine* (6 a year, in English), *Pashosh* (children's, 12 a year, in Hebrew), *Teva Va'aretz* (Nature & Land, 6 a year, in Hebrew).

Zoological Society of Israel: c/o Dept of Zoology, Tel-Aviv University, Ramat-Aviv; internet telem.openu.ac.il/zoosoc; f. 1940; 300 mems; Chair. B. S. GALIL.

Mathematical Sciences

Israel Mathematical Union: c/o Israel Mathematical Union, Dept of Mathematics, Bar-Ilan Univ., 31905 Haifa; e-mail imu@imu.org.il; internet imu.org.il; f. 1953; 210 mems; Pres. Prof. A. VAINSHTEIN; Sec. Dr Y. GINOSAR; Treas. Dr A. MELNIKOV.

Physical Sciences

Israel Chemical Society: POB 26, 76100 Rehovot; tel. (8) 9343829; e-mail ics.sec@gmail.com; internet www.weizmann.ac.il/ics; a scientific and professional asscn; holds two conventions each year and organizes lectures and symposia in various parts of Israel; the society represents Israel in the International Union of Pure and Applied Chemistry; Pres. Prof. HERBERT BERNSTEIN; Sec. Prof. MOSHE KOL.

Israel Geological Society: POB 1239, 91000 Jerusalem; e-mail gsi@igs.org.il; internet www.igs.org.il; f. 1951; 400 mems; Pres. ARIEL HEIMANN; Vice-Pres. DOV AVIGAD; publ. *Israeli Journal of Earth Sciences.*

Israel Physical Society: c/o Dept of Physics, Technion, 32000 Haifa; tel. (3) 5318431; e-mail dekel@phys.huji.ac; internet physics .technion.ac.il/~ips; f. 1954; 250 mems; Pres. Prof. AVISHAI DEKEL; Sec. Prof. AVRAHAM SCHILLER; publ. *Annals of the IPS.*

PHILOSOPHY AND PSYCHOLOGY

Israel Psychological Association: 74 Frishman St, POB 11497, 61114 Tel-Aviv; tel. (3) 5239393; e-mail psycho@zahav.net.il; internet www.psychology.org.il; f. 1958; 2,623 mems; Chair. DAN ZAKAY.

RELIGION, SOCIOLOGY AND ANTHROPOLOGY

Israel Oriental Society: The Hebrew University, Jerusalem; tel. (2) 5883633; f. 1949; aims to promote interest in and knowledge of history, politics, economics, culture and life in the Middle East; arranges lectures and symposia to study all aspects of contemporary Middle Eastern, Asian and African affairs; Chair. NEHEMIA LEVTZION; Sec. NIMROD GOREN; publ. *Hamizrah Hehadash* (The New East, 1 a year).

TECHNOLOGY

Association of Engineers and Architects in Israel: 200 Dizengoff Rd, POB 6429, 61063 Tel-Aviv; tel. (3) 5240274; e-mail eng-1@aeai.org.il; internet www.engineers .org.il; f. 1922; brs in Tel-Aviv, Jerusalem, Haifa, Beersheba; 20,000 mems; Pres. Prof. Y. NEEMAN; Chair. Eng. E. COHEN-KAGAN; publs *Chemical Engineering* (6 a year), *Electrical Engineers* (6 a year), *Journal of Engineering and Archaeology* (12 a year, in Hebrew with English summaries).

Israel Society of Aeronautics and Astronautics: POB 2956, 61028 Tel-Aviv; e-mail biaf@aerospace.org.il; internet www .aerospace.org.il; f. 1951 as Israel Soc. of Aeronautical Sciences, merged 1968 with Israel Astronautical Soc.; lectures and confs to foster the growth of aerospace science; 300 mems; Chair. EMANUEL BLASS; Sec.-Gen. YEHUDA BOROVIK; publ. *BIAF-Israel Aerospace e-Magazine* (4 a year).

Society of Electrical and Electronics Engineers of Israel: 200 Dizengoff St, Tel-Aviv; internet www.seeei.org.il; f. 1937; 120 mems; Pres. Ing. J. KOEN; Sec. Ing. J. KORNBLUM; publ. *Electricity and People* (6 a year, in Hebrew).

Research Institutes

GENERAL

Asper Centre for Entrepreneurship: Jerusalem School of Business Admin., Jerusalem; tel. (2) 5882994; e-mail shellyk@savion .huji.ac.il; internet bschool.huji.ac.il; attached to Hebrew Univ. of Jerusalem; Dir Prof. DAVID MAZUKSKY.

Center for the Study of Rationality: Givat Ram, Jerusalem; tel. (2) 6584514; e-mail elinorh@savion.huji.ac.il; internet www.ratio.huji.ac.il; f. 1991; attached to Hebrew Univ. of Jerusalem; Dir Prof. EYAL WINTER.

Centre for the Studies of Philanthropy in Israel: c/o Hebrew Univ. of Jerusalem, Mt Scopus, 91905 Jerusalem; tel. (2) 5882203; e-mail philanthropy@savion.huji.ac.il; internet http://www.sw.huji.ac.il/page/961; attached to Hebrew Univ. of Jerusalem; Dir Prof. HILLEL SCHMID.

Cherrick Centre for the Study of Zionism, the Yishuv and the State of Israel: Cherrick Centre, Mt Scopus, 91905 Jerusalem; tel. (2) 5882867; e-mail cherrick@mscc .huji.ac.il; internet cherrick.huji.ac.il; attached to Hebrew Univ. of Jerusalem; Dir Dr UZI REBHUN.

European Forum at the Hebrew University: c/o Hebrew Univ. of Jerusalem, Mt Scopus, 91905 Jerusalem; tel. (2) 5883286; e-mail mseuro@mscc.huji.ac.il; internet www .ef.huji.ac.il; attached to Hebrew Univ. of Jerusalem; Dir Prof. BIANCA KUHNEL.

Fishman-JEC Center for Finance, Entrepreneurship and Real Estate: Jerusalem School of Business Admin., Mt Scopus, 91905 Jerusalem; tel. (2) 5889453; e-mail mswiener@mscc.huji.ac.il; internet pluto.huji.ac.il/~fishman_rec/index.php; attached to Hebrew Univ. of Jerusalem; Dir Prof. ZVI WIENER.

Halbert Centre for Canadian Studies: c/o Hebrew Univ. of Jerusalem, Mt Scopus, 91905 Jerusalem; tel. (2) 5881344; e-mail mscanada@mscc.huji.ac.il; attached to Hebrew Univ. of Jerusalem; Dir Prof. NACHMAN BEN-YEHUDA.

Harry S. Truman Research Institute for the Advancement of Peace: c/o Hebrew Univ. of Jerusalem, Mt Scopus, 91905 Jerusalem; tel. (2) 5882300; e-mail truman@savion.huji.ac.il; internet truman.huji.ac.il; attached to Hebrew Univ. of Jerusalem; Dir Prof. MENAHEM BLONDHEIM; Exec. Dir NAAMA SHPETER.

Institute for Advanced Studies: Givat Ram, 91904 Jerusalem; tel. (2) 6584735; e-mail advance@vms.huji.ac.il; internet www.as.huji.ac.il; attached to Hebrew Univ. of Jerusalem; f. 1975; Dir Prof. ELIEZER RABINOVICI.

Lafer Centre for Women and Gender Studies: Room 4705, Faculty of Social Sciences, Hebrew Univ. of Jerusalem, Mt Scopus, 91905 Jerusalem; tel. (2) 5883455; e-mail mslaferc@mscc.huji.ac.il; internet new.huji.ac.il/en/page/908; attached to Hebrew Univ. of Jerusalem; Dir Prof. NURIT YERMIA.

Liverant Centre for the Study of Latin America, Spain, Portugal and their Jewish Communities: Rabin Bldg, Mt Scopus, 91905 Jerusalem; tel. (2) 5881633; e-mail liwerant_center@savion.huji.ac.il; internet www.hum.huji.ac.il/site/liwerant; attached to Hebrew Univ. of Jerusalem; Dir Prof. ISRAEL YUVAL.

Louis Frieberg Centre for East Asian Studies: c/o Hebrew Univ. of Jerusalem, Faculty of Humanities, Mt Scopus, 91905 Jerusalem; tel. (2) 5881371; e-mail eacenter@mscc.huji.ac.il; internet www.eacenter.huji .ac.il; f. 2006; attached to Hebrew Univ. of Jerusalem; Dir Dr GIDEON SHELACH.

Samuel Neaman Institute for Advanced Studies in Science and Technology: Technion City, 32000 Haifa; tel. (4) 8292329; e-mail info@neaman.org.il; internet www.neaman.org.il; f. 1978; ind. public policy institute researching nat. problems in science and technology, education, and economic, health and social devt; Dir Prof. MOSHE MOSHE.

Sturman Centre for Human Development: c/o Hebrew Univ. of Jerusalem, Mt Scopus, 91905 Jerusalem; tel. (2) 5883409; e-mail msmerava@mscc.huji.ac.il; attached to Hebrew Univ. of Jerusalem; Dir Prof. RAM FROST.

Swiss Centre for Conflict Research: c/o Hebrew Univ. of Jerusalem, Mt Scopus, 91905 Jerusalem; tel. (2) 5883056; e-mail crmr@savion.huji.ac.il; internet crmr.huji.ac

.il; f. 1999; attached to Hebrew Univ. of Jerusalem; studies sources and causes of domestic and external conflicts in gen. and in Israel in particular; explores methods, techniques and strategies to resolve these conflicts from different disciplinary points of view, incl. social psychology, int. relations and political science, communication and media studies, sociology, education and law; Dir Prof. IFAT MAOZ.

Technion Research and Development Foundation Ltd: Senate House, Technion City, 32000 Haifa; tel. (4) 8292497; e-mail oshmu@cs.technion.ac.il; internet www.trdf.co.il; f. 1952; operates Industrial Testing Laboratories (bldg materials, geodetic research, soils and roads, hydraulics, chemistry, metals, electro-optics and microelectronics, vehicles); administers sponsored research at Technion—Israel Institute of Technology (see under Univs) in aeronautical, agricultural, biomedical, chemical, civil, computer, electrical, food and biotechnology, industrial, management and mechanical engineering; biology, chemistry, mathematics and physics (sciences); and architecture and town planning, education in technology and science, general studies, medicine; 120 subsidiaries in fields of electronics, energy, agriculture, food and medicine; Man. Dir Prof. ODED SHMUELI.

AGRICULTURE, FISHERIES AND VETERINARY SCIENCE

Agricultural Research Organization: Volcani Center, POB 6, 50250 Bet-Dagan; tel. (3) 9683226; e-mail research@volcani.agri.gov.il; internet www.agri.gov.il; f. 1921; fundamental and applied research in agriculture; numerous scientific projects at 7 institutes and 3 experiment stations; part of the Min. of Agriculture and Rural Devt; library of 30,000 vols and periodicals; Dir Prof. YITZHAK SPIEGEL; publ. *Israel Agresearch* (Hebrew with English summaries and captions).

Attached Institutes:

Institute of Agricultural Engineering: tel. (3) 9683303; Dir Dr ZE'EV SCHMILOVITCH.

Institute of Animal Science: Volcani Center, POB 6, 50250 Bet-Dagan; tel. (8) 9484400; e-mail harpaz@volcani.agri.gov.il; internet www.agri.gov.il/en/units/institutes/3.aspx; basic and practical research to support Israeli animal breeders and farmers; depts (i) Poultry and Aquaculture, (ii) Ruminant Science and Genetics; Head of Institute Prof. SHEENAN HARPAZ.

Institute of Plant Protection: tel. (3) 9683437; e-mail frtir@volcani.agri.gov.il; Dir Prof. ABED GERA.

Institute of Plant Sciences: tel. (3) 9683482; e-mail vcfield@volcani.agri.gov.il; Dir Prof. ITAMAR GLAZER.

Institute of Soils, Water and Environmental Sciences: tel. (3) 9683640; e-mail etty@volcani.agri.gov.il; Dir Dr MENACHEM BEN-HUR.

Institute for Technology and the Storage of Agricultural Products: tel. (3) 9683588; e-mail gadit@volcani.agri.gov.il; Dir Prof. ELAZAR FALLIK.

Centre for Agricultural Economic Research: Hebrew Univ. of Jerusalem, POB 12, 76100 Rehovot; tel. (8) 9489230; e-mail ayal.kimhi@mail.huji.ac.il; attached to Hebrew Univ. of Jerusalem; Dir Prof. AYAL KIMHI; publ. *Journal of Rural Cooperation*.

Centre for Research in Plant Sciences in Agriculture: HU POB 12, 76100 Rehovot; tel. (8) 9489812; e-mail samach@agri.huji.ac.il; attached to Hebrew Univ. of Jerusalem; Dir Dr ALON SAMACH.

Hebrew University Center of Excellence in Agriculture and Environmental Health: POB 12, 76100 Rehovot; tel. (8) 9489340; e-mail chefetz@agri.huji.ac.il; internet www.ehf.org.il/en/generalpage/hebrew-university-center-excellence-agriculture-and-environmental-health; attached to Hebrew Univ. of Jerusalem; Dir Prof. BENNY CHEFETZ.

Herb and Frances Brody Center for Food Sciences: Hebrew Univ. of Jerusalem, POB 12, 76100 Rehovot; tel. (8) 9489292; e-mail fridman@agri.huji.ac.il; attached to Hebrew Univ. of Jerusalem; Dir Prof. RONNIE FRIEDMAN.

Otto Warburg Minerva Centre for Agricultural Biotechnology: Hebrew Univ. of Jerusalem, POB 12, 76100 Rehovot; tel. (8) 9489973; e-mail ingel@agri.huji.ac.il; internet departments.agri.huji.ac.il/biotech; Dir Prof. EDOUARD JURKEVITCH.

Research Centre for Agriculture, Environment and Natural Resources (RCAENR): HU POB 12, 76100 Rehovot; tel. (8) 9489401; e-mail shafir@agri.huji.ac.il; attached to Hebrew Univ. of Jerusalem; Dir Prof. SHARONI SHAFIR.

Research Centre for Sustainable Animal Health and Husbandry: HU POB 12, 76100 Rehovot; tel. (8) 9489988; e-mail sivan@agri.huji.ac.il; attached to Hebrew Univ. of Jerusalem; Dir Prof. BERTA LEVAVI-SIVAN.

ECONOMICS, LAW AND POLITICS

Gilo Citizenship, Democracy and Civil Education Centre: c/o Hebrew Univ. of Jerusalem, Mt Scopus, 91905 Jerusalem; tel. (2) 5882267; e-mail gilocenter@mscc.huji.ac.il; internet www.gilocenter.huji.ac.il; attached to Hebrew Univ. of Jerusalem; Dir Dr AVNER DE-SHALIT.

Harry and Michael Sacher Institute for Legislative Research and Comparative Law: c/o Hebrew Univ. of Jerusalem, Mt Scopus, 91905 Jerusalem; tel. (2) 5882535; e-mail sacher.institute@gmail.com; internet law.mscc.huji.ac.il/law1/sache; attached to Hebrew Univ. of Jerusalem; Dir Prof. MICHAEL KARAYANNI.

International Institute for Counter-Terrorism (ICT): Interdisciplinary Center Herzliya, POB 167, 46150 Herzliya; tel. (9) 9527277; e-mail webmaster@ict.org.il; internet www.ict.org.il; f. 1996; global research on terrorism and counter-terrorism; Chair. SHABTAI SHAVIT; Exec. Dir Dr BOAZ GANOR; Deputy Dir Dr EITAN AZANI.

Israel Matz Institute for Research in Jewish Law: Faculty of Law, Hebrew Univ. of Jerusalem, 91905 Jerusalem; tel. (2) 5882501; e-mail jewishlaw@savion.cc.huji.ac.il; internet law.huji.ac.il/merkazim.asp; attached to Hebrew Univ. of Jerusalem; Dir Prof. BERACHYAHU LIFSHITZ.

Jerusalem Institute for Israel Studies: 20 Radak St, 92186 Jerusalem; tel. (2) 5630175; e-mail internet@jiis.org.il; internet www.jiis.org.il; f. 1981; independent non-profit organization to study policy issues and social, economic and political processes in Jerusalem in order to facilitate and improve public policy-making; and to study and disseminate research and environmental policy issues in Israel; Dir ORA AHIMEIR; Exec. Dir Prof. JAACOV BAR SIMON TOV.

K Mart Center for Retail and International Marketing: Jerusalem School of Business Admin., Jerusalem; tel. (2) 5883224; e-mail shellyk@savion.huji.ac.il; internet bschool.huji.ac.il; f. 1991; attached to Hebrew Univ. of Jerusalem; Dir Prof. JACOB GOLDENBERG.

Krueger Centre for Finance: c/o Hebrew Univ. of Jerusalem, Jerusalem School of Business Admin., Mt Scopus, 91905 Jerusalem; tel. (2) 5883224; e-mail shellyk@savion.huji.ac.il; f. 1984; attached to Hebrew Univ. of Jerusalem; supports research in finance, banking and accounting; Dir Prof. YISHAY YAFEH.

Leonard Davis Institute for International Relations: Alfred Davis Bldg, Mt Scopus, 91905 Jerusalem; tel. (2) 5882312; e-mail davis.institute@mail.huji.ac.il; internet davis.huji.ac.il; attached to Hebrew Univ. of Jerusalem; promotes scientific research in the theory of int. relations in interdisciplinary perspective; Dir Dr PIKI ISH SHALOM.

Levi Eshkol Institute for Social, Economic and Political Research in Israel: c/o Hebrew Univ. of Jerusalem, Mt Scopus, 91905 Jerusalem; tel. (2) 5883032; e-mail eshkol@mscc.huji.ac.il; internet eshkol.huji.ac.il; attached to Hebrew Univ. of Jerusalem; Dir Prof. MICHAEL SHALEV.

Minerva Centre for Human Rights: Mt Scopus, 91905 Jerusalem; tel. (2) 5881156; e-mail mchr@savion.huji.ac.il; internet www.minerva.huji.ac.il; attached to Hebrew Univ. of Jerusalem; Dir Dr TOMER BROUDE.

Mordechai Zagagi Centre for Finance and Accounting: Jerusalem School of Business Admin., Jerusalem; tel. (2) 5883224; e-mail shellyk@savion.huji.ac.il; attached to Hebrew Univ. of Jerusalem; Dir Prof. MOSHE LEVY.

Recanati Centre for Research in Business Administration: Jerusalem School of Business Admin., Jerusalem; tel. (2) 5883224; e-mail shellyk@savion.huji.ac.il; internet bschool.huji.ac.il; attached to Hebrew Univ. of Jerusalem; Dir Prof. ZVI WIENER.

Shasha Centre for Strategic Studies: c/o Hebrew Univ. of Jerusalem, Mt Scopus, 91905 Jerusalem; tel. (2) 5881988; e-mail saritf@savion.huji.ac.il; attached to Hebrew Univ. of Jerusalem; Dir SHLOMO HASSON.

Weitz Center for Development Studies: POB 12, 76100 Rehovot; tel. (8) 9474111; e-mail training@netvision.net.il; internet www.weitz-center.org; f. 1963; research, training and planning activities related to the promotion of rural regional devt, tourism and entrepreneurship in Israel and the developing world; library of 50,000 vols, World Bank depository library; Gen. Dir JULIA MARGULIES.

Yitzchak Rabin Center: 77 Rokach Blvd, POB 17538, 61175 Tel-Aviv; tel. (3) 7453333; e-mail info@rabincenter.org.il; internet www.rabincenter.org.il; f. 1997; history, soc. and culture of the State of Israel; associated Rabin archive, library and museum; Chair. Board of Governors DALIA RABIN.

EDUCATION

Centre for Literary Studies: Faculty of Humanities, Mt Scopus, 91905 Jerusalem; tel. (2) 5883925; e-mail cis@savion.huji.ac.il; attached to Hebrew Univ. of Jerusalem; Dir Dr JON DAVID WHITMAN.

Goldie Rotman Centre for Cognitive Science in Education: School of Education, Mt Scopus, 91905 Jerusalem; tel. (2) 5882102; e-mail kareev@vms.huji.ac.il; attached to Hebrew Univ. of Jerusalem; Dir Prof. YAAKOV KAREEV.

**Henrietta Szold Institute—National Institute for Research in the Beha-

vioural Sciences: 9 Columbia St, Kiryat Menachem, 96583 Jerusalem; tel. (2) 6494444; e-mail szold@szold.org.il; internet www.szold.org.il; f. 1941; non-profit org. undertaking research in psychology, psychometry, sociology and education; information retrieval centre for the social sciences in Israel; database of 40,000 records; Dir Prof. ISAAC FRIEDMAN; publ. *Megamot—Behavioral Sciences Quarterly*.

International Center for University Teaching of Jewish Civilization: Faculty of Humanities, Mt Scopus, 91905 Jerusalem; tel. (2) 5881773; e-mail msjewciv@mscc.huji.ac.il; internet www.hum.huji.ac.il/site/jewish-civilization; attached to Hebrew Univ. of Jerusalem; Dir Prof. CYRIL ASLANOV.

National Council of Jewish Women Research Institute for Innovation in Education: c/o Hebrew Univ. of Jerusalem, Mt Scopus, 91905 Jerusalem; tel. (2) 5882016; e-mail ayalab@savion.huji.ac.il; internet innovate.educate.huji.ac.il; f. 1968; attached to Hebrew Univ. of Jerusalem; facilitates research and applied activities to address educational problems, challenges and needs of children and youth to promote their educational and social advancement; Dir Prof. YAIR GAD.

FINE AND PERFORMING ARTS

Centre for Jewish Art: Faculty of Humanities, Mt Scopus, 91905 Jerusalem; tel. (2) 5882281; e-mail cja@huji.me; internet cja.huji.ac.il; attached to Hebrew Univ. of Jerusalem; Dir Dr RINA TALGAM.

Folklore Research Centre: Rabin Bldg, Mt Scopus, 91905 Jerusalem; tel. (2) 5881797; e-mail hasan@mscc.huji.ac.uk; attached to Hebrew Univ. of Jerusalem; Dir Prof. GALIT HASAN-ROKEM.

Jewish Music Research Centre: POB 39105, 91390 Jerusalem; tel. (2) 6585059; e-mail jmrc_inf@savion.huji.ac.il; internet www.jewish-music.huji.ac.il; attached to Hebrew Univ. of Jerusalem; Dir Prof. EDWIN SEROUSSI.

HISTORY, GEOGRAPHY AND ARCHAEOLOGY

Centre for Research on Dutch Jewry: Rabin Bldg, Mt Scopus, 91905 Jerusalem; tel. (2) 5880242; e-mail dutchjew@cc.huji.ac.il; internet dutchjewry.huji.ac.il; attached to Hebrew Univ. of Jerusalem; conducts and fosters scientific research in Dutch-Jewish history; Dir Prof. YOSEF KAPLAN.

Centre for Research on Romanian Jewry: Rabin Bldg, Mt Scopus, 91905 Jerusalem; tel. (2) 5881672; e-mail rumjewry@vms.huji.ac.il; attached to Hebrew Univ. of Jerusalem; Dir Dr ODED IR-SHAI.

Dinur Centre for Research in Jewish History: Rabin Bldg, Mt Scopus, 91905 Jerusalem; tel. (2) 5884894; e-mail dinur.center@mail.huji.ac.il; internet jewishhistory.huji.ac.il; attached to Hebrew Univ. of Jerusalem; Dir Dr ODED IR-SHAI.

Eliezer Ben-Yehudah Research Centre for History of Hebrew: Faculty of Humanities, Mt Scopus, 91905 Jerusalem; tel. (2) 5883550; e-mail yreshef@mscc.huji.ac.il; internet www.hum.huji.ac.il/benyehuda; attached to Hebrew Univ. of Jerusalem; Dir Dr YAEL RESHEF.

Israel Exploration Society: 5 Avida St, POB 7041, 91070 Jerusalem; tel. (2) 6257991; e-mail ies@vms.huji.ac.il; internet israelexplorationsociety.huji.ac.il; f. 1913 as the Soc. for the Reclamation of Antiquities; excavations and allied research into the history, archaeology and geography of Israel; publishes excavation reports, books, research results; educates the public in these matters by means of congresses, general meetings, etc.; Pres. JOSEPH AVIRAM; Chair. of Exec. Cttee Prof. E. STERN; Dir HILLEL GEVA; Deputy Dir ALAN PARIS; publs *Eretz-Israel* (every 3 years, in Hebrew and English), *Israel Exploration Journal* (2 a year, in English), *Qadmoniot* (2 a year, in Hebrew).

Joe Alon Centre for Regional and Folklore Studies: Kibbutz Lahav, 85335 Negev; tel. (8) 9913322; e-mail joealon@lhv.org.il; internet www.joealon.org.il; f. 1972; centre for research, study and survey of the Southern Shefelah (the hilly region between Jerusalem and Beersheba); incl. an Archaeological Museum, a Museum of Bedouin Culture, a Museum for the New Jewish Settlement in the Negev, the Fehalin Exhibit, housed in a restored dwelling cave complex at the foot of a major site; awards grants for research in the region; library of 900 vols, 3,500 slides; Exec. Dir UZZI HALAMISH.

Kenyon Institute: POB 19283, 91192 Jerusalem; tel. (2) 5828101; e-mail kenyon@cbrl.org.uk; internet www.britac.ac.uk/institutes/cbrl/; f. 1920 as British School of Archaeology in Jerusalem; part of the Council for British Research in the Levant (see parent institution in Research Institutes in Jordan); undertakes and promotes study of all aspects of the archaeology, history and culture of the Levant from prehistoric times to the present; library and hostel; library of 10,000 vols, 100 periodicals; Dir Dr JAIMIE LOVELL; Research Scholar CHLOE MASSEY.

Leo Baeck Institute Jerusalem: 33 Bustenai St, Jerusalem; tel. (2) 5633790; e-mail leobaeck@leobaeck.org; internet www.leobaeck.org; f. 1955; research and publs on history and culture of Central European Jewry; academic and cultural events, maintenance of library and archives; library: library and archive of items in German, English and Hebrew; special colln: microfilm archive of Jewish newspapers; publs *Bridges*, *Innovations in the Study of German Jewry*, *Juedischer Almanach*, *Studies in the History of German and Central European Jewry*.

Leonid Nevzlin Research Centre for Russian and East European Jewry: Rabin Bldg, Mt Scopus, 91905 Jerusalem; tel. (2) 5881959; e-mail merkaznev@savion.huji.ac.il; internet www.nevzlin.huji.ac.il; attached to Hebrew Univ. of Jerusalem; promotes multidisciplinary research and teaching of Russian and E European Jewish history and heritage; Admin. Dir Dr SEMION GOLDIN.

Philip and Muriel Berman Centre for Biblical Archaeology: Institute of Archaeology, Hebrew Univ., 91905 Jerusalem; tel. (2) 5882403; attached to Hebrew Univ. of Jerusalem; Dir Prof. YOSEF GARFINKEL.

Richard Koebner Minerva Centre for German History: Faculty of Humanities, Mt Scopus, 91905 Jersualem; tel. (2) 5883766; e-mail koebner.minerva@mail.huji.ac.il; f. 1986; attached to Hebrew Univ. of Jerusalem; Dir Dr OFER ASCHKENAZI.

Robert H. and Clarice Smith Centre for Art History: Faculty of Humanities, Mt Scopus, 91905 Jerusalem; tel. (2) 5883872; e-mail rachelmilstein@mail.huji.ac.il; internet www.smithcenter.huji.ac.il; attached to Hebrew Univ. of Jerusalem; Dir Prof. RACHEL MILSTEIN.

Sidney M. Edelstein Centre for the History and Philosophy of Science, Technology and Medicine: Safra Campus, Givat Ram, 91904 Jerusalem; tel. (2) 6585652; e-mail edelstein.center@mail.huji.ac.il; internet edelstein.huji.ac.il; attached to Hebrew Univ. of Jerusalem; fosters research based on the resources of the Einstein Archives, the Yahuda Theological Colln of Isaac Newton, the Edelstein Library that incl. rare books in the history of science, technology and medicine, incl. the Edelstein Collns on the history of dyeing and chemical technology; offers post-doctoral fellowships and short-term graduate support; Dir Prof. ORLY SHENKER; publ. *Aleph: Historical Studies in Science and Judaism*.

W. F. Albright Institute of Archaeological Research: 26 Salah ed-Din St, POB 19096, Jerusalem; tel. (2) 6288956; e-mail director@albright.org.il; internet www.aiar.org; f. 1900 as the American School of Oriental Research; research projects in Semitic languages, literatures and history; archaeological surveys and excavations; library of 35,000 vols; Pres. SHARON HERBERT; Dir S. GITIN.

LANGUAGE AND LITERATURE

Centre for the Study of Jewish Languages and Literature: Rabin Bldg, Mt Scopus, 91905 Jerusalem; tel. (2) 5880244; e-mail otirosh@mscc.huji.ac.il; attached to Hebrew Univ. of Jerusalem; Dir Dr OFRA TIROSH-BECKER.

Chais Centre for Jewish Studies in Russian: Rabin Bldg, Mt Scopus, 91905 Jerusalem; tel. (2) 5881770; e-mail chais_center@savion.huji.ac.il; attached to Hebrew Univ. of Jerusalem; Dir Dr SEMION GOLDIN.

Franz Rosenzweig Centre for the Study of German Culture and Literature: Rabin Bldg, Mt Scopus, 91905 Jerusalem; tel. (2) 5881909; e-mail yfaatw@pluto.mscc.huji.ac.il; attached to Hebrew Univ. of Jerusalem; Dir Prof. YFAAT WEISS.

Orion Centre for the Study of the Dead Sea Scrolls and Associated Literature: Rabin Bldg, Mt Scopus, 91905 Jerusalem; tel. (2) 5881966; e-mail orioncenter@huji.ac.il; internet orion.mscc.huji.ac.il; f. 1995; attached to Hebrew Univ. of Jerusalem; Dir Prof. MENAHEM KISTER.

MEDICINE

Alex Grass Center for Drug Design and Synthesis of Novel Therapeutics: The School of Pharmacy, Hebrew Univ. of Jerusalem, POB 12065 Jerusalem; tel. (2) 6758683; e-mail malkan@savion.huji.ac.il; attached to Hebrew Univ. of Jerusalem; Dir Prof. GIL LEIBOWITZ.

Brettler Center for Research in Molecular Pharmacology and Therapeutics: Institute for Drug Research, Hebrew Univ. of Jerusalem, POB 12065 Jerusalem; tel. (2) 6758743; e-mail ruths@savion.huji.ac.il; internet pharmacy.huji.ac.il; attached to Hebrew Univ. of Jerusalem; Dir Prof. FRANCESCA LEVI-SHAFFER.

Centre for Diabetes Research: Hebrew Univ., Hdassah Medical Centre, 2nd Fl., Main Bldg; tel. (2) 6776788; e-mail gleib@hadassah.org.il; attached to Hebrew Univ. of Jerusalem; Chair. Prof. GIL LEIBOWITZ.

Centre for the Study of Pain: c/o Hebrew Univ. of Jerusalem, Mt Scopus, 91905 Jerusalem; tel. (2) 6758456; e-mail talm@ekmd.huji.ac.il; internet paincenter.huji.ac.il/tal.htm; attached to Hebrew Univ. of Jerusalem; Dir Prof. MICHAEL TAL.

D. Walter Cohen DDS Middle East Centre for Dental Education: c/o Hebrew Univ. of Jerusalem, Mt Scopus, 91905 Jerusalem; tel. (2) 6758596; e-mail hujident@cc.huji.ac.il; attached to Hebrew Univ. of Jerusalem; Dir Dr YAEL HOURI-HADDAD.

David R. Bloom Centre for Pharmacy: Institute for Drug Research, POB 12065,

Jerusalem; tel. (2) 6758743; e-mail ronk@ekmd.huji.ac.il; internet pharmacy.huji.ac.il; attached to Hebrew Univ. of Jerusalem; Dir Prof. RON KOHEN.

Hubert H. Humphrey Center for Experimental Medicine and Cancer Research: tel. (2) 6758470; e-mail ruthyn@savion.huji.ac.il; attached to Hebrew Univ. of Jerusalem; Dir Prof. ODED BEHAR.

Institute for Dental Sciences: c/o Hebrew Univ. of Jerusalem, Mt Scopus, 91905 Jerusalem; tel. (2) 6757595; e-mail apalmon@cc.huji.ac.il; attached to Hebrew Univ. of Jerusalem; Dir Prof. AARON PALMON.

Institute for Medical Research: POB 12272, 91120 Jerusalem; tel. (2) 6757527; e-mail davidli@ekmd.huji.ac.il; internet medicine.huji.ac.il; attached to Hebrew Univ. of Jerusalem; Dir Prof. DAVID LICHTSTEIN.

Israel Gerontological Data Center (IGDC): Paul Baerwald School of Social Work and Social Welfare, Hebrew Univ. of Jerusalem, Mt Scopus, 91905 Jerusalem; tel. (2) 5882194; e-mail igdc@savion.huji.ac.il; internet igdc.huji.ac.il; attached to Hebrew Univ. of Jerusalem; Dir Prof. HOWARD LITWIN.

Lautenberg Centre for General and Tumour Immunology: c/o Hebrew Univ. of Jerusalem, Faculty of Medicine, POB 12272, 91120 Jerusalem; tel. (2) 6758726; e-mail daniellak@savion.huji.ac.il; internet immunology.huji.ac.il; attached to Hebrew Univ. of Jerusalem; Dir Prof. EITAN YEFENOF.

Levin Centre for the Study of Normal Child and Adolescent Development: c/o Hebrew Univ. of Jerusalem, Mt Scopus, 91905 Jerusalem; tel. (2) 5883370; e-mail levinc@mscc.huji.ac.il; f. 1982; attached to Hebrew Univ. of Jerusalem; Dir Prof. ARIEL KNAFO.

Niznick Dental Implant and Research Centre: c/o Hebrew Univ. of Jerusalem, Mt Scopus, 91905 Jerusalem; tel. (2) 6776193; e-mail ervinw@cc.huji.ac.il; attached to Hebrew Univ. of Jerusalem; Dir Prof. E. WEISS.

Ronald E. Goldstein Center for Aesthetic Dentistry and Clinical Research: Bichacho Clinic 14, Weizmann St, 6423914 Tel Aviv; tel. (3) 6050060; e-mail nitzan@bichacho.net; attached to Hebrew Univ. of Jerusalem; Dir Prof. NITZAN BICHACHO.

Sanford F. Kuvin Centre for the Study of Infectious and Tropical Diseases: Institute for Medical Research, POB 12272, 91120 Jerusalem; tel. (2) 6758409; e-mail haimr@ekmd.huji.ac.il; internet kuvin.huji.ac.il; attached to Hebrew Univ. of Jerusalem; Dir Prof. HAIM ROSEN.

Scheinfeld Centre for Human Genetics in the Social Sciences: c/o Hebrew Univ. of Jerusalem, Mt Scopus, 91905 Jerusalem; tel. (2) 536855; e-mail ebstein@mscc.huji.ac.il; attached to Hebrew Univ. of Jerusalem; conducts research and teaching of human behaviour genetics; Dir Prof. ARIEL KNAFO.

Sheba Medical Center: 52621 Tel-Hashomer; tel. (3) 5302473; e-mail med-tour@sheba.health.gov.il; internet eng.sheba.co.il; f. 1948; research centres in regenerative medicine, neuroscience, cancer, heart disease and genetics; incl. Israel National Center for Health Policy and Epidemiology Research, Israel National Center for Medical Simulation, Middle East Pediatric Congenital Heart Center, Israel Center for Newborn Screening, Israel National Center for Rehabilitation; Dir Prof. ZEEV ROTSTEIN.

NATURAL SCIENCES

General

Centre for Integrated Pest Management: Hebrew Univ. of Jerusalem, POB 12, 76100 Rehovot; tel. (8) 9489223; e-mail coll@agri.huji.ac.il; attached to Hebrew Univ. of Jerusalem; Dir Dr MOSHE COLL.

Israel Science Foundation: Albert Einstein Sq., 43 Jabotinsky St, 91040 Jerusalem; tel. (2) 5885412; e-mail tamar@isf.org.il; internet www.isf.org.il; f. 1995; Dir Dr TAMAR JAFFE-MITTWOCH.

Biological Sciences

Alexander Silberman Institute of Life Sciences: Givat Ram, 91904 Jerusalem; tel. (2) 65854314; e-mail rnathan@cc.huji.ac.il; internet www.bio.huji.ac.il; attached to Hebrew Univ. of Jerusalem; Chair. Prof. RAN NATHAN.

Benjamin Triwaks Bee Research Centre: Hebrew Univ. of Jerusalem, POB 12, 76100 Rehovot; tel. (8) 9489401; e-mail shafir@agri.huji.ac.il; internet departments.agri.huji.ac.il/entomology/staff_pages/shafir.html; attached to Hebrew Univ. of Jerusalem; Dir Dr SHARONI SHAFIR.

Israel Institute for Biological Research: POB 19, 7410001 Ness-Ziona; tel. (8) 9381656; e-mail mambi@iibr.gov.il; internet www.iibr.gov.il; f. 1952; conducts biomedical research in drug design, synthesis of fine chemicals and devt of newly advanced products and processes in biotechnology; 3 research divs: Chemistry, Biology and Environmental Sciences; library of 50,000 vols and 800 periodicals; Head of Biology Division Dr SHMUEL YITZHAKI; Head of Medicinal Chemistry Division Dr NISSAN ASHKENAZI; Head of Environmental Sciences Division Dr AVRAHAM LACSER; publ. *OHOLO Annual International Scientific Conference*.

Kennedy Leigh Centre for Horticultural Research: Hebrew Univ. of Jerusalem, POB 12, 76100 Rehovot; tel. (8) 9489251; e-mail shimony@agri.huji.ac.il; internet departments.agri.huji.ac.il/horticulture/kennedy.html; attached to Hebrew Univ. of Jerusalem; Dir Prof. ADAM ZACH.

National Institute for Psychobiology in Israel: Hebrew University, Givat Ram Campus, 91904 Jerusalem; tel. (2) 6584086; e-mail psychobi@cc.huji.ac.il; internet www.psychobiology.org.il; f. 1971 with funds from the Charles E. Smith Family Foundation, to create a network of scientists engaged in research in psychobiology, to further co-operative programmes between existing institutions, and to train personnel in the field of psychobiology; administers Charles E. Smith Family Laboratory for Collaborative Research in Psychobiology; operates through the Research and Development Authority of the Hebrew University; Pres. DAVID BRUCE SMITH; Dir Prof. SHAUL HOCHSTEIN; Chair. Prof. ELLIOT GERSHON.

Nutrigenomics and Functional Food Research Centre: HU POB 12, 76100 Rehovot; tel. (8) 9489746; e-mail froy@agri.huji.ac.il; attached to Hebrew Univ. of Jerusalem; Dir Prof. OREN FROY.

Mathematical Sciences

Edmund Landau Minerva Centre for Research in Mathematical Analysis and Related Areas: Institute of Mathematics, Givat Ram, Jerusalem; tel. (2) 6586868; e-mail ylast@math.huji.ac.il; internet www.ma.huji.ac.il; attached to Hebrew Univ. of Jerusalem; Dir Prof. YORAM LAST.

Sudarsky Centre for Computational Biology: Edmond Safra Campus, Givat Ram, Jerusalem; tel. (2) 6585425; e-mail michall@cc.huji.ac.il; attached to Hebrew Univ. of Jerusalem; conducts and fosters research combining computer science and the medical sciences, life sciences and biotechnology; Dir Prof. MICHAL LINEAL.

Physical Sciences

Earth Sciences Research Administration: 30 Malkhei Israel St, 95501 Jerusalem; tel. (2) 5314246; e-mail mbeyth@gsi.gov.il; f. 1949; attached to Min. of National Infrastructure; defines scientific issues involved in energy, environment and infrastructure; Dir-Gen. HEZI KUGLER.

Subordinate Institutions:

Geological Survey of Israel: 30 Malkhei Israel St, 95501 Jerusalem; tel. (2) 5314211; e-mail ask_gsi@gsi.gov.il; internet www.gsi.gov.il; f. 1949; geological mapping, research and exploration of mineral, water and energy resources; environmental geology; mitigation of earthquake hazards; Dir Dr ORA SHAPIRA.

Geophysical Institute of Israel: POB 182, 71100 Lod; tel. (8) 9785888; internet www.gii.co.il; f. 1957; activities devoted chiefly to the exploration of petroleum, water and mineral resources and to engineering studies in Israel and abroad, using geophysical methods; documentation unit; data-processing centre; monitoring and mitigation of earthquake hazards; Dir Dr Y. ROTSTEIN.

Israel Oceanographic and Limnological Research: POB 1793, 31000 Haifa; tel. (4) 8526639; e-mail barak@ocean.org.il; internet www.ocean.org.il; f. 1967; physical, chemical and biological oceanography and limnology; aquaculture; Dir Prof. BARAK HERUT.

Israel Meteorological Service: POB 25, 50250 Bet-Dagan; tel. (3) 9682121; e-mail ims@ims.gov.il; internet www.ims.gov.il; f. 1936; provides general service to public and detailed service to various orgs; library; various publs; Dir Z. ALPERSON.

Knune Minerva Farkas Center for the Study of Light Induced Processes: Institute of Chemistry, Givat Ram, Jerusalem; tel. (2) 6585326; e-mail sandy@fh.huji.ac.il; internet www.chemistry.huji.ac.il; attached to Hebrew Univ. of Jerusalem; Dir Prof. SANFORD RUCHMAN.

Leo Picard Groundwater Research Centre: c/o Hebrew Univ. of Jerusalem, Mt Scopus, 91905 Jerusalem; tel. (8) 9489174; e-mail chefetz@agri.huji.ac.il; attached to Hebrew Univ. of Jerusalem; Dir Prof. BENNY CHEFETZ.

Moshe Shilo Centre for Marine Biogeochemistry: Faculty of Science, Givat Ram Campus, 91904 Jerusalem; tel. (8) 6585090; e-mail anton@vms.huji.ac.il; internet mosheshilo-center.huji.ac.il; attached to Hebrew Univ. of Jerusalem; Dir Prof. ANTON POST.

Ring Centre for Multi-Disciplinary Environmental Research: Safra Campus, 91904 Jerusalem; tel. (2) 6586055; e-mail msfeitel@mscc.huji.ac.il; internet ringcenter.huji.ac.il; f. 1993; attached to Hebrew Univ. of Jerusalem; Dir Prof. ERAN FEITELSON.

Seagram Centre for Soil and Water Sciences: Hebrew Univ. of Jerusalem, POB 12, 76100 Rehovot; tel. (8) 9489340; e-mail soil@agri.huji.ac.il; internet departments.agri.huji.ac.il/soils; attached to Hebrew Univ. of Jerusalem; Dir Prof. BENNY CHEFETZ.

PHILOSOPHY AND PSYCHOLOGY

S. H. Bergman Centre for Philosophical Studies: Faculty of Humanities, Mt Scopus, 91905 Jerusalem; tel. (2) 5883762; attached to Hebrew Univ. of Jerusalem; Dir Dr MICHAEL ROUBACH; publ. *Iyyun* (4 a year).

Sigmund Freud Centre for Study and Research in Psychoanalysis: c/o Hebrew Univ. of Jerusalem, Mt Scopus, 91905 Jerusalem; tel. (2) 5883380; e-mail msfreud@mscc.huji.ac.il; internet social.huji.ac.il/content/misc/freud/english.html; f. 1979; attached to Hebrew Univ. of Jerusalem; conducts psychoanalytic studies and research both in psychoanalysis and at the interfaces between psychoanalysis and other fields; Dir Prof. GABRIEL SHEFLER.

RELIGION, SOCIOLOGY AND ANTHROPOLOGY

Ben-Zvi Institute for the Study of Jewish Communities in the East: POB 7660, Jerusalem; tel. (2) 5398844; e-mail bzi@ybz.org.il; internet www.ybz.org.il; attached to Hebrew Univ. of Jerusalem; Chair. Prof. YOM TOV ASSIS.

Centre for the Study of Christianity: Faculty of Humanities, Mt Scopus, 91905 Jerusalem; tel. (2) 5883827; e-mail centerc@savion.cc.huji.ac.il; attached to Hebrew Univ. of Jerusalem; Dir Dr BROURIA BITTON-ASHKELONY.

Harry Fischel Institute for Research in Talmud and Jewish Law: Bucharim Quarter, 14 David St (cnr Fischel St), POB 5289, 91052 Jerusalem; tel. (2) 5322517; f. 1932; seminary for Rabbis and Rabbinical Judges; legislation and research publs; codification of Jewish law; Jewish adult education centre; 80 mems; Chancellor Chief Rabbi SHEAR-YASHUV COHEN.

Jewish Oral Traditions Research Centre: Rabin Bldg, Mt Scopus, 91905 Jerusalem; tel. (2) 5881828; e-mail dornirit@zahav.net.il; attached to Hebrew Univ. of Jerusalem; Dir Prof. AHARON MAMAM.

Misgav Yerushalaim Centre for the Study of Sephardi and Oriental Jewry: Rabin Bldg, Mt Scopus, 91905 Jerusalem; tel. (2) 5883962; e-mail yaronbn@mscc.huji.ac.il; attached to Hebrew Univ. of Jerusalem; Dir Dr YARON BEN-NAEH.

Nehemia Levzion Centre for Islamic Studies: c/o Hebrew Univ. of Jerusalem, Faculty of Humanities, Mt Scopus, 91905 Jerusalem; tel. (2) 5881541; e-mail islamic@mscc.huji.ac.il; internet islam-center.huji.ac.il; f. 2004; attached to Hebrew Univ. of Jerusalem; Dir Dr MEIR HATINA.

Scholion Interdisciplinary Research Centre in Jewish Studies: Rabin Bldg, Mt Scopus, 91905 Jerusalem; tel. (2) 5882430; e-mail scholion@savion.huji.ac.il; internet scholion.huji.ac.il; attached to Hebrew Univ. of Jerusalem; Dir Prof. ISRAEL J. YUVAL.

Shaine Centre for Research in the Social Sciences: c/o Hebrew Univ. of Jerusalem, Mt Scopus, 91905 Jerusalem; tel. (2) 5883032; e-mail msschein@mscc.huji.ac.il; attached to Hebrew Univ. of Jerusalem; Dir Prof. GUY STECKLOV.

Vidal Sassoon International Centre for the Study of Antisemitism: Faculty of Humanities, Mt Scopus, 91905 Jerusalem; tel. (2) 5882494; e-mail sicsa@mscc.huji.ac.il; internet sicsa.huji.ac.il; f. 1982; attached to Hebrew Univ. of Jerusalem; conducts research on antisemitism throughout the ages, focusing on relations between Jews and non-Jews, particularly in situations of tension and crisis; Dir Prof. ROBERT WISTRICH.

World Jewish Bible Center: POB 7024, Jerusalem; tel. (2) 6255965; f. 1957; aims to disseminate knowledge of the Bible and of Bible research through publs, lectures and exhibitions; Chair. S. J. KREUTNER; publ. *Beit Mikra* (4 a year, in Hebrew).

Yad Izhak Ben-Zvi: POB 7660, 91076 Jerusalem; tel. (2) 5398888; e-mail ybz@ybz.org.il; internet www.ybz.org.il; f. 1964; encourages research into the history of Israel and Jerusalem; promotes the study of Jewish communities in the Middle East, Izhak Ben-Zvi and the Zionist and labour movements of Israel; library of 65,000 vols; Dir Dr ZVI ZAMERET; publs *Cathedra* (4 a year), *Et-mol* (6 a year), *Pe'amim* (4 a year), *Sefunot* (irregular), *Shalem* (irregular).

Subordinate Institutions:

Ben-Zvi Institute for the Study of Jewish Communities in the East: POB 7660, 91076 Jerusalem; tel. (2) 5398844; e-mail mbz@ybz.org.il; internet www.ybz.org.il; f. 1947; operated jtly with the Hebrew Univ. of Jerusalem; sponsors research into the history and culture of Jewish communities in Muslim countries since the 7th century; maintains large colln of MSS, and other historical documents; library; Deputy Chair. MICHAEL GLATZER; publs *Ginzei Qedem—Genizah Research Annual* (1 a year, in Hebrew and English), *Jewish Communities in the East in the 19th and 20th centuries*, *Pe'amim—Studies in Oriental Jewry* (4 a year, in Hebrew), *Sefunot* (irregular, in Hebrew).

Institute for Research of Eretz Israel: POB 7660, 91076 Jerusalem; tel. (2) 5398888; e-mail ybz@ybz.org.il; internet www.ybz.org.il; promotes research on the history of Eretz Israel from Biblical times to the mid-20th century, and publishes studies on the history and culture of the Jewish people in Israel from the destruction of the Second Temple to the first decades of the State of Israel's existence; research and studies based on the work of scientists at the main univs; Dir Prof. MARC HIRSHMAN.

TECHNOLOGY

Fritz Haber Research Centre for Molecular Dynamics: Institute of Chemistry, Givat Ram, 91904 Jerusalem; tel. (2) 6586114; e-mail roi.baer@huji.ac.il; internet www.fh.huji.ac.il; f. 1980; attached to Hebrew Univ. of Jerusalem; Dir Prof. ROI BAER.

G. W. Leibnitz Minerva Centre for Research in Computer Sciences: c/o Hebrew Univ. of Jerusalem, School of Computer Science and Engineering, Jerusalem; tel. (2) 6585730; e-mail noam.nisan@gmail.com; internet www.cs.huji.ac.il; attached to Hebrew Univ. of Jerusalem; Dir Prof. NOAM NISAN.

Harvey M. Krueger Family Centre for Nanoscience and Nanotechnology: Edmond J. Safra Campus, Givat Ram, Jerusalem; tel. (2) 6586948; e-mail huj-nano@savion.huji.ac.il; internet www.nanoscience.huji.ac.il; attached to Hebrew Univ. of Jerusalem; Dir Prof. DANNY PORATH.

Israel Atomic Energy Commission: POB 7061, 61070 Tel-Aviv; 26 Rehov Chaim Levanon, Ramat-Aviv, Tel-Aviv; tel. (3) 6462922; internet www.iaec.gov.il; f. 1952; advises the Govt on long-term policies and priorities in the advancement of nuclear research and devt; supervises the implementation of policies approved by the Govt, incl. the licensing of nuclear power plants; promotion of technological industrial applications; represents Israel in relations with scientific instns and organizations abroad (Israel is a mem. of IAEA); Chair. The PRIME MINISTER; Dir-Gen. G. FRANK.

Attached Research Centres:

Negev Nuclear Research Centre: Dimona; natural uranium-fuelled and heavy water-moderated reactor IRR-2 of 26 MW thermal; Dir MICHA DAPHT.

Soreq Nuclear Research Centre: 81800 Yavne; tel. (8) 9434290; internet www.soreq.gov.il; f. 1958; swimming-pool research reactor IRR-1 of 5 MW thermal; Dir URI HALAVEE.

Lisa Meitner-Minerva Centre for Computational Quantum Chemistry: Institute of Chemistry, Givat Ram, Jerusalem; tel. (2) 6585909; internet alpha.ch.huji.ac.il/public_html/welcome.htm; f. 1997; attached to Hebrew Univ. of Jerusalem; Dir Prof. SASON SHAIK.

Office of the Chief Scientist—Industrial Research Administration, Ministry of Industry and Trade: 5 Bank Israel St, POB 3166, 91036 Jerusalem; tel. (2) 6662486; f. 1970; promotes industrial research and devt in industry, research institutes and higher education institutes by financing projects; encourages establishment of science-based industrial parks near universities and research institutes; proposes policies to promote innovative industry through legislation, developing physical and technical infrastructure and intergovernmental industrial research and development (R&D) agreements; Chief Scientist ELI OPER.

Associated Institutions:

Institutes for Applied Research, Ben-Gurion University of the Negev: POB 1025, 84110 Be'ersheva; tel. (8) 5778382; e-mail negev@negev.org; f. 1956; engages in applied research in water desalination, membrane and ion-exchange technologies, chemical technologies, irrigation with brackish and seawater, development of salt- and drought-resistant crops and ornamentals, natural products from higher plants and algae, devt of mechanical and electromechanical products, utilization of non-conventional energy sources; 120 staff; library of 13,200 vols; Dir Prof. A. SHANI; publ. *Scientific Activities* (2 a year).

Israel Ceramic and Silicate Institute: Technion City, 32000 Haifa; tel. (4) 8222107; e-mail isracer@actcom.co.il; internet www.isracer.org; f. 1962; provides the local ceramic industry with technical assistance and with research and devt into advanced and new fields in ceramics technology; 12 staff; Dir Dr ADRIAN GOLDSTEIN.

Israel Fiber Institute: POB 8001, 91080 Jerusalem; tel. (2) 5707377; attached to Technion—Israel Institute of Technology; f. 1953; advances textile, polymer, paper, leather and related industries; applied research and development (R&D), testing services, quality control, training courses for engineers and technicians, MSc and PhD courses in conjunction with the Hebrew Univ.; 45 staff; library of 4,000 vols and 30 periodicals; Dir Dr HILDA GUTTMAN.

Israel Institute of Metals: Technion City, 32000 Haifa; tel. (4) 8294473; f. 1962; serves industry in metallurgy and powder technology, foundry, corrosion and coating technology, vehicle and mechanical engineering; Dir Prof. A. ROSEN.

Israel Institute of Plastics: POB 7293, 31072 Haifa; tel. (4) 8225174; f. 1981; research and development (R&D) and information centre for promoting the plastic industry; Dir Dr S. ABRAHAMI.

Israel Wine Institute: 4 Ha-Raz St, POB 2329, 76310 Rehovot; tel. (8) 9475693; f. 1957; improves the country's wines by means of quality control and applied research and promotes their export; Dir SHLOMO COHEN.

National Physical Laboratory: Hebrew Univ., Danziger A Bldg, Givat Ram Campus, 91904 Jerusalem; tel. (2) 6303501; attached to Min. of Industry, Trade and Labour; f. 1950; applied research with industrial orientation, basic physical and chemical standards; Dir GRISHA DEUTCH.

Rubber Research Association Ltd: Technion City, 32000 Haifa; tel. (4) 8222124; f. 1951; the advancement of the rubber industry in Israel; Dir D. CZIMERMAN.

Standards Institution of Israel: POB 39020, 61390 Tel-Aviv; tel. (3) 5454154; internet www.iso.co.il; f. 1923; tests the compliance of commodities with the requirements of standards and specifications; grants standards mark; conducts technological research; publishes the Nat. Standards Specifications and Codes; 550 staff; library of 300,000 standards; Dir-Gen. ELI HADAR; publ. *Mati* (4 a year).

Smart Family Foundation Communication Institute: c/o Hebrew Univ. of Jerusalem, Mt Scopus, 91905 Jerusalem; tel. (2) 5883210; e-mail msmartc@mscc.huji.ac.il; f. 1987; attached to Hebrew Univ. of Jerusalem; promotes devt of links between academe and media professionals working in communications field and with policy and decision makers in the public sector; Dir Prof. IFAT MAOZ.

Libraries and Archives

Be'ersheva

Ben Gurion University of the Negev Aranne Library: POB 653, 84105 Be'er Sheva; tel. (8) 6461413; e-mail yaatz@bgu.ac.il; internet www.bgu.ac.il/aranne; f. 1966; 1,000,000 vols, 25,000 current periodicals incl. ejournals, 3,200 microfilms, 300 audiovisual cassettes, 76 DVDs, 1,200 CD-ROMs and books, 1,500 online theses; spec. collns: David Tuviyahu Archives of the Negev; Isaiah Berlin Room; Dir HAYA ASNER.

Haifa

Borochov Library: c/o Haifa Labour Council, POB 5226, Haifa; f. 1921; 40,000 vols in central library, 60,000 vols in 24 brs; Chief Librarian EZECHIEL OREN.

Haifa AMLI Library of Music: 23 Arlosoroff St, POB 4811/25, Haifa; tel. (4) 8644485; f. 1958; lending library incl. books, scores, records and cassettes; Librarian LEAH MARCUS.

Pevsner Public Library: 54 Pevsner St, POB 5345, Haifa; tel. (4) 8667766; f. 1934; 200,000 vols covering all fields of literature and science, in Hebrew, English and German; 15 brs; Chief Librarian Dr S. BACK.

Technion—Israel Institute of Technology, Library System: Technion City, 32000 Haifa; tel. (4) 8292507; e-mail ddalia@cl.technion.ac.il; internet library.technion.ac.il; f. 1925; science, technology, architecture and medicine; Elyachar (Central) Library, 16 departmental libraries; 1,000,000 vols, 12,700 current periodicals, 281 databases, 12,000 ebooks; Dir DALIA DOLEV.

University of Haifa Library: Mount Carmel, 31905 Haifa; tel. (4) 8240289; e-mail libmaster@univ.haifa.ac.il; internet lib.haifa.ac.il; f. 1963; 1,552,883 vols, 41,797 periodical titles (incl. 26,261 ejournals), 480,000 microfiches and films, 27,000 maps, 100,899 digital images, 9,829 video cassettes and 4,382 DVDs; spec. collns incl. integrated law colln, rare books, media centre, laboratory for children's librarianship; Dir PNINA EREZ; Deputy Dir NAOMI GREIDINGER; Academic Dir Prof. JOSEPH ZIEGLER; Admin. Dir HUMI REKEM; publ. *Index to Hebrew Periodicals*.

Jerusalem

Archive and Library of Ashkenaz House Synagogue Memorial: 58 King George St, POB 7440, 91073 Jerusalem; tel. (2) 6233225; e-mail synagog@netvision.net.il; internet www.ashkenazhouse.org; f. 1988; research into German communities and synagogues destroyed during 'Kristallnacht' in Germany, November 1938; collects material about Ashkenaz Jewry and docs relating to 'Kristallnacht'; ongoing compilation of a series of memorial books in German (of which 5 have already appeared in print), documenting the synagogues and Jewish communities destroyed in the early 20th century in greater Germany; preparation of English-language memorial books on the above subjects, for the American public; research into history of the ship *Exodus* and the subsequent deportation of Holocaust survivors back to Europe; Founder and Dir-Gen. Prof. Dr MEIER SCHWARZ.

Bibliothèque de l'Ecole Biblique et Archéologique Française de Jérusalem: 6 Nablus Rd, POB 19053, 91190 Jerusalem; tel. (2) 6264468; e-mail biblio@ebaf.edu; internet www.ebaf.edu; f. 1890; archaeology and epigraphy of the ancient Near East, biblical studies; photographic colln of 20,000 pictures taken in the Near East in late 19th and early 20th century; 150,000 vols; Dir Prof. MARCEL SIGRIST; Head Librarian Rev. PAWEL TRZOPEK; publs *Cahiers de la Revue Biblique*, *Etudes Bibliques*, *Revue Biblique* (4 a year).

Central Archives for the History of the Jewish People (formerly Jewish Historical General Archives): POB 39077, 91390 Jerusalem; tel. (2) 6586249; e-mail archives@vms.huji.ac.il; internet sites.huji.ac.il/archives; f. 1939, present name and status 1969; serves as central archives of Jewish people and history; 15,000 vols on Jewish history, 1,600 community archives, 12,000 photographs, 8,000 statutes; Dir HADASSAH ASSOULINE.

Central Zionist Archives: POB 92, Jerusalem; tel. (2) 6204860; e-mail cza@wzo.org.il; internet www.zionistarchives.org.il; f. 1919; official repository of the World Zionist Org., the Jewish Agency, the Jewish Nat. Fund Keren Hayesod and the World Jewish Congress; 70,000 vols incl. books, 1m. photographs and negatives, 70,000 maps and settlement plans, 26,000 posters and handbills, 6,000 newspaper titles; 500 audio recordings, 2m. genealogical records and 500 microfilms; Dir Dr YIGAL SITRY; Archivist ROCHELLE RUBINSTEIN.

Gulbenkian Library: Armenian Patriarchate, POB 14106, 91140 Jerusalem; tel. (2) 6282331; e-mail library@armenian-patriarchate.org; f. 1929; donated by the late Calouste Gulbenkian; one of the three great Armenian libraries in the diaspora, the others being the Mekhitarist Fathers' Library in Venice, Italy and another in Vienna, Austria; public library of 100,000 vols, of which one-third are in Armenian and the rest in foreign languages, primarily English and French; receives more than 360 newspapers, magazines, periodicals (of which more than one-half are Armenian) from foreign countries; collns of newspapers and magazines since the 1850s; a copy of the first printed Armenian Bible (1666); 3,890 Armenian MSS; Dir Rev. Fr NORAYR KAZAZIAN; Sec. RINA DJERNAZIAN; Librarian MALINA ZAKIAN LA-PORTA; publ. *Sion* (official organ of the Armenian Patriarchate, 12 a year).

Israel Antiquities Authority Archives Branch: POB 586, 91004 Jerusalem; tel. (2) 6204680; e-mail arieh@israntique.org.il; internet www.antiquities.org.il; f. 1920; written, computerized, photographic and digitized records, maps and plans; Head of Archives Br. KRAPIWKO SILVIA; Asst to Head of Archives Br. ARIEH ROCHMAN-HALPERIN.

Israel State Archives: Prime Minister's Office, Kiryat Ben-Gurion, 91950 Jerusalem; tel. (2) 5680680; e-mail research@archives.gov.il; internet www.archives.gov.il; f. 1949; comprises 7 sections: Dept of Files and Manuscripts, Library Dept, Records Management, Supervision Dept of Public and Private Archives, Services to the Public, Technical Services Dept and Publ. of State Papers; holdings incl. files occupying 30 km of shelving, 150,000 printed items and 25,000 books; admin. records, incl. foreign relations, are available after 30 years and records on defence after 50 years; State Archivist E. FRIESEL; Dir M. MOSSEK; publs *Documents on the Foreign Policy of Israel*, *Israel Government Publications* (bibliography, 1 a year).

Jerusalem City (Public) Library: POB 1409, Jerusalem; tel. (2) 6256785; f. 1961; 750,000 vols; 20 brs and 2 bookmobiles; Dir ABRAHAM VILNER.

Library of the Central Bureau of Statistics: 66 Kanfei Nesharm St, POB 34525, 95464 Jerusalem; tel. (2) 6592666; internet www.cbs.gov.il; f. 1948; 40,000 vols; spec. colln: all publs of (British) Palestine Dept of Statistics (due to be transferred to the Israel State Archives); most publs available for exchange; Librarian MARIAN ROMAN.

Library of the Knesset: Knesset, 91950 Jerusalem; tel. (2) 6753333; internet www.knesset.gov.il; f. 1949; principally for members' use; 150,000 vols, incl. books, bound periodicals and colln of all Israeli Govt publs, UN publs and foreign parliamentary papers; Librarian NAOMI KIMHI.

Library of the Studium Biblicum Franciscanum: Monastery of the Flagellation, Via Dolorosa, POB 19424, 91193 Jerusalem; tel. (2) 6270473; e-mail librarysbf_ofm@yahoo.com; f. 1924; 50,000 vols chiefly on archaeology, Judaeo-Christianism, biblical and patristic studies, 420 periodicals; Library Dir GOH LIONEL.

Muriel and Philip Berman Medical Library, Hebrew University of Jerusalem: POB 12272, 91120 Jerusalem; tel. (2) 6758795; e-mail mdlibinfo@savion.huji.ac.il; internet library.ekmd.huji.ac.il; f. 1919; serves faculty and students of the Hebrew Univ. of Jerusalem Faculty of Medicine, Faculty of Dental Medicine, School of Pharmacy, Nursing School and School of Public Health and the Hadassah-Hebrew Univ. Hospital; 400,000 vols, 45,000 print and ebook titles, 8,000 ejournals in health sciences; history of medicine colln and museum; Dir SHARON LENGA.

National Library of Israel: POB 39105, 91390 Jerusalem; tel. (2) 6584651; e-mail orenw@savion.huji.ac.il; internet www.jnul.huji.ac.il; f. 1892; 10,000 MSS; 49,000 microfilmed Hebrew MSS; microfilms of Jewish and Israeli newspapers; 200 incunabula (120 Hebrew and 80 in other languages); 15,000 current periodicals; special collns incl. the Abraham Schwadron Colln of Jewish Autographs and Portraits, the Harry Friedenwald Colln on the History of Medicine, the National Sound Archives and the Jacob Michael Colln of Jewish Music, the Sidney M. Edelstein Colln on the History of Chemistry, the Eran Laor Cartographic Colln, the Archives of Albert Einstein; 5,000,000 vols, incl. those in departmental libraries; Dir OREN WEINBERG; Chief Librarian RIVKA

SHVEIKY; publs *Index of Articles on Jewish Studies* (1 a year), *Kiryat Sefer* (4 a year, bibliography).

Schocken Library: 6 Balfour St, 92102 Jerusalem; tel. (2) 5631288; e-mail jtspress@schocken-jts.org.il; internet www.schocken-jts.org.il; f. 1900; 55,000 vols, 200 MSS, 20,000 photostats (Hebrew Liturgy and Poetry); Dir Dr SHMUEL GLICK; Bibliographer and Research Librarian DAVID KERSCHEN.

Supreme Court Library: Supreme Court of Israel, Rehov Sha'arei Mishpat, Kiryat Ben Gurion, 91950 Jerusalem; tel. (2) 6759665; e-mail liba@supreme.court.gov.il; internet www.court.gov.il; f. 1949; 85,000 vols; Dir LIBA BORCK.

Kfar Giladi

Kfar Giladi Library: 12210 Kfar Giladi, Upper Galilee; f. 1934; 35,000 vols, 110 periodicals; Librarian SHULAMIT ROSENTHAL.

Kiryat Shmona

Library of Tel-Hai Academic College: Upper Galilee, 12210 Kiryat Shmona; tel. (4) 8181785; internet www.telhai.ac.il; incl. the Calvary Colln, the Ofer colln, the Kapeliuk Middle East colln, Dvir colln in environmental studies, the Lubin art colln and the Gail Chasin art colln, Littauer Judaic colln, Silvia Sheim colln; 80,000 vols, 600 periodicals, 1,200 video cassettes, 4,200 ejournals; Library Dir IRIS CHAI.

Ramat-Gan

Bar-Ilan University Library System: Central Library, 52900 Ramat-Gan; tel. (3) 5318165; e-mail tchiya.dagan@mail.biu.ac.il; internet www.biu.ac.il/lib; f. 1955; serves faculties of humanities, Judaica, law, social sciences, exact sciences and life sciences; 1,000,000 vols, 4,500 current journals; spec. collns incl. the Mordecai Margulies colln of rare 16th and 17th century Hebrew books and 800 Hebrew Oriental MSS, Berman colln of early E European Hebrew imprints, rare Latin and German books on Jewish studies, Old Testament criticism, material on the Dead Sea Scrolls and the Samaritans; a colln of material on the devt of Religious Zionism; colln of Responsa and Jewish studies; Moussaieff colln of 220 Kabbalistic MSS; Head Periodicals Dept T. DAGAN; publs *Hebrew Subject Headings* (online), *Index to Literary Supplements of the Daily Hebrew Press* (online).

'Dvir Bialik' Municipal Central Public Library: Hibat-Zion St 14, Ramat-Gan; f. 1945; 400,000 vols, incl. special Rabbinic literature and Social Sciences colln; maintains 11 brs; Chief Librarian HADASSAH PELACH.

Rehovot

Hebrew University of Jerusalem, The Library of Agriculture, Food and Environment: POB 12, 76100 Rehovot; tel. (8) 9489906; e-mail suzanag@savion.huji.ac.il; internet www.agri.huji.ac.il/library/menu.html; f. 1960; br. in Koret School of Veterinary Medicine: The Lubetzky-Americus Library of Veterinary Medicine; FAO repository library in Israel; 300,000 vols; Dir SUSANA GURMAN.

Weizmann Archives: POB 26, 76100 Rehovot; tel. (8) 9343390; internet www.weizmann.ac.il/wis-library/archive.htm; f. 1973; contains assembled letters, papers, photographs, and other docs relating to political and scientific activities of Dr Chaim Weizmann, first President of Israel; approx. 180,000 items; Archivist ORNA ZELTZER.

Weizmann Institute of Science Libraries: POB 26, 76100 Rehovot; tel. (8) 9343295; e-mail hedva.milo@weizmann.ac.il; internet www.weizmann.ac.il/dis/library; f. 1934, as Ziff Institute Libraries, current name adopted 1949; central library, 3 faculty libraries, 1 departmental library and approx. 50 departmental collns; 260,000 vols incl. bound periodicals; Chief Librarian HEDVA MILO.

Tel-Aviv

Felicja Blumental Music Center and Library: 26 Bialik St, 61048 Tel-Aviv; tel. (3) 6201185; e-mail info@fbmc.co.il; internet www.fbmc.co.il; f. 1950; 75,920 vols, 64 periodicals, 18,000 records, 3,446 CDs, 170 video cassettes; Bronislav Huberman archive, Joachim Stutschewsky archive, Shulamith Conservatory (1910), Beit Levi'im (1919), etc.; Dir IRIT SCHÖNHORN.

General Archives of the City of Tel-Aviv-Yafo: City Hall, 69 Ibn Gvirol St, 64162 Tel-Aviv; tel. (3) 6438554; e-mail archive@mail.tel-aviv.gov.il; internet tel-aviv.millenium.org.il; f. 1967; Dir LARISA SHNITKIND.

Library of the Kibbutzim College of Education: 149 Namir Rd, 62507 Tel-Aviv; tel. (3) 6902323; e-mail miri_ker@smkb.ac.il; internet www.smkb.ac.il; f. 1940; 75,000 vols; Librarian EDNA NAAMAN.

Sourasky Central Library, Tel-Aviv University: POB 39038, Ramat-Aviv, 61930 Tel-Aviv; tel. (3) 6408745; e-mail naamas@tauex.tau.ac.il; internet www.cenlib.tau.ac.il; f. 1954; incl. the Pevsner colln of Hebrew Press, the Faitlovitch colln, the colln of Yiddish Literature and Culture in memory of Benzion and Pearl Margulies, the Wiener Library colln, which concerns the Second World War, esp. the Holocaust, and the history of anti-Semitism, the Herbert Cohen colln of rare books, the Dr Horodisch colln on the history of books and the Jaffe colln of Hebrew poetry; 7 specialized br. libraries; 1m. vols, 4,800 current periodicals, 96,000 microforms; Dir NA'AMA SCHEFTELOWITZ.

Tel-Aviv Central Public Library 'Shaar Zion': 25 King Saul Blvd, POB 33235, Tel-Aviv; tel. (3) 6910141; internet www.tel-aviv.gov.il/english/culture/ariela.htm; f. 1922; 900,000 vols (in 25 brs); General Library in 8 languages; spec. collns: Rambam Library, Ahad ha-Am Library (history and geography of Eretz Israel), Dance Library, Graphoteque (lending library of artist prints), Legal Library; Dir ORA NEBENZAHL.

Museums and Art Galleries

Acre

Okashi Art Museum, Acre: Old City of Akko, El-Jazz'ar St, Acre; permanent exhibition of works by Avsalom Okashi (1916–1980); temporary exhibitions by Israeli artists.

Be'ersheva

Negev Museum: 60 Ha'atsmaut Rd, POB 5188, 84100 Be'ersheva; tel. (7) 6206570; e-mail br7museum@br7.org.il; f. 1954; exhibits from regional excavations, mainly from the Chalcolithic, Israelite, Roman and Byzantine periods; exhibitions of Israeli contemporary art; Dir GALIA GAVISH.

Haifa

Haifa Museum of Art: 26 Shabbetai Levy St, 33043 Haifa; tel. (4) 8523255; e-mail curator@hma.org.il; internet www.hma.org.il; f. 1951; collns of Israeli and world contemporary art, prints, art posters, paintings and sculptures; library of 10,000 vols; Curator Dir TAMI KATZ-FREIMAN.

National Maritime Museum: 198 Allenby Rd, POB 44855, 31447 Haifa; tel. (4) 8536622; e-mail curator@nmm.org.il; internet www.nmm.org.il; f. 1954; large colln of artefacts and ship models illustrating 5,000 years of navigation and shipbuilding, old maps and engravings, undersea archaeology, a Hellenistic bronze ram, and stamps and ancient coins connected with seafaring and maritime symbols; archaeology and civilizations of ancient peoples; scientific instruments; library: research library of 6,000 vols; Dir-Gen. NISSIM TAL; publ. *Sefunim*.

Tikotin Museum of Japanese Art: 89 Hanassi Ave, 34642 Haifa; tel. (4) 8383554; e-mail curator@tmja.org.il; internet www.tmja.org.il; f. 1960; paintings, prints, drawings, textiles, netsuke, lacquer work, ceramics, metalwork, colln of Mingei (folk art); courses for children and adults; library of 3,000 vols; Chief Curator Dr ILANA SINGER.

Jerusalem

Archaeological (Rockefeller) Museum: POB 71117, 91710 Jerusalem; tel. (2) 6282251; e-mail fawziib@imj.org.il; internet www.imj.org.il; f. 1938; fmrly Palestine Archaeological Museum; archaeology of Israel from earliest times until the end of Islamic period; largely material found in excavations before 1948; Dir JAMES S. SNYDER.

Beit Ha'Omanim (Jerusalem Artists' House): 12 Shmuel Hanagid St, Jerusalem; tel. (2) 6253653; e-mail artists@zahav.net.il; f. 1965; Israeli and foreign contemporary art exhibitions and permanent gallery of works by Israeli artists; Dir RUTH ZADKA.

Bible Lands Museum Jerusalem: POB 4670, 91046 Jerusalem; 25 Granot St, 93706 Jerusalem; tel. (2) 5611066; e-mail contact@blmj.org; internet www.blmj.org; f. 1992; ancient Near Eastern history and Biblical archaeology; Chair. BATYA BOROWSKI; Dir AMANDA WEISS; Deputy Dir ORIT LEV-SEGEV.

Israel Museum: POB 71117, 91710 Jerusalem; tel. (2) 6708811; e-mail info@imj.org.il; internet www.imj.org.il; f. 1965; fine art, Judaica and archaeology from Biblical times to the present; Shrine of the Book housing Dead Sea Scrolls; Billy Rose Sculpture Garden; library of 65,000 vols; Dir JAMES S. SNYDER; publ. *Journal* (1 a year).

Mayer, L. A., Museum for Islamic Art: POB 4088, 2 Hapalmach St, 91040 Jerusalem; tel. (2) 5661291; e-mail islamart@netvision.net.il; internet www.islamicart.co.il; f. 1974; colln of Islamic art: metalwork, glass, miniatures, ceramics, ivories, jewellery; Sir David Salomons colln of antique clocks and watches; educational activities in Jewish and Arab sectors; photographs and slides; library of 14,000 vols, 50 periodicals; Dir RACHEL HASSON.

Museum of Prehistory, Institute of Archaeology, Hebrew University: Mt Scopus Campus, 91905 Jerusalem; tel. (2) 5882099; internet archaeology.huji.ac.il; f. 1955; large colln of objects from prehistoric sites in Israel; library.

Museum of Taxes: 42 Agripas St, POB 3100, 91036 Jerusalem; tel. (2) 6257597; e-mail misim@mof.gov.il; internet ozar.mof.gov.il/museum; f. 1964; 5 sections: artefacts from the Land of Canaan and environs, taxes levied specifically on Jews in the diaspora, gen. section for tax-related items from all over the world, taxation in Israel, prevention of smuggling and importation of illegal goods and other customs-related issues; Dir MIRA DROR; publ. *Israeli Tax Review* (4 a year).

Museum of the Studium Biblicum Franciscanum: Monastery of the Flagellation, Via Dolorosa, POB 19424, 91193 Jerusalem; tel. (2) 6270456; e-mail secretary@studiumbiblicum.org; f. 1902; Palestinian archaeology: city coins of Palestine, Roman-Byzantine-Crusader pottery and objects; ancient model of Holy Sepulchre, Bethlehem treasure, bronze objects, seals, Egyptian findings, Mesopotamian colln, glassware, weights, amulets, antiphonaries, picture gallery, Pharmacy of St. Saviour's, Numismatic colln and inscriptions; Curator Prof. EUGENIO ALLIATA; Sec. ROSARIO PIERRI; publ. *SBF Museum*.

Yad Vashem, Holocaust Martyrs' and Heroes' Remembrance Authority: Mount of Remembrance, POB 3477, 90435 Jerusalem; tel. (2) 6443400; e-mail general.information@yadvashem.org.il; internet www.yadvashem.org; f. 1953; the Jewish people's nat. memorial to the Holocaust; Holocaust History museum: permanent exhibition of photographs, documents, artefacts and testimonies; Hall of Names; Hall of Remembrance; Children's Memorial; Valley of the Communities; Memorial to the Deportees; Ave and Garden of the Righteous Among the Nations; Holocaust art museum; Int. Institute for Holocaust Research is responsible for expanding academic and research activities; Int. School for Holocaust Studies organizes seminars and develops teaching materials; library of 123,000 vols; world's largest repository of archival and documentary information on the Holocaust: approx. 68m. pages of documents, microfilms, testimonies, diaries, artefacts; Chair. AVNER SHALEV; publ. *Yad Vashem Studies*.

Kibbutz Hazorea

Wilfrid Israel Museum of Oriental Art and Studies: Kibbutz Hazorea, 30060 Post Hazorea; f. 1947; opened 1951 in memory of the late Wilfrid Israel; a cultural centre for study and art exhibitions incl. modern art and all areas of the plastic arts; houses the Wilfrid Israel colln of Near and Far Eastern art and cultural materials; local archaeological exhibits from neolithic to Byzantine times; art library; Dir EHUD DOR.

Kibbutz Lahav

Museum of Bedouin Culture: Joe Alon Centre, Kibbutz Lahav, 85335 Negev D. N.; tel. (8) 9913322; e-mail joealon@lhv.org.il; internet www.joealon.org.il; f. 1985; part of the Col Joe Alon Centre for Regional and Folklore Studies; exhibition of contemporary arts and crafts, educational lectures and guided tours, photographs, demonstrations of Bedouin life (weaving, cooking, etc.); museum of Jewish settlement in the Negev; art gallery; museum of the Bar-Kokba Rebellion; awards grants for research in Bedouin and regional studies; library of 150 vols, 3,000 slides; Gen. Dir RACHEL ALON-MARGALIT.

Kiryat Shmona

Tel-Hai Museum: 12210 Tel-Hai, Upper Galilee; tel. (4) 6951333; reconstruction of a Jewish settlement from the beginning of the 20th century; documents of Joseph Trumpeldor and his defence of the region in 1920.

Ma'ayan Baruch

Ma'ayan Baruch Prehistory Museum of the Huleh Valley: 12220 Ma'ayan Baruch, Upper Galilee; tel. (4) 523791649; f. 1952; prehistory of the Huleh Valley from the Palaeolithic (incl. large colln of Ashulian handaxes) to the Chalcolithic period; locally excavated Bronze Age and Roman-Byzantine objects; colln of stone grain mills and oil presses; the Earliest Dog in the World, buried with a woman from the Natufian period (10,000 BC); plaster skull from Neolithic era (7000 BC); world ethnographic exhibition of tools fashioned by people who still live as in prehistoric times; Dir A. ASSAF.

Nazareth

Terra Sancta Museum: Terra Sancta Monastery, POB 23, 96100 Nazareth; tel. (4) 6572501; f. 1920; Byzantine (and later) remains, coins, Roman and Byzantine glass; colln of antiquities from excavations made in the monastery compound; Vicar of Monastery Rev. P. JOSÉ MONTALVERNE DE LANCASTRE.

Safad

Israel Bible Museum: c/o POB 1396, Safed; tel. (4) 6999972; internet www.israelbiblemuseum.com; f. 1984; exhibition of the biblical art of Phillip Ratner; permanent and changing exhibitions incl. Kabbalah and art for children; Dir AMI SHOSHAN.

Tel-Aviv

Ben-Gurion House: 17 Ben-Gurion Blvds, 63454 Tel-Aviv; tel. (3) 5221010; e-mail bghouse@bezeqint.net; f. 1974; residence of David Ben-Gurion, first Prime Minister of the State of Israel; museum and research and study centre; library of 20,000 vols and periodicals on history of Zionist movement, land and state of Israel, ancient peoples, cultures, religions and philosophies, gen. and military history; Dir HANNI HERMOLIN.

Beth Hatefutsoth (Nahum Goldmann Museum of the Jewish Diaspora): POB 39359, 61392 Tel-Aviv; tel. (3) 7457890; e-mail armoni@bh.org.il; internet www.bh.org.il; f. 1978; permanent exhibition tells the story of Jewish survival and life in the diaspora; temporary exhibitions portray Jewish communities all over the world; seminars and youth educational activities; photographic and film archives; Jewish Genealogy and music centre; CEO AVINOAM ARMONI.

Eretz-Israel Museum: 2 Chaim Levanon St, POB 17068, Ramat-Aviv, 61170 Tel-Aviv; tel. (3) 6415244; internet www.eretzmuseum.org.il; Tel-Aviv region archaeology and history, Jewish ethnography and folklore, ceramics, ancient glass, numismatics, history of Jewish theatre, tools and technology, planetarium; library of 40,000 vols.

Tel-Aviv Museum of Art: 27 Shaul Hamelech Blvd, POB 33288, 64329 Tel-Aviv; tel. (3) 6077000; e-mail cliffs@tamuseum.com; internet www.tamuseum.com; f. 1932; art colln consisting of works since 16th century; Israeli art; library: art library of 60,000 vols, periodicals, microfiches, databases; Dir and Chief Curator Prof. MORDECHAI OMER.

Universities

BAR-ILAN UNIVERSITY

52900 Ramat-Gan

Telephone: (3) 5318111
E-mail: director-general.office@mail.biu.ac.il
Internet: www.biu.ac.il

Founded 1953, inaugurated 1955
State control
Language of instruction: Hebrew
Academic year: October to June

4 Regional colleges; Ashkelon College, Jordan Valley College, Safed College, Western Galilee College; 76 research centres

Pres.: Prof. MOSHE KAVEH
Vice-Pres. for Research: Prof. HAROLD BASCH
Assoc. Vice-Pres.: JUDITH HAIMOFF
Rector: Prof. JOSEPH MENIS
Dir-Gen.: HAIM GLICK
Academic Registrar: M. MISHAN
Librarian: (vacant)

Library: see under Libraries and Archives
Number of teachers: 1,400
Number of students: 31,700

Publication: *Philosophia* (4 a year)

DEANS

Faculty of Exact Sciences: Prof. A. AMIR
Faculty of Humanities: Prof. B. ABRAHAMOV
Faculty of Jewish Studies: Prof. M. ORFALI
Faculty of Law: Prof. A. REICH
Faculty of Life Sciences: Prof. H. BREITBART
Faculty of Social Sciences: Prof. S. SANDLER

PROFESSORS

Faculty of Exact Sciences (tel. (3) 5318585; e-mail exacts@mail.biu.ac.il; internet www.esc.biu.ac.il):

AGRONOVSKY, M., Mathematics
AMIR, A., Computer Science
BASCH, H., Chemistry
BERKOWITZ, R., Physics
DEUTSCH, M., Physics
EHRENBERG, B., Physics
EISENBERG, L., Mathematics
FREULIKHER, V., Physics
FREUND, Y., Physics
FRIEDMAN, L., Mathematics
FRIMER, A., Chemistry
GEDANKEN, A., Chemistry
GOLDSCHMIDT, Z., Chemistry
GORDON, A., Chemistry
HALPERN, H., Physics
HAVLIN, S., Physics
HOCHBERG, K., Mathematics
HOZ, S., Chemistry
KANTOR, I., Physics
KAVEH, M., Physics
KAY, K., Chemistry
KESSLER, D., Physics
KRAUSS, S., Computer Science
KRUSHKAL, S., Mathematics
MARGEL, S., Chemistry
MARGOLIS, S., Mathematics
MARZBACH, E., Mathematics
NUDELMAN, A., Chemistry
ORBACH, D., Chemistry
PERSKY, A., Chemistry
RABIN, I., Physics
RAPPAPORT, D., Physics
ROSENBLUH, M., Physics
ROWEN, L., Mathematics
SHAPIRA, B., Physics
SHLIMAK, I., Physics
SHNIDER, S., Mathematics
SUKENIK, H., Chemistry
TEICHER, M., Mathematics
ULMAN, A., Chemistry
YESHURUN, Y., Physics
ZALCMAN, L., Mathematics

Faculty of Humanities (tel. (3) 5318370; e-mail segalil@mail.biu.ac.il; internet www.biu.ac.il/hu):

ABRAHAMOV, B., Arabic
FINE, J., English
HALAMISH, M., Philosophy
HANDELMAN, S., English
HARVEY, S., Philosophy
HASSINE, J., Comparative Literature
KATZOFF, R., Classical Studies
KOREN, R., French Culture
LANGERMAN, Z., Arabic
PERL, J., English
REICHELBERG, R., Comparative Literature
ROTHSTEIN, S., English
SAGUY, A., Philosophy
SCHWARTZ, D., Philosophy
SPOLSKY, E., English
WIDOKER, D., Philosophy

Faculty of Jewish Studies (tel. (3) 5318233; e-mail jsfcty@mail.biu.ac.il; internet www.biu.ac.il/js):

BAR TIKVAH, B., Literature of the Jewish People
BAUMGARTEN, A., Jewish History
COHEN, M., General History
COHEN, T., Literature of the Jewish People
DISHON, Y., Literature of the Jewish People
FEINER, S., Jewish History
GENIZI, H., General History
HAVLIN, S. Z., Talmud and Information Sciences
HAZAN, E., Literature of the Jewish People
KASHER, R., Bible
KLONER, A., Land of Israel Studies
KOGEL, J., Bible
LIPSKER, A., Literature of the Jewish People
MICHMAN, D., Jewish History
MILIKOWSKI, H., Talmud
ORFALI, M., Jewish History
ROSMAN, M., Jewish History
SAFRAI, Z., Land of Israel Studies
SCHWARTZ, J., Land of Israel Studies
SCHWARTZWALD, O., Hebrew Language
SHARVIT, S., Hebrew Language
SOKOLOFF, M., Hebrew and Semitic Languages
SPERBER, D., Talmud
SPIEGEL, Y., Talmud
TABORI, Y., Talmud
TAUBER, E., History of the Middle East
TOAFF, A., Jewish History
VARGON, S., Bible
WEISS, H., Literature of the Jewish People

Faculty of Law (tel. (3) 5318417; e-mail olmertr@mail.biu.ac.il; internet www.law.biu.ac.il):

COHEN, Z.
LERNER, S.

Faculty of Life Sciences (tel. (3) 5318721; e-mail landmar@mail.biu.ac.il; internet life-sciences.biu.ac.il):

ACHITUV, Y.
BREITBART, H.
BRODIE, C.
COHEN, Y.
HAAS, E.
KISLEV, M.
MALIK, Z.
MAYEVSKY, A.
SAMPSON, S.
SHAINBERG, A.
SHOHAM, Y.
SREDNI, B.
STEINBERGER, J.
SUSSWEIN, A.

Faculty of Social Sciences (tel. (3) 5318452; e-mail socials@mail.biu.ac.il; internet www.biu.ac.il/soc):

ADAD, M., Criminology
ALPEROVITCH, G., Economics
BABKOFF, H., Psychology
COHEN, S., Political Science
DON-YEHIEH, E., Political Science
FRIEDMAN, M., Sociology
GAZIEL, H., School of Education
GOLDREICH, Y., Geography
GREILSAMMER, I., Political Studies
HALEVY-SPIRO, M., Social Work
HILLMANN, A., Economics
INBAR, E., Political Science
IRAM, Y., Education
JAFFE, E., Business Administration
KATZ, J., Geography
KLEIN, P., Education
KOSLOWSKY, M., Psychology
KRAWITZ, S., Psychology
LAUTERBACH, B., School of Business Administration
LAVEE, H., Geography
LEVI-SHIFF, R., Psychology
MENIS, J., Education
MEVARECH, Z., Education
MIKULINCER, M., Psychology
NACHSHON, I., Criminology
NITZAN, S., Economics
ORBACH, I., Psychology
RABINOWITZ, J., Social Work
SANDLER, S., Political Science
SCHWARZWALD, J., Psychology
SHULMAN, S., Psychology
SILBER, J., Economics
TAPIERO, C., Economics
TZURIEL, D., School of Education
VAKIL, E., Psychology
WELLER, A., Psychology
WOLF, Y., Criminology
YEHUDA, S., Psychology
YITZCHAKI, H., Social Work
ZIDERMAN, A., Economics
ZISSER, B., Political Science

BEN GURION UNIVERSITY OF THE NEGEV

POB 653, 84105 Be'ersheva
Telephone: (8) 6461223
E-mail: rector@bgu.ac.il
Internet: www.bgu.ac.il
Founded 1965
Languages of instruction: English, Hebrew
Academic year: October to June
Pres.: Prof. RIVKA CARMI
Rector: Prof. JIMMY WEINBLATT
Vice-Pres. and Dir-Gen.: DAVID BAREKET
Vice-Pres. and Dean for Research and Devt: Prof. MORDECHAY HERSKOWITZ
Vice-Pres. for External Affairs: Prof. AMOS DRORY
Dir of Public Affairs: NINA PERLIS
Librarian: AVNER SCHMUELEVITZ
Library: see under Libraries and Archives
Number of teachers: 1,000
Number of students: 17,000
Publications: *Geography Research Forum, HAGAR—International Social Science Review, Israel Social Science Research Journal, Israel Studies, JAMA'A—Interdisciplinary Journal for the Study of the Middle East, MIKAN—Research Journal of Hebrew Literature, Shvut—Studies in Russian and East European Jewish History and Culture*

DEANS

Faculty of Engineering Sciences: Prof. GABI BEN-DOR
Faculty of Health Sciences: Prof. SHAUL SOFER
Faculty of Humanities and Social Sciences: Prof. MOSHE JUSTMAN
Faculty of Natural Sciences: Prof. AMIR SAGI
Guilford Glazer School of Business and Management: Prof. ARIE REICHEL
Kreitman School of Advanced Graduate Studies: Prof. RAMY BRUSTEIN

PROFESSORS

Faculty of Engineering Sciences (tel. (8) 6479270; e-mail offcdean@bgumail.bgu.ac.il; internet cmsprod.bgu.ac.il/eng/engn):

AHARONI, H., Electrical and Computer Engineering
ALFASSI, Z., Nuclear Engineering
APELBLAT, A., Chemical Engineering
ARAZI, B., Electrical and Computer Engineering
BEN-DOR, G., Mechanical Engineering
BEN-YAAKOV, S., Electrical and Computer Engineering
CENSOR, D., Electrical and Computer Engineering
DARIEL, M., Materials Engineering
DINSTEIN, I., Electrical and Computer Engineering
DUBI, A., Nuclear Engineering
EILON, A., Electrical and Computer Engineering
ELIEZER, D., Materials Engineering
ELPERIN, T., Mechanical Engineering
FINGER, N., Industrial Engineering and Management
FUKS, D., Materials Engineering
GALPERIN, A., Nuclear Engineering
GOTTLIEB, M., Chemical Engineering
HAVA, S., Electrical and Computer Engineering
HERSKOWITZ, M., Chemical Engineering
IGRA, O., Mechanical Engineering
JACOB, I., Nuclear Engineering
KAPLAN, B., Electrical and Computer Engineering
KOPEIKA, N., Electrical and Computer Engineering
KOST, J., Chemical Engineering
LADANY, S., Industrial Engineering and Management
LETAN, R., Mechanical Engineering
MENIPAZ, E., Industrial Engineering and Management
MERCHUK, J., Chemical Engineering
MOND, M., Mechanical Engineering
PERL, M., Mechanical Engineering
PLISKIN, J., Industrial Engineering and Management
PLISKIN, N., Industrial Engineering and Management
PORTMAN, V., Mechanical Engineering
RONEN, Y., Nuclear Engineering
ROTMAN, S., Electrical and Computer Engineering
SCHULGASSER, K., Mechanical Engineering
SEGEV, R., Mechanical Engineering
SHACHAM, M., Chemical Engineering
SHANI, G., Nuclear Engineering
SHER, E., Mechanical Engineering
SHINAR, D., Industrial Engineering and Management
SHUVAL, P., Information Systems Engineering
SINUANI-STERN, Z., Industrial Engineering and Management
SLONIM, M., Electrical and Computer Engineering
TALYANKER, M., Materials Engineering
TAMIR, A., Chemical Engineering
VILNAY, O., Construction Engineering
VOLLICH, D., Electrical and Computer Engineering
WISNIAK, J., Chemical Engineering
ZARETSKY, E., Mechanical Engineering

Faculty of Health Sciences (tel. (8) 6477409; e-mail rtemes@bgumail.bgu.ac.il; internet www.fohs.bgu.ac.il):

ABOUD, M., Microbiology and Immunology
ALKAN, M., Internal Medicine
APPELBAUM, A., Cardiology
APTE, R., Microbiology and Immunology
BASHAN, N., Clinical Biochemistry
BENJAMIN, J., Psychiatry
BUSKILA, D., Internal Medicine
CARMEL, S., Health Sociology
CARMI, R., Clinical Genetics
CLARFIELD, M., Geriatrics
FRASER, D., Epidemiology
GROSSMAN, Y., Physiology
GURMAN, G., Anaesthesiology
HALEVI, S., Dermatology
HALLAK, M., Gynaecology
HELDMAN, E., Physiology
HERZANO, Y., Radiology
ILIA, R., Cardiology
ISAKOV, N., Microbiology and Immunology
KATZ, M., Gynaecology
LEVY, R., Biochemistry
LEVY, Y., Biochemistry
LUNENFELD, E., Gynaecology
MARGULIS, C., Medical Education
MAZOR, M., Gynaecology
MEYERSTEIN, N., Physiology
MORAN, A., Physiology

NAGGAN, L., Epidemiology
NEUMANN, L., Epidemiology
PIURA, B., Gynaecology
PORATH, A., Internal Medicine
POTASHNIK, G., Gynaecology
RAGER, B., Microbiology and Immunology
SCHLESINGER, M., Paediatrics
SCHVARTZMAN, P., Family Medicine
SEGAL, S., Microbiology and Immunology
SHARONI, Y., Clinical Biochemistry
SCHLAEFFER, F., Internal Medicine
SHANY, SH., Clinical Biochemistry
SIKULER, E., Internal Medicine
SOFER, S., Paediatrics
SUKENIK, S., Internal Medicine
TAL, A., Paediatrics
WEINSTEIN, J., Microbiology
WHITE, E., Morphology

Faculty of Humanities and Social Sciences (tel. (8) 6461105; e-mail henik@bgumail.bgu.ac.il; internet www.bgu.ac.il/html/academics.html):

ALEXANDER, T., Hebrew Literature
BAR-ON, D., Behavioural Sciences
BENZION, U., Economics
BLIDSTEIN, G., Jewish Thought
BORG, A., Hebrew Language
BOWMAN, D., Geography and Environmental Development
BRAVERMAN, A., Economics
BREGMAN, D., Hebrew Literature
CASPI, D., Communication Studies
DANZINGER, L., Economics
DREMAN, S., Behavioural Sciences
EINY, E., Economics
GELMAN, Y., Philosophy
GILAD, I., Bible and Ancient Near-Eastern Studies
GORDON, D., Education
GORDON, H., Education
GORODETSKY, M., Education
GRADUS, Y., Geography and Environmental Development
GRIES, Z., Jewish Thought
GRUBER, I., Bible and Ancient Near-Eastern Studies
HENIK, A., Behavioural Sciences
HOCHMAN, O., Economics
HUROWITZ, V., Bible and Ancient Near-Eastern Studies
ISRALOWITZ, R., Social Work
JUSTMAN, M., Economics
KRAKOVER, S., Geography and Environmental Development
KREISEL, H., Jewish Thought
LARONNE, J., Geography and Environmental Development
LASKER, D., Jewish Thought
LAZIN, F., Behavioural Sciences
LIBERLES, R., History
LURIE, Y., Philosophy
MEIR, A., Geography and Environmental Development
MORRIS, B., Middle East Studies
OREN, E., Bible and Ancient Near-Eastern Studies
PARUSH, A., Philosophy
POZNANSKI, R., Politics and Government
PRIEL, B., Behavioural Sciences
QIMRON, E., Hebrew Language
REGEV, U., Economics
ROSEN, S., Bible and Ancient Near-Eastern Studies
SALMON, Y., History
SHAROT, S., Behavioural Sciences
SHINAR, D., General Studies
SIVAN, D., Hebrew Language
STERN, E., Geography and Environmental Development
TALSHIR, Z., Bible and Ancient Near-Eastern Studies
TOBIN, I., Foreign Languages and Literature
TROEN, I., History
TSAHOR, Z., History
TSOAR, H., Geography and Environmental Development
TZELGOV, Y., Behavioural Sciences
VINNER, S., Science and Technology Education
WEINBLATT, J., Economics

Faculty of Natural Sciences (tel. (8) 6461633; e-mail mia@math.bgu.ac.il; internet www.bgu.ac.il/html/academics.html):

ABRAHAM, U., Mathematics
ABRAMSKY, Z., Life Sciences
ALPAI, D., Mathematics
ALTSHULER, A., Mathematics
AVISHAI, Y., Physics
BAHAT, D., Geological and Environmental Sciences
BAND, Y., Chemistry
BARAK, Z., Life Sciences
BECKER, J., Chemistry
BELITSKI, H., Mathematics
BEREND, D., Mathematics
BERNSTEIN, J., Chemistry
BITTNER, S., Chemistry
BRUSTEIN, R., Physics
CHIPMAN, D., Life Sciences
COHEN, M., Mathematics
DAVIDSON, A., Physics
EFRIMA, S., Chemistry
EICHLER, D., Physics
EISENBERG, T., Mathematics
FEINTUCH, A., Mathematics
FONF, V., Mathematics
FUHRMANN, P. A., Mathematics
GEDALIN, M., Physics
GERSTEN, A., Physics
GLASER, R., Chemistry
GOLDSHTEIN, V., Mathematics
GOREN, S., Physics
GORODETSKY, G., Physics
GRANOT, Y., Life Sciences
HODORKOVSKY, V., Chemistry
HOROVITZ, B., Physics
HOROWITZ, Y., Physics
KISCH, H., Geological and Environmental Sciences
KOJMAN, M., Mathematics
KOST, D., Chemistry
LIN, M., Mathematics
MEIR, Y., Physics
MIZRAHI, Y., Life Sciences
MOALEM, A., Physics
MORDECHAI, S., Physics
MOREH, R., Physics
OWEN, D., Physics
PAROLA, A., Chemistry
POLAK, M., Chemistry
PRIEL, Z., Chemistry
PROSS, A., Chemistry
RABINOVITSCH, A., Physics
ROSENWAKS, S., Physics
RUBIN, M., Mathematics
SCHARF, B., Chemistry
SEGEV, Y., Mathematics
SHOSHAN-BARMATZ, V., Life Sciences
SHUKER, R., Physics
TKACHENKO, V., Mathematics
ZARITSKY, A., Life Sciences

Guilford Glazer School of Business and Management (tel. (8) 6472190; e-mail sompr@nihul.bgu.ac.il; internet www.bgu.ac.il/som):

BAR-ELI, M., Business Administration
DRORY, A., Business Administration
GIDRON, B., Business Administration
MALACH-PINES, A., Business Administration
PREISS, K., Business Administration
REICHEL, A., Hotel and Tourism Management

ATTACHED RESEARCH INSTITUTES

Ben-Gurion Research Institute for the Study of Israel: tel. (8) 6596936; e-mail moreshet@bgu.ac.il; internet cmsprod.bgu.ac.il/eng/centers/bgi; f. 1976; publ. *Israel Studies* (3 a year), *Iyunim Bitkumat Israel* (1 a year); Dir MICHAL MOUYAL.

Homeland Security Research Institute: tel. (8) 6596936; e-mail doronhav@bgu.ac.il; internet cmsprod.bgu.ac.il/eng/centers/hsri; Dir Prof. DORON HAVAZALET.

Jacob Blaustein Institute for Desert Research: Sde Boker Campus, 84990 Be'er-sheva; tel. (8) 6596777; e-mail bidr@bgu.ac.il; internet www.bgu.ac.il/bidr; f. 1974; Dir Prof. AVIGAD VONSHAK.

National Institute for Biotechnology in the Negev: tel. (8) 6461963; e-mail vardasb@bgu.ac.il; internet cmsprod.bgu.ac.il/eng/centers/nibn; Dir Prof. VARDA SHOSHAN BARMATZ.

Research Institute for Jewish and Israeli Literature and Culture: tel. (8) 6596936; e-mail heksher@bgu.ac.il; internet cmsprod.bgu.ac.il/eng/centers/heksherim; f. 2001; Dir Prof. YIGAL SCHWARTZ

HEBREW UNIVERSITY OF JERUSALEM

Mt Scopus, 91905 Jerusalem
Telephone: (2) 6585111
E-mail: admission@savion.huji.ac.il
Internet: www.huji.ac.il
Founded 1918
Private control, partially supported by the Govt
Academic year: October to June
Language of instruction: Hebrew
Chair., Board of Govs: MICHAEL FEDERMANN
Pres.: Prof. MENACHEM BEN-SASSON
Vice-Pres. and Dir-Gen.: BILLY SHAPIRA
Vice-Pres. for External Relations: Prof. RONNIE FRIEDMAN
Vice-Pres. and Chair. of the Authority for Research and Devt: Prof. ISAIAH ARKIN
Rector: Prof. ASHER COHEN
Vice-Rector: Prof. ORON SHAGRIR
Vice-Rector: Prof. ORNA KUPFERMAN
Dean for Students: Prof. YEHUDA SHAVIT
Acad. Sec.: IRIT MAGORA-LEVI
Number of teachers: 1,200
Number of students: 23,250

Publications: *ACTA-Analysis of Current Trends in Antisemitism* (2–3 a year, in English), *Aleph: Historical Studies in Science and Judaism* (1 a year, in English), *Antisemitism International* (1 a year, in English), *Edah Velashon* (Publ. of the Hebrew Univ. Jewish Oral Traditions Research Centre, 1 a year, in Hebrew), *Hispania Judaica Bulletin* (History, Culture, Thought, Literature, Art and Language of Jews in the Iberian Peninsula, in English), *Hukim-journal on Legislation*, *Israel Journal of Mathematics* (6 a year, in English), *Israel Law Review* (3 a year, in English), *Italia* (History, Culture and Literature of the Jews of Italy, 1 a year, multilingual), *Iyyun* (Journal of Philosophy, 4 a year; 2 a year in Hebrew, 2 a year in English), *Jerusalem Review of Legal Studies*, *Jerusalem Studies in Arabic and Islam (JSAI)* (1 a year, mostly with English contributions but also Arabic, French and German), *Jerusalem Studies in Hebrew Language* (1 a year, in Hebrew), *Jerusalem Studies in Hebrew Literature* (1 a year, in Hebrew), *Jerusalem Studies in Jewish Folklore* (1 a year, in Hebrew), *Jerusalem Studies in Jewish Thought* (1 a year, in Hebrew), *Jewish Law Annual*, *Jews in Russia Eastern Europe* (in English, published in cooperation with the Leonid Nevzlin Research Centre), *Journal d'Analyse Mathématique* (3 a year, in English), *Journal of Experimental Criminology* (4 a year, in English), *Massorot*

(Studies in Language Traditions of Hebrew and Aramaic, 1 a year, in Hebrew), *Mishpatim* (Law, 3 a year, in Hebrew and English), *Partial Answers* (Journal of Literature and the History of Ideas, in English), *Perspectives* (Humanistic Studies, in particular Literature, History and Arts, 1 a year, in French), *Politika* (Journal of Israeli political science and int. relations, in Hebrew), *QAEDEM: Monographs of the Institute of Archaeology* (1–2 a year, in English), *QEDEM Reports* (Archaeology, 1–2 a year, in English), *Shnaton Hamishpat Haivri* (Jewish Law, in Hebrew), *Shnaton: Annual for Biblical and Ancient Near Eastern Studies* (1 a year, in Hebrew), *Studies in Contemporary Jewry* (1 a year, in English, published in conjunction with Oxford Univ. Press), *Studies in Jewish Education* (1 a year, in Hebrew and English), *Tarbiz* (Jewish studies, 4 a year, in Hebrew), *Yearbook of Jewish Law*

DEANS

Faculty of Dental Medicine: Prof. AARON PALMON
Faculty of Humanities: Prof. REUVEN AMITAI
Faculty of Law: Prof. YUVAL SHANY
Faculty of Mathematics and Natural Science: Prof. YGAL EREL
Faculty of Medicine: (vacant)
Faculty of Social Sciences: Prof. VERED VINITZKY-SEROUSSI
Jerusalem School of Business Administration: Prof. YISHAY YAFEH
Paul Baerwald School of Social Work and Social Welfare: Prof. JOHN GAL
Robert H. Smith Faculty of Agriculture, Food and Environment: Prof. SHMUEL WOLF

PROFESSORS

Faculty of Agricultural, Food and Environmental Science (POB 12, Rehovot; tel. (8) 9489111; e-mail dotanz@savion.huji.ac.il; internet www.agri.huji.ac.il):

ABBO, S., Plant Sciences and Genetics in Agriculture
ADAM, Z., Plant Sciences and Genetics in Agriculture
BANETH, G., Veterinary Medicine
CAHANER, A., Plant Sciences and Genetics in Agriculture
CZOSNEK, H., Plant Sciences and Genetics in Agriculture
FEINERMAN, E., Agricultural Economics
FRIEDMAN, A., Animal Sciences
HADAR, Y., Plant Pathology and Microbiology
HALEVY, O., Animal Sciences
MEIDAN, R., Animal Sciences
NUSSINOVITCH, A., Biochemistry, Food Science and Nutrition
SAGUY, I., Biochemistry, Food Science and Nutrition
SHOSEYOV, O., Plant Sciences and Genetics in Agriculture
TSUR, Y., Agricultural Economics
VAINSTEIN, A., Plant Sciences and Genetics in Agriculture
WALLACH, R., Soil and Water Sciences
WEISS, D., Plant Sciences and Genetics in Agriculture
WOLF, S., Plant Sciences and Genetics in Agriculture
WOLFENSON, D., Animal Sciences
YARDEN, O., Plant Pathology and Microbiology
YUVAL, B., Entomology
ZAMIR, D., Plant Sciences and Genetics in Agriculture

Faculty of Dental Medicine (En Kerem Campus, POB 12272, 91120 Jerusalem; tel. (2) 6158595; e-mail dentistry_sa@savion.huji.ac.il; internet dental.huji.ac.il):

(Hebrew Univ.—Hadassah School of Dental Medicine)

BAB, I., Oral Pathology
DEUTSCH, D., Dental Sciences
MANN, J., Community Dentistry
NITZAN, D., Oral and Maxillofacial Surgery
SELA, M., Oral Biology
SHAPIRA, L., Periodontics
STABHOLZ, A., Endodontics
STEINBERG, D., Oral Biology
TAL, M., Dental Sciences

Faculty of Humanities (Mt Scopus, 91905 Jerusalem; tel. (2) 6585111; e-mail admission@savion.huji.ac.il; internet www.huji.ac.il):

(the Joseph and Ceil Mazer Centre for the Humanities, incl. the Institute of Asian and African Studies; Archaeology; Contemporary Jewry; Jewish Studies; Western Cultures)

AMITAI, R., Islamic and Middle Eastern Studies
BARTAL, I., Jewish History
BAR YAFFE, Y., Spanish and Latin American Studies
BELFER-COHEN, A., Archaeology
BEN-SASSON, M., Jewish History
BRODY, R., Talmudic Studies
BUDICK, E., American Studies
BUNIS, D., Hebrew Language
COHEN, E., History
COHEN, R., Jewish History
COTTON, H., History and Classics
DINER, D., History
DORON, E., Linguistics
ELIZUR, S., Hebrew Literature
ENOCH, D., Philosophy and Law
FOX, D., Linguistics and Cognitive Science
GOLOMB, J., Philosophy
GOREN-INBAR, N., Archaeology
GORING-MORRIS, N., Archaeology
HALBERTAL, M., Jewish Thought and Philosophy
HERMAN, G., History
HEVER, H., Hebrew Literature
HIRSCHFELD, A., Hebrew Literature
HOPKINS, S. A., Arabic Language and Literature
KADISH, A., History
KAHANA, M., Talmudic Studies
KAPLAN, S., Comparative Religion and African Studies
KISTER, M., Jewish Studies
LECKER, M., Arabic Language and Literature
LEDERHENDLER, E., History
MAMAN, A., Hebrew Language
NAEH, S., Talmud and Jewish Thought
PATRICK, J., Archaeology
POZY, C., Philosophy
RAPPAPORT-HOVAV, M., English Literature
ROJTMAN, B., French Language and Literature, General and Comparative Literature
SCHULMAN, D., Indian Studies and Comparative Religion
SCHWARTZ, D., Jewish History
SEROUSSI, E., Musicology
SHINAN, A., Hebrew Literature
SZABAR, S., Hebrew Literature and Art
TAUBE, M., Linguistics and Slavic Studies
TIMENCHIK, R., Russian and Slavic Studies
TOCH, M., History
TOKER, L., English Literature
WAHRMAN, D., History
WEISS, Y., History
WEISS, Z., Archeology
WOLOSKY, S., English Literature
YUVAL, I., Jewish History
ZAKAI, A., History

Faculty of Law (tel. (2) 5882528; e-mail law_sa@savion.huji.ac.il; internet law.huji.ac.il):

(incl. the Harry Sacher Institute for Legislative Research and Comparative Law, the Israel Matz Institute for Research in Jewish Law, and the Minerva Center for Human Rights)

AJZENSTADT, M., Sociology of Law
DOTAN, Y., Public Law
ENOCH, D., Moral, Political and Legal Philosophy
FASSBERG, C., Private International Law, Comparative Law, Legal History
GUR-ARYE, M., Criminal Law
HAREL, A., Jurisprudence, Theory of Rights, Economic Analysis of Law
HIRSCH, M., International Law-Public/Trade/Environmental, European Community law
LEWINSOHN-ZAMIR, D., Property Law, Land Use and Planning Law
LIFSCHITZ, B., Jewish Law
SHANY, Y., International Law, Courts and Tribunals, Humanitarian, Human Rights
SHETREET, S., Public Law and the Judiciary
WEISBURD, D., White Collar Crime, Policing
ZAMIR, E., Contract Law

Faculty of Medicine (Mt Scopus, 91905 Jerusalem; tel. (2) 6585111; e-mail admission@savion.huji.ac.il; internet www.huji.ac.il):

(the Hebrew Univ.—Hadassah Medical School, incl. the Institute for Medical Research–Israel Canada (IMRIC), the Hadassah-Henrietta Szold School of Nursing, the School of Occupational Therapy, the School of Pharmacy, the Braun School of Public Health and Community Medicine)

ALTUVIA, S.
AMSTER-CHODER, O., IMRIC
ARGOV, A., Neurology
ARIEL, I., Pathology
BAR-SHAVIT, Z., Biochemistry, IMRIC
BELLER, U., Obstetrics
BEN-CHETRIT, E., Medicine
BEN-HUR, T., Neurology
BENITA, S., Pharmacy
BEN-NERIAH, Y., Immunology, IMRIC
BEN-YEHUDA, A., Internal Medicine
BEN-YEHUDA, D., Haematology
BERGMAN, H., Medicine Neurobiology, IMRIC
BERGMAN, Y., Developmental Biology, Cancer Research, IMRIC
BERRY, E., Public Health, Nutrition
BIALER, M., Pharmacology
BREUER, R., Medical Imaging
BREZIS, M., Medicine
BURSZTYN, M., Internal Medicine
CHISIN, R., Medical Biophysics and Nuclear Medicine
DOMB, A., Pharmacy
DRENGER, B., Anaesthesiology
ELPELEG, O., Paediatric Medicine
ENGELHARD, D., Paediatric Medicine
FAINSOD, A., Developmental Biology, Cancer Research, IMRIC
FIBACH, E., Experimental Haematology
FRIEDLANDER, Y.
FRIEDMAN, G., Medicine, Geriatrics
GABIZON, R., Neurology
GABIZON, A., Oncology
GALUN, E., Gene Therapy
GERTZ, D., Anatomy
GERTZ, D., IMRIC
GIBSON, D., Pharmacy
GILON, D., Cardiology
GLASER, B., Endocrinology

GOLDBERG, N., Medical Imaging
GOLDBLUM, A., Pharmacy
GOLOMB, G., Pharmacy
GOMORI, M., Radiology
GRANOT, E., Paediatrics
GRUNHAUS, L., Psychiatry
HAMMERMAN, C., Paediatrics
HANSKY, E., IMRIC
HEYMAN, S., Internal Medicine
HIG'AZI, A., Clinical Biochemistry
HOFFMAN, A., Pharmacy
ILAN, Y., Medicine
JAFFE, C., IMRIC
KALCHEIM, C., IMRIC
KANNER, B., Biochemistry, IMRIC
KAPLAN, M., Paediatrics
KEREM, E., Paediatrics
KEREN, A., Cardiology
KOHEN, R., Pharmacy
KOPOLOVIC, J., Pathology
LAUFER, N., Obstetrics and Gynaecology
LEITERSDORF, E., Internal Medicine
LERER, B., Psychiatry
LEV-TOV, A., IMRIC
LEVY-SHAFFER, F., Pharmacology
LIBSON, Y., Medical Imaging
LICHTENSTEIN, D., Physiology
LIEBERGALL, M., Orthopaedic Surgery
LOTAN, C., Cardiology
MANDELBOIM, O., Immunology and Cancer Research
MANOR, O., Public Health
MARGALIT, H., IMRIC
MEYUCHAS, O., Biochemistry
MITRANI-ROSENBAUM, S., Molecular Biology, Gene Therapy
MOSHEIFF, R., Orthopaedics
NAPARSTEK, J., Internal Medicine
NAVEH-MANY, T., Nephrology
OREN, R., Gastroenterology
PEER, J., Ophthalmology
PERETZ- YABLONSKI, T., Oncology
PINES, O., Microbiology, IMRIC
RAZ, I., Internal Medicine
RAZIN, E., Biochemistry, IMRIC
REUBINOFF, B., Obstetrics and Gynaecology
RIVKIND, A., Trauma Surgery
ROSENSHINE, I., Microbiology, IMRIC
ROTSHENKER, S., IMRIC
RUBINSTEIN, A., Pharmacy
SHAPIRA, O., Cardiothoracic Surgery
SHAPIRA, S., Medical Management
SCHATTNER, A., Internal Medicine
SHLOMAI, J., Molecular Biology
SIEGAL, T., Neurology and Neuro-Oncology
SMUELOF, A., Obstetrics
SPRUNG, C. L., Anaesthesiology
STERN, Z., Medical Management
STHOEGER, Z., Internal Medicine
VARON, D., Haematology
VLODAVSKY, I., Oncology
WEISSMAN, C., Anaesthesiology
YAARI, E., Physiology
YAGEL, S., Obstetrics and Gynaecology
YEFENOF, E., Immunology
YINNON, A., Internal Medicine

Faculty of Science (Edmond J. Safra Givat Ram Campus, 91904 Jerusalem; tel. (2) 6585111; e-mail admission@savion.huji.ac.il; internet www.huji.ac.il):

(incl. the Alexander Silberman Institute of Life Sciences; Benin School of Engineering and Computer Science; Hermann Institute of Earth Sciences; Einstein Institute of Mathematics, Institute of Chemistry; Racah Institute of Physics; Interuniversity Institute for Marine Sciences in Eilat; and the Amos de Shalit Science Teaching Centre)

AGAM, O., Physics
AGMON, N., Chemistry
AGNON, A., Earth Sciences
AGRANAT, A., Applied Physics
AHARONOV, D., Computer Science
ARKIN, I., Life Sciences
ASSCHER, M., Chemistry
AVIGAD, D., Earth Sciences
AVNIR, D., Chemistry
BAER, R., Chemistry
BANIN, U., Chemistry
BEKENSTEIN, Y., Theoretical Physics
BELKIN, S., Life Sciences
BEN-ARTZI, M., Mathematics
BEN-OR, M., Computer Science
BENVENISTY, N., Life Sciences
BIALI, S., Chemistry
BIHAM, O., Physics
BINO, A., Chemistry
COHN, D., Applied Chemistry
DARVASI, A., Life Sciences
DEKEL, A., Theoretical Physics
DE-SHALIT, E., Mathematics
DEVOR, M., Life Sciences
DOLEV, D., Computer Science
ENZEL, Y., Earth Sciences
EREL, Y., Earth Sciences
EREZ, J., Earth Sciences and Oceanography
FEINBERG, J., Physics
FELDMAN, Y., Applied Physics
FRIEDLAND, L., Theoretical Physics
FRIEDMAN, N., Computer Science
GALILI, I., Science Teaching Center
GARTI, N., Chemistry
GENIN, A., Life Sciences and Oceanography
GIVEON, A., Physics
GRUENBAUM, Y., Life Sciences
GVIRTZMAN, H., Earth Sciences
HART, S., Mathematics and Economics
HIRSCHBERG, J., Life Sciences
HRUSHOVSKI, E., Mathematics
JOSKOWICZ, L., Computer Science
KADMON, R., Life Sciences
KALAI, G., Mathematics
KAPLAN, A., Life Sciences
KEREM, B., Life Sciences
KHAIN, A., Earth Sciences
KHAZDAN, D., Mathematics
KIFER, Y., Mathematics
KOSLOFF, R., Chemistry
KUPFERMAN, O., Computer Science
KUPFERMAN, R., Mathematics
LAPID, E., Mathematics
LAST, Y., Mathematics
LAZAR, B., Earth Sciences
LEV, O., Life Sciences
LEVIATAN, A., Physics
LEVIN, G., Mathematics
LEWIS, A., Applied Physics
LINDENSTRAUSS, E., Mathematics
LINIAL, M., Life Sciences
LINIAL, N., Computer Science
LISCHINSKI, D., Computer Science
LIVNAH, O., Physics
LIVNE, R., Mathematics
LUBOTZKY, A., Mathematics
MAGDASSI, S., Applied Chemistry
MAGIDOR, M., Mathematics
MANDLER, D., Chemistry
MATTHEWS, A., Earth Sciences
MEERSON, B., Experimental Physics
MILO, O., Physics
MOZES, S., Mathematics
NATHAN, R., Life Sciences
NAVON, O., Earth Sciences
NECHUSHTAI, R., Life Sciences
NELKEN, I., Life Sciences
NEYMAN, A., Mathematics and Economics
NISAN, N., Computer Science
OREN, A., Life Sciences
ORLY, J., Biological Chemistry
OVADYAHU, Z., Experimental Physics
PALDOR, N., Earth Sciences
PAUL, M., Experimental Physics
PELEG, S., Computer Science
PIRAN, Z., Theoretical Physics
RABANI, Y., Computer Sciences
RABINOVICI, E., Theoretical Physics
RIPS, E., Mathematics
ROSENFELD, D., Plant Sciences
ROSENSCHEIN, J., Computer Science
ROTH, M., Applied Physics
RUHMAN, S., Chemistry
SAAR, A., Physics
SAGIV, Y., Computer Science
SAMORODNISKI, A., Computer Science
SARI, R., Physics
SASSON, Y., Applied Chemistry
SCHULDINER, S., Life Sciences
SEGEV, I., Life Sciences
SELA, Z., Mathematics
SHAIK, S., Chemistry
SHALEV, A., Mathematics
SHASHUA, A., Computer Science
SHMIDA, A., Botany
SOLOMON, S., Theoretical Physics
SOMPOLINSKY, H., Physics
SOREQ, H., Biological Chemistry
TISHBY, N., Computer Science
WEINSHALL, D., Computer Science
WEISS, Y., Computer Science
WERMAN, M., Computer Science
WILLNER, I., Chemistry
YAROM, Y., Neurobiology
ZIGLER, A., Physics
ZOHARY, E., Life Sciences

Faculty of Social Sciences (Mt Scopus, 91905 Jerusalem; tel. (2) 6585111; e-mail admission@savion.huji.ac.il; internet www.huji.ac.il):

AHISSAR, M., Psychology
BAR-SIMAN-TOV, Y., International Relations
BENSTOCK, M., Economics
BEN-YEHUDA, N., Sociology
COHEN, A., Psychology
DAYAN, U., Geography
DEOUELL, L., Psychology
DE-SHALIT, A., Political Science
FEITELSON, E., Geography
FROST, R., Psychology
FRUMKIN, A., Geography
GATI, I., Psychology and Education
GOULD, D., Economics
HART, S., Economics
HASSIN, R., Psychology
HAVIV, M., Statistics
HAZAN, R., Political Science
HIRSCH, M., International Relations and Law
ILOUZ, E., Sociology
KANDEL, E., Economics
KELLA, O., Statistics
KREMER, I., Economics
LACH, S., Economics
LAVY, V., Economics
MAOR, M., Political Science
MAOZ, I., Communication
MOAV, O., Economics
OLIVER-LUMERMAN, A., Sociology, Anthropology
OMAN, S., Statistics
POLLAK, M., Statistics
RINOTT, Y., Statistics
RITOV, Y., Statistics
RUBIN, R., Geography
SALOMON, I., Geography and Urban Studies
SCHUL, Y., Psychology
SHALEV, M., Sociology, Anthropology and Political Science
SHAMIR, B., Sociology, Anthropology
SHANON, B., Psychology
SHAVIT, Y., Psychology
SZNAJDER, M., Political Science
TOVIAS, A., International Relations
VERTZBERGER, Y., International Relations
VINITZKY-SEROUSSI, V., Sociology, Anthropology
WINTER, E., Economics
YAKIR, B., Statistics
YIRMIYA, R., Psychology
YIRMIYA, N., Psychology
ZEIRA, J., Economics
ZUCKER, D., Statistics

Jerusalem School of Business Administration (tel. (2) 5883235; internet bschool.huji.ac.il):

AVRAMOV, D., Finance
KANDEL, E., Finance
KREMER, I., Finance
MAZURZKY, O., Marketing
MOSHEIOV, G., Operations Research
OFIR, C., Marketing
YAFEH, Y., Finance

Paul Baerwald School of Social Work and Social Welfare (tel. (2) 5881477; e-mail social-work@savion.huji.ac.il; internet www.sw.huji.ac.il):

GAL, J.
HAJ-YHIA, M.
LITWIN, H.

School of Education (Mt Scopus, 91905 Jerusalem; tel. (2) 6585111; e-mail admission@savion.huji.ac.il; internet www.huji.ac.il):

BUTLER, R., Education
GATI, I., Education, Psychology
HIRSHMAN, M., Jewish Education
RITOV, I., Education
SCHWARZ, B., Education
TATAR, M., Education
ZOHAR, A., Education

OPEN UNIVERSITY OF ISRAEL

108 Ravutski St, POB 808, 43107 Raanana
Telephone: (9) 7780778
E-mail: president@openu.ac.il
Internet: www.openu.ac.il

Founded 1974, fmrly Everyman's Univ., current name adopted 1989
Language of instruction: Hebrew
Academic year: September to June (2 semesters) and summer semester
Courses in the arts, culture, cognition, computer science and natural sciences, communication, democracy, education, economics, management, history, Judaic studies, life sciences, literature, language, mathematics, philosophy, philosophy of science, political science, psychology, sociology, culture, technology; undergraduate and graduate degrees

Chancellor: Lord WOOLF
Deputy Chancellor: Lord ROTHSCHILD
Vice-Chancellor: Prof. ABRAHAM GINZBURG
Pres.: Prof. HAGIT MESSER-YARON
Vice-Pres. for Academic Affairs: Prof. JUDITH GAL-EZER
Dir-Gen.: AMIT SHTREIT
Dean for Academic Studies: Prof. SONIA ROCAS
Dean for Devt and Technology: Prof. YOAV YAIR
Dean for Research: Prof. ANAT BARNEA
Dean for Students: Dr HAIM SAADOUN
Dir of the Library: HAVA MUSTIGMAN

Library of 75,000 vols, 500 ebooks, 92 databases, 20,000 eperiodicals
Number of teachers: 1,693 (80 senior faculty members, 428 junior faculty mems and 1,210 tutors throughout Israel teaching in 50 study centres)
Number of students: 42,300

TEL-AVIV UNIVERSITY

POB 39040, 69978 Tel-Aviv
Telephone: (3) 6408111
E-mail: tauinfo@post.tau.ac.il
Internet: www.tau.ac.il

Founded 1953, inaugurated 1956
Private control, partially supported by the Govt
Language of instruction: Hebrew
Academic year: October to June (2 terms)

Pres.: Prof. JOSEPH KLAFTER
Vice-Pres. for Public Affairs: Dr GARY SUSSMAN
Vice-Pres. for Research and Devt: Prof. EHUD GAZIT
Vice-Pres.: Col (Res.) YEHIEL BEN-ZVI
Rector: Prof. DANY LEVIATAN
Vice-Rector: Prof. ARON SHAI
Dir-Gen.: MORDEHAI KOHN
Academic Sec.: SARA KINEL
Dean of Students: Prof. YOAV ARIEL

Library: see under Libraries and Archives
Number of teachers: 2,200
Number of students: 29,000

Publications: *Dinei Israel* (1 a year), *Hasifrut* (4 a year), *International Perspective on Education and Society* (1 a year), *Israeli Society* (in Hebrew), *Israel Yearbook in Human Rights* (1 a year), *Iunei Mishpat* (4 a year), *Jahrbuch des Instituts für Deutsche Geschichte* (1 a year), *Kesher*, *Mediterranean Historical Review* (2 a year), *Michael* (8 every 18 months), *Middle East Contemporary Survey* (1 a year), *Mideast File* (4 a year), *Poetics Today* (4 a year), *Shvut* (9 a year), *Studies in Educational Evaluation* (4 a year), *Studies in Zionism* (2 a year), *Theoretical Inquiries in Law* (2 a year), *Zemanim* (4 a year)

DEANS

Buchmann Faculty of Law: Prof. HANOCH DAGAN
Faculty of Management (Leon Recanati Graduate School of Business Administration): Prof. ASHER TISHLER
George S. Wise Faculty of Life Sciences: Prof. YOEL KLOOG
Gershon H. Gordon Faculty of Social Sciences: Prof. NOAH LEWIN-EPSTEIN
Iby and Aladar Fleischman Faculty of Engineering: Prof. EHUD HEYMAN
Lester and Sally Entin Faculty of Humanities: Prof. EYAL ZISSER
Raymond and Beverly Sackler Faculty of Exact Sciences: Prof. HAIM WOLFSON
Sackler Faculty of Medicine: Prof. YOSEPH MEKORI
Yolanda and David Katz Faculty of Arts: Prof. HANNAH NAVEH

PROFESSORS

AARONSON, J., Mathematics
ABBOUD, S., Biomedical Engineering
ABRAMOWICZ, H., Physics
AHARONOWITZ, Y., Microbiology
AHARONY, A., Physics
AHITUV, N., Management
AKSELROD, S., Physics
ALGOM, D., Psychology
ALON, N., Mathematics
ALONI, R., Botany
ALPERT, P., Geophysics and Planetary Sciences
AMIRAV, A., Chemistry
AMIT, Y., Bible
AMOSSY, R., French Literature
ANDELMAN, D., Physics
ANILY, S., Management
APTER, A., Psychiatry
ARBEL, A., Industrial Engineering
ARBEL, B., History
ARBER, N., Medicine
ARON, S., History
ASHKENAZI, S., Paediatrics
AVERBUCH, A., Computer Sciences
AVRON, A., Computer Sciences
AYALON, A., History of the Middle East and Africa
AZAR, Y., Computer Sciences
AZRIEL, P., Anaesthiology and Intensive Care
BANKS-SILLS, L., Mechanical Engineering
BAR-KOCHVA, B., History of the Jewish People
BAR-MEIR, S., Medicine
BAR-NAVI, E., History
BAR-NUN, A., Planetary Sciences
BAR-TAL, D., Education
BARBASH, G., Preventive Medicine, Social Medicine
BARKAI, R., History
BARNEA, D., Mechanical Engineering
BARZILAY, Z., Paediatrics
BATTLER, A., Cardiology
BE'ERY, Y., Electrical Engineering
BEER, S., Plant Sciences
BELHASSEN, B., Cardiology
BELKIN, A., Theatre Arts
BELKIN, M., Ophthalmology
BEN, E. S., Psychology
BEN-AVRAHAM, Z., Geophysics
BEN-BASSAT, I., Haematology
BEN-DAVID, Y., Anatomy and Anthropology
BEN-JACOB, E., Physics
BEN-RAFAEL, E., Sociology and Anthropology
BEN-RAFAEL, Z., Gynaecology and Obstetrics
BEN-ZVI, A., Political Science
BEN-ZVI, L., Theatre Arts
BENAYAHU, Y., Zoology
BENJAMINI, Y., Statistics
BENNINGA, S., Management
BENVENISTE, Y., Mechanical Engineering
BENVENISTI, E., Law
BERECHMAN, J., Urban Planning
BERGMAN, D., Physics
BERNHEIM, J., Medicine
BERNSTEIN, J., Mathematics
BIDERMAN, S., Philosophy
BIXON, M., Chemistry
BOXMAN, R., Electrical and Electronic Engineering
BRACHA, B., Law
BRAUNER, N., Mechanical Engineering
BREIMAN, A., Plant Sciences
BUCHNER, A., Oral Pathology
CARMELI, S., Physics
CASHER, A., Physics
CHEN, R., Physics
CHESHNOVSKY, O., Chemistry
CHESKIS, S., Chemistry
CHOR, B., Computer Sciences
COHEN, A., Communication
COHEN, G., Molecular Microbiology and Biotechnology
COHEN, J., History of the Jewish People
COHEN, N., Law
CUKIERMAN, A., Economics
DAGAN, H., Law
DASCAL, M., Philosophy
DASCAL, N., Physiology
DAVIDSON, M., Psychiatry
DAYAN, D., Oral Pathology
DAYAN, T., Zoology
DEKEL, E., Economics
DERSHOWITZ, N., Computer Sciences
DEUTCH, M., Law
DINARI, G., Paediatrics
DOR, J., Obstetrics and Gynaecology
DRAZEN, A., Economics
DREYFUS, T., Teaching of Science
DYN, N., Applied Mathematics
ECKSTEIN, Z., Economics
EDEN, D., Management
EINAV, S., Biomedical Engineering
ELAD, D., Biomedical Engineering
ELDAR, M., Cardiology
ENTIN, O., Physics
EPEL, B. L., Botany
ESHEL, I., Statistics
EVEN, U., Chemistry
EVEN-ZOHAR, I., Theory of Literature
FABIAN, I., Cell Biology and Histology
FAINARU, M., Medicine
FARBER, M., Mathematics
FARFEL, Z., Medicine
FEDER, M., Electrical Engineering
FERSHTMAN, CH., Economics
FIAT, A., Computer Sciences
FINKELBERG, M., Classics
FINKELSTEIN, I., Archaeology
FISHELSON, Z., Cell and Development Biology
FISHER, M., Classical Archaeology
FLEUROV, V., Physics
FRANKFURT, L. L., Physics

FREEMAN, A., Biotechnology
FRENK, H., Psychology
FRENKEL, J., Economics
FRENKEL, N., Cell Research and Immunology
FRIEDLAND, N., Psychology
FRIEDMAN, M. A., Talmud
FUCHS, C., Statistics
FUCHS, M., Mechanical Engineering
GADOTH, N., Neurology
GAFTER, U., Medicine
GANS, CH., Law
GANZACH, Y., Management
GAT, A., Political Sciences
GAZIT, A., Human Microbiology
GERCHAK, Y., Industrial Engineering
GERSHONI, I., History of the Middle East
GERSHONI, Y., Cell Research and Immunology
GILBOA, I., Management, Economics
GINSBURG, D., Mathematics
GITIK, M., Mathematics
GLASNER, S., Mathematics
GLAZER, J., Management
GLEZERMAN, M., Obstetrics and Gynaecology
GLUSKIN, E., Mathematics
GOFER, A., Archaeology
GOLANI, I., Zoology
GOLDBERG, I., Chemistry
GOLDBOURT, U., Preventive Medicine, Social Medicine
GOLDHIRSCH, I., Mechanical Engineering
GOLDMAN, B., Genetics
GORODETSKY, G., History
GOVER, A., Electrical and Electronic Engineering
GOZES, I., Clinical Biochemistry
GRAUR, D., Zoology
GREEN, M., Preventive Medicine, Social Medicine
GREENSTEIN, E., Bible
GRODEZINSKY, Y., Psychology
GROSSMAN, E., Medicine
GUREVITZ, M., Plant Sciences
GUTNIK, D., Microbiology
HALKIN, H., Medicine
HALPERN, Z., Medicine
HAMMEL, I., Pathology
HARAN, D., Mathematics
HARATS, D., Medicine
HARDY, A., Electrical and Electronic Engineering
HASSIN, R., Statistics
HATIVA, N., Education
HAZAN, H., Sociology and Anthropology
HEFETZ, A., Zoology
HENIG, M., Management
HENIS, Y., Biochemistry
HERSHKOVITZ, I., Anatomy and Anthropology
HEYMAN, E., Electrical Engineering
HILDESHEIMER, M., Communication Disorders
HIZI, A., Cell Biology
HOCHBERG, Y., Statistics
HOFFMAN, Y., Bible
HOLZMAN, A., Hebrew Literature
HOMBURG, R., Obstetrics and Gynaecology
HORNIK, J., Management
HOROWITZ, A., Geology
HOROWITZ, M., Cell Research and Immunology
HUPPERT, D., Chemistry
ICHILOV, O., Education
ISAAC, B., Classics
ITZCHAK, Y., Diagnostic Radiology
IZRE'EL, S., Semitic Linguistics
JARDEN, M., Mathematics
KAFFE, I., Oral Radiology
KAHANE, Y., Management
KALAY, A., Management
KALDOR, U., Chemistry
KANDEL, SH., Management
KANTOR, Y., Physics
KARLINER, M., Physics
KARNIOL, R., Psychology
KASHMAN, Y., Chemistry
KATZ, D., History
KATZIR, A., Physics
KAUFMAN, G., Biochemistry
KEISARI, Y., Human Microbiology
KENAAN-KEDAR, N., History of Arts
KEREN, G., Cardiology
KIT, E., Mechanical Engineering
KLAFTER, J., Chemistry
KLEIN, A., Mathematics
KLEIN, S., Jewish Philosophy
KLIEMAN, A., Political Science
KLOOG, Y., Biochemistry
KORCZYN, A., Neurology
KORENSTEIN, R., Physiology
KOSLOFF, D., Geophysics
KREITLER, S., Psychology
KRONFELD, I., Geophysics and Planetary Sciences
KUPIEC, M., Microbiology
LAMED, R., Biotechnology
LANDMAN, F., Linguistics
LANGHOLZ, G., Electrical Engineering
LAOR, D., Hebrew Literature
LAOR, N., Psychiatry
LASS, Y., Physiology
LAVI, S., Cell Biology
LEDERMAN, E., Law
LEHRER, E., Statistics
LEIBOWITZ, E., Physics and Astronomy
LEIDERMAN, L., Economics
LESSING, J., Gynaecology and Obstetrics
LEVANON, N., Electrical and Electronic Engineering
LEVIATAN, D., Mathematics
LEVIN, D., Applied Mechanics
LEVIN, E., Physics
LEVIN, Z., Atmospheric Sciences
LEVO, Y., Medicine
LEVY, A., Physics
LEVY, S., Theatre Arts
LEWIN, N., Sociology and Anthropology
LIBERMAN, U. A., Statistics
LICHTENBERG, D., Pharmacology
LICHTENSTADT, J., Physics
LITSYN, S., Electrical Engineering
LIVSHITS, Z., Anatomy and Anthropology
LOBEL, T., Psychology
LOTAN, I., Physiology
LOYA, Y., Zoology
MAIMON, O., Industrial Engineering
MALKIN, I., Ancient History
MANSOUR, Y., Computer Sciences
MAOZ, D., Physics and Astronomy
MAOZ, Z., Political Science
MARGALIT, M., Education
MARGALIT, R., Biochemistry
MATZKIN, H., Surgery
MAUTNER, M., Law
MAZEH, T., Physics
MEDIN, Z., History
MEILIJSON, I., Statistics
MEKORI, Y., Medicine
MELAMED, E., Neurology
MENASHIRI, D., History of the Middle East
MESSER, H., Electrical Engineering
MEVARECH, M., Microbiology
MICHAELSON, D., Biochemistry
MILMAN, V., Mathematics
MILOH, T., Engineering
MIMOUNI, F., Paediatrics
MINTS, R., Physics
MOHR, R., Surgery
MOTRO, M., Cardiology
MULLER, E., Management
NAAMAN, N., History of the Jewish People
NADLER, A., Psychology
NAOR, Z., Biochemistry
NAVON, R., Human Genetics
NELSON, N., Biochemistry
NETZER, H., Physics
NEVO, D., Education
NITZAN, A., Chemistry
NUSSINOV, R., Biochemistry
NUSSINOV, S., Physics
OFEK, I., Human Microbiology
OFER, A., Management
OLEVSKII, A., Mathematics
OPPENHEIMER, A., History of the Jewish People
OR, U. G., Surgery
ORON, U., Zoology
ORON, Y., Pharmacology
OVADIA, M., Zoology
PASSWELL, J., Paediatrics
PAZ, G., Physiology
PELED, E., Chemistry
PHILLIP, M., Paediatrics
PIASETZKY, E., Physics
PICK, E., Immunology
PITARU, S., Oral Biology
PODOLACK, M., Planetary Science
POLAK, F., Bible
POLTEROVICH, L., Mathematics
PORAT, A., Law
PORTUGALI, J., Geography
RABEY, M., Neurology
RABINOVICH, I., History of the Middle East
RABINOWITZ, B., Cardiology
RAK, Y., Anatomy and Anthropology
RAVID, M., Medicine
RAVIV, A., Psychology
RAZ, A., Biochemistry
RAZ, J., East Asian Studies
RAZ, T., Management
RAZI, Z., History
RAZIN, A., Economics
RECHAVI, G., Haematology
REHAVI, M., Pharmacology
REIN, R., History
REPHAELI, Y., Physics
RISHPON, J., Biotechnology
ROKEM, F., Theatre Arts
ROLL, I., Classical Archaeology
RON, E., Microbiology
RON-EL, R., Gynaecology and Obstetrics
RONEN, B., Management
ROSENAU, P., Applied Mathematics
ROSENBAUM, M., Psychology
ROSENBERG, M., Human Microbiology
ROSENMAN, G., Electrical Engineering
ROSSET, SH., Mathematics
ROZEN, S., Chemistry
RUBIN, U., Arabic Language and Literature
RUBIN, Z., History
RUBINSTEIN, A., Economics
RUBINSTEIN, E., Medicine
RUDNICK, Z., Mathematics
RUPIN, E., Computer Science
RUPIN, E., Physiology
RUSCHIN, SH., Electrical Engineering
SABAR, B., Education
SADAN, J., Islamic Culture, Arabic Literature
SADKA, E., Economics
SAFRA, Z., Management
SAMET, D., Management
SAND, SH., History
SARNE, Y., Physiology
SAVION, N., Clinical Biochemistry
SCHMEIDLER, D., Statistics and Economics
SCHWARTZ, M., Physics
SEMYONOV, M., Sociology
SHACHAM-DIAM, Y., Electrical Engineering
SHAI, A., History
SHAKED, U., Electrical and Electronic Engineering
SHALGI, R., Embryology
SHAMIR, M., Political Science
SHAMIR, R., Computer Sciences
SHAMIR, Z., Hebrew Literature
SHANI, M., Health Systems Management
SHAPIRA, A., History of the Jewish People
SHAPIRA, Y., Electrical and Electronic Engineering
SHAPIRO, Y., Physiology
SHARIR, M., Computer Sciences
SHAVIT, Y., History of the Jewish People
SHAVIT, Y., Sociology and Anthropology
SHAVIT, Z., Semiotics and Cultural Research
SHEMER, J., Medicine
SHEMER, L., Mechanical Engineering
SHENKMAN, L., Medicine
SHILOH, Y., Human Genetics
SHOENFELD, Y., Medicine
SHOHAMY, E., Education
SHOHAT, M., Paediatrics

SHUSTIN, E., Mathematics
SIDI, Y., Medicine
SINGER, I., Cultures of the Ancient East
SINGER, S., Electrical Engineering
SIVASHINSKY, G., Applied Mathematics
SKORNICK, Y., Surgery
SKUTELSKY, E., Pathology
SNEH, B., Botany
SNYDERS, I., Electrical Engineering
SODIN, M., Mathematics
SOLOMON, B., Biotechnology
SOLOMON, Z., Social Work
SOUDRY, D., Mathematics
SPIEGLER, I., Management
STAVY, R., Teaching of Science
STEINBERG, B., Electrical Engineering
STERN, N., Medicine
STERNBERG, A., Physics
STERNBERG, M., Theory of Literature
STONE, L., Zoology
STRAUSS, S., Educational Psychology
TAL, H., Periodontology
TAMARKIN, M., History of Africa
TAMIR, A., Statistics
TAMSE, A., Endodontology
TARSI, M., Computer Sciences
TAUMAN, Y., Management
TEBOULLE, M., Operation Research and Statistics
TE'ENI, D., Management
TEICHMAN, M., Psychology
TEICHMAN, Y., Psychology
TERKEL, J., Zoology
TIROSH, D., Teaching of Science
TISHLER, A., Management
TODER, V., Embryology
TOLEDANO, E., History of the Middle East
TOURY, G., Theory of Literature, Comparative Literature
TSAL, Y., Psychology
TSIRELSON, B., Statistics
TUR, M., Electrical and Electronic Engineering
TUR-KASPA, R., Medicine
TURKEL, E., Mathematics
TYANO, S., Psychiatry
URBAKH, M., Chemistry
VERED, Z., Cardiology
VIDNE, B., Surgery
VOLKOV, S., History
WEINER, I., Psychology
WEINSTEIN, E., Electrical and Electronic Engineering
WEISMAN, Y., Paediatrics
WEISS, A., Electrical Engineering
WEISS, Y., Economics
WEIZMAN, A., Psychiatry
WEIZMAN, R., Psychiatry
WIENTROUB, S. H., Orthopaedic Surgery
WOLFSON, H., Computer Sciences
YAKAR, J., Archaeology
YANKIELOWICZ, S., Physics
YAROSLAVSKY, L., Electrical Engineering
YASSIF, E., Hebrew Literature
YEHUDAI, A., Computer Sciences
YINON, U., Physiology
YOGEV, A., Sociology of Education
YOM-TOV, Y., Zoology
ZADOK, R., History of the Jewish People and Cultures of the Ancient East
ZAGAGI, N., Classical Studies
ZAHAVI, J., Management
ZAKAY, D., Psychology
ZALTZMAN, N., Law
ZANG, I., Management
ZILCHA, I., Economics
ZISAPEL, N., Biochemistry
ZONNENSCHEIN, J., Physics
ZWICK, U., Computer Sciences

TECHNION—ISRAEL INSTITUTE OF TECHNOLOGY

32000 Haifa
Telephone: (4) 8292111
E-mail: pard@tx.technion.ac.il
Internet: www.technion.ac.il

Founded 1912, inaugurated 1924
State control
Language of instruction: Hebrew
Academic year: October to July

Pres.: Prof. PERETZ LAVIE
Sr Exec. Vice-Pres.: Prof. PAUL D. FEIGIN
Exec. Vice-Pres. and Dir-Gen.: Dr AVITAL STEIN
Exec. Vice-Pres. for Academic Affairs: Prof. MOSHE SIDI
Exec. Vice-Pres. for Research: Prof. ODED SHMUELI
Vice-Pres. for Resource Devt and External Relations: Prof. RAPHAEL ROM
Dean for Undergraduate Studies: Prof. YAACOV MAMANE
Dean for Graduate School: Prof. MOSHE SHPITALNI
Dean for Students: Prof. MICHAL GREEN

Library: see under Libraries and Archives
Number of teachers: 1,000
Number of students: 12,665 (9,401 undergraduate, 3,264 postgraduate)

Publications: *HaTechnion* (3 a year), *Shlomo Kaplansky Memorial Series* (incl. in *Israel Journal of Technology*), *The Joseph Wunsch Lectures* (1 a year)

DEANS

Faculty of Aerospace Engineering: Prof. YORAM TAMBOUR
Faculty of Architecture and Town Planning: Prof. YERACH DOYTSHER
Faculty of Biology: Prof. GADI SCHUSTER
Faculty of Biotechnology and Food Engineering: Prof. BEN ZION LEVI
Faculty of Civil and Environmental Engineering: Prof. ARNON BENTUR
Faculty of Computer Science: Prof. ELI BIHAM
Faculty of Electrical Engineering: Prof. ADAM SHWARTZ
Faculty of Industrial Engineering and Management: Prof. BOAZ GOLANY
Faculty of Materials Engineering: Prof. WAYNE D. KAPLAN
Faculty of Mathematics: Prof. JACOB RUBINSTEIN
Faculty of Mechanical Engineering: Prof. PINHAS BAR-YOSEPH
Faculty of Physics: Prof. NOAM SOKER
Ruth and Bruce Rappaport Faculty of Medicine: Prof. IDO PERLMAN
Schulich Faculty of Chemistry: Prof. MORIS EISEN

PROFESSORS

Faculty of Aerospace Engineering (tel. (4) 8292308; e-mail aerdean@aerodyne.technion.ac.il; internet ae-www.technion.ac.il):

BAR-ITZHACK, I., Navigation, Guidance and Control
DURBAN, D., Aerospace Structures
GANY, A., Rocket Propulsion
GIVOLI, D., Aerospace Structures, Computational Mechanics
GREENBERG, B., Combustion Theory
GUELMAN, M., Space Engineering
KARPEL, M., Aeroelasticity, Optimization
RAND, O., Rotary Wings, Aerospace Structures
ROSEN, A., Rotary Wings, Aerospace Structures
TAMBOUR, Y., Combustion of Fuel Sprays
WEIHS, D., Fluid Mechanics, Bio-Mechanics and Stability Theory
WELLER, T., Aerospace Structures, Smart Structures Technology

Faculty of Architecture and Town Planning (tel. (4) 8294001; e-mail deanarc@tx.technion.ac.il; internet architecture.technion.ac.il):

ALTERMAN, R., Land Development
AMIR, S., Regional Planning
BURT, M., Ocean Architecture
CARMON, N., Social Policy
CHURCHMAN, A., Environmental Psychology
SHAVIV, E., Energy and Architecture
SHEFER, D., Urban and Regional Economics

Faculty of Biology (tel. (4) 8294211; e-mail ddafna@tx.technion.ac.il; internet biology.technion.ac.il):

CASSEL, D., G-Proteins and Membrane Traffic
SCHUSTER, G., Molecular Biology

Department of Biomedical Engineering (tel. (4) 8294129; e-mail office@bm.technion.ac.il; internet www.bm.technion.ac.il):

DINNAR, U., Cardiovascular Fluid Dynamics, Minimal Invasive Diagnosis
LANIR, Y., Tissues Mechanics and Structure, Cardiac Mechanics, Coronary Circulation
MIZRAHI, J., Orthopaedic and Rehabilitation Biomechanics

Faculty of Biotechnology and Food Engineering (tel. (4) 8293068; e-mail biotech@tx.technion.ac.il; internet biotech.technion.ac.il):

COGAN, U., Food Chemistry
LEVI, B. Z., Mammalian Cell Biotechnology, Transcriptional Regulation, Innate Immunity
MILTZ, J., Packaging Engineering
SHOHAM, Y., Biochemical Engineering, Industrial Microbiology, Applied Enzymology

Faculty of Chemical Engineering (tel. (4) 8292820; e-mail chemeng@technion.ac.il; internet chemeng.technion.ac.il):

COHEN, Y., Polymer Science and Engineering
GRADER, G., Ceramic Materials, Sol-Gel Systems
LEWIN, D. R., Process Design and Control
MARMUR, A., Interfaces and Colloids
NIR, A., Fluid Mechanics, Transport Phenomena
SEMIAT, R., Process Development, Separation Processes, Desalination, Electro-Optical Techniques for Fluid-Flow
SHEINTUCH, M., Chemical Reaction Engineering, Catalysis, Non-linear Dynamics
TALMON, Y., Complex Liquids, Electron Microscopy

Faculty of Chemistry (tel. (4) 8293727; e-mail chsabine@tx.technion.ac.il; internet schulich.technion.ac.il):

APELOIG, Y., Organosilicon and Computational Chemistry
BAASOV, T., Bio-organic Chemistry, Enzymology
EISEN, M., Polymer Chemistry, Organometallic Chemistry
GROSS, Z., Catalysis, Inorganic Chemistry, Bioinorganic Chemistry
KAFTORY, M., Chemical Crystallography
KEINAN, E., Biocatalysis, Organic Synthesis, Molecular Computing
KOLODNEY, E., Molecular Beams, Surface Chemistry
MAREK, I., Organic Synthesis
MOISEYEV, N., Quantum Chemistry
SCHLECTER, I., Analytical Chemistry
SPEISER, S., Laser Photophysics

Faculty of Civil and Environmental Engineering (tel. (4) 8293066; e-mail deansecr@technion.ac.il; internet cee.technion.ac.il):

BENTUR, A., Cementitious and Composite Building Materials
CEDER, A., Transportation Planning and Operation
DOYTSHER, Y., Mapping and Geo-Information Engineering

EISENBERGER, M., Computational Mechanics-Static, Dynamics, Stability Analysis
FROSTIG, Y., Sandwich Structures, Prestressed Concrete, Retrofitting of Concrete Structures, Tile-Wall Systems
FRYDMAN, S., Geotechnical Engineering
KIRSCH, U., Structural Engineering
LAUFER, A., Project Management
MAMANE, Y., Air Pollution Meteorology, Atmospheric Aerosols
MURAVSKI, G., Soil Structure Interaction
NEUMANN, P. M., Plant Physiology
POLUS, A., Traffic Flow and Congestion Modelling, Safety of Transportation Systems
RUBIN, H., Contaminant Hydrology
SHEINMAN, I., Post-Buckling, Dynamics, Static, Damage, Vibration Induced by People
STIASSNIE, M., Water Waves
UZAN, J., Pavement Engineering
YANKELEVSKY, D., Impact Engineering, Mechanics of Reinforced Concrete, Earthquake Engineering
ZIMMELS, Y., Environmental and Process Engineering

Faculty of Computer Science (tel. (4) 8294313; e-mail itai@cs.technion.ac.il; internet www.cs.technion.ac.il):

BARAM, Y., Pattern Recognition, Artificial Neural Network
BIHAM, E., Cryptology
BRUCKSTEIN, A., Image Processing
BSHOUTY, N., Computational Learning Theory
FRANCEZ, N., Semantics and Verification, Computational Linguistics
GRUMBERG, O., Formal Verification
ISRAELI, M., Scientific Computing, Numerical Methods, Computational Linguistics
ITAI, A., Analysis of Algorithms and Data Structures, Computational Linguistics
KUSHILEVITZ, E., Complexity and Cryptography
MAKOWSKY, J., Mathematical Logic Computability and Complexity, Combinatorial Algorithms, Database Theory
MORAN, S., Search Methods on the Web
ROTH, R., Coding Theory
SIDI, A., Theoretical Numerical Analysis and Scientific Computing
SHMUELI, O., Databases: Systems and Theory
UNGARISH, M., Modelling and Numerical Simulation of Fluid Flows
ZAKS, S., Distributed Computing and Communication Networks

Faculty of Electrical Engineering (tel. (4) 8294680; e-mail eedean@ee.technion.ac.il; internet www.ee.technion.ac.il):

CIDON, I., Communication Networks
EISENSTEIN, G., Optoelectronics
FEUER, A., Automatic Control
FINKMAN, E., Quantum Hetrostructure
FISCHER, B., Optoelectronics
LEVIATAN, Y., Electromagnetic Waves
MALAH, D., Digital Signal Processing of Speech and Images
MERHAV, N., Information Theory
ROM, R., Communication Networks
SALZMAN, J., Optoelectronics
SCHIEBER, D., Energy Conversion
SEGALL, A., Computer Networks
SHAMAI, S., Information Theory
SHWARTZ, A., Large Deviations Theory
SIDI, M., Computer Networks
TANNENBAUM, A., Robust Control Theory
ZEEVI, Y., Vision and Image Sciences
ZEITOUNI, Z., Large Deviations Theory
ZIV, J., Statistical Communication, Information Theory

Faculty of Industrial Engineering and Management (tel. (4) 8294444; e-mail iedean@ie.technion.ac.il; internet iew3.technion.ac.il):

ADLER, R., Stochastic Processes
BEN-TAL, A., Non-linear Optimization
EREV, I., Behavioural Sciences and Experimental Economics
EREZ, M., Organizational Psychology
DE-HAAN, U., Entrepreneurship
FEIGIN, P., Applied Statistics
GOLANY, B., Industrial Engineering
GOPHER, D., Human Factors
KASPI, H., Probability and Stochastic Processes
MANDELBAUM, A., Operations Research, Stochastic Processes and their Applications
MONDERER, D., Game Theory
NEMIROVSKY, A., Optimization Complexity Theory
NOTEA, A., Non-Destructive Testing
ROTHBLUM, U. G., Operations Research
RUBINSTEIN, R., Stochastic Systems
SHTUB, A., Project Management
TENNENHOLTZ, M., Artificial Intelligence
WEISSMAN, I., Probability and Statistics

Faculty of Materials Engineering (tel. (4) 8294591; e-mail oilana@tx.technion.ac.il; internet materials.technion.ac.il):

EIZENBERG, M., Electronic Materials
GUTMANAS, E., Processing of High-Performance Material
KOMEM, Y., Electronic Materials
LIFSHITZ, Y., Nanostructured Inorganic Materials
SHECHTMAN, D., Properties and Microstructure of Intermetallic Compounds
SIEGMANN, A., Polymers and Plastic Structuring
ZOLOTOYABKO, E., X-Ray Diffraction

Faculty of Mathematics (tel. (4) 8223071; e-mail mathsee@tx.technion.ac.il; internet www.math.technion.ac.il):

AHARONI, R., Combinatorics
AHARONOV, D., Complex Analysis
BENYAMINI, Y., Banach Spaces
BERMAN, A., Matrix Theory
BSHOUTY, D., Complex Analysis, Probability Theory, Mathematical Statistics
CHILLAG, D., Algebra Group Theory
CWIKEL, M., Functional Analysis and Interpolation Space
GOLDBERG, M., Numerical Analysis
GORDON, Y., Functional Analysis
HERSHKOWITZ, D., Matrix Theory
IOFFE, A., General Theory of Sub-differentials
KATCHALSKI, M., Combinatorial Geometry
LERER, L., Linear Algebra, Operator Theory
LIRON, N., Applied Mathematics
LOEWY, R., Linear Algebra
MARCUS, M., Partial Differential Equations, Non-linear Analysis
NEPOMNYASHCHY, A., Fluid Mechanics
PINKUS, A., Approximation Theory
PINSKY, R., Probability and Stochastic Processes, Partial Differential Equations
REICH, S., Non-linear Analysis
RUBINSTEIN, J., Applied Mathematics
SOLEL, B., Operator Theory, Functional Analysis
SONN, J., Algebraic Number Theory
WAJNRYB, B., Algebraic Geometry
ZEITOUNI, O., Probability and Stochastic Processes
ZIEGLER, Z., Theory of Approximation

Faculty of Mechanical Engineering (tel. (4) 8292079; e-mail iritg@technion.ac.il; internet meeng.technion.ac.il):

ALTUS, E., Micro-Mechanics of Solids
BAR-YOSEPH, P., Finite Element Analysis
BEN-HAIM, Y., Decisions under Uncertainty, Reliability
DEGANI, D., Computational Fluid Dynamics
ELIAS, E., Thermohydraulics, Nuclear Engineering
ETSION, I., Tribology, Lubrication
GROSSMAN, G., Thermodynamics, Heat Pumps, Cooling and Air-Conditioning
GUTMAN, S., Relative Stability of Linear Dynamic Systems
HABER, S., Particulate Systems
PALMOR, Z., Digital Control of Industrial and Mechanical Systems
RUBIN, M., Continuum Mechanics
SHAPIRO, M., Porous Media, Aerosols
SHITZER, A., Bio-Heat Transfer
SHOHAM, M., Robotics and Medical Robotics
SHPITALNI, M., CAD/CAM, Manufacturing
TIROSH, J., Fracture Mechanics
YARIN, A., Rheology, Fluid Mechanics
YARIN, L. P., Two-Phase Flow, Combustion
ZVIRIN, Y., Solar Energy, Internal Combustion Engines

Faculty of Medicine (POB 9649, Bat Galim, 31096 Haifa; tel. (4) 8292111; e-mail md@tx.technion.ac.il; internet md.technion.ac.il):

AVIRAM, M., Lipid Research Laboratory
BENJAMIN, B., Haematology
BEYAR, R., Invasive Cardiology
CIECHANOVER, A., Intercellular Breakdown of Proteins
ETZIONI, A., Paediatrics and Immunology
FINBERG, J., Neuropharmacology
FINSOD, M., Neurosurgery
FRY, M., Enzymology of DNA Replication
GAVISH, M., Molecular Pharmacology
HASIN, Y., Cardiology
HERSHKO, A., Intracellular Protein Degradation
ITSKOVITZ, J., Human Embryonic Stem Cells
KRAUSZ, M., General Surgery
LAVIE, P., Psychobiology, Sleep Research
LEWIS, B., Cardiology
NEUFELD, G., Angiogenesis
PALTI, Y., Physiology and Biophysics
PERLMAN, I., Vision Neurophysiology
PRATT, H., Behavioural Sciences
ROWE, Y., Haematology
SHALEV, E., Obstetrics and Gynaecology
SKORECKI, K., Nephrology, Molecular Medicine
VOLDAVSKY, I., Vascular and Tumour Biology, Biochemistry
YOUDIM, M., Neuropharmacology

Faculty of Physics (tel. (4) 8293909; e-mail office@physics.technion.ac.il; internet physics.technion.ac.il):

AKKERMANS, E., Theory of Condensed Matter Physics, Mesoscopic Quantum
AUERBACH, A., Condensed Matter Theory
AVRON, J., Mathematical Physics
BRAUN, E., Biophysics, Non-linear Dynamics of Systems out of Equilibrium
COHEN, E., Spectroscopic Properties of Laser Materials
DADO, S., High-Energy Physics Experimentation
DAR, A., Astroparticle Physics
EHRENFREUND, E., Semiconducting Quantum Structures and Polymers
EILAM, G., Elementary Particle Physics
FELSTEINER, J., Condensed Matter Physics, Plasma Physics
FISHMAN, S., Quantum Chaos
GERSHONI, D., Semiconducting Quantum Heterostructures
GRONAU, M., Theoretical High-Energy Physics
KALISH, R., Ion-Implantation—Hyperfine Interactions
KOREN, G., Superconductivity and Lasers
LIPSON, S., Low-Temperature Physics
MANN, A., Theoretical Physics
MOSHE, M., Theoretical High-Energy Physics

ORI, A., General Relativity, Black Holes, Gravitational Radiation
POLTURAK, E., High-Temperature Superconductors
REGEV, O., Astrophysics
RIESS, I., Solid State Electrochemistry
SEGEV, M., Nonlinear Optics
SHAPIRO, B., Theory of Condensed Matter
SHAVIV, G., Astrophysics
SIVAN, U., Mesoscopic Physics, Bio-Electronics
SOKER, N., Astrophysics Theory

UNIVERSITY OF HAIFA

199 Aba Hushi Ave. Mount Carmel, 3498838 Haifa
Telephone: (4) 8240111
E-mail: rector@univ.haifa.ac.il
Internet: www.haifa.ac.il

Founded 1963
Private control
Language of instruction: Hebrew
Academic year: October to June

Pres.: Prof. AMOS SHAPIRA
Rector: Prof. DAVID FARAGGI
Vice-Rector: Prof. PERLA WERNER
Vice-Pres. for Admin.: Prof. BARUCH MARZAN
Vice-Pres. for External Relations and Resource Devt: RACHEL KAVERMAN
Vice-Pres. and Dean for Research: Prof. MICHAL YERUSHALMY
Registrar: RUTH RABINOWITZ
Academic Sec.: SHOSHANA LANDMAN
Dean for Graduate Studies: Prof. YITZHAK HARPAZ

Number of teachers: 2,096
Number of students: 17,350

Publications: *Dappim—Research in Literature* (1 a year, in Hebrew with English abstracts), *Jewish History* (every 2 years), *JTD Haifa University Studies in Theatre and Drama* (1 a year), *Mishpat Umimshal Law and Government in Israel* (every 2 years, in Hebrew), *Studies in Children's Literature* (1 a year, in Hebrew), *Studies in Education* (every 2 years, in Hebrew)

DEANS

Faculty of Education: Prof. LILI ORLAND BARAK
Faculty of Humanities: Prof. REUVEN SNIR
Faculty of Law: Prof. GAD BRAZILAI
Faculty of Natural Sciences: Prof. EDI BRKAI
Faculty of Social Sciences: Prof. GUSTAVO MESH
Faculty of Social Welfare and Health Sciences: Prof. SHAI LINN
Graduate School of Management: Prof. YOSSI YAGIL
School of Political Sciences: Prof. MICHAEL GROSS GADOT
School of Social Work: Prof. FAISAL AZAIZA

PROFESSORS

Faculty of Education (tel. (4) 8240893; internet www.edu.haifa.ac.il):

ALEXANDER, H., Education
BARAK, A., Education
BEN-PERETZ, M., Education
BREZNITZ, Z., Education
COHEN, A., Education
EIZIKOVITS, R., Education
HERTZ-LAZAROWITZ, R., Education
KARNI, A., Education
KATRIEL, T., Education
KLINGMAN, A., Education
LINN, R., Education
NESHER, P., Education
REITER, S., Special Education
SALOMON, G., Education
SCHECHTMAN, Z., Education
SEGINER, R., Education
SFARD, A., Mathematics Education
SHARE, D., Education
SHIMRON, J., Education
YERUSHALMY, M., Mathematics Education
ZEIDNER, M., Education

Faculty of Humanities (tel. (4) 8240125; e-mail pfientu1@univ.haifa.ac.il; internet hcc.haifa.ac.il):

AVISHUR, Y., Hebrew Language
BALABAN, O., Philosophy
BAR ITZHAK, H., Hebrew and Comparative Literature
BARAM, A., Middle Eastern History
BARNAI, J., Land of Israel Studies
BEN ZE'EV, A., Philosophy
BEN-ARTZI, Y., Land of Israel Studies
BEN-DOV, N., Hebrew and Comparative Literature
CHETRIT, J., Hebrew Language
CHISICK, H., General History
DAVID, E., General History
DIMANT, D., Jewish History
DORCHIN, Y., Art
ELBAZ, R., Hebrew and Comparative Literature
ELDAR, I., Hebrew Language
ERDINAST-VULCAN, D., English
EVRON, M., Archaeology
FIRRO, K., Middle Eastern History
FREEDMAN, W., English
GALIL, G., Biblical Studies
GELBER, Y., Land of Israel Studies
GILBAR, G., Middle Eastern History
GILEAD, A., Philosophy
GOLDSTEIN, Y., Land of Israel Studies
HAHLILI, R., Archaeology
HOFFMAN, J., Hebrew Language
HON, G., Philosophy
KAGAN, Z., Hebrew and Comparative Literature
KANAZI, G., Arabic Language and Literature
KATZ, A., Art
KELLNER, M., Jewish History
KOCHAVI, A., General History
KURZON, D., English
KUSHNIR, D., Middle Eastern History
LAUFER, B., English
LUZ, E., Jewish Thought
MALUL, M., Biblical Studies
MANSOUR, Y., Hebrew Language
MELAMED, A., Jewish History
MENACHE, S., General History
MICHEL, J., French
MYHILL, J., English
NEVO, J., Middle Eastern History
ODED, B., Jewish History
ORKIN, M., Theatre, English Literature
PACHTER, M., Jewish History
RAPPAPORT, U., Jewish History
REICH, R., Archaeology
ROBIN, R., General History, Communication
RONEN, A., Archaeology
ROZEN, M., Jewish History
SANDLER, W., English
SCHATZKER, C., Jewish History
SEGAL, A., Archaeology
SHAPIRA, A., Music
SHENHAR, A., Hebrew and Comparative Literature
SHICHOR, Y., Asian Studies
SHOHAM, R., Hebrew and Comparative Literature
SHPAYEV-MAKOV, H., General History
SMILANSKY, S., Philosophy
SNIR, R., Arabic
SOBEL, M., General History
STATMAN, D., Philosophy
STEINBERG, E., Music
STOW, K., Jewish History
TOBI, J., Hebrew and Comparative Literature
WARBURG, G., Middle Eastern History
WEITZ, Y., Land of Israel Studies
YARDENI, M., General History
YEHOSHUA, A., Hebrew and Comparative Literature
ZEHAVI, O., Music
ZINGUER, I., French

Faculty of Law (tel. (4) 8240633; internet law.haifa.ac.il):

BARZILAI, G., Law
BEN-OLIEL, R., Law
EDREY, Y., Law
GAL, M., Law
GROSS, E., Law
SALZBERGER, E., Law

Faculty of Natural Sciences (tel. (4) 8288077; e-mail mgoldbe1@univ.haifa.ac.il; internet science.haifa.ac.il):

BARKAI, E., Neurobiology and Ethology
BLAUSTEIN, L., Evolutionary and Environmental Biology
BRAUN, A., Mathematics
CARO, Y., Mathematics
CENSOR, Y., Mathematics
DAFNI, A., Evolutionary and Environmental Biology
FAHIMA, T., Evolutionary and Environmental Biology
GOLAN, J., Mathematics
GORDON, A., Science Education—Physics
IZHAK, I., Evolutionary and Environmental Biology
KARNI, A., Human Biology
KOROL, A., Evolutionary and Environmental Biology
KOZENIKOV, A., Mathematics
LEV, S., Science Education—Biology
LEV-YADUN, S., Science Education—Biology
MORAN, G., Mathematics
NE'EMAN, G., Biology
NEVO, E., Biology
REISNER, S., Mathematics
RICHTER-LEVIN, G., Biology
ROITMAN, M., Mathematics
RUBINSTEIN, Z., Mathematics
SKOLNICK, A., Biology
TEMPLETON, A., Evolution
TRIPONOV, E., Evolutionary and Environmental Biology
VAISMAN, I., Mathematics
WASSER, S., Evolutionary and Environmental Biology
WEIT, Y., Mathematics
YUSTER, R., Mathematics
ZACKS, J., Mathematics
ZOLLER, U., Chemistry

Faculty of Social Sciences (tel. (4) 8240331; e-mail ssmooha@univ.haifa.ac.il; internet hevra.haifa.ac.il):

AL-HAJ, M., Sociology
ARAZY, J., Mathematics and Computer Science
AZARYAHU, M., Geography and Environmental Studies
BAR-GAL, Y., Geography
BAR-LEV, S., Statistics
BEIT-HALLAHMI, B., Psychology
BEN-DOR, G., Political Science
BEN-ZVI, A., Political Science
BERG, M., Statistics and Business Administration
BERMAN, E., Psychology
BRAUN, A., Mathematics and Computer Science
BREZNITZ, S., Psychology
CENSOR, Y., Mathematics and Computer Science
EDEN, B., Economics
FARAGGI, D., Statistics
FELZENTAL, D., Political Science
FISHMAN, G., Sociology
FROSTIG, E., Statistics
GOLAN, J., Mathematics and Computer Science
GOLDENSCHLUGER, A., Statistics
GOLOMBIC, M., Computer Science

GORDON, D., Computer Science
GROSS, M., Political Science
GUIORA, A., Psychology
HARPAZ, Y., Sociology and Business Administration
HAYUTH, Y., Geography
INBAR, M., Geography
ISHAI, Y., Political Science
KATRIEL, T., Communication
KELLERMAN, A., Geography
KEREN, G., Psychology
KIMCHI, R., Psychology
KIPNIS, B., Geography
KLIOT, N., Geography
KORIAT, A., Psychology
KRAUS, V., Sociology
KUTIEL, H., Geography and Environmental Studies
LANDAU, G., Computer Science
LANDSBERGER, M., Economics
LANDSMAN, Z., Statistics
LANGBERG, N., Statistics
LESHEM, M., Psychology
MAKOV, E., Statistics
MATTRAS, Y., Sociology
MELNIK, A., Economics
MILLER, B., Political Science
MORAN, G., Mathematics and Computer Science
NAVON, D., Psychology
NEVO, B., Psychology
NEWMAN, I., Computer Science
OPPENHEIM, D., Psychology
PERRY, D., Statistics
RAKOVER, S., Psychology
RATNER, A., Sociology and Anthropology
REISER, B., Statistics
RICHTER-LEVIN, G., Psychology
ROITMAN, M., Mathematics
ROSENFELD, H., Sociology
ROSNER, M., Sociology
RUBIN, S., Psychology
RUBINSTEIN, Z., Mathematics and Computer Science
SAFIR, M., Psychology
SAGI-SCHWARTZ, A., Psychology
SAMUEL, Y., Sociology
SHECHTER, M., Economics
SHITOVITZ, B., Economics
SMOOHA, S., Sociology
SOBEL, Z., Sociology
SOFFER, A., Geography
VAISMAN, I., Mathematics and Computer Science
VIGODA-GADOT, E., Political Science
WATERMAN, S., Geography
WEIMAN, G., Sociology and Communication
WEISS, G., Statistics
WEIT, I., Mathematics and Computer Science
ZAKS, J., Mathematics and Computer Science

Faculty of Social Welfare and Health Sciences (tel. (4) 8249950; e-mail werner@research.haifa.ac.il; internet hw.haifa.ac.il):

BEN-ARI, A., Social Work
CAREL, R., Public Health
DICKSTEIN, R., Physiotherapy
EISIKOVITS, Z., Social Work
GREEN, M., Public Health
GUTTMAN, D., Social Work
KATZ, R., Human Services
LOEWENSTEIN, A., Gerontology
RIMMERMAN, A., Social Work
ROW, D., Community Mental Health
WEISS, T., Occupational Therapy
WERNER, P., Gerontology

Graduate School of Management:

MESHULAM, I., Business Administration
RAFAELI, S., Business Administration

Leon H. Charney School of Marine Sciences (tel. (4) 8249950; internet marsci.haifa.ac.il):

ARTZI, M., Maritime Civilizations
BEN AVRAHAM, Z., Maritime Civilizations
MART, Y., Maritime Civilizations
RINKEVICH, B., Marine Biology
SPAINER, E., Maritime Civilizations

WEIZMANN INSTITUTE OF SCIENCE

POB 26, 76100 Rehovot
Telephone: (8) 9342111
E-mail: news@weizmann.ac.il
Internet: www.weizmann.ac.il

Founded 1949, incl. the Daniel Sieff Research Institute (f. 1934).

Private non-profit corporation for fundamental and applied research in the natural and exact sciences; the Feinberg Graduate School offers MSc and PhD courses

Pres.: Prof. DANIEL ZAJFMAN
Vice-Pres.: Prof. HAIM GARTY
Vice-Pres. for Admin. and Finance: Dr ISAAC SHARIV
Vice-Pres. for Resource Devt and Public Affairs: Prof. ISRAEL BAR-JOSEPH
Vice-Pres. for Technology Transfer: Prof. MORDECHAI SHEVES
Chief Librarian: Mrs I. POLLACK

Library: see under Libraries and Archives
Number of teachers: 300
Number of students: 800 postgraduates

DEANS

Faculty of Biochemistry: Prof. ZVI LIVNEH
Faculty of Biology: Prof. MICHAL NEEMAN
Faculty of Chemistry: Prof. YEHIAM PRIOR
Faculty of Mathematics and Computer Science: Prof. DAVID PELEG
Faculty of Physics: Prof. YOSEF NIR
Feinberg Graduate School: Prof. LIA ADDADI

DIRECTORS OF CENTRES

Faculty of Biochemistry:

Avron-Wilstätter Minerva Center for Research in Photosynthesis: Prof. A. SCHERZ
Charles W. and Tillie K. Lubin Center for Plant Biotechnology: Prof. AVRAHAM LEVY
Crown Human Genome Center: Prof. DORON LANCET
David and Fela Shapell Family Center for Genetic Disorders Research: Prof. YORAM GRONER
Dr Joseph Cohn Minerva Center for Biomembrane Research: Prof. EITAN BIBI
Harry and Jeanette Weinberg Center for Plant Molecular Genetics Research: Prof. AVRAHAM LEVY
Kekst Family Center for Medical Genetics: Prof. YORAM GRONER
Leo and Julia Forchheimer Center for Molecular Genetics: Prof. YOSEF SHAUL
M. D. Moross Institute for Cancer Research: Prof. YORAM GRONER
Mel Dobrin Center for Nutrition: Prof. AVRAHAM LEVY
Y. Leon Benoziyo Institute for Molecular Medicine: Prof. ZVI LIVNEH

Faculty of Biology:

Belle S. and Irving E. Meller Center for Biology of Ageing: Prof. YAIR REISNER
Carl and Micaela Einhorn-Dominic Institute for Brain Research: Prof. YADIN DUDAI
Gabrielle Rich Center for Transplantation Biology Research: Prof. YAIR REISNER
Helen and Martin Kimmel Institute for Stem Cell Research: Prof. DOV ZIPORI
Kirk Center for Childhood Cancer and Immunological Disorders: Prof. BENJAMIN GEIGER
Murray H. and Meyer Grodetsky Center for Research of Higher Brain Functions: Prof. AMIRAM GRINVALD
Nella and Leon Benoziyo Center for Neurological Diseases: Prof. ANTHONY H. FUTERMAN
Nella and Leon Benoziyo Center for Neurosciences: Prof. YADIN DUDAI
Norman and Helen Asher Center for Brain Imaging: Prof. YADIN DUDAI
Wilner Family Center for Vascular Biology: Prof. NAVA DEKEL
Women's Health Research Center: Prof. VARDA ROTTER
Yad Abraham Research Center for Cancer Diagnostics and Therapy: Prof. VARDA ROTTER

Faculty of Chemistry:

Center for Energy Research: Prof. JACOB KARNI
Fritz Haber Center for Physical Chemistry: Prof. LUCIO FRYDMAN
Gerhardt M. J. Schmidt Minerva Center for Supermolecular Architecture: Prof. DAVID CAHEN
Helen and Martin Kimmel Center for Archaeological Science: Prof. STEPHEN WEINER
Helen and Martin Kimmel Center for Molecular Design: Prof. DAVID MILSTEIN
Helen and Martin Kimmel Center for Nanoscale Science: Prof. RESHEF TENNE
Helen and Milton A. Kimmelman Center for Biomolecular Structure and Assembly: Prof. ADA E. YONATH
Ilse Katz Institute for Material Sciences and Magnetic Resonance Research: Prof. YEHIAM PRIOR
Joseph and Ceil Mazer Center for Structural Biology: Prof. ZIPPORA SHAKKED
Moskowitz Center for Nano and Bio-nano Imaging: Prof. ABRAHAM MINSKY
Sussman Family Center for the Study of Environmental Sciences: Prof. BRIAN BERKOWITZ

Faculty of Mathematics and Computer Science:

Arthur and Rochelle Belfer Institute of Mathematics and Computer Science: Prof. DAVID PELEG
Ida Kohen Centre for Mathematics: Prof. DAVID PELEG
John von Neumann Minerva Center for the Development of Reactive Systems: Prof. DAVID HAREL

Faculty of Physics:

Albert Einstein Minerva Center for Theoretical Physics: Prof. MORDEHAI MILGROM
Benoziyo Center for Astrophysics: Prof. ELI WAXMAN
Center for Experimental Physics: Prof. YOSEF NIR
Crown Photonics Center: Prof. YARON SILBERBERG
Joseph H. and Belle R. Braun Center for Submicron Research: Prof. MOTY HEIBLUM
Maurice and Gabriela Goldschleger Center for Nanophysics: Prof. MOTY HEIBLUM
Minerva Center for Non-linear Physics of Complex Systems: Prof. ITAMAR PROCACCIA
Nella and Leo Benoziyo Center for High Energy Physics: Prof. GIORA MIKENBERG

Feinberg Graduate School:

Aharon Katzir-Katchalsky Center: Prof. LIA ADDADI
Dwek Family Research School of Chemical Science: Prof. GILAD HARAN
Ekard Research School of Biological Science: Prof. ARI ELSON
Lorry I. Lokey Research School of Biochemical Science: Prof. ARI ELSON
Moross Research School of Mathematics and Computer Science: Prof. RAN RAZ
Research School of Physical Science: Prof. SHIMON LEVIT

Colleges and Higher Institutes

Academic Centre Ruppin: PO Academic Centre Ruppin, 40250 Emek Hefer; tel. (9) 8983005; e-mail rani@ruppin.ac.il; internet www.ruppin.ac.il; f. 1949; three-year degree courses in accounting, business administration and behavioural sciences, economics; two-year courses in architecture, basic trades, computers, electrical engineering, industrial management, landscape architecture, megatronics, soil and water engineering; short courses in accounting and mechanics, basic economics; school of engineering: electrical, industrial and computer science; library: 30,000 vols; 350 teachers; 5,000 students; Pres. Prof. SHOSH ARAD; Dir ZVIKA LEVIN.

Academic Centre of Law and Business: 26 Ben Gurion St, 52275 Ramat-Gan; tel. (3) 6000800; e-mail info@rg-law.ac.il; internet www.clb.ac.il; depts of communication and technology, criminal law and criminology and law, human rights; 1,000 students; Dean Prof. PINHAS SHIFMAN.

Academic College of Tel-Aviv-Yaffo: 4 Antokolsky St, POB 16131, 61161 Tel-Aviv; tel. (3) 5211840; e-mail mirsham@mta.ac.il; internet www.mta.ac.il; Bachelors of Arts degrees in computer science, behavioural science, management, society and politics.

Bezalel Academy of Arts and Design: Mt Scopus, POB 24046, 91240 Jerusalem; tel. (2) 5893333; e-mail mail@bezalel.ac.il; internet www.bezalel.ac.il; f. 1906; degree courses in architecture, design, animation, ceramics and glass design, fine arts, gold and silversmithing industrial design, jewellery and fashion accessories design, photography, visual communication, video and computer imaging; library: 35,000 vols; 300 teachers; 1,600 students; Pres. Prof. ARNON ZUCKERMAN.

Ecole Biblique et Ecole Archéologique Française: 6 Nablus Rd, POB 19053, 91190 Jerusalem; tel. (2) 6264468; e-mail directeur@ebaf.edu; internet ebaf.op.org; f. 1890; research, Biblical and Oriental studies, exploration and excavation in Palestine; 14 professors; library: see under Libraries and Archives; Dir PAULINE BOILARD; publs *Cahiers de la Revue Biblique*, *Etudes Annexes*, *Etudes Bibliques*, *Littératures anciennes du Proche Orient*, *Revue Biblique* (4 a year).

Hadassah College: 37 Hanevi'im St, POB 1114, 91010 Jerusalem; tel. (2) 6291911; e-mail info@hadassah.ac.il; internet www.hadassah.ac.il; f. 1970; comprises Hadassah Academic College (depts of communication disorders, computer sciences, medical laboratory sciences, optometry), Hadassah College of Technology (depts of dental technology, cinema and television production, hotel management, photography and digital media, industrial design, printing and computer graphics, technical software engineering), Tachlit Centre for Lifelong Learning; Pres. Prof. NAVA BEN ZVI.

Hebrew Union College—Jewish Institute of Religion: 13 King David St, 94101 Jerusalem; tel. (2) 6203333; e-mail mzakai@huc.edu; internet www.huc.edu; f. 1963; br. of the same instn in the USA; the first year of graduate rabbinic studies, Jewish education, cantorial training and programme in biblical archaeology, incl. summer excavations; Rabbinic programme for Israel Reform (Progressive); English 'Lehrhaus' study programmes in classical Jewish Literature for gen. public (Bet Midrash); Skirball Museum of Biblical Archaeology; library: Abramov library of 40,000 vols; microfilm colln from American Jewish Archives; 35 teachers; 150 students; Pres. Dr DAVID ELLENSON; Dean Rabbi MICHAEL MARMUR.

International Institute of Histadrut: Beit Berl, 44905 Kfar Saba; tel. (9) 7612303; e-mail info@peoples.org.il; internet www.peoples.org.il; f. 1958 to train labour and cooperative movements, professional assocs and women's and youth orgs; candidates nominated by trade unions, cooperatives, univs, int. labour orgs, etc.; courses and seminars in fields of labour, social and economic devt and cooperative studies in Arabic, English, French, Russian and Spanish; 41,400 graduates from 140 countries; library: 15,000 vols, and monographs and periodicals; 8 teachers; 1,400 students; Dir-Gen. MICHAEL FROHLICH; Academic Dir SERDIO GRYN.

Jerusalem Academy of Music and Dance: Givat Ram Campus, 91904 Jerusalem; tel. (2) 6759911; e-mail schul@jamd.ac.il; internet www.jamd.ac.il; f. 1947; performing arts, composition, conducting and theory, music education, dance; awards BMus., BEdMus., Dance and Artists' Diplomas; courses leading to BAMus., MAMus. and MMus. in cooperation with the Hebrew University; Conservatory and High School (Music and Dance); 190 teachers; 550 students; library: 60,000 vols; colln of musical instruments; electroacoustic laboratory; Pres. Prof. ILAN SCHUL; Dir-Gen. MICHA TAL.

Jerusalem College of Technology: 21 Havaad Haleumi St, POB 16031, 91160 Jerusalem; tel. (2) 6751111; e-mail pr@jct.ac.il; internet www.jct.ac.il; f. 1969; 4-year first degree courses; library: 20,000 vols; 106 teachers (66 full-time, 40 part-time); 2,660 students; Pres. Prof. JOSEPH S. BODENHEIMER; Rector Prof. MENACHEM STEINER; Librarian ZVI SOBEL.

Jerusalem University College: Mount Zion, POB 1276, 91012 Jerusalem; tel. (2) 6718628; e-mail paulwright@juc.edu; internet www.juc.edu; f. 1957; also known as American Institute of Holy Land Studies; Christian study centre at univ. level; graduate and undergraduate courses in the geography, history, languages, religions and cultures of Israel in the Middle East context; field trips and archaeological excavation programme; 20 teachers; 200 students; Pres. Dr PAUL WRIGHT.

Mosad Harav Kook: POB 642, Jerusalem; tel. (2) 6526231; internet www.mosadharavkook.com; f. 1937 to educate and train young men for research in the field of Torah Literature and to infuse the original Hebrew culture in all classes of the people; library: Rav Maimon Library of Judaica; religious Zionist Archives; publs Torah-Science books, incl. the printing of MSS of previously unpublished *Rishonim* works that are still retained in Genizah form, popular commentary to the entire Bible; incorporates Institute for Chasiduth; Dir Rabbi JOSEPH MOVSHOVITZ.

ORT Braude College: POB 78, 21982 Karmiel; tel. (4) 9901911; e-mail rishum@braude.ac.il; internet www.braude.ac.il; f. 1988; B.Tech. degree programmes in biotechnology engineering, electrical and electronics engineering, mechanical engineering, industrial and management engineering, and software engineering; also practical engineering 2-year degree programmes; library: 50,000 vols; 320 teachers; 1,200 undergraduate students; Pres. Prof. YOHANAN ARZI.

Pontifical Biblical Institute: 3 Paul-Emile Botta St, POB 497, 91004 Jerusalem; tel. (2) 6252843; e-mail admipib@gmail.com; internet www.biblico.it/jerusalem.html; f. 1913 as a br. of the Pontifical Biblical Institute of Rome, Italy; fosters the study of Biblical geography and archaeology; provides courses for students and graduates of Roman Institute; Prehistorical Museum containing discoveries of Teleilat Ghassul, a chalcolithic site in the Jordan valley, excavated by the Institute; library: 26,000 vols for biblical studies; Dir Rev. JOSEPH DOAN CÔNG NGUYÊN.

Shenkar College of Engineering and Design: 12 Anne Frank St, 52526 Ramat Gan; tel. (3) 6110045; e-mail info@shenkar.ac.il; internet www.shenkar.ac.il; f. 1970; Bachelors degrees and research in industrial management and marketing, computer science, plastics engineering, industrial chemistry, industrial engineering, fashion design, textile and interior design, jewellery design, industrial design; library: 20,000 vols, 250 periodicals; 50 teachers; 2,180 students (680 full-time, 1,500 part-time); Pres. Prof. AMOTZ WEINBERG; Man. Dir GUY PERETZ.

Studium Biblicum Franciscanum: Monastery of the Flagellation, POB 19424, 91193 Jerusalem; tel. (2) 6270485; e-mail secretary@studiumbiblicum.org; internet www.custodia.org/sbf; f. 1927; centre of archaeological research sponsored by the Franciscan Custody of the Holy Land, biblical and archaeological faculty of the *Pontificium Athenaeum Antonianum*, Rome, for degrees of Bachelors in theology, Licentiate and Doctorate in biblical sciences and archaeology, and diploma in oriental biblical studies and archaeology and in biblical formation; 15 teachers; 80 students; Dean G. C. BOTTINI; publs *Analecta*, *Collectio Maior*, *Collectio Minor*, *Liber Annuus*, *Museum*.

Tel-Hai Academic College: 12210 Upper Galilee; tel. (4) 8181785; e-mail telhai@telhai.ac.il; internet www.telhai.ac.il; f. 1957; Bachelors degree courses in biotechnology and environmental sciences, nutrition sciences, education, economics and management, social work, computer science, multidisciplinary studies; Diploma courses in architecture, construction, electronics and electricity, computers, mechanics and machinery, industrial management, telemedia and communication, drama therapy; art institute courses in sculpture, drawing, ceramics, photography and ethnic crafts; 500 teachers; 4,000 students; Pres. Prof. ZEKI BERK; Vice-Pres. for Academic Affairs Prof. SHMUEL SHAMAI.

Ulpan Akiva Netanya, International Hebrew Study Centre: POB 6086, 42160 Netanya; tel. (9) 8352312; e-mail ulpanakv@netvision.net.il; internet www.ulpan-akiva.org; f. 1951; basic and supplementary courses in Arabic and Hebrew; cultural studies; 45 teachers; Dir ESTHER PERRON.

Yeshivat Dvar Yerushalayim (Jerusalem Academy of Jewish Studies): 53 Katzenellenbogen, Har Nof, POB 34580, 91344 Jerusalem; tel. (2) 6522817; e-mail dvar@dvar.org.il; internet www.dvar.org.il; f. 1970; runs courses in English, French, Spanish, Russian and Hebrew on the Bible, Hebrew, Talmud, philosophy, ethics and Halacha; 500 mems; library: 5,000 vols; 7 teachers; 70 students; Dean Rabbi B. HOROVITZ; Exec. Dir Rabbi E. ALTHEIM; publ. *Jewish Studies Magazine* (1 a year).

Zinman College of Physical Education and Sport Sciences at the Wingate Institute: 42902 Netanya; tel. (9) 8639222; e-mail zinman@wincol.macam.ac.il; internet www.wincol.ac.il; f. 1944; 4-year BEd programme, M.P.E. programme at the college, MA programme in conjunction with Haifa Univ.; in-service training; library: 52,000 vols, 180 periodicals; 450 teachers; 950 regular students, 3,000 students on other courses; Rector Prof. Dr MICHAEL SAGIV.

ITALY

The Higher Education System

Italy's first universities were established during the 10th to the 13th century and are among the oldest in Europe; in fact, Università degli Studi di Parma (AD 962) is Europe's oldest university, and other long-established universities include Università di Bologna (founded 1088), Università degli Studi di Modena e Reggio Emilia (founded 1175) and Università degli Studi di Perugia (founded 1200). Several universities date from the 14th to the 16th century. In 2006/07 there were 1.82m. undergraduate students in higher education in Italy; the largest universities were Sapienza Università di Roma, with around 170,000 students, and Bologna, with more than 100,000 students. In 2007/08 there were 74 institutes of higher education (state-owned and privately owned). In 2010 the total number of students enrolled in tertiary education was 1.98m. Study allowances are awarded to students according to their means and merit; however, most students pay tuition fees. Italian universities operate on the European Credit Transfer and Accumulation System (ECTS), and Italy also participates in the Bologna Process to establish a European Higher Education Area. The Ministry of Universities and Research is the government agency responsible for higher education. In addition to universities, there are four other types of state-recognized institutions of higher education: academies of arts education, higher institutes of applied arts, the national school for cinema studies and national institutes or schools for cultural restoration and preservation.

In accordance with the Bologna Process, an Italian Qualifications Framework was officially published in late 2010 and a National Agency for the Evaluation of Universities and Research Institutes (Agenzia Nazionale di Valutazione del Sistema Universitario e della Ricerca—ANVUR) was in the process of being established.

Admission to higher education is primarily based on the higher secondary school certificate (Diploma di Esame di Stato), though institutions may also administer entrance examinations. Since the implementation of the Bologna Process in 1999 the universities have adopted a three-tier Bachelors/Masters/Doctorate degree system. The Bachelors degree (Laurea) is a three-year programme that requires 180 ECTS credits. Undergraduates in specialized or professional fields that require longer periods of study, such as medicine (six years), pharmacy, architecture and law (all five years), may carry credits over into the Laurea Magistrale. Alternatively, the Laurea Magistrale may be awarded as a conventional Masters-type degree after two years' study following the Laurea. Dottorato di Ricerca is the standard doctoral degree programme, and admission is on the basis of the Laurea Magistrale and institutional requirements. The Dottorato di Ricerca is a structured research-based programme which lasts for at least three years. Since 2009 all graduates are issued with a Diploma Supplement.

Technical and vocational education is provided at secondary through to tertiary level. In 2008 the post-secondary, non-tertiary level within the higher technical education system—the Istruzione e Formazione Tecnica Superiore (IFTS)—was reorganized and henceforth programmes were provided by the Istituti Tecnici Superiori, Higher Technical Institutes. The IFTS courses are free of charge, co-financed by the Ministry and the Regions. There are also two systems providing continuing and vocational education, the Istruzione degli adulti which falls under the responsibility of the Ministry of Education, University and Research and the Formazione Professionale Continua, which is overseen by the Ministry of Labour, Health and Social Policies.

A decree was made in 2008 allowing universities to become private sector foundations, though by early 2011 none had yet taken up the option.

Regulatory and Representative Bodies

GOVERNMENT

Ministry of Cultural Heritage and Activities and Tourism: Via del Collegio Romano 27, 00186 Rome; tel. 6-67232980; e-mail urp@beniculturali.it; internet www.beniculturali.it; Minister MASSIMO BRAY.

Ministry of Education, Universities and Research: *Education Section:* Viale Trastevere, 76A, 00153 Rome; *Universities and Research Section:* Piazza Kennedy 20, 00144 Rome; tel. 6-58491; e-mail urp@istruzione.it; internet www.istruzione.it; Minister STEFANIA GIANNINI.

ACCREDITATION

Comitato Nazionale per la Valutazione del Sistema Universitario (National Committee for the Evaluation of the University System): Piazzale Kennedy 20, 00144 Rome; tel. 06-97726401; internet www.cnvsu.it; Pres. Prof. LUIGI BIGGERI.

ENIC/NARIC Italy/Centro di Informazione sulla Mobilità e le Equivalenze Accademiche (Information Centre on Academic Mobility and Equivalence): Viale XXI Aprile 36, 00162 Rome; tel. 06-86321281; e-mail cimea@fondazionerui.it; internet www.cimea.it; f. 1984; Dir Dott. CARLO FINOCCHIETTI.

Istituto Nazionale per la Valutazione del Sistema Educativo di Istruzione e di Formazione (National Institute for the Assessment of the Educational System): Villa Falconieri, Via Borromini 5, 00044 Frascati; tel. 06-94185319; e-mail biblioteca@invalsi.it; internet www.invalsi.it; f. 1974; library of 9,500 vols, 235 current periodicals; Dir GIOVANNI BOCCHIERI; Head Librarian RITA MARZOLI.

NATIONAL BODIES

Conferenza dei Rettori delle Università Italiane (Italian University Rectors' Conference): Palazzo Rondanini, Piazza Rondanini 48, 00186 Rome; tel. 06-684411; e-mail segreteriacrui@crui.it; internet www.crui.it; f. 1963; Pres. Prof. ENRICO DECLEVA; Exec. Dir Dott. EMANUELA STEFANI.

Consiglio Universitario Nazionale (National University Council): Piazzale Kennedy 20, 00144 Rome; tel. 06-97727502; e-mail cun@miur.it; internet www.cun.it; f. 1997; 57 mem. univs; Pres. Prof. ANDREA LENZI; Sec. Dott. ANTONIO VALEO.

Fondazione Rui: Viale XXI Aprile 36, 00162 Rome; tel. 06-86321281; e-mail info@fondazionerui.it; internet www.fondazionerui.it; f. 1959; library of 3,000 vols; Pres. Prof. CRISTIANO CIAPPEI; Dir Dr FABIO MONTI; publs *Fondazione Rui* (4 a year), *Universitas*.

Istituto per la Cooperazione Universitaria Onlus (Institute for University Co-operation): Viale G. Rossini 26, 00198 Rome; tel. 06-93938367; e-mail info@icu.it; internet www.icu.it; f. 1967 to promote cultural relations between different countries, chiefly through univ. cooperation, int. meetings and study groups; int. technical cooperation by sending volunteers and experts to developing countries; Pres. GIOVANNI DIANA; Gen. Sec. ANDREA VIGEVANI; publs *Educazione e Sviluppo* (irregular), *SIPE—Servizio Stampa Educazione e Sviluppo* (6 a year).

Learned Societies

GENERAL

Accademia delle Scienze dell'Istituto di Bologna (Academy of Sciences of the Bologna Institute): Via Zamboni 31, 40126 Bologna; tel. 051-222596; e-mail accademiascienze@libero.it; internet www.unibo.it/portale/ateneo/divulgazione+scientifica/accademia/default.htm; f. 1711; organizes national and international conventions and conferences; promotes studies of art restoration and art history; 60 mems; 200

corresp. mems; Pres. Prof. ILLIO GALLIGANI; Sec. Prof. RUGGERO BORTOLAMI.

Accademia delle Scienze di Ferrara (Academy of Sciences of Ferrara): Via de Romei 3, 44100 Ferrara; tel. 0532-205209; e-mail info@accademiascienze.ferrara.it; internet www.accademiascienze.ferrara.it; f. 1823; sections of Medical Sciences, Mathematics, Physics, Chemistry and Natural Sciences, Law, Economics, History and Moral Sciences; 270 mems; library of 12,500 vols; Pres. Prof. ROBERTO TOMATIS; Sec. Avv. VINCENZO CAPUTO; publ. *Atti*.

Accademia delle Scienze di Torino (Academy of Sciences of Turin): Via Maria Vittoria 3, 10123 Turin; tel. 011-5620047; e-mail presidenza@accademia.csi.it; internet www.accademiadellescienze.it; f. 1783; sections of moral, historical and philological sciences, and physical, mathematical and natural sciences; 310 mems; library: see under Libraries and Archives; Pres. Prof. PIETRO ROSSI; publs *Atti* (edns for physical, mathematical and natural sciences, and for moral sciences, history and philology, 1 a year each), *Memorie* (edns for physical, mathematical and natural sciences, and for moral sciences, history and philology, 1 a year each), *Quaderni* (irregular).

Accademia Etrusca (Etruscan Academy): Palazzo Casali, Piazza Signorelli 9, 52044 Cortona; tel. 0575-637248; e-mail accademia@accademia-etrusca.org; internet www.accademia-etrusca.org; f. 1727; promotes knowledge of the culture and history of the Cortona area and of Etruscan archaeological discoveries; 210 mems (incl. 50 hon. and 80 corresp.); Pres. Dott. GIOVANNANGELO CAMPOREALE; Vice-Pres. and Sec. Dott. PAOLO BRUSCHETTI; publs *Annuario* (every 2 years), *Cortona Francescana*, *Fonti e Testi*, *Note e Documenti*.

Accademia Gioenia di Catania: Via Fragalà 10, 95100 Catania; e-mail malber@unict.it; internet www.unict.it/gioenia; f. 1824; sections of Natural Sciences, Physics, Chemistry and Mathematics, and Applied Sciences; 56 mems, 57 corresp. mems; library of 20,000 vols, 400 periodicals; Pres. Prof. SALVATORE FOTI; Gen. Sec. Prof. GIORGIO MONTAUDO; publs *Atti della Accademia Gioenia di Scienze Naturali in Catania*, *Bollettino delle Sedute della Accademia Gioenia di Scienze Naturali in Catania*.

Accademia Ligure di Scienze e Lettere (Ligurian Academy of Sciences and Letters): Piazza G. Matteotti 5, 16123 Genoa; tel. 010-565570; e-mail accademialigure@fastwebnet.it; f. 1798; 180 mems (30 ordinary and 50 corresp. in each class; 20 hon.); library of 60,000 vols; Pres. Profa PAOLA MASSA PERGIOVANNI; Sec.-Gen. Dott. G. P. PELOSO; publs *Atti* (1 a year), *Studi e Ricerche*.

Accademia Nazionale dei Lincei: Palazzo Corsini, Via della Lungara 10, 00165 Rome; tel. 06-680271; e-mail segreteria@lincei.it; internet www.lincei.it; f. 1603; sections of Physical, Mathematical and Natural Sciences (Academic Secs Prof. GIANCARLO SETTI, Prof. ANNIBALE MOTTANA), Moral, Historical and Philological Sciences (Academic Secs Prof. ANTONIO GIULIANO, Prof. FULVIO TESSITORE); 540 mems (180 nat., 180 corresp., 180 foreign); library: see under Libraries and Archives; Pres. Prof. LAMBERTO MAFFEI; Vice-Pres. Prof. ALBERTO QUADRIO CURZIO; Academic Administrator Prof. LUCIANO MARTINI; Academic Administrator Prof. PIETRO RESCIGNO; publs *Memorie: Classe di Scienze Morali, Storiche e Filologiche* (irregular), *Memorie Lincee, Classe di Scienze Morali, Storiche e Filologiche* (4 a year), *Memorie Lincee, Matematica e Applicazioni* (irregular), *Memorie Lincee, Scienze Fisiche e Naturali* (irregular), *Notizie degli Scavi di Antichità*, *Rendiconti: Classe di Scienze Morali, Storiche e Filologiche* (4 a year), *Rendiconti Lincei: Matematica e Applicazioni* (4 a year), *Rendiconti Lincei: Scienze Fisiche e Naturali* (4 a year).

Accademia Nazionale di San Luca (National Academy of San Luca): Piazza dell'Accademia di San Luca 77, 00187 Rome; tel. 06-6798850; e-mail segreteria@accademiasanluca.it; internet www.accademiasanluca.it; f. 14th century; sections of Painting, of Sculpture, of Architecture; 54 mems; 90 corresp. mems; 30 foreign mems; 47 cultural and hon. mems; library: see under Libraries and Archives; Pres. NICOLA CARRINO; Sec.-Gen. GIORGIO CIUCCI.

Accademia Nazionale di Santa Cecilia (National Academy of Santa Cecilia): Auditorium Parco della Musica, Largo Luciano Berio 3, 00196 Rome; tel. 06-80242501; e-mail info@santacecilia.it; internet www.santacecilia.it; f. 1566; promotes symphonic concert music, has own symphony orchestra and chorus, carries out professional music training; 100 mems (70 nat., 30 foreign); Pres. Prof. BRUNO CAGLI; publs *E. M. Rivista degli Archivi di Etnomusicologia* (1 a year), *Studi Musicali* (2 a year).

Accademia Nazionale Virgiliana di Scienze, Lettere e Arti (Virgilian National Academy of Sciences, Literature and Arts): Via dell'Accademia 47, 46100 Mantua; tel. 0376-320314; e-mail mantua@accademiavirgiliana.191.it; internet www.accademiavirgiliana.it; f. early 17th century, present name 1981; 170 mems (90 full, 20 hon., 60 corresp.); library: see under Libraries and Archives; Pres. GIORGIO ZAMBONI; Sec. EUGENIO CAMERLENGHI; publ. *Atti e Memorie N. S.* (1 a year).

Accademia Petrarca di Lettere, Arti e Scienze di Arezzo (Petrarch Academy of Literature, Arts and Science): Via dell'Orto 28, 52100 Arezzo; tel. 0575-24700; e-mail info@accademiapetrarca.it; internet www.accademiapetrarca.it; f. 1810; 413 mems; library of 15,000 vols; Pres. Prof. GIULIO FIRPO; Sec. Prof. ANTONIO BATINTI; publs *Atti e Memorie* (1 a year), *Studi Petrarcheschi* (1 a year).

Accademia Pugliese delle Scienze (Puglia Academy of Sciences): Palazzo dell'Ateneo, Piazza Umberto I, 70121 Bari; tel. 080-5714578; e-mail accademia.pugliese@ateneo.uniba.it; internet www.ateneo.uniba.it/accademiapugliese; f. 1925; divided into 2 classes: physical, medical and natural sciences, and moral sciences; library of 6,600 vols, 270 periodical titles; 120 ordinary mems, 200 corresp. mems and 20 hon. mems; Pres. Prof. VITTORIO MARZI; Sec. GIOVANNA PANEBIANCO; publ. *Atti e Relazioni* (1 a year).

Accademia Roveretana degli Agiati di Scienze, Lettere ed Arti: Piazza Rosmini 5, 38068 Rovereto; tel. 0464-436663; e-mail segreteria@agiati.org; internet www.agiati.org; f. 1750; fosters the development of sciences, literature and art; 330 mems; library of 50,000 vols; Pres. Prof. FABRIZIO RASERA; Sec. Dott. CARLO ANDREA POSTINGER; publs *Atti* (Series A (human sciences, literature, art), online), *Atti* (Series B (mathematics, physics, natural science), online).

Accademia Tiberina: Via del Vantaggio 22, 00186 Rome; tel. 06-3610212; e-mail info@accademiatiberina.it; internet www.accademiatiberina.it; f. 1813; 200 mems and 2,000 assoc., corresp., resident and hon. mems; applied sciences, psychology, arts, hygiene and health, anthropology, Yoga-Vedanta centre; library of 10,000 vols; Pres. Mgr Prof. FERNANDO MARIOTTI; Sec. FRANCO ANTONIO PINARDI.

Accademia Toscana di Scienze e Lettere 'La Colombaria' (La Colombaria Tuscan Academy of Science and Literature): Via S. Egidio 23, 50122 Florence; tel. 055-2396628; e-mail segreteria@colombaria.it; internet www.colombaria.it; f. 1735; library of 30,000 vols; Pres. Prof. DANILO TORRE; Administrator Prof. PIERO TANI; publs *Atti e Memorie* (1 a year), *Corpus dei Papiri Filosofici Greci e Latini* (irregular), *Studi* (4 or 5 a year).

Fondazione Internazionale Premio E. Balzan—'Premio': Piazzetta Umberto Giordano 4, 20122 Milan; tel. (2) 76002212; e-mail balzan@balzan.it; internet www.balzan.org; f. 1956; awards Balzan Prizes for worldwide promotion of arts and sciences; about 30 mems; library of 4,500 vols; Pres. Prof. ENRICO DECLEVA; Sec.-Gen. Dr S. WERDER; publs *Balzan Prizes* (1 a year), *Balzan Prizes Interdisciplinary Forum* (1 a year), *The Annual Balzan Lecure*, *The Balzan Prizewinners' Research Projects: An Overview* (every 2 years).

Istituto Lombardo Accademia di Scienze e Lettere: Via Borgonuovo 25, 20121 Milan; tel. 2-864087; e-mail istituto.lombardo@unimi.it; internet www.istitutolombardo.it; f. 1802; divided into 2 classes: Mathematics and Natural Sciences; 120 mems, 193 corresp. assocs, 80 foreign mems; library of 495,000 vols, 330 Italian periodicals, 600 foreign periodicals; Pres. Prof. GIANNANTONIO SACCHI LANDRIANI; publs *Cicli di Lezioni* (1 a year), *Memorie della Classe di Scienze Matematiche e Naturali*, *Memorie della Classe di Lettere e Scienze Morali*, *Rendiconti—Classe di Lettere e Scienze Morali e Storiche*, *Rendiconti—Classe di Scienze Matematiche e Naturali*, *Rendiconti—Parte Generale e Atti Ufficiali*.

Istituto Veneto di Scienze, Lettere ed Arti (Venetian Institute of Sciences, Literature and Arts): Campo S. Stefano 2945, 30124 Venice; tel. 041-2407711; e-mail ivsla@istitutoveneto.it; internet www.istitutoveneto.it; f. 1838; functions as academy; also organizes postdoctoral courses; sections of Physical, Mathematical and Natural Sciences (Academic Sec. Prof. ANDREA RINALDO), Moral Sciences, Literature and Arts (Academic Sec. Prof. GHERARDO ORTALLI); 221 mems (incl. 119 corresp. and 33 foreign); library of 200,600 vols; Pres. Prof. GIAN ANTONIO DANIELI; Administrator Prof. LORENZO FELLIN; publs *Atti* (Proceedings (moral sciences series), 4 a year), *Atti* (Proceedings (physical sciences series), 4 a year), *Memorie*.

Società di Letture e Conversazioni Scientifiche (Scientific Society): Palazzo Ducale ammezzato ala est, Piazza Matteotti 5, Genoa; tel. 010-565141; e-mail info@letturescientifiche.it; internet www.letturescientifiche.it; f. 1866; holds conferences and debates on scientific, historical, literary and political topics; library of 11,000 vols; Pres. UMBERTO COSTA.

Società Nazionale di Scienze, Lettere ed Arti in Napoli (National Society for Sciences, Literature and Art in Naples): Via Mezzocannone 8, 80134 Naples; tel. 81-5527549; e-mail socnazsla@virgilio.it; internet www.socnazsla.unina.it; f. 1808; sections of physical and mathematical sciences, moral and political sciences, archaeology, literature and fine arts, medical sciences and surgery; library of 35,000 vols; Pres. Prof. FULVIO TESSITORE; Sec.-Gen. Prof. CARLO SBORDONE.

UNESCO Office in Venice–UNESCO Regional Bureau for Science and Culture in Europe (BRESCE): 4930 Castello–

Palazzo Zorzi, 30122 Venice; tel. 041-2601511; e-mail veniceoffice@unesco.org; internet www.unesco.org/venice; f. 1988; science policy, education and research throughout SE Europe; environmental policy in local govt (incl. management of water resources and prevention of natural disasters); devt of cultural activities and identifying priorities in SE Europe, such as protection and promotion of cultural heritage; training programmes for cultural conservation; promotes cultural dialogue and artistic creation, and handicraft as a symbol of cultural diversity; library of 2,000 UNESCO publs; Dir Dr ENGELBERT RUOSS.

AGRICULTURE, FISHERIES AND VETERINARY SCIENCE

Accademia di Agricoltura di Torino (Academy of Agriculture of Turin): Via Andrea Doria 10, 10123 Turin; tel. 011-8127470; e-mail to0323@biblioteche.reteunitaria.piemonte.it; internet web.tiscali.it/accagri; f. 1785; 155 mems; library of 26,000 vols, 50 current periodicals; Pres. ORAZIO SAPPA; publs *Annali dell'Accademia di Agricoltura di Torino* (1 a year), *Nuovo Calendario Georgico* (1 a year).

Accademia dei Georgofili (Academy of Georgofili): Logge Uffizi Corti, 50122 Florence; tel. 055-212114; e-mail accademia@georgofili.it; internet www.georgofili.it; f. 1753; promotes the application of sciences to agriculture and environmental protection, and the development of rural areas; 522 mems; library of 70,000 vols; Pres. Prof. FRANCO SCARAMUZZI; publs *Atti* (1 a year), *Quaderni*, *Rivista di Storia della Agricoltura*.

Accademia Italiana di Scienze Forestali (Italian Academy of Forest Sciences): Piazza Edison 11, 50133 Florence; tel. 055-570348; e-mail info@aisf.it; internet www.aisf.it; f. 1951; 327 mems; library of 6,000 vols; Pres. Prof. O. CIANCIO; publs *Annali* (1 a year), *L'Italia Forestale e Montana* (6 a year).

Accademia Nazionale di Agricoltura (National Academy of Agriculture): Via Castiglione 11, 40124 Bologna; tel. 051-268809; e-mail segreteria@accademia-agricoltura.it; internet www.accademia-agricoltura.unibo.it; f. 1807; 80 mems and 140 corresponding mems; library of 20,000 vols; Pres. Prof. GIORGIO AMADEI; Sec. GUALTIERO BARALDI; publ. *Annali* (4 a year).

Istituto Agronomico per l'Oltremare (Agronomic Institute for Overseas): Via Antonio Cocchi 4, 50131 Florence; tel. 055-50611; e-mail iao@iao.florence.it; internet www.iao.florence.it; f. 1904; 50 mems; library of 133,000 vols, 800 current periodicals; Dir-Gen. GIOVANNI TOTINO; publ. *Journal of Agriculture and Environment for International Development* (4 a year).

Società Italiana delle Scienze Veterinarie (Italian Society of Veterinary Sciences): Via Istria 3B, 25125 Brescia; tel. 030-223244; e-mail sisvet@fondiz.it; internet www.sisvet.it; f. 1947; 1,700 mems; Pres. Prof. ANTONIO PUGLIESE; Gen. Sec. Prof. MASSIMO DE MAJO; publ. *Atti*.

Società Italiana di Economia Agraria (Italian Agrarian Economics Society): c/o Dott. Annalisa Zezza, INEA, Via Barberini 36, 00187 Rome; e-mail zezza@inea.it; internet ilo.unimol.it/sidea; f. 1962; 300 mems; Pres. Prof. GIOVANNI CANNATA; Sec. Dott. ANNALISA ZEZZA; publ. *Atti* (1 a year).

ARCHITECTURE AND TOWN PLANNING

Centro Internazionale di Studi di Architettura 'Andrea Palladio' (Andrea Palladio International Centre for the Study of Architecture): Palazzo Barbaran da Porto, contra' Porti 11, CP 835, 36100 Vicenza; tel. 0444-323014; e-mail segreteria@cisapalladio.org; internet www.cisapalladio.org; f. 1958 to make known the work of Andrea Palladio, born Padua 1508, and to encourage the study of Palladianism and of Venetian architecture of all ages; library of 30,000 vols; Pres. AMALIA SARTORI; Dir GUIDO BELTRAMINI; publ. *Annali* (1 a year, online).

Istituto Nazionale di Architettura (IN-ARCH) (National Architectural Institute): Via Crescenzio 16, 00193 Rome; tel. 06-68802254; e-mail inarch@inarch.it; internet www.inarch.it; f. 1959; organizes meetings, debates and exhibitions; 1,000 mems; Pres. Ing. ADOLFO GUZZINI.

Istituto Nazionale di Urbanistica (INU) (National Institute of Town Planning): Piazza Farnese 44, 00186 Rome; tel. 06-68801190; e-mail segreteria@inu.it; internet www.inu.it; f. 1930; 2,654 mems (960 ordinary, 1,694 assoc.); Pres. FEDERICO OLIVA; Sec. SIMONE OMBUEN; publs *Urbanistica* (3 a year), *Urbanistica Dossier* (12 a year), *Urbanistica Informazioni* (6 a year).

Italia Nostra—Associazione Nazionale per la Tutela del Patrimonio Storico, Artistico e Naturale della Nazione (Italia Nostra—National Association for the Preservation of the Historical, Artistic and Natural Heritage of the Nation): Viale Liegi 33, 00198 Rome; tel. 6-8537271; e-mail italianostra@italianostra.org; internet www.italianostra.org; f. 1955; brs in 206 towns; 20,000 mems, subscribers, delegates; library of 4,500 vols; Pres. ALESSANDRA MOTTOLA MOLFINO; Sec. Gen. ANTONELLO ALICI; publ. *Italia Nostra* (9 a year).

BIBLIOGRAPHY, LIBRARY SCIENCE AND MUSEOLOGY

Associazione Italiana Biblioteche (Italian Library Association): CP 2461, Ufficio Roma 158, Via Marsala 39, 00185 Rome; c/o Biblioteca nazionale centrale, Viale Castro Pretorio 105, 00185 Rome; tel. 06-4463532; e-mail aib@aib.it; internet www.aib.it; f. 1930; supports organization and devt of libraries and a library service in Italy; acts as professional rep. in all cultural, scientific, technical, legal and legislative spheres; 4,500 mems; library of 8,000 vols, 500 journals; Pres. STEFANO PARISE; Sec. GIOVANNA FRIGIMELICA; publs *AIB Notizie* (6 a year), *Bollettino AIB* (4 a year).

Associazione Nazionale dei Musei Italiani (National Association of Italian Museums): Piazza San Marco 49, 00186 Rome; tel. 06-6791343; Pres. Prof. D. BERNINI; Sec. Dott. L. BARBACINI; publ. *Musei e Gallerie d'Italia*.

Istituto Centrale per il Restauro e la Conservazione del Patrimonio Archivistico e Librario (Central Institute for the Restoration and Conservation of Archives and Libraries): Via Milano 76, 00184 Rome; tel. 06-482911; e-mail icapl@beniculturali.it; internet www.icpal.beniculturali.it; f. 2007 by merger of Istituto Centrale per la Patologia del Libro (ICPL) with Centro di Fotoriproduzione Legatoria e Restauro Degli Archivi di Stato (CFLR); attached to Italian Min. of Cultural Heritage and Activities; book and document restoration and preservation; research on the safeguarding and conservation of library and archival heritage; 77 mems; library of 15,000 vols, 170 current periodicals; Dir MARIA CRISTINA MISITI.

ECONOMICS, LAW AND POLITICS

Accademia Italiana di Economia Aziendale (Academy of Business Economics): Piazza De'Calderini 2, 40124 Bologna; tel. 051-558798; e-mail segreteria@accademiaaidea.it; internet www.accademiaaidea.it; f. 1813; research teaching advisory; reps from all Italian universities; 810 mems (750 nat., 50 foreign and 10 hon.); Pres. Prof. ALESSANDRO CARRETTA; Vice-Pres. Prof. DONATELLA DEPPERU; Vice-Pres. Prof. VINCENZO MAGGIONI.

CIRGIS (International Centre for Juridical Research and Scientific Initiatives): Via Manzoni 45, 20121 Milan; tel. 2-6552167; e-mail segreteria@cirgis.it; internet www.cirgis.it; f. 1979; aims for the realization of exchanges of thought and experience between Italian and foreign jurists, the knowledge of laws and institutions of different countries through meetings, publs, etc.; c. 400 mems; Pres. Avv. Prof. FRANCESCO OGLIARI; Int. Sec. Avv. GIUSEPPE AGLIALORO.

Istituto di Diritto Romano e dei Diritti dell'Oriente Mediterraneo (Institute of Roman Law and Laws of the Near East): Facoltà di Giurisprudenza, Piazzale Aldo Moro 5, 00185 Rome; tel. 06-49910232; e-mail marilena.zanatatritto@uniroma1.it; f. 1937; library of 70,000 vols, 80 current periodicals; Dir Prof. ANDREA DI PORTO; Academic Sec. Dott. MARILENA ZANATA TRITTO.

Società Italiana degli Economisti (Italian Economists' Society): Piazzale Martelli, 8, 60121 Ancona; tel. 071-2207111; e-mail sie@univpm.it; internet www.sie.univpm.it; f. 1950; 594 mems; Pres. Prof. ALESSANDRO RONCAGLIA; Gen. Sec. Prof. ALBERTO ZAZZARO; publs *Bollettino dei Soci*, *Lettera* (1 a year), *Rivista Italiana degli Economisti*.

Società Italiana di Economia, Demografia e Statistica: Piazza Tommaso de Cristoforis, 6, 00159 Rome; tel. 6-43589008; e-mail sieds@tin.it; internet www.sieds.it; f. 1938; 600 mems; Pres. GIOVANNI MARIA GIORGI; Sec.-Gen. GIOVANNI CARIANI; publ. *Rivista Italiana di Economia, Demografia e Statistica* (4 a year).

Società Italiana di Filosofia del Diritto: c/o Ist. di Filosofia del Diritto, Facoltà di Giurisprudenza, Università La Sapienza, 00185 Rome; tel. 06-490489; internet www.sifd.it; f. 1936; 200 mems; Pres. Prof. FRANCESCO VIOLA; publ. *Rivista Internazionale di Filosofia del Diritto* (4 a year).

Società Italiana di Statistica (Italian Statistics Society): Salita de' Crescenzi 26, 00186 Rome; tel. 06-6869845; e-mail sis@caspur.it; internet www.sis-statistica.it; f. 1939; 1,000 mems; 300 associates; statistics and demography; Pres. Prof. MAURIZIO VICHI; Sec. Profa CECILIA TOMASSINI; publs *Statistical Methods and Applications* (4 a year; in English), *Statistica e Società* (online), *SIS-magazine* (online), *SIS-Informazioni* (12 a year).

Società Italiana per l'Organizzazione Internazionale (SIOI) (UN Association for Italy): Piazza di S. Marco 51, 00186 Rome; tel. 06-6920781; e-mail sioi@sioi.org; internet www.sioi.org; f. 1944; sections in Milan, Naples, Turin; library: see under Libraries and Archives; Pres. Hon. FRANCO FRATTINI; Sec.-Gen. MARCELO SALIMEI; publ. *La Comunità Internazionale* (4 a year).

EDUCATION

Associazione Pedagogica Italiana (Italian Educational Association): Via Zamboni 34, 40126 Bologna; tel. 051-2098442; e-mail info@aspei.it; internet www.aspei.it; f. 1950; aims to promote the development of schools in general and all other institutions of education, also studies and research in education; 50 brs; 5,000 mems; Pres. SIRA SERENELLA MACCHIETTI; Sec.-Gen. ALDO D'ALFONSO; publ. *Bollettino* (4 a year).

FINE AND PERFORMING ARTS

Accademia di Francia (French Academy in Rome): Villa Medici, Viale Trinità dei Monti 1, 00187 Rome; tel. 06-67611; e-mail standard@villamedici.it; internet www.villamedici.it; f. 1666; organizes exhibitions, concerts, symposia and seminars on artistic and literary topics, and on their history; library of 32,000 vols; Dir ÉRIC DE CHASSEY; Gen. Sec. SIDNEY PEYROLES.

Accademia Raffaello: Via Cesare Battisti 54, 61029 Urbino; tel. 0722-329695; e-mail segreteria@accademiaraffaello.it; internet www.accademiaraffaello.it; f. 1869; promotes fine art; 260 mems; library of 16,000 vols; Pres. Prof. GIORGIO CERBONI BAIARDI; publs *Accademia Raffaello. Atti e Studi*, *Rivista Accademia Raffaello* (2 a year).

Fondazione Istituto Italiano per la Storia della Musica (Italian Institute for the History of Music): c/o Accademia Nazionale di Santa Cecilia, Via Vittoria 6, 00187 Rome; tel. 06-36000146; e-mail info@iism.it; internet www.iism.it; f. 1938; Pres. Prof. AGOSTINO ZIINO.

Istituto Nazionale di Studi Verdiani (National Institute of Verdi Studies): Via Melloni 1B, 43100 Parma; tel. 0521-285273; e-mail direzione@studiverdiani.it; internet www.studiverdiani.it; f. 1960 under the patronage of the Int. Music Ccl and the Italian Min. of Culture; studies the life and works of Giuseppe Verdi; library of 15,000 vols, archives of 16,000 documents; Pres. MARIA MERCEDES CARRARA VERDI; Dir EMILIO SALA; publs *Carteggi Verdiani*, *Premio Internazionale Rotary Club di Parma 'Giuseppe Verdi'*, *Proceedings of Congresses*, *Quaderni*, *Studi Verdiani* (1 a year).

Istituto Universitario Olandese di Storia dell'Arte (Dutch University Institute for the History of Art): Viale Torricelli 5, 50125 Florence; tel. 055-221612; e-mail iuo@iuo.iris.firenze.it; internet niki.meyson.net; f. 1958; library of 50,000 vols; Dir Dr MICHAEL W. KWAKKELSTEIN.

Kunsthistorisches Institut in Florenz–Max-Planck-Institut/Istituto di Storia dell'Arte di Firenze (Institute for History of Art): Via Giuseppe Giusti 44, 50121 Florence; tel. 55-249111; e-mail khi-presse@khi.fi.it; internet www.khi.fi.it; f. 1897, became Max-Planck Institute 2002; research on history of art and architecture in Italy; 60 mems; library of 310,000 vols, 2,600 periodicals and 610,000 reproductions; spec. collns incl. art in Italy; Man. Dir Prof. Dr GERHARD WOLF; Dir Prof. Dr ALESSANDRO NOVA; publs *Collana del KHI*, *Deutsche Ausgabe der 'Vite'*, *Die Kirchen von Siena*, *I Mandorli*, *Italienische Forschungen*, *Mitteilungen des KHI*, *Studi e Ricerche*.

Real Academia de España en Roma (Royal Spanish Academy in Rome): Piazza San Pietro in Montorio 3, 00153 Rome; tel. 06-5812806; e-mail info@raer.it; internet raer.it; f. 1873; Dir ENRIQUE PANÉS; Gen. Sec. FERNANDO VALERO.

Società d'Incoraggiamento d'Arti e Mestieri (Society for the Encouragement of Arts and Crafts): Via Santa Marta 18, 20123 Milan; tel. 02-86450125; e-mail segreteria@siam1838.it; internet www.siam1838.it; f. 1838; education in mechanics, electronics, electrotechnics, chemistry, information technology; library of 6,000 vols; Pres. BRUNO SORESINA; Gen. Sec. ALBERTO PIANTA.

Società Italiana di Musicologia (Italian Musicological Society): CP 7256, Ag. Roma Nomentano, 00162 Rome; Via dei Greci 18, 00187 Rome; tel. 338-1957796; e-mail segreteria@sidm.it; internet www.sidm.it; f. 1964; 800 mems; Pres. GUIDO SALVETTI; Sec. SARA CICCARELLI; publs *Bollettino* (2 a year), *Fonti Musicali Italiane* (1 a year), *Rivista Italiana di Musicologia* (2 a year).

Società Italiana Musica Contemporanea: Via Domenichino 12, 20149 Milan; tel. 02-468157; e-mail simc@fastwebnet.it; internet www.simc-italia.it; f. 1923; Pres. Prof. DAVIDE ANZAGHI; Sec. Prof. GABRIELE ROTA; publ. *Newsletter* (online).

HISTORY, GEOGRAPHY AND ARCHAEOLOGY

Associazione Archeologica Romana (Roman Archaeological Society): Piazza Benedetto Cairoli 117, 00186 Rome; tel. 06-6865647; e-mail assoarcheologicaromana@tin.it; internet www.associazionearcheologicaromana.it; f. 1902; 400 mems; library of 3,000 vols; Pres. Prof. CLAUDIO STRINATI; Sec. Dott. PAOLA MANETTO; publ. *Romana Gens* (4 a year).

Istituto Geografico Militare (Military Geographical Institute): Via Cesare Battisti 10, 50122 Florence; tel. 055-27321; e-mail info@geomil.esercito.difesa.it; internet www.igmi.org; f. 1872; geodetic and topographical surveying; official cartography; library of 120,000 vols, 700 atlases, 22,000 cartographic items; Dir-Gen. Gen. ANTONIO DE VITA; publs *Bollettino di Geodesia e Scienze Affini* (3 a year), *L'Universo* (6 a year).

Istituto Italiano di Numismatica (Italian Numismatics Institute): Palazzo Barberini, Via Quattro Fontane 13, 00184 Rome; tel. 06-4743603; e-mail istituto@istitutoitalianonumismatica.it; internet www.istitutoitalianonumismatica.it; f. 1936; library of 22,000 vols; Dir Prof. SARA SORDA; publ. *Annali* (1 a year).

Istituto Italiano di Paleontologia Umana (Italian Institute of Human Palaeontology): Via Aldrovandi 18, 00197 Rome; tel. 6-8557598; e-mail info@isipu.org; internet www.isipu.org; f. 1913; quaternary environment, geology, palaeontology, palaeoanthropology, archaeology; extensive offprints series; 250 mems; library of 5,800 vols, 31 periodicals; Pres. RAFFAELE SARDELLA; publs *Memorie* (irregular), *Quaternaria* (1 a year).

Istituto Italiano per la Storia Antica (Italian Institute for Ancient History): Via Milano 76, 00184 Rome; tel. 06-4880597; e-mail storia.antica@virgilio.it; internet www.storiaantica.eu; f. 1935; library of 18,000 vols, 82 current periodicals; Pres. Prof. ANDREA GIARDINA; publs *Miscellanea Greca e Romana*, *Studi pubblicati dall'Istituto Italiano per la Storia Antica*.

Istituto Nazionale di Archeologia e Storia dell'Arte (National Institute of Archaeology and History of Art): Piazza San Marco 49, 00186 Rome; tel. 06-6780817; e-mail inasa@inasa-roma.it; internet www.inasa-roma.it; f. 1918; library of 500,000 vols; Pres. Prof. ADRIANO LA REGINA; publ. *RIASA—Rivista dell'Istituto Nazionale di Archeologia e Storia dell'Arte* (1 a year).

Istituto Nazionale di Studi Etruschi ed Italici (National Institute for Etruscan and Italic Studies): Via Romana 37A, 50125 Florence; tel. 055-2207175; e-mail studietruschi@interfree.it; internet studietruschi.org; f. 1932; 233 mems; library of 16,000 vols; Pres. Prof. GIOVANNANGELO CAMPOREALE; Gen. Sec. Prof. LUIGI DONATI; publ. *Studi Etruschi* (1 a year).

Istituto per la Storia del Risorgimento Italiano (Institute for the History of the Italian Revival): Museo Centrale del Risorgimento, Complesso del Vittoriano, Piazza Venezia, 00186 Rome; tel. 06-6793598; e-mail ist.risorgimento@tiscalinet.it; internet www.risorgimento.it; f. 1936; 3,400 mems; Pres. Prof. ROMANO UGOLLINI; Gen. Sec. Prof. SERGIO LA SALVIA; publs *Atti* (irregular), *Edizione scritti Garibaldi* (irregular), *Fonti* (irregular), *Memorie* (irregular), *Rassegna Storica del Risorgimento dal 1914* (online).

Istituto Storico Italiano per il Medio Evo (Italian Institute of Medieval History): Piazza dell'Orologio 4, 00186 Rome; tel. 06-68802075; e-mail amministrazione@isime.it; internet www.isime.it; f. 1883; library of 100,000 vols; Pres. Prof. MASSIMO MIGLIO; publs *Bullettino*, *Fonti per la Storia dell'Italia Medievale*, *Nuovi Studi Storici*, *Repertorium Fontium Historiae Medii Aevi*.

Istituto Storico Italiano per l'Età Moderna e Contemporanea (Italian Historical Institute for the Contemporary and Modern Era): Via Michelangelo Caetani 32, 00186 Rome; tel. 06-68806922; e-mail iststor@libero.it; internet www.icbsa.it; f. 1934; historical research and publications; library of 35,000 vols; Pres. Prof. LUIGI LOTTI; publ. *Annuario*.

Società di Minerva: Piazza Hortis 4, 34123 Trieste; tel. 040-660245; e-mail societadiminerva@gmail.com; internet www.societadiminerva.it; f. 1810; studies history, art and culture of Trieste, Istria and Gorizia; 150 mems; Pres. Prof. GINO PAVAN; Sec. Dott. GIULIANA MARINI; publs *Archeografo Triestino* (1 a year), *Extra serie dell'Archeografo Triestino* (irregular), *Quaderni di Minerva* (irregular).

Società di Studi Geografici (Society for Geographical Studies): Via San Gallo 10, 50129 Florence; tel. 055-2757956; e-mail info@societastudigeografici.it; internet www.societastudigeografici.it; f. 1895; Devt of geographic, territorial and regional geography through seminars, workshops, int. confs, journal publs; 500 mems; library of 25,000 vols; Pres. Prof. LIDIA SCARPELLI; Vice-Pres. Prof. LEONARDO ROMBAI; Sec. Prof. CAPINERI CRISTINA; publs *Memorie geografiche Nuova Serie* (1 a year), *Rivista Geografica Italiana* (4 a year).

Società Geografica Italiana: Palazzetto Mattei in Villa Celimontana, Via della Navicella 12, 00184 Rome; tel. 06-7008279; e-mail segreteria@societageografica.it; internet www.societageografica.it; f. 1867; library: see under Libraries and Archives; Pres. Prof. FRANCO SALVATORI; publs *Bollettino* (4 a year), *Ricerche e Studi*.

Società Napoletana di Storia Patria (Neapolitan Society of Italian History): Maschio Angioino, Piazza Municipio, 80133 Naples; tel. 081-5510353; e-mail info@storiapatrianapoli.it; internet www.storiapatrianapoli.it; f. 1875; library of 350,000 vols, 900 current periodicals; 650 mems; Pres. Prof. RENATA DE LORENZO; Vice-Pres. Prof. AURELIO MUSI; Librarian LUIGI CERULLO; publ. *Archivo Storico per le Province Napoletane*.

Società Romana di Storia Patria (Roman Society of Italian History): Piazza della Chiesa Nuova 18, 00186 Rome; tel. 6-68307513; e-mail segreteria@srsp.it; internet www.srsp.it; f. 1876; 117 mems; Pres. LETIZIA ERMINI PANI; Sec. ALBERTO BARTOLA; publs *Archivio della Società* (1 a year), *Codice Diplomatico di Roma e della Regione Romana* (irregular), *Miscellanea della Società* (irregular).

Società Storica Lombarda (Lombardy Historical Society): Via Morone 1, 20121 Milan; tel. 02-860118; e-mail storica@tiscalinet.it; internet www.societastoricalombarda.it; f. 1873; 450 mems; library of 27,000 vols; Pres. GIAN BATTISTA ORIGONI DELLA CROCE; Sec. Dott.

Luigi Orombelli; publ. *Archivio Storico Lombardo* (1 a year).

LANGUAGE AND LITERATURE

Accademia della Crusca: Villa Medicea di Castello, Via di Castello 46, 50141 Florence; tel. 55-454277; e-mail edizioni@crusca.fi.it; internet www.accademiadellacrusca.it; f. 1583; library of 128,000 vols; scientific research dedicated to the study and enhancement of the Italian language; 61 mems; Pres. Prof. Nicoletta Maraschio; Vice-Pres. Prof. Paola Manni; Dir of Philological Studies Rosanna Bettarini; Dir of Lexicographical Studies Prof. Luca Serianni; Dir of Grammatical Studies Prof. Teresa Poggi Salani; Sec. Prof. Massimo L. Fanfani; publs *La Crusca per voi* (2 a year), *Studi di Filologia Italiana* (1 a year), *Studi di Grammatica Italiana* (1 a year), *Studi di Lessicografia Italiana* (1 a year).

Alliance Française: Via Giulia 250, 00186 Rome; tel. 06-6892461; e-mail assistant-dgaf@alliancefr.it; internet www .alliancefr.it; offers courses and exams in French language and culture and promotes cultural exchange with France; attached teaching centres in 30 locations incl. Aosta, Bari, Bologna, Catania, Catanzaro, Genoa, La Spezia, Lecce, Messina, Padua, Potenza, San Marino, Sassari, Trieste, Turin, Venice and Verona; Dir Charles de Tinguy de la Giroulière.

British Council: Via di San Sebastianello, 16, 00187 Rome; tel. 06-478141; e-mail corsi .roma@britishcouncil.it; internet www .britishcouncil.org/italy; teaching centre; offers courses and exams in English language and British culture and promotes cultural exchange with the UK; attached teaching centres in Milan and Naples; Dir, Italy Paul Docherty.

Goethe-Institut: Via Savoia 15, 00198 Rome; tel. 06-8440051; e-mail info@rom .goethe.org; internet www.goethe.de/it/rom/ deindex.htm; offers courses and exams in German language and culture and promotes cultural exchange with Germany; attached centres in Genoa, Milan, Naples, Palermo, Rome, Trieste and Turin; library of 29,000 vols; Dir Susanne Höhn.

Instituto Cervantes: Via di Villa Albani 14–16, 00198 Rome; tel. 06-8537361; e-mail cenrom@cervantes.es; internet roma .cervantes.es; f. 1992; offers courses and exams in Spanish language and culture and promotes cultural exchange with Spain and Spanish-speaking Latin and Central America; attached centres in Milan, Naples and Palermo; library of 32,000 vols; Dir Mario García del Castro.

PEN Club Italiano: Via Daverio 7, 20122 Milan; tel. 0335-7350966; e-mail segreteria@ penclub.it; internet www.penclub.it; promotes freedom of expression; 250 mems; Pres. Sebastiano Grasso; Sec.-Gen. Giorgio Mannacio; publ. *Rivista* (4 a year).

Società Dante Alighieri: Palazzo di Firenze, Piazza Firenze 27, 00186 Rome; tel. 06-6873694; e-mail segreteria@ladante.it; internet www.ladante.it; f. 1889; promotes Italian language and culture throughout the world; Sec.-Gen. Comm. Dott. Alessandro Masi; publ. *Pagine della Dante* (3 a year).

Società Dantesca Italiana (Italian Dante Society): Palagio dell'Arte della Lana, Via Arte della Lana 1, 50123 Florence; tel. 055-287134; e-mail sdi@dantesca.it; internet www.dantesca.it; f. 1888; library of 30,000 vols, 1,500 microfilms; Pres. Dott. Eugenio Giani; Librarian Laura Breccia; publs *Collana, Dantesca, Edizione Nazionale delle Opere di Dante Alighieri, Manoscritti Danteschi e d'Interesse Dantesco, Quaderni degli Studi Danteschi, Quaderni del Centro di Studi e Documentazione Dantesca e Medievale, Rivista Annuale, Studi Danteschi.*

Società Filologica Romana: Dipartimento di Studi Europei, Americani e Interculturali, Sapienza Università di Roma, Facoltà di Lettere e Filosofia, Piazzale Aldo Moro 5, 00185 Rome; tel. 06-49913071; e-mail roberto .antonelli@uniroma1.it; internet w3 .uniroma1.it/studieuropei/sfr; f. 1901; organizes confs, meetings, seminars; 130 mems; library of 8,000 vols; Pres. Prof. Roberto Antonelli; Sec. Giovannella Desideri; publ. *Studj Romanzi.*

Società Italiana degli Autori ed Editori (SIAE) (Italian Authors' and Publishers' Society): Viale della Letteratura 30, 00144 Rome; tel. 06-59901; e-mail sam.urp@siae.it; internet www.siae.it; f. 1882; protects authors' and publishers' rights; 90,000 mems; administers the Biblioteca e Museo Teatrale del Burcardo (35,000 vols); Pres. Gino Paoli (acting); Gen. Dir Dr Gaetano Blandini; publs *Annuario dello Spettacolo, SiaeNews, VivaVerdi.*

Società Letteraria di Verona (Literary Society of Verona): Piazzetta Scalette Rubiani 1, 37121 Verona; tel. 045-595949; e-mail societaletteraria@societaletteraria.it; internet www.societaletteraria.it; f. 1808; promotes appreciation of sciences, literature and art; 500 mems; library of 100,000 vols; Pres. Daniela Brunelli; publ. *Bollettino* (1 a year).

MEDICINE

Accademia delle Scienze Mediche di Palermo: c/o Policlinico Universitario Paolo Giaccone, Dip. di Biopatologia e Metodologie Biomediche, Corso Tukory 211, 90134 Palermo; tel. 91-6552456; e-mail accademiascienze@unipa.it; internet www .unipa.it/accademiascienze; f. 1621; library; Pres. Prof. A. Salerno; Sec. Prof. Alfredo Di Jesù; publ. *Atti* (1 a year).

Accademia di Medicina di Torino (Turin Academy of Medicine): Via Po 18, 10123 Turin; tel. 11-8179298; e-mail accademia .medicina@unito.it; internet www .accademiadimedicina.unito.it; f. 1846; 120 ordinary mems, 30 hon. mems, 29 corresp. mems; library of 11,761 vols; Pres. Prof. Nicola Riccardino; Sec.-Gen. Prof. Giovanni Carlo Isaia; publ. *Giornale* (2 a year).

Accademia Medica di Roma: Policlinico Umberto I, Viale del Policlinico, 00161 Rome; tel. 6-4957818; e-mail info@ accademiamedicadiroma.it; f. 1875; 400 mems; Pres. Prof. Andrea Sciacca; Sec. Prof. Luigi Travia; publ. *Bolletino ed Atti* (1 a year).

Associazione Italiana di Dietetica e Nutrizione Clinica (Italian Association for Dietetics and Clinical Nutrition): Via dei Sassoni 16, 01030 Monterosi (VT); tel. 0761-699511; e-mail adicentral@libero.it; internet www.adiitalia.com; f. 1950; education and training; application of research in nutrition; 200 mems; Pres. Prof. Maria Antonia Fusco; Gen. Sec. Dr Giuseppe Fatati; publs *ADI Magazine* (4 a year), *Attualità in Dietetica e Nutrizione Clinica* (2 a year), *Mediterranean Journal of Nutrition and Metabolism.*

Associazione Italiana di Medicina Aeronautica e Spaziale (Italian Association for Aeronautical and Space Medicine): Università degli Studi di Roma 'La Sapienza', Istituto di Medicina Legale, Viale Regina Elena 336, 00161 Rome; tel. 0347-9401715; e-mail segreteria@aimas.it; internet www .aimas.it; f. 1963; Pres. Manlio Carboni; Gen. Sec. Paola Verde.

Fondazione Luigi Villa: Via Pace 9, 20122 Milan; tel. 02-5510709; e-mail info@ fondazioneluigivilla.org; internet www .fondazioneluigivilla.org; f. 1969; prevention and treatment of the haemorrhagic and thrombotic diseases; library of 9,500 vols; Pres. Prof. Piermannuccio Mannucci; Sec. Prof. Flora Peyvandi.

Società Italiana di Anestesia, Analgesia, Rianimazione e Terapia Intensiva (Italian Society for Anaesthesia, Analgesia, Resuscitation and Intensive Therapy): Corso Bramante 83, 10126 Turin; tel. 011-678282; e-mail siaarti@unipg.it; internet www.siaarti .it; f. 1934; 2,000 mems; Pres. Vito Aldo Peduto; Sec. and Treas. Fabio Gori; publ. *Minerva Anestesiologica* (12 a year).

Società Italiana di Cancerologia (Italian Society of Cancerology): Via G. Venezian, 1, 20133 Milan; tel. 02-23902675; e-mail sic@ istitutotumori.mi.it; internet www .cancerologia.it; f. 1952; Pres. Alfredo Fusco; publ. *Tumori* (6 a year, online).

Società Italiana di Chirurgia (Italian Society for Surgery): Viale Tiziano, 19, 00196 Rome; tel. 06-3221867; e-mail sic@ sichirurgia.org; internet www.sichirurgia .org; f. 1882; Pres. Prof. Gianluigi Melotti; Gen. Sec. Prof. Rocco Bellantone; publ. *Chirurgia Italiana* (6 a year).

Società Italiana di Farmacologia (Italian Pharmacological Society): Viale Abruzzi 32, 20131 Milan; tel. 02-29520311; e-mail sifcese@comm2000.it; internet www.sifweb .org; f. 1939 to develop pharmacological studies and their applications; 1,152 mems (1,115 ordinary, 13 hon., 24 assoc.); Pres. Prof. Carlo Riccardi; Sec. Prof. Liberato Berrino; publs *Pharmacological Research* (12 a year), *Quaderni della SIF* (4 a year, online).

Società Italiana di Ginecologia ed Ostetricia (Italian Society for Gynaecology and Obstetrics): Via dei Soldati 25, 00186 Rome; tel. 06-6875119; e-mail federazione@sigo.it; internet www.sigo.it; f. 1892; 5,300 mems; Pres. Giorgio Vittori; Sec. Fabio Sirimarco; publs *Atti* (1 a year), *Italian Journal of Gynaecology and Obstetrics* (4 a year), *SIGO Notizie* (3 a year).

Società Italiana di Medicina Interna (Italian Society for Internal Medicine): Viale dell'Università 25, 00185 Rome; tel. 06-44340373; e-mail info@simi.it; internet www .simi.it; f. 1887; annual nat. congress; 2,710 mems; Pres. Prof. Gino Roberto Corazza; Sec. Prof. Antonello Pietrangelo; publ. *Internal and Emergency Medicine* (in English).

Società Italiana di Medicina Legale e delle Assicurazioni (Italian Society for Legal Medicine and Assurance): Dipartimento di Scienze Anatomiche, Istologiche, Medico Legali e dell'Apparato Locomotore, Università degli Studi di Roma 'La Sapienza', Piazzale Aldo Moro 5, 00185 Rome; e-mail paola.frati@fastwebnet.it; internet www .simlaweb.com; f. 1897; Pres. Prof. Paolo Arbarello; Sec. Prof. Paola Frati; publ. *Rivista Italiana di Medicina Legale.*

Società Italiana di Odontostomatologia e Chirurgia Maxillo-Facciale (Italian Society for Odontostomatology and Maxillofacial Surgery): Via Eugubina 42a, 06122 Perugia; tel. 075-5729867; e-mail siocmf@tin .it; internet main.netemedia.net/siocmf; f. 1957; 2,000 mems; Pres. Prof. Pierluigi Sapelli; Sec.-Gen. and Treas. Prof. Maurizio Procaccini; publ. *Minerva Stomatologica* (12 a year).

Società Italiana di Ortopedia e Traumatologia (Italian Society for Orthopaedics and Traumatology): Via Nicola Martelli 3, 00197

Rome; tel. 06-80691593; e-mail segreteria@siot.it; internet www.siot.it; f. 1906; 3,100 mems; Pres. Prof. PIETRO BARTOLOZZI; Sec. Dott. ANDREA PICCIOLI.

Società Italiana di Radiologia Medica: Via della Signora 2, 20122 Milan; tel. 02-76006094; e-mail segreteria@sirm.org; internet www.sirm.org; f. 1913; Pres. ANTONIO ROTONDO; Sec. LUCA BRUNESE; publ. *La Radiologia Medica* (in Italian and English).

Società Italiana di Reumatologia (Italian Society for Rheumatology): Via Turati 40, 20121 Milan; tel. 02-7382330; e-mail segreteria@reumatologia.it; internet www.reumatologia.it; f. 1950; 915 mems; Pres. CARLOMAURIZIO MONTECUCCO; Gen. Sec. SILVANA ZENI; publ. *Reumatismo* (4 a year, in Italian and English).

Società Italiana di Traumatologia della Strada (Italian Society for Road Accident Traumatology): Via Monte delle Gioie 1/D, 00199 Rome; tel. 06-49982399; e-mail socitras@socitras.org; internet www.socitras.org; f. 1984; studies on road trauma, safety campaigns, dissemination of knowledge, training courses; 200 mems; Pres. Prof. ANDREA COSTANZO; Sec.-Gen. Dr ROBERTO SAPIA.

Società Medica Chirurgica di Bologna (Society of Medicine and Surgery): Palazzo dell'Archiginnasio, Piazza Galvani 1, 40124 Bologna; tel. 051-231488; e-mail info@medchir.bo.it; internet www.medchir.bo.it; f. 1802; holds scientific meetings; 350 mems; library of 15,000 vols; Pres. Prof. ROBERTO CORINALDESI; Sec. and Dir of Library Prof. STEFANO ARIETI; publ. *Bullettino delle Scienze Mediche*.

NATURAL SCIENCES

General

Accademia Nazionale delle Scienze, detta dei XL (National Academy of Sciences, known as the Forty): Via L. Spallanzani 7, 00161 Rome; tel. 06-44250054; e-mail segreteria@accademiaxl.it; internet www.accademiaxl.it; f. 1782 as the Italian Society; 65 mems (40 Italian, 25 foreign); Pres. Prof. G. T. SCARASCIA MUGNOZZA; Sec. Profa EMILIA CHIANCONE; publs *Annuario* (every 2 years), *Memorie di Matematica* (1 a year), *Rendiconti: Memorie Scienze Fisiche e Naturali* (1 a year), *Scritti e Documenti* (irregular).

Federazione delle Associazioni Scientifiche e Tecniche (Federation of Scientific and Technological Associations): Piazzale R. Morandi 2, 20121 Milan; tel. 02-77790304; e-mail fast@fast.mi.it; internet www.fast.mi.it; f. 1897; aims at fostering cultural debate and promotion of the fields of science policy, technological and industrial research and development, with particular reference to: energy and resources, chemistry and materials, electronics and information, biotechnology, technological research and innovation, ecology and environment, training, professionalism and job organization; mems: 40 scientific orgs, 55,000 individuals; Pres. Prof. ADOLFO COLOMBO; Gen. Sec. Dr ALBERTO PIERI; publ. *Scienza e Tecnica* (4 a year, online).

Società Adriatica di Scienze (Adriatic Society of Sciences): CP 1029, 34100 Trieste; e-mail adriscie@univ.trieste.it; internet www.units.it/~adriscie; f. 1874; 200 mems; library of 27,000 vols; Pres. Prof. FRANCO CUCCHI; Sec. BERNARDINO CRESSERI; publ. *Bollettino* (1 a year).

Società Italiana di Scienze Naturali (Italian Society of Natural Sciences): Museo Civico di Storia Naturale, Corso Venezia 55, 20121 Milan; tel. 02-795965; e-mail info@scienzenaturali.org; internet www.scienzenaturali.org; f. 1857; organizes meetings to present and discuss members' research results; study groups on vertebrates in the wild, exobiology and biological optimization; 457 mems; library of 1,600 vols of periodicals; Pres. Prof. BRUNO COZZI; Sec. Dr GIORGIO CHIOZZI; Treas. Dr ROBERTA CASTIGLIONI; publs *Atti della Società Italiana di Scienze Naturali e del Museo Civico di Storia Naturale in Milano* (2 a year), *Memorie della Società Italiana di Scienze Naturali e del Museo Civico di Storia Naturale in Milano*, *Natura* (2 a year), *Paleontologia Lombarda*, *Rivista Italiana di Ornitologia* (2 a year).

Società Italiana per il Progresso delle Scienze SIPS-onlus (Italian Society for Scientific Progress): Via San Martino della Battaglia, 44, 00185 Rome; tel. 06-4451628; e-mail sips@sipsinfo.it; internet www.sipsinfo.it; f. 1839; library of 30,000 vols; Pres. Prof. MAURIZIO LUIGI CUMO; Sec.-Gen. FILOMENA ROCCA; publs *Atti Riunioni SIPS* (every two years), *Scienza e Tecnica* (12 a year).

Società Toscana di Scienze Naturali (Tuscan Society of Natural Sciences): Via S. Maria 53, 56126 Pisa; e-mail info@stsn.it; internet www.stsn.it; f. 1847; 412 mems; library of 75,000 vols, 300 current periodicals; Pres. Prof. STEFANO MERLINO; Gen. Sec. Prof. FRANCO RAPETTI; Librarian CHIARA SORBINI; publs *Atti—Memorie Serie A (Abiologica)* (1 a year, online), *Atti—Memorie Serie B (Biologica)* (1 a year, online), *Palaeontographia Italica* (1 a year).

Biological Sciences

Società Botanica Italiana Onlus (Italian Botanical Society): Via Giorgio La Pira 4, 50121 Florence; tel. 55-2757379; e-mail sbi@unifi.it; internet www.societabotanicaitaliana.it; f. 1888; promotes progressing and disseminates information of botanical culture and sciences and their applications; 1,200 mems; library of 9,000 vols; Pres. Prof. FRANCESCO MARIA RAIMONDO; Sec. Prof. CONSOLATA SINISCALCO; publs *Informatore Botanico Italiano (Bollettino della Società Botancia Italiana onlus)* (2 a year, with irregular supplements), *Plant Biosystems (Giornale Botanico Italiano)* (4 a year, with irregular supplements).

Società Entomologica Italiana (Italian Entomological Society): Via Brigata Liguria 9, 16121 Genova; tel. (10) 586009; e-mail info@societaentomologicaitaliana.it; internet www.societaentomologicaitaliana.it; f. 1869; pure and applied entomology; library (Corso Torino 19/4 sc. A. Genoa); 640 mems; library of 1,100 vols; Pres. Prof. FRANCESCO PENNACCHIO; Sec. GIOVANNI RATTO; publs *Bollettino* (3 a year), *Entomologia* (online), *Memorie* (1 a year, online).

Società Italiana di Biochimica Clinica e Biologia Molecolare Clinica (Italian Society of Clinical Biochemistry and Clinical Molecular Biology): Via Libero Temolo 4, 20126 Milan; tel. 02-87390041; e-mail segreteria@sibioc.it; internet www.sibioc.it; f. 1968; 2,500 mems; mem. of Int. Federation of Clinical Chemistry; Pres. Dott. COSIMO OTTOMANO; Sec. GIUSEPPE AGOSTA; publ. *Biochimica Clinica* (6 a year).

Società Italiana di Biochimica e Biologia Molecolare (Italian Society for Biochemistry and Molecular Biology): Centro di Cultura Scientifica 'Alessandro Volta', Villa Olmo, Via Cantoni 1, 22100 Como; tel. 031-579815; e-mail segreteriasib@centrovolta.it; internet www.biochimica.it; f. 1951; has 16 scientific interest groups; 1,100 mems; Pres. Prof. ANTONIO DE FLORA; Sec. Prof. LUCIANA AVIGLIANO.

Società Italiana di Ecologia (SItE) (Italian Ecological Society): c/o Dipartimento di Scienze Ambientali 'G. Sarfatti', Via Mattioli 4, 53100 Siena; tel. 0577-232887; e-mail info@ecologia.it; internet www.ecologia.it; f. 1976; aims to promote theoretical and applied ecological research, to disseminate knowledge of ecology, encourage the devt of cultural exchange among researchers, and to facilitate nat. and int. cooperation; operates working groups, congresses, etc.; 705 mems; Pres. Prof. PIERLUIGI VIAROLI; Sec. ANTONIO MAZZOLA; publ. *SITE Atti* (proceedings of congresses and symposia, 1 a year).

Società Italiana di Microbiologia (Italian Microbiological Society): Via Sannio 4, 20137 Milan; tel. 02-59902320; e-mail sim@societasim.org; internet www.societasim.org; f. 1962; promotes the study of microbiology, holds congresses and conventions; Pres. GIUSEPPE NICOLETTI; Sec. and Treas. S. RIPA.

Physical Sciences

Associazione Geofisica Italiana (Italian Geophysical Association): c/o ISAC-CNR, Via Fosso del Cavaliere 100, 00133 Rome; tel. 06-49937680; e-mail info@associazionegeofisica.it; internet www.associazionegeofisica.it; f. 1951; promotes, coordinates and disseminates knowledge, studies and research on pure and applied geophysics; 200 mems; library of 1,500 vols; Pres. Dr MARINA BALDI; Sec. Dr CLAUDIO RAFANELLI; publ. *Bollettino Geofisico* (4 a year).

Associazione Geotecnica Italiana (Italian Geotechnical Association): Viale dell'Università 11, 00185 Rome; tel. 06-44704349; e-mail agiroma@iol.it; internet www.associazionegeotecnica.it; f. 1947; ind.; aims to encourage, carry out and support geotechnical studies and research in Italy through publications, conferences, scholarships, etc.; 1,100 mems; Pres. Prof. Ing. STEFANO AVERSA; Sec. Dott. Ing. CLAUDIO SOCCODATO; publ. *Rivista Italiana di Geotecnica* (4 a year).

Società Astronomica Italiana (Italian Astronomical Society): Largo E. Fermi 5, 50125 Florence; tel. 055-2752270; e-mail sait@arcetri.astro.it; internet www.sait.it; f. 1920; 700 mems; Pres. Prof. ROBERTO BUONANNO; Sec. Dr FABRIZIO MAZZUCCONI; publs *Giornale di Astronomia* (4 a year, print and electronic), *Memorie* (4 a year).

Società Chimica Italiana (Italian Chemical Society): Viale Liegi 48/C, 00198 Rome; tel. 06-8549691; e-mail segreteria@soc.chim.it; internet www.soc.chim.it; f. 1909; organizes confs and publs; promotes chemical culture by any event able to put in contact chemists with civil society; 5,000 mems; library of 2,300 vols; Pres. Prof. RAFFAELE RICCIO; publs *La Chimica e l'Industria* (12 a year), *La Chimica nella Scuola* (6 a year).

Società Geologica Italiana (Italian Geological Society): c/o Dipartimento di Scienze della Terra, Università degli Studi di Roma 'La Sapienza', Piazzale Aldo Moro 5, 00185 Rome; tel. (6) 4959390; e-mail info@socgeol.it; internet www.socgeol.it; f. 1881; 1,400 mems; Pres. Prof. CARLO DOGLIONI; Sec. Dott. ALESSANDRO ZUCCARI; publs *Italian Journal of Geosciences* (3 a year), *Memorie* (irregular), *Rendiconti* (irregular).

Società Italiana di Fisica (Italian Physics Society): Via Saragozza 12, 40123 Bologna; tel. 051-331554; e-mail sif@sif.it; internet www.sif.it; f. 1897; 1,500 mems; library of 6,500 vols; Pres. LUISA CIFARELLI; publs *EPJ Plus* (online), *European Physical Journal A—Hadrons and Nuclei* (12 a year, print and online), *European Physical Journal B—Condensed Matter and Complex Systems* (24 a year, print and online), *European Physical*

Journal C—Particles and Fields (12 a year, print and online), *European Physical Journal D—Atomic, Molecular, Optical and Plasma Physics* (12 a year, print and online), *European Physical Journal E—Soft Matter and Biological Physics* (12 a year, print and online), *Europhysics Letters* (24 a year, print and online), *Giornale di Fisica* (4 a year, print and online), *Il Nuovo Cimento C—Colloquia on Physics* (6 a year, print and online), *Il Nuovo Saggiatore* (4 a year, print and online), *Quaderni di Storia della Fisica* (irregular, print and online), *Rivista del Nuovo Cimento* (12 a year, print and online).

PHILOSOPHY AND PSYCHOLOGY

Società Filosofica Italiana (Italian Philosophical Society): c/o ILIESI-CNR, Villa Mirafiori, Via Nomentana 118, 00161 Rome; tel. 06-8604360; e-mail sfi@sfi.it; internet www.sfi.it; f. 1902; ind. org.; promotes philosophical research on a scientific level; safeguards the professional status of philosophy lecturers; encourages contact and collaboration in Italy and internationally between philosophic disciplines; helps set up local centres of study; 1,350 mems; Pres. Prof. FRANCESCO CONIGLIONE; Sec. and Treas. Dott. FRANCESCA GAMBETTI; publ. *Bollettino* (3 a year).

Società Italiana di Psicologia: Via Tagliamento 76, 00198 Rome; tel. 06-8845136; e-mail info@sips.it; internet www.sips.it; f. 1910; carries out activities in conjunction with univ. instns for study and research; organizes nat. congresses every 3 years; Pres. ANTONIO LO IACONO; publ. *Psicologia Italiana* (3 a year).

RELIGION, SOCIOLOGY AND ANTHROPOLOGY

Fondazione Marco Besso (Marco Besso Foundation): Largo di Torre Argentina 11, 00186 Rome; tel. 06-6865611; e-mail segreteriadue@fondazionemarcobesso.it; internet www.fondazionemarcobesso.it; f. 1918; promotes development of Roman cultural world; library: see under Libraries and Archives; Pres. GLORIA SONAGLIA LUMBROSO; Dir ANTONIO MARTINI.

Dipartimento di Scienze Statistiche (Department of Statistical Sciences): Viale Regina Elena, 296, 00161 Rome; tel. 06-49255318; e-mail sgritta@uniroma1.it; f. 1937; Italian section of Int. Institute of Sociology; 54 mems; library of 80,000 vols, 100 current periodicals; Pres. Prof. AMMASSARI; publs *Genus*, *International Review of Sociology*.

Società Italiana di Antropologia e Etnologia: Via del Proconsolo 12, 50121 Florence; tel. 055-2396449; e-mail info@antropologiaetnologia.it; internet www.antropologiaetnologia.it; f. 1871; 200 mems; library of 5,760 vols, 70 periodicals; Pres. Prof. PIERO MANNUCCI; Librarian MARIA EMANUELA FRATI; publ. *Archivio per l'Antropologia e la Etnologia* (1 a year).

TECHNOLOGY

Associazione Idrotecnica Italiana (Italian Water Resources Association): Via di Santa Costanza 7, 00198 Rome; tel. 06-8845064; e-mail info@idrotecnicaitaliana.it; internet www.idrotecnicaitaliana.it; f. 1923; study of problems concerning the utilization and management of water resources, and the safeguarding of the environment; 1,500 mems; library of 200 vols; Pres. MASSIMO VELTRI; Gen. Sec. FRANCESCO BOSCO; publ. *L'Acqua* (6 a year).

Associazione Italiana di Aeronautica e Astronautica (Italian Association of Aeronautical and Space Sciences): CP 227, 00187 Rome; tel. (6) 88346460; e-mail info@aidaa.it; internet www.aidaa.it; f. 1920; promotes and coordinates research in aeronautical and space sciences; cooperates with nat. and int. bodies in this field; 400 mems in 8 sections; Pres. Prof. LEONARDO LECCE; Gen. Sec. Prof. CESARE CARDANI; Treas. Prof. LUIGI BALIS CREMA; publ. *Aerotecnica Missili e Spazio* (4 a year).

Associazione Italiana di Metallurgia (Italian Metallurgical Association): Piazza R. Morandi 2, 20121 Milan; tel. 02-76021132; e-mail aim@aimnet.it; internet www.metallurgia-italiana.net; f. 1946; promotes and develops all aspects of science, technology and use of metals and materials closely related to metals; 2,000 mems; Pres. VINCENZO CRAPANZANO; Gen. Sec. Dott. FEDERICA BASSANI; publ. *La Metallurgia Italiana* (12 a year).

Associazione Italiana Nucleare (Italian Nuclear Association): Corso Vittorio Emanuele II 244, 00186 Rome; tel. 06-94005401; e-mail info@associazioneitaliananucleare.it; internet www.associazioneitaliananucleare.it; f. 2005; Pres. Ing. ENZO GATTA; Gen. Sec. Ing. UGO SPEZIA.

Comitato Elettrotecnico Italiano (CEI) (Italian Electrotechnical Committee): Via Saccardo 9, 20134 Milan; tel. 02-210061; e-mail cei@ceiweb.it; internet www.ceiweb.it; f. 1909; Pres. Dr Ing. UGO NICOLA TRAMUTOLI; Gen. Dir Dr Ing. ROBERTO BACCI.

Comitato Termotecnico Italiano (CTI) (Italian Thermotechnical Committee): Via Scarlatti 29, 20124 Milan; tel. 02-2662651; e-mail cti@cti2000.it; internet www.cti2000.it; f. 1933; Pres. Prof. Ing. CESARE BOFFA; Gen. Sec. Prof. Ing. GIOVANNI RIVA; publ. *La Termotecnica* (10 a year).

Ente Nazionale Italiano di Unificazione (UNI) (Italian National Standards Association): Via Sannio 2, 20137 Milan; tel. 02-700241; e-mail uni@uni.com; internet www.uni.com; f. 1921; Pres. PAOLO SCOLARI; Exec. Vice-Pres. Dr Ing. ENRICO MARTINOTTI; publ. *Unificazione* (4 a year).

Federazione Italiana di Elettrotecnica, Elettronica, Automazione, Informatica e Telecomunicazioni (AEIT) (Italian Federation for Electrotechnology, Electronics, Automation, Information Technology and Telecommunications): Central Office, Via Mauro Macchi 32, 20124 Milan; tel. 02-87389960; e-mail aeit@federaeit.it; internet www.aei.it; f. 1896; Pres. Ing. GIANFRANCO VEGLIO; Sec. IVANA SARTORI; publs *AEIT—Federazione di Elettrotecnica, Elettronica, Automazione, Informatica e Telecomunicazioni* (12 a year), *L'Energia Elettrica* (6 a year), *Mondo Digitale* (12 a year).

Istituto di Studi Nucleari per l'Agricoltura (ISNA) (Institute of Nuclear Studies applied to Agriculture): Via IV Novembre 152, 00187 Rome; tel. 06-6784991; f. 1959; Pres. Avv. Prof. GIUSEPPE GESUALDI; Sec.-Gen. Prof. M. L. SCARSELLI; publs *Agricoltura d'Italia* (12 a year), *Il Corriere di Roma*, *Quaderni ISNA*.

Istituto Italiano del Marchio di Qualità (IMQ) (Italian Institute of the Quality Mark): Via Quintiliano 43, 20138 Milan; tel. 02-50731; e-mail luigi.paleari@imq.it; internet www.imq.it; f. 1951; tests electrical and gas products to grant the IMQ safety mark; undertakes EU Directives conformity assessment and certifies company quality and management systems as part of the CSQ scheme; Pres. Ing. GIORGIO SCANAVACCA; Man. Dir Ing. GIANCARLO ZAPPA; publs *Gruppo IMQ Informa* (1 a year, online), *IMQ Notizie* (News, 2 a year, online).

Istituto Italiano della Saldatura (Italian Welding Institute): Lungobisagno Istria 15, 16141 Genoa; tel. 010-83411; e-mail iis@iis.it; internet www.iis.it; f. 1948; consultancy training, research, standardization, certification, laboratory tests and diploma courses in welding; 800 mems; library of 15,000 vols; Sec.-Gen. Dott. Ing. MAURO SCASSO.

Research Institutes

GENERAL

Consiglio Nazionale delle Ricerche (CNR) (National Research Council of Italy): Piazzale Aldo Moro 7, 00185 Rome; tel. 6-49931; e-mail urp@urp.cnr.it; internet www.cnr.it; f. 1923; research is carried out by 110 institutes in 11 depts: Agri-Food, Cultural Heritage, Cultural Identity, Earth and Environmental Sciences, Energy and Transport, Information and Communications Technology, Life Sciences, Materials and Devices, Medicine, Molecular Design, Production Systems; Pres. Prof. LUCIANO MAIANI; Gen. Man. Dott. FABRIZIO TUZI; publs *Almanacco della Scienza* (26 a year, online), *Ricerca e Futuro* (4 a year, print and online), *Notiziario Neutroni e Luce di Sincrotrone* (2 a year, in English, print and online).

Agri-Food:

Istituto di Biologia e Biotecnologia Agraria (Institute of Agricultural Biology and Biotechnology): Via Edoardo Bassini 15, 20133 Milan; tel. 2-23699403; e-mail direttore@ibba.cnr.it; internet www.ibba.cnr.it; f. 2001; Dir Dott. ROBERTO BOLLINI.

Istituto di Biometeorologia (Institute for Biometeorology): Via Giovanni Caproni 8, 50145 Florence; tel. 55-3033711; e-mail a.raschi@ibimet.cnr.it; internet www.ibimet.cnr.it; f. 2000; Dir Dott. ANTONIO RASCHI.

Istituto di Diritto Agrario Internazionale e Comparato/Centro di Responsabilità Scientifica IDAIC (Institute of International and Comparative Agricultural Law): Via La Marmora 29, 50121 Florence; tel. 55-579558; e-mail idaic@fi.191.it; internet www.idaic.it; f. 1957; Man. Dir Prof. ALBERTO GERMANO; publ. *Rivista di Diritto Agrario*.

Istituto di Genetica Vegetale (Institute of Plant Genetics): Via Giovanni Amendola 165/A, 70126 Bari; tel. 80-5583400; e-mail domenico.pignone@igv.cnr.it; internet www.igv.cnr.it; f. 2001; Dir Dott. DOMENICO PIGNONE.

Istituto di Scienza dell'Alimentazione (Institute of Food Science): Via Roma 52, 83100 Avellino; tel. 825-299111; e-mail direttore@isa.cnr.it; internet www.isa.cnr.it; f. 2001; Dir Prof. RAFFAELE COPPOLA.

Istituto di Scienze delle Produzioni Alimentari (Institute of Food Production Sciences): Via Amendola 122/O, 70126 Bari; tel. 80-5929333; e-mail angelo.visconti@ispa.cnr.it; internet www.ispa.cnr.it; f. 2001; Dir Dott. ANGELO VISCONTI.

Istituto per la Protezione Sostenibile delle Piante (Institute for Sustainable Plant Protection): Strada delle Cacce 73, 10135 Turin; tel. 11-3977911; e-mail direttore@ivv.cnr.it; internet www.ivv.cnr.it; f. 2014; Dir Dott. GIAN PAOLO ACCOTTO.

Istituto per i Sistemi Agricoli e Forestali del Mediterraneo (Institute for Mediterranean Agriculture and Forest Systems): CP 101, 80040 S. Sebastiano al Vesuvio; Via Patacca 85, 80056 Ercolano; tel. 81-7717325; e-mail segreteria@isafom.cnr.it; internet www.isafom.cnr.it; f. 2001; Dir Dr RICCARDO D'ANDRIA.

Istituto per il Sistema Produzione Animale in Ambiente Mediterraneo (Institute for Animal Production in the Mediterranean Environment): Via Argine 1085, 80147 Naples; tel. 81-5966006; e-mail leopoldo.iannuzzi@ispaam.cnr.it; internet www.ispaam.cnr.it; f. 2001; Dir Prof. LEOPOLDO IANNUZZI.

Istituto per la Protezione delle Piante (Plant Protection Institute): Via Madonna del Piano 10, 50019 Sesto Fiorentino; tel. 55-5225589; e-mail f.loreto@ipp.cnr.it; internet www.ipp.cnr.it; f. 2001; Dir Dott. FRANCESCO LORETO.

Cultural Heritage:

Istituto di Studi sul Mediterraneo Antico, Consiglio Nazionale delle Ricerche (CNR-ISMA) (Institute for the Study on Ancient Mediterranean, National Research Council (CNR-ISMA)): Area della Ricerca Roma 1, Via Salaria km 29.3, CP10, 00015 Monterotondo; tel. 6-90672670; e-mail segreteria.direzione@isma.cnr.it; internet www.isma.cnr.it; f. 2013 by incorporation Istituto di Studi sulle Civiltà dell'Egeo e del Vicino Oriente (ICEVO) and Istituto di Studi sulle Civiltà Italiche e del Mediterraneo Antico (ISCIMA); research in archaeology, history, philology and epigraphy of the ancient Mediterranean civilizations; library of 28,000 vols; Dir Prof. ALESSANDRO NASO; Sec. Dr FRANCESCA AGOSTINI; publs *Archeologia e Calcolatori*, *Mediterranea*, *RFS—Rivista di Studi Fenici*, *SMEA—Studi Micenei ed Egeo-Anatolici*.

Istituto per i Beni Archeologici e Monumentali (Institute of Archaeological Heritage—Monuments and Sites): Prov.le Lecce-Monteroni, 73100 Lecce; tel. 832-422200; e-mail segreteria@ibam.cnr.it; internet www.ibam.cnr.it; f. 2001; Dir Dott. ANTONELLA PELLETTIERI.

Istituto per la Conservazione e Valorizzazione dei Beni Culturali (Institute for the Conservation and Valorization of Cultural Heritage): Via Madonna del Piano 10, Edificio C, 50019 Sesto Fiorentino; tel. 55-5225484; e-mail direttore@icvbc.cnr.it; internet www.icvbc.cnr.it; f. 2001; Dir Dr PIERO TIANO.

Istituto per le Tecnologie Applicate ai Beni Culturali (Institute for Technologies Applied to Cultural Heritage): Via Salaria Km. 29.3, CP 10, 00016 Monterotondo Stazione; tel. 6-90625274; e-mail itabc@itabc.cnr.it; internet www.itabc.cnr.it; f. 2001; Dir Dott. SALVATORE GARRAFFO.

Cultural Identity:

Istituto di Linguistica Computazionale 'Antonio Zampolli' (Institute of Computational Linguistics): Via Giuseppe Moruzzi 1, 56124 Pisa; tel. 50-3152872; e-mail direttore@ilc.cnr.it; internet www.ilc.cnr.it; f. 2001; Dir Dott. ANDREA BOZZI.

Istituto di Ricerca sui Sistemi Giudiziari (Institute for Research on Judicial Systems): Via Zamboni 26, 40126 Bologna; tel. 51-2756211; e-mail direttore@irsig.cnr.it; internet www.irsig.cnr.it; f. 2002; Dir Dott. MARCO FABRI.

Istituto di Ricerca sull'Impresa e lo Sviluppo (Institute of Research on Business Firms and Development): Via Real Collegio 30, 10024 Moncalieri; tel. 11-6824911; e-mail segreteria@ceris.cnr.it; internet www.ceris.cnr.it; f. 1956; Dir Dott. SECONDO ROLFO.

Istituto di Ricerche sulla Popolazione e le Politiche Sociali (Institute for Research on Population and Social Policies): Via Palestro 328, 00185 Rome; tel. 6-492724200; e-mail info@irpps.cnr.it; internet www.irpps.cnr.it; f. 2001; Dir Dott. SVEVA AVVEDUTO.

Istituto di Ricerche sulle Attività Terziarie (Institute for Service Industry Research): Via Michelangelo Schipa 91, 80122 Naples; tel. 81-2470953; e-mail a.morvillo@irat.cnr.it; internet www.irat.cnr.it; f. 2001; Dir Dott. ALFONSO MORVILLO.

Istituto di Scienze e Tecnologie della Cognizione (Institute of Cognitive Sciences and Technologies): Via S. Martino della Battaglia 44, 00185 Rome; tel. 6-44595246; e-mail direzione.istc@istc.cnr.it; internet www.istc.cnr.it; f. 2001; Dir Dott. ROSARIO FALCONE.

Istituto di Storia dell'Europa Mediterranea (Institute of Mediterranean European History): Via G. B. Tuveri 128, 09129 Cagliari; tel. 70-403635; e-mail codignola@isem.cnr.it; internet www.isem.cnr.it; f. 2001; Dir Prof. LUCA CODIGNOLA BO.

Istituto di Studi Giuridici Internazionali (Institute for International Legal Studies): Via dei Taurini 19, 00185 Rome; tel. 6-49937660; e-mail segreteria@isgi.cnr.it; internet www.isgi.cnr.it; f. 1986, present name 2001; research in int. law; the int. protection of human rights; int. environmental law; library of 2,000 vols; Dir Prof. SERGIO MARCHISIO.

Istituto di Studi sui Sistemi Regionali Federali e sulle Autonomie 'Massimo Severo Giannini' (Institute for the Study of Regionalism, Federalism and Self-Government): Via dei Taurini 19, 00185 Rome; tel. 6-49937740; e-mail segreteria@issirfa.cnr.it; internet www.issirfa.cnr.it; f. 2001; Dir Prof. STELIO MANGIAMELI.

Istituto di Studi sulle Società del Mediterraneo (Institute of Studies on Mediterranean Societies): Via Pietro Castellino 111, 80131 Naples; tel. 81-6134086; e-mail istituto@issm.cnr.it; internet www.issm.cnr.it; f. 2001; growth, convergence and divergence in Mediterranean economies in the past and present; library of 15,000 vols; Dir Prof. PAOLO MALANIMA; publ. *Global Environment*.

Istituto di Teoria e Tecniche dell'Informazione Giuridica (Institute of Legal Information Theory and Techniques): Via de' Barucci 20, 50127 Florence; tel. 55-43995; e-mail ittig@ittig.cnr.it; internet www.ittig.cnr.it; f. 1968; Dir Dott. COSTANTINO CIAMPI; publ. *Informatica e Diritto* (Information Science and the Law).

Istituto Opera del Vocabolario Italiano (The Italian Dictionary): Via di Castello 46, 50141 Florence; tel. 55-452841; e-mail beltrami@ovi.cnr.it; internet www.ovi.cnr.it; f. 2001; Dir Prof. PIETRO BELTRAMI.

Istituto per il Lessico Intellettuale Europeo e la Storia delle Idee (Institute for the European Intellectual Lexicon and the History of Ideas): Villa Mirafiori, Via Carlo Fea 2, 00161 Rome; tel. 6-86320527; e-mail iliesi@iliesi.cnr.it; internet www.iliesi.cnr.it; f. 1964; investigates history of cultural and scientific terminology using historical semantic tools considering technical uses and ambiguities, synchronic and diachronic inter-relations, translations and transpositions across lexical fields; publishes lexica, indices and concordances, and sets up databases and scientific data processing applied to technical terminology in the humanities; 25 mems; library of 4,600 microfilms; Dir Prof. GIOVANNI ADAMO (acting); publs *Bruniana and Campanelliana*, *Elenchos*, *Lexicon Philosophicum*.

Istituto per la Storia del Pensiero Filosofico e Scientifico Moderno (Institute for the History of Philosophical and Scientific Thought in the Modern Age): Via Porta di Massa 1, 80133 Naples; tel. 81-2535580; e-mail sanna@unina.it; internet www.ispf.cnr.it; f. 2001; Dir Dott. MANUELA SANNA.

Istituto per le Tecnologie Didattiche-Consiglio Nazionale delle Ricerche (Institute for Educational Technology-National Research Council of Italy): Via de Marini 6, 16149 Genova; tel. 10-6475303; e-mail itd@itd.cnr.it; internet www.itd.cnr.it; f. 2001 by merging of Istituto per le Tecnologie Didattiche (CNR), based in Genoa and founded in 1970, and the Istituto Tecnologie Didattiche e Formative (CNR), established in 1993 in Palermo; research in educational technology; computer science, engineering, mathematics, physics, pedagogy, psychology, languages; library of 5,000 vols; Dir Dr ROSA BOTTINO; publ. *TD—Tecnologie Didattiche* (3 a year, in Italian, abstract in English, online, www.tdjournal.itd.cnr.it).

Earth and Environment:

Istituto di Biologia Agro-ambientale e Forestale (Institute of Agro-environmental and Forest Biology): Viale Guglielmo Marconi 2, 05010 Porano; tel. 763-374911; e-mail ibaf@pec.cnr.it; internet www.ibaf.cnr.it; f. 2001; Dir Dott. ENRICO BRUGNOLI.

Istituto di Geologia Ambientale e Geoingegneria (Institute of Environmental Geology and Geoengineering): Via Salaria Km 29.3, CP 10, 00016 Monterotondo Stazione; tel. 6-90672600; e-mail giovannimaria.zuppi@igag.cnr.it; internet www.igag.cnr.it; f. 2001; Dir Prof. GIOVANNI MARIA ZUPPI.

Istituto di Geoscienze e Georisorse (Institute of Geosciences and Earth Resources): Via Giuseppe Moruzzi 1, 56124 Pisa; tel. 50-3152372; e-mail igg@igg.cnr.it; internet www.igg.cnr.it; f. 2001; Dir Dott. GIOVANNI GIANELLI.

Istituto di Metodologie per l'Analisi Ambientale (Institute of Methodologies for Environmental Analysis): Contrada S. Loja, CP 27, 85050 Tito Scalo (PZ) Basilicata; tel. 971-427111; e-mail maa@pec.cnr.it; internet www.imaa.cnr.it; f. 2001; Dir Dott. VINCENZO LAPENNA.

Istituto di Ricerca per la Protezione Idrogeologica (Research Institute for Geo-hydrological Protection): Via Madonna Alta 126, 06128 Perugia; tel. 75-5014411; e-mail segreteria@irpi.cnr.it; internet www.irpi.cnr.it; f. 2001; Dir Dott. FAUSTO GUZZETTI.

Istituto di Ricerca sulle Acque (Water Research Institute): Via Salaria Km 29, 300, CP 10, 00015 Monteredondo Stazione; tel. 6-90672850; e-mail direzione@irsa.cnr.it; internet www.irsa.cnr.it; f. 2001; Dir Dott. MAURIZIO PETTINE.

Istituto di Scienze dell'Atmosfera e del Clima (Institute of Atmospheric Sciences and Climate): Via Piero Gobetti 101, 40129 Bologna; tel. 51-6399619; e-mail direttore@isac.cnr.it; internet www.isac.cnr.it; f. 2000; Dir Dott. CRISTINA SABBIONI.

Istituto di Scienze Marine (Institute of Marine Sciences): Arsenale Tesa 104, Castello 2737/F, 30122 Venice; tel. 41-2407927; e-mail direttore@ismar.cnr.it; internet www.ismar.cnr.it; f. 2001; Dir Dott. FABIO TRINCARDI.

Istituto per la Dinamica dei Processi Ambientali (Institute for the Dynamics of Environmental Processes): Calle Larga Santa Marta 2, 30123 Venice; tel. 41-

2348547; e-mail pietro.mario.rossi@idpa.cnr.it; internet www.idpa.cnr.it; f. 2001; Dir Dott. PIETRO MARIO ROSSI.

Istituto per l'Ambiente Marino Costiero (Institute for the Coastal Marine Environment): Calata Porta di Massa, 80133 Naples; tel. 81-5423804; e-mail direttore@iamc.cnr.it; internet www.iamc.cnr.it; f. 2001; Dir Dott. SALVATORE MAZZOLA.

Istituto per la Valorizzazione del Legno e delle Specie Arboree (Tree and Timber Institute): Via Madonna del Piano 10, 50019 Sesto Fiorentino; tel. 55-52251; e-mail direttore@ivalsa.cnr.it; internet www.ivalsa.cnr.it; f. 2002; Dir Prof. ARIO CECCOTTI.

Istituto per lo Studio degli Ecosistemi (Institute of Ecosystem Study): Largo Vittorio Tonolli 50, 28922 Pallanza Verbania; tel. 323-518300; e-mail direzione@ise.cnr.it; internet www.ise.cnr.it; f. 2001; Dir Dott. ROSARIO MOSELLO.

Istituto sull'Inquinamento Atmosferico (Institute for Atmospheric Pollution Research): Via Salaria Km 29.3, CP 10, 00016 Monterotondo; tel. 6-90625349; e-mail pirrone@iia.cnr.it; internet www.iia.cnr.it; f. 2001; Dir Dott. NICOLA PIRRONE.

Energy and Transport:

Istituto di Fisica del Plasma 'Piero Caldirola' (Institute for Plasma Physics): Via Roberto Cozzi 53, 20125 Milan; tel. 2-66173238; e-mail direttore@ifp.cnr.it; internet www.ifp.cnr.it; f. 1974; library of 3,000 vols, 100 periodical titles; Dir Dott. MAURIZIO LONTANO.

Istituto di Ricerche sulla Combustione (Institute for Research on Combustion): Piazzale Vincenzo Tecchio 80, 80125 Naples; tel. 81-7682245; e-mail ciajolo@irc.cnr.it; internet www.irc.cnr.it; f. 2001; Dir Dott. ANNA CIAJOLO.

Istituto di Tecnologie Avanzate per l'Energia 'Nicola Giordano' (Institute for Advanced Energy Technologies): Via Salita S. Lucia sopra Contesse 5, 98126 Messina; tel. 90-624246; e-mail gaetano.cacciola@itae.cnr.it; internet www.itae.cnr.it; f. 2000; Dir Dott. Ing. GAETANO CACCIOLA.

Istituto Gas Ionizzati/Consorzio RFX (Institute of Ionized Gas): Corso Stati Uniti 4, 35127 Padua; tel. 49-8295000; e-mail segrgen@igi.cnr.it; internet www.igi.cnr.it; f. 2001; Dir Prof. FRANCESCO GNESOTTO.

Istituto Motori (Motors Institute): Via Marconi 8, 80125 Naples; tel. 81-7177131; e-mail direttore@im.cnr.it; internet www.im.cnr.it; f. 2001; Dir Ing. PAOLA BELARDINI.

Istituto per l'Energetica e le Interfasi (Institute for Energetics and Interphases): Corso Stati Uniti 4, 35127 Padua; tel. 49-8295850; e-mail s.daolio@ieni.cnr.it; internet www.ieni.cnr.it; f. 2000; Dir Dott. SERGIO DAOLIO.

Information and Communications Technology:

Istituto di Analisi dei Sistemi ed Informatica 'Antonio Ruberti' (Institute for Systems Analysis and Computer Science): Viale Manzoni 30, 00185 Rome; tel. 6-77161; e-mail bertolai@iasi.cnr.it; internet www.iasi.cnr.it; f. 2001; Dir Dott. PAOLA BERTOLAZZI.

Istituto di Calcolo e Reti ad Alte Prestazioni (Institute for High-performance Computing and Networking): Via Pietro Bucci, Cubo 41C, 87036 Rende (CS); tel. 984-831720; e-mail cosenza@icar.cnr.it; internet www.icar.cnr.it; f. 2001; Dir Prof. DOMENICO TALIA.

Istituto di Elettronica e di Ingegneria dell'Informazione e delle Telecomunicazioni (Institute of Electronics, Computer and Telecommunications Engineering): Corso Duca degli Abruzzi 24, 10129 Turin; tel. 11-5645400; e-mail direttore@ieiit.cnr.it; internet www.ieiit.cnr.it; f. 2001; Dir Dott. RICCARDO TASCONE.

Istituto di Informatica e Telematica (Institute for Informatics and Telematics): Via Giuseppe Moruzzi 1, 56124 Pisa; tel. 50-3152112; e-mail domenico.laforenza@iit.cnr.it; internet www.iit.cnr.it; f. 2001; Dir Dott. DOMENICO LAFORENZA.

Istituto di Matematica Applicata e Tecnologie Informatiche (Institute of Applied Mathematics and Information Technology): Via Ferrata 1, 27100 Pavia; tel. 382-548211; e-mail direttore@imati.cnr.it; internet www.imati.cnr.it; f. 2000; Dir Prof. FRANCO BREZZI; Librarian M. GRAZIA FUSARI.

Istituto di Scienza e Tecnologie dell'Informazione 'Alessandro Faedo' (Institute of Information Science and Technology 'Alessandro Faedo'): Via Giuseppe Moruzzi 1, 56124 Pisa; tel. 50-3152878; e-mail direttore@isti.cnr.it; internet www.isti.cnr.it; f. 2000; Dir Dr CLAUDIO MONTANI.

Istituto per il Rilevamento Elettromagnetico dell'Ambiente (Institute for Electromagnetic Sensing of the Environment): Via Diocleziano 328, 80124 Naples; tel. 81-5707999; e-mail bucci.om@irea.cnr.it; internet www.irea.cnr.it; f. 2001; active microwave remote sensing; passive remote sensing in optics; modelling of electromagnetic interaction processes; multi-source data fusion and integration for environmental monitoring; sensors and techniques for electromagnetic diagnostics; biological effects and clinical diagnostic and therapy applications related to electromagnetic fields; 36 mems; Dir Prof. OVIDIO MARIO BUCCI.

Life Sciences:

Istituto di Biochimica delle Proteine (Institute of Protein Biochemistry): Via Pietro Castellino 111, 80131 Naples; tel. 81-6132273; e-mail d.corda@ibp.cnr.it; internet www.ibp.cnr.it; f. 2001; Dir Dott. DANIELA CORDA.

Istituto di Biologia e Patologia Molecolari (Institute of Molecular Biology and Pathology): Piazzale Aldo Moro 5, 00185 Rome; tel. (6) 49910877; e-mail info@ibpm.cnr.it; internet www.ibpm.cnr.it; f. 2001; Dir Dr IDA RUBERTI.

Istituto di Biomembrane e Bioenergetica (Institute of Biomembrane and Bioenergetics): Via Giovanni Amendola 165/A, 70126 Bari; tel. 80-5443389; e-mail g.pesole@ibbe.cnr.it; internet www.ibbe.cnr.it; f. 2001; Dir Dott. GRAZIANO PESOLE.

Istituto di Genetica delle Popolazioni (Institute of Population Genetics): Traversa La Crucca 3, Reg. Baldinca, 07100 Sassari; tel. 79-2841301; e-mail c.lamon@igp.cnr.it; f. 2001; Dir Dott. MARIO PIRASTU.

Istituto di Genetica e Biofisica 'Adriano Buzzati Traverso' (Institute of Genetics and Biophysics): Via Pietro Castellino 111, 80131 Naples; tel. 81-6132698; e-mail baldini@igb.cnr.it; internet www.igb.cnr.it; f. 2000; Dir Prof. ANTONIO BALDINI.

Istituto per l'Endocrinologia e l'Oncologia 'Gaetano Salvatore' (Institute for Experimental Endocrinology and Oncology): Via Sergio Pansini 5, 80131 Naples; tel. 81-7463602; e-mail a.fusco@ieos.cnr.it; internet www.ieos.cnr.it; f. 2001; Dir Prof. ALFREDO FUSCO.

Materials and Devices:

Istituto dei Sistemi Complessi (Institute for Complex Systems): Via dei Taurini 19, 00185 Rome; tel. 6-49937495; e-mail segreteria@isc.cnr.it; internet www.isc.cnr.it; f. 2004; Dir Prof. LUCIANO PIETRONERO.

Istituto di Biofisica (Institute of Biophysics): Via De Marini 6, Torre di Francia, 16149 Genoa; tel. 10-6475577; e-mail direttore@ge.ibf.cnr.it; internet www.ibf.cnr.it; f. 2001; Dir Dott. FRANCO GAMBALE.

Istituto di Cibernetica 'Edoardo Caianiello' (Cybernetics Institute): Via Campi Flegrei 34, 80078 Pozzuoli; tel. 81-8675111; e-mail m.russo@cib.na.cnr.it; internet www.cib.na.cnr.it; f. 2001; Dir MAURIZIO RUSSO.

Istituto di Fisica Applicata 'Nello Carrara' (Institute of Applied Physics): Via Madonna del Piano, 10 50019 Sesto Fiorentino (FI); tel. 55-5226436; e-mail r.salimbeni@ifac.cnr.it; internet www.ifac.cnr.it; f. 2001; Dir Dott. RENZO SALIMBENI.

Istituto di Fotonica e Nanotecnologie (Institute for Photonics and Nanotechnologies): Via Cineto Romano 42, 00156 Rome; tel. 6-4152221; e-mail evangelisti@ifn.cnr.it; internet www.ifn.cnr.it; f. 2000; study and devt of photonics from points of view of radiation-matter interaction and of developing materials, devices and systems; study and devt of nanotechnologies for the fabrication of nanoscale-size devices; devt of microelectronic and micromechanical devices; Dir Prof. FLORESTANO EVANGELISTI.

Istituto di Metodologie Inorganiche e dei Plasmi (Institute of Inorganic Methodologies and Plasmas): Via Salaria Km 29.3, CP 10, 00016 Monterotondo Scalo; tel. 6-906721; e-mail direttore@imip.cnr.it; internet www.imip.cnr.it; f. 2000; Dir Dott. MARIO CACCIATORE.

Istituto di Struttura della Materia (Institute for the Structure of Matter): Via del Fosso del Cavaliere 100, 00133 Rome; tel. 6-49934476; e-mail direttore@ism.cnr.it; internet www.ism.cnr.it; f. 2000; Dir Dott. DINO FIORANI.

Istituto Nanoscienze (Nanoscience Institute): Piazza San Silvestro 12, 56127 Pisa; tel. 50-509418; e-mail segreteria@nano.cnr.it; internet www.nano.cnr.it; f. 2010; Dir Dott. LUCIA SORBA.

Istituto Nazionale di Ottica (INO) (National Institute of Applied Optics): Largo Enrico Fermi 6, 50125 Florence; tel. 55-23081; e-mail direttore@ino.it; internet www.ino.it; f. 1927; quantum, instrumental and physiological optics; library of 7,000 vols; Pres. Dott. PAOLO DE NATALE; Gen. Dir Dr CARLO CASTELLINI.

Istituto Nazionale per la Fisica della Materia/Centro di Responsabilità Scientifica INFM (National Institute for the Physical Sciences of Matter): Corso Perrone 24, 16152 Genoa; tel. 10-6598750; e-mail sede@infm.it; internet www.infm.it; f. 2005; Dir Prof. ELISA MOLINARI.

Istituto Officina dei Materiali (Institute of Materials Workshop): S.S. 14, Km. 163.5, 34149 Trieste; tel. 40-3756411; e-mail iom@pec.cnr.it; internet www.iom.cnr.it; f. 2010; conducts interdisciplinary research based on knowledge of the physical properties and functionality of materials and complex systems at the atomic scale; Dir Prof. ALBERTO MORGANTE.

Istituto per i Processi Chimico-Fisici (Institute for Chemical and Physical Processes): Viale Ferdinando Stagno d'Alcontres, n. 37, 98158 Messina; tel. 90-39762200; e-mail direttore@ipcf.cnr.it; internet www.ipcf.cnr.it; f. 2000; Dir Dott. CIRINO SALVATORE VASI.

Istituto per la Microelettronica e Microsistemi (Institute for Microelectronics and Microsystems): Ottava strada, 5 (Zona Industriale), 95121 Catania; tel. 95-5968211; e-mail corrado.spinella@imm.cnr.it; internet www.imm.cnr.it; f. 2000; Dir Dott. CORRADO SPINELLA.

Istituto per le Applicazioni del Calcolo 'Mauro Picone' (Institute for Applied Mathematics): Viale dei Taurini 19, 00185 Rome; tel. 6-49270921; e-mail bertsch@iac.rm.cnr.it; internet www.iac.cnr.it; f. 2000; Dir Prof. MICHIEL BERTSCH.

Istituto Superconduttori, Materiali Innovativi e Dispositivi (Institute for Superconductors, Innovative Materials and Devices): Corso F. Perrone 24, 16152 Genoa; tel. 10-6598750; e-mail segreteria@spin.cnr.it; internet www.spin.cnr.it; f. 2010; Dir Dr CARLO FERDEGHINI.

Medicine:

Istituto di Bioimmagini e Fisiologia Molecolare (Institute of Molecular Bioimaging and Physiology): Via Fratelli Cervi 93, 20090 Segrate; tel. 2-21717514; e-mail direzione@ibfm.cnr.it; internet www.ibfm.cnr.it; f. 2001; Dir Prof. MARIA CARLA GILARDI.

Istituto di Biologia Cellulare (Institute of Cell Biology): Via E. Ramarini 32, 00015 Monterotondo Scalo; tel. 6-90091207; e-mail emma@emmanet.org; internet www.emma.cnr.it; f. 1969; research areas in functional genomics, systems of signal transduction, molecular aspects of the construction logic and the functioning of complex organisms, RNA, molecular aspects of the relationship between parasite and host in tropical diseases, construction of mutant strains and phenocopies of mice, cryo-conservation, rederivation, distribution of mutant strains, production and telematic distribution of databases of mutant strains; Dir Prof. GLAUCO TOCCHINI-VALENTINI.

Istituto di Biomedicina e di Immunologia Molecolare 'Alberto Monroy' (Institute of Biomedicine and Molecular Immunology): Via Ugo La Malfa 153, 90146 Palermo; tel. 91-6809194; e-mail segreteria@ibim.cnr.it; internet www.ibim.cnr.it; f. 2001; Dir Dott. GIOVANNI VIEGI.

Istituto di Fisiologia Clinica (Institute of Clinical Physiology): Via Giuseppe Moruzzi 1, 56124 Pisa; tel. 50-3152216; e-mail picano@ifc.cnr.it; internet www.ifc.cnr.it; f. 2001; Dir Dott. EUGENIO PICATO.

Istituto di Genetica Molecolare (Institute of Molecular Genetics): Via Abbiategrasso 207, 27100 Pavia; tel. 382-5461; e-mail biamonti@igm.cnr.it; internet www.igm.cnr.it; f. 2000; Dir Dott. GIUSEPPE BIAMONTI.

Istituto di Ingegneria Biomedica (Institute of Biomedical Engineering): Corso Stati Uniti 4, 35127 Padua; tel. 49-8295702; e-mail mbox@isib.cnr.it; internet www.isib.cnr.it; f. 2001; Dir Dott. FERDINANDO GRANDORI.

Istituto di Neurobiologia e Medicina Molecolare (Institute of Neurobiology and Molecular Medicine): Via del Fosso di Fiorano 64, Località Prato Smeraldo, 00143 Rome; tel. 6-501703025; e-mail segreteria@inmm.cnr.it; f. 2000; Dir Dott. DELIO MERCANTI.

Istituto di Neurogenetica e Neurofarmacologia (Institute of Neurogenetics and Neuropharmacology): Cittadella Universitaria di Cagliari, 09042 Monserrato CA Sardinia; tel. 70-6754543; e-mail c.flore@inn.cnr.it; f. 2001; Dir Prof. FRANCESCO CUCCA (acting).

Istituto di Neuroscienze (Neuroscience Institute): Via Giuseppe Moruzzi 1, 56124 Pisa; tel. 50-3153207; e-mail segreteria@in.cnr.it; internet www.in.cnr.it; f. 2001; Dir Prof. TULLIO POZZAN.

Istituto di Scienze Neurologiche (Institute of Neurological Sciences): Contrada Burga 44, 87050 Mangone; tel. 984-98011; e-mail a.quattrone@isn.cnr.it; internet www.isn.cnr.it; f. 2001; Dir Prof. ALDO QUATTRONE.

Istituto di Tecnologie Biomediche (Institute of Biomedical Technologies): Via Fratelli Cervi 93, 20090 Segrate; tel. 2-26422702; e-mail luigi.zecca@itb.cnr.it; internet www.itb.cnr.it; f. 2001; Dir Dott. LUIGI ZECCA.

Istituto per i Trapianti d'Organo e Immunocitologia (Organ Tranplantation and Immunology Institute): Piazzale Collemaggio, 67100 L'Aquila; tel. 862-27129; e-mail d.adorno@itoi.cnr.it; f. 2001; Dir Prof. DOMENICO ADORNO.

Molecular Design:

Istituto di Biostrutture e Bioimmagini (Institute of Biostructure and Bioimaging): Via Tommaso de Amicis 95, 80145 Naples; tel. 81-2203187; e-mail direttore@ibb.cnr.it; internet www.ibb.cnr.it; f. 2001; research areas incl. biochemical technologies and biostructure, biochemical technologies for diagnostic imaging, diagnostic imaging and radiotherapy technologies, diagnostic imaging and radiotherapy; Dir Dott. BRUNO ALFANO.

Istituto di Chimica Biomolecolare (Institute of Biomolecular Chemistry): Via Campi Flegrei 34, 80078 Pozzuoli; tel. 81-8675018; e-mail direzione@icb.cnr.it; internet www.icb.cnr.it; f. 2001; Dir Dott. BARBARA NICOLAUS.

Istituto di Chimica dei Composti Organo Metallici (Institute of Organometallic Compounds Chemistry): Via Madonna del Piano 10, 50019 Sesto Fiorentino (Firenze); tel. 55-5225280; e-mail claudio.bianchini@iccom.cnr.it; internet www.iccom.cnr.it; f. 2001; Dir Dott. CLAUDIO BIANCHINI.

Istituto di Chimica del Riconoscimento Molecolare (Institute of Chemistry of Molecular Recognition): Via Mario Bianco 9, 20131 Milan; tel. 2-28500024; e-mail segreteria@icrm.cnr.it; internet www.icrm.cnr.it; f. 2001; Dir Dott. SERGIO RIVA.

Istituto di Chimica e Tecnologia dei Polimeri (Institute of Polymer Chemistry and Technology): Via Campi Flegrei 34, 80078 Pozzuoli; tel. 81-8675111; e-mail secr@ictp.cnr.it; internet www.ictp.cnr.it; f. 2001; Dir Prof. COSIMO CARFAGNA.

Istituto di Chimica Inorganica e delle Superfici (Institute of Inorganic and Surface Chemistry): Corso Stati Uniti 4, 35127 Padua; tel. 49-8295611; e-mail info@icis.cnr.it; internet www.icis.cnr.it; f. 2000; Dir Dott. GILBERTO ROSSETTO.

Istituto di Cristallografia (Institute of Crystallography): Via Giovanni Amendola 122/O, 70126 Bari; tel. 80-5929148; e-mail segreteria@ic.cnr.it; internet www.ic.cnr.it; f. 2001; Dir Dott. MICHELE SAVIANO.

Istituto di Metodologie Chimiche (Institute of Chemical Methodologies): Area della ricerca RM 1, Via Salaria Km 29, 300, Montelibretti RM; tel. 690625111; e-mail direttore@imc.cnr.it; internet www.imc.cnr.it; f. 2001; Dir Dott. GIANCARLO ANGELINI.

Istituto di Scienze e Tecnologie Molecolari (Institute of Molecular Science and Technologies): Via Camillo Golgi 19, 20133 Milan; tel. 2-50314276; e-mail s.alocci@istm.cnr.it; internet www.istm.cnr.it; f. 2000; Chair. Dott. RINALDO PSARO.

Istituto per i Materiali Compositi e Biomedici (Institute for Composite and Biomedical Materials): Piazzale Vincenzo Tecchio 80, 80125 Naples; tel. 81-7682508; e-mail segreteria@imcb.cnr.it; internet www.imcb.cnr.it; f. 2001; Dir Ing. LUIGI AMBROSIO.

Istituto per la Sintesi Organica e la Fotoreattività (Institute for Organic Syntheses and Photoreactivity): Via Piero Gobetti 101, 40129 Bologna; tel. 51-6399770; e-mail direzione@isof.cnr.it; internet www.isof.cnr.it; f. 2000; Dir Dott. ROBERTO ZAMBONI.

Istituto per la Tecnologia delle Membrane (Institute for Membrane Technology): Via P. Bucci, Cubo 17C, 87036 Rende (CS); tel. 984-492050; e-mail l.giorno@itm.cnr.it; internet www.itm.cnr.it; f. 2001; devt of membrane science and technology at nat. and int. level; Dir Dott. LIDIETTA GIORNO.

Istituto per lo Studio dei Materiali Nanostrutturati (Institute of Nanostructured Materials): Via dei Taurini 19, 00185 Rome; tel. 6-90672484; e-mail mariaester.moresi@ismn.cnr.it; internet www.ismn.cnr.it; f. 2000; Dir Dr GIUSEPPINA PADELETTI.

Istituto per lo Studio delle Macromolecole del CNR (Institute for Macromolecular Studies of CNR): Via Edoardo Bassini 15, 20133 Milan; tel. 2-23699370; e-mail bolognesi@ismac.cnr.it; internet www.ismac.cnr.it; f. 2000; Dir Dott. INCORONATA TRITTO.

Production Systems:

Istituto dei Materiali per l'Elettronica ed il Magnetismo (Institute of Materials for Electronics and Magnetism): Parco Area delle Scienze 37A, 43124 Parma; tel. 521-26911; e-mail direttore-imem@imem.cnr.it; internet www.imem.cnr.it; f. 2001; library of 1,300 vols; Dir Dott. SALVATORE IANNOTTA.

Istituto di Acustica e Sensoristica 'Orso Mario Corbino' (Institute of Acoustics and Sensors): Via del Fosso del Cavaliere 100, 00133 Rome; tel. 6-45488482; e-mail segreteria@idasc.cnr.it; internet www.idasc.cnr.it; f. 2001; Dir CLAUDIO RAFANELLI.

Istituto di Scienza e Tecnologia dei Materiali Ceramici (Institute of Ceramics Science and Technology): Via Granarolo 64, 48018 Faenza; tel. 546-699711; e-mail istec@istec.cnr.it; internet www.istec.cnr.it; f. 2001; Dir Dott. ALIDA BELLOSI.

Istituto di Studi sui Sistemi Intelligenti per l'Automazione (Institute of Intelligent Systems for Automation): Via Giovanni Amendola 122/D-O, 70126 Bari; tel. 80-5929429; e-mail distante@ba.issia.cnr.it; internet www.issia.cnr.it; f. 2001; Dir Dott. ARCANGELO DISTANTE.

Istituto di Tecnologie Industriali e Automazione (Institute of Industrial Technologies and Automation): Via Bassini 15, 20133 Milan; tel. 2-23699995; e-mail itia.milano@itia.cnr.it; internet www.itia.cnr.it; f. 2000; Dir Prof. TULLIO TOLIO.

Istituto per le Macchine Agricole e Movimento Terra (Institute for Agricultural and Earth-moving Machines): Via Canal Bianco 28, 44124 Ferrara; tel. 532-735611; e-mail info@imamoter.cnr.it; internet www.imamoter.cnr.it; f. 2001; Dir Ing. ROBERTO PAOLUZZI.

Istituto per le Tecnologie della Costruzione (Construction Technologies Institute): Viale Lombardia 49, 20098 San Giuliano Milanese; tel. 2-9806301; e-mail roberto.vinci@itc.cnr.it; internet www.itc.cnr.it; f. 2001; Dir Ing. ROBERTO VINCI.

AGRICULTURE, FISHERIES AND VETERINARY SCIENCE

Consiglio per la Ricerca e la Sperimentazione in Agricoltura (CRA) (Agricultural Research Council): Via Nazionale 82, 00184 Rome; tel. 06-478361; e-mail cra@entecra.it; internet sito.entecra.it; f. 1999; supervised by the Ministry of Agriculture, Food and Forests; gathers findings of 28 agricultural research institutes and 54 related operational units; depts of Vegetal Biology and Production, Animal Biology and Production, Transformation and Valorization of Agro-Industrial Products, Agronomy, Forestry and Land Use, Quality, Certification and Referenzation; Pres. Prof. GIUSEPPE ALONZO; Dir-Gen. Dr IDA MARANDOLA (acting).

Istituto Sperimentale per la Zoologia Agraria (Experimental Institute of Agricultural Zoology): Via Lanciola 12A, Cascine del Riccio, 50125 Florence; tel. 055-24921; e-mail isza@isza.it; internet www.isza.it; f. 1875; library of 55,000 vols; Dir Dott. MARCO VITTORIO COVASSI; publ. *Redia* (1 a year).

Ufficio Centrale di Ecologia Agraria (Meteorological and Ecological Centre): Via del Caravita 7A, 00186 Rome; tel. 06-695311; e-mail ucea@ucea.it; internet www.ucea.it; f. 1876; controls 100 observatories; 18 mems; Dir Dott. DOMENICO VENTO; publs *Bollettino Agrometeorologico Nazionale* (12 a year), *Bollettino Avversità Meteo*, *Indici Agroclimatici: Velocità e direzione del vento*, *Osservazioni Meteo Collegio Romano* (1 a year, electronic).

ECONOMICS, LAW AND POLITICS

Centre for Studies on Technologies in Distributed Intelligence Systems (TeDIS): Isola di San Servola, 30100 Venice; tel. 041-2719511; e-mail stefano.micelli@univiu.org; internet www.univiu.org/research-training/research-tedis; f. 1999; attached to Venice Int. Univ.; conducts research on industrial districts, technologies and networks, SMEs, local clusters and internationalization, creativity, design and innovation, innovation in public administration, e-government and e-democracy, transport logistics and supply chain management; Pres. ENZO RULLANI; Dir STEFANO MICELLI.

Centre for Thematic Environmental Networks (TEN): Isola de San Servolo, 30100 Venice; tel. 041-2719511; e-mail ten@univiu.org; internet www.univiu.org/research-training/research-ten; f. 2003; attached to Venice Int. Univ.; promotes the exchange of knowledge and information in the field of the environment and offers tools and supplementary approaches in order to solve environmental issues with specific reference to sustainable devt; Pres. Prof. IGNAZIO MUSU; Dir Dott. ALESSANDRA FORNETTI.

Centro di Ricerche Economiche e Sociali (CERES) (Centre for Economic and Social Research): Via Gianturco 11, 00195 Rome; tel. 06-8173016; e-mail info@ce-res.org; internet www.ce-res.org; f. 1970 as an autonomous body promoted by a trade union (CISL); improves economic and social conditions of workers; fosters contact and collaboration between nat. and int. centres and institutes interested in problems of economic and social devt; Pres. Prof. RENATA LIURAGHI; Sec.-Gen. Prof. GABRIELLA PAPPADA; publs *Benessere degli Anziani* (12 a year), *Quaderni di Economia del Lavoro* (2 a year).

Centro Speciale sulla Sicurezza Internazionale (Insubria Centre on International Security (ICIS)): Palazzo Natta, Via Natta 14, 22100 Como; tel. 031-579825; e-mail icis@uninsubria.it; attached to Università degli Studi dell'Insubria; Dir Prof. MAURIZIO MARTELLINI.

Fondazione Giangiacomo Feltrinelli: Via Romagnosi 3, 20121 Milan; tel. 02-874175; internet www.fondazionefeltrinelli.it/feltrinelli-cms; f. 1949; history of int. socialism, communism and the labour movement; economic and social history; library of 200,000 vols, 317 current periodicals, 2,500 microforms; Pres. CARLO FELTRINELLI.

Istituto Affari Internazionali (International Affairs Institute): Via Angelo Brunetti 9, 00186 Rome; tel. (6) 3224360; e-mail iai@iai.it; internet www.iai.it; f. 1965; promotes understanding of the problems of int. politics through studies, research, meetings and publs; library of 26,000 vols; Pres. STEFANO SILVESTRI; Exec. Vice-Pres. GIANNI BONVICINI; Vice-Pres. VINCENZO CAMPORINI; Dir and Legal Rep. ETTORE GRECO; Vice-Dir NATHALIE TOCCI; Librarian ALESSANDRA BERTINO; publs *AffarInternazionali* (online, in Italian), *IAI Research Papers/Quaderni IAI* (6 a year, in English and Italian), *IAI Working Papers/Documenti IAI* (40 a year, in English and Italian), *La Politica Estera dell'Italia* (yearbook, in Italian), *The International Spectator* (4 a year, in English).

Istituto di Studi Europei 'Alcide De Gasperi': Via Poli 29, 00187 Rome; tel. 06-6784262; e-mail kipsc@tin.it; internet www.ise-ies.org; f. 1953; promotes research and organizes meetings on legal, economic, political and social issues in the field of European co-operation and integration, and within a broader pan-European context; the Post-graduate School of European Studies organizes courses of varying duration and specialized seminars; courses are also held on the specialized English and French terminology of European int. orgs; library of 5,000 vols; Pres. Prof. Dott. GIUSEPPE SCHIAVONE; Admin. Officer CLAUDIA BATTISTI.

Istituto Italiano di Studi Legislativi (Italian Institute for Legislative Studies): Via del Corso 267, 00186 Rome; tel. 06-69941306; e-mail gianpierorsello@inwind.it; f. 1925 to promote the scientific and technical studies of legislation; Pres. Prof. GIAN PIERO ORSELLO; Gen. Sec. Dott. FRANCA CIPRIGNO; publs *L'Italia e l'Europa*, *Yearbook of Comparative Law and Legislative Studies*.

Istituto Nazionale di Statistica (National Institute of Statistics): Via Cesare Balbo 16, 00184 Rome; tel. 06-46731; e-mail dgen_s@istat.it; internet www.istat.it; f. 1926; library of 500,000 vols, 2,700 current periodicals; Pres. ENRICO GIOVANNINI; Gen. Dir GIOVANNI FONTANAROSA; publ. *Rivista di Statistica Ufficiale* (4 a year, print and online).

Istituto per gli Studi di Politica Internazionale (Institute for the Study of International Politics): Palazzo Clerici, Via Clerici 5, 20121 Milan; tel. 02-8633131; e-mail ispi.segreteria@ispionline.it; internet www.ispionline.it; f. 1934; public and private funding; aims to provide information and analysis of the great global issues of today, to identify opportunities for more effective Italian participation in int. affairs, to identify the domestic factors that constrain or enhance Italy's int. role; research in int. politics and economics, strategic problems and the history of foreign relations, European integration, int. economic cooperation, consolidation of peace and security among nations, strengthening of political freedoms and democratic instns; library of 80,000 vols, historical archive, press archive; postgraduate training courses; organizes conferences, lectures, etc.; Pres. BORIS BIANCHERI; Dir Dott. PAOLO MAGRI; publs *ISPI Relazioni Internazionali* (3 a year, online), *Quaderni di Relazioni Internazionali* (3 a year, online), *Annuario sulla Politica Estera Italiana* (1 a year).

Istituto per le Relazioni tra l'Italia e i Paesi dell'Africa, America Latina, Medio ed Estremo Oriente (IPALMO) (Institute for Relations between Italy and the Countries of Africa, Latin America and the Middle and Far East): Via Ennio Quirino Visconti 8, 00193 Rome; tel. 06-32699701; e-mail ipalmo@ipalmo.com; internet www.ipalmo.com; f. 1971; promotes and develops political, economic and cultural relations between countries in these regions; research and promotion of information at all levels of Italian society; to organize confs, seminars, etc.; library of 20,000 vols, 500 periodicals; Pres. GIANNI DE MICHELIS; Gen. Sec. CRISTINA GAGGIO; publ. *Politica Internazionale* (6 a year).

UNICEF Office of Research Innocenti: Piazza SS. Annunziata 12, 50122 Florence; tel. 055-20330; e-mail florence@unicef.org; internet www.unicef-irc.org; f. 1988; initiates, finances and conducts research vital to the work of the United Nations Children's Fund (UNICEF), esp. in the field of children's rights, child poverty, well-being and protection; addresses emerging issues in areas of social and economic policies and implementation of int. standards for children in all countries; incl. the fmr UNICEF Innocenti Research Centre; Dir GORDON ALEXANDER.

EDUCATION

Istituto per Ricerche ed Attività Educative (Institute for Educational Research and Activity): Riviera di Chiaia 264, 80121 Naples; tel. 081-2457074; e-mail ipe@ipeistituto.it; internet www.ipeistituto.it; f. 1979; aims to give young people access to education, culture and jobs; offers grants, promotes study and research in education; 32 mems; library of 6,500 vols; Pres. Prof. RAFFAELE CALABRÒ; Gen. Sec. Dott. LORENZO BURDO; publ. *IPEnews* (2 a year).

FINE AND PERFORMING ARTS

Istituto Internazionale per la Ricerca Teatrale (International Institute for Theatre Research): Casa di Goldoni, S. Tomà 2794, 30124 Venice; tel. 041-714883; f. 1953 by the Int. Fed. for Theatre Research; library of 30,000 vols; spec. collns: critical works, Italian and foreign dramatic works, Venetian musical theatre scores, periodicals, edns of the playwright Carlo Goldoni, Maddelena (miscellany), Ortolani miscellany, Vendramin Archive; Chair. Prof. CARMELO ALBERTI; Gen. Sec. Doc. MARIA IDA BIGGI.

Istituto Superiore per la Conservazione ed il Restauro (Institute for Conservation and Restoration): Via di San Michele 23, 00153 Rome; tel. 06-67236300; e-mail is-cr@beniculturali.it; internet iscr.beniculturali.it; f. 1939; research on the influence of environment on cultural property and on prevention of deterioration; studies formulation of rules on theory of conservation and restoration and on techniques to be used; advises institutes of the Min. of Cultural Assets and Activities, and regional organizations; in-service teaching and refresher courses; carries out restoration of complex works or those of interest in research and teaching; library of 35,000 vols, 650 periodicals; Dir GISELLA CAPPONI; publ. *Bollettino ICR* (2 a year).

Villa I Tatti/Harvard University Center for Italian Renaissance Studies: Via di Vincigliata 26, 50135 Florence; tel. 055-603251; internet itatti.harvard.edu; f. 1961; fmr residence of Bernard Berenson, who left his library and art colln to Harvard; offers postdoctoral study on aspects of the Italian Renaissance incl. historiography; library of 187,000 vols, 625 current periodicals, 250,000 photographs; Dir Prof. LINO PERTILE; publ. *I Tatti Studies in Renaissance History* (2 or 3 a year).

HISTORY, GEOGRAPHY AND ARCHAEOLOGY

Academia Belgica (Belgian Academy in Rome): Via Omero 8, 00197 Rome; tel. 06-203986303; e-mail walter.geerts@academiabelgica.it; internet www.academiabelgica.it; f. 1939; research centre and residence; congress centre; promotion of science and culture from Belgium and its regions; library of 80,000 vols; Dir Prof. WALTER GEERTS; publs *Belgian Historical Institute in Rome* (series and annual bulletin since 1919), *Bibliotheca Cumontiana*, *Etudes de Philologie, d'Archéologie et d'Histoire Anciennes* (irregular).

Accademia di Danimarca (Danish Institute of Science and Art in Rome): Via Omero 18, 00197 Rome; tel. 6-3265931; e-mail accademia@acdan.it; internet www.acdan.it; f. 1956; archaeology, philology, art and architecture, history of art, history of music, literature; library of 24,000 vols; Dir Prof MARIANNE PADE (acting); Sec. JANNE NIELSEN PENAZZI; publ. *Analecta Romana Instituti Danici*.

Accademia Tedesca (German Academy in Rome): Villa Massimo, Largo di Villa Massimo 1–2, 00161 Rome; tel. 06-4425931; e-mail info@villamassimo.de; internet www.villamassimo.de/it/demnaechst/index.html; Dir Dr JOACHIM BLÜHER.

American Academy in Rome: Via Angelo Masina 5, 00153 Rome; tel. 06-58461; e-mail info@aarome.org; internet www.aarome.org; f. 1894; fellowships for independent study and advanced research in fine arts, classical studies, art history, Italian studies and archaeology; library of 135,000 vols; Pres. and CEO ADELE CHATFIELD-TAYLOR; Dir CHRISTOPHER CELENZA.

British Institute of Florence: Piazza Strozzi 2, 50123 Florence; tel. 055-26778200; e-mail info@britishinstitute.it; internet www.britishinstitute.it; f. 1917; develops cultural understanding between the UK and Italy through the teaching of their respective languages and cultures; offers a range of Italian language and history of art courses, and an extensive programme of English language courses for the host population; a number of special programmes are run in conjunction with British and American univs; archive containing material relating to the British community in Tuscany in 19th and early 20th centuries incl. the Waterfield family, Susan Horner, Maquay family, Edward Gordon Craig and Edward Hutton; Vernon Lee colln contains a number of books from her library with her annotations; library of 50,000 vols; 1,700 students; Dir VANESSA HALL-SMITH.

British School at Rome: Via Gramsci 61, 00197 Rome; tel. 06-3264939; e-mail info@bsrome.it; internet www.bsr.ac.uk; f. 1901, inc. by Royal Charter 1912; postgraduate residential centre for higher research in the humanities and for the practice of the fine arts and architecture; 40 residents; library of 60,000 vols, 600 current periodicals; Dir Prof. CHRISTOPHER SMITH.

Canadian Academic Centre in Italy: Via Zara 30, 00198 Rome; tel. 06-4404329; e-mail caci@caspur.it; internet www.acadita.ca/caci.html; f. 1978; assists Canadian researchers and scholars in Italy and promotes their work through lectures, conferences and publications; fosters academic exchanges between Italy and Canada; library of 3,000 vols; Dir EGMONT LEE.

Centro Camuno di Studi Preistorici (Centre for Prehistoric Studies): Via Marconi 7, 25044 Capo di Ponte (Brescia); tel. 0364-42091; e-mail info@ccsp.it; internet www.ccsp.it; f. 1964; specializes in prehistoric rock art; archaeological research, early religions, anthropology and ethnology; seminars, int. symposia, individual tutoring in prehistoric and tribal art; coordinator of World Archives of Rock Art; provides advisers and consultants on conservation, exhibition and evaluation of prehistoric and tribal art; park and museum planning; field research in Europe, Asia and Australia; Valcamonica summer school; library of 40,000 vols, 300,000 photographs; Dir Prof. EMMANUEL ANATI; publs *Archivi*, *BCSP: The World Journal of Prehistoric and Tribal Art*.

Centro Italiano di Studi sul Basso Medioevo – Accademia Tudertina: Via Ciuffelli 31, 06059 Todi (Perugia); tel. 75-8942521; e-mail istituticulturali@librari.beniculturali.it; f. 1986; all aspects of late medieval civilization; Pres. Prof. TULLIO GREGORY; Dir Prof. ENRICO MENESTÒ.

Deutsches Archäologisches Institut Rom (German Archaeological Institute Rome): Via Curtatone, 4D, 00185 Rome; tel. 06-4888141; e-mail sekretariat.rom@dainst.de; internet www.dainst.org; f. 1829; library of 220,000 vols, 1,200 current periodicals; Dir Prof. Dr ORTWIN DALLY; Dir Prof. Dr KLAUS S. FREYBERGER; Sec. ALESSANDRA RIDOLFI; publs *Palilia*, *Römische Mitteilungen* (1 a year), *Sonderschriften des Deutschen Archäologischen Instituts Rom*.

Fondazione Centro Italiano di Studi sull'Alto Medioevo (Central Italian Foundation for Studies on Early Medieval Civilization): Palazzo Ancaiani, Piazza della Libertà 12, 06049 Spoleto; tel. 0743-225630; e-mail cisam@cisam.org; internet www.cisam.org; f. 1952; promotes research, conferences and scientific publications on all aspects of early medieval civilization; library of 3,000 vols; Pres. Prof. ENRICO MENESTÒ; publs *Bizantinistica* (1 a year), *Franciscana* (1 a year), *Medioevo e Rinascimento* (1 a year).

Ecole Française de Rome/Scuola Francese di Roma (French School in Rome): Piazza Farnese 67, 00186 Rome; tel. 06-68601333; e-mail dirsecr@efrome.it; internet www.efrome.it; f. 1875; French school of archaeology and history, specializing in Rome and medieval and modern Italy; library of 205,000 vols, 2,000 periodicals and 32,000 offprints; Dir CATHERINE VIRLOUVET; Dir for Studies FRANÇOIS DUMASY; Dir for Studies STÉPHANE GIOANNI; Dir for Studies STÉPHANE BOURDIN; publ. *Mélanges de l'Ecole Française de Rome* (series *Antiquité, Moyen Age, Italie et Méditerranée*).

Escuela Española de Historia y Arqueología, CSIC Roma (Spanish School of History and Archaeology in Rome): Via di Sant'Eufemia 13, 00187 Rome; tel. 6-68100021; e-mail escuela@csic.it; internet www.eehar.csic.es; f. 1910; history of Italian-Spanish interaction; organizes confs, seminars; research programmes and support for Spanish historians and archaeologists in Italy; library of 20,000 vols; spec. collns: Italica, Monumenta Albornotiana, documents on Spanish music in Italy, Serie Arqueológica and Serie Histórica; Dir Prof. FERNANDO GARCÍA SANZ; Vice-Dir Prof. LEONOR PEÑA CHOCARRO.

Institutum Romanum Finlandiae: Passeggiata del Gianicolo 10, 00156 Rome; tel. 06-68801674; e-mail info@irfrome.org; internet www.irfrome.org; f. 1954; Classical and Italian studies; library of 17,000 vols; Dir KATARIINA MUSTAKALLIO; publ. *Acta Instituti Romani Finlandiae*.

Istituto di Norvegia in Roma (Norwegian Institute in Rome): Viale Trenta Aprile 33, 00153 Rome; tel. 06-58391007; e-mail mejohansen@roma.uio.no; internet www.hf.uio.no/dnir; f. 1959; library of 25,000 vols; Head of Dept TURID KARLSEN SEIM; publ. *Acta ad Archaeologiam et Artium Historiam Pertinentia* (1 a year).

Istituto Ellenico di Studi Bizantini e Postbizantini di Venezia (Hellenic Institute of Byzantine and Post-Byzantine Studies of Venice): Castello 3412, 30122 Venice; tel. 041-5226581; e-mail info@istitutoellenico.org; internet www.istitutoellenico.org; f. 1951; library of 35,000 vols, archives containing 200,000 documents from 16th–19th centuries relating to Greek Orthodox community of Venice; Dir Prof. CHRYSSA MALTEZOU; Librarian Dr DESPINA VLASSI; publ. *Thesaurismata* (1 a year).

Istituto Italiano di Studi Germanici (Italian Institute for Germanic Studies): Via Calandrelli 25, 00153 Rome; tel. 06-588811; e-mail chiarini@studigermanici.it; internet www.studigermanici.it; f. 1932; library of 80,000 vols, 200 periodicals; Dir Prof. PAOLO CHIARINI; publs *Atti*, *Poeti e Prosatori Tedeschi*, *Strumenti*, *Studi e Ricerche*, *Studi Germanici* (3 a year), *Wissenschaftliche Reihen: Testi e Materiali*.

Istituto Italiano per gli Studi Storici (Italian Institute for Historical Studies): Via Benedetto Croce 12, 80134 Naples; tel. 081-5512390; e-mail istituto@iiss.it; internet www.iiss.it; f. 1947; organizes seminars and lessons; awards 20 student grants annually and offers scholarships to Italian and non-Italian students in history, philosophy and humanities; library of 135,000 vols, 1,500 periodicals, 400 current periodicals; Pres. Prof. NATALINO IRTI; Gen. Sec. Dott.ssa MARTA HERLING; Librarian Dott. ELLI CATELLO; publs *Annali* (1 a year), *Carteggi di Benedetto Croce* (2 a year), *Collana delle Monografie* (2 a year), *Inventari*, *Ristampe Anastatiche*, *Saggi e Studi*, *Testi Storici Filosofici e Letterari* (1 a year).

Istituto Nazionale di Studi Romani (National Institute of Roman Studies): Piazza dei Cavalieri di Malta 2, 00153 Rome; tel. 06-5743442; e-mail segreteria@studiromani.it; internet www.studiromani.it; f. 1925; promotes the study of Rome from ancient to modern times in all aspects; 120 mems; library of 26,000 vols, 1,500 periodicals; Pres. Prof. PAOLO SOMMELLA; Dir LETIZIA LANZETTA; publs *Rassegna d'Informazioni* (12 a year), *Studi Romani* (4 a year).

Istituto Nazionale di Studi sul Rinascimento (National Institute of Renaissance Studies): Palazzo Strozzi, 50123 Florence; tel. 055-287728; e-mail insr@iris.firenze.it; internet www.insr.it; f. 1938; publishes critical texts and results of research; 10-mem. ccl; library of 45,000 vols, 500 periodicals, special colln 'Machiavelli-Serristori', art photo library of 78,000 items, 700 microfilms; Pres. Prof. MICHELE CILIBERTO; publ. *Rinascimento* (1 a year).

Istituto Papirologico 'Girolamo Vitelli' (Papyrological Institute): Borgo degli Albizi

12–14, 50122 Florence; tel. 055-2757764; e-mail simona.russo@unifi.it; internet vitelli .ifnet.it; f. 1908; study of Greek and Latin papyri; library of 25,000 vols; colln of papyri; Scientific Dir Prof. GUIDO BASTIANINI; publs *Comunicazioni dell'Istituto Papirologico 'G. Vitelli'* (every 2 years), *Notiziario di Studi e Ricerche in Corso* (online), *Papiri Greci e Latini*.

Istituto Siciliano di Studi Bizantini e Neoellenici 'B. Lavagnini' (Sicilian Institute for Byzantine and Neo-hellenic Studies): Via Noto 34, 90141 Palermo; tel. 091-6259541; e-mail segreteria@issbi.org; internet www.issbi.org; f. 1952; 120 mems (60 ordinary, 60 corresp.); library of 10,000 vols; Pres. Prof. VINCENZO ROTOLO; Sec.-Gen. Prof. RENATA LAVAGNINI.

Istituto Storico Austriaco Roma (Austrian Historical Institute in Rome): Viale Bruno Buozzi 111–113, 00197 Rome; tel. 06-36082601; e-mail info@oehirom.it; internet www.oehirom.it; f. 1881; library of 87,000 items; Dir Univ. Doz. Dr. ANDREAS GOTTSMANN; publ. *Römische Historische Mitteilungen* (1 a year).

Istituto Storico Germanico di Roma/ Deutsches Historisches Institut in Rom (German Historical Institute in Rome): Via Aurelia Antica 391, 00165 Rome; tel. 06-6604921; e-mail verwaltung@dhi-roma.it; internet www.dhi-roma.it; f. 1888; medieval, modern and contemporary history; history of music; library of 231,745 vols, 867 current periodicals; Dir Prof. Dr MARTIN BAUMEISTER; Head Librarian Dr THOMAS HOFMANN; publs *Analecta musicologica, Bibliographische Informationen zur neuesten Geschichte Italiens, Bibliothek des Deutschen Historischen Instituts Rom, Quellen und Forschungen aus italienischen Archiven und Bibliotheken, Ricerche dell'Istituto Storico Germanico di Roma*.

Real Colegio Mayor de San Clemente de los Españoles (Royal College of Spain): Via Collegio di Spagna 4, 40123 Bologna; tel. 051-330408; e-mail segreteria@bolonios.it; internet www.bolonios.it; f. 1364 under Will of Cardinal Don Gil de Albornoz; study centre for 20 Spanish postgraduates; library of 25,000 vols; Rector JOSÉ GUILLERMO GARCÍA VALDECASAS; publ. *Studia Albornotiana* (irregular).

Reale Istituto Neerlandese a Roma (Royal Netherlands Institute): Via Omero 10–12, 00197 Rome; tel. 06-3269621; e-mail info@knir.it; internet www.knir.it; f. 1904; classical archaeology, history of art, history of Rome and Italy; residence for scholars from Dutch univs; library of 50,000 vols; Dir Prof. Dr BERNARD STOLTE; publ. *Fragmenta* (1 a year).

Svenska Institutet i Rom (Swedish Institute of Classical Studies in Rome): Via Omero 14, 00197 Rome; tel. 06-3201596; e-mail info@isvroma.org; internet www.isvroma.it; f. 1926; library of 65,000 vols, 300 current periodicals; Swedish courses for students of classical archaeology and history of art; fellowships in classical philology, archaeology, architecture, history of art and conservation; excavations at various sites in Italy; Dir KRISTIAN GÖRANSSON; Librarian ASTRID CAPOFERRO; publs *Acta Instituti Romani Regni Sueciae* (irregular), *Opuscula* (1 a year), *Suecoromana*.

MEDICINE

Istituto di Ricerche Farmacologiche 'Mario Negri' (Institute of Pharmacological Research): Via La Masa 19, 20156 Milan; tel. 02-390141; e-mail mnegri@marionegri.it; internet www.marionegri.it; f. 1961; non-profit org. for research and education in pharmacology and biomedicine; library of 5,000 vols, 250 periodicals; Chair. Dott. PAOLO MARTELLI; publs *Negri News* (12 a year), *Research and Practice* (6 a year).

Istituto Nazionale di Ricerca per gli Alimenti e la Nutrizione (National Institute for Research on Food and Nutrition): Via Ardeatina 546, 00178 Rome; tel. 06-514941; e-mail segreteriadg@inran.it; internet www .inran.it; f. 1936 as part of CNR, independent 1958 on budget of Min. of Agricultural Resources, supported by contracts and grants from Min. of Health, CNR and int. bodies; biological research in human nutrition, analyses and surveys on composition and nutritive value of foods; Gen. Dir Dott. SALVATORE PETROLI.

Istituto Nazionale per la Ricerca sul Cancro (National Institute for Cancer Research): Largo Rosanna Benzi 10, 16132 Genoa; tel. 010-56001; e-mail direzione .generale@istge.it; internet www.istge.it; f. 1978; research in all fields of cancer prevention, diagnosis, cure and rehabilitation; holds conferences, seminars, training courses; library of 1,808 books, 148 periodicals; Gen. Dir Dott. GIAN FRANCO CIAPPINA; Scientific Dir Prof. RICCARDO ROSSO.

Istituto Superiore di Sanità (Higher Institute of Health): Viale Regina Elena 299, 00161 Rome; tel. 06-49901; e-mail web@iss .it; internet www.iss.it; f. 1934; aims to promote public health through scientific research, surveys, controls and analytical tests in the various fields of health sciences; library of 200,000 vols, 3,500 current periodicals; Pres. Prof. ENRICO GARACI; Dir-Gen. MONICA BETTONI; publs *Annali* (4 a year, online), *Istisan Congressi* (5 a year, online), *Notiziario* (12 a year, online), *Rapporti ISTISAN* (40 a year, online), *Strumenti di Riferimento* (irregular, online).

NATURAL SCIENCES

General

Istituto per l'Interscambio Scientifico/ Fondazione ISI (Institute for Scientific Interchange): Viale S. Severo 65, 10133 Turin; tel. 011-6603090; e-mail isi@isi.it; internet www.isi.it; f. 1982; promotes basic research in molecular biology, chemistry, computer sciences, economics, mathematics, theoretical physics; Pres. MARIO RASETTI.

Biological Sciences

Herbarium Universitatis Florentinae—Sezione Botanica, Museo di Storia Naturale dell'Università di Firenze: Via La Pira 4, 50121 Florence; tel. 055-2757462; e-mail musbot@unifi.it; f. 1842; systematic botany, plant geography, history of botanical collns; Dir Dr CHIARA NEPI; publ. *Pubblicazioni del Museo Botanico*.

Stazione Zoologica 'Anton Dohrn' (Zoological Station 'Anton Dohrn'): Villa Comunale, 80121 Naples; tel. (81) 5833111; e-mail stazione.zoologica@szn.it; internet www.szn .it; f. 1872; conducts biological research on marine organisms and marine ecosystems; library of 90,000 vols, 159 periodicals, 1,000 electronic resources; Pres. Prof. ROBERTO DI LAURO; Gen. Dir Ing. MARCO CINQUEGRANI; publs *History and Philosophy of Life Sciences* (3 a year), *Marine Ecology*.

Mathematical Sciences

Istituto Nazionale di Alta Matematica Francesco Severi (National Institute of Higher Mathematics): Piazzale Aldo Moro 5, 00185 Rome; tel. 06-490320; e-mail indam@ altamatematica.it; internet www .altamatematica.it; f. 1939; promotes training of researchers in mathematics, conducts research in pure and applied mathematics; Pres. Prof. VINCENZO ANCONA.

Physical Sciences

Comitato Glaciologico Italiano (Italian Glaciological Committee): Corso Massimo D'Azeglio 42, 10125 Turin; tel. 011-3977251; e-mail comitato@glaciologia.it; internet www .glaciologia.it; f. 1895; glaciology and alpine climatology, glacier monitoring, cryosphere, glacial geology and geomorphology, glaciological hazard; library of 700 books, 15,000 photographs; Pres. Prof. CARLO BARONI; Gen. Sec. Prof. VALTER MAGGI; publ. *Geografia Fisica e Dinamica Quaternaria* (2 a year).

Dipartimento di Ingegneria Nucleare, Centro Studi Nucleari Enrico Fermi (CESNEF) (E. Fermi Centre for Nuclear Studies): Politecnico di Milano, Via Ponzio 34/3, 20133 Milan; tel. 02-23996300; e-mail dipnuc@polimi.it; internet www.cesnef .polimi.it; f. 1957; a division of the Department of Energy of the Politecnico di Milano; trains technical personnel in the fields of nuclear energy, physics of materials, and electronics; library of 7,000 vols, 31 current periodicals; Head of Dept Prof. CARLO BOTTANI.

Istituto Gemmologico Italiano (Italian Gemmological Institute): Piazza San Sepolcro, 1, 20123 Milan; tel. 02-80504992; e-mail info@igi.it; internet www.igi.it; f. 1973; courses in gemmology, laboratory analysis, research; 1,500 mems; Pres. PAOLO VALENTINI.

Istituto Idrografico della Marina (Italian Hydrographic Institute): Passo dell'Osservatorio 4, 16134 Genova; tel. 010-24431; e-mail iim.sre@marina.difesa.it; internet www .marina.difesa.it; f. 1872; library of 35,000 vols; Dir Contrammiraglio FRANCO FAVRE.

Istituto Italiano di Speleologia: Dip. Scienze della Terra e Geologico-Ambientali, Via Zamboni 67, 40126 Bologna; tel. 051-2094543; e-mail dewaele@geomin.unibo.it; f. 1929; exploration and scientific research in natural caves; library of 65,000 vols; Dir Prof. PAOLO FORTI; Librarian MICHELE SIVELLI; publ. *Memorie* (irregular).

Istituto Nazionale di Astrofisica: Viale del Parco Mellini 84, 00136 Rome; tel. 06-355331; e-mail inaf@inaf.it; internet www .inaf.it; promotes, carries out and co-ordinates research in the fields of astronomy, radioastronomy, spatial astrophysics and cosmic physics; has observatories in: Bologna, Cagliari, Catania, Florence, Milan, Naples, Padua, Palermo, Rome, Teramo, Trieste and Turin; finances the Telescopio Nazionale Galileo (*q.v.*) located on La Palma, Canary Islands; has a part ownership in the Large Binocular Telescope at the Mount Graham Int. Observatory (*q.v.*), AZ, USA; Chair. Prof. TOMMASO MACCACARO; Dir of Research Prof. ANTONIO NAVARRO.

Istituto Nazionale di Fisica Nucleare (INFN) (National Institute of Nuclear Physics): Via Enrico Fermi 40, 00044 Frascati (Rome); tel. 06-94031; e-mail prot_ac@inf .infn.it; internet www.infn.it; f. 1951; promotes and undertakes research in fundamental nuclear physics; consists of: Central Administration (Frascati), 19 divisions, 4 National Laboratories (Frascati, Legnaro, Gran Sasso (L'Aquila), Catania), the National Centre for Informatics and Networking (CNAF Bologna) and 11 groups; the divisions are at the Institutes of Physics at the Universities of Turin, Milan, Padua, Genoa, Trieste, Bologna, Pisa, Pavia, Florence, Rome, Rome II, Rome III, Naples, Bari, Catania, Cagliari, Ferrara, Perugia, Lecce; the groups are at the Institutes of Physics at the Universities of Alessandria, Trento,

Udine, Brescia, Parma, Siena, Salerno, Messina, L'Aquila, Cosenza, Sanità; Pres. Prof. ROBERTO PETRONZIO.

Istituto Nazionale di Geofisica e Vulcanologia (National Institute of Geophysics and Volcanology): Via di Vigna Murata 605, 00143 Rome; tel. 06-518601; e-mail info@ingv.it; internet www.ingv.it; f. 1936; seismology, tectonophysics, geomagnetism, aeronomy, environmental geophysics; has important additional facilities in Bologna, Catania, Milan, Naples, Palermo and Pisa; library of 8,000 vols, 150 current periodicals; Pres. Prof. ENZO BOSCHI; Gen. Dir Dott. TULLIO PEPE; publs *Annali di Geofisica* (6 a year), *Annuario Geomagnetico*, *Bollettino dei Valori Istantanei alle Ore 0*, *Bollettino Indici K* (12 a year), *Bollettino Ionosferico* (12 a year), *Bollettino Macrosismico* (1 a year), *Bollettino Sismico* (4 a year), *Tavole di Previsione Ionosferica* (26 a year), *2* (3 a year).

Istituto Nazionale di Oceanografia e di Geofisico Sperimentale (National Institute for Oceanography and Experimental Geophysics): Borgo Grotta Gigante 42/C, 34010 Sgonico (TS); tel. 040-21401; e-mail mailbox@ogs.trieste.it; internet www.ogs.trieste.it; f. 1958; library of 3,000 vols; Chair. Prof. IGINIO MARSON; Gen. Dir Dott. TIZIANA MAIER; publ. *Bollettino di Geofisica Teorica e Applicata* (4 a year).

PHILOSOPHY AND PSYCHOLOGY

Centro Superiore di Logica e Scienze Comparate (Centre for Logic and Comparative Science): Via Belmeloro 3, 40126 Bologna; f. 1969; promotes the study of logic and contributes to research in this field; 1,250 mems; library and archives; Pres. Prof. FRANCO SPISANI.

Istituto di Studi Filosofici 'Enrico Castelli' (Institute of Philosophy): Via Carlo Fea 2, 00161 Rome; tel. 06-44238062; e-mail pierluigi.valenza@uniroma1.it; internet www.filosofia.uniroma1.it; f. 1939; Pres. Prof. JEAN-LUC MARION; publs *Archivio di Filosofia* (2 a year), *Bibliografia Filosofica Italiana*, *Edizione Naz. A. Rosmini*, *Edizione Naz. dei Classici del Pensiero Italiano*, *Edizione Naz. V. Gioberti*, *Settimana di Studi Filosofici Internazionali* (1 a year).

RELIGION, SOCIOLOGY AND ANTHROPOLOGY

Centro Internazionale di Ricerca per le Storie Locali e le Diversità Culturali (International Research Centre for Local Histories and Cultural Diversities): Via Ravasi 2, 21100 Varese; tel. 0332-219800; e-mail centrostorielocali@uninsubria.it; internet www.cslinsubria.it; f. 1999; attached to Università degli Studi dell'Insubria; Pres. Prof. RENZO DIONIGI; Scientific Dir Prof. GIANMARCO GASPARI.

Fondazione di Ricerca 'Istituto Carlo Cattaneo' ('Istituto Carlo Cattaneo' Research Foundation): Via Santo Stefano 11, 40125 Bologna; tel. 51-239766; e-mail istitutocattaneo@cattaneo.org; internet www.cattaneo.org; f. 1965; studies and researches in the field of social science with particular regard to education, electoral behaviour, politics, crime, terrorism, family, immigration and public policy; Pres. Prof. ELISABETTA GUALMINI; Dir Dott. STEFANIA PROFETI; publs *Cattaneo* (irregular), *Cultura in Italia* (1 a year), *Elezioni, Governi, Democrazia* (irregular), *Italian Politics—A Review* (1 a year), *Misure/Materiali di ricerca dell'Istituto Carlo Cattaneo* (irregular), *Polis-Ricerche e Studi su Società e Politica in Italia* (3 a year), *Politica in Italia*, *Stranieri in Italia* (irregular).

Istituto Italiano di Antropologia (Italian Institute of Anthropology): Università di Roma 'La Sapienza', Dipart. di Biologia Animale e dell'Uomo, P.le Aldo Moro 5, 00185 Rome; tel. 06-49912273; e-mail isita@isita-org.com; internet www.isita-org.com; f. 1893 as Società Romana di Antropologia; adopted current name in 1937; promotes interdisciplinary approach to anthropology, which encompasses a synthesis of the biological, social and cultural aspects of human evolution; organizes scientific meetings; runs courses and seminars; 120 mems; library of 6,500 vols; Pres. BERNARDINO FANTINI; Sec. Assoc. Prof. GIOVANNI DESTRO-BISOL; publ. *Journal of Anthropological Sciences* (1 a year, print and online).

Istituto Italiano per l'Africa e l'Oriente (IsIAO) (Italian Institute for Africa and the East): Via Ulisse Aldrovandi 16, 00197 Rome; tel. 06-328551; e-mail info@isiao.it; internet www.isiao.it; f. 1995; a museum of oriental art is attached to the Institute; library of 140,000 vols, 500 current periodicals; Pres. Prof. GHERARDO GNOLI; Gen. Dir Dr UMBERTO SINATTI; publs *Africa* (4 a year), *Cina* (1 a year), *East and West* (4 a year, in English), *Il Giappone* (1 a year), *Reports and Memoirs*, *Rome Oriental Series*.

Istituto Luigi Sturzo: Via delle Coppelle 35, 00186 Rome; tel. 06-6840421; e-mail segretaria@sturzo.it; internet www.sturzo.it; f. 1951; sociological and historical research; library of 120,000 vols; Pres. Dott. ROBERTO MAZZOTTA; Sec.-Gen. Dott. FLAVIA NARDELLI; publs *Civitas* (3 a year), *Sociologia* (3 a year).

Istituto per l'Oriente C. A. Nallino: Via Alberto Caroncini 19, 00197 Rome; tel. (6) 8084106; e-mail ipocan@ipocan.it; internet www.ipocan.it; f. 1921; researches on modern and ancient Near East; library of 35,000 vols, 300 periodicals; Pres. Prof. CLAUDIO LO JACONO; publs *Eurasian Studies* (2 a year), *Oriente Moderno* (2 a year), *Quaderni di Studi Arabi* (1 a year), *Rassegna di Studi Etiopici* (1 a year).

TECHNOLOGY

Agenzia Nazionale per le Nuove Tecnologie, l'Energia e lo Sviluppo Economico Sostenible (ENEA) (National Agency for New Technology, Energy and Sustainable Economic Development): Lungotevere Thaon di Revel 76, 00196 Rome; tel. 06-36271; e-mail uffstampa@enea.it; internet www.enea.it; f. 1960; scientific research and technological devt, implementing advanced research programmes and conducting complex projects for Italy's social and economic devt; library of 250,000 vols; Commr Dott. GIOVANNI LELLI; publs *Energia, Ambiente e Innovazione* (6 a year), *Rapporto Energia e Ambiente* (1 a year, online).

Centro Radioelettrico Sperimentale 'Guglielmo Marconi' (Marconi Experimental Radio-electric Centre): Dipartimento di Ingegneria Elettronica, Università di Tor Vergata, Via del Politecnico 1, 00133 Rome; e-mail luglio@uniroma2.it; internet www.centromarconi.it; f. 1933; research on radio waves; Pres. GIOVANNI CANCELLIERI.

Centro Sviluppo Materiali SpA: Via di Castel Romano 100, 00128 Rome; tel. 06-50551; e-mail info@c-s-m.it; internet www.c-s-m.it; f. 1963; reference centre for innovation in materials and in related production, design and application technologies; library of 40,000 vols; Chair. Dott. ROBERTO BRUNO; CEO MAURO PONTREMOLI.

Fondazione Guglielmo Marconi (Guglielmo Marconi Foundation): Via Celestini 1, 40037 Pontecchio Marconi (BO); tel. 051-846121; e-mail fgm@fgm.it; internet www.fgm.it; f. 1938; research in telecommunications; library of 3,500 vols; Chair. Prof. GABRIELE FALCIASECCA.

Istituto Nazionale per Studi ed Esperienze di Architettura Navale (National Institute of Naval Architecture Studies and Experiments): Via di Vallerano 139, 00128 Rome; tel. 06-502991; e-mail secretary@insean.it; internet www.insean.it; f. 1927; library of 3,500 vols; Pres. GIANO PISI; Gen. Dir Dott. EMILIO F. CAMPANA; publ. *Quaderni* (1 a year).

SORIN Biomedica SpA: Via Benigno Crespi 17, 20159 Milan; tel. (2) 69969711; internet www.sorin.com; f. 1956; applied research in biomedicine; production and development of radiopharmaceuticals and immunodiagnostic kits (using radioactive and enzymatic tracers), pacemakers, artificial cardiac valves (mechanical and biological), oxygenators, dialysers, haemodialysis and haemoperfusion accessories; 3,600 staff; Chair. ROSARIO BIFULCO; CEO ANDRÉ-MICHEL BALLESTER.

Libraries and Archives

Alessandria

Biblioteca Civica: Piazza Vittorio Veneto 1, (ang. Via Machiavelli), 15100 Alessandria; tel. 0131-515911; e-mail biblioteca.civica@comune.alessandria.it; internet www.comune.alessandria.it; f. 1806; 180,000 vols, 217 current periodicals; Dir (vacant).

Ancona

Archivio di Stato di Ancona: Via Maggini 80, 60127 Ancona; tel. 071-2800356; e-mail as-an@archivi.beniculturali.it; internet archivi.beniculturali.it/asan; f. 1941; provincial archives dating from before Italian unification; 8,000 vols, 280 periodicals; Dir Dott. GIOVANNA GIUBBINI; publ. *Archivio di Stato-Ancona* (series, irregular).

Biblioteca Comunale Luciano Benincasa: Via Bernabei 32, 60121 Ancona; tel. 71-2225020; e-mail benincasa@comune.ancona.it; internet www.comune.ancona.it/ankonline/it/uffici/biblioteche/index.html; f. 1669; 170,700 vols, 62 incunabula, 124 periodicals, 343 MSS, 3,000 *cinquecentine*; Dir EMANUELA IMPICCINI.

Arezzo

Biblioteca della Città di Arezzo: Palazzo Pretorio, Via dei Pileati 8, 52100 Arezzo; tel. 0575-22849; e-mail direzione@bibliotecaarezzo.it; internet www.bibliotecarezzo.it; f. 1603; 265,000 vols, pamphlets and miscellanea, 548 MSS and 197 incunabula; Dir Dott. MANUELA FABBRINI.

Ascoli Piceno

Biblioteca Comunale 'Giulio Gabrielli': Polo Culturale S. Agostino, Corso Mazzini, 90, 63100 Ascoli Piceno; tel. 736-248650; e-mail protocollo@comune.ascolipiceno.it; internet www.comune.ascolipiceno.it; f. 1849; 200,000 vols, 300 incunabula, 900 MSS, 3,000 *cinquecentine*, 340 periodicals; Dir Dott. FABIO EMIDIO ZEPPILLI.

Avellino

Biblioteca Provinciale Scipione e Giulio Capone: Corso Europa 41, 83100 Avellino; tel. 0825-790513; e-mail info@mediateca.avellino.it; internet www.culturacampania.rai.it; f. 1913; 200,000 vols; Dir Dott. PASQUALE DI SALVIO.

Bari

Archivio di Stato di Bari: Via Pietro Oreste 45, 70125 Bari; tel. 080-099311; e-mail as-ba@beniculturali.it; internet www

.archiviodistatodibari.beniculturali.it; f. 1835; 6,192 vols, 224 periodicals, 139 MSS; Dir Dott. EUGENIA VANTAGGIATO.

Biblioteca Nazionale 'Sagarriga-Visconti-Volpi': Via Pietro Oreste 45, 70121 Bari; tel. 080-2173111; e-mail bn-ba@beniculturali.it; internet www.bibliotechepubbliche.it; f. 1865; 300,000 vols, 55 incunabula, 460 MSS, 2,196 *cinquecentini*, 450 current periodicals; Dir Dott. MARINA PANETTA.

Bergamo

Civica Biblioteca 'Angelo Mai': Piazza Vecchia 15, 24129 Bergamo; tel. 035-399430; e-mail info@bibliotecamai.org; internet www.bibliotecamai.org; f. 1760; 650,000 vols, 9,380 MSS, 22,000 parchments, 2,140 incunabula, 12,000 *cinquecentine*; Dir Dott. GIULIO ORAZIO BRAVI.

Bologna

Archivio di Stato di Bologna: Piazza dei Celestini 4, 40123 Bologna; tel. 051-223891; e-mail as-bo@beniculturali.it; internet www.archiviodistatobologna.it; f. 1874; 245,592 items; 23,000 vols, 331 periodicals; Dir ELISABETTA ARIOTI.

Biblioteca Carducci: Piazza Carducci 5, 40125 Bologna; tel. 051-347592; e-mail casacarducci@comune.bologna.it; internet www.casacarducci.it/htm/home.htm; given to the commune of Bologna in 1907 by Marguerite of Savoy, inaugurated in 1921; the library preserves the surroundings of the poet Giosuè Carducci and contains his collected works, as well as many rare editions of other works; 35,000 items; Dir PIERANGELO BELLETTINI.

Biblioteca Comunale dell'Archiginnasio: Piazza Galvani 1, 40124 Bologna; tel. 051-276811; e-mail archiginnasio@comune.bologna.it; internet www.archiginnasio.it; f. 1801; 951,535 vols (incl. 2,500 incunabula, 20,000 16th-century edns), 12,000 MSS, 500,000 letters and documents; Dir Dott. PIERANGELO BELLETTINI; publ. *L'Archiginnasio—Bollettino della Biblioteca Comunale di Bologna* (1 a year).

Biblioteca del Dipartimento di Scienze Giuridiche 'A. Cicu': Via Zamboni 27–29, 40126 Bologna; tel. 051-2099626; e-mail dipscgiur.biblioteca@unibo.it; internet www.giuridico.unibo.it; f. 1926; 215,000 vols, 1,042 current periodicals; Chief Librarian Dott. ANNA PRAMSTRAHLER.

Biblioteca San Domenico: Piazza San Domenico 13, 40124 Bologna; tel. 051-6400493; e-mail biblsand@iperbole.bologna.it; internet www.conventosandomenico.org/conventosandomenico/s2magazine/index1.jsp?idpagina=435; f. 1218; more than 85,000 vols, incunabula and MSS; spec. collns incl. philosophy and theology; Dir ANGELO PIAGNO.

Biblioteca Universitaria di Bologna: Via Zamboni 33–35, 40126 Bologna; tel. 51-2088300; e-mail direzione@bub.unibo.it; internet www.bub.unibo.it; f. 1712; 1,375,068 vols, 15,238 *cinquecentini*, 312,194 pamphlets, 12,875 MSS, 1,021 incunabula, 77,481 microforms, 743 current periodicals; Dir Dott. BIANCASTELLA ANTONINO; publs *BUBLife*, *In Bub: Ricerche e Cataloghi sui Fondi della Biblioteca Universitaria di Bologna* (1 a year).

Brescia

Biblioteca Queriniana: Via Mazzini 1, 25121 Brescia; tel. 030-2978200; e-mail queriniana@comune.brescia.it; internet queriniana.comune.brescia.it; f. 1747; 526,000 vols; Dir Dott. ENNIO FERRAGLIO.

Cagliari

Archivio di Stato di Cagliari: Via Gallura 2, 09125 Cagliari; tel. 070-669450; e-mail as-ca@beniculturali.it; internet www.archiviostatocagliari.it; f. 19th century; 29,525 vols, 2,690 periodicals, 21 MSS, 407,000 microfiches; Dir Dott.ssa ANNA PIA BIDOLLI.

Biblioteca Universitaria: Via Università 32A, 09123 Cagliari; tel. 070-661021; e-mail bu-ca@beniculturali.it; internet www.sardegna.beniculturali.it/index.php?it/267/biblioteche/22/biblioteca-universitaria-di-cagliari; f. 1792; 460,470 vols; 6,000 MSS, 236 incunabula, 5,000 *cinquecentini*, Gabinetto delle Stampe 'Anna Marongiu Pernis' contains 4,541 etchings; Dir ESTER GESSA.

Campobasso

Archivio di Stato di Campobasso: Via Orefici 43, 86100 Campobasso; tel. 0874-411488; e-mail as-cb@beniculturali.it; internet www.archivi.beniculturali.it/ascb; f. 1818; 19,658 vols, 935 periodicals, 29 MSS; Dir Dott. ANNALISA CARLASCIO.

Catania

Archivio di Stato di Catania: Via Vittorio Emanuele 156, 95131 Catania; tel. 095-7159860; e-mail as-ct@beniculturali.it; internet archivi.beniculturali.it/asct; f. 1854; 161,790 items; 11,700 vols; Dir Dott. ALDO SPARTI.

Biblioteca Regionale Universitaria: Piazza Università 2, 95124 Catania; tel. 095-7366111; f. 1755; 350,000 vols, 116 incunabula, 522 MSS, 2,710 *cinquecentini*; Dir MARIA GRAZIA PATANÈ.

Biblioteche Riunite Civica e A. Ursino Recupero: Via Biblioteca 13, 95124 Catania; tel. 095-316883; internet www.comune.catania.it; f. 1931 as municipal library, fmrly a Benedictine monastery library, nationalized in 1867; 210,000 vols, specializing in Sicily and Catania, 1,696 parchments, 2,000 MSS, 132 incunabula and 4,000 *cinquecentine*; Dir Dott. RITA ANGELA CARBONARO.

Cesena

Istituzione Biblioteca Malatestiana: Piazza Bufalini 1, 47521 Cesena; tel. 0547-610892; e-mail malatestiana@sbn.provincia.ra.it; internet www.malatestiana.it; f. 1452; 300,000 vols, 287 incunabula, 4,000 *cinquecentine*, 1,753 MSS; Dir Dott. MONICA ESPOSITO.

Como

Biblioteca Comunale: Piazzetta Venosto Lucati 1, 22100 Como; tel. 031-270187; e-mail biblioteca@comune.como.it; internet bibliotecacomunale.comune.como.it; f. 17th century; 380,000 vols; Dir RICCARDO TERZOLI.

Cremona

Biblioteca del Seminario Vescovile: Via Milano 5, 26100 Cremona; tel. 03-72458289; e-mail biblio.seminario@gmail.com; internet biblioseminariocremona.wordpress.com; f. 1592; 100,000 vols, 400 MSS, 20 incunabula, 1,300 *cinquecentine*; Dir ANDREA FOGLIA.

Biblioteca Statale: Via Ugolani Dati 4, 26100 Cremona; tel. 0372-495611; e-mail bs-cr@beniculturali.it; f. c. 1600; 700,000 vols, 2,380 MSS, 18,600 letters and documents, 374 incunabula, 6,000 16th-century editions; Dir Dr STEFANO CAMPAGNOLO; publs *Annali*, *Fonti e Sussidi*, *Mostre*.

Fermo

Biblioteca Civica 'Romolo Spezioli': Piazza del Popolo 63, 63023 Fermo; tel. 0734-284310; e-mail biblioteca.orientamento@comune.fermo.net; internet cultura.fermo.net; f. 1688; 350,000 vols and pamphlets, incl. 681 incunabula, 15,000 *cinquecentine*; 110 current periodicals, 3,000 MSS; Dir Dott. MARIA CHIARA LEONORI.

Ferrara

Biblioteca Comunale Ariostea: Via Scienze 17, 44121 Ferrara; tel. 0532-418200; e-mail info.ariostea@comune.fe.it; internet www.artecultura.fe.it; f. 1753; 430,257 vols; Dir Dott. ENRICO SPINELLI.

Florence

Archivio di Stato di Firenze: Viale Giovine Italia 6, 50122 Florence; tel. 055-263201; e-mail as-fi@beniculturali.it; internet www.archiviodistato.firenze.it; f. 1852; 790,000 items; 51,000 vols, 350 periodicals; Dir CARLA ZARRILLI.

Biblioteca degli Uffizi: Loggiato degli Uffizi, 50122 Florence; tel. 055-2388647; e-mail biblioteca@polomuseale.firenze.it; internet www.polomuseale.firenze.it/biblioteche/bib_uffizi.asp; f. 1770; 78,600 titles, incl. 470 MSS, 192 *cinquecentine*, 140 current periodicals; Dir Dott. CLAUDIO DI BENEDETTO.

Biblioteca del Gabinetto Scientifico Letterario G. P. Vieusseux: Palazzo Strozzi, Piazza Strozzi, 50123 Florence; tel. 055-288342; e-mail biblioteca@vieusseux.it; internet www.vieusseux.fi.it; f. 1819; 450,000 vols; Dir LAURA DESIDERE; publs *Antologia Vieusseux* (New Series, 4 a year), *Il Vieusseux* (4 a year).

Attached Archive:

Archivio Contemporaneo 'Alessandro Bonsanti': Palazzo Corsini-Suarez, Via Maggio 42, 50125 Florence; tel. 055-290131; e-mail archivio@vieusseux.it; internet www.vieusseux.fi.it/archivio_contemporaneo.html; f. 1975; 500,000 documents, 50,000 vols; Man. GLORIA MANGHETTI.

Biblioteca Marucelliana: Via Cavour 43–47, 50129 Florence; tel. 055-2722200; e-mail b-maru@beniculturali.it; internet www.maru.firenze.sbn.it; f. 1752; 630,000 vols and pamphlets, incl. 490 incunabula and 7,995 *cinquecentine*; 2,927 MSS, 3,200 drawings, 53,000 prints, 10,065 periodicals; Dir Dott. MONICA MARIA ANGELI.

Biblioteca Medicea-Laurenziana: Piazza S. Lorenzo 9, 50123 Florence; tel. 55-210760; e-mail b-mela@beniculturali.it; internet www.bmlonline.it; f. 1571; contains the private Medici Library, collns of MSS from the Medici family, the Grand Dukes of Lorena, S. Croce, S. Marco, Badia Fiesolana, cathedral of Florence, and private family collns; 15th- and 16th-centuries first edns; 14,000 MSS of the 5th–19th century; 2,500 papyri, 80 ostraca, 150,000 vols; Dir Dr VERA VALITUTTO.

Biblioteca Moreniana: Via dei Ginori 10, 50123 Florence; tel. 055-2760331; e-mail moreniana@provincia.fi.it; internet www.provincia.fi.it/palazzo-medici-ricciardi/biblioteca-moreniana; f. 1869; 34,000 vols, c. 2,000 MSS, specializing in ancient Tuscan history; Dir MASSIMO TARASSI.

Biblioteca Nazionale Centrale: Piazza Cavalleggeri 1, 50122 Florence; tel. 055-249191; e-mail info@bncf.firenze.sbn.it; internet www.bncf.firenze.sbn.it; f. 1747; 6,000,000 vols, pamphlets, 120,000 periodicals (15,000 current), 25,000 MSS, 4,000 incunabula, 29,000 *cinquecentine*; Dir Dott. MARIA LETIZIA SEBASTIANI; publ. *Bibliografia nazionale italiana* (12 a year, 1 a year accumulations, 4 a year CD-ROM).

Biblioteca Pedagogica Nazionale: c/o Biblioteca di Documentazione Pedagogica,

Palazzo Gerini, Via M. Buonarroti 10, 50122 Florence; tel. 055-2380364; e-mail biblioteca@indire.it; internet www.indire.it/chisiamo/biblio_patrimonio.html; f. 1941; 85,000 vols, 1,600 periodicals, rare books, drawings; data banks on education; Dir Dott. PAMELA GIORGI; publs *Schedario* (review of children's literature, 3 a year), *Segnalibro* (review of literature for young people, 1 a year).

Biblioteca Riccardiana: Via dei Ginori 10, 50123 Florence; tel. 055-212586; e-mail b-ricc@beniculturali.it; internet www.riccardiana.firenze.sbn.it; f. 1815; 63,833 vols, 4,450 MSS, 725 incunabula, 3,865 *cinquecentine*, 258 periodicals; Dir Dott. GIOVANNA LAZZI.

Biblioteca Umanistica dell' Università: Piazza Brunelleschi 4, 50121 Florence; tel. 055-2757811; e-mail floriana.tagliabue@unifi.it; internet www.sba.unifi.it/biblio/umanistica; f. 1959; 1,600,000 vols; sections on philosophy, geography, literature, psychology, education, art history, and N American history and literature; Dir Dott. FLORIANA TAGLIABUE.

Forlì

Biblioteca Comunale 'Aurelio Saffi': Corso della Repubblica 72, 47100 Forlì; tel. 0543-712600; e-mail biblioteca-saffi@comune.forli.fc.it; internet www.cultura.comune.forli.fc.it; 490,000 vols, 250 incunabula, 8,000 16th-century editions, 2,000 MSS, 2,200 periodicals; Dir Dr FRANCO FABBRI.

Genoa

Archivio di Stato di Genova: Piazza S. Maria in Via Lata, 7, 16128 Genoa; tel. 010-537561; e-mail as-ge@beniculturali.it; internet archivi.beniculturali.it/asge/asge.htm; f. 1817; 13,000 vols, 145 periodicals; Dir PAOLA CAROLI.

Biblioteca Durazzo Giustiniani: Via XXV Aprile 12, 16123 Genoa; tel. 010-2476232; f. 1760–1804; 20,000 17th- and 18th-century vols, 1,000 *cinquecentine*, 448 incunabula, 300 MSS; Curator Dott.ssa SANDRA MACCHIAVELLO.

Biblioteca di Storia dell'Arte: Via ai Quattro Canti di San Francesco 49/51, 16121 Genoa; tel. 010-5574957; e-mail biblarte@comune.genova.it; internet www.museidigenova.it/spip.php?article313; f. 1908; attached to Centro di Documentazione per la Storia, l'Arte, l'Immagine di Genova; 51,000 vols, 207 current periodicals; specialized library relating to Italian and Genoese fine arts (since 11th century); Dir Dr ELISABETTA PAPONE; publ. *Bollettino dei Musei Civici Genovesi*.

Biblioteca Universitaria: Via Balbi 3 e 38B, 16126 Genoa; tel. 010-254641; e-mail bu-ge@beniculturali.it; internet www.bibliotecauniversitaria.ge.it; f. 18th century; 617,109 vols, 1,039 incunabula, 1,949 MSS, 19,287 letters and documents; Dir Reg. SIMONETTA BUTTÒ.

Gorizia

Biblioteca Statale Isontina di Gorizia: Via Mameli 12, 34170 Gorizia; tel. 0481-580211; e-mail bs-ison@beniculturali.it; internet www.isontina.beniculturali.it; f. 1629; lending and reference library; bibliographical information service; 381,526 vols, 41 incunabula, 934 *cinquecentine*, 1,074 current periodicals, 862 MSS, 1,181 microfiches; Dir Prof. MARCO MENATO; publ. *Studi Goriziani* (2 a year).

Imola

Biblioteca Comunale: Via Emilia 80, 40026 Imola; tel. 0542-602636; e-mail bim@comune.imola.bo.it; internet bim.comune.imola.bo.it; f. 1761; 470,000 vols, 1,692 MSS, 140 incunabula; Dir Dott. MARINA BARUZZI.

L'Aquila

Biblioteca Provinciale 'Salvatore Tommasi': Via Niccolò Copernico, Bazzano, 67100 L'Aquila; tel. 0862-61964; e-mail biblioteca.reference@provincia.laquila.it; internet www.provincia.laquila.it/biblioteca; f. 1848; 260,000 vols, 230 current periodicals, 131 incunabula, 911 MSS, 3,500 *cinquecentine* (rare 16th-century editions); Dir Dott. PAOLO COLLACCIANI.

Livorno

Biblioteca Labronica—Villa Fabbricotti: Viale della Libertà 30, 57123 Livorno; tel. 0586-264511; e-mail labronica@comune.livorno.it; f. 1816; 120,000 vols incl. 2,000 *cinquecentine*, 1,500 MSS, 117 incunabula and 60,000 letters and documents; Dir Dott. DUCCIO FILIPPI; publ. *Quaderni della Labronica* (4 a year).

Attached Libraries:

Biblioteca Labronica—Bottini dell'Olio: Via del Forte di San Pietro 15, 57123 Livorno; tel. 0586-219265; e-mail bottinidellolio@comune.livorno.it; internet www.comune.livorno.it/_livo/pages.php?id=127; 61,000 vols; Dir Dott. DUCCIO FILIPPI.

Biblioteca Labronica—Sezione Emeroteca: Via del Toro 8, 57123 Livorno; tel. 0586-892059; e-mail emeroteca@comune.livorno.it; 3,950 periodicals, 750 current periodicals; Dir Dott. DUCCIO FILIPPI.

Lucca

Biblioteca Statale di Lucca: Via S. Maria Corteorlandini 12, 55100 Lucca; tel. 0583-491271; e-mail bs-lu@beniculturali.it; internet www.bslu.librari.beniculturali.it; f. 1794; 449,200 vols, 594 current periodicals, 10,000 *cinquecentine*, 835 incunabula, 4,321 MSS, 19,462 letters and documents; Dir Dott. MARCO PAOLI.

Macerata

Biblioteca Comunale Mozzi-Borgetti: Piazza Vittorio Veneto 2, 62100 Macerata; tel. 0733-256360; e-mail biblioteca@comune.macerata.it; internet www.comune.macerata.it/entra/engine/raservepg.php3/p/2508110417; f. 1773; 350,000 vols, 10,000 MSS, 300 incunabula, 20,000 photographs; Dir Dott.ssa ALESSANDRA SFRAPPINI.

Mantua

Biblioteca Comunale Teresiana: Via Roberto Ardigò 13, 46100 Mantua; tel. 0376-321515; e-mail bibliotecacomunale@comune.mantova.gov.it; internet www.bibliotecateresiana.it; f. 1780; 330,000 vols, 1,375 MSS, 1,425 incunabula, 8,500 *cinquecentine*; Dir Dr CESARE GUERRA; Librarian RAFFAELLA PERINI.

Biblioteca dell' Accademia Nazionale Virgiliana: Via dell'Accademia 47, 46100 Mantua; tel. 376-320314; e-mail info@accademianazionalevirgiliana.org; internet www.accademianazionalevirgiliana.org; f. early 17th century; 30,000 vols; Librarian Prof. ANNA MARIA LORENZONI; publs *Atti e Memorie* (1 a year), *Nuova Serie* (1 a year).

Messina

Biblioteca Regionale Universitaria di Messina: Via I Settembre 117, 98122 Messina; tel. 090-771908; e-mail brs.me@regione.sicilia.it; internet www.regione.sicilia.it/beniculturali/brum/index.htm; f. 1731; 449,926 vols, 461 current periodicals, 1,307 MSS, 423 incunabula, 3,637 *cinquecentine*; Dir Arch. ROCCO GIOVANNI SCIMONE.

Milan

Archivio di Stato di Milano: Via Senato 10, 20121 Milan; tel. 02-7742161; e-mail as-mi@beniculturali.it; internet www.archiviodistatomilano.it; f. 1886; 27,096 vols and pamphlets, 18,814 periodicals; Dir Dott. MARIA BARBARA BERTINI.

Archivio Storico Civico e Biblioteca Trivulziana: Castello Sforzesco, 20121 Milan; tel. 02-88463690; e-mail c.ascbibliotrivulziana@comune.milano.it; internet www.comune.milano.it; f. 1872 as Archivio Storico Civico, merged with Biblioteca Trivulziana in 1935; 170,000 vols, 1,500 MSS dating from the 8th century, 1,300 incunabula, rare works on history, literature, local historical artefacts; Dir Dott. ISABELLA FIORENTINI; publ. *Libri & Documenti* (1 a year).

Biblioteca Archeologica e Numismatica: Castello Sforzesco, 20121 Milan; tel. 02-88463772; e-mail c.bibliocasva@comune.milano.it; internet www.comune.milano.it/baac; f. 1808; prehistoric, Roman, Etruscan, Greek and Egyptian archaeology; coins and medals; library and historical archives; 26,930 vols, 17,650 periodicals, 240 current periodicals; Dir Dr SERGIO GRAFFI.

Biblioteca Centrale di Ingegneria–Leonardo: Piazza Leonardo da Vinci 32, 20133 Milan; tel. 02-23992550; internet www.biblio.polimi.it/biblioteche; f. 1863; 192,100 vols, 350 MSS, 3,780 periodicals, 173 current periodicals; Head of Library MARINELLA TRENTA.

Biblioteca Comunale 'Sormani': Palazzo Sormani, Corso di Porta Vittoria 6, 20122 Milan; tel. 02-88463397; e-mail c.bibliocentrale@comune.milano.it; internet www.comune.milano.it/biblioteche; f. 1886; 640,000 vols, 20,000 periodicals, 2,300 current periodicals, 32,500 audio and video items, 500 electronic resources; Dir Dott. ANNA MARIA ROSSATO.

Biblioteca d'Arte: Castello Sforzesco, 20121 Milan; tel. 02-88463737; e-mail c.biblioarte@comune.milano.it; internet www.comune.milano.it/casva; f. 1930; art history, applied arts, museology, graphics, design, visual arts; art library; 120,008 vols, 1,681 periodicals, 257 current periodicals; Dir SERGIO GRAFFI; Librarian ANNA BALDINI.

Biblioteca d'Ateneo dell'Università Cattolica del Sacro Cuore: Largo Gemelli 1, 20123 Milan; tel. 02-72342230; e-mail biblioteca.direzione-mi@unicatt.it; internet www.unicatt.it/library; f. 1921; linked to libraries in three other locations: Brescia, Piacenza and Cremona, and Rome and Campobasso; 1,373,000 vols and pamphlets, 32,520 periodicals, 12,800 electronic journals, 270 online and CD-ROM-based databases; Head of Library Dott. ELLIS SADA.

Biblioteca del Centro Nazionale di Studi Manzoniani: Via Morone 1, 20121 Milan; tel. 02-86460403; e-mail info@casadelmanzoni.it; f. 1937; 25,000 vols; Dir Prof. GIANMARCO GASPARI; Pres. Prof. ANGELO STELLA; publs *Annali*, *Bollettino Bibliografico*, *Edizione Nazionale ed Europea delle Opere di Alessandro Manzoni*.

Biblioteca del Conservatorio 'Giuseppe Verdi': Via Conservatorio 12, 20122 Milan; tel. 02-762110219; e-mail biblioteca@consmilano.it; internet www.consmilano.it; f. 1808; 500,000 items; 50,000 MSS, 30,000 books on music, 400 periodicals; Librarian LICIA SIRCH.

Biblioteca dell' Istituto Lombardo Accademia di Scienze e Lettere: Via Borgonuovo 25, 20121 Milan; tel. 02-864087; e-mail istituto.lombardo@unimi.it; internet www.istitutolombardo.it/biblioteca.html; f. 1802;

495,000 vols, 2,600 periodicals; Dir Dott. ADELE BIANCHI ROBBIATI.

Biblioteca dell' Università Commerciale Luigi Bocconi: Via Gobbi 5, 20136 Milan; tel. 02-58365027; e-mail library.staff@unibocconi.it; internet lib.unibocconi.it; f. 1903; ILL and Circulation Services, reference services, European documentation centre, information literacy workshops, electronic course reserves, copyright advising and support; 709,772 vols, 10,002 paper periodicals, 24,137 ejournals, 69,270 theses, 72 databases, 2,141 ancient books (from 16th to 18th centuries) and 312 ebooks; Head Librarian Dott. MARISA SANTARSIERO.

Biblioteca della Facoltà di Agraria: Università degli Studi di Milano, Via G. Celoria 2, 20133 Milan; tel. 02-50316428; e-mail bib.agraria@unimi.it; internet users.unimi.it/biblioteche/agraria; f. 1871; 35,000 vols and periodicals; Scientific Dir Profa VINCENTINA ANDREONI; Librarian Dott. ANGELO BOZZOLA.

Biblioteca delle Facoltà di Giurisprudenza e di Lettere e Filosofia dell' Università: Via Festa del Perdono 7, 20122 Milan; tel. 02-50312468; e-mail info.bglf@unimi.it; internet www.sba.unimi.it/biblioteche/bglf/1864.html; f. 1925; 360,000 vols, 1,379 current periodicals, 1,034 online periodicals; Dir LIDIA CATERINA DIELLA.

Biblioteca Nazionale Braidense: Via Brera 28, 20121 Milan; tel. 02-86460907; e-mail b-brai@beniculturali.it; internet www.braidense.it; f. 1770; 1,500,000 vols, 17,149 periodicals, 26,455 autographs, 2,107 MSS; Dir Dott. AURELIO AGHEMO.

Civiche Raccolte Storiche di Milano, Biblioteca e Archivio: Palazzo De Marchi, Via Borgonuovo 23, 20121 Milan; tel. 02-88464180; e-mail francesco.basile@comune.milano.it; internet www.civicheraccoltestoriche.mi.it/biblioteca.php; f. 1884; 130,000 vols, periodicals and pamphlets, 3,825 files of documents since 1750; Dir CLAUDIO SALSI.

Veneranda Biblioteca Ambrosiana: Piazza Pio XI 2, 20123 Milan; tel. 02-806921; e-mail info@ambrosiana.it; internet www.ambrosiana.eu; f. 1607, opened to the public in 1609; 900,000 vols and rare prints, 36,000 MSS mostly Latin, Greek, and Oriental, 3,0000 incunabula, 12,000 parchments, 22,500 prints, 20,000 letters, 22,000 engravings; Dir Dott. GIANANTONIO BORGONOVO; publ. *Accademia Ambrosiana:Studia Borromaica* (1 a year).

Modena

Biblioteca Estense Universitaria: Palazzo dei Musei, Largo Porta S. Agostino 337, 41121 Modena; tel. 059-222248; e-mail b-este@beniculturali.it; internet bibliotecaestense.beniculturali.it; 562,491 vols, 11,025 MSS, 1,662 incunabula, 15,996 *cinquecentine*, 129,181 pamphlets, 8,663 periodicals; Dir Dott. LUCA BELLINGERI; Librarian ANNALISA BATTINI.

Naples

Archivio di Stato di Napoli: Piazzetta del Grande Archivio, 80138 Naples; tel. 081-5638111; e-mail as-na@beniculturali.it; internet www.archiviodistatonapoli.it; f. 1808; 544,000 items; 25,000 vols; Dir Dott. IMMA ASCIONE.

Biblioteca del Conservatorio S. Pietro a Majella: Via S. Pietro a Majella 35, 80138 Naples; tel. (81) 5644427; e-mail biblioteca@sanpietroamajella.it; internet www.sanpietroamajella.it/it/bl_introduzione_w.html; f. 1791; 300,000 vols, 18,000 MSS, 10,000 costume designs, 8,000 opera libretti, 10,000 letters, 200 *cinquecentine*; Dir Dr FRANCESCO MELISI.

Biblioteca della Facoltà di Agraria dell' Università degli Studi di Napoli Federico II: Via Università 100, 80055 Portici; tel. 081-2539321; e-mail giovanna.ameno@unina.it; internet biblioteca.agraria.unina.it; f. 1872; 65,000 vols, 3,511 periodicals, 363 current periodicals; Dir Dott. GIOVANNA AMENO.

Biblioteca della Pontificia Facoltà Teologica dell' Italia Meridionale, sezione 'San Tommaso d'Aquino': Viale Colli Aminei 2, 80131 Naples; tel. 081-7410000; e-mail presidenzapftim@libero.it; internet www.teologia.it/pftim; f. 1687; 120,000 vols; 11 incunabula, 600 MSS, 1,000 periodicals, 450 current periodicals; Dir Prof. ANTONIO PORPORA.

Biblioteca della Società Napoletana di Storia Patria: Piazza Municipio, Maschio Angioino, 80133 Naples; tel. 081-5510353; e-mail bibl.snsp@libero.it; internet www.storia.unina.it/snsp; f. 1875; 350,000 vols, 2,400 MSS, 2,955 periodicals, 900 current periodicals, 1,300 *cinquecentine*, 59 incunabula; Librarian MARIA CONCETTA VILLANI; publ. *Archivio Storico per le Province Napoletane*.

Biblioteca di Castelcapuano: Piazza Tribunali 1, 80138 Naples; tel. 081-269416; e-mail info@bibliotecademarsico.it; f. 1848; 80,000 vols and pamphlets, 1,100 documents; Dir Dott. RAFFAELLO ROSSI BUSSOLA.

Biblioteca Nazionale 'Vittorio Emanuele III': Piazza del Plebiscito 1, 80132 Naples; tel. 081-7819111; e-mail bn-na@beniculturali.it; internet www.bnnonline.it; f. 1804; 1,800,000 vols, 19,000 MSS, 8,300 periodicals, 4,563 incunabula, 1,792 papyri from Herculaneum; Dir Dott. MAURO GIANCASPRO.

Biblioteca Statale Oratoriana del Monumento Nazionale dei Girolamini: Via Duomo 142, 80138 Naples; tel. 081-294444; e-mail bmn-gir@beniculturali.it; internet www.girolamini.it; f. 1586; 169,000 vols, 120 incunabula, 5,000 *cinquecentine*, 485 periodicals, 57 current periodicals; Dir GIOVANNI FERRARA.

Biblioteca Universitaria di Napoli: Via G. Paladino 39, 80138 Naples; tel. 081-5517025; e-mail bu-na@beniculturali.it; internet www.bun.unina.it; f. 1816; open to the public; 776,211 vols, 5,820 periodicals, 3,654 *cinquecentine*, 462 incunabula, 144 MSS; Dir Dott. ANNA BOLOGNESE.

Novara

Biblioteca Civica 'Carlo Negroni': Corso Felice Cavallotti 4, 28100 Novara; tel. 0321-3702800; e-mail biblioteca.negroni@comune.novara.it; internet www.comune.novara.it/citta/biblioteca/biblioteca.php; f. 1848; 300,000 vols, 3,052 periodicals, 2,000 *cinquecentine*, 130 incunabula, 771 microfilms, 420 MSS, maps, 6,500 discs, tapes and cassettes.

Padua

Biblioteca Civica: Via Altinate 71, 35121 Padua; tel. 049-8204811; e-mail biblioteca.civica@comune.padova.it; internet www.padovanet.it/biblioteche; f. 1858; art, Italian literature, history, local history (Padua and Veneto); 500,000 vols, 5,500 MSS, 385 incunabula, 2,000 periodicals, 1300 DVDs; Head Librarian Dr GILDA P. MANTOVANI; publ. *Bollettino del Museo Civico di Padova*.

Biblioteca del Seminario Vescovile di Padova-della Facoltà Teologica del Triveneto-dell'Istituto Filosofico Aloisianum: Via Seminario 29, 35122 Padua; tel. 049-8230013; e-mail biblioteca@fttr.it; internet www.seminariopadova.it; f. 1671; 300,000 vols, 1,135 MSS, 417 incunabula, 800 periodicals; Dir Prof. RICCARDO BATTOCCHIO; Librarian Dr CONCETTA ROCIOLA; Librarian Dr GIOVANNA BERGANTINO; Librarian Dr LAURA SCIMÒ.

Biblioteca Universitaria: Via S. Biagio 7, 35121 Padua; tel. 049-8240211; e-mail bu-pd@beniculturali.it; internet www.bibliotecauniversitariapadova.beniculturali.it; f. 1629; 676,982 vols; 2,798 MSS, 1,283 incunabula, 1,530 music scores, 1,055 maps, 6,681 periodicals, 592 current periodicals, 9,622 *cinquecentine*, 3,000 prints and engravings; Dir Dott. FRANCESCO ALIANO.

Pontificia Biblioteca Antoniana Basilica del Santo: Piazza del Santo 11, 35123 Padua; tel. 049-8751492; e-mail info@bibliotecaantoniana.191.it; internet biblioteca.antoniana.net; f. 13th century; 85,000 vols, 800 MSS; Head Librarian Dr ALBERTO FANTON.

Palermo

Archivio di Stato di Palermo: Corso Vittorio Emanuele 31, 90133 Palermo; tel. 091-2510634; e-mail as-pa@beniculturali.it; internet www.archiviodistatodipalermo.it; f. 1814; 386,918 items; 22,000 vols; Dir CLAUDIO TORRISI.

Biblioteca Centrale della Regione Siciliana: Corso Vittorio Emanuele 429–431, 90134 Palermo; tel. 091-7077642; e-mail bcrs@regione.sicilia.it; internet www.regione.sicilia.it/beniculturali/bibliotecacentrale; f. 1782; 682,000 vols; 1,930 MSS, 1,044 incunabula, 5,907 periodicals, 15,000 letters and documents, 5,066 rare books, 4,125 maps, prints and engravings, 47,664 microforms, 3,541 photographs and slides; Dir FRANCESCO VERGARA.

Biblioteca Comunale: Piazza Casa Professa 1, 90134 Palermo; tel. 091-7407940; e-mail sistemabibliotecario@comune.palermo.it; internet librarsi.comune.palermo.it; f. 1760; 376,571 vols, 5,000 MSS, 1,038 incunabula, 6,000 *cinquecentine*; Dir Dott. FILIPPO GUTTUSO.

Parma

Biblioteca Palatina: Strada alla Pilotta 3, 43121 Parma; tel. 0521-220411; e-mail b-pala@beniculturali.it; internet www.bibliotecapalatina.beniculturali.it; f. 1761; 715,000 vols, 6,671 MSS, 556 periodicals, 3,044 incunabula, 52,601 engravings and drawings; Dir SABINA MAGRINI; Librarian DANIELA MOSCHINI.

Biblioteca Palatina–Sezione Musicale presso il Conservatorio di Musica 'A. Boito': Via del Conservatorio 27, 43121 Parma; tel. 0521-289429; e-mail b-pala@beniculturali.it; internet www.bibliotecapalatina.beniculturali.it; f. 1889; 167,000 items; 167,000 vols, 16,288 MSS, 40 periodicals; Dir Dr SABINA MAGRINI.

Pavia

Biblioteca Civica 'Carlo Bonetta': Piazza Petrarca 2, 27100 Pavia; tel. 382-21635; e-mail fbonetta@comune.pv.it; internet www.comune.pv.it/site/home/canali-tematici/arte-e-cultura/biblioteca-civica-bonetta.html; f. 1887; Dir Dott. FELICE MILANI.

Biblioteca Universitaria: Corso Strada Nuova 65, 27100 Pavia; tel. 0382-24764; e-mail bu-pv@beniculturali.it; internet siba.unipv.it/buniversitaria; f. 1763; 497,077 vols, 2,556 MSS, 691 incunabula, 6,102 periodicals, 718 current periodicals, 7,000 *cinquecentine*, 11,021 microfilms, 4,000 engravings; Dir Dott. ALESSANDRA BRACCI.

Perugia

Biblioteca Augusta del Comune di Perugia: Palazzo Conestabile della Staffa, Via delle Prome 15, 06122 Perugia; tel. 075-5772500; e-mail augusta@comune.perugia

.it; internet www.comune.perugia.it/canale.asp?id=2822; f. 1615; 380,000 vols, 3,380 MSS, 1,330 incunabula, 3,800 periodicals, 16,500 *cinquecentine*; Dir Dott. MAURIZIO TARANTINO.

Pesaro

Biblioteca e Musei Oliveriani: Via Mazza Domenico 97, 61121 Pesaro; tel. 0721-33344; e-mail biblio.oliveriana@provincia.ps.it; internet www.oliveriana.pu.it/index.php?id=14525; f. 1793; 354,000 vols on general culture and local history; Dir MARCELLO DI BELLA; publ. *Studia Oliveriana* (1 a year).

Piacenza

Biblioteca Comunale Passerini Landi: Via Carducci 14, 29121 Piacenza; tel. 532-492410; e-mail biblio.reference@comune.piacenza.it; internet passerinilandi.biblioteche.piacenza.it; f. 1774; 50,000 vols, 1,000 incunabula, 5,000 *cinquecentine*; Dir Dott. ANTONELLA GIGLI.

Pisa

Biblioteca Universitaria: Via Santa Maria 5, 56126 Pisa; tel. 50-25194; e-mail bu-pi@beniculturali.it; internet www.pisa.sbn.it; f. 1742; 600,000 vols, 1,395 MSS, 24,087 documents, 162 incunabula, 117,130 periodicals, 7,083 *cinquecentine*; Dir Dott. ALESSANDRA PESANTE.

Pistoia

Biblioteca Comunale Forteguerriana: Piazza della Sapienza 5, 51100 Pistoia; tel. 0573-24348; e-mail forteguerriana@comune.pistoia.it; internet www.comune.pistoia.it/forteguerriana/index.html; f. 1696; 220,000 vols, 1,290 periodicals, 1,000 MSS, 126 incunabula, 3,000 *cinquecentine*; Dir MARIA STELLA RASETTI.

Portici

Biblioteca del Dipartimento di Entomologia e Zoologia Agraria, Università degli Studi di Napoli Federico II: Via Università 100, 80055 Portici; tel. 081-2539188; e-mail bibliodeza@unina.it; f. 1872; applied entomology and biological control; 100,000 vols; Dir CINZIA STELLATO; publ. *Bollettino del Laboratorio di Entomologia Agraria 'Filippo Silvestri'*.

Potenza

Archivio di Stato di Potenza: Via Nazario Sauro 1, 85100 Potenza; tel. 0971-56144; e-mail as-pz@beniculturali.it; internet aspz.it; f. 1818; 10,500 linear miles of records (since the 11th century); administrative and judicial archives since 1687; notarial archives since 1524; archives of religious houses dissolved in the 19th century; private and feudal archives since 1500; collns of parchments (since the 10th century) and municipal statutes; also archives of ecclesiastical bodies incl. those of the Venosa cathedral chapter (since the 11th century); 17,000 vols, 2,500 periodicals; Dir Dott.ssa VALERIA VERRASTRO.

Biblioteca Nazionale: Via del Gallitello 103, 85100 Potenza; tel. 0971-54829; e-mail bn-pz@beniculturali.it; internet www.bibliotecanazionale.potenza.it; f. 1985; functions as univ. library (Univ. della Basilicata) and regional library; 300,000 vols, 1,681 periodicals; Dir FRANCESCO SABIA.

Ravenna

Istituzione Biblioteca Classense: Via Baccarini 3, 48121 Ravenna; tel. 0544-482112; e-mail informazioni@classense.ra.it; internet www.classense.ra.it; f. 1707–11; 800,000 vols incl. 800 incunabula, 8,000 *cinquecentine*, 800 MSS, 10,000 prints; Dir Dott. MARIA GRAZIA MARINI; publ. *Letture Classensi*.

Reggio Emilia

Biblioteca Panizzi: Via Farini 3, 42121 Reggio Emilia; tel. 0522-456084; e-mail panizzi@municipio.re.it; internet panizzi.comune.re.it; f. 1796; 500,000 vols, 10,000 MSS; Dir GIORDANO GASPARINI.

Rimini

Biblioteca Civica Gambalunga: Via Gambalunga 27, 47921 Rimini; tel. 0541-704486; e-mail gambalunghiana@comune.rimini.it; internet www.bibliotecagambalunga.it; f. 1619; 220,000 vols (incl. 7,000 *cinquecentine*), 382 incunabula, 1,350 MSS, 2,545,periodicals, 400 current periodicals, 1,960 bound periodicals, 8,000 drawings and engravings, 80,000 photographs; Dir ORIETTA BAIOCCHI.

Rome

Archivio Centrale dello Stato: Piazzale degli Archivi 27, 00144 Rome; tel. 06-545481; e-mail acs@beniculturali.it; internet www.acs.beniculturali.it; f. 1875; 110 shelf-km of documents; political, administrative, cultural and judicial archives of the Kingdom of Italy and Italian Republic; 89,317 vols; Dir AGOSTINO ATTANASIO.

Archivio di Stato di Roma: Corso del Rinascimento 40, 00186 Rome; tel. 06-6819081; e-mail as-rm@beniculturali.it; internet www.archiviodistatoroma.beniculturali.it; f. 1871; conservation of archives produced by the central offices of the Papal State from the Middle Ages to 1870, together with documents produced by other agencies in the Rome area; papal provincial treasuries (incl. Avignon and Benevento); archives of religious orders since the 14th century and of brotherhoods, academies, corporate bodies, the University of Rome and notary registers since the 13th century; conservation of govt office records of the Italian State with seat in Rome; School of Archival Science, Latin Palaeography and Diplomatics; 52,000 vols, with 3 important collns: Statutes, MSS, Decrees; Dir Prof. EUGENIO LO SARDO.

Biblioteca Angelica: Piazza Sant'Agostino 8, 00186 Rome; tel. 06-6840801; e-mail b-ange@beniculturali.it; internet www.biblioangelica.it; f. 1605; 15th–18th-century literature; Augustinian, Jansenist, Reformation and counter-Reformation collns; 220,000 vols, 2,704 MSS, 1,156 incunabula; Dir Dott.ssa FIAMMETTA TERLIZZI.

Biblioteca Casanatense: Via S. Ignazio 52, 00186 Rome; tel. (6) 6976031; e-mail casanatense@biblioroma.sbn.it; internet www.casanatense.it; f. 1701; preserves and enhances the collns of Cardinal Girolamo Casanate; 400,000 vols; spec. collns: MSS colln, 6,000 vols of great value incl. exultet, liturgical codes, medical-scientific texts, Oriental and Hebraic codes, famous autographs incl. that of Niccolò Paganini; Incunabula colln, 2,200 vols incl. unique first edns and plaques; Engravings colln, 30,000 engravings incl. Abbot Antonio Ricci's donation and endowment of the Chamber of Calligraphy; Musical works colln, 1,700 MSS and 2,000 published works; Theatre colln, 7,000 copies of dramatic works and musical librettos, Edicts and Bans colln, 70,000 from 1550 to 1870, esp. from the Pontiff State; Periodicals: colln, 2,000 titles (220 current subscriptions) incl. Roman and Pontifical State journals; Heraldry colln, 1,200 works; Sanctification actions colln, Decisions of the Sacred Rota and other ecclesiastical tribunals; the library's holdings are currently being increased by the acquisition of antiquarian materials and new publs; Dir IOLANDA OLIVIERI.

Biblioteca Centrale del Consiglio Nazionale delle Ricerche (Central Library of National Research Council): Piazzale Aldo Moro 7, 00185 Rome; tel. 06-49933221; e-mail biblioce@bice.rm.cnr.it; internet www.bice.rm.cnr.it; f. 1927; 1,000,000 vols, 10,000 periodicals (6,000 online), EU depository library; scientific and technical subjects; Dir Prof. BRUNELLA SEBASTIANI.

Biblioteca Centrale del Ministero dell'Interno: Palazzo del Viminale, Via Agostino Depretis, 00184 Rome; tel. 06-46525703; internet www.interno.it/mininterno/export/sites/default/it/sezioni/ministero/biblioteche/la_biblioteca_centrale; f. 1872; 110,000 vols; Dir ARTURO LETIZIA.

Biblioteca Centrale Giuridica del Ministero della Giustizia: Palazzo di Giustizia, Piazza Cavour, 00193 Rome; tel. 06-68834900; e-mail bcg@giustizia.it; internet www.giustizia.it/giustizia/it/mg_7.wp; f. 1866; 200,000 vols, 2,300 periodicals, 1,000 current periodicals; Dir Dr ORAZIO FRAZZINI.

Biblioteca del Ministero degli Affari Esteri: Piazzale della Farnesina 1, 00194 Rome; tel. 06-36913279; e-mail giorgetta.troiano@esteri.it; internet www.esteri.it/mae/it/ministero/servizi/italiani/archivi_biblioteca/biblioteca.htm; f. 1850; 200,000 vols, 1,500 periodicals, 168 current periodicals; international relations, contemporary history; Dir Dott. MARIA ADELAIDE FRABOTTA.

Biblioteca del Senato 'Giovanni Spadolini': Piazza della Minerva, 38, 00186 Rome; tel. 6-67063717; e-mail bibliotecaminerva@senato.it; internet www.senato.it/biblioteca; f. 1848; chiefly works on law, history and politics; medieval statutes; 700,000 vols, 3,200 periodicals, 150 current periodical subscriptions, 630 newspapers, 80 current newspapers, 850 MSS, 80 incunabula, 2,000 *cinquecentine*; Dir Prof. RENATA GIANNELLA (acting).

Biblioteca dell'Accademia Nazionale dei Lincei e Corsiniana: Via della Lungara 10, 00165 Rome; tel. 06-6861983; e-mail biblioteca@lincei.it; internet www.lincei.it; f. 1883; 552,000 vols on history of arts, sciences and culture, 7,000 periodicals, 4,600 MSS, 2,307 incunabula; oriental section on Arabic and Islamic civilization, with 35,000 books, 350 periodicals, 500 MSS; online catalogue for modern collection; Dir Dott. MARCO GUARDO; Librarian (Ancient Printed Books) Dott. EBE ANTETOMASO; Librarian (Modern Printed Books) Dott. ALESSANDRO ROMANELLO; Librarian (Oriental Section) Dott. VALENTINA SAGARIA ROSSI; Librarian (Oriental Section and Interlibrary Loans) Dott. ANDREA TRENTINI; Librarian (Reading Room and Loan Service) ANDREA DIBITONTO.

Biblioteca della Camera dei Deputati: Via del Seminario 76, 00186 Rome; tel. 06-67603476; e-mail bib_segreteria@camera.it; f. 1848 in Turin; 1,000,000 vols, 10,000 bound periodicals, 2,500 current periodicals; Dir Dr ANTONIO CASU; publ. *Bollettino Nuove Accessioni* (12 a year).

Biblioteca della Fondazione Marco Besso: Largo di Torre Argentina 11, 00186 Rome; tel. 06-68192984; e-mail biblioteca@fondazionemarcobesso.it; internet www.fondazionemarcobesso.it/nuovobesso; f. 1918; 60,000 vols and 5,000 pamphlets; spec. collns: Rome, Dante, Proverbs, Tuscia; Curator ANTONIO MARTINI.

Biblioteca della Società Geografica Italiana: Villa Celimontana, Via della Navicella 12, 00184 Rome; tel. 06-7008279; e-mail biblioteca@societageografica.it; internet www.societageografica.it/archivio/biblioteca/

index.htm; f. 1867; 400,000 vols; Library Counsellor LINA MARIA VITALE; publs *Bollettino della Società Geografica Italiana*, *Memorie della Società Geografica Italiana*, *Ricerche e Studi*.

Biblioteca della Società Italiana per l'Organizzazione Internazionale (SIOI): Piazza di S. Marco 51, Palazzetto di Venezia, 00186 Rome; tel. 06-6920781; e-mail sioi@sioi.org; internet www.sioi.org/la_biblioteca.htm; f. 1944; 70,000 vols, 800 periodicals, 500,000 UN documents; Dir Dott. SARA CAVELLI.

Biblioteca della Soprintendenza alla Galleria Nazionale d'Arte Moderna e Contemporanea: Viale delle Belle Arti 131, 00196 Rome; tel. 06-32298246; e-mail s-gnam.biblio@beniculturali.it; internet www.gnam.beniculturali.it; f. 1945; 74,000 vols, 1,500 periodicals, 40,000 miscellaneous items on art since the 19th century; Dir Prof. LEANDRO VENTURA; Librarian Dott. GIULIA TALAMO; publ. *Bollettino Mensile delle Nuove Accessioni* (12 a year, online).

Biblioteca di Archeologia e Storia dell'Arte: Piazza Venezia 3, 00187 Rome; tel. 06-6977001; e-mail b-asar@beniculturali.it; internet www.archeologica.librari.beniculturali.it; f. 1922; 370,000 vols, 3,900 periodicals, 1,600 MSS, 16 incunabula, 66,000 microfiches, 740 *cinquecentine*, and 20,700 engravings, drawings and photographs; Dir MARIA CONCETTA PETROLLO.

Biblioteca di Storia Moderna e Contemporanea: Via M. Caetani 32, 00186 Rome; tel. 06-6828171; e-mail b-stmo@beniculturali.it; internet www.bsmc.it; f. 1917; 450,000 vols, 11,000 MSS, 7,200 bound periodicals, 600 current periodicals, 3,000 microfilms and microfiches; Dir STEFANIA MURIANNI.

Biblioteca Istituto Italo-Latino Americano: Via Giovanni Paisiello 24, 00198 Rome; tel. 06-68492215; e-mail biblioteca@iila.org; internet www.iila.org; f. 1966; specializes in contemporary Latin-American life; services offered: offsets of any item in library, in-service library loans, information service; 80,000 vols, 1,000 periodicals, 100 CD-ROMs; Librarian Prof. RICCARDO CAMPA.

Biblioteca Lancisiana: Borgo Santo. Spirito 3, 00193 Rome; tel. 06-68352449; e-mail segreteria.biblioteca@lancisiana.it; internet www.lancisiana.it; f. 1711; history of medicine, history of science; 18,013 vols, 374 MSS, 60 incunabula, 2,000 *cinquecentine*; Dir Dott. SAVERIO MARCO FIORILLA; Currently closed for repairs and renovation work.

Biblioteca Medica Statale: Viale del Policlinico 155, 00161 Rome; tel. 06-490778; e-mail bs-medi@beniculturali.it; internet bms.beniculturali.it; f. 1925; 145,000 vols, 1,193 periodicals; Dir Dr GIOVANNI ARGANESE; publ. *Bollettino Bimestrale Nuove Accessioni*.

Biblioteca Musicale del Conservatorio 'Santa Cecilia': Via dei Greci 18, 00187 Rome; tel. 06-36096736; internet www.conservatoriosantacecilia.it; f. 1875; 300,000 vols, 10,000 MSS, 100 current periodicals; Dir Prof. DOMENICO CARBONI.

Biblioteca Nazionale Centrale di Roma: Viale Castro Pretorio 105, 00185 Rome; tel. 06-4989318; e-mail bnc-rm@beniculturali.it; internet www.bncrm.librari.beniculturali.it; f. 1876; 6,000,000 vols, 8,000 MSS, 2,000 incunabula, 25,000 *cinquecentine*, 20,000 maps, 50,000 periodicals, 10,000 prints and drawings; Dir Dott. OSVALDO AVALLONE.

Biblioteca Storica e Centro Multimediale del Ministero dell'Economia e delle Finanze: Via XX Settembre 97, 00187 Rome; tel. 06-47613120; e-mail biblioteca.storica@tesoro.it; internet www.dag.mef.gov.it/le_persone/cittadini/biblioteca_storica_presentazione; f. 1857; 100,000 vols; Head Dott. PATRIZIA FEMORE.

Biblioteca Storica Nazionale dell'Agricoltura: Via XX Settembre 20, 00187 Rome; tel. 06-46652163; e-mail bibliotecastorica@politicheagricole.gov.it; internet www.politicheagricole.it; f. 1860; 500,000 vols, 300 current periodicals; Dir Dott. MASSIMO RAGUCCI.

Biblioteca Universitaria Alessandrina: Piazzale Aldo Moro 5, 00185 Rome; tel. 06-44740220; e-mail alessandrina@librari.beniculturali.it; internet www.alessandrina.librari.beniculturali.it; f. 1667; 1,000,000 vols, 452 MSS, 674 incunabula, 15,000 *cinquecentine*; Dir MARIA CRISTINA DI MARTINO.

Biblioteca Vallicelliana: Piazza della Chiesa Nuova 18, 00186 Rome; tel. 06-68802671; e-mail b-vall@beniculturali.it; internet www.vallicelliana.it; f. 1581; 150,000 vols, 2,659 MSS, 404 incunabula; also contains library of 'Società Romana di Storia Patria' (50,000 vols); Dir Dr GUGLIELMO BARTOLETTI.

Bibliotheca Hertziana—Max-Planck-Institut für Kunstgeschichte (Hertziana Library—Max Planck Institute for Art History): Via Gregoriana 30, 00187 Rome; tel. 06-69993227; e-mail institut@biblhertz.it; internet www.biblhertz.it; f. 1913; 300,000 vols on history of Italian art, 1,139 periodicals, 2,559 bound periodicals, 809,000 photographs of Italian art; Librarian Dr ANDREAS THIELEMANN; publs *Römische Forschungen der Bibliotheca Hertziana*, *Römisches Jahrbuch der Bibliotheca Hertziana*, *Römische Studien der Bibliotheca Hertziana*, *Studi della Biblioteca Hertziana*.

Cineteca Nazionale: Via Tuscolana 1524, 00173 Rome; tel. 06-72294278; e-mail biblioteca@fondazionecsc.it; internet www.snc.it/ct_home.jsp?id_link=129&area=29; f. 1935; includes the National Film Archive and the Luigi Chiarini Library; 92,000 vols and documents, 10,976 scenarios, 871 bound periodicals, 170 current periodicals; Gen. Dir MARCELLO FOTI; Library Dir Dott.ssa FIAMMETTA LIONTI; publ. *Bianco e Nero* (3 a year).

David Lubin Memorial Library, Food and Agriculture Organization (FAO) of the United Nations: Viale delle Terme di Caracalla, 00153 Rome; tel. 06-57053784; e-mail fao-library-reference@fao.org; internet www.fao.org/library; f. 1946; reference and information services, briefings and seminars, and electronic reproduction of FAO documents; technical services for institutional repository; 1,000,000 vols and more than 8,000 current journals, of which 2,500 electronic; Head Librarian PATRICIA MERRIKIN.

Istituto Centrale per i Beni Sonori ed Audiovisivi (Central Institute for Sound and Audiovisual Heritage): Via M. Caetani 32, 00186 Rome; tel. 06-68406901; e-mail ic-bsa@beniculturali.it; internet www.icbsa.it; f. 1928; collection of recordings of eminent Italians; 220,000 records of classical and light music, jazz; 25,000 records and tapes on anthropology and folklore; collection of sound reproduction equipment; 13,000 vols, 150 current periodicals, 2,000 opera librettos; Dir Dott. MASSIMO PISTACCHI; Librarian MARIA CARLA ZOU.

Istituto Centrale per il Catalogo Unico delle Biblioteche Italiane e per le Informazioni Bibliografiche (Central Institute of the Union Catalogue of Italian Libraries and Bibliographical Information): Viale Castro Pretorio 105, 00185 Rome; tel. 06-4989425; e-mail ic-cu@beniculturali.it; internet www.iccu.sbn.it; f. 1951; Dir ROSA CAFFO.

Rovigo

Pinacoteca dell'Accademia dei Concordi: Piazza V. Emanuele II 14, 45100 Rovigo; tel. 0425-27991; e-mail concordi@concordi.it; internet www.concordi.it; f. 1580; Egyptian and Roman colln; numismatic colln of 2,000 items; colln of paintings from 15th–19th centuries; 250,000 vols.

Sassari

Biblioteca Universitaria: Piazza Università 21, 07100 Sassari; tel. 079-235179; e-mail bu-ss@beniculturali.it; internet sba.uniss.it; f. between 1558 and 1562; 200,000 vols, 1,200 bound periodicals, 1,000 current periodicals, 1,500 MSS, 1,431 microfilms, 71 incunabula, 3,500 *cinquecentine*; Dir ELISABETTA PILIA.

Siena

Biblioteca Comunale degli Intronati: Via della Sapienza 1/7, 53100 Siena; tel. 0577-282972; e-mail biblioteca@biblioteca.comune.siena.it; internet www.bibliotecasiena.it; f. 1758; 386,419 vols, 3,679 bound periodicals, 1,091 current periodicals, 5,699 MSS, 1,038 incunabula, 20,000 prints, 5,810 microfiches, 32,500 slides; Dir Dott. DANIELE DANESI.

Teramo

Biblioteca Provinciale 'Melchiorre Dèlfico': Via Dèlfico 16, 64100 Teramo; tel. 0861-252744; e-mail biblioteca@provincia.teramo.it; internet www.provincia.teramo.it/biblioteca; f. 1814; 260,000 vols, 5,000 bound periodicals, 600 current periodicals, 1,200 *cinquecentine*, 55 incunabula, 15,000 MSS, 100,000 photographs; Dir LUIGI PONZIANI.

Trento

Biblioteca dell' Archivio di Stato di Trento: Via Maestri del Lavoro 4, 38100 Trento; tel. 0461-829008; e-mail as-tn@beniculturali.it; internet www.icar.beniculturali.it/biblio; f. 1919; administered by the Ministero per i Beni Culturali e Ambientali; cultural function and to promote historical research; 7,141 vols, 100 periodicals, holds archives of state offices from pre-unification Italy and single documents and archives belonging to or deposited with the State; Dir GIOVANNI MARCADELLA.

Biblioteca Comunale: Via Roma 55, 38100 Trento; tel. 0461-275521; e-mail tn.viaroma@biblio.infotn.it; internet www.bibcom.trento.it; f. 1856; 762,628 vols, 25,255 MSS, 8,760 periodicals, 10,440 maps, 175,351 vols on history and culture of Trentino-Alto Adige; 8,395 vols in the Austrian Library; Dir Dr FABRIZIO LEONARDELLI; publs *A TUTTO BIB—Novita per Ragazzi* (4 a year), *BIB—Notiziario della Biblioteca Comunale di Trento* (4 a year), *Pubblicazioni Trentine* (1 a year), *Studi Trentini* (4 a year), *Trentine* (1 a year).

Treviso

Biblioteca Borgo Cavour: Borgo Cavour 20, 31100 Treviso; tel. 0422-545342; e-mail info@bibliotecatreviso.it; internet www.bibliotecatreviso.it; f. 1770; 450,000 vols, 5,000 MSS, 800 incunabula, 13,000 prints; Dir Dott. EMILIO LIPPI; publ. *Studi Trevisani*.

Trieste

Archivio di Stato di Trieste: Via A. La Marmora 17, 34139 Trieste; tel. 040-647921; e-mail as-ts@beniculturali.it; internet www.archivi.beniculturali.it/asts; f. 1926; 45,711 vols, 1,116 periodicals; Dir Dott. GRAZIA TATÒ; Librarian CARMELO BIANCO.

Biblioteca Civica 'A. Hortis': Via Madonna del Mare 13, 34124 Trieste; tel. 40-6758200; e-mail bibcivica@comune.trieste.it; internet www.retecivica.trieste.it/

triestecultura/new/bibliotecacivica; f. 1793; 400,000 vols, 401 MSS, drawings and maps; Petrarch, Piccolomini, Svevo and Joyce sections and historical archives; Dir Dott. BIANCA CUDERI.

Biblioteca Statale di Trieste: Largo Papa Giovanni XXIII 6, 34123 Trieste; tel. 040-300725; e-mail bs-ts@beniculturali.it; internet www.bsts.librari.beniculturali.it; f. 1956; 200,000 vols; Dir Dott. SABINA MAGRINI.

Narodna in študijska knjižnica v Trstu (Slovene National Study Library): Via S. Francesco 20, 34133 Trieste; tel. 040-635629; e-mail bibslo@spin.it; internet www.knjiznica.it; f. 1947; 150,000 vols, 500 periodicals.

Turin

Archivio di Stato di Torino: Piazza Castello 209 and Via Piave 21, 10124 Turin; tel. (11) 540382; e-mail as-to@beniculturali.it; internet www.archiviodistatotorino.it; f. 8th century, bldg 1731; houses documents of House of Savoy (county, duchy, kingdom) up to 1861, and those of provincial state admins of 19th and 20th centuries; archives: 83 shelf-km; 50,000 vols, MSS collns; Dir Dr MARIA BARBARA BERTINI.

Biblioteca dell' Accademia delle Scienze di Torino: Via Maria Vittoria 3, 10123 Turin; tel. 011-5620047; e-mail biblioteca@accademia.csi.it; internet www.accademiadellescienze.it; f. 1783; a conservation library covering most fields of the sciences and humanities; rare books dating from the 15th–19th centuries; colln of books, letters and MSS from the late 18th–19th centuries; 200,000 vols, 418 current periodicals and 4,780 others, 35,000 letters, MSS; online catalogue; Head Librarian Dott. ELENA BORGI; publs *Atti della Accademia* (1 a year), *Memorie della Accademia* (1 a year), *Quaderni della Accademia* (1 a year).

Biblioteca Nazionale Universitaria: Piazza Carlo Alberto 3, 10123 Turin; tel. 011-8101111; e-mail bu-to@beniculturali.it; internet www.bnto.librari.beniculturali.it; f. 1723; 1,068,765 vols, 239,302 vols of periodicals, 4,500 MSS, 1,603 incunabula, 6,000 *cinquecentine*, 15,000 drawings and prints; Dir Dott. ROBERTO DI CARLO.

Biblioteca Reale: Piazza Castello 191, 10122 Turin; tel. 011-543855; e-mail b-real@beniculturali.it; internet www.bibliotecareale.beniculturali.it; f. 1831; 200,000 vols, 4,500 MSS, 1,500 parchments, 3,055 drawings, 1,112 periodicals, 187 incunabula, 5,019 *cinquecentine*; library of the Savoy family; historical documents on heraldry, military matters, the Sardinian States, the *Risorgimento* and the Piedmont; Dir CLARA VITULO.

Biblioteca Speciale di Matematica 'Giuseppe Peano': Dipartimento di Matematica, Università degli Studi di Torino, Via Carlo Alberto 10, 10123 Turin; e-mail biblioteca.peano@unito.it; f. 1883; 70,000 vols; Dir Prof. CATIERINA DAGNINO.

Biblioteche Civica Centrale: Via Cittadella 5, 10122 Turin; tel. 011-4429812; e-mail biblioteche.civiche@comune.torino.it; internet www.comune.torino.it/cultura/biblioteche; f. 1869; 524,553 vols, 67 incunabula, 2,000 MSS, 1,600 *cinquecentine*, 18,762 rare vols, 7,721 microfilms, 1,247 current periodicals; 14 br. libraries; Dir Dott. PAOLO MESSINA.

Sistema Bibliotecario del Politecnico di Torino: Corso Duca degli Abruzzi 24, 10129 Turin; tel. 011-0906709; e-mail direttore.bibli@polito.it; internet www.biblio.polito.it; 15,000 vols; Dir Dott. MARIA VITTORIA SAVIO.

Udine

Biblioteca Civica 'Vincenzo Joppi': Piazza Marconi 8, 33100 Udine; tel. 0432-271583; e-mail bcu@comune.udine.it; internet www.sbhu.it/udine; f. 1864; 526,000 vols, 10,000 MSS, 124 incunabula, 3,000 *cinquecentine*; Dir Dott. ROMANO VECCHIET.

Urbino

Biblioteca Universitaria: Via Aurelio Saffi 2, 61029 Urbino; tel. 0722-305212; e-mail fabio@uniurb.it; internet sba.uniurb.it; f. 1520; 850,000 vols, 5,300 periodicals, 3,950 *cinquecentine*; Dir Dott. SEBASTIANO MICCOLI; Dir Dott. MARCELLA PERUZZI.

Venice

Biblioteca dell' Accademia Armena di S. Lazzaro dei Padri Mechitaristi: Isola S. Lazzaro, 30126 Venice; tel. 041-5260104; f. 1701; 170,000 vols, 4,500 MSS; Dir Dr SAHAK DJEMDJEMIAN.

Biblioteca del Civico Museo Correr: Piazza S. Marco 52, Procuratie Nuove, 30124 Venice; tel. 041-2405211; e-mail biblioteca.correr@fmcvenezia.it; internet www.museiciviciveneziani.it; f. 1830; specializes in history of art and Venetian history; 150,000 vols, 76,000 ancient books, 752 incunabula, 12,000 MSS, 700 illuminated MSS; Dir GABRIELLA BELLI; Librarian PIERO LUCCHI.

Biblioteca Nazionale Marciana: Piazzetta San Marco 7, 30124 Venice; tel. 41-2407211; e-mail biblioteca@marciana.venezia.sbn.it; internet marciana.venezia.sbn.it; f. 1468; 1m. vols, 4,034 periodicals, 2,887 incunabula, 24,069 *cinquecentine*, 13,118 MSS; Dir Dott. MAURIZIO MESSINA.

Fondazione Scientifica Querini-Stampalia: Castello 5252, 30122 Venice; tel. (41) 2711411; e-mail biblioteca@querinistampalia.org; internet www.querinistampalia.it/biblioteca; f. 1869; 320,000 vols, 400 current periodicals; Dir MARIGUSTA LAZZARI.

Verona

Biblioteca Civica: Via Cappello 43, 37121 Verona; tel. 045-8079700; e-mail bibliotecacivica.segreteria@comune.verona.it; internet biblioteche.comune.verona.it; f. 1792; 700,000 vols, 1,200 incunabula, 3,477 MSS; Dir Dott. REN GABRIELE.

Vicenza

Biblioteca Civica Bertoliana: Contrà Riale 5, 36100 Vicenza; tel. 0444-578211; e-mail consulenza@bibliotecabertoliana.it; internet www.bibliotecabertoliana.it; f. 1696; 800,000 vols, 852 incunabula, 3,565 MSS, 750 periodicals, 8,000 *cinquecentine*; Librarian Dott. GIORGIO LOTTO.

Museums and Art Galleries

Ancona

Museo Archeologico Nazionale delle Marche: Palazzo Ferretti, Via Ferretti 6, 60121 Ancona; tel. 071-202602; e-mail mara.silvestrini@beniculturali.it; internet www.archeomarche.it/musarch.htm; f. 1906; prehistoric and Roman archaeology; large colln from Iron Age Picene and Celtic cultures; Dir Dott. MARA SILVESTRINI.

Aquileia

Museo Archeologico Nazionale: Via Roma 1, 33051 Aquileia; tel. 0431-91016; e-mail archeologico@museoarcheo-aquileia.it; internet www.museoarcheo-aquileia.it; f. 1882; collection of Roman architecture, sculpture, inscriptions, mosaics, etc. from excavations in the town; library of 10,000 vols; Dir Dott. FRANCA MASELLI SCOTTI; publ. *Aquileia Nostra* (1 a year).

Attached Museum:

Museo Paleocristiano: Via Monastero, 33051 Aquileia; tel. 0431-91035; e-mail paleocristiano@museoarcheo-aquileia.it; internet www.museoarcheo-aquileia.it; f. 1961; mosaics and inscriptions from the palaeo-Christian era; Dir Dott. FRANCA MASELLI SCOTTI.

Ardea

Raccolta Manzù: Via Laurentina Km 32.8, 00040 Ardea; tel. 06-9135022; e-mail mcossu@arti.beniculturali.it; internet www.museomanzu.beniculturali.it; f. 1969; paintings and sculptures by Giacomo Manzù (b. 1908 in Bergamo); part of Nat. Gallery of Modern Art in Rome; Chief Dir MARCELLA COSSU; Technical Dir ALESSANDRO MARIA LIGUORI.

Arezzo

Museo Archeologico Nazionale 'Gaio Cilnio Mecenate': Via Margaritone 10, 52100 Arezzo; tel. 0575-20882; internet www.mega.it/archeo.toscana/samuar.htm; f. 1832; Etruscan, Greek and Roman antiquities, coralline vases of Augustan period, sarcophagi, mosaics, coins and bronzes; Dir Dott. P. ZAMARCHI.

Museo Statale d'Arte Medievale e Moderna: Via San Lorentino 8, 52100 Arezzo; tel. 0575-409050; internet www.sbappsae-ar.beniculturali.it/index.php?it/179/museo-statale-darte-medievale-e-moderna; f. 1957; Italian paintings from 13th–19th centuries, Majolica ware, glass, ivories, seals and coins; Curator Dott. STEFANO CASCIU.

Assisi

Museo del Tesoro della Basilica di S. Francesco in Assisi: Piazza S. Francesco, 2, 06081 Assisi; tel. 075-819001; e-mail museosc@gmail.com; internet www.sanfrancescoassisi.org; f. 1927; historical and artistic collns relating to the Basilica church of St Francis, F. M. Perkins colln of 13th–15th-century European art; Dir Fr LUIGI MARIOLI.

Bari

Museo Archeologico: Palazzo dell'Ateneo, Piazza Umberto I, 70121 Bari; tel. 080-5211559; internet www.archeologia.beniculturali.it/pages/atlante/s89.html; f. 1882; library of 2,500 vols; Dir Dott. GIUSEPPE ANDREASSI.

Pinacoteca Provinciale: Via Spalato 19, 70121 Bari; tel. 080-5412421; e-mail pinacotecaprov.bari@tin.it; f. 1928; Apulian, Venetian and Neapolitan paintings and sculpture from 11th to 19th centuries; paintings from the 'Macchiaioli'; library of 3,000 vols; Dir Dott.ssa CLARA GELAO.

Bergamo

Accademia Carrara di Belle Arti–Museo: Accademia Carrara di Belle Arti, Piazza Giacomo Carrara 82/A, 24121 Bergamo; tel. 035-399640; e-mail amministrazione_accademiacarrara@comune.bg.it; internet www.accademiacarrara.bergamo.it; f. 1796; colln incl. paintings by Bellini, Raffaello, Pisanello, Mantegna, Botticelli, Beato Angelico, Previtali, Tiepolo, Lotto, Moroni, Baschenis, Galgario; drawings, prints and sculptures since 15th century; Dir FRANCESCO ROSSI.

Bologna

Museo Civico Archeologico: Via dell'Archiginnasio 2, 40124 Bologna; tel. 051-2757211; e-mail mca@comune.bologna.it; internet www.comune.bologna.it/museoarcheologico; f. 1881; collns incl. 200,000 works divided into several sections; prehistoric, Egyptian, Greek, Roman, Villanovan, Etruscan and Celtic antiquities; numismatic colln; educational activities; library of 20,750 vols, 320 periodicals, 149 current periodicals; Dir Dott. PAOLA GIOVETTI; Curator Dr ANNA DORE; Curator Dr DANIELA PICCHI; Curator Dr LAURA MINARINI; Curator Dr MARINELLA MARCHESI.

Pinacoteca Nazionale: Via Belle Arti 56, 40126 Bologna; tel. 051-4209411; e-mail sbsae-bo@beniculturali.it; internet www.pinacotecabologna.it; f. 1808; Bolognese paintings and other Italian schools from 14th–18th centuries; German and Italian engravings; Dir Dott. GIANPIERO CAMMAROTA.

Bolzano

Museo Archeologico dell'Alto Adige/ Südtiroler Archäologiemuseum (South Tyrol Museum of Archaeology): Via Museo 43, 39100 Bolzano; tel. 0471-320100; e-mail museo@iceman.it; internet www.iceman.it; history and archaeology of the S Tyrol region from the Palaeolithic to the Carolingian period (AD 800); also 'Ötzi', 5,000-year old mummified man discovered in the Schnalstal Glacier in 1991; Dir Dr ANGELIKA FLECKINGER.

Museo Civico di Bolzano: Via Cassa di Risparmio 14, 39100 Bolzano; tel. 471-997967; e-mail museo.civico@comune.bolzano.it; internet www.bolzano.net/museocivico.htm; f. 1902; history of art since medieval period; archaeology, numismatics, furniture, liturgical items; library of 30,000 vols, 428 periodicals; Dir Dott. STEFAN DEMETZ.

Brescia

Fondazione Brescia Musei: Via Musei 55, 25121 Brescia; tel. 30-2400640; e-mail info@bresciamusei.com; internet www.bresciamusei.com; Dir Dott. RENATA STRADIOTTI.

Constituent Museums and Galleries:

Museo delle Armi 'Luigi Marzoli': Via Castello 9, 25121, Brescia; tel. 30-293292; f. 1988; 14th- to 18th-century arms.

Museo del Risorgimento: Via Castello 9, 25121 Brescia; tel. 30-293292; e-mail info@museorisorgimentotorino.it; f. 1959; 19th-century historical exhibits.

Pinacoteca Tosio Martinengo: Piazza Moretto 4, 25121 Brescia; tel. 30-3774999; f. 1906; art from the 13th to 18th centuries.

Santa Giulia–Museo della Città: Via dei Musei 81/bis, 25121 Brescia; tel. 30-2977834; f. 1882; art and archaeology and 3 churches; incl. colln of the former Museo Romano (prehistoric, pre-Roman and Roman artefacts).

Museo Civico di Scienze Naturali: Via Ozanam 4, 25128 Brescia; tel. 030-2978672; e-mail museo.scienze@comune.brescia.it; internet www.comune.brescia.it/museoscienzenaturali; f. 1949; botanical, geological, zoological and palaeoethnographical collns; library of 60,000 vols, 150 current periodicals; Dir MARCO TONON; publs *Annuario Civica Specola Cidnea*, *Natura Bresciana*.

Museo Diocesano: Via Gasparo da Salò 13, 25122 Brescia; tel. 030-40233; e-mail seo@diocesi.brescia.it; internet www.diocesi.brescia.it/museodiocesano; f. 1978; Dir GIUSEPPE FUSARI.

Cagliari

Museo Archeologico Nazionale: Cittadella dei Musei, Piazza Arsenale 1, 09124 Cagliari; tel. 070-655911; e-mail sba-ca@beniculturali.it; f. 1806; Sardinian antiquities (prehistorical, Punic, Roman periods); library of 8,000 vols; Dir Dr MARCO EDOARDO MINOJA.

Capua

Museo Provinciale Campano: Via Roma, 81043 Capua; tel. 0823-620076; e-mail museocampano@provincia.caserta.it; internet www.museocampano.it; f. 1870; library of 70,000 vols, 2,956 MSS; Pres. ON. DOMENICO ZINZI; Dir MARIA LUISA NAVA.

Chieti

Museo Archeologico Nazionale d'Abruzzo: Via Villa Comunale 2, 66100 Chieti; tel. 0871-331668; e-mail maria.ruggeri-01@beniculturali.org; internet www.archeoabruzzo.beniculturali.it/manda1.html; f. 1959; pottery, weapons and ornaments from 9th to 4th century BC, burial sites, sculpture from 6th and 5th centuries BC; Dir Dott. MARIA RUGGERI.

Cividale

Museo Archeologico Nazionale: Piazza del Duomo 13, 33043 Cividale del Friuli; tel. 0432-700700; e-mail museoarcheocividale@beniculturali.it; f. 1817; prehistoric, Roman and medieval archaeology, jewellery and miniatures, MSS; library of 20,000 vols and archives; Dir Dott. FABIO PAGANO; publ. *Forum Iulii* (1 a year).

Faenza

Museo Internazionale delle Ceramiche: Viale Baccarini 19, 48018 Faenza; tel. 0546-697311; e-mail info@micfaenza.org; internet www.micfaenza.org; f. 1908; history, art and techniques of ceramics; library of 53,000 vols; Pres. Dr PIER ANTONIO RIVOLA; publ. *Faenza* (6 a year).

Ferrara

Gallerie d'Arte Moderna e Contemporanea: Corso Porta Mare 9, 44100 Ferrara; tel. 0532-243415; e-mail artemoderna@comune.fe.it; internet www.artecultura.fe.it; Dir Dott. ANDREA BUZZONI.

Constituent Galleries:

Palazzo dei Diamanti: Corso Ercole I d'Este 21, 44121 Ferrara; tel. 0532-244949; e-mail diamanti@comune.fe.it; internet www.palazzodiamanti.it; incl. Gallerie d'Arte Moderna e Contemporanea; opens in occasion of temporary exhibitions.

Palazzo Massari: Corso Porta Mare 9, 44100 Ferrara; tel. 0532-244949; e-mail artemoderna@comune.fe.it; incorporates Museo d'Arte Moderna e Contemporanea 'Filippo de Pisis', Museo dell'Ottocento, Museo G. Boldini, Padiglione d'Arte Contemporanea.

Museo Archeologico Nazionale di Ferrara: Via XX Settembre 122 (Palazzo di Ludovico il Moro), 44100 Ferrara; tel. 0532-66299; e-mail sba-ero.museoarchferrara@beniculturali.it; internet www.archeobo.arti.beniculturali.it/ferrara; f. 1935; Greco-Etruscan vases, statuettes, bronzes and gold ornaments from the graves of Spina; Dir Dott. CATERINA CORNELIO.

Florence

Comune di Firenze–Direzione Cultura–Servizio Musei: Via delle Conce 28, 50122 Florence; tel. 55-2625961; e-mail gestione.musei@comune.fi.it; internet www.museicivicifiorentini.it; Dir ELENA PIANEA.

Attached Museums and Galleries:

Cappella Brancacci: Piazza del Carmine 14, 50124 Florence; tel. 55-2382195; e-mail gestione.musei@comune.fi.it; frescoes in the Church of Santa Maria del Carmine painted by Masolino (1383–1447) and Masaccio (1401–28), and completed by Filippino Lippi (1457–1504).

Collezioni del Novecento: Forte di Belvedere, Via San Leonardo 1, Florence; tel. 55-2340849; c. 250 works donated by Alberto della Ragione in 1970; Italian art 1914–60.

Fondazione Salvatore Romano: Piazza Santo Spirito 29, 50125 Florence; tel. 55-287043; colln of sculptures given by Salvatore Romano; incl. 2 pieces by Tino di Camaino, and 2 fragments attributed to Donatello.

Galleria Rinaldo Carnielo: Piazza Savonarola 3, 50132 Florence; works by the sculptor Rinaldo Carnielo (1853–1910).

Museo Firenze com'era: Via dell'Oriuolo 24, 50122 Florence; tel. 55-2616545; depicts the history of the city.

Museo di Palazzo Vecchio: Quartieri Monumentali, Piazza della Signoria, 50122 Florence; tel. 55-2768325; paintings, furnishings; frescoes by Ghirlandaio, Salviati, Bronzino, Vasari; Michelangelo's 'Victory' statue.

Museo di Santa Maria Novella: Piazza S. Maria Novella, 50123 Florence; tel. 55-282187; museum built in part of a Dominican church; 15th-century frescoes of the Genesis story by Paolo Uccello, Dello Delli; 14th-century frescoes by Andrea di Bonaiuto depicting the Dominican order and the Church Triumphant.

Museo Stefano Bardini: Via dei Renai 37, 50125 Florence; tel. 55-2342427; f. 1925; paintings by Pollaiuolo, Beccafumi, Lucas Cranach, Mirabello Cavalori, Giovanni da S. Giovanni, Cecco Bravo, Guercino, Carlo Dolci, Luca Giordano, Il Volterano; sculptures by Nicola and Giovanni Pisano, Tino di Camaino, Andrea della Robbia, Donatello, Michelozzo; oriental rugs, bronzes, arms, furniture, medals, etc.

Gabinetto Disegni e Stampe degli Uffizi: Via della Ninna 5, 50122 Florence; tel. 055-2388671; e-mail ua@polomuseale.firenze.it; internet www.polomuseale.firenze.it/musei/disegni; Dir MARZIA FAIETTI.

Galleria d'Arte Moderna: Piazza Pitti 1, 50125 Florence; tel. 055-2388601; e-mail gam@polomuseale.firenze.it; internet www.polomuseale.firenze.it/musei/artemoderna; f. 1914; paintings and sculptures since the 19th century; library of 2,000 vols on the history of art; Dir ANNAMARIA GIUSTI.

Galleria degli Uffizi: Piazzale degli Uffizi, 50122 Florence; tel. 055-2388651; e-mail direzione.uffizi@polomuseale.firenze.it; internet www.polomuseale.firenze.it/uffizi; f. 16th century; Florentine Primitive and Renaissance paintings and sculpture, and paintings by German, Dutch and Flemish masters; library of 64,000 vols, 470 MSS relating to the Florentine collections, 5 incunabula, 996 bound periodicals, 140 current periodicals; Dir ANTONIO NATALI.

Galleria dell' Accademia: Via Ricasoli 58–60, 50122 Florence; tel. 055-2388609; e-mail galleriaaccademia@polomuseale.firenze.it; internet www.polomuseale.firenze.it; f. 1784; colln of Michelangelo's statues in Florence and works of art of 13th–19th-century masters, mostly Tuscan; colln of musical instruments from the Medici and Lorena families; Dir Dott. ANGELO TARTUFER.

Galleria Palatina e Appartamenti Reali: Piazza Pitti 1, 50125 Florence; tel. 055-2388614; e-mail galleriapalatina@polomuseale.firenze.it; internet www.polomuseale.firenze.it/musei/palatina; f. 18th and 19th centuries; Italian and European masterpieces from the 16th and 17th centuries, incl. works by Raphael, A. del Sarto, Carvaggio, Titian, Rubens, Correggio and Van Dyck; Dir ALESSANDRO CECCHI.

Museo Archeologico Nazionale: Piazza SS. Annunziata 9, 50121 Florence; tel. 055-23575; internet www.firenzemusei.it/archeologico; f. 1870; Egyptian, Etruscan and Greco-Roman archaeology; Dir Dott.ssa G. CARLOTTA CIANFERONI; Curator for Egyptian Section Dott.ssa MARIA CRISTINA GUIDOTTI; Curator for Greece Section Dott. MARIO IOZZO.

Museo degli Argenti: Piazza Pitti 1, 50125 Florence; tel. 055-2388709; e-mail argenti@polomuseale.firenze.it; internet www.polomuseale.firenze.it/musei/argenti; summer state apartments of the Medici Grand Dukes; collns of gold, silver, enamel, *objets d'art*, hardstones, ivory, amber, cameos and jewels, principally from the 15th–18th centuries; Dir MARIA SFRAMELI.

Attached Gallery:

Galleria del Costume: Piazza Pitti 1, 50125 Florence; tel. 055-2388763; e-mail costume.pitti@polomuseale.firenze.it; internet www.polomuseale.firenze.it/musei/costume; period costumes, principally since the 18th century, shown in the neo-classical Meridiana wing of the Pitti Palace; Dir CATERINA CHIARELLI.

Museo dell' Opera di Santa Maria del Fiore: Via della Canonica 1, 50122 Florence; tel. 055-2302885; e-mail opera@operaduomo.firenze.it; internet www.operaduomo.firenze.it; f. 1891; Administrator PATRIZIO OSTICRESI.

Museo della Casa Buonarroti: Via Ghibellina 70, 50122 Florence; tel. 055-241752; e-mail fond@casabuonarroti.it; internet www.casabuonarroti.it; f. 1858; works by Michelangelo and others; large collection of drawings by Michelangelo, sculptures, majolica and archaeological items from the Buonarroti family collections; library of 10,000 vols, 41 periodicals, 44 *cinquecentine*, Buonarotti Archive of 169 vols; Dir PINA RAGIONIERI.

Museo delle Porcellane: Piazza Pitti 1, 50125 Florence; tel. 055-2388709; e-mail argenti@polomuseale.firenze.it; internet www.polomuseale.firenze.it/musei/porcellane; collection of European porcelain from c. 1720–1850; Dir ORNELLA CASAZZA.

Museo di Palazzo Davanzati (Antica Casa Fiorentina): Via di Porta Rossa 13, 50122 Florence; tel. 055-2388610; e-mail museo.davanzati@polomuseale.firenze.it; internet www.polomuseale.firenze.it/davanzati; f. 1956; applied arts, specializing in lace and ceramics; Dir MARIA GRAZIA VACCARI.

Museo di San Marco (San Marco Museum): Piazza San Marco 3, 50121 Florence; tel. 55-2388608; e-mail museosanmarco@polomuseale.firenze.it; internet www.polomuseale.firenze.it/musei/sanmarco; f. 1869; colln of paintings by Fra Angelico; Dir Dott.ssa MAGNOLIA SCUDIERI.

Museo Galileo—Istituto e Museo di Storia della Scienza: Piazza dei Giudici 1, 50122 Florence; tel. 055-265311; e-mail info@museogalileo.it; internet www.museogalileo.it; f. 1927; museum of scientific instruments and institute dedicated to the research, documentation and dissemination of the history of science; library of 110,000 vols; Dir Prof. PAOLO GALLUZZI; publs *Galilaeana* (1 a year), *Nuncius Annali di Storia della Scienza* (Nuncius Journal of the Material and Visual History of Science, 2 a year).

Museo Horne: Via dei Benci 6, 50122 Florence; tel. 055-244661; e-mail info@museohorne.it; internet www.museohorne.it; furniture and works of art from the 14th–16th centuries; library of 5,000 vols; Dir Dott. ELISABETTA NARDINOCCHI.

Museo Marino Marini: Piazza San Pancrazio, 50123 Florence; tel. 055-219432; e-mail info@museomarinomarini.it; internet www.museomarinomarini.it; f. 1988; 183 sculptures, paintings, drawings by the sculptor Marino Marini (1901–80) in a permanent exhibition; Pres. CARLO SISI.

Museo Nazionale del Bargello: Via del Proconsolo 4, 50122 Florence; tel. 055-2388606; e-mail museobargello@polomuseale.firenze.it; internet www.polomuseale.firenze.it/musei/bargello; f. 1859; medieval and modern sculpture and *objets d'art*; organizes exhibitions, research and concerts; Dir BEATRICE PAOLOZZI STROZZI.

Museo Stibbert: Via F. Stibbert 26, 50134 Florence; tel. 055-486049; e-mail info@museostibbert.it; internet www.museostibbert.it/web.it; f. 1908; Etruscan, Roman and medieval arms and armour; European and Oriental arms from 15th to 19th centuries; holy objects and vestments; European and Oriental costumes, etc., from 18th to 19th centuries; Flemish tapestries from 15th to 17th centuries, Italian and foreign paintings and furniture from 14th to 19th centuries; library of 3,500 vols; Dir KIRSTEN ASCHENGREEN PIACENTI.

Forlì

Forlì Cultura—Musei e Gallerie: Comune di Forlì, Piazza Saffi 8, 47100 Forlì; tel. 0543-712111; internet www.cultura.comune.forli.fc.it.

Attached Museums and Galleries:

Armeria Albicini: Corso della Repubblica 72, 47121 Forlì; tel. 0543-712606; e-mail servizio.pinacoteca.musei@comune.forli.fc.it; 500 arms and pieces of armour from the 15th century to the 19th century; colln of arms from Congo.

Museo Archeologico: Palazzo del Merenda, Corso della Repubblica 72, 47121 Forlì; tel. 0543-712606; e-mail servizio.pinacoteca.musei@comune.forli.fc.it; f. late 19th century; exhibits from the Lower Palaeolithic to the seventh century AD.

Museo Etnografico Romagnolo 'B. Pergoli': Palazzo del Merenda, Corso della Repubblica 72, 47121 Forlì; tel. 0543-712609; e-mail servizio.pinacoteca.musei@comune.forli.fc.it; exhibits depicting rural work and crafts, home environments, workshops relating to various trades.

Museo del Risorgimento 'A. Saffi': Corso G. Garibaldi 96, 47121 Forlì; tel. 0543-712609; e-mail musei@comune.forli.fc.it; internet www.cultura.comune.forli.fc.it; artefacts from the Napoleonic era to World War II; Dir CRISTINA AMBROSINI.

Museo Romagnolo del Teatro: Corso Garibaldi, 96, 47121 Forlì; tel. 0543-21109; e-mail servizio.pinacoteca.musei@comune.forli.fc.it; theatrical memorabilia, musical instruments.

Museo Storico 'Dante Foschi': Via Piero Maroncelli 3, 47121 Forlì; tel. 0543-32328; e-mail servizio.pinacoteca.musei@comune.forli.fc.it; 20th-century uniforms, arms, medals, awards, coins, military decorations and badges, postcards, books, furniture.

Pinacoteca Civica 'Melozzo degli Ambrogi': Piazza Guido da Montefeltro 12, 47100 Forlì; tel. 0543-712659; e-mail museisandomenico@comune.forli.fc.it; f. 1838; paintings on wood and canvas, frescoes, sculptures and tapestries.

Istituti Culturali ed Artistici: Corso della Repubblica 72, 47100 Forlì; tel. 0543-712600; comprises a picture gallery, collection of prints and engravings, archaeological and ethnographical museums, ceramics, sculpture and local history; Piancastelli collection of paintings, medals and coins; Dir Dr FRANCO FABBRI.

Pinacoteca e Musei del Comune: Corso della Repubblica 72, 47100 Forlì; tel. 0543-712606; e-mail servizio.pinacoteca.musei@comune.forli.fc.it; internet www.cultura.comune.forli.fc.it; f. 1838; Dir LUCIANA PRATI.

Genoa

Comune di Genova Direzione Cultura, Sport e Turismo—Settore Musei: Largo Pertini 4, 16121 Genoa; tel. 010-5574700; e-mail museicivici@comune.genova.it; internet www.comune.genova.it/turismo/musei/welcome.htm; f. 1908; library of 40,000 vols; Dir GUIDO GANDINO; publ. *Bollettino dei Musei Civici Genovesi* (4 a year).

Attached Museums and Galleries:

Archivio Storico del Comune di Genova: Palazzo Ducale, Piazza Matteotti 10, 16123 Genoa; tel. 010-5574808; e-mail archiviostorico@comune.genova.it; internet www.archiviostoricogenova.it; f. 1906; documents since 15th century; coins, weights and measures; Curator RAFFAELLA PONTE.

Castello D'Albertis Museo delle Culture del Mondo: Corso Dogali 18, 16136 Genoa; tel. 010-2723820; e-mail castellodalbertis@comune.genova.it; internet www.castellodalbertis.museidigenova.it; f. 2004; housed in a Neo-Gothic castle with archaeological and ethnological collns from pre-Columbian civilizations of Central and S America, Indians of N American plains, Hopi of Arizona, cultures of Oceania and Africa; also houses Museo delle Musiche dei Popoli (Folk Music Museum) that preserves musical instruments from all over the world; Curator MARIA CAMILLA DE PALMA.

Centro di Documentazione per la Storia, l'Arte, l'Immagine di Genova: Via ai 4 Canti di San Francesco 59–61 r, 16124 Genoa; tel. 010-5574956; e-mail archiviofotografico@comune.genova.it; internet www.museidigenova.it; f. 2005; art library; topographic colln; 200,000 photographs (1860–1946) on Genoese customs and history, 19th-century landscapes, war damage, Italian and Genoese art and architecture 11th–19th centuries; photographs of museum collns; topographical and cartographical documents on Genoa and Liguria; library of 50,000 vols, 200,000 photos, 7,000 documents; Dir ELISABETTA PAPONE.

Civico Museo di Storia e Cultura Contadina Genovese e Ligure: Salita al Garbo 47, 16159 Genoa Rivarolo; tel. 010-7401243; f. 1983; colln of tools and utensils relating to local rural life since 19th century; Curator PATRIZIA GARIBALDI.

Galata Museo del Mare: Calata de Mari 1, Darsena, Porto Antico, 16128 Genoa; e-mail info@galatamuseodelmare.it; internet www.galatamuseodelmare.it; maritime history of the city; exhibits incl. 17th-century galleon, arsenal, docks, ancient atlases and naval instruments.

Galleria di Palazzo Bianco: Via Garibaldi 11, 16124 Genoa; tel. 010-5572193; e-mail museidistradanuova@comune.genova.it; internet www.museidigenova.it; f. 1889; paintings by Genoese and

Flemish masters and other schools (16th–18th centuries); Dir PIERO BOCCARDO; Curator RAFFAELLA BESTA.

Galleria di Palazzo Rosso: Via Garibaldi 18, 16124 Genoa; tel. 010-2476351; e-mail museopalazzorosso@comune.genova.it; internet www.museopalazzorosso.it; f. 1874; the fine art colln of a noble Genoese family: paintings and sculpture, frescoes and stuccos, nativity models, ceramics; also a colln of textiles; Curator PIERO BOCCARDO.

Museo di Archeologia Ligure: Villa Durazzo-Pallavicini, Via Pallavicini 11, 16155 Genoa–Pegli; tel. 010-6981048; e-mail archligure@mail.it; f. 1892; Ligurian archaeology of the periods up to the Roman era; colln of Greek and Roman antiquities; Curators PATRIZIA GARIBALDI, GUIDO ROSSI.

Museo d'Arte Contemporanea Villa Croce: Via Jacopo Ruffini 3, 16128 Genoa; tel. 010-585772; e-mail museocroce@comune.genova.it; internet www.museovillacroce.it; f. 1985; works by key Italian artists; documentation on artistic research in Genoa and Liguria from the Second World War onwards; sculpture by Genoese and Ligurian artists; specialized library and archive open to the public; library of 20,000 books and exposition catalogues; Curator SANDRA SOLIMANO.

Museo d'Arte Orientale 'Edoardo Chiossone': Villetta di Negro, Piazzale Mazzini 4N, 16122 Genoa; tel. 010-542285; e-mail museochiossone@comune.genova.it; internet www.chiossone.museidigenova.it; f. 1905; Japanese works of art from 11th–19th centuries (about 20,000 pieces), collected in Japan during the Meiji period by Edoardo Chiossone; Dir DONATELLA FAILLA.

Museo Civico di Storia Naturale 'Giacomo Doria': Via Brigata Liguria 9, 16121 Genoa; tel. 010-564567; e-mail museodoria@comune.genova.it; internet www.museodoria.it; f. 1867; zoology, botany and geology; library of 93,000 vols; Dir Dr GIULIANO DORIA; publs *Annali* (1 a year), *Doriana* (irregular).

Museo 'Giannettino Luxoro': Via Mafalda di Savoia 3, 16167 Genoa–Nervi; tel. 010-322673; f. 1945; Flemish and Genoese paintings of the 17th and 18th centuries, furniture, ceramics and pottery in the rooms of an early 20th-century villa; Curator LOREDANA PESSA.

Museo Navale: Villa Doria, Piazza Bonavino 7, 16156 Genoa–Pegli; tel. 010-6969885; f. 1930; models of ships, nautical instruments, navigation maps, prints; Curator PIERANGELO CAMPODONICO.

Museo del Risorgimento e Istituto Mazziniano: Casa di Mazzini, Via Lomellini 11, 16124 Genoa; tel. 010-2465843; e-mail museorisorgimento@comune.genova.it; internet www.istitutomazziniano.it; f. 1934; exhibits illustrating life and work of Mazzini, 19th-century documents and arms, specialized library containing works since 18th century; Curator LEO MORABITO.

Museo di Sant'Agostino: Piazza Sarzano 35r., 16128 Genoa; tel. 010-2511263; e-mail museosagostino@comune.genova.it; internet www.museosantagostino.it; f. 1939, closed due to damage sustained during the Second World War, reopened 1984; sculpture from 10th–18th centuries, architecture and paintings; Curator ADELMO TADDEI.

Museo del Tesoro della Cattedrale di San Lorenzo: Piazza San Lorenzo, 16123 Genoa; tel. 010-2471831; e-mail info@arti-e-mestieri.it; internet www.museosanlorenzo.it; f. 1892; gold and silver objects; Curator CLARIO DI FABIO.

Padiglione del Mare e della Navigazione: Porto Antico—Magazzini del Cotone, 16126 Genoa; tel. 010-2463678; f. 1996; maritime colln; works of art, models and reproductions; Curator PIERANGELO CAMPODONICO.

Raccolte Frugone in Villa Grimaldi: Villa Grimaldi Fassio, Via Capolungo 9, Nervi, 16167 Genoa; tel. 010-322396; e-mail raccoltefrugone@comune.genova.it; internet www.raccoltefrugone.it; f. 1993; colln of sculpture and paintings by Italian and int. artists since 19th century; Curator MARIA FLORA GIUBILEI.

Galleria Nazionale di Palazzo Spinola: Piazza Pellicceria 1, 16123 Genoa; tel. 010-2705300; e-mail palazzospinola@beniculturali.it; f. 1958; Dir Dott.ssa FARIDA SIMONETTI; publ. *Quaderni* (1 a year).

Soprintendenza per i Beni Archeologici della Liguria: Palazzo Reale, Via Balbi 10, 16126 Genoa; tel. 010-27181; e-mail sba-lig@beniculturali.it; internet www.archeoge.beniculturali.it; f. 1939; preservation of monuments and excavations of Liguria (prehistoric, Roman and medieval); conservation of the ancient city of Luni, prehistoric caves of Balzi Rossi and archeological area of Varignano Vecchio; library of 15,500 vols; Superintendent Dott. BRUNO MASSABÒ; Librarian MARTA PUPPO; publ. *Archeologia in Liguria* (every 2 years).

Grosseto

Museo Archeologico e d'Arte della Maremma: Piazza Baccarini 3, 58100 Grosseto; tel. 0564-488750; e-mail maam@gol.grosseto.it; internet www.gol.grosseto.it/puam/comgr/museo/museo.php; f. 1865; archaeological and medieval findings from the Maremma; library of 3,000 vols; Dir Dott. VALERIO FUSI.

L'Aquila

Museo Nazionale d'Abruzzo: Castello Cinquecentesco, Via Colecchi 1, 67100 L'Aquila; tel. 0862-633303; e-mail calcedonio.tropea@beniculturali.it; internet www.museonazionaleabruzzo.beniculturali.it; f. 1949; art from the early Middle Ages to contemporary times; Dir Dott. CALCEDONIO TROPEA.

Lecce

Museo Provinciale 'Sigismondo Castromediano': Viale Gallipoli 28, 73100 Lecce; tel. 0832-683503; e-mail acassiano@provincia.le.it; internet eneaportal.unile.it/sul_cammino_di_enea_it/lecce/cultura/musei; f. 1868; archaeology and art gallery; library of 5,500 vols, 2,500 pamphlets and offprints; Dir ANTONIO CASSIANO.

Lucca

Museo e Pinacoteca Nazionale di Palazzo Mansi: Via Galli Tassi 43, 55100 Lucca; tel. 583-55570; e-mail sbappsae-lu.museilucchesi@beniculturali.it; internet www.tuscanypass.com/tuscany_attractions/9281_museo-nazionale-di-palazzo-mansi-e-pinacoteca-nazionale.html; f. 1868; paintings by Titian, Tintoretto, etc., and Tuscan, Venetian, French and Flemish Schools; Dir Dott. MARIA TERESA FILIERI.

Museo Nazionale di Villa Guinigi: Villa Guinigi, Via della Quarquonia, 55100 Lucca; tel. 0583-496033; e-mail luccamuseinazionali@libero.it; internet www.luccamuseinazionali.it/content.php?p=vg_edificio; colln of Roman and late Roman sculptures and mosaics; Romanesque, Gothic, Renaissance and Neoclassical sculpture; paintings from the 12th–18th centuries incl. Fra Bartolomeo and Vasari; wood inlays, textiles, medieval goldsmiths' art; Dir Dott. MARIA TERESA FILIERI.

Mantua

Palazzo Ducale e Castello di San Giorgio: Piazza Sordello 40, 46100 Mantua; tel. 0376-352100; e-mail sbsae-mn@beniculturali.it; internet www.mantovaducale.beniculturali.it; incorporates Museo e Galleria di Pittura (13th–18th-century paintings) and Museo Statuario d'Arte Greca e Romana; Dir Dott. GIOVANNA PAOLOZZI STROZZI.

Matera

Museo Nazionale D. Ridola: Via D. Ridola 24, 75100 Matera; tel. 0835-310058; internet www.archeologia.beniculturali.it/pages/atlante/s201.html; f. 1910; local prehistory; funerary items from 6th–4th centuries BC, bronzes; Dir Dott. MARIA LUISA NAVA.

Messina

Museo Regionale: Viale della Libertà 465, 98121 Messina; tel. 090-361292; internet www.regione.sicilia.it/beniculturali/dirbenicult/database/page_musei/pagina_musei.asp?id=5&idsito=43; f. 1922; local art and culture from 12th–18th centuries; Dir Dott. CARMELA ANGELA DI STEFANO.

Milan

Circuito dei Musei del Centro di Milano: Palazzo De Marchi, Via Borgonuovo 23, 20121 Milan; tel. 2-88464180; internet www.museidelcentro.mi.it; f. 1884; library of 130,000 vols; Dir CLAUDIO SALSI.

Attached Museums and Galleries:

Casa del Manzoni: Via Moroni 1, 20121 Milan; tel. 2-86460403; internet www.casadelmanzoni.it; fmr home of the writer Manzoni.

Museo Bagatti Valsecchi: Via Gesù 5, 20121 Milan; tel. 2-76006132; e-mail segreteria@museobagattivalsecchi.org; internet www.museobagattivalsecchi.org; f. 1994; fmr 19th-century residence containing paintings, wood carvings, weapons and armour, ceramics, glassware, gold and ivory artifacts, decorative metal objects, tapestries.

Museo di Milano: Via Moroni 1, 20121 Milan; tel. 2-86460403; internet www.museodimilano.mi.it; colln of prints, paintings, sculpture; 18th-century home decoration, furniture and objects.

Museo del Risorgimento: Via Borgonuovo 23, 20121 Milan; tel. 2-88464180; internet www.museodelrisorgimento.mi.it; f. 1885; collns of prints, paintings, sculpture, drawings, arms and memorabilia illustrate the period 1796–1870 in Italian history.

Museo Teatrale alla Scala: Largo Ghiringhelli 1, Piazza Scala, 20121 Milan; tel. 2-88792473; e-mail lascalarisponde@teatroallascala.org; internet www.museidelcentro.mi.it/frameset_scala.htm; f. 1913; library of 140,000 vols; instruments from the 17th century, paintings, ceramics, memorabilia, costumes, posters.

Galleria d'Arte Moderna: Via Palestro 16, 20121 Milan; tel. 02-88445947; internet www.gam-milano.com; f. 1861; painting and sculpture from Neo-Classical period until late 19th century; incl. the Grassi and Vismara collns and Museo Marino Marini; Dir CLAUDIO SALSI.

Museo Civico di Storia Naturale di Milano: Corso Venezia 55, 20121 Milan; tel. 02-88463280; internet www.comune

.milano.it/museostorianaturale; f. 1838; all brs of natural history; depts of botany, entomology, invertebrate palaeontology, invertebrate zoology, mineralogy, vertebrate palaeontology, vertebrate zoology; library of 152,000 vols; Dir Dr DOMENICO PIRAINA; publs *Atti della Società Italiana di Scienze Naturali e del Museo Civico di Storia Naturale di Milano* (2 a year), *Memorie della Società Italiana di Scienze Naturali e del Museo Civico di Storia Naturale di Milano* (irregular), *Natura* (2 a year).

Raccolte Artistiche, Raccolte Grafiche e Fotografiche: Castello Sforzesco, 20121 Milan; tel. 02-88463700; f. 1878; sculpture from the Middle Ages to the 16th century, incl. the *Pietà* of Michelangelo; paintings, incl. works by Mantegna, Foppa, Lippi, Bellini, Lotto, Tintoretto, Tiepolo, Guardi; furniture, silver, bronzes, ivories, ceramics, musical instruments, tapestries by Bramantino, Bertarelli stamp colln; library of 41,000 vols; Dir for Engravings and Drawings Dr CLAUDIO SALSI; Dir for Art Collns Dr FRANCESCA TASSO.

Museo Nazionale della Scienza e della Tecnologia 'Leonardo da Vinci': Via San Vittore 21, 20123 Milan; tel. 02-485551; e-mail info@museoscienza.it; internet www.museoscienza.org; f. 1953; scientific and technical activities, displaying relics, models and designs, with particular emphasis on Leonardo's work; library of 45,000 vols, mostly history of science and technology, 150 *cinquecentine*, large section on Leonardo, including facsimile of every MS; Dir FIORENZO GALLI; publ. *Museoscienza* (2 a year).

Museo Poldi Pezzoli: Via A. Manzoni 12, 20121 Milan; tel. 02-796334; e-mail info@museopoldipezzoli.it; internet www.museopoldipezzoli.it; f. 1881; paintings from 14th–19th centuries; armour, tapestries, rugs, jewellery, porcelain, glass, textiles, furniture, clocks and watches, etc.; library of 5,500 vols; Dir Dott. ANNALISA ZANNI.

Pinacoteca Ambrosiana: Piazza Pio XI 2, 20123 Milan; tel. 02-806921; e-mail info@ambrosiana.it; internet www.ambrosiana.eu; f. 1618; paintings by Raphael, Botticelli, Titian, Luini, Jan Brueghel, Leonardo da Vinci, Jacobo Bassano, Bramantino, etc.; miniatures, enamels, ceramics and medallions; Dir Dott. FRANCO BUZZI.

Pinacoteca di Brera: Via Brera 28, 20121 Milan; tel. 02-722631; e-mail sbsae-mi.brera@beniculturali.it; internet www.brera.beniculturali.it; f. 1809; pictures of all schools, especially Lombard and Venetian; paintings by Mantegna, Bellini, Crivelli, Lotto, Titian, Veronese, Tintoretto, Tiepolo, Foppa, Bergognone, Luini, Piero della Francesca, Bramante, Raphael, Caravaggio, Rembrandt, Van Dyck, Rubens; also 20th-century works, mostly Italian; Dir SANDRINA BANDERA.

Modena

Galleria, Museo e Medagliere Estense: Palazzo dei Musei, Piazza Sant' Agostino 337, 41121 Modena; tel. 059-4395711; e-mail sbsae-mo@beniculturali.it; internet www.spsae-mo.beniculturali.it; f. 15th century in Ferrara, transferred to Palazzo Ducale, Modena, 1598, to Palazzo dei Musei 1894; collns incl. about 2,000 paintings and drawings from 14th to 18th centuries, sculpture, engravings, medals; library of 15,000 vols; Superintendent Dott. STEFANO CASCIU.

Museo Civico Archeologico Etnologico: Palazzo dei Musei, Viale Vittorio Veneto 5, 41100 Modena; tel. 059-2033100; e-mail museo.archeologico@comune.modena.it; internet www.comune.modena.it/museoarcheologico; f. 1871; prehistory and ethnology; library of 5,000 vols, 2,700 pamphlets; Curator Dott. ILARIA PULINI; publ. *Quaderni*.

Museo Civico d'Arte: Viale Vittorio Veneto 5, 41124 Modena; tel. 059-2033100; e-mail museo.arte@comune.modena.it; internet www.comune.modena.it/museoarte; f. 1871; paintings, sculpture, decorative arts; history and culture of Modena from 12th–20th centuries; library of 7,500 vols, 3,500 pamphlets; Dir Dott. FRANCESCA PICCININI.

Museo Lapidario Estense: Palazzo dei Musei, Piazza Sant' Agostino 337, 41121 Modena; tel. 059-4395711; e-mail sbsae-mo@beniculturali.it; internet www.spsae-mo.beniculturali.it; f. 1828; Roman and medieval archaeological collns; Superintendent Dott. STEFANO CASCIU.

Naples

Museo Archeologico Nazionale: Piazza Museo Nazionale 19, 80135 Naples; tel. 081-292823; e-mail ssba-na@beniculturali.it; internet museoarcheologiconazionale.campaniabeniculturali.it; f. 18th century; Greek, Roman, Italian and Egyptian antiquities; Superintendent Prof. Dr PIETRO GIOVANNI GUZZO; publ. *Rivista di Studi Pompeiani* (1 a year).

Museo Civico 'Gaetano Filangieri': Via Duomo 288, 80138 Naples; tel. 081-203211; internet filangieri.sbapsaena.campaniabeniculturali.it; f. 1888; paintings, furniture, archives, photographs, majolica, arms and armour; library of 30,000 vols, and coin collection of Neapolitan history; Dir ANTONIO BUCCINO GRIMALDI.

Museo 'Duca di Martina' alla Floridiana: Via Cimarosa 77, 80127 Naples; tel. 081-5788418; e-mail martina.artina@beniculturali.it; f. 1931; decorative art; exhibits donated by the Duke; spec. colln of oriental art; Dir Dr LUISA AMBROSIO.

Museo e Gallerie Nazionali di Capodimonte: Via Miano 2, 80131 Naples; tel. 081-7499111; e-mail capodimonte.artina@arti.beniculturali.it; internet museodicapodimonte.campaniabeniculturali.it; f. 1738; paintings from 13th–19th centuries; sculpture from 19th century; contemporary art; colln of arms and armour; medals and bronzes of the Renaissance; porcelain; library of 2,000 vols; Dir Prof. MARIELLA UTILI.

Museo Nazionale di San Martino: Largo San Martino 2, 80129 Naples; tel. 81-2294510; e-mail sspsae-na.sanmartino@beniculturali.it; f. 1872; ancient church of San Martino with 16th–18th century pictures, 13th–19th century sculpture, majolica and porcelain, Neapolitan historical records and topographical colln, naval colln, arms and military costumes, opaline glass, section of modern painting, prints and engravings; Dir Dott. ROSSANA MUZII.

Sorprintendza Speciale Per I Beni Archeologici Di Napoli E Pompei: Via Villa dei Misteri 2, 80045 Pompei; tel. 081-8575111; e-mail sba-pomp@beniculturali.it; internet www.pompeiisites.org; f. 1982; Superintendent Prof. TERESA ELENA CINQUANTAQUATTRO.

Supervised Sites:

Antiquarium Nazionale di Boscoreale: Via Settetermini 15, Loc. Villa Regina, 80041 Boscoreale; tel. 081-5368796; e-mail sba-pomp@beniculturali.it; internet www.pompeiisites.org; Dir Dott. GRETE STEFANI.

Scavi di Ercolano: Corso Resina, 80056 Ercolano; tel. 081-7324311; e-mail sba-pomp@beniculturali.it; internet www.pompeiisites.org; Dir Dott. MARIA PAOLA GUIDOBALDI.

Scavi di Oplontis: Via Sepolcri, 80058 Torre Annunziata; tel. 081-8621755; e-mail sba-pomp@beniculturali.it; internet www.pompeiisites.org; Dir Dott. LORENZO FERGOLA.

Scavi di Pompei: Via Villa dei Misteri 2, 80045 Pompei; tel. 081-8575111; e-mail sba-pomp@beniculturali.it; internet www.pompeiisites.org; f. 2008; Dir Prof. TERESA ELENA.

Scavi di Stabia: Via Passeggiata Archeologica, 80053 Castellammare di Stabia; tel. 081-8714541; e-mail sba-pomp@beniculturali.it; internet www.pompeiisites.org; Dir Dott. GIOVANNA BONIFACIO.

Padua

Musei Civici di Padova: Piazza Eremitani 8, 35121 Padua; tel. 049-8204551; e-mail musei@comune.padova.it; internet padovacultura.padovanet.it/it/musei/complesso-eremitani; f. 1825; Dir DAVIDE BANZATO; publ. *Bollettino del Museo Civico di Padova* (1 a year).

Constituent Institutions:

Cappella degli Scrovegni: Piazza Eremitani 8, 35121 Padua; tel. 49-8204551; e-mail musei@comune.padova.it; internet padovacultura.padovanet.it/it/musei/cappella-degli-scrovegni; f. 1300; hall with presbytery, on altar Madonna and child with 2 angels, by 14th-century sculptor Giovanni Pisano; Giotto frescoes; Dir Dr DAVIDE BANZATO.

Museo Archeologico: c/o Musei Civici, Piazza Eremitani 8, 35121 Padua; tel. 049-8204551; e-mail museo.archeologico@comune.padova.it; internet padovacultura.padovanet.it/homepage-6.0/2004/02/museo_archeologico_2.html; f. 1825; pre- and early historic and Roman finds; Dir DAVIDE BANZATO.

Museo d'Arte Medioevale e Moderna: c/o Musei Civici agli Eremitani, Piazza Eremitani 8, 35121 Padua; tel. 049-8204551; e-mail musei@comune.padova.it; internet padovacultura.padovanet.it/it/musei/museo-darte-medievale-e-moderna; f. 1825; works from 14th and 15th centuries; Venetian paintings from 14th to the 16th centuries; sculptures from 14th to the 18th centuries; decorative and architectural fragments of inscribed stone tablets; Dir DAVIDE BANZATO.

Museo d'Arte. Museo di Arti Applicate e Decorative: c/o Palazzo Zuckermann, Corso Garibaldi 33, 35121 Padua; tel. 049-8205664; e-mail museo.arte@comune.padova.it; internet padovacultura.padovanet.it/it/musei/museo-di-arti-applicate-e-decorative; glass, carvings, ceramics, silver, ivory, jewellery, textiles and furniture; paintings, architectural fragments from 9th to 10th centuries, coats of arms of Venetian families; Dir DAVIDE BANZATO.

Museo Bottacin: Palazzo Zuckermann, Corso Garibaldi 33, 35121 Padua; tel. 049-8205675; e-mail museo.bottacin@comune.padova.it; internet padovacultura.padovanet.it/homepage_06/2013/04/museo_bottacin_1.html; f. 1865; Graeco-Roman, Paduan, Venetian, Italian, Napoleonic coins, seals and medals, 19th-century sculptures and paintings; library of 50,000 vols; Librarian Dr MARCO CALLEGARI.

Palazzo della Ragione 'Il Salone': Piazza delle Erbe, 35122 Padua; tel. 049-8205006; e-mail musei@comune.padova.it;

internet padovacultura.padovanet.it/it/musei/palazzo-della-ragione; f. 1218; works by Fra Giovanni degli Eremitani, frescoes by Nicolò Miretto and Stefano Da Ferrara; Dir DAVIDE BANZATO.

Palermo

Museo Archeologico Regionale 'A. Salinas' ('A. Salinas' Regional Archaeological Museum): Piazza Olivella 24, 90100 Palermo; tel. 916116806; e-mail urpmuseopa@regione.sicilia.it; internet www.regione.sicilia.it/beniculturali/salinas; f. 1866; prehistoric, Egyptian, Greek, Punic, Roman and Etruscan antiquities; library of 25,000 vols and pamphlets; Dir FRANCESCA SPATAFORA.

Parma

Galleria Nazionale: Piazzale della Pilotta 15, 43100 Parma; tel. 0521-233309; e-mail sbaspr@libero.it; internet www.artipr.arti.beniculturali.it/htm/galleria.htm; f. 1752, later reconstructed and added to; paintings from 13th–19th centuries, incl. works by Correggio, Parmigianino, Cima, El Greco, Piazzetta, Tiepolo, Holbein, Van Dyck, Mor, Nattier, and several painters of the school of Parma; 19th-century paintings by Parmesan painters; library of 15,000 vols; Superintendent LUCIA FORNARI SCHIANCHI.

Museo Archeologico Nazionale: Piazza della Pilotta 5, 43100 Parma; tel. 0521-233718; e-mail sba-ero.museoarchparma@beniculturali.it; internet www.archeobologna.beniculturali.it/parma; f. 1760; archaeological colln of sculptures and other monuments from Veleia; Prehistoric and Bronze Age collns; Roman monuments from province of Parma; Egyptian, Greek, Etruscan and Roman art documents; Dir Dott. MARIA BERNABÒ BREA.

Museo Bodoniano: c/o Biblioteca Palatina, Palazzo della Pilotta 3A, 43121 Parma; tel. 0521-220411; e-mail museobodoni@beniculturali.it; internet www.museobodoni.beniculturali.it; f. 1963; dedicated to art of printing: punches, original matrices and moulds (approx. 80,000) from Bodoni's printing works; rare edns, technical manuals, press and tools of 'the prince of printers'; Pres. ORAZIO TARRONI; Curator CATERINA SILVA; publ. *Crisopoli. Bollettino del Museo Bodoniano di Parma* (1 a year).

Pavia

Civici Musei—Castello Visconteo: Viale XI Febbraio 35, 27100 Pavia; tel. 0382-33853; e-mail museicivici@comune.pv.it; internet www.museicivici.pavia.it; f. 1838; library of 24,800 vols; Dir Dott. SUSANNA ZATTI; Librarian ANGELA MACELLI.

Perugia

Galleria Nazionale dell'Umbria: Palazzo dei Priori, Corso Vannucci 19, 06123 Perugia; tel. 075-58668415; e-mail sbsae-umb@beniculturali.it; internet www.gallerianazionaleumbria.it; f. 1918; paintings of Umbrian school, 13th–19th centuries; also sculptures and jewellery; library of 5,300 vols; Dir Dott. FABIO DE CHIRICO; Curator FEDERICA ZALABRA.

Museo Archeologico Nazionale dell'Umbria: Piazza Giordano Bruno 10, 06121 Perugia; tel. 075-5727141; e-mail sba-umb@beniculturali.it; internet www.archeopg.arti.beniculturali.it; f. 1948; prehistoric, Roman, Hellenistic and Etruscan remains; primitive pottery, bone tools, funerary urns, amulets, archaic bronzes, coins; Dir MARISA SCARPIGNATO.

Pesaro

Musei Civici di Pesaro (Pinacoteca e Museo delle Ceramiche): Piazza Toschi Mosca 29, 61121 Pesaro; tel. (721) 387541; e-mail musei@comune.pesaro.ps.it; internet www.museicivicipesaro.it; f. 1936; art gallery and ceramics and decorative arts museum; Coordinator ERIKA TERENZI.

Pisa

Museo Nazionale di San Matteo: Piazza San Matteo in Soarta 1, 56126 Pisa; tel. 050-541865; e-mail sbapsae-pi.museosanmatteo@beniculturali.it; internet www.sbappsae-pi.beniculturali.it/index.php?it/146/pisa-museo-nazionale-di-san-matteo; f. 1949; sculptures by the Pisanos and their school; colln of the Pisan school from the 12th–14th centuries, and paintings and sculpture from the 15th to 17th centuries (works by Simone Martini, Masaccio, Beato Angelico, Benozzo Gozzoli, Ghirlandaio, Donatello, Della Robbia), 10th–17th-century ceramics, colln of coins and medals; Dir DARIO MATTEONI.

Portoferraio

Museo Napoleonico di Villa S. Martino: San Martino, 57037 Portoferraio; tel. 0565-914688.

Ravenna

Museo Nazionale di Ravenna: Via San Vitale, 17, 48121 Ravenna; tel. 0544-543711; e-mail sbap-ra.museonazionale@beniculturali.it; internet soprintendenzaravenna.beniculturali.it; f. 1885; state property since 1885; art, numismatics and archaeology; Dir ANTONELLA RANALDI.

Reggio Calabria

Museo Nazionale: Piazza De Nava 26, 89122 Reggio Calabria; tel. 0965-812255; e-mail sba-cal@beniculturali.it; internet www.museonazionalerc.it; f. 1958; archaeological objects from Calabria from prehistoric era to Roman times; also Antiquarium di Locri (Locri), Museo Archaeologico (Vibo Valentia), Museo Archaeologico (Crotone), Museo della Sibaritide (Sibari); art gallery; library of 10,000 vols; Dir Dott. ELENA LATTANZI; publ. *Klearchos* (1 a year).

Rome

Galleria Borghese: Piazzale del Museo Borghese, 5, 00197 Rome; tel. 06-8413979; e-mail info.servizimusei@libero.it; internet www.galleriaborghese.it; f. c. 1616; picture gallery, collections of classical and Baroque sculpture; Dir Dott. ALBA COSTAMAGNA.

Galleria Nazionale d'Arte Antica di Palazzo Barberini: Via delle Quattro Fontane 13, 00184 Rome; tel. 06-4824184; internet www.galleriaborghese.it; Italian and European paintings from 12th–18th centuries, Baroque architecture; Corsini colln at Galleria Corsini, Via della Lungara 10; Dir Dott. SIVIGLIANO ALLOISI.

Istituto Centrale per la Demoetnoantropologia Museo Nazionale delle Arti e Tradizioni Popolari: Piazza Marconi 8/10, 00144 Rome; tel. 06-5926148; e-mail ic-d@beniculturali.it; internet www.idea.mat.beniculturali.it; f. 1923; library of 30,000 vols; archives of musical, spoken and photocinematographic material; Dir Dott.ssa DANIELA PORRO.

Istituto Nazionale per la Grafica: Calcografia, Via della Stamperia 6, 00187 Rome; tel. 06-69980242; e-mail s.papaldo@inggrafica.it; internet www.grafica.arti.beniculturali.it; f. 1895; Italian and foreign prints and drawings from 14th century onwards; collection of matrices since 16th century; Dir Dott. SERENITA PAPALDO.

Keats-Shelley House: Piazza di Spagna 26, 00187 Rome; tel. (6) 6784235; e-mail info@ksh.roma.it; internet www.ksh.roma.it; f. 1903; access by appointment and dependent upon a letter of recommendation from an academic instn or publisher; Dir's permission required prior to consulting books published before 1900; library: reference library of 8,000 vols; Dir Dr GIUSEPPE ALBANO; publ. *The Keats-Shelley Review*.

Mausoleo di Cecilia Metella: Viale Appia Antica 161, 00179 Rome; tel. 06-39967700; internet www.medioevo.roma.it/html/architettura/torri-ext/tex-castello_caetani.htm#01; f. AD 20–30; funeral monument.

Musei Capitolini: Piazza del Campidoglio 1, 00186 Rome; tel. 06-67102475; e-mail info.museicapitolini@comune.roma.it; internet www.museicapitolini.org; f. 1471; archaeology, art history; Dir CLAUDIO PARISI PRESICCE.

Museo Barracco: Corso Vittorio Emanuele 168, 00186 Rome; tel. 06-68806848; e-mail info.museobarracco@comune.roma.it; internet en.museobarracco.it; f. 1905; evolution of sculpture from Egyptian to Roman styles; Dir Dott. MADDALENA CIMA.

Museo della Civiltà Romana: Piazza G. Agnelli 10, 00144 Rome; tel. 06-5926041; e-mail info.museociviltaromana@comune.roma.it; internet www.museociviltaromana.it; f. 1952; history of Rome from its origins; Curator CLAUDIO PARISI PRESICCE.

Museo di Palazzo Venezia: Via del Plebiscito 118, 00186 Rome; tel. 06-69994284; internet museopalazzovenezia.beniculturali.it; f. 1921; 13th–16th century paintings; bronze, marble and terracotta sculptures; medieval and Renaissance decorative art; 16th–17th century ceramics; furniture, prints, textiles; Dir ROSSELLA VODRET.

Museo di Roma: Piazza San Pantaleo 10 (Piazza Navona), 00186 Rome; tel. 06-67108346; e-mail museodiroma@comune.roma.it; internet www.museodiroma.it; f. 1930; topographic, cultural, social, historical and artistic devt of Rome since medieval times; Dir PIER LUIGI MATTERA.

Museo Nazionale d'Arte Orientale: Palazzo Brancaccio, Via Merulana 248, 00185 Rome; tel. 06-46974815; e-mail mn-ao.direzione@beniculturali.it; internet www.museorientale.beniculturali.it; f. 1957; library of 10,000 vols; Dir MARIAROSARIA BARBERA.

Museo Nazionale di Castel Sant'Angelo: Lungotevere Castello 50, 00193 Rome; tel. 06-6819111; e-mail sspsae-rm.santangelo@beniculturali.it; internet castelsantangelo.beniculturali.it; f. 1925; ancient armoury; architectural and monumental remains, frescoes, sculptures, pictures and period furniture; library of 13,000 vols, 60 periodicals; Dir MARIA GRAZIA BERNARDINI.

Museo Nazionale di Villa Giulia: Piazzale di Villa Giulia 9, 00196 Rome; tel. 06-3226571; e-mail sba-em@beniculturali.it; internet villagiulia.beniculturali.it; f. 1889; Etruscan and Italian antiquities; Dir Dott. ALFONSINA RUSSO.

Museo Nazionale Preistorico Etnografico 'Luigi Pigorini': Piazzale G. Marconi 14, 00144 Rome; tel. 06-549521; e-mail s-mnpe@beniculturali.it; internet www.pigorini.beniculturali.it; f. 1875; prehistory and ethnology; library of 70,000 vols, 500 bound periodicals, 500 current periodicals; Superintendent FRANCESCO DI GENNARO; publ. *Bullettino di Paletnologia Italiana* (1 a year).

Ostia Antica: Viale dei Romagnoli 717, 00119 Ostia Antica, Rome; tel. 6-56358099; internet archeoroma.beniculturali.it/siti-archeologici/ostia-antica; Roman antiquities, monuments, paintings, sculptures, mosaics; Dir Dr CINZIA MORELLI.

Soprintendenza alla Galleria Nazionale d'Arte Moderna e Contemporanea: Viale delle Belle Arti 131, 00196 Rome; tel. 06-322981; e-mail ss-gnam@beniculturali.it; internet www.ufficignam.beniculturali.it; Superintendent MARIA VITTORIA MARINI CLARELLI.

Attached Sites:

Galleria Nazionale d'Arte Moderna e Contemporanea: Viale delle Belle Arti 131, 00197 Rome; tel. 06-322981; e-mail s-gnam@beniculturali.it; internet www.gnam.beniculturali.it; f. 1883; art since 19th century; library of 70,000 vols, 1,500 periodicals; Dir MARIA VITTORIA MARINI CLARELLI.

Museo Boncompagni Ludovisi: Via Boncompagni 18, 00187 Rome; tel. (6)-42824074; e-mail museoboncompagni.info@beniculturali.it; internet www.museoboncompagni.beniculturali.it; f. 1995; modern decorative arts and fashion; Dir MARIASTELLA MARGOZZI.

Museo Hendrik Christian Andersen: Via Pasquale Stanislao Mancini, 20 (Piazzale Flaminio), 00196 Rome; tel. 06-3219089; e-mail s-gnam.museoandersen@beniculturali.it; internet www.museoandersen.beniculturali.it; f. 1999; paintings and sculpture by Hendrik Christian Andersen (1872–1940); Dir MATILDE AMATURO.

Museo Mario Praz: Palazzo Primoli, Via Zanardelli 1, 00186 Rome; tel. 06-6861089; e-mail museopraz@museopraz.191.it; internet www.museopraz.beniculturali.it; f. 1995; furniture, paintings, sculpture, carpets, miniatures and objects made of bronze, crystal, porcelain, silver and marble collected by Mario Praz (1896–1982); Dir PATRIZIA ROSAZZA.

Raccolta Manzù: Via Laurentina Km 32, 00040 Ardea; tel. 06-9135022; e-mail mcossu@arti.beniculturali.it; internet www.museomanzu.beniculturali.it; f. 1981; work by the sculptor Manzù; Chief Dir MARCELLA COSSU.

Soprintendenza Speciale per i Beni Archeologici di Roma: Piazza dei Cinquecento 67, 00185 Rome; tel. 06-48020205; e-mail ssba-rm@beniculturali.it; internet archeoroma.beniculturali.it; Superintendent Dott. ANNA MARIA MORETTI.

Attached Sites:

Il Colosseo (The Colosseum): Piazza del Colosseo 1, 00184 Rome; tel. 06-39967700; internet archeoroma.beniculturali.it/siti-archeologici/colosseo; f. AD 80; Dir ROSSELLA REA.

Domus Aurea (Golden House): Via della Domus Aurea 1, 00184 Rome; tel. 06-39967700; internet archeoroma.beniculturali.it/siti%20archeologici/centro/domus%20aurea; remains of Nero's villa built after the great fire of AD 64; Dir FEDORA FILIPPI.

Foro Romano e Palatino (Roman Forum and Palatine Hill): Piazza Santa Maria Nova 53, 00186 Rome; tel. 06-39967700; internet archeoroma.beniculturali.it/siti%20archeologici/centro/foro%20romano; history of Rome from 8th century BC; Dir MARIA ANTONIETTA TOMEI.

Museo Nazionale dell'Alto Medioevo (National Museum of the Early Middle Ages): Viale Lincoln 3, Esposizione Universale, 00144 Rome; tel. 06-54228124; internet archeoroma.beniculturali.it/musei/museo-nazionale-dell-alto-medioevo; f. 1967; exhibits dateable between the 4th and 14th centuries, coming mainly from Rome and central Italy; weapons, jewels, ivories, glassware and vessels in bronze and ceramic, marble reliefs, furnishings, Coptic colln of reliefs and textiles, marble inlay; Dir MARGHERITA TATA BEDELLO.

Museo della Via Ostiense (Via Ostiense Museum): Via Raffaele Persichetti, 00153 Rome; tel. 06-5743193; internet archeoroma.beniculturali.it/museo_della_via_ostiense; f. 1967; plastic reconstructions of the ancient city of Ostia, and of nearby ports in the 1st and 2nd centuries AD, paintings; Man. ANGELO PELLEGRINO.

Terme di Caracalla: Viale delle Terme di Caracalla, 00153 Rome; tel. 06-39967700; internet archeoroma.beniculturali.it/siti-archeologici/terme-caracalla; f. AD 216; remains of large complex of Roman baths; Dir MARINA PIRANOMONTE.

Villa dei Quintili: Via Appia Nuova 1092, 00178 Rome; tel. 06-39967700; internet archeoroma.beniculturali.it/siti%20archeologici/suburbio/villa%20dei%20quintili; f. 2nd century AD; extensive villa with rooms for masters and servants, bath quarters; Dir RITA PARIS.

Museo Nazionale Romano: Piazza dei Cinquecento 79, 00185 Rome; tel. 06-483617; internet archeoroma.beniculturali.it/museo-nazionale-romano; f. 1889; Greek, Hellenistic and Roman sculpture and bronzes, paintings and mosaics, numismatics; archaeological colln; Dir Prof. ADRIANO LA REGINA.

Constituent Centres:

Crypta Balbi: Via delle Botteghe Oscure 31, 00186 Rome; tel. 06-39967700; internet archeoroma.beniculturali.it/musei/museo-nazionale-romano-crypta-balbi; f. 13BC; remains of an arcaded courtyard and theatre; material and tools from a 7th-century workshop; Man. LAURA VENDITTELLI.

Palazzo Altemps: Piazza di Sant'Apollinare 46, 00186 Rome; tel. 06-39967700; internet archeoroma.beniculturali.it/musei/museo-nazionale-romano-palazzo-altemps; f. 1997; Greek and Roman sculpture; Mans ALESSANDRA CAPODIFERRO, MATILDE DE ANGELIS.

Terme di Diocleziano (Baths of Diocletian): Via Enrico de Nicola 79, 00185 Rome; tel. 06-39967700; internet archeoroma.beniculturali.it/musei/museo-nazionale-romano-terme-diocleziano; f. 3rd century AD; museum f. 1889; sculpture, sarcophagi, inscriptions, mosaics and frescoes; Man. ROSANNA FRIGGERI.

Palazzo Massimo: Largo di Villa Peretti, 00185 Rome; tel. 06-39967700; internet archeoroma.beniculturali.it/musei/museo-nazionale-romano-palazzo-massimo; f. 1998; statues, mosaic pavement, numismatics, frescoes, bronzes and jewellery from 1st century BC to 4th century AD; Man. RITA PARIS.

Villa Farnesina: Via della Lungara 230, 00165 Rome; tel. 6-68027268; e-mail farnesina@lincei.it; internet www.villafarnesina.it; now the property of the Accademia Nazionale dei Lincei; built 1509 by Peruzzi; decorated by Raphael, Peruzzi and others; Curator Geom. RODOLFO DONZELLI.

Rovereto

Museo Civico di Rovereto: Borgo Santa Caterina 41, 38068 Rovereto; tel. 0464-452800; e-mail museo@museocivico.rovereto.tn.it; internet www.museocivico.rovereto.tn.it; f. 1851; sections on archaeology, art history, astronomy, botany, earth sciences, numismatics and zoology; Dir FRANCO FINOTTI.

Rovigo

Pinacoteca dell'Accademia dei Concordi e del Seminario Vescovile: Palazzo Roverella, Via Laurenti 8/10, 45100 Rovigo; tel. 0425-460093; e-mail info@palazzoroverella.com; internet www.palazzoroverella.com/pinacoteca.php; contains 650 Venetian paintings from the 15th–18th centuries; colln of Flemish paintings.

Sarsina

Museo Archeologico Nazionale: Via Cesio Sabino 39, 47027 Sarsina; tel. 0547-94641; internet www.comune.sarsina.fo.it/museoarch/museo.htm; f. 1890; exhibition of archaeological remains from the Roman age; Dir Dott. CHIARA GUARNIERI.

Sassari

Museo Nazionale Archeologico Etnografico 'G. A. Sanna': Via Roma, 64 07100 Sassari; tel. 079-272203; e-mail museosanna@beniculturali.it; internet www.museosannasassari.it; f. 1931; archaeology, medieval and modern art, ethnography; Dir Dott.ssa GABRIELLA GASPERETTI.

Siena

Museo Archeologico: Piazza Duomo 1, 53100 Siena; tel. 0577-534511; e-mail infoscala@sms.comune.siena.it; internet www.santamariadellascala.com; antiquities from the local area; Etruscan section; numismatic colln; Curator ENRICO TOTI.

Museo Aurelio Castelli: Strada dell'Osservanza 7, 53100 Siena; tel. 0577-332444; internet www.sienaonline.it/aurelio_castelli.html; 14th–15th-century sculpture; paintings and drawings from the 15th–18th centuries; library of 25,000 vols.

Pinacoteca Nazionale: Palazzo Buonsignori, Via San Pietro 29, 53100 Siena; tel. 0577-286143; e-mail pinacoteca.siena@libero.it; internet www.spsae-si.beniculturali.it/index.php?it/77/musei; f. 1930; 650 Sienese paintings of the 13th–16th centuries; Dir Dott. ANNA MARIA GUIDUCCI.

Syracuse

Museo Archeologico Regionale 'Paolo Orsi': Viale Teocrito 66, 96100 Syracuse; tel. 0931-489511; e-mail museo.arche.orsi@regione.sicilia.it; internet www.regione.sicilia.it/beniculturali/museopaoloorsi; f. 1988; prehistory, statuary and antiques from the excavations of the Graeco-Roman city and from prehistoric and classical sites of Eastern Sicily; colln of coins and medals, created in the 1950s, by Luigi Bernabò Brea; archaeological exhibition of Christian hypogei, remains of an archaic necropolis, elements of Hellenistic dwellings in Syracuse; historical site of non-Catholic cemetery with the tomb of the German poet August von Platen; Dir Dr BEATRICE BASILE.

Taranto

Museo Archeologico Nazionale: Via Cavour 10, 74100 Taranto; tel. 099-4532112; e-mail museoarch.taranto@beniculturali.it; internet www.museotaranto.org; f. 1887; local prehistory and Greco-Roman remains; Dir ANTONIETTA DELL'AGLIO.

Tarquinia

Museo Archeologico Nazionale Tarquiniense: Palazzo Vitelleschi, Piazza Cavour, 01016 Tarquinia; tel. 0766-856036; e-mail info@tarquiniaturismo.it; f. 1924; Etruscan sarcophagi from the 4th and 3rd centuries BC, Etruscan and Greek vases, bronzes, ornaments; Etruscan paintings; Dir Dott. MARIA GABRIELLA SCAPATICCI.

Trento

Castello del Buonconsiglio–Monumenti e Collezioni Provinciali: Via Bernardo Clesio 5, 38122 Trento; tel. 0461-233770; e-mail info@buonconsiglio.it; internet www.buonconsiglio.it; f. 1924; ancient, medieval and modern art; Dir Dott. FRANCO MARZATICO.

Trieste

Civici Musei di Storia ed Arte: Via Rossini 4, IV Piano, 34121 Trieste; tel. 040-6754035; e-mail dugulin@comune.trieste.it; internet www.retecivica.trieste.it/triestecultura; Dir Dott. MARIA MASAU DAN.

Constituent Museums and Galleries:

Castello di San Giusto e Civico Museo del Castello, Lapidario Tergestino: Piazza della Cattedrale 3, 34121 Trieste; tel. 040-309362; e-mail cmsa@comune.trieste.it; internet www.retecivica.trieste.it/triestecultura/new/musei/sangiusto; f. 1936, Lapidario 2001; Dir Dott. MARIA MASAU DAN.

Civico Aquario Marino: Molo Pescheria 2, 34139 Trieste; tel. 040-306201; e-mail museisci@comune.trieste.it; internet www.retecivica.trieste.it/triestecultura/new/musei_scientifici/aquario; f. 1933; Dir Dott. MARIA MASAU DAN.

Civico Museo d'Arte Orientale: Via San Sebastiano 1, 34121 Trieste; tel. 040-6754068; e-mail museoarteorientale@comune.trieste.it; internet www.retecivica.trieste.it/triestecultura/new/musei/museo_orientale; f. 2001; Dir Dott. MARIA MASAU DAN.

Civico Museo di Guerra per la Pace 'Diego de Henriquez': Via delle Milizie 16, 34139 Trieste; tel. 040-948430; e-mail museodehenriquez@comune.trieste.it; internet www.retecivica.trieste.it/triestecultura/new/musei/museo_henriquez; f. 1998; Dir Dott. MARIA MASAU DAN.

Civico Museo del Mare: Via Campo Marzio 5, 34139 Trieste; tel. 040-304885; e-mail museomare@comune.trieste.it; internet www.retecivica.trieste.it/triestecultura/new/musei_scientifici/mare; f. 1968; Dir Dott. MARIA MASAU DAN.

Civico Museo Sartorio: Largo Papa Giovanni XXIII 1, 34123 Trieste; tel. 040-301479; e-mail cmsa@comune.trieste.it; internet www.retecivica.trieste.it/triestecultura/new/musei/museo_sartorio; f. 1947; Dir Dott. MARIA MASAU DAN.

Civico Museo di Storia ed Arte e Orto Lapidario: Piazza della Cattedrale 1, 34121 Trieste; tel. 040-308686; e-mail cmsa@comune.trieste.it; internet www.retecivica.trieste.it/triestecultura/new/musei/museo_storiaedarte; f. Orto Lapidario 1843, Civico Museo di Storia 1873; Dir Dott. MARIA MASAU DAN.

Civico Museo di Storia Naturale: Via dei Tominz 4, 34139 Trieste; tel. 040-6758658; e-mail sportellonatura@comune.trieste.it; internet www.retecivica.trieste.it/triestecultura/new/musei_scientifici/storia_naturale; f. 2010; Dir Dott. MARIA MASAU DAN.

Civico Museo di Storia Patria—Civico Museo Morpurgo de Nilma: Via Imbriani 5, 34122 Trieste; tel. 040-636969; e-mail cmsa@comune.trieste.it; internet www.retecivica.trieste.it/triestecultura/new/musei/museo_storiapatria; f. Museo Morpurgo 1947, Civico Museo di Storia Patria 1950; Dir Dott. MARIA MASAU DAN.

Civico Museo Teatrale 'Carlo Schmidl': Via Rossini, 4, 34122 Trieste; tel. 040-6754072; e-mail museoschmidl@comune.trieste.it; internet www.retecivica.trieste.it/triestecultura/new/musei/museo_schmidl; f. 1924; Curator STEFANO BIANCHI.

Civico Orto Botanico: Via Marchesetti 2, 34139 Trieste; tel. 040-360068; e-mail ortobotanico@comune.trieste.it; internet www.retecivica.trieste.it/triestecultura/new/musei_scientifici/orto_botanico; f. 1842; Curator MASSIMO PALMA.

Museo Ferroviario di Trieste Campo Marzio: Via Giulio Cesare 1, 34123 Trieste; tel. 040-3794185; e-mail info@museoferroviariotrieste.it; internet www.museoferroviariotrieste.it; Dir Dott. MARIA MASAU DAN.

Museo Joyce: Via Madonna del Mare 13, 34121 Trieste; tel. 040-3593606; e-mail museojoyce@comune.trieste.it; internet www.museojoycetrieste.it; f. 2004; Dir Dott. MARIA MASAU DAN.

Museo Petrarchesco Piccolomineo: Via Madonna del Mare 13, 34123 Trieste; tel. 040-6758184; e-mail museopetrarchesco@comune.trieste.it; internet www.retecivica.trieste.it/triestecultura/new/musei/museo_petrarchesco; f. 2003; Dir ALESSANDRA SIRUGO.

Museo Postale e Telegrafico della Mitteleuropa: Piazza Vittorio Veneto 1, 34132 Trieste; tel. 040-6764264; e-mail simonchi@posteitaliane.it; internet www.retecivica.trieste.it/triestecultura/new/musei/museo_postale; f. 1997, in association with Poste Italiane S.p.A.; Dir Dott. MARIA MASAU DAN.

Museo Revoltella – Galleria d'Arte Moderna: Via Diaz 27, 34123 Trieste; tel. 040-6754350; e-mail revoltella@comune.trieste.it; internet www.museorevoltella.it; f. 1872; library of 17,000 vols, 426 periodicals, 34 current periodicals; Dir Dott. MARIA MASAU DAN.

Museo della Risiera di San Sabba—Monumento Nazionale: Via Giovanni Palatucci 5, 34148 Trieste; tel. 040-826202; e-mail risierasansabba@comune.trieste.it; internet www.retecivica.trieste.it/triestecultura/new/musei/risiera_san_sabba; f. 1975; Dir Dott. MARIA MASAU DAN.

Museo del Risorgimento e Sacrario Oberdan: Via XXIV Maggio 4, 34133 Trieste; tel. 040-361675; e-mail cmsa@comune.trieste.it; internet www.retecivica.trieste.it/triestecultura/new/musei/museo_risorgimento; f. 1934; Dir Dott. MARIA MASAU DAN.

Museo Sveviano: Via Madonna del Mare 13, 34123 Trieste; tel. 040-6758182; e-mail museosveviano@comune.trieste.it; internet www.retecivica.trieste.it/svevo; f. 1997; library of 3,000 vols; Dir Dott. BIANCA CUDERI.

Turin

Armeria Reale: Piazza Castello 191, 10123 Turin; tel. 011-543889; e-mail armeriareale@artito.arti.beniculturali.it; internet www.artito.arti.beniculturali.it; f. 1837; colln of arms; includes the equestrian armour of Otto Heinrich and works by Pompeo della Chiesa, Etienne Delaune and the engravers of the Munich school, Emanuel Sadeler, Daniel Sadeler and Caspar Spät; Dir ALESSANDRA GUERRINI.

Fondazione Torino Musei: Corso Vittorio Emanuele II 78, 10121 Turin; tel. 011-4436901; e-mail info@fondazionetorinomusei.it; internet www.comune.torino.it/musei; Sec.-Gen. and Administrative Dir ADRIANO DA RE.

Attached Museums:

Borgo e Rocca Medioevale: Parco del Valentino, Viale Virgilio 107, 10126 Turin; tel. 011-4431701; e-mail borgomedievale@fondazionetorinomusei.it; internet www.borgomedievaletorino.it; Dir ENRICA PAGELLA.

Galleria Civica d'Arte Moderna e Contemporanea: Via Magenta 31, 10128 Turin; tel. 011-5629911; e-mail gam@fondazionetorinomusei.it; internet www.gamtorino.it; f. 1953; Dir DANILO ECCHER.

Museo d'Arte Orientale (Museum of Oriental Art): Via San Domenico 11, 10122 Turin; tel. 011-4436927; e-mail mao@fondazionetorinomusei.it; internet www.maotorino.it; f. 2008; Dir FRANCO RICCA.

Palazzo Madama—Museo Civico d'Arte Antica: Piazza Castello, 10122 Turin; tel. 011-4433501; e-mail palazzomadama@fondazionetorinomusei.it; internet www.palazzomadamatorino.it; f. 1863; Dir ENRICA PAGELLA.

Museo Civico Pietro Micca e dell'assedio di Torino del 1706 (Pietro Micca and 1706 Siege of Turin Civic Museum): Via Guicciardini 7A, 10121 Turin; tel. 011-546317; internet www.museopietromicca.it; f. 1961; Hon. Curator and Dir-Gen. SEBASTIANO PONSO.

Galleria Sabauda: Via Accademia delle Scienze 6, 10123 Turin; tel. 11-5617776; internet www.museitorino.it/galleriasabauda/index.html; f. 1832; one of principal Flemish and Dutch collns, and early Italian, also Bronzino, Veronese, Tiepolo and Lombard and Piedmontese schools, furniture, sculpture and jewellery; Dir Dott. PAOLA ASTRUA.

Museo di Antichità: Via XX Settembre 88C, 10122 Turin; tel. 011-5211106; e-mail info@museoarcheologico.it; internet www.museoantichita.it; f. 1940; Piedmontese prehistory; Etruscan, Sardinian and Gallo-Roman remains; Greek and Cypriot ceramics; Roman statues; silverware; Dir Dott. LILIANA MERCANDO.

Museo Egizio: Via Accademia delle Scienze 6, 10123 Turin; tel. 011-5617776; e-mail info@museoegizio.it; internet www.museoegizio.it; f. 1824; Pharonic, Ptolemaic and Coptic antiquities; entire furnishings of the tomb of architect Kha and his wife from Deir el-Medina, Temple of Ellesija (reconstructed Nubian temple of 18th dynasty) presented by the Egyptian Govt; objects from Droveth colln and Schiaparelli excavations in Egypt; Dir ELENI VASSILIKA.

Udine

Civici Musei e Gallerie di Storia ed Arte: Colle del Castello, Piazza Libertà, 33100 Udine; tel. 0432-271591; e-mail silvia.bianco@comune.udine.it; internet www.comune.udine.it/opencms/opencms/release/comuneudine/cittavicina/cultura/it/musei/civici_musei_e_gallerie_di_storia_ed_arte; f. 1866; history, art; Dir Dott. SILVIA BIANCO.

Urbino

Galleria Nazionale delle Marche—Palazzo Ducale: Piazza Duca Federico 107, 61029 Urbino; tel. 0722-2760; e-mail info.servizimusei@libero.it; internet www.galleriaborghese.it/nuove/einfourbino.html; f. 1912; medieval and Renaissance works of art originating in the town of Urbino and the provinces of Marche; Dir Dott. LORENZA MOCHI ONORI.

Venice

Biennale di Venezia: Ca' Giustinian, San Marco 1364/A, 30124 Venice; tel. 041-

5218711; e-mail info@labiennale.org; internet www.labiennale.org; f. 1895; organizes artistic and cultural events throughout the year: visual arts, architecture, cinema, theatre, music, dance; the Biennale also manages the historical archive of contemporary art; library of 130,000 vols and catalogues, photographs, art monographies, magazines etc.; Pres. PAOLO BARATTA; Gen. Dir ANDREA DEL MERCATO.

Gallerie dell'Accademia: Campo della Carità, Dorsoduro 1050, 30100 Venice; tel. 041-5222247; e-mail sspsae-ve.accademia@beniculturali.it; internet www.polomuseale.venezia.beniculturali.it/index.php?it/3/gallerie-dellaccademia; f. 1807; Venetian painting 1310–1700; Dir MATTEO CERIANA.

Galleria Giorgio Franchetti alla Ca' d'Oro: Cannaregio 3932, 30126 Venice; tel. (41) 5222349; e-mail sspsae-ve.franchetti@beniculturali.it; internet www.polomuseale.venezia.beniculturali.it/index.php?it/4/galleria-giorgio-franchetti-alla-ca-doro; f. 1928; sculpture, bronzes, medals, coins, tapestries, ceramics, and Venetian, central Italian and Flemish art; Deputy Dir Dott. CLAUDIA CREMONINI; Curator Dott. CLAUDIA CREMONINI; Ceramics Curator Dott. FRANCESCA SACCARDO; Paintings Restorer Dott. GLORIA TRANQUILLI.

Musei Civici Veneziani: Piazza San Marco 52, 30124 Venice; tel. 041-5225625; e-mail info@fmcvenezia.it; internet www.museiciviciveneziani.it; Dir Prof. GIANDOMENICO ROMANELLI.

Constituent Institutions:

Ca' Rezzonico: Dorsoduro 3136, 30123 Venice; tel. 041-2410100; e-mail info@fmcvenezia.it; internet www.museiciviciveneziani.it; f. 1935; 18th-century Venetian art, sculpture, etc.

Casa di Carlo Goldoni: San Polo 2794, 30125 Venice; tel. 041-2759325; e-mail mkt.musei@comune.venezia.it; internet www.museiciviciveneziani.it; house of the comic playwright (1707–93).

Galleria Internazionale d'Arte Moderna di Ca' Pesaro: Santa Croce 2076, 30135 Venice; tel. 041-5240695; e-mail mkt.musei@comune.venezia.it; internet www.museiciviciveneziani.it; f. 1897; works of art since the 19th century.

Museo Correr: Piazza San Marco 52, 30124 Venice; tel. 041-2405211; e-mail info@fmcvenezia.it; internet www.museiciviciveneziani.it; f. 1830 by Teodoro Correr who bequeathed his collns to the city; Venetian art (13th–16th centuries) and history of Serenissima, Renaissance coins, ceramics; publ. *Bollettino* (4 a year).

Museo Fortuny: San Marco 3780, 30124 Venice; tel. 041-5200995; e-mail mkt.musei@comune.venezia.it; internet www.museiciviciveneziani.it; closed for restoration.

Museo del Merletto: Piazza Galuppi 187, 30012 Burano; tel. 041-730034; e-mail mkt.musei@comune.venezia.it; internet www.museiciviciveneziani.it; f. 1981; examples of lace since 19th century in the former Lace School.

Museo di Storia Naturale: Santa Croce 1730, 30125 Venice; tel. 041-2750206; e-mail mkt.musei@comune.venezia.it; internet www.museiciviciveneziani.it; f. 1923; natural history; entomology, malacology, ornithology, icthyology, African ethnology; library of 10,000 vols.

Museo del Vetro: Fondamenta Giustinian 8, 30121 Murano; tel. 041-739586; e-mail mkt.musei@comune.venezia.it; internet www.museiciviciveneziani.it; f. 1861; Venetian glass from middle ages to the present; also collns of Roman glass from 1st century AD, Spanish, Bohemian and English collns; archives and photographic colln; spec. exhibitions and educational projects.

Palazzo Ducale (Doge's Palace): Piazza San Marco 1, 30124 Venice; tel. 041-2715911; e-mail mkt.musei@comune.venezia.it; internet www.museiciviciveneziani.it; f. 1340; doge's apartments, institutional chambers, armoury and prisons.

Palazzo Mocenigo: Santa Croce 1992, 30126 Venice; tel. 041-721798; e-mail mkt.musei@comune.venezia.it; internet www.museiciviciveneziani.it; palace of the noble Venetian family that provided several of the doges; colln of fabrics and costumes; library on history of fashion.

Planetario di Venezia: Ass.Astrofili Veneziani, CP 36, Venice Lido; tel. 041-731518; e-mail planetario@astrovenezia.net; internet www.astrovenezia.net.

Torre Civica di Mestre: Piazza Erminio Ferretto, 30174 Mestre; tel. 041-2749062; internet www.museiciviciveneziani.it/frame.asp?pid=996; f. 13th century.

Torre dell'Orologio (Clock Tower): Piazza San Marco, 30124 Venice; tel. 041-2715911; e-mail mkt.musei@comune.venezia.it; internet www.museiciviciveneziani.it; f. 15th century; closed for restoration.

Museo Archeologico Nazionale: Piazza S. Marco 52, 30124 Venice; tel. 041-5225978; e-mail sspsae-ve.archeologico@beniculturali.it; internet www.polomuseale.venezia.beniculturali.it/index.php?it/6/museo-archeologico-nazionale; f. 1523, reorganized 1923–26 and again after 1945; Greek and Roman sculpture, gems and coins, mosaics and sculptures from the 5th century BC–11th century AD; library of 3,000 vols; Curator MARIA CRISTINA DOSSI.

Museo d'Arte Orientale: Sestiere di Santa Croce 2076, 30100 Venice; tel. 041-5241173; e-mail sspsae-ve.orientale@beniculturali.it; internet www.polomuseale.venezia.beniculturali.it/index.php?it/5/museo-darte-orientale; 17th–19th-century decorative arts from the Far East; Dir Dott. FIORELLA SPADAVECCHIA.

Museo della Fondazione Querini Stampalia: Santa Maria Formosa, Castello 5252, 30122 Venice; tel. 041-2711411; e-mail museo@querinistampalia.org; internet www.querinistampalia.it; f. 1869; 14th- to 19th-century Italian paintings, 18th- and 19th-century furniture, china; library of 330,000 vols, 400 periodicals; Dir Dott. ENRICO ZOLA.

Museo Storico Navale: Riva S. Biasio Castello 2148, 30122 Venice; tel. 041-2441399; e-mail museostoriconavale@virgilio.it; f. 1929; library of 3,000 vols; Dir MARCO SANSONI; Curator LORENZO SFERRA.

Peggy Guggenheim Collection (Solomon R. Guggenheim Foundation, New York): Palazzo Venier dei Leoni, 701 Dorsoduro, 30123 Venice; tel. 041-2405411; e-mail info@guggenheim-venice.it; internet www.guggenheim-venice.it; f. 1980; permanent colln incl. masterpieces of Cubism, Futurism, metaphysical painting, European abstraction, surrealism, and American abstract expressionism; 80 masterpieces from the Hannelore B. and Rudolph B. Schulhof colln; Italian futurist works on loan from the Gianni Mattioli colln; Nasher Sculpture Garden; Dir Prof. PHILIP RYLANDS.

Pinacoteca Manfrediniana: Dorsoduro 1, 30123 Venice; tel. 041-2411018; e-mail seminario@patriarcato.venezia.it; internet www.marcianum.it; f. 1827; paintings and sculpture of the Roman, Gothic, Renaissance, Baroque, Neo-classical periods; library of 80,000 vols; Dir Prof. Mgr LUCIO CILIA.

Verona

Galleria d'Arte Moderna Palazzo Forti: Via A. Forti 1, 37121 Verona; tel. 045-8001903; e-mail palazzoforti@comune.verona.it; internet www.palazzoforti.it; f. 1982; Dir Prof. G. ROSSI CORTENOVA.

Musei Civici d'Arte di Verona: Corso Castelvecchio 2, 37121 Verona; tel. 045-8062611; e-mail castelvecchio@comune.verona.it; internet portale.comune.verona.it/nqcontent.cfm?a_id=582; f. 1857; Dir Dott. PAOLA MARINI.

Constituent Museums and Galleries:

Museo degli Affreschi 'Giovanni Battista Cavalcaselle' alla Tomba di Giulietta: Via del Pontiere 35, 37122 Verona; tel. 045-8000361; e-mail castelvecchio@comune.verona.it; f. 1973; Dir Dott. PAOLA MARINI.

Museo Archeologico al Teatro Romano: Regaste Redentore 2, 37129 Verona; tel. 045-8000360; e-mail castelvecchio@comune.verona.it; f. 1924; Dir Dott. PAOLA MARINI.

Museo di Castelvecchio: Corso Castelvecchio 2, 37121 Verona; tel. 045-8062611; e-mail castelvecchio@comune.verona.it; library of 42,000 vols, 500 periodicals; Dir Dott. PAOLA MARINI.

Museo Lapidario Maffeiano: Piazza Brà 28, 37121 Verona; tel. 045-590087; f. 1745; Curator Dott. MARGHERITA BOLLA.

Vicenza

Musei Civici Vicenza: Palazzo Chiericati, Piazza Matteotti 37–39, 36100 Vicenza; tel. 444-222811; e-mail museonatarcheo@comune.vicenza.it; internet www.museicivicivicenza.it; Dir Dott. MARIA ELISA AVAGNINA.

Attached Museums:

Museo Civico Pinacoteca: Palazzo Chiericati, Piazza Matteotti 37–39, 36100 Vicenza; tel. 444-321348; e-mail museocivico@comune.vicenza.it; internet www.museicivicivicenza.it/it/mcp/index.php; f. 1855; 13th–19th century paintings and sculpture by artists incl. Montagna, Veronese, Tintoretto and Tiepolo; MSS, drawings, prints and coins; Dir Dott. MARIA ELISA AVAGNINA.

Museo del Risorgimento e della Resistenza: Villa Guiccioli, Viale X Giugno 115, 36100 Vicenza; tel. 444-222820; e-mail museorisorgimento@comune.vicenza.it; internet www.museicivicivicenza.it/it/mrr/index.php; Dir Dott. MAURO PASSARIN.

Museo Naturalistico Archeologico: Chiostri di Santa Corona, contrà Santa Corona 4, 36100 Vicenza; tel. 444-320440; e-mail museonatarcheo@comune.vicenza.it; internet www.museicivicivicenza.it/it/mna/index.php; f. 1991; fossils, flora and fauna; Palaeolithic and local Roman remains; Dir Dott. ANTONIO DAL LAGO; publ. *Natura Vicentina* (1 a year).

Viterbo

Museo Civico: Piazza Francesco Crispi 2, 01100 Viterbo; tel. 0761-348275; e-mail museocivico@comune.viterbo.it; internet www.comune.viterbo.it/museocivico; f. 1912; archaeology, art history; Dir ORSOLA GRASSI.

Volterra

Museo Diocesano d'Arte Sacra: Palazzo Vescovile, Via Roma 13, 56048 Volterra; tel. 0588-86290; e-mail museoartesacravolterra@nemail.it; internet www.comune.volterra.pi

.it/museiit/musart.html; f. 1932; sculpture, paintings, costumes, ornaments; Dir Dott. UMBERTO BAVONI.

Museo Etrusco Guarnacci: Via Don Minzoni 15, 56048 Volterra; tel. 0588-86347; e-mail a.furiesi@comune.volterra.pi.it; internet www.comune.volterra.pi.it/english/museiit/metru.html; f. 1761; Roman and Etruscan coins, urns, bronzes, etc.; Dir Dr ALESSANDRO FURIESI.

State Universities

POLITECNICO DI BARI

Via E. Orabona 4, 70125 Bari
Telephone: 080-5962111
E-mail: rettore@poliba.it
Internet: www.poliba.it
Founded 1990
State control
Rector: Prof. NICOLA COSTANTINO
Deputy Rector: Prof. FRANCESCO SELICATO
Admin. Dir: Dott. ANTONIO DI GUARDO
Library of 200,000 and journals

DEANS

Faculty of Architecture: Prof. Arch. CLAUDIO D'AMATO GUERRIERI
I Faculty of Engineering (in Bari and Foggia): Prof. Ing. ANTONIO DELL'AQUILA
II Faculty of Engineering (in Taranto): Prof. Ing GREGORIO ANDRIA

POLITECNICO DI MILANO

Piazza Leonardo da Vinci 32, 20133 Milan
Telephone: 02-23991
Internet: www.polimi.it
Founded 1863
Language of instruction: Italian, English
Academic year: November to October
Rector: Prof. GIOVANNI AZZONE
Vice-Rector: Prof. ALESSANDRO BALDUCCI
Gen. Dir: GRAZIANO DRAGONI
Librarian: SONIA PASQUALIN
Number of teachers: 1,355
Number of students: 25,952
Publication: *Politecnico* (4 a year)

DEANS

First School of Architecture (Architecture and Society): Prof. PIERCARLO PALERMO
Second School of Architecture (Civil Architecture): Prof. ANGELO TORRICELLI
School of Design: Prof. ARTURO DELL'ACQUA BELLAVITIS
First School of Engineering (Civil, Environmental and Territorial Engineering): Prof. FEDERICO PEROTTI
Second School of Engineering (Systems Engineering): Prof. ALESSANDRO POZZETTI
Third School of Engineering (Industrial Process Engineering): Prof. MAURIZIO MASI
Fourth School of Engineering (Industrial Engineering): Prof. GIOVANNI LOZZA
Fifth School of Engineering (Information Engineering): Prof. ROBERTO NEGRINI
Sixth School of Engineering (Construction Engineering/Architecture): Prof. EMILIO PIZZI

POLITECNICO DI TORINO

Corso Duca degli Abruzzi 24, 10129 Turin
Telephone: 11-5646100
E-mail: rettore@polito.it
Internet: www.polito.it
Founded 1859
Public control
Languages of instruction: English, Italian
Academic year: November to October
Higher Institute of Engineering and Architecture
Rector: Prof. FRANCESCO PROFUMO
Vice-Rector: Prof. MARCO GILLI
Admin. Dir: ENRICO PERITI
Library Dir: Dott. MARIA VITTORIA SAVIO
Library of 382,898 vols
Number of teachers: 814
Number of students: 29,000

DEANS

First School of Architecture: Prof. FERRUCCIO ZORZI
First School of Engineering: Prof. DONATO FIRRAO
Fourth School of Engineering—Economics and Management: Prof. SERGIO ROSSETTO
Graduate School: Prof. MARIO RASETTI (Dir-Second School of Architecture—Architecture and Environment: Prof. ROCCO CURTO
Third School of Engineering—Information Technologies: Prof. PAOLO ENRICO CAMURATI

SAPIENZA UNIVERSITÀ DI ROMA

Piazzale Aldo Moro 5, 00185 Rome
Telephone: 06-49911
E-mail: rettore@uniroma1.it
Internet: www.uniroma1.it
Founded 1303 by Pope Boniface VIII, with the Papal Bull 'In Supremae praeminentia dignitatis'
Rector: Prof. LUIGI FRATI
Vice-Rector: Prof. FRANCESCO AVALLONE
Deputy Rector for Accomplishment and Implementation of the Rector's Programme and for Relations with the Admin.: Prof. ADRIANO REDLER
Deputy Rector for Applied Research, Technology Transfer and Relations with the Business World: Prof. LUCIANO CAGLIOTI
Deputy Rector for Cooperation and Int. Relations: Prof. ANTONELLO BIAGINI
Deputy Rector for Devt of Research and Educational Activities: Prof. BARTOLOMEO AZZARO
Deputy Rector for Relations with Confederate Univs: Prof. FULCO LANCHESTER
Deputy Rector for Strategic Planning: Prof. GIUSEPPINA CAPALDO
Head of Admin.: CARLO MUSTO D'AMORE
Librarian: Prof. GIOVANNI CICLOTTI
Number of teachers: 4,500
Number of students: 140,000

DEANS

Faculty of Architecture: Prof. RENATO MASIANI
Faculty of Civil and Industrial Engineering: Prof. FABRIZIO VESTRONI
Faculty of Economics: Prof. ATTILIO CELANT
Faculty of Engineering, Information Technology and Statistics: Prof. LUIGIA CARLUCCI AIELLO
Faculty of Jurisprudence: Prof. MARIO CARAVALE
Faculty of Mathematics, Physics and Natural Science: Prof. PIERO NEGRINI
Faculty of Medicine and Dentistry: Prof. ADRIANO REDLER
Faculty of Medicine and Psychology: Prof. VINCENZO ZIPARO
Faculty of Pharmacy and Medicine: Prof. EUGENIO GAUDIO
Faculty of Philosophy, Arts, Humanities and Oriental Studies: Prof. MARTA FATTORI
Faculty of Political Science, Sociology and Communication: Prof. GIANLUIGI ROSSI

ATTACHED CENTRES

Interdepartmental Research Centre of European and International Studies: internet www.eco.uniroma1.it/europe; Dir Prof. GIUSEPPE BURGIO.

Interuniversity Research Centre on Developing Countries (CIRPS): internet www.cirps.it; Dir Prof. VINCENZO NASO

SECONDA UNIVERSITÀ DEGLI STUDI DI NAPOLI

Viale Beneduce 10, 81100 Caserta
Telephone: 0823-274901
E-mail: rettoratoce@unina2.it
Internet: www.unina2.it
Founded 1991
State control
Rector: Prof. FRANCESCO ROSSI
Vice-Rector: Prof. MARIO DE ROSA
Admin. Dir: Dott. VINCENZO LANZA
Number of students: 30,000

DEANS

Faculty of Architecture: Prof. CARMINE GAMBARDELLA
Faculty of Economics: Prof. CLELIA MAZZONI
Faculty of Engineering: Prof. MICHELE DI NATALE
Faculty of Environmental Sciences: Prof. PAOLO VINCENZO PEDONE
Faculty of Law: Prof. LORENZO CHIEFFI
Faculty of Letters and Philosophy: Prof. ROSANNA CIOFFI
Faculty of Mathematical, Physical and Natural Sciences: Prof. AUGUSTO PARENTE
Faculty of Medicine and Surgery: Prof. GIUSEPPE PAOLISSO
Faculty of Political Studies: Prof. GIAN MARIA PICCINELLI
Faculty of Psychology: Prof. ALIDA LABELLA

UNIVERSITÀ CA' FOSCARI VENEZIA

Dorsoduro 3246, 30123 Venice
Telephone: 041-2348111
E-mail: help@unive.it
Internet: www.unive.it
Founded 1868, formerly Istituto Universitario di Economia e Commercio e di Lingue e Letterature Straniere
Academic year: November to October
Rector: Prof. CARLO CARRARO
Pro-Rector: Prof. ERASMO SANTESSO
Admin. Dir: Dott. STEFANIA TORRE
Librarian: EUGENIO BURGIO
Number of teachers: 494
Number of students: 17,427
Publications: *Annuario*, *Cafoscariappuntamenti* (6 a year), *Cafoscarinotizie* (4 a year)

DEANS

Faculty of Economics: Prof. ANTONELLA BASSO
Faculty of Foreign Languages and Literature: Prof. ALIDE CAGIDEMETRIO
Faculty of Letters and Philosophy: Prof. FILIPPO MARIA CARINCI
Faculty of Mathematical, Physical and Natural Sciences: Prof. ALVISE BENEDETTI

UNIVERSITY CENTRES AND SCHOOLS

Administrative Computer Centre: Dorsoduro 2169, Santa Marta, 30123 Venice; Pres. Dott. G. BUSETTO.

Computer Centre: Dorsoduro 3861, 30123 Venice; tel. 5229823; Pres. Prof. G. PACINI.

Interdepartmental Experimental Centre: Dorsoduro 2137, 30123 Venice; tel. 5298111; Pres. Prof. G. A. MAZZOCCHIN.

Interfaculty Linguistics Centre: Santa Croce 2161, 30125 Venice; tel. 5241642; Dir Prof. G. CINQUE.

Interuniversity Centre for Venetian Studies: San Marco 2945, Ca' Loredan, 30124 Venice; tel. 5200996; Dir Prof. G. PADOAN.

Statistical Documentation Centre: Dorsoduro 3246, 30123 Venice; tel. 5298111; Dir Prof. R. VEDALDI

UNIVERSITÀ DEGLI STUDI 'GABRIELE D'ANNUNZIO' CHIETI PESCARA

Via dei Vestini 31, 66013 Chieti Scalo
Telephone: 0871-3551
E-mail: segreteriarettore@unich.it
Internet: www.unich.it
Founded 1965 as a private univ.; became a state univ. 1982
State control
Rector: Prof. FRANCO CUCCURULLO
Gen. Dir: Dr MARCO NAPOLEONE
Number of students: 19,000

DEANS

Faculty of Architecture: Prof. ALBERTO CLEMENTI
Faculty of Arts: Prof. STEFANO TRINCHESE
Faculty of Economics: Prof. ANNA MORGANTE
Faculty of Education: Prof. GAETANO BONETTA
Faculty of Foreign Languages and Literature: Prof. CARLO CONSANI
Faculty of Management: Prof. GIUSEPPE PAOLONE
Faculty of Mathematical, Physical and Natural Sciences: Prof. LEANDRO D'ALESSANDRO
Faculty of Medicine and Surgery: Prof. CARMINE DI ILIO
Faculty of Pharmacy: Prof. MICHELE VACCA
Faculty of Psychology: Prof. RAFFAELE CIAFARDONE
Faculty of Social Sciences: Prof. MICHELE CASCAVILLA
Faculty of Sports Science: Prof. MARIO FELACO

UNIVERSITÀ DEGLI STUDI 'MAGNA GRÆCIA' DI CATANZARO

Viale Europa, Località Germaneto, 88100 Catanzaro
Telephone: 0961-3694001
E-mail: rettore@unicz.it
Internet: www.unicz.it
Founded 1998
State control
Rector: Prof. FRANCESCO SAVERIO COSTANZO
Vice-Rector: Prof. LUIGI VENTURA
Admin. Dir: Dott. LUIGI GRANDINETTI
Number of students: 11,000

DEANS

Faculty of Law: Prof. LUIGI GRANDINETTI
Faculty of Medicine and Surgery: Prof. GIOVAMBATTISTA DE SARRO
Faculty of Pharmacy: Prof. DOMENICANTONIO ROTIROTI

UNIVERSITÀ DEGLI STUDI DEL MOLISE

Via de Sanctis, 86100 Campobasso
Telephone: 0874-4041
E-mail: amministrazione@cert.unimol.it
Internet: www.unimol.it
Founded 1982
Academic year: October to September
Rector: Prof. GIOVANNI CANNATA
Vice-Rector: Prof. SALVATORE PASSARELLA
Admin. Dir: Dott. VINCENZO LUCCHESE
Library Dir: Dott. VINCENZO LUCCHESE
Number of students: 10,331

DEANS

Faculty of Agriculture: Prof. EMANUELE MARCONI
Faculty of Economics: Prof. PAOLO DE VITA
Faculty of Engineering: Prof. DONATELLA CIALDEA
Faculty of Health Sciences: Prof. MAURIZIO TAGLIALATELA
Faculty of Human and Social Sciences: Prof. PAOLO MAURIELLO
Faculty of Law: Prof. GIANMARIA PALMIERI
Faculty of Mathematical, Physical and Natural Sciences: Prof. VINCENZO DE FELICE
Faculty of Medicine: Prof. GIOVANNANGELO ORIANI

UNIVERSITÀ DEGLI STUDI DEL SANNIO

Piazza Guerrazzi 1, 82100 Benevento
Telephone: 824-305001
E-mail: rettore@unisannio.it
Internet: www.unisannio.it
Founded 1998
State control
Rector: Prof. FILIPPO BENCARDINO
Admin. Dir: Dott. GAETANO TELESIO
Library of 28,000 vols, 350 journals

DEANS

Faculty of Economics and Business: Prof. MASSIMO SQUILLANTE
Faculty of Engineering: Prof. FILIPPO DE ROSSI
Faculty of Law: Prof. ANNA CLARA MONTI
Faculty of Mathematical, Physical and Natural Sciences: Prof. FRANCESCO MARIA GUADAGNO

UNIVERSITÀ DEGLI STUDI DELL'AQUILA

Via Giovanni Falcone 25, 67100 Coppito (AQ)
Telephone: 0862-432030
E-mail: webmaster@cc.univaq.it
Internet: www.univaq.it
Founded 1952
Rector: Prof. FERDINANDO DI ORIO
Admin. Dir: Dott. FILIPPO DEL VECCHIO
Library of 171,356 vols
Number of teachers: 600
Number of students: 20,000

DEANS

Faculty of Arts: Prof. GIANNINO DI TOMMASO
Faculty of Biotechnologies: Prof. SILVIA BISTI
Faculty of Economics: Prof. FABRIZIO POLITI
Faculty of Education: Prof. ANTONELLA GASBARRI
Faculty of Engineering: Prof. PIER UGO FOSCOLO
Faculty of Mathematical, Physical and Natural Sciences: Prof. PAOLA INVERARDI
Faculty of Medicine and Surgery: Prof. MARIA GRAZIA CIFONE
Faculty of Psychology: Prof. FERNANDA AMICARELLI
Faculty of Sports Science: Prof. LEILA FABIANI

UNIVERSITÀ DEGLI STUDI DELL'INSUBRIA

Via Ravasi 2, 21100 Varese
Telephone: 0332-219001
E-mail: rettore@uninsubria.it
Internet: www.uninsubria.eu
Founded 1998
Rector: Prof. RENZO DIONIGI
Vice-Rector in Como: Prof. GIORGIO CONETTI
Administrative Director: Dr MARINO BALZANI
Library Dir: ALESSANDRA BEZZI
Library of 81,570 vols, 648 journals, 13,000 electronic journals
Number of teachers: 393
Number of students: 9,546

DEANS

Faculty of Economics: Prof. MATTEO ROCCA
Faculty of Law: Prof. MARIA PAOLA VIVIANI SCHLEIN
Faculty of Medicine in Varese: Prof. FRANCESCO PASQUALI
Faculty of Sciences in Como: Prof. STEFANO SERRA CAPIZZANO
Faculty of Sciences in Varese: Prof. ALBERTO COEN PORISINI

UNIVERSITÀ DEGLI STUDI DELLA BASILICATA

Via Nazario Sauro 85, 85100 Potenza
Telephone: 0971-201111
E-mail: segreteriarettore@unibas.it
Internet: www.unibas.it
Founded 1982
Rector: Prof. MAURO FIORENTINO
Vice-Rector: Prof. GIOVANNI CARLO DI RENZO
Admin. Dir: Dott. MARIO GIANNONE CODIGLIONE
Librarians: Prof. CARLO MARIA SIMONETTI, Prof. GABOR KORCHMAROS
Library of 85,000 vols
Number of teachers: 307
Number of students: 4,845
Publications: *Basilicata Università*, *Collana 'Atti e Memorie'*, *Collana 'Strutture e Materiali'*, *Quaderni*

DEANS

Faculty of Agriculture: Prof. MICHELE PERNIOLA
Faculty of Engineering: Prof. IGNAZIO MARCELLO MANCINI
Faculty of Humanities and Philosophy: Prof. PASQUALE FRASCOLLA
Faculty of Mathematical, Physical and Natural Sciences: Prof. ONOFRIO MARIO DI VINCENZO
Faculty of Pharmacy: Prof. FAUSTINO BISACCIA

UNIVERSITÀ DEGLI STUDI DELLA TUSCIA

Via. S. Maria in Gradi 4, 01100 Viterbo
Telephone: 0761-3571
E-mail: infoperme@unitus.it
Internet: www3.unitus.it
Founded 1979
State control
Academic year: November to October
Rector: Prof. MARCO MANCINI
Vice-Rector: Prof. STEFANO GREGO
Admin. Dir: Dr GIOVANNI CUCULLO
Number of teachers: 320
Number of students: 10,000

DEANS

Faculty of Agriculture: Prof. BRUNO RONCHI
Faculty of Conservation of Cultural Heritage: Prof. ALFIO. CORTONESI
Faculty of Economics: Prof. ALESSANDRO RUGGIERI
Faculty of Mathematics, Physics and Natural Sciences: Prof. LUIGI BOSCO
Faculty of Modern Languages and Literature: Prof. GAETAO PLATANIA
Faculty of Political Sciences: Prof. MAURIZIO RIDOLFI

UNIVERSITÀ DEGLI STUDI DI BARI 'ALDO MORO'

Piazza Umberto I 1, 70121 Bari
Telephone: 080-311111
E-mail: urp@urp.uniba.it
Internet: www.uniba.it
Founded 1924
Rector: Prof. CORRADO PETROCELLI

Vice-Rector: Prof. AUGUSTO GARUCCIO
Admin. Dir: Dott. GIORGIO DE SANTIS

Number of teachers: 700
Number of students: 42,439

DEANS

Faculty of Agriculture: Prof. VITO NICOLA SAVINO
Faculty of Arts: Prof. GRAZIA DISTASO
Faculty of Biotechnology: Prof. LUIGI PALMIERI
Faculty of Economics: Prof. VITTORIO DELL'ATTI
Faculty of Economics (Taranto): Prof. BRUNO NOTARNICOLA
Faculty of Education: Prof. GIUSEPPE ELIA
Faculty of Foreign Languages and Literature: Prof. PASQUALE GUARAGNELLA
Faculty of Law: Prof. MARIO GIOVANNI GAROFALO
Faculty of Law (Taranto): Prof. ANTONIO FELICE URICCHIO
Faculty of Mathematical, Physical and Natural Sciences: Prof. PAOLO SPINELLI
Faculty of Mathematical, Physical and Natural Sciences (Taranto): Prof. SILVIA ROMANELLI
Faculty of Medicine and Surgery: Prof. ANTONIO QUARANTA
Faculty of Pharmacy: Prof. ROBERTO PERRONE
Faculty of Politics: Prof. ENNIO TRIGGIANI
Faculty of Veterinary Medicine: Prof. BUONAVOGLIA CANIO

UNIVERSITÀ DEGLI STUDI DI BERGAMO

Via Salvecchio 19, 24129 Bergamo
Telephone: 035-2052111
E-mail: postmaster@unibg.it
Internet: www.unibg.it

Founded 1968

Rector: Prof. STEFANO PALEARI
Vice-Rector: Prof. VALERIA UGAZIO
Admin. Dir: Dott. GIUSEPPE GIOVANELLI
Librarian: Dott. ENNIO FERRANTE

Library of 200,000 vols, 1,200 journals
Number of teachers: 211
Number of students: 6,317

DEANS

Faculty of Economics: Prof. LAURA VIGNANÒ
Faculty of Education: Prof. IVO LIZZOLA
Faculty of Engineering: Prof. PAOLO RIVA
Faculty of Foreign Languages and Literature: Prof. BRUNO CARTOSIO
Faculty of Humanities: Prof. CLAUDIO VILLA
Faculty of Law: Prof. BARBARA PEZZINI

PROFESSORS

Faculty of Economics:
- AMADUZZI, A., Business Administration
- ARCUCCI, F., International Trade and Finance
- BERTOCCHI, M. I., Financial Mathematics
- BIFFIGNANDI, S., Statistics Applied to Economics
- FENGHI, F., Commercial Law
- FERRI, P. E., Economic Analysis
- GAMBARELLI, G., General Mathematics
- GRAZIOLA, G., Economics of Enterprise
- LEONI, R., Labour Economics
- MASINI, M., Banking
- RENOLDI, A., Value Management
- SACCHETTO, C., Tax Law
- SPEDICATO, E., Operations Research
- TAGI, G., Industrial Operations Management
- TAGLIARINI, F., Commercial Penal Law

Faculty of Engineering:
- BUGINI, A., Industrial Management of Quality
- COLOMBI, R., Statistics and Probability
- PERDICHIZZI, A., Energetic Powerplants
- RIVA, R., Theoretical and Applied Mechanics
- SALANTI, A., Economics

Faculty of Foreign Languages and Literature:
- BELLER, M., German Language and Literature
- CASTOLDI, A., French Language and Literature II
- CERUTI, M., Epistemology
- CORONA, M., Anglo-American Languages and Literature
- GOTTI, M., History of the English Language
- LOCATELLI, A., English Language and Literature
- MARZOLA, A., English Language and Literature
- MIRANDOLA, G., French Language and Literature I
- MOLINARI, M. V., Germanic Philology
- MORELLI, G., Spanish Language and Literature
- PAPA, E., Modern and Contemporary History
- VILLA, C., Medieval and Humanist Philology

UNIVERSITÀ DEGLI STUDI DI BRESCIA

Piazza del Mercato 15, 25121 Brescia
Telephone: 030-29881
E-mail: ammcentr@cert.unibs.it
Internet: www.unibs.it

Founded 1982

Rector: Prof. SERGIO PECORELLI
Vice-Rector: Prof. DANIELE MARIOLI
Admin. Dir: Dott. ENRICO PERITI
Librarians: EUGENIO PELIZZARI (Economics and Law), Dott. MARCO BAZZOLI (Engineering), ENRICA VERONESI (Medicine and Surgery)

Number of teachers: 573
Number of students: 14,132

DEANS

Faculty of Economics: Prof. CLAUDIO TEODORI
Faculty of Engineering: Prof. ALDO ZENONI
Faculty of Law: Prof. ANTONELLO CALORE
Faculty of Medicine and Surgery: Prof. STEFANO MARIA GIULINI

UNIVERSITÀ DEGLI STUDI DI CAMERINO

Piazza Cavour 19/f, 62032 Camerino
Telephone: 0737-4011
E-mail: segreteria.rettore@unicam.it
Internet: www.unicam.it

Founded 1336; University status 1727
Academic year: November to October

Rector: Prof. FULVIO ESPOSITO
Vice-Rector: Prof. IPPOLITO ANTONINI
Deputy Rector for Int. Research: Prof. FLAVIO CORRADINI
Deputy Rector for Teaching: Prof. LUCIANO MISICI
Deputy Rector for Student Affairs: Prof. DANIELA ACCILI
Admin. Dir: Dott. LUIGI TAPANELLI
Librarian: SONIA CAVIRANI

Number of teachers: 301
Number of students: 10,055

DIRECTORS

School of Advanced Studies: Prof. CRISTINA MICELI
School of Architecture and Design: Prof. UMBERTO CAO
School of Bioscience and Biotechnology: Prof. CLAUDIO GUALERZI
School of Environmental Science: Prof. CARLO RENIERI
School of Law: Prof. IGNAZIO BUTI
School of Pharmaceutical Sciences and Health Products: Prof. SAURO VITTORI
School of Science and Technology: Prof. ROBERTO BALLINI
School of Veterinary Medicine: Prof. GIACOMO RENZONI

ATTACHED INSTITUTES

School of Specialization in Animal Health, Livestock and Animal Production: Dir Prof. ANDREA SPATERNA.

School of Specialization in Civil Law: Dir Prof. LUCIA RUGGERI.

School of Specialization in Clinical Biochemistry: Dir Prof. ROSALIA TACCONI.

School of Specialization in Hospital Pharmacy: Dir Prof. CARLO POLIDORI.

School of Specialization for the Legal Professions: Dir Prof. Avv. MAURIZIO CINELLI

UNIVERSITÀ DEGLI STUDI DI CASSINO

Via G. Marconi 10, 03043 Cassino (Frosinone)
Telephone: 0776-2991
E-mail: info@unicas.it
Internet: www.unicas.it

Founded 1979
State control

Rector: CIRO ATTAIANESE
Vice-Rector: FRANCO DE VIVO
Admin. Dir: ASCENZO FARENTI

Number of teachers: 334
Number of students: 11,415

DEANS

Faculty of Arts and Philosophy: SEBASTIANO GENTILE
Faculty of Economics: Prof. ENRICA IANNUCCI
Faculty of Engineering: Prof. GIOVANNI BETTA
Faculty of Law: Prof. EDOARDO ALES
Faculty of Sports Sciences: Prof. GIOVANNI CAPELLI

UNIVERSITÀ DEGLI STUDI DI CATANIA

Piazza dell' Università 2, 95124 Catania
Telephone: 095-321112
E-mail: rettore@unict.it
Internet: www.unict.it

Founded 1434

Rector: Prof. ANTONINO RECCA
Vice-Rector: Prof. MARIA LUISA CARNAZZA
Admin. Dir: Dott. LUCIO MAGGIO

Number of teachers: 1,517
Number of students: 53,674

DEANS

Faculty of Agriculture: Prof. AGATINO RUSSO
Faculty of Architecture: Prof. CARLO TRUPPI
Faculty of Arts: Prof. ENRICO IACHELLO
Faculty of Economics: Prof. CARMELO BUTTÀ
Faculty of Education: Prof. FEBRONIA ELIA
Faculty of Engineering: Prof. LUIGI FORTUNA
Faculty of Foreign Languages and Literature: Prof. NUNZIO FAMOSO
Faculty of Law: Prof. VINCENZO DI CATALDO
Faculty of Mathematical, Physical and Natural Sciences: Prof. GUIDO LI VOLSI
Faculty of Medicine and Surgery: Prof. FRANCESCO BASILE
Faculty of Pharmacy: Prof. GIUSEPPE RONSISVALLE
Faculty of Political Science: Prof. GIUSEPPE BARONE

UNIVERSITÀ DEGLI STUDI DI FIRENZE

Piazza San Marco 4, 50121 Florence
Telephone: 055-27571
E-mail: urp@unifi.it
Internet: www.unifi.it

Founded 1321
Academic year: September to August

Rector: Prof. ALBERTO TESI
Vice-Rector for Finance: Prof. GIACOMO POGGI
Vice-Rector for Scientific Research: Prof. ELISABETTA CERBAI
Vice-Rector for Teaching and Student Affairs: Prof. ANNA NOZZOLI
Vice-Rector for Technological Transfer: Prof. MARCO BELLANDI
Admin. Dir: Dott. MICHELE OREFICE
Dir of Library System: Dott. GIULIA MARAVIGLIA

Number of teachers: 2,236
Number of students: 59,847

DEANS

Faculty of Agriculture: Prof. GIUSEPPE SURICO
Faculty of Architecture: Prof. SAVERIO MECCA
Faculty of Arts: Prof. RICCARDO BRUSCAGLI
Faculty of Economics: Prof. FRANCESCO GIUNTA
Faculty of Education: Prof. SIMONETTA ULIVIERI
Faculty of Engineering: Prof. STEFANO MANETTI
Faculty of Law: Prof. PAOLO CAPPELLINI
Faculty of Mathematical, Physical and Natural Sciences: Prof. EMILIO MARIO CASTELLUCCI
Faculty of Medicine and Surgery: Prof. GIAN FRANCO GENSINI
Faculty of Pharmacy: Prof. SERGIO PINZAUTI
Faculty of Political Sciences: Prof. FRANCA MARIA ALACEVICH
Faculty of Psychology: Prof. ANDREA SMORTI

UNIVERSITÀ DEGLI STUDI DI FOGGIA

Via A. Gramsci 89/91, 71122 Foggia
Telephone: 08831-338446
E-mail: urp@unifg.it
Internet: www.unifg.it

Founded 1999
State control

Rector: Prof. GIULIANO VOLPE
Deputy Rector: Prof. ANDREA DI LIDDO
Admin. Dir: Dott. COSTANTINO QUARTUCCI

Library of 80,000 vols, 780 journals, 4,300 online journals
Number of teachers: 198
Number of students: 11,000

DEANS

Faculty of Agriculture: Prof. AGOSTINO SEVI
Faculty of Arts and Philosophy: Prof. GIOVANNI CIPRIANI
Faculty of Economics: Prof. ISABELLA VARRASO
Faculty of Education: Prof. FRANCA PINTO MINERVA
Faculty of Law: Prof. MAURIZIO RICCI
Faculty of Medicine and Surgery: Prof. MATTEO DI BIASE

UNIVERSITÀ DEGLI STUDI DI GENOVA

Via Balbi 5, 16126 Genoa
Telephone: 010-20991
E-mail: orientamento@unige.it
Internet: www.unige.it

Founded 1670
Academic year: November to October

Rector: Prof. GIACOMO DEFERRARI
Vice-Rector: Prof. MAURIZIO MARTELLI
Admin. Dir: ROSA GATTI

Number of teachers: 1,719
Number of students: 40,125

Publications: *Annuario dell'Università di Genova* (sections on research and teaching units, each annual), *Genuense Atenaeum* (6 a year)

DEANS

Faculty of Architecture: STEFANO FRANCESCO MUSSO
Faculty of Arts: FRANCESCO SURDICH
Faculty of Economics: PIER MARIA FERRANDO
Faculty of Education: GUIDO FRANCO AMORETTI
Faculty of Engineering: PAOLA GIRDINIO
Faculty of Foreign Languages and Literature: SERGIO POLI
Faculty of Law: PAOLO COMANDUCCI
Faculty of Mathematical, Physical and Natural Sciences: GIANCARLO ALBERTELLI
Faculty of Medicine and Surgery: GIANCARLO TORRE
Faculty of Pharmacy: ALESSANDRO BALBI
Faculty of Political Sciences: GIOVANNI BATTISTA VARNIER

UNIVERSITÀ DEGLI STUDI DI MACERATA

Piaggia della Torre 8, 62100 Macerata
Telephone: 0733-2581
E-mail: rettorato@unimc.it
Internet: www.unimc.it

Founded 1290

Rector: Prof. LUIGI LACCHÈ
Vice-Rector: Prof. ROSA MARISA BORRACCINI
Admin. Dir: Dott. MAURO GIUSTOZZI

Number of teachers: 300
Number of students: 15,000

DEANS

Faculty of Communication Sciences: Prof. BARBARA POJAGHI
Faculty of Cultural Heritage: Prof. ENZO CATANI
Faculty of Economics: Prof. ANTONELLA PAOLINI
Faculty of Education: Prof. GIUSEPPE ROSSI
Faculty of Humanities and Philosophy: Prof. GIANFRANCO PACI
Faculty of Law: Prof. ALBERTO FEBBRAJO
Faculty of Political Science: Prof. FRANCESCO ADORNATO

UNIVERSITÀ DEGLI STUDI DI MESSINA

Piazza Salvatore Pugliatti 1, 98122 Messina
Telephone: 090-6761
E-mail: rettorato@unime.it
Internet: www.unime.it

Founded 1548
State control
Languages of instruction: Italian, English
Academic year: October to June

Rector: Prof. PIETRO NAVARRA
Deputy Vice-Rector: Prof. EMANUELE SCRIBANO
Admin. Dir: Prof. FRANCO DE DOMENICO

Number of teachers: 1,300
Number of students: 26,000

DEANS

Faculty of Arts and Humanities: Prof. VINCENZO FERA
Faculty of Economics: Prof. LUIGI FERLAZZO NATOLI
Faculty of Education: Prof. ANTONINO PENNISI
Faculty of Engineering: Prof. SIGNORINO GALVAGNO
Faculty of Law: Prof. SALVATORE BERLINGÒ
Faculty of Mathematics, Physics and Natural Sciences: Prof. MARIO GATTUSO
Faculty of Medicine: Prof. EMANUELE SCRIBANO
Faculty of Pharmacy: Prof. GIUSEPPE BISIGNANO
Faculty of Politics: Prof. ANDREA ROMANO
Faculty of Veterinary Medicine: Prof. VINCENZO CHIOFALO

UNIVERSITÀ DEGLI STUDI DI MILANO

Via Festa del Perdono 7, 20122 Milan
Telephone: 2-503111
E-mail: webmaster@unimi.it
Internet: www.unimi.it

Founded 1923
public control
Academic year: October to September

Rector: Prof. ENRICO DECLEVA
Vice-Rector: Prof. DARIO CASATI
Vice-Rector for Research: Prof. ALBERTO MANTOVANI
Pro-Rector for Postgraduate Education and Int. Affairs: Prof. MARINO REGINI
Pro-Rector for Research: Prof. ALBERTO MANTOVANI
Admin. Dir: ALBERTO SILVANI
Library Dir: Dott. MAURIZIO DI GIROLAMO

Number of teachers: 716
Number of students: 63,000

Publication: *Sistema Università* (4 a year, online, www.unimi.it/news/38106.htm)

DEANS

Faculty of Agriculture: Prof. MARISA PORRINI
Faculty of Arts: Prof. GIULIANA ALBINI
Faculty of Law: Prof. ALESSANDRO ALBISETTI
Faculty of Mathematical, Physical and Natural Sciences: Prof. PAOLA CAMPADELLI
Faculty of Medicine and Surgery: Prof. VIRGILIO FERRUCCIO FERRARIO
Faculty of Motor Sciences: Prof. ARSENIO VEICSTEINAS
Faculty of Pharmacy: Prof. CESARE SIRTORI
Faculty of Political Sciences: Prof. DANIELE CHECCHI
Faculty of Veterinary Medicine: Prof. GIORGIO POLI

PROFESSORS

Faculty of Agriculture (Via Celoria 2, 20133 Milan; tel. 02-50316500; e-mail preside .agraria@unimi.it; internet www.unimi.it/ ateneo/facol/agraria.htm):

ANDREONI, V., Agricultural Microbiology
BASSI, D., Fruit Farming
BELLI, G., Plant Pathology
BIANCO, P. A., Plant Pathology
BODRIA, L., Agricultural Mechanics
BONOMI, F., Biochemistry
CASATI, D., Agrofood Economy
CASTELLI, G., Agricultural Mechanics
CASTROVILLI, C. M., Zooculture
COCUCCI, M., Physiology of Farmed Plants
CORTESI, P., Plant Pathology
CROVETTO, G. M., Animal Nutrition and Foodstuffs
DE WRACHIEN, D., Irrigation and Drainage
DESIMONI, E., Analytical Chemistry
DURANTI, M. M., Biochemistry
ECCHER, T., General Arboriculture
ELIAS, G., Environmental Technical Physics
FRISIO, D. G., Rural Economics and Surveying
GALLI, A., Foods Microbiology
GANDOLFI, C., Agricultural and Forest Hydraulics
GARLASCHI, F. M., Vegetable Physiology
GASPARETTO, E., Agricultural Mechanization
GAVAZZI, G., Plant Genetic Improvement

GENEVINI, P., Soil Chemistry
GIURA, R., Agricultural Hydraulics
GREPPI, M., Hydraulic Systems, Forestry
LOCATELLI, D. P., General and Applied Entomology
LOZZIA, G. C., General and Applied Entomology
LUCISANO, M., Food Science and Technology
MAGGIORE, T., Herbaceous Farming
MANACHINI, P., General Microbiology
MANNINO, S., Chemico-Physical and Sensory Analysis of Food
MERLINI, L., Organic Chemistry
MONDELLI, R., Organic Chemistry
PAGANI, S., Enzymology
PELLEGRINO, L. M., Food Science and Technology
PIERGIOVANNI, L., Food Science and Technology
POLELLI, M., Rural Evaluation
POMPEI, C., Food Technology Processes
PORRINI, M., Physiology
PRETOLANI, R., Rural Economics and Surveying
QUARONI, S., Vegetable Pathology
RAGG, E. M., Organic Chemistry
RESMINI, P., Agricultural Industry
ROSSI, M., Food Science and Technology
SACCHI, G. A., Organic Chemistry
SALAMINI, F., Genetics and Biotechnology
SANGIORGI, F., Rural and Forest Construction
SCHIRALDI, A., Physical Chemistry
SCIENZA, A., General Arboriculture and Tree Cultivation
SORLINI, C., Agricultural and Forest Microbiology
SUCCI, G., Special Animal Husbandry
SÜSS, L., Agricultural Entomology
TANO, F., Herbaceous Farming
TATEO, F., Food Science and Technology
TESTOLIN, G., Human Food and Nutrition
TOCCOLINI, A., Rural and Forest Construction
VOLONTERIO, G., Agricultural Industry
ZOCCHI, G., Food Science and Technology

Faculty of Law (Via Festa del Perdono 7, 20122 Milan; tel. 02-50312400; e-mail presidenza.giurisprudenza@unimi.it; internet www.unimi.it/ateneo/facol/giurisp.htm):

ALBISETTI, A., Ecclesiastical Law
AMODIO, E., Procedural Penal Law
ANGIOLINI, V., Constitutional Law
BARIATTI, S., International Law
BENATTI, F., Institutions of Private Law
BOSCHIERO, N., International Law
CANDIAN, A., Comparative Private Law
CANTARELLA, E., Institutions of Roman Law
CARINCI, M. T., Labour Law
CARNEVALI, U., Institutions of Private Law
CASTAGNOLA, A., Civil Procedural Law
CASUSCELLI, G., Ecclesiastical Law
CAVALLONE, B., Civil Procedural Law
CONDINANZI, M., International Law
D'AMICO, M. E., Constitutional Law
DE NOVA, G., Civil Law
DENOZZA, F., Commercial Law
DI RENZO, M. G., History of Italian Law
DOLCINI, E., Penal Law
DOMINIONI, O., Procedural Penal Comparative Law
FERRARI, E., Administrative Law
FERRARI, S., Canon Law
FERRARI, V., Sociology of Law
FLORIDA, G., Comparative Public Law
FRASSI, P. A., Commercial Law
GAFFURI, G., Tributary Law
GALANTINI, M. N., Procedural Penal Law
GAMBARO, A., Comparative Private Law
GITTI, G., Institutions of Private Law
GNOLI, F., Roman Law
GOISIS, G., Political Economy
GRECO, G., Administrative Law
GREZZI, M. L., Philosophy of Law
GUERCI, C. M., Political Economy
JAEGER, P., Commercial Law
JORI, M., Philosophy of Law
LANCELLOTTI, E., Financial Science
LUZZATI, C. R., Philosophy of Law
LUZZATTO, R., International Law
MARINUCCI, G., Penal Law
MASSETTO, G., History of Italian Law
MERLIN, E., Civil Procedural Law
MORELLO, U. M., Private Law
NASCIMBENE, B., European Community Law
PADOA SCHIOPPA, A., History of Italian Law
PALIERO, C., Penal Law
PARISI, F., Institutions of Private Law
PELOSI, A. C., Institutions of Private Law
PERICU, G., Administrative Law
PISANI, M., Procedural Penal Law
POCAR, F., International Law
POLARA, G., Institutions of Roman Law
RICCI, E., Bankruptcy Law
RIMINI, E., Commercial Law
ROSSIGNOLI, B., Economics of Credit Institutions
SACCHI, R., Commercial Law
SALETTI, A., Civil Procedural Law
SANTA MARIA, A., International Law
SPAGNUOLO VIGORITA, L., Labour Law
TENELLA SILLANI, C., Institutions of Private Law
TREVES, T., International Private and Procedural Law
TRIMARCHI, F., Administrative Law
TRIMARCHI, P., Civil Law
VIGANÒ, F., Penal Law
VILLA, G., Institutions of Private Law
VILLATA, R., Administrative Law
VIOLINI, L., Constitutional Law
VITALI, E. G., Ecclesiastical Law
ZANON, N., Constitutional Law

Faculty of Letters and Philosophy (Via Festa del Perdono 7, 20122 Milan; tel. 02-50312701; e-mail elio.franzini@unimi.it; internet www.unimi.it/ateneo/facol/letfil.htm):

ALBINI, G., Medieval History
ANTONIELLI, L., History of Political Institutions
ANZI, A., History of the English Theatre
BARONI, M. F., Palaeography
BEJOR, G., Classical Archaeology
BERRA, C., Italian Literature
BIANCHI, E., Geography
BIGALLI, D., History of Philosophy
BIGNAMI, M., English Language and Literature
BOCCALI, G., Sanskrit Language and Literature
BOELLA, L., Moral Philosophy
BOLOGNA, M., Archives, Bibliography and Library Science
BOLOGNA, M. P., Glottology and Linguistics
BONOMI, A., Philosophy of Language
BONOMI, I., Italian Linguistics
BOSISIO, P., Dramatic Arts
BRAMBILLA, E., Modern History
BRIOSCHI, F., History of Literary Criticism
BROGI, G., History of the Russian Language
BRUTI LIBERATI, L., Modern History
CADIOLI, A. V., Contemporary Italian Literature
CAIZZI, F., History of Ancient Philosophy
CANAVERO, A., Modern History
CANZIANI, G., History of Philosophy
CAPRA, C., Modern History
CASALEGNO, P., Philosophy and Theory of Languages
CATTANEO, M. T., Spanish Language and Literature
CAVAJONI, G., Latin Language and Literature
CERCIGNANI, F., German Language and Literature
CHIAPPA, M. L., Medieval History
CHITTOLINI, G., Medieval History
CIANCI, G., English Language and Literature
CICALESE, M. L., Theory and History of Historiography
COLOMBO, M., French
COMBA, R., Medieval History
COMETTA, M., German Philology
CONCA, F., History of the Greek Language
CORDANO, F., Greek History
D'AGOSTINO, A., Romance Philology
DAVERIO, G., Greek History
DE ANGELIS, V., Humanistic Philology
DECLEVA, E., Contemporary History
DE FRANCESCO, A., Modern History
DEGRADA, F., History of Modern and Contemporary Music
DE MARINIS, R. C., Early and Recorded History
DEVECCHI, P., History of Modern Art
DI SALVO, M. G., Slavonic Philology
DOGLIO, M., French Literature
DONATI, C., History of the Ancient Italian States
DONINI, P., History of Ancient Philosophy
FIACCADORI, G., Christian and Medieval Archaeology
FORABOSCHI, D., Roman History
FRANZINI, E., Aesthetics
FUMAGALLI, M. J., History of Medieval Philosophy
GALLAZZI, C., Papyrology
GIACOMELLI, R., Glottology and Linguistics
GIORELLO, G., Philosophy of Science
GORI, G., History of Modern Philosophy
GUALANDRI, I., Latin Literature
IAMARTINO, G., English
LANARO, G. V., History of Philosophy
LEHNUS, L. A., Classical Philology
MARI, M., Italian Literature
MASINI, A., Italian Linguistics
MAZZOCCA, F., Museology, Art Criticism and Restoration Criticism
MENEGHETTI, M. L., Romance Philology
MERLO, G., History of the Medieval Church and Heresy
MERZARIO, R., Economic History
MICHELI, G., History of Science and Technology
MILANINI, C., Italian Literature
MODENESI, M., French Literature
MONTALEONE, C., Moral Philosophy
MONTECCHI, G., Bibliography and Archive and Library Science
MORGANA, S., Italian Language History
NEGRI, A., History of Modern Art
NISSIM, L., French Language and Literature
ORLANDI, G., Medieval Latin Literature
PAGETTI, C., English Language and Literature
PERASSI, E., Hispano-American Languages and Literatures
PETTOELLO, R., History of Philosophy
PEYRONEL, S., Medieval and Early Modern History
PIACENTINI, P., Egyptology and Coptic Civilization
PIRETTO, G. P., Slavic Studies
PIVA, P., History of Medieval Art
PUNZO, M., Modern History
RAMBALDI, E., Moral Philosophy
ROSA, G., Contemporary Italian Literature
RUMI, G., Contemporary History
SAMPIETRO, L., Anglo-American Languages and Literatures
SAPELLI, G., Economic History
SCARAMELLINI, G., Geography
SCARAMUZZA, G., Aesthetics
SCARAMUZZA, M. E., Spanish Literature
SINI, C., Theoretical Philosophy
SPAGGIARI, W., Italian Literature
SPERA, F., Italian Literature
TREVES, A. L., Geography
VALOTA, B., History of Eastern Europe

VISMARA, P., History of Christianity and the Churches
ZANETTO, G., Greek Language and Literature
ZECCHI, S., Aesthetics
ZERBI, M. C., Geography

Faculty of Medicine (Via Festa del Perdono 7, 20122 Milan; tel. 02-50312360; e-mail preside.medicina@unimi.it; internet www.unimi.it/ateneo/facol/medchir.htm):

AGUS, G. B., Vascular Surgery
ALESSI, E., Dermatology
ALLEGRA, L., Diseases of the Respiratory System
ALLEVI, P., Biochemistry
ALTAMURA, A. C., Psychiatry
ALTOMARE, G., Dermatology
ANASTASIA, M., Chemistry and Biochemical Propaedeutics
AUSTONI, E., Urology
AUXILIA, F., Hygiene
BA, G., Psychiatry
BALDISSERA, F. G., Human Physiology
BALSARI, A., General Pathology
BEK PECCOZ, P., Endocrinology
BELLINI, T., Applied Physics (Arts, Environment, Biology and Medicine)
BERTAZZI, P. A., Industrial Medicine
BIANCHI PORRO, G., Gastroenterology
BIGLIOLI, P., Cardiac Surgery
BLASI, F. B., Diseases of the Respiratory System
BOCK, G., History of Medicine
BOLIS, G., Obstetrics and Gynaecology
BORTOLANI, E., General Surgery
BRAGA, P., Pharmacology
BRESOLIN, N., Neurology
BRESSANI DOLDI, S., General Surgery
BRUSATI, R., Maxillofacial Surgery
BUSACCA, M., Obstetrics and Gynaecology
CABITZA, P., Orthopaedics and Traumatology
CAIRO, G., General Pathology
CAJONE, F., General Pathology
CANTALAMESSA, L., Internal Medicine
CAPETTA, P., Obstetrics and Gynaecology
CAPPELLINI, M. D., Internal Medicine
CAPUTO, R., Dermatology
CARACCIOLO, E., Clinical Psychology
CARRASSI, A., Special Odontostomatological Pathology
CARRUBA, M., Pharmacology
CATTANEO, M. N., Internal Medicine
CAVAGNA, G., Human Physiology
CAVAGNINI, F., Endocrinology
CAVALLARI, P., Physiology
CESARANI, A., Audiology
CESTARO, B. A., Biological Chemistry
CHIESARA, E., Toxicology
CHIGORNO, V. L., Clinical Biochemistry and Molecular Biology
CIANCAGLINI, R., Clinical Gnathology
CICARDI, M., Internal Medicine
CLEMENTI, F., Cellular and Molecular Pharmacology
CLERICI, M. S., General Pathology
COGGI, G., Pathological Anatomy and Histology
COLOMBI, A., Industrial Medicine
COLOMBO, M., Internal Medicine
COMI, P., General Pathology
CONTE, D., Gastroenterology
CORNALBA, G., Imaging and Radiotherapy Diagnostics
CORTELLARO, M., Internal Medicine
CORTI, M., Medical Physics
CROSIGNANI, P., Obstetrics and Gynaecology
CROSTI, C., Dermatology
CUSI, D. M., Nephrology
D'ANGELO, E., Human Physiology
DE FRANCHIS, R., Gastroenterology
DECARLI, A., Medical Statistics
DELLE FAVE, A., General Psychology
DESIDERIO, M. A., General Pathology
DI FIORE, P. P., General Pathology
DI GIULIO, A. M., Pharmacology
DONATELLI, F., Cardiac Surgery
DUBINI, F., Microbiology
FANTINI, F., Rheumatology
FARGION, S. R., Internal Medicine
FARNETI, A., Forensic Medicine
FARRONATO, G., Odontostomatological Diseases
FASSATI, L. R., General Surgery
FEDELE, L., Obstetrics and Gynaecology
FERRARIO, V. F., Human Anatomy
FERRERO, M. E., General Pathology
FIORENTINI, C., Cardiology
FOÀ, V., Industrial Hygiene
FOSCHI, D., General Surgery
GABRIELLI, L., Vascular Surgery
GAINI, S. M., Neurosurgery
GALLI, M., Infectious Diseases
GALLI, M. G., Hygiene
GALLUS, G. V., Medical Statistics and Biometrics
GATTINONI, L., Anaesthesiology and Resuscitation
GELMETTI, C., Dermatology
GHIDONI, R., Biological Chemistry
GIANNI, A., Medical Oncology
GINELLI, E., General Biology
GIOIA, M. A., Human Anatomy
GIOVANNINI, M., Paediatrics
GRANDI, M. A., Forensic Medicine
GROPPETTI, A., Pharmacology
GUAZZI, M., Cardiology
GUIDOBONO CAVALCHIN, F., Pharmacology
IAPICHINO, G., Anaesthesiology
INVERNIZZI, G., Psychiatry
LAMBERTENGHI DELILIERS, G., Internal Medicine
LARIZZA, L., Medical Genetics
LEDDA, M., Histology
LENTI, C., Child Neuropsychiatry
LEONETTI, G., Medical Semiology and Methodology
LODI, F., Forensic Toxicology
LUCIGNANI, G., Imaging and Radiotherapy Diagnostics
MAGRINI, F., Internal Medicine
MALCOVATI, M., Molecular Biology
MALLIANI, A., Internal Medicine
MANNUCCI, P. M., Internal Medicine
MANTOVANI, A., General Pathology
MARIANI, C., Neurology
MARIOTTI, M., Physiology
MARONI, M., Industrial Medicine
MASSIMINI, F., General Psychology
MATTINA, R., Microbiology
MATTURRI, L., Pathological Anatomy and Histology
MELZI D'ERIL, G., Clinical Biochemistry and Molecular Biology
MEOLA, G., Neurology
MERONI, P., Internal Medicine
MEZZETTI, M., Thoracic Surgery
MILANESI, G., Cellular Biology
MILANI, F., Radiotherapy
MOJA, E., General Psychology
MONTORSI, M., General Surgery
MORABITO, A., Medical Statistics
MORACE, G., Microbiology and Clinical Microbiology
MORGANTI, A., Internal Medicine
MORONI, M. E., Infectious Diseases
MÜLLER, E., Pharmacology
NICOLIN, A. N., Pharmacology
ORECCHIA, R., Radiotherapy
ORZALESI, N., Ophthalmology
OTTAVIANI, F., Otorhinolaryngology
PAGANI, M., Internal Medicine
PAGANO, A., Hygiene
PARDI, G., Obstetrics and Gynaecology
PELICCI, P. G., General Pathology
PERETTI, G., Orthopaedics and Traumatology
PERRELLA, M., Physical Biochemistry
PODDA, M., Internal Medicine
POLI, M., General Psychology
PONTIROLI, A., Internal Medicine
PRINCIPI, N., Paediatrics
RATIGLIA, R., Ophthalmology
RIVA, E., General and Specialist Paediatrics
ROCCO, F., Urology
RONCALLI, M., Pathological Anatomy
RONCHETTI, F., Chemistry and Biochemical Propaedeutics
RONCHI, E., Forensic Medicine
ROVIARO, G. C., General Surgery
SALVATO, A., Orthognathodontics
SAMBATARO, G., Otorhinolaryngology
SANTAMBROGIO, L., Thoracic Surgery
SANTANIELLO, E., Chemistry and Biochemical Propaedeutics
SANTORO, F., Odontostomatology
SCALABRINO, G., General Pathology
SCARONE, S., Psychiatry
SCORZA, R., Clinical Immunology and Allergology
SCORZA, R., General Surgery
SETTEMBRINI, P., Vascular Surgery
SICCARDI, A., General Biology
SMIRNE, S., Neurology
SONNINO, S., Biological Chemistry
SPINNLER, H., Neurology
STEFANI, M., Anatomy and Pathological Histology
STROHMENGER, L., Pedodontics
SURACE, A., Orthopaedics and Traumatology
TAROLO, G. L., Nuclear Medicine
TASCHIERI, A., General Surgery
TEALDI, D. G., Vascular Surgery
TENCHINI, M. L. G., General Biology
TETTAMANTI, G., Human Systematic Biochemistry
TRABUCCHI, E., General Surgery
VAGO, G., Pathological Anatomy
VERGANI, C., Gerontology and Geriatrics
VIALE, G., Pathological Anatomy and Histology
VICENTINI, L., Pharmacology
VILLA, M. L., Immunology
WEINSTEIN, R., Parodontology
ZANETTI, A., Hygiene
ZOCCHI, L., Physiology

Faculty of Motor Sciences (Via Kramer 4A, 20129 Milan; tel. 02-50315151; e-mail scienze.motorie@unimi.it; internet www.unimi.it/ateneo/facol/scmot.htm):

CARANDENTE, F., Internal Medicine
FIORILLI, A., Applied Dietetics
LUZI, L., Physiology
PETRUCCIOLI, M. G., Human Anatomy
PIZZINI, G., Human Anatomy
SFORZA, C., Human Anatomy
VEICSTEINAS, A., Physiology
VENERANDO, B., Biochemistry

Faculty of Pharmacy (Viale Balzaretti 9, 20133 Milan; tel. 02-50318402; e-mail presidenza.farmacia@unimi.it; internet www.unimi.it/ateneo/facol/farmacia.htm):

ABBRACHIO, M. P., Pharmacology
ALBINATI, A., General and Inorganic Chemistry
BARLOCCO, D., Pharmaceutical Chemistry
BECCALLI, E., Organic Chemistry
BERINGHELLI, T., General and Inorganic Chemistry
BERRA, B., Biological Chemistry
BOMBIERI, G., Drug Analysis
CARINI, M., Pharmaceutical Chemistry
CASTANO, P., Human Anatomy
CATAPANO, A. L., Pharmacology
CATTABENI, F., Applied Pharmacology
CATTANEO, E., Pharmacology
CELOTTI, F., General Pathology
CESAROTTI, E., General and Inorganic Chemistry
COLONNA, S., Organic Chemistry
CORSINI, A., Pharmacology
D'ALFONSO, G., General and Inorganic Chemistry

DALLA CROCE, P., Heterocyclic Chemistry
DE AMICI, M., Pharmaceutical Chemistry
DE GIULI MORGHEN, C., General Microbiology
DE MICHELI, C., Pharmaceutical and Toxicological Chemistry
DEL PRA, A., General and Inorganic Chemistry
FERRI, V., Pharmaceutical and Toxicological Chemistry
FOLCO, G., Pharmacology and Pharmacognosy
FRANCESCHINI, G., Pharmacology
GALLI, C., Pharmacological Tests and Measuring
GALLI, C. L., Pharmacology
GAVEZZOTTI, A., Physical Chemistry
GAZZANIGA, A., Applied Pharmaceutical Technology
GELMI, M. L., Organic Chemistry
MAFFEI FACINO, R., Drug Analysis
MAGGI, A. C., Pharmacology
MONTANARI, L., Pharmaceutical Technology, Socioeconomy and Legislation
MOTTA, M., General Physiology
PALLAVICINI, M., Pharmaceutical Chemistry
PIVA, F., Physiology
POCAR, D., Organic Chemistry
RACAGNI, G., Pharmacology and Pharmacognosy
SIRTORI, C., Clinical Pharmacology
SPARATORE, A., Pharmacological Chemistry
STRADI, R., Physical Methods in Organic Chemistry
TARAMELLI, D., General Pathology
TOMÈ, F., Pharmaceutical Biology
TREMOLI, E., Pharmacology
VALOTI, E., Pharmaceutical Chemistry

Faculty of Political Sciences (Via Conservatorio 7, 20122 Milan; tel. 02-50321000; e-mail presidenza.scienze.politiche@unimi.it; internet www.unimi.it/ateneo/facol/scpol.htm):

ALBERICI, A., Economics of Credit Institutions
ANTONIOLI, M., Contemporary History
BARBA NAVARETTI, G., Political Economy
BECCALLI, B. Z., Sociology of Economic and Labour Processes
BERNAREGGI, G. M., Public Economy
BESUSSI, A., Political Philosophy
BILANCIA, P., Institutions of Public Law
BOGNETTI, G., Financial Sciences
BORDOGNA, L., Sociology of Economic and Labour Processes
CAFARI PANICO, R., European Community Law
CALVI, M. V., Spanish Language and Translation
CELLA, G. P., Economic Sociology
CHECCHI, D., Political Economy
CHIARINI, R., History of Political Parties and Political Movements
CHIESI, A. M., General Sociology
CLERICI, R., International Private Law
DE CARLI, P. G., Economics and Law
DE MARCO, E., Institutions of Public Law
DONZELLI, F., Political Economy
ESCOBAR, R., Political Philosophy
FACCHI, A., Philosophy of Law
FERRARA, M., Political Science
FERRARI, A., Contemporary History
FERRARI, P. A., Statistics
FLORIO, M., Financial Science
FRIGO, M., International Law
GALEOTTI, M. D., Political Economy
GANINO, M., Comparative Public Law
GARAVELLO, O., Economic Politics
GARZONE, G. E., English
ICHINO, P., Labour Law
ISENBURG, T., Political and Economic Geography
ITALIA, V., Institutions of Public Law
JULLION, M. C., French Language and Translation
LACAITA, G. C., Contemporary History
LAMBERTI ZANARDI, P., International Law
LAVAGNINO, A., Chinese and South East Asian Languages and Literatures
LEONINI, L., Sociology of Cultural and Communicative Processes
LIVORSI, F., History of Political Doctrine
LUPONE, A. M. G., International Law
MARAFFI, M., General Sociology
MARTELLI, P., Political Science
MARTINELLI, A., Political Science
MAURI, A., Economics of Credit Institutions
MAZZOLENI, F., Sociology of Cultural and Communicative Processes
MISSALE, A., Political Economy
MOIOLI, A., Economic History
MOLTENI, C., Japanese and Korean Languages and Literatures
MOSS, D. M., Demo-Etno-Anthropology
NICOLINI, G., Statistics
OLLA, M. P., History of International Relations
PEDRAZZI, M., International Law
PILOTTI, L., Economics and Management Studies
REGALIA, I., Sociology of Economic and Labour Processes
REGINI, M., Industrial Relations
REGONINI, G., Political Science
RIMINI, C. P., Institutions of Private Law
RIOSA, A., Contemporary History
RIVOLTA, G. C., Commercial Law
RONFANI, P., Juridical Sociology of Deviance and Social Change
RUFFINI, M. L., Comparative Private Law
SALVATI, M. A., Political Economy
SANTONI, M., Public Economy
SEGATTI, P., Political Phenomena and Sociology
TURSI, A., Labour Law
VENTURINI, G., International Law
VIARENGO, I., International Law
VIVAN, I., English Literature
ZICCARDI, F. E., Comparative Private Law

Faculty of Sciences (Via Saldini 50, 20133 Milan; tel. 02-50316001; e-mail presidenza .scienze@unimi.it; internet www.unimi.it/ateneo/facol/smfn.htm):

ACERBI, E., Physics Experiments
ANNUNZIATA, R., Organic Chemistry
APOLLONI, B., Informatics
ARDIZZONE, S., Physical Chemistry
ARTIOLI, G., Mineralogy
BAMBUSI, D. P., Mathematical Physics
BELLINI, G., Physics Experiments
BELLOBONO, I. R., General and Inorganic Chemistry
BELLONE, E., History of Science and Technology
BERETTA, G. P., Applied Geology
BERTIN, G., Astronomy and Astrophysics
BERTINO, E., Database and Information Systems
BERTOLINI, M., Geometry
BERTONI, A., Theoretical Computer Science
BIRATTARI, C., Physics
BLASI, A., Mineralogy
BOLOGNESI, M., Biochemistry
BONETTI, R., Nuclear and Sub-Nuclear Physics
BONIFACIO, R., Institutions of Theoretical Physics
BORIANI, A., Petrography
BORTIGNON, P. F., Nuclear and Sub-Nuclear Physics
BOTTAZZINI, U., Complementary Mathematics
BRACCO, A., Physics Experiments
BROGLIA, R. A., Theory of Nuclear Structures
BRUSCHI, D., Informatics
CAMPADELLI, P., Informatics
CANDIA, M. D., Zoology
CANUTO, G., Geometry
CAPASSO, V., Mathematical Statistics
CARACCIOLO, S., Theoretical Physics and Mathematical Models and Methods
CASTANO, S., Computer Science
CAVALLINI, G., General Pedagogy
CENINI, S., General and Inorganic Chemistry
CESA BIANCHI, N. A., Informatics
CIANI, G. F., Inorganic Chemistry
CINQUINI, M., Organic Chemistry
COLOMBO, R., Cytology and Histology
COTTA RAMUSINO, P., Theoretical Physics and Mathematical Models and Methods
COZZI, F., Organic Chemistry
DAMIANI, E., Informatics
DANIELI, B., Physical Methods in Organic Chemistry
D'ANTONA, O., Informatics
DE BERNARDI, F., Zoology
DEDÒ, M., Geometry
DE FALCO, D., Calculus of Probability and Mathematical Statistics
DEGLI ANTONI, G., Applied Computer Science (Programming)
DEHÒ, G., Genetics
DEJANA, E., General Pathology
DE MICHELIS, M., Plant Physiology
D'ESTE, G., Algebra
DESTRO, R., Physical and Chemical Laboratory
DI FRANCESCO, D., General Physiology
ERBA, E., Palaeontology and Palaeoecology
FAELLI, A., General Physiology
FERRAGUTI, M., Zoology
FERRARI, R., Statistical Mechanics
FERRARIO, A., Mineral Deposits
FERRUTI, P., Macromolecular Chemistry
FOIANI, M., Molecular Biology
FORNI, L., Physical Chemistry
FORNILI, S. L., Physics
FORTE, S., Theoretical Physics and Mathematical Models and Methods
GADIOLI, E., Nuclear Physics
GAETANI, M., Geology
GALASSI, S., Ecology
GALGANI, L., Pure Mechanics
GALLI, E. A., General Microbiology
GARLASCHELLI, L., General and Inorganic Chemistry
GENNARI, C., Organic Chemical Laboratory
GHILARDI, S., Logic and Philosophy of Science
GIANINETTI, E., Theoretical Chemistry
GIAVINI, E., Comparative Anatomy
GIGLIO, M., Physics Experiments
GORLA, M., Genetics
GOSSO, G., Structural Geology
GRAMACCIOLI, C., Physical Chemistry
GREGNANIN, A., Petrography
HAUS, G., Computer Science
JADOUL, F., Regional Geology
JENNINGS, R., Photobiology
LANDINI, D., Industrial Chemistry
LANTERI, A., Geometry
LANZ, L., Institutions of Theoretical Physics
LICANDRO, E., Physical Chemistry
LONGHI, P., Electrochemistry
LONGO, C., Botany
LORENZI, A., Mathematical Analysis
MAIORANA, S., Organic Chemistry
MANDELLI, L., General Physics
MANITTO, P. M., Chemistry of Natural Organic Substances
MANTOVANI, R., Genetics
MARANESI, P., Electronics
MARTELLA, G., Information Systems
MERONI, E., Experimental Physics
MILANI, P., Material Structure
MILAZZO, M., Physical Methodology in the Arts
MOSCA, A., Clinical Biochemistry and Molecular Biology
MUSSINI, T., Electrochemistry
MUSSIO, P., Informatics
NALDI, G., Numerical Analysis
NICOLA, P. C., Mathematical Economics

NICORA, A., Palaeontology and Palaeoecology
ORSINI, F., Organic Chemistry
PAGANONI, L., Mathematical Analysis
PALLESCHI, M., Institutions of Advanced Geometry
PANERAI, A., Pharmacology
PAULMICHL, M., Physiology
PAVARINO, L. F., Numerical Analysis
PAVERI, F. S., Institutions of Mathematics
PEROTTI, M. E., Cytology and Histology
PESOLE, G., Molecular Biology
PIGHIZZINI, G., Computer Science
PIGNANELLI, M., Institutions of Nuclear and Subnuclear Physics
PIURI, V., Information Processing Systems
PIZZOTTI, M., General and Inorganic Chemistry
PLEVANI, P., Molecular Biology
POLI, S., Petrology and Petrography
POZZOLI, R., Material Structure
PREMOLI SILVA, I., Micropalaeontology
PROVINI, A., Ecology
RAGAINI, V., Chemical Industrial Processes and Systems
RAGUSA, F., Experimental Physics
RAIMONDI, M., Physical Chemistry
REATTO, L., Material Structure
RIGOLI, M., Geometry
ROSSI, G. P., Informatics
ROSSI, M., General and Inorganic Chemistry
RUF, B., Mathematical Analysis
RUSSO, G., Organic Chemistry
SABADINI, R., Terrestrial Physics
SAINO, N., Ecology
SALA, F., Botany
SAMARATI, P., Computer Science
SANNICOLÒ, F., Organic Chemistry
SCARABOTTOLO, N., Computer Science
SCOLASTICO, C., Organic Chemistry
SEGALE, A., Rural Economics and Surveying
SERRA, E., Mathematical Analysis
SIRONI, A., General and Inorganic Chemistry
SIRONI, G., Genetics
SMIRAGLIA, C., Physical Geography and Geomorphology
SOAVE, C., Plant Physiology
SPERANZA, G., Organic Chemistry
STURANI, E. P., Cellular Biochemistry
TANTARDINI, G. F., Physical Chemistry
TINTORI, A., Palaeontology and Palaeoecology
TONELLI, C., Genetics
TRASATTI, S., Electrochemistry
TUCCI, P., History of Physics
UGO, R., General Inorganic Chemistry
VALLE, G., Computer Science
VAN GEEMAN, L., Geometry
VANONI, M. A., Biochemistry
VERDI, C., Institutions of Mathematics
VITELLARO, L., Comparative Anatomy and Cytology
ZAMBELLI, V., Algebra
ZANETTI, G., Biological Chemistry
ZANON, D., Theory of Physics, Mathematical Models and Methods

Faculty of Veterinary Medicine (Via Celoria 10, 20133 Milan; tel. 02-50318002; e-mail presveter@unimi.it; internet www.unimi.it/ateneo/facol/medvet.htm):

ADDIS, F., Clinical Veterinary Surgery
BALDI, A., Animal Nutrition and Foodstuffs
BELLOLI, A. G., Medical Veterinary Semiology
BERETTA, C., Pharmacology, Pharmacodynamics and Veterinary Pharmacy
BONIZZI, L., Veterinary Microbiology and Immunology
BONTEMPO, V., Animal Nutrition and Diet
CAIROLI, F., Clinical Obstetrics and Veterinary Gynaecology
CANTONI, C. A., Animal Food Products Inspection and Control
CARENZI, C., Morpho-Functional Evaluation of Animal Production
CARLI, S., Veterinary Pharmacology and Toxicology
CATTANEO, P., Animal Food Products Inspection and Control
CLEMENT, M. G., Veterinary Physiology
CODAZZA, D. M., Infectious Diseases of Domestic Animals
CORINO, C., Animal Foodstuffs and Nutrition
CREMONESI, F., Veterinary Obstetrics and Gynaecology
CRIMELLA, C., Special Zootechnics
DE GRESTI DI SANLEONARDO, A., Surgical Veterinary Semiology
DELL' ORTO, V., Animal Foodstuffs and Nutrition
DOMENEGHINI, C., Systematic and Comparative Veterinary Anatomy
FERRANDI, B., Systematic and Comparative Veterinary Anatomy
FERRO, E., Clinical Veterinary Medicine
FINAZZI, M., Veterinary Pathological Anatomy
FONDA, D., Surgical Veterinary Semiology
GALLAZI, D., Infectious Diseases of Domestic Animals
GANDOLFI, F., Anatomy of Domestic Animals
GENCHI, C., Parasitic Diseases
GUIDOBONO CAVALCHINI, A., Mechanization of Farming Processes.
GUIDOBONO CAVALCHINI, L., Aviculture
LANFRANCHI, P., Veterinary Parasitology
LAURIA, A., Veterinary, Systematic and Comparative Anatomy
MORTELLARO, C., Veterinary Surgical Pathology
NAVAROTTO, P., Rural and Forest Construction
PAGNACCO, G., Animal Genetic Improvement and General Husbandry
PEZZA, F., Clinical Veterinary Medicine
PIRANI, A., Rural Economics and Surveying
POLI, G., Veterinary Microbiology and Immunology
POMPA, G., Veterinary Toxicology
PONTI, W., Infectious Diseases of Domestic Animals
PORCELLI, F., General and Special Histology and Embryology
POZZA, O., Pathology of Domestic Animals
RONCHI, S., Biochemistry
RUFFO, G., Infectious Diseases, Prophylaxis and Veterinary Inspection
SALA, V., Infectious Diseases of Domestic Animals
SARTORELLI, P., Veterinary General Pathology and Pathological Anatomy
SAVOINI, G., Foodstuffs Technology
SCANZIANI, E., General and Veterinary Anatomical Pathology
SECCHI, C. L., Biochemistry
VALFRÈ, F., Supply, Markets and Rural Industries
VERGA, M., Specialized Zootechnics
ZECCONI, A., Infectious Diseases of Domestic Animals

UNIVERSITÀ DEGLI STUDI DI MILANO-BICOCCA

Piazza dell'Ateneo Nuovo 1, 20126 Milan
Telephone: 02-64481
E-mail: international.office@unimib.it
Internet: www.unimib.it
Founded 1998
Academic year: October to September
Rector: Prof. MARCELLO FONTANESI
Vice-Rector: Prof. SUSANNA MANTOVANI
Admin. Dir: CANDELORO BELLANTONI
Number of teachers: 910
Number of students: 35,689

DEANS

Faculty of Economics: Prof. MASSIMO SAITA
Faculty of Education: Prof. SILVIA KANIZSA
Faculty of Law: Prof. BRUNO BOSCO
Faculty of Mathematical, Physical and Natural Sciences: Prof. FRANCESCO NICOTRA
Faculty of Medicine and Surgery: Prof. ANDREA STELLA
Faculty of Psychology: Prof. LAURA D'ODORICO
Faculty of Sociology: Prof. ANTONIO DE LILLO
Faculty of Statistics: Prof. GIOVANNI CORRAO

UNIVERSITÀ DEGLI STUDI DI MODENA E REGGIO EMILIA

Via Università 4, 41121 Modena
Telephone: 59-2056511
E-mail: rettore@unimore.it
Internet: www.unimore.it
Founded 1175
Academic year: November to October
Rector: Prof. ALDO TOMASI
Vice-Rector (Modena Campus): Prof. SERGIO PABA
Vice-Rector (Reggio Emilia Campus): Prof. LUIGI GRASSELLI
Admin. Dir: Dott. STEFANO RONCHETTI
Library Dir: Dott. MARIA RAFFAELLA INGROSSO
Library of 294,000 vols
Number of teachers: 700
Number of students: 14,564

DEANS

Faculty of Agriculture: Prof. DOMENICO PIETRO LO FIEGO
Faculty of Arts: Prof. MARINA BONDI
Faculty of Biosciences and Biotechnology: Prof. SERGIO FERRARI
Faculty of Communications and Economics: Prof. GIOVANNA GALLI
'Marco Biagi' Faculty of Economics: Prof. EUGENIO CAPERCHIONE
Faculty of Education: Prof. GIORGIO ZANETTI
'Enzo Ferrari' Faculty of Engineering: Prof. GIUSEPPE CANTORE
Faculty of Engineering (Reggio Emilia): Prof. EUGENIO DRAGONI
Faculty of Law: Prof. RENZO LAMBERTINI
Faculty of Mathematical, Physical and Natural Sciences: Prof. CARLO MARIA BERTONI
Faculty of Medicine and Surgery: Prof. GABRIELLA AGGAZZOTTI
Faculty of Pharmacy: Prof. ALBERTINO BIGIANI

PROFESSORS

Faculty of Agricultural Science and Technology (Via Kennedy 17, 42100 Reggio Emilia; tel. 0522-383232; internet www.rcs.re.it/corsi/agraria.htm):

BIANCHI, U., Genetics
GIUDICI, P., Agroalimentary and Environmental Microbiology
PELLEGRINI, M., Applied Geology
TONGIORGI, P., Zoology

Faculty of Arts and Philosophy (Via Berengario 51, 41100 Modena; tel. 059-2056911):

BONDI, M., English Linguistics
DRUMBL, J., German Linguistics
TOCCI, G., Modern History

Faculty of Economics (Via Berengario 51, 41100 Modena; tel. 059-2056911; e-mail preside.economia@unimo.it; internet www.economia.unimo.it):

BISONI, C., Professional and Banking Procedures
BOSI, P., Finance and Financial Law
BRUSCO, S., Economics and Industrial Policy

BURSI, T., Industrial and Commercial Techniques
FERRARI, A., Stock Exchange Techniques
GINZBURG, A., Economic and Financial Policy
GOLZIO, L. E., Work Study
GRANDORI, A., Personnel Management
LANE, D. A., Statistics
RICCI, G., Financial Mathematics

Faculty of Engineering (Via Campi 213/A, 41100 Modena; tel. 059-2055107; e-mail preside.ingegneria@unimo.it; internet www.ing.unimo.itViale Allegri 15, 42100 Reggio Emilia; tel. 0522-406356; e-mail preside.ingre@unimo.it; internet www.ingre.unimo.it):

ALBERIGI, A., Electronics
ANDRISANO, A. O., Industrial Design
BAROZZI, G. S., Technical Physics
BERGAMASCHI, S., Information Elaboration Systems
BISI, O., General Physics
CAMPI, S., Mathematical Analysis
CANALI, C., Applied Electronics
CANNAROZZI, M., Construction Theory
CANTORE, G.
CECCHI, R., Environmental Sanitary Engineering
FANTINI, F., Industrial Electronics
FRANCESCHINI, V., Rational Mechanics
GRASSELLI, L., Geometry
IMMOVILLI, G., Electronic Communications
NANNARONE, S., Physics
PELLACANI, G. C., General and Inorganic Chemistry
PILATI, F., Macromolecular Chemistry
RIMINI, B., Industrial Plant Mechanics
SANDROLINI, S., Hydraulic Machinery
STROZZI, A.
TIBERIO, P., Information Elaboration Systems
ZOBOLI, M.

Faculty of Jurisprudence (tel. 059-2056589; e-mail preside.giurisprudenza@unimo.it; internet www.giurisprudenza.unimo.it):

ALESSANDRINI, S., Economic Policy
ANTONINI, A., Navigation Law
BIONE, M., Commercial Law
BONFATTI, S., Banking Law
BORGHESI, D., Law of Civil Procedure
CALANDRA BUONAURA, V., Commercial Law
DONINI, M., Penal Law
GALANTINO, L., Labour Law
GASPARINI CASARI, V., Administrative Law
GIANOLIO, R. C., Administrative Law
GUERZONI, L., Ecclesiastical Law
LAMBERTINI, R., Institutions of Roman Law
LUBERTO, S., Anthropology and Criminology
MARANI, F., General Private Law
PANFORTI, M. D., Comparative Private Law
SILINGARDI, G., Transport Law
VIGNUDELLI, A., Constitutional Law

Faculty of Mathematics, Physics and Natural Sciences (Via Campi 213/A, 41100 Modena; tel. 059-371834; e-mail preside.scienze@unimo.it; internet www.scienze.unimo.it):

ACCORSI, C. A., Phytogeography
BERTOLANI, R., Zoology
BERTONI, C. M., Theoretical Physics
BONI, M., Mathematical Analysis
BORTOLANI, V., Solid State Physics
CALANDRA BUONAURA, C., Structure of Materials
CAPEDRI, S., Petrography
CAVICCHIOLI, A., Institutes of Advanced Geometry
CHITI, G., Mathematical Analysis
CREMA, R., Ecology
DEL PRETE, C., Botany
DIECI, G., Micropalaeontology
FANTIN, A. M., Histology and Embryology
FAZZINI, P., Geology
FUNARO, D., Numerical Analysis
GAGLIARDI, C., Geometry II
JACOBONI, C., Atomic Physics
LARATTA, A., Numerical Analysis and Programming
LAZZERETTI, P., Physical Chemistry
LEVONI, S., Foundations of Mathematical Physics
MAGHERINI, P. C., General Physiology
MARINI, M., Comparative Anatomy
MENABUE, L., General and Inorganic Chemistry
MESCHIARI, M., Geometry
MIRONE, P., Physical Chemistry
MOMICCHIOLI, F., Physical Chemistry
OTTAVIANI, E., Comparative Anatomy and Cytology
OTTAVIANI, G., Physics (Preparation of Experiments)
PAGLIAI, A. M., Zoology
PAGNONI, U. M., Organic Chemistry
PALYI, G., Chemical Composition
PANIZZA, M., Physical Geography
PASSAGLIA, E., Mineralogy
PRUDENZIATI, M., Applied Electronics
QUATTROCCHI, P., Advanced Elementary Mathematics
RIVALENTI, G., Metamorphic Petrography
RUSSO, A., Palaeoecology
SANTANGELO, R., Terrestrial Physics
SEGRE, U., Electrochemistry
SERPAGLI, E., Palaeontology
SIGHINOLFI, G., Geochemistry
TADDEI, F., Advanced Organic Chemistry
TORRE, G., Organic Chemistry

Faculty of Medicine and Surgery (Via del Pozzo 71, 41100 Modena; tel. 059-422398; e-mail preside.medicina@unimo.it; internet wwww.medicina.unimo.it):

AGGAZZOTTI, G., Hygiene and Dentistry
AGNATI, L. F., Human Physiology
ALBERTAZZI, A., Nephrology
ARTIBANI, W., Urology
BAGGIO, G. G., Pharmacology
BALLI, R., Otorhinolaryngology
BARBOLINI, G., Anatomy, Histology and Pathology
BEDUSCHI, G., Forensic Medicine
BERGOMI, M., Hygiene and Odontology
BERNASCONI, S., Paediatrics
BERTOLINI, A., Pharmacology
BLASI, E., Microbiology
BOBYLEVA, V., General Pathology
BON, L., Human Physiology
BORELLA, P., General and Applied Hygiene
CALANDRA BUONAURA, S., General Pathology
CANÉ, V.
CARULLI, N., Medical Pathology and Clinical Methodology
CAVAZZUTI, G. B., Clinical Paediatrics
CELLI, L., Orthopaedics and Traumatology
CONSOLO, U., Odontostomatological Special Surgery
CORAZZA, R., Human Physiology
CORTESI, N., General Clinical Surgery and Surgical Therapy
CORTI, A., Biological Chemistry
CURCI, P., Psychiatry
DE BERNARDINIS, G., General Surgery
DE FAZIO, F. A., Forensic and Insurance Medicine
DE GAETANI, C., Foundations of Medicine and Histological Pathology
DELLA CASA, L., Infectious Diseases
ESPOSITO, R., Infectious Diseases
FABBRI, L., Respiratory Diseases
FABIO, U., Microbiology
FAGLIONI, P., Clinical Neurology
FERRARI, F., Pharmacology
FERRARI, S., Applied Biology
FERRARI, S., Biological Chemistry
FORABOSCO, A., Histology and Embryology
GALETTI, G., Clinical Otorhinolaryngology
GIANNETTI, A., Clinical Dermatology
GUARALDI, G. P., Clinical Psychiatry
GUERRA, R., Clinical Ophthalmology
JASONNI, V. M., Obstetrics and Gynaecology
LODI, R. G., Thoracic Surgery
MANENTI, F., Gastroenterology
MAROTTI, G., Human Anatomy
MATTIOLI, G., Cardiology
MODENA, M. G., Cardiology
MONTI, M. G., Biological Chemistry
MORUZZI, M. S., Chemical Biology
MUSCATELLO, U., General Pathology
PASETTO, A., Anaesthesiology
PONZ DE LEON, M., Internal Medicine
PORTOLANI, M., Virology
ROMAGNOLI, R., Radiology
SALVIOLI, G., Surgical Pathology
SAVIANO, M., Surgical Pathology
SEIDENARI, S., Allergological Dermatology
SILINGARDI, V., Special Medical Pathology and Clinical Methodology
STELLA, A., Vascular Surgery
STERNIERI, E., Clinical Pharmacology
TOMASI, A., General Physiopathology
TORELLI, G., Haematology
TORELLI, U., General Clinical Medicine and Therapy
TRENTINI, G. P., Anatomy and Pathological History
VENTURA, E., General Clinical Medicine and Therapy
VIVOLI, G., Hygiene
VOLPE, A., Physiopathology of Human Reproduction
ZENEROLI, M. L., Semiotics
ZINI, I., Human Physiology

Faculty of Pharmacy (Via Campi 183, 41100 Modena; tel. 059-2055169; e-mail preside.farmacia@unimo.it; internet www.farmacia.unimo.it):

ALBASINI, A., Applied Pharmaceutical Chemistry and Toxicology
BARALDI, M., Pharmacology
BERNABEI, M. T., Pharmaceutical Procedures and Legislation
BRASILI, L., Pharmaceutical and Toxicological Chemistry
CAMERONI, R., Applied Pharmaceutical Chemistry
FORNI, F., Pharmaceutical Procedures and Legislation
GALLI, E., Mineralogy
GAMBERINI, G., Pharmaceutical Chemical Analysis
MELEGARI, M., Pharmaceutical Chemical Analysis II
MONZANI, V. A., Pharmaceutical Chemical Analysis
PECORARI, P., Pharmaceutical Chemical Analysis
PIETRA, P., General Physiology
QUAGLIO, G., Hygiene

UNIVERSITÀ DEGLI STUDI DI NAPOLI 'FEDERICO II'

Corso Umberto I, 80138 Naples
Telephone: 081-2531111
E-mail: webint@unina.it
Internet: www.unina.it
Founded 1224
Rector: Prof. MASSIMO MARRELLI
Pro-Rector: Prof. GAETANO MANFREDI
Admin. Dir: Dott. MARIA LUIGIA LIGUORI
Library of 1,200,000 vols, 18,000 journals
Number of teachers: 1,483
Number of students: 94,510

DEANS

Faculty of Agriculture: Prof. PAOLO MASSI
Faculty of Architecture: Prof. CLAUDIO CLAUDI DE SAINT MIHIEL
Faculty of Arts: Prof. ARTURO DE VIVO
Faculty of Biotechnology: Prof. GENNARO PICCIALLI

Faculty of Economics: Prof. ACHILLE BASILE
Faculty of Engineering: Prof. PIERO SALATINO
Faculty of Law: Prof. LUCIO DE GIOVANNI
Faculty of Mathematical, Physical and Natural Sciences: Prof. ROBERTO PETTORINO
Faculty of Medicine and Surgery: Prof. GIOVANNI PERSICO
Faculty of Pharmacy: Prof. GIUSEPPE CIRINO
Faculty of Political Science: Prof. MARCO MUSELLA
Faculty of Sociology: Prof. GIANFRANCO PECCHINENDA
Faculty of Veterinary Medicine: Prof. LUIGI ZICARELLI

UNIVERSITÀ DEGLI STUDI DI NAPOLI – L'ORIENTALE

Via Partenope 10/A, 80121 Naples
Telephone: 081-7643230
E-mail: ateneo@pec.unior.it
Internet: www.iuo.it
Founded 1732
Chancellor: Prof. LIDA VIGANONI
Vice-Chancellor: Prof. GIUSEPPE CATALDI
Pro-Rector for Teaching: Prof. ELDA MORTICCHIO
Admin. Dir: Dott. CLAUDIO BORRELLI
Library of 673,000 vols

DEANS

Faculty of Arabian-Islamic and Mediterranean Studies: Prof. AGOSTINO CILARDO
Faculty of Arts: Prof. AMNERIS ROSELLI
Faculty of Foreign Languages and Literature: Prof. AUGUSTO GUARINO
Faculty of Political Science: Prof. GIORGIO AMITRANO

UNIVERSITÀ DEGLI STUDI DI PADOVA

Via 8 Febbraio 2, 35122 Padua
Telephone: 049-8275111
E-mail: rettore@unipd.it
Internet: www.unipd.it
Founded 1222
Rector: Prof. GIUSEPPE ZACCARIA
Vice-Rector: Prof. FRANCESCO GNESOTTO
Admin. Dir: Arch. GIUSEPPE BARBIERI
Librarian: Dott. MAURIZIO VEDALDI
Number of teachers: 1,382
Number of students: 60,000

DEANS

Faculty of Arts: Prof. MICHELE CORTELAZZO
Faculty of Agriculture: Prof. GIANCARLO DALLA FONTANA
Faculty of Economics: Prof. ENRICO RETTORE
Faculty of Education: Prof. GIUSEPPE MICHELI
Faculty of Engineering: Prof. PIERFRANCESCO BRUNELLO
Faculty of Law: Prof. GHERARDO BERGONZINI
Faculty of Mathematical, Physical, and Natural Sciences: Prof. RENATO BOZIO
Faculty of Medicine and Surgery: Prof. GIORGIO PALÙ
Faculty of Pharmacy: Prof. GIULIANO BANDOLI
Faculty of Political Science: Prof. GIANNI RICCAMBONI
Faculty of Psychology: Prof. PIETRO BOSCOLO
Faculty of Statistical Sciences: Prof. GIANPIERO DALLA ZUANNA
Faculty of Veterinary Medicine: Prof. MASSIMO CASTAGNARO

UNIVERSITÀ DEGLI STUDI DI PALERMO

Piazza Marina 61, 90133 Palermo
Telephone: 091-270111
E-mail: info@unipa.it
Internet: www.unipa.it
Founded 1777
Rector: Prof. ROBERTO LAGALLA
Vice-Rector: Prof. ENNIO CARDONA
Admin. Dir: Dott. ANTONIO VALENTI
Number of teachers: 1,300
Number of students: 70,000
Publications: *Annali del Seminario Giuridico, Circolo Giuridico 'L. Sampolo'*

DEANS

Faculty of Agriculture: Prof. GIUSEPPE GIORDANO
Faculty of Arts: Prof. MARIO GANDOLFO GIACOMARRA
Faculty of Architecture: Prof. ANGELO MILONE
Faculty of Economics: Prof. FABIO MAZZOLA
Faculty of Education: Prof. MICHELE COMETA
Faculty of Engineering: Prof. Ing. FABRIZIO MICARI
Faculty of Law: Prof. ANTONIO SCAGLIONE
Faculty of Arts: Prof. MARIO GANDOLFO GIACOMARRA
Faculty of Mathematical, Physical and Natural Sciences: Prof. ROBERTO BOSCAINO
Faculty of Medicine and Surgery: Prof. GIACOMO DE LEO
Faculty of Pharmacy: Prof. GIROLAMO CIRRINCIONE
Faculty of Politics: Prof. ANTONELLO MIRANDA
Faculty of Sports Science: Prof. GIUSEPPE LIOTTA

UNIVERSITÀ DEGLI STUDI DI PARMA

Via Università 12, 43121 Parma
Telephone: 0521-032111
E-mail: protocollo@pec.unipr.it
Internet: www.unipr.it
Founded 962
Academic year: October to September
Rector: Prof. GINO FERRETTI
Deputy Rector: Prof. CARLO CHEZZI
Admin. Dir: Dott. RODOLFO POLDI
Number of teachers: 1,100
Number of students: 30,000

DEANS

Faculty of Agriculture: Prof. ERASMO NEVIANI
Faculty of Architecture: Prof. IVO IORI
Faculty of Economics: Prof. GIAN PIERO LUGLI
Faculty of Engineering: Prof. ANTONIO MONTEPARA
Faculty of Humanities: Prof. ROBERTO GRECI
Faculty of Law: Prof. LAURA PINESCHI
Faculty of Mathematical, Physical and Natural Sciences: Prof. GIAN LUIGI ROSSI
Faculty of Medicine and Surgery: Prof. LORIS BORGHI
Faculty of Pharmacy: Prof. PAOLO COLOMBO
Faculty of Politics: Prof. ALESSANDRO DUCE
Faculty of Psychology: Prof. SILVIA PERINI
Faculty of Veterinary Medicine: Prof. ATTILIO CORRADI

UNIVERSITÀ DEGLI STUDI DI PAVIA

Corso Strada Nuova 65, 27100 Pavia
Telephone: 0382-9811
E-mail: rettore@unipv.it
Internet: www.unipv.eu
Founded 1361 by Emperor Charles IV
Academic year: November to October
Rector: Prof. ANGIOLINO STELLA
Admin. Dir: Dr GIOVANNI COLUCCI
Number of teachers: 1,120
Number of students: 23,000
Publication: *Annuario* (online)

DEANS

Faculty of Arts and Philosophy: Prof. ELISA ROMANO
Faculty of Economics: Prof. CARLUCCIO BIANCHI
Faculty of Engineering: Prof. Ing. CARLO CIAPONI
Faculty of Law: Prof. ETTORE DEZZA
Faculty of Mathematical, Physical and Natural Science: Prof. LUCIO TOMA
Faculty of Medicine and Surgery: Prof. ANTONIO DAL CANTON
Faculty of Musicology: Prof. GIANCARLO PRATO
Faculty of Pharmacy: Prof. AMEDEO MARINI
Faculty of Political Sciences: Prof. FABIO RUGGE

UNIVERSITÀ DEGLI STUDI DI PERUGIA

Piazza dell' Università 1, 06100 Perugia
Telephone: 075-5851
E-mail: gestione@unipg.it
Internet: www.unipg.it
Founded 1276
State control
Academic year: November to October
Rector: Prof. FRANCESCO BISTONI
Admin. Dir: Dott.ssa ANGELA MARIA LACAITA
Pro-Rector: Prof. ANTONIO PIERETTI
Librarian: PAOLO BELLINI
Number of teachers: 312
Number of students: 31,746
Publications: *La Salute Umana*, *L'Università*, *Rivista di Biologia*, *Rivista di Dermatologia*, *Rivista di Idrobiologia*

DEANS

Faculty of Agriculture: Prof. FRANCESCO PENNACCHI
Faculty of Economics: Prof. PIERLUIGI DADDI
Faculty of Education: Prof. ROMANO UGOLINI
Faculty of Engineering: Prof. GIANNI BIDINI
Faculty of Law: Prof. MAURO BOVE
Faculty of Humanities: Prof. GIORGIO BONAMENTE
Faculty of Mathematical, Physical and Natural Sciences: Prof. FAUSTO ELISEI
Faculty of Medicine and Surgery: Prof. LUCIANO BINAGLIA
Faculty of Pharmacy: Prof. CARLO ROSSI
Faculty of Political Science: Prof. GIORGIO EDUARDO MONTANARI
Faculty of Veterinary Medicine: Prof. FRANCO MORICONI

PROFESSORS

Faculty of Agrarian Science:
ABBOZZO, P., Farm Evaluation
BENCIVENGA, M., Systematic Agricultural Botany
BERNARDINI BATTAGLINI, M., Animal Husbandry
BIANCHI, A. A., Herbaceous Cultivation
BIN, F., Biological Techniques
BONCIARELLI, F., Cultivation of Special Herbaceous Plants
BUSINELLI, M., Soil Chemistry
CIRICIOFOLO, E., Biology, Production and Technology of Seeds
COSTANTINI, F., Animal Nutrition and Feeding
COVARELLI, G., Weed Control
DURANTI, E., Physiology of Animals in Stockbreeding
FALCINELLI, M., Genetic Improvement in Cultivated Plants
FANTOZZI, P., Alimentation
FATICHENTI, F., Agrarian and Arboreal Microbiology
GIOVAGNOTTI, C.
LORENZETTI, F., Agrarian Genetics
MANNOCCHI, F., Agrarian Hydraulics
MARTE, M., Plant Pathology
MARTINI, A., Agrarian Microbiology

MARUCCHINI, C., Introductory Agrarian Chemistry
MENNELLA, V. G., Agricultural and Forestry Planning
MONOTTI, M., General Agriculture
MONTEDORO, G., Agricultural Industries
PENNACCHI, F., Agrarian Economics
RAGGI, V., Plant Pathology
ROMANO, B., Morphology and Plant Physiology
ROSSI, A. C., Economics and Agrarian Policy
ROSSI, J., Dairy Food Microbiology
SARTI, D. M., Stockbreeding
SCARPONI, L., Agrarian Biochemistry
SOLINAS, M., Agricultural Entomology
STANDARDI, A., Specialist Fruit Growing
TOMBESI, A., General Fruit Growing
VERONESI, F., Genetic Biotechnology
ZAZZERINI, A., Phytotherapy

Faculty of Economics:
BORGIA, R., Institutions of Private Law
BRACALENTE, B., Economics Statistics
CALZONI, G., Political Economy
CAVAZZONI, G., Accountancy
CHIARELLE, R., Institutions of Public Law
CICCHITELLI, G., Statistics
CORALLINI, S., Banking
FORCINA, A., Statistics
GRASSELLI, P. M., Political Economy
MEZZACAPO, V., Banking Legislation
MORICONI, F., Mathematics
PAGLIACCI, G., General Mathematics
PERONI, G., Marketing
RIDOLFI, M., Political Economy
SEDIARI, T., Agrarian Economics and Politics
SEVERINO, P., Commercial Penal Law

Faculty of Education:
BALDINI, M., History of Philosophy
BUCCI, S., General Education
DOTTI, U., Italian Language and Literature
FINZI, C., History of Political Doctrine
FISSI MIGLIORINI, R., Dantesque Philology
FURIOZZI, G. B., History of Umbria
MANCINI, F. F., History of Umbrian Art
MIRRI, E., Philosophy
PERUGI, M., Romance Philology
PETRONI, F., History of Modern and Contemporary Italian Literature
RICCIOLI, G., French Language and Literature
ROSATI, L., Teaching
SANTINI, C., Latin Language and Literature
SETAIOLI, A., Latin Grammar
UGOLINI, R., Contemporary History
ZURLI, L., Latin Philology

Faculty of Engineering:
BALLI, R., Applied Mechanics
BASILI, P., Electromagnetic Fields
BATTISTON, R., Physics
BERNA, L., Urban Technology
BIDINI, G., Machines
BORRI, A., Construction Theory
BRANDI, P., Mathematical Analysis
BURRASCANO, P., Electrotechnology
CANDELORO, D., Mathematical Analysis I
CONTI, P., Industrial Technical Drawing
CORRADINI, C., Technical Hydrology
FELLI, M., Technical Physics
LA CAVA, M., Automatic Controls
LIUTI, G., Chemistry
MAZZOLAI, F. M., Physics
PALMIERI, L., Physics
PARDUCCI, A., Construction Technology
PUCCI, E., Advanced Mechanical Engineering
SOCINO, G., Physics
SOLETTI, A. C., Design
SORRENTINI, R., Electromagnetic Fields
TACCONI, P., Applied Geology
VECCHIOCATTIVI, F., Chemistry

Faculty of Jurisprudence:
AZZARITI, G., Constitutional Law
BADIALI, G., International Law
BARBERINI, G., Ecclesiastical Law
CAPRIOLI, S., History of Modern Italian Law
CARDI, E., Procedural Law
CAVALAGLIO, A., Bankruptcy Law
CAVALLO, B., Administrative Law
CINELLI, M., Labour Law
DALLERA, G. F., Finance and Financial Law
GAITO, A., Penal Law
MIGLIORINI, L., Administrative Law
MORSELLI, E., Penal Law
PALAZZO, A., Institutions of Private Law
PALAZZOLO, N., History of Roman Law
PEPPE, L., Roman Law
SALVI, C., Civil Law
SASSANI, M., Civil Procedural Law
TALAMANCA, A., Canon Law
TINELLI, G., Tax Law
VOLPI, M., Constitutional Comparative Law

Faculty of Letters and Philosophy:
AGOSTINIANI, L., Linguistics
BONAMENTE, G., Roman History
CARANCINI, G. L., European Protohistory
COARELLI, F., Greek and Roman Antiquity
DI PILLA, F., French Language and Literature
FALASCHI, G., Italian Literature
FROVA, C., Medieval History
GIORDANI, R., Christian Archaeology
ISOLA, A., Ancient Christian Literature
MADDOLI, G., Greek History
MELELLI, A., Geography
MENESTÒ, E., Medieval Latin Literature
MORETTI, G., Italian Dialectology
PICCINATO, S., Anglo-American Literature
PIERETTI, A., Theoretical Philosophy
PIZZANI, U., Latin Literature
PRIVITERA, G. A., Greek Literature
RONCALLI DI MONTORIO, F., Etruscan Studies and Italic Antiquity
RUFINI, S., English Language and Literature
SANTACHIARA, U., Church History
SCARPELLINI PANCRAZI, P., History of Medieval Art
SEPPILLI, T., Cultural Anthropology
SPAGGIARI PERUGI, B., Romance Philology
TORELLI, M., Archaeology and History of Greek and Roman Art
TORTI, A., English Language and Literature

Faculty of Mathematical, Physical and Natural Sciences:
ALBERTI, G., Inorganic Chemistry
AMBROSETTI, P. L., Palaeontology
ANTONIELLI, M., Plant Physiology
AQUILANTI, V., General and Inorganic Chemistry
AVERNA, A.
BARSI, F., Theory and Application of Mechanical Calculation
BARTOCCI, U., Geometry
CATALIOTTI, R. S., Physical Chemistry
CIOFI DEGLI ATTI, C., Institutions of Nuclear Physics
CIONINI, P. G., Botany
CIROTTO, C., Cytology and Histology
CLEMENTI, S., Organic Chemistry
COLETTI, G., Institutions of Mathematics
DE TOLLIS, B. A., Institutions of Theoretical Physics
DI GIOVANNI, M. V., Zoology
FAINA, G., Geometry
FAVARO MAZZUCATO, G., Physical Chemistry
FRINGUELLI, F., Organic Chemistry
GAINO, E., Zoology
GIANFRANCHESCHI, G. L., General Physiology
GRANETTI, B., Botany
GUAZZONE, S., Algebra
IORIO, A. M., Virology
LAGANÀ, A., General and Inorganic Chemistry
LARICCIA, P., Physics Laboratory
MAFFEI, P., Astrophysics
MANTOVANI, G., General Physics
MARINO, G., Organic Chemistry
MAZZUCATO, U., Physical Chemistry
MONTANINI MEZZASOMA, I., Biochemistry
MOROZZI, G., Hygiene
MORPURGO, G. P., Genetics
NAPPI, A., General Physics
ONORI, G., Physics
ORLACCHIO, A., Biochemistry
PASCOLINI, R., Comparative Anatomy
PASSERI, L., Sedimentology
PECCERILLO, A., Petrography
PERUZZI, M. I., General Physics
PIALLI, G., Geology
PIOVESANA, O., General and Inorganic Chemistry
PUCCI, P., Mathematical Analysis
RINALDI, R., Mineralogy
SACCHETTI, F., Solid State Physics
SANTUCCI, S., Physics Laboratory
SAVELLI, G., Organic Chemistry
SGAMELLOTTI, A., Inorganic Chemistry
SRIVASTAVA YOGENDRA, N., Quantum Theory
TATICCHI, A., Organic Chemistry
TATICCHI, M. I., Ecology
TULIPANI, S., Computer Science
VERDINI, L., Structure of Matter
VOLPI, G., General and Inorganic Chemistry
ZANAZZI, P. F., Crystallography

Faculty of Medicine and Surgery:
ABBRITTI, G., Industrial Medicine
AMBROSIO, G., Cardiology
ARIENTI, G., Biological Chemistry
BARTOLI, A., General Surgery
BECCHETTI, E., Histology
BINAGLIA, L., Chemistry and Biomedicine
BISTONI, F., Microbiology
BOLIS, G. B., Anatomy and Pathological Histology
BOLLI, G., Metabolic Diseases
BORRI, P. F., Psychiatry
BRUNETTI, P., Internal Medicine
BUCCIARELLI, E., Anatomy and Pathological Histology
CALANDRA, P., Dermatology
CAPRINO, G., Radiology
CASALI, L., Diseases of the Respiratory System
DADDI, G., Surgical Pathology and Clinical Propaedeutics
DELOGU, A., Ophthalmology
D'ERRICO, P., Dental Prosthesis
DONATO, R. F., Neuroanatomy
FABRONI, F., Forensic Medicine
FALORNI, A., Paediatrics
FIORE, C., Physiopathological Optics
FRONGILLO, R. F., Infectious Diseases
FURBETTA, M., Preventive and Social Paediatrics
GALLAI, V., Neurology
GIOVANNINI, E., General Biology
GORACCI, G. F., Biological Chemistry
GRIGNANI, F., Internal Medicine
LATINI, P., Radiotherapy
LAURO, V., Gynaecology and Obstetrics
LIOTTI, F. S., General Biology
LISI, P., Dermatology
MAGNI, F., Human Physiology
MAIRA, G., Neurosurgery
MANNARINO, E., Internal Medicine
MARCONI, P., Immunology
MARTELLI, M. F., Haematology
MASTRANDREA, V., Hygiene
MODOLO, M. A., Hygiene
MOGGI, L., General Surgery
MORELLI, A., Gastroenterology
NEGRI, P. L., Paradontology

NENCI, G. G., Internal Medicine
NORELLI, G. A., Forensic Medicine
PALUMBO, R., Nuclear Medicine
PAULUZZI, S., Infectious Diseases
PECORELLI, F., Orthopaedics and Traumatology
PEDUTO, V. A., Anaesthesia and Resuscitation
PETTOROSSI, V. E., Human Physiology
PORENA, M., Urology
PUXEDDU, A., Internal Medicine
RIBACCHI, R., Anatomy and Pathological Histology
RICCARDI, C., Pharmacology
RINONAPOLI, E., Orthopaedics and Traumatology
ROSI BARBERINI, G., Cellular Biology
ROSSI, R., General Pathology
SALVADORI, P., Physics
SANTEUSANIO, F., Endocrinology
SENIN, U., Geriatrics and Gerontology
STAFFOLANI, N., Oral Surgery
STAGNI, G., Infectious Diseases
TRISTAINO, B., General Surgery
VACCARO, R., Paediatrics
VALORI, C., Internal Medicine
VILLANI, C., Oncological Gynaecology
VIOLA MAGNI, M. P., General Pathology

Faculty of Pharmacy:

CORSANO LEOPIZZI, S., Pharmaceutical and Toxicological Chemistry
COSTANTINO, U., General and Inorganic Chemistry
DAMIANI, P., Food Science Chemistry
FIORETTI CECCHERELLI, M. C., Pharmacology and Pharmacognosy
FLORIDI, A., Biochemistry
FRAVOLINI, A., Pharmaceutical and Toxicological Chemistry
GRANDOLINI, G., Socioeconomic Technology and Pharmaceutical Legislation
MENGHINI, A., Pharmaceutical Botany
PELLICCIARI, R., Pharmaceutical and Toxicological Chemistry
PUCCETTI, P., Pharmacology
ROSSI, C., Applied Pharmaceutical Chemistry
SCASSELLATI, S. G., Hygiene
TESTAFERRI, L., Organic Chemistry
TIECCO, M., Organic Chemistry
VECCHIARELLI, A., Microbiology

Faculty of Political Science:

BONO, S., History and Institutions of Afro-Asian Countries
CARINI, C., History of Political Doctrine
COMPARATO, V. I., Modern History
CRESPI, F., Sociology
D'AMOJA, F., History of International Relations
DI GASPARE, G., Economic Law
GALLI DELLA LOGGIA, E., History of Political Parties and Movements
GROHMANN, A., Economic History
MARCHISIO, S., International Law
MELOGRANI, P., Contemporary History
MERLONI, F., Administrative Justice
RAVERAIRA, M., Institutions of Public Law
TEODORI, M., American History
TOSI, L., History of Treaties and International Politics
TRAMONTANA, A., Finance

Faculty of Veterinary Medicine:

ASDRUBALI, G., Pathology of Birds
AVELLINI, G., Clinical Veterinary Medicine
BATTISTACCI, M., Clinical Veterinary Surgery
BEGHELLI, V., Veterinary Physiology and Ethology
BELLUCCI, M., Veterinary Radiology and Nuclear Medicine
BOITI, C., Veterinary Physiology and Ethology
CASTRUCCI, G., Infectious Diseases and Prophylaxis
CECCARELLI, P., Topographical Veterinary Anatomy
CHIACCHIARINI, P., Obstetrics and Gynaecology
DEBENEDETTI, A., Endocrinology of Domestic Animals
DI ANTONIO, E., Inspection and Control of Foodstuffs of Animal Origin
FRUGANTI, G., Veterinary Medical Pathology
GAITI, A., Biochemistry
GARGIULO BERSIANI, A. M., Histology and General Embryology
LORVIK, S., Anatomy of Domestic Animals
MALVISI, J., Pharmacology and Pharmacodynamics
MANGILI PECCI, V., Laboratory Diagnosis
MANOCCHIO, I., Pathological Anatomy
MORICONI, F., Veterinary Surgical Pathology
OLIVIERI, O., Animal Nutrition
POLIDORI GIROLAMO, A. B., Veterinary Parasitology
RANUCCI, S., Veterinary Medical Semiology and Clinical Methodology
SILVESTRELLI, M., Special Stockbreeding
VALENTE, C., Infectious Diseases
VITELLOZZI, G., Veterinary Pathological Anatomy

UNIVERSITÀ DEGLI STUDI DI PISA

Lungarno Pacinotti 43, 56126 Pisa
Telephone: 050-2212111
E-mail: rettore@unipi.it
Internet: www.unipi.it

Founded 1343
State control
Academic year: November to October

Rector: Prof. MASSIMO MARIO AUGELLO
Deputy Rector: Prof. NICOLETTA DE FRANCESCO
Vice-Rector for Applied Research and Innovation: Prof. PAOLO FERRAGINA
Vice-Rector for Budgetary Policy: Prof. ADA CARLESI
Vice-Rector for Infrastructure: Assoc. Prof. SANDRO PACI
Vice-Rector for Internationalization: Assoc. Prof. ALESSANDRA GUIDI
Vice-Rector for Legal Matters: Prof. FRANCESCO DEL CANTO
Vice-Rector for Research: Prof. PAOLO BARALE
Vice-Rector for Student Affairs: Dott. ROSALBA TOGNETTI
Vice-Rector for Teaching: Prof. PAOLO MANCARELLA
Vice-Rector for University Relations: Assoc. Prof. MARIA ANTONELLA GALANTI
Chief Admin. Officer: Dott. RICCARDO GRASSO
Librarian: Dott. RENATO TAMBURRINI

Number of teachers: 1,767
Number of students: 52,648

DEANS

Faculty of Agriculture: Dott. STEFANO FANTI
Faculty of Economics: Prof. DIANORA POLETTI
Faculty of Engineering: Prof. Ing. PIERANGELO TERRENI
Faculty of Foreign Languages and Literature: Prof. BRUNO MAZZONI
Faculty of Law: Prof. EUGENIO RIPEPE
Faculty of Letters and Philosophy: Prof. ALFONSO MAURIZIO IACONO
Faculty of Mathematical, Physical and Natural Sciences: Prof. PAOLO ROSSI
Faculty of Medicine and Surgery: Prof. MARIO PETRINI
Faculty of Pharmacy: Prof. CLAUDIA MARTINI
Faculty of Political Science: Prof. CLAUDIO PALAZZOLO
Faculty of Veterinary Medicine: ALESSANDRO POLI

UNIVERSITÀ DEGLI STUDI DI ROMA 'FORO ITALICO'

(Italian University of Sport and Movement)

Piazza Lauro de Bosis 15, 00194 Rome
Telephone: 06-36733599
E-mail: rettorato@iusm.it
Internet: www.uniroma4.it

Founded 1998
State control

Depts of human movement and sport sciences, training for physical activities and sports, health sciences

Rector: Prof. PAOLO PARISI
Vice-Rector: Prof. FABIO PIGOZZI
Admin. Dir: Dott. GIULIO GORIA

Number of teachers: 60
Number of students: 2,000

UNIVERSITÀ DEGLI STUDI DI ROMA 'TOR VERGATA'

Via Orazio Raimondo 18, 00173 Rome
Telephone: 06-72591
E-mail: rettore@uniroma2.it
Internet: web.uniroma2.it

Founded 1985

Rector: Prof. RENATO LAURO
Deputy Rector: Prof. GIUSEPPE SANTONI
Admin. Dir: Dr ERNESTO NICOLAI

Number of teachers: 1,538
Number of students: 43,000

Publications: *I Quaderni di Tor Vergata*, *L'Osservatorio*

DEANS

Faculty of Economics: Prof. MICHELE BAGELLA
Faculty of Engineering: Prof. VITTORIO ROCCO
Faculty of Law: Prof. GIAN PIERO G. MILANO
Faculty of Literature and Philosophy: Prof. LAZZARO CAPUTO
Faculty of Mathematical, Physical and Natural Sciences: Prof. MAURIZIO PACI
Faculty of Medicine and Surgery: Prof. GIUSEPPE NOVELLI

UNIVERSITÀ DEGLI STUDI DI SALERNO

Via Ponte don Melillo, 84084 Fisciano (Salerno)
Telephone: 089-961111
E-mail: urp@unisa.it
Internet: www.unisa.it

Founded 1970

Rector: Prof. RAIMONDO PASQUINO
Vice-Rector: Prof. MARIA GALANTE
Admin. Dir: Dott. GIUSEPPE PADUANO

DEANS

Faculty of Economics: Prof. DANIELA VALENTINO
Faculty of Education: Prof. LUIGI REINA
Faculty of Engineering: Prof. VITALE CARDONE
Faculty of Foreign Languages and Literature: Prof. ILEANA PAGANI
Faculty of Law: Prof. ENZO MARIA MARENGHI
Faculty of Letters and Philosophy: Prof. LUCA CERCHIAI
Faculty of Mathematical, Physical and Natural Sciences: Prof. MARIA TRANSIRICO
Faculty of Pharmacy: Prof. RAFFAELE RICCIO
Faculty of Political Science: Prof. LUIGINO ROSSI

UNIVERSITÀ DEGLI STUDI DI SASSARI

Piazza Università 21, 07100 Sassari, Sardinia
Telephone: 079-228211
E-mail: direzione@uniss.it
Internet: www.uniss.it

Founded 1562
State control
Academic year: November to October

Rector: Prof. Attilio Matino
Vice-Rector: Prof. Laura Manca
Admin. Dir: Dott. Guido Croci
Librarian: Dott. Elisabetta Pilia

Number of teachers: 604
Number of students: 16,319

DEANS

Faculty of Agriculture: Prof. Pietro Luciano
Faculty of Architecture: Prof. Giovanni Maciocco
Faculty of Economics: Prof. Enrico Grosso
Faculty of Foreign Languages and Literature: Prof. Giulia Pissarello
Faculty of Law: Prof. Francesco Sini
Faculty of Letters and Philosophy: Prof. Aldo Maria Morace
Faculty of Mathematical, Physical and Natural Sciences: Prof. Massimo Carpinelli
Faculty of Medicine and Surgery: Prof. Giuseppe Maeddu
Faculty of Pharmacy: Prof. Maria Antonietta Zoroddu
Faculty of Political Science: Prof. Virgilio Mura
Faculty of Veterinary Medicine: Prof. Salvatore Naitana

UNIVERSITÀ DEGLI STUDI DI SIENA

Via Banchi di Sotto 55, 53100 Siena
Telephone: 0577-232111
E-mail: info@unisi.it
Internet: www.unisi.it

Founded 1240

Rector: Prof. Angleo Riccaboni
Registrar: Dott. Ines Fabbro
Library Dir: Dott. Guido Badalamente

Number of teachers: 514
Number of students: 19,093

Publication: *Annuario Accademico*

DEANS

Faculty of Arts and Humanities: Prof. Roberto Venuti
Faculty of Arts and Humanities (Arezzo): Prof. Walter Bernardi
Faculty of Economics: Prof. Guido Ghellini
Faculty of Engineering: Prof. Enrico Martinelli
Faculty of Law: Prof. Roberto Guerrini
Faculty of Mathematical, Physical and Natural Sciences: Prof. Donato Donati
Faculty of Medicine and Surgery: Prof. Gian Maria Rossolini
Faculty of Pharmacy: Prof. Maurizio Botta
Faculty of Political Science: Prof. Luca Verzichelli

UNIVERSITÀ DEGLI STUDI DI TERAMO

Viale Crucioli 122, 64100 Teramo
Telephone: 0861-2661
E-mail: protocollo@pec.unite.it
Internet: www.unite.it

Founded 1993, upon independence of Teramo campus of Università degli Studi 'Gabriele D'Annunzio'

Rector: Prof. Rita Tranquilli Leali
Pro-Rector: Prof. Fulvio Marsilio
Admin. Dir: Dott. Luigi Renzullo
Librarian: Dott. Valeria de Bartolomeis

Library of 162,156 vols
Number of teachers: 250
Number of students: 8,242

Publication: *Trimestre* (2 a year)

DEANS

Faculty of Agriculture: Prof. Dino Mastrocola
Faculty of Communication Studies: Prof. Luciano D'Amico
Faculty of Law: Prof. Floriana Cursi
Faculty of Political Science: Prof. Enrico Del Colle
Faculty of Veterinary Medicine: Prof. Fulvio Marsilio

UNIVERSITÀ DEGLI STUDI DI TORINO

Via Verdi 8, 10124 Turin
Telephone: 011-6706111
E-mail: rettore@unito.it
Internet: www.unito.it

Founded 1404
Academic year: October to September

Rector: Prof. Ezio Pelizzetti
Pro-Rector: Prof. Sergio Roda
Admin. Dir: Loredana Segreto

Number of teachers: 4,000
Number of students: 70,000

DEANS

Faculty of Agriculture: Prof. Elisabetta Barberis
Faculty of Arts and Humanities: Prof. Lorenzo Massobrio
Faculty of Economics: Prof. Sergio Bortolani
Faculty of Education: Profa Renato Grimaldi
Faculty of Law: Prof. Gianmaria Ajani
Faculty of Mathematical, Physical and Natural Sciences: Prof. Alberto Conte
Faculty of Medicine and Surgery 'San Luigi Gonzaga': Prof. Pier Maria Furlan
Faculty of Modern Languages and Literature: Prof. Liborio Termine
Faculty of Pharmacy: Prof. Michele Trotta
Faculty of Political Sciences: Prof. Fabio Armao
Faculty of Psychology: Prof. Ferdinando Rossi
Faculty of Veterinary Medicine: Prof. Bartolomeo Biolatti

UNIVERSITÀ DEGLI STUDI DI TRENTO

Via Belenzani 12, 38122 Trento
Telephone: 461-881111
E-mail: direzione.generale@unitn.it
Internet: www.unitn.it

Founded 1962
State control (since 1982)
Academic year: October to September

Pres.: Dott. Innocenzo Cipolletta
Rector: Prof. Davide Bassi
Vice-Rector: Prof. Giovanni Pascuzzi
Deputy Rector for Admin. Staff Affairs, Collective Bargaining and Business Relationships: Prof. Alberto Molinari
Deputy Rector for Int. Relations: Prof. Carla Locatelli
Deputy Rector for Scientific Research: Prof. Antonio Schizzerotto
Gen. Dir: Dott. Giancarla Masè
Librarian: Dott. Paolo Bellini

Library of 416,655 vols and 13,035 periodicals
Number of teachers: 577
Number of students: 15,226

DEANS

Faculty of Arts and Philosophy: Prof. Maurizio Giangiulio
Faculty of Cognitive Science: Prof. Franco Fraccaroli
Faculty of Economics: Prof. Paolo Collini
Faculty of Engineering: Prof. Marco Tubino
Faculty of Law: Prof. Luca Nogler
Faculty of Mathematical, Physical and Natural Sciences: Prof. Andrea Caranti
Faculty of Sociology: Prof. Bruno Dallago
School of International Studies: Prof. Paolo Collini (Dir)
School on Local Development: Prof. Bruno Dallago (Dir)

UNIVERSITÀ DEGLI STUDI DI TRIESTE

Piazzale Europa 1, 34127 Trieste
Telephone: 040-5587111
E-mail: rettore@units.it
Internet: www.units.it

Founded 1924

Rector: Prof. Francesco Peroni
Vice-Rector: Prof. Sergio Paoletti
Admin. Dir: Dott. Antonino Di Guardo
Librarian: M. Luisa Nesbeda

Number of teachers: 1,200
Number of students: 24,500

Publication: *Piazzale Europa News* (3 a year, online)

DEANS

Advanced School of Modern Languages for Interpreters and Translators: Prof. Nadine Celotti
Faculty of Architecture: Prof. Giovanni Fraziano
Faculty of Economics: Prof. Gianluigi Gallenti
Faculty of Education: Prof. Giuseppe Battelli
Faculty of Engineering: Prof. Roberto Camus
Faculty of Humanities: Prof. Maria Cristina Benussi
Faculty of Law: Prof. Paolo Giangaspero
Faculty of Mathematics, Physics and Natural Sciences: Prof. Rinaldo Rui
Faculty of Medicine and Surgery: Prof. Nicolò De Manzini
Faculty of Pharmacy: Prof. Roberto Della Loggia
Faculty of Political Science: Prof. Roberto Scarciglia
Faculty of Psychology: Prof. Walter Gerbino

UNIVERSITÀ DEGLI STUDI DI UDINE

Palazzo Florio, Via Palladio 8, 33100 Udine
Telephone: 0432-556111
E-mail: urp@uniud.it
Internet: www.uniud.it

Founded 1978
State control
Language of instruction: Italian
Academic year: September to June

Rector: Prof. Alberto Felice De Toni
Pro-Rector: Prof. Angelo Vianello
Gen. Dir: Dott. Massimo di Silverio

Library of 839,000 vols, 2,518 journals, 48,028 ejournals
Number of teachers: 690
Number of students: 16,098

DEANS

Faculty of Agriculture: Prof. Roberto Pinton
Faculty of Economics: Prof. Marina Brollo
Faculty of Education: Prof. Gian Luca Foresti
Faculty of Engineering: Prof. Alberto Felice De Toni

Faculty of Humanities: Prof. ANDREA TABARRONI
Faculty of Law: Prof. DANILO CASTELLANO
Faculty of Mathematical, Physical and Natural Sciences: Prof. FRANCO PARLAMENTO
Faculty of Medicine and Surgery: Prof. MASSIMO BAZZOCCHI
Faculty of Foreign Languages and Literature: Prof. ANTONELLA RIEM NATALE
Faculty of Veterinary Medicine: Prof. BRUNO STEFANON

UNIVERSITÀ DEGLI STUDI DI URBINO 'CARLO BO'

Via Aurelio Saffi 2, 61029 Urbino
Telephone: 0722-3051
E-mail: rettore@uniurb.it
Internet: www.uniurb.it

Founded 1506
State control
Academic year: November to October

Rector: Prof. STEFANO PIVATO
Vice-Rector: Prof. GIANCARLO FERRERO
Admin. Dir: Dott. LUIGI BOTTEGHI

Library: see under Libraries and Archives
Number of teachers: 483
Number of students: 17,000

Publications: *Documents de Travail* (semiotics, in 6 series), *Fonti e Documenti* (history), *Hermeneutica* (philosophy), *Le Carte* (history), *Notizie da Palazzo Albani* (art review), *Quaderni dell'Istituto di Filosofia* (philosophy), *Quaderni di Hermeneutica* (philosophy), *Quaderni Urbinati di Cultura Classica* (philology), *Storie Locali* (history), *Studi Urbinati—A* (law and economics), *Studi Urbinati—B* (history, philosophy and literature)

DEANS

Faculty of Economics: Prof. MASSIMO CIAMBOTTI
Faculty of Education: Prof. DOMENICO LOSURDO
Faculty of Foreign Languages and Literature: Prof. ANNA TERESA OSSANI
Faculty of Law: Prof. EDUARDO ROZO ACUNA
Faculty of Letters and Philosophy: Prof. SETTIMIO LANCIOTTI
Faculty of Pharmacy: Prof. ORAZIO CANTONI
Faculty of Political Sciences: Prof. MARCO CANGIOTTI
Faculty of Science and Technology: Prof. STEFANO PAPA
Faculty of Sociology: Prof. BERNARDO VALLI
Faculty of Sports Science: Prof. VILBERTO STOCCHI

PROFESSORS

(Some staff serve in more than one faculty)

Faculty of Economics (Via Saffi 42, 61029 Urbino; tel. 0722-305500; e-mail presecon@uniurb.it; internet www.econ.uniurb.it):

- ANTONELLI, G., Marketing of Agroindustrial Products
- CIAMBOTTI, M., Economic Planning and Auditing
- FERRERO, G., Marketing
- GARDINI, L., Mathematics for Economic Applications
- GIAMPAOLI, A., Banking
- MARCHINI, I., Business Economics
- PAOLONI, M., General and Applied Accountancy
- PENCARELLI, T., Economics and Management
- POLIDORI, G., Transport Economics
- RINALDI, R., Financial Law
- STEFANINI, L., General Mathematics

Faculty of Education (Via Bramante 17, 61029 Urbino; tel. 0722-327628; e-mail lisa@uniurb.it; internet www.uniurb.it/sciform/home.htm):

- BALDACCI, M., General Pedagogy
- CUBELLI, R., General Psychology
- FILOGRASSO, N., General Pedagogy
- LOSURDO, D., History of Philosophy
- PERSI, P., Geography
- PIRANI, P., Educational Psychology
- RIPANTI, G., Theoretical Philosophy
- ROSSI, S., Theory and Techniques of Psychological Discourse
- SALA, G., Dynamic Psychology

Faculty of Environmental Sciences (Località Crocicchia, 61029 Urbino; tel. 0722-304271; e-mail sc.ambientali@uniurb.it; internet www.uniurb.it/sa/index.html):

- CECCHETTI, G., Principles of Environmental Protection
- CONFORTO, G., Laboratory of General Physics
- MAGNANI, F., Environmental Chemistry
- WEZEL FORESE, C., Stratigraphy
- ZUMINO, M. E., Biogeography

Faculty of Foreign Languages (Piazza Rinascimento 7, 61029 Urbino; tel. 0722-328506; e-mail pres.facolta.lingue@uniurb.it):

- BOGLIOLO, G., French Literature
- MORISCO, G., Anglo-American Languages and Literatures
- MULLINI, R., English Literature
- OSSANI, A. T., Italian Literature
- PIVATO, S., Contemporary History
- SAURIN DE LA IGLESIA, M. R., Spanish Literature
- VENTURELLI, A., History of German Culture
- ZAGANELLI, G., Romance Philology

Faculty of Law (Via Matteotti 1, 61029 Urbino; tel. 0722-3031; e-mail presidigiur@giur.uniurb.it; internet www.uniurb.it):

- DONDI, A., Civil Procedural Law
- FANTAPPIÈ, C., History of Canon Law
- FERRONI, L., Institutes of Private Law
- GILIBERTI, G., Roman Law
- MARI, L., International Law
- MOROZZO DELLA ROCCA, P., Civil Law
- ROZO ACUNA, E., Comparative Public Law

Faculty of Letters and Philosophy (Piano S. Lucia 6, 61029 Urbino; tel. 0722-320125; e-mail preslet@lettere.uniurb.it):

- ARBIZZONI ARTUSI, G., Philosophy of Italian Literature
- BERNARDINI, P., Greek Language and Literature
- BOLDRINI, S., Latin Language and Literature
- CECCHINI, E., Humanist Medieval Latin Literature
- CECCHINI, F. M., Contemporary History, History of the Risorgimento
- CERBONI BAIARDI, G., Italian Literature
- CUBEDDU, I., Theoretical Philosophy
- FRANCHI, A., Glottology and Linguistics
- GORI, F., History of Christianity and the Church
- GUERCIO, M., Archives, Bibliography and Librarianship
- ILLUMINATI, A., History of Philosophy
- LANCIOTTI, S., Latin Language and Literature
- PERINI, G., Museum Organization and Art and Restoration Criticism
- PERUSINO, F., Greek Language and Literature
- QUESTA, C., Classical Philology
- RAFFAELLI, R., Latin Language and Literature
- RINALDI TUFI, S., Classical Archaeology
- SCODITTI, G., Anthropological Demoethnic Studies
- TAROZZI, G., Logic and Philosophy of Science

Faculty of Mathematics, Physics and Natural Sciences (Località Crocicchia, 61029 Urbino; tel. 0722-304283; e-mail scienze.mmffnn@uniurb.it):

- ATTANASI, O. A., Organic Chemistry
- BALSAMO, M., Zoology
- BERETTA, E., Mathematical Analysis
- COCCIONI, R., Micropalaeontology
- COLANTONI, P., Sedimentology
- DEL GRANDE, P., Comparative Anatomy
- GAZZANELLI, G., Cytochemistry and Histochemistry
- GORI, U., Applied Geology
- MAGNANI, M., Biological Chemistry
- MICHELONI, M., General and Inorganic Chemistry
- NINFALI, P., Comparative Biochemistry
- PAPA, S., Human Anatomy
- PERRONE, V., Stratigraphic Geology

Faculty of Pharmacy (Via Saffi 2, 61029 Urbino; tel. 0722-329881; e-mail farmacia@uniurb.it):

- ACCORSI, A., Biological Chemistry
- CANTONI, O., Pharmacotherapy
- DACHÀ, M., Applied Biochemistry
- PIATTI, E., Food Science
- TARZIA, G., Pharmaceutical Chemistry and Toxicology
- VETRANO, F., Physics

Faculty of Physical Education and Health (Via Oddi 14, 61029 Urbino; tel. 0722-3517278; e-mail presid.smotorie@uniurb.it):

- FALCIERI, E., Human Anatomy
- STOCCHI, V., Applied Biochemistry

Faculty of Political Sciences (Via Bramante 17, 61029 Urbino; tel. 0722-328557; e-mail sc.politiche@uniurb.it):

- DELLA CANANEA, G., Administrative Law
- GREGOIRE, R., History of Christianity
- GUDERZO, M., History of International Relations
- MAZZONI, R., Political Economy
- PARLATO, V., Canon Law
- TENELLA-SILLANI, C., Institutes of Private Law

Faculty of Sociology (Via Saffi 15, 61029 Urbino; tel. 0722-327343; e-mail presidenza@soc.uniurb.it; internet www.soc.uniurb.it):

- ALFIERI, L., Political Philosophy
- DEI, M., Sociology of Education
- DEL TUTTO, L., General Linguistics
- DIAMANTI, I., Political Science
- FRANCI, A., Social Statistics
- GRASSI, P., Philosophy of Religions
- MAGGIONI, G., Sociology of Law
- MAZZOLI, G., Communication Sociology
- NEGROTTI, M., Methodology in Human Sciences
- PIAZZI, G., Sociological Theory
- VALLI, B., Mass-Media Sociology

UNIVERSITÀ DEGLI STUDI DI VERONA

Via dell'Artigliere 8, 37129 Verona
Telephone: 045-8028111
E-mail: sito@ateneo.univr.it
Internet: www.univr.it

Founded 1982

Rector: Prof. ALESSANDRO MAZZUCCO
Pro-Rector: Prof. BETTINA CAMPEDELLI
Admin. Dir: Dott. ANTONIO SALVINI
Library Dir: Dott. FABRIZIO BERTOLI

Number of teachers: 258
Number of students: 13,087

DEANS

Faculty of Economics: Prof. FRANCESCO ROSSI
Faculty of Education: Prof. MARIO LONGO
Faculty of Foreign Languages and Literature: Prof. ALESSANDRA TOMASELLI
Faculty of Humanities and Philosophy: Prof. GUIDO AVEZZÙ
Faculty of Law: Prof. STEFANO TROIANO
Faculty of Mathematical, Physical and Natural Sciences: Prof. ROBERTO GIACOBAZZI

Faculty of Medicine and Surgery: Prof. MICHELE TANSELLA
Faculty of Motor and Sports Science: Prof. CARLO MORANDI

UNIVERSITÀ DEGLI STUDI ROMA TRE

Via Ostiense 159, 00154 Rome
Telephone: 6-57332403
E-mail: segr_ret@uniroma3.it
Internet: www.uniroma3.it
Founded 1992
State control
Rector: Prof. GUIDO FABIANI
Deputy Rector: Prof. MARIO MORGANTI
Admin. Dir: Dott. PASQUALE BASILICATA
Library of 500,000 vols, 2,500 journals, 6,500 online journals
Number of teachers: 870
Number of students: 40,000

DEANS

Faculty of Architecture: Prof. FRANCESCO CELLINI
Faculty of Economics: Prof. CARLO MARIA TRAVAGLINI
Faculty of Education: Prof. GAETANO DOMENICI
Faculty of Engineering: Prof. PAOLO MELE
Faculty of Humanities: Prof. FRANCESCA CANTÙ
Faculty of Law: Prof. PAOLO BENVENUTI
Faculty of Mathematical, Physical and Natural Sciences: Prof. SETTIMIO MOBILIO
Faculty of Political Sciences: Prof. FRANCESCO GUIDA

UNIVERSITÀ DEL SALENTO

Piazza Tancredi N7, 73100 Lecce
Telephone: 0832-291111
E-mail: rettore@unisalento.it
Internet: www.unisalento.it
Founded 1956; current name 2006
Academic year: November to October
Rector: Prof. DOMENICO LAFORGIA
Admin. Dir: Dott. INNOCENZO SANTORO
Librarian: Dott. MARIA GRAZIA D'ALOISIO
Library of 1,000,000 vols, 600 journals
Number of teachers: 750
Number of students: 28,000

DEANS

Faculty of Cultural Heritage: Prof. REGINA POSO
Faculty of Economics: Prof. STEFANO ADAMO
Faculty of Education: Prof. GIOVANNI INVITTO
Faculty of Engineering: Prof. Ing. VITO DATTOMA
Faculty of Foreign Languages and Literature: Prof. ALIZIA ROMANOVIC
Faculty of Humanities: Prof. ROSARIO COLUCCIA
Faculty of Industrial Engineering: Prof. Ing. ANTONIO FICARELLA
Faculty of Law: Prof. RAFFAELE DE GIORGI
Faculty of Science: Prof. CARLO SEMPI
Faculty of Social and Political Science: Prof. MARCELLO STRAZZERI

UNIVERSITÀ DELLA CALABRIA

Via P. Bucci, 87036 Arcavacata di Rende
Telephone: 0984-4911
E-mail: diramm@unical.it
Internet: www.unical.it
Founded 1972
Academic year: November to October
Rector: Prof. GIOVANNI LATORRE
Admin. Officer: Dott. BRUNA ADAMO
Library of 400,000 vols
Number of teachers: 865 (incl. professors and researchers)
Number of students: 34,266

DEANS

Faculty of Economics: Prof. FRANCO RUBINO
Faculty of Engineering: Prof. PAOLO VELTRI
Faculty of Letters and Philosophy: Prof. RAFFAELE PERRELLI
Faculty of Mathematical, Physical and Natural Sciences: Prof. GINO MIROCLE CRISCI
Faculty of Pharmacy, Nutrition and Health: Prof. SEBASTIANO ANDÒ
Faculty of Political Sciences: Prof. GUERINO D'IGNAZIO

UNIVERSITÀ DI BOLOGNA

Via Zamboni 33, 40126 Bologna
Telephone: 51-2099111
Internet: www.unibo.it
Founded 1088
Languages of instruction: English, Italian, Spanish
Academic year: October to July
Rector: Prof. IVANO DIONIGI
Deputy Rector: Prof. EMILIO FERRARI
Vice-Rector for Financial Statements: Prof. SANDRO SANDRI
Vice-Rector for Int. Relations: Dr CARLA SALVATERRA
Vice-Rector for Research: Prof. DARIO BRAGA
Vice-Rector for the Romagna Campuses: Prof. GUIDO SARCHIELLI
Vice-Rector for Students and Institutional Communication: Prof. ROBERTO NICOLETTI
Vice-Rector for Teaching and Education: Prof. GIANLUCA FIORENTINI
Vice-Rector for Univ. Staff: Prof. PATRIZIA TULLINI
Dir-Gen.: Dott. GIUSEPPE COLPANI
Library of 1,250,000 vols and 400 video cassettes
Number of teachers: 2,881
Number of students: 87,418

DEANS

School of Agriculture and Veterinary Medicine: Prof. ANNA ZAGHINI
School of Arts, Humanities and Cultural Heritage: Prof. CONSTANTINO MARMO
School of Economics, Management and Statistics: Prof. RENZO ORSI
School of Engineering and Architecture: Prof. PIERPAOLO DIOTALLEVI
School of Foreign Languages and Literature, Interpreting and Translation: Prof. DANIELA GALLINGANI
School of Law: Prof. NICOLETTA SARTI
School of Medicine: Prof. LUIGI BOLONDI
School of Pharmacy, Biotechnology and Sport Science: Prof. CLAUDIO GALLETTI
School of Political Sciences: Prof. DANIELA GIANNETTI
School of Psychology and Education: Prof. BRUNA ZANI
School of Science: Prof. ANDREA BOTTONI

UNIVERSITÀ DI CAGLIARI

Via Università 40, 09124 Cagliari, Sardinia
Telephone: 070-6751
E-mail: rettore@unica.it
Internet: www.unica.it
Founded 1606 by Pope Paul V
Rector: Prof. GIOVANNI MELIS
Vice-Rector: Prof. GIOVANNA MARIA LEDDA
Admin. Dir: Dott. FABRIZIO CHERCHI
Librarian: Dott. DONATELLA TORE
Number of teachers: 1,000
Number of students: 18,000
Publication: *Studi Economico-Giuridici* and publs from each faculty

DEANS

Faculty of Architecture: Prof. ANTONELLO SANNA
Faculty of Economics: Prof. ERNESTINA GIUDICI
Faculty of Education: Prof. ANTONIO CADEDDU
Faculty of Engineering: Prof. GIORGIO MASSACCI
Faculty of Foreign Languages and Literature: Prof. GIUSEPPE MARCI
Faculty of Law: Prof. MASSIMO DEIANA
Faculty of Letters and Philosophy: ROBERTO CORONEO
Faculty of Mathematical, Physical and Natural Sciences: Prof. LUCA FANFANI
Faculty of Medicine and Surgery: Prof. MARIO PIGA
Faculty of Pharmacy: Prof. FILIPPO PIRISI
Faculty of Political Science: Prof. PAOLA PIRAS

UNIVERSITÀ DI FERRARA

Via Savonarola 9, 44121 Ferrara
Telephone: 0532-293111
E-mail: urp@unife.it
Internet: www.unife.it
Founded 1391
Academic year: November to October
Rector: Prof. PASQUALE NAPPI
Admin. Dir: Dott. CLARA COVIELLO
Number of teachers: 714
Number of students: 16,752
Publications: *Annali dell' Università*, *Ateneo* (6 a year)

DEANS

Faculty of Architecture: Prof. GRAZIANO TRIPPA
Faculty of Arts: Prof. MATTEO GALLI
Faculty of Economics: Prof. CATERINA COLOMBO
Faculty of Engineering: Prof. PIERO OLIVO
Faculty of Law: Prof. GIANGUIDO BALANDI
Faculty of Mathematical, Physical and Natural Sciences: Prof. ROBERTO CALABRESE
Faculty of Medicine and Surgery: Prof. ALBERTO LIBONI
Faculty of Pharmacy: Prof. SEVERO SALVADORI

PROFESSORS

Faculty of Architecture (Via Quartieri 8, 44100 Ferrara; tel. 0532-293613; e-mail faf@unife.it; internet architettura.fe.infn.it):

ACOCELLA, A., Architectural Technology
ALESSANDRI, C., Construction Theory
CECCARELLI, P., Urban Planning
DI FEDERICO, I., Industrial Technical Physics
LAUDIERO, F., Construction Methods
MINARDI, B., Urban and Architectonic Composition
TRIPPA, G., Architectural Technology

Faculty of Economics (Vicolo del Gregorio 13–15, 44100 Ferrara; tel. 0532-293000; internet www.economia.unife.it):

BIANCHI, P., Applied Economics
CALAMANTI, A., Economics of Financial Mediators
COCOZZA, F., Economic Law
PINI, P., Political Economy
POLA, G., Finance
SEGALA, F., Mathematical Analysis

Faculty of Engineering (Via Saragat 1, 44100 Ferrara; tel. 0532-974871; internet www.unife.it/facolta/facolta-300076.htm):

BEGHELLI, S., Automatic Controls
BETTOCCHI, R., Energy and Environmental Systems
DAL CIN, R., Stratigraphic and Sedimentological Geology

Dalpiaz, G., Applied Machine Mechanics
Del Piero, G., Construction Theory
Ferretti, P., Experimental Physics
Franchini, M., Hydraulic and Marine Hydraulic Engineering
Frontera, F., Experimental Physics
Lamma, E., Information Processing Systems
Olivo, P., Electronics
Padula, M., Mathematical Physics
Piva, S., Industrial Technical Physics
Pompoli, R., Environmental Technical Physics
Russo, P., Topography and Cartography
Tralli, A., Construction Theory
Zucchi, F., Chemical Foundations of Technology

Faculty of Law (Corso Ercole I d'Este 37, 44100 Ferrara; tel. 0532-205521; e-mail infogiur@unife.it; internet www.giuri.unife.it):

Adami, F. E., Canon and Ecclesiastical Law
Balandi, G. G., Labour Law
Bernardi, A., Penal Law
Bin, R., Constitutional Law
Borghi, P., Agrarian Law
Brunelli, G., Institutions of Public Law
Bruzzo, A., Political Economy
Cariello, V., Commercial Law
Casarotto, G., Agrarian Law
Cazzetta, G., History of Medieval and Modern Law
Ciaccia, B., Civil Procedure Law
Costato, L., Agrarian Law
De Giorgi, M. V., Private Law
Grippo, G., Commercial Law
Manfredini, A., Roman Law and Laws of Antiquity
Nappi, P., Agrarian Law
Pastore, B., Philosophy of Law
Pellizzer, F., Administrative Law
Pugiotto, A., Constitutional Law
Salerno, F., International Law
Scarano Ussani, V., Roman Law and Laws of Antiquity
Somma, A., Comparative Private Law
Zamorani, P., Roman Law and Laws of Antiquity

Faculty of Letters and Philosophy (Via Savonarola 38, 44100 Ferrara; tel. 0532-293416; internet www.unife.it/facolta/facolta-300035.htm):

Bellatalla, L., History of School and Educational Institutions
Bollini, M., Roman History
Campi, C. A., Geography
Cherchi, P., Italian Literature
Fabbri, P., Musicology and Musical History
Fava, E., Glottology and Linguistics
Folli, A., Contemporary Italian Literature
Galli, M., German Literature
Genovesi, G., General and Social Pedagogy
Matarrese, S., Italian Language
Mazzi, M. S., Medieval History
Mazzocchi, G., Spanish Literature
Merci, P., Romance Philology and Linguistics
Nespor, M. A., Glottology and Linguistics
Pancera, C., History of Schools and Educational Institutions
Ricci, G., Modern History
Sechi, S., Contemporary History
Tempera, M., English Literature
Trovato, P., Italian Language
Varese, R., History of Modern Art
Zanotti, A., General Sociology

Faculty of Mathematical, Physical and Natural Sciences (Via Luigi Borsari 46, 44100 Ferrara; tel. 0532-291347; internet www.unife.it/facolta/facolta-275017.htm):

Abelli, L., Comparative Anatomy and Cytology
Alberti, A., Mineralogy
Barbujani, G., Genetics
Beccaluva, L., Petrology and Petrography
Bernardi, F., Biochemistry
Biasini, L., Numerical Analysis
Bignozzi, C. A., General and Inorganic Chemistry
Bosellini, A., Stratigraphic and Sedimentological Geology
Broglio, A., Anthropologyy
Caneschi, L., Theoretical Physics and Mathematical Models and Methods
Cimiraglia, R., Physical Chemistry
Coltorti, M., Petrology and Petrography
Corallini, A., General Microbiology
Dalpiaz, P., General Physics
Del Centina, A., Geometry
Di Capua, E., Experimental Physics
Dondi, F., Analytical Chemistry
Dondoni, A., Organic Chemistry
Ellia, P., Geometry
Fagioli, F., Environmental and Conservation Chemistry
Fasulo, M. P., General Botany
Fiorentini, G., Nuclear and Subnuclear Physics
Foa', A. G., Zoology
Gerdol, R., Environmental and Applied Botany
Gilli, G., Physical Chemistry
Lascu, A., Geometry
Martinelli, G., Experimental Physics
Massari, U., Mathematical Analysis
Menini, C., Algebra
Nanni, T., Applied Geology
Nizzoli, F., Solid-State Physics
Pepe, L., Complementary Mathematics
Peretto, C., Anthropology
Piccolino, M., Physiology
Prodi, F., Earth Physics
Rossi, R., Ecology
Ruggiero, V., Numerical Analysis
Sacchi, O., Physiology
Sacerdoti, M., Mineralogy
Salvatorelli, G., Comparative Anatomy and Cytology
Scandola, F., General and Inorganic Chemistry
Schiffrer, G., Theoretical Physics and Mathematical Models and Methods
Siena, F., Petrology and Petrography
Solonnikov, V., Mathematical Physics
Traverso, O., General and Inorganic Chemistry
Tripiccione, R., Theoretical Physics and Mathematical Models and Methods
Zanghirati, L., Mathematical Analysis

Faculty of Medicine and Surgery (Via Fossato di Mortara 64/b, 44100 Ferrara; tel. 0532-291545; e-mail preside.medicina@unife.it; internet unife.it/facolta/medicina):

Avato, F. M., Forensic Medicine
Azzena, G. F., General Surgery
Bergamini, C., Clinical Biochemistry and Clinical Molecular Biology
Berti, G., General Pathology
Borea, P. A., Pharmacology
Borgna, C., General and Specialized Paediatrics
Calura, G., Odontostomatological Diseases
Calzolari, E., Medical Genetics
Capitani, S., Human Anatomy
Caruso, A., Histology
Cassai, E., Microbiology and Clinical Microbiology
Castoldi, G. L., Haematology
Cavazzini, L., Anatomical Pathology
Ciaccia, A., Diseases of the Respiratory Tract
Conconi, F., Biochemistry
Croce, C. M., Medical Oncology
Dallocchio, F. P. F., Biochemistry
De Rosa, E., Industrial Medicine
Degli Uberti, E., Endocrinology
Del Senno, L., Molecular Biology
Di Virgilio, F., General Pathology
Donini, I. G., General Surgery
Durante, E., General Surgery
Favilla, M., Physiology
Fellin, R., Internal Medicine
Ferrari, R., Cardiovascular Diseases
Granieri, E., Neurology
Grazi, E., Biochemistry
Gregorio, P., General and Applied Hygiene
Gualdi, E., Anthropology
Liboni, A., General Surgery
Longhini, C., Internal Medicine
Mannella, P., Imaging and Radiotherapy Diagnostics
Martini, A., Audiology
Molinari, S., Clinical Psychology
Mollica, G., Obstetrics and Gynaecology
Nenci, I., Anatomy and Pathological Histology
Pastore, A., Otolaryngology
Pinamonti, S., Applied Biology
Ramelli, E., Psychiatry
Regoli, D., Pharmacology
Sebastiani, A., Eyesight Diseases
Siciliani, G., Odontostomatological Diseases
Spidalieri, G., Physiology
Tognon, M., Applied Biology
Traina, G. C., Ambulatory Diseases
Trotta, F., Rheumatology
Turini, D., Urology
Vigi, V., General and Specialized Paediatrics
Virgili, A., Skin and Venereal Diseases

Faculty of Pharmacy (Via Fossato di Mortara 17/19, 44100 Ferrara; tel. 0532-291265; e-mail farmline@unife.it; internet web.unife.it/facolta/farmacia):

Baraldi, P. G., Pharmaceutical Chemistry
Bianchi, C., Pharmacology
Biondi, C., Physiology
Brandolini, V., Food Chemistry
Bruni, A., Pharmocological Biology
Gambaccini, M., Applied Physics (Conservation, Environmental, Biological and Medical)
Gambari, R., Biochemistry
Manfredini, S., Pharmaceutical Chemistry
Manservigi, R., Microbiology and Clinical Microbiology
Menegatti, E., Applied Pharmaceutical Technology
Pollini, G. P., Organic Chemistry
Rizzuto, R., General Pathology
Salvadori, S., Pharmaceutical Chemistry
Scatturin, A., Applied Pharmaceutical Chemistry
Simoni, D., Pharmaceutical Chemistry
Tanganelli, S., Pharmacology
Tomatis, R., Pharmaceutical Chemistry
Traniello, M. S., Biochemistry

UNIVERSITÀ IUAV DI VENEZIA

Santa Croce 191, Tolentini, 30135 Venice
Telephone: 041-2571750
E-mail: rettorato@iuav.it
Internet: www.iuav.it

Founded 1926
public control
Language of instruction: Italian
Academic year: November to October

Rector: Prof. Amerigo Restucci
Vice-Rector: Prof. Donatella Calabi
Admin. Dir: Anna Maria Cremonese
Librarian: Dott. Anna Tonicello

Library of 123,000 vols, 2,500 periodicals
Number of teachers: 517
Number of students: 12,000

DEANS

Dept of Architecture and Arts: Prof. Carlo Magnani

Dept of Architecture, Construction and Conservation: Prof. RENZO DUBBINI
Dept of Design and Planning in Complex Environments: Prof. MEDARDO CHIAPPONI

UNIVERSITÀ MEDITERRANEA DI REGGIO CALABRIA

Via Diana 3, 89125 Reggio Calabria
Telephone: 0965-872912
E-mail: amministrazione@pec.unirc.it
Internet: www.unirc.it
Founded 1982
Rector: Prof. MASSIMO GIOVANNINI
Pro-Rector: Prof. FRANCESCO RUSSO
Admin. Dir: ANTONIO ROMEO
Number of students: 9,697

DEANS
Faculty of Agriculture: Prof. SANTO MARCELLO ZIMBONE
Faculty of Architecture: Prof. FRANCESCA FATTA
Faculty of Engineering: Prof. ADOLFO SANTINI
Faculty of Law: Prof. ATTILIO GORASSINI

UNIVERSITÀ POLITECNICA DELLE MARCHE

Piazza Roma 22, 60121 Ancona
Telephone: 071-2201
E-mail: info@univpm.it
Internet: www.univpm.it
Founded 1969
State control
Academic year: November to October
Rector: Prof. SAURO LONGHI
Vice-Rector: Prof. GIAN LUCA GREGORI
Admin. Dir: Dott. LUISIANA SEBASTIANELLI
Librarian: Dott. SANDRO APIS
Library of 26,000 vols
Number of teachers: 534
Number of students: 16,900

DEANS
Department of Agriculture: Prof. BRUNO MEZZETTI
Department of Sciences: Prof. PAOLO MARIANI
Faculty of Economics: Prof. FRANCESCO MARIA CHELLI
Faculty of Engineering: Prof. DARIO AMODIO
Faculty of Medicine and Surgery: Prof. ANTONIO BENEDETTI

Other Universities, Colleges and Institutes

AMERICAN UNIVERSITY OF ROME

Via Pietro Roselli 4, 00153 Rome
Telephone: 06-58330919
E-mail: admissions@aur.edu
Internet: www.aur.edu
Founded 1969
Language of instruction: English
Academic year: August to July
Pres.: Dr ANDREW THOMPSON
Provost: Dr MAURIZIO MAMORSTEIN
Dir of First Year Program and Coordinator of Special Projects: DIANE FRANCES HYETT
Assoc. Dean of Enrolment Services and Registrar: STEFANIA IORIO
Dir of Library and Information Services: JAMES L. WEINHEIMER
Library of 15,000 vols
Number of teachers: 69
Number of students: 500

ENI CORPORATE UNIVERSITY—SCUOLA ENRICO MATTEI

Via S. Salvo 1, 20097 San Donato Milanese
Telephone: 02-52057907
E-mail: info.scuolamattei@eni.it
Internet: www.enicorporateuniversity.it/scuolamattei/
Founded 1957
Academic year: September to June
Economic and management studies; higher degrees in energy and environmental economics, and petroleum engineering.
Dean: Prof. PIERANGELO CIGNOLI
Library of 15,000 vols
Number of teachers: 50
Number of students: 55 new students per year
Publication: *Quaderni* (3 a year)

EUROPEAN UNIVERSITY INSTITUTE

Via dei Roccettini 9, 50014 San Domenico di Fiesole, Florence
Telephone: 055-46851
Internet: www.eui.eu
Founded 1972 by the mem. states of the European Communities (present-day EU)
Academic year: September to June
Language of instruction: EU languages
Depts of economics, history and civilization, law, and political and social sciences
Pres.: MARISE CREMONA
Sec.-Gen.: Dott. PASQUALE FERARA
Library Dir: VEERLE DECKMYN
Library of 500,000 vols, 3,000 journals
Number of teachers: 50 (full-time)
Number of students: 600 (postgraduate)
Publications: *EUI Review*, *EUI Working Papers*, *European Foreign Policy Bulletin*, *European Journal of International Law*, *European Law Journal*, *President's Annual Report*, *Robert Schuman Centre Newsletter*.

ATTACHED INSTITUTIONS
Academy of European Law: e-mail academy@eui.eu; internet www.eui.eu/departmentsandcentres/academyeuropeanlaw; Advanced-level summer courses in human rights law and EU law; Dirs Prof. LOÏC AZOULAI, Prof. MARISE CREMONA, Prof. FRANCESCO FRANCIONI.
Robert Schuman Centre for Advanced Studies: e-mail rscsecretariat@eui.eu; internet www.eui.eu/departmentsandcentres/robertschumancentre; Research on Europe and the processes of European integration. Core themes are: European instns, governance and democracy; migration; economic and monetary policy; competition policy and market regulation; energy policy; int. and transnational relations of the EU; Dir Prof. STEFANO BARTOLINI

FREIE UNIVERSITÄT BOZEN/LIBERA UNIVERSITÀ DI BOLZANO (Free University of Bozen/Bolzano)

Piazza Università 1, 39100 Bolzano
Telephone: 0471-011000
E-mail: info@unibz.it
Internet: www.unibz.it
Founded 1997
Provincial state control
Languages of instruction: German, Italian, English
President: Dr KONRAD BERGMEISTER
Rector: Prof. WALTER A. LORENZ
Vice-Rector for Intercultural Communication: Prof. JOHANN DRUMBL
Vice-Rector for Research: Prof. YURIY KANIOVSKYI
Head of Library: ELISABETH FRASNELLI
Library of 77,300 books, 1,036 periodicals, 4,250 online journals, 68 databases
Number of teachers: 25
Number of students: 1,965

DEANS
Faculty of Computer Science: Prof. GIANCARLO SUCCI
School of Economics and Management: Prof. MAURIZIO MURGIA
Faculty of Education: Prof. Dr FRANZ COMPLOI
Faculty of Design and Art: Prof. Dr phil. habil. GERHARD GLÜHER
Faculty of Science and Technology: Prof. MASSIMO TAGLIAVINI

IMT INSTITUTE FOR ADVANCED STUDIES

Piazza San Ponziano 6, 55100 Lucca
Telephone: 0583-4326561
E-mail: info@imtlucca.it
Internet: www.imtlucca.it
State control
Language of instruction: English
Academic year: February to January
Doctoral programmes: computer science and engineering, management and devt of cultural heritage, political systems and institutional change, and economics, markets, institutions
Dir: Prof. FABIO PAMMOLLI
Deputy Dir: Prof. ALBERTO BEMPORAD
Librarian: CATERINA TANGHERONI
Library of 4,200 vols
Number of teachers: 35
Number of students: 128

ISTITUTO ITALIANO DI SCIENZE UMANE (SUM)

Palazzo Strozzi, Piazza degli Strozzi, 50123 Florence
Telephone: 055-2673300
Internet: www.sumitalia.it
State control
Masters course in local govt; doctoral courses in political science, European private law; scholarships for post-doctoral research in humanities
Dir: Prof. MARIO CITRONI
Admin. Dir: Dott. ANTONIO CUNZIO

ISTITUTO REGIONALE DI STUDI E RICERCA SOCIALE

Piazza S. Maria Maggiore 7, 38100 Trento
Telephone: 0461-273611
E-mail: info@irsrs.tn.it
Internet: irsrs.isite.it
Founded 1947; until c. 1993, Scuola Superiore Regionale di Servizio Sociale
Two-year course for health workers
Pres.: Dott. ITALO MONFREDINI
Dir: Dott. LAURA RAVANELLI
Library of 15,000 vols, 825 journals, 300 current journals
Number of teachers: 350
Number of students: 6,000
Publication: *Annali* (1 a year).

CONSTITUENT INSTITUTE
Università della Terza Età e del Tempo Disponibile (Open University): internet irsrs.isite.it/area4; training for social workers, and adult education

ISTITUTO UNIVERSITARIO DI STUDI EUROPEI (IUSE)
(University Institute of European Studies)

Via Maria Vittoria 26, 10123 Turin
Telephone: 11-8394660
E-mail: info@iuse.it
Internet: www.iuse.it
Founded 1952
Language of instruction: English, French
Offers postgraduate courses, exec. courses and research in European and international law and economics
Pres.: Prof. MARIO COMBA
Library of 45,000 vols, incl. books, periodicals, official publs from EU and other int. orgs

ISTITUTO UNIVERSITARIO DI STUDI SUPERIORI (IUSS)

Viale Lungo Ticino Sforza 56, 27100 Pavia
Telephone: 0382-375811
E-mail: external.relations@iusspavia.it
Internet: www.iusspavia.it
Founded 1997
Languages of instruction: Italian, English
Courses in humanities, social sciences, science and technology, biomedical sciences; master's and higher education courses in management of complex systems, media science and technology, materials science, seismic engineering, nuclear technology, developmental cooperation, exec. programme in int. economic integration, int. design seminar; doctoral courses offered in asscn with the Università degli Studi di Pavia
Dir: Prof. ROBERTO SCHMID

ITALIAN UNIVERSITY LINE (IUL)

Via M. Buonarroti 10, 50122 Florence
E-mail: segreteria@iuline.it
Internet: www.iuline.it
Founded 2005
Private control
Offers distance learning
Rector: Prof. STEFANIA FUSCAGNI

JOHN CABOT UNIVERSITY

Via della Lungara 233, 00165 Rome
Telephone: 06-6819121
E-mail: info@johncabot.edu
Internet: www.johncabot.edu
Office in USA: 14100 Walsingham Rd, Suite 36, #10, Largo, FL 33774, USA
E-mail: usoffice@johncabot.edu
Founded 1972
Independent, four-year institution of liberal arts
President: FRANCO PAVONCELLO
Vice-President and Dean of Academic Affairs: MARY MERVA
Vice-President for Operations and Finance: ANDREA GIUMMARRA
Registrar: CARMEN SCARPATI
Head Librarian: ELISABETTA MORANI
Library: Frohring Library: reference material, curriculum-related items, newspapers, 1,000 online journals
Number of teachers: 100
Number of students: 850

PROFESSORS

CREAGAN, J. F., International Relations
GRAY, L. E., Political Science

JOHNS HOPKINS UNIVERSITY—SCHOOL OF ADVANCED INTERNATIONAL STUDIES EUROPE AT BOLOGNA

Via Belmeloro 11, 40126 Bologna
Telephone: 051-2917811
E-mail: sais.eu.admissions@jhu.edu
Internet: www.sais-jhu.edu
Founded 1955
Language of instruction: English
Academic year: September to May
Dir: Prof. KENNETH KELLER
Dir for Finance and Admin.: BART DRAKULICH
Registrar: BERNADETTE O'TOOLE
Head Librarian: GAIL MARTIN
Library of 85,000 vols
Number of teachers: 50
Number of students: 185
Publication: *Bologna Center Journal of International Affairs* (1 a year)

LIBERA UNIVERSITÀ DEGLI STUDI DI ENNA 'KORE' (UKE)

Cittadella Universitaria, 94100 Enna (SI)
Telephone: 0935-536342
E-mail: rettore@unikore.it
Internet: www.unikore.it
Founded 2004
Private control with public participation
Pres.: Prof. CATALDO SALERNO
Rector: Prof. SALVO ANDÒ
Admin. Dir: Dott. SALVATORE BERRITTELLA

DEANS

Faculty of Arts and Communication: Prof. LIBORIO TERMINE
Faculty of Economic and Social Sciences: Prof. GIACOMO MULÉ
Faculty of Engineering and Architecture: Prof. GIOVANNI TESORIERE
Faculty of Law: Prof. GIUSEPPE DI CHIARA
Faculty of Psychology and Educational Sciences: Prof. VALERIA SCHIMMENTI
Faculty of Sports Science and Wellbeing: Prof. MARIO LIPOMA

LIBERA UNIVERSITÀ DEGLI STUDI PER L'INNOVAZIONE E LE ORGANIZZAZIONI (LUSPIO)

Via delle Sette Chiese 139. 00145 Rome
Telephone: 06-5107771
E-mail: info@luspio.it
Internet: www.luspio.it
Founded 1996
Private control
Rector: Prof. GIUSEPPE ACOCELLA
Deputy Rector: Prof. GIANDOMENICO BOFFI
Admin. Dir: Dott. CRISTIANO NICOLETTI

DEANS

Faculty of Economics: Prof. GUIDO PAGGI
Faculty of Interpretation and Translation: Prof. NOVELLA NOVELLI
Faculty of Political Sciences: Prof. OLGA MARZOVILLA
Higher School of Advanced Studies: Prof. ROBERTO GUIDA (Dir)

LIBERA UNIVERSITÀ DI LINGUE E COMUNICAZIONE IULM

Via Carlo Bo 1, 20143 Milan
Telephone: 02-891411
E-mail: iulm.orienta@iulm.it
Internet: www.iulm.it
Founded 1968
Languages of instruction: English, Italian
Academic year: October to May
Rector: Prof. GIOVANNI A. PUGLISI
Vice-Rector: Prof. MARIO NEGRI
Library Dir: Prof. MARIA T. BETTETINI
Library of 190,000 vols, 1,350 journals
Number of teachers: 350
Number of students: 4,000

DEANS

Faculty of Arts, Tourism and Markets: Prof. ANGELO TURCO
Faculty of Communications, Public Relations and Advertising: Prof. GIAN BATTISTA CANOVA
Faculty of Interpreting, Translation, and Language and Cultural Studies: Prof. PAOLO PROIETTI

LIBERA UNIVERSITÀ INTERNAZIONALE DEGLI STUDI SOCIALI 'GUIDO CARLI'
(Independent International University of Social Studies)

Viale Pola 12, 00198 Rome
Telephone: 06-852251
E-mail: direzionegenerale@luiss.it
Internet: www.luiss.it
Founded 1945, recognized by the Government 1966
Languages of instruction: English, Italian
Pres.: Dott. EMMA MARCEGAGLIA
Rector: Prof. MASSIMO EGIDI
Gen. Dir: PIER LUIGI CELLI
Librarian: Dr BEATRIZ VILLAGRASA HERNANDEZ
Library of 128,000 vols, 1,975 journals, 63,733 ejournals, 13,798 ebooks, 75 databases
Number of teachers: 1,070
Number of students: 7,708

DEANS

Dept of Business and Management: Prof. GENNARO OLIVIERI
Dept of Finance and Economics: Prof. GIORGIO DI GIORGIO
Dept of Law: Prof. ANTONIO NUZZO
Dept of Political Science: Prof. SEBASTIANO MAFFETONE

LIBERA UNIVERSITÀ MARIA SS. ASSUNTA

Via della Traspontina 21, 00193 Rome
Telephone: 06-684221
E-mail: lumsa@lumsa.it
Internet: www.lumsa.it
Founded 1939
Academic year: October to July
Rector: Prof. GIUSEPPE DALLA TORRE DEL TEMPIO DI SANGUINETTO
Vice-Rector: Prof. GIUSEPPE IGNESTI
Admin. Dir: Dott. GIANNINA DI MARCO
Librarian: Dott. GIUSEPPINA D'ALESSANDRO
Library of 100,000 vols
Number of teachers: 350
Number of students: 5,200
Publications: *I Quaderni della Lumsa* (1 a year), *Nuovi Studi Politici* (4 a year)

DEANS

Faculty of Eduction: Prof. CONSUELO CORRADI
Faculty of Law: Prof. ANGELO RINELLA
Faculty of Letters and Philosophy: Prof. LOREDANA LAZZARI

LIBERA UNIVERSITÀ MEDITERRANEA 'JEAN MONNET'

S. S. 100 Km 18, Casamassima (BA)
Telephone: 080-6978111
E-mail: info@lum.it
Internet: www.lum.it
Founded 1995
Private control

Rector: EMANUELE DEGENNARO
Admin. Dir: FELICE GNAGNARELLA

Library of 11,000 vols, 160 journals, 30 online journals

DEANS

Faculty of Economics: Prof. ANTONELLO GARZONI
Faculty of Law: Prof. ROBERTO MARTINO

SCUOLA INTERNAZIONALE SUPERIORE DI STUDI AVANZATI

Via Bonomea 265, 34136 Trieste

Telephone: 040-3787111
Internet: www.sissa.it

Founded 1978; sponsored by the Italian Govt
public control
Languages of instruction: English, Italian
Academic year: November to October

Higher degrees in physics, mathematics and neuroscience; research; fellowships for students

Dir: Prof. GUIDO MARTINELLI
Admin. Dir: GABRIELE RIZZETTO

Library of 20,000 vols, 120 journals, 7,000 ejournals
Number of teachers: 62
Number of students: 230

SCUOLA NORMALE SUPERIORE DI PISA

Piazza dei Cavalieri 7, 56126 Pisa

Telephone: 50-509111
E-mail: info@pec.sns.it
Internet: www.sns.it

Founded 1810
State control

Dir: Prof. FABIO BELTRAM
Admin. Dir: Dott. ANNA MARIA GAIBISSO
Library Dir: Dott. ENRICO MARTELLINI

Library: 1m. vols
Number of teachers: 40
Number of students: 280

Publications: *Annali* (Arts series, Science series), *Appunti*, *Bibliotheca*, *Colloquia*, *CRM Series* (mathematical research), *Seminari e Convegni*, *Strumenti*, *Studi*, *Tesi*, *Testi e Commenti*

DEANS

Faculty of Arts: Prof. DANIELE MENOZZI
Faculty of Sciences: Prof. RICCARDO BARBIERI

SCUOLA SUPERIORE DI STUDI UNIVERSITARI E DI PERFEZIONAMENTO 'SANT'ANNA'

Piazza Martiri della Libertà 33, 56127 Pisa

Telephone: 50-883111
E-mail: urp@sssup.it
Internet: www.sssup.it

Founded 1987
Private control

Programmes in economics, law, political sciences, agriculture, medicine, industrial and information engineering; offers standard courses, univ. and int. Masters degree courses, PhD programmes and doctorates, and advanced education

Pres.: Prof. RICCARDO VARALDO
Dir: Prof. MARIA CHIARA CARROZZA
Admin. Dir: MARIO GARZELLA

Library of 70,000 vols, 200 current journals, 30,000 online journals
Number of teachers: 103
Number of students: 1,810

DEANS

Academic Class of Experimental Sciences: Prof. ENRICO BONARI
Academic Class of Social Sciences: Prof. EMANUELE ROSSI

UNIVERSITÀ CAMPUS BIO-MEDICO DI ROMA

Via Álvaro del Portillo, 21, 00128 Rome

Telephone: 06-225411
E-mail: info@unicampus.it
Internet: www.unicampus.it

Founded 1991
Private control

Pres.: Prof. PAOLO ARULLANI
Rector: Prof. VINCENZO LORENZELLI
Admin. Dir: Ing. PAOLO SORMANI

DEANS

Faculty of Engineering: Prof. LUIGI MARRELLI
Faculty of Medicine and Surgery: Prof. VINCENZO DENARO

UNIVERSITÀ CARLO CATTANEO—LIUC

Corso Matteotti 22, 21053 Castellanza (VA)

Telephone: 0331-5721
E-mail: info@liuc.it
Internet: www.liuc.it

Founded 1991
Private control

Rector: ANDREA TARONI
Gen. Dir: PIERLUIGI RIVA

DEANS

Faculty of Economics: Prof. VALTER LAZZARI
Faculty of Engineering: Prof. GIACOMO BUONANNO
Faculty of Law: Prof. MARIO ZANCHETTI

UNIVERSITÀ CATTOLICA DEL SACRO CUORE
(Catholic University of the Sacred Heart)

Largo A. Gemelli 1, 20123 Milan

Telephone: 2-72341
E-mail: seg.prorettori@unicatt.it
Internet: www.unicattolica.it

Founded 1920, recognized by the Govt 1924

Rector: Prof. LORENZO ORNAGHI
Admin. Dir: Prof. MARCO ELEFANTI
Librarian: Dott. ELLIS SADA

Library: 2m. vols, 32,000 journals, 12,000 online journals
Number of teachers: 1,400
Number of students: 42,000

Publication: various, published by individual faculties

DEANS

Faculty of Agriculture: Prof. LORENZO MORELLI
Faculty of Banking, Finance and Insurance Sciences: Prof. MARIO ANOLLI
Faculty of Economics (Milan and Rome): Prof. DOMENICO BODEGA
Faculty of Economics (Piacenza): Prof. MAURIZIO LUIGI BAUSSOLA
Faculty of Education: Prof. MICHELE LENOCI
Faculty of Law (Milan): Prof. GABRIO FORTI
Faculty of Law (Piacenza): Prof. ROMEO ASTORRI
Faculty of Letters and Philosophy: Prof. ANGLEO BIANCHI
Faculty of Linguistic Sciences and Foreign Literatures: Prof. LUISA CAMAIORA
Faculty of Mathematical, Physical and Natural Sciences: Prof. ALFREDO MARZOCCHI
Faculty of Medicine and Surgery: Prof. ROCCO BELLANTONE
Faculty of Political Sciences: Prof. CARLO BERETTA
Faculty of Psychology: Prof. EUGENIA SCABINI
Faculty of Sociology: Prof. MAURO MAGATTI

UNIVERSITÀ COMMERCIALE LUIGI BOCCONI

Via Sarfatti 25, 20136 Milan

Telephone: 2-58361
Internet: www.unibocconi.eu

Founded 1902
Private control
Academic year: November to October

Pres.: Prof. MARIO MONTI
Rector: Prof. GUIDO TABELLINI
Vice-Pres.: Prof. LUIGI GUATRI
Man. Dir: Dott. BRUNO PAVESI

Number of teachers: 971
Number of students: 12,600

Publications: *Azienda Pubblica*, *Commercio*, *Economia delle Fonti di Energia*, *Economia e Management*, *Economia e Politica Industriale*, *Finanza Marketing e Produzione*, *Giornale degli Economisti e Annali di Economia*, *Sviluppo e Organizzazione*

DEANS

Graduate School: Prof. FRANCESCO SAITA
PhD School: Prof. ALFONSO GAMBARDELLA
School of Law: Prof. GIOVANNI IUDUCA
SDA Bocconi School of Management: Prof. ALBERTO GRANDO
Undergraduate School: Prof. GIOVANNI VALOTTI

PROFESSORS

AIROLDI, G., Business Administration
ALESSANDRI, A., Commercial Law
AMATORI, F., Economic History
AMIGONI, F., Business Administration
ARTONI, R., Public Finance
BATTIGALLI, P., Economics
BELTRATTI, A., Economics
BERTONI, A., Corporate Finance
BIANCHI, L. A., Company and Business Law
BINI, M., Corporate Finance
BORGONOVI, E., Public Administration
BRUGGER, G., Corporate Finance
BRUNETTI, G., Business Administration
BRUNI, F., International Monetary Theory and Policy
BUSACCA, B., Business Administration and Management
CASTAGNOLA, A., Civil Law
CASTAGNOLI, E., Mathematics
CATTINI, M., Economic History
CIFARELLI, D. M., Statistics
CODA, V., Business Administration
DE PAOLI, L., Business Administration and Management
DEMATTÈ, C., Financial Intermediaries
FABRIZI, P. L., Securities Market
FAVERO, C. A., Monetary Economics
FERRARI, G., Monetary Economics
FILIPPINI, C., Economic Development
FORESTIERI, G., Financial Intermediaries
FRACCHIA, F., Administrative Law
FROVA, A., Corporate Finance
GIAVAZZI, F., Economics
GOLFETTO, F., Business Administration and Management
GRANDORI, A., Corporate Organization
GUARNERI, A., Comparative Civil Law
INVERNIZZI, G., Business Administration
IUDICA, G., Civil Law
LIEBMAN, S., Labour Law
MALERBA, F., Business Administration
MARCHETTI, P., Industrial Law
MASSARI, M., Capital Budgeting
MONTESANO, A., Economics
MONTI, M., Economics
MOTTURA, P., Financial Intermediaries
MULIERE, P., Statistics
ONIDA, F., International Economics
PACI, S., Management of Insurance Companies and Savings Institutions

PECCATI, L., Mathematics for Economics and Finance
PERRONE, V., Organization Theory
PEZZANI, F., Business Administration
PIVATO, S., Industrial Management
PODESTÀ, S., Commercial Management
PORTA, A., Monetary Theory and Policy
PROVASOLI, A., Cost Accounting and Management Control Systems
ROMANI, A., Economic History
RUOZI, R., Banking
SACERDOTI, G., International Law
SALVEMINI, S., Human Resources Management
SECCHI, C., Economics of the European Communities
SENN, L., Regional Economics
SITZIA, B., Econometrics
TABELLINI, G., Economics
URBANI, G., Political Science
VALDANI, E., Marketing
VALOTTI, G., Business Administration
VERONESE, P., Statistics
VICARI, S., Management of Industrial Companies
VIGANO, A., Cost Accounting and Management Control Systems

UNIVERSITÀ DEGLI STUDI DI SCIENZE GASTRONOMICHE
(University of Gastronomic Sciences)

Piazza Vittorio Emanuele 9, fraz. Pollenzo, 12042 Bra (CN)
Telephone: 0172-458511
E-mail: info@unisg.it
Internet: www.unisg.it
Founded 2004
Private control
Undergraduate course in gastronomic sciences; graduate course in gastronomy and food communications; Masters courses in Italian gastronomy and tourism, and food culture and communications; Advanced School in Sustainability and Food Policies
Rector: Prof. VALTER CANTINO
Vice-Rector: Prof. ALBERTO CAPATTI
Admin. Dir: CARLO CATANI
Number of teachers: 15

UNIVERSITÀ DEGLI STUDI E-CAMPUS

Via Isimbardi 10, 22060 Novedrate (CO)
Telephone: 031-7942500
E-mail: info@uniecampus.it
Internet: www.uniecampus.it
Founded 2006
Private control
Pres.: Prof. LANFRANCO ROSATI
Offers distance learning

COORDINATORS
Faculty of Arts: Prof. PAOLO TROVATO
Faculty of Economics: Prof. ELISABETTA BERTACCHINI
Faculty of Engineering: Prof. CARLO MARIA BARTOLINI

UNIVERSITÀ DEGLI STUDI SUOR ORSOLA BENINCASA

Corso Vittorio Emanuele 292, 80135 Naples
Telephone: 081-2522111
E-mail: f.desanctis@unisob.na.it
Internet: www.unisob.na.it
Founded 1864
Private control
Rector: Prof. FRANCESCO DE SANCTIS
Deputy Rector: Prof. LUCIO D'ALESSANDRO
Admin. Dir: Dott. ANTONIO CUNZIO

DEANS
Faculty of Arts: Prof. EMMA GIAMMATTEI
Faculty of Education: Prof. LUCIO D'ALESSANDRO
Faculty of Law: Prof. FRANCO FICHERA

UNIVERSITÀ DELLA VALLE D'AOSTA/ UNIVERSITÉ DE LA VALLÉE D'AOSTE

Strada Cappuccini 2A, 11100 Aosta
Telephone: 0165-306711
E-mail: info@univda.it
Internet: www.univda.it
Founded 2000
Private control
Languages of instruction: Italian, English, French, Spanish, German
Rector: Prof. PIETRO PASSERIN D'ENTRÈVES
Admin. Dir: Dott. FRANCO VIETTI

DEANS
Faculty of Economics and Management: Prof. CHIARA MAURI
Faculty of Education: Prof. TERESA GRANGE
Faculty of Languages and Communication: Prof. CARLO MARIA BAJETTA
Faculty of Political Sciences: Prof. MICHELE VELLANO
Faculty of Psychology: Prof. MARIA GRAZIA MONACI

UNIVERSITÀ EUROPEA DI ROMA

Via degli Aldobrandeschi 190, 00163 Rome
Telephone: 06-665431
E-mail: rettorato@unier.it
Internet: www.universitaeuropeadiroma.it
Founded 2004
Private control
Rector: Prof. Padre PAOLO SCARAFONI
Gen. Sec.: Padre JESÚS PARREÑO
Undergraduate courses in economics, history, law, psychology

UNIVERSITÀ PER STRANIERI 'DANTE ALIGHIERI'

Via del Torrione 95, 89125 Reggio di Calabria
Telephone: 0965-312593
E-mail: rettore@unistrada.it
Internet: www.unistrada.it
Founded 1984
Private control
Rector: Prof. SALVATORE BERLINGÒ
Pro-Rector: Prof. ANTONINO ZUMBO
Admin. Dir: ALESSANDRO ZOCCALI
Undergraduate courses in social sciences, literature, foreign languages and literature; graduate courses in planning and management of policies and social sciences, int. marketing; European Masters degree course

UNIVERSITÀ PER STRANIERI DI PERUGIA

Piazza Fortebraccio 4, 06123 Perugia
Telephone: 75-57461
E-mail: diramm@unistrapg.it
Internet: www.unistrapg.it
Founded 1921
Academic year: January to December
Rector: Prof. STEFANIA GIANNINI
Vice-Rector: Prof. MARCO IMPAGLIAZZO
Admin. Dir: Dott. ANTONELLA BIANCONI
Library of 70,000 vols
Number of teachers: 100
Number of students: 7,000
Publication: *Annali dell'Università*

DEANS
Faculty of Italian Language and Culture: Prof. PAOLA BIANCHI DE VECCHI

ATTACHED CENTRES
Centre for Language Evaluation and Certification: Dir Prof. GIULIANA GREGO BOLLI.
WARREDOC: e-mail warredoc@unistrapg.it; internet warredoc.unistrapg.it; Carries out teaching, research, organizational and documentation activities in the sphere of water resources, environment, natural disasters management and sustainable devt; Dir Prof. ROBERTO CHIONNE

UNIVERSITÀ PER STRANIERI DI SIENA

Piazza Carlo Rosselli 27–28, 53100 Siena
Telephone: 577-240100
E-mail: info@unistrasi.it
Internet: www.unistrasi.it
Founded 1917
State control
Rector: Prof. MASSIMO VEDOVELLI
Pro-Rector: Prof. MARINA BENEDETTI
Admin. Dir: Dott. ALESSANDRO BALDUCCI
Number of students: 4,599

DEANS
Faculty of Italian Language and Culture: Prof. MASSIMO PALERMO

UNIVERSITÀ TELEMATICA 'GIUSTINO FORTUNATO'

Viale Raffaele Delcogliano 12, 82100 Benevento
Telephone: 0824-316057
E-mail: info@unifortunato.eu
Internet: www.unifortunato.eu
Founded 2006
Private control
Rector: Prof. AUGUSTO FANTOZZI
Admin. Dir: Dott. MARIA VINCENZA RIVELLINI
Offers distance learning. Masters degrees in law, business law, Roman law, tax law

UNIVERSITÀ TELEMATICA 'LEONARDO DA VINCI'

Piazza San Rocco, 66010 Torrevecchia Teatina (CH)
Telephone: 0871-361658
E-mail: info@unidav.it
Internet: www.unidav.it
Founded 2004 jointly by the Università degli Studi 'Gabriele D'Annunzio' and the Fondazione Università 'Gabriele d'Annunzio'
Private control
Rector: Prof. FABIO CAPANI
Offers distance learning. Faculties of cultural heritage, education, law, management, medicine and surgery, psychology

UNIVERSITÀ TELEMATICA 'UNIVERSITAS MERCATORUM'

Via Appia Pignatelli 62, 00178 Rome
Telephone: 06-78052327
E-mail: segreteria@unimercatorum.it
Internet: www.unimercatorum.it
Founded 2006
Private control
Rector: Prof. GIORGIO MARBACH
Offers distance learning; undergraduate courses in company management, human resources management

UNIVERSITÀ TELEMATICA DELLE SCIENZE UMANE UNISU

Via Casalmonferrato 2B, 00182 Rome
Telephone: 06-70304302
E-mail: info@unisu.it

Internet: www.unisu.it
Founded 2006
Private control
Rector: Prof. Avv. GIOVANNI PUOTI
Gen. Dir: DANIELA SASANELLI
Admin. Dir: LUIGI PELUSO CASSESE
Offers distance learning. Faculties of economics, education, law, politics

UNIVERSITÀ TELEMATICA INTERNAZIONALE UNINETTUNO

Corso V. Emanuele II 39, 00186 Rome
Telephone: 06-69207670
E-mail: info@uninettunouniversity.net
Internet: www.uninettunouniversity.net
Founded 2005
Private control
Rector: Prof. MARIA AMATA GARITO
Admin. Dir: STEFANO FRIGERI
Offers distance learning

DEANS

Faculty of Arts: Prof. TATIANA KIROVA
Faculty of Communication Sciences: Prof. ALBERTO ABRUZZESE
Faculty of Economics: Prof. GENNARO OLIVIERI
Faculty of Engineering: Prof. BERNARDINO CHIAIA
Faculty of Law: Prof. GIOVANNI CABRAS
Faculty of Psychology: Prof. JOOST LOWYCK

UNIVERSITÀ TELEMATICA PEGASO

Via Vittoria Colonna 14, Angolo Piazza Amedeo, 80121 Naples
Telephone: 081-19567975
E-mail: direttore.generale@unipegaso.it
Internet: www.unipegaso.it
Founded 2006
Private control
Offers distance learning. Faculties of humanities, law
Rector: Prof. GIOVANNI DI GIANDOMENICO
Gen. Dir: Prof. ELIO PARIOTA

UNIVERSITÀ TELEMATICA SAN RAFFAELE ROMA

Via di Val Cannuta 247, 00166 Rome
Telephone: 06-52252552
E-mail: segreteria.didattica@unisanraffaele.gov.it
Internet: www.unisanraffaele.gov.it
Founded 2006
Private control
Language of instruction: Italian
Academic year: October to September
Offers distance learning; faculties of agriculture, architecture and industrial design, sport sciences
Rector: Prof. ENRICO GARACI

UNIVERSITÀ TELEMATICA UNITELMA

Viale Regina Elena 295, 00161 Rome
Telephone: 06-69190797
E-mail: segreteria@unitelma.it
Internet: www.unitelma.it
Founded 2004
Private control
Rector: Prof. ANIELLO CIMITILE
Admin. Dir: Dott. MICHELE OREFICE
Offers distance learning

DEANS

Faculty of Economics: Prof. SERGIO SCIARELLI
Faculty of Law: Prof. ANIELLO CIMITILE

UNIVERSITÀ VITA-SALUTE 'SAN RAFFAELE'

Via Olgettina, 58, 20132 Milan
Telephone: 2-26433802
E-mail: segreteria.studenti@unisr.it
Internet: www.unisr.it
Founded 1996
Private control
Rector: Sac. Prof. LUIGI M. VERZÉ
Gen. Dir: Dott. RAFFAELLA VOLTOLINI

DEANS

Faculty of Medicine and Surgery: Prof. MASSIMO CLEMENTI
Faculty of Philosophy: Prof. MICHELE DI FRANCESCO
Faculty of Psychology: Prof. LUCIO SARNO

VENICE INTERNATIONAL UNIVERSITY

Isola di San Servolo, 30100 Venice
Telephone: 041-2719511
E-mail: viu@univiu.it
Internet: www.univiu.org
Founded 1997
Academic year: September to May
Pres.: UMBERTO VATTANI
Dean: STEFANO MICELLI
Admin. Dir: ALESSANDRO SPEZZAMONTE
Dir of School of Humanities and Social Sciences: LUCA PES
Staff and students provided by the constituent univs

Schools of Music and Art

ART

Accademia Albertina delle Belle Arti di Torino: Via Accademia Albertina 6, 10123 Turin; tel. 011-889020; e-mail info@accademialbertina.torino.it; internet www.accademialbertina.torino.it; f. 1652; 70 teachers; 550 students; Pres. Dott. MARCO ALBERA; Dir Prof. GUIDO CURTO.

Accademia di Belle Arti di Bologna (Academy of Fine Arts of Bologna): Via Belle Arti 54, 40126 Bologna; tel. 051-4226411; e-mail info@accademiabelleartibologna.it; internet www.accademiabelleartibologna.it; f. 1710; library: 15,000 vols; Dir Prof. ADRIANO BACCILIERI; Librarian CRISTINA PRATI; publ. *Prontuario* (1 a year).

Accademia di Belle Arti di Brera (Academy of Fine Arts of Brera): Palazzo di Brera, Via Brera 28, 20121 Milan; tel. 02-869551; e-mail accademia@accademiadibrera.milano.it; internet www.accademiadibrera.milano.it; f. 1776; library: 25,000 vols; 400 teachers; 3,500 students; Pres. Dott. SALVATORE CARRUBBA; Dir Prof. GASTONE MARIANI.

Accademia di Belle Arti di Carrara (Academy of Fine Arts): Via Roma 1, 54033 Carrara; tel. 0585-71658; e-mail info@accademiacarrara.it; internet www.accademiacarrara.it; courses in painting, sculpture and scene-painting; Dir Prof. MARCO BAUDINELLI; Admin. Dir Dr GUIDO RAFFAELE.

Accademia di Belle Arti di Firenze (Academy of Fine Arts of Florence): Via Ricasoli 66, 50122 Florence; tel. 055-215449; e-mail segreteria@accademia.firenze.it; internet www.accademia.firenze.it; f. 1801; library: 22,000 vols; Pres. Avv. GAETANO VICICONTE; Dir Prof. GIULIANA VIDETTA.

Accademia di Belle Arti di Lecce (Academy of Fine Arts of Lecce): Via Libertini 3, 73100 Lecce; tel. 0832-258611; e-mail accademialecce@libero.it; internet www.accademiabelleartilecce.com; Dir Prof. Arch. GIACINTO LEONE.

Accademia di Belle Arti di Napoli (Academy of Fine Arts of Naples): Via Costantinopoli 107, 80138 Naples; tel. 081-444245; e-mail napoli_accademia@libero.it; internet www.accademianapoli.it; f. 1838; library: 7,000 vols; Dir Prof. ALFREDO SCOTTI.

Accademia di Belle Arti di Palermo (Academy of Fine Arts of Palermo): Via Papireto 1, 90134 Palermo; tel. 091-580876; e-mail amministrazione@accademiadipalermo.it; internet www.accademiadipalermo.it; f. 1780; Dir Prof. UMBERTO DE PAOLA.

Accademia di Belle Arti di Ravenna (Academy of Fine Arts of Ravenna): Via delle Industrie 76, 48122 Ravenna; tel. 0544-453125; e-mail accademia@comune.ra.it; internet www.accademiabellearti.ra.it; f. 1827; library: 10,000 vols; Dir Prof. MAURO MAZZALI; Admin. Dir Dott.ssa ORIELLA GARAVINI.

Accademia di Belle Arti di Roma (Academy of Fine Arts of Rome): Via Ripetta 222, 00186 Rome; tel. 06-3227025; e-mail direzione@accademiabelleartiroma.it; internet www.accademiabelleartiroma.it; f. 1873; 2,000 students; Pres. Dr CESARE ROMITI; Dir Prof. GERARDO LO RUSSO.

Accademia di Belle Arti di Venezia (Academy of Fine Arts of Venice): Dorsoduro 423, 30123 Venice; tel. 041-2413752; e-mail info@accademiavenezia.it; internet www.accademiavenezia.it; f. 1750; 96 teachers; 870 students; Dir CARLO DI RACO.

Accademia di Belle Arti 'Pietro Vannucci' di Perugia (Academy of Fine Arts of Perugia): Piazza San Francesco al Prato 5, 06123 Perugia; tel. 075-5730631; e-mail direzione@abaperugia.org; internet www.abaperugia.org; f. 1573; 96 Academicians, 143 Hon. Academicians; collections of paintings, engravings, drawings, etc.; library: 13,330 vols; Pres. Avv. MARIO RAMPINI; Dir Prof. GIULIANO GIUMAN.

Istituto Statale d'Arte: Via Bramante 20, 61029 Urbino; tel. 0722-329892; e-mail ia.scuolalibro@provincia.ps.it; internet www.isaurbino.it; f. 1865; engraving techniques, cartoon drawing, ceramics, photography, editorial graphics, publicity art; library: 20,000 vols; 110 teachers; 714 students; Pres. Prof. MAURIZIA RAGONESI.

Istituto Statale d'Arte 'Enrico e Umberto Nordio': Via di Calvola 2, 34143 Trieste; tel. 040-300660; e-mail info@isanordio.it; internet www.isanordio.it; f. 1955; courses in architecture, design and printing of textiles, interior decorating; library: 5,450 vols; Dir Prof. TEODORO GIUDICE.

Istituto Statale d'Arte 'Filippo Figari': Piazza d'Armi 16, CP 105, 07100 Sassari; tel. 079-234466; e-mail sssd020006@istruzione.it; f. 1935; woodwork, metalwork, weaving, painting, ceramics, graphic art and architecture; Pres. Prof. NICOLÒ MASIA.

Istituto Statale d'Arte 'G. Ballardini': Corso Baccarini 17, 48018 Faenza; tel. 0546-21091; e-mail iaballardini@provincia.ra.it; internet www.ceramicschool.it; f. 1916; basic courses in ceramic art and technology; higher courses in stoneware, ceramic building coatings, porcelain, restoration, technology of special ceramics, traditional ceramics.

DANCE AND DRAMA

Accademia Nazionale d'Arte Drammatica 'Silvio d'Amico': Via Vincenzo Bellini 16, 00198 Rome; tel. 06-8543680; e-mail segreteria.direttore@silviodamico.it; internet www.silviodamico.it; f. 1935; 45 teachers; 100 students; Dir Prof. LUIGI MARIA MUSATI.

Accademia Nazionale di Danza: Largo Arrigo VII 5, 00153 Rome; tel. 06-5717621; e-mail sd@accademianazionaledanza.it; internet www.accademianazionaledanza.com; f. 1948; Pres. BRUNO BORGHI; Dir MARGHERITA PARRILLA.

MUSIC

Accademia Filarmonica Romana (Rome Philharmonic Academy): Via Flaminia 118, 00196 Rome; tel. 06-3201752; e-mail info@filarmonicaromana.org; internet www.filarmonicaromana.org; f. 1821; library: 1,500 vols; Pres. PAOLO BARATTA; Artistic Dir SANDRO CAPPELLETTO.

Accademia Musicale Chigiana: Via di Città 89, 53100 Siena; tel. 0577-22091; e-mail accademia.chigiana@chigiana.it; internet www.chigiana.it; f. 1932; master classes, seminars, lectures, concerts, operas, international research conventions; 26 teachers; 351 students; Artistic Director Maestro ALDO BENNICI.

Conservatorio 'Claudio Monteverdi' di Bolzano: Piazza Domenicani 19, 39100 Bolzano; tel. 0471-978764; e-mail info@conservatoriobolzano.it; internet www.conservatoriobolzano.it; f. 1940; library: 10,000 vols; international Busoni Piano Competition held annually; Dir Prof. FELIX RESCH; Admin. Dir Dott. MARIO BELLI.

Conservatorio di Musica 'Arrigo Boito' di Parma: Via del Conservatorio 27A, 43121 Parma; tel. 0521-381911; e-mail direttore@conservatorio.pr.it; internet www.conservatorio.pr.it; f. 1825; library: 70,000 vols; 140 teachers; 800 students; Dir ROBERTO CAPPELLO.

Conservatorio di Musica 'Benedetto Marcello': Palazzo Pisani, San Marco 2810, 30124 Venice; tel. 041-5225604; e-mail direttoreamministrativo@conseve.it; internet www.conseve.it; f. 1877; 90 teachers; 480 students; library: 50,000 vols, 70 periodicals; Dir Prof. MASSIMO CONTIERO.

Conservatorio di Musica di Napoli 'San Pietro a Majella': Via San Pietro a Majella 35, 80138 Naples; tel. 081-5644411; e-mail direzioneamministrativa@sanpietroamajella.it; internet www.sanpietroamajella.it; Dir PATRIZIO MARRONE; Admin. Dir CLOTILDE PUNZO.

Conservatorio di Musica 'Giovan Battista Martini': Piazza Rossini 2, 40126 Bologna; tel. 051-221483; e-mail segreteria@conservatorio-bologna.com; internet www.conservatorio-bologna.com; f. 1804; Dir DONATELLA PIERI.

Conservatorio di Musica 'Giuseppe Tartini': Via Ghega 12, 34132 Trieste; tel. 040-6724911; e-mail rosanna.corsi@conts.it; internet www.conservatorio.trieste.it; f. 1903; 93 teachers; 630 students; Dir MASSIMO PAROVEL; Admin. Dir ROSANNA CORSI.

Conservatorio di Musica 'Giuseppe Verdi': Via Conservatorio 12, 20122 Milan; tel. 02-762110216; e-mail segreteriadirezione@consmilano.it; internet www.consmilano.it; f. 1808; library: see under Libraries and Archives; Dir SONIA BO.

Conservatorio di Musica 'Niccolò Piccinni': Via Cifarelli 26, 70124 Bari; tel. 080-5740022; e-mail diramm@conservatoriopiccinni.it; internet www.conservatoriopiccinni.it; f. 1959; library: 11,000 vols; Dir Maestro FRANCESCO MONOPOLI; Admin. Dir Dott. ANNAMARIA SFORZA.

Conservatorio di Musica 'Vincenzo Bellini' di Palermo: Via Squarcialupo 45, 90133 Palermo; tel. 091-580921; e-mail paconsediwin@hotmail.com; internet www.conservatoriobellini.it; f. 1721; library: 40,000 vols, collection of 18th- and 19th-century MSS; Dir Maestro CARMELO CARUSO; Admin. Dir Dott. RAIMUNDO CIPOLLA; publ. *Quaderni del Conservatorio* (irregular).

Conservatorio 'Santa Cecilia': Via dei Greci 18, 00187 Rome; tel. 06-36096720; internet www.conservatoriosantacecilia.it; Dir Maestro EDDA SILVESTRI.

Conservatorio Statale di Musica 'G. Rossini': Piazza Olivieri 5, 61100 Pesaro; tel. 0721-33671; e-mail segreteria@conservatoriorossini.it; internet www.conservatoriorossini.it; f. 1882; library: 25,000 vols; Dir MAURIZIO TARSETTI.

Conservatorio Statale di Musica 'Giovanni Pierluigi da Palestrina': Piazza E. Porrino 1, 09128 Cagliari; tel. 070-493118; e-mail dir.amministrativo@conservatoriocagliari.it; internet www.conservatoriocagliari.it; f. 1939; Dir Prof. M. GABRIELLA ARTIZZU; Admin. Dir Dott. FRANCESCA BASILONE.

Conservatorio Statale di Musica 'Giuseppe Verdi': Via Mazzini 11, 10123 Turin; tel. 011-8178458; internet www.conservatoriotorino.eu; f. 1867; Dir MARIA LUISA PACCIANI.

Conservatorio Statale di Musica 'Luigi Cherubini': Piazzetta delle Belle Arti 2, 50121 Florence; tel. 055-2989311; e-mail info@conservatorio.firenze.it; internet www.conservatorio.firenze.it; f. 1861; 107 teachers; 702 students; Dir Prof. PAOLO BIORDI; Chief Admin. Officer Dott. ROBERTO VOLPI.

JAMAICA

The Higher Education System

The University of Technology, Jamaica (formerly Jamaica Institute of Technology) was founded in 1958, while Jamaica was under British colonial administration. In 1962 Jamaica achieved full independence within the Commonwealth, and in the same year the University of the West Indies (UWI, founded 1948), which now has two campuses on the island (one at Mona and the other at Montego Bay in western Jamaica—the latter having been opened in 2008), was elevated to university status. There are two other universities in Jamaica—the privately controlled Northern Caribbean University, which was founded in 1907 as the West Indian Training School and was accorded university status in 1999. Other higher education establishments include teacher training colleges, community colleges, technical and vocational training institutes, and business colleges. In 2003/04 there were 15 institutions providing tertiary education with 11,600 students enrolled. By 2010 64,101 students were enrolled in tertiary education, and in 2012 the University Council of Jamaica reported that there were 62 accredited institutions operating. The Tertiary Unit of the Ministry of Education is the government agency responsible for higher education. Although the State subsidizes tertiary education, many students have to take out loans to cover the cost of their tuition fees; the largest provider of such loans is the Students' Loan Bureau.

Admission to higher education is on the basis of two or more GCE A-Levels (or equivalent qualifications, including Associate degrees). The Bachelors is the standard undergraduate degree and lasts three to four years, followed by the Masters, the first postgraduate degree. The UWI offers either a two-year, coursework-based Masters programme or a research-based Master of Philology (MPhil). The highest university degree is the Doctorate, which lasts for three years after award of the Masters.

Technical and vocational education at the post-secondary level is supervised by the Human Employment and Resource Training Agency and the National Council on Technical and Vocational Education and Training. The former body runs several academies and vocational training centres and the latter is the official body responsible for awarding the National Vocational Qualification of Jamaica (Levels 1–5). A three-year Associate in Science degree is offered by the College of Agriculture, Science and Education.

The University Council of Jamaica, which was established in 1987, is responsible for the registration, quality assurance and accreditation of higher education institutions and programmes.

Regulatory and Representative Bodies

GOVERNMENT

Ministry of Education: 2 National Heroes Circle, Kingston 4; tel. 922-1400; e-mail communications@moe.gov.jm; internet moe .gov.jm; Minister Rev. RONALD THWAITES.

Ministry of Science, Technology, Energy and Mining: PCJ Bldg, 36 Trafalgar Rd, Kingston 10; tel. 929-8990; e-mail info@mem .gov.jm; internet www.mem.gov.jm; Minister PHILLIP PAULWELL.

Ministry of Youth and Culture: 64 Knutsford Blvd, Third and Fifth Fl., Kingston 5; tel. 960-6427; e-mail info@mysc.gov.jm; Minister LISA HANNA.

ACCREDITATION

University Council of Jamaica: 6B Oxford Rd, Kingston 5; tel. 929-7299; e-mail info@ucj .org.jm; internet www.ucj.org.jm; f. 1987 to increase the availability of univ.-level training in Jamaica, through accreditation of instns, courses and programmes for recognition and acceptability; has the power to confer degrees, diplomas, certificates and other academic awards and distinctions on those who have pursued courses approved by the Council at associated tertiary instns; Chair. Dr BURCHELL WHITEMAN; Exec. Dir Dr YVONNETTE J. MARSHALL.

Learned Societies

GENERAL

Institute of Jamaica: 12–16 East St, Kingston; tel. 922-0620; e-mail info@ instituteofjamaica.org.jm; internet www .instituteofjamaica.org.jm; f. 1879; comprises the Nat. Library of Jamaica (see under Libraries and Archives); 2 Junior Cultural Centres; Natural History Div.; Arawak (Indian) Museum; Jamaica Folk Museum; Military Museum; Maritime Museum; the Nat. Gallery of Jamaica; the African-Caribbean Institute/Jamaica Memory Bank; Institute of Jamaica Publs; Exec. Dir VIVIAN CRAWFORD (acting); publ. *Jamaica Journal*.

UNESCO Office Kingston: 3rd Fl., The Towers, 25 Dominica Drive, Kingston 5; tel. 929-7087; e-mail kingston@unesco.org; internet www.unescocaribbean.org; designated Cluster Office for Antigua and Barbuda, Bahamas, Barbados, Belize, Dominica, Grenada, Guyana, Jamaica, St Christopher and Nevis, St Lucia, St Vincent and the Grenadines, Suriname, Trinidad and Tobago; Dir HELENE-MARIE GOSSELIN.

AGRICULTURE, FISHERIES AND VETERINARY SCIENCE

Jamaican Association of Sugar Technologists: c/o Sugar Industry Research Institute, Kendal Rd, Mandeville; tel. 962-2241; f. 1937 by the local sugar industry to conduct research and investigate technical problems of the Jamaican sugar industry; 266 mems; uses library of Sugar Industry Research Institute; Pres. MICHAEL G. HYLTON; Sec. H. M. THOMPSON; publ. *JAST Journal* (1 a year).

ARCHITECTURE AND TOWN PLANNING

Jamaican Institute of Architects: POB 251, Kingston 10; 5 Oxford Park Ave, Kingston 5; tel. 926-8060; e-mail jia@cwjamaica .com; internet www.jia.org.jm; f. 1957; 106 mems (81 full, 25 assoc.); Pres. LAURIE FERRON; Vice-Pres. FRANZ-JOSEPH REPOLE; Hon. Sec. DOUGLAS STIEBEL; publ. *Jamaica Architect* (1 a year).

BIBLIOGRAPHY, LIBRARY SCIENCE AND MUSEOLOGY

Library and Information Association of Jamaica: POB 125, Kingston 5; tel. 541-3990; e-mail liajapresident@yahoo.com; internet www.liaja.org.jm; f. 1950 as Jamaica Library Asscn; 227 mems; Pres. VIVIENE KERR-WILLIAMS; Sec. MARSHA-GAY ROBINSON.

HISTORY, GEOGRAPHY AND ARCHAEOLOGY

Jamaica National Heritage Trust: 79 Duke St, Kingston CSO; tel. 922-3990; e-mail jnht@cwjamaica.com; internet www .jnht.com; f. 1958; protection, preservation, restoration and promotion of Jamaica's material and cultural heritage, particularly through declaration of nat. monuments and designation of protected nat. heritage; Chair. AINSLEY HENRIQUES; Exec. Dir LALETA DAVIS-MATTIS.

LANGUAGE AND LITERATURE

Alliance Française: 12B Lilford Ave (off Lady Musgrave Rd), Kingston 10; tel. 978-4622; e-mail alliance.francaisekingston@ laposte.net; offers courses and examinations in French language and culture and promotes cultural exchange with France.

British Council: British High Commission, 28 Trafalgar Rd, Kingston 10; tel. 929-7090; e-mail bcjamaica@britishcouncil.org.jm; internet www.britishcouncil.org/caribbean; offers courses and examinations in English language and British culture; promotes cultural exchange with the UK; Man. NICOLA JOHNSON.

MEDICINE

Medical Association of Jamaica: 19A Windsor Ave, Kingston 5; tel. 946-1105; internet www.medicalassnjamaica.com; f. 1877 as br of British Medical Asscn; ind. body 1966; for the promotion of medical and allied sciences and of the medical profession; 707 mems; Pres. Dr ALVERSTON BAILEY; Hon. Sec. Dr ANN JACKSON-GIBSON; publ. *Journal* (1 a year).

TECHNOLOGY

Jamaica Institution of Engineers: 2 Winchester Rd, Kingston 10; tel. 929-6741; e-mail jie@cwjamaica.com; internet www.jiejamaica.org; f. 1960, present name 1977; promotes the advancement of the engineering profession and the practice and science of engineering, and facilitates the exchange of information and ideas on those subjects among the mems and others; 600 mems; Pres. Dr DAVID SMITH; Hon. Sec. HERMON EDMONSON; publ. *JIE Advisor* (12 a year).

Research Institutes

AGRICULTURE, FISHERIES AND VETERINARY SCIENCE

Sugar Industry Research Institute: Kendal Rd, Mandeville; tel. 962-2241; e-mail sirijam@jamaicasugar.org; internet www.jamaicasugar.org; f. 1973; research into sugar cane cultivation and environmental management; library of 660 vols, 2,500 bound vols of periodicals; Dir for Research EARLE ROBERTS.

ECONOMICS, LAW AND POLITICS

Planning Institute of Jamaica: 16 Oxford Rd, POB 634, Kingston 5; tel. 960-9339; e-mail info@pioj.gov.jm; internet www.pioj.gov.jm; f. 1955, fmrly the Central Planning Unit, current name adopted 1984; policy advice on economic, social and sustainable devt issues to the govt; Dir-Gen. COLIN BULLOCK; publs *Economic and Social Survey Jamaica* (1 a year), *Economic Update and Outlook* (4 a year), *JA People Magazine* (1 a year), *Jamaica Survey of Living Conditions* (1 a year).

MEDICINE

Caribbean Food and Nutrition Institute (CFNI): Jamaica Centre, POB 140, Mona, Kingston 7; tel. 927-1540; e-mail e-mail@cfni.paho.org; internet www.cfni.paho.org; f. 1967; conducts research and training courses and provides technical advisory services to 18 govts of the English-speaking Caribbean on matters relating to food and nutrition; library of 5,700 vols; there is a centre in Trinidad; Dir Dr FITZROY HENRY; publs *Cajanus* (4 a year), *Nyam News* (24 a year).

Medical Research Council Laboratories: University of the West Indies, Mona, Kingston 7; tel. 927-2471; e-mail grserjnt@uwimona.edu.jm; f. 1974; attached to Medical Research Council, London, United Kingdom; research into sickle-cell disease; 20 staff; Dir G. R. SERJEANT.

NATURAL SCIENCES

General

Scientific Research Council: POB 350, Kingston 6; tel. 927-1771; e-mail prinfo@src-jamaica.org; internet www.src-jamaica.org; f. 1960; undertakes, fosters and coordinates scientific research in the island; library of 10,000 vols; Exec. Dir Dr AUDIA BARNETT; publs *Conference Proceedings* (1 a year), *Jamaican Journal of Science and Technology* (1 a year).

Libraries and Archives

Kingston

Jamaica Library Service: 2 Tom Redcam Dr., POB 58, Kingston 5; tel. 926-3310; e-mail hq@jls.org.jm; internet www.jamlib.org.jm; f. 1948; provides an island-wide network of 656 service points, including 13 parish libraries, and 121 br. libraries; oversees 925 school and higher education libraries; total bookstock 2,711,000 vols, 70 periodicals; 1,121,000 vols in primary schools and 428,000 vols in secondary schools; Dir PATRICIA ROBERTS; publ. *Statistical Report of the Jamaica Library Service* (1 a year).

National Library of Jamaica: 12 East St, POB 823, Kingston; tel. 967-2494; e-mail nljresearch@cwjamaica.com; internet www.nlj.gov.jm; f. 1979; 47,000 printed items, 29,600 maps and plans, 4,400 serials, 27,100 photographs, 3,150 MSS, 2,550 items of audiovisual material on Jamaica and the West Indies; Exec. Dir WINSOME HUDSON; publs *Jamaica National Bibliography* (1 a year), *National Library News* (2 a year).

University of the West Indies Library: Mona, Kingston 7; tel. 512-3569; e-mail main.library@uwimona.edu.jm; internet www.mona.uwi.edu/library; f. 1948; 518,981 vols incl. 6,349 current and 6,495 non-current periodicals in the Main Library and 2 br. libraries for the Medical (32,896 vols) and Scientific (97,634 vols) Collns; Campus Librarian NORMA Y. AMENU-KPODO.

Spanish Town

Jamaica Archives and Records Department: cnr King and Manchester Sts, Spanish Town, St Catherine; tel. 984-2581; e-mail jarchives@jard.gov.jm; internet www.jard.gov.jm; f. 1659 as the admin. and record keeping arm of the Colonial Govt, present status 1955; nat. archives of Jamaica; spec. colln of ecclesiastical and private records of historical value; oversees the effective and efficient management and use of govt records; acquires, preserves and makes accessible records of nat. significance; Govt Archivist CLAUDETTE THOMAS; Sr Archivist RACQUEL STRATCHAN.

Museum

Kingston

Institute of Jamaica Museum: see Institute of Jamaica.

Universities

UNIVERSITY OF TECHNOLOGY, JAMAICA

237 Old Hope Rd, Kingston 6
Telephone: 927-16808
E-mail: regist@utech.edu.jm
Internet: www.utechjamaica.edu.jm

Founded 1958 as Jamaica Institute of Technology; became College of Arts, Science and Technology 1959; current name and status 1995
State control
Language of instruction: English
Academic year: August to May

Serves Antigua and Barbuda, Anguilla, Barbados, Bahamas, Belize, British Virgin Islands, Dominica, Grenada, Guyana, Jamaica, St Lucia, St Vincent, Trinidad and Tobago, Turks and Caicos Islands

Chancellor: EDWARD SEAGA
Pro-Chancellor: VIVIAN CRAWFORD
Pres.: ERROL MORRISON
Deputy Pres.: GOSSETT OLIVER
Vice-Pres. for Devt and Community Service: Prof. ROSALEA HAMILTON
Vice-Pres. for Graduate Studies, Research and Entrepreneurship: PAUL IVEY (acting)
Vice-Pres. for Human Resource & Admin.: JENNIFER ELLIS
Vice-Pres. for Planning and Operations: Dr KOFI NKRUMAH-YOUNG
Registrar: ELAINE WALLACE (acting)
Univ. Librarian: DAVID DRYSDALE

Library of 123,848 vols, 995 print periodicals and journals
Number of teachers: 557 (full-time)
Number of students: 12,000

Publication: *Journal*

DEANS

College of Business and Management: Dr PAUL GOLDING
College of Health Sciences: Dr ELLEN CAMPBELL-GRIZZLE
Faculty of Education and Liberal Studies: Dr ROHAN LEWIS
Faculty of Engineering and Computing: NILZA SMITH
Faculty of Law: Prof. ALFRED MCPHERSON
Faculty of Science and Sport: Prof. COLIN GYLES
Faculty of the Built Environment: Dr CAROL ARCHER

UNIVERSITY OF THE WEST INDIES, MONA CAMPUS

Mona, Kingston 7
Telephone: 927-1661
E-mail: campusregistraroffice@uwimona.edu.jm
Internet: www.mona.uwi.edu
Founded 1948, univ. status 1962
Academic year: August to July

Serves 16 territories: Jamaica, Anguilla, Bahamas, Belize, British Virgin Islands, Cayman Islands, Barbados, Antigua and Barbuda, Dominica, Grenada, Montserrat, St Christopher and Nevis, St Lucia, Turks and Caicos, St Vincent and the Grenadines, Trinidad and Tobago; faculties of humanities and education, medical sciences and social sciences are located on all 3 campuses; faculty of law is in Barbados, agriculture and engineering in Trinidad, and the faculties of pure and applied sciences in Barbados and Jamaica

Chancellor: Sir GEORGE ALLEYNE
Vice-Chancellor: Prof. NIGEL HARRIS
Prin.: Prof. KENNETH HALL
Univ. Registrar: GLORIA BARRETT-SOBERS
Librarian: STEPHNEY FERGUSON

Number of teachers: 400
Number of students: 11,000

Publications: *Arts Review* (2 a year), *Caribbean Journal of Criminology and Social Psychology* (2 a year), *Caribbean Journal of Education*, *Caribbean Law Bulletin* (2 a year), *Caribbean Law Review* (2 a year), *Caribbean Quarterly*, *Journal of Tropical Agriculture* (4 a year), *Social Economics Studies* (4 a year), *West Indian Journal of Engineering* (2 a year), *West Indian Law Journal* (1 a year), *West Indian Medical Journal* (4 a year)

DEANS AT MONA

Faculty of Humanities and Education: Prof. AGGREY BROWN
Faculty of Medical Sciences: Prof. ARCHIBALD MCDONALD
Faculty of Pure and Applied Sciences: Prof. RONALD YOUNG
Faculty of Social Sciences: MARK FIGUEROA

PROFESSORS

AHMAD, M., Biotechnology
BAILEY, W., Geography and Geology
BAIN, B., Community Health and Psychiatry
BENNETT, F., Pathology
BORNHOP, D., Applied Chemistry
BRANDAY, J., Surgery, Radiology, Anaesthesia and Intensive Care

BROWN, A., Mass Communication
BURTON, E., Medicine
CAMPBELL, C., History
CHEN, A., Physics
CHEVANNES, B., Social Anthropology
CHRISTIE, C., Obstetrics, Gynaecology and Child Health
DASGUPTA, T., Inorganic Chemistry
DENBOW, C., Medicine
DEVONISH, H., Language, Linguistics and Philosophy
DONOVAN, S., Palaeozoology
DURRANT, F., Library and Information Studies
FLETCHER, P., Clinical Surgery
FORRESTER, T., Tropical Medicine
FREEMAN, B., Ecology
HANCHARD, B., Anatomical Pathology
HICKLING, F., Psychiatry
JACKSON, T., Igneous Petrology
JACOBS, H., Chemistry
JONES, E., Public Administration
LENNARD, J., English and American Literature
LEO-RHYNIE, E., Women and Development Studies
LEWIS, R., Political Thought
MILLER, E., Teacher Education
MOORE, B., History
MORGAN, O., Medicine
MORRIS, M., Creative Writing and West Indian Literature
MORRISON, E., Biochemistry
MUNROE, T., Government and Politics
NETTLEFORD, R. N., Continuing Studies
REICHGELT, J., Computer Science
REID, H., Clinical Haemorheology
ROBINSON, E., Geology
SHIRLEY, G., Management Studies
SPENCER, H., Cardiothoracic Surgery
THOMAS-HOPE, E., Environmental Development
UCHE, C., Sociology and Social Work
WALKER, S., Epidemiology
WARNER-LEWIS, M., African Caribbean Language and Orature
WILKS, R., Epidemiology
WINT, A., International Business
YOUNG, R., Physiology

ATTACHED INSTITUTES

Biotechnology Centre: 2 St John's Close, Univ. of the West Indies, Mona Campus, Kingston 7; tel. 977-1828; internet www.myspot.mona.uwi.edu/biotech; Dir Prof. M. AHMAD.

Caribbean Institute of Media and Communication: e-mail carimac@uwimona.edu.jm; internet www.mona.uwi.edu/carimac; Dir Drs M. DE BRUIN.

Centre for Environment and Development: e-mail vcoffice@uwimona.edu.jm; Dir Prof. A. BINGER.

Centre for Gender and Development Studies: Dir Dr B. BAILEY.

Centre for Management Development: Dir Dr J. COMMA.

Centre for Marine Sciences: e-mail cms@uwimona.edu.jm; internet www.mona.uwi.edu/cms; Dir Dr G. WARNER.

Chronic Disease Research Centre: Dir Prof. H. FRASER.

Institute of Caribbean Studies: e-mail icsmona@uwimona.edu.jm; internet www.mona.uwi.edu/humed/ics; Dir J. PEREIRA.

Institute of Education: e-mail ioe@uwimona.edu.jm; internet www.mona.uwi.edu/ioe; Dir J. TUCKER.

International Centre for Environment and Nuclear Sciences: internet www.icens.org; Dir Prof. G. C. LALOR.

Philip Sherlock Centre for Creative Arts: Mona, Kingston 7; tel. 927-1047; f. 1967; offers credit courses at the undergraduate level in musical studies, theatre studies and applied drama; home for student cultural clubs and socs; annual Philip Sherlock Int. Arts Festival; Prin. Prof. GORDON SHIRLEY; Sec. CAROLYN ALLEN.

School of Business: e-mail msb@uwimona.edu.jm; internet www.mona.uwi.edu/msb; Dir Prof. G. SHIRLEY.

School of Continuing Studies: Mona, Kingston 7; Dir Prof. L. CARRINGTON.

Sir Arthur Lewis Institute for Social and Economic Studies: Mona, Kingston 7; tel. 927-2409; e-mail iserdoc@uwimona.edu.jm; applied research relating to the Caribbean; Dir Prof. N. DUNCAN (Mona; Dir Prof. A. DOWNES (Cave Hill; Dir Prof. S. RYAN (St. Augustine.

Trade Union Education Institute: Mona, Kingston 7; Dir of Studies Prof. L. CARRINGTON.

Tropical Medicine Research Institute: e-mail tmritmru@uwimona.edu.jm; internet www.uwi.edu/tmriMona, Kingston 7; Dir Prof. TERRENCE FORRESTER.

AFFILIATED INSTITUTIONS

Caribbean Institute for Meteorology and Hydrology: Dir Dr COLIN DEPRADINE.

Mico Teachers' College: Dir Dr CLAUDE PACKER.

St John Vianney and the Uganda Martyrs: Dir Rev. MICHAEL DE VERTEUIL.

St Michael's Seminary: Mona, Kingston 7; awards degrees of the Univ. of the West Indies; Director Sr THERESA LOWE CHING.

United Theological College of the West Indies: Mona, Kingston 7; e-mail unitheol@cwjamaica.com; internet www.utcwi.edu.jm; awards degrees and licentiates of the Univ. of the West Indies; Pres. Dr LEWIN WILLIAMS (acting)

College

College of Agriculture, Science and Education: POB 170, Passley Gardens, Port Antonio, Portland; tel. 993-3246; e-mail registrar@case.edu.jm; internet www.case.edu.jm; f. 1995 by merger of College of Agriculture and Passley Gardens Teachers' College; faculties of agriculture, education and science; community college and continuing education programmes; library: 35,000 vols, spec. collns: UN publs, West Indian works, Jamaica Govt publs; 643 students (533 full-time, 86 part-time and 24 evening); Pres. Dr PAUL IVEY (acting); Registrar PATRICIA WRIGHT-CLARKE.

JAPAN

The Higher Education System

Higher education in Japan consists of five basic categories of institution: universities (daigaku), junior colleges (tanki-daigaku), technology colleges (koto-senmongakko), professional graduate schools (the latter since 2003) and special training schools (senshu-gakko). Institutions are either publicly or privately administered; more than 70% of universities and more than 90% of junior colleges are in the private sector. In 2010 there were 778 universities and graduate schools, with 2.89m. students, 453 junior and technology colleges, with 214,542 students, and 3,311 special training schools with 638,000 students. There were, in addition, 1,466 miscellaneous vocational schools in 2010 with 130,000 students. Universities offer the full range of undergraduate and postgraduate degrees, and since incorporation in 2004 have become autonomous from the Ministry of Education, Culture, Sports, Science and Technology with regard to decisions about finance, staffing and self-assessment. Junior colleges specialize in two- or three-year Associate Degrees (Jun-Gakushi), credits from which may be accepted towards completion of the university Bachelors degrees. Technology colleges offer five-year training programmes in specialist fields of engineering and technology, and professional graduate schools, first established in 2003, offer two-year programmes of study aimed at bridging the gap between formal education and professional experience. Special training schools offer advanced courses in technical and vocational subjects, lasting for at least one year. The Ministry of Education, Culture, Sports, Science and Technology is responsible for education at all levels, sets the centrally compiled curriculum guidelines and authorizes textbooks. The Japan University Accreditation Association (JUAA) carries out the Certified Evaluation System, whereby all universities are evaluated periodically by a ministry-approved third party. (The JUAA was originally established in 1947 and had voluntary membership.) There are a number of other higher education evaluation/accreditation bodies, including the National Institution for Academic Degrees and University Evaluation, the Japan Institution for Higher Education Evaluation and the Japan Association for College Accreditation. Average annual costs (tuition, fees and living expenses) for a student are relatively high; consequently, students frequently work part-time or borrow money through the government-supported Japan Scholarship Association. Assistance is also offered by local governments, non-profit corporations and other institutions.

Admission to university is a three-stage process, based on completion of secondary education, results in the Unified First Stage Examination, administered by the National Centre for University Entrance, and each institution's entrance examination and/or interview. Applicants may only take an institution's entrance examination depending upon their results in the Unified First Stage Examination. The Bachelors (Gakushi) is the undergraduate degree, and is awarded on a 'credit' system following four (or up to six, for some subjects) years of study. Students must accrue at least 124 credits in 'major' and 'minor' subjects. The two-year Associate Degree offered by junior colleges requires a minimum of 62 credits and the three-year Associate Degree 93 credits. The first postgraduate degree is the Masters (Shūshi). Academic Masters degrees take two years, require 30 credits, the completion of a thesis and the passing of an examination. There are no Masters available in medical fields; graduates studying these subjects proceed directly to doctoral studies. Professional Masters degrees, which are offered by professional graduate schools, take between one and three years, depending on the subject. The minimum credit requirement is 30 credits and submission of a thesis is not necessary. The Doctorate (Hakushi) is the second postgraduate degree and the highest university-level qualification. The programme of study requires a further three to four years following the Masters, the accumulation of at least another 30 credits, the taking of an examination and the submission of a thesis. There are two types of doctorate available: doctorate by course work or doctorate by dissertation.

Technical and vocational education qualifications include the Special Training School Advanced Course Certificate (Senshu gakko Senmon-ka shuryo shosho), Special Training School Upper Secondary Certificate (Senshu gakko koto-ka sotsugyuo menjo), Technical Associate Degree or Diploma from a Special Training School (Senmonshi) and the Vocational Training Certificate or Diploma (awarded by Vocational Training College of the Ministry of Health, Labour and Welfare).

In 2005 a report entitled The Future of Higher Education in Japan was published. The report identified that as from 2007 university capacity would be at saturation point. It specified a number of goals including increased funding and quality assurance, a review of undergraduate liberal arts education and the introduction of a system for approving new institutions and departments.

The 2009 White Paper on Education, Culture, Sports, Science and Technology included plans to reduce government funding for national and city-controlled universities, greater use of English as the medium of instruction (the university of Tokyo began its first English-language undergraduate courses in 2012), the subsidization of private institutions, and a series of targeted programmes—including a university excellence initiative, an evolving quality assurance programme, and an effort to recruit more foreign students. In 2009, as part of the Global 30 'internationalization' project that was launched at an estimated cost of US $37m. that year, 13 universities were selected to function as core schools for receiving international students.

About 230 universities were affected by the earthquake and tsunami that hit the north-east of Japan in March 2011, causing severe damage to buildings and research and classroom facilities (as well as representing a major set-back for the ongoing plans for the further 'internationalization' of the Japanese higher education sector). According to government figures, the overall cost of the extensive destruction inflicted on universities by the disaster totalled approximately US $740m.

Regulatory and Representative Bodies

GOVERNMENT

Ministry of Education, Culture, Sports, Science and Technology: 3-2-2, Kasumigaseki, Chiyoda-ku, Tokyo 100-8959; tel. (3) 5253-4111; internet www.mext.go.jp; Minister HAKUBUN SHIMOMURA.

ACCREDITATION

Daigaku Kijun Kyokai (Japan University Accreditation Association): 2-7-13, Ichigaya Sadohara-cho, Sinjuku-ku, Tokyo 162-0842; tel. (3) 5228-2020; internet www.juaa.or.jp; f. 1947; promotes the qualitative improvement of univs in Japan through the voluntary efforts and mutual assistance of mem. univs; Pres. HIROMI NAYA.

Daigaku-hyoka Gakui-juyo Kiko (National Institution for Academic Degrees and University Evaluation—NIAD-UE): 1-29-1 Gakuen-nishimachi, Kodaira-shi, Tokyo 187-8587; tel. (42) 307-1500; e-mail dir-intl@niad.ac.jp; internet www.niad.ac.jp; f. 1991; ind. agency conducting evaluations of teaching and research activities at univs, junior colleges, colleges of technology and inter-univ. research institutes to raise the quality of education and research; awards academic degrees to learners recognized as having fulfilled required academic standards; Pres. TOMOYUKI NOGAMI.

Japan Association for College Accreditation (JACA): 4–2–11 Kudankita Chiyoda-ku, Tokyo 102-0073; tel. (3) 3261-3594; e-mail jimukyoku@jaca.or.jp; internet www.jaca.or.jp; f. 1994; sustains quality of junior college education by assisting and supporting mem. junior colleges in educational and research activities; formulates accreditation policies and procedures for junior colleges; Pres. OSAMU SEKIGUCHI; Vice-Pres. HIDEKAZU SEKINE; Vice-Pres. HIROAKI SUEOKA.

NATIONAL BODIES

Chuo Kyoiku Shingikai (Central Council for Education): Min. of Education, Culture, Sports, Science and Technology, 3-2-2, Kasumigaseki, Chiyoda-ku, Tokyo 100-8959; tel. (3) 5253-4111; internet www.mext.go.jp; f. 1952; advises the Minister; carries out research and considers issues relating to the promotion of education, lifelong learning and sports; has 5 working groups concerned with: education systems, lifelong learning, elementary and lower secondary education, univs, and sports and youth; Chair. MASAKAZU YAMAZAKI.

Japan Institution for Higher Education Evaluation: Daini-Seiko bldg 2F, 4–2–11, Kudan-kita, Chiyoda-ku, Tokyo 102-0073; tel. (3) 5211-5131; internet www.jihee.or.jp; f. 2005; assures quality and facilitates reform and improvement of educational and research activities conducted at univs.

Kokuritsu Daigaku Kyokai (Japan Association of National Universities): 4F, Nat. Center of Sciences Bldg, 1-2, Hitotsubashi 2-chome, Chiyoda-ku, Tokyo 101-0003; tel. (3) 4212-3506; e-mail info@janu.jp; internet www.janu.jp; Pres. HIROSHI KOMIYAMA.

Koritsu Daigaku Kyokai (Japan Association of Municipal and Prefectural Colleges and Universities): Toranomon-Yoshiara Bldg, 9th Floor, 1-6-13 Nishi-Shimbashi, Minato-ku, Tokyo 105-0003; tel. (3) 3501-3336; e-mail jimu@kodaikyo.jp; internet www.kodaikyo.jp; f. 1949; 74 mems; Pres. TAKAO KODAMA.

Nihon Shiritsu Daigaku Kyokai (Association of Private Universities of Japan): Shigakukaikan Bekkan 9F, 4-2-25 Kudankita, Chiyoda-ku, Tokyo 102-0073; tel. (3) 3261-7048; e-mail koei@shidaikyo.or.jp; internet www.shidaikyo.or.jp; f. 1946; 384 private univs and colleges; Chair. Dr SUNAO ONUMA; Sec.-Gen. HIDEBUMI KOIDE; publ. *Kyoikugakujutsu*.

Learned Societies

GENERAL

Nihon Gakujutsu Kaigi (Science Council of Japan): 22–34 Roppongi 7-chome, Minato-ku, Tokyo 106; tel. (3) 3403-6291; internet www.scj.go.jp; f. 1949; governmental org. coordinating Japan's scientific research; divs of agriculture, commerce and business administration, dentistry and pharmacology, economics, engineering, law and political science, literature, medicine, pedagogy, philosophy, psychology, pure science, sociology and history; 210 mems; library: see under Libraries and Archives; Pres. Dr ICHIRO KANAZAWA; Sec.-Gen. YASUHIKO NAGASHIMA.

Nihon Gakujutsu Shinko-kai (Japan Society for the Promotion of Science): 6 Ichibadncho, Chiyoda-ku, Tokyo 102-8471; tel. (3) 3263-1722; internet www.jsps.go.jp; f. 1932; independent admin. institution and funding agency; administers grants-in-aid for scientific research, research fellowships for young scientists, univ./industry cooperation, scientific outreach, etc.; has cooperative agreements with 82 overseas orgs; operates JSPS overseas offices in 10 cities; 99 mems; Pres. MOTOYUKI ONO; publs *Japanese Scientific Monthly*, *JSPS Quarterly*.

Nippon Gakushiin (Japan Academy): 7-32 Ueno Park, Taito-ku, Tokyo 110-0007; tel. (3) 3822-2101; e-mail international@japan-acad.go.jp; internet www.japan-acad.go.jp; f. 1879; 150 mems; Pres. Prof. TAKASHI SUGIMURA; Vice-Pres. Prof. HIROSHI SHIONA; Section Chair. (Humanities and Social Sciences) Prof. YOICHI HIGUCHI; Section Chair. (Pure and Applied Sciences) Prof. YOSHIHIDE KOZAI; publs *Proceedings* (2 series, 10 a year), *Nippon Gakushiin Kiyo* (3 a year).

AGRICULTURE, FISHERIES AND VETERINARY SCIENCE

Engei Gakkai (Japanese Society for Horticultural Science): Business Center for Academic Societies Japan, 16–9 Honkomagome 5-chome, Bunkyo-ku, Tokyo 113; tel. (3) 5814-5801; f. 1923; 2,795 mems; Pres. ICHIRO KAJIURA; Sec. TADASHI BABA; publ. *Journal* (6 a year).

Nihon Ikushu Gakkai (Japanese Society of Breeding): c/o Faculty of Agriculture, University of Tokyo, Bunkyo-ku, Tokyo 113-8657; tel. (3) 5841-5065; e-mail kishima@abs.agr.hokudai.ac.jp; internet www.nacos.com/jsb/e; f. 1951; 2,300 mems; Pres. ATSUCHI HIRAI; publs *Breeding Science* (4 a year), *Ikushugaku Kenkyu* (4 a year).

Nihon Ju-í Gakkai (Japanese Society of Veterinary Science): Tokyo RS Bldg, 8th Fl., 6-26-12 Hongo, Bunkyo-ku, Tokyo 113-0033; tel. (3) 5803-7761; e-mail office@jsvs.or.jp; internet www.soc.nii.ac.jp/jsvs; f. 1885; 4,100 mems; Pres. KUNIO DOI; publ. *The Journal of Veterinary Medical Science* (12 a year).

Nihon Oyo Toshitsu Kagaku Kai (Japanese Society of Applied Glycoscience): c/o National Food Research Institute, 2-1-2 Kannondai, Tsukuba, Ibaraki 305; tel. (298) 38-7991; e-mail jsag@mynavi.jp; internet www.soc.nii.ac.jp/jsag; f. 1952; 1,147 mems; Pres. YASUHITO TAKEDA; Vice-Pres HIROKAZU MATSUI, KENJI YAMAMOTO, TAKASHI KURIKI; publ. *Journal of Applied Glycoscience* (4 a year).

Nihon Sanshi Gakkai (Japanese Society of Sericultural Science): c/o Nat. Institute of Agrobiological Sciences, 1-2 Ohwashi, Tsukuba, Ibaraki 305-8634; tel. (29) 838-6056; e-mail jsss@silk.or.jp; internet www.soc.nii.ac.jp/jsss2; f. 1930; 557 mems; Pres. Prof. MICHIHIRO KOBAYASHI; Man. HIDETOSHI TERAMOTO; publs *Journal of Insect Biotechnology and Sericology* (3 a year), *Journal of Sericultural Science of Japan* (Sanshi Konchu Biotec, 3 a year).

Nippon Seibutsu-Kogaku Kai (Society for Biotechnology, Japan): c/o Faculty of Engineering, Osaka Univ., 2–1 Yamadaoka, Suita, Osaka 565-0871; tel. (6) 6876-2731; e-mail info@sbj.or.jp; internet www.sbj.or.jp; f. 1923; provides training and devt opportunities for students and young researchers; 3,500 mems; Pres. Prof. SATOSHI HARASHIMA; publs *Journal of Bioscience and Bioengineering* (12 a year, in English), *Seibutsu-kogaku Kaishi* (12 a year, in Japanese).

Nihon Shinringakkai (Japanese Forestry Society): c/o Japan Forest Technical Association, Rokubancho 7, Chiyoda-ku, Tokyo; tel. (3) 3261-2766; f. 1914; forestry research; 2,900 mems; Pres. KAZUMI KOBAYASHI; publs *Journal* (6 a year), *Shinrin Kagaku* (bulletin, 3 a year).

Nippon Chikusan Gakkai (Japanese Society of Animal Science): 201 Nagatani Corporas, Ikenohata 2-9-4, Taito-ku, Tokyo 110-0008; tel. (3) 3828-8409; e-mail tikusan@blue.ocn.ne.jp; internet www.soc.nii.ac.jp/jszs; f. 1924; animal science; 2,706 mems; Pres. HIDEO YANO; publs *Animal Science Journal* (6 a year), *Nihon Chikusan Gakkaihou* (4 a year).

Nippon Dojo-Hiryo Gakkai (Japanese Society of Soil Science and Plant Nutrition): 26-10-202 Hongo, 6-chome, Bunkyo-ku, Tokyo; tel. (3) 3815-2085; e-mail sfpoffice@jssspn.jp; internet jssspn.jp; f. 1914; 2,600 mems; Pres. MASAMI NANZYO; publs *Japanese Journal of Soil and Science Plant Nutrition*, *Journal* (6 a year), *Soil Science and Plant Nutrition* (6 a year).

Nippon Nougei Kagaku Kai (Japan Society for Bioscience, Biotechnology and Agrochemistry): 4–16 Yayoi 2-chome, Bunkyo-ku, Tokyo 113-0032; e-mail shomu-b@jsbba.or.jp; internet www.jsbba.or.jp; f. 1924; 12,546 mems; library of 742,010 vols; Pres. Prof. SAKAYU SHIMIZU; publs *Bioscience, Biotechnology and Biochemistry* (12 a year, in English), *Nippon Nōgeikagaku Kaishi* (12 a year, in Japanese), *Kagaku To Seibutsu* (12 a year, in Japanese).

Nippon Sakumotsu Gakkai (Crop Science Society of Japan): 2F Shin-Kyoritsu Bldg, Shinkawa 2-22-4, Chuo-ku, Tokyo 104-0033; e-mail cssj-jim@bridge.ocn.ne.jp; internet www.cropscience.jp; f. 1927; 1,500 mems; Pres. Dr SHIGEMI AKITA; Sec. YUSEKE GOTO; publs *Japanese Journal of Crop Science* (4 a year), *Plant Production Science* (4 a year).

Nippon Shokubutsu-Byori Gakkai (Phytopathological Society of Japan): Shokubo Bldg, Komagome 1-43-11, Toshima-ku, Tokyo 170; tel. (3) 3943-6021; e-mail byori@juno.ocn.ne.jp; internet www.ppsj.org; f. 1916; promotes research on plant diseases; 1,880 regular mems; Pres. SHINJI TSUYUMU; Vice-Pres. TOMONORI SHIRAISHI; publ. *Journal* (4 a year).

Nippon Suisan Gakkai (Japanese Society of Fisheries Science): c/o Tokyo University of Marine Science and Technology, 4-5-7 Konan, Minato-ku, Tokyo 108-8477; tel. (3) 3471-2165; e-mail fishsci@d1.dion.ne.jp; internet www.miyagi.kopas.co.jp/jsfs; f. 1932; research in fishing science and technology, mariculture, aquaculture, marine environmental science and related fields; 4,879 mems; library of 80 vols; Pres. Prof. S. WATABE; publs *Fisheries Science* (6 a year, in English), *Nippon Suisan Gakkaishi* (6 a year, in Japanese with English abstracts).

Nogyokikai Gakkai (Japanese Society of Agricultural Machinery): c/o BRAIN, 1-40-2 Nisshin-cho, Saitama 331-8537; tel. (48) 652-4119; e-mail jsam@iam.brain.go.jp; internet www.j-sam.org; f. 1937; 1,500 mems; Pres. TOMOHIKO ICHIKAWA; publ. *Journal of the Japanese Society of Agricultural Machinery* (6 a year).

ARCHITECTURE AND TOWN PLANNING

Nihon Zoen Gakkai (Japanese Institute of Landscape Architecture): Zoen Kaikan, 6th Fl., 1-20-11 Jinnan, Shibuya-ku, Tokyo 150-0041; tel. (3) 5459-0515; e-mail info@landscapearchitecture.or.jp; internet www.landscapearchitecture.or.jp; f. 1924; 1,800 mems; Pres. AKIRA HOMMA; publ. *Journal*.

Nihon Zosen Gakkai (Japanese Society of Naval Architects and Ocean Engineers):internet www.jasnoe.or.jp; f. 2005 by merger of Society of Naval Architects of Japan, Kansai Society of Naval Architects,

Japan, and the West-Japan Society of Naval Architects; publ. *Kanrin*.

Nippon Toshi Keikaku Gakkai (City Planning Institute of Japan): Ichibancho-West Building 6F, Ichibancho 10, Chiyoda-ku, Tokyo 102-0082; tel. (3) 3261-5407; internet wwwsoc.nii.ac.jp/cpij; f. 1951; 5,349 mems; Pres. TAKASHI ONISHI; publ. *City Planning Review* (6 a year).

BIBLIOGRAPHY, LIBRARY SCIENCE AND MUSEOLOGY

Gakujutsu Bunken Fukyu-Kai (Association for Science Documents Information): c/o Tokyo Institute of Technology, 2-12-1 Ookayama, Meguro-ku, Tokyo 152-8550; e-mail gakujyutubunken@mvd.biglobe.ne.jp; f. 1933; Pres. SHU KANBARA; publ. *Reports on Progress in Polymer Physics in Japan* (1 a year, in English).

Information Processing Society of Japan: Kagaku-kaikan (Chemistry Hall) 4F, 1–5 Kanda-Surugadai, Chiyoda-ku, Tokyo 101-0062; tel. (3) 3518-8374; e-mail somu@ipsj.or.jp; internet www.ipsj.or.jp; f. 1960; 30,000 mems; Pres. Dr HAJIME SASAKI; publ. *Journal of Information Processing*.

Joho-Jigyo, Kagaku-Gijutsu Shinko Kiko (S&T Information Services, Japan Science and Technology Agency (JST)): 5-3 Yonban-cho, Chiyoda-ku, Tokyo 102-8666; tel. (3) 5214-8402; e-mail sti@jst.go.jp; internet sti.jst.go.jp; f. 1957; an integrated org. of S&T; prepares abstracts, online and manual search services, translation and photo-duplication service, library service, computer processing; 470 mems; Pres. K. KITAZAWA; publs *Current Bibliography on Science and Technology* (Abstracts from about 16,200 journals, 12 series), *Current Science and Technology Research in Japan* (in English and Japanese), *Journal of Information Processing and Management* (12 a year), *JST Thesaurus*, *JST Holding List of Serials and Proceedings* (online).

Joho Kagaku Gijutsu Kyokai (Information Science and Technology Association): Sasaki Bldg, 5–7 Koisikawa 2, Bunkyo-ku, Tokyo 112; tel. (3) 3813-3791; e-mail infosta@infosta.or.jp; internet www.infosta.or.jp; f. 1950; 2,020 mems; Pres. T. GONDOH; publ. *Journal* (1 a year).

Nihon Hakubutsukan Kyokai (Japanese Association of Museums): Shoyu-Kaikan 3-3-1, Kasumigaseki, Chiyoda-ku, Tokyo 100-8925; tel. (3) 3591-7190; e-mail webmaster@j-muse.or.jp; internet www.j-muse.or.jp; f. 1928; Gen. Man. YOKO NIIZUMA; 1,280 mems; publ. *Museum Studies* (12 a year).

Nihon Toshokan Kyokai (Japan Library Association): 1-11-14, Shinkawa, Chuo-ku, Tokyo 104-0033; tel. (3) 3523-0811; e-mail info@jla.or.jp; internet www.jla.or.jp; f. 1892; all aspects of library development; 8,900 mems; library of 10,000 vols; Sec.-Gen. KATSURA YOKOYAMA; publs *Gendai no Toshokan* (4 a year), *Nihon no Sankotosho Shikiban* (4 a year), *Nihon no Toshokan* (1 a year), *Toshokan Nenkan* (1 a year), *Toshokan Zasshi* (12 a year).

Nippon Toshokan Joho Gakkai (Japan Society of Library and Information Science): c/o Graduate School of Library and Information Science, Univ. of Tsukuba, 1–2 Kasuga, Tsukuba-shi, Ibaraki-ken 305-8550; e-mail jslis-info@slis.tsukuba.ac.jp; internet www.soc.nii.ac.jp/jslis; f. 1953; 750 mems; Pres. SHUICHI UEDA; Sec. YUKO YOSHIDA; publ. *Journal* (4 a year).

ECONOMICS, LAW AND POLITICS

Aziya Seikei Gakkai (Japan Association for Asian Studies): c/o Ochanomizu University, 2-1-1 Otsuka, Bunkyo-ku, 112-8610; tel. 5976-1478; e-mail jaas-info@npo-ochanomizu.org; internet www.jaas.or.jp; f. 1953; 900 mems; Pres. SATOSHI AMAKO; publ. *Aziya Kenkyu* (Asian Studies, 4 a year).

Hikaku-ho Gakkai (Japan Society of Comparative Law): c/o Faculty of Law, Tokyo University, Hongo, Bunkyo-ku, Tokyo 113; internet www.asas.or.jp/jscl; f. 1950; studies in comparative law; holds confs; issues pubs; 780 mems; Pres. H. TANAKA; publ. *Hikakuhô Kenkyû* (Comparative Law Journal, 1 a year).

Hogaku Kyokai (Jurisprudence Association): Faculty of Law, University of Tokyo, Hongo, Bunkyo-ku, Tokyo; tel. (3) 3812-2111; f. 1884; 600 mems; Pres. TAKESHI SASAKI; publs *Hogaku Kyokai Zasshi*, *Journal*.

Hosei-shi Gakkai (Japan Legal History Association): Kyoto University, Yoshida-hommachi, Sakyo-ku, Kyoto 606-8501; tel. (75) 753-3235; e-mail jalha@wwwsoc.nii.ac.jp; internet wwwsoc.nii.ac.jp/jalha; f. 1949; 495 mems; Pres. H. TERADA; publ. *Legal History Review* (1 a year).

Hosokai (Lawyers' Association): 1, 1-chome, Kasumigaseki, Chiyoda-ku, Tokyo; tel. (3) 3581-2146; internet www.hosokai.or.jp; f. 1891; 20,000 mems; library of 30,000 vols; Pres. RYOHACHI KUSABA; Dir ISAO IMAI; publ. *Hoso Jiho*.

Japan Institute of International Affairs: Toranomon Mitsui Bldg, 3rd Fl., 3-8-1 Kasumigaseki, Chiyodaku, Tokyo 100-0013; tel. (3) 3503-7261; e-mail jiiajoho@jiia.or.jp; internet www.jiia.or.jp; f. 1956; 512 mems; Pres. YOSHIJI NOGAMI; Deputy Dir-Gen. NAOKO SAIKI; publ. *Kokusai Mondai* (International Relations, 4 a year, in Japanese).

Japan Institute of Public Finance: c/o Institute of Statistical Research, Japan Life Insurance Bldg, 7th Fl., 1-18-16 Shinbashi Minatoku, Tokyo 105-0004; tel. (3) 3591-8496; e-mail zaisei@isr.or.jp; internet wwwsoc.nii.ac.jp/jipf; f. 1940 as Japanese Association of Fiscal Science; 1,000 mems; publ. *Zaisei Kenkyu* (1 a year).

Keizai Riron Gakkai (Japan Society of Political Economy): Faculty of Economics, Rikkyo University, 3 Ikebukuro, Toshima-ku, Tokyo; e-mail secretariat@jspe.gr.jp; internet www.jspe.gr.jp; f. 1959; 865 mems; Pres. H. OOUCHI; publ. *Political Economy Quarterly*.

Keizaigaku-shi Gakkai (Japan Society for the History of Economic Thought): Dept of Economics, Tohoku University, Kawauchi, Sendai; tel. (22) 217-6275; e-mail mawatari@econ.tohoku.ac.jp; internet society.cpm.ehime-u.ac.jp/shet/shet.html; f. 1949; 810 mems; Pres. SHOHKEN MAWATARI; publ. *History of Economic Thought*, *Society Newsletter*.

Kokusaiho Gakkai (Association of International Law): Faculty of Law, Univ. of Tokyo, Hongo, Bunkyo-ku, Tokyo; tel. (3) 3812-2111; f. 1897; 804 mems; Pres. M. OTSUKA; publs *Kokusaiho Gaiko Zasshi*, *Journal of International Law and Diplomacy*.

Labour Lawyers Association of Japan: 4F Sohyo-Kaikan, 3-2-11 Kanda-Surugadai Chiyoda-ku, Tokyo; tel. (3) 3251-5363; f. 1957; 1,400 mems; publ. *Rodosha no Kenri* (Workers' Rights, 4 a year).

Nichibei Hougakukai (Japanese American Society for Legal Studies): c/o Faculty of Law, Univ. of Tokyo, Hongo, Bunkyo-ku, Tokyo 113-0033; e-mail yosaitoh@j.u-tokyo.ac.jp; f. 1964; seeks and develops mutual understanding of Japanese and American law and legal scholarship, esp. through cooperation of members of the legal profession; 800 mems; Dir Y. KAKISHIMA; publ. *Amerikaho* (Law in the USA, 2 a year).

Nihon Keizai Gakkai (Japanese Economics Association): Sankyo Bldg 703, 1-7-10, Iidabashi Chiyoda-ku, Tokyo 102-0072; tel. (3) 5211-5707; e-mail office@jeaweb.org; internet www.jeaweb.org; f. 1934; 3,414 mems; Pres. YOSHIO HIGUCHI; publ. *Japanese Economic Review* (4 a year).

Nihon Kinyu Gakkai (Japan Society of Monetary Economics): 1-2-1 Nihonbashi Hongokucho, Chuo-ku, Tokyo 103-0021; tel. (3) 3231-1372; e-mail jsme@d8.dion.ne.jp; internet www.jsmeweb.org; f. 1943; 1,365 mems; Pres. Prof. HIDEO FUJIWARA; publ. *Review of Monetary and Financial Studies* (2 a year).

Nihon Koho Gakkai (Japan Public Law Association): Univ. of Tokyo, 7-3-1 Hongo, Bunkyo-ku, Tokyo; e-mail shishido@j.u-tokyo.ac.jp; f. 1948; 1,200 mems; Pres. Prof. MITSUO KOBAYAKAWA; publ. *Koho-Kenkyu* (Public Law Review, 1 a year).

Nihon Minji Soshoho Gakkai (Japan Association of Civil Procedure Law): c/o Faculty of Law, Osaka City University, 3-3-138 Sugimoto, Sumiyoshi-ku, Osaka; tel. (6) 6605-2327; f. 1949; 815 mems; Pres. H. MATSUMOTO; publ. *Journal of Civil Procedure* (1 a year).

Nihon Tokei Gakkai (Japan Statistical Society): c/o SINFONICA, Nohgakushorin Bldg 5F, 3-6 Kanda Jimbouchо Chiyoda-ku, Tokyo 101-0051; tel. (3) 3234-7738; internet www.jss.gr.jp; f. 1931; 1,312 mems; Pres. Prof. AKIMICHI TAKEMURA; Pres. Prof. MANABU IWASAKI; publ. *Journal* (2 a year).

Nippon Hoshakai Gakkai (Japan Association of Sociology of Law): University of Tokyo, Hongo, Bunkyo-ku, Tokyo; internet wwwsoc.nii.ac.jp/hosha; f. 1947; 805 mems; Pres. N. TOSHITANI; publ. *Sociology of Law* (1 a year).

Nippon Hotetsu-Gakkai (Japan Association of Legal Philosophy): Chiba University, Faculty of Law and Economics, 1-33, Yayoi-cho, Inage-ku, Chiba-shi, Chiba 263-8522; tel. (43) 290-2362; e-mail jalp@wwwsoc.nii.ac.jp; internet wwwsoc.nii.ac.jp/jalp; f. 1948; 486 mems; Pres. Prof. ITARU SHIMAZU; publ. *The Annals of Legal Philosophy*.

Nihon Keiei Gakkai (Japan Academy of Business Administration): Hitotsubashi Univ., 2-1 Naka, Kunitachi, Tokyo 186-8601; tel. (42) 580-8571; internet www.keiei-gakkai.jp; f. 1926; 2,000 mems; Pres. N. KAIDO; publs *Annual Review of Business Administration*, *Journal of Business Management*.

Nippon Keiho Gakkai (Criminal Law Society of Japan): University of Tokyo, Hongo, Bunkyo-ku, Tokyo; f. 1949; 1,000 mems; Pres. K. SHIBAHARA; publ. *Journal* (4 a year).

Nippon Keizai Seisaku Gakkai (Japan Economic Policy Association): School of Political Science and Economics, Waseda University, 1-6-1 Nishiwaseda, Shinjuku-ku, Tokyo 169-8050; tel. (3) 5286-2193; e-mail jepa-mail@list.waseda.jp; internet wwwsoc.nii.ac.jp/jepa; f. 1940; 1,150 mems; Pres. Prof. YASUMI MATSUMOTO; publ. *International Economic Policy Studies*.

Nippon Seizi Gakkai (Japanese Political Science Association): Faculty of Law, Rikkyo University, 3-34-1, Nishi-Ikebukuro, Toshima-ku, Tokyo 171; e-mail ykobayas@hs.catv.ne.jp; internet www.jpsa-web.org; 820 mems; Sec.-Gen. Dr YOSHIAKI KOBAYASHI; publ. *Annals* (1 a year).

Nippon Shogyo Gakkai (Japan Society of Commercial Sciences): Meiji University, Surugadai Kanda, Chiyoda-ku, Tokyo; f. 1951; 980 mems; Pres. K. FUKUDA.

Private International Law Association: Chuo University Faculty of Law, 742-1 Higashinakano Hachioji-shi, Tokyo 192-0393; tel. (42) 674-3154; f. 1949; 244 mems; Pres. KORESUKE YAMAUCHI.

Tokyo Daigaku Keizai Gakkai (Society of Economics): Faculty of Economics, Univ. of Tokyo, 7-3-1 Hongo, Bunkyo-ku, Tokyo 113-0033; f. 1922; 200 mems; Pres. NAOTO KUNITOMO; publ. *Journal of Economics* (4 a year).

EDUCATION

Asia–Pacific Cultural Centre for UNESCO (ACCU): 6 Fukuromachi, Shinjuku-ku, Tokyo 162-8484; tel. (3) 3269-4435; e-mail general@accu.or.jp; internet www.accu.or.jp; f. 1971; adult learning materials, children's books, literacy materials devt, music, personnel exchange programmes, photo contest, protection of cultural heritage, training programmes and other regional cultural activities; library of 29,000 vols; Pres. KAZUO SUZUKI; Dir-Gen. KOJI NAKANISHI; publs *Activity Report* (1 a year), *ACCU News* (6 a year, in Japanese), *Asian/Pacific Book Development* (4 a year, in English).

Nihon Gakko-hoken Gakkai (Japanese Association of School Health): Dept of Health Education, Faculty of Education, University of Tokyo, Hongo 7-3-1, Bunkyo-ku, Tokyo 113; tel. (3) 3812-2111; e-mail jash@shobix.co.jp; internet www.soc.nii.ac.jp/jash; f. 1954; 1,500 mems; Pres. ATSUHISA EGUCHI; publ. *Gakko-hoken Kenkyu* (Japanese Journal of School Health, 12 a year).

Nihon Hikaku Kyoiku Gakkai (Japan Comparative Education Society): c/o Dept of Education, Graduate School of Human Environment Studies, Kyushu University, 6-19-1, Hakozaki, Higashi-ku, Fukuoka City, Fukuoka Prefecture 812-8581; tel. (92) 632-8426; f. 1965; 905 mems; Pres. K. MOCHIDA; Sec.-Gen. H. TAKEKUMA; publs *Comparative Education* (2 a year), *Newsletter* (2 a year).

Nihon Kyoiku Gakkai (Japanese Educational Research Association): 2-29-3-3F Hongo, Bunkyo-ku, Tokyo 113-0033; tel. (3) 3818-2505; e-mail jsse@oak.ocn.ne.jp; f. 1941; 3,300 mems; Pres. HIDENORI FUJITA; publs *Educational Studies in Japan: International Yearbook*, *The Japanese Journal of Educational Research* (4 a year).

Nihon Kyoiku-shakai Gakkai (Japan Society of Educational Sociology): Faculty of Education, University of Tokyo, Hongo 7-3-1, Bunkyo-ku, Tokyo 113; tel. (3) 3907-3750; e-mail g003jses-mng@ml.galileo.co.jp; internet www.gakkai.ne.jp/jses; f. 1949; 1,200 mems; Pres. HIDENORI FUJITA; publ. *Journal of Educational Sociology* (2 a year).

Nihon Kyoiku-shinri Gakkai (Japanese Association of Educational Psychology): Hongo Ohara Bldg, 7th Floor, Hongo 5-24-6, Bunkyo-ku, Tokyo 113-0033; tel. (3) 3818-1534; internet www.edupsych.jp; f. 1952; 7,100 mems; Pres. TOMOKAZU HAEBARA; publ. *Japanese Journal of Educational Psychology* (4 a year).

Nippon Kagaku Kyoiku Gakkai (Japan Society for Science Education): c/o Nakanishi Printing Co. Ltd., Shimotachiuri Ogawa-Higashi, Kamikyo-ku, Kyoto 602 8048; tel. (75) 41-53-661; e-mail jsse@nacos.com; internet www.jsse.jp; f. 1977; science and mathematics education and educational technology; 1,200 mems; Pres. J. YOSHIDA; publs *Journal* (4 a year), *Letter* (6 a year), *Proceedings of Annual Meeting*.

Nippon Sugaku Kyoiku Gakkai (Japan Society of Mathematical Education): POB 18, Koishikawa, Tokyo 112-8691; tel. (3) 3946-2267; internet www.sme.or.jp; f. 1919; 3,334 mems; Pres. Prof. T. SAWADA; publs *Journal* (12 a year), *Supplementary issue* (report on mathematical education, 2 a year), *Yearbook* (1 a year).

Nihon Taiiku Gakkai (Japan Society of Physical Education, Health and Sport Sciences): Kishi Memorial Hall, Jinnan 1-1-1, Shibuya-ku, Tokyo 150-8050; tel. (3) 3481-2427; e-mail ijshs@taiiku-gakkai.or.jp; internet taiiku-gakkai.or.jp; f. 1950; 6,000 mems; Pres. Prof. Dr MICHIYOSHI AE; publ. *International Journal of Sport and Health Science* (1 a year).

FINE AND PERFORMING ARTS

Bijutsu-shi Gakkai (Japanese Art History Society): c/o Tokyo National Research Institute of Cultural Properties, 13–27 Ueno Park, Taito-ku, Tokyo 110; e-mail jahs@univcoop.or.jp; internet www.soc.nii.ac.jp/jahs2; f. 1949; 2,300 mems; publ. *Journal* (4 a year).

Nihon Engeki Gakkai (Japanese Society for Theatre Research): Waseda University, 1-6-1 Nishi-Waseda, Shinjuku-ku, Tokyo 169-8050; tel. (3) 3203-4141; f. 1949; Pres. T. MORI.

Nippon Ongaku Gakkai (Musicological Society of Japan): 3-3-3-201 Iidabashi, Chiyoda-ku, 102-0072 Tokyo; tel. (3) 3288-5616; e-mail office@musicology-japan.org; f. 1952; 1,350 mems; Pres. T. ISOYAMA; publ. *Ongaku Gaku* (Journal, 3 a year).

HISTORY, GEOGRAPHY AND ARCHAEOLOGY

Keizai Chiri Gakkai (Japan Association of Economic Geographers): Institute of Economic Geography, Faculty of Economics, East Bldg, Hitotsubashi University, Naka 2-1, Kunitachi-shi, Tokyo 186; tel. (425) 72-1101; e-mail jimukyoku@economicgeography.jp; internet wwwsoc.nii.ac.jp/jaeg; f. 1954; 700 mems; Pres. K. TAKEUCHI; publ. *Annals* (4 a year).

Nihon Kokogakkai (Archaeological Society of Japan): c/o Tokyo National Museum, Ueno Park, Taito-ku, Tokyo; f. 1895; 2,200 mems; Pres. Dr FUJITA KUNIO; publ. *Kokogaku Zasshi* (4 a year).

Nippon Kokogaku Kyokai (Japanese Archaeological Association): 5-15-5, Hirai, Edogawa-ku, Tokyo 132-0035; tel. (3) 3618-6608; internet archaeology.jp; f. 1948; 4,253 mems; library of 47,009 vols; Pres. TETSUO KIKUCHI; publ. *Nihon Kōkogaku* (journal).

Nippon Oriento Gakkai (Society for Near Eastern Studies in Japan): Tokyo-Tenrikyokan 9, 1-chome 9, Kanda Nishiki-cho, Chiyoda-ku, Tokyo 101-0054; tel. (3) 3291-7519; f. 1954; 800 mems; Pres. KOJI KAMIOKA; publs *Oriento* (2 a year, in Japanese), *Orient* (1 a year, in European languages).

Nippon Seibutsuchiri Gakkai (Biogeographical Society of Japan): c/o Sadaharu Morinaka, 11–20 Totsukahasami-cho, Kawaguchi, Saitama 333-0805; tel. (48) 295-4574; e-mail qyv04336@nifty.ne.jp; internet wwwsoc.nii.ac.jp/tbsj; f. 1928; 300 mems; Pres. SADAHARU MORINAKA; publs *Bulletin*, *Biogeographica*, *Fauna Japonica*.

Nippon Seiyoshigakukai (Japanese Society of Western History): Dept of Western History, Graduate School of Letters, Osaka Univ., 1–5 Machikaneyama-cho, Toyonaka, Osaka 560-8532; tel. (6) 6850-5105; e-mail seiyousihgaku@mti.biglobe.ne.jp; f. 1948; 880 mems; Pres. Prof. A. EGAWA; publ. *Studies in Western History* (4 a year).

Shigaku-kai (Historical Society of Japan): University of Tokyo, Hongo, Bunkyo-ku, Tokyo 113; e-mail shigaku@l.u-tokyo.ac.jp; f. 1889; c. 2,470 mems; Pres. OSAMU NARUSE; publ. *Shigaku-Zasshi* (Historical Journal of Japan).

Tokyo Chigaku Kyokai (Tokyo Geographical Society): 12–2 Nibancho, Chiyoda-ku, Tokyo 102-0084; tel. (3) 3261-0809; e-mail chigaku@abox9.so-net.ne.jp; internet www.geog.or.jp; f. 1879; 810 mems; Pres. ISAMU KOBAYASHI; publ. *Journal of Geography* (6 a year, and 1 special issue a year).

Toyoshi-Kenkyu-Kai (Society of Oriental Researches): Kyoto University, Sakyo-ku, Kyoto City; tel. (75) 753-2790; e-mail orientalresearches@bun.kyoto-u.ac.jp; internet wwwsoc.nii.ac.jp/toyoshi/index.html; f. 1935; 1,400 mems; Pres. I. MIYAZAKI; publ. *Toyoshi-Kenkyu* (Journal of Oriental Researches, 4 a year).

LANGUAGE AND LITERATURE

Alliance Française: Imamura Bldg, 9th Fl., 2-2-11 Tenjinbashi, Kita-Ku, Osaka 530-0041; tel. (6) 358-7391; e-mail info@calosa.com; internet www.calosa.com; offers courses and examinations in French language and culture and promotes cultural exchange with France; attached teaching centres in Nagoya, Sapporo, Sendai and Tokushima; Dir ERIC GALMARD.

British Council: 1–2 Kagurazaka, Shinjuku-ku, Tokyo 162-0825; tel. (3) 3235-8031; e-mail enquiries@britishcouncil.or.jp; internet www.britishcouncil.org/japan; teaching centre; offers courses and examinations in English language and British culture and promotes cultural exchange with the UK; attached teaching centres in Kyoto, Nagoya and Osaka; Dir, Japan JOANNA BURKE.

Goethe-Institut: Doitsu Bunka Kaikan, 7-5-56 Akasaka, Minato-ku, Tokyo 107-0052; tel. (3) 3584-3201; e-mail info@tokyo.goethe.org; internet www.goethe.de/os/tok/deindex.htm; offers courses and examinations in German language and culture and promotes cultural exchange with Germany; attached centres in Kyoto and Osaka; library of 10,000 vols, 40 periodicals; Dir RAIMUND WOERDEMANN.

Japan Comparative Literature Association: Aoyamagakuin University, Shibuya-ku, Tokyo; tel. (3) 5421-3238; internet wwwsoc.nii.ac.jp/jcla; f. 1948; 400 mems; Pres. KEN INOUE; Sec.-Gen. Prof. TAKASHI ARIMITSU; publ. *Journal* (1 a year).

Japanese Centre of International PEN: 20-3 Kabuto-cho, Nihonbashi, Chuo-ku, Tokyo 103-0026; e-mail secretariat01@japanpen.or.jp; internet www.japanpen.or.jp; f. 1935; Pres. KAZUNARI YOSHIZAWA.

Kokugogakkai (Society for the Study of Japanese Language): Faculty of Letters, University of Tokyo, Hongo, Bunkyo-ku, Tokyo 113; e-mail office@jpling.gr.jp; internet wwwsoc.nii.ac.jp/jpling; f. 1944; 1,500 mems; Pres. ETSUTARO IWABUCHI; publ. *Studies in the Japanese Language* (4 a year).

Manyo Gakkai (Society for Manyo Studies): 3-3-138 Sugimotocho Sumiyoshiku, Osaka 558-0022; tel. (6) 6605-2414; f. 1951; 810 mems; publ. *The Manyo* (4 a year).

Nihon Dokubungakkai (Japanese Society of German Literature): c/o Ikubundo, Hongo 5-30-21, Bunkyo-ku, Tokyo 113-0033; tel. (3) 3813-5861; e-mail jgg@tokyo.email.ne.jp; internet wwwsoc.nii.ac.jp/jgg; f. 1947; 2,600 mems; Pres. Prof. TERUAKI TAKAHASHI; publs *Doitsu Bungaku/German Literature* (2 a year), *Doitsugo Kyoiku/Deutschunterricht in Japan* (1 a year).

Nihon Eibungakkai (English Literary Society of Japan): Kenkyusha Eigo-Center Bldg 1–2 Kagurazaka, Shinjuku-ku, Tokyo 162-0825; tel. (3) 5261-1922; e-mail ejimu@elsj.org; internet www.elsj.org; f. 1928; 3,600 mems; Pres. YOSHIYUKI FUJIKAWA; publ. *Studies in English Literature* (2 a year).

Nihon Esperanto Gakkai (Japan Esperanto Institute): Waseda-mati 12-3, Sinzyuku-ku, Tokyo 162-0042; tel. (3) 3203-4581; e-mail chb71944@biglobe.ne.jp; f. 1919; 1,435 mems; linguistics; Pres. YAMASAKI SEIKÔ; Sec. ISINO YOSIO; publ. *La Revuo Orienta* (12 a year).

Nihon Gengogakkai (Linguistic Society of Japan): Shimotachiuri Ogawa Higashi, Kami Kyoku, Kyoto 602-8048; tel. (75) 415-3661; e-mail lsj@nacos.com; internet www.tooyoo.l.u-tokyo.ac.jp/~lsj/jap; f. 1938; 2,050 mems; publ. *Gengo Kenkyu* (Journal, 2 a year).

Nippon Onsei Gakkai (Phonetic Society of Japan): National Institute for Japanese Language, 10–2 Midori-cho, Tachikawa, Tokyo 190-8561; tel. (42) 540-4515; e-mail psj@nacos.com; internet www.psj.gr.jp; f. 1926; study of sound phenomena of human speech; 780 mems; library of 30,000 vols; Pres. SHOSUKE HARAGUCHI; publ. *Journal* (3 a year).

Nippon Seiyo Koten Gakkai (Classical Society of Japan): Dept of Classics, Faculty of Letters, Kyoto Univ., Kyoto 606-8501; tel. (75) 753-2767; e-mail hiroyuki.takahashi@bun.kyoto-u.ac.jp; internet clsoc.jp; f. 1950; 500 mems; Pres. Dr TETSUO NAKATSUKASA; Sec. Prof. HIROYUKI TAKAHASHI; publs *Japan Studies in Classical Antiquity (JASCA)* (every 3 years, in English), *Journal of Classical Studies* (1 a year, in Japanese).

MEDICINE

Japanese Society for the Study of Pain: Department of Anaesthesiology, Nihon University School of Medicine, 30-1, Oyaguchi-kamicho, Itabashi-ku, Tokyo 173-8610; tel. (3) 3972-8111; e-mail s-ogawa@med.nihon-u.ac.jp; f. 1973; research into pain mechanism and pain management; 698 mems; Pres. Prof. K. IWATA; publ. *Pain Research* (4 a year).

Nihon Eisei Gakkai (Japanese Society for Hygiene): Laboratory of Environmental Health Sciences, Graduate School of Medicine, Univ. of Tokyo, 7–3–1 Hongo, Bunkyo-ku Tokyo 113-0033; tel. (6) 5841-1917; e-mail eisei_office@nacos.com; internet www.nihon-eisei.org; f. 1929; 2,000 mems; Pres. Prof. CHIHARU TOHYAMA; publs *Environmental Health and Preventive Medicine* (6 a year, in English), *Japanese Journal of Hygiene* (4 a year, in Japanese).

Nihon Hinyokika Gakkai: (Japanese Urological Association); Saito Bldg, 5F, 2-17-15 Yushima, Bunkyo-ku, Tokyo 113-0034; f. 1912; 8,000 mems; Pres. Prof. YUKIO HOMMA; publs *International Journal of Urology* (12 a year), *Japanese Journal of Urology* (5 a year).

Nihon Hotetsu Shika Gakkai (Japan Prosthodontic Society): 1-43-9 Komagome, Toshima-ku, Tokyo; tel. (3) 5940-5451; e-mail hotetsu-gakkai01@max.odn.ne.jp; internet www.hotetsu.com; f. 1931; meetings, confs, seminars; researches on new prosthodontics; liaisons with other prosthodontic societies worldwide; 6,611 mems; Pres. Prof. KEIICHI SASAKI; Vice-Pres. and Pres. Elect KIYOSHI KOYANO; Vice-Pres. YOSHINOBU TANAKA; Gen. Affairs HIDEO MATSUMURA; publs *Journal of Prosthodontic Research* (4 a year), *Nihon Hotetsu Shika Gakkai zasshi* (Journal of Japan Prosthodontic Society, 4 a year).

Nihon Ishi-Kai (Japan Medical Association): Bunkyo-ku, Tokyo 113; e-mail jmaintl@po.med.or.jp; f. 1916; 121,514 mems; Pres. Y. KARASAWA; publs *Japan Medical Association Journal* (6 a year, in English), *Journal* (12 a year, in Japanese).

Nihon Junkanki Gakkai (Japanese Circulation Society): 8th Fl., CUBE OIKE Bldg, 599 Bano-cho Karasuma Aneyakoji, Nakagyo-ku, Kyoto 604-8172; tel. (75) 257-5830; e-mail admin@j-circ.or.jp; internet www.j-circ.or.jp; f. 1935; cardiology; 21,096 mems; Chief Dir AKIRA TAKESHITA; publs *Circulation Journal* (12 a year, in English; 3 a year, supplement in Japanese), *Journal of Board of Certified Members of the Japanese Circulation Society* (2 a year, in Japanese).

Nihon Kakuigakukai (Japanese Society of Nuclear Medicine): c/o Japan Radioisotope Asscn, 2-28-45 Honkomagome, Bunkyo-ku, Tokyo 113-0021; tel. (3) 3947-0976; e-mail anm@xvg.biglobe.ne.jp; internet www.jsnm.org; f. 1963; 3,500 mems; Pres. Dr TOMIO INOUE; publs *Annals of Nuclear Medicine* (10 a year), *Japanese Journal of Nuclear Medicine* (4 a year).

Nihon Koku Eisei Gakkai (Japanese Society for Oral Health): c/o Koku Hoken Kyokai 43-9, Komagome 1-chome Toshima-ku, Tokyo 170-0003; tel. (3) 3947-8891; internet www.kokuhoken.or.jp/jsdh; f. 1952; 2,450 mems; Pres. MASAKI KAMBARA; publ. *Journal* (4 a year).

Nihon Koku Geka Gakkai (Japanese Society of Oral and Maxillofacial Surgeons): Seven-Ster Mansion Takanawa (2nd floor), 20-26-202 Takanawa 2-chome, Minato-Ku, Tokyo; tel. (3) 5791-1791; e-mail office@jsoms.or.jp; internet www.jsoms.org; f. 1952; 8,500 mems; Gen. Sec. Dr KANICHI SETO; publ. *Japanese Journal of Oral and Maxillofacial Surgery* (12 a year).

Nihon Kokuka Gakkai (Japanese Stomatological Society): Department of Oral Surgery, School of Medicine, University of Tokyo, 7-3-1 Hongo, Bunkyo-ku, Tokyo 113-8549; tel. (3) 5803-5400; f. 1947; 3,600 mems; Dir ICHIRO YAMASHITA; publ. *Journal* (4 a year).

Nihon Kyosei Shikagakkai (Japan Orthodontic Society): c/o Koku Hoken Kyokai, 1-44-2 Komagome, Toshima-ku, Tokyo 170-0003; tel. (3) 3947-8891; e-mail info@jos.gr.jp; internet www.jos.gr.jp; f. 1932; 4,200 mems; Pres. Dr KUNIMICHI SOMA; publ. *Orthodontic Waves* (6 a year, in English and Japanese).

Nihon Masuika Gakkai (Japan Society of Anaesthesiologists): TY Bldg 6F, 18-11 Hongo 3-chome, Bunkyo-ku, Tokyo 113-0033; tel. (3) 3815-0590; e-mail gakujyutu@anesth.or.jp; internet www.anesth.or.jp; f. 1954; 8,677 mems; Pres. K. HANAOKA; Sec. Y. SHIMIDA; publs *Masui* (12 a year), *Journal of Anaesthesia* (4 a year).

Nihon Naika Gakkai (Japanese Society of Internal Medicine): 28–8, 3-chome, Bunkyo-ku, Tokyo 113-8433; e-mail iminfo@naika.or.jp; internet www.naika.or.jp; f. 1903; 73,000 mems; Chief Dir ICHIRO KANAZAWA; publs *Internal Medicine* (12 a year, in Japanese), *Internal Medicine* (12 a year, in English).

Nihon No-Shinkei Geka Gakkai (Japan Neurosurgical Society): Ishikawa Bldg 4F, 5-25-16 Hongo, Bunkyo-ku, Tokyo; tel. (3) 3812-6226; e-mail jns@ss.iij4u.or.jp; internet jns.umin.ac.jp; f. 1948; 8,088 mems; Chair. TAKASHI YOSHIMOTO; publ. *Neurologia Medico-Chirurgica* (12 a year, in English).

Nihon Ronen Igakukai (Japan Geriatrics Society): Kyorin Bldg No 702, 4-2-1 Yushima, Bunkyo-ku, Tokyo 113; internet www.jpn-geriat-soc.or.jp; f. 1959; 4,500 mems; Chair. Prof. H. ORIMO; publ. *Japan Journal of Geriatrics* (6 a year).

Nihon Seishin Shinkei Gakkai (Japanese Society of Psychiatry and Neurology): Wing Bldg 52, 5-25-18 Hongo, Bunkyo-ku, Tokyo 113-0033; tel. (3) 3814-2991; e-mail info@jspn.or.jp; internet www.jspn.or.jp; 8,200 mems; Pres. Dr TAKUYA KOJIMA; publ. *Seishin Shinkeigaku Zasshi* (12 a year, in Japanese).

Nihon Shika Hoshasen Gakkai (Japanese Society for Oral and Maxillofacial Radiology): c/o Hitotsubashi Printing Co. Ltd, Gakkai Business Center, 2-4-11 Fukagawa, Koutou-ku, Tokyo 135-0033; tel. (3) 5620-1953; e-mail tsuchimochi@ngt.ndu.ac.jp; f. 1951; 1,200 mems; Sec.-Gen. S. KANDA; publs *Dental Radiology* (4 a year, in Japanese), *Oral Radiology* (2 a year, in English).

Nihon Shika Igakkai (Japanese Association for Dental Science): 4-1-20 Kudankita, Chiyoda-ku, Tokyo; tel. (3) 3262-9214; internet www.jads.jp; f. 1949; 94,000 mems; 39 mem. socs; Pres. Prof. K. ETO; publs *Journal of Japanese Association for Dental Science* (1 a year), *Japanese Dental Science Review* (2 a year).

Nihon Shokaki-byo Gakkai (Japanese Society of Gastroenterology): Ginza Orient Bldg, 8F, Ginza 8-9-13, Chuo-ku, Tokyo; tel. (3) 3573-4297; e-mail info@jsge.or.jp; internet www.jsge.or.jp; f. 1898; 25,000 mems; Pres. KENJI FUJIWARA; publs *Journal of Gastroenterology* (12 a year, in English), *Nihon Shokaki-byo Gakkai Zasshi* (12 a year, in Japanese).

Nihon Shonika Gakkai (Japan Paediatric Society): 4F Daiichi Magami Bldg, 1-1-5 Koraku, Bunkyo-ku, Tokyo 112-0004; tel. (3) 3818-0091; internet www.jpeds.or.jp; f. 1896; 16,311 mems; Pres. Dr SHUMPEI YOKOTA; Sec.-Gen. Dr MAKIKO OKUYAMA; publs *Paediatrics International* (6 a year, in English), *Journal of the Japan Paediatric Society* (12 a year, in Japanese).

Nihon Syoyakugakkai (Japanese Society of Pharmacognosy): Business Centre for Academic Societies, 4–16, Yayoi 2-chome, Bunkyo-ku, Tokyo 113; tel. (3) 5206-6007; e-mail shoyaku@asas.or.jp; internet www.jsphcg.gr.jp; f. 1946; 1,027 mems; Pres. M. KONOSHIMA; publ. *Japanese Journal of Pharmacognosy* (4 a year).

Nihon Teii Kinou Shinkei Geka Gakkai (Japan Society for Stereotactic and Functional Neurosurgery): c/o Dept of Neurological Surgery, School of Medicine, Nihon University, 30-1 Ohyaguchi Kamimachi, Itabashi-ku, Tokyo 173-8610; tel. (3) 3972-8111, ext. 2481; e-mail teii@med.nihon-u.ac.jp; internet jssfn.umin.ac.jp; f. 1963; 518 mems; Sec.-Gen. Dr C. FUKAYA; publ. *Functional Neurosurgery* (2 a year).

Nihon Yakuri Gakkai (Japanese Pharmacological Society): Yayoi 2-4-16, Bunkyo-ku, Tokyo 113-0032; tel. (3) 3814-4828; e-mail society@pharmacol.or.jp; internet www.pharmacol.or.jp; f. 1927; 5,000 mems; Chair. HIROSHI IWAO; publs *Folia Pharmacologica Japonica* (12 a year, in Japanese), *Journal of Pharmacological Sciences* (13 a year, in English).

Nippon Bitamin Gakkai (Vitamin Society of Japan): Nihon Italia kyoto Kaikan, Yoshida Ushinomiya, Sakyo-ku, Kyoto 606-8302; tel. (75) 751-0314; e-mail vsojkn@mbox.kyoto-inet.or.jp; internet web.kyoto-inet.or.jp/people/vsojkn; f. 1947; 2,000 mems; Pres. KENJI FUKUZAWA; Chief Sec. TAKESHI MATUMOTO; publs *Journal of Nutritional Science and Vitaminology* (6 a year, in English), *Vitamins* (12 a year, in Japanese).

Nippon Byorigakkai (Japanese Society of Pathology): New Akamon Bldg 4F, 2-40-9 Hongo, Bunkyo-ku, Tokyo 113-0033; tel. (3) 5684-6886; e-mail jsp-admin@umin.ac.jp;

internet jsp.umin.ac.jp; f. 1911; 4,200 mems; Chair. SHIGEO MORI; publs *Annual of Pathological Autopsy Cases in Japan* (in Japanese), *Pathology International* (12 a year, in English), *Proceedings* (in Japanese).

Nippon Gan Gakkai (Japanese Cancer Association): c/o Cancer Institute, Kami-Ikebukuro 1-37-1, Toshima-ku, Tokyo 170-0012; tel. (3) 3918-0111, ext. 4231; f. 1907; 16,976 mems; Pres. Dr TOMOYUKI KITAGAWA; publs *Japanese Journal of Cancer Research* (12 a year), *Gann Monograph on Cancer Research* (irregular).

Nippon Ganka Gakkai (Japanese Ophthalmological Society): 2-4-11-402, Sarugaku-cho, Chiyoda-ku, Tokyo 101-8346; internet www.nichigan.or.jp; f. 1897; 13,690 mems; Pres. MAKOTO ARAIE; publs *Japanese Journal of Ophthalmology* (6 a year), *Journal of Japanese Ophthalmological Society* (12 a year).

Nippon Geka Gakkai (Japan Surgical Society): World Trade Center Bldg, 2-4-1 Hamamatsu-cho, Minato-ku, Tokyo 105-6108; tel. (3) 5733-4094; e-mail info@jssoc.or.jp; internet www.jssoc.or.jp; f. 1899; 37,405 mems; Pres. TAKASHI KANEMATSU; publ. *Surgery Today* (12 a year).

Nippon Hifu-ka Gakkai (Japanese Dermatological Association): CosmosHongo Bldg 6F, 1-4, Hongo 4-chome, Bunkyo-ku, Tokyo 113-0033; tel. (3) 3811-5099; e-mail gakkai@dermatol.or.jp; internet www.dermatol.or.jp; f. 1901; 8,567 mems; Pres. S. HARADA; publs *Japanese Journal of Dermatology* (14 a year, in Japanese), *Journal of Dermatology* (12 a year, in English).

Nippon Hoi Gakkai (Medico-Legal Society of Japan): Dept of Forensic Medicine, Faculty of Medicine, Univ. of Tokyo, 7-3-1 Hongo, Bunkyo-ku, Tokyo 113; tel. (3) 5800-5416; e-mail legalmed@m.u-tokyo.ac.jp; internet web.sapmed.ac.jp/jslm; f. 1914; 1,400 mems; Pres. Dr KENJI KAMIYA; publs *Japanese Journal of Legal Medicine* (2 a year), *Legal Medicine* (4 a year).

Nippon Hoshasen Eikyo Gakkai (Japan Radiation Research Society): Nat. Institute of Radiological Sciences, 9-1 Anagawa-4, Inage-ku, Chiba 263-8555; tel. (43) 251-2111; f. 1959; 1,052 mems; Pres. MANABU FUKUMOTO; publ. *Journal of Radiation Research* (4 a year).

Nippon Igaku Hōshasen Gakkai (Japan Radiological Society): NP-II Bldg, 5-1-16 Hongo, Bunkyo-ku, Tokyo 113-0033; tel. (3) 3814-3077; e-mail qa@radiology.or.jp; internet www.radiology.jp; f. 1950; 7,500 mems; Pres. Dr OSAMU MATSUI; publ. *Radiation Medicine*.

Nippon Jibi-Inkoka Gakkai (Otorhinolaryngological Society of Japan, Inc.): 3-25-22 Takanawa, Minato-ku, Tokyo 108-0074; tel. (3) 3443-3085; e-mail office@jibika.or.jp; internet www.jibika.or.jp; f. 1893; 10,500 mems; Pres. TAKUYA UEMURA; publ. *Nippon Jibi-Inkoka Gakkai Kaiho (Tokyo)* (12 a year).

Nippon Kaibo Gakkai (Japanese Association of Anatomists): c/o Oral Health Institute, 1-43-9 Komagome, Toshima-ku, Tokyo; tel. (3) 3947-8891; e-mail gakkai24@kokuhoken.or.jp; internet www.anatomy.or.jp; f. 1893; 2,408 mems; Pres. Dr MITSUHIRO KAWATA; publ. *Anatomical Science International* (4 a year).

Nippon Kansenshoh Gakkai (Japanese Association for Infectious Diseases): Nichinai Bldg, 2F, 3-28-8, Hongo, Bunkyo-ku, Tokyo 113-0033; tel. (3) 5842-5845; e-mail info@kansensho.or.jp; internet www.kansensho.or.jp; f. 1926; 10,500 mems; Pres. AIKICHI IWAMOTO; publs *Journal of the Japanese Association for Infectious Diseases* (6 a year, online), *Journal of Infection and Chemotherapy* (online).

Nippon Kekkaku-byo Gakkai (Japanese Society for Tuberculosis): 1-24, Matsuyama 3-chome, Kiyose-shi, Tokyo 204-8533; tel. 424-92-2091; e-mail tb55@heart.ocn.ne.jp; f. 1923; 3,000 mems; Chair. Dr K. AOKI; publ. *Kekkaku* (12 a year).

Nippon Ketsueki Gakkai (Japanese Society of Haematology): c/o Kinki Chiho Invention Center, 14 Kawahara-cho, Yoshida, Sakyo-ku, Kyoto 606-8305; tel. (75) 752-2844; e-mail info@jshem.or.jp; internet www.jshem.or.jp; f. 1937; academic year September to August; supports basic and clinical research; promotes education and patient care in haematology; organizes meetings, symposia and so on; 7,500 mems; Pres. Prof. YUZURU KANAKURA; publs *International Journal of Hematology* (12 a year), *The Japanese Journal of Clinical Hematology* (12 a year).

Nippon Kisei-chu Gakkai (Japanese Society of Parasitology): Dept of Tropical Medicine and Parasitology, Keio University School of Medicine, 35 Shinanomachi Shinjuku-ku, Tokyo 160-8582; tel. (3) 3353-1211; e-mail jsp2011@gmail.com; internet jsp.tm.nagasaki-u.ac.jp; f. 1929; 998 mems; Pres. Prof. T. HORII; Chair Prof. T. TAKEUCHI; publ. *Parasitology International* (4 a year).

Nippon Koshu-Eisei Kyokai (Japan Public Health Association): Koei Bldg, 1-29-8, Shinjuku, Shinjuku-ku, Tokyo 160-0022; tel. (3) 3352-4281; e-mail info@jpha.or.jp; internet www.jpha.or.jp; f. 1883; 5,000 mems; Pres. MINORU SEIJO; publs *Japanese Journal of Public Health*, *Public Health Information* (12 a year).

Nippon Rai Gakkai (Japanese Leprosy Association): 4-2-1, Aoba-cho, Higashimurayama-shi, Tokyo 189-0002; tel. (42) 391-8085; e-mail jla-hp-admin@hansen-gakkai.jp; internet www.hansen-gakkai.jp; f. 1927; 355 mems; Pres. NORIHASA ISHII; publ. *Japanese Journal of Leprosy* (3 a year).

Nippon Saikingakkai (Japanese Society for Bacteriology): c/o Oral Health Association of Japan, 1-44-2 Komagome, Toshima-ku, Tokyo 170; tel. (3) 3947-8891; e-mail gakkai@kokuhiken.or.jp; internet wwwsoc.nii.ac.jp/jsb; f. 1927; 3,400 mems; Pres. Dr HIDEO HAYASHI; publs *Japanese Journal of Bacteriology* (4 a year), *Microbiology and Immunology* (12 a year).

Nippon Sanka-Fujinka Gakkai (Japan Society of Obstetrics and Gynaecology): Twin View Ochanomizu Bldg, 2-3-9 Hongo, Bunkyo-ku, Tokyo 113-0033; tel. (3) 5842-5452; e-mail nissanfu@jsog.or.jp; internet www.jsog.or.jp; f. 1949; 15,926 mems; Chair. Prof. I. KUO KONISHI; publ. *Acta Obstetrica et Gynaecologica Japonica* (12 a year).

Nippon Seikei Geka Gakkai (Japanese Orthopaedic Association): 2-40-18, Hongo, Bunkyo-ku, Tokyo 113-8418; tel. (3) 3816-3671; e-mail office@joa.or.jp; internet www.joa.or.jp; f. 1926; 20,742 mems; Pres. Prof. HIROSHI YAMAMOTO; publs *Journal* (12 a year, in Japanese), *Journal of Orthopaedic Science* (6 a year, in English).

Nippon Seiri Gakkai (Physiological Society of Japan): 3-30-10 Hongo, Bunkyo-ku, Tokyo 113-0033; tel. (3) 3815-1624; e-mail psj@qa2.so-net.ne.jp; internet int.physiology.jp; f. 1922; 3,700 mems; Pres. YASUNOBU OKADA; publs *Journal of the Physiological Society of Japan* (12 a year, in Japanese), *Journal of the Physiological Society of Japan* (6 a year, in English).

Nippon Shika Hozon Gakkai (Japanese Society of Conservative Dentistry): c/o Oral Health Association of Japan (Koku Hoken Kyokai), Komagome TS Bldg, 1-43-9 Komagome, Toshima-ku, Tokyo 170-0003; tel. (3) 3947-8891; e-mail gakkai8@kokuhoken.or.jp; internet wwwsoc.nii.ac.jp/jscd; f. 1955; 4,540 mems; Pres. HIDEAKI SUDA; publ. *Journal of Conservative Dentistry* (6 a year).

Nippon Shinkei Gakkai (Japanese Society of Neurology): Ichimaru Bldg 31-21, Yushima 2-chome, Bunkyo-ku, Tokyo 113-0034; tel. (3) 3815-1080; internet www.neurology-jp.org; f. 1960; 6,895 mems; Chair. ICHIRO KANAZAWA; publ. *Clinical Neurology* (12 a year).

Nippon Shinkeikagaku Gakkai (Japan Neuroscience Society): Hongo Bldg 9F 2-2, Hongo 7-chome, Bunkyo-ku, Tokyo 113-0033; tel. (3) 3813-0272; e-mail office@jnss.org; internet www.jnss.org; f. 1974; 4,000 mems; Pres. Dr YASUSHI MIYASHITA; publs *Neuroscience Research* (12 a year), *News*.

Nippon Tonyo-byo Gakkai (Japan Diabetes Society): 5-25-18, Hongo, Bunkyo-ku, Tokyo 113-0033; tel. (3) 3815-4364; f. 1958; 15,533 mems; Pres. KOICHI YOKONO; publ. *Journal* (12 a year).

Nippon Uirusu Gakkai (Society of Japanese Virologists): Business Centre for Academic Societies, 5-16-9 Honkomagome, Bunkyo-ku, Tokyo 113; f. 1953; 3,000 mems; Pres. Dr HIROSHI YOSHIKURA; publs *Microbiology and Immunology* (12 a year), *Virus* (2 a year, in Japanese with English summary).

Nippon Yakugaku-Kai (Pharmaceutical Society of Japan): 12-15, Shibuya 2-chome, Shibuya-ku, Tokyo 150-0002; tel. (3) 3406-3321; e-mail doi@pharm.or.jp; internet www.pharm.or.jp; f. 1880; 21,541 mems; Pres. O. YONEMITSU; Exec. Dir M. OHZEKI; publs *Biological and Pharmaceutical Bulletin* (12 a year), *Chemical and Pharmaceutical Bulletin* (12 a year), *Farumashia* (12 a year), *Japanese Journal of Toxicology and Environmental Health* (6 a year).

Nippon Yuketsu Gakkai (Japan Society of Blood Transfusion): Metropolitan Tokyo Red Cross Blood Centre, 1-31-4 Hiroo, Shibuya-ku, Tokyo; tel. (3) 5485-6020; internet www.yuketsu.gr.jp; f. 1954; 3,000 mems; Pres. TAKEO JUJI; publ. *Japanese Journal of Transfusion Medicine* (6 a year).

Oto-Rhino-Laryngological Society of Japan: 3-25-22 Takanawa, Minato-Ku, Tokyo 108-0074; tel. (3) 3443-3085; internet www.jibika.or.jp; f. 1893 as the Tokyo Oto-Rhino-Laryngological Society; 1947 present name; 10,604 mems; Chair GINICHIRO ICHIKAWA; publs *Auris Nasus Larynx*, *Nippon Jibiinkoka Gakkai Kaiho* (12 a year).

NATURAL SCIENCES

General

Nihon Kagakushi Gakkai (History of Science Society of Japan): Shimazu Bldg 202, 2-13-1 Hirakawa-cho, Chiyoda-ku, Tokyo 102-0093; tel. (3) 3239-0545; internet historyofscience.jp; f. 1941; 1,000 mems; Pres. TATSUMASA DOUKE; publs *Kagakushi Kenkyu* (4 a year), *Historia Scientiarum* (3 a year).

Biological Sciences

Nihon Hassei Seibutsu Gakkai (Japanese Society of Developmental Biologists): Center for Developmental Biology, RIKEN Kobe, 2–2–3 Minatojima-minami Chuo-ku, Kobe, Hyogo 650-0047; tel. (78) 306-3072; e-mail jsdbadmin@jsdb.jp; internet www.jsdb.jp; f. 1968; 1,400 mems; Pres. KIYOKAZU AGATA; publ. *Development, Growth and Differentiation* (9 a year, in English).

Nihon Jinrui Iden Gakkai (Japan Society of Human Genetics): Dept of Medical Genomics, Tokyo Medical and Dental University, 1-5-45 Yushima, Bunkyo-ku, Tokyo 113-

8510; tel. (3) 5803-5820; e-mail jshg@soteria.cc; internet jshg.jp; f. 1956; 1,046 mems; Pres. YU-SUKE NAKAMURA; publ. *Journal* (4 a year).

Nihon Kairui Gakkai (Malacological Society of Japan): National Science Museum, 3-23-1, Hyakunin-cho, Shinjuku-ku, Tokyo 169-0073; tel. (3) 3364-7124; e-mail msj_manager@hotmail.com; f. 1928; scientific research on molluscs; 900 mems; Pres. T. OKUTANI; publs *Chiribotan* (4 a year, in Japanese with English abstract), *Venus* (4 a year).

Nihon Kontyû Gakkai (Entomological Society of Japan): c/o Dept of Zoology, National Science Museum (Natural History), 3-23-1 Hyakunin-cho, Shinjuku, Tokyo 169; e-mail ueno@kintaro.grt.kyushu-u.ac.jp; f. 1917; 1,300 mems; Pres. HIROSHI SHIMA; publs *Entomological Science*, *Insects of Japan* (irregular).

Nihon Mendel Kyokai (Japan Mendel Society): Editorial and Business Office, Cytologia, c/o Toshin Bldg, Hongo 2-27-2, Bunkyo-ku, Tokyo 113-0033; e-mail mendel-cytologia@ib.k.u-tokyo.ac.jp; f. 1929; 1,100 mems; Pres. HIDEO HIROKAWA; publ. *Cytologia* (4 a year).

Nihon Seitai Gakkai (Ecological Society of Japan): 1–8 Nishihanaikecho, Koyama, Kitaku Kyoto 603-8148; tel. (75) 384-0250; e-mail office@mail.esj.ne.jp; internet www.esj.ne.jp/esj; f. 1953; research in all aspects of ecology; 4,000 mems; Pres. H. MATSUDA; Sec.-Gen. T. TAKADA; publs *Japanese Journal of Ecology* (3 a year, in Japanese), *Ecological Research* (6 a year, in English), *Japanese Journal of Conservation Ecology* (2 a year, in Japanese).

Nihon Shokubutsu Bunrui Gakkai (Japanese Society for Plant Systematics): Faculty of Symbiotic Systems Science, Fukushima University, Fukushima 960-1296; e-mail jimu@e-jsps.com; internet wwwsoc.nii.ac.jp/jsps; f. 2001; plant taxonomy and phytogeography; 900 mems; Pres. JIN MURATA; Sec. TAKAHIDAE KUROSAWA; publ. *Acta Phytotaxonomica et Geobotanica* (3 a year).

Nippon Chô Gakkai (Ornithological Society of Japan): c/o National Museum of Nature and Science, 3-23-1 Hyakunin-cho, Shinjuku-ku, Tokyo 169-0073; tel. (3) 3364-7131; e-mail nihon-chogakkai@lagopus.com; internet www.soc.nii.ac.jp/osj; f. 1912; 1,300 mems; library of 600 vols; Pres. HIROSHI NAKAMURA; Vice-Pres. ISAO NISHIUMI; publs *Japanese Journal of Ornithology* (2 a year, in Japanese), *Ornithological Science* (2 a year, in English).

Nihon Dobutsu Gakkai (Zoological Society of Japan): Toshin Bldg, Hongo 2-27-2, Bunkyo-ku, Tokyo 113-0033; tel. (3) 3814-5461; e-mail zsj-society@zoology.or.jp; internet www.zoology.or.jp; f. 1878; 2,500 mems; Pres. YOSHITAKA NAGAHAMA; Sec.-Gen. YUKO NAGAI; publ. *Zoological Science* (12 a year).

Nippon Eisei-Dobutu Gakkai (Japanese Society of Medical Entomology and Zoology): c/o Dept of Parasitology, School of Medicine, Aichi Medical University, Nagakute, Aichi 480-1195; tel. (561) 62-3311; e-mail ac038-jsmez@canpan.org; internet www.jsmez.gr.jp; f. 1943; 750 mems; Pres. Prof. YASUO CHINZEI; publ. *Medical Entomology and Zoology* (4 a year).

Nippon Iden Gakkai (Genetics Society of Japan): National Institute of Genetics, 1, 111 Yata, Mishima, Shizuoka 411-8540; tel. 55-981-6736; e-mail japgenet@lab.nig.ac.jp; internet wwwsoc.nii.ac.jp/gsj3; f. 1920; 1,500 mems; Pres. SADAO ISHIWA; publ. *Genes and Genetic Systems* (6 a year).

Nippon Kin Gakkai (Mycological Society of Japan): c/o Forest Health Group, Kansai Research Center, Forestry and Forest Products Research Institute, Nagai-Kyutaro 68, Momoyama-cho, Fushimi-ku, Kyoto 612-0855; tel. (75) 366-9912; e-mail msj_office@remach.kais.kyoto-u.ac.jp; internet wwwsoc.nii.ac.jp/msj7; f. 1956; 1,600 mems; Pres. MAKOTO KAKISHIMA; publ. *Mycoscience* (4 a year).

Nippon Kumo Gakkai (Arachnological Society of Japan): c/o Kyoto Women's Univ., 35 Kitahiyoshi-cho, Imakumano, Higashiyama-ku, Kyoto 605-8501; tel. (75) 531-9196; e-mail nakatake@kyoto-wu.ac.jp; f. 1936; 300 mems; Pres. Dr TADASHI MIYASHITA; Sec. KENSUKE NAKATA; publ. *Acta Arachnologica* (2 a year).

Nippon Oyo-Dobutsu-Konchu Gakkai (Japanese Society of Applied Entomology and Zoology): c/o Japan Plant Protection Association, 43-11, 1-chome, Komagome, Toshima-ku, Tokyo 170; internet odokon.org; f. 1957; 2,000 mems; Pres. Prof. KENJI FUJISAKI; Exec. Dir HIROSHI HONDA; publs *Applied Entomology and Zoology* (4 a year, in English), *Japanese Journal of Applied Entomology and Zoology* (4 a year, in Japanese with English synopsis).

Nippon Rikusui Gakkai (Japanese Society of Limnology): c/o School of Environmental Science, University of Shiga Prefecture, 2500 Hassaka-cho, Hikone, Shiga 522-8533; tel. (749) 28-8307; e-mail ban@ses.usp.ac.jp; internet wwwsoc.nii.ac.jp/jslim; f. 1931; 1,288 mems; Pres. Dr NORIO OGURA; Gen. Sec. Dr OSAMU MITAMURA; publs *Japanese Journal of Limnology* (3 a year), *Limnology* (3 a year).

Nippon Shokubutsu Gakkai (Botanical Society of Japan): c/o Toshin Bldg, 2-chome 27-2 Hongo, Bunkyo-ku, Tokyo; tel. (3) 3814-5675; e-mail bsj@bsj.or.jp; internet bsj.or.jp; f. 1882; 2,100 mems; Pres. H. FUKUDA; publ. *Journal of Plant Research* (6 a year).

Nippon Shokubutsu Seiri Gakkai (Japanese Society of Plant Physiologists): Shimotachiuri Ogawa Higashi, Kamikyoku, Kyoto 602-8048; tel. (75) 415-3661; e-mail jspp@nacos.com; internet www.nacos.com/jspp; f. 1959; 3,201 mems; Pres. KIYOTAKA OKADA; Sec.-Gen. AKIRA NAGATANI; publ. *Plant and Cell Physiology* (12 a year).

Mathematical Sciences

Nihon Sugaku Kai (Mathematical Society of Japan): 34–8, Taito 1-chome, Taito-ku, Tokyo 110-0016; tel. (3) 3835-3483; f. 1877; 5,000 mems; Pres. SADAYOSHI KOJIMA; publs *Journal* (4 a year), *Sugaku* (4 a year), *Sugaku-Tsushin* (bulletin, 4 a year), *Japanese Journal of Mathematics* (2 a year), *MSJ Memoirs* (irregular), *Advanced Studies in Pure Mathematics* (irregular).

Physical Sciences

Butsuri Tansa Gakkai (Society of Exploration Geophysicists of Japan): 2F MK5 Bldg, 1-5-6 Higashikanda, Chiyoda-ku, Tokyo 101-0031; tel. (3) 6804-7500; e-mail office@segj.org; internet www.segj.org; f. 1948; 1,420 mems; Pres. S. ROKUGAWA; publ. *Butsuri Tansa* (Geophysical Exploration, 6 a year).

Chigaku Dantai Kenkyu-kai (Association for Geological Collaboration in Japan): Kawai Bldg, 2-24-1, Minami-Ikebukuro, Toshima-ku, Tokyo 171-0022; tel. (3) 3983-3378; e-mail chidanken@tokyo.email.ne.jp; internet www.soc.nii.ac.jp/agcj/index.html; f. 1947; study of geology, mineralogy, palaeontology and related earth sciences; 1,500 mems; Pres. TSUTOMU OHTSUKA; Sec. YOSHIAKI KANAI; publs *Sokuhō* (News, 12 a year), *Chikyu-Kagaku* (Earth Science, 6 a year), *Senpō* (Monograph, irregular), *Chigaku Kyoiku To Kagaku-undo* (Education of Earth Science, 2 a year).

Chikyu-Denjiki Chikyu-Wakuseiken Gakkai (Society of Geomagnetism and Earth, Planetary and Space Science): Edocho 85-1, Kobe, Chuo-ku, Tokyo 650-0033; tel. (78) 332-3703; e-mail sgepss@pac.ne.jp; internet www.kurasc.kyoto-u.ac.jp/sgepss; f. 1947; frmly Nippon Chikyu Denki Ziki Gakkai; 695 mems; Pres. Prof. RYOICHI FUJII; publ. *Earth, Planets and Space* (12 a year).

Japan Weather Association: Sunshine 60 Bldg 3-1-1, Higashi-Ikebukuro, Toshima-ku, Tokyo 170-6055; tel. (3) 5958-8161; e-mail webmaster@jwa.go.jp; internet www.jwa.or.jp; f. 1950; Pres. MICHIHIKO MATSUO; publs *Geophysical Magazine*, *Journal of Meteorological Research* (12 a year), *Kisho*, *Oceanographical Magazine* (4 a year).

Japanese Society of Microscopy: Akihabara Konoike Bldg 3F, 1-25 Kanda-sakuma Cho, Chiyoda-ku, Tokyo 101-0025; e-mail kenbikyo@realize-se.co.jp; internet wwwsoc.nii.ac.jp/jsm; f. 1949; 2,690 mems; Pres. KAZUO OGAWA; publ. *Journal of Electron Microscopy* (4 a year).

Kobunshi Gakkai (Society of Polymer Science, Japan): Shintomicho Tokyu Bldg, 3-10-9 Irifune, Chuo-ku, Tokyo 104-0042; tel. (3) 5540-3771; e-mail intnl@spsj.or.jp; internet www.spsj.or.jp; f. 1951; 12,598 mems; Pres. MITSUO SAWAMOTO; publs *Kobunshi* (High Polymers, 12 a year), *Kobunshi Ronbunshu* (Journal of Polymer Science and Technology, 12 a year, abstracts in English), *Polymer Journal* (12 a year, in English), *Polymer Preprints* (2 a year, in English, CD-ROM).

Nihon Bunseki Kagaku-Kai (Japan Society for Analytical Chemistry): Gotanda Sanhaitsu, 26-2, Nishigotanda 1-chome, Shinagawa-ku, Tokyo 141-0031; tel. (3) 3490-3351; e-mail analytsci@jsac.or.jp; internet www.soc.nii.ac.jp/jsac; f. 1952; 9,108 mems; Pres. M. TANAKA; Sec.-Gen. Dr TADASHI FUJINUKI; publs *Bunseki Kagaku* (12 a year), *Analytical Sciences* (6 a year).

Nihon Kobutsu Kagaku Kai (Japan Association of Mineralogical Sciences): c/o Graduate School of Science, Tohoku Univ., Sendai 980-8578; tel. (22) 224-3852; e-mail kyl04223@nifty.ne.jp; internet jams.la.coocan.jp; f. 2007, by merger of Japanese Assoc. of Mineralogists, Petrologists and Economic Geologists (f. 1928) and Mineralogical Soc. of Japan (f. 1955); science, mineral science, geochemistry, petrology; 950 mems; library of 4,200 vols; Pres. Dr TAKASHI MURAKAMI; Vice-Pres. Dr YASUHITO OSANAI; Sec. MASUMI MIYACHI; publs *Japanese Magazine of Mineralogical and Petrological Sciences* (6 a year), *Journal of Mineralogical and Petrological Sciences* (6 a year).

Nihon Nensho Gakkai (Combustion Society of Japan): c/o Department of Mechanical Engineering, Osaka Prefecture University, 1-1 Gakuen-cho, Sakai, Osaka 599-8531; tel. (72) 255-7037; e-mail office@combustionsociety.jp; internet combustionsociety.jp; f. 1953; 700 mems; Pres. TOSHIKAZU KADOTA; publ. *Journal* (4 a year).

Nihon Nogyo-Kisho Gakkai (Society of Agricultural Meteorology of Japan): c/o Yokendo Co. Ltd., 5-30-15 Hongo, Bunkyo-ku, Tokyo 113-0033; tel. (3) 3814-0915; e-mail nogyo-kisho@yokendo.co.jp; internet www.soc.nii.ac.jp/agrmet; f. 1942; studies protected cultivation, agricultural meteorology and resources of food production; 787 mems; Pres. Prof. MASUMI OKADA; publs *Journal of Agricultural Meteorology* (4 a year), *Seibutsu to Kisho* (ejournal).

Nihon Seppyo Gakkai (Japanese Society of Snow and Ice): 3rd Fl., Kagaku-Kaikan, Kanda Surugadai 1-5, Chiyoda-ku, Tokyo 101-0062; tel. (3) 5259-5245; e-mail jimu@seppyo.org; internet www.seppyo.org; f. 1939; 950 mems; Pres. Dr MASAYOSHI NAKAWO; publs *Seppyo* (Journal of the Japanese Society of Snow and Ice, 6 a year, in Japanese and English), occasional papers and bibliography.

Nippon Bunko Gakkai (Spectroscopical Society of Japan): c/o Industrial Hall, 1-13, Kanda-Awaji-cho, Chiyoda-ku, Tokyo 101; tel. (3) 3253-2747; e-mail office@bunkou.or.jp; f. 1951; 1,300 mems; Pres. M. TASUMI; Sec. Y. F. MIZUGAI; publ. *Bunko Kenkyu* (6 a year).

Nippon Butsuri Gakkai (Physical Society of Japan): 5th Floor, Eishin-kaihatsu Bldg, 5-34-3 Shimbashi, Minato-ku, Tokyo 105-0004; tel. (3) 3434-2671; e-mail jps-office@jps.or.jp; internet wwwsoc.nii.ac.jp/jps; f. 1946; 18,223 mems; Pres. SUKEKATSU USHIODA; publs *Butsuri* (12 a year, in Japanese), *Journal of the Physical Society of Japan* (12 a year), *Physics Education in Universities* (3 a year, in Japanese), *Progress of Theoretical Physics* (12 a year).

Nippon Chishitsu Gakkai (Geological Society of Japan): Igeta Bldg, 8-15 Iwamoto-cho 2-chome, Chiyoda-ku, Tokyo 101-0032; tel. (3) 5823-1150; e-mail main@geosociety.jp; internet www.geosociety.jp; f. 1893; stratigraphy, petrology, tectonics, volcanology, etc; 5,000 mems; library of 10,000 vols; Pres. ASAHIKO TAIRA; publ. *Journal* (12 a year).

Nippon Dai-Yonki Gakkai (Japan Association for Quaternary Research): 3rd Fl., Rakuyo Bldg, Waseda-Tsurumaki-cho 519, Shinjuku, Tokyo 162-0041; tel. (3) 5291-6231; e-mail daiyonki@shunkosha.com; internet wwwsoc.nii.ac.jp/qr/index.html; f. 1956; 1,800 mems; Sec. of Exec. Cttee SUMIKO KUBO; publ. *Quaternary Research* (5 a year).

Nippon Kagakukai (Chemical Society of Japan): 1-5 Kanda-Surugadai, Chiyoda-ku, Tokyo 101-8307; tel. (3) 3292-6161; e-mail info@chemistry.or.jp; internet www.csj.jp; f. 1878; 31,000 mems; Pres. Prof. YASUHIRO IWASAWA; Man. HIROKO IHIDA; publs *Bulletin of the Chemical Society of Japan* (12 a year), *Chemistry: An Asian Journal* (12 a year), *Chemistry Letters* (12 a year), *Chemical Record* (6 a year).

Nippon Kaisui Gakkai (Society of Sea Water Science, Japan): c/o Sea Water Science Research Laboratory, Salt Industry Centre of Japan, 4-13-20, Sakawa, Odawara-shi, Kanagawa; e-mail office@swsj.org; f. 1950; 414 mems; Pres. SHINICHI NAKAO; publ. *Journal*.

Nippon Kaiyo Gakkai (Oceanographic Society of Japan): MACAS, 9th Fl., Palaceside Bldg, 1-1-1 Hitotsubashi, Chiyoda-ku, Tokyo 100-0003; tel. (3) 3211-1412; e-mail jos@mycom.co.jp; internet wwwsoc.nii.ac.jp/kaiyo; f. 1941; 2,379 mems; Pres. ISAO KOIKE; publs *Journal of Oceanography* (6 a year), *Umi no Kenkyu* (Oceanography in Japan, 6 a year).

Nippon Kazan Gakkai (Volcanological Society of Japan): c/o Earthquake Research Institute, University of Tokyo, 1-1-1 Yayoi, Bunkyo-ku, Tokyo 113-0032; tel. (3) 3813-7421; e-mail kazan@khaki.plala.or.jp; internet wwwsoc.nii.ac.jp/kazan; f. 1932; 1,200 mems; Pres. TADAHIDE UI; publ. *Bulletin* (6 a year).

Nippon Kessho Gakkai (Crystallographic Society of Japan): Nissei Bldg, 3-11-6 Otuka, Bunkyo-ku, Tokyo 112-0012; tel. (3) 5940-7640; e-mail crsj-post@bunken.co.jp; internet www.crsj.jp; f. 1950; 1,000 mems; Pres. KAZUMAZA OHSUMI; Sec.-Gen. MASAKI TAKATA; publ. *Journal* (6 a year).

Nippon Kisho Gakkai (Meteorological Society of Japan): c/o Japan Meteorological Agency, 1-3-4 Ote-machi, Chiyoda-ku, Tokyo 100-0004; tel. (3) 3212-8341; e-mail metsoc-j@aurora.ocn.ne.jp; internet www.metsoc.or.jp; f. 1882; 4,300 mems; Pres. T. ASAI; publs *Journal* (6 a year), *Tenki* (12 a year, in Japanese).

Nippon Kokai Gakkai (Japan Institute of Navigation): c/o Tokyo University of Mercantile Marine, 2-1-6 Etchujima, Koto-ku, Tokyo; tel. (3) 3630-3093; e-mail navigation@nifty.com; internet homepage2.nifty.com/navigation; f. 1948; 1,011 mems; Pres. Prof. S. KUWASIMA; publs *Journal* (2 a year), *Navigation* (4 a year).

Nippon Koseibutsu Gakkai (Palaeontological Society of Japan): 4th Fl., Hongo MT Bldg, Hongo 7-2-2, Bunkyo-ku, Tokyo 113-0033; tel. (3) 3814 5490; e-mail psj-office@world.ocn.ne.jp; internet www.palaeo-soc-japan.jp; f. 1935; 1,050 mems; Pres. TOMOKI KASE; publs *Fossils* (2 a year), *Paleontological Research* (4 a year).

Nippon Onkyo Gakkai (Acoustical Society of Japan): Nakaura 5th Bldg, 2-18-20 Sotokanda, Chiyoda-ku, Tokyo 101-0021; e-mail asj-www@asj.gr.jp; internet www.asj.gr.jp; f. 1936; 4,530 mems; Pres. T. SONE; publs *Acoustical Science and Technology* (12 a year, online), *Reports of Spring and Autumn Meetings* (2 a year).

Nippon Sokuchi Gakkai (Geodetic Society of Japan): c/o Japanese Association of Surveyors, 1-3-4 Koishikawa, Bunkyo-ku, Tokyo, 112-0002; tel. (3) 5684-3358; e-mail nihonsokuchi@jsurvey.jp; internet wwwsoc.nii.ac.jp/geod-soc; f. 1954; studies astronomy, crustal activity, earth tide, geodesy, geomagnetism, gravity; 600 mems; library of 5,000 vols; Pres. Dr SHUHEI OKUBO; publ. *Journal* (4 a year).

Nippon Temmon Gakkai (Astronomical Society of Japan): National Astronomical Observatory, 2-21-1 Osawa, Mitaka-shi, Tokyo 181-8588; tel. (422) 31-1359; e-mail jimu@asj.or.jp; internet www.asj.or.jp; f. 1908; 2,640 mems; Pres. Y. UCHIDA; publs *Publications* (6 a year), *The Astronomical Herald* (12 a year, in Japanese).

Nippon Yukagaku Kai (Japan Oil Chemists' Society): 7th Floor, Yushi Kogyo Kaikan, 13-11, Nihonbashi 3-chome, Chuo-ku, Tokyo 103-0027; tel. (3) 3271-7463; e-mail yukagaku@jocs-office.or.jp; internet www.jocs.jp; f. 1951; 2,426 mems; Pres. ISAO IKEDA; publ. *Journal of Oleo Science* (12 a year).

Sen-i Gakkai (Society of Fibre Science and Technology, Japan): 3-3-9-208 Kamiosaki, Shinagawa-ku, Tokyo 141; tel. (3) 3441-5627; e-mail office@fiber.or.jp; internet www.fiber.or.jp; f. 1943; c. 3,000 mems; Pres. HIROSHI INAGAKI; publ. *Journal* (12 a year).

Shokubai Gakkai (Catalysis Society of Japan): 1-5 Kanda Surugadai, Chiyoda-ku, Tokyo 101-0062; tel. (3) 3291-8224; e-mail catsj@pb3.so-net.ne.jp; internet www.shokubai.org; f. 1958; 2,370 mems; Pres. Y. MOROOKA; publ. *Shokubai* (Catalyst, 8 a year).

Zisin Gakkai (Seismological Society of Japan): 6-26-12 Tokyo RS Bldg, Hongo, Bunkyo-ku, Tokyo 113-0033; tel. (3) 5803-9570; e-mail zisin@tokyo.email.ne.jp; internet wwwsoc.nii.ac.jp/ssj; f. 1929; 2,000 mems; Chair. TERUYUKI KATO; publs *Earth Planets and Space* (12 a year), *Naifuru* (4 a year), *Zisin* (Journal, 4 a year).

PHILOSOPHY AND PSYCHOLOGY

Bigaku-Kai (Japanese Society for Aesthetics): Kyoto Univ., Graduate School of Human and Environmental Studies, Prof. Shinohara's Room, Yoshida-Nihonmatsu-Cho, Sakyo-ku, Kyoto 606-8501; e-mail bigakukai@nifty.ne.jp; internet www.bigakukai.jp; f. 1950; 1,500 mems; Pres. MOTOAKI SHINOHARA; Sec. TOMOKI YAMAUCHI; publs *Aesthetics* (every 2 years), *Bigaku* (2 a year, in Japanese).

Moralogy Kenkyusho (Institute of Moralogy): 2-1-1, Hikarigaoka, Kashiwa-shi, Chiba-ken 277-8654; tel. (4) 7173-3252; e-mail rc@moralogy.jp; internet rc.moralogy.jp; f. 1926; 236 mems; library of 70,753 vols; Gen. Sec. T. NAGAI; publ. *Studies in Moralogy* (2 a year).

Nihon Rinrigakukai (Japanese Society for Ethics): Dept of Ethics, Faculty of Letters, University of Tokyo, Bunkyo-ku, Tokyo 113; tel. (3) 727-147; e-mail jse@logos.tsukuba.ac.jp; internet jse.trustyweb.jp; f. 1950; 800 mems; Pres. YÔKICHI YAZIMA; Man. MASAHIRO NAKAGAWA; publ. *Rinrigakunenpo* (1 a year).

Nippon Dobutsu Shinri Gakkai (Japanese Society for Animal Psychology): c/o K. & U. Co. Ltd, MSK Bldg 3F, 3-32-7 Hongo, Bunkyo-ku, Tokyo 113-0033; tel. (3) 3815-4800; e-mail dousin-gakkai@umin.ac.jp; internet plaza.umin.ac.jp/dousin; f. 1933; 400 mems; Pres. MASATAKA WATANABE; publ. *The Japanese Journal of Animal Psychology* (2 a year).

Nippon Shakai Shinri Gakkai (Japanese Society of Social Psychology): c/o International Academic Printing Co. Ltd, 4-4-19 Takadanobaba, Shinjuku-ku, Tokyo 169-0075; tel. (3) 5389-6217; e-mail jssp-post@bunken.co.jp; internet www.socialpsychology.jp; f. 1950; 1,896 mems; Pres. IKUO DAIBO; publs *Japanese Journal of Social Psychology*, *Bulletin* (3 a year).

Nippon Shinri Gakkai (Japanese Psychological Association): 5-23-13-2F, Hongo, Bunkyo-ku, Tokyo 113-0033; tel. (3) 3814-3953; e-mail jpa@psych.or.jp; internet www.psych.or.jp; f. 1927; 7,900 mems; Pres. TAKAO SATO; publs *Japanese Journal of Psychology* (6 a year), *Japanese Psychological Research* (4 a year).

RELIGION, SOCIOLOGY AND ANTHROPOLOGY

Japanese Society of Cultural Anthropology: 2-1-1-813 Mita, Minato-ku, Tokyo 108-0073; tel. (3) 5232-0920; e-mail hoya@jasca.org; internet www.soc.nii.ac.jp/jasca; f. 1934; 2,000 mems; publ. *Bunkajinruigaku* (Japanese Journal of Cultural Anthropology, 4 a year).

Nihon Indogaku Bukkyôgakukai (Japanese Association of Indian and Buddhist Studies): Hongo Bldg 2F, 3-33-5 Hongo, Bunkyo-ku, Tokyo 113-0033; e-mail enquiry@jaibs.jp; internet www.jaibs.jp; f. 1951; 2,350 mems; Pres. KIYOTAKA KIMURA; publ. *Indogaku Bukkyôgaku Kenkyû* (Journal of Indian and Buddhist Studies).

Nihon Shūkyō Gakkai (Japanese Association for Religious Studies): 1-29-7-205 Hongo, Bunkyo-ku, Tokyo 113-0033; tel. (3) 5684-5473; internet www.soc.nii.ac.jp/jars; f. 1930; 2,100 mems; Pres. FUJIO IKADO; publ. *Journal of Religious Studies* (4 a year).

Nippon Dokyo Gakkai (Japan Society of Taoistic Research): Tokyo University, Faculty of Letters, 5-28-20 Hakusan, Bunkyo-ku, Tokyo 112-8606; tel. (3) 3945-7557; f. 1950; 650 mems; Pres. TOSHIAKI YAMADA; publ. *Journal of Eastern Religions* (2 a year).

Nippon Jinruigaku Kai (Anthropological Society of Nippon): 3-21-10 3F Urban Ootsuka, Kita Otsuka, Toshima, Tokyo 170-0004; tel. (3) 5814-5801; e-mail g002jinrui-mng@ml.galileo.co.jp; internet www.anthropology.jp; f. 1884; 700 mems; Pres. TASUKU KIMURA; publs *Anthropological Science* (3 a year), *Anthropological Science (Japanese Series)* (2 a year).

Nippon Shakai Gakkai (Japanese Sociological Society): Dept of Sociology, Faculty of Letters, Univ. of Tokyo, 7-3-1 Hongo, Bunkyo-ku, Tokyo 113-0033; tel. (3) 5841-8933; e-mail g009jss-mng@ml.gakkai.ne.jp; internet www.gakkai.ne.jp/jss; f. 1923; 3,600 mems; Pres. SHUJIRO YAZAWA; publs *International Journal of Japanese Sociology* (1 a year, in English), *Shakaigaku Hyóron* (4 a year).

Tōhō Gakkai (Institute of Eastern Culture): 4-1, Nishi Kanda 2-chome, Chiyoda-ku, Tokyo 101-0065; tel. (3) 3262-7221; e-mail iec@tohogakkai.com; internet www.tohogakkai.com; f. 1947; Asian studies; 1,600 mems; Chair. YOSHIO TOGAWA; Sec.-Gen. HIDEO KAWAGUCHI; publs *Acta Asiatica* (bulletin, 2 a year), *Tōhōgaku* (Eastern Studies, 2 a year), *Transactions of the International Conference of Eastern Studies* (1 a year).

TECHNOLOGY

Denki Gakkai (Institute of Electrical Engineers of Japan (IEEJ)): Homat Horizon Bldg, 6-2 Goban-cho, Chiyoda-ku, Tokyo 102-0076; tel. (3) 3221-7256; e-mail jimkyoku@iee.or.jp; internet www.iee.or.jp; f. 1888; 26,000 mems; Pres. HISAO OKA; publs *IEEJ Transactions on Electronics, Information and Systems* (12 a year, in English and Japanese), *IEEJ Transactions on Fundamentals and Materials* (12 a year, in English and Japanese), *IEEJ Transactions on Industry Applications* (12 a year, in English and Japanese), *IEEJ Transactions on Power and Energy* (12 a year, in English and Japanese), *IEEJ Transactions on Sensors and Micromachines* (12 a year, in English and Japanese), *Journal of the IEEJ* (12 a year, in Japanese).

Denshi Joho Tsushin Gakkai (Institute of Electronics, Information and Communication Engineers): Kikai-Shinko-Kaikan Bldg, 5-8, Shibakoen 3-chome, Minato-ku, Tokyo 105-0011; tel. (3) 3433-6691; e-mail member@ieice.org; f. 1917; 40,000 mems; Pres. HISASHI KANEKO; publs *Journal*, *Transactions* (9 series, incl. *Original Contributions in English and Abstracts in English from the Transactions*, 12 a year).

Doboku-Gakkai (Japan Society of Civil Engineers): Yotsuya 1-chome, Shinjuku-ku, Tokyo; tel. (3) 3355-3452; e-mail iad@jsce.or.jp; internet www.jsce-int.org; f. 1914; 40,742 mems; library of 45,000 vols; Pres. Dr TORU KONDO; Exec. Dir MORIYASU FURUKI; publs *Civil Engineering, JSCE* (1 a year), *Coastal Engineering in Japan* (2 a year, in English), *Journal* (12 a year), *Transactions* (12 a year).

Keikinzoku Gakkai (Japan Institute of Light Metals): Tukamoto-Sazan Bldg, 2–15, Ginza 4-chome, Chuo-ku, Tokyo 104-0061; tel. (3) 3538-0232; e-mail jilm1951@jilm.or.jp; internet www.jilm.or.jp; f. 1951; 2,222 mems; Pres. AKIHIKO KAMIO; publ. *Journal* (12 a year, in Japanese with English synopsis).

Keisoku Jidouseigyo Gakkai SICE (Society of Instrument and Control Engineers): 1-35-28-303, Hongo, Bunkyo-ku, Tokyo 113-0033; tel. (3) 3814-4121; e-mail member@sice.or.jp; internet www.sice.or.jp; f. 1962; 9,183 mems; Pres. SUSUMU TACHI; Vice-Pres RYOICHI TAKAHASHI, KAZUO KYUMA; publ. *Journal* (12 a year).

Kuki-Chowa Eisei Kogakkai (Society of Heating, Air-conditioning and Sanitary Engineers of Japan): 8-1, 1-chome, Kitashinjuku, Shinjuku-ku, Tokyo; f. 1917; 17,000 mems; Pres. M. KAMATA; publs *Journal* (12 a year), *Transactions* (12 a year).

Nihon Genshiryoku Gakkai (Atomic Energy Society of Japan): Shimbashi 2-3-7, Minato-ku, Tokyo 105-0004; tel. (3) 3508-1261; e-mail atom@aesj.or.jp; internet www.aesj.or.jp/en; f. 1959; peaceful uses of atomic energy; 7,700 mems; Pres. Dr M. TAKUMA; Sec. Gen. Y. TARUISHI; publs *Journal of Nuclear Science and Technology* (12 a year), *Nihon-Genshiryoku-Gakkai Shi* (12 a year), *Transactions of the Atomic Energy Society of Japan* (4 a year).

Nihon Kasai Gakkai (Japanese Association for Fire Science and Engineering): 3F Gakkai Center Bldg, 2-4-16 Yayoi, Bunkyo-ku, Tokyo 113-0032; tel. (3) 3813-8308; e-mail kasai50@sepia.ocn.ne.jp; f. 1951; 2,000 mems; Pres. TAKAO WAKAMATU; publ. *Kasai* (Fire, 6 a year).

Nihon Kikai Gakkai (Japan Society of Mechanical Engineers): Shinanomachi-Rengakan Bldg 5th Floor, Shinanomachi 35, Shinjuku-ku, Tokyo 160-0016; tel. (3) 5360-3500; e-mail wwwadmin@jsme.or.jp; internet www.jsme.or.jp; f. 1897; 40,000 mems; Pres. KANEKO SHIGEHIKO; publs *Journal* (12 a year), *JSME International Journal* (12 a year, in English, online), *Transactions* (12 a year).

Nippon Kinzoku Gakkai (Japan Institute of Metals): 1-14-32 Ichibancho, Aoba-ku, Sendai 980-8544; tel. (22) 223-3685; e-mail secgnl@jim.or.jp; f. 1937; 10,000 mems; Pres. KIYOHITO ISHIDA; publs *Bulletin* (12 a year), *Journal* (12 a year), *Materials Transactions* (12 a year, in English).

Nippon Kogakukai (Japan Federation of Engineering Societies): Kaikan Bldg 6th Fl., 5-26-20 Shiba, Minato-ku, Tokyo 108-0014; tel. (3) 5765-8002; internet www.jfes.or.jp; f. 1879.

Nippon Koku Ūchu Gakkai (Japan Society for Aeronautical and Space Sciences): c/o Meiko Bldg, Bekkan, 1-18-2 Shinbash, Minato-ku, Tokyo 105-0004; tel. (3) 3501-0463; e-mail office@jsass.or.jp; internet www.jsass.or.jp; f. 1934; 4,000 mems; Pres. Prof. JUNICHIRO KAWAGUCHI; publs *Journal* (12 a year), *Transactions* (6 a year).

Nippon Seramikusu Kyoukai (Ceramic Society of Japan): 22-17, 2-chome, Hyakunin-cho, Shinjuku-ku, Tokyo 169-0073; e-mail information@cersj.org; internet www.ceramic.or.jp; f. 1891; 5,546 mems; Pres. YOSHINORI KOKUBU; publs *Journal*, *Ceramics Japan* (Bulletin).

Nippon Shashin Gakkai (Society of Photographic Science and Technology of Japan): Tokyo Polytechnic Institute, 2-9-5 Hon-cho, Nakano-ku, Tokyo 164-8678; tel. (3) 3373-0724; internet www.spstj.org; f. 1925; 1,550 mems; Pres. T. WAKABAYASHI; publ. *Journal* (6 a year).

Nippon Tekko Kyoukai (Iron and Steel Institute of Japan): Niikura Building, 2-Kanda-Tsukasacho 2-chome, Chiyoda-ku, Tokyo 101-0048; tel. (3) 5209-7011; e-mail admion@isij.or.jp; internet www.isij.or.jp; f. 1915; 9,274 mems; Exec. Dir Dr AKIRA KOJIMA; publs *Ferrum* (bulletin, 12 a year, in Japanese), *ISIJ International* (12 a year, in English), *Tetsu-to-Hagané* (Iron and Steel, 12 a year, in Japanese).

Nippon Tribologi Gakkai (Japanese Society of Tribologists): c/o Kikai Shinko Kaikan No. 407-2, 3-5-8, Shibakoen, Minato-ku, Tokyo 105-0001; tel. (3) 3434-1926; e-mail jast@tribology.jp; internet www.tribology.jp; f. 1956; 3,044 mems; Pres. TAKASHI YAMAMOTO; publs *Journal of Japanese Society of Tribologists* (12 a year), *Tribology* (online).

Nogyo-Doboku Gakkai (Japanese Society of Irrigation, Drainage and Reclamation Engineering): Nogyo Doboku-Kaikan, 34-4 Shinbashi 5-chome, Tokyo 105-0004; tel. (3) 3436-3418; e-mail suido@jsidre.or.jp; internet www.jsidre.or.jp; f. 1929; 13,000 mems; Pres. Prof. TSUYOSHI MIYAZAKI; publs *Journal* (12 a year), *Journal of Rural and Environmental Engineering* (in English, 2 a year), *Transactions* (6 a year).

Seisan Gijutsu Kenkyusho (Institute of Industrial Science): c/o University of Tokyo, 4-6-1 Komaba, Meguro-ku, Tokyo 153-8505; tel. (3) 5454-6024; e-mail kokusai@iis.u-tokyo.ac.jp; internet www.iis.u-tokyo.ac.jp; f. 1949; Dir-Gen. Prof. S. NISHIO; publ. *Seisan-Kenkyu* (12 a year).

Shigen Sozai Gakkai (Mining and Materials Processing Institute of Japan): Nogizaka Bldg, 9-6-41 Akasaka, Minato-ku, Tokyo 107-0052; tel. (3) 3402-0541; e-mail info@mmij.or.jp; internet www.mmij.or.jp; f. 1885; 2,030 mems; Sec.-Gen. SUSUMU OKABE; publs *Journal of MMIJ* (9 a year), *MMIJ Proceedings* (2 a year).

Sisutemu Seigyo Jyouhou Gakkai (Institute of Systems, Control and Information Engineers): 14 Yoshidakawaharacho, Sakyo-ku, Kyoto City, Kyoto 606-8305; tel. (75) 751-6413; e-mail office@iscie.or.jp; internet www.iscie.or.jp; f. 1957; 2,744 mems; Pres. MINORU ABE; publ. *Systems, Control and Information* (12 a year).

Yosetsu Gakkai (Japan Welding Society): 1-11 Sakuma-cho, Kanda, Chiyoda-ku, Tokyo; tel. (3) 3253-0488; internet www.soc.nii.ac.jp/jws; f. 1925; 5,000 mems; Pres. Dr SHUZO SUSEI; publ. *Journal* (12 a year).

Research Institutes

GENERAL

Kokusai Nihon Bunka Kenkyu Center (International Research Center for Japanese Studies): 3–2 Oeyama-cho, Goryo, Nishikyo-ku, Kyoto 610-1192; tel. (75) 335-2222; e-mail www-admin@nichibun.ac.jp; internet www.nichibun.ac.jp/ja; f. 1987; attached to Nat. Institutes for the Humanities (an Inter-Univ. Research Institute Corp.); interdisciplinary and comprehensive research on Japanese studies, and research cooperation; library of 490,000 vols, 6,700 periodicals; Dir-Gen. Dr KAZUHIKO KOMATSU; publs *Japan Review* (in English), *Nihon Kenkyu* (in Japanese).

Sogo Kenkyu Kaihatsu Kiko (National Institute for Research Advancement): POB 5004, 34F Yebisu Garden Place Tower, 4-20-3 Ebisu, Shibuya-ku, Tokyo 150-6034; tel. (3) 5448-1700; e-mail info@nira.or.jp; internet www.nira.or.jp; f. 1974; conducts its own research, also comms and subsidizes research by other bodies; promotes int. exchange of research affecting policy-making around the world; research results are made public through lectures, symposia or publ. of reports; Chair. JIRO USHIO; Pres. MOTOSHIGE ITOH; publs *Almanac of Think Tanks in Japan*, *NIRA Kenkyu Hokokusho*, *NIRA Research Output* (in English), *NIRA Review* (in English), *NIRA Seisaku Kenkyu*, *NIRA's World Directory of Think Tanks* (in English).

AGRICULTURE, FISHERIES AND VETERINARY SCIENCE

Forest and Forest Products Research Institute: 1 Matsunosato, Tsukuba Ibaraki 305-8687; tel. (29) 873-3211; e-mail www@ffpri.affrc.go.jp; internet www.ffpri.affrc.go.jp; f. 1878; library of 386,000 vols (incl. br.

stations); Pres. KAZUO SUZUKI; publ. *Bulletin* (4 a year).

NARO Agricultural Research Center: 3-1-1 Kannondai, Tsukuba, Ibaraki 305-8666; tel. (29) 838-8481; e-mail www@narc.affrc.go.jp; internet www.naro.affrc.go.jp/narc; f. 1981; library of 63,000 vols, 5,800 periodicals; Dir KAZUO TERASHIMA.

National Food Research Institute: 2-1-12 Kannondai, Tsukuba, Ibaraki 305-8642; tel. (29) 838-7971; internet www.nfri.affrc.go.jp; f. 1934; food processing, chemistry, technology, storage, engineering, distribution, nutrition; applied microbiology, analysis, radiation, etc.; 121 mems; library of 40,000 vols; Dir Dr S. TANIGUCHI; publs *Report of the National Food Research Institute*, *Food Science and Technology*.

National Institute for Rural Engineering: 2-1-6 Kannondai, Tsukuba-shi, Ibaraki-ken 305-8609; tel. (298) 38-7513; internet www.nkk.affrc.go.jp; f. 1988; research on engineering technologies for agriculture and rural community areas; 115 mems; library of 38,000 vols; Dir-Gen. HIROSHI SATO; publs *Bulletin* (12 a year), *Technical Report* (irregular).

National Institute of Agrobiological Sciences (NIAS): 2-1-2 Kannondai, Tsukuba, Ibaraki 305-8602; tel. (298) 38-7406; e-mail niasl@nias.affrc.go.jp; internet www.nias.affrc.go.jp; f. 2001 by merger of National Institute of Agrobiological Resources (NIAR) and National Institute of Sericultural and Entomological Sciences (NISES); life science research on plants, animals and insects to facilitate the devt of Japan's domestic agricultural industry; 400 mems; library of 75,000 vols; Pres. TERUO ISHIGE; publ. *Gamma Field Symposia* (1 a year).

National Institute of Animal Health: 3-1-5, Kannondai, Tsukuba-shi, Ibaraki 305-0856; tel. (29) 838-7708; e-mail ref-niah@ml.affrc.go.jp; internet niah.naro.affrc.go.jp; f. 1921; animal husbandry, biology, veterinary medicine; 3 br. laboratories; library of 21,422 vols, 2,465 serial titles; Dir-Gen. Dr TAKAFUMI HAMAOKA; publs *Animal Health* (research report, 1 a year), *Bulletin* (1 a year).

National Institute of Crop Science: 2-1-18 Kannondai, Tsukuba, Ibaraki 305-8518; tel. (298) 38-8260; e-mail www-nics@naro.affrc.go.jp; internet nics.naro.affrc.go.jp; f. 1893; library of 130,000 vols; publ. *Bulletin* (irregular).

NARO Institute of Fruit Tree Science: 2-1 Fujimoto, Tsukuba, Ibaraki 305-8605; tel. (29) 838-6451; e-mail faq-fruit@ml.affrc.go.jp; internet www.naro.affrc.go.jp/english/index.html; f. 1902; library of 60,000 vols; Dir Dr YOSHINORI HASEGAWA.

National Institute of Livestock and Grassland Science: 2 Ikenodai, Kukizaki, Ibaraki 305-0901; tel. (298) 38-8612; e-mail nilgs-libchief@ml.affrc.go.jp; internet www.nilgs.naro.affrc.go.jp; f. 1916; library of 51,000 vols; Librarian KIRIKO HASHIMOTO; publ. *Bulletin* (irregular).

National Institute of Vegetable and Tea Science: 360 Kusawa, Ano, Age Mie 514–2392; tel. (59) 268-4621; internet vegetea.naro.affrc.go.jp; f. 1902; publ. *Bulletin* (1 a year).

Policy Research Institute, Ministry of Agriculture, Forestry and Fisheries: 2-2-1 Nishigahara, Kita-ku, Tokyo; tel. (3) 3910-3946; e-mail www@primaff.affrc.go.jp; internet www.primaff.affrc.go.jp; f. 1946; library of 331,495 vols; Dir T. SHINOHARA; publ. *Journal of Agricultural Policy Research* (in Japanese).

ECONOMICS, LAW AND POLITICS

Chuto Chosakai (Middle East Institute of Japan): Sanko Park Bldg, 5th Fl., 7-3-1 Nishi-Shinjuku-ku, Tokyo 160-0023; tel. (3) 3371-5798; internet www.meij.or.jp; f. 1960; government-aided; exchanges information with other countries; research activities in 4 areas: political and diplomatic affairs, industry, economy, natural resources; library in process of formation; Chair. KOSAKU INABA; publs *Chuto Kenkyu* (Journal of Middle East Studies, 12 a year), *Chuto Kitaafurika Nenkan* (Yearbook of the Middle East and North Africa).

Japan Center for International Exchange: 4-9-17 Minami-Azabu, Minato-ku, Tokyo 106-0047; tel. (3) 3446-7781; e-mail admin@jcie.or.jp; internet www.jcie.or.jp; f. 1971 to promote dialogue between Japan and the rest of the world; int. confs and seminars, overseas programme planning, promotion of policy studies and exchange programmes among philanthropic orgs; Japanese Secretariat of the Trilateral Comm.; Pres. TADASHI YAMAMOTO.

Japan Economic Research Institute: 6th Floor, Kowa 32 Bldg, 2-32, Minami-Azabu 5-chome, Minato-ku, Tokyo 106-0047; tel. (3) 3442-9400; e-mail web@nikkeicho.or.jp; internet www.nikkeicho.or.jp; f. 1962; research and study of domestic and foreign economic and business management; library of 8,000 vols; Exec. Dir KATSUZO YAMADA; Chair. KENJIRO NAGASAKA; publ. research reports.

Japan Maritime Development Association: Kaiun Bldg, 6-4, 2-chome, Hirakawa-cho, Chiyoda-ku, Tokyo; tel. (3) 3265-5231; e-mail info@jsmea.or.jp.

Kabushikikaisha Mitsubishi Sogo Kenkyusho (Mitsubishi Research Institute, Inc.): 3-6, Otemachi 2-chome, Chiyoda-ku, Tokyo 100-8141; tel. (3) 3270-9211; internet www.mri.co.jp; f. 1970; aims to meet new social, economic and industrial requirements in an age of advanced information systems and internationalization; research on nat. and int. scale to serve the needs of government agencies and industry in the fields of economic, political, industrial and management affairs, techno-economics, social engineering, technology and data processing; 900 mems; library of 63,000 vols, 1,000 periodicals; Chair. TAKESHI YANO; Pres. MASAYUKI TANAKA; publs *Outlook for the Japanese Economy* (2 a year), *Journal* (2 a year), *MRI Analysis of Japanese Corporations* (2 a year).

National Institute of Population and Social Security Research: 6th Fl., Hibiya Kokusai Bldg, 2-2-3 Uchisaiwaicyo, Chiyoda-ku, Tokyo 100-0011; tel. (3) 3595-2984; e-mail soumuka@ipss.go.jp; internet www.ipss.go.jp; f. 1939; part of Ministry of Health and Welfare; library of 16,000 vols; Dir TAKANOBU KYOGOKU; publ. *Journal of Population Problems* (4 a year).

Nihon Boeki Shinkokiko, Ajia Keizai Kenkyusho (Institute of Developing Economies, Japan External Trade Organization): 3-2-2 Wakaba, Mihama-ku, Chiba-shi, Chiba 261-8454; tel. (43) 299-9500; e-mail info@ide.go.jp; internet www.ide.go.jp; f. 1960; researches on economic, political and social issues in developing economies to support Japan's expansion of harmonious trade and investment; provision of int. economic cooperation focused on developing economies; 400 mems; library of 600,000 vols; Chair. and CEO HIROYUKI ISHIGE; Pres. TAKASHI SHIRAISHI; publs *Ajia Keizai* (4 a year, in Japanese), *The Developing Economies* (4 a year, in English), *Ajiken World Trend* (12 a year, in Japanese).

Nihon Keizai Kenkyu Center (Japan Center for Economic Research): Nikkei Kayabacho Bldg, 2-6-1 Nihombashi-kayabacho, Chuo-ku, Tokyo 103; tel. (3) 3639-2801; e-mail jcernet@jcer.or.jp; internet www.jcer.or.jp; f. 1963; 372 institutional, 280 individual mems; library of 45,813 vols, 920 periodicals; Pres. S. TOSHIDA; publ. *Asian Economic Policy Review*.

Nippon Keidanren (Japan Business Federation): 1-9-4, Otemachi, Chiyoda-ku, Tokyo 100-8188; tel. (3) 5204-1500; internet www.keidanren.or.jp; f. 2002 by merger of Keidanren (Japan Federation of Economic Organizations) and Nikkeiren (Japan Federation of Employers' Associations); 1,662 mems; library of 100,000 vols; Chair. FUJIO MITARAI.

Nippon Research Center Ltd: 2-7-1 Nihonbashi-honchou, Chuo-ku, Tokyo 103-0023; tel. (3) 6667-3400; internet www.nrc.co.jp; f. 1960 by interdisciplinary researchers and businessmen to meet the needs of industrial and economic circles; marketing and public opinion research, marketing consultancy, public relations, economic forecasting and urban and regional devt; 96 staff; library of 3,000 vols; Pres. INAHIRO SUZUKI; publ. *Bulletin of Marketing Research* (1 a year, in Japanese).

Rôdô Kagaku Kenkyusho (Institute for Science of Labour): 2-8-14, Sugao, Miyamae-ku, Kawasaki City, Kanagawa 216-8501; tel. (44) 977-2121; internet www.isl.or.jp; f. 1921; systems safety, chemical health risk management, employment and working life conditions, human–technology interaction, human work environment management, local industries, occupational epidemiology, systems safety, welfare support, work stress, participatory training for occupational safety and health; Pres. TAKAFUSA SHIOYA; Dir Dr KAZUHIRO SAKAI; publs *Rôdô Kagaku* (Journal of Science of Labour, 6 a year), *Rôdô no Kagaku* (Digest of Science of Labour, 12 a year).

EDUCATION

Kokuritsu Kyoiku Seisaku Kenkyu Sho (National Institute for Educational Policy Research): 3-2-2 Kasumigaseki, Chiyoda-ku, Tokyo 100-8951; tel. (3) 6733-6833; e-mail info@nier.go.jp; internet www.nier.go.jp; f. 1949; conducts basic research on specific issues for use in the planning and formulation of education policy and also pursues a wide range of activities such as providing academic sectors with information about educational studies, conducting research studies in conjunction with schools, pursuing practical research into social education, and conducting joint int. initiatives (incl. research studies) in the education field; library: see under Libraries and Archives; Dir-Gen. TATSUYA OTSUKI; publs *Kenkyushuroku* (2 a year, in Japanese), *Koho* (6 a year, in Japanese).

FINE AND PERFORMING ARTS

Tokyo Bunkazai Kenkyu-jo (Tokyo National Research Institute of Cultural Properties): 13-43 Ueno Park, Taito-ku, Tokyo 110-8713; tel. (3) 3823-2241; internet www.tobunken.go.jp; f. 1930; depts incl. Intangible Cultural Heritage, Research Programming; also Center for Conservation Science and Restoration Techniques, Japan Center for Int. Co-operation in Conservation and Div. of General Affairs; library of 110,000 vols; Dir-Gen. SUZUKI NORIO; publs *Bijutsu Kenkyu* (Journal of Art Studies, 4 a year), *Hozon Kagaku* (Science for Conservation, 1 a year), *Nihon Bijutsu Nenkan* (Year Book of Japanese Art), *Proceedings of the*

International Symposium on the Conservation and Restoration of Cultural Property (1 a year).

Tōyō Ongaku Gakkai (Society for Research in Asiatic Music): 307 Miharu Bldg, 3-6-3 Ueno, Taitô-ku, Tokyo 110-0005; tel. (3) 3823-5173; e-mail len03210@nifty.com; internet tog.a.la9.jp; f. 1936; aims to promote research in Japanese and other Asian music and ethnomusicology; 750 mems; Pres. ATSUMI KANESHIRO; publ. *Tōyō Ongaku Kenkyū* (1 a year).

HISTORY, GEOGRAPHY AND ARCHAEOLOGY

Geospatial Information Authority of Japan: Kitasato-1, Tsukuba, Ibaraki 305-0811; tel. (29) 864-1111; internet www.gsi.go.jp; f. 1869; National Survey and Mapping Org.; library of 32,000 vols; Dir YOSHIHISA HOSHINO; publ. *Bulletin* (1 a year).

LANGUAGE AND LITERATURE

Kokubungaku Kenkyu Siryokan (National Institute of Japanese Literature): Midorityou 10-3 Tachikawa, Tokyo 190-0014; tel. (50) 5533-2900; e-mail so-mu@nijl.ac.jp; internet www.nijl.ac.jp; f. 1972 by the Min. of Education, Science and Culture at the recommendation of the Japan Science Council and in response to requests for a centre for the preservation of Japanese classical literature; surveys, collects (largely in microfilm), studies, processes, preserves and provides access to MSS and old printed books relating to Japanese literature before 1868; also undertakes research in this field; provides scholarly community with facilities for consultation and reproduction of materials; historical documents division collects and preserves documents of *kinsei* (1600–1867); library: see under Libraries and Archives; Dir-Gen. Dr YUICHIRO IMANISHI; publs *Bulletin* (1 a year), *Bibliographic Reports* (1 a year), *Bibliography of Research in Japanese Literature* (1 a year), *Proceedings of the International Conference on Japanese Literature in Japan* (1 a year).

Kokuritu Kokugo Kenkyuzyo (National Institute for Japanese Language and Linguistics): 10-2 Midorimachi, Tachikawa, Tokyo; tel. (42) 540-4300; internet www.ninjal.ac.jp; f. 1948; depts of linguistic theory and structure, language change and variation, corpus studies, cross-linguistic studies; aims to promote linguistic studies of Japanese on int. levels and provides Japanese language corpora and databases online; library of 150,000 vols; Dir-Gen. Dr TARO KAGEYAMA; publs *Kokugo Nenkan* (Japanese Language Studies, 1 a year), *Nihongo Kagaku* (Japanese Linguistics), *Nihongo Kyouiku Ronshu* (Japanese Language Education, 1 a year).

MEDICINE

Cancer Institute, Japanese Foundation for Cancer Research: 3-10-6 Ariake, Koto-ku, Tokyo, 135-8550; tel. (3) 3520-0111; e-mail international@jfcr.or.jp; internet www.jfcr.or.jp; f. 1908; departments of biochemistry, cancer chemotherapy, cell biology, experimental pathology, gene research, human genome analysis, pathology, physics, molecular biotherapy and viral oncology; Cancer Chemotherapy Center, Cancer Institute Hospital and Genome Center attached; library of 5,000 vols, 10,000 periodicals; Dir Dr TETSUO NODA; publ. *Japan Journal for Cancer Research* (12 a year).

Institute of Brain and Blood Vessels: 6-23 Ootemachi, Isezaki City, Gumma; tel. (270) 24-3355; f. 1963; clinical and basic research on cerebrovascular disease; Dir Dr TATSURU MIHARA; publ. *Nosotchu No Kenkyu* (Studies on Apoplexy).

Institute of Chemotherapy: 6-1-14 Kohnodai, Ichikawa City, Chiba; tel. (473) 75-1111; f. 1939; Dir Prof. TSUGUO HASEGAWA; publ. *Bulletin of the Institute of Chemotherapy*.

Kekkaku Yobo Kai Kekkaku Kenkyujo (Research Institute of Tuberculosis, Japan Anti-Tuberculosis Association): 3-1-24 Matsuyama Kiyose-shi, Tokyo 204-8533; tel. (424) 93-5711; internet www.jata.or.jp; f. 1939; research on health education campaign against tuberculosis: information, surveillance and training centre: tuberculosis and respiratory diseases; 56 mems; library of 15,000 vols; Dir Dr NOBUKATSU ISHIKAWA; publs *Information and Review of Tuberculosis and Respiratory Disease Research* (4 a year, in Japanese), *Red Double-Barred Cross* (6 a year, in Japanese), *Review of Tuberculosis for Public Health Nurses* (2 a year, in Japanese).

Kitasato Institute Research Center for Biologicals: 6-111 Arai, Kitamoto-shi, Saitama 108; tel. (3) 3444-6161; internet www.kitasato.ac.jp; f. 1914; research on the cause, prevention and therapy of various diseases; 1,100 mems; library of 86,000 vols; Dir S. OMURA.

Kohno Clinical Medicine Research Institute: 1-28-15 Kita-Shinagawa, Shinagawa-ku, Tokyo; tel. (3) 472-4630; internet kcmi.or.jp; f. 1951; 62 staff; library of 3,000 vols; Dir M. KOHNO; publs *Archives*, *Bulletin*.

Miyake Medical Institute: 1-3 Tenjin-mae, Takamatsu City, Kagawa; internet www.miyake.or.jp; f. 1949; Dir T. MIYAKE.

National Cancer Center: 5-1-1 Tsukiji, Chuo-ku, Tokyo 104-0045; tel. (3) 3542-2511; e-mail www-admin@ncc.go.jp; internet www.ncc.go.jp; f. 1962; diagnosis, treatment and research of cancer and allied diseases; dept of Min. of Health, Labour and Welfare; 800 staff; library of 56,000 vols, 17,000 monographs, 500 periodicals; Pres. SETSUO HIROHASHI; Dir for Hospital RYOSUKE TSUCHIYA; Dir for Research Institute KEIJI WAKABAYASHI; publs *Collected Papers of Hospital* (1 a year, in English and Japanese, distributed free to libraries), *Collected Papers of Research Institute* (1 a year, in English, distributed free to libraries), *Tumour Registration of Bone, Lung, Stomach, Blood, Brain, etc.* (in Japanese, distributed free to libraries).

National Institute of Genetics: 1111, Yata, Mishima City, Shizuoka 411-8540; tel. (55) 981-6707; e-mail shomuka@lab.nig.ac.jp; internet www.nig.ac.jp/home.html; f. 1949; part of Ministry of Education, Culture, Sports, Science and Technology; library of 20,000 vols; Dir Dr YOSHIKI HOTTA.

National Institute of Health and Nutrition: 1-23-1 Toyama, Shinjuku-ku, Tokyo 162-8636; tel. (3) 3203-5721; e-mail eiken-office@nih.go.jp; internet www.nih.go.jp; f. 1920; part of Min. of Health, Labour and Welfare; library of 30,000 vols; Dir NOBUAKI SHIBAIKE; publ. *Japanese Journal of Nutrition* (6 a year, in Japanese).

National Institute of Health Sciences: 1-18-1 Kamiyoga, Setagaya, Tokyo 15-8501; tel. (3) 3700-1141; internet www.nihs.go.jp; f. 1874; research in connection with the cosmetics, drugs, environmental chemicals, medical devices and regulation of foods; Dir MASAHIRO NISHIJIMA; publ. *Bulletin* (1 a year).

National Institute of Occupational Safety and Health: 6-21-1, Nagao Tama-ku, Kawasaki City, Kanagawa 214-8585; tel. (44) 865-6111; e-mail info@niih.go.jp; internet www.jniosh.go.jp/en; f. 1956; part of Min. of Health, Labour and Welfare; library of 26,000 vols; Dir YUTAKA MAEDA; publ. *Industrial Health* (6 a year).

National Institute of Public Health: 2-3-6 Minami, Wako-shi, Saitama 351-0197; internet www.niph.go.jp; f. 2002; by merger of Institute of Public Health, National Institute of Health Services Management and part of the Dept of Oral Science in National Institute of Infectious Disease; depts of education and training technology, environmental health, epidemiology, facility sciences, health promotion, healthy building and housing, human resources development, management sciences, oral health, policy sciences, public health nursing, social services, technology assessment and biostatistics, water supply engineering; library of 80,000 books, 4,000 journals; publ. *Hoken Iryo Kagaku*.

National Institute of Infectious Diseases: Toyama 1-23-1, Shinjuku-ku, Tokyo 162-8640; tel. (3) 5285-1111; e-mail info@nih.go.jp; internet www.nih.go.jp/niid; f. 1947; part of Ministry of Health, Labour and Welfare; research on communicable diseases, including an AIDS Research Centre; assay of biological products and antibiotics; library of 30,000 vols; Dir TATSUO MIYAMURA; publ. *The Japanese Journal of Infectious Diseases* (6 a year).

National Institute of Mental Health, National Center of Neurology and Psychiatry: 4-1-1 Higashimaci, Kodaira-shi, Tokyo 187-8553; tel. (42) 341-2711; internet www.ncnp.go.jp/nimh; f. 1952; part of Ministry of Health, Labour and Welfare; Dir A. FUJINAWA; publ. *Journal of Mental Health* (1 a year).

Neuropsychiatric Research Institute: 91 Benten-cho, Shinjuku-ku, Tokyo; tel. (3) 3260-9171; internet www.seiwa-hp.com; f. 1951; research on sleep disorders, mood disorders; art therapy; Chief Dir NOBUMASA KATO.

Nukada Institute for Medical and Biological Research: 5-18 Inage-cho, Chiba-City, Chiba; f. 1939; Dir Dr H. NUKADA; publ. *Report* (irregular).

Ogata Institute for Medical and Chemical Research: 2-10-14 Higashi-Kanda, Chiyoda-ku, Tokyo 101-0031; tel. (3) 3865-7500; f. 1962; library of 12,000 vols; Pres. MASAHIDE ABE; publ. *Igaku to Seibutsugaku* (Medicine and Biology, 12 a year).

Tokyo Metropolitan Institute of Medical Science: Honkomagome 3-18-22, Bunkyo-ku, Tokyo 113-8613; tel. (3) 3823-2105; e-mail ui@rinshoken.or.jp; internet www.rinshoken.or.jp; f. 1975; research in aetiology and pathogenesis of intractable diseases and application of molecular and cellular biology to the aetiology of these diseases; library of 30,000 vols; Dir KEIJI TANAKA; publ. *Rinshoken News* (12 a year, in Japanese).

NATURAL SCIENCES

General

Kokuritsu Kyokuchi Kenkyujyo (National Institute of Polar Research): Midoricho 10–3, Tokyo 190-8518; tel. (42) 512-0648; e-mail shomu@nipr.ac.jp; internet www.nipr.ac.jp; f. 1973 fmrly Polar Research Centre of the National Science Museum; attached to Joho Shisutemu Kenkyu Kiko (Research Organization of Information Systems); govt-sponsored; implements programmes of the Japanese Antarctic Research Expeditions (JARE), organizes postgraduate courses in polar subjects, offers research facilities to nat. and foreign univs and individual researchers; library of 53,000 vols and bound periodicals, 4,600 ejournals;

Dir-Gen. Prof. KAZUYUKI SHIRAISHI; Librarian YORIKO HAYAKAWA; publs *Antarctic Geological Map Series* (irregular), *Antarctic Record* (3 a year), *Antarctic Special Map Series* (irregular), *Arctic Data Reports* (irregular), *JARE Data Reports* (8 a year), *Journal* (irregular), *Memoirs of the National Institute of Polar Research* (Special Issue, irregular), *Polar Science* (4 a year).

Biological Sciences

Kihara Institute for Biological Research: Yokohama City University, Maioka-cho 641, Totsuka-ku, Yokohama 244; tel. (45) 820-1900; f. 1942; library of 20,000 vols; Dir KAORU MIYAZAKI; publs *Seiken Ziho* (1 a year), *Wheat Information Service* (2 a year).

Osaka Bioscience Institute: 6-2-4 Furuedai, Suita-shi, Osaka 565-0874; tel. (6) 6872-4812; e-mail office@obi.or.jp; internet www.obi.or.jp; f. 1987; library of 15,000 vols; Dir Dr SHIGETADA NAKANISHI; Librarian ATSUKO TAKIKAWA.

Tokyo Biochemical Research Institute: Kyobashi NS Bldg, 2-5-21 Kyobashi, Chuo-ku, Tokyo 104-0031; tel. (3) 3562-5705; e-mail asia@tokyobrf.or.jp; internet www.tokyobrf.or.jp; f. 1950; Dir M. OKADA.

Mathematical Sciences

Institute of Statistical Mathematics: 4-6-7 Minami Azabu, Minato-ku, Tokyo 106-8569; tel. (3) 5421-8719; internet www.ism.ac.jp; f. 1944; Nat. Inter-Univ. Research Institute; research in statistics; library of 52,000 vols, 2,250 periodicals; Dir Prof. GENSHIRO KITAGAWA; publs *Annals* (4 a year), *Proceedings* (2 a year).

Physical Sciences

Fukada Geological Institute: 2-13-12 Hon-Komagome, Bunkyo-ku, Tokyo 113-0021; tel. (3) 3944-8010; e-mail fgi@fgi.or.jp; internet www.fgi.or.jp; f. 1954; Chair TADASHI SATO; publs *Fukadaken Library* (10 a year), *Nenpo* (1 a year, in English or Japanese, both with English abstract).

Institute of Physical and Chemical Research (RIKEN): 2–1 Hirosawa, Wako-shi, Saitama 351-0198; tel. (48) 462-1111; e-mail koho@riken.jp; internet www.riken.go.jp; f. 1917; studies related to science and technology; 621 mems; library of 100,000 vols; Pres. RYOJI NOYORI; publs *RIKEN Accelerated Progress Report* (1 a year), *RIKEN Review* (6 a year).

Japan Atomic Energy Agency (JAEA): 4–49 Muramatsu, Tokai-mura, Naka-gun, Ibaraki 319-1184; tel. (29) 282-1122; internet www.jaea.go.jp; f. 2005 by merger of Japan Atomic Energy Research Institute (JAERI) and Japan Nuclear Cycle Development Institute (JNC); library of 36,000 vols; Pres. TOSHIO OKAZAKI; Exec. Dir ICHIRO NAKAJIMA.

Kobayasi Institute of Physical Research: 3-20-41 Higashi-Motomachi, Kokubunji, Tokyo 185-0022; tel. (42) 321-2841; e-mail info@kobayasi-riken.or.jp; internet www.kobayasi-riken.or.jp; f. 1940; acoustics (noise and vibration, acoustic material, piezoelectric material); Pres. M. YAMASHITA; Dir K. YAMAMOTO.

Meteorological Research Institute: 1–1 Nagamine, Tsukuba, Ibaraki 3050052; tel. (29) 853-8546; www.mri-jma.go.jp; f. 1942; 174 mems; meteorology, geophysics, seismology, oceanography, geochemistry; Dir-Gen. H. ITOH; publ. *Papers in Meteorology and Geophysics* (4 a year).

National Astronomical Observatory, Mizusawa VERA Observatory: 2-12 Hoshigaoka-cho, Oshu-shi Mizusawa, Iwate-ken 023-0861; tel. (197) 22-7111; internet www.miz.nao.ac.jp; f. 1899; astronomy, geophysics, geodesy; part of Institute of Natural Sciences; library of 68,400 vols; Prof. H. KOBAYASHI; publ. *National Astronomical Observatory Technical Reports of the Mizusawa Kansoku Centre*.

National Institute for Materials Science: 1-2-1 Sengen, Tsukuba, Ibaraki 305-0047; tel. (29) 859-2000; e-mail info@nims.go.jp; internet www.nims.go.jp; f. 2001; management of basic research and devt of materials science and advancement of expertise in field; 1,450 mems; Pres. Prof. SUKEKATSU USHIODA.

Space Activities Commission: 2-2-1 Kasumigaseki, Chiyoda-ku, Tokyo 100-8966; tel. (3) 3581-5271; f. 1968; contributes to a comprehensive and streamlined execution of govt programmes on space devt, incl. organization of admin. agencies, planning of general policies and outlining training programmes for researchers and technicians; Chair. SADAKAZU TANIGAKI.

RELIGION, SOCIOLOGY AND ANTHROPOLOGY

Okura Institute for the Study of Spiritual Culture: 2-10-1 ookurayama, Kohoku-ku, Yokohama; tel. (45) 542-0050; e-mail okuraseishinbunka@js6.so-net.ne.jp; internet www.okuraken.or.jp; f. 1932; Dir R. TAKAI; publ. *Okuravama Ronshu*.

TECHNOLOGY

Building Research Institute: 1 Tachihara, Tsukuba-shi, Ibaraki Pref.; tel. (29) 864-2151; e-mail bri@kenken.go.jp; internet www.kenken.go.jp; f. 1946; 101 mems; building design and use, building economics, building materials, construction techniques, earthquake engineering, environmental engineering, fire safety, structural engineering, town planning; library of 50,000 vols; Chief Exec. Y. SAKAMOTO; publ. *BRI Research Papers*.

Civil Engineering Research Institute of Hokkaido/Hokkaido Development Agency: Hiragishi 1-3, Toyohira-ku, Sapporo 062-8602; e-mail mailinfo@ceri.go.jp; internet www.ceri.go.jp; f. 1937; library of 36,000 vols; Pres. TOMONORI SAITO; publ. *Report* (4 a year).

Communications Research Laboratory: 4-2-1 Nukui-Kitamachi, Koganei, Tokyo 184-8795; tel. (42) 327-5392; e-mail publicity@crl.go.jp; internet www.crl.go.jp; f. 1952; next-generation information-communication networks, radio, space and optical communication, space weather forecasting, and related fields; library of 160,000 vols; Dir T. IIDA; publs *CRL Annual Bulletin* (in Japanese), *CRL News* (12 a year, in Japanese), *Ionospheric Data in Japan* (12 a year), *Journal* (4 a year), *Review* (4 a year, in Japanese).

Engineering Research Institute: Faculty of Engineering, University of Tokyo, 11-16, Yayoi 2-chome, Bunkyo-ku, Tokyo; f. 1939; 67 staff; library of 6,747 vols; Dir YOICHI GOSHI.

Institute for Fermentation, Osaka: 17-85, Juso-honmachi 2-chome, Yodogawaku, Osaka 532; tel. (6) 6300-6555; e-mail desk@ifo.or.jp; internet www.ifo.or.jp; f. 1944; preservation and distribution of micro-organisms and animal cells; 23 staff; library of 800 vols; Dir Dr TORU HASEGAWA; publs *List of Cultures*, *IFO Research Communications* (every 2 years).

Institute for Future Technology: Tomiokabashi Bldg, 2-6-11 Fukagawa, Koto-ku, Tokyo; tel. (3) 5245-1011; e-mail info@iftech.or.jp; internet www.iftech.or.jp; f. 1971; research in the fields of technology forecasting, technology assessment and other socio-economic research in future technologies (electronics, telecommunications, space and energy); library of 15,000 vols; Pres. HIROEI FUJIOKA; Chief Sec. TAKAMITSU KOSHIKAWA; publ. *Kenkyu Seika Gaiyo* (research results, 1 a year, in Japanese).

Institute of Energy Economics, Japan: Inui Bldg, 13-1 Kachidoki 1-chome, Chuo-ku, Tokyo 104-0054; tel. (3) 5547-0211; e-mail otoiawase@tky.ieej.or.jp; internet eneken.ieej.or.jp; f. 1966; coordinates information related to energy, its use, supply, conservation and economic aspects; provides material as basis for planning and policy formation by govt and private business; int. cooperation on energy projects; library of 56,450 vols; Chair. and CEO MASAKAZU TOYODA; Man. Dirs MASAKI CHIBA, KOKICHI ITO, KENSUKE KANEKIYO KENJI KOBAYASHI HIDEKI OKAMOTO, TSUTOMU TOICHI, Dr KEN KOYAMA, Dr KOICHIRO TANAKA AKIHIRO KUROKI; publs *IEEJ Energy Journal* (4 a year, in English), *EDMC Energy Trend* (12 a year, in Japanese), *EDMC Handbook of Energy & Economic Statistics in Japan* (1 a year, in English).

Institute of Research and Innovation, Japan: 1-6-8 Yushima, Bunkyo-ku, Tokyo 113; tel. (3) 5689-6356; e-mail info@iri.or.jp; f. 1959; fmrly Industrial Research Institute, Japan; independent; research and devt in technology and socio-technology, incl. alternative energy sources, nuclear technologies and related innovative problems; 70 research staff; library of 2,000 vols; Pres. SHO NASU; Dir JIRO MIYAMOTO; publ. *Bulletin* (4 a year, in Japanese).

International Association of Traffic and Safety Sciences: 6-20, 2-chome, Yaesu, Chuo-ku, Tokyo 104-0028; e-mail pa_nyc_enquiries@pa.gov.sg; f. 1974; aims to contribute to the realization of a better traffic soc. through the practical application of research conducted in a variety of fields; research surveys on traffic and its safety; colln and retrieval of information on traffic-related sciences; sponsorship of domestic and int. symposia and study meetings; provision of awards; IATSS Forum, human resource devt programme for SE Asian countries; Exec. Dir HIROSHI ISHIZUKI; publs *IATSS Research* (2 a year, in English), *IATSS Review* (4 a year, in Japanese with English abstracts), *Statistics: Road Accidents in Japan* (1 a year, in English), *White Paper on Traffic Safety* (1 a year, in English).

Japan Aerospace Exploration Agency (JAXA): 1-6-4 Marunouchi, Chiyoda-ku, Tokyo 100-0005; tel. (3) 6266-6400; e-mail kibo-pao@jaxa.jp; internet www.jaxa.jp; f. 2003 by merger of Institute of Space and Astronautical Science (ISAS), National Aerospace Laboratory of Japan (NAL) and National Space Development Agency of Japan (NASDA); Pres. KEIJI TACHIKAWA.

Japan Construction Method and Machinery Research Institute: 3154 Obuchi, Fuji-shi, Shizuoka-ken; tel. (545) 35-0212; e-mail nakashima@cmi.or.jp; f. 1964; construction machine testing and associated research; Dir HIDESUKE NAKASHIMA.

Kokudo Gijyutsu Seisaku Sougou Kenkyujo (National Institute for Land and Infrastructure Management, Ministry of Land, Infrastructure and Transport): 1 Asahi, Tskuba-shi, Ibaraki-ken 305-0804; tel. (29) 864-4593; e-mail kokusaie@nilim.go.jp; internet www.nilim.go.jp; f. 2001; 43 research divisions; 386 staff; research on advanced information technology, airports, building, coastal and marine environments, disaster risk management, environment, harbours, housing, land and construction management, ports, rivers, roads, water quality control, and urban planning; library of 193,000 vols; Dir TSUNEYOSHI MOCHIZUKI; publ. *NILIM News Letter* (in English).

National Institute of Advanced Industrial Science and Technology: Tokyo Headquarters, 1-3-1, Kasumigaseki Chiyoda-ku, Tokyo 100-8921; tel. (3) 5501-0900; e-mail presec@m.aist.go.jp; internet www.aist.go.jp; f. 2001; government-sponsored research institute; Dir Dr HIROYUKI YOSHIKAWA.

National Marine Research Institute: 6-38-1, Shinkawa, Mitaka, Tokyo 181-0004; tel. (422) 41-3015; e-mail info2@nmri.go.jp; internet www.nmri.go.jp; f. 1916, present name 2001; attached to Min. of Transport; shipbuilding and marine engineering; library of 68,000 vols; Pres. SHIRO INOUE; publ. *Papers* (6 a year).

National Research Institute for Earth Science and Disaster Prevention (NIED): 3–1 Tennodai, Tsukuba, Ibaraki 305-0006; tel. (29) 851-1611; e-mail outreach@bosai.go.jp; internet www.bosai.go.jp; f. 1963; library of 71,232 vols; Pres. YOSHIMITSU OKADA; publs *Report of the NIED* (1 a year), *Technical Note of the NIED* (irregular), *Disaster Research Report of the NIED* (irregular).

Branches:

Nagaoka Institute of Snow and Ice Studies: 187-16, Maeyama, Suyoshi Omachi, Nagaoka-shi, Niigata-ken 940; study of techniques for the prevention of snow damage.

Shinjyo NIED Branch of Snow and Ice Studies: 1400, Takadan, Toka-machi, Shinjo-shi, Yamagata-ken 996; study of the prevention of disasters caused by snow and ice.

National Research Institute of Brewing: 2-6-30 Takinogawa, Kita-ku, Tokyo 114-0023; tel. (3) 3910-6237; e-mail info@nrib.go.jp; internet www.nrib.go.jp; f. 1904; Pres. JYUNICHI HIRAMATSU; Exec. Dir YASUZOU KIZAKI.

Noguchi Institute: 1-8-1 Kaga, Itabashi-ku, Tokyo 173-0003; tel. (3) 3961-3255; internet www.noguchi.or.jp; f. 1941; research into carbohydrate chemistry, solid-state catalysts for ecoprocess; Pres. KAGEYASU AKASHI.

Port and Airport Research Institute: 3-1-1 Nagase, Yokosuka, Kanagawa 239-0826; internet www.pari.go.jp; f. 1962 as Port and Harbour Research Institute; later reorganized into 2 institutes: National Institute for Land and Infrastructure Management and Port and Airport Research Institute; attached to Ministry of Transport; research on all aspects of port, harbour and airport construction technology; library of 20,000 vols; Exec. Researcher Dr SHIGEO TAKAHASHI; publs *Report* (4 a year), *Technical Notes* (4 a year).

Railway Technical Research Institute: 2-8-38 Hikari-cho, Kokubunji-shi, Tokyo 185-8540; tel. (425) 73-7258; internet www.rtri.or.jp; f. 1986; research and devt in railway technologies and labour science incl. investigation and preparation of drafts of railway technology standards; colln and release of railway-related documents; publs and lectures; diagnosis, advice; drafting of original plans and proposals for standardization with regard to int. railway standards; commissions testing and research projects; library of 170,277 vols; Chair. Prof. EISUKE MASADA; Pres. Dr HISASHI TARUMI.

Research Institute for Production Development: 15 Shimo Kamomori Honmachi, Sakyo-ku, Kyoto 606-0805; tel. (75) 781-1107; f. 1947; Pres. TAKAO YAMAMURO.

Research Institute of Printing Bureau: 6-4-20 Sakawa, Odawara, Kanagawa; tel. (465) 49-4246; f. 1891; Dir H. NONAKA; publ. *Research Bulletin* (2 a year).

Shobo-kenkyujo (National Research Institute of Fire and Disaster): 35-3, Jindaiji-Higashicho 4-chome, Chofu, Tokyo 182-8508; tel. (422) 44-8331; e-mail toiawase2008@fri.go.jp; internet www.fri.go.jp; f. 1948; library of 17,500 vols; Dir AKIRA TERAMURA; publs *Shobo-kenkyujo Hokoku*, *Shoken Syuho* (1 a year).

Tensor Society: c/o Kawaguchi Institute of Mathematical Sciences, Matsu-ga-oka 2-7-15, Chigasaki 253; e-mail tensorsociety@ybb.ne.jp; f. 1937; undertakes original research in the field of tensor analysis and its applications; library of 23,000 vols; Pres. Prof. Dr T. KAWAGUCHI; Sec. Prof. Dr H. KAWAGUCHI; publ. *Tensor* (3 a year).

Libraries and Archives

Akita

Akita Prefectural Library: 14-31 Sannousinmati, Akita-shi, Akita 010-0952; tel. (18) 866-8400; e-mail apl@apl.pref.akita.jp; internet www.apl.pref.akita.jp; f. 1899; 403,162 vols; Librarian N. FUJITA.

Chiba

Chiba Prefectural Central Library: 11-1 Ichibacho Chuo-ku, Chiba City 260-8660; tel. (43) 222-0116; internet www.library.pref.chiba.lg.jp; 268,488 vols; Librarian S. TATEISHI.

Hakodate

Hakodate City Library: 17-2 Aoyagi-cho, Hakodate City; tel. (138) 22-7447; 122,500 vols (including br. library); Librarian I. FUKUDA.

Hiroshima

Hiroshima Prefectural Library: 3-7-47 Senda-machi, Naka-ku, Hiroshima City; tel. (82) 241-4995; e-mail hirokento@hplibra.pref.hiroshima.jp; f. 1951; public library; 399,957 vols; Librarian K. HATAKEYAMA.

Ise

Jingu Bunko: 1711 Koda-kushimoto-cho, Ise, Mie Prefecture 516-0016; tel. (596) 222737; internet www.isejingu.or.jp/bunka/bunbody4.htm; 260,000 vols on Shinto; Dir and Chief of Cultural Section KUNIO KOHORI.

Kagoshima

Kagoshima Prefectural Library: 1-1 Shiroyama-machi, Kagoshima City; 222,357 vols; Librarian H. KUBOTA.

Kanazawa

Kanazawa City Libraries: 2-20 Tamagawa-cho, Kanazawa City 920; internet www.lib.kanazawa.ishikawa.jp; 510,000 vols; Librarian N. YOSHIMOTO.

Kanazawa Municipal Izumino Library: 22-22, 4-chome Izumino-machi, Kanazawa City 921-8034; tel. (76) 280-2345; e-mail m-m@lib.kanazawa.ishikawa.jp; internet www.lib.kanazawa.ishikawa.jp; f. 1995; 360,000 vols; Dir S. KIDO.

Kobe

Kobe City Library: 7-2 Kununoki-cho, Ikuta, Kobe; f. 1911; 240,000 vols; Librarian S. AKAI.

Kobe University Library: Rokkodai-cho, Nada-ku, Kobe; tel. (78) 803-7315; e-mail kikaku@lib.kobe-u.ac.jp; internet www.lib.kobe-u.ac.jp; f. 1908; 2,958,000 vols; Dir TAKESHI SASAKI.

Kochi

Kochi Prefectural Library: 3 Marunouchi, Kochi City; 141,927 vols; Librarian N. SHIMESHINO.

Kyoto

Institute for Research in Humanities Library: Yoshida-Honmachi, Sakyo-ku, Kyoto 606-8501; attached to Kyoto University; 564,000 vols; institute divided into 2 sections: humanities and oriental studies; Dir Prof. NAOKI MIZUNO.

Kyoto Prefectural Library and Archives: 1-4 Hangi-cho, Shimogamo, Sakyo-ku, Kyoto-shi, Kyoto 606-0823; tel. (75) 723-4831; internet www.pref.kyoto.jp/shiryokan; f. 1898; 350,000 vols; Dir MINORU SHIBATA.

Kyoto University Library: Yoshida Honmachi, Sakyo-ku, Kyoto 606-8501; tel. (75) 753-2613; e-mail kikaku@kulib.kyoto-u.ac.jp; internet www.kulib.kyoto-u.ac.jp; f. 1899; central library and 51 libraries of 18 graduate schools and 14 research institutes; 6,697,788 vols; Dir Dr TAKASHI HIKIHARA; publ. *Seishu* (4 a year).

Ryukoku University Library: 67 Tsukamoto-cho, Fukakusa, Fushimi-ku, Kyoto 612; tel. (75) 645-7885; e-mail f-lib@ad.ryukoku.ac.jp; internet opac.lib.ryukoku.ac.jp; f. 1639; 1,800,000 vols; 3 brs: Fukakusa, Omiya and Seta libraries; Librarian JITSUZO SHIGETA.

Matsuyama

Matsuyama University Library: 4-2 Bunkyo-cho, Matsuyama 790; tel. (89) 925-7111; e-mail mu-libs@matsuyama-u.jp; internet www.matsuyama.ac.jp; f. 1923; 540,000 vols; collection of rare books, including first editions of 18th- and 19th-century works on political economy; Librarian Prof. K. SHISHIDO.

Nagoya

Nagoya City Tsuruma Central Library: 43 Tsurumai-cho, Tsurumai 1-1-155, Showa-ku, Nagoya City; tel. (52) 741-3131; internet www.tsuruma-lib.showa.nagoya.jp; f. 1923; 1,040,400 vols; Librarian Y. WADA.

Nagoya University Library: Furo-cho, Chikusa-ku, Nagoya 464-8601; tel. (52) 789-3678; e-mail wwwadmin@nul.nagoya-u.ac.jp; internet www.nul.nagoya-u.ac.jp; f. 1939; central library and 24 libraries of 14 graduate schools and 3 institutes; 3,231,191 vols; Dir Prof. M. SANO; Dir for Admin. Dept KIYOHIKO SAKAI; publ. *Kanto* (4 a year).

Naha

Ryukyu Islands Central Library: Central Library Building, Naha, Okinawa; f. 1950; 45,926 vols; central deposit library.

Nara

Nara Prefectural Library and Information Center: 48 Nobori Ooji-cho, Nara City 630-8135; tel. (742) 34-2111; e-mail info@library.pref.nara.jp; internet www.library.pref.nara.jp; f. 1909; 296,000 vols; Dir Dr SENDA MINORU; publ. *Untei*.

Niigata

Niigata Prefectural Library: 3-1-2 Meike Minami, Niigata City; tel. (25) 284-6001; f. 1915; 610,000 vols; Librarian K. SHIBUYA.

Niigata University Library: 8050 Ikarashi 2-nocho, Nishi-ku, Niigata City 950-2181; f. 1949; 1,672,410 vols; Dir T. YATA.

Nishinomiya

Kwansei Gakuin University Library: 1-1-155 Uegahara, Nishinomiya, Hyogo 662-8501; tel. (798) 54-6121; e-mail library@kwansei.ac.jp; internet library.kwansei.ac.jp; f. 1889; br. libraries for 11 schools, 13 graduate schools, 2 satellite campuses; 1,500,000 vols; Dean for Univ. Library Services TAKUJI OKUNO.

Okayama

Okayama University Library: 1-1 Naka 3-chome, Tsushima, Okayama City 700-8530; tel. (86) 252-1111; internet www.lib.okayama-u.ac.jp; f. 1949; 2 br. libraries; 1,870,000 vols; Dir H. INOUE; publ. *Kai* (Library News, 2 a year).

Osaka

Kansai University Library: 3-3-35 Yamate-cho, Suita-shi, Osaka; tel. (6) 368-1157; e-mail ku-library@ml.kandai.jp; internet web.lib.kansai-u.ac.jp/library; f. 1914; 2,028,000 vols; Librarian K. KITAGAWA.

Osaka Prefectural Nakanoshima Library: 1-2-10 Nakanoshima, Kita-ku, Osaka 530-0005; tel. (6) 6203-0474; internet www.library.pref.osaka.jp; f. 1903; 545,000 vols; Head Librarian HIROKAZU OMOKI; publ. *Osaka Furitsu Tosyokan Kiyou* (1 a year).

Sapporo

Hokkaido University Library: Kita 8 Nishi 5, Kita-ku, Sapporo 060-0808; tel. (11) 716-2111; e-mail service@lib.hokudai.ac.jp; internet www.lib.hokudai.ac.jp/index_e.html; f. 1876; 20 br. libraries; 3,688,129 vols (incl. 1,798,649 foreign language texts); spec. collns on Slavic studies and N Eurasian culture studies; Librarian Dr MASAAKI HEMMI; publ. *Yuin* (4 a year).

Sendai

Tohoku University Library: Kawauchi, Aoba-ku, Sendai 980-77; internet www.library.tohoku.ac.jp; f. 1911; 2,247,000 vols, incl. Kano Colln (108,000 vols) in Japanese and Chinese, the Tibetan Buddhist Canons (6,652 vols), Wundt Colln (15,800 vols) and several other special collns; Dir Prof. KEICHI NOE.

Shizuoka

Shizuoka Prefectural Central Library: 53–1 Yada, Shizuoka City; tel. (54) 262-1242; e-mail mailmaster@tosyokan.pref.shizuoka.jp; internet www.tosyokan.pref.shizuoka.jp; f. 1925; 430,000 vols, 7,500 periodicals, 4,000 films and videotapes; Librarian YOSHIHIKO SUZUKI; publs *Aoi* (1 a year), *Toshokan-Dayori* (6 a year).

Tenri

Tenri Central Library: 1050 Somanouchi, Tenri, Nara 632-8577; tel. (743) 63-9200; e-mail info@tcl.gr.jp; internet www.tcl.gr.jp; f. 1930; spec. libraries: Yorozuyo Library on Christian Missions (incl. Jesuit mission printings in Japan), Kogido Library of Africana Colln (6,000 items), Ito Jinsai on Confucian Studies, Wataya Library on Renga and Haikai Collns (20,000 items); 2m. vols (incl. 480,000 in foreign languages); Dir Prof. KEIICHIRO MOROI; publ. *Biblia* (2 a year, in Japanese).

Tokyo

Chuo University Library: 742-1 Higashi-nakano, Hachioji-shi, Tokyo 192-0393; tel. (4) 2674-2511; f. 1885; 2m. vols (577,826 in foreign languages), 14,561 periodicals; Librarian Prof. NOBUO YASUI.

Hitotsubashi University Library: Naka 2-1, Kunitachi City, Tokyo 186-8601; tel. (42) 580-8237; internet www.lib.hit-u.ac.jp; f. 1885; houses br. library for Institute of Economic Research; 2,243,867 vols (incl. 404,946 vols of Institute of Economic Research library), 16,508 periodicals; Dir YOSHIKI ENATSU; Dir K. ASAKO; Librarian SHINOBU MURAI.

Imperial Household Agency Library: 1–1 Chiyoda, Chiyoda-ku, Tokyo; tel. (3) 3213-1111; e-mail information@kunaicho.go.jp; f. 1948; 87,946 vols; Librarian Mr MOMOTA.

International Christian University Library: 10-2 Osawa 3-chome, Mitaka-shi, Tokyo 181-8585; tel. (422) 33-3301; e-mail library@icu.ac.jp; internet www-lib.icu.ac.jp; f. 1953; 765,241 vols; Dir TAMAMI HATA-KEYAMA (acting).

Japan Meteorological Agency Library: 1-3-4 Ote-machi, Chiyoda-ku, Tokyo 100-8122; e-mail jma-library@met.kishou.go.jp; f. 1875; 110,000 vols; Chief Librarian YOSHIO SHINOHARA.

Keio University Media Center: 2-15-45 Mita, Minato-ku, Tokyo 108; Chair. S. SUGIYAMA.

Kokugakuin University Library: 4-10-28 Higashi, Shibuya-ku, Tokyo; f. 1882; 1,087,663 vols; Librarian Prof. TOSHIO SAWA-NOBORI; publ. *Kokugakuin Daigaku Toshokan Kiyo* (Library Journal).

Kokuritsu Kobunshokan (National Archives): 3-2 Kitanomaru Park, Chiyoda-ku, Tokyo 102-0091; tel. (3) 3214-0621; internet www.archives.go.jp; f. 1971; attached to Cabinet office; archives, Cabinet Library of 480,000 vols, and govt records of 725,000 vols; Pres. MASAYA TAKAYAMA; publs *Archives* (3 a year), *Kitanomaru* (1 a year).

Kokuritsu Kyoiku Seisaku Kenkyujo, Kyoiku Kenkyu Joho Senta, Kyoiku Toshokan (Library of Education, Educational Resources Research Centre, National Institute for Educational Research of Japan): 3-2-2 Kasumigaseki, Chiyoda-ku, Tokyo 100-8951; tel. (3) 6733-6536; e-mail library@nier.go.jp; internet www.nier.go.jp/library; f. 1949; 500,000 vols; Chief Librarian HISAO SUNAOSHI; publ. *Kyoiku Kenkyu Ronbun Sakuin* (Education Index, 4 a year, online).

Ministry of Foreign Affairs Library: 2-2 Kasumigaseki, Chiyoda-ku, Tokyo 100; 90,638 vols and 175 periodicals; Librarian YOSHIMASA KIMURA.

Ministry of Justice Library: 1-1, 1-chome, Kasumigaseki, Chiyoda-ku, Tokyo 100-8977; f. 1928; attached to Nat. Diet Library; 310,000 vols; Chief Librarian Y. MATSUMOTO.

National Diet Library: 1-10-1 Nagatacho, Chiyoda-ku, Tokyo 100-8924; tel. (3) 3581-2331; e-mail kokusai@ndl.go.jp; internet www.ndl.go.jp; f. 1948; deposit library for Japanese publs and publs of the UN, UNESCO, ILO, WHO, ICAO, WTO; IFLA PAC centre for Asia, ISSN centre for Japan, Japanese Nat. Agency for ISIL (the Int. Standard Identifier for Libraries and Related Orgs); 1 bureau and 5 depts: research and legislative reference bureau, admin., acquisitions and bibliography, reader services and collns, digital information, Kansai-kan and ILCL; consists of main library, detached library in the Diet, int. library of children's literature, Toyo Bunko (Oriental) Library and 27 br. libraries in the exec. and judicial agencies of the govt; 39,430,946 vols, 10,096,114 books, 546,379 maps, 681,338 recorded materials, 9,120,195 items of microform, 112,228 optical discs, 571,266 Japanese doctoral dissertations, 350,905 MSS, 15,407,485 serial subscriptions (periodicals and newspapers); Librarian NORITADA OTAKI; publs *Books on Japan* (4 a year, in English, online), *Current Awareness* (in Japanese and English, online and print).

National Institute of Japanese Literature Library: Midorityou 10-3, Tachikawa Tokyo 190-0014; tel. (50) 553-32926; e-mail service@nijl.ac.jp; internet www.nijl.ac.jp; f. 1972; 188,397 vols; microforms of woodcuts, old printed books and MSS; 46,434 reels of microfilm, 57,358 sheets of microfiche, 74,362 vols of paper copy, 6,773 titles of serials; archives for Japanese historical documents: 500,000 items; Dir N. YAMASHITA.

Norin Suisansho Toshokan: (Ministry of Agriculture, Forestry and Fisheries Library): 1-2-1, Kasumigaseki, Chiyoda-ku, Tokyo 100-8950; tel. (3) 3910-3978; e-mail ref-primaff@ml.affrc.go.jp; f. 1948; 275,000 vols; Librarian TATEKI ARAI; publs *Norin Suisan Tosho Shiryo Geppo* (12 a year, review of publs on agriculture, forestry and fisheries), *Norin Suisan Bunken Kaidai* (1 a year, annotated bibliography).

Ochanomizu University Library: 1-1 Otsuka 2-chome, Bunkyo-ku, Tokyo 112-8610; tel. (3) 5978-5839; e-mail lib-ref@cc.ocha.ac.jp; internet www.lib.ocha.ac.jp; f. 1874, reorganized 1949; 710,000 vols; Dir Prof. Dr KEIKO TAKANO.

Science Council of Japan Library: 22-34, Roppongi 7-chome, Minato-ku, Tokyo 106; tel. (3) 3403-6291; internet www.scj.go.jp; f. 1949; 54,000 vols; Librarian MASATO OKA-MOTO.

Seikado Bunko Library and Art Museum: 2-23-1 Okamoto, Setagaya-ku, Tokyo; tel. (3) 3700-0007; internet www.seikado.or.jp; 200,000 vols of Chinese and Japanese classics; Librarian MAKO NARI-SAWA.

Sophia (Jôchi) University Library: 7-1 Kioi-cho, Chiyoda-ku, Tokyo 102-8554; tel. (3) 3238-3511; f. 1913; 920,000 vols, 10,500 periodicals; Librarian MIKITO HAYASHI.

Statistical Library, Statistics Bureau, Management and Coordination Agency: 19-1, Wakamatsu-cho, Shimjuku-ku, Tokyo 162; tel. (3) 3202-1111; internet www.stat.go.jp; f. 1946; 400,000 vols; Librarian KENJI OKADA; publs numerous reports, statistical handbooks.

Supreme Court Library: 4-2 Hayabusa-cho, Chiyoda-ku, Tokyo 102-8651; f. 1949; 260,000 vols; Librarian M. UEMURA.

Tokyo Geijutsu Daigaku Toshokan (Tokyo University of the Arts Library): Ueno Park 12-8, Taito-ku, Tokyo 110-8714; tel. (50) 5525-2420; internet www.lib.geidai.ac.jp; f. 1887; over 330,699 vols, 1,378 microfilms, 3,704 microfiches; also music and audiovisual collns (57,765 scores, 10,235 records, 8,349 CDs, 2,289 video recordings); Dir KINYA OSUMI.

Tokyo Metropolitan Central Library: 5-7-13 Minami-Azabu, Minato-ku, Tokyo 106-8575; tel. (3) 3442-8451; internet www.library.metro.tokyo.jp; f. 1972; research and reference centre, centre of library co-operation in Tokyo; 1,471,000 vols and 10,000 periodicals; Morohashi Colln (Chinese classics), Sanetoh Colln (Chinese literature), Yedo Colln, Kaga Colln (rare books of the Yedo Era) and others; Dir TETSUYA SAITO; publs *Hibiya*, *Library Science Bulletin* (1 a year).

Tokyo University of Foreign Studies Library: 3-11-1 Asahicho, Fuchu-shi, Tokyo 183-8534; tel. (42) 330-5193; e-mail www-lib@tufs.ac.jp; internet www.tufs.ac.jp/common/library/index-e.html; f. 1899; 817,360 vols (incl. 440,673 foreign); Dir H. KURIHARA.

Tokyo University of Marine Science and Technology Library: Konan 4-5-7, Minato-ku, Tokyo 108-8477; tel. (3) 5463-0444; e-mail to-joho@s.kaiyodai.ac.jp; internet lib.s.kaiyodai.ac.jp; f. 1888; 296,000 vols (including 74,000 foreign); Chief Librarian HIROSHI OKADA; publ. *Journal* (1 a year).

Toyo Bunko (Oriental Library): Honkomagome 2-28-21, Bunkyo-ku, Tokyo 113-0021; tel. (3) 3942-0121; e-mail webmaster@

toyo-bunko.or.jp; internet www.toyo-bunko.or.jp; f. 1924; 898,542 vols; research library specializing in Asian studies; spec. collns: Iwasaki colln of old and rare Japanese and Chinese books and MSS, Kawaguchi colln of Tibetan and Buddhist classics, Morrison colln of Western books on Asia; Dir YOSHINOBU SHIBA; publs *Toyo Gakuho* (4 a year), *Memoirs of the Research Department of the Toyo Bunko* (1 a year, jt publ. with National Diet Library).

University of Tokyo Library System: Hongo 7-3-1, Bunkyo-ku, Tokyo 113-0033; tel. (3) 5841-2612; e-mail kikaku@lib.u-tokyo.ac.jp; internet www.lib.u-tokyo.ac.jp; f. 1877; general library, Komaba library, Kashiwa library and 52 faculty and institute libraries; 9,030,000 vols incl. Nanki colln (96,000 vols) and several other spec. collns; Dir M. FURUTA; publ. *Bulletin*.

Waseda University Library: 1-6-1 Nishiwaseda, Shinjuku-ku, Tokyo 169-8050; e-mail info@wul.waseda.ac.jp; internet www.wul.waseda.ac.jp; f. 1882; 5,624,351 vols; Dir SHOZO IIJIMA.

Toyonaka

Osaka University Library: 1-4, Machikaneyama-cho, Toyonaka, Osaka 560-0043; tel. (6) 6850-5045; e-mail db-inq@brary.osaka-u.ac.jp; internet www.library.osaka-u.ac.jp; f. 1931; 3,050,000 vols; main library and 2 br. libraries; Dir MINORU KAWAKITA.

Utsunomiya

Tochigi Prefectural Library: 1-2-23 Hanawada, Utsunomiya, Tochigi 320-0027; tel. (28) 622-5111; e-mail tochilib@lib.pref.tochigi.jp; internet www.lib.pref.tochigi.jp; 196,579 vols; Librarian T. IZUMI.

Yamaguchi

Yamaguchi Prefectural Library: 150–1 Matsue, Ushirogawa, Yamaguchi City 753-0083; tel. (3) 924-2111; internet library.pref.yamaguchi.lg.jp; f. 1903; 389,104 vols; Librarian TANAKA HIROSHI; publ. *Toshokan Yamaguchi*.

Yamaguchi University Library: 1667-1 Yoshida, Yamaguchi-shi, Yamaguchi 753-8511; tel. (3) 933-5177; e-mail li313@yamaguchi-u.ac.jp; f. 1949; 2 br. libraries; 1,552,323 vols, 29,501 periodicals.

Yokohama

Kanagawa Prefectural Library: 9-2 Momijigaoka, Nishi-ku, Yokohama City; f. 1954; 76 mems; 540,875 vols; Librarian M. ANDO; publ. *Kanagawa Bunka* (6 a year).

Yokohama National University Library: 79-6 Tokiwadai, Hodogayaku, Yokohama 240-8501; tel. (45) 339-3217; e-mail libref@ynu.ac.jp; internet www.lib.ynu.ac.jp/english/index.html; f. 1949; 1,401,234 vols; Dir Prof. YASUNORI FUKAGAI; Librarian M. YOSHINO.

Museums and Art Galleries

Abashiri

Abashiri Kyodo Hakubutsukan (Abashiri Municipal Museum): Katsuramachi 1-1-3, Abashiri-shi, Hokkaido 093-0041; tel. (152) 43-3090; f. 1936; 600 local products, 25,000 articles of historical, geographical and archaeological interest, and 1,800 ethnological objects; Dir HIDEAKI WADA.

Atami

MOA Museum of Art: 26-2, Momoyama, Atami 413-8511; tel. (557) 84-2511; internet www.moaart.or.jp; f. 1957, reorganized 1982 by Mokichi Okada Asscn; Japanese and Oriental fine arts: paintings, ceramics, lacquers, calligraphy and sculptures; library of 25,000 vols; Dir YOJI YOSHIOKA; publs *Digest Catalogue*, *MOA Museum Members Club* (4 a year), *Selected Catalogue* (5 vols).

Gora

Hakone Museum of Art: 1300 Gora, Kanagawa Pref.; tel. (460) 2-2623; internet www.moaart.or.jp/english/hakone; f. 1952; private collection of Japanese ceramic works of art belonging to Okada Mokichi; Dir YOJI YOSHIOKA (Director of MOA Foundation).

Hakodate

Hakodate City Museum: 21-7 Suehiro-cho, Hakodate City; tel. (138) 22-4128; f. 1879; oldest local museum in Japan; Dir M. ISHIKAWA.

Hiraizumi

Chuson-ji Sanko-zo (Chuson-ji Temple Sanko Repository): Hiraizumi-machi, Nishi-Iwai-gun; internet www.chusonji.or.jp; f. 1955 to preserve treasures and possessions of the Fujiwara family who were important in the late Heian period (801–1185).

Hiroshima

Hiroshima Children's Museum: 5-83, Moto-machi, Naka-ku, Hiroshima City 730; tel. (82) 222-5346; e-mail riyou-annai@pyonta.city.hiroshima.jp; internet www.pyonta.city.hiroshima.jp; f. 1980; scientific and cultural programmes; planetarium; exhibits on science, transport, astronomy; Dir HIROSHI OKIMOTO; publs *Kagakukan Dayori* (12 a year), *Planetarium* (4 a year).

Ikaruga

Hōryūji (Hōryūji Temple): Aza Hōryūji, Ikaruga-cho, Ikoma-gun, Nara Prefecture; a large number of Buddhist images and paintings; the buildings date from the Asuka, Nara, Heian, Kamakura, Ashikaga and Tokugawa periods.

Ise

Jingu Chokokan (Jingu Historical Museum): 1754-1 Koda-kushimoto, Ise City, Mie 516-0016; tel. (596) 22-1700; internet www.isejingu.or.jp/museum; 1,734 exhibits, incl. treasures of the Grand Shrine of Ise (Naiku Shrine and Geku Shrine) and many objects of historical interest; library of 1,082 vols, MSS and pictures; Dir and Chief of Cultural Section of the Grand Shrine of Ise KUNIO KOHORI.

Jingu Nogyokan (Agricultural Museum): 1754-1 Koda-kushimoto-cho, Ise, Mie 516-0016; tel. (596) 22-1700; internet www.isejingu.or.jp/museum; f. 1905; 9,583 exhibits connected with agriculture, forestry and fishing (incl. colln of over 40 species of shark); Dir KUNIO KOHORI.

Itsukushima

Itsukushima Jinja Homotsukan (Treasure Hall of the Itsukushima Shinto Shrine): Miyajima-cho, Saeki-gun; f. 1934; 4,000 exhibits of paintings, calligraphy, sutras, swords, and other ancient weapons; Curator and Chief Priest MOTOYOSHI NOZAKA.

Kamakura

Kamakura Kokuhokan (Kamakura Museum): 2-1-1 Yukinoshita, Kamakura City, Kanawaga; tel. (467) 22-0753; internet www.city.kamakura.kanagawa.jp/kokuhoukan/index.htm; f. 1928; Japanese art and history in the Middle Ages; 3,521 valuable specimens of Japanese fine arts; 12 mems; library of 6,587 vols; Dir TATSUTO NUKI; publ. *Kokuhokan-zuroku*.

Museum of Modern Art, Kamakura: 2-1-53 Yukinoshita, Kamakura, Kanagawa 248-0005; tel. (467) 22-5000; e-mail kamakura_hayama@moma.pref.kanagawa.jp; internet ww.moma.pref.kanagawa.jp; f. 1951; modern and contemporary art in Japan and Europe; Dir TADAYASU SAKAI.

Kobe

Hakutsuru Bijitsukan (Hakutsuru Fine Art Museum): 6-1-1 Sumiyoshiyamate, Higashinada-ku, Kobe 658-0063; tel. (78) 851-6001; f. 1934; 1,300 specimens of fine art, incl. noted Chinese ceramics, old bronze vases and silverware, and oriental carpets; library of 10,000 vols; Dir HIDEO KANO.

Kobe City Museum: 24 Kyo-machi, Chuo-ku, Kobe 650-0034; tel. (78) 391-0035; internet www.city.kobe.jp/cityoffice/57/museum; f. 1982; theme of museum is the historical view of international cultural intercourse, especially contact between Eastern and Western cultures; 38,000 items including 21 national treasure items, important collections of Namban and Kohmoh arts, 17th–19th-century maps, also historical and archaeological items; library of 55,000 vols; Sec.-Gen. KAZUO KOBAYASHI; publs *Yearbook*, *Museum Tayori* (newsletter, 3 a year), *Bulletin* (1 a year).

Kochi

Kochi Kaitokukan (Kochi Castle): 1-2-1 Marunouchi, 780-0850 Kochi City, Kochi Prefecture; tel. (888) 24-5701; internet www.pref.kochi.jp/~kochijo; f. 1913; 800 exhibits, including autographs and material of interest in Japanese historical research; Dir YUTAKA KONDO.

Kotohira

Kotohira-gü Hakubutsukan (Museum in the Kotohira Shrine): Kotohira-gü Shrine, Kotohira-machi, Nakatado-gun; 3,011 exhibits; Chair. MITSUSHIGE KOTOOKA; Sec. HAZIME HIRAO KOTOHIRA.

Kumamoto

Kumamoto Arts and Crafts Museum: 3–35 Chibajo-machi, Kumamoto City 860-0001; tel. (96) 324-4930; f. 1982; traditional arts and crafts; 3,000 ancient and contemporary items.

Kurashiki

Ohara Bijutsukan (Ohara Museum of Art): 1-1-15 Chuo, Kurashiki City; tel. (86) 422-0005; e-mail info@ohara.or.jp; internet www.ohara.or.jp; f. 1930; westernpaintings since the 19th century and contemporary arts; modern Japanese ceramics and fabrics; modern Japanese oil paintings; Asiatic art; artwork from Ancient Egypt and Medieval Islam; contemporary art; Dir SHUJI TAKASHINA.

Kushiro

Kushiro-shiritsu Hakubutsukan (Kushiro City Museum): Harutori Park 1-7, Shunkodai, Kushiro; tel. (154) 41-5809; e-mail ku7011@city.kushiro.hokkaido.jp; internet www.city.kushiro.hokkaido.jp; f. 1936; 12,130 earthenware articles, natural history museum; Dir FUMIO NISHIYAMA; publs *Memoirs of the Kushiro City Museum* (1 a year), *Science Report of the Kushiro City Museum* (4 a year).

Kyoto

Chishakuin (Treasure Hall of the Chishakuin Temple): 964 Higashi-Kawaramachi, Higashiyama-ku, Kyoto; tel. (75) 541-5361; Buddhist equipment and utensils, old documents, paintings, calligraphy, sutras, and books in Japanese and in Chinese.

Daigoji Reihokan (Treasure Hall of the Daigoji Temple): Daigo, Fushimi-ku, Kyoto; tel. (75) 571-0002; f. 1936; contains 1,500 old art objects and 120,000 historical documents relating chiefly to Buddhism.

Jishoji (Ginkakuji) (Silver Temple): Ginkakuji-cho, Sakyo-ku, Kyoto; f. 1482 by Yoshimasa, eighth Shogun of Ashikaga, as 12 separate bldgs in the grounds of his villa; only the Ginkaku or Silver Hall, and the Togudo are now left; Curator R. ARIMA.

Kitano Temmangu Homotsuden (Treasure Hall of Kitano-Temmangu shrine): Kitano Bakuro-cho, Kamigyo-ku, Kyoto; tel. (75) 461-0005; internet www.kitanotenmangu.or.jp; shrine dedicated to Michizane Sugawara, statesman and great scholar of Heian period; exhibits of treasure hall include the 'Kitano-Tenjin' history picture scrolls and an ancient copy of the 'Nihon Shoki'.

Korūji Reihōden (Treasure Museum of the Koryuji Temple): Koryuji Temple, Uzumasa, Ukyo-ku, Kyoto; f. 1922; many Buddhist images and pictures, including the two images of 'Miroku Bosatsu'; Curator EIKO KIYOTAKI.

Kyoto Kokuritsu Hakubutsukan (Kyoto National Museum): 527 Chaya-cho, Higashiyama-ku, Kyoto; tel. (75) 541-1151; e-mail welcome@kyohaku.go.jp; internet www.kyohaku.go.jp; f. 1897 as Imperial Museum of Kyoto; collects, preserves, manages and displays cultural properties from Heian to Edo period; research and educational programmes; library of 52,692 vols, 188,528 research photographs, 11,513 exhibits; Dir Dr JOHEI SASAKI; Chief Curator RYU MURAKAMI; publs *Bulletin* (Research journal, 1 a year, in Japanese), *Ueno Memorial Foundation for the Study of Buddhist Art* (1 a year, in Japanese).

Kyoto-shi Bijutsukan (Kyoto Municipal Museum of Art): Okazaki Park, Sakyo-ku, Kyoto 606-8344; tel. (75) 771-4107; internet www.city.kyoto.jp/bunshi/kmma; f. 1933; contemporary fine art objects (mostly Japanese); Dir MITSUGI UEHIRA.

Myōhōin (Treasure House of the Myōhōin Temple): Myohoin-maegawa-cho, Higashiyama-ku, Kyoto; possessions of Toyotomi-Hideyoshi and many other national treasures.

National Museum of Modern Art, Kyoto: Enshoji-cho, Okazaki, Sakyo-ku, Kyoto; tel. (75) 761-4111; e-mail info@momak.go.jp; internet www.momak.go.jp; f. 1963; Nihonga (Japanese-style painting), Yōga (Western-style painting), prints, sculpture, crafts (ceramics, textiles, metalworks, wood and bamboo works, lacquers and jewellery), photography and modern art; Dir MASAAKI OZAKI; Chief Curator HIDETSUGU YAMANO; publs *Museum News* (6 a year), *Membership* (4 a year).

Ninnaji Reihóden (Treasure Hall of the Ninnaji Temple): Ninnaji Temple, Omuro Daimon-cho, Ukyo-ku, Kyoto.

Rengeoin (Sanjusangendo) (Treasure House of the Rengeoin Temple): Mawari-cho, Higashiyama-ku, Kyoto; 'One Thousand Images' and many other Buddhist images.

Rokuonji (Treasures of the Rokuonji Temple): Kinkakuji-cho, Kita-ku, Kyoto; famed for its garden and gold pavilion.

Shoren-in (Treasure House of the Shōren-in Temple): Sanjōbō-machi, Awadaguchi, Higashiyama-ku, Kyoto; internet www.shorenin.com; f. 1153; Dir JIKO HIGASHIFUSHIMI; library of 5,000 vols; rare books, writings, paintings, etc.

Taiten Kinen Kyoto Shokubutsuen (Kyoto Prefectural Museum Botanical Garden): Hangi-cho, Shimogamo, Sakyô-ku, Kyoto 606-0823; tel. (75) 701-0141; 120,000 plants and 5,500 botanical specimens.

Toyokuni Jinja Hómotsuden (Treasure Hall of the Toyokuni Shrine): Shomen Chaya-machi Yamato-Ooji, Higashiyama-ku, Kyoto; treasures and possessions of Toyotomi-Hideyoshi, incl. paintings, painted screens, swords, etc.

Yogen-In (Treasure Hall of the Yōgen-In Temple): Sanju-sangendō-mae, Yamato-ōji Shichijō Higashi Iru, Higashiyama-ku, Kyoto.

Yūrinkan (Yurinkan Collection): 44 Okazaki-Enshōjichyô, Sakyō-ku, Kyoto 606-8344; tel. (75) 761-0638; f. 1926; privately owned by the Fujii Foundation; rare antique Chinese fine arts and curios, incl. bronze and jade ware, porcelain, seals, Buddhist images, pictures, and calligraphy; Dir Z. FUJII.

Matsue

Koizumi-Yakumo Kinenkan (Lafcadio Hearn Memorial Museum): 322 Okudani-machi, Matsue City 690-0872; tel. (852) 21-2147; f. 1933; collection of items belonging to Lafcadio Hearn; library of 492 vols (works by and on Hearn); Dir TOSHIO UCHIDA.

Shimane Prefectural Museum: 1 Tono-machi, Matsue City; tel. (852) 22-6727; e-mail kodai@izm.ed.jp; internet www2.pref.shimane.jp/kodai; f. 1959; bronze bells, bronze swords and other ancient heritage; Dir SYO KATSUBE; publs *Ancient Culture in Shimane* (1 a year), *News of the Institution for Ancient Study* (4 a year), *Studies of Ancient Culture* (1 a year).

Matsumoto

Matsumoto City Museum: 4-1 Marunouchi, Matsumoto City, Nagano 390-0873; tel. (263) 32-0133; e-mail mcmuse@city.matsumoto.nagano.jp; internet www.city.matsumoto.nagano.jp; f. 1906; folklore, history, archaeology, star festival dolls, popular belief tools, fine art, agricultural tools; Dir KENICHI KUMAGAI.

Minobu

Minobusan Homotsukan (Treasury of the Kuonji Temple): Kuonji Temple, Minobu-machi, Minami-Koma-gun; 300 articles, examples of the fine arts, and materials connected with the history of the Nichiren Sect of Buddhism, the biography of Saint Nichiren.

Mount Koya

Kōyasan Reihōkan (Museum of Buddhist Art on Mount Kōya): Kōyasan, Kōya-cho, Ito-gun; f. 1921; 50,000 exhibits, incl. Buddhist paintings and images, sutras and old documents, some of them registered National Treasures and Important Cultural Properties; a centre of Buddhism in Japan; Dir CHIKYŌ YAMAMOTO.

Nagoya

Nagoya Castle Donjon: 1-1 Hon-maru, Naka-ku, Nagoya; tel. (52) 231-1700; built in 1612 by Ieyasu Tokugawa; destroyed by fire 1945; restored to its original form 1959; exhibition rooms, galleries and observatory; 1,049 paintings of the Kano school on sliding doors and ceilings; armoury and swords.

Nara

Kasugataisha Homotsuden (Treasure Hall of the Kasugataisha Shrine): Kasugataisha Shrine, 160 Kasugano-cho, Nara City; f. 1934; the ancient, curvilinear style of architecture is called 'Kasuga Zukuri' after this shrine; Shrine Master CHIKATADA KASANNOIN.

Museum Yamato Bunkakan: 1-11-6 Gakuen-minami, Nara; tel. (742) 45-0544; internet www.kintetsu.jp/kouhou/yamato; f. 1960; art objects of East Asia, chiefly Japan, China and Korea; library of 20,000 vols; Dir Prof. SHUGO ASANO; publs *Yamato Bunka* (2 a year), *Catalogues of the Museum Collection* (in English), *Bi-no-Tayori* (4 a year).

Nara National Museum: 50 Nobori-oji-cho, Nara-shi 630-8213; tel. (742) 22-7771; internet www.narahaku.go.jp; f. 1895; Buddhist sculptures, paintings, applied arts, calligraphy, archaeological objects, etc.; also special exhibitions; library of 59,750 vols; Dir KENICHI YUYAMA.

Neiraku Museum: Isuien Park, 74 Suimon-cho, Nara City; tel. (742) 25-0781; f. 1939; ancient Chinese bronze mirrors, seals, etc., and Korean potteries; Dir KIKUKO NAKAMURA.

Todaiji: 406-1 Zōshi-cho, Nara; tel. (742) 22-5511; f. 752; HQ of Kegonshū Buddhist sect; Daibutsuden: Main Hall of the Todaiji Temple, the largest wooden edifice in the world, the world-famous Great Image of Buddha and 2 Bodhisattvas; attached bldgs are the Hokkedō, Kaidan-in, Nigatsudō, which contain many famous images of Buddha and Bodhisattva; library of 70,000 vols, 10,000 MSS; Dir K. KITAKAWARA; publ. *Nanto Bukkyō: Journal of the Nanto Society for Buddhist Studies* (1 a year).

Yakushiji (Yakushiji Temple): 457 Nishi-no-Kyō-machi, Nara City 630-8563; tel. (742) 33-6001; e-mail yksj8@mahoroba.or.jp; internet www.nara-yakushiji.com; f. 697; famous bronze images of the Yakushi Trinity; a pagoda 1,300 years old; Dir Lord Abbot S. MATSUKUBO.

Narita

Naritasan Reikokan Museum (Treasure Hall of the Naritasan-Shinshoji Temple): Narita Park, Narita City, Chiba Pref. 286-0023; tel. (476) 22-2111; internet www.naritasan.or.jp; f. 1947; contains treasures dedicated to the shrine and archaeological pieces from the region, 12,113 MSS and books, sculptures, botanical specimens; Curator SHOSEKI TSURUMI.

Omishima

Oyamazumi Jinja Kokuhokan (Treasure Hall of the Oyamazumi Shrine): Oyamazumi Shrine, Omishima Town, Ochigun; f. AD 1; 2,000 exhibits, incl. a large colln of ancient armour, swords, and the oldest mirrors in Japan; library of 20,000 vols; Curator YASUHISA MISHIMA.

Osaka

National Museum of Ethnology: 10-1 Senri Expo Park, Suita, Osaka 565-8511; tel. (6) 6876-2151; internet www.minpaku.ac.jp; f. 1974; 256,436 artefacts from Japan and abroad; conducts anthropological research and promotes general understanding and awareness of peoples, socs and cultures around the world; established as Inter-Univ. Research Institute; library of 643,925 vols, 16,635 journals, 70,456 audiovisual items; Dir-Gen. KEN'ICHI SUDO; publs *Bulletin* (in Japanese, English, French, Spanish, Russian, Chinese and German, 4 a year), *Minpaku Anthropology Newsletter* (2 a year, in English), *Senri Ethnological Reports* (irregular), *Senri Ethnological Studies* (in English and selected other European languages, irregular).

Osaka Municipal Museum of Art: 1–82 Chausuyama-cho, Tennoji-ku, Osaka 543-0063; tel. (6) 6771-4874; internet www.city.osaka.jp/museum-art; f. 1936; Chinese, Korean and Japanese fine art; library of 11,000 vols; Dir YUTAKA MINO; publ. *Miotsukushi* (Bulletin, 2 a year).

Osaka Museum of Natural History: Nagai Park, Higashisumiyoshi-ku, Osaka 546-0034; tel. (6) 6697-6221; internet www.mus-nh.city.osaka.jp; f. 1952; botany, entomology, geology, palaeontology and zoology; Dir TAKAYOSHI NASU; Head Curator MOTOHARU OKAMOTO; publs *Bulletin*, *Nature Study*, *Occasional Paper* (1 a year), *Special Publications* (1 a year).

Tenri

Tenri University Sankokan Museum: 250 Morimedo-cho, Tenri City, Nara Prefecture 632-8540; tel. (743) 63-8414; internet www.sankokan.jp; f. 1930; attached to Tenri Univ.; ethnographic and archaeological items from all parts of the world.

Tokyo

Ancient Orient Museum: 1–4 Higashi Ikebukuro 3-chome, Toshima-ku, Tokyo 170-8630; tel. (3) 3989-3491; e-mail museum@orientmuseum.com; internet www.sa.il24.net; f. 1978; archaeology and art history of Middle and Near East, Egypt, India and Central Asia; library of 19,000 vols; Dir Dr ICHIRO NAKATA; Curator K. ISHIDA; publ. *Bulletin of the Ancient Orient Museum* (1 a year).

Bridgestone Museum of Art, Ishibashi Foundation: 10-1, Kyobashi 1-chome, Chuo-ku, Tokyo 104-0031; tel. (3) 3563-0241; f. 1952 by Shojiro Ishibashi; private museum of 19th- and 20th-century European paintings and modern Japanese Western-style paintings; Dir NORIO SHIMADA.

Gotoh Museum: 9–25 3-chome Kaminoge, Setagaya-ku, Tokyo; tel. (3) 3703-0662; internet www.gotoh-museum.or.jp; f. 1960; Japanese, Chinese and Korean art; c. 5,000 exhibits, incl. the 'Tales of Genji' scroll and the 'Diary of Lady Murasaki' scroll; Curator FUKUSHIMA OSAMU.

Inokashira Onshi Koen Shizen Bunkaen (Natural Science Park in Inokashira Park): 1-17-6 Gotenyama, Musashinoshi, Tokyo; zoo, botanical garden, research room, marine biology room.

Kokuritsu Kagaku Hakubutsukan (National Museum of Nature and Science): 7-20 Ueno Park, Taito-ku, Tokyo 110-8718; tel. (3) 3822-0111; e-mail webmaster@kahaku.go.jp; internet www.kahaku.go.jp; f. 1877, merged with Research Institute for Natural Resources in 1971; exhibits of natural history, physical science and engineering; colln of over 4.0m. specimens; library of 112,062 vols; Dir SHINJI KONDO; publ. *Memoirs* (irregular).

Kotsu Hakubutsukan (Transportation Museum): 25 1-chome, Kanda-Sudacho, Chiyoda-ku, Tokyo; tel. (3) 3251-8481; e-mail gakugei@kouhaku.or.jp; internet www.kouhaku.or.jp; f. 1921; aircraft, electric equipment, locomotives, motor-cars, ships, etc.; Dir TATSUHIKO SUGA.

Meguro Parasitological Museum: 4-1-1 Shimomeguro, Meguro-ku, Tokyo 153-0064; tel. (3) 3716-1264; internet www.kiseichu.org; f. 1953; science of parasites; Dir KAZUO OGAWA.

Meiji Jingu Homotsuden (Meiji Shrine Treasure Museum): Yoyogi, Shibuya-ku, Tokyo; f. 1921; 102 treasures and possessions of Emperor Meiji and 74 objects belonging to Empress Shoken; there is also a Memorial Picture Gallery.

Mori Art Museum: 53rd Fl., Roppongi Hills, Mori Tower, 6-10-1 Roppongi, Minato-ku, Tokyo; tel. (3) 5777-8600; internet www.mori.art.museum; f. 2003; Dir FUMIO NANJO.

Museum of Contemporary Art, Tokyo: Metropolitan Kiba Park, 4-1-1 Miyoshi Koto-ku, Tokyo 135-0022; tel. (3) 5245-4111; internet www.mot-art-museum.jp; Japanese and foreign art since 1945.

National Museum of Modern Art, Tokyo: 3–1 Kitanomaru Koen, Chiyoda-ku, Tokyo 102-8322; tel. (3) 5777-8600; internet www.momat.go.jp; f. 1952; art museum and crafts gallery; colln of modern artworks, and related references dating from the beginning of the 20th century to present; art museum incls paintings, sculptures, prints, watercolours, drawings, photographs and other works; crafts gallery incls textiles, glass, lacquer, wood, bamboo and metalwork, dolls, industrial and graphic design; also nat. film centre holding films and non-film materials; Dir KAMOGAWA SACHIO; publs *Gendai no Me* (in Japanese, 6 a year), *National Film Center Newsletter* (in Japanese, 6 a year).

National Museum of Western Art: 7–7 Ueno Park, Taito-ku, Tokyo 110-0007; tel. (3) 5777-8600; e-mail wwwadmin@nmwa.go.jp; internet www.nmwa.go.jp; f. 1959 (bldg designed by Le Corbusier); 19th-century European paintings and sculptures collected by the late Kojiro Matsukata and new acquisitions of old masters; Dir Dr MASANORI AOYAGI.

Nezu Institute: 6-5-1 Minami-Aoyama Minato-ku, Tokyo 107-0062; tel. (3) 3400-2536; e-mail nezu@nezu-muse.or.jp; internet www.nezu-muse.or.jp; f. 1940; private colln by Nezu Kaichiro Sr. and donations of approx. 7,000 paintings, calligraphy, sculpture, swords, ceramics, lacquer-ware, archaeological exhibits; 7 items of nat. treasures, 87 items of cultural properties; Dir NEZU KOICHI; Chief Curator SHIRAHARA YUKIKO.

Nihon Mingeikan (Japan Folk Crafts Museum): 4-3-33 Komaba, Meguro-ku, Tokyo 153-0041; tel. (3) 3467-4527; internet www.mingeikan.or.jp; f. 1936; Japanese traditional folk craft and craft from around the world; spec. collns from founding mems of Mingei Movement: Soetsu Yanagi, Kanjiro Kawai, Shoji Hamada, Keisuke Serizawa, Bernard Leach, Shiko Munakata, Kenkichi Tomimoto and others; Dir NAOTO FUKASAWA; publ. *Mingei* (12 a year).

Okura Cultural Foundation Okura Shukokan Museum: 2-10-3, Toranomon, Minato-ku, Tokyo; f. 1917; 1,700 articles of fine arts; library of 36,000 vols of Chinese classics; Pres. NOBORU NISHITANI.

Shitamachi Museum: 2-1 Ueno Park, Taito-ku, Tokyo; tel. (3) 3823-7451; internet www.taitocity.net/taito/shitamachi; f. 1980; re-creation of the old commercial district of Tokyo; incl. typical street, wooden houses, life-size figures, furniture, pictures, books and letters, religious material, domestic utensils, Second World War items, games and musical instruments, cosmetics and accessories, etc.; Dir HIDENOBU HIROSE.

Shodo Hakubutsukan (Calligraphy Museum): 2-10-4 Negishi, Taito-ku, Tokyo 110-0003; tel. (3) 3872-2645; f. 1936; colln of the calligrapher, the late F. Nakamura; 1,000 rubbed copies of the stone tablets and 'hōjō', ancient texts of calligraphy (10,000 articles).

Tokyo Daigaku Rigaku Kenkyu-ka Fuzoku Shokubutsuen (Botanical Gardens, Graduate School of Science, University of Tokyo): 7-1, Hakusan 3, Bunkyo-ku, Tokyo 112; tel. (3) 3814-2625; f. 1684, transferred to Univ. 1877; Nikko br.; research in systematic botany and conservation of plants; 6,000 kinds of plants; 2,500 in Nikko; associated with the herbarium TI with approx. 700,000 specimens; library of 20,000 vols; Dir Prof. Dr JIN MURATA.

Tokyo Kokuritsu Hakubutsukan (Tokyo National Museum): 13-9 Ueno Park, Taito-ku, Tokyo 110-8712; tel. (3) 5405-8686; internet www.tnm.jp; f. 1872; largest museum in Japan; Japanese and E fine arts, incl. paintings, calligraphy, sculpture, metalwork, ceramic art, textiles, lacquer-ware, archaeological exhibits; Dir-Gen. MASAMI ZENIYA; publs *Museum* (12 a year), *Tokyo National Museum News* (12 a year).

Tokyo-to Bijutsukan (Tokyo Metropolitan Art Museum): 8-36 Ueno Park, Taito-ku, Tokyo; tel. (3) 3823-6921; e-mail tobi@tobikan.jp; internet www.tobikan.jp; f. 1926; ancient and modern art exhibition, educational service, art library and gallery for group exhibitions; closed from April 2010 to March 2012 for renovation; Dir YOSHITAKE MAMURO; Curator ATSUKO TAKEUCHI; publ. *Bulletin* (1 a year).

University Art Museum, Tokyo University of the Arts: Ueno Park, Taito-ku, Tokyo 110-8714; tel. (3) 5525-2200; internet www.geidai.ac.jp/museum; paintings, sculptures and applied art of Japan, China and Korea.

Waseda Daigaku Tsubouchi Hakase Kinen Engeki Hakubutsukan (Tsubouchi Memorial Theatre Museum, Waseda University): 1-6-1 Nishi-Waseda, Shinjuku-ku, Tokyo 169-8050; tel. (3) 5286-1829; e-mail enpaku@list.waseda.jp; internet www.waseda.jp/enpaku; f. 1928; library of 200,000 vols, 46,700 woodblock colour prints and 343,000 pictures; Dir MIKIO TAKEMOTO; publs *Studies in Dramatic Art*, *Theatre Museum*.

Yasukuni Jinja: Kudan Kita, 3-1-1, Chiyoda-ku, Tokyo 102-8246; tel. (3) 3261-8326; internet www.yasukuni.or.jp; f. 1869; nat. shrine dedicated to the war dead; museum displays items from wars fought by Japan since the establishment of the shrine.

Ueno

Iga-ryu Ninja Museum: 117-13-1 Ueno-marunouchi, Iga City, Mie Prefecture; tel. (595) 23-0311; e-mail ninpaku@ict.ne.jp; internet www.iganinja.jp; history and exhibits on Ninjas, spies who played an important role during periods of civil war in medieval Japan.

Yokohama

Kanagawa Prefectural Kanazawa Bunko Museum: 142 Kanazawa-cho, Kanazawa-ku, Yokohama; tel. (45) 701-9069; internet www.planet.pref.kanagawa.jp/city/kanazawa.htm; f. 1972; nat. treasures (figure of Hojo-Sanetoki, etc.); library: f. 1275; 20,000 old books and 4,149 documents; Curator MAKOTO NAGAMURA.

National Universities

AICHI PREFECTURAL UNIVERSITY

1522-3 Ibaragabasama, Kumabari, Nagakute-cho, Aichi-gun, Aichi 480-1198

Telephone: (561) 64-1111

E-mail: jim@bur.aichi-pu.ac.jp

Internet: www.aichi-pu.ac.jp

Founded 1947

Pres.: MASAO MORI

Library of 450,000 vols

PROFESSORS

Faculty of Foreign Studies:

HAYAMIZU, Y., Department of French Studies

HIOKI, M., Department of German Studies

KICHISE, S., Department of British and American Studies
KURAHASHI, M., Department of Chinese Studies
SHIGA, I., Department of Spanish and Latin American Studies

Faculty of Information Science and Technology:
HANDA, N., Department of Applied Information Science and Technology
SAKURAI, K., Department of Information Systems

Faculty of Letters:
KAWAGUCHI, A., Department of Childhood Education
KOTANI, S., Department of Japanese Language and Letters
SHIMIZU, K., Department of Social Welfare
TOUYAMA, I., Department of English
YAMADA, M., Department of Japanese History and Culture

ASAHIKAWA MEDICAL UNIVERSITY

2-1-1-1 Midorigaokahigashi, Asahikawa 078-8510
Telephone: (166) 65-2111
E-mail: somu-koho@jimu.asahikawa-med.ac.jp
Internet: www.asahikawa-med.ac.jp
Founded 1973
Independent (National University Corporation)
Academic year: April to March
Pres.: AKITOSHI YOSHIDA
Exec. Dir: TADAHIRO SASAJIMA
Exec. Dir: TAKEO MATSUNO
Exec. Sec.-Gen.: SUSUMU KUBO
Library Dir: HITOSHI FUJIO
Library of 139,000 vols
Number of teachers: 263
Number of students: 953 (845 undergraduate, 108 postgraduate)
Publication: *Asahikawa Medical University* (1 a year)

BUNKYO UNIVERSITY

3-2-17 Hatanodai, Shinagawa-ku, Tokyo 142-0064
Telephone: (3) 3783-5511
E-mail: iec@stf.bunkyo.ac.jp
Internet: www.bunkyo.ac.jp
Founded 1927
Faculties of culture, education, human science, information and communications, international studies, language and literature
Pres.: TSUNEYOSHI ISHIDA
Library of 546,000 vols
Number of teachers: 226
Number of students: 8,649

CHIBA UNIVERSITY

1-33 Yayoi-cho, Inage-ku, Chiba-shi, Chiba 263-8522
Telephone: (43) 251-1111
E-mail: kokusai@office.chiba-u.jp
Internet: www.chiba-u.jp
Founded 1949
State control
Languages of instruction: English, Japanese
Academic year: April to March
Pres.: Prof. YASUSHI SAITO
Vice-Pres. for Education and Student Affairs: Prof. SEIJI NAGASAWA
Vice-Pres. for General Affairs: TERUSHI IKEDA
Vice-Pres. for Planning Affairs: Prof. KEIJI YAMAMOTO
Vice-Pres. for Planning and Human Resources: Prof. ITARU SHIMAZU
Vice-Pres. for Research and Int. Affairs: Prof. TAKESHI TOKUHISA
Library Dir: Prof. HIROYA TAKEUCHI
Library of 1,395,415 vols
Number of teachers: 1,202
Number of students: 15,032

Publications: *Bulletin of the Faculty of Education* (1 a year), *Chiba University Social Sciences and Humanities* (1 a year), *Economics Journal* (4 a year), *HortResearch* (1 a year), *International Research and Education* (1 a year, in Japanese), *Journal of Humanities* (1 a year), *Journal of Law and Politics* (4 a year), *Journal on Public Affairs* (1 a year), *Journal of the School of Nursing* (1 a year), *Laboratory Waste Treatment Plant Bulletin* (1 a year), *Marine Biosystems Research* (1 a year), *Outline of the Research Centre for Pathogenic Fungi and Microbial Toxicoses* (every 2 years), *Record of Research Activities of the Faculty of Pharmaceutical Science*, *Research Activities and Interests of the Faculty of Engineering* (2 a year), *Research Report of the Centre for Co-operative Research*, *Studies on Humanities and Social Sciences of Chiba University* (2 a year, in Japanese), *Technical Bulletin of the Faculty of Horticulture* (1 a year), *Technical Reports of Mathematical Sciences* (1 a year), *The Outline of the Chemical Analysis Center*

DEANS

Faculty of Education: Prof. FUMIO TAKIZAWA
Faculty of Engineering: Prof. AKIHIDE KITAMURA
Faculty of Horticulture: Prof. TAKATO KOBA
Faculty of Law and Economics: Prof. SHOICHI OGANO
Faculty of Letters: Prof. MASARU YAMADA
Faculty of Pharmaceutical Sciences: Prof. YASUSHI ARANO
Faculty of Science: Prof. KAZUYO OHASHI
Graduate School of Advanced Integration Science: Prof. SHOJI TOMINAGA
Graduate School of Humanities and Social Sciences: Prof. HIROSHI NAKAGAWA
Graduate School of Medical and Pharmaceutical Sciences: Prof. TOMOKO YAMAMOTO
Law School: Prof. TSUTOMU YASUMURA
School of Medicine: Prof. HARUAKI NAKAYA
School of Nursing: Prof. HARUE MASAKI

PROFESSORS

Centre for Environment, Health and Field Sciences (6-2-1 Kashiwanoha, Kawashi-shi, Chiba 277-0882; tel. (4) 7137-8000):
IKEGAMI, F., Chemical, Biochemical and Pharmacological studies of Plant Secondary Metabolites used for Medical Purposes
MIYAZAKI, Y., Nature Therapy, Health Sciences

Centre for Environmental Remote Sensing (tel. (43) 290-3832; internet www.cr.chiba-u.jp):
MIWA, T., Dept of Geoinformation Analysis
NISHIO, H., Dept of Database Research
SUGIMORI, Y., Dept of Geoinformation Analysis
TAKAMURA, T., Dept of Sensor and Atmospheric Radiation
TAKEUCHI, N., Dept of Sensor and Atmospheric Radiation

Centre for Language Education:
DOI, M., Applied Linguistics, English Language Education, CALL (Computer-Assisted Language Learning)
HASHIMOTO, Y., Chinese Language
HONG, J., Chinese Language
IZUMI, T., French Language
KUBOTA, M., Linguistics
OHYAMA, K., English Language
SEINO, T., German Language
SHIINA, K., Methodology for English Teaching
TABATA, T., Linguistics, Phonology
TAKAHASHI, H., English Language
TAKAHASHI, N., French Language
TANAKA, S., German Language
ZHOU, F., Chinese Language

Centre for Frontier Science (1-33 Yayoi-cho, Inage-ku, Chiba-shi, Chiba 263-8522; tel. (43) 290-3522; e-mail info@cfs.chiba-u.jp; internet www.cfs.chiba-u.ac.jp):
HANAWA, T., Astrophysics
OHTAKA, K., Applied Physics

Faculty of Education (1-33 Yayoi-cho, Inage-ku, Chiba-shi, Chiba 263-8522; tel. (43) 290-2505; e-mail hag2505@office.chiba-u.jp; internet www.edu.chiba-u.jp):
AKASHI, Y., Sociology of Education
AMAGASA, S., School and Curriculum Management
ARARAGI, C., Educational Psychology, Social Psychology
FUJIKAWA, D., Educational Methods and Development of Classroom Instructions
FUJITA, T., Science Education
FUJITA, Y., Sport Physiology
FUSHIMI, Y., Psychology of Classroom Learning and Instructional Methods
GOTO, M., Composition and Construction, Basic Art and Design and Education of Basic Art and Design
HAMADA, H., Hydrology and Limnology
HANAZAWA, H., Psychopathology
HATANAKA, T., Neuroethology
HAZAMA, K., Psychology of Juvenile Delinquency and Clinical Psychology
HIDAKA, T., Sport Sociology
HIRAIDE, S., British and American Literature
HONDA, S., Music Education
HOSAKA, T., Guidance and Counselling
IIZUKA, M., Electric Device, Informational Education
INOUE, T., Sociology, Social Theory, Environmental Sociology
ISAKA, J., History of Japanese Language
ISHII, K., Cookery Science, Food Science and Home Economics
ISOZAKI, I., Policy Process, Japanese Politics, Policy Education
ITO, Y., Home Economics Education and Childhood Education
KAMBARA, M., Educational Psychology, Psychology of Motivation
KANAMOTO, M., Musicology, Research into Music Education
KATAOKA, Y., Study of Guidance and Gender Equality Education
KATO, S., Chinese Literature
KATO, T., Physics education, Experiments of Magnetic and Dielectric Crystals
KATO, O., Oil and Water Painting
KITAJIMA, Y., Physiological Psychology for Persons with SMID
KOMIYAMA, T., Modulation of Spinal Reflexes during Movement
KUBO, K., Family Relations and Family Resource Management
MARUYAMA, K., Algebraic Topology, Differential Topology, Homotopy Theory
MATSUO, N., Studies of Teaching Geometry, Mathematical Teaching and Learning, Mathematical Thinking
MISAWA, M., Environmental Geography, Climatology
MIYANO, M., Music Education
MIYASHITA, K., Adolescent Psychology, Personality Psychology
MIYAZAKI, K., Sculpture
MURAMATSU, S., Nutrition, Biochemistry, Physiology
NAGANE, M., Educational Psychology and Educational Physiology
NAGASAWA, S., Social Education

NAKAI, T., Mathematics Programming, Applied Mathematics
NAKAZAWA, J., Development Psychology
NARUKAWA, Y., Psychology of Children with Disabilities, Support
NISHIGAKI, C., English Language Education
NOMURA, J., Immunology and Enrironmental Medicine
OHKOUCHI, N., Horticulture Science, Method of Technology Education, Agriculture Education
OI, K., English Teaching Pedagogy and English Linguistics
OKADA, K., Yogo Educational Pedagogy, Sceence of School Health Promotion
OOTA, K., Curriculum Development
OOTA, M., Special Support Education (Study of Teaching)
SASAKI, T., Art Education
SATO, K., Ethics
SATO, M., Children's Literature, Comparative Literature
SATO, M., Movement Theory of Gymnastics
SHIMADA, K., Mathematics Education
SHUTO, H., Education of Japanese Language
SUGITA, K., Pediatric Neurology, Cognitive Neurology and School Health Science
SUGIYAMA, H., Theory of Physical Education, Contemporary Sport
SUZUKI, A., Physiology and Ecology of Fungi
SUZUKI, H., Japanese Classical Literature, Japanese Classical Poetry, Studies of the Tale of Genji
SUZUKI, T., Education of Technology and Manual Arts
TAKAHASHI, H., Health Education
TAKEUCHI, H., Geographical Education
TAKIZAWA, F., Philosophy of Physical Education
TERAI, M., Teaching of the National Language
TODA, Y., Social Studies Education (History Education)
TOKUYAMA, I., Physical Education
TOMITA, H., Science of Early Childhood Care and Education, Developmental Psychology
TOZAKI, K., Physics of Phase Transition, Scientific Instrumentation
TSURUOKA, Y., Studies of Science Curriculum Theory, Values of Science Education, Environmental Education
UESUGI, K., Moral Education
UKAWA, M., Piano Performance
WATANABE, S.
YAMADA, N., Morphological Study of a Molecular Assemblage formed from Amphiphilic Molecules
YAMAMOTO, J., Composition
YAMANO, Y., Electrical and Electronics Insulating Engineering, Electrostatic Engineering
YAMAZAKI, Y., Geology
YATAGAI, M., Textile Care and Textile Conservation
YOSHIDA, M., Distance Education, Educational Technology
YOSHIOKA, N., Sport Biomechanics

Faculty of Law and Economics (1-33 Yayoi-cho, Inage-ku, Chiba-shi, Chiba 263-8522; tel. (43) 290-2343; e-mail gae2343@office.chiba-u.jp; internet www.le.chiba-u.ac.jp):

AOYAMA, K., Fixed Point Theory, Convex Analysis, Nonlinear Functional Analysis
ENDOH, Y., Corporation Law, Commercial Law
FURUUCHI, H., Modern European Economic History
HIROI, Y., Welfare Policy
INABA, H., Food Demand Analysis, Food Supply Analysis, Measurement of Diet Patterns
ISHIDA, K., Origins of the Triple Alliance, History of the League of Nations and the United Nations, Decolonisation of the Mediterranean
ISHIDA, Y., French Culture
ISHII, T., Criminal Law
KAKIHARA, K., Macroeconomics
KOBAYASHI, M., Comparative Politics, Political Theory, Political Philosophy
KUDO, H., Ecological Economics
KURASAKA, H., Ecological Economics, Environment Policy
KUROKI, Y., Monetary Economics
MIYAZAKI, R., Japanese Politics, Urban-Rural Relations
NAKAHARA, H., International Research and Development, Company Management
NOMURA, Y., General Equilibrium Analysis, Welfare Economics, Incomplete Market Analysis
OGANO, S., Civil Law
OHTSUKA, S., Theory of Financial Reporting, Standard-Setting Process in Accounting, Accounting Information System
OISHI, A., Labour Economics
OKABAYASHI, N., Private Law
OKUMOTO, Y., Economic Statistics, Seasonal Adjustment Method of Time Series, System of National Accounts
SAKAKIBARA, K., Economic Theory
SATO, E., Marketing
SHIMAZU, I., Theory of Spontaneous Law, Law and Economics, Law and Ethical Consensus
TACHIBANA, T., Development Economics
UCHIMURA, H., German Culture and Philosophy
UOZUMI, H., Public Administration
YOSHIZUMI, Y., Accounting Policy Making, Accounting Disclosure

Faculty of Letters (1-33 Yayoi-cho, Inage-ku, Chiba-shi, Chiba 263-8522; tel. (43) 290-2343; e-mail gae2343@office.chiba-u.jp; internet www.l.chiba-u.ac.jp):

ABE, A., Science of Cognition Information
CHO, K., Modern Korean History of Grassroots Movement, History of Political Thought
DEN, Y., Spoken Discourse Analysis, Psycholinguistics, Computational Linguistics, Cognitive Science
GODO, K., Historical Studies of Japanese
HOSAKA, T., Studies of Relationship between Nation and Religion in the Roman Empire
ISHII, M., History of Language Culture for the Middle Ages German and Latin
IZUMI, C., Ancient Philosophy and Science
JITSUMOTI, M., Comparative Congnition, Animal Learning
KAJITA, S., Theory of Governance, Semantics and General Linguistic in Modern English
KANNO, K., Studies of Speech
KATAGIRI, M., Sociological Theory, Theory of Modern Society
KATO, T., Studies of Bible, Theory of Comparative Civilisation
KIMURA, E., Perceptual Psychology
KURITA, Y., Middle-East, North Africa Modern History
MITSUI, Y., 18th-Century French Literature, Philosophy of the Enlightenment
MIYAKE, A., Modern Japanese History, Labour History
MIYAKE, A., Labour History of Modern Japanese
MURAOKA, H., Japanese Language and Culture
NAKAGAWA, H., Eurasian Languages and Cultures
NISHIMURA, Y., Theory of France Culture, Theory of Comparative Literature
OGATA, T., Sociology of Labour
OZAWA, H., Modern and Contemporary History of Europe
SHIBA, K., Medieval Literature
SHINOZAKI, M., English Literature, Critical Theory
SUGAHARA, K., History of Tokugawa Shogunate
SUTO, N., Cognitive Psychology
SUZUKI, N., Behavioral Science
TAKAGI, G., Japanese Early Modern Literature
TAKAHASHI, K., Ancient Philosophy
TAKEI, H., Medical Anthropology, Cultural Anthropology, Amazonian Aboriginal Culture
TAKEUCHI, H., Library and Information Science
TOKIZANE, S., American Literature, Novel, Theory of Literature
TSUCHIDA, T., International Cultures and Languages
UEMURA, K., History of Image for Italian Sculpture
WAKABAYASHI, A., Psychology of Individual Difference, Psychographic Measurement Theory, Cognitive Neuroscience
YAMADA, M., Historical Studies
YANAGISAWA, S., Japanese Prehistoric Archaeology
YONEMURA, C., Family Sociology, Historical Sociology
YOSHIDA, A., Cultural Anthropology

Faculty of Science:

FUNABASHI, M., Carbohydrate Chemistry
HINO, Y., Mathematical Analysis
HIROI, Y., Metamorphic Petrology
IMAMOTO, T., Organic Chemistry
INOUE, A., Clay Mineralogy
ISEZAKI, N., Geophysics
ISIMURA, R.
ITO, M., Sedimentology
ITO, T., Structural Geology
KANEKO, K., Surface Solid State Chemistry, Molecular Science, Adsorption Science
KIMURA, T., High Energy Physics
KITAZUME, M., Finite Group Theory, Algebraic Combinatorics
KOBAYASHI, K., Cell Biology
KOHORI, Y., Low-temperature Physics
KOSHITANI, S., Algebra
KOYAMA, N., Biochemistry
KURASAWA, H., Nuclear Physics
MATSUMOTO, R., Astrophysics
NAGISA, M., Operator Algebra
NAKAGAMI, J., Statistics, Mathematical Programming
NAKAMURA, K., Coding Theory, Cryptography and Information Security
NAKANO, M., Biochemistry
NAKAYAMA, T., Nanoscience
NISHIDA, T., Mineralogy
NOZAWA, S., Algebra
OBINATA, T., Developmental Biology
OGAWA, K., Nuclear Physics
OHARA, S., Environmental Geology
OHASHI, K., Cell Physiology
SAKURA, Y., Hydrogeology
TAGURI, M., Statistics
TAKAGI, R., Geometry
TAKEDA, Y., Coordination Chemistry, Solution Chemistry
TSUJI, T., Computer Software, Theory of Programmes
TUTIYA, T., Echophysiology
YAMADA, I., Solid State Physics
YAMAMOTO, K., Molecular Physiology
YANAGISAWA, A., Organic Chemistry
YASUDA, M., Statistics
WATANO, Y., Plant Biosystems, Molecular Ecology

Graduate School of Engineering (1-33, Yayoi-cho, Inage-ku, Chiba-shi, Chiba 263-8522; tel. (43) 290-3034; e-mail mah3034@office.chiba-u.jp; internet www.eng.chiba-u.ac.jp):

AKAZOME, M., Solid-State Organic Chemistry, Synthetic Organic Chemistry, Metalorganic Chemistry

ANDO, M., Structural and Construction Systems Planning, Building Production Design, Project Management, Property Management

AOKI, H., Materials Planning, Industrial Design, Kansei (Emotion) Engineering

ASANUMA, H., Smart Materials, Intellectual Materials and Structural Systems, Composite Materials, Multi-Functional Materials, Self-Restoration

FUJINAMI, M., Analytical Chemistry, Instrumental Analysis, Surface Science, Radiation Chemistry, Positron Annihilation Spectroscopy, Laser Spectroscopy

FUKUKAWA, Y., Conservation of Historic Environments, Revitalisation of Central Urban Areas, Urban Planning Systems Theory, Approaches to Urban Design

HARADA, Y., Study of Building Construction, Steel Structures, Quake-Resistant Design of Architectural Structures

HASHIMOTO, K., Ultrasonic Engineering, Elastic Surface Wave Devices, High-Frequency Electronic Circuits, Communications Engineering, Micro-Processing, Optical Probes, Sensors

HIBINO, H., Design Psychology, Colour Psychology, Impression Evaluations, Psychophysics, Emotional Design

HIRATA, H., Systems Science and Engineering, Large-Scale Systems, Biological Systems, Optimization, Intelligence and Learning

HOSHI, N., Surface Electrochemistry, Well-Defined Surfaces, Shape-Controlled Nano-Particles, Fuel Cells, Surface Spectroscopy, Scanning Probe Microscopy

HOSHINO, K., Electrochemistry, Electrophotographic, Nano Structure Materials Chemistry

HU, N., Mechanics of Materials, Computational Mechanics, Materials Strength, Composite Materials, Damage Evaluation, Optimization

IGARASHI, T., Endoscopic Image Processing, Endoscopic Surgery, Surgical Equipments, Three-Dimensional and Panoramic Image for Endoscopy

ISHITANI, Y., Semiconductor Optical Physics, Semiconductor Optical Devices, Semiconductor Nanostructures, Nitride Semiconductors

ITO, K., Antennas, Medical Electromagnetic Engineering, Antennas for Medical Application, Body-Centric Wireless Communications, Human Body Phantoms

ITO, T., Computational Science, Exclusive Computers, Hardware, Numerical Computations, Electronic Holography, 3-D Moving Images

IWADATE, Y., Liquid Theory, Amorphous Materials Science, Structural Analysis and Control, High Energy Irradiation, Development and Modification of Environmentally Adaptable and Highly Functional Materials

IWANAGA, K., Microwave Engineering, Synthesis of Nonuniform Transmission Lines, Inverse Scattering, Filters, Scattering of Electromagnetic Waves, Numerical Analysis

IZUMI, N., Building Construction, Reinforced Concrete Structures, Quake-Resistant Design, Damping Structures, Architectural Structure Design

KAKEGAWA, K., Environmentally Sustainable Ceramics Materials, Ash Recycling, Nano-Organizational Materials, Amorphous Use Materials

KARATSU, T., Photochemistry, Organic Silicone Chemistry, Luminescent Materials, Organic Electro-Luminescence, Photochromic Materials

KATO, H., Production Systems, Machine Operations Assist, Virtual Reality, Skill Training and Inheritance, Sensory Feedback

KATSUURA, T., Human Life Engineering, Environmental Ergonomics, Physiological Anthropology, Design Humanomics

KAWASE, T., Environmental Facility Planning and Design, Energy-Efficient Planning, Workplace Productivity, Application of Solar Power Generation System

KISHIKAWA, K., Liquid Crystals, Soft Materials, Supramolecules, Suprastructures, Nanofunction Materials

KITAHARA, T., City Planning, Urban Design, Urban Landscape Planning, Urban Revitalization Planning, Community Building, Community Planning

KITAMURA, A., Photochemistry, Optical Function Materials, Energy Conversion Materials, Electron Transfer Reactions, Noninvasive Measurements

KOAKUTSU, S., Computer Engineering

KOBAYASHI, H., Housing and Residential Environment Planning, Community Design, Housing Policies, Community Building, Real Estate Systems, Architectural Planning

KOHMOTO, S., Supramolecular Chemistry, Molecular Recognition, Soft Materials, Optical Function Materials

KUBO, M., Design Morphology, Modelling Dynamics, Production Design, Materials Planning

KUDO, K., Organic Semiconductors, Organic Transistors, Ultra-Thin-Film Materials, Semiconductor Devices, Molecular Devices

KURYU, A., Urban Architecture, Underground Architecture, Landscapes, Collaboration

LIU, H., Biodynamics, Computational Dynamics, Biological Flight and Notation, Winged Flight Vehicles, Biomimetics, Physiological Flow, Circulatory System Simulations, Multi-Scale/Multi-Physics Modelling, Medical Imaging

LIU, K., Systems Control Engineering, Advanced Control Theory, Control of Power Electronics, Control of Power Systems, Smart-Grid

MACHIDA, M., Organic and Heavy Metal Pollutants, Aqueous Solution, Activated Carbon, Adsorption, Surface Chemistry, Water Environment

MAENO, K., Aerospace Thermal Flow, Applied Laser Measurement, Shock Waves, Compressible Fluids, Extremely Low Temperatures

MANABE, Y., Image Measurement, Computer Vision, Colour Image Engineering, Virtual Reality

MATSUBA, I., Neural Network

MISHINA, H., Tribology, Machine Element, Surface Engineering, Surface Physicality

MORITA, N., Precision Machining, Non-Traditional Machining, Micro Machining, Machine Tool, Cutting Tool, Surface Integrity

MORIYOSHI, Y., Thermofluid Engineering, Internal Combustion Engine, Modelling, Numerical Analysis, Laser Measurement Diagnostics

MORRIS, M., History of Architecture, Urban History, History of Artificial Environments, Conservation and Restoration of Historic Architecture, Architectural Design Based on Historical Learning

NAKAGOME, H., Thermal Engineering, Environmental and New Energies, Cryogenic Technologies, Waste and Recycling, Pyrolysis, Hydrogen, Magnetic Refrigeration

NAKAI, S., Earthquake Disaster Prevention, Quake-Resistant Design, Foundational Vibrations, Fundamental Structures, Dynamic Interactions, Microtopography, Traffic Vibration

NAKAMOTO, T., Micro-Processing, Machine Processing, 3-D Modelling, Laser Processing, Machine Elements

NAKAYAMA, S., Architectural Planning, Facilities Design Planning, Facilities Management, POE, Public Facilities Planning, Hospitals, Welfare Facilities

NONAMI, K., Unmanned Aerial Vehicles/Micro Aerial Vehicles, Six Legged Walking Robots, Dual Manipulator and Hand Robots, Autonomous Robotic Boats, Autonomous Intelligent Mobile Robots, Flywheel Energy Storage System and Electric Vehicles, Systems Control

OGURA, H., Effective Energy Utilization Systems, Energy Savings, Chemical Heat Storage, Chemical Heat Pumps, Environmental Energy Engineering, Chemical Engineering

OTSUBO, Y., Environmental Particle Technology, Soft Machines, Fluid Devices, Colloids, Rheology Control

SATO, K., Environmental Design, Spatial Design Planning, Environmental Psychology, Sound Environment Planning

SAITO, K., High-Speed Protein Purification, Bioreactors, Bioaffinity Reaction on Porous Adsorbents, Radiation Graft Polymerization, Polymer Brush

SATO, S., Catalytic Process, Dehydration of Polyols, Interconversion of Resources Derived from Plants, Porous Solids

SATO, Y., Power Electronics, Electronic Equipment, Motor Control, Electrical System Control, New Energies

SAKAMOTO, M., Organic Synthesis, Organic Photochemistry, Crystal Engineering, Asymmetric Synthesis, Heterocyclic Chemistry, Molecular Recognition

SAKATA, S., Ubiquitous Network / Machine-to-Machine Connection, Smart-Grid, Internet, Multimedia Connection, Mobile Computing

SEKI, M., Bioprocess Engineering, Chemical Reaction Engineering, Micro/Nanofluidics, Microreactors, Biochips, MicroTAS, Microfabrication, Bioreactors, Biocatalysts, Cell Culture and Separation

SHIMAZU, S., Catalysis, Chemistry of Metal Complexes, Green Chemistry, Nano-Structured Catalysts, Molecular Recognition, Layered Materials, Chemical Conversion of Biomass, Lignocellulose

SHIMOYAMA, I., Neuroscience

SHIODA, S., Communication Networks, Internet, Operations Research, Performance Evaluations, Probability Theory

SUGAI, Y., Systems Engineering, Analysis and Design of Large-Scale Networks, Optimization Engineering, Neural Networks

SUZUKI, N., Regional Design that Responds to Social Change, Lifestyle Building, Traditional Technologies, Poverty and Globalization

TAKAHASHI, H., Educational Engineering, CALL System, Information Equipment, Multimedia, Communication, English Education

TAKAHASHI, T., Building Construction, Design Load, Long-Period Seismic Waves, Statistics of Extremes, Structural Reliability, Target Standards, Performance Based Design

TAKANO, T., Electrical Wave Physical Engineering, Electromagnetic Wave Measurement, Radio Astronomy, Air Electricity, Cloud Physics

TAKEI, M., Multiphase Flow, Visualization, Two Phase Flow, Micro Channel, Artificial Heart, Plant
TATEDA, M., Light-Optic Communication
TERAUCHI, F., Materials Planning, Design Psychology, Kansei (emotion) Engineering, Touch, Smell
TOMINAGA, S., Visual Information, Colour Information Processing, Computer Colour Vision
TSUGE, K., Producing Urban Environments, Redevelopment of Urban Areas, Mixed Use Facilities Design
UEDA, A., Design Culture Planning, Utilization of Local Resources, Endogeneous Regional Development, Endogeneous Tourism Creation
UENO, T., Architectural Design, Architectural Planning, Urban Planning
WATANABE, M., Industrial Design, Design Systems, Design Management, Design Planning
YAGUCHI, H.
YAMAMOTO, E., Image Measurement System, MR Imaging, Ultrasonic Imaging, Image Simulator
YAMAZAKI, F., Urban Infrastructure, Earthquake Disaster Prevention, Lifeline Systems, Remote Sensing, Transportation Systems, Geographic Information Systems
YANAGISAWA, K.
YASHIRO, K., Microwave Engineering, Synthesis of Nonuniform Transmission Lines, Inverse Scattering, Filters, Scattering of Electromagnetic Waves, Numerical Analysis
YU, W., Biocontrol, Bioengineering, Medical Robotics, Rehabilitation Robotics (including Assistive Technology), Artificial Intelligence
ZEN, H., Image and Video Processing, Computer Vision, Multimedia, Sensing

Graduate School of Horticulture (648 Matsudo, Matsudo-shi, Chiba 271-8510; tel. (47) 308-8706; e-mail zaf8703@office.chiba-u.jp; internet www.h.chiba-u.ac.jp):

AKASAKA, M., Landscape Planning, Geschichte des Stadtgruens
AMEMIYA, Y., Plant Pathology
ANDO, A., Theory of Protein Engineering, Molecular Life Chemistry
EGASHIRA, Y., Food Chemistry, Nutritional Chemistry, Nutritional Molecular Biology, Nutritional Biochemistry
FUJII, E., Planting Environment
GOTO, E., Plant Biological Information Measurement, Biological Environment System Engineering
HARADA, K., Genetics and Plant Breeding
HONJO, T., Planting Design
IKEZAWA, K., Environment Landscape Design
INUBASHI, K., Soil Science
ISODA, A., Crop Science
KINOSHITA, I., City Planning, Citizen Participation
KOBA, T., Molecular Cytogenetics and Genome Sciences of Plants
KOBAYASHI, H., Policy and International Aspects
KOBAYASHI, T., Landscape and Restoration Ecology
KODAMA, H., Molecular Mechanisms for the Transgene-Induced Rna Silencing, Microarray Analyses of Tobacco, Torenia and Petunia Plants, Functional Analysis of Cysteine-Synthase Like Protein, Effects of Composting Products on Plant Growth and Nitrate Contents
KONDO, S., Roles of Physiological Active Substances in Fruit Growth
MASADA, M., Biochemistry
MATSUDA, T., Agricultural Economics
MATSUI, H., Fruit Science
MATSUOKA, N., Agricultural Meteorology, Natural Disaster Science
MII, M., Plant Cell Technology
MISAWA, M., Physiography (Climatology)
MIYOSHI, K., Floriculture
NAKAMUTA, K., Chemical Ecology, Animal behavior, Applied Entomology
NISHIDA, Y., Molecular Design of Sugar-Based Reagents and their Practical Use for Solving the Worldwide Problem of Infection Diseases and Bio-Terrorism
NISHINO, E., Leaf and Flower Development of Wild Type Plants and Mutants in Japanese Morning Glory, Garden Plants and Wild Plants. Comparative Anatomy and Development of Sesame Seeds
OHE, Y., Horticultural Information Science
OKITSU, S., Forest Ecology
SAITO, O., Farm Business Management
SANADA, H., Food and Nutrition
SAKAMOTO, K., Soil Microbiology, Rhizosphere Microbiology
SAKURAI, S., Direct Marketing by the Farm Sector, Role of Social Capital in Rural Community, Diversification of Rural Economy
SATO, T., Plant Molecular Physiology, Post Harvest Physiology of Fruits and Vegetables, Food Preservation, Regulation Mechanisms of Ethylene Biosynthesis in Higher Plant
SHINOHARA, Y., Vegetable Science
SUZUKI, A., Mycology
TAGAWA, A., Postharvest Engineering, Food Engineering, Food Physicality
TAKAGAKI, M., Agronomy of Tropical Agriculture
TANG, C., Water Cycle and Element Migration in Forestry Basin, Groundwater Flow, Geohydrochemistry, Contaminant Movement in Water, Hillslope Hydrology and Integrated Hydrological Processess in Arid, Semi-arid as well as Tropical Regions by Using Isotopes and Chemistry
TASHIRO, Y., Urban Landscape Design
WATANABE, Y., Plant Nutrition
YAMAUCHI, S., Humanistic Study on Environment
ZHANG, J., Research Survey in China on the Theme of Space Representation and Characteristics of Traditional Landscape Architecture Technologies

Graduate School of Medical and Pharmaceutical Sciences:

CHIBA, T., Neurobiology

Graduate School of Medicine (1-8-1 Inohana, Chuo-ku, Chiba-shi, Chiba 260-8670; tel. (43) 222-7171; e-mail g5004@office.chiba-u.jp; internet www.m.chiba-u.ac.jp):

BUJO, H., Genome Research and Clinical Application
FUJISAWA, T., Thoracic Surgery
FUKUDA, Y., Autonomic Physiology
HARIGAYA, K., Molecular and Tumour Pathology
HATA, A., Public Health
HATTORI, T., Neurology
HIRASAWA, H., Emergency and Critical Care Medicine
ICHINOSE, M., Plastic Surgery
ISHIKURA, H., Molecular Pathology
ITO, H., Radiology
ITO, H., Urology
IWASE, H., Legal Medicine
IYO, M., Psychiatry
KIMURA, S., Biochemistry and Molecular Pharmacology
KOHNO, Y., Paediatrics
KOMURO, I., Cardiovascular Science and Medicine
KOSEKI, H., Molecular Embryology
KURIYAMA, T., Respirology
KUWAKI, T., Molecular and Integrative Physiology
MIYAZAKI, M., General Surgery
MORI, C., Bioenvironmental Medicine
MORIYA, H., Orthopaedic Surgery
NAKAYA, H., Pharmacology
NAKAYAMA, T., Medical Immunology
NISHINO, T., Anaesthesiology
NODA, M., Molecular Infectology
NOGAWA, K., Occupational and Environmental Medicine
NOMURA, F., Molecular Diagnosis
OCHIAI, T., Academic Surgery
OHNUMA, N., Paediatric Surgery
OKAMOTO, Y., Otorhinolaryngology
SAISHO, H., Medicine and Clinical Oncology
SAITO, T., Molecular Genetics
SAITO, Y., Clinical Cell Biology
SEKIYA, S., Reproductive Medicine
SHINKAI, H., Clinical Biology of Extracellular Matrix
SHIRASAWA, H., Molecular Virology
SUZUKI, N., Environmental Biochemistry
TAKIGUCHI, M., Biochemistry and Genetics
TANIGUCHI, M., Molecular Immunology
TANZAWA, H., Clinical Molecular Biology
TOKUHISA, T., Developmental Genetics
TOSHIMORI, K., Anatomy and Developmental Biology
YAMAMOTO, S., Ophthalmology and Visual Science
YAMAURA, A., Neurological Surgery
YANO, A., Infection and Host Disease

Graduate School of Nursing (1-8-1 Inohana, Chuo-ku, Chiba-shi, Chiba 260-8672; tel. (43) 226-2377; e-mail taf5654@office.chiba-u.jp; internet www.n.chiba-u.jp):

FUNASHIMA, N., Nursing Education
IWASAKI, Y., Psychiatric Nursing
KITAIKE, T., Health Science
MAJIMA, T., Adult Nursing
MASAKI, H., Gerontological Nursing
MIYAZAKI, M., Community Health Nursing
MORI, M., Maternity Nursing
NAKAMURA, N., Child Nursing
NOJI, A., Nursing Care Development and Evaluation
OKADA, S., Pathobiology
SAKAI, I., Long-Term Care Facilities Nursing System Management
SUWA, S., Visiting Nursing
TESHIMA, M., Hospital Nursing Care
WAZUMI, Y., Nursing Policy and Education Development
YAMAMOTO, T., Theoretical Nursing
YOSHIMOTO, T., Geriatric Community Nursing, Care Systems Management

Graduate School of Pharmaceutical Sciences (1-33 Yayoi-cho, Inage-ku, Chiba-shi, Chiba 263-8522; tel. (43) 251-1111):

AIMI, N., Molecular Structure and Biological Function
ARANO, Y., Radiopharmaceutical Chemistry
CHIBA, K., Pharmacology and Toxicology
HAMADA, Y., Pharmaceutical Chemistry
HORIE, T., Biopharmaceutics
IGARASHI, K., Clinical Biochemistry
ISHIBASHI, M., Natural Products Chemistry
ISHIKAWA, T., Medicinal Organic Chemistry
KOBAYASHI, H., Biochemistry
MURAYAMA, T., Chemical Pharmacology
NEYA, S., Physical Chemistry
NISHIDA, A., Synthetic Organic Chemistry
SAITOH, K., Molecular Biology and Biotechnology
SUZUKI, K. T., Toxicology and Environmental Health
TOIDA, T., Bio-analytical Chemistry
UEDA, S., Drug Information and Communication
UENO, K., Geriatric Pharmacology and Therapeutics
YAMAGUCHI, N., Molecular Cell Biology
YAMAMOTO, K., Pharmaceutical Technology
YAMAMOTO, T., Microbiology and Molecular Genetics

YANO, S., Molecular Pharmacology and Pharmacotherapeutics

Graduate School of Science (1-33, Yayoi-cho, Inage-ku, Chiba-shi, Chiba 263-8522; tel. (43) 290-2872; e-mail iac2871@office.chiba-u.jp; internet www.s.chiba-u.ac.jp):

ARAI, T., Mathematical Informatics
ARAI, T., Organic Chemistry
ENDOH, T., Molecular Biology
FUJIKAWA, T., Physical Chemistry
HATTORI, K., Earth Interior Science
HIROI, Y., Metamorphic Petrology
INABA, T., Differential Topology
INOUE, A., Clay Mineralogy
ISHIMURA, R., Algebra Analysis
ITO, M., Earth Surface Sciences
KANEGAWA, K., Earth Interior Science
KANOH, H., Physical Chemistry
KIMURA, S., Molecular Physiology
KITAZUME, M., Finite Groups and related topics
KOHORI, Y., Condensed-Matter Physics
KOMORI, Y., Mathematical Informatics
KONDO, K., Elementary Partivle Physics
KOSHITANI, S., Algebra
KOTAKE, N., Earth Surface Science
KUGA, K., Topology
MATSUMOTO, R., Astrophysics, Computational Physics
MATSUYAMA, K., Semiparametric and Nonparametric Statistica Inferences
MIYAUCHI, T., Earth Surface Science
MURO, K., Condensed-Matter Physics
NAGISA, M., Functional Analysis
NAKADA, H., Nuclear Theory
NAKAGAMI, J., Mathematical Statistics, Mathematical Programming
NAKAYAMA, T., Physics of Quantum Many-body System
NISHIKAWA, K., Physical Chemistry
NOZAWA, S., Algebra
OHASHI, K., Cell Physiology
OHTA, Y., Theory of Strongly Correlated Electron System
OKADA, Y., Linear Partial Differential Equations, Microlocal Analysis
OTO, K., Condensed-Matter Physics
SAKANE, F., Life Chemistry
SAKURAI, T., Mathematical Informatics
SATO, T., Plant Moleclar Biology
SUGIYAMA, K., Differential Topology
TAKEUCHI, N., Earth Surface Science
TAMURA, T., Molecular Biology
TANEMURA, H., Probability Theory
TOGO, H., Organic Chemistry
TSUCHIYA, T., Ecology
TSUKUI, M., Earth Interior Science
WATANO, Y., Phylogenetics
YAMAMOTO, K., Molecular Biology
YANAGISAWA, A., Organic Chemistry

Health Sciences Centre (1-33 Yayoi-cho, Inage-ku, Chiba-shi, Chiba 263-8522; tel. (47) 290-2210; e-mail inf@hsc.chiba-u.ac.jp; internet hschome-gw.hsc.chiba-u.ac.jp):

NAGAO, K., Internal Medicine

Institute of Media and Information Technology (1–33 Yayoi-cho, Inage-ku, Chiba-shi, Chiba 263-8522; tel. (43) 290-3535; internet www.imit.chiba-u.jp):

KOMORI, Y., Mathematical Logic
SOHMIYA, Y., German Linguistics, Semantics, Corpus Linguistics
ZEN, H., Intelligent Information Media

International Student Centre (tel. (43) 290-2197; e-mail bm2198@office.chiba-u.jp):

HATA, H., Teaching Japanese as a Second Language
NIIKURA, R., Cross-cultural Psychology

Marine Biosystems Research Centre (1 Uchiura, Amatsu-kominato-cho, Awagun, Chiba 299-5502; tel. (47) 095-2201; e-mail bee3832@office.chiba-u.jp; internet marine.biosystems.chiba-u.jp):

MIYAZAKI, T., Aquatic Ecology
TOGASHI, T., Ecology

Research Centre for Frontier Medical Engineering:

HANEISHI, H., Processing, Analysis and Integration of CT, MRI and PET Images, Medical Application of Colour and Spectral Information
HAYASHI, H., Minimally Invasive Surgery, Near-Infrared Bioimaging, Sentinel lymph Node Navigation Surgery, Characteristic Analysis of Surgical Energy Devices
SHIMOYAMA, I., Human Neurophysiology
SUZUKI, M., Orthopaedic Surgery, Biomaterial, Biomechanics

Research Centre for Pathogenic Fungi and Microbial Toxicology (1-8-1 Inohana, Chuo-ku, Chiba 260-8670; tel. (43) 222-7171; internet www.pf.chibau.ac.jp; f. 1946; Dir: YUZURU MIKAMI):

FUKUSHIMA, K., Division of Fungal Resources and Development
KAMEI, K., Division of Fungal Infection
MIKAMI, Y., Division of Molecular Biology and Therapeutics
NISHIMURA, K., Division of Phylogenetics
TAKEO, K., Division of Ultrastructure and Function

University Hospital (1-8-1 Inohana, Chuo-ku, Chiba-shi, Chiba 260-8670; tel. (43) 222-7171; e-mail byoin-soumu@office.chiba-u.jp; internet www.ho.chiba-u.jp):

IKUSAKA, M., Dept of General Medicine
KITADA, M., Pharmacy
KOUZU, T., Dept of Endoscopic Diagnostics and Therapeutics
SATOMURA, Y., Medical Informatics
TANABE, M., Postgraduate Education Centre

CHUKYO UNIVERSITY

101-2 Yagoto Honmachi, Showa-ku, Nagoya-shi, Aichi-ken 466-8666
Telephone: (52) 835-7111
E-mail: ic@mng.chukyo-u.ac.jp
Internet: www.chukyo-u.ac.jp
Founded 1954
Pres.: KAORU KITAGAWA
Chancellor and Chair. of the Board of Dirs: KIYOHIRO UMEMURA
Dir of the Library: HITOSHI YASUMURA
Dir, Admin. Bureau: KAZUHIRO HANAMURA

DEANS

Faculty of English: HIROSHI YOSHIKAWA
Faculty of Economics: KIYOHIDE UMEMURA
Faculty of Law: YUKIO HIYAMA
Faculty of Letters: SUMIAKI MORISHITA
Faculty of Psychology: MAREHIRO MUKAI
Faculty of Sociology: NOBORU MATSUDA
School of Health and Sport Sciences: KAGEMOTO YUASA
School of Information Science and Technology: HIROYASU KOSHIMIZU
School of International Liberal Studies: SUSUMU ITO
School of Management: MASAAKI NAKAMURA
School of Policy Design: NOBUHIRO OKUNO

CHUO GAKUIN UNIVERSITY

451 Kujike, Abiko, Chiba 270-1196
Telephone: (4) 7183-6501
Internet: www.cgu.ac.jp
Founded 1900
Faculties of commerce, law
Pres.: TERUO OKUBO

EHIME UNIVERSITY

10-13 Dogo-Himata, Matsuyama City 790-8577
Telephone: (89) 927-9000
E-mail: hisyo@stu.ehime-u.ac.jp
Internet: www.ehime-u.ac.jp
Founded 1949
Independent
Academic year: April to March (2 terms)
Pres.: MASAYUKI KOMATSU
Admin. Officer: I. KUBONIWA
Dean of Students' Affairs Office: T. SAITO
Library Dir: KOJI SANUKI
Library of 1,144,000 vols
Number of teachers: 976 full-time
Number of students: 9,858

DEANS

Faculty of Agriculture: MASAYA SHIRAISHI
Faculty of Education: YASUNOBU KINTO
Faculty of Engineering: KOICHI SUZUKI
Faculty of Law and Arts: MOTOJI IMAIZUMI
Faculty of Medicine: KOJI HASHIMOTO
Faculty of Science: YASUNOBU YANAGISAWA
United Graduate School of Agricultural Sciences: TADAAKI WAKIMOTO

FUKUI UNIVERSITY

9-1 Bunkyo 3-chome, Fukui City 910-8507
Telephone: (776) 23-0500
E-mail: kaiho@sec.icpc.fukui-u.ac.jp
Internet: www.fukui-u.ac.jp
Founded 1949
Independent
Academic year: April to March
Pres.: SHINPEI KOJIMA
Dir of Admin.: YUZO SATO
Librarian: TOSHIYUKI KODAIRA
Library of 453,403 vols
Number of teachers: 367
Number of students: 4,159

DEANS

Faculty of Education and Regional Studies: YOSHIHIKO HAYATA
Faculty of Engineering: SHINGO TAMAKI

FUKUSHIMA UNIVERSITY

1 Kanayagawa, Fukushima 960-1296
Telephone: (24) 548-8084
E-mail: hpc@fukushima-u.ac.jp
Internet: www.fukushima-u.ac.jp
Faculties and graduate schools of administration and social sciences, economics and business administration, human development and culture, symbiotic systems science
Pres.: TOSHIO KONNO
Number of students: 4,309

FUKUYAMA UNIVERSITY

985-1 Aza-Sanzou, Higashimuracho, Fukuyama-shi, Hiroshima 729-0292
Telephone: (84) 936-2111
E-mail: soumu@fucc.fukuyama-u.ac.jp
Internet: www.fukuyama-u.ac.jp
Founded 1975
Chancellor: TAKASHI MIYACHI
Pres.: TAIZO MUTA
Vice-Pres: HIRAKU SHIMADA, RYUUSUKE YOSHIHARA
Librarian: TOSHIRO KATAOKA
Library of 222,700 vols
Number of teachers: 240
Number of students: 5,500

DEANS

Faculty of Economics: ISAO OOKUBO
Faculty of Engineering: KAZUO KOBAYASHI

Faculty of Human Cultures: FUMIKO MATSUDA
Faculty of Life Science and Biotechnology: KIYOSHI SATOUCHI
Faculty of Pharmacy: SATOSHI HIBINO

GIFU UNIVERSITY

1-1 Yanagido, Gifu-shi, Gifu-ken 501-1193
Telephone: (58) 230-1111
E-mail: gjea04007@jim.gifu-u.ac.jp
Internet: www.gifu-u.ac.jp
Founded 1949
Independent
Pres.: T. KINJOH
Sec.-Gen.: Y. KIJIMA
Librarian: T. UNO
Library of 822,409 vols, 13,000 periodicals
Number of teachers: 738 full-time
Number of students: 5,995

DEANS

Faculty of Agriculture: T. NAKAMURA
Faculty of Education: YOSHIMI SASAKI
Faculty of Engineering: H. SHIMIZU
Faculty of Regional Studies: Y. MATSUDA
School of Medicine: Y. NOZAWA

GUNMA UNIVERSITY

4–2 Aramaki-machi, Maebashi City, Gunma 371-8510
Telephone: (27) 220-7111
E-mail: s-research@jimu.gunma-u.ac.jp
Internet: www.gunma-u.ac.jp
Founded 1949
Academic year: April to March
President: MAMORU SUZUKI
Vice-Pres. for General, Financial Affairs and Facilities: HIROYUKI SHIRAI
Vice-Pres. for Research: SEIJI OZAWA
Vice-Pres. for Student Affairs: KIMIO NAKAMURA
Dir of University Hospital: YASUO MORISHITA
Dir of Management: MOTOHARU IUE
Admin.: TADEDNORI IKENOUE
Librarian: YOUICHI NAKAZATO
Library of 651,576 vols
Number of teachers: 849 full-time
Number of students: 7,021
Publication: *Journal of Social and Information Studies* (1 a year)

DEANS

Faculty of Education: TADASHI MATSUDA
Faculty of Engineering: TAKAYUKI TAKARADA
Faculty of Medicine: FUMIO GOTO
Faculty of Social and Information Studies: NOBUTAKA OCHIAI
Institute of Molecular and Cellular Regulation: ITARU KOJIMA

HIROSAKI UNIVERSITY

1 Bunkyo-cho, Hirosaki 036-8560
Telephone: (172) 36-2111
E-mail: webmaster@cc.hirosaki-u.ac.jp
Internet: www.hirosaki-u.ac.jp
Founded 1949
Independent
Academic year: April to March
Pres.: MASAHIKO ENDO
Vice-Pres.: Y. MIZUNE
Registrar: R. SHIBATA
Librarian: E. OKAZAKI
Dir of the Hospital: S. HARATA
Number of teachers: 692
Number of students: 5,512
Publication: *School Outline* (1 a year)

DEANS

Faculty of Agriculture and Life Science: K. TOYOKAWA
Faculty of Education: H. OZAWA
Faculty of Humanities: T. TANNO
Faculty of Science and Technology: H. OHNUKI
School of Medicine: M. ENDO

PROFESSORS

Faculty of Agriculture and Life Science (3 Bunkyo-cho, Hirosaki 036-8561; internet nature.cc.hirosaki-u.ac.jp):

ANDO, Y., Entomology
AOYAMA, M., Soil Science
ARAKAWA, O., Pomology
ASADA, Y., Applied Microbiology, Microbial Technology
BOKURA, T., Agricultural Meteorology
FUKUDA, H., Horticulture
HARADA, Y., Plant Pathology
ISHIGURO, S., Biochemistry of the Eye, Developmental Biology
KANDA, K., Cooperative Study
KUDO, A., Irrigation, Drainage and Hydraulic Engineering
MAKITA, H., Vegetation Geography, Environmental Science
MIYAIRI, K., Biochemistry
MOTOMURA, Y., Science of Horticultural Bioproducts
MUTO, A., Molecular Engineering
NAKAMURA, S., Biochemical Engineering
NIIZEKI, M., Plant Breeding and Genetics
OBARA, Y., Cytogenetics
OHMACHI, T., Molecular Biology, Applied Microbiology
OKUNO, T., Organic Chemistry and Biochemistry
SASAKI, C., Agricultural Land Engineering
SAWADA, S., Plant Ecophysiology
SAWARA, Y., Animal Behaviour
SHIOZAKI, Y., Pomology
SUGIYAMA, K., Virology, Molecular Biology
SUGIYAMA, S., Crop Science, Plant Evolutionary Biology
TAKAHASHI, H., Regional Economy
TAKAMURA, K., Morphogenesis
TAKEDA, K., Microbial Ecology
TANIGUCHI, K., Rural Planning
TOYOKAWA, K., Feeds and Feeding
UNO, T., Agricultural Economics
YURUGI, M., Structural Mechanics, Construction Materials, Concrete

Faculty of Education (internet siva.cc.hirosaki-u.ac.jp):

ANDO, F., Education for Children with Disabilities
ANNO, M., Japanese History
ASANO, K., Piano
FUMOTO, N., Psychology of Sport and Physical Activity
GION, Z., Social Studies Education
HAGA, T., Clothing Science
HANDA, S., Mathematics Education
HAYAKAWA, M., Health Education
HIKAGE, Y., Home Economics Education, Laundering and Finishing
HIRAKI, K.
HIRAOKA, K., Adolescent Development, Learning Theory
HONMA, M., Movement Theory
HORIUCHI, H., Earth Materials Science
HOSHI, K., Art Education
HOSHINO, H., Condensed Matter Physics
IMAI, T., Musicology
ITOH, S., Analysis
IWAI, Y., Oil Painting, Tempera and Etching
KAMADA, K., Sedimentology
KAMIYA, K., Rural Sociology
KATO, Y., Food Chemistry
KITADA, T., Harmonic Analysis
KON, M., Differential Geometry
MARUYAMA, M., Japanese Literature
MENZAWA, K., School Health Education and Safety Education, School Health Promotion
MORI, A., School Health Education
MORI, R., Home Economics Education
MURAKAMI, O., Animal Physiology
MURAYAMA, M., Educational Methodology
NANBA, K., Algebra, Foundations of Mathematics, Discrete Mathematics
OHSHIMA, Y., Biomechanics
OHTAKA, A., Animal Taxonomy
OKADA, K., Sculpture, Clay Working (Pottery)
OKUNO, T., English Linguistics
OTA, S., Mathematics Education
OTSUBO, S., Sociology of Education
OYAMA, S., Health and Physical Education
OZAWA, H., Educational System and Administration
SAITO, S., Science Education, Phycology, Limnology
SAITO, T., History of Medieval Japan
SATO, K., Exercise Physiology
SATO, S., Adult Education
SATO, Y., Paediatrics
SATOH, Y., Magnetics
SEKI, H., Photochemistry
TAKANASHI, T., English Teaching Methodology
TANDOH, S., Educational Psychology
TOYOSHIMA, A., Social Clinical Psychology
UEDA, K., Timber Engineering
WATANABE, K., Voice
YAJIMA, T., Philosophy
YAMAGUCHI, T., Sinology
YOSHINO, H., Developmental Psychology, Psychology of Personality

Faculty of Humanities (internet human.cc.hirosaki-u.ac.jp):

AKAGI, K., Public Economics, Law and Economics
ARAI, K., Behavioural Accounting
CARPENTER, V., International Politics
FUJINUMA, K., Japanese Archaeology
FUJITA, M., Business Behaviour, Public Utilities
FUNAKI, Y., Statistics and Operations Research
HASEGAWA, S., Early Modern Japanese History
HORIUCHI, T., Constitutional Law
HOSHINO, Y., Accounting and Control
IGARASHI, Y., Ethics
ISHIDOU, T., English, American Literature, American Studies, Robert Frost, Mark Twain, McCarthyism
KATORI, K., Science of Information and Systems
KITAJIMA, S., Regional Economy and Regional Policy
MOROOKA, M., Science of Religion
MURAMATSU, K., Political Theory
MURATA, S., English Literature
NAKAZAWA, K., Western Economic History
NITTA, S., Modern German Literature
OKAZAKI, E., Philosophy
OKUNO, K., Linguistics
PHILIPS, J. E., History of Africa, America and Islam
SAKUMICHI, S., Social Psychology, Anthropology
SATO, N., English Literature
SATOH, K., Japanese Linguistics
SHIMUZU, A., Philosophy of Information
SHINOMIYA, T., Business History
SUDO, H., History of Art
SUGIYAMA, Y., Cultural Anthropology
SUZUKI, K., Economic Theory
TANAKA, I., German Literary Arts
TERADA, M., French Literature
UEKI, H., Chinese Classical Literature
USUDA, S., Japanese Literature
WARASHINA, K., Japanese Language
YASUDA, M., Marketing

Faculty of Science and Technology (3 Bunkyo-cho, Hirosaki 036-8561; internet www.st.hirosaki-u.ac.jp):
AMENOMORI, M., Cognitive Science, Super-high Energy Physics
ARAKI, T., Applied Electronics
FUKASE, M., VLSI Computer
FURUYA, Y., Intelligent Materials Design and Systems, Materials Processing, Solid State Sensors and Actuators, Non-destructive Evaluation
GOTO, T., Applied Chemistry
IIKURA, Y., Instrumentation Physics, Remote Sensing
INAMURA, T., Spray Engineering and Combustion, Propulsion Engineering
ITO, A., Combustion, Fire Science, Multiple Phase Flow
ITO, S., Organic Syntheses
KATO, H., Solid State Physics, Synchrotron-Radiation Science
KAWAGUCHI, S., Cosmic-ray Physics
KURAMATA, S., Space Physics
KURATSUBO, S., Harmonic Analysis
MAKINO, E., Micro Electromechanical Systems
MASHITA, M., Thin Film and Surface Physics
MIYATA, H., Solid Mechanics, Fracture Mechanics, Strength Evaluation Systems
MORI, T.
MOTOSE, K., Algebra
NAKAZATO, H., Functional Analysis
NANJO, H., High Energy Astrophysics
NENCHEV, D. N., Robotics
OHZEKI, K., Analytical Chemistry
RIKIISHI, K., Physical Oceanography, Meteorology, Glaciology
SAITO, M., Computational Science Approach to Biomolecular Recognition
SAKISAKA, Y., Solid State Physics, Synchrotron-radiation Science
SASAKI, K., Surface Physics
SATO, H., Phase Transformation, Plastic Deformation
SATO, T., Raman Spectra
SATO, T., Seismology
SHIBA, M., Disaster Prevention Geology
SHIMIZU, T., Bioinformatics, Biophysics
SUDO, S., Physical Chemistry
SUTO, S., Physical Chemistry of Polymers
TAJIRI, A., Organic Physical Chemistry
TAKAGUCHI, M., Matrix Analysis
TAKEGAHARA, K., Theoretical Solid State Physics
TANAKA, K., Physical Vulcanology, Seismology
TSURUMI, M., Environmental Chemistry, Geochemistry
UJIIE, Y., Petroleum Geology, Organic Geology
YOSHIOKA, Y., Computer Networks, Computer Architecture
YOSHIZAWA, A., Organic Materials Science

School of Medicine (53 Hon-cho, Hirosaki 036-8563; internet hippo.med.hirosaki-u.ac.jp):
ABE, Y., Radiation Oncology
ENDO, M., Glycobiology of Glycoconjugates
HADA, R., Medical Informatics
HANADA, K., Sun Protection, Laser Therapy, Atopic Dermatitis, Photodynamic Therapy
ICHIMARU, T., Medical Apparatus and Engineering
ICHINOHE, T., Paediatric Nursing, Guidance in Nursing Practice
ITO, E., Paediatric Haematology and Oncology
IWASAKI, A., Medical (Radiation) Physics
KACHI, T., Anatomy
KAGIAYA, A., Obstetrics and Gynaecology
KAMIYA, H., Immunopathology of Parasitic Infection
KANEKO, S., Epiteptology, Clinical and Basic Neuropsychopharmacology
KAWAHARA, R., Gerontological Nursing
KIKUCHI, H., Endocrinology
KIMURA, H., Oral and Maxillo-facial Surgery
KIMURA, K., Nursing of Adults
KUDO, H., Tumour Pathology
KURATA, K., Neurophysiology
KURODA, N., Forensic Pathology
MATSUKI, A., Anaesthesiology, Intensive Care, Pain Clinic
MATSUMOTO, M., Neurophysiology
MATSUNAGA, M., Clinical Neurology, Neuroepidemiology
MINAGAWA, T., Cancer Nursing
MITA, R., Public Health
MIURA, H., Existence Philosophy, Medical Philosophy and Ethics
MIURA, T., Orthopaedic Surgery, Rehabilitation Medicine
MIZUSHIMA, Y., Respirology, Gerontology
MOTOMURA, S., Cardiovascular Pharmacology
MUNAKATA, A., Gastroenterology
MUNAKATA, H., Paediatric Surgery
NAKAMURA, T., Chronic Pancreatitis, Pancreatic Steatorrhoea, Pancreatic Diabetes, Gastric Emptying, Clinical Laboratory Medicine
NAKANE, A., Bacteriology, Immunology
NAKAZAWA, M., Basic and Clinical Research for Retinal Diseases
NIKARA, T., Physiology
OHGUSHI, Y., Nursing Science
OKUMURA, K., Internal Medicine, Cardiology
SASAKI, J., Tumour Immunology, Pathogenic Bacteriology, Food Science
SASAKI, M., Surgery for Digestive Diseases, Hepato-pancreaticobiliary Surgery, Liver Transplantation
SATO, T., Pathology
SATO, Y., Neuroscience
SATOH, K., Basic Studies on the Pathogenesis of Cerebrovascular Diseases
SATOH, K., Biochemistry, Enzymology, Chemical Larcinogenesis
SAWADA, Y., Study of Wound Healing, Burns, Hypertrophic Scan and Keloids, Microcirculation of the Flap
SEIMIYA, Y., Analysis of Daily Activity
SHINKAWA, H., Inner and Middle Ear Morphology, Middle Ear Surgery
SHOMURA, K., Neural Anatomy
SUDA, T., Endocrinology and Metabolism
SUGAMARA, K., Pharmacological and Pharmaceutical Drugs Interaction
SUGAWARA, K., Physical Fitness, Nutrition, Immunology
SUZUKI, S., Neurosurgery, Cerebrovascular Diseases
SUZUKI, T., Oncology of the Urogenital Region
TAKAHASHI, G., Microscopic Anatomy, Cell Biology
TATEISHI, T., Clinical Pharmacology, Pharmacokinetics and Pharmacodynamics
TSUCHIDA, S., Cancer Biochemistry, Biochemical Pharmacology
TSUSHIMA, H., Physical Therapy
WADA, K., Clinical Research in Adult Epilepsy
WAKABAYASHI, K., Neuropathology
WAKUI, M., Cellular Physiology
WAKUI, M., Physiology I
YAGIHASHI, S., Pathology
YAMABE, H., Nephrology
YAMADA, C., Community Health, Public Health, International Health, International Cooperation
YASUJIMA, M., Laboratory Medicine, Hypertension
YODONO, H., Research of Interventional Radiology
YONESAKA, S., Paediatric Cardiology

ATTACHED RESEARCH INSTITUTES

Center for Computing and Communications: 3 Bunkyo-Cho, Hirosaki 036-8561; Dir Y. YOSHIOKA.

Center for Education and Research of Lifelong Learning: 1 Bunkyo-cho, Hirosaki 036-8560; Dir S. SATO.

Center for Educational Research and Practice: 1 Bunkyo-cho, Hirosaki 036-8560; Dir K. FUKIGAI.

Center for Joint Research: 3 Bunkyo-cho, Hirosaki 036-8561; Dir A. TAJIRI.

Earthquake and Volcano Observatory: 3 Bunkyo-cho, Hirosaki 036-8561; Dir K. TANAKA.

Gene Research Center: 3 Bunkyo-cho, Hirosaki 036-8561; Dir M. NIIZEKI.

Institute of Brain Science: 5 Zaifu-cho, Hirosaki 036-8562; Dir M. MATSUNAGA.

Institute for Experimental Animals: 5 Zaifu-cho, Hirosaki 036-8562; Dir H. KAMIYA.

University Farms: 7-1 Shitafukuro, Fujisaki-machi, Aomori-ken 038-3802; Dir T. NOMURA

HIROSHIMA UNIVERSITY

3-2 Kagamiyama 1-chome, Higashi-Hiroshima 739-8511
Telephone: (82) 422-7111
E-mail: inquiry@office.hiroshima-u.ac.jp
Internet: www.hiroshima-u.ac.jp/index-j.html

Founded 1949
Private control
Academic year: April to March (2 semesters)
Pres.: TOSHIMASA ASAHARA
Exec. Vice-Pres. for Education: M. SAKAKOSHI
Exec. Vice-Pres. for Research: E. TSUCHIYA
Exec. Vice-Pres. for Public Relations and Academic Information: T. OKAMOTO
Exec. Vice-Pres. for International Affairs: Y. YAMANE
Exec. Vice-Pres. for Medical Affairs: M. OCHI
Exec. Vice-Pres. for Finance and General Affairs: T. KAWAMOTO
Vice-Pres. for Student Support: N. KAWASAKI
Vice-Pres. for Library: K. TOMINAGA

Library of 3,367,718 vols, incl. 1,305,786 in foreign languages
Number of teachers: 1,766
Number of students: 15,463

Publications: *Agricultural and Fisheries Economics of Hiroshima University*, *Bulletin of Setouchi Field Science Centre Graduate School of Biosphere Science Hiroshima University*, *Bulletin of the Department of Teaching Japanese as a Second Language*, *Bulletin of the Faculty of Education*, *Bulletin of the Faculty of School Education*, *Bulletin of the Graduate School of Education*, *Bulletin of the Graduate School of Engineering*, *Bulletin of the Graduate School of Integrated Arts and Sciences*, *Bulletin of the Institute for the Cultural Studies of the Seto Inland Sea*, *Bulletin of Training and Research Centre for Clinical Psychology*, *Bulletin of Research Centre for Educational Study and Practice*, *Bulletin of the Research Centre for the Technique of Representation*, *Daigaku ronshu: Research in Higher Education*, *Essay on Modern Literature*, *Etudes de Langue et Littérature françaises de l'Université de Hiroshima*, *Hiroshima Forum for Psychology*, *Hiroshima Interdisciplinary Studies in the Humanities*, *Hiroshima Journal of Ethnological Studies*, *Hiroshima Journal of Mathematics Education*, *Hiroshima Journal of Medical Sciences*, *Hiroshima Law Review*, *Hiroshima Papers on Society and Culture*, *Hiroshima Peace Science*, *Hir-*

oshima Psychological Research, Hiroshima Studies in English Language and Literature, Hiroshima Studies in Language and Language Education, Hiroshima University Management Review, IPSHU Research Report Series, Journal of Health Sciences, Journal of Hiroshima University Archives, Journal of International Cooperation in Education, Journal of International Development and Cooperation, Journal of Japan Academy of Neonatal Nursing, Journal of Learning and Curriculum Development, Journal of Learning Science, Journal of the Faculty of Applied Biological Science, Hiroshima University, Journal of the Graduate School of Biosphere Science, Journal of the Hiroshima University Curriculum Research and Development Association, The Annals of Educational Research, The Annals of the Research Project Centre for the Comparative Study of Logic, The Annual of Research on Early Childhood, The Bulletin of the Centre for Research on Regional Economic Systems, The Bulletin of the Centre for Special Needs Education Research and Practice, The Economic Studies, The Hiroshima Economic Review, The Hiroshima Economic Studies, The Hiroshima Law Journal, The Hiroshima University Studies, Faculty of Letters, The Hiroshima University Studies, Graduate School of Letters, The Journal of Ethical Studies, The Journal of Hiroshima University Dental Society, The Journal of Social and Cultural Studies on Asia, The Review of the Study of History, Medical Journal of Hiroshima University, Memoirs of the Faculty of Integrated Arts and Sciences, Reviews in Higher Education, Review of Japanese Studies, Scientific Report of the Laboratory for Amphibian Biology, Seikei Ronso: The Journal of Politics and Economics of Hiroshima University, Studies in European and American Culture

DEANS

Faculty of Dentistry: Prof. T. TAKATA
Faculty of Medicine: Prof. M. YOSHIZUMI
Faculty of Pharmaceutical Sciences: Prof. H. OTSUKA
Graduate School of Advanced Sciences of Matter: Prof. T. TAKABATAKE
Graduate School of Biomedical Sciences: Prof. M. KOBAYASHI
Graduate School of Biosphere Sciences: Prof. M. ESAKA
Graduate School of Education: Prof. K. TANAHASHI
Graduate School of Engineering: Prof. F. YOSHIDA
Graduate School of Health Sciences: Prof. S. KAWAMATA
Graduate School of of Integrated Arts and Sciences: Prof. O. KASHIHARA
Graduate School for International Development and Cooperation: Prof. H. IKEDA
Graduate School of Letters: Prof. H. YAMAUCHI
Graduate School of Science: Prof. H. DEGUCHI
Graduate School of Social Sciences: Prof. S. TOMIOKA
Hiroshima University Hospital: Prof. K. CHAYAMA (Dir)
Hiroshima University Law School: Prof. M. KINOSHITA

PROFESSORS

Faculty of Integrated Arts and Sciences (7-1 Kagamiyama 1-chome, Higashi-Hiroshima 739-8521; tel. (82) 422-7111; e-mail souka-bucho-sien@office.hiroshima-u.ac.jp; internet home.hiroshima-u.ac.jp/souka/e/ias.html):

Division of Area Studies:
FUJITA-SANO, M., Cultural Anthropology, American Studies
IIDA, M., English Literature and Culture
ITOH, S., American Literature and Culture
KASHIHARA, O., Modern Japanese Literature
KOHATA, F., Biblical Studies
KUSUNOSE, M., Modern Chinese History
MIKI, N., Contemporary Chinese Culture
OKAMOTO, M., American Social History
SATAKE, A., Japanese History and Culture
SATO, M., History of German Literature, Everyday Life and Customs in the Early Modern Age
TAKATANI, M., Cultural Anthropology, South-East Asian Studies

Division of Behavioural and Biological Sciences:
ANDO, M., Integrative Physiology
FURUKAWA, Y., Neurobiology
HORI, T., Psychophysiology
IWATA, K., Comparative Politics and Diplomacy
KAWAHARA, A., Developmental Biology
KUSUDO, K., History of Sport
SEIWA, H., Psychology of Personality
TSUTSUI, K., Brain Science
URA, M., Social Psychology
WADA, M., Biochemistry of Exercise
YAMASAKI, M., Exercise Physiology

Division of Creative Arts and Sciences:
GOLDSBURY, P. A., Philosophy of Language, Comparative Culture
HARA, M., Comparative Philosophy and Music Aesthetics
KOTOH, T., Comparative Philosophy
MURASE, N., French Theatre, French Studies
NAKAMURA, H., Shakespeare, Cinema Studies, Cultural Semiotics
SAITO, T., Modern Science and Mysticism
TAKAHASHI, N., Ancient Greek Philosophy

Division of Language and Culture:
ANIYA, S., Linguistics
HIGUCHI, M., English Philology
IMAZATO, C., History of the English Language, Lexicography
INOUE, K., Linguistics
KOBAYASHI, H., Applied Linguistics, TESOL
NISHIDA, T., Applied Linguistics
OGAWA, Y., Comparative Study of Japanese and Chinese
SKAER, P. M., Linguistics
TANAKA, S., German Literature
YAMADA, J., Psycholinguistics
YOON, K. B., Korean Literature
YOSHIDA, M., Linguistics

Division of Materials Science:
FUKAMIYA, N., Bioactive Natural Products Chemistry
HATAKENAKA, N., Theoretical Condensed Matter Physics
HIKOSAKA, M., Soft Materials Physics
HOSHINO, K., Condensed Matter Physics
ITOH, T., Molecular Spectroscopy and Quantum Chemistry
KOJIMA, K., Condensed Matter Physics
KOMINAMI, S., Biophysical Chemistry
NAGAI, K., Theoretical Solid State Physics
TAKEDA, T., Condensed Matter Physics
UDAGAWA, M., Condensed Matter Physics

Division of Mathematical and Information Sciences:
AGAOKA, Y., Differential Geometry
HARADA, K., Geometry Graphics
KUWADA, M., Experimental Design
MIZUTA, Y., Function Theory
YOSHIDA, K., Applied Analysis

Division of Natural Environmental Sciences:
FUKUOKA, M., Research of Earth Resources
HAYASE, K., Environmental Sciences
HONDA, K., Chemical Ecology
HORIKOSHI, T., Microbiology
KAIHOTSU, I., Hydrology
NAKAGOSHI, N., Landscape Ecology
NARISADA, K., Science Studies
OHO, Y., Environmental Geology
SAKURAI, N., Environmental Plant Physiology
TOGASHI, K., Applied Ecology

Division of Socio-Environmental Studies:
AKIBA, S., Rural Sociology
FUKIHARA, S., Regions and Economy
ICHIKAWA, H., History of Technology
YASUNO, M., Contemporary History

Graduate School of Biosphere Sciences:
NAKANE, K., Environmental Ecosystem Ecology
SAKUGAWA, H., Environmental Chemistry

Graduate School of Education (1-1 Kagamiyama 1-chome, Higashi-Hiroshima 739-8524; tel. (82) 422-7111; e-mail kyoiku-kyo-sien@office.hiroshima-u.ac.jp; internet www.ed.hiroshima-u.ac.jp/index.html):

Doctoral Programme in Learning and Curriculum Development; and Masters Programme in Learning Science—Learning Development Major:
DOBASHI, T., Lifespan Developmental Education
HIGUCHI, S., Philosophy and Aesthetics of Learning
ISHII, S., Environmental Psychology
MORI, T., Psychology of Learning
NISHINE, K., Sociology of Education
TAKAHASHI, S., Social Psychology

Doctoral Programme in Learning and Curriculum Development; and Masters Programme in Learning Science—Curriculum and Instruction Development Major:
KIHARA, S., Physical Education
KIMURA, H., Social Studies Education
KUROSE, M., Keyboard Music
MAEDA, S., Human Geography
MATSUDA, Y., Psychology of Physical Education
MOCHIZUKI, T., Food Science
MORITA, N., Japanese Language Education
SHIBA, K., Science Education
TAINOSHO, J., Home Economics Education
WAKAMOTO, S., Art Education

Doctoral Programme in Learning and Curriculum Development; and Masters Programme in Special Education:
FUNATSU, M., Psychology of Children with Disabilities
HAYASAKA, K., Speech and Language Pathology
OCHIAI, T., Special Educational Systems, Inclusive Education
SHIMIZU, Y., Audiology and Education of Children with Hearing Impairment
YAMANASHI, M., Methods of Teaching Children with Visual Impairment

Doctoral Programme in Arts and Science Education; and Masters Programme in Science, Technology and Science Education—Science Education Major:
FURUKAWA, Y., Solid State Chemistry, Magnetic Resonance
HAYASHI, T., Regional Geology, Geoinformatics, Earth Science Education
KADOYA, S., Science Education
MAEHARA, T., Particles and Fields, Physics Education
SUZUKI, M., Petrology
TANAKA, H., Inorganic Chemistry
TOKUNAGA, T., Solid State Physics
TORIGOE, K., Zoology, Biology Education
TSUTAOKA, T., Solid State Physics

YAMASHITA, Y., Nuclear Physics, Physics Education

Doctoral Programme in Arts and Science Education; and Masters Programme in Science, Technology and Science Education—Mathematics Education Major:

IMAOKA, M., Geometry
IWASAKI, H., Mathematics Education
KAGEYAMA, S., Statistics and Combinatorics
MARUO, O., Algebra
NAKAHARA, T., Mathematics Education

Doctoral Programme in Arts and Science Education; and Masters Programme in Science, Technology and Science Education—Technology and Information Education Major:

BANSHOYA, K., Woodworking
MONDEN, Y., Computer Science
TASHIMA, S., Mechanical Processing
UEDA, K., Technology Educations
YAMAMOTO, T., Computer Control Technology

Doctoral Programme in Arts and Science Education; and Masters Programme in Science, Technology and Science Education—Social Studies Education Major:

IKENO, N., Social Studies Education
KATAKAMI, S., Social Studies Education
KOBARA, T., Social Studies Education
MIYAKE, T., Modern Japanese History
NAKAYAMA, T., Medieval Japanese History
OBI, T., Eastern History
SATO, S., Western History
SHIMOMUKAI, T., Ancient and Medieval Japanese History
TANAHASHI, K., Social Studies Education

Doctoral Programme in Arts and Science Education; and Masters Programme in Language and Culture Education—Japanese Language and Culture Education Major:

EBATA, Y., Japanese Language
IWASAKI, F., Japanese Literature
TAKAHASHI, K., Linguistic Geography
TAKEMURA, S., Japanese Literature
YOSHIDA, H., Japanese Language Education

Doctoral Programme in Arts and Science Education; and Masters Programme in Language and Culture Education—English Language and Culture Education Major:

FUKAKAWA, S., Pragmatics, Classroom Research
HAMAGUCHI, O., American Literature
MIURA, S., English Language Education
NAKAO, Y., English Philology and Linguistics
TANAKA, M., Language Testing in English Language Teaching

Doctoral Programme in Arts and Science Education; and Masters Programme in Language and Culture Education—Japanese Pedagogy, Linguistics and Culture Studies Major:

KURACHI, A., Intercultural Education
MACHI, H., Study of Japanese Composition and Style
MIZUMACHI, I., Educational Language Technology
MIZUSHIMA, H., Comparative Cultures and Comparative Literature
NAKAMURA, S., Japanese Intellectual History
NUIBE, Y., Japanese Language Pedagogics
NUMOTO, K., Historical Study of Japanese Language
SAKODA, K., Second Language Acquisition
TAWATA, S., Japanese Linguistics and Japanese Language Education

Doctoral Programme in Arts and Science Education; and Masters Programme in Lifelong Activities Education—Health and Sports Sciences Education Major:

ESASHI, Y., Physical Education
KUROKAWA, T., Sports Training
KUSUDO, K., History of Sport
MATSUOKA, S., Physical Education
WATANABE, K., Physiology, Sports Biomechanics
YANAGIHARA, E., Kinematical Analysis in Sport (Ball Games)

Doctoral Programme in Arts and Science Education; and Masters Programme in Lifelong Activities Education—Human Life Sciences Education Major:

HIRATA, M., Management of Life
IKAWA, Y., Science of Food Preparation
IWASHIGE, H., House Environment Science
MIYAMOTO, S., Clothing Science
SHIBA, S., Home Economics Education

Doctoral Programme in Arts and Science Education; and Masters Programme in Lifelong Activities Education—Music Culture Education Major:

CHIBA, J., Musicology
KUROSE, M., Keyboard Music
OKANO, S., Piano
OKUDA, M., Vocal Music
YOSHITOMI, K., Music Education

Doctoral Programme in Arts and Science Education; and Masters Programme in Lifelong Activities Education—Art Education Major:

ESAKI, A., Product Design
SUGAMURA, T., Science of Arts (History of Japanese Arts)
UCHIDA, M., Drawing and Painting

Doctoral Programme in Education and Human Science; and Masters Programme in Educational Studies:

KOGA, K., Educational Administration and Policy
KOHNO, K., Studies of Educational Leadership
KOIKE, G., Adult and Continuing Education
NAKANO, K., Curriculum Research
NINOMIYA, A., Comparative Education
OKATO, T., Educational Management
OTSUKA, Y., Comparative Education
SAKAKOSHI, M., Educational Thought and Philosophy in Germany
SATOH, H., History of Japanese and Eastern Education
TORIMITSU, M., Early Childhood Education
YAMASAKI, H., Sociology of Higher Education
YASUHARA, Y., History of Western Education

Doctoral Programme in Education and Human Science; and Masters Programme in Psychology:

FUKADA, H., Social Psychology
KODAMA, K., Clinical Psychology
MAEDA, K., Developmental Psychology
MIYATANI, M., Cognitive Psychology
OKAMOTO, Y., Developmental Clinical Psychology
TOSHIMA, T., Neuropsychology
YAMAZAKI, A., Child Psychology

Doctoral Programme in Education and Human Science; and Masters Programme in Higher Education Research and Development:

ARIMOTO, A., Sociology of Higher Education
DAIZEN, T., Sociology of Higher Education
HATA, T., History of Higher Education in Japan
KITAGAKI, I., Education Technology, Fuzzy Science
YAMAMOI, A., Sociology of Higher Education

Graduate School of Advanced Sciences of Matter (3-1 Kagamiyama 1-chome, Higashi-Hiroshima 739-8530; tel. (82) 422-7111; internet www.hiroshima-u.ac.jp/en/adsm/):

Department of Molecular Biotechnology:

HIRATA, D., Molecular Biology
KATO, J., Molecular Environmental Biotechnology
KINASHI, H., Microbiology and Natural Product Chemistry
KURODA, A., Biochemistry
MIYAKAWA, T., Molecular Biotechnology in Yeast
NISHIO, N., Environmental Bioengineering
ONO, K., Molecular Biochemistry
TSUCHIYA, E., Molecular Cell Biology
YAMADA, T., Plant/Microbe Interactions

Department of Quantum Matter:

ENDO, I., Photon Physics
JO, T., Theory of Condensed Matters
KADOYA, Y., Solid State Quantum Optics
OGUCHI, T., Computational Physics
OKAMOTO, H., Beam Physics
SERA, M., Experimental Researches of Strongly Correlated Electron Systems
SUZUKI, T., Low Temperature Physics
TAKABATAKE, T., Magnetism and Magnetic Materials
TAKAHAGI, T., Nanotechnology

Department of Semiconductor Electronics and Integration Science:

IWATA, A., Integrated Circuits
MIURA-MATTAUSCH, M., Semiconductor Device Technology
MIYAZAKI, S., Semiconductor Electronics

Graduate School of Biomedical Sciences (2-3 Kasumi 1-chome, Minami-ku, Hiroshima 734-8513; tel. (82) 257-5555; e-mail bimes-kyou@office.hiroshima-u.ac.jp; internet www.hiroshima-u.ac.jp/bimes/):

Programmes for Applied Biomedicine:

AKAGAWA, Y., Advanced Prosthodontics, Implantology
EBOSHIDA, A., Public Health and Health Policy, Health Science, Epidemiology, Environmental Health
HAMADA, T., Geriatric Dentistry, Prosthodontics, Stomatognathic Dysfunction
HIRAKAWA, K., Otorhinolaryngology, Head and Neck Surgery and Oncology, Rhinology
INAI, K., Pathology, Tumour Pathology
ITO, K., Radiology, Diagnostic Imaging, Interventional Radiology
KAMATA, N., Oral and Maxillofacial Surgery
KANBE, M., Clinical Laboratory Medicine, Clinical Physiology, ME, Medical Informatics, Gene Engineering
KAWAHARA, M., Dental Anaesthesiology, Pain Clinic
KIMURA, K.
KOBAYASHI, M., Paediatrics, Child Health
KOHNO, N., Molecular and Internal Medicine, Respiratory Diseases, Cancer Therapeutics
KOZAI, K., Paediatric Dentistry
KUDO, Y., Obstetrics and Gynaecology
MAEDA, N., Oral Growth and Developmental Biology, Development of Masticatory System
MORIKAWA, N., Clinical Pharmacotherapy, Pharmacokinetics, Therapeutic Drug Monitoring
OCHI, M., Orthopaedic Surgery, Sports Medicine, Knee Surgery
OZAWA, K., Pharmacotherapy, Clinical Pharmacology
SUEDA, T., Surgery, Thoracic and Cardiovascular Surgery, Bioengineering

TAKAHASHI, I., Preventive Dentistry, Mucosal Immunology
TANIGAWA, K., Emergency and Critical Care Medicine, Cardiopulmonary Resuscitation, Airway Management, Free Radicals and Reperfusion Injury
TANIMOTO, K., Oral and Maxillofacial Radiology, Dysphagia
TANNE, K., Orthodontics and Craniofacial Developmental Biology, Biomechanics
YAJIN, K., Otorhinolaryngology, Head and Neck Surgery, Head and Neck Oncology, Rhinology
YOSHIZAWA, K., Infectious Disease Control and Prevention, Seroepidemiology of Viral Hepatitis
YUGE, O., Anaesthiology and Critical Care

Programmes for Biomedical Research:

AOYAMA, H., Anatomy and Developmental Biology
ASAHARA, T., Surgery, Gastroenterological Surgery, Organ Transplantation
CHAYAMA, K., Medicine and Molecular Science, Gastroenterology, Hepatology
DOHI, T., Dental Pharmacology
HAZEKI, O., Physiological Chemistry, Cellular Signal Transduction
HIDE, M., Dermatology, Allergology and Immunopharmacology in Skin
IDE, T., Cellular and Molecular Biology
KANNO, M., Immunology, Parasitology, Molecular Immunology
KATAOKA, K., Histology and Cell Biology, Histochemistry and Cell Biology of the Digestive Organs
KATO, Y., Dental and Medical Biochemistry, Biochemistry and Oral Biology
KIKUCHI, A., Biochemistry, Intracellular Signal Transduction
KURIHARA, H., Periodontal Medicine, Periodontal Tissue Regeneration, Endodontology
KURISU, K., Neurosurgery, Neuro-oncology, Neuroradiology, Surgery of Brain Tumours and Cerebro-vascular Disease, Skull Base Surgery
MASUJIMA, T., Analytical Molecular Medicine and Devices, Videonanoscopes, Cell Dynamics, Pharmaco-dynamics, Bioanalysis
MATSUMOTO, M., Clinical Neuroscience and Therapeutics, Neurology, Strokology, Gerontology
MISHIMA, H., Ophthalmology and Visual Science, Glaucoma, Ocular Cell Biology, Ocular Pharmacology, Retinal Disease
OGATA, N., Neurophysiology
OHTA, S., Xenobiotic Metabolism and Molecular Toxicology, Neurochemistry, Drug Metabolism
OKAMOTO, T., Molecular Oral Medicine and Maxillofacial Surgery
OKAZAKI, M., Biomaterials Science, Dental Materials
SAKAI, N., Molecular and Pharmacological Neuroscience, Molecular Neurobiology, Neuropharmacology
SHIBA, Y., Oral Physiology
SUGAI, M., Bacteriology, Oral Microbiology
SUGIYAMA, M., Molecular Microbiology and Biotechnology, Antibiotics, Enzymology, Molecular Genetics, Applied Microbiology
TAKATA, T., Oral Maxillofacial Pathobiology, Oral Oncology, Periodontal Tissue Engineering, Diagnostic Pathology
UCHIDA, T., Oral Biology, Oral Anatomy
USUI, T., Urology, Andrology, Oncology, Endo-urology
YAMAWAKI, S., Psychiatry and Neurosciences, Biological Psychiatry, Psychopharmacology, Affective Disorders, Neuroleptic Malignant Syndrome, Psychosomatic Medicine, Liaison Psychiatry, Psycho-oncology
YASUI, W., Molecular Pathology, Molecular Pathology of Gastrointestinal Cancer
YOSHIDA, T., Virology, Paramyxovirus, Bacteriology
YOSHIZUMI, M., Cardiovascular Physiology and Medicine, Cardiology and Vascular Biology

Programmes for Pharmaceutical Sciences:

KOIKE, T., Functional Molecular Sciences, Medicinal Chemistry, Bioinorganic Chemistry
NAKATA, Y., Pharmacology, Neuropharmacology, Molecular Pharmacology
OOTSUKA, H., Pharmacognosy and Natural Product Chemistry, Molecular Pharmaceutics
TAKANO, M., Pharmaceutics and Therapeutics, Drug Transporters and Metabolizing Enzymes, Drug Delivery Systems
TAKEDA, K., Synthetic Organic Chemistry, Mechanistic Organic Chemistry, Synthetic Methodology

Graduate School of Biosphere Sciences (4-4 Kagamiyama 1-chome, Higashi-Hiroshima 739-8528; tel. (82) 424-7905; e-mail sei-bucho-sien@office.hiroshima-u.ac.jp; internet home.hiroshima-u.ac.jp/gsbstop/english/top/index-e.html):

Department of Bioresource Science and Technology:

ESAKA, M., Function and Biosynthesis of Ascorbic Acid in Plants
FUJITA, M., Environmental Physiology of Farm Animals
FURASAWA, S., Basic and Applied Immunobiology
GOTO, N., Enology and Viticulture
GUSHIMA, K., Foraging Ecology of Coral Reef Fishes
HORI, K., Structures, Functions and Applications of Lectins from Marine Organisms
IEFUJI, H., Environmental and Food Biotechnology
IMABAYASHI, H., Larval Settlement of Benthic Organisms
KATO, N., Nutrition and Cancer
KONO, K., Cellular Immunology
MATSUDA, H., Chicken Monoclonal Antibodies
MITANI, K., Holistic Management of Farm Animals
MIZUTA, K., Molecular and Cellular Biology of Yeast
NAGAMATSU, Y., Applied Biochemistry of Microbial Proteins
NAKANO, H., Behaviour and Control of Foodborne Bacterial Pathogens
NISHIMURA, T., Structure and Function of Proteases in Muscle Foods
OHTA, T., Physiological Phenomena and Molecules, Identification and Mechanism Analysis
SATO, K., Physical Chemistry of Lipids
SUZUKI, K., Emulsifying Characteristics and Properties of Food Emulsions
SUZUKI, N., Bio-organic Chemistry, Active Oxygen, Antioxidative Activity, Bio- and Chemiluminescence
TANIGUCHI, K., Ruminant Nutrition and Feeding
TERADA, T., Nuclear Transfer in the Bovine and Porcine Embryo
TSUDUKI, M., Animal Breeding and Genetics
YOSHIMURA, Y., Endocrine Control of Avian Reproductive Functions

Department of Environmental Dynamics and Management:

FUJITA, K., Source–Sink Relationship
HOSHIKA, Y., Mechanism of Material Circulation and its Control in Coastal Seas
ISEKI, K., Marine Ecology and Biogeochemical Cycle
KONO, K., Biology and Fertility of Soils
MARAYAMA, T., Biology of Symbiotic Relationships between Marine Invertebrates and Micro-organisms, Biology of Hyperthermophiles
MASAOKA, Y., Enhancement of Metal Stress Tolerance in Plants
NAKANE, K., Environmental Chemistry
SAKUGAWA, H., Environmental Ecosystem Ecology
TAKASUGI, Y., Monitoring and Diagnosis of the Physical Environment in Semi-enclosed Sea
UYE, S., Production Ecology of Marine Zooplankton
YAMAMOTO, K., Microbial Ecology and Marine Ecology
YAMAMOTO, T., Aquatic Environmental Management
YAMAUCHI, M., Development of Ecophysiological Soil and Water Management Technology for Environmental Protection

Department of Sciences for Biospheric Co-existence:

NAKAI, T., Fish-pathogenic Bacteria and Viruses
TANAKA, H., Consumer Food Cooperatives
UEMATSU, K., Neural Basis for Fish Swimming
YAMAO, M., Locally Based Coastal Resource Management in Asia, Sustainable Coastal Fisheries Management and 'Code of Conduct for Responsible Production', People's Participation in Community Development and their Responsibility, Development and Export-oriented Food Production and its Impact on the Resource Environment

Graduate School of Engineering (4-1 Kagamiyama 1-chome, Higashi-Hiroshima 739-8527; tel. (82) 422-7111; internet www.eden.hiroshima-u.ac.jp):

Mechanical Systems Engineering:

ISHIZUKA, S., Combustion Science and Technology
KIKUCHI, Y., Heat Transfer, Biomass Energy, Carbon Nanotube
KUROKI, H., Powder Metallurgy and Ceramics
MAEKAWA, H., Fluid Engineering
NAGAMURA, K., Machine Elements, Gear Design and Vibration, Tribology
NAKAGAWA, N., Dynamics of Machines
NAKASA, K., Strength and Fracture of Materials, Vibration and Sound, Acoustic Energy
OBA, F., Manufacturing Systems
SAEKI, M., Automatic Control
SAWA, T., Strength of Material, Elasticity, Solid Mechanics
SHINOZAKI, K., Welding and Joining
SHIZUMA, K., Quantum Energy Applications
TAKI, S., Reactive Gas Dynamics
TAKIYAMA, K., Plasma Spectroscopy
YAMANE, Y., Machining, Machine Tools and Mechatronics
YANAGISAWA, O., Control of Material Properties
YOSHIDA, F., Engineering Elasto-Plasticity

Artificial Complex Systems Engineering:

HINAMOTO, T., Electronic Control, Digital Signal Processing
IWASE, K., Mathematical Statistics and Data Analysis
KADO, T., Nano-electronics
KANEKO, M., Robotics, Active Sensing
NAKANO, K., Computer Engineering
NISHIZAKI, I., Decision Analysis and Game Theory
SAKAWA, M., Systems Optimization
SHIBATA, T., Differential Equations and their Application

TAKAHASHI, K., Production Systems Engineering
TSUJI, T., Biological Systems Engineering
YOKOGAWA, K., Computational Materials Science
YORINO, N., Electric Power System Engineering

Information Engineering:

DOHI, T., Systems Reliability Engineering
HARADA, K., Graphics Geometry
HIRASHIMA, T., Computer-based Learning Environment
KUBO, F., Algebraic Deformation Theory
KUWADA, M., Experimental Designs
MORITA, K., Theoretical Computer Science
SHIBA, M., Complex Analysis and its Applications
WATANABE, T., Computer Science and Information Technology

Chemistry and Chemical Engineering:

ASAEDA, M., Separation and Purification Technology
HARIMA, Y., Materials Physical Chemistry
HIROKAWA, T., Applied Instrumental Analysis
KUNAI, A., Organic Materials Chemistry
OKADA, M., Environmental Chemical Engineering
OKUYAMA, K., Thermal Fluids Engineering
OTSUBO, T., Applied Organic Chemistry
SAKOHARA, S., Polymer Technology
SHIONO, T., Advanced Polymer Chemistry
TAKISHIMA, S., Chemical Engineering Thermodynamics
YAMANAKA, S., Applied Inorganic Materials Chemistry
YOSHIDA, H., Fine Particle Technology

Social and Environmental Engineering:

DOI, Y., Marine Hydrodynamics
FUJIKUBO, M., Strength of Structures
FUJIMOTO, Y., Reliability of Structures and Systems
KANEKO, A., Ocean–Atmosphere Environment
KAWAHARA, Y., Hydraulic Engineering
KITAMURA, M., Computational Mechanics for Structural Design
KOSE, K., Management of Human-Technology–Environment Systems
MATSUO, A., Building Structures
MIURA, K., Building Disasters Prevention
MURAKAWA, S., Community Environmental Science
NAKAMURA, H., Structural Engineering
OHKUBO, T., Building Materials and Components
SASAKI, Y., Soil Mechanics and Earthquake Geotechnical Engineering
SATO, R., Concrete and Concrete Structural Engineering
SUGANO, S., Earthquake Engineering
SUGIE, Y., Transportation Planning
SUGIMOTO, T., Architectural History and Design Theory
TAKAKI, M., Ocean Space Engineering
TSUCHIDA, T., Geotechnical and Geo-environmental Engineering
YASUKAWA, H., Naval Architecture
YOKOBORI, H., Architecture, Urban Planning and International Cooperation

Graduate School for International Development and Cooperation (5-1 Kagamiyama 1-chome, Higashi-Hiroshima 739-8529; tel. (82) 424-6905; e-mail idec@hiroshima-u.ac.jp; internet home.hiroshima-u.ac.jp/idec):

Division of Development Science:

FUJIWARA, A., Transportation Planning, Environmental Engineering
HIGO, Y., Ocean Engineering
KINBARA, T., Management and Organization
KOMATSU, M., Development Economics
MATSUOKA, S., Environmental Economics
NAKAZONO, K., International Relations
NOHARA, H., Comparative Study of Industrial Organizations
SAITO, K., Marine Development Technology
TOMINAGA, K., Disaster Prevention on Geotechnical Engineering

Division of Educational Development and Cultural and Regional Studies:

IKEDA, H., Content-based Science Education (Biology Education), International Cooperation in Science Education
KASAI, T., Motor Neurophysiology and Motor Rehabilitation Medicine
TABATA, Y., Educational Administration (Educational System, Teacher Education)
UEHARA, A., Intercultural Communication

Graduate School of Letters (2-3 Kagamiyama 1-chome, Higashi-Hiroshima 739-8522; tel. (82) 422-7111; e-mail bun-kyo-sien@office.hiroshima-u.ac.jp; internet home.hiroshima-u.ac.jp/bungaku/index.html):

ARIMOTO, N., Modern and Contemporary Japanese Literature
FURUSE, K., Archaeology
HARANO, N., French Language and Literature
ICHIKI, T., Chinese Philosophy
IMADA, Y., Linguistics
ITOH, K., Medieval Japanese Literature
ITOH, S., American Literature and Culture
IWAI, T., Ancient History of Europe
JIMURA, A., English Language Studies
KANO, M., Chinese Linguistics
KATSUBE, M., Japanese Modern History
KAWAHARA, T., German Plays and Opera
KISHIDA, H., Ancient and Medieval Japanese History
KONDO, Y., History of Ethical Thought
KUBOTA, K., Modern and Contemporary Japanese Literature
MATSUI, F., History of Ethical Thought, Bioethics
MATSUMOTO, M., Japanese Language Studies
MATSUMOTO, Y., French Language and Literature
MIURA, M., History of Japanese Architecture
MIZUTA, H., History of Western Philosophy
NAKAMURA, H., Shakespeare, Cinema Studies, Cultural Semiotics
NISHIBEPPU, M., Ancient History of Japan
NOMA, F., History of Ancient and Medieval Chinese Thought
OCHI, M., Ethics
OKAHASHI, H., Human Geography, Regional Geography
OKAMOTO, A., Modern and Contemporary Western History
OKUMURA, K., Physical Geography, Quaternary Geology
SATO, T., Chinese Literature
SODA, S., Modern Chinese History
TANAKA, H., Modern Contemporary American Literature
TOMINAGA, K., Chinese Literature
UEDA, Y., Linguistics
UEKI, K., English Literature
UEMURA, Y., Asian History
YAMASHIRO, H., Medieval Western History
YAMAUCHI, H., Western Philosophy
YOSHINAKA, T., English Literature

Graduate School of Medicine (2-3 Kasumi 1-chome, Minami-ku, Hiroshima 734-8553; tel. (82) 257-5555; e-mail bimes-kyou@office.hiroshima-u.ac.jp; internet www.hiroshima-u.ac.jp/hsc/):

Health Sciences:

INAMIZU, T., Sports Medicine and Sciences
INOUE, M., Gastroenterology, Gastrointestinal Physiology and Treatment of Acid-related Diseases
KAKEHASHI, M., Health Science, Health Statistics, Mathematical Modelling, Public Health
KATAOKA, T., Health Care for Adults
KAWAMATA, S., Anatomy of Musculoskeletal System, Anatomy of Calcified Tissue
KINJYO, T., Geriatric Nursing
KOBAYASHI, T., Health Development
MATSUKAWA, K., Physiology, Neural Control of the Cardiovascular System, Motor Control
MIYAGUCHI, H., Occupational Behavioural Science Laboratory
MIYAKOSHI, Y., Fundamentals of Nursing Theory and Practice, Nursing Management and Education
MORIYAMA, M., Medical–Surgical Nursing, Adult Health Nursing
MURAKAMI, T., Rheumatoid Surgery, Elbow Surgery, Sports Medicine
OKAMURA, H., Psycho-oncology, Psychosocial Rehabilitation
ONO, M., Community Health and Home Care Nursing
SHIMIZU, H., Science of Occupational Therapy
SHINKODA, K., Physical Therapy, Kinesiology
TANAKA, Y., Paediatrics, Health Science, Nursing Education
TOBIMATSU, Y., Rehabilitation Medicine and Science for the Elderly and People with Disabilities
TSUSHIMA, H., Community and School Health Nursing
URABE, Y., Athletic Rehabilitation
YAMAKATSU, H., Occupational Therapy for Physical Dysfunction and ADL Disorder
YOKOO, K., Neonatal Nursing, Maternal and Child Health Nursing, Midwifery
YUGE, R., Nerve and Muscle Regeneration

Graduate School of Science (3-1 Kagamiyama 1-chome, Higashi-Hiroshima 739-8526; tel. (82) 422-7111; e-mail ri-bucho-sien@office.hiroshima-u.ac.jp; internet www.sci.hiroshima-u.ac.jp/english):

Mathematics:

ENOMOTO, H., Graph Theory, Discrete Mathematics
KAMADA, S., Knots, Topology
MATSUMOTO, M., Galois Group, Arithmetic Fundamental Group, Random Number Generation
MATUMOTO, T., Topology
MIZUTA, Y., Potential Theory
MORITA, T., Dynamic Systems, Ergodic Theory
NAGAI, T., Differential Equations
TSUZUKI, N., Arithmetic Geometry, Number Theory
YOSHINO, M., Differential Equations

Physical Science:

HASHIMOTO, E., Physics of Perfect Crystals, Synchrotron Radiation Physics
HIRAYA, A., Molecular Photophysics and Photochemistry
HORI, T., Particle Accelerator Physics, Synchrotron Radiation Physics
KOJIMA, Y., Theory of Relativity and Astrophysics
MARUYAMA, H., Solid State Physics, X-Ray Spectroscopy
NAMATAME, H., Solid State Physics, Synchrotron Radiation Physics
OHSUGI, T., High Energy Particle Physics, Gamma-ray Astrophysics
OKAWA, M., Elementary Particle Theory, Lattice QCD
SUGITATE, T., High Energy Nuclear Physics
TANAKA, K., Photochemistry and Photophysics
TANIGUCHI, M., Solid State Physics, Synchrotron Radiation Science

Chemistry:

AIDA, M., Quantum Chemistry
EBATA, T., Laser Chemistry and Molecular Spectroscopy
FUJIWARA, T., Analytical Chemistry
FUKAZAWA, Y., Organic Stereochemistry
INOUE, K., Molecular Magnetism
MIYOSHI, K., Coordination and Organometallic Chemistry
OHKATA, K., Synthesis and Isolation of Natural Products
OHNO, K., Physical Chemistry and Vibrational Spectroscopy
YAMAMOTO, Y., Organic Main Group Element Chemistry
YAMASAKI, K., Chemical Kinetics and Dynamics

Biological Science:

DEGUCHI, H., Plant Taxonomy and Ecology, Bryology
HOSOYA, H., Cell Biology, Signal Transduction
MICHIBATA, H., Molecular Physiology
SUZUKI, K., Molecular Genetics, Yeast and Agrobacterial Genetics
TAKAHASHI, Y., Plant Molecular Biology
YOSHIZATO, K., Developmental Biology, Regeneration Biology

Earth and Planetary Systems Science:

HIDAKA, H., Isotope Geochemistry
SHIMIZU, H., Trace Element Geochemistry
TAJIMA, F., Solid Earth Geophysics
WATANABE, M., Ore Petrology and Ore Genesis

Mathematical and Life Sciences:

GEKKO, K., Physical Chemistry of Biopolymers
HIRATA, T., Biological Chemistry and Biotechnology
IDE, H., DNA Damage and Repair
KOBAYASHI, R., Self-organization in Material and Life Science
MORIKAWA, H., Molecular Plant Biology
NISHIMORI, H., Complex Systems and Nonlinear Dynamics
SAKAMOTO, K., Dynamical Systems
TANIMOTO, Y., Magneto-science
YAMAMOTO, T., Molecular Developmental Biology
YOSHIDA, K., Partial Differential Equations

Marine Biological Laboratory:

YASUI, K., Development and Bio-history of Marine Deuterostomes

Miyajima Natural Botanical Garden:

DEGUCHI, H., Plant Taxonomy and Ecology, Bryology

Institute for Amphibian Biology:

KASHIWAGI, A., Endocrine Disruptors, Space Biology, Apoptosis, Transgenesis
SUMIDA, M., Evolutionary Genetics, Molecular Phylogeny
YAOITA, Y., Developmental Biology, Metamorphosis, Programmed Cell Death

Laboratory of Plant Chromosome and Gene Stock:

KONDO, K., Plant Demography, Chromosome Science and Gene Resources

Graduate School of Social Sciences (Higashi-Hiroshima Campus: 2-1 Kagamiyama 1-chome, Higashi-Hiroshima 739-8525 Higashi-Senda Campus: 1-89 Higashisenda-machi 1-chome, Hiroshima 730-0053; tel. (82) 422-7111 (Higashi-Hiroshima), (82) 542-7014 (Higashi-Senda); e-mail syakai-bucho-sien@office.hiroshima-u.ac.jp):

AGAOKA, Y., Medieval Western History
AIZAWA, Y., Private International Law
EGASHIRA, D., Sociology
FUKIHARU, T., Microeconomics
FUTAMURA, H., Public Finance
GINAMA, I., Macroeconometrics
HINO, S., Product Development Theory
HOSHINO, I., Financial Accounting
INOUE, Z., Management (Strategy Theory)
ISHIDA, M., International Finance
ITOH, T., Economic Policy
KAN, T., Fiscal Policy
KANNO, R., Finance
KATOH, F., Occidental Economic History
KAWASAKI, N., Public Administration
MAEKAWA, K., Financial Econometrics
MAKINO, M., Political History
MATSUDA, M., Political Economy
MATSUMIZU, Y., World Economic Conditions
MATSUIKE, H., Criminal Law
MATSUURA, K., Finance and Econometrics
MORIBE, S., Japanese Politics
MORIOKA, T., Labour Economics
MORITA, K., Comparative Economic Systems
MURAMATSU, J., Marketing Theory
NISHIMURA, H., Constitutional Law
NISHITANI, H., International Law
NOMOTO, R., Industrial Organization
ODAKI, M., Statistics
OKAMURA, M., International Economics, Applied Microeconomics
OTANI, T., Sociology of Law
SAKAGUCHI, K., Management Accounting
SAKANE, Y., Economic History of Japan
TAKAHASHI, H., Civil Law
TAKI, A., Industrial Relations
TERAMOTO, Y., Diplomacy and Diplomatic History
TODA, T., Regional Development Policy
TOMIOKA, S., Economic History
TSUBAKI, Y., Information Resource Management
TSUJI, H., Labour Law
UEDA, Y., Public Choice and Institutional Economics
WAKIMOTO, S., Economic Policy
WATANABE, M., Social Policy
YAMADA, S., History of Political Thought
YANO, J., Macroeconomics
YOSHIDA, O., Asian Politics
YOSHIHARA, T., Legal History

Law School (1-89 Higashisenda 1-chome, Hiroshima 730-0053; tel. (82) 542-7014; e-mail senda-bk-sien@office.hiroshima-u.ac.jp; internet www.law.hiroshima-u.ac.jp/lawschool/ls-top.htm):

GOTOH, K., Commercial Law
HIRANO, T., Legal Philosophy
KAMITANI, Y., Civil Law
KATAGI, H., Commercial Law
KINOSHITA, M., Commercial Law
KOHAMA, S., Civil Law
KOHARI, Y., International Law
MITSUI, M., Labour Law
MONDEN, T., Constitutional Law
NAKA, T., Administrative Law
ODA, N., Criminal Law
OHKUBO, T., Criminal Procedure
OKAMOTO, T., Civil Law
SAEKI, Y., Administrative Law
TANABE, M., Civil Procedure
TORIYABE, S., Civil Law

Research Institute for Radiation Biology and Medicine (2-3 Kasumi 1-chome, Minami-ku, Hiroshima 734-8553; tel. (82) 257-5555; e-mail bimes-gen@office.hiroshima-u.ac.jp; internet www.rbm.hiroshima-u.ac.jp/index.html):

HONDA, H., Developmental Biology
HOSHI, M., Radiation Biophysics
INABA, T., Molecular Oncology, Haematology
KAMIYA, K., Radiation Biology, Oncology
KIMURA, A., Haematology and Oncology
MATSUURA, S., Human Genetics
MIYAGAWA, K., Molecular Oncology
NISHIYAMA, M., Molecular Oncology, Preclinical Development
OHTAKI, M., Biometrics, Environmetrics
SUZUKI, F., Radiation Biology
TAKIHARA, Y., Stem Cell Biology, Haematology, Regenerative Medicine
TASHIRO, S., Molecular Cell Biology

ATTACHED INSTITUTES

Beijing Research Centre: College of International Education, Capital Normal University, 105 Xisanhuan Beilu, Beijing 00037, China; Dir T. SATO.

Centre for the Study of International Cooperation in Education: 5-1 Kagamiyama 1-chome, Higashi-Hiroshima 739-8529; e-mail cice@hiroshima-u.ac.jp; internet home.hiroshima-u.ac.jp/cice; Dir A. NINOMIYA.

Collaborative Research Centre: 10-31 Kagamiyama 3-chome, Higashi-Hiroshima 739-0046; Dir Y. YAMANE.

Community Cooperation Centre: 3-2 Kagamiyama 1-chome, Higashi-Hiroshima 739-8511; Dir T. ANDO.

Environmental Research and Management Centre: 5-3 Kagamiyama 1-chome, Higashi-Hiroshima 739-8513; e-mail iwwt@hiroshima-u.ac.jp; Dir S. OTA.

Health Service Centre: 7-1 Kagamiyama 1-chome, Higashi-Hiroshima 739-8511; e-mail health@hiroshima-u.ac.jp; internet home.hiroshima-u.ac.jp/health; Dir M. YOSHIHARA.

Hiroshima Synchrotron Radiation Centre: 313 Kagamiyama 2-chome, Higashi-Hiroshima 739-8526; internet www.hsrc.hiroshima-u.ac.jp; Dir M. TANIGUCHI.

Information Media Centre: 4-2 Kagamiyama 1-chome, Higashi-Hiroshima 739-8526; internet www.media.hiroshima-u.ac.jp; Dir T. WATANABE.

Institute for Peace Science: 1-89, Higashisenda-machi 1-chome, Naka-ku, Hiroshima 730-0053; e-mail heiwa@hiroshima-u.ac.jp; internet home.hiroshima-u.ac.jp/heiwa; Dir M. MATSUO.

International Student Centre: 1-2 Kagamiyama 1-chome, Higashi-Hiroshima 739-8523; e-mail inquiry@office.hiroshima-u.ac.jp; internet www.hiroshima-u.ac.jp/en/international-center; Dir S. TAWADA.

Natural Science Centre for Basic Research and Development: 3-1 Kagamiyama 1-chome, Higashi-Hiroshima 739-8526; internet home.hiroshima-u.ac.jp/nbard; Dir I. YAMASHITA.

Research Centre for Nanodevices and Systems: 4-2 Kagamiyama 1-chome, Higashi-Hiroshima 739-8527; Dir A. IWATA.

Research Centre for Regional Geography: 2-3 Kagamiyama 1-chome, Higashi-Hiroshima 739-8522; Dir H. OKAHASHI.

Research Institute for Higher Education: 2-2 Kagamiyama 1-chome, Higashi-Hiroshima 739-8521; tel. (82) 424-6240; e-mail k-kokyo@office.hiroshima-u.ac.jp; internet en.rihe.hiroshima-u.ac.jp; Dir MASASHI FUJIMURA.

Saijo Seminar House: Misonou, Saijo-cho, Higashi-Hiroshima 739-0024; Dir S. TAKAHASHI

HITOTSUBASHI UNIVERSITY

2-1 Naka, Kunitachi City, Tokyo 186-8601
Telephone: (42) 580-8000
E-mail: pla-ko.g@dm.hit-u.ac.jp
Internet: www.hit-u.ac.jp

Founded 1875
Private control
Academic year: April to March

Pres.: HIROMITSU ISHI
Vice-Pres.: JYURO TERANISHI

Dir-Gen.: SAKASHI KAMATA
Dean of Students: TAKEHIKO SUGIYAMA
Librarian: MAKOTO IKEMA

Library of 1,739,884 vols
Number of teachers: 465 (full-time)
Number of students: 6,429

Publications: *Gengo Bunka—Cultura Philologica* (1 a year), *Hitotsubashi Arts and Sciences* (1 a year), *Hitotsubashi Journal of Commerce and Management* (1 a year), *Hitotsubashi Journal of Economics* (2 a year), *Hitotsubashi Journal of Law and Politics* (1 a year), *Hitotsubashi Journal of Social Studies* (2 a year), *The Hitotsubashi Review* (12 a year)

DEANS

Graduate School and Faculty of Commerce and Management: K. ITO
Graduate School and Faculty of Economics: E. TAJIKA
Graduate School and Faculty of Law: T. YAMAUCHI
Graduate School and Faculty of Social Sciences: N. TASAKI
Graduate School of International Corporate Strategy: H. TAKEUCHI
Graduate School of Language and Society: Y. SANO

ATTACHED INSTITUTES

Institute of Economic Research: Tokyo; e-mail www-info@ier.hit-u.ac.jp; internet www.ier.hit-u.ac.jp; f. 1940; 41 teachers; Dir M. KUBONIWA; publ. *Economic Review* (4 a year).

Institute of Innovation Research: Tokyo; e-mail iir.g@dm.hit-u.ac.jp; internet www.iir.hit-u.ac.jp; f. 1997; 11 teachers; Dir S. NAGAOKA; publ. *Hitotsubashi Business Review* (4 a year)

HOKKAIDO UNIVERSITY

Kita, 8 Nishi 5, Kita-ku, Sapporo 060-0808
Telephone: (11) 706-8027
E-mail: info@oia.hokudai.ac.jp
Internet: www.oia.hokudai.ac.jp

Founded 1876
Private control
Academic year: April to March

Pres.: Prof. KEIZO YAMAGUCHI
Vice-Pres.: Prof. KAZUSHIGE KAWABATA
Vice-Pres.: Prof. TAKASHI MIKAMI
Vice-Pres.: Prof. TAKAHIKO NITTA
Vice-Pres.: Prof. ICHIRO UYEDA
Vice-Pres.: Prof. KAZUNORI YASUDA
Dir: Prof. KENICHI IYAMA
Dir-Gen.: Prof. NAOKI MURATA
Dir for Univ. Library: Prof. TAKAHIKO NITTA

Library of 3,831,786 vols
Number of teachers: 2,030
Number of students: 18,043

Publications: *Hokudai Jiho* (12 a year), *Hokkaido University Magazine* (1 a year)

DEANS

Faculty of Advanced Life Science: MAKOTO DEMURA
Faculty of Pharmaceutical Sciences: MASABUMI MINAMI
Faculty of Science: Prof. MASAKANE YAMASHITA
Graduate School and Faculty of Education: YOICHI ANEZAKI
Graduate School and Faculty of Fisheries Sciences: NAOTSUNE SAGA
Graduate School and Faculty of Letters: KAZUYORI YUHAZU
Graduate School and Faculty of Science: HIROAKI TERAO
Graduate School and Research Faculty of Agriculture: TOMOMI MARUTANI
Graduate School of Chemical Sciences and Engineering: TOYOJI KAKUCHI
Graduate School of Dental Medicine: KUNIAKI SUZUKI
Graduate School of Economics and Business Administration: HIROSHI YOSHIMI
Graduate School of Engineering: NAOSHI BABA
Graduate School of Environmental Science and Faculty of Environmental Earth Science: KATSUAKI SHIMAZU
Graduate School of Health Sciences and Faculty of Health Sciences: HIROYUKI DATE
Graduate School of Information Science and Technology: MASAHITO KURIHARA
Graduate School of International Media, Communication and Tourism Studies and Research Faculty of Media and Communication: SHINKICHI USAMI
Graduate School of Law: TADASU WATARI
Graduate School of Life Science: TAKAYUKI TAKAHASHI
Graduate School of Medicine: MASANORI SASAHARA
Graduate School of Veterinary Medicine: MUTSUMI INABA
Graduate School and Faculty of Public Policy: MIKINE YAMAZAKI

PROFESSORS

Faculty and School of Fisheries Science (3-1-1 Minato-cho, Hakodate; tel. (13) 840-5505; e-mail shomu@fish.hokudai.ac.jp; internet www.fish.hokudai.ac.jp):

ABE, S., Aquagenomics and Resources Management
ADACHI, S., Molecular Cell Biology and Histology
ARAI, K., Genetics, Genomics and Developmental Biology
GOSHIMA, S., Marine Ecology; Behaviour; Benthos
GOTO, A., Evolutionary Biology of Fishes
HARA, A., Comparative Biochemistry of Fish Serum Protein
HIROYOSHI, K., Fisheries Business Economics
IIDA, K., Underwater Acoustics; Fisheries and Plankton Acoustics; Bio-Acoustics
IKEDA, T., Zooplankton Ecology
ISSHIKI, K., Food Safety; Food Protection
ITABASHI, Y., Lipid Chemistry and Chromatography
KAERIYAMA, M., Conservation Ecology; Salmonology; Fish Ecology
KAWAI, Y., Food Preservation; Food Chemistry; Food Hygiene
KIMURA, N., Fishing Informatics; Seakeeping Qualities of Fishing Vessels
KISHI, J., Numerical Modelling of Marine Ecosystems
KONNO, K., Marine Food Science
KUMA, K., Chemical Oceanography and Marine Biogeochemistry
MEGURO, T., Marine Biology
MIURA, T., Scientific Gears for Fish Sampling
MIYASHITA, K., Liquid Oxidation and Antioxidant
MONTANI, S., Biogeochemical Oceanography
NAKAYA, K., Phylogeny; Taxonomy; Sharks
OJIMA, T., Molecular Biology and Biotechnology of Marine Organisms
OKAMOTO, J., Fisheries Policy
SAEKI, H., Health Benefit of Marine Food Proteins and Marine Food Allergy
SAGA, N., Marine Biology; Developmental Biology
SAITOH, S., Satellite Oceanography
SAKURAI, Y., Marine Ecology; Reproductive Ecology of Marine Fish and Cephalopods
SIGA, N., Zooplankton Taxonomy and Ecology
TAKAGI, Y., Mechanism of Biomineralization
TAKAHASHI, K., Conversion of Fisheries By-products into Value Added Products
TAKAHASHI, T., Life History of Righteye Flounders
YABE, M., Systematic Ichthyology
YANADA, M., Marine Organic Chemistry
YOSHIMIZU, M., Viral and Bacterial Fish Diseases
YOSHIMURA, Y., Control and Design of Fishing Boats and Fisheries Machinery

Faculty of Advanced Life Science (Kita 10, Nishi 8, Kita-ku, Sapporo; tel. (11) 716-3026; e-mail shomu@sci.hokudai.ac.jp; internet www.lfsci.hokudai.ac.jp):

AYABE, T., Innate Intestinal Immunity
DEMURA, M., Membrane Protein NMR and Bioinformatics
IGARASHI, Y., Sphingolipid Biology and Biochemistry
KAMO, N., Biophysical Chemistry
KODA, T., Molecular Biology
KOIKE, T., Molecular and Cellular Neurobiology
NAITO, S., Molecular Genetics
NISHIMURA, S., Advanced Chemical Biology
OBUSE, C., Molecular and Cellular Biology
SEYA, T., Microbiology and Immunology
SUGAHARA, K., Glycoscience and Glycobiology
TAKAHASHI, T., Reproductive Biology
TANAKA, I., Protein Crystallography
YAMASHITA, M., Reproductive Biology
YAMAGUCHI, J., Plant Biology and Biochemistry
YAZAWA, M., Biochemistry

Faculty of Education (Kita 11, Nishi 7, Kita-ku, Sapporo; tel. (11) 707-6586; e-mail shomu@edu.hokudai.ac.jp; internet www.hokudai.ac.jp/educat):

ANEZAKI, Y., Higher and Continuing Education
AOKI, O., Education and Poverty
CHEN, S., Developmental Psychology of Infancy
KAWAGUCHI, A., Prevention and Health
MIYAZAKI, T., Adult Education
MIZUNO, M., Muscle Physiology
MUROHASHI, H., Clinical Cognitive Neuroscience
NISHIO, T., History of Physical Education and Sport
OHTSUKA, Y., Health Resort Medicine
ONAI, T., Sociology of Education
SATO, K., Psychology of Learning
SHINDO, S., Teaching Methods for Physical Education
SUDA, K., Teaching Methods for Mathematics
SUZUKI, T., Community Adult Education
TANAKA, Y., Developmental Psychopathology
TOKORO, S., Comparative History of Education
TSUBOI, Y., Educational Administration
YANO, T., Physiology of Exercise

Faculty of Environmental Earth Science (Kita 10, Nishi 5, Kita-ku, Sapporo; tel. (11) 728-4715; e-mail somu@ees.hokudai.ac.jp; internet www.ees.hokudai.ac.jp):

FUGETSU, B., Ion/Membrane Interactions
HASEBE, F., Weather/Oceanic Physics/Hydrology; Environmental Dynamic Analysis
HIGASHI, S., Animal Ecology
HIRAKAWA, K., Landform Development under Periglacial and Glacial Environment; Active Tectonics and Paleo-mega-tsunamis
IKEDA, M., Effects of Ocean and Sea Ice on Climate Variability

IWAKUMA, T., Ecology/Environment; Environmental Dynamic Analysis; Resource Maintenance Studies
KIMURA, M., Ecology/Environment; Animal Physiology/Behaviour Heredity/Genome Dynamics
KOHYAMA, T., Maintenance Mechanisms of Species Diversity; Scale Issue of Forest Ecosystem Response to Global Change
KUBOKAWA, A., Weather/Oceanic Physics/Hydrology
MATSUDA, F., Synthetic Organic Chemistry and Natural Product Chemistry
MINAGAWA, M., Isotope Biogeochemistry
MORIKAWA, M., Applied Microbiology; Living Organism Molecular Science
NAKAMURA, H., Organic Chemistry/Physical Chemistry/Analytical Chemistry
NORIKI, S., Analytical Chemistry; Earth Astrochemistry; Environmental Dynamic Analysis
OHARA, M., Evolution of Life History of Plants and Conservation
OKUHARA, T., Environmental Catalyst
ONO, Y., Environmental Geography
SAKAIRI, N., Synthetic Carbohydrate Chemistry
SHIMAZU, K., Environmental Chemistry; Functional Material Chemistry
SUGIMOTO, A., Environmental Dynamic Analysis; Earth Astrochemistry; Weather/Oceanic Physics/Hydrology
TANAKA, S., Analytical Chemistry; Environmental Technology/Environmental Material
TAKADA, T., Ecology/Environment
YAMAZAKI, K., Weather/Oceanic Physics/Hydrology
YOSHIKAWA, H., Environmental Dynamic Analysis; Weather/Oceanic Physics/Hydrology

Faculty of Pharmaceutical Sciences (Kita 12, Nishi 6, Kita-ku, Sapporo; tel. (11) 706-3486; e-mail shomu@pharm.hokudai.ac.jp; internet www.pharm.hokudai.ac.jp):

ARIGA, H., Molecular Biology
HARASHIMA, H., Molecular Design of Pharmaceutics
HASHIMOTO, S., Synthetic and Industrial Chemistry
INAGAKI, F., Structural Biology
ISEKI, K., Clinical Pharmaceutics and Therapeutics
KOBAYASHI, J., Natural Products Chemistry
MATSUDA, A., Medicinal Chemistry
MATSUDA, T., Hygienic Chemistry
MINAMI, M., Pharmacology
MIURA, T., Analytical Chemistry
SATO, Y., Fine Synthetic Chemistry
SHUTO, S., Organic Chemistry for Drug Development
SUZUKI, T., Neuroscience
YOKOSAWA, H., Biochemistry

Faculty of Public Policy (Kita 9, Nishi 7, Kita-ku, Sapporo; tel. (11) 706-3074; e-mail shomu@juris.hokudai.ac.jp; internet www.hops.hokudai.ac.jp):

ISHII, Y., Regional Policy
KEN ENDO, I., International Politics
KURATA, K., Technology Policy
MATSUURA, M., Japanese Political History
MIYAWAKI, A., Public Administration
NAKAMURA, K., International Politics
NAKATSUJI, T., Transportation and Traffic Engineering
SASAKI, T., International Political Economy
SHIBATA, F., Social Security Administration
SHUNJI KANIE, S., Structural Mechanics
WATARI, T., Administrative Law
YAMADA, H., Macroeconomic Policy
YAMAGUCHI, J., Public Administration
YAMAZAKI, M., Local Government and Politics
YOSHIDA, F., Environmental Economics

Faculty of Science (Kita 10, Nishi 8, Kita-ku, Sapporo; tel. (11) 716-3026; e-mail shomu@sci.hokudai.ac.jp; internet www.sci.hokudai.ac.jp):

AIKAWA, H., Potential Theory
AMITSUKA, H., Condensed Matter Physics
ARAI, A., Mathematical Physics
FUJIMOTO, M., Theoretical Physics
FUJINO, K., Mineralogy
GONG, J., Polymer Science
HAYASHI, M., Function Theory
HEKI, K., Space Geodesy
HINATSU, Y., Solid State Chemistry
HORIGUCHI, T., Phycology and Protistology
IDO, M., Solid State Physics
IKEDA, R., Geophysical Hydrology
INABE, T., Solid State Chemistry
ISHIKAWA, G., Geometry
ISHIKAWA, K., Theoretical Physics
ISHIMORI, K., Structural Chemistry
IZUMIYA, S., Geometry
JIMBO, S., Applied Analysis, Partial Differential Equations
KASAHARA, M., Seismology and Geodesy
KATAKURA, H., Speciation of Terrestrial Invertebrates
KATO, A., Plant Molecular Genetics
KATO, K., Nuclear Physics
KATO, M., Coordination Chemistry
KAWABATA, K., Biophysics
KAWAMOTO, N., Theoretical Physics
KAWANO, K., Structural Biology
KISHIMOTO, A., Operator Algebra
KITAMURA, N., Analytical Chemistry
KOIKE, K., Solid State Physics
KOYAMA, J., Solid Earth Science
KOZASA, T., Astrophysics and Planetary Science
KUMAGAI, K., Solid State Physics
KURAMOTO, K., Planetary Science
MATSUOU, M., Philosophy of Science
MAWATARI, S., Taxonomy of Invertebrates
MINOBE, S., Physical Oceanography, Climate and Meteorology
MOGI, T., Subsurface Geophysics
MURAKOSHI, K., Material Chemistry
NAGASAKA, Y., Theory of Function
NAKAGAWA, M., Volcanology and Petrology
NAKAMURA, G., Inverse Problems, Partial Differential Equations
NAKAMURA, I., Algebraic Geometry
NAKAZI, T., Functional Analysis
NOMURA, K., Solid State Physics
OHKAWA, F., Theoretical Physics
OIKAWA, H., Bio-organic Chemistry
ONO, K., Differential Geometry and Topology
ONODERA, A., Solid State Physics
OZAWA, T., Partial Differential Equations
SAKAGUCHI, K., Biological Chemistry
SASAKI, N., Tissue Science and Mechanobiology
SAWAMURA, M., Organometallic Chemistry
SUGIYAMA, S., History of Science
SUZUKI, N., Molecular Cell Biology
SUZUKI, N., Organic Geochemistry
SUZUKI, T., Physical Organic Chemistry
TAKAHATA, M., Behavioural Physiology
TAKEDA, S., Physical Chemistry
TAKESHITA, T., Structural Geology and Tectonics
TAKETSUGU, T., Quantum Chemistry
TANINO, K., Synthetic Organic Chemistry
TERAO, H., Combinatorics, Singularities
UOSAKI, K., Physical Chemistry
URANO, A., Neuroendocrinology
WATANABE, S., Planetary Atmosphere
YAMAGUCHI, K., Differential Geometry
YAMAMOTO, K., Plant Physiology
YAMAMOTO, S., Condensed-Matter Theory
YAMASHITA, H., Representation Theory
YOMOGIDA, K., Seismology
YOSHIDA, T., Group Theory and Combinatorics
YURI, M., Complex Systems and Ergodic Theory
YURIMOTO, H., Geochemistry

Graduate School of Dental Medicine (Kita 13, Nishi 7, Kita-ku, Sapporo 060-8586; tel. (11) 706-4313; e-mail d-syomu@jimu.hokudai.ac.jp; internet www.den.hokudai.ac.jp):

FUKUSHIMA, K., Oral Pathobiological Science
IIDA, J., Oral Functional Science
INOUE, N., Oral Health Science
KAWANAMI, M., Oral Health Science
KITAGAWA, K., Oral Pathobiological Science
MORITA, M., Oral Health Science
NAKAMURA, M., Oral Pathobiological Science
OHATA, N., Oral Functional Science
SANO, H., Oral Health Science
SHIBATA, K., Oral Pathobiological Science
SHINDOH, M., Oral Pathobiological Science
SUZUKI, K., Oral Pathobiological Science
TAMURA, M., Oral Health Science
TOTSUKA, Y., Oral Pathobiological Science
WATARI, F., Oral Health Science
YAWAKA, Y., Oral Functional Science
YOKOYAMA, A., Oral Functional Science

Graduate School of Economics and Business Administration (Kita 9, Nishi 7, Kita-ku, Sapporo; tel. (11) 706-4058; e-mail keizai@pop.econ.hokudai.ac.jp; internet www.econ.hokudai.ac.jp/en05):

HAMADA, Y., Money and Banking
HASEGAWA, H., Econometrics
INOUE, H., International Investment and Finance
ITAYA, J., Public Economics
IWATA, S., Corporate Behaviour
KANDA, K., Disclosure System and Financial Accounting
KANIE, A., Auditing
KIMURA, T., Operations Research
KOJIMA, H., Management of Non-Profit Organizations
KOYAMA, K., Public Finance
MACHINO, K., Applied Game Theory
MIYAMOTO, K., Economic History of Asia
MOHRI, S., Management by Networking
NISHIBE, M., Evolutionary Economics
OKABE, H., Social Economy
SASAKI, K., History of Economics
SEKIGUCHI, Y., Managerial Informatics
SONO, S., Foundations of Statistics
TANAKA, S., Socioeconomic History
UCHIDA, K., Macroeconomics
YONEYAMA, Y., Financial Accounting
YOSHIMI, H., Auditing and Public Sector Accounting
YOSHINO, E., Comparative Socioeconomic Systems

Graduate School of Engineering (Kita 13, Nishi 8, Kita-ku, Sapporo; tel. (11) 716-8832; e-mail shomu@eng.hokudai.ac.jp; internet www.eng.hokudai.ac.jp):

AKERA, H., Quantum Matter Physics
ARAI, M., Chemical Engineering
ASAKURA, K., Atmospheric and Terrestrial Engineering
BABA, N., Optical Science and Technology
CHIKAHISA, T., Applied Energy Systems
ENAI, M., Planning and Performances for Built Environment
FUJII, Y., Geoenvironmental Engineering
FUJIKAWA, S., Materials and Fluid Mechanics
FUJITA, O., Space Systems Engineering
FUNAMIZU, N., Water Metabolic System
FURUICHI, T., Policy for Engineering and Environment
FURUSAKA, M., Applied Quantum Beam Engineering
GOHARA, K., Complex Material Physics
GOTO, Y., Building Science and Space Planning

HABAZAKI, H., Functional Materials Chemistry
HARA, S., Industrial Organic Chemistry
HAYASHIKAWA, T., Sustainable Infrastructure System
HINO, T., Plasma Science and Engineering
ICHIKAWA, T., Functional Materials Chemistry
IGUCHI, M., Ecological Materials
IKEGAWA, M., Micromechanical Systems
ISHIMASA, T., Complex Material Physics
ITAGAKI, M., Plasma Science and Engineering
IZUMI, N., Hydraulic and Aquatic Environment Engineering
KADO, Y., Human Settlement Design
KAGAYA, S., Construction Engineering for Cold Regional Environment
KAGIWADA, T., Biomechanics and Robotics
KAKUCHI, T., Chemistry of Functional Molecules
KAMIDATE, T., Chemistry of Functional Molecules
KANEKO, K., Atmospheric and terrestrial Engineering
KIKKAWA, S., Inorganic Materials Chemistry
KIYANAGI, Y., Applied Quantum Beam Engineering
KOBAYASHI, H., Human Settlement Design
KOBAYASHI, Y., Biomechanics and Robotics
KONNO, H., Functional Materials Chemistry
KOSHIZAWA, A., Planning and Performances for Built Environment
KUDO, K., Micromechanical Systems
MASUDA, T., Chemical Engineering
MATSUI, Y., Water Metabolic System
MATSUTO, T., Solid Waste Resources Engineering
MATSUURA, K., Materials Design
MIDORIKAWA, M., Structural and Urban Safety Design
MIKAMI, T., Construction Engineering for Cold Regional Environment
MITACHI, T., Geoenvironmental Engineering
MIURA, S., Geoenvironmental Engineering
MIYAURA, N., Industrial Organic Chemistry
MOHRI, T., Materials Design
MORITA, R., Optical Science and Technology
MUKAI, S., Chemical Engineering
MUNEKATA, M., Biotechnology
MUTO, S., Solid State Physics and Engineering
NAGANO, K., Planning and Performances for Built Environment
NAGATA, H., Space Systems Engineering
NAKAMURA, T., Materials and Fluid Mechanics
NAKANO, T., Chemistry of Functional Molecules
NAKAYAMA, T., Quantum Matter Physics
NARABAYASHI, T., Nuclear and Environmental Systems
NARITA, Y., Micromechanical Systems
NAWA, T., Solid Waste Resources Engineering
OGAWA, H., Applied Energy Systems
OHKUMA, T., Industrial Organic Chemistry
OHNUKI, S., Energy Materials
OHNUMA, H., Construction Engineering for Cold Regional Environment
OHTA, S., Atmospheric and Terrestrial Engineering
OHTSUKA, T., Ecological Materials
ORIHARA, H., Complex Material Physics
OSHIMA, N., Space Systems Engineering
SASAKI, K., Materials and Fluid Mechanics
SASATANI, T., Structural and Urban Safety Design
SATO, S., Nuclear and Environmental Systems
SATOH, K., Policy for Engineering and Environment
SENBU, O., Building Science and Space Planning
SHIMADA, S., Inorganic Materials Chemistry
SHIMAZU, Y., Nuclear and Environmental Systems
SHIMIZU, Y., Policy for Engineering and Environment
SUGIYAMA, K., Nuclear and Environmental Systems
SUGIYAMA, T., Sustainable Infrastructure System
SUMIYOSHI, T., Applied Quantum Beam Engineering
SUZUKI, R., Ecological Materials
TADANO, S., Biomechanics and Robotics
TAGUCHI, S., Biotechnology
TAKAGI, M., Biotechnology
TAKAHASHI, H., Materials Design
TAKAHASHI, J., Inorganic Materials Chemistry
TAKAHASHI, M., Hydraulic and Aquatic Environment Engineering
TAKEDA, Y., Applied Energy Systems
TAMURA, S., Solid State Physics and Engineering
TANAKA, K., Solid State Physics and Engineering
TANDA, S., Quantum Matter Physics
TSUNEKAWA, M., Solid Waste Resources Engineering
UEDA, M., Structural and Urban Safety Design
UEDA, T., Sustainable Infrastructure System
UKAI, S., Energy Materials
WATANABE, Y., Water Metabolic System
WRIGHT, O., Quantum Matter Physics
YAMASHITA, M., Optical Science and Technology
YAMASHITA, T., Hydraulic and Aquatic Environment Engineering
YOKOYAMA, S., Planning and Performances for Built Environment
YONEDA, T., Geoenvironmental Engineering

Graduate School of Information Science and Technology (Kita 14, Nishi 9, Kita-ku, Sapporo; tel. (11) 706-6514; e-mail jimusitu@ist.hokudai.ac.jp; internet www.ist.hokudai.ac.jp):

AMEMIYA, Y., Integrated Systems Engineering
ARAKI, K., Information Media Science and Technology
ARIMURA, H., Knowledge Software Science
ENDO, T., Bioinformatics
FUKUI, T., Integrated Systems Engineering
FURUKAWA, M., Complex Systems Engineering
HARAGUCHI, M., Knowledge Software Science
HASEYAMA, M., Information Media Science and Technology
HOMMA, T., Informatics for System Synthesis
IGARASHI, H., Informatics for System Synthesis
KANAI, S., Informatics for System Creation
KANEKO, S., Informatics for System Creation
KAWAHARA, K., Biomedical Systems Engineering
KITA, H., Informatics for System Synthesis
KOSHIBA, M., Information Communication Systems
KUDO, M., Mathematical Information Science
KURIHARA, M., Complex Systems Engineering
MISHIMA, T., Advanced Electronics
MIYAKOSHI, M., Mathematical Information Science
MIYANAGA, Y., Information Communication Systems
MOTOHISA, J., Integrated Systems Engineering
NOJIMA, T., Information Communication Systems
OGASAWARA, S., Informatics for System Synthesis
OGAWA, Y., Information Communication Systems
OHUCHI, A., Complex Systems Engineering
ONOSATO, M., Informatics for System Creation
SAKAI, Y., Integrated Systems Engineering
SATO, Y., Mathematical Information Science
SHIMIZU, K., Biomedical Systems Engineering
SUEOKA, K., Advanced Electronics
TAKAHASHI, Y., Advanced Electronics
TANAKA, Y., Knowledge Software Science
WADA, M., Complex Systems Engineering
WATANABE, H., Bioinformatics
YAMAMOTO, K., Biomedical Systems Engineering
YAMAMOTO, M., Advanced Electronics
YAMAMOTO, T., Information Media Science and Technology
YAMASHITA, Y., Informatics for System Creation
ZEUGMANN, T., Knowledge Software Science

Graduate School of Law (Kita 9, Nishi 7, Kita-ku, Sapporo; tel. (11) 706-3074; e-mail shomu@juris.hokudai.ac.jp; internet www.juris.hokudai.ac.jp):

DOKO, T., Labour Law
FUJIWARA, M., Civil Law
GONZA, T., History of Political Theory
HASEGAWA, K., Philosophy of Law
HAYASHI, T., Commercial Law
HAYASHIDA, S., Economic Analysis of Law
HIENUKI, T., Economic Law
HITOMI, T., Administrative Law
ICHIRO OZAKI, S.
IKEDA, S., Civil Law
IMAI, H., Philosophy of Law
KOMORI, T., International Law
MACHIMURA, Y., Law of Civil Procedure
MATSUHISA, M., Civil Law
MIYAMOTO, T., Comparative Political Economy
MURAKAMI, H., Administrative Law
NAGAI, C., Criminal Law
NAKAYAMA, H., Law of Criminal Procedure
OHTSUKA, R., Commercial Law
OKADA, N., Constitutional Law
ONAGI, A., Criminal Law
SASADA, E., Constitutional Law
SEGAWA, N., Civil Law
SHIRATORI, Y., Law of Criminal Procedure
SORAI, M., Modern Political Analysis
SUZUKI, K., Asian Law
TAGUCHI, M., Western Legal History
TAKAMI, S., Law of Civil Procedure
TAMURA, Y., Intellectual Property Law
TANAKA, H., Legal Ethics
TSUJI, Y., Political Theory
TSUNEMOTO, T., Constitutional Law
YAMAMOTO, T., Commercial Law
YAMASHITA, R., Administrative Law
YOSHIDA, K., Civil Law

Graduate School of Letters (Kita 10, Nishi 7, Kita-ku, Sapporo; tel. (11) 726-7728; e-mail wwwadmin@let.hokudai.ac.jp; internet www.hokudai.ac.jp/letters):

ABE, J., Psychology
AKASHI, M., Occidental History
ANDO, A., Western Literature
ANZAI, M., Western Literature
CHIBA, K., Philosophy
FUJII, K., Religious Studies and Indian Philosophy
GOTO, Y., Japanology
HANAI, K., Philosophy

HISHITANI, S., Psychology
HOSODA, N., Religious Studies and Indian Philosophy
IKEDA, S., Linguistics Sciences
IKEDA, T., Regional Sciences
INOUE, K., Japanese History
IRIMOTO, T., Northern Culture Studies
KADOWAKI, S., Linguistic Sciences
KAMEDA, T., Behavioural Sciences
KANEKO, I., Sociology
KITAMURA, K., Theory and History of Art
KURYUZAWA, T., Occidental History
KUWAYAMA, T., History and Anthropology
MATSUOKA, M., Sociology
MIKI, S., Asian History
MISAKI, H., Japanology
MIYATAKE, K., History and Anthropology
MOCHIZUKI, T., Linguistics and Western Languages
NAKA, M., Psychology
NAKATOGAWA, K., Philosophy
NAMBU, N., Japanese History
NITTA, T., Ethics and Applied Philosophy
ONO, Y., Linguistics Sciences
OTA, K., History and Anthropology
SAKURAI, Y., Sociology
SATO, R., Sinology
SOTO, J., Filmology and Cultural Studies of Representation
SEKI, T., Regional Sciences
SHIMIZU, M., Linguistics and Western Languages
SHIRAKIZAWA, A., Japanese History
SUTO, Y., Sinology
TAKAHASHI, H., Linguistics and Western Languages
TAKAHEI, H., Philosophy
TAKEDA, M., Sinology
TAKIGAWA, T., Psychology
TAYAMA, T., Psychology
TOMITA, Y., Japanology
TSUMAGARI, T., Northern Culture Studies
TUDA, Y., Asian History
URAI, Y., Linguistics and Western Languages
UTSUNOMIYA, T., Religious Studies and Indian Philosophy
WADA, H., Psychology
YAMADA, T., Philosophy
YAMADA, T., Western Literature
YAMAGISHI, T., Behavioural Sciences
YUHAZU, K., Sinology

Graduate School of Medicine (Kita 15, Nishi 7, Kita-ku, Sapporo; tel. (11) 716-5003; e-mail shomu@med.hokudai.ac.jp; internet www.med.hokudai.ac.jp):

AKITA, H., Medical Oncology
ARIGA, T., Paediatrics
ARIKAWA, J., Infectious Disease
CHIBA, H., Biomedical Informatics
DAIGUJI, M., Clinical Occupational Therapy
DATE, H., Medical Engineering and Science
FUJITA, H., Environmental Biology
FUKUDA, S., Otolaryngology, Head and Neck Surgery
FUKUSHIMA, J., Basic Physical Therapy
FUKUSHIMA, K., Sensorimotor and Cognitive Research
GANDO, S., Acute and Critical Care Medicine
HATAKEYAMA, S., Medical Chemistry
HATTA, T., Clinical Occupational Therapy
HONMA, K., Chronobiology
IMAMURA, M., Haematology and Oncology
INOUE, K., Basic Occupational Therapy
ISHIZU, A., Clinical Pathophysiology
IWANAGA, T., Histology and Cytology
IWASAKI, Y., Neurosurgery
IWATA, G., Maternal Nursing and Child Nursing
KAMIYA, H., Neurobiology
KASAHARA, M., Pathology
KAWAGUCHI, H., Laboratory Medicine
KISHI, R., Public Health
KOBAYASHI, S., Biomedical Informatics
KOIKE, T., Clinical Immunology
KONDO, S., Surgical Oncology
KOYAMA, T., Psychiatry
MAEZAWA, M., Healthcare Research and Quality
MATSUNO, K., Clinical Pathophysiology
MATSUSHITA, M., Adult and Gerontological Nursing
MIKAMI, T., Clinical Pathophysiology
MINAKAMI, H., Obstetrics
MINAMI, A., Orthopaedic Surgery
MIWA, S., Cellular and Molecular Pharmacology
MIYAMOTO, K., Clinical Physical Therapy
MORIMOTO, Y., Anaesthesia and Perioperative Medicine
MORISHITA, S., Fundamental Nursing
MORIYAMA, T., Biomedical Informatics
MURATA, W., Basic Occupational Therapy
NISHIMURA, M., Respiratory Medicine
NISHIOKA, T., Radiological Technology
NONOMURA, K., Renal and Genito-urinary Surgery
OGASAWARA, K., Medical Engineering and Science
OHMIYA, Y., Photobiology
OHNO, S., Ophthalmology
SAEKI, K., Community Health Nursing
SAGAWA, T., Maternal Nursing and Child Nursing
SAITO, T., Community Health Nursing
SAKAI, M., Radiological Technology
SAKURAGI, N., Reproductive Endocrinology and Oncology
SAKURAI, T., Medical Informatics
SASAKI, F., Paediatric Surgery
SASAKI, H., Neurology
SATO, Y., Maternal Nursing and Child Nursing
SHIMIZU, H., Dermatology
SHIMIZU, T., Radiological Technology
SHIRATO, H., Radiology
TAKANAMI, S., Community Health Nursing
TAKEDA, N., Basic Physical Therapy
TAMAKI, N., Nuclear Medicine
TAMASHIRO, H., Global Health and Epidemiology
TERAZAWA, K., Forensic Medicine
TODO, S., General Surgery
TSUTSUI, H., Cardiovascular Medicine
WATANABE, M., Anatomy and Embryology
YAMAGUCHI, H., Biomedical Informatics
YAMAMOTO, T., Medical Engineering and Science
YAMAMOTO, Y., Plastic Surgery
YAMANAKA, M., Clinical Physical Therapy
YASUDA, K., Sports Medicine and Joint Reconstruction Surgery
YOKOSAWA, K., Medical Engineering and Science
YOSHIMURA, S., Fundamental Nursing
YOSHIOKA, M., Neuropharmacology

Graduate School of Veterinary Medicine (Kita 18, Nishi 9, Kita-ku, Sapporo; tel. (11) 706-5173; e-mail syomu@vetmed.hokudai.ac.jp; internet www.vetmed.hokudai.ac.jp):

AGUI, T., Disease Control
FUJINAGA, T., Veterinary Clinical Sciences
FUJITA, S., Environmental Veterinary Sciences
HABARA, Y., Biomedical Sciences
HORIUCHI, M., Prion Diseases
INABA, M., Veterinary Clinical Sciences
INANAMI, O., Environmental Veterinary Sciences
ITO, S., Biomedical Sciences
KATAKURA, K., Disease Control
KIDA, H., Disease Control
KIMURA, K., Biomedical Sciences
KON, Y., Biomedical Sciences
TAKAHASHI, Y., Veterinary Clinical Sciences
TAKASHIMA, I., Environmental Veterinary Sciences
TSUBOTA, T., Environmental Veterinary Sciences
UMEMURA, T., Veterinary Clinical Sciences

Research Faculty of Agriculture (Kita 9, Nishi 9, Kita-ku, Sapporo; tel. (11) 706-4123; e-mail shomu@agr.hokudai.ac.jp):

ARIGA, S., Environmental Molecular Bioscience
ASANO, K., Applied Microbiology
BANDO, H., Applied Molecular Entomology
DEMURA, K., Agricultural and Environmental Policy
FUJIKAWA, S., Woody Plant Biology
HARA, H., Nutritional Biochemistry
HASEGAWA, S., Soil Conservation
HASHIDOKO, Y., Ecological Chemistry
HATANO, R., Soil Science
HATTORI, A., Meat Science
HIRAI, T., Timber Engineering
HIRANO, T., Environmental Informatics
IIZAWA, R., Agricultural Marketing
IWAMA, K., Crop Science
KAKIZAWA, H., Forest Policy
KAWABATA, J., Food Biochemistry
KIMURA, A., Molecular Enzymology
KIMURA, T., Agricultural and Food Process Engineering
KITAMURA, K., Plant Genetics and Evolution
KOBAYASHI, Y., Animal Nutrition
KODA, Y., Crop Physiology
KOIKE, T., Silviculture and Forest Ecology
KONDO, S., Animal Production System
KONDO, T., Environmental Horticulture and Landscape Architecture
KUROKAWA, I., Farm Management
MARUTANI, T., Earth Surface Processes and Land Management
MASUDA, K., Plant Functional Biology
MASUTA, C., Cell Biology and Manipulation
MATSUDA, J., Agricultural Circulative Engineering
MATSUI, H., Biochemistry
MIKAMI, T., Genetic Engineering
NABETA, K., Natural Product Chemistry
NAGASAWA, T., Land Improvement and Management
NAITO, S., Molecular Biology
NAKAMURA, F., Animal By-product Science
NAKAMURA, F., Forest Ecosystem Management
NOGUCHI, N., Vehicle Robotics
OSAKI, M., Plant Nutrition
OSANAMI, F., Agricultural Development
SAITO, Y., Animal Ecology
SAKASHITA, A., Agricultural Cooperative
SANO, Y., Plant Breeding
SHIMAZAKI, K., Dairy Food Science
SUZUKI, M., Horticultural Science
UBUKATA, M., Wood Chemistry
URANO, S., Agricultural and Environmental Physics
UYEDA, I., Pathogen–Plant Interactions
WATANABE, T., Animal Breeding and Reproduction
YAJIMA, T., Forest Resource Biology
YOKOTA, A., Microbial Physiology

Research Faculty of Media and Communication (Kita 17, Nishi 8, Kita-ku, Sapporo; tel. (11) 716-2111; e-mail soumu@ilcs.hokudai.ac.jp; internet www.hokudai.ac.jp/imcts/rfmc.html):

Most of the Professors in this Faculty also belong to the Foreign Language Education Center.

EGUCHI, Y., German
HASHIMOTO, H., English
ISHIBASHI, M., German
ISHIKAWA, K., German
KOBAYAKAWA, M., International Public Relations
KOGA, H., Italian
MIYASHITA, M., English

NAGAI, Y., Chinese
NISHI, M., French
NOZAWA, Y., Chinese
OGAWA, Y., English
OHIRA, T., French
OHNO, K., English
SATOH, S., German
SONODA, K., English
STAPLETON, P., English
SUGIURA, S., Russian
TAKAHASHI, Y., German
TAKAI, K., Chinese
TAKEMOTO, K., English
TAKENAKA, M., French
TERADA, T., German
TSUKUWA, M., German
UEDA, M., English
USAMI, S., Russian
YAMADA, K., Russian
YAMADA, Y., English
YOSHIDA, T., German

ATTACHED RESEARCH INSTITUTES

Admission Center: f. 2005; Dir MINORU WAKITA.

Catalysis Research Center: internet www.cat.hokudai.ac.jp; f. 1989; Dir WATARU UEDA.

Center for Advanced Research of Energy Conversion Materials: internet labs.eng.hokudai.ac.jp/labo/carem; f. 2004; Dir KAZUYA KUROKAWA.

Center for Advanced Tourism Studies: internet www.cats.hokudai.ac.jp; f. 2006; Dir SHUZO ISHIMORI.

Center for Ainu and Indigenous Studies: e-mail ainu@let.hokudai.ac.jp; internet www.cais.hokudai.ac.jp; f. 2007; Dir TERUKI TSUNEMOTO.

Center for Experimental Research in Social Sciences: e-mail cerss@lynx.let.hokudai.ac.jp; internet lynx.let.hokudai.ac.jp/cerss; f. 2007; Dir TOSHIO YAMAGISHI.

Center for Instrumental Analysis: f. 1979; Dir TOSHIAKI MIURA.

Center for Research and Development in Higher Education: e-mail presiden@high.hokudai.ac.jp; f. 1995; Dir MINORU WAKITA.

Central Institute of Radioisotope Science: e-mail jimu-cis@ric.hokudai.ac.jp; internet www.hokudai.ac.jp/radiois; f. 1978; Dir NAGARA TAMAKI.

Creative Research Initiative 'Sousei': e-mail rso@cris.hokudai.ac.jp; internet www.cris.hokudai.ac.jp/cris; f. 2005; Dir HISATAKE OKADA.

Environmental Preservation Center: f. 1995; Dir MASAYA SAWAMURA.

Field Science Center for the Northern Biosphere: f. 2001; Dir KAICHIRO SASA.

Foreign Language Education Center: f. 2007; Dir YUTAKA EGUCHI.

Health Administration Center: f. 1972; Dir MANABU MUSASHI.

Hokkaido University Archives: internet www.hokudai.ac.jp/bunsyo; f. 2005; Dir MASAAKI HEMMI.

Hokkaido University Museum: f. 1999; Dir SHUNSUKE MAWATARI.

Information Initiative Center: e-mail unyo@iic.hokudai.ac.jp; internet www.iic.hokudai.ac.jp; f. 2003; Dir TSUYOSHI YAMAMOTO.

Institute for Genetic Medicine: internet www.igm.hokudai.ac.jp; f. 2000; Dir TOSHIMITSU UEDE; publ. *Collected Papers* (1 a year).

Institute of Low Temperature Science: internet www.lowtem.hokudai.ac.jp; f. 1941; Dir AKIRA KOUCHI.

International Student Center: internet www.isc.hokudai.ac.jp; f. 1991; Dir TAKEO HONDOH.

Meme Media Laboratory: e-mail nwada@meme.hokudai.ac.jp; internet www.meme.hokudai.ac.jp; f. 1996; Dir YUZURU TANAKA.

Research and Education Center for Brain Science: e-mail brain@med.hokudai.ac.jp; internet www.hokudai.ac.jp/recbs; f. 2003; Dir SHINYA KURIKI.

Research Center for Integrated Quantum Electronics: e-mail rciqeadmin@rciqe.hokudai.ac.jp; internet www.rciqe.hokudai.ac.jp; f. 2001; Dir TAKASHI FUKUI.

Research Center for Zoonosis Control: internet www.czc.hokudai.ac.jp; f. 2005; Dir HIROSHI KIDA.

Research Institute for Electronic Science: internet www.es.hokudai.ac.jp; f. 1943; Dir KEIJI SASAKI.

Slavic Research Center: e-mail src@slav.hokudai.ac.jp; internet src-h.slav.hokudai.ac.jp; f. 1990; Dir KIMITAKA MATSUZATO; publ. *Acta Slavica Iaponica* (1 a year)

IBARAKI UNIVERSITY

1-1, Bunkyo 2-chome, Mito-shi, Ibaraki-ken 310-8512
Telephone: (29) 228-8007
Internet: www.ibaraki.ac.jp

Founded 1949
Private control
Academic year: April to March

Pres.: TAKEO MIYATA
Admin.: T. MIYATA
Dean of Student Affairs: F. IKEYA
Librarian: Y. ASANO

Library of 939,000 vols
Number of teachers: 584 (full-time)
Number of students: 8,864

Publications: Bulletins (in Japanese), Journals of the faculties (in Japanese)

DEANS

Faculty of Education: R. KIKUCHI
Faculty of Engineering: K. YAMAGATA
Faculty of Humanities: T. MURANAKA
Faculty of Science: T. WATANABE
School of Agriculture: T. MATUDA

PROFESSORS

Faculty of Education:

ADACHI, K., School Education
AKISAKA, M., Clinical Medicine
AKUTA, N., Clinical Psychology
ARAKAWA, C., Housing and Domestic Science
EBATA, H., School Education
FUJIHIRA, S., German Literature
HASEGAWA, S., Vocal Music
HASHIURA, H., Japanese Literature
HATTORI, K., Physical Activity Science
HAYAKAWA, K., Composition
HAYAKAWA, T., Geomorphology
HONNDA, T., Information Education
IKEYA, F., European History
INABA, K.
INAMI, Y., Computer Science
KAIZU, S., Applied Mathematics
KAJIWARA, S., Instrumental Music
KANEKO, K., Art Education
KIKUCHI, R., Adult Education
KIMURA, K., Philosophy
KOIZUMI, S., Art History
KOJIMA, H., Information Education
KOMURO, K., Technical Education
KUSAKA, Y., Physical Education
MAEKAWA, Y., Sinology
MAKINO, Y., Geology
MATSUDA, M., Art Education
MATSUI, M., Information Sciences
MATSUMURA, T., Education for Handicapped Children
MATSUZAKA, A., Health and Physical Education
MIURA, T., Health and Physical Education
NAGASAWA, K., English Language Teaching
NAKAMURA, T., Health Education
NAMIKI, T., English Morphology
OGATA, T., Health and Physical Education
OKAMOTO, K., Physical Education
ONO, Y., Mycology
ONODERA, A., Historical Geography
OSHIMA, K., Earth Science
OTA, S., Physical Education
OTAKE, H., Women's Studies
OTANI, H., School Nursing
OTSUKI, I., Economic History of Modern Japan
OUCHI, Z., Language Ethics Education
OZAKI, H., Physiology for Handicapped Children
SASAKI, Y., Japanese Language Teaching
SATO, A., Musicology
SATO, E., Mathematical Education
SATO, H., Technical Education
SOGA, H., Mathematical Science
SOGO, M., Painting
SUGANUMA, K., Clinical Psychology
SUZUKI, E., Social Studies Teaching
TAKIZAWA, T., Hygienics
TANAKA, K., Music Education
TANIGUCHI, T., School Education
TASHIRO, T., School Education
TATSUMI, N., Physical Education
TERAMOTO, T., Industrial Arts
TOGASHI, T., Physical Education
TOSHIYASU, Y., Science Education
YAMAMOTO, H., Organic Chemistry
YAMAMOTO, K., Household Management Education
YAMANE, S., Insect Ecology
YAMASHITA, T., School Education
YANAGIDA, N., Mathematics
YASUDA, K., Home Economics Education
YOSHIDA, H., Home Economics Education

Faculty of Engineering:

ABE, O., Ceramics Engineering
ARAKI, T., Computer Science
EDA, H., Production Engineering and Machine Tools
ENOMOTO, M., Materials Physics
FUJII, K., Laser and Plasma
FUKUZAWA, K., Concrete Engineering
HAMAMATSU, Y., Modelling and Simulation
HARIU, T., Electronic Material Systems
HOSHI, T., Systems Information and Remote Sensing
ICHIMURA, M., Materials Physics
IGARASHI, S., Analytical Chemistry
IKEHATA, T., Plasma Science
IMAI, Y., Communication Engineering
INUI, M., Systems Engineering
ISHIGURO, M., Computer Applications
ITO, G., Plastic Working Science
KAGOSHIMA, K., Antennae
KAMINAGA, H., Energy Conversion
KANO, M., Discrete Mathematics and its Application
KAZITANI, S., Energy Conservation
KIKUMA, I., Electronic Materials
KISHI, Y., Intelligent Systems
KOBAYASHI, M., Systems Information
KOBIYAMA, M., Electromagnetic Systems
KOUNOSU, S., Design Engineering
KOYAMADA, Y., Photonic Systems
KOYANAGI, T., Landscape Planning and Design
KUROSAWA, K., Plasma Science
MAEKAWA, K., Materials Science and Engineering
MASUI, M., Electronic Materials
MASUZAWA, T., Dynamics of Machines
MIMURA, N., Global Environment Engineering
MOMOSE, Y., Surface Chemistry

Motohashi, Y., Materials Science and Engineering
Muranoi, T., Electronic Materials for Functionality
Naito, K., Analytical Chemistry
Nakamoto, R., Functional Analysis
Nara, K., Electrical Power Systems
Niimura, N., Physics
Nirei, H., Environmental Asset Science
Numao, T., Architecture
Oguchi, K., Dynamics of Machines
Okada, Y., Dynamics of Machines
Ono, K., Polymer Science
Onuki, J., Materials Technology
Ozawa, S., Computational Physics
Sasaki, Y., Foundation and Design of Precision Engineering
Senba, I., Computer Science
Shiraishi, M., Systems and Controls
Siohata, K., Design Engineering
Sugita, R., Electrical and Electronics Engineering
Suzuki, H., Mechanical Design
Suzuki, T., Energy Conversion
Takahashi, M., Organic Chemistry
Takeuchi, M., Electrical Materials
Tazuke, Y., Applied Physics
Tomoda, Y., Mechanical Metallurgy
Tozune, A., Electric Machines
Turuta, K., High Voltage and Plasma Science
Wu, Z., Structural Engineering
Yamanaka, K., Systems and Controls
Yasuhara, K., Geotechnical Engineering
Yokoyama, K., Structural Engineering
Zyou, M., CAD/CAM/CAE

Faculty of Humanities:

Aizawa, Y., English and American Culture
Amemiya, S., Politics
Aoki, K., French
Ariizumi, S., Economic Structure
Aritomi, M., Psychology
Asano, Y., Human Geography
Cheang, K., Linguistics
Fujii, F., Linguistics
Fukaya, N., Law
Fukazawa, Y., European History
Fushimi, K., German
Iizuka, K., Law
Iijima, H., Management Science
Kamata, A., Social Structure
Kamiya, T., Social Structure
Kanamoto, S., Japanese Education
Kanou, Y., Asian Culture
Katayama, Y., Philosophy
Kimura, M., South-East Asia Area Study
Kishimoto, N., Linguistics
Koido, M., French and European Culture
Koizumi, Y., English and American Culture
Komiyaji, M., Business Administration
Lieng, J., Sinology
Matumura, N., Social Structure
Mayanagi, M., Oriental History
Mogi, M., Comparative Culture
Moriya, S., Logic
Moriya, T., Sociology
Muranaka, M., Sociology
Nakura, B., Economic Structure
Nosaka, M., Law
Ohata, K., English and American Culture
Okubo, N., French Culture
Saito, M., Regional Societies
Saito, Y., Local Administration
Sano, H., Media Studies
Sasaki, H., History
Sasakura, S., English
Sato, K., Economic Structure
Sato, K., German Culture
Sibuya, A., Sociology
Simaoka, S., English
Sugii, K., Oriental History
Sugishita, T., International Cooperation Theory
Sumikawa, H., European and American Economy Theory
Suzuki, T., Communication
Suzuki, Y., Psychology
Suzuki, Y., German
Takahashi, T., English
Tamura, T., Law
Tanaka, S., Regional Societies
Tatewaki, I., Regional Societies
Tateyama, Y., International Economics
Tokue, K., Economic Policy
Ueno, H., Social Anthropology
Umeda, T., Law
Watanabe, K., European Culture
Yamamoto, H., Asian Economics

Faculty of Science:

Amano, T., Science of Cosmic Matter
Fujii, Y., Coordination Chemistry
Fujiwara, T., Physics
Hori, Y., Botany
Horiuchi, T., Analysis
Ichimasa, M., Cell Biology
Ichimasa, Y., Physiology
Ikeda, Y., Geochemistry
Imura, H., Analytical Chemistry
Isizuka, T., Astrophysics
Izuoka, A., Physical Chemistry
Kaneko, M., Chemistry
Kanno, S., Atomic Physics
Kawada, Y., Chemistry
Kimura, M., Geochemistry
Kojima, J., Entomology
Matsuda, R., Algebra
Mishima, S., Biology
Miwa, I., Biology
Morino, H., Systematics
Nakano, Y., Structural Chemistry
Nishihara, Y., Magnetism and Superconductivity
Noda, F., Theoretical High Energy
Ohashi, K., Analytical Chemistry
Onishi, K., Applied Mathematics
Onose, H., Statistics
Oriyama, T., Organic Chemistry
Oshima, H., Topology
Sakata, F., Mathematical Science
Sakuma, T., Solid-State Physics
Tagiri, M., Earth and Planetary Physics
Takano, K., Mathematics
Urabe, T., Geometry
Watanabe, T., Earth Science
Yamada, M., Physics
Yamagami, S., Quantum Physics
Yanagida, R., Cosmic Ray Physics
Yokosawa, M., Astrophysics

School of Agriculture:

Akutsu, K., Plant Pathology
Goto, T., Applied Physics
Karube, J., Farmland Engineering
Kashiwagi, M., Regional Planning Science
Kinose, K., Hydraulic Engineering
Kodama, O., Bio-regulation Chemistry
Kosugiyama, M., Animal Breeding
Kouno, Y., Chemical Ecology
Kubota, M., Soil Science and Plant Nutrition
Kurusu, Y., Industrial Microbiology
Machida, T., Agricultural Systems
Marubashi, W., Plant Breeding
Masaki, T., Enzymatic Chemistry
Matsuda, T., Horticulture
Matsuzawa, Y., Animal Husbandry and Behaviour
Moriizumi, S., Agricultural Machinery
Nakagawa, M., Agricultural Economics
Nakajima, M., Farm Science
Nakamura, Y., Feed Science
Nakane, K., Algebra
Nakasone, H., Agricultural and Environmental Engineering
Ota, H., Microbial Ecology
Sago, R., Cultivation Science
Shio, K., Information Science
Shirai, M., Molecular Microbiology
Takahara, H., Bioresource Engineering
Tsukihashi, T., Horticulture
Yonekura, M., Crop Production

IWATE UNIVERSITY

3-18-8 Ueda, Morioka, Iwate 020-8550
Telephone: (19) 621-6006
E-mail: ssomu@iwate-u.ac.jp
Internet: www.iwate-u.ac.jp

Founded 1949
Independent
Academic year: April to March

Pres.: Kenichi Hirayama
Chief Admin. Officer: Toshiaki Kikuchi
Librarian: Yoshiya Nakashima

Library of 760,434 vols
Number of teachers: 835
Number of students: 6,218

Publications: *Journal of the Faculty of Agriculture*, *Report on Technology of Iwate University*, *Artes Liberales*

DEANS

Faculty of Agriculture: Yoshinobu Ota
Faculty of Education: Takao Fujiwara
Faculty of Technology: Kunio Mori
College of Humanities and Social Sciences: Tatsuyuki Takatsuka

JAPAN ADVANCED INSTITUTE OF SCIENCE AND TECHNOLOGY

1-1 Asahidai, Nomi, Ishikawa 923-1292
Telephone: (761) 51-1111
E-mail: daihyo@jaist.ac.jp
Internet: www.jaist.ac.jp

Founded 1990
State control
Languages of instruction: English, Japanese
Academic year: April to March

Pres.: Takuya Katayama
Vice-Pres.: Yasushi Hibino
Vice-Pres.: Susumu Kunifuji
Vice-Pres.: Yusuke Kawakami
Vice-Pres.: Koichiro Ochimizu
Dir of the Library: Akira Shimazu

Library of 139,229 vols
Number of teachers: 179
Number of students: 902

Publication: *JAIST NOW* (2 a year)

DEANS

School of Information Science: Tetsuo Asano
School of Knowledge Science: Michitaka Kosaka
School of Materials Science: Masahiko Tomitori

KAGAWA UNIVERSITY

1-1 Saiwai-cho, Takamatsu-shi 760-8521
Telephone: (87) 832-1025
E-mail: kokusait@jimu.ao.kagawa-u.ac.jp
Internet: www.kagawa-u.ac.jp

Founded 1949
Independent
Academic year: April to March

Pres.: Dr Yoshitsugu Kimura
Vice-Pres: Dr Hiroaki Takeuchi, Dr Takumi Yoshizawa
Sec.-Gen.: Kunio Seki
Librarian: Masayuki Sato

Library of 650,000 vols
Number of teachers: 473 (incl. teachers at attached schools)
Number of students: 5,261

DEANS

Faculty of Agriculture: Masahiko Ichii
Faculty of Economics: Michiyo Ihara
Faculty of Education: Yoshimasa Kano
Faculty of Engineering: Hiroshi Ishikawa

Faculty of Law: SADAMI UEMURA
Faculty of Medicine: AKINOBU OKABE

KAGOSHIMA UNIVERSITY

1-21-24, Korimoto, Kagoshima 890-8580
Telephone: (992) 85-7111
E-mail: sbunsho@kuas.kagoshima-u.ac.jp
Internet: www.kagoshima-u.ac.jp

Founded 1949
State control

Pres.: HIROKI YOSHIDA
Dir-Gen.: CHIKARA MORIMOTO

Library of 1,338,169 vols
Number of teachers: 1,200 (full-time)
Number of students: 11,000

DEANS

Faculty of Agriculture: I. IWAMOTO
Faculty of Dentistry: K. SUGIHARA
Faculty of Education: A. TAKEKUMA
Faculty of Fisheries: T. NORO
Faculty of Law, Economics and the Humanities: H. ISHIKAWA
Faculty of Medicine: Y. EIZURU
Faculty of Science: S. KIYOHARA
Graduate School of Health Science: A. YOSHIDA
Graduate School of Medical and Dental Sciences: T. MATSUYAMA
Graduate School of Science and Engineering: Y. FUKUI
Law School: H. UNIEME
Professional Graduate School of Clinical Psychology: T. ABE
United Graduate School of Agricultural Sciences: T. SUGANUMA

KANAGAWA UNIVERSITY

3-27-1 Rokkakubashi, Kanagawaku, Yokohama 221-8686
Telephone: (45) 491-1701
E-mail: kohou-info@kanagawa-u.ac.jp
Internet: www.kanagawa-u.ac.jp

Founded 1949

Faculties of business administration, economics, engineering, foreign languages, law, science

Library of 1,110,000 vols
Number of students: 19,129

KANAZAWA UNIVERSITY

Kakuma-machi, Kanazawa-shi 920-1192
Telephone: (76) 264-5111
E-mail: now@kanazawa-u.ac.jp
Internet: www.kanazawa-u.ac.jp

Founded 1949
Independent
Academic year: April to March

Pres.: SHIN-ISHI NAKAMURA
Vice-Pres. for Finance and Hospital: M. FURUKAWA
Vice-Pres. for General Affairs and Human Resources: N. WAKISAKA
Vice-Pres. for Education and Student Affairs: Y. KASHIMI
Vice-Pres. for Information: S. SAKURAI
Vice-Pres. for Research and Int. Affairs: I. NAGANO

Library of 1,786,038 vols
Number of teachers: 1,082
Number of students: 10,443

DEANS

College of Human and Social Sciences: S. IKUTA
College of Medical, Pharmaceutical and Health Sciences: H. YAMAMOTO
College of Science and Engineering: K. YAMAZAKI
Graduate School of Education: H. OKUBO
Graduate School of Human and Socio-environmental Studies: H. INOUE
Graduate School of Medical Science: O. MATSUI
Graduate School of Natural Science and Technology: Y. FUKUMORI
Law School: S. OJIMA

PROFESSORS

Advanced Science Research Centre (13-1 Takara-machi, Kanazawa, Ishikawa; tel. (76) 265-2771; e-mail yamaguti@kenroku.kanazawa-u.ac.jp; internet web.kanazawa-u.ac.jp/~asrc):

ASANO, M., Experimental Animal Science
MORI, H., Nuclear Medicine
YAMAGUCHI, K., Molecular Genetics

Cancer Research Institute (13-1 Takara-machi, Kanazawa, Ishikawa; tel. (76) 265-2799):

HARADA, F., Molecular and Cellular Biology
HIRAO, A., Molecular and Cellular Biology
MINAMOTO, T., Basic and Clinical Oncology
MUKAIDA, N., Molecular Oncology
MURAKAMI, S., Molecular Genetics
SATO, H., Molecular Oncology
SAWABU, N., Basic and Clinical Oncology
SUDA, T., Molecular and Cellular Immunology
TAKAKURA, N., Molecular and Cellular Biology
YAMAMOTO, K., Molecular and Cellular Biology
YOSHIOKA, K., Molecular and Cellular Biology

Centre for Cooperative Research (tel. (76) 264-6111):

SERYO, K., Mechanical Engineering
YOSHIKUNI, N., Intellectual Property Management

Faculty of Economics (tel. (76) 264-5440):

BENNOU, S., Economic History of Modern China
GOKA, K., Labour Economics
HORIBAYASHI, T., Theory of Economic Planning
IKARIYAMA, H., Public Finance
KAMIJO, I., History of Economic Thought
MAEDA, T., Modern Economics
MARUYAMA, K., Comparative Social Philosophy
MIYATA, M., Banking and Financial Systems
MURAKAMI, K., Principles of Economics
NAKASHIMA, K., World-System Theory and the Financial History of Medieval and Modern Europe
NAMU, S., Education
NISHIDA, Y., Japanese Contemporary Agricultural History
NISHIJIMA, T., Contrastive Sociolinguistics
NOMURA, M., History of Social Thought
SAWADA, M., Industrial Relations and Human Resource Management in Japan and the USA, General Theory of Business Management
SHIRAISHI, H., Business Administration
TSURUZONO, Y., Korean History
UNNO, Y., Economic Policy
YOKOYAMA, T., Social Security
YOSHINO, Y., Sports Science

Faculty of Education (tel. (76) 264-5555):

DEMURA, S., Lifelong Sports
EMORI, I., Pedagogy
GOMI, T., Historical Geography
HATANAKA, H., Magnetic Resonance
IHARA, Y., Inorganic Chemistry
IKEGAMI, K., Developmental Psychology
ISHIMURA, U., Physical Education
ITOH, S., Geography and Planning
IZUMI, N., Dielectrics
KATAGIRI, K., Developmental Neuropsychology of Mental Retardation
KATOH, K., Japanese Linguistics
KAWABATA, K., Freshwater Biology
KAYAHARA, M., Clinical Psychology
KIMURA, M., Education for the Handicapped
KONDOH, A., Japanese Linguistics
KUJIRA, Y., Crop Science
KUROBORI, T., Applied Optics
MAEDA, H., Modern Japanese Literature
MATSUBARA, M., Teaching of Science
MATSUDAIRA, M., Textile Science
MATSUNAKA, H., Instrumental Music
MATSUSHITA, R., Philosophy of Education
MATSUURA, N., Graphic Design
MIYASHITA, T., History of European Art
MIYOSHI, Y., Information Science
MORI, E., Japanese Literature
MOROOKA, K., Teaching Methods
MURAI, A., Research on Methods of Teaching Social Studies
OHTSUKA, I., English Linguistics
OI, M., Communication Disorders
OKAZAKI, F., Philosophy
OKUBO, H., History of Physical Education and Sports
OKUDA, H., Japanese History
SAKAYORI, A., Igneous Petrology
SASAK, T., Materials Science and Engineering
SHINOHARA, H., Music Education
SUGIMOTO, M., Geology
SUNADA, R., Practice and Research for Clinical Psychology and Education
TANABE, S., Educational Administration and Management
UEDA, J., Chemistry
YAKURA, K., Plant Molecular Biology
YAMAGISHI, M., Housing Science
YAMAMOTO, H., Biomechanics in Sports
YAMAMOTO, H., Classic Japanese Literature
YAMAMOTO, T., Teaching Methods
YASUKAWA, T., History of Foreign Education

Faculty of Law (tel. (76) 264-5403):

CHEN, I., Conflict of Laws
INOUE, H., Social Security Law
KASHIMA, M., International Relations
KUSUNE, S., International Communication
MAEDA, T., Labour Law
NAKAMASA, M., Social Philosophy
NAKAMURA, M., Chinese Legal History
NAKAYAMA, H., Criminal Procedure
NISHIMURA, S., Political Sociology
SAKURAI, T., European Legal History
TAKAHASHI, R., Sociology
TOKUMOTO, S., Civil Law
UMEDA, Y., Japanese Legal History
YAMAGATA, K., Developmental Psychology

Faculty of Letters (tel. (76) 264-5360):

FUJII, S., Prehistory of the Near East
FURUHATA, T., Oriental History
HASHIMOTO, K., Sociology
HONMA, T., American Literature
IKUTA, S., English Literature
IWATA, R., Chinese Linguistics
KAGAMI, H., Cultural Anthropology
KAJIKAWA, S., Russian History
KAJIKAWA, Y., Geography
KAMIYA, H., Geography
KASAI, J., Japanese History
KASUYA, Y., French Literature
KIGOSHI, O., Japanese Literature
KUBOTA, I., German Literature
KUBUKI, S., Comparative Culture
MATSUKAWA, J., Cognitive Psychology
MIZOBE, A., Sociology
MOCHII, Y., Oriental History
MURAKAMI, K., American Literature
NAKABAYASHI, N., Cultural Anthropology
NAKAMURA, Y., English Language
NISHIMURA, S., Japanese Literature
NITTA, T., Linguistics

OHTAKI, S., Chinese Language
SASAKI, T., Archaeology
SHIBATA, M., Philosophy
SHIMA, I., Comparative Culture
SUNAHARA, Y., Philosophy
TAKADA, S., English Literature
TAKAHAMA, S., Archaeology
TAKEUCHI, Y., German Linguistics
TOHDA, M., British History
TSUGE, Y., Linguistics
UCHIDA, H., French Literature
UEDA, M., Japanese Literature
YASUMURA, N., Classical Greek and Latin Literature

Faculty of Medicine (5-11-80 Kodatsuno, Kanazawa, Ishikawa; tel. (76) 265-2500):

AMANO, R., Radiochemistry and Radiobiology
ASAI, H., Physical Therapy
HASEGAWA, M., Mental Health and Psychiatric Nursing
HOSO, M., Pathology and Anatomy
HOSOMI, H., Ethics and Bioethics
HOSONO, R., Neurobiology
IKUTA, M., Human Activity Analysis
INAGAKI, M., Fundamental Nursing and Division of Health Science
IZUMI, K., Gerontological and Rehabilitation Nursing
KARASAWA, T., Bacterial Pathogenesis
KAWAHARA, E., Pathology
KAWAI, K., Radiopharmaceutical Chemistry
KIDO, T., Occupational and Environmental Health
KIKUCHI, Y., Radiation Oncology
KIMURA, R., Child Development and Paediatric Nursing
KOJIMA, K., Medical Electronics and Information Sciences
KOSHIDA, K., Medical Radiation Protection
KOYAMA, Y., Psychiatry and Neuropsychology
MIZUKAMI, Y., Radiation Pathology
NAKASHIMA, H., Bioinformatics
NAKATANI, T., Anatomy and Biology of Cutaneous Wounds
NEMOTO, T., Medical Engineering, Bioengineering, Biomedical Measurement
NOTOYA, M., Neuropsychology and Speech Pathology
OGIWARA, S., Physical Therapy
OHTAKE, S., Haematology and Oncology
SAEKI, K., Community Health Nursing
SAKAI, A., Maternal and Child Nursing and Midwifery
SANADA, S., Radiological Technology and Medical Physics
SEKI, H., Child and Adolescent Health
SHIMADA, K., Women's Health and Midwifery
SHOSAKU, T., Neurophysiology
SOMEYA, F., Rehabilitation Medicine
SUZUKI, M., Neuroradiology
TACHINO, K., Rehabilitation Medicine
TAKATA, S., Clinical Physiology
TAKAYAMA, T., Nuclear Medicine Technology
TANAKA, J., Virology
YACHIE, A., Immunology and Host Defence

Graduate School of Medical Science (13-1 Takara-machi, Kanazawa, Ishikawa; tel. (76) 265-2100):

FUJIWARA, K., Human Movement and Health
FUKUDA, R., Molecular Genetics (Dept. of Biochemistry)
FURUKAWA, M., Otorhinolaryngology, Head and Neck Surgery
HASHIMOTO, T., Laboratory Medicine
HIGASHIDA, H., Biophysical Genetics
ICHIMURA, H., Viral Infection and International Health
INABA, H., Emergency Medical Science (Department of Emergency and Critical Care Medicine)
INOUE, M., Molecular Reproductive Biology
ISEKI, S., Histology and Embryology
KANEKO, S., Cancer Gene Regulation, Gastroenterology and Nephrology
KANO, M., Cellular Neurophysiology
KATO, S., Molecular Neurobiology
KOIZUMI, S., Angiogenesis and Vascular Development (Department of Paediatrics)
KOSHINO, Y., Psychiatry and Neurobiology
MATSUI, O., Radiology
NAKANISHI, Y., Molecular and Cellular Biochemistry
NAKANUMA, Y., Morpho-Functional Pathology (Department of Human Pathology)
NAKAO, S., Cellular Transplantation Biology (Haemato-oncology and Respiratory Medicine)
NAMIKI, M., Integrative Cancer Therapy and Urology
OGAWA, S., Biotargeting
OGINO, K., Environmental and Preventive Medicine
OHSHIMA, T., Forensic and Social Environmental Medicine
OOI, A., Molecular and Cellular Pathology
SAIJOH, K., Environmental and Molecular Bio-informatics
SHIMIZU, T., Bacteriology
SUGIYAMA, K., Ophthalmology
TAKEHARA, K., Angiogenesis and Connective Tissue Metabolism (Department of Dermatology)
TAKUWA, Y., Molecular Vascular Physiology
TANAKA, S., Anatomy and Neuroembryology
TOMITA, K., Restorative Medicine of Neuromusculoskeletal System (Department of Orthopaedic Surgery)
TONAMI, N., Biotracer Medicine (Department of Nuclear Medicine)
WATANABE, G., Thoracic, Cardiovascular and General Surgery (Department of Surgery I)
YAMADA, M., Neurology and Neurobiology of Ageing
YAMAMOTO, E., Oral and Maxillofacial Surgery
YAMAMOTO, H., Biochemistry and Molecular Vascular Biology
YAMAMOTO, K., Organ Function Restoratology (Department of Anaesthesiology and Intensive Care Medicine)
YOKOI, T., Drug Metabolism and Molecular Toxicology
YOKOTA, T., Stem Cell Biology
YOSHIMOTO, T., Molecular and Medical Pharmacology

Graduate School of Natural Science and Technology (tel. (76) 264-6821):

ADACHI, M., Optical Metrology
ANDO, T., Biophysics
AOKI, K., Theoretical Physics
ARAI, S., Petrology
CHIKATA, Y., Bridge Maintenance Management
ENDO, K., Theoretical Chemistry
FUJIMAGARI, T., Mathematical Analysis
FUJISHITA, H., Quantum Physics of Condensed Matter
FUJIWARA, N., Systems and Control
FUKUMORI, Y., Physiological Chemistry
FUNADA, T., Vehicle Automation
FURUMOTO, M., Geophysics
HASHIMOTO, H., Visual Communication, Video Coding, Multimedia Processing
HATANE, I., Numerical Analysis, Computational Physics and Mathematics
HAYAKAWA, K., Hygienic Chemistry
HAYASHI, Y., Separation Engineering
HIRAO, M., Production Engineering
HIROSE, Y., Computational Mechanics
HIWATARI, Y., Theory of Material Physics
HOJO, A., Strength of Materials
HONJO, T., Analytical Chemistry
ICHINOSE, T., Functional Analysis
IKEDA, O., Electrochemistry
INOMATA, K., Organic Chemistry
ISHIBASHI, H., Synthetic Organic Chemistry
ISHIDA, H., Coastal Engineering
ISHIWATARI, A., Geology and Petrology
ISOBE, K., Inorganic Chemistry
ITO, H., Differential Equations
ITO, S., Discrete Dynamical System and its Application
ITO, T., Algebraic Combinatorics
IWAHARA, M., Power Electronics, Applied Magnetics
IWATA, Y., Dynamics of Machinery
KAJIKAWA, Y., Structural Engineering
KAMIYA, Y., Robotics
KANJIN, Y., Harmonic Analysis
KANOH, S., Synthetic Polymer Chemistry
KASUE, A., Geometry
KATO, M., Stratigraphy and Palaeontology
KAWAKAMI, M., Urban and Regional Planning
KIHARA, K., Mineralogy and Crystallography
KIMATA, N., Infrastructure Planning, System Simulation
KIMURA, H., Artificial Intelligence
KIMURA, K., Drug Management and Policies
KIMURA, S., Fluid Mechanics and Thermal Sciences
KINOSHITA, H., Organic Chemistry
KITAGAWA, K., Mechanical Properties of Engineering Materials
KITAGAWA, M., Deformation and Strength of Man-made and Naturally Produced Materials
KITAURA, M., Earthquake Engineering
KODAMA, A., Geometry
KOMURA, A., Electrochemistry
KUBO, J., Theoretical Physics
KUMEDA, M., Electronic Materials
KUNIMOTO, K., Bio-organic Chemistry, Environmental Technology
MAEGAWA, K., Structural Engineering
MAGAI, T., Defects in Solids
MASUYA, H., Structural Engineering
MATSUDA, Y., Integrated Circuits
MATSUMOTO, T., Pile Foundations, Pile Dynamics, Numerical Analysis
MATSUNAGA, T., Molecular Human Genetics
MATSUURA, K., Instrumentation by Image Processing
MIKAGE, M., Herbal Medicine and Natural Resources
MIYAGISHI, S., Applied Physical Chemistry
MIYAJIMA, M., Earthquake Engineering
MIYAKAWA, T., Partial Differential Equations
MONZEN, R., Metallic Materials
MORI, S., Heat and Mass Transfer
MORIMOTO, A., Electronic Materials
MOTOI, M., Organic Chemistry of Polymers
MUKAI, C., Pharmaceutical and Organic Chemistry
MURAKAMI, T., Astrophysics
MURAMOTO, K., Image Information Systems
NAGANO, I., Radio Wave Engineering
NAKAGAKI, R., Physical Chemistry
NAKAMOTO, Y., Polymer Chemistry
NAKANISHI, T., Radiochemistry
NAKAO, S., Applied Mathematics
NAKAYAMA, K., Adaptive Systems
NAOE, S., Optical Properties of Materials
NISHIKAWA, K., Digital Signal Processing
NISHIKAWA, K., Theoretical Chemistry
NITTA, K., Polymer Physics
ODA, J., Bionic Design
OHASHI, N., Molecular Physics

OHGISHI, M., Cognitive Engineering
OHKUMA, S., Biochemistry and Molecular Cell Biology
OHTA, T., Pharmacognosy and Chemistry of Natural Products
OKUNO, M., Mineralogy and Non-crystalline Material Science
OMATA, S., Partial Differential Equations and Numerical Analysis
OTANI, Y., Aerosol Technology
SAITOU, M., Computational Materials Science
SAKURAI, S., Developmental Biology
SAKURAI, T., Biochemistry
SATO, H., Non-linear Vibration
SATO, Y., Organic Physical Chemistry
SEKI, H., Environmental Engineering
SEKIZAKI, M., Physical Chemistry of Crystals
SENDA, H., Coordination Chemistry
SHIMADA, K., Clinical Analytical Sciences
SHINTAKU, S., Textile Machinery
SOMEI, M., Chemistry
SUGANO, T., Algebra
SUZUKI, H., Solid State Physics
SUZUKI, M., Coordination Chemistry
SUZUKI, N., Holistic Pharmacotherapy
TAGO, Y., Computational Science
TAKAHASHI, K., Photo-function Material Chemistry
TAKAMIYA, S., Microwave/Optoelectronic Semiconductor Devices
TAKANOBU, S., Stochastic Analysis
TAKAYAMA, J., Traffic Engineering and Transport Planning
TAKIMOTO, A., Heat and Mass Transfer, Energy Conversion and Environmental Conservation
TAMAI, N., River Engineering, River Planning
TAMURA, K., Chemical Engineering Fundamentals and Thermodynamics
TANAKA, I., History of Science and Technology
TAZAKI, K., Environmental Earth Science
TORII, K., Civil Engineering Materials
TSUCHIYA, M., Mathematics (Theory of Stochastic Processes)
TSUJI, A., Innovative Pharmaceutics
UCHIYAMA, Y., Tribology (Friction and Wear Mechanisms of Rubbers and Plastics)
UEDA, K., Phylogenetics
UEDA, K., Separation and Analytical Chemistry
UEDA, T., Precision Machining, Laser Processing
UENO, H., Fluid Machinery, Fluid Power
UESUGI, Y., Plasma Science, Fusion Plasma Engineering
USUDA, M., Materials Working
YAJIMA, T., Ecology
YAMADA, K., Neuropsychopharmacology
YAMADA, M., Combinatorics
YAMADA, M., Opto-electronics
YAMADA, T., Polymer Processing, Reaction Engineering and Phase Equilibria
YAMADA, Y., Mechanical Properties of Materials
YAMAKOSHI, K., Biomedical Engineering
YAMANE, S., Computer Science
YAMAZAKI, K., Structural Optimization
YATOMI, C., Non-linear Continuum Mechanics
YOKOI, T., Drug Metabolism and Molecular Toxicology
YONEDA, Y., Molecular Pharmacology
YONEYAMA, T., Metal Forming, Machine Design

Law School (tel. (76) 264-5968):
ATARASHI, M., Constitutional Law
FURITSU, T., Criminal Law
HASEGAWA, T., Civil Law
HATA, Y., Comparative Constitutional Law
HIGASHI, I., Criminal Procedure
HOSOKAWA, T., Administrative Law
KASHIMI, Y., Civil Law
NAKAJIMA, F., Commercial Law
NAKO, M., Labour Law
NISHIMURA, S., Criminal Law
NOSAKA, Y., Civil Law
OJIMA, S., Family Law
SATO, M., Criminal Procedure
TAJIMA, J., Civil Law

Environmental Preservation Centre (tel. (76) 234-6893):
OHTA, T., Chemical Engineering Thermodynamics

Extension Institute (tel. (76) 264-5271):
HATTORI, E., Adult Education (Life-long Education), Extramural Education

Foreign Language Institute (tel. (76) 264-5760):
AISAWA, K., German
KANEKO, Y., German
KIKUCHI, E., German
KUWANO, H., English
MIKAMI (KIMURA), J., French
OYABU, K., English
SANBAI, R., English
SAWADA, S., English
WATANABE, A., English
YABUCHI, T., Chinese

Health Service Centre (tel. (76) 264-5251; e-mail nakabaya@kenroku.kanazawa-u.ac.jp):
NAKABAYASHI, H., Endocrinology and Metabolism

Information Media Centre (tel. (76) 264-6911):
SHAKO, M., Network Security
SUZUKI, T., Computational Physics, Particle Physics

Institute for Nature and Environmental Technology (tel. (76) 264-6141):
IWASAKA, Y.
KASHIWAYA, K., Hydro-geomorphology
KIMURA, S., Heat Transfer and Fluid Mechanics
KOMURA, K., Environmental Radioactivity
NAKAMURA, K., Ecology
SASAYAMA, Y., Biodiversity
SHIMIZU, N., Bioengineering
YAMADA, S., Magnetic Technology
YAMAMOTO, M., Nuclear Geochemistry

International Student Centre (tel. (76) 264-5188):
MATSUSHITA, M., Psychology
MIURA, K., Japanese Language Education
OKAZAWA, T., Insect Ecology

Research Centre for Higher Education (tel. (76) 264-5837):
AONO, T., Medical Law
HAYATA, Y., Evaluation

University Hospital (13-1 Takara-machi, Kanazawa, Ishikawa; tel. (76) 265-2000):
KOIZUMI, J., Department of General Medicine
MIYAMOTO, K., Department of Hospital Pharmacy

KITAMI INSTITUTE OF TECHNOLOGY

165 Koen-cho, Kitami, Hokkaido 090-8507
Telephone: (157) 26-9106
E-mail: soumu05@desk.kitami-it.ac.jp
Internet: www.kitami-it.ac.jp

Founded 1960
Independent
Academic year: April to March (2 semesters)

Pres.: HIDEYUKI TSUNEMOTO
Vice-Pres: KOICHI AYUTA, NOBUO TAKAHASHI
Dir of Admin.: AKIHIRO SHIBAZAKI
Library Dir: TOSHIYUKI OSHIMA

Number of teachers: 150 full-time
Number of students: 2,103

Publication: *Memoirs of Kitami Institute of Technology*

KOBE UNIVERSITY

1-1 Rokkodai-cho, Nada-ku, Kobe 657-8501, Hyogo
Telephone: (78) 881-1212
E-mail: www-admin@kobe-u.ac.jp
Internet: www.kobe-u.ac.jp

Founded 1902
Independent
Academic year: April to March

Pres.: TOMOYUKI NOGAMI
Dirs: KUNIO SAKAMOTO, MASAHIRO TAKASAKI, MASAYUKI SUZUKI, OSAMI NISHIDA, SADAO KAMIDONO, SHIGEYUKI MAYAMA, SHINZO KITAMURA, SHOJI NISHIJIMA
Dir of Admin.: KUNIO SAKAMOTO
Library Dir: KENICHI SUDO

Library of 3,365,000 vols
Number of teachers: 1,674 full-time
Number of students: 17,598

Publications: *Law Review* (1 a year), *Economic Review* (1 a year), *Business Research* (irregular), *Journal of Mathematics* (2 a year), *Kobe Journal of Medical Sciences* (6 a year), *Bulletin of Allied Medical Sciences* (1 a year), *Memoirs of the Graduate School of Science and Technology* (1 a year), *Journal of International Cooperation Studies* (3 a year), *Economic and Business Review* (1 a year), *Journal of Economics and Business Administration* (12 a year), *Kobe Economic and Business Review* (1 a year)

DEANS

Faculty of Agriculture: CHIHARU NAKAMURA
Faculty and Graduate School of Letters: TAKAJI MATSUSHIMA
Faculty of Cross-cultural Studies: SATOSHI MUNAKATA
Faculty of Human Development: SUSUMU WADA
Faculty and Graduate School of Law: EIJI TAKIZAWA
Faculty and Graduate School of Economics: TAKASHI NAKATANI
Faculty and Graduate School of Business Administration: HISAKATSU SAKURAI
School and Graduate School of Medicine: SAKAN MAEDA
Faculty of Engineering: HIROMOTO USUI
Faculty of Maritime Sciences: KINZO INOUE
Faculty of Science: HIROSHI TAKEDA
Graduate School of Cultural Studies and Human Science: SUSUMU WADA
Graduate School of Humanities and Social Sciences: TAKAJI MATSUSHIMA
Graduate School of International Cooperation Studies: YUTAKA KATAYAMA
Graduate School of Science and Technology: HIDEKI FUKUDA
Research Institute for Economics and Business Administration: HIDETOSHI YAMAJI

PROFESSORS

Biosignal Research Center (tel. (78) 803-5332; e-mail drkikaku@ofc.kobe-u.ac.jp; internet inherit:biosig.kobe-u.ac.jp/biosignal/english/index.html):
KIKKAWA, U., Biochemistry
ONO, Y., Biology of Living Functions
SAITO, N., Pharmacology
YONEZAWA, K., Biochemistry

Faculty of Agriculture (1-1 Rokkodai-cho, Nada-ku, Kobe 657-8501; tel. (78) 803-5921; e-mail ashomu@ofc.kobe-u.ac.jp; internet www.ans.kobe-u.ac.jp/indexe.html):
AE, N., Soil Science and Plant Nutrition
AOKI, K., Applied Biofunctional Chemistry

ASHIDA, H., Applied Biofunctional Chemistry
HASEGAWA, S., Animal Nutrition, Morphology and Microbiology
HATA, T., Regional and Environmental Engineering
HORIO, H., Biosystems Engineering
HOSAKA, K., Food Resources Education and Research Centre
HOSHI, N., Animal Nutrition, Morphology and Microbiology
INAGAKI, N., Horticultural Science
KAKO, T., Food and Environmental Economics
KAMIJIMA, O., Plant Breeding and Production Science
KANAZAWA, K., Biofunctional Molecules
KAWAMURA, T., Biosystems Engineering
MAYAMA, S., Plant Protection
MIYAKE, H., Biofunctional Chemistry
MIYANO, T., Animal Breeding and Reproduction
MIZUNO, M., Plant Resource Science
MUKAI, F., Animal Breeding and Reproduction
NAITO, T., Plant Protection
NAKAMURA, C., Plant Genetics and Physiology
NAKANISHI, T., Horticultural Science
OHNO, T., Biofunctional Molecules
OHSAWA, R., Animal Science
OKAYAMA, T., Applied Biofunctional Chemistry
SHIMIZU, A., Animal Nutrition, Morphology and Microbiology
SUGIMOTO, T., Genetics and Physiology
SUGIMOTO, Y., Applied Biofunctional Chemistry
TAKADA, O., Food and Environmental Economics
TANAKA, T., Regional and Environmental Science
TERAI, H., Horticultural Science
TOYODA, K., Biosystems Engineering
UCHIDA, K., Regional and Environmental Science
UCHIDA, N., Plant Breeding and Production Science
YAMAGATA, H., Biofunctional Molecules
YASUDA, T., Plant Genetics and Physiology

Faculty of Cross-cultural Studies (1-2-1 Tsurukabuto, Nada-ku, Kobe 657-8501; tel. (78) 803-7515; e-mail shomudai@ofc.kobe-u.ac.jp; internet ccs.cla.kobe-u.ac.jp/kohou/eigo):

AMANO, K., Comtemporary Culture and Society Division
CHO, S., Comtemporary Culture and Society Division
FUJINO, K., Contemporary Culture and Society Division
GODA, T., Intercultural Communication Division
HAYASHI, H., Human Communication and Information Science Division
ICHIDA, Y., Comtemporary Culture and Society Division
ISHIHARA, K., Area Studies Division
ISHIKAWA, T., Area Studies Division
ISHIZUKA, H., Area Studies Division
KABURAGI, M., Human Communication and Information Science Division
KAGEYAMA, S., Area Studies Division
KIBA, H., Intercultural Communication Division
KINOSHITA, M., Area Studies Division
KOMURASAKI, S., Intercultural Communication Division
LU, X., Area Studies Division
MIKAMI, T., Contemporary Culture and Society Division
MIKIHARA, H., Comtemporary Culture and Society Division
MIURA, N., Intercultural Communication Division
MIZUGUCHI, S., Human Communication and Information Science Division
MIZUTA, K., Comtemporary Culture and Society Division
MORIMOTO, M., Intercultural Communication Division
MORISHITA, J., Human Communication and Information Science Division
MUNAKATA, S., Comtemporary Culture and Society Division
NOTANI, K., Intercultural Communication Division
OHTSUKI, K., Human Communication and Information Science Division
SADANOBU, T., Human Communication and Information Science Division
SAKAMOTO, C., Area Studies Division
SAKANO, T., Intercultural Communication Division
SASAE, O., Area Studies Division
SHIBATA, Y., Intercultural Communication Division
SONE, H., Area Studies Division
SUDO, K., Area Studies Division
SUZAKI, S., Area Studies Division
TANIMOTO, S., Area Studies Division
TERAUCHI, N., Area Studies Division
TODA, M., Intercultural Communication Division
UCHIDA, M., Intercultural Communication Division
UOZUMI, K., Contemporary Culture and Society Division
UTSUKI, N., Human Communication and Information Science Division
WANG, K., Area Studies Division
YAMAZAKI, Y., Contemporary Culture and Society Division
YOKOYAMA, R., Area Studies Divison
YOSHIDA, N., Contemporary Culture and Society Division
YOSHIOKA, M., Intercultural Communication Division

Faculty of Engineering (tel. (78) 803-6333; e-mail kousyomu@ofc.kobe-u.ac.jp; internet www.eng.kobe-u.ac.jp/index.html):

ADACHI, H., Theory and History of Architecture
DEKI, S., Applied Inorganic Chemistry
FUJII, S., Energy Conversion Engineering
FUJITA, I., Hydraulic Engineering
HAYASHI, S., Mathematical Theory of Programming
HIRASAWA, S., Heat Transfer and Thermal Engineering
KAKUDA, Y., Mathematical Logic and Mathematical Design Theory
KANKI, H., Machine Dynamics and Control
KAWATANI, M., Structural Dynamics
KAYA, N., Space Solar Power Systems
KIKYO, H., Mathematical Logic and Computer Science
KONDO, A., Biochemical Engineering
KURODA, K., Transportation Engineering and Infrastructure Planning
MASUDA, S., Algorithms and Data Structures
MATSUYAMA, H., Membrane Technology
MICHIOKU, K., River Hydraulics
MITANI, I., Ultimate Design of Steel and Composite Structures
MIYOSHI, T., Quantum Electronics
MORII, M., Information Theory, Computer Networks, Internet Security and Cryptography
MORIMOTO, M., Environmental Acoustics
MORIWAKI, T., Intelligent Manufacturing Systems and Ultraprecision Machining
MORIYAMA, M., Architectural and Urban Environmental Engineering
NAGAO, T., Design and Performance of Building Structures
NAKAGIRI, S., Control and Identification of Distributed Systems
NAKAI, Y., Fatigue and Fracture of Engineering Materials
NAMBU, T., Control of PDE
NISHINO, T., Polymer Chemistry
NUMA, M., VLSI Design and CAD
OGAWA, M., Semiconductor Electronics
OHI, K., Quake-proof Structural Engineering
OHMAE, N., Micro- and Nano-Tribology and Surface Engineering
OHMURA, N., Transport Science
OHTA, Y., Control Engineering
OKUBO, M., Polymer Colloid Chemistry
OSUKA, K., Advanced Control Engineering
SHIBUYA, S., Geotechnical Engineering
SHIGEMURA, T., Urban and Architectural Design
SHIOZAKI, Y., Urban and Housing Study
SHIRASE, K., Autonomous Machine Tools and Intelligent Manufacturing Systems
TADA, Y., Optimum Design of Systems
TAKADA, S., Earthquake Engineering
TAKENAKA, N., Multiphase Flow Engineering
TAKI, K., Computer Science and Engineering
TOMITA, Y., Solid Mechanics
TOMIYAMA, A., Energy and Environmental Engineering
TSUKAMOTO, M., Computer Systems and Networking
TSURUYA, S., Catalytic Chemistry
UEDA, Y., Applied Physical Chemistry
USUI, H., Non-Newtonian Fluid Mechanics
WADA, O., Optoelectronic Materials and Devices
YASAKA, Y., Plasma Science and Power Engineering
YASUDA, C., Architectural Planning and Urban Design
YASUDA, H., Nanomaterials Science
YOSHIMOTO, M., VLSI System Engineering
YOSHIMURA, T., Applied Optics and Image Processing

Faculty of Letters (tel. (78) 803-5591; e-mail lsoumu@lit.kobe-u.ac.jp; internet www.lit.kobe-u.ac.jp):

DONOHASHI, A., Art History
EDAGAWA, M., French Literature
FUJI, M., Sociology
FUJITA, H., Geography
FUKUNAGA, S., Japanese Literature and Language
HASEGAWA, K., Geography
HISHIKAWA, E., British and American Literature
IWASAKI, N., Sociology
KAMATANI, T., Chinese Language and Literature
KAZASHI, N., Philosophy
KUBOZONO, H., Linguistics
MATSUDA, H., French Literature
MATSUDA, T., Philosophy
MATSUMOTO, Y., Linguistics
MATSUSHIMA, T., Psychology
MOHRI, A., European and American History
MORI, N., Asian History
NAGANO, J., Art Theory
NISHIMITSU, Y., Linguistics
OGURA, T., Psychology
OHTSURU, A., European and American History
RINBARA, S., Japanese Literature and Language
SAITO, S., British and American Literature
SASAKI, M., Sociology
SUZUKI, Y., Japanese Literature and Language
TAKAHASHI, M., Japanese History
YAMAGUCHI, K., German Literature
YAMAMOTO, M., Philosophy
YUI, K., Sociology

Faculty of Human Development (3-11 Tsurukabuto, Nada-ku, Kobe 657-8501; tel. (78)

803-7905; e-mail info@h.kobe-u.ac.jp; internet www.h.kobe-u.ac.jp):

AMAKAWA, T., Sciences for the Natural Environment
AOKI, T., Human Life Environment
ASANO, S., Studies of Social Environment
EBINA, K., Sciences for the Natural Environment
ENOMOTO, T., Sciences for the Natural Environment
FUNAKI, T., Educational Science
FUNAKOSHI, S., Childhood Development and Education
GOMI, K., Childhood Development and Education
HAMAGUCHI, H., Human Life Environment
HIRAKAWA, K., Sports Science
HIRAYAMA, Y., Human Life Environment
HIROKI, K., Childhood Development and Education
HOUNOKI, K., Adult Learning
ICHIHASHI, H., Human Life Environment
IMATANI, N., Studies of Social Environment
INAGAKI, N., Educational Science
ISHIKAWA, T., Health Education
ITO, K., Development Psychology
IWAI, M., Music
JOH, H., Human Life Environment
KAWABATA, T., Health Education
KAWABE, S., Sports Science
KISHIMOTO, H., Childhood Development and Education
MARUYA, N., Human Life Environment
MIKAMI, K., Educational Science
NAKABAYASHI, T., Developmental Psychology
NAKAGAWA, K., Sciences for the Natural Environment
NAKAMURA, K., Developmental Psychology
NAKAYAMA, S., Art and Design
NINOMIYA, A., Studies of Social Environment
ODA, T., Behavioural Development Studies
ODAKA, N., Art and Design
OGAWA, M., Educational Science
OKADA, S., Behavioural Development Studies
SAIDA, Y., Music
SAITO, K., Sciences for the Natural Environment
SATO, M., Developmental Psychology
SHIBA, M., Sports Performance
SHIRAKURA, T., Mathematics and Computer Studies
SUEMOTO, M., Adult Learning
SUGINO, K., Developmental Psychology
TAINOSHO, Y., Sciences for the Natural Environment
TAKAHASHI, J., Mathematics and Computer Studies
TAKAHASHI, M., Mathematics and Computer Studies
TAKAHASHI, T., Mathematics and Computer Studies
TANAKA, Y., Health Education
TERAKADO, Y., Sciences for the Natural Environment
TSUCHIYA, M., Educational Science
TSUKAWAKI, J., Art and Design
UEZI, S., Sciences for the Natural Environment
WADA, S., Studies of Social Environment
WAKAO, Y., Music
YAMAGUCHI, Y., Sport Sciences
YAMASAKI, T., Studies of Social Environment
YANAGIDA, Y., Sport Sciences
YANO, S., Human Life Environment

Faculty of Maritime Sciences (5-1-1 Fukaeminamimachi, Higashinada-ku, Kobe 658-0022; tel. (78) 431-6206; e-mail mssoumu@ofc.kobe-u.ac.jp; internet www.maritime.kobe-u.ac.jp):

AZUKIZAWA, T., Marine Mechatronics
FUKUDA, K., Maritime Energy Engineering
FUKUOKA, T., Machine Design Engineering
FUKUSHI, K., Analytical Chemistry
FURUSHO, M., Seamanship and Traffic Psychology at Sea
HASHIMOTO, M., Internal Combustion Engines
HAYASHI, Y., Ship Navigation
IMAI, A., Logistics Planning
INOUE, K., Marine Traffic Engineering and Maritime Safety Management
INOUE, T., Network and Communication Systems Engineering
ISHIDA, H., Marine Meteorology
ISHIDA, K., Disaster Science
ISHIDA, T., Marine Power and System Engineering
ISOGAI, T., Statistical Science and Quality Management
KATO, E., Functional Polymer Materials Science
KIMURA, R., Acoustical Engineering and Maintenance Engineering
KITAMURA, A., Particle Beam Engineering
KOBAYASHI, E., Maritime Science and Naval Architecture
KOGUCHI, N., Navigation
KOZAI, K., Satellite Oceanography
MARUO, K., Partial Differential Equations
NISHIDA, O., Energy and Environmental Engineering
NISHIO, S., Naval Architecture
NISHIOKA, T., Fracture Mechanics, Computational Mechanics, Experimental Mechanics
ODA, K., Radiation Dosimetry and Applications
OTSUJI, T.
SADAKANE, H., Naval Architecture
SAKAMOTO, K., Power Electronics
SATO, M., Material Chemistry for Transportation
SHIOTANI, S., Numerical Ship Hydrodynamics
SIMADA, H., Cognitive Science
SUGITA, H., Management for Marine Power Plants
SUZUKI, S., Marine Traffic Laws
TAKAHASHI, R., Statistics
TANAKA, S., Fluid Mechanics of Engineering
YAMAMURA, S., Information Engineering
YOSHIDA, S., Shipping Economics

Faculty of Science (tel. (78) 803-5761; e-mail rishomu@ofc.kobe-u.ac.jp; internet www.sci.kobe-u.ac.jp):

FUKE, K., Physical Chemistry
FUKUDA, Y., Optical Physics
FUKUYAMA, K., Analysis
GUNJI, Y., Planetary Science
HARIMA, H., Condensed Matter Theory
HAYASHI, F., Biology of Living Functions
HAYASHI, M., Organic Chemistry
HIGUCHI, Y., Applied Mathematics
HIMENO, S., Inorganic Chemistry
IKEDA, H., Applied Mathematics
KADONO, Y., Biology of Living Structures
LIM, C. S., High Energy Theory
MATSUDA, T., Planetary Science
MIMURA, T., Biology of Living Structures
MIYATA, T., Earth Science
NAKAGAWA, Y., Planetary Science
NAKAMURA, N., Planetary Science
NAKANISHI, Y., Algebra and Geometry
NORO, M., Applied Mathematics
ONISHI, H., Physical Chemistry
OTOFUJI, Y., Earth Science
SAITO, M., Algebra and Geometry
SAKAMOTO, H., Biology of Living Functions
SASAKI, T., Algebra and Geometry
SATO, H., Earth Science
SETSUNE, J., Inorganic Chemistry
TAKANO, K., Analysis
TAKAYAMA, N., Analysis
TAKEDA, H., Particle Physics
TOMEOKA, K., Planetary Science
TSUCHIYA, T., Biology of Living Functions
WADA, S., Condensed Matter Physics
WATANABE, K., Biology of Living Structures
YAMADA, Y., Analysis
YAMAMURA, K., Organic Chemistry
YAMAZAKI, T., Algebra and Geometry

Graduate School of Business Administration (2-1 Rokkodai-cho, Nada-ku, Kobe, 657-8501; tel. (78) 803-7256; e-mail bwebmstr@kobe-u.ac.jp; internet www.b.kobe-u.ac.jp):

DEI, F., International Economics, International Investments
FUJIWARA, K., Money and Financial Systems
GOTOH, M., Financial Reporting and Accounting Systems
HARADA, T., Industrial Organization
ISHII, J., Marketing Management and Business Strategy
KAGONO, T., Business Strategy and Corporate Behaviour
KANAI, T., Organizational Behaviour
KATO, H., Finance
KATO, Y., Management Accounting
KOGA, T., International Accounting
KOKUBU, K., Social and Environmental Accounting
KOMBAYASHI, N., Human Resource Management
KOU, L., Marketing
KUTSUNA, K., Entrepreneurial Finance
KUWAHARA, T., Business History
MARUYAMA, M., Applied Microeconomics, Distribution Systems
MATSUO, H., Supply Chain Management, Production Planning and Scheduling
MIZUTANI, F., Public Utility Economics and Regulatory Economics
NAITO, F., Financial Accounting and Auditing
NAKANO, T., Accounting Systems and History
OGAWA, S., Marketing
SAKAKIBARA, S., Corporate Finance and Portfolio Management
SAKASHITA, A., Organizational Behaviour and Corporate Culture
SAKURAI, H., Financial Accounting, Financial Statement Analysis
SHOJI, K., Transport Economics and Policy
TAKAO, A., Insurance Industry Analysis
TAKASHIMA, K., Marketing and Distribution Systems
TANI, T., Management Accounting and Control

Graduate School of Economics (2-1 Rokkodai-cho, Nada-ku, Kobe 657-8501; tel. (78) 803-7246; e-mail esoumu@ofc.kobe-u.ac.jp; internet www.econ.kobe-u.ac.jp):

ADACHI, M., Social Policy
AMANO, M., Modern Japanese Economic History
FUJITA, S., International Monetary System
FUKUDA, W., Economic System Theory
HAGIWARA, T., Contemporary Technology Theory
HAMORI, S., Statistical Analysis of Economic Time Series Data
HARA, M., International Investment Theory
HARUYAMA, T., Economic Growth Theory
IRITANI, J., Public Finance Policy
ISHIGURO, K., International Politics and Economics
ISHIKAWA, M., Environmental Economics
JINUSHI, T., American Economy
KATO, H., Chinese Economy
KUBO, H., European Economy
MARUYA, R., Theory of Economic Policy
MATSUBAYASHI, Y., Empirical Analysis of International Macroeconomy
MITANI, N., Labour Economics
NAKAMURA, T., Macroeconomics, Investment Theory
NAKANISHI, N., International Economics

Nakatani, T., Macrodynamic Theory
Ohkubo, H., Monetary Policy
Ohtani, K., Theory of Statistical Inference
Okunishi, T., European Economic History
Oshio, T., Social Security
Shigetomi, K., Economic History of Modern Britain
Takahashi, S., World Economic Geography
Takigawa, Y., Monetary Economics
Tanaka, Y., Theory of Economic Structure
Tanizaki, H., Estimation and Test in Simulation-base Econometrics
Uemiya, S., History of Economic Theory
Uranagase, T., Japanese Economic History
Yamaguchi, M., Agricultural Policy
Yanagawa, T., Industrial Organization
Yoshii, M., Comparative Economics

Graduate School of Cultural Studies and Human Science (3-1-1 Tsurukabuto, Nada-ku, Kobe 657-8501; tel. (78) 803-7905; e-mail inkouhou@ccs.cla.kobe-u.ac.jp; internet www.cla.kobe-u.ac.jp/sojinka):

Harima, T., Clinical Psychology
Hounoki, K., Human and Community Empowerment
Kawabata, T., Human and Community Empowerment
Suemoto, M., Human and Community Empowerment

Graduate School of Humanities and Social Sciences (1-1 Rokkodai-cho, Nada-ku, Kobe 657-8501; tel. (78) 803-5591; e-mail lsoumo@lit.kobe-u.ac.jp; internet www.lit.kobe-u.ac.jp/index_bunka.html):

Iwasaki, N., Theory of Social Risks

Graduate School of International Cooperation Studies (2-1 Rokkodai-cho, Nada-ku, Kobe 657-8501; tel. (78) 803-7265; e-mail kokusomu@ofc.kobe-u.ac.jp; internet www.kobe-u.ac.jp/~gsics/indexj.html):

Alexander, R. B., Endogenous Security
Chen, K., Economic Development and Regional Inequality
Fukui, S., Development Microeconomics
Igarashi, M., International Law
Katayama, Y., Political Development in South-East Asia
Kimura, K., Nation-building and State Formation in Korea
Matsunaga, N., International Trade and Economic Growth
Matsunami, J., Comparative Study on Deregulation, Privatization and Local Government
Mizuno, T., Review and Future Assessment on International Issues
Nishina, K., Development Finance
Ohta, H., Applied Microeconomics
Shibata, A., International Law
Suruga, T., Economic Development and Employment
Takada, H., Local Public Administration and Finance
Takahashi, M., African Economics
Tatebayashi, M., Policy Activities of Political Elites in Japan
Tosa, H., Critical Theory and its Application in International Relations
Uchida, Y., Social Sector Management in Developing Countries
Ueno, H., Transition Economy Policies

Graduate School of Law (2-1 Rokkodai-cho, Nada-ku, Kobe 657-850; tel. (78) 803-7232; e-mail j1shomu@ofc.kobe-u.ac.jp; internet www.law.kobe-u.ac.jp):

Akasaka, M., Constitutional Law
Amiya, R., Western Political History
Baba, K., Sociology of Law
Fujiwara, A., Japanese Legal History
Hamada, F., Labour Law
Hasunuma, K., Philosophy of Law
Hata, M., Civil Procedure
Iida, F., Political Theory
Inoue, N., Constitutional Law
Inoue, Y., Intellectual Property Law
Iokibe, M., Japanese Political History, Comparative Politics
Ishikawa, T., Professional Legal Education
Isomura, T., Civil Law
Ito, M., Comparative Politics
Ji, W. D., Chinese Law, Comparative Studies in Legal Culture
Kashimura, S., Sociology of Law
Kikkawa, G., International Relations
Komuro, N., International Economic Law
Kondo, M., Commercial Law, Securities Regulation
Kubota, A., Civil Law
Maruyama, E., Anglo-American Law, Medical Law
Masujima, K., International Relations
Morishita, T., Russian Law, Principles of Social Sciences
Nakagawa, T., Administrative Law
Nakanishi, M., Civil Procedure
Nakano, S., Private International Law, International Civil Procedure
Negishi, A., Economic Law
Oshima, S., Professional Legal Education
Otsuka, H., Criminal Law
Ouchi, S., Labour Law
Saito, A., International Trade Law, Private International Law
Sakamoto, S., International Law
Sato, H., Tax Law
Sensui, F., Economic Law
Shinada, Y., Political Data Analysis, Election System
Shitani, M., Commercial Law
Sudo, M., Professional Legal Education
Takizawa, E., Western Legal History, Roman Law
Tejima, Y., Civil and Medical Law
Tsukimura, T., International Relations
Ushima, K., Criminal Law
Yamada, S., Civil Law
Yamada, T., Professional Legal Education
Yamamoto, H., Civil Procedure
Yamamoto, K., Civil Law
Yasunaga, M., Civil Law
Yonemaru, T., Administrative Law
Yukizawa, K., Commercial Law, Commercial Transactions

Graduate School of Science and Technology (tel. (78) 803-5332; e-mail drkikaku@ofc.kobe-u.ac.jp; internet www.scitec.kobe-u.ac.jp/english/index.html):

Abe, S., Function Control
Arai, T., Information Mathematics
Asakura, Y., Space Formation Engineering
Boku, S., Environmental Science of Bioresource Production
Fukuda, H., Applied Molecular Assembly
Kanazawa, Y., Bioresource and Energy Creation
Kato, S., Material Production Process Engineering
Kitagawa, H., Relational Biosystems
Kojima, F., Structural Design
Maekawa, S., Bioinformation
Matsushita, T., Fire Safety Engineering, Thermal Environmental Engineering in Building
Miyake, M., Biosystem Applications
Mukai, T., Space and Planetary Materials
Nakayama, A., Regional Environment
Nanba, T., Material Functions
Noumi, M., Mathematical Structures
Nozaki, M., Material Structures
Odani, M., Urban Transportation Planning, Urban and Regional Planning
Ohkawa, T., Intelligent Bioinformatics
Ono, M., Food Marketing
Sasaki, M., Organic Chemistry
Tabuchi, M., Creation of Spatial Systems
Takeda, M., Molecular Cellular Science
Takeuchi, T., Molecular Structure and Function
Tanaka, S., Theoretical Life Science and Computational Molecular Biology
Taura, T., Intelligent Artificial Systems
Tsubaki, M., Functional Molecular Assembly
Tsutahara, M., Biological Resource Utilization
Uehara, K., Media Technology and its Production
Yamanaka, M., Earth Sciences

International Student Center (tel. (78) 803-5265; e-mail ryugaku@ofc.kobe-u.ac.jp; internet www.kobe-u.ac.jp/~kisc):

Nakanishi, Y., Education in Japanese Language
Seguchi, I., Intercultural and Transcultural Education

Medical Center for Student Health (tel. (78) 803-5245; e-mail healthy@kobe-u.ac.jp; internet www.kobe-u.ac.jp/medicalc):

Baba, H., Internal Medicine, Biosignal Pathophysiology

Molecular Photoscience Research Center (tel. (78) 803-5761; e-mail rishomu@ofc.kobe-u.ac.jp; internet www.kobe-u.ac.jp/mprc):

Ohta, H., Condensed Matter Physics
Tominaga, K., Condensed Phase Dynamics

Research Center for Environmental Genomics (tel. (78) 803-5332; e-mail drkikaku@ofc.kobe-u.ac.jp; internet www.rceg.biosig.kobe-u.ac.jp/hpj.html):

Fukami, Y., Biology of Living Structures
Nanmori, T., Plant Molecular Biology
Oono, K., Plant Cell Biology

Research Center for Inland Seas (tel. (78) 803-5761; e-mail rishomu@ofc.kobe-u.ac.jp; internet www.kobe-u.ac.jp/kurcis):

Hyodo, M., Earth Science
Kawai, H., Marine Biology
Nagata, S., Environmental Biochemistry

Research Center for Urban Safety and Security (tel. (78) 803-6437; e-mail rcuss@kobe-u.ac.jp; internet www.kobe-u.ac.jp/~tosi):

Ariki, Y., Media Engineering
Iizuka, A., Geo-environmental Engineering and Geoinformatics
Ishibashi, K., Seismotectonics
Kamae, I., Health Informatics and Decision Sciences
Okimura, T., Slope Stability and Geotechnical Engineering
Tanaka, Y., Soft Ground Engineering and Earthquake Geotechnical Engineering

Research Institute for Economics and Business Administration (2-1 Rokkodai-cho, Nada-ku, Kobe 657-8501; tel. (78) 803-7270; e-mail office@rieb.kobe-u.ac.jp; internet www.rieb.kobe-u.ac.jp):

Goto, J., International Economy and Business
Igawa, K., International Economy and Business
Isobe, T., International Economy and Business
Izawa, H., International Economy and Business
Kamihigashi, T., Information Economy and Business
Katayama, S., International Economy and Business
Kojima, K., Information Economy and Business
Konishi, Y., Information Economy and Business
Lee, H., Information Economy and Business
Miyao, R., RIEB Liaison Centre
Nishijima, S., International Economy and Business
Nobeoka, K., RIEB Liaison Centre
Shimomura, K., Information Economy and Business

TOMITA, M., International Economy and Business
YAMAJI, H., Information Economy and Business

Research Institute for Higher Education (1-2-1 Tsurukabuto, Nada-ku, Kobe 657-8501; tel. (78) 803-7522; e-mail dakaikei@ofc.kobe-u.ac.jp; internet www.kurihe.kobe-u.ac.jp):

KAWASHIMA, T., Sociology of Education
MAIYA, K., Experimental Psychology
YAMANOUCHI, K., Sociology of Education

School and Graduate School of Medicine (7-5-1 Kusunoki-cho, Chuo-ku, Kobe 650-0017; tel. (78) 382-5111; e-mail webmst@med.kobe-u.ac.jp; internet www.med.kobe-u.ac.jp/welcomej.html):

AIBA, A., Cell Biology
AKITA, H., General Medical Science
ANDO, H., Basic Allied Medicine
AZUMA, T., Polygenic Disease Research
CHIHARA, K., Endocrinology; Metabolism, Neurology and Haematology; Oncology
FUJIMARA, M., Urulogy
FURUKAWA, H., Applied Occupational Therapy
GU, E., Advanced Medical Research and Treatment
HASHIMOTO, T., Basic Occupational Therapy
HAYASHI, Y., Molecular Medicine and Medical Genetics
HOTTA, H., Microbiology and Genomics
ISHII, N., Disaster and Emergency Medicine
ISHIKAWA, Y., Health Sciences and Basic Nursing
KASUGA, M., Diabetes, Digestive and Kidney Diseases
KATAOKA, T., Molecular Biology
KAWABATA, M., International Health
KAWAGUCHI, Y., Psychiatric Nursing and Mental Health
KAWAMATA, T., Applied Occupational Therapy
KITA, A., Maternal Nursing and Midwifery
KOHMURA, E., Neurosurgery
KOMORI, T., Oral and Maxillofacial Functional Science
KUMAGAI, S., Clinical Pathology and Immunology
KUNO, T., Molecular Pharmacology and Pharmacogenomics
KURODA, Y., Gastroenterological Surgery
KUROSAKA, M., Orthopaedic Surgery
MAEDA, K., Psychiatry and Neurology
MAEDA, S., Molecular Pathology
MARUO, T., Women's Medicine
MATSUDA, N., Community Health Nursing
MATSUMURA, S., Biochemistry
MATSUO, H., Maternity Nursing
MATSUO, M., Paediatrics
MIKI, A., Basic Physical Therapy
MINAMI, Y., Biomedical Regulation and Parasitology
MURATA, K., Clinical Nursing
NAKAMURA, S., Biochemistry
NAKAZONO, N., Applied Medical Technology
NEGI, A., Ophthalmology
NIBU, K., Otorhinolaryngology—Head and Neck Surgery
NISHIGORI, C., Dermatology
NISHIO, H., Public Health
NISHIYAMA, K., Basic Medical Technology
OBARA, H., Perioperative Medicine and Pain Management
OKAMURA, H., Molecular Brain Science
OKITA, Y., Cardiovascular, Thoracic and Paediatric Surgery
OKUMURA, K., Clinical Pharmacokinetics
RYO, R., Applied Medical Technology, Haematology and Blood Transfusion Medicine
SAKAMOTO, N., Medical Informatics
SEINO, S., Cell Biology and Neurophysiology
SEKI, K., Applied Occupational Therapy
SHIMADA, T., Applied Physical Therapy
SHIOZAWA, S., Rheumatology
SUGIMURA, K., Radiology
TABUCHI, Y., Clinical Oncology and Surgical Nursing
TAHARA, S., Plastic Surgery
TAKADA, S., Maternal and Child Health Science
TAMURA, Y., Basic Nursing
TERASHIMA, T., Developmental Neurobiology
TSUTOU, A., Basic Allied Medicine
UENO, Y., Legal Medicine
UGA, S., Parasitology
USAMI, M., Basic Medical Technology, Surgical Metabolism and Nutrition
WATANABE, M., Applied Medical Technology
YADA, M., Clinical Nursing
YAMAGUCHI, M., Applied Occupational Therapy
YAMAMURA, H., Proteomics
YAMAZAKI, I., Applied Occupational Therapy
YOKONO, K., Internal and Geriatric Medicine
YOKOYAMA, M., Cardiovascular and Respiratory Internal Medicine
YOKOZAKI, H., Surgical Pathology

School of Languages and Communication (1-2-1 Tsurukabuto, Nada-ku, Kobe 657-8501; tel. (78) 803-7522; e-mail dakaikei@ofc.kobe-u.ac.jp; internet solac.cla.kobe-u.ac.jp):

GREER, T., Conversation Analysis, Applied Linguistics, Bilingualism
IGUCHI, J., Applied Linguistics
ISHIKAWA, S., Applied Linguistics
KASHIWAGI, H., English Language Education
KATO, M., English Education
MASUDA, Y., German Linguistics
MIKI, Y., European Maritime Culture
MURATA, R., The Later Enlightenment in Germany
NAKAGAWA, M., Contrastive Linguistics
OKIHARA, K., Applied Linguistics and English Language Education
SHIMAZU, A., American Literature
TSUJIMOTO, Y., British Journalism of the 18th and 19th Centuries
URITA, S., English Literature
YOKOKAWA, H., Psycholinguistics
ZHU, C., Phonetics and Foreign Language Education

KUMAMOTO UNIVERSITY

39-1 Kurokami 2-chome, Kumamoto-shi 860-8555
Telephone: (96) 344-2111
E-mail: message@svml.jimu.kumamoto-u.ac.jp
Internet: www.kumamoto-u.ac.jp
Founded 1949
Independent
Academic year: April to March (2 terms)
Pres.: Dr TATSURO SAKIMOTO
Dir of Admin. Bureau: MASAHARU CHOKI
Vice-Pres: Prof. CHIUCHI HIRAYAMA, Prof. TOMOMICHI ONO
Librarian: Prof. NAKAMASA IWAOKA
Number of teachers: 1,022
Number of students: 9,836
Publications: *Cryogenics Report of the Shockwave and Condensed Matter Research Center* (1 a year), *Kumamoto Journal of Culture and Humanities* (1 a year), *Kumamoto Journal of Mathematics* (1 a year), *Kumamoto Journal of Science (Earth Sciences)* (1 a year), *Kumamoto Law Review* (4 a year), *Kumamoto University Studies in Social and Cultural Sciences* (1 a year), *Memoirs of the Faculty of Engineering* (2 a year), *Physics Report of Kumamoto University* (every 2 years)

DEANS

Faculty of Education: Prof. SHOICHI ISHIHARA
Faculty of Engineering: Prof. ISAO TANIGUCHI
Faculty of Law: Prof. YATARO YOSHINAGA
Faculty of Letters: Prof. MASATO MORI
Faculty of Medical and Pharmaceutical Sciences: Prof. NOBUO SAKAGUCHI
Faculty of Science: Prof. MITSUHIKO KOHNO
Graduate School of Science and Technology: Prof. KATSUHIKO SUGAWARA
Graduate School of Social and Cultural Sciences: Prof. YASUTOSHI YUKAWA
School of Law: Prof. ITARU YAMANAKA

PROFESSORS

Faculty of Education (40-1 Kurokami 2-chome, Kumamoto 860-8555; tel. (96) 342-2514; e-mail kyo-somu@jimu.kumamoto-u.ac.jp; internet www.educ.kumamoto-u.ac.jp):

ASAKAWA, M., Food
BABA, K., Biology
CHIKUMA, Y., Educational Philosophy
FUKUSHIMA, K., Physics
HARADA, I., Electricity
HIGASHI, T., Electricity
HIRAMINE, Y., Algebra
HIRAWA, T., Vocal Music
HORIHATA, M., Japanese Linguistics
ICHIMURA, K., School Health
ISHIHARA, S., Sculpture
ITOH, J., Algebra
KAWAMINAMI, H., Teaching of Social Studies
KIMURA, M., School Health
KIYOZUMI, M., School Health
KOGA, N., Sociology
KUWAHATA, M., Teaching of Domestic Sciences
MAEDA, K., Teaching of Science
MASAMOTO, K., Biology
MIYAMOTO, M., Teaching of Social Studies
NAGATA, N., Teaching of School Health
NAKATA, Y., Educational Administration
NAKAYAMA, T., Theory and History of Music
NISHIKAWA, M., English Linguistics
OGATA, A., Psychology of Handicapped Children
OGAWA, K., Japanese Literature
OGO, K., Exercise and Hygiene
SHIBAYAMA, K., Clinical Psychology
SHIN, K., Education of Handicapped Children
SHINOHARA, H., Educational Psychology
SUGI, S., Teaching of Japanese
SUGOU, H., History of Handicraft Education
SUZUKI, R., English and American Literature
SUZURIKAWA, S., Social Welfare
TAKAGI, N., Teaching of English
TAKAMORI, H., Clothing
TANIGUCHI, K., Physiology of Exercise
TODA, T., English Linguistics
TORIKAI, K., Home Management
TSURUSHIMA, H., History
TSUZINO, T., Mechanics
UMEDA, M., Design and Crafts
WATANABE, K., Earth Science
YAMAMOTO, S., Teaching of Mathematics
YAMANAKA, M., Economics
YANAGI, H., Educational Sociology
YOKOYAMA, S., Geography
YONEMURA, K., Clinical Medicine and Nursing
YOSHIDA, M., Group Dynamics
YOSHIKAWA, N., Theory and History of Art
YOSHINAGA, S., Teaching of Music

Faculty of Engineering (39-1 Kurokami 2-chome, Kumamoto 860-8555; tel. (96) 342-

3513; internet www.eng.kumamoto-u.ac.jp/english/index.htm):

AKIYAMA, H., Electrical Energy Systems
EBIHARA, K., Electrical Energy Systems
FURUKAWA, K., Water Environmental Engineering
GOTO, M., Bio-related Molecular Science
HARADA, H., Intelligent Systems Engineering
HIROE, T., High Pressure Science and Materials Processing
HIROSE, T., Biochemical Engineering
IHARA, H., Bio-related Molecular Science
IKEGAMI, T., Advanced Technology of Electrical and Computer Systems
IKUNO, H., Electronic and Communication Systems
IMURA, H., Thermal and Fluid Energy Systems
INOUE, T., Electronic and Communication Systems
ISHIHARA, O., Regional Planning and Management
IWAI, Z., Intelligent Systems for Measurement and Control
JYO, A., Chemistry of Molecular Engineering
KASHIWAGI, H., Intelligent Systems for Measurement and Control
KAWAJI, S., Computer Science and Engineering
KAWAMURA, Y., Advanced Materials Technology
KITANO, T., Regional Planning and Management
KITAZANO, Y., Water Environmental Engineering
KOBAYASHI, I., Water Environmental Engineering
KURODA, N., Advanced Materials Technology
MACHIDA, M., Chemistry for Molecular Engineering
MAKINO, Y., Architectural Planning and Design
MAZDA, T., Structural Engineering
MITA, N., Advanced Technology of Electrical and Computer Systems
MITSUI, Y., Architectural Planning and Design
MIYAHARA, K., Electronic and Communication Systems
MIZOKAMI, S., Disaster Prevention Engineering
MOROZUMI, M., Regional Planning and Management
MURAYAMA, N., Advanced Technology of Electrical and Computer Systems
NAITOU, K., Mathematical Science
NAKAMURA, R., Intelligent Systems Engineering
NAKAMURA, Y., Advanced Technology of Electrical and Computer Systems
NISHIDA, M., Advanced Materials Technology
NONAKA, T., Chemistry for Material Science
OBARA, Y., Geotechnical Engineering
ODA, I., Intelligent Machine Design and Manufacturing
OGAWA, K., Architectural Planning and Design
OHMOTO, T., Water Environmental Engineering
OHNO, Y., Materials Development Systems
OHTANI, J., Water Environmental Engineering
OSHIMA, Y., Mathematical Science
SADATOMI, M., Thermal and Fluid Energy Systems
SAISHO, M., Disaster Prevention Engineering
SAKURADA, K., Disaster Prevention Engineering
SATONAKA, S., Intelligent Machine Design and Manufacturing
SHOSENJI, H., Chemistry for Molecular Engineering
SUEYOSHI, T., Computer Science and Engineering
SUZUKI, A., Geotechnical Engineering
TAKADA, Y., Mathematical Science
TANIGUCHI, I., Bio-related Molecular Science
TONDA, H., Materials Development Systems
TORII, S., Intelligent Machine Design and Manufacturing
UCHIYAMA, O., Architectural Planning and Design
UMENO, H., Computer Science and Engineering
USAGAWA, T., Intelligent Systems Engineering
WATANABE, J., Thermal and Fluid Energy Systems
YAMAO, T., Structural Engineering
YANO, T., Structural Engineering
YASUI, H., Intelligent Machine Design and Manufacturing
YOKOI, Y., Mathematical Science

Faculty of Law (40-1 Kurokami 2-chome, Kumamoto 860-8555; tel. (96) 342-2315; e-mail jsj-somu@jimu.kumamoto-u.ac.jp; internet www.law.kumamoto-u.ac.jp):

FUKAMATI, K., International Law
HAYASHI, I., International Law
INADA, T., Criminal Procedure
ITO, H., Politics
IWAOKA, N., Politics
KAWAMOTO, T., English Literature
KITAGAWA, K., Philosophy
KIZAKI, Y., Civil Law
MORI, M., German Literature
NAKAMURA, N., Philosophy of Law
OHSAWA, H., Politics
SATO, M., Economic Policy
SUZUKI, K., Politics
WAKASONE, K., European Legal History
YAMASHITA, T., Economics
YAMAZAKI, K., Tax Law
YOSHIDA, I., Sociology of Law
YOSHINAGA, Y., Social Law

Faculty of Letters (40-1 Kurokami 2-chome, Kumamoto 860-8555; tel. (96) 342-2313; e-mail bun-somu@jimu.kumamoto-u.ac.jp; internet www.let.kumamoto-u.ac.jp/let/index.html):

FUKAHORI, K., German Literature
FUKUZAWA, K., Linguistics
HOHGETSU, T., Geography
IHARA, S., Japanese Language
IKEDA, M., Cultural Anthropology and Medical Humanities
KAMIMURA, N., German Language
KINOSHITA, N., Archaeology
KOMATSU, H., Cultural History
KOMOTO, M., Archaeology
KUMAMOTO, S., English Language
MARUYAMA, S., Regional Sociology
MORI, M., Japanese Literature
OGINO, K., German Language
OKABE, T., Aesthetics
OOKUMA, K., French Literature
SAKATA, M., German Literature
SHINOZAKI, S., Ethics
SUGITANI, K., German Literature
TAGUCHI, H., Sociology
TAKAHASHI, T., Ethics
TANAKA, Y., German Literature
TANIKAWA, N., English Literature
TERADA, M., French Literature
TOKUNO, S., Regional Sociology
TONE, T., Psychology
WATANABE, I., Psychology
YASUDA, M., Folklore
YOSHIKAWA, E., Chinese Language
YOSIMURA, T., Japanese History

Faculty of Medical and Pharmaceutical Sciences (1-1 Honjo 1-chome, Kumamoto 860-8556; tel. (96) 373-5904; e-mail iys-somu@jimu.kumamoto-u.ac.jp; internet www.medphas.kumamoto-u.ac.jp):

ARAKI, E., Metabolic Medicine
EKINO, S., Histology
ENDO, F., Paediatrics
FUTATUKA, M., Public Health
GOTO, M., Structure-Function Physical Chemistry
HARADA, S., Medical Virology
HARANO, K., Computational Molecular Design
HORIUCHI, S., Medical Biochemistry
IMAI, T., Drug Metabolism and Disposition
INOMATA, Y., Paediatric Surgery
IRIE, T., Clinical Chemistry and Informatics
ITO, T., Pathology and Experimental Medicine
KAI, H., Molecular Medicine
KAMASUJI, M., Cardiovascular Surgery
KIKAWA, K., General Medicine
KINOSHITA, Y., Aggressology and Critical Care Medicine
KITAMURA, T., Clinical Behavioural Sciences
KODAMA, K., Anatomy
KURATSU, J., Neurosurgery
MIIKE, T., Child Development
MITSUYA, H., Haematology
MITSUYAMA, S., Pharmacology and Molecular Therapeutics
MIURA, R., Molecular Enzymology
MIYATA, T., Chemico-Pharmacological Sciences
MIZUSHIMA, T., Pharmaceutical Microbiology
MORI, M., Molecular Genetics
NAKAGAWA, K., Pharmacology and Therapeutics
NAKAJIMA, M., Organic Chemistry
NAKANISHI, H., Molecular Pharmacology
NAKAYAMA, H., Molecular Cell Function
NISHIMURA, Y., Immunogenetics
NOHARA, T., Natural Medicines
OGAWA, H., Cardiovascular Medicine
OGAWA, H., Sensory and Cognitive Physiology
OHTSUKA, M., Bio-organic Medicinal Chemistry
OKABE, H., Diagnostic Medicine
OKAMURA, H., Reproductive Medicine and Surgery
OTAGIRI, M., Biopharmaceutics
SAITO, H., Pharmacy
SAKAGUCHI, N., Immunology
SASAKI, Y., Gastroenterology and Hepatology
SAYA, H., Tumour Genetics and Biology
SHIGA, K., Molecular Physiology
SHINOHARA, M., Oral and Maxillofacial Surgery
SHOJI, S., Pharmaceutical Biochemistry
TAKAHAMA, K., Environmental and Molecular Health Sciences
TAKEYA, M., Cell Pathology
TANAKA, H., Developmental Neurobiology
TANIHARA, H., Ophthalmology and Visual Science
TERASAKI, H., Anaesthesiology
TOMITA, K., Nephrology
TSUNENARI, S., Forensic Medicine
UCHINO, M., Neurology
UEDA, M., Pharmaceutical Microbiology
UEDA, S., Urology
UEKAMA, K., Physical Pharmaceutics
UNO, T., Analytical and Biophysical Chemistry
YAMAGATA, Y., Structural Biology
YAMAMOTO, T., Molecular Pathology
YAMASHITA, Y., Diagnostic Imaging
YOSHIHARA, H., Medical Informatics

YUMOTO, E., Otolaryngology—Head and Neck Surgery

Faculty of Science (39-1 Kurokami 2-chome, Kumamoto 860-8555; tel. (96) 342-3314; e-mail rig-some@jimu.kumamoto-u.ac.jp; internet www.sci.kumamoto-u.ac.jp/index.html):

ABE, S. I., Developmental Biology
ANIYA, M., Fundamental Physics
ARAI, K., Fundamental Physics
FUJII, A., Solid State Spectroscopy
FURUSHIMA, M., Algebra and Geometry
HAMANA, Y., Probability Theory
HARAOKA, Y., Analysis and Applied Analysis
HASE, Y., Palaeobotany and Environmental Science
HASEGAWA, S., Palaeontology and Environmental Science
HASENAKA, T., Volcanology and Igneous Petrology
ICHIKAWA, F., Superconductivity
ICHIMURA, K., Physical Chemistry
IMAFUKU, K., Organic Chemistry
ISHIDA, A., Dynamics of Environments
ITOH, K., Magnetic Thin Films
KIMURA, H., Analysis and Applied Analysis
KOBAYASHI, O., Algebra and Geometry
KOHNO, M., Analysis and Applied Analysis
MATSUMOTO, N., Inorganic Chemistry
MATSUSAKA, T., Dynamics of Environments
MATSUZAKI, S., Physical Chemistry
MITSUNAGA, M., Quantum Optics
MOMOSHIMA, N., Environmental Analysis
MOTOYOSHI, A., Fundamental Physics
NISHINO, H., Organic Chemistry
NISHIYAMA, T., Petrology, Mineralogy and Geodynamics
NOHDA, S., Environmental Analysis
OHWAKI, S., Integrated Mathematics
SAKAMOTO, N., Polymer Chemistry
SANEMASA, I., Environmental Analysis
SHIBUYA, H., Palaeomagnetism and Geodynamics
SHIMADA, J., Groundwater Circulation
SHIODA, M., Molecular Cell Biology
TANI, T., Molecular Biology
UCHINO, A., Dynamics of Environments
WATANABE, A., Algebra and Geometry
YAMAKI, H., Algebra and Geometry
YOSHIASA, A., Geodynamics and Condensed Matter Physics

Graduate School of Social and Cultural Sciences (40-1 Kurokami 2-chome, Kumamoto 860-8555; tel. (96) 342-2313; e-mail bun-somu@jimu.kumamoto-u.ac.jp; internet www.let.kumamoto-u.ac.jp/gsscs/index_e.html):

YAMANAKA, S., Geography
YUKAWA, Y., Linguistics

Graduate School of Science and Technology (39-1 Kurokami 2-chome, Kumamoto 860-8555; tel. (96) 342-3013; e-mail dcjimu@gpo.kumamoto-u.ac.jp; internet 133.95.161.1/index-en.html):

HASEGAWA, S., Natural Environmental Sciences
HIYAMA, T., Energy Systems
ICHIMURA, K., Basic Chemistry and Physics for Materials Sciences
IKI, K., Human-Environmental Engineering
ISHITOBI, M., Intelligent Manufacturing Systems
KAWAHARA, M., Materials Science and Technology
KIDA, K., Applied Chemistry for Materials and Life Sciences
MATSUMOTO, Y., Applied Chemistry of Materials
OHBA, H., Mechanical Systems Design
OHTSU, M., Disaster-preventive Structural Engineering
OKUNO, Y., Electrical and Computer Engineering
SUGAWARA, K., Environmental Conservation Engineering
UCHIMURA, K., Intelligent Systems and Computer Science
YAMAKI, H., Mathematics
YOSHITAMA, K., Bioinformational Science

School of Law (40-1 Kurokami 2-chome, Kumamoto 860-8555; tel. (96) 342-2315; e-mail jsj-somu@jimu.kumamoto-u.ac.jp; internet www.kumamoto-ua.ac.jp/lawschool):

FUKUYAMA, M., Law
HARADA, T., Law
HASHIMOTO, M., Civil Law
HAYASHI, M., Local Government Law
HIRATA, H., Criminal Procedure
ISHIBASHI, H., Social Law
KUBOTA, M., Commercial Law
MATSUBARA, H., Civil Procedure Law
NAKAGAWA, Y., Administrative Law
NAKAMURA, S., Criminal Law
ONO, Y., Civil Law
ONODERA, M., Prosecutor
SAWATARI, K., Law
TADA, N., International Private Law
YAMAMOTO, E., Constitutional Law
YAMANAKA, I., Legal Theory and History

Center for AIDS Research (2-1 Honjo 2-chome, Kumamoto 860-0811; tel. (96) 373-6531; internet www.caids.kumamoto-u.ac.jp):

MATSUSHITA, S., Clinical Retrovirology and Infectious Diseases
OKADA, S., Haematopoiesis
TAKIGUCHI, M., Viral Immunology

Center for Marine Environment Studies (39-1 Kurokami, 2-chome, Kumamoto 860-8555; tel. (96) 342-3448; internet www.engan.dc.kumamoto-u.ac.jp/index.html):

HENMI, Y., Analysis of Cyclization Systems for Natural Resources
TAKIKAWA, K., Hydro- and Geosphere Environments
TAKIO, S., Conservation and Development of Natural Resources

Center for Multimedia and Information Technologies (39-1 Kurokami 2-chome, Kumamoto 860-8555; tel. (96) 342-3824; internet www.cc.kumamoto-u.ac.jp):

IRIGUCHI, N.
NAKANO, Y.
SUGITANI, K.

Cooperative Research Center (2081-7 Tabaru, Mashiki-machi, Kumamoto 861-2202; tel. (96) 286-1212; internet www.kcr.kumamoto-u.ac.jp/index-j.html):

HIROSUE, H., Liaison between University and Industry
MATSUSHITA, H., Technology Transfer between University and Industry

Institute of Molecular Embryology and Genetics (24-1 Kuhonji 4-chome, Kumamoto 862-0976; tel. (96) 344-2111; e-mail imeg@kaiju.medic.kumamoto-u.ac.jp; internet www.imeg.kumamoto-u.ac.jp):

KUME, S., Stem Cell Biology
NAGAFUCHI, A., Cellular Interactions
NAKAO, M., Organ Development
NISHINAKAMURA, R., Integrative Cell Biology
OGAWA, M., Cell Differentiation
OGURA, T., Molecular Cell Biology
OKUBO, H., Molecular Neurobiology
SHIMAMURA, K., Morphogenesis
TAGA, T., Cell Fate Modulation
YAMAIZUMI, M., Cell Genetics
YAMAMURA, K., Developmental Genetics
YOKOUCHI, Y., Pattern Formation

Institute of Resource Development and Analysis (2-2-1 Honjo, Kumamoto 860-0811; tel. (96) 373-6637; e-mail iys-senter@jimu.kumamoto-u.ac.jp):

NAKAGATA, N., Reproductive Engineering
URANO, T., Microbiology and Genetics
YAMADA, G., Transgenic Technology

International Student Center (40-1 Kurokami 2-chome, Kumamoto 860-8555; tel. (96) 342-2133; e-mail gji-ryugaku@jimu.kumamoto-u.ac.jp; internet center.ryu.kumamoto-u.ac.jp/index_e.html):

KOWAKI, M., Linguistics (Semitic Languages)

Research Center for Higher Education (40-1 Kurokami 2-chome, Kumamoto 860-8555; tel. (96) 342-2716; e-mail gak-kyomu@jimu.kumamoto-u.ac.jp; internet www.ge.kumamoto-u.ac.jp):

OHMORI, F., Education Policy
SUGAWARA, T., Educational Evaluation
YAMADA, M., Advanced and Applied Education of European History

Research Center for Lifelong Learning (40-1 Kurokami 2-chome, Kumamoto 860-8555; tel. (96) 342-3281; e-mail sos-tiiki@kumamoto-u.ac.jp; internet www.lifelong.kumamoto-u.ac.jp):

SAGA, T., Philosophy, Bio-ethics
UENO, S., Political Science
YANAGI, H., Educational Sociology

Shock Wave and Condensed Matter Research Center (39-1 Kurokami 2-chome, Kumamoto 860-8555; tel. (96) 342-3299; internet www.shocomarec.kumamoto-u.ac.jp):

FUJII, A., Low Temperature Science
ITO, S., Shock Processing and its Applications
KUBOTA, H., Solid State Physics under Multi-Extreme Conditions

KYOTO INSTITUTE OF TECHNOLOGY

Hashigami-cho, Matsugasaki, Sakyo-ku, Kyoto 606-8585
Telephone: (75) 724-7111
E-mail: webmaster@adm.kit.ac.jp
Internet: www.kit.ac.jp

Founded 1949
Public control
Academic year: April to March

Pres.: YOSHIMICHI EJIMA
Vice-Pres.: MASAO FURUYAMA
Vice-Pres.: MUTSUO TAKENAGA
Dir-Gen.: KIMIO MURAMATSU
Librarian: SHIGEYUKI YAMAGUCHI

Library of 378,000 vols
Number of teachers: 301
Number of students: 4,068

Publications: *Memoirs of the Faculty of Engineering and Design—JINBUN* (Series of Science and Technology, 1 a year), *Bulletin of the Faculty of Textile Science* (1 a year)

DEANS

Faculty of Engineering and Design: RIKUO OTA
Faculty of Textile Science: SHIGERU KUNUGI

KYOTO UNIVERSITY

Yoshida-Honmachi, Sakyo-ku, Kyoto 606-8501
Telephone: (75) 753-7531
E-mail: koryu52@mail.adm.kyoto-u.ac.jp
Internet: www.kyoto-u.ac.jp

Founded 1897
Private control
Academic year: April to March

Pres.: HIROSHI MATSUMOTO

Exec. Vice-Pres. for Student Affairs: AKIHIKO AKAMATSU
Exec. Vice-Pres. for Education: TOSHIYUKI AWAJI
Exec. Vice-Pres. for Finance and Facilities: NOBORU NISHISAKA
Exec. Vice-Pres. for Planning and Evaluation: NOBUYOSHI ESAKI
Exec. Vice-Pres. for Research: KIYOSHI YOSHIKAWA
Library: see under Libraries and Archives
Number of teachers: 5,448
Number of students: 22,707

DEANS

College of Medical Technology: (vacant)
Graduate School of Agriculture and Faculty of Agriculture: TAKASHI ENDO
Graduate School of Asian and African Area Studies: SHIGEKI KAJI
Graduate School of Biostudies: SHIN YONEHARA
Graduate School of Economics and Faculty of Economics: KAZUHIRO UEDA
Graduate School of Education and Faculty of Education: YASUSHI MAEHIRA
Graduate School of Energy Science: HIROHIKO TAKUDA
Graduate School of Engineering and Faculty of Engineering: MASAO KITANO
Graduate School of Global Environmental Studies: SHIGEO FUJII
Graduate School of Human and Environmental Studies and Faculty of Integrated Human Studies: YASUHIKO TOMIDA
Graduate School of Informatics: RYO SATO
Graduate School of Law and Faculty of Law: TAKASHI MURANAKA
Graduate School of Letters and Faculty of Letters: YOSHIHISA HATTORI
Graduate School of Management: YOSHIHIRO TOKUGA
Graduate School of Medicine and Faculty of Medicine: NAGAHIRO MINATO
Graduate School of Pharmaceutical Sciences and Faculty of Pharmaceutical Sciences: HIDEO SAJI
Graduate School of Science and Faculty of Science: JUICHI YAMAGIWA
Law School: YOSHIO SHIOMI
School of Government: TOMOHIRO OKADA
School of Public Health: (vacant)

PROFESSORS

Graduate School of Agriculture and Faculty of Agriculture (Kitashirakawa, Oiwake-cho, Sakyo, Kyoto, 606-8502; tel. (75) 753-6490; internet www.kais.kyoto-u.ac.jp):

ADACHI, S., Bioengineering
AOYAMA, S., Agricultural Facility Engineering
AZUMA, J., Forest Biochemistry
ENDO, T., Plant Genetics
FUJISAKI, K., Insect Ecology
FUJITA, M., Structure of Plant Cells
FUJIWARA, T., Fisheries, Oceanography
FUSHIKI, T., Nutrition Chemistry
FUTAI, K., Environmental Mycoscience
HIRATA, T., Marine Bioproducts Technology
HIROOKA, H., Animal Science
HORIE, T., Crop Science
IMAI, H., Animal Reproduction
INOUYE, K., Enzyme Chemistry
IWAI, Y., Forest Resources and Society
KAGATSUME, M., Regional Environmental Economics
KANO, K., Bioelectroanalytical Chemistry
KAWACHI, T., Water Resources Engineering
KAWADA, T., Food Biochemistry
KITA, K., Bioenergy Conversion
KITABATAKE, N., Food and Environmental Science
KOSAKI, T., Soil Science
KUME, S., Environmental Physiology
MATSUMOTO, T., Fibrous Biomaterials
MATSUMURA, Y., Quality Analysis and Assessment
MITSUNO, T., Irrigation, Drainage and Hydrological Environment Engineering
MIYAGAWA, H., Bioregulation Chemistry
MIZUYAMA, T., Erosion Control
MORIMOTO, Y., Landscape Architecture
MURATA, K., Molecular Biotechnology
NAKAHARA, H., Marine Microbial Ecology
NAKATSUBO, F., Chemistry of Biomaterials
NIIYAMA, Y., Farm Management
NISHIDA, R., Chemical Ecology
NISHIO, Y., Chemistry of Composite Materials
NISHIOKA, T., Biofunction Chemistry
NOBUCHI, T., Forest Utilization
NODA, K., Comparative Agricultural History
ODA, S., Farm Management Information and Accounting
OHIGASHI, H., Organic Chemistry in Life Science
OHNISHI, O., Crop Evolution
OHTA, S., Tropical Forest Resources and Environments
OIDA, A., Agricultural Systems Engineering
OKUMURA, S., Wood Processing
OKUNO, T., Plant Pathology
SAKO, Y., Marine Microbiology
SAKUMA, M., Behavioural Physiology and Chemical Ecology of Insects
SAKURATANI, T., Tropical Agriculture
SASAKI, Y., Animal Breeding and Genetics
SEKIYA, J., Plant Nutrition
SHIMIZU, S., Fermentation Physiology and Applied Microbiology
SUEHARA, T., Principles of Agricultural Science
TAKAFUJI, A., Ecological Information
TAKEBE, T., Agricultural and Environmental Policy
TAKEDA, H., Forest Ecology
TANAKA, M., Fish Biology
TANI, M., Forest Hydrology
TANISAKA, T., Plant Breeding
TOMINAGA, T., Weed Ecology
UEDA, K., Cellular Biochemistry
UEDA, M., Biomacromolecular Chemistry
UMEDA, M., Field Robotics
UTSUMI, S., Food Quality Design and Development
YAMADA, T., Plant Production Management
YAMASUE, Y., Physiological Aspects of Agricultural Systems
YANO, H., Animal Nutrition
YAZAWA, S., Vegetable and Ornamental Horticulture
YONEMORI, K., Pomology
YOSHIDA, M., Forest Policy and Economics
YOSHIKAWA, M., Physiological Function of Food

Graduate School of Asian and African Area Studies (46 Shimoadachi-cho, Yoshida, Sakyo-ku, Kyoto 606-8501; tel. (75) 753-7302; e-mail soumu@cseas.kyoto-u.ac.jp; internet www.asafas.kyoto-u.ac.jp):

ADACHI, A., The Hindu World
ARAKI, S., Agricultural Ecology
HIRAMATSU, K., Natural Hisory
ICHIKAWA, M., Socio-ecological History
KAJI, S., Culture and Ethnicity
KAKEYA, M., Livelihood and Economy
KOBAYASHI, S., Environmental Ecology
KOSUGI, Y., The Islamic World
OHTA, I., Nature–Human Interaction
SHIMADA, S., Socio-cultural Integration
SUGISHIMA, T., Comparative Social Transformation

Graduate School of Biostudies:

INABA, K., Laboratory of Science Communication and Bioethics
INOUE, T., Laboratory of Gene Biodynamics
ISHIKAWA, F., Laboratory of Cell Cycle Regulation
KAKIZUKA, A., Laboratory of Functional Biology
KOCHI, T., Laboratory of Plant Molecular Biology
KOZUTUMI, Y., Laboratory of Membrane Biochemistry and Biophysics
MINATO, N., Laboratory of Immunology and Cell Biology
NAGAO, M., Laboratory of Biosignals and Response
NEGISHI, M., Laboratory of Molecular Neurobiology
NISHIDA, E., Laboratory of Signal Transduction
SATO, F., Laboratory of Molecular and Cellular Biology of Totipotency
TAKEYASU, K., Laboratory of Plasma Membrane and Nuclear Signalling
UEMURA, T., Laboratory of Cell Recognition and Pattern Formation
YAMAMOTO, K., Laboratory of Molecular Biology of Bioresponse
YONEHARA, S., Laboratory of Molecular and Cellular Biology

Graduate School of Economics and Faculty of Economics (tel. (75) 753-3400; e-mail kyoumu@econ.kyoto-u.ac.jp; internet www.econ.kyoto-u.ac.jp):

FUJII, H., International Accounting
FURUKAWA, A., Money and Finance
HIOKI, K., Organization Theory
HISAMOTO, N., Labour Economics
HORI, K., Economic History
IMAKUBO, S., Economic Policy
IWAMOTO, T., International Economics
KAZUSA, Y., Managerial Accounting
KIJIMA, M., Financial Engineering
KOJIMA, H., Principles of Economics
MORIMUNE, K., Econometrics
MOTOYAMA, Y., World Economy
NARIU, T., Applied Economics
NEI, M., Modern Economics
NISHIMURA, S., Applied Economics
NISHIMUTA, Y., Business History
OHNISHI, H., Economic Statistics
OKADA, T., Regional Economy
SHIMOTANI, M., Japanese Economy
SHIOJI, H., Japanese Economy
TACHIBANAKI, T., Economic Policy
TANAKA, H., History of Social Thought
TAO, M., Business Policy
TOKUGA, Y., Accounting for Venture Business
UETA, K., Public Finance
UNI, H., Economic Theory
WAKABAYASHI, Y., Marketing
YAGI, K., Economic Theory
YAMAMOTO, H., Chinese Economy
YOSHIDA, K., Contemporary Economics

Graduate School of Education and Faculty of Education (tel. (75) 753-3010; e-mail kyoumu@kyoumu.educ.kyoto-u.ac.jp; internet www.educ.kyoto-u.ac.jp):

FUJIWARA, K., Clinical Psychology
INAGAKI, K., Sociology of Education
ITOH, Y., Clinical Psychology
IWAI, H., Sociology of the Course of Life
KAWAI, T., Clinical Psychology
KAWASAKI, Y., Library and Information Science
KOYASU, M., Cognitive Psychology in Education
MAEHIRA, Y., Lifelong Education
OKADA, Y., Clinical Personality Psychology
SUGIMOTO, H., Comparative Education
SUZUKI, S., Pedagogy
TAKAMI, S., Educational Finance
TANAKA, K., Curriculum Development and Assessment
TSUJIMOTO, M., Japanese History of Education
YAMADA, Y., Developmental Psychology
YANO, S., Clinical Pedagogy

YOSHIKAWA, S., Cognitive Psychology in Education

Graduate School of Energy Science (tel. (75) 753-4871; internet www.energy.kyoto-u.ac.jp/index-eng.html):

HOSHIDE, T., Fracture Mechanics for System Integrity
ISHIHARA, K., Social Engineering of Energy
ISHII, R., Space Energy and Resources
ISHIYAMA, T., Combustion Engine Technology
IWASE, M., Physical Chemistry of Iron- and Steelmaking and Related High-Temperature Processes
KASAHARA, M., Atmospheric Environmental Engineering
KONDO, K., Plasma Diagnostics
MABUCHI, M., Materials Science and Engineering
MAEKAWA, T., Plasma Physics
MATSUMOTO, E., Non-linear Continuum Mechanics
NOZAWA, H., Physics and Technology of VLSI
SAKA, S., Ecosystems of Biomass for Energy Use
SHIOJI, M., Combustion Science and Engineering
SHIOTSU, M., Thermal Hydraulics in Energy Systems
TAKUDA, H., Advanced Processing of Resources and Energy
TEZUKA, T., Energy Economics
YAO, T., Solid-state Energy Chemistry
YOSHIKAWA, H., Man–Machine Systems

Graduate School of Engineering and Faculty of Engineering:

AOKI, K., Rarefied Gas Dynamics
AOKI, K., Resources Development Engineering
AOYAMA, Y., Biorecognition
AOYAMA, Y., Urban and Regional Planning
ARAKI, M., Control Engineering
ASAKURA, T., Tunnel Engineering
ASHIDA, Y., Exploration Geophysics
AWAKURA, Y., Materials Electrochemistry
CHUJO, Y., Polymerization Chemistry
EGUCHI, K., Catalyst Science and Catalyst Design Engineering
FUJII, S., Division of Environmental Quality Control
FUKUYAMA, A., Basic Quantum Engineering
HAGIWARA, T., Automatic Control Engineering
HAMACHI, I., Bio-organic Chemistry
HASEBE, S., Process Systems Engineering
HAYASHI, Y., Disaster Risk Management of Built Environment
HIGASHITANI, K., Surface Control Engineering
HIGUCHI, T., Landscape and Environmental Planning
HIKIHARA, T., Power Conversion and Control Laboratory
HIRAO, K., Inorganic Structural Chemistry
HIYAMA, T., Organic Chemistry of Natural Products
HOJO, M., Continuum Mechanics
HOKOI, S., Thermal Analysis and Design
HOSODA, T., River Engineering
ICHIKAWA, A., Systems and Control
IEMURA, H., Earthquake Engineering
IMAHORI, H., Applied Molecular Science
IMANAKA, T., Biotechnology
INAMURO, T., Fluid Dynamics
INOUE, K., Space Development and Structural Systems
INOUE, M., Energy Conversion Chemistry
INUI, H., Intermetallic Alloys for Structural and Functional Uses
ISHIKAWA, J., Charged Particle Devices
ITO, S., Polymer Structure and Function
ITOH, A., Applied Beam Materials Engineering
ITOH, S., Urban Sanitary Engineering
KAKIUCHI, T., Functional Solution Chemistry
KATO, N., Architectural Information Systems
KAWAI, J., Process Chemical Physics
KIDA, S., Fluid Dynamics
KIMURA, K., Mesoscopic Materials Engineering
KIMURA, S., Design of Functional Materials
KITAGAWA, S., Functional Chemistry
KITAMURA, R., Transport Planning and Engineering
KITAMURA, T., Mechanical Behaviour of Materials
KITANO, M., Quantum Optical Engineering
KOBAYASHI, K., Civil Engineering Systems Analysis
KOBAYASHI, T., Biomedical Engineering
KOMORI, S., Fluids Engineering
KOTERA, H., Mechanical Systems
KUBO, A., Machine Design
MAE, K., Environmental Process Engineering
MAEDA, T., Theory of Architecture and Environmental Design
MAKI, T., Mechanical Properties of Steel
MAKINO, T., Thermophysical Properties of Materials
MASUDA, H., Powder Technology
MASUDA, T., Polymer Physics and Rheology
MATSUBARA, A., Precision Measurement and Machining
MATSUBARA, E., Structural Characterization by X-ray Diffraction
MATSUHISA, H., Vibration Engineering
MATSUMOTO, M., Wind Engineering
MATSUOKA, T., Engineering Geology
MATSUSHIGE, K., Molecular Nano-electronics
MITSUDO, T., Catalysis
MIURA, K., Environmental Process Engineering
MIYAGAWA, T., Durability of Reinforced Concrete
MIYAHARA, M., Fluids Confined in Nanospace Order Formation by Nano-colloids
MIYAZAKI, N., Computational Solid Mechanics
MONNAI, T., Architecture and Human Environmental Planning
MORI, Y., Molecular Biology
MORISAWA, S., Environmental Risk Analysis
MORISHIMA, N., Neutron Science
MORIYAMA, H., Nuclear Materials
MUNEMOTO, J., Architectural Planning
MURAKAMI, M., Organometallic Chemistry
MURAKAMI, M., Thin Film Metallurgy
NAGATA, M., Gas Dynamics
NAKATSUJI, H., Quantum Chemistry
NEZU, I., Fluid Mechanics and Hydraulics
NISHIMOTO, S., Excited-state Hydrocarbon Chemistry
NODA, S., Quantum Optoelectronics Engineering
OGUMI, Z., Electrochemistry
OHE, K., Organometallic Chemistry
OHNISHI, Y., Rock Mechanics
OHSAWA, Y., Electric Power System Engineering
OHSHIMA, M., Materials Process Engineering
OKA, F., Soil Mechanics
ONO, K., Propulsion Engineering
OSAMURA, K., Science of Materials
OSHIMA, K., Organic Reaction Chemistry
OTSUKA, K., Analytical Chemistry of Materials
SAITO, T., Mining and Rock Mechanics
SAKAI, T., Coastal Engineering
SAKAKI, S., Quantum Molecular Science and Technology
SAWAMOTO, M., Living Cationic Polymerization
SAWARAGI, T., Design Systems Engineering
SCAWTHORN, C., Natural Hazard Risk Management
SERIZAWA, A., Nuclear Reactor Engineering
SHIMA, S., Engineering Plasticity
SHIMASAKI, M., Computational Electromagnetic Field Analysis
SHIRAKAWA, M., Biophysical Chemistry
SUGIMURA, H., Nanoscopic Surface Architecture
SUGINOME, M., Organic Synthesis and System Design
SUZUKI, M., Integrated Function Engineering
TABATA, O., Micro Electro-Mechanical Systems
TACHIBANA, A., Quantum Theory of Condensed Matter
TACHIBANA, K., Plasma Physics and Technology
TAKADA, M., Housing and Environmental Design
TAKAHASHI, H., Architectural Design and Theory
TAKAHASHI, Y., History of Architecture
TAKAMATSU, S., Architectural Design
TAKAOKA, G., Ion Engineering, Cluster Science
TAKEDA, N., Solid Waste Management
TAKEWAKI, I., Earthquake Resistant Engineering
TAKIGAWA, T., Physics of Polymer Materials
TAMON, H., Separation Engineering
TAMURA, K., Structural Properties of Materials
TAMURA, M., Environmental Remote Sensing
TAMURA, T., Applied Mechanics
TANAKA, F., Polymer Core Physical Chemistry
TANAKA, H., Environmental Evaluation
TANAKA, I., Ceramic Materials Science
TANAKA, K., Inorganic Solid-State Chemistry
TANAKA, K., Molecular Energy Conservation
TANAKA, T., Molecular Science and Technology of Catalysis
TANIGUCHI, E., Urban Infrastructure Systems
TSUCHIYA, K., Dynamics and Control of Space Vehicles
TSUNO, H., Water Quality Conservation
UCHIYAMA, I., Environmental Health
UETANI, K., Mechanics of Building Structures
WADA, O., Circuit Theory and Applications
WATANABE, F., Reinforced and Pressed Concrete Structures
YAMAMOTO, K., Quantum Physics
YAMASHINA, H., Computer-integrated Manufacturing
YOSHIDA, H., Urban Environment and Safety Engineering
YOSHIDA, J., Organic Chemistry
YOSHIKAWA, T., Robotics
YOSHIMURA, M., Knowledge and Information Systems
YOSHIZAKI, T., Polymer Statistical Mechanics
YOSIDA, H., Thermal Systems Engineering

Graduate School of Global Environmental Studies (tel. (75) 753-9167; internet www.adm.kyoto-u.ac.jp/ges):

KAMON, M., Environmental Infrastructure Engineering
KAWASAKI, M., Environmental Atmospheric Chemistry
KOBAYASHI, M., Global Environment Architecture
KOBAYASHI, S., Regional Planning
KOSAKI, T., Terrestrial Ecosystems Management
MATSUI, S., Environmentally Friendly Industries for Sustainable Development

MATSUOKA, Y., Global Integrated Assessment Modelling
MATSUSHITA, K., Global Environmental Policy
MIMURO, M., Environmental Biotechnology
MORIMOTO, Y., Landscape Ecology and Planning
NAKAHARA, H., Conservation of Coastal Ecosystems
OGAWA, T., Philosophical Theory of Human and Environmental Symbiosis
SHIIBA, M., Circulation of Environmental Resources
TAKEBE, T., Global Resource Economics
TAMURA, R., Environmental Materials Science
UETA, K., Global Ecological Economics
YOKOYAMA, T., Towards a Theory of Global Civilization

Graduate School of Human and Environmental Studies and Faculty of Integrated Human Studies (Yoshida Nihonmatsu-cho, Sakyo, Kyoto; tel. (75) 753-2950; internet www.adm.kyoto-u.ac.jp/jinkan):

ADACHI, Y., Socio-cultural Environments
ATSUJI, T., Chinese Linguistics
BECKER, C., Comparative Religion, Ethics, Death and Dying
EDA, K., History of Modern China
FUKUI, K., Cultural Anthropology of Ethiopia
FUKUOKA, K., American Literature
FUNAHASHI, S., Neurophysiology
HATTORI, F., Linguistics and Slavonic Languages
HORI, T., Natural Environments
INAGAKI, N., Modern French Literature
ISHIDA, A., Modern German Philology and Literature
ISHIHARA, A., Neurochemistry and Physiology
IYORI, T., Common Environmental System
KAMATA, H., Volcanology
KANASAKA, K., Human Societies
KATO, M., Coexisting Systems of Nature and Human Beings
KAWASHIMA, A., Modern British History
KIMURA, T., Russian Literature
KIWAMOTO, Y., Plasma Physics
KOYAMA, S., History of Japanese Education
KUJIRAOKA, T., Human Development
MAEGAWA, S., Low Temperature Magnetism
MAMIYA, Y., Common Environmental System
MARUHASHI, Y., English Drama
MATSUDA, K., History of Western Learning in Japan
MATSUI, M., Systematic Zoology
MATSUMARU, M., Neurophysiology
MATSUURA, S., History of North-Eastern Asia
MICHIHATA, T., German Literature
MIHARA, O., German Literature
MITANI, K., Slavic Linguistics
MIYAMOTO, Y., Polymer Physics
MORIMOTO, Y., Theory of Partial Differential Equations
MORITANI, T., Environmental Conservation and Development
MOTOKI, Y., Medieval History of Japan
MURANAKA, S., Solid State Chemistry
NAGAYA, M., History and Theory of Social Statistics
NAKANISHI, T., International Relations
NISHII, M., Environmental Conservation and Development
NISHIMURA, M., History of Western Law
NISHIWAKI, T., History of Chinese Philosophy
NISHIYAMA, R., Ancient History of Japan
NIWA, T., American Literature
OKADA, A., Art History and Criticism
OKADA, K., Pedagogy
OKI, M., Linguistics and French Language
ONO, S., Middle High German Literature
OTAGI, H., History of Medieval China
SAEKI, K., Social-environmental System
SAITO, H., Comparative Linguistics and German Language
SAKAGAMI, M., Gravity and Relativity
SHIKAYA, T., Philosophy of Aesthetics
SHIMADA, M., Contemporary History of the United States
SHINGU, K., Fundamental Human Ontology
SHINOHARA, M., Aesthetics and Philosophy
SUGAWARA, K., Social Anthropology and Communication
SUGIMAN, T., Group Dynamics
SUZUKI, M., 18th-century English Culture and Literature
TAKAHASHI, Y., Environmental Conservation and Development
TAKASAKI, K., Algebraic Analysis and Mathematical Physics
TAMADA, O., Environmental Conservation and Development
TANABE, R., German Literature
TOGO, Y., French Linguistics
TOMIDA, Y., Philosophy and History of Philosophy
TOMITA, H., Statistical Physics
TORISSEN, E., Comparative Culture
TSUDA, K., Internal Medicine
UCHIDA, M., Grammar of the Japanese Language
USHIKI, S., Coexisting Systems of Nature and Human Beings
YAMADA, M., Urban Geography
YAMADA, T., Anthropology and Cognition, Shamanism and Ethnicity
YAMAGUCHI, R., Coexisting Systems of Nature and Human Beings
YAMAMOTO, Y., Organic Chemistry
YAMANASHI, M., Cognitive Linguistics
YASUI, K., Human Development
YODA, Y., Shakespeare

Graduate School of Informatics (tel. (75) 753-3599; e-mail jimu-soumu@i.kyoto-u.ac.jp; internet www.i.kyoto-u.ac.jp):

EIHO, S., Image Processing Systems
FUJISAKA, H., Non-equilibrium Dynamics
FUKUSHIMA, M., Systems Optimization
FUNAKOSHI, M., Nonlinear Dynamics
GOTOH, O., Bioinformatics
INUI, T., Cognitive Science
ISHIDA, T., Global Information Network
ISO, Y., Analysis of Inverse Problems
IWAI, T., Dynamical Systems Theory
IWAMA, K., Logic Circuits, Algorithms and Complexity Theory
KATAI, O., Symbiotic Systems
KATAYAMA, T., Control Systems Theory
KIGAMI, J., Nonlinear Analysis
KOBAYASHI, S., Biological Information
KUMAMOTO, H., Human Systems
MATSUDA, T., Biomedical Engineering
MATSUYAMA, T., Visual Information Processing
MORIHIRO, Y., Integrated-media Communications
MORIYA, K., Bioresource Informatics
MUNAKATA, T., Physical Statistics
NAKAMURA, Y., Applied Mathematical Analysis
NAKAMURA, Y., Processor Architecture and Systems Synthesis
NISHIDA, T., Artificial Intelligence
NOGI, T., Fundamentals of Complex Systems
OKUNO, H. G., Speech Media Processing
ONODERA, H., Integrated Circuits Design Engineering
SAKAI, H., Mathematical Systems Theory
SAKAI, T., Environmental Informatics
SATO, M., Foundations of Software Science
SATO, T., Advanced Signal Processing
SUGIE, T., Mechanical Systems Control
TAKAHASHI, T., Intelligent Communication Networks
TAKAHASHI, Y., Information Systems
TANAKA, K., Digital Library
TOMITA, S., Computer Architecture
YAMAMOTO, A., Foundations of Artificial Intelligence
YAMAMOTO, Y., Intelligent and Control Systems
YOSHIDA, S., Digital Communications
YUASA, T., Computer Software

Graduate School of Law and Faculty of Law (internet www.kyodai.jp/i-english.htm):

AKIZUKI, K., Public Administration
ASADA, M., International Law
DOI, M., Constitutional Law
HATTORI, T., German Law
HAYASHI, N., Roman Law
IDA, R., Law of International Organizations
ITO, T., Japanese Legal History
ITO, Y., Political and Diplomatic History of Japan
KAMEMOTO, H., Legal Philosophy
KARATO, T., Political and Diplomatic History
KASAI, M., Law of Civil Procedure
KAWAHAMA, N., Economic Law
KAWAKAMI, R., European Legal History
KIMURA, M., Comparative Politics
KINAMI, A., Anglo-American Law
KITAMURA, M., Commercial Law
MABUCHI, M., Public Policy
MAEDA, M., Commercial Law
MATOBA, T., Political Science
MATSUOKA, H., Civil Law
MORI, T., Constitutional Law
MORIMOTO, S., Commercial Law
MURANAKA, T., Labour Law
NAKAMORI, Y., Criminal Law
NAKANISHI, H., International Politics
NISHIGORI, S., Civil Law
NISHIMURA, K., Social Security Law
OISHI, M., Constitutional Law
OKAMURA, S., Administrative Law
OKAMURA, T., Tax Law
ONO, N., History of Political Thought
OTAKE, H., Political Process
SAKAI, H., International Law
SAKAMAKI, T., Criminal Law
SAKUMA, T., Civil Law
SAKURADA, Y., Private International Law
SHIBAIKE, Y., Administrative Law
SHINKAWA, T., Political Process
SHIOMI, J., Criminal Law
SHIOMI, Y., Civil Law
SHIYAKE, M., Constitutional Law
SUZAKI, H., Commercial Law
SUZUKI, M., International Politics and Economy
TAKAYAMA, K., Criminal Law
TANAKA, S., Legal Philosophy
TANASE, T., Sociology of Law
TERADA, H., Oriental Legal History
TOKUDA, K., Law of Civil Procedure
YAMAMOTO, K., Civil Law
YAMAMOTO, K., Law of Civil Procedure
YAMAMOTO, Y., Civil Law
YOKOYAMA, M., Civil Law
YOSHIOKA, K., Criminology

Graduate School of Letters and Faculty of Letters:

AKAMATSU, A., History of Indian Philosophy
FUJII, J., Japanese History
FUJITA, K., Psychology
FUJITA, M., Japanese Philosophy
FUMA, S., Oriental History
HAMADA, M., Asian History
HATTORI, Y., European History
HAYASHI, S., Humanistic Informatics
HIRATA, S., Chinese Language and Literature
IKEDA, S., History of Chinese Philosophy
ISHIKAWA, Y., Geography

ITO, K., Philosophy
ITO, K., Sociology
IWAKI, K., Aesthetics and Art History
IZUMI, T., Archaeology
KAMADA, M., Japanese History
KATAYANAGI, E., Christian Studies
KATSUYAMA, S., Japanese History
KAWAI, K., Chinese Language and Literature
KAWAZOE, S., History of Western Medieval Philosophy
KETA, M., Philosophy of Religion
KIDA, A., Japanese Language and Literature
KIHIRA, E., Contemporary History
KINDA, A., Geography
KOBAYASHI, M., History of Western Philosophy
MATSUDA, M., Sociology
MIMAKI, K., Buddhist Studies
MINAMIKAWA, T., European History
MIYAUCHI, H., English Language and Literature
NAGAI, K., Contemporary History
NAKAMURA, K., American Literature
NAKAMURA, T., Art History
NAKATSUKASA, T., Greek and Latin Classics
NEDACHI, K., Aesthetics and Art History
NISHIMURA, M., German Language and Literature
OCHIAI, E., Sociology
OSAKA, N., Psychology
OTANI, M., Japanese Language and Literature
SAITO, Y., Italian Language and Literature
SAKURAI, Y., Psychology
SATO, A., Slavic Languages and Literature
SHOGAITO, M., Linguistics
SUGIMOTO, Y., 20th-Century Studies
SUGIURA, K., Geography
SUGIYAMA, M., Oriental History
TAGUCHI, N., French Language and Literature
TAKAHASHI, H., Greek and Latin Classics
TAKUBO, Y., Linguistics
TOKUNAGA, M., Sanskrit Language and Literature
UCHII, S., Philosophy and History of Science
UEHARA, M., Archaeology
WAKASHIMA, T., English Language and Literature
YOSHIDA, J., French Language and Literature
YOSHIDA, K., Linguistics
YOSHIMOTO, M., Oriental History

Graduate School of Medicine and Faculty of Medicine (Yoshida konoe-cho, Sakyo-ku, Kyoto 606-8501; tel. (75) 753-4300; e-mail shomu06@mail.adm.kyoto-u.ac.jp; internet www.med.kyoto-u.ac.jp):

CHIBA, T., Gastroenterology and Hepatology
FUJII, S., Gynaecology and Obstetrics
FUJITA, J., Clinical Molecular Biology
FUKUDA, K., Anaesthesia
FUKUHARA, S., Epidemiology and Health Care Research
FUKUI, T., Clinical Epidemiology
FUKUSHIMA, M., Pharmacoepidemiology
FUKUYAMA, H., Functional Brain Imaging
HASHIMOTO, N., Neurosurgery
HAYASHI, T., Psychiatry
HIRAIDE, A., Center for Medical Education
HIRAOKA, M., Radiation Oncology and Image-applied Therapy
HONJO, T., Immunology and Genomic Medicine
ICHIYAMA, S., Clinical Laboratory Medicine
IDE, C., Anatomy and Neurobiology
IMANAKA, Y., Healthcare Economics and Quality Management
INAGAKI, M., Metabolism and Clinical Nutrition
INUI, K., Pharmacy
ITO, J., Otolaryngology, Head and Neck Surgery
KANEKO, T., Morphological Brain Science
KAWANO, K., Integrative Brain Science
KIHARA, M., Global Health and Socio-Epidemiology
KITA, T., Cardiovascular Medicine
KOIZUMI, A., Health and Environmental Sciences
KOMEDA, M., Cardiovascular Surgery
KOSUGI, S., Biomedical Ethics
MAEKAWA, T., Transfusion Medicine and Cell Therapy
MANABE, T., Diagnostic Pathology
MATSUDA, F., Genome Epidemiology
MIMORI, T., Rheumatology and Clinical Immunology
MINATO, N., Immunology and Cell Biology
MISHIMA, M., Respiratory Medicine
MITSUYAMA, M., Microbiology
MIYACHI, Y., Dermatology
NABESHIMA, Y., Pathology and Tumour Biology
NAKAHARA, T., Public Health and International Health
NAKAHATA, T., Paediatrics
NAKAMURA, T., Orthopaedic and Musculoskeletal Surgery
NAKANISHI, S., Biological Sciences
NAKAO, K., Medicine and Clinical Science
NARUMIYA, S., Cell Pharmacology
NODA, M., Molecular Oncology
NOMA, A., Physiology and Biophysics
OGAWA, O., Urology
OHMORI, H., Physiology and Neurobiology
SAKAMOTO, J., Epidemiological and Clinical Research Information Management
SATO, T., Biostatistics
SERIKAWA, T., Laboratory Animals
SHIMIZU, A., Human Genome Analysis
SHINOHARA, T., Molecular Genetics
SHIOTA, K., Anatomy and Developmental Biology
SHIRAKAWA, T., Health Promotion and Human Behaviour
SUZUKI, S., Plastic and Reconstructive Surgery
TAKAHASHI, R., Neurology
TAKEDA, S., Radiation Genetics
TAKETO, M., Pharmacology
TAMAKI, K., Legal Medicine
TANAKA, K., Transplantation and Immunology
TOGASHI, L., Diagnostic Imaging and Nuclear Medicine
TSUKITA, S., Cell Biology
UCHIYAMA, T., Haematology and Oncology
WADA, H., Thoracic Surgery
YOKODE, M., Clinical Innovative Medicine
YOSHIHARA, H., Medical Informatics
YOSHIMURA, N., Ophthalmology and Visual Sciences

Graduate School of Pharmaceutical Sciences and Faculty of Pharmaceutical Sciences (46-29 Yoshida Shimoadachi-cho, Sakyo-ku, Kyoto 606-8501; tel. (75) 753-4510; internet www.pharm.kyoto-u.ac.jp):

AKAIKE, A., Pharmacology
FUJII, N., Bio-organic Medicinal Chemistry
HANDA, T., Biosurface Chemistry
HASHIDA, M., Drug Delivery Research
HONDA, G., Pharmacognosy
ITOH, N., Genetic Biochemistry
KANEKO, S., Molecular Pharmacology
KATO, H., Structural Biology
KAWAI, A., Molecular Microbiology
SAJI, H., Patho-Functional Bioanalysis
TAKAKURA, Y., Biopharmaceutics and Drug Metabolism
TAKEMOTO, Y., Organic Chemistry
TOMIOKA, K., Synthetic Medicinal Chemistry
TSUJIMOTO, G., Genomic Drugs Discovery

Graduate School of Science and Faculty of Science:

AGATA, K., Developmental Biology
AOYAMA, H., Theory of Elementary Particles
ARUGA, T., Surface Chemistry
AWAJI, T., Physical Oceanography
FUJIYOSHI, Y., Molecular Biophysics
FUKAYA, K., Geometry
HANADA, T., Inorganic Materials Chemistry
HARA-NISHIMURA, I., Plant Cell Biology
HATA, H., Theoretical Particle Physics
HAYASHI, T., Organic Chemistry
HIRAJIMA, T., Petrology
HIRANO, T., Neurobiology
HORI, M., Animal Ecology
HORIUCHI, H., Theoretical Nuclear Physics
IKAWA, M., Partial Differential Equations
IMAFUKU, M., Ethology
IMAI, K., Experimental Nuclear Physics
IMANISHI, H., Foliation and Symplectic Geometry
INAGAKI, S., Astrophysics
IYEMORI, T., Solar Terrestrial Physics
KAJIMOTO, O., Physical Chemistry
KATAYAMA, K., Biological Anthropology
KATO, K., Number Theory
KATO, S., Representation Theory
KATO, S., Theoretical Chemistry
KAWAI, H., Theoretical Particle Physics
KIDA, H., Climate Physics
KITAMURA, M., Mineralogy
KONO, A., Topology
KOYAMA, K., Cosmic Ray Physics
KUROKAWA, H., Solar Physics
MACHIDA, S., Geomagnetism and Space Physics
MAIHARA, T., Astrophysics
MARUOKA, K., Synthetic Organic Chemistry
MARUYAMA, M., Algebraic Geometry
MASUDA, F., Stratigraphy and Sedimentology
MATSUDA, Y., Solid State Physics
MATSUKI, T., Lie Groups
MIKI, K., Structural Biochemistry and Protein Crystallography
MIWA, T., Algebraic Analysis
MIZUSAKI, T., Low-Temperature Physics
MORI, K., Molecular Biology
MORIWAKI, A., Algebraic Geometry
NAGATA, T., Astrophysics
NAGATANI, A., Plant Physiology
NAKAJIMA, H., Representation Theory and Geometry
NAKAMURA, T., Nuclear Astrophysics
NISHIDA, G., Algebraic Topology
NISHIKAWA, K., Experimental High Energy Physics
NISHIWADA, K., Differential Equations, Financial Mathematics
OBATA, M., Petrology
OIKE, K., Seismology and Physics of the Earth's Interior
OKADA, A., Active Tectonics and Geomorphology
OKADA, K., Plant Molecular Genetics
ONUKI, A., Statistical Physics
OSUKA, A., Organic Chemistry
SAITO, G., Organic Solid State Chemistry
SAITO, H., Number Theory
SASAO, N., Experimental High-Energy Physics
SATOH, N., Developmental Genomics
SETOGUCHI, T., Vertebrate Palaeontology
SHIBATA, K., Solar and Cosmic Plasma Physics
SHICHIDA, Y., Molecular Physiology
SHIGEKAWA, I., Probability Theory
SHIMAMOTO, T., Structural Geology and Rock Rheology
SHIRAYAMA, Y., Marine Biology
SHISHIKURA, M., Dynamical System

SUGIYAMA, H., Chemical Biology, Bioorganic Chemistry
TAKEMOTO, S., Geodesy
TAKEMURA, K., Quaternary Geology and Geothermal Sciences
TAKADA, S., Developmental Biology
TANAKA, K., Solid State Spectroscopy, Laser Spectroscopy
TANAKA, Y., Volcano Magnetism
TANIMORI, T., Cosmic Ray Physics
TANIMURA, Y., Theoretical Chemical Physics
TERAO, T., Chemical Physics
TERAZIMA, M., Physical Chemistry, Biophysical Chemistry
TOBE, H., Plant Systematics and Evolution
TSUTSUMI, Y., Nonlinear Partial Differential Equations
UE, M., Low-dimensional Topology
UEDA, T., Complex Analysis in Several Variables
UEMATSU, T., Theory of Elementary Particles
UENO, K., Theory of Complex Manifolds
YAMADA, K., Theory of Condensed Matter
YAMAGIWA, J., Primatology and Anthropology
YAMAUCHI, J., Physical Chemistry and Electron Spin Resonance
YAMAUCHI, M., Number Theory
YAO, M., Physics of Disordered Systems
YODEN, S., Meteorology
YONEI, S., Radiation Biology
YOSHIDA, H., Number Theory
YOSHIKAWA, K., Chemical Physics, Biological Physics
YOSHIMURA, K., Inorganic Chemistry, Solid State Chemistry and Physics, Nuclear Magnetic Resonance
YUSA, Y., Hydrology and Geothermal Sciences

School of Health Sciences, Faculty of Medicine (53 Syogoin Kawahara-cho, Sakyo-ku, Kyoto 606-8507):

AMANO, S., Experimental Epileptology and Neuropathology
EGAWA, T., Diabetes, Teaching Renal Failure, Foot Care
FUJITA, M., Cardiology
FUKUDA, K., Nuclear Magnetic Resonance
FUKUDA, Y., Hepatology, Clinical Immunology
FUNATO, T., Laboratory Medicine and Molecular Diagnostics
HAYASHI, Y., Adult Health Nursing
HINOKUMA, F., Maternal Nursing, Midwifery
INAMOTO, T., Surgery and Clinical Oncology
KABEYAMA, K., Midwifery, Mother and Child Nursing, Women's Health
KATSURA, T., Preventive Nursing, Community Health Nursing
KAWASAKI, N., Biochemistry and Glycobiology
KONISHI, N., Occupational Therapy, Developmental Delay
MITANI, A., Rehabilitation and Brain Science
MIYAJIMA, A., Environmental Health Nursing
NARUKI, H., Community Health Nursing
NOMURA, S., Neuroanatomy and Functional Human Anatomy
SAITO, Y., Basic Nursing, Hospital Infection Control
SAKURABA, S., Psychiatric and Mental Health Nursing
SASADA, M., Haematology and Infectious Diseases
SUGA, S., Clinical Psychology
TOICHI, M., Psychiatry, Cognitive Neuroscience
TSUBOYAMA, T., Orthopaedics, Musculoskeletal Oncology, Bone Metabolism
TSUKITA, S., Cell Biology
UMEMURA, S., Biomedical Ultrasonics
YAMANE, H., Occupational Therapy for Mental Disorders

Law School (internet www.kyodai.jp/i-ls.htm):

ASADA, M., International Law
DOI, M., Constitutional Law
ENDO, K., Law Practice Unit
HAMAMOTO, S., Law Practice Unit
HATTORI, T., German Law
HAYASHI, N., Roman Law
HONDA, M., Law Practice Unit
IDA, R., International Law
IIMURA, Y., Law Practice Unit
ITO, T., Japanese Legal History
ITO, Y., Political and Diplomatic History of Japan
KAMEMOTO, H., Legal Philosophy
KAMIKO, A., Law Practice Unit
KASAI, M., Law of Civil Procedure
KAWAHAMA, N., Economic Law
KAWAKAMI, R., European Legal History
KINAMI, A., Anglo-American Law
KITAGAWA, K., Law Practice Unit
KITAMURA, M., Commercial Law
MAEDA, M., Commercial Law
MATSUDA, K., Law Practice Unit
MATSUOKA, H., Civil Law
MORI, T., Constitutional Law
MORIKAWA, S., Law Practice Unit
MORIMOTO, S., Commercial Law
MURAKAMI, K., Law Practice Unit
MURANAKA, T., Labour Law
NAKAGAWA, H., Law Practice Unit
NAKAMORI, Y., Criminal Law
NISHIGORI, S., Civil Law
NISHIMURA, K., Social Security Law
OISHI, M., Constitutional Law
OKAMURA, S., Administrative Law
OKAMURA, T., Tax Law
SAKAI, H., International Law
SAKAMAKI, T., Criminal Law
SAKUMA, T., Civil Law
SAKURADA, Y., Private International Law
SHIBAIKE, Y., Administrative Law
SHIMIZU, M., Law Practice Unit
SHIOMI, J., Criminal Law
SHIOMI, Y., Civil Law
SHIYAKE, M., Constitutional Law
SUZAKI, H., Commercial Law
TAKAYAMA, K., Criminal Law
TANASE, T., Sociology of Law
TERADA, H., Oriental Legal History
TOKUDA, K., Law of Civil Procedure
YAMAGAMI, K., Law Practice Unit
YAMAMOTO, K., Law of Civil Procedure
YAMAMOTO, K., Civil Law
YAMAMOTO, Y., Civil Law
YASUKI, K., Law Practice Unit
YOKOYAMA, M., Civil Law
YOSHIOKA, K., Criminology

ATTACHED RESEARCH INSTITUTES

Academic Center for Computing and Media Studies: Yoshida-Honmachi, Sakyo-ku, Kyoto; internet www.media.kyoto-u.ac.jp; f. 2002; Dir Prof. T. MATSUYAMA.

Center for African Area Studies: Shimoadachi-cho 46, Yoshida, Sakyo-ku, Kyoto; e-mail caas@jambo.africa.kyoto-u.ac.jp; internet www.africa.kyoto-u.ac.jp; f. 1986; Dir Prof. Dr S. ARAKI.

Center for Archaeological Operations: Yoshida Honmachi, Sakyo-ku, Kyoto; f. 1977; Dir Prof. Dr M. UEHARA.

Center for Ecological Research: 509-3 2-chome, Hirano, Otsu, Shiga 520-2113; internet www.ecology.kyoto-u.ac.jp; f. 1991; Dir Prof. Y. TSUBAKI.

Center for Southeast Asian Studies: Shimoadachi-cho 46, Yoshida, Sakyo-ku, Kyoto; e-mail editorial@cseas.kyoto-u.ac.jp; internet www.cseas.kyoto-u.ac.jp; f. 1965; Dir Prof. Dr K. TANAKA; publ. *Southeast Asian Studies* (4 a year), *Kyoto Review of Southeast Asia* (in English).

Center for the Promotion of Excellence in Higher Education: Yoshida-nihonmatsu-cho, Sakyo-ku, Kyoto; e-mail 730center@@@mail2.adm.kyoto-u.ac.jp; internet www.highedu.kyoto-u.ac.jp; f. 2003; Dir Prof. Dr T. TANAKA.

Disaster Prevention Research Institute: Gokasho, Uji City, Kyoto; internet www.dpri.kyoto-u.ac.jp; f. 1951; Dir Prof. K. ISHIHARA.

Environment Preservation Center: Yoshida Honmachi, Sakyo-ku, Kyoto; internet eprc.kyoto-u.ac.jp; f. 1977; Dir Prof. K. OSHIMA.

Field Science Education and Research Center: Oiwake-cho, Kitashirakawa, Sakyo-ku, Kyoto; e-mail joho@kais.kyoto-u.ac.jp; f. 2003; Dir Prof. M. TANAKA.

Fukui Institute for Fundamental Chemistry: Takanonishihiraki-cho, Sakyo-ku, Kyoto; f. 2002; Dir Prof. H. NAKATSUJI.

Institute of Advanced Energy: Gokasho, Uji City, Kyoto; e-mail office@iae.kyoto-u.ac.jp; internet www.iae.kyoto-u.ac.jp; f. 1941; Dir Prof. A. KOHYAMA.

Institute for Chemical Research: Gokasho, Uji City, Kyoto; internet www.kuicr.kyoto-u.ac.jp; f. 1926; Dir Prof. N. ESAKI.

Institute of Economic Research: Yoshida Honmachi, Sakyo-ku, Kyoto; internet www.kier.kyoto-u.ac.jp; f. 1962; library of 75,722 vols; Dir Prof. Dr T. SAWA.

Institute for Frontier Medical Sciences: 53 Kawahara-cho, Shogoin, Sakyo-ku, Kyoto 606-8507; internet www.frontier.kyoto-u.ac.jp; f. 1998; Dir Prof. N. NAKATSUJI.

Institute for Research in Humanities: Ushinomiya-cho, Yoshida, Sakyo-ku, Kyoto; e-mail annai@zinbun.kyoto-u.ac.jp; internet www.zinbun.kyoto-u.ac.jp; f. 1939; Dir Prof. B. KIN; publ. *Journal of Oriental Studies* (1 a year), *Journal of Humanities Studies* (1 a year, in Japanese), *Annual Bibliography of Oriental Studies*, *Annals ZINBUN* (irregular, in European languages).

Institute for Virus Research: Kawara-cho, Shogoin, Sakyo-ku, Kyoto; internet www.virus.kyoto-u.ac.jp; f. 1956; Dir Prof. R. KAGEYAMA.

Kyoto University Archives: Yoshida Honmachi, Sakyo-ku, Kyoto; e-mail archives@mail2.adm.kyoto-u.ac.jp; f. 2000; Dir Prof. Dr J. SASAKI.

Kyoto University International Innovation Center: Kyoto-Daigaku-katsura, Nishikyo-ku, Kyoto; f. 2001; Dir Prof. K. MAKINO.

Kyoto University Museum: Yoshida Honmachi, Sakyo-ku, Kyoto; f. 1997; Dir Prof. Dr I. YAMANAKA.

Primate Research Institute: Kanrin 41-2, Inuyama City, Aichi Prefecture; internet www.pri.kyoto-u.ac.jp; f. 1967; Dir Prof. N. SHIGEHARA.

Radiation Biology Center: Yoshida Konoecho, Sakyo-ku, Kyoto; internet www.rbc.kyoto-u.ac.jp; f. 1976; research and postgraduate training in radiation biology; Dir Prof. T. MATSUMOTO.

Radioisotope Research Center: Yoshida Konoecho, Sakyo-ku, Kyoto; f. 1971; Dir Prof. Dr Y. ISOZUMI.

Research Center for Low Temperature and Materials Science: Oiwake-cho, Kitashirakawa, Sakyo-ku, Kyoto; f. 2002; Dir Prof. T. MIZUSAKI.

Research Institute for Mathematical Sciences: Kitashirakawa, Sakyo-ku, Kyoto; f. 1963; research and postgraduate training in mathematical sciences; library of 91,198 vols; Dir Prof. SHIGEFUMI MORI.

Research Institute for Sustainable Humanosphere: Gokasho, Uji City, Kyoto; f. 2004; Dir Prof. S. KAWAI.

Research Reactor Institute: Kumatori-cho, Sennan-gun, Osaka; internet www.rri.kyoto-u.ac.jp; f. 1963; library of 45,300 vols; Dir Prof. S. SHIROYA.

Yukawa Institute for Theoretical Physics: Kitashirakawa, Sakyo-ku, Kyoto; internet www.yukawa.kyoto-u.ac.jp; f. 1953; Dir Prof. T. KUGO; publ. *Progress of Theoretical Physics* (12 a year)

KYUSHU INSTITUTE OF DESIGN

Shiobaru 4-9-1, Minami-ku, Fukuoka-shi 815-8540
Telephone: (92) 553-4407
E-mail: syomuka@kyushu-id.ac.jp
Internet: www.kyushu-id.ac.jp

Founded 1968
Independent
Academic year: April to March (2 semesters)

Pres.: SHO YOSHIDA
Dir-Gen.: MAKOTO OHYA
Dean of Students: MASAMICHI OHKUBO
Library Dir: RYUZO TAKIYAMA

Number of teachers: 96
Number of students: 1,208 (929 undergraduate, 279 postgraduate)

PROFESSORS

Department of Environmental Design:
- DOI, Y., History of Architecture and Industrial Design
- HIROKAWA, S., Theory of Environmental Design
- ISHII, A., Environmental Systems, Building and Environment Engineering
- KATANO, H., Environmental Systems and Building Construction
- KATO, H. M., Environmental Planning and Design
- MIYAMOTO, M., Environmental Planning and Design
- OHKUBO, M., Environmental Systems and Structural Engineering
- SHIGEMATSU, T., Theory of Environmental Design

Department of Industrial Design:
- FUKATA, S., Intelligent Mechanics and Control
- ISHIMURA, S., Industrial History
- ITOI, H., Industrial Design
- MORITA, Y., Public Space and Element Design
- SAKATA, T., Mathematical Statistics
- SAKI, K., Tribology
- SATO, H., Ergonomics
- TOCHIHARA, Y., Environmental Ergonomics
- YASUKOUCHI, A., Physiological Anthropology

Department of Visual Communication Design:
- FUKUSHIMA, S., Artificial Intelligence
- GENDA, E., Image Design
- NAGASHIMA, K., Image Engineering
- SATO, M., Research and Design on Sign Communication
- URAHAMA, K., Image Information Processing
- WAKIYAMA, S., Visual Image Design
- YAMASHITA, S., Vision Science and Neurobiology
- YAMASHITA, Y., Vision Science and Psychophysics

Department of Acoustic Design:
- FUJIEDA, M., Science of Sound Culture
- FUJIWARA, K., Science of Acoustical Environment
- IWAMIYA, S., Science of Acoustical Environment
- KAWABE, T., Science of Acoustical Environment
- NAKAJIMA, Y., Science of Acoustic Information
- NAKAMURA, S., Science of Sound Culture
- YOSHIKAWA, S., Science of Acoustic Information

Department of Art and Information Design:
- FUJIMURA, N., Media Design
- KUROSAWA, S., Media Art and Culture
- OHNISHI, S., Media Art and Culture
- OTA, S., Information Environment Sciences
- SASABUCHI, S., Information Environment Sciences

KYUSHU INSTITUTE OF TECHNOLOGY

1-1 Sensui-sho, Tobata-ku, Kitakyushu-shi, Fukuoka 804-8550
Telephone: (93) 884-3008
E-mail: kok-ryugaku@jimu.kyutech.ac.jp
Internet: www.kyutech.ac.jp

Founded 1909
Independent
Language of instruction: Japanese
Academic year: April to March

Pres.: TERUO SHIMOMURA
Registrar: MAKOTO YOSHIDA
Librarian: MORIO MATSUNAGA

Library of 489,867 vols
Number of teachers: 636 full-time
Number of students: 6,307

Publications: *Bulletin*, *Memoirs*

DEANS

Faculty of Computer Science and Systems Engineering: T. KODAMA
Faculty of Engineering: T. KOBAYASHI
Graduate School of Computer Science and Systems Engineering: H. TSUKAMOTO

KYUSHU UNIVERSITY

6-10-1 Hakozaki, Higashi-ku, Fukuoka 812-8581
Telephone: (92) 642-2111
Internet: www.kyushu-u.ac.jp

Founded 1911
Private control
Languages of instruction: English, Japanese
Academic year: April to March

Pres.: Dr SETSUO ARIKAWA
Exec. Vice-Pres.: Dr KATSUMI IMAIZUMI
Exec. Vice-Pres.: Dr HIDETOSHI OCHIAI
Exec. Vice-Pres.: Dr RITSUKO KIKUKAWA
Exec. Vice-Pres.: Dr RYOICHI TAKAYANAGI
Exec. Vice-Pres.: Dr YUKIO FUJIKI
Exec. Vice-Pres.: Dr SHUNICHI MARUNO
Exec. Vice-Pres.: Dr HIROTO YASUURA
Exec. Vice-Pres. and Dir-Gen.: AKIYOSHI MOTOKI
Librarian: YOSHIAKI KAWAMOTO

Library of 4,057,788 vols, 93,921 serials
Number of teachers: 2,327
Number of students: 18,967

DEANS

Faculty of Agriculture: A. YOSHIMURA
Faculty of Dental Science: A. AKAMINE
Faculty of Design: S. ISHIMURA
Faculty of Economics: K. YAMAMOTO
Faculty of Engineering: S. YAMADA
Faculty of Engineering Sciences: H. NAKASHIMA
Faculty of Human–Environment Studies: Y. HAKODA
Faculty of Humanities: M. TAKAYAMA
Faculty of Information Science and Electrical Engineering: R. TANIGUCHI
Faculty of Languages and Cultures: M. TOKUMI
Faculty of Law: I. SAKO
Faculty of Mathematics: M. KANEKO
Faculty of Medical Sciences: M. KATANO
Faculty of Pharmaceutical Sciences: K. INOUE
Faculty of Sciences: M. ARATONO
Faculty of Social and Cultural Studies: H. HATTORI
Graduate School of Integrated Frontier Sciences: Y. MORITA
Graduate School of Systems Life Sciences: K. IRAMINA
Law School (Professional Graduate School): H. AKAMATSU
School of Education: H. MINAMI

MIE UNIVERSITY

1515 Kamihama-cho, Tsu-shi, Mie 514
Telephone: (592) 32-1211
E-mail: webmast.en@ab.mie-u.ac.jp
Internet: www.mie-u.ac.jp

Founded 1949
Independent
Academic year: April to March

Pres.: RYUICHI YATANI
Chief Admin. Officer: KATSUYUKI KUROSAKI
Librarian: HIROYUKI NODA

Library of 783,000 vols
Number of teachers: 1,740
Number of students: 7,505

Publications: *Outline of Mie University* (every 2 years), *The Journal of Law and Economics* (Hōkei Ronsō), various faculty bulletins

DEANS

Faculty of Bioresources: HITOSHI OBATA
Faculty of Education: TAKESHI KINOSHITA
Faculty of Engineering: GORO SAWA
Faculty of Humanities and Social Sciences: HIDEKAZU HIROSE
School of Medicine: RYUICHI YATANI
College of Medical Sciences: KATSUMI DEGUCHI

MURORAN INSTITUTE OF TECHNOLOGY

Mizumoto-cho 27-1, Muroran 050-8585, Hokkaido
Telephone: (143) 46-5022
E-mail: koho@mmm.muroran-it.ac.jp
Internet: www.muroran-it.ac.jp

Founded 1949
Independent
Academic year: April to March

Pres.: HIROAKI TAGASHIRA
Admin. Officer: YASHUTO UEMARA
Chief Librarian: KEN-ICHI MATSUOKA

Library of 284,300 vols
Number of teachers: 360
Number of students: 3,500

Publication: *Memoirs* (1 a year)

NAGAOKA UNIVERSITY OF TECHNOLOGY

1603-1 Kamitomioka, Nagaoka, Niigata 940-2188
Telephone: (258) 46-6000
E-mail: syomugroup@jcom.nagaokaut.ac.jp
Internet: www.nagaokaut.ac.jp

Founded 1976
State control
Languages of instruction: English, Japanese
Academic year: April to March

Depts of bioengineering, civil and environmental engineering, electrical engineering, management and information system science, materials science and technology, mechanical engineering, system safety

Pres.: Prof. YO KOJIMA
Vice-Pres. for Academic Affairs: Prof. YASUNORI MIYATA
Vice-Pres. for Evaluation: Prof. IKUZO NISHIGUCHI
Vice-Pres. for Graduate School: Prof. YASUNOBU INOUE
Vice-Pres. for Industry–Academia Cooperation and Information: ATSUSHI KAWASAKI
Vice-Pres. for Int. Affairs: Prof. KOZO ISHIZAKI
Vice-Pres. for Research, Admission and Student Affairs: Prof. KYUICHI MARUYAMA
Dir for Admin.: SATO MASARU

Library of 140,000 vols
Number of teachers: 212
Number of students: 2,469

DEANS

Graduate School of Engineering: Prof. YASUNOBU INOUE
Graduate School of Management of Technology: Prof. YASUNORI MIYATA
School of Engineering: Prof. YASUNOBU INOUE

NAGASAKI UNIVERSITY

1-14 Bunkyo-machi, Nagasaki 852-8521
Telephone: (95) 819-2042
E-mail: www_admin@ml.nagasaki-u.ac.jp
Internet: www.nagasaki-u.ac.jp

Founded 1949
Academic year: April to March
Independent

Pres.: HIROSHI SAITO
Vice-Pres: TSUYOSHI SAKIYAMA, HARUHIKO MASAKI, SHIGERU KATAMINE
Dir-Gen.: SYUSUKE MORITA
Library Dir: TAKATOSHI OKABAYASHI

Library of 1,078,347 vols
Number of teachers: 1,067 full-time
Number of students: 8,935

Publications: *Bulletin of the Faculty of Education*, *Journal of Business and Economics* (4 a year), *Annual Review of South East Asian Studies*, *Annual Review of Economics*, *Nagasaki Medical Journal* (4 a year), *Acta Medica Nagasakiensia* (2 a year), *Report of the Faculty of Engineering* (2 a year), *Journal of Environmental Studies* (2 a year), *Bulletin of the Faculty of Fisheries*, *Bulletin of the School of Allied Medical Sciences*, *Seasonal Report of the Education and Research Centre for Life-long Learning*

DEANS

Faculty of Economics: Prof. TOSHIO SUGIHARA
Faculty of Education: Prof. TATEO HASHIMOTO
Faculty of Engineering: Prof. JUN OYAMA
Faculty of Environmental Studies: Prof. YOSHIHIKO INOUE
Faculty of Fisheries: Prof. MUTSUYOSHI TSUCHIMOTO
Graduate School of Biomedical Sciences: Prof. KOHTARO TANIYAMA
Graduate School of Science and Technology: Prof. TADASHI ISHIHARA
Institute of Tropical Medicine: Prof. YOSHIKI AOKI
School of Allied Medical Sciences: Prof. AKEMI TERASAKI
School of Dentistry: Prof. MITSURU ATSUTA
School of Medicine: Prof. TAKASHI KANEMATSU
School of Pharmaceutical Sciences: Prof. KENICHIRO NAKASHIMA

DIRECTORS

Animal Research Center: Prof. MICHIO NAKAMURA
Atomic Bomb Disease Institute: Prof. MASAO TOMONAGA
Center for Educational Research and Training: Prof. AKIFUMI FUKUI
Center for Frontier Life Sciences: Prof. HIROSHI SATO
Center for Instrumental Analysis: Prof. SUSUMI HATAKEYAMA
Division of Comparative Medicine: HIROSHI SATO
Division of Functional Genomics: NORIO NIIKAWA
Division of Radiation Biology and Protection: Prof. YUTAKA OKUMURA
Education and Research Center for Life-long Learning: Prof. KAGEHIRO ITOYAMA
Environmental Protection Center: Prof. TAKEHIRO TAKEMASA
Garden for Medicinal Plants: Prof. ISAO KONO
Health Center: Prof. NOBUKO ISHII
International Student Center: Prof. YOSHIHIRO MATSUMURA
Joint Research Center: Prof. MAKOTO EGASHIRA
Marine Research Institute: Prof. HIDEAKI NAKATA
Research and Development Center for Higher Education: Prof. SHIGERU KATAMINE
Research Center for Tropical Infectious Diseases: Prof. MASAAKI SHIMADA
Science Information Center: Prof. HIDEO KURODA
University Hospital attached to School of Dentistry: Prof. HIROYUKI FUJII
University Hospital attached to School of Medicine: Prof. KOJI SUMIKAWA

PROFESSORS

Faculty of Economics (4-2-1 Katafuchi, Nagasaki 850-8506; tel. (95) 820-6300; internet www.econ.nagasaki-u.ac.jp):

AOYAMA, S., Development Economics
BASU, D., International Economics
FUJINO, T., Japanese Corporations and Management
FUJITA, W., Economics of Natural Resources and Energy
FUKAURA, A., Monetary Economics
FUKUZAWA, K., Labour Economics
FURUYAMA, M., Law and Finance
GUNN, G., International Relations
IDE, K., Modern Asian Economies
IMADA, T., Accounting
KANKE, M., Business Management
KASAHARA, T., Business Enterprise and Human Evolution
KAWAMURA, Y., Corporate Planning of Financial Institutions, Investment Banking
KIHARA, T., Cooperation Among Nations and International Economics
KOREEDA, M., Microeconomics
MARUYAMA, Y., Decision Making
MATSUMOTO, M., Economic History of the British Empire
MATSUNAGA, A., Small Business Administration
MIHARA, Y., Human Resource Management
MURATA, S., Microeconomics
MURATA, Y., Mathematics
OKADA, H., Financial Accounting
SHIBATA, K., Japanese Economic History
SUGIHARA, T., Management Engineering
SUSAI, M., International Finance
TAGUCHI, N., International Investment
TAKAHASHI, Y., Intellectual Property and Licensing
TAKAKURA, Y., Political Economy
TATEYAMA, S., Business Enterprises and Asian Economics
UCHIDA, S., Monetary Economics
UENO, K., Financial Accounting
UNOTORO, Y., Japanese Economy
YAJIMA, K., Derivative Securities

Faculty of Education (internet www.edu.nagasaki-u.ac.jp):

ADACHI, K., Analysis and Applied Mathematics
AIKAWA, K., School for Intellectually Impaired Children
AKASAKI, M., Teaching of Home Economics
ARITA, Y., Teaching of Social Studies
AZUMA, M., Biology
FUKUI, A., Music Education
FUKUYAMA, Y., Physics
FUNAKOE, K., Law
FURUYA, Y., Materials Science and Engineering
GOTO, Y., Early Childhood Education and Care
HAMASAKI, K., German Literature
HARADA, J., Educational Psychology
HASHIMOTO, T., Science Education
HIGUCHI, S., Analytical Chemistry
HORIUCHI, I., Pianoforte Playing
IIZUKA, T., Philosophy
IKAWA, S., Painting
INOUE, I., American Literature
ITOYAMA, K., Teaching of Technology
IYAMA, K., Social Education
JINNO, N., Biology
KABASHIMA, S., Physics
KAMIZONO, K., Moral and Philosophy Education
KATSUMATA, T., Japanese Literature
KITAMURA, Y., Analysis
KOGA, M., Solid State Physics
MATUNAGA, J., Teaching of Health and Physical Education
MIYAZAKI, M., Developmental Psychology
MURATA, Y., Developmental Psychology
NAKAMURA, M., American Literature
NAKAMURA, Y., English and American Literature
NAKANISHI, H., Biology
NISHIZAWA, S., Physical Fitness
OBARA, T., Exercise Physiology
ODA, M., Design
OSAKI, Y., Astronomy
OTSUBO, Y., Teaching of English
SATO, K., Sculpture
SINNO, T., Psychological Study of Preschool Children's Play
SINOHARA, S., Philosophy
SUGAWARA, M., Exercise Physiology
SUGAWARA, T., Geometry
SUGIYAMA, S., Woodworking
TAHARA, Y., School Health and Sports Physiology
TAKAHASHI, S., International Law, Constitutional Law
TAKAHASHI, S., Sociology
TAMARI, M., Food and Nutritional Chemistry
TANIGAWA, M., Politics
TOMONAGA, S., Psychology
WASHIO, T., Algebra
YAMAGUCHI, T., History
YAMAMOTO, T., Teaching of Japanese
YAMANO, S., Theory of Music
YAMAUCHI, M., Physical Education
YANAGIDA, Y., Educational Sociology
YASUKOUCHI, Y., Teaching of Japanese
YOKOYAMA, M., Politics
YOSHIOKA, H., Educational Psychology

Faculty of Engineering (internet www.eng.nagasaki-u.ac.jp):

AOYAGI, H., Biochemistry
EGASHIRA, M., Materials Chemistry
FUJIYAMA, H., Plasma Science
FUKUNAGA, H., Magnetics
FURUMOTO, K., Hydraulics
HARADA, T., Reinforced and Prestressed Concrete Structures
HASAKA, M., Materials Physics and Engineering
IMAI, Y., Fracture Mechanics
ISHIMATSU, T., Measurement and Control Engineering

IWANAGA, H., Analysis of Crystal Structure
IWAO, M., Synthetic Organic Chemistry
KAGAWA, A., Metal Science
KANEMARU, K., Heat Transfer
KAWAZOE, T., Tribology
KISU, H., Computational Mechanics
KOBAYASHI, K., Network Systems
KODAMA, Y., Fluid Dynamics
KUDO, A., Algebra
KUDO, T., Solid State Electrochemistry
MATSUDA, H., Structural and Engineering Mechanics
MATSUO, H., High-voltage Engineering
MIYAHARA, S., Pattern Recognition and Information Retrieval Systems
NOGUCHI, M., Hydraulics
OGURI, K., Computer and Information Science
OKABAYASHI, T., Dynamics and Control of Structures
ONISHI, M., Coordination Chemistry
OYAMA, J., Electrical Machinery
SAKIYAMA, T., Structural Analysis
SETOGUCHI, K., Fatigue
SHIGECHI, T., Thermal Engineering
SHUGYO, M., Inelastic Behaviour of Steel Structures
TAKAHASHI, K., Structural Vibration
TAKENAKA, T., Electromagnetic Wave Theory
TAMARU, Y., Organic Chemistry
TANABASHI, Y., Soil Mechanics
TANAKA, K., Engineering Optics
TSUJI, M., Electrical Control Systems
UCHIYAMA, Y., Ceramics Science and Technology

Faculty of Environmental Studies (internet www.env.nagasaki-u.ac.jp/mainj.shtml):

ARAO, K., Meteorology and Climatology
FUKUSHIMA, K., Anthropology of Religion
GOTO, N., Solid State Physics
HAMA, T., Labour Environment
HAYASE, T., Environmental Politics
HIMENO, J., History of Economics
IDE, Y., Environmental Business Management
IKENAGA, T., Plant Functional Science
IKUNO, M., Civil Law
INOUE, Y., Philosophy
ISHIZAKI, K., Environmental Engineering
KOHRA, S., Environmental Chemistry
MASAKI, H., Oriental Philosophy and Bioethics
MIYA, Y., Crustacean Taxonomy
NAKAMURA, T., Biostatistics and Risk Analysis
NAKAMURA, T., Coastal Oceanography
ONO, T., Environment Economics
SAKUMA, T., Japanese Intellectual History
SONODA, N., German Literature
TAIMURA, A., Exercise Physiology
TAKAZANE, Y., French Culture and Culture Exchange
TAKEMASA, T., Soil Physics
TANIMURA, K., Living Environment
TSUCHIYA, K., Environmental Physiology
UEDA, K., Peptide Chemistry
WAKAKI, T., Japanese Literature
YAMAZAKI, S., Environmental Biochemistry
YOSHIDA, M., Greek Philosophy
YOSHIKAWA, I., Radiation Genetics

Faculty of Fisheries (internet www.fish .nagasaki-u.ac.jp/index.htm):

ARAKAWA, O., Marine Food Hygiene
GODA, M., Navigation, Nautical Instruments
HARA, K., Biochemistry
HASHIMOTO, J., Deep-sea Biology
ISHIHARA, T., Aquatic Biochemistry
ISHIMATSU, A., Fish Physiology
ISHIZAKA, J., Biological Oceanography, Ocean Colour Remote Sensing
KATAOKA, C., Marine Social Science
KITAMURA, H., Marine Chemical Ecology, Effects of Pollution on Marine Life
MATSUBAYASHI, N., Colloid and Interface Science
MATSUOKA, K., Micropalaeontology and Coastal Environment Science
MATSUYAMA, M., Limnology and Oceanography
MORII, H., Ecology and Physiology of Marine and Food Bacteria
NAKATA, H., Fisheries Oceanography and Coastal Oceanography
NATSUKARI, Y., Fisheries Biology, Invertebrates, Cephalopoda
NISHINOKUBI, H., Fishing Boat Seamanship, Fishing Gear Engineering
NOZAKI, Y., Chemistry and Technology of Marine Food Materials
ODA, T., Marine Biochemistry
TACHIBANA, K., Nutritional Chemistry of Marine Food
TAKEMURA, A., Acoustical Behaviour of Marine Animals, Life History of Marine Mammals and Sharks
TAMAKI, A., Ecology of Marine Benthos
TSUCHIMOTO, M., Nutritional Physiology of Marine Food
YAMAGUCHI, Y., Fishing Technology Science, Fishing Ground Ecology
YOSHIKOSHI, K., Fish Pathology

Graduate School of Science and Technology (internet www.seisan.nagasaki-u.ac.jp):

FUJITA, Y., Marine Phycology
FURUKAWA, M., Polymer Science
GOTOH, K., Remote Sensing
HAGIWARA, A., Marine Invertebrate Zoology, Live Food Science, Applied Planktology
ISHIDA, M., Diesel Combustion Engineering
KURODA, H., Computer and Information Science
MATSUO, H., Electronic and Digital Control
NAKASHIMA, N., Chemistry and Materials Science of Nanocarbons
YOSHITAKE, Y., Vibration of Structures

Institute of Tropical Medicine (1-12-4 Sakamoto, Nagasaki 852-8523; tel. (95) 849-7800; internet www.tm.nagasaki-u.ac.jp):

AOKI, Y., Parasitology
HIRAYAMA, K., Molecular Immunogenetics
HIRAYAMA, T., Bacteriology
IWASAKI, T., Pathology
KANBARA, H., Protozoology
MIZOTA, T., Social Environment
MOJI, K., Human Ecology
MORITA, K., Virology
NAGATAKE, T., Internal Medicine
NAKAMURA, M., Biochemistry
SHIMADA, M., Eco-epidemiology
TAKAGI, M., Medical Entomology
YAMAMOTO, N., Preventive Medicine and AIDS Research

School of Dentistry (1-7-1 Sakamoto, Nagasaki 852-8588; tel. (95) 849-7600; internet www.de.nagasaki-u.ac.jp):

ATSUTA, M., Fixed Prosthodontics
FUJII, H., Removable Prosthodontics
FUJIWARA, T., Paediatric Dentistry
HARA, Y., Periodontology
HAYASHI, Y., Endodontics and Operative Dentistry
HISATSUNE, K., Dental Materials Science
INOKUCHI, T., Oral and Maxillofacial Surgery II
KATO, Y., Dental Pharmacology
MIZUNO, A., Oral and Maxillofacial Surgery I
NAKAMURA, T., Radiology and Cancer Biology
NAKAYAMA, K., Oral Bacteriology
NEMOTO, T., Oral Biochemistry
OI, K., Dental Anaesthesiology
ROKUTANDA, A., Oral Anatomy
SHINSHO, F., Preventive Dentistry
TAKANO, K., Oral Histology
TODA, K., Oral Physiology
YAMAGUCHI, A., Oral Pathology
YOSHIDA, N., Orthodontics

School of Medicine (1-12-4 Sakamoto, Nagasaki 852-8523; tel. (95) 849-7000; internet www.med.nagasaki-u.ac.jp):

AIKAWA, T., Physiology of Visceral Function and Body Fluid
AOYAGI, K., Preventive Health Sciences and Community Health
EGUCHI, K., Immunology, Endocrinology and Metabolism
EISHI, K., Cardiovascular Surgery
FUNASE, K., Human Motor Control, Exercise Physiology
HAMANO, K., Foundations of Nursing
HAYASHI, K., Radiological Science
ISHIHARA, K., Adult Nursing, Cancer Nursing
ISHIMARU, T., Obstetrics and Gynaecology
ITO, T., Biochemistry
KAMIHIRA, S., Laboratory Medicine
KANEMATSU, T., Surgery
KANETAKE, H., Nephro-urology
KATAMINE, S., Cellular and Molecular Biology
KATAYAMA, I., Dermatology
KATO, K., Anatomy of Locomotor Systems, Physical Anthropology
KOHNO, S., Molecular and Clinical Microbiology
KOJI, T., Histology and Cell Biology
KONDO, T., Clinical Biochemistry and Molecular Biology in Ageing-related Vascular Diseases and Cancer
MATSUMOTO, T., Paediatrics
MATSUSAKA, N., Rehabilitation Medicine, Orthopaedic Surgery
MATSUYAMA, T., Cytokine Signalling
MIYASHITA, H., Child Nursing, Rehabilitation
MORISHITA, M., Community Health Nursing
MORIUCHI, H., Medical Virology
NAGAO, T., Occupational Therapy, Assistive Technology
NAGASHIMA, S., Macroscopic Morphology
NAGATA, I., Clinical Neuroscience, Neurology and Neurosurgery
NAKAGOMI, O., Molecular Epidemiology
NAKAJIMA, H., Gynaecological Oncology, Obstetrics
NAKAZONO, I., Forensic Pathology and Science
NIIKAWA, N., Human Genetics
NIWA, M., Neurosensory Pharmacology
OHISHI, K., Midwifery
OHTA, Y., Psychiatry, Mental and Physical Health
OKUMURA, Y., Radiation Biophysics
SATO, H., Comparative Medicine
SEKINE, I., Molecular Pathology
SENJYU, H., Physical Therapy, Pulmonary Rehabilitation
SHIBATA, Y., Radiation Epidemiology
SHIMOKAWA, I., Pathology and Gerontology
SHINDO, H., Orthopaedic Pathomechanism
SHINOHARA, K., Physiology
SUMIKAWA, K., Anaesthesiology
TAGAWA, Y., Thoracic Surgery and Cytometry
TAGUCHI, T., Pathology
TAHARA, H., Physical Therapy, Quality of Life
TAKAHASHI, H., Otorhinolaryngology
TANIYAMA, K., Pharmacology and Therapeutics
TASHIRO, T., Respirology, Infectious Diseases
TERASAKI, A., Adult Health Nursing
TOKUNAGA, M., Public Health Nursing
TOMONAGA, M., Molecular Medicine and Haematology
URATA, H., Adult Nursing, Surgical Nursing
YAMASHITA, S., Molecular Medicine

YANO, K., Cardiovascular Medicine
YOSHIMURA, T., Neurology (Morphology in Neuromuscular Diseases)
YUI, K., Immunology

School of Pharmaceutical Sciences (internet www.ph.nagasaki-u.ac.jp/indexj.html):

FUJITA, K., Pharmaceutical Chemistry
HATAKEYAMA, S., Pharmaceutical Organic Chemistry
KAI, M., Chemistry of Biofunctional Molecules
KOBAYASHI, N., Molecular Biology of Diseases
KOHNO, M., Cell Regulation
KOUNO, I., Pharmacognosy
KURODA, N., Analytical Chemistry for Pharmaceutics
MURATA, I., Pharmacotherapeutics
NAKAMURA, J., Pharmaceutics
NAKASHIMA, K., Analytical Research for Pharmacoinformatics
NAKAYAMA, M., Hygienic Chemistry
NATSUMARA, Y., Synthetic Chemistry for Pharmaceutics
UEDA, H., Molecular Pharmacology and Neuroscience
WATANABE, M., Radiation and Life Science
YOSHIMOTO, T., Biotechnology

NAGOYA INSTITUTE OF TECHNOLOGY

Gokiso-cho, Showa-ku, Nagoya 466-855
Telephone: (52) 735-5000
E-mail: kouhou@adm.nitech.ac.jp
Internet: www.nitech.ac.jp

Founded 1949
Independent
Language of instruction: Japanese
Academic year: April to March

Pres.: HIROAKI YANAGIDA
Vice-Pres: IWATA AKIRA, NOBUYUKI MATSUI, TETSUMI HORIKOSHI
Dir-Gen.: HIDESHI SUDA
Dir for Univ. Library: KOICHIRO KAWASHIMA

Library of 463,169 vols
Number of teachers: 372
Number of students: 6,516

Publication: *Bulletin* (1 a year).

ATTACHED INSTITUTES

Center for Information and Media Studies: Gokiso-cho, Showa-ku, Nagoya 466-8555; e-mail staff@center.nitech.ac.jp; Dir YUKIE KOYAMA.

Ceramics Research Laboratory: 6–29 Asahigaoka 10-chome, Tajimi, Gifu; e-mail ota@crl.nitech.ac.jp; internet www.crl.nitech.ac.jp; Dir SUGURU SUZUKI.

Cooperative Research Center: Gokiso-cho, Showa-ku, Nagoya; Dir KOICHI NAKAMURA.

Instrument and Analysis Center: Gokiso-cho, Showa-ku, Nagoya 466-8555; Dir YOSHIHARU TSUJITA.

Research Center for Micro-structure Devices: Gokiso-cho, Showa-ku, Nagoya; Dir MASAYOSHI UMENO

NAGOYA UNIVERSITY

Furo-cho, Chikusa-ku, Nagoya 464-8601
Telephone: (52) 789-2044
E-mail: ised@post.jimu.nagoya-u.ac.jp
Internet: www.nagoya-u.ac.jp

Founded 1939
Independent
Language of instruction: Japanese
Academic year: April to March (two semesters)

Pres.: MICHINARI HAMAGUCHI
Vice-Pres and Trustees: TAKASHI MIYATA, HARUO SABURI, HIROYUKI SUGIYAMA, ICHIRO YAMAMOTO, RYOICHI FUJII
Vice-Pres. for Hospital Management: SEIICHI MATSUO
Vice-Pres. for Research and Int. Planning: YOSHIHITO WATANABE
Vice-Pres. for Evaluation and Gen. Planning: YUSHU MATSUSHITA
Dir-Gen. for Admin.: MAKOTO TAKAHASHI
Dir of the Library: YOSHITO ITOH

Library: see under Libraries and Archives
Number of teachers: 1,716 full-time
Number of students: 14,977 full-time

Publication: *Nagoya University Bulletin*

DEANS

Graduate School of Bioagricultural Sciences: T. MATSUDA
Graduate School of Economics: MAKOTO TAWADA
Graduate School of Education and Human Development: MISAO HAYAKAWA
Graduate School of Engineering: N. SAWAKI
Graduate School of Environmental Studies: YASUSHI YAMAGUCHI
Graduate School of Information Science: NOBUAKI KOGA
Graduate School of International Development: KATSUFUMI NARITA
Graduate School of Languages and Culture: K. KONDO
Graduate School of Law: H. SABURI
Graduate School of Letters: TOSHIHIRO WADA
Graduate School of Mathematics: Y. NAMIKAWA
Graduate School of Medicine: M. HAMAGUCHI
Graduate School of Science: I. OHMINE
School of Agricultural Sciences: T. MATSUDA
School of Economics: MAKOTO TAWADA
School of Education: MISAO HAYAKAWA
School of Engineering: N. SAWAKI
School of Informatics and Sciences: M. SANO
School of Law: H. SABURI
School of Letters: TOSHIHIRO WADA
School of Medicine: M. HAMAGUCHI
School of Science: I. OHMINE

DIRECTORS

Bioscience and Biotechnology Center: TSUKASA MATSUDA
Center for Asian Legal Exchange: MASANORI AIKYO
Center for Chronological Research: TOSHIO NAKAMURA
Center for Cooperative Research in Advanced Science and Technology: G. OBINATA
Center for Developmental Clinical Psychology and Psychiatry: S. HONJO
Center for Gene Research: M. ISHIURA
Center for Information Media Studies: I. YAMAMOTO
Center for Studies of Higher Education: MOTOKAZU KIMATA
EcoTopia Science Institute: TSUNEO MATSUI
Education Center for International Students: YUKIO ISHIDA
Hydrospheric Atmospheric Research Center: HIROSHI UYEDA
Information Technology Center: T. WATANABE
Institute for Advanced Research: KONDO TAKAO
International Cooperation Center for Agricultural Education: AKIRA YAMAUCHI
Kobayashi–Maskawa Institute for the Origin of Particles and the Universe: TOSHIHIDE MASKAWA (Dir-Gen.)
Nagoya University Museum: M. ADACHI
Radioisotope Research Center: K. NISHIZAWA
Research Center for Materials Science: RYOJI NOYORI (Supervisor)
Research Center of Health, Physical Fitness and Sports: K. SHIMAOKA
Research Institute of Environmental Medicine: I. KODAMA
Solar–Terrestrial Environment Laboratory: YUTAKA MATSUMI
University Hospital: A. IGUCHI

PROFESSORS

Center for Gene Research (Furo-cho, Chikusa-ku, Nagoya 464-8602; tel. (52) 789-3080; internet www.gene.nagoya-u.ac.jp/index-e.html):

ISHIURA, M., Genome Biology, Molecular Biology
SUGITA, M., Plant Molecular Biology

Center for Studies of Higher Education (tel. (52) 789-5696; e-mail webmaster@cshe.nagoya-u.ac.jp; internet www.cshe.nagoya-u.ac.jp):

NATSUME, T., Comparative Study on Higher Education

Radioisotope Research Center (Furo-cho, Chikusa-ku, Nagoya 464-8602; tel. (52) 789-2563; internet www.ric.nagoya-u.ac.jp):

NISHIZAWA, K., Radiation Protection

Nagoya University Museum (Furo-cho, Chikusa-ku, Nagoya 464-8601; tel. (52) 789-5767; internet www.num.nagoya-u.ac.jp):

ADACHI, M., Sedimentation and Tectonics
NISHIKAWA, T., Taxonomy and Phylogeny of Marine Invertebrates

Center for Cooperative Research in Advanced Science and Technology (tel. (52) 789-3921; internet www.ccrast.nagoya-u.ac.jp):

IWATA, S., Magnetic Materials and Magnetic Devices
KASAHARA, K., Quantum Electronics, Optical Communication
MORI, S., Environment Process Technology
OBINATA, G., Modelling and Control in Robotics, Human–Robot Interfaces, Biocybernetics
OGAWA, M., Semiconductor Devices
TAKAHASHI, H., Copyright

Center for Information Media Studies (tel. (52) 789-3903; internet www.media.nagoya-u.ac.jp):

NAGAO, K., Digital Content Technology, Media Informatics, Image and Language Processing, Agent Technology, Artificial Intelligence

Center for Chronological Research (Furo-cho, Chikusa-ku, Nagoya 464-8602; tel. (52) 789-2579; internet www.nendai.nagoya-u.ac.jp/en/index.html):

NAKAMURA, T., Geochemistry and Radiochronometry
SUZUKI, K., Petrology and Geochronology

Bioscience and Biotechnology Center (tel. (52) 789-5194; internet www.agr.nagoya-u.ac.jp/~nubs/index.html):

HATTORI, T., Plant Cell Function
KITAJIMA, K., Animal Cell Function
KITANO, H., Plant Bioresources
MATSUOKA, M., Plant Molecular Breeding
UOZUMI, T., Molecular Biosystems
WAKAMATSU, Y., Freshwater Fish Stocks

Hydrospheric–Atmospheric Research Center (tel. (52) 789-3466; e-mail koho@hyarc.nagoya-u.ac.jp; internet www.hyarc.nagoya-u.ac.jp/hyarc):

NAKAMURA, K., Satellite Meteorology
SAINO, T., Ocean Climate Biology
UYEDA, H., Meteorology
YASUNARI, T., Meteorology, Climate System Study

Center for Asian Legal Exchange (tel. (52) 789-2325; e-mail cale@nomolog.nagoya-u.ac.jp; internet www.nomolog.nagoya-u.ac.jp):

AIKYO, M., Asian Law

Information Technology Center (tel. (52) 789-4352; internet www.itc.nagoya-u.ac.jp):

- ISHII, K., Computational Fluid Dynamics
- MASE, K., Computer Mediated Communication
- MIYAO, M., Ergonomics
- YOSHIKAWA, M., Database Systems

Center for Developmental Clinical Psychology and Psychiatry (tel. (52) 789-2656):

- HONJO, S., Child Psychiatry
- TSURUTA, K., School Counselling
- UJIIE, T., Clinical Support of the Mother–Child Relationship

Education Center for International Students (tel. (52) 789-2198; internet www.ecis.nagoya-u.ac.jp):

- KASHIMA, T., Phonetics, Teaching Pronunciation of Japanese as a Foreign Language
- MATSUURA, M., International Student Advisory and Resource Services
- MURAKAMI, K., Teaching Japanese as a Foreign Language
- NOMIZU, T., Instrumental Analytical Chemistry, Student Exchange Programme Education
- OZAKI, A., Teaching Japanese as a Foreign Language

EcoTopia Science Institute (tel. (52) 789-5262; e-mail jimu@esi.nagoya-u.ac.jp; internet www.esi.nagoya-u.ac.jp):

- ENOKIDA, Y., Nuclear Fuel Engineering
- FUJISAWA, T., High-Temperature Physical Chemistry
- HASEGAWA, T., Environmental Thermo-Fluid Technologies
- HASEGAWA, Y., Energy Science
- ICHIHASHI, M., Electron Optics
- ITHO, H., Solid Waste Treatment
- KATAYAMA, A., Bioremediation and Bioreclamation
- KATAYAMA, M., Communication and Information Systems
- KITAGAWA, K., Advanced Energy Conversion Systems and Technologies
- NAGASAKI, T., Materials Science
- OKUBO, H., Electric Power Engineering
- SUZUKI, K., Environmental Research
- TAKAI, O., Materials Science and Engineering
- TANAKA, N., High Resolution Electron Microscopy and Electron Diffraction of Clusters, Wires and Think-Film Related to Nanotechnology
- TATEISHI, K., Structural Engineering
- TONOIKE, T., Linguistics, Lexicology and Optimality Theory
- WATANABE, T., Fluid Informatics and Computational Fluid Dynamics
- YOGO, T., Materials Chemistry

Graduate School of Environmental Studies (tel. (52) 789-3454; internet www.env.nagoya-u.ac.jp):

- AGETA, Y., Glaciology
- ANDO, M., Seismology and Geodesy
- ENAMI, M., Metamorphic Petrology and Rock-forming Mineralogy
- FUJII, N., Volcanology and Planetary Physics
- FUKUWA, N., Earthquake Engineering
- HATTA, T., Neuropsychology
- HAYASHI, N., Economic and Urban Geography
- HAYASHI, Y., Sustainable Transport and Spatial Development
- HIBINO, T., Electrochemistry
- HIRAHARA, K., Seismology
- HIROSE, Y., Environmental Social Psychology
- HOSHINO, M., Surface Material Systems
- IKADATSU, Y., Jurisprudence
- IMURA, H., Environmental Systems Analysis and Planning
- ISHII, K., Associative Learning
- ITAKURA, T., Sociology
- ITO, Y., Counselling and Clinical Psychology (Person-centered Approach and Focusing-oriented Psychotherapy)
- KAI, K., Meteorology, Climatology and Remote Sensing
- KAINUMA, J., Sociology
- KANZAWA, H., Meteorology
- KATAGI, A., Architectural Design and Theory
- KAWABE, I., REE Geochemistry, Geochemical Earthquake Prediction
- KAWADA, M., History of Political Thought in Japan
- KAWAGUCHI, J., Cognitive Psychology, Human Memory
- KAWAI, T., Environmental Science
- KAWASAKI, S., Economics
- KUNO, S., Environmental Engineering, Environmental Psychology
- KURODA, T., Urban Economics, Regional Science, Economic Theory
- MASUZAWA, T., Inorganic Biogeochemistry
- MATSUBARA, T., Environmental Science, Microbiology, Biochemistry
- MATSUMOTO, E., Geochemistry
- MIZOGUCHI, T., Historical Geography, Regional Study of South Asia
- MORIKAWA, T., Transport Planning
- MORIMOTO, H., Mathematical Biology
- MURATA, S., Organic Chemistry, Physical Organic Chemistry, Environmental Materials Science
- NISHIHARA, K., Sociology, Phenomenological Sociology, Social Theory
- OHKAWA, M., Constitutional Law, Environmental Law
- OHMORI, H., Structural Mechanics and Computational Analysis
- OKAMOTO, K., Geography, Behavioural Geography, Urban Geography
- OKUMIYA, M., Optimization of Energy Supplies in Building and Urban Scale
- OZAWA, T., Geobiology, Evolutionary Biology
- SANO, M., Fuel Cell, Secondary Battery, Energy Systems
- SHIMIZU, H., Architectural Planning and Design, Theatre Planning and Administration
- SUGIMOTO, T., Heterocyclic Chemistry
- SUZUKI, Y., Active Tectonics
- TANAKA, S., Urban Sociology
- TANAKA, T., Isotope Geochemistry
- TANOUE, E., Marine Biogeochemistry
- TESHIGAWARA, M., Reinforced Concrete Structures
- UMITSU, M., Geomorphology, Quaternary Geology, Geo-environmental Studies
- YAMADA, I., Seismology and Planetary Physics
- YAMADA, K., Structural Engineering, Bridge Engineering
- YAMAGUCHI, Y., Remote Sensing for Environmental Monitoring

Graduate School of International Development (tel. (52) 789-4952; e-mail webmaster@gsid.nagoya-u.ac.jp; internet www.gsid.nagoya-u.ac.jp):

- EZAKI, M., Development Information Systems
- FUTAMURA, H., Drug Trafficking in Latin America
- HIROSATO, Y., Educational Development
- KIMURA, H., Dynamics of Regional Politics, International Cooperation Policy I, II, Dynamics of Regional Politics
- KINOSHITA, T., Second Language Acquisition, Learning, Language Assessment, TESOL and Applied Linguistics
- NAKANISHI, H., International and Regional Politics, Organization for International Cooperation
- NISHIMURA, Y., Development Management
- OHASHI, A., South-East Asian Studies
- OMURO, T., Dynamic Theory of Language
- OSADA, H., Integrated Development Planning
- OTSUBO, S., International Development Economics
- SAKURAI, T., Theory of Intercultural Communication
- SUGIURA, M., Second Language Acquisition
- TAKAHASHI, K., Multiculturalism I, Social Change During Modernization
- YASUDA, N., Comparative Asian Legal Systems, Introduction to Law and Development Studies

Graduate School of Languages and Cultures (tel. (52) 789-4881; e-mail lcoffice@lang.nagoya-u.ac.jp; internet www.lang.nagoya-u.ac.jp):

- ANDO, S., 16th- and 17th-Century English Poetry
- ARIKAWA, K., German Literature in the Age of the Enlightenment
- FUKUDA, M., Comparative Literature and Culture, Medical History
- HIGH, P., Intellectual History of Japanese Film
- IIDA, H., Contrastive Study of Japanese, Korean and English
- INOUE, I., English Linguistics
- KAMIYA, O., Modern Chinese Language
- KATO, S., American Literature, Japanese and American Environmental Literature
- KONDO, K., Language Typology
- KOSAKA, K., Contrastive Linguistics
- MAENO, M., Cultural History of Early Modern Europe
- MATSUMOTO, I., Women's Studies
- MATSUOKA, M., Victorian Literature
- MURANUSHI, K., William Shakespeare
- NAGAHATA, A., American Literature
- NAKAI, M., Trend of Thought in Modern Chinese Literature
- NAKAJIMA, T., German Lyric Poems of the 19th Century
- OCHI, K., Obliteration of Feminine in the Western Culture
- SHIBATA, S., Modern Literature in Japan and Germany
- SUZUKI, S., Emblems and Religious Poetry in the 16th and 17th Centuries
- TADOKORO, M., Comparative Literature and Culture
- TANO, I., Modern American Literature and Culture
- YANAGISAWA, T., Language Typology, North-Western Caucasian Languages
- YOSHIMURA, M., English Romanticism

Graduate School of Mathematics (Furo-cho, Chikusa-ku, Nagoya 464-8602; tel. (52) 789-2429; internet www.math.nagoya-u.ac.jp/en):

- FUJIWARA, K., Algebraic Geometry
- GYOJA, A., Representation Theory
- KANAI, M., Geometry and Dynamic Systems
- KANNO, H., Mathematical Physics
- KIMURA, Y., Fluid Dynamics
- KOBAYASHI, R., Differential Geometry
- KONDO, S., Algebraic Geometry
- MATSUMOTO, K., Number Theory
- MIYAKE, M., Partial Differential Equations
- NAMIKAWA, Y., Algebraic Geometry
- NAYATANI, S., Conformal Geometry
- OHSAWA, T., Complex Analysis
- SATO, H., Geometry
- SHIOTA, M., Real Algebraic Geometry
- SHOJI, T., Representational Theory
- TSUCHIYA, A., Geometry and Mathematical Physics
- UMEMURA, H., Algebraic Geometry
- UZAWA, T., Representational Theory

International Cooperation Center for Agricultural Education (tel. (52) 789-4225; e-mail iccae@agr.nagoya-u.ac.jp; internet www.agr.nagoya-u.ac.jp/~iccae/index-j.html):

ASANUMA, S., Network Development
MATSUMOTO, T., Project Development

Research Center for Materials Science (Furo-cho, Chikusa-ku, Nagoya 464-8602; tel. (52) 789-5902; internet www.rcms.nagoya-u.ac.jp/intro/):

IMAE, T., Physical Chemistry
KITAMURA, M., Synthetic Organic Chemistry
SEKI, K., Physical Chemistry
TATSUMI, K., Inorganic Chemistry

Research Center of Health, Physical Fitness and Sports (tel. (52) 789-3946; internet www.htc.nagoya-u.ac.jp):

HIRUTA, S., Workload in Care Services
IKEGAMI, Y., Biomechanical Analysis of Human Movement
ISHIDA, K., Cardio-respiratory Responses during Exercise
IZUHARA, Y., Class Work Study of Physical Education
KONDO, T., Exercise and Gastrointestinal Function, Pancreatic Diseases, Breath and Skin Gas in Health and Diseases
NISHIDA, T., Achievement Motivation in Physical Education and Sports
OGAWA, T., Phenomenological Psychopathology, Psychoanalytic Psychotherapy of Adolescents
OSHIDA, Y., Exercise for Insulin Resistance
SHIMAOKA, K., Teaching of Exercise in Health Promotion Programmes
SHIMAOKA, M., Health and Physical Fitness in Workers
YAMAMOTO, Y., Motor Control and Learning from a Dynamical System Approach

Research Institute of Environmental Medicine (tel. (52) 789-3886; internet www.riem.nagoya-u.ac.jp/e/index.html):

KAMIYA, K., Molecular and Genomic Regulation of the Heart
KODAMA, I., Molecular and Cellular Cardiology
KOMATSU, Y., Synaptic Plasticity in the Visual Cortex
MIZUMURA, K., Neurophysiology of Pain
MURATA, Y., Molecular Genetics
SAWADA, M., Molecular and Cellular Neuroscience
SEO, H., Molecular Mechanism of Hormone Action
SUZUMURA, A., Neuroimmunology
YASUI, K., Bioinformation Analysis

School of Agricultural Sciences and Graduate School of Bioagricultural Sciences (tel. (52) 789-5266; e-mail info@agr.nagoya-u.ac.jp; internet www.agr.nagoya-u.ac.jp):

AOI, K., Polymer Chemistry
DOKE, N., Plant Pathology
EBIHARA, S., Animal Behavioural Physiology
FUKUSHIMA, K., Forest Chemistry
FUKUTA, K., Animal Morphology and Function
HATTORI, K., Plant Genetics and Breeding
HATTORI, S., Forest Resources Utilization
HIRASHIMA, Y., Biomaterials Engineering
ISOBE, M., Organic Chemistry
KIMURA, M., Soil Biology and Chemistry
KITAGAWA, Y., Stem Cell Engineering
KOBAYASHI, M., Biodynamics of Insect–Virus Interactions
KOBAYASHI, T., Gene Regulation
MAEDA, K., Reproductive Science
MAESHIMA, M., Cell Dynamics
MAKI, M., Molecular and Cellular Regulation
MATSUDA, T., Molecular Bioregulation
MIYAKE, H., Plant Resources and Environment
MIZUNO, T., Molecular Biology and Molecular Genetics
MORI, H., Developmental Signalling Biology
NAKAMURA, K., Biological Chemistry
NAKANO, H., Molecular Biotechnology
NAMIKAWA, T., Animal Genetics
NOGUCHI, T., Molecular Physiological Chemistry
OHTA, T., Forest Meteorology and Hydrology
OJIKA, M., Molecular Function Modelling
OMATA, T., Molecular Plant Physiology
OSAWA, T., Food and Biodynamics
SAKAGAMI, Y., Bioactive Natural Products Chemistry
SHIBATA, E., Forest Protection
SHIMADA, K., Animal Physiology
SOMIYA, H., Animal Information Biology
TAKABE, T., Biosphere Symbiosis
TAKENAKA, C., Forest Environment and Resources
TAKEYA, H., Socioeconomic Science of Food Production
TANAKA, T., Applied Entomology
TOMARU, N., Forest Ecology and Physiology
TSUCHIKAWA, S., Mechanical Engineering for Biological Materials
TSUGE, T., Microbes and Plant Production
YAGINUMA, T., Sericulture Entomological resources
YAMAUCHI, A., Biosphere Resources Cycling
YAMAKI, S., Horticultural Science
YOKOTA, H., Animal Feeds and Production
YOSHIMURA, T., Biomacromolecules

School and Graduate School of Economics (tel. (52) 789-4920; internet www.soec.nagoya-u.ac.jp):

ANDO, T., History of European Economic Thought
ARAYAMA, Y., Agricultural Policy and Economic Growth
HIRAKAWA, H., Asian Economics
KANAI, Y., British Monetary History during the Inter-war Period
KIMURA, S., Management Accounting
KISIDA, T., Organization
MINAGAWA, T., Microeconomic Foundations of Macroeconomics
NABESHIMA, N., History of Economic Thought, Political Economy
NAGAO, S., History of Economic and Social Thought, Political Economy
NAKANISHI, S., Japanese Economic History
NEMOTO, J., Applied Econometrics and Productivity Analysis
NOGUCHI, A., Financial Accounting
OHTA, S., Labour Economics
OKUMURA, R., Intertemporal Open-economy Macroeconomics
SATO, M., Conceptual Framework of Business Accounting
TAKAKUWA, S., Business Administration
TAKEUCHI, J., Comparative Study on Economic Development
TAKEUCHI, N., Stabilization Policy
TAMARU, M., Globalization and Japanese Economy
TAWADA, M., International Trade Theory
TOMOSUGI, Y., Management Audit
TSUKADA, H., Mathematical Finance
WAGO, H., Econometrics Analysis
YAMAMOTO, T., Financial Statement Analysis
YAMORI, N., Monetary Economics and Banking Theory

School and Graduate School of Education and Human Development (tel. (52) 789-2602; internet www.educa.nagoya-u.ac.jp):

HAYAKAWA, M., Philosophy of Human Becoming
HAYAMIZU, T., Psychology of Personality
IMAZU, K., Sociology of Education
KAGEYAMA, H., School Psychology
KANAI, A., Clinical Psychology
KATOH, S., History of Education
MATOBA, M., Methods of Education
MATUSHITA, H., Philosophy of Human Becoming
MORITA, M., Family Psychology
MURAKAMI, T., Psychometrics
NAKAJIMA, T., Educational Administration
NISHINO, S., Comparative Education
NOGUCHI, H., Psychometrics
OKADA, T., Cognitive Psychology
OTANI, T., Technologies in Education
TAKAGI, Y., School Environment
TERADA, M., Vocational and Technical Education
UEDA, T., Educational Management
YOSHIDA, T., Social Psychology

School and Graduate School of Engineering (Furo-cho, Chikusa-ku, Nagoya 464-8603; tel. (52) 789-3405; internet www.engg.nagoya-u.ac.jp):

ANDO, H., Mathematical Information Systems
ASAI, S., Electromagnetic Processing of Materials
ASAOKA, A., Soil Mechanics
BABA, Y., Applied Analytical Chemistry
FUJIMAKI, A., Integrated Quantum Devices Engineering
FUKUDA, T., Micro-nano System Control Engineering
FURUHASHI, T., Complex Systems
HAYAKAWA, Y., Intelligent Mechatronics
HIRASAWA, M., Nano-integration Engineering
HONDA, H., Bio-process Engineering
HOSOE, S., Mechatronics Control
ICHIMIYA, A., Fundamental Quantum Engineering
IGUCHI, T., Quantum Beam Measurement and Instrumentation
IIDA, T., Energy Environmental Safety Engineering
IIJIMA, S., Molecular Biology and Genetic Engineering
IKUTA, K., Biomedical Micro- and Nano-mechatronics
INOUE, J., Solid State Engineering
IRITANI, E., Mechanical Separation Process Engineering
ISHIDA, Y., Intelligent Manufacturing Machinery
ISHIHARA, K., Chemistry of Biologically Active Materials
ISHIKAWA, T., Deformation Processing of Materials
ITOH, Y., Infrastructure System Design
KAMIGAITO, M., Organic Chemistry of Macromolecules
KANEDA, Y., Computational Fluid Mechanics
KANETAKE, N., Structure and Morphology Control Engineering
KAWAIZUMI, F., Diffusional Process Engineering
KITANO, T., Radiation Chemistry
KODA, S., Chemical Physics of Condensed Matters
KONO, A., Optical Electronics
KOUMOTO, K., Solid State Materials
KUKITA, Y., Energy Transport Engineering
KURODA, K., Nano-material Characterization
KURODA, S., Quantum Material Physics and Engineering
KUWABARA, M., Materials Reaction Process Engineering
MATSUDA, H., Thermal Energy Engineering
MATSUDA, I., Design of Catalytic Reactions
MATSUI, M., Magnetism of Materials and Magnetics

MATSUI, T., Energy Functional Materials Engineering
MATSUMOTO, T., Knowledge-based Design
MATSUMURA, T., High Current and Power Engineering
MATSUSHITA, Y., Physical Chemistry of Materials
MITAKU, S., Biophysical Engineering
MITSUYA, Y., Micro- and Nano-instrumentation Engineering
MIYATA, T., Fatigue and Fracture of Materials
MIZUTANI, N., Coastal and Maritime Engineering
MIZUTANI, T., Quantum Nano-devices Engineering
MORINAGA, M., Materials Design
MURAMATSU, N., Human System Engineering
MUTO, S., Energy Materials Science under Extreme Conditions
NAKAMURA, A., Optical Physics
NAKAMURA, H., Concrete Materials and Structures
NAKAMURA, M., Resources and Environment
NAKAMURA, Y., Fluid Dynamics
NAKAZATO, K., Intelligent Devices
NIIMI, T., Micro Thermofluid Engineering
NISHIYAMA, H., Selective Organic Synthesis
NOMURA, H., Casting and Solidification Process Engineering
OHNO, N., Computational Solid Mechanics
OKIDO, M., Surface-interface Engineering
OKUMA, S., Information and Control Systems
ONOGI, K., Process Systems Engineering
SAITO, Y., Nano-structure Analysis
SAKAI, Y., Statistical Fluid Engineering
SAKATA, M., Structural Physics Engineering
SATO, K., Micro- and Nano-process Engineering
SATO, K., Communication Networks
SATSUMA, A., Catalyst Design
SAWADA, Y., Disaster Prevention, Geotechnical Engineering
SAWAKI, N., Semiconductor Electronics
SEKI, T., Molecular Assembly, Systems Engineering
SHAMOTO, E., Ultra-precision Engineering
SHIMADA, T., Super-microcomputing
SHINODA, T., Fabrication of Materials Engineering
SODA, K., Quantum Beam Materials Engineering
SOGA, T., Physical Gas Dynamics
SUGAI, H., Plasma Electronics
SUZUOKI, Y., Energy System and Engineering
TAGAWA, T., Chemical Reaction Engineering
TAKAGI, K., Functional Crystalline Chemistry
TAKAI, Y., Energy Device Engineering
TAKAMURA, S., Plasma Science and Technology
TAKEDA, K., Physical Chemistry of Materials
TAKEDA, Y., Nano-materials and Devices
TANAKA, E., Biomechanics
TANAKA, K., Materials and Mechanics
TANIGUCHI, G., Architectural Planning
TANIMOTO, M., Visual Information
TORIMOTO, T., Material Design Chemistry
TSUBAKI, J., Processes for the Functional Development of Materials
TSUJIMOTO, T., River, Coastal and Estuarine Hydro-morphodynamics
TSUNASHIMA, S., Spin Electronics
UEDA, T., Structural Mechanics
UMEHARA, N., Manufacturing Process Technology
UMEMURA, A., Propulsion Energy Systems Engineering
URITANI, A., Applied Nuclear Physics
USAMI, T., Structural Analysis
YAMADA, K., Control Systems Engineering
YAMAMOTO, I., Energy Materials Recycling Engineering
YAMANE, T., Protein Crystallography and Structural Biology
YAMANE, Y., Reactor Physics and Engineering
YAMASHITA, H., Heat Transfer and Combustion
YAMAZAKI, K., Energy Materials Science Engineering
YASHIMA, E., Polymer Materials Design
YOSHIKAWA, N., Aerospace Microsystems
ZAIMA, S., Nano-structured Electronic Device Engineering

School and Graduate School of Law (tel. (52) 789-4910; e-mail info@nomolog.nagoya-u.ac.jp; internet www.nomolog.nagoya-u.ac.jp):

AIKYO, K., Constitutional Law
AKANE, T., Criminal Procedure
CHIBA, E., Civil Law
FUJITA, S., Role of the Attorney in Legal Practice
FUKE, T., Public Finance Law and Tax Law
HACHISUKA, T., Role of the Attorney in Legal Practice
HAMADA, M., Corporate Law
HASEGAWA, Y., Civil Procedure
HASHIDA, H., Criminal Law
HONMA, Y., Civil Procedure
ICHIHASHI, K., Administrative Law
ISHII, M., Western Legal History
ISOBE, T., History of Western Political Thought
JIMBO, F., Japanese Legal History
KAGAYAMA, S., Civil Law
KAMINO, K., Administrative Law
KATO, H., Environmental Law
KATO, M., Civil Law
KAWANO, M., Civil Procedure
KITAZUMI, K., Western Political History
KOBAYASHI, R., Commercial Law
MAKINO, J., Business Law Practice
MASUDA, T., Japanese Political History
MATSUURA, Y., Legal Informatics, History of Legal Thought
MORI, H., Constitutional Law
MORIGIWA, Y., Jurisprudence
MOTO, H., Constitutional Law
NAKAHIGASHI, M., Corporate Law
NAKAYA, H., Civil Law
OBATA, K., International Law
OHSAWA, Y., Criminal Procedure
ONO, K., Political Science
SABURI, H., International Law
SADAKATA, M., International Politics
SINDO, H., Urban Politics
SUGAWARA, I., Sociology of Law
SUGIURA, K., Russian Law
SUZUKI, M., Intellectual Property Law
URABE, N., Constitutional Law
USHIRO, F., Public Administration
WADA, H., Labour Law
YAMAMOTO, T., Criminal Law

School and Graduate School of Letters (tel. (52) 789-2202; internet www.lit.nagoya-u.ac.jp):

ABE, Y., Anthropology, Study of Religions and the History of Japanese Thought
AMANO, M., English Linguistics
EMURA, H., Asian History
HAGA, S., Japanese History
IKEUCHI, S., Japanese History
INABA, N., Japanese History
INOUE, S., Asian History
KAMIO, M., English and American Literature
KAMITSUKA, Y., Chinese Philosophy
KANAYAMA, Y., Philosophy
KASUGA, Y., Japanese Culture
KIMATA, M., Aesthetics and Art History
KUGINUKI, T., Japanese Linguistics
MACHIDA, K., Linguistics
MATSUZAWA, K., French Literature
MIYAJI, A., Aesthetics and Art History
ODA, Y., Japanese Culture
OGAWA, M., Classics
SATO, S., Western History
SHIMADA, Y., Anthropology, Study of Religions and the History of Japanese Thought
SHIMIZU, S., German Literature
SHIOMURA, K., Japanese Literature
SUGIYAMA, H., Chinese Literature
SUTO, Y., Western History
TAKAHASHI, T., Japanese Literature
TAKEUCHI, H., Chinese Philosophy
TAKIKAWA, M., English and American Literature
TAMURA, H., Philosophy
TSUBOI, H., Japanese Culture
WADA, T., Indian Studies
WAZAKI, H., Anthropology, Study of Religions and the History of Japanese Thought
YAMADA, H., Philosophy
YAMAMOTO, N., Archaeology
YOSHIDA, J., Chinese Philosophy

School and Graduate School of Medicine (65 Tsurumai-cho, Showa-ku, Nagoya 466-8550; tel. (52) 744-2500; internet www.med.nagoya-u.ac.jp):

ANDO, H., Paediatric Surgery
ANDO, S., Clinical Nursing
AOYAMA, A., International Health
AOYAMA, T., Basic Radiological Technology
ASANO, M., Human Development Nursing and Midwifery
BAN, N., Family and Community Medicine
FUJIMOTO, T., Molecular Cell Biology
FURUKAWA, K., Molecular and Cellular Biology
GOTO, H., Therapeutic Medicine
GOTO, S., Fundamentals of Nursing
HAMAGUCHI, M., Molecular Pathogenesis
HAMAJIMA, N., Preventive Medicine
HIRAI, M., Public Health and Home Care Nursing
HIROSE, K., Cell Physiology
HOSHIYAMA, M., Basic Occupational Therapy
IDA, K., Basic Physical Therapy
IGUCHI, A., Geriatrics
IKEMATSU, Y., Clinical Nursing
ISHIGAKI, T., Radiology
ISHIGURE, N., Medical Radiological Technology
ISHIGURO, N., Orthopaedics
ISOBE, K., Immunology
ITO, H., Basic Medical Technology
ITO, K., Medical Administration and Politics
ITO, S., Basic Radiological Technology
KAIBUCHI, K., Cell Pharmacology
KAJITA, E., Public Health and Home Care Nursing
KATSUMATA, Y., Legal Medicine and Bioethics
KAWAMURA, M., Basic Physical Therapy
KAWATSU, Y., Fundamentals of Nursing
KIKKAWA, F., Obstetrics and Gynaecology
KIKUCHI, A., Molecular Mycology and Medicine
KIUCHI, T., Transplant Surgery
KOBAYASHI, K., Basic Physical Therapy
KODERA, Y., Medical Radiological Technology
KOIKE, Y., Medical Laboratory Technology
KOJIMA, S., Paediatrics
KOJIMA, T., Medical Laboratory Technology
KOMORI, K., Vascular Surgery
MAEDA, H., Medical Radiological Technology
MAEKAWA, A., Public Health and Homecare Nursing
MATSUMURA, Y., Clinical Nursing
MATSUO, S., Clinical Immunology
MIYATA, T., Cell Biology
MIZUTANI, M., Clinical Nursing

MORI, N., Biological Response
MORITA, S., Human Development Nursing and Midwifery
MURATE, T., Medical Laboratory Technology
MUROHARA, T., Cardiology
NABESHIMA, T., Clinical Pharmacy
NAGASE, F., Medical Laboratory Technology
NAKAMURA, S., Clinical Pathophysiology
NAKAO, A., Gastroenterological Surgery
NAKASHIMA, T., Otorhinolaryngology
NAOE, T., Haematology
NARAMA, M., Human Development Nursing and Midwifery
NASU, T., Occupational and Environmental Health
NIMURA, Y., Surgical Oncology
NISHIYAMA, Y., Molecular Virology
OBATA, Y., Medical Radiological Technology
OHNO, K., Neurogenetics and Bioinformatics
OHTA, M., Molecular Bacteriology
OISO, Y., Diabetology and Endocrinology
OTA, K., Fundamentals of Nursing
OZAKI, N., Psychiatry
SAKAKIBARA, H., Public Health and Home Care Nursing
SHIMADA, Y., Anaesthesiology
SHIMAMOTO, K., Medical Radiological Technology
SHIMOKATA, K., Clinical Preventive Medicine
SOBUE, G., Neurology
SOKABE, M., Cell Biophysics
SUGIMURA, K., Basic Occupational Therapy
SUZUKI, K., Basic Occupational Therapy
SUZUKI, K., Human Development Nursing and Midwifery
SUZUKI, S., Applied Physical Therapy
TABUSHI, K., Basic Radiological Technology
TACHIKAWA, K., Hospital and Healthcare Business Management
TAGAWA, Y., Applied Occupational Therapy
TAKAGI, K., Basic Medical Technology
TAKAHASHI, M., Tumour Pathology
TAKAHASHI, T., Molecular Carcinogenesis
TAKAMATSU, J., Transfusion Medicine
TAKEZAWA, J., Emergency and Critical Care Medicine
TERASAKI, H., Protective Care for Sensory Disorders
TOMITA, Y., Dermatology
TORII, S., Plastic and Reconstructive Surgery
TOYOSHIMA, H., Public Health
UEDA, M., Maxillofacial Surgery
UEDA, Y., Cardio-thoracic Surgery
WAKUSAWA, S., Basic Medical Technology
WATANABE, N., Clinical Nursing
YAMADA, S., Applied Physical Therapy
YAMAUCHI, K., Medical Information and Management Science
YAMAUCHI, T., Fundamentals of Nursing
YOKOI, T., Medical Laboratory Technology
YOSHIDA, J., Neurosurgery

School and Graduate School of Science (Furo-cho, Chikusa-ku, Nagoya 464-8602; tel. (52) 789-2394; internet www.sci.nagoya-u.ac.jp/index.html):

AIBA, H., Molecular Biology
AWAGA, K., Materials Chemistry
ENDO, T., Biochemistry
FUKUI, Y., Astrophysics
HIRASHIMA, D., Condensed Matter Physics
HOMMA, M., Bioenergetics
HORI, H., Evolutionary Genetics
IIO, T., Biophysics
ISHII, K., Theoretical Biology
ITOH, M., Solid State Physics
ITOH, S., Biophysics, Bioenergetics
KATOU, K., Physiology of Plant Growth
KONDO, S., Pattern Formation
KONDO, T., Plant Physiology
KOUYAMA, T., Biophysics
KUNIEDA, H., Astrophysics
KUROIWA, A., Developmental Biology
MACHIDA, Y., Molecular Biology
MATSUMOTO, K., Molecular Biology
MORI, I., Molecular Neurobiology
NAKANISHI, T., Nuclear and Particle Physics
NISHIDA, Y., Animal Development
NIWA, K., Nuclear and Particle Physics
NOZAKI, K., Nonlinear Physics
ODA, Y., Developmental Biology
OHMINE, I., Physical Chemistry
OHSAWA, Y., Plasma Physics
OHSHIMA, T., Nuclear and Particle Physics
OKAMOTO, Y., Theoretical Biophysics
OWARIBE, K., Cell Adhesion and Cytoskeleton
SANDA, I., Particle Physics and Fields
SATO, M., Solid State Physics
SATO, S., Astrophysics
SAWADA, H., Marine Biochemistry
SHIBAI, H., Astrophysics
SHINOHARA, H., Physical Chemistry
SUGAI, S., Solid State Physics
SUZUMURA, Y., Solid State Physics
TOMIMATSU, A., Theory of Gravitation
UEMURA, D., Organic Chemistry
WADA, N., Low Temperature Physics
WATANABE, Y., Bioinorganic Chemistry
YAMAGUCHI, S., Organic Chemistry
YAMAWAKI, K., Elementary Particle Physics and Fields

School of Informatics and Sciences and Graduate School of Information Science (tel. (52) 789-4716; e-mail syomuk@info.human.nagoya-u.ac.jp; internet www.is.nagoya-u.ac.jp):

AGUSA, K., Information Engineering
ARITA, T., Complex Systems Science
AZEGAMI, H., Complex Systems Science
HAYAKAWA, Y., Complex Systems Science
HIRATA, T., Computer Science and Mathematical Informatics
HIROKI, S., Complex Systems Science
ISHII, K., Systems and Social Informatics
JINBO, M., Computer Science and Mathematical Informatics
KOGA, N., Complex Systems Science
MATSUBARA, Y., Computer Science and Mathematical Informatics
MATSUMOTO, H., Computer Science and Mathematical Informatics
MATSUO, S., Complex Systems Science
MITSUI, T., Computer Science and Mathematical Informatics
MIWA, K., Media Science
MORI, M., Complex Systems Science
MORI, T., Complex Systems Science
MURASE, H., Media Science
NAGAOKA, M., Complex Systems Science
OHNISHI, N., Media Science
SAITO, H., Media Science
SAKABE, T., Information Engineering
SAKAI, M., Computer Science and Mathematical Informatics
SASAI, M., Complex Systems Science
SUENAGA, Y., Media Science
SUGIYAMA, Y., Complex Systems Science
TAKADA, H., Information Engineering
TAKAGI, N., Information Engineering
TAKAHAMA, M., Information Engineering
TAKEDA, K., Media Science
TODAYAMA, K., Systems and Social Informatics
WATANABE, T., Systems and Social Informatics
YASUDA, T., Systems and Social Informatics
YASUMOTO, M., Computer Science and Mathematical Informatics
YOKOI, S., Systems and Social Informatics
YOKOSAWA, H., Complex Systems Science
YONEYAMA, M., Systems and Social Informatics

Solar–Terrestrial Environment Laboratory (Honohara 3-13, Toyokawa, Aichi Pref., 442-8507; tel. (533) 86-3154; internet www.stelab.nagoya-u.ac.jp):

FUJII, R., Space Science (Magnetosphere and Ionosphere Physics
ITOW, Y., Cosmic Ray, Dark Matter and Neutrino Physics
KAMIDE, Y., Solar–Terrestrial Physics
KIKUCHI, T., Solar–Terrestrial Physics
KOJIMA, M., Interplanetary Space Physics
MATSUMI, Y., Atmospheric Photochemistry and Chemical Kinetics
MIZUNO, A., Atmospheric Chemistry and Radio Astronomy
MURAKI, Y., Solar Cosmic Ray Physics
OGAWA, T., Upper Atmosphere Physics
OGINO, T., Space Plasma Physics

NARA WOMEN'S UNIVERSITY

Kita-Uoya-Higashi-Machi, Nara City 630-8506

Telephone: (742) 20-3736
E-mail: iec@cc.nara-wu.ac.jp
Internet: www.nara-wu.ac.jp

Founded 1908

Language of instruction: Japanese
Academic year: April to March

Pres.: HARUKI IMAOKA
Sec.-Gen.: HIROSHI SAITO

Library of 533,000 vols
Number of teachers: 197
Number of students: 2,682

Publications: *Studies in Home Economics*, *Graduate School of Human Culture*

DEANS

Faculty of Human Life and Environment: Prof. K. MIKI
Faculty of Letters: Prof. Y. YANAGISAWA
Faculty of Science: Prof. K. IWAI
Graduate School of Human Culture (Doctorate Course): Prof. M. NAKAJIMA

NIIGATA UNIVERSITY

8050 Ikarashi Ni-no-cho, Nishi-ku, Niigata 950-2181

Telephone: (25) 262-6246
E-mail: kokusai@adm.niigata-u.ac.jp
Internet: www.niigata-u.ac.jp

Founded 1949
Independent
Academic year: April to March

Pres.: AKIRA HASEGAWA
Vice-Pres: MASAHIRO SHIMADA, SHOJI KOHNO, SUKEO FUKASAWA, TADAO ITO, TAKEHIKO BANDO
Dir of Univ. Library: TAKASHI OOKUMA

Library: see under Libraries and Archives
Number of teachers: 1,226
Number of students: 12,901

DEANS

Faculty of Agriculture: T. OHYAMA
Faculty of Dentistry: T. MAEDA
Faculty of Economics: Y. SUGAHARA
Faculty of Education and Human Sciences: T. MORITA
Faculty of Engineering: H. OHKAWA
Faculty of Humanities: H. HONDA
Faculty of Law: T. KATO
Faculty of Medicine: M. UCHIYAMA
Faculty of Science: K. SHUTO
Graduate School of Education: T. MORITA
Graduate School of Health Sciences: M. TAKAHASHI
Graduate School of Management of Technology: M. MASUDA
Graduate School of Medical and Dental Sciences: M. UCHIYAMA

Graduate School of Science and Technology: T. HASEGAWA
Graduate School of the Study of Modern Society and Culture: Y. SUZUKI
School of Law: K. HONMA

OBIHIRO UNIVERSITY OF AGRICULTURE AND VETERINARY MEDICINE

Inada-cho, Obihiro, Hokkaido 080-8555
Telephone: (155) 49-5111
E-mail: soumu@obihiro.ac.jp
Internet: www.obihiro.ac.jp

Founded 1941
Independent
Academic year: April to March

Pres.: NAOYOSHI SUZUKI
Dir of Admin. Bureau: M. KIKUCHI
Dir of Univ. Library: T. KAWABATA

Library of 190,426 vols
Number of teachers: 149
Number of students: 1,431

Department of Agro-Environmental Science: JUNKO MARUYAMA
Department of Applied Veterinary Science: TOSHIKAZU SHIRAHATA
Department of Basic Veterinary Science: JUNZO YAMADA
Department of Clinical Veterinary Science: TAKAO SARASHINA
Department of Pathobiological Science: MASAKAZU NISHIMURA
Research Unit of Animal Physiology and Function: IKICHI ARAI
Research Unit of Animal Production Science: MIKAMI MASAYUKI
Research Unit of Engineering in Agricultural and Biological Systems: KENICHI ISHIBASHI
Research Unit of Environmental and Rural Engineering: FUJIO TSUCHIYA
Research Unit of Farm Management: ICHIO SASAKI
Research Unit of Food and Resource Economics: SHIGERU ITO
Research Unit of Molecular Cell-Regulation Science: HIROSHI MASUDA
Research Unit of Plant Bioscience: SOUHEI SAWADA
Research Unit of Socio-Environmental Science: MASARU UMETSU

Publication: *Research Bulletin* (on Natural Sciences and on Humanities and Social Sciences, each 2 a year)

OCHANOMIZU UNIVERSITY

2-1-1 Otsuka, Bunkyo-ku, Tokyo 112-8610
Telephone: (3) 5978-5106
E-mail: soumu2@cc.ocha.ac.jp
Internet: www.ocha.ac.jp

Founded 1874, reorganized 1949 as Nat. Univ.
Private control
Language of instruction: Japanese
Academic year: April to March

Pres.: Dr SAWAKO HANYU
Admin.: HIDEYASU YAMAZAKI
Librarian: SARUMARU MAKIKO

Library of 686,063 vols
Number of teachers: 364
Number of students: 3,117

Publications: *Natural Science Report of the Ochanomizu University* (2 a year), *Ochanomizu University Studies in Art and Culture* (1 a year)

DEANS

Faculty of Human Life and Environmental Sciences: MUNEKAZU FUJITA
Faculty of Letters and Education: TOSHIHIKO YONEDA
Faculty of Science: AKIO SUGAMOTO
Graduate School of Humanities and Sciences: YOSHIHIRO MOGAMI

OITA UNIVERSITY

700 Dannoharu, Oita City
Telephone: (97) 569-3311
E-mail: webmaster@ad.oita-u.ac.jp
Internet: www.oita-u.ac.jp

Founded 1949
Independent
Language of instruction: Japanese
Academic year: April to March (2 semesters)

Pres.: IWAO NAKAYAMA
Dir-Gen. of Admin. Bureau: TAKANOBU IRIE
Dir of Univ. Library: KOICHI OBA

Library of 541,000 vols
Number of teachers: 569
Number of students: 5,802

DEANS

Faculty of Economics: MINORU UNO
Faculty of Education and Welfare Science: MAKOTO OSHIMA
Faculty of Engineering: TADAO EZAKI
Graduate School of Social Service Administration: TAKATOMI NINOMIYA

ATTACHED INSTITUTE

Tsurumi Seaside Research Institute: Aza-Hirama, Oaza-Ariakeura, Tsurumi-machi, Minamiamabe-gun, Oita 876-1204; tel. (972) 33-1133

OKAYAMA UNIVERSITY

1-1-1, Tsushima-Naka, Okayama 700-8530
Telephone: (86) 252-1111
E-mail: ace7038@adm.okayama-u.ac.jp
Internet: www.okayama-u.ac.jp

Founded 1949
Independent
Academic year: April to March (2 semesters)

Pres.: ICHIRO KONO
Vice-Pres: KYOZO CHIBA, KIICHI MATSUHATA, HIROKAZU OSAKI, HAJIME INOUE
Dir-Gen.: T. ABE

Library: see under Libraries and Archives
Number of teachers: 1,341 full-time
Number of students: 14,091

Publication: *Okayama University Bulletin*

DEANS

Dental School: T. WATANABE
Faculty of Agriculture: T. SHIRAISHI
Faculty of Economics: T. MATSUMOTO
Faculty of Education: N. MORIKAWA
Faculty of Engineering: H. TOTSUJI
Faculty of Environmental Science and Technology: T. ADACHI
Faculty of Law: S. TANI
Faculty of Letters: F. TAKAHASHI
Faculty of Pharmaceutical Sciences: T. KIMURA
Faculty of Science: K. KASE
Graduate School of Environmental Science (Doctorate Course): F. NAKASUJI
Graduate School of Humanities and Social Sciences (Doctorate Course): T. TAKAHASHI
Graduate School of Medicine, Dentistry and Pharmaceutical Science (Doctorate Course): H. KUMON
Medical School: K. OGUMA
School of Law: M. OKADA, Graduate School of Natural Science and Technology (Doctorate Course): J. TAKADA

PROFESSORS

Faculty of Agriculture (tel. (86) 251-8273):
BABA, N., Chemistry of Biological Functions
ICHINOSE, Y., Genetic Engineering
INABA, A., Postharvest Agriculture
INAGAKI, K., Applied Biochemistry and Biotechnology
IZUMIMOTO, M., Animal Food Technology
KAMIMURA, K., Microbial Function
KANZAKI, H., Chemistry and Biochemistry of Bioactive Compounds
KIMURA, Y., Bioapplied Enzymology
KOMATSU, Y., Farm Management and Data Processing Methods
KONDO, Y., Animal Physiology and Pharmacology
KUBOTA, N., Horticultural Crop Production
KUNIEDA, T., Animal Genetics
KURODA, T., Crop Production Science
MASUDA, M., Olericulture
MIYAMOTO, T., Animal Food Function
NAKAJIMA, S., Chemistry and Biochemistry of Bioactive Compounds
NAKASUJI, F., Integrated Pest Management
NIWA, K., Animal Reproduction
OIKAWA, T., Animal Genetics and Breeding
OKAMOTO, G., Pomology
OKUDA, K., Animal Reproduction
SAKAGUCHI, E., Animal Nutrition
SAKAMOTO, K., Applied Plant Ecology
SASAKAWA, H., Rhizosphere Biological Chemistry
SATO, K., Animal Genetics and Breeding
SATOH, T., Resources Management
SHIMOISHI, Y., Biological Information of Chemistry
SHIRAISHI, T., Plant Pathology
SUGIO, T., Microbial Function
TADA, M., Biological Chemistry of Foods
TAHARA, M., Cell Engineering
TSUDA, M., Crop Whole-plant Physiology
YOKOMIZO, I., Farm Management and Date Processing Methods
YOSHIKAWA, K., Physiological Plant Ecology

Faculty of Economics (tel. (86) 251-7345):
CHINO, T., Health Economics
ENOMOTO, S., Strategic Management
GENKA, T., Comparative Economic Systems
HARUNA, S., Industrial Organization
HIRANO, M., Local Public Finance
KONISHI, N., Accounting
KOYAMA, Y., Financial Management
KUROKAWA, K., Economic History of the United States
MATSUDA, Y., Organizational Behaviour and Organizational Change
MATSUMOTO, T., Economic History of Modern Asia
NAGAHATA, H., Statistics, Information Science
NAKAMURA, R., Urban and Regional Economics
NIIMURA, S., History of Economic Thought
OTA, Y., History of Economic Thought
SHIMONO, K., Economic History of Modern Japan
TAKEMURA, S., Theory of the Firm, Industrial Organization
WADA, Y., Social Economics
YOSHIDA, T., Social Statistics, Econometrics
ZHANG, X., Economic Statistics

Faculty of Education (tel. (86) 251-7584):
ARIYOSHI, H., Teacher Training
DOI, Y., Algebra
FUCHIGAMI, K., School Organizational Psychology
FUJITA, R., Housing and Living Design
FUKUNAGA, S., British Literature
FURUICHI, Y., Educational Psychology
IDO, K., Music Education
IKEDA, A., Geometry
INADA, T., Japanese Literature
INOUE, S., Educational Psychology
KAGA, M., Biomechanics
KANETA, Y., Composition
KANI, K., Material Engineering
KASAI, Y., Science of Food Preparation
KAWATA, T., Food Science
KISHIMOTO, H., Political Science

KITA, H., Chemistry
KITAGAMI, M., School Management
KONDO, I., Information Technology
KOSAKO, M., English Philology
KUSACHI, I., Mineralogy
MATSUOKA, Y., Clinical Psychology
MIZUNO, M., Developmental Psychology
MONDEN, S., Education for School Health Care
MORI, K., Chinese Philosophy
MORIKAWA, N., Pedagogy
MUSHIAKI, M., Vocal Music
NAKAO, Y., Chemistry
NII, I., Arts and Crafts Education
NISHIYAMA, M., Paintings
NOBE, M., Sociology
OGAWA, T., Paintings
OGURA, H., Biology
OHASHI, K., Manufacturing Education
OHASHI, Y., Physical Education
OKU, S., Music Education
ONO, H., Curriculum Development
ONOYAMA, K., Ceramics
SAKATA, N., Physical Education
SANADA, S., Education for Handicapped Children
SANEKATA, N., Mathematical Analysis
SUGAHARA, M., Japanese Education
SUGIHARA, R., Clothing Science
TAKAHASHI, K., Medicine for School Health Care
TAKAHASHI, T., Mathematics Education
TAKATSUKA, S., English Language Teaching
TAKAYAMA, Y., Social Studies Education
TANAKA, K., Science Education
TANAKA, K., Social Psychology
TANAKA, M., European History
TOKUNAGA, T., Sport Education
UEHARA, K., History
YAMAGUCHI, H., Computer Education
YAMAGUCHI, S., Psychology of Pre-school Children
YAMAMOTO, H., Musicology
YAMAMOTO, H., Systems Engineering
YAMAMOTO, T., Clinical Psychology
YAMANAKA, Y., History of Japanese Education
YAMASHITA, N., Solid State Spectroscopy
YANAGIHARA, M., Psychology of Handicapped Children
YOSHIDA, N., Japanese Language

Faculty of Engineering (tel. (86) 251-8004):

FUNABIKI, N., Distributed Systems
GOFUKU, A., Systems Applications
GOTO, K., Functional Materials Chemistry
HASHIGUCHI, K., Foundations of Information Science
HATA, M., Distributed Systems
INABA, H., Energy Engineering
INOUE, A., Systems Theory
KAMIURA, Y., Electronics
KANATANI, K., Foundations of Information Science
KISHIMOTO, A., Functional Materials Chemistry
KOGA, R., Network Architecture
KONISHI, M., Electrical Engineering
MASAKI, A., Information-based Engineering Systems
MIYAZAKI, S., Systems Intelligence
MORIKAWA, Y., Foundations of Information and Communication
NAKANISHI, K., Biotechnology
NARA, S., Electronics
NOGI, S., Electronics
NORITSUGU, T., Systems Control
OHMORI, H., Applied Bioscience
OSAKA, A., Bioactive Materials
SAITO, S., Bioactive Materials
SAKAI, H., Biotechnology
SAKAI, T., Molecular Transformation Chemistry
SAKATA, Y., Functional Materials Chemistry
SENUMA, T., Control of Material Properties
SHAKUNAGA, T., Artificial Intelligence
SHIMAMURA, K., Functional Materials Chemistry
SISHIDO, M., Biomolecular Engineering
SUGIYAMA, Y., Foundations of Information and Communication
SUZUKI, K., Systems Theory
SUZUMORI, K., Systems Control
TADA, N., Material Engineering
TAKADA, J., Functional Materials Chemistry
TAKAHASHI, N., Electrical Engineering
TAKAI, K., Molecular Transformation Chemistry
TANAKA, H., Molecular Transformation Chemistry
TANAKA, Y., Systems Applications
TANIGUCHI, H., Information-based Engineering Systems
TOMITA, E., Energy Engineering
TORAYA, T., Applied Bioscience
TORII, T., Materials Engineering
TOTSUJI, H., Electronics
TUKADA, K., Electronics
TUKAMOTO, S., Manufacturing Engineering
UNEYAMA, K., Molecular Transformation Chemistry
UNO, Y., Design and Manufacturing Technology
WASHIO, S., Engineering Measurement
YAMADA, H., Biomolecular Engineering
YAMASAKI, S., Artificial Intelligence
YANASE, S., Engineering Measurement
YOKOHIRA, T., Network Architecture
YOSHIDA, A., Design and Manufacturing Technology

Faculty of Law (tel. (86) 251-7345):

ARAKI, M., Western Political History
ATAKA, K., Local Tax and Finance Law
HARANO, A., Administrative Law
HATANO, S., European Legal History
KAWAHARA, Y., International Politics
KOYAMA, H., Administrative Law
KUROKAMI, N., Law of International Organizations
NAKAMURA, M., Information Law and Policy
NAKATOMI, K., Constitutional Law
NISHIHARA, J., Civil Law
OBATA, T., Japanese Political History
SANO, H., Private International Law
TANI, S., Political Process
TONAI, K., Labour Law
YAMAGUCHI, K., Constitutional Law
YONEYAMA, K., Commercial Law
ZHANG, H., Chinese Law

Faculty of Letters (tel. (86) 251-7345):

EGUCHI, Y., Japanese Linguistics
HASEGAWA, Y., Psychology
HISANO, N., History of Japanese Culture
INADA, T., Archaeology
INAMURA, S., Ethics
JIANG, K., Modern History of Japanese Culture
KANASEKI, T., Comparative Study of Cultures
KITAMURA, K., Cultural Anthropology
KITAOKA, T., Religious Philosophy
KOBAYASHI, T., Sociology
KURACHI, K., History of Japanese Culture
MATSUMOTO, M., English Historical Linguistics
MIYAKE, S., Operatic Studies
NAGASE, H., French Literature
NAGATA, R., European History
NIIMURA, Y., History of Chinese Culture
NIIRO, I., Archaeology
NISHIMAE, T., American Literature
SHIMOSADA, M., Chinese Literature
TAKAHASHI, F., Ethics
TAKAHASHI, T., Old German Language and Literature
TAKUMA, F., Modern German History
TANAKA, T., Psychology
TAYA, R., Psychology
TERAOKA, T., History of German Literature
TSUJI, S., Linguistics
UCHIDA, K., Geography
WADA, M., Linguistics
WATANABE, M., Japanese Literature
YAMAGUCHI, K., Aesthetics
YAMAGUCHI, N., History of French Thought
YOSHIOKA, F., English Literature

Faculty of Pharmaceutical Sciences (tel. (86) 251-7913):

HARAYAMA, T., Synthetic and Medicinal Chemistry
HIROTA, T., Pharmaceutical Chemistry
KAMEI, C., Pharmacology
KAWASAKI, H., Clinical Pharmaceutical Science
KIMURA, T., Pharmaceutics
KUROSAKI, Y., Pharmaceutics
MORIYAMA, Y., Neurochemistry
NARIMATSU, S., Health Chemistry
OKAMOTO, K., Bio-organic Chemistry
SAITO, Y., Pharmaceutical Analytical Chemistry
SASAKI, K., Pharmaceutical Fundamental Science
SHINODA, S., Environmental Hygiene
TAMAGAKE, K., Pharmaceutical Physical Chemistry
TSUCHIYA, T., Microbiology
WATAYA, Y., Medicinal Information
YAMAMOTO, I., Immunochemistry
YAMAMOTO, S., Molecular Microbiology
YOSHIDA, T., Pharmacognosy

Faculty of Science (tel. (86) 251-7764):

ASAMI, M., Petrology
CHIBA, H., Isotope Geochemistry
HARADA, I., Theoretical Physics
HIROKAWA, M., Mathematical Physics
ISHIDA, H., Structural Chemistry
IWAMI, M., Thin Films and Surface Physics
KAGAWA, H., Molecular Biology
KAMADA, T., Molecular Cell Biology
KASE, K., Resources Geology
KAWAGUCHI, K., Molecular Spectroscopy
KIMURA, M., Organic Function Chemistry
KIYOHARA, K., Differential Geometry
KOBAYASHI, T., Physics of Strongly Correlated Systems
KOJIMA, M., Coordination Chemistry
KURODA, Y., Inorganic Chemistry
KUTSUKAKE, K., Molecular Genetics
MACHIDA, K., Mathematical Physics
MOTOMIZU, S., Analytical Chemistry
NAGAO, M., Surface Chemistry
NAKAMURA, H., Number Theory
NAKANO, I., High Energy Physics
NARAOKA, H., Organic Cosmogeochemistry
NOGAMI, Y., Low Dimensional Material Physics
ODA, H., Seismology
OSHIMA, K., Physics of Quantum Materials
ONO, F., Physics of Materials under Extreme Conditions
SAKAI, T., Differential Geometry
SAKAMOTO, T., Marine Biology
SAKUDA, M., Neutrino Physics
SATAKE, K., Organic Chemistry
SATO, R., Analysis
SAWADA, A., Quantum Electromagnetic Physics
SHEN, J.-R., Plant Physiology and Structural Biology
SHIBATA, T., Geology
SHIMAKAWA, K., Petrology and Marine Geology
SUZUKI, I., Geophysics
TAKAGI, K., Synthetic Organic Chemistry
TAKAHASHI, S., Endocrinology
TAKAHASHI, T., Plant Molecular Genetics
TAKAHASHI, Y., Plant Physiology and Plant Molecular Biology
TAMURA, H., Analysis
TANAKA, H., Theoretical Chemistry
TOMIOKA, K., Chronobiology

TSUKAMOTO, O., Atmospheric Science
UEDA, H., Molecular and Developmental Biology
YAMADA, H., Representation Theory
YAMAMOTO, H., Organic Chemistry
YAMAMOTO, S., Physical Chemistry
YAMAMOTO, Y., Plant Physiology and Biochemistry
YOKOYA, T., Photo-emission Condensed Matter Physics
YOSHIKAWA, Y., Inorganic Chemistry
YOSHIMURA, H., Particle Physics-based Cosmology
YOSHINO, Y., Algebra
ZHENG, G.-Q., Low-Temperature Condensed-Matter Physics

Graduate School of Medicine, Dentistry and Pharmaceutical Sciences:
ABE, K., Neuroscience
AWAYA, T., Legal Medicine and Bioethics
DATE, I., Neuroscience
FUKUI, K., Oral Pathobiology
GOHDA, E., Immunochemistry
HARAYAMA, T., Synthetic and Medicinal Chemistry
HATANO, T., Natural Product Chemistry
HIRAMATSU, Y., Obstetrics and Gynaecology
HIROTA, T., Pharmaceutical Chemistry
HUH, N., Basic Oncology
ISHIZU, H., Legal Medicine and Bioethics
IWATSUKI, K., Sensory and Locomotory Function Medicine
KAMEI, C., Pharmacology
KANAZAWA, S., Radiology and Laboratory Medicine
KATO, N., Basic Oncology
KATSU, T., Pharmaceutical Physical Chemistry
KAWAKAMI, N., Social Medicine and Environmental Health Sciences
KAWASAKI, H., Clinical Pharmaceutical Science
KIMATA, Y., Sensory and Locomotory Function Medicine
KIMURA, T., Pharmaceutics
KISHI, K., Oral and Maxillofacial Surgery and Diagnostic Medicine
KITAYAMA, S., Oral Pathobiology
KOIDE, N., Radiology and Laboratory Medicine
KUBOKI, T., Oral Functional Reconstruction
KUMON, H., Basic and Clinical Pathophysiology
KURODA, S., Basic and Clinical Neuroscience
KUROSAKI, Y., Pharmaceutics
MAKINO, H., Basic and Clinical Pathophysiology
MATSUI, H., Basic and Clinical Neuroscience
MATSUO, R., Oral Biology
MINAGI, S., Oral Functional Reconstruction
MIYOSHI, S., Environmental Hygiene
MORISHIMA, T., Obstetrics and Gynaecology
MORITA, K., Anaesthesiology and Emergency Medicine
MORIYAMA, Y., Neurochemistry
NAGAI, N., Oral Pathobiology
NAKAYAMA, E., Infection and Immunology
NARIMATSU, S., Health Chemistry
NINOMIYA, Y., Human Biology
NISHIZAKI, K., Sensory and Locomotory Function Medicine
OGAWA, N., Basic and Clinical Neuroscience
OGUMA, K., Infection and Immunology
OHE, T., Cardiovascular Medicine
OHTSUKA, A., Human Biology
OHTSUKA, Y., Basic and Clinical Neuroscience
OKAMOTO, K., Bio-organic Chemistry
SAITO, Y., Pharmaceutical Analytical Chemistry
SANO, S., Cardiovascular Pathophysiology
SASAKI, A., Oral and Maxillofacial Surgery and Diagnostic Medicine
SASAKI, J., Anatomy
SASAKI, K., Pharmaceutical Fundamental Science
SHIMADA, M., Oral and Maxillofacial Surgery and Diagnostic Medicine
SHIMIZU, K., Basic Oncology
SHIMIZU, N., Basic and Clinical Pathophysiology
SHIMONO, T., Oral Health, Growth and Development
SHIRATORI, Y., Basic and Clinical Pathophysiology
SUGAHARA, T., Oral and Maxillofacial and Diagnostic Medicine
SUGIMOTO, T., Oral Biology
SUZUKI, K., Oral Functional Reconstruction
TAKASHIBA, S., Oral Health, Growth and Development
TAKEI, K., Human Biology
TAKIGAWA, M., Oral Biology
TANAKA, N., Basic and Clinical Pathophysiology
TANIMOTO, M., Basic and Clinical Pathophysiology
TSUCHIYA, T., Microbiology
TSUTSUI, K., Human Biology
WATANABE, T., Oral Health, Growth and Development
WATAYA, Y., Medicinal Information
YAMADA, M., Infection and Immunology
YAMAMOTO, S., Molecular Microbiology
YAMAMOTO, T., Oral Biology
YAMAMOTO, T., Oral Health, Growth and Development
YASUDA, T., Basic and Clinical Pathophysiology
YOSHINO, T., Basic and Clinical Pathophysiology
YOSHIYAMA, M., Oral Functional Reconstruction

Medical School:
AKIMOTO, N., Adult Nursing
ARAO, Y., Clinical Biology
ASARI, S., Adult Nursing
FUJINO, F., Adult Nursing
FUKAI, K., Human Nursing
IKEDA, S., Clinical Pathology
JOJA, I., Medical Radiotechnology
KAGEYAMA, J., Adult Nursing
KANDA, A., Community Health Nursing
KATAOKA, M., Clinical Biology
KATO, H., Medicinal Radioscience
KATO, K., Human Nursing
KAWASAKI, S., Medical Radioscience
KURAZONO, H., Clinical Biology
KUSACHI, S., Clinical Pathology
NAKAGIRI, Y., Medical Radiotechnology
NAKATA, Y., Clinical Pathology
NISHIDA, M., Adult Nursing
ODA, M., Maternal and Child Health Nursing
OHTA, N., Maternal and Child Health Nursing
OKA, H., Clinical Biology
OKAMOTO, M., Clinical Biology
OKANO, H., Community Health Nursing
OKUDA, H., Maternal and Child Health Nursing
ONO, K., Maternal and Child Health Nursing
SENDA, Y., Adult Nursing
SUMIMOTO, T., Medical Radioscience
TAKAHASHI, K., Clinical Pathology
TAGUCHI, T., Medical Radiotechnology
TAKEDA, Y., Medical Radiotechnology
YAMAMOTO, Y., Medical Radioscience
YAMAOKA, K., Medical Radioscience
YOKOYAMA, Y., Community Health Nursing

School of Law (tel. (86) 251-7345):
AKAMATSU, H., Civil Law
FUJITA, H., Civil Law
FUJIWARA, K., Criminal Procedure
HAGA, R., Commercial Law
HAGIWARA, S., Criminal Law
IGUCHI, F., Constitutional Law
KITAGAWA, K., Criminal Law
MATSUMURA, K., Civil Procedure
MIURA, O., Commercial Law
OKADA, M., Administrative Law
SATO, S., Investigative Law
UEDA, S., Criminal Procedure

ATTACHED INSTITUTES

Institute for Study of the Earth's Interior: 827, Yamada, Misasa-cho, Tohaku-gun, Tottori 682-0193; tel. (858) 43-1215; internet www.misasa.okayama-u.ac.jp; f. 1985; Dir Prof. E. NAKAMURA.

Research Institute for Bioresources: 2-20-1, Chuo, Kurashiki, Okayama 710-0046; tel. (86) 424-1661; internet www.rib.okayama-u.ac.jp; f. 1914; affiliated 1951; Dir Prof. K. TAKEDA

OPEN UNIVERSITY OF JAPAN

2-11 Wakaba, Mihama-ku, Chiba City 261-8586
Telephone: (43) 276-5111
E-mail: eng-web@ouj.ac.jp
Internet: www.ouj.ac.jp

Founded 1983

Chair.: YASUSHI MITARAI
Pres.: HIROMITSU ISHI
Vice-Pres: YOICHI OKABE, HIROSHI OGINO, HIROFUMI HONMA
Dir-Gen.: MITSUHIRO IKEHARA
Librarian: HITOSHI ABE

Library of 630,643 vols
Number of teachers: 94
Number of students: 87,169

OSAKA UNIVERSITY

1-1 Yamadaoka, Suita, Osaka 565-0871
Telephone: (6) 6877-5111
E-mail: kokusai-ina@ml.office.osaka-u.ac.jp
Internet: www.osaka-u.ac.jp

Founded 1931, merged with Osaka Univ. of Foreign Studies 2007
State control
Academic year: April to March

Pres.: TOSHIO HIRANO
Exec. Pres.: SABURO AIMOTO
Exec. Pres.: AKIO BABA
Exec. Pres.: SHIGEYUKI EBISU
Exec. Pres.: KIYOSHI HIGASHIJIMA
Exec. Pres.: TAKAHITO OHKI
Exec. Pres.: FUMIO OHTAKE
Exec. Pres.: YASUYUKI OKAMURA
Vice-Pres.: MASAO IKEDA
Vice-Pres.: TOSHIYA HOSHINO
Vice-Pres.: YUZURU KANAKURA
Vice-Pres.: YASUSHI NAGATA
Vice-Pres.: TADASHI SHIMODA

Library: see under Libraries and Archives
Number of teachers: 4,230
Number of students: 23,404

Publications: *International Public Policy Studies* (2 a year), *Memoir of Graduate School of Human Sciences* (1 a year), *Memoirs of the Graduate School of Letters* (1 a year), *Memoirs of the Institute of Scientific and Industrial Research* (1 a year), *Osaka Economic Papers* (4 a year), *Osaka Journal of Mathematics* (4 a year), *Studies in Language and Culture* (1 a year), *Transactions of JWRI* (2 a year)

DEANS

Graduate School and Faculty of Medicine: YASUFUMI KANEDA
Graduate School and School of Dentistry: SATOSHI WAKISAKA

Graduate School and School of Economics: MASAMITSU OHNISHI
Graduate School and School of Engineering: TOMOYUKI KAKESHITA
Graduate School and School of Engineering Science: GENTA KAWAHARA
Graduate School and School of Human Sciences: MASAYUKI NAKAMICHI
Graduate School and School of Letters: AKIO WADA
Graduate School and School of Pharmaceutical Sciences: YASUO TSUTSUMI
Graduate School and School of Science: ATSUSHI SHINOHARA
Graduate School of Frontier Biosciences: TORU NAKANO
Graduate School of Information Science and Technology: KATSURO INOUE
Graduate School of Language and Culture: HIROYUKI WAGATA
Graduate School of Law and Politics: YUTAKA TAKENAKA
Osaka School of International Public Policy: MASANAO MURAKAMI
Osaka University Law School: YOSHIHIRO MISAKA
School of Foreign Studies: AKIHIKO AZUMA
United Graduate School of Child Development: TAIICHI KATAYAMA

PROFESSORS

Graduate School and Faculty of Medicine (2-2 Yamadaoka, Suita, Osaka 565-0871; internet www.med.osaka-u.ac.jp):

AOZASA, K., Molecular Pathology
ARAKIDA, M., Health Promotion Science
ASO, Y., Health Promotion Science
BEPPU, S., Functional Diagnostic Physics
FUJIKADO, T., Applied Visual Science
FUJIWARA, C., Child and Reproductive Health
FUJIWARA, H., Medical Physics and Engineering
FUKUZAWA, M., Paediatric Surgery
HARUNA, M., Medical Physics and Engineering
HATAZAWA, J., Nuclear Medicine
HAYAKAWA, K., Health Promotion Science
HAYASHI, N., Molecular Therapeutics
HIRANO, T., Immunology and Molecular Biology
HORI, M., Cardiovascular Medicine
HOSOKAWA, K., Plastic Surgery
INAGAKI, S., Bioinformatics
INOUE, O., Medical Physics and Engineering
INOUE, T., Radiation Oncology
IWATANI, Y., Bioinformatics
JOHKOH, T., Functional Diagnostic Science
KANAKURA, Y., Haematology and Oncology
KANEDA, Y., Gene Therapy Science
KANOH, M., Cellular Neuroscience
KATAYAMA, I., Dermatology
KAWANO, S., Functional Diagnostic Science
KAWASE, I., Respirology
KIDO, Y., Evidence-based Clinical Nursing
KINOSHITA, H., Biomechanic and Motor Control
KUBO, T., Otorhinolaryngology
KURACHI, Y., Pharmacology
KUROKAWA, N., Pharmacy
MAKIMOTO, K., Evidence-based Clinical Nursing
MASHIMO, T., Anaesthesiology and Critical Care Medicine
MATOBA, R., Legal Medicine
MATSUURA, N., Functional Diagnostic Science
MIKAMI, H., Health Promotion Science
MIYASAKA, M., Immunodynamics
MIYAZAKI, J., Stem Cell Regulation Research
MONDEN, M., Surgery
MORIMOTO, K., Hygiene and Preventive Medicine
MURASE, K., Medical Physics and Engineering
MURATA, Y., Obstetrics and Gynaecology
NAGAI, T., Child and Reproductive Health
NAGATA, S., Genetics
NAKAMURA, H., Radiology
NAKAMURA, T., Molecular Regenerative Medicine
NAKANO, T., Stem-cell Biology
NOGUCHI, S., Surgical Oncology
OGASAWARA, C., Health Promotion Science
OGIHARA, T., Geriatric Medicine
OGINO, S., Evidence-based Clinical Nursing
OHASHI, K., Child and Reproductive Health
OHIRA, Y., Applied Psychology
OHNO, Y., Health Promotion Science
OKAMOTO, M., Molecular Physiological Chemistry
OKUMIYA, A., Evidence-based Clinical Nursing
OKUYAMA, A., Urology
OZONO, K., Paediatrics
SAKODA, S., Neurology
SATO, H., Cognitive Neuroscience
SHIMADA, M., Child and Reproductive Health
SHIMOMURA, I., Internal Medicine
SHIRAKURA, R., Organ Transplantation
SOBUE, K., Neuroscience
SUGIMOTO, H., Traumatology and Acute Critical Medicine
SUGIMOTO, N., Applied Bacteriology
SUGIYAMA, H., Functional Diagnostic Science
SUZUKI, S., Evidence-based Clinical Nursing
TODA, T., Clinical Genetics
TAKAI, Y., Molecular Biology and Biochemistry
TAKEDA, H., Medical Information Science
TAKEDA, J., Environmental Genetics
TAKEDA, M., Psychiatry
TAMURA, S., Interdisciplinary Image Analysis
TANIGUCHI, N., Biochemistry
TANO, Y., Ophthalmology
TESHIMA, T., Medical Physics and Engineering
TOHYAMA, M., Anatomy and Neuroscience
TSUJIMOTO, Y., Molecular Genetics
UCHIYAMA, Y., Cell Biology and Neuroscience
YAMAMOTO, Y., Bioinformatics
YAMAMURA, T., Bioinformatics
YAMATODANI, A., Medical Physics and Engineering
YANAGIDA, T., Physiology and Biosignalling
YONEDA, Y., Anatomy and Cell Biology
YORIFUJI, S., Functional Diagnostic Science
YOSHIDA, T., Applied Psychology
YOSHIKAWA, H., Orthopaedic Surgery
YOSHIMINE, T., Neurosurgery

Graduate School and School of Dentistry (1-8 Yamadaoka, Suita, Osaka 565-0871; internet www.dent.osaka-u.ac.jp/index-e.html):

AMANO, A., Oral Science Methodology
EBISU, S., Endodontology
FURUKAWA, S., Oral and Maxillofacial Radiology
KAMISAKI, Y., Pharmacology
KAN, Y., Oral Physiology
KOGO, M., Management of Oral and Maxillofacial Diseases
MAEDA, Y., Interdisciplinary Dentistry
MORISAKI, I., Nursing Dentistry
MURAKAMI, S., Periodontology
NIWA, H., Dental Anaesthesiology
NOKUBI, T., Oromaxillofacial Prosthodontics
OHSHIMA, T., Paediatric Dentistry
SHIZUKUISHI, S., Preventive Dentistry
TAKADA, K., Orthodontics and Dentofacial Orthopaedics
TOYOSAWA, S., Oral Pathology
WAKISAKA, S., Oral Anatomy and Developmental Biology
YATANI, H., Occlusion, TMD and Advanced Prosthodontics
YONEDA, T., Molecular and Cellular Craniofacial Biology
YOSHIDA, A., Oral Anatomy and Neurobiology
YURA, Y., Oral and Maxillofacial Oncology

Graduate School and School of Economics (1-7 Machikaneyama-cho, Toyonaka, Osaka 560-0043; tel. (6) 6850-6111):

ABE, K., Economics
ABE, T., Historical Analysis
ASADA, T., Business Information
BAN, K., Economics
DOME, T., Political Analysis
FUKUSHIGE, M., Management of Technology
FUTAGAMI, K., Economics
HONDA, Y., Policy Analysis
HONMA, M., Economics
IMAI, Y., Theoretical Analysis
KANAI, K., Business Information
KOBAYASHI, T., Business Information
MINO, K., Theoretical Analysis
MIYAMOTO, M., Historical Analysis
NAGATANI, H., Theoretical Analysis
NAKAJIMA, N., Business
OHNISHI, M., Business
OHYA, K., Business Analysis
SAITO, S., Policy Analysis
SAMURA, T., Historical Analysis
SAWAI, M., Historical Analysis
SUGIHARA, K., Economics
TABATA, Y., Business Analysis
TAKAO, H., Business
TAKEDA, E., Business Analysis
YAMADA, M., Theoretical Analysis

Graduate School and School of Engineering (2-1 Yamadaoka, Suita, Osaka 565-0871; internet www.eng.osaka-u.ac.jp):

Department of Advanced Science and Biotechnology:

AONO, M., Applied Surface Science
FUKUI, K., Dynamic Cell Biology
FUKUZUMI, S., Physical Chemistry for Life Science
HARASHIMA, S., Molecular Genetics
ITO, K., Applied Optics and Optical Information Processing
KANAYA, S., Biological Extremity Engineering
KOBAYASHI, A., Cell Technology
MIYATA, M., Molecular Recognition Chemistry
OHTAKE, H., Biochemical Engineering
SHIOYA, S., Bioprocess Systems Engineering
TAKAI, Y., Theoretical Computation Physics
URABE, I., Enzyme Engineering
YOKOYAMA, M., Molecular System Engineering

Department of Applied Chemistry:

AKASHI, M., Industrial Organic Chemistry
BABA, A., Resources Chemistry
CHATANI, N., Molecular Interaction Chemistry
HIRAO, T., Material Synthetic Chemistry
IMANAKA, N., Material Synthetic Chemistry
INOUE, Y., Molecular Interaction Chemistry
KAI, Y., Structural Physical Chemistry
KAMBE, N., Synthesis and Catalysis
KOMATSU, M., Synthetic Organic Chemistry
KUROSAWA, H., Organometallic Chemistry
KUWABATA, S., Applied Chemistry
OHSHIMA, T., Theoretical Organic Chemistry
UYAMA, H., Theoretical Organic Chemistry

Department of Materials Chemistry:
HIRAO, T., Materials Synthetic Chemistry
IMANAKA, N., Materials Synthetic Chemistry
KAI, Y., Structural Physical Chemistry
KOMATSU, M., Synthetic Organic Chemistry
KUWABATA, S., Applied Electrochemistry
OSHIMA, T., Theoretical Organic Chemistry
UYAMA, H., Structural Organic Chemistry

Department of Biotechnology:
FUKUI, K., Dynamic Cell Biology
HARASHIMA, S., Molecular Genetics
KOBAYASHI, A., Cell Technology
OTAKE, H., Biochemical Engineering
SHIOYA, S., Bioprocess Systems Engineering
URABE, I., Enzyme Engineering

Department of Precision Science, Technology and Applied Physics:
HIROSE, K., Computational Physics
KASAI, H., Materials Physics Theory
KATAOKA, T., Quantum Measurement and Instrumentation
KAWAKAMI, N., Condensed Matter Physics and Statistical Physics
MASUHARA, H., Laser Photochemistry and Microspectroscopy
MORITA, M., Scientific Hardware Systems
SUGAWARA, Y., Engineering Physics
YAGI, A., Non-linear Analysis and its Applications
YAMAUCHI, K., Ultra-precision Machining
YASUTAKE, K., Atomically Controlled Processes
YOSHII, K., Functional Materials

Department of Applied Physics:
KASAI, H., Materials Physics Theory
KAWAKAMI, N., Condensed Matter Physics and Statistical Physics
MASUHARA, H., Laser Photochemistry and Microspectroscopy
SUGAWARA, Y., Engineering Physics
YAGI, A., Nonlinear Analysis and its Applications

Department of Adaptive Machine Systems:
ASADA, M., Emergent Robotics
ISHIGURRO, H., Evolution Dynamics
MINAMINO, Y., Intelligent Materials
NAKATANI, A., Microdynamics
OHJI, T., Advanced Materials Processing
YASUDA, H., Materials Processing and Devices

Department of Mechanophysics Engineering:
FUJITA, K., Design and Manufacturing Engineering
HURUSHO, J., Real-world Active Intelligence
IKEDA, M., Control Engineering
INABA, T., Morphology in Machine Phenomena
KAJISHIMA, T., Fluid Engineering and Thermohydrodynamics
KATAOKA, I., Quantum Measurement
KUBO, S., Materials and Structures Evaluation
MINOSHIMA, K., Intelligent Materials
MIYOSHI, T., Production and Measurement Systems Engineering
MORI, N., Complex Fluid Mechanics
OTA, Y., Control Engineering
SHIBUTANI, Y., Solid Mechanics
TAKEISHI, K., Thermal Science and Engineering
TAKEUCHI, Y., Design and Manufacturing Engineering
TANAK, T., Mechanical Systems Analysis and Solid Mechanics
TSUJI, Y., Complex Fluid Mechanics
UMEDA, Y., Design and Manufacturing Engineering

Department of Mechanical Engineering and Systems:
KUBO, S., Materials and Structures Evaluation
MINOSHIMA, K., Materials and Structures Evaluation
MIYOSHI, T., Production and Measurement Systems Engineering
SHIBUTANI, Y., Solid Mechanics
TANAKA, T., Mechanical Systems Analysis and Solid Mechanics

Department of Computer-controlled Mechanical Systems:
FUJITA, K., Design and Manufacturing Engineering
FURUSHO, J., Real-world Active Intelligence
IKEDA, M., Control Engineering
OTA, Y., Control Engineering
SHIRAI, Y., Real-world Active Intelligence
TAKEUCHI, Y., Design and Manufacturing Engineering

Department of Materials Science and Processing:
ARAI, E., Advanced Manufacturing Systems
FUJIMOTO, K., Micro-nano Systems
FUJIMOTO, S., Environmental Materials and Surface Processing
FUJIWARA, Y., Crystal Growth
HIRATA, Y., Intelligent Materials Processing Systems
HIROSE, K., Computational Physics
HUJIMOTO, S., Environmental Materials and Surface Processing
KAKESHITA, T., Quantum Physics of Solids
KOBAYASHI, K., Smart Materials Processing
MATSUO, S., Intelligent Materials Processing
MINAMI, F., Materials Evaluation for Structuring
NISHIMOTO, K., Materials Joining
TANAKA, T., Interface Science and Technology
TOYODA, M., Strength/Fracture Evaluation for Manufacturing
USUI, T., Materials Processing and Metallurgy
YAMAMOTO, M., Physics of Surface and Interface
YAMASHITA, H., Thermophysics of Materials

Department of Materials Science and Engineering:
FUJIWARA, Y., Crystal Growth
KAKESHITA, T., Quantum Physics of Solids
YAMAMOTO, M., Physics of Surface and Interface

Department of Manufacturing Science:
ARAI, E., Advanced Manufacturing Systems
FUJIMOTO, K., Micro-nano Systems
HIRATA, Y., Intelligent Materials Processing Systems
KOBAYASHI, K., Smart Materials Processing
MINAMI, F., Materials Evaluation for Structuring
MIYAMOTO, I., Intelligent Materials Processing Systems
NISHIMOTO, K., Materials Joining
TOYODA, M., Strength/Fracture Evaluation for Manufacturing

Department of Communications Engineering:
BABAGUCHI, N., Telecommunications and Systems Engineering
IIDA, T., Fusion Engineering
ISE, T., Systems and Electric Power Engineering
ITO, T., Electro-materials Engineering
KAWASAKI, Z., Fundamentals for Communications Engineering
KODAMA, R., Laser Engineering
KOMAKI, S., Microwave and Optical Communication Systems
KUMAGAI, S., Control Engineering
MORITA, S., Microscopic Quantum Engineering
NISHIKAWA, M., Supra-high-temperature Engineering
SANPEI, S., Telecommunication and Systems Engineering
SASAKI, T., Applied Electrophysics
SUGINO, T., Science and Technology of Electrical Materials
SUHARA, T., Integrated Electronic Engineering
TAKINE, T., Advanced Communications and Photonic Networks
TANAKA, K., Laser Engineering
TANIGUCHI, K., Quantum Devices
TANINO, T., Systems Analysis and Optimization
TSUJI, K., Systems Engineering
YAGI, T., Control System Engineering

Department of Sustainable Energy and Environmental Engineering:
HORIIKE, H., Neutronics and Nuclear Instrumentation
KAGA, A., Engineering for the Atmospheric Environment
MIZUNO, M., Environment and Energy Systems
MORIOKA, T., Environmental Management
NISHIJIMA, S., Nuclear Chemical Engineering
SAWAKI, M., Environmental Management
TAKEDA, T., Nuclear Reactor Physics
YAMANAKA, S., Nuclear Fuels

Department of Global Architecture:
DEGUCHI, I., Social Systems Engineering
HASEGAWA, K., Naval Architecture
IMAI, K., Regional Environment and Global Transport
KATO, N., Naval Architecture
KOHZU, I., Structural Engineering
MATSUI, S., Structural and Geotechnical Engineering
NAITO, S., Marine Systems Engineering
NAKATSUJI, K., Social Systems Engineering
NITTA, Y., Social Systems Engineering
OHNO, Y., Structural Engineering
SAGARA, K., Architectural Design
TACHIBANA, E., Structural Engineering
TANIMOTO, C., Sustainable Development and Strategy
TOKIDA, K., Structural and Geotechnical Engineering
YAMAGUCHI, K., Sustainable Development and Strategy
YAO, T., Naval Architecture

Department of Environmental Engineering:
FUJITA, M., Water Science and Environmental Biotechnology
KAGA, A., Engineering for the Atmospheric Environment
MIZUNO, M., Environment and Energy Systems
MORIOKA, T., Environmental Management

Department of Management for Industry and Technology:
NARUMI, S., Management of Technology Knowledge
SATO, T., Technology Design
YAMAMOTO, T., Management of Technology Knowledge
ZAKO, M., Technology Design

Science Center for Atoms, Molecules and Ions Control:
FUKUDA, T., Plasma Particle Control Division
HAMAGUCHI, S., Plasma Particle Control Division
NAKATANI, R., Micro-composite Research Division

OKADA, S., Plasma Particle Control Division
SHIRAI, Y., Micro-structures Division

Research Center for Ultra-Precision Science and Technology:
ENDO, K., Precision Science and Technology

Graduate School and School of Engineering Science (1-3 Machikaneyama-cho, Toyonaka, Osaka 560-8531; tel. (6) 6850-6111; internet www.es.osaka-u.ac.jp/index-e.html):

Department of Materials Engineering Science:
HIRAI, T., Solar Energy Chemistry
HIRATA, Y., Environment and Energy System
HIYAMIZU, S., Quantum Physics of Nanoscale Materials
IMOTO, N., Quantum Physics of Nanoscale Materials
INOUE, Y., Environment and Energy System
ITOH, T., Dynamics of Nanoscale Materials
IWAI, S., Molecular Organization Chemistry
KANEDA, K., Chemical Reaction Engineering
KITAOKA, Y., Frontier Materials
KITAYAMA, T., Synthetic Chemistry
KUBOI, R., Bioprocess Engineering
MASHIMA, K., Synthetic Chemistry
MATSUMURA, M., Solar Energy Chemistry
MIYAKE, K., Electron Correlation Physics
MIYASAKA, H., Dynamics of Nanoscale Materials
NAKANO, M., Chemical Reaction Engineering
NAKATO, Y., Molecular Organization Chemistry
NAOTA, T., Synthetic Chemistry
OHGAKI, K., Environment and Energy System
SHIMIZU, K., Quantum Science in Extreme Conditions
SUGA, S., Electron Correlation Physics
SUZUKI, N., Frontier Materials
SUZUKI, Y., Electron Correlation Physics
TADA, H., Quantum Physics of Nanoscale Materials
TAYA, M., Bioprocess Engineering
TOBE, Y., Frontier Materials
UEYAMA, K., Chemical Reaction Engineering
YOSHIDA, H., Quantum Science in Extreme Conditions

Department of Mechanical Science and Bioengineering:
ARAKI, T., Biomedical and Biophysical Measurements
HIRAO, M., Mechanics of Solid Materials
KOBAYASHI, H., Mechanics of Solid Materials
MIYAZAKI, F., Mechano-informatics
NOMURA, T., Biophysical Engineering
OHSHIRO, O., Biomedical and Biophysical Measurements
OSAKADA, K., Mechano-informatics
SUGIMOTO, N., Mechanics of Fluids and Thermo-fluids
TANAKA, M., Biomedical Engineering
TSUJIMOTO, Y., Propulsion Engineering
WAKABAYASHI, K., Biophysical Engineering

Department of Systems Innovation:
AIDA, S., Mathematical and Statistical Finance
AKASAKA, Y., Solid-State Electronics
ARAI, T., Intelligent Systems
FUJII, T., System Theory
IIGUNI, Y., System Theory
INAGAKI, N., Mathematical and Statistical Finance
INUIGUCHI, M., Theoretical Systems Science
ITOSAKI, H., Advanced Quantum Devices and Electronics
KANO, Y., Statistical Science
KITAGAWA, M., Advanced Quantum Devices and Electronics
KOBAYASHI, T., Optical Electronics
NAGAI, H., Mathematical and Statistical Finance
NAWA, H., Mathematical Modelling
NISHIDA, S., Intelligent Systems
OKAMOTO, H., Solid-State Electronics
OKAMURA, Y., Optical Electronics
OKUYAMA, M., Solid-State Electronics
SATO, K., Intelligent Systems
SHIRAHATA, S., Statistical Science
SUZUKI, T., Mathematical Modelling
URABE, S., Optical Electronics
USHIO, T., Theoretical Systems Science
YACHIDA, M., Intelligent Systems

Graduate School and School of Human Sciences (1-2 Yamadaoka, Suita, Osaka 565-0871; tel. (6) 6877-5111; internet www.hus.osaka-u.ac.jp/english):
ABE, A., Educational Policy and Administration
ADACHI, K., Behavioural Data Science
DAIBO, I., Social Psychology
FUJIOKA, J., Educational Psychology
FUJITA, A., Clinical Thanatology and Geriatric Behavioural Science
HINOBAYASHI, T., Comparative and Developmental Psychology
HIRASAWA, Y., Lifelong Education
IMURA, O., Clinical Psychology
KASUGA, N., People and Culture
KAWABATA, A., Advanced Empirical Sociology
KIMAE, T., Sociology of Modern Society
KOIZUMI, J., Cultural and Social Anthropology
KONDO, H., Sociology of Education
KOTO, Y., Sociological Theory
KUGIHARA, N., Social Psychology
KUMAKURA, H., Biological Anthropology
KURIMOTO, E., Cultural and Social Anthropology
KUWANO, S., Environmental Psychology
MAESAKO, T., Communication and Media
MINAMI, T., Comparative and Developmental Psychology
MIURA, T., Applied Cognitive Psychology
MIYATA, K., Clinical Psychology
MORIKAWA, K., Fundamental Psychology
MUTA, K., Sociology of Communication
NAKAGAWA, S., Cultural and Social Anthropology
NAKAMURA, T., Quantitative Psychology of Expression and Cognition
NAKAMURA, Y., International Collaboration
NAKAYAMA, Y., Logical Studies, Foundation of Science
NAOI, A., Information Technology and Human Sciences
OIMATSU, K., Clinical Psychology
ONODA, M., Educational Policy and Administration
SHIMIZU, K., Cultural Studies of Education
SUGAI, K., Educational Technology
SUGENO, T., Philosophical Anthropology
TSUTSUMI, S., Social Policy and Community Empowerment Studies
USUI, S., Human Risk Studies
UTSUMI, S., International Collaboration
YAMAMOTO, T., Behavioural Physiology

Graduate School and School of Letters (1-5 Machikaneyama-cho, Toyonaka, Osaka 560-8532; tel. (6) 6850-6111; e-mail web-admin@www.let.osaka-u.ac.jp; internet www.let.osaka-u.ac.jp):
AKITA, S., Western History
AMANO, F., Theatre Studies
AOKI, N., Japanese Linguistics
ARAKAWA, M., Central Asian History
EGAWA, A., Western History
ENOMOTO, F., Indian Philosophy and Buddhist Studies
FUJIKAWA, T., Western History
FUJITA, H., Environmental Aesthetics
FUKUNAGA, S., Archaeology
GOTO, A., Japanese Language and Literature
HACHIYA, M., Japanese Language and Literature
HAYASHI, M., German Literature
IIKURA, Y., Japanese Language and Literature
IKAI, T., Japanese History
IRIE, Y., Philosophy and History of Philosophy
IZUHARA, T., Japanese Language and Literature
KAMIKURA, T., Aesthetics
KASHIWAGI, T., French Literature
KATAYAMA, T., Asian History
KAWAMURA, K., Historical Studies of Cultural Exchanges
KINSUI, S., Japanese Language and Literature
KOBAYASHI, S., Human Geography
KODERA, T., Art History
KUDO, M., Japanese Linguistics
MOMOKI, S., Asian History
MORIOKA, Y., American Literature
MORIYASU, T., Central Asian History
MURATA, M., Japanese History
NAGATA, Y., Theatre Studies
NAITO, T., Comparative Literature
NAKAOKA, N., Clinical Philosophy and Ethics
NEGISHI, K., Musicology
OBA, Y., English Linguistics
OHASHI, R., Philosophy and Aesthetics
OKUDAIRA, S., Art History
SANADA, S., Japanese Linguistics
SUGIHARA, T., Historical Studies of Cultural Exchanges
SURO, N., Philosophy, Modern Thought and Cultural Studies
TAIRA, M., Japanese History
TAKAHASHI, B., Chinese Literature
TAKENAKA, T., Western History
TAMAI, A., English Literature
TOKI, S., Japanese Linguistics
UENO, O., Philosophy and History of Philosophy
UMEMURA, T., Japanese History
WADA, A., French Literature
WAKAYAMA, E., Art History
WASHIDA, K., Clinical Philosophy and Ethics
YUASA, K., Chinese Philosophy

Graduate School and School of Pharmaceutical Sciences (1-6 Yamadaoka, Suita, Osaka 565-0871; internet www.phs.osaka-u.ac.jp):
AZUMA, J., Clinical Evaluation of Medicines and Therapeutics
BABA, A., Molecular Neuropharmacology
DOI, T., Protein Molecular Engineering
HIRATA, K., Environmental Bioengineering
IMANISHI, T., Bio-organic Chemistry
KITA, Y., Synthetic Organic Chemistry
KOBAYASHI, M., Natural Product Chemistry
MAEDA, M., Biochemistry and Molecular Biology
MATSUDA, T., Medicinal Pharmacology
MURAKAMI, N., Medicinal Plant Resource Exploration
NAKAGAWA, S., Biopharmaceutics
NASU, M., Environmental Science and Microbiology
NISHIKAWA, J., Environmental Biochemistry
OHKUBO, T., Biophysical Chemistry
TAKAGI, T., Pharmaceutical Information Science
TANAKA, K., Toxicology
TANAKA, T., Medicinal and Organic Chemistry
UNO, T., Analytical Chemistry

YAGI, K., Bio-functional Molecular Chemistry
YAMAMOTO, H., Immunology

Graduate School and School of Science (1-1 Machikaneyama-cho, Toyonaka, Osaka 560-0043; tel. (6) 6850-6111; internet www.sci.osaka-u.ac.jp):

AKAI, H., Quantum Physics
AKUTSU, Y., Quantum Physics
AOSHIMA, S., Polymer Synthesis
ASAKAWA, M., Hadronic Physics
DOI, S., Analysis
FUJIKI, A., Global Geometry and Analysis
FUKASE, K., Natural Product Chemistry
FUKUYAMA, K., Structural Biology
HARADA, A., Supermolecular Science
HASE, S., Organic Biochemistry
HAYASHI, N., Applied Mathematics
HIGASHIJIMA, K., Particle Physics
HOSOTANI, Y., Fundamental Physics
IBUKIYAMA, T., Algebra
INABA, A., Structural Thermodynamics
KAIZAKI, S., Inorganic Chemistry
KANAZAWA, H., Molecular Biology
KASAI, T., Reaction Dynamics, Molecular Thermodynamics
KATAKUSE, I., Interdisciplinary Physics
KAWAMURA, H., Solid-State and Statistical Physics
KAWARAZAKI, S., Solid-State Physics
KISHIMOTO, T., Particle and Nuclear Physics
KOISO, N., Geometry
KONNO, K., Algebra
KONNO, T., Coordination Chemistry
KOTANI, S., Analysis
KUNO, Y., Elementary Particle Physics
KURAMITSU, S., Biophysical Chemistry
MABUCHI, T., Global Mathematics
MASUKATA, H., Molecular Genetics
MATSUDA, J., Planetary Science
MUNAKATA, T., Chemistry
MURATA, M., Biomolecular Chemistry
NAKASHIMA, S., Physical Geochemistry
NAKAZAWA, Y., Condensed Matter Physical Chemistry
NAMIKAWA, Y., Algebra
NISHIDA, H., Development Biology
NISHITANI, T., Analysis
NOMACHI, M., Quark Nuclear Physics
NORISUYE, T., Polymer Solutions
NOZUE, Y., Condensed Matter Physics
OGAWA, T., Quantum Physics
OGIHARA, S., Cell Biology
OHSHIKA, K., Geometry
ONUKI, Y., Condensed Matter Physics
SATO, T., Polymer Chemical Physics
SHIMODA, T., Nuclear Physics
SHINOHARA, A., Nuclear Chemistry
SUGITA, H., Analysis
SUZUKI, S., Bioinorganic Chemistry
TAJIMA, S., Condensed Matter Physics
TAKAHARA, F., Theoretical Astrophysics
TAKEDA, S., Condensed Matter Physics
TAKISAWA, H., Molecular Cell Biology
TERASHIMA, I., Plant Ecophysiology
TOKUNAGA, F., Extreme-environment Biology
TSUCHIYAMA, A., Experimental Planetology
TSUNEKI, K., Comparative Zoology
TSUNEMI, H., Astrophysics
UMEHARA, M., Global Mathematics
USUI, S., Algebra
WATANABE, T., Algebra
WATARAI, H., Analytical Chemistry
YAMAGUCHI, K., Quantum Chemistry, Physical Chemistry of Condensed Matter
YAMANAKA, T., High Energy Physics
YAMANAKA, T., Physics of Matter
YONESAKI, T., Microbial Genetics

Graduate School of Information Science and Technology (1-5 Yamadaoka, Suita, Osaka 565-0871; tel. (6) 6877-5111; internet www.ist.osaka-u.ac.jp):

Department of Pure and Applied Mathematics:

DATE, E., Mathematical Science
HIBI, T., Combinatorics
KAWANAKA, N., Discrete Structures
MATSUMURA, A., Applied Analysis
ODANAKA, S., Computer-assisted Mathematics
SAKANE, Y., Applied Geometry

Department of Information and Physical Sciences:

ISHII, H., Operations Research
MORITA, H., Computing with Complexity and Nonlinearity
NUMAO, M., Architecture for Intelligence
TANIDA, J., Physical Sciences
UOSAKI, K., Nonlinear Systems, Modelling and Optimization

Department of Computer Science:

HAGIHARA, K., Supercomputing Engineering
INOUE, K., Software Engineering
KUSOMOTO, S., Software Science
MASUZAWA, T., Algorithm Engineering
YAGI, Y., Intelligent Media Systems

Department of Information Systems Engineering:

CHIBA, T., Advanced System Architecture
IMAI, M., Integrated System Design
KAWATA, T., Advanced Systems Architecture
KIKUNO, T., Dependability Engineering
ONOYE, T., Information Systems Synthesis
TAKEMURA, H., Integrated Media Environment

Department of Information Networking:

HIGASHINO, T., Mobile Computing
IMASE, M., Information Sharing Platform
MURAKAMI, K., Intelligent Networking Systems
NAKANO, H., Advanced Network Architecture
OBASHI, Y., Cyber Communication
SATO, T., Cyber Communication

Department of Multimedia Engineering:

FUJIWARA, T., Information Security Engineering
KATAGIRI, Y., Multimedia Agent Systems
KISHINO, F., Human Interface Engineering
KOGURE, K., Multimedia Agent Systems
KOMODA, N., Business Information Systems
NISHIO, S., Multimedia Data Engineering
SHIMOJO, S., Applied Media Engineering

Department of Bioinformatic Engineering:

AKAZAWA, K., Human Information Engineering
KASHIWABARA, T., Bio-network Engineering
MATSUDA, H., Genome Information Engineering
SHIMIZU, H., Metabolic Engineering

Graduate School of Language and Culture (1-8 Machikaneyama-cho, Toyonaka, Osaka 560-0043; tel. (6) 6850-6111):

DYUBOVSKI, A., Language and Technology
HARUKI, Y., Language and Communication
HAYASHI, Y., Language and Information Science
HUKAZAWA, Y., Language and Communication
IWANE, H., Language and Technology
KANASAKI, H., Area Studies in Language and Culture
KANEKO, M., Area Studies in Language and Culture
KIMURA, K., Area Studies in Language and Culture
KIMURA, S., Interdisciplinary Cultural Studies
KITAMURA, T., Interdisciplinary Cultural Studies
NAKA, N., Language and Culture in International Relations
NAKANO, Y., Language and Culture in International Relations
NARITA, H., Education in Language and Culture
OKADA, N., Education in Language and Culture
OKITA, T., Education in Language and Culture
SENBA, Y., Language and Technology
TAKAOKA, K., Language and Culture in International Relations
TSUDA, A., Language and Communication
TSUKUI, S., Area Studies in Language and Culture
WATANABE, S., Language and Information Science
YOKOTA, G., Interdisciplinary Cultural Studies

Graduate School of Law (1-6 Machikaneyama-cho, Toyonaka, Osaka 560-0043; tel. (6) 6850-6111):

AOE, H., Legal Practice
AOTAKE, S., Legal Practice
CHAEN, S., Legal Practice
HIRATA, K., Legal Practice
IKEDA, T., Legal Practice
KOJIMA, N., Legal Practice
KOSUGI, S., Legal Practice
MATSUI, S., Legal Practice
MATSUKAWA, T., Legal Practice
MATSUMOTO, K., Legal Practice
MISAKA, Y., Legal Practice
MIZUTANI, N., Legal Practice
MURAKAMI, T., Legal Practice
SAKUMA, O., Legal Practice
SHIMOMURA, M., Legal Practice
SUENAGA, T., Legal Practice
SUZUKI, H., Legal Practice
TANIGUTCHI, S., Legal Practice
YOSHIDA, M., Legal Practice
YOSHIMOTO, K., Legal Practice

Graduate School of Frontier Biosciences (1-3 Yamadaoka, Suita, Osaka 565-0871; internet www.fbs.osaka-u.ac.jp):

FUJITA, I., Neuroscience
HAMADA, H., Organismal Biosystems
HANAOKA, F., Integrated Biology
HIRANO, T., Organismal Biosystems
KAWAMURA, S., Nanobiology
KINOSHITA, S., Biophysical Dynamics
KONDOH, H., Biomolecular Networks
KURAHASHI, T., Biophysical Dynamics
MURAKAMI, F., Neuroscience
NAGATA, S., Integrated Biology
NAKANO, T., Integrated Biology
NAMBA, K., Nanobiology
NORIOKA, S., Biophysical Dynamics
OGURA, A., Neuroscience
OHZAWA, I., Neuroscience
OKAMOTO, M., Biomolecular Networks
SHIMOMURA, I., Organismal Biosystems
SUGINO, A., Biomolecular Networks
TANAKA, K., Organismal Biosystems
YAGI, T., Integrated Biology
YAMAMOTO, N., Neuroscience
YANAGIDA, T., Nanobiology
YONEDA, Y., Biomolecular Networks

Graduate School of Law and Politics and School of Law (1-6 Machikaneyama-cho, Toyonaka, Osaka 560-0043; tel. (6) 6850-6111):

HAYASHI, T., Comparative Law and Politics
KAWATA, J., Center for Legal and Political Practice
KUNII, K., Comparative Law and Politics
MITSUNARI, K., Independent Study Center
NAKAO, T., Comparative Law and Politics
NAKAYAMA, R., Governance and Law
OKUBO, N., Governance and Law
SAKAMOTO, K., Governance and Law
TAGO, K., Governance and Law
TAKADA, A., Governance and Law

TAKAHASHI, A., Independent Study Course
TAKENAKA, Y., Independent Study Course
TAKIGUCHI, T., Comparative Law and Politics
YAMASHITA, M., Comparative Law and Politics
YOON, K. C., International and Comparative Law Course

Osaka School of International Public Policy (1-31 Machikaneyama-cho, Toyonaka, Osaka 560-0043; tel. (6) 6850-6111):

HASHIMOTO, Y., Comparative Public Policy
HOSHINO, T., Systems Integration
KOHSAKA, A., Systems Integration
KOJIMA, N., Comparative Corporate Behaviour
KUROSAWA, M., International Public System
MATSUSHIGE, H., Systems Integration
MURAKAMI, M., International Public System
NAKANO, T., Comparative Corporate Behaviour
NOMURA, Y., Systems Integration
SAITO, S., Comparative Economic Development
SAWAI, M., Comparative Economic Development
SUGIHARA, S., Contemporary Japanese Law and Economy
TAKENAKA, H., International Trade Relations
TANIGUCHI, S., International Trade Relations
TOKOTANI, F., Comparative Public Policy
YAMAUCHI, N., Contemporary Japanese Law and Economy
YONEHARA, K., Contemporary Japanese Law and Economy

ATTACHED INSTITUTES

Institute for Protein Research: Suita Campus, Yamadaoka, Suita, Osaka; e-mail toiawase@protein.osaka-u.ac.jp; internet www.protein.osaka-u.ac.jp; Dir HIDEO AKUTSU.

Institute of Scientific and Industrial Research: Suita Campus, Mihogaoka, Ibaraki, Osaka; e-mail kouhou@sanken.osaka-u.ac.jp; internet www.sanken.osaka-u.ac.jp; Dir TOMOJI KAWAI.

Institute of Social and Economic Research: Suita Campus, Mihogaoka, Ibaraki, Osaka; internet www.iser.osaka-u.ac.jp; Dir SHINSUKE IKEDA.

Joining and Welding Research Institute: Suita Campus, Mihogaoka, Ibaraki, Osaka; internet www.jwri.osaka-u.ac.jp; Dir KIYOSHI NOGI.

Research Institute for Microbial Diseases: Suita Campus, Yamadaoka, Suita, Osaka; internet www.biken.osaka-u.ac.jp; Dir TAROH KINOSHITA

OTARU UNIVERSITY OF COMMERCE

3-5-21, Midori, Otaru 047-0851, Hokkaido
Telephone: (134) 27-5200
E-mail: inl@office.otaru.ac.jp
Internet: www.otaru-uc.ac.jp

Founded 1949
Independent

Depts of economics, commerce, law, information and management sciences, teacher-training programme in commerce and graduate school

Pres.: IEMASA YAMADA
Chief Admin. Officer: HIROSHI AIBA
Librarian: YOICHIRO YUKI

Library of 420,000 vols
Number of teachers: 134
Number of students: 2,260

PROFESSORS

Department of Commerce: HAJIME ITOH
Department of Economics: HAJIME IMANISHI
Department of Information Technology: HARUHIKO OGASAWARA
Department of Law: MASAHIRO MICHINO

SAGA UNIVERSITY

Honjo-cho 1, Saga City 840
Telephone: (952) 28-8168
E-mail: sagakoho@mail.admin.saga-u.ac.jp
Internet: www.saga-u.ac.jp

Founded 1949
Academic year: April to March

Pres.: HARUO UEHARA
Vice-Pres: GUNJI ARAMAKI, YASUHISA SHINTOMI
Dir of Gen. Admin. Bureau: TOSHIJI UEDA
Dir of Univ. Library: KEIICHI MIYAJIMA

Library of 600,341 vols
Number of teachers: 471
Number of students: 595 graduate, 5,808 undergraduate

Publication: various faculty reports and bulletins

DEANS

Faculty of Agriculture: TAKAYUKI KOJIMA
Faculty of Culture and Education: KENJI TSUJI
Faculty of Economics: KAZAFUMI KOGA
Faculty of Science and Engineering: AKIRA HASEGAWA

DIRECTORS

Analytical Research and Development Center: KEIICHI WATANABE
Coastal Bioenvironment Center: OSAMU KATO
Computer and Network Center: YOSHIAKI WATANABE
Institute of Lowland Technology: SHIGENORI HAYASHI
Institute of Ocean Energy: MASANORI MONDE
International Student Center: TATSUYA KOMOTO
Joint Research and Development Center: KOHEI ARAI
Synchrotron Light Application Center: HIROSHI OGAWA
Venture Business Laboratory: MASAYOSHI AIKAWA

SAITAMA UNIVERSITY

255 Shimo-Okubo, Sakura-ku, Saitama 338-8570
Telephone: (48) 858-9624
E-mail: kokusai@gr.saitama-u.ac.jp
Internet: www.saitama-u.ac.jp

Founded 1949
Private control
Academic year: April to March

Pres.: YOSHIHIKO KAMII
Exec. Dir: HIROKI YAMAGUCHI
Exec. Dir: MAKOTO HORI
Exec. Dir: MITSUHIRO IKEHARA
Exec. Dir: YASUTAKE KATO

Library of 852,037 vols, 21,198 periodicals
Number of teachers: 553
Number of students: 8,932

Publications: *Asian Economy and Social Environment* (1 a year), *Research Report of Department of Civil and Environmental Engineering* (1 a year), *Saitama Mathematical Journal* (1 a year)

DEANS

Faculty of Economics: KAZUO USUI
Faculty of Education: KYOJI SAITO
Faculty of Liberal Arts: HIROAKI ITO
Graduate School of Cultural Science: HIROAKI ITO
Graduate School of Economic Science: KAZUO USUI
Graduate School of Education: KYOJI SAITO
Graduate School of Science and Engineering: AKIRA NAGASAWA
School of Engineering: YUICHI SATO
School of Science: TAKAFUMI SAKAI

SHIGA UNIVERSITY

1-1-1 Banba, Hikone, Shiga 522-8522
Telephone: (749) 27-1172
E-mail: koho@biwako.shiga-u.ac.jp
Internet: www.shiga-u.ac.jp

Founded 1949
Independent
Academic year: April to March

Pres.: KENICHI MIYAMOTO
Vice-Pres: SEIJI OGURI, HIDEKI SUMIOKA
Admin. Dir: OSAHIRO TODOROKI
Librarian: TAKEO TERAYOKO

Library of 550,208 vols
Number of teachers: 315
Number of students: 3,981

Publications: *Fuzoku-shiryo-kan Kenkyu-Kiyo* (Bulletin of the Archival Museum, 1 a year), *Kenkyu-Nenpo* (Annals of Human and Social Sciences, 1 a year), *The Hikone Ronso* (economics, irregular), *Kyoiku-Gakubu Kiyo* (Memoirs of the Faculty of Education, 1 a year), *Shiga-Eibun-Gakkai-Ronbunshu* (English Studies Review, every 2 years)

DEANS

Faculty of Economics: HIROAKI KITAMURA
Faculty of Education: SHOBU SATO
Graduate School of Economics: HIROAKI KITAMURA
Graduate School of Education: SHOBU SATO

ATTACHED RESEARCH INSTITUTES

Archives Museum: Dir HIDEKI USAMI.

Center for Educational Research and Practice: 2-5-1 Hiratsu, Otsu, Shiga 520-0862; Dir TSUTOMU KUBOSHIMA.

Center for Environmental Education and Lake Science: 2-5-1 Hiratsu, Otsu, Shiga 520-0862; internet rcse.edu.shiga-u.ac.jp; Dir SHUICHI ENDO.

Institute for Economic and Business Research: Dir NAOKI UMEZAWA.

Information Processing Center: Dir SABURO HORIMOTO.

Joint Research Center: Dir ISAO OGAWA.

Research Center for Lifelong Learning: 2-5-1 Hiratsu, Otsu, Shiga 520-0862; Dir OSAMU UMEDA

SHIMANE UNIVERSITY

1060 Nishikawatsu-cho, Matsue-shi, Shimane-ken 690-8504
Telephone: (852) 32-6100
E-mail: webinfo@jn.shimane-u.ac.jp
Internet: www.shimane-u.ac.jp

Founded 1949
Independent
Academic year: April to March

Pres.: YUICHI HONDA
Registrar: T. KAMADA
Librarian: S. WATANABE

Library of 692,000 vols
Number of teachers: 500
Number of students: 5,550

DEANS

Faculty of Education: M. YAMASHITA
Faculty of Law and Literature: Y. MATSUI

Faculty of Life and Environmental Sciences: H. Yamamoto
Faculty of Science and Engineering: A. Takuna

SHINSHU UNIVERSITY

Asahi 3-1-1, Matsumoto, 390-8621 Nagano-ken
Telephone: (263) 35-4600
E-mail: shinhp@shinshu-u.ac.jp
Internet: www.shinshu-u.ac.jp

Founded 1949
Independent

Pres.: Kiyohito Yamasawa

Number of teachers: 1,150 full-time
Number of students: 11,446 (9,364 undergraduates, 2,082 in Graduate School)

DEANS

Faculty of Agriculture: Soichiro Nakamura
Faculty of Arts: Hideo Watanabe
Faculty of Economics: Joji Tokui
Faculty of Education: Yoshinao Hirano
Faculty of Engineering: Masayuki Okamoto
Faculty of Science: Mitsuo Takeda
Faculty of Textile Science and Technology: Kunihiro Hamada
School of Medicine: Keishi Kubo

SHIZUOKA UNIVERSITY

Ohya 836, Shizuoka-shi 422-8529
Telephone: (54) 238-4407
E-mail: koho@gene1.adb.shizuoka.ac.jp
Internet: www.shizuoka.ac.jp

Founded 1949
Independent

Pres.: Yoshimitsu Amagishi
Vice-Pres: Nobuyuki Araki, Hirokazu Nakai
Dir-Gen.: Shigenobu Mori
Dir of Univ. Library: Kimio Bamba

Number of teachers: 744 full-time
Number of students: 11,112

DEANS

Faculty of Agriculture: Kiyoshi Okawa
Faculty of Education: Shoji Kanai
Faculty of Engineering: Hitoshi Ishii
Faculty of Humanities and Social Sciences: Yoshihiko Yamamoto
Faculty of Information Sciences: Hiroyuki Tokuyama
Faculty of Science: Katsutoshi Ishikawa

DIRECTORS

Center for Education and Research Lifelong Learning: Kinji Taki
Center for Joint Research: Naomichi Okamoto
Information Processing Center: Naokazu Yamaki
Institute for Genetic Research and Biotechnology: Koichi Yoshinaga
International Student Center: Takashige Honda
Research Institute of Electronics: Kenzo Watanabe
Satellite Venture Business Laboratory: Norihiro Inagaki

TOHOKU UNIVERSITY

1-1 Katahira, 2-chome, Aoba-ku, Sendai 980-8577
Telephone: (22) 217-4844
E-mail: kokusai@bureau.tohoku.ac.jp
Internet: www.tohoku.ac.jp/english

Founded 1907
State control
Languages of instruction: English, Japanese
Academic year: April to March

Pres.: Susumu Satomi
Exec. Vice-Pres. for Education, Student Support and Student International Exchange: Kimio Hanawa
Exec. Vice Pres. for Financial Affairs and Campus Planning: Yoshihiko Tsukuda
Exec. Vice-Pres. for General Affairs, International Relations and Academic Affairs: Toshiya Ueki
Exec. Vice-Pres. for Human Resources and Personnel Admin., Facilities: Kimikazu Iwase
Exec. Vice-Pres. for Industry University Collaboration: Hiroshi Kazui
Exec. Vice-Pres. for Research and Environmental Security: Sadayoshi Ito
Vice-Pres. for Legal Affairs: Eiji Hyodo
Vice-Pres. for Public Relations, Alumni Association and Information Systems: Takafumi Aoki

Library: see under Libraries and Archives
Number of teachers: 2,992
Number of students: 18,073

Publications: *Annals of nanoBME* (1 a year), *Annual Research Bulletin of the Graduate School of Pharmaceutical Sciences* (1 a year), *Bulletin of the Tohoku University Museum* (1 a year), *CYRIC annual report / Cyclotron and Radioisotope Center, Tohoku University* (1 a year), *Discussion paper / Tohoku Management & Accounting Research Group. Department of Economics. Tohoku University* (irregular), *Explorations in English linguistics: EEL / Tohoku University. Department of English Linguistics* (1 a year), *Graduate School of Engineering and Faculty of Engineering* (1 a year), *Interdisciplinary Information Science* (2 a year), *Journal of Integrated Field Science* (1 a year), *Reports of the Institute of Fluid Science* (1 a year), *Research Report of the Laboratory of Nuclear Science* (1 a year), *The science reports of the Tohoku University* (2 a year), *Tohoku Journal of Agricultural Research* (2 a year), *Tohoku Journal of Experimental Medicine* (12 a year), *Tohoku Mathematical Journal. Second Series* (4 a year), *Tohoku Mathematical Publications* (irregular), *Tohoku Psychologica Folia* (1 a year)

DEANS

Graduate School of Agricultural Science: Michio Komai
Graduate School of Arts and Letters: Ken-ichi Ohbuchi
Graduate School of Biomedical Engineering: Hidetoshi Matsuki
Graduate School of Dentistry: Keiichi Sasaki
Graduate School of Economics and Management: Seiichi Ohtaki
Graduate School of Education: Kazuo Hongo
Graduate School of Educational Informatics, Research Division: Shinichi Watabe
Graduate School of Engineering: Hiroshi Kanai
Graduate School of Environmental Studies: Kazuyuki Tohji
Graduate School of Information Sciences: Michitaka Kameyama
Graduate School of International Cultural Studies: Takashi Kuroda
Graduate School of Law: Tatsunori Watanabe
Graduate School of Life Sciences: Hideyuki Takahashi
Graduate School of Medicine: Noriaki Ohuchi
Graduate School of Pharmaceutical Sciences: Yoshiteru Oshima
Graduate School of Science: Hiroshi Fukumura

PROFESSORS

Botanical Gardens (12-2 Kawauchi, Aoba-ku, Sendai 980-0862; tel. (22) 795-6760; e-mail garden-tu@biology.tohoku.ac.jp; internet www.biology.tohoku.ac.jp/garden):

Suzuki, M., Plant Anatomy

Center for Interdisciplinary Research (Aoba, Aramaki, Aoba-ku, Sendai 980-8578; tel. (22) 795-5757; e-mail office@cir.tohoku.ac.jp; internet www.cir.tohoku.ac.jp):

Kasuya, A., Materials Science
Suemitsu, M., Materials Science
Yamane, H., Solid-state Chemistry
Yao, T., Department of Applied Physics

Center for Low-temperature Science (2-1-1 Katahira, Aoba-ku, Sendai 980-8577; tel. (22) 215-2181; e-mail ltcenter@imr.tohoku.ac.jp; internet www.clts.tohoku.ac.jp):

Aoki, H., Low-temperature Physics

Center for North-East Asian Studies (41 Kawauchi, Aoba-ku, Sendai 980-8576; tel. (22) 795-6009; e-mail asiajimu@cneas.tohoku.ac.jp; internet www.cneas.tohoku.ac.jp/index-j.html):

Hirakawa, A., Political Economy
Isobe, A., Cultural Studies
Kikuchi, E., Regional Ecosystem Studies
Kudoh, J., North Asian Societies
Kuribayashi, H., Linguistic Studies
Miyamoto, K., Socio-economic Studies on the Environment
Sato, M., Environmental and Resources Survey
Segawa, M., Social Ecology
Taniguchi, H., Geochemistry
Yamada, K., Social Structure

Center for the Advancement of Higher Education (41 Kawauchi, Aoba-ku, Sendai 980-8576; tel. (22) 795-7551; e-mail center@high-edu.tohoku.ac.jp; internet www.he.tohoku.ac.jp/index.html):

Hida, W., Respiratory Medicine
Horie, K., Linguistic Typology and Japanese–Korean Contrastive Linguistics
Nawata, T., Applied Research Section
Saitoh, K., Applied Research Section
Sekiuchi, T., Basic Research Section
Shizuya, H., Theoretical Computer Science
Suzuki, T., Applied Clinical Psychology
Yoshimoto, K., Formal Linguistics, Cognitive Science

Cyclotron Radioisotope Center (6-3 Aoba, Aramaki, Aoba-ku, Sendai 980-8578; tel. (22) 795-7800; e-mail admin@cyric.tohoku.ac.jp; internet www.cyric.tohoku.ac.jp):

Baba, M., Radiation Physics
Itoh, M., Nuclear Medicine
Iwata, R., Radioisotope Production and Radiopharmaceutical Chemistry
Okamura, H., Nuclear Physics

Graduate School of Educational Informatics, Research Division (Kawauchi, Aoba-ku, Sendai 980-8576; tel. (22) 795-6103; internet www.ei.tohoku.ac.jp):

Hagihara, T., Theory of an Open University
Iwasaki, S., Information Technology Educational Architecture
Muraki, E., Information Technology Education System Theory
Watabe, S., Information Technology Cognitive Science

Graduate School of Environmental Studies (Aobayama, Sendai 980-8579; tel. (22) 795-4504; e-mail s-ara@bureau.tohoku.ac.jp; internet www.kankyo.tohoku.ac.jp):

Arai, K., Environmental Chemical Engineering
Asano, Y., East Asian Philosophy
Chida, T., Geoenvironmental Remediation
Enomoto, H., Environmental Processing for Energy Resources
Hattori, T., Environmentally Benign Sythesis

HOSHINO, H., Analytical Environmental Chemistry
ISHIDA, H., Environmentally Harmonized Materials
KAYA, K., Environmental Ecology Design
KIMUTA, Y., Middle Eastern and Central Asian Studies
MARUYAMA, K., Structural Materials for Eco-friendly Systems
MATSUE, T., Environmental Bioengineering
MATSUKI, K., Environmental Geomechanics
NAGASAKA, T., Environmental Impact Assessment
NARISAWA, M., Korean Ethnoculture
NIITSUMA, H., Earth System Monitoring and Instrumentation
SAITO, T., Urban Environment
SAKAIDA, K., Physical Environmental Geography
SATAKE, M., International Economic and Environmental Studies
TAKAHASHI, H., Earth Exploitation Environmental Studies
TANIGUCHI, S., Materials Process for Circulatory Society
TOHJI, K., Design of Eco-nanomaterials
TSUCHIYA, N., Environmental Geochemistry
YAMASAKI, N., Environmental Hydrothermal Processes
YOSHIOKA, T., Recycling Chemistry

Graduate School of Information Sciences (Aoba, Aramaki, Aobu-ku, Sendai 980-8579; tel. (22) 795-5813; e-mail is-syom@bureau.tohoku.ac.jp; internet www.is.tohoku.ac.jp):

ADACHI, Y., Media and Semiotics
AKAMATSU, T., Road Transportation and Traffic
ANDO, A., Econometric System Analysis
AOKI, T., Computer Structures
DEGUCHI, K., Image Analysis
EBISAWA, H., Physical Fluctuomatics
FUKUCHI, H., Verbal Text Analysis
HASHIMOTO, K., Intelligent Control Systems
HIAI, F., Mathematical Systems Analysis III
HIDA, W., Health Informatics
HORIGUCHI, S., Firmware Science
INAMURA, H., International and Intermodal Transportation
ITOI, K., Information Biology
IWASAKI, S., Cognitive Psychology
KAMEYAMA, M., Intelligent Integrated Systems
KANEKO, M., Mathematical Structures II
KATO, N., Information Technology
KINOSHITA, T., Communication Software Science
KOBAYASHI, H., Ultra-high-speed Information Processing Algorithm
KOBAYASHI, K., Theory of Social Structure and Change
KOBAYASHI, N., Foundations of Software Science
KUDOH, J., Environmental Informatics
MARUOKA, A., Computation Theory
MORISUGI, H., Regional and Urban Planning
MUNEMASA, A., Mathematical Structures I
NAKAJIMA, K., Brain Function Integration
NAKAMURA, T., Computer Architecture
NAKAO, M., Biomodelling
NEMOTO, Y., Communication Science
NISHIZEKI, T., Algorithm Theory
NUMASAWA, J., Information Storage Systems
OBATA, N., Mathematical Systems Analysis II
OBAYASHI, S., Fusion Flow Informatics
OHORI, A., Logic for Information Science
OZAWA, M., Mathematical Structures III
SASAKI, K., Socio-economic Analysis of Urban Systems
SASOH, S., Flow System Informatics
SEKIMOTO, E., Media and Culture
SHINOHARA, A., System Information Sciences
SHIOIRI, S., Visual Recognition and Systems
SHIRATORI, N., Communication Theory
SHIZUYA, H., Information Security
SONE, H., Information Network Systems
SUNOUCHI, C., Mathematical Structures IV
SUZUKI, Y., Acoustic Information
TADOKORO, S., Human–Robot Informatics
TAKEUCHI, O., Philosophy of Human Information
TOKUYAMA, T., Design and Analysis of Information Systems
TOYAMA, Y., Logic for Information Science
TSUBOKAWA, H., Life Fluctuomatics
URAKAWA, H., Mathematical Systems Analysis I
YAMAMOTO, H., Political Analysis of the Information Society
YAMAMOTO, S., Mathematical Modelling

Graduate School of International Cultural Studies (Kawauchi, Aoba-ku, Sendai 980-8576; tel. (22) 795-7541; internet www.intcul.tohoku.ac.jp):

ASAKAWA, T., Language System
ASANO, Y., Asian Cultural Studies
FUJITA, M., Comparative Cultural Studies
FUJIWARA, I., Comparative Cultural Studies
HOLDEN, T., Multicultural Societies
ICHIKAWA, M., Cultural Uses of Language
IGAWA, M., American Studies
ISHIHATA, N., Cultural Uses of Language
ISHIKAWA, H., Asian Cultural Studies
KAWAHIRA, Y., Language Generation
KITAGAWA, S., Islamic Areas and Cultural Studies
KOBAYASHI, F., European Cultural Studies
KUSUDA, I., Language Systems
NUNOTA, T., European Cultural Studies
SASAKI, K., Linguistic Communication
SATO, K., Language Systems
SATO, S., Language Generation
SHIGAKI, M., Language Education
SUZUKI, M., Cultural Uses of Language
TAKAHASHI, R., Science, Technology and Environment
TAKENAKA, K., American Studies
TANAKA, T., Multicultural Societies
TATSUYOSHI, T., Monetary Economics
YAMAGUCHI, N., Linguistic Function
YAMASHITA, H., Multicultural Societies
YOKOKAWA, K., International Economic Relations
YONEYAMA, C., Linguistic Function

Graduate School of Life Sciences (tel. (22) 795-5702; internet www.lifesci.tohoku.ac.jp/index.html):

ARIMOTO, H., Biostructrual Chemistry
HIGASHITANI, A., Genomic Reproductive Biology
IDE, H., Organogenesis
IIJIMA, T., Systems Neuroscience
KATOW, H., Developmental Biology
KAWATA, M., Evolutionary Biology
KUMAGAI, T., Genetic Ecology in Critical Environments
KUSANO, T., Plant Molecular and Cellular Biology
MAEDA, Y., Control of Growth and Differentiation
MINAMISAWA, K., Environmental Microbiology
MIZUNO, K., Molecular Cell Biology
MURAMOTO, K., Functional Biomolecules
NAKAMURA, H., Molecular Neurobiology
NISHITANI, K., Plant Physiology
OHSHIMA, Y., Bio-organic Chemistry
SASAKI, M., Biostructural Chemistry
SOGAWA, K., Gene Regulation
TAKAGI, T., Molecular Diversity
TAKAHASHI, H., Space and Adaptation Biology
TSUDA, M., Microbial Genetics
URABE, J., Community and Ecosystem Ecology
WATANABE, M., Plant Reproductive Biology
WATANABE, T., Organella Research
YAMAMOTO, D., Neurogenetics
YAMAMOTO, K., Molecular Genetics
YAWO, H., Molecular and Cellular Neurosciences

Information Synergy Center (6-3 Aoba, Aramaki, Aoba-ku, Sendai 980-8578; tel. (22) 795-3407; internet www.isc.tohoku.ac.jp):

KINOSHITA, T., Knowledge Engineering
KOBAYASHI, H., High-performance Computer Systems
SONE, H., Communication Networks
YOSHIZAWA, M., Communication Networks

Institute for Materials Research (2-1-1 Katahira, Aoba-ku, Sendai 980-8577; tel. (22) 215-2181; e-mail imr-som@imr.tohoku.ac.jp; internet www.imr.tohoku.ac.jp):

CHEN, M., International Frontier Center for Advanced Materials
FUKUYAMA, H., International Frontier Center for Advanced Materials
GOTO, T., Multifunctional Materials Science
HASEGAWA, M., Irradiation Effects in Nuclear and Related Materials
INOUE, A., Non-equilibrium Materials
IWASA, Y., Low-temperature Condensed State Physics
KAWASAKI, M., Superstructured Thin Film Chemistry
KAWAZOE, Y., Materials Design by Computer Simulation
KOBAYASHI, N., Low-temperature Physics
MAEKAWA, S., Theory of Solid State Physics
MATSUI, H., Nuclear Materials Engineering
MATSUOKA, T., Advanced Electronic Materials
NAKAJIMA, K., Crystal Physics
NOJIRI, H., Magnetism
SAKURAI, T., Surface and Interface Research
SATO, Y., Non-equilibrium Materials
SHIKAMA, T., Nuclear Materials Science
SHIOKAWA, Y., Radiochemistry of Metals
TAKANASHI, K., Magnetic Materials
UDA, S., Crystal Chemistry
WAGATSUMA, K., Analytical Science
WATANABE, K., High Field Laboratory for Superconducting Materials
YAMADA, K., Neuron and Gamma-ray Spectroscopy on Condensed Matters

Institute of Development, Ageing and Cancer (4-1 Seiryo-machi, Aoba-ku, Sendai 980-8575; tel. (22) 717-8443):

FUKUDA, H., Radiation Medicine
FUKUMOTO, M., Pathology
ISHIOKA, C., General Internal Medicine, Gastroenterology, Molecular Biology
KONDO, T., Thoracic Surgery, Lung Cancer, Lung Transplantation
MATSUI, Y., Developmental Biology
NUKIWA, T., Chest Physician, Molecular Biology
OBINATA, M., Cell Biology
OGURA, T., Developmental Neurobiology, Developmental Biology, Molecular Biology
SATAKE, M., Molecular Biology
SATO, Y., Vascular Biology
TAKAI, T., Experimental Immunology
TAMURA, S., Biochemistry and Molecular Biology
TSUCHIYA, S., Paediatrics
YAMAMOTO, T., Molceular Biology, General Medical Chemistry, Pathological Medical Chemistry

YAMBE, T., Artificial Organs, Cardiovascular Medicine
YASUI, A., DNA Repair and Ageing

Institute of Fluid Science (2-1-1 Katahira, Aoba-ku, Sendai 980-8577; tel. (22) 795-5302; e-mail shomu@ifs.tohoku.ac.jp; internet www.ifs.tohoku.ac.jp):

FUJISHIRO, I., Complex Dynamics
HAYASE, T., Super-real-time Medical Engineering
HAYASHI, K., Molten Geomaterials
IKOHAGI, T., Complex Flow Systems
INOUE, O., Advanced Computational Fluid Dynamics
ISHIMOTO, J., Reality-coupled Computation
KOBAYASHI, H., Complex Dynamics
KOHAMA, Y., Ultimate Flow Environment
MARUYAMA, S., Heat Transfer Control
NANBU, K., Gaseous Electronics
NISHIYAMA, H., Electromagnetic Intelligent Fluids
OBAYASHI, S., Integrated Fluid Informatics
OHARA, T., Molecular Heat Transfer
OHIRA, K., Cryogenic Flow
OTA, M., Biofluids Control
QIU, J., Intelligent Systems
SAMUKAWA, S., Intelligent Nano-process
SASOH, A., Ultra-high Enthalpy Flow
SUN, M., Interdisciplinary Shockwave Research
TAKAGI, T., Advanced Systems and Materials Evaluation
TAKEUCHI, S., Advanced Systems
TOKUYAMA, M., Theoretical Fluid Dynamics
TSUCHIYAMA, T., Advanced Technology for Environment and Energy

Institute of Multidisciplinary Research for Advanced Materials (2-1-1 Katahira, Aoba-ku, Sendai 980-8577; tel. (22) 795-5202; internet www.tagen.tohoku.ac.jp):

AJIRI, T., Organic Resources Chemistry
ARIMA, T., Strongly Correlated Electron Systems
HARADA, N., Chemistry of Molecular Chirality
ISSHIKI, M., High Purity Materials
ITAGAKI, K., Nonferrous Chemical Metallurgy
ITO, O., Photochemistry
KAINO, T., Materials Chemistry
KAKIHANA, M., Chemical Engineering
KASAI, E., Iron and Steel Engineering
KAWAMURA, J., Solid State Ion Physics
KITAKAMI, O., Magnetic Materials and Devices
KITAMURA, S., Ferrous Process Metallurgy
KOMEDA, T., Molecular Chemistry
KONO, S., Surface Physics
KOYAMA, T., Biochemistry
KURIHARA, K., Surface Forces
KYOTANI, T., Applied Chemistry
MIYASHITA, T., Materials Chemistry
MIZUSAKI, J., Solid State Ion Devices
MURAMATSU, A., Solid State Chemistry
NAKAMURA, T., Physical Process Engineering
NAKANISHI, H., Materials Chemistry
NODA, Y., Electronic Properties of Solids
OKA, Y., Solid State Spectroscopy
OTSUKA, Y., Catalytic and Chemical Processes
SAITO, F., Chemical Engineering, Powder Technology
SAITO, M., Chemistry
SATO, S., Metal Industrial Engineering
SATO, T., Inorganic Materials Chemistry
SHIMIZU, T., Bio-inorganic Chemistry
SINDO, D., Atomic Scale Morphology Analysis
SODEOKA, M., Chemistry
SUITO, H., Physico-chemical Metallurgy
SUZUKI, S., Physical Metallurgy
TERAUCHI, M., Electronic Diffraction and Spectrology
TERO, S., Physical Chemistry
TOCHIYAMA, O., Atomic Energy Engineering
TSAI, A., Materials Control
UDAGAWA, Y., X-ray Physics
UEDA, K., Molecular Physics
UMETSU, Y., Aqueous Processing, Physical Chemistry of Metals
YAMAMOTO, M., Soft X-ray Microscopy
YAMAUCHI, S., Physical Chemistry
YANAGIHARA, M., Soft X-ray Microscopy
YOKOYAMA, T., Chemical Engineering

International Exchange Center (Kawauchi, Aoba-ku, Sendai 980-8576; tel. (22) 795-7776; e-mail ryugaku@bureau.tohoku.ac.jp; internet www.insc.tohoku.ac.jp):

HORIE, K., Linguistic Typology and Japanese–Korean Comparative Linguistics
KASUKABE, Y., Development of the Short-term Student Exchange Programme
SATO, S., Japanese Language Teaching
SHIGENO, Y., Technologies of Resource and Material Processing
UEHARA, S., Linguistics and Phonetics
YOSHIMOTO, K., Formal Syntax and Japanese Intonation

New Industry Creation Hatchery Center (Aoba 6-6-10, Aramaki, Aoba-ku, Sendai 980-8579; tel. (22) 795-7105; e-mail liaison-office@niche.tohoku.ac.jp; internet www.niche.tohoku.ac.jp):

ICHIE, M., Music and Acoustical Medicine
ISHIDA, K., Advanced Materials based on Computer-aided Design and Microstructural Control
KAWASHIMA, R., Functional Brain Imaging
KOHNO, M., Research and Development on Genomics-protemics Technology and Free Radical Control
MIYAMOTO, A., Quantum Design of Nano-functional Materials
OHMI, T., DIIN (New Intelligence for IC Differentiation) Project
TAKAHASHI, M., Development of Self-assembled Monodisperse Nano-particles, Thin-film Media for Terabit Recording
TERASAKI, T., Drug Discovery and Development
UEMATSU, Y., Development of Technology for Preserving the Environment and Reducing Wind-induced Disaster
YAMANAKA, K., Advanced Ultrasonic Non-destructive Evaluation and Sensing
YOKOYAMA, H., Ultrabroadband Coherent Light Sources

Research Institute of Electrical Communication (2-1-1 Katahira, Aobaku, Sendai 980-8577; tel. (22) 795-5420; e-mail shomu@jm.riec.tohoku.ac.jp; internet www.riec.tohoku.ac.jp/index-j.html):

AOI, H., Information Storage Systems
CHO, Y., Dialectric Nano-devices
EDAMATSU, K., Quantum Optics and Optical Spectroscopy
HANYU, T., Next-generation VLSI Computing
ITO, H., Quantum and Optoelectronics
MASUOKA, F., Electron Devices
MATSUOKA, H., Advanced Practical Information Technology Development
MIZUNO, K., Electron Devices
MURAOKA, H., Information Recording Devices
MUROTA, J., Atomically Controlled Processing
NAKAJIMA, K., Intelligent Integrated Systems
NAKAMURA, Y., Information Storage Engineering
NAKAZAWA, M., Ultra-High-Speed Optical Communication
NIWANO, M., Molecular Electronics, Silicobioelectronics
NUMAZAWA, J., Video Storage Systems
OHNO, H., Compound Semiconductors, Quantum Structures and Spintronics
OHORI, A., Computer Science
OTSUJI, H., Ultrafast and Ultrabroadband Electronics
SHIRAI, M., Advanced Functional Materials
SHIRATORI, N., Information Communication Systems
SIOIRI, S., Visual Cognition and Systems
SUGIURA, A., Electromagnetic Compatibility
SUZUKI, Y., Acoustic Signal Processing
TAKAGI, T., Wireless Mobile Systems
TANEICHI, M., Advanced Practical Information Technology Development
TOYAMA, Y., Computer Science
TSUBOUCHI, K., Wireless Internet System, Circuits and Devices
YANO, M., Informatics in Biological Systems

School and Graduate School of Arts and Letters (Kawanchi, Aoba-ku, Sendai 980-8576; tel. (22) 795-6003; e-mail art-syom@bureau.tohoku.ac.jp; internet www.sal.tohoku.ac.jp/index-j.html):

ABE, H., Western Literature and Languages
AKOSHIMA, K., Japanese History and Archaeology
CHIGUSA, S., Linguistics
GOTO, H., Linguistics
GOTO, T., Indology and History of Indian Buddhism
GYOBA, J., Psychology
HANATO, M., Sinology
HARA, E., Western Literature and Languages
HARA, J., Behavioural Science
HARA, K., Western Literature and Languages
HASEGAWA, K., Sociology
IMAIZUMI, T., Japanese History and Archaeology
KANEKO, Y., Western Literature and Languages
KAWAI, Y., Oriental History
KOBAYASHI, T., Japanese Linguistics
KUMAMOTO, T., Oriental History
MASAMURA, T., Sociology
MATSUMOTO, N., European History
MIURA, S., Sinology
MORIMOTO, K., Western Literature and Languages
NAKAOKA, R., History of Fine Arts
NAKAJIMA, R., Sinology
NAKAMURA, M., Western Literature and Languages
NIHEI, M., Japanese Literature and History of Japanese Philosophy
NIHEI, Y., Psychology
NOE, K., Philosophy and Ethics
NUMAZAKI, I., Cultural Anthropology and Science of Religions
OHBUCHI, K., Psychology
OHTO, O., Japanese History and Archaeology
ONO, Y., European History
OZAKI, A., History of Fine Arts
SAITA, I., Applied Japanese Linguistics
SAITO, M., Japanese Linguistics
SAITO, Y., Western Literature and Languages
SAKURAI, M., Indology and History of Indian Buddhism
SATO, H., Japanese Literature and History of Japanese Philosophy
SATO, M., European History
SATO, N., Japanese Literature and History of Japanese Philosophy
SATO, Y., Behavioural Science
SHIMA, M., Cultural Anthropology and Science of Religions
SHIMIZU, T., Philosophy and Ethics
SHINO, K., Philosophy and Ethics

SUTO, T., Japanese History and Archaeology
SUZUKI, A., Applied Japanese Linguistics
SUZUKI, I., Cultural Anthropology and Science of Religions
TAKAGI, K., Sociology
UMINO, M., Behavioural Science
YOSHIHARA, N., Sociology
ZAKOTA, Y., Philosophy and Ethics

School and Graduate School of Dentistry (4-1 Seiryo-machi, Aoba-ku, Sendai 980-8575; tel. (22) 717-8244; e-mail den-syom@bureau.tohoku.ac.jp; internet www.ddh.tohoku.ac.jp/index.html):

ECHIGO, S., Oral Surgery
HAYASHI, H., Oral Physiology
IGARASHI, K., Oral Dysfunction Science
KAWAMURA, H., Maxillofacial Surgery
KIKUCHI, M., Oral and Craniofacial Anatomy
KIMURA, K., Fixed Prosthodontics
KOMATSU, M., Operative Dentistry
KOSEKI, T., Preventive Dentistry
MAYANAGI, H., Paediatric Dentistry
OKUNO, O., Dental Biomaterials
ŌOYA, K., Oral Pathology
OSAKA, K., International Oral Health
SASAKI, K., Advanced Prosthetic Dentistry
SASANO, T., Oral Diagnosis and Radiology
SASANO, Y., Craniofacial Development and Regeneration
SHIMAUCHI, H., Periodontology and Endodontology
SHINODA, H., Dental Pharmacology
SUGAWARA, S., Oral Molecular Bioregulation
SUZUKI, O., Craniofacial Function Engineering
TAKADA, H., Oral Microbiology
TAKAHASHI, M., Dento-oral Anaesthesiology
TAKAHASHI, N., Oral Ecology and Biochemistry
WATANABE, M., Ageing and Geriatric Dentistry

School and Graduate School of Economics and Management (27-1 Kawauchi, Aoba-ku, Sendai 980-8576; tel. (22) 795-6263; e-mail webmaster@econ.tohoku.ac.jp; internet www.econ.tohoku.ac.jp/indexj.html):

AKITA, J., International Finance
AOKI, K., Comparative Economic Systems
AOKI, M., Cost Accounting
DOLAN, D., Business Communication
FUJII, T., International Accounting
FUKAI, T., Auditing
HASEBE, H., History of Japanese Economy
HAYASHIYAMA, Y., Environmental Economics
HINO, S., Modern Political Economy
HIRAMOTO, A., Japanese Economy
HOSOYA, Y., Econometrics
IPPOSHI, N., Accounting
ITO, T., Information Systems Management
KAMOIKE, O., Money and Banking
KANAZAKI, Y., Financial Management
KOHNO, D., Business Administration
KOHNO, S., Personnel Administration
KWEON, K. C., Research and Development Management
MASUDA, S., Regional Planning
MIYAKE, M., Macroeconomics
MORI, K., Political Economy
NAKAGAWA, T., International Management
NISHIZAWA, A., Policies for New Venture Creation
NOMURA, M., Social Policy
ODONAKA, N., Socio-intellectual History
OMURA, I., Political Economy
OTAKI, S., Business Policy
OTOMASA, S., Corporate Governance
SARUWATARI, K., Comparative Business Studies
SATO, H., International Economics
SEKITA, Y., Welfare Information System
SHIMOMURA, H., Tax Law
SUZUKI, T., Business History
TANIGUCHI, A., Types of Business Enterprise
TERUI, N., Marketing
TSUGE, N., Agricultural Economics
TSUKUDA, Y., Business Statistics
YASUDA, K., Management Information System

School and Graduate School of Education (Kawauchi, Aoba-ku, Sendai 980-8576; tel. (22) 795-6103; internet www.sed.tohoku.ac.jp/index-j.html):

AKINAGA, Y., Sociology of Education
ARAI, K., Educational Policy and Planning
HASEGAWA, K., Clinical Psychology
HONGO, K., Psychology and Disability
HOSOKAWA, T., Developmental Disorders
IKUTA, K., Philosophy of Education
KAJIYAMA, M., History of Japanese Education
KATO, M., History of Foreign Education
KAWASUMI, R., Compensation and Welfare of Disabilities
KIKUCHI, T., Developmental Psychology
KOIZUMI, S., Educational Process Studies
MIYAKOSHI, E., Comparative Educational Systems
MIZUHARA, K., Curriculum Studies
NAKAZIMA, N., Socio-cultural Study of Sport
OMOMO, T., Educational Administration
ONODERA, T., Educational Psychology
TAKAHASHI, M., Adult Education
UENO, T., Clinical Community Psychology
UNO, S., Educational Psychology

School and Graduate School of Engineering (6-6-04, Aramaki Aza Aoba, Aoba-ku, Sendai 980-8579; tel. (22) 795-5817; e-mail dean@eng.tohoku.ac.jp; internet www.eng.tohoku.ac.jp):

ABE, H., Urban Design
ABE, K., Fusion Reactor Engineering
ADACHI, F., Communication Systems
ANZAI, K., Casting and Advanced Solidification Processing
ASAI, H., Experimental Aerodynamics
ASAI, K., Solid State Physical Chemistry
ASO, H., Network Theory
CHONAN, S., Biomechatronics
EMURA, T., Intelligent Mechatronics
ESASHI, M., Micromachines
FUKINISHI, Y., Fluid Mechanics
FUKUNAGA, H., Space Structures
GALSTER, W., Energy Physics Engineering
HAMAJIMA, T., Applied Power Systems Engineering
HANE, K., Mechanoptics Design
HARA, N., Materials Electrochemistry
HARAYAMA, Y., Technology Policy
HASHIDA, T., Complex Fracture Systems Design
HASHIZUME, H., Fusion and Electromagnetic Engineering
HATAKEYAMA, R., Basic Plasma Engineering
HINO, M., Ferrous Process Metallurgy
HOKKIRIGAWA, K., Intelligent Systems Engineering
HOSHIMIYA, N., Biomedical Electronics
ICHINOKURA, O., Power Electronics
IGUCHI, Y., Socio-engineering
IIBUCHI, K., History of Architecture
IKEDA, K., Mathematical Systems Design
IMAMURA, F., Tsunami Engineering
INOMATA, H., Supercritical Fluid Technology
INOMATA, K., Spin-electronics Materials
INOUE, K., Machine Design
INOUE, N., Structural Engineering
INOUE, Y., Applied Organic Synthesis
INUTAKE, M., Magneto-Plasma-Dynamics Engineering
ISHIDA, K., Computational Microstructure Design
ISHII, K., Radiation Science and Engineering
ITAYA, K., Electrochemical Science and Technology
ITO, T., Solid State Electronics
IWAKUMA, T., Structural Mechanics
IWASAKI, S., Engineers Education and Educational Informatics
KAJITANI, T., Applied X-ray and Neutron Spectroscopy
KANAI, H., Electronic Control Engineering
KANNO, M., Architectural Planning
KATO, K., Tribology
KAWAMATA, M., Intelligent Electronic Circuits
KAWASAKI, A., Micro-power Processing and Systems
KAZAMA, M., Geotechnical Engineering
KISHINO, Y., Mechanics of Materials
KIYONO, S., Nanosystem Engineering
KOIKE, J., Device Reliability Science and Engineering
KOIKE, Y., Low Temperature Physics and Superconductivity Physics
KOKAWA, H., Interface Science and Engineering of Joining
KONNO, M., Material Processing
KOSUGE, K., System Robotics
KOYANAGI, M., Advanced Bio-nano Devices
KUMAGAI, I., Protein Technology
KURIYAGAWA, T., Nanoprecision Mechanical Fabrication
KUSHIBIKI, J., Instrumentation and Ultrasonic Micro-spectroscopy Network
KUWANO, H., Informative Nanotechnology
MAKINO, S., Intelligent Communication Engineering
MANO, A., Disaster Potential Research
MASUYA, G., Aerospace Systems
MATSUBARA, F., Applied Mathematical Physics
MATSUKI, H., Bio-electromagnetics
MATSUMOTO, S., Process Control
MIHASHI, H., Building and Materials Science
MIMURA, H., Nuclear Energy Flow, Environmental Engineering
MIURA, H., Fracture Control of Microstructures
MIURA, T., Energy Process Engineering
MIYAZAKI, T., Magnetism and Magnetic Materials
MIZOGUCHI, T., Environmental Chemistry
MOTOSAKA, M., Earthquake Engineering
NAGAHIRA, A., Management of Technology
NAKAHASHI, K., Aerodynamic Design
NAKAMURA, K., Acoustic Physics Engineering
NISHIMURA, O., Ecological Engineering
NISHIZAWA, M., Biomicromachine Engineering
NISINO, T., Applied Life Chemistry
NOIKE, T., Environmental Protection Engineering
NITTA, J., Materials Quantum Science
OHMI, T., Urban Planning and Analysis
OHTSU, H., Applied Nuclear Medical Engineering
OKADA, M., Energy Materials
OMURA, T., Water Quality Engineering
OOJI, A., Energy Conversion Technology
OTA, T., Control of Heat Transfer
OUCHI, C., Biomedical Materials
OYAMA, Y., Opto-electronic Materials
SAHASHI, M., Magnetic Microelectronics
SAITOH, H., Engineering for Information Society
SAKA, M., Mechanics of Materials Systems
SAKUMA, A., Solid-state Physics
SASAO, M., Fusion Plasma Diagnostics
SATO, M., Cell Biomechanics
SAWADA, K., Computational Aerodynamics
SAWAMOTO, M., Hydro-environment Systems
SAWAYA, K., Electromagnetic Wave Engineering

SEKINE, H., Smart System for Materials and Structures
SHINDO, Y., Mechanics and Design of Material Systems
SHODA, S., Functional Macromolecular Chemistry
SHOJI, K., Precision Machining
SMITH, R. L., Supercritical Fluid Technology
SOYAMA, H., Intelligent Sensing of Materials
SUGAWA, S., Advanced Functional Systems Engineering
SUGIMURA, Y., Structural Mechanics
SUZUKI, M., Structural Design Engineering
SUZUKI, M., Physicochemistry of Biomolecular Systems
TAKIZAWA, H., Synthetic Chemistry of Advanced Materials
TANAKA, H., Environmental Hydrodynamics
TOCHIYAMA, O., Nuclear Fuel Engineering
UCHIDA, S., Science and Engineering of Particle Beams
UCHIDA, T., Image Electronics
UCHIYAMA, M., Science and Engineering of Particle Beams
UEMATSU, Y., Wind Engineering
WADA, H., Biomechanical Engineering
WAKABAYASHI, T., Foundation of Risk Assessment and Management
WAKABAYASHI, T., Nuclear Energy Systems Safety Engineering
WATANABE, T., Material Design and Interface Engineering
YAMADA, M., Hydrocarbon Chemistry
YAMADA, M., Architectural Disaster Prevention Engineering
YAMADA, Y., Particle-beam Substance Reaction Engineering
YAMAGUCHI, M., Electromagnetic Theory
YAMAGUCHI, T., Computational Biomechanics
YAMAMURA, T., Physics and Chemistry of Fluids
YAMANAKA, K., Materials Evaluation and Sensing
YOKOBORI, T., Materials Design and Interface Engineering
YONEMOTO, T., Reaction Process Engineering
YOSHIDA, K., Space Exploration
YOSHINO, H., Building Environmental Engineering
YOSHINOBU, T., Biomedical Electronics
YUGAMI, H., New Energy Engineering

School and Graduate School of Law (27-1 Kawauchi, Aoba-ku, Sendai 980-8576; tel. (22) 795-6173; e-mail law-jm@bureau.tohoku.ac.jp; internet www.law.tohoku.ac.jp):

AOI, H., Jurisprudence
ARIKAWA, T., Constitutional Law
HIRATA, T., European Political History
IKUTA, O., Land Law
INABA, K., Administrative Law
KAISE, Y., International Civil Procedure
KAWAKAMI, S., Civil Law
KAWATO, S., Political Science, Modern Political Analysis
KOGAYU, T., Civil Law
MIZUNO, N., Civil Law, Family Law
MORITA, K., Administrative Law
OHNISHI, H., International Politics
OKAMOTO, M., Criminal Law
OUCHI, T., Western Legal History
OZAKI, K., International Law
SAITO, T., Criminology
SAKATA, H., Civil Procedure
SERIZAWA, H., Anglo-American Law, Transnational Law of Information
SHIBUYA, M., Tax Law
TSUJIMURA, M., Constitutional Law, Comparative Constitutional Law
UEKI, T., International Law
UEMURA, T., Current Japanese Administration
YAGYU, K., History of Political Theory
YAMAMOTO, H., Constitutional Law, Comparative Constitutional Law
YOSHIDA, M., Japanese Legal History
YOSHIHARA, K., Commercial Law, Commercial Law

School and Graduate School of Medicine (2-1 Seiryo-machi, Aoba-ku, Sendai 980-8575; tel. (22) 717-8005; e-mail med-som@bureau.tohoku.ac.jp; internet www.med.tohoku.ac.jp/index-j.html):

ABE, T., Clinical Cell Biology
AIBA, S., Dermatology
ARAI, Y., Urology
DODO, Y., Anatomy and Anthropology
DOHURA, K., Prion Biology
FUKUDO, S., Behavioural Medicine
FUNAYAMA, M., Forensic Medicine
HANDA, Y., Restorative Neuromuscular Rehabilitation
HATTORI, T., Allergy and Infectious Diseases
HAYASHI, Y., Paediatric Surgery
HONGO, M., Comprehensive Medicine (University Hospital)
HORII, A., Molecular Pathology
IGARASHI, K., Biochemistry
ITOH, S., Nephrology, Endocrinology and Vascular Medicine
ITOH, T., Immunology and Embryology
ITOYAMA, Y., Neurology
IZUMI, S., Physical Medicine and Rehabilitation
KAKU, M., Molecular Diagnostics
KASAI, N., Institute for Animal Experimentation
KATAGIRI, H., Advanced Therapeutics for Metabolic Diseases
KATOH, M., Anaesthesiology
KITAMOTO, T., Creutzfeldt–Jakob Disease Science and Technology
KOBAYASHI, T., Otolaryngology, Head and Neck Surgery
KOHZUKI, M., Internal Medicine and Rehabilitation Science
KOINUMA, N., Health Administration and Policy
KOKUBUN, S., Orthopaedic Surgery
KONDO, H., Histology
KONDO, Y., Medical Informatics
MARUYAMA, Y., Physiology I
MATSUBARA, Y., Medical Genetics
MATSUOKA, H., Psychiatry
MORI, E., Behavioural Neurology and Cognitive Neuroscience
NAGATOMI, R., Medicine and Science in Sport and Exercise
NAKAYAMA, K., Developmental Genetics
NODA, T., Molecular Genetics
OHUCHI, N., Surgical Oncology
OKA, Y., Molecular Metabolism and Diabetes
OKAMURA, K., Obstetrics
ONO, T., Genome and Radiation Biology
OSUMI, N., Developmental Neuroscience
SAIJO, Y., Molecular Medicine
SASAKI, I., General Surgery, Biological Regulation and Oncology
SASAKI, T., Rheumatology and Haematology
SASANO, H., Anatomical Pathology
SATOH, H., Environmental Health Sciences
SATOMI, S., Advanced Surgical Science and Technology
SHIBAHARA, S., Molecular Biology and Applied Physiology
SHIMOSEGAWA, T., Gastroenterology
SHINOZAWA, Y., Emergency and Critical Care Medicine
SHIRATO, K., Cardiovascular Medicine
SORA, I., Psychobiology
SUGAMURA, K., Immunology
TABAYASHI, K., Cardiovascular Surgery
TAKAHASHI, A., Neuroendovascular Therapy
TAKAHASHI, S., Diagnostic Radiology
TAKESHIMA, H., Biochemistry and Molecular Biology
TOMINAGA, T., Neurosurgery
TSUJI, I., Epidemiology
UEHARA, N., International Health
YAEGASHI, N., Gynaecological Oncology
YAMADA, A., Plastic and Reconstructive Surgery
YAMADA, S., Therapeutic Radiology
YAMAMURO, M., Pain Control
YANAGISAWA, T., Molecular Pharmacology
YANAI, K., Pharmacology
YOSHIMOTO, T., Neurosurgery

School and Graduate School of Pharmaceutical Sciences (Aoba, Aramaki, Aoba-ku, Sendai 980-8578; tel. (22) 795-6801; e-mail ph-som@bureau.tohoku.ac.jp; internet www.pharm.tohoku.ac.jp):

ANZAI, J., Pharmaceutical Physicochemistry
ENOMOTO, T., Molecular Cell Biology
FUKUNAGA, K., Pharmacology
IHARA, M., Medicinal Chemistry
IMAI, Y., Clinical Pharmacology and Therapeutics
IWABACHI, Y., Synthetic Chemistry
KONDO, Y., Molecular Transformation
KOSUGI, H., Organoreaction Chemistry
NAGANUMA, A., Molecular and Biochemical Toxicology
NAKAHATA, N., Cellular Signaling
OHIZUMI, Y., Pharmaceutical Molecular Biology
OHUCHI, K., Pathophysiological Biochemistry
OSHIMA, Y., Natural Products Chemistry
SAKAMOTO, T., Heterocyclic Chemistry
TAKEUCHI, H., Bio-structural Chemistry
TERASAKI, T., Membrane Transport and Drug Targeting
YAMAGUCHI, M., Organometallic Chemistry
YAMOZOE, Y., Drug Metabolism and Molecular Toxicology

School and Graduate School of Science (6-3 Aoba, Aramaki, Aoba-ku, Sendai 980-8578; tel. (22) 795-6346; e-mail sci-syom@bureau.tohoku.ac.jp; internet www.sci.tohoku.ac.jp):

AOKI, S., Atmospheric Physics
ASANO, S., Atmospheric Radiation, Physical Climatology
BANDO, S., Differential Geometry
CHIBA, M., Astrophysics
EZAWA, Z. F., Theoretical High Energy Physics, Condensed Matter Physics
FUJIMAKI, H., Geochemistry and Petrology
FUJIMOTO, H., Geodynamics of Subduction Zones
FUJIMURA, Y., Theoretical Chemistry
FUKUMURA, H., Physical Chemistry
FUKUNISHI, H., Upper Atmosphere Physics
FUTAMASE, T., Cosmology, General Relativity
HAMA, H., Beam Physics
HANAMURA, M., Algebraic Geometry
HANAWA, K., Physical Oceanography
HASEGAWA, A., Seismology
HASHIMOTO, O., Experimental Nuclear Physics
HATTORI, T., Mathematical Physics
HIKASA, K., Theoretical High Energy Physics
HINO, M., Human Geography
HIRAMA, M., Organic Chemistry
IGARASHI, G., Volcanology and Planetary Science
IMAIZUMI, T., Active Tectonics
INOUE, K., Experimental Particle Physics
ISHIDA, M., Algebraic Geometry
ISHIHARA, T., Solid State Photophysics
IWASAKI, T., Atmospheric Science
KABUTO, K., Organic Chemistry
KAIHO, K., Palaeontology

KASAGI, J., Nuclear Physics
KAWAKATSU, T., Physics of Soft Materials
KAWAMURA, H., Satellite Oceanography
KENMOTSU, K., Differential Geometry
KIRA, M., Organometallic Chemistry
KOBAYASHI, N., Functional Molecular Chemistry
KOBAYASHI, T., Experimental Nuclear Physics
KOZONO, H., Functional Analysis
KUDOH, Y., Mineralogy and Crystallography
KURAMOTO, Y., Theoretical Condensed Matter Physics
MIKAMI, N., Physical Chemistry
MINOURA, K., Palaeontology
MIYASE, H., Experimental Nuclear Physics
MORIOKA, A., Planetary Space Science
MORITA, N., Organic Chemistry
MORITA, Y., Number Theory
MURAKAMI, Y., Solid State Physics
NAKAMURA, T., Number Theory
NAKAZAWA, T., Atmospheric Physics
NIIZEKI, K., Theoretical Condensed Matter Physics
NISHIKAWA, S., Differential Geometry
ODA, M., Micropalaeontology
OGAWA, T., Partial Differential Equations and Applied Analysis
OHKI, K., Biophysics
OHNO, K., Physical Chemistry
OHTANI, E., Geochemistry and Planetology
OKAMOTO, H., Atmospheric Radiation
OKANO, S., Planetary Spectroscopy
ONO, T., Planetary Plasma Physics
ONODERA, H., Microscopic Research on Magnetism
OTSUKI, K., Tectonics and Structural Geology
SAIKAN, S., Non-linear Laser Spectroscopy
SAIO, H., Astrophysics
SAITO, R., Solid State Theory Nanotube
SATO, H., Seismology
SATOH, T., Experimental Ultra Low Temperature Physics
SEKI, M., Astrophysics
SHIMIZU, H., Nuclear Physics
SUTO, S., Surface Physics
SUZUKI, A., Experimental Particle Physics
SUZUKI, M., Plant Anatomy
TAKAGI, I., Partial Differential Equations
TAKAHASHI, T., Photoemission Solid State Physics
TAKAHASHI, T., Number Theory
TAKEDA, M., Probability Theory
TAKIGAWA, N., Theoretical Nuclear Physics
TAMURA, S., Astronomy
TANAKA, K., Mathematical Logic and Foundations of Mathematics
TANIGAKI, K., Solid State Physics
TERAMAE, N., Analytical Chemistry
TOBITA, H., Inorganic Chemistry
TOSA, M., Astronomy
TOYOTA, N., Molecular Metals
TSUBOTA, H., Experimental Nuclear Physics
UEDA, M., Natural Product Chemistry
UMINO, N., Seismotectonics
YAMAGUCHI, A., Experimental High Energy Physics
YAMAMOTO, H., Experimental High Energy Physics
YAMAMOTO, Y., Organic Chemistry
YAMASHITA, M., Coordination Chemistry
YANAGIDA, E., Partial Differential Equations
YASUDA, N., Meteorology
YOSHIDA, T., Volcanology and Petrology
YOSHIFUJI, M., Organic Chemistry
YUKIE, A., Number Theory

School of Agriculture and Graduate School of Agricultural Science (1-1 Tsutsumidori-Amamiyamachi, Aoba-ku, Sendai 981-8555; tel. (22) 717-8603; e-mail agr-syom@bureau.tohoku.ac.jp; internet www.agri.tohoku.ac.jp):

AKIBA, Y., Animal Nutrition
GOMI, K., Microbial Biotechnology
HASEBE, T., Environmental Economics
IKEDA, I., Food and Biomolecular Science
IKEGAMI, M., Plant Pathology
KAMIO, Y., Applied Microbiology
KANAHAMA, K., Horticultural Science
KATSUMATA, R., Animal Microbiology
KIJIMA, A., Ecological Genetics (Field Science Center)
KOKUBUN, M., Crop Science
KOMAI, M., Nutrition
KUDO, A., Farm Business Management
KUWAHARA, S., Applied Bio-organic Chemistry
MAE, T., Plant Nutrition and Function
MATSUDA, K., Insect Science and Bioregulation
MINAMI, T., Fisheries Biology and Ecology
MIYAZAWA, T., Biodynamic Chemistry
MOROZUMI, K., Regional Planning
MUROGA, K., Aquacultural Biology
NAKAI, Y., Animal Health and Management
NANZYO, M., Soil Science
NISHIDA, A., Animal Breeding and Genetics
NISHIMORI, K., Molecular Biology
NISHIO, T., Plant Breeding and Genetics
OBARA, Y., Animal Physiology
OHKAMA, K., Agricultural and Resource Economics
OMORI, M., Fisheries Biology and Ecology
SAIGUSA, M., Environmental Crop Science (Field Science Center)
SAITO, G., Remote Sensing (Field Science Center)
SAITO, T., Animal Products Chemistry
SATO, E., Animal Reproduction
SATO, M., Marine Biochemistry
SATO, S., Land Ecology
SEIWA, K., Forest Ecology
SUZUKI, T., Marine Biotechnology
TANIGUCHI, A., Biological Oceanography
TANIGUCHI, K., Applied Aquatic Botany
TANIGUCHI, N., Applied Population Genetics
TORIYAMA, K., Environmental Biotechnology
YAMAGUCHI, T., Functional Morphology
YAMASHITA, M., Biophysical Chemistry
YAMAYA, T., Plant Cell Biochemistry
YONEKURA, H., Resource Management and Development Policy

School of Health Science, Faculty of Medicine (2-1 Seiryo-machi, Aoba-ku, Sendai 980-8575; tel. (22) 717-7903; e-mail cms-syom@bureau.tohoku.ac.jp; internet www.cms.tohoku.ac.jp):

HAYASHI, S., Molecular Oncology
ISHIDA, M., Management of Nursing
ITAGAKI, K., Fundamental Nursing
KOBAYASHI, K., Clinical Investigation
KUROKAWA, T., Microbiology
MARUOKA, S., Nuclear Medicine
MASUDA, T., Pathology
MORI, I., Medical Imaging
NEMOTO, R., Adult Nursing
OISHI, M., Image Engineering
OOTAKA, T., Haematology
SAITO, H., Community Health Nursing
SAITO, H., Psychiatry
SAITO, K., Midwifery
SHINDOH, C., Respiratory Physiology
SHIWAKU, H., Child Health Nursing
TAKABAYASHI, T., Maternity Investigation
TAMURA, H., Neuroradiology
ZUGUCHI, M., Diagnostic Radiology

Tohoku University Museum (Aoba 6-3, Aramaki, Aoba-ku, Sendai 980-8578; tel. (22) 795-6767; e-mail staff@museum.tohoku.ac.jp; internet www.museum.tohoku.ac.jp):

EHIRO, M., Geology and Palaeontology
YANAGIDA, T., Archaeology

TOKYO INSTITUTE OF TECHNOLOGY

2-12-1, Ookayama, Meguro-ku, Tokyo 152-8550

Telephone: (3) 5734-3827
E-mail: kenkyusha@jim.titech.ac.jp
Internet: www.titech.ac.jp

Founded 1881
Independent
Academic year: April to March

Pres.: KENICHI IGA
Exec.Vice-Pres. for Education: AKIO SAITO
Exec.Vice-Pres. for Finance: HIROMITSU MUTA
Exec.Vice-Pres. for Planning: ICHIRO OKURA
Exec.Vice-Pres. for Research: TATSUO IZAWA
Dir-Gen. of Admin. Bureau: DAISUKE IKEDA
Dir of Institute Library: EIJI FUJIWARA

Library of 886,484 vols
Number of teachers: 1,149
Number of students: 6,477

DEANS

School of Bioscience and Biotechnology: TOMOYA KITAZUME
School of Engineering: KEN OKAZAKI
School of Science: MAKOTO OKA
Graduate School of Bioscience and Biotechnology: TOMOYA KITAZUME
Graduate School of Decision Science and Technology: HIROMITSU MUTA
Graduate School of Engineering: KEN OKAZAKI
Graduate School of Information Science and Engineering: YUKIO TAKAHASHI
Graduate School of Innovation Management: TAKAO ENKAWA
Graduate School of Science and Engineering: MAKOTO OKA
Interdisciplinary Graduate School of Science and Engineering: SACHIHIKO HARASHINA

PROFESSORS

Graduate School of Bioscience and Biotechnology:

AKAIKE, T., Biomaterial Design
AONO, R., Microbial Physiology, Genetic Engineering
FUJIHIRA, M., Biomolecular Processes
HAMAGUCHI, Y., Cell Biology
HANDA, H., Biotechnology
HASHIMOTO, H., Bio-organic Chemistry
HIROSE, S., Biochemistry
ICHINOSE, H., Neurochemistry and Neuropharmacology
IKAI, A., Biodynamics
INOUE, Y., Enzyme Functions
ISHIKAWA, T., Biofunctional Engineering
KISHIMOTO, T., Cell and Developmental Biology
KITAMURA, N., Molecular Biology
KITAZUME, T., Bio-organic Chemistry
KUDO, A., Molecular Immunology
MOTOKAWA, T., Animal Physiology
NAKAMURA, S., Genetic Engineering
OKADA, N., Molecular Evolution
OKAHATA, Y., Fundamentals of Biomolecules
OKURA, I., Biophysical Chemistry, Enzyme Chemistry
SATO, F., Molecular Design of Biological Importance
SEKINE, M., Bio-organic Chemistry
SHISHIDO, K., Molecular Biology
TAKAMIYA, K., Plant Physiology
TANAKA, N., Protein Crystallography
UENO, A., Bio-organic Chemistry, Molecular Recognition
UNNO, H., Biochemistry

Graduate School of Decision Science and Technology:

ENKAWA, T., Production Management
HASHIZUME, D., Sociology

HAYASAKA, M., History of Politics (Slavic Studies)
HIDANO, N., Regional Planning and Infrastructure Project Appraisal
HIGUCHI, Y., Socioeconomic Networks
IGUCHI, T., Japanese Literature
IIJIMA, J., Systems Theory
IMADA, T., International Relations
ISHII, M., Sports Psychology
ITO, K., Ergonomics, Production Control
KIJIMA, K., Management Systems
KIMOTO, T., History of Technology
KUWAKO, T., Philosophy
KYOMOTO, N., Intellectual Property Strategy, Licensing, Software Protection
MAYEKAWA, S., Psychometrics, Educational Statistics, Multivariate Data Analysis
MIYAJIMA, M., Industrial Management
MIYAKAWA, M., Applied Statistics, Quality Control
MIZUNO, S., Operations Research
MURAKI, M., Process Management
MUTA, H., Educational Planning, Economics of Education
MUTO, S., Game Theory
NAKAGAWA, M., Educational Psychology
NAKAHARA, Y., Exercise Physiology
NAKAI, N., Urban Planning
SAIKI, T., Patenting of Pharmaceutical Inventions
SAITO, T., Sociometrics
SAITO, U., Regional Landscape Planning and Design
TANAKA, Z., Political Science
WARAGAI, T., Philosophy, Logic
WATANABE, C., Technology Policy, Technology Management
YAMAMURO, K., Document Analysis
YAMATO, T., Economic Theory
YAMAZAKI, M., History of Science
YANO, M., Social Planning

Graduate School of Information Science and Engineering:
FUJII, S., Environmental Engineering
FUJIWARA, E., Coding Theory, Computer Systems
FURUI, S., Speech Recognition, Human Interfaces
HIGUCHI, Y., Socioeconomic Networks
HIROSE, S., Applied Solid Mechanics, Ultrasonic Nondestructive Evaluation, Numerical Analysis using Boundary Element Method
KIMEI, H., Geophysical Prospecting
KIMURA, K., Vibration, Stochastic Dynamics, Nonlinear Dynamics
KOJIMA, M., Mathematical Programming
KOJIMA, S., Geometry and Topology
MASE, S., Spatial Statistics
MORI, K., Computer Systems, Distributed Computing
NADAOKA, K., Environmental Systems Analysis, Coastal and Ocean Engineering, Mesoscale Meteorology, Applied Remote Sensing, Coastal-space Design, Applied Fluid Dynamics
NAKAJIMA, M., Computer Graphics, Image Processing
NAKAMURA, H., Strength of Materials
OGAWA, H., Pattern Recognition, Image Processing
SAEKI, M., Software Engineering
SASAJIMA, K., Precision Engineering, Measuring Systems
SASSA, M., Computer Software, Programming Environments
SATO, T., Artificial Intelligence and Logic Programming
SHIBAYAMA, E., Software Science, Parallel and Distributed Computing
SHIMIZU, M., Biomechanics, Fluid Dynamics
TAKAHASHI, W., Functional Analysis and its Applications
TAKAHASHI, Y., Applied Probability, Operations Research
TAKIGUCHI, K., Mechanics of Building Structures, Disaster Prevention Systems, Concrete Engineering
TANAKA, H., Natural Language Processing
TOKUDA, T., Software Engineering
UJIHASHI, S., Biomechanics, Sports Engineering, Safety Engineering
WATANABE, O., Theory of Computation
YONEZAKI, N., Applied Logic, Software Science

Graduate School of Science and Engineering:
ABE, M., Electronic Properties of Matter
AKAGI, H., Power Engineering, Power Electronics, Electrical Machines
ANDO, I., Polymer Structure, NMR Spectroscopy, Electronic Structure of Polymers
ANDO, M., Antennas, Electromagnetic Wave Theory
ANDO, T., Physics, Condensed Matter Theory, Quantum Hall Effect, Semiconductor Quantum Structures
AOKI, Y., Urban Planning
ARAKI, K., Coding Theory, Digital Communication Systems
ASAHI, K., Experimental Nuclear Physics
DAIMON, M., Cement Chemistry, Porous Materials, Hydrochemical Synthesis
ENDO, M., Solid Vibrations
ENOKI, T., Physical Chemistry
FUJII, N., Electronic Circuits and Networks
FUJIMOTO, Y., Bio-organic Chemistry
FUJIOKA, H., History of Architecture, Architectural Design
FUJITA, T., Algebraic Geometry
FURUYA, K., Optical and Quantum Electronics
FUTAKI, A., Differential Geometry
HAGIWARA, I., Collaboration Engineering
HANNA, J., Imaging Materials
HASHIMOTO, T., Polymer Processing, Thermal Properties of Polymers
HIGUCHI, Y., Exercise Physiology
HINODE, H., Inorganic Synthesis of Solids, Inorganic Industrial Chemistry
HIRAO, A., Polymer Syntheses
HIROSE, S., Robotics, Biomechanics
HONKURA, Y., Geophysics
HOSOYA, A., Theoretical Cosmology
ICHIMURA, T., Molecular Spectroscopy
IGUCHI, I., Condensed Matter Physics and Superconducting Electronics
IIO, K., Experimental Condensed Matter Physics
IKARIYA, T., Homogeneous Catalysis, Synthetic Organic Chemistry
IKEDA, S., Hydraulics and Environmental Fluid Mechanics
INOU, N., Biomechanics, Autonomous Decentralized Systems, Robotics
INOUE, A., Singularity, Algebraic Geometry
INOUE, T., Physical Chemistry of Polymer Materials
ISHII, S., Singularity and Bifurcation
ISHII, S., Electric Power Engineering, Plasma
ISHIZU, K., Polymer Syntheses, Polymer Reactions
IWAMOTO, M., Electronic Materials
IWASAWA, N., Synthetic Organic Chemistry
IWATSUKI, N., Robotics
KAIZU, Y., Coordination Chemistry
KAJIUCHI, T., Biochemical Engineering, Environmental Chemical Engineering
KAKIMOTO, F., Experimental Cosmic Ray Physics
KAKIMOTO, M., Polymer Syntheses, Thin Polymer Films
KAKINUMA, K., Bio-organic Chemistry
KAWAI, N., Astrophysics
KAWAMURA, K., Physics, Inorganic Chemistry, Mineral Physics
KAWASAKI, J., Mass Transfer Operations
KAWASHIMA, K., Earthquake Engineering
KIKUTANI, T., Fibre and Polymer Processing, Physical Properties of Polymers
KISHIMOTO, K., Strength of Materials, Computational Mechanics
KITAGAWA, A., Fluid Power Control
KOBAYASHI, A., Industrial Measurement
KOBAYASHI, H., Fracture Mechanics and Fatigue
KONAGAI, M., Semiconductors
KOSHIHARA, S., Materials Science
KOUCHI, N., Physical Chemistry of Atomic and Molecular Processes
KUMAZAWA, I., Human Interface
KUNIEDA, H., Integrated Circuits, Signal Processing
KURODA, C., Process Information Systems
KUROKAWA, N., Number Theory
KUSAKABE, O., Geotechnical Engineering
KYOGOKU, K., Tribology, Machine Elements
MARUYAMA, S., Geology, Tectonics
MARUYAMA, T., Physical Chemistry in Advanced Materials
MATSUI, Y., Advanced Thermo-fluid Dynamics
MASUKO, M., Tribology, Applied Surface Chemistry
MATSUO, T., Physical Metallurgy of Iron and Steels, High Temperature Deformation in Alloys
MATSUO, Y., Mechanical Properties of Ceramics
MATSUZAWA, A.
MIKI, C., Structural Mechanics and Engineering
MIMACHI, K., Special Functions, Material Physics, Representation Theory, Holonomic Systems
MINAMI, F., Solid State Physics and Laser Spectroscopy
MITA, T., Control Theory, Applications of Control Theory, Robotics
MIYAUCHI, T., Fluid Dynamics, Reactive Gas Dynamics
MIYAZAKI, K., Technology Strategy and Diffusion
MIZUTANI, N., Advanced Ceramics, Ceramic Processing, Electro-ceramics, Thin Films
MOCHIMARU, Y., Computational Fluid Dynamics
MORIIZUMI, T., Bioelectronics
MUNEKATA, H., Applied Physics of Property and Crystallography
MURAI, T., Wanderology
MURAKAMI, H., Workshop Processes and Production Engineering
MURATA, M., Differential Equations
NAGAHASHI, H., Image Processing
NAGAI, T., Solar–Terrestrial Physics
NAGATA, K., High-Temperature Physical Chemistry and Electronic Materials
NAKAHARA, T., Lubrication Technology, Two-Phase Flow, Oil Hydraulics
NAKAJIMA, K., Chemical Engineering
NAKAMURA, Y., Diffraction Crystallography, Magnetic Thin Film
NAKASHIMA, S., Experimental Physical Geochemistry, Geochemical Spectroscopy and Kinetics, Physicochemical Properties of Water in the Earth, Organic–Inorganic Interactions and the Origin of Life, Geochemistry of Resources and the Environment
NAKAZAWA, K., Planetary Physics
NISHI, T., Polymer Alloys, Soft Materials, Polymer Nanotechnology
NISHIDA, N., Experimental Condensed Matter Physics, Low-Temperature Physics
NISHIMORI, H., Statistical Physics
NIWA, J., Structural Concrete
OBIKAWA, T., Machining, Materials Science, Mechanical Processing Systems
OGAWA, K., Mechanical Operations

OGAWA, T., Steel and Shell Structures
OGUNI, M., Physical Inorganic Chemistry
OHASHI, H., Power Semiconductor Devices
OHASHI, Y., Crystal Chemistry
OHTA, H., Geotechnical Engineering
OHTAGUCHI, K., Biochemical Reaction Engineering
OKA, M., Theoretical Nuclear Physics
OKADA, K., Ceramic Raw Materials, Mineralogical Science
OKADA, T., Analytical Chemistry
OKAZAKI, K., Thermal and Environmental Engineering
OKUDA, Y., Low-Temperature Physics
OKUI, N., Organic Thin Films, Physical Properties of Polymers
OKUMA, M., Dynamics, Optimum Design
OKUTOMI, M., Computer Vision
ONO, K., Dynamics of Machinery
ONZAWA, T., Welding and Materials Science
OTSUKA, K., Heterogeneous Catalysis, Electrocatalysis
OTSUKI, N., Construction Materials, Environmental Materials Design
SAITO, A., Thermal Engineering
SAITO, S., Theoretical Condensed Matter Physics
SAITO, Y., Manufacturing Engineering, CAD, CAM, Computer Intelligent Manufacturing
SAJI, T., Electrochemistry, Surface Chemistry
SAKAI, N., Theoretical Elementary Particle Physics
SAKAI, Y., Communication Systems
SAKAMOTO, K., Architectural Design
SAKANIWA, K., Communication Theory
SAMPEI, M., Control Theory (Linear and Non-linear) and its Application, Nonholonomic Systems
SATO, T., Materials Development, Magnetic Materials, Amorphous Metals
SATOH, I., Thermal Engineering, Heat Transfer Measurement
SENDA, M., Environmental Design
SHIBATA, S., Inorganic Materials Engineering
SHIBATA, T., Experimental Nuclear Physics
SHIBUYA, K., Physical Chemistry
SHIGA, H., Complex Analysis
SHIGA, T., Stochastic Processes
SUMITA, M., Solid Structure and Physical Properties of Organic Materials, Polymer Composites
SUSA, M., Physical Chemistry of Materials
SUZUKI, H., Organometallic Chemistry
SUZUKI, H., Radio Communications Engineering
SUZUKI, K., Organic Chemistry
SUZUKI, M., Plasma Engineering, Nuclear Chemical Engineering
SUZUMURA, A., Joining, High-Temperature Materials
TAKAGI, S., Analogue Integrated Circuits, Analogue Signal Processing
TAKAHASHI, E., Petrology, Geochemistry, Solid Geophysics
TAKAHASHI, T., Synthetic Organic Chemistry, Synthetic Processes for Natural Products
TAKATA, T., Supramolecular and Polymer Chemistry
TAKAYANAGI, K., Diffraction, Crystal Physics, Surface Physics
TAKEZOE, H., Optical and Electrical Properties of Organic Materials
TANIOKA, A., Physical Chemistry of Organic Materials, Membrane Science
TOKIMATSU, K., Geotechnical Engineering
TOKURA, H., Processing Technologies
TSUDA, K., Chemical Plant Materials
TSUNAKAWA, H., Geophysics
TSURU, T., Chemistry of Metal Surfaces, Electrochemistry, Corrosion and Passivity of Metals
TSURUMI, T., Electrical Properties and Structure of Inorganic Materials
UCHIYAMA, K., Stochastic Processes and Applied Probability
UEDA, M., Condensed Matter Theory, Quantum Optics
UEDA, M., Polymer Syntheses
UEDA, M., Wave Information Processing
UENO, S., Theory of Parallel and VLSI Computation
UYEMATSU, T., Information Theory, Data Compression
WAKIHARA, M., Inorganic Solid-State Chemistry
WATANABE, J., Structure and Properties of Polymer Liquid Crystals
WATANABE, Y., Experimental Particle Physics
YABE, T., Laser Nuclear Fusion, Computational Fluid Dynamics
YAGI, K., Experimental Condensed Matter Physics, Crystal and Surface Physics
YAI, T., Transport Planning and Engineering
YAMAJI, A., Materials Science
YOSHIDA, T., Topology
YOSHINO, J., Experimental Condensed Matter Physics

Interdisciplinary Graduate School of Science and Engineering (4259 Nagatsuta-cho, Midori-ku, Yokohama 226-8502; tel. (45) 922-1111):

AOYAGI, Y., Information Devices
ASADA, M., Quantum Electronics
DEGUCHI, H., Polymer Synthesis
DOI, Y., Polymer Synthesis
FUCHIGAMI, T., Catalytic Chemistry
HARA, M., Nanotechnology
HARASHINA, S., Environmental Planning, Conflict Resolution
HATORI, Y., Visual Communication System, Network Interface
HIROTA, K., Information Systems
HORIOKA, K., High Power Beam Technology, Laser Engineering
HOTTA, E., Plasma Engineering, Pulsed Power Technology
HOYANO, A., Urban and Building Environment
ISHIKAWA, T., Hydraulics and Hydrology
ISHIWARA, M., Nanomaterials
ITO, K., Computational Brain Science, Design and Control of Robotics and Prostheses
KABASHIMA, Y., Information and Communication Engineering
KANNO, R., Lithium Battery, Solid-State Ionics, Inorganic Materials Chemistry, Solid State Electrochemistry, High-Pressure and Thin-film Synthesis
KATO, M., Fracture and Deformation
KINUGASA, Y., Earthquake Geology, Environmental Geology
KOBAYASHI, S., Knowledge Information Processing
KOBAYASHI, T., Digital Signal Processing
KOHNO, T., Nuclear Physics, Heavy Ion-Beam Science
KOSUGI, Y., Neural Networks
KUMAI, S., Nano-electronics
MAEJIMA, H., Microprocessors, Special Purpose Processors, On-chip Systems
MIDORIKAWA, S., Earthquake Engineering
MISHIMA, Y., Physical Metallurgy and Alloy Design
NAKAMURA, K., Computational Neuroscience
NAKANO, Y., Environmental Engineering, Separation Process Engineering
NITTA, K., Artificial Intelligence, Regal Reasoning
ODAWARA, O., Electrochemistry of Metals
OHMACHI, T., Earthquake Engineering
OHNO, R., Architectural Design and Planning, Environmental Psychology
OHSAKA, T., Molten Salt Chemistry, Electrochemistry, Electroanalytical Chemistry, Bioelectrochemistry
OHTSU, M., Opto-quantum Electronics
OKAMURA, T., Cryogenic and Energy Conversion Engineering
ONAKA, S., Mechanical Properties of Materials
SAKAI, T., Semiconductor Devices
SASANO, S., History of Urban and Architectural Design
SATO, A., Strengthening Mechanism and Lattice Imperfections
SEO, K., Engineering Seismology
TAMURA, T., Environmental Atmospheric Turbulence, Urban Wind Climate, Aerodynamic Control
TEHRANO, T., Intelligent Informatics
UCHIKAWA, K., Visual Information Processing
WATANABE, M., Physical Geography
YAI, T., Transport Planning and Engineering
YAMAMURA, M., DNA Computing
YAMASAKI, H., Energy Conversion Engineering
YAMAZAKI, Y., Solid-State Physics and Chemistry
YOKOYAMA, M., Automated Machine Design
YOSHIKAWA, K., High-Temperature Energy Conversion, Environmental Fluid Dynamics

Chemical Resources Laboratory:

AKITA, M., Organometallic Chemistry
DOMEN, K., Surface Chemical Reaction
FUJII, M.
IKEDA, T., Polymer Chemistry and Photochemistry
ISHIDA, M., Chemical Engineering and Chemical Environmental Process Design
IWAMOTO, M., Heterogeneous Catalysis
IYODA, T., Functional Molecular Materials, Nano-structured Materials, Materials Electrochemistry
NAKA, Y., Process Systems Engineering
OSAKADA, K., Coordination and Organometallic Chemistry
SHODA, M., Biochemical Engineering, Applied Microbiology
TANAKA, M., Industrial Organic Chemistry
YAMAMOTO, T., Inorganic and Organometallic Chemistry
YAMASE, T., Photochemistry and Photoelectrochemistry
YOSHIDA, M., Biochemistry

Materials and Structures Laboratory:

ATAKE, T., Materials Science, Physical Chemistry
HAYASHI, S., Structural Engineering
ITOH, M., Physical Properties of Inorganic Materials
KASAI, K., Structural Engineering, Earthquake Engineering
KONDO, K., Inorganic Materials and Properties, Applied Physics of Property and Crystallography
SASAKI, S., Synchotron Radiation Science, X-ray Crystallography, Solid-State Physics
TANAKA, K., Inorganic Materials and Properties, Building Materials
WAKAI, F., Inorganic Materials and Properties
YAMAUCHI, H., Materials Science, Applied Physics of Property and Crystallography, Strongly Correlated Electron Materials, Superconducting Oxides
YASUDA, E., Ceramic Base Composites, Carbon Alloys and Materials
YOSHIMURA, M., Inorganic Materials and Properties, Soft Processing, Advanced Ceramics

Precision and Intelligence Laboratory:
- HATSUZAWA, T., Precise Measurement
- HIGO, Y., Physical Metallurgy, Nondestructive Evaluation
- HORIE, M., Kinematics of Machinery
- HOUJOH, H., Acoustic Measurement, Machine Dynamics
- KAGAWA, T., Process Control
- KOBAYASHI, K., Opto-electronics, Optical Communications, Photonic Integrated Semiconductor Devices
- KOYAMA, F., Optical Semiconductor Devices
- MASU, K., Advanced Microdevices
- OHTSUKI, S., Bio-medical Ultrasonics, Acoustic Engineering
- SATO, M., Pattern Recognition Image Processing
- SHINNO, H., Ultraprecision Machining, Machine Tool Engineering
- SIMOKOBE, A., Dynamics and Control of Precision Mechanisms
- UEHA, S., Ultrasonic Engineering, Applied Optics
- WAKASHIMA, K., Materials Science, Micromechanics of Composites
- WATANABE, S., Mathematics and Information Science
- YOKOTA, S., Fluid Power Control

Research Laboratory for Nuclear Reactors:
- ARITOMI, M., Nuclear Thermal Engineering
- FUJII, Y., Fusion Fuel Chemistry, Tritium Chemistry
- HATTORI, T., Accelerator Physics, Heavy Ion Inertial Fusion
- KATO, Y., Advanced Nuclear Reactor Systems Design, Complex Flow Computer Simulation
- NINOKATA, H., Reactor Safety, Reactor Physics
- OGAWA, M., Beam Plasma Sciences, Nuclear Fusion, Nuclear Physics
- SEKIMOTO, H., Neutronics, Nuclear Reactor Design
- SHIMADA, R., Fusion Reactor Control, Plasma Engineering
- TORII, H., Energy Policy
- YANO, T., Composite Materials and their Properties
- YOSHIZAWA, Y., Thermal Engineering, Energy System, Combustion

TOKYO MEDICAL AND DENTAL UNIVERSITY

5-45, Yushima 1-chome, Bunkyo-ku, Tokyo 113

Telephone: (3) 3813-6111

E-mail: kouhou.adm@tmd.ac.jp

Internet: www.tmd.ac.jp

Founded 1946

Independent

Academic year: April to March (2 semesters)

Pres.: AKIO SUZUKI

Dir-Gen.: O. KIKUKAWA

Dir for Univ. Library: KEIICHI OHYA

Library of 334,132 vols

Number of teachers: 696

Number of students: 2,921

Publications: *Bulletin*, *Bulletin of the Department of General Education*, *Reports of the Medical Research Institute*, *Reports of the Institute for Medical and Dental Engineering*

DEANS

College of Liberal Arts and Sciences: SAKUMI ITABASHI

Faculty of Dentistry: KAZUHIRO ETO

Faculty of Medicine: KATSUIKU HIROKAWA

Graduate School of Allied Health Sciences: RYUICHI KAMIYAMA

ATTACHED INSTITUTES

Institute for Medical and Dental Engineering: 3-10, Kandasurugadai 2-chome, Chiyoda-ku, Tokyo 101; Dir T. TOGAWA.

Medical Research Institute: 3-10, Kandasurugadai 2-chome, Chiyoda-ku, Tokyo 101; e-mail webmaster.mri@tmd.ac.jp; internet www.tmd.ac.jp/mri; Dir A. SAKUMA

TOKYO NATIONAL UNIVERSITY OF FINE ARTS AND MUSIC

12-8 Ueno Park, Taito-ku, Tokyo 110-8714

Telephone: (3) 5685-7500

E-mail: toiawase@ml.geidai.ac.jp

Internet: www.geidai.ac.jp

Founded 1949

Pres.: IKUO HIRAYAMA

Dir of Univ. Library: HIROMICHI UENO

Sec.-Gen.: YOSHIYUKI OTAWA

Library: see under Libraries and Archives

Number of teachers: 218 full-time

Number of students: 2,785

DEANS

Faculty of Fine Arts: KIJO ROKKAKU

Faculty of Music: AKIO SONODA

TOKYO UNIVERSITY OF AGRICULTURE AND TECHNOLOGY

2-8-1 Harumi-cho, Fuchu-shi, Tokyo 183

Telephone: (423) 64-3311

E-mail: koho2@cc.tuat.ac.jp

Internet: www.tuat.ac.jp

Founded 1949

Independent

Language of instruction: Japanese

Academic year: April to March

Pres.: HIDEFUMI KOBATAKE

Vice-Pres: TADASHI MATSUNAGA, TAKAHIKO ONO, AKIRA SASAO, HIROFUMI TAKEMOTO

Library Dir: HIROYUKI OHNO

Library of 524,018 vols

Number of teachers: 442

Number of students: 5,966 (4,032 undergraduate, 1,934 graduate)

Publication: faculty bulletins (1 a year)

DEANS

Faculty of Agriculture: YASUHISA KUNIMI

Faculty of Technology: AKINORI KOKITSU

Graduate School of Bio-applications and Systems Engineering: MASANORI OKAZAKI

Graduate School of Technology Management: HIDEO KAMEYAMA

United Graduate School of Agricultural Science: YUTARO SENGA

TOKYO UNIVERSITY OF FISHERIES

5–7 Konan 4, Minato-ku, Tokyo 108-8477

Telephone: (3) 5463-0400

E-mail: www-master@tokyo-u-fish.ac.jp

Internet: www.tokyo-u-fish.ac.jp

Founded 1888

Academic year: April to March

Pres.: Dr FUMIO TAKASHIMA

Vice-Pres: Dr K. SATO, Dr R. TAKAI

Admin. Dir: M. SATO

Librarian: Dr E. WATANABE

Library of 268,000 vols

Number of teachers: 171

Number of students: 1,745

Publication: *Journal of the TUF* (2 a year)

HEADS OF LABORATORIES

Aquatic Biosciences:
- Aquatic Biology: Dr K. FUJITA, Prof. M. OMORI, Dr S. SEGAWA, Prof. J. TANAKA, Dr S. WATANABE
- Aquaculture: Dr T. TAKEUCHI, Dr M. NOTOYA, Dr N. OKAMOTO, Dr T. WATANABE, Dr H. FUKUDA
- Genetics and Biochemistry: Dr T. AOKI

Fisheries Resource Management:
- Fisheries Resource Management System: Dr T. KITAHARA, Dr S. YAMADA, Dr K. TAYA, Y. SATO, Dr K. UENO, Prof. Y. SATO
- Ecology and Economics of Fisheries Resources: Dr Y. NAKAI, Dr A. OHNO, Dr R. ISEDA, Dr N. KOIWA, Prof. Y. NAKAI
- International Economics of Fisheries and Food Industries: Dr K. SAKURAI

Food Science and Technology:
- Food Chemistry: Dr T. SUZUKI, Dr T. FUJII, Dr S. WADA, Dr M. TANAKA
- Food Engineering: Dr H. WATANABE, Prof. T. MIHORI, Dr R. TAKAI
- Marine Biochemistry: Dr S. KIMURA, Dr K. SHIOMI, Dr H. YAMANAKA, Dr T. HAYASHI, Dr T. WATANABE
- Applied Microbiology: Dr E. WATANABE

International and Interdisciplinary Studies:
- English: Dr S. MIURA
- Ethics: T. AMEMIYA
- French: T. SHIMANO
- History: O. KANAMORI
- Psychology: Dr K. NAKAMURA

Marine Science and Technology:
- Fishing Science and Technology: Dr T. ARIMOTO, Dr C. ITOSU, Dr H. KANEHIRO, Dr T. TOKAI
- Ocean Systems Engineering: Dr T. AKITA, Prof. Y. NAKAMURA, Dr K. SATOHH, Dr M. FURUSAWA, Dr S. YADA, Dr S. MURAMATSU

Ocean Sciences:
- Marine Ecosystem Studies: Dr T. ISHIMARU, Dr M. MAEDA, Dr M. NAMIKOSHI, Dr Y. YAMAGUCHI
- Physics and Environmental Modelling: Prof. Y. ANDO, Dr K. KIHARA, Dr M. MATSUYAMA, Dr T. MORINAGA, Dr H. NAGASHIMA, Dr H. OHASHI, Dr N. SHIOTANI

TOKYO UNIVERSITY OF FOREIGN STUDIES

3-11-1 Asahicho, Fuchu-shi, Tokyo 183-8534

Telephone: (42) 330-5126

E-mail: ml-zhenhp@tufs.ac.jp

Internet: www.tufs.ac.jp/index-j.html

Founded 1899, reorganized 1949

Semi-private instn

Pres.: SETSUHO IKEHATA

Dir-Gen.: M. KOTANI

Library Dir: N. TOMIMORI

Library: see under Libraries and Archives

Number of teachers: 241 full-time

Number of students: 4,282

Publication: *Area and Culture Studies* (2 a year)

DEANS

Faculty of Foreign Studies: AKIRA BABA

ATTACHED INSTITUTE

Research Institute for Languages and Cultures of Asia and Africa: 3-11-1 Asahicho, Fuchu-shi, Tokyo 183-8534; tel. (42) 330-5600; e-mail ilcaa@aa.tufs.ac.jp; internet www.aa.tufs.ac.jp; f. 1964; Dir Dr K. MIYAZAKI; publ. *Journal of Asian and African Studies* (2 a year), *Newsletter* (3 a year)

TOKYO UNIVERSITY OF MERCANTILE MARINE

2-1-6 Etchujima, Koto-ku, Tokyo 135-8533

Telephone: (3) 5245-7312

Internet: www.tosho-u.ac.jp

Founded 1875

Independent
Pres.: Akio M. Sugisaki
Dir of Admin. Bureau: Takao Oka
Library Dir: Suushin Sato

Number of teachers: 110 full-time
Number of students: 1,093

Publication: *Journals* (natural sciences, humanities and social sciences)

PROFESSORS

Electric Power: Yoshihiro Hatanaka
Floating Facilities: Kuniaki Shoji
Information Systems Engineering and Navigation Systems: Hayama Imazu
Internal Combustion Engines: Hiroshi Okada
International Cultural Studies: Takako Niwa
Logistics Engineering: Iwao Taminaga
Machinery and Equipment: Toshihiko Fujita
Marine Engineering and Guidance Control: Kohei Ohtsu
Marine Science and Technology: Hiroshi Yamagishi
Mathematical Science: Osamu Matsushita
Navigational Electronics: Shogo Hayashi
Nuclear Power: Tomoji Takamasa
Power Systems Engineering and Steam Power: Masahiro Osakabe

TOTTORI UNIVERSITY

4-101 Minami, Koyama-cho, Tottori City 680-0945
Telephone: (857) 31-5010
E-mail: net_adm@jim.tottori-u.ac.jp
Internet: www.tottori-u.ac.jp

Founded 1949
Academic year: April to March

Pres.: Masanori Michiue
Dir-Gen. of Admin.: Y. Suzuki
Librarian: K. Kosaka

Number of teachers: 762 full-time
Number of students: 6,090

DEANS

Faculty of Agriculture: M. Iwasaki
Faculty of Education and Regional Sciences: M. Nagayama
Faculty of Engineering: H. Kiyama
Faculty of Medicine: T. Nose

TOYAMA UNIVERSITY

3190 Gofuku, Toyama City 930-8555
Telephone: (764) 45-6011
E-mail: info@toyama-u.ac.jp
Internet: www.toyama-u.ac.jp

Founded 1949; Toyama Medical and Pharmaceutical University, Takaoka National College and Toyama University merged May 2003
Academic year: April to March (2 terms)

Pres.: Hiroshi Takizawa
Chief Admin. Officer: O. Imada
Librarian: H. Fujita

Library of 965,300 vols
Number of teachers: 445 full-time
Number of students: 7,400

DEANS

Faculty of Economics: S. Yoshihara
Faculty of Education: M. Kase
Faculty of Engineering: M. Tokizawa
Faculty of Humanities: N. Kotani
Faculty of Science: K. Matsumoto

TOYOHASHI UNIVERSITY OF TECHNOLOGY

Tempaku, Toyohashi, Aichi 441-8580
Telephone: (532) 47-0111
Internet: www.tut.ac.jp

Founded 1976
Private control
Academic year: April to March

Pres.: Dr Yoshiyuki Sakaki
Vice-Pres.: Yasuyoshi Inagaki
Vice-Pres.: Dr Kiyokatsu Jinno
Vice-Pres.: Dr Yo Kikuchi
Vice-Pres.: Dr Kazuhiko Terashima
Vice-Pres.: Dr Mitsuteru Ishida
Vice-Pres.: Dr Makoto Ishida
Dir-Gen. of Admin. Bureau: Toshiaki Tsuji
Librarian: Dr Noriyoshi Kakuta

Library of 170,000 vols
Number of teachers: 213
Number of students: 2,144

DEANS

Dept of Architecture and Civil Engineering: Hiroshi Matsumoto
Dept of Computer Science and Engineering: Jun Miura
Dept of Electrical and Electronic Information Engineering: Mitsuo Fukuda
Dept of Environmental and Life Sciences: Shinichi Itsuno
Dept of Knowledge-based Information Engineering: Yoshimasa Takahashi
Dept of Materials Science: Katsuyuki Aoki
Dept of Mechanical Engineering: Masao Uemura
Dept of Production Systems Engineering: Masahiro Kawakami
Institute of Liberal Arts and Sciences: Kiyokatsu Jinno

UNIVERSITY OF ELECTRO-COMMUNICATIONS

1-5-1 Chofugaoka, Chōfu City, Tokyo 182-8585
Telephone: (424) 43-5017
E-mail: kenkyo-k@office.uec.ac.jp
Internet: www.uec.ac.jp

Founded 1949
independent control
Language of instruction: Japanese
Academic year: April to March

Pres.: Takashi Fukuda
Library Dir: T. Miki

Number of teachers: 302 full-time
Number of students: 5,074 (3,758 undergraduate, 1,316 postgraduate)

DEANS

Informatics and Engineering: Kazuhiko Honjo
Information and Communications Systems: Hiroki Honda

UNIVERSITY OF MIYAZAKI

1-1 Gakuen Kibanadai Nishi, Miyazaki-shi, Miyazaki 889-2192
Telephone: (985) 58-7104
E-mail: kokusai@of.miyazaki-u.ac.jp
Internet: www.miyazaki-u.ac.jp

Founded 1949; present name and status 2003 following integration of Miyazaki Medical College
Independent
Academic year: April to March (2 semesters)

Pres.: A. Sumiyoshi
Registrar: K. Ohtani
Librarian: C. Tamura

Number of teachers: 624
Number of students: 5,450

Publications: Bulletins and memoirs of the faculties

DEANS

Faculty of Agriculture: S. Kobaye
Faculty of Education and Culture: T. Iwamoto
Faculty of Engineering: K. Hirano
Miyazaki Medical College: H. Kannan

UNIVERSITY OF THE RYUKYUS

1 Senbaru, Nishihara-cho, Okinawa 903-0213
Telephone: (98) 895-2221
E-mail: webmaster@www.u-ryukyu.ac.jp
Internet: www.u-ryukyu.ac.jp

Founded 1950
Academic year: April to March
Independent
Language of instruction: Japanese

Pres.: Teruo Iwamasa
Vice-Pres. for Financial, Facilities and Hospital Management: Hayao Miyagi
Vice-Pres. for Gen. Affairs: Takashi Maruyama
Vice-Pres. for Planning and Management Strategy: Hajime Oshiro
Vice-Pres. for Research Education and Student Affairs: Rishun Shinzato
Vice-Pres. for Research Outreach and Int. Affairs: Keisuke Taira
Dean of Students: Katsuma Yagasaki
Library Dir: K. Oyakawa

Library of 930,000 vols
Number of teachers: 879
Number of students: 8,195

DEANS

Faculty of Agriculture: S. Gibo
Faculty of Education: T. Nakamura
Faculty of Engineering: T. Yamakawa
Faculty of Law: K. Uezato
Faculty of Medicine: Y. Sato
Faculty of Science: M. Tsuchiya
Faculty of Tourism Sciences and Industrial Management: T. Heshiki
Graduate School of Health Sciences: T. Hokama
Graduate School of Law: T. Takara

PROFESSORS

Faculty of Agriculture:

Akinaga, T., Postharvest Handling
Chinen, I., Applied Biochemistry
Gibo, S., Land Conservation
Hayashi, H., Woody Materials and Processing
Higa, T., Tropical Horticulture
Higoshi, H., Animal Hygiene
Hirata, E., Forestry Measurement
Hongo, F., Chemistry of Animal Products and Applied Bioresource Utilization
Ishimine, Y., Economic Plants
Iwahashi, O., Insect Ecology
Kawashima, Y., Comparative Anatomy
Kobamoto, N., Applied Biophysics
Koki, Z., Preventive Forestry Engineering
Kuroda, T., Environmental Information Sciences
Miyagi, N., Soil Engineering
Murayama, S., Crop Science
Nakada, T., Animal Reproduction
Nakasone, Y., Food Chemistry
Oshiro, S., Animal Science, Environmental Physiology
Sato, S., Genetics and Breeding of Rice Plants
Shinjo, A., Animal Breeding
Shinjo, T., Geomechanics
Shinohara, T., Forest Policy and Economics
Tawata, S., Pesticide Chemistry
Tokashiki, Y., Soil Science
Ueno, M., Agricultural Engineering
Uesato, K., Floricultural Plant Science
Yaga, S., Wood Chemistry and Wood Preservation
Yamashiro, S., Agricultural Engineering
Yasuda, M., Food Microbiology
Yonaha, T., Plant Pathology

YOSHIDA, S., Agricultural Marketing Theory

Faculty of Education:

AIZAWA, T., Chinese Literature
ARATA, Y., Biophysics Engineering
FUJIE, T., Homemaking Education, Aesthetics in Costume
FUJIWARA, Y., Didactics
HAMAMOTO, M., Sports Methodology
HANASHIRO, R., Consumer Education
HIGA, Z., Technical Education
HIGASIMORI, K., Food Science
HIRATA, E., Education for the Handicapped
IKEDA, K., Judo
INOUE, K., Lifelong Education
ISHIGURO, E., Optics
ISHIKAWA, K., Social Development in Children
ITOKAZU, T., Educational Music of Wind Instruments
IZUMI, K., Vocal Music
KAKAZU, T., Psychology
KAMIYAMA, T., Woodcut
KAMIZONO, S., Developmental Psychology of Mentally and Physically Disabled Children
KATO, M., Complex Analysis
KAWANA, T., Physical Geography
KINJO, M., Mathematics Education
KINJO, S., Culinary Science
KINJO, Y., Inorganic Chemistry
KOBASHIGAWA, H., Sports Psychology
KOBAYASHI, M., Theory and History of Art
KOJIMA, Y., Japanese Literature
KOYANAGI, M., Physical Chemistry
MAEHARA, H., Discrete Geometry
MAEHARA, T., Psychology
MAESHIRO, R., Regional Economics
MATSUMOTO, S., Mathematical Physics
MIZUNO, M., Criminal Law
NAGAYAMA, T., Piano Playing
NAKAMURA, I., Meteorology
NAKAMURA, T., Education for the Handicapped
NAKAMURA, T., Theory of Music
NAKASONE, Y., Ecology
NAKAZATO, H., Algebra
NISHIMURA, S., Sculpture
NISHIZATO, K., History of East Asia
NOHARA, T., Palaeontology
OKUDA, M., Ceramic Art
OZAWA, Y., Japanese Literature
SEKINE, H., Electricity and Electrical Engineering
SHIMABUKURO, Z., English Linguistics
SHIMOJANA, M., Animal Ecology and Taxonomy (especially spiders)
SHINZATO, R., Clinical Psychology
SHINZATO, S., Kinematics and Dynamics of Mechanisms
SIMABUKURO, T., Psychology of Personality
TAIRA, K., Health Promotion
TAIRA, T., Physical Education
TAKASHIMA, N., Social Studies
TAKEDA, H., International Peace Studies
TAMAKI, A., Physical Education
TOMINAGA, D., Psychophysiology
UEZU, E., Nutrition and Physiology
YAMAUTI, S., TESL/TEFL
YONEMORI, T., Educational Information Technology

Faculty of Engineering:

AMANO, T., Wind Engineering for Building Structures
ASHARIF, M. R., Adaptive Digital Signal Processing, Speech in Images
FUKUSHIMA, S., Architectural Planning
IKEDA, T., Urban and Regional Planning
KANESHIRO, H., Fatigue Fracture
KINA, S., Sanitary Engineering
KODAMA, M., Microwave
MEKARU, S., Plastic Working
MIYAGI, H., Intelligent Systems
MIYAGI, K., High-Velocity Impact
MORITA, D., Conservation Science and Environmental Planning for Architecture
NAGAI, M., Mechanics and Fluid Engineering
NAGATA, T., Thermal Engineering
NAKAMURA, I., Electronic Circuits
NAKAO, Z., Mathematical Informatics
OSHIRO, T., Structural Analysis and Materials
OYAKAWA, K., Heat Transfer Augmentation
SHINZATO, T., Thermal Engineering
TAKAHASHI, H., Power Systems Engineering and Surge Analysis
TAKARA, T., Spoken Language Processing
TAMAKI, S., Digital Control
TOGUCHI, M., Electronic Materials
TSUKAYAMA, S., Coastal Engineering
TSUTSUI, S., Coastal Engineering
UEZATO, K., Electric Machinery
YABUKI, T., Bridge and Structural Engineering
YAFUSO, T., Strength of Materials
YAMAKAWA, T., Reinforced Concrete Structures
YAMAMOTO, T., Neuro-control
YAMASHIRO, Y., Electrical Materials
YARA, H., Welding Engineering
YOSHIYA, K., Intelligent Information Processing
ZUKERAN, C., Multiple-valued Logic Circuit

Faculty of Law and Letters:

AKAMINE, K., American Literature
AKAMINE, M., Japanese Folklore
AKAMINE, M., Modern Chinese History, Modern Okinawa History
ANDO, Y., Sociology
ARAKAKI, S., Civil Law
ASHITOMI, T., Civil Law
CHINEN, S., Monetary Economics
CHINEN, Y., Public Finance
EGAMI, T., Science of Public Administration, Comparative Politics
ENDO, M., Cognitive Psychology
GABE, M., International Relations
HAMASAKI, M., Greek Philosophy
HESHIKI, T., International Marketing
HIYANE, T., History of Political Thought, Political Science
HOSAKA, H., Journalism
IHA, M., Marketing
IKEDA, Y., Japanese Archaeology, Museography
IKEMIYA, M., Ryukyuan Literature
IMURA, O., Clinical Psychology
INABA, Y., Criminal Procedure
IREI, T., Human Resources Management, Business Administration
ISHIKAWA, T., Regional Geography, Human Geography
ISHIMINE, K., Constitutional Law
KABIRA, N., Economic History
KARIMATA, S., Japanese Linguistics, Study of Ryukyuan Dialects
KAWASOE, M., Social Services for the Aged
KOMATSU, M., Economic History
KUDEKEN, K., Community Development in Social Welfare
MACHIDA, M., Settlement Geography, Geographical Information Systems
MAEKADO, A., Geomorphology
MIYARA, S., Linguistics
NAKACHI, H., Administrative Law
NAKACHI, K., American Literature
NAKAHARA, T., Business and Corporation Laws
NAKAHODO, M., Modern Japanese Literature
NAKAMURA, T., Social Psychology
NAMIHIRA, T., Political Philosophy and Theory, Political Science
NISHIKAWA, H., Contemporary Philosophy
OSABE, Y., Asian History
OSHIRO, H., International Economics
OSHIRO, I., Theoretical Economics
OSHIRO, M., Managerial Finance
OSHIRO, T., Regional Development Policy
OYAKAWA, T., Linguistics
SAKIMA, N., European History
SHIMABUKURO, S., Human Geography
SHIMABUKURO, T., Commercial Law, Law of Securities Regulation
SHIMIZU, K., Criminal Law
SHIMOJI, Y., English Linguistics
SHIMURA, K., Quality Management
SUZUKI, N., International Sociology
TAIRA, M., American Literature
TAIRA, T., Applied Linguistics
TAKARA, K., Ryukyuan History
TAKARA, T., Constitutional Law, Administrative Law
TAMAKI, I., Civil Procedure Law
TAMAKI, M., Ryukyuan Literature
TANAKA, H., Economic Statistics
TOMA, S., Theoretical Economics
TOMINAGA, H., Econometrics
TOYOOKA, T., Accounting Information Theory, Accounting Systems
TSUHA, T., Social Anthropology
TSUNODA, M., Civil Law, European Private Law
UEZATO, K., Chinese Literature
UEZU, Y., Accounting
YAMAZATO, J., Japanese History
YAMAZATO, K., American Literature
YOGI, K., Linguistics
YONAHARA, T., Strategic Management
YOSHII, K., German
YOSHIMURA, K., English Literature
YOSHIZAWA, T., Sociology of Education

Faculty of Medicine:

ANIYA, Y., Biochemical Pharmacology
ARAKI, K., Haematology
ARIIZUMI, M., Preventive Medicine
FUKUNAGA, T., Virology
HOKAMA, T., Health Care
IMAMURA, T., Bacteriology
ISHIZU, H., Mental Health Science
ISIDA, H., Anatomy
ITO, E., Pathology
IWAMASA, T., Pathology
IWANAGA, M., Bacteriology
KANAYA, F., Hand Surgery, Microsurgery
KANAZAWA, K., Gynaecological Oncology, Reproductive Immunology
KARIYA, K., Biochemistry
KOJA, K., Surgery
KONO, S., Obstetrics and Gynaecology, Endocrinology
KOSUGI, T., Physiology, Haematology
MAEHIRA, F., Clinical Biochemistry, Biochemistry
MIYAGI, I., Medical Entomology
MIYAZAKI, T., Forensic Medicine
MURAYAMA, S.
MUTO, Y., Digestive Surgery
NAKA, K., Health Administration
NODA, Y., Otorhinolaryngology, Head and Neck Surgery
NONAKA, S., Dermatology, Photobiology
OGAWA, Y., Urology
OGURA, C., Neuropsychiatry
OHTA, T., Paediatrics
SAITO, A., Internal Medicine
SAKANASHI, M., Pharmacology
SAKIHARA, S., Health Sociology, Community Health
SATO, Y., Parasitology
SAWAGUCHI, S., Ophthalmology
SHIMADA, K., Human Pathology
SHIMAJIRI, S., Maternal Nursing
SUGAHARA, K., Anaesthesiology
SUNAGAWA, Y., Adult Nursing, Geriatric Nursing
SUNAKAWA, H., Oral and Maxillofacial Surgery
TAKASU, N., Internal Medicine
TANAKA, T., Biochemistry
TERASHIMA, S., Physiology
UZA, M., Health Care

YAMANE, N., Laboratory Medicine
YASUZUMI, F., Anatomy
YOSHII, Y., Neurosurgery

Faculty of Science:

FUKUHARA, C., Inorganic Chemistry
GINOZA, M., Condensed Matter Physics
GOYA, E., Functional Analysis
HAGIHARA, A., Forest Ecophysiology
HAYASHI, D., Structural Geology
HENNA, J., Mathematical Statistics
HIDAKA, M., Coral Biology
HIGA, M., Organic Chemistry
HIGA, T., Marine Natural Products Chemistry
HOSOYA, M., Computer Physics
IKEHARA, N., Physiology and Biochemistry
ISA, E., Calcification
ISHIJIMA, S., Atmospheric Science
KAKAZU, K., Mathematical Physics
KATO, Y., Petrology
KIMURA, M., Marine Geology
KODAKA, K., Functional Analysis
KUNIYOSHI, M., Marine Natural Products Chemistry
MAEDA, T., Algebraic Geometry
MAEHARA, R., Topology
MATAYOSHI, S., Quantum Physics
MIYAGI, Y., Molecular Spectroscopy
NAKAMURA, S., Cytology
NIKI, H., Solid State Physics
NISHISHIRAHO, T., Approximation Theory
OHMURA, Y., Condensed Matter Physics
OOMORI, T., Marine Geochemistry
SHIGA, H., Topology
SHOKITA, S., Fisheries Biology
SUZUKI, T., Number Theory
TAIRA, H., Analytical Chemistry
TAKUSHI, E., Solid State Optics
TEZUKA, M., Topology
TOKUYAMA, A., Environmental Chemistry
TOMOYOSE, T., Solid State Physics
TSUCHIYA, M., Ecology
UEHARA, T., Embryology
UEHARA, Y., Physical Chemistry
YAGASAKI, K., Solid State Physics
YAMAGUCHI, M., Coral-reef Biology
YAMAMOTO, S., Sedimentology
YAMAZATO, M., Probability Theory
YOGI, S., Organic Chemistry
YONASHIRO, K., Condensed Matter Physics

Education and Research Center for Lifelong Learning (Senbaru, Nishihara-cho, Okinawa):

DAIZEN, T., Sociology of Schooling, Sociology of Higher Education

Okinawa–Asia Research Center of Medical Science (Uehara, Nishihara-cho, Okinawa):

JINNO, Y., Molecular Genetics
TANAKU, Y.

Tropical Biosphere Research Center:

ARAMOTO, M., Terrestrial Resources
FUJIMORI, K., Cell Biology
KUMAZAWA, N., Environmental Microbiology Epidemiology
MURAI, M., Animal Ecology
NAKAMURA, M., Reproductive Biology
TAKASO, T., Plant Morphology

University Hospital (Uehara, Nishihara-cho, Okinawa):

HIROSE, Y., Hospital Information System, Knowledge-base System
HOBARA, N., Pharmacokinetic Drug Interaction, Quality Control of Medicine

ATTACHED INSTITUTES

Academic Museum (Fujukan): Senbaru, Nishihara-cho, Okinawa; e-mail fujukan@agr.u-ryukyu.ac.jp; internet fujukan.lib.u-ryukyu.ac.jp; Dir Y. KAWASHIMA.

Center for Cooperative Research: Senbaru, Nishihara-cho, Okinawa; Dir H. YARA.

Center for Educational Research and Practice: Senbaru, Nishihara-cho, Okinawa; Dir T. YONEMORI.

Center for Educational Research and Training of Handicapped Children: Senbaru, Nishihara-cho, Okinawa; Dir S. KAMIZONO.

Computing and Networking Center: Senbaru, Nishihara-cho, Okinawa; e-mail la-query@osn.u-ryukyu.ac.jp; internet www.cnc.u-ryukyu.ac.jp; Dir H. MIYAGI.

Education and Research Center for Lifelong Learning: Senbaru, Nishihara-cho, Okinawa; Dir T. YOSHIZAWA.

Environmental Science Center: Senbaru, Nishihara-cho, Okinawa; Dir Y. MIYAGI.

Gene Research Center: Senbaru, Nishihara-cho, Okinawa; internet www.tbc.u-ryukyu.ac.jp/comb; Dir N. KOBAMOTO.

Health Administration Center: Senbaru, Nishihara-cho, Okinawa; Dir H. TAKARA.

Institute for Animal Experiments: Uehara, Nishihara-cho, Okinawa; Dir E. ITO.

Instrumental Research Center: Senbaru, Nishihara-cho, Okinawa; e-mail irc@lab.u-ryukyu.ac.jp; internet irc1.lab.u-ryukyu.ac.jp; Dir Y. UEHARA.

Language Center: Senbaru, Nishihara-cho, Okinawa; Dir Y. SHIMOJI.

Low Temperature Center: Senbaru, Nishihara-cho, Okinawa; Dir H. NIKI.

Okinawa–Asia Research Center of Medical Science: Uehara, Nishihara-cho, Okinawa; Dir K. NARITOMI.

Radioisotope Laboratory: Senbaru, Nishihara-cho, Okinawa; Dir E. ISA.

Research Laboratory Center: Uehara, Nishihara-cho, Okinawa; Dir M. SAKANASHI.

Tropical Biosphere Research Center: Senbaru, Nishihara-cho, Okinawa; e-mail knkuodor@to.jim.u-ryukyu.ac.jp; internet www.tbc.u-ryukyu.ac.jp; Dir K. FUJIMORI.

Attached Stations:

Iriomote Station: Uehara Taketomi-cho, Yaeyama Okinawa; internet www.tbc.u-ryukyu.ac.jp/iriomote; Chief T. TAKASO.

Sesoko Station: Sesoko Motobu-cho, Okinawa; internet www.tbc.u-ryukyu.ac.jp/sesoko; Chief M. MURAI.

University Education Center: Senbaru, Nishihara-cho, Okinawa; Dir H. NAKACHI.

University Experimental Farm: Senbaru, Nishihara-cho, Okinawa; Dir Y. ISHIMINE.

University Experimental Forest: Yona, Kunigami-son, Okinawa; Dir E. HIRATA.

University Hospital: Uehara, Nishihara-cho, Okinawa; Dir K. KANAZAWA

UNIVERSITY OF TOKUSHIMA

2-24 Shinkura-cho, Tokushima 770-8501
Telephone: (88) 656-7000
E-mail: hibunsyok@jim.tokushima-u.ac.jp
Internet: www.tokushima-u.ac.jp

Founded 1949
National University Corporation
Academic year: April to March

Pres.: TOSHIHIRO AONO
Vice-Pres: HIROSHI NAKAMURA, HIROSHI KAWAKAMI, HISASHI KITAJIMA, MASAYUKI SHIBUYA, YASUHIRO KURODA
Sec.-Gen.: HIROSHI NAKAMURA
Dir of Univ. Library: KAZUO HOSOI

Number of teachers: 895 full-time
Number of students: 7,744

Publications: *Bulletin of the Faculty of Engineering* (1 a year), *Journal of Human Sciences* (1 a year), *Journal of Human Sciences and Arts* (1 a year), *Journal of Language and Literature* (1 a year), *Journal of Mathematics* (1 a year), *Journal of Medical Investigation* (2 a year), *Natural Science Research* (1 a year), *Social Sciences Research* (1 a year)

DEANS

Faculty of Dentistry: EIICHI BANDO
Faculty of Engineering: YONEO YANO
Faculty of Integrated Arts and Sciences: MAKOTO WADA
Faculty of Medicine: SABURO SONE
Faculty of Pharmaceutical Sciences: TAKSAHI YAMAUCHI
Institute of Health Biosciences, Graduate School: SABURO SONE

PROFESSORS

Faculty of Dentistry, Graduate School of Oral Sciences and Institute of Health Biosciences (3-18-15 Kuramoto-cho, Tokushima 770-8504; tel. (88) 633-9100; e-mail isysoumu2k@jim.tokushima-u.ac.jp):

ASAOKA, K., Biomaterials and Bio-engineering
BANDO, E., Fixed Prosthodontics
HANEJI, T., Anatomy and Histology
HAYASHI, Y., Oral Molecular Pathology
HONDA, E., Oral and Maxillofacial Radiology
HOSOI, K., Molecular Oral Physiology
ICHIKAWA, T., Removable Prosthodontics and Oral Implantology
KAWANO, F., Oral Care and Clinical Education
KITAMURA, S., Anatomy
MATSUO, T., Conservative Dentistry
MIYAKE, Y., Microbiology
MORIYAMA, K., Orthodontics and Dentofacial Orthopaedics
NAGATA, T., Periodontology and Endodontology
NAGAYAMA, M., Oral and Maxillofacial Surgery
NAKAJO, N., Dental Anaesthesiology
NISHINO, M., Paediatric Dentistry
NOMA, T., Molecular Biology
SATO, M., Oral and Maxillofacial Surgery and Oncology
YOSHIMOTO, K., Molecular Pharmacology

Faculty of Engineering (2-1 Minamijosanjima-cho, Tokushima 770-8506; tel. (88) 656-7304; e-mail kgsoumuk@jim.tokushima-u.ac.jp; internet www.e.tokushima-u.ac.jp/english/main.html):

AKAMATSU, N., Neural Networks and Speech Recognition
AOE, J., Intelligent Systems Engineering
FUKUI, M., Optoelectronics
FUKUTOMI, J., Fluid Engineering and Turbomachinery
HANABUSA, T., Production Systems Engineering
HASHIMOTO, C., Construction Materials
HASHINO, M., Stochastic Hydrology, Water Resources Engineering
HIRAO, K., Structural Engineering and Seismic Design
HORI, H., Biological Science
IMAEDA, M., Process Dynamics and Control
IMAI, H., Mathematics and Applied Mathematics
INOUE, K., Applied Superconductivity and High-Field Generation
INOUE, T., Crystal Growth and Crystal Engineering
IRITANI, T., Spread Spectrum Communications
ISAKA, K., Electric Energy Engineering
IWATA, T., Applied Spectroscopy and Optical Measurement
KAIEDA, Y., Plastic Forming and Powder Metallurgy
KANESHINA, S., Biological Science
KAWAMURA, Y., Organic Chemistry

KAWASHIRO, K., Enzyme Engineering
KINOUCHI, Y., Biomedical Electronics
KITAYAMA, S., Digital Signal Processing
KONAKA, S., Integrated Circuits
KONDO, A., Geotechnical Engineering
KONISHI, K., Robot and Computer Vision
KORAI, H., Microbiology and Microbiological Control
MASUDA, S., Synthetic and Polymer Chemistry
MIWA, K., Combustion Engineering and Energy Conversion
MIZUGUCHI, H., Urban Planning and Landscape Design
MOCHIZUKI, A., Foundations Engineering and Soil Mechanics
MORIOKA, I., Heat Transfer
MOTONAKA, J., Analytical Chemistry
MURAKAMI, H., Risk and Environmental Assessment
MURAKAMI, R., Metal Fatigue, Surface Modification
NAGAMACHI, S., Mathematics and Applied Mathematics
NIKI, N., Medial Imaging, Pattern Recognition
NISHIDA, N., Optical Information Science
NOJI, S., Molecular Biology and Devlopmental Biology
OHNO, T., Nuclear Magnetic Resonance
OHNO, Y., Electron Devices
OKABE, T., River Engineering, Environmental Hydraulics
ONISHI, T., Power Engineering
ONO, N., Multi-agent Systems and Reinforcement Learning
OOSHIMA, T., Enzymology and Genome Engineering
OUSAKA, A., Thermal Engineering, Multiphase Flow
OYA, K., Particle-surface Collisions and Nuclear Fusion
REN, F., Computer Science Technology, Natural Language Processing
SAKAI, S., Semiconductor Photonic Devices
SAWADA, T., Structural Engineering, Earthquake Engineering
SHIMOMURA, T., Soft Engineering, Algorithic Debugging
SUEDA, O., Well-being Engineering and Assistive Engineering
TAJIMA, K., All-optical Devices
TAKEUCHI, T., Numerical Analysis
TAMESADA, T., Design and Test of Electronic Circuits
TAMURA, K., Biophysical Chemistry
TANAKA, H., Polymer Synthesis and Functional Organic Materials
TOMIDA, T., Chemical Processes Engineering
TSUJI, A., Biochemistry and Protein Engineering
TSUKAYAMA, M., Synthetic and Polymer Chemistry
YAMADA, K., Elasticity and Micromechanics
YAMAGAMI, T., Geotechnical and Landslide Engineering
YAMANAKA, H., Urban Transport Planning and Design
YANO, Y., Intelligent Systems Engineering
YOSHIDA, K., Material Evaluation and Acoustic Emission
YOSHIMURA, T., Vehicle Suspensions and Fuzzy Control

Faculty of Integrated Arts and Sciences (1-1 Minamijosanjima-cho, Tokushima 770-8502; tel. (88) 656-7103; e-mail sksoumks@jim.tokushima-u.ac.jp; internet www.ias.tokushima-u.ac.jp):

ABE, E., Kimono Cloth Shrinkage and Repair
ANDO, M., Chinese Literature
ARAKI, H., Motor and Behavioural Physiology
ARIMA, T., Philosophy of the Qin and Han Dynasties
AZUMA, K., Calligraphy
AZUMA, U., Asian Archaeology
BABA, T., German Language and Literature
GOTO, T., Comparative Biochemistry and Physiology
HAMADA, J., Visual Perception
HARAMIZU, T., Japanese Literature
HAYASHI, H., Environmental Biology
HAYASHI, K., Constitutional Law
HIOKI, Z., Theoretical High-Energy Physics
HIRAI, S., Historical Geography
HIRAKI, M., Study of Painting Expression
IMAI, S., Applied Spectrocopy, Atomic Spectrometry and Trace Analysis
INOUE, N., English Corpus Linguistics, English Lexicography
ISHIDA, K., Microfossil Geology
ISHIDA, M., Philosophy of the Mind–Body Problem
ISHIHARA, T., Differential Geometry
ISHII, K., Image Conservation Techniques
ISHIKAWA, E., German Language and Literature
ITO, M., Partial Differential Equations
ITO, T., Computational Mathematics and Sciences
ITO, Y., Functional Analysis
KATAOKA, K., Musicology
KATAYAMA, S., Algebraic Number Theory
KATSURA, S., German Language and Literature
KAWAKAMI, S., German Language and Literature
KISHIE, S., Japanese Dialects
KOORI, N., Nuclear Physics
KOYAMA, K., Solid-State Physics
KUWABARA, M., Japanese History
KUWABARA, R., Global Analysis
MAEDA, S., Applied Mathematics
MASUDA, T., Bio-organic Chemistry
MATOBA, H., Exercise Physiology
MATSUMOTO, M., Physical Chemistry
MATSUO, Y., Genetics
MATSUSHITA, M., English Literature
MAYUMI, K., Environmental Economics
MIKI, M., Financial Accounting
MITSUI, A., Industrial Technology
MIURA, T., Physical Education
MIYAZAKI, T., English Literature
MIYAZAWA, K., Composition, Music using Computers
MIZUSHIMA, T., Middle Eastern Economics
MORI, Y., Psychotherapy
MORIOKA, Y., English Linguistics
MOTOKI, Y., English Linguistics
MURATA, A., Geology
NAKAGAWA, H., Marine Physiology and Biochemistry
NAKAJIMA, M., Economic History
NAKAMURA, H., Physical Education
NAKAYAMA, S., Nuclear Physics
NISHIDE, K., American History
OBARA, S., Exercise Physiology
OHASHI, M., Mathematical Programming
OHASHI, M., Immunobiology
OHBUCHI, A., Algebraic Geometry
OYAMA, Y., Analytical Cytology
SAKUMA, R., Social and Imperial History of Modern Britain
SANO, K., Physiological Psychology
SEKIZAWA, J., Risk Assessment for Environmental Protection and Safety
SENBA, M., Japanese Linguistics
SEO, I., English Literature
SHIOTA, T., Geology
TACHIBANA, Y., Economic Theory
TAJIMA, T., French Literature
TAKEDA, Y., Natural Products Chemistry
TERAO, H., Inorganic Chemistry
UENO, K., Sociology of Social Problems
WADA, M., Organic Chemistry
YAMADA, K., Labour Law
YAMAMOTO, M., Developmental Disorders
YOKOIGAWA, K., Applied Microbiology
YOSHIDA, H., Theoretical Sociology
YOSHIDA, S., Ancient Greek Philosophy
YOSHIMORI, K., Chinese Medieval History

Faculty of Medicine, Graduate School of Medical Sciences and Institute of Health Biosciences (3-18-15 Kuramoto-cho, Tokushima 770-8503; tel. (88) 633-9116; e-mail isysoumu1k@jim.tokushima-u.ac.jp; internet www.hosp.med.tokushima-u.ac.jp/university/servlet/index):

ADACHI, A., Virology
ARASE, S., Dermatological Science
DOI, T., Clinical Biology and Medicine
FUKUI, Y., Anatomy and Developmental Neurobiology
IRAHARA, M., Gynaecology and Obstetrics
ISHIMURA, K., Anatomy and Cell Biology
ITO, S., Digestive and Cardiovascular Medicine
IZUMI, K., Molecular and Environmental Pathology
KAJI, R., Clinical Neuroscience
KITAGAWA, T., Cardiovascular Surgery
KISHI, K., Nutritional Physiology
KUBO, S., Legal Medicine
MATSUMOTO, T., Medicine and Bioregulatory Sciences
MIYAMOTO, K., Nutritional Biochemistry
MORITA, Y., Integrative Physiology
NAGAHIRO, S., Neurosurgery
NAKAHORI, Y., Human Genetics and Public Health
NAKANISHI, H., Plastic and Reconstructive Surgery
NAKAYA, Y., Nutrition and Metabolism
NISHITANI, H., Radiology
OHMORI, T., Psychiatry
OSHITA, S., Anaesthesiology
OTA, F., Food Microbiology
SANO, T., Human Pathology
SASAKI, T., Biochemistry
SHIOTA, H., Ophthalmology and Visual Science
SONE, S., Internal Medicine and Molecular Therapeutics
TAKEDA, E., Clinical Nutrition
TAKEDA, N., Otorhinolaryngology and Communicative Neuroscience
TAMAKI, T., Pharmacology
TASHIRO, S., Digestive and Paediatric Surgery
TERAO, J., Food Science
YAMAMOTO, S., Applied Nutrition
YASUI, N., Orthopaedic Surgery
YASUMOTO, K., Immunology and Parasitology
YOSHIZAKI, K., Physiology

Faculty of Pharmaceutical Sciences and Graduate School of Pharmaceutical Sciences (1-78-1 Shomachi, Tokushima 770-8505; tel. (88) 633-7245; e-mail isysoumu3k@jim.tokushima-u.ac.jp; internet www.ph.tokushima-u.ac.jp):

ARAKI, T., Drug Metabolism and Therapeutics
BABA, Y., Molecular and Pharmaceutical Biotechnology
CHUMAN, H., Molecular and Analytical Chemistry
FUKUI, H., Molecular Pharmacology
FUKUZAWA, K., Health Chemistry
HIGUCHI, T., Molecular Cell Biology and Medicine
ITO, K., Medicinal Biotechnology
KIHARA, M., Pharmaceutical Information Science
KIWADA, H., Pharmacokinetics and Biopharmaceutics
KUSUMI, T., Marine Medicinal Resources
NAGAO, Y., Molecular Medicinal Chemistry
OCHIAI, M., Pharmaceutical Organic Chemistry
SHIMABAYASHI, S., Physical Pharmacy
SHISHIDO, K., Organic Synthesis

TAKAISHI, Y., Pharmacognosy
TAKIGUCHI, Y., Clinical Pharmacology
YAMAUCHI, T., Biochemistry

School of Health Sciences (3-18-15 Kuramoto-cho, Tokushima 770-8503; tel. (88) 633-9003; e-mail isysoumu4k@jim.tokushima-u.ac.jp; internet www2.medsci.tokushima-u.ac.jp):

FUJII, M., Neuroradiology
HARADA, M., Neuroradiology
KAGAWA, N., Human Pathology
KAWANISHI, C., Fundamental Nursing
KONDO, H., Fundamental Nursing
KONDO, T., Nutritional Biochemistry
MAEZAWA, H., Radiation Medicine
MORIMOTO, T., Breast Surgery
NAGAMINE, I., Clinical Neurpsychiatry
NAGASHINO, H., Biomedical Engineering
NINOMIYA, T., Psychosomatic Medicine
ONISHI, C., Adult and Gerontological Nursing
ONO, T., Bacterial Genetics
SAITOH, K., Cardiology
SEKIDO, K., Dermatological Science
TADA, T., Gerontological Nursing
TAKEGAWA, Y., Radiotherapy
TAMURA, A., Adult Nursing
TERAO, T., Maternal Health
UENO, J., Diagnostic Radiology
YAMANO, S., Artificial Reproductive Technology
YOSHINAGA, T., Medical Image Reconstruction

Center for Advanced Information Technology (2-1 Minamijosanjima-cho, Tokushima 770-8506; tel. (88) 656-7555; e-mail kokusai1@jim.tokushima-u.ac.jp; internet www.ait.tokushima-u.ac.jp):

KITA, K., Computer Science, Information Retrieval, Natural Language Processing
OE, S., Image Processing and Visual Pattern Processing

Center for University Extension (1-1 Minamijosanjima-cho, Tokushima 770-8502; tel. (88) 656-7276; e-mail kygakusk@jim.tokushima-u.ac.jp; internet www.cue.tokushima-u.ac.jp):

HIROWATARI, S., Adult and Continuing Education
MORITA, H., Analytical Chemistry
SODA, K., Function of Narrative
WAKAIZUMI, S., High-Energy Physics
YOSHIDA, A., Educational Technology

Institute for Animal Experimentation, Institute of Health Biosciences (3-18-15 Kuramoto-cho, Tokushima 770-8503; tel. (88) 633-9116; e-mail isysoum1k@jim.tokushima-u.ac.jp; internet www.anex.med.tokushima-u.ac.jp):

SASAKI, T., Biochemistry

Institute for Enzyme Research (3-18-15 Kuramoto-cho, Tokushima 770-8503; tel. (88) 633-9420; e-mail kenkyu@jim.tokushima-u.ac.jp; internet mms1.ier.tokushima-u.ac.jp/index2.html):

EBINA, Y., Molecular Genetics
FUKUI, K., Gene Regulatorics
KIDO, H., Molecular Enzyme Chemistry
MATSUMOTO, M., Informative Cytology
SUGINO, H., Molecular Cytology
TANIGUCHI, H., Molecular Enzyme Physiology

Institute for Genome Research (3-18-15 Kuramoto-cho, Tokushima 770-8503; tel. (88) 633-9420; e-mail kenkyu@jim.tokushima-u.ac.jp; internet www.genome.tokushima-u.ac.jp):

HARA, E., Division of Protein Information
ITAKURA, M., Division of Genetic Information
SHINOHARA, Y., Division of Gene Expression
SIOMI, H., Division of Gene Function Analysis
TAKAHAMA, Y., Division of Experimental Immunology

Institute for Medicinal Resources, Institute of Health Biosciences (1-78-1 Shomachi, Tokushima 770-8505; tel. (88) 633-7245; e-mail isysoum3k@jim.tokushima-u.ac.jp; internet www.ph.tokushima-u.ac.jp):

ITO, K., Medicinal Biotechnology

International Student Center (1-1 Minamijosanjima-cho, Tokushima 770-8502; tel. (88) 656-7082; e-mail ryugakuk@jim.tokushima-u.ac.jp; internet www.isc.tokushima-u.ac.jp):

JIN, C. H., Computing Science
MISUMI, T., Teaching Japanese as a Foreign Language
OISHI, Y., Teaching Japanese as a Foreign Language

Radioisotope Center (3-18-15 Kuramoto-cho, Tokushima 770-8503; tel. (88) 633-9416; e-mail kenkyu@jim.tokushima-u.ac.jp; internet ricb.ri.tokushima-u.ac.jp/rirc.html):

ADACHI, A., HIV/AIDS treatment

UNIVERSITY OF TOKYO

7-3-1 Hongo, Bunkyo-ku, Tokyo 113-8654
Telephone: (3) 3812-2111
E-mail: kokusai@ml.adm.u-tokyo.ac.jp
Internet: www.u-tokyo.ac.jp
Founded 1877
Independent
Academic year: April to March
Pres.: Dr JUNICHI HAMADA
Univ. Librarian: KAZUHIKO SAIGO
Library: see under Libraries and Archives
Number of teachers: 4,165
Number of students: 29,000

DEANS

Graduate School of Agricultural and Life Sciences and Faculty of Agriculture: SHINICHI SHOGENJI
Graduate School of Arts and Sciences and College of Arts and Sciences: SUSUMU YAMAKAGE
Graduate School of Economics and Faculty of Economics: HIROSHI YOSHIKAWA
Graduate School of Education and Faculty of Education: M. SATOH
Graduate School of Engineering and Faculty of Engineering: TAKEHIKO KITAMORI
Graduate School of Frontier Sciences: HIROYUKI YAMATO
Graduate School of Humanities and Sociology and Faculty of Letters: KAZUHISA TAKAHASHI
Graduate School of Information Science and Technology: M. TAKEICHI
Graduate School for Law and Politics: MASAHITO INOUYE
Graduate School of Mathematical Sciences: TOSHIO OSHIMA
Graduate School of Medicine and Faculty of Medicine: TAKAO SHIMIZU
Graduate School of Pharmaceutical Sciences and Faculty of Pharmaceutical Sciences: TETSUO NAGANO
Graduate School of Public Policy: KUNIAKI TANABE
Graduate School of Science and Faculty of Science: TOSHIO YAMAGATA
Interfaculty Initiative in Information Studies and Graduate School of Interdisciplinary Information Studies: T. HANADA

PROFESSORS

Graduate School of Agricultural and Life Sciences and Faculty of Agriculture (1-1-1 Yayoi, Bunkyo-ku, Tokyo 113-8657; tel. (3) 5841-5486; e-mail oice@ofc.a.u-tokyo.ac.jp; internet www.a.u-tokyo.ac.jp/english/index.html):

ABE, H., Biochemistry of Aquatic Animals
ABE, K., Biological Function Development
AIDA, K., Fish Physiology
AKASHI, H., Veterinary Microbiology
ANDO, N., Wood-based Materials and Timber Engineering
AOKI, I., Fisheries Biology
CHIDA, K., Cell Regulation
DOI, K., Veterinary Pathology
FUKUDA, K., Biological Function Development
FUKUI, Y., Biological Chemistry
FUKUYO, Y., Aquatic Biology
FURUYA, K., Fisheries Oceanography
HAYASHI, Y., Veterinary Anatomy
HIGUCHI, H., Wildlife Biology
HINO, A., Aquaculture Biology
HOGETSU, T., Plant Physiology and Plant Ecology, Silviculture
HONMA, M., Economics
HORI, S., Landscape and Sustainable Tourism
HORINOUCHI, S., Microbiology and Fermentation
IDE, Y., Forestry Gene Science
IGARASHI, Y., Applied Microbiology
INOUE, M., Forest Policy
ISOGAI, A., Pulp and Paper Sciences
ITOH, K., Veterinary Public Health
IWAMOTO, N., Agricultural History and History of Agricultural Sciences
IZUMIDA, Y., International Food System
KISHINO, H., Biometrics and Statistical Genetics
KITAHARA, T., Organic Chemistry
KOBAYASHI, H., Forest Utilization
KOBAYASHI, K., Agricultural Ecosystems
KUGA, S., Structural Biopolymers
KUMAGAI, S., Veterinary Public Health
KUMAGAI, Y., Evaluation of the Natural Environment
KURATA, K., Bio-environmental Engineering
KUROHMARU, M., Veterinary Anatomy
KUROKURA, H., Aquatic Biology
MASAKI, H., Molecular and Cellular Breeding
MATSUNAGA, S., Aquatic Natural Products Chemistry
MESHITSUKA, G., Wood Chemistry and Pulping Chemistry
MIYAZAKI, T., Soil Physics and Soil Hydrology
MORI, Y., Veterinary Ethology
NAGASAWA, H., Bio-organic Chemistry
NAGATA, S., Forest Ecology and Society
NAGATO, Y., Plant Breeding and Genetics
NAKANISHI, T. M., Radio–Plant Psychology
NANBA, S., Bioresource Technology
NISHIHATA, M., Veterinary Physiology
NISHIYAMA, M., Cell Biotechnology
NISHIZAWA, N. K., Plant Nutrition and Biotechnology
OGAWA, H., Veterinary Emergency Medicine
OGAWA, K., Fish Pathology
OHSHITA, S., Bioprocess Engineering
OHSUGI, R., Crop Physiology
OHTA, A., Cellular Genetics
OHTA, M., Wood-based Materials and Timber Engineering, Wood Physics
OMASA, K., Biological and Environmental Information Engineering
ONO, H., Polymeric Materials
ONO, K., Veterinary Clinical Pathobiology
ONODERA, T., Molecular Immunology
OYAIZU, H., Soil Science
OZAKI, H., Veterinary Pharmacology
SAGARA, Y., Food Informatics and Engineering
SAKAI, H., Forest Utilization
SAKAI, S., Animal Breeding
SAMEJIMA, M., Forest Chemistry

SASAKI, N., Veterinary Surgery
SATO, R., Food Chemistry
SENOO, K., Soil Microbiology
SHIMADA, T., Insect Genetics and Bioscience
SHIMIZU, K., Bioinformation Engineering
SHIMIZU, M., Food Chemistry
SHIMOMURA, A., Forest Landscape Planning and Design
SHIOTA, K., Cellular Biochemistry
SHIOZAWA, S., Physical Planning and Environmental Engineering
SHIRAISHI, N., Forest Management
SHIRAKO, Y., RNA Virology
SHOGENJI, S., Food and Resource Economics
SHOUN, H., Enzymology and Applied Microbiology
SUGIYAMA, N., Horticultural Science
SUZUKI, M., Forest Hydrology and Erosion Control
TAKAHASHI, N., Nutritional Biochemistry
TAKEUCHI, K., Landscape Ecology and Planning
TANAKA, T., Water Environmental Engineering
TANGE, T., Forest Ecophysiology
TANIGUCHI, N., Agricultural Structure and Policy
TANOKURA, M., Food Engineering
TATSUKI, S., Applied Entomology
TOJO, H., Applied Genetics
TSUBONE, H., Comparative Pathophysiology
TSUJIMOTO, H., Veterinary Internal Medicine
TSUTSUMI, N., Plant Molecular Genetics
WASHITANI, I., Conservation Ecology
WATABE, S., Aquatic Molecular Biology and Technology
WATANABE, H., Organic Chemistry
YAGI, H., Farm Business Management
YAMAGUCHI, I., Pesticide and Natural Products Chemistry
YAMAGUCHI-SHINOZAKI, L., Plant Molecular Biology
YAMAMOTO, H., Forest Planning
YAMANE, H., Environmental Biochemistry
YATAGAI, M., Plant Material Sciences
YODA, K., Microbiology Biotechnology
YOKOYAMA, S., Biomass Energy Conversion Technology
YONEYAMA, T., Plant Nutrition and Fertilizers
YOSHIKAWA, Y., Laboratory Animal Science
YOSHIMURA, E., Plant Molecular Physiology

Graduate School of Arts and Sciences and College of Arts and Sciences (3-8-1 Komaba, Meguro-ku, Tokyo 153-8902; tel. (3) 5454-6827; e-mail info-komaba@adm.c.u-tokyo.ac.jp; internet www.c.u.-tokyo.ac.jp):

ADACHI, H., History of Japanese Technology
ADACHI, N., Area Studies
AIZAWA, T., German, German History
AOKI, M., German
ARAI, Y., Human Geography
ARAMAKI, K., International Finance
ASASHIMA, M., Developmental Biology
ATOMI, Y., Sports Sciences
BOCCELLARI, J., English, Comparative Literature
ELLIS, T., Japanese as a Foreign Language
ENDO, Y., American Studies
ENDO, Y., Physical Chemistry
ERIGUCHI, Y., Astrophysics
FUKAGAWA, Y., Development Studies, Korean Studies
FUNABIKI, T., Cultural Anthropology
GOTO, N., Environmental Economics
HASEGAWA, T., Behavioural Ecology
HAYAKAMA, S., Law
HAYASHI, F., American Literature
HIKAMI, S., Statistical Physics
HIROMATSU, T., Statistics
HYODO, T., Physics
IKEDA, N., German
IKEGAMI, S., European Medieval History
IKEUCHI, M., Biology
IMAI, T., Philosophy
ISHIDA, A., International Relations
ISHIDA, Y., German History, Comparative Genocide Studies
ISHII, A., International Relations
ISHII, N., Sports Sciences
ISHII, Y., French
ISHIMITSU, Y., German Literature
ISHIURA, S., Neuroscience
ISOZAKI, Y., Earth Science
ITO, A., Cultural Anthropology
ITOH, T., English
IWASA, T., French, Contemporary Art
IWASAWA, Y., International Law
KADOWAKI, S., Philosophy
KAGOSHIMA, S., Solid-State Physics
KAJI, T., German
KANEKO, K., Nonlinear Physics, Statistical Physics
KARIMA, F., Chinese
KATO, M., Architectural Composition Theory
KAWAI, S., Graphics
KAWANAGO, Y., German, History of Christian Thought
KAWATO, S., Biophysics
KAZAMA, Y., Theory of Elementary Particles
KIBATA, Y., English, British History
KIMURA, H., Anthropology
KITAGAWA, S., Philosophy
KOBAYASHI, K., Sports Sciences
KOBAYASHI, Y., French, Modern Thought
KODA, K., German
KOJIMA, N., Chemistry
KOJO, Y., Political Science
KOMAKI, K., Radiation Physics
KOMIYAMA, S., Theory of Solid-State Physics
KOMORI, Y., Japanese Literature
KONDOH, A., Japanese
KONOSHI, T., Japanese Literature
KOTERA, A., International Law
KUBOTA, S., Sports Science
KUGA, T., Quantum Electronics, Quantum Optics
KURODA, R., Biochemistry of DNA
KUROZUMI, M., Ethics, Japanese Intellectual History
LAMARRE, C., Linguistic Analysis
MABUCHI, I., Biochemistry and Biophysics
MARUYAMA, M., Economics
MASUDA, K., French, French Philosophy
MASUDA, S., Chemistry
MATSUBARA, R., Economic Thought, Social Economics
MATSUI, T., Theoretical Nuclear Physics
MATSUO, M., Environmental and Analytical Chemistry
MATSUOKA, S., Japanese Literature
MATSUURA, H., Multimedia Analysis
MISUMI, Y., Japanese Literature
MITANI, H., Japanese History
MIYAMOTO, H., Philosophy
MIYASHITA, S., French
MORI, M., Political and Social Philosophy
MOTOMURA, R., European History
MURATA, J., Philosophy
MURATA, M., Cell Biology and Biophysics
MURATA, Y., China Studies
NAGATA, T., Physical Chemistry
NAKAI, K., International Relations
NAKANISHI, T., Economics
NAKAZAWA, H., Crosscultural Communication
NAMIKI, Y., Chinese History
NISHINAKAMURA, H., Russian
NIWA, K., Research Management
NOMURA, T., Japanese
NOTOJI, M., American Literature
OE, H., International Relations, Human Security
OGOSHI, N., Korean
OHTA, K., Theoretical Nuclear Physics
OKA, H., English
OKABE, Y., German, Comparative Literature
OKOSHI, Y., Criminal Law
ONAKA, M., Catalysis Chemistry
ONUKI, T., Hellenistic and Early Christian Literature
OTSUKI, T., Sports Sciences
ROSSITTER, P., English
SAKAHARA, S., French
SAKAI, T., Political Science
SASAKI, C., History and Philosophy of Science
SATO, N., Plant Biology
SATO, Y., English, American Literature
SATO, Y., Law, Dispute Processing, Peace Building
SATOMI, D., Biology
SHIBA, N., Serbo-Croat, History
SHIBATA, T., History of Political Thought
SHIGEMASU, K., Bayesian Statistics
SHIMADA, M., Population and Evolutionary Ecology
SHIMOI, M., Inorganic Chemistry, Coordination Chemistry
SHIROTA, T., Chinese Literature
SUGAWARA, K., English
SUGAWARA, T., Physical Organic Chemistry
SUGIHASHI, Y., German, Literature and Aesthetics
SUGITA, H., Arabic
SUTOH, K., Molecular Cell Biology
SUYAMA, A., Biophysics
SUZUKI, H., English and Music
SUZUKI, K., French
SUZUKI, K., Graphics
TAJIRI, M., German
TAKADA, Y., English Literature
TAKAHASHI, H., History
TAKAHASHI, N., Political Science
TAKAHASHI, S., German Literature
TAKAHASHI, T., Philosophy
TAKATSUKA, K., Theoretical Molecular Science
TAKEUCHI, N., French, Comparative Literature
TAKITA, Y., English
TAMAI, T., Software Engineering
TANIUCHI, T., Human Geography
TANJI, A., English Literature
TOMODA, S., Organic Chemistry
TSUNEKAWA, K., Political Science
UCHIDA, R., Contemporary Society
UEDA, H., Spanish
URA, M., Russian Literature
USUI, R., German
WAKABAYASHI, M., Chinese, Modern History of East Asia
WILSON, B., English
YAMADA, H., French Literature, Psychoanalytic Criticism
YAMAKAGE, S., International Relations
YAMAMOTO, S., English
YAMAMOTO, T., Philosophy
YAMAMOTO, Y., Culture and Social Change
YAMASHITA, S., Cultural Anthropology
YAMAUCHI, M., Asian History
YAMAWAKI, N., History of Social Thought
YAMAZAKI, Y., Atomic Physics
YONEYA, T., Theoretical Physics
YOSHIE, A., Japanese History
YOSHIOKA, D., Theory of Solid-State Physics
YUASA, H., French
YUI, D., American and International History

Graduate School of Economics and Faculty of Economics (7-3-1 Hongo, Bunkyo-ku, Tokyo 113-0033; tel. (3) 5841-5543; e-mail advisefs@e.u-tokyo.ac.jp; internet www.e.u-tokyo.ac.jp):

ABE, M., Marketing

ARAI, T., Corporate Finance, Securities Investment
BABA, S., Economic History of the Western World, History of Industrialization and Urbanization in Germany
DAIGO, S., Financial Accounting
FUJIMOTO, T., Technology and Operations Management
FUJIWARA, M., Applied Microeconomics
FUKUDA, S., Money and Banking, Macroeconomics
HANNAH, L., Comparative Business History
HAYASHI, F., Applied Econometrics, Macroeconomics
HIROTA, I., Economic History of Modern France
ICHIMURA, H.
IHORI, T., Public Finance and Economics
ITO, T., International Finance, Finance and Macroeconomics
ITOH, MASANAO, Japanese Economy, Financial History in Japan
ITOH, MOTOSHIGE, International Economics
IWAI, K., Economic Theory
IWAMI, T., International Economics
IWAMOTO, Y., Public Economics, Macroeconomics
JINNO, N., Public Finance
KAMIYA, K., Microeconomics, Mathematical Programming
KANDORI, M., Microeconomic Theory, Game Theory
KANEMOTO, Y., Urban Economics
KOBAYASHI, T., Theory of Investments and Capital Markets
KUBOKAWA, T., Mathematical Statistics
KUNITOMO, N., Statistics, Econometrics and Financial Econometrics
MATSUI, A., Game Theory, Information Economics, Monetary Theory
MATSUSHIMA, H., Microeconomics, Game Theory, Theory of Finance, Informational Economics
MIWA, Y., Economics of Regulations, Corporate Governance, Law and Economics
MOCHIDA, N., Public Finance, Intergovernmental Fiscal Relations
MORI, T., Industrial Relations
OBATA, M., Economic Theory
OKAZAKI, T., Japanese Economic History
OKUDA, H., Russian Economic History
ONOZUKA, T., Economic History of the Western World
SAGUCHI, K., Industrial Relations
SHIBATA, T., Modern Capitalism, Institutional Economics
TABUCHI, T., Urban Economics
TAKAHASHI, N., Organization Theory
TAKEDA, H., Japanese Economic History
TAKENOUCHI, M., International Economics
UEDA, K., Macroeconomics, Financial Theory, Theory of International Finance
WADA, K., Comparative Business History
YAJIMA, Y., Statistics and Econometrics
YOSHIKAWA, H., Macroeconomics

Graduate School of Humanities and Sociology and Faculty of Letters (7-3-1 Hongo, Bunkyo-ku, Tokyo 113-0033; tel. (3) 5841-3705; e-mail shomu@l.u-tokyo.ac.jp; internet www.l.u-tokyo.ac.jp):

AKIYAMA, H., Social Psychology of Ageing
AMANO, M., Philosophy
FUJII, S., Modern Chinese Literature
FUJITA, K., Aesthetics
FUJITA, S., Early Modern Japanese History
FUJIWARA, K., Japanese Literature of Heian Era
FUKASAWA, K., History of Early Modern Europe
GOMI, F., Medieval Japanese History
GOTO, T., Japanese Archaeology
HASEMI, K., Russian and Polish Literature
HATTORI, T., Korean Studies (Sociology)
HAYASI, T., Turkic Languages
HIRAISHI, T., American Literature
HIRANO, Y., German Language and Literature
ICHIKAWA, H., History of Religion, the Bible and Judaism
IKEDA, K., Political Behaviour and Communication, Social Reality and Mediated Communication
IMAMURA, K., Japanese and Asian Archaeology
IMANISHI, N., English Linguistics and Syntax Theory
ISHII, N., History of Modern Europe
ITUMI, K., Classical Languages and Literature
KANAZAWA, M., Russian Literature
KANNO, K., Japanese Ethical Thoughts
KATAYAMA, H., Classical Languages and Literature
KAWAHARA, H., History of the Science of Chance
KIMURA, H., Chinese Language
KINOSHITA, N., Cultural Resource Studies
KISHIMOTO, M., Chinese History
KOJIMA, T., Medieval Japanese Literature
KOMATSU, H., Central Asian History
KONDO, K., History of Modern Europe
KONO, M., History of Japanese Art
KUMAMOTO, H., Indo-European Linguistics
MARUI, H., Indian Philosophy
MATSUMOTO, M., Sociology of Science and Technology, Environmental Sociology
MATSUMURA, K., Uralic Linguistics
MATSUNAGA, S., Philosophy
MATSUURA, J., German Language
MIZUSHIMA, T., South Asian History
MURAI, S., Medieval Japanese History
NAGAMI, S., Italian Language and Literature
NAGASHIMA, H., Early Modern Japanese Literature
NAKAJI, Y., French Language and Literature
NISHIMURA, K., Aesthetics
NITAGAI, K., Urban Sociology
NUMANO, M., Russian and Polish Literature
OHASI, Y., English Literature
ONUKI, S., East Asian Archaeology
OSANO, S., History of Western Art
SAITO, A., Indian Philosophy
SAKURAI, M., Ancient Greek History
SAKURAI, Y., South-East Asian History
SATO, M., Ancient Japanese History
SATO, S., Intellectual History of Modern China
SATO, T., Visual Perception
SATO, Y., Ethics and Social Thought
SATO, Y., History of Japanese Art
SEIYAMA, K., Mathematical Sociology
SEKINE, S., Occidental Ethical Thought
SHIBATA, M., American Literature
SHIGETO, M., German Linguistics
SHIMAZONO, S., Japanese Religious Thought
SHIOKAWA, T., French Language and Literature
SHITOMI, Y., West Asian History
SUEKI, F., Japanese Buddhism
SUZUKI, T., Japanese Language
TACHIBANA, M., Visual Neuroscience
TADA, K., Ancient Japanese Literature
TAKAHASHI, K., English Literature
TAKAHASHI, T., Dravidian Language and Literature
TAKANO, Y., Cognitive Psychology
TAKAYAMA, H., Medieval European History
TAKAYAMA, M., Philosophy
TAKEGAWA, S., Sociology of Social Policy
TAKESHITA, M., Islamic Studies
TAKEUCHI, S., Japanese Ethical Thought
TAMURA, T., French Language and Literature
TOKURA, H., Chinese Literature
TSUCHIDA, R., Sanskrit Language and Literature
TSUKIMURA, T., French Language and Literature
TSUNODA, T., Australian Aboriginal Linguistics
TSURUOKA, Y., Christian Mysticism
UENO, C., Family and Gender Studies
UTAGAWA, H., East Asian Archaeology
UWANO, Z., Accentology and Dialectology
WATANABE, H., Aesthetics
YAMAGUCHI, S., Experimental Social Psychology
YOSHIDA, M., Korean History
YOSHIDA, N., Early Modern Japanese History

Graduate School of Education and Faculty of Education (7-3-1 Hongo, Bunkyo-ku, Tokyo 113-0033; tel. (3) 5841-3904; e-mail edushomu@p.u-tokyo.ac.jp; internet www.p.u-tokyo.ac.jp/index-j.html):

AKITA, K., Action Research on Training
ETO, T., Health Education
HAEBARA, T., Educational Measurement
HIJIKATA, S., History of Japanese Education
HIROTA, T., Sociology of Education
ICHIKAWA, S., Cognitive Psychology
KAMEGUCHI, K., Clinical Psychology
KANAMORI, O., Methods of Education
KANEKO, M., Higher Education
KARIYA, T., Sociology of Education
KAWAMOTO, T., History of Western Education
MUTOH, Y., Physical Education
NAKADA, M., Methods of Education
NEMOTO, A., Library and Information Science
OGAWA, M., Educational Administration
SASAKI, M., Methods of Education
SATOH, K., Lifelong Learning
SATOH, M., Action Research on Teaching
SHIMOYAMA, H., Clinical Psychology
SHIOMI, T., Science of Education
SHIRAISHI, S., Anthropology of Education
TANAKA, C., Clinical Psychology
WATANABE, H., Educational Measurement
YAMAMOTO, Y., Physiology of Education
YANO, M., Higher Education

Graduate School of Engineering and Faculty of Engineering (7-3-1 Hongo, Bunkyo-ku, Tokyo 113-8656; tel. (3) 5841-7662; e-mail octo@t-adm.t.u-tokyo.ac.jp; internet www.t.u-tokyo.ac.jp):

AIDA, T., Macromolecular Chemistry, Supramolecular Chemistry, Bioinorganic Chemistry
AOKI, T., Aerospace Structures, Mechanics of Composite Materials, Smart Structures
ARAI, T., Automatic Assembly, Robotics, Artificial Intelligence and Service Engineering
ARAKAWA, Y., Electric Propulsion
DOI, M., Soft Matter Physics, Polymer Physics, Rheology
DOMEN, K., Heterogeneous Catalysis
FUJIMOTO, K., Deformation and Fracture of Solids, Tribology
FUJINO, Y., Structural Engineering, Dynamics, Control and Monitoring of Structures and Bridges, Wind and Earthquake
FUJITA, M., Organic Coordination Chemistry
FUJITA, T., Mineral and Material Processing, Recycling Technology, Intelligent Fluid
FUJIWARA, T., Solid-State Physics, Electronic Structure in Condensed Matter
FURUMAI, H., Urban Drainage and Water Quality Management
FURUTA, K., Cognitive Systems Engineering, Technology for Safe and Secure Society

GONOKAMI, M., Non-linear Optics, Quantum Optics, Quantum Electronics, Optical Processes in Solids
HANAKI, K., Urban and Global Environmental Management, Urban Environment Systems
HARATA, N., Urban Transport Planning
HASHIMOTO, K., Intelligent Materials
HASHIMOTO, T., Science and Technology Studies
HIDAKA, K., High Voltage Engineering, Electrical Insulation, Electrical Discharge and Plasma Physics
HIGUCHI, T., Mechatronics, Micro Electromechanical Systems
HIRAO, K., Theoretical Chemistry and Electronic Structure Theory
HORI, K., Artificial Intelligence
HORII, H., Sociotechnology, Rock Mechanics, Applied Mechanics
HOTATE, K., Photonic Sensing, Photonic Signal Processing, Optical Devices
ICHIKAWA, M., Semiconductor Nano-science and Technology
IEDA, H., Transport and City Planning
IIZUKA, Y., Systems Analysis and Design, Structured Knowledge Engineering, Health Care Social System Engineering
IKUHARA, Y., Interface and Grain Boundary Engineering
ISHIHARA, K., Biomaterials
ISHIHARA, S., Nanomechanics, Nanofabrication
ITO, T., Urban and Architectural History
KAGEYAMA, K., Composite Materials Engineering, Smart Material and Structure Systems
KAMATA, M., Equipment and Environmental Engineering
KAMATA, M., Noise and Vibration Control, Vehicle Engineering, Assistive Technology
KANEKO, S., Flow-induced Vibration, Vibration Control, Micro Gas Turbine Engineering
KANNO, M., Metallic Materials
KANODA, K., Experimental Physics of Low-dimensional Correlated Electronic Systems
KASAGI, N., Thermal and Fluids Engineering, Energy Systems Engineering, Turbulence Engineering
KATAOKA, K., Biomaterials and Drug Delivery Systems
KATO, T., Materials Chemistry, Polymer Chemistry, Supramolecular Chemistry
KATO, T., Surface Engineering, Tribology, Nanotribology
KATSUMURA, Y., Radiation Chemistry, Applied Radiation Chemistry
KAWACHI, K., Flight Dynamics, Biokinetics, Helicopter Engineering
KIMURA, F., Design Engineering, CAD/CAM, Manufacturing Systems, Computer-aided Technology in Manufacturing Engineering
KISHIO, K., Solid-State Chemistry, Ionic and Electronic Transport in Solids, Superconductivity
KITAMORI, T., Integration of Micro Chemical Systems, Micro Space Chemistry
KOBAYASHI, I., Environmental Information Network, Light Communications
KOIDE, O., Evaluation of Regional Risks and Multimedia Database System for Historical Disasters
KOIKE, T., Hydrology and Water Resources, Remote Sensing
KOMIYAMA, H., Global Environmental Engineering, Materials Science and Engineering
KOSAKO, T., Radiation Safety, Radiation Shielding, Radiation Dosimetry
KOSEKI, T., Metals and Alloys
KOSHI, M., Chemical Reaction Kinetics, Laser-induced Chemistry
KOSHIZUKA, S., Computational Fluid Dynamics
KUBO, T., Structural and Earthquake Engineering, Reinforced Concrete Structures
KUWAMURA, H., Structural Engineering, Steel Structures, Welding Mechanics, Reliability Analysis and New Materials
MABUCHI, K., Advanced Biomedical Engineering and Life Sciences
MADARAME, H., Nuclear Safety
MAEDA, K., Defects in Solids, Nanoscopic Analysis
MAEKAWA, K., Concrete Engineering, Modelling of Concrete Performance
MARUYAMA, S., Science and Technology of Carbon Nanotubes, Nanoscale Thermal Engineering
MATSUMOTO, Y., Fluid Engineering, Molecular Dynamics
MATSUSHIMA, K., Business and Innovation Modelling
MITSUISHI, M., Intelligent Manufacturing Systems, Network-based Manufacturing Systems, Active Thermal Compensation for High-speed Machine Tools
MIYATA, H., Computational Fluid Dynamics, Systems Design, Technology Management
MIZUNO, N., Catalytic Chemistry, Inorganic Chemistry
MOHRI, N., Manufacturing Systems Control, Precision Machining
MORISHITA, E., High-speed Gas Dynamics
NAGAMUNE, T., Biotechnology, Biochemical Engineering, Protein Engineering
NAGAOSA, N., Condensed Matter Theory, Superconductivity
NAGASAKI, S., Safety Research on the Nuclear Fuel Cycle
NAGASAWA, Y., Architectural Planning and Design
NAGASHIMA, T., Aerospace Propulsion
NAGASUKA, S., Space Engineering
NAITO, H., Architectural Design, Landscape Design
NAKAO, M., Nano-micro Manufacturing, Information Instrument Design, Mechanical Engineering for Science
NAKAO, S., Membrane Science and Technology
NAKAZAWA, M., Radiation Measurement, Quantum Beam Engineering
NAMBA, K., Sustainable Design in Architecture and Urban Space
NAWATA, K., Econometrics, Statistics
NISHIMURA, Y., Urban Conservation Planning, Urban Design
NITTA, T., Applied Superconductivity, Electrical Machinery, Power Systems
NOZAKI, K., Organometallic Chemistry, Homogeneous Catalysis
ODA, T., Electrostatics, Plasma Application for Environmental Protection and Magnetic Separation
OHASHI, H., Thermal Hydrodynamics, Advanced Models for Complex Phenomena
OHBA, Z., Education Systems Project
OHGAKI, S., Environmental Engineering
OHTSU, M., Nanophotonics
OKA, Y., Nuclear Reactor Design and Analysis
OKABE, A., Urban and Regional Analysis, Geographical Information Science
OKABE, Y., Information Devices, Superconductive Electronics, Brain Computer
OKAMOTO, K., Visualization, Micro,-Nano- and Biofluids
OKATA, J., Urban Planning
OKUBO, S., Mining Machinery, Rock Mechanics
OKUDA, H., Computational Mechanics, Digital Value Engineering
OSHIMA, M., Semiconductor Surface Chemistry, Synchrotron Radiation Science
OZAWA, K., Construction, Project and Infrastructure Management
RINOIE, K., Aircraft Design, Separated Flow Aerodynamics
ROKUGAWA, S., Exploration Geophysics, Earth Observing Systems
SAKAI, S., Strength of Materials, Life Cycle Assessment, Fracture Mechanics
SAKAMOTO, I., Building Construction, Timber Structures
SAKAMOTO, Y., Environmental Control Engineering, Air Conditioning
SATO, K., Petroleum Engineering
SATO, S., Coastal and Environmental Engineering
SEKIMURA, N., Maintenance Engineering, Nuclear Materials, Effects of Radiation on Materials
SHIBATA, T., Semiconductor Devices and Integrated Circuits, Integrated Human Intelligence Systems
SHIMIZU, E., Geoinformatics, Regional Planning
SHINOHARA, O., Landscape Planning and Civic Design
SHIOYA, T., Aerospace Materials, Mechanical Behaviour of Materials
SUGA, T., Microsystem Integration and Packaging, Eco-design
SUZUKI, H., Computer-aided Design and Manufacture, Geometric Modelling
SUZUKI, H., History of Architecture, History of Modern Architecture
SUZUKI, H., Structural Engineering, Ocean Engineering
SUZUKI, S., Flight Mechanics, Control Engineering
SUZUKI, T., Systems Engineering in Materials Science
TAIRA, K., RNA as Origin of Life and RNA Technology
TAKADA, T., Structural Reliability, Earthquake Engineering, Computational Mechanics, Risk Analysis, Decision Theory
TAKAHASHI, H., Digital Signal Processing
TAKAMASU, K., Precision Metrology, Nanometer Measurement, Coordinate Metrology
TAMAKI, K., Marine Geology
TANAKA, M., Materials and Device Physics, Spintronics
TANAKA, S., Fusion Engineering, Nuclear Waste Management
TARUCHA, S., Electronic Properties of Semiconductor Nanostructures
TERAI, T., Materials Science for Nuclear Systems, Fusion Reactor Engineering, Synthesis and Property Control of Advanced Materials by High-energy Particle Processing
TOKURA, Y., Materials Physics
TORIUMI, A., Advanced Devices Engineering
TOWHATA, I., Geotechnical Engineering
UEDA, T., Cost-Benefit Analysis, Infrastructure Economics
UESAKA, M., Quantum Beam Engineering and Applied Electro-Magnetics
WADA, K., Microphotonics
WASHIZU, M., Bio-nanotechnology
WATANABE, S., Computational Engineering of Nanomaterials
YAGI, O., Applied Microbiology
YAMADA, I., Lifestyle and Environmental Information Technology, Network Sensing, Telecommunication Energy Systems
YAMAGUCHI, H., Polar Environment Engineering, Cavitation
YAMAGUCHI, S., Solid-State Ionics
YAMAGUCHI, Y., Nanomaterials Technology, Chemical System Engineering
YAMAJI, K., Energy Systems Engineering
YAMASHITA, K., Theoretical Chemistry and Chemical Reaction Dynamics, Computational Molecular Engineering

YAMATOMI, J., Rock Engineering and Mining Engineering
YOKOYAMA, A., Power Systems Engineering, Control Engineering
YOSHIDA, M., Education Systems Project
YOSHIDA, T., Plasma Materials Engineering
YUHARA, T., Energy Engineering and Policy, Engineering for Naval Architecture and Ocean Engineering, Management of Engineering Projects

Graduate School of Frontier Sciences (5-1-5 Kashiwanoha, Kashiwa-shi, Chiba 277-8562; tel. (4) 7136-5506; e-mail souiki@k.u-tokyo.ac.jp; internet www.k.u-tokyo.ac.jp):

AIDA, H., High-quality Networking, Parallel and Distributed Processing
AIZAWA, K., Image Processing, Multimedia Technologies
AMEMIYA, Y., X-ray Physics and Instrumentation
ASAI, K., Stochastic Models in Bioinformatics
CHIKAYAMA, T., Information Engineering
FUJIMORI, A., Condensed Matter Physics
FUJIWARA, H., Insect Molecular Biology
HAMANO, Y., Content Production
HARATA, N., Urban Transport Planning, Environmental Information Systems in Spatial Planning and Policy
HASEZAWA, S., Plant Cell Biology
HIHARA, E., Refrigeration Engineering, Heat Transfer, Multi-phase Flows
HIROSE, K., Speech Information Processing
HISADA, T., Finite Element Method, Biomechanics
HOSAKA, H., Information Mechatronics and Microdynamics
IBA, H., Evolutionary Computation, Evolutionary Robotics, Genome Informatics
ISOBE, M., Coastal Environment
ITO, K., Polymer Physics
ITO, T., Functional Genomics
IWATA, S., Design Science, Environmental Studies
KAGEMOTO, H., Environmental Hydrodynamics
KAJI, M., Forest Ecology
KANDA, J., Structural Engineering
KATAOKA, H., Biochemistry
KAWAI, M., Surface Science, Nano-Science
KAWANO, S., Molecular Cell Biology
KIMURA, K., Nano-space Function Design, Applied Solid-State Physics
KITOH, S., Environmental Ethics
KOBAYASHI, I., Laboratory of Social Genome Sciences
KOJI, O., Environmental Visualization
KONO, M., Energy Conversion, Aerospace Propulsion
KUMAGAI, Y., Landscape Architecture, Forest Landscape Planning and Design
KUNISHIMA, M., International Infrastructure Development and Management
MATSUHASHI, R., Environment Systems and Economics
MATSUI, T., Comparative Planetology
MINO, T., Water Environment Control, Environmental Biotechnology
MITANI, H., Molecular Genetics, Radiation Biology
MIYAMOTO, Y., Molecular Physiology
MORISHITA, S., Computational Biology, Bioinformatics, Data Mining, Database Systems, Computational Logic
NAGATA, M., Insect Pathology
NAKAYAMA, M., Weather Resources Management and Regional Planning
NAMBA, S., Molecular Plant-Microbe Interactions
NISHITA, T., Computer Graphics
OHMORI, H., Natural Environmental Structures
OHNO, H., Living Environmental Design
OHSAWA, M., Plant Ecology
OHYA, Y., Signal Transduction
OKADA, M., Brain Science Information Theory and Physics
ONABE, K., Semiconductor Materials Engineering
SAIGO, K., Synthetic Organic Chemistry, Synthetic Macromolecular Chemistry
SAIKI, K., Surface Science
SAKUMA, I., Biomedical Engineering, Computer-aided Surgery, Precision Engineering
SASAKI, K., Mechatronics, Signal Processing
SHIBATA, T., Semiconductor Electronics
SUGANO, S., Functional Genomics
SUGIURA, S., Cardiology, Physiology of Cardiac Muscle
TAKAGI, H., Solid-State Physics and Chemistry
TAKAGI, S., Semiconductor Device Engineering
TAKAGI, T., Computational Biology
TAKAGI, Y., Development Economics
TAKASE, Y., Plasma Physics
TAKEDA, N., Smart Structures and Composite Materials
TAKEDA, T., Brain Science
TORIUMI, M., Petrology, Structural Geology
TORO, S., Ocean Environmental Engineering
TSUJI, S., Environmental Archaeology and Ethnology
TSUJI, T., Biomedical Engineering, Cardiovascular Surgery, Biomaterials
TSUKIHASHI, F., Physical Chemistry of Materials
UEDA, T., Molecular Biology
WADA, H., Magneto-Science and Technology
WATANABE, S., Natural Environment Formation
WATANABE, T., Molecular Oncology, Human Retrovirology
YAMAJI, E., Agro-environmental Engineering
YAMAJI, K., Energy Systems Analysis
YAMAMOTO, H., Information Theory and Cryptology
YAMAMOTO, K., Glycobiology
YAMATO, H., Industrial Information Systems and Environment
YANAGISAWA, Y., Chemical Analysis of Air and Indoor Air Pollution, Systems Analysis of Global Environment
YANAGITA, T., International Monetary Economics
YOSHIDA, T., Transnational Infrastructure Management
YOSHIDA, Z., Plasma Physics and Nonlinear Sciences
YOSHIMURA, S., Simulation and Virtual Environment

Graduate School of Information Science and Technology (7-3-1 Hongo, Bunkyo-ku, Tokyo 113-8656; tel. (3) 5841-7662; e-mail octo@t-adm.t.u-tokyo.ac.jp; internet www.i.u-tokyo.ac.jp):

ANDO, S., Sensors, Measurement, Image Processing
AOYAMA, T., Communication Networks and Systems
DOHI, T., Computer-aided Surgery
ESAKI, H., Computer Networks, Internet Architecture
FUJII, M., Economics and Finance
HAGIYA, M., Formal Verification, Programming Languages, Biocomputing
HARA, S., Control Theory, Learning and Optimization
HARASHIMA, H., Human Communications Engineering
HIRAKI, K., Parallel Processing, Computer Architecture, High Speed Networks
HIROSE, K., Speech Information Processing
HIROSE, M., Virtual Reality, Human Interface
IMAI, H., Alogorithms, Optimization, Complexity, Quantum Computing
ISHIKAWA, M., Robotics, Vision, VLSI, Optics in Computing
ISHIZUKA, M., Artificial Intelligence, Multimodal Lifelike Agents, WWW Intelligence
KANZAKI, R., Neural Mechanisms of Behaviour
MABUCHI, K., Advanced Biomedical Engineering and Life Science
MUROTA, K., Discrete Mathematics
NAKAMURA, Y., Robotics, Mechatronics, Automatic Control
NANYA, T., Dependable Computing and VLSI Design
OKABE, Y., Time Series Analysis and Financial Technology
OTSU, N., Real-world Intelligence, Pattern Recognition
OYANAGI, Y., Numerical Analysis, Parallel Processing
SAGAYAMA, S., Speech Recognition, Signal Processing, Spoken Dialogue System, Music Information Processing
SAKAI, S., Computer Systems and Applications
SATO, T., Intelligent Mechanics Human Machine Systems, Human Cooperative Robotics
SHIMOYAMA, I., Micro Electromechanical Systems, Robotics
SUGIHARA, K., Computational Geometry, Robust Scientific Computation
SUGIHARA, M., Numerical Analysis
TACHI, S., Advanced Robotics, Virtual Reality, Telexistence and Retro-reflective Projection Technology
TAKEICHI, M., Programming Language Theory and its Implementation
TAKEUCHI, I., Real-time Distributed Cooperative Systems
TAKEMURA, A., Statistical Science
YONEZAWA, A., Foundation for Computer Software, Programming Language, Software Security

Graduate School for Law and Politics (7-3-1 Hongo, Bunkyo-ku, Tokyo 113-0033; tel. (3) 5841-3104; e-mail jshomu@j.u-tokyo.ac.jp; internet www.j.u-tokyo.ac.jp):

AIHARA, R., Litigation, Finance and Corporate Law
ARAKI, T., Labour and Employment Law
ASAKA, K., Anglo-American Law
BABA, Y., European Political History
CH'EN, P. H.-C., Principles of Comparative Law, Chinese Legal System
DOGAUCHI, H., Civil Law, Trust Law
EBIHARA, A., German Law
EGASHIRA, K., Commercial Law
FOOTE, D. H., Sociology of Law
FUJITA, T., Commercial Law
FUJIWARA, K., International Politics, Southeast Asian Studies
FURUE, Y., Criminal Procedure
HASEBE, Y., Constitutional Law
HIBINO, T., Constitutional Theory
HIGUCHI, N., Anglo-American Law
HIROSE, H., Consumer Law
IGARASHI, T., Comparative Politics
INOUE, T., Philosophy of Law
INOUYE, M., Criminal Procedure
ISHIGURO, K., Private International Law, Conflict of Laws
ISHIKAWA, K., Constitutional Law
ITO, M., Civil Procedure
ITO, Y., European Law
IWAHARA, S., Corporation Law, Regulation of Financial Institutions
IWAMURA, M., Social Security Law
KABASHIMA, I., Japanese Politics
KANDA, H., Commercial Law
KANSAKU, H., Commercial Law

KATO, J., Comparative Politics
KAWAIDE, Y., History of Western Political Thought
KITAMURA, I., French Law
KOBA, A., Roman Law
KOBAYAKAWA, M., Administrative Law
KOKETSU, H., Administrative Law
KUBO, F., American Government and History
MASUI, Y., Tax Law
MATSUSHITA, J., Insolvency Law
MIYASAKO, Y., International Business Law
MORITA, A., Public Administration
MORITA, H., Civil Law
MORITA, O., Civil Law
NAKATANI, K., International Law
NAKAYAMA, N., Intellectual Property Law
NAKAZATO, M., Tax Law
NISHIDA, N., Criminal Law
NISHIKAWA, Y., Occidental Legal History
NITTA, I., Japanese Legal History
NOMI, Y., Civil Law, Trust Law
NOZAKI, K., General Legal Practice
OBUCHI, T., Intellectual Property Law
OCHIAI, S., Commercial Law
OHGUSHI, K., Latin American Politics
OKUWAKI, N., International Law
OMURA, A., Civil Law
ONUMA, Y., International Law
OTA, S., Law and Social Science, Law and Economics, Civil Dispute Resolution, Legal Negotiation
SAEKI, H., Criminal Law
SAITO, M., Administrative Law, Law of Local Government
SHIOKAWA, N., Russian and Post-Soviet Politics
SHIRAISHI, T., Competition Law
TAKAHARA, A., Politics of East Asia
TAKAHASHI, H., Civil Procedure
TAKAHASHI, K., Constitutional Law
TAKAHASHI, S., History of International Politics
TAKATA, H., Civil Procedure
TANABE, K., Policy Studies
TERAO, Y., Anglo-American Law
UCHIDA, T., Civil Law
UGA, K., Administrative Law
USUI, M., Public Finance Law
WATANABE, H., History of Japanese Political Thought
YAMAGUCHI, A., Criminal Law
YAMAMOTO, R., Administrative Law
YAMAMURO, M., Criminal Procedure
YAMASHITA, T., Commercial Law

Graduate School of Science and Faculty of Science (7-3-1 Hongo, Bunkyo-ku, Tokyo 113-0033; tel. (3) 5841-4570; e-mail shomu@adm.s.u-tokyo.ac.jp; internet www.s.u-tokyo.ac.jp):

AIHARA, H., High Energy Physics
AKASAKA, K., Evolutional and Developmental Biology
AOKI, H., Theoretical Condensed-matter Physics
AOKI, K., Population Biology
EGUCHI, T., Theoretical Particle Physics
FUKADA, Y., Biochemistry and Molecular Biology
FUKUDA, H., Plant Cell Biology
GELLER, R., Seismology
HAMAGUCHI, H., Physical Chemistry
HAMANO, Y., Earth Dynamics
HASEGAWA, T., Solid-State Chemistry
HATSUDA, T., Theoretical Hadron Physics
HAYANO, R., High Energy Nuclear Physics Experiment
HIBIYA, T., Ocean Dynamics
HIRANO, H., Evolutionary Genetics
HOSHINO, M., Space Physics
IWASAWA, Y., Surface Chemistry and Catalysis
KAMIYA, R., Cell Biology
KAWASHIMA, T., Organic Chemistry
KIMURA, G., Tectonics, Structural Geology
KOBAYASHI, A., Materials Chemistry, Structural Chemistry
KOBAYASHI, T., Quantum Electronics
KOMAMIYA, S., Experimental Elementary Particle Physics
KOMEDA, Y., Plant Molecular Genetics
KUBO, T., Physiological Chemistry, Molecular Biology
KUBONO, S., Nuclear Physics, Nuclear Astrophysics
KUWAJIMA, K., Biophysics
MAKISHIMA, K., Experimental High Energy Astrophysics
MATSUMOTO, R., Sedimentology and Geochemistry
MATSU'URA, M., Earthquake Physics, Tectonics
MINOWA, M., Experimental Particle Physics without Accelerators
MIYAMOTO, M., Evolution of Planetary Material
MIYASHITA, S., Statistical Mechanics, Magnetism, Condensed Matter
MURAKAMI, T., Environmental Mineralogy
MURATA, J., Plant Systematics
NAGAHARA, H., Petrology, Planetary Science
NAGAO, K., Geochemistry
NAGATA, T., Plant Physiology and Plant Molecular Biology
NAKADA, Y., Stellar Astrophysics
NAKAMURA, E., Organic Chemistry
NAKANO, A., Developmental Cell Biology
NARASAKA, K., Synthetic Organic Chemistry
NISHIHARA, H., Inorganic Chemistry
NOMOTO, K., Theoretical Astrophysics
NONAKA, M., Molecular Immunology
NOTSU, K., Geochemistry
OHTA, T., Solid-State Physical Chemistry
OKA, Y., Neurobiology
OKAMURA, S., Extragalactic Astronomy
ONAKA, T., Astrophysics
OTSUKA, T., Nuclear Theory
OZAWA, K., Petrology
SAIGO, K., Molecular Biology
SAKAI, H., Nuclear Physics
SAKANO, H., Molecular Biology
SANO, M., Nonlinear Dynamics, Fluid Dynamics
SATO, K., Astrophysics and Cosmology
SHIBAHASHI, H., Theoretical Astrophysics
SHIMOURA, S., Nuclear Physics
SHIONOYA, M., Bioinorganic Chemistry
SOFUE, Y., Radio Astronomy
SUGIURA, N., Planetary Science
TACHIBANA, K., Chemistry of Natural Products
TADA, R., Sedimentology and Palaeoceanography
TAJIMA, F., Molecular Population Genetics
TAKEDA, H., Developmental Genetics
TANABE, K., Palaeontology
TERASAWA, T., Space and Magnetospheric Physics
TOHE, A., Yeast Genetics
TSUBONO, K., Experimental Relativity
UCHIDA, S., Solid-State Physics, High-Temperature Superconductivity
UEDA, S., Human Molecular Evolution
UMEZAWA, Y., Analytical Chemistry
URABE, T., Chemical Geology, Economic Geology
WADATI, M., Statistical Physics and Condensed-matter Physics
YAMAGATA, T., Ocean–Atmosphere Dynamics
YAMAGISHI, A., Clay Mineralogy
YAMAMOTO, M., Molecular Genetics
YAMAMOTO, S., Astrophysics, Astrochemistry, Molecular Spectroscopy
YAMANOUCHI, K., Physical Chemistry
YANAGIDA, T., Elementary Particle Physics
YOKOYAMA, J., Cosmology and Astrophysics
YOKOYAMA, S., Biophysics, Biochemistry and Molecular Biology
YOSHII, Y., Galactic Astronomy

Graduate School of Mathematical Sciences (3-8-1 Komaba, Meguro-ku, Tokyo 153-8914; tel. (3) 5465-7014; e-mail suriso@ms.u-tokyo.ac.jp; internet www.ms.u-tokyo.ac.jp):

ARAI, H., Real Analysis, Harmonic Analysis, Theory of Function Spaces
FUNAKI, T., Probability Theory
FURUTA, M., Global Analysis, Low-dimensional Topology
GIGA, Y., Nonlinear Analysis
HORIKAWA, E., Algebraic Geometry
JIMBO, M., Integrable Systems, Representation Theory
KATAOKA, K., Partial Differential Equations
KATSURA, T., Algebraic Geometry
KAWAHIGASHI, Y., Operator Algebras
KAWAMATA, Y., Algebraic Geometry and Complex Manifolds
KIKUCHI, F., Numerical Analysis
KOHNO, T., Three-manifolds, Quantum Groups
KUSUOKA, S., Probability Theory and its Application
MATANO, H., Nonlinear Partial Equations, Dynamical Systems
MATSUMOTO, Y., Topology
MIYAOKA, Y., Algebraic Geometry
MORITA, S., Topology of Manifolds
NAKAMURA, S., Differential Equations and Mathematical Physics
NOGUCHI, J., Complex Analysis in Several Variables, Complex Geometry
ODA, T., Number Theory
OKAMOTO, K., Differential Equations Complex Analysis
OSHIMA, T., Algebraic Analysis, Theory of Unitary Representations
SAITO, S., Arithmetic Geometry, Algebraic Geometry
SAITO, T., Arithmetic Geometry
TOKIHIRO, T., Mathematical Physics, Solid-State Physics
TSUBOI, T., Foliations, Diffeomorphism Groups
YOSHIDA, N., Mathematical Statistics, Stochastic Analysis

Graduate School of Medicine and Faculty of Medicine (7-3-1 Hongo, Bunkyo-ku, Tokyo 113-0033; tel. (3) 5841-3303; e-mail liaison@m.u-tokyo.ac.jp; internet www.m.u-tokyo.ac.jp):

AKABAYASHI, A., Biomedical Ethics
ANDO, J., Systems Physiology
ARAIE, M., Ophthalmology
ETO, F., Rehabilitation Medicine
FUJITA, T., Nephrology and Endocrinology
FUKAYAMA, M., Human Pathology and Diagnostic Pathology
HANAOKA, K., Anaesthesiology and Pain Medicine
HASHIZUME, K., Paediatric Surgery
HIROKAWA, N., Cell Biology and Anatomy
IGARASHI, T., Paediatrics
IHARA, Y., Neuropathology
IINO, M., Cellular and Molecular Pharmacology
KADOWAKI, T., Nutrition and Metabolism
KAGA, K., Otorhinolaryngology, Head and Neck Surgery
KAI, I., Social Gerontology
KAMINISHI, M., Gastrointestinal Surgery, Surgical Sensory Motor Neuroscience, Metabolic Care and Endocrine Surgery
KANDA, K., Nursing Administration
KATO, N., Neuropsychiatry
KAZUMA, K., Adult Nursing; Terminal and Long-term Care Nursing
KIRINO, T., Neurosurgery
KITA, K., Biomedical Chemistry
KITAMURA, T., Urology
KIUCHI, T., Medical Information Network Research
KOBAYASHI, Y., Public Health

KOIKE, K., Infection Control and Prevention
KOSHIMA, I., Plastic and Reconstructive Surgery
KURIHARA, H., Physiological Chemistry and Metabolism
MAKUUCHI, M., Hepatobiliary Pancreatic Surgery, Artificial Organ and Transplantation
MATSUSHIMA, K., Molecular Preventive Medicine
MISHINA, M., Molecular Neurobiology
MIYASHITA, Y., Physiology
MIYAZONO, K., Molecular Pathology
MORI, K., Cellular and Molecular Physiology
MURASHIMA, S., Community Health Nursing
NAGAI, R., Cardiology
NAGASE, T., Respiratory Medicine
NAGAWA, H., Surgical Oncology
NAKAMURA, K., Orthopaedic Surgery
NOMOTO, A., Microbiology
OHASHI, Y., Biostatistics; Epidemiology and Preventive Health Sciences
OHE, K., Medical Informatics and Economics
OHTOMO, K., Diagnostic Radiology
OKAYAMA, H., Molecular Biology
OMATA, M., Gastroenterology
OUCHI, Y., Ageing Science, Geriatric Medicine
OYAMA, H., Clinical Bioinformatics
SANADA, H., Gerontological Nursing
SHIMIZU, T., Cellular Signalling
SUZUKI, H., Pharmaceutical Services
TAKAHASHI, K., Transfusion Medicine
TAKAHASHI, T., Neurophysiology
TAKAMOTO, S., Cardiothoracic Surgery
TAKATO, T., Oral and Maxillofacial Surgery
TAKETANI, Y., Obstetrics and Gynaecology
TAMAKI, K., Dermatology
TANIGUCHI, T., Immunology
TOHYAMA, C., Disease Biology and Interpretative Medicine
TOKUNAGA, K., Human Genetics
TSUJI, S., Neurology
TSUTSUMI, O., Obstetrics and Gynaecology
UENO, S., Bioimaging and Biomagnetics
USHIDA, T., Biomedical Materials and Systems
USHIJIMA, H., Developmental Medical Sciences
WAKAI, S., International Community Health
WATANABE, C., Human Ecology
YAHAGI, N., Emergency and Critical Care Medicine
YAMAMOTO, K., Allergology and Rheumatology
YAMAZAKI, T., Clinical Bioinformatics
YATOMI, Y., Clinical Laboratory Medicine
YOSHIDA, K., Forensic Medicine

Graduate School of Pharmaceutical Sciences and Faculty of Pharmaceutical Sciences (7-3-1 Hongo, Bunkyo-ku, Tokyo 113-0033; tel. (3) 5841-4878; e-mail adviser@mol.f.u-tokyo.ac.jp; internet www.f.u-tokyo.ac.jp/index-e.html):

ARAI, H., Health Chemistry
EBIZUKA, Y., Natural Products Chemistry
FUKUYAMA, T., Synthetic Natural Products Chemistry
FUNATSU, T., Biophysics
ICHIJO, H., Cell Signalling
IRIMURA, T., Cancer Biology and Molecular Immunology
IWATSUBO, T., Neuropathology and Neuroscience
KATADA, T., Physiological Chemistry
KIRINO, Y., Neurobiophysics
KOBAYASHI, S., Organic and Organometallic Chemistry
MATSUKI, N., Neuropharmacology and Neuroscience
MIURA, M., Molecular Neurobiology
NAGANO, T., Chemical Biology and Medicinal Chemistry
OHWADA, T., Organic and Medicinal Chemistry
SATOW, Y., Protein Structural Biology
SEKIMIZU, K., Biochemistry, Molecular Biology
SHIBASAKI, M., Synthetic Organic Chemistry
SHIMADA, I., Structural Biology, NMR Spectroscopy, Physical Chemistry
SUGIYAMA, Y., Molecular Pharmacokinetics

Graduate School of Public Policy (7-3-1 Hongo, Bunkyo-ku, Tokyo 113-0033; tel. (3) 5841-3104; e-mail ppin@j.u-tokyo.ac.jp; internet www.pp.u-tokyo.ac.jp):

HAYASHI, R., Economic Policy
ICHIMURA, H., Econometrics
IHORI, T., Public Finance, Public Economics
ITO, T., International Finance, Macroeconomics
KANEMOTO, Y., Urban Economics
KAWAI, M., Basic Macroeconomics
MORITA, A., Public Management
OKUWAKI, N., International Law and Organization, Law of the Sea, Air and Outer Space
TANABE, K., Politics, Policy Analysis, Policy Process

Interfaculty Initiative in Information Studies and Graduate School of Interdisciplinary Information Studies (7-3-1 Hongo, Bunkyo-ku, Tokyo 113-0033; tel. (3) 5841-5900; e-mail info@iii.u-tokyo.ac.jp; internet www.iii.u-tokyo.ac.jp):

ARAKAWA, C., Computational Fluid Dynamics, Simulation
BABA, A., Historical Informatics, Japanese Early Modern Economic History, Digital Archive Science
EINCO, S., Indian Philology, Ritual and Religion in India
HAMADA, J., Information Law and Policy
HANADA, T., Media Studies
HARA, Y., Economic Development Theory, Southeast Asian Economics
HARASHIMA, H., Communication Engineering and Face Studies
HASHIMOTO, Y., Social Psychology
HIROI, O., Social Psychology, Sociology of Disasters
IKEUCHI, K., Computer Vision
ISHIDA, H., Information Semiotics
KAN, S., Investigation of Possibilities for Regional Union in North-East Asia
KAWAGUCHI, Y., Computer Art
KUNIYOSHI, Y., Intelligent Systems and Informatics
NISHIGAKI, T., Information and Media Studies
SAKAMURA, K., Computer Architecture
SASAKI, M., Ecological Psychology
SUDOH, O., Economics of the Knowledge-based Society
TSUJII, J., Computational Linguistics, Natural Language Processing
YAMAGUCHI, Y., Graphics
YOSHIMI, S., Popular Culture and Media Events

ATTACHED RESEARCH INSTITUTES

Asian Natural Environmental Science Center: 1-1-1 Yayoi, Bunkyo-ku, Tokyo 113-8657; f. 1995; Dir K. TAKEUCHI.

Atmosphere and Ocean Research Institute: Kashiwanoha 5-1-15, Kashiwa 277-8564; internet www.aori.u-tokyo.ac.jp/english/index.html; f. 1962; Dir Dr HIROSHI NIINO; publ. *Coastal Marine Science* (1 a year), *Preliminary Cruise Report* (irregular).

Biotechnology Research Center: 1-1-1 Yayoi, Bunkyo-ku, Tokyo 113-8657; f. 1993; Dir S. HORINOUCHI.

Center for Climate System Research: 5-1-5 Kashiwanoha, Kashiwa-shi, Chiba 277-8568; f. 1991; Dir T. NAKAJIMA.

Center for Collaborative Research: 4-6-1 Komaba, Meguro-ku, Tokyo 153-8505; f. 1996; Dir H. YOKOI.

Center for Research and Development of Higher Education: 7-3-1 Hongo, Bunkyo-ku, Tokyo 113-0033; f. 1996; Dir K. OKAMOTO.

Center for Spatial Information Science: 5-1-5 Kashiwanoha, Kashiwa-shi, Chiba 277-8568; f. 1998; Dir R. SHIBASAKI.

Cryogenic Center: 2-11-16 Yayoi, Bunkyo-ku, Tokyo 113-0032; f. 1967; Dir M. MINOWA.

Earthquake Research Institute: 1-1-1 Yayoi, Bunkyo-ku, Tokyo 113-0032; internet www.eri.u-tokyo.ac.jp; f. 1925; Dir S. OKOBU; publ. *Bulletin of the Earthquake Research Institute* (4 a year).

Environmental Science Center: 7-3-1 Hongo, Bunkyo-ku, Tokyo 113-0033; f. 1975; Dir K. YAMAMOTO.

Health Service Center: 7-3-1 Hongo, Bunkyo-ku, Tokyo 113-0033; f. 1967; Dir (vacant); publ. *Kenko Kanri Gaiyo* (1 a year).

High Temperature Plasma Center: 5-1-5 Kashiwanoha, Kashiwa-shi, Chiba 277-8568; f. 1999; Dir Y. OGAWA.

Historiographical Institute: 7-3-1 Hongo, Bunkyo-ku, Tokyo 113-0033; internet www.hi.u-tokyo.ac.jp; f. 1869; Dir M. HOTATE; publ. *Shiryo Hensan—Sho Ho* (1 a year), *Shiryo Hensan—Jo Kenkyu Kiyo* (1 a year).

Information Technology Center: 2-11-16 Yayoi, Bunkyo-ku, Tokyo 113-8658; f. 1999; Dir Y. ISHIKAWA.

Institute for Advanced Studies on Asia: 7-3-1 Hongo, Bunkyo-ku, Tokyo 113-0033; e-mail webadmin@ioc.u-tokyo.ac.jp; internet www.ioc.u-tokyo.ac.jp; f. 1941; Dir YASUSHI OKI; publ. *International Journal of ASIAN STUDIES* (2 a year), *Memoirs* (2 a year), *Oriental Culture* (1 a year).

Institute for Cosmic Ray Research: 5-1-5 Kashiwanoha, Kashiwa-shi, Chiba 277-8582; f. 1953; Dir T. KAJITA; publ. *ICRR Report* (irregular), *ICRR News* (4 a year), *ICRR Hokoku*.

Institute of Industrial Science: 4-6-1 Komaba, Meguro-ku, Tokyo 153-8505; e-mail kokusai@iis.u-tokyo.ac.jp; internet www.iis.u-tokyo.ac.jp; f. 1949; Dir M. MAEDA; publ. *Seisan-Kenkyu* (12 a year).

Institute of Medical Science: 4-6-1 Shirokanedai, Minato-ku, Tokyo 108-8639; e-mail www-admin@ims.u-tokyo.ac.jp; internet www.ims.u-tokyo.ac.jp; f. 1892; Dir T. YAMAMOTO.

Institute of Molecular and Cellular Biosciences: 1-1-1 Yayoi, Bunkyo-ku, Tokyo 113-0032; e-mail iam-support @ iam.u-tokyo.ac.jp; internet www.iam.u-tokyo.ac.jp; f. 1953; Dir A. MIYAJIMA.

Institute of Social Science: 7-3-1 Hongo, Bunkyo-ku, Tokyo 113-0033; e-mail webmaster@iss.u-tokyo.ac.jp; internet www.iss.u-tokyo.ac.jp; f. 1946; Dir A. KOMORIDA; publ. *Shakai Kagaku Kenkyu* (Journal of Social Science, 6 a year), *Social Science Japan Journal* (2 a year), *Social Science Japan* (newsletter, 3 a year).

Institute for Solid-State Physics: 5-1-5 Kashiwanoha, Kashiwa-shi, Chiba 277-8581; e-mail ilo@issp.u-tokyo.ac.jp; internet www.issp.u-tokyo.ac.jp; f. 1957; Dir K. UEDA; publ. *Technical Report* (irregular).

Intelligent Modelling Laboratory: 2-11-16 Yayoi, Bunkyo-ku, Tokyo 113-8656; f. 1996; Dir K. HIRAO.

International Center: 7-3-1 Hongo, Bunkyo-ku, Tokyo 113-8654; f. 1990; Dir G. MESHITSUKA; publ. *Bulletin* (1 a year), *News* (4 a year).

International Center for Elementary Particle Physics: 7-3-1 Hongo, Bunkyo-ku, Tokyo 113-0033; f. 2004; Dir S. KOMAMIYA.

International Research Center for Medical Education: 7-3-1 Hongo, Bunkyo-ku, Tokyo 113-0033; e-mail ircme@m.u-tokyo.ac.jp; f. 2000; Dir KAZUHIKO YAMAMOTO; publ. *Newsletter* (2 a year).

Komaba Open Laboratory: 4-6-1 Komaba, Meguro-ku, Tokyo 153-8904; f. 1998; Dir T. NANYA.

Molecular Genetics Research Laboratory: 7-3-1 Hongo, Bunkyo-ku, Tokyo 113-0033; f. 1983; Dir M. YAMAMOTO.

Radioisotope Center: 2-11-16 Yayoi, Bunkyo-ku, Tokyo 113-0032; f. 1970; Dir Y. MAKIDE.

Research Center for Advanced Science and Technology: 4-6-1 Komaba, Meguro-ku, Tokyo 153-8904; f. 1987; Dir T. FUJITA.

Research into Artifacts Center for Engineering: 5-1-5 Kashiwanoha, Kashiwa-shi, Chiba 277-8568; f. 1992; Dir K. UEDA.

VLSI Design and Education Center: 2-11-16 Yayoi, Bunkyo-ku, Tokyo 113-8656; f. 1996; Dir K. ASADA.

University Museum: 7-3-1 Hongo, Bunkyo-ku, Tokyo 113-0033; f. 1965; Dir S. TAKAHASHI; publ. *Ouroboros* (newsletter, 3 a year), *Bulletin* (irregular), *Material Reports* (irregular), *UMUT Monograph* (irregular)

UNIVERSITY OF TSUKUBA

1-1-1 Tennodai, Tsukuba, Ibaraki-ken 305-8577
Telephone: (29) 853-2056
E-mail: global@un.tsukuba.ac.jp
Internet: www.tsukuba.ac.jp
Founded 1973
public control
Language of instruction: Japanese
Academic year: April to March

Pres.: KYOSUKE NAGATA
Vice-Pres.: YASUO MIAKE
Vice-Pres.: CAROLINE FERN BENTON
Vice-Pres.: KAZUHIKO SHIMIZU
Vice-Pres.: AKIRA YOSHIKAWA
Vice-Pres.: MICHIYOSHI AE
Vice-Pres.: TERUO HIGASHI
Vice-Pres.: YUICHI OHTA
Dir of Univ. Hospital: AKIRA MATSUMURA
Vice-Pres. and Dir of Education Bureau of the Laboratory Schools: TOSHINORI ISHIKUMA
Dir of Univ. Library: NAKAYAMA SHINICHI

Library of 2,596,533 vols, 29,847 periodicals
Number of teachers: 3,030
Number of students: 16,459

PROVOSTS

Undergraduate Programmes:
- School of Art and Design: Prof. NOBUO NAKAMURA
- School of Health and Physical Education: Prof. HISASHI SANADA
- School of Humanities and Culture: Prof. MAKOTO ITO
- School of Human Sciences: Prof. TAKAO ANDO
- School of Informatics: Prof. HIROAKI NISHIKAWA
- School of Integrative and Global Majors: Prof. MICHIYOSHI AE
- School of Life and Environmental Sciences: Prof. SACHIO MARUYAMA
- School of Medicine and Medical Sciences: Prof. AKIRA HARA
- School of Science and Engineering: Prof. MASAHIKO MIYAMOTO
- School of Social and International Studies: Prof. TOMOICHI SHINOZUKA

Masters Degree Programmes:
- TOUJI TANAKA (Provost)

Doctoral Degree Programmes:
- Graduate School of Business Sciences: Prof. CHIZURU NISHIO
- Graduate School of Comprehensive Human Sciences: Prof. YASUNORI KANAHO
- Graduate School of Humanities and Social Sciences: Prof. SHIGEO OSONOI
- Graduate School of Library, Information and Media Studies: Prof. SHIGEO SUGIMOTO
- Graduate School of Life and Environmental Sciences: Prof. HIROSHI EZURA
- Graduate School of Pure and Applied Sciences: Prof. HIDEO KIGOSHI
- Graduate School of Systems and Information Engineering: Prof. TOSHIYUKI INAGAKI

Faculties:
- Faculty of Art and Design: Prof. SHINICHI TAMAGAWA (Provost)
- Faculty of Business Sciences: Prof. YASUFUMI SARUWATARI (Provost)
- Faculty of Engineering, Information and Systems: Prof. HIDEAKI TAKAGI (Provost)
- Faculty of Health and Sport Sciences: Prof. AKIRA NAKAGAWA (Provost)
- Faculty of Humanities and Social Sciences: Prof. YOSHIKI TSUBOI (Provost)
- Faculty of Human Sciences: Prof. SHINYA MIYAMOTO (Provost)
- Faculty of Library, Information and Media Science: Prof. MAKOTO MATSUMOTO (Provost)
- Faculty of Life and Environmental Sciences: Prof. YOSHIHIRO SHIRAIWA (Provost)
- Faculty of Medicine: Prof. HIROYUKI YOSHIKAWA (Provost)
- Faculty of Pure and Applied Sciences: Prof. KAZUYUKI KANAYA (Provost)

UNIVERSITY OF YAMANASHI, NATIONAL UNIVERSITY CORPORATION

4-4-37 Takeda, Kofu, Yamanashi 400-8510
Telephone: (55) 220-8004
E-mail: soumuk@yamanashi.ac.jp
Internet: www.yamanashi.ac.jp
Founded 1949
Independent
Academic year: April to March

Pres.: YOJI YOSHIDA
Registrar: KENJI TAMARU
Dean of Students: KUNIO OOHARA
Librarian: TOSHIAKI OTOMO

Library of 556,439 vols
Number of teachers: 600
Number of students: 5,150

Publications: *Bulletin of the Faculty of Education and Human Sciences* (2 a year), *Report of the Faculty of Engineering* (1 a year), *Journal of Applied Educational Research* (1 a year), *Report of the Faculty of Medicine*

DEANS

Faculty of Education: TETSUO HORI
Faculty of Engineering: KOKI YOKOTSUKA
Faculty of Medicine: HIDEAKI NUKUI

ATTACHED INSTITUTES

Center for Crystal Science and Technology: attached to the Faculty of Engineering.

Center for Instrumental Analysis: 4-3-11 Takeda, Kofu 400-8511.

Center for Life Science Research: 1110 Shimokato, Tamaho-cho, Nakakoma-gun 409-3898.

Clean Energy Research Center: 7 Miyamae-cho, Kofu 400-0021; internet www.clean.yamanashi.ac.jp.

Cooperative Research and Development Center: 4-3-11 Takeda, Kofu 400-8511.

Institute of Enology and Viticulture: internet www.wine.yamanashi.ac.jp; attached to the Faculty of Engineering.

Integrated Information Processing Center: 4-3-11 Takeda, Kofu 400-8511; Dir KOJI IWANUMA.

International Student Center: 4-4-37 Takeda, Kofu 400-8510; e-mail yu-study-abroad@yamanashi.ac.jp

UTSUNOMIYA UNIVERSITY

350 Mine-machi, Utsunomiya-shi, Tochigi 321-8505
Telephone: (286) (36) 1515
E-mail: plan@miya.jm.utsunomiya-u.ac.jp
Internet: www.utsunomiya-u.ac.jp
Founded 1949
Independent
Language of instruction: Japanese
Academic year: April to March

Pres.: HIROTO TABARA
Vice-Pres: HIDEKI KASUYA, SHIGERU KITAJIMA
Dir of Univ. Library: HIROTAKA KOIKE

Library of 551,376 vols
Number of teachers: 476
Number of students: 5,411

DEANS

Faculty of Agriculture: TADATAKE MIZUMOTO
Faculty of Education: KIYOSHI NAKAMURA
Faculty of Engineering: YASUSHI NISHIDA
Faculty of International Studies: KAZUKO FUJITA

WAKAYAMA UNIVERSITY

Sakaedani 930, Wakayama-shi 640-8510
Telephone: (73) 454-0361
E-mail: koho@center.wakayama-u.ac.jp
Internet: www.wakayama-u.ac.jp
Founded 1949
Academic year: April to March

Pres.: S. MORIYA
Chief Admin. Officer: M. TANIGUCHI
Librarian: H. TACHIBANA

Library of 741,765 vols
Number of teachers: 371
Number of students: 4,460

Publications: *Bulletin of the Faculty of Education, The Wakayama Economic Review*

DEANS

Faculty of Economics: T. KINOUCHI
Faculty of Education: K. MORISUGI
Faculty of Systems Engineering: O. OTSUKI

YAMAGATA UNIVERSITY

1-4-12, Koshirakawa-machi, Yamagata 990-8560
Telephone: (23) 628-4006
E-mail: sombun@jm.kj.yamagata-u.ac.jp
Internet: www.yamagata-u.ac.jp
Founded 1949
Independent
Academic year: April to March (2 semesters)

Pres.: FUJIRO SENDO

Sec.-Gen.: DAISUKE IKEDA
Librarian: MASANOBU HAYAKAWA

Library of 991,330 vols
Number of teachers: 1,800
Number of students: 9,436

Publications: *Bulletin of Humanities* (1 a year), *Bulletin of Social Sciences* (2 a year), *Bulletin of Educational Science* (1 a year), *Bulletin of Natural Sciences* (1 a year), *Medical Journal* (2 a year), *Bulletin of Engineering* (1 a year), *Bulletin of Agricultural Science* (1 a year)

DEANS

Faculty of Agriculture: TAKESHI SASSA
Faculty of Education: TSUNEO ISHIJIMA
Faculty of Engineering: TAKESHI ENDO
Faculty of Literature and Social Sciences: KOICHI TAKAGI
Faculty of Science: SEIGO KATO
School of Medicine: MASAO ENDOH

YAMAGUCHI UNIVERSITY

1677-1 Yoshida, Yamaguchi 753-8511
Telephone: (83) 933-5026
E-mail: sh033@office.cc.yamaguchi-u.ac.jp
Internet: www.yamaguchi-u.ac.jp

Founded 1949
National University Corporation
Academic year: April to March

Pres.: HIROSHI KATO
Vice-Pres: KYOSUKE SAKATE, OSAMU FUKUMASA, SHINYA KAWAI TAKUYA MARUMOTO YOSHIKAZU SUGIHARA
Sec.-Gen.: YUTAKA MATSUYAMA
Dir of Univ. Library: OSAMU FUKUMASA

Library: see under Libraries and Archives
Number of teachers: 889
Number of students: 10,785 (9,099 undergraduates, 1,686 postgraduates)

DEANS

Faculty of Agriculture: DAIZO KOGA
Faculty of Economics: OSAMU TAKIGUCHI
Faculty of Education: ISSEI YOSHIDA
Faculty of Engineering: TOSHIKATSU MIKI
Faculty of Humanities: SUSUMU TANAKA
School of Medicine: TOKUHIRO HIROSHI ISHIHARA
Faculty of Science: HIROYUKI MASHIYAMA
Graduate School of East Asian Studies: NORIKO OTANI
Graduate School of Innovation and Technology Management: KEN KAMINISHI
United Graduate School of Veterinary Science: TOSHIHARU HAYASHI

YOKOHAMA NATIONAL UNIVERSITY

79-1 Tokiwadai, Hodogaya-ku, Yokohama 240-8501
Telephone: (45) 339-3036
E-mail: international@ynu.ac.jp
Internet: www.ynu.ac.jp

Founded 1949
Language of instruction: Japanese
Academic year: April to March (2 semesters)

Pres.: KUNIO SUZUKI
Exec. Dir and Exec. Vice-Pres.: YASUO KOKUBUN
Exec. Dir and Exec. Vice-Pres.: SHUJI MIZOGUCHI
Exec. Dir and Exec. Vice-Pres.: HITOSHI YAMADA
Exec. Dir and Sec. Gen.: AKIRA SHIMIZU

Library: see under Libraries and Archives
Number of teachers: 606
Number of students: 10,023

DEANS

College of Business Administration: H. NAKAMURA
College of Economics: E. TOMIURA
College of Education and Human Sciences: M. TAKAGI
College of Engineering Science: A. KAWAMURA
Faculty of Environment and Information Sciences: S. MORISHITA
Faculty of Urban Innovation: F. NAKAMURA
Graduate School of Education: M. TAKAGI
Graduate School of Engineering: A. KAWAMURA
Graduate School of International Social Sciences: K. YAMAKURA

PROFESSORS

College of Business Administration (79-4 Tokiwadai, Hodogayaku, Yokohama 240-8501; tel. (45) 339-3654; e-mail int.somu@nuc.ynu.ac.jp; internet www.business.ynu.ac.jp):

CHO, D., Business Admin.
MOGAKI, H., International Personnel Management
MORITA, H., Fiscal Studies, Finance Theory
NAKAMURA, H., Strategic Accounting, Capital Budgeting
OHTSUKA, E., Game Theory
SHIRAI, H., Management Information Systems, Business Modelling
TORII, A., Economic Policy
YAGI, H., Ecological Accounting
YAMAKURA, K., Management
YAMASHITA, S., Natural Economic Accounting
YOSHIKAWA, T., Cost Accounting, Management Accounting

College of Economics (79-3 Tokiwadai, Hodogayaku, Yokohama 240-8501; tel. (45) 339-3510; e-mail int.somu@nuc.ynu.ac.jp; internet www.econ.ynu.ac.jp):

AKIYAMA, T., Theoretical Economics
FUKAGAI, Y., History of Economic Thought, Economic Ethics
HAGIWARA, S., US Economic Policy
HASEBE, Y., Input–Output Analysis
KAMIKAWA, T., International Finance, Money and Banking
KANAZAWA, F., Public Finance, Local Finance
KIZAKI, M., Modern Chinese Economy, Corporate Governance in China, Chinese Labour Affairs
KOBAYASHI, M., Statistical Science
OKADO, M., Japanese Economic History
OMORI, Y., Labour Economics
TOMIURA, E., International Economics
UI, T., Theoretical Economics
YAMAZAKI, K., Economic Policy

College of Education and Human Sciences (79-2 Tokiwadai, Hodogayaku, Yokohama 240-8501; tel. (45) 339-3253; e-mail edu.somu@nuc.ynu.ac.jp; internet www.edhs.ynu.ac.jp):

ARAI, H., Pedagogy
ARAI, M., Production Engineering, Processing Studies
BABA, Y., General Mathematics
CHOMABAYASHI, T., Exercise Physiology
EBIHARA, O., Sociology of Physical Education and Sport
ETO, T., Geology
FUJIMORI, T., Sculpture
FUKAWA, G., Subject Pedagogy
FUKUDA, S., Experimental Psychology
HARADA, H., Soil Zoology
HASHIMOTO, Y., Science Education
HAYASHIBE, H., Developmental Psycholinguistics
HORI, M., Environmental Chemistry
ICHIYANAGI, H., Japanese Modern Literature, Japanese Modern Culture
IMOTO, S., German Literature, European Culture History
INOUE, K., Clinical Psychology
ISHIDA, J., Primary Mathematics Education
KANAI, Y., Ethics
KANAZAWA, H., Japanese Linguistics
KANEKO, K., Eating Habits Studies
KASAHARA, M., Cultural Anthropology
KATO, C., Japanese Modern History
KIKUCHI, T., Ecology, Environment
KIMURA, M., Sports Science
KITAGAWA, Y., Constitutional Law
KOBAYASHI, K., History of Thought
KOBAYASHI, N., Form, Structure
KOBAYASHI, Y., Movement Education Therapy
KOIZUMI, H., Teaching Methods
MAEDA, M., Geometry
MAJIMA, R., Palaeontology
MATSUISHI, T., Neuropsychiatric Studies
MIYAKE, A., Japanese Literature
MIYAZAKI, T., Philosphy, Ethics
MOCHIDA, Y., Ecology, Environment
MORIMOTO, S., Physiology and Applied Physiology, Exercise Physiology
MORIMOTO, S., Science Education
MOTEKI, K., Applied Musicology
MURATA, T., Modern Chinese History
MUROI, H., Aesthetics, Semiotics, Cultural Studies, Philosophy
NAKAGAWA, T., Education for the Hearing-impaired
NAKAMURA, E., Analytical Chemistry
NEGAMI, S., Topological Graph Theory
NISHIMURA, T., Consumer Policy
NISHIMURA, T., Geometry
NISHIWAKI, Y., Geographic Education
NUKATA, J., Cognitive Engineering
NUSHI, A., Educational Psychology
OCHIAI, M., Subject Pedagogy
OGAWA, M., Music Education
OKADA, M., Classical Chinese Literature
ONO, Y., Aesthetics, History of Art
OOISHI, A., Commutative Algebra
OSATO, T., Musicology
OSHIMA, A., Educational Technology
OTAKI, F., Piano Performance
SAKAI, Y., Computer Science
SANO, F., Outdoor Recreation
SASAKI, H., Pedagogy
SATO, Y., Form, Structure
SHIMOJO, H., Ethics
SHIROUZU, N., Modern Chinese Literature
SUGIMURA, H., Organic Chemistry
SUGIYAMA, T., Piano Performance
SUKAWA, H., Korean Economic History
SUZUKI, K., Weather, Oceanic Physics, Hydrology
SUZUKI, T., Home Economics Education, Family Studies
TAJIMA, F., Optical Measurement
TAKAGI, H., Adolescent Psychology
TAKAGI, M., Curriculum Studies
TAKAGI, N., Teaching Methodology
TAKAHASHI, K., Dance Education
TAKAHASHI, K., English Linguistics
TAKAHASHI, M., Educational Anthropology
TAKAYAMA, Y., Psychology of the Disabled
TAKUSARI, D., Aesthetics, History of Art
TANAKA, H., Environmental Physiology
TANEDA, Y., Colony Specificity
TANJI, Y., American Literature, Realism, Naturalism, Women's Studies
TANISHO, S., Biochemical Engineering
UMEMOTO, Y., History of French Theatre, Cinema Theory
WATABE, M., Sociology
YAMAMOTO, I., Experimental Condensed Matter Physics, Physics Education
YANAI, K., Philosophy
YOKOYAMA, N., Physical Education, Sports Science, Budo, Kendo

College of Engineering Science (79-5 Tokiwadai, Hodogayaku, Yokohama 240-8501; tel. (45) 339-3804; e-mail eng.somu@nuc.ynu.ac.jp; internet www.eng.ynu.ac.jp):

ADACHI, T., Electronic Devices, Electronic Equipment
AMEMIYA, N., Electric Power Engineering, Electronic Equipment Engineering
ANDO, K., Structural Ceramics
ARAI, H., Electromagnetics
ARAI, M., Ship Marine Engineering
ASAMI, M., Synthetic Chemistry
AZUSHIMA, A., Material Processing, Treatment
BABA, T., Applied Optics, Quantum Optical Engineering
FUKUTOMI, H., Structural/Functional Materials
HABUKA, H., Applied Physical Properties, Crystal Engineering
HANEJI, N., Electronic Device, Electronic Equipment
HIRAYAMA, T., Aeronautics
HIROSE, Y., Electronic Device, Electronic Equipment
IIDA, Y., Architectural History, Design
ISHIHARA, O., Plasma Science
ISHII, R., Digital Signal Processing
ITOH, K., Physical Chemistry
KAMEMOTO, K., Fluidics
KAMINOYAMA, M., Chemical Engineering
KAWAI, K., Metal Forming and Numerical Simulation
KAWAMURA, A., Power Electronics
KIMISHIMA, Y., Applied Solid-State Physics
KITADA, Y., Differential Topology
KITAYAMA, K., Architectural History, Design
KOBAYASHI, K., Earth Astrochemistry
KOBAYASHI, S., City Planning
KOHNO, R., Information Communication Technology
KOIZUMI, J., Bio-function, Bioprocessors
KOKUBUN, Y., Opto-electronics
KONNO, N., Mathematics
KUROKAWA, J., Fluid Engineering
MAEKAWA, T., Computer-aided Design
MATSUMOTO, K., Chemical Engineering, Material Properties, Transfer Operation, Unit Operation, Separation Engineering
MIURA, K., Metallic Physical Properties
MIZUGUCHI, J., Electronic Properties of Organic Semiconductors and Oxide Semiconductors
NAITO, A., Biophysics
NAKAMURA, F., Urban Transportation Planning
NISHINO, K., Thermal Engineering
OGINO, T., Surface Science and Nanotechnology of Semiconductors
OHARA, K., Theory of Architecture
OHNO, K., Mathematical Physics, Fundamental Theory of Physical Properties
OKUYAMA, K., Heat Transfer
ONO, T., Mathematical Physics, Fundamental Theory of Physical Properties
OTA, K., Energy
OYAMA, T., Power Systems Engineering
SAKAKIBARA, K., Physical Organic Chemistry
SANADA, K., Control Engineering
SASAKI, K., Elementary Particle Physics
SHIBATA, M., Elementary Particle Physics, Atomic Nucleus, Cosmic Ray, Space Physics
SHIBAYAMA, T., Civil Engineering
SHIRATORI, M., Machine Material, Material Mechanics
SUMI, Y., Naval Architecture and Ocean Engineering
SUZUKI, K., Naval Architecture and Ocean Engineering
SUZUKI, K., Physical Properties II
TAGAWA, Y., Building Construction/Material
TAKADA, H., Intelligent Mechanics, Mechanical Systems
TAKAGI, J., Production Engineering, Processing Studies
TAKAHASHI, A., Organic Polymer Chemistry, High Performance Polymers for Microelectronics
TAKANO, S., Mathematics
TAKEDA, J., Physical Properties II
TAKEMURA, Y., Magnetics
TAMANO, K., Geometry
TAMURA, A., Architectural Environment/ Equipment
TANAKA, H., Machine Element
TANAKA, M., Thin Film and Surface Interface Physical Properties
TANI, K., Rock Engineering
TASAI, A., Building Structure
TSUBAKI, T., Concrete Engineering
TSUBOI, T., Thermal Engineering
UEDA, K., Polymer/Textile Materials
UMEZAWA, O., Structural/Functional Materials
UTAKA, Y., Thermal Engineering
WATANABE, M., Carcinogenesis
WATANABE, M., Polymer Structure
YABUTA, T., Sensitivity Informatics, Soft Computing
YAGI, M., Physical Chemistry
YAKOU, T., Strength of Materials
YAMAMOTO, M., Architecture
YAMAZAKI, Y., Earthquake Engineering
YOKOYAMA, Y., Organic Industrial Materials
YOSHIDA, K., Architectural History, Design
YOSHIKAWA, N., Electronic Device, Electronic Equipment

Faculty of Environmental and Information Sciences (79-7 Tokiwadai, Hodogayaku, Yokohama 240-8501; tel. (45) 339-4422; e-mail env-inf.somu@nuc.ynu.ac.jp; internet www.eis.ynu.ac.jp):

ARIMA, M., Petrology
ARISAWA, H., Media Informatics, Database
FUJIWARA, K., Ecology, Environment
GOTOH, T., Perception Information Processing, Intelligent Robotics
HARA, T., Catalysis by Metal Complexes
HIRANO, N., Functional Analysis
HIRATSUKA, K., Applied Molecular Cell Biology
INOUE, S., Synthetic Chemistry
INOUE, Y., Naval Architecture and Ocean Engineering
KAGEI, S., Fuzzy Control
KANEKO, N., Ecology
KONDO, M., Industrial Technology Policy
MASUNAGA, S., Environmental Dynamic Analysis
MATSUDA, H., Environmental Ecology
MATSUMOTO, T., Information Security
MEGURO, T., Inorganic Materials
MITSUI, I., Regional Industrial Policy
MIYAKE, A., Safety Engineering
MORI, T., Natural Language Processing
MORISHITA, S., Machine Mechanics, Control
NAGAO, T., Biological/Living Body Informatics
NAKAI, S., Environmental Health
OGAWA, T., Safety Engineering
OHNO, K., Landscape Ecology
OHTANI, H., Safety Engineering
OKUTANI, T., Inorganic Material, Physical Properties
SADOHARA, S., Social System Engineering, Safety Systems
SASAMOTO, H., Plant Physiology
SEKINE, K., Material Processing, Treatment
SHIDA, K., Mathematical Sociology
SHUSA, Y., Globalization of Firms
SUZUKI, A., Materials Science
TAKEDA, Y., Management Information Systems
TAMURA, N., Natural Language Processing
TERADA, T., Mathematics
UENO, S., Control Engineering
UESUGI, S., Molecular Biology
YAMADA, H., Structural Engineering
YAMADA, T., Computational Mechanics

Graduate School of Education (79-2 Tokiwadai, Hodogayaku, Yokohama 240-8501; tel. (45) 339-3253; e-mail edu.somu@nuc.ynu.ac.jp; internet www.edhs.ynu.ac.jp):

INUZUKA, F., Guidance

Graduate School of International Social Sciences (79-4 Tokiwadai, Hodogayaku, Yokohama 240-8501; tel. (45) 339-3602; e-mail int.somu@nuc.ynu.ac.jp; internet www.igss.ynu.ac.jp):

ABE, S., Marketing, Consumer Behaviour
ARAKI, I., International Law
ARIE, D., Economic Doctrine, Economic Thought
ASANO, Y., Finance
DOI, H., Economic Theory
FUJIMORI, T., Resolution Process in Interpersonal Conflicts
HAMAMOTO, M., Accounting
HARADA, K., Constitutional Law
HIGASHIDA, A., Economic Statistics
IGARASHI, A., International Accounting, International Auditing
IKEDA, T., Development Economics
IMAMURA, Y., Civil Law
INOWE, T., Finance, Macroeconomics
ISHIYAMA, Y., Economic History
IWASAKI, M., Tax Law
IZUMI, H., Accounting and Book-keeping Systems
KATO, M., Environmental Law
KAWABATA, Y., Public Law
KAWASHIMA, K., General Civil and Commercial Practice
KIMIZUKA, M., Public Law
KOBAYASHI, M., Linguistics
KODA, K., Macroeconomics
KOIKE, O., Politics
KURASAWA, M., Theoretical Economics
KURUSHIMA, T., Commercial Law
MATSUI, Y., Business Administration
MITO, H., Business Administration
MIZOGUCHI, S., Management Accounting
MORIKAWA, T., International Law
NAGAI, K., Mathematical Statistics
NAKAMURA, K., Regional and Local Political Economy
NAKAMURA, Y., English Studies
NAKAMURA, Y., General Theory of Economics
NEMOTO, Y., International Law
NOMURA, H., Civil Law
OKABE, J., Economic Statistics
OKADA, E., Business Administration
OKUMURA, T., Monetary Economics
OKUYAMA, K., Sociology of Law
OSAWA, Y., Commercial Law
SAINO, H., Criminal Law
SAITO, S., Accounting
SANBE, N., Administrative Law
SATO, M., Criminal Law
SHIBATA, H., International and Comparative Human Resource Management
SUGIHARA, M., Financial, Commercial and Civil Law
TAKAHASHI, J., Civil Law, Land Law, Sociology Law
TAKAHASHI, M., Fiscal Studies, Finance Theory
TANAKA, M., Business Administration
TANAKA, T., Criminal Law
TASHIRO, Y., Agricultural Policy
TOKUE, Y., Criminal and Procedure Law
UEMURA, H., Theoretical Economics
YAMAGUCHI, O., Pension Mathematics
YOO, H., Int. Law

ATTACHED RESEARCH INSTITUTES

Center for Economic Growth and Strategy: 79-4 Tokiwadai, Hodogayaku, Yokohama; tel. (45) 339-3593; e-mail csegcseg@ynu.ac.jp; internet www.cseg.ynu.ac.jp; Dir Prof. Dr HIROYUKI YAGI.

Center for Future Medical Social Infrastructure Based on Information Communications Technology: 79-7 Tokiwadai, Hodogayaku, Yokahama; tel. (45) 339-4490; e-mail mict@ynu.ac.jp; internet www.mict-ynu.ac.jp; Dir RYUJI KOHNO.

Center for Health Service Science: 79-8 Tokiwadai, Hodogaya-ku, Yokohama 240-8501; tel. (45) 339-3153; e-mail healths@ynu.ac.jp; internet www.hoken.ynu.ac.jp; Dir KENJI OHSHIGE.

Center for Oceanic Studies and Integrated Education: 79-5 Tokiwadai, Hodogayaku, Yokohama; tel. (45) 339-3067; e-mail kaiyo@ynu.ac.jp; internet www.cosie.ynu.ac.jp/index.html; Dir Prof. Dr HIROYUKI MATSUDA.

Center for Risk Management and Safety Sciences: 79-5 Tokiwadai, Hodogayaku, Yokohama 240-8501; tel. (45) 339-3776; e-mail anshin@ynu.ac.jp; internet www.anshin.ynu.ac.jp; Dir KAZUYOSHI SEKINE.

Cooperative Research and Development Center: 79-5 Tokiwadai, Hodogayaku, Yokohama 240-8501; tel. (45) 339-4381; e-mail cordec@nuc.ynu.ac.jp; internet www.crd.ynu.ac.jp; Dir SHIN MORISHITA.

Education Center: 79-1 Tokiwadai, Hodogayaku, Yokohama 240-8501; tel. (45) 339-3135; e-mail kyomu.gakumu@nuc.ynu.ac.jp; internet www.yec.ynu.ac.jp; Dir KUNIO SUZUKI.

Facility of RI Research and Education: 79-5 Tokiwadai, Hodogayaku, Yokohama 240-8501; tel. (45) 339-4410; internet www.ric.ynu.ac.jp; Dir SHIGEMARU TANISHO.

Global–Local Education Research Center: 79-3 Tokiwadai, Hodogayaku, Yokohama 240-8501; tel. (45) 339-3579; e-mail chiki-ct@ynu.ac.jp; internet www.crd.ynu.ac.jp/chiki-ct; Dir SHIGETAKA KOBAYASHI.

Information Technology Service Center: 79-5 Tokiwadai, Hodogayaku, Yokohama 240-8501; tel. (45) 339-4390; e-mail joho.kikaku@nuc.ynu.ac.jp; internet www.ipc.ynu.ac.jp; Dir EISAKU OTSUKA.

Instrumental Analysis Center: 79-5 Tokiwadai, Hodogayaku, Yokohama 240-8501; tel. (45) 339-4406; e-mail iac@nuc.ynu.ac.jp; internet www.iac.ynu.ac.jp; Dir YASUSHI YOKOYAMA.

International Student Center: 79-1 Tokiwadai, Hodogayaku, Yokohama 240-8501; tel. (45) 339-3186; e-mail ryugakusei.center@nuc.ynu.ac.jp; internet www.isc.ynu.ac.jp; Dir TOMOYA SHIBAYAMA.

Support Center for Gender Equity: 79-4 Tokiwadai, Hodogayaku, Yokohama; tel. (45) 339-3234; internet www.sankaku.ynu.ac.jp; Dir HITOSHI YAMADA.

Venture Business Laboratory: 79-5 Tokiwadai, Hodogayaku, Yokohama 240-8501; tel. (45) 339-4280; e-mail ec-kanri@ynu.ac.jp; internet www.vbl.ynu.ac.jp; Dir AKIHIRO TAMURA

Municipal Institutions

AOMORI UNIVERSITY OF HEALTH AND WELFARE

Mase 58-1 Hamadate, Aomori 030-8505
Telephone: (17) 765-2000
E-mail: webmaster@auhw.ac.jp
Internet: www.auhw.ac.jp

Founded 1999

Faculty of health sciences, incl. divs of human sciences, nursing, social welfare, therapy

Pres.: SACHIE SHINDO

DAIDO INSTITUTE OF TECHNOLOGY

10-3 Takiharu-cho, Minami-ku, Nagoya
Internet: www.daido-it.ac.jp

Founded 1961

Schools of informatics, engineering, liberal arts and sciences; Graduate School of Technology

Pres.: AKIRA SAWAOKA

Library of 170,000 vols
Number of teachers: 97
Number of students: 3,530

EDOGAWA UNIVERSITY

Komaki 474, Nagareyama-shi, Chiba-ken 270-0198
Telephone: (4) 7152-0661
E-mail: webmaster@edogawa-u.ac.jp
Internet: www.edogawa-u.ac.jp

Founded 1990

College of Sociology

FUJI WOMEN'S UNIVERSITY

Kita 16-jo Nishi 2, Kita-ku, Sapporo-shi, Hokkaido 001-0016
Telephone: (11) 736-0311
E-mail: somu@fujijoshi.ac.jp
Internet: www.fujijoshi.ac.jp

Founded 1961

Faculties of humanities, life sciences

Pres.: YOSHIKO NAGATA

Library of 300,000 vols
Number of teachers: 89
Number of students: 2,250

FUJITA HEALTH UNIVERSITY

1–98 Dengakugakubo, Kutsukake-cho, Toyoake, Aichi-ken 470-1192
Telephone: (562) 93-2504

Founded 1964

Faculties of medical technology, nursing, radiological technology, rehabilitation

Pres.: HIROSHI NAKANO

Library of 172,000 vols, 1,068 periodicals

FUKUI UNIVERSITY OF TECHNOLOGY

3-6-1 Gakuen, Fukui City, Fukui 910-8505
Telephone: (776) 29-2620
E-mail: kouhou@fukui-ut.ac.jp
Internet: www.fukui-ut.ac.jp

Depts of applied nuclear technology, architecture and civil engineering, electrical and electronic engineering, environmental and biotechnological frontier engineering, management information science, mechanical engineering, space communication engineering

Pres.: Prof. MASAHIRO JOHNO
Chancellor: Prof. KEN KANAI

Number of teachers: 160

FUKUOKA INSTITUTE OF TECHNOLOGY

3-30-1 Wajiro-Higashi, Higashi-ku, Fukuoka 811-0295
Telephone: (92) 606-0607
E-mail: www-staff@fit.ac.jp
Internet: www.fit.ac.jp

Faculties of engineering, information engineering, social and environmental studies

Pres.: KAORU YAMAFUJI

FUKUSHIMA MEDICAL UNIVERSITY

1 Hikariga-oka, Fukushima 960-1295
Telephone: (24) 547-1111
Internet: www.fmu.ac.jp

Founded 1950

Academic year: April to March

Pres.: SHINICHI KIKUCHI
Dir for Library: H. OOHIRA
Sec.: Y. YOSHIDA

Library of 220,765 vols
Number of teachers: 722
Number of students: 1,205

Publications: *Fukushima Igaku Zasshi* (Fukushima Medical Journal, 4 a year), *Fukushima Journal of Medical Science* (2 a year)

DEANS

Faculty of Medicine: HITOSHI OHTO
Faculty of Nursing: JUNZO SUZUKI

GIFU PHARMACEUTICAL UNIVERSITY

5-6-1, Mitahora-higashi, 5-chome, Gifu 502-8585
Telephone: (58) 237-3931
E-mail: iinuma@gifu-pu.ac.jp
Internet: www.gifu-pu.ac.jp

Founded 1932

Municipal Control

Academic year: April to March

Pres.: Prof. MASAYUKI KUZUYA
Chief Admin. Officer: TAKASHI SHINODA
Library Dir: Prof. HIROICHI NAGAI

Library of 59,000 vols
Number of teachers: 70
Number of students: 649

Publications: *Bulletin of Liberal Arts, Proceedings* (1 a year)

DEANS

Faculty of Manufacturing Pharmacy: Prof. TADASHI KATAOKA
Faculty of Pharmaceutical Science: Prof. KAZUYUKI HIRANO

PROFESSORS

FURUKAWA, S., Molecular Biology
GOTO, M., Pharmaceutical Analytical Chemistry
HARA, A., Biochemistry
HIRANO, K., Pharmaceutics
HIROTA, K., Medicinal Chemistry
INOUE, K., Pharmacognosy
KATAOKA, T., Pharmaceutical Chemistry
KAWASHIMA, Y., Pharmaceutical Engineering
KUZUYA, M., Pharmaceutical Physical Chemistry
MASAKI, Y., Pharmaceutical Synthetic Chemistry
MORI, H., Microbiology
NAGAI, H., Pharmacology
NAGASE, H., Hygienics

HACHINOHE INSTITUTE OF TECHNOLOGY

88-1 Ohbiraki Myo, Hachinohe, Aomori 031-8501
Telephone: (178) 25-3111
E-mail: www-admin@hi-tech.ac.jp
Internet: www.hi-tech.ac.jp

Founded 1972

Faculties of architectural engineering, chemical engineering on biological environments, electronic intelligence and systems, environmental and civil engineering, mechanical systems on information technology, system and information engineering, liberal arts and technology

Pres.: Dr SHOYA MASAMI

Library of 100,000 vols, 300 periodicals
Number of students: 5,000

HAKUOH UNIVERSITY

1117 Daigyoji, Oyama City, Tochigi Prefecture 323-8585
Telephone: (285) 22-1111
E-mail: nyuushi@hakuoh.ac.jp
Internet: www.hakuoh.ac.jp
Pres.: MAYUMI MORIYAMA
Founded 1915
Faculties of business management, education and law
Number of students: 4,000
Library of 175,000 vols

HAMAMATSU UNIVERSITY SCHOOL OF MEDICINE

1-20-1 Handayama Hamamatsu-shi Sizuoka, Hamamatsu City 431-3192
Telephone: (53) 435-2111
Internet: www.hama-med.ac.jp
Founded 1974
Medical school
Number of teachers: 273

HANNAN UNIVERSITY

5-4-3 Amami, Higashi, Matsubara, Osaka 580-8502
Telephone: (72) 332-1224
E-mail: webmaster@hannan-u.ac.jp
Internet: www.hannan-u.ac.jp
Founded 1965
Faculties of business, economics, int. communication, management information
Pres.: SHINICHI OTSUKI

HEALTH SCIENCES UNIVERSITY OF HOKKAIDO

1757 Kanazawa, Tobetsu-cho, Ishikari-gun, Hokkaido 061-0293
Telephone: (1332) 3-1211
E-mail: nice@hoku-iryo-u.ac.jp
Internet: www.hoku-iryo-u.ac.jp
Founded 1974
Library of 145,000 vols
Number of students: 2,400

HIMEJI INSTITUTE OF TECHNOLOGY

2167 Shosha, Himeji City, Hyogo 671-2201
Telephone: (792) 66-1661
E-mail: www-adm@cnth.himeji-tech.ac.jp
Internet: www.himeji-tech.ac.jp
Founded 1944 as Hyogo Prefectural Special College of Technology, 1949 under present name
Academic year: April to March
President: TADAO HAKUSHI
Dean of Students: HIROSHI NAKAYAMA
Dir of Administration: TOSHIAKI SUZUKI
Library Dir: HIDEHIKO NAKANO
Library of 173,000 vols
Number of teachers: 354
Number of students: 3,222
Publication: *Reports of Himeji Institute of Technology* (1 a year)

DEANS

Department of General Education: YASUKAGE ODA
Faculty of Engineering: MOTOYOSHI HASEGAWA
Faculty of Science: SHIGERU TERABE
School of Humanities for Environmental Policy and Technology: JUNJI KIHARA

HOSHI UNIVERSITY

2-4-41 Ebara, Shinagawa, Tokyo 142-8501
Telephone: (3) 5498-5821
E-mail: www@hoshi.ac.jp
Internet: www.hoshi.ac.jp
Faculty of pharmaceutical sciences
Library of 85,000 vols, 716 periodicals
Number of students: 1,200

IWATE PREFECTURAL UNIVERSITY

152-52 Takizawa-aza-sugo, Takizawa, Iwate 020-0193
Telephone: (19) 694-2012
Internet: www.iwate-pu.ac.jp
Founded 1988
President: TANIGUCHI MAKOTO
Vice-President: (vacant)

DEANS

Faculty of Nursing: TSUBOYAMA MICHIKO
Faculty of Policy Studies: KOMARU MASAAKI
Faculty of Social Welfare: SATO TADASHI
Faculty of Software and Information Science: SUGAWARA MITSUMASA

KITAKYUSHU UNIVERSITY

4-2-1 Kitagata, Kokuraminami-ku, Kitakyushu-shi, Fukuoka 802-8577
Telephone: (93) 962-1837
E-mail: shomu@kitakyu-u.ac.jp
Internet: www.kitakyu-u.ac.jp
Founded 1946, university status 1950
Library of 379,000 vols
Number of students: 5,456

KOBE CITY UNIVERSITY OF FOREIGN STUDIES

9-1 Gakuen-higashi-machi, Nishi-ku, Kobe 651-2187
Telephone: (78) 794-8121
E-mail: info@office.kobe-cufs.ac.jp
Internet: www.kobe-cufs.ac.jp
Founded 1946
Academic year: April to March
Pres.: EIICHI KIMURA
Registrar: MASAAKI OMORI
Librarian: SHIRO WADA
Library of 390,000 vols
Number of teachers: 90
Number of students: 2,300

KOBE UNIVERSITY OF COMMERCE

Gakuen-nishimachi, Nishi-ku, Kobe 651-2197
Telephone: (78) 794-6161
E-mail: shomuka@kobuec.ac.jp
Internet: www.kobeuc.ac.jp/index_e.htm
Founded 1929
State control
Language of instruction: Japanese
Academic year: April to March
President: YASUO SAKAMOTO
Registrar: NOBUHIDE FUJIWARA
Librarian: KENTARO NOMURA
Library of 406,000 vols
Number of teachers: 103
Number of students: 2,050

KUMAMOTO PREFECTURAL UNIVERSITY

3-1-100 Tsukide, Kumamoto City 862-8502
Telephone: (96) 383-2929
E-mail: www-admin@pu-kumamoto.ac.jp
Internet: www.pu-kumamoto.ac.jp
Founded 1947
Faculties of administration, cultural studies, environmental and symbiotic sciences, letters
Library of 300,000 vols

KYOTO PREFECTURAL UNIVERSITY OF MEDICINE

465 Kajii-cho, Kawaramachi, Hirokoji, Kamikyo-ku, Kyoto 602-8566
Telephone: (75) 251-5111
E-mail: kikaku01@koto.kpu-m.ac.jp
Internet: www.kpu-m.ac.jp
Founded 1873
President: IBATA YASUHIKO
Dean of Students: MARUNAKA YOSHINORI
Director of University Hospital: YAMAGISHI HISAKAZU
Director of Library: NISHIMURA TSUNEHIKO
Library of 218,000 vols
Number of teachers: 304
Number of students: 649 undergraduate, 193 postgraduate
Publication: *Kyoto Furitsu Ikadaigaku Zasshi* (Journal)

DEANS

College of Medical Technology: T. REIKO
Faculty of Culture and Education: M. SANO
Graduate School: F. SHINJI

KYOTO SANGYO UNIVERSITY

Motoyama, Kamigamo, Kita-ku, Kyoto City 603-8555
Telephone: (75) 705-1408
E-mail: info-adm@star.kyoto-su.ac.jp
Internet: www.kyoto-su.ac.jp
Founded 1965
Faculties of business administration, cultural studies, economics, engineering, foreign languages, law, science
Pres.: TOYOH SAKAI
Number of teachers: 297
Number of students: 12,949 undergraduates, 301 graduates

KYUSHU SANGYO UNIVERSITY

3-1 Matsukadai 2-chome, Higashi-ku, Fukuoka 813-8503
Telephone: (92) 673-5050
Internet: www.ip.kyusan-u.ac.jp
Founded 1960
Faculties of commerce, economics, engineering, fine arts, information science, int. culture, management
Chair.: YAMASHITA HIROHIKO
Pres.: SAGO TAKASHI
Library of 712,310 vols
Number of teachers: 330
Number of students: 15,200

NAGANO UNIVERSITY

Shimonogo 658-1, Ueda-shi, Nagano-ken 386-1298
Telephone: (268) 39-0001
E-mail: kouhou@nagano.ac.jp
Internet: www.nagano.ac.jp
Founded 1966
Pres.: RIKIO SHIMADA
Faculties of social science and social welfare
Library of 127,000 vols
Number of teachers: 120
Number of students: 1,656

NAGASAKI PREFECTURAL UNIVERSITY

123 Kawashimo-cho, Sasebo-shi, Nagasaki-ken 858-8580

Telephone: (956) 47-2191

Internet: www.nagasakipu.ac.jp

Founded 1967

Depts of Distributive Science and Business Administration, Economics, Regional Policy; Graduate School of Economics

NAGOYA CITY UNIVERSITY

1 Kawasumi, Mizuho-cho, Mizuho-ku, Nagoya

Telephone: (52) 841-6201

E-mail: ncu_website@sec.nagoya-cu.ac.jp

Internet: www.nagoya-cu.ac.jp

Founded 1950

Pres.: YOSHIRO WADA

Sec.-Gen.: S. ISOBE

Library Dir: S. SAITO

Library of 502,973 vols

Number of teachers: 536

Number of students: 3,500

Publications: *Nagoya Medical Journal* (in English, 4 a year), *NCU* (in Japanese), *Oikonomika* (in Japanese, 4 a year)

DEANS

Faculty of Economics: Y. NAITO

Faculty of Pharmaceutical Sciences: H. IKEZAWA

Medical School: M. SASAKI

School of Design and Architecture: T. YANAGISAWA

School of Humanities and Social Sciences: T. KIDO

OSAKA CITY UNIVERSITY

3-3-138, Sugimoto, Sumiyoshi-ku, Osaka-shi 558-8585

Telephone: (6) 6605-3410

E-mail: t-koho@ado.osaka-cu.ac.jp

Internet: www.osaka-cu.ac.jp

Founded 1949

State control

Language of instruction: Japanese

Academic year: April to March

Pres.: Y. NISHIZAWA

Vice-Pres.: T. KIRIYAMA

Vice-Pres.: M. MIYANO

Vice-Chair.: T. KASHIWAGI

Head of Bureau for Admissions and Education: K. TAMAI

Head of Bureau for Students' Affairs: O. TOMIZAWA

Dir for Media Centre: H. HASHIMOTO

Library of 2,500,000 books, 9,000 periodicals

Number of teachers: 720

Number of students: 8,407

Publications: *City, Culture and Society (Urban Research Plaza)* (4 a year), *Memoirs of the Faculty of Engineering* (1 a year), *Osaka Journal of Mathematics* (4 a year), *Research Journal for Creative Cities (Graduate School for Creative Cities)* (2 a year), *Urban Scope (ejournal of the Urban-Culture Research Center)* (1 a year)

DEANS

Graduate School and Faculty of Business: Y. SUZUKI

Graduate School and Faculty of Economics: M. MORI

Graduate School and Faculty of Engineering: Y. HINO

Graduate School and Faculty of Law: F. NAGAI

Graduate School and Faculty of Literature and Human Science: T. IKEGAMI

Graduate School and Faculty of Human Life Science: M. HATANAKA

Graduate School and Faculty of Science: T. HOSON

Graduate School for Creative Cities: Y. HIROTA

Graduate School of Medicine: T. ARAKAWA

Graduate School of Nursing: M. IMANAKA

OSAKA GAKUIN UNIVERSITY

2-36-1 Kishibe-Minami, Suita-shi, Osaka 564-8511

Telephone: (6) 6381-8434

E-mail: www-admin@uta.osaka-gu.ac.jp

Internet: www.osaka-gu.ac.jp

Faculties of business administrative sciences, corporate intelligence, distribution and communication sciences, economics, foreign languages, informatics, int. studies, law

Pres.: YOSHIYASU SHIRAI

Library of 990,000 vols

OSAKA PREFECTURE UNIVERSITY

1-1 Gakuen-cho, Sakai, Osaka 599-8531

Telephone: (72) 252-1161

Internet: www.osakafu-u.ac.jp

Founded 1949 as Naniwa University; present name 1955

Prefectural control

Academic year: April to March

Pres.: TSUTOMU MINAMI

Admin.: TOSHIHIKO HONDA

Dir of Library and Science Information Centre: YOJI HIMENO

Library of 1,072,033 vols

Number of teachers: 871

Number of students: 6,332

Publications: *British and American Language and Culture*, *DMSIS Research Report*, *Journal of Economics, Business and Law*

DEANS

College of Agriculture: MITSUNORI KIRIHATA

College of Economics: KATSUHIRO MIYAMOTO

College of Engineering: YOJI TAKEDA

College of Integrated Arts and Sciences: SIGEMITSU NAKANISI

College of Social Welfare: YOICHI DOI

SAPPORO MEDICAL UNIVERSITY

Nishi 17-chome, Minami 1-jo, Chuo-ku, Sapporo, Hokkaido 060

Telephone: (11) 611-2111

E-mail: icccj@sapmed.ac.jp

Internet: web.sapmed.ac.jp

Founded 1945 as Hokkaido Prefectural School of Medicine; became Sapporo Medical College 1950; current name adopted 2014

Academic year: April to March

Pres.: K. SHIMAMOTO

Chief Admin. Officer: H. SAITO

Librarian: N. TOUSE

Library of 214,000 vols

Number of teachers: 388

Number of students: 1,482

Publication: *Sapporo Igaku Zassi* (Sapporo Medical Journal, with English summaries, 6 a year)

DEANS

School of Health Sciences: Y. INUI

School of Medicine: Y. KUROKI

SHIMONOSEKI UNIVERSITY

2-1-1 Daigakucho, Shimonoseki City, Yamaguchi Prefecture 751-8510

Telephone: (832) 52-0288

E-mail: www-admin@shimonoseki-cu.ac.jp

Internet: www.shimonoseki-cu.ac.jp

Founded 1962

Schools of economics and int. commerce

Library of 171,200 vols

Number of students: 2,270

TOKYO METROPOLITAN UNIVERSITY

Minami-Ohsawa 1-1, Hachioji-shi, Tokyo 192-0397

Telephone: (426) 77-1111

E-mail: info@jmj.tmu.ac.jp

Internet: www.tmu.ac.jp

Founded 1949

Municipal control

Language of instruction: Japanese

Academic year: April to March (2 terms)

Pres.: K. OGIUE

Dir. of Admin. Bureau: T. MORUOKA

Librarian: M. MAEDA

Library: see under Libraries and Archives

Number of teachers: 646

Number of students: 6,540

Publications: *Bulletin* (1 a year), *Daigaku-hiroba* (6 a year), *Gakuhou* (2 a year)

DEANS

Center for Urban Studies: TOSHIHIKO MOGI

Faculty of Economics: TOSHINAO NAKATSUKA

Faculty of Engineering: KOHEI SUZUKI

Faculty of Law: MASAHIDE MAEDA

Faculty of Science: HIDEYUKI SATO

Faculty of Social Sciences and Humanities: SATORU NAGUMO

PROFESSORS

Center for Urban Studies:

AKIYAMA, T., City Transportation Planning
HAGAI, M., Comparative Urban Public Administration
HAGIHARA, K., Urban and Regional Economics
HOSHI, T., Health Science
MATSUMOTO, Y., Social Network Theory
NAKABAYASHI, I., Urban Geography and City Planning
TAMAGAWA, H., Urban Space Analysis

Faculty of Economics:

ASANO, H., Marketing Science
ASANO, S., Econometrics
CHIBA, J., Financial Accounting
FUKAGAI, Y., History of Economic Thought
FUKUSHIMA, T., Public Economics, International Economics
HIGANO, M., Money and Banking
KANAYA, S., Fiscal and Monetary Policy
KUWATA, K., Management Strategy
MIYAKAWA, A., Marxian Economic Theory, History of Economic Thought
MURAKAMI, N., Chinese Enterprise Location
NAKAMURA, J., Labour Economics
NAKATSUKA, T., Business Administration, Operations Research
OMORI, Y., Econometrics
TODA, H., Econometrics
WAKITA, S., Japanese Labour Market
YAGO, K., French Economic History
YAMATO, T., Distribution Mechanism
YAMAZAKI, S., Distribution Policy

Faculty of Engineering:

ANDO, Y., River Engineering, Applied Hydrology
ASAKO, Y., Heat and Mass Transfer
CHIKAZAWA, M., Physical Chemistry of Solid Surfaces
FUKAO, S., Building Construction

FURUKAWA, Y., Precision Machining and Computer-Aided Manufacturing Systems
HOBO, T., Analytical Chemistry and Instrumental Analysis
IGOSHI, M., Computer-Aided Design and Manufacturing
IKUTA, S., Parallel Algorithms
INOUE, H., Physical Organic Photochemistry
ISHIKAWA, H., e-Business Model and Database
ISHINO, H., Building Service Engineering
ITO, D., Superconductors and their Applications
IWASAKI, K., Computer Architecture
IWATATE, T., Geomechanics
IYODA, T., Molecular Functional Materials
KATAKURA, M., Traffic Engineering and Infrastructure Planning
KAWAI, T., Organic Chemistry
KAWATA, S., Control Engineering
KIMURA, G., Electrical Machinery and Power Electronics
KITSUTAKA, Y., Building Material Engineering
KIYA, T., Digital Signal Management
KOBAYASHI, K., Architectural Theory and Design
KOIZUMI, A., Sanitary Engineering
KOKUBU, K., Concrete Technology
MAEDA, K., Bridge and Structural Engineering
MASUDA, H., Electrical Chemistry
MISAWA, H., Strength of Materials
MORIYA, T., Applications of Ultrasonics
NAGAHAMA, K., Chemical Engineering, Phase Equilibrium and Related Properties
NAGAOKA, S., Functional Materials
NAGASAWA, S., Applications of Lasers and Remote Sensing
NAKAMURA, I., Robotics and Mechatronics
NISHIKAWA, T., Structural Engineering
NISHIMURA, K., Geomechanics
NISHIMURA, H., Plasticity and New Materials Processing
OKUMURA, T., Semiconductor Physics, Optoelectric Devices
OTA, M., Power Engineering
SAKAKI, T., Strength of Metals and Alloys
SEKIMOTO, H., Piezo-electrical Vibrations and their Applications
SUZUKI, K., Structural Dynamics
TAKAMIZAWA, K., City Planning
TAKI, M., Bioelectromagnetics, Noise Control Engineering
UENO, J., Architectural Planning
UMEGAKI, T., Ceramics, Inorganic Phosphate Chemistry
UMEYAMA, M., Water Environmental Engineering
WATANABE, K., Hydrodynamics, Hydraulic Machinery
WATANABE, T., Environment and Energy Saving
YAMADA, M., Chemical Sensing and Instrumentation
YAMAGISHI, T., Synthetic Organic Chemistry
YAMAZAKI, S., Structural Engineering
YOKOYAMA, R., Control and Optimization of Large-Scale Systems
YOSHIBA, M., High Temperature Material

Faculty of Law:
ASAKURA, M., Labour Law, Social Security Law
FUCHI, M., European Legal History
HITOMI, T., Decentralization and Local Autonomy
IKEDA, T., Civil Law, Law of Land Property
ISHIDA, A., Domestic Politics and International Politics
ISHII, M., Civil Law, Medical Law
ISHIKAWA, K., Constitutional Law
ISOBE, T., Administrative Law
KIMURA, M., Criminal Law
MAEDA, M., Criminal Law
MIYAMURA, H., History of Japanese Political Thought
MIZUBAYASHI, T., Japanese Legal History
MORIYAMA, S., East Asian Politics
MORITA, A., Outside Application of National Control
NAKAJIMA, H., Civil Procedure
NAWATA, Y., Philosophy of Law
NOGAMI, K., Political History of Western Countries
NOMURA, Y., Civil Law, Environmental Law
SHIBUYA, T., Commercial Law, Intellectual Property Law, Competition Law

Faculty of Science:
ABE, T., Physical Training
ACHIBA, Y., Laser Chemistry
AIHARA, Y., Ageing and Temperature Regulation
EBIHARA, M., Space Chemistry
FUKUSAWA, H., Classical Oceanography
GUEST, M., Geometry
HIROSE, T., Experimental High-Energy Physics
HISANAGA, S., Cell Biology
HORI, N., Environmental Geography
HUYAMA, Y., Genetics
IKEMOTO, I., Solid-State Chemistry
IMANAKA, K., Human Motor Behaviour, Perception and Motor Control
ISOBE, T., Biological Chemistry
ISOZAKI, H., Partial Differential Equations
IWATA, S., Glacial Geomorphology
IYODA, M., Organic Chemistry
IZAWA, T., Biochemistry and Physiology of Exercise
KACHI, N., Botanical Ecology
KAINOSHO, M., Biochemistry
KAMIGATA, N., Organic Chemistry
KAMISHIMA, Y., Topology
KATADA, M., Physical Inorganic Chemistry and Radiochemistry
KATO, T., Physical Chemistry
KIKUCHI, T., Topography
KOBAYASHI, N., Atomic and Molecular Physics (Experimental)
KOMANO, T., Molecular Genetics
KORANAGA, T., Micro-nano System
KOUGI, M., Neutron Scattering and Solid-State Physics
KUWASAWA, K., Neurobiology
MIKAMI, T., Climatology, Climate Change, Urban Climate
MINAKATA, H., High-energy Physics
MIYAHARA, T., Solid-State Spectroscopy
MIYAKE, K., Number Theory
MIZOGUCHI, K., Solid-State Physics and Magnetic Resonance
MOCHIZUKI, K., Partial Differential Equations
NAKAMURA, K., Algebraic Number Theory and Algorithms
OHASHI, T., X-ray Astronomy
OHNITA, Y., Differential Geometry and Lie Groups
OKA, M., Singularity Theory and Algebraic Geometry
OKABE, Y., Theoretical Condensed-Matter Physics
OKADA, M., Harmonious Analysis
OKUNO, K., Atomic Physics
PRICE, W. S., Biochemistry
SAITO, S., Elementary Particle Basic Theory
SAKAI, M., Analytic Functions
SATO, H., Electron Theory of Metals
SHIMADA, K., Bacteriology
SUGIURA, Y., Human Geography
SUZUKI, T., Atomic Nuclear Physics
TAKII, S., Microbial Ecology
TERAO, H., Singularities and Combinatorics
WADA, M., Photobiology
WAKABAYASHI, M., Systematic Botany
WATANABE, Y., Aquatic Ecology
YAMASAKI, H., Seismo-tectonics, Quaternary Geology
YAMASAKI, T., Systematic Zoology
YASUGI, S., Developmental Biology
YOMASHITA, M., Inorganic Chemistry

Faculty of Social Sciences and Humanities:
EBARA, Y., Theoretical Sociology
FUKUI, A., French Philosophy
FUKUMA, K., Modern English Poetry
FUKUMOTO, Y., German Linguistics
FUKUSHIMA, F., African Literature
HARA, K., European Culture
HIRAI, H., Modern Chinese Literature
ICHIHARA, S., Psychology of Perception
IDE, H., English Novels
INADA, A, Classical Literature
INUI, A., Secondary Education and Educational Practice
ISHIHARA, K., Family Studies, Social Research
ISHIKAWA, T., French Philosophy of the 17th Century
ISHINO, K., French Semantics
ITO, C., English Novels
JIN, K., Comparative Linguistics
JITSUKAWA, T., French Philosophy
KAI, H., Ethics
KANZAKI, S., Ancient Greek Philosophy
KATO, M., Modern English Poetry
KIMURA, M., Ancient Korean History
KISHI, Y., German Literature
KOBAYASHI, K., History of Japanese Language
KOBAYASHI, R., Social Studies and Administration
KOTANI, H., Indian History
KUROSAKI, I., Educational Administration
MANZAWA, M., Modern German Literature
MOGI, T., Educational Psychology
MORIOKA, K., Urban Sociology, Comparative Sociology
MURAYAMA, K., American Novels
NAGAI, T., Clinical Psychology
NAGUMO, S., Modern Chinese Literature
NAKAJIMA, H., Theoretical Linguistics
NAKANO, T., Modern French History
NARASAKI, H., Contemporary American Novel
NISHIKAWA, N., French Poetry of the 19th Century
OCHIAI, M., Chinese Dialectology
OGINO, T., Sociolinguistics
OHGUSHI, R., Adult Education
OKABE, H., Modern German Literature
OKABE, T., Social Welfare System
OKADA, E., History of Social Welfare
OKADA, M., Middle French Literature
OKADA, N., German Philosophy
OKAZAWA, S., Contemporary German Literature
OKUBO, Y., French Literature of the 16th Century
OKUMURA, S., Capitalism in Pre-Communist China
ONO, A., Archaeology
ORISHIMA, M., American Novels
OTSUKA, K., Social Anthropology
PEARSON, H. E., Applied Linguistics, TESOL
SATAKE, Y., Federal Chinese History
SATO, S., Chinese Philology
SEO, I., German Literature of the 20th Century
SOEDA, A., Social Methodology
SUDA, O., Developmental Study of Communication
SUZUKI, T., Contemporary Austrian Literature
TAKAHASHI, K., Political Sociology
TAKAYAMA, H., English Poetry of the 18th Century
TANJI, N., Philosophy of Science

UENO, Y., Shakespearian Studies
WATANABE, Y., Social Anthropology
YASUDA, T., Reading Process Research
YOSHIKAWA, K., French Literature of the 20th Century

WAKAYAMA MEDICAL UNIVERSITY

811-1 Kimiidera, Wakayama City 641-8509
Telephone: (73) 447-2300
E-mail: waidai@wakayama-med.ac.jp
Internet: www.wakayama-med.ac.jp
Founded 1945
President: HIROYUKI YAMAMOTO
Library of 63,250 vols
Number of teachers: 260
Number of students: 399
Publications: *Wakayama Igaku* (in Japanese, 4 a year), *Wakayama Medical Reports* (in English, 4 a year)

YOKOHAMA CITY UNIVERSITY

22-2 Seto, Kanazawa-ku, Yokohama 236-0027
Telephone: (45) 787-2311
E-mail: netadmin@yokohama-cu.ac.jp
Internet: www.yokohama-cu.ac.jp
Founded 1928
Municipal control
Academic year: April to March
Chancellor and Pres.: KEICHI OGAWA
Chief Admin. Officer: ROKUROU TAKAI
Library Dir: MASATAKA OZAKI
Library of 677,610 vols
Number of teachers: 640
Number of students: 5,480
Publications: *Yokohama Shiritu Daigaku Ronso* (Bulletin, 8 a year), *Yokohama Shiritu Daigaku Kiyo* (Journal, 1 a year), *Keizai-to-Boeki* (Industry and Trade, 2 a year), *Yokohama Medical Bulletin* (in English, 1 a year), *Yokohama Igaku* (Medical Journal, 6 a year), *Yokohama Mathematical Journal* (in English, 2 a year)

DEANS

Faculty of Economics and Business Administration: KAWAUCHI YOSHITADA
Faculty of Humanities and International Studies: FUNIO KANEKO
Faculty of Science: MAKI KUNISUKE
School of Medicine: OKUDA KENJI

Private Universities and Colleges

AICHI UNIVERSITY

4-60-6, Hiraike-cho, Nakamura-ku, Aichi Prefecture 453-8777
Telephone: (525) 64-6116
E-mail: inted@aichi-u.ac.jp
Internet: www.aichi-u.ac.jp
Founded 1946
Academic year: April to March
Pres.: NOBUTERU TAKEDA
Library of 1,458,362 vols
Number of teachers: 714 (254 full-time, 460 part-time)
Number of students: 10,084

DEANS

Faculty of Business Administration: KAZUHIKA TOMIMASU
Faculty of Economics: TETSU CHIN
Faculty of International Communication: MICHIHISA TSUKAMOTO
Faculty of Law: YUUKI HIROSE
Faculty of Letters: TOSHIKATSU ITO
Faculty of Modern Chinese Studies: SATORU ABE
Faculty of Regional Policy: YOICHI NIINO
Graduate School of Business Administration: MITSUSHI TAMAKI
Graduate School of Chinese Studies: AKIRA MIYOSHI
Graduate School of Economics: SHIGEMI YABUUCHI
Graduate School of Humanities: ZENICHI EBISAWA
Graduate School of International Communication: TAKASHI TAKAHASHI
Graduate School of Law: HUMITOSHI OBAYASHI
Junior College: TAKAO KUROYANAGI

AICHI GAKUIN UNIVERSITY

12 Araike, Iwasaki-cho, Nisshin-shi, Aichi-ken 470-0195
Telephone: (5617) 3-1111
E-mail: nyushi@dpc.agu.ac.jp
Internet: www.agu.ac.jp
Founded 1876
Private control
Language of instruction: Japanese
Academic year: April to March
Pres.: HIDETO OONO
Registrar: TAICHI HAYAKAWA
Librarian: KUNIHIRO TAKARADA
Library of 1,151,388 vols
Number of teachers: 506
Number of students: 13,273
Publications: *Transactions of the Institute for Cultural Studies* (1 a year), *Business Review of Aichi Gakuin University* (1 a year), *Aichi Gakuin Law Review* (4 a year), *Journal of the Research Institute of Zen* (1 a year), *The Journal of Aichi Gakuin University* (4 a year), *Foreign Languages and Literature* (1 a year), *Journal of Aichi Gakuin University Dental Society* (4 a year), *Regional Analysis* (2 a year)

DEANS

Faculty of Business and Commerce: MAKOTO OZAKI
Faculty of Dentistry: TOSHIHIDE NOGUCHI
Faculty of General Education: MASAMI INAGAKI
Faculty of Law: KEIICHI TAKAGI
Faculty of Letters: MITSURU ANDO
Faculty of Management: ICHIRO MUKAI
Faculty of Pharmacy: TAKUMA SASAKI
Faculty of Policy Studies: TSUDZUKI TAKAHIKO
Faculty of Psychological and Physical Science: YUZOU SATOU
Japanese Language Course for Foreign Students: KATSUSHI KONDO
Junior College: MASASHI MUKAI

UNIVERSITY OF AIZU

Aizu-Wakamatsu, Fukushima-ken 965-8580
Telephone: (242) 37-2500
E-mail: daigakuin@u-aizu.ac.jp
Internet: www.u-aizu.ac.jp
Founded 1993
Public control
Languages of instruction: English, Japanese
Academic year: April to March
Pres.: SHIGEAKI TSUNOYAMA
Number of teachers: 112
Number of students: 1,283

DEANS

Computer Science and Engineering: RYUICHI OKA

AOYAMA GAKUIN UNIVERSITY

4-4-25 Shibuya, Shibuya-ku, Tokyo 150-8366
Telephone: (3) 3409-8111
E-mail: iec-office@iec.aoyama.ac.jp
Internet: www.aoyama.ac.jp
Founded 1874
Academic year: April to March
Chancellor: M. FUKAMACHI
President: Dr M. HANDA
Vice-Pres: Dr M. NISHIZAWA, Dr M. TSUJI
Admin. Officer: T. MUNEKATA
Library Dir: Dr H. TAKAMORI
Library of 1,442,666 vols, 16,262 periodicals
Number of teachers: 1,422 (including 976 part-time)
Number of students: 19,372
Publications: *Aoyama Journal of Business* (4 a year), *Aoyama Journal of Economics* (4 a year), *Aoyama Law Review* (4 a year), *Aoyama Journal of General Education*, *Thought Currents in English Literature*, *Educational Inquiry*, *KIYO* (Journal of Literature), *Aoyama Gobun* (Journal of Japanese Literature), *Aoyama Shigaku* (Journal of History), *Aoyama Business Review*, *Aoyama Journal of International Politics, Economics and Business*, *Etudes Françaises*, *Aoyama International Communication Studies*, *Aoyama Management Review*

DEANS

College of Economics: Dr Y. YOSHIZOE
College of Law: Dr T. YAMAZAKI
College of Literature: H. ISHIZAKI
College of Science and Engineering: Dr K. UOZUMI
Graduate School of International Management: Dr F. ITOH
School of Business Administration: S. HASEGAWA
School of International Politics, Economics and Business Administration: S. HAKAMADA

CHAIRS OF DEPARTMENTS

College of Economics (internet www.econ.aoyama.ac.jp):
- Department of Economics: N. HIRASAWA
- Department of Economics (Evening Division): S. SUGIURA

College of Law (internet www.als.aoyama.ac.jp):
- Department of Law: T. DOBASHI

College of Literature (internet www.cl.aoyama.ac.jp):
- Department of Education: Y. SAKAI
- Department of Education (Evening Division): Dr M. KITAMOTO
- Department of English: M. AKIMOTO
- Department of English (Evening Division): Y. SAKUMA
- Department of French: Dr T. TSUYUZAKI
- Department of Japanese: Y. HIJIKATA
- Department of History: Dr S. WATANABE
- Department of Psychology: K. ENDO

College of Science and Engineering (internet www.agnes.aoyama.ac.jp):
- Department of Physics: Dr I. NISHIO
- Department of Chemistry: Dr H. ITOH
- Department of Mechanical Engineering: Dr S. OHISHI
- Department of Electrical Engineering and Electronics: Dr A. SAWABE
- Department of Industrial and Systems Engineering: Dr M. KURODA
- Deparment of Integrated Information Technology: Dr S. NINOMIYA

School of Business Administration (internet www.agub.aoyama.ac.jp):
- Department of Business Administration: Dr O. SATO

Department of Business Administration (Evening Division): Dr N. IWATA

School of International Politics, Economics and Business (internet www.sipeb.aoyama.ac.jp):

Department of International Politics: Dr J. TSUCHIYAMA

Department of International Economics: K. SENBA

ASIA UNIVERSITY

5-24-10 Sakai, Musashino-shi, Tokyo 180-8629

Telephone: (422) 36-3255

E-mail: koryu@asia-u.ac.jp

Internet: www.asia-u.ac.jp/english

Founded 1941

Academic year: April to March

President: SHINICHI KOIBUCHI

Librarian: SEIJI NAKAMURA

Library of 548,000 vols

Number of teachers: 466 (174 full-time, 292 part-time)

Number of students: 8,029

DEANS

Asia University Junior College: S. USUI

Faculty of Business Administration: H. OSHIMA

Faculty of Economics: T. KATO

Faculty of International Relations: H. OGAWA

Faculty of Law: H. NAKANO

Faculty of Liberal Arts: T. WATANABE

Graduate School of Business Administration: K. KASAI

Graduate School of Economics: Y. TOZAWA

Graduate School of Law: T. MORIMOTO

AZABU UNIVERSITY

1-17-71 Fuchinobe, Sagamihara City, Kanagawa 229-8501

Telephone: (42) 754-7111

E-mail: koho@azabu-u.ac.jp

Internet: www.azabu-u.ac.jp

Founded 1890

President: TSUNENORI NAKAMURA

Librarian: HIDEO FUJITANI

Library of 135,000 vols

Number of teachers: 182

Number of students: 2,300

Publication: *Bulletin*

DEANS

College of Environmental Health: TSUYOSHI HIRATA

School of Veterinary Medicine: TOSHIO MASAOKA

BUKKYO UNIVERSITY

96 Kitahananobo-cho, Murasakino, Kita-ku, Kyoto 603-8301

Telephone: (75) 491-2141

E-mail: mmc-info@bukkyo-u.ac.jp

Internet: www.bukkyo-u.ac.jp

Founded 1868

Private control

Academic year: April to March

Pres.: RYUZEN FUKUHARA

Vice-Pres.: E. NAKAMURA

Registrar: H. OHKITA

Librarian: Y. YAMADA

Library of 684,000 vols

Number of teachers: 164

Number of students: 6,457

Publications: *Journal of the Faculty of Letters* (1 a year), *Journal of the Faculty of Education* (1 a year), *Journal of the Faculty of Sociology* (1 a year), *Bukkyo University Graduate School Review* (1 a year)

DEANS

Faculty of Letters: M. SHIMIZU

Faculty of Education: J. KAKUMOTO

Faculty of Sociology: M. HAMAOKA

Postgraduate Programmes in Literature: M. SHIMIZU

Postgraduate Programmes in Education: J. KAKUMOTO

Postgraduate Programmes in Sociology: M. HAMAOKA

Independent Postgraduate Programmes in Buddhism: S. ONODA

Training Programme for the Jodo Priesthood: T. TODO

CHIKUSHI JOGAKUEN UNIVERSITY

2-12-1 Ishizaka, Dazaifu City, Fukuoka Prefecture 818-0192

Telephone: (92) 925-3511

Internet: www.chikushi.ac.jp

Founded 1988

Depts of Asian Studies, Clinical Psychology, English, English and Multimedia Studies, Human Welfare, Japanese Language and Literature

CHUBU UNIVERSITY

1200 Matsumoto-cho, Kasugai-shi, Aichi-ken 487-8501

Telephone: (568) 51-1111

E-mail: cucip@office.chubu.ac.jp

Internet: www.chubu.ac.jp

Founded 1964

Language of instruction: Japanese

Academic year: April to March

Chancellor: KAZUO YAMADA

Pres.: ATSUO IIYOSHI

Library of 427,000 vols

Number of teachers: 491 (incl. 244 part-time)

Number of students: 8,000 (incl. 200 postgraduate)

Publications: *Memoirs of the College of Engineering* (1 a year), *Sogo Kogaku* (Journal of the Research Institute for Science and Technology, 1 a year), *Journal of the College of Business Administration and Information Science* (2 a year), *Journal of the College of International Studies* (2 a year), *Journal of the Research Institute for International Studies* (1 a year), *Journal of the Research Institute for Industry and Economics* (1 a year), *Journal of Information Science* (1 a year), *Journal of the College of Humanities* (1 a year)

DEANS

College of Business Administration and Information Science: Dr NOBUO KAMATA

College of Engineering: Dr MAKOTO WATANABE

College of Humanities: YUKIO AKATSUKA

College of International Studies: Dr NOBUHIRO NAGASHIMA

Graduate School of Business Administration and Information Science: Dr NOBUO KAMATA

Graduate School of Engineering: Dr MAKOTO WATANABE

Graduate School of International Studies: Dr NOBUHIRO NAGASHIMA

CHUO UNIVERSITY

742-1 Higashinakano, Hachioji-shi, Tokyo 192-0393

Telephone: (426) 74-2111

E-mail: intlcent@tamajs.chuo-u.ac.jp

Internet: www.chuo-u.ac.jp

Founded 1885

Academic year: April to March (2 semesters)

Pres. and Chancellor: KOJI SUZUKI

Sec.-Gen.: SHUNSUKE HODOSHIMA

Dean of Students: HISAO FUKUCHI

Library Dir: KEN NAGASAKI

Library: see under Libraries and Archives

Number of teachers: 2,009

Number of students: 29,573 (3,171 evening course), 1,833 graduates

Publications: various faculty bulletins, journals

DEANS

Correspondence Division, Faculty of Law: M. SUGAWARA

Faculty of Commerce: K. KITAMURA

Faculty of Economics: A. ICHII

Faculty of Law: K. NAGAI

Faculty of Literature: S. HAYASHI

Faculty of Policy Studies: M. KONO

Faculty of Science and Engineering: N. OKUBO

Graduate School of Commerce: M. TATEBE

Graduate School of Economics: H. TANAKA

Graduate School of Law: T. SHIIBASHI

Graduate School of Literature: S. MUTO

Graduate School of Policy Studies: T. MASUJIMA

Graduate School of Science and Engineering: K. SUGIYAMA

DIRECTORS

Computer Center: T. SEKIGUCHI

Health Center: T. TSUKADA

Institute of Accounting Research: Y. WATABE

Institute of Business Research: T. ISHIZAKI

Institute of Comparative Law in Japan: T. KINOSHITA

Institute of Cultural Science: M. IRINODA

Institute of Economic Research: Y. KOGUCHI

Institute of Health and Physical Science: A. NISHITANI

Institute of Science and Engineering: M. IRI

Institute of Social Science: Y. KAWASAKI

International Center: H. HAYASHIDA

DAITO BUNKA UNIVERSITY

1-9-1 Takashimadaira, Itabashi-ku, Tokyo 175-8571

Telephone: (3) 5399-7323

E-mail: info@ic.daito.ac.jp

Internet: www.daito.ac.jp

Founded 1923

Private control

Academic year: April to March

Chair. of Board: T. TAKEUCHI

Pres.: M. WADA

Managing Dirs: K. SOEDA, S. TSUJINO

Dir of Admin. Office: S. TSUJINO

Dir of Academic Affairs: S. WATABE

Librarian: I. MIYOSHI

Library of 1,204,490 vols

Number of teachers: 1,070

Number of students: 13,315

Publications: *Daito Bunka Daigaku* (Bulletin), *Daito Bunka News* (10 a year)

DEANS

Faculty of Business Administration: Y. OKADA

Faculty of Economics: M. NAKAMURA

Faculty of Foreign Languages: K. NAKAMURA

Faculty of International Relations: H. MATSUI

Faculty of Law: H. TOKI

Faculty of Literature: J. SHIMOYAMA

Faculty of Social–Human Environmentology: Y. TAKAYAMA

Faculty of Sports and Health Science: J. OKADA

HEADS OF GRADUATE SCHOOLS

Asian Area Studies: K. OKADA

Business Administration: M. AMAGASA

Economics: Y. FUJIWARA

Foreign Languages: E. NISHIKAWA
Law: T. SONOHARA
Law School: T. HIRAGI
Literature: T. KAWACHI

JAPANESE LANGUAGE PROGRAMME FOR FOREIGN STUDENTS

Japanese Language Course: T. MIKAMI

DOHTO UNIVERSITY

149 Nakanoswawa, Kitahiroshima-shi, Hokkaido 061-1196
Telephone: (11) 372-3111
E-mail: kokusai@dohto.ac.jp
Internet: www.dohto.ac.jp
Founded 1964
Faculties of fine arts, management, social welfare
Chancellor: Dr JUN SAKURAI

DOKKYO UNIVERSITY

1-1 Gakuen-cho, Soka-shi, Saitama-ken 340-0042
Telephone: (489) 46-1635
E-mail: kouhou@stf.dokkyo.ac.jp
Internet: www.dokkyo.ac.jp
Founded 1964
Private control
Pres.: KO KAJIYAMA
Vice-Pres.: TAKAHIRO AZUMA
Vice-Pres.: TSUNEHISA YAMADA
Head Admin.: KAORU DOMON
Librarian: HEIZABURO SHIBATA
Library of 830,000 vols
Number of teachers: 646
Number of students: 8,892
Publications: *Dokkyo Law Journal, Dokkyo Law Review, Dokkyo Studies in Data Processing and Computer Science, Dokkyo Studies in Japanese Language Teaching, Dokkyo-Universität Germanistische Forschungsbeiträge, Dokkyo University Studies in English, Dokkyo University Studies in Foreign Language Teaching, Dokkyo University Studies of Economics, Études de Langue et Culture, Multidisciplinary Research for Regions, Studies on Environmental Symbiosis*

DEANS

Faculty of Economics: TADASHI INUI
Faculty of Foreign Languages: YOSHITAKA KAKINUMA
International Liberal Arts: KAZUHIKO IIJIMA
Faculty of Law: FUMIO FUKUNAGA
Graduate School of Economics: RUMI TATSUTA
Graduate School of Foreign Languages: TERUAKI EBANA
Graduate School of Law: TAKESHI KATADA

DOSHISHA UNIVERSITY

Karasuma Imadegawa, Kamigyo-ku, Kyoto 602-580
Telephone: (75) 251-3110
E-mail: ji-shomu@mail.doshisha.ac.jp
Internet: www.doshisha.ac.jp
Founded 1875
Academic year: April to March
Chancellor: M. OYA
President: E. HATTA
Dean of Academic Affairs: N. TABATA
Dean of Student Affairs: A. MORITA
Administrative Officer: I. HARA
Library: Libraries with 715,027 vols
Number of teachers: 489 full-time
Number of students: 24,166
Publications: *Studies in Christianity, Studies in Humanities, Doshisha Studies in English, Social Science Review, Doshisha Law Review, Economic Review, Doshisha Business Review, Science and Engineering Review of Doshisha University, Doshisha American Studies, The Social Sciences, The Humanities, The Study of Christianity and Social Problems, Shuryu, Doshisha Literature, L.L.L., Studies in Cultural History, Annual of Philosophy, Philosophical Review, Journal of Education and Culture, Doshisha Psychological Review, Bigaku Geijutsugaku, Doshisha Kokubungaku, Doshisha Review of Sociology, Doshisha Kogaku Kaiho, Doshisha Studies in Language and Culture, Doshisha Policy and Management Review, Doshisha Hokentaiiku, Doshisha Danso, Neesima Studies*

DEANS

Faculty of Commerce: T. UKAI
Faculty of Economics: T. NISHIMURA
Faculty of Engineering: M. SENDA
Faculty of Law: A. SEGAWA
Faculty of Letters: Y. KUROKI
Faculty of Theology: K. MORI
Graduate School of American Studies: T. KAMATA
Graduate School of Policy and Management: S. OTA

DIRECTORS

Center for American Studies: N. YAMAUCHI
Institute for Language and Culture: I. KOIKE
Institute for the Study of Humanities and Social Sciences: T. TAKITA
Science and Engineering Research Institute: O. YAMAGUCHI

DOSHISHA WOMEN'S COLLEGE OF LIBERAL ARTS

Kodo, Kyotanabe-shi, Kyoto-fu 610-0395
Telephone: (774) 65-8411
E-mail: somu-t@dwc.doshisha.ac.jp
Internet: www.dwc.doshisha.ac.jp
Founded 1876
Academic year: April to March
Chancellor: M. OYA
Pres.: J. MORITA
Registrar: Y. HONMA
Librarian: Y. YODEN
Library of 445,983 vols
Number of teachers: 750
Number of students: 5,948

DEANS

Academic Affairs: Y. HONMA
Academic Research Promotion Center: K. MOROI
Accounting and Finance: S. TAKAMOTO
Admissions Center: N. YOSHIKAI
Career Support Center: N. MORISHITA
Contemporary Social Studies: T. KONO
General Affairs: K. KOSAKA
Human Life and Science: N. NISHIMURA
International Exchange Center: T. TAGUCHI
Liberal Arts: M. TERAKAWA
Library and information Services Center: Y. YODEN
Pharmaceutical Sciences: K. MORITA
Religious Affairs: J. KONDO
Student Affairs: Y. KOMOTO

FUKUOKA UNIVERSITY

8-19-1, Nanakuma, Jonan-ku, Fukuoka 814-0180
Telephone: (92) 871-6631
E-mail: fupr@adm.fukuoka-u.ac.jp
Internet: www.fukuoka-u.ac.jp
Founded 1934
Private control
Academic year: April to March
Pres.: HIROYUKI YAMASHITA
Vice-Pres: KENROU KAWAIDA, KUNIHIDE MIHASHI, MASAHIRO KIKUCHI
Sec.-Gen.: K. SUETSUGU
Librarian: H. NAGATA
Library of 1,400,000 vols
Number of teachers: 928 full-time
Number of students: 22,319
Publication: *Bulletin*

DEANS

Faculty of Commerce: T. ETO
Faculty of Economics: T. TANAKA
Faculty of Engineering: H. YAMASHITA
Faculty of Humanities: S. MAMOTO
Faculty of Law: N. ASANO
Faculty of Pharmaceutical Sciences: H. SHIMENO
Faculty of Science: M. SAIGO
Faculty of Sports and Health Science: K. KANAMORI
School of Medicine: Y. IKEHARA

DIRECTORS

Animal Care Unit: S. KASHIMURA
Central Research Institute: Y. TOMINAGA
Computer Centre: K. SHUDO
Fukuoka University Chikushi Hospital: T. YAO
Fukuoka University Hospital: A. ARIYOSHI
Language Training Centre: K. TACHIBANA
Radioisotope Centre: S. TASAKI
Takamiya Evening School: M. MORI

GAKUSHUIN UNIVERSITY

1-5-1 Mejiro, Toshima-ku, Tokyo 171-8588
Telephone: (3) 3986-0221
E-mail: webmaster@gakushuin.ac.jp
Internet: www.gakushuin.ac.jp/univ
Founded 1949
Private control
Language of instruction: Japanese
Academic year: April to March
Chancellor: Y. HATANO
Pres.: N. FUKUI
Chief Admin. Officer: M. MIYAZAKI
Dean of Students: Y. KUSANO
Librarian: T. TAKANO
Library of 1,600,000 vols
Number of teachers: 281 full-time, 663 part-time
Number of students: 8,652 (8,066 undergraduate, 586 postgraduate)
Publications: *Gakushuin Daigaku Bungaku-Bu Kenkyu Nenpo* (Annual Collection of Essays and Studies, Faculty of Letters), *Gakushuin Daigaku Hogakkai Zasshi* (Gakushuin Review of Law and Politics, 2 a year), *Gakushuin Daigaku Keizai Ronshu* (Gakushuin Economic Papers, 4 a year), *Gakushuin Daigaku Kenkyusosho* (Gakushuin University Studies, 1 a year)

DEANS

Faculty of Economics: T. UEDA
Faculty of Law: M. KAMIYA
Faculty of Letters: T. KANDA
Faculty of Sciences: T. TAKAHASHI

CHAIRMEN

Graduate School of Economics: S. KAMBE
Graduate School of Humanities: T. KANDA
Graduate School of Law: T. TSUNEOKA
Graduate School of Management: T. SUZUKI
Graduate School of Politics: Y. NAKAI
Graduate School of Sciences: T. TAKAHASHI
Professional School of Law: Y. NOSAKA

PROFESSORS

Faculty of Economics:

AOKI, Y., Consumer Behaviour
ARAI, K., Stochastic Processes and Statistics

ASABA, S., Business Economics and Strategic Management
ENDO, H., Health Economics and Business Policy
FUKUCHI, J., Statistics, Statistical Finance
HOSONO, K., Macroeconomics
IMANO, K., Human Resource Management
ISHII, S., Economic History of Japan
ITSUMI, Y., Public Finance
IWATA, K., Japanese Economic Studies, Land and Housing Economics
KAMBE, S., Microeconomic Theory and Game Theory
KANEDA, N., Accounting
KATSUO, Y., Financial Accounting
KAWASHIMA, T., Special Economics and Econometrics
KOYAMA, A., Business Finance and International Management
MITSUI, K., Public Economics
MIYAGAWA, T., Macroeconomics, Japanese Economy
MORITA, M., Management Science and Strategic Management
MUKUNOKI, H., International Economics
NAMBU, T., Industrial Economics
OKUMURA, H., Japanese Economic Studies, International Finance
SHIROTA, Y., Computer Science
SUGITA, Y., Marketing Science
SUZUKI, T., Business History
TANAKA, N., Systems and Simulation
TATSUMI, K., Financial Markets and Investment
UCHINO, T., Management and Organization Theory
UEDA, T., Marketing
WADA, T., Business Economics and Strategic Management
WAKISAKA, A., Economics of Work and Pay
WAKOH, J., Game Theory, Mathematical Economics
YUZAWA, T., Business History

Faculty of Law:

ENDO, K., Sociology
FUKUMOTO, K., Politics
HASEBE, Y., Law of Civil Procedure
HASHIMOTO, Y., Labour and Employment Law
HIRANO, H., Social Psychology
IIDA, Y., Political History of Europe
INOUE, T., History of Politics and Diplomacy in Japan
ISOZAKI, N., Political Change in East Asia
KAMIYA, M., Anglo-American Law
KANZAKI, T., Conflict of Laws
KATSUNAGI, T., Public Policy and Jurisprudence
MAEDA, A., Commercial Law
MIZUNO, K., Civil Law
MORINAGA, T., History of Western Political Thought
MURAMATSU, M., Public Administration
MURANUSHI, M., International Politics
NAKAI, Y., Comparative Politics
NOMURA, T., Civil Law
NONAKA, N., Principles of Political Science
NOSAKA, Y., Constitutional Law
OKA, T., Civil Law
OKINO, M., Civil Law
SAKAMOTO, K., Political Process of Japan
SAKURAI, K., Administrative Law
SASAKI, T., Political Theory
SHIBAHARA, K., Criminal Law
SHIZUMI, M., Criminal Law
SUDO, N., Sociology
SUNADA, I., American Government and Politics
TAKAGI, H., Administrative Law
TOMATSU, H., Constitutional Law
TSUMURA, M., Law of Criminal Procedure
TSUNEOKA, T., Administrative Law

Faculty of Letters:

ABE, S., History of Japanese Language and Dialectology
ARIKAWA, H., History of European Art
CHUJOH, S., 19th-Century French Novel
FITZSIMMONS, A., Irish Literature, Modern British Poetry
FUKUI, N., Contemporary European History
HARADA, Y., French 17th-Century Philosophy and Literature
HASHIMOTO, M., Modern English Literature, Irish Literature
HOSAKA, Y., Semantics, Syntax (German)
HYODO, H., Japanese Medieval Literature, Culture of Japanese Performing Arts
IENAGA, J., Medieval Japanese History
INOUE, I., Modern Japanese History
ITOH, K., Clinical Psychology, Supportive Psychotherapy
IWASAKI, H., 20th-Century French Novel
KAMENAGA, Y., Medieval European History
KAMIOKA, N., Contemporary American Novels
KANDA, T., Medieval Japanese Literature
KANEGAE, H., Ancient Japanese History
KAWAGUCHI, Y., Educational Methodology
KAWASAKI, Y., Psychotherapy, Transference
KOBAYASHI, T., History of Japanese Art
KOMATSU, E., Linguistics
MAEDA, N., Modern Japanese Linguistics
MANO, Y., British Novels
MARÉ, T., French Literature
MATSUSHIMA, S., English Romantic Poetry
MIYASHITA, S., German Poetry
MURANO, R., Cross-cultural Communication, Teaching Japanese as a Foreign Language
NAGANUMA, Y., Volunteer Learning
NAGASHIMA, Y., Linguistics (Semantics)
NAGATA, Y., Social Psychology
NAKAJIMA, H., English Linguistics
NAKAMURA, I., History of Japanese Thought
NAKANO, H., Elizabethan Drama
NINOMIYA, R., 17th- and 18th-Century French Literature
NOMURA, R., 17th- and 18th-Century French Literature
OHNUKI, A., Cultural Studies
OKAMOTO, J., German Linguistics, Cognitive Semantics, Linguistic Theory
PEKAR, T., German Literature, Cultural Studies
SAEKI, T., French Drama
SAITOH, T., Educational History
SAKAI, K., Comparative Philosophy, Modern (18th- and 19th-Century) Philosophy, Phenomenology
SAKONJI, S., Greek Philosophy, Neoplatonism, Renaissance Philosophy
SANO, M., History of Japanese Art
SASAKI, T., Ancient Japanese Linguistics
SHIMADA, M., Ancient Roman History
SHIMOKAWA, K., British Philosophy (Locke and Hume), Ethics and Political Philosophy
SHINKAWA, T., Medieval Thought and Buddhism in Japan
SHINODA, A., Comparative Psychology
SHINOHARA, S., Learning Theories
SHIOTANI, K., 18th- and 19th-century English Literature
SUGIYAMA, N., French Philosophy
SUWA, T., Cultural Geography
TAKADA, H., German Linguistics, History of the German Language, Historical Pragmatics
TAKAHASHI, H., History of European Art
TAKAMI, K., Linguistics (Syntax and Semantics)
TAKANO, T., Early Modern Japanese History
TAKETSUNA, S., Educational Psychology
TAKEUCHI, F., Modern Asian History
TANABE, C., American Literature
TOGAWA, S., Modern Japanese Literature
TOYAMA, M., Social Cognition, Causal Attribution
TSURUMA, K., Ancient Chinese History
UCHIDA, T., American Literature
WATANABE, M., History of German Linguistics, Sociolinguistics, Comparative Linguistics
YAHAGI, S., 19th-Century American Literature
YAMAMOTO, M., Child Development, Developmental Disorder
YAMAMOTO, Y., Modern Japanese Literature
YOSHIDA, K., French Poetry and Poets
YOSHIKAWA, M., Clinical Psychology, Clinical Assessment

Faculty of Science (tel. (3) 3986-0221 ext. 6450; e-mail sci-off@gakushuin.ac.jp):

AKAO, K., Complex Manifolds
AKAOGI, M., Science of the Earth's Materials under High Pressure
AKIYAMA, T., Synthetic Organic Chemistry
ARAKAWA, I., Surface and Vacuum Science
FUJIWARA, D., Functional Analysis, Theory of Partial Differential Equations
HIRANO, T., Quantum Optics
IDA, D., Gravity and Relativistic Cosmology
IITAKA, S., Algebraic Geometry, Birational Geometry
ISHII, K., Vibrational Spectroscopy of Molecular Systems
KATASE, K., Differential Topology, Complex Dynamic Systems
KAWABATA, A., Theory of Solid-State Physics, Mesoscopic Physics
KAWASAKI, T., Topology and Geometry of Surfaces
KOTANI, M., Photochemistry and Photophysics of Organic Solids
MIZOGUCHI, T., Materials Science, Spin-polarized Electron Spectroscopy, Magnetism, Amorphous Materials
MIZUTANI, A., Numerical Analysis
MOCHIDA, K., Organometallic Chemistry of Group 14 Elements
MURAMATSU, Y., Geo- and Environmental Chemistry of Trace Elements and Isotopes
NAKAJIMA, S., Number Theory
NAKAMURA, H., Organic Synthesis
NAKANO, S., Number Theory
NISHIZAKA, T., Biophysics of Macromolecular Motion
TAKAHASHI, T., Electronic Properties of Small-dimensional Conductors, Organic Conductors and Superconductors
TASAKI, H., Theoretical Physics and Mathematical Physics
WATANABE, M., Physics of Crystal Growth
YAJIMA, K., Mathematical Physics, Partial Differential Equations

Center for Sports and Health Science (tel. (3) 3971-8989):

HANEDA, Y., Sports Biomechanics
HIRO, N., Sports Methodology
ONO, T., Exercise Physiology
SATO, Y., Applied Physiology, General Principle of Ball Game Strategy and Tactics
TAKAMARU, Y., Coaching Sciences
YAGI, Y., Sports Psychology

HAKODATE UNIVERSITY

5-1 Takaoka-cho, Hakodate 042-0955
Telephone: (138) 57-1181
E-mail: post@hakodate-u.ac.jp
Internet: www.hakodate-u.ac.jp

Founded 1938

Faculty of commerce

Pres.: HAKUSHI KAWAMURA

Number of students: 1,200

HIROSHIMA JOGAKUIN UNIVERSITY

4-13-1, Ushita-higashi, Higashi-ku, Hiroshima 732-0063
Telephone: (82) 228-0386
E-mail: kokusai@gaines.hju.ac.jp
Internet: www.hju.ac.jp

Founded 1886, as college 1949
Academic year: April to March

Depts of English studies, environmental culture, environmental science, nGraduate School of Language and Culture, human and cultural studies, human life science, Japanese language and literature

Pres.: Hiroshi Imada
Vice-Pres.: Shigeki Satoh
Registrar: Yuji Maewaka
Chief Admin. Officer: Shigenobu Hatakeyama

Library of 200,000 vols
Number of teachers: 75
Number of students: 2,062

Publication: *Bulletin* (1 a year)

HIROSHIMA UNIVERSITY OF ECONOMICS

5-37-1 Gion, Asaminami-ku, Hiroshima 731-0192
Telephone: (82) 871-1002
E-mail: int-sc@hue.ac.jp
Internet: www.hue.ac.jp

Founded 1967
Languages of instruction: English, Japanese
Academic year: April to March

Pres.: Koichi Maekawa
Chief Admin. Officer: Toshitsugu Matsui
Librarian: Sachio Kataoka

Library of 439,549 vols
Number of teachers: 240 (114 full-time, 126 part-time)
Number of students: 4,000

DEANS

Faculty of Economics: Mikio Aso
Graduate School of Economics: Koichi Maekawa

HIROSHIMA SHUDO UNIVERSITY

1-1-1 Ozuka-higashi, Asaminami-ku, Hiroshima 731-3195
Telephone: (82) 830-1103
Internet: www.shudo-u.ac.jp

Faculties of commercial sciences, economic sciences, human environmental sciences, humanities and human sciences and law

Pres.: Masanori Kodama

Library of 640,594 vols in Japanese and other languages; 4,999 periodicals, 655,112 other items
Number of teachers: 179
Number of students: 6,204

Publications: *Monographs of the Institute for Advanced Studies, Papers of the Research Society of Commerce and Economics, Studies in the Humanities and Sciences, Shudo Hogaku: Shudo Law Review, Journal of Human Environmental Studies, Journal of Economic Sciences*

HOKKAI-GAKUEN UNIVERSITY

4-1-40, Asahi-machi, Toyohira-ku, Sapporo 062-8605
Telephone: (11) 841-1161
Internet: www.hgu.jp

Founded 1952
Academic year: April to March

Chair.: Masao Morimoto
Pres.: K. Kimura
Librarian: T. Yasukata

Library of 1,040,889 vols
Number of teachers: 234 full-time
Number of students: 8,354

Publications: *Keizai Ronshu* (Journal of Economics, 4 a year), *Hogaku Kenkyu* (Journal of the Faculty of Law, 4 a year), *Gakuen Ronshu* (Journal of Hokkai-Gakuen University, 4 a year), *Jinbun Ronshu* (Studies in Culture, 3 a year), *Keiei Ronshu* (Journal of Business Administration, 4 a year)

DEANS

Faculty of Business Administration: J. Sato
Faculty of Economics: H. Morishita
Faculty of Engineering: H. Sugimoto
Faculty of Humanities: J. Gunshi
Faculty of Law: H. Kusama

ATTACHED INSTITUTES

Center for Academic Affairs: Dir H. Morishita.

Center for Development Policy Studies: f. 1957; Dir K. Takahara; publ. *Kaihatsu Ronshu* (Journal of Policy Studies, 2 a year)

HOKURIKU UNIVERSITY

1-1 Taiyogaoka, Kanazawa City, Ishikawa Prefecture 920-1180
Telephone: (76) 229-1161
E-mail: koho@hokuriku-u.ac.jp
Internet: www.hokuriku-u.ac.jp

Founded 1975
Academic year: April to March

Pres.: S. Kawashima
Librarian: Y. Kitano

Library of 209,000 vols
Number of teachers: 144
Number of students: 3,000

Publications: *Hokuriku Daigaku Kiyo* (bulletin, 1 a year), *Hokuriku Hogaku* (journal of law and political science, 4 a year)

DEANS

Faculty of Future Learning: S. Sonoyama
Faculty of Pharmaceutical Sciences: T. Sawanishi
Graduate School of Pharmaceutical Research: T. Sawanishi (Chair.)

HOSEI UNIVERSITY

2-17-1, Fujimi, Chiyoda-ku, Tokyo 102-8160
Telephone: (3) 3264-9662
E-mail: ic@hosei.ac.jp
Internet: www.hosei.ac.jp

Founded 1880
Private control
Language of instruction: Japanese
Academic year: April to March

Pres.: Toshio Masuda
Vice-Pres: Akira Hamamura, Yoshiro Fukuda, Jun Nakamura, Akira Tokuyasu
Registrar: (vacant)
Library Dir: Mitsuo Nesaki

Library of 1,620,000 vols
Number of teachers: 2,740 (746 full-time, 1,994 part-time)
Number of students: 36,302, incl. graduate 2,268, correspondence education 6,375

Publications: *Daigakuin Kiyo* (Graduate School Bulletin, 2 a year), *Gendaifukushi Kenkyu* (Bulletin of the Faculty of Social Policy and Administration, 1 a year), *Hogaku-Shirin* (Law and Political Sciences Review, 4 a year), *Hosei Daigaku Bungakubu Kiyo* (Bulletin of Faculty of Letters, 1 a year), *Hosei Daigaku Kogakubu Kenkyu Shuho* (College of Engineering Bulletin, 1 a year), *Hosei Daigaku Kyariadezaingakubu Kiyo* (Bulletin of the Faculty of Lifelong Learning and Career Studies, 1 a year), *Ibunka* (Journal of Intercultural Communication, 1 a year), *Keiei Shirin* (Business Journal, 4 a year), *Keizai-Shirin* (Economic Review, 4 a year), *Ningen Kankyo Ronshu* (Journal of Humanity and the Environment, 2 a year), *Shakai Shirin* (Sociology and Social Sciences, 4 a year)

DEANS

Business School of Accountancy: Kikuya Masato
Business School of Innovation Management: Kosuke Ogawa
Faculty of Bioscience and Applied Chemistry: Toshiyuki Nagata
Faculty of Business Administration: Masao Yokouchi
Faculty of Computer and Information Sciences: Hiroshi Hanaizumi
Faculty of Economics: Michiki Kikuchi
Faculty of Engineering: Yasuhiro Yamamoto
Faculty of Engineering and Design: Yutaka Tanaka
Faculty of Global and Interdisciplinary Studies: Mitsutoshi Somura
Faculty of Humanity and the Environment: Kazuo Sekiguchi
Faculty of Intercultural Communication: Yasushi Suzuki
Faculty of Law: Yasuko Kono
Faculty of Letters: Tadashi Miyakawa
Faculty of Lifelong Learning and Career Studies: Koichiro Komikawa
Faculty of Science and Engineering: Kiyotaka Sakino
Faculty of Social Policy and Administration: Ikuji Ishikawa
Faculty of Social Sciences: Mizuhito Kanehara
Faculty of Sports and Health Studies: Haruo Kariya
Graduate School Committee: Yasuaki Kumata (Chair.)
Graduate School of Art and Technology: Norio Takeuchi
Graduate School of Business Administration: Yoshio Okunishi
Graduate School of Computer and Information Sciences: Nobuhiko Koike
Graduate School of Economics: Toshiyuki Okuyama
Graduate School of Engineering: Yasuhiro Yamamoto
Graduate School of Environmental Management: Ryo Fujikura
Graduate School of Humanities: Tadashi Kanou
Graduate School of Intercultural Communication: Yoshiaki Oshima
Graduate School of Law: Akimasa Yanagi
Graduate School of Policy Sciences: Masahide Majima
Graduate School of Politics: Yoshihiko Nawata
Graduate School of Regional Policy Design: Yoshiyuki Okamoto
Graduate School of Social Well-Being Studies: Kenichi Baba
Graduate School of Sociology: Mafumi Fujita
International Japan-Studies Institute: Yuko Tanaka
Law School: Akimichi Iwama

ATTACHED INSTITUTES

Boissonade Institute of Modern Laws and Politics: 2-17-1 Fujimi, Chiyoda-ku, Tokyo 102-8160; f. 1977; Dir T. Ohno.

Computational Science Research Centre: 3-7-2 Kajino-cho, Koganei-shi, Tokyo 184-8584; e-mail cms@ml.hosei.ac.jp; internet www.media.hosei.ac.jp; f. 1969; Dir M. Kusakabe.

Information Research Institute, California: 800 Airport Blvd, Suite 504, Burlingame, CA 94010, USA; f. 2000; Dir K. Yana.

Information Research Technology Centre: 2-17-1 Fujimi, Chiyoda-ku, Tokyo 102-8160; f. 2000; Dir G. SHIRAI.

Institute of Comparative Economic Studies: 4342 Aihara-machi, Machida-shi, Tokyo 194-0298; e-mail ices@adm.hosei.ac.jp; internet www.hosei.ac.jp/ices; f. 1984; Dir K. ODAKA; publ. *Journal* (1 a year).

Institute of Nogaku Studies: 2-17-1 Fujimi, Chiyoda-ku, Tokyo 102-8160; f. 1952; Dir H. NISHINO; publ. *Catalogue Noh Drama Collections*.

Institute of Okinawan Studies: 2-17-1 Fujimi, Chiyoda-ku, Tokyo 102-8160; e-mail okiken@adm.hosei.ac.jp; internet www.hosei.ac.jp/fujimi/okiken; f. 1972; Dir T. YASUE; publ. *Bulletin*.

Japan Statistics Research Institute: 4342 Aihara-machi, Machida-shi, Tokyo 194-0298; internet www.hosei.ac.jp/toukei; f. 1946; Dir H. MORI; publ. *Bulletin* (1 a year).

Ohara Institute for Social Research: 4342 Aihara-machi, Machida-shi, Tokyo 194-0298; e-mail oharains@adm.hosei.ac.jp; internet oohara.mt.tama.hosei.ac.jp; f. 1919; Dir S. HAYAKAWA; publ. *Labour Yearbook of Japan* (1 a year), *Report* (12 a year).

Research and Service Centre for Tama Community: 2-17-1 Fujimi, Chiyoda-ku, Tokyo 102-8160; Dir C. HIRABAYASHI; publ. *Newsletter* (4 a year).

Research Centre of Ion Beam Technology: 3-7-2 Kajino-cho, Koganei-shi, Tokyo 184-8584; e-mail ion-info@ml.hosei.ac.jp; internet www.ionbeam.hosei.ac.jp; f. 1979; Dir T. NAKAMURA.

Sports and Physical Education Research Centre: 2-17-1 Fujimi, Chiyoda-ku, Tokyo 102-8160; e-mail tarnatai@hosei.ac.jp; internet www.hosei.ac.jp/taiku/rpes; f. 1976; Dir K. GOMYO

INTERNATIONAL CHRISTIAN UNIVERSITY

10-2, Osawa 3-chome, Mitaka-shi, Tokyo 181-8585

Telephone: (422) 33-3038
E-mail: webmaster@icu.ac.jp
Internet: www.icu.ac.jp

Founded 1949
Languages of instruction: Japanese, English
Academic year: April to March or September to June

Pres.: JUNKO HIBIYA
Vice-Pres. for Academic Affairs: ANRI MORIMOTO
Vice-Pres. for Financial Affairs: ICHIRO NISHIDA
Dean for Int. Affairs: S. MALARNEY
Library Dir: YUKI NAGANO

Library: see under Libraries and Archives
Number of teachers: 149 (full-time)
Number of students: 2,929

Publications: *Asian Cultural Studies, Educational Studies, Humanities—Christianity and Culture, Language Research Bulletin, Social Science*

DEANS

College of Liberal Arts: T. ITOH
Graduate School: T. SASAKI
Student Affairs: Y. SHIMIZU

ATTACHED INSTITUTES

Hachiro Yuasa Memorial Museum: internet subsite.icu.ac.jp/yuasa_museum; f. 1982; collections of Japanese archaeology and folk art; Dir ANRI MORIMOTO.

Institute of Asian Cultural Studies: e-mail asian@icu.ac.jp; internet subsite.icu.ac.jp/iacs; f. 1971, replacing Committee f. 1958; Dir W. STEELE; publ. *Asian Cultural Studies* (1 a year).

Institute of Educational Research and Service: internet web.icu.ac.jp/iers; f. 1953; Dir J. MAHER; publ. *Educational Studies* (1 a year).

Institute for the Study of Christianity and Culture: e-mail icc@icu.ac.jp; internet subsite.icu.ac.jp/icc; f. 1963; Dir A. TANAKA; publ. *Humanities—Christianity and Culture* (1 a year).

Peace Research Institute: e-mail icupri@icu.ac.jp; internet subsite.icu.ac.jp/pri; f. 1991; Dir J. WASILEWSKI.

Research Center for Japanese Language Education: e-mail scj@icu.ac.jp; internet subsite.icu.ac.jp/rcjle; f. 1991; Dir M. HIROSE.

Social Science Research Institute: e-mail ssri@icu.ac.jp; internet subsite.icu.ac.jp/ssri; f. 1953; Dir S. ISHIWATA; publ. *The Journal of Social Science* (2 a year)

ISHINOMAKI SENSHU UNIVERSITY

1 Shinmito, Minamisakai, Ishinomaki-shi, Miyagi 986-8580

Telephone: (225) 22-7711
Internet: www.isenshu-u.ac.jp

Faculties of business administration and science

Chair.: Dr MASAYOSHI DEUSHI
Pres.: RYOUJI KOBAYASHI

Library of 100,000 vols

IWATE MEDICAL UNIVERSITY

19-1 Uchimaru, Morioka, Iwate 020-8505

Telephone: (19) 651-5111
E-mail: webmaster@iwate-med.ac.jp
Internet: www.iwate-med.ac.jp

Founded 1928, University 1952
Private control

President: SHIGERU ONO
Librarian: TOKIO NAWA

Library of 249,221 vols
Number of teachers: 500
Number of students: 1,037

Publications: *Journal of the Iwate Medical Association* (6 a year), *Dental Journal* (4 a year)

DEANS

School of Dentistry: KIMIO SAKAMAKI
School of Liberal Arts and Sciences: KOKI KANNO
School of Medicine: CHUICHI ITO

JAPAN WOMEN'S UNIVERSITY

2-8-1 Mejirodai, Bunkyo-ku, Tokyo 112-8681

Telephone: (3) 3943-3131
E-mail: n-abroad@atlas.jwu.ac.jp
Internet: www.jwu.ac.jp

Founded 1901
Private control
Academic year: April to March

Pres.: YOSHIKO ARIKAWA
Vice-Pres.: IKUKO KOYABE
Vice-Pres.: TAKAMASA KOYAMA

Library of 806,842 vols
Number of teachers: 258
Number of students: 6,143

DEANS

Faculty of Human Sciences and Design: TAKASHIGE ISHIKAWA
Faculty of Humanities: YASUYUKI SHIMIZU
Faculty of Integrated Arts and Social Sciences: KIICHIRO IINAGA
Faculty of Science: RYOKO IMAICHI

JIKEI UNIVERSITY

3-25-8 Nishi-Shinbashi, Minato-ku, Tokyo 105-8461

Telephone: (3) 3433-1111
Internet: www.jikei.ac.jp

Founded 1881
Private control
Academic year: April to March

President: SATOSHI KURIHARA

Library of 227,036 vols
Number of teachers: 2,151
Number of students: 1,545

Publications: *Tokyo Jikeikai Medical Journal* (in Japanese, 6 a year), *Jikeikai Medical Journal* (in English, 4 a year), *Kyoiku Kenkyu Nenpo* (in Japanese, 1 a year), *Research Activities* (in English, 1 a year)

DEANS

School of Medicine and School of Nursing: S. KURIHARA

KANSAI UNIVERSITY

3-3-35 Yamate-cho, Suita-shi, Osaka 564-8680

Telephone: (6) 6368-1121
E-mail: www-adm@www.kansai-u.ac.jp
Internet: www.kansai-u.ac.jp

Founded 1886
Academic year: April to March

Pres.: TEIICHI KAWATA
Chair. of Board of Trustees: SEIICHIRO MORIMOTO
Dir of Educational Affairs Bureau: YASUHIRO KONISHI
Librarian: NOBORU TANAKA

Library: see under Libraries and Archives
Number of teachers: 1,827
Number of students: 26,674

Publications: *Bungaku Ronshu* (Literary Essays, 3 a year), *Hogaku Ronshu* (Law Review, 4 a year), *Shakaigaku Kiyo* (Journal of Sociological Research, 2 a year), *Keizai Ronshu* (Economic Review, 6 a year), *Shogaku Ronshu* (Business Review, 5 a year), *Kogaku Kenkyu Hokoku* (Technology Reports, 1 a year), *Keizai-Seiji Kenkyusho Kenkyu Shoho* (Economic and Political Studies), *Tozaigakujutsu Kenkyusho Kiyo* (Bulletin of Institute of Oriental and Occidental Studies), *Kogaku to Gijutsu* (Engineering and Technology), *Hogaku Kenkyusho Kenkyu Shoho*, *Gien* (Industrial Technology), *Review of Law and Politics*, *Review of Economics*, *Review of Business and Commerce*, *Joho Kenkyu* (Informatics Research), *Senri eno Muchii* (Journal of Graduate School of Foreign Language Education and Research, 1 a year), *Hakubatsukan Kiyo* (1 a year), *Kokogakutsu Shiryoshitsu Kiyo* (1 a year), *Jinken Mondai Kenkyu Kiyo* (1 a year)

DEANS

Faculty of Commerce: Prof. HIROMI TSURUTA
Faculty of Economics: Prof. KANJI MORIOKA
Faculty of Engineering: Prof. TETSUAKO TSUCHIDO
Faculty of Informatics: Prof. TAKASHI KATO
Faculty of Law: Prof. KUMIHIRO OHNUMA
Faculty of Letters: Prof. KEIJI SHIBAI
Faculty of Sociology: Prof. ICHIRO MATSUHARA
Institute of Foreign Language Education and Research: Prof. TAICHI USAMI
School of Law: Prof. KEIICHI YAMANAKA

PROFESSORS

Faculty of Law

Department of Jurisprudence:

FUKUTAKI, H., Commercial Law
GOTO, M., Civil Law

ICHIHARA, Y., History of Legal Thought
ICHIKAWA, K., Japanese Legal History
IKEDA, T., Administrative Law
IWASAKI, K., Insurance Law and Shipping Law
KAMEDA, K., Administrative Law II
KOCHU, N., Constitutional Law
KOIZUMI, Y., Constitutional Law
KOKUBU, T., Family Law and Succession Law
KURITA, K., Maritime Law
KURITA, T., Debtors' and Creditors' Rights
KUZUHARA, R., Criminal Law
NAGATA, S., Civil Law
OHNUMA, K., Labour Law
OHNUMA, K., Labour Law II
OKA, T., European Legal History
SASAMOTO, Y., Insurance Law
SATO, Y., Private International Law
SENTO, Y., Family Law and Succession Law
TSUKIOKA, T., Law of Real Property
YOSHIDA, E., Comparative Constitutional Law
YOSHIDA, N., Emancipation of Buraku

Department of Politics:

MANABE, S., Diplomatic History
MORIMOTO, T., Political and Governmental Organization
OTSURU, C., International Politics
TERAJIMA, T., Political Philosophy
TOKURA, K., European Politics
WAKATA, K., Political Psychology
YAMAMOTO, K., Information Processing
YAMANO, H., Political History of Modern Japan

Faculty of Letters

Course of English Language and Literature:

AKIMOTO, H., American Literature
AOYAMA, T., Linguistics
HASEGAWA, A., English Linguistics
HOSHII, Y., Introductory Seminar
IRIKO, F., Study of American Literature
ISHIZAKA, K., Middle English
KAMIMURA, T., Modern British Novels
KIRWAN, J.
MAKIN, P. J., Modern British and American Poetry
SAKAMOTO, T., History of English Literature
SHIMAZAKI, M., British and American Prose
TANIGUCHI, Y., Modern American Literature
TSUTSUI, O., British and American Drama

Course of Japanese Language and Literature:

ENDO, K., Japanese Linguistics
FUJITA, S., Japanese Literature (Edo Period)
KAMITANI, E., Japanese Linguistics
OHHAMA, M., Early Ancient Japanese Literature
SEKIYA, T., Textual Criticism of Noh Plays
TANAKA, N., Literature in the Heian Period
URANISHI, K., Modern and Contemporary Japanese Literature
YAMAMOTO, T., Early Modern Japanese Fiction
YAMAMOTO, T., Literature in the Heian Period
YOSHIDA, N., History of Modern Japanese Literature

Course of Philosophy:

INOUE, K., Comparative Study of Eastern and Western Thought
KIOKA, N., Philosophy
NAKATANI, N., History of Art in the Far East
ODA, Y., History of Religions
SHINAGAWA, T., Ethics
YAMAMOTO, I., Philosophy

Course of French Language and Literature:

HIRATA, S., Modern French Literature
HONDA, T., French Linguistics
ITOH, M., French Philology
KASHIWAGI, O., French Literature
KAWAKAMI, M., Modern French Literature
NONAMI, T., French Literature
OKU, J., History of French Literature

Course of German Language and Literature:

HAMAMOTO, T., German Cultural Studies
KUDO, Y.
SHIBATA, T., German Literature
TAKEICHI, O., German Linguistics
USAMI, Y., Modern German Literature
WATANABE, Y., German Linguistics
YAKAME, T., German Literature

Course of History and Geography:

ASAJI, K., European Medieval History
FUJITA, T., History of Early China
HASHIMOTO, S., Human Geography
ITOH, O., Human Geography
KOBA, M., Physical Geography
MATSUURA, A., History of Early Modern China
MORI, T.
NAKAMURA, H., History of Modern Russia
NISHIMOTO, M., History of Ancient Japan
NOMA, H., Human History
OHYA, W., History of Modern Japan
SHIBAI, K., History of Modern and Contemporary Europe
SHINTANI, H., History of West Asia
SUITA, H., History of Ancient Orient
TAKAHASHI, S., Human Geography
TAKAHASHI, T., History of Medieval Japan
YABUTA, Y., History of Early Modern Japan
YONEDA, F., Archaeology

Course of Chinese Language and Literature:

AZUMA, J., History of Chinese Philosophy
HAGINO, S., Modern and Contemporary Chinese Literature
INOUE, T., Early Modern Chinese Literature
KAWATA, T., History of Chinese Philosophy
KITAOKA, M., Modern Chinese Literature
KUSAKA, T., Chinese Linguistics
MORISE, T., Classical Chinese Poetry
NIKAIDO, Y., Chinese Popular Religion
TAKEUCHI, Y., Sociology of Education
TAO, D., History of Chinese Philosophy
UCHIDA, K., Chinese Linguistics

Course of Education:

AKAO, K., Adult Education Theory
FUJII, M., Psychology
HATASE, N., Clinical Psychology
MATSUMURA, N., Developmental Psychology
NAKATA, Y., Psychology
NOMURA, Y., Experimental Psychology
OKAMURA, T., Public Administration of Education
TAMADA, K., Pedagogy
TANAKA, T., Psychology
TANAKA, Y., Sociology of Education
YAMAMOTO, F., Pedagogy
YAMAZUMI, K., Educational Research

Inter-Departmental Course:

HAZAMA, K., Social Welfare
KURAHASHI, E., Library and Information Science
SAWAI, S.
SHIBATA, H., Information Processing
UEDA, Y., Liberation of Buraku

Course of Physical Arts:

AOKI, S., Health and Physical Education
BAN, Y., Health and Physical Education
KAWAMOTO, T., Health and Physical Education
KIMURA, S., Health and Physical Education
MIURA, T., Health and Physical Education
MIZOHATA, K., Health and Physical Education
OITA, K., Health and Physical Education
SHIRAFUJI, I., Health and Physical Education
TAKECHI, H., Health and Physical Education
TAMURA, N., Health and Physical Education
ZAKO, T., Health and Physical Education

Faculty of Economics:

AKIOKA, H., Microeconomics
HAMANO, K., Economic History of Japan
HASHIMOTO, K., Public Finance
HASHIMOTO, N., Econometrics
HASHIMOTO, S., History of Economic Theories
HAYASHI, H., Public Finance
HIROE, M., Monetary Policy
ICHIEN, M., Social Security
ICHIKAWA, K., Commercial Economics
ISHIDA, H., Economics of Modern China
IWAI, H., Economic Statistics
KASEDA, H., Economic History
KASHIHARA, M., Agricultural Economics
KASUGA, J., Principles of Economics
KITAGAWA, K., European Economic History
KOIKE, H., Introduction to Political Economy
KUSUNOKI, S., International Economics
LEE, Y., Social Economics
MATSUO, A., Mathematical Statistics
MATSUSHITA, K., Demography
MORIOKA, K., Introduction to Political Economy
MOTOKI, H., Macrodynamics
NAGAHISA, R., Principles of Economics
OTSUKA, T., Social Policy
SATO, M., Macroeconomics
TAKESHITA, K., Theory of Economic Systems
TANIDA, N., Information Processing
UEMURA, K., History of Social Thought
WAKAMORI, F., Political Economy
YASUKI, H., Industrial Organization
YOSHINAGA, K., Economic Statistics

Faculty of Commerce:

ABE, S., Public Sector Economics
ARAKI, T., Information Processing Practice
HABARA, K., Non-Life Insurance
HATORI, Y., International Relations
HIROSE, M., General Management
HIROTA, T., Corporate Strategy
IKEJIMA, M., Securities Markets
INOUE, S., Business History
ITO, K., Human Resources Management
IWASA, Y., Financial Intermediation and Institutions
KATO, Y., Distribution Theory
MATSUMOTO, Y., Monitoring Theory for Fair Disclosure
MATSUO, N., Financial Accounting
MIKAMI, H., Economics of Transport and Communication
MIZUNO, I., Management Accounting
MYOJIN, N., Book-keeping
NAGANUMA, H., History of Commerce
NAKAJIMA, M., Cost Accounting and Accounting History
NAKAMURA, M., Business Communication
OKU, K., Theory of International Trade
OKURA, Y., Tax Accounting
SASAKURA, A., International Accounting
SHIBA, K., Accounting Information Theory
SUYAMA, K., Marketing Management
TAKAHASHI, N., International Transport
TAKAYA, S.
TSURUTA, H., Public Finance
UE, K., Monetary Theory
YOKOTA, S., European and American Economy
YOSHIDA, T., Management of International Trade

Faculty of Sociology

Major in Sociology:

ISHIMOTO, K., Theory of Buraku Liberation
IWAMI, K., Understanding Modern Societies
KAKEBA, H., Sociology of Knowledge

KATAGIRI, S., Theoretical Sociology
KUMANO, T., Cultural Anthropology
MATSUHARA, I., Social Policy and Planning
NAGAI, Y., Urban Studies
SUGINO, A., Social Welfare Policy and Planning
YAMAMOTO, Y., Sociology of Knowledge
YAMATO, R., Sociology of Family

Major in Industrial Psychology:

AMEMIYA, T., Ergonomics
ENDO, Y., Social Cognition
HIGASHIMURA, T., Information Processing
IIDA, N., Psychiatry
KAWASAKI, T., Vocational Guidance
KURATO, Y., Clinical Psychology
SEKIGUCHI, R., Experimental Psychology
SHIMIZU, K., Psychometrics
TAKAGI, O., Interpersonal Psychology
TERASHIMA, S., Clinical Psychology
TSUCHIDA, S., Social Psychology

Major in Mass Communication:

FUJIOKA, S., Journalism
KIMURA, Y., Social Communication
KURODA, I., Sociology of Broadcasting Culture
MIZUNO, Y.
OGAWA, H., Media and Culture
SENO, G., Human Communication
TSUNEKI, T., Communication Behaviour
YOSHIOKA, I., Communication Theory

Major in Industrial Sociology:

ASADA, M., Policy for Economic Stabilization
FUNABA, T., Human Resource Studies
HASHIMOTO, K., Philosophy of Science
MORITA, M., Personnel Management
OH, Y., Industrial Information Theory
ONISHI, M., Labour–Management Relations
SAITOU, Y., Industrial Technology
TAKASE, T., Industrial Sociology
WAKABAYASHI, M., Business Administration
YANO, H., Economic Theory
YOSANO, A., Mathematical Sociology

Faculty of Informatics:

AOYAMA, C., Global Environmentology
ATSUJI, S., Organizational Decision Making
COOK, N. D., General Systems Theory
EZAWA, Y., Computer Science
FUKADA, Y., Image Processing and Pattern Recognition
FUKE, H., International Networks
FURUTA, H., Fuzzy Logic, Theory and Application
HAYASHI, I., Information Systems Management
HAYASHI, T., Computer Graphics
HIJIKATA, H., Mathematics
HIROKAME, M., Mathematics
HORI, M., File Structure
ITO, T., Computer Simulation
KAMEI, K., Management
KATO, M., Philosophy
KATO, T., Cognitive Science
KATO, T., Computer Crime
KITAJIMA, O., Business Behaviour
KITANI, S., Public Administration
KOMATSU, Y., Business Administration
KUBOTA, K., Audiovisual Media Production
KUBOTA, M., Communication
KUROKAMI, H., Multimedia Education
KUROKUZU, H., Accounting Information Systems
KUWABARA, T., Psychology
MIYASHITA, F., Computer Science
NAKAGAWA, Y., Data Structure and Algorithm
NOGUCHI, H., Business Information
OKAMOTO, T., Public Policy
SANO, M., Community Networks
SHIOMURA, T., Microeconomic Models
SHYI, S. C., Management Information Systems
SUGA, T., Computer-based Communication
TANAKA, S., Knowledge Information Processing
TSUJI, M., Software Architecture
UESHIMA, S., Principles of Database Management
UKAI, Y., Economic Policy
YAMAGUCHI, S., Cultural Studies of Information Society
YAMANA, T., Macroeconomic Models
YOSHIDA, N., Principles of Computer Electronics

Faculty of Engineering

Department of Mechanical Engineering:

ARAI, Y., Measurement Systems
ISHIHARA, I., Thermal Engineering
KITAJIMA, K., Manufacturing Processes
SHINGUABARA, S., Nanophysics and Nanofabrication Technology
SHINKE, N., Strength of Materials
TAGAWA, N., Micromechatronics
TAKUMA, M., Experiments on Mechanical Engineering

Department of Mechanical Systems Engineering:

BANDO, K., Computational Fluid Dynamics
FUJITA, T., Analytical Dynamics
HIGUCHI, M., Production Engineering
IWATSUBO, T., Measurement Systems
MORI, A., Machine Design and Engineering Tribology
OHBA, K., Fluids Engineering and Biomechanics
OZAWA, M., Engineering Thermodynamics
UCHIYAMA, H., Control Engineering

Department of Electrical Engineering and Computer Science:

HARA, T., Theory of Electricity and Magnetism
HORIBA, Y., System LSI
KUMAMOTO, A., Flexible and Intelligent Image Processing
MAEDA, Y., Control Theory and Neural Computation
OHNISHI, M., Study of Ion Beam Colliding Fusion Neutron Source
TAMURA, H., Applied Systems Science
YAMAMOTO, M., Computer Networking

Department of Electronics:

IIDA, Y., Microwave and Millimetre-Wave Engineering
KOJIMA, T., Optical and Electromagnetic Engineering
MUNEYASU, M., Image Processing
MURAMAKA, N., Computer Systems Engineering
NOMURA, Y., Information and Intelligent Systems
OKADA, H., Information Networks
OMURA, Y., Device Physics and Modelling
YOKOTA, K., Semiconductor Engineering

Department of Chemical Engineering:

MIYAKE, T., Catalyst Engineering
MIYAKE, Y., Separation Engineering
MUROYAMA, K., Chemical Reaction Engineering
ODA, H., Physical Chemistry
OKADA, Y., Nanoparticle Engineering
SHIBATA, J., Physical Chemistry
SUZUKI, T., Catalyst Engineering
YAMAMOTO, H., Experimental Chemical Engineering

Department of Applied Chemistry:

ARAKAWA, R., Analytical Chemistry
ISHII, Y., Organometallic Chemistry
ISHIKAWA, T., Electrochemistry and Electrochemical Devices
MATSUMOTO, A., Polymer Chemistry
OCHI, M., Polymer Engineering
OUCHI, T., Functional Polymers
TANEKA, K., Organic Supramolecular Chemistry

Department of Materials Science and Engineering:

AKAMATSU, K., Functional Materials
IKEDA, M., Environmental Conscious Materials Laboratory
KOBAYASHI, T., Processing of Molten Metals
KOMATSU, S., Strength of Materials
KOZUKA, H., Ceramic Engineering
MIYAKE, H., Foundry Engineering
OISHI, T., Physical Chemistry of Materials Processing
SUGIMOTO, T., Nonferrous Metallic Materials

Department of Systems Management Engineering:

AOYAGI, S., Automatic Control Theory
FUYUKI, M., Production Systems Engineering
HORII, K., Human Factors Engineering
MORI, K., Production Management
NAKAI, T., Operations Research
UEMURA, T., Visual Information Engineering

Department of Civil and Environmental Engineering:

DOGAKI, M., Structural Mechanics
ISHIGAKI, T., Hydraulic Engineering for Environment and Disaster Prevention
KAWAKAMI, S., Traffic Engineering
KUSUMI, H., Rock Mechanics and Geological Engineering
MIKAMI, I., Design of Civil Engineering Structures
SAKANO, M., Structural Engineering
TOYOFUKU, T., Construction Materials
WADA, Y., Sanitary Engineering

Department of Architecture:

ASANO, K., Structural Engineering
EGAWA, N., Architectural Environmental Design Laboratory
KAWAI, Y., Environmental Engineering
KAWAMICHI, R., Architectural Theory and Design
MARUMO, H., Urban Design
NAGAI, N., History of Architecture
NOGUCHI, T., Environmental Engineering
YAO, S., Structural Engineering

Department of Biotechnology:

HASEGAWA, Y., Genetic Engineering
OBATA, H., Microbial Technology
TSUCHIDO, T., Biocontrol Technology
UESATO, S., Pharmaceutical Technology
YAGI, H., Biochemical Engineering
YOSHIDA, M., Food Biotechnology

General Education in Natural Sciences:

AKI, S.
FUKUSHIMA, M., Probability Theory
ICHIHARA, K., Probability Theory
IKEUCHI, I., Intracellular Signals Transduction Mechanism of Neuronal Cells
KURISU, T., Game Theory
KURIYAMA, A., Mathematical Physics
KUSUDA, M., Functional Analysis
SAITO, T.
SEKI, M., Fluid Dynamics
SHIRAIWA, T., Chiral Molecular Chemistry
TAJITSU, Y.
TAMURA, H., Naturally Occurring Polymer Chemistry
TATSUMI, M., Applied Analytical Chemistry
URAGAMI, T., Functional Polymer Science
YAMAMURA, M., Quantum Many-body Physics
YAMAUCHI, O., Bio-inorganic Chemistry
YANAGAWA, T., Knot Group Theory

Institute of Foreign Language Education and Research:

FUKUI, N., Study of Japanese Culture and Ruth Benedict

GEN, YUKIKOI, Diachronic Study of Colloquial Chinese
GIBBS, A. S., Approach to Foreign Language Communication through Pragmatics, Stylistics and Discourse Analysis, Reading and Writing for Academic Purposes
HIRATA, W., Spanish and Latin American Literature
ISHIHARA, T., American Literature
JOHNSON, G. S., Presentation, Oral Interpretation
KAWAI, T., English Education, English Linguistics
KIKUCHI, A., Linguistics
KIKUCHI, U., Experimental Phonetics
KITAMURA, Y., Cognitive Science, Education Technology
KITE, Y., Sociolinguistics, Second Language Acquisition
KONDO, M., Russian Literature
KUMATANI, A., Korean Linguistics, Sociolinguistics
MOCHIZUKI, M., Applied Linguistics, Japanese Linguistics
NISHIKAWA, K., Chinese Linguistics
SAITO, E., English Education
SCHAUWECKER, D. F., Japanese–German Relationships
SHEN, G., Chinese Language Education
SUGITANI, M., German Language, Education and Intercultural Communication
TAKAHASHI, H., Sociolinguistics
TAKAHASHI, T., English Language Education
TAKEUCHI, O., Applied Linguistics, Educational Technology
USAMI, T., English Literature, English Education
WADA, Y., Medieval Manuscript Studies
YAMAMOTO, E., English Linguistics
YAMANE, S., English Phonetics
YASHIMA, T., Applied Linguistics, Intercultural Communication
YOSHIZAWA, K., Applied Linguistics

School of Law:
FUJITA, H., International Law
HAYAKAWA, T., Commercial Law
IMANISHI, Y., Civil Law
ISHII, K., Criminal Procedure
KAMEDA, K., Administrative Law
KAWAGUCHI, M., Labour Law
KIMURA, T., Civil Law
KINOSHITA, S., Constitutional Law
KITAGAWA, T., Law of International Transactions
KUBO, H., Civil Law
MURATA, H., Constitutional Law
MUROTA, G.
NOVO, M., Administrative Law
ODO, Y., Civil Law
SHIMADA, R., Civil Procedure
TAKESHITA, K., Philosophy of Law
TAKIGAWA, T., Economic Law, International Economic Law
TATSUMI, N., Intellectual Property Law
WAKAMATSU, Y., Civil Law
YAMANAKA, K., Criminal Law
YAMATO, M., Commercial Law

KEIO UNIVERSITY

2-15-45 Mita, Minato-ku, Tokyo 108-8345
Telephone: (3) 5427-1517
E-mail: www@info.keio.ac.jp
Internet: www.keio.ac.jp/index-en.html
Founded 1858
Private control
Academic year: April to March
Pres.: ATSUSHI SEIKE
Vice-Pres. for Education, Student Affairs, Facilities and Admin.: AKIRA HASEYAMA
Vice-Pres. for Environment: TADASHI KASAHARA
Vice-Pres. for Financial Affairs and Accounting, Management Reform: MASAHIKO SHIMIZU
Vice-Pres. for Gen. and Legal Affairs, Public Relations, Alumni Relations, Procurement, Strategic Planning, Crisis Management: MAKOTO IDA
Vice-Pres. for Human Resource Management, Community and Regional Affairs, Gender Equality: NAOKI WATANABE
Vice-Pres. for Int. Collaboration: NAOYUKI AGAWA
Vice-Pres. for Keio Univ. Hospital: YOSHIAKI TOYAMA
Vice-Pres. for Research, Academic-Industry Collaboration, IT: TOSHIAKI MAKABE
Sec. Gen.: MASAHIRO KOYA
Registrar: BUNJI KURIYA
Dir for Library: KAZUO SHIIKI (Information and Media Center for Science and Technology)
Dir for Library: YOSHIKAZU SUGIMOTO (Information and Media Center for Pharmaceutical Sciences)
Dir for Library: YUKIO ITO (Hiyoshi Media Centre)
Dir for Library: SHINYA SUGIYAMA (Mita Media Centre)
Dir for Library: ATSUKO KOISHI (SFC Media Center)
Dir for Library: KEIICHI FUKUDA (Shinanomachi Media Center)
Library of 4,783,740 vols
Number of teachers: 2,177
Number of students: 33,827 (regular course), 9,266 (correspondence course)
Publications: *Keio Business Review* (1 a year), *Keio Communication Review* (1 a year), *Keio Economic Observatory* (irregular), *Keio Economic Studies* (2 a year), *Keio Journal of Medicine* (4 a year), *Okajima's Folia Anatomica Japonica* (4 a year)

DEANS

Faculty of Business and Commerce: YOSHIO HIGUCHI
Faculty of Economics: MASAMICHI KOMURO
Faculty of Environment and Information Studies: JUN MURAI
Faculty of Law: RYOSEI KOKUBUN
Faculty of Letters: KEN SEKINE
School of Medicine: MAKOTO SUEMATSU
Faculty of Nursing and Medical Care: KIKUKO OTA
Faculty of Pharmacy: TADAHIKO MASHINO
Faculty of Policy Management: JIRO KOKURYO
Faculty of Science and Technology: TOJIRO AOYAMA

CHAIRPERSONS

Graduate School of Business Administration: KYOICHI IKEO
Graduate School of Business and Commerce: YOSHIO HIGUCHI
Graduate School of Economics: SHINSUKE NAKAMURA
Graduate School of Health Management: SHOHEI ONISHI
Graduate School of Human Relations: NORIYUKI SUGIURA
Graduate School of Law: RYOSEI KOKUBUN
Graduate School of Letters: AKIO USHIBA
Graduate School of Media and Governance: IKUYO KANEKO
Graduate School of Media Design: MASA INAKAGE
Graduate School of Medicine: HIDEYUKI OKANO
Graduate School of Pharmaceutical Sciences: TADASHI KASAHARA
Graduate School of Science and Technology: TOSHIAKI MAKABE
Graduate School of System Design and Management: YOSHIAKI OHKAMI
Law School: KANTARO TOYOIZUMI

DIRECTORS

Fukuzawa Memorial Center for Modern Japanese Studies: MASAMICHI KOMURO
Institute of Cultural and Linguistic Studies: SUMIO NAKAGAWA
Institute for Economic and Industry Studies (Sangyo Kenkyujo): HITOSHI HAYAMI
Institute for Media and Communications Research: YUTAKA OISHI
Institute of Physical Education: FUMIO UEDA
Keio Institute of East Asian Studies: YOSHIHIDE SOEYA
Keio Research Center for Foreign Language: KAZUMI SAKAI
Sports Medicine Research Center: SHOHEI ONISHI

KINKI UNIVERSITY

Kowakae 3-4-1, Higashiosaka-shi, Osaka 577-8502
Telephone: (6) 6721-2332
E-mail: koho@msa.kindai.ac.jp
Internet: www.kindai.ac.jp
Founded 1925
Private control
Language of instruction: Japanese
Academic year: April to March
Pres.: HIROYUKI HATA
Head Administrator: HIROAKI SEKOH
Library of 1,200,000 vols
Number of teachers: 1,563
Number of students: 29,794
Publications: *Acta Medica Kinki University* (2 a year), *Annals of the Molecular Engineering Institute* (1 a year), *Bulletin of the Fisheries Laboratory of Kinki University* (irregular), *Bulletin of the Pharmaceutical Research and Technology Institute* (1 a year), *Bulletin of the School of Literature, Arts and Cultural Studies* (1 a year), *Ikoma Journal of Economics* (2 a year), *Journal of Business Administration and Marketing Strategy* (3 a year), *Journal of the Faculty of Science and Engineering at Kinki University* (1 a year), *Law Review of Kinki University* (4 a year), *Medical Journal of Kinki University* (2 a year), *Memoirs of the Faculty of Agriculture of Kinki University* (1 a year), *Memoirs of the Institute of Advanced Technology* (2 a year), *Memoirs of the School of Biology-Oriented Science and Technology* (1 a year), *Multimedia Education* (1 a year), *Research Journal of the Department of Teacher Education* (2 a year), *Research Reports of the Faculty of Engineering of Kinki University* (1 a year), *Science and Technology* (1 a year)

DEANS

School of Agriculture: KOICHIRO KOMAI
School of Biology-Oriented Science and Technology: KAZUO YAMAMOTO
School of Business Administration: HIROYASU OKITSU
School of Economics: KYOUZOU TAKECHI
School of Engineering: HIROSHI TSUBAKIHARA
School of Humanity-Oriented Science and Engineering: MASAYUKI ONO
School of Law: HIDEJIRO ISHIDA
School of Literature, Arts and Cultural Studies: YUTAKA ARAMAKI
School of Medicine: HARUMASA OYANAGI
School of Pharmaceutical Sciences: KAZUAKI KAKEHI
School of Science and Engineering: MEGUMU MUNAKATA

KOBE GAKUIN UNIVERSITY

518 Arise, Ikawadani-cho, Nishiku, Kobe 651-2180

Telephone: (78) 974-1551
E-mail: kgu@j.kobegakuin.ac.jp
Internet: www.kobegakuin.ac.jp

Founded 1966
Academic year: April to March
Campuses at Nagata and Port Island

Pres.: Yoshio Okada
Dir-Gen. for Admin.: Ttetsuaki Takenaka
Librarian: Hiromi Yoshida

Library of 955,062 vols
Number of teachers: 284
Number of students: 10,172

Publications: *Kobe Gakuin Hogaku* (Law and Politics Review), *Kobe Gakuin Economic Papers, Memoirs of the Faculty of Pharmaceutical Sciences, Journal of Business Management*

DEANS

Faculty of Business Admin.: Nobuo Tsuno
Faculty of Economics: Yoshio Tanaka
Faculty of Humanities and Sciences: Hironori Mizumoto
Faculty of Law: Toyoki Okada
Faculty of Nutrition: Kiyoshi Goda
Faculty of Pharmaceutical Sciences: Hiroshi Okamoto
Faculty of Rehabilitation: Isao Nara
Graduate School of Economics: Yoshio Tanaka
Graduate School of Food and Medicinal Sciences: Kiyoshi Goda
Graduate School of Humanities and Sciences: Hironori Mizumoto
Graduate School of Law: Toyoki Okada
Graduate School of Law Practices: Kenji Sanekata
Graduate School of Nutrition: Kiyoshi Goda
Graduate School of Pharmaceutical Sciences: Hiroshi Okamoto

KOGAKUIN UNIVERSITY

1-24-2, Nishi-shinjuku, Shinjuku-ku, Tokyo 163-8677

Telephone: (3) 3342-1211
E-mail: gakuen_koho@sc.kogakuin.ac.jp
Internet: www.kogakuin.ac.jp

Founded 1887, present status 1949
Private control
Language of instruction: Japanese
Academic year: April to March

Pres.: Prof. Dr Akisato Mizuno
Vice-Pres. for Univ. Reform: Prof. Dr Yasushi Nagasawa
Vice-Pres. for Placement Affairs: Prof. Dr Yasushi Nozawa
Dean for Education Support Functions: Prof. Dr Takashi Watanabe
Library Dir: Prof. Dr Kiyoshi Kato

Library of 338,163 vols, incl. 60,635 bound magazines
Number of teachers: 694 (221 full-time, 473 part-time)
Number of students: 6,653 (full-time 5,984 undergraduate, 453 postgraduate, 17 doctoral, 199 part-time)

Publications: *Kogakuin University Bulletin* (2 a year), *Research Reports of Kogakuin University* (2 a year)

DEANS

Faculty of Engineering: Prof. Dr Jun-ichi Arai
Faculty of Global Engineering: Prof. Dr Takashi Saika
Faculty of Informatics: Prof. Dr Noboru Sugamura
Graduate School of Engineering: Prof. Dr Yasutada Imamura
School of Architecture: Prof. Dr Yasushi Nagasawa

KOKUGAKUIN UNIVERSITY

4-10-28, Higashi, Shibuya-ku, Tokyo 150-8440

Telephone: (3) 5466-0111
E-mail: kokusai@kokugakuin.ac.jp
Internet: www.kokugakuin.ac.jp

Founded 1882
Academic year: April to March

Pres.: Prof. Masahiko Asoya
Sec.-Gen.: Shozo Sanagi
Librarian: T. Sawanobori

Library: see under Libraries and Archives
Number of teachers: 790
Number of students: 10,319

Publications: *Kokugakuin Zasshi* (Journal of Kokugakuin University), *Kokugakuin Keizaigaku* (Kokugakuin University Economic Review), *Kokugakuin Hogaku* (Journal of the Faculty of Law and Politics), *Kokugakuin Daigaku Kiyo* (Transactions of Kokugakuin University), *Kokugakuin Daigaku Daigakuin Bungaku Kenkyuka Ronshu* (Journal of the Graduate School, Kokugakuin University), *Kokugakuin Daigaku Kenzaigaku Kenkyuka Kiyo* (Kokugakuin University Economic Studies), *Kokugakuin Hokenronso* (Journal of Law and Politics, Graduate School of Law), *Nihonbunka-Kenkyusho-Kiyo* (Transactions of the Institute for Japanese Culture and Classics)

DEANS

Faculty of Economics: Hironori Kon'i
Faculty of Law: Seiichi Nagamori
Faculty of Letters: Shuhei Aoki
Faculty of Shinto Studies: Soji Okada
Graduate School: Tsuyoshi Fujimoto
Law School: Katsumasa Hirabayashi

ATTACHED RESEARCH INSTITUTE

Institute for Japanese Culture and Classics: 4-10-28, Higashi, Shibuya-ku, Tokyo 150-8440

KOKUSHIKAN UNIVERSITY

4-28-1 Setagaya, Setagaya-ku, Tokyo 154-8515

Telephone: (3) 5481-3112
E-mail: wwwadmin@kiss.kokushikan.ac.jp
Internet: www.kokushikan.ac.jp

Founded 1917
Private control
Academic year: April to March

Chair.: Haruo Nishihara
Pres.: Hideo Osawa
General Dir: Atsushi Matsumoto
Librarian: Shoichi Yamamoto

Library of 630,638 vols
Number of teachers: 310
Number of students: 12,677

Publications: *Politics and Economics Review, Kokushikan Law Review*, various faculty journals and reviews

DEANS

Faculty of Engineering: Katsuhiko Wakabayashi
Faculty of Law: Noriyoshi Watanabe
Faculty of Letters: Akira Abe
Faculty of Political Science and Economics: Hiroyuki Yamazaki
Faculty of Political Science and Economics (Evening Session): Ryozo Shirogane
Faculty of Physical Education: Kazuyuki Nishyama
Junior College: Hiroshi Tashiro
School of Asia 21: Kageaki Kajiwara

KOMAZAWA UNIVERSITY

1-23-1 Komazawa, Setagaya-ku, Tokyo 154-8525

Telephone: (3) 3418-9011
E-mail: info-soumu@komazawa-u.ac.jp
Internet: www.komazawa-u.ac.jp
Academic year: April to March

Pres.: Ryoko Hirose
Vice-Pres.: Masaki Kubota
Vice-Pres.: Noriaki Kuwata
Registrar: Yoshihiro Saruyama
Librarian: Kanji Hikasa

Library of 1,217,082 vols
Number of teachers: 324
Number of students: 15,539

Publications: *Business Studies, Journal of Buddhist Economic Research, Journal of Buddhist Studies, Journal of Comparative Buddhist Literature, Journal of Global Media Studies, Journal of Health Sciences of Komazawa University, Journal of Historical Studies, Journal of Radiological Sciences of Komazawa University, Journal of the Faculty of Arts and Sciences, Journal of the Faculty of Buddhism, Journal of the Faculty of Law, Journal of the Faculty of Letters, Komazawa Annual Reports of Psychology, Komazawa Business Review, Komazawa Educational Review, Komazawa Japanese Literature, Komazawa Journal of Geography, Komazawa Journal of Japanese Culture, Komazawa Journal of Sociology, Komazawa Law and Political Science Review, Komazawa Law Journal, Komazawa University Bunka, Regional Views, Studies in British and American Literature, The Economic Review of Komazawa University, The Semiannual Periodical of The faculty of Arts and Sciences*

DEANS

Faculty of Arts and Sciences: Yoshimasa Ikegami
Faculty of Buddhism: Atsushi Kanazawa
Faculty of Business Administration: Nobuo Katagiri
Faculty of Economics: Takashi Oguri
Faculty of Global Media Studies: Kenichi Kawasaki
Faculty of Health Sciences: Yasutsugu Seo
Faculty of Law: Reiko Oyama
Faculty of Letters: Yasutomi Taniguchi
Graduate Division of Global Media: Hidenori Fuke

KONAN UNIVERSITY

8-9-1 Okamoto, Higashinada-ku, Kobe 658-8501

Telephone: (78) 431-4341
E-mail: kiec@adm.konan-u.ac.jp
Internet: www.konan-u.ac.jp

Founded 1918

President: Y. Sugimura

Library of 775,000 vols
Number of teachers: 240 full-time
Number of students: 9,578

Publications: *Journal of Konan University Faculty of Letters* (irregular), *Memoirs of Konan University* (science and engineering series, 2 a year), *Konan Economic Papers* (irregular), *Konan Hogaku* (Konan Law Review, irregular), *Konan Business Review* (irregular), *Journal of the Institute for Language and Culture* (irregular)

DEANS

Faculty of Business Administration: Y. Nakata
Faculty of Economics: H. Kobayashi
Faculty of Law: T. Maeda
Faculty of Letters: T. Hisatake

Faculty of Science and Engineering: T. SHIGEMATSU

KOSHIEN UNIVERSITY

Momijigaoka, Takarazuka, Hyogo 665-0006
Telephone: (797) 87-5111
E-mail: nyuushi@koshien.ac.jp
Internet: www.koshien.ac.jp

Founded 1967

Colleges of business administration, humanities, information sciences, nutrition

Pres.: TOMIO KINOSHITA

Library of 106,942 vols
Number of teachers: 170
Number of students: 1,428

KURUME UNIVERSITY

67 Asahi-Machi, Kurume 830-0011
Telephone: (942) 35-3311
E-mail: soumu@med.kurume-u.ac.jp
Internet: www.kurume-u.ac.jp

Founded 1928

Faculties of commerce, economics, law, literature and medicine

Pres.: KYOZO KOKETSU
Dir for Admin. Office: KATSUMI YOSHIHISA

Library of 415,000 vols
Number of teachers: 534
Number of students: 5,808

Publications: *The Kurume Medical Journal* (4 a year), *The Journal of the Kurume Medical Association* (12 a year), *The Journal for Studies on Industrial Economics* (4 a year)

KWANSEI GAKUIN UNIVERSITY

1-1-155 Uegahara, Nishinomiya, Hyogo 662-8501
Telephone: (798) 51-0952
E-mail: ciec@kwansei.ac.jp
Internet: www.kwansei.ac.jp

Founded 1889
Academic year: April to March

Chancellor: MICHIYA HATA
Pres.: KAZUO HIRAMATSU
Vice-Pres.: KOHEI ASANO
Vice-Pres.: TOKUTOSHI INOUE
Vice-Pres.: HIDEKI MINE
Library Dir: TAKUTOSHI INOUE

Library: see under Libraries and Archives
Number of teachers: 435 full-time
Number of students: 18,702

Publications: *Economic Review, Humanities Review, Journal of Business Administration, Journal of Economics, Journal of Law and Politics, Journal of Policy Studies, Journal of the School of Sociology, Language and Culture, Law Review, Natural Sciences Review, Review of Economics and Business Management, Social Sciences Review, Studies in Computer Science, Studies in Teacher Development, Theological Studies*

DEANS

School of Business Administration: AKIRA MIYAMA
School of Economics: SHIN NEGISHI
School of Humanities: ATSUHIDE SAKAKURA
School of Law and Politics: YOZO SAWADA
School of Policy Studies: TOYOO FUKUDA
School of Science: YAICHI SHINOHARA
School of Sociology: MICHIHITO TSUSHIMA
School of Theology: ETSURO KINOWAKI
Graduate School of Language, Communication and Culture: TAKAAKI KANZAKI
Institute of Business and Accounting: MARTIN COLLICK
Law School: TOORU KATO

KYOTO NOTRE DAME UNIVERSITY

1–2 Minami Nonogami-cho, Shimogamo, Sakyo-ku, Kyoto 606-0847
Telephone: (75) 781-1173
E-mail: international@notredame.ac.jp
Internet: www.notredame.ac.jp

Founded 1961
Private control
Language of instruction: Japanese
Academic year: April to March

Pres.: M. YABUUCHI
Vice-Pres.: N. MAKINAI

Library of 200,000 vols
Number of teachers: 223 (70 full-time, 153 part-time)
Number of students: 1,792

DEANS

Dept of Cross-Cultural Studies: KATSUHIRO HORI
Dept of English Language and Literature: YASUTOMO ARAI
Faculty of Home Sciences and Welfare: YASUKO YONEDA
Faculty of Psychology: ETSUKO UEDA
Graduate School for Applied English and Intercultural Studies: IZUMI SUGAWA
Graduate School for Clinical Psychology: YOKO FUJIKAWA
Graduate School for Home Sciences and Welfare: HISAYUKI MURATA

KYOTO PHARMACEUTICAL UNIVERSITY

5, Misasagi-Nakauchi-cho, Yamashina-ku, Kyoto 607-8414
Telephone: (75) 595-4600
E-mail: kpu-koho@mb.kyoto-phu.ac.jp
Internet: www.kyoto-phu.ac.jp

Founded 1884

Pres.: MASAZUMI IKEDA
Registrar: Dr NORIAKI FUNASAKI
Librarian: Dr TAKESI NISINO

Library of 91,260 vols
Number of teachers: 104
Number of students: 1,821

PROFESSORS

FUJIMOTO, S., Environmental Biochemistry
FUNASAKI, N., Physical Chemistry
HAMAZAKI, H., Health and Sports Sciences
HATAYAMA, T., Biochemistry
HIRAYAMA, T., Public Health
KAMBE, T., Mathematics
KIM, J., Cell Biology
KISO, Y., Medicinal Chemistry
KITAMURA, K., Analytical Chemistry
KOHNO, S., Pharmacology
KOIKE, C., Physics Laboratory
KONOSHIMA, T., Pharmaceutical Sciences and Natural Resources
MURANISHI, S., Pharmaceutics
NAKATA, T., Clinical Pharmacology
NISHINO, T., Microbiology
NODE, M., Pharmaceutical Manufacturing Chemistry
OHTA, S., Chemistry of Functional Molecules
OKABE, S., Applied Pharmacology
SAKURAI, H., Analytical and Bioinorganic Chemistry
SATO, T., Pathological Biochemistry
TAKADA, K., Pharmacokinetics
TAKEUCHI, K., Pharmacology and Experimental Therapeutics
TANIGUCHI, T., Neurobiology
UENISHI, J., Pharmaceutical Chemistry
YAMAMOTO, A., Biopharmaceutics
YOKOYAMA, T., Hospital Pharmacy
YOSHIKAWA, M., Pharmacognosy

MATSUYAMA UNIVERSITY

4–2 Bunkyo-cho, Matsuyama, Ehime 790-8578
Telephone: (89) 925-7111
E-mail: mu-koho@matsuyama-u.ac.jp
Internet: www.matsuyama-u.ac.jp

Founded 1923
Academic year: April to March

Pres.: Prof. SATORU KANIMORI
Registrar: SANIMOTU OCHI

Library: see under Libraries and Archives
Number of teachers: 308
Number of students: 5,730

Publications: *Matsuyama Daigaku Ronshu* (6 a year), *Studies in Language and Literature* (2 a year)

DEANS

Faculty of Business Administration: Prof. N. IDIIDA
Faculty of Economics: Prof. J. IRIE, Prof. Y. SEINO
Faculty of Humanities: Prof. T. KANAMURA
Faculty of Law: Prof. T. TAKEMIYA
Junior College: Prof. K. YAGI

MEIJI UNIVERSITY

1-1 Kanda-Surugadai, Chiyoda-ku, Tokyo 101-8301
Telephone: (3) 3296-4545
E-mail: koho@isc.meiji.ac.jp
Internet: www.meiji.ac.jp

Founded 1881
Private control
Academic year: April to March (2 semesters)

Pres.: Prof. HIROMI NAYA
Dir of Library: Prof. MASAHIKO YOSHIDA

Library of 2,350,000 vols
Number of teachers: 2,803 (1,002 full-time, 1,801 part-time)
Number of students: 32,713 (29,944 undergraduate, 2,769 postgraduate)

DEANS

Graduate School: TAKEHIKO YOSHIMURA
School of Agriculture: FUMITAKA HAYASE
School of Arts and Letters: YOSHIKATSU HAYASHI
School of Business Admin.: ETSUO ABE
School of Commerce: KATSUHIKO YOKOI
School of Global Japanese Studies: SEIICHI KANISE
School of Information and Communication: HARUMI HOSONO
School of Law: SHIGEYO TAKACHI
School of Political Science and Economics: KOSAKU DAIROKUNO
School of Science and Technology: ICHIRO MIKI

GRADUATE SCHOOL CHAIRMEN

Dept of Agriculture: KOSUKE NOBORIO
Dept of Arts and Letters: MASATO GODA
Dept of Advanced Mathematical Science: MASAYASU MIMURA
Dept of Business Administration: MASAYASU TAKAHASHI
Dept of Commerce: TOSHIHIRO SARUWATARI
Dept of Global Business: YUKIHIKO UEHARA
Dept of Governance Studies: HIROO ICHIKAWA
Dept of Humanities: SUSUMU YAMAIZUMI
Dept of Information and Communication: TAKEHIKO DAIKOKU
Dept of Law: KAZUHIRO MURAKAMI
Dept of Law School: TAKASHI KAWACHI
Dept of Political Science and Economics: OSAMU OGO
Dept of Professional Accountancy: NOBUHIKO SATO
Dept of Science and Technology: ICHIRO MIKI

MEIJI GAKUIN UNIVERSITY

1-2-37 Shirokanedai, Minato-ku, Tokyo 108-8636
Telephone: (3) 5421-5165
E-mail: koho@mguad.meijigakuin.ac.jp
Internet: www.meijigakuin.ac.jp
Founded 1877
Private control
Language of instruction: Japanese
Academic year: April to July, September to March
Chancellor: Prof. SATORU KUZE
Pres.: Prof. YOSHIKAZU WAKITA
Vice-Pres: Prof. MIKIKO YAMAZAKI, Prof. TOMOYOSHI KOIZUMI, Prof. TOSHIO HASHIMOTO
Admin. Officer: SHUJI SHIBASAKI
Librarian: Prof. KUNIO IWAYA
Library of 825,000 vols
Number of teachers: 256
Number of students: 13,639
Publications: *Meiji Gakuin Review*, *English Language and Literature*, *Papers and Proceedings of Economics*, *Proceedings of Integrated Arts and Sciences*, *Law Review* (3 a year), *International and Regional Studies* (2 a year), *French Literature*, *Art Studies*, *Psychology*, *Sociology and Social Welfare Review* (1 a year)

DEANS

Faculty of Economics: Prof. TAKESHI OSHIO
Faculty of General Education: Prof. YASUO IKEGAMI
Faculty of International Studies: Prof. NOZOMO AKIZUKI
Faculty of Law: Prof. MITSURU ABE
Faculty of Literature: Prof. RYUUICHI HIGUCHI
Faculty of Sociology and Social Work: Prof. KATSUYOSHI KAWAI
Graduate School of Economics: Prof. MASAAKI TAKAMATSU
Graduate School of International Studies: Prof. SHIGEMOCHI HIROSHIMA
Graduate School of Law: Prof. AKIRA OKI
Graduate School of Literature: Prof. MASAAKI TSUTSUI
Graduate School of Sociology and Social Work: Prof. KIYOSHI MATSUI

MEIJO UNIVERSITY

1-501 Shiogamaguchi, Tempaku-ku, Nagoya, Aichi 468-8502
Telephone: (52) 832-1151
E-mail: kikaku@meijo-u.ac.jp
Internet: www.meijo-u.ac.jp
Founded 1949
Private control
Academic year: April to March
President: MASAKI AMINAKA
Administrative Officer: RYOICHI ARAI
Library Director: YUICHIROU OZAKI
Library of 735,994 vols, 7,047 periodicals
Number of teachers: 431 (full-time)
Number of students: 15,495
Publications: *Meijo Hogaku*, *Meijo Ronsou*, faculty bulletins and reports

DEANS

Faculty of Agriculture: NAOSUKE NII
Faculty of Business: HITOSHI IMAI
Faculty of Economics: UMEGAKI
Faculty of Education: KOUJI ITOU
Faculty of Law: YUZOU KIMURA
Faculty of Pharmacy: YOSHIO SUZUKI
Faculty of Science and Technology: TETSO HUJIMOTO
Faculty of Urban Science: TODASHI USHIJIMA
Junior College: SHINJI MORITA

MEISEI UNIVERSITY

2-1-1 Hodokubo, Hino-shi, Tokyo 191-8506
Campuses at Hino and Ome
Telephone: Hino: (42) 591-5111; Ome: (428) 25-5111
E-mail: office@flc.meisei-u.ac.jp
Internet: www.meisei-u.ac.jp
Founded 1964
Private control
Academic year: April to March
Pres.: JUN'ICHI UJIHARA
Vice-Pres: TAKEHIKO MARUYAMA, TETSUO OGAWA
Dirs of Student Affairs: TOSHIAKI UEDA, KAZUYOSHI YAMANAKA
Sec.-Gen.: KATSUNORI KANATANI
Library Dir: YOSHIAKI FIUNATSU
Library of 880,305 vols, 4,300 periodicals
Number of teachers: 243
Number of students: 8,651 (correspondence courses 8,152)
Publications: *Research Bulletin of Meisei University. Humanities and Social Sciences* (1 a year), *Research Bulletin of Meisei University. Physical Sciences and Engineering* (1 a year), *Bulletin of Meisei University. Department of Arts, Faculty of Japanese Culture* (1 a year), *Research Bulletin of Meisei University. Faculty of Informatics* (1 a year), *Annual Bulletin of the Graduate School of Humanities and Social Sciences, Meisei University*

DEANS

Faculty of Economics (Hino): Prof. YOSHIHIKO NISHINO
Faculty of Humanities (Hino): Prof. KOICHI TSUKADA
Faculty of Informatics (Ome): Prof. KANJI OTSUKA
Faculty of Japanese Culture (Ome): Prof. KENJI IKAWA
Faculty of Physical Sciences and Engineering (Hino): Prof. MUNEKAZU TAKANO

MEJIRO UNIVERSITY

4-31-1 Nakaochiai, Shinjuku-ku, Tokyo 161-8539
Telephone: (3) 5996-3121
E-mail: webmaster@mejiro.ac.jp
Internet: www.mejiro.ac.jp
Founded 1923
Pres.: KOKI SATO

DEANS

Faculty of Business Administration: (vacant)
Faculty of Human and Social Sciences: OSAMI HUKUSHIMA
Faculty of Humanities: KISAKU KUDO

MOMOYAMA GAKUIN UNIVERSITY (St Andrew's University)

1-1 Manabino, Izumi, Osaka 594-1198
Telephone: (725) 54-3131
E-mail: kokusai@andrew.ac.jp
Internet: www.andrew.ac.jp
Founded 1959
Languages of instruction: English, Japanese
Academic year: April to March
Pres.: MICHIO MATSUURA
Vice-Pres.: AKIRA HASEGAWA
Vice-Pres.: YOJI IWATSU
Vice-Pres.: JIRO KIMURA
Library Dir: NORIO KITAGAWA
Library of 646,000 vols
Number of teachers: 156
Number of students: 7,387
Publications: *Economic & Business Review*, *English Review*, *Human Sciences Review*, *Intercultural Studies*, *Journal of Christian Studies*, *Pan-Pacific Business Review*, *Research Institute Bulletin*, *St. Andrew's University Law Review*, *Sociological Review*

DEANS

Faculty of Business Administration: KICHIZO AKASHI
Faculty of Economics: NORIO TAKEHARA
Faculty of Law: NORIYUKI HONMA
Faculty of Letters: NATSUKI KUNIMATSU
Faculty of Sociology: YOSHIFUMI SHIMIZU

MIYAGI GAKUIN WOMEN'S COLLEGE

9-1-1 Aoba-ku, Sendai Miyagi 981-8557
Telephone: (22) 279-1311
E-mail: www-admin@mgu.ac.jp
Internet: www.mgu.ac.jp
Founded 1886
Private control
Language of instruction: Japanese
Academic year: April to March
Chancellor: K. MATSUZAKI
President: M. ANBE
Librarian: T. ONODERA
Library of 320,000 vols
Number of teachers: 100
Number of students: 3,094
Publications: *Bulletin of English Department* (1 a year), *Christianity and Culture* (1 a year), *Japanese Literature Note* (1 a year), *Journal of Miyagi College for Women* (1 a year), *Annals of the Institute for Research in Humanities and Social Sciences* (1 a year)

DEANS

Department of Cultural Studies: W. TAKAHASHI
Department of Developmental and Clinical Studies: T. ADAOHI
Department of Domestic and Cultural Sciences: N. OKABO
Department of English Literature: K. ISOZAKI
Department of Food and Nutritional Science: H. HIRAMOTO
Department of Intercultural Studies: M. KUROTAKI
Department of Japanese Literature: M. HAKAZAWA
Department of Music: T. SUMIKAWA

NAGOYA UNIVERSITY OF COMMERCE AND BUSINESS

4-4 Sagamine, Komenoki-cho, Nisshin-shi, Aichi 470-0193
Telephone: (561) 73-2111
Internet: www.nucba.ac.jp
Founded 1953
Private control
Language of instruction: Japanese
Academic year: April to February (2 terms)
Pres.: HIROSHI KURIMOTO
Dir: MASAHIDE KURIMOTO
Dir of Library: (vacant)
Library of 70,000 vols
Number of teachers: 160 (102 full-time, 58 part-time)
Number of students: 3,389
Publications: *Journal of Economics and Management* (2 a year), *Journal of Language, Culture and Communication* (2 a year), *Bulletin of the Yuichi Kurimoto Memorial Graduate School of Business Administration* (1 a year)

DEANS

Faculty of Accounting and Finance: Prof. AKIRA KOBASHI
Faculty of Business Administration: Prof. HIROKO KAKITANI

Faculty of Foreign Languages and Asian Studies: Prof. GEORGE WATT
Faculty of Management Information Science: Prof. NAMIO HONDA

NANZAN UNIVERSITY

18 Yamazato-cho, Showa-ku, Nagoya 466-8673
Telephone: (52) 832-3111
E-mail: webmaster@nanzan-u.ac.jp
Internet: www.nanzan-u.ac.jp

Founded 1949
Private control
Language of instruction: Japanese
Academic year: April to March

Pres.: MICHAEL CALMANO
Vice-Pres.: K. AOKI, N. KINOSHITA, M. NORO
Chief of Gen. Affairs Section: S. SAWAGUCHI
Librarian: H. HOSOYA

Library of 745,014 vols, 16,655 periodicals, 7,425 audiovisual titles
Number of teachers: 805 (320 full-time, 485 part-time)
Number of students: 10,011

Publications: *Academia (Humanities and Natural Sciences)* (2 a year, in English and Japanese), *Academia (Information Sciences and Engineering)* (1 a year, in English and Japanese), *Academia (Literature and Language)* (2 a year, in English and Japanese), *Academia (Social Sciences)* (2 a year, in English and Japanese), *Nanzan Journal of Theological Studies* (1 a year, in English and Japanese), *Nanzan Law Review* (4 a year, in Japanese), *Nanzan Management Review* (3 a year, in English and Japanese), *Nanzan Studies on Japanese Language and Culture* (1 a year, in Japanese), *The Nanzan Journal of Economic Studies* (3 a year, in English and Japanese)

DEANS

Faculty of Business Administration: Y. KAORU
Faculty of Economics: Y. ARAI
Faculty of Foreign Studies: H. FUJIMOTO
Faculty of Humanities: S. SAKAI
Faculty of Information Sciences and Engineering: A. SUZUKI
Faculty of Law: T. SOEDA
Faculty of Policy Studies: T. MATSUDO
General Education: Y. NAKA

ATTACHED INSTITUTES

Center for American Studies: 18 Yamazato-cho, Showa-ku, Nagoya; tel. (52) 832-3111; e-mail center-as@ic.nanzan-u.ac.jp; internet www.ic.nanzan-u.ac.jp/america/index.html; study of American politics, economics, diplomacy, culture and society and US-Japan relations; library of 17,454 vols, 327 periodicals, 19 audiovisual items; Dir Prof. T. SUZUKI; publ. *Nanzan Review of American Studies* (1 a year, in English).

Center for Asia-Pacific Studies: 18 Yamazato-cho, Showa-ku Nagoya; tel. (52) 832-3111; e-mail cfes-cfas-all@nanzan-u.ac.jp; internet www.ic.nanzan-u.ac.jp/asiapacific; interdisciplinary study of the politics, int. relations, economics, society, history, culture, and literature of the Asia-Pacific region; library of 6,452 vols, 251 periodicals, 83 audiovisual items; Dir Prof. T. HAYASHI; publ. *Bulletin* (1 a year, in Japanese).

Center for European Studies: 18 Yamazato-cho, Showa-ku, Nagoya; tel. (52) 832-3111; e-mail cfes-cfas-all@nanzan-u.ac.jp; internet www.ic.nanzan-u.ac.jp/europe; interdisciplinary study of European politics, economics and society; library of 4,580 vols, 204 periodicals, 9 audiovisual items; Dir Prof. R. MANO; publ. *Bulletin* (1 a year, in Japanese).

Center for Japanese Studies: 18 Yamazato-cho, Showa-ku, Nagoya; tel. (52) 832-3123; e-mail cjs@ic.nanzan-u.ac.jp; internet www.nanzan-u.ac.jp/english/cjs; one-semester or one-year programme in language-related studies, area studies and practical courses in traditional arts; library of 790,000 vols; Dir Prof. MASAHIRO HOSHINO.

Center for Latin American Studies: 18 Yamazato-cho, Showa-ku, Nagoya; tel. (52) 832-3111; e-mail centro-latino@ic.nanzan-u.ac.jp; internet www.ic.nanzan-u.ac.jp/latin/index.html; study of Latin America, particularly the humanities and social sciences (history, anthropology, education, economics, literature, philosophy, politics, archaeology and linguistics); library of 11,417 vols, 313 periodicals, 45 audiovisual items; Dir Prof. T. KATO; publ. *Perspectivas Latinoamericanas* (1 a year, in English, Portuguese and Spanish).

Center for Legal Practice-Education and Research: 18 Yamazato-cho, Showa-ku, Nagoya; tel. (52) 832-8197; e-mail housou-jitsumu@nanzan-u.ac.jp; internet www.ic.nanzan-u.ac.jp/housou; research and practice of legal practical education; implement business studies and lectures about legal practice; Dir Prof. Y. KATO.

Center for Linguistics: 18 Yamazato-cho, Showa-ku, Nagoya; tel. (52) 832-3110; e-mail ling@ic.nanzan-u.ac.jp; internet www.ic.nanzan-u.ac.jp/linguistics; research in comparative syntax and language acquisition: int. jt research projects with Cambridge, Siena, Connecticut, Hyderabad, and Tsing Hua; library of 5,000 vols; Dir Prof. M. SAITO; publ. *Nanzan Linguistics* (1 or 2 a year, in English).

Center for Management Studies: 18 Yamazato-cho, Showa-ku, Nagoya; tel. (52) 832-3111; e-mail mcenter@ic.nanzan-u.ac.jp; specializing in the study of management issues; Dir Prof. H. GANKOJI.

Center for Research in Mathematical Sciences and Information Engineering: 27 Seirei-cho, Seto; tel. (561) 89-2081; e-mail liaison-msie@nanzan-u.ac.jp; internet www.seto.nanzan-u.ac.jp/msie; research into information engineering and quantitative sciences; coordination of collaboration between industry and academia; Dir Prof. S. OSAKI; publ. *Academia (Information Sciences and Engineering)* (1 a year, in English and Japanese).

Center for the Study of Human Relations: 18 Yamazato-cho, Showa-ku, Nagoya; tel. (52) 832-5002; e-mail ninkan-c@nanzan-u.ac.jp; internet www.ic.nanzan-u.ac.jp/ninkan; Dir Prof. T. TSUMURA; publ. *The Nanzan Journal of Human Relations* (1 a year, in Japanese).

Institute for Social Ethics: 18 Yamazato-cho, Showa-ku, Nagoya; tel. (52) 832-3111; e-mail sharink@ic.nanzan-u.ac.jp; internet www.ic.nanzan-u.ac.jp/ise/index.html; research on the principles of social ethics and the ethical problems of contemporary society; library of 21,893 vols; Dir Prof. M. MARUYAMA; publ. *Society and Ethics* (1 a year, in Japanese).

Nanzan Anthropological Institute: 18 Yamazato-cho, Showa-ku, Nagoya; tel. (52) 832-3111; e-mail ai-nu@ic.nanzan-u.ac.jp; internet www.ic.nanzan-u.ac.jp/jinruiken/index.html; research in cultural anthropology, mainly in SE, E and S Asia; library of 11,246 vols, 682 periodicals, 24 audiovisual titles; Dir Prof. A. GOTO; publ. *Nanzan Studies in Cultural Anthropology* (irregular, in Japanese).

Nanzan Institute for Religion and Culture: 18 Yamazato-cho, Showa-ku, Nagoya; tel. (52) 832-3111; e-mail nirc-office@ic.nanzan-u.ac.jp; internet nirc.nanzan-u.ac.jp; research in the area of world religions with spec. reference to the religions of Asia and to the dialogue between religions; library of 20,772 vols, 570 periodicals, 104 audiovisual titles; Dir Prof. MICHIAKI OKUYAMA; publ. *Nanzan Symposia* (irregular, in Japanese), *Religious Studies Today* (irregular, in Japanese), *Bulletin* (1 a year, in Japanese and English), *Japanese Journal of Religious Studies* (2 a year, in English), *Asian Ethnology* (fmrly Asian Folklore Studies, 2 a year, in English), *Nanzan Library of Asian Religion and Culture* (irregular, in English), *Nanzan Studies in Asian Religions* (irregular, in English), *Nanzan Studies in Religion and Culture* (irregular, in English)

NIHON UNIVERSITY

8–24, Kudan-Minami 4-chome, Chiyoda-ku, Tokyo 102-8275
Telephone: (3) 5275-8116
E-mail: ils@nihon-u.ac.jp
Internet: www.nihon-u.ac.jp

Founded 1889 as Nihon Law School, present status 1903
Private control
Languages of instruction: English, Japanese
Academic year: April to March

Chair. of Board: H. TANAKA
Pres.: K. OTSUKA
Vice-Pres.: S. MAKIMURA
Vice-Pres.: Dr M. SUGIMOTO
Vice-Pres.: Dr T. KUSAMA

Library of 5,838,526 vols
Number of teachers: 2,905 (full-time)
Number of students: 80,063

Publications: *Johokagaku Kenkyu* (information science studies), *Journal of Oral Science*, *Kaikeigaku Kenkyu* (accounting), *Kenkyu Kiyo* (humanities and social sciences), *Kenkyu Kiyo* (proceedings of the Institute of Natural Sciences), *Kenkyu Kiyo Nihon Daigaku Shigakubu (Ippan Kyouiku)* (transactions of the School of Dentistry (General Studies)), *Kokusai Kankei Gakubu Nenpo* (international relations), *Kokusai Kankei Kenkyu* (international relations), *Kokusai Chiiki Kenkyujo Shoho* (RRIAP proceedings of symposium), *Nichidai Igaku Zasshi* (journal of Nihon University Medical Association), *Nihon Daigaku Geijutsu Gakubu Kiyo Ronbunhen* (research in fine art at the College of Art), *Nihon Daigaku Geijutsu Gakubu Kiyo Sousakuhen* (artistic works of the College of Art), *Nihon Daigaku Kokusai Kankei Gakubu Seikatsu Kagaku Kenkyujo Hokoku*, *Nihon Daigaku Kou Gakubu Kiyo* (journal of the College of Engineering), *Nihon Daigaku Kyouiku Seido Kenkyujo Kiyo* (bulletin of the Educational Systems Research Institute), *Nihon Daigaku Igakubu Kiyo* (bulletin of the liberal arts and sciences), *Nihon Daigaku Seibutsushigenkagakubu Sogokenkyujo Kenkyugyosekishu* (proceedings of the General Research Institute, College of Bioresource Sciences), *Nihon Daigaku Seibutsushigenkagakubu ei Kenkyu* (proceedings of the Life Science Research Center, College of Bioresource Sciences), *Nihon Daigaku Seisanko Gakubu Kenkyu Houkoku* (journal of the College of Industrial Technology, in editions A and B), *Nihon Daigaku Seisankogaku Kenkyujo Shohou* (journal of the College of Industrial Technology), *Nihon Daigaku Seishin Bunka Kenkyujo Kiyo* (bulletin of the Culture Research Institute), *Nihon Daigaku*

Tsushinkyoikubu Kenkyu Kiyo (bulletin of the Correspondence Division of Nihon University), *Nihon Daigaku Yakugakubu Kenkyu Kiyo* (bulletin of the College of Pharmacy), *Nihon Hogaku* (law), *Nihon University Comparative Law*, *Rikogaku Kenkyu Shoho* (journal of the Institute of Science and Technology), *PRIAP Circular*, *Sou-Ka-Ken Nyusu* (URC news), *Seikei Kenkyu* (political science and economics), *Shogaku Kenkyu* (business and industry), *Nihon University Journal of Medicine*

DEANS

College of Art: Y. NODA (acting)
College of Bioresource Sciences: E. KOUNO
College of Commerce: I. KOSEKI
College of Economics: H. ONAGI
College of Engineering: K. IDEMURA
College of Humanities and Sciences: N. KATO
College of Industrial Technology: I. MATSUI
College of International Relations: S. SATO
College of Law: M. SUGIMOTO (acting)
College of Pharmacy: T. KUSAMA
College of Science and Technology: T. TAKIDO
Distance Learning Division: Y. FUKUDA
Junior College: K. OTSUKA
School of Dentistry: N. KOSHIKAWA
School of Dentistry at Matsudo: K. SHIBUTANI
School of Medicine: Y. KATAYAMA

NIPPON DENTAL UNIVERSITY

1-9-20 Fujimi, Chiyoda-ku, Tokyo 102-8159
Telephone: (3) 3261 8311
E-mail: web-master@tokyo.ndu.ac.jp
Internet: www.ndu.ac.jp

Founded 1907
Academic year: April to March

Pres.: SEN NAKAHARA
Deans: SEN NAKAHARA (Niigata Faculty), SHIGEO YOKODUKA (Tokyo Faculty)
Registrars: KENEI OHBA (Niigata), SHINICHI TAKIZAWA (Tokyo)
Librarians: KAN KOBAYASHI (Niigata Faculty), TAKEJI AYUKAWA (Tokyo Faculty)

Library of 96,822 vols (Tokyo Faculty), 89,217 vols (Niigata Faculty)
Number of teachers: 1,000
Number of students: 2,000

Publication: *Odontology* (6 a year)

PROFESSORS

Tokyo:

AIYAMA, S., Anatomy
AOBA, T., Pathology
FURUTA, Y., Anatomy
FURUYA, H., Anaesthesiology
ISHIKAWA, H., Orthodontics
KAMOI, K., Periodontology
KATSUUMI, I., Conservative Dentistry
KOBAYASHI, Y., Prosthodontics
MATSUMOTO, S., Physiology
NAKAHARA, S., Dentistry in Society
NIWA, M., Hygiene
OGIWARA, K., Paedodontics
SANADA, K., Biochemistry
SATO, T., Anatomy
SIRAKAWA, M., Oral Surgery
SUZUKI, T., Surgery
TANAKA, H., Conservative Dentistry
TSUTSUI, T., Pharmacology
UCHIDA, M., Oral and Maxillofacial Surgery
YOKOZUKA, S., Prosthodontics
YOSHIDA, T., Dental Materials Science
YOSIKAWA, M., Microbiology
YOSUE, T., Radiology

Niigata

1-8 Hamauracho, Niigata-shi, Niigata 951; tel. (25) 267-1500; fax (25) 267-1134

HASEGAWA, A., Periodontology
HATA, Y., Prosthodontics
HATATE, S., Prosthodontics
IGARASHI, F., Otorhinolaryngology
KAMEDA, A., Orthodontics
KANRI, T., Anaesthesiology
KATAGIRI, M., Oral Pathology
KATOH, Y., Conservative Dentistry
KAWASAKI, K., Conservative Dentistry
KIMURA, T., Dental Pharmacology
KOBAYASHI, K., Oral Anatomy
MATAGA, I., Oral Surgery
MATSUKI, H., Surgery
MORITA, O., Prosthodontics
MURAKAMI, T., Oral Physiology
NAKAHARA, S., Dentistry in Society
OGURA, H., Dental Materials Science
NISHIMURA, K., Oral Surgery
SAITO, K., Oral Microbiology
SHIBAZAKI, K., Internal Medicine
SHIMAMURA, H., Oral Biochemistry
SHIMOOKA, S., Paedodontics
SUETAKA, T., Oral Hygiene
TSUCHIKAWA, K., Oral Surgery
TSUCHIMOTO, M., Radiology

NIPPON SPORT SCIENCE UNIVERSITY

Tokyo Campus: 1-1 Fukasawa 7-chome, Setagaya-ku, Tokyo 158-8508
Telephone: (3) 5706-0900
Yokohama Campus: 1221-1 Kamoshida-cho, Aoba-ku, Yokohama, Kanagawa 227-0033
Telephone: (45) 963-7900
E-mail: international@nittai.ac.jp
Internet: www.nittai.ac.jp

Founded 1891, present status 1949
Private control
Language of instruction: Japanese
Academic year: April to March (2 semesters)

Pres.: Prof. Dr RYOSHO TANIGAMA
Vice-Pres. for Academic and Student Affairs: Prof. DAIZO HAKAMADA
Vice-Pres. for Management and Planning: Prof. SHIGEAKI ABE
Exec. Dir, Admin. Office: MASAHIRO FUJINO

Library of 435,000 vols, 6,367 periodicals
Number of teachers: 130
Number of students: 6,000

DEANS

Faculty of Medical Science: KENJI HIRANUMA
Faculty of Sport Science: KOJI GUSHIKEN
Graduate School of Health and Sport Science: Prof. Dr NAOTO KIMURA
School of Childhood Sport Education: TAKESHI KUBO
Women's Junior College of NSSU: KUMIKO TOKIMOTO

PROFESSORS

ABE, S., Physical Education (Graduate School)
AKIYAMA, A., Cultural Education (Graduate School)
ARAKI, T., Physical Education
ENDA, Y., Physical Education
FUJIMOTO, H., Physical Education
FUJITA, S., Cultural Education
FUJIWARA, S., Physical Education
FUNATO, K., Physical Education (Graduate School)
GUSHIKEN, K., Physical Education
HAKAMADA, D., Martial Arts
HIRANUMA, K., Health Science (Graduate School)
HONMA, K., Cultural Education
HOSOKAWA, S., Early Child Education
IGAWA, S., Health Science (Graduate School)
IRIE, K., Health Science (Graduate School)
ITO, N., Physical Education (Graduate School)
ITO, T., Health Science (Graduate School)
IWASA, K., Physical Education
KENMOTSU, E., Lifelong Sports and Recreation (Graduate School)
KIBAMOTO, H., Physical Education
KIMURA, N., Health Science (Graduate School)
KIYOTA, H., Health Science (Graduate School)
KOBAYAKAWA, Y., Health Science
KOIZUMI, N., Lifelong Sports and Recreation
KUBO, T., Physical Education
KURODA, M., Cultural Education
KUSUMOTO, Y., Cultural Education (Graduate School)
MATSUI, K., Physical Education (Graduate School)
MATSUMOTO, S., Physical Education (Graduate School)
MIYAKE, K., Martial Arts (Graduate School)
MORISHIMA, A., Cultural Education
MORITA, J., Physical Education
MURAKAMI, O., Physical Education (Graduate School)
MURAMOTO, K., Physical Education
NARITA, K., Cultural Education
NISHIDA, T., Physical Education
NISHIO, S., Lifelong Sports and Recreation (Graduate School)
OCHIAI, T., Cultural Education
ODE, K., Lifelong Sports and Recreation (Graduate School)
OGAWA, K., Physical Education
OKADA, A., Cultural Education
OKUIZUMI, K., Early Childhood Education
ONO, M., Health Science
OSAFUNE, T., Cultural Education
OSAKABE, H., Cultural Education
OUCI, T., Physical Education
SAIJO, O., Physical Education (Graduate School)
SAKAI, H., Early Childhood Education
SAKURAI, T., Health Science (Graduate School)
SEKIGUCHI, O., Physical Education
SEKINE, Y., Physical Education
SHIMZU, Y, Physical Education
SUGAWARA, I., Physical Education
TAKADA, R., Physical Education
TAKAHASHI, K., Health Science (Graduate School)
TAKAHASHI, T., Physical Education (Graduate School)
TAKIZAWA, K., Physical Education (Graduate School)
TANIGMA, R., Martial Arts
TOKIMOTO, K., Early Childhood Education
UEDA, Y., Lifelong Sports and Recreation
UENO, J., Health Science (Graduate School)
WATANABE, I., Physical Education
YAMADA, T., Health Science (Graduate School)
YAMAMOTO, I., Health Science
YASUHIRO, Y., Physical Education

OBIRIN UNIVERSITY

3758 Tokiwa-machi, Machida-shi, Tokyo 194-0294
Telephone: (42) 797-5419
E-mail: cis@obirin.ac.jp
Internet: www.obirin.ac.jp

Founded 1966

Colleges of business and public administration, economics, humanities, int. studies

Pres.: TOYOSHI SATOW
Number of students: 7,000

OSAKA MEDICAL COLLEGE

2–7 Daigakumachi, Takatsuki City, Osaka 569-8686
Telephone: (72) 683-1221
E-mail: hp-info@poh.osaka-med.ac.jp
Internet: www.osaka-med.ac.jp

Founded 1927
Private control

Language of instruction: Japanese
Academic year: April to March
Chair.: TADAHIRO TANAKA
Pres.: MASAHISA SHIMADA
Sec.-Gen: (vacant)
Librarian: AKIRA SHIMIZU
Library of 221,160 vols
Number of teachers: 362
Number of students: 601
Publications: *Journal* (in Japanese, 1 a year), *Bulletin* (in English, 1 a year)

OSAKA SANGYO UNIVERSITY

3-1-1 Nakagaito, Daito-shi, Osaka 574-8530
Telephone: (72) 875-3001
Internet: www.osaka-sandai.ac.jp
Founded 1965
Faculties of business management, economics, engineering, human environment; college of general education; Graduate School
Chair. of the Board of Trustees: SHIMEJI FURUTANI
Pres.: JUNICHIRO SEJIMA
Number of teachers: 250
Number of students: 15,634

OTEMON GAKUIN UNIVERSITY

1-15 Nishiai 2-chome, Ibaraki, Osaka 567-8502
Telephone: (72) 641-9631
E-mail: kokusai@jimu.otemon.ac.jp
Internet: www.otemon.ac.jp
Founded 1966
Faculties of economics, int. liberal arts, management, psychology, sociology
Pres.: TAKASHI SUZUKI
Library of 450,000 vols

RIKKYO UNIVERSITY (St Paul's University)

3-34-1 Nishi-Ikebukuro, Toshima-ku, Tokyo 171-8501
Telephone: 3985-2204
E-mail: cis@grp.rikkyo.ne.jp
Internet: www.rikkyo.ne.jp
Founded 1874
Private control
Academic year: April to March
Chancellor: Rev. TOSHIHIKO HAYAMI
President: TERUO OSHIMI
Registrar: Prof. Y. HIKITA
Librarian: Prof. H. SENGOKU
Library of 1,540,558 vols
Number of teachers: 1,110
Number of students: 15,000
Publications: *Rikkyo* (4 a year), *Rikkyo Daigaku Toshokan Dayori* (library news), *Rikkyo Daigaku Shokuin Kiyo* (administrative staff research proceedings, 1 a year), *Kiristokyo Kyoiku Kenkyu* (Studies in Christian Education), *Rikkyo University Bulletin* (every 2 years), *Rikkyo Koho* (Rikkyo news bulletin, 6 a year), and numerous faculty journals

DEANS

Faculty of Arts: H. MAEDA
Faculty of Community and Human Services: M. SEKI
Faculty of Economics: N. OIKAWA
Faculty of General Curriculum Development: Y. SHOJI
Faculty of Law and Politics: T. AWAJI
Faculty of Science: T. MOTOBAYASHI
Faculty of Social Relations: N. SHIRAISHI
Faculty of Tourism: N. OKAMOTO

RISSHO UNIVERSITY

4-2-16 Osaki, Shinagawa-ku, Tokyo 141
Telephone: (3) 3492-5262
E-mail: kint@ris.ac.jp
Internet: www.ris.ac.jp
Founded 1872
Private control
Language of instruction: Japanese
Academic year: April to March
Chancellor: N. TANAKA
President: H. SAKAZUME
Vice-President: Z. KITAGAWA
Registrar: (vacant)
Chief Librarians: H. FUJITA (Osaki), Y. IKOMA (Kumagaya)
Number of teachers: 700 (217 full-time, 483 part-time)
Number of students: 11,900
Publications: *Bulletin* (1 a year), *Journal of Buddhist Studies*, *Journal of Nichiren Buddhism* (1 a year), *Quarterly Report of Economics*

DEANS

Faculty of Buddhist Studies: K. MITOMO
Faculty of Business and Management: Y. KATO
Faculty of Economics: K. FUKUOKA
Faculty of Geo-Environmental Science: Y. YOSHIDA
Faculty of Law: S. IWAI
Faculty of Letters: S. TEGAWA
Faculty of Social Welfare: T. HOSHINO
Graduate School (Business Administration): T. OKUMURA
Graduate School (Economics): K. FUKUOKA
Graduate School (Law): T. SUZUKI
Graduate School (Literature): Y. TAKAGI

RITSUMEIKAN UNIVERSITY

56-1 Tojiin Kitamachi, Kita-ku, Kyoto 525-8577
Telephone: (75) 465-1111
E-mail: kokusai@st.ritsumei.ac.jp
Internet: www.ritsumei.ac.jp
Founded 1900
Private control
Academic year: April to March
Pres.: TOYO OMI NAGATA
Vice-Pres.: SADAO KAWAMURA
Vice-Pres.: KIMIO YAKUSHIJI
Dean for Academic Affairs: MITSURU SATO
Dean for Graduate Affairs: YOSHINOBU KUSAKABE
Dean for Research Affairs: MAKOTO SATO
Dean for Student Affairs: KATSUO NAKAGAWA
Dean for Library: YOSHIHIRO TANIGUCHI
Library of 2,532,945 vols
Number of teachers: 1,312 full-time
Number of students: 35,604 full-time
Publications: *Art Research*, *Core Ethics*, *Journal of Human Science*, *Journal of Ritsumeikan Geographical Society*, *Memoirs of Research Institute of Humanities and Social Science*, *Memoirs of the Institute of Humanities, Human and Social Science*, *Memoirs of the SR Center*, *Ritsumeikan University*, *Proceedings of the Philosophical Society of Ritsumeikan University*, *Ritsumeikan Annual Review of International Studies* (in English), *Ritsumeikan Bungaku*, *Ritsumeikan Business Review*, *Ritsumeikan Economic Review*, *Ritsumeikan Eibei Bungaku*, *Ritsumeikan Gakurin*, *Ritsumeikan International Affairs*, *Ritsumeikan Journal of International Relations and Area Studies*, *Ristumeikan Journal of International Studies*, *Ritsumeikan Law Review*, *Ritsumeikan Ronkyu Nihon Bungaku*, *Ritsumeikan Shigaku*, *Ritsumeikan Torena Haiho*, *Ritsumeikan Toyoshigaku*, *Ritsumeikan Sangyo Shyakaironsyu*, *Ritsumeikan Seisaku Kagaku*, *Social Systems Studies*, *Studies in Language and Culture*

DEANS

College and Graduate School of Business Administration: TERUYOSHI TANAKA
College and Graduate School of International Relations: HIROFUMI OGI
College and Graduate School of Policy Science: KIYOFUMI KAWAGUCHI
College and Graduate School of Science and Engineering: HIDEYUKI TAKAKURA
College and Graduate School of Social Sciences: KUNIHIRO TOSHIFUMI
College of Economics: JUNICHI HIRATA
College of Information Science and Engineering: TAKEO IIDA
College of Law: RYOICHI YOSHIMURA
College of Letters: KAZUAKI KIMURA
Graduate School for Core Ethics and Frontier Sciences: KOZO WATANABE
Graduate School of Economics: SHUJI MATSUKAWA
Graduate School of Language Education and Information Science: JUNSAKU NAKAMURA
Graduate School of Science for Human Services: CHUICHIRO TAKAGAKI
Graduate School of Law: SHIRO AKAZAWA
Graduate School of Letters: HIROHIDE TAKEYAMA
Law School: MASATO ICHIKAWA

PROFESSORS

College and Graduate School of Business Administration:

ANDO, T., Technology Transfer
BAILEY, A., English
CHIYODA, K., Accounting
DOI, Y., Transportation
ENNO, B., Corporate Culture and Governance
FUJITA, T., Business Accounting
HARA, Y., International Corporations
HASHIMOTO, T., Business Administration History
HATTORI, Y., Modern Financial Markets
HIRAI, T., Environmental Accounting Theory
HYOUDO, T., Contemporary Science and Technology
IDA, T., English
IKEDA, S., Cultural Studies, Total Quality Management
IMADA, O., Production Management
ITO, T., Politics and Literature in the Weimar Republic
IWATA, N., Japanese Language Education and Linguistics
KINOSHITA, A., Distribution Procedures
KOEZUKA, H., Product Planning, Marketing Channels
KOKUBO, M., Industrial and Social Psychology
KOSAKA, K., Communicative and Cognitive Mechanisms
MATSUI, T., Medium Enterprises
MATSUMURA, K., Business Financial Management
MIURA, I., Japanese Retail Business
MIURA, M., Health Science
MIYOSAWA, T., Managerial Accounting
MUKAI, J., International Finance
MURAYAMA, T., International Investment
NAGASHIMA, O., Japanese Economy
NAKAMURA, M., Multinationals
NAKANISHI, I., Industrial Economics, Comparative Economic Studies
NAKATA, M., General Business Administration
NAMIE, I., Labour Problems
OKAMOTO, N., Physical Fitness
OKUMURA, Y., Business Strategies
SAITO, M., Business Administration

SASABE, A., History of Science and Engineering
SATO, N., Design Management
SCHLUNZE, R. D., International Management, Economic Geography
SHIOMI, K., Cross-cultural Communication
SUZUKI, Y., French
TAKEDA, M., Management Organization and Information Systems
TAKI, H., Corporations and Accounting
TAMAMURA, H., Privatization
TANAKA, A., Asian Enterprises
TANAKA, T., History of Business Thought
TANAKA, T., Statistics
TANEDA, Y., Managerial Accounting
WATANABE, T., Business Management
YAMAZAKI, S., Spanish
YAMAZAKI, T., Business Administration
YANAGASE, K., Public Finance, Public Economics, Development Policy
YOSHIDA, K., Mathematical Programming

College and Graduate School of Economics:
AGATSUMA, N., Economic Policy
ASADA, K., Public Finance, Money and Banking
FUJIOKA, A., Economic Analysis of Nuclear-based Military Expansion
FURUKAWA, A., Economic Policy
HAMADA, S., Corporate Law
HATANAKA, T., Early Modern Japanese History
HIRATA, J., Economic Statistics
INABA, K., Economic Statistics
IWATA, K., International Economics
IZAWA, H., Economic Theory
KAJIYAMA, N., Currency Exchange System and Economic Development
KAKIHARA, H., Economic Policy, Medicine
KAKUTA, S., Economic Theory
KANEMARU, Y., East Asian Economic History and Modern Chinese History
KASAI, T., International Economic Cooperation
MATSUBARA, T., Agricultural Economics
MATSUI, S., Political Economy, Economic Philosophy
MATSUKAWA, S., General Theory of Economics
MATSUMOTO, A., Political, Financial and Monetary Economics
MATSUNO, S., East Asian Economic Relations
NISHIGUCHI, K., Economic Theory of Developing Nations
NOZAWA, T., Phonology, Psycholinguistics
OHKAWA, M., Economic Theory, International Economics
OHKAWA, T., Industrial Organization
OKAO, K., History of Modern Sports
SAITO, T., Modern Chinese Literature
SAKAMOTO, K., Economic Policy
SATO, T., Social Policy
SATOU, Y., Sport Psychology
SHIMADA, Y., Area Environmental Systems
SHIMIZU, Y., Educational Technology, Intercultural Communication
TAKAGI, A., Contemporary Capitalism
TANAKA, H., Russian and Eastern European Economic Studies
TANAKA, Y., International Economics
TANIGAKI, K., International Trade Theory
TOMATSURI, T., Tourism
TSUJII, E., English
UCHIYAMA, A., Public Finance
WAKABAYASHI, H., Comparative Research of Policy Theories, Regional Policy
YAMADA, H., Econometrics
YAMAI, T., German Economics
YAMAMOTO, S., Actuarial Economics, Insurance, US–Japanese Comparative Economics and Portfolio Theory
YOKOYAMA, M., International Economics
YOSHIDA, C., International Economics
ZHENG, X., Urban and Regional Economics

College and Graduate School of Law:
AKAZAWA, S., Politics, History
ARAKAWA, S., Civil Law, Sociology of Law
DEGUCHI, M., Civil Procedure Law
HANATATE, F., Civil Law
HIRANO, H., Basic Science of Law
HISAOKA, Y., Criminal Law, Criminal Procedure Law
HONDA, M., German Criminal Law
HORI, M., Politics
IKUTA, K., Criminal Law, Criminal Procedure Law
ISHIHARA, H., English Literature
KATSUI, H., Civil Law
KOBORI, M., Modern British Politics
KOYAMA, Y., Civil Law
KURATA, M., Human Rights Theory, Constitutional Law
KUZUNO, H., Criminal Justice and Juvenile Justice
MIKI, Y., Taxation Law
MIYAI, M., International Economic Law
MIZUGUCHI, N., Public Administration, Regional Autonomy
MOTOYAMA, A., Family Law
MURAKAMI, H., Political Science
NAKAJIMA, S., Public Law
NAKAMURA, Y., French Modern Legal History, French Criminal Procedure
NAKATANI, Y., Politics
NISHIMURA, M., International Politics
NOGUCHI, M., English
OHGAKI, H., Financial Law
OHIRA, Y., Japanese Legal History
OKAWA, S., Civil Law
SATO, K., Social Law
SO, S., East Asian Law and Human Rights
SUTO, Y., Proportional Doctrines
TAKEHAMA, O., Insurance
TAKEHARU, S., German, German Literature
TANIMOTO, K., German Language and Literature
TOKUGAWA, S., Civil Law
UNOKI, Y., Chinese Language and Literature
YAKUSHIJI, K., International Law
YAMAMOTO, T., Social Security Law
YASUMOTO, N., Public Administrative Law
YOSHIDA, M., Labour Law
YOSHIMURA, R., Law of Damage
YOSHIOKA, K., Literary Theory

College and Graduate School of Letters:
AKAMA, R., Modern Drama, Literature and Ukiyoe
ASAO, K., Applied Linguistics
EGUCHI, N., Caribbean Studies
FOX, C. E., Modern Japanese Verse
FUJI, K., Experimental Analysis of Behaviour
FUJIMAKI, M., Human Geography, Urban Social Geography
HATTORI, K., Philosophy of Nature and Social Philosophy
HAYASHI, N., Study of True Human Education
HIEDA, Y., Comparative Literature
HIGASHIYAMA, A., Psychology of Sensation and Perception, Geometry of Visual Space
HIKOSAKA, Y., History of Japanese Dialects
HONDA, O., History of Agricultural Development
HONGO, M., National Law of Ancient Japan, Royal Authority and Religion
HOSHINO, Y., Human Memory and Learning, Cognitive Processes
HOSOI, K., Personality
IKEDA, Y., Modern Philosophy
IKUTA, M., Comparative Study of Large Asian Cities
ISE, T., Philosophy
ISHII, F., German Literature in the Pre-March Revolution Period
KASUGAI, T., Clinical Education
KATAHIRA, H., Land Use in the Semi-arid Regions of Australia, Landscape Reproduction
KATSURAJIMA, N., Japanese Early Modern History, Tokugawa Intellectual History
KAWAGUCHI, Y., The English Novel: Forster, Austen, Golding
KAWASHIMA, K., Study of Artisan Guilds and the Rural Traditional Handicraft Industry
KAWASHIMA, M., Life and Culture in Late Medieval Japan
KIDACHI, M., Archaeology
KIMURA, K., Modern Japanese Literature
KITAMURA, M., Political and Cultural Development in the Republic of China
KITANO, K., Film Studies
KITAO, H., Ethics and Philosophy
KO, J. Y., Korean Archaeology
KOBAYASHI, K., Poetry and Painting of William Blake
KUSAKABE, Y., Greek Philosophy, History of Ontology
MACLEAN, R., English and American Literature since the 18th Century
MARUYAMA, M., 20th-Century American Literature
MASHIMO, A., Ancient Japanese Literature, Manyoshu and Oral Literature
MATSUDA, K., English Romantic Poets of the 18th and 19th Centuries
MATSUDA, T., Perception and Cognition
MATSUMOTO, H., Late 19th- to Early 20th-Century Politics
MATSUMOTO, Y., Medieval Chinese History, Political System of the Tang Dynasty
MOCHIZUKI, A., Applied Behaviour Analysis, Behavioural Human Serviceology
MUKAI, T., Hegelian Philosophy, Culture and Ideology
MURASHIMA, Y., Educational Philosophy, Moral Education
NAGATA, T., Modern and Contemporary American History
NAKAGAWA, S., Modern Japanese Literature
NAKAGAWA, Y., American Literature, Women's Studies
NAKAGAWA, Y., Holistic Education, Women's Studies
NAKANISHI, K., Heian Literature
ODA, M., Cognitive Science, Concept and Imagery
ODAUCHI, T., Religious Movements and Heresy in Medieval Europe
OHTO, C., Greek and Hellenistic History
OKADA, H., Contemporary Chinese Literature
OUJI, T., Area Studies
OZEKI, M., Political Thought and History in Modern Japan, Cultural Theory
PEATY, D., English Language Education
SAITO, T., Research on Altered States of Consciousness
SANO, M., Generative-grammatical Analyses of Japanese and English
SATO, T., Educational and Social Psychology, Experimental Psychology
SHIMA, H., Studies in Tang Dynasty Thought
SHIMIZU, Y., Medieval Chinese Literature and Criticism
SHIMOKAWA, S., Life and Works of Stendhal
SUGIHASHI, T., History of the Warrior Government Formation
TADAI, T., Evidence-based Clinical Psychology and Psychiatry
TAKAGI, K., Developmental Psychology
TAKAHASHI, H., Contemporary German History
TAKAHASHI, M., Natural Environmental Changes and Relationship to Human Lifestyles
TAKASHIMA, K., 19th-Century American Literature

TAKEYAMA, H., Italian Literature, Ethnography and Comparative Culture
TAKIMOTO, K., Modern Japanese Literature, Mori Ogai
TANI, T., Phenomenology and Contemporary Philosophy
TOBINO, K., Philosophical Study in Education and Human Relations
TSUCHIDA, N., Developmental Psychology
TSUKAMA, Y., Linguistics, Phonetics, Foreign Language Education
UEDA, H., Meiji Japanese Literature
UEDA, T., History of Contemporary Western Art, Art Criticism
UENO, R., Classical Chinese Literature
WADA, S., Archaeological Research of the Yayoi and Kofun Peirods
WELLS, K., American Poetry, Folklore and Folksong, Comparative Culture
YAGI, Y., Psychology of Self; Personality and Social Psychology
YAMAMOTO, M., Psychotherapy and Psychoanalysis
YANO, K., Archaeology
YANO, K., Human Geography
YONEYAMA, H., American History, Japanese American History
YOSHIDA, H., Learning Psychology
YOSHIKOSHI, A., Human Impact on the Hydrological Environment
YOSHIMURA, H., Chinese Tang Dynasty Literature
YUKAWA, E., Applied Linguistics and Bilingualism

College and Graduate School of International Relations:

ANDO, T., Western Political History
ANZAI, I., International Peace Theory
ASAHI, M., Contemporary Global Economics
HARA, T., South American Anthropology
HOSHINO, K., European Economics, Monetary Integration
INOUE, J., Cultural Sociology
ITAKI, M., Social Science Methodology
KA, G., Japanese and Chinese Comparative Studies
KANEKO, H., Contemporary German Poetry
KATO, T., Black African-American Literature
KATSURA, R., Asian and International Social Welfare, Family Welfare and Policy
KIMIJIMA, A., Peace Studies, Constitutional Law
KIYOMOTO, O., Contemporary South-East Asian History
KOBAYASHI, M., Political Science
KOYAMA, M., International Relations
MATSUSHITA, K., Politics of Developing Countries
MINAMINO, Y., Comparative Politics, Political History, Irish Political History
MIYAKE, M., Linguistic Analysis
MUN, G. S., North-East Asian History
NAGASU, M., Japanese Development Assistance, International Cooperation
NAKAGAWA, R., Asian Economics
NAKAMURA, Y., French Thought and Literature, Contemporary Japanese Literature
NAKATSUJI, K., Modern Political History
ODAIRA, K., International Cooperation Law, Francophone and EU Studies
OGI, H., Asian Studies, Chinese Education and Literature
OIKAWA, M., Contemporary American Theatre
OKUDA, H., International Finance
OZORA, H., Mass Media
SATO, M., Comparative Sociology, African Politics
SHAWBACK, M., Foreign Languages, General Studies
TAKAHASHI, N., Japanese Economy
TAKEUCHI, T., Comparative Analysis of Family Structure
TATSUZAWA, K., International Law Relations, Islamic Law, Space Law
WAKANA, M., American Literature
WASSERMAN, M., Theatrical Arts of the West and Japan
YAMADA, H., Japanese Language
YAMAMOTO, S., American Drama

College and Graduate School of Policy Science:

HIRAO, H., Use of Computers in English Education
HONDA, Y., Econometrics
HOSOI, K., Modern Management Theory
JIDOU, Y., History of Industrial Technology
KAWAGUCHI, K., Citizen Participation, Cooperatives and NPOs
KISHIMOTO, T., International Politics and Economics
MIKAMI, T., Artificial Intelligence, Memory and Decision-Making
MIKAMI, T., Administrative Law, Planning Law
MURAYAMA, H., Political Attitude and Political Behaviour
OBATA, N., Environmental Policy
SATOH, M., Policy Formation
SHIGEMORI, T., Political Theory
SHIRAKAWA, I., Economic Policy, International Economics
TAKADA, S., Urban and Regional Planning
TAKAO, K., Environmental Policies, Development Economics
TONEGAWA, K., System Simulation and Management Problems
YAMAMOTO, R., Obligation, Medical Malpractice and Consumer Law
YAMANE, H., Post-war German Literature
YASUE, N., EU and Other International Organizations
ZHOU, W., Environmental Policy, Energy Systems Engineering

College and Graduate School of Science and Engineering:

ABE, A., Technology Management
AKISHITA, S., Active Noise Control in Machinery, Robotics
AMANO, K., Environmental Systems Analysis
AMASAKI, S., Concrete Engineering
AMEYAMA, K., Physical Metallurgy, Microstructure Control, Electron Microscopy
AOYAMA, A., Life-Cycle Engineering
ARAI, M., Spectral Theory of Differential Operators
ARAKI, Y., Educational Technology
ARASE, M., Linguistics, English, Japanese, Substance-Dependence Research
ARIMOTO, S., Robotics, Mechatronics, Machine Intelligence
CHEN, E., Image-Processing, Radioactive Rays Image Measurement, Soft Computing
EGASHIRA, S., Solid Particle and Water Tow Phase Flows, Watercourse and Riverbed Variations
ENDO, A., Community Structure of Terrestrial Invertebrate Animals
FUJIEDA, I., Graphic Information Machinery
FUJIMURA, S., Riemannian Geometry
FUJINO, T., Electrical Engineering
FUKAGAWA, R., Geomechanics, Geomechatronics
FUKUI, M., System LSIs
FUKUMOTO, T., Soil Mechanics and Geotechnical Engineering
FUKUYAMA, T., Elementary Particles, High Energy Astrophysics
HARUNA, M., Urban and Regional Planning Systems
HAYAKAWA, K., Traffic-induced Ground Vibration Propagation and Reduction Measures
HIRAI, S., Robotic Manipulation
IIDA, T., Ergonomics
IKEDA, K., Nonlinear Physical Phenomena
IMAI, S., Atomic Layer CVD and Fabrication of Single Electron Devices
IMAMURA, N., Chemistry of Bio-active Compounds produced by Micro-organisms
ISAKA, T., Sports Biomechanics, Analysis of Human Movement
ISHII, A., Robot Vision, Sensors and Image Analysis
ISHII, H., Number Theory of Automorphic Forms
ISONO, Y., Computational Material Science
ITO, M., Strength and Design of Steel Structures
IWASHIMIZU, Y., Solid Mechanics, Ultrasonic Materials Evaluation
IZUNO, K., Earthquake Resistant Design of Structures
KAITO, C., Quantum Dots Formation
KASAHARA, K., Optical Communication Devices
KATO, M., Physical Chemistry
KAWABATA, T., Power Electronics
KAWAGUCHI, A., Preparation of Functional Polymer Materials Using Epitaxies, and Study of their Properties
KAWAMURA, S., Robotics
KIDO, Y., Investigation of Surface and Interface Structures
KIMATA, M., Engineering
KITAZAWA, T., Numerical Analysis of Electromagnetic Wave Problems
KOBAYASHI, H., Wind-tunnel Experiments and Analyses of Long Bridges Subject to Wind Load
KOJIMA, K., Material and Inorganic Chemistry, Optical Materials
KOJIMA, T., FEM Analysis of Hybrid Concrete Structures Using Discrete Elements
KOMATSU, Y., Online Parameter Estimations of the Induction Machine Utilizing Extension Slip Method
KONDO, K., Synthesis of Functional Polymers
KONISHI, S., Micronanomechatronics and Micromachines, Systems Engineering, Electronic Devices
KOYANAGI, S., Parallel Computation, Database Computer Engineering, Data Mining
KUBO, M., Applied Microbiology
KURATSUJI, H., Quantum Phenomenology
KUSAKA, T., Fracture Mechanics
MAEDA, H., Robot Intelligence for Action and Tasks
MAKIKAWA, M., Biomedical Engineering, Application of Human Motion for Engineering
MATSUDA, T., Separation Analysis, Electroanalysis, Environmental Analysis Chemistry
MATSUOKA, M., Nickel-hydride Batteries, Solar Cells Electrocatalysis, Titanium Dioxide Photocatalysis
MIKI, H., Semiconductor Materials, Solid-state Devices
MIYANO, T., Complex Systems Science, Artificial Intelligence
MIZOSHIRI, I., Medical Electronics and Biological Engineering
MORIMOTO, A., Ultrafast Photonics, Ultrafast Laser Technology, and Terahertz Optoelectronics
MORISAKI, H., Analysis of the Surface Characteristics of Microbial Cells, and the Interaction between Micro-organisms and Interfaces
MURAHASHI, M., Regional and Urban Structure Analyses and Development Techniques
NAKADA, T., Surface Properties

NAKAJIMA, H., Theoretical Analysis of the Interaction Structures of Multi-component Systems
NAKAJIMA, J., Waste Water Treatment Systems, Nitrogen and Phosphorus Removal
NAKAJIMA, K., Homogeneous Kähler Manifolds
NAKAMURA, N., Structure and Physical Properties of Normal Long Chain Compounds, Ionomers and Liquid Crystals
NAKANISHI, T., Measurement and Estimation of Automobile Traffic Flow
NAKAYA, Y., Human Interface, Artificial Intelligence, Recognition Engineering
NAMBA, H., Surfaces as New Materials, Surface Chemical Dynamics
NANISHI, Y., Semiconductor Optoelectronic Devices, Physical Properties of Quantum Structures, Plasma-excited Semiconductor Processes
NARUKI, I., Analysis and Geometry of Complex Manifolds
NISHIO, S., Surface Science
NISHIWAKI, K., Gas Flow, Turbulence, Heat Transfer and Combustion in Combustion Chambers
NUMAI, T., Optical Electronics
OGAMI, Y., Fluid Dynamics
OGASAWARA, H., Geophysics
OGAWA, H., Intelligence Information Science
OGAWA, S., Analysis of Moduli Spaces
OGURA, T., Si System Architecture
OIKAWA, K., Architectural and Urban Space Planning, Environmental Design
OKADA, M., Magnetic and Dielectric Materials, Semiconductor Lasers
ONO, B., Cellular and Molecular Study of the Biological Functions of the Budding Yeast
ONO, Y., Optical Periodic Microstructure
OSAKA, H., Operator Algebras
OZUTSUMI, K., Structural and Thermodynamic Studies of Metal Complexes in Solution
SAITO, S., Optical Communications
SAKAI, J., Optical Fibre Communications and Optical Information Processing
SAKAI, T., Statistical Research on Reliability Engineering
SAKANE, M., Strength Evaluation of Heat-resistant Materials at High Temperatures
SATOMI, J., Basic Physiological and Biochemical Study of Sports Training
SAWAMURA, S., High-pressure Physical Chemistry of Solutions
SHIMAKAWA, H., Social Systems, Computer Software, Information Systems
SHINODA, H., Environmental Studies
SHINYA, H., Functional Analysis
SHIRAISHI, H., Electro-analytical Chemistry
SUGIMOTO, S., Systems and Control Engineering
SUGINO, N., Teaching English as a Foreign Language
SUGIYAMA, S., Microsystem Technology
SUZUKI, K., MEMS for Information and Telecommunication
SUZUKI, K., Pharmaceutical Development, Molecular Biology
TACHIKI, T., Physiology, Biochemistry and the Breeding of Useful Micro-organisms
TAKAKURA, H., High-efficiency Solar Cell Research
TAKANO, N., Computational Mathematics
TAKAYAMA, S., Advanced Sensing Systems and Measurement Science
TAKAYAMA, Y., Computative Algebra
TAKENAKA, A., Properties of Elementary Particles and their Interactions
TAMAKI, J., Design of Functional Interface between Inorganic Materials for Gas-sensing Devices
TAMIAKI, H., Bio-organic Chemistry
TAMURA, H., Information Engineering, Virtual Reality
TANAKA, H., Computer Vision, Visual Communication, Intelligent Information Systems
TANAKA, K., Micro-electric Machine Systems
TANAKA, S., Computer Graphics Systems
TANAKA, T., Precision Processing
TANIGUCHI, Y., High-pressure Physical Chemistry of Liquids, Solutions and Biological Materials
TANIKAGA, R., Organic Synthesis Using Biocatalysts and Organic Sulphurous Reagents
TATEYAMA, K., Construction Engineering
TERAI, H., Research into Computer and LSI Design Automation Systems
THAWONMAS, R., Artificial Intelligence, Entertainment Computing
TOKI, K., Earthquake Engineering, Natural Disaster Science
TORIYAMA, T., Optical Applied Measurements
TSUDAGAWA, M., Analysis and Application of Space Filters
TSUKAGUCHI, H., Transport System Planning and Management
UKITA, H., Optomechatronics
WAKAYAMA, M., Food and Nutrition
WAKAYAMA, M., Food and Nutrition, Micro-organisms
WATANABE, T., Control Engineering
XU, G., Pattern Recognition, Computer Science, Robotics
YAMADA, H., Development of Free-electron Laser
YAMADA, K., Water Demand Analyses and Predictions
YAMADA, O., Mathematical Analysis
YAMADA, T., Probability and Statistics
YAMADA, T., Telecommunication
YAMAMOTO, N., Biomechanics and Function of Living Systems
YAMASAKI, M., Urban Landscape Planning
YAMAUCHI, H., System VLSI Architecture and Implementation
YAMAZAKI, K., Parallel Computing, Computer Graphics, Case-based Reasoning
YOSHIDA, M., Ecology, Ethology
YOSHIHARA, Y., Formation Mechanisms of Harmful Combustion Products and Methods for their Reduction
YOSHIMURA, Y., Structural Phase Transition in Alkali Metal Cyanide

College and Graduate School of Social Sciences:

AKAI, S., Sociology
ARAKI, H., Human Development
ARUGA, I., Turn-Verein
FUKASAWA, A., French Labour and Social History
HIGASHI, J., Critical Applied Linguistics, Sociology of Education
HOGETSU, M., Sociology of Deviance and Sociological Theories
IIDA, T., Sociology
IKEUCHI, Y., American Playwrights
IKUTA, M., Welfare and Information Technology
INUI, K., Social Planning
ISHIKURA, Y., Welfare Sociology, Child and Clinical Psychiatry
JINBO, T., Alternative Media, Media Ethics and Journalism
KANAI, J., Sports Sociology
KIDA, A., Japanese Sociology
KOIZUMI, H., Advertising
KUNIHIRO, T., Political Sociology
KUSAFUKA, N., Physical Education
KUTSUNAI, K., French Literature
LIM, B., Urban Planning
MAEDA, N., Welfare Sociology and Comparative Research in Welfare
MATSUBA, M., German Capitalism
MATSUDA, H., History of Modern Social Thought
MINESHIMA, A., Welfare of the Disabled
MIYASHITA, S., History of Science and Technology
MONDEN, K., History of Science and Technology
MORINISHI, M., History of the Performing Arts
NAGASAWA, K., General Theory of Economics, Economical Statistics
NAKAFUMI, S., Chinese Language and Study of the Tale of the Heike
NAKAGAWA, K., Sociology
NAKAMA, Y., Art History
NAKAMURA, T., Cultural Anthropology
NODA, M., Judicial Welfare
OGAWA, E., Elderly Home Care
OKADA, M., Health Education and Social Work
OKUGAWA, O., Cross-cultural Communication
OZAWA, W., Cross-cultural Communication
SAKAMOTO, T., Sociology
SAKATA, K., Local Media Theory, Broadcast Media Theory
SAKURADANI, M., Sociology
SASAKI, K., Cultural Anthropology
SATO, Y., Sociology, Philosophy
SATOU, H., Sociology, Social Security
SHIBATA, H., Social Security
SHINODA, T., Theory of Political Economy
SUDO, Y., Modern Capitalism
SUZUKI, M., Social Consciousness
TAKAGAKI, C., Mass Communication
TAKAGI, M., Clinical Psychology
TAKAHASHI, M., Sociology
TAKEHAMA, A., Consumer Behaviour
TSUDA, M., Public Access
TSUDOME, M., Social Welfare
TSUJI, K., Disaster Behaviour
WADA, T., Labour Sociology
WEN, C., the Tale of the Heike, Chinese Language
YAMAMOTO, T., Welfare Budget and Administration
YAMASHITA, T., Leisure and Sports Sociology
YANAGISAWA, S., Sociology
YOSHIDA, M., Psycholinguistics

College of Information Science and Engineering:

ASANO, S., Bioscience and Bio-informatics
CHEN, Y. W., Media Technology
ENDO, H., Computer Science
FUJITA, N., Bioscience and Bio-informatics
FUKUMOTO, J., Natural Language Processing
FUSAOKA, A., Human and Computer Intelligence
HACHIMURA, K., Media Technology
HAGIWARA, H., Human and Computer Intelligence
HATTORI, F., Information and Communication Science
HAYANO, T., Proteomics, Molecular Biology, Biochemistry
HAYASHI, T., Media Technology
HIGUCHI, N., Media Technology
IIDA, T., Human and Computer Intelligence
IKEDA, H., Computer Science
INOUE, Y., Information Systems Engineering
KAMEI, K., Human and Computer Intelligence
KAWAI, M., Wireless and Network Systems
KAWAGOE, K., Information and Communication Science
KIKUCHI, M., Bioscience and Bio-informatics
KIKUCHI, T., Bioscience and Bio-informatics
KISHIMOTO, R., Information and Communication Science

KITAMOTO, S., Computer-Generated Animation
KOTSUKI, S., Genetic Informatics
KUNIEDA, Y., Computer Science
KUWABARA, K., Knowledge Processing, Communication Science
MAEDA, T., Electromagnetic Waves and Data Transmission
NAGANO, S., Systems Biology
NAKATANI, Y., Information and Communication Science
NISHIKAWA, I., Human and Computer Intelligence
NISHIO, N., Computer Science
NOZAWA, K., Educational Technology, Inter-cultural Communication
OGAWA, E., Knowledge Engineering
OHNISHI, A., Operating Systems
OKUBO, E., Computer Science
OSHIMA, T., Artificial Reality
OYANAGI, S., Computer Science
RINALDO, F. J., Artificial Intelligence, Expert Systems and Knowledge Information Processing
SHIMAKAWA, H., Computer Science
SHINODA, H., Human and Computer Intelligence
SHIRAI, Y., Robot Intelligence
SUGINO, N., Teaching English as a Foreign Language
SUZUKI, K., Bioscience and Bio-informatics
TAMURA, H., Media Technology
TANAKA, H., Human and Computer Intelligence
TANAKA, S., Media Technology
THAWONMAS, R., Intelligent Entertainment Computing
XU, G., Media Technology
YAMASHITA, Y., Media Technology
YOSHIKAWA, T., Mechatronics, Control Engineering and Robotics

Graduate School for Core Ethics and Frontier Sciences:

AKAMA, R., Japanese Literature
DUMOUCHEL, P., Economic Philosophy
ENDO, A., Symbiosis Theory
GOTO, R., Economic Philosophy
KAMBAYASHI, T., Aesthetics, Art
KOIZUMI, Y., Philosophy
MATSUBARA, Y., History of Science, Scientific Theory
NISHI, M., Comparative Literature
NISHIKAWA, N., French Language, Japanese History, European History
TATEIWA, S., Ethics
UEMURA, M., Television Gaming
WATANABE, K., Cultural Anthropology, African Studies, History of Anthropology

Graduate School of Sciences for Human Services:

AKIRA, H., Genetic Psychology
DAN, S., Family Medical Treatment Methods
FUJI, N., Clinical Psychology
HAYASHI, N., Education, Theory of Character Building
MOCHIZUKI, A., Experimental Action Analysis
MURAMOTO, K., Clinical Psychology, Trauma
NAKAGAWA, Y., Clinical Pedagogics
NAKAMURA, J., Intelligence Development, Life-Span Development, Counselling
NAKAMURA, T., Sociology, Social Welfare
NODA, M., Administration of Welfare Justice, Child Welfare
TADAI, T., Clinical Psychology, Psychiatry
TAKAGAKI, C., Clinical Psychology
TAKINO, I., Clinical Psychology
TOKUDA, K., Clinical Psychology

Graduate School of Language Education and Information Science:

AZUMA, S., Code-switching, Socio-linguistic Significance
LEE, N., Linguistics
KAWAMURA, K., English as a Foreign or Second Language
MATSUDA, K., English Literature
NAKAMURA, J., English Corpus Linguistics
NOZAWA, K., Teaching English as a Foreign Language
OHNO, Y., Japanese Pedagogics, Formal Language Studies
OKURA, M., Japanese Language Teaching Methodology
RATZLAFF, G., Second Language Pedagogy and Acquisition
SHIMIZU, Y., Teaching English as a Foreign Language
SUGIMORI, M., Applied Linguistics
TSUKUMA, Y., Linguistics, Phonetics
UMESAKI, A., English Education
YAMADA, H., Linguistics, Phonetics
YOSHIDA, S., Psychology Linguistics

Law School:

DANBAYASHI, K., Women and Law, Trial Procedure
FUJITA, M., Criminal Practice Law
HANATATE, F., Civil Law
HIRAI, T., Civil, Merchant and Medical Law
IBUSUKI, M., Legal Informatics, Criminal Procedure
ICHIKAWA, M., Constitutional Case Law
KATSUI, H., Civil Law
KITAMURA, K., Public Law
KOMATSU, Y., Bankruptcy Law, Consumer Law and Intellectual Property Law
KURONO, Y., Civil Law
MATSUI, Y., International Law
MATSUMIYA, T., Criminal Law
MATSUMOTO, K., Civil Liability, Limitation Act
MORISHITA, H., Criminal Law and Criminal Defence
NINOMIYA, S., Civil Law
OKAHARA, F., Civil Law
OKAMOTO, M., Real Estate Law
OKAWA, S., Civil Case Law, Criminal Case Law
OKUBO, S., Public Law
SAGAMI, Y., Civil Law
SAKAI, H., International Civil Procedure
SHINATANI, T., Corporate Law, Securities Regulation
TANAKA, T., Enterprise Law
UEDA, K., Criminology
WADA, S., Civil Law
WATANABE, S., International Private Law and Civil Procedure
YAMAGUCHI, K., Consumer Protection and International Trade
YAMAMOTO, T., International Conflict Management
YAMANA, T., Tax and Inheritance Tax Law
YASUMOTO, N., Administrative Law, Tax Law

RITSUMEIKAN ASIA PACIFIC UNIVERSITY

1-1 Jumonjibaru, Beppu-shi, Oita 874-8577
Telephone: (977) 78-1111
Internet: www.apu.ac.jp

Founded 2000
Private control
Languages of instruction: English, Japanese
Academic year: September to February

Pres.: Prof. SHUN KORENAGA
Vice-Pres.: Prof. MASAO HOMMA
Vice-Pres.: Prof. JUNICHI HIRATA
Vice-Pres.: Prof. SUSUMU YAMAGAMI
Vice-Pres.: Prof. A. MANI
Dean for Academic Affairs: Prof. JUNICHI HIRATA
Dean for Admissions: Prof. YUICHI KONDO
Dean for Student Affairs: Prof. CHAN HOE KIM

Library of 65,000 vols
Number of teachers: 120
Number of students: 6,040 (5,708 undergraduate, 254 postgraduate)
Publications: *Journal of Asia Pacific Studies* (3 a year), *Polyglossia* (2 a year)

DEANS

College of Asia Pacific Studies: JEREMY EADES
College of International Management: KENJI YOKOYAMA
Graduate School of Asia Pacific Studies: JEREMY EADES
Graduate School of International Management: KENJI YOKOYAMA

RYUKOKU UNIVERSITY

67 Tsukamoto-cho, Fukakusa, Fushimi-ku, Kyoto 612-8577
Telephone: (75) 642-1111
E-mail: ric@rnoc.fks.ryukoku.ac.jp
Internet: www.ryukoku.ac.jp

Founded 1639
Private control
Academic year: April to March

Chancellor: KOSHO FUJIKAWA
Pres.: DOSHO WAKAHARA
Vice-Pres: TAKESHI HORIKAWA
Vice-Pres: YOSHIO KAWAMURA
Sec.-Gen.: CHIKO IWAGAMI
Librarian: JITSUZO SHIGETA

Library: see under Libraries and Archives
Number of teachers: 501
Number of students: 19,830
Publications: *Ryukoku Law Review* (4 a year), *Journal of Economic Studies* (4 a year), *Journal of Ryukoku University* (2 a year), *Ryukoku Journal of Humanities and Sciences* (2 a year), *Journal of Intercultural Communication* (1 a year)

DEANS

Faculty of Business Administration: RINPACHI MISHIMA
Faculty of Economics: HIROKUNI TERADA
Faculty of Intercultural Communication: MASANORI HIGA
Faculty of Law: KEIJI NAGARA
Faculty of Letters: EGUN MIKOGAMI
Faculty of Science of Technology: YOUICHI KOBUCHI
Faculty of Sociology: KAZUNORI KOGA
Japanese Culture and Language Programme: ITSUYO HIGASHINAKA
Junior College: DOSHO WAKAHARA

PROFESSORS

Faculty of Business Administration:

ABE, D., Theoretical Economics
FUJITA, N., Japanese Business History
HARA, M., International Accounting Theory
HAYASHI, A., Corporate Accounting
HAYASHI, K., Cost Accounting
HITOMI, K., Manufacturing Systems Engineering
HONDA, H., Corporate Finance Theory
INOUE, H., Business Management
INOUE, K., Finance Theory
KAMEI, M., International Business Management
KANEKO, A., Insurance Theory
KATAGIRI, M., Marketing Theory
KAWASHIMA, M., Marketing Theory
KITAZAWA, Y., Small Business Management
KOIKE, T., Information Processing Management
KONNO, T., Information Processing Management
MASAOKA, M., Managerial Accounting
MISHIMA, R., Business Administration Psychology
MORIYA, H., Merchandise Studies
NAKAYAMA, J., German Literature

NATSUME, K., International Business Strategy
NISHIHARA, J., Japanese Language Education
NISHIKAWA, K., Labour Management
NOMA, K., Marketing Research
OHGAI, T., International Business
OHNISHI, K., Information Industry
OHSUGI, M., International Finance Theory
ONO, K., Accounting
SATO, K., Marketing
SHIGEMOTO, N., Business Organization Theory
SHIMADA, H., Business Management
SHIMADA, M., English Linguistics
SUGIMURA, M., French Literature
TAKADA, S., Religion
TERASHIMA, K., Information Management
TOGAMI, M., Sociology
TOYOSHIMA, M., Engineering Management
YAMASHITA, A., Macroeconomics
YOKOYAMA, K., Regional Sociology
YOSHIHIRO, S., Primate Ecology
YUI, H., Industrial Engineering

Faculty of Economics:
AZUMA, T., Applied Physiology
HATA, N., Health Industry Economics
HIGUCHI, M., Middle Spanish Literature
IGUCHI, T., Industrial Organization
ISHIKAWA, R., Labour Economics
ITOH, T., Mathematics
KANEKO, H., Economic Theory
KAWAMURA, T., German Literature
KAWAMURA, Y., Development Sociology
LAKSHMAN, W. D., Economic Theory
MATSUOKA, K., Economic Policy
MATSUOKA, T., Theory of Modern Capitalism
MISAKI, S., Economic Theory
MIZUHARA, S., Economic Thought
NAKAMURA, H., Regional Economics
NISHIBORI, F., Theoretical Economics
OBAYASHI, M., African American Development
OISHI, M., English Language
OKACHI, K., International Economic Theory
OMAE, S., Social Policy
OTSUKI, M., German Economic History
SHIMUZU, K., American Literature
TAJIRI, E., Teaching Japanese
TAKADA, M., Public Finance
TAKENAKA, E., Labour Economics
TANAKA, Y., Economic Systems Theory
TERADA, H., Financial Theory
TSUBOUCHI, R., Sociology
YAMAMOTO, S., International Economics
YOSHIMURA, H., Indian Mahayanist Buddhist Thought
YUNO, T., International Finance

Faculty of Intercultural Communication:
AKAGI, H., Japanese Industrial Arts
FUKUDA, K., The United Nations and Japan
FURMANOVSKY, M., American History, TESOL
HABITO, R., Indian and Buddhist Philosophy
HAMANO, S., Human Rights Law, Western Political Thought
HIGA, M., Applied Linguistics
KIGLICS, I., Economics
KIMURA, B., Psychiatry
KOIZUMI, T., Comparative Study of Civilizations
KWON, O., Education
MACADAM, J., Comparative Culture
MATSUBARA, H., Western History
MATSUI, K., Energy Economics
MIYAKAWA, C., French Literature and Language
MURATA, S., Comparative Study of Educational Systems
NAGASAKI, N., Modern South Asian History
PANG, C., Japanese Language, Chinese Language
SAKAMOTO, S., Food Culture, Ethnobotany
SIMPSON, J., World Agriculture
SUDO, M., Comparative Study of Folklore
SUEHARA, T., Cultural Anthropology, Economic Anthropology
SUGIMURA, T., History of Middle Eastern Art
TOH, N., International Communications and Relations
TSURUTA, K., Comparative Literature
UEYAMA, D., Buddhist Studies

Faculty of Law:
FUJIWARA, H., Civil Law
FUKUSHIMA, I., Criminal Law
HAYASHI, T., Buddhism
HIGASHI, F., Physical Education
HIRANO, T., Political Processes
HIRANO, T., The Constitution; Religious Law
HONMA, Y., Civil Proceedings Act
ISHIDA, T., Political Theory
ISHII, K., Philosophy of Law
ISHIZUKA, S., Criminology
IWATA, N., Chinese Language
KATSURA, F., English Language and Literature
KAWABATA, M., African Politics
KAWASUMI, Y., Civil Law
KIM, D., International Human Rights Laws
KISAKA, J., Japanese Political History
KONDO, H., 18th-Century English Novel
KUBOTA, M., Sports Sociology
MIKAMI, T., Administrative Law
MIZUNO, T., Tax Law
NAGARA, K., Administrative Law
NISHIO, Y., Commercial Law
SAKAI, S., Current Middle East Politics
SAKAMOTO, M., Administration
SHIRAISHI, K., Public Administration
TAKAHASHI, S., Italian Fascism
TAKEHISA, S., Commercial Law
TAKITA, R., Commercial Politics
TANAKA, N., International Law
TODORIKI, K., Sports Sociology
TOMINO, K., Regional Autonomy
TSUJITA, J., Astrophysics
UEDA, K., Constitutional Law
WAKITA, S., Labour Law
YOROI, T., Labour Law

Faculty of Letters:
AKAMATSU, T., History of Japanese Buddhism
AKIMOTO, M., Japanese Language and Literature
ASADA, M., Japanese Tendai Sect
ASAI, N., Shin Buddhism
CHIN, K., Chinese Language and Literature
DOI, J., Modern Japanese Literature
ECHIZENYA, H., Modern Japanese Culture
FUJIMOTO, M., American Culture
FUKUSHIMA, H., Modern Japanese History
FUROMOTO, T., Anglo-Irish Literature
HAYASHIDA, Y., Eastern History
HIGASHINAKA, I., English Romantic Literature
HIRATA, A., Modern Japanese Thought
ICHIMURA, T., Psychology
INOUE, Y., English Language
ITOI, M., Japanese Language
IZUMOJI, O., Japanese Literature
KAGOTANI, M., Japanese History
KATSUBE, M., Japanese Archaeology
KIDA, T., Modern Chinese History
KITANO, A., Modern Japanese Literature
KODAMA, D., History of Indian Buddhism
KODAMA, S., History of Japanese Religion
KODANI, S., English Literature
KOJIMA, M., Intercultural Pedagogy
KUDARA, K., Buddhism
LAZARIN, M., Philosophy
MARUYAMA, T., Philosophy
MASUDA, R., English Literature
MIKOGAMI, E., Indian Philosophy
MIKOGAMI, E., Modern Western Philosophy
MITSUKAWA, T., Indian Buddhism
MIYAMA, Y., Japanese Literature of the Edo Period
MIYAMOTO, S., Modern English Novels
MIZOGUCHI, K., Philosophy
NAGAKAWA, H., American Literature
NAKAYAMA, S., Chinese Buddhism
NISHIYAMA, R., Mathematics
ODA, Y., Eastern History
OHMINE, A., Philosophy
OHTA, T., Shin Buddhism
OHTORI, K., Tanka Poetry in the Middle Ages
OKA, R., Thought of Shiran
OKAZAKI, K., Japanese Archaeology
SHIYOUBO, T., English Linguistics
TAKEDA, H., History of Indian Buddhism
TAKEDA, R., Buddhism
TANAKA, M., Educational Psychology
TANAKA, S., Psychology
TATSUGUCHI, M., Buddhist Theology
TOKUNAGA, D., Shin Buddhism
TOMITA, M., Educational Technology
TSUNEYOSHI, K., Methods and Curriculum of Education
TSUZUKI, A., East Asian History
UESUGI, T., Philosophy of Education
UMITANI, N., Philosophy of Education
UWAYOKOTE, M., Japanese History
WATANABE, K., History of Sports Philosophy
WATANABE, T., Chinese Buddhist Theory
YAMADA, Y., English Literature
YATA, R., History of Shin Buddhism

Faculty of Science and Technology:
ABE, H., Plasma Physics
ARIKI, Y., Pattern Recognition
DOHSHITA, S., Speech and Audio Media Processing
ENAMI, K., Materials Science and Engineering
FUJIMOTO, Y., Information Engineering
GOTOH, Y., Materials Science
HARADA, T., Catalytic Chemistry
HAYASHI, H., Polymer Science
HORIKAWA, T., Mechanical Engineering and Materials Science
IIDA, S., Solid State Physics
IKEDA, T., Applied Analysis and Computational Science
IWAMOTO, T., Robot Engineering
JIKU, F., Environmental Engineering
KAIYOH, H., Communications Engineering
KAMIJOH, E., Inorganic Functional Materials
KATOH, K., Multivariable Functions
KAWASHIMA, H., Mechanical Engineering
KOBAYASHI, K., Metallic Materials Chemistry
KOBUCHI, Y., Information Science
KOKUBU, H., Mathematics and Dynamic Systems
KONDOH, H., Germanic Literature and Languages
KUNIHIRO, T., Nuclear and Elementary Particle Physics
KUTSUNA, H., Mechanical Engineering
MATSUMOTO, W., Mathematics (Analysis)
MATSUSHITA, T., Coordination Chemistry
MIYASHITA, T., Mechanical Physics
MORITA, Y., Nonlinear Differential Equations
NAKAMURA, T., Computer Science
NAKANISHI, S., Mechanical Engineering
NISHIHARA, H., Superconductivity; Physics
OHJI, K., Mechanical Engineering
OHTSUKA, N., Materials Strength and Fracture Mechanics
OKADA, Y., Information Processing
OKAMOTO, Y., Anglo-Irish Literature
OZAWA, T., Information Technology
SAITOH, M., Optics
SOHMA, K., Buddhism

TAGUCHI, T., Health and Physical Education
TAKAHASHI, T., Science Education and Educational Technology
TAKAYANAGI, K., Astronomy
TSUBOI, Y., Mechatronics and Electronic Control
TSUTSUMI, K., Intelligent Robotic Systems
UDO, A., Systems Engineering
URABE, K., Ceramics
WADA, T., Inorganic Materials Chemistry
YOTSUTANI, S., Mathematics (Analysis)
YUKIMOTO, Y., Semiconductor Electronics

Faculty of Sociology:

FUKUZAKI, S., Health Science
FUNAHASHI, K., Community and Regional Studies
FUSHIMI, Y., Social Welfare Finance
HAYASE, K., Senior Citizens' Welfare
KAMEYAMA, Y., Sociology
KANBAYASHI, S., Social Technology for the Disabled
KASAHARA, S., Industrial Sociology
KISHIDA, H., Clinical Psychology
KODAMA, N., Sociology
KOGA, K., Religion
KOSHII, I., Social Psychology
KUCHIBA, M., Comparative Sociology
MATSUSHITA, K., Population Economics
MATSUTANI, N., Social Security Theory
MORI, Y., Social Welfare Institutions
MUKAI, T., Rural Sociology
MURAI, R., Welfare for the Disabled
NORIKUMO, S., Information Engineering
ODA, K., Social Welfare
OGASAWARA, M., Theoretical Sociology
OSHIDA, E., Mass Media Civilization
SASAKI, M., Social Work
SEKIGUCHI, S., Psychology
SHIMIZU, H., Everyday Life and Religion
SHIMIZU, K., Social Welfare
TAKEHARA, H., Principles of Education
TANAKA, S., Industrial Sociology
TANO, T., Health and Physical Education
TERAKAWA, Y., Religious Psychology
WATARI, H., English Philology

Junior College:

ASAEDA, Z., History of Japanese Buddhism
HAMAGAMI, Y., Child Welfare
IHARA, K., Nursing Technology
IIDA, K., International Social Welfare
IKUTA, M., Social Welfare for the Elderly
KATOH, H., History of Social Welfare Policy
KAWAZOE, T., Shin Buddhism
NAGAI, T., Developmental Psychology
OHNISHI, M., Community Health
TANIMOTO, M., Philosophy
TATSUDANI, A., History of Shin Buddhism
WAKAHARA, D., Pedagogy
YAMADA, M., Indian Buddhism
YAMADA, Y., Shin Buddhism
YOSHIDA, K., Discrimination Problems

ATTACHED RESEARCH INSTITUTES

Institute of Buddhist Cultural Studies: Shichijo Ohmiya, Shimogyo-ku, Kyoto 600; Dir KYOSHIN ASANO.

Joint Research Centre for Science and Technology: 1-5 Yokoya, Seta Ohe-cho, Otsu, Shiga 520-21; Dir KEISUKE KOBAYASHI.

Research Institute for the Social Sciences: 67 Tsukamoto-cho, Fukakusa, Fushimi-ku, Kyoto; Dir TAKESHI HIRANO.

Socio-cultural Research Institute: 1-5 Yokoya, Seta Ohe-cho, Otsu, Shiga 520-21; e-mail setaken@ad.ryukoku.ac.jp; internet scri.rec.ryukoku.ac.jp; Dir KENICHI MATSUI

UNIVERSITY OF THE SACRED HEART, TOKYO

Hiroo 4-chome 3-1, Shibuya-ku, Tokyo 150-8938
Telephone: (3) 3407-5811
E-mail: wwwadmin@u-sacred-heart.ac.jp
Internet: www.u-sacred-heart.ac.jp

Founded 1948
Private control
Academic year: April to March

Pres.: Prof. HEIJI TERANAKA
Vice-Pres. for Graduate Studies: YOSHIKO OKAZAKI
Vice-Pres. for Students: MITSUKO KANEKO
Vice-Pres. for Studies: KENSUKE SUGAWARA
Business Chief: KIMIO MURAMATSU
Registrar: YORIKO YOSHIDA
Librarian: Prof. HITOSHI OBARA

Library of 390,000 vols
Number of teachers: 68 full-time, 318 part-time
Number of students: 2,241

Publications: *Seishin Ronso* (Seishin Studies, 2 a year), *Religion and Civilization* (Bulletin of the Research Institute for the Study of Christian Culture, 1 a year)

SANNO INSTITUTE OF MANAGEMENT

6-39-15 Todoroki, Setagaya, Tokyo 158-8630
Telephone: (3) 3704-1111
Internet: www.sanno.ac.jp

Founded 1925

Consists of SANNO Graduate School (MBA Programme), SANNO University Isehara (4-year degree course in Management and Informatics, and distance education course), SANNO College Jiyugaoka (2-year degree course, and distance education course)
Academic year: April to March

Chair.: SHUNICHI UENO
Pres., Sanno University: MASAAKI HARADA
Exec. Dir: TOSHIKAZU TAMURA

Library of 345,000 vols
Number of teachers: 126
Number of students: 7,410 (excluding distance education course students)

Publications: *SANNO College Bulletin* (2 a year), *SANNO College Jiyugaoka Bulletin* (1 a year), *Journal of the Management Research Centre* (irregular)

DEANS

Business Administration: MICHIKO MORIWAKI
Graduate School: TOSHIKAZU TAMURA
School of Management and Information Science: MINAMI MIYAUCHI

SAPPORO GAKUIN UNIVERSITY

11-Banchi, Bunkyodai, Ebetsu, Hokkaido 069-8555
Telephone: (11) 386-8111
E-mail: kouhou@ims.sgu.ac.jp
Internet: www.sgu.ac.jp

Founded 1946

Faculties of commerce, economics, humanities, law, social information

Pres.: AKIKO FUSE

SAPPORO UNIVERSITY

3-7-3-1 Nishioka, Toyohira-ku, Sapporo 062-8520
Telephone: (11) 852-1181
E-mail: koho@ofc.sapporo-u.ac.jp
Internet: www.sapporo-u.ac.jp

Founded 1967
Private control
Academic year: April to March

Pres.: MASAYUKI KIMURA
Head Administrator: K. KUROSAWA
Librarian: N. TAKAMATSU

Library of 426,000 vols
Number of teachers: 162
Number of students: 6,700

Publications: *Sapporo Law Review* (2 a year), *Journal of Comparative Cultures* (2 a year), *Sapporo University Journal* (2 a year), *Industrial and Business Journal* (2 a year)

DEANS

Faculty of Business Administration: J. ARAKAWA
Faculty of Cultural Studies: M. YAMAGUCHI
Faculty of Economics: K. MOTODA
Faculty of Foreign Languages: M. KATO
Faculty of Law: H. TANAKA
Graduate School of Law: K. SAKAI
Women's Junior College: A. TODA

SEIJO UNIVERSITY

6-1-20 Seijo, Setagaya-ku, Tokyo 157-8511
Telephone: (3) 3482-6020
E-mail: info@seijo.ac.jp
Internet: www.seijo.ac.jp

Founded 1950
Private control
Academic year: April to March

Pres.: YUJI YUI
Admin. Sec.: M. SHIMANO
Librarian: H. FUKUMITSU

Library of 688,395 vols
Number of teachers: 584 (148 full-time, 436 part-time)
Number of students: 5,999

DEANS

Faculty of Arts and Literature: EIJI UENO
Faculty of Economics: YOSHIO ASAI
Faculty of Law: HIROYUKI KONNO
Faculty of Social Innovation: MITSUNOBU SHINOHARA
Junior College: MASUMI ISHINABE

SEIKEI UNIVERSITY

3-3-1 Kichijoji-Kitamachi, Musashino City, Tokyo 180-8633
Telephone: (422) 37-3517
E-mail: koho@jim.seikei.ac.jp
Internet: www.seikei.ac.jp/university/index.html

Founded 1949
Private control
Language of instruction: Japanese
Academic year: April to March

Pres.: YOICHI KAMEJIMA
Librarian: MITSUO MIYAMOTO

Library of 742,000 vols
Number of teachers: 243 (full-time)
Number of students: 8,144 (7,745 undergraduate, 399 postgraduate)

Publications: *Journal of the Faculty of Economics, Journal of the Faculty of Science and Technology, Journal of the Graduate School of Humanities, Review of Asian and Pacific Studies, Seikei Daigaku Rikogaku-kenkyu Hokoku, Seikei Eigo Eibungaku Kenkyu, Seikei Hogaku, Seikei Jinbunkenkyu, Seikei Kokubun, Seikei Review of English Studies*

DEANS

Faculty of Economics: YOSHIFUMI FUJIGAKI
Faculty of Humanities: MITSUNORI KADOGUCHI
Faculty of Law: NOBORU KOBAYASHI
Faculty of Science and Technology: IKUO ITO
Law School: TOMOMICHI WATANABE

SENSHU UNIVERSITY

8 Kandajimbo-cho 3-chome, Chiyoda-ku, Tokyo 101-8425
Telephone: (44) 911-1250

E-mail: iaffairs@acc.senshu-u.ac.jp
Internet: www.senshu-u.ac.jp

Founded 1880
Academic year: April to March

Pres.: YOSHIHIRO HIDAKA
Librarian: T. OBA

Library of 1,110,000 vols
Number of teachers: 400 full-time
Number of students: 20,472

DEANS

School of Business Administration: K. UOTA
School of Commerce: K. ONISHI
School of Economics: S. SAKAI
School of Law: B. KOHATA
School of Literature: T. ARAKI
School of Network and Information: M. SAKAMOTO
Graduate School of Business Administration: N. TAKEMURA
Graduate School of Commerce: N. OGUCHI
Graduate School of Economics: M. YABUKI
Graduate School of Humanities: T. SUZUKI
Graduate School of Law: T. TAKAGAI
Professional School of Legal Affairs: Y. HIRAI

SETSUNAN UNIVERSITY

17-8 Ikedanakamachi, Neyagawa-shi, Osaka 572-8508
Telephone: (72) 839-9450
E-mail: kikakuka@ofc.setsunan.ac.jp
Internet: www.setsunan.ac.jp

Founded 1975
Private control
Academic year: April to March

Chair.: TETSUROU KURE
Pres.: MITSUNORI IMAI

Library of 550,000 vols
Number of teachers: 298
Number of students: 8,090

DEANS

Faculty of Business Administration: KANJU HANEISHI
Faculty of Economics: KIICHIRO YAGI
Faculty of Foreign Studies: KAORI IWAMA
Faculty of Law: NOBORU KOYAMA
Faculty of Nursing: KIYOKAZU OGITA
Faculty of Pharmaceutical Sciences: YOKO GOKAN
Faculty of Science and Engineering: TOSHIMICHI MORIWAKI

SHIKOKU UNIVERSITY

Ojin-cho, Tokushima-shi, Tokushima 771-1192
Telephone: (88) 665-9911
Internet: www.shikoku-u.ac.jp

Founded 1966

Faculty of literature; graduate school of management and information science

Pres.: NOBORU FUKUOKA

Library of 317,470 vols
Number of teachers: 163
Number of students: 3,114

SOKA UNIVERSITY

1-236, Tangi-cho, Hachioji, Tokyo 192-8577
Telephone: (426) 91-8200
E-mail: adm@j.soka.ac.jp
Internet: www.soka.ac.jp

Founded 1971
Private control
Academic year: April to March

Pres.: Prof. Dr MASAMI WAKAE
Vice-Pres: Prof. KATSUHIKO FUKUSHIMA, Prof. MASASUKE NIHEI
Librarian: Prof. EIICHI IMAGAWA

Library of 1,005,000 vols
Number of teachers: 295
Number of students: 7,842

Publication: *SUN* (Soka University News, 4 a year)

DEANS

Division of Correspondence Education: Prof. TADASHIGE TAKAMURA
Faculty of Business Administration: Prof. KAORU YAMANAKA
Faculty of Economics: Prof. Dr HIDETAKA HASEBE
Faculty of Education: Prof. RIKIO KIMATA
Faculty of Engineering: Prof. YOSHIMI TESHIGAWARA
Faculty of Law: Prof. AKIRA KIRIGAYA
Faculty of Letters: Prof. YUTAKA ISHIGAMI
Graduate School of Economics: Prof. KINJI UEDA
Graduate School of Engineering: Prof. KOJIRO KOBAYASHI
Graduate School of Law: Prof. KAZUO KAWASAKI
Graduate School of Letters: Prof. KAZUNORI KUMAGAI
Institute of Japanese Language: Prof. KEIKO ISHIKAWA

DIRECTORS

Institute for the Comparative Study of Cultures: M. KITA
Institute of Asian Studies: E. IMAGAWA
Institute of Life Science: M. WAKAE
Institute of Systems Science: M. WAKAE
International Research Institute for the Advanced Study of Buddhism: H. KANNO
Peace Research Institute: T. TAKAMURA

SOPHIA UNIVERSITY/JÔCHI DAIGAKU

Kioicho 7–1, Chiyoda-ku, Tokyo 102-8554
Telephone: (3) 3238-3111
Internet: www.sophia.ac.jp

Founded 1913
Private control (Society of Jesus)
Languages of instruction: English, Japanese
Academic year: April to March

Chancellor: TOSHIAKI KOSO
Pres.: YOSHIAKI ISHIZAWA
Vice-Pres.: J. HOLLERICH
Vice-Pres.: J. KOBAYASHI
Vice-Pres.: M. YAJIMA
Registrar: M. FUJIMURA

Library: see under Libraries and Archives
Number of teachers: 505
Number of students: 11,963 (1,182 graduates, 10,509 undergraduates, 272 law school)

Publications: *Monumenta Nipponica* (4 a year, in English), *Sophia* (4 a year, in Japanese)

DEANS

Faculty of Comparative Culture: Y. OKADA
Faculty of Economics: K. YAMADA
Faculty of Foreign Studies: T. UENO
Faculty of Humanities: Y. OHASHI
Faculty of Human Sciences: I. TOCHIMOTO
Faculty of Law: N. TSUJI
Faculty of Science and Technology: T. HAYASHITA
Faculty of Theology: T. SAKUMA

DIRECTORS

European Institute: M. NAKAMURA
Iberoamerican Institute: M. NEVES
Institute for Global Concern: K. NAKANO
Institute for Studies of the Global Environment: H. KITO
Institute of American and Canadian Studies: K. OSHIO
Institute of Asian Cultures: T. TERADA
Institute of Christian Culture: T. SAKUMA
Institute of Comparative Culture: J. FARRER
Institute of Medieval Thought: N. SATO
Life Science Institute: K. KUMAKURA
Linguistic Institute for International Communication: K. YOSHIDA

TAKUSHOKU UNIVERSITY

3-4-14 Kohinata, Bunkyo-ku, Tokyo 112
Telephone: (3) 3947-2261
E-mail: web_int@ofc.takushoku-u.ac.jp
Internet: www.takushoku-u.ac.jp

Founded 1900

Campuses at Hachioji and Bunkyo

Chancellor: S. ODAMURA
Pres.: TOSHIO WATANABE
Chair. of Board of Directors: T. FUJITO
Librarian: S. KORI

Library of 440,000 vols
Number of teachers: 528
Number of students: 10,377

Publications: *Hokoku* (1 a year), *Kaigai Jijo* (Journal of World Affairs, 12 a year), *Takushoku Daigaku Ronshu* (6 a year)

DEANS

Faculty of Commerce: T. TAKAHASHI
Faculty of Engineering: M. SAKATA
Faculty of Foreign Languages: T. WADA
Faculty of Political Science and Economics: K. KOBAYASHI
Graduate School: T. OSAKAI
Hokkaido Takushoku Junior College: T. ISHIKAWA
Special Japanese Language Course for Foreign Students: M. ARAKI
Takushoku Junior College: T. GOTO

TAMAGAWA UNIVERSITY

6-1-1 Tamagawa Gakuen 6-chome, Machida, Tokyo 194-8610
Telephone: (427) 39-8111
E-mail: webmaster@tamagawa.ac.jp
Internet: www.tamagawa.ac.jp

Founded 1929
Private control
Language of instruction: Japanese
Academic year: April to March

Pres.: YOSHIAKI OBARA
Registrar: TAKASHI URATA
Librarian: HARUA TODA

Library of 860,000 vols, 8,000 periodicals
Number of teachers: 787 (351 full-time, 436 part-time)
Number of students: 7,774

Publications: *Mitsubachi Kagaku* (4 a year), *Shoho* (1 a year), *Zenjin Education* (12 a year)

DEANS

Associate Degree Junior College for Women: TOMIO OZAWA
Department of Education by Correspondence: HIROSHI YONEYAMA
Faculty of Agriculture: TADAYUKI ISHIYAMA
Faculty of Arts and Education: HIROSHI YONEYAMA
Faculty of Engineering: HIDETAKE TANIBAYASHI
Graduate School for Agriculture: MITSUO MATSUKA
Graduate School for Education and Letters: YASUTADA TAKAHASHI
Graduate School for Engineering: TAKURO KOIKE
Junior College for Women: MICHIAKI NAGAI

TEZUKAYAMA UNIVERSITY

7-1-1 Tezukayama, Nara City 631-8501
Telephone: (742) 48-9122
E-mail: webmaster@tezukayama-u.ac.jp

Internet: www.tezukayama-u.ac.jp
Founded 1941
Faculties of business administration, economics, humanities, law and policy
Library of 280,000 vols
Number of teachers: 109
Number of students: 4,166

TOHOKU GAKUIN UNIVERSITY

1-3-1 Tsuchitoi, Aoba-ku, Sendai 980-8511
Telephone: (2) 264-6425
E-mail: ico@tscc.tohoku-gakuin.ac.jp
Internet: www.tohoku-gakuin.ac.jp
Founded 1886
Private control
Language of instruction: Japanese
Academic year: April to March
Library of 1,200,000 vols
Pres.: Nozomu Hoshimiya
Vice-Pres.: Makoto Saito
Vice-Pres.: Yoshitaka Shibata
Number of teachers: 511
Number of students: 12,518
Publications: *Church and Theology* (2 a year), *Economics* (3 a year), *History and Geography* (2 a year), *Human, Jurisprudence* (2 a year), *Linguistic and Information Sciences* (3 a year), *Science and Engineering Report* (2 a year), *Tohoku Gakuin University Review English Language and Literature* (2 a year)

DEANS
Faculty of Economics: Yoshinori Harada
Faculty of Engineering: Ginro Endo
Faculty of Fitness and Administration: Nobumasa Yamamoto
Faculty of Law: Ryuichiro Takagi
Faculty of Letters: Kenichi Endo
Faculty of Liberal Arts: Masahiro Sakuma

TOKAI UNIVERSITY EDUCATIONAL SYSTEM

2-28-4 Tomigaya, Shibuya-ku, Tokyo 151-8677
Telephone: (3) 3467-2211
E-mail: pr@yyg.u-tokai.ac.jp
Internet: www.tokai.ac.jp
Founded 1942
Private control
Language of instruction: Japanese
Academic year: April to March
Chair. and Pres.: Prof. Tatsuro Matsumae
Vice-Chair. and Vice-Pres.: Prof. Yoshiaki Matsumae.

CONSTITUENT UNIVERSITIES

Tokai University

4-1-1 Kitakaname, Hiratsuka-shi, Kanagawa, 259-1292
Telephone: (463) 58-1211
E-mail: kikaku@tsc.u-tokai.ac.jp
Internet: www.u-tokai.ac.jp
Founded 1946
Private control
Language of instruction: Japanese
Academic year: April to March
Campuses in Hokkaido, Kanagawa, Kumamoto, Shizuoka, Tokyo
Chancellor: Prof. Jiro Takano
Vice-Chancellor: Prof. Hiromu Hashimoto
Vice-Chancellor: Prof. Kiyoshi Yamada
Vice-Chancellor: Prof. Masafumi Kato
Vice-Chancellor: Tateo Adachi
Vice-Chancellor: Prof. Yasuhiro Yamashita
Vice-Chancellor: Prof. Yasuo Tanaka
Librarian: Yasuo Tanaka
Library of 2,647,482 vols
Number of teachers: 1,736 full-time
Number of students: 29,637
Publication: *Tokai Journal of Experimental and Clinical Medicine*

DEANS
Agriculture: Tatsuro Murata
Art and Technology: Takumi Hayashi
Biological Science and Engineering: Kenji Yano
Biology: Prof. Sen Takenaka
Business Studies: Jinichi Okuyama
Engineering: Prof. Katsumi Hiraoka
Foreign Language Centre: Ryoji Okuda (Exec. Dir)
Health Sciences: Michiko Mizoguchi
High Technology for Human Welfare: Kiyoshi Nozu
Humanities and Culture: Ryutaro Kajii
Industrial Engineering: Tsutomu Ichikawa
Information and Telecommunication Engineering: Toshio Nakashita
Information Sciences and Technology: Toshio Nakashita
International Cultural Relations: Satoru Mabuchi
Japanese Language Course for Foreign Students: Harumi Murakami (Head)
Law: Kazuhiro Yoshikawa
Letters: Michiko Saito (Dean)
Marine Science and Technology: Noboru Kato
Medicine: Yutaka Imai
Physical Education: Yasuhiro Yamashita
Political Science and Economics: Akira Konakayama
Science: Yasuyuki Miura
Tokai Institute of Global Education and Research: Hirohisa Uchida (Exec. Dir)
Tourism: Ryozo Matsumoto

TOKIWA UNIVERSITY

1-430-1 Miwa, Mito-shi, Ibaraki Prefecture 310-8585
Telephone: (29) 232-2511
E-mail: kouhou@tokiwa.ac.jp
Internet: www.tokiwa.ac.jp
Founded 1983
Colleges of applied international studies, community development, human science; graduate school of human science
Chair.: Hidemichi Morosawa
Pres.: Isato Takagi

TOKYO UNIVERSITY OF PHARMACY AND LIFE SCIENCES

1432-1 Horinouchi, Hachioji, Tokyo 192-03
Telephone: (426) 76-5111
Internet: www.toyaku.ac.jp
Founded 1880
Schools of life sciences and pharmacy
Pres.: Dr T. Yamakawa
Librarian: Prof. A. Ohta
Library of 100,000 vols, 500 periodicals
Number of teachers: 200
Number of students: 2,200

TOKYO DENKI DAIGAKU (Tokyo Denki University)

2-2 Kanda-Nishiki-cho, Chiyoda-ku, Tokyo 101-8457
Telephone: (3) 5280-3555
E-mail: gakuchoshitsu@jim.ac.jp
Internet: www.dendai.ac.jp
Founded 1907
Academic year: April to March
President: Dr Yoshihiro Toma
General Director of Multimedia Resource Centre and Library: Dr T. Saito
Library of 321,481 vols, 2,975 periodicals
Number of teachers: 748 (355 full-time, 393 part-time)
Number of students: 11,563

DEANS
Graduate School of Engineering: J. Iwamoto
Graduate School of Science and Engineering: M. Takizawa
School of Engineering: T. Ibamoto
School of Engineering (Evening Programme): S. Murakami
School of the Information Environment: S. Nakamura
School of Science and Engineering: Y. Kashimura

DIRECTORS
Applied Superconductivity Research Laboratory: I. Nemoto
Centre for Research Collaboration: H. Tomita
Frontier Research and Development Centre: Y. Uchikawa
Research Institute for Construction Technology: M. Tachibana
Research Institute for Technology: H. Inaba

TOKYO DENTAL COLLEGE

1-2-2 Masago, Mihama-ku, Chiba 261-8502
Telephone: (43) 270-3764
E-mail: int@tdc.ac.jp
Internet: www.tdc.ac.jp
Founded 1890
Academic year: April to March
Dean: Prof. Yuzuru Kaneko
Vice-Deans: Prof. Masashi Yakushiji
Library of 198,000 vols
Number of teachers: 306
Number of students: 983 (802 undergraduate, 181 postgraduate)
Publications: *Bulletin* (in English, 4 a year), *Shikwa Gakuho* (research journal, in Japanese, every 2 months)

TOKYO KEIZAI UNIVERSITY

1-7-34 Minami-cho, Kokubunji-shi, Tokyo 185-8502
Telephone: (42) 328-7711
Internet: www.tku.ac.jp
Founded 1900 as Okura Commerce School
Private control
Academic year: April to March
Pres.: Prof. Shigekazu Kukita
Chief Admin. Officer: Akira Funaki
Dir of Library: Prof. Kenji Omori
Library of 700,000 vols
Number of teachers: 356
Number of students: 6,335
Publications: *Journal of Communication Studies* (2 a year), *Journal of Humanities and Natural Sciences* (2 a year), *Journal of Tokyo Keizai University* (3 a year), *Tokyo Kezai Law Review* (2 a year)

DEANS
Faculty of Business Administration: Makoto Takewaki
Faculty of Communication Studies: Yasuyuki Kawaura
Faculty of Contemporary Law: Yoshitomo Ode
Faculty of Economics: Tadashi Hamano
Graduate School of Business Administration: Seishi Nakamura (Chair.)
Graduate School of Communication Studies: Ryosuke Kawai (Chair.)
Graduate School of Contemporary Law: Yayoi Isono (Chair.)
Graduate School of Economics: Takeshi Kojima (Chair.)

TOKYO UNIVERSITY OF AGRICULTURE

1-1-1 Sakuragaoka, Setagaya-ku, Tokyo 156-8502

Telephone: (3) 5477-2560
E-mail: tuacip@nodai.ac.jp
Internet: www.nodai.ac.jp

Founded 1891
Languages of instruction: Japanese, English
Academic year: April to March

Pres.: Dr KANJU OHSAWA
Chief Admin. Officer: YUJI FURUYA

Library of 665,000 vols
Number of teachers: 354
Number of students: 13,598

Publication: *Journal of Agricultural Science*

DEANS

Faculty of Agriculture: Dr TOSHIRO SUZUKI
Faculty of Applied Bioscience: Dr HARUKAZU SUZUKI
Faculty of Bio-Industry: Dr MICHINARI YOKOHAMA
Faculty of Int. Agriculture and Food Studies: Dr HISAMITSU TAKAHASHI
Faculty of Regional Environmental Science: Dr SHIGEYUKI MIYABAYASHI
Graduate School of Agriculture: Dr TOSHIYUKI MONMA
Graduate School of Bio-Industry: Dr TOHRU OHYAMA
Junior College: Dr HIROSHI TACHI

TOKYO UNIVERSITY OF SCIENCE

1-3 Kagurazaka, Shinjuku-ku, Tokyo 162-8601

Telephone: (3) 3260-4271
E-mail: intlexchg@admin.tus.ac.jp
Internet: www.tus.ac.jp

Founded 1881
Private control
Language of instruction: Japanese
Academic year: April to March

Pres.: AKIRA FUJISHIMA
Librarian: MASAAKI UEKI

Library of 1,007,422 vols
Number of teachers: 732
Number of students: 20,755

Publication: *Science Forum* (12 a year)

DEANS

Faculty of Engineering Division I: SEIICHIRO HANGAI
Faculty of Engineering Division II: TOSHIAKI YACHI
Faculty of Industrial Science and Technology: YASUHIRO AKIRA
Faculty of Pharmaceutical Sciences: SEIICHI TANUMA
Faculty of Science Division I: YOSHIHIRO MARUYAMA
Faculty of Science Division II: AKIRA YOSHIOKA
Faculty of Science and Technology: YASUHIRO HIRAKAWA
School of Management: HITOTORA HIGASHIKUNI

ATTACHED INSTITUTES

Research Education Organization for Information Science and Technology: 1–3 Kagurazaka, Shinjuku-ku, Tokyo 162-8601; tel. (3) 3260-4271; Prin. MASANORI OHYA.

Research Institute for Biological Sciences: 2641 Yamazaki, Noda-shi, Chiba 278-8510; tel. (4) 7124-1501; internet www.ribs.tus.ac.jp; Prin. TAKACHIKA AZUMA.

Research Institute for Science and Technology: 2641 Yamazaki, Noda-shi, Chiba 278-8510; tel. (4) 7124-1501; e-mail rsc-ml@tusml.ac.jp; internet www.tus.ac.jp/rist; Prin. YOSHIMASA NIHEI

TOKYO WOMEN'S CHRISTIAN UNIVERSITY

2-6-1, Zempukuji, Suginami-ku, Tokyo 167-8585

Telephone: (3) 5382-6340
E-mail: iec@office.twcu.ac.jp
Internet: www.twcu.ac.jp

Founded 1918
Private control
Language of instruction: Japanese
Academic year: April to March

Pres.: AKIKO MINATO
Librarian: SHINSUKE MUROFUCHI

Library of 600,000 vols
Number of teachers: 142
Number of students: 4,208 (incl. 78 graduates)

Publications: *Annals of Institute for Comparative Studies of Culture* (1 a year), *Essays and Studies in British and American Literature* (2 a year), *Historica* (1 a year), *Japanese Literature* (2 a year), *Science Reports* (1 a year), *Sociology and Economics* (1 a year)

DEANS

College of Arts and Sciences: SANAE INOUE
College of Culture and Communication: YUKO KOBAYASHI
Graduate School: HIROSHI IMAI

CHAIRMEN

Graduate School of Culture and Communication: RYOICHI SATO
Graduate School of Humanities: HIROSHI IMAI
Graduate School of Science: MASAHIKO SHINOHARA

TOKYO WOMEN'S MEDICAL UNIVERSITY

8-1 Kawada-cho, Shinjuku-ku, Tokyo 162-8666

Telephone: (3) 3353-8111
E-mail: kouhou.bm@twmu.ac.jp
Internet: www.twmu.ac.jp

Founded 1900
Private control
Language of instruction: Japanese
Academic year: April to March

President: K. TAKAKURA
Registrar: H. YOSHIOKA
Librarian: M. KOBAYASHI

Library of 227,850 vols
Number of teachers: 2,178
Number of students: 961

Publication: *Journal of Tokyo Women's Medical University* (in English or Japanese, 12 a year)

TOYO UNIVERSITY

28-20 Hakusan 5-chome, Bunkyo-ku, Tokyo 112-8606

Telephone: (3) 3945-7557
E-mail: ipo@hakusrv.toyo.ac.jp
Internet: www.toyo.ac.jp

Founded 1887
Private control
Academic year: April to March

Pres.: TOMONORI MATSUO
Dir of Academic Affairs: MIKIO AKIYAMA
Librarian: TAKITARO MORIKAWA

Library of 1,101,256 vols
Number of teachers: 1,269 (523 full-time, 746 part-time)
Number of students: 29,819

Publications: faculty bulletins, journals, etc.

DEANS

Undergraduate School of Business Administration: YOUICHI KAKIZAKI
Undergraduate School of Economics: SHUNICHI KIGAWA
Undergraduate School of Engineering: MASAHIDE YONEYAMA
Undergraduate School of Law: HIDETOSHI KOBAYASHI
Undergraduate School of Life Sciences: AKIRA SAKURAI
Undergraduate School of Literature: TASHIAKI YAMADA
Undergraduate School of Regional Development Studies: HAJIME NAGAHAMA
Undergraduate School of Sociology: MAMORA FUNATSU
Graduate School of Business Administration: YASUHIRO OGURA
Graduate School of Economics: KIYOSHI ASUNO
Graduate School of Engineering: TOHRU IUCHI
Graduate School of Law: MASUO IMAGAMI
Graduate School of Life Sciences: AKIRA INOUE
Graduate School of Literature: KAZUO ARITA
Graduate School of Regional Development Studies: TOMONORI MARSUO
Graduate School of Sociology: KOJUN FURUKAWA

TSUDA COLLEGE

2-1-1 Tsuda-machi, Kodaira-shi, Tokyo 187-8577

Telephone: (42) 342-5111
E-mail: cie@tsuda.ac.jp
Internet: www.tsuda.ac.jp

Founded 1900

Faculty of liberal arts, depts of English language and literature, int. and cultural studies, mathematics and computer science; postgraduate schools of int. and cultural studies, literary studies, mathematics
Academic year: April to March

Chair.: REIJIROU HATTORI

Library of 350,000 vols, 3,400 periodicals
Number of teachers: 83 full-time
Number of students: 2,830 (incl. 85 postgraduate)

Publications: *Journal of Tsuda College* (1 a year), *The Study of International Relations* (1 a year), *The Tsuda Review* (1 a year)

TSURU UNIVERSITY

3-8-1 Tahara, Tsuru, Yamanashi 402-8555

Telephone: (554) 43-4341
E-mail: gakusei@tsuru.ac.jp
Internet: www.tsuru.ac.jp

Founded 1955

Teacher training college
Number of teachers: 74 (full-time)
Number of students: 3,000

WASEDA UNIVERSITY

1-104 Totsukamachi, Shinjuku-ku, Tokyo 169-8050

Telephone: (3) 3203-4141
E-mail: intl-ac@list.waseda.jp
Internet: www.waseda.jp

Founded 1882
Private control
Academic year: April to February

Pres.: KATSUHIKO SHIRAI
Vice-Pres. for Fundraising Promotion (Head), Alumni Relations, Management Planning, and Research Promotion: KENJI HORIGUCHI

Vice-Pres. for Legal Affairs and Operational Audit: TERUAKI TAYAMA
Vice-Pres. for Academic Affairs (Head), Cultural Program, and Honjo Project: KENJIRO TSUCHIDA
Vice-Pres. for Personnel and Labour Affairs: SATOSHI SHIMIZU
Vice-Pres. for Int. Affairs (Head): KATSUICHI UCHIDA
Vice-Pres. for Public Relations, Affiliated Schools: TOMOKI WARAGAI
Vice-Pres. for Academic Affairs, Int. Affairs and Fundraising Promotion: MASATAKA OTA
Vice-Pres. for Campus Planning, Promotion of IT and Fundraising Promotion: AKIRA NISHITANI
Vice-Pres. for Research Promotion (Head) and Fundraising Promotion: YOSHIJI HORIKOSHI
Vice-Pres. for Student Affairs, Career Support and Affiliated Schools: EI'ICHIRO NOJIMA
Vice-Pres. for General Affairs, Affiliated Companies (Head), and Personnel of Admin. Staff: HIDEAKI TAUCHI
Vice-Pres. for Finance: EI'ICHIRO KOBAYASHI
Vice-Pres. for Sports Promotion: ISAO MURAOKA (Exec. Dir)
Vice-Pres. for Strategic Management Planning, Alumni Relations, Fundraising Promotion: SEIJI HONDA
Vice-Pres. for Devt of Univ.-Local Relations, Honjo Project, Strategic Management Planning, Holding Company and Cultivation of Human Resources (Admin. Staff): KUNIO TANIGUCHI
Vice-Pres. for Alumni Relations: EIKO KONO
Vice-Pres. for Research Promotion and Alumni Relations: YASUMASA UMESATO
Vice-Pres. for Alumni Relations and Alumni Assen.: AKIHIDE FUKUDA
Dir of Library: NOBUYUKI KAMIYA

Library of 5,100,000 vols
Number of teachers: 6,560
Number of students: 53,522 (44,829 undergraduate, 8,693 postgraduate)

DEANS

Graduate School of Accountancy: YOSHITAKA KOBAYASHI
Graduate School of Advanced Science and Engineering: ATSUSHI ISHIYAMA
Graduate School of Asia-Pacific Studies: MICHIO YAMAOKA
Graduate School of Commerce: MASATAKA OTA
Graduate School of Creative Science and Engineering: HIROSHI YAMAKAWA
Graduate School of Economics: RYO NAGATA
Graduate School of Education: TSUGIYOSHI YUKAWA
Graduate School of Environment and Energy Engineering: KATSUYA NAGATA
Graduate School of Finance, Accounting and Law: MEGUMI SUTO
Graduate School of Global Information and Telecommunication Studies: YOSHIYORI URANO
Graduate School of Human Sciences: HIROYUKI TORIGOE
Graduate School of Information Production, and Systems: KOTARO HIRASAWA
Graduate School of Japanese Applied Linguistics: HIROSHI KABAYA
Graduate School of Law: KOJI OHMI
Graduate School of Letters, Arts and Sciences: KOICHI OUCHI
Faculty of Science and Engineering: SHUJI HASHIMOTO (Sr Dean)
Graduate School of Fundamental Science and Engineering: SUNAO KAWAI
Graduate School of Political Science: SEISHI SATO
Graduate School of Social Sciences: YASUHIRO ONISHI
Graduate School of Sport Sciences: TETSUO FUKUNAGA
School of Advanced Science and Engineering: ATSUSHI ISHIYAMA
School of Commerce: NAOTO ONZO
School of Creative Science and Engineering: HIROSHI YAMAKAWA
School of Culture, Media and Society: SUMIO OBINATA
School of Education: TATSUYUKI KAMIO
School of Fundamental Science and Engineering: SUNAO KAWAI
School of Human Sciences: MIHO SAITO
School of Humanities and Social Sciences: SUMIO OBINATA
School of International Liberal Studies: PAUL SNOWDEN
School of Law: TATSUO UEMURA
School of Letters, Arts and Sciences I: TERUHISA TAJIMA
School of Letters, Arts and Sciences II: TERUHISA TAJIMA
School of Political Science and Economics: SHOZO IIJIMA
School of Science and Engineering: SHUJI HASHIMOTO
School of Social Science: HIDETOSHI TAGA
School of Sport Sciences: ISAO MURAOKA
The Okuma School of Public Management: KOICHIRO AGATA
Waseda Law School: KAORU KAMATA

Schools of Art and Music

Elizabeth University of Music: 4-15 Noboricho, Naka-ku, Hiroshima; tel. (82) 221-0918; internet www.eum.ac.jp; f. 1952; library: 88,750 vols, 18,000 sound recordings; 117 (47 full-time, 70 part-time) teachers; 709 (656 undergraduate, 53 postgraduate) students; Pres. HIDEAKI NAKAMURA; Dean of Academic Affairs K. NAGAI; publ. *Kenkyuu Kiyoo* (1 a year).

Kanazawa College of Art: 5-11-1, Kodatsuno, Kanazawa, Ishikawa 920-8656; tel. (76) 262-3531; e-mail admin@kanazawa-bidai.ac.jp; internet www.kanazawa-bidai.ac.jp; f. 1946; depts of Fine Art, Design, Crafts; Graduate School; Research Institute of Art and Craft, f. 1972; library: 72,000 vols; 67 full-time staff, 200 part-time staff; 665 students; Pres. YOSHIAKI INUI.

Kunitachi College of Music: 5-5-1 Kashiwa-cho, Tachikawa-shi, Tokyo 190-8520; tel. (42) 536-0321; internet www.kunitachi.ac.jp; f. 1950; library: 155,000 books, 120,000 vols of sheet music, 170,000 audiovisual items; 417 teachers; 2,439 students; Pres. NORIKO TAKANO; publs *Kenkyu Kiyo* (Memoirs, 1 a year), *Daigakuin Nempo* (publication of the postgraduate school, 1 a year), *Ongaku Kenkyujo Nempo* (publication of the research institute, 1 a year).

Kyoto City University of Arts: 13-6 Kutsukake-cho, Ohe, Nishikyo-ku, Kyoto 610-1197; tel. (75) 332-0701; internet w3.kcua.ac.jp; Faculties of fine arts and music; 740 undergraduate students, 134 graduates; Pres. Dr YASUNORI NISHIJIMA.

Musashino Academia Musicae: 1-13-1 Hazawa, Nerima-ku, Tokyo 176-8521; tel. (3) 3992-1121; internet www.musashino-music.ac.jp; f. 1929; library: 200,000 vols; 382 teachers; 2,269 students; Pres. NAOKATA FUKUI; Librarian HACHIRO CHIKURA; publ. *Review of Studies* (1 a year, in Japanese).

Osaka College of Music: 1-1-8, Shonaisaiwaimaohi, Toyonaka City, Osaka 561-8555; tel. (6) 6334-2131; e-mail info@daion.ac.jp; internet www.daion.ac.jp; f. 1915; courses in composition, vocal music and instrumental music; library: 123,500 vols; 376 teachers; 1,171 students; Pres. NOBUO NISHIOKA.

Tama Art University: 3-15-34 Kaminoge, Setagaya-ku, Tokyo 158; tel. (3) 3702-1141; e-mail pro@tamabi.ac.jp; internet www.tamabi.ac.jp; f. 1935; undergraduate division est. 1953; depts within the Faculty of Art and Design: ceramic, glass and metal works; environmental design; graphic design; information design; art science; painting; product and textile design; sculpture; 415 teachers; 4,718 students, incl. 3,491 undergraduates and 235 graduates; Pres. SHIRO TAKAHASHI.

Toho Gakuen School of Music: 41-1 1-chome, Wakaba-cho, Chofu-shi, Tokyo 182-8510; tel. (3) 3307-4101; internet www.tohomusic.ac.jp; f. 1961; library: 133,000 vols; 83 teachers; 1,400 students; Pres. T. TSUTSUMI.

Tokyo College of Music: 3-4-5, Minami-Ikebukuro, Toshima-ku, Tokyo 171-8540; tel. (3) 3982-3186; internet www.tokyo-ondai.ac.jp; f. 1907; library: 130,000 vols, 11,300 CDs; 1,702 students; Pres. YOSHIO UNNO.

Ueno Gakuen University: Department of Music, Faculty of Music and Cultural Studies, 24-12 Higashi-Ueno 4-chome, Taito-ku, Tokyo 110-8642; tel. (3) 3842-1021; e-mail info@uenogakuen.ac.jp; internet www.uenogakuen.ac.jp; f. 1904; library: 175,000 vols; 184 teachers; 580 students; Pres. Prof. HIRO ISHIBASHI.

JORDAN

The Higher Education System

In 1920 Jordan (formerly Transjordan) became a League of Nations mandate under British administration. The mandate was terminated in 1946 and Jordan became an independent sovereign state. Wars with Israel in 1948 and 1967 led to an influx of Palestinian refugees; moreover, after the Six Day War (1967) Jerusalem and the West Bank fell wholly under Israeli control. Until 1967 the oldest institution of higher education in Jordan was Birzeit University in the West Bank, which was founded as a school in 1924, added post-secondary courses in 1953 and became a two-year junior college in 1961. However, after 1967 Birzeit University came under Israeli jurisdiction and since 1994 has been part of the Palestinian (National) Authority (PA). The oldest university is now the University of Jordan (founded 1962). The Ministry of Higher Education and Scientific Research and the Council of Higher Education (founded 1982) are the bodies responsible for higher education, which consists of public and private universities (of which there were 10 and 20 respectively in 2011, compared with a total of only four in 1991). In addition, there are currently some 54 community colleges offering diploma-level post-secondary programmes of study. The total number of students in tertiary education increased from around 40,000 in 1991 to some 246,928 in 2010. In general, the medium of instruction is Arabic, although the majority of scientific, medical and technological university courses are conducted in English.

Universities admissions operate on the basis of the General Secondary Examination (Tawjihi). Jordanian universities operate a US-style 'credit semester' system, under which students are required to accumulate a given number of credits each semester in order to graduate. The standard undergraduate Bachelors degree is a four-year programme of study and requires at least 132 credits. Degrees in professional fields of study, such as medicine, engineering and dentistry, may last from five to six years. In 2005 the Council of Higher Education introduced the University Achievement Examination, to be taken by all undergraduates in the final year of the Bachelors degree. The purpose of this examination is to develop a standard measure for evaluating students and courses at both public and private institutions on a subject by subject basis. Success in this examination leads to the award of the University Achievement Examination Qualification Certificate. There are three postgraduate degrees: the Higher Diploma, Masters and Doctor of Philosophy. The Higher Diploma is a one- to three-year course in a professional field of study. The Masters is generally a two-year course requiring at least 33 credits. Finally, the Doctor of Philosophy lasts for three to five years, and is a combination of both coursework and original research. The full scope of postgraduate degrees is only available at public universities.

Post-secondary vocational and technical education is serviced in the main by community colleges. There are also accredited workplace-based training schemes, which are administered by the Vocational Training Corporation (under the authority of the Ministry of Labour). Courses at community colleges last two to three years, require at least 66 credits for completion and lead to the award of a Diploma. All public community colleges are affiliated to Al-Balqa' Applied University. In 1999 a law was passed establishing a five-tier framework for post-secondary non-university education, graded Semi-Skilled, Skilled, Craftsman, Technician and Professional. To ensure the maintenance of educational standards, the Ministry of Higher Education and Scientific Research evaluates all community college courses. Consequently, most community colleges have now obtained general and professional accreditation.

As a part of the Ministry of Higher Education and Scientific Research, the Accreditation Council was responsible for quality assurance until June 2007 when it was dissolved and the Higher Education Accreditation Commission (consisting of a president, a vice-president, two full-time members, and three part-time members) was set up in its place. In 2006 Jordan signed the Catania Declaration to put into place a 'Euro-Mediterranean Higher Education Area' which seeks to carry out the directives of the Barcelona Declaration of 1995, which later became the Bologna Process. In 2007 a number of priorities were highlighted to bring Jordan's higher education system into line with the European model.

The second stage of the Education Reform for the Knowledge Economy, a 12-year project (2003–15) to improve all levels of the education system in Jordan through policy reforms, was launched in 2009. In August 2011 the Ministry of Higher Education and Scientific Research (working in collaboration with university presidents) drew up a three-year higher education reform plan (2012–15) aimed at improving the quality of higher education and producing graduates who could meet market requirements and compete on an international level. The plan included proposals to give public universities greater autonomy regarding student admissions (through examinations and interviews); to classify community colleges into two types—academic and technical; to establish more laboratories and to allocate 5% of each university's budget for research purposes; and to give universities more independence by providing their boards of trustees with greater academic, administrative and financial authority.

Regulatory and Representative Bodies

GOVERNMENT

Council of Higher Education: Ministry of Higher Education and Scientific Research, POB 35262, Amman; tel. (6) 5347671; e-mail mohe@mohe.gov.jo; internet www.mohe.gov.jo; f. 1982; controls the devt of private higher education and ensures that minimum standards are maintained; Chair. THE MINISTER OF HIGHER EDUCATION AND SCIENTIFIC RESEARCH.

Ministry of Culture: POB 6140, Amman; tel. (6) 5696218; e-mail info@culture.gov.jo; internet www.culture.gov.jo; Minister Dr LANA MAMKEGH.

Ministry of Education: POB 1646, Amman 11118; tel. (6) 5607181; e-mail moe@moe.gov.jo; internet www.moe.gov.jo; Minister Dr MUHAMMAD THNEIBAT.

Ministry of Higher Education and Scientific Research: POB 35262, Amman 11180; tel. (6) 5347671; e-mail mohe@mohe.gov.jo; internet www.mohe.gov.jo; Minister AMIN MAHMOUD.

ACCREDITATION

Higher Education Accreditation Commission: POB 138, Amman 11941; tel. (6) 5347671; e-mail a_hunaiti@mohe.gov.jo; f. 2007; Pres. ABDELRAHIM A. HUNAITI.

Learned Societies

GENERAL

Aal al-Bayt Foundation for Islamic Thought: POB 950361, Amman 11195; tel. (6) 4633642; e-mail aalal-bayt@rhc.jo; internet www.aalalbayt.org; f. 1980; research is divided into 2 main categories: long-term projects such as the issuing of the *Encyclopedia of Arab Islamic Civilization*, the *Comprehensive Catalogue of Arab Islamic MSS*, the *Annotated Bibliographies of Islamic Economy and Islamic Education* and the Great Tafsirs project; and medium-term projects dealing with contemporary Muslim life and thought; 130 mems from 42 countries; library of 26,146 vols, 562 periodicals; special collns: Hashemite and Jordanian Collns; Dir FARUK JARRAR; Librarian NOUZAT ABU LABAN.

UNESCO Office Amman: POB 2270, Amman 11181; Wadi Saqra St, Amman 11181; tel. (6) 5516559; e-mail amman@unesco.org; f. 1973; Dir MOHAMED DJELID.

BIBLIOGRAPHY, LIBRARY SCIENCE AND MUSEOLOGY

Jordan Library and Information Association: POB 6289, Amman; tel. (6) 4629412; internet www.jorla.org; f. 1963; 600 mems; Pres. FADIL KLAYB; Sec. YOUSRA ABU AJAMIEH; publs *Directory of Periodicals in Jordan, Directory of the Libraries in Jordan, Jordanian National Bibliography 1979–, Palestinian Bibliography, Palestinian-Jordanian Bibliography, Rissalat al-Maktaba* (The Message of the Library, 4 a year).

LANGUAGE AND LITERATURE

British Council: First Circle, Jebel Amman, POB 634, Amman 11118; tel. (6) 4603420; e-mail info@britishcouncil.org.jo; internet www.britishcouncil.org/jordan.htm; teaching centre; offers courses and examinations in English language and British culture and promotes cultural exchange with the UK; Dir TIM GORE.

Goethe Institut Jordanien: POB 1676, Amman 11118; 5 Abdel Mun'im Al Rifa'i St, Amman 11118; tel. (6) 4641993; e-mail info@amman.goethe.org; internet www.goethe.de/na/amm/enindex.htm; offers courses and exams in German language and culture and promotes cultural exchange with Germany; library of 3,000 vols; Dir Dr CHRISTIANE KRÄMER-HUS-HUS.

Instituto Cervantes: Mohammad Hafiz Ma'ath St 10, POB 815467, Amman 11180; tel. (6) 4610858; e-mail cenamm@cervantes.es; internet amman.cervantes.es; offers courses and examinations in Spanish language and culture and promotes cultural exchange with Spain and Spanish-speaking Latin and Central America; library of 14,000 vols; Dir MARÍA CARMEN ORDÓÑEZ CARVAJAL.

NATURAL SCIENCES

Biological Sciences

Royal Marine Conservation Society of Jordan: POB 831051, Amman 11183; tel. (6) 5676173; e-mail information@jreds.org; internet www.jreds.org; f. 1993; conservation and sustainable use of the marine environment through conservation programmes, advocacy, education, outreach and empowerment; 250 mems; Exec. Dir FADI F. SHARAIHA.

Research Institutes

AGRICULTURE, FISHERIES AND VETERINARY SCIENCE

National Center for Agricultural Research and Extension: POB 226, Amman; internet www.ncartt.gov.jo; f. 1958 as Dept of Agricultural and Scientific Research and Extension; 1985 became the National Center for Agricultural Research and Technology Transfer; present name 2007; covers all brs of agricultural research, information and extension; library of 18,500 vols; Dir SAID GHEZAWI.

HISTORY, GEOGRAPHY AND ARCHAEOLOGY

Council for British Research in the Levant: POB 519, Jubaiha, Amman 11941; tel. (6) 5341317; e-mail cbrl@britac.ac.uk; internet www.cbrl.org.uk; f. 1996 by merger of the British Institute in Amman for Archaeology and History and the British School of Archaeology in Jerusalem; supports British post-doctoral research in social sciences and the contemporary Levant; provides some limited grant funding and a hostel, library and laboratory facilities to members; library of 24,000 vols, divided between Amman and Jerusalem; Dir Prof. BILL FINLAYSON; publ. *Levant* (3 a year).

TECHNOLOGY

Royal Scientific Society: POB 1438, Al-Jubaiha 11941; tel. (6) 5344701; e-mail rssinfo@rss.gov.jo; internet www.rss.gov.jo; f. 1970; independent, non-profit industrial research and development centre; electronic services and training centre, computer systems, mechanical engineering, chemical industry, building research centre, economics, wind and solar energy research centre; 10 technical centres housing 38 specialized laboratories; Exec. Vice-Pres. Dr SEYFEDDIN MUAZ.

Libraries and Archives

Amman

Abdul Hameed Shoman Public Library: POB 940255, Amman 11194; tel. (6) 4633627; e-mail library@shoman.org.jo; internet www.shoman.org; f. 1986; 140,000 vols, 1,000 periodicals; Dir GHALEB AL MASOUD.

Amman Public Libraries Department: POB 182181, Amman; tel. (6) 4627718; e-mail subeihi@hotmail.com; f. 1960; 500,000 vols, 257,179 vols in Arabic and English, 256 current periodicals; 31 brs for adults and children, Deposit Library for UNESCO (5,000 vols); Jordanian publs; Dir MOHAMMAD SUBEIHI.

El Hassan Library and Media Centre, Princess Sumaya University for Technology: POB 1438, Amman; tel. (6) 5359949; e-mail info@psut.edu.jo; internet www.psut.jo/main/units/library-and-media-center.html; f. 2004; core colln incl. energy, civil engineering, construction, industrial chemistry, mechanical engineering, computer science, economics, electronics; 56,000 vols, 913 periodical titles, 200 theses, 2,000 non-print media, 450 maps, 15,000 specifications; Library Dir Dr NERMEEN SHUQOM.

National Library: POB 6070, Amman 11118; 9 Haroun al-Rasheed St, Amman 11118; tel. (6) 5662845; e-mail nl@nl.gov.jo; internet www.nl.gov.jo; f. 1994; prepares and issues the nat. bibliography and union catalogue; responsible for copyrights and legal deposits; responsible for enforcing Jordanian copyright law; depository for nat., UNESCO and WIPO publs; 140,439 vols, 52,000 titles; Dir-Gen. MOHAMMAD AMIN ALFALEH ALABADI.

University of Jordan Library: Univ. of Jordan, Amman; tel. (6) 5355000; e-mail library@ju.edu.jo; internet library.ju.edu.jo; f. 1962; 789,000 vols, 350 current Arabic periodicals, 19,977 online periodicals, mainly in English; 15 reading rooms; legal depository for UN, WHO, FAO, World Bank, UNESCO, IMF, SIPRI, UNU, ILO, Institute for Peace Research documents; legal deposit for dissertations from all Arab universities; Dir Dr MOHAMMAD RAQAB; publs *Bibliographical list and indexes* (irregular), Directory for Theses Deposited at University Library (2 a year), *Library Guide* (1 a year).

Museums and Art Galleries

Amman

Folklore Museum: POB 88, Amman; f. 1972; housed by the Dept of Antiquities; colln of nat. traditional costumes; Curator Mrs SA'DIYA AL-TEL.

Jordan Archaeological Museum: POB 88, Amman; tel. (6) 46319768; e-mail doa@nic.net.jo; f. 1951; 13,000 objects, 36,000 coins; 20 staff; library of 3,560 vols; Curator AIDA NAGHAURY.

Museum of Popular Traditions: POB 88, Amman; f. 1971; local domestic history; brs in Petra, Madaba, Salt and Kerak; Curator IMAN QUDA.

Universities

AL-AHLIYYA AMMAN UNIVERSITY

Al-Ahliyya Amman Univ., POB 19328, Amman
Telephone: (5) 3500211
E-mail: info@ammanu.edu.jo
Internet: www.ammanu.edu.jo

Founded 1990
Private control
Languages of instruction: Arabic, English
Pres.: Prof. Dr MAHER SALIM

DEANS

Faculty of Administrative and Financial Science: Dr HUSSEIN EL-YASEEN
Faculty of Arts: Dr WAFA EL-KHADRA
Faculty of Engineering: Prof. Dr SADIQ HAMED
Faculty of Information Technology: Dr MUSTAFA YASEEN
Faculty of Law: Dr OMAR EL-BOURINI
Faculty of Nursing: Prof. Dr WASEELA PETRO
Faculties of Pharmacy and Medical Sciences: Dr MAHER SHORBAJI

AL AL-BAYT UNIVERSITY

POB 130040, Mafraq 25113
Telephone: (2) 6297000
E-mail: programmer@aabu.edu.jo
Internet: www.aabu.edu.jo

Founded 1992
public control
Languages of instruction: Arabic, English
Academic year: September to June
Pres.: Prof. NABIL T. SHAWAGFEH
Vice-Pres. for Admin. and Finance: Prof. JIHAD SHAHER AL-MAJALI
Registrar: QFTAN AL-MONANI

Library: 122,005 Arabic Books, 36,019 English books, 23,000 ebooks
Number of teachers: 317
Number of students: 11,897

Publications: *Al-Manara* (Journal of Academic Research, 4 a year, in English and Arabic), *Al-Zahra* (12 a year, in English and Arabic)

DEANS

Faculty of Arts and Humanities: Prof. MOHAMMAD AL DROBI
Faculty of Educational Sciences: Dr AWATIF ABU SHAOR
Faculty of Engineering: Dr ALI ABU KANEEMAH
Faculty of Finance and Business Administration: Dr JAMAL AL-SHARAIRI
Faculty of Law: Dr EID AL-HUSSBAN
Faculty of Nursing: Dr OMAR RAWAJFEH
Faculty of Science: Dr EQAB RABIE
Faculty of Shari'a: Dr MOHAMMAD AL-ZUGHOL

Prince Hussein Bin Abdullah College for Information Technology: Dr ISMAIL ABABNEH

AL-BALQA' APPLIED UNIVERSITY

POB 19117, Al-Salt, Al-Balqa' Governorate
Telephone: (5) 3491111
E-mail: davana@bau.edu.jo
Internet: www.bau.edu.jo

Founded 1997
State control
There are 14 affiliated univ. colleges and around 36 affiliated private, military and UN-operated colleges
Pres.: Prof. Dr OMAR ABDALKARIM RIMAWI
Vice-Pres.: Prof. ABDALLAH S. AL-ZOUBI
Vice-Pres.: Prof. NAIM M. ALJOUNI
Dean of Student Affairs: Dr HAMDAN AWAMLEH
Librarian: NIDAL AL-AHMAD
Library of 38,500 vols
Number of teachers: 1,460
Number of students: 45,000

DEANS

Faculty of Agricultural Technology: Dr YASIN ALZU'BI
Faculty of Engineering: Dr MAHER KHAKISH
Faculty of Graduate Studies and Scientific Research: Dr GHANDI ANFOKA
Faculty of Planning and Management: JIHAD ABU AL SONDOS
Faculty of Science and Information Technology: Dr IBRAHIM HAMARNEH

AL-HUSSEIN BIN TALAL UNIVERSITY

POB 20, Ma'an
Telephone: (3) 2179000
E-mail: ahu@go.com.jo
Internet: www.ahu.edu.jo

Founded 1999
State control
Pres.: ALI KHALAF AL-HROOT
Dean of Academic Research: Prof. KAMAL AYOUB MOMANI
Number of teachers: 58
Number of students: 1,948
Publication: *Al-Haq Ya'lu* (2 a year)

DEANS

College of Archaeology, Tourism and Hotel Management: Prof. HANI HAYAJNEH
College of Arts: Dr TAISIR KHALIL EL-ZAWAREH
College of Business Administration and Economics: (vacant)
College of Computer Engineering and Information Technology: Dr FARES FRAIJ
College of Education: Dr MONA ALI ABU DARWESH
College of Mining and Environmental Engineering: Dr MARWAN BATIHA
College of Science: Dr ALI MAHMUD ATEIWI

AL-ISRA PRIVATE UNIVERSITY

POB 22/33, Amman 11622
Telephone: (6) 4711710
E-mail: info@isra.edu.jo
Internet: www.isra.edu.jo

Founded 1991
Private control
Languages of instruction: Arabic, English
Pres.: ABDUL BARI DURA
Vice-Pres.: NAYEF KHARMA
Dean of Research: GHANEM EL-HASAWI
Dean of Student Affairs: HOSNI AL-SHEYYIB

DEANS

Faculty of Administrative and Financial Sciences: MUSA ALMADHOON
Faculty of Engineering: AHMAD AL-FAHED NUSEIRAT
Faculty of Law: AHMED ABU SHANAB
Faculty of Pharmacy and Medical Sciences: MAZEN QATTO
Faculty of Science and Information Technology: AYMAN AL-NSOUR

AL-ZAYTOONAH UNIVERSITY

POB 130, Amman 11733
Telephone: (6) 4291511
E-mail: information@alzaytoonah.edu.jo
Internet: www.alzaytoonah.edu.jo

Founded 1993
Private control
Languages of instruction: Arabic, English
Pres.: Prof. NASR SALEH
Number of teachers: 300
Number of students: 8,000

DEANS

Faculty of Arts: ISAM MAHMOOD ABU SALEEM
Faculty of Economics and Administrative Science: GHALIB AWAD RIFA'I
Faculty of Law: HUSSEIN ATTA HAMDAN
Faculty of Nursing: AHLAM YOUSSEF HAMDAN
Faculty of Pharmacy: SAYYED ISMAIL MOHAMMAD
Faculty of Science: ABDEL FATAH ARIF TAMIMI

APPLIED SCIENCE UNIVERSITY

POB 166, Amman 11931
Telephone: (6) 5609999
E-mail: info@aspu.edu.jo
Internet: www.aspu.edu.jo
Private control
Languages of instruction: Arabic, English
Academic year: September to June
Chair.: ABDALLAH ABU KHADEJEH
Pres.: ZEYAD RAMADAN
Number of teachers: 319
Number of students: 8,000
Publication: *Jordanian Journal of Applied Sciences* (2 a year)

DEANS

Faculty of Allied Medical Sciences: KAYED QUR'OUSH
Faculty of Art and Design: AHMAD MURSI
Faculty of Arts and Humanities: KAYED QUR'OUSH
Faculty of Economics and Administrative Sciences: MAHFOUZ JUDEH
Faculty of Engineering: YEHYA ABDELLATIF
Faculty of Information Technology: NAEL HIRZALLAH
Faculty of Law: TALIB MOUSA
Faculty of Nursing: SAMIHA JARRAH
Faculty of Pharmacy: SUHAIR SALEH

JORDAN UNIVERSITY OF SCIENCE AND TECHNOLOGY (JUST)

POB 3030, Irbid 22110
Telephone: (2) 7201000
E-mail: just@just.edu.jo
Internet: www.just.edu.jo

Founded 1986
State control
Languages of instruction: Arabic, English
Academic year: September to September
Pres.: Prof. WAJIH M. OWAIS
Dean of Research: Prof. FAWZI BANAT
Dir of Public Relations: MUHANNAD MALKAWI
Registrar: FAISAL AL RIFAIE
Librarian: ISSA LELLO
Library of 90,000 vols
Number of teachers: 750
Number of students: 20,409 (18,850 undergraduate and 1,559 graduate)

DEANS

College of Architecture and Design: Dr NATHEER ABU OBEID
Faculty of Agriculture: Prof. MUNIR J. RUSAN
Faculty of Applied Medical Sciences: Prof. LAILA NIMRI
Faculty of Computer Information Technology: Dr MOHAMMAD AL-ROUSAN
Faculty of Dentistry: Prof. ANWAH BATAINEH
Faculty of Engineering: Prof. KHALED A. MAYYAS
Faculty of Medicine: Prof. KAMAL E. BANI-HANI
Faculty of Nursing: Dr MUNTAHA GHARAIBEH
Faculty of Pharmacy: Dr KHOULOUD ALKHAMIS
Faculty of Science and Arts: Prof. AHMED M. ELBETIEHA
Faculty of Veterinary Medicine: Prof. SAEB AL-SUKHON

MU'TAH UNIVERSITY

POB 7, Mu'tah, Al-Karak 61710
Telephone: (3) 2372380; (6) 4617860
E-mail: hunaiti@hu.edu.jo
Internet: www.mutah.edu.jo

Founded 1981
State control
Languages of instruction: Arabic, English
Academic year: September to June
Pres.: Prof. Dr ABDEL RAHIM A. HUMAITI
Vice-Pres. for Academic Affairs: Prof. MOHAMMAD ABBADI
Vice-Pres. for Admin. Affairs: Prof. QUBLAN AL-MAJALI
Vice-Pres. for Humanities and Science: Prof. MOHANNAD AMIN ABBADI
Vice-Pres. for Military Affairs: ESMAEL E. AL-SHOBAKI
Dean for Academic Research: Prof. MOHAMMAD AL-TARAWNEH
Dean for Graduate Studies: Prof. NIDAL HAWAMDEH
Dean for Student Affairs: Prof. AHMAD BATTAH
Dir of Cultural and Public Affairs: JAZA' MOHAMMAD AL-MASARWEH
Registrar: YASER KASASBEH
Librarian: Dr ABDEL WAHAB MOBIDEEN
Library of 534,753 vols
Number of teachers: 530
Number of students: 16,000
Publication: *Mu'tah Journal for Research and Studies*

DEANS

Faculty of Agriculture: Dr AMER MAMKAGH
Faculty of Arts: Prof. HUSSAM ALDEEN MUBAIDEEN
Faculty of Business Administration: Dr FAHAD S. KHATEEB
Faculty of Education: Prof. MOHAMMAD RABABAA
Faculty of Engineering: Prof. AYMAN AL-MAAYTEH
Faculty of Law: Dr NIZAM AL-MAJALI
Faculty of Medicine: Prof. ADEL ABU AL-HAIJA
Faculty of Nursing: Prof. SAMEER AL-TAWEEL
Faculty of Physical Education: Prof. MOUTASEM SHATNAWI
Faculty of Sciences: Prof. MAHDI LATAIFEH
Faculty of Shari'a: Prof. NAEL ABU ZAID
Faculty of Social Sciences: Prof. IBRAHIM AL-OROUD

PHILADELPHIA UNIVERSITY

POB 1, Amman 19392
Telephone: (6) 4799000
E-mail: info@philadelphia.edu.jo
Internet: www.philadelphia.edu.jo

Founded 1989
Private control

Languages of instruction: Arabic, English
Vice-Pres. for Academic Affairs: Prof. MOHAMMAD AWWAD
Vice-Pres. for Admin. and Financial Affairs: Prof. SALEH ABU OSBA
Dean of Academic Research and Graduate Studies: Prof. MAHMOUD KISHTA
Dean of Student Affairs: Dr MOUSTAFA AL-JALABNEH
Dir for Admissions and Registration: Dr KHALDOUN BATIHA

Number of teachers: 300
Number of students: 5,000

DEANS

Faculty of Admin. and Financial Sciences: Prof. KHALID AL-SARTAWI
Faculty of Arts: Dr MOHAMMAD OBAIDELLAH
Faculty of Engineering: Prof. KASIM AL-AUBAIDY
Faculty of Information Technology: Dr KHALDOUN BATIHA
Faculty of Law: Dr BASSAM AL-TRAWNEH
Faculty of Nursing: Dr FADIA HASNA
Faculty of Pharmacy: Dr JALAL AL-JAMAL
Faculty of Science: Dr RIYAD JABRI

PRINCESS SUMAYA UNIVERSITY FOR TECHNOLOGY

POB 1438, Al-Jubaiha 11941
Telephone: (6) 5359967
E-mail: info@psut.edu.jo
Internet: www.psut.edu.jo

Founded 1991
Private control
Pres.: Prof. HISHAM GHASSIB
Librarian: NERMEEN SHUQOM

Library: see under Libraries and Archives
Number of teachers: 10
Number of students: 120

DEANS

King Abdullah II School for Electrical Engineering: Prof. BASSAM KAHHALEH
King Hussein School for Information Technology: Prof. YAHIA AL-HALABI

THE HASHEMITE UNIVERSITY

POB 330127, Zarqa 13115
Telephone: (5) 3903333
E-mail: huniv@hu.edu.jo
Internet: www.hu.edu.jo

Founded 1992
State control
Languages of instruction: Arabic, English
Academic year: August to June
Pres.: Prof. KAMAL BANI HANI
Vice-Pres.: Prof. MARWAN OBEIDAT
Vice-Pres.: Prof. MOHAMMAD MISMAR
Dean for Student Affairs: Dr YUSIF OLEIMAT
Librarian: Dr MU'ATH BATAINEH

Library of 250,000 vols, 26,367 periodicals
Number of teachers: 510
Number of students: 28,000

Publications: *Jordan Journal of Biological Sciences*, *Jordan Journal of Earth and Environmental Sciences*, *Jordan Journal of Mechanical and Industrial Engineering*

DEANS

Faculty of Allied Health Sciences: Dr SALEM R. Y. AL-MALOUL
Faculty of Arts: Dr ABDUL-BASIT AL-ZYUD
Faculty of Childhood: Dr SUHA (M. H) S. AL HASSAN
Faculty of Economics and Admin. Science: Dr HUSAM KHADDASH
Faculty of Educational Sciences: Dr AIMAN AL-OMARI
Faculty of Engineering: Dr SHAHER RABAB'AH
Faculty of Information Technology: Dr AHMAD KHASAWNEH
Faculty of Medicine: Prof. KAMAL BANI-HANI
Faculty of Natural Resources and Environment: Prof. EID A. E. AL TARAZI
Faculty of Nursing: Prof. NIJMEH AL-ATIYYAT
Faculty of Physical Education and Sports Sciences: Dr MAHER AL-KILANI
Faculty of Research and Graduate Studies: Prof. SADI ABDUL-JAWAD
Faculty of Sciences: Prof. ALI ELKARMI

UNIVERSITY OF JORDAN

Amman 11942
Telephone: (6) 5355000
E-mail: admin@ju.edu.jo
Internet: www.ju.edu.jo

Founded 1962
state and autonomous control
Languages of instruction: Arabic, English
Academic year: September to August (2 semesters and a summer session)
Pres.: KHALED AL-KARAKI
Dir of Registration and Admission: GHALEB AL-HOURANI
Dir of Library: Dr HANI AL-AMAD

Library: see under Libraries and Archives
Number of teachers: 931
Number of students: 23,623

Publication: *Dirasat* (scientific research)

DEANS

Faculty of Agriculture: Prof. MOHAMMED ISAM YAMAMI
Faculty of Arts: Dr SALAMEH NAIMT
Faculty of Arts and Design: Dr ABDUL-HAMEED HAMAM
Faculty of Business: Prof. HANI AL-DMOUR
Faculty of Dentistry: Prof. LAMIS RAJAB
Faculty of Educational Sciences: Prof. MOHAMMAD NAZIH HAMDI
Faculty of Engineering and Technology: Prof. RAED M. SAMRA
Faculty of Foreign Languages: Prof. AHMAD MAJDOUBEH
Faculty of Graduate Studies: Prof. MUNA S. AL-HADIDI
Faculty of International Studies: Prof. ABDULLAH NAGRASH
Faculty of Law: Prof. GEORGE HAZBOUN
Faculty of Medicine: Dr SLAM SALEH DARADKEH
Faculty of Nursing: Dr INAAM KHALAF
Faculty of Pharmacy: Dr KHALED M. AIEDEH
Faculty of Physical Education: Prof. SUHA ADEEB DAOUD
Faculty of Rehabilitation Sciences: Prof. BASSAM AMMARI
Faculty of Science: Dr HALA KHYAMI-HORANI
Faculty of Shari'a (Islamic Studies): Prof. MOHAMMAD KHAZER AL-MAJALI
King Abdullah II Faculty for Information Technology: Dr FAWAZ AHMAD M. MASOUD AL-ZAGHOUL

UNIVERSITY OF PETRA

POB 961343, Amman 11196
Telephone: (6) 5799555
E-mail: registrar@uop.edu.jo
Internet: www.uop.edu.jo

Founded 1991 as Jordan Univ. for Women
Languages of instruction: Arabic, English
Private control
Pres.: Prof. ADNAN BADRAN
Vice-Pres. for Academic Affairs and Dean of Research and Graduate Studies: Prof. NIZAR EL-RAYYES
Dean of Admissions and Registration: Dr NASER AL-JARNAL
Dean of Student Affairs: Dr MOUHAMAD EL-KASASBEH

Library of 91,411 vols, 65,387 titles, 52,000 ebooks
Number of teachers: 266
Number of students: 6,000

Publications: *Al-Basair* (scientific journal, 2 a year), *Awraq Jamie'ya* (2 a year)

DEANS

Faculty of Administrative and Financial Services: Dr RAFIQ OMAR
Faculty of Architecture and Arts: Dr AHMAD ABDEL-JAWAD
Faculty of Arts and Sciences: Prof. MOHAMMAD ISHAQ AL-ANANI
Faculty of Information Technology: Dr GASSAN ISSA
Faculty of Pharmacy and Medical Sciences: Prof. TAWFEEQ ARAFAT

YARMOUK UNIVERSITY

POB 566, Irbid 21163
Telephone: (2) 7211111
E-mail: yarmouk@yu.edu.jo
Internet: www.yu.edu.jo

Founded 1975
national and autonomous control
Languages of instruction: Arabic, English
Academic year: October to June
Pres.: Prof. Dr FAYEZ I. KHASAWNEH
Vice-Pres. for Academic Affairs: Prof. Dr HISHAM S. GHARAIBEH
Vice-Pres. for Admin. Affairs: Prof. Dr MOHAMMED S. SUBBARINI
Registrar: ZACHARIAH ABU-ALDAHAB
Librarian: Dr MOHAMMAD SARAYRAH

Library: Central Library of 300,000 vols, 800 current periodicals
Number of teachers: 687
Number of students: 21,205

Publications: *Abhath al-Yarmouk* (Yarmouk Research Journal), *Yarmouk Numismatics* (journal)

DEANS

Faculty of Archaeology and Anthropology: Prof. ZAIDON AL-MUHASIN
Faculty of Arts: Prof. FAHMI GHAZWI
Faculty of Economics and Administrative Sciences: Prof. WALEED HMEDAT
Faculty of Education: Prof. YOUSEF SAWALMEH
Hijjawi Faculty of Engineering Technology: Prof. FAROQ AL-OMARY
Faculty of Fine Arts: Prof. KHALID AL-HAMZEH
Faculty of Information Technology: Prof. SULEIMAN MUSTAFA
Faculty of Law: Dr AYMEN MASADEH
Faculty of Physical Education: Prof. Dr ALI AL-DEIRY
Faculty of Science: Prof. IBRAHIM ABU AL-JARAIESH
Faculty of Shari'a (Islamic Law): Dr MUHAMMAD AL-OMARI

PROFESSORS

ABDUL-ALMAJED, M., Usul al-Din
ABDUL-HAFEZ, S., Biology
ABDULHAY, W., Political Science
ABDUL-RAHMAN, A., Arabic
ABO-ZEID, M., Electronic Engineering
ABU AL-JARAYESH, I., Physics
ABU HELOU, Y., Education
ABU-HILAL, A., Geology
ABU-RAHMAH, K., Arabic
ABU-SALEH, M., Statistics
ABUL-UDOUSS, Y., Arabic
ADWAN, Y., Public Administration
AL-ADWAN, S., Chemistry
AL-AHMADI, A., Usul al-Din
AL-ARAIBI, M., Fine Arts
AL-AWNEH, S., Education Psychology
AL-FAYOUMI, I., Arabic
AL-HAQ, F., Linguistics

AL-HASSAN, K., Chemistry
AL-HASSAN, S., English
AL-HIARY, H., Education
AL-JUBOORY, K., Epigraphy
AL-KATIB, R., Education
AL-KAYSI, M., Islamic Studies
AL-MUHEISEN, Z., Archaeology
AL-NOURI, Q., Anthropology
AL-QUDAH, M., Chemistry
AL-QURAISH, T., Semitic and Oriental Languages
AL-SAADI, W., Public Law
AL-SALEM, H., Physical Education
AL-SALIM, M., Business Administration
AL-SHEIKH, K., Arabic
AL-SHMAI, F., Private Law
AL-TELL, SH., Education
ARAJI, A., Public Administration
AREDAH, F., Sports Science
ASFAR, O., Engineering Science and Mechanics
ATHAMNEH, N., English
ATIYYAT, A., Chemistry
ATOUM, A., Education
AWAD, A., History
AYYOUB, N., Physics
BADER, Y., Linguistics
BAKKAR, Y., Arabic
BANI HANI, A., Economics
BARQAWI, K., Chemistry
BATAYNEH, M., History
DAIRY, A., Physical Education
DARABSEH, M., Arabic
DWAIRI, I., Geology
ESMADI, F., Chemistry
FAOURI, R., Public Administration
FARGHAL, M., English
FATAFTAH, Z., Chemistry
FORA, A., Mathematics
GHARAIBEH, H., Banking and Finance
GHARAIBEH, S., Geology
GHAWANMEH, Y., History
GHAZWI, F., Sociology
GHAZZAWI, M., Education
HADDAD, H., Arabic
HADDAD, M., Anthropology
HADDAD, N., Arabic
HAJ-HUSSEIN, A. T., Chemistry
HAMAD, A., Arabic
HAMAM, A., Music
HAMDAN, A., Linguistics
HAMMAD, KH., Economics
HIJAZI, M., Usul al-Din
HIJJEH, M., Mathematics
HMEDAT, W., Economics
HUNAITI, A., Biology
IDRES, A., Fiqh
JIBRIL, I., Chemistry
KAFAFI, Z., Archaeology
KHARBUTLI, M., English
KHASAWNEH, F., Biology
KHASAWNEH, I., Chemistry
KHATEEB, A., Education
KHAWALDEH, M., Education
KHRAIWISH, H., Arabic
KOFAHI, M., Physics
KURDI, Z., Physical Education
LAHAM, N., Physics
LAHHAM, J., Biology
MADAN, K., Statistics
MAHADIN, R., Linguistics
MAHMOUD, S., Physics
MAKKI, A., Electrical Power Engineering
MARI, T. A., Education
MASHAGBAH, F., English
MOMANI, Q., Arabic
MOMANI, R., Economics
MOMANI, R., Islamic Economy
MRYYAN, N., Economics
NAFI, A., Arabic
NAJJAR, M., Anthropology
NUSAIR, N., Public Administration
ODEH, A., Education
OGLAH, A., Biology
OLAIMAT, M., Education
OLWAN, M., Law
OMARI, M, Usul al-Din
OWEIS, W., Biology
QASSEM, W., Biomechanics
QUDAH, S., Arabic
QUTTOUS, B., Arabic
RABABAH, M., Arabic
RABBA'I, A., Arabic
RASHID, M., Chemistry
RAWI, Z., Statistics
RAYYAN, M., History
REFAI, M., Mathematics
REFAIE, S., Electronic Engineering
RHAYYEL, A., Mathematics
SABBAGH, Z., Business Administration
SADEDDIN, W., Geology
SADIQ, M., Fine Arts
SAFA, F., Arabic
SALEM, A., Physics
SALHIEH, M., History
SARI, S., Archaeology
SERYANI, M., Geography
SHARE'E, M., Economics
SHARI, A., Arabic
SHAYEB, F., Arabic
SHORFAT, M., Linguistics
SMADI, A., Education Psychology
STATIYYEH, S., Arabic
SUBBARINI, M., Education
SULEIMAN, I., Journalism
TALAFHA, H., Economics
TALIB, M., Chemistry
TASHTOUSH, H., Chemistry
THALJI, A., English
UGAILI, S., Computer Science
UGLAH, M., Fiqh and Islamic Studies
WARDAT, R., Linguistics
WAZARMAS, I., Physical Education
YOUNIS, M., Mathematics
YUSUF, N., Physics
ZAGHAL, A., Sociology
ZAGHAL, M., Chemistry
ZIADAT, A., Journalism
ZUBI, A., Arabic
ZUGHOUL, M., English

ZARQA UNIVERSITY

POB 132222, Al-Zarqa 13132
Telephone: (5) 3821100
E-mail: info@zu.edu.jo
Internet: www.zu.edu.jo

Founded 1994
Private control
Languages of instruction: Arabic, English
Academic year: October to June

Pres.: Prof. YOUSEF ABU ADDOUS
Vice-Pres.: Prof. ZAKARIA SIAM
Dean for Scientific Research and Graduate Studies: Prof. SAMI AL-ALI
Dean for Student Affairs: Dr MAJED MASADEH
Head of Library: Dr AWNI MANSOUR

Library of 110,000 vols, 956 periodicals
Number of teachers: 280
Number of students: 7,470

Publications: *The International Arab Journal of Information Technology* (6 a year, in English, print and online (www.iajit.org)), *Zarqa Journal for Research and Studies in Humanities*

DEANS

Faculty of Art: Prof. ABDULHAMEED GHUNAIM
Faculty of Arts and Designs: Dr HUSNI ABU KRAIEM
Faculty of Economics and Administrative Sciences: Prof. MOHAMMAD AL-TAAI
Faculty of Educational Sciences: Dr YOUSEF ABU SHINDI
Faculty of Engineering: Dr OMAR AL-OMARI
Faculty of Journalism and Mass Communication: Prof. ADEL ZIADAT
Faculty of Law: MUSTAFA AL-KHASAWNEH
Faculty of Nursing: Dr MANAL ZEINHOM
Faculty of Pharmacy: NANCY HAKOOZ
Faculty of Science and Information Technology: Dr HAMMED FAWAREH
Faculty of Shari'a (Islamic Studies): Dr MUHAMMAD BANI-SALEH
Faculty of Supporting Medical Sciences: MOUSA AL-QTAM

PROFESSORS

ABOUDI, A., English Literature
ABU-ODDOUS, Y., Arabic Language
ABU SAFIEH, H., Physics
AHMAD, M., Mathematics
AL-ALI, S., Physics
AL-ATHARI, F., Statistics
AL-AZZAWI, M., Psychological Science
AL-BADRI, A., Psychological Science
AL JABBALI, I., English Literature
AL-JMAILY, H., Economics
AL-KASASBEH, R., Electrical Engineering
AL-TAEE, M., Business Management
AQEL, M., Computer Science
AQTAM, M., Biology
EL KHATTAT, M., Interior Design
GUNAIM, A. H., Human Geography
HAKOUZ, N., Chemistry
MAIDEH, I., Accounting
MIRO, U., Civil Engineering
SIAM, Z., Arabic Literature
ZIADAT, A., Political Sociology

Colleges

Department of Statistics: POB 2015, Amman 11181; tel. (6) 5300700; e-mail j.s.t.c@dos.gov.jo; internet www.dos.gov.jo; f. 1964 for the training of govt employees and other applicants in statistical methods; library: 700 vols; Dir ABDULHADI ALAWIN.

National Institute of Training: POB 960383, Amman; tel. (6) 4664155; f. 1968 as the Jordanian Institute for Public Administration; present name and status 2001; administrative training, research and consultation; library: 5,386 vols; Dir-Gen. ABDULLAH ELAYYAN.

KAZAKHSTAN

The Higher Education System

The Kazakh (formerly Kyrgyz) Autonomous Soviet Socialist Republic was founded in 1920 and became a full Union Republic of the USSR in 1936. In 1991 Kazakhstan declared independence from the USSR, and was renamed the Republic of Kazakhstan. The oldest institutions of higher education date from the Soviet period, and include Kazakh National Pedagogical University, Abai (founded 1928), West Kazakhstan State University named after M. Utemisov (founded 1932; current name and status 2000) and Al-Farabi Kazakh National University (founded 1934; current name and status 1994). For the most part, the Ministry of Education and Science oversees higher education, which is governed according to the Law on Higher Education (1993 and 2007). The languages of instruction are Kazakh and Russian, although Kazakhs constitute the majority of students in higher education and ethnic Russians mostly choose to attend institutions outside Kazakhstan. Among institutions offering higher education are universities, academies, institutes, conservatories, higher schools and higher vocational schools. In 2003/04 there were 134 non-governmental higher education institutes with 297,900 students. In 2008/09 there were 108,000 students enrolled in professional-technical schools, and in 2010/11 a total of 620,400 students were undertaking tertiary education at 149 state-run higher schools, including universities. Since the early 1990s the number of higher education institutions has risen substantially (particularly in the private sector, with more than 100 establishments having been founded since independence). Kazakhstan ratified the Lisbon Convention in 1998 and signed up to the Bologna Process in 2010. A new Law on Higher Education was implemented in 2007 which outlines the Bologna principles (including the adoption of a credit-based system of comparable degrees with two main cycles—undergraduate and graduate).

Since 2004 admission to higher education has been on the basis of both the old Diploma of Completed Secondary Education and the new Unified National Testing Examination. Since 1995/96 the university awards system has moved away from the Soviet-era Specialist Diploma (undergraduate), Candidate of Sciences and Doctor of Sciences (both postgraduate) and towards the European-style Bachelors, Masters and Doctor of Philosophy (PhD) degrees. The undergraduate-level Specialist Diploma continues to be offered in a number of disciplines, particularly professional areas such as military studies, medicine and engineering, and lasts five to six years. Graduates with this degree (which is considered to be equivalent to a Masters) may advance straight to doctoral-level studies. The Bachelors is a four-year degree; students pursue a general programme of studies in the first two years before majoring in one subject in the final two years. Graduates with a Bachelors may then study for a Masters degree, a one-and-a-half- to two-year course of study, which requires the presentation of a thesis. The Soviet-style Candidate of Sciences and the Bologna-style PhD are research-based degrees lasting two to three years, following which the student must defend a thesis. Entrance to these courses requires either the Specialist Diploma or the Masters. Finally, the highest university-level degree is the Doctor of Sciences, a period of study with no fixed duration, which allows the student to pursue a career in academia or research.

Technical and vocational education at post-secondary level is offered by vocational schools, technical schools and colleges. The standard entry requirement is 11–12 years of completed education or the Diploma of Completed Secondary Education. Courses leading to the award of the Diploma of Completed Vocational Secondary Education last between six months to one year. There are also vocational colleges that administer courses of two to three years leading to the award of the Diploma of Specialized Secondary Education in a single professional field of study. In 2011 a State Programme of Education Development was adopted for 2011–20. Amongst its objectives are to introduce a 12-year education system, develop a public–private partnership model of education financing, modernize the technical and vocational education sector, ensure lifelong education and fully integrate into the European higher education space.

The National Accreditation Centre at the Ministry of Education and Science is responsible for quality assurance and accreditation, which consists of a three-stage process: licensing, attestation and accreditation. First, an institution's legal status is affirmed by the award of an operational licence. Second, a process of attestation assesses the institution's compliance with minimum educational standards defined by the Ministry of Education and Science. Third, and finally, institutions that have met the appropriate standards of quality assurance receive full accreditation, which is then dependent on future five-yearly attestation processes.

Regulatory Bodies

GOVERNMENT

Ministry of Culture and Information: Orynbor kosh. 8, Astana 010000; tel. (717) 2740429; e-mail mki@mki.gov.kz; internet www.mki.gov.kz; Minister MUKHTAR KUL-MUKHAMMED.

Ministry of Education and Science: Orynbor kosh. 8, Astana 010000; tel. (717) 2912790; e-mail info@edu.gov.kz; internet www.edu.gov.kz; Minister SARINZHIPOV ASLAN BAKENOVICH.

ACCREDITATION

National Accreditation Centre: Office 504, 19 Imanova St, Astana; tel. (717) 2787611; e-mail nac.edu@bk.ru; internet nac.edu.kz; f. 2005; develops nat. model of quality assurance in education; conducts institutional and specialized accreditation of educational instns; organizes and performs training studies regarding accreditation processes; Dir Dr RIMMA GANIEVNA SEIDAKHMETOVA.

Learned Societies

GENERAL

National Academy of Sciences of the Republic of Kazakhstan: Shevchenko 28, Almaty 050021; tel. (727) 2695593; f. 1946; sections of biological and medical sciences, chemical engineering, earth sciences, humanities and social sciences, physical and mathematical sciences; Pres. MURAT ZHURINOV.

UNESCO Almaty Office: 67 Tole Bi St, Almaty 050000; tel. (727) 2582643; e-mail almaty@unesco.org; internet www.unesco.kz; f. 1994; designated Cluster Office for Kazakhstan, Kyrgyzstan, Tajikistan, Uzbekistan; Dir SERGEY LAZAREV.

LANGUAGE AND LITERATURE

British Council: 97 Zholdasbekov St, Samal–2, Samal Towers, Block A–2, 11th Fl., Almaty 050051; tel. (727) 2444144; e-mail almaty@kz.britishcouncil.org; internet www.britishcouncil.org/kazakhstan; offers courses and examinations in English language and British culture; promotes cultural exchange with the UK; attached office in Astana; responsible for British Council work in Kyrgyzstan; library of 10,000 vols; Dir LENA MILOSEVIC.

Goethe-Institut: Dschandosowa 2, Almaty, 050040; tel. (727) 3922259; e-mail info@almaty.goethe.org; internet www.goethe.de/oe/alm/deindex.htm; offers courses and examinations in German language and culture and promotes cultural exchange with Germany; library of 5,000 vols; Dir BARBARA FRAENKEL-THONET.

Taraz Association of Teachers of English (TATE): 9 Suleimanova St, Taraz, Zhambyl; tel. (726) 2344137; e-mail tate@

hotbox.ru; f. 1996; promotes learning of English, professional devt of teachers, exchange of knowledge and information; 100 mems; Pres. GULMIRA YEMKULOVA.

NATURAL SCIENCES

Biological Sciences

Kazakh Physiology Society: Al-Farabi Ave 93, Almaty 480060; tel. (727) 2783659; e-mail i.physiology@nursat.kz; attached to Institute of Human and Animal Physiology; Head Prof. I. K. KOLBAY.

TECHNOLOGY

National Academy of Engineering of the Republic of Kazakhstan: 80 Bogenbay Batyra St, Almaty 480100; tel. (727) 2911793; e-mail btzh@netmail.kz; provides forum for scientists, engineers, experts in the field of natural, technical and economic sciences; supports industrial and innovative devt of Kazakhstan; 150 mems; Pres. BAKYTZHAN TURSYNOVICH ZHUMAGULOV.

Research Institutes

AGRICULTURE, FISHERIES AND VETERINARY SCIENCE

A. I. Barayev Research Institute of Grain Farming: Nauchniy Village, Shorthandy, Akmola 021600; tel. (716) 3121059; e-mail kanal@kepter.kz; f. 1956; library of 56,000 vols; Dir ZHEKSENBAY KASKARBAYEV.

Akmola Agricultural Research Institute: Charlinka, Zerendinsky raion, Selo Akmola 021231; tel. (711) 7224186; f. 1984; Dir BAKYTZHAN ZHANAIDAROVICH KHAMZIN.

Aral Scientific and Research Institute of Agroecology and Agriculture: Abaja 29B, Kyzylorda 467018; f. 1995; Dir MEIRMAN GALIOLLA TOLENDYULY.

Atyrau Scientific and Research Institute of Agriculture: Shelesnodoroshnaja 2, Atyrau 060002; tel. (710) 2229046; f. 1995; Dir KARIMOV SHAIDOLLA KARIMOVICH.

Central Kazakhstan Scientific and Research Institute of Agriculture: Buchar Zhyrau raion Selo Centralnoe, Karagandy 472384; tel. (721) 3831251; f. 1937; Dir KHRISTENKO ALEXANDR FJODOROVICH.

East Kazakhstan Scientific and Research Institute of Agriculture: Ul. Nagornaya 3A, Glubokovsky raion, Pos., Opytnoye Pole Eastern Kazakhstanv 070512; tel. (727) 2295654; Dir ZHEKSEKENOV SAINELCHAN ZHEKSEKENOVICH.

Kazakh Scientific and Research Institute of Astrakhan Breeding: pr. Lenina 3, Shymkent 160019; tel. (725) 2120409; f. 1962; Dir ABDRACHMAN MOLDANASAROVICH OMBAEV.

Kazakh Scientific and Research Institute of Economy and Organization of Agroindustrial Complex: ul. Tsatpaeva 30B, Almaty 050057; tel. (727) 2436411; f. 1934; Dir GANI ALIMOVICH KALIEV.

Kazakh Scientific and Research Institute of Feeding-stuff Production and Pasture: ul. Dzhandosova 51, Almaty 050035; tel. (727) 2214586; f. 1969; Dir KASYM ABUOVICH ASANOV.

Kazakh Scientific and Research Institute of Forestry JSC KazAgroInnovation: Kirov Str. 58, Shchuchinsk 021704; tel. (716) 3641153; e-mail kafri50@mail.ru; f. 1957; library of 160,000 vols; Dir-Gen. Prof. Dr BOLAT MAZHITOVICH MUKANOV.

Kazakh Scientific and Research Institute of Fruit Growing and Viticulture: pr. Gagarina 238A, Almaty 050035; tel. (727) 2482890; f. 1978; Dir DUISENBAY SAILAUBAEVICH IZBASAROV.

Kazakh Scientific and Research Institute of Grain and Processed Grain Products: ul. Ugolnaya 26, Astana 478000; tel. (717) 2310193; f. 1953; Dir KOMYSCHNIK LEONID DMITRIEVICH.

Kazakh Scientific and Research Institute of Mechanization and Electrification in Agriculture: pr. Raimbeka 312, Almaty 050005; tel. (727) 2404800; f. 1978; Dir ASAN BEKENOVICH OSPANOV.

Kazakh Scientific and Research Institute of Poultry: Pos. 50 Let Kazakhskoi SSR, Ul. Maslieva 8, Karasaisky raion, Almaty, 040933; tel. (727) 7195631; f. 1966; Dir JEGOROV NICOLAY PETROVICH.

Kazakh Scientific and Research Institute of the Fishing Industry: ul. Suyunbay 89A, Almaty 050016; Dir SHOKAN ASHENOVICH ALPEYISOV.

Kazakh Scientific and Research Institute of Water Management: Koigeldy St 12, Taraz, Zhambyl 080003; tel. (726) 2426071; e-mail iwre@nursat.kz; internet www.kaziwr.isd.kz; f. 1950; research in field of water resources management, land reclamation and irrigation, agricultural water supply; Dir MUCHAMEDZHANOV VALIACHMET NURIACHMETOVICH.

Kazakh Scientific and Research Technological Institute of Exploitation and Maintenance of Agricultural Machinery: Lenina 176, Akkol, Akmola 020100; tel. (716) 3821275; e-mail kazniti@mail.kz; f. 1962; Dir SOLOMKIN ALEXANDR PROKOPJEVICH.

Kazakh Scientific, Research and Design Institute of the Meat and Milk Industry: ul. Baitursunova 29, Semipalatinsk 490035; tel. (722) 2442615; e-mail nikimmp@ok.kz; f. 1958; Dir KUSMANOV KAISAR KUSMANOVICH.

Kazakh Veterinary Scientific and Research Institute: pr. Raimbeka 222, Almaty 480029; tel. (727) 2321755; f. 1925; Dir ABYLAI RYSBAIULY SANSYZBAI.

Kostanai Scientific and Research Institute of Agriculture: 50 Let Oktobra 94, Kostanai 485000; tel. (714) 2278034; f. 1984; Dir DVURECHENSKIY VALENTIN IVANOVICH.

National Academic Centre of Agrarian Research: 79 Abylai Khan, Almaty 480091; tel. (727) 2625217; depts of economics and information in agriculture, crop science and plant breeding, farming, agrochemistry, water and forest production and agroecology, livestock production and veterinary science, mechanization of agricultural production, processing and storing agricultural produce.

Northern Kazakhstan Research Institute of Animal Breeding and Veterinary Science: Ul. Institutskaya 1, Bishkul raion, Northen Kazakhstan 150700; tel. (715) 3821344; f. 1962; library of 41,000 vols; Dir KANAT ISMAILOVICH MYNZHASOV.

Pavlodar Scientific and Research Institute of Agriculture: Pavlodarskij raion, pos. Krasnoarmeika, Pavlodar 140909; tel. (718) 4553003; e-mail nii07@inbox.ru; f. 1993; Gen. Dir BAKYT IRMULATOV.

Research Institute for Plant Protection: Karasai raion, Selo Rakhat, Almaty 040924; e-mail kazniizr@nursat.kz; f. 1958; library of 29,134 vols; Dir TLEU NURMURATOVICH NURMURATOV.

Research Institute of Potato and Vegetable Growing: Karasai raion, Pos. Kainar, Almaty 040917; tel. (727) 2983706; f. 1945; Dir BABAEV SAILAU AKHMETOVICH.

Research Institute of Sheep Raising: Zhambulsky raion, Mynbaevo, Almaty 040622; tel. (727) 222002; e-mail aklima@kaznet.kz; f. 1933; sheep, goat, horse and camel breeding; library of 100,000 vols; Dir K. U. MEDEUBEKOV; publ. *Proceedings* (1 a year).

South Kazakhstan Scientific and Research Institute of Agriculture: Soviyetskaya 111, Shymkent 160813; tel. (725) 2222098; f. 1988; Dir MUHTAR ZHANBYRBAYEVICH ZHANBYRBAYEV.

Taldykorgan Agricultural Research Institute: Taldykorgan raion, Pos. Zarya, Almaty 040000; tel. (728) 2299445; f. 1992; Dir MARAT KARIBAYEVICH KOZHAHMETOV.

Tselinny Scientific and Research Institute of Mechanization and Electrification in Agriculture: pr. Abaya 34, Kostanai 110011; e-mail celin@mail.kz; Dir VLADIMIR LEONIDOVICH ASTAFEV.

Uspanov Institute of Soil Science: Akademgorodok, Almaty 050060; e-mail soil@nursat.kz; f. 1945; attached to Nat. Acad. of Sciences of Kazakhstan; Dir A. S. SAPAROV.

ECONOMICS, LAW AND POLITICS

Institute of Economics: Kurmangazy 29, Almaty 480100; tel. (727) 2930175; e-mail ieconom@academset.kz; f. 1952; attached to Min. of Education and Science; Dir Dr A. K. KOSHANOV.

Institute of Economics and Business: 22 Satpaev str., Almaty 480013; tel. (727) 2577138; f. 1966, present status 2000; attached to Kazakh National Technical University after K. I. Satpaev; depts of assessment, accountancy and auditing, economics of industry, finance, management and marketing in industry; Dir BEKEN B. MANANOV.

Institute of State and Law: Kurmangazy 29, Almaty 050000; tel. (727) 2695911; f. 1961; attached to Min. of Education and Science; Dir E. K. NURPEISOV.

Institute of State and Law: 71 Al-Farabi Ave, Almaty 050040; tel. (727) 3773548; e-mail kz_instituta@mail.ru; internet kaznu.kz/en/10439/page; f. 1946, current name adopted 1991; attached to Al-Farabi Kazakh Nat. Univ.; fundamental and practical research on contemporary issues of state and law devt; Dir Dr ARON AMANZHOLOVICH SALIMGEREI.

Kazakhstan Institute for Strategic Studies under the President of the Republic of Kazakhstan: Dostyk Ave 87B, Almaty 050010; tel. (727) 2643404; e-mail office@kisi.kz; internet www.kisi.kz; f. 1993; maintains analytical and research support for Pres. of Kazakhstan; Dir SULTANOV BULAT KLYCHBAYEVICH.

HISTORY, GEOGRAPHY AND ARCHAEOLOGY

Ch. Ch. Valikhanov Institute of History and Ethnology: ul. Shevchenko 28, Almaty 050021; tel. (727) 2629237; f. 1945; attached to Min. of Education and Science; Dir S. F. MAZHITOV.

Institute of Geography: 67/99 Kabanbai batyr str./Pushkin str., Almaty 050010; tel. (727) 2918129; e-mail ingeo@mail.kz; internet www.ingeo.kz; f. 1938; attached to Min. of Education and Science; research areas incl. physical and social economics, geography, geomorphology, hydrology, geoecology, GIS-mapping; Dir N. K. MUKITANOV.

Margulan Institute of Archaeology: pr. Dostyk Ave 44, Almaty 480100; tel. (727) 2618585; e-mail margulan@freenet.kz; f. 1991; attached to Nat. Acad. of Sciences; Dir Prof. K. BAIPAKOV.

LANGUAGE AND LITERATURE

A. Baitursynov Institute of Linguistics: ul. Kurmangazy 29, Almaty 050021; tel. (727) 2615635; e-mail tilbilimi@bk.ru; f. 1961; attached to Dept of Science of Min. of Education and Science; conducts research in Kazakh linguistics; library of 500,000 vols; Dir Dr SHERUBAI KURMANBAIULY; publ. *Linguistic*.

M. Auezov Institute of Literature and Art: 29 Kurmangazy str., Almaty 050010; tel. (727) 2727411; e-mail lit_art@academset.kz; internet litart.academset.kz; f. 1934, fmrly Institute of Language and Literature, present name and status 1961; attached to Min. of Education and Science and Nat. Acad. of Sciences of Kazakhstan; research fields incl. art history, Kazakh literary studies, folklore; Dir SEIT ASKAROVICH KASKABASOV; Deputy Dir GULNAR TAZABEKOVNA ZHUMASEITOVA; publ. *Keruen* (4 a year).

MEDICINE

Central Asian Plague Prevention Research Institute: Kopalskaya ul. 14, Almaty 050034; tel. (727) 2357548; Dir V. M. STEPANOV.

Institute of Microbiology, Epidemiology and Infectious Diseases: ul. Pastera 34, Almaty 050002; tel. (727) 2330426; Dir I. K. SHURATOV.

Institute of Nutrition: ul. Klochkova 66, Almaty 050008; tel. (727) 2429203; f. 1974; attached to Min. of Education and Science; Dir T. SH. SHARMANOV; publs *Voprosy pitaniya, Zdravookhranenie Kazakhstana* (8–10 a year).

Kazakh Paediatrics Research Institute: Al-Farabi Ave 146, Almaty 050000; tel. (727) 2488121; f. 1932; library of 36,000 vols; Dir ORMANTAEV KAMAL SARUAROVICH.

Kazakh Research Institute of Skin and Venereal Diseases: Rayimbek 60, Almaty 050002; tel. (727) 3974223; e-mail kaznikvi@mail.ru; internet www.dsnikvi.kz; f. 1931; attached to Min. of Health; library of 250,000 vols; Dir ALEXANDER EDRISOVICH ESHIMOV.

National Centre for Tuberculosis Problems: Bekhozhin ul. 5, Almaty 050000; tel. (727) 2918657; e-mail ncpt@itte.kz; f. 1932; library of 11,000 vols; Dir Prof. SH. ISMAILOV.

National Centre of Labour Hygiene and Occupational Diseases: 15 Mustafina, Karaganda 100012; tel. (721) 2565263; e-mail ncgtpz@gmail.com; internet ncgtpz.kz; f. 1958 as Institute of Physiology and Occupational Diseases; present name 2002; attached to Min. of Health; Dir Dr ZHAMILYA BATTAKOVA; publ. *Occupational Hygiene and Medical Ecology* (4 a year).

NATURAL SCIENCES

Biological Sciences

Institute of Botany: Timiryazeva 44, Almaty 050029; tel. (727) 2476692; e-mail adm@botan.academ.alma-ata.su; f. 1995; attached to Nat. Acad. of Sciences of Kazakhstan; Dir S. A. ABIYEV.

Institute of Experimental Biology: pr. Abaya 38, Almaty 050022; tel. (727) 2923717; attached to Min. of Education and Science; Dir A. M. MURZAMADIEV.

Institute of General Genetics and Cytology: 75 Al–Farabi St, Almaty 050040; tel. (727) 2498217; e-mail adm@iggc.academ.alma-ata.su; f. 1995; attached to Nat. Acad. of Sciences of Kazakhstan.

Institute of Human and Animal Physiology: Akademgorodok, Al-Farabi Ave 93, Almaty 480060; tel. (727) 2783659; e-mail i.physiology@nursat.kz; f. 1945; attached to Nat. Acad. of Sciences of Kazakhstan; studies the interaction and interrelation between different elements of organisms of living creatures; Dir BOLAT MAHATOV.

Institute of Microbiology and Virology: 103 Bogenbai Batyr str, Almaty 050010; tel. (727) 2618497; e-mail ber@imv.academ.alma-ata.su; f. 1956; attached to Min. of Education and Science; Dir S. A. AITKELDIEVA.

Institute of Zoology: Al-Farabi 93, Akademgorodok, 050060 Almaty; tel. (727) 2694876; e-mail instzoo@nursat.kz; f. 1943; attached to Min. of Education and Science; Dir Prof. ALIKHAN MELBEKOV.

Kazakh Academy of Nutrition: Klochkov St 66, Almaty 050000; tel. (727) 2422640; e-mail asalkhanova@caffproject.net; internet kan-kaz.org; f. 1974; fundamental and applied biomedical researches on nutrition problems; devt of sanitary norms and standards; quality assurance and safety of food; promotion of healthy nutrition; Dir Prof. Dr SHARMANOV TOREGELDY; publ. *Health and Illness*.

M. A. Aitkhozhin Institute of Molecular Biology and Biochemistry: ul. Michurina 80, Almaty 050012; tel. (727) 2671852; f. 1983; attached to Min. of Education and Science; Dir Prof. N. A. AITKHOZHIN (acting).

Mathematical Sciences

Institute of Mathematics and Mathematical Modeling: Pushkin St 125, Almaty 050010; tel. (727) 2727093; e-mail rgpimim@mail.ru; internet www.math.kz; f. 1965 as Institute of Mathematics and Mechanics, current name adopted 2012; attached to Min. of Education and Science; conducts fundamental and applied research in mathematics; Dir Prof. TYNYSBEK S. KALMENOV; Deputy Dir GULMIRA K. ZAKIRYANOVA; publ. *Mathematical Journal*.

Institute of Theoretical and Applied Mathematics: ul. Pushkina 125, Almaty 050021; tel. (727) 2613740; e-mail bliev@itpm.alma-ata.su; f. 1965; attached to Nat. Acad. of Sciences of Kazakhstan; Dir N. K. BLIEV.

Physical Sciences

Chemical-Metallurgical Institute: Ermekov 63, Karaganda 100009; tel. (721) 2433161; e-mail hmi@mail.krg.kz; f. 1958; attached to Nat. Acad. of Sciences of Kazakhstan; Dir Dr BOLAT KHASSEN.

Fesenkov Astrophysical Institute: Kamenskoe plato, Almaty 480068; tel. (727) 2650040; e-mail adm@afi.academ.alma-ata.su; f. 1950; attached to Nat. Acad. of Sciences of Kazakhstan; observational, theoretical and numerical researches; Dir Prof. LEONID CHECHIN.

Institute of Ionosphere: Kamenskoe plato, Almaty 050020; tel. (727) 3803054; e-mail admion1@mail.ru; f. 1983; attached to Nat. Center of Space Researches and Technologies; research fields incl. geodynamics, geophysics, space physics, solar-terrestrial physics, physics of plasma cosmic rays, magnetosphere, ionosphere, physics of atmosphere, electric field, land and space geodynamic and geophysical monitoring of earth crust; Dir BAUYRZHAN KURMANOV; Scientific Sec. MUKASHEVA SAULE.

Institute of Nuclear Physics: 1 Ibragimova St, Almaty 050032; tel. (727) 3866800; e-mail morzhic@mail.ru; internet www.inp.kz; f. 1957; attached to Nat. Nuclear Centre; research into acceleration technologies, applied nuclear physics, nuclear physics, reactor research, solid state physics; Dir Prof. NASSURLLA BURTEBAYEV (acting); Sec. Dr AKTORGYN ZHANKADAMOVA.

Institute of Organic Catalysis and Electrochemistry: 142 Kunaev str., Almaty 050010; tel. (727) 2615808; e-mail orgcat@nursat.kz; f. 1969; attached to Min. of Education and Science; Dir ZAKUMBAEVA GAUKHAR DAULENOVNA.

Institute of Organic Synthesis and Carbon Chemistry: ul. 40–let Kazakhstana, Karaganda 100000; tel. (727) 2526085; f. 1983; attached to Nat. Acad. of Sciences of Kazakhstan; Dir S. M. MOLDAKHMETOV.

Institute of Petroleum Chemistry and Natural Salts: ul. Lenina 2, Atyrau 060002; tel. (712) 2222674; f. 1960; attached to Nat. Acad. of Sciences of Kazakhstan; Dir N. R. BUKEIKHANOV.

Institute of Physics and Technology: Ibragimova 11, Almaty 050032; tel. (727) 3865536; e-mail info@sci.kz; internet www.sci.kz; f. 1991; attached to Nat. Acad. of Sciences of Kazakhstan; depts of condensed matter physics, material science and nanotechnology, spectroscopic methods of research, high-energy physics and cosmic rays, information technology; Dir Dr B. N. MUKASHEV.

Institute of Seismology: pr. Al-Farabi 75, Almaty 050060; tel. (727) 2482134; e-mail adm@seism.academ.alma-ata.su; f. 1976; attached to Nat. Acad. of Sciences of Kazakhstan; Dir TANATKAN ABAKAN.

Institute of Space Research: Shevchenko st. 15, Almaty 480021; tel. (727) 2615853; e-mail zak@kaziki.alma-ata.su; f. 1991; attached to Nat. Acad. of Sciences of Kazakhstan; Dir UMIRZAK MACHMUTOVICH SULTANGAZIN.

JSC Bekturov Institute of Chemical Sciences: Walikhanov str. 106, Almaty 050010; tel. (727) 2912457; e-mail info@chemistry.kz; internet www.chemistry.kz; f. 1945; attached to Min. of Education and Science; library of 83,000 vols; Dir Prof. Dr E. E. ERGOZHIN; publ. *Chemical Journal of Kazakhstan* (4 a year).

JSC International Research and Production Holding 'Phytochemistry': str. Gazaliev, 4, Karaganda 100009; tel. (721) 2433127; e-mail phyto_pio@mail.ru; internet www.phyto.kz; carries out research and devt work to create high-end technology and equipment for the manufacture of medical products; study of natural plant materials; f. 1995.

K. I. Satpaev Institute of Geological Sciences: 69A Kabanbai Batyr str., Almaty 480091; tel. (727) 2915608; e-mail adm@geol.academ.alma-ata.su; f. 1940; attached to Nat. Acad. of Sciences of Kazakhstan; Dir GEROI ZHOLTAYEV.

National Nuclear Centre of the Republic of Kazakhstan: St Tauelsizdik 6, Kurchatov 071100; tel. (722) 5123333; e-mail nnc@nnc.kz; internet www.nnc.kz; f. 1992; Dir S. T. TUKHVATULIN.

Physical Technical Institute: Alatau, Almaty 050032; tel. (727) 2690566; e-mail mukashev@sci.kz; f. 1991; attached to Nat. Acad. of Sciences of Kazakhstan; Dir Prof. B. N. MUKASHEV.

U. M. Akhmedsafin Institute of Hydrogeology and Hydrophysics: ul. Krasina 94, Almaty 050010; tel. (727) 2615051; f. 1965; attached to Min. of Education and Science; Dir V. V. VESELOV.

PHILOSOPHY AND PSYCHOLOGY

Institute of Philosophy and Political Science: ul. Kurmangazy 29, Almaty 050021; tel. (727) 2695911; e-mail data@itte.kz; f. 1991; attached to Nat. Acad. of Sciences of Kazakhstan; Dir Prof. ABDIMALIK N. NASYNBAYEV; publ. *Farabi*.

RELIGION, SOCIOLOGY AND ANTHROPOLOGY

R. B. Suleimenov Institute of Orient Studies: 29 Kurmangazy St., Almaty 050010; tel. (727) 2611601; f. 1996; attached to Nat. Acad. of Sciences of Kazakhstan; Dir Dr MERUERT KH. ABUSSEITOVA.

TECHNOLOGY

Eastern Mining and Metallurgical Research Institute for Non-ferrous Metals: 1 Promyshlennaya str., Ust-Kamenogorsk 070002; tel. (723) 2753773; e-mail vcmnauka@mail.east.telecom.kz; internet vcm.ukg.kz; f. 1950; attached to Min. of Industry and New Technologies; carries out research and semi-commercial scale tests; provides scientific and technical assistance in the introduction of technologies and equipment in the fields of polymetal ores mining and dressing, heavy non-ferrous metals metallurgy, applied and analytical chemistry, environment protection; library of 169,500 vols; Dir Dr NIKOLAY N. USHAKOV; Deputy Dir A. I. ANANIN; Deputy Dir V. A. SHUMSKIY.

Institute of Informatics and Control Problems: Pushkina str. 125, Almaty 050010; tel. (727) 2723711; e-mail office@ipic.kz; f. 1991; attached to Science Cttee of MES RK; Dir M. N. KALIMOLDAYEV.

Institute of Metallurgy and Ore Enrichment: 29/33 Shevchenko St., Almaty 050010; tel. (727) 2915781; e-mail imo-almaty@nursat.kz; internet www.imo.nursat.kz; f. 1945; attached to Min. of Education and Science; Dir Prof. Dr BAGDAULET KENZHALIEV; publ. *Kompleksnoe Ispolzovanie Mineralnogo Siria* (6 a year).

Kunayev Institute of Mining: Ave Abai 191, Almaty 050046; tel. (727) 3765300; e-mail info@igd.kz; internet www.igd.kz; f. 1944; attached to Nat. Centre for Integrated Minerals Recycling of the Republic of Kazakhstan; scientific and research activity in mining; devt of rational methods of design and management of production processes at mining companies; creation of effective and environmentally safe technologies and minerals mining equipment; postgraduate training of scientific personnel, training of mining specialists, scientific and technical popularization of latest achievements of science and equipment; editorial activity; int. cooperation; economic activity; library of 46,138 vols, incl. 21,860 periodicals; Dir Prof. Dr BUKTUKOV NIKOLAI SADVAKASOVICH; publ. *Scientific and Technical Provision of Mining Production* (2 a year).

National Centre for Complex Processing of Mineral Raw Materials: Dzhandosov 67, Almaty 050036; tel. (727) 2590070; e-mail cmrp@itte.kz; f. 1993; attached to Nat. Academy of Sciences of Kazakhstan; Dir Prof. Dr ABDURASUL ZHARMENOV.

Scientific and Technological Centre of Machinery Construction: pr. Abaya 191, Almaty 480064; tel. (727) 2469750; e-mail mntc@mail.ru; f. 1998; Dir Prof. Dr SKANDERBEK U. JOLDASBEKOV.

Libraries and Archives

Almaty

Central Scientific Library of Scientific Committee of the Ministry of Education and Science of the Republic of Kazakhstan: 28 Shevchenko str., Almaty 050010; tel. (727) 2610037; e-mail cnb@library.kz; internet www.library.kz; f. 1932, present name and status 1999; 5.5m. vols, 2,041 MSS; Dir KARLIGASH KAIMAKBAEVA; publ. *Kitapkhana Alemi* (Library World, 4 a year).

Central State Archives of the Republic of Kazakhstan: 39 Abay Ave, Almaty 050000; tel. (727) 2671462; e-mail cga_rk@mail.ru; 1.5m. archive cases; documents of pre-Soviet period; Dir LYAZZAT AKTAYEVA.

National Library of the Republic of Kazakhstan: Abai Ave 14, Almaty 050013; tel. (727) 2672883; e-mail intrel@nlrk.kz; internet www.nlrk.kz; f. 1931; legal deposit library; 6m. vols; Dir-Gen. GULISSA BALABEKOVA.

President's Archives of the Republic of Kazakhstan: 87-B Dostyk Ave, Almaty 050021; tel. (727) 2646907; e-mail arcobotd@mail.ru; internet www.aprk.kz; f. 1994; 700,000 units of storage for the period of 1918–2006; br. in Astana; Dir VLADIMIR N. SHEPEL.

Republican Scientific and Technical Library: 233 Mukanov str., Almaty; tel. (727) 2682679.

Republican Youth Library named after Zhambyl: 43 Furmanov str., Almaty; tel. (727) 2711499.

Scientific and Technical Library of Kazakhstan: S. Mukanov 223B, Almaty 050026; tel. (727) 3784195; e-mail rntb@nursat.kz; internet www.rntb.kz; f. 1960; 35.3m. vols (incl. patents); Dir-Gen. K. G. URMURZINA.

Scientific Library of Al-Farabi Kazakh National University: Timiryazeva ul. 42, Almaty 050010; tel. (727) 2472761; e-mail guljan_m@kazsu.kz; internet lib.kazsu.kz; f. 1934; 1.5m. vols; Dir MUSAGALIEVA GULZHAN MUSAEVNA.

Astana

National Academic Library of the Republic of Kazakhstan: St Dostyk 11, Astana 010000; tel. (717) 2446180; e-mail info@nabrk.kz; internet nabrk.kz; f. 2004; 600,000 vols, 1,500 periodicals; Dir-Gen. SHAIMUKHANBETOVA ZHANNA KAKIBAYEVNA; Deputy Dir-Gen. for Cultural Events ISAKANOVA GALIYA BUKEEVNA; Deputy Dir-Gen. for Library and Information Technologies DARIBAEVA GULSHAT GABDULLAEVNA; publ. *Kitap Patshalygy*.

Republican Library for the Blind and Visually Impaired Citizens of the Republic of Kazakhstan: 2/1 Tashenov str., Astana; tel. (717) 2937080; e-mail rbnsg@rambler.ru; internet www.blindlib.kz; f. 1969; Dir GULBARFIN BALGOZHINA.

Karaganda

Central City Library named after M. Auezov: Mir Blvd 43, Karaganda; tel. (721) 2421226.

Karaganda Regional Universal Research Library named after N. V. Gogol: 44 S. Erubaev str., Karaganda 100000; tel. (721) 2567655; e-mail info@karlib.kz; internet www.karlib.kz; f. 1934, present status 1938; 400,000 vols, 23,562 periodicals; Dir DINA AMANZHOLOVA.

Karaganda State University Library: ul. Universitetskaya 28, Karaganda 100026; tel. (721) 2770416; e-mail rootlib@ksu.kz; internet library.ksu.kz; 400,000 vols; Dir ALMAGAMBETOVA DAMETKEN RAYEVNA.

Kostanay

Kostanay Branch of the Republican Scientific and Technical Library: Taran St 105, Kostanay; tel. (714) 2541746; e-mail kf_rntb@mail.ru; internet www.kstntb.kz.

Regional Universal-Scientific Library named after L. N. Tolstoy: 111 Altinsarin str., Kostanay 110000; tel. (714) 25003548; e-mail kst.tolstovka@mail.kz; internet kstounb.kz; 550,044 vols; Dir KAZINA GULZHAMERIA GALIASKAROVNA.

Kyzylorda

Kyzylorda Regional Library named after A. Tazhibayev: Abai Ave 27, Kyzylorda; tel. (724) 2239801.

Pavlodar

Toraigyrov Oblast Universal Scientific Library: 104 Akademik Satpayev St, Pavlodar; tel. (718) 2320802; e-mail library@pavlodar.kz; internet www.pavlodarlibrary.kz; f. 1896; depository of local documents; coordinates work of all libraries; 900,000 vols; Dir MAYA ABDRAKHMANOVNA ZHIENBAYEVA.

Museums and Art Galleries

Akmola

Literary Museum named after I. Esenberlin: Kuanyshev St 3A, Atbasar, Akmola; tel. (716) 4341428.

Museum named after M. Gabdullin: Aulbekov St 123, Kokshetau, Akmola; tel. (716) 2257627; e-mail mgabdullin@mail.ru; Dir KENZHEAKHMET MARYAM.

Museum of City History: Chapayev St 32, Kokshetau, Akmola; tel. (716) 2269890.

Museum of Literature and Art: Chapayev St 32, Kokshetau, Akmola; tel. (716) 2269793.

Regional History and Local Lore Museum: Kalinin St 33, Kokshetau, Akmola; tel. (716) 2255861.

Aktobe

Aktobe Regional History and Local Lore Museum: Altynsarin St 14, Aktobe; tel. (713) 2211367.

Museum named after A. Moldagulova: A. Moldagulova Ave 47, Aktobe; tel. (713) 2521598.

Almaty

Abylkhan Kasteev State Museum of Arts of the Republic of Kazakhstan: ul. Satpayeva 30A, Almaty 050040; tel. (727) 3945519; e-mail kazart@nursat.kz; internet www.gmirk.kz; f. 1976; attached to Min. of Culture; Kazakh art, folk art, Russian art, Western-European art; library of 24,333 vols; Dir B. SERALIYEV.

Almaty History and Local Lore Museum: Nauryzbai Batyr 108, Almaty; tel. (727) 2617301.

Central State Museum of Kazakhstan: Samal–1, 44, Almaty 480099; tel. (727) 2645577; e-mail csmrk@hn.freenet.kz; internet www.unesco.kz/heritagenet/kz/hn-english/csmrk/engl/index_en.htm; archaeology, ethnography, history, natural history of Kazakhstan; Dir ALIMBAY NURSAN.

House Museum named after D. Kunayev: Tulebayev 117, Almaty; tel. (727) 2614269.

Literary and Memorial House Museum named after M. Auezov: Tulebayev St 185, Almaty; tel. (727) 2612277.

Museum of Archaeology: Dostyk Ave 44, Almaty 050013; tel. (727) 2939880; internet www.museumalmaty.kz; f. 2002; organizes exhibitions, int. confs, round tables on historical and cultural heritage; displays objects dating from Bronze Age to present; Dir ERBOLAT K. AUEZOV.

Museum of Art 'Umai' named after Zh. Shardenov: Nauryzbai Batyr St 108, Almaty; tel. (727) 2729216.

Republican Literary Memorial Museum Complex named after S. Mukanov and G. Musrepov: Tulebayev St 125KB 3; tel. (727) 2725912.

Republican Museum of Book: Kabanbai Batyr St 94, Almaty 480100; tel. (727) 2622213; f. 1977; exhibits history of devt of Kazakh writing, of press, of books and modern publs; colln incl. 20,000 exhibits, incl. rare original MSS, current periodical editions, ancient drawings, booklets, emblems and charts; Dir SH. ESMURZAYEV.

Republican Museum of Folk Musical Instruments named after Ykylas: Zenkov St 24, Almaty; tel. (727) 2916316.

Astana

Museum named after S. Seifullin: Auezov St 78, Astana; tel. (717) 2321590.

Museum of Modern Art: 3 Respublika Ave; tel. (717) 2440261; e-mail msi_astana@mail.ru; internet www.msi-astana.kz; f. 1980, fmrly Museum of Fine Arts; colln incls works by artists from Armenia, Belarus, Estonia, Georgia, Kazakhstan, Latvia, Lithuania, Russia, Tajikistan, Ukraine, Uzbekistan; Dir N. SHIVRINA.

Museum of the First President of the Republic of Kazakhstan: Beibitshilik St 11, Astana; tel. (717) 2751214; e-mail museum_08@mail.ru; internet www.prezidentsmuseum.kz; f. 2005; exhibits 7,420 units; collns incl. art, clothes, soft stock, carpet and felt goods, highest state orders, jewellery and oriental stones, material culture, souvenirs and decorative dishes, weapons and numismatics; 97,180 archives; library of 15,356 vols; Dir ALMA SAGYNGALI; publ. *Miras* (4 a year).

Presidential Centre of Culture of the Republic of Kazakhstan: Republic Ave 2, Astana 010000; tel. (717) 2443265; internet www.pmo.kz; f. 2000; represents history and culture of Kazakhstan; library of 600,189 vols, 345 journals; Dir MYRZATAI ZHOLDASBEKOV; publ. *Madeni Mura*.

'Shezhire' Gallery of Modern Art: Abai Ave 47, Astana; tel. (717) 2391000; f. 2001.

State Museum of Gold and Precious Metals of the Republic of Kazakhstan: Baraev St 1, Astana 000010; tel. (717) 2443266; e-mail astana@museumofgold.kz; internet www.museumofgold.kz; f. 1990; preserves, restores valuable artefacts from precious metals and stones; collns incl. archaeological objects, foleristics, jewellery and vessels, horse-riding equipment, numismatics, weapons; Dir SADYBAI GAUHAR KASIEVNA.

Atyrau

Makat History and Local Lore Museum: Dossor, 2nd Microdistrict, Makat, Atyrau; tel. (712) 3521816.

Makhambet History and Local Lore Museum: Abai St 14, Makhambet, Atyrau; tel. (712) 3621908.

Regional History and Local Lore Museum: B. Momyshuly St 3, Atyrau; tel. (712) 2355305.

Regional Museum—Reserve 'Khan Ordaly Saraishyk': Saraishyk, Makhambet, Atyrau; tel. (712) 3625506.

Karaganda

Aktogay Archaeological and Ethnographic Museum: Zh. Akbai St 1, v. Aktogay, Karaganda; tel. (710) 3721051; f. 1986; archaeology, ethnography, decorative and applied arts.

Balkhash History Museum: Sh. Uallikhanov St 12, Balkhash, Karaganda; tel. (710) 3651484; f. 1970; 39,531 exhibits displaying archaeology, ethnography and life, history of Balkhash, nature and environment.

Egindybulaksky History Museum: v. Egindybolak, Tattimbet St 29, Karaganda; f. 1989; displays objects of local history, ethnography, decorative art.

Karaganda Regional History and Local Lore Museum: Yerubayev St 38, Karaganda; tel. (721) 2571279; e-mail muzeumkz@mail.ru; f. 1932.

Karaganda Regional Museum of Fine Arts: Bukhar Zhyrau St 76, Karaganda; tel. (721) 2432993; e-mail izo@karaganda.kz; f. 1988; displays objects of applied arts, graphics, painting, sculptures.

Karkaraly History Museum: Lenin St 34, Karkaralinsk, Karaganda; tel. (721) 4632788; f. 1974; exhibits objects of ethnography, decorative art of Kazakhstan.

Literary Memorial Museum named after Abai Kunanbaev: Abai St 32, Abai, Karaganda; f. 1980.

Osakarovsky History Museum: t. Oskarovka, Novaya St 43, Karaganda; tel. (721) 4931640; f. 1985.

Zhanarkin Local History Museum named after S. Seifullin: t. Atasu, S. Seifullin Ave 13, Zhanarkin, Karaganda; f. 1994; displays objects depicting archaeology, culture, ethnography, history of Kazakhstan.

Zhezkazgan History and Local Lore Museum: Lenin Ave 22, Zhezkazgan, Karaganda; tel. (710) 233555.

Pavlodar

History and Local Lore Museum: Gornyakov St 34, Ekibastuz, Pavlodar; tel. (718) 3549692.

History and Local Lore Museum named after G. N. Potanin: Lenin St 147, Pavlodar; tel. (718) 2325924.

Memorial Museum named after K. I. Satpayev: K. Satpayev St 38, Bayanaul, Pavlodar; tel. (718) 4091344.

Pavlodar Regional Art Museum: Toraigyrov St 44/1, Pavlodar; tel. (718) 2327111; Dir SHESTOPALOVA GALINA PAVLOVNA.

South Kazakhstan

Regional History and Local Lore Museum: Kazybek bi St 13, Shymkent, S Kazakhstan.

Zhambyl

Regional History and Local Lore Museum: Tole bi St 55, Taraz, Zhambyl; tel. (726) 2432585.

Universities

ABAY MYRZAKHMETOV KOKSHETAU UNIVERSITY

189A Auezov St, Kokshetau, Akmola
Telephone: (716) 2230278
E-mail: kuam-kokchetau@mail.ru
Internet: kuam.kz
Private control

Rector: Prof. Dr IRINA SUBBOTINA
Vice-Chancellor for Academic and Methodic Work: Prof. MADIE YELUBAYEV
Vice-Chancellor for Educational Work: DINARA ABDULMANOVA
Vice-Chancellor for Scientific Work: DMITRY LEPESHEV

AKHMET BAITURSYNOV KOSTANAY STATE UNIVERSITY

Baitursinov str. 47, Kostanai 110000
Telephone: (714) 2511195
E-mail: ksu47@mail.kz
Internet: www.ksu.kst.kz
Founded 1939, present status 1992
State control
Languages of instruction: English, Kazakh, Russian

Faculties of agrarian-biology, economics, engineering, information technologies, humanitarian and social sciences, journalism, law, veterinary and food products processing; Social-technical College

Rector: Prof. Dr NAMETOV ASKAR MYRZAKHMETOVICH
First Pro-Rector: Prof. IBRAGIMOV PRIMKUL SHOLPANKULOVICH
Pro-Rector for Academic Studies and New Technologies Training: Prof. MAIYER FYODOR FYODOROVICH
Pro-Rector for Finance and Social Affairs: Prof. SEITKAZINOV DUSEMBAI TEMIRZHANOVICH
Pro-Rector for Science and Int. Contacts: P KIM NATALYA PAVLOVNA

Number of students: 8,000
Number of teachers: 200

Publications: *Mezhvuzovskii nauchnyi zhurnal* (Intercollegiate Scientific Journal), *Vestnik Nauki* (Herald of Science, 4 a year), *Zharsken-Kostanai* (6 a year), *Zhas Orken*

AKTOBE STATE PEDAGOGICAL INSTITUTE

A. Moldagulova str. 34, Aktobe
Telephone: (713) 2568280
E-mail: aktobegpi@mail.ru
Internet: www.aktobe-gpi.kz
Founded 2004
State control
Language of instruction: Kazakh
Academic year: September to June

Rector: Prof. Dr AMANTAY ABILKHAIROVICH NURMAGAMBETOV
Vice-Rector for Academic and Educational Work: Prof. Dr TULEGEN AMIRZHANOVICH BOTAGARIEV
Vice-Rector for Educational Work: ANATOLY VLADMROVICH USOV
Vice-Rector for Science and Int. Relations: NURTAZA SATYMOVICH KADIRNIYAZOV
Library Dir: AYAGOZ KADESHOVNA KAZHIYAKPAROVA

Library of 450,000 vols
Number of teachers: 351
Number of students: 5,144

DEANS

Faculty of Foreign Languages: ZAMZAGUL YESSENOVNA SULEIMENOVA
Faculty of History: SAMAT AMANGELDINOVICH YESSKALIEV
Faculty of Mathematics, Physics and Natural Sciences: AMINA AKZATOVNA MUKHAMBETOVA
Faculty of Pedagogy and Psychology: LYAZZAT BISENBAEVNA ALEKESHOVA
Faculty of Philology: SABYRZHAN SAGIDOLLAEVICH MUKHTAROV
Professional and Creative Faculty: VICTOR VASILYEVICH PROSYANKIN

PROFESSORS

ABDRAKHMANOVICH, A. A.
ABILKHAIROVICH, N. A.
AGISZHANOVICH, A. N.
ALMAGAMBETOVICH, S. Z.
AMIRZHANOVICH, B. T.
GEORGIEVICH, T. I.

IGOR FELIKSOVICH, S.-L.
NURMANOVICH, N. I.
ORYNBASAROVNA, T. Z.
SHUNKEEVICH, S. K.
TAIZHANOVICH, T. A.
TYNYSHTYKBAEVNA, S. G.

AKTOBE STATE UNIVERSITY NAMED AFTER K. ZHUBANOV

Molgagulova 34, Aktobe 030000
Telephone: (713) 2553756
E-mail: zhubanov@mail.ru
Internet: www.agu.kz
Founded 1966 as Aktobe State Pedagogical Institute, current name adopted 1990, current status 2001
State control
Depts of economy, education, science and culture, technology
Rector: Dr KENZHEGALI KENZHEBAEV
Vice-Rector for Science and Int. Relations: Prof. KUANTAY ABDIKALYKOV

AL-FARABI KAZAKH NATIONAL UNIVERSITY

71 Al-Farabi Ave, Almaty 050040
Telephone: (727) 3773333
E-mail: icd.kaznu@gmail.com
Internet: kaznu.kz
Founded 1934, fmrly Kazakh S. M. Kirov State Univ., present name and status 1994
State control
Languages of instruction: Kazakh, Russian
Academic year: September to June (2 semesters)
Rector: Dr MUTANOV GALIMKAIR MUTANOVICH
First Vice-Rector: BURKITBAYEV MUKHAMBETKALI MYRZABAEVICH
Vice-Rector for Academic Affairs: BALAKAEVA GULNAR TULTAEVNA
Vice-Rector for Economic and Production Affairs: EVGENIY ALEXEEVICH AN
Vice-Rector for Research-Innovation Affairs: RAMAZANOV TLEKKABUL SABITOVICH
Vice-Rector for Social Devt: SHOLPAN ERBOLOVNA DZHAMANBALAYEVA
Librarian: MUSAGALIEVA GULZHAN MUSAEVNA
Library: see under Libraries and Archives
Number of teachers: 2,500
Number of students: 19,000
Publication: *Vestnik KazNU* (1 a year)

DEANS

Faculty for Pre-College Education: Dr T. O. MOLDAKHANOV
Faculty of Biology and Biotechnology: Prof. Dr TAMARA MINAZHEVNA SHALAKHMETOVA
Faculty of Chemistry and Chemical Technology: Prof. YERDOS KALIMULLAULY ONGARBAYEV
Faculty of Geography and Nature Management: Prof. Dr V. GRIGORYEVICH SALNIKOV
Faculty of History, Archaeology and Ethnology: Prof. Dr ZHAKEN KOZHAKHMETOVICH TAIMAGAMBETOV
Faculty of International Relations: KARIMZHAN NURUMOVICH SHAKIROV
Faculty of Journalism: ESBERGEN ORAZULY ALAUKHNOV
Faculty of Law: Prof. DAULET LAIKOVICH BAIDELDINOV
Faculty of Mechanics and Mathematics: Prof. D. ZH AHMED-ZAKI
Faculty of Oriental Studies: Dr B. N. ZHUBATOVA
Faculty of Philology, Literary Studies and World Languages: Prof. Dr KANSEYT A. ABDEZULY
Faculty of Philosophy and Political Science: Prof. Dr ALIYA RIMGAZYKYZY MASSALIMOVA
Faculty of Physics and Technics: Prof. B. A. ALIYEV
High School of Economy and Business: Prof. BAYAN ZHUNDIBAEVNA ERMEKBAYEVA
Physico-Technical Faculty: ALIYEV BAKHODIR AZIYMZHANOVYCH

ALMATY TECHNOLOGICAL UNIVERSITY

Tole bi str. 100, Almaty 050012
Telephone: (727) 2935289
E-mail: rector@atu.kz
Internet: www.atu.kz
Founded 1957
State control
Rector: Prof. Dr KURALBEK SADIBAEVICH KULAZHANOV
Pres.: Prof. Dr TALGAT KURALBEKOVICH KULAZHANOV
First Vice-Rector: Prof. Dr OSPANOV ASSAN BEKESHOVICH
Vice-Rector for Science and Innovation: SERIK NIYAZBEKOVICH TUMENOV
Number of teachers: 470
Number of students: 9,000

DEANS

Economics and Business Faculty: Prof. Dr GULNAR ZHANGUTTINA
Faculty of Distance Learning: Prof. Dr MEDVEDKOV EVGENIY BORISOVICH
Faculty of Engineering and Information Technology: Prof. Dr ABDRAHIMOV URAL TUTKABAEVICH
Faculty of Food Productions: Prof. Dr KIZATOVA MAYGUL ZHALELOVNA
Faculty of Light Industry and Design: KURMANALIEV MUSREPBEK KURMANALIEVICH

ALMATY UNIVERSITY OF POWER ENGINEERING AND TELECOMMUNICATION

126 Baytursynova str., Almaty 050013
Telephone: (727) 2925740
E-mail: aipet@aipet.kz
Internet: www.aipet.kz
Founded 1975 as Almaty Energy Institute, present name 2010
State control
Faculties of power engineering, radio engineering, thermal engineering; part-time courses and retraining; pre-institutional training; ENTEL College; br. in Ust Kamenogorsk
Rector: Prof. GUMARBEK ZH. DAUKEYEV
Library of 465,000 vols
Number of teachers: 284
Number of students: 4,856
Publications: *Collections of Postgraduate Works* (1 a year), *Collections of Scientific Works* (2 a year)

ASTANA MEDICAL UNIVERSITY

49A Beibitshilik St, Astana
Telephone: (717) 2539453
E-mail: rektorat@amu.kz
Internet: www.amu.kz
Founded 1964, fmrly Kazakh Medical Academy, present name and status 2009
Private control
Rector: SHAIDAROV MAZHIT ZEINULLOVICH
Pro-Rector for Academic Activities: ZHAKSYLYKOVA GULNAR ADILKHANOVNA
Number of teachers: 700
Number of students: 5,249

ATYRAU INSTITUTE OF OIL AND GAS

Azattyk Ave 1, Atyrau 060002
Telephone: (7122) 354654
E-mail: aing-atr@nursat.kz
Internet: www.aing.kz
Founded 1998
State control
Depts of distance education, economy, mechanics, oil, technology
Rector: DYUSSEMBEK U. KULZHANOV
Library of 738,333 vols
Number of teachers: 264
Number of students: 3,734

ATYRAU UNIVERSITY NAMED AFTER KHALEL DOSMUKHAMEDOV

Studencheskiy Ave 212, Atyrau 060011
Telephone: (712) 2276305
E-mail: atyrauuniv@nursat.kz
Internet: www.atyrauuniv.kz
State control
Rector: K. ZHAULIN

DEANS

Faculty of Physics, Mathematics And Information Technologies: IDRISOV SALAMAT NURMUHANOVICH

CASPIAN STATE UNIVERSITY OF TECHNOLOGY AND ENGINEERING NAMED AFTER SH. YESENOV

14 microdistrict 50, Aktau 466200
Telephone: (729) 2438568
E-mail: aktsu@nursat.kz
Founded fmrly Aktau Sh. Yesenov University
State control
Rector: Prof. ABDUMUTALIP ABZHAPPAROV

D. SERIKBAEV EAST KAZAKHSTAN STATE TECHNICAL UNIVERSITY

69 A. K. Protozanov St, Ust-Kamenogorsk 070004
Telephone: (723) 2267409
E-mail: kanc_ekstu@mail.ru
Internet: www.ektu.kz
Founded 1958
State control
Depts of architectural and civil engineering, economics and management, informational technology and power engineering, mechanical engineering and transport, mining and metallurgy
Rector: Prof. Dr NURLAN MUKHANVICH TEMIRBEKOV
First Vice-Rector: ZHENIS ORAZHANOVICH KULSEITOV
Vice-Rector for Educational and Methodical Work: LINOK NIKOLAY NIKOLAEVICH
Vice-Rector for Production and Economic Affairs: RAKHMETZHANOV ERLAN UATAEVICH
Vice-Rector for Science and Int. Cooperation: ABULHAIROV DARMEN KARATAYEICH
Vice-Rector for Social Issues: NAZBIYEV ZHAKSYGELDY DYUSUPKANOVICH
Library: 1m. vols
Number of teachers: 660
Number of students: 10,400
Publications: *Collections of Scientific Works* (1 a year), *Vestnik* (scientific journal, 4 a year), *Za znanie!* (To Knowledge!, 12 a year)

DEUTSCH-KASACHISCHE UNIVERSITÄT
(Kazakh-German University)

ul. Pushkina 111/113, Almaty 050010
Telephone: (727) 3550551
E-mail: info@dku.kz
Internet: www.dku.kz
Founded 1999
Private control

Faculties of economics, engineering and ecology, engineering and economics, social and political sciences

Rector: Dr JOHANN WILHELM GERLACH

Pro-Rector: Dr MOSKOWTSCHENKO

DZHAMBUL UNIVERSITY

16A, Taraz, Zhambyl 080003

Telephone: (726) 2231978

State control

GOVERNMENT SEMIPALATINSK STATE MEDICAL UNIVERSITY

Abaya ul. 103, Semipalatinsk 490050

E-mail: info@gssmu.com

Internet: www.gssmu.com

Founded 1952 as Semipalatinsk State Medical Univ.; attached to Min. of Health

State control

Regional office in Pakistan

Library of 330,000 vols

Number of teachers: 900

Number of students: 3,500

Publication: *Science & Health Services*

HODJA AHMET YESEVI KAZAKH-TURKISH INTERNATIONAL UNIVERSITY

Maydan Yesim-Khan 2, Turkistan 487010

Telephone: (725) 3363636

E-mail: yeseviun@mktu.turkistan.kz

Internet: www.yesevi.edu.kz

Founded 1991 jtly by Govts of Kazakhstan and Turkey

State control

Languages of instruction: English, Kazakh, Russian, Turkish

Academic year: September to July

Faculties of art, art studies, ecology, economics, history, history and philology, languages and literature, law, mathematics and economics, medicine, natural sciences, oriental studies

Pres.: Prof. Dr OSMAN HORATA

Rector: Prof. Dr LESBEK TAŞIMOV

Library of 480,000 vols

Number of teachers: 700

Number of students: 10,200

Publication: *Scientific Methodological Articles* (24 a year)

INNOVATIVE UNIVERSITY OF EURASIA

45 Lomov str., Pavlodar 140003

Telephone: (718) 2345172

E-mail: dir_biblio@ineu.edu.kz

Internet: ineu.edu.kz

Private control

Academies of education, engineering, management

Rector: ASKAR USYPOVICH KAMERBAEV

Library of 500,000 vols

Number of teachers: 700

Number of students: 11,000

INTERNATIONAL ACADEMY OF BUSINESS

Rozibakieva St 227, Almaty 050060

Telephone: (727) 2496446

E-mail: info@iab.kz

Internet: www.iab.kz

Founded 1988 as Almaty School of Management, present name and status 1996

Private control

Languages of instruction: English, Kazakh, Russian

Accounting and audit, business, economy, finance, information science, management, marketing

Rector: ASSYLBEK KOZHAKHMETOV

Dean: Prof. NURZHAMAL DUISENGULOVA

INTERNATIONAL BUSINESS ACADEMY

12 Tulepov St, Karaganda 100027

Telephone: (721) 2421435

Internet: www.kubup.edu.kz

Founded 1991, fmrly Karaganda University of Business, Management and Law, present name and status 2008

Private control

Pres.: Dr SAGINOV KAZBEK ABYLKASOVICH

Vice-Pres. of Academic and Economic Work: TSAI YURI SERGEEVICH

Vice-Pres. of Innovations and Information Technologies: LEONOV VYACHESLAV VALENTINOVICH

Librarian: GULENKOVA NADEZHDA ALEKSANDROVNA

Library of 70,000 vols

DEANS

Business Faculty: BAIKENZHIN YANVARBEK ASYLBEKOVICH

Foreign Languages Faculty: PECHERSKIH THALIYA FAYAZOVNA

KARAGANDA 'BOLASHAK' UNIVERSITY

16 Yerubayev str., Karaganda

Telephone: (721) 2420425

E-mail: kubolashak@gmail.com

Internet: www.kubolashak.kz

Founded 1995

Private control

Languages of instruction: English, German, Kazakh, Russian

Faculties of economics and information science, law, humanities-pedagogy, pharmacy

Rector: NURLAN ORYNBASAROVICH DULATBEKOV

Library of 400,000 vols

Publications: *Learning Kazakh language*, *Syr men Symbat*

KARAGANDA ECONOMICAL UNIVERSITY OF KAZPOTREBSOYUZ

Akademicheskaya str. 9, Karaganda 100009

Telephone: (721) 2441624

E-mail: rector@keu.kz

Internet: www.keu.kz

Founded 1966, present name and status 1995

Private control

Rector: Prof. Dr ERKARA BALKARAEVICH AYMAGAMBETOV

First Vice-Rector: ROSA OLZHABAEVNA BUGUBAEVA

Pro-Rector for Research: ANWAR MUHAMETOVICH NEVMATULIN

Pro-Rector for Social Affairs: COSMAN ZHAKUPBAEVICH ABILOV

Library of 580,000 vols

Number of teachers: 400

Number of students: 8,500

DEANS

Faculty of Accounting and Finance: Prof. Dr GULMIRA NAKIPOVA

Faculty of Business And Law: FARHIYA MOMUSHEVA

Faculty of Economics And Management: GALIYA GIMRANOVA

KARAGANDA STATE MEDICAL UNIVERSITY

Gogol str. 40, Karaganda 100008

Telephone: (721) 2513897

E-mail: info@kgmu.kz

Internet: kgma.kz

Founded 1950

State control

Languages of instruction: English, Kazakh, Russian

Rector: Dr RAUSHAN SULTANOVNA DOSMAGAMBETOVA

Pro-Rector for Academic and Educational Effort: KUSAINOVA ARMAN SAILAUBEKOVNA

Pro-Rector for Scientific Effort: AZIZOV ILYA SULEIMANOVICH

Library Dir: SHEGAI LUDMILA ANATOLIEVNA

Library of 500,000 vols, 186 periodicals

Number of teachers: 520

Number of students: 5,000

Publication: *Medicine and Ecology* (6 a year)

DEANS

Faculty of Continuous Professional Devt: Prof. Dr OSPANOVA KADISHA BAZARBAEVNA

Faculty of General Medicine and Stomatology: TOLEUBEKOV KUATBEK KUANSHBEKOVICH

Faculty of Medical Business, Paediatrics, Eastern Medicine and Internship: Dr TASHKENBAEVA VENERA BAZARBEKOVNA

Faculty of Social Health Protection, Nurse Business, Pharmacy, Medical and Prophylactic Effort: Dr SHAIZADINA FATIMA MEIRHANOVNA

KARAGANDA STATE TECHNICAL UNIVERSITY

56 Mira Blvd, Karaganda 100027

Telephone: (721) 2564422

E-mail: kargtu@kstu.kz

Internet: www.kstu.kz

Founded 1953 as Karaganda Mining Institute; present name and status 1996

State control

Faculties of business management, civil engineering, economics and management, electromechanical engineering, geoecology, information technology, machine building, mining, transport and road engineering

Rector: Prof. ARSTAN MAULENOVICH GAZALIYEV

First Vice-Rector: Prof. Dr MARAT KENESOVICH IBATOV

Vice-Rector for Academic Affairs: Prof. VICTOR VLADIMIROVICH EGOROV

Vice-Rector for Admin. and Exec. Work: BAUYRZHAN KUSHERBAYEVICH URBISINOV (acting)

Vice-Rector for Education Affairs: Dr GULZHAKHAN ABZHANOVNA BAIZHABAGINOVA (acting)

Librarian: B. O. BEYSEMBAEVA

Library: 1.5m. vols

Number of teachers: 762

Number of students: 8,166

KARAGANDA STATE UNIVERSITY NAMED AFTER ACADEMICIAN E. A. BUKETOV

Universitetskaya ul. 28, Karaganda 100028

Telephone: (721) 2770389

E-mail: office@ksu.kz

Internet: www.ksu.kz

Founded 1972, present name 1992

State control

Academic year: September to June

Rector: Prof. Dr YERKIN KINAYATOVICH KUBEYEV

Library: 1.7m. vols

Number of teachers: 1,200
Number of students: 13,000
Publication: *Vestnik* (4 a year)

DEANS

Faculty of Biology and Geography: AITKULOV AIDAR MURATOVICH
Faculty of Chemistry: TAZHBAYEV YERKEBLAN MURATOVICH
Faculty of Economics: YESENGELDIN BAUYRZHAN SATYBALDINOVICH
Faculty of History: SAKTAGANOVA ZAURESH GALYMZHANOVNA
Faculty of Law: KOZHAKHMETOV GALYM ZEINEKENOVICH
Faculty of Mathematics: Prof. N. G. ABDRAKHMANOV
Faculty of Physics: NUSUPBEKOV BEKBOLAT RAKISHEVICH

KAZAKH ABLAI KHAN UNIVERSITY OF INTERNATIONAL RELATIONS AND WORLD LANGUAGES

Muratbayeva 200 str., Almaty 050022
Telephone: (727) 2922363
E-mail: kazumo@ablaikhan.kz
Internet: www.ablaikhan.kz
Founded 1941 as Kazakh State Teacher's Institute of the Foreign Languages, present name 1944
State control
Rector: SALIMA S. KUNANBAEVA
Vice-Rector for Scientific and Research Work: KUSAYIN T. RYSSALDY
Vice-Rector for Social Work: ZHUMAGUL A. ISMAGAMBETOVA
Vice-Rector for Study and Methodical Work: SATIMA S. ZHUMAGULOVA
Vice-Rector for Study Dept: NAGIMA A. SARSEMBAEVA
Library of 630,000 vols
Number of teachers: 668
Number of students: 5,000

DEANS

Faculty of Oriental Studies: Prof. Dr A. B. NAYRZBAEVA
Pedagogical Faculty of Foreign Languages: Prof. Dr AYBARSHA ISLAM
Translation Faculty: FAIZOVA K. KAMILYA (acting)

KAZAKH ACADEMY OF SPORTS AND TOURISM

Almaty
Telephone: (727) 22001133
E-mail: info@kazacademsport.kz
Internet: www.kazacademsport.kz
Founded 1944
State control
Pres.: Prof. KAIRAT ZAKIRYANOV

DEANS

Faculty of Olympic Sports: DINARA NURMUKHANBETOVA
Faculty of Postgraduate and Additional Education: DUSKAEVA NAZIMA
Faculty of Professional Sports and Arts: BOLDYREV BORIS
Faculty of Tourism: VUKOLOV VLADIMIR

KAZAKH ACADEMY OF TRANSPORT AND COMMUNICATIONS NAMED AFTER M. TYNYSHBAYEV

Shevchenko str. 97, Almaty 050012
Telephone: (727) 2920986
E-mail: info@kazatk.kz
Internet: www.kazatk.kz
State control
Rector: ALPYSBAYEV SERIK AITAKHYNOVICH

KAZAKH-AMERICAN FREE UNIVERSITY

Bazhova str. 68, Ust-Kamenogorsk 070018
Telephone: (723) 2222324
E-mail: kafu_ukg@mail.ru
Internet: www.kafu.kz
Founded 1994
Private control
Languages of instruction: English, Kazakh, Russian
Academic year: September to June
Faculties of foreign languages, information systems, law, management
Pres.: Dr EREZHEP A. MAMBETKAZIYEV
Number of students: 5,465

KAZAKH-AMERICAN UNIVERSITY

Toraigirov str. 29, Almaty 050043
Telephone: (727) 2268000
E-mail: info@kau.kz
Internet: www.kau.kz
Founded 1997
Private control
Pres.: AMIRLAN A. KUSAINOV
Library of 200,000 vols

KAZAKH-BRITISH TECHNICAL UNIVERSITY

Toli bi 59, Almaty 050000
Telephone: (727) 2504658
E-mail: kbtu@kbtu.kz
Internet: www.kbtu.kz
Founded 2001
State control
Rector: ISKANDER K. BEISEMBETOV
Library of 307,616 vols

DEANS

Faculty of Economics and Finance: ABDRAHMANOVA T. GULNAR
Faculty of General Education: TOKMAGAMBETOV ALKEN SHUGAIBEKOVICH
Faculty of Information Technology: TIMUR F. UMAROV
International School of Economics: ZOYA TUIEBAKHOVA

KAZAKH ECONOMICS UNIVERSITY NAMED AFTER T. RYSKULOV

ul. Dzhandosova 55, Almaty 050035
Telephone: (727) 3095973
E-mail: kazsam@pisem.net
Internet: www.kazeu.kz
Founded 1963 as Alma-Ata Institute of National Economy, present status 1991, present name 2000
State control
Depts of accounting and statistics, business management and social service, economics and management, engineering, finance; military dept
Rector: Dr ALI AZHIMOVICH ABISHEV
Library: 1.2m. vols
Number of teachers: 600
Number of students: 12,000

KAZAKH HUMANITARIAN LAW UNIVERSITY

pr. Abaya 50A, Almaty 050008
Telephone: (727) 2425225
E-mail: info@kazguu.kz
Founded 1994
State control
Languages of instruction: Kazakh, Russian
Academic year: September to June
Rector: MAKSUT NARIKBAYEV
Vice-Rector: BOLAT BEYEKENOV
Library of 100,237 vols
Number of teachers: 545
Number of students: 1,883
Publication: *State and Law* (3 a year)

DEANS

Commercial Law: SERGEY MARKIN
Criminal Law and Trial Investigation Law: RAMASAN NURTAYEV
Int. Law: IRINA KHAN
Judicial and State Prosecution Law: OMIRBAY KYSTAUBAY

KAZAKH NATIONAL AGRARIAN UNIVERSITY

Abaya Ave 8, Almaty 050010
Telephone: (727) 2641948
E-mail: info@kaznau.kz
Internet: www.kaznau.kz
Founded 1996 by merger of Kazakh State Institute of Agriculture (f. 1929) and Alma-Ata Veterinary Institute (f. 1910)
State control
Languages of instruction: English, Kazakh, Russian
Academic year: September to May
Rector: T. I. YESPOLOV
Depts of agricultural biology, economy and law, engineering, forestry and horticulture, microbiology, production of animal breeding, veterinary medicine
Library of 800,000 vols
Number of teachers: 716
Number of students: 7,600

KAZAKH NATIONAL MEDICAL UNIVERSITY NAMED AFTER S. D. ASFENDIYAROV

ul. Tole-bi 88, Almaty 050012
Telephone: (727) 2927937
E-mail: kaznmu@arna.kz
Internet: www.kaznmu.kz
Founded 1930 as Kazakh State Medical Institute, present name and status 2001
State control
Faculties of dentistry, gen. medicine, health sciences, paediatrics, pharmacy, public health, stomatology, therapeutics
Rector: ASFENDIYAROV A. A. AKANOV
Library of 221,000 vols
Number of teachers: 1,500
Number of students: 5,349

KAZAKH NATIONAL PEDAGOGICAL UNIVERSITY, ABAI

13 Dostyk Ave, Almaty 050010
Telephone: (727) 2916339
E-mail: rector@kaznpu.kz
Internet: www.kaznpu.kz
Founded 1928 as Kazakh State Univ.
State control
Languages of instruction: Kazakh, Russian
Academic year: September to June
Rector: PRALIYEV SERIK ZHAILAUOVICH
First Vice-Rector: Prof. Dr MUBARAK ERMAGANBETOV
Vice-Rector for Admin. Affairs: TEMIRBOLAT EDILBAYEV
Vice-Rector for Int. Relations: Dr DANA MEDEUOVA
Vice-Rector for Science: Prof. Dr VLADIMIR KOSSOV
Librarian: NURGUL IMANSYDYKOVA
Library of 2,500,000 vols
Number of teachers: 730
Number of students: 15,000

DEANS

Faculty of Arts and Graphics: Prof. Dr BERIKZHAN ALMUHAMBETOV
Faculty of Chemistry and Biology: Prof. KHAIRULLA ZHANBEKOV
Faculty of Finance and Economics: Prof. Dr ARDAK SAHANOVA
Faculty of Geography and Ecology: Prof. Dr O. B. MAZBAYEV
Faculty of History: GABIT KENZHEBAYEV
Faculty of Int. Relations and Jurisprudence: Dr TALGAT BALASHOV
Faculty of Philology: Prof. Dr BALTABAI ABDIGAZIULY
Faculty of Physics and Mathematics: Dr MURAT BEKPATSHAYEV
Faculty of Physical Training and Initial Military Preparation: Prof. Dr KAIRAT ADAMBEKOV
Faculty of Psychology and Pedagogy: Prof. Dr ROZALINDA SHAHANOVA

KAZAKH NATIONAL TECHNICAL UNIVERSITY AFTER K. I. SATPAEV

Satbayev 22, Almaty 050013
Telephone: (727) 2926025
E-mail: allnt@kazntu.sci.kz
Internet: www.kazntu.kz

Founded 1934 as Kazakh Polytechnic Institute; present name and status 1996
State control
Languages of instruction: Kazakh, Russian
Academic year: September to July

Institutes of architecture and building, base education, distance learning, economics and business, geology and oil gas business, industrial engineering, information and telecommunication technologies, mountain metallurgy

Rector: Prof. Dr ZHEKSENBEK MAKEYEVICH ADILOV
Hon. Rector: DOSYM KASYMULY SULEEV
First Vice-Rector and Vice-Rector for Teaching Work: Prof. Dr BAIYSBEKOV SHYNYBAY BAIYSBEKOVICH
Vice-Rector for Academic Affairs: SARSEN S. ZHUSUPBEKOV
Vice-Rector for Academic and Educational Work: Prof. Dr SYDYKOV ULYKPAN ESILHANOVICH
Vice-Rector for Infrastructure Devt: TYNYBEKOV RISHAT IMELOVICH
Vice-Rector for Science and Int. Relations: Prof. Dr DYUSSEMBAYEV IZIM NASIEVICH
Vice-Rector for Social Work: MUKANOV KANATBEK NURTAZINOVICH

Library of 2,000,147 vols
Number of teachers: 1,268
Number of students: 12,086

Publication: *KazNTU Herald* (scientific magazine)

KAZAKH-RUSSIAN UNIVERSITY

Kabanbay Batyra St 8, Astana 010000
Telephone: (717) 2240403
E-mail: muh-astana@rambler.ru
Internet: www.kru.kz

Founded 1998
Private control

Depts of economics, business and tourism, information and design, pedagogy and psychology, political science and law

Rector: MULDAKHMETOV ZEINOLLA MULDAKHMETOVICH

Library of 109,550 vols

KAZAKHSTAN ENGINEERING-TECHNOLOGICAL UNIVERSITY

Al-Farabi Ave 93A, Almaty 050060
Telephone: (727) 3000777
E-mail: kazetu@kazetu.kz
Internet: www.kazetu.kz

Founded 2001
Private control
Languages of instruction: Kazakh, Russian

KAZAKH STATE WOMEN'S PEDAGOGICAL INSTITUTE

Aiteke-bi 99, Almaty 050000
Telephone: (727) 2394283
E-mail: zhenpi@mail.online.kz

Founded 1944
State control
Languages of instruction: Kazakh, Russian
Academic year: September to July

Rector: SHAMSHA BERKIMBAYEVA

Faculties of economics, education, history, library science, modern languages, music education, natural sciences, philology, philosophy, primary education, sports, teacher training

Library of 860,000 vols
Number of teachers: 650
Number of students: 2,600

KAZAKH UNIVERSITY OF COMMUNICATIONS

Samal. Zhetysu-1, d. 32A, Almaty 050063
Telephone: (727) 3767478
E-mail: kups1@mail.ru
Internet: www.kups.kz

Founded 2000, fmrly Kazakh Univ. of Railway Transport
State control

Rector: Prof. Dr AMANGELDY DZHUMAGALIEVICH OMAROV
Vice-Rector for Academic Affairs: Prof. Dr A. K. KAYNARBEKOV
Vice-Rector for Educational Work: R. A. KASHABAEVA
Vice-Rector for Scientific and Educational Work: A. A. SHALKAROV

Publication: *Industrial Vehicles Kazakhstan*

DEANS

Organization of Transportation and Economy: Prof. Dr SARZHANOV TAYZHAN SADYHANOVICH
Transportation Engineering, Construction and Automation: KASIMOV BAUYRZHAN RAHMEDIEVICH

KAZAKH UNIVERSITY OF ECONOMICS, FINANCE AND INTERNATIONAL TRADE

Zhubanov str. 7, Astana
Telephone: (717) 2373904
E-mail: mailbox@kuef.kz
Internet: www.kuef.kz

Founded 1999, present name and status 2007
Private control
Languages of instruction: Kazakh, Russian
Academic year: September to June

Depts of accounting and finance, economy, management and law, postgraduate education, distance education

Rector: Prof. Dr SARSENGALI ABDYMANAPOV

Library of 500,000 vols
Number of teachers: 311
Number of students: 4,075

KOKSHETAU STATE UNIVERSITY NAMED AFTER SH. UALIKHANOV

ul. Karla Marksa 76, Kokshetau, Akmola 020000
Telephone: (716) 2255583
E-mail: universi@kokshetau.online.kz
Internet: kgu.kz

Founded 1996, current name adopted 2001
State control
Languages of instruction: Kazakh, Russian
Academic year: September to July

Rector: Prof. Dr KALABAYEV NAYMAN BUBEEVICH
First Deputy Rector: Prof. Dr PERNEHAN IBADULLAEVICH SADYKOV
Deputy Rector for Academic Work and Methodology: Dr AIGUL DOSZHANOVNA ZHAKUPOVA
Deputy Rector for Research and Int. Relations: ABAI MUKHAMEDIYAROVICH DOSTIYAROV
Deputy Rector for Social and Educational Work: AMANAY ASYLBAYEVICH SEYTKASSYMOV
Librarian: TOKPERDINOVA AIGUL MUKASHEVNA

Library of 600,000 vols
Number of teachers: 450
Number of students: 4,900

DEANS

Dept of Economics Information Technologies: RAKHIMOVA GULMIRA AKHMETOVNA
Dept of Natural Sciences and Pedagogy: KHAMITOVA AINA SULTANSEITOVNA
Dept of Tourism, Sport and Design: SHAHARBEK TULEGENOVICH TULEGENOV
Faculty of Agriculture and Technology: ALEKSANDR PODDUBNY
Faculty of History and Law: BEKSEITOVA AKBOTA TASTANBEKOVNA
Faculty of Philology: BAYMANOVA LAZZAT SEITZIEVNA
Faculty of Physics and Mathematics: KHAMZINA BOTAGOZ ERKENOVNA

KOSTANAI STATE PEDAGOGICAL INSTITUTE

Tarana str. 118, Kostanay 11000
Telephone: (714) 2530455
E-mail: kgpi118@mail.ru
Internet: www.kspi.kz

Founded 1939
State control

Depts of applied linguistics, distance learning, foreign languages, history and art, pedagogy, natural science, physical education and sport, psychology and education, social sciences

Rector: Prof. Dr BAIMIRZAEV KUAT MARATULY
Pro-Rector for Educational Methodological Work: KUANISHBAEV SEITBEK BEKENOVICH
Pro-Rector for Scientific Work and Int. Relations: ZHARKOVA VALENTINA IVANOVNA

Library of 500,000 vols

KOSTANAY ENGINEERING PEDAGOGICAL UNIVERSITY

Chernyshevsky St. 5, Kostanay 110000
Telephone: (714) 2280257
E-mail: adm@kineu.kz
Internet: kineu.kz

Founded 2007
Private control

Faculties of agricultural technology and energy, distance learning, economics, engineering and transport, postgraduate education

Rector: Prof. S. B. ISMURATOV

Number of teachers: 139

KYZYLORDA HUMANITARIAN UNIVERSITY NAMED AFTER KORKYT ATA

Zheltoksan 40, Kyzylorda 120000
State control

KYZYLORDA STATE UNIVERSITY NAMED AFTER KORKYT ATA

Aiteke-bi 29A, Kyzylorda 120014
Telephone: (724) 2261716
E-mail: ksu@korkyt.kz
Internet: www.korkyt.kz

Founded 1937, present name and status 1998
State control
Languages of instruction: Kazakh, Russian
Academic year: September to June

Faculties of correspondence and evening courses, economics and ecology, economics and engineering, history and law, natural sciences, philology and arts, physics and mathematics

Rector: KYLYSHBAI A. BISSENOV

Library: 1.8m. vols
Number of teachers: 460
Number of students: 8,000

Publications: *Syr Tulegu* (news), *Vestnik* (sciences, 4 a year)

L. N. GUMILYOV EURASIAN NATIONAL UNIVERSITY

5 Munaitpasov Str., Astana 010008
Telephone: (717) 2353806
E-mail: root@lceu.ricc.kz
Internet: enu.kz

Founded 1996, present status 2001
State control
Languages of instruction: Kazakh, Russian
Academic year: September to June

Rector: Prof. Dr ERLAN B. SYDYKOV
First Vice-Rector: Prof. Dr ZHAMILYA N. NURMANBETOVA
Vice-Rector for Education: LAURA A. YESMUKHANOVA
Vice-Rector for Educational and Methodical Affairs and Strategic Devt: Prof. Dr DIKHAN KAMZABEKULY
Vice-Rector for Research: Prof. Dr RAKHMETKAZHI I. BERSIMBAYEV

Library: 1.4m. vols
Number of teachers: 900
Number of students: 9,042

DEANS

Faculty of Information Technologies: Prof. Dr ZHANAT KUNAPIANOVNA NURBEKOVA
Faculty of International Relations: SOMZHUREK BAUBEK ZHUMASHULY
Faculty of Journalism and Political Science: Prof. SAK KAIRAT

M. AUEZOV SOUTH KAZAKHSTAN STATE UNIVERSITY

pr. Tauke-Khan 5, Shymkent 160012
Telephone: (725) 2535048
E-mail: biblioteka@ukgu.kz
Internet: www.ukgu.kz
State control

Rector: BISHIMBAEV VALIHAN KOZIKEEVICH
First Pro-Rector: SABIRHANOV DARHAN SABIRHANOVICH
Pro-Rector for Admin. Activity: TAGIBAEV DAUREN DOSMAHAMBETOVICH
Pro-Rector for Scientific Research and Int. Relations: BAKHOV ZHUMABEK KUBEEVICH
Pro-Rector for Social Problems and Educational Work: ISKAKOV TURLIBEK UTESHEVICH
Pro-Rector for Study and Information Technology: BAIBOLOV KANAT SEITJANOVICH

Number of teachers: 1,500
Number of students: 20,000

DEANS

Agro-Industrial Faculty: Dr A. K. ZHYLKYBAEV
Faculty of Building and Transport: SADYKOV ZHENIS ABZHANOVICH
Faculty of Chemical Technology: Prof. Dr ANARBAEV ABIBULLA ABILDAEVICH
Faculty of Economics and Finance: RAKHMETULINA ZHIBEK BERLIBEKOVNA
Faculty of Information Technology, Telecommunications and Automated Systems: BESBAEV GANI ABZELBEKOVICH
Faculty of Light and Food Industries: BAIZHANOVA SULUSHASH BOLABIEVNA
Faculty of Jurisprudence and Int. Relations: SARYKULOV KURMANGALI RAKHMANBERDIEVICH
Faculty of Mechanical and Petroleum Engineering: MYRZALIEV DARKHAN SAPARBAEVICH
Faculty of Pedagogy and Culture: ALIMA BALTABAEVNA NURLIBEKOVA
Faculty of Philology: TLEUBERDIEV BOLATBEK MAKULBEKOVICH
Faculty of Sport and Tourism: DEMEUOV AKHAN KALYBAIULY
Natural-Pedagogical Faculty: MADIAROV NURLIBY

MIRAS UNIVERSITY

Kurnakova St 2, Shymkent 160000
Telephone: (725) 2438266
E-mail: info@miras.edu.kz
Internet: www.miras.edu.kz

Founded 1997
Private control

Library of 150,000 vols

NATIONAL DEFENCE UNIVERSITY

Shuchinsk, Akmola 476410
Telephone: (716) 3641819

Founded 2002, fmrly Military Academy of the Armed Forces; attached to Min. of Defence of the Republic of Kazakhstan
State control

Offers postgraduate courses in logistics management, military and state management, military and admin. management, military education management, moral and welfare management, technical provision management

Chief: NIKOLAY KUATOV

NAZARBAYEV UNIVERSITY

53 Kabanbay batyr Ave, Astana 010000
Telephone: (717) 2706180
E-mail: info@nu.edu.kz
Internet: nu.edu.kz

Founded 2009 as New Univ. of Astana, present name 2010
State control
Language of instruction: English

Rector: SHIGEO KATSU
Provost: ANNE LONSDALE

DEANS

School of Engineering: Prof. STEFAAN SIMONS
School of Science and Technology: Dr RON BULBULIAN

NORTH KAZAKHSTAN STATE UNIVERSITY NAMED AFTER MANASH KOZYBAEV

Pushkin St 86, Petropavlovsk 150000
Telephone: (152) 493352
E-mail: mail@nkzu.kz
Internet: www.nkzu.kz

Founded 1937
State control
Languages of instruction: Kazakh, Russian
Academic year: September to August

Rector: Prof. Dr ASHIMOV UNDASSYN BAIKENOVICH
Vice-Rector for Academic Work: KAIRZHANOVA LAURA SOVETOVNA
Vice-Rector for Scientific Work and External Relations: TUKACHYOV ALEXANDER ANDREEVICH
Vice-Rector for Educational Work: TAIZHANOVA MUKARAM MURZATOVNA
Vice-Rector for House-Keeping Unit: KUSHUMBAEV AKBAY BAGYTKEREEVICH

Library: 1m. vols
Number of teachers: 440
Number of students: 13,000

DEANS

Faculty of Economics: D. N. SHAIKIN
Faculty of Energetic and Mechanical Engineering: N. K. NABIEV
Faculty of History and Law: SABYR I. IBRAEV
Faculty of Information Technologies: B. E. BATYROV
Faculty of Music: N. I. PYSTOVALOVA
Faculty of Natural-Geographic Sciences: I. V. GOLODOVA
Faculty of Physical Education: D. U. ZERNOV
Faculty of Transport-Building Engineering: R. S. IMAMBAEVA
Institute of Language and Literature: ZH. S. TALASPAEVA
Qualification Development Institute: A. SH. YASHKINA

PAVLODAR STATE PEDAGOGICAL INSTITUTE

Mira St 60, Pavlodar 140002
Telephone: (718) 2552476
E-mail: priem@ppi.kz
Internet: www.ppi.kz

Founded 1962
State control

Faculties of philology, natural science, psychology and pedagogy, physics and mathematics, economics and law, physical education

Rector: Dr NURGALI R. ARSHABEKOV

Library of 437,241 vols

PAVLODAR STATE UNIVERSITY NAMED AFTER S. TORAIGHYROV

Ul. Lomova 64, Pavlodar 140008
Telephone: (718) 2451110
E-mail: rector@psu.kz
Internet: www.psu.kz

Founded 1962
State control

Institutes of humanities, natural sciences, power engineering and automation, economics and law, construction, transport and machine-building, teacher-training; institute for the improvement of qualifications

Rector: ERLAN ARYN

Library of 870,000 vols
Number of teachers: 810
Number of students: 13,000

Publications: *Biological Sciences of Kazakhstan* (4 a year), *Regional Studies* (4 a year), *Science and Technology of Kazakhstan* (4 a year)

SARSEN AMANZHOLOV EAST KAZAKHSTAN STATE UNIVERSITY

30 Gvardeiskoi Divizii St 34, Ust-Kamenogorsk 070002
Telephone: (723) 2541411
E-mail: rector@vkgu.kz
Internet: www.vkgu.kz

Founded 1952
State control
Languages of instruction: Kazakh, Russian
Academic year: September to June

Rector: Prof. Dr Beibit Baimagambetovitch Mamrayev
First Vice-Rector: Gainelgazy Adilgazinov
Pro-Rector for Economic Affairs and Facilities: Borambayev Gafur Maratovich
Pro-Rector for Educational and Methodological Activities: Kalenova Bakitgul Sovetovna
Pro-Rector for Strategic Devt and Science: Kasabekov Sailau Amanzholovich
Pro-Rector for Students Social Affairs: Orazalin Slyambek Kalibekovich (acting)
Library of 992,710 vols
Number of teachers: 700
Number of students: 11,079

DEANS

Faculty of Distance Learning: Bairkenova Gulmira Toulebekovna
Faculty of Ecology And Natural Science: Mirzagalieva Anar Bazarovna
Faculty of Economics and Business: Kakimzhanov Zainel Rakimovich
Faculty of History and International Policy Studies: Ahmetova Gulzhan Mirzamuhambetovna
Faculty of Mathematics, Physics And Technology: Temirbekov Nurlykhan Mukanuli
Faculty of Philology: Dr Kurmanbayeva Shinar Kapantakizi
Faculty of Psychology and Pedagogy: Apishev Orazbek Demesinovich
Faculty of Sports and Culture: Sarmuldinov Rizabek Barievich
Faculty of State Management and Law: Seitembetov Ermek Zhakenovich

SEMEY STATE UNIVERSITY NAMED AFTER SHAKARIM

St Glinka 20a, Semey 490035
Telephone: (722) 2422937
E-mail: dst@semgu.kz
Internet: www.semgu.kz
Founded 1995
State control
Languages of instruction: Kazakh, Russian
Academic year: September to June
Rector: Amirbekov Sharipbek
Pro-Rector: Berdan Abdazimovich Rskeldiyev
Provost for Research, Innovation and Int. Activities: Amirkhanov Kumarbek Zhunusbekovich
Library: 1m. vols
Number of teachers: 648
Number of students: 8,682

DEANS

Agrarian Faculty: Zejnolla Kalymbekovich Tokayev
Faculty of Engineering and Technology: Serik Tumenov
Faculty of Finance and Economics: Kozhageldiev Begman Kadyrovich
Faculty of Humanities: Arap Slyamovich Espenbetov
Faculty of Information and Communicative Technology: Utedzhanova Bibatpa Keshenovna
Faculty of Natural Sciences: Benur Musabalina
Faculty of Philology: Farida Zhaksybayeva

SEMIPALATINSK STATE PEDAGOGICAL INSTITUTE

Tanibergenov str. 1, Semey 071410
Telephone: (722) 2359433
E-mail: oo@sgpi.kz
Internet: sgpi.kz
Founded 1934
State control
Library of 320,000 vols, 300 periodicals

SIRDARIYA UNIVERSITY

St Auezov 11, Maktaaral Dist, S Kazakhstan
Telephone: (725) 3463000
E-mail: sirdariya@mail.ru
Internet: www.sirdariya.narod.ru
Founded 1998
Private control
Faculties of chemistry and biology, design and music education, distance learning, history and law, humanitary education, physical culture and sports, physics and mathematics
Rector: Ashirov Abdimalik Manapuly
Library of 200,000 vols
Number of students: 5,000

SOUTHERN KAZAKHSTAN AUZEV HUMANITIES UNIVERSITY

Beibitshilik 3, Shymkent 160018
Telephone: (725) 2449988
E-mail: ukrgi-smh@nursat.kz
State control

SOUTHERN KAZAKHSTAN MEDICAL ACADEMY

Lenina 1, Shymkent 160000
Founded 1944
State control

S. SEIFULLIN KAZAKH AGRO TECHNICAL UNIVERSITY

62 pr. Pobedy, Astana 473032
Telephone: (717) 2317547
E-mail: agun.katu@gmail.com
Internet: www.agun.kz
Founded 1957 as Akmola Agricultural Institution,
State control
Depts of agronomy, architecture, computer systems and vocational training, energy, economy, land-use planning, technology, veterinary medicine
Rector: Prof. Dr Akhylbek K. Kurishbaev
First Vice-Rector: Prof. Dr Aitzhan M. Abdyrov
Vice-Rector for Research and Int. Relations: Prof. Dr Balgabay S. Maikanov
Vice-Rector for Students Welfare and Social Problems: Alexander V. Mayer
Library: 1m. vols
Number of teachers: 402
Number of students: 2,043

STATE FINANCIAL INSTITUTE

ul. Shugajeva 159, Semipalatinsk 071403
Telephone: (722) 2635920
Founded 1995
State control
Rector: Gennadi N. Garmanić

SULEYMAN DEMIREL UNIVERSITY

Abilay Khan str. 3, Kaskelen, Almaty 040900
Telephone: (727) 3079565
E-mail: info@sdu.edu.kz
Internet: www.sdu.edu.kz
Founded 1996
Private control
Languages of instruction: English, Kazakh
Academic year: September to August
Rector: Prof. Dr Mesut Akgül
Vice-Rector: Mehmet Izol
Vice-Rector for Academic Affairs: Prof. Dr Nurlibek Seitkulov
Vice-Rector for Student Affairs: Prof. Dr Saltanat Amirgaliyeva
Gen. Sec.: Ali Kocak
Librarian: Abdullah Askari
Library of 55,000 vols
Number of teachers: 300
Number of students: 2,500
Publications: *SDU Impressions*, *SDU Khabarshisi*

DEANS

Faculty of Economics: Prof. Dr Saltanat Amirgaliyeva
Faculty of Engineering: Prof. Dr Humbat Aliyev
Faculty of Law: Prof. Dr Nurlibek Seitkulov
Faculty of Philology: Prof. Dr Davran Gaipov

TARAZ STATE PEDAGOGICAL UNIVERSITY

ul. Tole-bi 62, Taraz, Zhambyl 080000
Telephone: (726) 2435806
E-mail: targpi@mail.ru
Internet: www.tarmpi.kz
Founded 1967
State control
Languages of instruction: Kazakh, Russian
Teacher training and research
Rector: Prof. Dr Machmetgaly N. Sarybekov
Number of teachers: 319

TARAZ STATE UNIVERSITY NAMED AFTER M. KH. DULATY

Tole Bi str. 60, Taraz, Zhambyl
Telephone: (726) 2453664
E-mail: info@tarsu.kz
Internet: www.tarsu.kz
Founded 1998
State control
Institutes of distance learning, economics and business, environment and construction, general engineering, humanities-social sciences, law, oil and gas mechanics, postgraduate education and professional training, technology and information systems, water resources
Rector: Prof. Dr Ashimzhan Suleimenuly Akhmetov
First Vice-Rector: Prof. Dr Omarbekuly Tiribolsyn
Vice-Rector for Educational and Methodical Work: Prof. Dr Daria Perneshovna Kozhamzharova
Vice-Rector for Educational Work and Public Relations: Almara Erkinovna Nauryzbekova
Vice-Rector for Research and Int. Relations: Prof. Seytkhan Meldebekovich Koybakov
Number of teachers: 600
Number of students: 15,000

'TURAN-ASTANA' UNIVERSITY

Dukenuly St 29, Astana
Telephone: (717) 2395110
E-mail: info@turan-astana.kz
Internet: www.turan-astana.kz
Founded 1998
Private
Rector: Prof. Dzhaparova Gulzhamal Alkenovna
Library of 300,000 vols
Number of teachers: 180

DEANS

Dept of Engineering and Economics: Aisakova Bakhytzhan Aitmagambetovna
Dept of Humanities and Law: Shakishev Kazbek Danagulovich

TURAN UNIVERSITY

L. Chaikina str 12, Almaty 050020
Telephone: (727) 3873232
E-mail: turpost@list.ru
Internet: www.turan.edu.kz
Private control
Rector: Prof. R. A. ALSHANOV

UNIVERSITY KAINAR

Satpaev str. 7A, Almaty
Telephone: (727) 2558633
E-mail: kainar@university.com
Internet: kainar-edu.kz
Founded 1991
Private control
Rector: Prof. YERENGAIP S. OMAROV
Library of 253,018 vols

DEANS
Economics and Information Systems: KULYASH SYZDYKOVA
History, Law and International Relations: NURLAN APAKHAYEV
Languages, Journalism and Tourism: ANIPA MUKHTAROVA
Pedagogics and Social Sciences: OLESSYA FEDOROVICH

UNIVERSITY OF INTERNATIONAL BUSINESS

Abay Ave 8A, Almaty
Telephone: (727) 2500505
E-mail: gamarnik@uib.kz
Internet: www.uib.kz
Founded 1992 as Republic Business School, present name and status 2001
Private control
Pres.: YERLAN K. SAGADIEV
Rector: Prof. Dr GENNADIY N. GAMARNIK
Vice-Rector for Admin. and Economic Work: AMANDOS K. KENESBAYEV
Vice-Rector for Pedagogical Work and Public Relations: GULFIYA R. NAZYROVA
Vice-Rector for Teaching and Scientific Work: GULNARA ZH. NURMUKHANOVA
Library Dir: GULNAZ K. BUTKO
Number of teachers: 179

DEANS
Faculty of Economics and Accounting: Prof. Dr ABU U. MUKHAMEMEDOV
Faculty of Information Technology and Finance: KENESBAYEVA DINARA ZHUMAGALIEVNA
Postgraduate and Vocational Training Faculty: Dr GULNARA T. DEMEUOVA

WEST KAZAKHSTAN AGRARIAN—TECHNICAL UNIVERSITY NAMED AFTER ZHANGIR KHAN

ul. Krasnoarmejskaja 19, Uralsk 090000
Telephone: (711) 2501374
E-mail: zapkazgu@wkau.kz
Internet: www.wkau.kz
Founded 1932, present name and status following merger of Western Kazakhstan Agrarian Univ., Western Kazakhstan Humanities Univ. and Western Kazakhstan Dauletkerey Institute of Arts 2003
Faculties of agribusiness and ecology, culture and library science, economics, finance and accountancy, fine arts, geography and natural sciences, history and human rights, musical arts, oil and gas, pedagogy, philology, physics and mathematics, polytechnic, sports and physical training, veterinary medicine and biotechnology
Rector: BOZYMOV KAZYBAI KARAEVICH
First Vice-Rector: TAUBAEV UTEGEN BAIRGALIEVICH
Vice-Rector for Additional Education and Int. Cooperation: Prof. Dr GUMAROV GALI SAGINGALIEVICH
Vice-Rector for Educational Work: SULTANOV AKYLBEK UZAKBAEVICH
Vice-Rector for Scientific Work: TRAISOV BALUASH BAKISHEVICH
Library: 1.2m. vols
Number of teachers: 899
Number of students: 17,052

WEST KAZAKHSTAN GOVERNMENT MEDICAL UNIVERSITY OF M. OSPANOV

Maresyev St 68, Aktobe 030019
Telephone: (713) 2563425
E-mail: biblioteka.zkgma@mail.ru
Internet: zkgmu.kz
State control
Languages of instruction: English, Kazakh, Russian
Rector: BEKMUHAMBETOV ERBOL ZHASULANOVICH
Library of 500,000 vols, 200 journals

WEST KAZAKHSTAN STATE UNIVERSITY NAMED AFTER M. UTEMISOV

Dostyk prospect, 162, Uralsk, West Kazakhstan
Telephone: (711) 512632
E-mail: zapkazgu@rambler.ru
Internet: wksu.kz
Founded 1932, current name and status 2000
State control
Depts of art and culture, economics and management, history and law, natural and mathematical sciences, pedagogy, philology
Rector: Prof. Dr I. A. SALIMOVICH
Library: 1.2m. vols

ZHETYSU STATE UNIVERSITY NAMED AFTER I. ZHANSUGUROV

ul. I. Zhansugurova 187A, Taldykorgan 040009
Telephone: (727) 2220020
E-mail: tk_jgu@mail.ru
Internet: zhgu.edu.kz
Founded 1972
State control
Languages of instruction: Kazakh, Russian
Academic year: September to June
Rector: Prof. Dr BEKTURGANOV ABDIMANAP ELIKBAEVICH
Pro-Rector: ASKHAT SARSENBAYEV
Vice-Rector for Scientific Research Work and Int. Relations: Dr NURGABYL DUISEBEK NURGABYLULY
Number of teachers: 307
Number of students: 6,985

DEANS
Faculty of Finance and Economics: Dr KANTUREEV MANSUR TASYBAEVICH
Faculty of Humanities: ZARIKBEK ZH. SLANBEKOV
Faculty of Mathematics and Natural Science: ANDASBAEV ERLAN SULEYMENOVICH
Faculty of Pedagogics and Psychology: HAPIZA TANIRBERGENOVNA NAUBAEVA

ZHEZKAZGAN UNIVERSITY NAMED AFTER O. A. BAIKONUROVA

Alashahana 1B, Zhezkazgan, Karaganda 100600
Telephone: (710) 2736324
E-mail: univer_zhez@mail.ru
Internet: www.zhezu.kz
Founded 1956
State control
Languages of instruction: English, Kazakh, Russian
Rector: Prof. ABDILMALIK ARGYNOVICH TAKISHOV
Vice-Rector: KALI KISHAUOV
Library of 950,578 vols
Number of teachers: 1,035
Number of students: 3,061

DIRECTORS
Institute of Economics and Law: G. A. DAUKENOVA
Institute of Mining Engineering: D. ZH. SARSEMBAYEV
Institute of Natural Sciences: OMITRAI ZHALELOV
Institute of Philology and Arts: MURAT ABEUOV

Other Higher Educational Institutes

Academy of Civil Aviation: Zakarpaskaya St 44, Almaty 050039; tel. (727) 3838979; internet www.agakaz.kz; f. 1994, present name and status 1995; library: 147,000 vols; 130 teachers; aviation, automotive engineering, technology; Rector Prof. Dr ALDAMZHAROV KAZBEK BAHITOVICH.

Academy of Public Administration under The President of the Republic of Kazakhstan: 33A Abay Ave, Astana 010000; tel. (717) 2753023; e-mail info@apa.kz; internet pa-academy.kz; f. 1994, present name and status 2008; offers Masters and doctorate courses in economics, law, int. relations, political science, public and local admin., social work, translation major; attached instns: Institute of Diplomacy, Institute of Justice, Institute for Public Admin. Modernization, Institute of Civil Servants' Retraining and Skills Upgrading, Institute of Public and Local Admin., Nat. School of Public Policy; 69 teachers; 285 students; Rector Dr ARYN ORSARIYEV; Vice-Rector for Academic Work Prof. Dr MUKHAMEDZHANOVA ALIYA GAFUROVNA; Vice-Rector for Economic and Admin. Issues AYGUL NADIROVA; Vice-Rector for Science and Int. Relations Dr RUSTEM ZHOLAMAN.

Academy of the Financial Police: Central Post Office, POB 53, Astana 010000; Tselinograd Dist., Kosshy Settlement, Akmola; tel. (716) 5199402; e-mail afp@abekp.kz; internet www.academfinpol.kz; f. 1999; faculty of internal education and magistracy; depts of criminal and criminal-procedural rights, customs affairs, foreign languages, military, physical and spec. training chair, operative-detective activity and org. of preliminary inquiry's chair, social and economic-legal disciplines, state-legal disciplines; 436 students; Head IBRAIMOV RUSTAM ANVAROVICH; Vice-Chief of Combatant Forces IBRAGYMOV NURLAN KUSHANTAYEVICH; Vice-Chief of Educational Work BAYMURZIN MANARBEK SAPARBEKOVICH; Vice-Chief of Teaching and Methodological Work SMAGULOV ASILBEK AYJARYKOVICH; publ. *Vestnik of the Financial Police Academy* (4 a year).

Academy of the Ministry of Interior Affairs of the Republic of Kazakhstan: Almaty; f. 1999; trains new recruits for law enforcement and legislative bodies; 257 teachers; Head D. T. KENZHETAYEV.

Aktobe State Medical Institute: ul. Lenina 52, Aktobe 463022; tel. (713) 2543904; library: 62,000 vols.

Almaty Academy of Economics and Statistics: Zhandosova str. 59, Almaty 050035; tel. (727) 3414141; e-mail info@aesa.kz; internet www.aesa.kz; f. 1999; computer science, economics, finance, statistics, management; library: 342,160 vols; 235 teachers; 9,414 students; Pres. D. S. RAIMOV; Rector V. A. KORVYAKOV.

Almaty State Theatrical and Cinema Institute: ul. Bogenbai Batyr 136, Almaty 480091; tel. (727) 2636652; f. 1992; acting and directing apprenticeship; library: 400 vols; 10 teachers.

Arkalyk State Pedagogical Institute named after I. Altynsarin: R. Mayasov St 34, Arkalyk, Kostanay; e-mail argpi@mail.kz.

Astana State Medical Academy: pr. Mira 51A, Astana 473013; tel. (717) 22607829; e-mail akma@asdc.kz; f. 1964, present name and status 1997; faculties of medicine and biological sciences, medicine, paediatrics; library: 381,500 vols; 370 teachers; 2,100 students; Rector R. K. TULEBAYEV.

Fashion Business Academy 'Symbat': Alimzhanov St, Almaty; tel. (727) 2731441; e-mail president@symbat.kz; internet www.symbat.kz; f. 1996; offers courses in art designing (design), technologies and designing of garments, decorative art, economy and business, hairdressing art and decorative cosmetics; Rector ASSANOVA SABYRKUL ZHAYLAUBEKOVNA; First Pro-Rector ASSANOVA AINUR ESMUKHAMBETOVNA; Pro-Rector for Educational and Methodical Activity TAIPOVA MARIYAM KAKHARMANOVNA; Pro-Rector for Official Language Devt AITULENOVA KYDYR TURSYNOVNA; Librarian NUSSIPBEKOVA GULBANU; publ. *Industry of Design and Technology*.

'Financial Academy' JSC: 25 Esenberlin St, Astana 010011; tel. (717) 2383308; e-mail mailbox@fin-academy.kz; internet www.fin-academy.kz; f. 2009; business accounting and audit, assessment, economics, finance, natural and technical disciplines, social sciences and humanities; Rector Prof. Dr SARSENGALI A. ABDYMANAPOV; Vice-Rector for Educational and Social Work IDIRISOV ZHUMABAY MOLDAKADIROVICH; Vice-Rector on Financial and Economic Activities RYSKELDINOVA GULNARA MANAPOVNA.

Karaganda Metallurgical Institute: Respublika Ave 30, Temirtau 101400; tel. (721) 2915626; e-mail karmeti@mail.kz; f. 1963; faculties of chemical eng., mechanical eng., metallurgy; library: 288,000 vols; 175 teachers; 2,500 students; Rector Prof. ABDRAKHMAN NAIZABEKOV.

Kazakh Kurmangazy National Conservatoire: 86 Abylai Khan Ave, Almaty 050000; tel. (727) 2627640; e-mail info@conservatoire.kz; internet www.conservatoire.kz; f. 1944; music teaching and psychology; music theory; instrumental performance (piano, organ, string instruments, wind instruments, and drums); composition; vocal (opera singing, chamber singing); music conducting (orchestra conducting and choir conducting); folk music art (folk instruments, folk singing); library: 579,038 vols; 240 teachers; 800 students.

Kazakh Leading Academy of Architecture and Civil Engineering: 28 Ryskulbekov str., Almaty 050043; tel. (727) 3096143; e-mail info@kazgasa.kz; internet www.kazgasa.kz; f. 1957 as Kazakh State Academy of Architecture and Civil Engineering, present name and status 2001; undergraduate and postgraduate courses and scientific research, PhD programmes; faculties of architecture, civil engineering, environmental engineering, economics and management in construction, social sciences; 309 teachers; 4,262 students; Pres. AMIRLAN A. KUSSAINOV; Vice-Pres. SERIC D. SYKHYMBAEV; publ. *Messenger of KazGASA* (4 a year).

Kazakh Road-Transport Institute named after L. B. Goncharov: Gogol St 84A, Almaty; Rector KABASHEV RAKHYMZHAN ABYLKASYMOVICH.

Kazakhstan Institute of Management, Economics and Strategic Research (KIMEP): 2 Abay Ave, Office 209, Almaty 050010; tel. (727) 2704200; internet www.kimep.kz; f. 1992; colleges of business, continuing education, social sciences; library: 97,000 vols; 184 teachers; 4,000 students; Pres. Dr CHAN YOUNG BANG.

Military Institute of Air Forces named after twice hero of Soviet Union T. Y. Begeldinov: 16 Moldagulova Ave, Aktobe; tel. (713) 2522845; f. 1996; attached to Min. of Defence of the Republic of Kazakhstan; electrical engineering, electromechanical engineering, mechanical engineering, navigator engineering, pilot engineering, radio engineering; Rector ALMUKHAMBETOV ORAZBEK KHAMITOVICH.

Military Institute of Land Forces: Krasnogorskaya St 35, Almaty 480094; f. 1970 as Almaty Higher General Command School, present name and status 2003; attached to Min. of Defence of the Republic of Kazakhstan; offers higher military professional education; Chair. SABIT KUDAYBERGENOV.

Military Institute of Radio Electronics and Communication: 53 Zhandosov str., Almaty; tel. (727) 2998797; f. 2002; attached to Min. of Defence of the Republic of Kazakhstan; offers higher education courses incl. communication network and switching system, radio communication and radio navigation, radio engineering for anti-aircraft and missile troops units and formations, radio engineering for air defence anti-aircraft and missile troops units and formations, radio engineering for radio technical troops units and formations, engineering for automated control systems.

Naval Institute: 24 Microdistrict, Aktau; tel. (729) 2429945; f. 2001 as Higher Naval School, present name 2003; attached to Min. of Defense of the Republic of Kazakhstan; courses incl. navigation and visual connection, ship communication facilities, ship engine with internal combustion and electrical facilities.

Rudnyi Industrial Institute: ul. 50 let Oktyabrya 38, Rudnyi 111500; tel. (714) 3150703; e-mail rii@krcc.kz; internet www.rii.kz; f. 1958; faculties of automation of production processes, construction, economics, mining; attached institute in Lisakovsk; library: 5,000 vols; 200 teachers; 3,189 students; Rector Prof. U. T. ABDRAKHIMOV.

South Kazakhstan Technical University: Tauke-han 5, Shymkent 160018; tel. (725) 2535048; f. 1943; faculties of chemical technology, economics, mechanical technology; library: 524,000 vols; Rector T. SH. KALMENOV; publ. *Science and Education in South Kazakhstan*.

KENYA

The Higher Education System

Until independence was achieved in 1963 Kenya was part of British East Africa. The oldest institutions of higher education were established during British colonial rule, such as Egerton University (founded 1939; current name and status 1987), the University of Nairobi (founded 1956; current name and status 1970) and Strathmore University (founded 1961; current name and status 1993). In 2012 there were seven public universities and 20 private universities. In 2009 an estimated 155,000 students were enrolled in Kenya's universities (and recently established constituent colleges). In both public and private universities the senior officer is the Chancellor, who in public universities is appointed by the President and in private universities in accordance with their individual Charters. University governance is handled by the Governing Council or Board of Trustees, the University Senate, which is responsible for academic affairs, and the Management Board, which, with the aid of the Vice-Chancellor, oversees the University administration. The Ministry of Higher Education, Science and Technology is the government ministry in charge of higher education, acting under the aegis of the Commission for Higher Education and the Directorate of Higher Education. Public universities operate with autonomy, but are funded by the State (as well as by students' tuition fees). The Higher Education Loans Board disburses loans to university students on behalf of the Government. Private institutions are supervised and accredited by the Commission for Higher Education.

Admission to university undergraduate degree programmes is on the basis of at least an average C+ score in the Kenya Certificate of Secondary Education. Admission to Diploma or Certificate programmes requires at least C– or D+, respectively. Diplomas and Certificates are awarded after up to a year of intensive study at universities and polytechnics or through 'open' and distance-learning schemes. Students who have been awarded the Diploma or Certificate may be admitted to degree-level programmes. In 2008, in order partially to compensate for the inadequate number of university places, 13 polytechnics were upgraded to the status of constituent colleges (affiliated to public universities) to enable them to offer degree-level courses. The standard undergraduate Bachelors degree lasts for four years, except in professional disciplines such as veterinary medicine (five years), architecture and medicine (both six years). Upon completion of the Bachelors degree, students may take either a one-year Postgraduate Diploma course or a one- to three-year Masters degree. The most advanced university-level degree programme is the Doctorate, which usually requires three years of study following award of the Masters.

Post-secondary vocational and technical education is available through a number of different institutions, including craft training institutes, youth polytechnics, institutes of technology and polytechnics. Although there is not yet a uniform national framework for vocational qualifications, they are roughly separated into four levels: artisan, craftsman, technician and technologist. The Kenya Institute of Education and Kenya National Examinations Council are responsible for developing curricula and testing at these four levels. Qualifications offered include Higher Diploma, Higher Technician Diploma, Ordinary Diploma and Ordinary Technician Diploma. In 2012 a reform of the sector was proposed by the Technical and Vocational Education and Training Bill to regulate and provide autonomy for institutions operating in this area, and harmonize training qualifications under the Technical and Vocational Education and Training Authority.

In the late 2000s and early 2010s Kenya's higher education, science and technology sector was preparing for major legislative and institutional reforms aimed at promoting a knowledge-based economy to improve national prosperity and global competitiveness. In mid-2010 the Government announced plans to spend US $56m. in donor funding to strengthen vocational and technical training and to help boost the country's skills base by increasing student enrolment by at least 20,000. The plans envisaged the construction of 13 new polytechnics and the upgrading of existing youth polytechnics to national polytechnic status. Plans are also under way to establish a National Open University of Kenya—the country's eighth public university—enabling students to undertake degree courses through online learning. In January 2011, as part of a campaign to rid the country of substandard education providers, the Government ordered the closure of around 110 unaccredited colleges. In 2012 the Universities Bill was passed. Under the new law the Commission for Higher Education was replaced by the Commission for University Education, which became the body responsible for establishing, accrediting and governing both public and private universities. A Universities Fund was also created to provide finance for public universities through a mixture of government funding and income generated from investments made by the Board of Trustees.

Regulatory and Representative Bodies

GOVERNMENT

Ministry of Education: POB 30040, 00100 Nairobi; Jogoo House 'B', Harambee Ave, Nairobi; tel. (20) 318581; e-mail info@education.go.ke; internet www.education.go.ke; Cabinet Sec. JACOB KAIMENYI.

Ministry of Sports, Culture and the Arts: POB 49849, 00100 Nairobi; Second Fl., Kencom House Bldg, Moi Ave, Nairobi; tel. (20) 2250576; e-mail csoffice@minspoca.go.ke; internet www.minspoca.go.ke; Cabinet Sec. Dr HASSAN WARIO ARERO.

ACCREDITATION

Commission for University Education: POB 54999, 00200 Nairobi; Red Hill Rd, off Limuru Rd, Gigiri; tel. (20) 7205000; e-mail info@cue.or.ke; internet www.cue.or.ke; f. 1985; plans for the establishment and devt of higher education and training; organizes resources for higher education and training; accredits and regularly inspects univs; coordinates and regulates admission to univs; 28 mems; library of 4,284 vols; Sec. and CEO Prof. DAVID K. SOME.

Learned Societies

GENERAL

African Network of Scientific and Technological Institutions (ANSTI): UNESCO Nairobi Office, POB 30592, 00100 Nairobi; tel. (20) 622620; e-mail info@ansti.org; internet www.ansti.org; f. 1980 under the auspices of UNESCO and UNDP, aided by Germany and based at the UNESCO Regional Bureau for Science and Technology (*q.v.*); aims to bring about collaboration between African engineering, scientific and technological institutions involved in post-graduate training, and to undertake research and development in areas of developmental significance in the region; mems: 85 institutions in 32 countries; Coordinator Prof. J. G. MASSAQUOI; publs *African Journal of Science and Technology*, *Directory of ANSTI Institutions*.

Kenya National Academy of Sciences: POB 39450, Nairobi; tel. (20) 311714; e-mail secretariat@knascience.org; internet www.knascience.org; f. 1983; advancement of learning and research; 200 mems; Chair. Prof. RAPHAEL M. MUNAVU; Hon. Sec. Prof. RATEMO MICHIEKA; publs *Kenya Journal of Science and Technology* (2 a year), *Post Magazine*, *Proceedings of Symposia*.

National Council for Science and Technology: POB 30623, 00100 Nairobi; tel. (20) 241349; e-mail info@ncst.go.ke; internet www.ncst.go.ke; f. 1977; attached to Min. of Higher Education, Science and Technology;

semi-autonomous government agency; provides advisory services to the Government; 27 council mems; library of 3,000 vols, collection of research reports; Sec. Prof. SHAUKAT ABDULRAZAK.

UNESCO Nairobi Regional Bureau for Science and Technology for Sub-Saharan Africa and Cluster Office: POB 30592, Nairobi 00100 GPO; United Nations Offices, Gigiri, Block C, United Nations Ave, Gigiri, Nairobi; tel. (20) 621234; e-mail nairobi@unesco.org; internet www.unesco-nairobi.org; f. 1965; regional office for 47 African countries; designated Cluster Office for Burundi, Kenya, Rwanda and Uganda; library of 10,000 vols, 400 periodicals; Dir MOHAMMED DJELID; publ. *African Journal of Science and Technology* (2 a year).

AGRICULTURE, FISHERIES AND VETERINARY SCIENCE

Agricultural Society of Kenya: POB 21340, 00505 Nairobi; tel. (20) 2641067; e-mail info@nitf.ask.co.ke; internet www.ask.co.ke; f. 1901; encourages and assists agriculture in Kenya; holds 12 shows a year and farming competitions; sponsors Young Farmers' Clubs of Kenya; 12,000 mems; Chair. ALICE C. KALYA; Chief Exec. BATRAM M. MUTHOKA; publ. *The Kenya Farmer* (12 a year).

BIBLIOGRAPHY, LIBRARY SCIENCE AND MUSEOLOGY

Kenya Library Association: POB 46031, 00100 Nairobi; tel. (20) 625237; e-mail ekobachi@yahoo.com; internet www.klas.or.ke; f. 1956; organizes, unites and represents the professions concerned with information work in Kenya; promotes professional integrity and governs the members of the assn in all matters of professional practice; 200 mems; Chair. Prof. NYAMBOGA; Nat. Sec. HELLEN AMUNGA; Nat. Sec. ESTHER K. OBACHI; publs *Kelias News* (6 a year), *Maktaba—Official Journal* (2 a year).

ECONOMICS, LAW AND POLITICS

Law Society of Kenya: POB 72219, 00200 Nairobi; Professional Centre, First Floor, Parliament Rd, Nairobi; tel. (20) 625391; e-mail lsk@lsk.or.ke; internet www.lsk.or.ke; f. 1949; 4,000 mems; Sec. APOLLO MBOYA; publ. *The Advocate* (4 a year).

HISTORY, GEOGRAPHY AND ARCHAEOLOGY

Historical Association of Kenya: c/o Prof. B. A. Ogot, Moi University, POB 3900, Eldoret; f. 1966; Chair. Prof. BETHWELL A. OGOT; Sec. Dr KARIM K. JANMOHAMED; publs *Hadith Series* (1 a year), *Kenya Historical Review* (2 a year).

LANGUAGE AND LITERATURE

Alliance Française: Maison Française Monrovia, Loila St, POB 45475, 0100 Nairobi; tel. (20) 340054; e-mail info@alliancefrnairobi.org; internet www.afkenya.or.ke; offers courses and examinations in French language and culture and promotes cultural exchange with France; attached teaching centre in Mombasa; Exec. Dir HERVÉ BRANEYRE.

British Council: Upperhill Rd, POB 40751, 00100 Nairobi; tel. (20) 2836000; e-mail information@britishcouncil.or.ke; internet www.britishcouncil.co.ke; teaching centre; offers courses and examinations in English language and British culture; promotes cultural exchange with the UK; Country Dir ALISON COUTTS; Regional Dir ALLAN CURRY.

Goethe-Institut: Maendeleo House, POB 49468, 00100 Nairobi; tel. (20) 2211381; e-mail info@nairobi.goethe.org; internet www.goethe.de/nairobi; offers courses and examinations in German language and culture and promotes cultural exchange with Germany; provides information on Germany's cultural, social and political life; library of 6,000 vols; Dir JOHANNES HOSSFELD.

MEDICINE

Kenya Medical Association: Chyulu Rd, Upper Hill, POB 48502, 00100 Nairobi; tel. (20) 275695; e-mail nec@kma.co.ke; internet www.kma.co.ke; f. 1968; 2,000 mems; Chair. Dr ELLY NYAIM; Sec. Dr KAVOO KILONZO; publs *East African Medical Journal* (12 a year), *Medicus* (12 a year).

NATURAL SCIENCES

Biological Sciences

East African Wildlife Society: POB 20110, 00200 City Sq., Riara Rd, off Ngong Rd, Nairobi; tel. (20) 3874145; e-mail info@eawildlife.org; internet www.eawildlife.org; f. 1961; non-profit org.; safeguards and promotes the conservation and sustainable management of wildlife resources and their natural habitats in East Africa; 6,000 mems; Exec. Dir MICHAEL GACHANJA; publs *African Journal of Ecology* (4 a year), *Swara* (4 a year), *Wildlife Info* (4 a year).

Nature Kenya, the East Africa Natural History Society: POB 44486, GPO, 00100 Nairobi; tel. (20) 3749957; e-mail office@naturekenya.org; internet www.naturekenya.org; f. 1909; 1,000 mems; library of 10,000 vols; Chair. ALAN CARLES; publs *Journal of East African Natural History* (2 a year), *Kenya Birds* (2 a year), *Nature East Africa (the EANHS Bulletin)* (2 a year).

Physical Sciences

Kenya Astronomical Society: POB 59224, Nairobi.

RELIGION, SOCIOLOGY AND ANTHROPOLOGY

Theosophical Society: 55A Third Parklands Ave, POB 45928, Nairobi; Gen. Sec. C. P. ROBERTSON-DUNN; publ. *The Theosophical Light* (2 a year).

TECHNOLOGY

Institution of Engineers of Kenya: KRBC Annex, First Floor, POB 41346, 00100 Nairobi; tel. (20) 2729326; e-mail secretariat@iekenya.org; internet www.iekenya.org; f. 1945, present name 1973; 2,100 mems; Chair. Eng. JULIUS M. RIUNGU; Hon. Sec. Eng. MWAMZALI SHIRIBWA; publ. *Kenya Engineer* (6 a year).

Research Institutes

AGRICULTURE, FISHERIES AND VETERINARY SCIENCE

Coffee Research Foundation: CRF Coffee Research Station, POB 4, Ruiru; tel. (151) 2100972; e-mail director@crf.co.ke; internet www.crf.co.ke; f. 1949; research on coffee cultivation, agronomy and management, marketing and economics of production; Dir JOSEPH K. KIMEMIA; publ. *Kenya Coffee Bulletin*.

Ministry of Livestock Development, Department of Veterinary Services: Private Bag, Kangemi, 00625 Nairobi; e-mail info.livestock@kenya.go.ke; internet www.livestock.go.ke; f. 1903; control and diagnosis of animal diseases, advisory service to farmers, animal health policy formulation, veterinary research and investigation services, veterinary regulation services; library of 27,500 vols; Dir Dr PETER ITHONDEKA.

Pyrethrum Board of Kenya: POB 420, Nakuru; tel. (51) 2211567; e-mail pbk@kenya-pyrethrum.com; internet www.kenya-pyrethrum.com; f. 1948; research and information on pyrethrum as a natural insecticide; Dir SAMUEL KIHIU; publ. *Pyrethrum Post* (2 a year).

Tea Research Foundation of Kenya: POB 820, 20200 Kericho; tel. (52) 20598; e-mail lib-trfk@kenyaweb.com; internet www.tearesearch.or.ke; f. 1951; research and technology devt on the production and manufacture of tea, with spec. emphasis on agronomic, botanical, environmental and physical parameters; pests and diseases management; tea biochemistry and processing of tea, technology, knowledge and information transfer, training and advisory services; value addition, product diversification and market research; library of 12,000 vols; Man. Dir Dr ELIUD KIPLIMO KIREGER; Deputy Dir Dr JOHN KIPKOECH BORE; publs *Tea Growers' Handbook*, *Tea Journal* (2 a year), *TRFK Quarterly Bulletin*.

HISTORY, GEOGRAPHY AND ARCHAEOLOGY

British Institute in Eastern Africa: POB 30710, GPO 0100 Nairobi; tel. (20) 4343190; e-mail office@biea.ac.uk; internet www.biea.ac.uk; f. 1960; library of 5,000 vols, 100 periodicals; research into the history and archaeology of Eastern Africa, for which occasional grants and studentships are offered; Dir Prof. AMBREENA MANJI; publs *Azania: Archaeological Research in Africa* (4 a year), *Journal of Eastern African Studies* (4 a year).

MEDICINE

Kenya Medical Research Institute (KEMRI): Mbagathi Rd, POB 54840, 00200, Nairobi; tel. (20) 2713349; internet www.kemri.org; f. 1979; under the Min. of Public Health and Sanitation; research in biomedical sciences, cooperates with other instns in training programmes and research, cooperates with the relevant ministries, the Nat. Ccl for Science and Technology and the Medical Science Advisory Research Cttee; 11 centres: Centre for Biotechnology Development Research, Centre for Clinical Research, Centre for Geographic Medicine Research, Centre for Infections and Parasitic Diseases Research, Centre for Microbiology Research, Centre for Public Health Research, Centre for Respiratory Diseases Research, Centre for Traditional Medicines and Drugs Research, Centre for Vector Biology and Control Research, Centre for Virus Research, Eastern and Southern Africa Centre of International Parasite Control (ESACIPAC); coordinates the annual African Health Sciences Congress and is secretariat for African Forum for Health Sciences (AFHES); library of 3,000 vols, colln of scientific reprints, theses and dissertations; Dir Dr SOLOMON MPOKE; publs *African Journal of Health Sciences* (4 a year), *AIDS Update* (6 a year), *KEMRI Abstracts*.

NATURAL SCIENCES

Biological Sciences

Institute of Primate Research: National Museums of Kenya, POB 24481, Nairobi; tel. (20) 882571; e-mail info@primateresearch.org; internet www.primateresearch.org; research in ecology and conservation, infectious diseases, primate medicine, reproductive biology and virology; Dir Dr THOMAS M. KARIUKI; publ. *IPR Report* (1 a year).

TECHNOLOGY

Kenya Industrial Research and Development Institute: Lusaka Rd, Dunga, POB 30650, 00100, Nairobi; tel. (20) 6003842; e-mail info@kirdi.go.ke; internet www.kirdi.go.ke; f. 1948; provides advice for established local industrial concerns and gives assistance in the establishment of new industries on the utilization of local materials; Dir Prof. TUIKONG D. K. SEREM.

Mines and Geological Department: Madini House, Machakos Rd, POB 30009, 00100 Nairobi; tel. (20) 558034; e-mail cmg@bidii.com; f. 1933; geological survey and research; mineral resources development; administers mineral and explosives laws; library of 32,000 vols, 10,000 periodicals; Commr MOSES MASIBO; publs *Mineral Statistics Data*, statistics.

Libraries and Archives

Mombasa

British Council Library: Jubilee Insurance Bldg, Moi Ave, POB 90590, Mombasa; 3,000 vols, 32 periodicals; Information Centre Man. MARY STEVENS.

Nairobi

Desai Memorial Library: POB 1253, Nairobi; e-mail info@desaimemorial.org; f. 1942; public library and reading room; 31,800 vols; books in Swahili, English, Gujarati, Gurumukhi, Hindi and Urdu; reference, newspaper and periodical sections; Pres. A. M. SADARUDDIN; Sec. HARSHAD JOSHI.

High Court of Kenya Library: Law Courts, POB 30041, Nairobi; f. 1935; comprises High Court Library and Court of Appeal Library in Nairobi and 10 major br. libraries at Bungoma, Eldoret, Kakamega, Kisii, Kisumu, Machakos, Mombasa, Nakuru and Nyeri; 100,000 vols, 65 periodicals on practitioner's law, with special emphasis on Kenyan and English law; Head Librarian E. N. JUMA.

Ismail Rahimtulla Trust Library: POB 40333, Nairobi; f. 1953; 7,200 vols; Librarian P. GITAU.

Kenya Agricultural Research Institute Library: POB 57811, Nairobi; e-mail resource.centre@kari.org; internet www.kari.org; f. 1928; extends current scientific awareness service to all agricultural research and academic centres and official depts within Kenya; 150,000 vols; Asst Dir Information and Documentation Services REGE RACHEL; Librarian PATRICK MAINA; publ. *East African Agricultural and Forestry Journal* (4 a year).

Kenya National Archives and Documentation Service: POB 49210, Moi Ave, 00100 Nairobi; tel. (20) 2228959; internet www.archives.go.ke; f. 1965; preservation and custodian of public records; assists govt offices in the maintenance of public records; over 1m. items, incl. reports, maps, films, microfilms, photographs, slides; archival materials accessible to nat. and int. researchers; 5 records centres in Mombasa, Nairobi, Nakuru, Kisumu and Kakamega; 50,000 vols and periodicals, incl. 9,000 govt monographs; 600 annual reports from govt ministries and depts; Kenya Gazette, Laws of Kenya and parliamentary debates; 20,000 general and Africana vols; 700 theses and dissertations; 5,000 legal deposit collns; 1,600 periodicals and journals, incl. 30 current titles; Dir JOHN G. M'RERIA.

Kenya National Library Services: Ngong Rd, POB 30573, 00100 Nairobi; tel. (20) 2725550; e-mail nld@knls.ac.ke; internet www.knls.ac.ke; f. 1965; public library services through Nat. Lending Library in Nairobi, 19 brs and 8 mobile units; Nat. Reference and Bibliographic Dept f. 1980; 621,000 vols, 120 periodicals; Chair. Archbishop STEPHEN ONDIEKI; Dir S. K. NG'ANG'A; publs *Kenya National Bibliography* (1 a year), *Kenya Periodical Directory* (every 2 years).

McMillan Memorial Library: Banda St, POB 40791, Nairobi; f. 1931; 2 br. libraries at Kaloleni and Eastlands; comprises Nairobi City Library Services; collns of old photographs, microfilms of East Africa, serial publs; Africana colln of 20,000 vols; 400,000 vols; Chief Librarian A. O. ESILABA.

University of Nairobi Libraries: POB 30197, 00100 Nairobi; tel. (20) 318262; e-mail librarian@uonbi.ac.ke; internet uonlibrary.uonbi.ac.ke; f. 1959; 850,000 vols, 600 periodicals, 7,000 electronic journals; 11 brs; acts as legal nat. depository and UN deposit library; Librarian SALOME N. MUNAVU (acting).

Museums and Art Galleries

Nairobi

National Museums of Kenya: Museum Hill, POB 40658, 00100 Nairobi; tel. (20) 742131; internet www.museums.or.ke; f. 1910 by the E African Natural History Soc.; all brs of natural sciences, prehistory, geology, education, ethnography; library: joint library with E African Natural History Soc., 30,000 vols; Dir Dr IDLE OMAR FARAH; Librarian A. H. K. OWANO; publs *Horizons*, *Journal of East Africa Natural History*, *Kenya Past and Present*.

Attached Museums:

Fort Jesus Museum: POB 82412, Mombasa; e-mail nmkfortj@swiftmombasa.com; f. 1960; inside 16th-century Portuguese fortress overlooking Mombasa harbour; finds from various coastal Islamic sites, from Fort Jesus, and from a 17th-century Portuguese wreck illustrate the history of the Kenyan coast; library of 1,000 vols and numerous offprints; Curator ALI BAAKABE.

Kisumu Museum: POB 1779, Kisumu; e-mail kisumuse@africaonline.co.ke; Curator PETER NYAMENYA.

Kitale Museum: POB 1219, 30200 Kitale; e-mail jogega@museums.or.ke; f. 1926; natural and cultural museum; history and science, emphasis on education; library of 5,000 vols; Sr Curator JULIAS JUMA OGEGA.

Lamu Museum: POB 48, Lamu; internet www.museums.or.ke; Curator ATHMAN HUSSEIN.

Universities

ADVENTIST UNIVERSITY OF AFRICA

Private Bag Mbagathi, 00503 Nairobi
Telephone: (20) 6603073
E-mail: info@aua.ac.ke
Internet: www.aua.ac.ke
Founded 2006
Private control
Language of instruction: English

AFRICA NAZARENE UNIVERSITY

POB 53067, 00200 Nairobi
Telephone: (20) 2527170
Internet: www.anu.ac.ke
Founded 1994
Private control
Academic year: September to August (3 trimesters)
Depts of commerce, computer science and theology
Vice-Chancellor: Prof. LEAH T. MARANGU
Deputy Vice-Chancellor for Academic Affairs: Prof. MARY JONES
Number of teachers: 50
Number of students: 850

AFRICAN VIRTUAL UNIVERSITY

POB 25405, 00603 Nairobi
Cape Office Park, Ring Rd, Kilimani, Nairobi
Telephone: (20) 2528333
E-mail: contact@avu.org
Internet: www.avu.org
Founded 1997
Languages of instruction: English, French
Ind. distance-learning institution sponsored by the World Bank, providing education in 18 African countries through a network of 33 Learning Centres
Rector: Dr BAKARY DIALLO

CATHOLIC UNIVERSITY OF EASTERN AFRICA

POB 62157 00200 Nairobi
Telephone: (20) 2525811
Internet: www.cuea.edu
Founded 1984 as Catholic Higher Institute of Eastern Africa; present name and status 1992
Private control
Language of instruction: English
Academic year: August to July
Vice-Chancellor: Rev. PIUS RUTECHURA
Deputy Vice-Chancellor for Academics: Prof. JUSTUS MBAE
Deputy Vice-Chancellor for Admin.: Rev. Prof. JUVENALIS BAITU
Deputy Vice-Chancellor for Finance: OCBAMARIAM BEKIT
Univ. Librarian: Rev. M. KISENYI
Library of 61,705 vols, 11,553 periodicals
Number of teachers: 362
Number of students: 7,000
Publications: *African Christian Studies* (4 a year), *Eastern Africa Journal of Humanities and Science* (2 a year)

DEANS

Faculty of Arts and Social Sciences: FREDERICK N. MVUMBI
Faculty of Commerce: Dr ALOYS B. AYAKO
Faculty of Education: Dr SIMON KANG'ETHE
Faculty of Law: EMILIUS NDIRITU
Faculty of Science: Prof. GENEVIEVE MWAYULI
Faculty of Theology: Rev. Prof. CONSTANCE BANSIKIZA

DAYSTAR UNIVERSITY

Athi River Campus, POB 17, 90145 Athi River
Mombasa Campus, POB 99483, Kilindini, 80107 Mombasa
Nairobi Campus, POB 44400, 00100 Nairobi
Telephone: (45) 6622601 (Athi River)
E-mail: info@daystar.ac.ke
Internet: www.daystar.ac.ke
Founded 1974
Private control
Vice-Chancellor: Dr TIMOTHY WACHIRA

Deputy Vice-Chancellor for Academic Affairs: Prof. JAMES KOMBO
Deputy Vice-Chancellor for Finance and Admin.: JOMO GATUNDU
Deputy Vice-Chancellor for Institutional Advancement: Dr JON MASSO
Library of 73,600 vols, 365 audiovisual resources, 13,600 electronic journals, 40 print journals
Number of teachers: 230
Number of students: 3,937

DEANS

School of Arts and Humanities: PURITY KIAMBI
School of Business and Economics: MUTURI WACHIRA
School of Communication, Language and Performing Arts: Prof. LEVI OBONYO
School of Human and Social Sciences: Dr ALICE MUNENE
School of Science, Engineering and Health: Dr PETER NGURE

EGERTON UNIVERSITY

POB 536, 20115 Egerton
Telephone: (51) 2217891
E-mail: info@egerton.ac.ke
Internet: www.egerton.ac.ke

Founded 1939, university status 1987
State control
Language of instruction: English
Academic year: August to May

Chancellor: BETHUEL ADBU KIPLAGAT
Vice-Chancellor: Prof. J. K. TUITOEK
Deputy Vice-Chancellor for Academic Affairs: Prof. ROSE A. MWONYA
Deputy Vice-Chancellor for Admin. and Finance: Prof. JOHN NJENGA MUNENE
Deputy Vice-Chancellor for Research and Extension: Prof. J. G. MWANGI
Academic Registrar: Prof. S. F. OWIDO
Prin. of Chuka Constituent College: E. M. NJOKA
Prin. of Kisii Constituent College: Prof. JOHN AKAMA
Prin. of Laikipia Campus: Prof. F. K. LELO
Dean of Students: J. K. KIBET (acting)
Librarian: JANEGRACE K. KINYANJUI

Library of 77,439 vols
Number of teachers: 570
Number of students: 10,149

Publications: *Egerton Journal of Education and Human Resources* (2 a year), *Egerton Journal of Humanities, Social Sciences and Education* (2 a year), *Egerton Journal of Science and Technology* (2 a year), *Journal of Environment, Natural Resources Management and Society* (2 a year)

DEANS

Faculty of Agriculture: Prof. Dr ALEXANDER KAHI
Faculty of Arts and Social Sciences: Dr FUGICH WAKO
Faculty of Commerce: P. A. C. KAPSOOT
Faculty of Education: Dr S. W. WACHANGA
Faculty of Engineering and Technology: B. M. MUTUA
Faculty of Environment and Resources Development: Prof. K. N ONDIMU
Faculty of Health Sciences: Dr PAMELA FEDHA TSIMBIRI
Institute of Gender, Women and Development Studies: Dr R. A. O. ODHIAMBO (Dir)

GREAT LAKES UNIVERSITY OF KISUMU

POB 2224, 40100 Kisumu
Telephone: (57) 2023972
E-mail: info@gluk.ac.ke
Internet: www.gluk.ac.ke

Founded 1998
Private control
Language of instruction: English

Faculties of arts and sciences, health sciences; tropical institute of community health and devt

Vice-Chancellor: Prof. DAN C. O. KASEJE

GRETSA UNIVERSITY

POB 3, 0100 Thika
Telephone: (20) 2308997
E-mail: info@gretsauniversity.ac.ke
Internet: www.gretsauniversity.ac.ke

Founded 2006
Private control
Language of instruction: English

Schools of business, hospitality and tourism management, science and technology and education, humanities and social sciences

Vice-Chancellor: Dr J. KURIA THUO
Academic Registrar: WANYIRI KAGIRI
Librarian: ESTHER MUKUNDI

INOORERO UNIVERSITY

Inoorero Center, Luhya Lane Limuru Rd, Parklands, POB 60550, 00200 Nairobi
Telephone: (22) 323819
E-mail: info@iu.ac.ke
Internet: www.iu.ac.ke

Founded 2009
Private control
Language of instruction: English

Schools of ICT, business and law

Chancellor: Hon. F. T. NYAMMO
Vice-Chancellor: Prof. H. M. THAIRU
Deputy Vice-Chancellor for Academics, Research and Student Affairs: Prof. KOI MUCHIRA TIRIMA
Deputy Vice-Chancellor for Admin., Planning and Devt: WAMUYU KAMBO
Univ. Librarian: BERNARD KAMANDA

Library of 9,000 vols, 25,000 ejournal titles

INTERNATIONAL LEADERSHIP UNIVERSITY

Mtito Andei Rd, Kilimani, Nairobi
Telephone: (20) 2720837
E-mail: info@kenya.ilu.edu
Internet: www.kenya.ilu.edu

Founded 1993
Private control
Language of instruction: English
Academic year: August to June

Chancellor: Dr DELANYO ADADEVOH
Vice-Chancellor: Prof. ERIC ASEKA
Deputy Vice-Chancellor for Academic Affairs: Prof. MARTA BENETT
Deputy Vice-Chancellor for Planning and Devt: Prof. DAVID NGARUIYA
Academic Dean: JOHN K. MUNGANIA
Univ. Registrar: ROSEMARY GITONGA

JOMO KENYATTA UNIVERSITY OF AGRICULTURE AND TECHNOLOGY

POB 62000, City Sq., 00200 Nairobi
Telephone: (67) 52124
E-mail: info@jkuat.ac.ke
Internet: www.jkuat.ac.kec

Founded 1981 as a middle-level college, present status 1994
State control
Language of instruction: English
Academic year: May to April

Chancellor: Prof. FRANCIS JOHN GICHAGA
Vice-Chancellor: Prof. MABEL O. IMBUGA
Deputy Vice-Chancellor for Academic Affairs: Prof. ROMANUS ODHIAMBO
Deputy Vice-Chancellor for Research, Production and Extension: Prof. ESTHER MURUGI KAHANGI
Librarian: LAWRENCE M. WANYAMA

Library of 87,000 vols
Number of teachers: 588
Number of students: 22,000

Publications: *JKUAT Scientific Proceedings*, *Journal of Agriculture Science and Technology* (2 a year), *Journal of Civil Engineering* (1 a year)

DEANS

Faculty of Agriculture: E. OLUOCH ASHER
Faculty of Science: Dr MARY NDUNG'U
School of Architecture and Building Sciences: Dr SUSAN KIBUE
School of Civil, Environmental and Construction Engineering: GEOFFREY MANG'URIU
School of Electrical, Electronics and Information and Engineering: Dr JOHN NDERU
School of Human Resource Development: Dr ELEGWA MUKULU
School of Mechanical, Manufacturing and Materials Engineering: Dr BERNARD IKUA

KABARAK UNIVERSITY

Nakuru-Eldama Ravine Highway, POB 20157, Kabarak
Telephone: (20) 2114658
E-mail: registrar@kabarak.ac.ke
Internet: www.kabarak.ac.ke

Founded 2002

Chancellor: H. E. DANIEL ARAP MOI
Vice-Chancellor: Rev. Prof. JACOB KIBOR
Dean of Students: Dr MOSES ALELA
Univ. Librarian: SYLVESTER OTENYA

DEANS

School of Business: Prof. ALLAN MULENGANI KATWALO
School of Law: Prof. P. L. O. LUMUMBA
School of Science, Engineering and Technology: Prof. JACKSON KITETU

KCA UNIVERSITY

Thika Rd, POB 56808, 00200 Ruaraka
Telephone: (20) 8070408
E-mail: corporate@kca.ac.ke
Internet: www.kca.ac.ke

Founded 1989
Private control
Language of instruction: English

Chancellor: Prof. ARTHUR ESHIWANI
Vice-Chancellor: Prof. NOAH O. MIDAMBA
Registrar: JOHN KAMAU
Dir for Finance: MICHAEL INGUTIA
Librarian: BENJAMIN MUTUNGI

Number of teachers: 198
Number of students: 12,215

DEANS

Faculty of Computing and Information Management: Dr ALICE NJUGUNA
Faculty of Education and Arts: Dr CALEB GUDO
School of Business and Public Management: Prof. SILAS ONYANGO
School of Graduate Studies and Research: Dr MUCHIRI MWANGI

KENYA METHODIST UNIVERSITY

POB 267, Meru
Telephone: (64) 31229
E-mail: info@kemu.ac.ke
Internet: www.kemu.ac.ke

Founded 1997
Private control

Chancellor: Rev. Dr STEPHEN KANYARU M'IMPWI

Vice-Chancellor: Prof. ALFRED MUTEMA
Deputy Vice-Chancellor for Academic Affairs: Rev. Dr KOBIA ATAYA
Deputy Vice-Chancellor for Admin. and Finance: Prof. JOTHAM MICHENI
Librarian: NANCY KAMAU

DEANS
Faculty of Computing and Informatics: Dr SALESIO KIURA
Faculty of Education and Social Sciences: Prof. BONAVENTURE KEERE
Faculty of Science and Technology: Prof. ELLIS NJOKA
School of Business and Economics: Prof. KINUTHIA NGANGA
School of Medicine and Health Sciences: Prof. ALICE MUTUNGI

KENYATTA UNIVERSITY

POB 43844, 00100 Nairobi
Telephone: (20) 8710901
E-mail: info@ku.ac.ke
Internet: www.ku.ac.ke

Founded 1972 as constituent college of Univ. of Nairobi, present status 1985
State control
Language of instruction: English
Academic year: September to July

Chancellor: ONESMUS MUTUNGI
Vice-Chancellor: Prof. OLIVE M. MUGENDA
Deputy Vice-Chancellor for Academic Affairs: Prof. JOHN OKUMU
Deputy Vice-Chancellor for Admin.: Prof. P. K. WAINAINA
Deputy Vice-Chancellor for Finance, Planning and Devt: Prof. KEREN MBURUGU
Registrar for Academic Affairs: Dr STEPHEN N. NYAGA
Registrar for Admin.: Dr DANIEL M. MUINDI
Registrar for Finance, Planning and Devt: Dr NELSON M. KARAGU
Librarian: GEORGE GITAU NJOROGE (acting)

Library of 352,361 vols, 108,000 print and electronic periodicals
Number of teachers: 945
Number of students: 61,000

Publications: *African Journal of Educational Studies*, *Chemchemi*, *International Journal of the School of Humanities and Social Sciences*, *East African Journal of Life Sciences*, *East African Journal of Physical Sciences*

DEANS
School of Agriculture and Enterprise Development: Prof. WACHEKE WANJOHI
School of Applied Human Sciences: Dr ANDANJE MWISUKHA
School of Business: Dr GERALD ATHERU
School of Economics: Dr NELSON WAWIRE
School of Education: Prof. FATUMA CHEGE
School of Engineering and Technology: Eng. S. M. MAMBO
School of Environmental Studies: Prof. J. B. KUNG'U
School of Graduate Studies: Prof. P. O. OKEMO
School of Health Sciences: Dr B. M. OKELLO-AGINA
School of Hospitality and Tourism: Dr ALICE ONDIGI
School of Humanities and Social Sciences: Prof. C. A. SHISANYA
School of Law: Dr NZUKI MWINZI
School of Pure and Applied Sciences: Dr J. NGERANWA
School of Visual and Performing Arts: Dr BEATRICE DIGOLO

MASENO UNIVERSITY

Private Bag, Maseno
Telephone: (57) 351620
E-mail: vc@maseno.ac.ke
Internet: maseno.ac.ke

Founded 2000 upon independence of Moi University's Maseno Univ. College
State control

Chancellor: FLORIDAH KARANI
Vice-Chancellor: Prof. DOMINIC MAKAWITI
Deputy Vice-Chancellor for Academic Affairs: Prof. MADARA OGOT
Deputy Vice-Chancellor for Admin. and Finance: Prof. J. O. NYABUNDI
Deputy Vice-Chancellor for Planning, Research and Extension Services: Prof. GEORGE MARK ONYANGO
Librarian: SYLVIA OGOLA

Library of 150,000 vols
Number of teachers: 320
Number of students: 5,250

Publications: *Equator News* (4 a year), *General Information Booklet* (1 a year), *Graduation Bulletin* (1 a year), *Maseno Journal of Education, Arts and Science* (1 a year), *Maseno University Calendar* (every 5 years)

DEANS
School of Agriculture and Food Security: Prof. J. O. NYABUNDI
School of Arts and Social Sciences: Prof. SUSSY GUMO KURGAT
School of Biological and Physical Science: Prof. AGURE JOHN OGONJI
School of Business: Dr PATRICK BONIFACE OJERA
School of Development and Strategic Studies: Prof. FREDRICK O. WANYAMA
School of Education: Dr EDWARDS JOASH KOCHUNG
School of Environment and Earth Sciences: Prof. JOSEPHINE K. W. NGAIRA
School of Medicine: Prof. WILSON ODERO
School of Planning and Architecture: Dr GEORGE G. WAGAH
School of Public Health and Community Development: Prof. ROSEBELLA O. ONYANGO

MASINDE MULIRO UNIVERSITY OF SCIENCE AND TECHNOLOGY

POB 190, Kakamega
Telephone: (56) 31375
E-mail: vc@mmust.ac.ke
Internet: www.mmust.ac.ke

Founded 1972 as Western College of Arts and Applied Sciences
State control

Vice-Chancellor: Prof. B. C. CLEOPHAS WANGILA
Deputy Vice-Chancellor for Admin. and Finance: Prof. S. K. MAKHANU
Univ. Librarian: RAYMOND OCHOGGIA

MOI UNIVERSITY

POB 3900, Eldoret 30100
Telephone: (53) 43620
E-mail: vcmu@mu.ac.ke
Internet: www.mu.ac.ke

Founded 1984
State control
Language of instruction: English
Academic year: September to June

Chancellor: Prof. BETHWEL ALLAN OGOT
Vice-Chancellor: Prof. R. K. MIBEY
Deputy Vice-Chancellor for Planning and Development: Prof. J. SANG (acting)
Deputy Vice-Chancellor for Research and Extension: Prof. B. E. L. WISHITEMI
Chief Academic Officer: Prof. K. OLE KAREI
Finance Officer: MILCA MUTWOL
Librarian: TIRONG ARAP TANUI

Library of 200,000 vols, 50,000 periodicals
Number of teachers: 844
Number of students: 34,477

DEANS
School of Aerospace Sciences: Prof. P. K. TORONGEY
School of Arts and Social Sciences: Prof. NATHAN O. OGECHI
School of Biological and Physical Sciences: Dr AMBROSE K. KIPROP
School of Dentistry: Dr C. KIBOSIA
School of Economics and Business Management: MARY J. KIPSAT
School of Education: Prof. PETER L. BARAZA
School of Engineering: Prof. PAUL M. WAMBUA
School of Environmental Sciences: Prof. WILSON K. YABANN
School of Human Resources Development: Prof. J. KWONYIKE
School of Information Sciences: Prof. JAPHETH OTIKE
School of Law: HENRY J. A. LUGULU
School of Medicine: Prof. PAUL AYUO
School of Nursing: I. I. MBAI
School of Public Health: Dr G. ETTYANG
School of Tourism, Hospitality and Event Management: Dr DAMIANNAH M. KIETI

MOUNT KENYA UNIVERSITY

POB 342, Thika
Telephone: (20) 2088310
E-mail: info@mku.ac.ke
Internet: www.mku.ac.ke

Founded 2006
Private control

Chancellor: Prof. Dr VICTORIA WULSIN

STRATHMORE UNIVERSITY

Madaraka Estate, Ole Sangale Rd, POB 59857, City Sq., 00200 Nairobi
Telephone: (703) 034000
E-mail: admissions@strathmore.edu
Internet: www.strathmore.edu

Founded 1961 as Strathmore College; present name c. 1993
Private control
Academic year: July to June

Vice-Chancellor: Prof. JOHN ODHIAMBO
University Sec.: Dr CHARLES SOTZ
Deputy Vice-Chancellor for Academic Affairs: Dr FLORENCE OLOO
Librarian: GEORGE GITAU

Library of 80,000 vols
Number of teachers: 130
Number of students: 4,737

DEANS
Faculty of Information Technology: Dr REUBEN MARWANGA
Faculty of Tourism and Hospitality: Dr JOSEPH WADAWI
School of Accountancy: Dr JAMES BOYD MCFIE
School of Graduate Studies: Prof. RUTH KIRAKA
School of Humanities and Social Sciences: Prof. CHRISTINE GICHURE
School of Management and Commerce: DAVID WANG'OMBE
Strathmore Business School: Dr EDWARD MUNGAI

UNIVERSITY OF EASTERN AFRICA, BARATON

POB 2500, 30100 Eldoret
Telephone: (20) 8023084
E-mail: dvc@ueab.ac.ke
Internet: ueab.ac.ke

Founded 1980
Private control
Language of instruction: English
Academic year: September to July
Chancellor: BLASIUS RUGURI
Vice-Chancellor: Prof. MIRIAM MWITA
Deputy Vice-Chancellor for Academics: Dr KORSO GUDE
Dean of Students: Dr PAUL WAHONYA
Library of 50,000 vols
Number of teachers: 89
Number of students: 1,502 (1,286 full-time, 216 part-time)

DEANS

School of Business: ABRAHAM IDOWU
School of Education: Dr LAZARUS NDIKU
School of Health Sciences: Dr DIXON ANJEJO
School of Humanities and Social Sciences: Dr LAMECK MIYAYO
School of Science and Technology: Prof. ZACHARIAH NGALO

UNIVERSITY OF NAIROBI

POB 30197, Nairobi
Telephone: (20) 318262
E-mail: postmaster@unics.gn.apc.org
Internet: www.uonbi.ac.ke

Founded 1956 as Royal Technical College of E Africa, current name adopted 1970
State control
Language of instruction: English
Academic year: October to July
Chancellor: JOSEPH B. WANJUI
Vice-Chancellor: Prof. GEORGE A. O. MAGOHA
Deputy Vice-Chancellor for Academic Affairs: Prof. JACOB T. KAIMENYI
Deputy Vice-Chancellor for Admin. and Finance: Prof. PETER M. F. MBITHI
Deputy Vice-Chancellor for Research, Production and Extension: Prof. LUCY W. IRUNGU
Deputy Vice-Chancellor for Student Affairs: Prof. ISAAC MBECHE
Librarian: SALOME N. MUNAVU
Number of teachers: 1,662
Number of students: 45,548

DEANS

Faculty of Agriculture: Prof. SOLOMON IGOSANGWA SHIBAIRO
Faculty of Arts: Prof. PRESTON O. CHITERE
Faculty of Veterinary Sciences: Prof. MULEI CHARLES MATIKU
School of Arts and Design: Dr WALTER H. ONYANGO (Dir)
School of Biological Sciences: Dr ELIJAH AKUNDA (Dir)
School of Built Environment: Prof. T. J. C. ANYAMBA
School of Business: Prof. STEPHEN NZUVE
School of Continuing and Distance Education: Dr HARRIET J. KIDOMBO
School of Dental Sciences: Prof. LOICE WARWARE GATHECE
School of Economics: Prof. MARIARA JANE WANJIKU KABUBO
School of Education: Prof. SAMSON GUNGA OKURO
School of Engineering: Dr ODIRA PATTIS M. AKUMU (acting)
School of Law: Prof. PATRICIA KAMERI-MBOTE
School of Mathematics: Dr WERE IAMEN HUDSON
School of Medicine: Prof. OMWANDHO CHARLES O. A.
School of Nursing: Dr GRACE M. OMONI (Dir)
School of Pharmacy: Prof. ANASTASIA GUANTAI
School of Physical Sciences: Prof. LYDIA W. NJENGA

PROFESSORS

Faculty of Agriculture (POB 29053, Nairobi; tel. (20) 631340):
IMUNGI, J. K., Food Technology and Nutrition
KANYARI, P. W. N., Veterinary Pathology and Microbiology
KARUE, C. N., Range Management
LARMAT, NANCY K. KARANJA
MARIBEI, JAMES M., Clinical Studies
MBUGUA, SAMUEL K., Food Technology and Nutrition
MICHIEKA, R. W., Crop Protection
MITARU, B., Animal Production
MUKUNYA, D. M., Crop Protection
MWANGOMBE, A., Crop Protection
OGUTU, A., Agricultural Economics
WAITHAKA, K., Crop Science

Faculty of Architecture (tel. (20) 2724521):
ROSTOM, R. S., Geospatial and Space Technology
SYAGGA, P. M., Land Development

Faculty of Arts (tel. (20) 318362; e-mail arts@uonbi.ac.ke):
ABDULAZIZ, M. H., Linguistics and African Languages
CHESAINA, C., Literature
INDANGASI, H., Literature
KIMUYU, PETER K.
MUGAMBI, J. N. K., Religious Studies
MUREITHI, L. P., Economics
MURIUKI, G., History
MWABU, G. M., Economics
NYASANI, J., Philosophy
ODINGO, R. S., Geography
OJANY, F. F., Geography
OMONDI, L. N., Linguistics and African Languages
OYUGI, W. O., Political Science and Public Administration
WANYANDE, PETER, Political Science and Public Administration

Faculty of Veterinary Sciences (POB 29053, Nairobi; tel. (20) 631007; e-mail deanfvm@uonbi.ac.ke):
AGUMBAH, G. J. O., Clinical Studies
GATHUMA, J. M., Public Health, Pharmacology and Toxicology
KIPTOON, J. C., Clinical Studies
MAINA, J. N., Veterinary Anatomy
MAITHO, T. E., Public Health, Pharmacology and Toxicology
MALOIY, G. M. O., Physiology
MITEMA, S. E. O., Public Health, Pharmacology and Toxicology
MUNYUA, W. K., Veterinary Pathology
MUTIGA, E. R., Clinical Studies
NYAGA, P. N., Veterinary Pathology
ODUOR-OKELLO, D., Veterinary Anatomy

School of Business (tel. (20) 2059163):
KIBERA, F. N., Business Administration

School of Dental Sciences (tel. (20) 2720322):
GUTHUA, S. W., Oral Surgery
KAIMENYI, J. T., Periodontology and Community Dentistry
MAKAWITI, DOMINIC W., Biochemistry
MWANG'OMBE, JOSEPH K., Community Health
OPINYA, G. N., Paediatric Dentistry, Orthodontics

School of Education (POB 97, Kikuyu; tel. (66) 6750940; e-mail deanedu@uonbi.ac.ke):
KARANI, F. A., Educational Communication and Technology
MACHARIA, D., Education
OKOMBO, O., Linguistics and Literature
WANJALA, Linguistics and Literature

School of Engineering (tel. (20) 339061):
ADUOL, F. W. O., Surveying
GICHAGA, F. J., Civil Engineering
LUTI, F. M., Mechanical Engineering
OBUDHO, R. A., Urban and Regional Planning
OTIENO, A. V., Electrical and Electronics Engineering
SHARMA, T. C., Agricultural Engineering

School of Law (tel. (20) 3740366):
MUTUNGI, O. K., Commercial Law
OJWANG, J. B., Private Law

School of Medicine (tel. (20) 2726300):
ATINGIA, J. E. U., Orthopaedic Surgery
BHATT, S. M., Medicine
BWIBO, N. O., Paediatrics
KIGONDU, C., Clinical Chemistry
KUNGU, A., Human Pathology
KYAMBI, J. M., Surgery
MALEK, A. K., Human Anatomy
MATTA, W. M., Human Anatomy
MEME, J. S., Paediatrics
NDELE, J., Pharmacology
NDETEI, D. M., Psychiatry
ODHIAMBO, P. A., Surgery
OJWANG, S. B. O., Obstetrics and Gynaecology
OLIECH, J. S., Surgery
OTIENO, L. S., Medicine
PAMBA, H. O., Medical Microbiology
SINEI, S. K., Obstetrics and Gynaecology
THAIRU, K., Physiology
WAMOLA, I. A., Medical Microbiology
WASUNA, A. E. U., Surgery

School of Pharmacy (tel. (20) 2726771):
GUANTAI, A.
KOKWARO, G. O., Pharmaceutics and Pharmacy Practice
MAITAI, C. K., Pharmacology and Pharmacognosy
MWANGI, J. W., Pharmacology and Pharmacognosy

School of Physical Sciences (tel. (20) 4443181; e-mail deanscience@uonbi.ac.ke):
GENGA, R., Physics
GITU, P. M., Chemistry
JUMBA, ISAAC, Chemistry
KAMAU, G. N., Chemistry
KHAMALA, C. P. M., Zoology
KOKWARO, J. O., Botany
MAVUTI, KENNETH M., Zoology
MIBEY, R. K., Botany
MIDIWO, J. O., Chemistry
MUKIAMA, T. K., Botany
MUNAVU, R. M., Chemistry
MWANGI, R. W., Zoology
NYAMBOK, I. O., Geology
ODADA, E., Geology
ODHIAMBO, J. W., Mathematics
OGALLO, L. T., Meteorology
OGANA, B. W., Mathematics
ONYANGO, F. N., Physics
OTIENO-MALO, J. B., Physics
PATEL, P. J., Physics
POKHRIYAL, G. P., Mathematics
WANDIGA, S. O., Chemistry

Institutes:
ALILA, P., Institute for Development Studies
OCHOLLA-AYAYO, A. B. C., Population Studies and Research Institute
OKIDI, C. O., Institute for Development Studies
RODRIGUES, A. J., School of Informatics and Computing
SUDA, C., Institute of African Studies
WANDIBBA, S. B. A., Institute of African Studies

Colleges

Eldoret Polytechnic: POB 4461, Eldoret; tel. (53) 32661; e-mail eldopoly@africaonline.co.ke; offers certificate and diploma courses in library and information studies; Prin. Cleophas Lagat.

Kenya Conservatoire of Music: POB 41343, Nairobi; tel. (720) 962288; e-mail info@conservatoire.co.ke; internet conservatoire.co.ke; f. 1944; library of instrumental and vocal scores; Chair. Isaac O. Awuondo; Dir Corrine Towett; Sec. Rosemary Kilonzi.

Kenya Medical Training College: POB 30195, Nairobi; tel. (20) 725711; e-mail info@kmtc.ac.ke; internet www.kmtc.ac.ke; f. 1927, present name 1994; clinical medicine, community health nursing, pharmacy, medical laboratory sciences, food science and inspection; library: 18,000 vols, 150 periodicals; 1,500 teachers; 18,000 students; Chair. Hon. Joe Donde; Dir Dr Charles Olang'o Onudi.

Kenya School of Government: POB 23030, Lower Kabete, Nairobi; tel. (20) 2375340; e-mail info@ksg.ac.ke; internet www.ksg.ac.ke; f. 1961; residential training for the Kenya Public Service in public admin., project devt and management, senior management seminars, research and consultancy, computer courses, effective management communication, management information systems, policy analysis, management of public enterprises, French courses, finance management, environmental management, performance improvement programmes, human resource management, customer care and ethics, disaster management, training for trainers; library: 47,067 vols, 30 current periodicals and a fully equipped audiovisual aids centre; 30 teachers; 280 students; Chair. Francis N. Kibera; Dir Gen. Elijah K. Wachira; publs *K. I. A. Occasional Papers* (12 a year), *Newsline* (3 a year).

Kenya School of Law: POB 30369, Nairobi; tel. (20) 8890044; e-mail lawschool@ksl.ac.ke; internet www.ksl.ac.ke; f. 1963; library: 4,730 vols; 13 teachers; 400 students; Prin. Prof. W. Kulundu-Bitonye; Sr Principal Lecturer Anthony Munene; Librarian Roselyn Nyamato-Kwenda.

Kiambu Institute of Science and Technology: POB 414, Kiambu; internet www.kist.ac.ke; f. 1973; depts of bakery technology, building, business education, computer studies, electrical engineering, electronics; library: 10,000 vols; 61 teachers; 600 students; Prin. Simon Irungu.

Kisumu Polytechnic: POB 143, Kisumu; tel. (57) 2020071; e-mail info@kisumupoly.ac.ke; internet www.kisumupoly.ac.ke; f. 1997; courses offered in accounting and business administration, analytical chemistry, automotive engineering, building, computer studies, electrical engineering, electronics, food and beverage management, mechanical engineering, personnel management; 112 teachers; 2,000 students; Prin. Joyce Nyanjom.

Mombasa Polytechnic University College: POB 90420, Mombasa; Tom Mboya Ave, Tudor Area, Mombasa; tel. (41) 2492222; e-mail principal@mombasapoly.ac.ke; internet www.mombasapoly.ac.ke; f. 1948; full-time, 'sandwich', block-release and day-release courses; library: 20,000 vols; 200 teachers; 4,037 students; Chair. Prof. Shellamiah Okoth Keya; Prin. Prof. Josphat Kazungu Ziro Mwatela.

Rift Valley Institute of Science and Technology: POB 7182, Nakuru; tel. (37) 2079754; e-mail principal@rvist.ac.ke; internet www.rvist.ac.ke; f. 1979; agricultural mechanical engineering, building and civil engineering, computer studies, business studies, electrical and electronics, hospitality and tourism studies and liberal studies; library: 9,000 vols; 125 teachers; 1,200 students; Prin. E. K. Koimet; Registrar Paul Langat.

KIRIBATI

The Higher Education System

In 1979 the Gilbert Islands became an independent republic within the Commonwealth, under the name of Kiribati. Higher education primarily consists of a branch of the University of the South Pacific (USP). A USP Centre was first opened in Kiribati in 1976 and was upgraded to the status of a USP Campus in 2006. The Kiribati Campus currently has an enrolment of more than 3,000 students and offers a range of courses, including Preparatory, Foundation, Certificate, Diploma and Degree studies. In addition to the USP Campus, there are the Kiribati Teachers' College, the Marine Training Centre and the Kiribati Institute of Technology (founded in 1970 as the Tarawa Technical Institute), all of which are operated by the Government and are located on Tarawa Atoll. Courses at the Kiribati Institute of Technology (KIT) cover areas such as carpentry, engineering and accountancy and last for a maximum of one year. KIT participates in the Technical Vocational Education and Training Sector Strengthening Programme and as such all courses are delivered to theAustralian Vocational Education and Training Quality Framework. Courses at the Marine Training Centre train Kiribati seamen (enrolling 150 each year) to work for overseas shipping companies; and the Kiribati Teachers' College offers a two-year teacher training course, which enables successful students to teach pupils between the ages of six and 14 years. Students from Kiribati also attend establishments of higher education in Australia, New Zealand, Fiji and Canada. The Ministry of Education, Youth and Sport Development is responsible for tertiary education. The Ministry of Health and Medical Services runs a School of Nursing, also based on Tarawa. There were 198 students enrolled in teacher training and 1,303 in other vocational training in 2001.

Regulatory Body

GOVERNMENT

Ministry of Education: POB 263, Bikenibeu, Tarawa; tel. 28091; Minister MAERE TEKANENE.

Research Institute

NATURAL SCIENCES

Biological Sciences

Atoll Research Activities: POB 206, Bikenibeu, Tarawa; attached to Univ. of the South Pacific, Kiribati Campus; marine science and biology; Programme Man. TEMAKEI TEBANO; publ. *Atoll Bulletin*.

Library

Bairiki

National Library and Archives: POB 6, Bairiki, Tarawa; tel. 21337; f. 1979, fmrly Gilbert Islands Nat. Archives; nat. colln (housed in Archives) of 3,500 published items; archives records of 70,000 items; spec. collns incl. 600 rolls of microfilm and 4,000 microfiches; small philatelic, photograph, and sound recording collns; 50,000 vols; Librarian and Archivist KUNEI ETEKIERA.

Museum

Bairiki

Te Umanibong/Kiribati Cultural Museum: Bikenibeu, Tarawa; artefacts and other items of cultural and historic significance; Cultural Affairs Officer BWERE ERITAIA.

College

University of the South Pacific, Kiribati Campus: POB 59, Bairiki, Tarawa; tel. 21085; e-mail mackenzie_u@usp.ac.fj; internet www.usp.ac.fj; f. 1976, present location 1978, present status 2006; courses offered: English, computer science, education, science, management and accounting; library: 5,000 vols; 5 teachers; 3,000 students; Dir UEANTABO MACKENZIE (acting); Library Officer TEEWATA ROKETE.

DEMOCRATIC PEOPLE'S REPUBLIC OF KOREA

The Higher Education System

The Democratic People's Republic of Korea (North Korea) occupies the northern part of the Korean peninsula. In 1945 Korea was divided into military occupation zones, with Soviet forces in the North and US forces in the South. A provisional People's Committee, led by Kim Il Sung of the Korean Communist Party, was established in the North in 1946 and accorded government status. In 1948 the Democratic People's Republic of Korea was proclaimed. Education at all levels is strictly controlled by the Government. Institutions of higher education include colleges and universities, teacher training colleges (offering four-year courses), colleges of advanced technology (offering two- or three-year courses), medical schools (offering six-year courses), special colleges for science and engineering, art, music and foreign languages, and military colleges and academies. The oldest university is Kim Il Sung University, which was founded in 1946 and which is the only university in North Korea to provide Bachelors, Masters and doctoral degrees. Competition for admission into Kim Il Sung University is intense and is based not only on senior middle school grades but also on political criteria. Other notable universities include Kim Chaek University of Technology, which focuses on computer science, Pyongyang University of Foreign Studies, which trains diplomats and trade officials, and Kim Hyong-Jik University of Education, which trains teachers. Any individual who wishes to be admitted to any institution of higher education has to be nominated by the local 'college recommendation committee' prior to approval by county- and provincial-level committees. Furthermore, 20%–30% of the enrolment of every university in North Korea has to consist of discharged soldiers (who have served longer than three years) or workers (who have been employed for longer than five years). A report submitted to UNESCO by the North Korean Government in 2000 stated that there were more than 300 universities and colleges with 1.89m. students and academics. In March 2001 the Ministry of Education announced plans for the establishment of a university of information science and technology in Pyongyang, in cooperation with a South Korean education foundation (together with contributions from groups and individuals from other countries, notably the People's Republic of China and the USA). The new university, named the Pyongyang University of Science and Technology (PUST), officially opened in September 2009 (although classes did not commence until October 2010), and 250 faculty members, from South and North Korea (as well as from other countries), were expected to teach an annual intake of around 200 North and South Korean postgraduate students. The planning and construction of the PUST, which is North Korea's first joint-venture higher education establishment, was largely funded by South Korean evangelical Christian movements. Student numbers are predicted eventually to increase to 2,000 undergraduates and 600 graduates. None of the students were to pay tuition fees, the cost of which was to be borne by the North Korean Government.

There is a considerable emphasis on adult/continued education in North Korea and practically everyone in the country participates in some educational activity, usually in the form of 'small study groups'. Adult education institutions in the early 1990s reportedly included 'factory colleges' and 'farm colleges', at which workers were able to acquire new skills and techniques without having to leave their jobs.

In June 2010 it was reported that the Ministry of Education was to be reorganized as the Education Commission, comprising the Ministry of Higher Education and the Ministry of Common Education.

Regulatory Bodies

GOVERNMENT

Ministry of Culture: Pyongyang; Minister HONG KWANG-SUN.

Ministry of Education: Pyongyang; Minister (vacant).

Ministry of Higher Education: Pyongyang; Minister SONG JA RIP.

Learned Societies

GENERAL

Academy of Sciences: Ryonmotdong, Jangsan St, Sosong District, Pyongyang; tel. (2) 51956; f. 1952; brs of biology (Pres. SON KYONG NAM), construction and building materials (Pres. KIM MAN HYONG), electronics and automation design (Pres. LI SON BONG), light industry (Pres. PYON SOK CHON), and brs in Pyongsong (Chair. HAN BYONG HUI) and Hamhung (Pres. RI HYO SON); attached research institutes: see under Research Institutes; libraries: see under Libraries and Archives; Pres. JANG CHOL; publs *Bulletin* (6 a year), journals for analysis (4 a year each), biology, mathematics, mechanical engineering, metals, physics, and for chemical engineering and chemistry, electronic and automatic engineering, mining, geography and geology (6 a year each).

Academy of Social Sciences: Central District, Pyongyang; f. 1952; attached research institutes: see under Research Institutes; library: see under Libraries and Archives; Pres. KIM SOK HYONG.

AGRICULTURE, FISHERIES AND VETERINARY SCIENCE

Academy of Agricultural Science: Ryongsong District, Pyongyang; f. 1948; attached to Acad. of Sciences; attached research institutes: see under Research Institutes; Pres. KYE YONG SAM.

Academy of Fisheries: Namgangdong, Sung Ho District, Pyongyang; attached to Acad. of Sciences; f. 1969; 6 attached research institutes; Chair. SO GYONG HO.

Academy of Forestry: Samsindong, Taesong District, Pyongyang; f. 1948; attached to Acad. of Sciences; 5 attached research institutes; Pres. IM ROK JAE.

LANGUAGE AND LITERATURE

Goethe-Informationszentrum: Chollima Cultural House, 8-33 Jonggwang St, Central Area, Pyongyang; internet www.goethe.de/seoul; library of 4,000 vols; promotes cultural exchange with Germany; Dir Dr UWE SCHMELTER (based in Seoul).

MEDICINE

Academy of Medical Sciences: Saemauldong, Pyongchon District, POB 305, Pyongyang; tel. (2) 46924; attached to Acad. of Sciences; attached research institutes: see under Research Institutes; Pres. RI CHOL.

TECHNOLOGY

Academy of Light Industry Science: Kangan 1-dong, Songyo District, Pyongyang; f. 1954; 7 attached research institutes; Chair. LI JU UNG.

Academy of Railway Sciences: Namgyodong, Hyongjaesan District, Pyongyang; attached to Acad. of Sciences; 5 attached research institutes; Chair. MAENG YUN CHOL.

Research Institutes

AGRICULTURE, FISHERIES AND VETERINARY SCIENCE

Agricultural Chemical Research Institute: Ryongsong District, Pyongyang; attached to Acad. of Agricultural Science; Dir PAK JAE KUN.

Agricultural Irrigation Research Institute: Onchon County, S Pyongan Province; attached to Acad. of Agricultural Science; Dir HWANG CHANG HONG.

Agricultural Mechanization Research Institute: Sadong District, Pyongyang; attached to Acad. of Agricultural Science; Dir KANG SONG RYONG.

Crop Cultivation Research Institute: Ryongsong District, Pyongyang; attached to Acad. of Agricultural Science; Dir RYEM DOK SU.

Crop Science Research Institute: Sunchon City, S Pyongan Province; attached to Acad. of Agricultural Science; Dir PAK BYONG MUK.

Fruit Cultivation Research Institute: Sukchon County, S Pyongan Province; attached to Acad. of Agricultural Science; Dir JANG HY KUNG.

Poultry Science Research Institute: Hyongjaesan District, Pyongyang; attached to Acad. of Agricultural Science; Dir CHOI MAN SANG.

Reed Research Institute: Haeju City, S Hwanghae Province; attached to Acad. of Agricultural Science; Dir KIM IN SU.

Rice Research Institute: Ryongsong District, Pyongyang; attached to Acad. of Agricultural Science; Dir KIM SANG RYEN.

Sericulture Research Institute: Dongrim County, N Pyongan Province; attached to Acad. of Agricultural Science; Dir KIM SUN JONG.

Soil Science Research Institute: Ryongsong District, Pyongyang; attached to Acad. of Agricultural Science; Dir LI KUN HAENG.

Vegetable Science Research Institute: Sadong District, Pyongyang; attached to Acad. of Agricultural Science; Dir KIM HAK SON.

Veterinary Science Research Institute: Ryongsong District, Pyongyang; attached to Acad. of Agricultural Science; Dir PAK WON KUN.

Zoology Research Institute: Sariwon City, N Hwanghae Province; attached to Acad. of Agricultural Science; Dir KIM KYANG JUNG.

ARCHITECTURE AND TOWN PLANNING

Institute of Architecture and Building Engineering: c/o Academy of Sciences, Namgangdong, Sung Ho District, Pyongyang; Dir SIN DONG CHOL.

ECONOMICS, LAW AND POLITICS

Institute of International Affairs: c/o Academy of Social Sciences, Central District, Pyongyang; Dir KIM HYONG U.

Institute of Law: c/o Academy of Social Sciences, Central District, Pyongyang; Dir SIM HYONG IL.

Institute of Trade and Economics: c/o Academy of Social Sciences, Central District, Pyongyang; Dir (vacant).

HISTORY, GEOGRAPHY AND ARCHAEOLOGY

Institute of Archaeology: c/o Academy of Social Sciences, Central District, Pyongyang; Dir KIM MYONG NAM.

Institute of Geography: Ryonmotdong, Jangsan St, Sosong District, Pyongyang; attached to Acad. of Sciences; Dir KIM JONG RAK.

Institute of History: c/o Academy of Social Sciences, Central District, Pyongyang; Dir CHON YONG RYUL.

LANGUAGE AND LITERATURE

Institute of Ethnic Classics: c/o Academy of Social Sciences, Central District, Pyongyang; Dir KIM SUNG PHIL.

Institute of Juche Literature: c/o Academy of Social Sciences, Central District, Pyongyang; Dir KIM HA MYONG.

Institute of Linguistics: c/o Academy of Social Sciences, Central District, Pyongyang; Dir JONG SUN GI.

MEDICINE

Industrial Medicine Institute: Sapodong, Sapo District, Hamhung City; tel. (850) 2810; attached to Acad. of Medical Sciences; Dir JO UN HO.

Research Institute for the Cultivation of Medicinal Herbs: Wonjudong, Sariwon City, N Hwanghae Province; attached to Acad. of Medical Sciences; Dir KIM KWANG SOP.

Research Institute of Antibiotics: Ryonpodong, Sunchon City, Pyongan Province; attached to Acad. of Medical Sciences; Dir CHOE SUN JONG.

Research Institute of Biomedicine: Dongsandong, Rangnang District, Pyongyang; tel. (2) 23545; attached to Acad. of Medical Sciences; Dir PAK YUI SUN.

Research Institute of Child Nutrition: Dangsandong, Mangyongdae District, Pyongyang; tel. (2) 73430; attached to Acad. of Medical Sciences; Dir KIM YONG KWANG.

Research Institute of Endocrinology: Mirimdong, Sadong District, Pyongyang; tel. (2) 623828; attached to Acad. of Medical Sciences; Dir JANG HON CHOL.

Research Institute of Experimental Therapy: c/o Academy of Medical Sciences, Chonsongdong, Haesang District, Hamhung City, S Hamgyong Province; Dir NAM ON GIL.

Research Institute of Hygiene: Dangsandong, Mangyongdae District, Pyongyang; tel. (2) 44925; attached to Acad. of Medical Sciences; Dir JE HYONG DO.

Research Institute of Microbiology: Pyongsong City, S Pyongan Province; attached to Acad. of Medical Sciences; Dir KIM CHANG JIN.

Research Institute of Natural Drugs: Somundong, Donghumsan District, Hamhung City, S Hamgyong Province; tel. (850) 53905; attached to Acad. of Medical Sciences; Dir LI HWAI SU.

Research Institute of Oncology: Saemauldong, Pyongchon District, Pyongyang; tel. (2) 42208; attached to Acad. of Medical Sciences; Dir KIM CHUN WON.

Research Institute of Pharmacology: Daehungdong, Songyo District, Pyongyang; tel. 623868; attached to Acad. of Medical Sciences; Dir RYU GYONG HUI.

Research Institute of Psychoneurology: Uiju County, N Pyongan Province; attached to Acad. of Medical Sciences; Dir LI GYUN.

Research Institute of Radiological Medicine: Saemauldong, Pyongchon District, Pyongyang; tel. (2) 45347; attached to Acad. of Medical Sciences; Dir O SOK ROK.

Research Institute of Respiratory Ducts and Tuberculosis: c/o Academy of Medical Sciences, Chongsongdong, Haesang District, Hamhung City, S Hamgyong Province; Dir LI CHU WAN.

Research Institute of Surgery: c/o Academy of Medical Sciences, Chongsongdong, Haesang District, Hamhung City, South Hamgyong Province; Dir HAN BYONG GAP.

Research Institute of Synthetic Pharmacy: Sapodong, Sapo District, Hamhung City, S Hamgyong Province; attached to Acad. of Medical Sciences; Dir LI GI SOP.

NATURAL SCIENCES

General

Central Institute of Experimental Analysis: c/o Academy of Sciences, Kwahak-Idong, Unjong District, Pyongsong City, S Pyongan Province; tel. (2) 422-5044; f. 1983; attached to Acad. of Sciences; Dir RIM CHUN RYOB; publs *Bulletin*, *Punsok* (analysis, 4 a year).

Institute of Environmental Protection: Ryusongdong, Central District, Pyongyang; attached to Acad. of Sciences; Dir KIM YONG CHAN.

Biological Sciences

Institute of Botany: Kosandong, Daesong District, Pyongyang; attached to Acad. of Sciences; Dir GUAK JONG SONG.

Institute of Genetics: c/o Academy of Sciences, Ryonmotdong, Jangsan St, Sosong District, Pyongyang; Dir BAEK MUN CHAN.

Institute of Molecular Biology: c/o Academy of Sciences, Ryonmotdong, Jangsan St, Sosong District, Pyongyang; Dir KO GWANG UNG.

Institute of Plant Physiology: c/o Academy of Sciences, Ryonmotdong, Jangsan St, Sosong District, Pyongyang; Dir KIM SONG OK.

Institute of Zoology: Daesongdong, Daesong District, Pyongyang; attached to Acad. of Sciences; Dir BAEK JONG HWAN.

Mathematical Sciences

Institute of Mathematics: c/o Academy of Sciences, Doksandong, Pyongsong City, S Pyongan Province; Dir HO GON.

Physical Sciences

Institute of Analytical Chemistry: c/o Academy of Sciences, Chongsongdong, Hoesang District, Hamhung City, S Hamgyong Province; Dir RIM CHUN RYOP.

Institute of Ferrous Metals: Sae Goridong, Chollima District, Nampo City; attached to Acad. of Sciences; Dir LI BANG GUN.

Institute of Geology: c/o Academy of Sciences, Doksandong, Pyongsong City, S Pyongan Province; Dir KIM ZONG HUI.

Institute of Inorganic Chemistry: c/o Academy of Sciences, Chongsongdong, Hoesang District, Hamhung City, S Hamgyong Province; Dir CHU SUNG.

Institute of Macromolecular Chemistry: c/o Academy of Sciences, Chongsongdong, Hoesang District, Hamhung City, S Hamgyong Province; Dir LI JANG HYOK.

Institute of Non-Ferrous Metals: Jungdaedudong, Hangku District, Nampo City; attached to Acad. of Sciences; Dir KIM MYONG RIN.

Institute of Physical Chemistry: c/o Academy of Sciences, Chongsongdong, Hoesang District, Hamhung City, S Hamgyong Province; Dir KIM JUNG BAE.

Institute of Physics: c/o Academy of Sciences, Doksandong, Pyongsong City, S Pyongan Province; Dir RYO IN KWANG.

Institute of Pure Metals: Kumbitdong, Ryongsong District, Hamhung City, S Hamgyong Province; attached to Acad. of Sciences; Dir LI SANG BOM.

Pyongyang Astronomical Observatory: Daesongdong, Daesong District, Pyongyang; attached to Acad. of Sciences; Dir KIM YONG HYOK.

Research Centre for Atomic Energy: Mangyongdae District, Pyongyang; attached to General Dept of Atomic Energy; Pres. RIM PONG SIK.

PHILOSOPHY AND PSYCHOLOGY

Institute of Philosophy: c/o Academy of Social Sciences, Central District, Pyongyang; Dir KIM CHANG WON.

TECHNOLOGY

Institute of Chemical Engineering: c/o Academy of Sciences, Chongsongdong, Hoesang District, Hamhung City, S Hamgyong Province; Dir LI JAE OP.

Institute of Constructional Mechanization: c/o Academy of Sciences, Namgangdong, Sung Ho District, Pyongyang; Dir PAK RYANG SOP.

Institute of Electricity: c/o Academy of Sciences, Doksandong, Pyongsong City, S Pyongan Province; Dir CHOE WON GYONG.

Institute of Fuel: Dongsandong, Songrim City, N Hwanghe Province; attached to Acad. of Sciences; Dir KO YONG JIN.

Institute of Hydraulic Engineering: c/o Academy of Sciences, Namgangdong, Sung Ho District, Pyongyang; Dir KIM RYONG GYUN.

Institute of Industrial Biology: c/o Academy of Sciences, Doksandong, Pyongsong City, S Pyongan Province; Dir LI CHUN HO.

Institute of Mechanical Engineering: c/o Academy of Sciences, Doksandong, Pyongsong City, S Pyongan Province; Dir KIM UNG SAM.

Institute of Ore Dressing Engineering: c/o Academy of Sciences, Doksandong, Pyongsong City, S Pyongan Province; Dir LI WON SOK.

Institute of Organic Building Materials: c/o Academy of Sciences, Namgangdong, Sung Ho District, Pyongsong; Dir PAK CHANG SUN.

Institute of Paper Engineering: Songdori, Anju City, S Pyongan Province; attached to Acad. of Sciences; Dir RYU SAM JIP.

Institute of Silicate Engineering: Sijonggu, Taedong County, S Pyongan Province; attached to Acad. of Sciences; Dir KIM UNG SANG.

Institute of Thermal Engineering: c/o Academy of Sciences, Doksandong, Pyongsong City, S Pyongan Province; Dir HAN DONG SIK.

Institute of Tideland Construction: c/o Academy of Sciences, Namgangdong, Sung Ho District, Pyongyang; Dir CHO SOK.

Institute of Welding: Ponghwadong, Chollima District, Nampo City; attached to Acad. of Sciences; Dir CHAE HON MUK.

Research Centre of Electronics and Automation: c/o Academy of Sciences, Doksandong, Pyongsong City, S Pyongan Province; incorporates institutes of electronics, of computer science, of automation, of technical cybernetics, of electronic materials; Gen. Dir LI SON BONG.

Research Institute of Medical Instruments: Daesindong, Dongdaewon District, Pyongyang; tel. (2) 623839; attached to Acad. of Medical Sciences; Dir JO MYONG SAM.

Libraries and Archives

Chongjin

Chongjin City Library: Chongjin; Librarian KANG CHAE GUM.

Chongjin Historical Library: Chongjin; Curator EU JAI GYONG.

North Hamgyong Provincial Library: Chongjin; Librarian CHOI MYONG OK.

Haeju

South Hwanghae Provincial Library: Haeju; Librarian CHOI CHI DO.

Hamhung

South Hamgyong Provincial Library: Hamhung; Librarian KIM SOOK JONG.

Hesan

Ryanggang Provincial Library: Hesan; Librarian KIM CHOL WOO.

Kaesong

Kaesong City Library: Kaesong; Librarian HAN IL.

Kaesong Historical Library: Kaesong; Curator CHOI SAE YONG.

Kangge

Chagang Provincial Library: Kangge; Librarian SONG AAI GUN.

Pyongsong

South Pyongan Provincial Library: Pyongsong; Librarian KIM DUK KWAN.

Pyongyang

Academy of Sciences Library: Kwahakdong 1, Unjong District, POB 330, Pyongyang; tel. (2) 32353968; f. 1952; 3.2m. vols; Dir Prof. KIM HYON OK; Chief Librarian Assoc. Prof. HONG SANG SU; publ. *Bulletin*.

Academy of Social Sciences Library: Central District, Pyongyang; Chief Librarian KIM SAE SONG.

Grand People's Study House/State Central Library: Central District, POB 200, Pyongyang; tel. (2) 3215614; f. 1982; in charge of nat. bibliography; also functions as correspondence univ.; 20m. vols; Dir CHOE HUI JONG.

Pyongyang Scientific Library: Central District, POB 109, Pyongyang; tel. (2) 321-2314; f. 1978.

Sariwon

North Hwanghae Provincial Library: Sariwon; Librarian KIM HYO DAL.

Shinuiju

North Pyongan Provincial Library: Shinuiju; Librarian LI YONG SIK.

Wonsan

Kangwon Provincial Library: Wonsan; Librarian JI GYU HYOK.

Museums and Art Galleries

Haeju

Haeju Historical Museum: Haeju, South Hwanghae Province.

Hamhung

Hamhung Historical Museum: Hamhung, S Hamgyong Province; Curator KIM IK MYON.

Hyangsan County

Mt Myohyang-san Museum: Hyangsan County, N Pyongan Province; Curator CHOI HYONG MIN.

Pyongyang

Korean Art Gallery: opposite Korean Central History Museum, Central Dist., Pyongyang; f. 1954; mural paintings from 4th century, modern Korean paintings, oil paintings, prints, jewel paintings, sculptures, handicrafts and other colins; Curator KIM SANG CHOL.

Korean Central History Museum: Taedongmun-dong, Central District, Pyongyang; f. 1945; prehistory to early 20th century; Curator JANG JONG SIN.

Korean Ethnographic Museum: Central District, Pyongyang; Curator JON MOON JIN.

Korean Revolution Museum: Mansu Hill, Central District, Pyongyang; f. 1948; history from second half of 19th century to the present; anti-Japanese revolutionary armed struggle, Pochonbo Battle, Battle on Height 1211 of the Korean War; Dir HWANG SUN HUI.

Victorious War Museum: Sosong Dist., Pyongyang; f. 1974; history from second half of the 19th century to the present; Fatherland Liberation War; Dir THAE PYONG RYOL.

Shinchon County

Shinchon Museum: Shinchon County, S Hwanghae Province; Curator PAK IN CHAIK.

Shinuiju

Shinuiju Historical Museum: Shinuiju, N Pyongan Province; Curator PAK YONG GWAN.

Wonsan

Wonsan Historical Museum: Wonsan, Kangwon Province; Curator JO GANG BAIK.

Universities and Colleges

Kim Chaek University of Technology: Waesong District, Pyongyang; faculties of geology, mining, metallurgy, mechanical and electrical engineering, shipbuilding, electronics, nuclear technology; Pres. HONG SO HON.

Kim Hyong-Jik University of Education: Pyongyang; f. 1946; faculties of revolutionary history, pedagogy, history and geography, language and literature, foreign languages, mathematics, physics, biology, music, fine arts, physical education; 5-year degree course, short-term courses for teachers, correspondence and postgraduate courses; 2,500 students; Pres. HONG IL CHON.

KIM IL SUNG UNIVERSITY

Daesong District, Pyongyang
Telephone: (2) 54946
Founded 1946
State control
Academic year: September to August
Faculties of atomic energy, biology, chemistry, computer science, economics, foreign literature, geography, geology, history, law, philosophy, physics and mathematics, religion
Pres.: SONG JA RIP
Vice-Pres: CHOE JAND RYONG, JO CHOL, KIM IL GWANG, O KIL BANG, PAEK CHOL, PAEK JAE UK, RI JAE MYON, RI SONG CHOL, RO SONG CHAN
Number of teachers: 2,000
Number of students: 12,000
Publications: natural science magazine, social science magazine.

ATTACHED RESEARCH INSTITUTES

Computer Science College: Dir KIM YONG JUN.

Doctoral Institute: Dir HAN YONG GU.

Literature College: Dir UN JONG SOP

Pyongyang University of Agriculture: Pyongyang; f. 1981; depts of fruit and vegetable cultivation, poultry, stockbreeding; Pres. CHON SI GON.

Pyongyang University of Medicine: Woesong District, Pyongyang; colleges of higher and professional education (engineering, agriculture, fisheries, teacher training) situated in all the main towns; also Factory (Engineering) Colleges; Pres. RI WON GIL.

REPUBLIC OF KOREA

The Higher Education System

The country's oldest institutions of higher education were founded during the final years of the Joseon dynasty (1392–1910), among them Yonsei and Paichai Universities (both founded 1885), Ewha Women's University (founded 1886), Korea University (founded 1905; formerly Posung College) and Dongguk University (founded 1906). Several were established during the early years of the Japanese occupation of the Korean peninsula (1910–45), including Jinju National University (founded 1910), Seoul Theological University (founded 1911), Chung-Ang University (founded 1918) and Miryang National University (founded 1923). Consequently, the Korean education system at all levels displayed strong Japanese influences. Following the Allied defeat of Japan in 1945, Korea was divided at latitude 38°N into military occupation zones, with Soviet forces in the north and US forces in the south. In 1948 the US-administered south became the independent Republic of Korea, while the Democratic People's Republic of Korea was proclaimed in the Soviet-administered north. A three-year war between north and south ended in 1953, and the two countries remain divided at the ceasefire line, separated by a UN-supervised demilitarized zone. Post-1945 education in the south became influenced by the US system and since 1945 has been structured with six years of primary education, six years of secondary education and four years of higher education. A consequence of military control from the 1960s, and particularly during the 1980s, was that specialized and technical education became more respected than the general cultural knowledge traditionally held in high esteem. In recent years a high value has been placed upon scientific education, which resulted in South Korea becoming one of the world's most technologically advanced countries by the 1980s.

Overall responsibility for education (including higher education) resides with the Ministry of Education. Higher education consists of seven types of institution (which may all be either publicly or privately operated): junior colleges, colleges and universities, broadcast and correspondence universities, industrial universities, universities of education, technical colleges and miscellaneous colleges. Degrees are awarded on the basis of the US-style 'credit semester' system. Junior colleges, which were established in 1979 as a direct result of the growing demand for a technically trained workforce in the increasingly industrialized country, are distinguished from the other types of institution by the fact that they do not offer four-year undergraduate Bachelors degree programmes. Instead, they offer two- to three-year mainly technical and professionally orientated programmes in a wide variety of subjects leading to the award of Associate degrees (which require the accumulation of 80–120 credits and which were previously known as Junior College Diplomas or Certificates). The Associate degree permits access into the third year of a comparable Bachelors degree programme, although graduates often proceed directly into employment. Junior colleges are regulated and monitored by the Korean Council for College Education. The remaining six types of institution can all essentially be grouped under the general term colleges and universities, and are coordinated by the Korean Council for University Education (KCUE, founded 1982), which is responsible for improving institutional autonomy, flexibility and standards. All nationally recognized universities are required by law to become members of the KCUE. The Centre for University Accreditation of the KCUE is responsible for the evaluation and accreditation of all universities every five years; as well as institutional accreditation, this body also conducts programme accreditation. Furthermore, since 2009 university self-review has been required every two years. The acronym 'SKY' is used to denote the three most prestigious universities: Seoul National University, Korea University and Yonsei University. In 2007 there were 175 colleges and universities (the vast majority of which were in the private sector), with a student enrolment of 1,919,504. A further 296,576 students were enrolled in 1,042 graduate schools. In 2010, according to figures issued by UNESCO, 3,269,509 students were enrolled in tertiary education. Tuition fees in South Korean institutions of higher education are among the highest in the world and the Korea Student Aid Foundation was established to handle student loans. In mid-2011, following widespread student protests at recent large increases in tuition fees, the South Korean Government offered to reduce fees by up to 30% by 2014. However, in effect only 110 out of 334 universities reduced their tuition fees at the beginning of 2012 and then only by an overall average of 5%.

Since 1993 the US-style College Scholastic Aptitude Test has been the main basis for admission to higher education. Applicants are also assessed on their scholastic record and institutions may set their own entrance examination. The College Scholastic Aptitude Test is administered by the Institute of Curriculum and Evaluation. The main undergraduate degree is the four-year Bachelors (Haksa), although programmes in professional disciplines last longer (the architecture course takes five years and dentistry and medicine six years). Students usually need to accrue 140 credits for award of the Bachelors, of which 35 must be in a designated 'major' subject. Following the Bachelors, the postgraduate (or graduate), Masters (Suksa) and Doctorate (Paksa) degrees are offered primarily by graduate schools, which are generally part of research-orientated universities. The Masters lasts two years and requires 24–36 credits, the Doctorate at least two years and 36 credits; both of these degrees require the submission of a thesis.

Junior colleges, specialist vocational schools and technical high schools are among the leading institutions of vocational and technical education. Students at the schools usually work towards a vocational qualification and then sit the examination for the National Technical Certificate, while students at the junior colleges work towards an Associate degree (see above). In recent years technical colleges have been established to provide further education to high school or junior college graduates who are employed within industry. At both entry levels students study for two years and are awarded an Associate degree or Technical degree. Bachelors degree courses are also available at technical colleges.

The Government is faced with persistent problems in the higher education sector: a declining student population (owing to the overall fall in the birth rate), an oversupply of private institutions, concerns over the quality of degree programmes, and questions over whether universities can produce the requisite economic workforce for the growing number of technology-based companies. In September 2011, as part of the Government's attempts to restructure and improve the higher education sector, it was announced that 43 poorly managed private universities, colleges and vocational institutions would no longer be eligible for state subsidies.

Regulatory and Representative Bodies

GOVERNMENT

Ministry of Culture, Sports and Tourism: 215 Changgyeonggung-ro, Jongno-gu, Seoul 110-360; tel. (44) 203-2000; internet www.mcst.go.kr; Minister YOO JINRYONG.

Ministry of Education: 408 Galmae-ro, 77–6, Sejong-no, Jongno-gu, Seoul 110-760; tel. (44) 203-6060; internet www.moe.go.kr; Minister SEO NAMSOO.

Ministry of Science, ICT and Future Planning: 47 Govt Complex, Gyeonggi, Gwacheon 427-700; internet www.msip.go.kr; Minister CHOI MUN-KEE.

ACCREDITATION

Korean Council for University Education (KCUE): KGIT Sangam Centre, 11 Fl., Mapo-gu, Sangam-dong 1601, Seoul 121-270; tel. (2) 6393-5225; e-mail intl@kcue.or.kr; internet english.kcue.or.kr; f. 1982; 201 mems, incl. most 4-year univs in Republic of Korea; Chair. LEE BAE YONG; Sec.-Gen. Prof. PARK CHONG YUL; publ. *Daehak Gyoyuk* (Higher Education, in Korean).

NATIONAL BODY

Korean Federation of Teachers' Associations: 114-1 Taebongno, Seocho-Ku, Seoul 137-715; tel. (2) 570-5500; e-mail kfta2@kfta.or.kr; internet www.kfta.or.kr; f. 1947; Pres. Prof. AHN YANGOK.

Learned Societies

GENERAL

Korea Foundation: 10-11F Diplomatic Centre Bldg, 2558 Nambusunhwanno, Seocho-gu, Seoul 137-863; 1F Joongang Ilbo Bldg, Sunhwa-dong 7, Jung-gu, Seoul 100-759; tel. (2) 2046-8500; e-mail kfcenter@kf.or.kr; internet www.kf.or.kr; f. 1991, fmrly Int. Cultural Soc. of Korea; promotes mutual understanding and friendship between Korea and the rest of the world; 60 mems; library of 8,000 vols; Pres. YIM SUNG-JOON; publs *Korea Focus* (6 a year, in English), *Koreana* (4 a year, in English and Chinese).

National Academy of Sciences: San-94-4, Banpo 4-dong, Seocho-gu, Seoul 137-044; tel. (2) 534-0737; e-mail academy@mest.go.kr; internet www.nas.go.kr; f. 1954; 150 mems; library of 15,000 vols; Pres. KIM SANG-JOO; Vice-Pres. PARK YOUNG-SIK; publs *Development of Science Study in Korea* (1 a year, in Korean), *Journal of NAS* (1 a year, in Korean), *NAS Annual Bulletin* (in Korean), *NAS Bulletin* (every 2 years, in English), *Proceedings of the International Symposium* (1 a year, in Korean).

Royal Asiatic Society Korea Branch: Korean Christian Bldg, Room 611, 136–46, Yunji-dong, Chongno-ku, Seoul; tel. (2) 763-9483; e-mail royalasiatickorea@gmail.com; internet raskb.com; f. 1900; encourages interest in, and promotes study and dissemination of knowledge about, the arts, history, literature and customs of Korea and the neighbouring countries; lectures, excursions, spec. study groups, publs; 600 mems; library of 3,000 vols; Pres. AN SONJAE; Sec. JENNIFER FLINN; Treas. JACCO ZWETSLOOT; publ. *Transactions* (1 a year).

AGRICULTURE, FISHERIES AND VETERINARY SCIENCE

Korean Forestry Society: c/o Dept of Forest Resources, Seoul National University, Suwon, Kyonggido Seoul 441-744; tel. (331) 290-2330; f. 1960 to foster the study of all aspects of forestry, to promote cooperation among members; 800 mems; Pres. Prof. JONG HWA YOUN; Sec. Assoc. Prof. JOO SANG CHUNG; publ. *Journal* (4 a year).

BIBLIOGRAPHY, LIBRARY SCIENCE AND MUSEOLOGY

Korean Library Association: San 60-1, Banpo-dong, Seocho-gu, Seoul 137-702; tel. (2) 535-4868; e-mail klanet@hitel.net; internet www.korla.or.kr; f. 1945; a social and academic instn comprising all the libraries and librarians in Korea; 1,115 institutional, 1,865 individual mems; Pres. KI-NAM SHIN; Exec. Dir KYUNG-KU LEE; publs *KLA Bulletin* (6 a year), *Statistics on Libraries in Korea* (1 a year).

Korean Museum Association: c/o National Museum of Korea, 168-6 Yongsan-dong, Yongsan-gu, Seoul 140-026; tel. (2) 795-0937; e-mail webmaster@museum.or.kr; internet www.museum.or.kr; f. 1976; devt of museums through collaborative networking and of institutional museum policies for the benefits of the preservation of culture and education; Pres. KIDONG BAE.

Korean Research and Development Library Association: Room 0411, KIST Library, POB 131, Cheongryang, Seoul; tel. (82) 967-3692; f. 1979; Pres. KE HONG PARK; Sec. KEON TAK OH.

ECONOMICS, LAW AND POLITICS

Korean Association of Sinology: c/o Asiatic Research Centre, Korea University, Anam-dong, Seoul; f. 1955; 100 mems; Chair. JUN-YOP KIM; publ. *Journal of Chinese Studies*.

Korean Economic Association: 45, 4-ga, Namdae-mun-ro, Chung-gu, Seoul; tel. (2) 3210-2522; e-mail kea1952@kea.ne.kr; internet www.kea.ne.kr; f. 1952; theory, policy and history of economics and business administration; 2,800 mems; library of 3,000 vols; Pres. PYUNG-JOO KIM; Sec.-Gen. JOON-WOO NAHM; publ. *Korean Economic Review* (2 a year).

FINE AND PERFORMING ARTS

Music Association of Korea: Bldg 1-117, Dongsung-dong, Chongro-gu, Seoul 110-765; tel. (2) 744-8060; e-mail music@mak.or.kr; internet www.mak.or.kr; f. 1961 to develop Korean nat. music and to promote and protect Korean musicians; organizes concerts, encourages musical composition and nationwide singing; is active in the int. musical exchange and in music education; awards the Prize of Musical Culture; 700 mems; small library; Pres. Dr KIM YONG-JIN.

HISTORY, GEOGRAPHY AND ARCHAEOLOGY

Korean Geographical Society: Dept of Geography, College of Social Sciences, Seoul National University, Seoul 151-746; tel. (2) 875-1463; e-mail geography77@daum.net; internet www.kgeography.or.kr; f. 1945 to promote mutual cooperation in academic work and int. understanding; 772 individual mems, 69 institutional mems; Pres. LEE JEONG ROCK; Sec.-Gen. YONG-CHUL SHIN; publ. *Journal* (5 a year).

LANGUAGE AND LITERATURE

Alliance Française: 63-2 Hoehyun-dong 1-ga, Jung-gu, Seoul 100-873; tel. (2) 755-5702; e-mail alliance@nuri.net; internet www.afcoree.co.kr; offers courses and examinations in French language and culture and promotes cultural exchange with France; attached teaching centres in Busan, Chonju, Daegu, Daejon, Gwangju, Jeonju; Dir MARC SARRAZIN.

British Council: 4th Fl., Hungkuk Life Insurance Bldg, 226 Shinmunro 1-ga, Jongro-gu, Seoul 110-786; tel. (2) 3702-0600; e-mail info@britishcouncil.or.kr; internet www.bckorea.or.kr; teaching centre; offers courses and examinations in English language and British culture; promotes cultural exchange with the UK; Dir ROLAND DAVIES.

Goethe-Institut: 339-1 Huam-dong, Yongsan-ku, Seoul 140-901; tel. (2) 754-9831; e-mail info@seoul.goethe.org; internet www.goethe.de/os/seo/deindex.htm; offers courses and examinations in German language and culture and promotes cultural exchange with Germany; library of 12,000 vols; Dir JURGEN KEIL.

MEDICINE

Korean Medical Association: 302-75 Ichon 1-dong, Yongsan-gu, Seoul 140-721; tel. (2) 794-2474; e-mail intl@kma.org; internet www.kma.org; f. 1908; develops medical sciences and medical education by encouraging research and investigation; 59,292 mems; library of 10,000 vols; Pres. KYUNG MAN HO; publs *Journal* (12 a year), *The KMA News* (104 a year).

PHILOSOPHY AND PSYCHOLOGY

Korean Psychological Association: Dept of Psychology, Seoul National University, Shinrim 2-dong, Kwanak-gu, Seoul; tel. 877-0101; e-mail kpa0102@chol.com; internet www.koreanpsychology.or.kr; f. 1946; 420 mems; Pres. KIM MYUNG UN; Sec.-Gen. JUNGOH KIM; publs *Korean Journal of Clinical Psychology* (2 a year), *Korean Journal of Developmental Psychology* (1 a year), *Korean Journal of Industrial Psychology* (1 a year), *Korean Journal of Psychology* (2 a year), *Korean Journal of Social Psychology* (1 a year).

Research Institutes

GENERAL

Academy of Korean Studies: 110 Haogogae-gil, Bundang-gu, Seongnam-si, Gyeonggi-do, Seoul 463-791; tel. (31) 709-8111; internet www.aks.ac.kr; f. 1978 to research and re-evaluate traditional Korean culture; library of 361,000 vols incl. 35,000 in Western languages; Pres. KIM JEONG-BAE; publ. *Chongsin Munhwa / Academy News* (3–4 a year).

AGRICULTURE, FISHERIES AND VETERINARY SCIENCE

Rural Development Administration: Suin-ro, 150 (250 Seodun-dong), Gwonseon-gu, Suwon Gyeonggi-do, Seoul 441-707; tel. (31) 299-2200; e-mail rda@rda.go.kr; internet www.rda.go.kr; f. 1906 to carry out agricultural research and rural community devt; 11 subordinate research orgs, 9 provincial offices, 34 regional specialized crop stations; library of 190,000 vols; Administrator KIM JAE-SOO; publs *Agricultural Technology* (12 a year, in Korean), *Annual Research Report* (Korean and English edns), *Research and Extension* (12 a year, in Korean).

ECONOMICS, LAW AND POLITICS

Korea Development Institute: Hoegiro 47 Dongdaemun-gu, Seoul 130-740; tel. (2) 958-4114; e-mail kdiweb@kdi.re.kr; internet www.kdi.re.kr; f. 1971; conducts policy-oriented research relating to individual sectors of the economy; provides consultation on policy issues relating to short-term economic management and planning; library of 100,000 vols, 39,000 research reports, govt documents, also data bank; Pres. KIM JOON-KYUNG; publs *KDI Economic Outlook* (2 a year, in Korean), *KDI Journal of Economic Policy* (4 a year, in Korean), *KDI Monthly Economic Trends* (in Korean).

Korea Institute for Industrial Economics and Trade (KIET): 66 Hoegiro, Dong-daemun-gu, Seoul 130-742; tel. (2) 3299-3114; internet www.kiet.re.kr; f. 1976 as Korea Foundation for Middle East Studies, present name and status 1991; advises govt on industrial, trade and commercial policies; analyses Korean industry, int. economies, new technology and promotion of trade; library of 45,000 vols, 1,500 periodicals; Pres. OH SANG-BONG; publs *Journal of Industrial Competitiveness* (1 a year), *KIET Economic Outlook* (2 a year), *KIET Real Economy* (24 a year).

Korean Research Center: 228 Pyong-dong, Chongno-gu, Seoul; f. 1956; research in social sciences; maintains library; Pres. MUNAM CHON; publs *Journal of Social Sciences and Humanities*, *Korean Studies Series*.

EDUCATION

Korean Educational Development Institute: 92–6 Umyeon-dong, Seocho-gu, Seoul 137-791; tel. (2) 3460-0216; e-mail international@kedi.re.kr; internet eng.kedi.re.kr; f. 1972; ind., govt-funded research and devt institute; undertakes research and devt activities on education; assists govt in formulation of educational policies and in long-term devt of education; library of 121,197 vols, 88 periodicals, 499,018 microfiches; Pres. TAE-WAN KIM; publs *KEDI Journal of Education Policy* (2 a year, in English), *Research Abstracts* (1 a year, in English), *Statistical Yearbook of Education* (in English and Korean).

National Institute for Training of Educational Administrators: c/o Ministry of Education, 77-6 Sejong-ro, Jongno-gu, Seoul 110-760; tel. (2) 733-2741; f. 1970; govt institute; attached to Min. of Education; library of 21,000 vols; Dir CHONG-TAEK CHANG.

NATURAL SCIENCES

Physical Sciences

Korea Meteorological Administration: 45 Gisangcheong-gil, Dongjak-gu, Seoul 156-720; tel. (2) 836-2385; e-mail pb_int@kma.go.kr; internet web.kma.go.kr; under the control of the Min. of Environment; Administrator KO YUNHWA.

PHILOSOPHY AND PSYCHOLOGY

Korean Institute for Research in the Behavioural Sciences: 1606-3 Socho-Dong, Kangnam-gu, Seoul 137-071; tel. (2) 581-8611; f. 1968; basic and applied research in 5 areas: social, child, learning, organization, and psychological testing; library of 5,000 vols; Dir SUNG JIN LEE; publs *Research Bulletin*, *Research Notes*.

TECHNOLOGY

Electronics and Telecommunications Research Institute (ETRI): 138 Gajeongno, Yuseong-gu, Daejeon City, Seoul 305-700; tel. (42) 860-6114; e-mail sloh@etri.re.kr; internet www.etri.re.kr; f. 1976; undertakes research and devt in field of advanced information technology; library of 40,000 vols, 30,000 technical reports, and ETLARS databases; Pres. CHOI MUN-KEE; publs *Electronics and Telecommunications Trends* (4 a year), *ETRI Journal* (4 a year), *Patent Announcement* (26 a year), *Patent Information* (12 a year), *Weekly Technology Trends* (52 a year).

Korea Atomic Energy Research Institute (KAERI): POB 105, Yu-seong, Daejeon, Seoul 305-600; tel. (42) 868-2000; internet www.kaeri.re.kr; f. 1959; reactor-related research and devt, security and R&D of nuclear fuel, nuclear policy research, radiation application technology devt and research and treatment of nuclear radiation, nuclear personnel training and other aspects of nuclear energy; library of 61,000 vols, 700,000 technical reports and 950 periodicals; Pres. MYUNG SEUNG YANG; publs *Journal*, *KAERI Research Papers* (1 a year), *Won Woo* (6 a year).

Korea Institute of Energy Research: 102 Gajeong-ro, Yuseong-gu, Daejeon, Seoul 305-343; tel. (42) 860-3114; e-mail webadmin@kier.re.kr; internet www.kier.re.kr; f. 1977 to conduct research on energy and technology; supported by Min. of Science, ICT and Future Planning; 500 mems; library of 30,000 vols; Pres. HAN MOON-HEE; publs *Energy R&D*, *Technical Trends on NRSE*.

Korea Institute of Science and Technology (KIST): Hwarangno 14-gil 5, Seongbuk-gu, Seoul 136-791; tel. (2) 958-6124; e-mail cglee@kist.re.kr; internet www.kist.re.kr; f. 1966; research in applied science, chemical engineering, polymer engineering, materials science and engineering, mechanical and control systems, electronics and information technology, environment and CFC alternatives technology, systems engineering, genetic engineering, science and technology policy; library of 50,000 vols, 15,000 technical reports; Pres. Dr KIL-CHOO MOON; publ. *Collection of Abstracts* (1 a year, in English and Korean).

Libraries and Archives

Busan

Banyeo Library: San 129-9, Banyeo 3-dong, Haeundae-gu, Busan; tel. (51) 749-5731; internet www.banyeolib.or.kr.

Dong-Eui University Central Library: Kaya-dong, Pusanjin-ku, Busan, Seoul 614-714; tel. (51) 890-1155; e-mail hkyyh@deu.ac.kr; internet lib.deu.ac.kr; f. 1979; 810,000 vols; Library Dean Dr NAM SOO-HYUN.

Gang Seo Public Library: 2011-2 Daeju 2-dong, Ganseo-gu, Busan 618-807; tel. (51) 973-5274; e-mail gslibrary@korea.kr; internet library.bsgangseo.go.kr.

Pusan National University Library: 30 Jangjeon-dong, Keumjeong-gu, Pusan 609-735; tel. (51) 510-1800; e-mail info@pusan.ac.kr; internet pulip.pusan.ac.kr; f. 1946; depository library of the UN and IMF; 2,090,000 vols, 50,000 periodicals, 30,000 domestic and foreign ebooks; Dir DONG-HYUN JUNG.

Daegu

Bukbu Library: 447-10 Chimsan 3-dong, Buk-gu, Daegu, Seoul 702-857; tel. (53) 350-0800; internet www.bukbu-lib.daegu.kr; f. 1982.

Daebong Library: Daebong-dong, Jung-gu, Daegu; tel. (53) 422-0958; internet www.db.dblib.daegu.kr.

Dongbu Library: 664-19 Sinam 4-dong, Dong-gu, Daegu, Seoul 701-014; tel. (53) 603-6100; internet www.dongbu-lib.daegu.kr.

Duryu Public Library: 154 Duryu 3-dong, Dalseo-gu, Daegu; tel. (53) 650-0200; internet www.duryu-lib.daegu.kr.

Jungang Library: 42 Dongin-dong 2-ga, Munhwa-gil, Jung-gu, Daegu, Seoul 700-422; tel. (53) 420-2700; internet www.tglnet.or.kr; f. 1918 as Daegu Bu Library, renamed in 1995; Dir HONG-MAN KIM.

Kyungpook National University Library: 1370 Sankyuk-dong, Puk-ku, Taegu 702-701; tel. (53) 950-6510; e-mail mspark@kyungpook.ac.kr; internet kudos.knu.ac.kr; f. 1952; 2.1m. vols; Dir SEO JONG-MOON.

Nambu Metropolitan Library: San 192-4 Daemyeong 9-dong, Nam-gu, Daegu; tel. (53) 620-5511; e-mail nbl@edunavi.kr; internet www.nbl.or.kr; f. 1995; Curator JOHOSIK.

Seobu Public Library: 1230-1 Pyeongni 3-dong, Seo-gu, Daegu; tel. (53) 560-8800; internet www.seobu-lib.daegu.kr.

Suseong Library: 54 Art Gallery park-route (gil), Manchon 1 (il)-dong, Suseong-gu, Daegu, Seoul 706-707; tel. (53) 740-5532; internet www.hyomok-lib.daegu.kr; f. 1988. as Hyomok Library; present name in 2008.

Daejeon

Daejeon Student Education and Culture Centre: 701 Jung-gu, Daejeon, Seoul 301-807; tel. (42) 229-1490; internet www.djsecc.or.kr.

Daejeon University Library: Daejeon, Seoul 300-718; tel. (42) 280-2681; internet libweb.dju.ac.kr.

Hanbat Library: Daejeon, Seoul 301-711; tel. (42) 580-4114; e-mail hanbat@its.daejeon.kr; internet hanbat.metro.daejeon.kr; 568,028 vols.

National Archives of Korea: Govt Complex, Seonsaro, 139 (920 Dusan 2-Dong), Seo-gu, Daejeon 302-701; tel. (42) 481-6300; f. 1969, relocated from Seoul in 1998; 336,275 vols, 1.2m. diagrams, 1.5m. cards, 181,311 rolls of microfilm, 740,463 audiovisual items; colln of records of the Yi dynasty.

Branches:

National Archives, Busan: 2-dong, Geoje-dong San 126, Girokgwan 1st Fl., Busan; tel. (51) 550-8025.

National Archives, Seoul: Gwanghwamun Jeokseon-dong Platinum 201, 156-dong, Jongro-gu, Seoul; tel. 720-2721.

Gwangju

Chonnam University Library: Buk-gu, Yongbong to 77 Daechulbannap-sil, Gwangju, Seoul 500-757; tel. (62) 530-3571; e-mail yosulib@chonnam.ac.kr; internet library.chonnam.ac.kr; f. 1953; 2m. vols, 680,000 books, 20,000 journals and periodicals.

Honam University Library: Gwangsan Seobongdong 59-1, Gwangju, Seoul 506-714; tel. (62) 940-5185; e-mail bss@honam.ac.kr; internet library.honam.ac.kr; f. 1979.

Gyeonggi-do

Gamgol Library: 83-8 Sa-dong, Sangrok-gu, Ansan-si, Gyeonggi-do, Seoul 425-170.

Gwacheon Provincial Library of Gyeonggi: 12 Dosegwangil, Gwacheon, Gyeonggi-do; tel. (2) 3677-0371; e-mail webmaster@kwalib.or.kr; internet eng.kwalib.kr; f. 1984; 298,587 vols, 778 periodicals and magazines; Dir LEE WOON SUN.

Seoul

Chung-Ang University Library: 221 Huksuk-dong, Dongjak-ku, Seoul; e-mail international@cau.ac.kr; internet library.cau

.ac.kr; f. 1949; 1m. vols, 4,000 nat. and int. periodicals; Chief Librarian JANG HYEOK LIM.

Dongguk University Library: 263-ga, Pil-dong, Seoul; internet lib.dongguk.edu; f. 1906; Buddhist and Oriental studies; 350,000 vols, 1,100 periodicals; Dir Dr JAE HO SHIN.

Ewha Womans University Library: 11–1, Daehyun-dong, Sudaemun-gu, Seoul 120-750; tel. 3277-3124; e-mail jnam@mm.ewha.ac.kr; internet lib.ewha.ac.kr; f. 1923; 1.7m. vols; Dir BONG HEE KIM.

Korea Foundation and Cultural Centre Library: Joogang Ilbo Bldg, 1st Fl., Sunhwa-dong 7, Jung-gu, Seoul 100-759; tel. (2) 2151-6500; e-mail kfcenter@kf.or.kr; f. 2005; 9,200 vols, 5,200 periodicals and multimedia materials, 170 CDs, 240 DVDs, 320 cassettes.

Korea University Library: 1 Anam-dong, Sungbuk-gu, Seoul 136-701; tel. (2) 3290-1470; e-mail libweb@korea.ac.kr; f. 1937; 400,132 vols; Dir SUNG GI JON.

Korean Braille Library: 510-23 Amsa-dong, Kang dong-ku, Seoul 134-052; tel. (2) 3426-7411; e-mail kbl@kbll.or.kr; internet www.infor.kbll.or.kr; f. 1969; Dir KEUN HAE YOUK.

National Assembly Library: 1 Yoido-dong, Seoul; tel. (2) 784-3565; e-mail webw3@nanet.go.kr; internet www.nanet.go.kr; f. 1952; library service for members of the Nat. Assembly, the Executive, the Judiciary, and for scholars and legislative research activities and int. book exchange with 360 instns worldwide; 900,000 vols, 12,101 current periodicals, 700 newspapers; Librarian JONG PIL YOO; publs *Acquisitions List* (1 a year), *Index to Korean-Language Periodicals* (6 a year and 1 a year), *Index to Korean Laws and Statutes* (2 a year), *Index to National Assembly Debates* (irregular), *Issue Briefs* (irregular), *Legislative Information Analysis* (4 a year), *National Assembly Library Review* (12 a year), *National Masters and Doctorate Theses Bibliography* (1 a year).

National Library of Korea: Banpo-ro 664, Seocho-gu, Seoul 137-702; tel. (2) 535-4142; e-mail nlkpc@www.nl.go.kr; internet www.nl.go.kr; f. 1945; 3.9m. vols; legal deposit library for Korean publications, ISBN, ISSN nat. centre, KOLIS-NET (Korean Library Information System Network) centre, international exchange, research in library and information science, publishes nat. bibliographies, operates National Digital Library (www.dlibrary.go.kr) and training centre for librarians; Dir GI-YOUNG JEONG; publ. *Doseogwan* (4 a year).

Seoul National University Library: San 56-1, Shillim-dong, Kwanak-gu, Seoul 151-742; tel. (2) 880-5284; e-mail libdb@snu.ac.kr; internet library.snu.ac.kr; f. 1946; 2.1m. vols, 13,000 periodicals, incl. Agricultural Library (121,000 vols), Medical Library (123,000 vols), Law Library (65,000 vols), Business Library (11,000 vols), Social Sciences Library (20,000 vols), Dental Library (9,000 vols) and Kyujang-gak Archives (spec. colln on Choseon Dynasty, 152,000 vols); collns on the arts, sciences, law, education, music, medicine, engineering, economics and commerce; Dir CHONG SUH KIM; publs *Ko-munseo* (1 a year), *Kyujang-gak* (1 a year).

Transport Library: 168, 2-ka, Bongnae-dong, Seoul; f. 1920; 32,000 vols; Dir CHO WOO HYUN; Chief Librarian KIM DOO HO; publ. *Korean National Railroad Bulletin* (12 a year).

United Nations Depository Library: Korea University, 1 An-Am-dong, Sungbuk-gu, Seoul; tel. (2) 3290-1492; f. 1957; 38,000 vols; Dir HWA-YOUNG KIM; Librarian MI-GYOUNG CHO.

Yonsei University Library: Yonsei University, 134 Sinchon-dong, Sudaemoon-gu, Seoul; tel. (2) 361-3308; e-mail leehg@yonsei.ac.kr; internet library.yonsei.ac.kr; f. 1915; 1.5m. vols, incl. Korean archives, 10,700 periodicals; Dir JONG CHUL HAN; publs *Abstracts of Faculty Research Report*, *Dong Bang Hak Chi* (Journal of Korean Studies), *Inmun Kwahak* (Journal of Humanities), *International Journal of Korean Studies*, *Journal of East and West Studies*, *Kyo Yuk Non Jib* (Journal of Education), *Yonsei Magazine*, *Yonsei Non-Chong* (Journal of Graduate School), *Yonsei Social Science Review*.

Museums and Art Galleries

Busan

Busan Museum: 48-1 Daeyeon 4-dong, Namgu, Busan, Seoul 608-092; tel. (51) 610-7111; e-mail museum@metro.busan.kr; internet museum.busan.kr; f. 1978, renovated in 2002; collns from prehistoric period to the present.

Attached Museums:

Bokcheon Museum: 50 Bokcheon-dong Dongnae-gu, Busan, Seoul 607-020; tel. (51) 554-4263; f. 1996; displays artefacts excavated from the tumulus group in Bokcheon-dong that show the history of Busan from the prehistoric age to the Three Kingdoms Era.

Busan Modern History Museum:.

Dongsam-dong Shell Midden Museum: 750-1 Dongsam-dong, Yeongdo-gu Busan.

Busan Museum of Modern Art: 1413 Woo 2 dong, Haeundae-gu, Busan; tel. (51) 744-2602; internet www.busanmoma.org; f. 1998; exhibitions, scholastic research, archive and presentation, int. exchange, education, cultural events; Dir CHO IL SANG.

Pusan National University Museum: San 30, Jangjeon-dong, Geumjeong-gu, Busan, 609-735; internet www.pnu-museum.org; tel. (51) 510-1838; tel. (51) 581-2455; f. 1956; Korean archaeology with spec. colln of historical remains of Kyongsang-Namdo province, arts, ethnology, etc.; Dir Prof. GYEONGCHEOL SHIN; publ. *Research Reports* (irregular).

Daegu

Daegu Bangjja Yugi Museum: 399 Dohak-dong, Dong-gu, Daegu; tel. (53) 606-6171; internet artcenter.daegu.go.kr/bangjja; f. 2000, opened in 2007; built to preserve Bangjja Yugi (Korean Bronzewear) considered a traditional cultural property; major items of the Bangjja Yugi incl. musical instruments, utensils and other items for religious services, tableware and living goods.

Daegu National Museum: San 41, Hwang-geum-dong, Suseong-gu, Daegu; tel. (53) 768-6051; e-mail webadmin@daegu.museum.go.kr; internet daegu.museum.go.kr; f. 1994; 30,000 items, art and archaeology; main collns on the material culture of Daegu, and western and northern parts of the Gyeong-sangbuk-do province.

Daegu University Central Museum: Daegu University Museum, 15 Naeri, Jil-lyang, Daegu, Gyeongbuk 712-714; tel. (53) 850-5621; internet museum.daegu.ac.kr; f. 1981; 19 cultural property excavations, 33 cultural property surfaces and 37 academic reports.

Daejeon

Daejeon Metropolitan Museum of Arts: near 396 Mannyeon-dong, Seo-gu, Expo Park Daejeon; tel. (42) 602-3225; e-mail mintae@daejeon.go.kr; internet dmma.metro.daejeon.kr; f. 1998; features modern art from both domestic and foreign artists; outdoor sculpture park.

Daejeon Prehistoric Museum: Oeun-dong, Yuseong-gu, Daejeon, Seoul 305-330; tel. (42) 826-2814; internet museum.daejeon.go.kr; f. 2007; prehistory of the Daejeon region, collns and artefacts.

Geological Museum: Daejeon, Seoul 305-350; tel. (42) 868-3797; internet museum.kigam.re.kr; history of the earth, fossils, evolution; rocks and geological structures, minerals and human, environment and geology.

Ungno Lee Museum: 396 Mannyon-dong, Seo-gu, Daejeon; tel. (42) 602-3270; internet www.ungnolee-museum.daejeon.kr; f. 2007, in memory of late Korean painter Goam Ungno Lee.

Yeojin Buddhist Art Gallery and Museum: 442-1 Tablib-dong, Yuseong-gu, Daejeon, Seoul 450-702; tel. (42) 934-8466; internet www.yeojingallery.co.kr.

Gwangju

Gwangju Museum of Art: 48 Bagmulgwan, Ro Buk-gu, Gwangju, Seoul 500-170; tel. (62) 510-0113; internet www.artmuse.gjcity.net; f. 1992.

Gwangju National Museum: 114 Bak-mulgwan-lo St, Maegok-dong, Buk-gu, Gwangju, Seoul 500-150; tel. (62) 570-7014; e-mail webadmin@gwangju.museum.go.kr; internet gwangju.museum.go.kr; f. 1978; cultural heritage of Gwangju.

Gyeonggi-do

Ansan Fishing Village Folk Museum: 717 Seongam-dong, Danwon-gu, Ansan-si, Gyeonggi-do; tel. (32) 886-0126; preserves and exhibits traditional folk customs and fishing culture of Ansan fishing village.

Bucheon Museum of Bow: 8 Sports Complex, Chunui-dong, Wonmi-gu, Bucheon-si, Gyeonggi-do; tel. (32) 614-2678; internet www.bcmuseum.or.kr; f. 2004; preserving traditional bow kukgung culture.

Chunghyeon Museum: 1085-16 Soha 2-dong, Gwangmyeong-si, Gyeonggi-do 423-828; tel. (2) 898-0505; e-mail manager@chunghyeon.org; internet www.chunghyeon.org; f. 2003; Dir HAM GEUMJA.

Deung-Jan Museum: 258-9 Nyeoungwon, Myonhun-myeon, Yongin-si, Gyeonggi-do 449-850; tel. (31) 334-0797; e-mail deungjan@deungjan.or.kr; internet www.deungjan.or.kr; f. 1997; colln of ethnic antique lamps.

Gyeonggi Museum of Modern Art: Dong-sangil 36, 667-1 Choji-Dong, Danweon-gu, Ansan-si, Gyeonggi-do 425-866; tel. (31) 481-7007; e-mail minerva8@hanmir.com; internet www.gma.or.kr; f. 2006; Dir KIN HONG-HEE.

Gyeonggi Provincial Museum: 85 Sang-gal-dong, Giheung-gu, Yongin-si, Gyeonggi-do, Seoul 446-905; tel. (31) 288-5300; e-mail museum@kg21.net; internet www.musenet.or.kr; f. 1996; spec. exhibitions on culture of Gyeonggi province; Dir KIM JAE-YEOL.

Haegang Ceramics Museum: 330-1 Suwang-li, Shintun-myeon, Icheon, Gyeonggi-do; tel. (31) 634-2266; internet www.haegang.org; f. 1990; Korean ceramics; offers ceramic production courses.

Ho-Am Art Museum: 204 Gasil-ri, Pogok-eup, Cheoin-gu, Yongin-si, Gyeonggi-do 449-

811; tel. (31) 320-1801; e-mail juliana.park@samsung.com; internet hoam.samsungfoundation.org; f. 1982; largest privately owned museum in S Korea; colln of over 1,200 Korean works of art; sculpture garden of works by French sculptor Bourdelle.

Woljeon Museum of Art: 467-020, Expo-gil 48, Gwango-dong 378, Icheon-si, Gyeonggi-do; tel. (31) 637-0033; e-mail iwoljeon@iwoljeon.org; internet www.iwoljeon.org; f. 1991 in Seoul, moved to Icheon in 2007; commemorates work of Korean painter Woljeon Chang Woo-Soung; 1,532 artworks.

Gyeongsangbuk-do

Andongsoju and Traditional Food Museum: 280 Susang-dong, Andong, Gyeongsangbuk-do; tel. (54) 858-4541; internet www.andongsoju.net; f. 2000; museum of traditional Andong distilled liquor.

Gyeongju National Museum: 118 Iljeongno, Gyeongju, Gyeongsangbuk-do, Seoul 780-150; tel. (54) 740-7500; internet gyeongju.museum.go.kr; f. 1945; preserves culture of the Silla Kingdom; Dir YOUNG-HOON YI.

Gyeongsangbuk-do Forest Science Museum: tel. (54) 855-8681; internet www.gbfsm.or.kr; preserves historical material and data on forests and conducts academic research; outdoor facilities divided by themes into hydroponics zone, landscaping zone, wooded zone, clean zone, ecological zone, botanical communities, traditional culture practice zone (mountain village culture), ornithological facility and greenhouse zone.

Hahoe Mask Museum: 287 Hahoe-ri, Pungchun-myun, Andong Gyeongsangbuk-do; tel. (571) 853-2288; internet www.tal.or.kr; hahoe masks and Korean masks.

Silla Art and Science Museum: Gyeongju Folk Hand Craft Village, Gyeongju, Gyeongsangbuk-do; tel. (54) 745-4998; internet www.sasm.or.kr; f. 1988; represents the scientific advancements and achievement of the Silla period; incl. spec. exhibits on the Sokkuram Grotto and Chomsongdae observatories.

Jeollabuk-do

Gangam Calligraphy Museum: 197-2 Gyo-dong, Wansan-gu, Jeonju-si, Jeollabuk-do; tel. (63) 285-7442; f. 1995; 1,000 works by Korean calligraphers Jeong-hui Kim (1786–1856), Sam-man Lee (1770–1845) and Yak-yong Jeong (1762–1836).

Jeonju National Museum: 900 Hyoja-dong 2 Ga, Wansa-Gu, Jeonju, Jeollabuk-do, Seoul 560-859; tel. (63) 223-5651; internet jeonju.museum.go.kr; 24,000 artefacts; history and culture of Jeollabuk-do; Buddhist art works, pottery, gold artefacts and folk material; Dir HYUNG SIK YOO.

Jeollanam-do

Mokpo Natural History Museum: 9-28 Yonghae-dong, Mokpo-si, Jeollanam-do; tel. (61) 274-3655; internet museum.mokpo.go.kr; f. 2004; natural history; 40,000 artefacts.

National Maritime Museum: 8 Yonghae-dong, Mokpo, Jeollanam-do; tel. (61) 270-2000; internet www.seamuse.go.kr; f. 1994; exhibits underwater cultural heritage from the Korean waters and maritime culture incl. nautical traditions and Korean traditional boats.

Seoul

Chiwoo Craft Museum: 610-11 Woomyun-dong, Seocho-gu, Seoul; internet www.chiwoocraftmuseum.org; f. 2002; modern crafts; Curator LEE IN BEOM.

National Museum of Contemporary Art: Deoksugung, 5-1 Jeong-dung, Jung-gu, Seoul 100-120; e-mail miaya@mct.go.kr; internet www.moca.go.kr; exhibitions; educational programmes for art professionals and school liaison; general programmes, programmes for children and youth.

National Museum of Korea: 135 Seobinggo-ro, Yongsan-gu, Seoul 140-026; tel. (2) 2077-9000; internet www.museum.go.kr; f. 1908; Korean archaeology, culture and folklore; 100,000 artefacts representing over 5,000 years of human endeavour on the Korean peninsula; education centre; library of 20,000 vols; brs in 8 other towns; Dir CHOE KWANG-SHIK; publs *Bakmulkwan Sinmun* (Museum News, 12 a year), *Misul Charyo* (Materials in Art, 2 a year), *Report of Researches of Antiquities*, *The International Journal of Korean Art and Archeology*.

National Science Museum: 2 Waryong-dong, Jongno-gu, Seoul 110-360; tel. (2) 3668-2200; internet www.ssm.go.kr; f. 1926; holds National Science Fair, exhibitions, science classrooms, film service, etc.; library of 2,000 vols on science and technology; Dir CHI-EUN KIM; publ. *Bulletin*.

Seoul National University Museum: 599 Gwanak-ro, Gwanak-gu, Seoul 151-742; tel. (2) 880-5333; internet museum.snu.ac.kr; f. 1941; exhibition of Korean culture totalling 8,058 artefacts; library specializing in Korean archaeology, art history, anthropology and folklore; Dir Dr NAK-KYU PARK; publ. *Bulletin* (1 a year).

Yonsei University Museum: Shinchon-dong, Sudaemun-gu, Seoul; tel. (2) 123-3335; e-mail art@yonsei.ac.kr; internet museum.yonsei.ac.kr; f. 1965; research; prehistory, history, fine arts, ethnic customs, medicine, geology, etc.; Curator YOUNG CHEOL BAK; publs occasional papers, excavation reports.

Universities

PUBLIC UNIVERSITIES

ANDONG NATIONAL UNIVERSITY

388 Songcheon-dong, Andong-si, Gyeongsangbuk, Seoul 460-380
Telephone: (54) 820-5114
E-mail: w3master@andong.ac.kr
Internet: www.andong.ac.kr

Founded 1979

Pres.: LEE HEE JAE
Registrar: KIM JONG-SIK
Librarian: KU SANG-MAN

Library of 55,000 vols
Number of teachers: 113
Number of students: 2,900

CHANGWON NATIONAL UNIVERSITY

9 Sarim-dong, Changwon, Gyeongnam, Seoul 641-773
Telephone: (55) 213-3000
E-mail: admission@changwon.ac.kr
Internet: www.changwon.ac.kr

Founded 1969 as Masan Jr College of Education; became Changwon Nat. College 1984; present name 1991

Pres.: HO PARK SEONG

CHONBUK NATIONAL UNIVERSITY

567 Baekju-daero, deokjin-gu, Jeonju-si 561-756
Telephone: (63) 270-2098
Internet: www.chonbuk.ac.kr

Founded 1947
State control
Academic year: March to February (2 semesters)

Colleges of agricultural sciences, arts, commerce, education, engineering, environmental and bioresource sciences, human ecology, liberal arts, natural science, nursing, public service, social sciences, veterinary medicine; graduate schools of engineering, humanities and social sciences, natural sciences; medical school

Pres.: SUH GEO-SUK

Library of 385,000 vols
Number of teachers: 800
Number of students: 24,000

CHONNAM NATIONAL UNIVERSITY

300 Yongbong-dong, Buk-gu, Gwangju, Seoul 500-757
Telephone: (62) 530-1271
Gwangju Campus: 77 Yongbong-ro, Buk-gu, Gwangju, Seoul 500-757
Telephone: (62) 530-5114
Yeosu Campus: San 96-1 Doondeok-dong, Jeonnam, Seoul
Telephone: (61) 659-2114
E-mail: cnupr@chonnam.ac.kr
Internet: www.chonnam.ac.kr

Founded 1952
State control
Languages of instruction: English, Korean
Academic year: March to February (2 semesters)

Pres.: Dr YOON SOO KIM
Dean of Academic Affairs: Dr KYUNG-AN SONG
Dean of Planning and Research: Dr MOON SOO BOK
Dean of Student Affairs: Dr WOO YANG CHUNG
Dean of Int. Affairs: Dr GYONGGU SHIN
Librarian: Dr YOON JUNG HAN

Library of 600,000 vols, 6,000 periodicals
Number of teachers: 2,435
Number of students: 37,314

Publications: *Chonnam Medical Journal*, *Chonnam Review of American Studies*, *Industrial Relations Research*, *Journal of Agricultural Science and Technology*, *Journal of Arts*, *Journal of Drug Development*, *Journal of Humanities Studies*, *Journal of Natural Science*, *Journal of Regional Development*, *Journal of Research Institute for Catalysis*, *Journal of Sciences for Better Living*, *Journal of Sports Science*, *Journal of Unification Studies*, *Language Teaching*, *Research on Honam Culture*, *Rural Development Review*, *Social Science Review*, *Technological Review*, *Yongbong Review*

DEANS

College of Agriculture: SEUNG JU MOON
College of Arts: AE-SOON SUNG
College of Business Admin.: TAEGI KIM
College of Dentistry: SUN HEON KIM
College of Education: JONG BAIK REE
College of Engineering: MAN JUNG
College of Human Ecology: SOOK LEE
College of Law: CHANG SUN SHIN
College of Medicine: MINCHUL LEE
College of Natural Sciences: MIN HUH
College of Pharmacy: SEUNG HOON CHEON
College of Social Sciences: SUNG SUK YOON
College of Veterinary Medicine: BONG JOO PARK
Graduate School: YONG NAM LEE
Graduate School of Business Admin.: SUNG-CHANG JUNG
Graduate School of Education: JONG BAEK LEE
Graduate School of Industry: HI-SEAK YOON

Graduate School of Public Admin.: DOO TAEK IM

CHUNGBUK NATIONAL UNIVERSITY

410 Seongbong-ro, Heungdeok-gu, Cheongju, Chungbuk, Seoul 361-763
Telephone: (43) 261-3172
E-mail: webmaster@chungbuk.ac.kr
Internet: www.chungbuk.ac.kr

Founded 1951 as Agricultural College, univ. status 1970
Academic year: March to December (semesters)

Pres.: LIM DONG CHOL
Dir of Admin.: KEE UN CHUNG
Dean of Academic Affairs: YOUNG SOO JEONG
Dean of Planning and Research Affairs: SOON SEOP KWAK
Dean of Student Affairs: SUNG HOO HONG
Dir of Library: SOON KEY JUNG

Library of 520,000 vols
Number of teachers: 700
Number of students: 18,000

Publications: *Journal of Agricultural Science Research, Journal of Genetic Engineering Research, Journal of Humanities, Journal of Language and Literature, Journal of Pharmaceutical Science, Journal of Social Science, Journal of the Industrial Science and Technology Institute, Journal of the Institute of Construction Technology, Journal of the Research Institute for Computer and Information Communication, Jungwon Munhwa Nonchong, Juris Forum, Law Journal, Review of Industry and Management*

DEANS

College of Commerce and Business Administration: DO WON SUH
College of Education: SHEON JOO CHIN
College of Engineering: LEE JAE KI
College of Home Economics: KI NAM KIM
College of Humanities: JANG SUNG JOONG
College of Law: JUN HUR
College of Medicine: YOUNG JIN SONG
College of Natural Science: BYUNG CHOON LEE
College of Pharmacy: HAN KUN
College of Social Science: HEE KYUNG KANG
College of Veterinary Medicine: YOUNG WON YUN

CHUNGNAM NATIONAL UNIVERSITY

79 Daehangno, Yuseong-gu, Daejon, Seoul 305-764
Telephone: (42) 821-5013
Internet: www.chungnam.ac.kr

Founded 1952
Academic year: March to June, September to December

Pres.: SONG YONG-HO
Dean of Academic Affairs: CHUL KYU CHOI
Dean of Student Affairs: KUN MOOK CHOI
Registrar: MYUNG KYUN KIM
Librarian: JONG UP CHO

Number of teachers: 880
Number of students: 20,000

DEANS

College of Agriculture: JONG WOO KIM
College of Economics and Management: CHUL HWAN CHUN
College of Engineering: SOO YOUNG CHUNG
College of Fine Arts and Music: CHEOL NAM
College of Home Economics: YOUNG JIN CHUNG
College of Humanities: HAE KIL SUH
College of Law: KANG YONG LEE
College of Medicine: JIN SUN BAI
College of Natural Sciences: JONG SUK CHOI
College of Pharmacy: BYUNG ZUN AHN
College of Social Sciences: TONG HOON KIM
College of Veterinary Medicine: MOO HYUNG JUN
Graduate School: CHONG HOE PARK
Graduate School of Business Administration: KEAN SHIK LEE
Graduate School of Education: SANG CHUL KANG
Graduate School of Industry: GUNG SUCK NAM
Graduate School of Public Administration: JAE CHANG KA
Graduate School of Public Health: SAE JIN CHOI

GANGNEUNG–WONJU NATIONAL UNIVERSITY

Gangneung Campus: 120 Gangneung Daehangno, Gangneung City, Gangwon-do, Seoul 210-702
Telephone: (33) 642-7001
Wonju Campus: 901 Namwon-ro, Wonju City, Gangwon-do, Seoul 220-711
Telephone: (33) 760-8114
E-mail: ciec@nukw.ac.kr
Internet: www.gwnu.ac.kr

Founded 1968 as Kangnung Educational College, became Kangnung Junior College 1977 and Kangnung Nat. College 1979, present name 1991
State control
Academic year: March to December (2 semesters)

Colleges of humanities, social sciences, natural sciences, engineering, life sciences, arts and physical education, dentistry; 17 research institutes, museum, gallery

Pres.: Dr HAN SONG
Dean of Center for Int. Exchange and Cooperation: CHI SUNG-PA

Library of 250,000 vols, 9,044 periodicals
Number of teachers: 628 (258 full-time, 370 part-time)
Number of students: 7,321

GYEONGSANG NATIONAL UNIVERSITY

900 Gazwa-dong, Jinju, Seoul 660-701
Telephone: (55) 751-6229
E-mail: belle@gshp.gsnu.ac.kr
Internet: www.gsnu.ac.kr

Founded 1948 as Gyeongnam Provincial Junior Agricultural College; became Gyeongnam Nat. College 1968 and Gyeongsang Nat. College 1972; present name 1979

Colleges of agriculture and life science, business administration, education, engineering, humanities, law, marine science, medicine, natural sciences, social sciences, veterinary medicine

Pres.: HA WOO-SONG

Number of teachers: 670
Number of students: 23,300 (21,100 undergraduate, 2,200 postgraduate)

JEJU NATIONAL UNIVERSITY

Jejudaehakno 66, Jeju, Jeju-si 690-756
Telephone: (64) 754-2114
E-mail: webmaster@jejunu.ac.kr
Internet: www.jejunu.ac.kr

Founded 1952 as Jeju Provincial Junior College; became Jeju Nat. College 1962; present name 1982
Academic year: March to February

Pres.: Dr CHOONG-SUK KOH

Number of teachers: 600
Number of students: 10,000

KANGWON NATIONAL UNIVERSITY

192-1 Hyoja-dong, Chuncheon-si, Gangwon-do, Seoul 200-701
Telephone: (33) 250-6114
E-mail: intn@cc.kangwon.ac.kr
Internet: www.kangwon.ac.kr

Founded 1947

Pres.: KWON YONG JUNG
Registrar: LIM HYUNG-SIK
Librarian: PARK KYUNG-HO

Library of 206,000 vols
Number of teachers: 378
Number of students: 16,000

DEANS

College of Agriculture: LEE SANG-YOUNG
College of Business Administration: SHIM JONG-SEOP
College of Education: CHOI KEUN-SEONG
College of Engineering: PARK JE-SEON
College of Forestry: KIM SU-CHANG
College of Humanities and Social Science: PARK HAN-SEOL
College of Law: KIM JEUNG-HU
College of Natural Sciences: LEE CHONG-HYEOK

KONGJU NATIONAL UNIVERSITY

182 Shinkwan-dong, Kongju, Chungnam
Telephone: (416) 850-8114
Internet: www.kongju.ac.kr

Founded 1948 as Kongju Provincial Teachers' College; became Kongju Nat. Teachers' College 1950; present name 1991

Pres.: Dr SUCK-WON CHOI
Dean for Academic Affairs: HYUNG-TAE MOON
Dir-Gen.: CHANG-YONG PARK

Library of 360,000 vols
Number of teachers: 602
Number of students: 13,560

DEANS

College of Education: BYUNG-MOO KIM
College of Engineering: KUM-BAE LEE
College of Humanities and Social Sciences: PIL-YOUNG LEE
College of Industrial Sciences: SEONG-MIN KIM
College of Sciences: YOUNG-KYUN WOO

KOREA ADVANCED INSTITUTE OF SCIENCE AND TECHNOLOGY (KAIST)

335 Gwahak-ro (373-1 Guseong-dong), Yuseong-gu, Daejeon, Seoul 305-701
Telephone: (42) 350-2114
E-mail: sugyeng@kaist.ac.kr
Internet: www.kaist.ac.kr

Founded 1981 by merger of Korea Advanced Institute of Science (KAIS) and Korea Institute of Science and Technology (KIST); KIST separated from KAIST 1989; Korea Institute of Technology (KIT) merged with KAIST 1989
State control
Academic year: March to February

Colleges of business, cultural science, engineering, information science and technology, interdisciplinary studies, life science and bioengineering, natural science

Pres.: NAM PYO SUH

Number of teachers: 541
Number of students: 8,217

KOREA MARITIME UNIVERSITY

1 Dongsam-dong, Yeongdo-gu, Busan, Seoul 606-791
Telephone: (51) 410-4114
E-mail: webmaster@hhu.ac.kr
Internet: www.hhu.ac.kr

Colleges of engineering, international studies, maritime sciences, ocean science and technology

Pres.: OH KEO DON

KOREA NATIONAL OPEN UNIVERSITY

169 Dongsung-dong, Chongro-ku, Seoul 110-791
Telephone: (2) 744-114
E-mail: webmaster@knou.ac.kr
Internet: www.knou.ac.kr

Founded 1972
State control
Academic year: March to February

Pres.: CHANG SEE WOM
Registrar: KIM EUI-DONG
Library Dir: KIM SUNG-KIH

Library of 412,000 vols
Number of teachers: 112
Number of students: 199,000

Publications: *Distance Education*, *KNOU Journal*, *KNOU Weekly*

DEANS

College of Education: CHOI CHONG-SOOK
College of Liberal Arts: LEE YONG-HAK
College of Natural Science: KIM HYE-SEON
College of Social Science: KIM SOO-SIN
School of General Education: LEE YUNG-HO

ATTACHED RESEARCH INSTITUTES

Educational Media Development Centre: Dir KWAK DUK-HUN.

Institute of Distance Education: Dir HONG SOON-JEONG

KOREA NATIONAL UNIVERSITY OF THE ARTS

120-3 Yesuk-gil, Seongbuk-gu, Seoul 136-716
Telephone: (2) 746-9042
E-mail: admissions@knua.ac.kr
Internet: www.knua.ac.kr

Founded 1993

Colleges of dance, drama, film, Korean traditional arts, music, television and multimedia, visual arts

Pres.: LEE GEON-YONG
Provost: KIM BONG-RYOL

Number of teachers: 730
Number of students: 2,600

KUNSAN NATIONAL UNIVERSITY

1170 Daehangno, Gunsan, Seoul 573-701
Telephone: (63) 469-4134
E-mail: inter@kunsan.ac.kr
Internet: www.kunsan.ac.kr

Founded 1979
Languages of instruction: Korean, English
Academic year: March to February

Pres.: Dr LEE HEE-YEON

Library of 280,000 vols
Number of teachers: 327
Number of students: 11,065

PROFESSORS

College of Arts, School of Fine Arts and Design:

- CHO, Y. B., Department of Industrial Design
- KIM, S. T., Department of Industrial Ceramic Arts
- KIM, Y. O., Department of Music

College of Engineering, Faculty of Electronic and Information Engineering:

- HEO, B. M., Department of Mechanical Design Engineering
- KIM, S. G., Materials Science and Engineering
- LEE, H. Y., Department of Chemical Engineering
- LEE, J. I., Electronic and Information Engineering
- LIM, B. Y., Department of Civil Engineering
- MOON, C. H., Department of Architectural Engineering

College of Humanities, Faculty of Oriental Language and Literature:

- CHO, S. H., Department of Korean Language and Literature
- LEE, H. H., Department of History
- LIM, K.-J., Department of Philosophy
- MOON, C.-S., Department of Japanese Language and Literature
- PAE, B. H., Department of German Literature and Language
- PARK, B.-S., Department of Chinese Language and Literature
- SEO, H. S., Department of English Language and Literature

College of Natural Sciences:

- CHOI, H. S., Department of Chemistry
- HANG, T. S., Department of Mathematics
- KIM, A. S., Department of Clothing and Textiles
- KIM, S. Y., Department of Food Science and Nutrition
- LEE, K. S., Department of Biological Science
- PARK, Y. S., Department of Informatics and Statistics
- RYOU, O. S., Department of Human Ecology
- YOON, C. S., Department of Physics

College of Ocean Science and Technology:

- CHANG, S. H., Department of Food Science and Technology
- CHUNG, E. Y., Department of Aquaculture and Biotechnology
- JEONG, K. J., Department of Marine Engineering
- KIM, Y. G., Department of Marine Life Science
- LEE, K. R., Department of Marine Science and Production
- SEO, S. W., Department of Ocean System Engineering
- YIH, W. H., Department of Ocean Information Science

College of Social Sciences:

- HWANG, H. M., International Trade
- KIM, Y.-J., Public Administration
- KWON, E. M., Business Administration and Accounting
- LIM, H. J., Economics and Trade

KWANGJU UNIVERSITY

Kwangju, Seoul 503-703
Telephone: (80) 670-2600
E-mail: ssyeom@gwangju.ac.kr
Internet: kwangju.ac.kr

Founded 1981 as Kwangju Kyung Sang Jr College; became Kwangju Open College 1984; present name 1989

Colleges of arts, commerce and social welfare, engineering, humanities and social sciences, management; graduate school

Pres.: Dr LEE JAE-WOON

Library of 230,000 vols

KYUNGPOOK NATIONAL UNIVERSITY

1370 Sankyuk-dong, Buk-gu, Daegu, Seoul 702-701
Telephone: (53) 950-6091
E-mail: kunglobal@knu.ac.kr
Internet: www.knu.ac.kr

Founded 1946
State control
Academic year: March to February (2 semesters)

Pres.: NOH DONGIL
Dean for Academic Affairs: Dr KIM KEE CHAN
Dean for General Affairs: Dr PARK SEUNG TAE
Dean for Planning and Research Support: Dr SOHN JAE KEUN
Dean for Student Affairs: LEE MIN HYUNG

Library: see under Libraries and Archives
Number of teachers: 825
Number of students: 24,504

Publication: *Research Review* (1 a year)

DEANS

College of Agriculture and Life Sciences: Dr CHOI JONG-UCK
College of Dentistry: Dr KYUNG HEE-MOON
College of Economics and Commerce: Dr SOHN BYEONG-HAE
College of Engineering: Dr LEE DONG-HO
College of Human Ecology: Dr YOO YOUNG-SUN
College of Humanities: Dr KIM KEE-CHAN
College of Law: Dr KANG TAE-SEONG
College of Medicine: Dr KWAK JOUNG-SIK
College of Music and Visual Arts: Dr KWON KI-DUCK
College of Natural Sciences: Dr MOON BYUNG-JO
College of Social Sciences: Dr KIM JAE-HONG
College of Veterinary Medicine: Dr LEE CHA-SOO
Graduate School: Dr KWON YON-UNG
School of Electrical Engineering and Computer Science: Dr LEE YONG-HYUN

PROFESSORS

College of Agriculture and Life Sciences (#223 College of Agriculture and Life Sciences Building I, Kyungpook National University, Daegu, Seoul 702-701; tel. (53) 950-5700):

- CHEONG, S.-T., Fruit Science, Plant Propagation
- CHO, R.-K., Food Chemistry
- CHOI, J., Soil Science
- CHOI, J.-U., Food Preservation Engineering
- CHOI, K., Forest Management and Economics
- CHOI, K.-S., Animal Breeding
- CHOI, K.-S., Economic Statistics
- CHOI, S.-T., Floriculture, Protected Cultivation
- CHOI, Y.-H., Food Engineering
- CHUNG, J.-D., Plant Tissue Culture
- CHUNG, M.-S., Tree Cultivation
- CHUNG, S.-K., Food Analysis and Sanitation
- CHUNG, S.-O., Irrigation and Drainage Engineering
- EOM, T.-J, Woody Plant Biochemistry
- HONG, S.-C., Forest Ecology
- HWANG, Y.-H., Plant Genetics
- JANG, I.-J., Agricultural Robot for Control Measurements
- JO, J.-K., Grass Physiology
- JUNG, S.-K., Landscape Construction
- KIM, B.-S., Vegetable Cultivation, Pepper Cultivation
- KIM, C.-S., Agricultural Policy
- KIM, D.-S., Dairy Microbiology
- KIM, D.-U., Plant Molecular Biology
- KIM, J.-E., Environmental Chemistry
- KIM, K.-U., Weed Science
- KIM, S.-G., Agricultural Marketing
- KIM, S.-K., Maize Breeding
- KIM, T.-H., Agricultural Power Energy Conservation
- KIM, Y.-S., Landscape Planning

KWON, M.-N., Geotechnical and Foundation Engineering
KWON, Y.-J., Systematic Entomology
LEE, H.-C., Agricultural Economic History
LEE, H.-T., Landscape Design
LEE, J.-T., Fungal Plant Pathology
LEE, J.-Y., Wood Chemistry
LEE, K.-C., Landscape Management
LEE, K.-M., Terramechanics, Greenhouse Controls
LEE, K.-W., Viral Plant Pathology
LEE, S.-C., Crop Production and Management
LEE, S.-G., Agricultural Buildings
NOH, S.-K., Insect Genetic Resources
PARK, I.-H., Landscape Plants
PARK, K.-K., Post-Harvest Process, Systems Mechanics
PARK, S.-J., Wood Anatomy
PARK, W.-C., Plant Nutrition
PARK, Y.-G., Forest Genetics
RHEE, I.-J., Fibre Materials Science
RHEE, I.-K., Biochemistry
RYU, J.-C., Agricultural Crops
SOHN, H.-R., Sericulture
SOHN, J.-K., Rice Cultivation
SON, D.-S., Forest Cultivation
SUH, S.-D., Hydrology, Land Engineering
SYN, Y.-B., Fruit Science, Plant Physiology
UHM, J.-Y., Bacterial Plant Pathology
YEO, Y.-K., Lipid Chemistry

College of Dentistry (#211 College of Dentistry, Kyungpook National University, Daegu, Seoul 702-701; tel. (53) 420-6801):

BAE, Y.-C., Oral Anatomy
CHO, S.-A., Prosthodontics
CHOI, J.-K., Oral Medicine
JO, K.-H., Prosthodontics
KIM, C.-S., Oral and Maxillofacial Surgery
KIM, K.-H., Dental Materials
KIM, Y.-J., Paediatric Dentistry
KWON, O.-W., Orthodontics
KYOUNG, H.-M., Orthodontics
LEE, S.-H., Oral and Maxillofacial Surgery
NAM, S.-H., Paediatric Dentistry
SONG, S.-B., Preventive Dentistry and Public Health Dentistry
SUNG, J.-H., Orthodontics

College of Economics and Commerce (#213 College of Economics and Commerce, Kyungpook National University, Daegu, Seoul 702-701; tel. (53) 950-5403):

BAE, B.-H., Managerial Accounting
CHANG, H.-S., Marketing
CHANG, J.-S., Industrial Organization
CHO, S.-P., Financial Accounting
CHOE, J.-M., Managerial Accounting
CHOI, Y.-H., Korean Economy
HA, I.-B., Macroeconomics
HAN, D.-H., International Economics
JUNG, C.-Y., Operations Management
KANG, H.-Y., Managerial Accounting
KIM, H.-K., Labour Economics
KIM, J.-J., Marketing
KIM, S.-H., Monetary Economics, International Economics
KIM, Y.-H., Economic Development, Korean Economic History
KWON, C.-T., Financial Accounting
KWON, S.-C., Financial Accounting
KWON, S.-K., Financial Accounting
LEE, D.-M., Management Information Systems
LEE, H.-W., Operations Management
LEE, J.-D., Financial Management
LEE, J.-K., International Commercial Law
LEE, J.-W., Income Distribution, Comparative Economics
LEE, J.-W., Personnel and Organization Management
LEE, S.-D., Personnel and Organization Management
LEE, S.-H., Marketing
LEE, Y.-S., International Transportation and Logistics
MOON, S.-H., Operations Management
NAH, K.-S., Economic History
PARK, C.-S., Financial Management
PARK, J.-H., Macroeconomics
SHIN, M.-S., Financial Management
SOHN, B.-H., International Economics

College of Engineering (#211 College of Engineering Building VI, Kyungpook National University, Daegu, Seoul 702-701; tel. (53) 950-5500):

AHN, K.-S., Digital Engineering
BAE, K.-S., Digital Signal Processing, Speech Signal Processing, Digital Communication
BAE, S.-K., Geochemical Engineering
BAEK, Y.-S., Power Systems Analysis
CHIEN, S.-I., Vision
CHO, J.-H., Bioelectronics, Electronic Measurements
CHO, S.-H., Ceramics for Electronics
CHO, Y.-J., Computer Networks
CHO, Y.-K., Antenna and Propagation, Ultrasonics
CHOI, H.-C., Wave Propagation
CHOI, H.-M., Parallel Distributed Processing, Processors, Logic Design
CHOI, M.-H., Architectural Planning and Design
CHOI, S.-J., Water Supply and Waste Water Treatment Engineering
CHOI, S.-Y., Semiconductor Engineering
CHOI, T.-H., Robotics
CHUNG, I.-S., Mechanical Metallurgy
HA, J.-M., Urban Design and City Planning
HA, Y.-H., Image Processing and Computer Vision Digital Signal Processing
HAN, K.-J., Computer Networks
HAN, K.-Y., Water Resources Engineering
HEO, N.-H., Zeolite Chemistry, Physical Chemistry
HONG, J.-K., Speech Signal Processing
HONG, S.-M., Control Theory
HWANG, C.-S., Visual Communication
JEON, G.-J., Intelligent Control, Systems Engineering
JI, B.-C., Polymer and Fibre Physics
JOO, E.-K., Digital Communication
KANG, I.-K., Biopolymers
KANG, M.-M., Architectural Structure
KIM, C.-H., Applied Mechanics
KIM, C.-J., Architectural Design
KIM, C.-Y., Microwave Engineering
KIM, D.-G., Power Electronics
KIM, D.-H., Reaction Engineering
KIM, D.-R., Surface Science and Engineering
KIM, H.-G., Power Electronics
KIM, H.-J., Pattern Recognition
KIM, H.-S., Synthetic Organic Chemistry
KIM, J.-J., Structural Ceramics
KIM, N.-C., Digital Communications, Image Communications
KIM, N.-K., Dielectric Materials
KIM, S.-H., Computational Geometry
KIM, S.-H., Synthetic Functional Dyes
KIM, S.-J., Geometry, Numerical Analysis
KIM, S.-J., Optical Signal Processing, Circuits and Systems
KIM, S.-M., Automata Theory
KIM, S.-S., Tribology
KIM, T.-J., Inorganic and Organometallic Chemistry, Homogeneous Catalysis
KIM, W.-J., Architectural Construction
KIM, W.-S., Architectural Construction
KIM, W.-S., Polymer Synthesis
KIM, Y.-M., Computer Graphics, Image Processing
KIM, Y.-S., Geotechnical Engineering
KWON, O.-J., Powder Metallurgy
KWON, S.-B., Fluid Mechanics
KWON, W.-H., Powder Electronics
KWON, Y.-D., Structural Analysis
KWON, Y.-H., Architectural Structure
LEE, B.-K., Powder Synthesis
LEE, C.-W., Combustion
LEE, D.-D., Semiconductor Engineering
LEE, D.-H., Polymerization Catalysis
LEE, J.-H., Semiconductor Technology
LEE, J.-T., Process Control
LEE, K.-I., Audio and Video Engineering, Electronic Measurements
LEE, K.-K., Non-linear Control Theory
LEE, M.-H., Instrumental Analysis, NMR Spectroscopy
LEE, S.-J., Natural Language
LEE, S.-R., Control and Automation
LEE, T.-J., Process and Property Thermodynamics
LEE, Y.-H., Semiconductor Engineering
LEE, Y.-M., Precision Machining
LIM, Y.-J., Dyeing Chemistry
MIN, K.-E., Physical Properties of Solid Polymers
MIN, K.-S., Water Quality Engineering
MOON, J.-D., Applied Electrostatics and High Voltage Applications
OH, C.-S., Computation, Analysis and Design of Electrical Machinery
OH, T.-J., Polymer and Fibre Chemistry
PARK, B.-O., Composite Materials
PARK, H.-B., Robust Control Theory
PARK, J.-K., Biochemical Engineering and Transport Phenomena
PARK, J.-S., Instrumentation, CAD, VLSI Design
PARK, K.-C., Joining and Metal Forming
PARK, K.-H., Robotics and Control
PARK, L.-S., Physical Properties of Polymer Solutions
PARK, M.-H., Structural Engineering
PARK, S.-K., Microelectronics
PARK, S.-T., Computer Networks, Databases
RIU, K.-J., Heat Transfer
RYU, K.-W., Parallel Algorithms
SEO, B.-H., Automatic and Digital Control, Computer Applications
SEO, K.-H., Polymer Processing
SHIM, S.-C., Petroleum Chemistry, Organic and Organometallic Chemistry
SHIN, S.-K., Semiconductor Engineering
SOHN, B.-K., Semiconductor Engineering
SOHN, J.-R., Catalytic Chemistry, Inorganic Material
SOHNG, K.-I., Video Engineering, Multiple Valued Logic Systems
SONG, D.-I., Polymer Rheology
SONG, J.-W., Optical Communication
SUH, C.-M., Materials and Mechanics
YE, B.-J., Casting, Solidification
YOO, K.-Y., Parallel Processing
YU, S.-D., Integrated Circuits

College of Human Ecology (#212 College of Human Ecology, Kyungpook National University, Daegu, Seoul 702-701; tel. (53) 950-6200):

CHOI, B.-G., Child Development
CHOI, M.-S., Nutritional Biochemistry
KANG, M.-Y., Nutrition
LEE, H.-S., Nutrition

College of Humanities (#209 College of Humanities, Kyungpook National University, Daegu, Seoul 702-701; tel. (53) 950-5100):

BANG, I., Oriental Philosophy
CHEON, K.-S., Korean Syntax
CHO, M.-H., British and American Drama
CHOI, S.-S., German Literature, Classical Literature
CHOY, C.-H., Korean History
CHUNG, I.-S., Chinese Linguistics
CHUNG, J.-S., English Linguistics, Syntax
EUN, J.-N., Modern Anglo-American Literature
HAN, S.-Z., German Literature
HONG, S.-M., Korean Linguistics
HWANG, W.-Z., Korean Literature
JANG, T.-W., Chinese Linguistics
JU, B.-D., Korean History

KIM, C.-D., Political and Economic Anthropology
KIM, C.-G., Western History
KIM, C.-S., British Poetry
KIM, C.-W., German Drama
KIM, D.-M., Oriental Philosophy
KIM, I.-L., Korean Classical Literature
KIM, K.-C., English Linguistics
KIM, K.-S., Korean Classical Literature
KIM, S.-W., Korean Chinese Literature
KIM, Y.-D., Western Philosophy
KIM, Y.-K., Western Philosophy
KWON, K.-H., Modern Korean Literature
KWON, T.-R., Chinese Linguistics
KWON, Y.-U., Korean History
LEE, C.-S., Chinese Literature
LEE, D.-H., German Literature
LEE, E.-Y., French Phonology
LEE, H.-J., Archaeology
LEE, H.-J., Chinese Literature
LEE, J.-H., Japanese Literature
LEE, K.-E., Russian Literature
LEE, K.-J., German Idealism
LEE, P.-S., French Syntax
LEE, S.-G., Korean Dialectology
LEE, W.-K., English Literature
PAEK, D.-H., Korean Philology
PARK, C.-B., English Literature
PARK, J.-G., French Literature
PARK, S.-W., German Linguistics
PARK, Y.-H., Korean Chinese Literature
SHIN, O.-H., Western Philosophy
SOHN, H.-S., English Linguistics
YI, B.-K., Bronze Age Archaeology, Museology
YI, K.-S., Chinese History
YOO, K.-S., Western History

College of Law (#305 College of Law, Kyungpook National University, Daegu, Seoul 702-701; tel. (53) 950-5456):

CHANG, J.-H., Civil Law
KANG, T.-S., Civil Law
KIM, S.-T., Local Public Administration and Finance
KIM, Y.-S., Land Policy
LEE, Y.-J., Financial Administration
MOON, K.-S., Policy Sciences, Financial Management
PARK, J.-H., Urban Planning
PARK, J.-T., Commercial Law
RHEE, W.-W., Urban Administration

College of Medicine (#208 College of Medicine, Kyungpook National University, Daegu, Seoul 702-701; tel. (53) 420-6901; internet med.knu.ac.kr):

BAEK, W.-Y., Intensive Care Therapy
BAIK, B.-S., Craniofacial Surgery
CHAE, J.-M., Forensic Pathology
CHAE, S.-C., Cardiology
CHANG, S.-I., Surgery, Paediatric Surgery
CHANG, S.-K., Transplantation, Tumours
CHO, D.-K., Nephrology
CHO, D.-Y., Molecular Genetics
CHO, H.-J., Neuroanatomy
CHO, T.-H., Oncology
CHO, Y.-L., Gynaecological Oncology
CHOI, Y.-H., Gastroenterology
CHUN, B.-Y., Health Care Administration and Health Policy
CHUN, S.-S., Reproductive Endocrinology and Infertility
CHUNG, B.-Y., Adult Nursing, Cancer Nursing
CHUNG, J.-M., Gastroenterology
CHUNG, S.-L., Dermatology, Leprosy
CHUNG, T.-H., Immunology
DOH, B.-N., Psychiatric and Mental Health Nursing
HAMM, I.-S., Cerebrovascular Disease, Neuro-Oncology
HONG, H.-S., Anatomy, Medical Genetics
HONG, J.-G., Pain Clinic
HWANG, S.-K., Paediatric Neurosurgery
IHN, J.-C., Joint Reconstructive Surgery
JUN, J.-B., Dermatology, Mycology, Dermatopathology
JUN, J.-E., Cardiology
JUN, S.-H., Surgery, Colorectal Surgery
JUNG, M.-S., Women's Health Nursing
JUNG, S.-K., Paediatric Urology, Traumatology
KANG, D.-J., Psychiatry, Psychopharmacology
KANG, D.-S., Thoracic Radiology
KIM, B.-W., Endocrinology, Metabolism
KIM, B.-W., Tumours
KIM, C.-Y., Cardiovascular Pharmacology
KIM, D.-W., Dermatology
KIM, H.-M., Paediatrics, Neonatology
KIM, I.-T., Vitreous Humour and Retina
KIM, J.-C., Cellular and Molecular Immunology
KIM, K.-T., Paediatric Cardiovascular Surgery
KIM, M.-Y., Paediatric Nursing
KIM, N.-S., Allergology, Rheumatology
KIM, P.-T., Hand Surgery
KIM, S.-L., Cerebrovascular Disease
KIM, S.-Y., Vitreous Humour and Retina
KIM, T.-H., Diagnostic Radiology
KIM, Y.-I., Surgery
KIM, Y.-J., Interventional Radiology
KIM, Y.-W., Vascular Surgery
KOO, J.-H., Paediatrics, Nephrology
KWAK, J.-S., Forensic Pathology
KWAK, Y.-S., Pharmacy
KWON, J.-Y., Paediatric Ophthalmology
LEE, J.-B., Family Medicine
LEE, J.-T., Cardiovascular Surgery
LEE, J.-Y., Occupational Neurology
LEE, K.-B., Nuclear Medicine
LEE, K.-S., Paediatrics, Haemato-Oncology and Genetics
LEE, M.-G., Neuropsychological Pharmacology
LEE, S.-B., Paediatrics, Cardiology
LEE, S.-H., Otology, Neuro-Otology
LEE, S.-K., Biostatistics and Nutritional Epidemiology
LEE, S.-N., Psychiatry, Psychotherapy
LEE, W.-J., Renal Physiology
LEE, W.-K., Clinical Microbiology
LEE, Y.-C., Virology
LEE, Y.-H., Surgery, Head and Neck Endocrine Surgery
PARK, B.-C., Paediatric and Spinal Surgery
PARK, I.-H., Oncology and Infection
PARK, I.-K., Radiation Oncology, Radiation Biology
PARK, I.-S., Gynaecological Oncology
PARK, J.-H., Fundamentals of Nursing
PARK, J.-S., Cardiovascular Physiology
PARK, J.-S., Head and Neck Oncology
PARK, J.-W., Vascular Pharmacology and Anaesthesia
PARK, J.-Y., Health Care Administration and Health Policy
PARK, S.-Y., Adult Nursing
PARK, W.-H., Cardiology
PARK, Y.-K., Andrology
PARK, Y.-M., Spinal Neuro-Oncology, Neurotrauma
RIM, H.-D., Psychiatry, Psychosomatics
SEOL, S.-Y., Molecular Epidemiology
SOHN, Y.-K., Neuropathology
SUH, C.-K., Neurology
SUH, I.-S., Pathology of the Gastrointestinal Tract
SUH, J.-S., Diagnostic Haematology
SUH, S.-R., Adult Nursing
YEO, M.-H., Epidemiology and Population Dynamics
YU, W.-S., Surgery, Surgical Oncology
YUN, Y.-K., Surgery, Hepatobiliary Surgery

College of Music and Visual Arts (#217 College of Music and Visual Arts, Kyungpook National University, Daegu, Seoul 702-701; tel. (53) 950-5650):

BYUN, Y.-B., Sculpture
CHONG, H.-I., Kayagum (12-Stringed Zither)
CHUNG, H.-C., Composition
JUNG, W.-H., Piano
KANG, C.-S., Piano
KIM, G.-J., Voice (Soprano)
KIM, J.-W., Voice (Baritone)
KIM, K.-I., Piano
KIM, W.-S., Korean Painting
KU, Y.-K., Komungo (6-Stringed Zither)
KWON, K.-D., Visual Design
LEE, D.-C., Oil Painting
LEE, E.-S., Piano
LEE, K.-J., Kayagum (12-Stringed Zither)
LEE, W.-S., Visual Design
LIM, H.-S., Clarinet
OH, H.-C., Oil Painting
PARK, N.-H., Art History
SHIM, S.-H., Voice (Tenor)
YI, T.-B., Theory of Korean Music and Taegum (Korean Transverse Flute)
YOO, H., Korean Painting
YOON, J.-R., Cello
YUN, M.-G., Piri (Korean Oboe)

College of Natural Sciences (#201 College of Natural Sciences, Kyungpook National University, Daegu, Seoul 702-701; tel. (53) 950-5300):

BAE, Z.-U., Analytical Chemistry
CHANG, T.-W., Structural Geology
CHO, K.-H., Statistical Inference
CHOI, J.-K., Probability, Stochastic Processes
CHOI, S.-D., Condensed Matter Theory
HA, J.-H., Microbial Genetics
HUH, T.-L., Molecular Genetics
JEE, J.-G., Physical Chemistry
JEONG, J.-H., Inorganic Chemistry
JIN, I.-N., Enzymology
JO, S.-G., High Energy Physics Theory
JUNG, I.-B., Analysis
KANG, H.-D., Experimental Nuclear Physics
KANG, S.-S., Biochemistry and Animal Physiology
KIM, E.-S., Algebra
KIM, H.-S., Analysis
KIM, I.-S., Biochemistry
KIM, J.-G., Microbial Genetics
KIM, K.-E., Precipitation Mechanism
KIM, S.-W., Computer Languages
KIM, S.-W., Petrology
KIM, Y.-H., Cellular Immunobiology
KOH, I.-S., Sedimentology, Sedimentary Petrology
KWAK, Y.-W., Organic Chemistry
LEE, E.-W., Surface and Thin Films Experiments
LEE, H.-H., Analysis
LEE, H.-L., Analytical Chemistry
LEE, H.-R., Condensed Matter Theory
LEE, I.-S., Statistical Inference, Theoretical Statistics
LEE, J.-K., Organic Chemistry
LEE, J.-Y., Virology
LEE, K.-M., Radiative Transfer, Upper Atmosphere
LEE, S.-H., Analysis
LEE, S.-K., Information Visualization
LEE, S.-Y., Thin Film and Electroluminescence Experiments
LEE, Y.-H., Biochemical Engineering
LEE, Y.-S., Cellular Biochemistry
MIN, K.-D., Atmospheric Energetics
MOON, B.-J., Biochemistry
PARK, B.-G., Reliability Analysis
PARK, C.-Y., Topology
PARK, H.-C., Animal Taxonomy
PARK, J.-H., Plant Systematics
PARK, J.-W., Biochemical Carcinogenesis
PARK, W., Molecular Biology
PARK, Y.-B., Biochemistry
PARK, Y.-C., Database Systems
PARK, Y.-C., Inorganic Chemistry

PARK, Y.-S., Algebra
PARK, Y.-T., Organic Chemistry
SEO, B.-B., Genetics
SOHN, J.-K., Bayesian Decision Theory, Statistical Computing
SOHN, K.-S., Condensed Matter Theory
SOHN, U.-I., Molecular Biology
SON, D.-C., Experimental High Energy Physics
SONG, J.-K., Multivariate Data Analysis
SONG, S.-D., Plant Physiology
SUH, Y.-J., Geometry

College of Social Sciences (#315 College of Social Sciences, Kyungpook National University, Daegu, Seoul 702-701; tel. (53) 950-5200):

CHIN, S.-M., Industrial Sociology
CHO, H.-C., Counselling Psychology
CHOI, C.-M., Social Welfare Administration
CHOI, K.-S., Social Psychology
HAN, N.-J., Sociology of Family
JIN, Y.-S., Cognitive Psychology
KIM, J.-H., Ethics and Legal Studies in Mass Communication
KIM, W.-H., International Relations
KIM, Y.-H., Clinical Psychology
KIM, Y.-H., Social Policy
LEE, J.-H., Regional Geography
LEE, Y.-J., Information Science
NAM, K.-H., Bibliography
NOH, D.-I., Korean Politics
PARK, B.-S., Clinical Social Work
PARK, J.-S., Political Communication Theory
PARK, J.-W., Population Studies
PARK, K.-S., Broadcasting
PARK, S.-D., Social Security
PARK, Y.-C., Regional Development, Economic Geography
SHON, J.-P., Library Management
YOON, Y.-H., Comparative Politics

College of Veterinary Medicine (#205 College of Veterinary Medicine, Kyungpook National University, Daegu, Seoul 702-701; tel. (53) 950-5950):

BYUN, M.-D., Veterinary Obstetrics
CHOI, W.-P., Veterinary Microbiology
JANG, I.-H., Veterinary Surgery, Veterinary Obstetrics
KIM, B.-H., Veterinary Microbiology
KIM, Y.-H., Veterinary Obstetrics
LEE, C.-S., Veterinary Pathology
LEE, J.-H., Veterinary Medicine
MOON, M.-H., Veterinary Parasitology
PARK, C.-K., Veterinary Microbiology
TAK, R.-B., Veterinary Public Health
YU, C.-J., Veterinary Physiology

Teachers' College:

AHN, B.-H., Space Physics
BAE, H.-D., Politics, Political Thought
BAE, J.-E., English Literature
CHAE, H.-W., Training
CHANG, D.-I., Medieval Korean History
CHUNG, D.-H., German Linguistics
CHUNG, H.-P., Philosophy of Education
CHUNG, H.-S., Cell Biology, Photosynthesis
CHUNG, S.-T., Sport Psychology
CHUNG, W.-W., Mineralogy
HONG, Y.-P., Politics, Political Thought
HWANG, B.-S., French Linguistics
HWANG, S.-G., Algebra
IM, J.-R., Korean Linguistics
JANG, H.-S., Nutrition
JANG, Y.-O., Home Management
JO, P.-G., Clothing
JO, W.-R., Geomorphology
JUN, B.-Q., English Linguistics
KANG, Y.-H., Astronomy
KI, U.-H., Geometry
KIM, B.-K., Counselling
KIM, H.-K., Economic Development
KIM, H.-S., Early Modern East Asian History
KIM, J.-J., Dance
KIM, J.-T., Korean Linguistics
KIM, J.-W., Contemporary Western History
KIM, K.-H., Measurement and Evaluation for Physical Education
KIM, M.-H., Educational Administration
KIM, M.-K., Korean Literature
KIM, M.-N., Philosophy of Education
KIM, S.-H., Educational Psychology
KIM, Y.-H., Geometry
KOH, J.-K., Particle Physics, Physics Education
LEE, A.-H., Educational Psychology
LEE, B.-H., Early Modern Korean History
LEE, J.-H., Korean Literature
LEE, J.-H., Politics, International Politics
LEE, J.-W., Population Geography, Geographical Education
LEE, M.-H., Biomechanics
LEE, M.-J., Educational Psychology
LEE, M.-K., Ancient Korean History
LEE, M.-S., Physical Chemistry
LEE, N.-G., Rural Sociology
LEE, O.-B., Social Education
LEE, S.-B., Statistics and Critical Phenomena
LEE, S.-C., Sports Nutrition
LEE, S.-T., Korean Linguistics
LEE, W.-B., Organic Chemistry
LEE, Y.-J., Petrology
LIM, C.-K., German Literature
MOON, S.-H., Western Philosophy
OH, C.-H., Optics, Quantum Electronics
OH, D.-S., History of Physical Education
OH, Y.-S., Public Economics
PAK, J.-S., Geometry
PARK, C.-Y., Educational Administration
PARK, D.-K., Plasma Physics
PARK, J.-Y., English Literature
PARK, K.-S., Teaching English as a Second Language
PARK, T.-H., Urban Geography
RIM, S.-H., Algebra
RYU, S.-E., German Drama
SEO, J.-M., Korean Literature
SHIN, K.-J., French Literature
SHIN, Y.-G., Teaching of Physical Education
SOHN, J.-K., Animal Physiology
SONG, B.-H., Microbiology, Molecular Biology
SONG, W.-C., Politics, Political Thought
YANG, H.-J., Animal Morphology, Ecology
YANG, J.-S., Climatology
YANG, S.-Y., Palaeobiology
YI, M.-S., French Linguistics
YOH, S.-D., Organic Chemistry
YOO, Y.-J., Analysis
YOON, I.-H., Micrometeorology
YOON, J.-L., Educational Psychology

MOKPO NATIONAL MARITIME UNIVERSITY

Haeyangdaehang-Ro 91, Mokpo-si, Jeollanam-do 530-729

Telephone: (631) 240-7045
E-mail: ryujb@mmu.ac.kr
Internet: www.mmu.ac.kr

Founded 1950

Faculties of marine electronic and communication engineering, marine engineering, maritime transportation system, ocean system engineering; liberal arts centre

Pres.: Dr BYUNGJU OH

Library of 130,000 vols
Number of teachers: 97
Number of students: 2,417

MOKPO NATIONAL UNIVERSITY

61 Dorim-ri, Chonggye-myeon, Muan-gun 534-729

Telephone: (61) 450-2114
Internet: www.mokpo.ac.kr

Founded 1946 as Mokpo Teacher-Training School, present name and status 1990

Colleges of business administration, education, engineering, human ecology, humanities, music and fine arts, natural sciences, pharmacy, physical education, social sciences

Pres.: KO SEOK-KYU

Number of teachers: 810
Number of students: 12,900

NATIONAL FISHERIES UNIVERSITY OF BUSAN

599-1 Daeyun-dong, Nam-gu, Busan 608-737

Telephone: (51) 622-3951

Founded 1941 as Busan Fisheries College, attained university status 1990

Pres.: SUN-DUCK CHANG
Dean of Academic Affairs: YONG RHIM YANG
Dean of General Affairs: SE WHA SONG
Dean of Planning Research: YONG JOO KANG
Dean of Student Affairs: HYUN WOO CHUNG
Librarian: JAI YUL KONG

Library of 130,000 vols
Number of teachers: 306
Number of students: 7,700

Publications: *Bulletin*, *Natural Sciences* (2 a year), *Publication of Institute of Marine Sciences* (1 a year), *Social Sciences* (2 a year), *The Theses Collection of the Faculty Members*

DEANS

College of Business Administration: CHUNG YUL YU
College of Engineering: CHUNG KIL PARK
College of Fisheries Sciences: CHUL HYUN SOHN
College of Marine Sciences and Technology: YONG QUIN KANG
College of Natural Sciences: MAN DONG HUR
College of Social Sciences: CHARLES KIM

PUKYONG NATIONAL UNIVERSITY

559-1 Daeyon-dong, Nam-gu, Busan Seoul

Telephone: (51) 620-6114
E-mail: web@pknu.ac.kr
Internet: www.pknu.ac.kr

Founded 1996 by the amalgamation of Nat. Fisheries Univ. of Pusan and Pusan Nat. Univ. of Technology

Pres.: PARK MAENG EON
Dean of Academic Affairs: NAM SONG-WOO
Dean of Gen. Affairs: HWANG IN-CHUL
Dean of Planning Office: JUNG HYUN-CHAN
Dean of Student Affairs: HEUNG IL-PARK
Dir of Library: PYO YONG-SOO

Number of teachers: 664
Number of students: 23,671 (23,336 undergraduates, 335 graduates)

DEANS

Faculty of Business Administration: HA JONG-WOOK
Faculty of Engineering: LEE HYUNG-GI
Faculty of Environmental and Marine Science and Technology: KIM DAE-CHOUL
Faculty of Fisheries Science: BYUN DAE-SEOK
Faculty of Humanities and Social Sciences: SEUNG RAE-LEE
Faculty of Natural Sciences: KIM SE-KWON

PUSAN NATIONAL UNIVERSITY

30 Jangjeon-dong, Kumjeong-ku, Pusan 609-735

Telephone: (51) 510-1293
E-mail: pnuadmin@pusan.ac.kr
Internet: www.pusan.ac.kr

Founded 1946
Academic year: March to February

Pres.: INN-SE KIM
Dean of Academic Affairs: SANG-WOOK PARK
Dean of Planning and Research: JUNG-DUK LIM
Dean of Student Affairs: IN-BO SIM
Dir of General Affairs: SANG-WOO HAN
Dir of Library: DONG-HYUN JUNG
Library: see under Libraries and Archives
Museum: see Museums
Number of teachers: 967
Number of students: 24,670
Publications: *College Academic Journal*, *University Academic Journal* (annual collection of theses)

DEANS

College of Arts: EUL-MEE PARK
College of Business: BEUNG-GEUN MUN
College of Dentistry: LI-HEE YUN
College of Education: HONG-WOOK HUH
College of Engineering: MAN-HYUNG LEE
College of Human Ecology: YEONG-OK SONG
College of Humanities: JIN-NONG CHUNG
College of Law: BAE-WON KIM
College of Medicine: YONG-KI KIM
College of Natural Sciences: SANG-JOON LEE
College of Pharmacy: JEE-HYUNG JUNG
College of Social Sciences: HYUN-JUNG SHIN
Graduate School: JUNG-KEUN KIM
Graduate School of Education: HONG-WOOK HUH
Graduate School of Environment: MAN-HYUNG LEE
Graduate School of Industry: MAN-HYUNG LEE
Graduate School of Management: BEUNG-GEUN MUN
Graduate School of Public Administration: KI-HYUNG RYU

SEOUL NATIONAL UNIVERSITY

599 Gwanak-ro, Gwanak-gu, Seoul 151-742
Telephone: (2) 880-5114
E-mail: webmaster@snu.ac.kr
Internet: www.snu.ac.kr
Founded 1946
State control
Academic year: March to February
Pres.: JANG-MOO LEE
Vice-Pres.: SHIN BOK KIM
Vice-Pres. and Dean of Graduate School: HASUCK KIM
Dean for Academic Affairs: MYUNG HWAN KIM
Dean for Planning and Devt: CHONG NAM CHU
Dean for Research Affairs: JIN-HO SEO
Dean for Student Affairs: CHAE-SEONG CHANG
Chief of Gen. Admin.: IN-CHEOL HWANG
Dir-Gen. of Library: NAM JIN HUH
Library: see under Libraries and Archives
Number of teachers: 4,063
Number of students: 26,030
Publication: *University Gazette* (52 a year)

DEANS

College of Agriculture and Life Sciences: MOO HA LEE
College of Business Administration: TAE SIK AHN
College of Dentistry: PILL HOUN CHOUNG
College of Education: CHUNG-IL YUN
College of Engineering: TAI JIN KANG
College of Fine Arts: YOUNG GULL KWON
College of Human Ecology: IN KYEONG HWANG
College of Humanities: CHANG-KU BYUN
College of Law: JONG-SUP CHONG
College of Medicine: JUNG-GI IM
College of Music: TAI-BONG CHUNG
College of Natural Sciences: JONG SEOB LEE
College of Nursing: MI SOON SONG
College of Pharmacy: YOUNG-GER SUH
College of Social Sciences: HYUN-CHIN LIM
College of Veterinary Medicine: OH KYEONG KWEON
Graduate School: TAE SOO LEE
Graduate School of Business: TAE SIK AHN
Graduate School of Dentistry: PILL-HOON CHOUNG
Graduate School of Environmental Studies: KEE WON HWANG
Graduate School of Int. Studies: TAEHO BARK
Graduate School of Public Administration: JONGWON CHOI
Graduate School of Public Health: HAI WON CHUNG

SUNCHON NATIONAL UNIVERSITY

315 Maegok-dong, Sunchon, Chonnam 540-742
Telephone: (661) 750-3114
E-mail: webmaster@sunchon.ac.kr
Internet: www.sunchon.ac.kr
Founded 1935
State control
Academic year: March to December
Pres.: Dr JAE-KI KIM
Deans: Dr WON-OG YANG (Academic Affairs), Dr JONG-CHUN CHOI (Student Affairs), Dr NAM-HOON CHO (University Planning and Research), DOO-HEE LEE (General Affairs)
Librarian: Dr JIN-IL DOO
Library of 211,000 books
Number of teachers: 340
Number of students: 12,560 (11,117 undergraduate, 1,443 postgraduate)

DEANS

College of Agriculture and Life Science: Dr DONG-HWAN OH
College of Education: Dr SANG-WOOK HAN
College of Engineering: Dr BONG-CHAN BAN
College of Humanities and Social Sciences: Dr JUNG-SUN SHIM
College of Natural Sciences: Dr MAN-CHAI JANG

SUWON UNIVERSITY

San 2-2 Wawoo-ri, Bongnam-myun, Hwasung-si, Gyeonggi-do 445-743
E-mail: info@suwon.mail.co.kr
Internet: www.suwon.ac.kr
Founded 1982
Chair.: IN-SOO LEE
Pres.: D. Y. YOON

YOSU NATIONAL UNIVERSITY

96-1 Dundeok-dong, Yosu-shi, Chollanam-do 550-749
Telephone: (662) 659-2114
Internet: www.yosu.ac.kr
Founded 1917 as Yosu Public Fisheries School; became Yosu Public Fisheries Middle School 1946, Yosu National Fisheries High School 1963, Yosu National Fisheries Junior College 1979, Yosu National Fisheries College 1987, Yosu National Fisheries University 1993; present name 1998
Colleges of engineering, fisheries and ocean science, humanities and social science, natural science; graduate schools of education, and industry and technology
Pres.: HA-JOON KIM
Number of teachers: 212
Number of students: 5,064

PRIVATE UNIVERSITIES

AJOU UNIVERSITY

5 Woncheon-dong, Yeongtong-gu, Suwon, Seoul 443-749
Telephone: (2) 231-7121
E-mail: inter@ajou.ac.kr
Internet: www.ajou.ac.kr
Founded 1973
Colleges of business administration, engineering, humanities, medicine, natural sciences, social sciences; graduate school
Pres.: SUH MOON HO
Registrar: JOON YOP KIM
Librarian: JAE SUK LEE
Library of 230,000 vols
Number of teachers: 750
Number of students: 10,954

CATHOLIC UNIVERSITY OF DAEGU

13-13 Hayang-ro, Hayang-eup, Gyeongsan-si 712-702
Telephone: (53) 850-3052
E-mail: presid@cuth.cataegu.ac.kr
Internet: www.cu.ac.kr
Founded 1914
Private control
Colleges of design, economics and commerce, education, engineering, fine arts, foreign studies, health and medical science, hospitality and tourism administration, home economics, humanities, law, liberal arts, medicine, music, natural sciences, nursing, pharmacy, social sciences, theology
Pres.: CHUL HONG
Library of 410,000 vols
Number of teachers: 780
Number of students: 17,000
Publication: *Research Bulletin* (1 a year)

CATHOLIC UNIVERSITY OF KOREA

Songeui Campus: 505 Banpo-dong, Socho-gu, Seoul 137-701
Telephone: (2) 590-1081
Songsim Campus: 43-1 Yeokgok 2-dong, Wonmi-gu, Bucheon City, Gyeonggi-do 420-743
Telephone: (2) 2164-4000
Songsin Campus: 90-1 Hyehwa-dong, Jongro-gu, Seoul 110-758
Telephone: (2) 740-9704
E-mail: webmaster@catholic.ac.kr
Internet: www.cuk.ac.kr
Founded 1995 by merger of Catholic Univ. (f. c. 1984 from existing colleges) with Songsim Women's Univ. (f. 1957)
Songeui Campus: incl. Colleges of Medicine, and Nursing; Graduate Schools of Occupational Health, and Health Management; Songsim Campus: incl. Colleges of Humanities, Social Sciences, Science and Technology, and Human Ecology; Songsin Campus: incl. College of Theology
Pres.: Rev. PAHK JOHAN YEONG-SIK
Library of 160,000 vols
Number of teachers: 914
Number of students: 8,075 (6,772 undergraduate, 1,303 postgraduate)
Publication: *Catholic Theology and Thoughts* (1 a year)

CHEONGJU UNIVERSITY

36 Naedok-dong, Sangdang-ku, Cheongju 360-764
Telephone: (43) 229-8114
Internet: www.cheongju.ac.kr
Founded 1946 as Cheongju Commercial College; became Cheongju College 1951; present name 1981
Pres.: KIM YOON BAE

CHOSUN UNIVERSITY

375 Seosuk-dong, Dong-gu, Gwangju, Seoul 501-759

Telephone: (62) 230-7114
E-mail: webmaster@chosun.ac.kr
Internet: www.chosun.ac.kr

Founded 1946
Private control
Language of instruction: Korean
Academic year: March to February

Pres.: JEON HO-JONG
Dean of Academic Affairs: CHAI-KYUN PARK
Dean of Finance: JEI-WON KOH
Dean of General Affairs: PYUNG-JOON PARK
Dean of Student Affairs: YANG-SOO SON
Librarian: KI-SANG KIM

Library of 597,032 vols
Number of teachers: 556
Number of students: 26,164

DEANS

College of Arts: YONG-HYUN KUK
College of Business Administration: BYUNG-KYU KIM
College of Dentistry: CHANG-KEUN YOON
College of Education: HONG-WON PARK
College of Engineering: WHAN-KYU PARK
College of Foreign Languages: YONG-HERN LEE
College of Humanities: JEONG-SEOK KANG
College of Industry: HEUNG-KYU JOO
College of Law and Political Science: CHANG-HYEON KOH
College of Medicine: YO-HAN JUNG
College of Natural Science: HAK-JIN JUNG
College of Pharmacy: YEONG-JONG YOO
College of Physical Education: DONG-YOON CHOE
Evening College: JEONG-JOO CHOE
Graduate School: JOON-CHAE PARK
Graduate School of Education: SEOK-CHEOL PARK
Graduate School of Industry: SEONG-HYU JO

CHUNG-ANG UNIVERSITY

221 Heukseok–dong, Dongjak-gu, Seoul 156-756

Telephone: (2) 820-6202
E-mail: interedu@cau.ac.kr
Internet: www.cau.ac.kr

Founded 1918
Private control
Academic year: March to February (2 semesters)

Chair. and Chancellor: KIM HEE SU
Pres.: PARK BUM HONN
Vice-Pres.: HWANG YUN-WON
Vice-Pres. (Ansung Campus): SANG YOON LEE
Vice-Pres. (Seoul Campus): SIK KIM DAE
Provost of Medical Centre: CHANG KWUN HONG
Dir of Library (Ansung Campus): YANG HYUN LEE
Dir of Library (Seoul Campus): TAE WOO NAM

Library: 1.2m. vols
Number of teachers: 2,127
Number of students: 26,634 (22,071 undergraduate, 4,563 graduate)

Publications: *Chung-Ang Herald* (12 a year), *Chung-Ang Press* (52 a year), *College Journals* (1 a year), *Journal of Chung-Ang Pharmacy* (1 a year), *Journal of Economic Development* (1 a year), *Korean Education Index* (1 a year), *Korean Journal of Comparative Law* (1 a year), *Korean Studies Journal* (4 a year), *Theses Collection*

DEANS

College of Arts: SANG JUE SHIN
College of Construction Engineering: KI BONG KIM
College of Education: YOUNG DUCK CHOI
College of Engineering: SUNG SUN KIM
College of Foreign Languages: SUNG MOO YANG
College of Home Economics: YANG HEE KIM
College of Industrial Studies: KWANG RO YOON
College of Law: YOUNG SOL KWON
College of Liberal Arts: NAM JOON CHANG
College of Medicine: IM WON CHANG
College of Music: LEE SUK CHEH
College of Pharmacy: IN HOI HUH
College of Political Science and Economics: IN KIE KIM
College of Sciences: SUK YONG LEE
College of Social Sciences: CHI SOON JANG
Graduate School: JO SUP CHUNG
Graduate School of Construction Engineering: SUNG SUN KIM
Graduate School of Education: JAE WOO LEE
Graduate School of International Management: HUN CHU
Graduate School of Mass Communication: SANG CHUL LEE
Graduate School of Public Administration: SANG YOON REE
Graduate School of Social Development: KYONG SUH PARK
Graduate School of the Information Industry: YOUNG CHAN KIM

DAEBUL UNIVERSITY

72 Samho-ri, Samho-myeun, Yangam-gun, Chonnam, Seoul 526-702

Telephone: (61) 469-1114
E-mail: webmaster@mail.daebul.ac.kr
Internet: www.daebul.ac.kr

Founded 1994 as Daebul Institute of Technology and Science; present name 1996
Private control

Pres.: LEE GYEONG-SU

DAEGU UNIVERSITY

Jillyang, Gyeongsan, Gyeongbuk, Seoul 712-714

Telephone: (53) 850-5681
E-mail: oia@daegu.ac.kr
Internet: www.daegu.ac.kr

Private control
Languages of instruction: English, Korean
Academic year: March to February

Pres.: Dr DUCKRYUL HONG

Number of teachers: 1,682
Number of students: 30,885

DAEJON UNIVERSITY

96-3 Yongun-dong, Tong-gu, Daejon, Seoul 300-716

Telephone: (42) 282-0231
E-mail: parkjh@dju.kr
Internet: www.dju.ac.kr

DANKOOK UNIVERSITY

Jukjeon Campus: 126 Jukjeon-dong, Suji-gu, Yongin-si, Gyeonggi-do, Seoul 448-701
Cheonan Campus: San 29, Anseo-dong, Dongnam-gu, Cheonan-si,Chugnam, Seoul 330-714

Telephone: (31) 8005-2102
E-mail: webmaster@dankook.ac.kr
Internet: www.dankook.ac.kr

Founded 1947, univ. status 1967
Private control
Language of instruction: Korean
Academic year: March to February

Chancellor: CHANG CHOONG-SIK
Pres.: CHANG HOSUNG
Registrar: YONG-WOO LEE

Library of 140,000 vols
Number of teachers: 321
Number of students: 13,557

DEANS

College of Commerce and Economics: KIM HAENG-XUH
College of Education: KIM SEUNG-KOOK
College of Engineering: KO MYUNG-WON
College of Law: KIM YOO-HYUK
College of Liberal Arts and Sciences: CHA MOON-SUP

DONG-A UNIVERSITY

840 Hadan 2-dong, Saha-gu, Busan, Seoul 604-714

Telephone: (51) 200-6442
E-mail: president@donga.ac.kr
Internet: www.donga.ac.kr

Founded 1946
Private control
Language of instruction: Korean
Academic year: March to February

Pres.: CHOI JAE-RONG
Vice-Pres.: CHO BYUNG-TAE
Head of Secretariat: LEE YEONG-GI
Dean of Academic Affairs: CHOI CHANG-OCK
Dean of Admin.: KIM LI-KYOO
Dean of Financial Affairs: HWANG YOON-SIK
Dean of Research: CHOI SOON-KYU
Dean of Student Affairs: LEE DAE-KYU
Dir of Library: HAHN KUN-BAE

Library of 582,134 vols
Number of students: 17,217

DEANS

College of Agriculture: CHUNG DAE-SOO
College of Arts: PARK SOO-CHUL
College of Business Administration: JUN TAE-YOON
College of Engineering: PARK CHUN-KEUN
College of Human Ecology: KIM SEOK-HWAN
College of Humanities: CHUNG SANG-BAK
College of Law: JEONG MAN-HEE
College of Medicine: CHUNG DUCK-HWAN
College of Natural Sciences: UHM TAE-SEOP
College of Physical Education: PARK CHEOL-HO
College of Social Sciences: SUL KWANG-SUK
Graduate School: RYOO WOONG-DAL
Graduate School of Business Administration: KIM YONG-DAE
Graduate School of Education: TCHOI CHONG-IL
Graduate School of Industry: HAN KUN-MO
Graduate School of Mass Communication: KIM MIN-NAM

DIRECTORS

Agricultural Resources Research Institute: KIM YOUNG-KIL
Basic Science Research Institute: KIM WAN-SE
Business Management Research Institute: KIM SEONG-HWAN
Environmental Problems Research Institute: KIM JANG-HO
German Studies Institute: RHIE SANG-UG
Industrial Medicine Research Institute: KIM JUNG-MAN
Industrial Technology Research Centre: JUN TAE-OK
Institute for the Study of Law: KIM SANG-HO
Institute of Data Communication: HONG CHANG-HI
Institute of Korean Resources Development: CHUNG SUNG-GYO
Language Research Institute: HA CHI-GUN
Life Science Research Institute: CHOI YONG-CHUN
MIS Research Institute: HAN KAY-SEOB
Ocean Resources Research Institute: KIM JIN-HOO
Plastic Arts Research Institute: BACK SUNG-DO

Population Research Centre: CHOI SOON
Research Institute for Clinical Medicine: KIM JEONG-MAN
Research Institute for Genetic Engineering: CHUNG CHUNG-HAN
Research Institute for Human Ecology: PARK EUN-JOO
Research Institute for Humanities: CHUNG YOUNG-DO
Research Institute of Sports Science: AN YOUNG-PIL
Social Science Research Institute: KIM JAE-GYONG
Sokdang Academic Research Institute of Korean Culture: HYENG-JU KIM
Tourism and Leisure Research Institute: AHN YUNG-MYUN

DONG-EUI UNIVERSITY

24 Kaya-dong, Pusanjin-ku, Busan 614-714
Telephone: (51) 890-1114
E-mail: wwwadmin@www.dongeui.ac.kr
Internet: www.dongeui.ac.kr

Founded 1976 as Kyungdong Engineering Technical College; became Dong-Eui College 1979; present name 1983
Private control
Pres.: Dr KEUN-WU PAK
Library of 336,000 vols
Number of students: 3,704 (3,420 undergraduate, 284 postgraduate)

DONG YANG UNIVERSITY

1 Kyochon-dong, Punggi, Youngju, Kyungbuk, Seoul 750-711
Telephone: (572) 630-1114
E-mail: wwwadmin@dyu.ac.kr
Internet: www.dyu.ac.kr

Founded 1994
Private control
Academic year: March to December
Colleges of arts, human and social science, science and engineering; graduate schools of education and information
Pres.: Dr CHOI SUNG-HAE
Vice-Pres.: Dr PARK YOUNG-HWAN
Librarian: BYUN BOK-SOO
Library of 150,000 vols
Number of teachers: 80
Number of students: 3,100 (3,000 undergraduate, 100 postgraduate)

DONGDUK WOMEN'S UNIVERSITY

23-1 Wolgok-dong, Sungbuk-ku, Seoul 136-714
Telephone: (2) 940-4000
E-mail: master@dongduk.ac.kr
Internet: www.dongduk.ac.kr

Founded 1950
Private control
Language of instruction: Korean
Academic year: March to February (2 semesters)
Chancellor: WON-YOUNG CHO
Vice-Chancellor: YOUNG-YON YOON
Registrar: DO-SEOK CHANG
Librarian: YOON-SIK KIM
Library of 232,000 vols
Number of teachers: 154
Number of students: 6,155
Publications: *Dongduk News Letter* (2 a year), *Dongduk Women's Newspaper* (52 a year), *Journal of Dongduk Women's University*, *Treatise* (1 a year)

DEANS

College of Arts: SUN-BAEK JANG
College of Computer and Information Sciences: YANG-HEE LEE
College of Design: DONG-JO KOO
College of Humanities: SANG-GI CHO
College of Natural Sciences: SANG-SOON LEE
College of Performing Arts: (vacant)
College of Pharmacy: IN-KOO CHUN
College of Social Sciences: SAE-YOUNG OH
General Studies and Teaching Profession Division: HONG-TAE PARK

DONGGUK UNIVERSITY

26, Pil-dong, 3-ga Jung-gu, Seoul 100-715
Telephone: (2) 2260-3114
E-mail: iie@dongguk.edu
Internet: www.dongguk.ac.kr

Founded 1906, univ. status 1953
Private control
Colleges of agriculture and forestry, Buddhism, economics and commerce, education, engineering, law and political science, liberal arts and sciences, medical science; graduate schools of business administration, public administration, education, information industry; colleges on Kyongju Campus
Research Institutes: agriculture and forestry, Buddhist culture, business management, comparative literature, computer science, industrial technology, Korean studies, landscape art, law and political science, Middle Eastern and East European affairs, national security, overseas development, Saemaul research, statistical science, translation of Buddhist scriptures
Chair.: OH IN-GAB
Pres.: Dr SONG SUK-KU
Librarian: Dr KIM BO HWAN
Library: see under Libraries and Archives
Number of teachers: 500
Number of students: 16,050
Publications: *Dongguk Journal*, *Dongguk Post* (12 a year), *Dongguk Sasang* (Dongguk Thought), *Dongguk Shinmun* (52 a year), *Pulgyo Hakpo* (Journal of Buddhist Studies), and 20 others

DONGSEO UNIVERSITY

San 69-1, Churye-2-Dong, Sasang-gu, Busan, Seoul 617-716
Telephone: (51) 320-2092
E-mail: anna1974@dongseo.ac.kr
Internet: www.dongseo.ac.kr

Founded 1991 as Dongseo College of Technology; present name 1996
Pres.: Dr PARK DONG-SOON
Exec. Dir of Int. Cooperation Cttee: CHANG JEKUK
Number of students: 7,000

DONGSHIN UNIVERSITY

252 Daeho-hong, Naju, Jeonnam, Seoul 520-714
Telephone: (61) 330-3114
Internet: www.dongshinu.ac.kr

Colleges of arts, engineering, humanities and social science, information and science, oriental medicine
Pres.: LEE KYUM-BUM
Library of 500,000
Number of students: 1,604

DUKSUNG WOMEN'S UNIVERSITY

19 Geunhwagyo-gil, 419 Ssangmoon-dong, Dobong-gu, Seoul 132-714
Telephone: (2) 901-8691
E-mail: djsuk@duksung.ac.kr
Internet: www.duksung.ac.kr

Founded 1950
Private control
Language of instruction: Korean
Academic year: March to February
Pres.: CHI EUN HEE
Registrar: LIM SOOK-JA
Librarian: CHUNG YOUNG-HWAN
Library of 328,000 vols
Number of teachers: 310 (148 full-time, 162 part-time)
Number of students: 5,250
Publications: *Duksung Women's University Journal*, *Duksung Women's University Newsletter* (24 a year), *Duksung Women's University Newsletter*, *Geunmack* (1 a year)

DEANS

College of Fine Arts: KIM AIE-YUNG
College of Humanities: YOON JUNG-BOON
College of Natural Science: YOON SUK-IM
College of Pharmacy: JUNG KI-HWA
College of Social Sciences: KIM SUNG-CHUL

EWHA WOMEN'S UNIVERSITY

11-1 Daehyun-dong, Seodaemun-gu, Seoul 120-750
Telephone: (2) 3277-2114
E-mail: master@ewha.ac.kr
Internet: www.ewha.ac.kr

Founded 1886
Languages of instruction: English, Korean
Academic year: March to December (2 semesters)
Chancellor: YOON HOO-JUNG
Pres.: Dr SHIN IN-RYUNG
Librarian: KIM BONG-HEE
Library: see under Libraries and Archives
Number of teachers: 800
Number of students: 21,000 (6,000 graduate, 15,000 undergraduate)
Publications: *Edae Hakbo* (52 a year, in Korean), *Ewha News* (12 a year, in Korean), *Ewha Voice* (12 a year, in English)

DEANS

College of Arts and Design: Prof. KIM YOUNG-KI
College of Business Administration: Dr SUH YOON-SUK
College of Education: Dr JU YOUNG-JU
College of Engineering: Dr SHIN YEONG-SOO
College of Home Science and Management: Dr PARK SEONG-YEON
College of Human Movement and Performance: Dr KIM KEE-WOONG
College of Law: Dr YANG MYEONG-CHO
College of Liberal Arts: Dr KIM HYUN-JA
College of Medicine: Dr CHUNG HWA-SOON
College of Music: Prof. LEE KYU-DO
College of Natural Sciences: Dr LEE NAM-SOO
College of Nursing: Dr BYUN YOUNG-SOON
College of Pharmacy: Dr KIM CHOON-MI
College of Social Sciences: Dr AHN HONG-SIK
Graduate School: Dr CHANG PIL-WHA
Graduate School of Business Administration: Dr SUH YOON-SUK
Graduate School of Clinical Health Sciences: Dr KIM CHOON-MI
Graduate School of Design: Dr KIM YOUNG-KI
Graduate School of Education: Dr CHOI WOUN-SIK
Graduate School of Information Science: Dr AHN HONG-SIK
Graduate School of International Studies: Dr YOO JANG-HEE
Graduate School of Policy Sciences: Dr AHN HONG-SIK
Graduate School of Practical Music: Dr CHOI YOO-RI
Graduate School of Social Welfare: Dr CHOI WOUN-SIK
Graduate School of Theology: Dr YANG MYUNG-SU
Graduate School of Translation and Interpretation: Dr CHOI YOUNG

Institute of Science and Technology: Dr KIM WON

HALLYM UNIVERSITY

39 Hallymdaehak-gil, Chunchon, Kangwon-do, Seoul 200-702
Telephone: (33) 248-1000
E-mail: parkphil@hallym.ac.kr
Internet: www.hallym.ac.kr

Founded 1982
Private control
Academic year: March to December

Pres.: LEE YOUNG-SUN
Vice-Pres.: Dr HAN SIL
Dean for Academic Affairs: Dr CHOI SOO-YOUNG
Dean for Gen. Affairs: SUNG NAK-SUNG
Dean for Planning and Coordination: Dr LEE KI-WON
Dean for Student Affairs: Dr LEE CHOONG-IL
Library Dir: Dr BAK GEUN-GAB

Library of 373,000 books
Number of teachers: 591
Number of students: 10,119 (9,353 undergraduate, 766 postgraduate)

Publication: *Hallym News* (26 a year)

DEANS

College of Humanities: Prof. OH CHUN-TAEK
College of Information and Electronics Engineering: Prof. SONG CHANG-GEUN
College of Medicine: Prof. PARK HYOUNG-JIN
College of Natural Sciences: Prof. KIM RAK-JOONG
College of Social Sciences: Prof. KIM YUNG-MYUNG

HAN NAM UNIVERSITY

133 Ojeong-dong, Daedeok-gu, Daejon, Seoul 306-791
Telephone: (42) 629-7739
E-mail: webmaster@hannam.ac.kr
Internet: www.hannam.ac.kr

Founded 1956
Academic year: March to December

Colleges of economics and business administration, education, engineering, law, liberal arts, natural sciences, social sciences

Pres.: KIM HYUNG-TAE
Dir of Int. Relations Centre: Dr KYU TAE JUNG

Library: Univ. possesses Central Library, Central Museum, Natural History Museum, Academic Information Centre
Number of teachers: 965
Number of students: 11,441

HANKUK UNIVERSITY OF FOREIGN STUDIES

270 Imun-dong, Dongdaemun-gu, Seoul 130-791
Telephone: (2) 2173-2063
E-mail: gyoh@hufs.ac.kr
Internet: www.hufs.ac.kr

Founded 1954
Private control

Pres.: PARK CHUL
Dean for Academic Affairs: Prof. PAK SUNG RAE
Dean for Student Affairs: Prof. LEE CHANG BOK
Chief Admin. Officer: SEOK JOO YOON
Librarian: Prof. CHO KYU CHUL

Library of 303,900 vols
Number of teachers: 292
Number of students: 12,838

Publications: *Argus* (12 a year, in English and other foreign languages), *Journal* (1 a year), *Oe-Dae Hakbo* (52 a year, in Korean)

DEANS

Academic and Student Affairs (Evening Courses): Prof. WOO DUCK YONG
College of Education: Prof. OH HAN-JIN
College of Foreign Languages: Prof. CHOI JONG SOO
College of Law and Political Science: Prof. KIM DEOK
College of Liberal Arts and Sciences: Prof. KIM JIK HYUN
College of Occidental Languages: Prof. LEE YOUNG GUL
College of Oriental Languages: Prof. CHUNG KI IOB
College of Social Sciences: Prof. PARK BYUNG HO
College of Trade and Economics: Prof. LEE HEE JOON
Graduate School: Prof. REW JOUNG YOLE
Graduate School of Education: Prof. RHIM JIN KWON
Graduate School of International Trade: Prof. LEE HEE JOON
Graduate School of Interpretation and Translation: Prof. KIM I BAE
Graduate School of Management Information Systems: Prof. JUNG JAE SEOK

DIRECTORS

Audio-Visual Education Institute: Prof. PARK SOON-HAM
Chinese Studies Institute: Prof. CHOI KWAN-JANG
Foreign Language Training and Research Centre: Prof. KIM JAI MIN
Institute for Research in Languages and Linguistics: Prof. REW SEONG JOON
Institute of African Studies: Prof. PARK WON TAK
Institute of Foreign Language Studies: Prof. KIM YOUNG JO
Institute of History: Prof. PAK SUNG RAE
Institute of Humanities: Prof. KANG SUNG WI
Institute of International Communication: Prof. KIM JONG KI
Institute of Korean Regional Studies: Prof. AHN BYONG MAN
Institute of Latin-American Studies: Prof. MIN MAN SHIK
Institute of the Middle East: Prof. HONG SOON NAM
Interpretation and Translation Centre: Prof. KIM I-BAE
Research Institute for Economics and Business Administration: Prof. MIN BYUNG KWOON
Russian and East European Institute: Prof. CHO KYU WHA
Student Guidance Centre: Prof. YOON JONG GEON

HANSEO UNIVERSITY

360 Daegok-ri, Haemi-Myun, Seosan City, Chungcheongnam, Seoul 360-706
Telephone: (41) 660-1144
E-mail: webmaster@hanseo.ac.kr
Internet: www.hanseo.ac.kr

Colleges of aeronautical engineering, arts, engineering, graduate school, health science, liberal arts, science, social science

Founded 1989
Number of students: 1,927
Pres.: HAM KEE-SUN

HANSHIN UNIVERSITY

Hanshin, Seoul
Telephone: (31) 379-0103
Internet: www.hs.ac.kr

Founded 1980

Colleges of humanities, information sciences, management and trade, social sciences, theology

Number of students: 6,000
Pres.: YOON EUNG JIN

HANSUNG UNIVERSITY

389 Samseon-Dong 2-ga, Seongbuk-gu, Seoul
Telephone: (2) 760-4114
E-mail: getsmile@hansung.ac.kr
Internet: www.hansung.ac.kr

Founded 1945

Colleges of arts, engineering, humanities, liberal arts and science, social sciences

Pres.: CHUNG JOO-TAEK

HANYANG UNIVERSITY

17 Haengdang-dong, Seongdong-gu, Seoul 133-791
Telephone: (2) 2220-0114
E-mail: w3master@hanyang.ac.kr
Internet: www.hanyang.ac.kr

Founded 1939 as Hanyang Institute of Technology; present status 1959
Private control
Academic year: March to July, September to December

Colleges of commerce and economics, education, engineering (incl. architectural engineering), law and political science, liberal arts and sciences (incl. journalism and cinema), medicine, music, physical education; evening engineering college; graduate school of industrial management

Pres.: Dr KIM CHONG YANG
Academic Dean: Dr SONG CHANG SEOP

Library of 350,000 vols
Number of teachers: 958
Number of students: 24,508

Publications: *Hanyang Nonmun Dzip*, *Journal of Economic Studies*, *Journal of Korean Studies*, *Journal of Student Guidance Research*, *Sino-Soviet Affairs*, and numerous others

HONAM UNIVERSITY

Gwangsan Campus: 59-1 Seobong-Dong, Gwangsan-gu, Gwangju City, Seoul 506-714
Telephone: (62) 940-5114
Ssangchom Campus: 148 Ssangchon-dong, Seo-Ku, Gwangju City, Seoul 502-791
Telephone: (62) 370-8114
Internet: www.honam.ac.kr

Founded 1978

Colleges of arts and physical education, business administration, engineering, internet and media, humanities, natural science, social sciences

Chair.: Dr PARK KI-IN
Pres.: CHUNG BYOUNG-WAN

Library of 400,000 vols

HONG-IK UNIVERSITY

Seoul Campus: 72-1 Sangsu-dong, Mapo-gu, Seoul 121-791
Jochiwon Campus: Jochiwon-eup, Yeongi-gun, Chungcheongnam-do 339-701
Telephone: (2) 320-1114
E-mail: webm@wow.hongik.ac.kr
Internet: www.hongik.ac.kr

Founded 1946
Private control
Language of instruction: Korean
Academic year: March to June, September to December

Chair.: Dr LEE MYEON YOUNG
Pres.: KWON MYUNG KWANG
Vice-Pres: CHANG YOUNG TAE, LIM HAE CHULL
Vice-Pres. for Jochiwon Campus: LEE KI BOK

Dir of Univ. Library: KIM KUN HO
Library: 1m. vols
Number of teachers: 853 (463 full-time, 390 part-time)
Number of students: 16,679
Publications: *Hong-Ik Economic Review* (1 a year), *Hong-Ik University Journal* (1 a year), *Journal of Student Life* (1 a year), *Management Review* (1 a year), *Papers on the Study of Education* (1 a year)

DEANS
College of Architecture: KIM UK
College of Business Administration: KIM DONG HUN
College of Business Management (Jochiwon Campus): CHOI YEON
College of Design and Arts (Jochiwon Campus): PARK YON SUN
College of Education: KIM MIN JAE
College of Engineering: CHUNG JOON KI
College of Fine Arts: CHOI BYUNG HOON
College of Law: MIN KYOUNG-DO
College of Law and Economics: BAEK SEUNG GWAN
College of Liberal Arts: CHIN HYUNG JOON
College of Science and Technology (Jochiwon Campus): SHIN PAN SEOK
Graduate School: YOUNG TAE JANG
Graduate School of Advertising and Public Relations: CHANG DON RYUN
Graduate School of Architecture and Urban Design: CHUNG MYUNG WON
Graduate School of Business: LEE KWANG CHUL
Graduate School of Education: PARK SANG OK
Graduate School of Educational Management: PARK SANG OK
Graduate School of Film and Digital Media: KIM JONG DEOK
Graduate School of Fine Arts: KIM TAE HO
Graduate School of Industrial Arts: BYUN KUN HO
Graduate School of Industry (Jochiwon Campus): CHANG HO SUNG
International Design School for Advanced Studies: KIM CHUL HO

HOSEO UNIVERSITY

Asan Campus: 165 Sechul-ri, Baebang-myun, Asan, Chungnam, Seoul 336-795
Cheonan Campus: 268, Anseo-dong, Cheonan, Chungnam, Seoul 330-713
Telephone: (41) 540-5017
Internet: www.hoseo.ac.kr
Founded 1978
Private control
Pres.: KANG IL-KU
Library of 300,000 vols
Number of teachers: 520
Number of students: 12,000

INHA UNIVERSITY

253 Yonghyun-dong, Nam-gu, Inchon, Seoul 402-751
Telephone: (32) 860-7030
E-mail: orir@inha.ac.kr
Internet: www.inha.ac.kr
Founded 1954
Private control
Academic year: March to February
Pres.: Dr LEE BON-SU
Vice-Pres.: Dr CHOI BYUNG-HA
Registrar: Dr KIM CHONG-BO
Librarian: Dr YUN MYUNG-KOO
Library of 350,000 vols
Number of teachers: 644
Number of students: 18,116
Publications: bulletins of the research institutes

DEANS
College of Business and Economics: Dr KIM KI-MYUNG
College of Education: Dr KIM CHANG-GEOL
College of Engineering: Dr KANG BYUNG-HEE
College of Home Economics: (vacant)
College of Humanities: Dr KIM WOO-JIN
College of Law and Political Science: Dr LEE YOUNG-HEE
College of Medicine: Dr KIM SEH-HWAN
College of Natural Sciences: Dr PARK DAE-YOON
Graduate School: Dr CHOI JI-HOON
Graduate School of Business Administration: Dr SHINN YONG-HWI
Graduate School of Education: Dr CHUNG KI-HO
Graduate School of Engineering: Dr KIM DONG-IL
Graduate School of Public Administration: Dr SHIN YOUNG-SANG

INJE UNIVERSITY

Kimhae Campus, 607 Obang-dong, Gimhae, Gyeongnam, Seoul 621-749
Telephone: (55) 334-7111
Internet: www.inje.ac.kr
Founded 1983
Colleges of biomedical science and engineering, design, engineering, humanities and social sciences, medicine, music, natural sciences
Chair.: PAIK NAK WHAN
Pres.: LEE KYEONGHO
Library of 500,000 vols

JEONJU UNIVERSITY

1200 Hyoja-dong, Wansangu, Chonju Jeollabukdo, Seoul 520-759
Telephone: (652) 220-2122
Internet: www.jeonju.ac.kr
Colleges of architecture, arts, athletics, business administration, Christian studies, culture and tourism, economics and information, engineering, information technology and computer science, language and culture, law and public administration, natural sciences, social sciences, visual communication; teachers' college

KANGNAM UNIVERSITY

111 Gugal-dong, Gihoung-gu, Yongin-si, Gyeonggi-do, Seoul 449-702
Telephone: (31) 280-3500
E-mail: master@kangnam.ac.kr
Internet: www.kangnam.ac.kr
Founded 1946
Private control
Academic year: March to December
Chair.: YOON DO-HAN
Pres.: YOON SHINIL
Chief Librarian: KIM SEUNG-HWAN
Library of 240,000 vols
Number of teachers: 170
Number of students: 6,534 (6,433 undergraduate, 101 postgraduate)

DEANS
College of Art and Physical Education: Prof. YANG JAE-YONG
College of Humanities: Prof. JO SUNG-MO
College of Management and Economics: Prof. JAE-HA HWANG, Prof. HWANG JAE-HA
College of Science and Engineering: Prof. PARK KI-SUNG
College of Social Sciences: Prof. LEE CHANG-SUK
College of Social Welfare: Prof. KIM YOUNG-HO
College of Theology: Prof. LEE SOOK-JONG

Graduate School: NO SANG-HAK (Pres.)

KAYA UNIVERSITY

1103 Daegaya-ro, Goryeong-gun 717-801
Telephone: (54) 956-3100
E-mail: webmaster@kaya.ac.kr
Internet: www.kaya.ac.kr
Founded 1993
Private control
Languages of instruction: English, Korean
Academic year: February to December
Faculties of applied arts, commerce, education, health and medical science, humanities
Pres.: Dr SANG HEE LEE
Library: 2.8m. vols
Number of teachers: 100
Number of students: 4,120 (4,000 undergraduate, 120 postgraduate)

KEIMYUNG UNIVERSITY

2800 Dalgubeoldaero, Dalseo-gu, Daegu 704-701
Telephone: (53) 580-6023
E-mail: intl@kmu.ac.kr
Internet: www.kmu.ac.kr
Founded 1954
Private control
Languages of instruction: English, Korean
Academic year: March to December
Pres.: SYNN ILHI
Vice-Pres. for Academic Affairs: PAEK SEUNG KYUN
Vice-Pres. for Medical Affairs: KANG JIN-SUNG
Dean of Dongsan Library: PARK JOON-SHIK
Library: 1.2m. vols
Number of teachers: 1,284 (604 full-time, 680 part-time)
Number of students: 25,000
Publications: *Accounting Information Review*, *Asian Journal of Business and Entrepreneurship*, *Bulletin of the Institute for International Science*, *Business Management Review*, *Journal of Art and Culture*, *Journal of International Studies*, *Journal of Life Science Research*, *Journal of Nakdonggang Environmental Research Institute*, *Journal of Social Sciences*, *Journal of the Institute for Cross-Cultural Studies*, *Journal of the Institute for Japanese Studies*, *Journal of the Institute of Natural Sciences*, *Keimyung Journal of Nursing Science*, *Keimyung Law Review*, *Keimyung University Medical Journal*, *Proceedings of Mathematical Science*

DEANS
College of Education: SIM HO TACK
Faculty of Applied Sciences: MIN HYUNG-JIN
Faculty of Automotive Engineering: SHIN SUNG-HEON
Faculty of Basic Sciences: UHM JAE-KUK
Faculty of Business Administration: PARK MYUNG-HO
Faculty of Chemical and Materials Engineering: SYNN DONG-SU
Faculty of Commerce: OH SEI-CHANG
Faculty of Computer and Electronic Engineering: SON YOO-EK
Faculty of Environmental Studies: KIM IN-HWAN
Faculty of Fashion: JON KYONG-TAE
Faculty of Fine Arts: HUR YONG
Faculty of Humanities: JIN WON-SUK
Faculty of Human Life Sciences: JOO KWANG JEE
Faculty of International Studies: LI JONG-KWANG
Faculty of Language and Literature: KIM JONG SUN
Faculty of Law: CHOI SANG-HO
Faculty of Music: KIM JEONG GIL

Faculty of Nursing: KIM JEONG NAM
Faculty of Physical Education: KIM SANG HONG
Faculty of Police Sciences: CHOI EUNG RYUL
Faculty of Politics and Economics: CHO YONG SANG
Faculty of Social Sciences: KIM SE SHUL
Graduate School: PARK YOUNG CHOON
Graduate School of Arts: KIM JEONG GIL
Graduate School of Business Administration: KIM JIN TAK
Graduate School of Education: KIM KI-HAN
Graduate School of Industrial Design: HUR YONG
Graduate School of Industrial Technology: KIM HONG YOUNG
Graduate School of International Studies: OH SEI-CHANG
Graduate School of Medical Management: PARK YOUNG NAM
Graduate School of Pastoral Theology: CHONG JOONG-HO
Graduate School of Policy Development: CHOI BONG KI
Graduate School of the Sports Industry: KIM SANG-HONG
School of Medicine: PARK YOUNG NAM

KON-KUK UNIVERSITY

1 Hwayang-dong, Gwangjin-gu, Seoul 143-701
Telephone: (2) 450-3259
Internet: www.konkuk.ac.kr
Founded 1946, university status 1959
Private control
Academic year: March to February
Chair.: KYUNG-HEE KIM
Pres.: KIL-SAENG CHUNG
Vice-Pres: YUNG-KYE KANG (Seoul Campus): MOON-JA UM (Chungju Campus)
Registrar: HYEON-LYONG KIM
Librarian: YUNG-KWON KIM
Library: 1.1m. vols
Number of teachers: 589 (full-time)
Number of students: 17,177
Publications: *English Newspaper* (12 a year), *Newspaper* (52 a year)

DEANS

College of Agriculture: CHONG-CHON KIM
College of Animal Husbandry: CHANG-WON KANG
College of Architecture: YONG-SIK KIM
College of Art: HO-CHANG RYU
College of Arts and Design: HYUNG-JAE MAENG
College of Arts and Home Economics: WON-JA LEE
College of Business Administration: THOMAS T. H. JOH
College of Commerce and Economics: JEONG-PYO CHOL
College of Education: II HWANG
College of Engineering: KWANG-SOO KIM
College of Humanities: SOON-BONG PACK
College of Information and Telecommunication: SUN-YOUNG HAN
College of Law: SEUNG-HO LEE
College of Liberal Arts: OH-HYUN CHO
College of Life Environment: SUK-HUN KYUNG
College of Medicine: TAE-KYU PACK
College of Natural Sciences: LEE-CHOI CHANG
College of Political Science: SUNG-BOK LEE
College of Sciences: JUNE-TAK RHEE
College of Social Sciences: YOUNG-BOON LEE
College of Veterinary Medicine: BYUNG-JOO KIM
Graduate School: JOO-YOUNG LEE
Graduate School of Agriculture and Animal Science: SUN-JOO KIM
Graduate School of Architecture: BYOUNG-KEUN KANG
Graduate School of Business Administration: DAE-HO KIM
Graduate School of Design: LEE-SANG EUN
Graduate School of Education: DONG-OK LEE
Graduate School of Engineering: JOONG-RIN SHIN
Graduate School of Information and Telecommunication: CHUN-HYON CHANG
Graduate School of Mass Communication: DAE-IN KANG
Graduate School of Medicine: KYUNG-YUNG LEE
Graduate School of Public Administration: EUN-JAE LEE
Graduate School of Real Estate Studies: CHO-JOO HYUN
Graduate School of Social Sciences: NAM-KYU PARK

KONYANG UNIVERSITY

26 Nae-dong, Nonsan, Chungnam, Seoul 320-711
Telephone: (41) 730-5114
E-mail: webmaster@konyang.ac.kr
Internet: www.konyang.ac.kr
Founded 1991
Pres.: KIM HEE-SOO
Library of 250,000 vols

KOOKMIN UNIVERSITY

Jeongneung-gil 77, 861-1 Chongnung-dong, Songbuk-ku, Seoul 136-702
Telephone: (2) 910-4115
E-mail: caee@kookmin.ac.kr
Internet: www.kookmin.ac.kr
Founded 1946
Pres.: LEE SUNG WOO
Dean of Academic Affairs: Prof. KIM YOUNG-JEON
Dean of Student Affairs: Prof. LEE JONG-EUN
Dean of Gen. Affairs: KIL YEONG-BAE
Dean of Planning and Devt Affairs: Prof. KANG SIN-DON
Library of 200,000 vols
Number of teachers: 370 (159 full-time, 211 part-time)
Number of students: 15,000
Publications: *Design Review, Economic and Business Administration Review, Education Review, Journal of Language and Literature, Journal of Sports Science Research, Journal of the Scientific Institute, Kookmin Tribune* (12 a year, in English), *Kookmin University Bulletin* (1 a year), *Kookmin University Press* (52 a year), *Law and Political Review, Papers in Chinese Studies, Theses* (1 a year), *Theses of Engineering, Theses of Korean Studies*

DEANS

College of Architecture and Design: Prof. KIM CHUL-SOO
College of Economics and Business Administration: NAH OH-YOUN
College of Education: SHIN JOONG-SHIK
College of Engineering: Prof. YOON TAI-YOON
College of Forestry: KO YUNG-ZU
College of Law and Political Science: LEE YONG-SUN
College of Liberal Arts: Prof. LEE JUNG-KEE
Graduate School: CHOI HWAN-YOL
Graduate School of Business Administration: CHOI HWAN-YOL
Graduate School of Education: CHOI HWAN-YOL
Graduate School of Public Administration: LEE YOUNG-SUN

KOREA UNIVERSITY

1 5-ga, Anam-dong, Sungbuk-gu, Seoul 136-701
Telephone: (2) 3290-1152
Internet: www.korea.ac.kr
Founded 1905 as Posung College
Private control
Language of instruction: Korean
Academic year: March to February (2 semesters)
Pres.: EUH YOON-DAE (acting)
Dean for Academic Affairs: AHN CHANG-YIL
Dean for Construction and Facility Management: PAIK YOUNG-HYUN
Dean for Gen. Affairs: YOUN SA-SOON
Dean for Planning and Public Relations: PARK MANN-JANG
Dean for Students: KIM SONG-BOK
Librarian: SHIN IL-CHUL
Library: see under Libraries and Archives
Number of teachers: 1,408 (627 full-time, 781 part-time)
Number of students: 21,685
Publications: *Gyongyong Shinmoon* (52 a year, in Korean), *Kodai Moonwha* (1 a year, in Korean), *Kodai Shinmoon* (52 a year, in Korean), *Korea University Bulletin* (1 a year, in English), *Phoenix* (1 a year, bilingual), *The Granite Tower* (26 a year, in English)

DEANS

College of Agriculture: KWACK BEYOUNG-HWA
College of Business Administration: LEE JANG RHO
College of Economics and Commerce (Jochiwon campus): KIM JUNG-BAI
College of Education: YOU IN-JONG
College of Engineering: HONG JONG-HWI
College of Law: BAE JONG-DAE
College of Liberal Arts: HAN PONG-HEUM
College of Liberal Arts and Science (Jochiwon campus): KIM JUNG-BAI
College of Medicine: PARK SUNG-YONG
College of Political Science and Economics: CHO YONG-BUM
College of Science: KIM SI-JOONG
Graduate School: LAU BONG-WHAN
Graduate School of Business Administration: KIM DONG-KI
Graduate School of Education: KIM SUNG-TAI
Graduate School of Food and Agriculture: YANG HAN-CHUL

KOSIN UNIVERSITY

149-1 Dongsam-dong, Yeongdo-gu, Busan, Seoul 606-701
Telephone: (51) 990-2114
E-mail: logos@kosin.ac.kr
Internet: www.kosin.ac.kr
Founded 1946
Colleges of arts, computer sciences, health sciences, human ecology, humanities and social sciences, medicine, natural sciences, theology
Pres.: KIM SUNG-SOO
Library of 120,000 vols

KWANDONG UNIVERSITY

522 Naegok-dong, Kangnung-si, Gangwon-do, Seoul 210-701
Telephone: (33) 641-1011
Internet: www.kwandong.ac.kr
Founded 1959
Colleges of arts, education, humanities, law and politics, medicine, science and engineering
Pres.: PARK HUI-JONG
Number of students: 8,000

KWANGWOON UNIVERSITY

447-1 Wolgye-dong, Nowon-gu, Seoul 139-701

Telephone: (2) 940-5114

Internet: www.kwangwoon.ac.kr

Colleges of business, electronics and information, engineering, humanities and social sciences, law, natural sciences

Pres.: PARK YOUNG-SHIK

KYONGGI UNIVERSITY

San 94-6 Iui-dong, Yeongtong-gu, Suwon-si, Gyeonggi-do, Seoul 443-760

Telephone: (31) 249-8770

E-mail: oia@kgu.ac.kr

Internet: www.kgu.ac.kr

Founded 1947

Private control

Colleges of arts, economics and business administration, engineering, humanities, int. studies, law, natural sciences, physical education, social sciences, tourism sciences; graduate schools of alternative medicine, architecture, art and design, business administration, construction, culture and arts, education, engineering and industry, politics and policy, public administration, social welfare, sports science, tourism and hospitality

Chair.: CHU CHEONG-SOO

Chancellor: Dr HO JOON CHOI

Library of 1,500,000 vols

Number of teachers: 800

Number of students: 16,000

KYUNG HEE UNIVERSITY

Seoul Campus: Hoegi-dong, Dongdaemun-gu, Seoul 130-701

Telephone: (2) 961-0031

E-mail: cie@khu.ac.kr

Global Campus: Seocheon-Dong, Seoul 446-701

Telephone: (31) 201-3177

E-mail: intlctr@khu.ac.kr

Internet: www.kyunghee.ac.kr

Founded 1949, renamed 1952

Private control

Academic year: March to December (2 terms)

Founder-Chancellor: Dr CHOUE INWON

Pres.: KIM BYUNG-MOOK

Vice-Pres.: KIM BYUNG-MOOK (Seoul Campus): PARK KYU HONG (Suwon Campus): PARK MYUNG KWAN (Devt)

Registrars: CHOO DONG JOON (Seoul Campus): CHO WON-KYUNG (Suwon Campus)

Librarians: KIM JAE HONG (Seoul Campus): KIM HAN WON (Suwon Campus)

Library of 1,200,000 vols, separate medical library of 15,000 vols

Number of teachers: 2,300

Number of students: 29,080

Publications: *Kohwang* (1 a year, in Korean), *Peace Forum* (every 2 years, in English), *University Life* (12 a year, in English), *University Weekly* (in Korean), research bulletins for each college

DEANS

Seoul Campus:

College of Dentistry: LEE SANG RAE

College of Human Ecology: PARK HYUN-SUH

College of Law: LEE SHIYOON

College of Liberal Arts and Sciences: CHUNG BOK-KEUN

College of Medicine: CHO YOUG HO

College of Music: HWANG SUN

College of Oriental Medicine: LEE HYUNG KOO

College of Pharmacy: RHO YOUNG SOO

College of Political Science and Economics: SUH SUNG-HAN

College of Tourism and Hotel Management: YOO KON-JO

Graduate School: SOHN KWANG SHIK

Graduate School of Business Administration: LEE KEUN SOO

Graduate School of East–West Medicine: RYU KI-WON

Graduate School of Education: PARK KEE-SAW

Graduate School of International Legal Affairs: YUN MYUNG-SUNG

Graduate School of Journalism and Mass Communication: LEE SUK-WOO

Graduate School of NGO: PARK KUN WOO

Graduate School of Peace Studies: SOHN JAE-SHIK

Graduate School of Physical Education: KOH KI CHAE

Graduate School of Public Administration: OH SEI DEUK

Graduate School of Tourism: YOO KONG-JO

Suwon Campus:

College of Engineering and Department of Electronics and Information Technology: JUN KYE SUK

College of Foreign Languages: HUH JONG

College of Industry and Department of Life Science: JO JAE SUN

College of Natural Sciences and Department of the Environment and Applied Chemistry: CHOUNG SUK JIN

College of Social Sciences and Department of Management and International Relations: PARK WON-KYU

College of Sports Science and Department of Physical Education: KIM JIN HO

Department of Art and Design: LEE HEON LOOK

Department of Civil and Architectural Engineering: ON YOUNG TAE

Department of Mechanical and Industrial Systems Engineering: PARK KYOUNG SUK

Graduate School of Information and Communication: CHIN YONG-OHK

Graduate School of Industry and Information Science: LEE KYE TAK

Graduate School of Pan-Pacific International Studies: KIM CHONGSOO

KYUNGIL UNIVERSITY

33 Puho-ri, Hayang-up, Kyungsan-si, Kyungsangpuk-do, Seoul 712-701

Telephone: (53) 853-8001

E-mail: webmaster@kiu.ac.kr

Internet: www.kyungil.ac.kr

Founded 1963 as Technical High School attached to Chunggu College; renamed Jr Technical College attached to Yeungnam Univ. 1967; separated from Yeungnam Univ. as Yeungnam Jr Technical College 1975; renamed Kyungpook Jr Technical College 1976; renamed Kyungpook Jr College of Technology 1978; became Kyungpook Open Univ. 1985; renamed Kyungpook Sanup Univ. 1988; became Kyungil Univ. 1997

Private control

Academic year: March to December

Pres.: LEE NAM-KYO

Dir for Gen. Affairs: KIM JONG-SEOK

Dir of the Office for Planning and Devt: LEE WEON-SIK

Chief Librarian: PARK HA-YONG

Number of teachers: 250

Number of students: 10,000

DEANS

College of Engineering: YOON MYUNG-JIN

College of Formative Arts: KIM JUNG-WON

College of Humanities and Social Sciences: ANH YOOL-CHONG

College of Information Technology: KIM LEE-KOK

Graduate School: KIM JIN-HO

Graduate School of Design: KIM JIN-HO

Graduate School of Industry: KIM JIN-HO

School of General Education: SUH BO-GUN

KYUNGNAM UNIVERSITY

449 Wolyoung-dong, Masan, Kyungnam, Seoul 631-701

Telephone: (55) 245-5000

E-mail: aadm@kyungnam.ac.kr

Internet: www.kyungnam.ac.kr

Founded 1946

Private control

Pres.: Dr PARK JAE KYU

Registrar: Dr YANG JAE IN

Librarian: Dr YOUN DOCK JOUNG

Library of 537,887 vols

Number of teachers: 674

Number of students: 15,000

DEANS

College of Arts: Dr CHO JIN KI

College of Business Administration: Dr KOH HYUN WOOK

College of Education: Dr LEE SEOK ZOO

College of Engineering: Dr LEE SOO HEUM

College of Law and Political Science: Dr RA KYUNG SIK

College of Science: Dr LEE SUE DAE

Graduate School: Dr CHONG CHOONG KYUN

KYUNGSUNG UNIVERSITY

314–79 Daeyeon-dong, Nam-gu, Pusan 608-736

Telephone: (51) 663-4114

Internet: ks.ac.kr

Founded 1955 as Kyungnam Teacher's College, present name and status 1988

Colleges of arts, commerce and economics, engineering, law and political science, liberal arts, multimedia, pharmacy, science, theology; graduate schools of clinical pharmacology, digital design, education, international business, multimedia, social welfare

Chair.: KIM DAE-SUNG

Pres.: SONG SOO-GEUN

Library of 500,000 vols

Number of teachers: 700

Number of students: 13,000

KYUNGWON UNIVERSITY

San 65 Bokjeong-dong, Sujeong-gu, Seongnam, Gyeonggi-do 461-701

Telephone: (31) 750-5901

E-mail: webmaster@kyungwon.ac.kr

Internet: www.kyungwon.ac.kr

Founded 1982

Chair.: MEN JEONG GWANG-MO

Colleges of arts, business and economics, engineering, human ecology, humanities, law and science, music, natural science, Oriental medicine, software

Pres.: LEE GIL-YA

Number of teachers: 165

Number of students: 8,609

MOKWON UNIVERSITY

88 Doan-dong, Seo-gu, Daejeon 302-729

Telephone: (42) 829-7131

E-mail: inter@mokwon.ac.kr

Internet: www.mokwon.ac.kr

Founded 1954

Colleges of arts and design, education, engineering, humanities, music, natural sciences, social sciences, techno-sciences, theology, TV and film; graduate school of industrial information, journalism and public relations, theology

Pres.: KIM WUENBAE

Library of 340,000 vols

PAICHAI UNIVERSITY

155–40 Baejae-ro (Doma-Dong), Seo-gu, Daejeon 302-735

Telephone: (42) 520-5243

E-mail: inter@mail.pcu.ac.kr

Internet: www.paichai.ac.kr

Founded 1885

Academic year: September to June (2 terms)

Colleges of arts, business administration, engineering, fashion, foreign studies, humanities, law, natural sciences, social sciences, tourism

Chair.: HWANG BANG-NAM

Pres.: Dr KIM YOUNG-HO

POHANG UNIVERSITY OF SCIENCE AND TECHNOLOGY

San 31, Hyoja-dong, Nam-gu, Pohang, Gyungbuk, Seoul 790-784

Telephone: (54) 279-0114

E-mail: webmaster@postech.edu

Internet: www.postech.ac.kr

Founded 1986

Academic year: March to January

Pres.: Prof. SUNGGI BAIK

Vice-Pres.: Prof. IN-SIK NAM

Dean of Policy and Planning (Int. Affairs): Prof. YUSHIN HONG

Number of teachers: 243

Number of students: 3,097 (1,360 undergraduate, 1,737 postgraduate)

PUSAN UNIVERSITY OF FOREIGN STUDIES

55-1 Uan-dong, Nam-gu, Pusan 608-738

Telephone: (51) 640-3000

E-mail: webmaster@www.pufs.ac.kr

Internet: www.pufs.ac.kr

Colleges of commerce and business, humanities and social sciences, information and sciences, leisure sports studies, Occidental studies, Oriental studies

Library of 320,000 vols

SANGJI UNIVERSITY

660 Woosan-dong, Wonju, Kangwon-do

Telephone: (371) 730-0182

E-mail: webmaster@mail.sangji.ac.kr

Internet: www.sangji.ac.kr

Founded 1962

Colleges of art, economics and business administration, humanities and social sciences, life science and natural resources, Oriental medicine, science and engineering, and sports

Pres.: Dr SUNG-HOON KIM

Number of teachers: 473

SANGMYUNG UNIVERSITY

20 Hongjimun 2-gil, Jongno-gu, Seoul 110-743

Telephone: (2) 2287-5196

E-mail: oip@smu.ac.kr

Internet: www.smu.ac.kr

Founded 1965

Private control

Languages of instruction: English, Korean

Academic year: March to December

Pres.: Prof. TAE-BEOM KANG

Vice-Pres. for Cheonan Campus: DUCHEOL KIM

Vice-Pres. for Seoul Campus: YONGSEONG PARK

Library of 1,031,742 vols, 4,561 vols of periodicals

Number of teachers: 368

Number of students: 19,681 (17,749 undergraduate, 1,416 postgraduate, 516 int. students)

DEANS

College of Arts: JONGIN CHOI

College of Business: SEONGTAE HONG

College of Design: GYEONGHAN KIM

College of Education: Prof. GEOYONG PARK

College of Engineering: YEONGBEOM JANG

College of Humanities and Social Sciences: JINO JOO

College of Industry: JUNHYEON OH

College of Language and Literature: JONGBEOM YOON

College of Music: EUNHUI YANG

College of Natural Sciences: SEONGHO LEE

College of Software: YUNCHEOL BAEK

College of Visual Arts: JIYOUNG NA

SEJONG UNIVERSITY

98 Kunja-dong, Kwangjin-gu, Seoul

Telephone: (2) 3408-3499

E-mail: semyaje@sejong.ac.kr

Internet: sejong.ac.kr

Founded 1947

President: Dr CHUL-SU KIM

Vice-Presidents: Dr SUK-MO KOO (Academic Affairs, and Provost), Dr HYUN-JU SHIN (International Programmes and Christian Ministry), YOUNG-HWAN CHOI (Research and Development)

Dean of Academic Affairs: Dr YONG-U SOK

Dean of Student Support: Dr EUI-JANG KO

Dean of Finance: KWANG-HO PARK

Dean of Admissions and Planning: Dr JA-MO KANG

Number of students: 7,337

DEANS

College of Business Administration: Dr SOO-SUP SONG

College of Engineering: Dr HOON-IL OH

College of Liberal Arts: Dr CHON-SUN IHM

College of Music, Fine Arts and Physical Education: Dr DUCK-BOON LEE

College of Natural Sciences: Dr SUNG-CHUNG AN

College of Social Sciences: Dr KI-SANG LEE

College of Tourism: Dr SO-YOON CHO

Graduate School: Dr YANG-JA YOO

Graduate School of Business: Dr B. J. YANG

Graduate School of Education: Dr HYUN-WOOK NAM

Graduate School of Information and Communication: Dr JOUNG-WON KIM

Graduate School of Mass Communication: DON-SHIK CHOO

Graduate School of Public Administration: Dr KYUNG-SHIK JOO

Graduate School of Tourism: Dr CHOL-YONG KIM

SEOKYEONG UNIVERSITY

16-1 Jungneung-dong, Sungbuk-ku, Seoul 136-704

Telephone: (2) 940-7006

E-mail: skuinfo@skuniv.ac.kr

Internet: www.skuniv.ac.kr

Founded 1947

Colleges of arts, humanities, natural science and engineering, social science

Pres.: CHUL-CHOI YOUNG

Library of 381,120 vols, 46,120 ebooks, 219 current journals, 177 ejournal subscriptions, 2,283 cassettes, 1,894 CDs

SEOUL THEOLOGICAL UNIVERSITY

101 Sosabon 3-dong, Sosa-gu, Bucheon City 422-742

Telephone: (32) 340-9114

E-mail: admin@stu.ac.kr

Internet: www.stu.ac.kr

Founded 1911

Depts of childcare education, Chinese, Christian education, church music, early childhood, education, mission English, social welfare, theology

Pres.: SUK-SUNG YU

Library of 150,000 vols

SEOUL WOMEN'S UNIVERSITY

126 Kongnung 2-dong, Nowon-gu, Seoul 139-144

Telephone: (2) 970-5114

E-mail: webmaster@mail.swu.ac.kr

Internet: www.swu.ac.kr

Founded 1961

Private control

Academic year: March to February

Pres.: Dr KWANG-JA LEE

Dean for Academic Affairs: Dr KI SUK PARK

Dean for Gen. Affairs: Dr HEI JUNG CHUN

Dean for Planning and Budget: Dr EON HO CHOI

Dean for Student Affairs: Dr JU HAN PARK

Chief Librarian: Dr ON ZA PARK

Number of teachers: 136

Number of students: 5,911

Publications: *Journal of Art and Design* (1 a year), *Journal of Child Studies* (1 a year), *Journal of Student Guidance and Counselling* (1 a year), *Journal of the Graduate School of Seoul Women's University* (1 a year), *Journal of the Institute of Humanities* (1 a year), *Journal of the Natural Science Institute* (1 a year), *Journal of the Social Science Research Institute* (1 a year), *Journal of Women's Studies* (1 a year), *Seoul Women's University News* (26 a year)

DEANS

College of Humanities: Prof. YOUNG CHUL LEE

College of Information and Communication: Dr MOON HEE KANG

College of Natural Sciences: Dr JONG SUK LEE

College of Social Sciences: Dr MOON HEE KANG

Division of Fine Arts: Prof. BOK HEE CHEON

SEOWON UNIVERSITY

377-3 Musimseoro, Heungdeok-gu, Cheongju 361-742

Telephone: (43) 299-8114

E-mail: juns@seowon.ac.kr

Internet: www.seowon.ac.kr

Founded 1968 as Cheongju Women's Junior College, present name and status 1992

Faculties of business administration, education; schools of convergence bioscience and technology, design and environmental science, fusion arts, health and welfare, information technology, law and political science

Chair.: YONGKI SON

Pres.: SEOK-MIN SON

Number of teachers: 500

Number of students: 8,800

SILLA UNIVERSITY

617-736 San 1-1 Gwaebop-dong, Sasang-gu, Busan

Telephone: (51) 999-5000

E-mail: felix7@silla.ac.kr

Internet: www.silla.ac.kr

Founded 1954 as Busan Women's Junior College, present name and status 1997

Colleges of arts, economics and business administration, education, engineering, humanities and social sciences, IT design, medical and life sciences; graduate schools of business administration, education, social welfare

Chair.: HEA-GON PARK
Pres.: TAE-HAK PARK

SOGANG UNIVERSITY

CPO 1142, Seoul 100-611
Telephone: (2) 705-8114
E-mail: interrel@sogang.ac.kr
Internet: www.sogang.ac.kr

Founded 1960
Private control
Languages of instruction: English, Korean
Academic year: March to December (2 semesters)

Pres.: CHANG-SUP CHOI (acting)
Man. of Academic Affairs: MOON-SEOB YOUM
Man. of Student Affairs: MYEONG-HOON CHEON
Dir of Library: SEOG PARK

Number of teachers: 302
Number of students: 10,900

Publications: *Sogang Hakbo* (52 a year), *Sogang Herald* (12 a year)

DEANS

College of Engineering: YOUNG GOO LEE
College of Humanities: IN CHAI CHUNG
College of Natural Sciences: KWAE HI LEE
College of Social Science: KAP YUN LEE
General Education Division: HEE NAM CHOI
Graduate School: CHUL AN
Graduate School of Business: WOON YOUL CHOI
Graduate School of Economics: YOUNG GOO LEE
Graduate School of Education: JUNG TAEK KIM
Graduate School of Information and Technology: JUNG YUN SEO
Graduate School of International Studies: SE YOUNG AHN
Graduate School of Mass Communication: HAK SOO KIM
Graduate School of Media Communications: KAK YOON
Graduate School of Public Policy: KAP YUN LEE
Graduate School of Theology: TAE SU HA
School of Business Administration: JANG HO LEE
School of Economics: BOK UNG KIM

PROFESSORS

College of Engineering:

AN, C., Electronic Engineering
CHANG, I. S., Electronic Engineering
CHANG, J. H., Computer Science
CHOI, C. S., Chemical Engineering
CHOI, J.-W., Chemical Engineering
CHOI, M., Computer Science
HONG, D.-H., Electronic Engineering
HUR, N., Mechanical Engineering
HWANG, S. Y., Electronic Engineering
IHM, I., Computer Science
JANG, J. W., Electronic Engineering
JEE, Y., Electronic Engineering
JEON, D., Mechanical Engineering
JEONG, S., Mechanical Engineering
KIM, N., Mechanical Engineering
KIM, S. C., Computer Science
KOO, K. K., Chemical and Biomolecular Engineering
LEE, H. Y., Mechanical Engineering
LEE, J. W., Chemical Engineering
LEE, K. H., Electronic Engineering
LEE, K. S., Chemical Engineering
LEE, S. H., Electronic Engineering
LEE, T. S., Mechanical Engineering
NANG, J., Computer Science
OH, K. W., Computer Science
OH, S. Y., Chemical and Biomolecular Engineering
PARK, H. M., Chemical and Biomolecular Engineering
PARK, H. S., Chemical and Biomolecular Engineering
PARK, R. H., Electronic Engineering
PARK, S., Computer Science
RHEE, H. W., Chemical and Biomolecular Engineering
RIM, C. S., Computer Science
SEO, J., Computer Science
YOO, K.-P., Chemical and Biomolecular Engineering
YUN, S. W., Electronic Engineering

College of Humanities:

AN, S. J., English Language and Literature
BAIK, I. H., History
BAK, J. S., French Language and Literature
CHANG, S. N., German Language and Literature
CHANG, Y. H., English Language and Literature
CHO, B. H., History
CHO, S. W., English Language and Literature
CHOI, H.-M., French Language and Literature
CHUNG, D. H., History
CHUNG, I. C., Philosophy
JEONG, Y. I., Korean Language and Literature
KANG, Y. A., Philosophy
KEEL, H. S., Religious Studies
KIM, G., Chinese Culture
KIM, H. G., History
KIM, S. H., Religious Studies
KIM, S. N., Religious Studies
KIM, W. S., Philosophy
KIM, Y. H., History
KIM, Y. S., English Language and Literature
KWAK, C. G., Korean Language and Literature
LEE, J. D., German Language and Literature
LEE, J. W., History
LEE, S. B., English Language and Literature
LIM, S. W., History
PAK, C. T., Philosophy
SEONG, Y., Philosophy
SHIN, K., English Language and Literature
SHIN, S. W., English Language and Literature
SONG, H. S., Korean Language and Literature
SONG, W. Y., German Language and Literature
SPALATIN, C. A., Philosophy
SUH, C. M., Korean Language and Literature
SUNG, H. K., Korean Language and Literature
UM, J., Philosophy

College of Natural Sciences:

CHIN, C. S., Chemistry
CHO, K., Physics
CHO, S. H., Mathematics
CHUNG, D. M., Mathematics
CHUNG, S. Y., Mathematics
HONG, S. S., Mathematics
KANG, J., Chemistry
KIM, D. H., Chemistry
KIM, D. S., Mathematics
KIM, J., Mathematics
KIM, S. R., Life Science
KIM, W. S., Life Science
KIM, W. T., Physics
LEE, B. H., Physics
LEE, D., Chemistry
LEE, H., Chemistry
LEE, J. B., Mathematics
LEE, J. G., Mathematics
LEE, J. K., Life Science
LEE, W. K., Chemistry
PARK, G. S., Physics
PARK, S. A., Mathematics
PARK, S. H., Mathematics
PARK, Y. J., Physics
RHEE, B. K., Physics
SHIN, C. E., Mathematics
SHIN, W., Chemistry
SO, H., Chemistry
YANG, J. M., Life Science
YOON, K. B., Chemistry

College of Social Science:

CHANG, Y. H., Mass Communication
CHO, H., Sociology
CHO, O., Sociology
CHOI, C. S., Mass Communication
CHOI, O. C., Law
CHUNG, H.-J., Law
EOM, D. S., Law
HONG, S. B., Law
KANG, J. I., Political Science
KIM, H. S., Mass Communication
KIM, K. M., Sociology
KIM, Y. S., Political Science
LEE, K. Y., Political Science
OH, B. S., Law
PARK, H. S., Political Science
PARK, S. T., Sociology
SHIN, Y. H., Political Science
SONN, H. C., Political Science
SUH, K. M., Law
YOON, Y. D., Sociology

General Education Division:

CHO, G. H., General Education
CHOI, H. N., General Education
KIM, J.-W., General Education
KIM, O. S., General Education

Graduate School of International Studies:

AHN, S. Y.
CHO, Y. J.

Graduate School of Media Communications:

BYUN, D. H.
JUNG, M.-R.
KIM, C. H.
KIM, Y. Y.
LEE, S. W.
SHIN, H. C.
YOON, K.

Graduate School of Theology:

CHUNG, W. S.
MOON, J. Y.
SIM, J. H.

School of Business Administration:

CHEE, Y. H.
CHOI, J. H.
CHOI, S. J.
CHOI, W. Y.
CHUN, S. B.
HA, Y. W.
JON, J. S.
KANG, H. S.
KIM, S. K.
KOOK, C. P.
LEE, C.
LEE, D. S.
LEE, J. B.
LEE, J. H.
LEE, J. J.
LEE, K. L.
LEE, N. J.
LEE, W. Y.
LIM, C. U.
MIN, J. H.
PARK, K. K.
PARK, N. H.
PARK, Y. S.

RHO, B. H.
SUH, C. J.

School of Economics:
CHO, C. O.
GILL, I. S.
JEON, S. H.
KIM, B. U.
KIM, K. D.
KIM, K. H.
KIM, S. Y.
KWACK, T.
LEE, D. S.
LEE, H. K.
LEE, H. S.
LEE, Y. G.
NAHM, J. W.
NAM, S. I.
SONG, E. Y.
SUH, J. H.
WANG, G. H.

SOOKMYUNG WOMEN'S UNIVERSITY

53-12 Chungpa-dong 2-ka, Yongsan-gu, Seoul 140-742
Telephone: (2) 710-9114
E-mail: kslee@sookmyung.ac.kr
Internet: www.sookmyung.ac.kr

Founded 1906
Private control
Language of instruction: Korean
Academic year: March to February

Pres.: KYUNG-SOOK LEE
Dean for Academic Affairs: EUN-GYUN MOK
Dean for Admin. Affairs: CHUN-HAK OH
Dean for Planning: MOO-SEUCK CHO
Dean for Student Affairs: YOUNG-SOOK SUH
Library Dir: HEE-JAE LEE

Library of 628,688 vols
Number of teachers: 370
Number of students: 13,315

Publications: *Asian Women* (in English), *Bulletin* (1 a year, in English and Korean), *Sookdae Shinbo* (52 a year, in Korean), *Sookmyung Times* (12 a year, in English)

DEANS
College of Economics and Commerce: WON-BAE YOON
College of Fine Arts: HAK-SEONG KIM
College of Home Economics: SUN-JAE LEE
College of Liberal Arts: JUNG-SHIN HAN
College of Music: MAN-BANG YI
College of Natural Sciences: YOUNG-HEE HONG
College of Pharmacy: AN-KEUN KIM
College of Political Science and Law: SANG-KWANG LEE
Graduate School: JUNG-WOO LEE
Graduate Schools of Special Subjects: SOOK-HEE PARK

SOONGSIL UNIVERSITY

369 Sangdo-ro, Dongjak-gu, Seoul 156-743
Telephone: (2) 820-0777
Internet: eng.ssu.ac.kr

Founded 1897
Private control
Languages of instruction: English, Korean
Academic year: March to December

Chancellor: Dr CHONG-SOON PARK
Pres.: Dr DAE-KEUN KIM
Vice-Pres. for Academic Affairs: Dr SANG-WON LEE
Vice-Pres. for External Affairs: Dr INSUNG LEE
Librarian: Dr SANG-HO LEE

Library of 795,271 vols
Number of teachers: 586 (252 full-time, 334 part-time)
Number of students: 16,406

DEANS
College of Business Administration: KEUNBAE KIM
College of Core and Specialized Education: SUNWOOK KIM
College of Economics and International Commerce: JOONSUNG HWANG
College of Engineering: JAECHUL KIM
College of Humanities: EUNSOO CHOI
College of Information Technology: HUNSOO HANS
College of Law: SIYOUNG OH
College of Natural Sciences: TAEHOON LEE
College of Social Sciences: SEONGBAE KIM
Graduate School: JEONGSIK HA

SUNGKYUL CHRISTIAN UNIVERSITY

147-2 Anyang 8-dong, Manan-gu, Anyang, Kyungki-do 430-742
Telephone: (343) 467-8114
Internet: www.sungkyul.ac.kr

Founded 1962 as a seminary; present name 1992

Pres.: Dr KEE-HO SUNG

Library of 170,000 vols

SUNGKYUNKWAN UNIVERSITY

Humanities and Social Sciences Campus: 53 Myongnyun-dong 3-ga, Chongo-gu, Seoul 110-745
Natural Sciences Campus: 300 Chunchun-dong, Changan-gu, Suwon, Kyonggi-do 440-746
Telephone: (2) 760-0114
E-mail: webmaster@www.skku.ac.kr
Internet: www.skku.ac.kr

Founded 1398, univ. status 1953
Private control
Academic year: March to February

Chair. of the Board of Trustees: E-HOUCK KWON
Pres.: JUNG DON SEO
Vice-Pres.: CHAE-WOONG LEE (Humanities and Social Sciences Campus), YUN-HEUM PARK (Natural Sciences Campus)
Academic Affairs Officer: HYUK KIM
Librarian: PYUNG-U PARK

Library: 1.4m. vols
Number of teachers: 980
Number of students: 24,098

Publications: *Journal of Eastern Culture* (1 a year, in Korean), *Journal of Humanities Sciences* (1 a year, in Korean), *Journal of Human Life Sciences* (1 a year, in Korean), *Journal of Korean Economics* (1 a year), *Journal of Modern China* (1 a year, in Korean), *Journal of Social Sciences* (1 a year, in Korean), *Learned Papers in Science and Technology* (2 a year, in Korean), *Learned Papers in the Natural Sciences* (2 a year, in Korean), *Sung Kyun Law Review* (2 a year, in Korean), *Suson Learned Papers* (1 a year, in Korean)

DEANS
College of Education: YOUNG-EUN CHIN
College of Law: KYU-SANG JUNG
School of Architecture, Landscape Architecture and Civil Engineering: SANG-HAE CHOI
School of Art: HAK-SUN LIM
School of Business Administration: YOUNG-KYU KIM
School of Chemical, Polymer and Textile Engineering: BOONG-SOO JEON
School of Confucian and Oriental Studies: YOUNG-JIN CHOI
School of Economics: SUNG-SOON LEE
School of Electrical and Computer Engineering: CHIL-GEE LEE
School of Humanities: HAN-GU LEE
School of Human Life Sciences: YANG-HEE LEE
School of Language and Literature: BONG-WON CHOI
School of Life Sciences and Technology: KYU-SEUNG LEE
School of Mechanical Engineering: HYUN-SOO KIM
School of Medicine: DAY-YONG UHM
School of Metallurgical and Materials Engineering: JOEN-GEON HAN
School of Natural Sciences: SANG-TAE LEE
School of Pharmacy: WON-HUN HAM
School of Social Sciences: CHANG-SOO CHUNG
School of Sports Science: EUNG-NAM AHM
School of Systems Management Engineering: HOO-GON CHOI

SUNGSHIN WOMEN'S UNIVERSITY

249-1 Dongseon-dong 3-ga, Seongbuk-gu, Seoul 136-742
Telephone: (2) 920-7114
E-mail: www@cc.sungshin.ac.kr
Internet: www.sungshin.ac.kr

Founded 1936

Colleges of arts, education, human ecology, humanities, music, natural sciences, social sciences; graduate schools of culture industry, education, human resources management, plastic arts

Pres.: KOO YANG-KEUN

Library of 600,000 vols
Number of teachers: 680
Number of students: 13,000

UNIVERSITY OF ULSAN

POB 18, Ulsan, Seoul 680-049
Telephone: (52) 277-3101
E-mail: webmaster@mail.ulsan.ac.kr
Internet: uou.ulsan.ac.kr

Founded 1970
Private control
Academic year: March to December

Chair.: MONG-JOON CHUNG
Pres.: CHUNG-KIL CHUNG
Head of Academic Information Centre: Prof. JEONG-SEOK HEO

Library of 700,000 books, 909 periodicals
Number of teachers: 723
Number of students: 11,659 (6,121 undergraduate, 5,538 postgraduate)

DEANS
College of Business Administration: HI-KYOON LEE
College of Design: SANG-HYE HAN
College of Engineering: DONG-KEE LEE
College of Fine Arts: PYUNG-HUI PARK
College of Human Ecology: HYE-KYUNG KIM
College of Humanities: CHUNG-HOO SUH
College of Industry and Management: KYU-CHO LEE
College of Medicine: WON-DONG KIM
College of Music: HYUN-KYUNG CHAE
College of Natural Sciences: TAE-SOO KIM
College of Social Sciences: YEON-JAE SHIN
Graduate School: KANG-MOON KOH
Graduate School of Business Administration: JOONG-HEON NAM
Graduate School of Education: MYEUNG-HAK YANG
Graduate School of Industrial Technology: SEONG-DEUK KIM I
Graduate School of Information and Communications Technology: KYUNG-SUP PARK
Graduate School of Regional Development: WOO-SUNG KIM

WONKWANG UNIVERSITY

460 Iksandae-ro, Iksan, Jeonbuk 570-749
Telephone: (63) 850-5114
Internet: www.wonkwang.ac.kr

Founded 1946
Private control

Colleges of business and economics, dentistry, education, engineering, fine arts and design, human environmental sciences, humanities, life science and natural resources, medical sciences, natural sciences, Oriental medicine, pharmacy, social sciences; divs of fire service administration, interdisciplinary studies in humanities, interdisciplinary studies in natural science, military services, police administration; graduate schools of administration, complementary and alternative medicine, education, health and environment, industry and business, law, Oriental medicine, Oriental studies

Pres.: JEONG SE-HYUN

Number of teachers: 460

Number of students: 23,200

YEUNGNAM UNIVERSITY

280 Daehak-Ro, Gyeongsan 712-749

Telephone: (53) 810-7884

E-mail: yuiss@yu.ac.k

Internet: www.yu.ac.kr

Founded 1947

Private control

Academic year: March to February (2 semesters)

Pres.: Dr NOH SEOK-KYUN

Library: 1.6m. vols

Number of teachers: 1,036 (751 full-time, 285 part-time)

Number of students: 27,194 (23,752 undergraduate, 3,442 postgraduate)

PROFESSORS

College of Agriculture and Animal Sciences:

- BYUN, J. K., Horticulture
- CHOI, C., Food Technology and Science
- CHUNG, H. D., Horticulture
- CHUNG, Y. G., Food Science and Technology
- JUNG, K. J., Animal Science
- KIM, B. D., Community Development
- KIM, J. K., Applied Microbiology
- LEE, H. C., Animal Science
- PARK, C. H., Agronomy
- SON, J. Y., Animal Science
- SYE, Y. S., Animal Science
- YOON, W., Community Development

College of Commerce and Economics:

- BAE, Y. S., Economics
- HAR, C. D., Business Policy
- KIM, J. H., Foreign Trade
- KIM, K.-T., Economics
- KIM, T. W., Business Administration
- KWON, B. T., Economics
- LEE, W.-D., Economics
- PARK, S.-K., Business Administration
- RYU, C. O., Foreign Trade
- SANG, M. D., Business Administration
- SHIN, H. J., International Theory and Policy
- YI, Y. W., Economics
- YOON, I. H., Economics
- YU, H. K., Economics

College of Education:

- AHN, Y. T., Business Education
- BAEK, U. H., Developmental Psychology
- CHO, D. B., Personality and Education
- CHUN, B. K., Audiovisual Method
- CHUNG, S. M., History of Korean Education
- CHUNG, Y. K., Linguistics
- KIM, H., Evaluation
- KIM, J. R., Physical Education
- KWON, J. W., Educational Psychology
- LEE, J. H., Physical Education
- LEE, K. T., English Language Education
- LEE, S. B., Mathematics Education
- LIM, M. S., Physical Education
- PARK, B. M., Philosophy of Education
- PARK, Y. B., Curriculum and Instruction
- SONG, B. S., Educational Psychology

College of Engineering:

- BAE, J. H., Electrical Engineering
- BYUN, D. K., Civil Engineering
- CHANG, D. H., Textile Engineering
- CHO, B., Chemical Engineering
- CHO, H., Textile Engineering
- CHOI, S.-G., Electronic Engineering
- CHOI, S.-H., Mechanical Design
- CHUNG, K.-H., Electronic Engineering
- CHUNG, W.-G., Textile Engineering
- HA, Z.-H., Mechanical Engineering
- JOO, H., System Engineering
- KANG, S. H., Chemical Engineering
- KIM, D. O., Traffic Engineering
- KIM, G.-C., Civil Engineering
- KIM, H. S., Architectural Engineering
- KIM, I.-J., Architectural Engineering
- KIM, J. Y., Mechanical Engineering
- KIM, K. S., Industrial Chemistry
- KIM, S.-K., Textile Engineering
- LEE, D. H., Control Engineering
- LEE, D.-I., Electrical Engineering
- LEE, J. H., Industrial Chemistry
- LEE, K. S., Mechanical Engineering
- LEE, M. H., Industrial Chemistry
- LEE, M. Y., Electronic Communication
- LEE, S. T., Civil Engineering
- LEE, T.-S., Marine Engineering
- PARK, J. Y., Civil Engineering
- PARK, W.-K., Chemical Engineering
- PARK, Y.-K., Industrial Chemistry
- RO, C. K., Electrical Engineering
- RO, H. J., Architectural Engineering
- SOHN, Y. K., Computer Engineering
- SONG, J. S., Textile Engineering
- UM, W.-T., Urban Engineering
- WU, M. J., Civil Engineering

College of Fine Arts:

- HONG, S. M., Sculpture
- KIM, Y. Z., Painting

College of Home Economics:

- CHO, S. Y., Food and Nutrition
- HAN, J. S., Food Preparation
- KIM, K. S., Food Science
- LEE, J. O., Clothing Science
- LEE, J. S., Home Management
- LEE, K. R., Food and Nutrition
- PARK, J. R., Food Science

College of Law and Political Science:

- BYUN, J.-O., Constitutional and Administrative Law
- CHANG, T.-O., Public Administration
- CHEUNG, W. J., International Law
- CHO, C.-H., Civil Law
- CHOI, J.-C., Public Administration
- KIM, J.-S., Public Administration
- KIM, K.-D., Civil Law
- KWON, H. K., Political Science and Diplomacy
- LEE, W. S., Political Science and Diplomacy
- PAIK, S. K., Public Administration
- PARK, S.-W., Criminal Law
- RHEE, C.-W., Political Science and Diplomacy
- YOON, B. T., Public Administration

College of Liberal Arts:

- CHAE, S. H., Buddhist Philosophy
- CHANG, H. K., Psychology
- CHO, K.-S., Korean Language and Literature
- CHUNG, Y. W., Archaeology
- HU, J. W., Western Philosophy
- HUH, C. Y., European History
- HWANG, S.-M., English and Linguistics
- KEWN, S.-H., English Drama
- KIM, B. K., Western Philosophy
- KIM, C. S., Korean Language and Literature
- KIM, S. H., English Novels
- KIM, S. J., Korean History
- KIM, S. K., English Literature
- KIM, S. M., English Poetry
- KIM, T. K., Anthropology
- KIM, W.-W., English Poetry
- KWON, Y. G., English Language and Literature
- LEE, B. J., Asian History
- LEE, B. L., Korean Language and Literature
- LEE, C. H., Western Philosophy
- LEE, J. W., Chinese Prose, Phonology
- LEE, S.-D., English Poetry
- LEE, S. K., Korean History
- LEE, S.-T., English Literature
- LEE, W. J., Philosophy
- LEE, Y. K., Philosophy of History, Social Philosophy
- LIM, B.-J., French Language
- MUN, C.-B., English Philosophy
- O, S. C., Korean History
- OH, M.-K., Sociology
- SUH, I., American Literature
- SUH, K. B., Chinese Poetry
- YOH, K. K., English Language
- YOUN, Y.-O., Korean Literature

College of Medicine:

- CHUNG, J. H., Preventive Medicine
- CHUNG, J. K., Microbiology
- CHUNG, W. Y., Obstetrics and Gynaecology
- HAH, Y. M., Dermatology
- HAHN, D. K., Ophthalmology
- HAM, D. S., Anatomy
- IHIN, J. C., Orthopaedic Surgery
- KIM, C. S., Internal Medicine
- KIM, C. S., Pathology
- KIM, S. H., General Surgery
- KIM, W. J., Pharmacology
- KWUN, K. B., General Surgery
- LEE, S. K., Physiology
- LEE, T. S., Pathology
- LEE, Y. C., Anatomy
- PARK, C. S., Neurology
- SONG, K. W., Otorhinolaryngology

College of Music:

- KIM, S. W., Vocal Music

College of Pharmacy:

- CHANG, U. K., Pharmacy
- CHUNG, K. C., Pharmacy
- CHUNG, S. R., Pharmacy
- DO, J. C., Industrial Pharmacy
- HAN, B. S., Industrial Pharmacy
- HUH, K., Pharmacy
- JIN, K. D., Pharmacy
- KIM, J. Y., Industrial Pharmacy
- LEE, M. K., Industrial Pharmacy
- LEE, S. W., Pharmacology
- SEOH, B. C., Industrial Pharmacy

College of Science:

- CHANG, G. S., Physics
- CHANG, K., Mathematics
- CHO, H. S., Physics
- CHO, Y., Mathematics
- CHOE, O.-S., Physics
- DOH, M. K., Inorganic Chemistry
- KANG, S. G., Physics
- KIM, D. S., Analytical Chemistry
- KIM, J.-C., Mathematics
- KIM, J. D., Organic Chemistry
- KIM, M. M., Physics
- KIM, Y. H., Physics
- PAHK, G.-H., Mathematics
- PARK, B. K., Physical Chemistry
- PARK, H.-S., Mathematics
- PARK, W. H., Biology
- RO, H. K., Physics
- WOO, J., Statistics

YONSEI UNIVERSITY

Room 217B Baekyang Hall, 262 Seongsanno, Seodaemun-gu, Seoul 120-749

Telephone: (2) 2123-3488

E-mail: oia@yonsei.ac.kr

Internet: www.yonsei.ac.kr

Founded 1885

Private control

Languages of instruction: English, Korean
Academic year: March to February (2 semesters)

Pres.: HAN-JOONG KIM
Vice-Pres. for Academic Affairs: KYUNG-DUCK MIN
Vice-Pres. for External Affairs and Alumni: HAN-JOONG KIM
Vice-Pres. for Medical Affairs: JIN-KYUNG KANG
Vice-Pres. for Wonju Campus: DAI-WOON LEE
Dir of University Planning and Public Relations: IN-KI JOO
Dean for Academic Affairs: HI-SOO MOON
Dean for Admissions: YONG-HAK KIM
Dean for Student Affairs and Services: TAE-SEUNG PAIK
Dir for Gen. Affairs: HYUK-GEUN CHOI
Dir of the Central Library: YOUNG-SOO SHIN

Library: see under Libraries and Archives
Number of teachers: 3,324
Number of students: 28,409

Publications: *Abstracts of Faculty Research Reports, Business Review, Engineering Review, Focus on Genetic Science, Global Economic Review, Infection Control Newsletter, Journal of East and West Studies, Journal of Education Science, Journal of Engineering Research, Journal of Far Eastern Studies, Journal of Humanities, Journal of Korean Informatics, Journal of Korean Studies, Journal of Medical Technology, Journal of Nursing Science, Journal of the Institute of Basic Science, Journal of the Natural Science Research Institute, Journal of the Radio Communication Research Centre, Journal of the Research Institute of ASIC Design, Journal of the Research Institute of Information and Telecommunications, Journal of the Yonsei Institute for Cancer Research, Korean Journal of Health Science, Korean Journal of Nursing Questions, New Energy and Environmental Systems, Social Science Review, Theological Forum, Theology and Modern Times, Tropical Medicine News, Yonsei Annals, Yonsei Biochemistry, Yonsei Chunchu, Yonsei Communication, Yonsei Economics Review, Yonsei Engineering Magazine, Yonsei Health Science, Yonsei Journal of Clinical Orthodontics, Yonsei Journal of Dental Science, Yonsei Journal of Human Ecology, Yonsei Journal of Language and Literature, Yonsei Journal of Medical Education, Yonsei Journal of Medical History, Yonsei Journal of Public Administration, Yonsei Journal of Social Science, Yonsei Journal of Sport and Leisure Studies, Yonsei Journal of Women's Studies, Yonsei Law Journal, Yonsei Law Review, Yonsei Medical Journal, Yonsei Non-Chong, Yonsei Nursing Journal, Yonsei Philosophy Review, Yonsei Review of Educational Research, Yonsei Review of Theology and Culture, Yonsei Social Welfare Review, Yonsei Unification Studies, Yonsei University Counselling Centre Research Review*

DEANS

College of Business and Economics: SUNG-KUN HA
College of Dentistry: MOON KYU CHUNG
College of Engineering: DAE-HEE YOON
College of Government and Business: PYEONG-JUN YU
College of Health Sciences: SOO-HONG NOH
College of Human Ecology: YOUNG LEE
College of Humanities and Arts: (vacant)
College of Law: SANG-KI PARK
College of Liberal Arts: YOUNG MEE CHUNG
College of Life Science and Biotechnology: (vacant)
College of Medicine: NAM-SIK CHUNG
College of Music: MYUNG-JA CHO
College of Nursing: SO YA JA KIM
College of Science: YOUNG-MIN KIM
College of Science and Technology: (vacant)
College of Sciences in Education: INTACK OH
College of Social Sciences: WOO-SUH PARK
College of Theology: YANG-HO LEE
EastAsia Int. College: INSUNG LEE
Graduate School: TAE-YOUNG LEE
Graduate School of Communication and Arts: YOUNG-SEOK KIM
Graduate School of Economics: SUNG-KUN HA
Graduate School of Education: SANG-WAN HAN
Graduate School of Engineering: JINHO LEE
Graduate School of Government and Business: KYUNG-SIHK AHN
Graduate School of Health and Environment: SOO-HONG NOH
Graduate School of Human Environmental Science: CHUNG-SOOK YOON
Graduate School of Information: KAP-YOUNG JEONG
Graduate School of International Studies: CHUNG MIN LEE
Graduate School of Journalism and Mass Communication: YANG-SOO CHOI
Graduate School of Nursing: SO YA JA KIM
Graduate School of Public Administration: MYUNG-SOON SHIN
Graduate School of Public Health: P. H. OHRR HEECHOUL
Graduate School of Social Welfare: JAE-YOP KIM
Underwood Int. College: JUNG HOON LEE
United Graduate School of Theology: YANG-HO LEE
University College: KYUNG-CHAN MIN
Wonju College of Medicine: SEONG-JOON KANG
Yonsei Law School: HYUN YOON SHIN
Yonsei School of Business: SANG YONG PARK

PUBLIC UNIVERSITIES OF EDUCATION

CHEONGJU NATIONAL UNIVERSITY OF EDUCATION

135 Sugok-dong, Heung Duk-gu, Cheongju, Chungbuk 361-712
Telephone: (43) 279-0800
Internet: www.chongju-e.ac.kr

Founded 1941

Depts of ethics education, Korean education, fine arts, mathematics, music, physical education, practical arts, science, social studies; graduate school of education

Pres.: YONG-WOO LIM
Library of 100,000 vols

DAEGU NATIONAL UNIVERSITY OF EDUCATION

1797-6 Daemyung 2-dong, Namgu, Daegu, Seoul
Telephone: (53) 620-1114
E-mail: abc@dnue.ac.kr
Internet: www.dnue.ac.kr

Founded 1950

Teacher-training univ.

Pres.: SOHN SEOKRAK

Number of teachers: 112
Number of students: 3,512 (2,775 undergraduates, 737 graduates)

KOREA NATIONAL UNIVERSITY OF EDUCATION

7 Darak-ri, Kangnae-myon, Chongwon-gun, Chungbuk, Seoul 363-791
Telephone: (43) 230-3114
E-mail: internat@knuecc-sun.knue.ac.kr
Internet: www.knue.ac.kr

Founded 1984

Pres.: PARK BAE-HUN

Library of 300,000 vols
Number of teachers: 331
Number of students: 6,060

PUSAN NATIONAL UNIVERSITY OF EDUCATION

Pusan
Internet: www.pusan-e.ac.kr

Founded 1946 as Pusan Normal School, present name 1993

Pres.: Dr CHI-YUL OK

SEOUL NATIONAL UNIVERSITY OF EDUCATION

Seocho-dong 1650, Seocho-gu, Seoul 137-742
E-mail: center@snue.ac.kr
Internet: www.snue.ac.kr

Founded 1945

Pres.: KWANG-YONG SONG

PUBLIC UNIVERSITIES OF TECHNOLOGY

CHUNGJU NATIONAL UNIVERSITY

72 Daehak-ro, Chungju-si, Chungbuk 380-702
Telephone: (43) 841-5011
Internet: www.chungju.ac.kr

Founded 1962 as Chungju Technical Junior College, present status 1999
Public Control

Colleges of advanced science and technology, engineering, humanities, social sciences and fine arts, health, biology and aeronautical engineering; graduate schools of business administration, public administration and foreign languages, industry; division of liberal arts; campuses in Chungju and Jeungpyeong

Pres.: Dr JANG BYUNG-JIB

Number of teachers: 295
Number of students: 8,200

HANKYONG NATIONAL UNIVERSITY

67 Sukjong-dong, Ansung-City, Kyonggi-do, Seoul 456-749
Telephone: (31) 670-5114
E-mail: master@hnu.hankyong.ac.kr
Internet: www.hankyong.ac.kr

Founded 1939
State control
Academic year: March to February

Pres.: Dr KIM SUNG-JIN
Dir of the Office for Academic Affairs: CHOE IL-SHIN
Dir of the Office of Gen. Affairs: LEE JONG-NAM
Dir of the Office of Strategy Dept: RYU HO-SANG
Dir of the Office of Student Affairs: AN JAE-HO
Library Dir: YOU SHI-GYUN

Library of 82,000 books, 175 periodicals
Number of teachers: 458
Number of students: 7,718 (7,558 undergraduate, 160 postgraduate)

DEANS

College of Agriculture and Life Science: KIM YOUNG-HO
College of Humanities and Social Sciences: HONG WAN-PYO
College of Science and Engineering: LEE HAK-YOUNG
Graduate School of Industry: RHEE SONG-KAP

JINJU NATIONAL UNIVERSITY

150 Chilamdong, Jinju, Kyongnam, Seoul 660-758
Telephone: (55) 751-3114
Internet: www.chinju.ac.kr
Founded 1910
Colleges of agriculture, humanities and social services, science and engineering
Pres.: JUNG HAE-JU

KUMOH NATIONAL UNIVERSITY OF TECHNOLOGY

Sanho-to 77 (Yangho-dong), Gumi, Gyeongbuk, Seoul 730-701
Telephone: (54) 478-7114
Internet: www.kumoh.ac.kr
Founded 1979 as Kumoh Institute of Technology; became Kumoh Nat. Institute of Technology 1990; present name 1993
Pres.: Dr HWAN CHOI

MIRYANG NATIONAL UNIVERSITY

1025-1 Naei-dong, Miryang, Kyungnam 627-702
Telephone: (527) 354-3181
E-mail: sdlee@arang.miryang.ac.kr
Internet: www.miryang.ac.kr
Founded 1923 as a public school of agricultural sericulture
Pres.: TAE-KIL CHOI

DEANS AND CHAIRMEN
Graduate School: YON-GYU PARK
School of Architecture: KANG-GEUN PARK
School of Computer, Information and Communication Engineering: SUN-JONG KIM
School of Food Science and Environmental Engineering: DONG-SEOP KIM
School of Materials Engineering: SU-CHAK RYU

SAMCHOK NATIONAL UNIVERSITY

253 Gyodong, Samchok, Kangwon-do, Seoul 245-080
Telephone: (397) 572-8611
E-mail: webadmin@samchok.ac.kr
Internet: www.samchok.ac.kr
Founded 1939 as Samchok Public Vocational School; became Samchok Public Industrial School 1944, Samchok Public Industrial Middle School 1946 and Samchok Industrial High School 1950; present name 1991
Pres.: Dr TAE-YUN CHANG

SANGJU NATIONAL UNIVERSITY

Sangju, Gyeongsangbuk-do
E-mail: jkang@sangju.ac.kr
Internet: www.sangju.ac.kr
Founded 1921
Public
Pres.: KIM JONG-HO
Number of teachers: 104
Number of students: 4,350

PRIVATE UNIVERSITIES OF TECHNOLOGY

CHODANG UNIVERSITY

419 Muan-goon, Muan-eup, Seonnam-ree, Jeonnam, Seoul 534-701
Telephone: (61) 450-1012
E-mail: president@chodang.ac.kr
Internet: www.chodang.ac.kr
Founded 1979
Private control
Colleges of arts and physical education, humanities and social sciences, science and engineering; graduate divs of business and public administration, computer and information engineering, culinary arts, environmental engineering, information design, nursing science, ophthalmic optics, social welfare, social physical education
Pres.: JIN-YOUNG NOH

HANKUK AVIATION UNIVERSITY

100, Hanggongdae gil, Hwajeon-dong, Gyeonggi-do Goyang City, Seoul 412-791
Telephone: (2) 300-0114
Internet: www.hangkong.ac.kr
Founded 1952 as Nat. Aviation College, became Hankuk Aviation College 1968
Pres.: YUH JUNKU
Dean for Academic Affairs: LEE YEONG-HOOK
Dean for Planning and Int. Affairs: BOO JOON-HONG
Dean for Research Affairs and Faculty Evaluation: HWANG SOO-CHAN
Dean for Student Affairs: KIM CHIL-YOUNG
Library of 247,000 vols

DEANS
Graduate School: LEE YUN-HYUN
Graduate School of Aviation and Information Industry: HONG SOON-KIL
Graduate School of Business Administration: CHA GUN-HO

HANLYO UNIVERSITY

199-4 Deongrae-ri, Gwangyang-eup, Gwangyang-si, Jeollanam-do, Seoul 545-704
Telephone: (61) 761-6700
E-mail: ipsimast@hanlyo.ac.kr
Internet: www.hanlyo.ac.kr
Founded 1993
Private control

HOWON UNIVERSITY

727 Wolha-ri, Impi, Kunsan, Chonbuk, Seoul 573-718
Telephone: (63) 450-7114
Internet: www.howon.ac.kr
Founded 1977 as Kunsan Technical Advanced School; renamed Sohae Technical Jr College 1979; became Chonbuk Sanup Univ. 1988; present name 1998
Private control
Academic year: March to February
Pres.: KANG HEE-SUNG

WOOSONG UNIVERSITY

17-2 Jayang-dong, Dong-gu, Daejeon 300-718
Telephone: (42) 630-9600
E-mail: international@wsu.sc.kr
Internet: english.wsu.ac.kr
Founded 1954
Private control
Schools of Asia management, health and welfare, hotel and culinary arts, railroad and transportation, technomedia; SolBridge Int. School of Business
Chair.: KIM SUNG KYUNG
Pres.: JOHN E. ENDICOTT
Library of 275,063 vols, 3,152 reference books, 367 periodicals
Number of teachers: 212 full-time
Number of students: 7,037

MUNICIPAL UNIVERSITIES

UNIVERSITY OF INCHEON

319 Incheondae gil, Nam-gu, Incheon, Seoul
Telephone: (32) 770-8114
E-mail: sysop@incheon.ac.kr
Internet: www.incheon.ac.kr
Colleges of arts and physical education, economics and business administration, engineering, humanities, law, natural sciences, North-East Asian studies, social sciences
Pres.: AHN KYUNG SOO

UNIVERSITY OF SEOUL

90 Jeonnong-dong, Dongdaemun-gu, Seoul 130-743
Telephone: (2) 2210-2114
E-mail: w3adm@uos.ac.kr
Internet: www.uos.ac.kr
Founded 1918, Seoul City Univ. until 1996
Maintained by Seoul Metropolitan Govt
Language of instruction: Korean
Academic year: March to February
Pres.: Dr SANG-BUM LEE
Provost of Academic Affairs: Dr HYUN-SOO MIN
Provost of General Admin.: IN-SONG CHANG
Provost of Planning and Devt: Dr EUI-YOUNG SON
Provost of Student Affairs: Dr KEUN-HEE CHOI
Dir of Central Library: Dr YONG-GUN KIM
Library of 554,895 vols
Number of teachers: 302
Number of students: 14,867
Publication: *University Press* (26 a year)

DEANS
College of Economics and Business Administration: Dr JONG-DAE LEE
College of Engineering: Dr SUNG-IL CHO
College of Law and Public Administration: Dr YONG-CHAN PARK
College of Liberal Arts and Natural Sciences: Dr JUN-HO SONG
College of Urban Sciences: Dr HYUNG-SU HAN
Liberal Arts Division: Dr DONG-HA LEE
Graduate School: Dr JAE-BOK PARK
Graduate School of Business Administration: Dr JONG-DAE LEE
Graduate School of Engineering: Dr SUNG-IL CHO
Graduate School of Urban Administration: Dr HYUNG-SU HAN

DISTANCE LEARNING UNIVERSITIES (CYBER AND DIGITAL UNIVERSITIES)

BUSAN DIGITAL UNIVERSITY

167, Jurei-dong, Sasang-gu Bang Busan Seoul 617-701
Telephone: (51) 320-1919
Internet: www.bdu.ac.kr
Founded 2002
Private control
Divs of digital contents, hospitalities and tourism, social welfare, society and management
Pres.: KIM MIN-SIK

CYBER UNIVERSITY OF KOREA

1-21 Gye-dong, Bukchon-ro, Jongno-gu, Seoul 110-800
Telephone: (2) 6361-1810
E-mail: webmaster@cuk.edu
Internet: www.cuk.edu
Founded 2001
Depts of business administration, business convergence, child studies, computer and information communication, continuing education, counselling psychology, electricity and electronic engineering, English education, healthcare administration, information management and security, Korean, law, mechanical and control engineering, media design, media studies, practical foreign lan-

guages, real estate, social welfare, taxation and accounting, youth studies
Pres.: Dr KIM CHOONG SOON

DAEGU CYBER UNIVERSITY

15 Naeri-ri, Jillyang-eup, Gyeongsan-si 712-714
Telephone: (53) 850-4000
E-mail: idaegu@dcu.ac.kr
Internet: english.dcu.ac.kr
Founded 2001
Private control
Pres.: LEE YOUNG SAE

GUKJE DIGITAL UNIVERSITY

950-12 Ingye-dong, Paldal-gu, Suwon Gyeonggi-do, Seoul 442-832
Telephone: (31) 229-6200
E-mail: admin@gdu.ac.kr
Internet: eng.gdu.ac.kr
Founded 2003
Private control
Schools of business administration, lifelong education, physical and health arts, social sciences
Pres.: PARK YOUNG-KYU
Vice-Pres.: LEE KYOUNG-WOO

KYUNG HEE CYBER UNIVERSITY

26 Kyunghee-daero, Dongdaemun-gu, Seoul 130-739
Telephone: (2) 968-2233
E-mail: cyber@khcu.ac.kr
Internet: khcu.ac.kr
Founded 2001
Schools of business management; hotel, tourism and restaurant; information, culture and arts; international and regional studies; social science
Pres.: Dr INWON CHOUE
Number of students: 10,000

SEOUL CYBER UNIVERSITY

60 Solmae-ro 49-gil, Gangbuk-gu, Seoul 142-700
Telephone: (2) 944-5000
E-mail: apply@iscu.ac.kr
Internet: www.iscu.ac.kr
Founded 2000
Schools of business and international management, general education, human welfare, information technology and design, psychology and counselling, social science
Pres.: Dr IN KANG
Number of students: 8,000

SEOUL DIGITAL UNIVERSITY

320 Dokmak-ro, Mapo-gu, Seoul 121-040
Telephone: (2) 1544-0981
E-mail: go@sdu.ac.kr
Internet: www.sdu.ac.kr
Founded 2001
Divs of information and technology and cultural arts, liberal arts and social science
Pres.: JEONG OH-YOUNG
Number of teachers: 400
Number of students: 19,640 (12,340 full-time, 7,300 part-time)

WONKWANG DIGITAL UNIVERSITY

344-2 Sinyong-dong, Iksank-si
Telephone: (2) 1588-2854
Internet: www.wdu.ac.kr
Founded 2001
Divs of health, Korean culture, utility and welfare
Pres.: SEONG SI-JONG

Colleges

PUBLIC COLLEGES

Busan Women's College: 74 Yangjung-dong, Pusan Jin-ku, Pusan 614-734; tel. (51) 852-0081; internet www.bwc.ac.kr; f. 1954; divs of applied art, art, business and management, child education, tourism, welfare and health.

Iksan National College: Seoul 570-752; tel. (63) 850-0500; e-mail w3master@iksan.ac.kr; internet www.iksan.ac.kr; f. 1922.

Korea National College of Rehabilitation and Welfare: 5-3 Jangan-dong, Pyongtaek-si, Gyeonggi-do; tel. (31) 610-4600; internet www.hanrw.ac.kr; f. 2002.

Korea National Railroad College: 374-18 Wolam-dong, Uiwang-si, Gyeonggi-do; tel. (31) 461-4011; internet english.krc.ac.kr; f. 1905; depts of introduction to liberal art, railroad electrical control, railroad facility engineering, railroad management information, railroad operation mechanism, railroad transportation management, railroad vehicle machine, railroad vehicle electricity; 27 teachers; 610 students.

National Medical Centre College of Nursing: Euljiro 6 St, 18-79 Jongno-gu, Seoul 100-196; tel. (2) 2265-6339.

PRIVATE COLLEGES

Agricultural Cooperative College: San 38-27, Goyang, Seoul 412-038; tel. (31) 960-4117; e-mail hanaok@nonghyup.or.kr; internet www.nonghyup.or.kr; f. 1962; courses in agricultural technology, computer science, marketing and MBA.

Andong Institute of Information and Technology: Andong, Gyeongsangbuk-do, Seoul 760-833; tel. (54) 820-8053; e-mail info@ait.ac.kr; internet www.ait.ac.kr; f. 1972; library: 18,500 vols.

Ansan College of Technology: 671 Chojidong, Danwon-gu, Ansan Gyeonggi-do; tel. (31) 490-6191; e-mail sysop@act.ac.kr; internet eng.ansantc.ac.kr; f. 1979; Degree programmes in arts and sports, liberal arts and social sciences, natural sciences, technology; Pres. KANG SUNG NAK.

Busan Gyeongsang College: 277-4 Yeonsan 8-dong, Yeonje-gu, Busan; tel. (51) 850-1000; e-mail busybee@bsks.ac.kr; internet www.cwc.ac.kr; f. 1977; depts of advertising and interior design, advertising and public relations, airline services, child studies, distribution and logistics, early childhood education, hotel and tourism English, hotel and tourism management, international trade by air and sea, management, real estate management, social welfare and medical health administration, tax accounting; Pres. LEE DAL-DUK.

Cheju Tourism College: Seoul 690-791; tel. (64) 740-8700; internet www.cjtour.ac.kr; f. 1993 as Jeju Tourism Technical College, current name adopted 1998; depts of airline and convention management, art, business and social service, casino management, Chinese, engineering, English, food service and culinary arts, hotel management, Japanese, leisure and sports, public health, tourism management; Pres. KIM CHANG-HU.

Chungkang College of Cultural Industries: Icheon, Seoul 467-810; tel. (31) 639-5743; e-mail mjkang@chungkang.ac.kr; internet www.chungkang.ac.kr; f. 1996; divs of games and animation, human care, industrial design, information communications, performing arts; Pres. LEE SU-HYEONG.

Daedong College: 373-4 Bugok 2-dong, Keumjeong-gu, Busan, Seoul 609-715; tel. (51) 518-5444; internet www.daedong.ac.k; f. 1971 as Daedong Nursing School, jr college in 1979, full college status 1998; programmes in child welfare, cosmetology, leisure tourism management, nursing; Pres. KIM KYUNGHEE.

Daegu Mirae College: Mirae-gil 13, Gyeongsan, Gyeongbuk, Seoul 712-716; tel. (53) 810-9200; internet www.dmc.ac.kr; f. 1981; Depts of engineering, fine arts, humanities and society, natural sciences, physical education; Pres. YONG BUM-KWON.

Gangneung Yeongdong College: 1009 Hongje-dong, Gangneung, Kangwon-do, Seoul 210-792; tel. (33) 610-0114; internet www.yeongdong.ac.kr; f. 1963; programmes in nursing and health, depts of social welfare, tourism; Pres. KIM MYUNG HYUN.

Inha Technical College: 253 Yonghyun-dong, Nam-ku, Incheon, Seoul 402-752; tel. (32) 870-2114; internet english.inhatc.ac.kr; f. 1958; 6,500 students; Pres. PARK CHOON-BAE.

Kaywon School of Art and Design: 66 Kaywondaehangno (Naeson-dong), Uiwang, Gyeonggi-do, Seoul 437-712; tel. (31) 420-1700; e-mail choihs@kaywon.ac.kr; internet foreign.kaywon.ac.kr; f. 1979 as Institute Foundation Kaywon School, present status 1990; faculties of design, fine arts and information technology; Pres. KANG YOUNG-JIN.

KDI School of Public Policy and Management: 87 Hoegiro Dondaemun, Seoul 130-868; tel. (2) 3299-1114; e-mail admissions@kdischool.ac.kr; internet kdischool.ac.kr; f. 1997; Masters degree programme, PhD programme, and non-degree programmes; Dean SANG-MOON HAHM.

Seoul Institute of the Arts: 640 Gojan 2-dong, Dwang-gu, Ansan, Gyeonggi-do; tel. (31) 412-7100; e-mail mschoi@seoularts.ac.kr; internet www.seoularts.ac.kr; f. 1958; programmes in applied music, broadcasting, creative advertising, creative writing, dance, digital arts and humanities, film, interior design, Korean traditional music, photography, playwriting, theatre, visual design; Chair. LEE GI HUNG.

Taekyeung College: 24 Tanpuk-ri, Chainmyun, Kyungsan, Gyeongsangbuk-do, Seoul 712-851; tel. (53) 850-1361; e-mail clsfae@tk.ac.kr; internet www.tk.ac.kr; f. 1993; offers 3-year programmes in early childhood education, entertainment and event management, film and broadcasting, nursing, theatre, visual optics; 2-year programmes in baking technology, beauty design and modelling, hotel culinary arts, police administration, real-estate management, security administration, social welfare, sports science, tourism and hotel management; Pres. YOO JIN-SUN.

Yeungnam College of Science and Technology: 274 Hyeonchung-ro, 1737 Daemyeong 7-dong, Nam-gu, Daegu, Seoul 705-703; tel. (53) 650-9114; internet eng.ync.ac.kr; f. 1968; schools of civil engineering-architecture, cosmetics-chemistry, design, food-tourism, information technology, mechanical and automotive engineering technology, nursing, health, practical sociology; divs of electronics and information engineering, health science; Pres. LEE HO-SUNG.

KOSOVO

The Higher Education System

On 17 February 2008 the Serbian province of Kosovo unilaterally declared independence from the Republic of Serbia. By December 2011 86 UN member states, including 22 European Union (EU) member states and the USA, had formally recognized the Republic of Kosovo as an independent sovereign state. However, several countries, including the People's Republic of China and Russia, continue to withhold recognition. Russian opposition to independence for Kosovo has prevented the approval of a resolution on the status of Kosovo by the UN Security Council.

Higher education in Kosovo is regulated by the Ministry of Education, Science and Technology. The Universiteti i Prishtinës (University of Prishtina), which was founded in 1969 is the only internationally recognized public university; the language of instruction at this establishment is Albanian. In 2009/10 there were 37,839 undergraduate students and 3,544 Masters students enrolled at the University of Prishtina. The Univerzitet u Prištini (or University of Mitrovica, as it is recognized by the United Nations Mission in Kosovo—UNMIK), which is situated in the northern city of Kosovska Mitrovica and uses Serbian as its language of instruction, broke away from the University of Prishtina in 1999. Private universities have been permitted to operate in Kosovo since 1999.

Individual universities have specific entrance requirements as well as admission examinations organized by each institution. Kosovo, although not currently eligible for direct membership to the Bologna Process as it has not ratified the European Cultural Convention, attends Bologna ministerial meetings on an observer basis. The University of Prishtina began using the European Credit Transfer and Accumulation System (ECTS) in 2001/02 and the Ministry of Education, Science and Technology is working to implement ECTS in all higher education institutions. As a result of higher education reforms introduced in 2003–04, the University of Prishtina adopted the Bologna-compliant system of three-cycle degree structure, which includes the Bachelors, the Masters and Doctorate. Exceptions to this are the Faculty of Medicine, the Department of Albanian Language and Literature, and the newly established Faculty of Education. During 2004/05 the university enrolled the first students of the second cycle (Master of Arts or Science—two-year programme) in 45 departments across 11 faculties. Since 2006/07 the new programmes have been introduced gradually across all institutions of higher education (in parallel with the old degree system).

According to the new degree structure, the undergraduate Bachelors qualification requires the completion of 180–240 ECTS credits over a period of three to four years. At postgraduate level the Masters represents one year of postgraduate study (60 ECTS credits) after a four-year Bachelors programme or two years of postgraduate study (120 ECTS credits) after a three-year Bachelors programme, making a total of 300 ECTS credits in the first and second cycles. The third cycle—the Doctorate—requires at least three years of full-time study and the completion of 180 ECTS credits following a Masters degree. According to the old, pre-Bologna system of degrees in Kosovo, the following undergraduate qualifications are offered: Professional Baccalaureus—awarded with a professional title, requiring completion of 180–240 ECTS credits over a period of three to four years; Diplomirani (Graduation Diploma)—offered by universities after four to six or more years of full-time study following completion of secondary school; Diplomirani (Graduation Diploma)—awarded by higher schools after two to three years of full-time study; Professor—awarded after four years of full-time study following completion of the Secondary School Leaving Certificate; and Doktor (Medical Science)—awarded after six years of full-time study upon completion of 360 ECTS credits. At postgraduate level the following old-style degrees are available: Magistar Umjetnosti/Znanosti (Master of Arts/Science)—awarded upon completion of two or more years of full-time study following a four-year Diplomirani; Specijalista—Specialist Diploma (professional or academic studies)—representing one year of full-time study following a Baccalaureus and requiring the completion of all examinations and a thesis; and Doktor Znanosti (Doctor of Science)—awarded after at least four years of full-time study following a Magistar.

The Kosovo Accreditation Agency for (KAA) was founded by the Ministry of Education, Science and Technology, in accordance with the Law on Higher Education (2003/14), to provide external evaluation of both institutions and programmes and to assist institutions to carry out self-evaluation. The KAA, which comprises three overseas and six Kosovo experts, also guarantees the quality of educational and scientific research work carried out by both public and private institutions of higher education.

The Law on Vocational Education and Training was passed in April 2006. The new legislation aimed to regulate formal vocational education and training and ensure that it met the future needs of the labour market and complied with EU standards. The law, which specified the Ministry of Education, Science and Technology to be the highest authority regarding the approval and issuing of curricula for formal vocational education and training, envisaged a combination of school-based education with in-company training.

In 2010 the Government announced plans to open new universities in Peja and Gjilan, and the following year, in an attempt to increase enrolment, the University of Prishtina raised its student admission limit.

Regulatory and Representative Bodies

GOVERNMENT

Ministry of Culture, Youth and Sport: Sheshi Nëna Terezë, 10000 Prishtina; tel. (38) 211-637; e-mail info@mkrs-ks.org; internet www.mkrs-ks.org; Minister MEMLI KRASNIQI.

Ministry of Education, Science and Technology: Rruga Agim Ramadani, 10000 Prishtina; tel. (38) 213-327; e-mail masht@ks-gov.net; internet www.masht-gov.net; Minister Prof. Dr RAMË BUJA.

ACCREDITATION

Agjencia e Akreditimit te Kosovës (Kosovo Accreditation Agency): Rruga Agim Ramadani, 10000 Prishtina; tel. (38) 213-722; internet www.akreditimi-ks.org; established by the Ministry of Education, Science and Technology (MEST); public agency for the evaluation of quality at public and private institutions of higher education; Pres. Dr FERDIJE ZHUSHI ETEMI; Dir BASRI MUJA (acting).

Learned Societies

GENERAL

Akademia e Shkencave dhe e Arteve e Kosovës (Kosovo Academy of Sciences and Arts): Rruga Agim Ramadani, 10000 Prishtina; tel. (38) 249-303; e-mail ashak@ashak.org; internet www.ashak.org; f. 1975, present name and status 1978; promotes research in arts, linguistics and literature, natural sciences and social sciences; Pres. HIVZI ISLAMI; Vice-Pres. PAJAZIT NUSHI; publs *Kërkime* (Research, English and foreign), *Studimet* (Studies, English, French and German), *Vjetari* (1 a year).

Fondacionin e Kosovës për Shoqëri të Hapur (Kosovo Foundation for Open Society): Imzot Nike Prela, Vila 13, 10000 Prishtina; tel. (38) 542-157; e-mail info@kfos.org; internet www.kfos.org; f. 1993, present status and name 1999; non-governmental org.; focuses on minority rights, civic participation, European integration, governance and education; Exec. Dir LUAN SHLLAKU; publ. *European Magazine*.

BIBLIOGRAPHY, LIBRARY SCIENCE AND MUSEOLOGY

Shoqata e Bibliotekarëve të Kosovës (Association of Libraries of Kosovo): Sheshi 'Hasan Prishtina', 10000 Prishtina; tel. (38) 212-419; f. 1971; protects the rights of library employees; creates better working conditions; raises professionalism and expands professional activity of the libraries.

Research Institutes

GENERAL

Iniciativa Kosovare për Stabilitet (Kosovar Stability Initiative): Garibaldi St, H11/6, Prishtina; tel. (38) 222-321; e-mail info@iksweb.org; internet www.iksweb.org; f. 2004; empirical research and analysis of socio-economic devts in Kosovo; focuses on issues of corruption in post-war reconstruction, economic devt, education, environmental issues, governance, Kosovo's image problem and urban planning; Exec. Dir FLORINA DULI.

Instituti GAP (GAP Institute): Mbreti Zog St, 31/1, 10000 Prishtina; tel. (38) 224-145; e-mail info@institutigap.org; internet www.gapinstitute.org; f. 2007; professional research and devt institute; addresses the country's pressing economic, political and social challenges; Exec. Dir AGRON DEMI.

Instituti Kosovar për Kërkime dhe Zhvillime të Politikave (Kosovar Institute for Policy Research and Development): Rexhep Mala St 5A, 10000 Prishtina; tel. (38) 227-778; e-mail info@kipred.org; internet www.kipred.org; f. 2002; promotes and consolidates democracy and democratic values in Kosovo and the region through ind. research, capacity devt and instn building; Exec. Dir ILIR DEDA.

Qendra për Arsim e Kosovës (Kosovo Education Centre): Third Millennium School Complex, Isa Kastrati St, 10000 Prishtina; tel. (38) 244-257; e-mail office@kec-ks.org; internet www.kec-ks.org; f. 2000; NGO; conducts research in children rights, education and minority issues; Exec. Dir DUKAGJIN PUPOVCI.

Riinvest Instituti për Hulumtime Zhvillimore (Riinvest Institute for Development Research): Lidhja e Prizrenit No 42, 10000 Prishtina; tel. (38) 244-320; e-mail riinvest@riinvestinstitute.org; internet www.riinvestinstitute.org; f. 1995; non-profit org.; research on policies and policy advocacies on expansion of the business environment and construction of conditions towards economic viability; Pres. SEJDI OSMANI; Exec. Dir LUMIR ABDIXHIKU.

ECONOMICS, LAW AND POLITICS

Demokraci për Zhvillim (Democracy for Development): Nëna Terezë St, Block 30/A, Entry 2/1, Prishtina; tel. (38) 224-143; e-mail info@d4d-ks.org; internet www.d4d-ks.org; think-tank org.; public policy research in the fields of inter-ethnic, regional and int. relations, political parties, governance and socioeconomic devt; Exec. Dir LEON MALAZOGU.

Instituti i Kosovës për Drejtësi (Kosovo Law Institute): Gj. Kastrioti 1, Magjistralja Prishtina-Fushe, 12000 Kosove; e-mail info@kli-ks.org; internet kli-ks.org; non-governmental org.; focuses on legal education reform and continuing legal education, legal researches, legal commentaries and articles related to judiciary in Kosovo, drafting legislation, monitoring of courts system; Exec. Dir ADEM GASHI.

MEDICINE

Instituti Kombëtar i Shëndetësisë Publike te Kosovës (National Institute of Public Health of Kosovo): Rr. Nëna Tereze St, Rrethi i Spitalit, 10000 Prishtina; tel. (38) 550-585; e-mail info@niph-kosova.org; internet www.niph-kosova.org; f. 1925; prepares and implements nat. public health strategy through scientific research; Exec. Dir Dr NASER RAMADANI.

Libraries

Prishtina

Biblioteka 'Hivzi Sulejmani' (Hivzi Sulejmani Library): Rr. UÇK 10, 10000 Prishtina; tel. (38) 245-523; e-mail info@biblioteka-pr.org; internet www.biblioteka-pr.org; f. 1945; 74,719 vols; Dir MUNISH HYSENI; publ. *OAZA Revisitë Letrare* (in Albanian).

Biblioteka Kombëtare dhe Universitare e Kosovës (National and University Library of Kosovo): Hasan Prishtina Sq., 10000 Prishtina; tel. (38) 212-206; e-mail bkuk@biblioteka-ks.org; internet www.biblioteka-ks.org; f. 1944, present location 1946; 200,000 vols; Dir Prof. Dr SALI BASHOTA.

Museums and Art Galleries

Prishtina

Galeria e Arteve e Kosovës (Kosovo Art Gallery): Agim Ramadani 60, Prishtina; tel. (38) 227-833; e-mail gak@kujtesa.com; internet www.galeriaarteve.com; f. 1979; attached to Min. of Culture, Youth and Sport; promotes traditional and contemporary art; exhibits 2-D work of young local artists; organizes workshops and lectures.

Muzeu i Kosovës (Kosovo Museum): Sheshi Adam Jashari, Prishtina; tel. (38) 249-964; f. 1949, built 1898, served as HQ for Yugoslav Nat. Army 1945–75; colln of prehistoric objects uncovered in Kosovo; exhibits incl. clay statue of sitting goddess from the late Neolithic period found in Tjerrtorja in 1955, also featured in Prishtina city emblem; archaeological and ethnological artefacts, approx. 1,250 items moved to Belgrade for an exhibition are still to be returned.

Prishtina Ethnological Museum: Emin Gjik Complex, Rr. Zija 1, Prishtina; tel. (7) 4487-0672; e-mail isopjani@gmail.com; f. 1957 as home to Emin Gjinolli's family, used as Natural Museum until 1990, renovated with int. donations 2003, opened in present form 2006; attached to Dept of Culture, Ministry of Culture, Youth and Sport; displays the urban oda (saloon), folk dresses, folk instruments, Kosovo's heritage of filigree jewellery influenced by Sephardic Jews and practised in Prizren and Gjakova, carpet work, locally produced weapons of the time and religious objects dating back to the Illyrian ancestors.

Universities

AMERICAN UNIVERSITY IN KOSOVO

Nazim Gafurri 21, 10000 Prishtina
Telephone: (38) 608-608
E-mail: info@aukonline.org
Internet: www.aukonline.org
Founded 2002
Private control
Language of instruction: English
Academic year: September to August (4 semesters)

In partnership with the Rochester Institute of Technology (RIT), New York (accredited by the Middle States Association of Colleges and Schools); offers undergraduate and graduate courses; faculties of applied sciences, economics, English, general education, management, mathematics, media and information technology, public policy and governance

Library of 900 books, magazines, daily newspapers, reference materials, classroom materials, electronic technology resources, video cassettes and DVDs

Pres.: CHRISTOPHER HALL
Vice-Pres. and Chief Operating Officer: ILIR IBRAHIMI
Chief Financial Officer: ILIR KRASNIQI
Dir for Admissions: LAVON BAJRAMI
Head for Library: IVANA STEVANOVIC
Publication: *Academic Bulletin* (1 a year)

UNIVERSITETI AAB (AAB University)

Zona Industriale Prishtinë-Fushë Kosovë, 10000 Prishtina
Telephone: (38) 247-524
E-mail: info@universitetiaab.com
Internet: www.universitetiaab.com
Founded 2001 as Academy of Liberal Arts
Private control
Rector: Dr UROS LIPUSCEK
Library: scientific and academic publs, electronic study material

DEANS

Faculty of Applicative and Figurative Arts: BUJAR DEMJAHA
Faculty of Criminological Sciences: Prof. Dr RAMO MASLESA
Faculty of Economics: Prof. Dr FETAH REÇICA
Faculty of Education: Dr ISMAIL HASANI
Faculty of Foreign Languages: Prof. Dr MASAR STAVILECI
Faculty of Law: Dr MERSIM MAKSUTI
Faculty of Mass Communication: Dr RRAHMAN PAÇARIZI
Faculty of Music Arts: Prof. BAKI JASHARI
Faculty of Sport: Prof. Dr MEHDI JASHARI

UNIVERSITETI I PRISHTINËS (University of Prishtina)

Sheshi Nëna Tereze, 10000 Prishtina
Telephone: (38) 244-183
E-mail: rektorati@uni-pr.edu
Internet: www.uni-pr.edu
Founded 1969
State control
Academic year: September to June
Rector: Prof. Dr MUJË RUGOVA
Vice-Rector for Int. Cooperation: Prof. Dr NASER MRASORI
Vice-Rector for Resources and Infrastructure: Prof. Dr ENVER KUTLLOVCI
Vice-Rector for Teaching and Scientific Research: Prof. Dr BAJRAM BERISHA
Sec.-Gen.: MILAIM MAZREKU
Library: see under Libraries and Archives
Number of teachers: 756

Number of students: 41,383 (37,839 undergraduate, 3,544 postgraduate)

Publications: *Acta Biologiae et Medicinae Experimentalis, Pregled Predavanja, Univerzitetska Misao*

DEANS

Faculty of Agriculture and Veterinary Science: Dr SKENDER MUJI
Faculty of Applied Sciences in Business: Dr ARMAND KRASNIQI
Faculty of Applied Technical Sciences (Ferizaj): Dr AGRON BAJRAKTARI
Faculty of Applied Technical Sciences (Mitrovica): Dr AVDI SALIHU
Faculty of Arts: Prof. ADEM RUSTINOVCI
Faculty of Economics: Prof. Dr SKENDER AHMETI
Faculty of Education: Prof. HASAN MUJI
Faculty of Electrical Engineering and Computing: Dr MYZAFERE LIMANI
Faculty of Engineering and Architecture: Dr NASER KABASHI
Faculty of Law: Prof. Dr BAJRAM UKA
Faculty of Mathematics and Natural Sciences: Prof. Dr MINIR EFENDIJA
Faculty of Mechanical Engineering: Dr MUSLI BAJRAKTARI
Faculty of Medicine: Prof. NAIM HALITI (acting)
Faculty of Mining and Metallurgy: IZET ZEQIRI
Faculty of Philology: Prof. Dr OSMAN GASHI
Faculty of Philosophy: Prof. Dr RAMUSH MAVRIQI
Faculty of Sport Sciences: AJVAZ BERISHA

PROFESSORS

AHMEDI, I.
BAJRAKTARI, M.
BEHLULI, I.
EFENDIJA, M.
HAXHIBEQIRI, Q.
KABASHI, N.
KRASNIQI, F.
RESHANI, S.
RUGOVA, M.

UNIVERSITETI I PRISHTINËS—KOSOVSKA MITROVICA
(University of Prishtina—Kosovska Mitrovica)

Filip Visnjic St bb, 38220 Kosovska Mitrovica, Serbia
Telephone: (28) 422-340
E-mail: rektorat@pr.ac.rs
Internet: www.pr.ac.rs

Founded 1969
State control
Language of instruction: Serbian
Academic year: October to September

Rector: Dr SRECKO MILACIC
Vice-Rector for Education and Students Matters: Dr TOMISLAV TRIFIC
Vice-Rector for Int. and Inter-Univ. Relations: Dr ZDRAVKO VITOSEVIC
Sec.-Gen.: RENKA SCEPANOVIC

Library of 13,200 vols
Number of teachers: 746
Number of students: 10,000

DEANS

Faculty of Agriculture: Dr BOZIDAR MILOSEVIC
Faculty of Arts: ZORAN FURUNDZIC
Faculty of Economy: Dr ZVEZDICA SIMIC
Faculty of Law: Prof. Dr DUSANKA JOVOVIC
Faculty of Medical Science: Dr RADE GRBIC
Faculty of Philosophy: Prof. Dr BRANKO JOVANOVIC
Faculty of Science and Mathematics: Prof. Dr DRAGOMIR KICOVIC
Faculty of Sports and Physical Education: Prof. Dr DRAGAN POPOVIC
Faculty of Teacher Training: Prof. Dr ALIJA MANDAK
Faculty of Technical Science: Prof. Dr NEBOJSA ARSIC

PROFESSORS

ADROVIC, F., Experimental Physics
ANDJELKOVIC, Z., Histology
ANDREJEVIC, D., History of Serbian Literature
ANDRIC, V., Otorhinolaryngology
ARSIC, N., Energetics
ATLAGIC, M., History of Middle Age
BABIC, R., Telecommunication
BABIC, S., Plastic Anatomy
BACEVIC, M., Social Geography
BACOVIC, V., History of Serbian Literature
BAJMAK, S., Thermotechnics and Thermoenergetics
BARAC, M., Chemical Engineering
BARAC, S., Agricultural Mechanization
BASIC, S., Social Medicine
BIBERDZIC, M., Crop Husbandry
BJELIC, S., Electroenergetics
BOZINOVIC, M., Economic Statistics and Decision-making Methods
BUKUMIRIC, M., Contemporary Serbian Language
CATOVIC, E., Drawing
COVIC, L., Russian Language
DELETIC, Z., History of Serbian People in the 19th and 20th Centuries
DIMITRIJEVIC, B., Acting
DJEKIC, S., Production Mechanics
DJUZA, P., Painting
DOGANDZIC, A., Finances and Financial Institutions
ERCEVIC, L., Methodology of Art Education
FOLIC, L., Designing
FURUNOVIC, Z., Painting
GARIC, M., Viticulture
GLIGORIJEVIC, S., Morphology, Systematics and Phylogeny of Higher Plants
HOSEK, A., Applied Sociology
ISAILOVIC, Z., Financial Law
JANICIJEVIC, S., Pharmacology and Toxicology
JEVRIC, M., South-Slavic Literature
JEVTIC, M., Electroenergetics
JOVANOVIC, A., Internal Medicine
JOVANOVIC, B., General Pedagogy
JOVICEVIC, J., Physical Chemistry
JOVOVIC, D., Macroeconomical Theory and Politics
KACAPOR, S., General Pedagogy
KARAFERIC, A., Counterpoint
KICOVIC, D., Tourismology
KIKOVIC, D., Morphology, Systematics and Phylogeny of Lower Plants
KNEZEVIC, D., Husbandry
KOSANOVIC, K., Animal Physiology
KOSTIC, P., Methodology of Psychological Research
KOSTIC, S., Theoretical Subjects
KRSTIC, N., Dermatovenereology
KRVAVAC, M., International Private Law
KULIC, R., Science of Education
MALIKOVIC, D., New Age History of Serbian People
MANDAK, A., Mathematics
MARICIC, N., Applied Mechanics
MEMOVIC, E., Petrology
MIHAJLOVIC, V., Constitutional Law
MILACIC, S., Finances and Financial Institutions
MILANOVIC, B., Commercial Law
MILANOVIC, Z., Physiology
MILENKOVIC, M., Livestock Farming
MILETIC, S., Marketing
MILINIC, S., Internal Medicine
MILOJEVIC, A., Psychology in Education
MIRIC, M., Pathophysiology
MITIC, N., Pathology
MITROVIC, J., Business Informatics
MITROVIC, L., Macroeconomical Theory and Politics
MUSOVIC, A., Russian Language
NEDELJKOVIC, B., Rock and Soil Mechanics
NENADOVIC, M., Psychiatry
NESIC, B., Developmental Psychology
NESIC, V., Harmony and Study of Harmony
NIKCEVIC, P., Sculpture—Sculpture in the Material
NOVAKOVIC, T., Internal Medicine
OBRADOVIC, D., Sculpture—Modelling
PATROVIC, B., Gynaecology and Obstetrics
PAVLOVIC, A., Anaesthesiology
PEJCIC, H., Agriculture Economics and Cooperative Movements
PERIC, M., Paediatrics
PETKOVIC, D., Applied Physics
PETKOVIC, M., Sports and Sports Training
PETROVIC, M., Telecommunication
PETROVIC, N., Neurology
PETROVIC, R., Middle Age
PLECAS, M., Acting
POPOVIC, D., Martial Arts with Exploring Methods
RADOVIC, D., Physiology
RAICEVIC, S., Middle Age
RAICEVIC, V., Theoretical Mechanics
RAJOVIC, V., 'Evening Act'
REDZEPAGIC, S., Children's and Preventive Stomatology
RELIC, G., Gynaecology and Obstetrics
RISTANOVIC, D., Chemistry
RISTIC, J., Computing and Informatics
SAMARDZIC, S., Epidemiology
SAVIC, G., Genetics
SAVIC, L., Construction of Underground Spaces
SEKULIC, S., Surgery
SIMIC, Z., Economic Theory and Macroeconomic Analysis
SIMONOVIC, R., Analytical Chemistry
SOFTIC, S., Internal Medicine
SPALEVIC, L., Mathematics for Economists
STAMENKOVIC, S., Plant Protection
STANIMIROVIC, N., Agricultural Mechanization
STANISIC, S., Gynaecology and Obstetrics
STANOJEVIC, P., Criminal Procedural Law
STOJKOVIC, J., Livestock Farming and Domestic Animal Nutrition
STOSIC, N., Market Analysis and Prices
SUBARIC-GORGIEVA, G., Internal Medicine
TAHIRBEGOVIC, K., Thermotechnics and Thermoenergetics
TODIC, T., Production Mechanics
TOMIC, M., Mathematics
TOMIC, S., Internal Medicine
TRAJKOVIC, S., Business Informatics
TRIFIC, T., Graphics
UZELAC, M., Philosophy
VASIC, A., Surgery
VASIC, Z., Applied Mechanics
VEKOVIC, V., Criminology
VITOSEVIC, Z., Anatomy
VUCKOVIC, Z., Technology of Painting
ZAJMI, F., Graphical Design
ZELENOVIC, J., Marketing
ZIVKOVIC, M., Dental Illness
ZIZIC, M., Theory of Law
ZORIC, L., Ophthalmology

UNIVERSITETI I PRIZRENIT
(University of Prizren)

Tirana St, 20000 Prizren
Telephone: (29) 631-403
E-mail: info@uni-pz.org
Internet: www.uni-pz.org

Founded 2006
State control
Academic year: October to May

Faculties of architecture, computer science, economy, English literature, law, political science, psychology

Rector: Dr MAZLLUM BARALIU

Vice-Rector: Dr BEHXHET MUSTAFA
Library of 10,000 vols, 3,600 periodicals
Number of teachers: 77

UNIVERSITETI MBRETËROR ILIRIA (Iliria Royal University)

Rr. Gamend Zajmi 75, 10060 Prishtina
Telephone: (38) 233-951
E-mail: info@uiliria.org
Internet: www.uiliria.org
Private control
Languages of instruction: Albanian, English
Academic year: September to July
Under the royal patronage; offers Bachelors, Masters and doctoral courses
Pres.: Prof. Dr MIXHAIT REÇI
Rector: PAJAZIT NUSHI
Number of teachers: 150
Number of students: 6,000
Publications: *ILIRIA International Review*, *Revista Elektronike Studentore*

UNIVERSITETI PËR BIZNES DHE TEKNOLOGJI (University for Business and Technology)

Lagjja Kalabria, 10000 Prishtina
Telephone: (38) 541-400
E-mail: info@ubt-uni.net
Internet: www.ubt-uni.net
Private control
Languages of instruction: Albanian, English, French, German
Academic year: October to June
Courses in architecture and spatial planning, business and economy, computer science and engineering, information systems, law, management, mechatronics management; attached institute: Institute for European Studies and Int. Relations
Pres.: Dr EDMOND HAJRIZI

Colleges

Kolegji Dardania—Universiteti Dardania (Dardania College—Dardania University): Rr. Nazim Gafurri 17, Prishtina; tel. (38) 247-587; e-mail kolegjidardania@gmail.com; internet kolegjidardania.eu; f. 2004; depts of economics, economy of regional development, foreign languages, law, psychology and public administration; Rector Dr GJYLDANE MULLA.

Kolegji Evropian Dukagjini (European College Dukagjini): Rr. Wesley Clark, 30000 Peja; tel. (39) 431-684; e-mail info@dukagjinicollege.eu; internet www.dukagjinicollege.eu; f. 2006 as European Vision Univ., temporarily merged with the College Iliria in Prishtina, as the Peja Br.; offers Bachelors and Masters courses in applied informatics, banking, financing and accounting, law, management and informatics; Sec. MENTOR KAÇI; Dir for Admin. VIOLETA BEQIRI; Dir for Finance KASTRIOT GJOCAJ; Librarian SERVETE SHALA; publs *Buletini Shkencor* (Scientific Bulletin, 1 a year), *Revista Kerkime Zhvillimore* (Development Research Journal), *Revista Studentore* (Student Magazine).

Kolegji Fama (Fama College): Rr. Gustav Majer 7, 10000 Prishtina; tel. (38) 222-212; e-mail info@kolegjifama.eu; internet www.kolegjifama.eu; f. 2003; offers courses in banking, finance and accounting, criminology, management, law, political science and public administration, psychology, sociology; campuses in Prishtina, Prizren and Gjilan; Rector Dr FAIK BRESTOVC.

Kolegji Universi (Universe College): Bardhosh, 10100 Prishtina; tel. (38) 515-896; e-mail info@kolegjiuniversi.com; internet www.kolegjiuniversi.com; f. 2005; offers Bachelors and Masters programmes in physical culture, sport and recreation, nursing, sports medicine; library: 1,000 vols; 350 students; Dean ENVER GJINOLLI.

Kolegji Universitar Biznesi (Business University College): Rr. Motrat Qiriazi 29, Ulpianë, 10000 Prishtina; tel. (38) 500-878; internet uni-biznesi.com; f. 2004; offers Bachelors and Masters courses in banking and finance in business, emergency management, general law, management and economics, management and finance; library: 3,000 vols; Chair. Prof. Dr RESHAT KADRIU; Dean Prof. Dr SHYQERI KABASHI; 950 students; publ. *Modern Business*.

Kolegji Universitar Gjilani (Gjilani University College): Gjilan; tel. (280) 325-420; internet www.kugjilani.com; f. 2006; offers courses in banking, finance and accounting, general law, management; Dean NAIM MUSTAFA.

Kolegji Universitar Humanistica (Humanistica University College): Rr. Deshmorët e Kombit, Ferizaj; tel. (29) 326-070; e-mail info@humanistica-ks.net; internet www.humanistica-ks.net; library: 500 vols; Dir-Gen. Dr ISMAIL HASANI.

Kolegji Universitar ISPE (ISPE University College): Adrian Krasniqi St 9, 10000 Prishtina; tel. (38) 221-744; e-mail info@ispe-institut.org; internet www.kolegji-ispe.org; offers Bachelors programmes in economics, European integrated studies, law and security studies; Masters programme in European studies; Dir Prof. Dr AVNI MAZREKU.

Kolegji Universitar 'Pjetër Budi' (Pjeter Budi University College): Rr. Isa Kastrati, Prishtina; tel. (38) 234-566; e-mail info@universitetipjeterbudi.com; internet www.pjeterbudi.com; f. 2005; college of insurance, faculties of business administration, customs and forwarding, tourism and hotel management; Rector Dr SOFRONIJA MILADINOSKI; publ. *LOGOS*.

Kolegji Universitar Victory (University College Victory): Perandori Justinian 3, 10000 Prishtina; tel. (38) 248-445; e-mail info@kolegjivictory.com; internet www.kolegjivictory.com; f. 2005; offers undergraduate and postgraduate courses in business economics—foreign trade, international policy and diplomacy, law and international relations; Rector Dr BEDRI SELMANI.

Kolegji Universum (Universum College): Veterniku (përball Grand Store), Prishtina; tel. (38) 544-210; e-mail info@universum-ks.org; internet www.universum-ks.org; depts of business and management, and political science; mem. of European Assoc. for Int. Education; library: 4,000 vols; 403 (358 full-time, 45 part-time) students; Rector Dr ISAK SHEMA; publ. *Working Paper Series*.

Kolegji Vizioni Për Arsim (Vizioni Per Arsim College): Rr. Ahmet Kaçiku, 70000 Ferizaj; tel. (44) 583-573; e-mail vizionipa@gmail.com; internet www.vizioniperarsim.com; faculties of computer sciences and economy.

KUWAIT

The Higher Education System

Kuwait University (founded 1966) is the sole public university. In 2005/06 it had some 19,711 students enrolled out of an estimated total of 37,521 students in tertiary education. Kuwait University, which comprises 16 colleges located across five campuses, provides scholarships for a number of Arab, Asian and African students. By 2008/09 the total number of students enrolled in tertiary education in Kuwait had risen to an estimated 61,920. In 2011 there were 16 private higher education institutions. Although all the 16 institutions were licensed by the Private Universities Council of the Ministry of Higher Education, only eight had received official accreditation from the same body; these were American College of the Middle East, American University of the Middle East, American University of Kuwait, Arab Open University, Australian College of Kuwait, Box Hill College Kuwait (women's college), Gulf University for Science and Technology, and Kuwait–Maastricht Business School. The language of instruction at all of these private institutions is English and a number of them follow foreign curricula and degree systems. It is government policy to provide free education for all Kuwaiti citizens from primary to tertiary level. Students wishing to undertake courses not offered by Kuwait University are offered scholarships to study abroad (mainly in Egypt, Lebanon, the United Kingdom and the USA). In May 1996 the National Assembly approved a draft law to regulate students' behaviour, dress and activities, with regard to observance of the teachings of Shari'a (Islamic) law, and to eradicate coeducational classes at Kuwait University over a five-year period. Gender segregation was extended to private universities with the implementation of further legislation in January 2008. A KD 1,000m. project to build a large new modern campus ('University City') for the University of Kuwait to gather the institution's dispersed facilities on to one site was in the planning stages in early 2005 and was expected to be completed by 2015.

Admission to university-level undergraduate courses is on the basis of the General Secondary Education Certificate (Shahadat-al-thanawia-al-a'ama). The Bachelors degree is arranged on a US-style 'credit semester' system and usually lasts four years, except for professional programmes such as engineering and medicine, which last five and seven years, respectively. Masters degrees at Kuwait University last up to two years and are available in most subjects. Doctoral studies (in a limited range of subject areas) have only recently been offered at Kuwait University. In addition, postgraduate diplomas (known as Higher Diplomas) are offered in three specialist subjects at Kuwait University—Public Administration, Islamic Finance, and Marriage and Family Counselling.

The Public Authority for Applied Education and Training, which was established in 1982, oversees technical and vocational education. There are currently four colleges and seven institutes that offer tertiary-level courses in applied subjects. Most of these establishments offer two-year programmes leading to the Diploma in Applied Science Technology or the Diploma in Applied Business Science. The College of Basic Education offers a four-year Bachelors of Education.

Regulatory and Representative Bodies

GOVERNMENT

Ministry of Education: POB 7, 13001 Safat, Hilali St, Kuwait City; tel. 24839452; internet www.moe.edu.kw; Minister AHMAD ABD AL-MOHSIN AL-MULAIFI.

Ministry of Higher Education: Safat; tel. 24925177; e-mail info_minister@mohe.edu.kw; internet www.mohe.edu.kw; Minister AHMAD ABD AL-MOHSIN AL-MULAIFI (acting).

ACCREDITATION

Private Universities Council: POB 26166, 13122 Safat; tel. 22240591; e-mail imad@puc.edu.kw; internet www.puc.edu.kw; f. 2001; affiliated to Higher Education Council; ensures conformity with all rules and stipulations for licensing private educational instns; Chair. MINISTER OF HIGHER EDUCATION; Sec.-Gen. IMAD ALATIQI.

NATIONAL BODY

Public Authority for Applied Education and Training: POB 23167, 13092 Safat; tel. 22564960; e-mail bscg@paaet.edu.kw; internet www.paaet.edu.kw; f. 1982; autonomous body supervising technical and vocational training; the applied education sector comprises College of Basic Education, College of Business Studies, College of Technological Studies and College of Health Sciences; institutes in operation are Telecommunications and Navigation Institute, Electricity and Water Institute, Industrial Training Institute (brs in Shuwaikh and Subbah al-Salem), Nursing Institute, Constructional Training Institute and Vocational Training Institute.

Learned Societies

GENERAL

National Council for Culture, Arts and Letters: POB 23996, 13100 Safat; tel. 22469090; internet www.kuwait-info.com/a_culture/culture_nccal.asp; f. 1973; guidance and support in all fields of culture; sponsors art exhibitions, drama, publishes books and periodicals; Sec.-Gen. ALI AL YOHA; publs *Alam al-Fikr*, *Alam Al-Ma'arifa*, *Al-Fonon*, *Al-Thaqafa al-'Alamiyah*, *Ibda'at 'Alamiyah*.

LANGUAGE AND LITERATURE

British Council: 2 Al Arabi St, Block 2, POB 345, 13004 Safat, Mansouria, Kuwait City; tel. 22520067; e-mail info@kw.britishcouncil.org; internet www.britishcouncil.org/kuwait; teaching centre; offers courses and exams in English language and British culture and promotes cultural exchange with the UK; library of 9,000 vols; Dir, Teaching Centre Man. JOHN PARE (acting).

MEDICINE

Kuwait Medical Association: POB 1202, 13013 Safat; tel. 25312630; e-mail kmj@kma.org.kw; internet www.kma.org.kw; f. 1967; library of 46 vols; Pres. Dr ALI ALMUKAIMI; Sec.-Gen. Dr SHEHAB A. S. AKROOF; publ. *Kuwait Medical Journal* (4 a year).

Kuwait Medical Genetics Centre: tel. 24814328; e-mail rhjorge@kmgc.com.kw; internet www.kmgc.gov.kw; Chair. Dr SADIKA AL-AWADI.

Research Institutes

ECONOMICS, LAW AND POLITICS

Arab Planning Institute, Kuwait: POB 5834, 13059 Safat; tel. 24843130; e-mail api@api.org.kw; internet www.arab-api.org; f. 1966 with assistance from the UN Devt Programme, and since 1972 financed by 15 Arab mem. states; trains personnel in economic and social devt planning; undertakes research and advisory work and organizes confs and seminars on problems affecting economic and social devt in the Arab world; library of 70,000 vols (28,000 Arabic, 42,000 English), 400 periodicals; Dir-Gen. Dr BADER O. MALALLAH; Deputy Dir-Gen. Dr ALI ABDELGADIR ALI; publs *API working paper series* (in Arabic and English, irregular), *Development Bridge* (in Arabic, 10 a year), *Journal of Development and Economic Policies* (in Arabic and English, 2 a year).

EDUCATION

Gulf Arab States Educational Research Centre: POB 12580, 71656 Shamia; tel. 24835203; e-mail gaserc@kuwait.net; internet www.gaserc.edu.kw; f. 1978 as part of Arab Bureau of Education for the Gulf States; research on all educational topics; also provides training courses in developed curricula, educational statistics, educational evaluation, and educational research; Dir Prof. MARZOUG Y. AL-GHOUNIAM; Librarian MOHEI A. HAK; publ. *Al-Hasaad Al-Terbawi (Arabic Text)* (6 a year).

MEDICINE

Arabization Centre for Medical Sciences: POB 5225, 13053 Safat; tel. 25338610; e-mail acmls@acmls.org; internet www.acmls.org; f. 1983; part of Council of Arab Ministers of Health—Arab League; aims: the Arabization of medical literature and translation into Arabic of medical sciences, development of a current bibliographic database, issuing of Arabic medical directories, training of manpower in the field of medical information and library science; library of 1,000 vols; Sec.-Gen. Dr ABDEL RAHMAN AL-AWADI; publs *Arab Medical Doctors' Directory*, *Directory of Health Education and Research Organizations in Arab Countries*, *Directory of Hospitals and Clinics in Arab World*.

Kuwait Institute for Medical Specialization: POB 1793, 13018 Safat; tel. 22418782; e-mail info@kims.org.kw; internet www.kims.org.kw; f. 1984; attached to Min. of Health; publ. *Journal*.

NATURAL SCIENCES

General

Kuwait Foundation for the Advancement of Science: POB 25263, 13113 Safat; tel. 22425898; internet www.kfas.com; f. 1976; promotes scientific and technological advancement, provides financial aid for research projects, organizes symposia and conferences, develops Arabic-language publications; Dir ALI A. AL-SHAMLAN; publs *Al-Taqaddum al-Ilmi* (Scientific Advancement, 4 a year), *Majallat Al-Oloom* (12 a year).

Kuwait Institute for Scientific Research: POB 24885, 13109 Safat; tel. 24989360; e-mail public_relations@safat.kisr.edu.kw; internet www.kisr.edu.kw; f. 1967; promotes and conducts scientific research in the fields of economics and applied systems, environmental studies, food resources, infrastructure services and urban devt, oil sector support and water resources; Dir-Gen. Dr NAJI MOHAMED AL-MUTAIRI; publ. *Science and Technology*.

Libraries and Archives

Kuwait City

Kuwait University Libraries: POB 23558, Kuwait City; e-mail jac.lib@kuniv.edu; internet library.kuniv.edu.kw; f. 1966; 233,733 vols, 2,445 periodicals, 1,298 electronic journals, 20,000 audiovisual items; Dir DHIYA' ALJASIM.

Safat

National Library of Kuwait: POB 26182, 13122 Safat; tel. 22415181; e-mail library@nlk.gov.kw; internet www.nlk.gov.kw; f. 1936; nat. and UN depository library; nat. ISBN agency; nat. bibliographic centre; special colln *Kuwaitiana*; over 300,000 vols in Arabic and English, 750 periodicals; Dir-Gen. IMAD ABULBANAT.

National Scientific and Technical Information Centre: Kuwait Institute for Scientific Research, POB 24885, 13109 Safat; tel. 4818713.

Museums and Art Galleries

Safat

Department of Antiquities and Museums: POB 23996, 13100 Safat; tel. 22426521; Dir Dr FAHED AL-WOHAIBI.

Museums Controlled by the Department:

Failaka Island Archaeological Museum:exhibits from excavations.

Failaka Island Ethnographic Museum:colln of material from Failaka Island, housed in the old residence of the island's Sheikh.

Kuwait National Museum: Arabian Gulf St, Kuwait City; tel. 22432020; f. 1957; antiquities from late Bronze Age to Hellenistic period found at Failaka Island; ethnographic material.

Educational Science Museum: Ministry of Education, POB 7, 13001 Safat; tel. 22421268; f. 1972; lectures, exhibitions, film shows, etc.; sections on natural history, science, space, oil, health; planetarium, meteorology; library of 2,000 vols; Dir ADNAN AL-ALI.

Salmiya

Scientific Centre: POB 3504, 22036 Salmiya; tel. 1848888; e-mail info@tsck.org.kw; internet www.tsck.org.kw; educational facility with architectural design reflecting Islamic art and culture; walls contain ceramic depictions of Kuwait's history; bldg comprises aquarium, Discovery Place and IMAX theatre.

Universities

AMERICAN UNIVERSITY OF KUWAIT

POB 3323, 13034 Safat
Telephone: 2224399
E-mail: president@auk.edu.kw
Internet: www.auk.edu.kw

Founded 2003, accredited in 2006
Private control

Liberal arts, coeducational

Pres.: Dr TIM SULLIVAN
Exec. Dir: ERNEST E. COKLIN
Dean for Academic Affairs: Dr NIZAR HAMZEH
Dean for Student Affairs: Dr CAROL ROSS
Dir for Public Relations: AMAL AL-BINALI
Registrar: JILL ALLGIER
Librarian: AMNA AL-OMARE

Number of teachers: 125

AMERICAN UNIVERSITY OF THE MIDDLE EAST

POB 220, 15453 Dasman
Block 3, Bldg 1, Egaila Area
Telephone: 22251400
E-mail: info@aum.edu.kw
Internet: www.aum.edu.kw

Colleges of business, engineering; offers Masters in business administration programme; affiliated with Purdue Univ. and Univ. of Calgary in Canada

ARAB OPEN UNIVERSITY

POB 32004, Al-Jabria
Telephone: 24767291
E-mail: director@aou.edu.kw
Internet: www.aou.edu.kw

Founded 2003
Private control, in partnership with Open University, UK

Faculties of business administration, education, general studies, IT and computing, language studies

Pres. and Chair.: HRH Prince TALAL BIN ABDULAZIZ
Dir: Prof. ISMAIL TAQI

AUSTRALIAN COLLEGE OF KUWAIT

POB 1411, 13015 Safat
Telephone: 25376111
Internet: www.ack.edu.kw

Founded 2004
Private control

Depts of business studies and engineering

Pres.: ABDULLAH ABDUL MOHSEN AL SHARHAN

GULF UNIVERSITY FOR SCIENCE AND TECHNOLOGY

POB 7207, 32093 Hawally
Telephone: 25307000
E-mail: info@gust.edu.kw
Internet: www.gust.edu.kw

Founded 2002
Private control

Pres.: Dr ABDUL-RAHMAN SALEH AL-MUHAILAN
Dean for Student Affairs: Dr SABAH AL-QUADDOOMI
Librarian: SHOBHITA KOHLI

Library of 8,500 vols, 170 periodicals

DEANS

College of Arts and Sciences: Dr RAY WEISBORN
College of Business Administration: Prof. HUSSEIN AL-TALAFHA

PROFESSORS

AL-TALAFHA, H., Business Administration
ANKLI, R., Economics and Management
SAVAGE, A. J., Management and Marketing

KUWAIT UNIVERSITY

POB 5969, 13060 Safat
Telephone: 24845839
E-mail: info@kuniv.edu
Internet: www.kuniv.edu.kw

Founded 1966
State control
Languages of instruction: Arabic, English
Academic year: September to June (2 semesters)

Chancellor: HE THE MINISTER OF HIGHER EDUCATION
Pres.: Prof. NADER AL-JALLAL
Vice-Pres. for Academic Affairs: Prof. HASSAN AL-ALAWI
Vice-Pres. for Planning and Evaluation: Dr MOUDI AL-HUMOUD
Vice-Pres. for Research and Graduate Studies: Dr ASSAD ISMAEL
Dean for Admissions and Registration: Dr ABDULLA AL-FUHAID
Sec.-Gen.: Dr AHMED AL-DEKHIL (acting)
Library Dir: Dr HUSEIN AL-ANSARI

Library: see under Libraries and Archives
Number of teachers: 4,530
Number of students: 19,320

Publications: *Annals of the Faculty of Arts* (12 a year), *Arab Journal for the Humanities* (4 a year), *Arab Journal of Linguistics*, *Arab Journal of Management Sciences* (3 a year), *Educational Journal* (4 a year), *Islamic Studies Magazine* (3 a year), *Journal of Gulf and Arabian Peninsula* (4 a year), *Journal of Law* (4 a year), *Journal of Palestine Studies*, *Journal of Science* (2 a year), *Journal of the Social Sciences* (4 a year), *Medical Principles and Practice* (4 a year)

DEANS

College of Allied Health Sciences and Nursing: Dr HABIB ABUL
College of Arts: Dr SHAFIQA BASTAKI
College of Business Administration: Dr ADEL AL-HUSSAINAN
College of Dentistry: Dr JAWAD BEHBEHANI

College of Education: Dr RASHID ALI AL-SAHEL
College of Engineering and Petroleum: Prof. ABDUL-LATEEF AL-KHALEEFI
College of Graduate Studies: Dr ABDULLA AL-SHEIKH
College of Law: Dr FADEL NASRALLAH
College of Medicine: Dr JAWAD BEHBEHANI
College of Pharmacy: Dr LADISLAV NOVOTNY
College of Science: Prof. REDHA AL-HASAN
College of Shari'a and Islamic Studies: Dr MOHAMMED AL-TABTABAIE
College of Social Sciences: Dr ALI A. AL-TARRAH
Women's College: Dr AHMET YIGIT

KUWAIT–MAASTRICHT BUSINESS SCHOOL

Block 3, Kazima St, Dasma
Telephone: 22517091
E-mail: info@kmbs.edu.kw
Internet: www.kmbs.edu.kw

Founded 2003
Private control

Pres.: KHALEEL AL-ABDULLAH
Dir: ROSEMARY LLOYD
Head of Academic Affairs: Prof. HERNAN RIQUELME

PROFESSORS

MAGALHAES, R., Information Systems and Organization
NIKOLIK, D. A., e-Business
RIQUELME, H., Entrepreneurship and Strategy
RWEGASIRA, K. S. P., Financial Management and Accounting
SYBRANDY, A., Marketing
TUNINGA, R. S. J., International Business and Marketing

Colleges

Box Hill College Kuwait: POB 29192, 13152 Safat; tel. 22471703; e-mail info@bhck.edu.kw; internet www.bhck.edu.kw; attached to Box Hill Institute TAFE, Melbourne, Australia; Pres. EISA AL-REFAI; Exec. Vice-Pres. for Admin. JOE ALBAYATI.

College of Basic Education: *Female Campus*: POB 34053, 73251 Adailiya; tel. 24816044; e-mail bscg@paaet.edu.kw; f. 1973; attached to Public Authority for Applied Education and Training; BA degree courses in education; depts of Arabic language, education, educational technology, home economics, library sciences, interior design, Islamic sciences, mathematics, music education, physical education, psychology, sciences, social studies, teaching of arts.

College of Business Studies: *Male Campus*: POB 43197, 32046 Hawalli; tel. 22633622; e-mail bim@paaet.edu.kw; *Female Campus*: POB 44069, 32055 Hawalli; tel. 26169913; e-mail bif@paaet.edu.kw; f. 1975; attached to Public Authority for Applied Education and Training; depts of accountancy, administration and secretarial studies, economics, English language, insurance and banking, office training, typewriting.

College of Health Sciences: *Female Campus*: POB 14281, 72853 Shuwaikh; tel. 24837056; e-mail chsh@paaet.edu.kw; *Male Campus*: POB 33496, 73455 Rawda; tel. 22570115; e-mail chsm@paaet.edu.kw; f. 1974; attached to Public Authority for Applied Education and Training; Assoc. Degree courses; depts of environmental health, food sciences and nutrition, medical records, natural sciences, nursing, oral and dental health, pharmaceutical and medical sciences.

College of Technological Studies: POB 42325, 70654 Shuwaikh; tel. 24816122; internet www.paaet.edu.kw/cts; f. 1976; attached to Public Authority for Applied Education and Training; Assoc. Degree courses; depts of air conditioning and refrigeration, applied sciences, chemical engineering, civil engineering, electrical engineering, and power engineering, electronic engineering, motor vehicle and marine engineering, production engineering and welding; library: 6,510 vols, 180 periodicals; 322 teachers; 1,950 students; Dean Dr ADEL S. AL-JIMAZ.

Constructional Training Institute: POB 23167, 13092 Safat; tel. 4833186; f. 2000; attached to German Institute for Technical Cooperation; training programmes in building construction, civil engineering, interior finishing, mechanics.

Electricity and Water Institute: POB 15196, 35452 Daiyah; tel. 22570252; 2-year courses aimed at fulfilling requirements of Ministry of Electricity and Water in electrical power stations, water distillation plants, water pumps, operation of reverse osmosis units, maintenance of electrical networks.

Industrial Training Institute: POB 1236, 44000 Subbah al-Salem; tel. 25520037; f. 1992; 3-year courses to technician level.

Institute of Banking Studies: POB 1080, 13011 Safat; tel. 22458460; internet www.kibs.edu.kw; f. 1970 as Banking Studies Center; present name and Specialized Institute status 1982; accredited certificates in Islamic banking and financial services, credit management, investment management; Dir RIDHA M. AL KHAYYAT.

Nursing Institute: Al-Sabah Hospital, POB 22195, 13098 Safat; tel. 24819036; f. 1962; General Nursing Programme.

Vocational Training Institute: Sharq, POB 23167, 13092 Safat; tel. 22422116; 4-year courses in automotive electrics, refrigeration and air conditioning maintenance, automotive mechanics, cabinet work and decoration, formwork and reinforced concrete, electrical installation, offset printing, welding and metal casting.

KYRGYZSTAN

The Higher Education System

Following the Russian revolution in 1917, Kyrgyzstan was established as an autonomous region within the Russian Soviet Federated Socialist Republic (RSFSR). In 1936 it was recognized as a full Union member of the Soviet Union and became the Kyrgyz Soviet Socialist Republic. The oldest institutions of higher education were founded during the early years of Soviet rule, among them Jalal-Abad State University (founded 1926), Kyrgyz National University 'Zhusup Balasagyn' (founded 1925; current name 1993) and Kyrgyz Agrarian Academy (founded 1933). In August 1991 Kyrgyzstan declared its independence from the Soviet Union. The Ministry of Education and Science is responsible for the administration of higher education, which in 2011 consisted of 28 public and 23 private universities. The same year a total of 258,869 students were enrolled in tertiary education. Higher education is governed according to the Law on Education (1992). Since independence a number of reforms have given higher education institutions a greater level of autonomy for defining their academic programmes (within the framework of the state educational standards) and their methods of teaching. Some institutions of a specialist or professional nature are administered by the appropriate government ministry, and several universities are run on a cooperative basis between the Kyrgyz Government and governments of other countries, such as Kyrgyz-Russian Slavic University (founded 1993) and Kyrgyzstan-Turkey Manas University (founded 1995). The principal language of instruction at higher education institutions is Russian. The State Licensing and Attestation Inspectorate Service for Educational Institutions was established in 1994 under the authority of the Ministry of Education and Science and is the accrediting agency for higher education. Higher education institutions have to renew their accreditation every five years.

Admission to higher education is on the basis of the Certificate of Completed Secondary Education and success in university entrance examinations (which have been administered as a unified system—the National Scholarship Test—since 2003 by the independent Centre for Educational Assessment and Teaching Methods). Although Kyrgyzstan ratified the Lisbon Recognition Convention in 2004, it is not a state party to the European Cultural Convention of the Council of Europe, and is therefore not eligible to join the Bologna Process. None the less, the Education Development Strategy of the Kyrgyz Republic (2007–10) included plans to bring the country's education system in line with the key aspects of the Bologna Declaration. Kyrgyzstan currently operates a dual system of the old Soviet-style degrees alongside Bologna-style Bachelors and Masters degrees. The old, Soviet-style Specialist Diploma is a five- to six-year professionally orientated programme of study, followed by the two-year Candidate of Science and research-based Doctor of Science postgraduate programmes. Alternatively, an undergraduate may study for four years for the Bachelors degree, followed by a two-year Masters degree, before progressing onto the Candidate of Science and Doctor of Science programmes. The decision over whether to apply the European Credit Transfer and Accumulation System (ECTS) and to issue the Diploma Supplement is taken independently by each university.

In 2002 the Ministry of Education and Science established a quality assurance department and universities are now required to introduce measures for quality assurance. Under the second stage of the Education Development Strategy (2012–20) an accreditation commission was to be set up in the course of 2012, to license those universities capable of delivering Bachelors and Masters degrees; all other institutions were to be designated as colleges.

Responsibility for post-secondary technical and vocational education lies with the Ministry of Education and Science.

Regulatory Bodies

GOVERNMENT

Ministry of Culture and Tourism: Pushkina 78, 720040 Bishkek; tel. (312) 62-0482; e-mail info@mincultinfo.kg; internet www.minculture.gov.kg; Minister SULTAN RAYEV.

Ministry of Education and Science: Tynystanova 257, 720040 Bishkek; tel. (312) 66-2442; e-mail minedukg@gmail.com; internet edu.gov.kg; Minister KANAT SADYKOV.

ACCREDITATION

State Licensing and Attestation Inspectorate Service for Educational Institutions: Bishkek; tel. (312) 66-2287; e-mail bakul@yandex.ru; Head BAKTYHBEK ISKAKOVICH ISMAILOV.

Learned Societies

GENERAL

National Academy of Sciences of the Kyrgyz Republic: Chui Ave 265A, 720071 Bishkek; tel. (312) 65-8066; e-mail interdep_nas@mail.ru; internet www.nas.aknet.kg; f. 1943, present name and status 1993; depts of Physical-Engineering, Mathematical and Mining-Geological Sciences, Chemical-Technological, Medical-Biological and Agricultural Sciences, Humanities; 123 mems (40 permanent, 54 corresp., 7 foreign); attached research institutes: see Research Institutes; library: see under Libraries and Archives; Pres. Prof. Dr SHARIPA J. JOROBEKOVA.

BIBLIOGRAPHY, LIBRARY SCIENCE AND MUSEOLOGY

Kyrgyzstan Library Information Consortium: Abdrakhmanov St 208, R 26, 720040 Bishkek; tel. (312) 66-1826; e-mail kalyevna@mail.ru; internet bik.org.kg; f. 2002; promotes automation and integration of libraries resources in Kyrgyzstan; 120 mems; Pres. ROZA SULTANGAZIEVA; Vice-Pres. SANIA BATTALOVA.

Library Association of Kyrgyzstan: pr. Tynchtyk 27, 720044 Bishkek; tel. (312) 48-4134; Pres. T. SHAYMERGENOVA.

ECONOMICS, LAW AND POLITICS

Association of Microfinance Institutions: Toktogul str. 87A, Bishkek; tel. (312) 69-6286; e-mail executive@amfi.kg; internet www.amfi.kg; promotes devt of non-banking sector of Kyrgyzstan; 33 mems; Exec. Dir NARGIZA JOLDOSHOVA.

EDUCATION

Kyrgyz Adult Education Association: Manas pr. 40, Room 201, Bishkek; tel. (312) 96-13742; e-mail td_center@mail.ru; internet kaea.kg; f. 2006; establishes and develops effective system of adult education providers; 14 mems; Exec. Dir TATIANA SOLOMYKINA.

HISTORY, GEOGRAPHY AND ARCHAEOLOGY

Kyrgyz Geographical Society: bul. Erkindik 30, 720081 Bishkek; tel. (312) 26-4721; Chair. S. U. UMURZAKOV.

LANGUAGE AND LITERATURE

Alliance Française de Bichkek: Isanova str. 143/1, 720040 Bishkek; tel. (312) 32-3952; e-mail af.bichkek@gmail.com; f. 1993; offers courses and examinations in French language and culture and promotes cultural exchange with France; 488 mems; library of 4,000 vols.

British Council: see entry in Kazakhstan chapter.

Confucius Institute: c/o Bishkek Humanities Univ., pr. Mira 27, 720044 Bishkek; tel. (312) 21-8659; f. 2007; attached to Bishkek Humanities Univ.; promotes understanding of China and Chinese culture; holds scientific conferences, competitions; conducts qualification tests on Chinese language.

RELIGION, SOCIOLOGY AND ANTHROPOLOGY

Association of Civil Society Support Centres: Bishkek; e-mail ainura@acssc.kg; internet www.acssc.kg; f. 2002; maintains cooperation between NGOs; promotes interests of civil society and protects rights of people of Kyrgyzstan; creates conditions and mobilizes resources to foster effective civil society; 12 mems; Exec. Dir AYDAR MAMBETOV.

National Red Crescent Society of the Kyrgyz Republic: Erkindik Ave 10, Bishkek; tel. (312) 30-0190; e-mail redcross@elcat.kg; internet www.redcrescent.kg; f. 1926; prevents and mitigates human suffering in compliance with complete impartiality and non-discrimination based on ethnicity, race, age, gender, religious beliefs, class and political views; promotes mutual understanding and friendship among people; contributes to peace all over the world.

Research Institutes

AGRICULTURE, FISHERIES AND VETERINARY SCIENCE

Institute of Forest and Walnut Studies named after Gan, P. A.: Karagachovaya rosha 15, 720015 Bishkek; tel. (312) 67-9082; e-mail institute@lesik.elcat.kg; f. 1992; attached to Nat. Acad. of Sciences of the Kyrgyz Republic; research in forestry, forest soil science, entomology, phytopathology, forestry economy fields; Dir ESHALY TURDUKULOV.

ECONOMICS, LAW AND POLITICS

Institute for Public Policy: Business Centre, Third Fl., Isanov str. 42/1, 720017 Bishkek; tel. (312) 90-6240; e-mail office@ipp.kg; internet www.ipp.kg; f. 2005; promotes analysis and research in public policy; Pres. MURATBEK IMANALIEV; Dir-Gen. Prof. CHINARA JAKYPOVA.

Institute of Economics named after Alyshbaev J.: Chui Ave 265A, 720071 Bishkek; tel. (312) 64-6299; e-mail cer49@mail.ru; f. 1956; attached to Nat. Acad. of Sciences of the Kyrgyz Republic; research areas incl. theoretical fundamentals of developing market economy, study of devt problems of regional economy and real sector, capitalization of monetary assets, improvement of economical mechanisms and leverage of operation of the agrarian sector, enterprises, problems and prospects of Kyrgyzstan's interaction with int. economical and financial instns, improvement of social policy and justification of social standards.; Dir T. S. DYIKANBAYEVA; publ. *Economy* (4 a year).

Institute of Philosophy and Political and Legal Studies: Chui Ave 265A, 720071 Bishkek; tel. (312) 64-6312; e-mail togusakov2003@mail.ru; f. 1958; attached to Nat. Acad. of Sciences of the Kyrgyz Republic; research areas incl. philosophy of continuity of folk wisdom, traditions and customs, logic of developing public consciousness in new socially economic conditions, phenomenology and immanent logic of philosophical thought of the Kyrgyz people, spiritual culture of the Kyrgyz people and its ethical basics; Dir O. A. TOGUSAKOV.

HISTORY, GEOGRAPHY AND ARCHAEOLOGY

Institute of History and Cultural Heritage: Chui Ave 265A, 720071 Bishkek; tel. (312) 65-5495; e-mail inst_history@hotmail.kg; f. 1954; attached to Nat. Acad. of Sciences of the Kyrgyz Republic; research areas incl. formation and devt of Kyrgyzstan, democratization processes of sovereign Kyrgyzstan and devt of civil society and its instns, exploration problems of the Issyk-Kul sunken monuments, preservation, use and devt of Kyrgyzstan people's cultural heritage, genesis of the ancient and medieval settlements, towns and communications; Dir J. JUNASHALIYEV.

LANGUAGE AND LITERATURE

Institute of Kyrgyz Language and Literature named after Ch. Aitmatov: Chui Ave 265A, 720071 Bishkek; tel. (312) 65-7925; attached to Nat. Acad. of Sciences of the Kyrgyz Republic; research into Epos Manas and problems of artistic culture devt; analyses theoretical problems of Kyrgyz nat. literature and art; devt of Kyrgyz literary language; publ. *Issues of Language, Literature and Art* (2 a year).

Institute of Linguistics: Chui Ave 265A, 720071 Bishkek; tel. (312) 24-3495; f. 1924; attached to Nat. Acad. of Sciences of the Kyrgyz Republic; Dir T. AHMATOV.

MEDICINE

Institute of Medical Problems: 130A, Uzgenskaya str., 714018 Osh; tel. (3222) 21-395; e-mail impnankr@rambler.ru; f. 1994; attached to Nat. Acad. of Sciences of the Kyrgyz Republic; diseases prevention measures and maintenance of human physiological balances and pathology; preservation of genetic human resources; devt and introduction of import substituting and export oriented technologies in pharmacology and medicine; Dir R. TOYCHUYEV.

Kyrgyz Scientific Research Institute of Obstetrics and Paediatrics: Togolok Moldo Str. 1, 720040 Bishkek; tel. (312) 66-2413; e-mail comd@mail.kg; f. 1961; library of 14,000 vols; Dir DUYSHA KUDAYAROV.

Research and Development Institute of Molecular Biology and Medicine: Togolok Moldo 3, 720040 Bishkek; e-mail cardio@elcat.kg; f. 2002; library of 5,000 vols; Dir A. ALDASHEV.

Scientific and Production Centre for Preventive Medicine: Baitik Baatyr 34, 720005 Bishkek; tel. (312) 54-4578; e-mail npopm@mail.ru; f. 1938; researches into public health, and environment and health; library of 13,500 vols; Dir Prof. Dr OMOR T. KASYMOV.

NATURAL SCIENCES

Biological Sciences

Institute of Biology and Soil Sciences: 265 Chui Ave, 720071 Bishkek; tel. (312) 65-5511; f. 1994; attached to Nat. Acad. of Sciences of the Kyrgyz Republic; Dir S. KASIYEV.

Institute of Biotechnology: 265 Chui Ave, 720071 Bishkek; tel. (312) 39-2014; e-mail junushov@mail.ru; f. 1964; attached to Nat. Acad. of Sciences of the Kyrgyz Republic; creation of genetic resource bank of plants, livestock and microorganisms; devt of vaccine and other biological defence technology to protect farm animals against infectious diseases; creation and maintenance of manufacturing strains and microorganisms; research of natural nidality of infectious diseases common for humans and livestock; Dir ASANKADYR ZHUNUSHOV.

Mathematical Sciences

Institute of Theoretical and Applied Mathematics: 265A Chui Ave, 720071 Bishkek; tel. (312) 24-3561; e-mail mathnas@aknet.kg; internet www.math.aknet.kg; f. 1955; attached to Nat. Acad. of Sciences of the Kyrgyz Republic; fields of research incl. integro-differential equations, singular perturbations, reverse and ill-posed problems, computer proof of theorems, economical-mathematical methods; 55 mems; Dir MURZABEK I. IMANALIEV; Scientific Sec. MARYAM A. ASANKULOVA.

Physical Sciences

Institute of Energy Resources and Geoecology: 43 Toktogul str., 715600 Jalal-Abad; tel. (3722) 55-485; research into devt and introduction of renewable energy sources technology; attached to Nat. Acad. of Sciences of the Kyrgyz Republic.

Institute of Geology named after M. M. Adyshev: 30 Erkendik Ave, 720481 Bishkek; tel. (312) 66-4737; e-mail geol_kg@mail.ru; f. 1943; attached to Nat. Acad. of Sciences of the Kyrgyz Republic; research areas incl regional geology, geography, geoecology, mineral resources of Tien-Shan; Dir A. B. BAKIROV.

Institute of Geomechanics and Subsoil Development: 98 Mederova str., 720017 Bishkek; tel. (312) 54-1115; e-mail ifmgp@yandex.ru; internet www.nas.aknet.kg; attached to Nat. Acad. of Sciences of the Kyrgyz Republic; research areas incl. assessment, prediction and prevention of consequences of natural and technological disasters, geomechanics of rock mass, technology of subsoil devt.

Institute of Mountain Physiology: ul. Gorkogo 1/5, 720048 Bishkek; tel. (312) 44-9216; e-mail ifepv@mail.ru; internet www.nas.aknet.kg/index.php?menu=49; f. 1954; attached to Nat. Acad. of Sciences of the Kyrgyz Republic; Dir Prof. ALMAZ SHANAZAROV.

Institute of Physics: Chui Ave 265, 720071 Bishkek; tel. (312) 25-5259; e-mail interdep@aknet.kg; f. 1984; attached to Nat. Acad. of Sciences of the Kyrgyz Republic; Dir Prof. Dr TOKTOSUN OROZOBAKOV.

Institute of Rocks, Physics and Mechanics: ul. Mederova 98, 720815 Bishkek; tel. (312) 54-1115; e-mail ifmgp@totel.kg; f. 1960; attached to Nat. Acad. of Sciences of the Kyrgyz Republic; library of 500,000 vols; Dir I. T. AITMATOV; publ. *Proceedings* (every 2 years).

Institute of Seismology: 52/1 Asanbai Microdistrict, 720060 Bishkek; tel. (312) 52-3826; e-mail kanat53@rambler.ru; f. 1975; attached to Nat. Acad. of Sciences of the Kyrgyz Republic; assesses potential seismic hazard in Kyrgyzstan; Dir A. TURDULKULOV.

Kyrgyz Research Institute of Mineral Raw Materials: c/o Kyrgyz State Technical Univ. named after I. Razzakov, pr. Mira 66, 720044 Bishkek; tel. (312) 61-3485; attached to Kyrgyz State Technical Univ. named after I. Razzakov; Dir Prof. OMURKUL KABAEV.

RELIGION, SOCIOLOGY AND ANTHROPOLOGY

Centre of Science Methodology and Social Research: 265A Chui Ave, 720071 Bishkek; tel. (312) 64-6342; e-mail nurbekcsr@mail.ru; attached to Nat. Acad. of Sciences of the Kyrgyz Republic; sociological research, analysis and monitoring of sustainable devt, inter-ethnic conflicts, etc.; Dir Dr NURBEK OMURALIYEV.

Institute of Social Sciences: Mominova 11, 714000 Osh; tel. (3222) 29-244; f. 1994; attached to Nat. Acad. of Sciences of the Kyrgyz Republic; Dir E. SULAYMANOV.

TECHNOLOGY

Educational Scientific Technological Centre 'Vostok-Mir' for Textile and Light Industry: c/o Kyrgyz State Technical Univ. named after I. Razzakov, pr. Mira 66, 720044 Bishkek; e-mail ias52@mail.ru; attached to Kyrgyz State Technical Univ. named after I. Razzakov; Dir Prof. AIYM IMANKULOVA.

Innovation Centre of Phytotechnology: 267 Chui Ave, 720071 Bishkek; e-mail alhor64@yandex.ru; attached to Nat. Acad. of Sciences of the Kyrgyz Republic; conducts research in natural plant resources.

Institute of Automatics and Information Technology: 265 Chui Ave, 720071 Bishkek; tel. (312) 65-5522; e-mail automatics@aknet.kg; f. 1960; attached to Nat. Acad. of Sciences of the Kyrgyz Republic; Dir T. OMOROV.

Institute of Chemistry and Chemical Technology: 267 Chui Ave, 720071 Bishkek; tel. (312) 39-1948; e-mail icctkr@inbox.ru; f. 1994; attached to Nat. Acad. of Sciences of the Kyrgyz Republic; research on devt of technology of reworking of metallic ores, mineral and organic raw material; creation of new materials (high effective plant growth stimulators and protection means, organic and organo-mineral fertilizers on the base of acid amides, natural polymers, carbohydrates, amine acids, vitamins, nanomaterials); library of 65,000 vols (incl. scientific journals, books and preprints); Dir Prof. SH. ZHOROBEKOVA.

Institute of Machinery Sciences: 23 Skryabina str., 720055 Bishkek; tel. (312) 54-1113; e-mail shakirt1995@mail.ru; attached to Nat. Acad. of Sciences of the Kyrgyz Republic; research areas incl. scientific basis of mechanic and graded structure machines with power pulse systems; theory of power pulse systems and impact action machines; creation of highly productive and energy and material saving machines, equipment used in mining industry and construction; Dir Prof. M. DZHUMATAEV; publ. *Collected Scientific Articles of the Institute of Machinery Research* (every 2 years).

Institute of Natural Resources named after Djamanbaev A. S.: 31 A. Karimov str., 723500 Osh; tel. (3222) 24-532; e-mail ipr09@rambler.ru; f. 1988; attached to Nat. Acad. of Sciences of the Kyrgyz Republic; f. 1988; Dir ARZIEV JOROMAMAT.

Institute of Physical and Technological Problems and Materials Science named after J. J. Jeenbayev: 265 Chui Ave, 720071 Bishkek; tel. (312) 65-7698; attached to Nat. Acad. of Sciences of the Kyrgyz Republic; research areas incl. atmosphere physics and ozone layer researches, plasma, laser and nano-information technologies, predetermined properties material receipt, radio-physics.

Institute of Power Engineering and Microelectronics: Toktogul 43, 715600 Jalal-Abad; tel. (3722) 52-485; f. 1993; attached to Nat. Acad. of Sciences of the Kyrgyz Republic; Dir S. KYDYRALIYEV.

Institute of Water Problems and Hydropower: 533 Frunze St, 720033 Bishkek; tel. (312) 21-4572; e-mail iwp@istc.kg; internet www.caresd.net/iwp; f. 1992; attached to Nat. Acad. of Sciences of the Kyrgyz Republic; researches on water resources of Central Asia; Dir Prof. Dr DUISHEN M. MAMATKANOV.

Scientific and Research Institute for Chemical and Technical Problems: c/o Kyrgyz State Technical Univ. named after I. Razzakov, pr. Mira 66, 720044 Bishkek; tel. (312) 54-5129; e-mail mb051@jandex.ru; attached to Kyrgyz State Technical Univ. named after I. Razzakov; Dir Prof. MINARA BATKIBEKOVA.

Scientific and Research Institute for Energy and Communications: c/o Kyrgyz State Technical Univ. named after I. Razzakov, pr. Mira 66, 720044 Bishkek; tel. (312) 54-9035; e-mail suerkul@mail.ru; attached to Kyrgyz State Technical Univ. named after I. Razzakov; Dir Prof. SUERKUL KADYRKULOV.

Scientific and Research Institute for Physical and Technical Problems: c/o Kyrgyz State Technical Univ. named after I. Razzakov, pr. Mira 66, 720044 Bishkek; tel. (312) 54-5786; e-mail jenishtur@yahoo.com; attached to Kyrgyz State Technical Univ. named after I. Razzakov; Dir Prof. JENISHBEK TURGUMBAEV.

Libraries and Archives

Bishkek

Central Research Library of the National Academy of Sciences of the Kyrgyz Republic: 265A Chui Ave, 720071 Bishkek; tel. (312) 64-2693; e-mail tokonovatt@hotmail.kg; f. 1943; 985,000 vols; Dir IBRAIMOVA SHIRIN ZHAPAROVNA.

Scientific Library of the KNU Balasagina: Ave. Zhibyek Zholoo, 394, 720033 Bishkek; tel. (312) 32-2234; e-mail lib@university.kg; internet www.lib.university.kg; 931,500 vols; Dir MAYYA KADIRAKOONOVNA JAILKANOVA.

National Library of the Kyrgyz Republic: ul. Abdrakhmanova 208, 720040 Bishkek; tel. (312) 30-4675; e-mail library@nlpub.bishkek.gov.kg; internet www.nlkr.gov.kg; f. 1934; 5.8m. vols; Dir JULDYZ K. BAKASHOVA.

Scientific and Technical Library of Kyrgyzstan: 106 Chui Ave, 720302 Bishkek; tel. (312) 62-366; f. 1967; 5,817,000 vols (not incl. patents); Dir S. I. MAKAROV.

Museums and Art Galleries

Bishkek

Botanical Garden named after Gareev A. Z.: 1A Akhunbayev St, 720064 Bishkek; tel. (312) 51-7355; e-mail bgardennaskg@mail.ru; f. 1938; attached to Nat. Acad. of Sciences of the Kyrgyz Republic; maintains colins of local and foreign wild-growing and cultivated species of higher vascular plants; develops innovation technology for regulating plant growth and devt; library of 15,000 vols; Dir I. SODOMBEKOV; publ. *Introduktsiya i Akklimatizatsiya Rastenii v Kyrgyzstane* (1 a year).

Gapar Aitiev Kyrgyz National Museum of Fine Arts: Abdrahmanov str. 196, 720000 Bishkek; tel. (312) 66-4959; e-mail knmii@mail.ru; internet www.knmii.kg; f. 1935; paintings, drawings, sculptures and works of decorative and applied art, based on Kyrgyz and world art; modern Kyrgyz culture; works of S. Chuikov; 18,000 items: about 4,000 exhibits of fine arts-painting fund, 9,600 black-and-white arts, 1,000 sculptures, more than 3,000 decorative and applied arts; Dir Prof. YURISTANBEK SHYGAEV; Chief Curator AIGUL MAMBETKAZIEVA.

State Historical Museum of Kyrgyzstan: Krasnooktyabrskaya ul. 236, Bishkek; f. 1925; Dir N. M. SEITKAZIYEVA.

Universities

ACADEMY OF MANAGEMENT UNDER THE PRESIDENT OF THE KYRGYZ REPUBLIC

237 Panfilovs St, 720040 Bishkek
Telephone: (312) 62-3100
E-mail: marketing.amp@gmail.com
Internet: www.amp.aknet.kg
Founded 1992 as Bishkek Int. School of Management and Business
State control
Languages of instruction: English, Russian
Academic year: September to June
Faculties of international relations and world economy, public administration, law and business
Rector: Prof. Dr AKMATALIYEV ALMAZBEK AKMATALIEVICH
Vice-Rector for Academic Affairs: Prof. Dr FREYUK GRIGORY VASILEVICH
Vice-Rector for Additional Professional Education: MAMYTOVA AINA OSKOMBAEVNA
Vice-Rector for Finance and Devt: SYDYKOV BAKYTBEK KADYRALIEVICH
Dean: ANARBEK ADYJAPAROV
Library of 25,000 vols
Number of teachers: 300
Number of students: 678

ACADEMY OF THE MINISTRY OF INTERIOR OF THE KYRGYZ REPUBLIC NAMED AFTER E. ALIEV

1A Cholpon-Atinskaya str., 720083 Bishkek
Telephone: (312) 63-1451
E-mail: polacade@mail.ru
State control
Rector: BAZARBAEV ALMAZ SATYBALDIEVICH
Deputy Rector: DJOROBEKOVA ARZYGUL MAMAYUNUSOVNA

ACADEMY OF TOURISM

99 Chui Ave, 720022 Bishkek
Telephone: (312) 53-3386
E-mail: chormon@elcat.kg
Private control
Rector: CHORMONOV MELIS BAKASOVICH
Vice-Rector: CHORMONOV ARSLANBEK BAKASOVICH

AMERICAN UNIVERSITY OF CENTRAL ASIA

205 Abdymomunov St, 720040 Bishkek
Telephone: (312) 66-3309
E-mail: pr@mail.auca.kg
Internet: www.auca.kg
Founded 1993
Private control
Academic year: August to May (2 semesters)
Offers Bachelors and Masters degrees in liberal arts
Pres.: ANDREW B. WACHTEL
Registrar: ASEL KYRGYZBAEVA
Dean for Academic Affairs: ELIDA NOGOIBAEVA
Dean for Student Affairs: NIKOLAY SHULGIN
Library Dir: SAFIA RAFIKOVA
Library of 70,000 vols
Number of teachers: 124
Number of students: 1,181
Publication: *AUCA Magazine*

BALYKCHY SOCIAL-ECONOMIC INSTITUTE

51 Manasa str., Balykchy
Telephone: (3944) 25-875
Private control

Rector: ADENOV TALGAR ADENOVICH

BATKEN STATE UNIVERSITY

21 Djusupova St, 715100 Batken
Telephone: (3622) 36-226
State control
Rector: MATURAIMOV KIYAZIDIN OSORBAEVICH
Deputy Rector: MUSURMANOVA GULMIRA SADIROVNA

BISHKEK HIGHER MILITARY COLLEGE NAMED AFTER K. USENBEKOV

5 Lumumby str., Bishkek
Telephone: (312) 24-2726
State control
Rector: T. K. MOLDOBAEV

BISHKEK HUMANITIES UNIVERSITY NAMED AFTER K. KARASAEV

pr. Mira 27, 720044 Bishkek
Telephone: (312) 21-8659
E-mail: bhu@bhu.kg
Internet: bhu.kg
Founded 1979
State control
Rector: A. I. MUSAEV
Librarian: ROSA TURDUKEEVA
Faculties of administration and sociology, ecology and management, German philology, information, social work and psychology, Kyrgyz and Russian philology, Oriental Studies and international relations, Turkish relations
Library of 300,000 vols
Number of teachers: 600
Number of students: 10,000

BISHKEK STATE INSTITUTE OF ECONOMICS AND COMMERCE

58 Togolok Moldo str., 720033 Bishkek
E-mail: bsue@infotel.kg
State control

CHUI UNIVERSITY

187 Kievskaya str., 720300 Bishkek
Telephone: (312) 64-4795
E-mail: chu-univer@mail.ru
Private control
Rector: MAMBETKALIEV SULTAN MAMBETKALIEVICH
Vice-Rector: CHODONOV AIBEK KUBANYCHOVICH

DIPLOMATIC ACADEMY OF THE MINISTRY OF FOREIGN AFFAIRS OF THE KYRGYZ REPUBLIC

36 pr Erkindik, 720040 Bishkek
Telephone: (312) 62-1155
E-mail: dipacadem@ktnet.kg
Internet: www.dipacademy.com.kg
Founded 2001
State control
Depts of diplomatic and consular service, state and foreign languages, world politics and international relations
Rector: SADANBEKOV DJUMAGUL SADANBEKOVICH
Vice-Rector: OSMONALIEV KAIRAT MEDERBEKOVICH

EAST UNIVERSITY NAMED AFTER MAHMUD KASHGARI-BARSKANI

6A Volgogradskaya str., Bishkek
Telephone: (312) 63-1264
E-mail: vostok04@rambler.ru
Private control
Rector: ORMUSHEV ASAN SULAIMANOVICH
Vice-Rector: KOCHKUNOV AIDARBEK SULAIMANKULOVICH

I. ARABAEV KYRGYZ STATE UNIVERSITY

Razakov St 51, Block 2, 720026 Bishkek
Telephone: (312) 66-0347
E-mail: taku55@mail.ru
Founded 1952; attached to Min. of Education and Science
State control
Languages of instruction: Arabic, Chinese, English, French, German, Japanese, Kyrgyz, Russian
Academic year: September to June
Rector: Prof. TOLOBEK ABYLOVICH ABDYRACHMANOV
Vice-Rector for Academic Affairs: Doc. TUUGANBAI ABDYRACMANOVICH KONURBAEV
Librarian: DAVLETYAROVA NURILYA AITBAEVNA
Library of 500,000 vols
Number of teachers: 1,200
Number of students: 15,000
Publication: *Vestnik*

DEANS

Economics and Management Institute: FELIKS TURDUKULOV
Faculty of Oriental Studies and International Relations: ZAMIR ALYMKULOV
Humanities Institute: JUMAN BEGIMATOV
Institute of History and Socio-legal Education: GULNARA KURUMBAEVA
Institute of Innovation and Communication Technologies: KADYRBEK KALDYBAEV
Institute of In-service Teacher Training: GULDANA AKIEVA
Institute of Linguistics: Prof. SYRTBAI MUSAEV
Institute of Pedagogies: JOOMART BAISALOV
State Language and Culture Institute: AIGUL DUISHEMBIEVA

PROFESSORS

AKIEVA, G.
AKMATALIEV, A.
ALIEV, SH.
ARTYKBAEV, M.
ASANKANOV, A.
BAIGAZIEV, S.
BAISALOV, J.
BEKBOEV, A.
BEKBOLOTOVA, A.
BORUBAVA, A.
CHOROV, M.
DABAEV, K.
DYUSHALIAEV, K.
RAKHIMOVA, M.
SATYVALDIEV, A.

INSTITUTE OF SOCIAL DEVELOPMENT AND BUSINESS UNDER THE MINISTRY OF LABOUR AND SOCIAL DEFENCE

22A pr Manasa, 720010 Bishkek
Telephone: (312) 21-3863
State control
Rector: TABYSHOV RYSKELDI TABYSHEVICH
Vice-Rector: OSMONKULOVA GULDANA OROSHBEKOVNA

INSTITUTE OF STRATEGICAL INFORMATIONAL TECHNOLOGIES IN EDUCATION

27 pr. Molodoy Gvardii, Bishkek
Telephone: (312) 65-0684
E-mail: kgisito@mail.ru
Private control
Rector: KUBAEV BORIS HAMIDOVICH

INTERNATIONAL ACADEMY OF MANAGEMENT, LAW, FINANCE AND BUSINESS

St Bellorusskaya 6A, 720031 Bishkek
Telephone: (312) 53-1793
E-mail: akademy@hotmail.kg
Internet: maupfib.aknet.kg
Founded 1996
Private control
Depts of accounting and audit, business and finance, humanities, information technology, languages, law, management, natural sciences
Rector: NAZARMATOVA KASIRA MUKASHEVNA
Vice-Rector: AMANKULOV TOKTOGAZY AMANKULOVICH

INTERNATIONAL ATATURK ALATOO UNIVERSITY

M. Gorky St, Tunguch, Bishkek
Telephone: (312) 63-1425
E-mail: info@iaau.edu.kg
Internet: www.iaau.edu.kg
Founded 1996
Private control
Academic year: October to June (2 semesters)
Rector: Dr EROL ORAL
Library Dir: SANJAR ERDOLATOV
Publication: *Eurasian Journal of Business and Economics (EJBE)* (2 a year)

DEANS

Faculty of Economic and Administration Sciences: Prof. Dr MARIAM EDILOVA
Faculty of New Technologies: Dr VEDAT KIRAY

INTERNATIONAL UNIVERSITY OF KYRGYZSTAN

Chui pr. 255, 720001 Bishkek
Telephone: (312) 31-0471
E-mail: iuk@elcat.kg
Internet: www.iuk.kg
Founded 1993
State control
Language of instruction: Russian
Academic year: September to June
Pres.: ASYLBEK A. AIDARALIEV
Librarian: GULMIRA T. ABDYRAKOVNA
Library of 45,000 vols
Number of teachers: 670
Number of students: 6,215

DEANS

Faculty of Law, Business and Computer Technology: AINURA A. ADIEVA
Faculty of Social-Humanitarian and Natural Science Disciplines: KUBAN B. AMANALIEV
High School of Magistracy: RAHAT BEKBOEVA
International Educational Centre: TAKEN AKYLBEKOVA
Polytechnic College: AMAN TOHLUKOV (Dir)
Virtual Academy of IUK: TILEK A. ASANALIEV

ISSYK-KUL STATE UNIVERSITY NAMED AFTER K. TYNYSTANOV

Abdrahmanova str. 103, 722200 Karakol
Telephone: (3922) 50-1-23
E-mail: indepiksu@gmail.com
Founded 1940
State control
Language of instruction: Russian
Rector: Dr KURMANBEK ABDYLDAEV
Number of teachers: 382
Number of students: 6,710

DEANS

Faculty of Art and Culture: TYNCHYLYK KULCHUNOV
Faculty of Environmental Sciences and Tourism: RAHAT KERMALIEV
Faculty of Foreign Languages: SAYFULLA ABDULLAEV
Faculty of History: JENISHBEK KERIMKULOV
Faculty of Mathematics and Computer Science: RYSPEK ISKAKOV
Faculty of Natural Sciences: GULMIRA SARIEVA
Faculty of Philology, Pedagogy and Journalism: MURAT SADYROV
Faculty of Physical-Technical Studies: DAMIR ABDYLDAEV
Institute of Economics and Management: SALAMAT JOLDOSHEV

JALAL-ABAD STATE TECHNICAL INSTITUTE

St Frunze 32, 715600 Jalal-Abad
Telephone: (3722) 54-414
State control
Rector: SEITOV BOLOT MUKASHEVICH

JALAL-ABAD STATE UNIVERSITY

57 Lenin St, 715600 Jalal-Abad
Telephone: (3722) 33-900
E-mail: jasu@infotel.kg
Founded 1926
State control
Language of instruction: Kyrgyz, Russian
Academic year: September to June
Rector: Dr TURSUNBEK BEKBOLOTOV
Vice-Rector: Dr NURMAT JAILOBAEV
Library of 58,000 vols
Number of teachers: 600
Number of students: 16,000

DEANS

Faculty of Agriculture and Biology: TALCHA AMANKULOVA
Faculty of Economics: BEKMAMAT JOOSHBAYEV
Faculty of Engineering and Technology: EGEMBERDI UMETOV
Faculty of Foreign Languages: ASKAR MURZAKULOV
Faculty of Medicine: SHAIRBEK SULAIMANOV
Faculty of Philology: ANARA KADYROVA
Faculty of Technology: MANAS SOORONBAYEV

JALAL-ABAD UNIVERSITY OF ECONOMICS AND BUSINESS

30 Jenijok str., 715600 Jalal-Abad
Telephone: (3722) 50-804
E-mail: jaki@netmail.kg
Private control
Rector: TOKTOMATOV KANTORO SHARIPOVICH
Deputy Rector: MAMASYDYKOV ABDILBAET ASANOVICH

KIRGIZISTAN-TÜRKIYE MANAS ÜNIVERSITESI
(Kyrgyzstan-Turkey Manas University)

Mira Ave 56, 720044 Bishkek
Telephone: (312) 54-1942
E-mail: library@manas.edu.kg
Internet: web.manas.kg
Founded 1995 by govts of Kyrgyzstan and Turkey
State control
Languages of instruction: Kyrgyz, Turkish
Academic year: September to June
Pres.: Prof. Dr SEBAHATTIN BALCI
Co-Pres.: Prof. Dr ASYLBEK KULMIRZAYEV
Vice-Pres.: Prof. Dr ANVARBEK MOKEEV
Vice-Pres.: Prof. Dr MAHMUT İZCILER
Gen. Sec.: Asst Prof. Dr HIDAYET TUNCAY
Library Man.: MAKSATBEK INAKBEKOV
Library of 80,000 vols, 85 journals
Number of teachers: 96
Number of students: 4,038
Publications: *Fen Bilimleri Dergisi* (Journal of Science and Engineering, 2 a year), *Sosyal Bilimler Dergisi* (Journal of Social Sciences, 2 a year)

DEANS

Faculty of Agriculture: Prof. Dr A. İRFAN İLBAS
Faculty of Communication: Prof. Dr MEHMET KUCUKKURT
Faculty of Economics and Management: Prof. Dr MUHSIN HALIS
Faculty of Engineering: Prof. Dr ULAN BIRİMKULOV
Faculty of Fine Arts: Dr MEHMET BAŞBUĞ
Faculty of Letters: Prof. Dr LAYLI ÜKÜBAYEVA
Faculty of Science: Prof. Dr ALI OSMAN SOLAK
Faculty of Veterinary Science: Prof. Dr HÜSEYIN KARADAĞ

KYRGYZ NATIONAL AGRARIAN UNIVERSITY NAMED AFTER K. I. SKRIABIN

68 Mederova str, 720005 Bishkek
Telephone: (312) 54-5210
E-mail: knau-info@mail.ru
State control
Rector: NURGAZIEV RYSBEK ZARYLBEKOVICH
Vice-Rector: IRGASHEV ALMAZBEK SHUKURBAEVICH

KYRGYZ NATIONAL CONSERVATORY

115 Djantosheva str., 720005 Bishkek
Telephone: (312) 57-0225
State control
Rector: BEGALIEV MURATBEK
Vice-Rector: IMANALIEV URAZ

KYRGYZ NATIONAL UNIVERSITY 'ZHUSUP BALASAGYN'

ul. Frunze 547, 720024 Bishkek
Telephone: (312) 32-3126
E-mail: rector@university.kg
Internet: www.university.kg
Founded 1925, as Kyrgyz State Pedagogical Univ.; became Kyrgyz State Univ. 1951; present name 1993
State control
Academic year: September to June
Rector: AALYBEK AKUNOV
First Vice-Rector: KENESHBEK ALYMBEKOV
Number of teachers: 1,819
Number of students: 22,000

KYRGYZ-RUSSIAN ACADEMY OF EDUCATION

210 Leo Tolstoy St, 720009 Bishkek
Telephone: (312) 41-8262
E-mail: krao@elcat.kg
Internet: krao.web.kg
Founded 1997
Private control
Language of instruction: Russian
Academic year: September to July
Rector: Prof. CHINARA ASANOVNA SHAKEEVA
Library of 27,244 vols
Number of teachers: 68
Number of students: 2,040

PROFESSORS

ABLAEVNA, A. K., Chemistry
AKMATALIEVNA, M. B., History
AKULKERIMOVICH, B. A., Medical Sciences
ASANOVNA, A. A., Economics
ASANOVNA, S. C., Psychology
BOBUEVNA, S. R., Social Sciences
EGEMBERDIEVICH, U. T., Pedagogical Sciences
KAIYPBEKOVICH, T. B., Physics and Mathematics
KARYPBAEVICH, K. C., Legal Sciences
MEDERKULOVICH, S. C., Technical Sciences
MEKISHEVNA, K. G., Physics and Mathematics
MUKANGALIEVNA, K. M., Economics
NADZHMUDINOVNA, K. K., Psychology
OBOSBEKOVICH, M. A., Economics
RIFOVNA, B. A., History
SABENOVNA, A. S., Pedagogical Sciences
SADIEVICH, S. K., Legal Sciences
SAPARBEKOVNA, Z. Z., Economics
SATAROVICH, I. D., History
SHARSHEKEEVICH, I. K., Philosophy
STANBEKOVICH, S. A., Economics
SUYUMBAEVICH, B. S., Economics
SUYUNBAI, T., Legal Sciences
TURDUGAZIEVICH, A. N., Legal Sciences
USENOVNA, K. N., Economics
ZABIRDINOVICH, Z. A., History

KYRGYZ-RUSSIAN SLAVIC UNIVERSITY

ul. Kievskaya 44, 720000 Bishkek
Telephone: (312) 28-2859
E-mail: krsu@krsu.edu.kg
Internet: www.krsu.edu.kg
Founded 1993
State control
Rector: Prof. VLADIMIR I. NIFADEV
Pro-Rector for Academic Affairs: Prof. IMIL A. AKKOZIEV
Pro-Rector for Int. Relations: Prof. EDNAN O. KARABAEV
Pro-Rector for Scientific Affairs: Prof. VALERI M. LELEVKIN
Number of teachers: 1,973
Number of students: 11,000

DEANS

Faculty of Distance Education: Asst. Prof. YURI D. SURODIN
Faculty of Economics: Prof. VICKTOR K. GAIDAMAKO
Faculty of Humanities: Prof. ABDYKADYR O. ORUSBAEV
Faculty of International Relations: (vacant)
Faculty of Law: Asst. Prof. LEILA CH. SYDYKOVA
Faculty of Medicine: Prof. ANES G. ZARUFYAN
Faculty of Science and Technology: Asst. Prof. VLADIMIR A. YURIKOV

KYRGYZ STATE ACADEMY OF LAW

180A Chui Ave, 720001 Bishkek
Telephone: (312) 39-2093
E-mail: office@ua.kg
State control
Rector: KEREZBEKOV KANATBEK KEREZBEKOVICH
Vice-Rector: DMITRIENKO IRINA ANATOLYEVNA

KYRGYZ STATE INSTITUTE OF ARTS NAMED AFTER B. BEISHENALIEVA

115 Djantosheva str., 720005 Bishkek
Telephone: (312) 57-0979
State control
Rector: SUBANALIEV SAGYNALY SUBANALIEVICH
Vice-Rector: ABDYLDAEV OZBEK

KYRGYZ STATE INSTITUTE OF PHYSICAL TRAINING

97 Ahunbaeva str., 720064 Bishkek
Telephone: (312) 57-0968
State control
Rector: IMANALIEV TOKTOBEK TYBYNOVICH

Vice-Rector: Naraliev Askaraly Madaliévich

KYRGYZ STATE TECHNICAL UNIVERSITY NAMED AFTER I. RAZZAKOV

pr. Mira 66, 720044 Bishkek
Telephone: (312) 54-5125
E-mail: rector@ktu.aknet.kg
Internet: ktu.aknet.kg
Founded 1954 as Frunze Polytechnic Institute; present name 2005
State control
Academic year: September to July
Rector: Prof. Murataly Djamanbaev
First Vice-Rector for Academic Affairs: Prof. Dr Bekjan Torobekov
Vice-Rector for Economics and Finance: Prof. Dr Jalaladin Galbaev
Vice-Rector for Science and External Connections: Prof. Dr Turatbek Duishenaliev
Vice-Rector for Social Affairs and Devt of State Language: Gulmira Belekova
Library Dir: Nurila Sarybaeva
Library of 550,000 vols
Number of teachers: 900
Number of students: 17,000
Publications: *Herald* (2 a year), *Science and New Technologies* (4 a year)

DEANS
Faculty of Energy: Dr Manas Suerkulov
Faculty of Information Technology: Ryspek Akmatbekov
Faculty of Technology: Prof. Dr Tamara Djunushalieva
Faculty of Transport and Machine Building: Shadybek Djumakadyrov

KYRGYZ STATE UNIVERSITY OF CONSTRUCTION, TRANSPORT AND ARCHITECTURE NAMED AFTER N. ISANOV

Maldybaeva St 34-b, 720020 Bishkek
Telephone: (312) 54-3561
E-mail: ksucta@elcat.kg
Internet: www.ksucta.kg
Founded 1992
State control
Academic year: January to December
Faculties of humanities, Kyrgyz and Arabic, military studies
Rector: Prof. Dr Akymbek A. Abdykalykov
Vice-Rector for Educational Innovation and Investment: Prof. E. K. Boronbaev
Vice-Rector for Science and State Language: Dr N. J. Madanbekov
Academic Sec.: Dr N. A. Rajapova
Library of 300,000 vols
Number of teachers: 600
Number of students: 14,500
Publication: *Vestnik KSUCTA*

KYRGYZ-UZBEK UNIVERSITY

27 Gapar Aitiev Str., 714000 Osh
Telephone: (3222) 59-215
E-mail: kenjaevig@rambler.ru
Founded 1994
State control
Languages of instruction: Kyrgyz, Russian
Academic year: September to June
Rector: Prof. Dr Idris Kenzhaev
Vice-Rector: Topchubai Isakov
Vice-Rector: Ashirali Borboev
Vice-Rector: Mederbek Ismanov
Library of 196,380 vols
Number of teachers: 274
Number of students: 10,950
Publication: *Science, Education, Technic* (4 a year)

DEANS
Dept of Economics and Finances: Shaidilla Shakiev
Dept of Engineering and Technology: Kutmanaly Abdrakhmanov
Dept of Foreign Languages and Foreign Affairs: Arstan Kulnazarov
Dept of History and Languages: Prof. Aida Baltabaeva
Dept of Law and Customs: Almagul Kokoeva
Dept of Nature and Geography: Bolotbek Murzabaev
Dept of Physics and Mathematics: Altyn Zulpukarov
Russian Kyrgyz Dept: Rodima Toldieva

NARYN STATE UNIVERSITY

Sagynbay Orozbak Uulu St 47, 722600 Naryn
Telephone: (3522) 50-797
E-mail: nsu@ktnet.kg
Founded 1996
State control
Languages of instruction: Kyrgyz, Russian
Rector: Prof. Almaz Akmataliyev
Vice-Rector: Tashtanbek Siyayev
Number of teachers: 240
Number of students: 4,500

DEANS
Faculty of Agro-Technology: Kubanyebbek D. Duishekeyev
Faculty of Economics, Business and Admin.: Dr Damira K. Omuraliyeva
Faculty of Foreign Languages: N. A. Chorobaeva
Faculty of Natural Sciences and Humanities: Dr Yrys J. Jakeyeva
Faculty of New Information Technologies: Omurov N. K.
Faculty of Law: Salidin Kaldybayev
Faculty of Philology: Dr Ali Turdugulov
Faculty of Social and Political Science: G. Esenalieva

NATIONAL ACADEMY OF ARTS OF THE KYRGYZ REPUBLIC NAMED AFTER T. SADYKOV

98 Ciolkovskogo str., 720027 Bishkek
Telephone: (312) 49-3244
State control
Rector: Sadykov Turgunbay Sadykovich

OSH HUMANITY-PEDOGOGICAL INSTITUTE NAMED AFTER A. MYRSABEKOV

73 Isanova str., 714017 Osh
Telephone: (322) 25-4877
E-mail: osh.ogpi@mail.ru
State control
Rector: Isakov Kanybek Abduvasitovich
Vice-Rector: Rayimbekov Kanybek Turgunovich

OSH STATE UNIVERSITY

ul. Lenina 331, 723500 Osh
Telephone: (322) 22-2912
E-mail: oshsu@mail.ru
Internet: www.oshsu.kg
Founded 1951 as Osh Pedagogical Institute, present name and status 1992
State control
Academic year: September to July
Rector: Prof. Dr Muhtar Orozbekov
First Vice-Rector: Prof. Dr Turdumamat Kadyrov
Vice-Rector for Part-Time Education: Prof. Abdimalik Omoraliev
Vice-Rector for Science: Prof. Tasylkan Jumabaeva
Number of teachers: 1,600
Number of students: 30,000
Publication: *Vestnik* (research, 4 a year)

DEANS
Faculty of Business and Management: Asanov Avazbek Raimzhanovich
Faculty of Economy and Finance: Kupuev Pirmat
Faculty of Education: Attokurov Asamidin
Faculty of Kyrgyz Philology: Jamgyrchieva Gulina Tolobaevna
Faculty of Law and History: Kuldysheva Gulsara Kenjeevna
Faculty of International Relations and State Services: Sulaimanov Joomart Myrzaevich
Faculty of Mathematics and Information Technology: Abduvaliev Abdygany
Faculty of Medicine: Jeenbaev Jolbors
Faculty of Natural Science: Kolanov Orunbek
Faculty of Nature Use and Geography: Nizamiev Abdurashit
Faculty of Pedagogy: Akmatova Tanavar
Faculty of Physics and Technics: Kenzhaev Idirisbek
Faculty of Russian Philology: Attokurov Asamidin
Faculty of Theology: Aliev Asylbek
Faculty of Uzbek Humanities and Education: Tursunov Ravshanbek
Faculty of World Languages: Anarbaev Arap Anarbaevich
Financial-Juridical College: Erkebaev Tazhimamat
Medical College in Osh: Berkmamatov Shamyrbek Toktosunovich
Medical College in Uzgen: Stanbaev Ozgonbai Tillebaevich

OSH TECHNOLOGICAL UNIVERSITY

Isanov St 81, 714018 Osh
Telephone: (322) 25-4087
E-mail: musa_adyshev@rambler.ru
Internet: www.oshtu.kg
Founded 1993, fmrly Osh Higher College of Technology, present name and status 1996
State control
Faculties of construction engineering, cybernetics and information technology, ecology and geology, energetics and new energy technology, finance and economics, language technology, law, social sciences, state administration and business, technological engineering, transport and service technology; basic and professional education; evening and correspondence education
Rector: Prof. Toktomamatov Abdibali Toktomamatovich
Vice-Rector: Sopuev Adahimjan Sopuevich
Library of 206,000 vols
Number of teachers: 482
Number of students: 12,000
Publication: *Izvestiya OshTU*

PEOPLE'S FRIENDSHIP UNIVERSITY NAMED AFTER A. BATYROV

Lenin St, Jalal-Abad
Telephone: (372) 25-6590
Private control
Rector: Ahmedov Dilmurat
Vice-Rector: Mullaahunov Ibrahim

TALAS STATE UNIVERSITY

ul. Karla Marksa 25, 722720 Talas
Telephone: (342) 25-2015
E-mail: tsu1exrel@hotmail.kg

Founded 1996
State control
Languages of instruction: English, Kyrgyz, Russian
Academic year: September to June
Rector: Dr ASKARBEK ISAEVICH DZHYLKICHIEV
Library of 101,000 vols
Number of teachers: 248
Number of students: 2,983

DEANS

Faculty of Ecology and Agronomy: AIBEK UPENOV
Faculty of Economics and Law: ESENGUL OMUSHEV
Faculty of Education: ERKIN ABDRAIMOV
Faculty of Modern Languages: MANAS KALMANBETOV
Faculty of Technology: NURLAN ASYLBEKOV

Other Higher Educational Institutes

Asian Medical Institute: Gagarin St 58, Kant; tel. (312) 93-2645; e-mail asmiedu@yahoo.com; internet www.asmi.edu.kg; f. 2004; faculties of dentistry, medicine, nursing, preparatory courses; Rector MAMYTOV MITALIP MAMYTOVICH; Vice-Rector Dr ABAEVA TAMARA SURANALIEVNA.

Bishkek Academy of Finance and Economics: 55 Molodaya Gvardia Ave, 720010 Bishkek; tel. (312) 65-0486; e-mail bishkekacademy@hotmail.kg; f. 1994; 53 teachers; 567 students; Rector Prof. ABDRAKHMAN S. MAVLYANOV.

Bishkek branch of International Slavic University: pr. Manasa 1, 720017 Bishkek; tel. (312) 54-0865; e-mail msiukp@elcat.kg; Rector PODBELSKI EVGENI MIHAILOVICH; Vice-Rector KISLISINA SVETLANA NIKOLAEVNA.

Bishkek branch of Moscow Institute of Business and Law: 36 B. Batyra str., Bishkek; tel. (312) 54-7955; Rector ABDYLDAEV TAALAI ABDULDAEVICH.

Bishkek Institute of Moscow State University of Economics, Statistics and Informatics: 122 Sovetskaya str., Bishkek; tel. (312) 54-5571; e-mail biteci@nm.ru; Rector R. K. SULTANOV.

Karakol branch of Moscow Institute of Business and Law: 49 Jakypova str., 722360 Karakol; Rector ADYLDAEV TAALAI ADYLDAEVICH; Vice-Rector SHATEMIROVA IRINA CHONOEVNA.

Kyrgyz State Medical Academy: Akhunbaeva 92, 720020 Bishkek; tel. (312) 54-58-81; e-mail is@ksma.elcat.kg; internet www.ksma.edu.kg; f. 1939; faculties of general medicine, sanitation and hygiene, paediatric medicine, stomatology, pharmaceutics, and foreign and contract students; 408 teachers; 2,646 students; Rector (vacant).

OSCE Academy: 1A Botanichesky pereulok, Bishkek; tel. (312) 54-3200; e-mail info@osce-academy.net; internet www.osce-academy.net; f. 2002; postgraduate studies in economic governance and devt, politics and security; Dir MAXIM RYABKOV; Deputy Dir VIOLETTA YAN.

Osh branch of Moscow State Social University: 161 Karasuiskaya St, 714000 Osh; tel. (3222) 32-545; e-mail rgsuof@mail.ru; internet osh.rgsu.net; f. 1996; offers higher education in finance, law, business management, social work; library: 8,000 vols; Dir SALY K. TURDUBAEV.

LAOS

The Higher Education System

In 1946 the French Indo-China provinces of Luang Prabang, Vientiane and Champasak were united as the Kingdom of Laos, which became independent within the French Union in 1949 and achieved sovereignty in 1953. Sisavangvong University, the country's first university and named after the King, was founded in 1958. However, in 1975 the insurgent Neo Lao Haksat (Lao Patriotic Front) gained control of the country, abolished the monarchy and established the Lao People's Democratic Republic; Sisavangvong University was dissolved into separate colleges. In 1995 the National University of Laos (NUOL) was created from a merger of various institutions of higher education; the NUOL currently has 11 faculties across eight campuses. In 2009/10 there were 54,000 students enrolled at four university-level institutions and 59,000 at 96 other institutions of higher education. The Ministry of Education and Sports has overall responsibility for higher education.

Admission to higher education requires the main secondary school certificate (Baccalauréat), and the applicant is required to sit an entrance examination. The undergraduate degree is the Bachelors and the course lasts four years; however, some disciplines, notably pharmacy, dentistry, engineering (all five years) and medicine (six years), require longer. The NUOL also offers a number of postgraduate Masters programmes (of two to three years' duration) and is preparing to introduce doctoral degree programmes in the near future.

Vocational and technical education is provided by three kinds of institution: Vocational Schools, specializing in accountancy, teaching and nursery teaching; Middle Technical Schools, for training middle-level technicians; and Higher Technical Schools/Institutes, providing training for higher-level technicians. Both the Middle and Higher Technical Schools offer Diploma courses.

The Ministry of Education and Sports has established a formal accreditation and quality assurance process, which is administered by the Accreditation and Quality Assurance Centre. In 2006 a wide-ranging education reform was begun, of which the second stage, from 2011–15, concentrated on the development of higher education; one of the reforms under discussion was to implement a system of tuition fees for all higher education students.

Regulatory Bodies

GOVERNMENT

Ministry of Education and Sports: 1 rue Lanxang, BP 67, Vientiane; tel. (21) 216013; e-mail esitc@moe.gov.la; internet www.moe.gov.la; Minister Dr PHANKHAM VIPHAVANH.

Ministry of Information, Culture and Tourism: rue Setthathirat, Ban Xiengnyeun, Chanthaboury, BP 122, Vientiane; tel. (21) 212406; e-mail email@mic.gov.la; Minister Prof. Dr BOSENGKHAM VONGDARA.

Ministry of Science and Technology: POB 2279, Vientiane; tel. (21) 217706; e-mail most_info@most.gov.la; internet www.most.gov.la; Minister Dr BOVIENGKHAM VONGDARA.

Learned Society

RELIGION, SOCIOLOGY AND ANTHROPOLOGY

Lao Buddhist Fellowship Organization: POB 775, 01000 Vientiane; tel. (21) 412193; f. 1976; manages, develops and educates the Buddhist sangha and ensures that its members observe the laws of the country; 8,796 monks, 13,376 novices, 450 nuns and 563 sanghali; Pres. Rev. VICHIT SINGHARAJ.

Libraries and Archives

Vientiane

Bibliothèque Nationale du Laos (National Library of Laos): POB 704, Ministry of Information, Culture and Tourism, Vientiane; tel. (21) 212452; e-mail bailane@laotel.com; internet bnlaos.org; f. 1956; compiles nat. bibliography; spec. collns incl. palm-leaf MSS; 300,000 vols, 120 periodicals, 250 maps, 6,000 MSS; Dir KONGDEUANE NETTAVONGS; publs *Khao Bailan* (3 a year), *Lao Literature Series* (1 a year), *Siengkhene* (3 a year), *Vannasinh* (3 a year).

National University of Laos Central Library: Dongdok Campus, POB 7322, Dongdok, Vientiane; tel. (21) 770068; e-mail nuol@nuol.edu.la; internet www.nuol.edu.la; f. 1995; 26,165 vols; Dir CHANSY PHUANGSOUKETH; Pres. Assoc. Prof. SOUKKONGSENG SAIGNALEUTH.

Museums and Art Galleries

Luang Prabang

Haw Kham Royal Palace Museum (Lao National Museum): Luang Prabang; tel. (71) 212122; e-mail sisavath64@yahoo.com; f. 1976 as National Museum; Man. SISAVATH NHILATCHAY.

Pakse

Champasak Provincial Museum: Nat. Highway, 13S, Champasak, Pakse; tel. (31) 212501; f. 1995; archaeological, historical, ethnological artefacts; Dir THONGTINH PHOMPAKDY; Deputy Dir OUTHAI SENERATH; Deputy Dir PHOMMA NOYKHOUNSAVANH.

Vientiane

Ho Phra Keo: Setthathirat Rd, 01000 Vientiane; tel. (21) 212618; f. 1565 by King Setthathirat, became national museum 1965; colln of consecrated art objects; bronze statues of the Buddha in various positions of meditation; Dir THONGKHOUN SENGDALA.

Lao National Museum: Samsenthai Rd, 01000 Vientiane; tel. (21) 212460; f. 1985 as Lao Revolutionary Museum, present status 2000; colln of historical and revolutionary exhibits; Dir PENGSAVANH VONGCHANDEE; Deputy Dir BOUNHUANG SISENGPASETH; Deputy Dir PHETMALAYVANH KEOBOUNMA.

Pha That Luang: Saysettha District, 01000 Vientiane; tel. (21) 212618; f. 1566 by King Setthathirat, restored 1930; exhibits incl. a hair from the Buddha; built on the ruins of an 11th–13th-century Khmer temple; Dir THONGKHOUN SENGDALA.

Wat Si Saket: Lane Xang Ave, 01000 Vientiane; tel. (21) 212618; f. 1818 by King Anouvong; constructed in the early Bangkok style; temple and nat. museum; colln of miniature statues and images of Buddha; Dir THONGKHOUN SENGDALA.

University

NATIONAL UNIVERSITY OF LAOS

POB 7322, Dongdok, 01000 Vientiane
Telephone: (21) 770068
E-mail: nuol@nuol.edu.la
Internet: www.nuol.edu.la
Founded 1995 by merger of 10 existing institutions of higher education and a centre of agriculture
State control
Language of instruction: Lao
Academic year: September to June
Pres.: Assoc. Prof. SOUKKONGSENG SAIGNALEUTH
Rector: Dr SOMKOT MANGNOMEK
Vice-Rector for Academic Affairs: SAYAMANG VONGSAK
Vice-Rector for Planning and International Cooperation: TUYEN DONGVAN
Vice-Rector for Student Affairs: LAMMAY PHIPHAKKHAVONG
Chief Administrative Officer and Director of Rectorate Cabinet: Dr KONGSY SENGMANY
Dir of Central Library: CHANSY PHUANGSOUKET
Library of 120,000 vols
Number of teachers: 1,986
Number of students: 26,673
Publication: *Mahavithagnalay Heang Xath Lao* (Activities in the National University of Laos, 4 a year)

DEANS

Faculty of Agriculture: THONGPHANH KOUSONSAVATH
Faculty of Architecture: BOUALINH SOYSOUVANH

Faculty of Economics and Business Administration: KHAMLUSA NOUANSAVANH
Faculty of Education: KHAM-ANE SAYASONE
Faculty of Engineering: BOUALINH SOYSOUVANH
Faculty of Forestry: SOUCKONGSENG SAYALEUT
Faculty of Laws and Political Science: KHAMSONE SOULIYASENG
Faculty of Letters: Assoc. Prof. Dr PHETSAMONE KHOUNSAVATH
Faculty of Sciences: Assoc. Prof. Dr SOMKIAT PHASY
Faculty of Social Sciences: PHOUT SIMMALAVONG

Colleges

Lao-American College: Phonkeng Rd, Ban Phonkeng, Xaysettha Dist., 01000 Vientiane; tel. (21) 900454; e-mail lac@laopdr.com; internet www.lac.edu.la; f. 1993; Dir GINNY VAN OSTRAND.

Sangkha College: Muang Chanthaburi, 01000 Vientiane; tel. (21) 212141; f. 1929 as Pariyatti Dhamma School, present name 1996; attached to Min. of Education and Sports; faculties of arts, education; Dir Rev. BOUAKHAM SARIBOUT.

Sengsavanh College: 124 Dongmieng Rd, Sisavath Neua, Chanthabuli Dist., 01000 Vientiane; tel. (21) 223822; e-mail info@sengsavanh.net; internet www.sengsavanh.net; f. 1997 as language centre, present status 2000; Dir KHAMSENE SISAVONG.

LATVIA

The Higher Education System

Until Latvia first achieved independence in 1921, it was under Russian Tsarist and then Russian Bolshevik rule. The earliest surviving institutions of higher education were established during the period (1918–20) of de facto civil war involving the Latvian provisional Government, the Russian Bolsheviks, German volunteers and White Russians (Mensheviks). Institutions dating from this period include the University of Latvia, the Latvian Academy of Music, and the Transport and Telecommunication Institute (all founded in 1919). Institutions founded during the early independent period include Art Academy of Latvia (founded in 1919) and Daugavpils University (founded in 1921). In June 1940 the USSR invaded and occupied Latvia, which then became a Soviet Socialist Republic until regaining independence in 1991. The higher education system is administered according to the Education Act (1991), the Law on Higher Education Institutions (1995) and the Law on Vocational Education and Training (1999, revised 2001). A legal distinction is made between 'academic' and 'professional' higher education: university-level institutions offer both academic and professional qualifications; however, non-university level institutions of higher education offer only professional qualifications. The Ministry of Education and Science is the government body responsible for higher education. Latvia participates in the Bologna Process to establish a European Higher Education Area, the first phase of which was to adopt a credit-based system of comparable degrees with two main cycles (undergraduate and graduate). In 2010/11 higher education was offered at 58 institutions, with a total enrolment of 103,856 students. In 1994 an independent Higher Education Quality Evaluation Centre was established to oversee the accreditation and quality assurance (based on self-evaluation) of all higher education institutions and programmes in Latvia.

Since 2006 admission to all higher education levels is based on the results of central state examinations. Individual institutions, with authorization from the Council of Higher Education, may also stipulate additional specific enrolment requirements. In 2000 Latvia ratified the Bologna Process, and a two-tier Bachelors (Bakalaurs) and Masters (Magistrs) degree system has been established for both the academic and professional streams of higher education (although some old-style professional diplomas are still offered by non-university-level institutions). Degrees are awarded on the basis of an eight-level Latvian Qualifications Framework (LQF), with levels 6, 7 and 8 referring to Bachelors, Masters and Doctorate levels. The standard undergraduate Bachelors degree course lasts three to four years and requires the writing of a thesis and the acquisition of 120–160 credits. Only a four-year Bachelors programme is regarded as a complete degree; a three-year course is regarded as an intermediate qualification. Degree courses in professional fields may last longer, such as dentistry (five years) and medicine (six years), and are regarded as equivalent to the Masters. The Masters is either a one- to two-year degree course requiring the writing of a thesis and the accumulation of 40–80 credits, taken after the Bachelors, or a five-year undergraduate and postgraduate combined professional degree requiring 200 credits for completion. The Doctorate (Doktors)—entrance to which is through the Masters—is the highest university-level degree and involves three to four years of full-time study (120–160 credits), culminating with the public defence of a thesis.

The Vocational Education Law provides for a system of five professional qualification levels; these are not to be confused with the LQF system which defines vocational education as Levels 4 and 5. Technical and vocational education is principally available at post-secondary vocational colleges. The main award is the First Level Higher Vocational Diploma (or Level IV qualification equivalent to LQF Level 5), which requires two to three years of study. The second level of professional higher education (two to three years in duration) leads to the professional Level V qualification (either a professional qualification or a professional Bachelors degree, equivalent to LQF Level 6). This can be followed by a further one to two years of studies resulting in the award of a professional Masters degree (LQF Level 7). In 2009/10 there were 36,660 students enrolled in 96 vocational schools.

In 2010, in an effort to make the Latvian higher education sector more globally competitive, the Government proposed significant reforms to the national system of higher education, including the closure of some of the country's universities and research institutes and the merging of others.

Regulatory and Representative Bodies

GOVERNMENT

Ministry of Culture: K. Valdemara St 11A, Rīga 1364; tel. 67330200; e-mail pasts@km.gov.lv; internet www.km.gov.lv; Minister ZANETA JAUNZEME-GRENDE.

Ministry of Education and Science: Vaļņu St 2, Rīga 1050; tel. 67226209; e-mail pasts@izm.gov.lv; internet www.izm.gov.lv; Minister VJAČESLAVS DOMBROVSKIS.

ACCREDITATION

Nodibinājums Augstākās Izglītības Kvalitātes Novērtēšanas Centrs (Foundation Higher Education Quality Evaluation Centre): Vaļņu St 2, Rīga 1050; tel. 67213870; e-mail aiknc@aiknc.lv; internet www.aiknc.lv; f. 1994; assessment and accreditation of specific higher education instns and study programmes following recommendations of the Rectors' Ccl and EU requirements; Chair. Dr JURIS DZELME; Exec. Dir INITA ZAĻKALNE.

Akadēmiskās Informācijas Centrs (Academic Information Centre): Valnu St 2, Rīga 1050; Smilšu St 2, Fourth fl., Rīga; tel. 67225155; e-mail aic@aic.lv; internet www.aic.lv; f. 1994; rep. of the Latvian Centre for European recognition network ENIC/NARIC; provides information on the evaluation of foreign body recognition of professional qualifications in regulated professions; Dir BAIBA RAIMINA.

NATIONAL BODIES

Augstākās Izglītības Padome (Council of Higher Education): Zigfrīda Annas Meierovica Blvd 12, Rīga 1050; tel. 67223392; e-mail aip@latnet.lv; internet www.aip.lv; plans the devt of higher education and higher education establishments; 12 mems; Chair. Dr JANIS VETRA; Vice-Chair. TATJANA VOLKOVA.

Latvijas Rektoru Padome (Latvian Rectors' Council): Raiņa Blvd 19, Rīga 1586; tel. 67034338; e-mail rp@lanet.lv; internet www.rektorupadome.lv; f. 1991; promotes cooperation among higher education instns; represents the Latvian higher education sector in Latvia and abroad; prepares suggestions for devt and funding of higher education for Min. of Education and Science; 32 mems; Pres. Prof. ARVIDS BARSEVSKIS; Sec.-Gen. Prof. ANDREJS RAUHVARGERS.

Learned Societies

GENERAL

Latvijas Zinātņu Akadēmija (Latvian Academy of Sciences): Akadēmijas laukums 1, Rīga 1050; tel. 67225361; e-mail lza@lza.lv; internet www.lza.lv; f. 1946; divs of agriculture and forestry sciences, physical and technical sciences, social sciences and humanities; 384 mems (114 full, 55 hon., 126 corresp., 89 foreign); library: see under Libraries and Archives; Pres. Prof. Dr Hab. OJĀRS SPĀRĪTIS; Sec.-Gen. VALDIS KAMPARS; publs *Automātika un Skaitlošanas Tehnika* (Automation and Computer Engineering), *Heterociklisko Savienojumu Ķīmija* (Chemistry of Heterocyclic Compounds), *Kompozītmateriālu Mehānika* (Mechanics of Composite Materials), *Latvijas Fizikas un Tehnisko Zinātnu Žurnāls* (Latvian Journal of Physical and Technical Sciences), *Latvijas Ķīmijas Žurnāls* (Latvian Chemical Journal), *Magnitnaya Gidrodinamika* (Magnetic Hydrodynamics), *Proceedings of the Latvian Academy of Sciences* (in 2 sections: humanitarian sciences, and natural, exact and applied sciences).

LANGUAGE AND LITERATURE

Alliance Française: Merkela iela 13, Rīga 1050; tel. 67140175; offers courses and examinations in French language and culture and promotes cultural exchange with France.

British Council: Blaumana iela 5A-2, Rīga 1011; tel. 67281730; e-mail mail@britishcouncil.lv; internet www.britishcouncil.lv; offers courses and examinations in English language and British culture and promotes cultural exchange with the UK in arts, science and education; library; Dir SANDRA PRINCE.

Goethe-Institut: Torna iela 1, via Klostera iela, Rīga 1050; tel. 67508194; e-mail info@riga.goethe.org; internet www.goethe.de/ins/lv/rig/deindex.htm; offers courses and examinations in German language and culture and promotes cultural exchange with Germany; library of 7,000 vols; Dir ULRICH EVERDING; Librarian ZIGRIDA MUROVSKA.

Research Institutes

GENERAL

Management and Leadership Research Centre: Imantas 7. līnija 1, Rīga 1083; tel. 67860664; e-mail vzpc@rpiva.lv; f. 2011; attached to Rīga Teacher Training and Education Management Academy; facilitates research activities; facilitates cooperation among other educational instns; Dir INETA DAIKTERE; publ. *Scientia Regiminis*.

AGRICULTURE, FISHERIES AND VETERINARY SCIENCE

Latvijas Valsts Agrārās Ekonomikas Institūts (Latvian State Institute of Agrarian Economics): Struktoru iela 14, Rīga 1039; tel. 67552909; e-mail lvaei@lvaei.lv; internet www.lvaei.lv; f. 1998; promotes rural economic and social devt by providing scientific and research work to obtain objective and reliable information on rural and agricultural and food industry devt processes; Dir VIJA ANČUPĀNE.

Valsts Priekuļu Laukaugu Selekcijas Institūts (State Priekuli Plant Breeding Institute): Zinātnes St 2, Priekule 4126; tel. 64130162; e-mail pr_sel@apollo.lv; internet www.priekuliselekcija.lv; f. 1913; scientific research in fields of crop production, provision of scientific basis and expertise in various sectors of crop production to develop; provides seed propagation of 16 crop species; organizes int. conf.; Dir Dr ARTA KRONBERGA.

ECONOMICS, LAW AND POLITICS

Latvijas Zinātņu akadēmijas Ekonomikas institūts (Institute of Economics, Latvian Academy of Sciences): Akadēmijas laukums 1, Rīga 1050; tel. 67222830; e-mail ei@lza.lv; internet www.ei.lza.lv; f. 1997; Sec. DZINTRA POPOVIČA.

EDUCATION

Educator Training Support Centre: Brivibas iela 72, Rīga 1011; tel. 67312081; f. 1995; responsible for implementing and supporting govt policy on teacher-training and the devt of teaching skills; attached to Min. of Education and Science; Dir Dr SARMIS MIKUDA; publ. *Skolotājs*.

Lu Pedagogijas Zinātniskais Institūts (Institute of Pedagogical Sciences): Jūrmalas gatve 74/76, Rīga 1083; tel. 67034042; e-mail pzi@lu.lv; internet www.pzi.lu.lv; f. 2007; attached to Univ. of Latvia; provides scientific and applied research in pedagogy; Dir Prof. Dr Hab. IRINA MASLO; Scientific Sec. Dr TAMĀRA PĪGOZNE.

Pedagogijas un Psihologijas Zinātniski Pētnieciskais Institūts (Scientific Research Institute of Pedagogy and Psychology): Imantas 7. līnija 1, Rīga 1083; tel. 67860679; e-mail ppi@rpiva.lv; f. 2011; attached to Rīga Teacher Training and Education Management Academy; promotes the study of pedagogy, psychology and science; Dir DIANA VOITA.

HISTORY, GEOGRAPHY AND ARCHAEOLOGY

Institute of Geodesy and Geoinformatics: Raiņa Blvd 19, Rīga 1586; tel. 67034436; e-mail slr_jb@latnet.lv; f. 1994; attached to Univ. of Latvia; provides research on geoinformatics, global navigation and satellite systems and construction and application of satellite laser ranging systems; Dir Dr JĀNIS BALODIS; Scientific Sec. MADARA CAUNĪTE.

Latvijas Universitates Latvijas vēstures institūts (Institute of Latvian History at University of Latvia): Akadēmijas laukums 1, Rīga 1050; tel. 65223715; e-mail lvi@lza.lv; internet www.lvi.lv; f. 1936; depts of medieval and modern history, research on the Soviet and Nazi regimes, archaeology, ethnology, bioarchaeology; dendrochronological laboratory; repositories of archaeological, bioarchaeologica, ethnographic materials; library of 4,000 vols; Dir Dr GUNTIS ZEMITIS; Academic Sec. Dr VIKTORIJA BEBRE; publ. *Latvijas Vestures Institūta Žurnāls* (Journal, 4 a year).

LANGUAGE AND LITERATURE

Child's Language Research Centre: Imantas 7. līnija 1, Rīga 1083; tel. 67860682; e-mail bvpc@rpiva.lv; f. 2006; attached to Rīga Teacher Training and Education Management Academy; Dir ANNA VULĀNE.

Latvijas Universitātes Latviešu Valodas Institūts (Latvian Language Institute of the University of Latvia): Akadēmijas laukums 1, Rīga 1050; tel. 67227696; e-mail latv@lza.lv; internet www.lulavi.lv; f. 1992; research on dialectology and history of language, onomastics, grammar, lexicology and lexicography, sociolinguistics, terminology and studies of language culture; Dir Dr Hab. ILGA JANSONE; publ. *Linguistica Lettica* (2 a year).

Latvijas Universitates Literatūras, Folkloras un Mākslas Institūts (Institute of Literature, Folklore and Art of the University of Latvia): Akadēmijas laukums 1, Rīga 1050; tel. 67229017; e-mail litfom@lza.lv; internet www.lfmi.lu.lv; f. 1992, present status 2006; examines Latvian literature in the contexts of the historical Baltic space and of comparative literature; studies Latvian folklore and analyses historical and current trends in the devt of Latvian theatre, cinema and music; organizes 2 annual scholarly confs; Dir Dr DACE BULA; Research Sec. PAULS DAIJA; publ. *Letonica* (2 a year).

Rīgas Tehniskās universitātes Lietiškās Valodniecības Institūts (Institute of Applied Linguistics): Meza St 1, Rīga 1048; tel. 67089501; e-mail valodu.institus@rtu.lv; internet www.lvi.rtu.lv; f. 1958, present name 2011; conducts research on technical translation and terminology; contrastive linguistics; English linguistic aspects of the study; the new technologies of foreign language training; foreign language learning creative innovative methodologies; German language learning strategies in higher education; technical literature, translation problems; Dir Prof. Dr LARISA ILJINSKA; publ. *The Journal of Technical Translation* (1 a year).

MEDICINE

Institute of Experimental and Clinical Medicine: Ojara Vaciesa St 4, Rīga 1004; tel. 67613027; e-mail ekmi@lu.lv; internet www.lu.lv/eng/general/administrative/institutes/scientific/medicine/; f. 1946; attached to Univ. of Latvia; Dir Dr TALIVALDIS FREIVALDS; Scientific Sec. Dr LIGA PLAKANE.

NATURAL SCIENCES

Biological Sciences

Augusts Kirhenšteins Institute of Microbiology and Virology: Ratsupites iela 5, Rīga 1067; tel. 67426197; f. 1946, re-f. 1993; attached to Rīga Stradiņs Univ.; Dir Dr MODRA MUROVSKA (acting).

Biotehnologijas un Veterinārmedicīnas Zinātniskais Institūts 'Sigra' (Institute of Biotechnology and Veterinary Medicine): Institūta St 1, Sigulda 2150; tel. 67976307; e-mail sigra@lis.lv; internet www.sigra.lv; f. 1946; attached to Latvia Univ. of Agriculture; organizes scientific confs; devt of scientific justification for production of high quality, unpolluted, safe and healthy animal food; Dir Dr ALEKSANDRS JEMEĻJANOVS; Scientific Sec. Dr INESE ZĪTARE.

Institute of Biology, University of Latvia: Miera St 3, Salaspils 2169; tel. 67944988; e-mail office@email.lubi.edu.lv; internet www.lubi.edu.lv; f. 1951; 12 laboratories and 1 research group; provides theoretical basis for sustainable devt of natural resources; library of 23,673 vols; Dir Dr VIESTURS MELECIS; Deputy Dir Dr HENRIKS ZENKEVIČS.

Institute of Cardiology, University of Latvia: Pilsonu Str. 13, Rīga 1002; tel. 67069575; provides research on epidemiology and prevention of CVD; invasive cardiology; atherosclerosis of coronary and peripheral vessels; evaluation of gene polymorphisms in the devt of coronary heart disease and secondary CVD risk factors; Dir ANDREJS ERGLIS; Exec. Dir Dr ALDIS ROZENBERGS.

Latvijas Biomedicīnas Pētījumu un Studiju Centrs (Latvian Biomedical Research and Study Centre): Rātsupītes Str. 1, Rīga 1067; tel. 67808200; e-mail bmc@biomed.lu.lv; internet bmc.biomed.lu.lv; f. 1993; performs basic and applied research in molecular genetics, vaccine devt, genomics and proteomics, cancer biology, immunology, biotechnology, stem cell biology, structure biology; Dir Dr JĀNIS KLOVIŅŠ; Scientific Dir Dr Hab. PAULS PUMPĒNS.

Latvijas Hidroekologijas Institūts (Latvian Institute of Aquatic Ecology): Daugavgrīvas Str. 8, Rīga 1048; tel. 67601995; e-mail hydro@latnet.lv; internet www.lhei.lv; f. 1995; marine environment monitoring and research on long-term changes in the Baltic sea, seasonal cycles in estuarine planktonic and benthic communities, vertical fluxes and benthic-pelagic coupling, coastal biodiversity, invasive species, ecological modelling, toxic algae and algal toxins, biotests, ecological risk determination; Dir Dr ANDA IKAUNIECE.

Latvijas Organiskās Sintēzes Institūts (Latvian Institute of Organic Synthesis): Aizkraukles iela 21, Rīga 1006; tel. 67014801; e-mail sinta@osi.lv; internet www.osi.lv; f. 1957; attached to Latvian Acad. of Sciences; performs research in organic chemistry, molecular biology, bioorganic chemistry; Dir Prof. IVARS KALVIŅŠ; publ. *Chemistry of Heterocyclic Compounds* (12 a year, in Russian and English).

Latvijas Valsts Koksnes Ķīmijas Institūts (Latvian State Institute of Wood Chemistry): Dzērbenes Str. 27, Rīga 1006; tel. 67553063; e-mail koks@edi.lv; internet www.kki.lv; f. 1946; devt of technologies for obtaining materials and products from wood and wood biomass; science-based sustainable utilization of Latvia's wood resources for economic, social and environmental benefits; library of 10,000 vols; Dir Dr UGIS CĀBULIS.

Mathematical Sciences

Latvijas Universitātes Matemātikas un Informātikas Institūts (Institute of Mathematics and Computer Science, University of Latvia): Raiņa Blvd 29, Rīga 1459; tel. 67224730; e-mail imcs@lumii.lv; internet www.lumii.lv; f. 1959; main areas of research are mathematical foundations of computer science, complex systems modelling languages and tools devt, graph theory and processing of visual information, semantic web technologies, computational linguistics, bioinformatics, real time systems, information technologies and computer networks, mathematical modelling for technologies, natural sciences and theoretical problems of mathematical methods; Dir RIHARDS BALODIS-BOLUŽS; Exec. Dir INARA OPMANE.

Physical Sciences

Atomfizikas un Spektroskopijas Institūts (Institute of Atomic Physics and Spectroscopy): Raiņa Blvd 19, Rīga 1586; Skunu 4, Rīga; tel. 67225493; e-mail asi@lu.lv; internet www.asi.lv; f. 1994; attached to Univ. of Latvia; conducts fundamental and applied research in atomic physics, spectroscopy, photonics and related areas; Dir Dr AIGARS EKERS; Exec. Dir ULDIS JANSONS.

Centre for Sustainable Business: Strelnieku iela 4A, Rīga 1010; tel. 26114496; internet www.sseriga.edu/en/centres/centre-for-sustainable-business/centre-for-sustainable-business-at-sse-riga.html; f. 2012; attached to Stockholm School of Economics; research areas incl. waste of human, energy, and environmental resources, unjust and openly illicit business practices, governance, tax related behaviour, sponsorship and corporate citizenship and corporate social responsibility; Dir MAIJA KĀLE.

Institute of Astronomy University of Latvia: Raiņa Blvd 19, Rīga 1586; tel. 67034580; e-mail astra@latnet.lv; internet www.astr.lu.lv; f. 1946; satellite laser ranging; low dispersion spectral and photometric studies of carbon stars; digitalization of wide field Schmidt camera astro plates covering time-span from 1966 to 2005; updating of Catalog of Carbon stars (CGCS); optical system design and calculation; Dir Dr ILGMĀRS EGLĪTIS; Scientific Sec. KALVIS SALMIŅŠ; publ. *Zvaigžņotā Debess* (4 a year).

Institute of Microbiology and Biotechnology: Kronvalda Blvd 4, Rīga 1586; tel. 67034887; e-mail lumbi@lanet.lv; internet www.lu.lv/mbi; f. 1993; attached to Univ. of Latvia; conducts research on biology, biotechnology, microbiology; Dir Prof. Dr ULDIS KALNENIEKS.

Institute of Physical Energetics: Aizkraukles iela 21, Rīga 1006; tel. 67552011; e-mail fei@edi.lv; internet www.innovation.lv/fei; f. 1946; regional energy sector analysis and optimization; energy saving management; energy environmental policy studies; renewable energy resources; energy efficiency; electrical networks and electricity supply systems; clean fossil energy technologies; electrical devices and machines; research into advanced materials and solid state physics problems; Dir Prof. JURIS EKMANIS; publ. *Latvian Journal of Physics and Technical Sciences* (6 a year, print and online).

Institute of Physics of University of Latvia: Miera iela 32, Salaspils 2169; tel. 67944700; e-mail fizinst@sal.lv; internet ipul.lv; f. 1946, present status 1997; engineering physics and liquid metal technologies; Dir Dr JĀNIS ERNESTS FREIBERGS; publ. *Magnetohydrodynamics* (4 a year).

Latvijas Universitātes Cietvielu Fizikas Institūts (Institute of Solid State Physics, University of Latvia): Kengaraga St 8, Rīga 1063; tel. 67187816; e-mail issp@cfi.lu.lv; internet www.cfi.lu.lv; f. 1978, present status 2006; Dir Dr ANDRIS ŠTERNBERGS; Deputy Dir for Education Dr ANATOLIJS SARAKOVSKIS; Deputy Dir for Science Dr MARTINS RUTKIS.

Latvijas Universitates Ķīmiskās Fizikas Institūts (University of Latvia Institute of Chemical Physics): Raiņa Blvd 19, Rīga 1586; 4 Kronvalda Blvd, Rīga; tel. 67033875; internet www.kfi.lu.lv; f. 1988; provides research on nanostructured materials; quantum chemistry of molecules, clusters, nanostructures and solid state; devt of instrumentation for investigation of nanointeractions and radiation processes in solids; Dir Dr DONĀTS ERTS.

Latvijas Valsts Augļkopības Institūts (Latvia State Institute of Fruit-Growing): Graudu St 1, Dobele 3701; tel. 63722294; e-mail lvai@lvai.lv; internet www.lvai.lv; f. 1995, present status 2006; attached to Min. of Agriculture; research in the field of fruit growing; preservation of fruit tree, small fruit and lilac genetic resources; cooperation with interest groups in the field of agriculture and with individual fruit-growing and food processing enterprises; organizes scientific confs, seminars, lectures, exhibitions; Dir Dr EDĪTE KAUFMANE.

Latvijas Valsts Mežzinātnes Institūts 'Silava' (Latvian State Forest Research Institute 'Silava'): Rīgas Str. 111, Salaspils 2169; tel. 67942555; e-mail inst@silava.lv; internet www.silava.lv; f. 1946; conducts research on forest ecosystems and their components; works out recommendations for sustainable forest management and a rational and effective utilization of forest resources and forest products; Dir JURĢIS JANSONS; Sec. SIGNE ZOMMERE; publ. *Mežzinātne* (2 a year).

Nuclear Research Centre: Miera iela 31, Salaspils 2169; tel. 67901210; e-mail brzs@lanet.lv; f. 1992; attached to Latvian Acad. of Sciences; Dir A. LAPENAS.

Rīgas Tehniskā Universitāte Humanitarais Instituts (Rīga Technical University Institute of Humanities): Āzenes St 16/20, Rīga 1048; tel. 67089250; e-mail huminst@rtu.lv; internet www.huminst.rtu.lv; f. 1993; Dir Dr ALVARS BALDIŅŠ.

Rīgas Tehniskās Universitāte Neorganiskās Ķīmijas Institūts (Rīga Technical University Institute of Inorganic Chemistry): Miera iela 34, Salaspils 2169; tel. 67944711; e-mail nki@nki.lv; internet www.nki.lv; f. 1946; conducts theoretical and applied research in areas of inorganic chemistry, chemical technology, materials sciences; library of 26,161 vols; Dir Dr Hab. Ing. JANIS GRABIS; Scientific Sec. Dr ELGA SILIŅA; publ. *Latvijas kīmijas žurnāls* (Latvian Journal of Chemistry, 4 a year).

PHILOSOPHY AND PSYCHOLOGY

Latvijas Universitates Filozofijas un Sociologijas Instituts (University of Latvia Institute of Philosophy and Sociology): Akadēmijas laukums 1, Rīga 1940; tel. 67229208; e-mail fsi@lza.lv; internet www.fsi.lu.lv; f. 1981 as Latvia Acad. of Sciences Philosophy and Law Institute, current name and status 2006; research in the humanities and social sciences; Dir Prof. Dr MAIJA KŪLE; Scientific Sec. Dr VANDA DOMBROVSKA; publs *Etnicity*, *Religiski–filozofiski Raksti*.

TECHNOLOGY

Elektronikas un Datorzinātņu Institūts (Institute of Electronics and Computer Science): Dzērbenes St 14, Rīga 1006; tel. 67554500; e-mail info@edi.lv; internet www.edi.lv; f. 1960; carries out fundamental and applied research in computer science, information, communications and electronic technology and engineering areas; library of 10,000 vols; Dir Dr MODRIS GREITANS; publ. *Automatika i vychislitelnaya technika* (Automatic Control and Computer Sciences, 6 a year).

Institute of Polymer Mechanics, University of Latvia: Aizkraukles St 23, Rīga 1006; tel. 67551145; internet www.pmi.lv; f. 1963; theoretical and experimental studies of deformation and fracture of materials; mechanics of composite structure, numerical estimation methods and optimization; prediction of long-term deformation and strength of materials, effect of environmental factors on their exploitation properties; non-destructive testing methods for determining physical and mechanical properties; Dir EGILS PLUME; publ. *Mechanics of Composite Materials* (6 a year).

Lauksaimniecības Tehnikas Zinātniskais Institūts (Research Institute of Agricultural Machinery): Institūta St 1, Stopiņu novads, Ulbroka 2130; tel. 67910879; e-mail uzc@apollo.lv; internet www.llu-ltzi.lv; f. 1960 as Scientific Research Institute for the Mechanization and Electrification of Agriculture, present name and status 2004; attached to Latvia Univ. of Agriculture; carries out fundamental and material research of technical means and technological processes in agriculture; studies rational use of energy resources, acquisition of renewable kinds of energy; organizes confs, seminars, exhibitions; library of 16,000 vols; Dir SEMJONS IVANOVS; Sec. TATJANA PAVLOVIČA.

Rīga Informācijas Tehnoloģijas Institūts (Rīga Information Technology Institute): Meža iela 1/3, Rīga 400; tel. 67089594; internet iti.rtu.lv; f. 1990; attached to Rīga Technical Univ.; depts of management information and modelling and simulation; Dir Prof. Dr Ing. JĀNIS GRABIS.

Scientific Research Institute of Microdevices: Maskavas iela 240, Rīga 1063; tel. 67251619; f. 1962; semiconductor devices and integrated circuits; Dir ARNIS KUNDZINS.

Libraries and Archives

Rīga

Latvijas Nacionala Biblioteka (National Library of Latvia): Kr. Barona iela 14, Rīga 1423; tel. 67365250; e-mail lnb@lnb.lv; internet www.lnb.lv; f. 1919; 4,500,000 vols; Dir ANDRIS VILKS; Exec. Dir DZINTRA MUKĀNE; publs *Bibliotēku zinātnes aspekti* (irregular), *Latviešu Zinātne un Literatūra* (irregular).

Latvijas Universitātes Akadēmiskā bibliotēka (Academic Library of the University of Latvia): Rūpniecības Str. 10, Rīga 1235; tel. 67323649; e-mail acadlib@lib.acadlib.lv; internet www.acadlib.lv; f. 1524; 3.44m. vols (incl. 1.3m. vols of books, 1.7m. periodical copies, 263,000 items of ephemera, 32,700 vols of rare books, 20,500 items of MSS, 826 CD-ROMs); spec. collns incl. Latvian literature; Dir VENTA KOCERE.

Library of the University of Latvia: Raina Blvd 19, Rīga 1586; tel. 67551286; e-mail info-bibl@lu.lv; internet www.lu.lv/eng/library; f. 1862; 2m. vols; Dir Dr IVETA GUDAKOVSKA; Head of the Dept RUTA GARKLAVA.

Patentu Tehniskā Bibliotēka (Patent and Technology Library): K. Valdemāra Str. 33–6, Rīga 1010; tel. (7) 67226628; e-mail patbib@lrpv.gov.lv; internet www.lrpv.gov.lv; f. 1949; part of Patent Office of the Republic of Latvia; 39m. patents; Dir AGNESE BUHOLTE; Prin. Librarian NATALIA BOGDANOVA.

Rīgas Centrālajā bibliotēkā (Rīga Central Library): Brīvības St 49/53, Rīga 1010; tel. 67037121; e-mail rcb@rcb.lv; internet www.rcb.lv; f. 1978; 26 brs; Dir DOLORESA VEILANDE.

Museums and Art Galleries

Bauska

Bauska Castle Museum: Pilskalns, Bauska 3901; tel. 63922280; e-mail bauska.pils@e-apollo.lv; internet www.bauskaspils.lv; f. 1990; Bauska Castle history of the 15th-18th century; Dir M. SKANIS.

Cēsis

Cēsis Museum of History and Art: Pils laukums 9, Cēsis 4100; tel. 64122615; e-mail info@cesis.lv; f. 1925; history, ethnography of Cesis from ancient history to freedom of Latvia (early 20th century); library of 8,000 vols; Dir A. VANADZIŅŠ.

Rīga

Latvijas Dabas Muzejs (Natural History Museum of Latvia): K. Barona iela 4, Rīga 1050; tel. 67356023; e-mail ldm@dabasmuzejs.gov.lv; internet www.dabasmuzejs.gov.lv; f. 1845; colln of zoology, entomology, botany, mycology, palaeontology, geology, anthropology, environmental science, pedagogy and museology; library of 18,000 vols; Dir SKAIDRĪTE RUSKULE; publ. *Daba un Muzejs* (1 a year).

Latvijas Etnogrāfiskais Brīvdabas Muzejs (Ethnographic Open Air Museum of Latvia): Brīvības gatve 440, Rīga 1024; tel. 67994515; e-mail info@brivdabasmuzejs.lv; internet www.brivdabasmuzejs.lv; f. 1924; 118 folk architecture objects; wooden architecture since 17th century; archive of 70,000 units; Dir JURIS INDĀNS.

Latvijas Nacionālais Mākslas Muzejs (Latvian National Museum of Art): K. Valdemāra St 10A, Rīga 1010; tel. 67325051; e-mail lnmm@lnmm.lv; internet www.lnmm.lv; f. 1905, present name 2005; holds art exhibitions and scientific confs, diverse art and cultural events; incl. Arsenāls Exhibition Hall, Museum of Romans Suta and Aleksandra Beļcova, Museum of Decorative Art and Design, Art Museum Rīga Bourse; Dir MĀRA LĀCE.

Latvijas Nacionālā Vēstures Muzeja (National History Museum of Latvia): Pils laukums 3, Rīga 1050; tel. 67223004; e-mail museum@history-museum.lv; internet www.history-museum.lv; f. 1869; one million artefacts of archaeological digs, jewellery and coins, folk costumes, traditional tools, applied art, domestic items, photographs, documents, maps, engravings, paintings and other Latvian historical material; depts of archaeology, ethnography, history, numismatics, research and replicas; Dir ARNIS RADIŅŠ.

Museum of the History of Rīga and Navigation: Palasta iela 4, Rīga 1050; tel. 67211358; e-mail direct@rigamuz.lv; internet www.rigamuz.lv; f. 1773; 500,000 artefacts organized in 80 collns; depts of archaeology, history, navigation, numismatics; 3 br. museums: Museum of Ainaži Naval School in Ainaži (f. 1969), Rīga-Mentzendorff's House (1992), Latvian Museum of Photography (1993); library of 24,000 vols; Dir KLĀRA RADZIŅA.

Pauls Stradiņs Museum for History of Medicine: Antonijas iela 1, Rīga 1360; tel. 67220477; e-mail info@mvm.lv; internet www.mvm.lv; f. 1957; 199,000 artefacts of ethnomedicine, middle ages and renaissance, 18th-20th century medicines, space medicine; awards Pauls Stradiņš Prize in partnership with Latvian Acad. of Sciences for outstanding work in the area of medical studies or research into the history of medicine; library of 36,600 vols; Dir EDĪTE BĒRZIŅA; publ. *Acta Medico-Historica Rigensia*.

Rainis Museum of the History of Literature and Arts: Pils laukums 2, Rīga 1047; tel. 67227901; e-mail pumpurs@acad.latnet.lv; f. 1925; Dir I. ZUKULIS.

Salaspils

Nacionālais Botāniskais Dārzs (National Botanic Garden of Latvia): Miera St 1, Salaspils 2169; tel. 67945460; e-mail nbd@nbd.gov.lv; internet www.nbd.gov.lv; f. 1956; attached to Min. of the Environment and Regional Devt; library of 24,000 vols; Dir Dr ANDREJS SVILĀNS; publs *Index Seminum* (1 a year), *The Baltic Botanical Gardens* (every 2 years).

Universities

DAUGAVPILS UNIVERSITĀTE (Daugavpils University)

Vienības St 13, Daugavpils 5400
Telephone: 65422922
E-mail: du@du.lv
Internet: www.du.lv/lv

Founded 1921 as Daugavpils Pedagogical Secondary School, present name and status 2001
State control
Academic year: September to June (2 semesters)

Rector: Prof. Dr ARVĪDS BARŠEVSKIS
Vice-Rector for Research: Dr INESE KOKINA
Vice-Rector for Studies: Prof. Dr IRĒNA KAMINSKA
Dir for Library: REGĪNA TEREŠČENKOVA

Library of 400,000 vols
Number of teachers: 260
Number of students: 4,942

Publications: *Acta Biologica Universitatis Daugavpiliensis*, *Acta Latgalica*, *Baltic Journal of Coleopterology* (online (www.bjc.sggw.pl)), *Discourse and Communication for Sustainable Education*, *Humanitāro Zinātņu Vēstnesis*, *Journal of Teacher Education for Sustainability*, *Komparatīvistikas Institūta Almanahs*, *Literatūra un kultūra: process, mijiedarbība un problēmas*, *Mūzikas vēstures un teorijas mijiedarbe*, *Person. Color. Nature. Music.*, *Problems in music pedagogy*, *Regionālais Ziņojums*, *Sociālo Zinātņu Vēstnesis*

DEANS

Faculty of Education and Management: Prof. Dr JELENA DAVIDOVA
Faculty of Humanities: Dr VALENTĪNA LIEPA
Faculty of Music and Arts: Prof. Dr ĒVALDS DAUGULIS
Faculty of Natural Sciences and Mathematics: Prof. Dr VALFRĪDS PAŠKEVIČS
Faculty of Social Sciences: Prof. Dr VLADIMIRS MEŅŠIKOVS

LATVIJAS LAUKSAIMNIECĪBAS UNIVERSITĀTE (Latvia University of Agriculture)

Lielā St 2, Jelgava 3001
Telephone: 63022584
E-mail: rector@llu.lv
Internet: www.llu.lv

Founded 1939 as Jelgava Agricultural Acad., present name and status 1991
State control
Languages of instruction: English, German, Latvian, Russian

Rector: Prof. Dr JURIS SKUJĀNS
Vice-Rector for Science: PĒTERIS RIVŽA
Vice-Rector for Studies: ARNIS MUGURĒVIČS

Library of 426,073 vols
Number of teachers: 347
Number of students: 5,142

Publications: *Plesums*, *Works* (1 a year)

DEANS

Faculty of Agriculture: Dr ZINTA GAILE
Faculty of Economics: Prof. Dr IRINA PILVERE
Faculty of Engineering: Prof. Dr Eng. MĀRIS ĶIRSIS
Faculty of Food Technology: INGA CIPROVIČA
Faculty of Information Technologies: Dr Eng. ULDIS ILJINS
Faculty of Rural Engineering: Prof. Dr Eng. RITVARS SUDĀRS
Faculty of Social Sciences: Dr VOLDEMĀRS BARISS
Faculty of Veterinary Medicine: Dr ILMĀRS DŪRĪTIS
Forest Faculty: DAGNIS DUBROVSKIS
Technical Faculty: Prof. Dr Ing. KASPARS VĀRTUKAPTEINIS

LATVIJAS UNIVERSITATE (University of Latvia)

Raiņa Blvd 19, Rīga 1586
Telephone: 67034334
E-mail: lu@lu.lv
Internet: www.lu.lv

Founded 1919
State control
Language of instruction: Latvian
Academic year: September to June

Rector: Prof. Dr MĀRCIS AUZIŅŠ
Vice-Rector for Academic Affairs: Prof. ANDRIS KANGRO
Vice-Rector for Research: Prof. INDRIĶIS MUIŽNIEKS
Dir for Library: IVETA GUDAKOVSKA

Library: see under Libraries and Archives
Number of teachers: 980
Number of students: 17,625

Publications: *Acta Universitatis Latviensis* (10 a year), *Agora* (2 a year), *Ceļš* (theology, 1 a year), *History of Latvia* (4 a year), *Journal of Baltic Psychology* (1 a year), *Journal of the Latvian Institute of*

History (4 a year), *Lettonics* (every 2 years), *Linguistica Lettica* (every 2 years), *Magnetohydrodynamics* (4 a year), *Mechanics of Composite Materials* (6 a year), *The Baltic International Yearbook of Cognition, Logic and Communication* (online (cognition.lu.lv)), *Zvaigznota Debess* (The Starry Sky, 4 a year)

DEANS

Faculty of Biology: Dr NILS ROSTOKS
Faculty of Computing: Prof. JURIS BORZOVS
Faculty of Chemistry: ANDA PRIKSANE
Faculty of Economics and Management: MĀRIS PURGAILIS
Faculty of Education, Psychology and Art: Prof. ANDRIS GRINFELDS
Faculty of Geography and Earth Sciences: Prof. OLGERTS NIKODEMUS
Faculty of History and Philosophy: Prof. ANDRIS SNE
Faculty of Humanities: Prof. ILZE RŪMNIECE
Faculty of Law: Prof. KRISTĪNE STRADA-ROZENBERGA
Faculty of Medicine: Prof. INGRĪDA RUMBA-ROZENFELDE
Faculty of Physics and Mathematics: LEONĪDS BULIGINS
Faculty of Social Sciences: Prof. JURIS ROZENVALDS
Faculty of Theology: Dr RALFS KOKINS

LIEPĀJAS UNIVERSITĀTE
(Liepāja University)

Lielā iela 14, Liepāja 3401
Telephone: 63423568
E-mail: liepu@liepu.lv
Internet: www.liepu.lv

Founded 1954 as Liepaja Pedagogical Institute, present name and status 2008
State control
Rector: Dr JANIS RIMSANS
Vice-Rector for Science: Dr IEVA OZOLA
Vice-Rector for Studies: Dr ILMA NEIMANE
Dir for Library: AIJA KAIRENA
Library of 100,000 vols
Number of teachers: 74
Number of students: 1,762 (incl. 1,409 full-time and 353 part-time)

DEANS

Faculty of Humanities and Art: Dr ZANDA GUTMANE
Faculty of Natural and Social Sciences: Dr MARA ZELTINA
Faculty of Pedagogy and Social Work: Dr ILZE MIKELSONE

RĪGAS STRADIŅA UNIVERSITĀTE
(Rīga Stradiņs University)

Dzirciema St 16, Rīga 1007
Telephone: 67409105
E-mail: rsu@rsu.lv
Internet: www.rsu.lv

Founded 1950 as Rīga Medical Institute, present name and status 2002
State control
Languages of instruction: English, Latvian
Academic year: September to June
Rector: Prof. JĀNIS GARDOVSKIS
Vice-Rector for Admin.: JURIS LĀCIS
Vice-Rector for Devt: TOMS BAUMANIS
Vice-Rector for Education: Prof. ILZE AKOTA
Vice-Rector for Science: Prof. IVETA OZOLANTA
Dir for Library: INĀRA APLOKA
Library of 294,000 vols
Number of teachers: 519
Number of students: 7,412
Publications: *Dentistry* (1 a year), *Kirurģija* (Surgery, 2 a year), *Zinātniskie raksti* (medicine and pharmacy)

DEANS

Faculty of Communications: TAŅA LĀCE
Faculty of Continuing Education: JEVGĒNIJA LIVDĀNE
Faculty of Dentistry: Prof. INGRĪDA ČEMA
Faculty of European Studies: Prof. Dr ILGA KREITUSE
Faculty of Law: Prof. ANDREJS VILKS
Faculty of Medicine: ARDIS PLATKĀJIS
Faculty of Nursing: INGA MILLERE
Faculty of Pharmacy: BAIBA MAURIŅA
Faculty of Public Health: ANITA VILLERUŠA
Faculty of Rehabilitation: Prof. AIVARS VĒTRA

RĪGAS TEHNISKĀ UNIVERSITĀTE
(Rīga Technical University)

Kaļķu St 1, Rīga 1658
Telephone: 67089333
E-mail: info@rtu.lv
Internet: www.rtu.lv

Founded 1862 as Rīga Polytechnium, present name and status 1990
State control
Rector: Dr Ing. LEONĪDS RIBICKIS
Vice-Rector for Academic Affairs: Prof. Dr Ing. ULDIS SUKOVSKIS
Vice-Rector for Science: Prof. Dr Ing. TĀLIS JUHNA
Deputy Rector for Academic Policy and Quality Affairs: Dr GITA RĒVALDE
Deputy Rector for Business Relations and Devt: MODRIS OZOLIŅŠ
Deputy Rector for Infrastructure Management: AIGARS LOČMELIS
Deputy Rector for Int. Students: Dr IGORS TIPĀNS
Deputy Rector for Strategic Devt: MAREKS ZELTIŅŠ
Dir for Library: AIJA JANBICKA
Library of 2,300,000 vols
Number of teachers: 479
Number of students: 14,686
Publications: *Jaunais Inzenieris* (newspaper), *Scientific Proceedings of RTU* (4 a year)

DEANS

Faculty of Architecture and Urban Planning: UGIS BRATUŠKINS
Faculty of Civil Engineering: Prof. JURIS SMIRNOVS
Faculty of Computer Science and Information Technology: Prof. JANIS GRUNDSPENKIS
Faculty of Electronics and Telecommunications: Prof. GUNTARS BALODIS
Faculty of Engineering Economics and Management: Prof. REMIGIJS POČS
Faculty of Materials Science and Applied Chemistry: Prof. Dr VALDIS KOKARS
Faculty of Power and Electrical Engineering: Prof. Dr Ing. OSKARS KRIEVS
Faculty of Transport and Mechanical Engineering: Prof. ĒRIKS GERIŅŠ

Other Higher Educational Institutions

Baltic International Academy: Lomonosova St 4, Rīga 1003; tel. 67100610; e-mail info@bsa.edu.lv; internet www.bsa.edu.lv; f. 1992, present name 2006; 200 teachers; 4,500 students; Chair. STANISLAV BUKA; Dir for Library OLGA ZDEBSKA.

Ekonomikas un Kulturas Augstskola (University College of Economics and Culture): Lomonosova iela 1, korp. 5, Rīga 1019; tel. 20009051; e-mail sic@eka.edu.lv; internet www.eka.edu.lv; f. 1998; depts of culture, economics, foreign languages; library: 12,000 vols; Rector GUNTA VEISMANE; Vice-Rector Prof. Dr INETA KRISTOVSKA; Vice-Rector for Scientific Affairs Prof. Dr STAŅISLAVS KEIŠS; Head of Library RŪTA KORE.

Information Systems Management Institute: Lomonosov Str. 1, Bldg 6, Rīga 1019; tel. 67100607; e-mail isma@isma.lv; internet isma.lv; f. 1996; depts of computer technologies and natural sciences, culture, law, international business communications, management and economics, management and marketing; Pres. Prof. Dr ROMANS DJAKONS; Rector Prof. Dr MARGA ŽIVITERE; Vice-Rector for Academic Affairs Prof. Dr YURI SHUNIN; Vice-Rector for Admin. AIVARS STANKEVIČS; Vice-Rector for Int. Relations DENISS DJAKONS; Vice-Rector for Research Prof. Dr VIKTORS GOPEJENKO; Vice-Rector for Studies IVARS LINDE.

Jāzepa Vītola Latvijas Mūzikas Akadēmija (Jāzeps Vītols Latvian Academy of Music): Krishyana Barona iela 1, Rīga 1050; tel. 67228684; e-mail academy@jvlma.lv; internet www.jvlma.lv; f. 1919; depts of accompanists, choir conducting, choreography, composition, early music, humanities, jazz music, music education, music technology, musicology, orchestral instruments, piano, singing, string instruments, vocal music, wind instruments; library: 150,000 vols (incl. 54,000 audio and video cassettes, 92,000 scores, 4,500 books); 246 teachers; 426 students; Rector Prof. ARTIS SĪMANIS; Vice-Rector for Academic Work Prof. NORMUNDS VĪKSNE; Vice-Rector for Admin. ARMANDS LAPIŅŠ; Vice-Rector for Foreign Affairs Dr MAIJA SĪPOLA; Vice-Rector for Scientific and Creative Work Prof. Dr ANDA BEITĀNE; Head of Library EVITA STANKEVIČA.

Latvian Christian Academy: Fifth line 3, Bulduri, Jūrmala 2010; tel. 67753360; e-mail rektore@kra.lv; internet www.kra.lv; f. 1993; study programmes incl. Bible art, caritative social work, public relations, theology; Rector Prof. Dr SKAIDRĪTE GŪTMANE.

Latvijas Juras Akademija (Latvian Maritime Academy): Flotes iela 5B, Rīga 1016; tel. 67161125; e-mail info@latja.lv; internet www.latja.lv; f. 1993; study programmes in marine transport and engineering, port and shipping management; library: 45,000 vols; 300 students; 68 teachers; Rector JĀNIS BĒRZIŅŠ; Pro-Rector ILMĀRS LEŠINSKIS; Pro-Rector for Science ANATOLIJS SARAKOVSKIS; publ. *Journal of Maritime Transport and Engineering*.

Latvijas Kulturas Akademija (Latvian Academy of Culture): Ludzas St 24, Rīga 1003; tel. 67140175; e-mail admin@lka.edu.lv; internet www.lka.edu.lv; f. 1990; depts of cultural theory and history of culture, intercultural communication and foreign languages, sociology and management of culture, theatre and audiovisual arts; library: 55,000 vols; 65 teachers; 647 students; Rector Prof. JĀNIS SILIŅŠ; Vice-Rector Dr ZANE ŠILIŅA; Library Man. JURITA SIFERE.

Latvijas Mākslas Akadēmija (Art Academy of Latvia): Kalpaka Blvd 13, Rīga 1867; tel. 67332202; e-mail info@lma.lv; internet www.lma.lv; f. 1919; faculties of art history and theory, audiovisual media, design, visual arts, visual plastic arts; library: 30,000 vols; 100 teachers; 638 students; Rector Prof. ALEKSEJS NAUMOVS; Pro-Rector for Admin. and Creative Work Prof. KRISTAPS ZARIŅŠ; Pro-Rector for Study and Research Work ANDRIS TEIKMANIS; Head of Library JĀNIS PUTĀNS.

Latvijas Nacionālā Aizsardzības Akadēmija (National Defence Academy of Latvia): Ezermalas iela 8, Rīga 1014; tel. 67076881; e-mail intars.vascenkovs@mil.lv; internet www.naa.mil.lv; f. 1992; offers professional Bachelors degree in land force, naval force, air force military leadership; professional Masters study programme in military leadership and security; Rector EGILS LEŠČINSKIS; Pro-Rector GEORGS KERLINS; Head of Library LAILA TĪGERE; publs *Kadets, Militārais Apskats, Militārā Zinātne, Tēvijas Sargs* (12 a year).

Latvijas Sporta Pedagoģijas Akadēmija (Latvian Academy of Sport Education): Brīvības gatve 333, Rīga 1006; tel. 67543410; e-mail akademija@lspa.lv; internet www.lspa.lv; f. 1921 as Latvian Institute of Physical Education, present name 1991; depts of anatomy, athletics, gymnastics, heavy athletics, informatics, management, skiing, sport games, sport medicine, swimming, theory; library: 251,000 vols; 78 teachers; Rector Prof. Dr JĀNIS ŽĪDENS; Vice-Rector Prof. Dr ANDRA FERNATE; Vice-Rector Prof. Dr JURIS GRANTS; Vice-Rector Prof. Dr ULDIS SVINKS; Head of Library MARGARITA ZAĻŪKSNE; publ. *LASE Journal of Sport Science* (2 a year, in English).

Rēzeknes Augstskola (Rezekne Higher Education Institution): Atbrīvošanas aleja 90, Rēzekne 4601; tel. 64623709; e-mail ru@ru.lv; internet www.ru.lv; f. 1993; 402 students; Rector Prof. Dr Ing. EDMUNDS TEIRUMNIEKS; Vice-Rector for Cooperation and Devt IVETA GRAUDIŅA; Vice-Rector for Studies Dr ANGELIKA JUŠKO-ŠTEKELE.

Rīga Business School: Skolas St 11, Rīga 1010; tel. 67089800; e-mail info@rbs.lv; internet www.rbs.lv; f. 1991; attached to Rīga Technical Univ.; offers Bachelors, professional and executive MBA; Dir Dr JĀNIS GRĒVIŅŠ; Dir for Admin. AIRA TEREŠKO; Librarian UNA LUKJANOVA.

Rīga International School of Economics and Business Administration: Meža iela 3, Rīga 1048; tel. 67500265; e-mail riseba@riseba.lv; internet www.riseba.lv; f. 1992; campuses in Rīga and Daugavpils; Rector Dr IRINA SENNIKOVA; Vice-Rector for Science Prof. Dr VULFS KOZLINSKIS; Vice-Rector for Teaching and Learning Dr ILMARS KREITUSS; Chief Librarian INA MOKEROVA; publ. *Journal of Business Management*.

Rīgas Juridiskās Augstskolas (Rīga Graduate School of Law): Strēlnieku iela 4K-2, Rīga 1010; tel. 67039230; e-mail office@rgsl.edu.lv; internet www.rgsl.edu.lv; f. 1998 as Rīga Graduate School of Law, present status 2006; library: 8,000 vols; Rector Prof. Dr GEORGE ULRICH; Pro-Rector Dr MĀRTIŅŠ MITS; Head of Library LIGITA GJORTLERE.

Rīgas Pedagoģijas un Izglītības Vadības Akadēmija (Rīga Teacher Training and Education Management Academy): Imantas 7, linija 1, Rīga 1083; tel. 67808010; e-mail rpiva@rpiva.lv; internet www.rpiva.lv; f. 1994; 160 teachers; 3,500 students; Rector Prof. Dr Hab. DACE MARKUS; Vice-Rector Prof. Dr MĀRA MARNAUZA; Vice-Rector for Studies Prof. Dr RITA SPALVA; publs *Ad Verba Liberorun, Scientia Regiminis, Signum Temporis*.

Sociālo Tehnologiju Augstskola (Higher School of Social Technologies): Bezdeligu Str. 12, Rīga 1048; tel. 67461001; e-mail sta@sta-edu.lv; internet www.sta-edu.lv; f. 1991; depts of economics, law, languages; library: 20,000 vols; Rector JURIS ZAĶIS; Librarian LUDMILA GERASIMOVA.

Starptautiskā Praktiskās Psiholoģijas Augstskola (International Higher School of Practical Psychology): Bruņinieku St 65, Rīga 1011; tel. 67506257; e-mail sppa@sppa.lv; internet www.sppa.lv; f. 1988; faculties of advertisement and public relations, computer design, enterprise activity, psychology, translation, visual art; Pres. JĀNIS MIHAILOVS; Rector DZIDRA MEIKŠĀNE.

Stockholm School of Economics in Riga: Strelnieku iela 4A, Rīga 1010; tel. 67015800; e-mail office@sseriga.edu; internet www.sseriga.edu; f. 1994; depts of business and management, economics, languages; library: 25,000 vols; Rector Prof. Dr ANDERS PAALZOW; Pro-Rector Dr DIĀNA PAUNA; Head of Library DACE CĪRULE; publ. *Baltic Journal of Economics* (2 a year).

Transport and Telecommunication Institute: Lomonosova St 1, Rīga 1019; tel. 67100661; e-mail info@tsi.lv; internet www.tsi.lv; f. 1919, fmrly Rīga Aviation Univ., present status 1999; library: 36,000 vols, 200 journals; 220 teachers; 3,000 students; Rector Dr Ing. BORIS MISHNEV; First Vice-Chancellor Prof. Dr Ing. IRINA YATSKIV; Vice-Chancellor for Admin. Affairs JURIS KANELS; Vice-Chancellor for Economic Affairs NATALIA PODOLYAKINA; publs *Computer Modelling and New Technologies, Journal of Air Transportation, Nature and Computer World, Research and Technology-Step into the Future, Transport and Telecommunication, TTI Students Proceedings*.

Ventspils Augstskola (Ventspils University College): Inženieru St 101A, Ventspils 3601; tel. 63629657; e-mail venta@venta.lv; internet www.venta.lv; f. 1997; 60 teachers; 890 students; Rector Dr JĀNIS EGLĪTIS; Vice-Rector for Admin. and Finance ALEKSANDRS DUPATS; Vice-Rector for Science Dr AIGARS KRAUZE; Vice-Rector for Studies Dr ARNIS SAUKA; Library Man. DACE KREICBERGA.

Vidzemes Augstskola (Vidzeme University of Applied Sciences): Cesu St 4, Valmiera 4201; tel. 64207230; e-mail info@va.lv; internet www.va.lv; f. 1996, present name and status 2001; library: 19,000 vols; 1,423 students; Rector Dr VIJA DAUKŠTE; Vice-Rector for Academic Work Dr SARMĪTE ROZENTĀLE; Vice-Rector for Admin. ILGVARS ĀBOLS; Dir for Library INESE TAURĪTE.

LEBANON

The Higher Education System

The two oldest universities in Lebanon are private institutions founded by Christian denominations in the 19th century while Lebanon was still under Ottoman Turkish rule; they are the American University of Beirut (founded 1866; formerly Syrian Protestant College) and the Université Saint-Joseph (founded 1875; Jesuit control). Following the dissolution of the Ottoman Empire after the First World War (1914–18), a Greater Lebanese state was created by the Allied powers, administered by France under a League of Nations mandate from 1920 until independence was declared in 1941. Institutions of higher education established in this period include the Lebanese American University (founded 1835 by the United Presbyterian Church, USA), the Near East School of Theology (founded 1932) and the Académie Libanaise des Beaux-Arts (founded 1937). The higher education system, which is administered by the Ministry of Education and Higher Education, displays strong French and US influences, which vary from institution to institution reflecting whether they were set up by US missionaries or the French authorities. The language of instruction is Arabic, English or French, depending on the area of study and the system of education followed by the institution. Furthermore, higher education is dominated by private institutions; only the Université Libanaise (founded 1951) is under state control. Non-university institutions of higher education include religious institutes, university colleges and technology institutes. Some 216,851 Lebanese students were enrolled in higher education in the 2011/12 academic year.

Admission to university undergraduate courses is generally on the basis of the secondary school qualification (Baccalauréat Libanais or comparable qualification), and students may also be required to sit an entrance examination. Depending on the institution, the main undergraduate degree is known as the Licence, Bachelors, Maîtrise or Diploma, and is usually three to five years in duration. Medical students are awarded a professional degree called the Doctorat after seven years. A range of degrees is also available at the first stage of postgraduate study, including Masters, Maîtrise or Diplôme d'Etudes Supérieures. The final stage of university-level degrees is the Doctorat d'Etat.

The principal qualifications available in the post-secondary vocational and technical education sector are the Technicien Supérieur and the Licence Technique (requiring three years and four years of study, respectively). In 1998 Lebanon secured a loan of US $60m. from the World Bank, in order to restructure the country's system of technical and vocational education.

Institutions of higher education are accredited by the Ministry of Education and Higher Education and the Equivalence Committee (attached to the Ministry). The Université Libanaise is the only institution accredited solely by the Ministry, being the only public university in the country. Other institutions must be individually accredited by the Equivalence Committee. Accreditation is given in the form of a government decree. Each decree has a number and a date (for example, the Faculty of Arts and Social Sciences at the University of Balamand is accredited according to edict 4885 from 4/6/1988). Although the American University of Beirut is accredited by the US agency the Middle States Association of Schools and Colleges, it is, none the less, still recognized by the Government of Lebanon. In October 2011, in an attempt to strengthen the competitiveness of Lebanon's sole state university and numerous private universities, the Government announced plans to establish a national quality assurance agency, which would oversee a monitoring system for institutional performance.

Regulatory Bodies

GOVERNMENT

Ministry of Culture: Hatab Bldg, Madame Curie St, Verdun, Beirut; tel. (1) 744250; e-mail amalm@culture.gov.lb; internet www.culture.gov.lb; Minister GABY LAYOUN.

Ministry of Education and Higher Education: UNESCO Palace Quarter, Habib Abi Chahla Sq., Sixth Floor, Beirut; tel. (1) 772500; e-mail info@higher-edu.gov.lb; internet www.higher-edu.gov.lb; Minister HASSAN DIAB.

Learned Societies

GENERAL

UNESCO Office Beirut and Regional Bureau for Education in the Arab States: POB 5244, Beirut; located at: Cité Sportive Blvd, Beirut; tel. (1) 850013; e-mail beirut@unesco.org; internet www.unesco.org.lb; designated Cluster Office for Iraq, Jordan, Lebanon, Syria and Palestinian Autonomous Territories; Regional Bureau for Education in the Arab States; Dir RAMZI SALAMÉ.

BIBLIOGRAPHY, LIBRARY SCIENCE AND MUSEOLOGY

Lebanese Library Association (LLA): POB 113-5367, Beirut; tel. (9) 600372; e-mail randachidiac@usek.edu.lb; internet www.llaweb.org; f. 1960; 210 individual mems and 35 institutional mems; Pres. RANDA AL-CHIDIAC; Sec. RUDAYNAH SHOUJAH; Treas. DOMINGUA ABBOUD.

ECONOMICS, LAW AND POLITICS

Association Libanaise des Sciences Juridiques: Faculté de Droit et des Sciences politiques, Université Saint-Joseph, POB 17-5208, Beirut; tel. (1) 421000; f. 1963; represents Lebanon in the Int. Assen of Legal Science; study of legal problems in Lebanon, confs, etc.; 40 mems; Pres. PIERRE GANNAGÉ; Sec.-Gen. NABIL MAAMARY; publ. *Proche-Orient* (Judicial Studies).

LANGUAGE AND LITERATURE

British Council: Sadat/Sidani St, Azar Bldg, Ras Beirut; tel. (1) 740123; e-mail general.enquiries@lb.britishcouncil.org; internet www.britishcouncil.org/lebanon; teaching centre; offers courses and exams in English language and British culture and promotes cultural exchange with the UK; Dir Dr KEN CHURCHILL; Teaching Centre Man. ANDREW MACKENZIE.

Goethe-Institut: Damascus Rd, Berythech Bldg, 7th Floor, Beirut; tel. (1) 422291; e-mail info@beirut.goethe.org; internet www.goethe.de/beirut; offers courses and exams in German language and culture and promotes cultural exchange with Germany; library of 9,000 vols; Dir FAREED C. MAJARI.

Instituto Cervantes: Centre Ville, 287 A/B Maarad St, POB 11-1202, Beirut; tel. (1) 970253; e-mail cenbei@cervantes.es; internet beirut.cervantes.es; offers courses and exams in Spanish language and culture and promotes cultural exchange with Spain and Spanish-speaking Latin and Central America; library of 5,000 vols; Dir ANDRÉS PÉREZ SÁNCHEZ-MORATE.

Research Institutes

GENERAL

Institut Français du Proche-Orient: c/o Abou Roumaneh, 11, rue Chukri Al-Assali (à côté de l'ambassade du Japon), 344 Damas, Syria; tel. (1) 420291; e-mail contact@ifporient.org; internet www.ifporient.org; f. 2003; study of Middle East in all its aspects: economy, history, human geography, physical geography, sociology, towns; library of 125,000 vols; Dir FRANÇOIS BURGAT.

Orient-Institut der Deutschen Morgenländischen Gesellschaft Beirut (Orient Institute of the German Institute of Oriental Studies, Beirut): POB 11-2988, Riad el-Solh 1107 2120, Beirut; tel. (1) 359424; e-mail dir@oidmg.org; internet www.oidmg.org; f. 1961 by the Deutsche Morgenländische Gesellschaft (DMG); since 2002 part of DIGA (German Institutes for Humanities Abroad); activities in the field of Oriental research (Islamic, Arabic, Persian, Turcological, Semitic), philology, and contemporary history, incl. field research, history of the eastern Churches; cooperation with univs in the Middle East and Germany; library of 133,000 vols; Dir Prof. Dr MANFRED KROPP; publs *Beiruter Blätter* (every 2 years), *Bibliotheca Islamica—Beiruter Texte und Studien*.

ECONOMICS, LAW AND POLITICS

Centre for Arab Unity Studies: Beit Al-Nahda Bldg, Basra Str., Hamra Hamra, POB 113-6001, Beirut 2034 2407; tel. (1) 750084; e-mail info@caus.org.lb; internet www.caus.org.lb; f. 1975; an ind., non-political centre for scientific research on all aspects of Arab soc. and Arab unity, particularly in the fields of economics, politics, sociology and education; activities are governed and implemented by 3 bodies: Board of Trustees, Exec. Cttee and Gen. Secretariat; library of 18,000 vols, 1,657 periodicals; Dir-Gen. Dr YOUSSEF CHOUEIRY; publ. *Al-Mustaqbal Al-Arabi* (The Arab Future, 12 a year).

Lebanese Center for Policy Studies: POB 55-215, Vanlian Center, 8th Fl., Mkalles, Beirut; tel. (1) 486429; e-mail info@lcps-lebanon.org; internet www.lcps-lebanon.org; f. 1989; research into political, social and economic development; library facilities; Dir Dr OUSSAMA SAFA.

HISTORY, GEOGRAPHY AND ARCHAEOLOGY

Institut Français d'Archéologie du Proche Orient: rue de Damas, POB 11-1424, Beirut; tel. (1) 615844; e-mail ifapo@lb.refer.org; f. 1946; Dir JEAN-LOUIS HUOT; library of 45,000 vols; brs in Syria and Jordan; publs *Bibliothèque Archéologique et Historique*, *Revue d'Art et d'Archéologie, Syria*.

Libraries and Archives

Beirut

American University of Beirut Libraries: POB 11/0236, Riad El-Solh 1107 2020, Beirut; tel. (1) 340460 ext. 2600; e-mail library@aub.edu.lb; internet www.aub.edu.lb/libraries; f. 1866; 469,881 vols, 1,366 MSS, 305 periodicals, 1,139,346 audiovisual items, 1,948 maps; Librarian Dr LOKMAN MEHO.

Beirut Arab University Library: POB 11-5020, Beirut; tel. (1) 300110; e-mail library@bau.edu.lb; internet www.bau.edu.lb/library-home1; f. 1960; incl. 8 libraries, collns on Lebanese, Arabic and Islamic studies; 110,000 vols and 1,500 periodicals; Chief Librarian SAID TAYARA.

Bibliothèque Nationale du Liban: Immeuble Hatab, 6th Fl., rue Madame Curie, Beirut; tel. (1) 756321; e-mail info@bnlb.org; internet www.bnlb.org; f. 1921; library closed and collections put in storage 1979, due to civil war; restoration and reconstruction of the library began 2003; 150,000 vols, 2,500 MSS.

Bibliothèque Orientale: Rue de l'Université Saint-Joseph, POB 166-775, Achrafieh, Beirut 1100-2150; tel. (1) 421810; e-mail bo@usj.edu.lb; internet www.bo.usj.edu.lb; f. 1875; attached to Université Saint-Joseph; 230,000 titles, 1,800 periodicals, 3,500 MSS, 60,000 photographs, 3,000 maps; Dir MICHELINE SAINTE-MARIE BITTAR; publ. *Mélanges de L'Universités Saint-Joseph* (1 a year).

Bibliothèques de l'Université Saint-Joseph: POB 17 5208, Beirut; incl. specialized libraries of engineering sciences, letters and human sciences, medical sciences, social sciences; Library of Faris Zoghbie Cultural Foundation, Oriental Library.

Attached Library:

Bibliothèque de la Faculté des Lettres et des Sciences Humanies: rue de Damas, POB 17-5208, Beirut 1104 2020; tel. (1) 421000 ext. 5105; e-mail flsh.biblio@usj.edu.lb; f. 1977; 118,000 vols; Librarian LEILA BOU NADER ELIAN.

Near East School of Theology Library: POB 13-5780, Chouran, Beirut 1102 2070; tel. (1) 354194; e-mail library@theonest.edu.lb; internet www.theonest.edu.lb; f. 1932; 50,000 vols; colln of MSS, colln of The American Press; 135 religious periodicals (of which 80 are current); Librarian HILDA T. NASSAR; publ. *Theological Review* (2 a year).

Daroon-Harissa

Library of the Syrian Patriarchal Seminary: Seminary of Charfet, Daroon-Harissa; tel. (9) 260750; f. 1786; 55,000 vols, 2,100 MSS; Rector Fr ANTOINE NASSIF; publ. *Trait d'Union* (1 a year).

Khonchara

Library of the St John Monastery: Khonchara; f. 1696; Basilian Shweiriet Order, first printing press in the Middle East with Arabic and Greek letters (first book 1734); 12,000 vols, 372 MSS; Abbot-General Rt Rev. Mgr ATHANASE HAGE.

Saïda

Library of the Monastery of Saint-Saviour: Saïda; tel. 7975064; e-mail makarioshaidamous@gmail.com; f. 1711; Basilian Missionary Order of Saint-Saviour; 40,000 vols and 3,000 MSS; Librarian MAKARIOS HAIDAMOUS; Librarian FAYEZ FREIJAT; publs *An-Nahlat* (4 a year), *Nafhat Al-Moukhalles* (4 a year).

Museums and Art Galleries

Beirut

American University Museum: Ras, Beirut; tel. (1) 340549; e-mail museum@aub.edu.lb; internet www.aub.edu.lb/museum_archeo; f. 1868; Neolithic flint implements; bronze tools and implements from the Early Bronze Age to the Byzantine period; pottery and other artefacts from the Bronze and Iron Ages, and Classical, Hellenistic, Roman and Byzantine periods; Arabic pottery from the 8th to the 16th century; Phoenician glassware; Egyptian artefacts from the Neolithic to the Dynastic period; pottery from the Neolithic period of Mesopotamia and cylinder seals and cuneiform tablets from Sumer and Akkad; numismatics of the countries in the eastern basin of the Mediterranean; Dir Dr LEILA BADRE; publ. *Berytus* (1 a year).

Daheshite Museum and Library: POB 202, Beirut; contains watercolours, gouaches, original paintings, engravings, sculptures in marble, bronze, ivory and wood carvings; library of 30,000 vols (20,000 Arabic, 10,000 English and French), on arts, philosophy, history, literature, religions, etc.; Dir Dr A. S. M. DAHESH.

Musée des Beaux-Arts: POB 3939, Beirut; Dir Dr DAHESH.

Musée National de Beyrouth (National Museum of Beirut): rue de Damas, Beirut; e-mail info@beirutnationalmuseum.com; internet www.beirutnationalmuseum.com; f. 1919; collns from Prehistoric, Bronze Age, Iron Age, Hellenistic period, Roman period, Byzantine period, the Arab conquest, Mamluk period; Dir-Gen. Dr CAMILE ASMAR.

Nicolas Sursock Museum: Sursock St, Ashrafieh, Beirut; tel. (1) 334133.

Besharre

Musée Gibran Khalil Gibran: Besharre; dedicated to the life and works of the author.

Universities

AL-IMAM AL-OUZAI UNIVERSITY

POB 14-5355, Beirut 2802-1105
Telephone: (1) 704454
E-mail: islamic-studies@ouzai.org
Internet: www.ouzai.org

Founded 1979
Private control
Language of instruction: Arabic
Academic year: October to June

Chair.: TOUFIC EL-HOURI
Library Admin.: JOUMANA BA'YOUN

Library of 115,000 vols
Number of teachers: 120
Number of students: 4,716

DEANS

Imam Ouzai College of Islamic Studies: Prof. Dr KAMEL MOUSA
Islamic College of Business Administration: Prof. Dr MOHAMED ISKANDARANI

DIRECTORS

Documentation Centre for Bibliographic Information on Islam and the Muslim World: Dr BASSAM ABDEL HAMID
Documentation Centre on World Countries and Major Cities: Dr IBRAHIM ASSAL
Documentation Centre on World Leading Banks: HODA AL-KHARSA
Islamic Institute for the Supervision of Food Products: Dr IBRAHIM ADHAM

AMERICAN UNIVERSITY OF BEIRUT

POB 11-0236/31, Riad El-Solh, Beirut
Telephone: (1) 350000
E-mail: communications@aub.edu.lb
Internet: www.aub.edu.lb

Founded 1866
Private control
Language of instruction: English
Academic year: October to June

Pres.: PETER F. DORMAN
Vice-Pres. for Legal Affairs: PETER MAY
Vice-Pres. for Medical Affairs: MOHAMED SAYEGH
Vice-Pres. for Univ. Advancement: RICHARD BROW
Provost: AHMAD DALLAL
Registrar: Dr MOUEEN SALAMEH (acting)
Dean for Student Affairs: TALAL NIZAMEDDIN
Librarian: Dr LOKMAN MEHO

Library of 600,000 (923 subscribed periodicals, 1,200,000 audiovisual items)
Number of teachers: 817 (531 full-time, 286 part-time)
Number of students: 7,982 (6,400 undergraduate, 1582 graduate)

Publications: *Al-Abhath* (Arab Studies, 1 a year, in English and Arabic), *Berytus Archaeological Studies* (1 a year), *Research Report* (2 a year)

DEANS

Faculty of Agricultural and Food Sciences: NAHLA HWALLA
Faculty of Arts and Sciences: PATRICK MCGREEVY
Faculty of Engineering and Architecture: MAKRAM SUIDAN

Faculty of Health Sciences: IMAN NUWAYHID
Faculty of Medicine: MOHAMED SAYEGH
Suliman S. Olayan School of Business: SALIM CHAHINE (acting)

BEIRUT ARAB UNIVERSITY

POB 11-5020, Riad El-Solh 1107 2809, Beirut
Telephone: (1) 300110
E-mail: bau@bau.edu.lb
Internet: www.bau.edu.lb
Founded 1960 by the El-Ber Wa El-Ehsan Asscn, academically associated with the Univ. of Alexandria, Egypt
Private control
Languages of instruction: Arabic, English, French
Academic year: September to June
Pres.: Prof. Dr AMR AL ADAWI
Sec.-Gen.: ISSAM HOURY
Dir for Student Affairs: MOHAMED HAMOUD
Dir for Information Systems: Prof. WALID SHATILA
Chief Librarian: SAEED TAYARA
Library of 125,000 vols
Number of teachers: 784
Number of students: 12,194
Publications: *Architecture and Planning Journal* (1 a year), *Human Sciences Journal* (2 a year), *Journal of Commercial Research and Studies* (2 a year), *Revue des Études Juridiques* (2 a year)

DEANS

Faculty of Architecture: Prof. Dr RAMADAN ABDEL MAKSOUD
Faculty of Arts: Prof. Dr OLGA MATTAR MOHAMED GHAZI
Faculty of Commerce: Prof. Dr SAID ABDEL AZIZ OSMAN
Faculty of Dentistry: Prof. Dr MOSTAFA FAKHRI KHALIL
Faculty of Engineering: Prof. Dr IBRAHIM ABDEL-SALAM AWAD
Faculty of Health Sciences: Prof. Dr HIND MITWALLI
Faculty of Law: Prof. Dr HAFIZA EL-HADDAD
Faculty of Medicine: Prof. Dr MOUNIR MOHAMED ZEERBAN
Faculty of Pharmacy: Prof. Dr FAWZI ALI YAZIBI
Faculty of Science: Prof. Dr SAMY HAMED CHAABAN

PROFESSORS

Faculty of Architecture:
- ABDEL MAKSOUD, R., Building Science and Technology
- HAMDI, E. F., Environmental Design

Faculty of Arts:
- ABDUL RAHMAN, A. M., Sociology
- EBRAHEEM, E. A., Geography
- FAHMI, N. A., English Language and Literature
- GHAZI, O. M. M., General and Applied Linguistics

Faculty of Commerce:
- OSMAN, S. A., Public Economics

Faculty of Dentistry:
- AMER, W. A.-A., Oral Medicine, Periodontics and Diagnosis
- EL-MULHALLAWI, A. S., Oral and Maxillofacial Surgery
- KHALIL, M. F., Dental Biomaterials
- MOSTAFA, A. M. M., Conservative Dentistry, Operative Dentistry
- SEGAAN, G. I., Prosthodontics

Faculty of Engineering:
- AWAD, I. A., Computer Engineering and Systems
- BAGHDADI, K. H., River Engineering
- ELGHAMMAL, M. A., Electrical Systems
- EL-GHAZOULY, H. G., Surveying and Geodesy
- EL-SHERBINY, M. M., Electrical and Computer Engineering
- FARROUKH, O. O., Electromagnetics and Optics
- FATAH EL-BAB, F. A. I., Stability and Analysis of Space Structures
- GHABASHI, M. A-L., Theoretical Physics and Materials Science
- HASAB, M. A. H., Design of Thermal Systems
- KHALIL, M. F., Fluid Mechanics
- MOSTAFA, M. A. F., Mechanical Vibrations
- RAJAB, M. M. E., Microelectronics
- RASHED, A. M. H., Power Systems Analysis
- SOROUR, M. K., Thermal Engineering

Faculty of Law:
- ABD AL-WAHHAB, M. A., Public Law
- AL-HADDAD, H. S. A., Private International Law
- DWIDAR, M. H. I., Economy Planning
- EL-MAGZOUB, M. M., Public International Law
- KHALIL, A. A. S., Procedure Law

Faculty of Medicine:
- ABOU AL-OLA, M. M., Histology: Histochemistry and Electron Microscopy
- AHMED, S. I., Internal Medicine—Gastrointestinal
- EL-BAHEI, N. M., Clinical Pharmacology
- EL-GEBALY, F. F., Embryology and Genetics
- EL-SAWWA, E. A.-K., Anatomy: Embryology and Genetics
- KHEDR, M. M. S., Clinical Pharmacology
- MADWAR, A., Histology: Histochemistry and Electron Microscopy
- MASHALI, N. A.-R., Gynaecological Pathology and Haematopathology
- SALEH, M. N.-D. A., Anatomy: Genetics of Development
- ZEERBAN, M. M., Cardiothoracic Surgery

Faculty of Pharmacy:
- BORAI, N. A., Pharmaceutics
- EL-KHODAIRY, K. A.-H., Microencapsulation and Drug Delivery Systems
- EL-LAKANY, A. M., Chemistry of Natural Products
- EL-YAZBI, F. A., Pharmaceutical Analysis and Drug Quality Control
- MOHYEEDIN, M. M., Neurohumoral Transmission in Pharmacology
- OSHBA, N. H. M., Synthetic Medicinal Chemistry

Faculty of Science:
- ABD EL-JAWAD, N. M. A., Enzymology
- ALI, A. M. A. M., Nuclear Physics
- BADAWI, N. S. A., Cell Biology
- DUKAINESH, S. I. A., Invertebrate Ecology
- FALTAS, M. S., Fluid Dynamics
- HAMAD, H. H. A., Fluid Dynamics
- IBRAHIM, H. I., Solid State Physics
- KOREK, M., Molecular Physics
- MANSOUR, S. M. S., Organic Chemistry
- SHAALAN, S. H., Phycology

HAIGAZIAN UNIVERSITY

POB 11-1748, Beirut
Telephone: (1) 349230
E-mail: rartinian@haigazian.edu.lb
Internet: www.haigazian.edu.lb
Founded 1955
Private control
Academic year: October to June
Pres.: Rev. PAUL HAIDOSTIAN
Librarian: ZEVART TANIELIAN
Library: libraries (Armenian, Arabic and English) of 66,000 vols
Number of teachers: 63 (23 full-time, 40 part-time)
Number of students: 743
Publications: *Armenological Review* (1 a year), *Haigazian Focus* (1 a year), *Haigazian Herald* (4 a year), *In Spirit* (2 a year)

DEANS

Faculty of Arts and Sciences: ARDA EKMEKJI
Faculty of Business and Economics: FADI ASRAWI

LEBANESE AMERICAN UNIVERSITY

Beirut Campus: POB 13-5053, Chouran, Beirut 1102 2801
Telephone: (1) 786456
Byblos Campus: POB 36, Byblos
Telephone: (9) 547254
Internet: www.lau.edu.lb
Founded 1835 as American School for Girls, present name 1994
Private control
Language of instruction: English
Academic year: October to September
Pres.: Dr JOSEPH G. JABBRA
Provost: Dr GEORGES NAJJAR
Vice-Pres. for Advancement and Devt: ROY MAJDALANI
Vice-Pres. for Finance: EMILE LAMAH
Vice-Pres. for Student Enrolment and Management: Dr ELISE SALEM
Vice-Pres. (Gen. Counsel and Spec. Advisor to the Pres.): Dr CEDAR MANSOUR
Dean for Student Affairs for Beirut Campus: Dr RAED MOHSEN
Dean for Student Affairs for Byblos Campus: Dr MARS SEMAAN
Registrar for Beirut Campus: ANNIE LAJINIAN MAGARIAN
Registrar for Byblos Campus: Dr FOUAD SALIBI
Librarian for Beirut Campus: CINDERELLA HABRE
Librarian for Byblos Campus: JOSEPH HAJJ
Library of 392,670 vols, 2,447 periodicals, 97,077 ebooks, 130 databases (all campuses)
Number of teachers: 891 (337 full-time, 554 part-time)
Number of students: 8,273
Publications: *Al-Raida magazine* (4 a year), *Alumni Bulletin* (4 a year), *LAU magazine* (4 a year)

DEANS

School of Architecture and Design: Dr ELIE HADDAD
School of Arts and Sciences: Dr PHLIPPE FROSSARD
School of Business: Dr SAID EL FAKHANI
School of Engineering and Architecture: Dr GEORGES NASR
School of Medicine: Dr YOUSSEF COMAIR
School of Nursing: Dr NANCY HOFFART
School of Pharmacy: Dr PIERRE ZALLOUA

MIDDLE EAST UNIVERSITY

POB 90481, Jdeidet El Matn 1202-2040
Telephone: (1) 685800
E-mail: meu@meu.edu.lb
Internet: www.meu.edu.lb
Founded 1939
Private control
Language of instruction: English
Academic year: September to June
Offers degrees in business administration, computer science, education (elementary and secondary), religion; MBA; also diploma courses
Pres.: Dr L. HONGISTO
Registrar: S. ISSA
Library of 20,000 vols
Number of teachers: 29 (13 full-time, 16 part-time)

Number of students: 200

NOTRE DAME UNIVERSITY LOUAIZE

POB 72, Zouk Mikael
Telephone: (9) 208000
E-mail: webm@ndu.edu.lb
Internet: www.ndu.edu.lb
Founded 1987
Private control
Language of instruction: English
Academic year: October to September
Pres.: Rev. Walid Moussa
Vice-Pres. for Academic Affairs: Dr Antoine Farhat
Vice-Pres. for Admin.: Rev. Dr Ziad Antoun
Vice-Pres. for Communication and Public Relations: Dr Souheil Matar
Vice-Pres. for Finance: Rev. Dr Bechara Khoury
Dir for Admissions: Dr Vivian Nakhle
Dean for Students: Dr Ziad Fahed
Registrar: Lea Eid
Dir for Libraries: Leslie A. Hage
Library of 180,000 vols
Number of teachers: 695 (240 full-time and 455 part-time)
Number of students: 7,410
Publications: *PALMA Journal* (1 a year), *Spirit* (3 a year)

DEANS

Faculty of Architecture, Art and Design: Dr Jean-Pierre Asmar
Faculty of Business Administration and Economics: Dr Elie Menassa
Faculty of Engineering: Dr Michel Hayek
Faculty of Humanities: Dr Mary-Angela Willis
Faculty of Law and Political Science: Dr Maan Bou Saber
Faculty of Natural and Applied Sciences: Dr Georges Eid
Faculty of Nursing and Health Sciences: Dr Antoine Farhat

UNIVERSITÉ ANTONINE

POB 40016, Hadath Baabda
Telephone: (5) 924076
E-mail: contact@upa.edu.lb
Internet: www.upa.edu.lb
Founded 1996
Private control
Academic year: October to July
Faculties of biblical studies, computer studies, ecumenical and religious studies, multimedia and telecommunications engineering, nursing and theology, pastoral studies; higher institute of music; institute of physical education and sport; university technical institute of laboratory science and dental prosthetics
Number of teachers: 120
Number of students: 850
Publications: *Al-Antouniyah* (1 a year), *Our Liturgic Life* (2 series: research, 2 a year; celebrations, 4 a year)

UNIVERSITÉ LIBANAISE

place du Musée, Beirut
Telephone: (1) 612830
E-mail: sgul@ul.edu.lb
Internet: www.ul.edu.lb
Founded 1951
State control
Languages of instruction: Arabic, English, French
Academic year: October to June
Rector: Dr Zoheir Chokr
Sec.-Gen.: Mohamad El Baba
Head of Administrative Services: Rita Wehbeh
Librarian: Dina Succar
Library of 750,000 vols, 27,932 electronic journals, 55,722 electronic books
Number of teachers: 4,404
Number of students: 72,500
Publications: *Art and Architecture* (1 a year), *Dirassat* (1 a year), *Hannoun* (1 a year), *Pedagogic Research* (1 a year), *Social Sciences* (1 a year), *Tourism and Hospitality* (1 a year)

DEANS

Doctoral School of Literature, Humanities and Social Sciences: Dr Ibrahim Mohsen
Doctorate School of Science and Technology: Dr Zeinab Saad
Faculty of Agronomy: Dr Tayssir Hamieh
Faculty of Dentistry: Dr Mounir Doumit
Faculty of Economics and Business Administration: Dr Kameel Habib
Faculty of Engineering: Dr Mohamed Zoaeter
Faculty of Information and Documentation: Dr George Khatoura
Faculty of Law, Political and Administrative Sciences: Dr Felomen Naser
Faculty of Literature and Humanities: Dr Zoheir Chokr
Faculty of Medical Sciences: Dr Pierre Yard
Faculty of Pedagogy: Dr Mazen El Khatib
Faculty of Pharmacy: Dr Marie Toueiny
Faculty of Public Health: Dr Nina Saadallah
Faculty of Sciences: Dr Ali Mneimneh
Faculty of Tourism and Hospitality Management: Dr Kamal Hammad
Institute of Fine Arts: Dr Maamoun Chaaban
Institute of Social Sciences: Dr Fredrick Maatouk
University Institute of Technology: Dr Ali Ismail

UNIVERSITÉ SAINT-ESPRIT DE KASLIK

POB 446, Jounieh
Telephone: (9) 934444
E-mail: rectorat@usek.edu.lb
Internet: www.usek.edu.lb
Founded 1950
Languages of instruction: Arabic, English, French
Academic year: October to July
Chancellor: Abbé Élias Khalife
Rector: Père Antoine Al Ahmar
First Vice-Rector: Abbé Paul Naaman
Vice-Rector for Admin.: Père Antoine Al-Ahmar
Vice-Rector for External Relations and Research: Père Georges Hobeika
Sec.-Gen.: Père Pierre Bou Zeidan
Librarian: Père Joseph Moukarzel
Library of 250,000 vols
Number of teachers: 620
Number of students: 5,180
Publications: *Actes de Colloques tenus à l'Université Saint-Esprit de Kaslik*, *Annales de Philosophie et des Sciences Humaines* (1 a year), *Annales de Recherches Scientifiques* (1 a year), *Bibliothèque de l'Université Saint-Esprit de Kaslik*, *Bulletin de l'Université Saint-Esprit de Kaslik* (2 a year), *Cahiers Annuels* (1 a year), *Parole de l'Orient* (1 a year), *Revue de la Faculté des Beaux Arts* (1 a year), *Revue Juridique* (1 a year)

DEANS

Faculty of Agricultural Sciences: Fr Joseph Wakim
Faculty of Business Administration and Commercial Sciences: Fr Karam Rizk
Faculty of Fine Arts: Alexis Mouzarkel
Faculty of Law: Dr Joseph Chaoul
Faculty of Literature: Dr Antoine Noujaim
Faculty of Medicine: Fr Gédéon Mohasseb
Faculty of Music: Fr Louis Hajje
Faculty of Philosophy and Human Sciences: Fr Jean Akiki
Faculty of Sciences and Computer Engineering: Fr Antoine Al-Ahmar
Pontifical Faculty of Theology: Fr Thomas Mouhanna

UNIVERSITÉ SAINT-JOSEPH

rue de Damas, POB 17-5208, Mar Mikhaël, Beirut 1104 2020
Telephone: (1) 421000
E-mail: rectorat@usj.edu.lb
Internet: www.usj.edu.lb
Founded 1875
Private control
Languages of instruction: Arabic, English, French
Academic year: September to June (2 semesters)
Rector: Rev. Fr Salim Daccache
Vice-Rector: Rev. Fr Michel Scheuer
Vice-Rector for Academic Affairs: Henri Awit
Vice-Rector for Admin.: Wajdi Najem
Vice-Rector for Int. Relations: Dr Antoine Hokayem
Vice-Rector for Research: Dolla Karam Sarkis
Sec.-Gen.: Fouad Maroun
Library: see under Libraries and Archives
Number of teachers: 1,944
Number of students: 11,509
Publications: *ACES—Actualités Cliniques et Scientifiques* (2 a year), *Annales de Géographie—Géosphères* (1 a year), *Annales d'Histoire—Tempora* (1 a year), *Annales de la Faculté de Droit* (irregular), *Annales de Lettres Françaises—Acanthe* (1 a year), *Annales de l'Institut de Langues et de Traduction—Al-Kimiya* (1 a year), *Annales de l'Institut de Lettres Orientales* (1 a year), *Annales de Philosophie—Iris* (1 a year), *Annales de Psychologie et des Sciences de l'Education—Psy-écho* (1 a year), *Annales de Sociologie et d'Anthropologie* (1 a year), *Chroniques du CEMAM* (1 a year), *Chroniques Politiques* (1 a year), *Chroniques Sociales* (irregular), *Conférences de l'ALDEC* (1 a year), *Enseignement Continu Post-universitaire* (1 a year), *Études de droit libanais* (irregular), *Hommes et Sociétés du Proche-Orient* (1 a year), *Journées d'Études Post-universitaires* (1 a year), *L'Orient des Dieux* (1 a year), *Mélanges de l'Université Saint-Joseph* (1 a year), *Proche Orient Chrétien* (2 a year), *Proche Orient, Études Économiques* (irregular), *Proche Orient, Études en Management* (irregular), *Proche Orient, Études Juridiques* (irregular), *Publications Techniques et Scientifiques de l'École Supérieure d'Ingénieurs de Beyrouth* (irregular), *Regards* (1 a year), *Revue de l'Institut Libanais d'Éducateurs* (1 a year), *Travaux et Jours* (2 a year)

DEANS AND DIRECTORS

Centre of Banking Studies: Fadwa Mansour
Faculty of Arts and Human Sciences: Christine Babikian Assaf
Faculty of Business Administration: Toni Gibeily
Faculty of Dentistry: Dr Nada Naaman
Faculty of Economics: Joseph Gemayel
Faculty of Education Sciences: Fadi El Hage
Faculty of Engineering: Fadi Geara
Faculty of Languages: Henri Awaiss
Faculty of Law and Political Science: Léna Gannage
Faculty of Medicine: Dr Roland Tomb

Faculty of Nursing: RIMA SASSINE KAZAN
Faculty of Pharmacy: MARIANNE ABI FADEL
Faculty of Religious Studies: Rev. Fr THOM SICKING
Faculty of Sciences: TOUFIC RIZK
Higher Institute of Insurance Sciences: MELHEM EL KIK
Higher Institute of Religious Studies: Rev. Fr. EDGARD EL HAIBY
Higher Institute of Sciences of Insurance: MELHEM EL KIK
Higher Institute of Speech Therapy: CAMILLE MOITEL MESSARA
Institute of Business Administration: PHILIPPE FATTAL
Institute of Health and Social Protection Management: WALID KHOURY
Institute of Islamic-Christian Studies: Rev. Fr JOSEPH GEBARA
Institute of Oriental Literature: Rev. Fr SALAH ABOU JAOUDE
Institute of Physiotherapy: NISRINE ABDELNOUR LATTOUF
Institute of Political Science: FADIA KIWAN
Institute of Psychomotricity: CARLA ABI ZEID DAOU
Institute of Theatrical, Audiovisual and Cinema Studies: ELIE YAZBECK
Lebanese Institute of Educators: DUNIA AL MUKKADAM
Lebanese School of Social Work: MARYSE TANNOUS JOMAA
National Institute of Communication and Information: HADY SAWAYA
Open University: GÉRARD BEJJANI
School of Agro-Industrial Engineers: MAYA KHARRAT SARKIS
School of Laboratory Technicians in Medical Analysis: MARIE-GABRIELLE GHORRA HINDI
School of Mediterranean Agricultural Engineers: FADI GEARA
School of Midwifery: YOLLA ATALLAH
School of Translators and Interpreters of Beirut: GINA ABOU FADEL

UNIVERSITY OF BALAMAND

POB 100, Tripoli, Kelhat-Koura
Telephone: (6) 930250
E-mail: pr@balamand.edu.lb
Internet: www.balamand.edu.lb
Founded 1988
Private control
Languages of instruction: Arabic, English,, French, Greek
Academic year: September to June
Pres.: ELIE A. SALEM
Vice-Pres. for Devt and Public Affairs: MICHEL NAJJAR
Vice-Pres. for Health and Community Relations: NADIM KARAM
Vice-Pres. for Medical Affairs in the USA: TALI' BASHOUR
Vice-Pres. for Planning and Educational Relations: GEORGES N. NAHAS
Dean of Admissions and Registration: WALID MOUBAYED
Dean of Student Affairs: ANTOINE GERJESS
Dir for Devt: HAISSAM HAIDAR
Librarian: SAMEERA BASHIR
Library of 70,000 vols
Number of teachers: 800 (incl. full-time and part-time)
Number of students: 5,090
Publications: *Al-Inaa* (irregular), *Al-Marquab* (1 a year), *ALBAtros* (2 a year), *Chronos* (2 a year), *Hawliyat* (Theology, 1 a year), *Revue Médicale Libanaise* (4 a year)

DEANS

Faculty of Arts and Social Sciences: GEORGE BAHR
Faculty of Business Administration: KARIM NASR (acting)
Faculty of Engineering: MICHEL NAJJAR (acting)
Faculty of Health Sciences: NADIM KARAM
Faculty of Sciences: JIHAD ATTIEH
Faculty of Library and Information Studies: GEORGES N. NAHAS
Faculty of Medicine: CAMILLE NASSAR
Lebanese Academy of Fine Arts: ANDRE BEKHAZI
St George Faculty of Postgraduate Medical Education: CAMILLE NASSAR
St John of Damascus Institute of Theology: Bishop KHATTAS HAZIM

Colleges

Académie Libanaise des Beaux-Arts (Lebanese Academy of Fine Arts): POB 55251, Sin-El-Fil, Beirut; Ave Emile Edde, Sin-El-Fi, Beirut; tel. (1) 480056; e-mail alba@alba.edu.lb; internet www.alba.edu.lb; f. 1937; attached to Univ. of Balamand; schools of architecture, decorative arts, film and audiovisual, visual arts; planning institute; library: 4,300 vols; 180 teachers; 600 students; Dean Prof. ANDRÉ BEKHAZI; Sec.-Gen. CHRISTINE ZACHARIOU; publ. *L'Albatros* (3 a year, print and online, www.alba.edu.lb/french/albatros).

Near East School of Theology: POB 13-5780, Beirut 1102 2070; tel. (1) 354194; e-mail nest.adm@inco.com.lb; internet www.pcusa.org/pcusa/wmd/globaled/institutes/nest.htm; f. 1932; Protestant ecumenical institution of higher learning; offers theological education and pastoral training to qualified candidates for church ministries, as well as to lay candidates regardless of church affiliation, sex, race or nationality; library: 40,000 vols; 7 teachers; 36 students; Pres. Dr MARY MIKHAEL; publ. *Theological Review*.

LESOTHO

The Higher Education System

The Roman Catholic Hierarchy of South Africa founded Pius XII College in 1945, while Lesotho was part of the British protectorate of Basutoland. Pius XII College became known as the University of Basutoland, Bechuanaland and Swaziland in 1963, and after the Kingdom of Lesotho was declared an independent state in 1966 it was renamed the University of Botswana, Lesotho and Swaziland. In 1975 the University of Botswana, Lesotho and Swaziland was divided into separate national universities, and the branch at Roma, Lesotho, was reconstituted as the National University of Lesotho (NUL). Higher education is funded by the central Government, which accounts for about 90% of the NUL's income. Some 11,425 students were enrolled at the NUL in 2010/11. The medium of instruction at the university, which currently has seven faculties, is English. According to the Council of Higher Education (CHE), which was signed into law in 2004, in 2012 there were eight public higher education institutions and five private institutions, with a total enrolment for 2010/11 of 23,987 students.

Governance of the NUL consists of the Council (appointed by the Head of State), Senate, Congregation, Student Union, non-academic staff and external members. The Head of State is the Chancellor of the University, and the Vice-Chancellor, Pro-Vice Chancellor, Registrar, Bursar and Librarian are the primary management staff, responsible for the day-to-day affairs of the university. Overall responsibility for policy lies with the Council, and the Senate oversees all academic affairs. Deans of Faculty and Directors of Institutes are the heads of academic units.

Admission to the NUL is on the basis of the Cambridge Overseas School Certificate in the first or the second division. A Diploma is awarded in theology and agriculture after two years, otherwise the undergraduate Bachelors degree last four years, divided into two two-year cycles. Award of the Bachelors of Law requires a further two years of study. The postgraduate Masters degree lasts two years and is awarded in arts, science and education. Doctoral degree programmes are available in agriculture, education and the humanities, and last for two years after the award of the Masters. In order to complete the Doctorate, students are required to write a thesis and take an oral examination.

Technical and vocational education consists of a College Certificate, Diploma or City & Guilds qualification. Courses are offered by a number of different institutions, including home economics and craft schools, nursing colleges, trade schools, Lesotho Agricultural College and Lerotholi Polytechnic College (founded c. 1906). In 2011 the Government announced plans to transform Lerotholi Polytechnic College into a university of science and technology by 2015.

Regulatory Bodies

GOVERNMENT

Ministry of Communications, Science and Technology: Moposo House, Third Fl., POB 36, Maseru 100; tel. (22) 324-715; internet www.gov.ls/comms; Minister Hon. TŠELISO MOKHOSI.

Ministry of Education and Training: Cnr of Constitution and Pioneer Road, POB 47, Maseru 100; tel. 22313045; e-mail letsoelam@education.gov.ls; internet www.education.gov.ls; Minister MAKABELO PRISCILLA MOSOTHOANE.

Ministry of Tourism, Environment and Culture: POB 52, Maseru 100; tel. 22313034; internet www.gov.ls/tourism; Minister MAMAHELE RADEBE.

Learned Societies

BIBLIOGRAPHY, LIBRARY SCIENCE AND MUSEOLOGY

Lesotho Library Association: Private Bag A26, Maseru; tel. 22213420; f. 1978; 60 individual mems, 22 institutions; Chair. S. M. MOHAI; Sec. N. TAOLE; publ. *Journal* (1 a year).

LANGUAGE AND LITERATURE

Alliance Française: cnr Pioner Rd and Kingsway, Private Bag A106, Maseru 100; tel. 22325722; e-mail maseru@alliance.org.za; internet www.alliancefrancaise.co.za/lesotho; offers courses and exams in French language and culture, and promotes cultural exchange with France.

Research Institutes

AGRICULTURE, FISHERIES AND VETERINARY SCIENCE

Department of Agricultural Research: POB 829, Maseru 100; tel. 22312395; e-mail agricres@leo.co.ls; research station at Maseru and field experimental stations.

NATURAL SCIENCES

Physical Sciences

Geological Survey Department: Dept of Mines and Geology, POB 750, Maseru 100; tel. 22323750; Dir MATSEPO C. RAMAISA.

Libraries and Archives

Maseru

Lesotho National Archives: POB 52, Maseru 100; tel. 22312047; f. 1958; undertakes research and preservation of nat. documents since 1869; Sr Archivist M. QHOBOSHEANE.

Lesotho National Library Service: POB 985, Maseru 100; tel. 22323100; f. 1976; 30,000 vols; Sr Librarian M. MABATHOANA (acting).

University

NATIONAL UNIVERSITY OF LESOTHO

PO Roma 180
Telephone: 22340601
E-mail: registrar@nul.ls
Internet: www.nul.ls

Founded 1945 as Pius XII College, became campus of Univ. of Botswana, Lesotho and Swaziland 1966; present name 1975
Language of instruction: English
Academic year: August to May

Chancellor: HM King LETSIE III
Vice-Chancellor: Dr T. H. MOTHIBE
Pro-Vice-Chancellor: Dr N. L. MAHAO
Registrar: J. M. HLALELE
Librarian: A. M. LEBOTSA

Library of 205,150 vols, 500 periodicals
Number of teachers: 171
Number of students: 11,425

Publications: *Announcer*, *Lesotho Law Journal*, *Light in the Night*, *Mohlomi Journal* (History), *Mophatlatsi*, *NUL News*, *NUL Research Journal*

DEANS

Faculty of Agriculture: Prof. P. M. SUTTON
Faculty of Education: Dr E. M. MARUPING
Faculty of Health Science: Prof. P. O. ODONKOR
Faculty of Humanities: Rev. J. KHUTLANG
Faculty of Law: O. M. OWORI
Faculty of Science and Technology: Prof. K. K. GOPINATHAN
Faculty of Social Sciences: Prof. S. G. HOOHLO

DIRECTORS

Institute of Education: S. T. MOTLOMELO
Institute of Extra-Mural Studies: Prof. D. BRAIMOH, Prof. Y. D. BWATWA, Dr A. M. SETSABI
Institute of Labour Studies: S. SANTHO (acting)
Institute of Southern African Studies: Dr M. MOCHEBELELE

PROFESSORS

Faculty of Agriculture:
BRAIDE, F. G.
EBENENE, A. C.
OKELW-UMA, I.
SUTTON, P. M.

Faculty of Education:
MATS'ELA, Z. A., Language and Social Education

Faculty of Law:
KUMAR, U., Private Law

Faculty of Postgraduate Studies:
BALOGUN, T. A.

Faculty of Science and Technology:
GOPINATHAN, K. K., Physics
MALU, O.

Faculty of Social Sciences:
EJIGOU, A., Statistics

Institute of Southern African Studies:
PRASAD, G.

College

Lesotho Agricultural College: POB 139, Maseru; tel. 22322484; f. 1955; State control; language of instruction: English; academic year August to May (2 semesters); library: 60,000 vols; Prin. Dr S. L. RALIT-S'OELE.

LIBERIA

The Higher Education System

From 1821 onwards emancipated slaves from the southern states of the USA were resettled along the West Guinean coast, and in 1847 the independent, sovereign state of Liberia was declared, with a Constitution based on that of the USA. Liberia College, the first institution of higher education, was founded in 1862 and became a university in 1951. In 1889 Cuttington University College was founded by the Episcopal Church in the USA, by whom it is still maintained in conjunction with the Episcopal Church in Liberia. Other institutions of higher education include the William V. S. Tubman University (founded 1970; formerly Harper Technical College and subsequently William V. S. Tubman College of Technology) and the Booker Washington Institute (founded 1929). There are also junior colleges offering two-year degree programmes. In the academic year 1999/2000 there were 44,107 students enrolled in university-level institutions and 15,631 students enrolled in post-secondary technical and vocational education. In 2009 there was a total of 17,620 students enrolled at the University of Liberia, which is located across three campuses and which consists of six colleges, three professional schools (including a law school and medical school), three graduate programmes and the Institute for Population Studies. A Commission on Higher Education was established in 1989 to evaluate, accredit and monitor the quality of performance of Liberia's tertiary institutions.

Degree-awarding establishments must be chartered by the national legislature, but higher education in Liberia is decentralized in that each institution is autonomous and governed by a Board of Trustees. Each institution of higher education sets its own standards (under the authority of the Ministry of Education). The Minister of Education is the government representative on each Board of Trustees, which is advised by an Administrative Council, comprising all academic and administrative staff, two elected faculty members and two elected student representatives. The Council also advises the President of the University and coordinates the day-to-day running of the institution. The State provides funding to both public and private institutions and also offers financial aid to students, which covers one-half of the cost of tuition and study materials.

The higher education system is based on the US system and the medium of instruction is English. Applicants must hold the Senior High School certificate to gain admission to higher education and are also required to sit entrance examinations in English and mathematics. Students at junior colleges study for the two-year Associate degree, and university undergraduates take a four-year Bachelors degree. The Bachelor of Law degree is awarded after five years and medical degrees after seven years. Postgraduate degrees, such as the Masters, are available on a limited basis.

In addition to junior colleges, post-secondary technical and vocational education is offered by technical colleges.

In 2007 the Government consulted with the American Association of State Colleges and Universities for help and advice in rebuilding Liberia's post-secondary education system, which had been severely affected by 14 years of civil war (1989–2003). In 2011 USAID funded the Excellence in Higher Education for Liberian Development project in order to create two academic centres of excellence, in agriculture at Cuttington University and engineering at the University of Liberia.

Regulatory Bodies

GOVERNMENT

Ministry of Education: E. G. N. King Plaza, Broad St, POB 10-1545, 1000 Monrovia 10; tel. 226216; internet www.moe.gov.lr; Minister ETMONIA DAVID TARPEH.

Ministry of Information, Culture and Tourism: Capitol Hill, POB 10-9021, 1000 Monrovia 10; tel. 226269; e-mail info@micat.gov.lr; internet www.micatliberia.com; Minister LEWIS G. BROWN, II.

Learned Societies

LANGUAGE AND LITERATURE

Alliance Française: 28 Payne Ave, POB 10, 3016 Sinkor 14th/15th Sts, 1000 Monrovia 10; tel. 226888; e-mail alliancefr_monrovia@yahoo.com; offers courses and exams in French language and culture, and promotes cultural exchange with France.

Society of Liberian Authors: POB 2468, Monrovia; f. 1959; aims to encourage general interest in writing and encourage literature in local vernacular; publ. *Kaafa* (2 a year).

TECHNOLOGY

Geological, Mining and Metallurgical Society of Liberia: POB 902, Monrovia; f. 1964; 78 mems; Pres. CLETUS S. WOTORSON; Sec. Dr MEDIE-HEMIE NEUFVILLE; publ. *Bulletin* (2 a year).

Liberia Arts and Crafts Association: POB 885, Monrovia; f. 1964; 14 mems; aims to encourage artists and craftsmen through exhibitions, sales, workshops; Pres. R. VANJAH RICHARDS.

Research Institutes

AGRICULTURE, FISHERIES AND VETERINARY SCIENCE

Central Agricultural Research Institute: Mailbag 3929, Suakoko, Bong County; tel. 223443; f. 1946; under Min. of Agriculture; programmes in 4 key areas: infrastructure and manpower devt, crop improvement and urban agriculture, livestock and fisheries improvement, natural resource management and value addition; library of 8,700 vols; Dir-Gen. Dr J. QWELIBO SUBAH; publ. *CARI News*.

MEDICINE

Liberian Institute for Biomedical Research: POB 10-1012, 1000 Monrovia 10; f. 1952, renamed 1975; Dir Dr ALOYSIUS P. HANSON.

NATURAL SCIENCES

Biological Sciences

Nimba Research Laboratory: c/o Lamco J. V. Operating Co, Grassland, Nimba, Robertsfield; POB 69, Monrovia; f. 1962; under supervision of Nimba Research Committee of International Union for Conservation of Nature and Natural Resources, in conjunction with UNESCO; biological and ecological exploration and conservation in the Mount Nimba region; library of 100 vols and access to LAMCO library, Yekepa; Chair. KAI CURRY-LINDAHL.

Libraries and Archives

Monrovia

Government Public Library: Ashmun St, POB 10-9046, 1000 Monrovia 10; tel. 450465; e-mail liberianationalpubliclibrary@yahoo.com; f. 1959; attached to Centre for Nat. Documents and Records Agency; 15,000 vols; Dir FORKPA H. KEMAH.

Liberian Information Service Library: POB 9021, Monrovia; reference.

University of Liberia Libraries: Univ. of Liberia, POB 9020, Monrovia; tel. 517986; f. 1862; gen. library and separate law library; 107,384 vols, 2,118 periodicals; Dean for Libraries (vacant); Dir THELMA C. DOE (acting).

Museums and Art Galleries

Cape Mount

Tubman Centre of African Cultures: Cape Mount; local art, history and ethnology.

Monrovia

Africana Museum: Cuttington Univ. College, c/o Episcopal Church Office, POB 277, Monrovia; f. 1960; items from Liberia and neighbouring countries; traditional arts and crafts, ethnographical material; depository for archaeological collns; serves as a teaching colln for the college and as a research facility for visiting scholars; Dir Dr ADETOKUNBO K. BORISHADE.

National Museum: Broad and Buchanan Sts, POB 3223, Monrovia; f. 1962; Liberian history, art and ethnography; Dir BURDIE UREY-WEEKS.

Universities

CUTTINGTON UNIVERSITY

POB 10-0277, 1000 Monrovia 10

Telephone: 227413

E-mail: info@cuttingtonuniversity.edu.lr

Internet: www.cuttingtonuniversity.edu.lr

Colleges of agriculture and integrated development studies, business and public administration, education, health sciences, liberal arts and social sciences, natural sciences, theology; institute for peace and conflict resolution; research and devt institute

Pres.: Dr HENRIQUE F. TOKPA

Vice-Pres. for Academic Affairs: THEODORE V. K. BROWN, SR (acting)

Vice-Pres. for Admin.: JACKSON T. DUMOE (acting)

Vice-Pres. for Graduate School and Professional Studies: Dr FREDRICK GBEGBE

Vice-Pres. for Public Relations: Dr JOSHUA D. B. GIDDINGS

Vice-Pres. for Research and Planning: Dr CHARLES K. MULBAH

Assoc. Vice-Pres. for Management and Internal Control: Dr JOSHUA D. B. GIDDINGS

Vice-Pres. for Public Relations: Dr JOSHUA D. B. GIDDINGS

Number of teachers: 110

Number of students: 1,770 (1545 undergraduate, 225 graduate)

UNIVERSITY OF LIBERIA

POB 9020, Monrovia

Telephone: 224670

E-mail: alconteh@yahoo.com

Internet: www.universityliberia.org

Founded 1862 as Liberia College, univ. status 1951

State control

Language of instruction: English

Academic year: March to December (2 semesters)

Pres.: Dr BEN ROBERTS

Vice-Pres. for Academic Affairs: Dr FREDERICK S. GREGBE

Vice-Pres. for Admin.: Dr WINGROVE C. DWAMINA (acting)

Dean for Admissions: MOORE T. WORRELL

Libraries: see under Libraries and Archives

Publications: *Liberian Law Journal*, *This Week on Campus*, *University of Liberia Catalogue and Announcements*, *University of Liberia Journal*, *Varsity Pilot*

DEANS

A. M. Douglas College of Medicine: Dr TAIWO DARAMOLA

College of Agriculture and Forestry: Dr BISMARCK REEVES

College of Business and Public Administration: Prof. WILLIE BELLEH, Jr

College of Science and Technology: Prof. FREDERICK D. HUNDER (acting)

College of Social Sciences and Humanities (Liberia College): Dr BEN A. ROBERTS

Louis Arthur Grimes School of Law: Cllr LUVENIA ASH-THOMPSON

Student Affairs: HARRISON MLE-SIE WOART

William V. S. Tubman Teachers' College: Dr JOSHUA D. CLEON

COORDINATORS OF SCHOOLS

Graduate School of Education Administration: Dr HENRY KWEKWE

Graduate School of Regional Planning: Dr JAMES N. KOLLIE, Sr

School of Pharmacy: Dr ARTHUR S. LEWIS

WILLIAM V. S. TUBMAN UNIVERSITY

Harper Office: POB 3570, Harper Maryland 15th St Sinkor, Monrovia

Telephone: 720692

E-mail: admin@tubmanu.edu.lr

Internet: www.tubmanu.edu.lr

Founded 1978 as William V. S. Tubman College of Technology; univ. status 2008

State control

Language of instruction: English

Academic year: March to December

Pres.: Dr ELIZABETH DAVIS-RUSSELL

Vice-Pres. for Academic Affairs: Dr ELIZABETH Q. ENANORIA-CARBAJOSA

Vice-Pres. for Admin.: Dr SYRULWA SOMAH

Vice-Pres. for Institutional Advancement: Rev. RITA TOWNSEND

Vice-Pres. for Research and Sponsored Programs: Dr RICHARD A. NISBETT

Vice-Pres. for Student Affairs: Rev. Dr ANTHONY G. DIOH

Librarian: JENNIFER G. DIOH

DEANS

College of Agriculture and Food Sciences: Dr THERESA C. FEROLINO

College of Arts and Sciences: Dr ELLIOT WREH-WILSON

College of Education: Dr COLEEN CLAY

College of Engineering and Technology: GERALD B. COLEMAN

College of Health Sciences: Dr LUCKY OSARHIEMEN EHIGIATOR

College of Management and Public Administration: Rev. RITA TOWNSEND (acting)

College

Booker Washington Institute: POB 273, Kakata; tel. 331048; f. 1929; State control; 52 teachers; 750 students; agricultural and industrial courses; secondary high school courses; basic computer literacy; Principal MULBAH JACKOLLIE.

LIBYA

The Higher Education System

All current institutions of higher education have been founded since Libya became an independent kingdom in 1951. (Following a military coup in 1969, it became known as the Libyan Arab Republic, between 1977 and 1986 it was called the Socialist People's Libyan Arab Jamahiriya and from 1986 until the downfall of the regime of Col Muammar al-Qaddafi in the latter half of 2011 it was known as the Great Socialist People's Libyan Arab Jamahariya. In September 2011, citing the Libyan interim Constitutional Declaration of 3 August 2011, the UN recognized the new name of the country as simply Libya.) The University of Libya was founded in 1955 with the establishment of a Faculty of Arts and Education on a campus in Benghazi, followed the next year by a Faculty of Science on a campus near Tripoli. The university was subsequently enlarged with the addition of faculties of economics, law, agriculture, medicine, engineering, and Arabic language and Islamic studies. In 1973 the University of Libya was divided into two parts, to form the Universities of Tripoli and Benghazi (later renamed Al-Fateh University and the University of Garyounis, respectively—although the former was reported to have unofficially reverted to the title of University of Tripoli following the fall of al-Qaddafi's regime in 2011). In 2002/03 there were an estimated 375,028 students in recognized institutions of higher education. In 2007 the Government launched a scholarship programme whereby Libyan students could undertake graduate and postgraduate studies abroad. The Secretariat for Education and Research is the responsible body for higher education, which is financed from the state budget. However, due to the expansion in student numbers and growing pressure on government funding, greater autonomy has been granted to local public administrations in allowing the establishment of new, mostly private, universities. Since 1997 some five private universities have been set up, all of which have been given provisional official accreditation.

A People's Committee, headed by a Dean (who acts as the Secretary), is the management body of each University. The main academic units are the Faculty and the Department. Faculties are also governed by a People's Committee, the Secretary of which represents the Faculty on the University People's Committee. Heads of Department are members of the Faculty People's Committee. Students sit on University and Faculty People's Committees.

Admission to higher education is on the basis of the Secondary Education Certificate, with different pass marks depending on the type of institution or degree applied for. Most undergraduate Bachelors degrees from universities require four years of study, but architecture, engineering (both five years) and medicine (six years, including a one-year residency) require longer. The main postgraduate degrees, which are generally offered at the larger universities, are the Higher Diploma, Masters and Doctorate. The Higher Diploma and Masters are both two-year programmes of study following award of the Bachelors, and study for the Doctorate also lasts two years, culminating in public defence of a thesis.

Technical and vocational training at post-secondary level is offered by higher institutes, which were established mainly in the 1980s (to reduce enrolment rates at university faculties of science, engineering and technology). Programmes are three years in duration and, upon successful completion, lead to the Higher Technician Diploma. Holders of this qualification are then entitled, if they so wish, to complete a further one or two years in the same subject to obtain a Bachelors degree.

The Centre for Quality Assurance and Accreditation of Higher Education Institutions, which was founded in 2006 and is part of the Secretariat for Education and Research, is the body responsible for the quality assurance and accreditation of all higher education providers in Libya (mandatory by law).

The civil conflict in 2011 severely disrupted the higher education sector, with many buildings being damaged, looted or destroyed, students abandoning their studies to join the rebel movement, and universities and institutes closing down completely. Following the collapse of al-Qaddafi's regime, the new Government—the National Transitional Council—promised to reopen all educational institutions as soon as possible and to make wide-ranging improvements to the education sector (including the provision of more and better equipment, the revision of syllabuses and changes to admission criteria). In 2012 it was reported that the Ministry of Higher Education and Scientific Research was prepared to provide substantial financial backing for construction of 20 new campuses, support for students wishing to study abroad in nursing, medicine, engineering, and other priority areas, primarily in the United Kingdom, but also in Germany and Canada, and for postgraduate research collaboration on subjects of water conservation, irrigation and farming techniques, and environmental sciences.

Regulatory Body

GOVERNMENT

Ministry of Culture and Civil Society: Tripoli; tel. (21) 4900391; e-mail info@culture.ly; internet www.culture.ly; Minister HABIB MUHAMMAD AL-AMIN.

Ministry of Education: Tripoli; e-mail info@edu.gov.ly; internet edu.gov.ly; Minister ALI OBAID.

Ministry of Higher Education and Scientific Research: Tripoli; tel. (21) 4630209; e-mail info@edu.gov.ly; internet www.higheredu.gov.ly; Minister MUHAMMAD HASSAN ABUBAKER.

ACCREDITATION

Centre for Quality Assurance and Accreditation of Higher Education and Training Institutions: Ben Ashur St, 80767 Tripoli; tel. (21) 3617328; e-mail elkabir@qaa.ly; internet www.qaa.ly; f. 2006; dept in the Min. of Higher Education and Scientific Research; accredits all basic, vocational and higher education providers in Libya; evaluation of qualification from overseas for Libyan and non-Libyan; Dir Prof. MOHAMMED ELKABIR.

Learned Societies

LANGUAGE AND LITERATURE

British Council: POB 6797, Tripoli; Casablanca St, Hey El Wihda El Arabia, Siyahia, Tripoli; tel. (21) 4843164; e-mail info.libya@ly.britishcouncil.org; internet www.britishcouncil.org/libya; offers courses and exams in English language and British culture and promotes cultural exchange with the UK; Dir CARL REUTER.

Research Institutes

GENERAL

National Academy for Scientific Research: POB 12312, Tripoli; tel. (21) 3339101; f. 1981 to conduct, finance and support scientific studies and research in all brs of knowledge; 330 mems; library of 19,000 vols; Dir-Gen. Dr TAHER H. JEHEMI; publs *Al-Fikr Al-Arabi*, *Al-Fikr Al-Istratiji Al-Arabi*, *Al-Ilm Wa Atteknolojia*.

National Scientific Research and Study Centre: POB 84662 Shara Azawia, Tripoli; tel. (21) 3602783; f. 1995; centres of scientific research and studies; library and documentation; publishing and information; documentation and information; publ. *Al Jadeed* (4 a year).

Tajoura Nuclear Research Center: POB 30878, Tajoura; tel. (21) 3614130; e-mail admin@tnrc.org; internet www.tnrc.org; f. 1995; research in basic and applied science, nuclear energy, renewable sources of energy, desalination of water; publ. *Al Nawah*.

HISTORY, GEOGRAPHY AND ARCHAEOLOGY

Libyan Studies Centre: POB 5070, Sidi Munaider, Tripoli; tel. (21) 3333996; e-mail libyanjihad@libsc.org.ly; internet www.libsc.org.ly; f. 1978; historical studies and documentation; 140 mems; library of 100,000 vols, 700 periodicals, 3,000 MSS, 60,000 photographs; Dir Dr MOHAMED T. JERARY; publs *Al-Insaf* (1 a year), *Al-Kunnasha* (The Scrap Book, 2 a year), *Al-Wathaiq wa Al-Makhtutat* (1 a year), *As-Shahid* (The Martyr, 1 a year), *Index of Libyan Periodicals* (1 a year), *Majallat Al-Buhuth At-Tarikhia* (2 a year).

Libraries and Archives

Benghazi

National Library of Libya: POB 9127, Benghazi; tel. (61) 9096379; e-mail nat-lib-libya@hotmail.com; internet www.nllnet.net; f. 1973; Gen. Sec. MOHAMMAD A. ESHOWEIHDI.

University of Garyounis Library: POB 1308, Benghazi; tel. (61) 87633; f. 1955; 294,844 vols; 2,170 periodicals; 7 depts, including 2,360 MSS, 70,000 documents, 10,000 microfilms and rare books; Chief Librarian AHMED GALLAL; publs available for exchange.

Tripoli

Agricultural Research Centre Library: POB 2480, Tripoli; tel. (21) 3616865; e-mail taherazzabi@mailcity.com; f. 1973; 6,000 vols, 220 periodicals; Librarian LAMIS AL-GABSI.

Government Library: 14 Shar'a Al-Jazair, Tripoli; f. 1917; 35,500 vols; Librarian BASHIR AL-BADRI.

National Archives: Castello, Tripoli; tel. (21) 40166; internet www.nllnet.net; f. 1928; controlled by Department of Antiquities, General People's Committee for Education, Tripoli; extensive colln of documents relating to the history of Libya, mostly in Turkish from the Ottoman period; 5 libraries, 55,000 vols; Curator ABDULAALI OWN; publ. *Libya Antiqua*.

Museums and Art Galleries

Shahat

Department of Antiquities, Shahat (Cyrene): responsible for archaeological sites from Shahat west to the frontiers of Tocra, east to Msa'd; Controller BRAYEK ATTIYA.

Tripoli

Department of Antiquities: Assarai Al-Hamra, Tripoli; responsible for all museums and archaeological sites in Libya; Pres. Dr ABDULLAH SHAIBOUB.

Museums controlled by the Department:

Apollonia Museum: Marsa Soussa.

Archaeological, Natural History, Epigraphy, Prehistory and Ethnography Museums: Assarai Al-Hamra, Tripoli.

Benghazi Museum: Benghazi; mausoleum of Omar El Mukhtar.

Cyrene Museum: Cyrene (Shahat).

Gaigab Museum: Gaigab (near Cyrene).

Germa Museum: Germa (Fezean).

Islamic Museum: Tripoli.

Leptis Magna Museum: Leptis Magna.

Ptolemais Museum: Tolmeitha.

Sabratha Museum of Antiquities: Sabratha.

Tauchira Museum: Tokra.

Zanzur Museum: Zanzur (Tripoli).

Universities

AL-ARAB MEDICAL UNIVERSITY

POB 18251, Benghazi
Telephone: (61) 225007
Founded 1984
State control
Languages of instruction: Arabic, English
Academic year: September to May
Pres.: Dr AMER RAHIL
Registrar: ABU-BAKER AMMARI
Librarian: MOHAMMED EL-SAID
Library of 30,000 vols, 600 periodicals
Number of teachers: 256
Number of students: 1,615
Publication: *Garyounis Medical Journal* (2 a year)

DEANS

Faculty of Dentistry: Dr ABDULLA OMAR DOURDA
Faculty of Medicine: Dr ABDUL HADI MOUSSA
Faculty of Pharmacy: Dr ABDUSALAM A. AL-MAYHOUB

AL-FATEH UNIVERSITY

POB 3601381, Tripoli
Telephone: (22) 605441
E-mail: n.bazina@alfateh.edu.ly
Internet: www.alfateh.edu.ly
Founded 1957
State control
Language of instruction: Arabic
Academic year: September to June
Pres.: Dr MOHAMED L. FARHAT
Vice-Pres.: Dr NAJAH S. ELGABSI
Sec.-Gen.: Dr YOUNIS ALAGILI
Gen. Registrar: Dr AWEDAT GANDOUR
Librarian: Dr MOHAMED ABDUL JALEEL
Number of teachers: 3,200
Number of students: 75,000
Publications: *Bulletin of the Faculty of Education, Bulletin of the Faculty of Engineering, Bulletin of the Faculty of Law, Libyan Journal of Agriculture, Libyan Journal of Sciences*

DEANS

Faculty of Agriculture: Dr AMER ELMIGRI
Faculty of Economics and Political Science: Dr HAFAD SHAILI
Faculty of Education: Dr TOHAMI TARHOUNI
Faculty of Engineering: Dr ABDULHAMID ASHOUR
Faculty of Fine Arts: Dr HAMID
Faculty of Law: Dr OMAR HUSSIN
Faculty of Physical Education: Dr SADDIK EL KABOLI
Faculty of Science: Dr OMAR ELHAJI
Faculty of Veterinary Medicine: Dr SALAH ZWAI (acting)

AL-FATEH UNIVERSITY FOR MEDICAL SCIENCES

POB 13040, Tripoli
Telephone: (21) 4625060
E-mail: info@aums.edu.ly
Internet: www.aums.edu.ly
Founded 1986
State control
Languages of instruction: Arabic, English
Faculties of dentistry, medical technology, medicine, pharmacy

BRIGHT STAR UNIVERSITY OF TECHNOLOGY

POB 58158, Ajdabia
Telephone: (64) 23012
Founded 1981
State control
Language of instruction: Arabic
Academic year: October to June
Chancellor: Eng. ALI SALEH ELFAZZANI
Registrar: Eng. MANSOOR MASOOD FARAJ
Chief of Admin.: Eng. ABD ELSALAM ELZAROUG
Librarian: IBRAHIM MOHAMED AMIR
Number of teachers: 67
Number of students: 1,160

DERNA UNIVERSITY

Derna
Founded 1995
State control
Languages of instruction: Arabic, English
Faculties of accountancy and economics, fine arts and architecture, law, medical technology, social sciences

NASIR UNIVERSITY

POB 48222, Al-Khums Tripoli
Telephone: (325) 660080
Founded 1986
State control
Academic year: September to July
Faculties of arts, economics and political science, education and science, engineering, law, science

OMAR AL-MUKHTAR UNIVERSITY

POB 991, Al-Bayda
Telephone: (84) 6310719
E-mail: info@omulibya.org
Founded 1985
State control
Faculties of agriculture, engineering, literature and education, science and veterinary medicine
Pres.: ABDALLA A. M. ZAIED

OPEN UNIVERSITY

POB 13375, Tripoli
Telephone: (21) 4874000
E-mail: info@libopenuniv-edu.org
Internet: www.libopenuniv-edu.org
Founded 1987
State control
Language of instruction: Arabic
Academic year: September to July
Faculties of accountancy, administration, Arabic, economics, education and psychology, geography, history, Islamic studies, law, political science, sociology and social work; dept of continuing education
Pres.: IBRAHIM ABU-FARWA
Number of teachers: 52
Number of students: 8,410

SEBHA UNIVERSITY

POB 18758, Sebha
Telephone: (71) 626012
E-mail: info@sebhau.edu.ly
Internet: www.sebhau.edu.ly
Founded 1983 from the Faculty of Education of Al-Fateh University

State control
Languages of instruction: Arabic, English
Academic year: October to August

Chancellor: Dr MOHAMED MUFTAH SALEH
Vice-Chancellor: SALEM ABDULLAH SAID
Registrar: MISBAH AL-GHAWIL
Librarian: ZIDAN AL-BREIKY

Number of teachers: 646
Number of students: 9,403

Publications: *Al-Shifa* (medicine, 1 a year), *Physical Education Magazine* (2 a year)

DEANS

Faculty of Agriculture: Dr MOHAMMAD ABDUL KARIM
Faculty of Arts and Education: HAMED MASHMOOR
Faculty of Dentistry: Dr HASAN AL-BUSAIFY
Faculty of Economics and Accountancy: Dr BASHIR ABU-QILA
Faculty of Engineering and Technology: MOHAMMAD ARAHOOMA
Faculty of Medicine: Dr OMAR IBRAHIM AL-SHAIBANI
Faculty of Physical Education: ABDUL RAHMAN AL-ANSARI
Faculty of Science: Dr MOHAMMAD BASHIR HASAN

SEVENTH OF APRIL UNIVERSITY

POB 16418, Al-Zawia
Telephone: (23) 24035
E-mail: 7april_univ@mail.lttnet.net

Founded 1988
State control
Languages of instruction: Arabic, English

Faculties of education, engineering, physical education (women only), science

Pres.: Prof. SHABAN T. AL ASWAD

SEVENTH OF OCTOBER UNIVERSITY

POB 2478, Misurata
Telephone: (51) 2627201
Internet: www.7ou.edu.ly

Founded 2004
State control

Faculties of agriculture, arts, education, engineering, information technology, law, medical technology, medicine, nursing, pharmacy, science; MSc in information technology in partnership with Nottingham Trent University, UK

Number of teachers: 961
Number of students: 20,000

UNIVERSITY OF GARYOUNIS

POB 1308, Benghazi
Telephone: (61) 2220147
E-mail: uni.office@benghazi.edu.ly
Internet: www.uob.edu.ly

Founded 1955 as the Faculty of Arts and Education, Benghazi; became Univ. of Benghazi 1973; present name 1976
State control
Language of instruction: Arabic

Chancellor: Dr MUHAMID A. ALMAHDAWI
Registrar: MAHMUD M. FAKHRI
Library: see under Libraries and Archives
Number of teachers: 1,300
Number of students: 35,230

DEANS

Faculty of Arts and Education: Dr FATHI AL-HARIM
Faculty of Economics: Dr ABDELGADIR AMIR
Faculty of Engineering: Dr BELAID EIKWARI
Faculty of Law: Dr SULMAN AL-GURISH
Faculty of Science: Dr MUHAMID EL-AWIME

UNIVERSITY OF SIRT

POB 674, Sirt
Telephone: (54) 5260363
E-mail: info@su.edu.ly
Internet: www.su.edu.ly

Founded 1989
State control

Faculties of agriculture, arts, dentistry, economics, education, engineering, law, medical, medicine, nursing, science, technology

Pres.: Dr MOHAMMED A. A. ABDULLA

Colleges

African Centre for Applied Research and Training in Social Development (ACARTSOD): POB 80606, Tripoli; tel. (21) 4835103; e-mail fituri_acartsod@hotmail.com; f. 1977 as an intergovernmental instn under the auspices of the UN Economic Comm. for Africa and the OAU; aims to promote and coordinate applied research and training in the field of social devt at regional and sub-regional levels, organizes seminars, etc.; Deputy Exec. Dir Dr AHMED SAID FITURI; publ. *African Social Challenges* (1 a year).

Faculty of Islamic Call: POB 71771, Tripoli; tel. (21) 4801472; e-mail mu_dyab@yahoo.com; internet www.islamic-call.org/web_fic.html; f. 1974; 4-year courses in Koranic and Arabic studies; 300 students.

Higher Institute of Industry: Misurata; internet www.hii.edu.ly; f. 1988; HNDs, Bachelors of Technology, Masters of Technology; Dean Dr MAJDI A. ASHIBANI.

Higher Institute of Mechanical and Electrical Engineering: POB 61160, Hoon; tel. (57) 602841; e-mail aisa_jadi@yahoo.com; f. 1976; BSc-level studies; library: 22,000 vols, 100 periodicals; 48 teachers; 336 students; Dean AISA S. JADI.

Higher Institute of Technology: POB 68, Brack; tel. (71) 45300; f. 1976; first degree courses in general sciences, medical technology, food technology and environmental sciences; library: 10,000 vols; 60 teachers; 500 students; Dean Dr ABDUSSALAM M. ALMETHNANI.

Islamic Arts and Crafts School: Shar'a 1 September, Tripoli; tel. (21) 3334315.

National Institute of Administration: POB 3651, Tripoli; tel. (21) 4623420; f. 1953; offers higher diploma in administration and accounting; library: 10,000 vols; 30 teachers; publ. *National Magazine of Administration*.

National Posts and Telecommunications Institute: POB 2428, Tripoli; f. 1963; library: 510 vols; Dir K. MARABUTACI.

LIECHTENSTEIN

The Higher Education System

The Principality's first university was not founded until 1992 when the former Liechtensteinische Ingenieurschule (founded 1961; formerly Abendtechnikum Vaduz) achieved university status as the Fachhochschule Liechtenstein (Liechtenstein University of Applied Sciences); it subsequently became the Hochschule Liechtenstein in 2005 and the Universität Liechtenstein in 2008, offering Bachelors, Masters and Doctoral degrees in architecture and business sciences. In November 2010 the Liechtenstein Parliament adopted the amended law on the Universität Liechtenstein, which was ratified on 1 February 2011. A private university, the Private Universität im Fürstentum Liechstenstein, which provides postgraduate-level courses in human sciences and jurisprudence, was founded in Triesen in 2000. Other establishments of higher education include the publicly funded Liechtensteinische Musikschule (Liechtenstein Music School) in Vaduz, the private postgraduate-level International Akademie für Philosophie im Fürstentum Liechstenstein and the Liechtenstein-Institut (a privately run research and academic teaching centre). Many Liechtensteiners continue their studies at universities in Austria and Switzerland. In 2004/2005 there were 527 students in higher education in Liechtenstein and 931 attending institutions abroad. All levels of the education system are under the jurisdiction of the central Government. In addition, the State provides funding for the establishment of some private institutions as well as sponsorship for foreign institutions in Liechtenstein. The main medium of instruction is German.

The Fachhochschule Liechtenstein (as it was at that date) commenced implementation of the Bologna Process in 2003. The 2005 Act on Higher Education regulates the compulsory use of ECTS (European Credit Transfer and Accumulation System) with both Masters and Bachelors degrees; it also stipulates that Diploma Supplements should be issued in both German and English. A draft national qualifications framework was prepared in 2010 and presented to national stakeholders and relevant qualifications authorities in German-speaking neighbouring countries throughout 2011; it was expected to be integrated into the European Qualifications Framework at the beginning of 2013. Liechtenstein is affiliated to the European Network for Quality Assurance in Higher Education and is committed to the quality standards targeted by that organization. Higher education institutions are obliged to internal quality assurance and, according to the Act on Higher Education, an external evaluation of each institution has to take place at least once every six years. A national quality assurance body does not exist in Liechtenstein itself, but there is a close cooperation with quality assurance agencies in neighbouring countries.

Admission to higher education depends upon completion of secondary education and award of the Matura or Berufsmatur. The undergraduate degree is the Bachelors, a three-year programme of study (comprising 180 ECTS credit units). Following the Bachelors, postgraduate students may be awarded the Masters, which takes one-and-a half years (90 ECTS credit units), and finally Doctor of Philosophy, which takes at least three years and requires the defence of a thesis.

Vocational and technical training in Liechtenstein consists of workplace-orientated apprenticeship schemes.

Regulatory and Representative Bodies

GOVERNMENT

Ministry of External Affairs, Education and Culture: Vaduz; tel. 236-60-19; Minister Dr AURELIA FRICK.

ACCREDITATION

ENIC/NARIC Liechtenstein: Schulamt, Europark, Austr. 79, Postfach 684, 9490 Vaduz; tel. 236-67-82; e-mail eva-maria .schaedler@llv.li; internet www.sa.llv.li; Head of Upper Secondary and Higher Education Div. EVA-MARIA SCHÄDLER.

NATIONAL BODY

Schulamt (Education Office): Austr. 79, Postfach 684, 9490 Vaduz; tel. 236-67-70; e-mail info@sa.llv.li; internet www.sa.llv.li; undertakes the devt of education in kindergartens, schools and colleges; drafts and refines curricula; supervises and manages teaching staff; administers educational programmes; Chief Officer GUIDO WOLFINGER.

Learned Societies

HISTORY, GEOGRAPHY AND ARCHAEOLOGY

Historischer Verein für das Fürstentum Liechtenstein (Historical Society for the Principality of Liechtenstein): Plankner Str. 39, 9494 Schaan; tel. 392-17-47; e-mail info@historischerverein.li; internet www.historischerverein.li; f. 1901; 850 mems; library of 3,000 vols; Pres. GUIDO WOLFINGER; publ. *Jahrbuch*.

NATURAL SCIENCES

General

Liechtensteinische Gesellschaft für Umweltschutz (Liechtenstein Society for Environmental Protection): Im Bretscha 22, 9494 Schaan; tel. 232-52-62; e-mail info@lgu.li; internet www.lgu.li; f. 1973; 750 mems; Pres. RAINER KÜHNIS; Man. Dir MORITZ RHEINBERGER; publs *LGU-Liewoseiten* (irregular), *Mitteilungen* (4 a year).

Research Institute

ECONOMICS, LAW AND POLITICS

Liechtenstein-Institut: Auf dem Kirchhügel, St Luziweg 2, 9487 Gamprin-Bendern; tel. 373-30-22; e-mail admin@liechtenstein-institut.li; internet www.liechtenstein-institut.li; f. 1986; research on topics related to Liechtenstein in the fields of law, political science, history, economics and social science; library of 8,000 vols; Pres. Dr Iur. GUIDO MEIER; Dir Dr WILFRIED MARXER.

Libraries and Archives

Vaduz

Amt für Kultur-Landesarchiv (Office of Cultural Affairs-National Archives): Peter-Kaiser-Pl. 2, Postfach 684, 9490 Vaduz; tel. 236-63-40; e-mail info.aku@llv.li; internet www.aku.llv.li; f. 1961; nat. archives; reference library of 9,000 linear m of documents; Dir Mag. Phil. RUPERT TIEFENTHALER; Deputy Archivist Dr DOROTHEE PLATZ; publ. *Veröffentlichungen des Liechtensteinischen Landesarchivs*.

Liechtensteinische Landesbibliothek (National Library of Liechtenstein): Gerberweg 5, Postfach 385, 9490 Vaduz; tel. 236-63-63; e-mail info@landesbibliothek.li; internet www.landesbibliothek.li; f. 1961; public, academic and nat. library; 250,000 vols; Dir BARBARA VOGT.

Museums and Art Galleries

Vaduz

Kunstmuseum Liechtenstein: Städtle 32, Postfach 370, 9490 Vaduz; tel. 235-03-00; e-mail mail@kunstmuseum.li; internet www.kunstmuseum.li; f. 2000; museum of modern and contemporary art; nat. colln; Dir Dr FRIEDEMANN MALSCH; Curator CHRISTIANE MEYER-STOLL.

Liechtensteinisches Landesmuseum (Liechtenstein National Museum): Städtle 43, 9490 Vaduz; tel. (423) 239-68-20; e-mail info@landesmuseum.li; internet www.landesmuseum.li; f. 1954; incl. items from collns of the Prince, the State and the Liechtenstein Historical Soc.; Dir Prof. Dr RAINER VOLLKOMMER.

Postmuseum des Fürstentums Liechtenstein: Städtle 37, 9490 Vaduz; tel. 239-68-46; internet www.llm.li/d/postmuseum.asp; f. 1930; Liechtenstein stamps, historical postal documents, postal machinery; Dir NORBERT HASLER.

Universities

INTERNATIONAL AKADEMIE FÜR PHILOSOPHIE IM FÜRSTENTUM LIECHTENSTEIN
(International Philosophy Academy in the Principality of Liechtenstein)

Im Schwibboga 7B, 9487 Bendern

Telephone: 265-43-43
E-mail: admin@iap.li
Internet: www.iap.li
Private control

Rector: JOSEF SEIFERT
Gen. Sec.: HUBERTUS DESSLOCH
Chief Librarian: MECHTHILD WEISS-RAICHLE

Library of 14,000 vols

PROFESSORS

MCCORMICK, P.
POREBSKI, C.
SEIFERT, J.

UFL PRIVATE UNIVERSITÄT IM FÜRSTENTUM LIECHTENSTEIN
(UFL Private University of the Principality of Liechtenstein)

Dorfstr. 24, 9495 Triesen

Telephone: 392-40-10
E-mail: info@ufl.li
Internet: www.ufl.li

Founded 2000
Private control

Rector: Prof. Dr KARL M. SUDI
Dir of Studies: Prof. Dr PATRICIA SCHIESS

DEANS

Faculty of Law: (vacant)
Faculty of Medical Science: Prof. Dr HEINZ DREXEL

UNIVERSITÄT LIECHTENSTEIN
(University of Liechtenstein)

Fürst-Franz-Josef-Str., 9490 Vaduz

Telephone: 265-11-11
E-mail: info@uni.li
Internet: www.uni.li

Founded 1961 as Abendtechnikum Vaduz, present name and status 2008
State control
Languages of instruction: German, English

Rector: KLAUS NÄSCHER
Vice-Rector: Prof. Dipl. Ing. HANSJÖRG HILTI
Librarian: ELISABETH EMMA WEILER

Number of students: 1,000

Publication: *Denkfabrik* (magazine, 2 a year)

DEANS

Institute of Architecture and Planning: Prof. Dipl. Ing. HANSJÖRG HILTI
Institute of Business Information Systems: Prof. Dr JAN VOM BROCKE
Institute of Entrepreneurship: Prof. Dr URS BALDEGGER
Institute of Financial Services: Prof. Dr MARTIN WENZ

PROFESSORS

BALDEGGER, U., Entrepreneurship
EISINGER, A., Urban Construction and Development
HILTI, H., Design and Woodwork
KÄFERSTEIN, J., Design and Construction
MEISTER, U., Design and Construction
MENICHETTI, M. J., Business Economics
WEINMANN, S, Information Technology for Business
WENZ, M., Business Management and International and Liechtenstein Tax Law
WINNING, H.-H., Urban Construction, Planning and Transport

College

Liechtensteinische Musikschule: St Florinsgasse 1, Postfach 435, 9490 Vaduz; tel. 235-03-30; e-mail info@musikschule.li; internet www.musikschule.li; f. 1963; int. masterclasses June to September; library: 12,000 vols, special colln of works of composer Josef Gabriel Rheinberger; 100 teachers; 2,600 students; Dir KLAUS BECK.

LITHUANIA

The Higher Education System

The oldest existing institution of higher education in Lithuania is Vilniaus Universitetas (Vilnius University), founded in 1579 when Lithuania was united in a Commonwealth with Poland. The next oldest institution is Vilniaus Dailes Akademija (Vilnius Academy of Arts), founded in 1793. In 1795 Lithuania was annexed by the Russian Empire and remained under Russian (and later, Bolshevik) rule until 1920, when the USSR recognized Lithuanian independence. In 1922 Lithuania was declared a parliamentary democracy under the terms of its first Constitution. Several university-level institutions date from this year, among them Kauno Medicinos Universitetas (Kaunas Medical University), Kauno Technologijos Universitetas (Kaunas University of Technology) and Vytauto Didžiojo Universitetas (Vytautas Magnus University). According to the 'Secret Protocols' to the 1939 Treaty of Non-Aggression signed by the USSR and Nazi Germany, Lithuania was to come under German influence. However, the subsequent Nazi-Soviet Treaty on Friendship and Existing Borders granted the USSR control of Lithuania. In 1940 the Lithuanian Government was forced to resign and a Soviet Socialist Republic was established. In 1990 Lithuania was the first Soviet republic to declare independence, although this was not recognized by the USSR State Council until 1991. In February of that year the Supreme Council of the Republic of Lithuania adopted the Law on Science and Studies, which established the guidelines of higher education reform, with the intention of bringing Lithuania's research and higher education system closer to that of Western Europe. Following the introduction of the Law on Education in 2000, Lithuania participated in the Bologna Process to establish a European Higher Education Area, the first phase of which was to adopt a credit-based system of comparable degrees with two main cycles (undergraduate and graduate). From 2003 a uniform tuition fee was introduced for students in higher education, although there were exemptions for the highest achievers. In 2010/11 total enrolment in higher education was an estimated 186,861. In 2011/12 there were 23 universities (of which 14 are public) and 24 colleges (of which 13 are public). The Ministry of Education and Science is responsible for formal education at all levels and private higher education is strictly regulated by the State. The principal medium of instruction is Lithuanian. External evaluation of higher education studies is carried out by the independent Centre for Quality Assessment in Higher Education, which was founded in 1995.

The main requirement for admission to higher education is the Certificate of Maturity (Brandos Atestatas), the main secondary school qualification. Institutions receiving more applications than places available set competitive entrance examinations. Lithuania has established a two-tier Bachelors (Bakalauras) and Masters (Magistras) degree system in accordance with the principles of the Bologna Process. The two-tier system has been implemented for most degree programmes with the exception of law and medicine and related fields, which involve a long, single-cycle integrated study period. The Bachelors is a four- to five-year programme of study and students are required to accrue 160–240 European Credit Transfer and Accumulation System (ECTS) credits for award of the degree. A 2006 amendment to the Law on Higher Education enabled colleges to award a Professional Bachelor degree (Profesinis Bakalauras) from 2007 onwards. Following the Bachelors is the Masters, the first postgraduate-level degree. This is a programme of study lasting one-and-a-half to two years, and may be awarded in conjunction with a professional title. Since 2007 college graduates wishing to undertake Masters studies at university do not first have to complete university Bachelors programmes. The Doctorate (Daktaras) follows the Masters and requires up to four years of study, covering classroom-based instruction and original thesis research. Since 2006, as part of the Bologna Process, all higher education graduates, with the exception of doctoral and art postgraduate students, are issued with a Diploma Supplement. The Supplement is issued free of charge and in two languages—Lithuanian and English.

Technical and vocational education at post-secondary level is available at junior colleges, and vocational schools (Aukstesnioji mokykla), of which there were 78 in 2010, with a total student enrolment of 47,900 in that academic year. Qualifications offered include the Higher Education Diploma (Aukštojo Mokslo Diplomas) and College Diploma (Aukštesniojo Mokslo Diplomas).

In 2009 the Ministry of Education and Science launched wide-ranging reforms to public sector higher education institutes with the implementation of the Law on Higher Education and Research. Among the key objectives of the programme, which was to be financed by European Union Structural Funds, were the reform of the legal status, management and funding of state academic institutions. Ultimately all state higher education establishments were to be granted full administrative autonomy, admission procedures were to be improved, greater accessibility to higher education was to be ensured for all levels of society, government funding to students was to be substantially increased and a number of research institutes were to be incorporated into certain universities.

Regulatory and Representative Bodies

GOVERNMENT

Ministry of Culture: J. Basanavičiaus g. 5, 01118 Vilnius; tel. (5) 219-3400; e-mail culture@lrkm.lt; internet www.lrkm.lt; Minister ŠARŪNAS BIRUTIS.

Ministry of Education and Science: A. Volano Str. 2/7, 01516 Vilnius; tel. (5) 219-1190; e-mail smmin@smm.lt; internet www.smm.lt; Minister DAINIUS PAVALKIS.

ACCREDITATION

Lithuanian ENIC/NARIC: A. Goštauto g. 12, 01108 Vilnius; tel. (5) 210-4772; e-mail enicnaric@skvc.lt; internet www.skvc.lt/enic-naric; Deputy Dir AURELIJA VALEIKIENE.

NATIONAL BODIES

Lietuvos kolegijų direktorių konferencija (Lithuanian College Directors' Conference): J. Jasinskio g. 15, 01111 Vilnius; tel. (5) 219-1600; internet www.kolegijos.lt; f. 2002; 24 mems; Pres. Dr GINTAUTAS BRAŽIŪNAS; Exec. Dir KRISTINA LAKICKAITĖ.

Lietuvos Mokslo Taryba (Research Council of Lithuania): Gedimino pr. 3, 01103 Vilnius; tel. (5) 212-4933; e-mail info@lmt.lt; internet www.lmt.lt; f. 1991; advises on the formulation and implementation of science, education, research and devt policy; funds programme- based research and devt; promotes the devt of researcher resources; fosters research activities of science and higher education instns; 29 mems; Chair. Prof. DAINIUS H. PAUŽA; Dir AUŠRA VILUTIENĖ.

Lietuvos Respublikos Valstybinis Patentų Biuras (State Patent Bureau of the Republic of Lithuania): Kalvarijų Str. 3, 09310 Vilnius; tel. (5) 278-0290; e-mail info@vpb.gov.lt; internet www.vpb.lt; carries out the state legal protection of industrial property incl. inventions, designs, trademarks and service marks, semiconductor product topographies; Dir RIMVYDAS NAUJOKAS.

Lietuvos Universitetų Rektorių Konferencija (Lithuanian University Rectors' Conference): Laisves al 13, 44238 Kaunas; tel. (6) 186-8019; e-mail lurkbiuras@lurk.lt; internet www.lurk.lt; promotes scientific, educational, cultural and economic devt, cooperation between higher education instns and int. networking, cooperation with governmental authorities and local self-govt bodies; Pres. Prof. Dr Hab. REMIGIJUS ŽALIŪNAS; Sec.-Gen. Prof. Dr Hab. KĘSTUTIS KRIŠČIŪNAS.

Mokslo, Inovacijų ir Technologijų Agentūra (Agency for Science, Innovation and Technology): A. Goštauto Str. 12–219, 01108 Vilnius; tel. (5) 264-4708; e-mail info@mita.lt; internet www.mita.lt; f. 1999 as Eureka Information Center, present name 2010; provides qualitative and professional services to develop science, industry and services sectors based on advanced technologies and innovation; Dir ARŪNAS KARLONAS.

Nacionalinis egzaminų centras (National Examination Centre): M. Katkaus Str. 44, 09217 Vilnius; tel. (5) 275-6180; e-mail centras@nec.lt; internet www.egzaminai.lt; f. 1996; provides assistance to pupils, teachers, school; organizes and performs basic education attainments and examinations; conducts int. research; Dir DANUTĖ ŠUKIENĖ.

Studijų kokybės vertinimo centras (Centre for Quality Assessment in Higher Education): A. Goštauto g. 12, 01108 Vilnius; tel. (5) 210-4772; e-mail skvc@skvc.lt; internet www.skvc.lt; f. 1995; promotes quality of higher education activities through external evaluation, evaluation of foreign qualifications; Dir ARTŪRAS GREBLIAUSKAS.

Valstybinis Studijų Fondas (State Studies Foundation): A. Goštauto Str. 12–407, 01108 Vilnius; tel. (5) 263-9152; e-mail fondas@vsf.lt; internet www.vsf.lt; f. 1993 as Lithuanian State Science and Studies Foundation, present name and status 2010; administers state loans and state-supported loans to students; implements measures assigned by the Min. of Education and Science to ensure quality and accessibility of higher education; Dir Dr SIGITAS RENČYS.

Learned Societies

GENERAL

Lietuvos Mokslu Akademija (Lithuanian Academy of Sciences): 3 Gedimino pr., LT-01103 Vilnius; tel. (5) 261-3651; e-mail prezidiumas@lma.lt; internet lma.lt; f. 1941; divs of agricultural and forestry sciences, biological, medical and geosciences, humanities and social sciences, mathematical, physical and chemical sciences, technical sciences; 209 mems (incl. 96 full, 46 emeritus, 1 expert, 66 foreign); library: see under Libraries and Archives; Pres. Prof. VALDEMARAS RAZUMAS; Sec.-Gen. Prof. VYTAUTAS BASYS; publs *Acta medica Lituanica* (3 or 4 a year), *Arts Studies* (5 a year), *Journal of Agricultural Sciences* (4 a year), *Journal of Biology* (4 a year), *Journal of Chemistry* (4 a year), *Journal of Ecology* (3 or 4 a year), *Journal of Geography* (4 a year), *Journal of Geology* (4 a year), *Journal of Philosophy and Sociology* (3 or 4 a year), *Journal of Power Engineering* (4 a year), *Lithuanian Science* (5 or 6 a year), *Lituanistica* (3 or 4 a year), *Science and Technology* (12 a year).

BIBLIOGRAPHY, LIBRARY SCIENCE AND MUSEOLOGY

Lietuvos Mokslinių Bibliotekų Asociacija (Lithuanian Research Library Consortium): Gedimino Ave 51, 01504 Vilnius; tel. (5) 239-8684; e-mail lmba@lnb.lt; internet www.lmba.lt; f. 2001; subscribes to electronic databases for consortium mems and other libraries; enhancement of professional competencies of librarians; encourages participation in EU programmes and projects; 56 mems; Pres. EMILIJA BANIONYTĖ.

Lietuvos Mokslo Periodikos Asociacija (Association of Lithuanian Serials): Taikos g. 4–33, 05255 Vilnius; tel. (5) 237-0686; e-mail info@moksloperiodika.lt; internet www.serials.lt; f. 2010; an ind. asscn of Lithuanian instns, agencies, companies, orgs and persons related to serials publishing; organizes seminars and confs on journal publishing and scientometrics; 19 mems; Pres. ELEONORA DAGIENE.

LANGUAGE AND LITERATURE

Alliance Française: Mykolo Romerio Universitetas, Ateities g. 20-118, 08303 Vilnius; tel. (5) 271-4672; offers courses and exams in French language and culture and promotes cultural exchange with France.

British Council: Antakalnio St 2, 10308 Vilnius; tel. (5) 264-4890; e-mail mail@britishcouncil.lt; internet www.britishcouncil.org/lithuania; f. 1992; offers courses and exams in English language and British culture and promotes cultural exchange with the UK; library of 5,201 vols; Dir ARTŪRAS VASILIAUSKAS.

Goethe-Institut: Gedimino pr. 5, 01103 Vilnius; tel. (5) 231-4433; e-mail info@vilnius.goethe.org; internet www.goethe.de/ins/lt/vil/deindex.htm; offers courses and exams in German language and culture and promotes cultural exchange with Germany; Dir JOHANNA M. KELLER.

PEN Centre of Lithuania: K. Sirvydo 6, 2600 Vilnius; tel. (6) 104-0020; f. 1989; promotes friendship and cooperation among writers internationally; campaigns for freedom of expression, human rights and democratic causes; 34 mems; Pres. HERKUS KUNCIUS; Sec. LAIMANTAS JONUSYS.

Research Institutes

GENERAL

Inovacinis Specialiųjų Konstrukcijų ir Statinių Mokslo Institutas 'Kompozitas' (Innovatory Scientific Institute of Special Structures 'Kompozitas'): Saulėtekio al.11, SRL-II, Room 29, 10223 Vilnius; tel. (5) 274-5227; e-mail kmi@vgtu.lt; internet www.isksmi.st.vgtu.lt; f. 1992; attached to Vilniaus Gedimino Technikos Universitetas; construction process of scientific technical expertise; innovative actions; engineering and consultancy work; building, engineering, construction, technology and lifting machinery construction surveys; Dir Prof. Dr Hab. AUDRONIS KAZIMIERAS KVEDARAS.

Institute of Open Source Research: Naugarduko Str. 41, 00223 Vilnius; tel. (5) 274-4765; e-mail info@aki.lt; attached to Vilniaus Gedimino Technikos Universitetas; Dir ZILVINAS JANČORAS.

Mokslininkų Sąjungos Institutas (Institute of Lithuanian Scientific Society): J. Basanaviciaus St 6, 01118 Vilnius; tel. (5) 261-6775; e-mail mokslasplius@itpa.lt; internet msi.lms.lt; f. 1995; facilitates and develops fundamental and applied research for economy and culture; Dir Dr VALENTAS DANIUNAS.

AGRICULTURE, FISHERIES AND VETERINARY SCIENCE

Lietuvos Agrarinės Ekonomikos Institutas (Lithuanian Institute of Agrarian Economics): V. Kudirkos St 18–2, 03105 Vilnius; tel. (5) 261-4525; e-mail laei@laei.lt; internet www.laei.lt; f. 1990; conducts and implements scientific research and experimental devt in agriculture, food economy and rural devt; Dir Dr RASA MELNIKIENĖ; Scientific Sec. Dr VIRGILIJUS SKULSKIS.

Lietuvos Agrarinių ir Miškų Mokslų Centras (Lithuanian Research Centre for Agriculture and Forestry): Instituto aleja 1, 58344 Akademija Kėdainių Dist.; tel. (3) 473-7057; e-mail lammc@lammc.lt; internet www.lammc.lt; f. 2009; focuses on energy crops and their devt; 3 research institutes; library of 60,000 vols; Dir Prof. Dr Hab. ZENONAS DABKEVIČIUS; Scientific Sec. Dr VITA TILVIKIENĖ.

Lietuvos Agrarinių ir Miškų Mokslų Centro Filialas Sodininkystės ir Daržininkystės Institutas (Institute of Horticulture, Lithuanian Research Centre for Agriculture and Forestry): Kauno St 30, 54333 Babtai Kauno Dist.; tel. (3) 755-5395; e-mail institutas@lsdi.lt; internet www.lsdi.lt; f. 1938 as Horticulture Test Station, present name and status 2010; develops theoretical basis for breeding of horticultural plants; creates new varieties, accumulates and preserves genetic resources of horticultural plants; investigates biological regularities of horticultural plants, model agrobiological systems for quality and productivity; Dir ČESLOVAS BOBINAS; Deputy Dir for Admin. JONAS OLKŠTINAS; Deputy Dir for Science AUDRIUS SASNAUSKAS.

Lietuvos Agrarinių ir Miškų Mokslų Centro Filialas Žemdirbystės Institutas (Institute of Agriculture, Lithuanian Research Centre for Agriculture and Forestry): Instituto al. 1, 58344 Akademija; tel. (4) 737-271; e-mail lzi@lzi.lt; internet www.lzi.lt; f. 1956, present name and status 2010; carries out research and devt work in the fields of soil science, soil and crop management, agrochemistry, crop production, plant protection, apiculture, plant genetics, plant breeding, biotechnology, agroecology and rural devt; collects and disseminates the scientific knowledge, plant gene resources, seed production, agrochemical research; trains scientists; Dir Dr VYTAUTAS RUZGAS; Scientific Sec. Dr VITA TILVIKIENĖ; publ. *Zemdirbyste-Agriculture* (4 a year).

Miškų institutas Lietuvos Agrarinių ir Miškų Mokslų Centras (Institute of Forestry, Lithuanian Research Centre for Agriculture and Forestry): Liepų str. 1, 53101 Girionys; tel. (37) 547-221; e-mail miskinst@mi.lt; internet www.mi.lt; f. 1950, present name and status 2010; conducts fundamental and applied forest research to obtain new knowledge for social, ecological and economical devt; disseminates scientific and technical information about forest and environment; library of 61,000 vols; Dir Prof. Dr Hab. REMIGIJUS OZOLINČIUS; Scientific Sec. Dr DIANA MIZARAITE; publs *Baltic Forestry* (2 a year, in English, online (www.balticforestry.mi.lt)), *Miskininkyste* (Forestry, 2 a year, in Lithuanian, online (www.miskininkyste.mi.lt)).

ARCHITECTURE AND TOWN PLANNING

Architektūros Institutas (Institute of Architecture): Pylimo g. 26/1, AR-I, Room 1.1, 01132 Vilnius; tel. (5) 274-5214; e-mail archinst@vgtu.lt; internet www.ai.ar.vgtu.lt; f. 1999; attached to Vilniaus Gedimino Technikos Universitetas; Dir Dr JONAS JAKAITIS.

ECONOMICS, LAW AND POLITICS

Institute for Social Research: Saltoniškių 58, 08105 Vilnius; tel. (5) 275-8667; e-mail sti@ktl.mii.lt; f. 1977; conducts research in the fields of theory and methodology of social science, social welfare, social stratification, demographic processes, ethnic studies; Dir Prof. ARVYDAS VIRGILIJUS MATULIONIS; publs

Humanistika, Logos, Philosophy and Sociology (4 a year).

Institute of Economics of the Lithuanian Academy of Sciences: Gostauto 12, 2600 Vilnius; tel. 262-3502; e-mail ejvilkas@ktl.mii.lt; f. 1941; research in mathematical modelling; devt of Lithuanian economy; integration into EU; history of economic thought; library of 5,000 vols; Dir Prof. EDUARDAS VILKAS.

Lietuvos Teisės Institutas (Law Institute of Lithuania): Ankštoji g. 1A, 01109 Vilnius; tel. (5)249-7591; e-mail info@teise.org; internet teise.org; f. 1991; conducts interdisciplinary legal theory and social practice research; Dir Dr MARGARITA DOBRYNINA (acting); Research Dir Dr INGRIDA MAČERNYTĖ-PANOMARIOVIENĖ; publ. *Legal Issues*.

FINE AND PERFORMING ARTS

Lietuvos Kultūros Tyrimų Institutas (Lithuanian Culture Research Institute): Saltoniškių g. 58, 08105 Vilnius; tel. (5) 275-1898; e-mail lkti@lkti.lt; internet www.lkti.lt; studies Lithuanian culture, devt of art and philosophy, peculiarities and links with presence and contemporary world cultural changes; Dir JOLANTA ŠIRKAITE; Scientific Sec. SANDRA KULIEŠIENĖ; publs *Art Critics, Philosophy and Sociology*.

HISTORY, GEOGRAPHY AND ARCHAEOLOGY

Geodezijos Institutas (Research Institute of Geodesy): Saulėtekio al. 11, 10223 Vilnius; tel. (5) 274-4705; e-mail gi@vgtu.lt; internet www.gi.ap.vgtu.lt; f. 1992; attached to Vilniaus Gedimino Technikos Universitetas; researches on gravity field, magnetic field, on geodetic coordinate systems; establishment of GPS precision networks, Lithuanian nat. gravity network, Lithuanian nat. geodetic vertical network; investigates geoid of Lithuanian territory, permanent GPS stations network devt (LitPOS), geodynamic processes, aero photogrammetric methods; devt of information system for geodetic reference, preparation of aero navigation data in WGS 84 coordinate system; researches and improves surveying instruments and calibration methods; Dir Prof. Dr EIMUNTAS KAZIMIERAS PARŠELIŪNAS.

Geologijos ir Geografijos Institutas (Institute of Geology and Geography): T. Ševčenkos Str. 13, 03223 Vilnius; tel. (5) 210-4690; e-mail info@geo.lt; internet www.geo.lt; f. 1941, present name and status 2010; attached to Gamtos Tyrimų Centras; researches structure, composition and evolution of the Earth's crust and its surface and subsurface resources; structure, state and dynamics of climate, hydrosphere and geological environment; analysis and prediction of processes for conservation, sustainable devt and geotechnologies; geosystems in the Baltic Sea and the coastal zone and prediction of their future devt; analysis, cartographic modelling and prediction of landscape and human geographic processes for territorial planning; Dir Dr MIGLĖ STANČIKAITĖ; Head of Library SIGITA DAGIENĖ; publs *Annales Geographicae* (Geografijos metraštis, Geographical Yearbook, 1 a year), *Baltica* (2 a year).

Lietuvos Istorijos Institutas (Lithuanian Institute of History): Kražių g. 5, 01108 Vilnius; tel. (5) 261-4436; e-mail istorija@istorija.lt; internet www.istorija.lt; f. 1941; promotes study of archaeology, ethnology (and social anthropology), heraldry, sigillography, numismatics, palaeography and genealogy; library of 145,128 vols; Dir Dr RIMANTAS MIKNYS; Scientific Sec. Dr SAULĖ URBANAVIČIENĖ; publs *Archaeological Investigations in Lithuania, Archaeologija Baltica* (Lithuanian Archaeology), *Lietuvos archeologija* (Lithuanian Archaeology), *Lithuanian Ethnology, Lithuanian Historical Studies, Lithuanian Metrica, Urban Past, Yearbook of Lithuanian History* (2 a year).

Teritorijų Planavimo Mokslo Institutas (Research Institute of Territorial Planning): Saulėtekio al. 11, 10223 Vilnius; tel. (5) 237-0576; e-mail tpmi@vgtu.lt; internet www.tpi.vgtu.lt; f. 1992; attached to Vilniaus Gedimino Technikos Universitetas; prepares planning documents; advises planning issues; develops residential projects, urban digital plans, storing information in databases; prepares landscape architectural projects; Dir Prof. Dr MARIJA BURINSKIENĖ; publs *Baltic Journal of Road and Bridge Engineering, Technological and Economic Development of Economy*.

LANGUAGE AND LITERATURE

Lietuviu Kalbos Institutas (Institute of the Lithuanian Language): P. Vileisio str. 5, 10308 Vilnius; tel. (5) 234-6472; e-mail lki@lki.lt; internet www.lki.lt; f. 1939; research into the Lithuanian language: lexicology, lexicography and grammatical structure, dialects, sociolinguistic and historical, operation of the Lithuanian language in soc., terminology, Lithuanian onomastics; Dir Dr JOLANTA ZABARSKAITE; Research Sec. VIOLETA MEILIŪNAITĖ; Sec. VIRGINIJA GAIDYTĖ; publs *Acta Linguistica Lithuanica* (2 a year), *Archivum Lithuanicum* (1 a year), *Kalbos Kultūra* (1 a year), *Terminologija* (1 a year).

Lietuvių literatūros ir tautosakos institutas (Institute of Lithuanian Literature and Folklore): Antakalnio 6, 10308 Vilnius; tel. (5) 262-1943; e-mail direk@llti.lt; internet www.llti.lt; f. 1939; carries out long-term investigations and studies of the Lithuanian literature, folklore and literary heritage; fundamental studies; comparative studies; int. devt of Lithuanian culture and heritage studies; analysis and evaluation of contemporary Lithuanian literature; education of young promising scientists; library of 272,000 vols and other printed matter; Dir Dr MINDAUGAS KVIETKAUSKAS; publs *Colloquia* (2 a year), *Senoji Lietuvos literatūra* (Old Lithuanian Literature, 2 a year), *Tautosakos darbai* (Folklore Studies, 2 a year).

MEDICINE

Higienos Institutas (Institute of Hygiene): Didžioji St 22, 01128 Vilnius; tel. (5) 262-4583; e-mail institutas@hi.lt; internet www.hi.lt; f. 1808; library of 8,000 vols; Dir REMIGIJUS JANKAUSKAS; publ. *Public Health* (4 a year).

Valstybinis mokslinių tyrimų institutas Inovatyvios medicinos centras (State Research Institute Centre for Innovative Medicine): Žygimantų g. 9, 01102 Vilnius; tel. (5) 262-8636; e-mail imc@imcentras.lt; internet www.imcentras.lt; f. 2010; rheumatology, regenerative medicine, immunology, immunotechnology, molecular biology; Dir Prof. Dr Hab. ALGIRDAS VENALIS; Scientific Sec. Dr ALMANTAS SIAURYS.

Vilniaus Universiteto Onkologijos Institutas (Institute of Oncology, Vilnius University): Santariškių 1, 08660 Vilnius; tel. (5) 278-6700; e-mail administracija@vuoi.lt; internet www.vuoi.lt; f. 1990; performs fundamental and applied scientific oncological research; trains scientists and specialists of oncology; provides personal health care services for oncological patients; Dir Prof. Dr Hab. NARIMANTAS EVALDAS SAMALAVIČIUS.

NATURAL SCIENCES

Biological Sciences

Aplinkos Apsaugos Institutas (Research Institute of Environment Protection): Saulėtekio ave 11, Faculty of Environmental Engineering, SRK-II, Room 211, 10223 Vilnius; tel. (5) 274-4726; e-mail aai@vgtu.lt; internet www.aai.ap.vgtu.lt; f. 2002; attached to Vilniaus Gedimino Technikos Universitetas; environmental investigations, evaluation, education and training; devt of new technologies; organizes scientific meetings, seminars, workshops; Dir Prof. Dr Hab. PRANAS BALTRĖNAS.

Fizinių ir Technologijos Mokslų Centras (Center for Physical Sciences and Technology): Savanorių Ave 231, 02300 Vilnius; tel. (5) 264-9211; e-mail office@ftmc.lt; internet www.ftmc.lt; f. 2010 by merger of the Institute of Physics, Semiconductor Physics Institute, the Institute of Chemistry; carries out long-term fundamental and experimental research in the fields of physics, chemistry and technologies; Dir VIDMANTAS REMEIKIS; Scientific Sec. MINDAUGAS DAGYS.

Gamtos Tyrimų Centras (Nature Research Centre): Akademijos g. 2, 08412 Vilnius; tel. (5) 272-9257; e-mail sekretoriatas@gamtostyrimai.lt; internet www.gamtostyrimai.lt; f. 2009 by merger of Institute of Ecology, Institute of Botany, Institute of Geology and Geography; attached to Vilnius Univ.; researches preservation, restoration and sustainable use of natural and biological resources; library of 90,000 vols; Dir Prof. Dr Hab. VINCAS BŪDA; publs *Annales Geographicae* (2 a year), *Baltica* (2 a year, in English), *Botanica Lithuanica* (4 a year, in English), *Ekologija, Zoology and Ecology*.

Gamtos Tyrimų Centro Botanikos Institutas (Institute of Botany of Nature Research Centre): Žaliųjų Ežerų g. 49, 08406 Vilnius; tel. (5) 271-1618; e-mail botanika@botanika.lt; internet www.botanika.lt; f. 1959, present name and status 1992; conducts scientific studies in botany, mycology, virology, phytopathology, biodeterioration and bioremediation, phytosociology, vegetation science and vegetation mapping, plant physiology and genetics; Dir Dr JUOZAS LABOKAS; publ. *Botanica Lithuanica* (4 a year).

Vilniaus Universitetas Biochemijos Institutas (Vilnius University Institute of Biochemistry): Mokslininkų Str. 12, 08662 Vilnius; tel. (5) 272-9144; e-mail biochemija@bchi.vu.lt; internet www.bchi.lt; f. 1967; investigates structure, function and application of biocatalysts; signals pathways and epigenetic regulation of tumour and stem cells; studies structure and function of self-assembled structures of lipids and proteins; Dir Prof. Dr Hab. VALDAS LAURINAVICIUS; Sec. JEKATERINA JURKŠAITYTĖ.

Mathematical Sciences

Vilniaus Universiteto Matematikos ir Informatikos Institutas (Vilnius University Institute of Mathematics and Informatics): Akademijos Str. 4, 08663 Vilnius; tel. (5) 210-9300; e-mail info@mii.vu.lt; internet www.mii.lt; f. 1956, present name and status 2010; conducts scientific research and experimental devt for the economy of Lithuania and int. cooperation; Dir Prof. Dr Hab. GINTAUTAS DZEMYDA; publs *Informatica* (4 a year), *Informatics in Education* (2 a year), *Lithuanian Mathematical Journal* (4 a year, in English), *Mathematical Modelling and Analysis, Nonlinear Analysis: Modelling and Control* (4 a year).

Physical Sciences

Lietuvos geologijos tarnyba (Lithuanian Geological Survey): S. Konarskio 35, 03123 Vilnius; tel. (5) 233-2889; e-mail lgt@lgt.lt; internet www.lgt.lt; f. 1940; attached to Min. of Environment; acts on behalf of the govt in areas of geological investigation, groundwater monitoring of economic entities, regulation of subterranean resources, accumulation of geological data; mem. of Forum of European Geological Surveys since 1994; Dir. JONAS SATKUNAS.

Teorinės Fizikos ir Astronomijos Institutas Vilniaus Universitetas (Institute of Theoretical Physics and Astronomy Vilnius University): A. Goštauto St 12, 01108 Vilnius; tel. (5) 219-3251; e-mail tfai@tfai.vu.lt; internet www.tfai.vu.lt; f. 1990; investigations of atoms, subatomic particles, molecules, their structures and plasma spectroscopy, their application in nanophysics and astrophysics; incl. astronomical observatory, planetarium; library of 250,000 vols; Dir and Head of Astronomical Observatory Dr Hab. GRAŽINA TAUTVAIŠIENĖ; publs *Baltic Astronomy* (4 a year, online (www.tfai.vu.lt/balticastronomy)), *Lietuvos dangus* (Sky of Lithuania, 1 a year, in Lithuanian), *Lithuanian Journal of Physics* (4 a year, online (www.itpa.lt/~lfd/Lfz/LFZ.html)).

TECHNOLOGY

Biotechnologijos Institutas Vilniaus Universitetas (Institute of Biotechnology Vilnius University): V. A. Graičiūno st 8, 02241 Vilnius; tel. (5) 260-2103; e-mail office@ibt.lt; internet www.ibt.lt; f. 1975; conducts research and training in the fields of biotechnology and molecular biology; research and devt of recombinant biomedical proteins, genetic and molecular studies of restriction modification phenomenon, developing of viruses diagnostics, epigenetics study of small RNA, drug design and synthesis and bioinformatics; Dir Prof. KESTUTIS SASNAUSKAS.

Internetinių ir Intelektualiųjų Technologijų Institutas (Research Institute of Internet and Intelligent Technologies): Saulėtekio al. 11, 10223 Vilnius; tel. (5) 274-5002; e-mail edmundas.zavadskas@vgtu.lt; attached to Vilniaus Gedimino Technikos Universitetas; develops web-based intelligent systems, intelligent tutoring systems, computer learning systems, audio and visual aids, ebooks for distance learning; analysis of electronic city systems; knowledge management; electronic commerce, e-business; smart technologies; biometric technologies; Dir Prof. Dr Hab. ARTŪRAS KAKLAUSKAS.

Kelių Tyrimo Institutas (Road Research Institute): Saulėtekio al. 11, 10223 Vilnius; tel. (5) 275-3520; e-mail kti@vgtu.lt; internet www.kti.ap.vgtu.lt; f. 2009; attached to Vilniaus Gedimino Technikos Universitetas; carries out int. research on street and road design, construction, reconstruction, repair and maintenance areas; Dir Dr AUDRIUS VAITKUS.

Kosmoso Mokslo ir Technologijų Institutas (Space Science and Technology Institute): Sauletekio Ave 15, 10224 Vilnius; e-mail kmti@kmti.lt; internet www.space-lt.eu/kmti; f. 2010; conducts research for scientific tasks, technologies demonstrations, educational purposes and popularization of science; Dir Dr DOMANTAS BRUCAS; Dir for Development SAULIUS LAPIENIS.

Lietuvos Energetikos Institutas (Lithuanian Energy Institute): Breslaujos g. 3, 44403 Kaunas; tel. (3) 740-1805; e-mail rastine@mail.lei.lt; internet www.lei.lt; f. 1956, current name adopted 1992; research activities incl. security of energy supply and risk assessment, nuclear energy and radioactive waste management, metrology, hydrology, fuel cells and hydrogen, renewable energy, energy efficiency combustion, plasma engineering; library of 59,758 vols; Dir Prof. Dr Hab. EUGENIJUS UŠPURAS; Scientific Sec. Dr ROLANDAS URBONAS; publs *Energetika* (4 a year), *Environmental Research, Engineering and Management* (4 a year), *Lietuvos Energetika* (1 a year).

Scientific Institute of Thermal Insulation: Linkmenų Str. 28, 08217 Vilnius; tel. (5) 275-0001; e-mail termo@aiva.lt; attached to Vilniaus Gedimino Technikos Universitetas; Dir Dr Hab. ANTANAS LAUKAITIS.

Suvirinimo ir Medžiagotyros Problemų Institutas (Research Institute of Welding and Materials Science): Basanavičiaus str. 28, Second block, Room 103, 03224 Vilnius; tel. (5) 274-5053; e-mail suvirinimo-institutas@vgtu.lt; internet www.smpi.me.vgtu.lt; f. 1994; attached to Vilniaus Gedimino Technikos Universitetas; develops welding technologies, modern materials, dangerous welding design reliability, durability and ageing; Dir Dr NIKOLAJ VIŠNIAKOV.

Transporto Institutas (Transport Research Institute): Plytinės Str. 27, 10105 Vilnius; tel. (5) 274-4981; e-mail tmi@vgtu.lt; internet www.tmi.vgtu.lt; f. 1998; attached to Vilniaus Gedimino Technikos Universitetas; forecasts transport system devt; methodology and strategy of transport infrastructure devt and modernization; develops intermodal transport; researches on innovative transport technologies; interaction, harmonization of transport networks and transportation technologies; structural changes of transport system; modelling of transport processes; modernization, devt of different transport modes; drafts regulations for transport system activities and harmonization; Dir Prof. Dr Hab. ADOLFAS BAUBLYS.

Libraries and Archives

Vilnius

Lietuvos Mokslų Akademijos Vrublevskių Biblioteka (Wroblewski Library of the Lithuanian Academy of Sciences): Žygimantu g. 1, 01102 Vilnius; tel. (5) 262-9537; e-mail biblioteka@mab.lt; internet www.mab.lt; f. 1941; 3,755,249 vols; Dir Dr SIGITAS NARBUTAS; Scientific Sec. LEOKADIJA KAIRELIENĖ.

Lietuvos Nacionaline Martyno Mažvydo Biblioteka (Martynas Mažvydas National Library of Lithuania): Gedimino ave 51, 01504 Vilnius; tel. (5) 249-7023; e-mail biblio@lnb.lt; internet www.lnb.lt; f. 1919, incorporated Nat. Printing Archive 1992; 6,700,000 vols; Dir-Gen. Prof. Dr RENALDAS GUDAUSKAS; Scientific Sec. BIRUTĖ PEČIULEVIČIŪTĖ; publ. *Tarp Knygų* (12 a year).

Lietuvos Technikos Biblioteka (Lithuanian Technical Library): Šv. Ignoto g. 6, 01144 Vilnius; tel. (5) 261-0379; e-mail info@tb.lt; internet www.tb.lt; f. 1957; patent information centre; publishes official bulletins and patent documents of the State Patent Bureau; 45,844,100 vols; Dir KAZYS MACKEVIČIUS.

Vilniaus Universiteto Biblioteka (Vilnius University Library): Universiteto g. 3, 01122 Vilnius; tel. (5) 268-7100; e-mail mb@mb.vu.lt; internet www.mb.vu.lt; f. 1570; 5,382,344 vols; Dir-Gen. IRENA KRIVIENĖ.

Museums and Art Galleries

Kaunas

Kaunas Botanical Garden: Ž. E. Žilibero g. 6, 46324 Kaunas; tel. (37) 390-033; e-mail bs@bs.vdu.lt; internet botanika.vdu.lt; f. 1923; attached to Vytautas Magnus University; research into botany, ecology and the natural environment; 5 depts of medicinal plants, plant pathology, dendrology, pomology, floriculture; library of 10,000 vols; Dir Prof. VIDA MILDAŽIENĖ.

National M. K. Čiurlionis Art Museum: Vlado Putvinskio 55, 44248 Kaunas; tel. (37) 229-475; e-mail mkc.info@takas.lt; internet www.ciurlionis.lt; f. 1921, present name 1997; Lithuanian and European art, folk art, oriental and ancient Egyptian art, numismatics; subdivs: Mykolas Žilinskas Art Gallery, Kaunas Picture Gallery, Antanas Žmuidzinavičius Memorial Museum and Devil's Museum, Historical Presidential Palace of Lithuania, Museum of Ceramics, Adelė and Paulius Galaunė House, Liudas Truikys and Marijona Rakauskaitė Memorial Museum, Juozas Zikaras Memorial Museum, Mikalojus Konstantinas Čiurlionis Memorial Museum, Vytautas Kazimieras Jonynas Gallery in Druskininkai; library of 30,000 vols; Dir OSVALDAS DAUGELIS; Chief Curator NIJOLĖ ADOMAVIČIENĖ.

Vytautas the Great War Museum: K. Donelaičio g. 64, 44248 Kaunas; tel. (37) 320-765; e-mail vdkaromuziejus@kam.lt; f. 1921; archaeological finds, weapons, firearms, ammunition, army uniforms, objects and documents relating to the transatlantic flight of the 'Lituanica'; colln of ethnographic photographs by Balys Buracas (1897–1972); Dir KĘSTUTIS KURŠELIS.

Trakai

Trakai Historical Museum: Kęstučio Str.4, 21104 Trakai; tel. (5) 285-5297; e-mail info@trakaimuziejus.lt; internet www.trakaimuziejus.lt; f. 1948; 16th- and 17th-century tiles, coins, pottery, bone chessmen and other artefacts discovered during excavations at Trakai Castle; ethnographic and applied art collns; Dir VIRGILIJUS POVILIŪNAS.

Vilnius

Lietuvos Nacionalinis Muziejus (National Museum of Lithuania): Arsenalo Str. 1, 01143 Vilnius; tel. (5) 262-7774; e-mail muziejus@lnm.lt; internet www.lnm.lt; f. 1855; archaeology, ethnography, history, iconography, numismatics; library of 55,000 vols; Dir BIRUTE KULNYTE; Chief Curator HALINA PASKEVICIENE; publs *Archaeology*, *Ethnography* (1 a year), *Museum* (1 a year), *Numismatics* (1 a year).

Lithuanian Art Museum: Str. Bokšto 5, 01126 Vilnius; tel. (5) 262-8030; e-mail muziejus@ldm.lt; internet www.ldm.lt; f. 1933 as Vilnius City Museum, present name and status 1997; Lithuanian and foreign works of fine and applied art; br. museums incl. Clock Museum, Foreign Art Gallery, Juodkrant Exhibition Hall, Klaipėda Picture Gallery, Museum of Applied Art, Palanga Amber Museum, Pranas Gudynas Restoration Centre of Museum Treasures, Vilnius Picture Gallery; library of 25,166 vols; Dir ROMUALDAS BUDRYS; publ. *Issues of the Museum* (1 a year).

Universities

ALEKSANDRO STULGINSKIO UNIVERSITETAS (Aleksandras Stulginskis University)

Studentu g. 11, 53361 Kaunas
Telephone: (37) 752-300
E-mail: asu@asu.lt
Internet: www.asu.lt
Founded 1924
State control
Languages of instruction: English, Lithuanian, Russian
Academic year: September to June
Rector: Prof. Dr ANTANAS MAZILIAUSKAS
Vice-Rector for Management and Strategic Planning: Dr VIDMANTAS BUTKUS
Vice-Rector for Research: Dr LAIMA TAPARAUSKIENE
Vice-Rector for Studies: Dr JONAS ČAPLIKAS
Dir for Library: AUŠRA RAGUCKAITĖ
Library of 514,434 vols, 157,316 publication titles, 174 printed serials, 26,000 electronic scholarly serials in 24 subscribed databases
Number of teachers: 200
Number of students: 5,517
Publications: *Agricultural Engineering* (4 a year), *Baltic Forestry* (2 a year, online, www.balticforestry.mi.lt), *Economics and Rural Development*, *Environmental Research, Engineering and Management*, *Management Theory and Studies for Rural Business and Infrastructure Development* (4–5 a year), *Miskininkyste* (Journal on Forest Science, 2–4 a year, online, www.miskininkyste.mi.lt), *Water Management Engineering*, *Žemdirbystė* (Agriculture, 4 a year), *Žemės ūkio mokslai* (Agricultural Sciences, 4 a year, in English and Lithuanian)

DEANS
Faculty of Agricultural Engineering: Dr ROLANDAS DOMEIKA
Faculty of Agronomy: Dr VIKTORAS PRANCKIETIS
Faculty of Economics and Management: Prof. Dr NERINGA STONČIUVIENĖ
Faculty of Forestry and Ecology: Dr EDMUNDAS BARTKEVIČIUS
Faculty of Water and Land Management: Dr VIDMANTAS GURKLYS

EUROPOS HUMANITARINIS UNIVERSITETAS (European Humanities University)

Tauro g. 12, 01114 Vilnius
Valakupių g. 5, 10101 Vilnius
Telephone: (5) 263-9650
E-mail: office@ehu.lt
Internet: www.ehu.lt
Founded 1992, present status 2006
Languages of instruction: Belarusian, English, Russian
Rector: Dr ANATOLI MIKHAILOV
Vice-Rector for Academic Affairs: ALIAKSANDR KALBASKA
Vice-Rector for Admin. and Infrastructure: IRENA VAIŠVILAITĖ
Vice-Rector for Devt and Int. Relations: DARIUS UDRYS
Provost and Chief Operating Officer: G. DAVID POLLICK
Dean of the School of Graduate Studies: ALLA SOKOLOVA
Dean of the School of Undergraduate Studies: RYHOR MINIANKOU
Library of 16,000 vols
Number of teachers: 150
Number of students: 1,660
Publication: *Jus Gentium*

KAUNO TECHNOLOGIJOS UNIVERSITETAS (Kaunas University of Technology)

K. Donelaičio St 73, 44029 Kaunas
Telephone: (37) 300-011
E-mail: rastine@ktu.lt
Internet: www.ktu.lt
Founded 1922
State control
Academic year: September to June
Rector: Prof. PETRAS BARŠAUSKAS
Vice-Rector for Int. Relations and Devt: Prof. SIGITAS STANYS
Vice-Rector for Research: Prof. ASTA PUNDZIENĖ
Vice-Rector for Studies: Prof. PRANAS ŽILIUKAS
Dir for Library: GENOVAITE DUOBINIENĖ
Library of 1,328,211 vols
Number of teachers: 880
Number of students: 10,991
Publications: *Chemical Technology* (4 a year, online (www.chemtech.ktu.lt)), *Economics and Management* (1 a year), *Electronics and Electrical Engineering* (8 a year, online (www.eejournal.ktu.lt)), *Engineering Economics* (5 a year, online (www.inzeko.ktu.lt)), *Environmental Research, Engineering and Management* (4 a year, online (www.erem.ktu.lt)), *European Integration Studies* (1 a year, online (www.eis.ktu.lt)), *Information Technology and Control* (4 a year, online (www.itc.ktu.lt)), *Journal of Sustainable Architecture and Civil Engineering* (4 a year, online (www.sace.ktu.lt)), *Language Teaching and Learning in the Context of Social Changes* (2 a year), *Materials Science* (4 a year, online (www.matsc.ktu.lt)), *Mechanics* (6 a year, online (www.mechanika.ktu.lt)), *Public Policy and Administration* (4 a year, online (www.vpa.ktu.lt)), *Social Sciences* (4 a year, online (www.socsc.ktu.lt)), *Studies about Languages* (2 a year, online (www.kalbos.ktu.lt)), *Ultragarsas* (Ultrasound, 4 a year, online (www.ultragarsas.ktu.lt))

DEANS
Faculty of Chemical Technology: Dr EUGENIJUS VALATKA
Faculty of Civil Engineering and Architecture: Dr ŽYMANTAS RUDZIONIS
Faculty of Design and Technologies: Prof. EUGENIJA STRAZDIENE
Faculty of Economics and Management: Prof. Dr GRAZINA STARTIENE
Faculty of Electrical and Control Engineering: Prof. Dr JONAS DAUNORAS
Faculty of Fundamental Sciences: Dr VYTAUTAS JANILIONIS
Faculty of Humanities: Dr DALIA STAPONKUTĖ
Faculty of Informatics: Prof. Dr EDUARDAS BAREIŠA
Faculty of Mechanical Engineering and Mechatronics: ANDRIUS VILKAUSKAS
Faculty of Social Sciences: Prof. Dr MONIKA PETRAITĖ
Faculty of Telecommunications and Electronics: Prof. ALGIMANTAS VALINEVICIUS
International Studies Centre: Dr ARVYDAS PALEVICIUS (Dir)
Panevėžys Institute: Prof. ŽILVINAS BAZARAS (Dir)

KAZIMIERO SIMONAVIČIAUS UNIVERSITETAS (Kazimieras Simonavičius University)

J. Basanavičiaus g. 29A, 03109 Vilnius
Telephone: (5) 213-5172
E-mail: ksu@ksu.lt
Internet: www.ksu.lt
Founded 2003 as Vilnius Acad. of Business Law, present name and status 2012
Private control
Rector: Prof. Dr ARŪNAS AUGUSTINAITIS
Vice-Rector: Dr AUSTĖ KIŠKIENĖ
Chancellor: DARIUS VERBYLA
Librarian: NATALIJA ACHREMČIKAITĖ
Number of teachers: 75
Number of students: 500

DEANS
Klaipėda Faculty: Prof. Dr RIMANTAS STAŠYS
Law Faculty: Prof. Dr KAZIMIERAS LIUDVIKAS VALANČIUS

KLAIPĖDOS UNIVERSITETAS (Klaipėda University)

Herkaus Manto Str. 84, 92294 Klaipėda
Telephone: (4) 639-8900
E-mail: klaipedos.universitetas@ku.lt
Internet: www.ku.lt
Founded 1991
State control
Academic year: September to June
Rector: Prof. Dr VAIDUTIS LAURĖNAS
Vice-Rector for Infrastructure and Devt Affairs: Prof. Dr RIMANTAS DIDŽIOKAS
Vice-Rector for Research and Academic Affairs: Prof. Dr INGA DAILIDIENĖ
Dir for Library: JANINA PUPELIENĖ
Library of 459,383 vols
Number of teachers: 600
Number of students: 6,500
Publications: *Acta Historica Universitatis Klavpeolencis* (1 a year), *Andragogy*, *Archaeologia Baltica*, *Jura ir aplinka* (Sea and Environment, 4 a year), *Regionų formavimosi ir plėtros tyrimai* (Regional Formation and Development Studies), *Res Humanitariae*, *Tiltai* (Bridges, 4 a year), *Tradicija ir dabartis* (Tradition and the Present, 1 a year)

DEANS
Faculty of Arts: Prof. VYTAUTAS TETENSKAS
Faculty of Health Sciences: Prof. Dr ARTŪRAS RAZBADAUSKAS
Faculty of Humanities: Prof. Dr RIMANTAS BALSYS
Faculty of Marine Engineering: Dr RIMA MICKEVIČIENĖ
Faculty of Natural Sciences and Mathematics: Prof. Dr PETRAS GRECEVIČIUS
Faculty of Pedagogy: Dr POVILAS ŽAKAITIS
Faculty of Social Sciences: Prof. Dr ANTANAS BUČINSKAS

LCC TARPTAUTINIS UNIVERSITETAS (LCC International University)

Kretingos g. 36, 92307 Klaipėda
Telephone: (46) 310-745
E-mail: info@lcc.lt
Internet: www.lcc.lt
Founded 1991 as Lithuania Christian Fund College
Language of instruction: English
Pres.: Dr MARLENE WALL
Academic Vice-Pres.: Dr LOWELL GRETEBECK
Student Life Vice-Pres.: MARGARITA PAVLOVIČ
Head Librarian: JOLANTA KAUN
Library of 20,000 vols
Number of students: 650

LIETUVOS EDUKOLOGIJOS UNIVERSITETAS (Lithuanian University of Educational Sciences)

Studentų g. 39, 08106 Vilnius
Telephone: (5) 279-0281
E-mail: stojimas@leu.lt

Internet: www.leu.lt
Founded 1935 as Nat. Pedagogical Institute in Klaipėda, present name and status 2011
State control
Languages of instruction: English, Lithuanian, Russian
Academic year: September to June
Rector: Prof. Dr Hab. ALGIRDAS GAIŽUTIS
Vice-Rector for Devt: Prof. Dr AIVAS RAGAUSKAS
Vice-Rector for Research: Prof. Dr Hab. RIMANTAS ŽELVYS
Vice-Rector for Studies: Dr VYTAUTAS BERNOTAS
Dir for Library: EMILIJA BANIONYTĖ
Library of 644,525 vols
Number of teachers: 552
Number of students: 9,000
Publications: *Istorija* (History, 4 a year, in English and Lithuanian), *Pedagogika* (Pedagogy Studies, in English, German, Lithuanian and Russian), *Socialinis Ugdymas* (Social Education, 3 a year, in English and Lithuanian), *Žmogus ir Zodis* (Man and the Word, in English, French, German, Italian, Lithuanian, Polish and Russian)

DEANS
Faculty of Education: Prof. Dr ONA MONKEVIČIENĖ
Faculty of History: Prof. Dr EUGENIJUS JOVAISA
Faculty of Lithuanian Philology: Prof. Dr VILIJA SALIENE
Faculty of Philology: Prof. Dr GINTAUTAS KUNDROTAS
Faculty of Science and Technology: Prof. Dr VIRGINIJUS SRUOGA
Faculty of Social Sciences: Assoc. Prof. Dr VYTAS NAVICKAS
Faculty of Sports and Health Education: Prof. Dr AUDRONIUS VILKAS

LIETUVOS SPORTO UNIVERSITETAS
(Lithuanian Sports University)

Sporto 6, 44221 Kaunas
Telephone: (37) 302-621
E-mail: lsu@lsu.lt
Internet: www.lkka.lt
Founded 1945 as Lithuanian State Institute of Physical Education, present name and status 2012
State control
Rector: Prof. Dr Hab. ALBERTAS SKURVYDAS
Vice-Rector: Prof. Dr ARVYDAS STASIULIS
Vice-Rector for Studies: Prof. Dr RASA JANKAUSKIENĖ
Head of Library: ASTA CHARŽEVSKIENĖ
Number of teachers: 193
Number of students: 2,456
Publications: *Rehabilitation Sciences*, *Ugdymas. Kno Kultūra. Sportas* (Education. Physical Training. Sport, 4 a year)

DEANS
Faculty of Sports Biomedicine: Dr NERIJUS MASIULIS
Faculty of Sports Education: Dr ARŪNAS ARŪNAS

LIETUVOS SVEIKATOS MOKSLŲ UNIVERSITETAS
(Lithuanian University of Health Sciences)

A. Mickevičiaus str. 9, 44307 Kaunas
Telephone: (37) 327-201
E-mail: info@lsmuni.lt
Internet: lsmuni.lt
Founded 2010 by merger of Kaunas Medical Univ. and Lithuanian Veterinary Academy
State control
Rector: Prof. Dr Hab. REMIGIJUS ŽALIŪNAS
Vice-Rector for Research: Prof. Dr Hab. VAIVA LESAUSKAITĖ
Vice-Rector for Studies: Prof. Dr Hab. RENALDAS JURKEVIČIUS
Vice-Rector for Univ. Clinics: Prof. Dr Hab. JUOZAS PUNDZIUS
Vice-Rector for Veterinary: Prof. Dr ANTANAS SEDEREVIČIUS
Dir for Library: MEILĖ KRETAVIČIENĖ
Library of 640,697 vols
Number of teachers: 1,300
Number of students: 7,000

DEANS
Faculty of Animal Husbandry Technology: Dr PAULIUS MATUSEVIČIUS
Faculty of Medicine: Prof. ALGIMANTAS TAMELIS
Faculty of Nursing: Prof. Dr JŪRATĖ MACIJAUSKIENĖ
Faculty of Odontology: Prof. Dr Hab. RIČARDAS KUBILIUS
Faculty of Pharmacy: Prof. VITALIS BRIEDIS
Faculty of Public Health: Prof. RAMUNĖ KALĖDIENĖ
Faculty of Veterinary Medicine: Prof. Dr ALBINA ANIULIENĖ

MYKOLO ROMERIO UNIVERSITETAS
(Mykolas Romeris University)

Ateities St 20, 08303 Vilnius
Telephone: (5) 271-4625
E-mail: roffice@mruni.eu
Internet: www.mruni.eu
Founded 1990 as Law Univ. of Lithuania, present name 2004
State control
Academic year: September to June
Chancellor: SAULIUS SPURGA
Rector: Prof. Dr ALVYDAS PUMPUTIS
Vice-Rector for Devt: Dr STASYS VAITKEVIČIUS
Vice-Rector for Education: GIEDRIUS VILIŪNAS
Vice-Rector for Infrastructure: VLADAS BRAKAUSKAS
Vice-Rector for Research and Int. Relations: Prof. Dr INGA ŽALĖNIENĖ
Deputy Dir for Library: NIJOLĖ LIATUKIENĖ
Library of 191,141 vols, 188 periodicals
Number of teachers: 828
Number of students: 20,000

DEANS
Faculty of Economics and Finance Management: Prof. Dr RIMA ŽITKIENĖ
Faculty of Law: Prof. Dr RIMA AŽUBALYTĖ
Faculty of Politics and Management: Dr ALGIRDAS MONKEVIČIUS
Faculty of Public Security: Prof. SAULIUS GREIČIUS
Faculty of Social Policy: Prof. Dr LETA DROMANTIENE
Faculty of Social Technologies: Prof. Dr AELITA SKARŽAUSKIENĖ

ŠIAULIŲ UNIVERSITETAS
(Šiauliai University)

Vilniaus St 88, 76285 Šiauliai
Telephone: (41) 595-800
E-mail: all@cr.su.lt
Internet: www.su.lt
Founded 1997 by merger of Šiauliai Pedagogical Institute and Siauliai Polytechnical Faculty of Kaunas Univ. of Technology
State control
Rector: DONATAS JURGAITIS (acting)
Vice-Rector for Research and Art: Prof. Dr STEFANIJA ALIŠAUSKIENĖ
Vice-Rector for Studies: Dr JUOZAS PABRĖŽA
Dir for Library: GRAŽINA LAMANAUSKIENĖ
Library of 459,527 vols
Number of teachers: 840
Number of students: 6,000
Publications: *Acta Humanitarica Universitatis Saulensis*, *Archivum Lituanicum* (1 a year), *Ekonomika ir Vadyba: Aktualijos ir Perspektyvos* (Economics and Management: Current Issues and Perspectives, 3 a year), *Filologija* (Philology), *Inter-Studia Humanitatis*, *Jaunųjų Mokslininkų Darbai* (Journal of Young Scientists, 3 a year), *Kūrybos erdvės* (Spaces of Creation, 2 a year), *Lyciu studijos ir tyrimal* (Gender Studies and Research, in Lithuanian), *Siauliai Mathematical Seminar*, *Socialiniai Tyrimai* (Social Research), *Special Education*, *Teacher Education*

DEANS
Continuing Studies Institute: Dr LIDIJA UŠECKIENĖ
Faculty of Arts: Prof. V. JANULIS
Faculty of Education: Dr AUŠRA KAZLAUSKIENĖ
Faculty of Humanities: Prof. Dr BRONIUS MASKULIŪNAS
Faculty of Mathematics and Informatics: Dr DARIUS ŠIAUČIŪNAS
Faculty of Natural Sciences: Dr ALFREDAS LANKAUSKAS
Faculty of Social Sciences: Dr TEODORAS TAMOŠIŪNAS
Faculty of Social Welfare and Disability Studies: Dr INGRIDA BARANAUSKIENĖ
Faculty of Technology: Dr SERGĖJUS RIMOVSKIS

VILNIAUS GEDIMINO TECHNIKOS UNIVERSITETAS
(Vilnius Gediminas Technical University)

Saulėtekio al. 11, 10223 Vilnius
Telephone: (5) 274-5030
E-mail: rastine@vgtu.lt
Internet: www.vgtu.lt
Founded 1956
State control
Languages of instruction: English, Lithuanian
Academic year: September to June
Chancellor: ARŪNAS KOMKA
Rector: Prof. ALFONSAS DANIŪNAS
Vice-Rector for Int. Relations: Dr ASTA RADZEVIČIENĖ
Vice-Rector for Research: Prof. ANTANAS ČENYS
Vice-Rector for Strategic Devt: Prof. ALFREDAS LAURINAVIČIUS
Vice-Rector for Studies: Prof. ROMUALDAS KLIUKAS
Dir for Library: RIMUTĖ ABRAMČIKIENĖ
Library of 542,112 vols, 104,639 titles
Number of teachers: 930
Number of students: 13,000
Publications: *Aviation* (4 a year), *Business Management and Education* (2 a year), *Engineering Structures and Technologies* (4 a year), *Geodesy and Cartography* (4 a year), *International Journal of Strategic Property Management* (4 a year), *Journal of Business Economics and Management* (4 a year), *Journal of Civil Engineering and Management* (4 a year), *Journal of Environmental Engineering and Landscape Management* (4 a year), *Limes: Borderland Studies* (2 a year), *Mathematical Modelling and Analysis* (4 a year), *Mokslas—Lietuvos Ateitis / Science—Future of Lithuania* (6 a year), *Mokslo ir Technikos Raida / Evolution of Science and Technology* (2 a year), *Santalka: Filologija, Edukologija / Coactivity: Philology, Education*, *Santalka: Filosofija, Komunikacija / Coactivity: Philosophy, Communication* (4 a year), *Technological and Economic Development of Economy* (4 a year), *The Baltic Journal of Road and Bridge Engineering*

(4 a year), *The Journal of Architecture and Urbanism* (4 a year), *Town Planning and Architecture* (4 a year), *Transport* (4 a year), *Verslas: Teorija ir Praktika/Business: Theory and Practice* (4 a year)

DEANS

Antanas Gustaitis' Aviation Institute: Prof. Dr Hab. JONAS STANKŪNAS (Dir)
Faculty of Architecture: Prof. Dr RIMANTAS BUIVYDAS
Faculty of Business Management: Dr JELENA STANKEVIČIENĖ
Faculty of Civil Engineering: Dr ALGIRDAS JUOZAPAITIS
Faculty of Creative Industries: Prof. Dr Hab. POVILAS TAMOŠAUSKAS
Faculty of Electronics: Prof. Dr Hab. ROMA RINKEVIČIENĖ
Faculty of Environmental Engineering: Prof. Dr DONATAS ČYGAS
Faculty of Fundamental Sciences: Prof. Dr Hab. RIMANTAS BELEVIČIUS
Faculty of Mechanics: Prof. Dr Hab. ALGIRDAS VACLOVAS VALIULIS
Faculty of Transport Engineering: Dr VILIUS BARTULIS

PROFESSORS

Antanas Gustaitis' Aviation Institute (Rodūnios Kelias 30, 02187 Vilnius; tel. (5) 274-4809; e-mail avinst@vgtu.lt; internet www.agai.vgtu.lt):

PILECKAS, E.
STANKŪNAS, J.
ŽILIUKAS, A.

Faculty of Architecture (Pylimo g. 26/1, 03227 Vilnius; tel. (5) 274-5212; e-mail archdek@vgtu.lt; internet www.ar.vgtu.lt):

ANUŠKEVIČIUS, J.
BUIVYDAS, R.
ČAIKAUSKAS, G
ČEREŠKEVIČIUS, S.
DAUNORA, Z. J.
DIČIUS, V.
DINEIKA, A.
JUREVIČIENĖ, J.
PALEKAS, R.
ŠEIBOKAS, J.
STAUSKIS, V. J.
VYŠNIŪNAS, A.
ZIBERKAS, L. P.

Faculty of Business Management (Saulėtekio al. 11, 10223 Vilnius; tel. (5) 274-4888; e-mail management@vgtu.lt; internet www.vv.vgtu.lt):

BIVAINIS, J.
CHLIVICKAS, E.
DUBAUSKAS, G.
GINEVIČIUS, R.
MELNIKAS, B.
MITKUS, S.
PALIULIS, N.
RAKAUSKIENĖ, O. G.
RUTKAUSKAS, A. V.
STAŠKEVIČIUS, J.
TVARONAVIČIENĖ, M.

Faculty of Civil Engineering (Saulėtekio al. 11, 10223 Vilnius; tel. (5) 274-5239; e-mail stfdek@vgtu.lt; internet www.st.vgtu.lt):

ANDRUŠKEVIČIUS, A.
ATKOČIŪNAS, J.
ČYRAS, P.
GAILIUS, A.
JUOZULYNAS, J.
KAKLAUSKAS, A.
KAKLAUSKAS, G.
KALANTA, S.
KARKAUSKAS, R.
KVEDARAS, A.
LAUKAITIS, A.
MAČIULAITIS, R.
MARČIUKAITIS, J.
NORKUS, A.
PARASONIS, J.
RASLANAS, S.
ŠAPALAS, A.
TURSKIS, Z.
USTINOVIČIUS, L.
VADLŪGA, R.
VAIDOGAS, E.
VAINIŪNAS, P.
VALIVONIS, J.
ZAVADSKAS, E.

Faculty of Electronics (Naugarduko g. 41, 03227 Vilnius; tel. (5) 274-4753; e-mail elfdekanatas@vgtu.lt; internet www.el.vgtu.lt):

BALEVIČIUS, S.
BAŠKYS, A.
DAMBRAUSKAS, A.
GALDIKAS, A.
JANKAUSKAS, Z.
KAJACKAS, A.
KIRVAITIS, R.
KVEDARAS, V.
MARCINKEVIČIUS, A.
MARTAVIČIUS, R.
NAVAKAUSKAS, D.
NAVICKAS, R.
NICKELSON, L.
NOVICKIJ, J.
PAULIKAS, Š.
POŠKA, A.
RINKEVIČIENĖ, R.
SKUDUTIS, J.
ŠMILGEVIČIUS, A.
ŠTARAS, S.
URBANAVIČIUS, V.

Faculty of Environmental Engineering (Saulėtekio al. 11, 10223 Vilnius; tel. (5) 274-4727; e-mail apf@vgtu.lt; internet www.ap.vgtu.lt):

BALTRĖNAS, P.
BURINSKIENĖ, M.
BUTKUS, D.
ČESNA, B.
ČESNULEVIČIUS, A.
ČYGAS, D.
GINIOTIS, V.
JAKOVLEVAS-MATECKIS, K.
JANKAUSKAS, V.
JUODIS, E.
LAURINAVIČIUS, A.
LUKIANAS, A.
MARTINAITIS, V.
MATUZEVIČIUS, A.
PARŠELIŪNAS, E.
PETKEVIČIUS, K.
PETROŠKEVIČIUS, P.
ŠAKALAUSKAS, K.
ŠAULYS, V.
SKEIVALAS, J.
VAIKASAS, S.
VAITIEKŪNAS, P.
VASAREVIČIUS, S.
ZAKAREVIČIUS, A.

Faculty of Fundamental Sciences (Saulėtekio al. 11, 10223 Vilnius; tel. (5) 274-4843; e-mail fmf@vgtu.lt; internet www.fm.vgtu.lt):

ADOMĖNAS, P.
BAUŠYS, R.
BELEVIČIUS, R.
BUSILAS, A.
ČENYS, A.
ČIEGIS, R.
ČIŽAS, A.
DZEMYDA, G.
GEDVILAITĖ, A.
GIRGŽDYS, A.
JUKNA, A.
KAČIANAUSKAS, R.
KAZRAGIS, A.
KERIENĖ, J.
KIRJACKIS, E.
KLEIZA, J.
KLIUKAS, R.
KRENEVIČIUS, A.
KRYLOVAS, A.
KUBILIUS, K.
KULVIETIS, G.
KULYS, J.
LAURINAVIČIUS, V.
LEONAVIČIUS, M.
LIPEIKA, A.
MIŠKINIS, P.
MOCKUS, J.
NAVAKAUSKIENĖ, R.
PODVEZKO, V.
PRAGARAUSKAS, H.
RADAVIČIUS, M.
RUDZKIS, R.
RUTKAUSKAS, S.
ŠABLINSKAS, V.
ŠAKALAUSKAS, L.
ŠATKOVSKIS, E.
SAULIS, L.
STYRO, D.
SUNKLODAS, J.
SUŽIEDĖLIS, A.
VASILECAS, O.
ŽILINSKAS, J.
ŽURAUSKIENĖ, N.

Faculty of Mechanics (J. Basanavičiaus g. 28, 03224 Vilnius; tel. (5) 274-4745; e-mail mechanik@vgtu.lt; internet www.me.vgtu.lt):

AUGUSTAITIS, V.
KASPARAITIS, A.
MARCINKEVIČIUS, A. H.
MARIŪNAS, M.
MASKELIŪNAS, R.
SIDARAVIČIUS, D. J.
TURLA, V.
VALIULIS, A.
VASILIONKAITIS, V.
VEKTERIS, V.

Faculty of Transport Engineering (J. Basanavičiaus g. 28, 03224 Vilnius; tel. (5) 274-4797; e-mail tif@vgtu.lt; internet www.ti.vgtu.lt):

BAUBLYS, A.
BAUBLYS, J.
BOGDEVIČIUS, M.
BUTKEVIČIUS, J.
BUTKUS, A.
JARAŠŪNIENĖ, A.
LINGAITIS, L.
PALŠAITIS, R.
PIKŪNAS, A.
SIVILEVIČIUS, H.
SPRUOGIS, B.
ŽVIRBLIS, A.

VILNIAUS UNIVERSITETAS (Vilnius University)

Universiteto g. 3, 01513 Vilnius
Telephone: (5) 268-7001
E-mail: infor@cr.vu.lt
Internet: www.vu.lt

Founded 1579
State control
Language of instruction: Lithuanian
Academic year: September to June

Rector: Prof. Dr Hab. JŪRAS BANYS (acting)
Pro-Rector for Academic Affairs: Dr JUOZAS GALGINAITIS
Pro-Rector for Admin.: Dr ALEKSAS PIKTURNA
Pro-Rector for Int. Affairs: Dr RIMANTAS VAITKUS
Pro-Rector for Research: Prof. Dr Hab. JŪRAS BANYS
Dir for Library: Prof. IRENA KRIVIENĖ

Library: see under Libraries and Archives
Number of teachers: 1,351
Number of students: 22,264

Publications: *Acta Orientalia Vilnensia* (1 a year), *Acta Paedagogica Vilnensia* (2 a year), *Archaeologica Lituana* (1 a year), *Baltic Astronomy* (4 a year), *Book Science* (2 a year), *Economics* (4 a year), *Informatica* (4 a year), *Informatics in Education* (2 a year), *Information Sciences* (4 a year), *Journal of Baltic Linguistics (Baltistica)* (3 a year), *Journal of Political Sciences* (4 a year), *Law* (4 a year), *Linguistics* (2 a year), *Literature* (4 a year), *Lithuanian Foreign Policy Review* (2 a year), *Lithuanian Mathematical Journal*, *Lithuanian Political Science Yearbook* (1 a year), *Nonlinear Analysis: Modelling and Control* (4 a year), *Olympiads in Informatics*, *Organizations and Markets in Emerging Economies* (2 a year), *Problems* (2 a year), *Psychology* (2 a year), *Respectus Philologicus* (1–2 a year), *Sociology, Thought and Action* (2 a year), *STEP: Social Theory, Empirics, Policy and Practice* (2 a year), *Studies of Lithuanian History* (2 a year), *Transformation in Business and Economics* (1 a year), *Vertimo Studijos* (Translations Studies, 2 a year)

DEANS

Faculty of Chemistry: Prof. Dr Hab. AIVARAS KAREIVA
Faculty of Communication: ANDRIUS VAIŠNYS
Faculty of Economics: Dr JONAS MARTINAVIČIUS
Faculty of History: Prof. Dr RIMVYDAS PETRAUSKAS
Faculty of Humanities in Kaunas: Prof. Dr SAULIUS GUDAS
Faculty of Law: Prof. Dr TOMAS DAVULIS
Faculty of Mathematics and Informatics: Prof. GEDIMINAS STEPANAUSKAS
Faculty of Medicine: Prof. Dr ALGIRDAS UTKUS
Faculty of Natural Sciences: Prof. Dr Hab. OSVALDAS RUKŠĖNAS
Faculty of Philology: Dr ANTANAS SMETONA
Faculty of Philosophy: Dr KĘSTUTIS DUBNIKAS
Faculty of Physics: Prof. Dr VYTAUTAS BALEVIČIUS

PROFESSORS

Faculty of Chemistry (Naugarduko g. 24, 03225 Vilnius; tel. (5) 219-3103; e-mail chf@chf.vu.lt; internet www.chf.vu.lt):

ABRUTIS, A., Inorganic Chemistry
ARMALIS, S., Analytical Chemistry
BALTRŪNAS, G., Electrochemistry
BARKAUSKAS, J., Inorganic Chemistry
DAUJOTIS, V., Surface and Boundary-layer Chemistry
KAREIVA, A., Inorganic Chemistry
KAZLAUSKAS, R., Analytical Chemistry
MAKUŠKA, R., Polymer Chemistry
PADARAUSKAS, A., Analytical Chemistry
RAMANAVIČIUS, A., Biochemistry, Immunology
TAUTKUS, S., Analytical Chemistry
TUMKEVIČIUS, S., Organic Chemistry
VAINILAVIČIUS, P., Organic Chemistry

Faculty of Communication (Saulėtekio ave 9, 10222 Vilnius; tel. (5) 236-6115; e-mail info@kf.vu.lt; internet www.kf.vu.lt):

KAUNAS, D., Book History, Book Science

Faculty of Economics (Saulėtekio 9, 10222 Vilnius; tel. (5) 236-6126; e-mail ef@ef.vu.lt; internet www.ef.vu.lt):

BERŽINSKAS, G., Quality Management
GYLYS, P., Economics Theory
LAKIS, V., Audit
MACKEVIČIUS, J., Accounting and Audit
MARČINSKAS, A., Management
MARTIŠIUS, S., Econometrics
PRANULIS, V., Marketing
RUŽEVIČIUS, J., Quality Management
SIMANAUSKAS, L., Economic Informatics
VENGRAUSKAS, P. V., Research in field of Cooperative Trade
ŽEBRAUSKAS, A., Chemical Technology

Faculty of History (Universiteto g. 7, 01513 Vilnius; tel. (5) 268-7280; e-mail if@if.vu.lt; internet www.if.vu.lt):

BUMBLAUSKAS, A., Theory of History and History of Culture
BUTKUS, Z., Contemporary History since 1914
GUDAVIČIUS, E., Medieval History
LUCHTANAS, A., Archaeology
MICHELBERTAS, M., Archaeology, Numismatics
VALIKONYTĖ, J., Medieval History

Faculty of Humanities in Kaunas (Muitinės g. 8, 44280 Kaunas; tel. (37) 422-523; e-mail info@khf.vu.lt; internet www.khf.vu.lt):

ČIEGIS, R., Economics
GRONSKAS, V., Economics
POLIAKOVAS, O., Diachronic Balto-Slavic Linguistics

Faculty of Law (Saulėtekio al. 9, 10222 Vilnius; tel. (5) 236-6185; e-mail teises_fakultetas@tf.vu.lt; internet www.tf.vu.lt):

MARCIJONAS, A., Environmental Law
NEKROŠIUS, V., Civil Proceedings, Roman Law
ŠILEKIS, E., Constitutional Law
VANSEVIČIUS, S., History of Lithuanian State and Law

Faculty of Mathematics and Informatics (Naugarduko St 24, 03225 Vilnius; tel. (5) 219-3050; e-mail mif@mif.vu.lt; internet mif.vu.lt):

BAGDONAVIČIUS, V., Probability Theory and Mathematical Statistics
BIKELIS, A., Probability Theory and Mathematical Statistics
BLOZNELIS, M., Probability Theory
ČEKANAVIČIUS, V., Probability Theory and Mathematical Statistics
IVANAUSKAS, F., Numerical Analysis
KUBILIUS, J., Probabilistic Number Theory, History of Mathematics
LAURINČIKAS, A., Probabilistic Number Theory
LEIPUS, R., Probability Theory and Mathematical Statistics
MACKEVIČIUS, V., Theory of Probability
MANSTAVIČIUS, E., Probabilistic Number Theory
PAULAUSKAS, V., Theory of Probability
RAČKAUSKAS, A., Theory of Probability

Faculty of Medicine (M. K. Čiurlionio g. 21, 03101 Vilnius; tel. (5) 239-8700; e-mail mf@mf.vu.lt; internet www.mf.vu.lt):

AMBROZAITIS, A., Infectious Diseases
BALČIŪNIENĖ, I., Cardiology
BARKAUSKAS, E. V., Vascular Surgery
BAUBINAS, A., Environmental Hygiene, Paediatric Hygiene
BUBNYS, A., Surgery
ČESNYS, G., Anatomy, Anthropology
DAINYS, B., Transplantation, Urology, Nephrology
DEMBINSKAS, A., Psychiatry
DUBAKIENĖ, R., Allergology
IRNIUS, A., Gastroenterology
IVAŠKEVIČIUS, J., Anaesthesiology, Intensive Care
JANILIONIS, R., Pulmonology
KALIBATIENĖ, D., Gastroenterology, Therapy, Nursing
KALTENIS, P., Paediatrics, Paediatric Nephrology
KUČINSKAS, V., Human Genetics
KUČINSKIENĖ, Z. A., Medical Biochemistry
LAUCEVIČIUS, A., Cardiology
NOREIKA, L. A., Surgery
PARNARAUSKIENĖ, R., Neurology, Neurophysiology
PLIUŠKYS, J. A., Internal Medicine
PORVANECKAS, N., Traumatology-Orthopaedics
PRONCKUS, A., Surgery
RAMANAUSKAS, J., Pharmacology
RAUGALĖ, A., Paediatrics
SIAURUSAITIS, B. J., Paediatric Surgery
SIRVYDIS, V., Cardiac Surgery
STRUPAS, K., Surgery
TRIPONIS, V. J., Vascular Surgery
USONIS, V., Paediatric Infectology
UŽDAVINYS, G., Cardiac Surgery
VAIČEKONIS, V., Pulmonology
VALANTINAS, J., Hepatology
VALIULIS, A., Paediatric Pulmonology
VENALIS, A., Rheumatology
VITKUS, K., Reconstructive Surgery
ŽVIRONAITĖ, V., Cardiology

Faculty of Natural Sciences (M. K. Čiurlionio g. 21/27, 03101 Vilnius; tel. (5) 239-8200; e-mail gf@gf.vu.lt; internet www.gf.vu.lt):

BUKANTIS, A., Climatology
ČESNULEVIČIUS, A., Geomorphology
ČITAVIČIUS, D. J., Molecular Genetics of Microorganisms
DUNDULIS, K. J., Engineering Geology
GAIGALAS, A. J., Lithology
JANKAUSKAS, T. R., Palaeontology and Stratigraphy
JUODKA, B., Molecular Biology
JURGAITIS, A., Lithology and Mineral Deposits
KABAILIENĖ, M., Palaeontology and Stratigraphy
KAVALIAUSKAS, P., Land Management
KILKUS, K., Hydrology
KIRVELIENĖ, V., Cell Biochemistry
LAZUTKA, J. R., Human Cytogenetics
MOKRIK, R., Palaeohydrogeology, Hydrochemistry, Groundwater Formation
NAUJALIS, J. R., Botany
PODĖNAS, S., Entomology
RAKAUSKAS, R., Entomology
RANČELIS, V. P., Genetics
SLAPŠYTĖ, G., Animal Genetics
TRIMONIS, A. E., Oceanology
VALENTA, V. J., Biology
ŽAROMSKIS, R. P., Oceanology

Faculty of Philology (Universiteto g. 5, 01513 Vilnius; tel. (5) 268-7207; e-mail flf@flf.vu.lt; internet www.flf.vu.lt):

GIRDENIS, A. S., General Linguistics, Baltic Linguistics
JAKAITIENĖ, E. M., Lexicology, Semantics
KOSTIN, E., Russian Literature
KOŽENAUSKIENĖ, R., Stylistics
LASSAN, E., Syntax, Cognitive Linguistics
NASTOPKA, K. V., Literary Theory, Lithuanian Literature
NORKAITIENĖ, I. N., History of German Language, German Philology, Semantics, Semiotics
PAKERIENĖ-DAUJOTYTĖ, V., History and Philosophy of Literature
PAULAUSKIENĖ, A., Grammar
ROSINAS, A., Comparative Linguistics, History of Baltic Languages
STUNDŽIA, B., Phonetics, Phonology
TEMČINAS, S., Old Church Texts, Balto-Slavic Linguistics
ULČINAITĖ, E., Neo-Latin Literature
USONIENĖ, A., English Linguistics, Semantics, Syntax

Faculty of Philosophy (Universiteto Str. 9/1, 01513 Vilnius; tel. (5) 266-7606; e-mail fsf@fsf.vu.lt; internet www.fsf.vu.lt):

BAGDONAS, A., Developmental Psychology
DOBRYNINAS, A., Philosophy of Social Sciences, Criminology
GAILIENĖ, D., Differential and Individual Psychology
KALENDA, C., Ethics
KOČIŪNAS, R. A., Clinical Psychology
NORKUS, Z., History of Philosophy
PLEČKAITIS, R., History of Philosophy
PŠIBILSKIS, V., Political Science
ŠAULAUSKAS, M. P., Contemporary Philosophy, Theories of Social Change, Postmodern Theories
ŠLIOGERIS, M. A., Metaphysics

VAITKEVIČIUS, P. H., Applied and Experimental Psychology
VALICKAS, G., Social Psychology

Faculty of Physics (Saulėtekio ave 9, 10222 Vilnius; tel. (5) 236-6000; e-mail ff@ff.vu.lt; internet www.ff.vu.lt):

ARLAUSKAS, K., Solid State Physics, Noncrystalline Materials
BALEVIČIUS, V., Theoretical Physics, Optics, Spectroscopy
BANDZAITIS, A., Atomic Physics
BANYS, J., Solid State Physics, Ferroelectrics
DIKČIUS, G., Optics, Spectroscopy
GADONAS, R. E., Optics
GARŠKA, E., Acoustics
GAVRIUŠINAS, V., Semiconductor Physics
GRIGAS, J., Ferroelectrics and Phase Transitions
IVAŠKA, V., Electromagnetism
JARAŠIUNAS, K., Semiconductor Physics
JURŠĖNAS, S. A., Semiconductor Physics
JUŠKA, G., Solid State Physics, Noncrystalline Materials
KAŽUKAUSKAS, V., Semiconductor Physics
KIMTYS, L., Magnetic Resonance, Relaxation, Spectroscopy
MONTRIMAS, E., Semiconductor Physics, Electronics Structure
ORLIUKAS, A. F., Solid State Ionics
PALENSKIS, V., Superconductor Physics
PISKARSKAS, A., Optics
ROTOMSKIS, R., Biophysics
SAKALAUSKAS, S., Electronics and Physical Instrumentation
SIRUTKAITIS, V., Optics
SMILGEVIČIUS, V., Optics
STABINIS, A. P., Optics
STORASTA, J., Semiconductor Physics
TAMULAITIS, G., Semiconductor Physics
VAITKUS, J. V., Semiconductor Physics
VALKŪNAS, L., Clinical Physics, Biophysics
ŽILINSKAS, P. J., Metrology, Physical Instrumentation
ŽUKAUSKAS, A., Semiconductor Physics

VYTAUTO DIDŽIOJO UNIVERSITETAS (Vytautas Magnus University)

K. Donelaičio g. 58, 44248 Kaunas
Telephone: (37) 222-739
E-mail: info@vdu.lt
Internet: www.vdu.lt
Founded 1922, closed 1950, reopened 1989
State control
Languages of instruction: English, Lithuanian
Academic year: September to June
Rector: Prof. Dr ZIGMAS LYDEKA
Vice-Rector for Devt: Prof. NATALIJA MAŽEIKIENĖ
Vice-Rector for Public Communication: Prof. AUKSĖ BALČYTIENĖ
Vice-Rector for Research: Prof. JUOZAS AUGUTIS
Vice-Rector for Studies: Dr KĘSTUTIS ŠIDLAUSKAS
Dir for Library: LINA BLOVEŠČIŪNIENĖ
Library of 279,169 vols
Number of teachers: 550
Number of students: 10,000

Publications: *Agora: Politinių Komunikacijų Studijos* (Agora: Political Communication Studies), *Aukštojo Mokslo Kokybė* (The Quality of Higher Education, 1 a year), *Baltic Journal of Law & Politics* (2 a year), *Česlovo Milošo Skaitymai* (Czeslaw Milosz's Readings, 1 a year), *Culture and Society: Journal of Social Research* (2 a year), *Darbai ir Dienos* (Works and Days), *Grupės ir Aplinkos* (Groups and Environments), *Humanitariniai Mokslai Naujojoje Europoje* (Humanities in New Europe), *International Journal of Psychology: A Biopsychosocial Approach* (2 a year), *Kauno Istorijos Metraštis* (1 a year), *Laikas ir Zodis: Studentų Mokslo Darbai*, *Meno Istorija ir Kritika* (Art History and Criticism, 1 a year), *Oikos: Lietuvių Migracijos ir Diasporos Studijos* (Lithuanian Migration and Diaspora Studies, 2 a year), *Organizacijų Vadyba: Sisteminiai Tyrimai* (Management of Organizations: Systematic Research, 4 a year), *Politikos Mokslų Almanachas* (2 a year), *Profesinis Rengimas: Tyrimai ir Realijos* (Vocational Training: Research and Realities), *Sesija*, *Socialinis Darbas. Patirtis ir Metodai* (2 a year), *SOTER* (4 a year), *Taikomoji Ekonomika: Sisteminiai Tyrimai* (Applied Economics: Systematic Research, 2 a year), *Vytauto Didžiojo Universiteto Botanikos Sodo Raštai* (Scripta Horti Botanici Universitatis Vytauti Magni), *Žiniasklaidos Transformacijos* (Media Transformations)

DEANS

Faculty of Arts: INA PUKELYTĖ
Faculty of Catholic Theology: BENAS ULEVIČIUS
Faculty of Economics and Management: Prof. PRANAS ŽUKAUSKAS
Faculty of Humanities: INETA DABAŠINSKIENĖ
Faculty of Informatics: DAIVA VITKUTĖ-ADŽGAUSKIENĖ
Faculty of Law: Prof. JULIJA KIRŠIENĖ
Faculty of Natural Sciences: Prof. ALGIMANTAS PAULAUSKAS
Faculty of Political Science and Diplomacy: Prof. Dr ŠARŪNAS LIEKIS
Faculty of Social Sciences: Prof. JONAS RUŠKUS
Music Academy: SAULIUS GERULIS

PROFESSORS

Faculty of Arts:

LEVANDAUSKAS, V.
STAUSKAS, V.
VAŠKELIS, B.

Faculty of Catholic Theology:

MOTUZAS, A.
NARBEKOVAS, A.
PUZARAS, P.
ŽEMAITIS, K.

Faculty of Economics and Management:

CEPINSKIS, J.
KVEDARAVIČIUS, P.
ZAKAREVIČIUS, P.
ZUKAUSKAS, P.

Faculty of Humanities:

ALEKSANDRAVIČIUS, E.
APANAVIČIUS, R.
DONSKIS, L.
GAMZIUKAITE-MAŽIULIENĖ, R.
GENZELIS, B.
GUDAITIS, L. F.
KARALIŪNAS, S.
KERBELYTE, B.
KIAUPA, Z.
MARCINKEVICIENE, R.
SKRUPSKELYTE, V.

Faculty of Informatics:

AUGUTIS, J.
KAMINSKAS, V.
SAPAGOVAS, M.
SKUČAS, I.

Faculty of Natural Sciences:

GRAŽULEVIČIENE, R.
JUKNYS, R.
KAMUNTAVIČIUS, G.
MARUSKA, A.
MILDAŽIENE, V.
PRANEVIČIUS, L.
STRAVINSKIENE, V.

Faculty of Political Sciences and Diplomacy:

PRAZAUSKAS, A.

Faculty of Social Sciences:

GOŠTAUTAS, A.
LAUŽACKAS, R.
PUKELIS, K.
TERRESEVIČIENE, M.
VAŠTOKAS, R.

Colleges

Alytaus Kolegija (Alytus College): 17 Studentu St, 62256 Alytus; tel. (315) 79-075; e-mail rastal@akolegija.lt; internet www.akolegija.lt; f. 2000; Dir DANUTE REMEIKIENE; Deputy Dir for Academic Affairs JURGITA MERKEVIČIENĖ; Deputy Dir for Strategic Devt and Infrastructure NERIJUS CESIULIS.

Kauno Kolegija (Kaunas University of Applied Sciences): Pramones pr. 20, 50468 Kaunas; tel. (37) 352-324; e-mail rastine@go.kauko.lt; internet www.kaunokolegija.lt; f. 2000; 558 teachers; 7,600 students; Dir Dr MINDAUGAS MISIŪNAS.

Kauno Miškų ir Aplinkos Inžinerijos Kolegija (Kaunas Forestry and Environmental Engineering University of Applied Sciences): Liepu St 1, 53101 Girionys, Kaunas dist.; tel. (37) 383-082; e-mail info@kmaik.lm.lt; internet www.kmaik.lt; f. 1927, present name and status 2002; faculties of environmental engineering, forestry and landscape architecture; Dir Dr ALBINAS TEBĖRA; Deputy Dir for Academic Affairs Dr LORETA SEMAŠKIENĖ; Deputy Dir for Devt and Innovation KRISTINA BUTKIENĖ; Head of Library ZITA PETRAITYTĖ.

Kauno Technikos Kolegija (Kaunas Technical College): Tvirtovės ave 35, 50155 Kaunas; tel. (37) 308-320; e-mail ktk@ktk.lt; internet www.ktk.lt; f. 1920, present name 1990; library: 100,000 vols; Deputy Dir for Academic Affairs Dr MARIJA JOTAUTIENE; Dean of the Faculty of Civil Engineering NERIJUS VARNAS.

Klaipėdos Valstybinė Kolegija (Klaipeda State College): Jaunystes Str. 1, 91274 Klaipėda; tel. (46) 489-266; e-mail office@kvk.lt; internet www.kvk.lt; f. present name 2009; 300 teachers; 3,939 students; Dir VALERIJUS KUZNECOVAS; Dir for Academic Affairs ŠARŪNAS BERLINSKAS; Dir for Infrastructure ADOMAS MAŽEIKA; Dir for Strategic Devt NIJOLĖ GALDIKIENĖ.

Klaipėdos Verslo Aukštoji Mokykl (Klaipeda Business School): Tilzes str. 46A, 91112 Klaipėda; tel. (46) 310-214; e-mail administracija@kvam.lt; internet www.kvam.lt; f. 1997, present status 2001; study programmes in accounting, banking, business management, English, English for business communication, finance, international business, law; Dir Dr IRENA SABALIAUSKAITE; Deputy Dir for Infrastructure TENGIZ DZIBLADZE; Deputy Dir for Studies Dr RASA LEKAVICE.

Kolpingo Kolegija (Kolping University of Applied Sciences): Raguvos g. 7, 44275 Kaunas; tel. (37) 201-528; e-mail info@kolping.lt; internet kolegija.kolping.lt; f. 2001; programs of studies incl. English business language, ecotourism, finances, financial accounting in public sector, international management, social work, law; Dir LINA KALIBATAITĖ.

Lietuvos Verslo Kolegija (Lithuania Business University of Applied Sciences): Turgaus str. 21, 91246 Klaipėda; tel. (46) 311-099; e-mail vlvk@vlvk.lt; internet www.vlvk.lt; f. 1994, present status 2001; depts of economics, general subjects, informatics, management, recreation and tourism, technologies; Dir Dr ANGELĖ LILEIKIENĖ; Vice-Dir for Studies Dr GENOVAITĖ AVIŽONIENĖ; Head of Library VILMA PIPIRIENĖ.

Marijampolės Kolegija (Marijampole College): P. Armino g. 92, 68125 Marijampolė; tel. (343) 50-750; e-mail direkcija@mkolegija.lt; internet www.marko.lt; f. 2001; Dir Dr VAIDOTAS VILIŪNAS; Deputy Dir for Academic Affairs IRENA SVILIUVIENĖ; Deputy Dir for Infrastructure and Devt JONAS DOVYDĖNAS; publ. *Homo-Societas-Technologiae*.

Panevėžio Kolegija (Panevėžys College): Laisvės a. 23, 35200 Panevėžys; tel. (45) 460-322; e-mail kolegija@panko.lt; internet www.panko.lt; f. 2002; study programmes in biomedical sciences, technological sciences, social sciences, art studies; 162 teachers; 1,995 students; Dir EGIDIJUS ŽUKAUSKAS; Deputy Dir for Academic Affairs Dr RASA GLINSKIENĖ; Deputy Dir for Infrastructure Dr GEDIMINAS SARGŪNAS.

Šiaulių Valstybinė Kolegija (Šiauliai State College): Aušros al. 40, 76241 Šiauliai; tel. (41) 523-768; e-mail administracija@svako.lt; internet www.svako.lt; f. 2002; 260 teachers; 2,300 students; Prin. Dr NATALIJA SEDŽIUVIENĖ.

Šiaurės Lietuvos Kolegija (Northern Lithuania College): Tilzes str. 22, 78243 Siauliai; tel. (41) 525-100; e-mail info@slk.lt; internet www.slk.lt; f. 2002; study programmes in business management, computer network administration, economics of financial institutions, event business management, law, multimedia technologies; Dir Dr MYKOLAS DROMANTAS; Deputy Dir for Academic Affairs ŽIVILE NAKCIUNIENE; Deputy Dir for Devt DAINORA SAMCENKIENE; Librarian LAIMA JUZULENIENE.

Socialinių Mokslų Kolegija (University of Applied Social Sciences): Nemuno g. 2, 91199 Klaipėda; tel. (46) 397-077; e-mail priemimas@smk.lt; internet www.smk.lt; f. 1994, present name and status 2001; 2,000 students; Dir GABIJA SKUČAITĖ; Deputy Dir for Academic Affairs NERINGA ČEKANAVIČIENĖ; Head of Library VIRGINIJA JONIKIENĖ.

Tarptautinė Teisės ir Verslo Aukštoji Mokykla (International School of Law and Business): Laisvės pr. 58, 05120 Vilnius; tel. (5) 242-6000; e-mail info@ttvam.lt; internet www.ttvam.lt; study programmes incl. accounting, advertising management, business management, finance, law, tourism and hotel management, transport management; 300 teachers; 2,500 students; Dir Dr GITANA JURGELAITIENĖ; Deputy Dir for Academic Affairs Dr IZOLDA JOKŠIENĖ; Deputy Dir for Quality AURELIJA RUDAITIENĖ; Dean of Faculty of Management and Law LIUDMILA ZUMERIENĖ; publs *Issues of Business and Law* (online (www.ibl.ttvam.lt)), *Verslo ir teisės aktualijos / Current Issues of Business and Law* (online (www.vta.ttvam.eu)).

Utenos Kolegija (Utena University of Applied Sciences): Maironio 7 str., 28142 Utena; tel. (389) 51-662; e-mail direktorius@utenos-kolegija.lt; internet www.utenos-kolegija.lt; Rector Prof. Dr GINTAUTAS BUŽINSKAS; Deputy Rector for Academic Affairs ANTANAS PANAVAS; Deputy Rector for Science and Devt Dr VITALIJA BARTUŠEVIČIENĖ; Head of Library KRISTINA GOGELIENĖ.

V. A. Graičiūno Vadybos Mokyklos (V. A. Graičiūnas School of Management): Kęstučio g. 57A, 44303 Kaunas; tel. (37) 320-281; e-mail avm@avm.lt; internet www.avm.lt; f. 1993; campus in Vilnius; study programmes incl. business law, international business and communication, logistics business management, marketing and sales management, office management and international communication, tourism and hospitality; Dir EUGENIJA VAGNERIENĖ.

Vilniaus Dizaino Kolegija (Vilnius College of Design): Kauno g. 34, 03202 Vilnius; tel. (5) 261-1121; e-mail vdk@dizainokolegija.lt; internet www.dizainokolegija.lt; f. 1997 as Giedrė Fledžinskienė Higher School of Arts, present name and status 2005; faculties of applied photography, design for creative industries, fashion design, graphic design, interior design; 60 teachers; 500 students; Chancellor GIEDRĖ FLEDŽINSKIENĖ; Dir ALDIS FLEDŽINSKAS; Deputy Dir for Academic Affairs UGNĖ MARIJA ŠIUGŽDINYTĖ.

Vilniaus Kolegija (Vilnius University of Applied Sciences): J. Jasinskio g. 15, 01111 Vilnius; tel. (5) 219-1600; e-mail viko@viko.lt; internet www.viko.lt; f. 2000; 7,500 students; 465 teachers; Dir Dr GINTAUTAS BRAŽIŪNAS; Dir for Academic Affairs ANGELĖ GRASĖ MILEVSKIENĖ; Dir for Infrastructure VYTAUTAS LAUCIŪNAS; Dir for Finance ANA ŽILĖNIENĖ; Head of Library VIDA SUŠINSKIENĖ.

Vilniaus Kooperacijos Kolegija (Vilnius Cooperative University of Applied Sciences): Konstitucijos pr. 11, 09308 Vilnius; tel. (5) 275-0183; e-mail info@vkk.lt; internet www.vkk.lt; f. 2000; campus in Kaunas; study programmes incl. accounting, business economics, business management, catering business organization, communication management, information systems implementation and support, retail banking economics, sales management; Prin. JONAS JAKUBAUSKAS.

Vilniaus Technologijų Ir Dizaino Kolegija (Vilnius University of Applied Engineering Sciences): Antakalnio St 54, 10303 Vilnius; tel. (5) 234-1524; e-mail info@vtdko.lt; internet www.vtdko.lt; 400 teachers; 4,000 students; Dir NIJOLĖ KIKUTIENĖ; Deputy Dir for Academic Affairs ANNA LIMANOVSKAJA; Deputy Dir for Finance TATJANA VOLYNCEVA; Library Man. JŪRATĖ MALAŠAUSKIENĖ.

Vilniaus Universiteto Tarptautinio Verslo Mokykla (International Business School at Vilnius University): Sauletekio ave 22, 10225 Vilnius; tel. (5) 236-6888; e-mail info@tvm.vu.lt; internet www.tvm.vu.lt; f. 1989; Dir JULIUS NIEDVARAS; Deputy Dir for Executive Training LAIMA URBŠIENĖ; Deputy Dir for Science, Innovation and Quality Dr ERIKA VAIGINIENĖ; Deputy Dir for Studies and Int. Relations DIANA ILEVIČIENĖ; publ. *International Business: Innovations, Psychology, Economics*.

Vilniaus Verslo Kolegija (Vilnius Business College): Kalvariju str. 125, 08221 Vilnius; tel. (5) 215-4884; e-mail info@kolegija.lt; internet www.kolegija.lt; f. 1989, present name and status 2001; applied English, business management, finance, hospitality industry, media and computer games and programming and internet technology; Man. Dir JOLANTA RASTENIENĖ; Sec. JOANA SAMBORSKAJA.

Žemaitijos Kolegija (Zemaitija College): L. Ivinskio g. 5, 90311 Rietavas; tel. (448) 68-471; e-mail zemko@zemko.lt; internet www.zemko.lt; f. 2002; study programmes in business management, financial accounts, business information systems, land management and geodesy, landscape gardening and design, agricultural technologies, vehicle technical maintenance, electrical engineering, pedagogy of arts, pedagogy of music, pedagogy of dance, rural tourism, management of cultural activities, social work; Dir JONAS EUGENIJUS BAČINSKAS; Vice-Dir for Academic Activities ALMA LENGVENIENĖ; Dean of Mazeikiai Faculty MARIJA LABŽENTIENĖ; Dean of Rietavas Faculty NARŪNAS MARTINKUS; Dean of Telsiai Faculty JANINA REINIENĖ.

Other Higher Educational Institutes

Generolo Jono Žemaičio Lietuvos Karo Akademija (General Jonas Zemaitis Military Academy of Lithuania): Šilo Str. 5A, 10322 Vilnius; tel. (5) 212-6923; e-mail lka@mil.lt; internet www.lka.lt; f. 1994 as Military Academy of Lithuania, present name 1998; depts of applied sciences, engineering management, foreign languages, humanities, management, political science; military depts of tactics, combat support and physical training; Centre of Science; Military History Centre; Strategic Research Centre; library: 250,000 vols; 424 students; Commandant Col EUGENIJUS VOSYLIUS; Vice-Rector for Studies and Research Prof. Dr VALDAS RAKUTIS; Head of Library JANINA TUPENIENE; publ. *Cadet*.

ISM University of Management and Economics: E. Ozeskienes St 18, 44254 Kaunas; tel. (37) 302-405; e-mail ism@ism.lt; internet www.ism.lt; f. 1999; library: 7,518 vols; 60 teachers; 2,000 students; Pres. Dr NERIJUS PAČĖSA; Head of Library JURGITA KUNIGIŠKYTĖ; publ. *Business Training Centre News* (12 a year).

Lietuvos Aukštoji Jūreivystės Mokykla (Lithuanian Maritime Academy): I. Kanto Str. 7, 92123 Klaipėda; tel. (46) 397-240; e-mail lajm@lajm.lt; internet www.lajm.lt; f. 1948 as Klaipėda Maritime School, present name 2008; study programmes in marine navigation, marine engineering, port and shipping management, finances of port and shipping companies and maritime transport logistics technologies; Dir VIKTORAS SENČILA; Head of Libraries MARINA ŠABALOVA.

Lietuvos Muzikos ir Teatro Akademija (Lithuanian Academy of Music and Theatre): Gedimino pr. 42, 01110 Vilnius; tel. (5) 261-2691; e-mail rektoratas@lmta.lt; internet lmta.lt; f. 1933, present name 2004; library: 213,000 vols, 29,000 records; 274 teachers; 1,167 students; Rector Prof. ZBIGNEVAS IBELGAUPTAS; Vice-Rector for Art Prof. Dr RAMUNĖ MARCINKEVIČIŪTĖ; Vice-Rector for Science Dr JUDITA ŽUKIENĖ; Vice-Rector for Studies Dr VIDA UMBRASIENĖ; Head of Library EGLĖ KRIŠČIŪNAITĖ; publ. *Menotyra* (Science of Art, 1 a year).

Telšių Vyskupo Vincento Borisevičiaus Kunigų Seminarija (Bishop Vincentas Borisevicius Priest Seminary): Katedros a. 6, 87131 Telšiai; tel. (444) 60-622; e-mail seminarija@telsiai.lcn.lt; internet tks.lt; Rector VIKTORAS AČAS; Vice-Rector REMIGIJUS SAUNORIUS.

Vilniaus Dailes Akademija (Vilnius Academy of Arts): Maironio g. 6, 01124 Vilnius; tel. (5) 210-5430; e-mail vda@vda.lt; internet www.vda.lt; f. 1793; depts of architecture, art theory and history, ceramics, design, fashion design, industrial art, interior and furnishing, monumental and decorative arts, painting, printmaking, sculpture, textiles; faculties at Kaunas, Klaipėda, Vilnius; 280 teachers; 1,928 students; Rector Prof. AUDRIUS KLIMAS (acting); Pro-Rector for Arts ARVYDAS ŠALTENIS; Pro-Rector for Science Prof. ADOMAS BUTRIMAS; Pro-Rector for Strategic Devt SAULIUS VENGRIS; Pro-Rector for Studies EGLĖ GANDA BOGDANIENĖ.

Vilniaus Šv. Juozapo Kunigų Seminarija (Vilnius St. Joseph Seminary): Kalvarijų g. 325, 08420 Vilnius; tel. (5) 270-1602; e-mail rastine@vks.lcn.lt; internet www.seminarija.lt; f. 1582, reopened 1993; Rector ŽYDRŪNAS VABUOLAS; Vice-Rector ANDŽEJ ŠUŠKEVIČ; Dir for Library IRENA ALEKSANDRAVIČIENĖ.

LUXEMBOURG

The Higher Education System

In 1867 the London Congress declared Luxembourg to be an independent, sovereign state, although it remained under Dutch hegemony until 1890. The oldest existing institution of higher education is the Conservatoire de Musique de la Ville de Luxembourg (founded 1906), but the first university-level institution, the Université du Luxembourg, was not established until 2003. Prior to the foundation of the Université du Luxembourg, an Act of 1969 permitted the recognition of qualifications awarded by overseas universities in Luxembourg; one such institution is Sacred Heart University in Luxembourg (founded 1991; attached to Sacred Heart University, CT, USA). The Centre Universitaire de Luxembourg (CUL) was established in 1969, offering one-, two- or three-year courses in the humanities, sciences and law and economics, as well as training courses for lawyers and teachers, following which the students generally attended other European universities. In 2003 the CUL merged with the Institut d'Etudes Educatives et Sociales, the Institut Supérieur d'Etudes et de Recherches Pédagogiques and the Institut Supérieur de Technologie to form the Université du Luxembourg. The university operates from three campuses—Kirchberg, Limpertsberg and Walferdange—and offers a full range of degrees and postgraduate qualifications taught in French, German and English. In December 2005 the Government announced that a single site was to be developed at Belval-Ouest, near Esch-sur-Alzette, to accommodate the Université du Luxembourg, eventually regrouping the existing, dispersed faculties; the Luxembourg Centre for Systems Biomedicine opened there in 2011 and other faculties were to follow from 2014 onwards. Aside from the Université du Luxembourg, the other main higher education establishment in Luxembourg is the Institut Universitaire International, which was founded in 1974 and which focuses on vocational training (to diploma, Bachelors or Masters level and specializes in the fields of business, law and management) in collaboration with academic and economic partners from Luxembourg and other countries.

The Board of Governors decides upon the general policies and strategies of the Université du Luxembourg and controls the University's activities. The Rectorate is the executive body of the University and is assisted by the Scientific Consultancy Commission (which is primarily consulted on issues relating to the direction of research policies and educational programmes) and the University Council (which helps the Rectorate to draft a multi-annual development plan and also considers educational and scientific matters relating to the University). Each of the University's three Faculties is headed by a Dean. Higher education is overseen by the Ministry of Higher Education and Research.

The Université du Luxembourg participates in the Bologna Process to establish a European Higher Education Area, the first phase of which was to adopt a credit-based system of comparable degrees with two main cycles (undergraduate and postgraduate). The university uses European Credit Transfer and Accumulation System (ECTS) credit units and issues the Diploma Supplement free of charge and in English, French and German. The Bachelors is the primary undergraduate degree and requires three to four years of study (180–240 ECTS credits); the first postgraduate degree is the Masters, and lasts one to two years (60–120 ECTS credits); and the Doctorate is the highest university degree, lasting three to four years. Students at Bachelors level are required to spend a period studying abroad during which at least 30 ECTS credits have to be accrued. There are several non-university institutions offering a variety of two- to four-year diploma courses. In 2005/06 some 9,227 students were enrolled at university-level institutions, including 6,063 who were studying abroad. In 2010 5,376 students were enrolled in tertiary education within Luxembourg.

The Université du Luxembourg offers short-cycle courses with ECTS credit units and vocational and professional courses (in the areas of judiciary, chartered accountancy and secondary school teaching). These were previously offered by the CUL but have been adapted to Bologna standards. The programmes are generally two years in duration and result in the award of a Diplôme. Technical and vocational education also takes the form of adult and continuing programmes, and is offered by a range of institutions and agencies, including Centres of Continuing Vocational Training, the Ministry of National Education and Vocational Training, Chambers of Commerce and Trades, the Communes and Private Associations. In 2002 a new centre was established by the then Ministry of Education, Vocational Training and Sport and the Ministry of Health to cater for the demand for vocational training in the health sector.

Regulatory and Representative Bodies

GOVERNMENT

Ministry of Culture: 4 bd F. D. Roosevelt, 2450 Luxembourg; tel. 24786600; e-mail info@mc.public.lu; internet www.mc.public.lu; Minister MAGGY NAGEL.

Ministry of Higher Education and Research: 20 montée de la Pétrusse, 2327 Luxembourg; tel. 24786619; internet www.mesr.public.lu; Minister CLAUDE MEISCH.

Ministry of National Education and Vocational Training: 29 rue Aldringen, 1118 Luxembourg; tel. 24785100; e-mail info@men.lu; internet www.men.public.lu; Minister CLAUDE MEISCH.

ACCREDITATION

ENIC/NARIC Luxembourg: Min. of Higher Education and Research, 18–20 montée de la Pétrusse, 2912 Luxembourg; tel. 4785139; e-mail jean.tagliaferri@mcesr.etat.lu; internet www.cedies.public.lu; Contact Prof. JEAN TAGLIAFERRI.

Learned Societies

GENERAL

Institut Grand-Ducal: 2A rue Kalchesbruck, 1852 Luxembourg; tel. 24788640; e-mail sekretariat@igd-leo.lu; internet www.igd-leo.lu; incl. 6 sections: arts and literature, history, linguistics, ethnology and place names, medicine, moral and political sciences, natural sciences; Pres. Dr PAUL DOSTERT.

LANGUAGE AND LITERATURE

Institut Pierre Werner: Bâtiment Robert Bruch, 2e étage, 28 rue Münster, 2162 Luxembourg; tel. 490443; e-mail info@ipw.lu; internet www.ipw.lu; f. 2003 jtly by the Centre Culturel Français, Goethe-Institut (Germany) and Ministère de la Culture Luxembourgeois; named after fmr Luxembourgeois Prime Minister; promotes cultural diversity and exchange in Europe; Dir MARIO HIRSCH.

MEDICINE

Collège Médical: 7–9 ave Victor Hugo, 1750 Luxembourg; tel. 24785514; e-mail info@collegemedical.lu; internet www.collegemedical.lu; f. 1818; governmental consultative body; 12 mems; Pres. Dr PIT BUCHLER; Sec. ROGER HEFTRICH.

NATURAL SCIENCES

Biological Sciences

Société des Naturalistes Luxembourgeois (Society of Naturalists Luxembourg): BP 327, 2013 Luxembourg; e-mail info@snl.lu; internet www.snl.lu; f. 1890; promotes nature conservation and studies natural environment of Luxembourg and modifications of animal and plant communities caused by environmental changes; working groups: botany, mycology, and entomology; organizes confs and guided excursions; 385 mems; Pres. Dr CHRISTIAN RIES; Sec. YVES KRIPPEL.

Research Institutes

ECONOMICS, LAW AND POLITICS

Institut National de la Statistique et des Études Économiques: BP 304, Luxembourg 2013; 13 rue Erasme, 1468 Luxembourg; tel. 24784219; e-mail info@statec.etat.lu; internet www.statec.lu; f. 1962; attached to Min. of the Economy; library of 20,000 vols, 5,500 monographs, 15,000 periodicals; Dir SERGE ALLEGREZZA; publs *Bulletin du STATEC* (5 a year), *Cahiers Économiques* (irregular), *Conjoncture Flash* (12 a year), *Economie et Statistiques* (irregular), *Indicateurs Rapides* (15 series), *Kaléidoscope* (irregular), *Luxembourg en Chiffres* (1 a year), *Note de Conjoncture* (3 a year), *Regards* (irregular), *Répertoire des Entreprises*.

EDUCATION

Commission Grand-Ducale d'Instruction: 29 rue Aldringen, 2926 Luxembourg; tel. 4785254; f. 1843; Pres. FRANCIS JEITZ; Sec. PAUL KLEIN.

MEDICINE

Centre de Recherche Public de la Santé: 1 A-B rue Thomas Edison, 1445 Strassen; tel. 26970880; e-mail aurelia.derischebourg@crp-sante.lu; internet www.crp-sante.lu; f. 1988; applied, clinical and public health research; Pres. FRANK GANSEN; CEO JEAN-CLAUDE SCHMIT.

TECHNOLOGY

Centre de Recherche Public Henri Tudor: 29 ave John F. Kennedy, 1855 Luxembourg-Kirchberg; tel. 4259911; e-mail info@tudor.lu; internet www.tudor.lu; f. 1988; applied science; Pres. GEORGES BOURSCHEID; Dir Dr MARC LEMMER; publ. *Les Cahiers de l'Innovation* (irregular).

Libraries and Archives

Esch-sur-Alzette

Bibliothèque Municipale (Municipal Library): 26 rue Emile Mayrisch, 4240 Esch-sur-Alzette; tel. 547383; e-mail bibliotheque@villeesch.lu; internet www.esch.lu; f. 1919; English, French, German, Luxembourgish and Portuguese literature; non-fiction books, multimedia, spec. colln: Luxemburgensia; 60,000 vols; Chief Librarian HENRI LUTGEN.

Luxembourg

Archives Nationales: plateau du Saint Esprit, BP 6, 2010 Luxembourg; tel. 24786660; e-mail archives.nationales@an.etat.lu; internet www.anlux.lu; f. 19th century; 40,000 vols; Dir JOSÉE KIRPS.

Bibliothèque Nationale: 37 blvd F. D. Roosevelt, 2450 Luxembourg; tel. 2297551; e-mail info@bnl.etat.lu; internet www.bnl.lu; f. 1798, reorganized 1897, 1945, 1958, 1973, 1988 and 2010; nat. and research library open to the gen. public; 1.4m. items; Dir Dr MONIQUE KIEFFER.

Mersch

Centre National de Littérature/Lëtzebuerger Literaturarchiv (National Centre for Literature): 2 rue Emmanuel Servais, 7565 Mersch; tel. 3269551; e-mail info@literaturarchiv.lu; internet www.literaturarchiv.lu; f. 1986; spec. colln of works published in Luxembourg: Luxembourgish literatures, edits literary reference books, re-edits Luxembourgish texts, evaluates archives; 40,000 vols, 530 periodicals, author archives, posters, audiovisual items, spec. collns; Dir CLAUDE D. CONTER; Librarian CHARLOTTE ZIGER; Librarian DAPHNÉ BOEHLES; publ. *Bibliographie Courante de la Littérature Luxembourgeoise* (1 a year).

Museum

Luxembourg

Musée National d'Histoire et d'Art: Marché-aux-Poissons, 2345 Luxembourg; tel. 4793301; e-mail musee@mnha.etat.lu; internet www.mnha.public.lu; f. 1845; archaeology, fine arts, industrial and popular arts, weaponry, history of Luxembourg; library of 25,000 vols; archive of photographs dating from 1865; Dir MICHEL POLFER; publ. *L'Annuaire* (1 a year).

University

UNIVERSITÉ DU LUXEMBOURG

Limpertsberg Campus: 162A ave de la Faïencerie, 1511 Luxembourg
Kirchberg Campus: 6 rue Richard Coudenhove-Kalergi, 1359 Luxembourg
Walferdange Campus: route de Diekirch, 7220 Walferdange
Telephone: 4666445000
E-mail: seve.infos@uni.lu
Internet: www.uni.lu
Founded 1969, present name and status 2003
State control
Languages of instruction: English, French, German
Academic year: October to June
Rector: ROLF TARRACH
Vice-Rector for Academic Affairs: Prof. Dr LUCIEN KERGER
Vice-Rector for Int. Relations and Special Projects: Prof. Dr FRANCK LEPRÉVOST
Vice-Rector for Research: Prof. Dr LUCIÈNNE BLESSING
Dir for Admin.: Prof. Dr ERIC TSCHIRHART
Library Dir: MARIE-PIERRE PAUSCH
Library of 220,000 vols, 900 periodicals
Number of teachers: 350 (mostly part-time)
Number of students: 1,600
Publications: *Avis de la CNE*, *Cahiers d'Economie*, *Cahiers d'Histoire*, *Cahiers de Pédagogie*, *Cahiers de Philosophie—série A*, *Cahiers de Philosophie—série B*, *Cahiers de Physique*, *Cahiers ISIS*, *Editions Spéciales*, *English Studies*, *Etudes Classiques*, *Etudes de Biologie*, *Etudes de Géographie*, *Etudes de Philosophie*, *Etudes Romanes*, *Germanistik*, *Les Droits de l'Homme*, *Travaux de Linguistique*, *Travaux de Mathématiques*

DEANS

Faculty of Language and Literature, Humanities, Arts and Education: Prof. Dr MICHEL MARGUE
Faculty of Law, Economics and Finance: Prof. Dr ANDRÉ PRÜM (acting)
Faculty of Science, Technology and Communication: Prof. Dr PAUL HEUSCHLING

Colleges

Conservatoire de Musique d'Esch-sur-Alzette: BP 310, 4004 Esch-sur-Alzette; 50 rue d'Audun, 4218 Esch-sur-Alzette; tel. 549725; e-mail contact@conservatoire-esch.lu; internet www.esch.lu/culture/conservatoire; f. 1926 as École Municipale de Musique; present status 1969; 60 teachers; 1,000 students; Prin. Prof. FRED HARLES; publ. *Annuaire* (1 a year).

Conservatoire de Musique de la Ville de Luxembourg: 33 rue Charles Martel, 2134 Luxembourg; tel. 47965555; e-mail cml@vdl.lu; internet www.cml.lu; f. 1906; 136 teachers; 2,600 students; Dir FERNAND JUNG; publ. *Compte rendu* (1 a year).

Institut Universitaire International de Luxembourg: Château de Munsbach, 31 rue du Parc, 5374 Luxembourg; tel. 26159212; internet www.iuil.lu; f. 1974; Dir POL WAGNER.

Lycée Technique pour Professions Educatives et Sociales: rue de Bettembourg, 3378 Livange; tel. 5235251; e-mail secretariat@ltpes.lu; internet www.iees.lu; f. 2005; library: 24,000 vols; 800 students; Dir HENRY R. WELSCHBILLIG.

Sacred Heart University in Luxembourg: 7 rue Alcide de Gasperi, 2981 Luxembourg; tel. 227613; e-mail arech@shu.lu; internet www.shu.lu; f. 1991; attached to Sacred Heart Univ., Connecticut, USA; US-accredited MBA programme; 80 students; Dir Dr PETRA GARNJOST.

FORMER YUGOSLAV REPUBLIC OF MACEDONIA

The Higher Education System

After the First World War (1914–18) Vardar Macedonia, the area now known as the Former Yugoslav Republic of Macedonia (FYRM), became part of the new Kingdom of Serbs, Croats and Slovenes (formally named Yugoslavia in 1929). Following the Second World War (1939–45) Macedonia became part of the new communist-led Federative People's Republic of Yugoslavia. In 1991 the Macedonian Sobranie (Assembly) declared the republic of Macedonia to be a sovereign territory. Macedonian secession was effectively acknowledged by the Federal Republic of Yugoslavia in 1992. Univerzitet 'Sv. Kiril I Metodij' (Sts Cyril and Methodius University in Skopje—founded 1949) is the oldest of the eight universities in Macedonia; among the others are Univerzitet 'Sv. Kliment Ohridski' Bitola (St. Clement of Ohrid University of Bitola—founded 1979) and Universiteti I EJL (South-East European University—founded 2001). The last of these was established in the north-western city of Tetovo following new legislation in 2000 that permitted the use of Albanian and other languages in private tertiary institutions, and in 2004, under further amendments to legislation on higher education, it became the third state-funded university. In 2003/04 there were 46,637 students enrolled at the universities at Skopje and at Bitola. By 2010 student enrolment in tertiary education had risen to 61,764.

The Republic of Macedonia became a member of the Bologna Process in 2003 and began the introduction of the European Credit Transfer and Accumulation System (ECTS); study and subject programmes were henceforth also designed according to the principles of the three-tier (Bachelors/Masters/Doctorate) Bologna Process. A new Law on Higher Education was passed in 2008, in order to formalize the final reforms and structures needed to achieve full compliance with the Bologna Process. New Statutes were adopted by the public universities to broaden the responsibilities of the Senate and Rectors, and to allow for a University Council to be created. Furthermore, a strategy was put into place to open decentralized higher education units of dispersed studies in most towns to improve access to universities in rural areas.

Admission to higher education is on the basis of the Secondary Leaving Diploma and entrance examinations. Higher education is divided between universities/university faculties and colleges. Universities and university faculties offer three-year Bachelors degree programmes (although medical courses last longer). The first postgraduate degree is the Masters (Magister) and is a two-year research degree culminating in public defence of a thesis. The final university-level degree is the Doctorate, which takes at least three years after the Masters and requires the completion of a minimum of 180 ECTS credit units. Colleges specialize in two- to three-year diploma courses leading to a professional title.

The Board for Accreditation of Higher Education (Odbor za Akreditacija vo Vissokoto Obrazovanie) is the national body responsible for all higher education institutions. Staff are externally evaluated by the Higher Education Evaluation Agency (Agencija za evaluacija na visokoto obrazovanie). However, under the 2008 Law on Higher Education these two bodies were merged into one national Quality Assurance Agency. A National Qualifications Framework was also being established in cooperation with Tempus, the European programme charged with modernizing the higher education system in partner countries.

Regulatory and Representative Bodies

GOVERNMENT

Ministry of Culture: ul. Gjuro Gjakovik 61, 1000 Skopje; tel. (2) 324-0500; e-mail info@kultura.gov.mk; internet www.kultura.gov.mk; Minister Elizabeta Kancheska-Milevska.

Ministry of Education and Science: Mito Hadzivasilev Jasmin bb, 1000 Skopje; tel. (2) 311-7896; e-mail contact@mon.gov.mk; internet www.mon.gov.mk; Minister Abdilaqim Ademi.

ACCREDITATION

ENIC/NARIC Macedonia: Information Centre, Ministry of Education and Science, Mito Hadzivasilev Jasmin bb, 1000 Skopje; tel. (2) 311-7896; e-mail nadezda.uzelac@mofk.gov.mk; internet www.mon.gov.mk; Head of Information Centre Nadezda Uzelac.

Learned Societies

GENERAL

Makedonska Akademija na Naukite i Umetnostite (Macedonian Academy of Sciences and Arts): Blvr Krste Misirkov 2, POB 428, 1000 Skopje; tel. (2) 323-5400; e-mail manu@manu.edu.mk; internet www.manu.edu.mk; f. 1967; sections of arts, linguistics and literary sciences, mathematical and technical sciences, social sciences; 72 mems (43 ordinary, 29 foreign); library of 145,000 vols, incl. 52,000 monographs, 1,500 journals and magazines; Pres. Georgi Stardelov; Vice-Pres. Vlado Kambovski; Vice-Pres. Bojan Šoptrajanov; Sec. Ljupčo Kocarev; publs *Letopis* (1 a year), *Prilozi na Oddelenieto za biološki i medicinski nauki* (Contributions of the Dept of Biological and Medical Sciences, 2 a year), *Prilozi na Oddelenieto za lingvistika i literaturna nauka* (Contributions of the Dept of Linguistics and Literary Sciences, 2 a year), *Prilozi na Oddelenieto za matematičko-tehnički nauki* (Contributions of the Dept of Mathematical and Technical Sciences, 2 a year), *Prilozi na Oddelenieto za opštestveni nauki* (Contributions of the Dept of Social Sciences, 2 a year).

Makedonsko Naucno Drustvo—Bitola (Macedonian Scientific Association—Bitola): POB 145, 7000 Bitola; tel. (47) 222-683; e-mail mnd-bitola@t-home.mk; internet www.mnd-bitola.mk; f. 1960 as Asscn for Science and Art (ASA), present name and status 2002; scientific meetings, symposia, research; 8 depts: social sciences, law sciences, natural sciences, medical and applied sciences, technical sciences, arts, linguistics and literature, history and geography; 7 centres: training and application of safety and quality of food systems, lobbying, ethnology and folklore, applied arts, energy and ecology, public relations and journalism, applied medicine; 320 mems; library of 3,500 vols; Pres. Prof. Dr Boris Angelkov; Vice-Pres. Prof. Dr Violeta Manevska; Sec. Aleksandra Sokaroska; publ. *Prilozi* (Contributions, 2 a year).

AGRICULTURE, FISHERIES AND VETERINARY SCIENCE

Sojuz na Društvata na Veterinarnite Lekari i Tehničari na Makedonija (Union of Associations of Veterinary Surgeons and Technicians of Macedonia): Veterinaren institut, c/o Faculty of Veterinary Medicine, Lazar Pop-Trajkov 5, POB 95, 1000 Skopje; tel. (2) 324-0700; f. 1950; attached to Sts Cyril and Methodius Univ.; 450 mems; Pres. Siljan Zaharievski; Sec. Adžievski Blaže; publ. *Makedonski veterinaren pregled* (Macedonian Veterinary Review).

Združenie na Zemjodelski Inženeri na Makedonija (Association of Agricultural Engineers of Macedonia): Zemjodelski fakultet, POB 297, 1000 Skopje; tel. (2) 311-5277; f. 1994; 3,000 mems; Sec. Prof. Dragoslav Kocevski; publ. *Macedonian Agriculture Review* (1 a year).

BIBLIOGRAPHY, LIBRARY SCIENCE AND MUSEOLOGY

Bibliotekarsko Zdruzenie na Makedonija (Macedonian Library Association): c/o Narodna i univerzitetska biblioteka 'St Kliment Ohridski', Blvr Goce Delčev 6, 1000 Skopje; tel. (2) 7026-2120; e-mail bzm@bzm.org.m; internet www.bzm.org.mk; f. 1949; 500 mems; Pres. NIKOLCE VELJANOVSKI; Sec. ROZITA PETRINSKA; publ. *Bibliotekarstvo* (2 a year).

Društvo na Muzejskite Rabotnici na Makedonija (Museum Society of Macedonia): Muzej na grad Skopje, Mito Hadži-Vasilev-Jasmin bb, 1000 Skopje; f. 1951; 100 mems; Pres. KUZMAN GEORGIEVSKI; Sec. GALENA KUCULOVSKA.

Sojuz na društvata na arhivskite rabotnici na Makedonija (Union of Societies of Archivists of Macedonia): Gligor Prličev 3, POB 496, 1000 Skopje; tel. (2) 323-7211; f. 1954; 340 mems; publ. *Makedonski arhivist* (1 a year).

ECONOMICS, LAW AND POLITICS

Sojuz na Ekonomistite na Makedonija (Union of Economists of Macedonia): Ekonomiski fakultet, K. Misirkov bb, 1000 Skopje; tel. (2) 322-4311; f. 1950; 3,000 mems; Pres. Prof. Dr TAKI FITI; Sec. ACO SPASOVSKI; publ. *Stopanski pregled* (Economic Review).

FINE AND PERFORMING ARTS

Društvo na Likovnite Umetnici na Makedonija (Association of Artists of Macedonia): Makedonija str. 12, POB 438, 1000 Skopje; tel. (2) 321-1533; e-mail dlum.makedonija@hotmail.co.uk; internet www.dlum.org.mk; f. 1944; 450 mems; Pres. TANJA BALAC; Sec. BRANISLAV MIRČEVSKI.

Sojuz na Kompozitorite na Makedonija (Composers Association of Macedonia): Maksim Gorki 18, 1000 Skopje; tel. (2) 311-9824; e-mail socom@socom.com.mk; internet www.socom.com.mk; f. 1950; preserves the tradition of folk music; collects and processes folk music material; 49 mems; Pres. MARKO KOLOVSKI; Gen. Sec. LAZAR MOJSOVSKI; publ. *Informer*.

HISTORY, GEOGRAPHY AND ARCHAEOLOGY

Geografsko Društvo na R. Makedonija (Geographical Society of Macedonia): Geografski institut pri Prirodnomatematički fakultet, POB 146, 1000 Skopje; f. 1949; 600 mems; Pres. Prof. VASIL GRAMATNIKOVSKI; Sec. Asst NIKOLA PANOV; publ. geographical surveys and outlooks.

Makedonsko Arheološko Naučno Društvo (Macedonian Archaeological Research Society): Čurčiska bb, 1000 Skopje; tel. (2) 311-6044; e-mail contact@mand.org.mk; internet www.mand.org.mk; f. 1972 as Archaeological Soc. of the Republic of Macedonia; symposia, lectures, publs; 150 mems; Chair. MARINA ONCHEVSKA TODOROVSKA; Pres. IRENA KOLISTRKOSKA NASTEVA; Sec. SILVANA BLAZEVSKA; publ. *Macedoniae acta archaeologica*.

Sojuz na Istoricarite na Republika Makedonija (Association of the Historians of Republic of Macedonia): Institut za nacionalna istorija, ul. Grigor Prličev 3, POB 591, 1000 Skopje; tel. (2) 311-4078; e-mail kotlarn@yahoo.com; f. 1952; 120 mems; Pres. Dr NATASHA KOTLAR-TRAJKOVA; Sec. TEON DZINGO; Treas. DRAGAN ZAJKOVSKI; publ. *Spisanie Istorija* (History).

LANGUAGE AND LITERATURE

Alliance Française: NUUB. 'Sv. Kliment Ohridski', Leninova 39, 7000 Bitola; tel. (47) 232-363; e-mail afbitola@yahoo.fr; f. 2001; library of 400 vols; offers courses and examinations in French language and culture and promotes cultural exchange with France; Dir MARIE-CLEMENCE VATELOT.

British Council: Blvr Goce Delcev 6, POB 562, 1000 Skopje; tel. (2) 313-5035; e-mail info@britishcouncil.org.mk; internet www.britishcouncil.org/macedonia; f. 1996; offers courses and examinations in English language and British culture and promotes cultural exchange with the UK; library of 6,000 vols; Dir ANDREW HADLEY.

Društvo na Literaturnite Preveduvači na Makedonija (Society of Literary Translators of Macedonia): POB 3, 1000 Skopje; f. 1955; 102 mems; Pres. Prof. Dr STEFAN SIMOVSKI; Sec. TAŠKO ŠIRILOV.

Društvo na Pisatelite na Makedonija (Writers' Association of Macedonia): Maksim Gorki 18, 1000 Skopje; tel. (2) 322-8039; f. 1947; 269 mems; Pres. JOVAN PAVLOVSKI; Sec. PASKAL GILOVSKI; Sec. SVETLANA HRISTOVA-JOCIĆ.

Združenie na Folkloristite na Makedonija (Association of Folklorists of Macedonia): Institut za folklor, Ruzveltova 3, 1000 Skopje; tel. (2) 323-3876; f. 1952; 60 mems; Pres. GORGI SMOKVARSKI; Sec. ERMIS LAFAZANOVSKY; publ. *Narodno Stvaralaštvo* (1 or 2 a year).

MEDICINE

Farmaceutsko Društvo na Makedonija (Pharmacological Society of Macedonia): Ivo Ribar Lola MI/6, 1000 Skopje; Pres. LAZAR TOLOV; Sec. GALABA SRBINOVSKA; publ. *Bilten* (Bulletin).

Makedonsko Lekarsko Društvo (Macedonian Medical Association): Dame Gruev 3, 1000 Skopje; tel. (2) 316-2577; e-mail mld@unet.com.mk; internet www.mld.org.mk; f. 1945; promotes medical and related sciences; conserves and protects the interests of doctors; 4,490 mems; Pres. Prof. JOVAN TOFOSKI; publ. *Makedonski Medicindki Pregled*.

NATURAL SCIENCES

General

Makedonsko Ekološko Društvo (Macedonian Ecological Society): Blvd Kuzman Josifovski Pitu, 28/III-7, 1000 Skopje; tel. (2) 240-2773; e-mail contact@mes.org.mk; internet www.mes.org.mk; f. 1972; devt of ecology, promotion of environmental science and protection of environment and nature; Pres. Dr LJUPČO MELOVSKI; publ. *Macedonian Journal of Environment and Ecology* (2 a year).

Mathematical Sciences

Sojuz na Matematičari na Makedonija (Society of Mathematicians of Macedonia): Blvr Aleksandar Makedonski bb, POB 10, 1000 Skopje; tel. (2) 311-6053; e-mail vesname@iunona.pmf.ukim.edu.mk; internet www.smm.org.mk; f. 1950; Chief Officer Prof. Dr BORKO ILIEVSKI; Chief Officer Prof. Dr NIKOLA PANDESKI; publ. *Matematički Bilten* (Mathematical Bulletin).

Physical Sciences

Društvo na Fizičarite na Republika Makedonija (Society of Physicists of Macedonia): Gazi Baba bb, POB 162, 1000 Skopje; tel. (2) 324-9999; e-mail irina.petreska@pmf.ukim.edu.mk; internet www.dfrm.org; f. 1949; promotes research in physics, natural sciences and protection of environment; 159 mems; Pres. STOJAN MANOLEV; Sec. Dr IRINA PETRESKA; Treas. LIHNIDA STOJANOVSKA-GEORGIEVSKA; publs *Impuls* (jt publ. with Institute of Physics, Faculty of Natural Sciences, 2 a year), *Macedonian Physics Teacher*.

Makedonsko Geološko Društvo (Macedonian Geological Society): Geološki zavod, POB 28, 1000 Skopje; tel. (2) 323-0873; f. 1954; 300 mems; library of 20,000 vols; Pres. NIKOLA TUDŽAROV; Sec. ROZA PETROVSKA.

Research Institutes

GENERAL

Institutot za Životna Sredina i Zdravje (Institute for Environment and Health): Ilindenska nn, Campus Bldg 201.01/1, 1200 Tetovo; tel. (44) 356-114; e-mail ieh@seeu.edu.mk; internet ieh.seeu.edu.mk; f. 2005; attached to SEE Univ.; programmes in education, research, building partnerships and environmental awareness; 30 research students, 5 external research assocs.

AGRICULTURE, FISHERIES AND VETERINARY SCIENCE

Institut za Južni Zemjodelski Kulturi (Institute of Southern Crops): Goce Delčev bb, 2400 Strumica; tel. (34) 345-096; e-mail admin@isc.ukim.edu.mk; f. 1956; attached to Dept of Plant Protection, Sts Cyril and Methodius Univ.; Dir Dr SAŠA MITREV; publ. *Zbornik* (Collected Papers).

Institut za Ovoštarstvo (Institute of Pomology): Prvomajska 5, 1000 Skopje; tel. (2) 323-0557; f. 1953; attached to Sts Cyril and Methodius Univ.; fruit research; library of 3,670 vols; Dir Dr IVAN KUZMANOVSKI.

Institut za Tutun Prilep (Scientific Tobacco Institute Prilep): Kičevkso Džade, 7500 Prilep; tel. (48) 412-760; e-mail tobacco_institute_prilep@yahoo.com; internet www.tip.edu.mk; f. 1924; attached to St Clement of Orhid Univ. of Bitola; scientific research investigations, education, application and production activities in tobacco breeding; tobacco museum and meteorological station; depts of agrotechnics, chemistry of tobacco, tobacco smoke, residues from pesticides and biochemistry; economic planning and programming; genetics, selection and seed control; technology, fermentation and fabrication; library of 4,211 books, 125 titles of scientific and research publs; Pres. Dr JORDAN TRAJKOSKI; Vice-Pres. Dr VERA DIMESKA; Dir Prof. Dr KIRIL FILIPOSKI; publ. *Tutun* (Tobacco, 6 a year).

Univerzitet Sv. Kiril i Metodij Institut za Stočarstvo (Sts Cyril and Methodius University Institute of Animal Science): Bul. Ilinden br. 92, A 1000 Skopje; tel. (2) 306-5120; e-mail institut-za-stocarstvo@live.com; f. 1952; attached to Sts Cyril and Methodius Univ.; Gen. Man. Prof. Dr VASIL KOSTOV; Sec. ALEN SALIU.

Zemjodelski institut (Institute of Agriculture): Blvr Aleksandar Makedonski bb, 1000 Skopje; tel. (2) 3230-910; e-mail d.mukaetov@zeminst.edu.mk; attached to Sts Cyril and Methodius Univ.; Dir Dr DUSKO MUKAETOV; Sec. VIKTORIJA KALAJDZISKA.

ECONOMICS, LAW AND POLITICS

Ekonomski Institut—Skopje Univerzitet Sv. Kiril i Metodij (Institute of Economics—Sts Cyril and Methodius University in Skopje): Prolet 1, POB 250, 1000 Skopje; tel. (2) 311-5076; e-mail eis@ek-inst.ukim.edu.mk; internet www.ek-inst.ukim.edu.mk; f. 1952; attached to Sts Cyril and Methodius Univ.; scientific research and educational instn; offers postgraduate studies in agrobusiness, entrepreneurship, financial management, international economics, international management; organizes confs on economic issues; library of 13,861 vols, 327 internal projects and 431 periodicals; Dir Prof. Dr BILJANA ANGELOVA; Librarian SRETANKA GJORGJIEVSKA; publ. *Economic Development-Journal of the Institute of Economics* (3 a year).

HISTORY, GEOGRAPHY AND ARCHAEOLOGY

Institut za Nacionalna Istorija (Institute of National History): ul. Gligor Prličev br. 3, 1000 Skopje; tel. (2) 311-4078; e-mail inimak@on.net.mk; internet www.makedonika.org/ini; f. 1948; attached to Sts Cyril and Methodius Univ.; history of the Macedonian and Balkan peoples and ethnic communities; 56 mems; library of 27,350 vols, 37,500 periodicals, 1,300 vols of newspapers; Dir Prof. Dr NOVICA VELJANOVSKI; Sec. TATIANA DOJCINOVSKA; publ. *Glasnik* (Journal).

LANGUAGE AND LITERATURE

Institut za Folklor 'Marko Cepenkov' (Marko Cepenkov Institute of Folklore): Ruzveltova 3, POB 319, 1000 Skopje; tel. (2) 338-0176; e-mail ifmarkocepenkov@mt.net.mk; internet www.ifmc.ukim.mk; f. 1950 as Folklore Institute of the Republic, present status 1979; attached to Sts Cyril and Methodius Univ.; study of the spiritual and material culture of the Macedonian people: people's literature, ethnology, vernacular architecture, textile ornaments, traditional arts and crafts and skills; Dir Dr SEVIM PILICKOVA; Sec. TODOR ANDREEV; publ. *Makedonski folklor* (2 a year).

Institut za Makedonska Literatura (Institute of Macedonian Literature): Gligor Prlicev 5, 1000 Skopje; tel. (2) 322-0309; e-mail maclit@iml.ukim.edu.mk; internet iml.ukim.edu.mk; f. 1998; attached to Sts Cyril and Methodius Univ.; continuous and systematic research, adherence and interpretation of literature and its tradition in Macedonia; training of young personnel for scientific work; depts of contributing scientific activities—bibliography, documentation, library and informatics, medieval Macedonian literature, Macedonian folk literature, Macedonian literature of the 19th and 20th centuries, Macedonian–Balkan literary-historical relations, literatures of the nationalities in Macedonia, theory of literature and comparative literature; Dir LORETA GEORGIEVSKA-JAKOVLEVA; Sec. SARITA TRAJANOVA; Treas. VESELA KRALJEVA; publs *Spectrum* (scientific magazine), *Literary Context* (scientific publ. for comparative literature).

Institut za Makedonski Jazik 'Krste Misirkov' (Krste Misirkov Institute of Macedonian Language): Grigor Prličev 5, 1000 Skopje; tel. (2) 311-4733; e-mail kontakt@imj.ukim.edu.mk; f. 1953; attached to Sts Cyril and Methodius Univ.; depts of contemporary Macedonian, dialectology, history of the Macedonian language, Macedonian lexicology and lexicography, onomastics; Dir Dr GOCE CVETANOVSKI; Sec. MARIJA GJOSHEVA; publs *Makedonistika*, *Makedonski Jazik*, *Stari Tekstovi*.

Research Centre for Areal Linguistics: Blvr Krste Misirkov 2, 1000 Skopje; tel. (2) 323-5400; e-mail ical@manu.edu.mk; internet www.manu.edu.mk; f. 2000; attached to Macedonian Acad. of Sciences and Arts; researches the role of spatial factors in the devt and function of language; archives rare books and MSS; organizes meetings and lectures; library of 10,000 vols, spec. colln of rare books, 40 CDs, 2,000 minutes of audio material; Dir Prof. ZUZANNA TOPOLINSKA; Deputy Dir Prof. MARJAN MARKOVIC.

NATURAL SCIENCES

Institut za Zemjotresno Inženerstvo i Inženerska Seizmologija (Institute of Earthquake Engineering and Engineering Seismology): Salvador Aljende str. 73, POB 101, 1000 Skopje; tel. (2) 3107-701; e-mail garevski@pluto.iziis.ukim.edu.mk; internet www.iziis.edu.mk; f. 1965; attached to Sts Cyril and Methodius Univ.; supervises post-earthquake reconstruction, revitalization and devt of Skopje; depts of building structures and materials, dynamic testing laboratory and informatics, engineering structures, geotechnics and special structures and informatics, natural and technological hazards ecology, risk disaster management and strategic planning; Dir MIHAIL GAREVSKI; Deputy Dir GOLUBKA NECEVSKA-CVETANOVSKA.

RELIGION, SOCIOLOGY AND ANTHROPOLOGY

Institut za Sociološki i Političko-pravni Istražuvanja (Institute of Sociological, Political and Juridical Research): Blvr Partizanski odredi bb, 1000 Skopje; tel. (2) 3061-119; e-mail jakjor@isppi.ukim.edu.mk; internet www.isppi.ukim.edu.mk; f. 1965; attached to Sts Cyril and Methodius Univ.; study of sociological, political and juridical phenomena; research; collaboration with instns and orgs engaged in research in sociology, political science and law; depts of information and documentation, political science, sociology; centres for ethnic relations, management and human resource devt, public policy and public admin., criminology, crime prevention and law enforcement policy, communication, media, and culture, human rights and nat. security, strategic studies; Dir Prof. JORDE JAKIMOVSKI.

TECHNOLOGY

Geološki Zavod (Geology Institute): POB 28, 1000 Skopje; tel. (2) 230-873; f. 1944; geological mapping, exploration of mineral deposits, drilling, mining, grouting; 700 mems; library of 10,000 vols; Gen. Dir DRAGAN ANGELESKY; publ. *Trudovi*.

Research Centre for Energy, Informatics and Materials: Blvr Krste Misirkov 2, 1000 Skopje; tel. (2) 323-5400; e-mail jpj@manu.edu.mk; internet www.manu.edu.mk/icei; f. 1986; attached to Macedonian Acad. of Sciences and Arts; initiates and coordinates nat. research programmes; conducts research; divs of energy, environment, materials and neuroinformatics; Dir Acad. JORDAN POP-JORDANOV.

Zavod za Ispituvanje na Materijali i Razvoj na novi Tehnologii (Institution for Research of Materials and Development of New Technologies): Rade Koncar 16, 1000 Skopje; tel. (2) 311-6610; e-mail zimad@mt.net.mk; internet www.zim.com.mk; f. 1956, present status 2007; attached to Sts Cyril and Methodius Univ.; comprises 3 instns: Institute of Materials, Institute for Transport and Environment, Institute to Develop New Technologies; scientific research; publishing scientific achievements; Dir BORCE TANEVSKI.

Hidro Energo In'enering Skopje R. Makedonija (Hydro Energo Engineering DOO Skopje—Republic of Macedonia): Blvr Jane Sandanski 76, 1000 Skopje; tel. (2) 245-4333; e-mail hei@hei.com.mk; internet www.hei.com.mk; f. 2008; design and devt of investment and technical documentation from the fields of hydro-technical engineering, hydro-energetics, hydro-informatics and geotechnical engineering; library of 1,800 vols; Dir Ing. METODI BOEV; Man. Dr Ing. KAEVSKI IVANCO; publ. *Vodostopanski problemi* (Water Development Problems, every 5 years).

Libraries and Archives

Bitola

Nacionalna Ustanova Univerzitetska Biblioteka 'Kliment Ohridski' (National Institution University Library 'St Kliment Ohridski'): Leninova 39, 7000 Bitola; tel. (47) 220-208; e-mail nuub@nuub.mk; internet www.nuub.mk; f. 1945; 500,000 vols; Dir NAUME GORGIEVSKI; publ. *Library Trend* (1 a year).

Skopje

Biblioteka 'Braka Miladinovci' (City Library 'Braka Miladinovci'): Partizanski odredi 22, 1000 Skopje; tel. (2) 323-2544; e-mail direktor@gbiblsk.edu.mk; internet www.gbiblsk.edu.mk; f. 1945 as City Library, present name 1963; 27 brs; 800,000 vols; Pres. PETRE M. ANDREEVSKI; Dir FILIP PETROVSKI (acting).

Državen Arhiv na Republika Makedonija (State Archives of the Republic of Macedonia): Gligor Prličev 3, 1000 Skopje; tel. (2) 311-5783; e-mail arhiv@unet.com.mk; internet www.arhiv.gov.mk; f. 1951; 9 regional depts: Skopje, Bitola, Prilep, Tetovo, Shtip, Strumica, Kumanovo, Ohrid and Veles; 70m. documents; Dir Dr ZORAN TODOROVSKI; publ. *Makedonski archivist*.

Attached Departments:

Oddelenie Bitola (Department of Bitola): Blvr 1 Maj 55, 7000 Bitola; tel. (47) 241-740; f. 1954 as municipal archive, present status 1990; conservation, colln and printing of archive materials; 3,823 books, 163 magazines and 155 newspapers; Dir JOVAN KOCHANKOVSKY.

Oddelenie Kumanovo (Department of Kumanovo): Goce Delchev Str. 25, 1300 Kumanovo; tel. (31) 420-464; f. 1954; 543 archive groups and 8 archival collns; documents on economics, sociology, culture and politics.

Oddelenie Ohrid (Department of Ohrid): Nikola Karev Str. 6, 6000 Ohrid; tel. (46) 252-104; f. 1955, since 1990 as dept of Ohrid of the State Archives of the Republic of Macedonia; spec. collns: Old Church Slavonic MSS (14th–19th centuries), early Greek and Arabic books; 598 record groups and 17 archival collns; 3,000 vols; Dir DIMITAR SMILESKI.

Oddelenie Prilep (Department of Prilep): Aleksandar Makedonski Str. 134, 7500 Prilep; tel. (48) 424-192; f. 1955; jurisdiction over municipalities of Prilep, Dolneni, Krivogashtani, Krushevo, Zhitoshe, Makedonski Brod and Plasnica; 594 archive funds and 8 archival collns; Head MIHAJLO ATANASOSKI.

Oddelenie Skopje (Department of Skopje): Moskovska 1, 1000 Skopje; tel. (2) 307-6461; f. 1952; 3,000 vols, 1.5 km of archive records, 333,152 units of published information, 675 record groups and 10 archival collns, 30,000 photographs from 1928 to 1983; Dir Dr MILOŠ KONSTANTINOV; publ. *Dokumenti i materiali za istorijata na Skopje* (irregular).

Oddelenie Stip (Department of Stip): Sane Georgiev Str. 35, 2000 Stip; tel. (32) 391-337; f. 1956; jurisdiction over municipalities of Stip, Karbinci, Sveti Nikole, Lozovo, Probishtip, Kochani, Chreshinovo-Obleshevo, Zrnovci, Vinica, Delchevo,

Makedonska Kamenica, Radovish and Konche; working with 275 archive owners; 523 record groups and 22 archival collns.

Oddelenie Strumica (Department of Strumica): 27 Mart Str. 2, 2400 Strumica; tel. (34) 322-083; internet www.arhiv.gov.mk; f. 1956; jurisdiction over municipalities of Strumica, Berovo, Novo Selo, Pehchevo, Vasilevo and Bosilovo; working with 225 archive owners; 453 record groups and 8 archival collns.

Oddelenie Tetovo (Department of Tetovo): Cvetan Dimov Str. 1, 1220 Tetovo; tel. (44) 332-209; f. 1961 as Historical Archives of the Municipalities of Tetovo and Gostivar; jurisdiction over municipalities of Gostivar, Tetovo, Brvenica, Bogovinje, Zhelino, Yegunovce, Tearce, Vrapchtishte, Mavrovi Anovi-Rostushe; working with 183 archive owners; 701 record groups and archival collns; colln of documents in Old Turkish from the Casa of Tetovo (1705–1924).

Oddelenie Veles (Department of Veles): Naum Naumovski, Borche Str., 1400 Veles; tel. (43) 234-784; f. 1954 as Archiv na Veles (Archives of Veles); jurisdiction over municipalities of Veles, Chashka, Gradsko, Rosoman, Negotino, Kavadarci, Demir Kapiya, Valandovo, Gevgeliya, Bogdanci and Doyran; working with 267 archive owners; 538 record groups and 8 archival collns.

Nacionalna i univerzitetska biblioteka 'Sv. Kliment Ohridski' (St Clement of Orhid National and University Library): Blvr Goce Delčev 6, POB 566, 1000 Skopje; tel. (2) 311-5177; e-mail kliment@nubsk.edu.mk; internet www.nubsk.edu.mk; f. 1944; state copyright, central and deposit library; nat. centre for ISSN (international standard serial number) and nat. agency for ISBN (international standard book number), int. agency for ISMN (int. standard music number), centre for int. lending of library materials, ECRIS—scholars and scientific workers in European CRIS database; coordinates work of all libraries; 3m. vols, spec. collns: Slav MSS, incunabula and rare books, oriental, music, cartography, doctoral theses, fine art; Dir MILE BOSHESKI; Head of Dept VIKTORIJA KOSTOSKA; publ. *Makedonska bibliografija* (in 3 series, each 4 a year).

Museums and Art Galleries

Bitola

NU Zavod i Muzej Bitola (NI Institute and Museum Bitola): ul. Kliment Ohridski bb, 7000 Bitola; tel. (47) 233-187; e-mail muzej@muzejbt.org.mk; internet www.muzejbt.org.mk; f. 1948 as The Museum of the town of Bitola, as the Art Gallery of Bitola 1958, given status nat. instn of culture 2003; archaeology, art, ethnology, history; library of 10,000 vols; Dir IVAN JOLEVSKI.

Kratovo

Centar za Karpesta umetnost, Kratovo (Centre of Rock Art, Kratovo): Planinska 1, 1360 Kratovo; tel. (31) 481-572; e-mail lcfrockart@yahoo.com; internet www.rock-art.mk; f. 2004; protects rock engravings; exhibits artefacts and rock engravings; organizes scientific excursions, expeditions and lectures; field research; collns of engravings, 500 images, 200 photographs, 12 documentaries, written documents about St Georgi Kratovski, objects made from stones, bones, wood and pottery; handmade crafts; Pres. STEVCE DONEVSKI.

Ohrid

National Workshop for Handmade Paper 'St. Kliment Ohridski': Samoilova 60, 6000 Ohrid; tel. (46) 253-610; e-mail panevski@ohridpaper.com.mk; internet www.ohridpaper.com.mk; f. 2002; paper produced in original Chinese tradition of 2nd century BC; presents procedure of making paper, with knowledge of the history of paper and method of first printing on Gutenberg press (15th century).

Skopje

Muzej na Grad Skopje (Museum of Skopje): Mito Hadživasilev Jasmin bb, 1000 Skopje; tel. (2) 311-5367; f. 1949; 21,950 exhibits incl. 12,000 archaeological, 2,965 historical, 5,010 ethnographic and 2,965 history of art exhibits and 182 photographs; Dir JOVAN SHURBANOVSKI; Sr Curator MILOS BILBIJA.

Muzej na Makedonija (Museum of Macedonia): ul. Ćurčiska bb, 1000 Skopje; tel. (2) 311-6044; e-mail musmk@mt.net.mk; internet www.musmk.org.mk; f. 1924; anthropology, archaeology, art history and conservation, history, ethnology; exhibits folk costumes, jewellery, traditional architecture, textiles, crafts, economy, customs and traditional musical instruments, fresco replicas, icons from 14th–19th centuries; library of 19,000 vols; Dir MARY ANICIN PEJOSKA; Programme Dir PERO JOSIFOVSKI; publs *Numizmatičar* (1 a year), *Zbornik* (Collected Papers, 1 a year).

Nacionalna Ustanova Muzej na Sovremena Umetnost vo Skopje (National Institution Museum of Contemporary Art Skopje): Samoilova bb, POB 482, 1000 Skopje; tel. (2) 311-7734; e-mail msu-info@msuskopje.org.mk; internet www.msuskopje.org.mk; f. 1964, present bldg 1970; depts of collns and exhibitions, education and conservation and restoration, research and documentation; organizes exhibitions and events of Macedonian and foreign art, discussions with artists, panels, film and video presentations and lectures; library of 20,000 titles (research and documentation dept); Dir ELIZA SULEVSKA; publs *Large Glass Magazine*, catalogues and monographs and spec. edns of *Psyce*, *Playtime*, *Macedonian Critic* and *Dossier MoCA Skopje*.

Prirodonaučen muzej na Makedonija (Macedonian Museum of Natural History): Blvr Ilinden 86, 1000 Skopje; tel. (2) 311-7669; e-mail macmusnh@unet.com.mk; f. 1926; collects, studies and exhibits natural resources of Macedonia; 4,000 original exhibits on display in glass showcases and dioramas; displays fossils that date back 8m.–10m. years; library of 44,000 vols; Dir Dr SVETOZAR PETKOVSKI; Curator GUTE MLADENOOVSKI; publs *Acta*, *Fauna na Makedonija*, *Fragmenta Balcanica*.

Umetnička Galerija (Art Gallery): Kruševska 1A, POB 278, 1000 Skopje; tel. (2) 323-3904; f. 1948; modern art; Dir VIKTORIJA VASEVA-DIMESKA.

Universities

DRŽAVNIOT UNIVERZITET VO TETOVO
(State University of Tetova)

Rruga e Ilindenit pn, 1200 Tetova
Telephone: (44) 356-500
E-mail: international@unite.edu.mk
Internet: www.unite.edu.mk

Founded 1994, officially recognized as State Univ. 2004
State control
Languages of instruction: Albanian, English, Macedonian

Faculties of applied sciences, arts, business administration, economics, food technology, law, mathematics and natural sciences, medical sciences, philology, philosophy, physical education

Rector: Prof. Dr AGRON REKA

FON UNIVERZITET
(FON University)

Str. Vojvodina bb, 1000 Skopje
Telephone: (2) 244-5555
E-mail: info@fon.edu.mk
Internet: www.fon.edu.mk

Founded 2003 as Faculty of Social Studies FON
Private control

Chancellor: Prof. Dr ALEKSANDAR NIKOLOVSKI
Vice-Chancellor for Science and Technology: Prof. Dr SIME ARSENOVSKI
Vice-Chancellor for Science and Technology: Prof. Dr BAJRAM POLOZANI
Vice-Chancellor for Studies: Prof. Dr RISTO MALCESKI
Pres.: FIJAT CANOSKI
Gen. Sec.: BILJANA KAROVSKA-ANDONOVSKA

DEANS

Faculty of Applied European Languages: Prof. Dr ALEKSA POPOSKI
Faculty of Design and Multimedia: Assoc. Prof. ALEKSANDAR NOSPAL
Faculty for Detectives and Security: Prof. Dr ALEKSANDAR DONCEV
Faculty of Economics: Prof. Dr MIRKO TRIPUNOSKI
Faculty of Information and Communication Technology: Prof. Dr OLIVER ILIEV
Faculty of Law: Prof. Dr GJORGI TONOVSKI
Faculty of Politics and International Relations: Prof. Dr NANO RUZIN
Faculty of Sport and Sport Management: Prof. Dr VANGEL SIMEV

MEGUNARODEN BALKANSKI UNIVERZITET
(International Balkan University)

Tashko Karadza bb, 1000 Skopje
Telephone: (2) 321-4831
E-mail: info@ibu.edu.mk
Internet: www.ibu.edu.mk

Founded 2006
Private control
Language of instruction: English
Academic year: September to August

Rector: Prof. Dr SINASI GÜNDÜZ
Vice-Rector: Prof. Dr ABDURAUF PRUTHI
Vice-Rector: Prof. Dr LILJANA MARKOVSKA
Sec.-Gen.: VISAR RAMADANI

Library of 3,000 (2,000 English, 1,000 Turkish) reference books
Number of teachers: 40
Number of students: 504

DEANS

Faculty of Communications: Prof. Dr DONA KOLAR-PANOV
Faculty of Economics and Administrative Sciences: Asst Prof. Dr SNEZANA BILIC-SOTIROSKA
Faculty of Fine Arts: Prof. Dr LIDIJA PETKOVSKA
Faculty of Languages: Asst Prof. Dr YILDIRAY CEVIK
Faculty of Technical Sciences: Prof. Dr VERKA MESHKO

UNIVERSITETI I EJL
(South East European University)

Ilindenska bb, 1200 Tetovo
Telephone: (44) 356-000
E-mail: t.selimi@seeu.edu.mk
Internet: www.seeu.edu.mk
Founded 2001
State control
Languages of instruction: Albanian, English
Academic year: August to June
Rector: Dr ALAJDIN ABAZI
Pro-Rector for Academic Issues: Prof. Dr ZAMIR DIKA
Pro-Rector for Finance Planning and Devt: Prof. Dr ABDYLMENAF BEXHETI
Pro-Rector for Research and Quality Assurance: Prof. Dr MURTEZAN ISMAILI
Sec.-Gen: XHEVAIR MEMEDI
Library of 26,000 books, 11,350 titles
Number of teachers: 300
Number of students: 7,000

DEANS

Faculty of Business Administration: Prof. Dr IZET ZEQIRI
Faculty of Contemporary Sciences and Technologies: Dr BEKIM FETAJI (acting)
Faculty of Languages, Cultures and Communication: Prof. Dr VEBI BEXHETI
Faculty of Law: Prof. Dr ISMAIL ZENNELI
Faculty of Public Administration: Prof. Dr ETEM AZIRI
Faculty of Teacher Training: Dr TEUTA ARIFI

UNIVERZITET 'GOCE DELČEV' ŠTIP
(Goce Delcev University of Stip)

Krste Misirkov bb, POB 201, 2000 Stip
Telephone: (32) 550-000
E-mail: contact@ugd.edu.mk
Internet: www.ugd.edu.mk
Founded 2007
State control
Languages of instruction: English, Macedonian
Academic year: September to June
Rector: Prof. Dr SASA MITREV
Vice-Rector for Education: Prof. Dr EMILIJA JANEVIK IVANOVSKA
Vice-Rector for Devt, Investments and Maintenance: Asst. Prof. Dr KIRIL BARBAREEV
Vice-Rector for Science: Prof. Dr BLAZO BOEV
Sec.-Gen.: RISTO KOSTURANOV
Library of 5,000 vols
Number of teachers: 600
Number of students: 17,000

DEANS

Faculty of Agriculture: Prof. Dr ILIJA KAROV
Faculty of Computer Sciences: Prof. Dr VLADO GICEV
Faculty of Economics: Prof. Dr RISTO FOTOV
Faculty of Education: Prof. NIKOLA SMILKOV
Faculty of Electrical Engineering: Prof. Dr TATJANA ATANASOVA PACEMSKA
Faculty of Law: Prof. Dr JOVAN ANANIEV
Faculty of Mechanical Engineering: Prof. Dr DEJAN MIRAKOVSKI
Faculty of Medicine: Prof. Dr NIKOLA KAMCEV
Faculty of Music: Prof. Dr ILCO JOVANOV
Faculty of Natural and Technical Sciences: Prof. Dr ZORAN PANOV
Faculty of Philology: Prof. Dr VIOLETA DIMOVSKA
Faculty of Technology: Prof. Dr VINETA SREBRENKOSKA
Faculty of Tourism and Business Logistics: Prof. Dr NAKO TASKOV

UNIVERZITET 'SV. KIRIL I METODIJ' VO SKOPJE
(Sts Cyril and Methodius University in Skopje)

Blvr Krste Misirkov bb, 1000 Skopje
Telephone: (2) 329-3293
E-mail: ukim@ukim.edu.mk
Internet: www.ukim.edu.mk
Founded 1949
State control
Language of instruction: Macedonian
Academic year: September to May
Rector: Prof. Dr VELIMIR STOJKOVSKI
Vice-Rector for Finance, Investments and Devt: Prof. Dr PECE NEDANOVSKI
Vice-Rector for Int. Cooperation: Prof. Dr MOME SPASOVSKI
Vice-Rector for Science: Prof. Dr KOLE VASILEVSKI
Vice-Rector for Teaching: Prof. Dr ELENA DUMOVA-JOVANOSKA
Sec.-Gen.: ILIJA PIPERKOSKI
Number of teachers: 2,700
Number of students: 50,000
Publications: *Univerzitetski bilten, Univerzitetski vesnik i Studentski zbor*

DEANS

Faculty of Agricultural Sciences and Food: Prof. DRAGI DIMITRIEVSKI
Faculty of Architecture: Prof. Dr TIHOMIR STOJKOV
Faculty of Civil Engineering: Prof. Dr PETER CVETANOVSKI
Faculty of Dentistry: Prof. Dr ALEKSANDAR GRCEV
Faculty of Dramatic Arts: Prof. KIRIL RISTOSKI
Faculty of Economics: Prof. Dr LJUBOMIR KEKENOVSKI
Faculty of Education (Skopje): Prof. Dr NIKOLA PETROV
Faculty of Education (Stip): Prof. SPASKO SIMONOVSKI
Faculty of Electrical Engineering and Information Technologies: Prof. Dr MILE STANKOVSKI
Faculty of Fine Arts: Prof. DIMITAR MALIDANOV
Faculty of Forestry: Prof. Dr BRANKO RABADZISKI
Faculty of Law: Prof. Dr BORCE DAVITKOVSKI
Faculty of Mechanical Engineering: Prof. Dr ATANAS KOCOV
Faculty of Medicine: Prof. Dr NIKOLA JANKULOVSKI (acting)
Faculty of Mining and Geology: Prof. Dr TODOR DELIPETROV
Faculty of Music: Prof. Dr EVUSKA ELEZOVIC-TRPKOVA
Faculty of Natural and Mathematical Sciences: Prof. Dr DONE GERSHANOVSKI
Faculty of Pedagogy: Prof. Dr VLADO TIMOVSKI
Faculty of Pharmacy: Prof. Dr ALEKSANDAR DIMOVSKI
Faculty of Philology: Prof. Dr MAKSIM KARANFILOVSKI
Faculty of Philosophy: Prof. Dr GORAN AJDINSKI
Faculty of Physical Education: Prof. Dr GINO STREZOVSKI
Faculty of Technology and Metallurgy: Prof. Dr ALEKSANDAR DIMITROV
Faculty of Veterinary Medicine: Prof. Dr DINE MITROV

PROFESSORS

Faculty of Agricultural Sciences and Food (Blvr Aleksandar Makedonski bb, 1000 Skopje; tel. (2) 311-5277; e-mail d.dimitrievski@fznh.ukim.edu.mk; internet www.fznh.ukim.edu.mk):

ANCEV, E.
AZDERSKI, J.
BELIČOVSKI, S.
BELKOVSKI, N.
BOZINOVIK, Z.
CUKALIEV, O.
DZABIRSKI, V.
EGUMENOVSKI, P.
GICEV, A.
GORGEVSKI, G.
GOŠEVSKI, D.
HADŽI PECOVA, S.
HRISTOV, P.
ILIK-POPOVA, S.
IVANOVSKI, P.
JANKULOVSKI, D.
MARINKOVIK, L.
MARTINOVSKI, G.
MIHAJLOVSKI, M.
MITRIKESKI, J.
NAUMOVSKI, M.
PEJKOVSKI, C.
PEŠEVSKI, M.
POSTOLOVSKI, M.
SIVAKOV, L.
STOJKOVSKI, C.
TANEVSKI, D.
USALESKI, V.
VASILEVSKI, G.
VIDOJA, T.
ŽIBEROSKI, J.
ŽIVKO, D.

Faculty of Electrical Engineering and Information Technologies (Karpos II bb, 1000 Skopje; tel. (2) 306-2224; e-mail dekan@feit.ukim.edu.mk; internet www.feit.ukim.edu.mk):

ACKOVSKI, R.
ARSENOV, A.
ARSOV, D.
ARSOV, G.
ARSOV, L.
BOGDANOVA, S.
CEKREDZI, N.
CUNDEV, M.
DAVCEV, D.
FILIPOSKI, V.
FUSTIC, V.
GAVRILOVSKA, L.
GAVROVSKI, C.
GEORGIEVA, V.
GLAMOCANIN, V.
GRCEV, L.
HANDZISKI, B.
JANEV, L.
KAMILOVSKI, M.
KARADZINOV, L.
KOCAREV, L.
KOCEV, K.
KOLEMISEVSKA-GUGULOVSKA, T.
KUJUMDZIEVA-NIKOLOSKA, M.
LAZOV, P.
LOSKOVSKA, S.
MIHAJLOV, D.
MIRCEVSKI, S.
NIKOLOVSKI, L.
PANOVSKI, L.
PIPEREVSKI, B.
POPOVSKI, B.
TALESKI, R.
TENTOV, A.
ULCAR STAVROVA, T.
ZLATANOVSKI, M.

Faculty of Forestry (Blvr Aleksandar Makedonski bb, 1000 Skopje; tel. (2) 316-5777; e-mail sumarski@sf.ukim.edu.mk; internet www.sf.ukim.edu.mk):

DIMESKA, J.
DINA KOLEVSKI, D.
EFREMOVSKI, V.
MALETIKJ, V.
MANE, T.
NACEVSKA, M.
NACHESKI, S.
NIKOLOV, N.
RABADZHISKI, B.

RISTEVSKA, P.
RIZOVSKA ATANASOVSKI, J.
ROSE, A.
SIMAKOSKI, N.
TRAJKOV, P.
TRPOSKI, Z.
VASILEVSKI, K.

Faculty of Law (Blvr Krste Petkov Misirkov bb, 1000 Skopje; tel. (2) 311-7244; e-mail dekan@pf.ukim.edu.mk; internet www.pf.ukim.edu.mk):

BAJALDZIEV, D.
BELICANEC, T.
DAVITKOVSKI, B.
FRCKOSKI, L.
GAVROSKA, P.
GEORGIEVSKI, S.
GRADISKI-LAZAREVSKA, E.
IVANOV, G.
JANEVSKI, A.
KALAMATIEV, T.
KAMBOVSKI, V.
KANDIKJAN, V.
KANEVCEV, M.
KLIMOVSKI, S.
MALESKI, D.
MANOLEVA-MITROVSKA, D.
MICAJKOV, M.
MUKOSKA-CINGO, V.
PENDOVSKA, V.
PETRUSEVSKA, T.
POLENAK-AKIMOVSKA, M.
POPOVSKA, B.
SILJANOVSKA-DAVKOVA, G.
STAROVA, G.
TODOROVA, S.
TUPURKOVSKI, V.
ZIVKOVSKA, R.

Faculty of Physical Education (ul. Zeleznicka bb, 1000 Skopje; tel. (2) 311-3654; e-mail kontakt@ffk.ukim.edu.mk; internet www.ffk.ukim.edu.mk):

DZHAMBAZOVSKI, A.
IVANOV, D.
JOVANOVSKI, J.
NASTEVSKA, V.
NAUMOVSKI, A.
PETROVSKI, V.
RADIC, Z.
STREZOVSKI, G.
TUFEKCHIEVSKI, A.

UNIVERZITET 'SV. KLIMENT OHRIDSKI' BITOLA
(St Clement of Orhid University of Bitola)

Blvr 1 Maj bb, 7000 Bitola
Telephone: (47) 223-788
E-mail: rektorat@uklo.edu.mk
Internet: www.uklo.edu.mk

Founded 1979
State control
Language of instruction: Macedonian

Rector: Prof. Dr ZLATKO ZHOGLEV
Vice-Rector for Academic Affairs: SASHO ATANASOSKI
Vice-Rector for Financial Issues and Devt: LUPCO TREPEZANOVSKI
Vice-Rector for Student Affairs: PERE ASLIMOSKI
Sec.-Gen.: OFELIJA HRISTOVKSA

Library of 160,000 vols, 500 periodicals, 1,000 microforms
Number of teachers: 337
Number of students: 11,644

Publication: *Scientific Review* (1 a year)

DEANS

Faculty of Administration and Management of Information Systems: Prof. Dr VIOLETA MANEVSKA
Faculty of Economics: Prof. Dr GORDANA TRAJKOSKA
Faculty of Education: Prof. Dr JOVE DIMITRI TALEVSKI
Faculty of Law: Prof. Dr ILIJA TODOROVSKI
Faculty of Technical Sciences: Dr VESNA MIKAROVSKA

PROFESSORS

Faculty of Administration and Management of Information Systems (Partizanska bb (Kompleks Kasarni), 7000 Bitola; tel. (47) 259-921; internet famis.edu.mk):

PANOVSKA-BOSKOSKA V.

Faculty of Economics (Gorče Petrov bb, 7500 Prilep; tel. (48) 427-020; internet www.eccfp.edu.mk):

ATANASOSKI, S.
BASESCU-GJORGJIESKA, M.
DIMKOV, D.
GEORGIEVSKI, M.
ILIESKA, C.
JANESKA, M.
KOKAROSKI, D.
LASHKOSKA, V.
PECHIJARESKI, L.
RISTESKA, A.
ROCHESKA, S.
SOKOLOSKI, B.
SOTIROSKI, K.
STOJANOSKI, L.
TALESKA, S.
TRAJKOSKA, G.

Faculty of Education (ul. Vasko Karangelevski bb, 7000 Bitola; tel. (47) 253-652; e-mail contact@pfbt.uklo.edu.mk; internet www.pfbt.uklo.edu.mk):

ASLIMOVSKI, P.
GRUEVSKI, T.
KOLONDZHOVSKI, B.
METHODS, P.
RISTOVSKI, D.
SMILEVSKI, C.
STOILKOVA-KAVKALESKA, M.

Faculty of Law (ul. Prilepska bb, Bitola; tel. (47) 221-115; e-mail pfk@uklo.edu.mk; internet www.pfk.uklo.edu.mk):

TODOROVSKI, E.

Faculty of Technical Sciences (I. L. Ribar bb, 7000 Bitola; tel. (47) 207-702; e-mail info.tfb@uklo.edu.mk; internet www.tfb.edu.mk):

ANDREEVSKA, A.
BOMBOL, C.
DESKOVSKI, S.
DONEVSKI, B.
EMS, I.
GERAMITCIOSKI, T.
JOLEVSKI, T.
KANEVCE, G.
KANEVCE, L.
KRSTANOSKI, N.
MIJAKOVSKI, E.
MIKAROVSKA, V.
PANOVSKI, S.
PAVLOV, V.
POPNIKOLOVA-RADEVSKA, M.
POPOVSKI, D.
POPOVSKI, K.
STOJANOVSKA, L.
TALEVSKI, J.
TRAJKOVSKI, D.
TROMBEV, G.
ZLATKOVSKI, S.

UNIVERZIȚET ZA TURIZAM I MENADŽMENT SKOPJE
(Skopje University of Tourism and Management)

ul. Partizanski Odredi br. 99, 1000 Skopje
Telephone: (2) 309-3209
E-mail: contact@utms.edu.mk
Internet: www.utms.edu.mk

Private control

Faculties of economy, entrepreneurial business, international marketing and management, management of human resources, public relations, sport tourism, tourism

Chancellor: Prof. Dr ACE MILENKOVSKI

MADAGASCAR

The Higher Education System

In 1896 Madagascar came under French colonial rule and in 1958 it became an autonomous state (as the Malagasy Republic) within the French Community; full independence was achieved in 1960. The Université d'Antananarivo (founded 1961) is the oldest current institution of higher education; it was formed from a merger of pre-existing colleges. It was reorganized in 1976 as a decentralized institution and the six regional centres acquired the status of independent universities in 1988. The Ministry of Higher Education and Scientific Research has overall responsibility for higher education, which consists of universities, technical higher institutes, teacher training colleges and a number of private institutions (the majority of which offer professional training programmes in fields of management, engineering and agriculture leading to the award of various diplomas). In 2011 there were 52,028 students enrolled at the six public universities, 1,349 at the three technical higher institutes, 58 at the National Institute of Science and Nuclear Technology, 21,199 at private accredited higher education institutions, and a further 10,914 students were registered for university-level distance education. The old degree system was based upon the French cyclical model. However, in 2008 a new higher education system was launched in Madagascar based on the Bologna-style Licence/Masters/Doctorate (LMD) system and including the adoption of transferable credits. The new three-tier system, which was intended to harmonize the country's higher education programmes according to international standards, was scheduled to be fully implemented by the end of 2012. At the beginning of the 2013/14 academic year all higher education programmes were to be LMD compliant.

The Rector or President is the head of the University, governing in conjunction with Councils for administrative and academic affairs. The Administrative Council oversees the institutional budget, stipulates rules and regulations and ensures good governance. The Academic Council is responsible for matters of teaching and research.

The secondary school Baccalauréat is required for admission to university. The new LMD system of higher education consists of three cycles. The first cycle lasts for three years (comprising at least 180 credits) and leads to the award of the Licence degree (which is issued with a Diploma Supplement). The second-cycle postgraduate Masters degree (either professionnelle or de recherche) requires two years of study and the accumulation of another 120 credits, and the third-cycle Doctorate degree is awarded three years after the Masters and requires the defence of a thesis. All accredited higher institutions providing doctoral programmes are organized under the Consortium d'Ecoles Doctorales de Madagascar (CEDM), which was established in 2010 by the Ministry of Higher Education and Scientific Research in collaboration with the Agence Universitaire de la Francophonie. The CEDM is responsible for the coordination and development of doctoral education in Madagascar.

The main post-secondary qualification for technical and vocational education is the Brevet de Technicien Supérieur, awarded after two years' study at technical higher institutes. Three-year post-secondary courses lead to the Diplôme de Technicien Supérieur Spécialisé.

The body responsible for conducting the external evaluation of higher education providers as part of the established accreditation process is the Commission Nationale d'Habilitation (National Accreditation Commission), which replaced the Agence Nationale d'Evaluation (AGENATE, National Agency for Evaluation) in 2010. Aside from the external evaluation, each higher education institution is also required to monitor the quality of their own programmes using internal quality assurance processes.

Regulatory and Representative Bodies

GOVERNMENT

Ministry of Culture and Heritage: Antananarivo 101; e-mail ministre@mcp.gov.mg; internet www.mcp.gov.mg; Minister ELIA RAVELOMANANTSOA.

Ministry of Higher Education and Scientific Research: Antananarivo 101; internet www.mesupres.gov.mg; Minister AMETTE ETIENNE HILAIRE RAZAFINDEHIBE.

Ministry of National Education: BP 247, Anosy, Antananarivo 101; tel. (20) 22-243-08; e-mail mlraharimalala@yahoo.fr; internet www.education.gov.mg; Minister REGIS MANORO.

Ministry of Technical Education and Professional Training: BP 793, Antananarivo 101; internet www.metfp.gov.mg; Minister JEAN ANDRÉ NDREMANJARY.

NATIONAL BODY

Maison de la Communication des Universités (Universities' Communication Centre): Immeuble Ex-Super bazar Analakely, 28 rue Andrianampoinimerina, Antananarivo; tel. (20) 22-636-19; e-mail contact@mcumadagascar.org; internet enduma.africa-web.org; f. 1993; acts as an intermediary between the univs and public life; 12 mems; Pres. of Admin. Council ARMAND RASOAMIARAMANANA; Gen. Dir MICHEL NORBERT REJELA.

Learned Societies

GENERAL

Académie Nationale Malgache: BP 6217, Tsimbazaza, Antananarivo; f. 1902; studies in human and natural sciences; four sections: language, literature and arts, moral and political sciences, basic sciences, applied sciences; 140 mems, 60 foreign mems in each section; library of 100,000 vols; Pres. Dr C. RABENORO; publs *Bulletin de l'Académie* (1 a year), *Bulletin d'Information et de Liaison*, *Mémoires*.

BIBLIOGRAPHY, LIBRARY SCIENCE AND MUSEOLOGY

Association des Bibliothécaires, Documentalistes, Archivistes et Muséographes de Madagascar: Bibliothèque Nationale, BP 257, Antananarivo; tel. (20) 22-258-72; f. 1976; promotion, devt, preservation and conservation of nat. collns; Pres. CHRISTIANE ANDRIAMIRADO; Sec. SAMOELA ANDRIANKOTONIRINA; Sec. FRANÇOISE RAMANANDRAISOA; publ. *Haren-tsaina* (2 a year).

LANGUAGE AND LITERATURE

Alliance Française: Ambavamamba 101, BP 916, Antananarivo; tel. (20) 22-232-63; e-mail webmaster@alliancefr.mg; internet www.alliancefr.mg; offers courses and exams in French language and culture and promotes cultural exchange with France; attached teaching centres in Ambanja, Ambatondrazaka, Ambilobe, Ambositra, Ambovombe, Andapa, Antalaha, Antananarivo, Antsahabe, Antsalova, Antsirabé, Antsiranana, Antsohihy, Fandriana, Farafangana, Fianarantsoa, Fort Dauphin, Mahajanga, Maintirano, Manakara, Mananjary, Moramanga, Morombe, Morondava, Nosy Be, Sainte Marie, Sambava, Toamasina, Tolagnaro, Toliara, Tsiroanomandidy, and Vohemar; Dir of Operations HERVÉ LE PORZ.

British Council: see chapter on Mauritius.

Research Institutes

GENERAL

Institut de Recherche pour le Développement (IRD): BP 434, Antananarivo 101; tel. (20) 22-330-98; e-mail irdmada@ird.mg; internet www.ird.mg; research into economics, statistics, fisheries, environment, health, deforestation, biodiversity and water; see main entry under France; library of 200 vols; Dir CHRISTIAN FELLER.

AGRICULTURE, FISHERIES AND VETERINARY SCIENCE

Centre National de Recherche Appliquée au Développement Rural (CENRADERU): BP 1690, Antananarivo; internet www.fofifa.mg; f. 1994; research into agriculture, forestry and fisheries, zoology, veterinary studies and rural economy; publ. *Rapport d'Activité* (1 a year).

Département de Recherches Agronomiques de la République Malgache: Centre National de Recherche Appliquée au Développement Rural, BP 1444, Ambatobe, Antananarivo 101; tel. (20) 22-527-07; e-mail rag@fofifa.mg; internet www.fofifa.mg; stations at Alaotra, Ambanja, Ambovombe, Antalaha, Fianarantsoa, Ilaka Est, Ivoloina, Kianjasoa, Kianjavato, Mahajanga, Tanandava; Dept Chief LÉA RANDRIAMBOLANORO.

Institut d'Elevage et de Médecine Vétérinaire des Pays Tropicaux: Antananarivo; central laboratory, research stations at Kianjasoa and Miadana; see main entry under France.

HISTORY, GEOGRAPHY AND ARCHAEOLOGY

Institut Géographique et Hydrographique National (National Geographic and Hydrographic Institute): rue Dama-Ntsoha, Ambanidia, BP 323, Antananarivo 101; tel. (20) 22-229-35; e-mail ftm@moov.mg; internet www.ftm.mg; f. 1945; Dir ANDRIANJAFIMBELO RAZAFINAKANGA.

NATURAL SCIENCES

Biological Sciences

Institut Pasteur: BP 1274, Antananarivo 101; tel. (20) 22-412-72; e-mail ipm@pasteur.mg; internet www.pasteur.mg; f. 1898; biological research; library of 6,200 vols; Dir Dr MAUCLÈRE; publ. *Archives* (2 a year).

Physical Sciences

Institute and Observatory of Geophysics: Univ. of Antananarivo, POB 3843, Antananarivo 101; tel. (20) 22-301-82; f. 1889, affiliated to the Univ. 1967; study of seismology, geomagnetism, exploration geophysics, time service, remote sensing, instrumentation, meteorological and astronomical observation; library of 3,000 vols, 800 periodicals; Dir RAMBOLAMANANA GÉRARD; publs *Bulletin Magnetique* (13 a year), *Bulletin Méteorologique* (12 a year), *Bulletin Sismique* (1 a year), *Mada–Geo* (4 a year).

Service Géologique: BP 322, Antananarivo 101; tel. (20) 22-400-48; internet www.cite.mg/mine; f. 1926; library of 3,000 vols; Dir A. RANANDARIVELO; publs *Annales géologiques, Atlas des fossiles caractéristiques de Madagascar, Documentation du Service Géologique, Travaux du Bureau Géologique.*

TECHNOLOGY

Bureau de Recherches Géologiques et Minières (BRGM): BP 458, Antananarivo; see main entry under France; Dir G. BOURNAT.

Libraries and Archives

Antananarivo

Archives Nationales: BP 3384, Antananarivo; tel. (20) 22-235-34; e-mail rijandriamihamina@malagasy.com; f. 1958; historical library of 30,000 vols; Dir SAHONDRA ANDRIAMIHAMINA.

Bibliothèque Municipale: Ave Analakely, Antananarivo; f. 1961; 22,600 vols.

Bibliothèque Nationale: Anosy, BP 257, Antananarivo; tel. (20) 22-258-72; f. 1961; 236,800 books, 2,660 periodicals, 2,912 MSS, 2,600 maps; spec. collns: history, literature, the arts, applied sciences, information on Madagascar; Dir L. RALAISAHOLIMANANA; publ. *Bibliographie Nationale de Madagascar* (1 a year).

Bibliothèque Universitaire d'Antananarivo: Campus Universitaire Ambohitsaina, BP 908, Antananarivo 101; tel. (20) 22-612-28; e-mail bu@univ-antananarivo.mg; internet www.bu.univ-antananarivo.mg; f. 1960; spec. MSS colln: Madagascar and Indian Ocean; 350,452 vols; Dir JEAN-MARIE ANDRIANIAINA.

Médiathèque de l'Institut Français de Madagascar: 14 ave de l'Indépendance, BP 488, Antananarivo 101; tel. (20) 22-236-47; e-mail info@institutfrancais-madagascar.com; internet www.institutfrancais-madagascar.com; f. 1964; 32,140 vols, 35 periodicals, 418 CD-ROMs, 2,704 CDs, 4,451 video cassettes and DVDs; Dir PHILIPPE GEORGEAIS; Librarian CHRISTIANE LAROCCA.

Museums and Art Galleries

Antananarivo

Institut de Civilisations/Musée d'Art et d'Archéologie Université d'Antananarivo: Isoraka, 17 rue Dr Villette, BP 564, Antananarivo 101; tel. 2422165; e-mail musedar@gmail.com; f. 1970; attached to Institut de Civilisations; art, archaeology and social sciences; library of 2,000 vols; Dir Dr RADIMILAHY CHANTAL; publs *Taloha* (1 a year), *Travaux et Documents* (irregular).

Musée Historique et Ethnographique: Palais Andafiavaratra, rue Pasteur Ravelojaona, Antananarivo; tel. (20) 22-200-91; f. 1897; history and arts; Curator JEAN CLAUDE ANDRIANIMANANA.

Universities

UNIVERSITÉ D'ANTANANARIVO (University of Antananarivo)

Campus Universitaire Ambohitsaina, BP 566, Antananarivo 101
Telephone: (20) 22-326-39
E-mail: presidence@univ-antananarivo.mg
Internet: www.univ-antananarivo.mg
Founded 1961
State control
Language of instruction: French
Academic year: March to November
Rector: Prof. PANJA RAMANOELINA
Vice-Rector: Prof. ROGER RANDRIANJA
Vice-Rector: Prof. JOELISON RATSIRARSON
Vice-Rector: Prof. MARIE LYDIA AGNÈS RAVALISOA
Library: see under Libraries and Archives
Number of teachers: 739
Number of students: 27,000

DEANS

Agriculture: JEAN RASOARAHONA
Higher Normal School: JEAN CLAUDE OMER ANDRIANARIMANANA
Law, Economy, Gestion and Sociology: Dr DAVID OLIVANIAINA RAKOTO
Literature and Human Sciences: RICHARD RANARIVONY
Medicine: MAMY LALATIANA ANDRIAMANARIVO
Polytechnic: PHILIPPE ANDRIANARY
Sciences: MARSON RAHERIMANDIMBY

UNIVERSITÉ D'ANTSIRANANA

BP 0, Antsiranana 201
Telephone: (20) 82-92-596
E-mail: presidence@univ-antsiranana.org
Internet: www.univ-antsiranana.org
Founded 1976
State control
Academic year: January to September
Pres.: Prof. CHARLES BERNARD ANDRIANIRINA
Admin. Dir: BEBOTSY
Campus Man. Dir: FRANÇOIS MANDRAVA
Librarian: SYLVANA ROSIE RAKOTOVAO
Number of teachers: 145 (85 permanent, 60 temporary)
Number of students: 3,000

DEANS

Faculty of Arts and Humanities: JEAN LEWIS BOTOUHELY
Faculty of Science: BRIANT KALL

DIRECTORS

École Normale Supérieure pour l'Enseignement Technique: HONORÉ EUGÈNE RAKOTONDRASOA
École Supérieur Polytechnique: TEFY RAKOTOBE RAOELIVOLOLONA
Institut Supérieur en Administration d'Entreprises: RAYMONDE MARY MAHO

UNIVERSITÉ DE FIANARANTSOA

BP 1264, 301 Fianarantsoa
Telephone: (20) 7550802
E-mail: ufianara@syfed.refer.mg
Internet: www.univ-fianar.mg
Founded 1988
State control
Language of instruction: French
Academic year: November to July
Rector: MARIE DIEUDONNÉ MICHEL RAZAFINDRANDRIATSIMANIRY
Admin. and Financial Dir: DOMINIQUE RAZAFIMANAMPY
Dir of Studies and Research: RIVO RAKOTOZAFY
Librarian: BRUNO JEAN ROMUALD RANDRIAMORA
Number of teachers: 63
Number of students: 1,836

DEANS

Faculty of Law: PATRICE GOUSSOT
Faculty of Letters and Human Sciences: CLAIRE RASOMALALAVAO
Faculty of Sciences: BENJAMIN RANDRIANIRINA

UNIVERSITÉ DE MAHAJANGA

BP 652, Mahajanga 401
Telephone: (20) 62-908-34
Founded 1977
State control
Language of instruction: French
Academic year: March to October
Rector: Prof. ANTOINE ZAFERA RABESA
Registrar: DIANA VOAHANGINIRINA RAHARINIAINA
Librarian: JUSTINE RAZANAMANITRA
Library of 8,054 vols
Number of teachers: 83 full-time
Number of students: 2,129
Publication: *JSPM* (2 a year)

DEANS

Faculty of Dentistry and Stomatology: HENRI MARTIAL RANDRIANARIMANARIVO
Faculty of Medicine: LISY RAVOLAMANANA
Faculty of Natural Sciences: JOHNSON CHRISTIAN MILADERA

UNIVERSITÉ DE TOAMASINA

BP 591, Toamasina

Telephone: (20) 53-322-44

Internet: www.univ-toamasina.mg

Founded 1977 as Centre Universitaire Régional de Toamasina, present status 1988

State control

Language of instruction: French

Rector: ROGER RAJAONARIVELO

Sec.-Gen.: ANDRÉ BIAS RAMILAMANANA

Librarian: ELIANE JOSÉPHINE RENÉ

Number of teachers: 54

Number of students: 3,391

DEANS

School of Arts and Research: ABRAHAM LATSAKA

School of Economics and Management: SETH ARSÈNE RATOVOSON

UNIVERSITÉ DE TOLIARA

BP 185, Maninday, Toliara 601

Telephone: (20) 94-410-33

E-mail: presidence@univ-toliara.mg

Internet: www.univ-toliara.mg

Founded 1977 as Regional Centre of Université de Madagascar; independent university status 1988

State control

Languages of instruction: French, Malagasy

Academic year: November to July

Rector: M. THEODORET

Library of 8,000 vols

DEANS

École Normale Supérieure: JEAN RAKOTOARIVELO

Faculty of Arts and Humanities: MARC JOSEPH RAZAFINDRAKOTO

Faculty of Science: HERY ANTENAINA RAZAFIMANDIBY

Colleges

Collège Rural d'Ambatobe: BP 1629, Antananarivo; Dir M. ROGER RAJOELISOLO.

Institut National des Sciences Comptables et de l'Administration d'Entreprises: Maison des Produits, 67 Ha, BP 946, Antananarivo 101; tel. (20) 22-660-65; e-mail drinscae@simicro.mg; f. 1986; 4-year courses and in-service training in accountancy, management and banking; library: 17,230 vols, 24 periodicals; 24 teachers; 1,051 students (325 full-time, 726 in-service); Dir-Gen. VICTOR HARISON.

Institut National des Sciences et Techniques Nucléaires: BP 4279, Antananarivo 101; tel. (20) 22-355-84; f. 1976 as laboratory; institute status 1992; depts of dosimetry and radiation protection, x-ray fluorescence techniques and environment, nuclear techniques and analysis, theoretical physics, instrumentation and maintenance, computer science, renewable energies; Dir RAOELINA ANDRIAMBOLOLONA; publ. *Journal des Sciences et Techniques Nucléaires*.

Institut National des Télécommunications et des Postes: Antanetibe, Antananarivo 101; f. 1968; 200 students.

MALAWI

The Higher Education System

The former British protectorate of Nyasaland gained independence, as Malawi, in 1964 and became a republic in 1966. Higher education consists of two state universities, the University of Malawi (founded 1964) and the Mzuzu University (founded 1997 and first students admitted in 1999), and some five private tertiary education institutions with the authority to award Diplomas and Bachelors degrees. All of the private higher education institutions have been granted university status within the last 10 years or so. The medium of instruction is English. As part of its ambitious initiative to open five new institutions of higher learning by 2020 in an effort to meet growing demand, in mid-2009 the Government announced plans to start the construction of the country's third state-run institution of higher learning—a science and technology university in the capital of Lilongwe. The new university was to be funded by a large loan from the People's Republic of China. Among the other proposed new institutions were the University of Bangula in the south of the country, which would focus on cotton research and water resources management, and the University of Marine Biology, which was to be built in the district of Mangochi. It was intended that the opening of the five new higher education institutions would lead to the abolition of the controversial quota system according to which entry into university is determined by place of origin rather than merit.

The University of Malawi has a federal structure, consisting of five colleges (Domasi College of Education, Chancellor College, College of Medicine, Kamuzu College of Nursing and Malawi Polytechnic), each headed by a Principal, assisted by a Vice-Principal, Registrar and Deans of Faculty. The Head of State is the Chancellor of the University, and the Vice-Chancellor is the senior governing officer, overseeing the day-to-day running of the institution. The Chancellor is guided by the University Council, the university policy-making body. In mid-2011 Parliament approved an amendment to the 1964 University of Malawi Act allowing for the Bunda College of Agriculture to be delinked from the University of Malawi to become the Lilongwe University of Agriculture and Natural Resources. The University of Malawi had a total of 7,371 students in 2014, while 1,350 students were enrolled at Mzuzu University, 358 at the Catholic University of Malawi (founded 2004) and 148 at the University of Livingstonia (founded 2003). In addition, there was a small number of students enrolled at the Marine Training College at Monkey Bay, established in 1998. In 2009/10 a total of 10,296 students were enrolled in tertiary education. Some students attend institutions in the United Kingdom and the USA. The Ministry of Education, Science and Technology is responsible for providing higher education.

Admission to university is mainly on the basis of the Malawi School Certificate of Education (MSCE), but O-Levels and the Cambridge Overseas Higher School Certificate are also accepted. The University of Malawi requires applicants to pass the University Entrance Examination in addition to the MSCE. The colleges of the University of Malawi used to offer three-year Diploma courses, but these have now been almost completely phased out. The main undergraduate degree is the standardized four-year Bachelors, but the University of Malawi also offers a five-year Bachelors of Science and a five-year Bachelors of Medicine Bachelors of Surgery. On completion of the Bachelors, postgraduates can study for a further two years for the Masters. Postgraduate diplomas, which take one to two years, are also offered at the University of Malawi. The final university-level degree is the PhD, lasting three to four years and requiring the defence of a thesis and an oral examination.

The National Apprenticeships Scheme is the principal form of post-secondary technical and vocational education; the Scheme is regulated by the Technical, Entrepreneurial and Vocational Education and Training Authority (TEVETA, founded 1999). Programmes, entrance to which requires the MSCE, last for four years and are offered in a number of professional fields. The main qualifications are the Craft/Advanced Craft Certificate (coordinated by the Malawi National Examination Board) and the Trade Test Certificate (awarded by the Ministry of Labour). Malawi Polytechnic and technical colleges offer technician training courses to pupils who hold the MSCE; the former also offers City & Guilds qualifications. TEVETA is currently in the process of implementing a four-level National Qualifications Framework. The Malawi College of Health Sciences, functioning under the Ministry of Health, offers three-year Diploma programmes in allied health subjects, including clinical medicine, pharmacy and radiography. Holders of the nursing Diploma may undertake a further year's study leading to the University Certificate in Midwifery. There are a number of other post-secondary institutions offering vocational training in specific areas administered by various government ministries. These include Magomero College (under the Ministry of Gender, Child Development and Community Development), which provides training for social workers, the Malawi Institute of Tourism (under the Ministry of Tourism, Wildlife and Culture) and the Police Training College (under the Ministry of National Defence).

In June 2011 a bill was passed to establish a National Council for Higher Education, which was to oversee the regulation, quality assurance and accreditation of the country's universities.

Regulatory Body

GOVERNMENT

Ministry of Education, Science and Technology: Private Bag 328, Capital Hill Circle, Capital City, Lilongwe 3; tel. (1) 789422; e-mail education@education.gov.mw; Minister Dr LUCIO KANYUMBA.

Ministry of Tourism, Wildlife and Culture: Lilongwe 3; tel. (1) 772702; e-mail tourism@malawi.net; Minister MOSES KUNKUYU KALONGASHAWA.

Learned Societies

GENERAL

Society of Malawi: POB 125, Blantyre; tel. (1) 872617; e-mail societyofmalawi@africa-online.net; internet www.societyofmalawi.org; f. 1946; study and records of history and natural sciences; 250 mems; library of 3,000 vols, 2,000 periodicals, 5,000 photographs; Chair. CARL BRUESSOW; Hon. Sec. MIKE BAMFORD; publ. *Journal* (2 a year).

BIBLIOGRAPHY, LIBRARY SCIENCE AND MUSEOLOGY

Malawi Library Association: POB 429, Zomba; tel. (1) 524265; e-mail fkachala@sobomw.com; f. 1976; trains library assistants, provides professional advice, holds seminars and workshops; 340 mems; Pres. GEOFFREY F. SALANJE; Sec.-Gen. FRANCIS F. C. KACHALA; publs *MALA Bulletin* (1 a year), *MALA Trends* (every 2 years), *MALA Update*.

LANGUAGE AND LITERATURE

British Council: Plot no. 13/20 City Centre, POB 30222, Lilongwe 3; tel. (1) 773244; e-mail info@britishcouncil.org.mw; internet www.britishcouncil.org/malawi; offers courses and exams in English language and British culture and promotes cultural exchange with the UK; library of 5,991 vols; Dir MARC JESSEL.

MEDICINE

Medical Association of Malawi: Private Bag 360, Chichiri, Blantyre 3; tel. (1) 630333; f. 1967; 265 mems; 100 assoc. mems; Chair. Dr B. MWALE; Sec. Dr E. MTITIMILA; publ. *Malawi Medical Journal*.

Research Institutes

AGRICULTURE, FISHERIES AND VETERINARY SCIENCE

Agricultural Research and Extension Trust: PMB 9, Lilongwe; tel. (1) 761148; e-mail iphiri@aret.org.mw; f. 1995; attached to Tobacco Asscn of Malawi; applied research on improvement of burley, flue-cured and fire-cured tobacco in Malawi; Dir Dr IBRAHIM PHIRI; publs *Coresta Bulletin* (4 a year), *Tobacco Science*.

Baka Agricultural Research Station: POB 97, Karonga; f. 1974; attached to Min. of Agriculture and Food Security; applied research on the general agronomy of the Karonga and Chitipa regions.

Bvumbwe Agricultural Research Station: POB 5748, Limbe; tel. (1) 662206; e-mail agric-research@sdnp.org.mw; f. 1940; attached to Min. of Agriculture and Food Security; conducts applied research into tree and horticultural crops, especially tung, macadamia, cashew, vegetables, spices, coffee, mushrooms, roots and tubers, and the general agronomy of the Southern uplands; library of 1,500 vols; Deputy Dir of Agricultural Research Services T. G. CHILANGA.

Central Veterinary Laboratory: POB 527, Lilongwe; tel. (1) 766341; e-mail dahi.cvl@malawi.net; f. 1974; attached to Min. of Agriculture and Food Security; research into endemic diseases.

Chitala Agricultural Research Station: Private Bag 13, Salima; e-mail agric-research@sdnp.org.mw; f. 1978; attached to Min. of Agriculture and Food Security; part of Lakeshore Rural Development Programme; conducts research on cereals, cotton, groundnuts, mango, roots and tubers, livestock; Station Man. L. R. NTUANA.

Chitedze Agricultural Research Station: POB 158, Lilongwe; tel. (1) 773252; e-mail agri-research@sdnp.org.mw; internet dars.gov.mw; f. 1948; attached to Min. of Agriculture and Food Security; conducts applied research into cereals, grain legumes, oil seeds, pasture and the general agronomy of the Central Region and into livestock improvement, especially of local Zebu cattle; library of 10,000 vols, 300 periodicals; Head Dr P. SIBALE.

Fisheries Research Station: POB 27, Monkey Bay; tel. (1) 587249; e-mail fru2015@gmail.com; f. 1954; attached to Min. of Agriculture and Food Security; research into fisheries of Lake Malawi; socio-economic surveys; Chief Fisheries Research Officer Dr M. C. BANDRA; publs *Fisheries Bulletin* (12 a year), *Survey Reports* (4 a year), *Technical Reports* (12 a year).

Forest Research Institute of Malawi: POB 270, Zomba; govt institute; research into silviculture, tree breeding, pathology, entomology, soils, mycorrhizae and wood products.

Kasinthula Agricultural Research Station: POB 28, Chikwawa; tel. (1) 423207; e-mail agric-research@sdnp.org.mw; f. 1976; attached to Min. of Agriculture and Food Security; irrigation research; Officer in Charge JULIAN W. MCHOWA.

Lifuwu Agricultural Research Station: POB 102, Salima; tel. (26) 5829661; e-mail lifuwu@malawi.net; f. 1973; attached to Dept of Agricultural Research Services; rice research; Asst Dir T. R. MZENGEZA.

Lunyangwa Agricultural Research Station: POB 59, Mzuzu; tel. (1) 312962; e-mail lunyangwa@sdnp.org.mw; f. 1968; attached to Min. of Agriculture and Food Security; research on livestock, pasture, coffee, root and tuber crops; conducts applied research into the general agronomy of the N Region; Head Dr ALLAN CHILIMBA.

Makoka Agricultural Research Station: Private Bag 3, Thondwe; tel. (881) 198635; e-mail entomology@broadbandmw.com; f. 1967; research into cotton, cassava, sweet potato, maize, groundnuts, soya beans, pigeon peas, cowpeas, sunflowers, sorghum and rice; agroforestry species and domestication of wild fruits; library of 1,600 vols; Head KETULO SALIPIRA; Deputy Head ROSE MKANDAWIRE; publs *Makoka Agricultural Research Station*, *Malawi Journal of Agricultural Sciences*, *Report*.

Mbawa Agricultural Research Station: POB 8, Embangweni; tel. (1) 342362; e-mail agric-research@sdnp.org.mw; internet www.agricresearch.gov.mw; f. 1936; attached to Dept of Agricultural Research Services, Min. of Agriculture and Food Security; applied research into livestock, cereals, grain legumes and technology transfer initiatives; publs *Quarterly Report*, *Station Guide* (1 a year).

Mikolongwe Livestock Improvement Centre: POB 5193, Limbe; f. 1955; attached to Min. of Agriculture and Food Security; seeks to improve productive capacity of local Zebu cattle and fat-tailed sheep; the station also contains the Poultry Improvement Unit and the Veterinary Staff training school.

Mwimba Tobacco Research Station: POB 224, Kasungu; f. 1979; attached to Min. of Agriculture and Food Security; applied research on improvement and production of flue-cured and oriental tobacco in Malawi.

Tea Research Foundation (Central Africa): POB 51, Mulanje; tel. (1) 467277; e-mail trfca@africa-online.net; f. 1966; conducts research on the genetic improvement of tea and associated agronomic research and training for the tea industry in southern Africa; Dir Dr A. S. KUMWENDA.

NATURAL SCIENCES

Physical Sciences

Geological Survey of Malawi: POB 27, Zomba; tel. (1) 524166; e-mail gsdmalawi2012@gmail.com; f. 1921; attached to Min. of Mining; geological mapping and surveys; mineral investigation, engineering, geology, geophysics, drilling, seismology; library of 10,000 vols; Deputy Dir J. W. SALIMA.

Libraries and Archives

Lilongwe

Malawi National Library Service: POB 30314, Lilongwe 3; tel. (1) 773700; e-mail gnyali@nlsmw.org; f. 1968; provides public library services; publishes children's books; 1,000,000 vols; Nat. Librarian G. L. NYALI; publ. *Accessions Bulletin*.

Zomba

National Archives of Malawi: Mkulichi Rd, POB 62, Zomba; tel. (1) 525240; e-mail archives@sdnp.org.mw; internet chambo.sdnp.org.mw/ruleoflaw/archives; f. 1947 as br. of Central African Archives, current name adopted 1964; public archives, records management, historical MSS, legal deposit library, films, tapes, microfilms, gramophone records, philatelic colln, maps, and plans; nat. ISBN agency; 30,000 vols, 240 periodicals; Dir PAUL LIHOMA; Librarian STANLEY S. GONDWE; publ. *Malawi National Bibliography* (1 a year).

University of Malawi Chancellor College Library: POB 280, Zomba; tel. (1) 524222; e-mail dbvphiri@cc.ac.mw; f. 1965; 475,000 vols; Librarian D. B. VUWA PHIRI.

Museums

Blantyre

Museums of Malawi: POB 30360, Chichiri, Blantyre 3; tel. (1) 672438; e-mail museums@malawi.net; f. 1959; Dir of Museums Dr M. E. D. NHLANE.

Universities

UNIVERSITY OF MALAWI

POB 278, Zomba
Telephone: (1) 524282
E-mail: uniregistrar@usdnp.org.mw
Internet: www.unima.mw
Founded 1964
Language of instruction: English
State control
Academic year: June to September
Number of teachers: 710
Number of students: 7,371
Chancellor: THE PRES. OF MALAWI
Vice-Chancellor: Dr E. FABIANO
Registrar: BEN WOKOMAATANI MALUNGA
Librarian: F. G. HOUSE (acting)
Publications: *Journal of Humanities*, *Journal of Social Science*, *Malawi Journal of Science and Technology*, *Research Report to Senate*.

CONSTITUENT INSTITUTES

Bunda College of Agriculture: POB 219, Lilongwe; tel. (1) 277226; library of 50,000 vols; 131 teachers; 681 students; Prin. Prof. M. B. KWAPATE; Registrar M. CHIMOYO.

Chancellor College: POB 280, Zomba; tel. (1) 524222; library of 300,000 vols; 250 teachers; 1,812 students; Prin. Prof. C KUMLONGERA; Registrar U JEDEGWA.

College of Medicine: Private Bag 360, Chichiri, Blantyre 3; tel. (1) 871911; e-mail registrar@medcol.mw; internet www.medcol.mw; library of 18,000 vols; 135 teachers; 1,067 students; Prin. Assoc. Prof. KENNETH MALETA; Registrar CHIFUNDO TRIGU-LEMANI; publ. *Malawi Medical Journal*.

Kamuzu College of Nursing: PB 1, Lilongwe; tel. (1) 751622; library of 24,000 vols; 66 teachers; 300 students; Prin. Dr ADDRESS MALUTA; Registrar MARY WASIN.

Malawi Polytechnic: PB 303, Chichiri, Blantyre 3; tel. (1) 670411; library of 38,745 vols; 176 teachers; 2,549 students; Prin. Y. A. ALIDE (acting); Registrar A. KUMWENDA

MZUZU UNIVERSITY

Private Bag 201, Luwinga, Mzuzu 2
Telephone: (1) 320575
E-mail: registrar@mzuni.ac.mw

Founded 1999
State control

Chancellor: THE PRES. OF MALAWI
Vice-Chancellor: Prof. LANDSON MHANGO
Deputy Vice-Chancellor: Prof. ORTON MSISKA
Registrar: REGINALD MUSHANI
Librarian: Prof. JOSEPH UTA

Library of 27,000 vols, 250 periodicals
Number of teachers: 132
Number of students: 1,350

DEANS

Faculty of Education: GOLDEN MSILIMBA

Faculty of Environmental Sciences: JARRET MHANGO

Faculty of Information Science and Communication: Prof. JOSEPH J. UTA

Faculty of Health Sciences: Prof. YOHANE NYASULU

Faculty of Tourism and Hospitality Management: BRIGHT M.C. NYIRENDA

MALAYSIA

The Higher Education System

The country's oldest existing institution of higher education is Universiti Teknologi Malaysia (Malaysia University of Technology), Johor, which was founded in 1904 (current name and status 1972) when Johor was still an independent Malay state (it came under British control in 1914). The next oldest institution is Universiti Pendidikan Sultan Idris (Sultan Idris Education University—founded 1922). Malaya was granted independence, within the Commonwealth, in 1957 and Malaysia was established in 1963, through the union of the independent Federation of Malaya (renamed the States of Malaya), Singapore, and the former British colonies of Sarawak and Sabah. Subsequently, Singapore left the federation and the States of Malaya were styled Peninsular Malaysia. In October 1994, in an attempt to improve standards and to reduce the cost of sending Malaysian students abroad to study, the Government introduced a bill that would allow foreign universities to establish branch campuses in Malaysia. From the end of that year the Government permitted the use of English as a medium of instruction in science and engineering subjects at tertiary level. In 1998 the Government's incorporation of higher education gave greater powers of autonomy to the universities, which are each governed by an executive body (Board of Governors) and academic council (Senate). At the seventh ASEAN summit meeting in November 2001 it was decided that the town of Bandar Nusajaya in Johor would be the location for the first ASEAN university. It would be Malaysia's second international university. In 2009 there were 1,000,694 students enrolled in tertiary education; by 2011 the total number of students enrolled in private institutions alone was more than 541,000. In 2012 there were 20 public universities, 33 private universities and university colleges, and four foreign university branch campuses. Responsibility for the provision of higher education in Malaysia rests with the Ministry of Higher Education. Legislation covering the higher education sector includes: the Universities and University Colleges Act (1971), which lays down the regulations for the establishment and management of public universities and university colleges; the Education Act (1996), which relates to the establishment and management of community colleges and polytechnic institutions; the Private Higher Education Institutions Act (1996), which deals with the registration, regulation and quality control of private higher education institutions; and the National Council on Higher Education Act (1996), which led to the creation of a National Council to formulate education policies and assist in developing the higher education sector. The language of instruction in public institutions of higher education is primarily Malaysian, while private establishments use mainly English. Both public and private higher education institutions charge tuition fees in Malaysia, although the fees at public institutions are generally much lower than at their private counterparts.

The main criteria for admission to higher education are the Malaysia Higher Certificate of Education (Sijil Tinggi Persekolahan Malaysia) and Matriculation Certificate. Applications are made through the central Bahagian Pengurusan Kemasukan Pelajaran (Division of Student Admission—formerly known as the Unit Pusat Universiti). The Malaysian University English Test, which was first launched in 1999 and is administered by the Malaysian Examinations Council (Majlis Peperiksaan Malaysia), is a test to measure a prospective student's English language proficiency for access to tertiary education. This test is mandatory to gain entry to Bachelors programmes at all public universities. Racial quotas, a highly politicized and controversial issue in Malaysia, exist for university admission. However, in 2002 the Government announced a reduction of reliance on racial quotas, instead leaning more towards meritocracy. The undergraduate Bachelors degree course lasts three to four years, though some disciplines require longer periods of study, such as medicine and dentistry (which both require five years). Following the Bachelors, the Masters is the first postgraduate degree, requiring one to three years' further study; finally, after award of the Masters, study for a PhD lasts a minimum of two years. This three-tier system of degrees is supplemented by undergraduate and postgraduate Certificate and Diploma programmes.

Post-secondary vocational and technical education leading to the award of various certificates and diplomas is available at specialist schools and institutes, including polytechnics, the Universiti Tunku Abdul Rahman (a government-sponsored institution mainly serving the Chinese community), training institutions of the Majlis Amanah Rakyat (MARA, Council of Trust for the Indigenous People), community colleges and industrial training institutes. A five-level National Skill Certification system was introduced in 1993 by the National Vocational Training Council.

The Malaysian Qualification Agency (MQA) was established under the Malaysian Qualifications Agency Act 2007 by the merger of the previous National Accreditation Board (LAN) and the Quality Assurance Division of the Ministry of Higher Education. The merger was approved in December 2005 and the MQA was launched in November 2007. Before the merger, LAN (founded in 1998) acted as a statutory body under the Ministry of Education to ensure the standard and quality of certificates, diplomas and degree courses run by the private higher education institutions. There are two processes involved in the current MQA accreditation system: Provisional Accreditation—this initial process helps private higher education providers to achieve accreditation by enhancing the standards and quality set in the provisional accreditation evaluation; and Accreditation—this is a formal recognition that the certificates, diplomas and degrees awarded by private higher education institutions are in accordance with the standards set. Long-established, well-functioning higher education providers with accredited study programmes may apply for self-accrediting status.

Regulatory and Representative Bodies

GOVERNMENT

Ministry of Education: Block E8, Complex E, Fed. Govt Admin. Centre, 62604 Putrajaya; tel. (3) 80008000; e-mail 80008000@1mocc.gov.my; internet www.moe.gov.my; Minister Y. A. B. Tan Sri Dato' Haji MUHYIDDIN BIN HAJI MOHD YASSIN; Minister Y. B. Dato' Seri IDRIS BIN JUSOH.

Ministry of Science, Technology and Innovation: Level 1–7, Block C4 and C5, Complex C, Fed. Govt Admin. Centre, 62662 Putrajaya; tel. (3) 88858000; e-mail info@mosti.gov.my; internet www.mosti.gov.my; Minister Y. B. Datuk Dr EWON EBIN.

Ministry of Tourism and Culture: No 2, Tower 1, Jl P5/6, Precinct 5, 62200 Putrajaya; tel. (3) 80008000; e-mail info@motac.gov.my; internet www.motac.gov.my; Minister Dato' Seri MOHAMED NAZRI BIN ABDUL AZIZ.

ACCREDITATION

Malaysian Qualifications Agency: Tingkat 14B, Menara PKNS-PJ, 17, Jl Yong Shook Lin, Petaling Jaya, 46050 Selangor Darul Ehsan; tel. (3) 79687002; e-mail akreditasi@mqa.gov.my; internet www.mqa.gov.my; f. 2007 by merger of National Accreditation Board (LAN) and the Quality Assurance Division; attached to Min. of Higher Education; responsible for quality assurance of higher education for both private and public sectors to maintain Malaysian qualification standards; facilitates articulation and recognition of qualifications; Chair. Dr MOHAMED SALLEH MOHAMED YASIN; Deputy Chair. Prof. Dr MOHAMAD ZAWAWI ISMAIL.

NATIONAL BODY

Malaysian Association of Private Colleges and Universities: c/o International Medical University, 126 Jalan 19/155B, Bukit Jalil, 57000 Kuala Lumpur; tel. (3) 86569980; e-mail info@mapcu.com.my; internet www.mapcu.com.my; f. 1997; promotes and coordinates the devt of private higher education in Malaysia; 70 mems (45 ordinary mems, 15 assoc. mems, 10 br. mems); Pres. Dr PARMJIT SINGH; Sec.-Gen. Y. Bhg. Dato' PETER NG.

Learned Societies

ARCHITECTURE AND TOWN PLANNING

Malaysian Institute of Architects: 4–6 Jl Tangsi, POB 10855, 50726 Kuala Lumpur; tel. (3) 26934182; e-mail info@pam.org.my; f. 1967; 3,005 mems; library of 1,000 vols; Pres. Ar Dr TAN LOKE MUN; publs *Berita Akitek* (12 a year), *Majalah Akitek* (Architecture Malaysia, 6 a year), *PAM Directory* (1 a year), *Panduan Akitek* (1 a year).

BIBLIOGRAPHY, LIBRARY SCIENCE AND MUSEOLOGY

Librarians' Association of Malaysia: POB 12545, 50782 Kuala Lumpur; Perpustakaan Negara Malaysia, 232 Jl Tun Razak, 50572 Kuala Lumpur; tel. (3) 26947390; e-mail pustakawan55@gmail.com; internet www.ppm55.org; f. 1955; organizes workshops, visits, confs/seminars, demonstrations of technological innovations and community services; 600 mems; Pres. Assoc. Prof. Dr MOHD SHARIF MOHD SAAD; Sec. BALQIS SUJAK; publ. *Jurnal PPM* (1 a year).

HISTORY, GEOGRAPHY AND ARCHAEOLOGY

Malaysian Historical Society: Aras 3, Anjung Wisma Sejarah, 230 Jl Tun Razak, 50400 Kuala Lumpur; tel. (3) 26815388; e-mail sej@psm.org.my; internet www.psm.org.my; f. 1953; activities incl. restoration and preservation of historical sites; 200 individual and institutional mems; Pres. Dato' Seri MUHYIDDIN BIN MOHD YASSIN; publs *Malaysia Dari Segi Sejarah* (1 a year), *Malaysia in History*.

LANGUAGE AND LITERATURE

Alliance Française de Kuala Lumpur: 15 Lorong Gurney, 54100 Kuala Lumpur; tel. (3) 26947880; e-mail info@alliancefrancaise.org.my; internet www.alliancefrancaise.org.my; f. 1961; offers courses and exams in French language and culture and promotes cultural exchange with France; 3 centres in Kuala Lumpur and Alliance Française de Penang in Georgestown; 2,300 mems; library of 5,500 vols; Dir BRUNO PLASSE.

British Council: POB 10539, 50916 Kuala Lumpur; Ground Fl., West Block, Wisma Selangor Dredging, 142C Jl Ampang, 50450 Kuala Lumpur; tel. (3) 27237900; e-mail kualalumpur@britishcouncil.org.my; internet www.britishcouncil.org.my; teaching centre; offers courses and exams in English language and British culture and promotes cultural exchange with the UK; attached offices in Kota Kinabalu, Kuching, Penang (teaching centre) and Subang Jaya (teaching centre); library of 14,000 vols, 100 periodicals; Dir GERRY LISTON; Dir, English Language STEVE BATES.

Dewan Bahasa dan Pustaka (National Language and Literary Agency): POB 10803, 50926 Kuala Lumpur; tel. (3) 21481011; internet www.dbp.gov.my; f. 1956; develops and enriches the Malay language; develops literary talent; standardizes spelling and pronunciation and devises technical terms, etc., in Malay; prints or assists in the production of publs in Malay and the translation of books into Malay; 1,171 mems; library: see under Libraries and Archives; Dir-Gen. Dato' Hj. TERMUZI HJ. ABDUL AZIZ; publs *Dewan Bahasa* (12 a year), *Dewan Budaya* (12 a year), *Dewan Sastera* (12 a year), *Pelita Bahasa* (12 a year).

Goethe-Institut: Suite 06–07, 6th Fl., Menara See Hoy Chan, 374 Jl Tun Razak, 50400 Kuala Lumpur; tel. (3) 21642011; e-mail info@kualalumpur.goethe.org; internet www.goethe.de/malaysia; offers courses and exams in German language and culture and promotes cultural exchange with Germany; Dir ROLF STEHLE.

Tamil Language Society: c/o Dept of Indian Studies, University of Malaya, 50603 Kuala Lumpur; tel. (3) 79675510; e-mail sas_india@um.edu.my; internet www.nustls.org; f. 1957; 350 mems; promotes Tamil language and Indian culture; Pres. THIRUVALAGU JAYA SEELAN; Hon. Sec. L. KRISHNAN; publ. *Tamil Oli* (1 a year, in English, Malay and Tamil).

MEDICINE

Academy of Family Physicians of Malaysia: Room 6, 5th Fl., MMA House, 124 Jl Pahang, 53000 Kuala Lumpur; tel. (3) 40417735; e-mail afpm@po.jaring.my; f. 1973; 800 mems; Pres. Dr M. K. RAJAKUMAR; Chair. (vacant); publ. *The Family Physician* (3 a year).

Malaysian Medical Association: 4th Fl., MMA House, 124 Jl Pahang, 53000 Kuala Lumpur; tel. (3) 40411375; e-mail info@mma.org.my; internet www.mma.org.my; f. 1959; 10,000 mems; Pres. Dr DAVID QUEK KWANG LENG; Man. RISSA SOETAMA; publ. *Medical Journal of Malaysia* (4 a year).

NATURAL SCIENCES

General

Malaysian Scientific Association: Room 1, 2nd Fl., Bangunan Sultan Salahuddin Abdul Aziz Shah, 16 Jl Utara, POB 48, 46700 Petaling Jaya; tel. (3) 79578930; e-mail malsci@tm.net.my; f. 1955; 388 mems, engaged in scientific and technological works; Pres. Dr SOON TING KUEH; Hon. Sec. Dr ZURAINEE MOHD NOR.

Biological Sciences

Malaysian Nature Society: POB 10750, 60724 Kuala Lumpur; tel. (3) 22879422; e-mail natsoc@po.jaring.my; internet www.mns.org.my; f. 1940; promotes the study, appreciation and conservation of nature; 5,000 mems; Pres. Dato' Dr SALLEH MOHD NOR; Exec. Dir Dr LOH CHI LEONG; publs *Malaysian Naturalist* (4 a year), *The Malayan Nature Journal* (4 a year).

Malaysian Society for Biochemistry and Molecular Biology: d/a Pusat Pengajian Biosains dan Bioteknologi Fakulti Sains dan Teknologi, Universiti Kebangsaan Malaysia, 43600 Selangor; f. 1973; lectures, workshops and seminars, annual conf.; 120 mems; Pres. Prof. PERUMAL RAMASAMY; Sec. Dr SHEILA NATHAN; publs *Malaysian Journal of Biochemistry and Molecular Biology*, *Proceedings of Annual Conference*.

Malaysian Zoological Society/Zoo Negara: Hulu Kelang, 68000 Ampang, Selangor Darul Ehsan; tel. (3) 41083422; e-mail pa_m@zoonegaramalaysia.my; internet www.zoonegaramalaysia.my/mzs.html; f. 1961; Pres. Dato' Sr ZAHARIN MD. ARIF (acting).

RELIGION, SOCIOLOGY AND ANTHROPOLOGY

Royal Asiatic Society, Malaysian Branch: 130M Jl Thamby Abdullah, off Jl Tun Sambanthan, Brickfields, 50470 Kuala Lumpur; tel. (3) 22748345; e-mail mbras@tm.net.my; internet www.mbras.org.my; f. 1877; 935 mems; history, literature, sociology, anthropology; Pres. Datuk ABDULLAH BIN ALI; Sec. Datuk BURHANUDDIN BIN AHMAD TAJUDIN; publ. *Journal* (2 a year).

Research Institutes

AGRICULTURE, FISHERIES AND VETERINARY SCIENCE

Department of Agriculture: Min. of Agriculture, Aras 7-17, Wisma Tani, No 30 Persiaran Perdana, Persint 4, Federal Govt Admin. Centre, 62624 Putrajaya; tel. (3) 88703007; e-mail pro@doa.gov.my; internet www.doa.gov.my; f. 1905; undertakes all aspects of research and extension for improvement of crops; pest forecasting and surveillance; establishing Agricultural Information System; library of 15,000 vols; Dir-Gen. Dato' MUSTAFA KAMAL BIN BAHARUDDIN; publs *Malaysian Agricultural Journal*, *Statistical Digest*.

Forest Research Institute Malaysia (FRIM): Kepong, 52109, Selangor Darul Ehsan; tel. (3) 62797000; e-mail feedback@frim.gov.my; internet www.frim.gov.my; f. 1929; consists of 485.2 ha of experimental plantations, 5 arboreta, a nursery, a museum, a herbarium of 300,000 sheets of tree species, a wood colln of nearly 10,000 specimens, and a library (see under Libraries and Archives); 9 substations consisting of 2,988 ha; Rattan Information Centre est. 1982; Dir-Gen. Dato' Dr ABDUL LATIF MOHMOD; publs *Bamboo Bulletin*, *Conservation Malaysia Bulletin*, *FRIM in Focus*, *FRIM Technical Information*, *Journal of Tropical Forest Products*, *Journal of Tropical Forest Science*, *Malayan Forest Records*, *Research Pamphlets*, *Research Programme*, *RIC Bulletin*, *Siri Alam & Rimba*, *Timber Technology Bulletin*, *Tree Flora of Sabah and Sarawak*, *Urban Forestry Bulletin*.

Freshwater Fisheries Research Division: Fri Glami Lemi, Jelebu, Titi, 71650 Negeri Sembilan; tel. (6) 6133000; e-mail pppat@po.jaring.my; internet www.fri.gov.my/frigl; f. 1957 as Tropical Fish Culture Research Institute; current name adopted 1996; attached to Dept of Fisheries, Malaysia; library of 3,800 vols; Chief Officer JAMALUDIN IBRAHIM.

Malaysian Agricultural Research and Development Institute (MARDI): POB 12301, GPO, 50774 Kuala Lumpur; tel. (3) 89437111; e-mail enquiry@mardi.gov.my; internet www.mardi.my; f. 1969; an autonomous organization that conducts scientific, technical, economic and sociological research in Malaysia with respect to the production, utilization and processing of all crops (except rubber and oil palm) and livestock; library of 50,000 vols; Dir-Gen. Dr SAHARAN BIN ANANG; Librarian KHADIJAH IBRAHIM; publs *Agromedia* (4 a year), *Journal of Tropical Agriculture and Food Sciences* (2 a year).

Malaysian Rubber Board: POB 10150, 50450 Kuala Lumpur; tel. (3) 92062000; e-mail general@lgm.gov.my; f. 1998; consists of a directorate, 5 depts and 34 units, 2 research centres namely Tun Abdul Razak Research Centre in Hertford, England and RRIM in Sungai Buloh, Selangor, Malaysia; engaged in rubber research and devt; technical advisory service and information on all aspects of rubber production; library: see under Libraries and Archives; Dir-Gen. Dr SALMIAH AHMAD; publs *Journal of Rubber Research* (4 a year), *Malaysian Rubber Technology Development* (4 a year).

ECONOMICS, LAW AND POLITICS

Asian and Pacific Development Centre: Pesiaran Duta, POB 12224, 50770 Kuala Lumpur; tel. (3) 6511088; e-mail info@apdc.po.my; f. 1980; promotes and undertakes research and training, acts as a clearing house for information on devt, offers consultancy services; current programme: to overcome poverty, to assist devt instns to manage nat. devt and change, to increase the policy-making capacity of Asian-Pacific countries, to increase the capacity of the region to adjust to the changing world environment; 19 full mem. govts, 1 assoc. mem., 1 contributing non-mem.; library of 43,200 vols; Dir Dr MOHD NOOR HAJI HARUN; publs *Asia-Pacific Development Monitor* (2 a year), *Issues in Gender and Development*.

MEDICINE

Institute for Medical Research (IMR): Jl Pahang, 50588 Kuala Lumpur; tel. (3) 26162666; e-mail portal@imr.gov.my; internet www.imr.gov.my; f. 1900; attached to Min. of Health; researches into biomedical and social aspects of tropical diseases, provides specialized diagnostic, consultative and information services, trains medical and paramedical staff, also WHO Centre for Research and Training in Tropical Diseases for the Western Pacific Region, and SEAMEO-TROPMED National Centre, WHO Collaborating Centre for Taxonomy and Immunology of Filariasis and Screening and Clinical Trials of Drugs against Brugian Filariasis, and WHO Collaborating Centre for Ecology, Taxonomy and Control of Vectors of Malaria, Filariasis and Dengue; library of 20,000 vols; Dir Dr SHAHNAZ BINTI MURAD (acting); publs *International Medical Journal*, *Study of the Institute for Medical Research* (irregular).

NATURAL SCIENCES

Physical Sciences

Minerals and Geoscience Department Malaysia: Locked Bag 2042, 88999 Kota Kinabalu, Sabah; tel. (88) 260311; e-mail jmgsbh@jmg.gov.my; internet www.jmg.gov.my; f. 1949; geological mapping, minerals research, engineering geology, hydrogeology, geophysics, mineralogy and petrology, laboratory analysis; library of 3,500 vols; Dir N. K. ANG; publs *Malaysian Mineral Yearbook*, industrial mineral production statistics and directory of producers in Malaysia.

Minerals and Geosciences Department Malaysia: 20th Fl., Bangunan Tabung Haji, Jl Tun Razak, 50658 Kuala Lumpur; tel. (3) 21611033; e-mail jmgkll@jmg.gov.my; internet www.jmg.gov.my; f. 1903; attached to Min. of Natural Resources and Environment; brs in Perak, Sabah and Sarawak; basic geological information on E and W Malaysia with spec. emphasis on mineral resources; library of 18,720 vols (E Malaysia), 34,000 vols (W Malaysia); Dir-Gen. Dato' YUNUS ABD. RAZAK; publ. regional memoirs, map reports, economic bulletins, geochemical reports.

Minerals and Geoscience Malaysia, Sarawak Department: POB 560, 93712 Kuching, Sarawak; tel. (82) 244666; e-mail jmgswk@jmg.gov.my; f. 1949; geological mapping, mineral investigations, engineering geology, hydrogeology; library of 18,000 vols; Dir Dato' Hj. YUNUS BIN ABD. RAZAK; publ. bulletins, geological papers, technical papers, maps, memoirs, reports.

TECHNOLOGY

Malaysian Institute of Microelectronic Systems (MIMOS): MIMOS Berhad, Technology Park Malaysia, 57000 Kuala Lumpur; tel. (3) 89965000; e-mail info@mimos.my; internet www.mimos.my; f. 1985; research and devt in microelectronics, IT and related areas; provides advisory and technical services to the govt and the private sector; encourages and supports the creation of new industries based on high technology and modern microelectronics; library of 6,200 vols, 202 periodicals; Pres. and CEO Datuk ABDUL WAHAB ABDULLAH; COO ABD. AZIZ ABD. KADIR; publs *MIMOS IT Paper* (2 a year), *MOSMEDIA* (4 a year).

Standards and Industrial Research Institute of Malaysia (SIRIM): POB 7035, 40700 Shah Alam, Selangor;; tel. (3) 55446000; e-mail web@sirim.my; internet www.sirim.my; f. 1975 by merger of National Institute of Scientific and Industrial Research and the Standards Institution of Malaysia; research into existing and future problems relating to engineering and production of processed and fabricated industrial products; provides technical services incl. quality assurance, metrology, industry testing, technology modification and improvement, technology transfer, consultancy, industrial information and extension services; undertakes the drafting and publication of Malaysian standards and standards testing; library of 13,000 vols, 165,000 standards and specifications, 400 periodicals; Chair. Datuk HAJAH JAMALIAH KAMIS; publ. *Malaysian Standards*.

Libraries and Archives

Alor Setar

Kedah State Public Library Corporation: Jl Kolam Air, 05100 Alor Setar, Kedah Darul Aman; tel. (4) 7333592; e-mail pengarah@kdhlib.gov.my; internet www.kdhlib.gov.my; f. 1974; incl. Alor Setar Public Library, 8 br. libraries, 6 mobile libraries and 88 village libraries; 675,677 vols; Dir Dr ZAHIDI BIN DATO' HAJI ZAINOL RASHID.

Ipoh

Tun Razak Library: Jl Panglima Bukit Gantang Wahab, 30000 Ipoh, Perak Darul Ridzuan; tel. (5) 2436008; e-mail librarytunrazak_ipoh@yahoo.com; internet ptripoh.mbi.gov.my; f. 1931; spec. collns on Malaysia and Singapore; UNESCO depository; spec. language section; 278,993 vols in English, Chinese, Malay and Tamil; Asst Librarian NOOR AFITZA HJ. PAWAN CHIK; publ. *Malaysiana Collection*.

Johor Baharu

Perpustakaan Sultan Ismail: Jl Datin Halimah, 80350 Larkin, Johor Baharu; tel. (7) 2391799; e-mail info@psi.gov.my; f. 1964; 40,600 vols in Chinese, English, Malay and Tamil; Librarian (vacant).

Perpustakaan Sultanah Zanariah: 81310 Skudai, Johor Baharu; tel. (7) 5533333; e-mail psz-lib-opac@groups.utm.my; internet ent.library.utm.my; f. 1972; attached to Universiti Teknologi Malaysia; also in Kuala Lumpur; 344,000 vols, 9,300 periodicals; Chief Librarian KAMARIAH NOR MOHD DESA; publ. *Library Handbook* (1 a year, in Malay and English).

Kota Baharu

Perbadanan Perpustakaan Awam Kelantan (Kelantan Public Library Corporation): Jl Mahmood, 15200 Kota Baharu, Kelantan; tel. (9) 7444522; e-mail ppak@kelantan.gov.my; internet www.kelantanlibrary.gov.my; f. 1938, current name adopted 1974; 7 brs and 3 rural libraries; 261,000 vols; spec. colln: Kelantan Colln; Dir RUSLAN BIN HAJI HASSAN; Librarian MOHD AZIZI BIN ZAINUDIN.

Kota Kinabalu

Sabah State Library/Perpustakaan Negeri Sabah: Jl Tasik, off Jl Maktab Gaya, 88300 Luyang, Sabah; tel. (88) 231623; e-mail hq.ssl@sabah.gov.my; internet www.ssl.sabah.gov.my; f. 1953; state dept within Min. of Social Welfare; 24 brs, 13 mobile, 8 cyber vans and 75 village libraries; 2,503,980 vols; Dir WONG VUI YIN.

Kuala Lumpur

Arkib Negara Malaysia (National Archives of Malaysia): Jl Duta, 50568 Kuala Lumpur; tel. (3) 62090600; e-mail webmaster@arkib.gov.my; internet www.arkib.gov.my; f. 1957; public records, archives, audiovisual records, private and business records; Prime Minister's archives; 10,471 vols; Dir-Gen. (vacant); publs *Hari ini Dlm. Sejarah* (4 a year), *National Archives of Malaysia*.

Library, Forest Research Institute Malaysia: Kepong, 52109 Selangor; tel. (3) 62797497; e-mail zaki@frim.gov.my; internet www.frim.gov.my; f. 1929; 62,000 vols on forestry and related subjects, incl. medicinal plants, biodiversity, the environment; colln consists of books, scientific and technical reports, reprints, standards, conf. papers, theses, newspaper clippings, gazettes, maps; services incl. SDI, Rattan Information Centre, current awareness services, literature searches, OPAC, etc.; Library Head MOHAMAD ZAKI HAJI MOHD ISA; publs *FRIM in Focus* (4 a year), *FRIM Reports* (irregular), *FRIM Research Pamphlet* (irregular), *FRIM Technical Information* (irregular), *Journal of Tropical Forest Science* (4 a year), *Timber Technology Bulletin* (irregular).

Rubber Information Online System: RRIM Jl Ampang, 50450 Kuala Lumpur; tel. (3) 6039206; e-mail fauziah@lgm.gov.my; internet rios.lgm.gov.my; f. 1925; attached to Malaysian Rubber Board; 150,000 vols, mainly science and technology, particular emphasis on subjects relating to rubber research; Head of Library and Publications Unit PUAN FAUZIAH HAJI ABD. RAHMAN.

Ministry of Agriculture Library: Wisma Tani, Number 28, Persiaran Perdana, Presint 4, 62624 Putrajaya; tel. (3) 88701786; internet www.moa.gov.my; f. 1906; 80,000 vols.

Perpustakaan Kuala Lumpur (Kuala Lumpur Public Library): 1 Jl Raja, 50050 Kuala Lumpur; tel. (3) 26123500; e-mail kllibrary@dbkl.gov.my; internet kllibrary.dbkl.gov.my; f. 1966; 45,000 vols; Librarian SOONG WAN YOONG.

Perpustakaan Negara Malaysia (National Library of Malaysia): 232 Jl Tun Razak, 50572 Kuala Lumpur; tel. (3) 26871700; e-mail webmaster@pnm.gov.my; internet www.pnm.gov.my; f. 1966; nat. bibliographic centre, nat. depository, nat. centre for Malay MSS, nat. centre for ISBN and ISSN; depository for UN publs; 1,413,348 vols; Dir SALBIAH MOHAMMAD YUSOF; publs *Jurnal Filologi Melayu* (1 a year), *Selitan Perpustakaen* (2 a year).

Pusat Dokumentasi Melayu (Dewan Bahasa dan Pustaka) (Malay Documentation Centre, Institute of Language and Literature): POB 10803, 50926 Kuala Lumpur; tel. (3) 21481030; e-mail azlina@dbp.gov.my; internet www.dbp.gov.my; f. 1956; directory of Malaysian writers; bibliography of modern Malaysian literature; 141,105 vols, 80 periodicals, 5,107 audiovisual items; Head AIZAN MOHD ALI; publs *Mutiara Pustaka* (1 a year), *Subject Bibliography* (Bulletin, irregular).

University of Malaya Library: Pantai Valley, 50603 Kuala Lumpur; tel. (3) 7575887; e-mail query_perpustakaan@um.edu.my; f. 1957; 1,239,749 vols, 8,040 periodicals; spec. collns incl. medical, law, Malay language and culture, E Asian studies and Tamil studies; Chief Librarian Assoc. Prof. Dr NOR EDZAN CHE NASIR; publ. *Kekal Abadi* (2 a year).

Kuching

Sarawak State Library: Jalan Pustaka, Petra Jaya, 93050 Kuching; tel. (82) 442000; e-mail librarian@sarawak.gov.my; internet www.pustaka-sarawak.com/pustaka-sarawak; f. 2000; 258,102 vols; CEO RASHIDAH HAJI BOLHASSAN.

Melaka

Malacca Public Library Corporation: 242-1 Jl Bukit Baru, 75150 Melaka; tel. (6) 2824859; e-mail admin@perpustam.edu.my; internet www.perpustam.edu.my; f. 1977; 526,375 vols; Librarian RIZA FEISAL BIN SHEIK SAID.

Penang

Perbadanan Perpustakaan Awam Pulau Pinang (Penang Public Library Corporation): JKR 2118 Jl Perpustakaan, Seberang Jaya, 13700 Prai Penang; tel. (4) 3902387; e-mail webmaster@penanglib.gov.my; internet www.penanglib.gov.my; f. 1817, reorganized 1973; 6 brs, 2 town libraries and 12 mobile library units; 415,000 vols; Librarian NORLINA BINTI HAJI AHMAD.

Perpustakaan Universiti Sains Malaysia: Minden, 11800 Penang; tel. (4) 6577888; e-mail chieflib@usm.my; internet www.lib.usm.my; f. 1969; 809,000 vols (main library 644,000 vols, 5,500 periodicals; medical library 87,000 vols, 1,370 periodicals; engineering library 78,000 vols, 487 periodicals), media 122,916 items, 9,969 reels microfilm, 105,809 sheets microfiche; Chief Librarian Hon. Datin MASRAH HAJI ABIDIN; publ. *MIDAS Bulletin* (6 a year).

Serdang

Perpustakaan Sultan Abdul Samad (Sultan Abdul Samad Library): UPM Serdang, 43400 Selangor Darul Ehsan; tel. (3) 89468601; e-mail lib@lib.upm.edu.my; internet www.lib.upm.edu.my; f. 1971 by merger of College of Agriculture, Malaya and the Faculty of Agriculture, Universiti Putra Malaysia; renamed Universiti Putra Malaysia Library in 1997; current name adopted 2002; attached to Universiti Putra Malaysia; brs in Faculty of Medicine and Health Sciences, Faculty of Veterinary Medicine, Faculty of Engineering and the UPM Campus Bintulu in Sarawak; 601,663 vols and bound periodicals; colln of maps, sound recordings, microforms, video cassettes and slides; subscribes to 3,000 print journals and 60 online databases providing access to 56,000 full-text online journals; Chief Librarian AMIR HUSSAIN MOHD ISHAK (acting); Deputy Chief Librarian HAFIZAH HASSAN.

Shah Alam

Selangor Public Library Corporation: c/o Perpustakaan Raja Tun Uda, Persiaran Bandaraya, 40572 Shah Alam, Selangor; tel. (3) 55197667; e-mail jothi@ppas.org.my; internet www.ppas.org.my; f. 1971; 1,435,803 vols; main library; 8 brs, 4 township libraries; 55 village libraries and 13 mobile units; Dir SHAHANEEM HANOUM; publ. *Accession List* (12 a year).

Tun Abdul Razak Library: MARA Institute of Technology, 40450 Shah Alam, Selangor; tel. (3) 55443714; e-mail faizar@salam.uitm.edu.my; internet library.uitm.edu.my; f. 1957; 900,000 vols; Chief Librarian NOOR HIDAYAT BIN ADNAN.

Sintok

Perpustakaan Sultanah Bahiyah, Universiti Utara Malaysia: Universiti Utara Malaysia, 06010 Sintok, Kedah; tel. (4) 9283318; e-mail libuum@uum.edu.my; internet www.lib.uum.edu.my; f. 1984; 183,000 vols, 6,000 periodicals; Chief Librarian SALLEH HUDIN MUSTAFFA.

Museums and Art Galleries

Kota Kinabalu

Sabah Museum: Jl Muzium, 83000 Kota Kinabalu, Sabah; tel. (88) 225033; e-mail muzium.sabah@sabah.gov.my; internet www.museum.sabah.gov.my; f. 1886; anthropological, archaeological, ethno-botanical and ethnological, natural history and historical collns; Agop Batu Tulug Museum, Islamic Civilization Museum, Kinabatangan, Sandakan Heritage Museum, Kinarut Panoramic Mansion House, Sandakan Agnes Keith House, Sandakan Memorial Tun Abdul Razak, Semporna Bukit Tengkorak, Tambunan Datu Paduka Mat Salleh Memorial, Tenom Murut Culture Museum; Keningau Heritage Museum, Lahad Datu Mansuli archaeological site, Penampang Pogunon Burial Ancient Site, Tambunan Mat Sator Monument, Tenom Antoros Antenom Monument, Tenom Ulu Tomani Lamuyu Rock Carving; library of 7,000 vols; Dir JOANNA KITINGAN; publ. *Journal* (1 a year).

Kuala Lumpur

Islamic Arts Museum Malaysia: Jl Lembah Perdana, 50480 Kuala Lumpur; tel. (3) 22742020; e-mail info@iamm.org.my; internet www.iamm.org.my; f. 1998; art and culture of Islam from the 7th century to the present; incl. 12 permanent galleries; architecture, Qu'rans and manuscript, India, China, Malay World, textiles, jewellery, arms and armour, coins and seals, metalwork, ceramics and glasses, living with Wood; 2 spec. galleries; Dir SYED MOHAMAD ALBUKHARY.

National Museum of Malaysia/Muzium Negara: Jl Damansara, 50566 Kuala Lumpur; tel. (3) 22826255; e-mail info@jma.gov.my; internet www.jma.gov.my; f. 1963; houses collections of ethnographical, archaeological and zoological materials; comprehensive reference library on Malaysia and many Asian subjects, reference collections of archaeology, zoology and ethnography are also preserved in the Perak Museum, Taiping; Dir-Gen. Dr ADI HAJI TAHA; publ. *Federation Museums Journal* (1 a year).

Kuching

Sarawak Museum Department: Jl Tun Abang Haji Openg, 93566 Kuching; tel. (82) 244232; e-mail webmaster@museum.sarawak.gov.my; internet www.museum.sarawak.gov.my; f. 1886; ethnographic, archaeological, natural history and historical collns; reference library; state archives; Dir IPOI DATAN; publ. *Sarawak Museum Journal*.

Penang

Penang Museum and Art Gallery: No 57, Macalister Rd, Georgetown, 10400 Penang; tel. (4) 2261462; e-mail enquiries@penangmuseum.gov.my; internet www.penangmuseum.gov.my; f. 1963; Chair. Y. B. TUAN WONG HON WAI; Curator HARYANY MOHAMAD.

Taiping

Perak Museum: Jl Taming Sari, 34000 Taiping, Perak; tel. (5) 8072057; e-mail hanisah@jmm.gov.my; internet www.jmm.gov.my/en/museum/perak-museum; f. 1883; antiquities, Perak archives, ethnography, zoology and a library; Head NOR HANISAH BINTI AHMAD.

Universities

INTERNATIONAL ISLAMIC UNIVERSITY MALAYSIA

Jalan Gombak, 53100 Kuala Lumpur
Telephone: (3) 20564000
E-mail: pro@iiu.edu.my
Internet: www.iiu.edu.my

Founded 1983
State control
Languages of instruction: Arabic, English
Constitutional Head: HRH THE SULTAN OF PAHANG
Pres.: Y. B. Tan Sri Dato' SERI SANUSI BIN JUNID
Rector: Prof. Dr MOHD KAMAL HASSAN
Deputy Rector for Academic Affairs: Assoc. Prof. Dato' Haji JAMIL HAJI OSMAN
Deputy Rector for Planning and Development: Prof. Dr ISMAWI HAJI ZEN
Deputy Rector for Student Affairs and Discipline: Assoc. Prof. Dr SIDEK BABA
Chief Librarian: Assoc. Prof. SYED SALIM AGHA BIN SYED AZAMTHULLA

Library of 356,700 vols
Number of teachers: 1,166
Number of students: 16,649

Publications: *At-Tajdid* (2 a year, in Arabic), *Gombak Review* (2 a year, in English), *IIUM* (in English, 2 a year), *IIUM Journal of Economics and Management* (2 a year, in English), *IIUM Law Journal* (2 a year, in English), *Intellectual Discourse* (2 a year, in English)

DEANS OF KULLIYYAH

Ahmad Ibrahim Kulliyyah of Laws: Assoc. Prof. Dr NIK AHMAD KAMAL NIK MAHMOD
Kulliyyah of Architecture and Environmental Design: Assoc. Prof. Dr CHE MUSA CHE OMAR
Kulliyyah of Economics and Management Sciences: Assoc. Prof. Dr MOHD AZMI OMAR
Kulliyyah of Education: Assoc. Prof. Dr MOHD SAHARI NORDIN
Kulliyyah of Engineering: Assoc. Prof. Dr AHMAD FARIS ISMAIL
Kulliyyah of Information and Communications Technology: Dr MOHD ADAM SUHAIMI
Kulliyyah of Islamic Revealed Knowledge and Human Sciences: Prof. Dr MOHAMED ARIS HAJI OSMAN
Kulliyyah of Medicine: Prof. Dato' Dr MD. TAHIR AZHAR
Kulliyyah of Pharmacy: Prof. Dr TARIQ ADBUL RAZAK
Kulliyyah of Science: Assoc. Prof. Dr TORLA HAJI HASSAN

ATTACHED INSTITUTE

International Institute of Islamic Thought and Civilization (ISTAC): 205A Jl Damansara, Bukit Damansara, 50480 Kuala Lumpur; tel. (3) 2544444; e-mail admistac@iiu.edu.my; internet www.iium.edu.my/istac; f. 1991; financed by Min. of Education; postgraduate research and teaching in fields of Islamic thought and civilization; library of 149,686 vols; Dir Prof. Dr SYED MUHAMMAD NAQUIB AL-ATTAS

MALAYSIA UNIVERSITY OF SCIENCE AND TECHNOLOGY (MUST)

GL 33 (Ground Fl.), Block C, Kelana Sq., 17 Jl SS 7/26, 47301, Kelana Jaya, Petaling Jaya, Selangor Darul Ehsan
Telephone: (3) 78801777
E-mail: admin@must.edu.my
Internet: www.must.edu.my
Private control
Academic year: September to June
Postgraduate research univ.

Pres.: Dr OMAR ABDUL RAHMAN
Provost: Dr MOHD NIZAM ISA
Vice-Pres. for Finance and Business Affairs: BADLY SHAH BIN ARIFF SHAH
Registrar and Head of Admin.: STEPHEN JOHN LEE
Chief Librarian: JOHARI AFFANDI OMAR

DEANS

Biotechnology: Assoc. Prof. Dr LIM SAW HOON
Construction Engineering and Management: Assoc. Prof. Dr CHAN TOONG KHUAN
Energy and Environment: Asst Prof. Dr SCOTT KENNEDY
Information Technology: Assoc. Prof. Dr NOR ADNAN YAHYA
Materials Science and Engineering: Prof. Dr ZANULDIN AHMAD
Systems Engineering and Management: Asst Prof. Dr ASGARI BEHROOZ
Transportation and Logistics: Assoc. Prof. Dr LEONG CHOON HENG

MULTIMEDIA UNIVERSITY

Cyberjaya Campus: Jalan Multimedia, 63100 Cyberjaya, Selangor
Telephone: (3) 83125018
Melaka Campus: Jl Ayer Keroh Lama, 75450 Melaka
Telephone: (6) 2523460
E-mail: info@mmu.edu.my
Internet: www.mmu.edu.my

Chancellor: Tun Dato' Seri ZAKI TUN AZMI
Pres.: Prof. Dato' Dr MUHAMAD RASAT MUHAMAD
Vice-Pres. for Academic Affairs: Prof. Dr ONG DUU SHENG
Vice-Pres. for Research and Devt: Prof. Dr HENG SWEE HUAY
Librarian: KAMAL SUJAK

DEANS

Faculty of Business (Melaka Campus): Dr HISHAMUDDIN BIN ISMAIL
Faculty of Computing and Informatics (Cyberjaya Campus): Dr HO CHIN KUAN
Faculty of Creative Multimedia (Cyberjaya Campus): Assoc. Prof. Dr NEO TSE KIAN
Faculty of Engineering (Cyberjaya Campus): Prof. Dr HIN-YONG WONG
Faculty of Engineering and Technology (Melaka Campus): Dr ALAN TAN WEE CHIAT
Faculty of Information Science and Technology (Melaka Campus): Assoc. Prof. Dr LAU SIONG HOE
Faculty of Law (Melaka Campus): Dr MANIQUE APSARA EPHRANELLA COORAY
Faculty of Management (Cyberjaya Campus): Assoc. Prof. Dr DAVID YONG GUN FIE
Graduate School of Management (Cyberjaya Campus): Assoc. Prof. WAN FADZILAH WAN YUSOFF

UNIVERSITI KEBANGSAAN MALAYSIA (National University of Malaysia)

43600 UKM Bangi, Selangor
Telephone: (3) 89214187
E-mail: kbha@pkrisc.cc.ukm.my
Internet: www.ukm.my
Founded 1970
State control
Languages of instruction: Malay, English, Arabic
Academic year: May to April

Chancellor: Tuanku JAAFAR IBNI AL-MARHUM ABDUL RAHMAN
Vice-Chancellor: Prof. Dato' Dr MOHD SALLEH MOHD YASIN
Deputy Vice-Chancellor for Academic and International Affairs: Prof. Dr SUKIMAN SARMANI
Deputy Vice-Chancellor for Students and Alumni Affairs: Prof. Dato' Dr MOHD WAHID SAMSUDIN
Registrar: Hj. MOHAMED MUSTAFA MOHTAR
Bursar: Hj. MOHD ABDUL RASHID MOHD FADZIL
Chief Librarian: PUTRI SANIAH MEGAT ABDUL RAHMAN

Library of 945,000 vols, 4,000 journals
Number of teachers: 1,781
Number of students: 24,487

Publications: *Journal of Language Teaching, Linguistics and Literature, Jurnal Akademika, Jurnal Ekonomi Malaysia, Jurnal Islamiyyat, Jurnal Jebat, Jurnal Kejuruteraan* (2 a year), *Jurnal Pendidikan, Jurnal Pengurusan, Jurnal Perubatan UKM, Jurnal Psikologi Malaysia, Jurnal Sari, Jurnal Undang-Undang and Masyarakat, Sains Malaysiana* (4 a year)

DEANS

Centre for General Studies: Prof. Dr ABDUL LATIF SAMIAN
Faculty of Allied Health Sciences: Prof. Dr MOHD AZMAN ABU BAKAR
Faculty of Dentistry: Prof. Dato' Dr Hj. MOHD ARIFFIN HJ. MOHAMED
Faculty of Economics and Business: Prof. Dr NOOR AZLAN GHAZALI
Faculty of Education: Assoc. Prof. Dr LILIA HALIM
Faculty of Engineering: Prof. Ir. Dr HASSAN BASRI
Faculty of Islamic Studies: Prof. Dr ZAKARIA SETAPA
Faculty of Law: Assoc. Prof. KAMAL HALILI HASSAN
Faculty of Medicine: Prof. Dr LOKMAN SAIM
Faculty of Social Sciences and Humanities: Prof. Dr YUSOF ISMAIL
Faculty of Science and Information Technology: Prof. AZIZ DERAMAN
Faculty of Science and Technology: Prof. Dr ABDUL JALIL ABDUL KADER
Institute for Environment and Development (LESTARI): Prof. Dr IBRAHIM KOOMOO
Institute of Malay World and Civilization (ATMA): Prof. Dato' Dr SHAMSUL AMRI BAHARUDDIN
Institute of Malaysian and International Studies (IKMAS): Prof. Dr ROGAYAH HJ. MAT ZIN
Institute of Medical Molecular Biology (UMBI): Prof. Dr A. RAHMAN A. JAMAL
Institute of Microengineering and Nanoelectronics (IMEN): Prof. Dr BURHANUDDIN YEOP MAJLIS
Institute of Occidental Studies (IKON): Prof. Dato' Dr SHAMSUL AMRI BAHARUDDIN
Institute of Space (ANGKASA): Prof. Dr BAHARUDDIN YATIM
National Institute for Genomics and Molecular Biology—Malaysia: Prof. Dr NOR MUHAMMAD MAHADI

PROFESSORS

ABDUL HAMID, Z., Genetics and Plant Biotechnology
ABDUL KADER, A. J., Microbial Physiology
ABDUL KADIR, K., Endocrinology and Metabolism
ABDUL RAHMAN, R., Environmental Engineering
ABDUL RASHID, A. H., Anatomy
ABDULLAH, A., Food Science and Nutrition
ABDULLAH, I., Structural Geology and Tectonics
ABDULLAH, M., Statistics
ABDULLAH, P., Analytical and Environmental Chemistry
ABU BAKAR, M. A., Lipid Biochemistry
ABU TALIB, I., Material Physics
AHMAD, I., Virology
AHMAD, Z., Political Science
ALI, A., Industrial Planning and Strategies
ALI, O., Community Health
ALI JAMAL, A. R., Paediatric Haematology
ALI RAHIM, S., Development Communications
AZMAN ALI, R., Neurology, Epilepsy and Stroke Medicine
BABA, I., Inorganic Chemistry
BABJI, A. S., Food Science
BAHARUDDIN, S. A., Anthropology and Sociology
BASRI, H., Civil and Environmental Engineering
BIDIN, A. A., Toxonomy of Lower Plants
BOO NEM YUN, Neonatology
CHOO, O. L., Child Neurology and Development Paediatrics
DAUD, W. R. W., Drying, Separation and Fuel Cell Technology
DIN, L., Organic Chemistry
EMBI, M. N., Protein Biochemistry
GEORGE, E., Haematology
HADI, A. S., Urbanization, Industrialization and Migration
HAMDAN, A. R., Artificial Intelligence
HASAN, M. N. H., Zoology
HASAN, Z. A. A., Parasitology
HASSAN, H. R., Psychiatry
HASSAN, S. Z. S., Anthropology of Religion, Gender Studies
ISKANDAR, T. M., Internal Control and Auditing
ISMAIL, M. Y., Minority and Sub-culture Studies
ISMAIL, N. M. N., Obstetrics and Gynaecology
IZHAM CHEONG, Medicine
JAHI, J. M., Physical Geography
JAMAL, F., Clinical Bacteriology
JASIN, B., Micropalaeontology
KADRI, A., Zoology
KAMIS, A., Animal Physiology, Comparative Endocrinology
KENG, C. S., Haematology
KOMOO, I., Engineering Geology and Conservation Geology
KONG, C. T. N., Nephrology
KRISHNASWAMY, S., Psychiatry
LAZAN, H., Plant Physiology and Biochemistry
LIEW, C. G., Family Medicine
LIM, A., Clinical Microbiology and Antimicrobial Chemotherapy
LONG, J., Education
MAHADI, N. M., Environmental Microbiology
MAJLIS, B. Y., Integrated Circuit Technology
MAJZUB, R. M., Pre-school and Adolescent Education and Development
MANSOR, M., Cytogenetics, Cytology
MAT SALLEH, M., Solid State Physics
MEAH, F. A., Surgery
MEERAH, T. S. M., Science Education

Md. Hashim Merican, Z. M., Neuromuscular Pharmacology
Misiran, K., Anaesthesiology
Mohamad, A. L., Plant Systematics
Mohamad, H., Petrology and Geochemistry
Mohamed, M. A., Oral Health
Mohamed, R., Bacterial Serology
Mohamed Yasin, M. S., Medical Mycology
Mohammed Zain, S. bin, Mathematics
Mohd Noor, N., Plant Tissue Culture
Mohd Salleh, K., Science and Society
Ngah, W. Z. W., Medical Biochemistry
Nik Abd. Rahman, N. H. S., Archaeology
Noor, M. I., Nutrition
Nor, G. M., Oral Surgery
Othman, A. H., Coordination Chemistry
Othman, B. H. R., Marine Biology
Othman, M., Signals Processing
Othman, M. Y. H., Energy Physics
Pihie, A. H. L., Clinical Biochemistry
Sahid, I., Weed and Environmental Science
Said, I. M., Organic Chemistry
Saim, L., Otology and Neuro-otology
Salleh, A. R., Algebraic Topology, Ethnomathematics
Salleh, Ramli Md, Malay Syntax and Translation
Salleh, S. H. H., Traditional Malay Literature
Samsudin, A. R., Geophysics
Samsudin, M. W., Organic Chemistry
Sarmani, S., Radiochemistry
Shah, F. H., Molecular Biology
Shamsudin, A. H., Mechanical Engineering
Siwar, C., Rural Economics
Sulaiman, N. A., Bioscience and Clinical Pharmacology
Sulaiman, S., Vector Control, Vectorecology
Syed Hussain, S. N. A., Histopathology, Cytopathology
Tahir, U. M. M., Modern Malay Literature, Literary Criticism
Tamin, N. M., Eco-engineering Restoration
Tap, A. O. M., Pure Mathematics
Teh, W. H. W., Rural Culture and Society
Tengku Sembok, T. M., Information Retrieval
Yahaya, Muhammad, Physics
Yamin, B. M., Chemistry
Yatim, B., Applied Physics
Yong, O., Investment
Yusoff, K., Cardiology
Yusuf, M. Hj., Social Psychology
Zaman, H. B., Information Technology Policy and Strategic Studies

UNIVERSITI MALAYA
(University of Malaya)

50603 Kuala Lumpur
Telephone: (3) 79677022
E-mail: icr@um.edu.my
Internet: www.um.edu.my

Founded 1962
State control
Languages of instruction: Malay, English
Academic year: May to April (2 semesters)

Chancellor: HRH Sultan Azlan Muhibbuddin Shah Ibni Almarhum Sultan Yussuf Izzuddin Shah Ghafarullahu-Lah
Pro-Chancellor: HRH Raja Dr Nazrin Shah Ibni Sultan Azlan Muhibbuddin Shah
Pro-Chancellor: Toh Puan Datuk Hajjah Dr Aishah Ong
Pro-Chancellor: Tan Sri Dato' Seri Siti Norma Yaakob
Vice-Chancellor: Dr Ghauth Jasmon
Deputy Vice-Chancellor for Academic and Int. Affairs: Prof. Dr Hamzah Hj. Abdul Rahman
Deputy Vice-Chancellor for Devt: Prof. Datuk Dr Khaw Lake Tee
Deputy Vice-Chancellor for Research and Innovation: Prof. Dato' Dr Mohd Jamil Maa
Deputy Vice-Chancellor for Student Affairs and Alumni: Assoc. Prof. Datuk Dr Azarae Hj. Idris
Registrar: Norilah Salam
Librarian: Assoc. Prof. Dr Nor Edzan Hj. Che Nasir

Number of teachers: 2,613
Number of students: 25,474

Publications: *Budiman* (4 a year), *University of Malaya Gazette* (1 a year)

DEANS

Academic Devt Centre: Prof. Dr Raja Maznah Raja Hussain (Dir)
Academy of Islamic Studies: Prof. Dr Ahmad Hidayat Buang (Dir)
Academy of Malay Studies: Assoc. Prof. Datuk Zainal Abidin Borhan (Dir)
Asia-Europe Institute: Prof. Datuk Dr Roziah Omar (Exec. Dir)
Centre for Civilisational Dialogue: Prof. Datin Dr Azizan Baharuddin (Dir)
Centre for Foundation Studies in Science: Assoc. Prof. Dr Azilah Abdul Rahman (Dir)
Cultural Centre: Assoc. Prof. Dr Mohd Nasir bin Hashim (Dir)
Faculty of Arts and Social Sciences: Prof. Dr Mohammad Redzuan Othman
Faculty of Built Environment: Assoc. Prof. Dr Sir Noor Rosly Hanif
Faculty of Business and Accountancy: Assoc. Prof. Dr M. Fazilah Abd. Samad
Faculty of Computer Science and Information Technology: Prof. Dr Wan Ahmad Tajuddin Wan Abdullah (acting)
Faculty of Dentistry: Prof. Dr Ishak Abdul Razak
Faculty of Economics and Administration: Prof. Rajah Rasiah
Faculty of Education: Prof. Saedah Siraj
Faculty of Engineering: Assoc. Prof. Dr Mohd Hamdi Abd. Shukor
Faculty of Languages and Linguistics: Prof. Zuraidah Md Don
Faculty of Law: Prof. Dr Choong Yeow Choy
Faculty of Medicine: Prof. Dr Ikram Shah Ismail
Faculty of Science: Prof. Dr Mohd Sofian bin Azirun
Institute of China Studies: Assoc. Prof. Dr Yeoh Kok Kheng
Institute of Graduate Studies: Prof. Dr Norhanom Abdul Wahab
Institute of Principalship Studies: Prof. Dr Shahril Charil Marzuki (Dir)
Institute of Research Management and Monitoring: Prof. Dr Noorsaadah Abd. Rahman (Dir)
Int. Institute of Public Policy and Management: Dr Khadijah Md Khalid (Dir)
Sports Centre: Dr Abdul Halim Mokhtar (Dir)
University of Malaya Centre of Continuing Education: Prof. Datuk Dr Mansor Md Isa (Dir)

PROFESSORS

Academy of Islamic Studies:
Abdullah Alwi, H., Syariah and Economics
Mahfodz, M., Syariah and Law
Mahmood Zuhdi, A. M., Figh and Usul

Academy of Malay Studies:
Abu Hassan, M. S., Malay Literature
Asmah, O., Malay Linguistics
Hashim, M., Linguistics
Norazit, S., Economic Anthropology
Rahmah, B., Malay Culture and Arts
Wan Abdul Kadir, W. Y., Popular Culture Studies
Yaacob, H., Development Studies and Change

Faculty of Arts and Social Sciences:
Abdullah Zakavia, G., History
Ali, S. H., Sociology
Azizah, K., Anthropology and Sociology
Cheng, G. N., Chinese Studies
Fatimah Hasnah, D., Anthropology and Sociology
Lee, B. T., Geography
Lim, C. S., English Studies
Mohd Fauzi, Y., Anthropology and Sociology
Mohd Yusoff, H., History
Nathan, K. S.
Ramlah, A., History
Ranjit Singh, D. S., History
Shaharil, T. R., Southeast Asia Studies
Voon, P. K., Land Use Studies
Zainal, K., Anthropology and Sociology

Faculty of Business and Accountancy:
Mansor, M. I., Financial Management
Sieh, M. L., Business Administration

Faculty of Computer Science and Information Technology:
Mashkuri, Y., Computer Science

Faculty of Dentistry:
Hashim, Y., Oral Pathology and Oral Medicine
Ishak, A. R., Preventive Dentistry
Lian, C. B., Oral Surgery
Ling, B. C., Prosthetics
Lui, J. L., Conservative Dentistry
Rahimah, A. K., Community Dentistry
Siar, C. H., Periodontology
Toh, C. G., Conservative Dentistry
Zubaidah Abd., R., Oral Biology

Faculty of Economics and Administration:
Firdaus, A., Administration and Political Science
Jahara, Y., Development Studies
Jamilah, M. A., Development Studies
Jomo, K. S., Applied Economics
Kok, K. L., Applied Economics
Lee, K. H., Analytical Economics
Nagaraj, S., Applied Statistics
Naidu, G., Applied Economics
Tan, P. C., Applied Statistics

Faculty of Education:
Chew, S. B., Sociology of Education
Chiam, H. K., Social Psychology of Education
Gaudart, H. M., Language Education
Ishak, H., Pedagogy and Educational Psychology
Nik Azis, N. P., Mathematics and Science Education
Rahimah Hj., A., Educational Development
Ramiah, A. L., Educational Development
Safiah, O., Language Education
Suradi, S., Pedagogy and Educational Psychology
Yong, M. S. L., Pedagogy and Educational Psychology

Faculty of Engineering:
Abdul Ghani, K., Computer-aided Design and Manufacturing
Ezrin, A., Built Environment
Faisal, A., Civil and Environmental Engineering
Goh, S. Y., Mechanical and Material Engineering
Khalid, M. N., Electrical and Telecommunications Engineering
Lu, S. K. S., Electrical Engineering
Masitah, H., Chemical Engineering
Mohd Ali, H., Chemical Engineering
Mohd Zaki, A. M., Mechanical and Material Engineering
Ramachandran, K. B., Biochemical Engineering
Wan Abu Bakar, W. A., Mechanical Engineering
Woods, P. C., Built Environment

Faculty of Law:
- BALAN, P., Company Law and Civil Procedure
- HARI, C., Jurisprudence and Legal Philosophy
- KHAW, L. T., Law of Intellectual Property and Land Law
- MIMI KAMARIAH, A. M., Family Law and Criminal Procedure
- SOTHI RACHAGAN, N. S., Environmental and Consumer Law
- SURYA, P. S., International Law

Faculty of Medicine:
- ALJAFRI, A. M., Surgery
- ANUAR ZAINI, M. Z., Medicine
- ASMA, O., Paediatrics
- CHANDRA, S. N., Parasitology
- CHUA, C. T., Medicine
- DELLIKAN, A. E., Anaesthesiology
- DEVA, M. P., Psychological Medicine
- EL-SABBAN, F. M. F., Physiology
- GOH, K. L., Medicine
- KHAIRULL, A. A., Parasitology
- KULENTHRAN, A., Obstetrics and Gynaecology
- LAM, S. K., Medical Microbiology
- LANG, C. C., Medicine
- LIM, C. T., Paediatrics
- LIM, Y. C., Surgery
- LIN, H. P., Paediatrics
- LOOI, L. M., Pathology
- MENAKA, N., Pathology
- NGEOW, Y. F., Medical Microbiology
- ONG, S. Y. G., Anaesthesiology
- PARAMSOTHY, M., Medicine
- PERUMAL, R., Biochemistry
- PRASAD, U., Oto-rhino-laryngology
- PUTHUCHEARY, S. D., Medical Microbiology
- RAMAN, A., Physiology
- RAMANUJAM, T. M., Surgery
- ROKIAH, I., Medicine
- RUBY, H., Physiology
- SENGUPTA, S., Orthopaedic Surgery
- SIVANESARATNAM, V., Obstetrics and Gynaecology
- SUBRAMANIAM, K., Anatomy
- TAN, C. T., Medicine
- TAN, N. H., Biochemistry
- TEOH, S. T., Social and Preventive Medicine
- YAP, S. F., Pathology
- YEOH, P. N., Pharmacy

Faculty of Science:
- ANSARY, A., Microbiology and Bacteriology
- HAMID, A. H. A., Natural Product Chemistry
- HARITH, A., Physics
- KOH, C. L., Genetics
- LIM, M. H., Multilinear Algebra
- LOW, K. S., Lasers and Optoelectronics
- MAK, C., Plant Breeding
- MOHAMED, A. M., Taxonomy and Ecology
- MUHAMAD RASAT, M., Molecular Electronics
- MUHAMAD, Z., Botany
- MUKHERJEE, T. K., Genetics
- NAIR, H., Plant Physiology
- OSMAN, B., Philosophy of Science
- RAHIM, S., Semiconductor Physics
- RAJ, J. K., Engineering Geology
- RAMLI, A., Zoology
- WONG, C. S., Plasma Physics
- YEAP, E. B., Geology

UNIVERSITI MALAYSIA SABAH

Tingkat 9, Gaya Centre, Jl Tun Fuad Stephens, Locked Bag 2073, 88999 Kota Kinabalu, Sabah
Telephone: (88) 320789
E-mail: pejcslor@ums.edu.my
Internet: www.ums.edu.my

Founded 1994
Academic year: June to March

Vice-Chancellor: Prof. Datuk Seri Panglima Dr ABU HASSAN OTHMAN
Deputy Vice-Chancellor for Academic Affairs: Prof. Dr MOHD ZAHEDI DAUD
Deputy Vice-Chancellor for Research and Devt: Prof. Datuk Dr KAMARUZZAMAN AMPON
Deputy Vice-Chancellor for Student Affairs: Prof. Datuk Dr MOHD NOH DALIMIN
Registrar: HELA LADIN BIN MOHD DAHALAN
Librarian: CHE SALMAH MEHAMOOD

Number of teachers: 476
Number of students: 8,300

Publications: *Borneo Science* (2 a year), *Kinabalu* (1 a year), *Manu* (1 a year)

DEANS

Centre for Postgraduate Studies: Prof. Dr ZAINODIN HJ. JUBOK
Centre for the Promotion of Knowledge and Language Learning: Prof. Dr AHMAT ADAM
School of Arts Studies: Assoc. Prof. Haji INON SHAHARUDDIN ABD. RAHMAN
School of Business and Economics: Assoc. Prof. SYED AZIZI SYED WAFA
School of Business and Finance, Labuan: Assoc. Prof. Dr ZAINAL ABIDIN SAID
School of Education and Social Development: Prof. Dr SHUKERY MOHAMED
School of Engineering and Information Technology: Assoc. Prof. Dr SAZALI YAACOB
School of Food Science and Nutrition: Assoc. Prof. Dr MOHD ISMAIL ABDULLAH
School of Informatic Sciences, Labuan: AWANG ASRI AWANG IBRAHIM (acting)
School of International Forestry: Assoc. Prof. Dr AMINUDDIN MOHAMED
School of Psychology and Social Work: Prof. Dato' Dr ABDUL HALIM OTHMAN
School of Science and Technology: Assoc. Prof. Dr AMRAN AHMED
School of Social Sciences: Assoc. Prof. HASSAN BIN MAT NOR

UNIVERSITI MALAYSIA SARAWAK (UNIMAS)

Jl Dato' Mohd Musa, 94300 Kota Samarahan, Sarawak
Telephone: (82) 581000
E-mail: info@iad.unimas.my
Internet: www.unimas.my
State control
Language of instruction: English
Academic year: September to February

Chair.: Datu Dr HATTA SOLHI
Chancellor: Tun Yang Terutama Tun Datuk Patinggi ABANG HAJI MUHAMMAD SALAHUDDIN
Pro-Chancellor: Yang Amat Berhormat Pehin Sri Dr Haji ABDUL TAIB MAHMUD
Vice-Chancellor: Prof. Dato' Dr MOHD KADIM SUAIDI
Deputy Vice-Chancellor for Academic and Int.: Prof. Dr FATIMAH ABANG
Deputy Vice-Chancellor for Research and Innovation: Prof. Dr PETER SONGAN
Deputy Vice-Chancellor for Student Affairs and Alumni: Prof. MOHD FADZIL ABD. RAHMAN
Dir for Devt and Asset Management: HUMPHREY RAYANG JAYANG
Registrar: ABU BAKAR IBRAHIM (acting)
Chief Librarian: MARGARET SIMENG

Library of 108,000 vols, 10,000 journals
Number of teachers: 763
Number of students: 15,210 (13,956 undergraduate, 1,254 postgraduate)

DEANS

Faculty of Applied and Creative Arts: Assoc. Prof. Dr HASNIZAM ABD. WAHID
Faculty of Cognitive Science and Human Development: Assoc. Prof. Dr SHAHREN AHMAD ZAIDI ADRUCE
Faculty of Computer Science and Information Technology: JOHARI ABDULLAH
Faculty of Economy and Business: Dr MOHAMMAD AFFENDY ARIP
Faculty of Engineering: Prof. Dr WAN HASHIM WAN IBRAHIM
Faculty of Medicine and Health Sciences: Prof. Dr AHMAD HATA RASIT
Faculty of Resource Science and Technology: Assoc. Prof. Dr MOHD HASNAIN MD HUSSAIN
Faculty of Social Sciences: Assoc. Prof. Dr NEILSON ILAN MERSAT

PROFESSORS

- ABDULLAH, M. S., Medicine and Health Sciences
- AB HAMID, K., Engineering
- ABU MANSOR, S., Engineering
- AL MASHOOR, S. H., Medicine and Health Sciences
- BOHARI, H., Medicine and Health Sciences
- GUDUM, H., Medicine and Health Sciences
- HADI, Y., Resource Science and Technology
- HARUN, W. S. W., Resource Science and Technology
- LONG, P. K., Medicine and Health Sciences
- MAHFOZ, N., Cognitive Science and Human Development
- MALIK, A. S., Medicine and Health Sciences
- NGIDANG, D., Social Sciences
- SAID, S., Engineering
- SINGH, B., Medicine and Health Sciences
- THAMBYRAJAH, V., Medicine and Health Sciences

UNIVERSITI PENDIDIKAN SULTAN IDRIS
(Sultan Idris Education University)

35900 Tanjong Malim, Perak Darul Ridzuan
Telephone: (5) 4506332
E-mail: akademik@upsi.edu.my
Internet: www.upsi.edu.my

Founded 1922

Chancellor: HRH RAJA PERMAISURI PERAK DARUL RIDZUAN TUANKU BAINUN
Vice-Chancellor: Y. Bhg. Prof. Dato' AMINAH AYOB
Deputy Vice-Chancellor for Academic and Int. Affairs: Prof. Dr ZAKARIA KASA
Deputy Vice-Chancellor for Student Affairs and Alumni: Y. Bhg. Prof. Dr SHAHARUDIN ABDUL AZIZ
Deputy Vice-Chancellor for Research and Innovation: Y. Bhg. Prof. Dr MOHD MUSTAMAM ABD. KARIM
Registrar: Y. Bhg. Dato' RUSLEY BIN TAIB
Chief Bursary: HAJJAH KHADIJAH HAMDAN
Chief Librarian: CIK ZAHARIAH BINTI MOHAMED SHAHAROON

DEANS

Faculty of Art and Music: Dr MOHD HASSAN ABDULLAH
Faculty of Business and Economics: Dr NORLIA MAT NORWANI
Faculty of Cognitive Science and Human Development: Assoc. Prof. Dr ABDUL LATIF HJ. GAPOR
Faculty of Information and Communication Technology: Prof. Dr MOHAMAD IBRAHIM
Faculty of Languages: Dr ABDUL GHANI ABU
Faculty of Science and Technology: Assoc. Prof. Dr MUSTAFFA AHMAD
Faculty of Social Sciences and Humanities: IBRAHIM HASHIM
Faculty of Sports Sciences: Dr MOHD SANI MADON
Institute of Graduate Studies: Prof. Dr OMAR ABDULL KAREEM

UNIVERSITI PUTRA MALAYSIA
(Putra University, Malaysia)

43400 Serdang, Selangor Darul Ehsan
Telephone: (3) 89486101
E-mail: cans@admin.upm.edu.my
Internet: www.upm.edu.my

Founded 1971
State control
Languages of instruction: Malay, English
Academic year: May to November (2 semesters)

Chancellor: THE GOVERNOR OF PENANG
Vice-Chancellor: Prof. Dato' Dr MOHD ZOHADIE BARDAIE
Deputy Vice-Chancellor for Academic Affairs: Prof. Dr MUHAMAD AWANG
Deputy Vice-Chancellor for Devt: Assoc. Prof. Dr MAKHDZIR MARDAN
Deputy Vice-Chancellor for Student Affairs: Assoc. Prof. Dr Haji IDRIS ABDOL
Registrar: KAMALUL ARIFFIN MUSA
Librarian: KAMARIAH BT ABDUL HAMID

Number of teachers: 1,074
Number of students: 33,566

Publication: *Tribun Putra* (12 a year)

DEANS

Faculty of Agriculture: Prof. Dr MOHD YUSOF HUSSEIN
Faculty of Computer Science and Information Technology: Dr ABD. AZIM BIN ABD. GHANI
Faculty of Design and Architecture: Assoc. Prof. Dr MUSTAFA KAMAL
Faculty of Economics and Management: Prof. Dr NIK MUSTAFA RAJA ABDULLAH
Faculty of Educational Studies: Assoc. Prof. KAMARIAH BT ABU BAKAR
Faculty of Engineering: Prof. Dr Ir. RADIN UMAR RADIN SOHADI
Faculty of Food Science and Biotechnology: Prof. Dr GULAM RUSUL BIN RAHMAT ALI
Faculty of Forestry: Prof. Dato' Dr NIK MUHAMAD NIK MAJID
Faculty of Human Ecology: Prof. Dr ABDULLAH AL-HADI HJ. MUHAMED
Faculty of Medicine and Health Sciences: Assoc. Prof. Dr JAMMAL AHMAD ESSA
Faculty of Modern Languages and Communication: Prof. Dr SHAIK MOHD NOOR ALAM SHAIK MOHD HUSSEIN
Faculty of Science and Environmental Studies: Prof. Dr WAN ZIN WAN YUNUS
Faculty of Veterinary Medicine: Prof. Dato' Dr Sheik OMAR ABDUL RAHMAN
Graduate School of Management: Assoc. Prof. ZAINAL ABIDIN KIDAM
School of Graduate Studies: Prof. Dr AINI IDERIS

UNIVERSITI SAINS MALAYSIA
(University of Science, Malaysia)

Minden, 11800 Penang
Telephone: (4) 6533888
E-mail: pro@notes.usm.my
Internet: www.usm.my

Founded 1969
federal control
Languages of instruction: English, Malay
Academic year: September to August

Chancellor: HRH TUANKU SYED SIRAJUDDIN IBNI AL-MARHUM TUANKU SYED PUTRA JAMALULLAIL
Pro-Chancellor: Hon. Tan Sri RAZALI ISMAIL
Pro-Chancellor: Hon. Tan Sri Dato' Dr JEGATHESAN MANIKAVASAGAM
Vice-Chancellor: Hon. Prof. Dato' DZULKIFLI ABDUL RAZAK
Deputy Vice-Chancellor: Hon. Dato' Prof. OMAR OSMAN
Deputy Vice-Chancellor: Prof. AHMAD SHUKRI MUSTAPA KAMAL
Deputy Vice-Chancellor: Prof. ASMA ISMAIL
Registrar: JAMAHYAH BASIRON

Library: see under Libraries and Archives
Number of teachers: 1,938
Number of students: 26,837 (18,295 undergraduate, 8,542 postgraduate)

Publications: *Frontiers* (3 a year), *Graduate Infolink* (3 a year), *Kejuruteran* (3 a year), *Mediskop* (3 a year), *Perantara* (3 a year)

DEANS

Biomedical and Health Sciences Platform: Prof. SYED MOHSIN SYED SAHIL JAMALULLAIL
Clinical Sciences Research Platform: Prof. Dr NOR HAYATI OTHMAN
Engineering and Technology Research Platform: Prof. ZAINAL ARIFFIN MOHD ISHAK
Fundamental Sciences Research Platform: Prof. ABDUL LATIF AHMAD
Information and Communication Technology Research Platform: Assoc. Prof. BAHARI BELATON
Institute of Postgraduate Studies: Prof. ROSHADA HASHIM
Life Sciences Research Platform: Prof. MOHD NAZALAN MOHD NAJIMUDIN
School of Aerospace Engineering: Hon. Prof. HASNAH HJ. HARON
School of Arts: Assoc. Prof. A. RAHMAN HJ. MOHAMED
School of Biological Sciences: Prof. ABU HASSAN AHMAD
School of Chemical Engineering: Prof. AZLINA HARUN KAMARUDDIN
School of Chemical Sciences: Prof. WAN AHMAD KAMIL MAHMOOD
School of Civil Engineering: Prof. HAMIDI ABDUL AZIZ
School of Communication: Assoc. Prof. ADNAN HUSSEIN
School of Computer Sciences: Prof. ROSNI ABDULLAH MUSTAFA
School of Dental Sciences: Dr ADAM HUSEIN
School of Distance Education: OMAR MAJID
School of Education Studies: Assoc. Prof. ANNA CHRISTINA ABDULLAH
School of Electrical and Electronic Engineering: Prof. MOHD ZAID ABDULLAH
School of Health Sciences: Prof. AHMAD ZAKARIA
School of Housing, Building and Planning: Prof. Ir. MAHYUDDIN RAMLI
School of Humanities: Hon. Prof. Dr ABU TALIB AHMAD
School of Industrial Technology: Prof. ROZMAN HJ. DIN
School of Languages, Literacy and Translation: Prof. AMBIGAPATHY PANDIAN
School of Management: Hon. Dato' Assoc. Prof. ISHAK ISMAIL
School of Materials and Mineral Resources Engineering: Prof. AHMAD FAUZI MOHD NOOR
School of Mathematical Sciences: Assoc. Prof. AHMAD IZANI MD ISMAIL
School of Mechanical Engineering: Assoc. Prof. ZAIDI MOHD RIPIN
School of Medical Sciences: Prof. Dr ABDUL AZIZ BABA
School of Pharmaceutical Sciences: Prof. SYED AZHAR SYED SULAIMAN
School of Physics: Prof. ZAINURIAH HASSAN
School of Social Sciences: Assoc. Prof. ISMAIL BABA
Social Transformation Research Platform: Prof. BADARUDDIN MOHAMED

PROFESSORS

ABDUL AZIZ, B., Medical Oncology, Haematology and Palliative Medicine
ABDUL AZIZ, T., Radiation Biophysics, Medical Physics
ABDUL GHANI, S., Urban and Regional Planning
ABDUL RASHID, A. R., Clinical Pharmacology and Therapeutics
ABDUL WAHAB, A. R., Vector Ecology
AB RANI, S., Maxillofacial Surgery, Tissue Banking, Bone Banking
ABU HASSAN, A., Mosquito and Urban Pest Control, Aquatic Insects, Insect Ecology
ABU TALIB, A., South-East Asian History
AHMAD PAUZI, M. Y., Physiology
AHMAD SHUKRI, M. K., Radiation Biophysics, Medical Physics
AHMAD YUSOFF, H., Mechanical Computer-Aided Engineering, CAD-CAM
AISHAH, A. L., Pharmacology
AMBIGAPATHY, P., English as a Second Language and Sociolinguistics
AMINAH, A., Science Education
AMIR HUSSIN, B., Economics
ASMA, I., Medical Microbiology, Molecular Biology of Infectious Diseases, Rapid Diagnosis of Infectious Diseases esp. Typhoid and Paratyphoid Fevers
BAHARUDDIN, S., Plant Pathology
BAHRUDDIN, S., Chemical Resistance Measurements
BOEY, P. L., Palm Oil Chemistry and Technology
CHAN, K. L., Pharmaceutical Chemistry
CHAN, N. W., Water Resources, Hydrology and Flood Hazard Management, Climatology
CHONG, C. S., Biophysics
DAING MOHD NASIR, D. I., Accounting, Business Administration
DZULKIFLI, A. R., Pharmacology
FARID, G., Digital and Data Communication
FUN, H. K., Solid State Physics
GOON, W. K., Environmental Studies, Mangrove Ecosystem, Tropical Rain Forest
HANAFI, I., Plastic Composite and Rubber
HARBINDAR JEET SINGH, G. S., Calcium Metabolism
HASSAN, S., Applied Mathematics
IBRAHIM, C. O., Biotechnology
IBRAHIM, W., Transport Planning
ILYAS, M., Geophysics
ITAM, S., Medical Parasitology and Entomology
JAFRI MALIN, A., Neurosurgery
JAMIL, I., Polymers
JEYARATNAM, K., Policy Studies
JUNAIDAH, O., Scattering of Electromagnetic Waves
KAMARULAZIZI, I., Semiconductor Energy Studies, Clean Room Fabrication Technology
KOH, H. L., Environmental and Ecosystem Modelling EIA Simulation
LEE, C. Y., Geophysics Exploration, Applied Geophysics
LIM, K. O., Biophysics
LIM, P. E., Waste Water Treatment
LOH, K. W., Economics
MAFAUZY, M., Endocrinology, Effect of Natural Products on Diabetes
MAHYUDDIN, R., Building Technology
MASHHOR, M., Botany
MASHUDI, K., Linguistics
MD SALLEH, Y., Literature
MOHAMAD AZEMI, M. N., Food Technology
MOHAMAD, S., Literature
MOHAMED, S., Marketing
MOHAMED GHOUSE, N., Theatre and Dance
MOHAMED ISA, A. M., Biodegradable Plastics, Biotechnology
MOHAMED OMAR, K., Environmental Technology
MOHAMED RAZALI, S., Social Psychiatry and Rehabilitation
MOHAMED SHUKRI, S., Planning and Development Management
MOHAMMAD MAHFOOZ, A. A., Management
MORSHIDI, S., Urban Planning and Development
MUHAMAD, J., Management Science, Statistics, Operations Management

MUHAMMAD IDIRIS, S., Analytical Chemistry
MUSTAFFA, E., Medicine
NAVARATNAM, V., Clinical Pharmacology
NOR HAYATI, O., Surgical Pathology with special interest in Gynaepathology, Dermatopathology and Oncopathology
NORZAMI, M. N., Immunology
OMAR, S., Inorganic Chemistry
ONG, B. H., Computer-aided Geometric Design
OSMAN, M., Marketing
PLOTNIKOV IOURI, P., Flight Dynamics and Control Systems, Applied Optimal Control
POH, B. L., Organic Chemistry
QUAH, S. H., Applied Mathematics
RADZALI, O., Materials and Bioceramics Engineering
RAHMAT, A., Clinical Pharmacy and Toxicology
RAMLI, M., Persuasive Communication
ROGAYAH, J., Curricular Development and Problem-based Learning
ROSHADA, H., Biomedical Analysis
ROSHIHAN, M. A., Quality Control
ROZHAN, M. I., Solid State Physics
ROZMAN, D., Chemistry of Wood
RUSLAN, R., Geographic Information Systems
RUSLI, N., Public Health, Islamic Occupational and Health Medicine, AIDS Prevention and Counselling, Islamic Perspectives in Medicine and Health, Occupational Health and Safety
SARINGAT, B., Quality Control Tablets, Capsules, Herbal Formulations
SEETHARAMU, K. N., Heat Transfer, Computational Fluid Dynamics, Stress Analysis
SHARIF MAHSUFI, M., Pharmacokinetics, Drug Metabolism
SITI ZURAINA, A. M., Anthropology and Sociology
SUBASH, B., Chemical Reaction Engineering, Zeolite Catalysis, Environmental Catalysis, Process Design and Development
SUKOR, K., Poverty-focused Micro-credit Programme
SURESH, N., Economics
SYED IDRIS, S. H., Communications, Radar Systems, Microwave, Antenna and Propagation
SYED MOHSIN, S. S. J., Pharmacology
TENG, C. S., Chemical Engineering
TEOH, S. G., Inorganic and Organo-metallic Chemistry
WAN ABDUL MANAN, W. M., Nutrition, Public Health and Quality of Life
WAN MOHAMAD, W. B., Endocrinology, Impaired Glucose Tolerance Test
WAN ROSLI, W. D., Paper Technology
YUEN, K. H., Pharmaceutical Technology
ZABIDI AZHAR, H., Paediatric Neurology
ZAHARIN, Y., Computational Linguistics and Algebraic Geometry
ZAINAL ABIDIN, A., Electroplating, Waste Water Treatment
ZAINAL ARIFIN, A., Materials, Ceramics
ZAINAL ARIFIN, M. I., Polymer Technology
ZAINUL FADZIRUDDIN, Z., Molecular Biology
ZAKARIA, M. A., Colloid Surface and Cement Sciences
ZHARI, I., Pharmaceuticals
ZUBIR, D., Pollution
ZULFIGAR, Y., Coral and Marine Biology
ZULMI, W., Hand and Reconstructive Surgery

UNIVERSITI TEKNOLOGI MALAYSIA (University of Technology Malaysia)

Skudai, 81310 Johor
Telephone: (7) 5530222
E-mail: pendaftar@utm.my
Internet: www.utm.my

Founded 1904; univ. status 1972
State control
Languages of instruction: English, Malay
Academic year: June to March

Vice-Chancellor and Pres.: Dato' Prof. Ir. Dr ZAINI BIN UJANG
Deputy Vice-Chancellor for Academic and Int. Affairs: Prof. Dr Ir. MOHD AZRAAI BIN KASSIM
Deputy Vice-Chancellor for Research and Innovation: Prof. Dr MARZUKI BIN KHALID
Deputy Vice-Chancellor for Student Affairs and Alumni: Prof. Datuk Dr MOHD TAJUDIN BIN HJ. NINGGAL
Registrar: WAN MOHD ZAWAWI BIN WAN ABD. RAHMAN
Librarian: KAMARIAH BINTI NOR MOHD DESA
Library: see under Libraries and Archives
Number of teachers: 1,633
Number of students: 31,529
Publication: *Journal of Technology* (in 6 series, each 2 a year)

DEANS

Faculty of Bioscience and Bioengineering: Prof. Dr ROSLI BIN MD ILLIAS
Faculty of Built Environment: Assoc. Prof. Dr AHMAD NAZRI BIN MUHAMAD LUDIN
Faculty of Chemical Engineering: Prof. Dr ZAINUDDIN BIN ABDUL MANAN
Faculty of Civil Engineering: Assoc. Prof. Dr Ir. SHAHRIN BIN MOHAMMAD
Faculty of Computer Science and Information Systems: Prof. Dr ABDUL HANAN BIN ABDULLAH
Faculty of Education: Assoc. Prof. Dr MOHAMAD BIN BILAL ALI
Faculty of Electrical Engineering: Prof. Ir. Dr ABDUL HALIM BIN MOHD YATIM
Faculty of Geoinformation and Real Estate: Prof. Dr ALIAS BIN ABD. RAHMAN
Faculty of Health Science and Biomedical Engineering: Prof. Dr JASMY BIN YUNUS
Faculty of Islamic Civilisation: Assoc. Prof. AZMI SHAH BIN SURATMAN
Faculty of Management and Human Resources Development: Assoc. Prof. Dr AMRAN BIN MD. RASLI
Faculty of Mechanical Engineering: Prof. Dr ROSLAN BIN ABDUL RAHMAN
Faculty of Petroleum and Renewable Energy Engineering: Prof. Dr ARIFFIN BIN SAMSURI
Faculty of Science: Prof. Dr MADZLAN BIN AZIZ
Malaysian-Japan International Institute of Technology: Prof. Ir. MEGAT JOHARI BIN MEGAT MOHD NOR
School of Graduate Studies: Prof. Dr ROSE ALINDA BINTI ALIAS
UTM Advanced Informatics School: Prof. Dr SHAMSUL BIN SHAHIBUDIN
UTM International Business School: Assoc. Prof. Dr MOHD HASSAN BIN MOHD. OSMAN
UTM Perdana School of Science, Technology and Innovation Policy: Prof. ZAMRI BIN MOHAMED
UTM Razak School of Engineering and Advanced Technology: Prof. Dr AWALUDDIN BIN MOHAMED SHAHAROUN
UTM School of Professional and Continuing Education: Assoc. Prof. Dr KHAIRUL ANUAR ABDULLAH

UNIVERSITI TEKNOLOGI MARA

40450 Shah Alam, Selangor Darul Ehsan
Telephone: (3) 55442000
E-mail: webadmin@www.uitm.edu.my
Internet: www.uitm.edu.my

Founded 1956 as Dewan Latihan RIDA, became Maktab MARA 1965 and Institut Teknologi MARA 1967, present name 1999
Academic year: May to April

Vice-Chancellor: Dato' Seri Prof. Dr IBRAHIM ABU SHAH
Number of teachers: 4,200
Number of students: 100,000
Publications: *Accountancy Newsletter*, *Info UiTM*, *International Research Journal*

DEANS

Centre for Graduate Studies: Datin ZUBAIDAH ALSREE
Faculty of Accountancy: Prof. Dr Hj. IBRAHIM KAMAL ABDUL RAHMAN
Faculty of Administration and Law: Prof. Madya RAMLA BINTI MOHD NOH
Faculty of Applied Science: Prof. Madya Dr AHMAD SAZALI HAMZAH
Faculty of Architecture, Planning and Surveying: Prof. Madya Dr MOHAMED YUSOFF ABBAS
Faculty of Art and Design: Prof. Madya Dr BAHARUDIN UJANG
Faculty of Business and Management: Prof. Madya Dr JAMIL HAMALI
Faculty of Chemical Engineering: Prof. Madya Dr SHARIFAH AISHAH AYED A. KADIR
Faculty of Civil Engineering: Prof. Madya Ir Dr Hj. MOHD YUSOF ABD. RAHMAN
Faculty of Communication and Media Studies: Prof. Madya ALIAS MD SALLEH
Faculty of Education: Prof. Dr HAZADIAH MOHD DAHAN
Faculty of Electrical Engineering: Prof. Madya Dr YUSOF MD SALLEH
Faculty of Health Science: Prof. Dr ABD. RAHIM MD NOOR
Faculty of Hotel and Tourism Management: EN ABDUL AZIZ ABDUL MAJID
Faculty of Information Science: Prof. Madya Dr LAILI HJ HASHIM
Faculty of Information Technology and Quantitative Science: Prof. Madya AZIZI NGAH TASIR
Faculty of Mechanical Engineering: Prof. Madya Dr SHANRANI ANUAR
Faculty of Medicine: Y. Bhg. Dato' Prof. Dr KHALID YUSOF
Faculty of Office Management and Technology: Prof. Madya Dr HALIMATON HJ. KHALID
Faculty of Performing Arts: Prof. Madya Md RUSHDIE KUBON MD SHARIFF
Faculty of Pharmacy: Prof. Dr ABU BAKAR ABD MAJEED (acting)
Faculty of Sports Science and Recreation: Prof. Madya Dr Muhd KAMIL IBRAHIM

UNIVERSITI TEKNOLOGI PETRONAS

31750 Bandar Seri Iskandar, Tronoh, Perak Darul Ridzuan
Telephone: (5) 3688000
E-mail: utp@petronas.com.my
Internet: www.utp.edu.my

Founded 1995 as Institute of Technology Petronas; present name 1997

UNIVERSITI TENAGA NASIONAL

Km 7 Jl IKRAM-UNITEN, Kajang-Puchong, 43009 Kajang, Selangor
Telephone: (3) 89212113
E-mail: rusmala@uniten.edu.my
Internet: www.uniten.edu.my

Founded 1976 as Institut Latihan Sultan Ahmad Shah, renamed Tenaga Nasional Berhad 1990 and Institut Kerjuruteraan Teknologi Tenaga Nasional 1994, current name adopted 1997
Private control
Languages of instruction: English, Malay
Academic year: July to June

Vice-Chancellor: Prof. Ir Dr MASHKURI YAACOB
Deputy Vice-Chancellor for Academics: Prof. Ir Dr IBRAHIM HUSSEIN
Deputy Vice-Chancellor for Student Affairs, Alumni and Management: Dr MOHAMED NASSER MOHAMED NOOR
Deputy Vice-Chancellor for KSHAS: Assoc. Prof. Dr SHAARI MD NOR
Int. Relations Office: RUSMALA MOHD DAUD
Librarian: SAZALI SULAIMAN

Library of 80,000 vols
Number of teachers: 418
Number of students: 8,614

Publications: *Electronic Journal of Computer Science and Information Technology* (2 a year), *Journal of Business Management* (2 a year), *Journal of Energy & Environment* (2 a year)

DEANS

College of Business Management: Dr Hj. SHAARI MOHD NOR

College of Engineering: Dr IBRAHIM HUSSEIN

College of Information Technology: Dr ZAINUDDIN HASSAN (Deputy Dean)

Institute of Liberal Studies: Prof. Datin Dr Hj. KOBKUA SUWANNATHAT-PIAN

UNIVERSITI UTARA MALAYSIA
(Northern University of Malaysia)

06010 UUM Sintok, Kedah Darul Aman

Telephone: (4) 9284000
E-mail: ukkuum@uum.edu.my
Internet: www.uum.edu.my

Founded 1984
State control
Languages of instruction: Malay, English
Academic year: September to August (2 semesters)

Chancellor: HRH THE SULTAN OF KEDAH
Pro-Chancellor: Yang Amat Berbahagia Tun Dato' Sri Dr AHMAD FAIRUZ DATO' SHEIKH ABDUL HALIM
Pro-Chancellor: Yang Berbahagia Tan Sri Dato' Seri Dr ABDUL HAMID PAWANTEH
Vice-Chancellor: Yang Berbahagia Prof. Dato' Dr MOHAMED MUSTAFA ISHAK
Deputy Vice-Chancellor for Academic and International Affairs: Prof. Dr ROSNA AWANG HASHIM
Deputy Vice-Chancellor for Research and Innovation: Prof. Dr ABDUL RAZAK SALEH
Deputy Vice-Chancellor for Student Affairs and Alumni Relations: Datuk Dr AHMAD FAIZ HAMID
Bursar: AMRON MAN
Registrar: MOHAMAD AKHIR HAJI YUSUF
Chief Librarian: SALLEH HUDIN MUSTAFFA

Library of 1,136,803 vols
Number of teachers: 1,321
Number of students: 34,424

Publications: *International Journal of Banking and Finance* (2 a year), *International Journal of Management Studies* (2 a year), *Journal of Information and Communication Technology* (1 a year), *Journal of International Studies* (1 a year), *Journal of Law, Government and Social Science* (1 a year), *Journal of Legal Studies* (1 a year), *Journal of Technology and Operations Management* (1 a year), *Jurnal Pembangunan Sosial* (Journal of Social Development, 1 a year), *Malaysian Journal of Language and Communication* (1 a year), *Malaysian Journal of Learning and Instruction* (1 a year), *Malaysian Management Journal* (2 a year)

DEANS

Awang Had Salleh Graduate School of Arts and Sciences: Assoc. Prof. Dr ABDUL MALEK ABDUL KARIM

Ghazali Shafie Graduate School of Government: Assoc. Prof. Dr AHMAD MARTADHA MOHAMED

Othman Yeop Abdullah Graduate School of Business: Prof. Dr NOOR AZIZI ISMAIL

UUM College of Arts and Sciences: Assoc. Prof. AZMI SHAARI

UUM College of Business Studies: Assoc. Prof. Dr NASRUDDIN ZAINUDIN

PROFESSORS

ABAS, Z.
ABD KARIM, MOHD Z.
ABDUL AZIZ, A. R.
ABDULLAH, C. S.
AHMAD, N. H.
CHIK, A. R.
HIAU ABDULLAH, N. A.
KU MAHAMUD, KU R.
LEBAI DIN, A. K.
MAHMOOD, R.
MOHAMAD, M. H.
OMAR, Z.
YAAKUB, A. R.
YUSOFF, R. Z.

Colleges

Maktab Koperasi Malaysia (Cooperative College of Malaysia): 103 Jl Templer, 46700 Petaling Jaya, Selangor; tel. (3) 79649000; e-mail mkm@mkm.edu.my; internet www.mkm.edu.my; f. 1956; academic centres of accounting and finance, business, cooperative consultancy, cooperative governance and law, information technology and communications, international and corporate communication, research management and innovation; library: 30,000 vols; 2,900 students; Dir-Gen. Dr AHMAD ZAHIRUDDIN YAHYA; Dir for Library Encik KHAIRUL AKMAL SAIM; publ. *Dimensi Koop* (in Malay).

Institut Bahasa Melayu Malaysia (Malaysian Institute of the Malay Language): Lembah Pantai, 59990 Kuala Lumpur; tel. (3) 22822389; internet www2.moe.gov.my/ibmm; f. 1958; 81 teachers; 778 students; offers a 3-year pre-service diploma course, a 14-week in-service course in the teaching of the Malay language by trained teachers; students are selected by the Min. of Education; also offers short courses of Malay language as a foreign and second language; Prin. ENCIK SALLEH BIN MOHD HUSEIN.

KDU College: Jl SS 22/41, 47400 Petaling Jaya, Selangor; tel. (3) 77288123; e-mail best@kdu.edu.my; internet www.kdu.edu.my; f. 1983 as Kolej Damansara Utama; library: 25,300 vols; 250 teachers; 6,000 students; pre-university and foundation courses, diploma courses in business administration, computer science, engineering, hotels and tourism; degrees in business, accounting and finance, economics; CEO Dr YAP CHEE SING; Registrar TAN JING KUAN.

Tunku Abdul Rahman University College: POB 10979, 50932 Kuala Lumpur;; tel. (3) 4214977; e-mail info@mail.tarc.edu.my; internet www.tarc.edu.my; f. 1969; campuses in Johor, Penang and Perak; library: 230,000 vols and 11,000 units of electronic and audio-visual materials; 290 teachers; 8,100 students; Pres. Datuk Dr TAN CHIK HEOK; Registrar PHOONG HUEI LING.

Ungku Omar Polytechnic: Dairy Rd, 31400 Ipoh, Perak; tel. (5) 5457656; f. 1969 with UNESCO aid; library: 33,300 vols, 60 periodicals; 549 teachers; 6,451 students; Prin. Mej. Ir HAJI MOHAMED ZAKARIA B. MOHD NOOR; Admin. Officer ROFBIAH BT KAMARUDDIN; Librarian NOR AINON B. ZAKARIA.

Yayasan Pengurusun Malaysia (Malaysian Institute of Management): 227 Jl. Ampang, 50450 Kuala Lumpur; tel. (3) 2425255; f. 1966; MBA, BA, diploma and certificate courses; Pres. Raja Tun MOHAR BIN RAJA BADIOZAMAN; CEO Dr TARCISIUS CHIN; publs *Malaysian Management Review* (2 a year), *Management Newsletter* (4 a year).

MALDIVES

The Higher Education System

A system of non-formal, traditional education based on learning the Koran and arithmetic was developed in the Maldives during the 1950s in response to the widespread literacy requirements of those Maldivians with little or no access to schooling. The Maldives became fully independent, outside the Commonwealth, on 26 July 1965. The present structure of education was implemented following the establishment of the Ministry of Education in 1968. In 1989 the Government established a National Council on Education, under the chairmanship of the President, to oversee the development of education in the Maldives. The first institution of higher education, the Maldives College of Higher Education (MCHE), was founded in 1998 as part of a restructuring and rationalization of all government-operated post-secondary education (research and training) in the country. The first Bachelors degree programme was launched at the MCHE in 1999 and in 2001 the Ministry of Education established the Maldives National Qualifications Framework. Following the passage of a National University Act in December 2010, the MCHE was redesignated as the country's first university: the Maldives National University was officially inaugurated in February 2011. In 2011 4,095 students enrolled for full-time courses of longer than one year, and 795 students registered for short-term courses. Operating under the aegis of the Department of Higher Education and Training, the university is the only public degree-granting institution on the island. The university, which offers a range of degrees, diplomas and certificates, currently has eight faculties (health sciences, education, engineering technology, arts, Shari'a and law, hospitality and tourism studies, Islamic studies, and management and computing), three campuses and two centres. The Maldives Qualifications Authority (as the Maldives Accreditation Board was renamed in May 2010) is responsible for quality assurance, accreditation of higher education programmes of study and for developing and implementing a National Qualifications Framework.

Bachelors degrees are three-year programmes of study. Until 2012 the only postgraduate award was the Graduate Certificate; however, at the beginning of the 2013 academic year Masters and PhD programmes in Education and a PhD programme in Shari'a were introduced. Technical and vocational education consists of Certificate and Diploma courses run by the Maldives National University.

Regulatory and Representative Bodies

GOVERNMENT

Ministry of Education: Velaanaage 8–9 Fl., Ameer Ahmed Magu, Malé 20-096; tel. 3333262; e-mail media@moe.gov.mv; internet www.moe.gov.mv; Minister Dr AISHATH SHIHAM.

Ministry of Tourism: 5th Fl., Velaanaage Ameeru Ahmed Magu, Block 20096, Malé 20-05; tel. 3323224; e-mail info@tourism.gov.mv; internet www.tourism.gov.mv; Minister Dr AHMED ADHEEB ABDUL GHAFOOR.

ACCREDITATION

Maldives Qualifications Authority: Second Fl., H. Velaanaage, Malé 20027; tel. 3344077; e-mail info@mqa.gov.mv; internet www.mqa.gov.mv; f. 2000 as Maldives Accreditation Board, present name 2010; attached to Min. of Education; assures quality of post-secondary qualifications; 12 mems; CEO Dr ABDUL MUHSIN MOHAMED.

Learned Societies

GENERAL

Care Society: M. Fiyaathoshi Mage, Fiyaathoshimagu, Malé; tel. 3312491; e-mail info@caresociety.org.mv; internet www.caresociety.org.mv; f. 1998; promotes rights of people with disabilities; promotes formal and non-formal education, training opportunities for men, women and children with disabilities; 409 mems.

Maldivian Red Crescent Society: tel. 3341009; e-mail rasheeda.ali@redcrescent.org.mv; f. 2004; prevents and mitigates human suffering in compliance with complete impartiality and non discrimination based on ethnicity, race, age, gender, religious beliefs, class and political views; promotes mutual understanding and friendship among people; contributes to peace all over the world; Pres. IBRAHIM SHAFEEG; Sec-Gen. RASHEEDA ALI.

BIBLIOGRAPHY, LIBRARY SCIENCE AND MUSEOLOGY

Maldives Library Association: Nat. Library, Museum Building A, Majeedhee Magu, Malé; tel. 7767707; e-mail info.malias@gmail.com; f. 1987; aims to develop libraries and the field of librarianship in Maldives; automation of local libraries and creation of a Union catalogue; digitization of local collns; advocacy and consultancy for local libraries; Pres. AMINATH RIYAZ; Sec. AMINATH SHAZINA; Treas. SHAFEEA SHAKIR; publ. *Meet.Learn.Acquire* (Newsletter, every 3 years).

EDUCATION

Community Education Development Association: Jawahiru Bldg, First Fl., Ma. Haveeree Manzar, Shaheed Ali Hingun, Malé; tel. 3327436; e-mail info@cedassociation.org; internet www.cedassociation.org; f. 2005; promotes education, economic and social devt, healthcare in Maldives; protects human rights; Chair. JEFFREY SALIM WAHEED; Vice-Chair. Dr ISMAIL SHAFEEU.

FINE AND PERFORMING ARTS

Maldives Photographers Association: e-mail admin@mvphotographers.org; internet www.mvphotographers.org; f. 2008; promotes and develops art and profession of photography in Maldives; 98 mems; Pres. MOHAMED SHAFY.

HISTORY, GEOGRAPHY AND ARCHAEOLOGY

Oriental Society for Literature, Ancestral Studies, and History: H. New Happiness, Malé; e-mail info@orientalsociety.org; internet orientalsociety.org; promotes cultural activities and education in Asian literature, genealogy, history; interest areas incl. philology, literary criticism, paleography, epigraphy, linguistics, biography, genealogy, archaeology and philosophy, religion, folklore, art of Oriental civilizations.

LANGUAGE AND LITERATURE

Maldives Journalist Association: Malé; tel. 7785669; e-mail admin@mja.org.mv; internet maldivesjournalistassociation.org; f. 2009; promotes cooperation and professionalism among journalists; works towards establishing free and independent journalism; advocates rights and protection of journalists.

MEDICINE

Diabetes Society of Maldives: H. Bandosge, Dhubugasmagu, Malé; tel. 3328987; e-mail info@dsmaldives.org; internet www.dsmaldives.org; f. 2000 as Diabetes and Cancer Society of Maldives; generates awareness about diabetes; acts as a centre of information on diabetes; conducts screening programmes, presentation, consultation and health education.

NATURAL SCIENCES

Maldives Science Society: Fourth Fl., Ma. Uthuruvehi, Kenerее Magu, Malé 20191; tel. 7781650; e-mail aadhu@sciencemaldives.org.

TECHNOLOGY

National Centre for Information Technology: 64 Kalaafaanu Hingun, Malé 20064; tel. 3344000; e-mail secretariat@ncit.gov.mv; internet www.ncit.gov.mv; f. 2003; develops and promotes information technology in Maldives.

Research Institutes

GENERAL

National Centre for Linguistic and Historical Research: Sosun Magu, Henveiru, Malé 20-05; tel. 3323206; e-mail nclhr@dhivehinet.net.mv; internet www.qaumiyyath.gov.mv; f. 1982; research on history, culture and language of the Republic of Maldives; restoration and preservation of the nation's heritage; preservation and promotion of the Dhivehi language; Dir IBRAHIM ZUHOOR; publs *Dhivehinge Tharika* (2 a year), *Faiythoora* (12 a year).

AGRICULTURE, FISHERIES AND VETERINARY SCIENCE

Marine Research Centre: H. White Waves Moonlight Higun, Malé 20025; tel. 3322328; e-mail msadam@mrc.gov.mv; internet www.mrc.gov.mv; f. 1984; attached to Min. of Fisheries and Agriculture; research areas incl. coral reefs, mariculture, pelagic fisheries, reef fisheries; Dir Dr M. SHIHAM ADAM.

ECONOMICS, LAW AND POLITICS

Maldives Law Institute: Level II, Orchid-maagé, Ameer Ahmed Magu, Malé 0095; tel. 3344911; e-mail info@maldiveslawinstitute.org; internet www.maldiveslawinstitute.org; f. 2011; research into Maldivian law; promotes and assists devt of laws and regulations in the Maldives; Gen. Sec. MOHAMED IYAS; publ. *Maldives Law Review*.

Libraries and Archives

Malé

Islamic Library: Islamic Centre, Medhuziyaaraiy Magu, Malé 20-02; tel. 3323623; f. 1985; Islamic studies and literature; 4,500 vols; Dir AHMED SHATHIR.

Maldives National University Central Library: Rahdhebai Higun, Malé; tel. 3345164; e-mail mchelib@gmail.com; 60,000 vols; Chief Librarian AIMINATH RIYAZ.

National Library of Maldives: 59 Medhuziyaarai Magu, Malé 20158; tel. 3323943; e-mail info@nlm.gov.mv; internet www.nationallibraryofmaldives.com; f. 1945, as the State Library of Maldives, renamed Majeedi Library 1948, present name 1982; attached to Min. of Tourism; nat. library colln; public library facilities; recreation and research support; preserves nat. literature; 62,520 vols, spec. collns in Dhivehi, English, Arabic, Urdu; Dir-Gen. IBRAHIM SHIYAM; Chief Librarian FATHMATH SHIHAM; publs *Bibliography of Dhivehi Publications*, *Bibliography of English Publications*, *Mathifushuge Mauloomaathu* (information on Maldivian family trees).

Museums and Art Galleries

Malé

National Art Gallery: Museum Bldg–Block A, Medhuziyaraiy Magu, Malé; tel. 3343832; e-mail nationalartgallery@tourism.gov.mv; internet artgallery.gov.mv; f. 2005; organizes regular exhibitions, workshops, seminars; promotes colln of art works representing Maldivian culture.

National Centre for the Arts: Olympus Complex, Han'dhuvarudhey Hingun, Malé; tel. 3313456; e-mail nca@tourism.gov.mv; f. 2005.

National Museum: National Centre for Linguistic and Historical Research, Malé 20-05; tel. 3322254; e-mail nclhr@dhivehinet.net.mv; f. 1952; conservation and display of historical items; Senior Curator ALI WAHEED.

University

MALDIVES NATIONAL UNIVERSITY

Malé 20-04
Rahdhebai Higun, Machangolhi, Malé
Telephone: 3345101
E-mail: vc@mnu.edu.mv
Internet: mnu.edu.mv

Founded 1998 as Maldives College of Higher Education, present status 2011
State control

Chancellor: Dr MUSTAFA LUTFI
Vice-Chancellor: Dr HASSAN HAMEED
Deputy Vice-Chancellor for Academic Affairs: Dr ALI FAWAZ SHAREEF
Deputy Vice-Chancellor for Admin. and Finance: HUSSAIN HALEEM
Deputy Vice-Chancellor for Information and Innovation: FAYYAZ ALI MANIK
Registrar: AISHATH ALI
Chief Librarian: AMINATH RIYAZ

Library: see under Libraries and Archives

DEANS

Faculty of Arts: ABDUL RASHEED ALI
Faculty of Education: ASIM ABDUL SATTAR
Faculty of Engineering Technology: MOHAMED RIFFATH SIDHGEE
Faculty of Health Sciences: AISHATH SHAHEEN ISMAIL
Faculty of Hospitality and Tourism Studies: ZEENAZ HUSSAIN (acting)
Faculty of Islamic Studies: ALI ZAHIR
Faculty of Management and Computing: SHATHIF ALI (acting)
Faculty of Shari'a and Law: Dr ABDUL SATTAR ABDUL RAHMAN (acting)

Colleges

Clique College: Third Fl., M. Uthuruvehi Keneree Magu, Malé; tel. 3334036; e-mail info@cliquecollege.com; internet www.cliquecollege.com; f. 2000 as Clique Training Centre, present name and status 2009; offers higher education in accounting, business management, human resource management, information technology and financial management, marketing, tourism; library: 600,000 vols; Vice-Pres. MASTHOOR HUSNEE.

College of Islamic Studies: Malé; tel. 3322718; e-mail kulliyya@live.com; f. 1980; attached to Min. of Education; aims to provide educational opportunities for the country's young people, to encourage the spread of the Arabic language, to provide training and refresher courses for imams, lawyers, judges, and teachers of the Koran and Islamic studies, to promote study of the Koran, to upgrade the Islamic curriculum in accordance with the needs of the country, to publish and translate books on all aspects of Islam; library: 19,000 vols; Rector IBRAHIM ZAKARIYYA MOOSA; publ. *Al-Manhaj* (1 a year).

Cyryx College: M. Kothanmaage, Maaveyo Magu, Malé; tel. 3315870; e-mail info@cyryxcollege.edu.mv; internet www.cyryxcollege.edu.mv; f. 1993, present status 2009; schools of business, information technology, multimedia arts and design; Chair. AHMED SHAREEF; Academic Dir IBRAHIM WAHEED (acting).

Mandhu College: Falhumathee Magu, Malé; tel. 3330055; e-mail info@mandhu.com; internet www.pywork.com/mandhu; f. 1998 as Mandhu Learning Centre; schools of general studies, humanities and social sciences, information sciences and management.

MAPS College: First Fl., H. Vaifilaa–aage, Janavaree Magu, Malé; tel. 3314621; e-mail info@maps.edu.mv; internet www.maps.edu.mv; f. 1999 as MAPS Insitute, present name and status 2011; faculties of humanities, information science, management studies, tourism studies; library: 26,000 vols.

MALI

The Higher Education System

Mali, the former French colony of Soudan, became an independent state in 1960, following the secession of Senegal from the Federation of Mali, founded in 1959. Tertiary education facilities include the two state-operated universities—the Université de Bamako (founded 1996 following the merger of several higher education institutions as the Université de Mali; renamed 2002) and the Université de Ségou (founded 2009)—and several colleges of higher education. The medium of instruction in the higher education sector is French. Many students also receive higher education abroad, mainly in France and Senegal. In 2009 there were more than 60,000 students enrolled at the Université de Bamako, and in 2010 a total of 81,118 students were enrolled in tertiary education. The higher education system currently is undergoing wide-reaching reforms. In June 2011 all higher education institutions were closed and the Université de Bamako was divided into four separate units, each with university status: Université des Sciences, des Techniques et des Technologies; Université des Sciences Sociales et de Gestion; Université des Lettres et Sciences Humaines; and the Université des Sciences Juridiques et Politiques, known collectively as the Universités de Bamako. Other higher education providers were the École Normale Supérieure, École Normale de l'Enseignement Technique et Professionnel, École Nationale d'Ingénieurs Abderhamane Baba Touré, the Institut Polytechnique Rural de Formation et de Recherche Appliquée de Katibougou and the Institut Supérieur de Formation et de Recherche Appliquée. The Université de Ségou also had its first intake of 362 students in 2012.

The Ministry of Higher Education and Scientific Research controls higher education, but the two state-run universities are financially autonomous. The University Council is the policy-making body at both universities and the Rector acts as chief executive. The main academic divisions are the Colleges, Schools and Institutes.

The secondary school Baccalauréat is the main requirement for admission to higher education. The Bologna-style three-tier Licence/Master/Doctorat (LMD) degree system has recently been introduced in Mali. The undergraduate Licence degree is generally awarded after three years of study; in the fields of management, engineering and teacher training, however, the first stage of higher education lasts four years and courses in medicine and pharmacy last five to six years. Admission to postgraduate courses is selective and is often based on an entrance examination. Upon the successful completion of a one-year course following the Licence, students receive the Masters. To study towards a Doctorat, students must complete at least three years of further study.

Post-secondary technical and vocational education consists of programmes of study and professional training leading to the award of Brevet de Technicien, Diplôme de Technicien Supérieur, Diplôme des Sciences Appliquées and Diplôme Universitaire de Technologie.

Mali is a member of the African Quality Assurance Network (AfriQAN), which was established in 2007 (in collaboration with the Association of African Universities and the Global Initiative for Quality Assurance Capacity) to provide assistance to institutions concerned with quality assurance in higher education in Africa.

Regulatory Bodies

GOVERNMENT

Ministry of Culture: BP E4075, Cité Admin., Bâtiment N° 05, Bamako; tel. 2079-42-03; e-mail malibiennale@yahoo.fr; internet www.culture.gouv.ml; Minister Bruno Maïga.

Ministry of Higher Education and Scientific Research: BP 71, Bamako; tel. 2022-57-80; e-mail info@education.gov.ml; internet www.education.gov.ml; Minister Moustapha Dicko.

Ministry of National Education: Bamako; e-mail malieducation2010@gmail.com; internet www.education.gov.ml; Minister Jacqueline Nana Togola.

Ministry of Employment and Professional Training: BP 3298, Hamdallaye ACI 2000, Bamako; tel. 2029-51-36; internet www.mefp.gov.ml; Minister Mahamane Baby.

Learned Society

GENERAL

UNESCO Office Bamako: Badalabougou Est, BP E1763 Bamako; tel. 223-34-92; internet www.unesco-bamako.org; designated Cluster Office for Burkina Faso, Mali and Niger; Dir Ahmed Ould Deida.

Research Institutes

GENERAL

Centre National de la Recherche Scientifique et Technologique: BP 3052, Bamako; tel. 2021-90-85; internet www.cnrst.edu.ml; f. 1986; coordinates all research activity in Mali; 57 research instns; Chair. Dr Moussa Kante; publs *Revue Malienne de Science et de Technologie* (1 a year), *Vie de la Recherche* (4 a year).

Institut de Recherche pour le Développement (IRD): BP 2528, Bamako; tel. 221-05-01; e-mail granjon@sahel.ird.ml; environmental and social sciences for development; library of 4,000 books and journals; see main entry under France; Dir Joseph Brunet-Jailly; publ. *Actualités de la Recherche au Mali* (6 a year).

AGRICULTURE, FISHERIES AND VETERINARY SCIENCE

Centre National de Recherches Fruitières: BP 30, Bamako; f. 1962; controls experimental plantations, phytopathological laboratory, technological laboratory and pilot schemes; Dir P. Jeanteur.

Centre National de Recherches Zootechniques: BP 262, Bamako; tel. 355055; f. 1927; experimental farm with sections on genetics (bovine, swine, poultry), nutrition and biochemistry, pasture, veterinary medicine; library of 1,000 vols; Dir Dr Fernand Traore.

Institut du Sahel: BP 1530, Bamako; tel. 222-21-48; e-mail administration@insah.org; internet www.insah.org; f. 1976; a specialized instn of the Comité de Lutte contre la Sécheresse dans le Sahel (CILSS); aims to combat effects of drought and achieve food security in the Sahel (consisting of Burkina Faso, Cape Verde, Chad, The Gambia, Guinea-Bissau, Mali, Mauritania, Niger, Senegal) through the promotion and coordination of research, circulating scientific and technical information; library of 12,000 vols, 240 periodicals; Dir-Gen. Moustapha Amadou; publs *Actes, Études & Travaux, Etudes et Recherches, Recherche et Développement*.

Office du Niger: BP 106, Ségou; tel. 232-02-92; f. 1932, taken over by Mali govt 1958; research stations at Bougomi and Sahel (cotton), Kayo (rice), Soninkoura (fruit); Dir-Gen. Nancoma Keita.

MEDICINE

Centre National d'Appui à la Lutte contre la Maladie: Rue Raoul Follereau, BP 251, Bamako; tel. 222-51-31; f. 1935; part of Organisation de Co-ordination et de Coopération pour la Lutte contre les Grandes Endémies; medical research, teaching, treatment and epidemiology, specializing in leprosy; Chair. Samba Ousmane Sow.

Institut d'Ophtalmologie Tropicale de l'Afrique de l'Ouest Francophone: BP 248, Bamako; tel. 222-27-22; e-mail iota@malinet.ml; f. 1953; research in tropical eye diseases and prevention of blindness, training courses for technicians and doctors specializing in ophthalmology; Dir Prof. Abdoulaye Diallo.

NATURAL SCIENCES

Physical Sciences

Direction Nationale de la Météorologie: BP 237, Bamako; tel. 2020-62-04; e-mail dnm@afribone.net.ml; library of 1,265 vols; Dir K. KONARE.

Libraries and Archives

Bamako

Bibliothèque Nationale du Mali: BP E4473, ave Kassé Keïta, Bamako; tel. 2029-94-23; e-mail dnbd@afribone.net.ml; f. 1913; 60,000 vols, 2,000 current periodicals; Librarian MAMADOU DEMBA SISSOKO.

Centre Culturel Français: blvd de l'Indépendance, BP 1547, Bamako; tel. 222-40-19; e-mail ccfmedia@afribone.net.ml; internet www.ccfbamako.org; f. 1962; public library of 27,000 vols; Dir NICOLE SEURAT.

Timbuktu

Centre d'Études, de Documentation et de Recherches Historiques 'Ahmed Baba' (CEDRAB): BP 14, Timbuktu; tel. 292-10-81; f. 1973; preserves the historical heritage of the region; collects and conserves Arabic MSS; 15,000 archives; Dir MOHAMED GALLAH DICKO.

Museum

Bamako

Musée National du Mali: BP 159, Bamako; tel. 2022-34-86; e-mail musee@malinet.ml; internet www.musee-national-mali.org; f. 1953; library of 1,900 vols; Dir Dr SAMUEL SIDIBE.

University

UNIVERSITÉ DES SCIENCES JURIDIQUES ET POLITIQUES DE BAMAKO (USJPB)

BP E2528, site Universitaire de Badalabougou, Bamako

Telephone: 2022-19-33

E-mail: u-bamako@ml.refer.org

Internet: www.ml.refer.org/u-bamako

Founded 2011

State control

Language of instruction: French

Academic year: October to June

Rector: Prof. SALIF BERTHE

Number of teachers: 400 (165 full-time)

Number of students: 30,000

Publication: *Recherches Africaines*

DEANS

Faculty of Economics and Management: CHEICK HAMALLA FOFANA

Faculty of Law and Politics: AMADOU KEITA

Faculty of Letters, Languages, Arts and Humanities: SALIF BERTHE

Faculty of Medicine, Pharmacy and Dentistry: ANATOLE TOUNKARA

Faculty of Science and Technology: HAMIDOU DOUCOURE

Colleges

École des Hautes Études Pratiques: BP 242, Bamako; tel. 222-21-47; f. 1974, current name adopted 1979; diploma courses in accountancy, business studies; 35 teachers; 471 students; Dir-Gen. SIDI MOHAMED TOURE.

École Nationale d'Ingénieurs: BP 242, Bamako; tel. 222-21-47; Dir MAMADOU DIAKITE.

École Normale Supérieure: BP 241, Bamako; tel. 222-21-89; f. 1962; 150 teachers; 1,754 students; Dir SÉKOU B. TRAORÉ; publ. *Cahiers de l'ENSup*.

Faculté de Médecine, de Pharmacie et d'Odonto-Stomatologie: BP 1805, Bamako; tel. 222-52-77; f. 1969 (fmrly École Nationale de Médecine et de Pharmacie); library: 6,800 vols, 289 periodicals; 100 teachers; 1,800 students; Dir Prof. ISSA TRAORE; publ. *Mali Médical*.

Institut de Productivité et de Gestion Prévisionnelle: BP 1300, Bamako; tel. 222-55-11; f. 1971; library: 3,000 vols; in-service training, business advice; 15 staff; Dir-Gen. SIDIKI TRAORE.

MALTA

The Higher Education System

In 1592 the Jesuit Order founded the Collegium Melitense and in 1769 it was elevated to university status by Grandmaster Manoel Pinto de Fonseca; it is now known as the University of Malta (L-Università ta' Malta). From 1814 Malta was a Crown Colony of the United Kingdom, before becoming an independent sovereign state, within the Commonwealth, in 1964. Malta became a republic in 1974. Education is governed by the Education Act (1988), which is the responsibility of the Education Division of the Ministry of Education and Employment is free at all levels (although non-European Union students pay high university tuition fees). The principal language of instruction at post-secondary and tertiary level is English. The Council and the Senate are the supreme governing bodies of the University, which is an autonomous institution mainly funded by the Government. In 2012/13 there were some 11,000 students enrolled at the University (which has 14 faculties located across three campuses and more than 20 multi-disciplinary teaching and research institutes/centres). Malta participates in the Bologna Process to establish a European Higher Education Area, the first phase of which was to adopt a credit-based system of comparable degrees with two main cycles (undergraduate and graduate). European Credit Transfer and Accumulation System (ECTS) credits are now used for most programmes at the University of Malta. Other institutions such as the Institute of Tourism Studies and the Malta College of Arts, Science and Technology (MCAST, founded 2001) have their own credit system.

Admission to the University is mainly on the basis of the Matriculation Certificate Examination. Non-degree university studies last one to two years and result in award of either a Certificate or Diploma; the latter requires the accumulation of 60 (ECTS) credits. The undergraduate Bachelors degree is classified as either 'General' or 'Honours': the former requires three years of study (180 ECTS credits), and the latter usually four (240 ECTS credits). Degrees in professional fields of study may last longer, such as medicine (five years) and law (six years). The first postgraduate-level degree at the University is the Masters, which is open to anyone with a Bachelors degree. A Masters lasts one to two years (60–120 ECTS credits) and may be either a 'research' or a 'taught' degree. Finally the second postgraduate and highest university-level degree is the Doctor of Philosophy, awarded after around four years of original research and submission of a thesis; entrance to the PhD course is generally open to students holding the Masters. From late 2010 the Diploma Supplement was issued to all students graduating from the University of Malta.

The main institutions offering vocational education and training are the MCAST (comprising 11 institutes), the Institute of Tourism Studies and the Malta Institute of Conservation and the Management of Cultural Heritage. MCAST offers a range of courses, including all levels of BTEC Diplomas, Certificates and Bachelors (Honours). Alternatively, after completion of secondary school, students may choose to follow an apprenticeship scheme. There are two types available: the Extended Skill Training Scheme (ESTS) and the Technician Apprenticeship Scheme (TAS). Both schemes last four years and include practical training through work placements, which students find with the assistance of the Employment Training Corporation. Apprentices are trade tested by an independent board and, upon successful completion, are awarded a Journeyman's Certificate at either Craftsman level (for ESTS apprentices) or Technician level (for TAS apprentices).

The Office for Standards and Qualifications within the Kunsill Malti gall Kwalifiki (Malta Qualifications Council) is responsible for the development, promotion and maintenance of the Malta Qualifications Framework (MQF) and the National Occupational Standards related to sectors in vocational education and training (VET). In 2012 the 'Education Act: Further and Higher Education (Licensing, Accreditation and Quality Assurance) Regulations' was passed by which the Commission for Further and Higher Education was established as the competent authority for licensing, accreditation and quality assurance of higher education providers and programmes.

Regulatory and Representative Bodies

GOVERNMENT

Ministry of Education and Employment: Great Siege Rd, Floriana, Valletta VLT 2000; tel. 25980000; e-mail education@gov.mt; internet www.education.gov.mt; Minister EVARIST BARTOLO.

ACCREDITATION

ENIC/NARIC Malta: Malta Qualification Recognition Information Centre (Malta QRIC), 16–18 Tower Promenade, St Lucia SLC 1019; tel. 27540051; e-mail qric.malta@gov.mt; internet www.mqc.gov.mt; CEO EDEL CASSAR.

Kunsill Malti għall Kwalifiki (Malta Qualifications Council): 16–18 Tower Promenade, St Lucia SLC 1019; tel. 27540051; e-mail mgc@gov.mt; internet www.mqc.gov.mt; f. 2005; Chair. JOSEPH ABELA FITZPATRICK.

Learned Societies

AGRICULTURE, FISHERIES AND VETERINARY SCIENCE

Agrarian Society: Palazzo de la Salle, 219 Triq ir-Republika, Valletta VLT 1116; tel. 21244339; agrarja@gmail.com; f. 1844; 200 mems; Pres. JOSEPH BORG.

ARCHITECTURE AND TOWN PLANNING

Kamra tal-Periti Malta (Chamber of Architects and Civil Engineers): The Professional Centre, Triq Tas-Sliema, Gzira GZR 1633; tel. 21314265; e-mail info@ktpmalta.com; internet www.ktpmalta.com; f. 1920; mem. of Malta Fed. of Professional Asscns, Architects Ccl of Europe and Union Internationale des Architectes; 600 mems; Pres. VINCENT CASSAR; Hon. Sec. SIMONE VELLA LENICKER; publ. *The Architect* (4 a year).

BIBLIOGRAPHY, LIBRARY SCIENCE AND MUSEOLOGY

Malta Library and Information Association (MaLIA): c/o Univ. of Malta Library, Msida MSD 2080; tel. 22012262; e-mail info@malia-malta.org; internet www.malia-malta.org; f. 1969; promotes legislation concerning libraries; holds training courses in library and information science; one of the founding mems of the Commonwealth Library Asscn; 100 mems; Chair. MARY SAMUT-TAGLIAFERRO; Deputy Chair. ROBERT MIZZI.

ECONOMICS, LAW AND POLITICS

Malta Society of Arts, Manufactures and Commerce: Palazzo de la Salle, 219 Triq ir-Repubblika, Valletta VLT 1116; tel. 21244339; e-mail info@artsmalta.org; internet www.artsmalta.org; f. 1852; Pres. JOSEPH J. MIFSUD; Hon. Sec. STEPHEN SANT'ANGELO.

FINE AND PERFORMING ARTS

Malta Cultural Institute: 'La Paloma', 16 Triq Sant'Enriku, Sliema SLM 1321; tel. 21338923; e-mail maltacultinst@gmail.com; internet maltaculturalinstitute.yolasite.com; f. 1949; concerts, ballet, book presentations, painting and sculpture and ceramic exhibitions; 200 mems; Dir and Concert Coordinator MARIE THERESE VASSALLO; Sec. and Legal Advisor VANESSA MAGRO.

LANGUAGE AND LITERATURE

British Council: Exchange Bldgs, Triq ir-Repubblika, Valletta VLT 1117; tel. 21226377; e-mail mt.information@britishcouncil.org; internet www.britishcouncil.org/malta; f.

1937; offers examinations services for British univs; organizes cultural and educational events; promotes cultural exchange with the UK; Dir Dr PETRA BIANCHI.

NATURAL SCIENCES

Biological Sciences

Malta Ecological Foundation (ECO): Dar ECO, 10B Triq Sant' Andrija, Valletta VLT 1341; tel. 21641486; e-mail eco@ecomalta.org; internet www.ecomalta.org; f. 1992; 4,018 mems; library of 5,100 vols; Dir DUNSTAN HAMILTON; publ. *Stakeholder*.

Research Institutes

LANGUAGE AND LITERATURE

Institute of Linguistics: University of Malta, Msida, MSD 2080; tel. 23403081; internet www.um.edu.mt/linguistics; f. 1988; attached to Univ. of Malta; aims to teach as well as promote and coordinate research in both general and applied linguistics, furthers research involving the description of particular languages, not least Maltese, fosters the study of the various sub-fields of linguistics, and promotes interdisciplinary research; Dir Dr MARTIN R. ZAMMIT.

TECHNOLOGY

Institute for Sustainable Development: University of Malta, Msida, MSD 2080; tel. 23402147; internet www.um.edu.mt/isd; f. 2009; attached to University of Malta; aims to promote sustainability through interdisciplinary research, focusing on the deployment of information technology to support decision-making and strategy, while encouraging science and technology commercialization to enhance infrastructures, productivity and entrepreneurship; Dir Dr MARIA ATTARD.

Libraries and Archives

Gozo

Gozo Public Library: Triq Vajringa, Victoria, Gozo VCT 105; tel. 21556200; e-mail gozo.libraries@gov.mt; internet www.libraries.gov.mt/gpl; f. 1853, merged with the Royal Malta (now Nat.) Library 1948; nat. and reference library; copyright deposit library; 35,000 vols; Librarian GEORGE V. BORG.

Msida

University of Malta Library: Msida MSD 2080; tel. 23402317; e-mail dls@um.edu.mt; internet www.um.edu.mt/library; f. 1954 at the Old Univ. bldgs in Valletta; present location 1967; 850,000 vols, 650 print and 59,990 electronic journals; Dir KEVIN J. ELLUL; Deputy Dir JOANNA FELICE.

Valletta

National Library of Malta: Valletta VLT 1410; tel. 21243297; e-mail customercare.nlm@gov.mt; internet www.libraries.gov.mt; f. 1555; incorporates the archives of the Order of St John of Jerusalem until 1798; 1,000,000 vols, 1,600 historical MSS, 60 incunabula; Nat. Librarian and CEO OLIVER MAMO; Deputy Librarian JOANNE SCIBERRAS; publ. *Bibljografija Nazzjonali Malta / Malta National Bibliography* (1 a year).

Museums and Art Galleries

Gozo

Archaeology Museum of Gozo: Triq Bieb i-Imdina, The Citadel, Victoria, Gozo VCT 104; tel. 21556144; f. 1960 as Gozo Museum; present name 1986; illustrates the cultural history of Gozo from the prehistoric era to the early modern period.

Valletta

National Museum of Archaeology: Auberge de Provence, Triq ir-Repubblika, Valletta VLT 1117; tel. 21239375; e-mail vanessa.ciantar@gov.mt; internet www.maltavoyager.com/moa; artefacts dating back to the Neolithic period; library of 5,000 vols; Curator VANESSA CIANTAR.

National Museum of Fine Arts: South St, Valletta VLT 11; tel. 21225769; f. 1974; colln ranges from early Renaissance period to 20th century; exhibits incl. paintings by Guido Reni, Valentin de Boulogne, Jusepe Ribera, Albert Bierstadt and William Turner.

Sovrintendenza Tal-Patrimonju Kulturali (Superintendence of Cultural Heritage): 173 St Christopher St, Valletta VLT 2000; tel. 23950000; e-mail heritage.superintendence@gov.mt; internet www.culturalheritage.gov.mt; f. 2002 to replace Museums Dept (f. 1903); govt agency; fulfils duties of the state in ensuring the protection and accessibility of Malta's cultural heritage; responsible for all scientific investigation regarding cultural assets such as the conducting of field work and archaeological excavation, and for the full record keeping and management of documentation resulting from such interventions; evaluates art objects, objects of cultural value and collns of such items; advises and coordinates with the Malta Environment and Planning Authority on issues regarding land use and devt to safeguard cultural heritage when considering applications for planning permission; monitors and controls import and export of goods that are of cultural significance, whether the movement is temporary (for example, for exhibition or restoration purposes) or permanent; issues permits needed for such movements; has a number of direct commitments with regional and int. instns relating to the conservation and promotion of Malta's cultural heritage on int. basis; liaises with UNESCO, the Council of Europe and the European Union; participates in European and Euro-Med programmes; responsible for policy, standards, and guidelines related to cultural heritage and regulates heritage management plans; advises govt on heritage matters; Superintendent ANTHONY PACE.

University

UNIVERSITY OF MALTA

Msida, MSD 2080
Telephone: 23402340
E-mail: comms@um.edu.mt
Internet: www.um.edu.mt
Founded 1592 as Collegium Melitense, present status 1769
Language of instruction: English
Academic year: October to July
Chancellor: Prof. DAVID J. ATTARD
Pro-Chancellor: Dr MICHAEL SCIRIHA
Rector: Prof. JUANITO CAMILLERI
Pro-Rector for Academic Affairs: Prof. ALFRED J. VELLA
Pro-Rector for Research and Innovation: Prof. RICHARD MUSCAT
Pro-Rector for Student and Institutional Affairs: Prof. MARY ANNE LAURI
Registrar: VERONICA GRECH
Dir for Finance: MARK DEBONO
Dir for Library Services: KEVIN ELLUL
Library of 950,000 vols, 63,000 print and online periodicals
Number of teachers: 903 (778 full-time, 125 part-time)
Number of students: 11,000
Publications: *Journal of Anglo-Italian Studies, Journal of Baroque Studies, Journal of Education, Journal of Maltese Studies, Journal of Mediterranean Studies, Malta Medical Journal, Mediterranean Human Rights Journal, Mediterranean Journal of Educational Studies*

DEANS

Faculty for the Built Environment: Prof. A. TORPIANO
Faculty for Social Wellbeing: Dr M. COLE
Faculty of Arts: Prof. D. FENECH
Faculty of Dental Surgery: Prof. NIKOLAI ATTARD
Faculty of Economics, Management and Accountancy: Prof. J. FALZON
Faculty of Education: Prof. V. SOLLARS
Faculty of Engineering: Dr JOHN BETTS
Faculty of Information and Communication Technology: Prof. E A. CACHIA
Faculty of Health Sciences: Prof. A. XUEREB
Faculty of Laws: Prof. KEVIN AQUILINA
Faculty of Media and Knowledge Sciences: Prof. S. CHIRCOP
Faculty of Medicine and Surgery: Prof. G. LAFERLA
Faculty of Science: Prof. C. V. SAMMUT
Faculty of Theology: Rev. Prof. E. AGIUS

College

Malta College of Arts, Science and Technology (MCAST): Triq Kordin, Paola PLA 9032; tel. 23987100; e-mail information@mcast.edu.nt; internet www.mcast.edu.mt; f. 2001; Bachelors, diploma and certificate courses; Principal and CEO Prof. MAURICE GRECH; Dir EMANUEL ATTARD.

MARSHALL ISLANDS

The Higher Education System

The Republic of the Marshall Islands lies within the area of the Pacific Ocean known as Micronesia. In 1947 the UN authorized the USA to administer the Islands within a Trust Territory of the Pacific Islands. The 1986 Compact of Free Association between the Marshall Islands and the USA was renewed in May 2003. In 1993 the University of the South Pacific opened an extension centre on Majuro. The Fisheries and Nautical Training Centre offers vocational courses for Marshallese seeking employment in the fishing industry or on passenger liners, cargo ships and tankers. The College of the Marshall Islands, which became independent from the College of Micronesia in 1993, is based on Majuro, and offers a range of associate degree courses in liberal arts, business administration, nursing and elementary education. In 2003 there were an estimated 919 students enrolled in tertiary education. The Ministry of Education is responsible for providing higher education.

Regulatory Body

GOVERNMENT

Ministry of Education: POB 3, Majuro 96960; tel. 625-5262; e-mail rmimoe@rmimoe.net; Minister Dr Hilda C. Heine.

Learned Societies

NATURAL SCIENCES

Biological Sciences

Marshall Islands Conservation Society: POB 123, Majuro 96960; tel. 625-6427; e-mail miconservationsociety@gmail.com; internet www.kobedia.org; f. 2004; aims to help Marshallese manage and protect their atoll environments and sustainable use of resources; promotes community-based fisheries management, protection for endangered species (humphead wrasse, giant groupers, turtles and sharks); organizes community awareness workshops, conservation practitioner and fisheries observer training; monitors live reef food fish trade and aquarium trade exports; 3 programmes: marine, terrestrial, and public awareness and education; Exec. Dir Albon Ishoda.

Republic of the Marshall Islands Environmental Protection Authority (RMIEPA): POB 1322, Majuro 96960; tel. 625-3035; internet www.rmiepa.org; f. 1984; protects the natural environment of the Marshall Islands; ensures sustainability of resources and balance between economic devt and environment; Gen. Man. Deborah Barker-Manase.

Research Institutes

AGRICULTURE, FISHERIES AND VETERINARY SCIENCE

Marshall Islands Marine Resources Authority (MIMRA): POB 860, Majuro 96960; tel. 625-8262; e-mail petej@mimra.com; internet www.mimra.com; research and devt to generate awareness and promote involvement of the local population in sustainable management of coastal resources; incl. outer island fish market, community based fisheries management projects; grant aid projects in partnership with Japanese govt; Exec. Dir Glen Joseph; Exec. Sec. Kiko Andrike.

HISTORY, GEOGRAPHY AND ARCHAEOLOGY

Historic Preservation Office: POB 1454, Majuro 96960; tel. 625-4476; e-mail rmihpo@ntamar.com; internet alelemuseum.tripod.com/hpo.html; f. 1991 by the Historic Preservation Act of 1991 (amended in 1992) to preserve Marshallese culture; attached to Cultural Affairs Div., Min. of Internal Affairs; operates with advice and assistance from Advisory Ccl on Historic Preservation; conducts archaeological survey and inventory, outer island surveys, underwater surveys, oral history and ethnography; maintains RMI Register of Historic Places; Historic Preservation Officer Frederick deBrum; Chief Archaeologist Richard Williamson.

Nuclear Institute: Oscar deBrum Memorial Hall, Majuro; f. 1997; promotes research on and public understanding of history of nuclear weapons and their effects on culture and diplomacy, incl. US nuclear testing programme in the Marshall Islands; partnership with Nuclear Studies Institute of the American Univ. (Washington, DC, *q.v.*); incl. exchange programme for students and faculty; attached to College of the Marshall Islands; Dir Mary Silk.

Museum and Art Gallery

Majuro

Alele Museum, Library and National Archives: POB 629, Majuro 96960; tel. 625-3372; e-mail alele@ntamar.com; internet alelemuseum.tripod.com/index.html; f. 1981; Joachim deBrum Colln of over 2,500 glass-plate negatives of Marshallese life and landscapes during 1880–1930; Bogan Colln of Marshallese crafts from 1940s; recordings of traditional oral literature, video documentaries on cultural and community themes; organizes annual cultural festival (*Lutok Kobban Alele*); incorporates Nat. Archives, 2,500 microfilms covering Trust Territory of the Pacific Islands, Marshall Islands High Court Proceedings, Congress and *Nitijela* legislation, journal colln, Joachim deBrum Memorial Trust Corpn colln, birth and death certificates; Curator Kim Kowata.

University

UNIVERSITY OF THE SOUTH PACIFIC, MARSHALL ISLANDS CAMPUS

POB 3537, Majuro 96960

Telephone: 625-7279

E-mail: taafaki@usp.ac.fj

Internet: www.usp.ac.fj

Founded 1993

Offers Masters programme in business administration

Dir: Dr Irene Taafaki

Sec.: Marissa Note

Number of teachers: 10

College

Fisheries and Nautical Training Centre: POB 860, Majuro 96960; tel. 625-7449; e-mail mimra@ntamar.com; offers vocational courses for Marshallese seeking employment in the fishing industry or on passenger liners, cargo ships and tankers; attached to Marshall Islands Marine Resources Authority; Instructor William Sokomi.

MAURITANIA

The Higher Education System

Mauritania, formerly part of French West Africa, achieved full independence on 28 November 1960 (having become a self-governing member of the French Community two years earlier). The earliest institution of higher education was the Institut National des Hautes Etudes Islamiques (founded 1961). The state-operated Université de Nouakchott, the main university-level institution, was founded in 1981. In 2008/09 there were 11,794 students enrolled in the country's higher education institutions; by 2010 this had risen to 14,141. In 2008 the privately run Lebanese International University opened a campus in Nouakchott offering courses in arts, education, engineering, pharmacy, business administration and law, and in 2010 another private university, the University of Abdullah ibn Yasin, which has faculties of Shari'a, engineering, economics and administration, and arts and the media, was opened in the capital. The Ministry of National Education is the responsible government body for higher education, which is free (barring a nominal registration fee). The languages of instruction are French and Arabic.

Université de Nouakchott, which has four faculties, is governed by an Administrative Council, the membership of which consists of the staff, students and government officials. The Administrative Council is headed by the university President, who is aided by two Vice-Presidents and a Secretary. The senior academic officers are the Deans, Vice-Deans and General Secretary.

The secondary school Baccalauréat is the main requirement for admission to tertiary education. The university degree system was traditionally based on the old-style French model and consisted of two cycles. However, the implementation of the three-tier Bologna-style Licence/Masters/Doctorat (LMD) degree system commenced in 2008/09. The undergraduate Licence degree course lasts for three years and the postgraduate Masters and Doctorat for two and three years, respectively. From 2009/10 the Université de Nouakchott also offered a number of Masters degree programmes (including the Masters en Santé Publique) in cooperation with overseas institutions. The Diplôme de Docteur en Médecine is awarded upon successful completion of at least seven years of study (organized in three successive cycles). Prior to the commencement of the LMD system of degrees in 2008/09, there were no postgraduate-level degrees available in Mauritania; students usually completed their higher education abroad.

The Centre Supérieur d'Enseignement Technique is the leading institution of technical and vocational education, and specializes in mechanical and electrical engineering. The institution offers a three-year course to holders of the Brevet de Technicien leading to the award of the Brevet de Technicien Supérieur. The Ecole Nationale de la Santé Publique, entrance to which is based on the Baccalauréat and additional entrance examinations, provides a three-year course leading to the award of the Diplôme d'Etat de Technicien de Santé. At the same institution, the Diplôme de Brevet d'Infirmier is awarded after two years of study following the Brevet d'Etudes du Premier Cycle. In 2010 the Université de Nouakchott also opened an institute of professional education offering three-year specialized courses.

In November 2010 a government commission (the États généraux de l'Éducation nationale) was established in Mauritania with the aim of reforming the country's ailing higher education system. In November 2012 the commission began local public debates throughout the country with all stakeholders.

Regulatory Bodies

GOVERNMENT

Ministry of Culture, Youth and Sports: BP 223, Nouakchott; tel. 525-11-30; internet www.culture.gov.mr; Minister LALLA MINT CHERIF HACHEM.

Ministry of National Education: BP 387, Nouakchott; tel. 525-12-37; internet www.education.gov.mr; Minister B. A. OUSMANE.

Learned Societies

BIBLIOGRAPHY, LIBRARY SCIENCE AND MUSEOLOGY

Association Mauritanienne des Bibliothécaires, Archivistes et Documentalistes: c/o Bibliothèque Nationale, BP 20, Nouakchott; f. 1979; Pres. O. DIOUWARA; Sec. SID'AHMED FALL.

LANGUAGE AND LITERATURE

Alliance Française: BP 5022, Nouakchott; tel. 525-31-48; e-mail afm@mauritel.mr; offers courses and exams in French language and culture and promotes cultural exchange with France; attached teaching centres in Atar, Kaedi and Nouadhibou.

Research Institutes

GENERAL

Institut Mauritanien de Recherche Scientifique: BP 196, Nouakchott; Dir Prof. MOHAMED LEMINE OULD HAMMADI.

AGRICULTURE, FISHERIES AND VETERINARY SCIENCE

Institut Supérieur des Sciences et Techniques Halieutiques: Nouadhibou-Cansado; tel. 554-90-47; f. 1983; part of Economic Community of West Africa; research and training in the fisheries industry; Dir-Gen. D. SOGUI.

TECHNOLOGY

Direction des Mines et de la Géologie: Ministère des Mines et de l'Industrie, BP 199, Nouakchott; tel. 225-30-83; internet www.mines.gov.mr/mci/left/directions/dmg.htm; f. 1968; 17 mems; library of 3,000 vols; Dir WANE IBRAHIMA LAMINE.

Libraries and Archives

Nouakchott

Archives Nationales: BP 77, Ave de l'Indépendenance, Nouakchott; tel. 523-17-32; f. 1955; documentation centre; 3,000 vols, 1,000 periodicals; Dir NAGI OULD MOHAMED MAHMOUD.

Bibliothèque Nationale de Mauritanie: BP 20, Nouakchott; tel. 525-18-62; f. 1965; deposit library; documentation centre for W Africa; 10,000 vols, 4,000 old MSS; Dir MOHAMED MAHMOUD OULD.

University

UNIVERSITÉ DE NOUAKCHOTT

BP 798, Nouakchott

Telephone: 525-13-82

E-mail: webmaster@univ-nkc.mr

Internet: www.univ-nkc.mr

Founded 1981

State control

Languages of instruction: Arabic, French, English

Academic year: October to June

President: SIDI OULD MOHAMED ABDELLAHI

Librarian: ISSA OULD MOHAMED AHMED

Library of 20,059 vols

Number of teachers: 254

Number of students: 10,000

Publications: *Annales de la Faculté des Lettres et Sciences Humaines* (1 a year), *Revue d'Études Juridiques et Économiques* (1 a year)

DEANS

Faculty of Arts and Humanities: (vacant)

Faculty of Law and Economics: SIDI MOHAMED ABDELLAHI

Faculty of Medicine: (vacant)

Faculty of Science and Technology: AHMEDOH OULD HAOUBA

Colleges

Ecole Nationale d'Administration: BP 252, Nouakchott; tel. 525-32-22; f. 1966; library: 8,000 vols; a documentation and research centre for the study of admin. and politics in Mauritania; first degree courses; 30 teachers; 270 students; Dir CHEIK MOHAMED SALEM OULD MOHAMED LEMINE; Librarian YARBA FALL; publs *Annales*, *Futurs Cadres* (3 a year).

Institut National des Hautes Etudes Islamiques: Boutilimit; f. 1961; 300 students.

Institut Supérieur Scientifique: BP 5026, Nouakchott; tel. 525-11-68; f. 1986; mathematics, physics, chemistry, biology, geology, computer studies, natural resources, ecology; library: 30,000 vols; Dir AHMEDOU OULD HAMED.

MAURITIUS

The Higher Education System

Mauritius became independent, within the Commonwealth, in 1968. In 1992 the Republic of Mauritius was proclaimed. The University of Mauritius (founded 1965) is the oldest existing institution of higher education in Mauritius and is composed of five faculties—agriculture, engineering, science, law and management, and social studies and humanities—and a number of centres. In 2011/12 some 11,239 students were enrolled at the University of Mauritius. The total number of students enrolled in both public and private institutions for that academic year was 45,969, while a further 10,063 students were pursuing their studies abroad. In 2010, 7,442 students were enrolled in technical and vocational institutions. Government funding accounts for an estimated 85% of the University of Mauritius's running costs; the rest is made up from students' tuition fees, consultancy work and commercial rent. The University of Technology, Mauritius (UTM) was established in 2000 following the merger of two state institutions—the Mauritius Institute of Public Administration and Management and the State Information Training Centre. The UTM comprises three schools—the School of Innovative Technologies and Engineering, the School of Business Management and Finance, and the School of Sustainable Development and Tourism—and offers a range of course, including Diplomas, Bachelors and Masters. In November 2009 the Mauritian Government approved legislation to establish an Open University of Mauritius (OUM) and in 2010 the OUM formally took over the activities of the former Mauritius College of the Air. In 2012 the Université des Mascareignes came into existence through the merger of the Institut Supérieur de Technologie and the Swami Dayanand Institute of Management. The University has three Faculties: Business Management, Information and Communication Technology, and Sustainable Development and Engineering. In all there are 10 state-funded tertiary institutions in Mauritius. The number of private institutions, which has grown significantly in recent years, stands at 64, most of which are local branches of overseas institutions and offer courses to postgraduate level in a mixed-mode system of distance and conventional teaching. In 2012 it was announced that the Indian Institute of Technology (Delhi) would open an International Institute of Technology to offer higher level engineering courses in the near future. The Government's ultimate ambition is to transform the island into a regional 'knowledge hub', attracting about 100,000 foreign students by 2020. The Ministry of Tertiary Education, Science, Research and Technology is responsible for the higher education sector.

The Council is the policy-making body of the University of Mauritius with control of administration and finance, and the Senate is the highest academic body. The Court is a body that meets annually to discuss general plans. The five Faculty Boards coordinate all teaching and research, administer examinations and evaluate programmes of study, and act on the instructions of the Vice-Chancellor and Senate.

Two GCE A-Levels are the minimum requirement for admission to degree-level higher education, although for one- to three-year Certificate and Diploma courses the minimum requirement is the Cambridge Overseas School Certificate. Certificate courses are now being phased out. Undergraduate Bachelors degree courses at the country's four universities last three to four years, depending on the subject, but students wishing to study for professional degrees in dentistry or medicine must attend institutions outside the country. (Aside from the four universities, the Mahatma Gandhi Institute also offers Bachelors degree courses.) Following the Bachelors, the first postgraduate degree is the Masters, which lasts two to three years. There are two types of Masters: the Masters of Business Administration (MBA), which is a coursework-based degree, and the Masters of Philosophy (MPhil), which is a research-based degree available in a number of subject areas. Finally, the Doctor of Philosophy (PhD) is the highest university-level degree and is a research-based period of study lasting at least three years.

Post-secondary vocational and technical qualifications include several Brevets and Diplomas. The Mauritius Institute of Training and Development was established in 2009 through the merger of the Industrial and Vocational Training Board and the Technical School Management Trust Fund.

The Tertiary Education Commission (TEC) aims to promote, plan, develop and coordinate post-secondary education in Mauritius and implement a regulatory framework to achieve an international-quality education system. It is also responsible for allocating government funds to the tertiary education institutions under its purview and ensuring accountability and optimum use of resources. Since 2005 the TEC has had the mandate to regulate private post-secondary education institutions through institutional registration and programme accreditation to ensure the provision of good quality education. The TEC also determines the recognition and equivalence of post-secondary qualifications.

Regulatory and Representative Bodies

GOVERNMENT

Ministry of Arts and Culture: Renganaden Seeneevassen Bldg, 7th Fl., cnr Pope Hennessy and Maillard Sts, Port Louis; tel. 212-2112; e-mail moac@mail.gov.mu; internet culture.gov.mu; Minister MOOKHESSWUR CHOONEE.

Ministry of Education and Human Resources: MITD House, Pont Fer, Phoenix; tel. 601-5200; e-mail moeps@mail.gov.mu; internet ministry-education.gov.mu; Minister Dr VASANT KUMAR BUNWAREE.

Ministry of Tertiary Education, Science, Research and Technology: Level 4, Wing A, Cyber Tower One, Ebene; tel. 454-1450; e-mail tertiary@mail.gov.mu; internet tertiary.gov.mu; Minister Dr RAJESHWAR JEETAH.

NATIONAL BODY

Tertiary Education Commission: Réduit; tel. 467-8800; e-mail mohadeb@tec.mu; internet www.tec.mu; f. 1988; allocates funds to tertiary education instns from govt and other sources; oversees quality of educational provision in these instns; accredits tertiary-level programmes offered by the private sector; 9 mems; Chair. Prof. DONALD AH-CHUEN; Exec. Dir Dr PRAVEEN MOHADEB (acting).

Learned Societies

GENERAL

Royal Society of Arts and Sciences of Mauritius: c/o Mauritius Sugar Industry Research Institute, Réduit; tel. 454-1061; e-mail rsas@msiri.mu; f. 1829; Royal title 1847; 208 mems; Pres. Dr ASHA DOOKUN-SAUMTALLY; Hon. Sec. ROSEMAY NG KEE KWONG; publ. *Proceedings* (irregular).

AGRICULTURE, FISHERIES AND VETERINARY SCIENCE

Société de Technologie Agricole et Sucrière de Maurice: Mauritius Sugar Industry Research Institute, Réduit; tel. 454-1061; e-mail rngcheong@msiri.intnet.mu; f. 1910; 390 mems; Pres. Dr K. F. NG KEE KWONG; Hon. Sec. Dr R. NG CHEONG; publ. *Revue Agricole et Sucrière de l'Ile Maurice*.

HISTORY, GEOGRAPHY AND ARCHAEOLOGY

Société de l'Histoire de l'Ile Maurice: rue Chateauneuf, Curepipe, BP 150, Port Louis;

tel. 670-4811; e-mail societehistoire@intnet.mu; internet www.soc-histoire-maurice.org; f. 1938; 810 ordinary mems; Hon. Sec. MILDRED CARMAGNOLE; publ. *Dictionary of Mauritian Biography*.

LANGUAGE AND LITERATURE

Alliance Française: 1 rue Victor Hugo, Bell Village, Port Louis; tel. 212-2949; e-mail afim@intnet.mu; internet www.afmccf.com; offers courses and examinations in French language and culture and promotes cultural exchange with France; six attached teaching centres in Port Louis.

British Council: Royal Rd, POB 111, Rose Hill, Mauritius; tel. 403-0200; e-mail general.enquiries@mu.britishcouncil.org; internet www.britishcouncil.org/mauritius; offers courses and examinations in English language and promotes cultural exchange with the UK; also responsible for British Council work in Madagascar and the Seychelles; Dir ROSALIND BURFORD.

Research Institutes

AGRICULTURE, FISHERIES AND VETERINARY SCIENCE

Mauritius Sugar Industry Research Institute: 1 Moka Rd, Réduit; tel. 454-1061; e-mail contact@msiri.mu; internet www.msiri.mu; f. 1953; research on cane breeding, agronomy, soils, diseases, pests, weeds, botany, mechanization, biotechnology, sugar manufacture, by-products, also on food crops cultivated in association with sugar-cane and between cane cycles; library: see under Libraries and Archives; Dir Dr SALEM SAUMTALLY; publs *Flore de Mascareignes* (irregular), *Occasional Papers* (irregular), *Occasional Reports & Monographs* (irregular), *Research Reports* (irregular).

NATURAL SCIENCES

Biological Sciences

Research Centre for Mauritius Flora and Fauna: c/o Mauritius Institute, POB 54, Port Louis; tel. 212-0639; attached to Mauritius Institute.

Libraries and Archives

Coromandel

National Archives: Devt Bank of Mauritius Complex, Coromandel; tel. 233-4211; e-mail arc@mail.gov.mu; f. 1815; Conservation Unit for repairing damaged records, incl. a Photographic Section, Microfilm Section, Bindery, Oral History Unit and Paper Restoration Unit; 500,000 vols, records of the French (1721–1810) and British (1810–1968) Administrations incl. MSS and printed matters, notarial papers, Land Court registers, maps and plans; Chief Archives Officer PIERRE ROLAND CHUNG SAM WAN; Archivist DIANA ISOBELLE BABLEE.

Curepipe

Carnegie Library: Queen Elizabeth II Ave, Curepipe; tel. 674-2287; f. 1920; spec. colln on Indian Ocean islands; 90,000 vols; Senior Librarian T. K. HURRYNAG-RAMNAUTH.

Port Louis

City Library: City Hall, POB 422, Port Louis; tel. 212-0831 ext. 163; internet mpl.intnet.mu/library.htm; f. 1851; 110,000 vols; important collections on Mauritius and archives of Port Louis Municipal Council; music scores; depository for WHO publications; Head Librarian BENJAMIN SILARSAH; publs *Subject Bibliography on Mauritius* (1 a year), *Subject Index to Local Newspapers* (2 a year).

Réduit

Mauritius Sugar Industry Research Institute (MSIRI) Library: Réduit; tel. 454-1061; e-mail library@msiri.mu; internet www.msiri.mu; f. 1953; rep. colln on all aspects of sugar cane cultivation and sugar manufacture, and expanding colln on food crops; wide coverage of technical periodical literature; colln of prints and drawings and early publs on sugar cane; in-house databases and int. colln of CD-ROM databases and full texts; 31,875 vols; Man. of Scientific Information and Publs Dept ROSEMAY NG KEE KWONG.

University of Mauritius Library: Réduit; tel. 403-7915; e-mail uomlibrary@uom.ac.mu; internet www.uom.ac.mu; f. 1965; important collns in fields of management, social sciences, agriculture, science and technology, law, textile engineering, medical research and Mauritiana; partial depository for UN and World Bank publs; 185,000 vols (150,000 books, 35,000 bound vols of periodicals); Chief Librarian ISHWARDUTH DASSYNE.

Museums and Art Galleries

Mahebourg

National Historical Naval Museum: Royal Rd, Mahebourg; tel. 631-9329; f. 1950; br. of the Mauritius Institute; comprises colln of old maps, engravings, watercolours and naval relics of local interest, exhibited in an 18th-century French house; Dir R. GAJEELEE.

Port Louis

Port Louis Museum: Mauritius Institute, Port Louis; tel. 212-2815; e-mail mimuse@intnet.mu; f. 1880; comprises a Natural History Museum, collections of fauna, flora and geology of Mauritius and of the other islands of the Mascarene region; Dir S. ABDOOLRAHAMAN.

Réduit

Mauritius Herbarium: c/o Mauritius Sugar Industry Research Institute, Réduit; tel. 454-1061; e-mail cbaider@msiri.intnet.mu; internet www.msiri.mu; f. 1960; public herbarium for education and research about native flora; specializes in flora of Mascarene Islands; Herbarium Officer Dr CLAUDIA BAIDER; Librarian ROSEMARY NG KEE KWONG; publ. *Flore des Mascareignes* (irregular).

Universities

OPEN UNIVERSITY OF MAURITIUS

Réduit, Moka

Telephone: 403-8200

E-mail: openuniversity@open.ac.mu

Internet: www.open.ac.mu

Founded 2012

State control

Bachelors honours degrees in business accounting and finance, business management, commerce, English, finance with taxation; masters degrees in business administration, finance and investment, financial management and taxation, public administration; doctoral degree in business administration

Dir-Gen.: Dr KAVIRAJ SHARMA SUKON

UNIVERSITY OF MAURITIUS

Réduit

Telephone: 454-1041

E-mail: website@uom.ac.mu

Internet: www.uom.ac.mu

Founded 1965

Languages of instruction: English, French

partly State funded

Academic year: August to July

Chancellor: Sir RAMESH JEEWOOLALL

Pro-Chancellor: Prof. S. JUGESSUR

Vice-Chancellor: Prof. HARRY C. S. RUGHOOPUTH

Pro-Vice-Chancellor for Research, Consultancy and Innovation: Prof. SOONIL RUGHOOPUTH

Pro-Vice-Chancellor for Teaching and Learning: Prof. B. AMEENATH GURIB-FAKIM

Registrar: S. REKHA ISSUR-GOORAH

Chief Librarian: I. DASSYNE (acting)

Library: see under Libraries and Archives

Number of teachers: 510 (248 full-time, 262 part-time)

Number of students: 11,239

Publications: *Calendar* (1 a year), *Research Journal* (1 a year), *Vice-Chancellor's Report*

DEANS

Faculty of Agriculture: Assoc. Prof. Dr D. PUCHOOA (acting)

Faculty of Engineering: Prof. Dr R. MOHEE

Faculty of Law and Management: Assoc. Prof. T. D. JUWAHEER

Faculty of Science: Prof. H. T. Y. LI KAM WAH

Faculty of Social Studies and Humanities: Assoc. Prof. Dr S. K. SOBHEE

PROFESSORS

BAHORUN, T., Applied Biochemistry

BHURUTH, M., Computational Mathematics

BUNWAREE, S. S., Computational Mathematics (Gender and Development Studies)

JHURRY, D., Computational Mathematics (Chemistry)

MOHEE, R., Chemical and Environmental Engineering

RAMJEAWON, T., Computational Mathematics (Environmental Engineering)

RUGHOOPUTH, H. C. S., Electrical and Electronic Engineering

SOBHEE, S. K., Applied Economics and Development Studies

SOYJAUDAH, K. M. S., Communication Engineering

SUBRATTY, A. H., Biochemistry

UNIVERSITY OF TECHNOLOGY, MAURITIUS

La Tour Koenig, Pointe-aux-Sables

Telephone: 207-5250

E-mail: registrar@umail.utm.ac.mu

Internet: www.utm.ac.mu

Founded 2000

State control

Language of instruction: English

Academic year: August to June

Dir-Gen.: DHARMANAND GUPT FOKEER

Registrar: MAHENDRA CHUTTURDHARRY (acting)

Librarian: SAVITA BHOOABUL

Library of 21,893 vols

Number of teachers: 407 (48 full-time, 359 part-time)

Number of students: 4,568 (2,324 full-time, 2,244 part-time)

Colleges

Mahatma Gandhi Institute: Moka; tel. 403-2000; e-mail vkoonjal@intnet.mu; internet mgi.intnet.mu; f. 1970; serves as a centre for the study of Indian culture and traditions, and the promotion of education and culture; courses in Indian music and dance, fine arts, Indian languages, Mandarin and Indian philosophy; research in Indian and immigration studies, culture and civilization, Bhojpuri, folklore and oral traditions and Mauritian history, geography and literature; spec. collns: Gandhi, Mauritius, archives relating to Indian immigration to Mauritius 1842–1912; library: 100,000 vols; 218 secondary teachers, 76 in tertiary sector; 2,336 students; Chair. L. NUCKCHADY; Dir-Gen. S. NIRSIMLOO GAYAN (acting); Registrar Dr V. D. KOONJAL; publs *Journal of Mauritian Studies* (2 a year, in English), *Rimjhim* (4 a year, in Hindi), *Vasant* (4 a year, in Hindi).

Robert Antoine Sugar Industry Training Centre: Royal Rd, Réduit; tel. 454-7024; e-mail rasitc@intnet.mu; internet pages .intnet.mu/rasitc; f. 1980; courses in sugar cane agronomy, cane sugar manufacture and chemical control in sugar factories, mechanization of field operations, power generation for sugar factories, management skills, supervisory skills, leadership development, communications; courses in English and French at various levels; 100 part-time specialists; 800 part-time students; Dir Dr LINDA MAMET.

MEXICO

The Higher Education System

From the 1520s until independence in 1821 Mexico was under Spanish rule. The oldest current institutions of higher education date from this period, among them Universidad Nacional Autónoma de México (founded 1551), Universidad de Guanajuato (founded 1732; current name 1945), Universidad Autónoma de Campeche (founded 1756) and Universidad de Guadalajara (founded 1792). The Secretaría de Educación Pública (SEP) is the government ministry responsible for the administration of education at all levels, and since 2005 the Dirección General de Educación Superior Universitaria (DGESU) is the sub-department of the SEP which regulates higher education. In 2008/09 there were an estimated 5,560 institutes of higher education, attended by 2,705,200 students (including postgraduates). In 2010/11 enrolment at tertiary level had risen to 2,773,088 undergraduate and 208,225 postgraduate students.

Following legislation enacted in 1992 granting greater autonomy to the Federal States, there has been a considerable increase in the number of privately run institutions of higher education. In an attempt to remedy the large differences in the quality of programmes offered at higher education institutions, in early 2006 the Congreso de la Unión (Parliament) passed legislation requiring all public and private institutions of higher education that offered degree programmes to be accredited; prior to this there had been no national standards for accreditation or quality assurance. Institutions awarding degrees that did not meet the required national standards would have their licences suspended. In 2008 the Asociación Nacional de Universidades e Instituciones de Educación Superior (National Association of Universities and Higher Education Institutions) which currently represents 146 public and 29 private higher education institutions approved a preliminary document entitled The Evaluation, Certification and Accreditation of Higher Education in Mexico: Towards Integrating the System to Evaluate Higher Education. Since 2000 the Consejo para la Acreditación de la Educación Superior (COPAES—Council for Higher Education Accreditation) has been the sole body authorized by the SEP to confer formal recognition of higher education establishments; it operated as part of the Comités Interinstitucionales para la Evaluación de la Educación Superior (CIEES—Inter-institutional Committees for the Evaluation of Higher Education). However, as required by the education programme, Programa Sectorial de Educación 2007–12, in 2010 COPAES and CIEES were separated into two agencies overseeing accreditation and evaluation respectively in preparation for the implementation of a Sistema Nacional de Evaluación, Acreditación y Certificación de la Educación Superior (National System for Assessment, Accreditation and Certification in Higher Education). The Consejo para la Acreditación de la Educación Superior (COPAES) is the third agency that consults in the process of accreditation and evaluation and coordinates a system of university self-assessment and independent assessors.

Institutions of higher education are classified as follows: public federal universities, public state universities, technological universities, technological institutes, polytechnic universities, intercultural universities (established to promote the development of education among indigenous peoples and communities), public centres of research, higher teacher training schools, other public institutions and private institutions. The medium of instruction is generally Spanish.

To gain admission to a first degree programme, an applicant must possess the certificate for completion of secondary school, the Bachillerato, and, in most cases, sit an entrance examination. The technological universities have introduced a specialist two-year course (Técnico Superior Universitario or Profesional Asociado), which can either be used to transfer to the four-year Licenciado (see below) or as a complete qualification in its own right. The Licenciado is offered at undergraduate level by all institutions of higher education and usually lasts four years, although degrees awarded in conjunction with a professional title may last five or six years. New regulations since 2005 divide postgraduate studies into two main categories: those targeted at professional development—the one-year Diploma de Especialización and the two-year Maestría, and those targeted at scientific research—the two-year Maestría en Ciencias and the three- or four-year Doctorado en Ciencias. Both the Maestria and the Doctorado require the submission and defence of a thesis.

Post-secondary awards for vocational and technical education include the Salida Lateral or Carrera Corta (one to two years) leading to a Diploma or Titulo Técnico.

Regulatory and Representative Bodies

GOVERNMENT

Secretariat of State for Public Education: Argentina 28, 2°, Of. 3011 Col. Centro, 06020 México, DF; tel. (55) 3601-1000; e-mail educa@sep.gob.mx; internet www.sep.gob.mx; Sec. of Public Education ALONSO LUJAMBIO IRAZÁBAL.

ACCREDITATION

Asociación Nacional de Universidades e Instituciones de Educación Superior (ANUIES) (National Association of Universities and Institutions of Higher Education): Tenayuca 200, Col. Sta Cruz Atoyac, 03310 México, DF; tel. (55) 5420-4900; e-mail editor@anuies.mx; internet www.anuies.mx; f. 1950; coordinates and represents instns of higher education, studies academic and admin. problems of the nat. higher education system; promotes exchange of personnel, information and services between the affiliated instns; 145 affiliated univs, centres and colleges; library of 11,500 vols; Exec. Sec. Gen. Dr RAFAEL LÓPEZ CASTAÑARES; publ. *Revista de la Educación Superior* (4 a year).

Consejo para la Acreditación de la Educación Superior (COPAES) (Higher Education Accreditation Council): Cádiz Norte 35. Entre Carracci y Empresa (entrada por Carracci), Col. Extremadura Insurgentes, Del. Benito Juáre, 03740 México, DF; tel. (55) 5615-7281; e-mail comunicación@copaes.org; internet www.copaes.org.mx; f. 2000; non-profit NGO contributing towards the quality assurance of academic programmes in public and private instns by recognizing official accrediting orgs that in turn accredit undergraduate degree programmes in many study areas; Gen. Dir Ing. LUIS EDUARDO ZEDILLO PONCE DE LEÓN.

Federación de Instituciones Mexicanas Particulares de Educación Superior (FIMPES) (Federation of Mexican Higher Education Institutions): Río Guadalquivir 50, 4° Col. Cuauhtémoc, 06500 México, DF; tel. (55) 5514-5514; e-mail fimpes@fimpes.org.mx; internet www.fimpes.org.mx; f. 1981; comprises 114 HEIs incl. the principal private univs; works to improve communication and collaboration between its mems and the other educational instns in the country; promotes high academic standards; Exec. Sec. Lic. RODRIGO GUERRA BOTELLO.

NATIONAL BODIES

Centro de Cooperación Regional para la Educación de Adultos en América Latina y el Caribe (CREFAL)/Centre for Regional Cooperation for Adult Education in Latin America and the Caribbean: Avda Lázaro Cárdenas 525, Col. Revolución, 61609 Pátzcuaro, MICH; tel. (434) 342-8200; e-mail crefal@crefal.edu.mx; internet www.crefal.edu.mx; f. 1951 by UNESCO and OAS, now administered by a Board of Dirs from mem. countries; regional technical assistance, specialist training in literary and adult education, research; library of 80,416 vols; CEDEAL/CREFAL

Adult Education documentation centre for Latin America: database of 17,347 entries; Dir-Gen. MERCEDES CALDERÓN GARCÍA; publs *Decisio—Saberes para la Acción en Educación de Adultos* (4 a year, print and online, tumbi.crefal.edu.mx/decisio), *Revista Interamericana de Educación de Adultos* (2 a year, print and online, rieda.edu.mx).

Dirección General de Relaciones Educativas, Científicas y Culturales (Board of Educational, Scientific and Cultural Relations): Secretaría de Educación Pública, Argentina 28, Centro Histórico, 06029 México, DF; tel. (55) 3601-1000; f. 1960; comprises Sections of Technical Assistance, Int. Relations in the fields of education, science and culture and exchange; serves as coordinating agency between the UN, UNESCO, the OAS and the Mexican Govt; Dir Dr ENRIQUE G. LEÓN LÓPEZ.

Learned Societies

GENERAL

Colegio Nacional (National College): Luis González Obregón 23, Centro Histórico, 06020 México, DF; tel. (55) 5789-4330; e-mail colnal@mx.inter.net; internet www.colegionacional.org.mx; f. 1943; disseminates nat. culture; 34 mems; library of 39,694 vols, 25,146 periodicals; Sec./Administrator Lic. FAUSTO VEGA Y GÓMEZ; publ. *Memoria* (1 a year).

UNESCO Office Mexico: Pte Masaryk No 526, 3°, Col. Polanco, 11560 México, DF; tel. (55) 5280-7071; e-mail mexico@unesco.org; internet www.unesco.org/new/es/mexico; f. 1967; Dir NURIA SANZ.

AGRICULTURE, FISHERIES AND VETERINARY SCIENCE

Confederación Nacional Agronómica (National Agricultural Confederation): Mariano Azuela 121, 2°, Col. Sta Maria la Ribera, Del. Cuauhtémoc, 06400 México, DF; tel. (55) 5547-6442; internet www.agronomicanacional.mx; f. 1921 as Sociedad Agronómica Mexicana; current name adopted 1979; Pres. ARTURO VILLARINO PÉREZ.

ARCHITECTURE AND TOWN PLANNING

Asociación de Ingenieros y Arquitectos de México (Association of Mexican Engineers and Architects): Avda Constituyentes 800 (Oficina AIAM), Col. Belén de las Flores, México, DF; f. 1868; 560 mems; library of 7,565 vols; Pres. Ing. LUIS RAMOS LIGNÁN; Sec. Ing. JOSÉ ACOSTA SÁNCHEZ; publ. *Revista Mexicana de Ingeniería y Arquitectura* (4 a year).

BIBLIOGRAPHY, LIBRARY SCIENCE AND MUSEOLOGY

Asociación Mexicana de Bibliotecarios, AC (Mexican Library Association): Apdo 12-792, Administración de Correos 12, 03001 México, DF; Angel Urraza 817-A, Col. Del. Valle, 03100 México, DF; tel. (55) 5575-3396; e-mail correo@ambac.org.mx; internet www.ambac.org.mx; f. 1924; 1,061 mems; Pres. MARÍA ASUNCIÓN MENDOZA BECERRA; Sec.-Gen. CARMEN YASMINA LÓPEZ MORALES; publs *Memorias* (1 a year), *Noticiero de la AMBAC* (4 a year), *Revista Liber*.

Dirección General de Bibliotecas (Main Directorate of Libraries): Universidad Nacional Autónoma de México, Ciudad Universitaria, Apdo 70–392, 04510 México, DF; tel. (55) 5622-1603; e-mail sinfo@dgb.unam.mx; internet dgb.unam.mx; f. 1966; documentation service, current awareness and SDI services, computerized bibliographical searches; digital library of 6,000 periodical titles with full text; 140 specialized databases; library of 3,485 vols; spec. colln of 230 titles of abstracting and indexing periodicals; 2,500 Latin American periodicals; Dir Dr ADOLFO RODRÍGUEZ GALLARDO; publ. *Biblioteca Universitaria* (2 a year, print and online, revistas.unam.mx/index.php/rbu).

ECONOMICS, LAW AND POLITICS

Barra Mexicana—Colegio de Abogados (Mexican Bar Association—College of Advocates): Varsovia No 1, Col. Juárez, 06600 México, DF; tel. (55) 5208-3115; e-mail primeravicepresidenciabma@gmail.com; internet www.bma.org.mx; f. 1922; 1,732 mems; library of 5,260 vols; Pres. GABRIEL ORTIZ GOMEZ; Sec. RODRIGO ZAMORA ETCHARREN; publs *El Foro* (2 a year), *La Barra* (6 a year).

Instituto Nacional de Estadística y Geografía (National Institute of Statistics and Geography): Avda Héroe de Nacozari sur 2301, Fraccionamiento Jardines del Parque, Puerta 10 basamento, Departamento de Comunicación Social, 20276 Aguascalientes, AGS; tel. (449) 910-5300; e-mail comunicacionsocial@inegi.org.mx; internet www.inegi.org.mx; f. 1983; integrates and develops the Nat. System of Statistics and the Geographic Information System; undertakes the Nat. Census; library of 15,000 vols; Pres. Dr EDUARDO SOJO GARZA ALDAPE; publs *Cuaderno Estadístico de la Zona Metropolitana de la Ciudad de México* (1 a year), *La Minería en México* (1 a year), *México en el Mundo*, 4 statistical yearbooks; industry journals on automotive, chemical, food, steel, and textiles and clothing.

FINE AND PERFORMING ARTS

Asociación Musical Manuel M. Ponce, AC (Manuel M. Ponce Musical Association): Espíritu Santo 75, Col. Coyoacán 0400, México, DF; tel. (55) 5554-4028; e-mail isoldahc@hotmail.com; f. 1949; promotes annual concert seasons of traditional, modern and contemporary Mexican and foreign music; library of musical scores, tapes, records and books; Hon. Pres. LUIS HERRERA DE LA FUENTE; Pres. MARIA TERESA CASTRILLÓN; Sec. JUAN CARLOS CHACÓN.

Instituto Nacional de Bellas Artes y Literature (National Institute of Fine Arts and Literature): Paseo de la Reforma y Campo Marte s/n, Col. Chapultepec Polanco, Del. Miguel Hidalgo, 11560 México, DF; tel. (55) 5283-4600; e-mail dsi@inba.gob.mx; internet www.bellasartes.gob.mx; f. 1947; consists of depts of architecture, artistic education and admin., dance, literature, music, opera, theatrical production, visual arts; responsible for cultural insts throughout Mexico; Dir Lic. TERESA VICENCIO ALVAREZ; publs *Revista de Educación Artística* (4 a year), *Revista Hetereofonía* (3 a year), *Revista Pauta* (6 a year).

Affiliated institution:

Centro Nacional de Conservación y Patrimonio Artístico Mueble (National Centre for Conservation and Registry of Movable Art Heritage): San Ildefonso 60, Col. Centro, Del. Cuauhtémoc, México DF; tel. (55) 5702-2323; e-mail dsi@inba.gob.mx; f. 1958; restoration of works of art; Dir LUCIA GARCIA NORIEGA Y NIETO.

HISTORY, GEOGRAPHY AND ARCHAEOLOGY

Academia Mexicana de la Historia (Mexican Academy of History): Plaza Carlos Pacheco 21, Col. Centro, Cuauhtémoc, 06070 México, DF; tel. (55) 5518-2708; e-mail informes@acadmexhistoria.org.mx; internet www.acadmexhistoria.org.mx; f. 1919; 30 mems; corresp. of Real Academia, Madrid; library of 10,000 vols; Dir Dr MIGUEL LEÓN-PORTILLA; Sec. Dr GISELA VON WOBESER; publ. *Memorias* (2 a year).

Academia Nacional de Historia y Geografía (National Academy of History and Geography): Londres 60, Col. Juárez, Del. Cuauhtémoc, 06600 México, DF; tel. (55) 5533-4149; f. 1925; 179 mems; Pres. LUIS MALDONADO VENEGAS; Vice-Pres. Dr ULISES CASAB; publ. *Revista*.

Sociedad Mexicana de Geografía y Estadística (Mexican Society of Geography and Statistics): Calle de Justo Sierra 19, Apdo 10739, Del. Cuauhtémoc, 06020 México, DF; tel. (55) 5542-7341; e-mail ismge@prodigy.net.mx; internet www.smge.com.mx; f. 1833; 1,204 active mems, 640 corresp. mems; library of 450,000 vols; Pres. Lic. JULIO ZAMORA BÁTIZ; Sec.-Gen. Ing. LUIS BOLLAND CARRERE.

Sociedad Mexicana de Historia de la Ciencia y la Tecnología (Mexican Society for History of Science and Technology): Edif. de las Sociedades Científicas, Avda Cipreses s/n, Col. San Andrés Totoltepec, Tlalpan, 14400 México, DF; tel. (55) 5849-6830; e-mail ilm.smhct@gmail.com; f. 1964; Pres. Dr ISMAEL LEDESMA MATEOS; Sec.-Gen. Dr RAFAEL GUEVARA FEFER; publs *Anales*, *Memorias*, *Quipu*.

LANGUAGE AND LITERATURE

Academia Mexicana de la Lengua (Mexican Academy of Letters): Liverpool 76, Col. Juárez, 06600 México, DF; tel. (55) 5208-2526; e-mail academia@academia.org.mx; internet www.academia.org.mx; f. 1875; corresp. of the Real Academia Española (Madrid); 178 mems; Dir JAIME LABASTIDA OCHOA; Sec. GONZALO CELORIO BLASCO.

Alliance Française Mexique (French Alliance Mexico): Calle Socrates No 156, Esq. Homero Col. Los Morales Polanco Del. Miguel Hidalgo, 11510 México, DF; tel. (55) 1084-4190; e-mail comunicacion@alianzafrancesa.org.mx; internet www.alianzafrancesa.org.mx; f. 1884; offers courses and examinations in French language and culture and promotes cultural exchange with France; attached teaching centres in 43 other cities; Gen. Dir PHILIPPE PALADE; Dir MARIE-JOSE LEDUC.

British Council: Lope de Vega 316, Col. Chapultepec Morales, 11570 México, DF; tel. (55) 5263-1900; e-mail info@britishcouncil.org.mx; internet www.britishcouncil.org.mx; f. 1943; teaching centre; offers courses and exams in English language and British culture and promotes cultural exchange with the UK; also in Monterrey; Dir LENA MILOSEVIC.

Goethe-Institut: Apdo 7–992 Tonalá 43, Col. Roma (Entre Durango und Colima), 06700, México, DF; tel. (55) 5207-0487; e-mail info@mexiko.goethe.org; internet www.goethe.de/mexiko; f. 1966; offers courses and exams in German language and culture and promotes cultural exchange with Germany; attached centre in Guadalajara; library of 13,000 vols, 35 periodicals; Dir REINHARD MAIWORM.

PEN Club de México (PEN Club of Mexico): Heriberto Frías 1452–407, Col. del Valle, 03100 México, DF; tel. (55) 5564-5078; e-mail presidencia@penmexico.org.mx; internet www.penmexico.org.mx; f. 1924; 62 mems; Pres. ALINE DAVIDOFF; Sec. ALICIA QUIÑONES; publ. *Directory of Writers* (1 a year).

MEDICINE

Academia Mexicana de Cirugía (Mexican Academy of Surgery): Avda Cuauhtémoc 330, 3° Bloque B de la Unidad de Congresos del Centro Médico Nacional Siglo XXI, Col. Doctores, 06720 México, DF; tel. (55) 5761-2581; e-mail acameci@amc.org.mx; internet www.amc.org.mx; f. 1933; Pres. Dr ALEJANDRO REYES FUENTES; Sec. Dr FELIPE CRUZ VEGA; publ. *Revista Cirugía y Cirujanos* (2 a year, print and online, revistacirugiaycirujanos.com.mx).

Academia Mexicana de Dermatología (Mexican Academy of Dermatology): Georgia 114, Despacho 503, Col. Nápoles, Del. Benito Juárez, 03810 México, DF; tel. (55) 5682-2545; e-mail academiadermatologia@prodigy.net.mx; internet www.amd.org.mx; f. 1952; Pres. Dra ROSA ELBA BENUTO AGUILAR; Sec. Dra HEIDI MUÑOZ HINK; publ. *Gaceta Academia Mexicana de Dermatología*.

Academia Nacional de Medicina de México (National Academy of Medicine of Mexico): Apdo 7–813, Avda Cuauhtémoc 330, Bloque B planta baja, Col. Doctores, 06725 México, DF; tel. (55) 5519-8679; e-mail contacto@anmm.org.mx; internet www.anmm.org.mx; f. 1865; 14 sections; 340 mems; library of 20,000 vols; Pres. Dr ENRIQUE RUELAS BARAJAS; Gen. Sec. Dr JAVIER MANCILLA RAMÍREZ; publ. *Gaceta Médica de México*.

Asociación Mexicana de Facultades y Escuelas de Medicina (Mexican Association of Faculties and Schools of Medicine): López Cotilla 754, Col. del Valle, Del. Benito Juárez, 03100 México, DF; tel. (55) 5682-9482; e-mail amfem@amfem.edu.mx; internet www.amfem.edu.mx; f. 1957; mems 30 medical schools; Pres. Dr VÍCTOR MANUEL GARCÍA ACOSTA; Exec. Sec. Dra DIANA RIVERA GRADOS.

Asociación Nacional de Médicas Mexicanas, AC (Mexican Association of Women Doctors): Bruselas 10 Int. 403, Col. Juárez, 06600 México, DF; tel. (55) 5591-0159; internet medicasmexicanasac.tripod.com; f. 1926; 3,000 mems; represents members' interests as doctors, citizens and women; Pres. Dra IRENE TALAMAS V.; publ. *Revista*.

Consejo Mexicano de Dermatología, AC (Mexican Dermatological Council): Hospital Central 'Dr Ignacio Morones Prieto', Avda Venustiano Carranza 2395, Zona Universitaria, Col. Los Filtros, 78210 San Luis Potosí, SLP; tel. (444) 834-2795; e-mail consejomexicanodedermatologia@hotmail.com; internet www.consejomexicanodermatologia.org.mx; f. 1974; 349 mems; qualifies specialists as part of Nat. Academy of Medicine Comm. of Postgraduate Studies; Pres. Dr SERGIO GONZÁLEZ GONZÁLEZ; Sec. Dra MARÍA BERTHA TORRES ALVAREZ; publ. *Roster*.

Federación Mexicana de Colegios De Ginecología y Obstetricia (Mexican Federation of Gynaecology and Obstetrics Schools): Nueva York 38, Col. Nápoles, 03810 México, DF; tel. (55) 5669-0211; e-mail buzon@femecog.org.mx; internet www.femecog.org; f. 1961; 4,600 mems; Pres. Dr ERNESTO CASTELAZO MORALES; Sec. Dr MIGUEL A. MANCERA; publ. *Ginecología y Obstetricia de México*.

Sociedad Mexicana de Cardiología (Mexican Cardiological Society): Juan Badiano 1, Sección XVI Tlalpan, 14080 México, DF; tel. (55) 5655-7694; e-mail info@smcardiologia.org.mx; internet www.smcardiologia.org.mx; f. 1935; 1,250 mems; Pres. Dr JUAN VERDEJO-PARÍS; Sec. Dr SANTIAGO NAVA-TOWNSEND; publs *Archivos de Cardiología de México* (online, www.archivos-cardiologia.org.mx), *Revista Mexicana de Enfermería Cardiológica* (3 a year).

Sociedad Mexicana de Nutrición y Endocrinología, AC (Mexican Society for Nutrition and Endocrinology): Ohio 27, Col. El Rosedal, Del. Coyoacán, 04330 México, DF; tel. (55) 5336-9072; e-mail lcortes@endocrinologia.org.mx; internet www.endocrinologia.org.mx; f. 1960; 660 mems; Pres. Dr J. JORGE ESPINOZA CAMPOS; Sec. Dr FRANCISCO JAVIER VELÁZQUEZ CHÁVEZ; publ. *Revista de Endocrinología y Nutrición* (1 a year).

Sociedad Mexicana de Parasitología, AC (Mexican Parasitological Society): Casa Tlalpan, Avda Cipreses s/n, km 23.5 de la Antigua Carretera México-Cuernavaca, Col. San Andrés Totoltepec, 14400 México, DF; tel. (55) 5747-3348; e-mail mineko@cinvestav.mx; f. 1960; 51 mems (20 active; 31 hon.) from 14 countries; organizes congresses and symposia; Pres. Dr MINEKO SHIBAYAMA; Sec. Dr ROSAMARIA BERNAL.

Sociedad Mexicana de Pediatría (Mexican Paediatrics Society): Tehuantepec 86–503, Col. Roma Sur, Del. Cuauhtémoc, 06760 México, DF; tel. (55) 5564-8371; e-mail smp1930@socmexped.org.mx; internet www.socmexped.org.mx; f. 1930; 1,200 mems; Pres. Dr LÁZARO BENAVIDES; Gen. Sec. Dr MARIO GONZÁLEZ VITE; publ. *Revista Mexicana de Pediatría* (6 a year).

Sociedad Mexicana de Salud Pública (Mexican Society of Public Health): Herschel 109, Col. Anzures, Del. Miguel Hidalgo, 11590 México, DF; tel. (55) 5203-4291; e-mail smsp@prodigy.net.mx; internet www.smsp.org.mx; f. 1944; small library; 6,000 mems; Pres. Dra SILVIA GUILLERMINA ROLDAN FERNÁNDEZ; Gen. Sec. Dr IGNACIO F. VILLASEÑOR RUÍZ; publ. *Higiene* (3 a year).

NATURAL SCIENCES

General

Academia Mexicana de Ciencias (Mexican Academy of Sciences): Calle Cipreses s/n, km 23.5 de la Carretera federal México-Cuernavaca, San Andrés Totoltepec, Tlalpan, 14400 México, DF; tel. (55) 5849-4905; e-mail academia@amc.edu.mx; internet www.amc.unam.mx; f. 1959; research in fields of exact, natural and social sciences, humanities and engineering; encourages communication and collaboration between the various orgs responsible for research in Mexico; strengthening int. presence; consultancy services and performance evaluations for fed. and local govt, legislative and judicial brs and other orgs in civil soc.; 2,156 mems; library of 1,000 vols; Pres. JOSÉ FRANCO; Exec. Coordinator RENATA VILLALBA COHEN; publ. *Ciencia* (4 a year).

Biological Sciences

Asociación Mexicana de Microbiología, AC (Mexican Microbiological Association): Avda Instituto Politécnico Nacional 2508, San Pedro Zacatenco Del. Gustavo A. Madero, 07360 México, DF; tel. (55) 5747-3990; e-mail asoc_mex_micro@yahoo.com.mx; internet ammicrobiologia.cell.cinvestav.mx; f. 1949; Pres. Dr FERNANDO NAVARRO GARCÍA; Sec. Dra MARÍA GUADALUPE GUERRA SÁNCHEZ.

Sociedad Botánica de México (Mexican Botanical Society): Centro de Investigaciones en Ecosistemas, Universidad Nacional Autónoma de México, Campus Morelia, Antigua Carretera a Pátzcuaro 8701, Col. San José de La Huerta, 58190 Morelia, MICH; e-mail sbm@socbot.org.mx; internet www.socbot.org.mx; f. 1941; promotes the study, teaching and technology of botany; organizes National Botanic Congress every 3 years; 1,000 mems; library of 850 vols, 350 periodicals; Pres. Dr JORGE ARTURO MEAVE DEL CASTILLO; Exec. Sec. Dra MARTHA JUANA MARTÍNEZ GORDILLO; publs *Botanical Sciences* (4 a year, in Spanish and English, print and online, www.botanicalsciences.com.mx), *Macpalxochitl*.

Sociedad Mexicana de Bioquímica, AC (Mexican Society of Biochemistry): Avda Cipreses s/n, Col. San Andrés Totoltepec, Del. Tlalpan, 14400, Mexico, DF; tel. (55) 5622-5742; e-mail amanjarr@ifc.unam.mx; internet www.smb.org.mx; f. 1957; promotes education of biochemistry and biochemical research; organizes confs and seminars on biochemical topics; 600 mems; Pres. Dra ALICIA GONZÁLEZ MANJARREZ; Sec. Dra MARÍA EUGENIA GONSEBATT BONAPARTE.

Sociedad Mexicana de Entomología (Mexican Entomological Society): Apdo 63, 91000 Jalapa, VER; e-mail entomologia_2012@yahoo.com.mx; internet sme.colpos.mx; f. 1952; 650 mems; Pres. ALFONSO PESCADOR RUBIO; Sec. JESÚS ALBERTO ACUÑA SOTO; publ. *Folia Entomológica Mexicana* (3 a year).

Sociedad Mexicana de Fitogenética (Mexican Society of Plant Genetics): Apdo 21, 56230 Chapingo, MEX; Km 38.5 carretera México-Texcoco, 56230 Chapingo, MEX; tel. (595) 954-6652; e-mail presidentesomefi2013@gmail.com; internet www.somefi.mx; f. 1965; 1,000 mems; Pres. RAMÓN GARZA GARCÍA; Sec. Dr IVÁN RAMÍREZ RAMÍREZ; publs *Revista Fitotecnia Mexicana* (4 a year, print and online, www.revistafitotecniamexicana.org), *Revista Germen*.

Sociedad Mexicana de Fitopatología, AC (Mexican Society of Phytopathology): Apdo postal 85, 56230 Chapingo, MEX; tel. (595) 952-0200; e-mail smfpresidencia@hotmail.com; internet www.socmexfito.org; f. 1958; 400 mems; holds 1 nat. meeting per year; Pres. Dra MARÍA DE JESÚS YÁÑEZ MORALES; Sec.-Gen. Dr LUCIANO MARTÍNEZ BOLAÑOS; publs *El Vector*, *Revista Mexicana de Fitopatología* (2 a year, print and online, infit.org.mx/socmexfito/RevistaSMF).

Sociedad Mexicana de Historia Natural (Mexican Natural History Society): Avda Dr Vertiz 724, Col. Vertiz Narvarte, 03020 México, DF; tel. (55) 5519-4505; e-mail info@smhn.org.mx; internet smhn.org.tripod.com; f. 1868, refounded 1936; 400 mems; library of 5,000 vols; Pres. Dr RAUL GIO ARGAEZ; publ. *Revista*.

Sociedad Mexicana de Micología (Mexican Society of Mycology): Apdo 41, 67700 Linares, NL; tel. (55) 5541-1333; e-mail smdm@tap-ecosur.edu.mx; internet www.sociedadmexicanademicologia.org.mx; f. 1965; 400 mems; library of 12,000 vols; Pres. Dr MARTÍN ESQUEDA; Sec. Dr RICARDO VALENZUELA GARZA (acting); publ. *Revista Mexicana de Micología* (1 a year, print and online, revistamexicanademicologia.org).

Mathematical Sciences

Sociedad Matemática Mexicana (Mexican Mathematical Society): Apdo 70–450, Coyoacán, 04510 México, DF; Avda Cipreses s/n km 23.5 Carretera Federal México-Cuernavaca, Col. San Andrés Totoltepec, Del. Tlalpan, 14400 México, DF; tel. (55) 5849-6710; e-mail smm@smm.org.mx; internet sociedadmatematicamexicana.org.mx; f. 1943; 1,100 mems, 20 institutional mems; promotes mathematics, sponsors National Congresses and Regional Assemblies of mathematicians, and The National Mathematical Olympics; Pres. Dr ISIDORO GITLER GOLDWAIN; Gen. Sec. Dr GELASIO SALAZAR ANAYA; publs *Aportaciones Matemáticas*, *Boletín de la SMM* (2 a year, print and online, smm.org.mx/boletin), *Miscelánea Matemática* (2 a year, print and online, www.miscelaneamatematica.org).

Physical Sciences

Asociación Mexicana de Geólogos Petroleros (Mexican Association of Petroleum Geologists): Torres Bodet 176, 06400 México, DF; Edif. 8 departamento No 102, Fraccionamiento Carrizal, Villahermosa, Tabasco, 86035 México, DF; tel. (993) 314-8610; e-mail presidencia@amgp.org; internet www.amgp.org; f. 1949; 600 mems; Pres. JAIME PATIÑO RUIZ; Sec. MARÍA DE LOURDES CLARA VALDÉS.

Sociedad Astronómica de México, AC (Mexican Astronomical Society): Apdo M 9647, Jardín Felipe Xicoténcatl, Col. Alamos, 03400 México, DF; tel. (55) 5519-4730; e-mail sociedadastronomica@gmail.com; internet www.sociedadastronomica.org.mx; f. 1902; library of 5,000 vols; 500 mems; Pres. MARTE TREJO SANDOVAL; Sec.-Gen. JORGE RUBÍ GARZA; publ. *El Universo* (4 a year).

Sociedad Geológica Mexicana, AC (Mexican Geological Society): Torres Bodet 176, Del. Cuauhtémoc, 06400 México, DF; tel. (55) 5541-0879; e-mail publigl@geologia.igeolcu.unam.mx; internet www.sociedadgeologica.org.mx; f. 1904; 1,000 mems; library of 4,500 vols; Pres. Ing. BERNARDO MARTELL ANDRADE; Vice-Pres. Ing. HERIBERTO PALACIOS; Sec. Ing. LUIS VELÁZQUEZ AGUIRRE; publ. *Revista Mexicana de Ciencias Geológicas* (jtly, 3 a year).

Sociedad Química de México (Mexican Chemical Society): Barranca del Muerto 26, Esq. Hércules, Col. Crédito Constructor, Del. Benito Juárez, 03940 México, DF; tel. (55) 5662-6837; e-mail soquimex@prodigy.net.mx; internet www.soquimex.com.mx; f. 1956; 2,300 mems; Pres. Dra LENA RUIZ AZUARA; Sec. Dr EDUARDO GONZÁLEZ ZAMORA; publ. *Revista de la SQM* (4 a year, print and online, www.jmcs.org.mx).

RELIGION, SOCIOLOGY AND ANTHROPOLOGY

Sociedad Mexicana de Antropología (Mexican Anthropological Society): Apdo 100, C. A. P. Polanco, 11550 México, DF; Instituto de Investigaciones Antropológicas Ciudad Universitaria, 04510 Mexico, DF; tel. (55) 5622-9557; e-mail somedean@yahoo.com.mx; internet www.smamexico.org; f. 1937; 480 mems; Pres. FERNANDO NAVA; publ. *Revista Mexicana de Estudios Antropológicos* (1 a year).

TECHNOLOGY

Sociedad Mexicana de Ingeniería Sísmica, AC (Mexican Society of Seismic Engineering): Camino de Sta Teresa 187, Col. Parques del Pedregal, Tlalpan, 14020 México, DF; tel. (55) 5665-8377; e-mail smis@smis.org.mx; internet www.smis.org.mx; f. 1962; library of 82 vols; 350 mems; Pres. M. I. SEBASTIÁN SERRANO VEGA; Sec. Ing. GERARDO CORONA CARLOS; publ. *Revista de Ingeniería Sísmica* (2 a year).

Research Institutes

GENERAL

Institut de Recherche pour le Développement (IRD) (Development Research Institute): Anatole France No 17, Col. Chapultepec Polanco, 11560 México, DF; tel. (55) 5280-7688; e-mail mexique@ird.fr; internet www.mx.ird.fr; see main entry under France; Rep. PASCAL RENAUD.

AGRICULTURE, FISHERIES AND VETERINARY SCIENCE

Campo Agrícola Experimental Río Bravo (Río Bravo Agricultural Research Station): Apdo 172, Río Bravo, TAMPS; f. 1965; research into regional problems and diversification; Dir Ing. Agr. MANUEL CARNERO HERNÁNDEZ.

Instituto Nacional de Investigaciones Forestales, Agrícolas y Pecuarias (National Institute of Forestry, Agriculture and Livestock Research): Avda Progreso No 5, Col. Barrio de Sta Catarina, Del. Coyoacán, 04010 México, DF; tel. (55) 3871-8700; e-mail webmaster@inifap.gob.mx; internet www.inifap.gob.mx; f. 1985 through the integration of Instituto Nacional de Investigaciones Agrícolas, Instituto Nacional de Investigaciones Pecuarias and Instituto Nacional de Investigaciones Forestales; conducts research in all aspects of agricultural devt and production; agronomy library, livestock library and forestry library; Gen. Dir Dr PEDRO BRAJCICH GALLEGOS; publs *Revista Mexicana de Ciencias Agrícolas* (8 a year, print and online, www.remexca.org.mx), *Revista Mexicana de Ciencias Forestals* (4 a year, print and online, www.cienciasforestales.org.mx), *Revista Mexicana de Ciencias Pecuarias* (4 a year, print and online, revistacienciaspecuarias.mx).

BIBLIOGRAPHY, LIBRARY SCIENCE AND MUSEOLOGY

Instituto de Investigaciones Bibliográficas (Institute of Bibliographical Research): c/o Biblioteca Nacional de México and Hemeroteca Nacional de México, Centro Cultural Universitario, Ciudad Universitaria, Del. Coyoacán, 04510 México, DF; tel. (55) 5622-6827; e-mail webiib@iib.unam.mx; internet www.iib.unam.mx; f. 1899, current name adopted 1967; compiles national bibliographies and books on bibliographical subjects; Dir Dra GUADALUPE CURIEL DEFOSSÉ; Admin. Sec. Lic. BIBIANO CAMACHO MIRANDA; publ. *Nueva Gaceta Bibliográfica* (4 a year).

ECONOMICS, LAW AND POLITICS

Centro de Estudios Demográficos, Urbanos y Ambientales (Centre for Demographics, Urban and Environmental Studies): Camino al Ajusco 20, 14200 México, DF; tel. (55) 5449-3000; e-mail sgiorguli@colmex.mx; internet cedua.colmex.mx; f. 1964; attached to El Colegio de México, AC; library of 500,000 vols; Dir Dra SILVIA ELENA GIORGULI SAUCEDO; publ. *Revista de Estudios Demográficos y Urbanos* (3 a year).

Centro de Estudios Económicos (Centre for Economic Studies): Camino al Ajusco 20, Col. Pedregal de Sta Teresa, Apdo 20671, 10740 México, DF; tel. (55) 5449-3000; e-mail economia@colmex.mx; internet cee.colmex.mx; f. 1981; attached to El Colegio de México, AC; research areas incl. economic development, environmental economics, game theory, industrial organization, international economics, macroeconomics, microeconomics, public finance, statistics; masters and doctorate programmes; also PROCIENTEC; library of 8,000 vols; Dir Dr JOSÉ ROMERO TELLAECHE; publ. *Estudios Económicos* (2 a year, print and online, estudioseconomicos.colmex.mx).

Centro de Estudios Internacionales (Centre for International Studies): Camino al Ajusco 20, Col. Pedregal de Sta Teresa, 10740 México, DF; tel. (55) 5449-3000; e-mail ancova@colmex.mx; internet cei.colmex.mx; f. 1960; attached to El Colegio de México, AC; research areas include international relations, politics, federal and local public administration, Mexico's political system and foreign policy, and regional studies of N America, Europe and Latin America; Dir ANA COVARRUBIAS; publ. *Foro Internacional* (4 a year).

Centro de Relaciones Internacionales (Centre for International Relations): Edif. E, Planta Baja en la Facultad de Ciencias Políticas y Sociales, Circuito Mario de la Cueva s/n, frente a TV-UNAM, Ciudad Universitaria, Del. Coyoacán, 04510 México, DF; tel. (55) 5622-9412; f. 1970; attached to Faculty of Political and Social Sciences of the Universidad Nacional Autónoma de México; coordinates and promotes research in all aspects of international relations and Mexico's foreign policy, and training of researchers in different fields: disciplinary construction problems, cooperation and international law, developing nations, actual problems in world society, Africa, Asia, peace research; 30 full mems; library of 6,000 vols, 35 spec. collns, 16,000 journals; Dir Lic. FERNANDO CASTAÑEDA SABIDO; Gen. Sec. ROBERTO PEÑA GUERRERO; publ. *Revista de Relaciones Internacionales* (4 a year).

EDUCATION

Centro de Estudios Educativos, AC (Centre for Educational Studies): Avda Revolución 1291, Col. Tlacopac–San Angel, Del. Alvaro Obregón, 01040 México, DF; tel. (55) 5593-5719; e-mail cee@cee.edu.mx; internet www.cee.edu.mx; f. 1963; scientific research on educational problems in Mexico and Latin America; library of 36,553 vols, 1,930 audiovisual items, 11,100 journals, 2,603 serial titles, 556 theses; Dir-Gen. FERNANDO MEJIA BOTERO; publ. *Revista Latinoamericana de Estudios Educativos* (4 a year).

HISTORY, GEOGRAPHY AND ARCHAEOLOGY

Centro de Estudios de Asia y África (Centre for Asian and African Studies): Camino al Ajusco 20, Col. Pedregal de Sta Teresa, 10740 México, DF; tel. (55) 5449-3000; e-mail jramirez@colmex.mx; internet ceaa.colmex.mx; f. 1964; attached to El Colegio de México, AC; studies of and research on Africa, China, Korea, Japan, S Asia, SE Asia, Middle East and N Africa; library of 400,000 vols, 8,000 journal titles, 130 periodicals; Dir HILDA VARELA; publs *Anuario Asia Pacífico* (1 a year), *Cuadernos de Trabajo*, *Revista Estudios de Asia y África* (3 a year).

Centro de Estudios Históricos (Centre for Historical Studies): Coordinación Académica, Centro de Estudios Históricos, Camino al Ajusco 20, 10740 México, DF; tel. (55) 5449-3000; e-mail hsoto@colmex.mx; internet ceh.colmex.mx; f. 1941; attached to El Colegio de México, AC; history of Mexico and Latin America; Dir Dr ARIEL RODRÍGUEZ KURI; Sec. HORTENCIA SOTO; publ. *Revista Historia Mexicana* (4 a year).

Instituto Nacional de Estudios Históricos de las Revoluciones de México (INEHRM) (National Institute for Historical Studies of the Mexican Revolutions): Francisco I. Madero 1, Col. San Ángel, 01000 México, DF; tel. (55) 5616-3808; e-mail contactoinehrm@sep.gob.mx; internet www.inehrm.gob.mx; f. 1953; library of 82,000 vols; Man. Dra PATRICIA GALEANA.

LANGUAGE AND LITERATURE

Centro de Estudios Lingüísticos y Literarios (Centre for Linguistic and Literary Studies): Coordinación Académica, Centro de Estudios Lingüísticos y Literarios, Camino al Ajusco 20, 10740 México, DF; tel. (55) 5449-3018; e-mail eserralde@colmex.mx; internet cell.colmex.mx; f. 1947; attached to El Colegio de México, AC; Spanish linguistics and literature (PhD degrees), Indian languages, translation; Dir Dra LUZ ELENA GUTIÉRREZ DE VELASCO; Sec. ERIKA NASHELLY SERRALDE; publ. *Nueva Revista de Filología Hispánica* (2 a year).

MEDICINE

Instituto de Diagnóstico y Referencia Epidemiológicos (Institute of Epidemiological Diagnosis and Reference): Calle de Carpio 470, Santo Tomás, Miguel Hidalgo, 11340 México, DF; tel. (55) 5342-7550; e-mail ens_capacitacion_indre@hotmail.com; internet www.cenavece.salud.gob.mx/indre/interior/intd_index.html; f. 1938; performs epidemiological laboratory reference services nationwide; carries out technological devt and research in laboratory for support of epidemiological surveillance; trains and supervises laboratory personnel and performs quality control procedures for the National Laboratory Network; library of 3,930 vols, 603 journals. MEDLINE terminal; Dir Dr JOSÉ ALBERTO DÍAZ QUIÑONEZ.

Instituto Nacional de Cardiología 'Ignacio Chávez' (National Cardiological Institute Ignacio Chávez): Juan Badiano 1, Col. Sección XVI, Del. Tlalpan, 14080 México, DF; tel. (55) 5573-2911; e-mail dirgral@cardiologia.org.mx; internet www.cardiologia.org.mx; f. 1944; 390 medical mems; library of 8,465 vols, 569 periodicals; Dir Dr MARCO ANTONIO MARTINEZ RIOS; publ. *Archivos de Cardiología de México* (1 a year).

Instituto Nacional de Neurología y Neurocirugía (National Institute of Neurology and Neurosurgery): Insurgentes Sur 3877, Col. La Fama, Del. Tlalpan, 14269 México, DF; tel. (55) 5606-3822; e-mail dirmedica@innn.edu.mx; internet www.innn.salud.gob.mx; f. 1964; library of 2,700 vols, 270 periodicals; Dir-Gen. Dr MIGUEL ÁNGEL CELIS LÓPEZ.

Instituto Nacional de Salud Pública (National Institute of Public Health): Avda University 655, Col. Sta María Ahuacatitlán, 62100 Cuernavaca, MOR; tel. (777) 329-3000; e-mail mhernan@insp.mx; internet www.insp.mx; f. 1987; incl. School of Public Health in Mexico (f. 1922) and research centres on public health, health systems: infectious diseases, malaria, and nutrition and health; also in Cuernavaca, Tapachula and Tlalpan; library of 35,000 vols; Dir-Gen. Dr MAURICIO HERNÁNDEZ ÁVILA; publ. *Salud Pública de México* (6 a year).

NATURAL SCIENCES

General

Centro de Investigación y de Estudios Avanzados del Instituto Politécnico Nacional (Centre for Research and Advanced Studies of the National Polytechnic Institute): Apdo 14–740, 07000 México, DF; Avda Instituto Politécnico Nacional 2508, Col. San Pedro Zacatanco, Del. Gustavo A. Madero, 07360 México, DF; tel. (55) 5747-3800; e-mail portal@cinvestav.mx; internet www.cinvestav.mx; f. 1961; postgraduate research and training centre in sciences; integrates the work of 31 science and mathematics related depts; library of 256,000 vols, 3,200 spec. collns; Dir-Gen. Dr RENE ASOMOZA PALACIO; publs *Avance y Perspectiva* (4 a year), *Morfismos* (2 a year).

Consejo Nacional de Ciencia y Tecnología (CONACYT) (National Council for Science and Technology): Avda Insurgentes Sur 1582, Col. Crédito Constructor, Del. Benito Juárez, 03940 México, DF; tel. (55) 5322-7700; e-mail contacto@conacyt.mx; internet www.conacyt.mx; f. 1970; coordinates scientific research and devt and formulates policy; Dir ENRIQUE CABRERO MENDOZA; publ. *Ciencia y Desarrollo* (12 a year).

Biological Sciences

Instituto de Ecología, AC (Institute of Ecology): Apdo Postal 63, Carretera Antigua a Coatepec No 351, El Haya, 91070 Xalapa, VER; tel. (228) 842-1800; internet www.ecologia.edu.mx; f. 1975; plant and animal ecology and taxonomy, biogeography, dynamics and structure of ecosystems, conservation and management of natural resources; postgraduate programmes in ecology and natural resources management, wildlife management; library of 24,000 vols, 4,000 current periodicals incl. maps and databases; Dir-Gen. Dr MARTIN R. ALUJA SCHUNEMAN-HOFER; publs *Acta Botánica Mexicana* (4 a year, print and online, www1.inecol.edu.mx/abm), *Acta Zoológica Mexicana* (4 a year, print and online, www1.inecol.edu.mx/azm), *Flora del Bajío y de Regiones Adyacentes* (print and online, www1.inecol.edu.mx/publicaciones/FLOBA.htm), *Flora de Veracruz* (irregular, print and online, www1.inecol.edu.mx/floraver), *Madera y Bosques* (2 a year, print and online, www1.inecol.edu.mx/myb/MB2.htm), *Revista Mexicana de Micología* (2 a year, in Spanish and English, print and online, revistamexicanademicologia.org).

Instituto Nacional de la Pesca (National Fishery Institute): Pitágoras 1320, Col. Santa Cruz Atoyac, Del. Benito Juárez, 03310 México, DF; tel. (55) 3871-9500; e-mail contacto.siap@siap.gob.mx; internet www.inapesca.gob.mx; f. 1962; research in marine biology; library of 3,000 vols; Dir Dr PATRICIA ORNELAS RUÍZ.

Instituto Tecnológico del Mar (Institute of Marine Technology): km 12 Carretera Veracruz-Córdoba, Apdo Postal 68, 94290 Boca del Río, VER; tel. (229) 986-0189; internet www.itmar1.edu.mx; f. 1975, current name adopted 1981; 150 mems; library of 4,500 vols; Dir ALMILCAR SUÁREZ ALLEN.

Mathematical Sciences

Instituto de Matemáticas (Institute of Mathematics): Area de la Investigación Científica, Circuito Exterior, Ciudad Universitaria, Coyoacán, 04510 México, DF; tel. (55) 5622-4520; e-mail contacto@matem.unam.mx; internet www.matem.unam.mx; f. 1942; 59 mems; library of 20,000 vols; Dir Dr JAVIER BRACHO CARPIZO; Sec. BEATRIZ CAUDILLO; publs *Anales* (1 a year), *Aportaciones Matemáticas* (irregular), *Monografías* (irregular), *Publicaciones Preliminares*.

Physical Sciences

Instituto de Astronomía (Institute of Astronomy): Apdo postal 70–264, 04510 México, DF; Circuito de la Investigación Científica, Ciudad Universitaria, 04510 México, DF; tel. (55) 5622-3906; e-mail direc@astro.unam.mx; internet www.astroscu.unam.mx; f. 1878; attached to Universidad Nacional Autónoma de México; library of 10,000 vols, 1,550 journals; Dir Dr WILLIAM HENRY LEE ALARDIN; publs *Anuario del Observatorio Astronómico Nacional* (1 a year), *Revista Mexicana de Astronomía y Astrofísica* (2 a year).

Instituto Nacional de Astrofísica, Optica y Electrónica (National Institute of Astrophysics, Optics and Electronics): Luis Enrique Erro 1, Apdos 216 y 51, 72840 Tonantzintla, PUE; tel. (222) 266-3100; e-mail astrofi@inaoep.mx; internet www.inaoep.mx; f. 1971 fmrly Observatorio Nacional de Astrofísica, f. 1942; 22 research mems; library of 7,000 vols, 144 periodicals; Gen. Dir Dr ALBERTO CARRAMIÑANA ALONSO; Gen. Academic Sec. Dr MARÍA LUISA HERNÁNDEZ SIMÓN; publ. *Boletín del Instituto de Tonantzintla*.

Instituto Nacional de Investigaciones Nucleares (National Institute of Nuclear Research): km 36.5, Carretera México-Toluca s/n, La Marquesa, 52750, Ocoyoacac, MEX; tel. (55) 5329-7200; e-mail webmaster@inin.gob.mx; internet www.inin.mx; f. 1979 previously part of Instituto Nacional de Energía Nuclear, f. 1955; planning, research and devt of atomic technology, incl. non-military use of atomic energy; library of 41,500 vols (incl. theses), 75,000 periodicals, 7,300 consulting works, 6,000 pamphlets, 1,000 official publs, 125 video cassettes, 835,000 reports on microfiche and 25,000 in printed form; Gen. Dir LYDIA CONCEPCION PAREDES GUTIERREZ; Technical Sec. Dr JULIÁN SÁNCHEZ GUTIERREZ; publ. *Contacto Nuclear* (4 a year).

Servicio Meteorológico Nacional (National Weather Service): Avda Observatorio 192, Col. Observatorio, Del. M. Hidalgo, 11860 México, DF; tel. (55) 2636-4600; e-mail webmaster.smn@conagua.gob.mx; internet smn.cna.gob.mx; f. 1915; library of 80,000 vols, 90,180 pamphlets; Gen. Coordinator JUAN MANUEL CABALLERO G.

RELIGION, SOCIOLOGY AND ANTHROPOLOGY

Centro Co-ordinador y Difusor de Estudios Latinoamericanos (Coordinating and Information Centre for Latin American Studies): 8°, Torre II de Humanidades, Ciudad Universitaria, 04510 México, DF; tel. (55) 5623-0211; e-mail asantana@unam.mx; internet www.ccydel.unam.mx; f. 1978; attached to Universidad Nacional Autónoma de México; study of Latin America and the Caribbean in all disciplines (history, literature, philosophy, etc.); library of 22,000 vols of books and 300 periodical titles; Dir Dr ADALBERTO SANTANA HERNÁNDEZ; publs *Revista Archipiélago* (4 a year), *Revista Cuadernos Americanos*, *Revista Latinoamérica* (1 a year, in Spanish and English), *Publicaciones CIALC*.

Centro de Estudios Sociológicos (Centre for Sociological Studies): Camino al Ajusco 20, Pedregal de Sta Teresa, Tlalpan, 10740 México, DF; tel. (55) 5449-3000; e-mail coord.acad.ces@colmex.mx; internet ces.colmex.mx; f. 1973; attached to El Colegio de México, AC; research areas include sociological theory, economic sociology and the sociology of work, social movements and civil organizations, class and family, political parties, elections and politics, education, etc; Dir ARTURO ALVARADO MENDOZA; publ. *Revista Estudios Sociológicos* (1 a year).

Comisión Nacional para el Desarrollo de los Pueblos Indígenas (National Commission for the Development of Indigenous Peoples): Avda México-Coyoacán 343, Col. Xoco, Del. Benito Juárez, 03330 México, DF; tel. (55) 9183-2100; e-mail dirgral@cdi.gob.mx; internet www.cdi.gob.mx; f. 1948; forms links with indigenous communities of Mexico; organs incl. 23 coordinating centres in the interior, radio stations transmitting in 31 indigenous languages, 29 regional documentation and information centres; library of 25,000 vols; Dir-Gen. NUVIA MAYORGA DELGADO; publs *Colección Historia de los Pueblos Indígenas de México*, *México Indígena*.

Instituto Indigenista Interamericano (Inter-American Indian Institute): Avda de las Fuentes 106, Col. Jardines de Pedregal, Del. Álvaro Obregón, 01900 México, DF; tel. (55) 5595-8410; e-mail ininin@prodigy.net.mx; internet www.indigenista.org; f. 1940; supplies technical assistance to mem. govts for the Indian population of the continent; library of 40,000 vols; Dir GUILLERMO ESPI-

NOSA VELASCO; publ. *América Indígena* (4 a year).

Instituto Nacional de Antropología e Historia (National Institute of Anthropology and History): Insurgentes Sur No 421, Col. Hipódromo, 06100 México, DF; tel. (55) 4040-4624; e-mail direccion.dgeneral@inah.gob.mx; internet www.inah.gob.mx; f. 1939; govt organization for research, conservation and promotion of Mexican cultural heritage, controls 105 museums, incl. Galería de Historia, Museo del Templo Mayor, Museo Nacional de Antropología, Museo Nacional de Historia and Museo Nacional de las Culturas; Dir-Gen. MARÍA TERESA FRANCO; publs *Alquimia* (3 a year), *Arqueología* (2 a year), *Dimensión Antropológica* (3 a year), *Historias* (3 a year), *Museos de México y del Mundo* (2 a year, in Spanish and English).

TECHNOLOGY

Centro de Investigación en Computación (Computing Research Centre): Avda Juan de Dios Batiz s/n, Esq. Miguel Othón de Mendizabal, Unidad Profesional Adolfo López Mateos, Col. Nueva Industrial Vallejo, Del. Gustavo A. Madero, 07738 México, DF; tel. (55) 5729-6000 ext. 56604; e-mail webmaster@cic.ipn.mx; internet www.cic.ipn.mx; f. 1996; 250 mems; library of 14,000 vols; Dir Dr OSCAR CAMACHO NIETO; publs *Computación y Sistemas* (4 a year), *Research on Computing Science* (6 a year).

Instituto de Investigaciones Eléctricas (Institute of Electrical Research): Calle Reforma No 113, Col. Palmira, 62490 Cuernavaca, MOR; tel. (777) 362-3811; e-mail difusion@iie.org.mx; internet www.iie.org.mx; f. 1975; promotes and undertakes research and experimental devt in the electrical industry; consulting service; also in Monterrey and La Ventosa; library of 61,284 vols; Gen. Dir JOSÉ LUIS FERNÁNDEZ ZAYAS; publs *Folleto Corporativo*, *Informe Anual*.

Instituto Mexicano del Petróleo (Mexican Petroleum Institute): Eje Central Norte Lázaro Cárdenas 152, Col. San Bartolo Atepehuacan, Apdo 14–805, 07730 México, DF; tel. (55) 9175-6000; e-mail ranaya@imp.mx; internet www.imp.mx; f. 1965; research on petroleum products and equipment, petrochemical industries, economic studies, exploration, refining; training and specialist courses; library of 48,000 vols, 270 journal titles; Gen. Dir Dr VINICIO SURO PÉREZ; publ. *Gaceta IMP*.

Libraries and Archives

Chapingo

Biblioteca Central—Universidad Autónoma Chapingo (Central Library—Chapingo Autonomous University): Km 38.5 Carretera México-Texcoco, 56230 Texcoco, MEX; tel. (595) 952-1500; e-mail ramsestexcoco@yahoo.com; internet www.ceres.chapingo.mx; f. 1854, current name adopted 1977; interlibrary loans, digital library, reproduction; 250,000 vols, 4,000 periodicals, 9,000 maps; specializes in agricultural and forestry sciences, 4,000 theses; Dir Lic. RAMÓN SUÁREZ ESPINOSA; publs *Revista Chapingo Ingeniería Agrícola y Biosistemas*, *Revista Chapingo Serie Ciencias Forestales y del Ambiente*, *Revista Chapingo Serie Horticultura*, *Revista Chapingo Serie Zonas Aridas*.

Guadalajara

Coordinación de Bibliotecas, Universidad de Guadalajara (University of Guadalajara Library Services): Avda Juárez 976, Edif. Cultural y Administrativo, 7°, 44100 Guadalajara, JAL; tel. (33) 3134-2277; e-mail sergiolr@redudg.udg.mx; internet www.rebiudg.udg.mx; f. 1861, current name adopted 1994; depository for UNESCO publs; 1,995,164 vols, 15,261 periodicals (1,761 print, 13,500 electronic); Man. Dir SERGIO LÓPEZ RUELAS.

Mexico City

Archivo General de la Nación (General Archives of the Nation): Avda Eduardo Molina y Albañiles s/n, Col. Penitenciaría Ampliación, Del. Venustiano Carranza, 15350 México, DF; tel. (55) 5133-9900; e-mail argena@segob.gob.mx; internet www.agn.gob.mx; f. 1795; documents relating to vice-regal admin. of New Spain, the Inquisition, independence 1821–40, the 19th century, the Mexican Revolution 1910, and the years up to 1976 (50 km of documents); 49,000 vols; 1,050 pre-hispanic paintings; newspaper colln of 1,272,000 copies; microfilm service and library; Dir-Gen. Dra MARÍA DE LAS MERCEDES DE VEGA ARMIJO.

Biblioteca Central de la Universidad Nacional Autónoma de México (Central Library of the National Autonomous University of Mexico): Ciudad Universitaria, 04510 México, DF; tel. (55) 5622-1603; e-mail serviciosbc@dgb.unam.mx; internet bc.unam.mx; f. 1924; 527,000 vols, 3,586 periodicals, 4.5m. theses; Dir-Gen. of Libraries Dr ADOLFO RODRÍGUEZ GALLARDO; Sub Dir of the Central Library Lic. EUGENIO ROMERO HERNÁNDEZ.

Biblioteca de la Secretaría de Comunicaciones y Transportes (Library of the Ministry of Communications and Transport): Avda Xola, Esq. con Eje Central s/n, Col. Narvarte, Del. Benito Juárez, 03020 México, DF; tel. (55) 5723-9300; e-mail webmaster@sct.gob.mx; internet www.sct.gob.mx/carreteras/direccion-general-de-servicios-tecnicos/publicaciones/biblioteca; f. 1891; 10,000 vols; 3 sections on civil aviation, roads, ports and marines; Dir RENATO MOLINE ENRÍQUEZ.

Biblioteca del Honorable Congreso de la Unión (Library of the Honourable Congress of the Union): Biblioteca Unidad Centro Histórico, Edif. de la ex-Iglesia de Sta Clara, Tacuba 29, 06000 México, DF; tel. (55) 5510-3866; e-mail francisco.osornio@congreso.gob.mx; internet www.diputados.gob.mx/cedia/biblio/bibgen.htm; f. 1936; 110,000 vols, 95 periodicals; Dir Lic. FRANCISCO JAVIER OSORNIO VARGAS.

Biblioteca del Instituto Nacional de Salud Pública (Library of the National Institute of Public Health): Insp-Biblioteca, Avda Universidad 655, Cerrada los Pinos y Caminera, Col. Sta Maria Ahuacatitlán, 62100 Cuernavaca, MEX; tel. (777) 329-3000; e-mail mmorales@insp.mx; internet www.insp.mx/bibliotecas; f. 1922; spec. collns in air, behavioural sciences, epidemiology, hygiene, industrial hygiene and water, mental hygiene; spec. colln in health economics 'Julio Frenk Mora', historical documentary colln in public health from 1826; 45,000 vols, 800 periodicals; Librarian Lic. NATALIA LÓPEZ LÓPEZ; publs *Atlas de la Salud*, *Revista Salud Pública de México* (6 a year).

Biblioteca 'José Ma. Lafragua' ('José Ma. Lafragua' Library): Ex Colegio de la Santa Cruz de Tlatelolco, Plaza de las Tres Culturas, Avda R. Flores Magón 1, Col. Guerrero, 06995 México, DF; tel. (55) 3686-5100; e-mail bibliotecajmlafragua@sre.gob.mx; f. 19th century; 125,000 vols; specializes in history of Mexican diplomacy, int. relations and social sciences; Dir Dra MERCEDES DE VEGA ARMIJO.

Biblioteca 'Miguel Lerdo de Tejada' de la Secretaría de Hacienda y Crédito Público (Library 'Miguel Lerdo de Tejada' of the Ministry of Finance and Public Credit): Avda República de El Salvador 49, Centro Histórico, Del. Cuauhtémoc, 06080 México, DF; tel. (55) 3688-9837; e-mail biblioteca_lerdo@hacienda.gob.mx; internet www.shcp.gob.mx/difusion_cultural/biblioteca_miguel_lerdo_tejada; f. 1928; 250,000 vols; Dir Lic. JUAN MANUEL HERRERA.

Biblioteca Nacional de Antropología e Historia 'Dr Eusebio Dávalos Hurtado' (National Library of Anthropology and History): Avda Paseo de la Reforma y Calzada Gandhi s/n, 1°, Col. Polanco, 11560 México, DF; tel. (55) 4040-5300; e-mail contacto.bnah@inah.gob.mx; internet www.bnah.inah.gob.mx; f. 1888 as library of the Instituto Nacional de Antropología e Historia de México (see Research Institutes); 85,081 vols, 8,000 periodicals and 55,584 titles; Dir BALTAZAR BRITO GUADARRAMA; publs *Alquimía* (4 a year), *Arqueología* (4 a year), *Arqueología Mexicana* (6 a year), *Dimensión Antropológica* (3 a year), *Historias* (2 a year).

Biblioteca Nacional de México (National Library of Mexico): Centro Cultural Universitario, Ciudad Universitaria, Del. Coyoacán, 04510 México, DF; tel. (55) 5622-6800; e-mail webbnm@iib.unam.mx; internet www.bnm.unam.mx; f. 1867; run by Bibliographic Research Institute of the National University of Mexico; 1.25m. vols, and other items relating to the political, social, artistic, literary and historical devt of Mexico; Dir Dra GUADALUPE CURIEL DEFOSSÉ.

Biblioteca Vasconcelos (Vasconcelos Library): Eje 1 Norte s/n Esq. Aldama, Col. Buenavista, Del. Cuauhtémoc, 06350 México, DF; tel. (55) 9157-2800; e-mail contactobvasconcelos@conaculta.gob.mx; internet www.bibliotecavasconcelos.gob.mx; f. 1946; 67,000 vols, spec. collns; hall for the blind and visually impaired; Dir DANIEL GOLDIN HALFON; publ. *Biblioteca de México* (6 a year).

Centro de Documentación de la Secretaría de Economía y Sector Coordinado (CEDOCS) (Documentation Centre of the Ministry of Economy and Coordinated Sector (CEDOCS)): Avda Insurgentes Sur N° 1940, Col. Florida, Del. Álvaro Obregón, 01030 México, DF; tel. (55) 5229-6100; e-mail biblioteca.virtual@economia.gob.mx; internet www.economia.gob.mx/conoce-la-se/atencion-ciudadana/centro-de-documentacion; f. 1918; int. business, business guides, statistics on foreign investment, legislation; trade statistics; 42,250 vols; Head Lic. LAURA LORENA MÉNDEZ AGUILAR.

Coordinación Nacional de Literatura (National Coordination of Literature): Casa de Leona Vicario República de Brasil 37, Planta Baja, esq. Colombia Centro Histórico, Del. Cuauhtémoc México, DF; tel. (55) 5526-0219; e-mail diccionario@inba.gob.mx; internet www.literatura.bellasartes.gob.mx/acervos/index.php/acervos/nosotros; f. 1993; attached to Instituto Nacional de Bellas Artes; specializes in Mexican literature; 18,000 vols, 5,650 audio recordings, 5,550 vols of literary magazines and 13,000 photographs; Coordinator STASIA DE LA GARZA.

Hemeroteca Nacional de México (National Library of Periodicals): Centro Cultural Universitario, Ciudad Universitaria, Del. Coyoacán, 04510 México, DF; tel. (55) 5622-6827; e-mail webhnm@biblional.bibliog.unam.mx; internet www.hnm.unam.mx; f. 1912; run by Bibliographic Research Institute of the National University of Mexico; 250,000 vols; newspapers and periodicals; Mexican Gazette of 18th century; Coordinator GUADALUPE CURIEL DEFOSSÉ.

Subdirección General de Educación e Investigación Artísticas (General Division of Art Education and Research): Londres No 16, Col. Juárez, Del. Cuauhtémoc, 06600 México, DF; tel. (55) 5141-1100; e-mail sgeia@inba.gob.mx; internet www.sgeia.bellasartes.gob.mx; f. 1947; attached to Instituto Nacional de Bellas Artes; incl. 5 centres, each of which inherited specialist material from the fmr Biblioteca Ibero-Americana y de Bellas Artes; Sub Dir-Gen. JORGE S. GUTIÉRREZ.

Incorporated Centres:

Centro de Investigación para el Desarrollo Cultural y la Educación Artística (Research Centre for Cultural Development and Arts Education): Circuito Tecnopolo Norte s/n, Col. Hacienda Nueva, Aguascalientes, AGS; tel. (44) 9994-5150; e-mail ccb@inba.gob.mx; internet www.cidcea.bellasartes.gob.mx; Dir EUDORA FONSECA YERENA.

Centro Nacional de Investigación de Información y Documentación de la Danza José Limón ('José Limón' National Centre for Research, Information and Documentation on Dance): Calzada de Tlalpan y Río Churubusco s/n Col. Country Club, Torre de Investigacion 3°, 04220 México, DF; tel. (55) 4155-0000; e-mail difusioncenidid@conaculta.gob.mx; internet www.cenididanza.bellasartes.gob.mx; f. 1983; Dir ELIZABETH CÁMARA.

Centro Nacional de Investigación e Información Teatral 'Rodolfo Usigli' ('Rodolfo Usigli' National Centre for Research and Theatre Information): Torre de Investigación 5° y 6° Río Churubusco No 79 Esq. Calzada de Tlalpan, Col. Country Club, 04220 México, DF; tel. (55) 4155-0000; e-mail citru.difusion@inba.gob.mx; internet www.citru.bellasartes.gob.mx; f. 1981; Dir RICARDO GARCÍA.

Centro Nacional de Investigación y Documentación de las Artes Plásticas (National Centre for Research and Documentation on the Plastic Arts): Torre de Investigación Centro Nacional de las Artes, Río Churubusco No 79 Esq. Calzada de Tlalplan, Col. Country Club Coyoacán, 04220 México, DF; tel. (55) 4155-0000; e-mail direccion.cenidiap@conaculta.gob.mx; internet www.cenidiap.bellasartes.gob.mx; f. 1985; Dir CARLOS GUEVARA MEZA.

Centro Nacional de Investigación y Documentación Musical Carlos Chávez (Carlos Chávez National Centre for Research and Music Documentation): Torre de Investigación 7°, Centro Nacional de las Artes, Río Churubusco No 79 Esq. Calzada de Tlalplan, Col. Country Club Coyoacán, 04220 México, DF; tel. (55) 4155-0000; e-mail cenidim@conaculta.gob.mx; internet www.cenart.gob.mx/centros/cenidim; f. 1974; Dir JOSÉ ANTONIO ROBLES CAHERO.

Puebla

Biblioteca de la Universidad de las Américas (Library of University of the Americas): POB 100, Sta Catarina Mártir, San Andrés, 72820 Cholula, PUE; tel. (222) 229-2257; e-mail pregunta.biblio@udlap.mx; internet biblio.udlap.mx; f. 1940; humanities, science and technology; 400,000 vols, 2,200 periodicals; spec. colln; M. Covarrubias archives, R. Barlow archives, Herrera Carrillo archives, Porfirio Díaz archives; Dir Mtro ARTURO ARRIETA AUDIFFRED.

Toluca

Biblioteca Pública Central Estatal (Central State Public Library): Blvd Eduardo Monrroy Cardenas s/n, Centro Cultural Mexiquense, (Ex-Hacienda La Pila), Col. San Buenaventura, 50110 Toluca, MEX; tel. (722) 274-1131; e-mail bpcemex@conaculta.gob.mx; f. 1987; 40,012 vols, 128 periodicals; Dir MARÍA CRISTINA PÉREZ GÓMEZ.

Tuxtla Gutiérrez

Biblioteca Pública Central Estatal Centro Cultural Jaime Sabines (Central Public Library State Cultural Centre Jaime Sabines): Centro Cultural De Chiapas, Centro, 29000 Tuxtla Gutiérrez, CHIS; tel. (961) 612-5199; e-mail mtoledo@conecultachiapas.gob.mx; internet www.chiapas.gob.mx; f. 2000; Dir AURA ALICIA FERRA RIVERA.

Zacatecas

Coordinación Estatal De Bibliotecas Públicas de Zacatecas (State Coordination of Public Libraries of Zacatecas): Calzada Cerro del Grillo No 100, Complejo Vial Quebradilla, 98000 Zacatecas, ZAC; tel. (492) 924-0562; e-mail cebpzacatecas@hotmail.com; internet www.seczac.gob.mx/cebzac; f. 1832; current name adopted 1986; consists of the following libraries: Biblioteca Central Estatal 'Mauricio Magdaleno', Biblioteca de Colecciones Especiales 'Elias Amador' and 233 other units; State Coordinator Prof. EDUARDO MENDOZA VILLALPANDO.

Museums and Art Galleries

Campeche

Museo Regional de Campeche (Campeche Regional Museum): Calle 59 entre 16 y 14, 24000 Campeche, CAM; e-mail direccion.camp@inah.gob.mx; f. 1986; archaeology and history; Dir Arq. JOSÉ E. ORTÍZ LAN.

Guadalajara

Casa Taller José Clemente Orozco (House and Studio of José Clemente Orozco): Calle Aurelio Aceves 27, Col. Arcos Vallarta, 44120 Guadalajara, JAL; tel. (33) 3616-8329; e-mail cabanas@jalisco.gob.mx; f. 1951; paintings and sketches by the artist; Dir MARGARITA V. DE OROZCO.

Museo de las Artes Populares de Jalisco (Museum of Popular Arts in Jalisco): San Felipe 211, Esq. con Pino Suárez, Col. Guadalajara Centro, 44100 Guadalajara, JAL; tel. (33) 3030-9779; e-mail mapjsc@yahoo.com; colln incl. pieces related to music, horsemanship, ethnic groups and traditions of the region.

Museo del Periodismo y las Artes Gráficas (Museum of Journalism and Graphic Arts): Alcalde 225, Centro Histórico, 44100 Guadalajara, JAL; tel. (33) 3613-9286; e-mail museodelperiodismo@hotmail.com; f. 1994; colln of historical artifacts.

Museo Palacio de Gobierno (Palace Museum of the Government): Calle Corona No 31, Centro Histórico, 44100 Guadalajara, JAL; tel. (33) 3614-4038; e-mail museodepalacio@jalisco.gob.mx; internet capturaportal.jalisco.gob.mx/wps/portal/pj/jalisco/museopalacio; history of Jalisco; Dir CÉSAR SALVADOR RUIZ LÓPEZ.

Museo Regional de Guadalajara (Guadalajara Regional Museum): Liceo 60, Sector Hidalgo, Zona Centro, 44100 Guadalajara, JAL; tel. (33) 3613-2703; e-mail museoregionalguadalajara@hotmail.com; f. 1918 as Museo de Bellas Artes; current name adopted 1923; spec. collns of pre-Spanish and Colonial period art and paintings; archaeological and palaeontological colln; Dir Lic. CRISTINA SÁNCHEZ DEL REAL.

Guanajuato

Museo de Historia Natural 'Alfredo Dugès' (Natural History Museum Alfredo Dugès): Planta baja, del Edif. Central de la Universidad de Guanajuato, Calle Lascuráin de Retana No 5, zona centro, 36000 Guanajuato, GTO; tel. (473) 732-0006; e-mail duges@ugto.mx; internet www.museoduges.ugto.mx; f. 1870; attached to Universidad de Guanajuato; natural history colln of Alfredo Dugès with rare specimens; Curator GLORIA E. MAGAÑA COTA.

Madero

Museo de la Cultura Huasteca (Museum of Huastec Culture): Blvd Adolfo López Mateos s/n, Tampico, 89050 Madero, TAMPS; tel. (833) 210-2217; f. 1960; attached to Instituto Nacional de Antropología e Historia; library of 1,750 vols, 95 discs; Dir C. P. MARIA ALEJANDRINA ELÍAS ORTIZ.

Mérida

Museo Regional de Antropología de Yucatán (Regional Museum of Anthropology of Yucatán): Palacio Canton, Calle 43 por Paseo de Montejo, Mérida, YUC; tel. (999) 923-0557; e-mail palacio.canton@inah.gob.mx; f. 1959; attached to Instituto Nacional de Antropología e Historia; collns of pre-Hispanic Mayan and Olmec culture, precious stones, ceramics, jade, objects in copper and gold; Dir GIOVANA JASPERSEN GARCÍA; Curator PETER SCHMIEDT; Curator BLANCA GONZÁLEZ.

Mexico City

Laboratorio Arte Alameda (Alameda Laboratory of Arts): Dr Mora 7, Col. Centro Histórico, 06050 México, DF; tel. (55) 5510-2793; e-mail info.artealameda@gmail.com; internet www.artealameda.bellasartes.gob.mx; f. 1962 as Pinacoteca Virreinal de San Diego, present name and collns 2000; attached to Instituto Nacional de Bellas Artes; collns of new media and electronic art; Mexican colonial arts; library of 5,000 vols; Dir TANIA AEDO; Curator KARLA JASSO.

Museo de Arte 'Alvar y Carmen T. de Carrillo Gil' (Alvar and Carmen T. de Carrillo Gil Museum of Art): Avda Revolución 1608, Esq. Altavista, Col. San Angel, Del. Alvaro Obregón, 01000 México, DF; tel. (55) 5550-3983; e-mail macg.prensa@inba.gob.mx; internet www.museodeartecarrillogil.com; f. 1974; attached to Instituto Nacional de Bellas Artes; contemporary Mexican art; 1,775 pieces of collages, drawings, engravings, art objects, lithography, paintings, photography, sculptures, silk screens and videos; library of 3,500 vols; Dir VANIA ROJAS; publ. *Gazeta del Museo* (12 a year).

Museo de Arte Moderno (Museum of Modern Art): Bosque de Chapultepec, Paseo de la Reforma y Gandhi s/n, 11560 México, DF; tel. (55) 5553-6233; e-mail info@mam.org.mx; internet www.mam.org.mx; f. 1964; Mexican colln of modern and contemporary art and temporary exhibitions of modern Mexican and foreign art; organizes symposiums, temporary exhibitions, conversations with artists, confs, cultural activities, book presentations, workshops; library of 30,000 vols; Dir MAGDALENA ZAVALA BONACHEA; publ. *Critical Gazette*.

Museo de Historia Natural y Cultural Ambiental (Museum of Natural History and Environmental Culture): 2a Sección del Bosque de Chapultepec s/n, Apdo 18–845, Del. Miguel Hidalgo, 11800 México, DF; tel. (55) 5515-6304; e-mail mhn_mex@sma.df.gob.mx; internet www.museodehistorianatural.df.gob.mx; f. 1964; exhibitions on the universe, the earth, the origin of life, plant and animal taxonomy, evolution and adaptation of species, biology, man and bio-geographical areas; contains replicas of prehistoric creatures; library of 6,000 vols; Dir María Guadalupe Fragoso García.

Museo Estudio Diego Rivera (Museum of Diego Rivera's Studio): Calle Diego Rivera s/n Esq. Avda Altavista, Col. San Angel Inn, Del. Álvaro Obregón, 01060 México, DF; tel. (55) 5550-1518; e-mail medr.difusion@inba.gob.mx; internet www.estudiodiegorivera.bellasartes.gob.mx; f. 1986; attached to Instituto Nacional de Bellas Artes; permanent exhibition 'Estudio Taller de Diego Rivera'; Dir Luis Rius Caso.

Museo Nacional de Antropología (National Museum of Anthropology): Avda Paseo de la Reforma y Calzada Gandhi s/n, Col. Chapultepec Polanco, Del. Miguel Hidalgo, 11560 México, DF; tel. (55) 4040-5300; e-mail atencion.mna@inah.gob.mx; internet www.mna.inah.gob.mx; f. 1940; attached to Instituto Nacional de Antropología e Historia; anthropological, ethnological, and archaeological subjects relating to Mexico; 6,000 exhibits; library of 300,000 vols; Dir Antonio Saborit; publs *Cuadernos*, *Guides*.

Museo Nacional de Arquitectura (National Museum of Architecture): Palacio de Bellas Artes 3° nivel, Avda Juárez y Eje Central Lázaro Cárdenas, Centro Histórico, Del. Cuauhtémoc, 06050 México, DF; tel. (55) 5510-2853; e-mail mnalarq@inba.gob.mx; internet www.museonacionaldearquitectura.bellasartes.gob.mx; f. 1984; attached to Instituto Nacional de Bellas Artes; examples of Mexican architecture through the ages; photographic archive; original plans by Adamo Boari, Federico Mariscal, Juan O'Gorman, Carlos Obregón Santacilia, Mario Pani, Enrique del Moral, José Villagrán, Juan Segura, Francisco Centeno and Francisco J. Serrano; original drawings of the Palacio de Bellas Artes; Dir Xavier Guzmán.

Museo Nacional de Arte (National Museum of Art): Tacuba 8, Centro Histórico, Del. Cuauhtémoc, 06010 México, DF; tel. (55) 5130-3400; e-mail contacto@munal.inba.gob.mx; internet www.munal.com.mx; f. 1982; attached to Instituto Nacional de Antropología e Historia; permanent exhibitions of Mexican art from 16th century to 1950; library of 39,000 vols, 11,000 journals; Dir Augstín Arteaga; publ. *Revista Memoria*.

Museo Nacional de Artes e Industrias Populares (National Museum of Popular Arts and Industries): Avda Mexico Coyoacán No 343, Del. Benito Juárez, México, DF; tel. (55) 5521-6679; f. 1951; attached to Instituto Nacional Indigenista; examples of traditional Mexican art of all periods, conservation and encouragement of traditional handicrafts; Dir María Teresa Pomar.

Museo Nacional de Historia (National Museum of History): Primera Sección del Bosque de Chapultepec, Del. Miguel Hidalgo, 11580 México, DF; tel. (55) 4040-5228; e-mail difusion.mnh@inah.gob.mx; internet www.mnh.inah.gob.mx; f. 1944; attached to Instituto Nacional de Antropología e Historia; history of Mexico since the 16th century; historical paintings, flags, weapons, documents, jewellery, textiles, ceramics, furniture, clothing and other objects of social and cultural history; Dir-Gen. María Teresa Franco González Salas.

Museo Nacional de la Estampa (National Museum of Print): Avda Hidalgo 39, Plaza de la Santa Veracruz, Col. Centro, Del. Cuauhtémoc, 06050 México, DF; tel. (55) 5521-2244; e-mail munae.servicioseducativos@yahoo.com.mx; internet www.museonacionaldelaestampa.bellasartes.gob.mx; f. 1986; 12,000 works; engravings, graphic arts; permanent exhibition 'Proceso Histórico de la Estampa en México'; documentation centre; Dir Santiago Pérez Garci.

Museo Nacional de las Culturas (National Museum of Cultures): Calle de Moneda 13, Col. Centro Histórico, Del. Cuauhtémoc, 06010 México, DF; tel. (55) 5512-7452; e-mail direccion.cmuseo@inah.gob.mx; internet www.museodelasculturas.mx; attached to Instituto Nacional de Antropología e Historia; f. 1965; 14,000 objects; collns of archaeology and ethnology from all over the world; public lectures, spec. courses for teachers, training in plastic arts; library of 11,900 vols; Pres. Rafael Tovar y de Teresa; Dir María Teresa Franco González.

Museo Nacional de las Intervenciones (National Museum of the Interventions): General Anaya y 20 de Agosto, Del. Coyoacán, 04100 México, DF; tel. (55) 5604-0699; e-mail difusionmni@inah.gob.mx; internet www.cnca.gob.mx/cnca/inah/museos/munaint.html; f. 1981; attached to Instituto Nacional de Antropología e Historia; exhibits history of foreign interventions and Mexican independence; library of 800 vols; Dir Cecilia Genel Velasco.

Museo Nacional de San Carlos (San Carlos Museum): Puente de Alvarado 50, Col. Tabacalera, 06030 México, DF; e-mail mnsancarlos@mail.com; internet www.mnsancarlos.com; f. 1968; attached to Instituto Nacional de Bellas Artes; colln of 14th–19th century European panels, paintings, sculpture, drawings and prints; housed within the Palace of the Counts of Buenavista; library of 2,633 vols; Dir Carmen Gaitán Rojo; publ. *Gaceta de San Carlos* (4 a year).

Museo Tamayo (Tamayo Museum): Paseo de la Reforma No 51 Esq. Gandhi, Col. Bosque de Chapultepec, Del. Miguel Hidalgo, 11580 México, DF; tel. (55) 5286-6519; e-mail prensa@museotamayo.org; internet www.museotamayo.org; f. 1981; permanent colln of contemporary art, permanent exhibition of Rufino Tamayo's work; temporary exhibits of int. artists; library specializing in Rufino Tamayo, contemporary art and artists; Dir Carmen Cuenca Carrara.

Monterrey

Museo Regional de Nuevo León (Regional Museum of Nuevo León): Rafael José Verger s/n, Col. Obispado, 64010 Monterrey, NL; tel. (81) 8333-9588; internet dti.inah.gob.mx; f. 1956; regional and Mexican history, archaeology and painting; Dir Ing. Francisco Aguilar Moreno.

Morelia

Museo Regional Michoacano 'Dr Nicolás León Calderón' (Michoacan Regional Museum 'Dr Nicolás León Calderón'): Calle de Allende 305 Esq. con Abasolo, Centro, 58000 Morelia, MICH; tel. (443) 312-0407; e-mail inahmich@inah.gob.mx; f. 1886; archaeological, ecological, ethnographical and prehistoric collns of the dist.; library of 10,000 vols; Head Amalia Villalobos Díaz; publ. *Anales*.

Oaxaca

Museo de las Culturas de Oaxaca (Museum of the Cultures of Oaxaca): Apdo 68000, 'Ex-Convento de Santo Domingo de Guzmán', Macedonio Alcalá y Adolfo Gurrión s/n, Oaxaca, OAX; tel. (951) 516-2991; e-mail sdomingo@prodigy.net.mx; f. 1933; anthropology, archaeology, ethnography and religious art; contains archaeological treasures from Tomb No 7, Monte Albán, jewellery; Dir Karina Romero Rodríguez.

Patzcuaro

Museo de Artes e Industrias Populares de Pátzcuaro (Museum of Popular Arts and Industries of Patzcuaro): Enseñanza s/n Centro, 61600 Pátzcuaro, Michoacán; tel. (434) 342-4400; e-mail patricia_teran@inah.gob.mx; f. 1935; ancient and modern ethnographical exhibits relating to the Tarascan Indians of Michoacán; colonial and contemporary native art; Dir Patricia Terán Escobar.

Puebla

Museo de Arte 'José Luis Bello y González' (José Luis Bello y González Museum of Art): 3 Poniente No 302, Centro Histórico, Heróica Puebla de Zaragoza, 72000 Puebla, PUE; tel. (222) 232-9475; e-mail amhcastillo@yahoo.com.mx; f. 1938, opened to the public 1944; contains: ivories, porcelain, wrought iron, furniture, clocks, watches, musical instruments, etc., Mexican, Chinese and European paintings, sculptures, pottery, vestments, tapestries, ceramics, miniatures, etc.

Museo Regional de Puebla (Regional Museum of Puebla): Avda Ejercitos de Oriente s/n, Centro Civico 5 de Mayo, Los Fuertes, 72270 Puebla, PUE; tel. (222) 235-9702; e-mail murep.inah@gmail.com; internet murep-inah.jimdo.com; f. 1974; Dir Prof. Delia del Consuelo Domínguez Cuanalo; Sec. C. Graciela Sánchez Valencia.

Museo Regional de Santa Mónica (Santa Monica Regional Museum): Calle 18, Avda Poniente 103, Col. Centro, 72000 Puebla, PUE; tel. (222) 232-0178; e-mail santamonicapuebla@gmail.com; f. 1940; religious art; comprises collns of various disbanded convents; Dir Arq. Claudia Reyes Flores.

Puerto Vallarta

Museo Histórico Naval de Puerto Vallarta (Naval History Museum of Puerto Vallarta): Zaragoza 4 Centro, 48300 Puerto Vallarta, JAL; tel. (322) 223-5357; e-mail musnavllarta1@hotmail.com; f. 2006; colln incl. paintings, models, photographs, documents, maps, scale models and navigation instruments.

Querétaro

Museo Regional de Querétaro (Querétaro Regional Museum): Calle Corregidora Sur 3, 76000 Querétaro, QRO; tel. (442) 212-2031; e-mail museoregional.qro@inah.gob.mx; f. 1936; local history and art; Dir Gina Patricia Ulloa Cristoforo.

Tepotzotlán

Museo Nacional del Virreinato (National Museum of the Vice-Royalty): Plaza Hidalgo 99, Barrio San Martín, 54600 Tepotzotlán, MEX; tel. (55) 5876-0245; e-mail virreinato.museo@inah.gob.mx; internet www.virreinato.inah.gob.mx; f. 1964; attached to Instituto Nacional de Antropología e Historia; collns on the art and culture of the Colonial period; housed in 17th- and 18th-century bldgs; library of 4,000 vols from the 16th–19th century, 3,000 periodical titles, pamphlets and 125 CD titles; Dir Miguel Emigdio Fernández Félix.

Toluca

Museo de las Bellas Artes (Museum of Fine Arts): Calle de Santos Degollado 102, 50000 Toluca, MEX; tel. (722) 215-5329; e-mail gemimcda@edomex.gob.mx; paintings, sculptures, Mexican colonial art; Dir Lic. Leonel Sánchez Maldonado.

Tuxtla Gutiérrez

Museo Regional de Chiapas (Chiapas Regional Museum): Calzada de los Hombres Ilustres s/n, Parque Madero, 29000 Tuxtla Gutiérrez, CHIS; tel. (449) 916-5228; e-mail museoregionaldechiapas@hotmail.com; f. 1939; archaeological and historical colins; Dir ROBERTO LÓPEZ BRAVO.

Tzintzuntzan

Museo Etnográfico y Arqueológico (Ethnographical and Archaeological Museum): 58440 Tzintzuntzan, MICH; e-mail olgrom@hotmail.com; f. 1944; ethnographical and archaeological collns on the Tzintzuntzan and Tarascan zones of Lake Pátzcuaro.

Xalapa

Museo de Antropología de Xalapa (Xalapa Museum of Anthropology): Avda Xalapa s/n, 91010 Xalapa, VER; tel. (228) 815-0920; e-mail museo@uv.mx; internet www.uv.mx/max; f. 1959; attached to Universidad Veracruzana; spec. regional archaeological colins of the Olmec, Totonac and Huastec cultures of ancient Mexico; Dir Dra MAURA ORDOÑEZ VALENZUELA.

Universities

Higher education institutions in Mexico fall into one of 10 categories: public federal universities, public state universities, intercultural universities, technological universities, polytechnic universities, federal institutes of technology (hereafter simply referred to as federal institutes), state institutes of technology (hereafter state institutes), public centres of research (hereafter research centres), other public institutions, and private tertiary institutions (hereafter private institutions). All told there are over 1,600 institutions. Owing to space limitations we cannot list them all, and so have restricted our listings to the first five aforesaid categories and private tertiary institutions that are accredited universities. The numbers of other types of higher education institutions will be given for each state.

Aguascalientes

In Aguascalientes, there is one federal institute, one other public institution and four private institutions.

UNIVERSIDAD AUTÓNOMA DE AGUASCALIENTES
(Autonomous University of Aguascalientes)

Avda Universidad 940, Ciudad Universitaria, 20131 Aguascalientes, AGS
Telephone: (449) 910-7400
E-mail: atencionrectoria@correo.uaa.mx
Internet: www.uaa.mx
Founded 1973
State control
Language of instruction: Spanish
Academic year: August to June (2 semesters)
Rector: MARIO ANDRADE CERVANTES
Sec.-Gen.: Dr FRANCISCO JAVIER AVELAR GONZÁLEZ
Dir-Gen. for Educational Services: JOSÉ ANTONIO MARTÍNEZ MURILLO
Dir-Gen. for Finance: RICARDO GONZÁLEZ ÁLVAREZ
Dir-Gen. for Planning and Devt: JOSÉ ANTONIO MARTÍNEZ MURILLO
Dir-Gen. for Research and Postgraduate Affairs: Dr FERNANDO JARAMILLO JUÁREZ
Dir-Gen. for Undergraduate Teaching: Dr ARMANDO SANTACRUZ TORRES
Dir-Gen. for Univ. Infrastructure: MARIO HERNÁNDEZ PADILLA
Chief Librarian: IRMA GRACIELA DE LEON GARCÍA
Library of 152,200 vols
Number of teachers: 1,500
Number of students: 11,500
Publications: *Caleidoscopio* (2 a year), *Evaluación* (1 a year), *Gaceta Universitaria* (12 a year), *Investigación y Ciencia* (2 a year), *Scientiae Naturae* (2 a year)

ACADEMIC DIRECTORS

Centre for Agricultural Sciences: GABRIEL ERNESTO PALLÁS GUZMÁN
Centre for Arts and Culture: JORGE H. GARCÍA NAVARRO
Centre for Basic Sciences: JOSÉ DE JESÚS RUIZ GALLEGOS
Centre for Business Sciences (Sur Campus): JOSÉ JORGE SAAVEDRA GONZÁLEZ
Centre for Design and Construction Sciences: MARIO EDUARDO ZERMEÑO DE LEÓN
Centre for Economics and Administration: Dra MARÍA DEL CARMEN MARTÍNEZ SERNA
Centre for Engineering Sciences (Sur Campus): LUIS ENRIQUE ARÁMBULA MIRANDA
Centre for Health Sciences: Dr RAÚL FRANCO DÍAZ DE LEÓN
Centre for Social Sciences and Humanities: Dr DANIEL EUDAVE MUÑOZ

UNIVERSIDAD CUAUHTÉMOC
(Cuauhtémoc University)

Avda Independencia No 101, Col. Trojes de Alonso, 20100 Aguascalientes, AGS
Telephone: (449) 973-1122
E-mail: informes@ucuauhtemoc.edu.mx
Internet: www.ucuauhtemoc.edu.mx
Founded 1993
Private control
1 Programme accredited by COPAES (*q.v.*)
Rector: JUAN CAMILO MEZA JARAMILLO

UNIVERSIDAD PANAMERICANA
(Pan American University)

Josemaría Escrivá de Balaguer No 101, Fraccionamiento Rústicos Calpulli, 20290 Aguascalientes, AGS
Telephone: (449) 910-6209
E-mail: rpublicas@up.edu.mx
Internet: www.up.edu.mx
Founded 1967
Private control
2 Programmes accredited by COPAES (*q.v.*)
Rector: ALFONSO BOLIO ARCINIEGA
Library Head: Lic. VICENTA GARCIA VELÁZQUEZ

UNIVERSIDAD POLITÉCNICA DE AGUASCALIENTES
(Polytechnic University of Aguascalientes)

Calle Paseo San Gerardo No 207, Fraccionamiento San Gerardo, 20342 Aguascalientes, AGS
Telephone: (449) 442-1400
E-mail: comunicacion@upa.edu.mx
Internet: www.upa.edu.mx
Founded 2002
State control
Language of instruction: Spanish
Academic year: September to August
Rector: EULOGIA MONREAL ÁVILA
Librarian: ALEJANDRO SANTANA

UNIVERSIDAD TECNOLÓGICA DE AGUASCALIENTES
(Technological University of Aguascalientes)

Blvd Juan Pablo II No 1302, Fraccionamiento Ex Hacienda la Cantera, 20206 Aguascalientes, AGS
Telephone: (449) 910-5000
Internet: www.utags.edu.mx
Founded 1991
State control
Language of instruction: Spanish
Rector: JORGE ARMANDO LLAMAS ESPARZA
Academic Sec.: PABLO DE JESÚS MEDINA LLAMAS
Dir for Admin. and Finance: GERARDO LOYOLA BALLESTEROS
Sub-Dir for Planning and Evaluation: Lic. ANA MATILDE SAN JOSÉ ZELEDÓN
Sub-Dir for School Services: Ing. SANDRA MARTÍNEZ HERNÁNDEZ
Sub-Dir for Univ. Extension: BEATRIZ EMILIA MEDINA MARÍN
Librarian: MARLENE HERRERA CASTÁN
Library of 17,550 vols, 28 periodical titles, 75 online periodicals, 21 electronic libraries

Baja California

In Baja California, there are three federal institutes, two research centres and 22 private institutions.

UNIVERSIDAD AUTÓNOMA DE BAJA CALIFORNIA
(Autonomous University of Baja California)

Avda Álvaro Obregón y Julian Carrillo s/n, 21100 Mexicali, BC
Telephone: (686) 553-4461
E-mail: rector@uabc.edu.mx
Internet: www.uabc.mx
Founded 1957
State control
Language of instruction: Spanish
Academic year: August to June
Rector: Dr FELIPE CUAMEA VELÁZQUEZ
Vice-Rector: RENÉ ANDRADE PETERSON
Vice-Rector for Ensenada Campus: Dr ÓSCAR ROBERTO LÓPEZ BONILLA
Vice-Rector for Mexicali Campus: Dr MIGUEL ÁNGEL MARTÍNEZ ROMERO
Sec.-Gen.: Lic. RICARDO DAGNINO MORENO
Librarian: MARIANA BECERRA VALENZUELA
Publications: *Calafia*, *Ciencias Marinas*, *Cuaderno de Taller Literario*, *Cuadernos de Ciencias Sociales*, *Divulgare*, *Estudios Fronterizos*, *Paradigmas*, *Revista de Investigación Educativa*, *Revistas Universitarias*, *Semillero*, *Yubai*

UNIVERSIDAD DE TIJUANA
(University of Tijuana)

Avda J. Lucrecia Torriz No 1010, Col. Altamira, 22054 Tijuana, BC
Telephone: (664) 687-9454
Internet: www.udetijuana.edu.mx
Founded 1992
Private control
Accredited by FIMPES (*q.v.*)
Rector: JESÚS RUIZ BARRAZA

UNIVERSIDAD IBEROAMERICANA TIJUANA
(Ibero American University of Tijuana)

Avda Centro Universitario No 2501, Playas de Tijuana, 22200 Tijuana, BC
Telephone: (664) 630-1577
Internet: www.iberotijuana.edu.mx
Founded 1943
Private control
Accredited by FIMPES (*q.v.*)
Rector: Dr Rubén Arceo López
Sec.: Juan José Esquivias López
Publication: *El Bordo*

UNIVERSIDAD POLITÉCNICA DE BAJA CALIFORNIA
(Polytechnic University of Baja California)

Calle de la claridad SN, Col. Plutarco Elias Calles, 21376 Mexicali, BC
Telephone: (686) 104-2727
E-mail: rectoria@upbc.edu.mx
Internet: www.upbc.edu.mx
Founded 2006
State control
Language of instruction: Spanish
Academic year: September to August
Rector: Navor Rosas González
Academic Sec.: Abelardo Mercado Herrera
Admin. Sec.: Pedro Salazar Monroy

Baja California Sur

In Baja California Sur, there are two federal institutes, two state institutes, one research centre and two private institutions.

UNIVERSIDAD AUTÓNOMA DE BAJA CALIFORNIA SUR
(Autonomous University of Baja California Sur)

Carretera al Sur km 5.5, Apdo Postal 19-B, 23080 La Paz, BCS
Telephone: (612) 123-8800
E-mail: rectoria@uabcs.mx
Internet: www.uabcs.mx
Founded 1975
State control
Language of instruction: Spanish
Depts of agronomy, animal husbandry, computer systems, economics, humanities, marine biology, marine engineering, marine geology, political science and public administration
Rector: Gustavo Rodolfo Cruz Chávez
Academic Sec.: Dr Dante Arturo Salgado González
Sec. for Admin. and Finance: Dr José Isabel Urciaga García
Dir for Culture and Univ. Extension: Magda Dinorah Valdez Ceseña
Dir for Research and Postgraduate Affairs: Alba Eritrea Gámez Vázquez
Library Dir: José Alfredo Verdugo Sánchez
Publication: *Revista Científica Trayectos*

Campeche

In Campeche, there are three federal institutes, three state institutes, one research centre and 10 private institutions.

UNIVERSIDAD AUTÓNOMA DE CAMPECHE
(Autonomous University of Campeche)

Avda Agustín Melgar s/n entre Calle 20 y Juan de la Barrera, Col. Buenavista, 24039 San Francisco de Campeche, CAM
Telephone: (981) 811-9800
E-mail: webmaster@etzna.uacam.mx
Internet: www.uacam.mx
Founded 1965 as Universidad del Sudeste, current name adopted 1989
State control
Language of instruction: Spanish
Academic year: September to June
Centres for biomedical research, corrosion research, foreign languages, historical and social research, legal research, Spanish and Maya, sustainable development and utilization of wildlife; faculties of accounting and administration, chemical and biological sciences, dentistry, engineering, humanities, law, medicine, nursing, social sciences; school of agricultural sciences; institute of ecology, fisheries and oceanography of the Gulf of Mexico
Rector: Licda Adriana del Pilar Ortiz Lanz
Sec.-Gen.: Lic. Gerardo Montero Pérez
Dir for Admin. Services: Juan Carlos Limón López
Dir for Educational Support Service: Lic. José Manuel Caballero Alejandro
Dir for Human Resources: Lic. José A. Falcón Sánchez
Dir for Information Technology: Gerardo Elias Navarrete Teran
Dir for Planning and Quality: Ing. Mario Pérez Cervera
Dir for Postgraduate Studies and Research: Dr Benjamín Otto Ortega Morales
Library Dir: Lic. Enna Verónica Lara Gamboa
Number of teachers: 450
Number of students: 4,800
Publications: *Panorama* (6 a year), *Pinceladas* (6 a year)

UNIVERSIDAD AUTÓNOMA DEL CARMEN
(Autonomous University of Carmen)

Calle 56 No 4 Esq. Avda Concordia Col. Benito Juárez, 24180 Ciudad del Carmen, CAM
Telephone: (938) 381-1018
E-mail: controlescolar@delfin.unacar.mx
Internet: www.unacar.mx
Founded 1967
State control
Language of instruction: Spanish
Faculties of chemistry, commerce and administration, education, law
Rector: Dr José Antonio Ruz Hernández
Sec.-Gen.: Dr Miguel Jesús Medina Escalante
Academic Dir for Higher Secondary Education: Catalina Massa Casanova
Dir for Admin.: José Ramón Díaz Cicler
Dir for Finance: Gustavo Fuentes Benítez
Dir for Human Resources: Nancy Verónica Sánchez Sulú
Dir for Public Relations and Social Communication: María Elena Márquez Almazán
Dir for Libraries: Juan Ángel Vázquez Martínez
Library of 69,429 vols
Number of teachers: 340
Number of students: 4,500
Publication: *UNACAR Tecnociencia* (2 a year)

UNIVERSIDAD TECNOLÓGICA DE CAMPECHE
(Technological University of Campeche)

Carretera Federal 180 s/n, San Antonio Cárdenas, 24381 Carmen, CAM
Telephone: (938) 131-3290
Internet: www.utcam.edu.mx
Founded 1997
State control
Language of instruction: Spanish
Rector: Ing. Manuel Jesús Cordero Rivera
Academic Sec.: Lic. Oresbia Abreu Peralta
Dir for Admin. and Finance: Wilberth de Jesús González Ek
Dir for External Affairs, Dissemination and Univ. Extension: Lic. Georgina del Carmen Ordóñez Casanova

Chiapas

In Chiapas, there are three federal institutes, one state institute, one research centre and 29 private institutions.

UNIVERSIDAD AUTÓNOMA DE CHIAPAS
(Autonomous University of Chiapas)

Blvd Belisario Domínguez km 1081 s/n, 29050 Tuxtla Gutiérrez, CHIS
Telephone: (961) 617-8000
E-mail: rectoria@unach.mx
Internet: www.unach.mx
Founded 1975
State control
Language of instruction: Spanish
Academic year: September to July (2 semesters)
Rector: Dr Jaime Valls Esponda
Sec.-Gen.: Hugo Armando Aguilar Aguilar
Academic Sec.: Marcela Iturbe Vargas
Admin. Sec.: Miguel Ángel Cigarroa Torres
Dir-Gen. for Planning: Juan Carlos Rodríguez Guillén
Dir-Gen. for Research and Postgraduate Affairs: Dr Lorenzo Franco Escamirosa Montalvo
Dir-Gen. for Univ. Extension: Lic. Victor Fabian Rumaya Farrera
Library Dir: Dra Rosa Elba Chacón Escobar
Number of teachers: 900
Number of students: 12,000
Publication: *Gaceta Universitaria*

ACADEMIC DIRECTORS

Campus I (Tuxtla Gutiérrez):
Faculty of Accounting and Administration: Dr Rafael T. Franco Gurria
Faculty of Architecture: Arq. José Alberto Colmenares Guillen
Faculty of Engineering: Dr Francisco Alberto Alonso Farrera

Campus II (Tuxtla Gutiérrez):
Faculty of Human Medicine: Dr Roberto Fernando Solís Hernández
Faculty of Veterinary Medicine and Zootechnics: José Alfredo Castellanos Coutiño

Campus III (San Cristóbal de las Casas):
Faculty of Law: Dr Oswaldo Chaco Rojas
Faculty of Social Sciences: Mauro Jorge Robledo Cossío

Campus IV (Tapachula):
Faculty of Accounting: Enrique Yasusi Barroso Yoshikawa
Faculty of Administration Sciences: Mónica Juárez Ibarias
Faculty of Agriculture: Carlos Gumaro García Castillo

Faculty of Chemical Sciences: DANIEL MARCOS MINA

Campus V (Villaflores):

Faculty of Agronomy: JAIME LAVEN MARTÍNEZ

Campus VI (Tuxtla Gutiérrez):

Faculty of Humanities: GONZALO ESTEBAN GIRÓN AGUILAR

UNIVERSIDAD DE CIENCIAS Y ARTES DE CHIAPAS
(University of Arts and Sciences of Chiapas)

1A Sur Poniente 1460, Col. Centro, 29000 Tuxtla Gutiérrez, CHIS

Telephone: (961) 617-0400

E-mail: secgral@unicach.edu.mx

Internet: www.unicach.edu.mx

Founded 1893 as Industrial School of Chiapas; current name and status 1995

State control

Language of instruction: Spanish

Faculties of biological sciences, nutrition and food sciences; schools of arts, dentistry, engineering and topography, psychology; languages centre

Rector: Ing. ROBERTO DOMÍNGUEZ CASTELLANOS

Sec.-Gen.: JOSÉ RODOLFO CALVO FONSECA

Academic Sec.: FLORENTINO PÉREZ PÉREZ

Dir for Admin.: Lic. RICARDO CRUZ GONZÁLEZ

Dir for IT and Communication: Ing. BRENDA MARÍA VILLARREAL ANTELO

Dir for Planning: PASCUAL RAMOS GARCÍA

Dir for Research and Postgraduate Affairs: Dra MARÍA ADELINA SCHLIE GUZMÁN

Dir for Univ. Extension: Lic. MARÍA DE LOS ÁNGELES VÁZQUEZ AMANCHA

Library Dir: NOÉ FERNANDO GUTIÉRREZ GONZÁLEZ

UNIVERSIDAD INTERCULTURAL DE CHIAPAS
(Intercultural University of Chiapas)

Corral de Piedra No. 2, Ciudad Universitaria Intercultural, 29299 San Cristóbal de Las Casas, CHIS

Telephone: (967) 631-6151

E-mail: contacto@unich.edu.mx

Internet: www.unich.edu.mx

Founded 2004

Private control

Rector: JAVIER ÁLVAREZ RAMOS

Publication: *Gaceta Universitaria* (3 a year)

UNIVERSIDAD POLITÉCNICA DE CHIAPAS
(Polytechnic University of Chiapas)

Calle Eduardo J. Selvas s/n y Avda Manuel de J. Cancino, Col. Magisterial, 29082 Tuxtla Gutiérrez, CHIS

Telephone: (961) 612-0484

E-mail: rectoria@upchiapas.edu.mx

Internet: www.upchiapas.edu.mx

Founded 2004

State control

Language of instruction: Spanish

Academic year: August to July

Rector: NAVOR FRANCISCO BALLINAS

Academic Sec.: REBECA GUADALUPE BLANCO CARRILLO

Admin. Sec.: RIGOBERTO JIMÉNEZ JONAPÁ

UNIVERSIDAD VALLE DEL GRIJALVA
(Valle del Grijalva University)

Carretera Internacional km 1002, Rancho El Murray, Cintalapa, CHIS

Telephone: (968) 684-3873

Internet: www.uvg.edu.mx

Founded 1989

Private control

4 Programmes accredited by COPAES (*q.v.*)

Rector: Lic. FREDDY CLEMENTE COUTIÑO

Publication: *Conexxión*

Chihuahua

In Chihuahua, there are eight federal institutes, one state institute, one research centre, one other public institution and 26 private institutions.

UNIVERSIDAD AUTÓNOMA DE CHIHUAHUA
(Autonomous University of Chihuahua)

Avda Escorza 900, Zona Centro, 31000 Chihuahua, CHIH

Telephone: (614) 439-1500

E-mail: webmaster@uach.mx

Internet: www.uach.mx

Founded 1954

State control

Language of instruction: Spanish

Academic year: August to June

Faculties of accounting and administration, agricultural and forestry science, agricultural engineering, animal science and ecology, arts, chemistry, dentistry, engineering, international economics, law, medicine, nursing and nutrition, philosophy and letters, physical education and sports science, political and social sciences

Rector: JESÚS ENRIQUE SEÁÑEZ SÁENZ

Sec. Gen.: SAÚL ARNULFO MARTÍNEZ CAMPOS

Dir for Academic Affairs: Dr ALEJANDRO CHÁVEZ GUERRERO

Dir for Admin.: HORACIO JURADO MEDINA

Dir for Extension and Culture: Lic. SERGIO REAZA ESCÁRCEGA

Dir for Planning and Institutional Devt: ROSENDO MARIO MALDONADO ESTRADA

Dir for Research and Postgraduate Affairs: JAVIER MARTÍNEZ NEVÁREZ

Gen. Coordinator for Libraries: CLAUDIA PÉREZ AGUILAR

Publications: *Revista Tecnociencia*, *Synthesis*

ACADEMIC DIRECTORS

Faculty of Accountancy and Administration: LILIANA ALVAREZ LOYA

Faculty of Agricultural Technology: Dr JAIME JAVIER MARTÍNEZ TÉLLEZ

Faculty of Agriculture and Forestry: FRANCISCO MÁRQUEZ SALCIDO

Faculty of Arts: RAÚL SÁNCHEZ TRILLO

Faculty of Chemical Sciences: Ing. ALFREDO R. URBINA VALENZUELA

Faculty of Dentistry: Dr GUSTAVO ALATORRE VALLARINO

Faculty of Engineering: Ing. ARTURO LEAL BEJARANO

Faculty of International Economics: HERIK GERMÁN VALLES BACA

Faculty of Law: ENRIQUE ANTONIO CARRETE SOLÍS

Faculty of Medicine: Dr JESÚS GUADALUPE BENAVIDES OLIVERA

Faculty of Nursing and Nutrition Science: Lic. ELVIRA SÁENZ LÓPEZ

Faculty of Philosophy and Literature: LUIS ALBERTO FIERRO RAMÍREZ

Faculty of Physical Education and Sport Science: FRANCISCO JAVIER FLORES RICO

Faculty of Political and Social Sciences: ELOY DÍAZ UNZUETA

Faculty of Zootechnics: LUIS RAÚL ESCÁRCEGA PRECIADO

UNIVERSIDAD AUTÓNOMA DE CIUDAD JUÁREZ
(Autonomous University of Ciudad Juárez)

Avda Plutarco Elías Calles 1210, Fovissste Chamizal, 32310 Ciudad Juárez, CHIH

Telephone: (656) 688-2100

E-mail: daramire@uacj.mx

Internet: www.uacj.mx

Founded 1973

State control

Language of instruction: Spanish

Academic year: August to June

Attached campuses in Ciudad Cuauhtémoc and Nuevo Casas Grandes

Rector: Lic. RICARDO DUARTE JÁQUEZ

Sec.-Gen.: DAVID RAMÍREZ PEREA

Academic Sec.: Lic. MANUEL LOERA DE LA ROSA

Dir-Gen. for Admin. Services: RITA ILEANA OLIVAS LARA

Dir-Gen. for Extension and Student Services: HUGO STAINESS OROZCO

Dir-Gen. for Planning and Institutional Devt: ÁNGEL FERNANDO GÓMEZ MARTÍNEZ

Coordinator for Research and Postgraduate Studies: Dr LUIS ENRIQUE GUTIÉRREZ CASAS

Coordinator for Libraries: Dra CONSUELO PEQUEÑO RODRÍGUEZ

Number of teachers: 700

Number of students: 12,200

Publications: *Entorno*, *Nóesis*

ACADEMIC DIRECTORS

Institute of Architecture, Design and Art: Dr ERICK SÁNCHEZ FLORES

Institute of Biomedical Sciences: DANIEL CONSTANDSE CORTEZ

Institute of Engineering and Technology: FRANCISCO LÓPEZ HERNÁNDEZ

Institute of Social Sciences and Administration: JUAN IGNACIO CAMARGO NASSAR

UNIVERSIDAD TECNOLÓGICA DE CHIHUAHUA
(Technological University of Chihuahua)

Avda Montes Americanos No 501, Sector 35, 31216 Chihuahua, CHIH

Telephone: (614) 432-2000

E-mail: informes@utch.edu.mx

Internet: www.utch.edu.mx

Founded 2000

State control

Rector: VICTOR MANUEL MENDOZA SALCEDO

Number of teachers: 65

Number of students: 1,374

UNIVERSIDAD TECNOLÓGICA DE CIUDAD JUAREZ
(Technological University of Ciudad Juarez)

Avda Universidad Tecnológica No 3051, Lote Bravo II, 32695 Ciudad Juárez, CHIH

Telephone: (656) 649-0600

Internet: www.utcj.edu.mx

Founded 1999

State control

Academic year: September to August

Rector: RICARDO ANTONIO GARCÍA PARRA

Academic Sec.: ARMANDO VELOZ GRAJEDA

Publication: *Revista Digital UTCJ*

Coahuila

In Coahuila, there are four federal institutes, two state institutes, one research centre, two other public institutions and 25 private institutions.

UNIVERSIDAD AUTÓNOMA AGRARIA 'ANTONIO NARRO'
(Antonio Narro Agrarian Autonomous University)

Buenavista, 25315 Saltillo, COAH
Telephone: (844) 411-0275
E-mail: docencia@uaaan.mx
Internet: www.uaaan.mx

Founded 1923, univ. status 1975
federal control
Language of instruction: Spanish
Academic year: August to June

Depts of agricultural economics, agricultural machinery, agricultural management, animal science, breeding, forestry, horticulture, nutrition and food, parasitology, sociology, soil sciences

Rector: Dr ELADIO HERIBERTO CORNEJO OVIEDO
Sec.-Gen.: LORENZO CASTRO GOMEZ
Dir-Gen. for Academic Affairs: Dr RAÚL VILLEGAS VIZCAÍNO
Dir-Gen. for Admin.: MARÍA ELENA GÓNGORA
Dir for Communications: HERIBERTO MARTINEZ LARA
Dir for Planning and Evaluation: JESUS RODOLFO VALENZUELA GARCIA
Dir for Research: ALFREDO SÁNCHEZ LÓPEZ
Dir for Teaching: MARIO ERNESTO VAZQUEZ BADILLO
Librarian: LUZ ELENA PEREZ MATA (acting)

Number of teachers: 500
Number of students: 2,500

UNIVERSIDAD AUTÓNOMA DE COAHUILA
(Autonomous University of Coahuila)

Blvd V. Carranza y Salvador González Lobo s/n, Col. República Oriente, 25280 Saltillo, COAH
Telephone: (844) 438-1620
E-mail: portal@uadec.edu.mx
Internet: www.uadec.mx

Founded 1957
State control
Language of instruction: Spanish
Academic year: August to July (2 terms)

Rector: Lic. BLAS JOSÉ FLORES DÁVILA
Sec.-Gen.: Ing. SALVADOR HERNÁNDEZ VÉLEZ
Dir for Academic Affairs: Lic. FLAVIA JAMIESON AYALA
Dir for Planning: Ing. RICARDO H. MUÑOZ VAZQUEZ
Librarian: ANTONIO MALACARA

Number of teachers: 900
Number of students: 14,000

Publications: *Acta Química Mexicana* (2 a year), *Cienciacierta* (4 a year), *Ciencias de la Salud de la UAdeC* (3 a year), *Equilibrio Económico* (2 a year), *La Humildad Premiada* (2 a year)

UNIVERSIDAD AUTONOMA DE LA LAGUNA
(Autonomous University of La Laguna)

Avda Universidad s/n Col. El Tajito, 27100 Torreón, COAH
Telephone: (871) 718-5533
E-mail: rector@ual.mx
Internet: www.ual.mx

Founded 1988
Private control

Rector: JORGE YAMIL DARWICH RAMÍREZ
Dir-Gen. for Academic Affairs: JOSÉ GERARDO MARTÍN SARABIA
Dir-Gen. for Educational Admin.: MANUEL MORALES SALAZAR
Dir-Gen. for Planning and Educational Devt: PEDRO CÁRDENAS MÉNDEZ
Sec.-Gen.: MARÍA TERESA DÍAZ AGUILERA

UNIVERSIDAD AUTÓNOMA DEL NORESTE
(Autonomous University of the Northeast)

Blvd Enrique Reyna y Américas Unidas, 25100 Saltillo, COAH
Telephone: (844) 438-4000
Internet: www.uane.edu.mx

Founded 1974
Private control
Academic year: January to December (2 terms)

Rector: HIGINIO GONZÁLEZ CALDERÓN
Vice-Rector for Academic Affairs: Lic. MARÍA DEL CARMEN RUÍZ ESPARZA
Vice-Rector for Admin. Affairs: GABRIEL DURÁN MALTOS
Librarian: Lic. NELLY BERMÚDEZ ARRAZATE

Number of teachers: 708
Number of students: 5,000

UNIVERSIDAD AUTÓNOMA DE PIEDRAS NEGRAS
(Autonomous University of Piedras Negras)

Padre de las Casas, entre Rayón y Guerrero, 26000 Piedras Negras, COAH
Telephone: (878) 782-2035
E-mail: uapn@uapn.edu.mx
Internet: www.uapn.edu.mx

Founded 1929
Private control

Faculties of nursing and midwifery, pharmaco-chemical laboratory, pharmacy, social work

Rector: Prof. XAVIER N. MARTÍNEZ AGUIRRE

UNIVERSIDAD IBEROAMERICANA TORREÓN
(Ibero American University of Torreón)

Calzada Iberoamericana No 2255, 27020, Torreón, COAH
Telephone: (871) 705-1010
E-mail: webmaster@iberotorreon.edu.mx
Internet: www.itzel.lag.uia.mx

Founded 1984
Private control

Accredited by FIMPES (*q.v.*)

Rector: Ing. HÉCTOR ACUÑA NOGUEIRA

UNIVERSIDAD TECNOLÓGICA DE COAHUILA
(Technological University of Coahuila)

Avda Industria Metalúrgica No 2001, Parque Industrial Ramos Arizpe, 25900 Ramos Arizpe, COAH
Telephone: (844) 288-3803
E-mail: rectoria@utc.edu.mx
Internet: www.utc.edu.mx

Founded 1995
State control
Language of instruction: Spanish

Colima

In Colima, there is one federal institute and six private institutions.

UNIVERSIDAD DE COLIMA
(University of Colima)

Avda Universidad 333, Col. Las Víboras, 28040 Colima, COL
Telephone: (312) 316-1000
E-mail: rector@ucol.mx
Internet: www.ucol.mx

Founded 1940 as Universidad Popular de Colima, reorganized 1962
State control
Language of instruction: Spanish
Academic year: July to August

Faculties of accountancy and administration, architecture and design, arts and communications, biological sciences and agronomy, chemical sciences, civil engineering, economics, education, electromechanical engineering, foreign languages, law, marine sciences, medicine, nursing, philosophy, psychology, social and political sciences, social work, telematics, veterinary medicine and zoology; institute of fine arts; schools of foreign trade, marketing, tourism and gastronomy

Rector: JOSÉ EDUARDO HERNÁNDEZ NAVA
Sec.-Gen.: CHRISTIAN JORGE TORRES ORTÍZ ZERMEÑO
Gen. Coordinator for Admin. and Finance: JUAN CARLOS VARGAS LEPE
Gen. Coordinator for Extension: LUIS MIGUEL BUENO SÁNCHEZ
Gen. Coordinator for IT: Dra LOURDES GALEANA DE LA O
Gen. Coordinator for Research: Dr ALFREDO ARANDA FERNÁNDEZ
Gen. Coordinator for Social Communication: Licda MARÍA GUADALUPE CARRILLO CÁRDENAS
Gen. Coordinator for Teaching: Dra MARTA ALICIA MAGAÑA ECHEVERRÍA
Dir-Gen. for Libraries: Dra EVANGELINA SERRANO BARREDA

Number of teachers: 1,200
Number of students: 19,000

Publication: *Estudios Sobre las Culturas Contemporáneas*

Distrito Federal

In Distrito Federal, there are six research centres, 19 other public institutions and 163 private institutions.

EL COLEGIO DE MÉXICO
(The College of Mexico)

Camino al Ajusco No 20, Col. Pedregal de Sta Teresa, 10740 México, DF
Telephone: (55) 5449-3000
E-mail: coord.acad.ceh@colmex.mx
Internet: www.colmex.mx

Founded 1940
federal control
Language of instruction: Spanish
Academic year: August to May

Pres.: Dr JAVIER GARCIADIEGO DANTAN
Sec.-Gen.: MANUEL ORDORICA MELLADO
Gen. Coordinator for Academic Affairs: JEAN FRANÇOIS PRUD'HOMME
Academic Sec.: ALBERTO MARIO PALMA CABRERA
Admin. Sec.: ÁLVARO BAILLET GALLARDO
Librarian: MICAELA CHÁVEZ VILLA

Library of 650,000 vols, 8,000 periodical titles, 3,000 theses, 8,000 microfilms, 800 maps

Publications: *Estudios de Asia y África* (3 a year), *Estudios Demográficos y Urbanos* (3 a year), *Estudios Económicos* (2 a year), *Estudios Sociológicos* (3 a year), *Foro Internacional* (4 a year), *Historia Mexicana*

(4 a year), *Nueva Revista de Filología Hispánica* (2 a year)

INSTITUTO POLITÉCNICO NACIONAL
(National Polytechnic Institute)

Avda Luis Enrique Erro s/n, Unidad Profesional 'Adolfo López Mateos', Zacatenco, Del. Gustavo A. Madero, 07738 México, DF
Telephone: (55) 5729-6000
E-mail: cca@ipn.mx
Internet: www.ipn.mx
Founded 1936
State control
Language of instruction: Spanish
Academic year: August to July
Dir-Gen.: Dra YOLOXÓCHITL BUSTAMANTE DÍEZ
Sec.-Gen.: FERNANDO ARELLANO CALDERÓN
Academic Sec.: DAFFNY JESÚS ROSADO MORENO
Sec. for Research and Postgraduate Courses: Dra NORMA PATRICIA MUÑOZ SEVILLA
Dir for Libraries: Lic. BEATRIZ ELIZUNDIA BALCÁZAR
Number of teachers: 17,000
Number of students: 162,496
Publications: *Cronista Politécnico* (4 a year), *Innovación Educativa* (4 a year, print and online, www.innovacion.ipn.mx), *Polibits* (2 a year), *Polibotánica* (irregular)

UNIVERSIDAD ANÁHUAC
(Anahuac University)

No 46, Col. Lomas Anáhuac, Huixquilucan, 52786 Mexico City, DF
Telephone: (55) 5627-0210
E-mail: anahuac@anahuac.mx
Internet: www.anahuac.mx
Founded 1964
Private control
Academic year: August to June (2 terms)
8 Programmes accredited by COPAES (*q.v.*)
Rector: JESÚS QUIRCE ANDRÉS
Sec.-Gen.: Arq. JOSÉ MATEOS
Gen. Academic Dir: Dr CRISTIAN NAZER
Librarian: Mtro DANIEL MATTES
Library of 227,774 vols
Number of teachers: 1,593
Number of students: 11,527
Publications: *Carta Económica—Boletín Instituto Desarrollo Empresarial Anáhuac (IDEA)* (6 a year), *Generación Anáhuac* (6 a year), *Iuris Tantum* (1 a year), *Medicina y Etica* (4 a year)

DEANS

Faculty of Bioethics: Dr ANTONIO CABRERA CABRERA (Dir)
Faculty of Communication Sciences: Dr CARLOS GÓMEZ PALACIO (Dir)
Faculty of Education: Dra LUZ DEL CARMEN DÁVALOS (Dir)
Faculty of Engineering: Dr ALEJANDRO MONTANO
School of Actuarial Sciences: OLIVA SÁNCHEZ
School of Architecture: BERNARDO GÓMEZ-PIMIENTA (Dir)
School of Economics and Business: Dr RAMÓN LECUONA VALENZUELA
School of Industrial and Graphic Design: Lic. LEONOR AMOZURRUTIA
School of Law: Dr JOSÉ ANTONIO NÚÑEZ
School of Medicine: Dr TOMÁS BARRIENTOS
School of Psychology: Mtro JOSÉ MARÍA LÓPEZ
School of Tourism Administration: Prof. LOUIS PASCAL

UNIVERSIDAD AUTÓNOMA DE LA CIUDAD DE MÉXICO
(Autonomous University of the City of México)

Dr García Diego No 168, Col. Doctores, Del. Cuauhtémoc, 06720 México, DF
Telephone: (55) 1107-0280
E-mail: rectoria@uacm.edu.mx
Internet: www.uacm.edu.mx
Founded 2001
State control
Language of instruction: Spanish
Academic year: August to May
Colleges of humanities and social sciences, science and technology, sciences and humanities; campuses in Casa Talavera, Centro Vlady, Cuautepec, Del Valle, San Lorenzo Tezonco
Rector: Dr ENRIQUE DUSSEL AMBROSINI
Sec.-Gen.: ERNESTO ARECHIGA
Coordinator for Academic Affairs: MARÍA DEL RAYO RAMÍREZ FIERRO
Coordinator for Admin.: PATRICIA FUENTES RANGEL
Coordinator for Cultural Dissemination and Univ. Extension: MIGUEL ÁNGEL GODÍNEZ
Coordinator for Planning: Lic. CARMEN ALICIA PINEDA
Librarian: Lic. BLANCA ESTELA VELÁZQUEZ MORALES
Publications: *Acercate*, *Andamios* (3 a year), *Cultura Urbana*, *Genómicas Hoy* (3 a year), *PalaBrijes*

UNIVERSIDAD AUTÓNOMA METROPOLITANA
(Metropolitan Autonomous University)

Prolongación Canal de Miramontes 3855, Col. Ex Hacienda San Juan de Dios, Del. Tlalpan, 14387 Mexico City, DF
Telephone: (55) 5483-4000
E-mail: admision@correo.uam.mx
Internet: www.uam.mx
Founded 1973
federal control
Language of instruction: Spanish
Academic year: August to July
Rector Gen.: Dr SALVADOR VEGA Y LEÓN
Sec.-Gen.: NORBERTO MANJARREZ ÁLVAREZ
Gen. Coordinator for Admin.: RAÚL FEDERICO LEYVA FRANCO
Gen. Coordinator for Extension: WALTERIO FRANCISCO BELLER TABOADA
Gen. Coordinator for Institutional Devt: VICTOR MANUEL SOSA GODÍNEZ
Gen. Coordinator for Institutional Information: FERNANDO RAFAEL BAZÚA SILVA
Librarian: KAMILA KNAP ROUBAL
Number of teachers: 3,700
Number of students: 45,000
Publications: *Alegatos* (3 a year), *Argumentos* (3 a year), *Casa del Tiempo* (12 a year), *Contactos* (6 a year), *Diseño UAM* (3 a year), *Economía*, *El Cotidiano* (6 a year), *Pauta*, *Reencuentro* (irregular), *Revista A* (2 a year), *Revista Iztapalapa* (2 a year), *Semanario de la UAM* (52 a year), *Teoría y Práctica Sociológica*, *Topodrilo* (6 a year), *Universidad Futura* (irregular).

CONSTITUENT CAMPUSES

Unidad Azcapotzalco

Avda San Pablo 180, Col. Reynosa-Tamaulipas, Delegación Azcapotzalco, 02200 México, DF
Telephone: (55) 5485-9510
E-mail: comunicacion@correo.azc.uam.mx
Internet: www.azc.uam.mx
Rector: ROMUALDO LÓPEZ ZÁRATE
Sec.: ABELARDO GONZÁLEZ ARAGON
Librarian: FERNANDO VELÁZQUEZ MERLO

Unidad Cuajimalpa

Avda Vasco de Quiroga 4871, Col. Santa Fe Cuajimalpa, Delegación Cuajimalpa de Morelos, 05300 México, DF
Telephone: (55) 2636-3800
E-mail: rectoria@correo.cua.uam.mx
Internet: www.cua.uam.mx
Rector: Dr EDUARDO ABEL PEÑALOSA CASTRO

Unidad Iztapalapa

San Rafael Atlixco 186, Col. Vicentina, Delegación Iztapalapa, 09340 México, DF
Telephone: (55) 5612-4665
Internet: www.iztapalapa.uam.mx
Rector: Dr JAVIER VELÁZQUEZ MOCTEZUMA
Sec.: Dr MIGUEL ÁNGEL GÓMEZ FONSECA
Librarian: ALFONSO ROMERO SÁNCHEZ

Unidad Lerma

Avda de las Garzas 10, Col. El Panteón, Lerma de Villada, 52005 Municipio de Lerma, MEX
Telephone: (728) 282-7002
E-mail: rectoria@correo.ler.uam.mx
Internet: www.uam-lerma.mx
Rector: Dr JAVIER VELÁZQUEZ MOCTEZUMA
Sec.: Dr JORGE EDUARDO VIEYRA DURÁN

Unidad Xochimilco

Calzada del Hueso 1100, Col. Villa Quietud, Delegación Coyoacán, 04960 México, DF
Telephone: (55) 5483-7000
Internet: www.xoc.uam.mx
Rector: Dra PATRICIA EMILIA ALFARO MOCTEZUMA
Sec.: Lic. GUILLERMO JOAQUÍN JIMÉNEZ MERCADO
Librarian: Lic. HELIA ELENA TERREROS MADRIGAL
Librarian for Documentation: JULIO IBARRA MARTÍNEZ
Library of 25,000 vols

UNIVERSIDAD DEL CLAUSTRO DE SOR JUANA
(University of the Cloister of Sor Juana)

92, Centro Histórico, 06080, Mexico City, DF
Telephone: (55) 5130-3300
E-mail: rectoria@elclaustro.edu.mx
Internet: www.ucsj.edu.mx
Founded 1975
Private control
Accredited by FIMPES (*q.v.*)
Rector: CARMEN B. LÓPEZ-PORTILLO ROMANO
Publication: *Claustronomía*

UNIVERSIDAD DEL DESARROLLO EMPRESARIAL Y PEDAGÓGICO
(University of Business Development and Teaching)

Miguel Laurent 719, Col. del Valle, 03100 Mexico City, DF
Telephone: (55) 5688-8315
E-mail: admision@univdep.edu.mx
Internet: www.univdep.edu.mx
Private control
Rector: ROBERTO C. ÁNGELES LEMUS
Vice-Rector for Academics: MARÍA DEL CARMEN CONTRERAS JUÁREZ
Vice-Rector for Admin and Finance: ILIANA ANGELES MIRANDA
Vice-Rector for Institutional Devt: ROBERTO ANGELES MIRANDA

UNIVERSIDAD DEL PEDREGAL
(Pedregal University)

Avda Transmisiones 51, Col. Ex Hacienda San Juan Huipulco, Tlalpan, 14370 Mexico City DF
Telephone: (55) 8502-0101
E-mail: sriarectoria@upedregal.edu.mx
Internet: www.upedregal.edu.mx
Founded 1990
Private control
Accredited by FIMPES (*q.v.*)
Rector: Armando Martínez

UNIVERSIDAD DEL TEPEYAC
(University of Tepeyac)

Casi Esq. con Callao, Lindavista s/n, Lindavista, Gustavo A. Madero, 07300 Mexico City, DF
Telephone: (55) 5577-6024
E-mail: rectoría@tepeyac.edu.mx
Internet: www.tepeyac.edu.mx
Founded 1975
Private control
Accredited by FIMPES (*q.v*)
Rector: C. P. Rodrigo Valle Sánchez
Vice-Rector: Carlos Pelaez Casabianca
Sec. for Academics: Alma Arcella Esquivel Sandoval

UNIVERSIDAD DEL VALLE DE MÉXICO
(Mexico Valley University)

San Juan de Dios 6, Lázaro Cárdenas, Tlalpan, 14370 Mexico City, DF
Telephone: (55) 5671-1018
E-mail: jnajera@uvmnet.edu
Internet: www.uvmnet.edu
Founded 1960
Private control
Languages of instruction: Spanish, English, French
Academic year: August to June
10 Programmes accredited by COPAES (*q.v.*); Campuses also in Chapultepec and San Rafael
Rector: José Raúl Ayala Magdaleno
Vice-Rector for Academic Affairs: Lic. Sergio Linares
Head of Admin: Lic. Jesús Carranza
Registrar: Lic. Edith Terán
Librarian: Lic. Salvador Cipres
Publications: *Academias* (12 a year), *Adelante* (12 a year), *Lince* (12 a year)

DEANS OF CAMPUSES
Chapultepec: Lic. Elizabeth Manning
Guadalupe Insurgentes: Lic. Martha Anides
Lago Guadalupe: Lic. Gabriela Mota
Lomas Verdes: Lic. Patricia Puente
Querétaro: Lic. Silvia Rivera
Roma: Lic. Guadalupe Zuñiga
San Angel: Lic. Griselda Vega Tato
San Miguel de Allende: Dr Francisco Martínez
San Rafael: Lic. María de la Luz Díaz Miranda
Tlalpan: Lic. Luis Silva Guerrero
Xochimilco: Lic. Salvador Silva

UNIVERSIDAD DE NEGOCIOS ISEC
(ISEC University of Business)

Mier y Pesado No 227, Col. Del Valle, 03100 Mexico City, DF
Telephone: (55) 5687-9000
Internet: www.uneg.edu.mx
Founded 1954
Private control
Accredited by FIMPES (*q.v.*)
Rector: Rodrigo Mora Fernández

UNIVERSIDAD HEBRAICA
(Hebrew University)

Prolongación Avda de los Bosques No 292-A 5° Col. Lomas de Chamisal, Mexico City, DF
Internet: universidadhebraica.edu.mx
Founded 1992
Private control
Accredited by FIMPES (*q.v.*)
Pres.: Esther Nehmad
Vice-Pres.: Abel Puszkar
Librarian: Arsenio Raudry
Publication: *Jadashot*

UNIVERSIDAD IBEROAMERICANA
(Ibero American University)

Prolongación Paseo de la Reforma 880, Col. Lomas de Santa Fe, 01210 Mexico City, DF
Telephone: (55) 5950-4000
E-mail: vicerrectoria.academica@uia.mx
Internet: www.uia.mx
Founded 1943 as Centro Cultural Universitario, present status 1954
Private control
Language of instruction: Spanish
Academic year: August to July
22 Programmes accredited by COPAES (*q.v.*)
Rector: Dr José Morales Orozco
Vice-Rector for Academic Affairs: Dr Javier Prado Galán
Librarian: Teresa Matabuena
Library of 343,426 vols, 1,167 periodicals
Number of teachers: 1,859 (301 full-time, 1,558 part-time)
Number of students: 11,373 (10,538 undergraduate, 835 postgraduate)
Publications: *AlterTexto* (2 a year), *ArquiTectónica* (2 a year), *Boletín de Apoyos Académicos* (3 a year), *Boletín Ingenierías UIA* (3 a year), *Boletín Investigación UIA* (6 a year), *Didac* (2 a year), *Historia y Grafía* (2 a year), *Jurídica* (1 a year), *Psicología Iberoamericana* (2 a year), *Revista de Filosofía* (2 a year), *Revista Iberoamericana de Comunicación* (2 a year), *Revista Iberoamericana de Teología* (2 a year)

DEANS
Architecture: Carolyn Aguilar-Dubose
Art History: Dr José Francisco López Ruíz
Biomedical Engineering: Jorge Andrés Martínez Alarcón
Business Administration and Accounting: Jorge Smeke Swaiman
Chemical Engineering: Dr Jorge Ibañez Cornejo
Civil Engineering: Jorge Andrés Martínez Alarcón
Communication: Dr Manuel Alejandro Guerrero Martínez
Computing and Telecommunications Engineering: Jorge Andrés Martínez Alarcón
Design: Jorge Meza Aguilar
Economics: Dr Pablo Cotler Ávalos
Education: Dr Javier Loredo Enríquez
Finance: Jorge Smeke Swaiman
Food Engineering: Dr Jorge Ibañez Cornejo
Food Nutrition: Ana Bertha Pérez Lizaur
Foreign Affairs: Dra Laura Zamudio González
History: Dra Jane Dàle Lloyd Daley
Industrial Engineering: Jorge Andrés Martínez Alarcón
International Business Management: Jorge Smeke Swaiman
Latin American Literature: Dra Gloria María Prado Garduño
Law: Dr Victor Manuel Rojas Amandi
Marketing: Jorge Smeke Zwaiman
Mechanical and Electrical Engineering: Jorge Andrés Martínez Alarcón
Philosophy: Dr Luis Ignacio Guerrero Martínez
Physics Engineering: Dr Alfredo Sandoval
Political Sciences and Public Administration: Dra Helena Varela Guinot
Psychology: Dr Edgar Antonio Tena Suck
Religious Sciences: Dr Humberto José Sánchez Zariñaña

REGIONAL CAMPUSES

Universidad Iberoamericana—León

Libramiento Norte km 3, Apdo Postal 26, 37000 León, GTO
Telephone: (477) 11-38-60
Founded 1978
Private control
Language of instruction: Spanish
Academic year: August to July
Rector: Ing. Carlos Alberto Sebastián Serra Martínez
Dir-Gen. for Academic Affairs: Biol. Arturo Mora Alva
Dir-Gen. for Univ. Educational Services: Lic. David Martínez Mendizábal
Registrar: Quím. Mario Alberto Arredondo Morales
Librarian: Ing. Amador Cendejas Melgoza
Library of 41,000 vols, 691 periodicals
Number of teachers: 86 (48 full-time, 38 part-time)
Number of students: 2,319 (1,864 undergraduate, 455 postgraduate)
Publication: *Presencia Universitaria* (12 a year)

Universidad Iberoamericana—Puebla

Blvd del Niño Poblano 2901, U. Territorial Atlixcayotl, 72430 Puebla, PUE
Telephone: (222) 229-0700
E-mail: webmaster@uiagc.pue.uia.mx
Internet: www.pue.uia.mx
Founded 1983
Private control
Academic year: August to July
Rector: Arq. Carlos Velasco Arzac
Dir-Gen. for Academic Affairs: Mtro Javier Sánchez Díaz de Rivera
Dir-Gen. for Univ. Educational Services: Mtro Ramiro Bernal Cuevas
Registrar: Lic. Francisco Javier García García
Librarian: Lic. Luisa González Gardea
Library of 66,000 vols, 480 periodicals
Number of teachers: 132 (126 full-time, 6 part-time)
Number of students: 5,139 (4,181 undergraduate, 958 postgraduate)
Publications: *Comunidad* (3 a year), *Magistralis* (every 2 years)

Universidad Iberoamericana—Tijuana

Apdo 185, 22200 Tijuana, BC
Located at: Avda Centro Universitario 2501, Playas de Tijuana, 22200 Tijuana, Baja California
Telephone: (664) 630-1577
Internet: www.tij.uia.mx
Founded 1982
Private control
Language of instruction: Spanish
Academic year: August to July
Rector: Mtro Humberto Barquera Gómez
Dir-Gen. for Academic Affairs: Dr Alberto Odriozola
Dir-Gen.: Lic. Ariel García
Registrar: Lic. Isabel Huerta
Library of 29,000 vols, 465 periodicals

Number of teachers: 328
Number of students: 1,221 (823 undergraduate, 398 postgraduate)

Universidad Iberoamericana—Torreón

Calz. Iberoamericana No. 2255, C.P. 27010, Sucursal Torreón, COAH
Telephone: (871) 729-1010
Internet: www.lag.uia.mx
Founded 1982
Private control
Academic year: August to July
Rector: Ing. Hector Acuña Nogueira
Dir-Gen. for Academic Affairs: Ing. Gabriel Monterrubio Alvarez
Dir-Gen. for Univ. Educational Services: Mtro Felipe Espinoza Torres
Registrar: C.P. Claudia Rodríguez Torres
Librarian: Lic. Martha I. McAnally Salas
Library of 23,000 vols, 307 periodicals
Number of teachers: 387
Number of students: 2,299 (2,125 undergraduate, 174 graduate)
Publications: *Acequias* (4 a year), *Notilaguna* (12 a year)

UNIVERSIDAD INSURGENTES
(Insurgentes University)

Avda Revolución 1836, San Angel, Álvaro Obregón, 01000 Mexico City, DF
Telephone: (55) 5550-1431
Internet: www.universidadinsurgentes.edu.mx
Private control
Accredited by FIMPES (*q.v.*)
Rector: Argelia Hernández Espinoza
Publications: *Sodalitas* (24 a year), *Equidad* (24 a year)

UNIVERSIDAD INTERCONTINENTAL
(Intercontinental University)

Insurgentes Sur 4303 and 4135, Tlalpan, 14420 Mexico City, DF
Telephone: (55) 5487-1370
Internet: www.uic.edu.mx
Founded 1976
Private control
Language of instruction: Spanish
Academic year: August to July
2 Programmes accredited by COPAES (*q.v.*)
Rector: Juan José Corona López
Gen. Sec.: José-Luis Vega Arce
Admin. Officer: C.P. José Luis Leon Zamudio
Head Librarian: Miguel Ángel León Fabela
Number of teachers: 800
Number of students: 4,500
Publications: *Boletín Jurídico, Extensiones, Intersticios, Psicología y Educación Turismo, Traduic, Voces*

UNIVERSIDAD LA SALLE
(La Salle University)

Benjamin Franklin 47, Col. Hipódromo Condesa, 06140 Mexico City, DF
Telephone: (55) 5278-9508
Internet: www.ulsa.edu.mx
Founded 1962
Private control
Language of instruction: Spanish
Academic year: August to June
15 Programmes accredited by COPAES (*q.v.*)
Rector: Enrique González Alvarez
Vice-Rector for Academics: Jorge Manuel Iturbe Bermejo
Vice-Rector for Welfare and Training: Jose Noriega Manuiel Gironés
Registrar: Raul Hauser Luna
Librarian: María Asunción Mendoza Becerra
Library of 150,000 vols
Number of teachers: 996
Number of students: 10,000
Publications: *Boletín Agora de la Facultad de Derecho, Boletín de Biblioteca, Colección Jurídica Posiciones de la Facultad de Derecho, Diez Días, Gaceta ULSA, Humanitas, La Luciérnaga (Preparatoria), Logos, Reflexiones Universitarias, Revista Académica de la Facultad de Derecho, Revista Dirección, Revista Médica La Salle, Serie Cultura de la Facultad de Derecho, Siempre Unidos, Vera Humanitas*

UNIVERSIDAD NACIONAL AUTÓNOMA DE MÉXICO
(National Autonomous University of Mexico)

Ciudad Universitaria, Del. Coyoacán, 04510 México, DF
Telephone: (55) 5622-0958
E-mail: lal@hp.fciencias.unam.mx
Internet: www.unam.mx
Founded 1551
federal control
Language of instruction: Spanish
Academic year: August to May
Rector: Dr José Narro Robles
Sec.-Gen.: Dr Eduardo Bárzana García
Admin. Sec.: Ing. Leopoldo Silva Gutiérrez
Sec. for Community Services: Enrique Balp Díaz
Sec. for Institutional Devt: Dr Francisco José Trigo Tavera
Coordinator for Cultural Dissemination: Dra María Teresa Uriarte Castañeda
Coordinator for Humanities: Dra Estela Morales Campos
Coordinator for Planning, Budgeting and Evaluation: Dr Héctor Hiram Hernández Bringas
Coordinator for Scientific Research: Dr Carlos Arámburo de la Hoz
Dir-Gen. for Social Communication: Renato Dávalos López
Librarian: Dra Silvia González Marín
Library: in addition to the National Library and Central Library (see under Libraries and Archives), there are 142 specialized libraries
Number of teachers: 35,000
Number of students: 314,600
Publications: *Acta Poética* (1 a year), *Acta Sociológica* (3 a year), *Anales de Antropología* (1 a year), *Anales del Instituto de Biología: Serie Botánica* (2 a year), *Anales del Instituto de Biología: Serie Zoología* (2 a year), *Anales del Instituto de Investigaciones Estéticas* (2 a year), *Antropología Física Latinoamericana* (1 a year), *Antropológicas* (3 a year), *Anuario de la Historia del Derecho Mexicano* (1 a year), *Anuario de Letras* (1 a year), *Anuario de Letras Modernas* (1 a year), *Anuario Jurídico* (1 a year), *Archivos Hispanoamericanas de Sexología* (2 a year), *Atmósfera* (4 a year), *Bibliografía Filosófica Mexicana* (1 a year), *Bibliografía Latinoamericana* (2 a year), *Biblioteca Universitaria* (2 a year), *Bien: Boletín de Investigación, Educación y sus Nexos* (3 a year), *Carrizos* (4 a year), *Chicomóztoc: Boletín del Seminario de Estudios para la Descolonización de México* (1 a year), *Ciencias* (4 a year), *Clase: Citas Latinoamericanas en Ciencias Sociales y Humanidades* (4 a year), *¿Cómo Ves?* (12 a year), *Contaduría y Administración* (4 a year), *Crítica Jurídica* (2 a year), *Crítica: Revista Hispanoamericana de Filosofía* (3 a year), *Cuadernos Americanos* (6 a year), *Demos: Carta Demográfica sobre México* (1 a year), *Desde el Sur: Humanismo y Ciencia* (4 a year), *Dianoia: Anuario de Filosofía* (1 a year), *Diógenes* (4 a year), *Discurso: Cuadernos de Teoría y Análisis* (2 a year), *Economía Informa* (12 a year), *Educación Química* (6 a year), *Emprendedores* (6 a year), *Estudios de Antropología Biológica* (every 2 years), *Estudios de Cultura Maya* (every 2 years), *Estudios de Cultura Náhuatl* (every 2 years), *Estudios de Cultura Otopame* (every 2 years), *Estudios de Historia Moderna y Contemporánea de México* (1 a year), *Estudios de Historia Novohispana* (1 a year), *Estudios de Lingüística Aplicada* (2 a year), *Estudios Latinoamericanos* (2 a year), *Estudios Políticos* (3 a year), *Experiencia Literaria* (irregular), *Ingeniería, Investigación y Tecnología* (4 a year), *Investigación Bibliotecológica* (2 a year), *Investigación Económica* (4 a year), *Investigaciones Geográficas* (2 a year), *La Experiencia Literaria* (irregular), *Latinoamérica: Anuario de Estudios Latinoamericanos* (irregular), *Los Universitarios* (6 a year), *Mathesis* (4 a year), *Medievalia* (2 a year), *Momento Económico—Información y Análisis de la Conjuntura Económica* (6 a year), *Nova Tellus: Anuario del Centro de Estudios Clásicos* (2 a year), *Nuevo Consultorio Fiscal-Laboral y Contable-Financiero* (26 a year), *Omnia* (4 a year), *Perfiles Educativos* (4 a year), *Periódica: Indice de Revistas Latinoamericanas en Ciencias* (4 a year), *Pluralitas* (12 a year, online), *Poligrafías—Revista de Literatura Comparada* (1 a year), *Problemas del Desarrollo: Revista Latinoamericana de Economía* (4 a year), *Punto de Partida* (6 a year), *Relaciones Internacionales* (3 a year), *Revista CIHMECH* (1 a year), *Revista de Derecho Privado* (3 a year), *Revista de la Facultad de Medicina* (6 a year), *Revista de Zoología* (2 a year), *Revista Especializada en Ciencias Químicas Biológicas* (2 a year), *Revista Especializada en Ciencias Sociales y la Educación* (2 a year), *Revista Mexicana de Astronomía y Astrofísica* (2 a year), *Revista Mexicana de Ciencias Geológicas* (2 a year), *Revista Mexicana de Ciencias Políticas y Sociales* (4 a year), *Revista Mexicana de Sociología* (4 a year), *Revista Veterinaria—México* (4 a year), *Sinopsis* (1 a year), *Tempus* (irregular), *Theoría: Revista del Colegio de Filosofía* (3 a year), *Tip: Tópicos de Investigación y Posgrado* (3 a year), *Trabajo Social* (4 a year), *UNAM Hoy* (6 a year), *Universidad de México* (12 a year), *Vertientes—Revista Especializada en Ciencias de la Salud* (2 a year), *Voices of México* (4 a year)

ACADEMIC DIRECTORS

Faculty of Accounting and Administration: Juan Alberto Adam Siade
Faculty of Architecture: Arq. Marcos Mazari Hiriart
Faculty of Chemistry: Jorge Manuel Vázquez Ramos
Faculty of Dentistry: José Arturo Fernández Pedrero
Faculty of Economics: Dr Leonardo Lomelí Vanegas
Faculty of Engineering: José Gonzalo Guerrero Zepeda
Faculty of Law: Dra María Leoba Castañeda Rivas
Faculty of Medicine: Dr Enrique Luis Graue Wiechers
Faculty of Philosophy and Letters: Dra Gloria Villegas Moreno
Faculty of Political and Social Sciences: Fernando Campos Cázares
Faculty of Psychology: Dr Javier Nieto Gutiérrez

Faculty of Sciences: Dra ROSAURA RUIZ GUTIÉRREZ
Faculty of Veterinary Medicine and Zootechnics: MARÍA ELENA TRUJILLO ORTEGA

UNIVERSIDAD PANAMERICANA
(Pan American University)

Augusto Rodin 498, Col. Insurgentes Mixcoac, Del. Benito Juárez, 03920 Mexico City, DF
Telephone: (55) 5482-1600
E-mail: contacto@up.edu.mx
Internet: www.mixcoac.upmx.mx
Founded 1968
Private control
Academic year: August to June
8 Programmes accredited by COPAES (*q.v.*)
Rector Gen.: ALFONSO BOLIO ARCINIEGA
Vice-Rector: JESÚS MAGAÑA BRAVO
Vice-Rector: Lic. SERGIO RAIMOND-KEDILHAC NAVARRO
Admin. Dir: Dr VÍCTOR MANUEL PIZÁ
Librarian: ELISA RIVA PALACIO
Library of 160,000 vols
Number of teachers: 450
Number of students: 5,000
Publications: *Ars Juris* (2 a year), *Revista Istmo* (6 a year), *Tópicos Journal of Philosophy* (2 a year)

DIRECTORS

School of Accounting: CLAUDIO M. RIVAS
School of Administration: Ing. AMADEO VÁZQUEZ
School of Economics: Lic. FLAVIA RODRÍGUEZ
School of Education: Dra CARMEN RAMSO
School of Engineering: Ing. PEDRO CREUHERAS
School of Law: Dr ROBERTO IBÁÑEZ MARIEL
School of Philosophy: Dr ROCIO MIER Y TERÁN

AFFILIATED INSTITUTIONS

Instituto de Capacitación de Mandos Intermedios (Training Institute for Middle Management): Mar Mediterráneo 183, Col. Popotla, 11400 México, DF; tel. (55) 5399-7272; f. 1966; 170 teachers; 2,400 students; library of 1,200 vols; Dir CONRADO ANTONIO LARIOS.

Instituto de Desarrollo para Operarios (Institute of Development Workers): Norte 182, No 477, Col. Peñón de los Baños, 15520 México, DF; tel. (55) 5760-3464; f. 1968; 45 teachers; 550 students; library of 500 vols; courses for worker-management; Dir ENRIQUE SIERRA.

Instituto Panamericano de Alta Dirección de Empresa (Pan American Institute of Higher Business Studies): Floresta 20, Col. Clavería, 02080 México, DF; tel. (55) 5527-0260; f. 1967; library of 8,000 vols; 40 teachers; 1,900 students; Dir SERGIO RAIMOND-KEDILHAC NAVARRO.

Instituto Panamericano de Ciencias de la Educación (Pan American Institute of Sciences of Education): Augusto Rodin 498, Col. Mixcoac, 03920 México, DF; Dir Dra MARCELA CHAVARRÍA

UNIVERSIDAD PEDAGÓGICA NACIONAL
(National Pedagogic University)

Carretera al Ajusco No 24, Col. Héroes de Padierna, Del. Tlalpan, 14200 Mexico City, DF
Telephone: (55) 5630-9700
E-mail: rectoria@upn.mx
Internet: www.upn.mx
Founded 1978
federal control
Language of instruction: Spanish
Academic year: August to May
Academic units of educational policy, management and institutional processes, diversity and indigenous education, science, humanities and arts, information technology and alternative models, pedagogical theory and teacher training
Rector: TENOCH ESAÚ CEDILLO ÁVALOS
Academic Sec.: EVA FRANCISCA AUGUSTA RAUTENBERG Y PETERSEN
Admin. Sec.: FEDERICO VALLE RODRÍGUEZ
Dir for Cultural Diffusion and Univ. Extension: MARÍA TERESA BRINDIS PÉREZ
Dir for Planning: ALEJANDRA JAVIER JACUINDE
Dir for Library and Academic Support Services: FERNANDO VELÁZQUEZ MERLO
Number of teachers: 4,000
Number of students: 69,300

UNIVERSIDAD WESTHILL
(Westhill University)

Domingo García Ramos 56, Col. Prados de la Montaña 1 Santa Fé Cuajimalpa, 05610 Mexico City, DF
Telephone: (55) 8851-7000
E-mail: admisiones@uw.edu.mx
Internet: www.uw.edu.mx
Founded 1994
Private control
1 Programme accredited by COPAES (*q.v.*)
Rector: JOSÉ MARÍA RIOBÓO MARTÍ

UNIVERSIDAD YMCA
(YMCA University)

Lago Alberto No 337, Col. Anáhuac, Del. Miguel Hidalgo, Mexico City, DF
Telephone: (55) 5531-0574
E-mail: informes@uniymca.edu.mx
Internet: www.uniymca.edu.mx
Founded 2000
Private control
Accredited by ANUIES (*q.v.*)
Rector: JUAN BAQUÉ GONZÁLEZ

Durango

In Durango, there are two federal institutes, two state institutes and six private institutions.

UNIVERSIDAD JUÁREZ DEL ESTADO DE DURANGO
(Juárez University of the State of Durango)

Constitución 404 sur, Zona Centro, 34000 Durango, DGO
Telephone: (618) 812-0044
E-mail: ujed@ujed.mx
Internet: www.ujed.mx
Founded 1856 as a Civil College, univ. status 1957
State control
Language of instruction: Spanish
Academic year: January to December (2 terms)
Faculties of chemical sciences, dentistry, economics, accountancy and administration, forestry, law and political sciences, medicine and nutrition, nursing and obstetrics, psychology, social work, veterinary medicine and zootechnics; schools of applied mathematics, languages, music, painting, sculpture and crafts, physical education and sports
Rector: OSCAR ERASMO NÁVAR GARCÍA
Sec.-Gen.: JOSÉ VICENTE REYES ESPINO
Dir-Gen. for Admin.: MANUEL GUTIÉRREZ CORRAL
Dir for Devt and Human Resource Management: MANUEL DE JESÚS MARTÍNEZ AGUILAR
Dir for Planning and Academic Devt: JACINTO TOCA RAMÍREZ
Dir for School Services: Dr ALFONSO GUTIÉRREZ ROCHA
Dir for Univ. Extension: ALMA PATRICIA PIÑA GRISSMAN
Librarian: JOSÉ LINO HERNÁNDEZ CAMPOS
Number of teachers: 1,100
Number of students: 20,200
Publication: *Revista Enlaces Académicos* (2 a year)

UNIVERSIDAD LA SALLE LAGUNA
(La Salle Laguna University)

Canatlán No 150, Col. Parque Industrial Lagunero, 35078 Gómez Palacio, DGO
Telephone: (871) 750-2490
E-mail: promocion@ulsalaguna.edu.mx
Internet: www.ulsalaguna.edu.mx
Founded 1962
Private control
Accredited by FIMPES (*q.v.*)
Rector: Lic. LUIS ARTURO DÁVILA DE LEÓN
Dir for Academic Affairs: GUILLERMO VAZQUEZ MALDONADO
Dir for Economic and Administrative Affairs: ALMA LETICIA LÓPEZ BASALDÚA
Library of 21,500 vols

UNIVERSIDAD POLITÉCNICA DE GÓMEZ PALACIO
(Polytechnic University of Gómez Palacio)

Carretera el Vergel, Torreña km 0–820, Localidad el Vergel, 35120 Gómez Palacio, DGO
Telephone: (871) 192-2700
E-mail: contacto@upgop.edu.mx
Internet: www.upgop.edu.mx
Founded 2005
State control
Language of instruction: Spanish
Academic year: September to April
Rector: SILVIA ADRIANA JÁQUEZ CERVANTES
Academic Dir: MIGUEL ÁNGEL SERRANO GARCÍA
Admin. Dir: DIANA CATALINA HERNÁNDEZ LARA
Dir for External Affairs: MARTHA EUGENIA SEAÑEZ MARTÍNEZ
Dir for Planning and Institutional Evaluation: MAGALY LONGORIA DE LA TORRE
Dir for Library Services: RAÚL SEGUNDO AGUILAR

Estado de México

In Estado de México, there are two federal institutes, 16 state institutes, two other public institutions and 73 private institutions.

UNIVERSIDAD ANÁHUAC—ESTADO DE MÉXICO
(Anahuac University)

Avda Universidad Anáhuac s/n, Lomas Anáhuac, 52786 Huixquilucan, MEX
Telephone: (55) 5627-0210
E-mail: anahuac@anahuac.mx
Internet: www.anahuac.mx
Founded 1964
Private control
22 Programmes accredited by COPAES (*q.v*)
Rector: JESÚS QUIRCE ANDRÉS
Library of 227,774 vols

Number of teachers: 1,593
Number of students: 11,527
Publications: *Carta Económica—Boletín Instituto Desarrollo Empresarial Anáhuac (IDEA)* (6 a year), *Generación Anáhuac* (6 a year), *Iuris Tantum* (1 a year), *Medicina y Etica* (4 a year)

UNIVERSIDAD AUTÓNOMA CHAPINGO
(Chapingo Autonomous University)

Km 38.5 Carretera México-Texcoco, 56230 Chapingo, MEX
Telephone: (595) 952-1500
E-mail: relacionespublicas@correo.chapingo.mx
Internet: www.chapingo.mx
Founded 1854 as Escuela Nacional de Agricultura, current name adopted 1978
federal control
Language of instruction: Spanish
Academic year: August to June
Rector: Dr CARLOS ALBERTO VILLASEÑOR PEREA
Dir-Gen. for Academic Affairs: Dr RAMÓN VALDIVIA ALCALA
Dir-Gen. for Admin.: Ing. J. GUADALUPE GAYTÁN RUELAS
Dir-Gen. for Cultural Diffusion and Services: RAÚL REYES BUSTOS
Dir-Gen. for Research and Postgraduate Affairs: Dr J. REYES ALTAMIRANO CÁRDENAS
Librarian: RAMON SUAREZ ESPINOSA
Library: see under Libraries and Archives
Number of teachers: 1,200
Number of students: 6,800 (6,500 undergraduate, 300 graduate)
Publications: *Revista Chapingo* (6 a year), *Revista de Geografía Agrícola* (6 a year), *Textual* (2 a year)

ACADEMIC DIRECTORS

Agricultural Mechanical Engineering: Ing. MARCO ANTONIO ROJAS MARTÍNEZ
Agricultural Parasitology: Ing. LUIS OTHÓN ESPINOSA CARRILLO
Agroecology: JORGE DUCH GARY
Agroindustrial Engineering: Dr SALVADOR VALLE GUADARRAMA
Economic and Administrative Science: Dr JOSÉ MARÍA CONTRERAS CASTILLO
Forestry: Dr JORGE ANTONIO TORRES PÉREZ
Irrigation: FRANCISCO RAÚL HERNÁNDEZ SAUCEDO
Phytotechnics: Dr RAÚL NIETO ÁNGEL
Rural Sociology: Ing. JORGE TORRES BRIBIESCA
Zootechnics: Dr SERGIO IBAN MENDOZA PEDROZA

REGIONAL UNIVERSITY CENTRES

Centro Regional Universitario Centro Norte (Regional University Centre of North Central): Cruz del Sur No 100, Constelaciones, 98060 Zacatecas, ZAC; tel. (492) 924-6147; e-mail frijol_uach@msn.com; internet www.chapingo.mx/scru/crucen; f. 1985; Sub-Dir Dr LUIS MANUEL SERRANO COVARRUBIAS; Academic Coordinator JUAN MANUEL ZEPEDA DEL VALLE.

Centro Regional Universitario de la Península de Yucatán (Regional University Centre of the Peninsula of Yucatán): Ex Hacienda Temozón Norte, 97310 Mérida, YUC; tel. (999) 924-0054; internet www.crupy-uach.org.mx; f. 1981; Sub-Dir JORGE FLORES TORRES; Academic Coordinator Dr JULIO BACA DEL MORAL.

Centro Regional Universitario Occidente (Regional University Centre of the West): Periferico Independencia Poniente No 1000, 58170 Morelia, MICH; tel. (443) 316-1489; internet www.chapingo.mx/scru/cruco; f. 1987; Chief Admin. Officer Lic. EULALIA GARCÍA PÉREZ.

Centro Regional Universitario Oriente (Regional University Centre of the East): Km 3 Carretera Huatusco-Jalapa, 94100 Huatusco, VER; tel. (273) 734-0846; internet www.chapingo.mx/scru/cruo; f. 1980; Sub-Dir JOSÉ DOMINGO ROBLEDO MARTÍNEZ; Research Coordinator GUILLERMO CRUZ CASTILLO.

Centro Regional Universitario Sur (Regional University Centre of the South): Km 6.5 Carretera Oaxaca-México Crucero San Pablo Etla, 68000 Oaxaca, OAX; tel. (951) 518-7774; e-mail crus_academica@yahoo.com.mx; internet www.chapingo.mx/scru/crus; f. 1979; Sub-Dir RENATO ZARATE BAÑOS; Academic Coordinator MARIO SUMANO GIL.

Unidad Regional Universitaria de Zonas Aridas (Regional University Unit of Arid Zones): Domicilio Conocido, km 38 Carretera Torreón-Ciudad Juárez, 35230 Bermejillo, DGO; tel. (872) 776-0043; e-mail academica@chapingo.uruza.edu.mx; internet www.chapingo.uruza.edu.mx; f. 1974; Dir BERNARDO LÓPEZ ARIZA; Sub-Dir for Academic Affairs JOSÉ MANUEL CISNEROS VÁZQUEZ; Sub-Dir for Admin. Dr MIGUEL ANGEL MATA ESPINOSA; Sub-Dir for Research Dr AURELIO PEDROZA SANDOVAL.

Unidad Regional Universitaria SurSureste (Regional University Unit of the South-Southeast): Km 7 Carretera Teapa, Vicente Guerrero, 86800 Teapa, TAB; tel. (595) 952-1500; e-mail urusse@chapingo.mx; internet www.chapingo.mx/urusse; f. 1974; Dir JUAN ANGEL ALVAREZ VAZQUEZ; Sub-Dir for Academic Affairs Ing. FRANCISCO URIBE CRUZ; Sub-Dir for Admin. Lic. MIGUEL GONZALO VAZQUEZ LOPEZ

UNIVERSIDAD AUTÓNOMA DEL ESTADO DE MÉXICO
(Autonomous University of Mexico State)

Avda Instituto Literario 100, Col. Centro, 50000 Toluca, MEX
Telephone: (722) 226-2300
E-mail: rectoria@uaemex.mx
Internet: www.uaemex.mx
Founded 1956
State control
Language of instruction: Spanish
Academic year: September to August
Schools of accountancy and administration, agricultural sciences, anthropology, art and architecture, behavioural sciences, chemistry, dentistry, economics, engineering, geography, humanities, law, medicine, nursing, political sciences and public administration, sciences, tourism, urban and regional planning, veterinary medicine
Rector: JOSÉ BENJAMÍN BERNAL SUÁREZ
Sec. for Admin.: JAVIER GONZÁLEZ MARTÍNEZ
Sec. for Culture: IVETT TINOCO GARCÍA
Sec. for Int. Cooperation: YOLANDA BALLESTEROS SENTÍES
Sec. for Planning and Institutional Devt: MANUEL HERNÁNDEZ LUNA
Sec. for Research and Advanced Studies: Dra ÁNGELES DEL ROSARIO PÉREZ BERNAL
Sec. for Teaching: Dr ALFREDO BARRERA BACA
Dir-Gen. for Univ. Communication: Lic. JUAN PORTILLA ESTRADA
Librarian: RUPERTO RETANA RAMIREZ
Library of 292,000 vols
Number of teachers: 3,000
Number of students: 36,700
Publications: *Ciencias Agrícolas Informa*, *Convergencia* (3 a year), *Culinaria* (2 a year), *El Periplo Sustentable* (2 a year, print and online, www.psus.uaemex.mx), *Enlace Químico*, *Revista de Medicina e Investigación* (2 a year)

UNIVERSIDAD DEL VALLE DE MÉXICO—ESTADO DE MÉXICO
(Valle de México University, State of Mexico)

Avda de las palmas No 439 Poniente, Col. San Jorge Pueblo Nuevo, 52164 Metepec, MEX
Telephone: (722) 275-8666
Internet: www.toluca.uvmnet.edu
Founded 1976
Private control
Rector: GABRIELA MOTTA RAMÍREZ

UNIVERSIDAD DEL VALLE DE TOLUCA
(Valle de Toluca University)

Mariano Matamoros Sur No 1069, Col. Universidad, 50130 Toluca, MEX
Telephone: (722) 270-3279
Internet: www.uvt.edu.mx
Founded 1978
Private control
Accredited by ANUIES (*q.v.*)

UNIVERSIDAD EMILIO CÁRDENAS
(Emilio Cardenas University)

Avda Atlacomulco No. 191 y 193 Col. La Loma, Tlalnepantla, MEX
Telephone: (55) 5565-1020
E-mail: contacto@udec.com.mx
Internet: web.udec.com.mx
Founded 1974
Private control
Accredited by FIMPES (*q.v.*)
Rector: ALFONSO MALPICA

UNIVERSIDAD ESTATAL DEL VALLE DE ECATEPEC
(State University of the Valley of Ecatepec)

Avda Central s/n, Esq. Leona Vicario, Col. Valle de Anáhuac, 55210 Ecatepec, MEX
Telephone: (55) 5001-1400
E-mail: uneve@uneve.edu.mx
Internet: www.uneve.edu.mx
Founded 2001
State control
Language of instruction: Spanish
Academic year: September to August
Rector: JOSÉ ÁNGEL FERNÁNDEZ GARCÍA
Academic Sec.: JOSÉ LUIS HERNÁNDEZ OLVERA
Admin. Sec.: LUZ ROCIO HERNÁNDEZ VÉLEZ
Dir for Information, Planning, Programmes and Evaluation: ADOLFO FRANCISCO VOORDUIN FRAPPE

UNIVERSIDAD INTERCULTURAL DEL ESTADO DE MÉXICO
(Intercultural Mexico State University)

Libramiento Francisco Villa, s/n, Col. Centro, San Felipe del Progreso MEX
Telephone: (712) 123-5963
E-mail: correo@uiem.edu.mx
Internet: www.uiem.edu.mx
Founded 2004
Private control
Rector: JOSÉ FRANCISCO MONROY GAYTÁN

UNIVERSIDAD POLITÉCNICA DEL VALLE DE MÉXICO
(Polytechnic University of Valle de México)

Avda Mexiquense s/n, Esq. Avda Universidad Politécnica, Col. Villa Esmeralda, 54910 Tultitlán, MEX
Telephone: (55) 5062-6460
E-mail: informes@upvm.edu.mx
Internet: www.upvm.edu.mx

Founded 2004
State control
Language of instruction: Spanish
Academic year: September to August

Rector: ALBERTO SÁNCHEZ FLORES
Academic Sec.: JOSE MANUEL GUILLERMO GARCIA MACIAS
Admin. Sec.: HUGO ISRRAEL ZEPEDA LOPEZ
Dir for Univ. Extension and External Affairs: Lic. LUZ MARINA GALICIA LOPEZ
Library Dir: JUAN BECERRA HERNANDEZ

Publication: *Revista Innovación Tecnológica*

UNIVERSIDAD POLITÉCNICA DEL VALLE DE TOLUCA
(Polytechnic University of Valle de Toluca)

Km 5.6, Carretera Toluca-Almoloya de Juárez, Santiaguito Tlalcilalcali, 50904 Almoloya de Juárez, MEX
Telephone: (725) 276-6060
E-mail: vinculacion@upvt.edu.mx
Internet: www.upvt.edu.mx

Founded 2006
State control
Language of instruction: Spanish

Rector: LUIS CARLOS BARROS GONZÁLEZ
Dir for Admin. and Finance: RICARDO FELIX ONIEL JIMENEZ HERNANDEZ
Dir for Planning and External Affairs: VALENTIN ALFREDO PALMA BERNAL

UNIVERSIDAD TECNOLÓGICA DEL VALLE DE TOLUCA
(Technological University of Valle de Toluca)

Carretera del Departamento del DF Km 7.5, Santa Maria Atarasquillo, Lerma, MEX
Telephone: (728) 285-9552
E-mail: rectoria@utvtol.edu.mx
Internet: www.utvtol.edu.mx
State control

Rector: FAUSTO RIVEROS ACOSTA
Dir for Academic Devt: SERGIO TORRES PACHECO
Dir for Admin. and Finance: VERÓNICA MATHUS THOMÉ
Dir for Broadcasting and Univ. Extension: PEDRO GAYTÁN SEGURA

UNIVERSIDAD TECNOLÓGICA DE MÉXICO
(Technological University of Mexico)

Avda Marina Nacional No 162, Col. Anáhuac, 11320 Mexico City, DF
Telephone: (11) 020-022
E-mail: atencion@mail.unitec.mx
Internet: www.unitec.mx

Founded 1966
Private control

Rector: MANUEL CAMPUZANO TREVIÑO

Number of students: 34,080

UNIVERSIDAD TECNOLÓGICA DE NEZAHUALCÓYOTL
(Technological University of Nezahualcóyotl)

Centro Universidad Tecnologica s/n Col. Benito Juarez, 57000 Nezahualcóyotl, MEX
Telephone: (55) 5716-9700
E-mail: rector@utn.edu.mx
Internet: www.utn.edu.mx

Founded 1991
State control
Academic year: January to December

Rector: NOE MOLINA RUSILES
Dir for Admin. and Finance: JORGE ARTURO CASTANO HERNANDEZ

UNIVERSIDAD TECNOLÓGICA DE TECÁMAC
(Technological University of Tecámac)

Carretera Federal México, Pachuca Km 37.5, Col. Sierra Hermosa, 55740 Tecámac, MEX
Telephone: (55) 5938-8400
E-mail: uttecamac@uttecamac.edu.mx
Internet: www.uttecamac.edu.mx

Founded 1996
State control
Academic year: January to December

Rector: Ing. JESÚS G. ARROYO GARCÍA
Academic Sec.: SERGIO AGUILAR ROSALES
Dir for Admin. and Finance: LUIS ERNESTO RODOLFO CASTANEDA ZETINA
Dir for Univ. Extension: JORGE GRANADOS MARTINEZ

Number of students: 6,100

UNIVERSIDAD TECNOLÓGICA FIDEL VELÁZQUEZ
(Fidel Velázquez Technological University)

Ex. Hacienda de la Encarnación, Emiliano Zapata s/n, Col. El Tráfico, 54400 Nicolás Romero, MEX
Telephone: (55) 2649-3130
Internet: www.utfv.edu.mx

Founded 1993
State control

Rector: ENRIQUE RIVA PALACIO GALICIA
Academic Sec.: SERGIO DIEZ SERUR
Dir for Admin. and Finance: JOSE JORGE SAUCEDO HERRERA

Guanajuato

In Guanajuato, there are four federal institutes, two state institutes, three research centres, one other public institution and 52 private institutions.

UNIVERSIDAD DE GUANAJUATO
(University of Guanajuato)

Lascuráin de Retana 5, Col. Centro, 36000 Guanajuato, GTO
Telephone: (473) 732-0006
E-mail: rectoria@ugto.mx
Internet: www.ugto.mx

Founded 1732 as Colegio de la Purísima Concepción; renamed Colegio del Estado 1928; current name adopted 1945
State control
Language of instruction: Spanish
Academic year: August to June

Rector Gen.: Dr JOSÉ MANUEL CABRERA SIXTO
Sec.-Gen.: Dr MANUEL VIDAURRI ARÉCHIGA
Academic Sec.: ROSA ALICIA PÉREZ LUQUE
Sec. for Management and Devt: BULMARO VALDÉS PÉREZ GASGA
Librarian: Mtra ROSALÍA DEL CARMEN MACÍAS RODRÍGUEZ

Publications: *Acta Universitaria* (6 a year), *Azogue* (2 a year), *Centro, Textos de la Historia Guanajuatense* (1 a year), *Colmena Universitaria* (2 a year), *Gaceta Naturaleza* (2 a year), *Investigaciones Jurídicas* (2 a year), *Regiones* (2 a year), *Tarea Universitaria* (6 a year), *Voces, Laboratorio de Historia Oral* (2 a year).

CAMPUSES

Celaya-Salvatierra Campus

Eje Juan Pablo II Sur 201, Col. Santa María, Celaya, GTO
Telephone: (461) 598-5922
E-mail: rectoria.ccs@ugto.mx
Internet: www.celayasalvatierra.ugto.mx

Rector: Dra GUADALUPE OJEDA VARGAS

Guanajuato Campus

Fraccionamiento 1 s/n, Col. El Establo, 36250 Guanajuato, GTO
Telephone: (473) 735-2900
E-mail: mgallegos@ugto.mx
Internet: www.ugto.mx/campusgto

Divs of architecture, art and design, economics and administrative sciences, engineering, natural and exact sciences, social sciences and humanities, law, politics and governance

Rector: Dr LUIS FELIPE GUERRERO AGRIPINO
Academic Sec.: Dr ELOY JUÁREZ SANDOVAL

Irapuato-Salamanca Campus

Carretera Salamanca, Valle de Santiago km 3.5+1.8, Comunidad de Palo Blanco, Salamanca, GTO
Telephone: (464) 647-9940
E-mail: rectoriacis@ugto.mx
Internet: www.irapuatosalamanca.ugto.mx

Divs of engineering and life sciences

Rector: Dr ERNESTO ALFREDO CAMARENA AGUILAR
Academic Sec.: Dr OSCAR GERARDO IBARRA MANZANO

León Campus

Blvd Puente Milenio 1001, Fracción del Predio San Carlos, 37670 León, GTO
Telephone: (477) 104-0300
E-mail: rectorialeon@ugto.mx
Internet: www.campusleon.ugto.mx

Divs of health sciences, science and engineering, social sciences and humanities

Rector: Dr JOSÉ LUIS LUCIO MARTÍNEZ
Academic Sec.: Dr ENRIQUE VARGAS SALADO

UNIVERSIDAD DE LA SALLE BAJÍO
(La Salle Bajio University)

Ave Universidad 602, Col. Lomas del Campestre, 37150 Léon, GTO
Telephone: (477) 710-8500
E-mail: informes@delasalle.edu.mx
Internet: www.delasalle.edu.mx

Founded 1968
Private control
Academic year: August to December, February to June
17 Programmes accredited by COPAES (*q.v.*)

Rector: Lic. ANDRÉS GOVELA GUTIÉRREZ
Vice-Rector: Lic. FELIPE AURELIO PELCASTRE ARENAS
Registrar: Lic. LUIS ERNESTO RÍOS PÉREZ
Librarian: Lic. ISIDRO CONDE GONZÁLEZ

Library of 108,529 vols
Number of teachers: 1,230
Number of students: 13,000

Publications: *Cuadernos* (2 a year), *Entornos* (6 a year), *Espíritu Lasallista* (12 a year), *Magazine Lasalle* (6 a year).

CAMPUSES

Américas Campus: 860 students; Dir Lic. FERNANDO MONROY VIVAS.

Juan Alonso de Torres Campus: 1,300 students; Dir Lic. JOSÉ AMONARIO ASIÁIN DÍAZ DE LEÓN.

Salamanca Campus: 1,300 students; Dir Mtra ESTEBAN MARTÍNEZ HERNÁNDEZ.

San Francisco del Rincón Campus: 1,000 students; Dir Ing. MARTHA ELENA BERMÚDEZ FUNES

UNIVERSIDAD IBEROAMERICANA LEÓN
(Iberoamericana University, León)

Blvd Jorge Vértiz Campero No 1640, Col. Cañada de Alfaro, 37238, León, GTO
Telephone: (477) 710-0600
E-mail: international@leon.uia.mx
Internet: www.leon.uia.mx
Founded 1978
Private control
6 Programmes accredited by COPAES (*q.v.*)
Rector: P. MARCO ANTONIO FLORES BRAN
Asst Rector: Prof. SILVIA ANGÉLICA SÁNCHEZ GUZMÁN
Dir-Gen. for Academics: Prof. ISABEL JAIME VAZQUEZ
Dir-Gen. for Educational Services: ROGELIO HERNÁNDEZ TERÁN
Dir-Gen. for Support Services: SERGIO HERNÁNDEZ CABALLERO
Dir for Institutional Devt: SAGRARIO GUADALUPE REYES ESPINOSA
Dir for Management and Institutional Communication: IVONNE PÉREZ WILSON
Library of 80,002 vols

UNIVERSIDAD POLITÉCNICA DE GUANAJUATO
(Polytechnic University of Guanajuato)

Avda Universidad Norte s/n, Comunidad Juan Alonso, 38483 Cortazar, GTO
Telephone: (461) 441-4300
E-mail: contacto@upgto.edu.mx
Internet: www.upgto.edu.mx
Founded 2005
State control
Language of instruction: Spanish
Academic year: September to August
Rector: Ing. DANIEL JIMÉNEZ RODRIGUEZ

UNIVERSIDAD QUETZALCÓATL
(Quetzalcoatl University)

Blvd Arandas 975, 36615, Irapuato, GTO
Telephone: (462) 624-5025
E-mail: uqi@uqi.edu.mx
Internet: www.uqi.edu.mx
Founded 1982
Private control
1 Programme accredited by COPAES (*q.v.*)
Rector: Prof. AGUSTÍN GASCA CHÁVEZ

Guerrero

In Guerrero, there are five federal institutes, two state institutes and 16 private institutions.

UNIVERSIDAD AUTÓNOMA DE GUERRERO
(Autonomous University of Guerrero)

Avda Javier Méndez Aponte 1, Fraccionamiento Servidor Agrario, 03900 Chilpancingo, GRO
Telephone: (747) 471-9310
E-mail: rector@uagro.mx
Internet: www.uagro.mx
Founded 1869
State control
Language of instruction: Spanish
Academic year: August to June
Rector: Dr ASCENCIO VILLEGAS ARRIZÓN
Sec.-Gen.: ALBERTO SALGADO RODRIGUEZ
Dir-Gen. for Planning and Institutional Evaluation: JAVIER SALDANA ALMAZÁN
Librarian: Lic. ROBERT ALEXANDER ENDEAN GAMBOA
Number of teachers: 1,600
Number of students: 49,000
Publications: *Gaceta Popular*, *Otatal*, *Revista de la UAG*

UNIVERSIDAD HIPOCRATES
(Hipocrates University)

Avenida Urdaneta 360 Fraccionamiento Horn, 39355 Acapulco, GRO
Telephone: (744) 485-7991
E-mail: contacto@uhipocrates.edu.mx
Internet: www.uhipocrates.edu.mx
Founded 1986
Private control
Accredited by ANUIES (*q.v.*)
Rector: Prof. M. ARMANDO HERNÁNDEZ TORRES

UNIVERSIDAD INTERCULTURAL DEL ESTADO DE GUERRERO
(Intercultural University of the State of Guerrero)

Km 54, Carretera Tlapa-Marquelia, la Ciénega, Muncipality de Malinaltepec, GRO
E-mail: rectoria@uieg.edu.mx
Internet: www.uieg.edu.mx
Private control
Rector: Dr FLORIBERTO GONZÁLEZ GONZÁLEZ
Academic Sec.: Dr JAIME VIVAR MARTÍNEZ
Dir for Admin. and Finance: MINERVA MORENO ANTUNEZ
Dir for Planning: Dr SERGIO ALEJANDRO PASTRANA PELAEZ

Hidalgo

In Hidalgo, there are two federal institutes, four state institutes and 15 private institutions.

UNIVERSIDAD AUTÓNOMA DEL ESTADO DE HIDALGO
(Autonomous University of Estado de Hidalgo)

Telephone: (771) 717-2000
E-mail: subdidce@uaeh.edu.mx
Internet: www.uaeh.edu.mx
Founded 1869 as the Instituto Científico y Literario, present status 1961
State control
Language of instruction: Spanish
Academic year: September to June
Institutes of agricultural sciences, arts, basic and engineering sciences, economic and administrative sciences, health sciences, social sciences and humanities
Rector: HUMBERTO AUGUSTO VERAS GODOY
Sec.-Gen.: ADOLFO LOYOLA PONTIGO
Dir-Gen. for Academic Services: ARTURO FLORES ALVAREZ
Dir-Gen. for Evaluation: Dra PATRICIA BEZIES CRUZ
Dir-Gen. for Legal Affairs: Lic. FRANCISCO G. FONSECA ARELLANO
Dir-Gen. for Planning: Lic. GONZALO VILLEGAS DE LA CONCHA
Dir-Gen. for Social Communication and Public Relations: ALFREDO DÁVALOS MORENO
Dir-Gen. for Student Services: JUAN CARLOS MUÑOZ MEDINA
Dir for Libraries: JORGE PEÑA ZEPEDA
Library of 105,720 vols, 5,000 maps, bibliographies and CDs
Number of teachers: 700
Number of students: 9,000
Publications: *Mexican Journal of Medical Research* (2 a year), *Revista Técnica de Información*

UNIVERSIDAD LA SALLE PACHUCA
(La Salle University of Pachuca)

Belisario Domínguez No 202, Col. Centro, 42000 Pachuca, HGO
Telephone: (771) 717-0213
E-mail: rectoria@lasallep.edu.mx
Internet: www.lasallep.edu.mx
Founded 1994
Private control
Accredited by FIMPES (*q.v.*)
Rector: JOSÉ HORACIO MEJÍA GUTIÉRREZ
Vice-Rector: MARÍA DE LOS ÁNGELES CORONEL PEREA
Publications: *Mujer en Cuadro*, *Revista Xihmai*

UNIVERSIDAD POLITÉCNICA DE FRANCISCO I. MADERO
(Polytechnic University of Francisco I. Madero)

Domicilio conocido, Tepatepec, 42660 Francisco I. Madero, HGO
Telephone: (738) 724-1171
E-mail: rector@upfim.edu.mx
Internet: www.upfim.edu.mx
State control
Language of instruction: Spanish
Academic year: September to August
Rector: Ing. JUAN DE DIOS NOCHEBUENA HERNÁNDEZ
Academic Sec.: JULIO ANTONIO PÉREZ ESPINOSA
Admin. Sec.: Lic. JOSÉ HUMBERTO ÁNGELES HERNÁNDEZ
Dir for Planning and Evaluation: Ing. JAIME SALINAS PÉREZ
Publication: *Identidades* (3 a year)

UNIVERSIDAD POLITÉCNICA DE PACHUCA
(Polytechnic University of Pachuca)

Domicilio Carretera Pachuca-Ciudad Sahagún, km 20, Col. o Fraccionamiento Ex-Hacienda de Santa Bárbara, 43830 Municipio de Zempoala, HGO
Telephone: (771) 547-7510
E-mail: upp@upp.edu.mx
Internet: www.upp.edu.mx
Founded 2003
State control
Language of instruction: Spanish
Academic year: September to August
Rector: SERGIO ALEJANDRO ARTEAGA CARREÑO
Academic Sec.: Dr SERGIO ALEJANDRO MEDINA MORENO
Admin. Sec.: JORGE ALFREDO FERNÁNDEZ SALAS
Dir for External Affairs: Lic. JOSÉ FRANCISCO MORELOS FERNÁNDEZ
Dir for Planning: ELIMAR OCAMPO ALBA
Dir for Social Communication: ALFREDO PÉREZ MÁXIMO
Librarian: Lic. EDUARDO MENDOZA ESPINOZA

UNIVERSIDAD POLITÉCNICA DE TULANCINGO
(Polytechnic University of Tulancingo)

Calle Ingenierías No 100, Col. Huapalcalco, 43629 Tulancingo, HGO
Telephone: (775) 755-8202
Internet: www.upt.edu.mx

Founded 2002
State control
Language of instruction: Spanish
Academic year: September to August

Rector: GERARDO TÉLLEZ REYES
Academic Sec.: MARÍA DE JESÚS ESPINO GUEVARA
Admin. Sec.: LUÍS ALBERTO TÉLLEZ SOTO
Dir for External Affairs and Extension: Ing. CARLOS M. SUBERBIEL GONZÁLEZ
Dir for Open and Distance Education: FELIPE DURÁN ROCHA
Dir for Planning and Evaluation: ARTURO CALDERÓN HERNÁNDEZ
Dir for Social Communication: Lic. NELLY UBALDO MEJÍA
Librarian: BELÉM HERNÁNDEZ ESCOBEDO
Number of students: 2,066

Jalisco

In Jalisco, there are four federal institutes, nine state institutes, two research centres, two other public institutions and 77 private institutions.

UNIVERSIDAD AUTÓNOMA DE GUADALAJARA
(Autonomous University of Guadalajara)

Avda Patria 1201, Lomas del Valle, 45129 Zapopan, JAL
Telephone: (33) 3648-8824
E-mail: uag@uag.mx
Internet: www.uag.mx

Founded 1935
Private control
Language of instruction: Spanish
Academic year: August to May

1 Programme accredited by COPAES (*q.v.*)

Rector: ANTONIO LEAÑO REYES
Vice-Rector: Ing. JUAN JOSÉ LEAÑO ALVAREZ DEL CASTILLO
Chief Academic Officer: Dr NÉSTOR VELASCO P.
Chief Admin. Officer: Lic. RUBÉN QUIROZ V.
Librarian: Lic. ALBERTO OLIVARES DUARTE

Library of 178,000 vols, 3,760 maps, 3,400 periodicals

Publications: *Academia* (6 a year), *Actas de la Facultad de Medicina* (2 a year), *Docencia* (3 a year), *Item Histórico* (12 a year)

DEANS

College of Architecture and Design: Arq. RAÚL MENDOZA R.
College of Business: C. P. JAVIER GONZÁLEZ C.
College of Engineering: Ing. RAFAEL JAIME A.
College of Health Sciences: Dr NÉSTOR VELASCO P.
College of Humanities and Social Sciences: Lic. ISMAEL ZAMORA TOVAR
College of Law: Lic. HUMBERTO LÓPEZ DELGADILLO
College of Sciences: Ing. JAIME HERNÁNDEZ O.
Continuing Education: Dr JOSÉ MORALES G. (Dir)
Postgraduate Studies: Dr MAURICIO ALCOCER RUTHLING (Dir)
Research Administration: Dr RODOLFO CASILLAS V. (Dir)
Universidad en la Comunidad (UNICO, Junior College): Lic. PEDRO RODRÍGUEZ L. (Dir)

UNIVERSIDAD DE GUADALAJARA
(University of Guadalajara)

Avda Juárez 976, Col. Centro, 44100 Guadalajara, JAL
Telephone: (33) 3134-2222
E-mail: webudg@cencar.udg.mx
Internet: www.udg.mx

Founded 1791, restructured 1925
State control
Language of instruction: Spanish
Academic year: March to February

Rector Gen.: ITZCÓATL TONATIUH BRAVO PADILLA
Exec. Vice-Rector: Dr MIGUEL ÁNGEL NAVARRO NAVARRO
Sec.-Gen.: JOSÉ ALFREDO PEÑA RAMOS
Coordinator for Libraries: SERGIO LÓPES RUELAS

Library: see under Libraries and Archives
Number of teachers: 15,200
Number of students: 235,780

Publications: *Gaceta*, *Jures*, *Revista Universidad de Guadalajara* (4 a year).

UNIVERSITY CENTRES

Centro Universitario de Arte, Arquitectura y Diseño (University Centre for Art, Architecture and Design): Calzada Independencia Norte No 5075, Huentitán El Bajo, S. H., 44250 Guadalajara, JAL; tel. (33) 1202-3000; internet www.cuaad.udg.mx; Rector ERNESTO FLORES GALLO.

Centro Universitario de Ciencias Biológicas y Agropecuarias (University Centre for Biological Sciences and Agriculture): Camino Ramón Padilla Sánchez No 2100 Nextipac, Zapopan, JAL; tel. (33) 3777-1180; e-mail secadmin@cucba.udg.mx; internet www.cucba.udg.mx; Rector Dr SALVADOR MENA MUNGUÍA.

Centro Universitario de Ciencias de la Salud (University Centre for Health Sciences): Sierra Mojada 950, Col. Independencia, 44350 Guadalajara, JAL; tel. (33) 1058-5200; internet www.cucs.udg.mx; Rector Dr JAIME ANDRADE VILLANUEVA.

Centro Universitario de Ciencias Económico-Administrativas (University Centre for Economic and Administrative Sciences): Periférico Norte No 799, Núcleo Universitario Los Belenes, 45100 Zapopan, JAL; tel. (33) 3770-3300; e-mail rector@cucea.udg.mx; internet www.cucea.udg.mx; Rector JOSÉ ALBERTO CASTELLANOS GUTIÉRREZ.

Centro Universitario de Ciencias Exactas e Ingenierías (University Centre for Exact and Engineering Sciences): Blvd Marcelino García Barragán 1421, Esq. Calzada Olímpica, 44430 Guadalajara, JAL; tel. (33) 1378-5900; e-mail rector@cucei.udg.mx; internet www.cucei.udg.mx; Rector Dr CESAR OCTAVIO MONZÓN.

Centro Universitario de Ciencias Sociales y Humanidades (University Centre for Social Sciences and Humanities): Guanajuato No 1045, Col. Alcalde Barranquitas, 44260 Guadalajara, JAL; tel. (33) 3819-3300; internet www.cucsh.udg.mx; Rector Dr HÉCTOR RAÚL SOLÍS GADEA.

REGIONAL UNIVERSITY CENTRES

Centro Universitario de la Cienega (University Centre of the Cienega): Avda Universidad No 1115, Col. Lindavista, 47820 Ocotlán, JAL; tel. (392) 925-9400; internet www.cuci.udg.mx; Rector MARÍA FELICITAS PARGA JIMÉNEZ.

Centro Universitario de la Costa (University Centre of the Coast): Avda Universidad No 203, Del. Ixtapa, 48280 Puerto Vallarta, JAL; tel. (322) 226-2200; e-mail rectoria@cuc.udg.mx; internet www.cuc.udg.mx; Rector Dr MARCO ANTONIO CORTÉS GUARDADO.

Centro Universitario de la Costa Sur (University Centre of the South Coast): Avda Independencia Nacional No 151, 48900 Autlán de Navarro, JAL; tel. (317) 382-5010; internet www.cucsur.udg.mx; Rector ALFREDO TOMÁS ORTEGA OJEDA.

Centro Universitario del Norte (University Centre of the North): Carretera Federal No 23, km 191, 46200 Colotlán, JAL; tel. (499) 992-1333; internet www.cunorte.udg.mx; Rector GERARDO ALBERTO MEJÍA PÉREZ.

Centro Universitario de los Altos (University Centre of the Highlands): Carretera a Yahualica, km 7.5, Tepatitlán de Morelos, JAL; tel. (378) 782-8033; internet www.cualtos.udg.mx; Rector Dra I. LETICIA LEAL MOYA.

Centro Universitario de los Lagos (University Centre of the Lakes): Avda Enrique Díaz de León No 1144, Col. Paseos de la Montaña, 47460 Lagos de Moreno, JAL; tel. (474) 742-4314; e-mail comsocial@lagos.udg.mx; internet www.lagos.udg.mx; Rector Dr ARMANDO ZACARÍAS CASTILLO.

Centro Universitario de los Valles (University Centre of the Valleys): Carretera Guadalajara-Ameca km 45.5, 46600 Ameca, JAL; tel. (375) 758-0148; internet www.cuvalles.udg.mx; Rector Dr JOSÉ LUIS SANTANA MEDINA.

Centro Universitario del Sur (University Centre of the South): Avda Enrique Arreola Silva No 883, Col. Centro, 49000 Ciudad Guzmán, JAL; tel. (341) 575-2222; internet www.cusur.udg.mx; Rector RICARDO XICOTÉNCATL GARCÍA CAUZOR.

Centro Universitario de Tonalá (University Centre of Tonalá): Morelos No 180, Zona Centro, 45400 Tonalá, JAL; tel. (33) 3540-3020; internet cutonala.udg.mx; Rector Dra RUTH PADILLA MUÑOZ

UNIVERSIDAD DEL VALLE DE ATEMAJAC
(Atemajac Valley University)

Avda Tepeyac 4800, Col. Prados Tepeyac, 45050 Zapopan, JAL
Telephone: (33) 3628-7681
E-mail: informes.univa@univa.mx
Internet: www.univa.mx

Founded 1962
Private control

7 Programmes accredited by COPAES (*q.v.*)

Rector: Lic. FRANCISCO RAMÍREZ YÁÑEZ

Publication: *Revista CIF*

UNIVERSIDAD DEL VALLE DE MÉXICO—JALISCO
(University of the Mexican Valley, Jalisco)

Anillo Periférico Poniente No 7900, Col. Jardines del Colli, 45010 Zapopan, JAL
Telephone: (33) 3777-3400
Internet: www.zapopan.uvmnet.edu

Founded 2000
Private control

Rector: GABRIELA MOTTA RAMÍREZ

UNIVERSIDAD GUADALAJARA LAMAR
(Guadalajara Lamar University)

:Avda Inglaterra, Vallarta Poniente, Guadalajara, JAL
Telephone: (33) 3121-7793
Internet: www.lamar.edu.mx

Founded 1792
Private control

Accredited by ANUIES (*q.v.*)
Rector: Dr RICARDO RAMÍREZ ANGULO
Publication: *Revista Comunicarte—Arte, Cultura y Vida Lamar*

UNIVERSIDAD PANAMERICANA—JALISCO
(Pan American University, Jalisco)

Campus Guadalajara Calzada, Circunvalación Poniente No 49, Ciudad Granja 45010 Zapopan, JAL
Telephone: (33) 1368-2200
E-mail: ariverad@up.edu.mx
Internet: www.up.edu.mx/sede.aspx?doc=19
Founded 1989
Private control
Rector: Dr JUAN G. DE LA BORBOLLA RIVERO
Vice-Rector for Academics: RAFAEL HERNANDEZ CÁZARES
Vice-Rector for Admin: Dr JAVIER CASTAÑEDA IBARRA
Sec.-Gen. for Campus: JORGE E. FRANCO LÓPEZ

UNIVERSIDAD POLITÉCNICA DE LA ZONA METROPOLITANA DE GUADALAJARA
(Polytechnic University of the Guadalajara Metropolitan Area)

Carretera Tlajomulco, Santa Fe km 3.5 No 595, Col. Lomas de Tejeda, 45640 Tlajomulco de Zúñiga, JAL
Telephone: (33) 3040-9900
E-mail: informes@upzmg.edu.mx
Internet: www.upzmg.edu.mx
Founded 2004
State control
Language of instruction: Spanish
Academic year: September to August
Rector: JOSÉ ALFREDO LIZÁRRAGA DÍAZ
Academic Sec.: SERGIO BARRERA ELIZONDO
Admin. Sec.: JAIME JOSEMARÍA RANGEL HUERTA

UNIVERSIDAD TECNOLÓGICA DE JALISCO
(Technological University of Jalisco)

Luis J. Jiménez 577, Col. Primero de Mayo, 44979 Guadalajara, JAL
Telephone: (33) 3030-0900
E-mail: informes@utj.edu.mx
Internet: www.utj.edu.mx
Founded 1999
State control
Language of instruction: Spanish
Academic year: September to August
Rector: Ing. JOSÉ ANTONIO HERRERA LOMELÍ
Academic Sec.: (vacant)
Dir for Admin. and Finance: Lic. ADRIANA CIBRIÁN SUÁREZ
Dir for External Affairs: Lic. JENNIFER ARAMBURO MENDIVIL
Dir for Univ. Extension: Ing. FABIOLA MEDINA VILLASEÑOR
Librarian: Lic. SAGRARIO ESTHELA ROMERO DOMÍNGUEZ

Michoacán

In Michoacán, there are five federal institutes, five state institutes, one research centre, one other public institution and 17 private institutions.

UNIVERSIDAD INDÍGENA INTERCULTURAL DEL ESTADO DE MICHOACÁN
(Intercultural Indigenous University of the State of Michoacán)

Finca 'La Tsipekua' Carretera Pátzcuaro-Erongaricuaro km 3, 61614 Pátzcuaro, MICH
Telephone: (434) 342-5532
E-mail: contacto@uiim.edu.mx
Internet: www.uiim.edu.mx
Private control
Rector: Dr IRENEO ROJAS HERNÁNDEZ
Dir for Academics: Dr JOSE JUAN IGNACIO CARDENAS
Dir for Planning: TERESA BAUTISTA HERNÁNDEZ
Dir for Admin: JORGE BARRETO FLORES

UNIVERSIDAD LA SALLE MORELIA
(La Salle University of Morelia)

Avda Universidad No 500, Municipio de Tarímbaro, 58880 Morelia, MICH
Telephone: (443) 321-2102
Internet: www.lasallemorelia.edu.mx
Founded 1962
Private control
Accredited by FIMPES (*q.v.*)
Rector: Ing. HÉCTOR FRANCISCO GIORDANO COURCELLE
Publication: *La Revista Mímixekua*

UNIVERSIDAD LATINA DE AMÉRICA
(Latin University of America)

Manantial Cointzio Norte No 355, Fraccionamiento Los Manantiales, 58170 Morelia, MICH
Telephone: (443) 322-1500
E-mail: informes@unla.edu.mx
Internet: www.unla.mx
Founded 1992
Private control
3 Programmes accredited by COPAES (*q.v.*)
Rector: LUIS ROBERTO MANTILLA SAHAGÚN

UNIVERSIDAD MICHOACANA DE SAN NICOLÁS DE HIDALGO
(Michoacan University of San Nicolás of Hidalgo)

Avda Francisco J. Múgica s/n, Ciudad Universitaria, 58030 Morelia, MICH
Telephone: (443) 322-3500
E-mail: rectoria@umich.mx
Internet: www.umich.mx
Founded 1543 as Real Colegio de San Nicolás Obispo, univ. status 1917
State control
Language of instruction: Spanish
Academic year: August to July
Faculties of chemical and biological sciences, economic and administrative sciences, engineering and architecture, social and historical sciences
Rector: Lic. SALVADOR JARA GUERRERO
Sec.-Gen.: Dr JOSÉ EGBERTO BEDOLLA BECERRIL
Academic Sec.: Dr JOSÉ GERARDO TINOCO RUIZ
Admin. Sec.: CARLOS SALVADOR RODRÍGUEZ CAMARENA
Sec. for Culture: TEODORO BARAJAS RODRÍGUEZ
Librarian: MARÍA DE LA LUZ PÉREZ CRUZ
Library of 150,000 vols
Number of teachers: 2,200
Number of students: 31,800
Publications: *Cuadernos de Centro de Investigación de la Cultura Puehépecha*, *Cuadernos de Derecho*, *Polemos*, *Saber Más* (6 a year, print and online, www.sabermas.umich.mx), *Tzintzun: Revista de Estudios Históricos* (2 a year, print and online, tzintzun.iih.umich.mx)

UNIVERSIDAD VASCO DE QUIROGA
(Vasco de Quiroga University)

Avda Juan Pablo II No 555, Col. Sta Maria de Guido, 58090 Morelia, MICH
Telephone: (443) 323-5171
E-mail: rectoria@uvaq.edu.mx
Internet: www.uvaq.edu.mx
Founded 1979
Private control
Academic year: August to July
Accredited by FIMPES (*q.v.*)
Rector: RAÚL MARTÍNEZ RUBIO
Academic Sec.: JOSÉ DE JESÚS CASTELLANOS LÓPEZ
Admin. Sec.: MARÍA INÉS PÉREZ ALFARO
Dir for Communications and Public Relations: LAILA MAGALI MONTES NIETO
Library of 18,000 vols

Morelos

In Morelos, there are three federal institutes, one other public institution and 28 private institutions.

UNIVERSIDAD AUTÓNOMA DEL ESTADO DE MORELOS
(Autonomous University of the State of Morelos)

Avda Universidad 1001, Col. Chamilpa, 62209 Cuernavaca, MOR
Telephone: (777) 329-7000
E-mail: rectoria@uaem.mx
Internet: www.uaem.mx
Founded 1953
State control
Language of instruction: Spanish
Academic year: September to July
Centres for biological research, chemical research, research in biodiversity and conservation, research in biotechnology, research in engineering and applied sciences; faculties of accounting, administration and informatics, agricultural sciences, architecture, arts, biological sciences, chemical and engineering sciences, human communication, humanities, law, medicine, pharmacy, psychology; institute of educational sciences
Rector: Dr JESÚS ALEJANDRO VERA JIMÉNEZ
Sec.-Gen.: Dr JOSÉ ANTONIO GÓMEZ ESPINOZA
Academic Sec.: Dra PATRICIA CASTILLO ESPAÑA
Sec. for Extension: Dra LORENA NOYOLA PIÑA
Sec. for Research: Dr GUSTAVO URQUIZA BELTRÁN
Dir for Libraries: Lic. ANTONIO JAVIER GONZÁLEZ MUÑOZ
Number of teachers: 1,500
Number of students: 17,500
Publication: *Revista Inventio*

UNIVERSIDAD TECNOLÓGICA 'EMILIANO ZAPATA' DEL ESTADO DE MORELOS
(Emiliano Zapata Technological University of Estado de Morelos)

Avda Universidad Tecnológica No 1, Col. Palo Escrito, 62760 Emiliano Zapata, MOR
Telephone: (777) 368-1165
E-mail: rectoria@utez.edu.mx
Internet: www.utez.edu.mx
Founded 2000
State control

Language of instruction: Spanish
Academic year: September to August
Divs of economics and administration, industrial mechanics, information technology and communication
Rector: Lic. BEATRIZ RAMÍREZ VELÁZQUEZ
Academic Sec.: ALEJANDRO RAFAEL CABALLERO MORALES
Dir for Admin. and Finance: LUIS ANTONIO GUTIÉRREZ AGUILAR
Library of 12,000 vols

Nayarit

In Nayarit, there are three federal institutes and seven private institutions.

UNIVERSIDAD AUTÓNOMA DE NAYARIT
(Autonomous University of Nayarit)

Ciudad de la Cultura 'Amado Nervo', 63155 Tepic, NAY
Telephone: (311) 211-8800
E-mail: contacto@uan.edu.mx
Internet: www.uan.edu.mx
Founded 1930 as Instituto de Ciencias y Letras de Nayarit, univ. status 1969
Academic units of agriculture, basic sciences and engineering, biochemical sciences and pharmaceuticals, commerce and administration, dentistry, economics, law, medicine, nursing, veterinary medicine, zoology
Rector: JUAN LÓPEZ SALAZAR
Sec.-Gen.: CECILIO OSWALDO FLORES SOTO
Sec. for Academic Services: ARTURO SÁNCHEZ VALDÉS
Sec. for Extension and External Affairs: EDGAR RAYMUNDO GONZÁLEZ SANDOVAL
Sec. for Finance and Admin.: MARCELA LUNA LÓPEZ
Sec. for Higher Secondary Education: JOSÉ RICARDO CHÁVEZ GONZÁLEZ
Sec. for Research and Postgraduate Affairs: RUBÉN BUGARÍN MONTOYA
Sec. for Teaching: JORGE IGNACIO PEÑA GONZÁLEZ
Dir for Library: CLARA ORIZAGA RODRÍGUEZ
Library of 174,000 vols
Publications: *Revista Tamé*, *Revista Waxapa*

UNIVERSIDAD TECNOLÓGICA DE BAHÍA DE BANDERAS
(Technological University of Bahía de Banderas)

Blvd Nuevo Vallarta No 65, 63735 Nuevo Vallarta, NAY
Telephone: (322) 226-8300
Internet: www.utbb.edu.mx
Founded 2004
State control
Language of instruction: Spanish
Academic year: September to August
Divs of engineering, gastronomy, tourism
Rector: Lic. JOSÉ GÓMEZ PÉREZ
Academic Sec.: GUILLERMO MERINO TORRES
Dir for Admin. and Finance: GERARDO GANGOITI MIRAMONTES
Dir for External Affairs: ALVINO OCHOA TORRES
Sub-Dir for School Services: MARÍA DE GUADALUPE AMBRIZ MEZA

Nuevo Leon

In Nuevo Leon, there are two federal institutes, one other public institution and 46 private institutions.

UNIVERSIDAD AUTÓNOMA DE NUEVO LEÓN
(Autonomous University of Nuevo León)

Pedro de Alba s/n, San Nicolás de los Garza, NL
Telephone: (81) 8329-4000
E-mail: comentarios@uanl.mx
Internet: www.uanl.mx
Founded 1933
State control
Language of instruction: Spanish
Academic year: August to July
Rector: Dr JESÚS ANCER RODRÍGUEZ
Sec.-Gen.: ROGELIO GARZA RIVERA
Academic Sec.: JUAN MANUEL ALCOCER GONZÁLEZ
Sec. for Economic Devt: CARMEN DEL ROSARIO DE LA FUENTE GARCÍA
Sec. for Extension and Culture: ROGELIO VILLARREAL ELIZONDO
Sec. for Int. Relations: DANIEL GONZÁLEZ SPENCER
Sec. for Research, Innovation and Postgraduate Affairs: MARIO CÉSAR SALINAS CARMONA
Sec. for Sustainable Devt: ESTHELA MARÍA GUTIÉRREZ GARZA
Sec. for Univ. Affairs: LUZ NATALIA BERRÚN CASTAÑÓN
Capilla Alfonsina Univ. Library Dir: MINERVA MARGARITA VILLARREAL RODRÍGUEZ
Raúl Rangel Frías Univ. Library Dir: Lic. PORFIRIO TAMEZ SOLÍS
Library: 2.24m. vols
Number of teachers: 6,400
Number of students: 153,000
Publications: *Armas y Letras* (4 a year, print and online, www.armasyletras.uanl.mx), *Ciencia UANL* (4 a year, print and online, www.cienciauanl.uanl.mx), *Contexto* (2 a year, print and online, contexto.uanl.mx), *Ensayos* (irregular), *Imaginario Visual* (print and online, artesvisuales.uanl.mx/imaginario), *Perspectiva Social* (Social Perspectives, 2 a year, in Spanish and English, print and online, www.perspectivassociales.uanl.mx), *Química Hoy* (4 a year), *Trayectorias* (2 a year, print and online, trayectorias.uanl.mx)

ACADEMIC DIRECTORS
Faculty of Agronomy: Dr FRANCISCO ZAVALA GARCÍA
Faculty of Architecture: FRANCISCO FABELA BERNAL
Faculty of Biological Sciences: Dr ANTONIO GUZMÁN VELASCO
Faculty of Chemical Sciences: Ing. EDUARDO SOTO REGALADO
Faculty of Civil Engineering: PEDRO LEOBARDO VALDEZ TAMEZ
Faculty of Communication Sciences: LUCINDA SEPÚLVEDA GARCÍA
Faculty of Dentistry: ROSA ISELA SÁNCHEZ NÁJERA
Faculty of Earth Sciences: FRANCISCO MEDINA BARRERA
Faculty of Economics: JULIO CÉSAR ARTEAGA GARCÍA
Faculty of Forestry Sciences: Dr JAVIER JIMÉNEZ PÉREZ
Faculty of Law and Criminology: JOSÉ LUIS PRADO MAILLARD
Faculty of Mechanical and Electrical Engineering: Ing. ESTEBAN BÁEZ VILLARREAL
Faculty of Medicine: Dr SANTOS GUZMÁN LÓPEZ
Faculty of Music: LUIS GERARDO LOZANO LOZANO
Faculty of Nursing: MARÍA DIANA RUVALCABA RODRÍGUEZ
Faculty of Performing Arts: OLIVIA JANNETH VILLARREAL ARIZPE
Faculty of Philosophy and Letters: MARÍA LUISA MARTÍNEZ SÁNCHEZ
Faculty of Physical and Mathematical Sciences: ROGELIO JUVENAL SEPÚLVEDA GUERRERO
Faculty of Political Science and Public Administration: Dr GERARDO TAMEZ GONZÁLEZ
Faculty of Psychology: JOSÉ ARMANDO PEÑA MORENO
Faculty of Public Accounting and Administration: MARÍA EUGENIA GARCÍA DE LA PEÑA
Faculty of Public Health and Nutrition: HILDA IRENE NOVELO HUERTA
Faculty of Social Work and Human Development: MARÍA TERESA OBREGÓN MORALES
Faculty of Sports Administration: OSWALDO CEBALLOS GURROLA
Faculty of Veterinary Medicine and Zootechnics: JUAN JOSÉ ZÁRATE RAMOS
Faculty of Visual Arts: MARIO ALBERTO MÉNDEZ RAMÍREZ
Institute for Social Research: ESTHELA MARÍA GUTIÉRREZ GARZA

UNIVERSIDAD DE MONTEMORELOS
(University of Montemorelos)

Avda Libertad 1300 Poniente, 67530 Montemorelos, NL
Telephone: (826) 263-0900
E-mail: promocion@um.edu.mx
Internet: www.um.edu.mx
Founded 1942
Private control
Language of instruction: Spanish
Academic year: August to May
Schools of administrative sciences, arts and communication, education, engineering, health sciences, music, psychology, theology
Rector: Prof. ISMAEL CASTILLO OSUNA
Vice-Rector for Academic Affairs: Dra RAQUEL B. DE KORNIEJCZUK
Vice-Rector for Finance: JOEL SEBASTIÁN ESCUDERO
Vice-Rector for Student Affairs: EKEL COLLINS
Library Dir: Dr THERLOW HARPER
Number of teachers: 162
Number of students: 2,350
Publications: *Logos* (1 a year), *Memorias del Centro de Investigaciones Educativas* (1 a year), *Perspectivas Teológicas* (1 a year), *Revista Internacional de Estudios en Educación* (2 a year)

UNIVERSIDAD DE MONTERREY
(University of Monterrey)

Avda Ignacio Morones Prieto 4500 Pte., 66238 San Pedro Garza García, NL
Telephone: (81) 8125-1000
E-mail: rectoria@udem.edu.mx
Internet: www.udem.edu.mx
Founded 1969
Private control
Languages of instruction: English, Spanish
Academic year: January to December
Schools of art, architecture and design, business, education and humanities, engineering and technology, health sciences, law and social sciences
Rector: Dr ANTONIO J. DIECK ASSAD
Vice-Rector for Academic Affairs: Dr FERNANDO MATA CARRASCO
Vice-Rector for Admin.: PATRICIO EUGENIO DE LA GARZA CADENA
Vice-Rector for Institutional Devt: Ing. AGUSTÍN LANDA GARCÍA TÉLLEZ
Vice-Rector for Integral Education: Lic. ISABELLA NAVARRO GRUETER
Librarian: SAUL HIRAM SOUTO FUENTES
Library of 409,796 vols

Number of teachers: 704
Number of students: 11,673

UNIVERSIDAD METROPOLITANA DE MONTERREY
(Monterrey Metropolitan University)

Washington 424-A Oriente Centro, 64000 Monterrey, NL
Telephone: (81) 8130-7900
E-mail: info@umm.edu.mx
Internet: www.umm.edu.mx

Founded 1996
Private control

Accredited by FIMPES (*q.v.*)

UNIVERSIDAD REGIOMONTANA
(Regiomontana University)

Villagrán 238 Sur, Centro, 64000 Monterrey, NL
Telephone: (81) 8220-4620
E-mail: informes@mail.ur.mx
Internet: www.ur.mx

Founded 1969
Private control
Language of instruction: Spanish
Academic year: September to August

Faculties of business, engineering and architecture, humanities and social sciences

Pres. and Rector: ÁNGEL CASÁN MARCOS
Admin. Dir: Ing. GUILLERMO CHARLES LOBO
Registrar: Ing. GERARDO GONZÁLEZ
Librarian: Ing. JORGE MERCADO SALAS

Library of 43,000 vols
Number of teachers: 450
Number of students: 4,500

Publications: *Espresión* (52 a year), *Revista Innovación*, *Veritas* (1 a year)

Oaxaca

In Oaxaca, there are 11 federal institutes and 17 private institutions.

UNIVERSIDAD ANÁHUAC OAXACA
(Anáhuac University of Oaxaca)

Blvd Guadalupe Hinojosa de Murat No 1100, Cuilapam de Guerrero, Oaxaca de Juarez, OAX
Telephone: (951) 501-6250
E-mail: uao@anahuac.mx
Internet: www.anahuacoaxaca.edu.mx

Founded 2000
Private control

Accredited by FIMPES (*q.v.*); schools of business, communication, engineering, law and social sciences, psychology, tourism administration and gastronomy

Rector: Dr RODRIGO DEL VAL MARTIN

UNIVERSIDAD AUTÓNOMA 'BENITO JUÁREZ' DE OAXACA
(Benito Juárez Autonomous University of Oaxaca)

Avda Universidad s/n, Ex-Hacienda de 5 Señores, 68120 Oaxaca, OAX
Telephone: (951) 502-0700
E-mail: rector@uabjo.mx
Internet: www.uabjo.mx

Founded 1827 as Instituto de Ciencias y Artes, univ. status 1955
State control
Language of instruction: Spanish
Academic year: August to July

Rector: Lic. EDUARDO MARTÍNEZ HELMES
Sec.-Gen.: LETICIA EUGENIA MENDOZA TORO
Academic Sec.: CÉSAR ROBERTO TRUJILLO REYES
Admin. Sec.: SILVIANO CABRERA GÓMEZ
Sec. for Finance: Dr SAÚL ZENTENO JUÁREZ
Sec. for Interrelations: ROMUALDO TOLEDO AMBROSIO
Sec. for Planning: Dr ARISTEO SEGURA SALVADOR
Technical Sec.: ROBERTO VALDIVIESO SUASTEGUI
Library Dir: JUAN MANUEL GARCÍA MARTEL

Library of 77,200 vols
Number of teachers: 1,000
Number of students: 15,000

Publications: *El Cotidiano*, *Negocios y Desarrollo*

ACADEMIC DIRECTORS

Faculty of Accounting and Administration: ABEL MORALES SANTIAGO
Faculty of Architecture: Arq. JESÚS PABLO HENÁNDEZ
Faculty of Architecture—City University Campus: Arq. ENRIQUE MAYORAL GUZMÁN
Faculty of Chemistry: LEOBARDO REYES VELASCO
Faculty of Languages: GUADALUPE ÁNGELA RAMÍREZ VICTORIA
Faculty of Law and Social Sciences: REYNEL VASQUEZ ZARATE
Façulty of Medicine and Surgery: Dr MIGUEL ÁNGEL REYES FRANCO
Faculty of Nursing and Obstetrics: (vacant)
Faculty of Dentistry: MARÍA ELENA HERNÁNDEZ AGUILAR
School of Fine Arts: FIDEL TORREZ GONZÁLEZ
School of Economics: ARACELI ESCOBAR MÉNDEZ
School of Sciences: ISHTAR GEMMA HERNÁNDEZ CALVO
School of Veterinary Studies and Zootecnics: JORGE MORÍN RUBIO

UNIVERSIDAD DE LA SIERRA SUR
(University of the South Sierra)

Calle Guillermo Rojas Mijangos s/n, Esq. Avda Universidad, Col. Ciudad Universitaria, 70800 Miahuatlán de Porfirio Díaz, OAX
Telephone: (951) 572-4100
E-mail: serves@unsis.edu.mx
Internet: www.unsis.edu.mx

Founded 2000
State control
Language of instruction: Spanish
Academic year: October to September

Rector: Dr MODESTO SEARA VÁZQUEZ
Vice-Rector for Academic Affairs: SANDRA KARINA RAMÍREZ VÁSQUEZ
Vice-Rector for Admin.: Lic. ERICK ALEXIS OCHOA VALENCIA
Head of Postgraduate Studies: Dr PEDRO DURÁN FÉRMAN
Librarian: Lic. GEORGINA CERVANTES RÍOS

Publication: *Revista Salud y Administración* (3 a year)

UNIVERSIDAD DEL ISTMO
(Istmo University)

Carretera Chihuitan Ixtepec s/n, 70110 Ixtepec, OAX
Telephone: (971) 712-7050
E-mail: servesc@bianni.unistmo.edu.mx
Internet: www.unistmo.edu.mx

Founded 2002
State control
Language of instruction: Spanish
Academic year: October to September

Campuses in Juchitán and Tehuantepec

Rector: Dr MODESTO SEARA VÁZQUEZ
Vice-Rector for Academic Affairs: VÍCTOR MANUEL MARTÍNEZ RODRÍGUEZ
Vice-Rector for Admin.: HÉCTOR MANUEL CASTILLO SOSA
Head of Postgraduate Studies: Dr VÍCTOR IVÁN MORENO OLIVA
Librarian: Lic. NORMA CARRILLO HERRERA

UNIVERSIDAD DEL MAR
(University of the Sea)

Ciudad Universitaria, 70902 Puerto Ángel, Distrito de San Pedro Pochutla, OAX
Telephone: (958) 584-3078
E-mail: vicadem@angel.umar.mx
Internet: angel.umar.mx/campus

Founded 1992
State control
Language of instruction: Spanish
Academic year: October to September

Institutes for ecology, industries, resources; campuses in Puerto Escondido and Huatulco

Rector: Dr MODESTO SEARA VAZQUEZ
Vice-Rector for Academic Affairs: GERARDO ESTEBAN LEYTE MORALES
Vice-Rector for Admin.: JOSÉ LUIS RAMOS ESPINOZA
Vice-Rector for Relations and Research: Lic. MARTHA ISABEL PÉREZ HERNÁNDEZ
Head of Postgraduate Studies: Dr JUAN FRANCISCO MERAZ HERNANDO
Head Librarian: Lic. URSULA NAVARRO ALVARADO

Publication: *Ciencia y Mar*

UNIVERSIDAD REGIONAL DEL SURESTE
(Southeast Regional University)

Eulalio Gutiérrez 1002 Col. Miguel Alemán, 68120 Oaxaca, OAX
Telephone: (951) 514-1410
E-mail: rectoria@urse.edu.mx
Internet: www.urse.edu.mx

Founded 1977
Private control
Academic year: August to June

Accredited by FIMPES (*q.v.*)

Rector: Dr BENJAMÍN ALONSO SMITH ARANGO

UNIVERSIDAD TECNOLÓGICA DE LA MIXTECA
(Technological University of the Mixteca)

Carretera Huajuapan-Acatlima, km 2.5, 69000 Huajuápan de León, OAX
Telephone: (919) 532-0214
E-mail: escolar@mixteco.utm.mx
Internet: www.utm.mx

Founded 1990
State control
Language of instruction: Spanish
Academic year: October to September

Institutes of agroindustry, computer engineering, design, electronic and mechatronic engineering, humanities and social sciences, hydrology, mining, physics and mathematics

Rector: Dr MODESTO SEARA VÁZQUEZ
Vice-Rector for Academic Affairs: Dr RAÚL SALAS CORONADO
Vice-Rector for Admin.: JAVIER JOSÉ RUIZ SANTIAGO
Vice-Rector for Univ. Relations and Research: MARÍA DE LOS ÁNGELES PERALTA ARIAS
Librarian: Lic. MIGUEL ÁNGEL GONZÁLEZ VEGA

Publication: *Temas de Ciencia y Tecnología* (3 a year)

Puebla

In Puebla, there are three federal institutes, nine state institutes, one research centre, one other public institution and 90 private institutions.

BENEMÉRITA UNIVERSIDAD AUTÓNOMA DE PUEBLA
(Meritorious Autonomous University of Puebla)

4 Sur No 104, Centro Histórico, 72000 Puebla, PUE
Telephone: (222) 229-5500
E-mail: sg.direccion@correo.buap.mx
Internet: www.buap.mx

Founded 1937
State control
Language of instruction: Spanish
Academic year: August to May

Faculties of agro-hydraulic engineering, architecture, business administration, chemical engineering, chemical sciences, computer sciences, culture, economics, electronic sciences, languages, law and social sciences, medicine, philosophy and letters, physics and mathematics, psychology, public accounting, stomatology, veterinary medicine and zootechnics; institutes of government sciences and strategic development, physiology, science; schools of arts, biology

Rector: José Alfonso Esparza Ortiz
Sec.-Gen.: Dr René Valdiviezo Sandoval
Admin. Sec.: Juan José Oroza Pérez
Technical Sec.: Rosa Isela Ávalos Méndez
Dir-Gen. for Libraries: Silvia Jaime Hernández

Number of teachers: 3,600
Number of students: 42,000

Publication: *Revista Latinoamericana el Ambiente y las Ciencias*

UNIVERSIDAD BENITO JUAREZ GARCIA
(University Benito Juarez Garcia)

36 Norte 1609 América Norte, 72340 PUE
Telephone: (222) 235-3331
E-mail: inscripciones@ubj.edu.mx
Internet: www.ubj.edu.mx

Founded 1995
Private control

Accredited by FIMPES (*q.v.*)

Rector: Jorge Sánchez Zacarías
Vice-Rector: Aurora Martínez Álvarez
Dir-Gen of Human Resources and Finance: Raúl Vanthroy Sánchez Martínez
Dir of Admin: David Rosales Candía

Library: 8,903 magazines, 4,102,443 documents

UNIVERSIDAD DE LAS AMÉRICAS—PUEBLA
(University of the Americas—Puebla)

Sta Catarina Mártir, Apdo Postal 100, 72810 Cholula, PUE
Telephone: (222) 229-2000
E-mail: informes.nuevoingreso@udlap.mx
Internet: www.udlap.mx

Founded 1940 as Mexico City College, current name adopted 1963
Private control
Languages of instruction: Spanish, English
Academic year: August to May

29 Programmes accredited by COPAES (*q.v.*)

Rector: Dr Luis Ernesto Derbez Bautista
Academic Vice-Rector: Dra Cecilia Anaya Berrios
Admin. Vice-Rector: Prof. Monica Ruiz Huerta
Vice-Rector for Student Affairs: Prof. Maria del Carmen Palafox Ramos
Vice-Rector for Extension and Institutional Devt: Francisco Javier Mariscal Magdaleno
Librarian: Dr Alfredo Sánchez Hultrón Santos

Library: see under Libraries and Archives

Publications: *La Catarina*, *UDLA Informa*

DEANS

Faculty of Administration: Dr Francisco Guerra Vázquez
Faculty of Arts and Humanities: Dr Roberto Solano Méndez
School of Business and Economics: Dr José Angel Raynal
School of Engineering: Dr Andrés Ramos Ramírez
School of Social Sciences: Dr Isidro Morales Moreno
Research and Graduate Studies: Dr Gerardo Ayala San Martín

UNIVERSIDAD DE LA SIERRA
(University of the Sierra)

Universidad de la Sierra A.C. Avenida de los Técnicos s/n 73160 Huauchinango, PUE
Telephone: (776) 712-0491
E-mail: idiomas@usac.edu.mx
Internet: www.usac.edu.mx

Founded 1980
Private control

Accredited by ANUIES (*q.v.*)

Rector: Dr Hugo Jiménez Arroyo
Vice-Rector: Prof. Lorena Vargas Madrid
Vice-Rector for Academics: (vacant)

Library: 25 magazine titles; digital library

UNIVERSIDAD DEL VALLE DE MÉXICO—PUEBLA
(Valle de México University)

Camino Real a San Andrés Cholula No 4002 Col. Emiliano Zapata, 72810 San Andrés Cholula, PUE
Telephone: (222) 225-9171
E-mail: opinión@puebla.uvmnet.edu
Internet: www.puebla.uvmnet.edu

Founded 1960 as Institution Harvard; current name adopted 1968
Private control

6 Programmes accredited by COPAES (*q.v.*)

Rector: Gabriela Motta Ramírez

UNIVERSIDAD DE ORIENTE—PUEBLA
(University of the East—Puebla)

21 Oriente 1816 Azcárate, 72501 Puebla, PUE
Telephone: (222) 211-1698
Internet: www.puebla.uo.edu.mx

Founded 1996
Private control

Rector: Martha Patricia Agüera Ibáñez
Vice-Rector: José Fernando López Olea
Dir for Academics: Adriana del Villar Ayala
Dir for Admin: Gema Silva Vargas

UNIVERSIDAD INTERCULTURAL DEL ESTADO DE PUEBLA
(Intercultural University of the State of Puebla)

Juárez Nte No 40, Lipuntahuaca, 73475 Huehuetla, PUE
Telephone: (233) 488-1608
E-mail: informatica@uiep.edu. mx
Internet: www.uiep.edu.mx

Founded 2006
Private control

Rector: Alibert Sánchez Jiménez

UNIVERSIDAD POLITÉCNICA DE PUEBLA
(Polytechnic University of Puebla)

Tercer Carril del Ejido 'Serrano' s/n, San Mateo Cuanalá, Juan C. Bonilla, 72640 Puebla, PUE
Telephone: (222) 774-6640
E-mail: rector@uppuebla.edu.mx
Internet: www.uppuebla.edu.mx

State control
Language of instruction: Spanish

Rector: Alberto Sánchez Serrano
Academic Sec.: Dr Luis Huerta González
Admin. Sec.: Arturo Salcedo del Moral
Dir for Teaching and Postgraduate Affairs: Dr Antonio Benítez Ruiz

UNIVERSIDAD POPULAR AUTÓNOMA DEL ESTADO DE PUEBLA
(Popular Autonomous University of the State of Puebla)

21 sur 1103 Barrio Santiago, 72410, PUE
Telephone: (222) 229-9400
E-mail: admisiones@upaep.mx
Internet: www.upaep.mx

Founded 1973
Private control

Rector: Emilio José Baños Ardavín

UNIVERSIDAD TECNOLÓGICA DE HUEJOTZINGO
(Technological University of Huejotzingo)

Camino Real a San Mateo s/n, Santa Ana Xalmimilulco, 74169 Huejotzingo, PUE
Telephone: (227) 275-9302
E-mail: rectoria@uth.edu.mx
Internet: www.uth.edu.mx

Founded 1998
State control

Rector: Dr Juan Ramón Erosa Pineda
Academic Sec.: Ing. Arturo Benito Vásquez Ortiz

UNIVERSIDAD TECNOLÓGICA DE PUEBLA
(Technological University of Puebla)

Antiguo Camino a la Resurrecion No 1002-a, Zona Industrial Puebla Oriente, 72300 Puebla, PUE
Telephone: (222) 309-8858
Internet: www.utpuebla.edu.mx

Founded 1994
State control
Academic year: September to August

Rector: Dr Jorge Alfredo Guillén Muñoz

Academic Sec.: SERGIO FERNANDO AGUILAR ESCOBAR
Dir for Admin. and Finance: TOMÁS ESTEBAN SILVA LIMÓN
Dir for Univ. Extension: Lic. SERGIO RAÚL ORTIZ SAUCEDO

UNIVERSIDAD TECNOLÓGICA DE TECAMACHALCO
(Technological University of Tecamachalco)

Avda Universidad Tecnológica No 1, Col. El Montecillo, Tecamachalco, PUE
Telephone: (249) 422-3301
Internet: www.uttecam.edu.mx
Founded 1996
State control
Academic year: August to August
Rector: Dr JOSÉ ANTONIO GARRIDO NATAREN

Querétaro

In Querétaro, there are two federal institutes, two research centres, one other public institution and 14 private institutions.

UNIVERSIDAD ANÁHUAC QUERÉTARO
(Anáhuac University of Querétaro)

Circuito Universidades I Km 7 Fraccionamiento 2, Municipio El Marqués, 76246 Querétaro, QRO
Telephone: (442) 245-6742
Internet: www.anahuacqro.edu.mx
Founded 2005
Private control
Accredited by FIMPES (*q.v.*)
Rector: LUIS EDUARDO ALVERDE

UNIVERSIDAD AUTÓNOMA DE QUERÉTARO
(Autonomous University of Querétaro)

Centro Universitario, Avda Hidalgo s/n, Col. Las Campanas, 76010 Santiago de Querétaro, QRO
Telephone: (442) 192-1200
E-mail: rectoria@uaq.mx
Internet: www.uaq.mx
Founded 1951
State control
Language of instruction: Spanish
Academic year: July to June
Campuses in Aeropuerto, Cadereyta, Jalpan
Rector: GILBERTO HERRERA RUIZ
Academic Sec.: Dr CÉSAR GARCÍA RAMÍREZ
Admin. Sec.: JAIME ÁNGELES ÁNGELES
Sec. for Finance: Dr JOSÉ ANTONIO ROBLES HERNÁNDEZ
Sec. for Univ. Extension: MAGALI ELIZABETH AGUILAR ORTIZ
Dir-Gen. for Libraries: Dr IGNACIO RODRÍGUEZ SÁNCHEZ
Library of 240,000 vols, 150 journal titles, 20,000 ejournals, 17,000 theses, 600 CDs, cassettes and DVDs
Number of teachers: 1,500
Number of students: 18,000
Publications: *Autonomía*, *Revista Auriga*, *Revista Bellas Artes*, *Revista de Egresados de Contabilidad*, *Revista de Informática*, *Revista de Investigación*, *Revista de Medicina*, *Revista de Sociología*, *Revista Extensión Universitaria*

ACADEMIC DIRECTORS

Faculty of Accounting and Administration: Dr ARTURO CASTAÑEDA OLALDE
Faculty of Chemistry: SERGIO PACHECO HERNANDEZ
Faculty of Computer Science: RUTH ANGÉLICA RICO HERNÁNDEZ
Faculty of Engineering: Dr DOMÍNGUEZ GONZÁLEZ AURELIO
Faculty of Fine Arts: VICENTE LÓPEZ VELARDE FONSECA
Faculty of Languages and Letters: Lic. VERÓNICA NÚÑEZ PERUSQUÍA
Faculty of Law: Dra GABRIELA NIETO CASTILLO
Faculty of Medicine: Dr JAVIER ÁVILA MORALES
Faculty of Natural Sciences: MARGARITA TERESA DE JESÚS GARCÍA GASCA
Faculty of Philosophy: Dra BLANCA ESTELA GUTIÉRREZ GRAGEDA
Faculty of Political and Social Sciences: CARLOS PRAXEDIS RAMÍREZ OLVERA
Faculty of Psychology: JAIME ELEAZAR RIVAS MEDINA
Preparatory Faculty: ROSA MARÍA VÁZQUEZ CABRERA

UNIVERSIDAD MARISTA DE QUERÉTARO
(Marist University of Querétaro)

Marte No 2 Esq. Avda Universidad Col. Centro, 7600 Querétaro, QRO
Telephone: (442) 214-5929
Internet: www.umq.edu.mx
Founded 2001
Private control
Accredited by FIMPES (*q.v.*)
Number of students: 1,245

UNIVERSIDAD POLITÉCNICA DE QUERÉTARO
(Polytechnic University of Querétaro)

Carretera Estatal 420 s/n, 76240 El Marqués, QRO
Telephone: (442) 101-9000
Internet: www.upq.mx
State control
Language of instruction: Spanish
Academic year: September to August
Rector: CARLOS ALBERTO PACHECO LOUSTAUNAU
Academic Sec.: LARA NACIF SILICEO
Admin. Sec.: Lic. ERICK LEONARDO CORONA GARCÍA
Publication: *Revista UPQ*

UNIVERSIDAD TECNOLÓGICA DE QUERÉTARO
(Technological University of Querétaro)

Avda Pie de la Cuesta No 2501, Col. Unidad Nacional, 76148 Querétaro, QRO
Telephone: (442) 209-6100
Internet: www.uteq.edu.mx
Founded 1994
State control
Language of instruction: Spanish
Academic year: August to July
Rector: SALVADOR LECONA URIBE
Academic Sec.: Dr SALVADOR FRANCISCO ACUÑA GUZMÁN
Sec. for Admin. and Finance: Lic. RAÚL IGLESIAS FLORES
Sec. for External Affairs: MARTÍN LARIOS OSORIO
Dir for Academic Devt: IGNACIO ESCALERA CASTILLO
Dir for Planning and Evaluation: JUDITH VIDIMARA DEL PINO FLORES
Library of 29,800 vols, 38 periodical titles

Quintana Roo

In Quintana Roo, there are three federal institutes, one state institute, one research centre and four private institutions.

UNIVERSIDAD ANÁHUAC CANCÚN
(Anáhuac University of Cancún)

Blvd Cancún-Aeropuerto Km 13, 77565 Cancún, Q ROO
Telephone: (998) 881-7750
E-mail: informacion.cancun@anahuac.mx
Internet: www.anahuaccancun.edu.mx
Founded 2000
Private control
Accredited by FIMPES (*q.v.*)
Rector: Ing. MIGUEL PÉREZ GÓMEZ
Dir for Academic Affairs: ALDO CHÁVEZ CEREZO
Dir for Admin. and Finance: DEYBER HEREDIA CHABLÉ
Librarian: CECILIA SALAZAR SALAS

UNIVERSIDAD DEL CARIBE
(University of the Caribbean)

Lote 1, Manzana 1, Region 78, Esq. Fraccionamiento Tabachines, 77528 Cancún, Q ROO
Telephone: (998) 881-4400
E-mail: rectoria@unicaribe.edu.mx
Internet: www.unicaribe.edu.mx
Founded 2000
State control
Languages of instruction: English, Spanish
Academic year: August to May
Depts of culinary arts, economics and business, tourism and sustainable development
Pres.: SARA LATIFE RUIZ CHÁVEZ
Rector: TIRSO JUAN ORTIZ CORAL
Academic Sec.: HILARIO LÓPEZ GARACHANA
Sec. for Planning and Institutional Devt: RODOLFO RIVAS CHAVOYA
Librarian: LORENA CAREAGA VILIESID
Library of 17,000 vols
Number of teachers: 600
Number of students: 2,500

UNIVERSIDAD DE QUINTANA ROO
(University of Quintana Roo)

Blvd Bahía s/n, Esq. Ignacio Comonfort, Col. del Bosque, 77019 Chetumal, Q ROO
Telephone: (983) 835-0300
E-mail: lhmena@uqroo.mx
Internet: www.uqroo.mx
Founded 1991
State control
Language of instruction: Spanish
Academic divs of health sciences, political sciences and humanities, science and engineering, social sciences and business administration, sustainable development
Rector: ELINA ELFI CORAL CASTILLA
Sec.-Gen.: NANCY ANGELINA QUINTAL GARCÍA
Dir-Gen. for Academic Services: JORGE ALBERTO CHAN COB
Dir-Gen. for Admin. and Finance: Lic. JULIO HAN CHAN
Dir-Gen. for Extension: Lic. HUGO ESQUINCA FARRERA
Dir-Gen. for Planning: WILLIAM ALFREDO RAMÍREZ ROMERO
Dir-Gen. for Research and Postgraduate Affairs: Dr RAÚL ARÍSTIDES PÉREZ AGUILAR
Dir-Gen. for Student Welfare: MARÍA DE GUADALUPE CUÉLLAR ESPADAS
Technical Dir: ANA MARLENY RIVERO CANCHÉ
Head Librarian: DANIEL VARGAS ESPINOSA
Library of 30,500 vols
Publication: *Revista* (2 a year)

UNIVERSIDAD INTERCULTURAL MAYA DE QUINTANA ROO
(Maya de Quintana Roo Intercultural University)

Calle Primavera, s/n, entre Avda José María, Jacinto Canek Q ROO
Telephone: (997) 978-0371
Internet: www.uimqroo.edu.mx
Private control
Rector: Dr FRANCISCO JAVIER ROSADO MAY

UNIVERSIDAD LA SALLE CANCÚN
(La Salle University, Cancún)

Carretera Cancún-Playa del Carmen, km 11.5 Manzana 1 lote 1 SM, 77565, Cancún, Q ROO
Telephone: (998) 886-2201
Internet: www.lasallecancun.edu.mx
Founded 1978
Private control
Accredited by FIMPES (*q.v.*)
Rector: FERNANDO MAINOU CERVANTES
Vice-Rector: EFRAIN CALDERON AMAYA
Publication: *Revista Horizontal*

UNIVERSIDAD TECNOLÓGICA DE CANCÚN
(Technological University of Cancún)

Carretera Cancún-Aeropuerto, km 11.5, 77565 Cancún, Q ROO
Telephone: (998) 881-1900
Internet: utcancun.edu.mx
Founded 1998
State control
Language of instruction: Spanish
Divs of economics and administration, engineering and technology, gastronomy, tourism
Rector: LESLIE ANGELINA HENDRICKS RUBIO
Academic Sec.: Dra ELVA ISABEL GUTIÉRREZ CABRERA
Dir for Admin. and Finance: Ing. LANDI FUENTES BATES
Dir for External Affairs: Ing. LUIS ALBERTO GONZÁLEZ CABRERA
Dir for Univ. Extension and Student Services: Lic. ELENA MÚGICA SILVA
Sub-Dir for Planning and Evaluation: Lic. LIGIA MENDEZ CURIEL
Librarian: Lic. MARÍA E. BRAUER MENENDEZ
Library of 16,027 vols

San Luis Potosí

In San Luis Potosí, there are three federal institutes, two state institutes, two research centres and 10 private institutions.

UNIVERSIDAD AUTÓNOMA DE SAN LUIS POTOSÍ
(Autonomous University of San Luis Potosí)

Alvaro Obregón 64, Centro, 78000 San Luis Potosí, SLP
Telephone: (444) 826-1380
E-mail: rectoria@uaslp.mx
Internet: www.uaslp.mx
Founded 1826 as Instituto Cientifico y Literario
State control
Language of instruction: Spanish
Academic year: August to July
Faculties of accountancy and administration, agronomy, chemical sciences, economics, engineering, habitation, law, medicine, nursing, psychology, sciences, stomatology; schools of communication sciences, information sciences, social sciences and humanities; preparatory school in Matehuala
Rector: Arq. MANUEL FERMIN VILLAR RUBIO
Sec.-Gen.: Arq. DAVID VEGA NIÑO
Academic Sec.: LUZ MARÍA NIETO CARAVEO
Admin. Sec.: MARÍA MAGDALENA MIRANDA HERRERA
Sec. for Research and Postgraduate Affairs: Dr JORGE FERNANDO TORO VÁZQUEZ
Dir-Gen. for Libraries: Dr LUIS DEL CASTILLO MORA
Library: 3m. vols in 28 libraries
Number of teachers: 2,300
Number of students: 19,400
Publications: *Alfa y Omega* (2 a year), *Convergencia* (2 a year), *Escenario* (2 a year), *Espaciotiempo* (2 a year, in Spanish, English, French and Portuguese), *Hábitat* (1 a year), *Horizonte Administrativo* (3 a year), *La Rueda* (2 a year), *Revista del Instituto de Investigaciones Jurídicas* (2 a year), *Themis*

ACADEMIC DIRECTORS

Faculty of Accountancy and Administration: Dr CARLOS GONZÁLEZ LÓPEZ
Faculty of Agronomy: Dr JOSÉ LUIS LARA MIRELES
Faculty of Chemical Sciences: Dr FRANCISCO JAVIER MEDELLÍN RODRÍGUEZ
Faculty of Communications: ANA ISABEL MÉNDEZ ORTIZ
Faculty of Economics: Lic. JAIME HERNÁNDEZ ZAMARRÓN
Faculty of Engineering: JORGE ALBERTO PÉREZ GONZÁLEZ
Faculty of Habitat: Dr ANUAR ABRAHAM KASIS ARICEAGA
Faculty of Law: Lic. FERNANDO SÁNCHEZ LÁRRAGA
Faculty of Library Science: Dr GUADALUPE PATRICIA RAMOS FANDIÑO
Faculty of Medicine: Dr ALEJANDRO JAVIER ZERMEÑO GUERRA
Faculty of Nursing: CLAUDIA ELENA GONZÁLEZ ACEVEDO
Faculty of Psychology: Dr AGUSTÍN ZÁRATE LOYOLA
Faculty of Sciences: JORGE ALEJANDRO OCHOA CARDIEL
Faculty of Stomatology: Dr LUIS ARMANDO LEAL TOBÍAS

UNIVERSIDAD DEL CENTRO DE MÉXICO
(University of Central Mexico)

Capitán Caldera No 75, 78250 San Luis Potosi, SLP
Telephone: (444) 813-1923
E-mail: rectoria@ucem.edu.mx
Internet: www.ucem.edu.mx
Founded 1985
Private control
Academic year: August to July
Accredited by FIMPES (*q.v.*)
Publications: *Revista Alter Enfoques Criticos* (2 a year), *Revista Soy UCEM*

UNIVERSIDAD POLITÉCNICA DE SAN LUIS POTOSÍ
(Polytechnic University of San Luis Potosí)

Urbano Villalón No 500, Col. La Ladrillera, 78363 San Luis Potosí, SLP
Telephone: (444) 870-2100
E-mail: politecnica@upslp.edu.mx
Internet: www.upslp.edu.mx
Founded 2001
State control
Language of instruction: Spanish
Academic year: August to July
Rector: Dr JOSÉ ANTONIO LOYOLA ALARCÓN

UNIVERSIDAD TANGAMANGA
(Tangamanga University)

Avda Fray Diego de la Magdalena No 42, 78110 San Luis Potosi, SLP
Telephone: (444) 823-4900
E-mail: sanluis@utan.edu.mx
Internet: www.utan.edu.mx
Founded 1997
Private control
Accredited by FIMPES (*q.v.*)
Rector: Lic. GUILLERMO ARTURO CASTO PÉREZ
Publication: *Palabras Claras* (online)

Sinaloa

In Sinaloa, there are three federal institutes and 20 private institutions.

UNIVERSIDAD AUTÓNOMA DE SINALOA
(Autonomous University of Sinaloa)

Angel Flores y Riva Palacio s/n, 80000 Culiacán, SIN
Telephone: (667) 712-5441
E-mail: secgral@uas.uasnet.mx
Internet: www.uas.edu.mx
Founded 1874
State control
Languages of instruction: English, Spanish
Academic year: August to June
Rector: Dr JUAN EULOGIO GUERRA LIERA
Sec.-Gen.: JESÚS MADUEÑA MOLINA
Academic Sec.: Dr JUAN IGNACIO VELÁZQUEZ DIMAS
Admin. and Finance Sec.: MANUEL DE JESÚS LARA SALAZAR
Dir for External Affairs and Int. Relations: AMÉRICA MAGDALENA LIZÁRRAGA GONZÁLEZ
Dir-Gen. for Libraries: Ing. JOSÉ SAMUEL HIGUERA VALENZUELA
Library of 70,530 vols
Number of teachers: 4,478
Number of students: 128,077
Publication: *Buelna* (52 a year)

UNIVERSIDAD AUTÓNOMA INDÍGENA DE MÉXICO
(Autonomous Indigenous University of México)

Juárez 39, Mochicahui, 81890 El Fuerte, SIN
Telephone: (698) 892-0654
E-mail: secretariageneral@uaim.edu.mx
Internet: www.uaim.edu.mx
Founded 2001
State control
Language of instruction: Spanish
Academic campuses in Choix, Mochicahui, Los Mochis
Rector: GUADALUPE CAMARGO ORDUÑO
Sec.-Gen.: ROSA MARTÍNEZ RUIZ
Gen. Coordinator for Academic Affairs: Lic. MARIO ANTONIO FLORES FLORES
Gen. Coordinator for Admin.: MANUEL LÓPEZ ARMENTA
Gen. Coordinator for Research and Postgraduate Affairs: GUSTAVO ENRIQUE ROJO MARTÍNEZ
Librarian: ERNESTO GAXIOLA ENCINAS
Publications: *Juyyaania* (print and online, juyyaania.net), *Ra Ximhai* (3 a year, print and online, raximhai.com.mx)

UNIVERSIDAD DE OCCIDENTE
(Western University)

Avda Gabriel Leyva No 169 Sur, 81200 Los Mochis, SIN
Telephone: (668) 816-1050
Internet: www.udo.mx

Founded 1978
State control
Language of instruction: Spanish
Academic year: September to August

Campuses in Culiacan, El Fuerte, Guamuchil, Guasave, Mazatlan

Rector: GUILLERMO AARÓN SÁNCHEZ
Vice-Rector for Academic Affairs: RUBÉN FÉLIX GASTELUM
Vice-Rector for Admin. and Finance: EZEQUIEL AVILÉS OCHOA
Dir for Extension and External Affairs: MAGDA KARINA RIVERA MENDIOLA
Dir for Planning and Evaluation: SERGIO ALVARADO ALTAMIRANO
Dir for Research and Postgraduate Affairs: JOSE JAIME ZEPEDA RODRIGUEZ
Librarian: DELPHA DELLA ROCCA KING

Publications: *Ciencia Jurídica*, *Los Mochis, Un Sueño del Paraíso*

UNIVERSIDAD POLITÉCNICA DE SINALOA
(Polytechnic University of Sinaloa)

Carretera Municipal Libre Mazatlán Higueras km 3, Col. Genaro Estrada, 82199 Mazatlán, SIN
Telephone: (669) 180-0695
Internet: www.upsin.edu.mx

Founded 2005
State control
Language of instruction: Spanish

Rector: Dr LEONARDO GERMÁN GANDARILLA
Academic Sec.: JOSÉ ISIDRO OSUNA LÓPEZ
Admin. Sec.: Lic. BEATRIZ GUADALUPE ZUÑIGA VIZCARRA
Univ. Librarian: Lic. MARTHA ZAZIL LIZÁRRAGA GRAVE

Library of 6,830 vols

Sonora

In Sonora, there are six federal institutes, three state institutes, two research centres and nine private institutions.

UNIVERSIDAD DE NAVOJOA
(University of Navojoa)

Km 13 Carretera, 85800 Navojoa, SON
Telephone: (642) 423-3085
E-mail: info@unav.edu.mx
Internet: www.unav.edu.mx

Founded 1948
Private control

Rector: Prof. ORLEY SANCHEZ
Vice-Rector for Academic Affairs: MAR B. ELIZONDO SMITH
Librarian: Lic. SANDRA BALTAZAR JIMENEZ

UNIVERSIDAD DE SONORA
(University of Sonora)

Blvd Luis Encinas y Rosales s/n, Col. Centro, 83000 Hermosillo, SON
Telephone: (662) 259-2100
E-mail: rectoria@guaymas.uson.mx
Internet: www.uson.mx

Founded 1942
State control
Language of instruction: Spanish
Academic year: August to June

Academic divs of administrative sciences, accounting and agriculture, biological and health sciences, business management, economic and social sciences, engineering, exact and natural sciences, humanities and fine arts, social sciences

Rector: Dr HERIBERTO GRIJALVA MONTEVERDE
Sec.-Gen. for Academic Affairs: MARÍA MAGDALENA GONZÁLEZ AGRAMÓN
Sec.-Gen. for Admin.: MARÍA MAGDALENA GONZÁLEZ AGRAMÓN
Sec.-Gen. for Finance: MARÍA GUADALUPE SÁNCHEZ SOTO
Librarian: ADRIANA MADONIA

Library of 72,200 vols, 9,605 periodical titles, 10,386 theses, 525 cassettes, 476 CDs
Number of teachers: 1,100
Number of students: 18,000

Publications: *Biotecnia* (3 a year, print and online, www.biotecnia.uson.mx), *ConNotas* (2 a year, print and online, www.connotas.uson.mx), *Poemarios* (6 a year), *Reconstitución de Instituciones* (2 a year, print and online, www.ri.uson.mx), *Revista de Economía* (2 a year), *Revista de Física* (2 a year), *Sonora Agropecuario* (6 a year)

UNIVERSIDAD KINO
(Kino University)

Calzada Presbítero Pedro Villegas Ramirez, Final Oriente, Col. Casa Blanca, Hermosillo, SON
Telephone: (800) 822-4744
Internet: www.unikino.mx

Founded 1985
Private control

Accredited by FIMPES (*q.v.*)

Rector: Dr JOSÉ GUADALUPE RENTERIA TORRES
Dir-Gen.: JORGE ALBERTO COTA ENCINAS

UNIVERSIDAD LA SALLE NOROESTE
(La Salle University of the Northwest)

Veracruz s/n Norte, Col. Fraccionamiento Obregón Norte, 85019 Obregón, SON
Telephone: (644) 410-6000
Internet: www.ulsa-noroeste.edu.mx

Founded 1987
Private control

Accredited by FIMPES (*q.v.*)

Rector: JOSÉ RAMÓN CUBILLAS ROMERO
Academic Dir: FRANCISCO JESÚS LEYVA QUINTERO
Librarian: MARÍA LAURA FERRÉ VEGA

UNIVERSIDAD TECNOLÓGICA DE HERMOSILLO
(Technological University of Hermosillo)

Blvd de los Seris Final s/n, Parque Industrial Hermosillo, Hermosillo, SON
Telephone: (662) 251-1100
E-mail: editorial@uthermosillo.edu.mx
Internet: www.uthermosillo.edu.mx

Founded 1991
State control
Academic year: September to August

Rector: Ing. MIGUEL ÁNGEL SALAZAR CANDIA
Academic Sec.: Ing. ANTONIO QUINTAL BERNY
Dir for Admin. and Finance: JESÚS FRANCISCO VALENCIA TERÁN
Dir for Planning and Evaluation: Ing. LUIS FLORES GARCIA
Dir for Univ. Extension: CARLOS M. BONNAFOUX GÓMEZ

Publication: *Voces Universitarias*

Tabasco

In Tabasco, there are two federal institutes, five state institutes, one research centre and seven private institutions.

UNIVERSIDAD INTERCULTURAL DEL ESTADO DE TABASCO
(Intercultural University of the State of Tabasco)

Gregorio Mendez 6, Centro, 86870 Tacotalpa, TAB
Telephone: (932) 324-2221
E-mail: rectoria@uiet.edu.mx
Internet: www.uiet.edu.mx

Founded 2006
Private control

Rector: LUIS ALBERTO MÉNDEZ MAY

UNIVERSIDAD JUÁREZ AUTÓNOMA DE TABASCO
(Juárez Autonomous University of Tabasco)

Avda Universidad s/n, Zona de la Cultura, Col. Magisterial, 86040 Villahermosa, TAB
Telephone: (993) 358-1500
E-mail: rectoria@ujat.mx
Internet: www.ujat.mx

Founded 1958
State control
Language of instruction: Spanish
Academic year: September to August

Academic divs of agricultural sciences, basic sciences, biological sciences, economic and administrative sciences, education and arts, engineering and architecture, health sciences, informatics and systems, social sciences and humanities; campuses in Comalcalco and Los Ríos

Rector: JOSÉ MANUEL PIÑA GUTIÉRREZ
Sec. for Academic Services: Dra DORA MARÍA FRÍAS MÁRQUEZ
Sec. for Admin. Services: RUBICEL CRUZ ROMERO
Sec. for Finances: MARINA MORENO TEJERO
Sec. for Research, Postgraduate and External Affairs: Dr WILFRIDO MIGUEL CONTRERAS SÁNCHEZ
Dir for Libraries: ROSA VIRGINIA GÓMEZ SÁNCHEZ

Library of 174,608 vols
Number of teachers: 1,050
Number of students: 20,470

Publications: *Gaceta Juchiman*, *Perspectivas Docentes*, *Revista de la División de Ciencias Sociales y Humanidades*, *Revista Hitos de la División de Ciencias Economico-Administrativas/Centro*, *Revista Temas Biomédicos*, *Revista Zenzontle de la División de Educación y Artes*, *Universidad y Ciencias*

UNIVERSIDAD MUNDO MAYA
(Mundo Maya University)

Carretera Villahermosa-Buenavista km 4.5, Col. Miguel Hidalgo, 86126 Villahermosa, TAB
Telephone: (993) 350-3037
Internet: www.umma.com.mx
Private control

Accredited by FIMPES (*q.v.*)

UNIVERSIDAD OLMECA
(Olmeca University)

Km 14 Carretera Villahermosa-Macuspana Dos Montes, Municipio del Centro de Tabasco, 86280 Villahermosa, TAB
Telephone: (993) 187-9700
Internet: www.olmeca.edu.mx

Founded 1991
Private control

Accredited by FIMPES (*q.v.*)

Rector: Dr LÁCIDES GARCÍA DETJEN

UNIVERSIDAD POLITÉCNICA DEL GOLFO DE MÉXICO
(Polytechnic University of the Gulf of Mexico)

Carretera Federal Malpaso-El Bellote km 171, Monte Adentro, 86600 Paraíso, TAB
Telephone: (933) 333-2613
E-mail: informes@upgm.edu.mx
Internet: www.updelgolfo.edu.mx
Founded 2005
State control
Language of instruction: Spanish
Academic year: September to August
Rector: EDDY ARQUIMEDES GARCÍA ALCOCER

UNIVERSIDAD POLITÉCNICA MESOAMERICANA
(Mesoamerican Polytechnic University)

Carretera Tenosique-El Ceibo km 43.5 s/n, 86928 Tenosique, TAB
Telephone: (934) 342-4671
E-mail: rectoria@upm.edu.mx
Internet: www.upm.edu.mx
State control
Language of instruction: Spanish
Rector: JOSÉ ARMANDO PAZ MORALES
Academic Sec.: VICTOR GUILLERMO CASTRO
Sec. for Admin. and Finance: Lic. CARLOS CARAVEO ORDAZ
Librarian: ANA KRISTEL FONZ GUZMÁN

UNIVERSIDAD POPULAR DE LA CHONTALPA
(Popular University of Chontalpa)

Carretera Cárdenas-Huimanguillo km 2, 86500 Cárdenas, TAB
Telephone: (937) 372-7050
E-mail: contacto@upch.edu.mx
Internet: www.upch.edu.mx
Founded 1998
State control
Language of instruction: Spanish
Rector: JOSÉ LUIS HERNÁNDEZ LAZO
Sec. for Academic Affairs: BENJAMIN ALBERTO COCOM CANTÚ
Sec. for Admin. and Finance: ROGELIO RUIZ BASTOS
Sec. for Univ. Extension and Social Services: Dr MARTÍN ORTÍZ ORTÍZ
Publications: *Expresión Universitaria*, *Gaceta Enlace Universitaria*, *Revista Tecnociencia Universitaria*

Tamaulipas

In Tamaulipas, there are six federal institutes, one other public institution and 20 private institutions.

UNIVERSIDAD AUTÓNOMA DE TAMAULIPAS
(Autonomous University of Tamaulipas)

Matamoros 8 y 9, Col. Centro, 87000 Victoria, TAMPS
Telephone: (834) 318-1800
E-mail: prensa@uat.edu.mx
Internet: www.uat.edu.mx
Founded 1955
State control
Language of instruction: Spanish
Academic year: August to June
Faculties of commerce and business management, education and humanities. engineering and sciences, law and social sciences, music, nursing, veterinary medicine
Rector: Ing. JOSÉ MARIA LEAL GUTIÉRREZ
Sec.-Gen.: Dra OLGA HERNÁNDEZ LIMÓN
Academic Sec.: Ing. JOSÉ ANDRÉS SUÁREZ FERNÁNDEZ
Technical Sec.: Ing. JULIO GÓMEZ HERNÁNDEZ
Number of students: 36,000
Publications: *Biotam* (2 a year), *Sociotam* (2 a year)

UNIVERSIDAD DEL GOLFO
(Gulf University)

A. Obregón 203 Poniente, Zona Centro, 89000 Tampico, TAMPS
Telephone: (833) 212-9222
E-mail: publicidad@unigolfo.edu.mx
Internet: www.unigolfo.edu.mx
Founded 1971
Private control
Languages of instruction: English, German, Spanish
Academic year: September to July
Rector: Dr LEONARD TOSTEVIN
Sec.-Gen.: Lic. RAÚL MARTÍNEZ MEZA
Librarian: Lic. GERARDO JUÁREZ VALLE
Library of 25,000 vols
Number of teachers: 116
Number of students: 4,800

PROFESSORS
ACOSTA LACORTE, F., Physical Education
ACOSTA MERIDA, K.
ACOSTA TURRUBIATES, C., Psychology
AGUILAR ORTIZ, M., Engineering
AGUILLÉN BANDA, V., Nutrition
ALATORRE ZACARIAS, J.
ALVARADO ALMARAZ, S., Medicine
ALVAREZ ALARCÓN, A., Engineering
ALVAREZ TAPIA, J.
ALVIZO HERNÁNDEZ, M., Psychology
ARGUELLO RODRÍGUEZ, E., Nutrition
ARREOLA PÉREZ, M.
ARRIAGA RAMÍREZ, J.
BAUTISTA SAN JUAN, F.
BAZARTE CIBRIÁN, E., Economics
BLAS CHEE, D., Pedagogy
CABALLERO ACOSTA, J.
CABRALES PIÑEIRO, O., Psychology
CALDERAS MENDOZA, L.
CALDERÓN NICHOLS, A., Engineering
CALZADA HERNÁNDEZ, M., Psychology
CAMACHO DIAZ, A., Law
CAÑEDO OBESO, M., Systems Engineering
CANO CONTRERAS, M., English
CAÑÓN SÁNCHEZ, A., Medicine
CANTÚ CANTÚ, T., Economics
CASTELÁN CRUZ, J., Pedagogy
CASTLLO GONZÁLEZ, M.
CASTILLO LUNA, N., Law
CASTILLO PALENCIA, O.
CATALÁN DE LEÓN, A.
CHAVEZ FLORENTINO, R.
CHIMELY ALVAREZ, A.
CIBRIÁN GONZÁLEZ, N., Physical Education
CONTRERAS GONZÁLEZ, P., Psychology
COSTANTINO GUERRERO, N.
CRUZ CEBALLOS, I., Systems Engineering
CRUZ GONZÁLEZ, I., Systems Engineering
CRUZ HERNÁNDEZ, Z., Law
CRUZ POLANCO, A., Law
CUERVO CRUZ, M., Medicine
DEL ÁNGEL CISNEROS, V.
DEL ÁNGEL JERONIMO, A., Accounting
DELGADO CASTILLO, C., Medicine
DELGADO GARCÍA, M.
DEL VALLE LOMAS, J., English
DISODADO OLIVER, J., Medicine
ESCOBEDO MARTÍNEZ, V.
ESPINOZA HERNÁNDEZ, P., Nutrition
FLORENCIA ALEJANDRE, A., Law
FLORENCIA MEZA, J.
FLORES MELÉNDEZ, A.
FUENTES SAUCEDO, E., Physical Education
GALAVIZ BENITES, J., Engineering
GÁMEZ BLANCO, D., Engineering
GARCÍA MAYA, J.
GARCÍA TELLEZ, J.
GARZA BUENTELLO, J.
GARZA MAYA, M., Pedagogy
GAYTÁN HERNÁNDEZ, P.
GODÍNEZ ALLENDE, A., Psychology
GÓMEZ GUTIÉRREZ, E.
GÓMEZ SAGAOÓN, H., English
GONZÁLEZ ALONSO, H., Engineering
GONZÁLEZ ARMENTA, R.
GONZÁLEZ AZUA, A., Engineering
GONZÁLEZ GONZÁLEZ, M., Pedagogy
GONZÁLEZ SÁNCHEZ, M., Psychology
GONZÁLEZ VALDERRAMA, O.
GUERRERO NAVOR, S.
HERNÁDEZ BORREGO, O., Pedagogy
HERNÁNDEZ ARTEAGA, C., Law
HERNÁNDEZ DAVID, R.
HERNÁNDEZ GONZÁLEZ, R., English
HERNÁNDEZ HERNÁNDEZ, N.
HERNÁNDEZ MARTÍNEZ, M., Nutrition
HERNÁNDEZ NEIRA, X., Systems Engineering
HERNÁNDEZ NEIRA, M.
HERNÁNDEZ OROZCO, O., Law
HERNÁNDEZ ORTEGA, G.
HERNÁNDEZ PINEDA, X.
HERNÁNDEZ RAMÍREZ, A., Engineering
HERNÁNDEZ VÁSQUEZ, S., Economics
JASSO PÉREZ, H., English
JIMÉNEZ ALVARADO, V., Medicine
JUÁREZ FONSECA, D., Nutrition
LARA PADRÓN, F.
LEAL MARTÍNEZ, L., Medicine
LICONA MORALES, M., Law
LÓPEZ ALANÍS, J., Psychology
LOYA AVILES, T.
MALDONADO GONZÁLEZ, H., Engineering
MÁRQUEZ MARTÍNEZ, M.
MARTÍNEZ DIAZ, B.
MARTINEZ GONZÁLEZ, F.
MARTÍNEZ INFANTE, C.
MARTÍNEZ PONCE, E.
MAR ZUMAYA, E.
MEDINA REYES, A., Nutrition
MELLADO LÁZARO, L., Medicine
MENDOZA VÁZQUEZ, I.
MONTELONGO BRIONES, J.
MONTEMAYOR RODRÍGUEZ, Y., Pedagogy
MORENO ALFARO, G.
MORENO LÓPEZ, Y.
MORENO RIVERA, O.
NORIEGA DOÍNGUEZ, G.
ORTEGA GUZMÁN, V.
PADILLA GONZÁLEZ, N.
PADRÓN MELÉNDEZ, J.
PADRÓN SAN MARTÍN, J., Psychology
PALENCIA CRUZ, G.
PEÑA MALDONADO, R.
PÉREZ PALACIOS, R., Economics
PÉREZ RIVERA, B.
POU AGUILAR, A.
QUEVEDO HERNÁNDEZ, R.
QUINTANILLA GONZALEZ, J.
QUINTERO MALDONADO, R., Engineering
RAMÍREZ SEGURA, N., Mathematics
RENAS BAUTISTA, J.
RODRÍGUEZ GUTIÉRREZ, R., Engineering
ROSALES HERNÁNDEZ, I.
RUELAS FRAIRE, R.
SAAVEDRA CASTILLO, M.
SALDAÑA AMARO, F., Engineering
SÁNCHEZ GONZÁLEZ, G., Medicine
SÁNCHEZ RUIZ, N., Pedagogy
SANDOVAL SÁNCHEZ, J., Systems Engineering
SILVA MATOVICHE, A., Pedagogy
SILVA MAYA, D., Psychology
SOTO SANTILLANA, F., Law
TIJERINA BERMÚDEZ, J., Law
TOLEDANO DÁVILA, A.
TORRES JAUREGUI, G., Economics
TORRES VÉLEZ, O., Systems Engineering
TREJO MARTÍNEZ, E.
VALDIVIESO LÓPEZ, H.
VALENCIA ESTRELLA, S., Law
VÁZQUEZ URTIZ, I.
VÁZQUEZ URTIZ, J.
VERA REYNAGA, J.

VILLALÓN MARTÍNEZ DEL CAMPO, S., Systems Engineering
ZAMORA CRUZ, N., Nutrition
ZAPOTE TORIBIO, J.

UNIVERSIDAD DEL NORESTE
(Northeastern University)

Prolongación Avda Hidalgo No 6315, Col. Nuevo Aeropuerto, 89337 Tampico, TAMPS
Telephone: (833) 230-3830
E-mail: informes@une.edu.mx
Internet: www.une.edu.mx
Founded 1970
Private control
4 Programmes accredited by COPAES (*q.v.*)
Rector: FERNANDO R. CHUNG HERNANDEZ
Publications: *Revista de Medicina de la UNE*, *Revistas Digitales*, *Revista 'New England Journal of Medicine'*

UNIVERSIDAD LA SALLE VICTORIA
(La Salle University of Victoria)

Avda 5 de Mayo No 3506, Fraccionamiento Ampliación Villarreal, 87027 Ciudad Victoria, TAMPS
Telephone: (834) 314-6956
E-mail: webmaster@ulsavictoria.edu.mx
Internet: www.ulsavictoria.edu.mx
Founded 1999
Private control
Accredited by FIMPES (*q.v.*)
Rector: Dr MIGUEL ÁNGEL VALDEZ GARCÍA
Dir for Academic Affairs: FERNANDO ARRIAGA MARTÍNEZ
Dir for Admin.: MANUEL DE JESÚS PADILLA MUÑOZ

UNIVERSIDAD MÉXICO AMERICANA DEL NORTE
(Mexico University of North America)

Calle Primera s/n, Col. Círculo, 88640 Reynosa, TAMPS
Telephone: (899) 922-2002
Internet: www.uman.edu.mx
Founded 1983
Private control
Accredited by FIMPES (*q.v.*)
Rector: Dra EDITH CANTÚ DE MORETT
Sec.-Gen.: FRANCISCO ARMANDO NORATO LARA
Academic Sec.: ADRIÁN RAMOS BARRÓN

UNIVERSIDAD POLITÉCNICA DE ALTAMIRA
(Polytechnic University of Altamira)

Carretera Tampico-Mante, Entronque con Libramiento Corredor Industrial km 1.5, Altamira, TAMPS
Telephone: (833) 304-0474
Internet: www.upalt.edu.mx
Founded 2008
State control
Language of instruction: Spanish
Academic year: September to August
Rector: OSCAR JAVIER ALONSO BANDA

UNIVERSIDAD POLITÉCNICA DE VICTORIA
(Polytechnic University of Victoria)

Avda Nuevas Tecnologías 5902, Parque Científico y Tecnológico de Tamaulipas Carretera Victoria-Soto la Marina km 5.5, 87138 Ciudad Victoria, TAMPS
Telephone: (834) 171-1100
Internet: www.upvictoria.edu.mx
State control
Language of instruction: Spanish
Rector: SONIA MARICELA SÁNCHEZ MORENO

UNIVERSIDAD TECNOLÓGICA DE ALTAMIRA
(Technological University of Altamira)

Blvd de los Ríos km 3.100, Puerto Industrial Altamira, 89608 Altamira, TAMPS
Telephone: (833) 260-0252
E-mail: uta@utaltamira.edu.mx
Internet: www.utaltamira.edu.mx
Founded 2002
State control
Language of instruction: Spanish

Tlaxcala

In Tlaxcala, there are two federal institutes and six private institutions.

UNIVERSIDAD AUTÓNOMA DE TLAXCALA
(Autonomous University of Tlaxcala)

Avda Universidad 1, 90000 Tlaxcala, TLAX
Telephone: (246) 462-1167
E-mail: rectoria@cci.uatx.mx
Internet: www.uatx.mx
Founded 1976
State control
Language of instruction: Spanish
Academic year: July to June
Depts of biomedical sciences, education, humanities, social sciences; research centres of animal physiology and behaviour, animal reproduction, biological sciences and biotechnology, genetics and environment, regional development
Rector: RENÉ GRADA YAUTENTZI
Admin. Dir: DOROTEO NAVA
Librarian: OSVALDO RAMÍREZ ORTIZ
Number of teachers: 700
Number of students: 10,000

UNIVERSIDAD DEL ALTIPLANO
(University of Altiplano)

Eucaliptos No 1, Col. El Sabinal, Tlaxcala, TLAX
Telephone: (246) 462-1458
E-mail: informes@universidaddelaltiplano.com
Internet: www.universidaddelaltiplano.com
Founded 1991
Private control
Academic year: August to July
Language of instruction: Spanish
Rector: Lic. SUSANA FERNANDEZ ORDOÑEZ
Vice-Rector: PATRICIA FERNÁNDEZ ORDÓÑEZ
Dir-Gen. for Admin.: HÉCTOR CISNEROS VÁZQUEZ

UNIVERSIDAD DEL VALLE DE TLAXCALA
(University of Valley of Tlaxcala)

Avda Universidad s/n San Andrés Ahuashuatepec, Tzompantepec, 90491 Tlaxcala, TLAX
Telephone: (241) 417-7377
E-mail: rectoria@univalletlax.edu.mx
Internet: www.univalletlax.edu.mx
Founded 1993
Private control
Academic year: August to July
Rector: MIGUEL MÉNDEZ GARCÍA SALAZAR
Dir-Gen. for Academic Affairs: Lic. GUSTAVO CARPINTERO VEGA

UNIVERSIDAD POLITÉCNICA DE TLAXCALA
(Polytechnic University of Tlaxcala)

Avda Universidad Politécnica No 1, Col. San Pedro Xalcaltzinco, 90180 Tepeyanco, TLAX
Telephone: (246) 465-1300
E-mail: upt@uptlax.edu.mx
Internet: www.uptlax.edu.mx
Founded 2004
State control
Language of instruction: Spanish
Rector: NARCISO XICOHTÉNCATL ROJAS
Academic Sec.: LUIS ÁLVAREZ OCHOA
Admin. Sec.: IMELDA SILVA SAMPEDRO
Dir for External Affairs: RICARDO SÁNCHEZ ESQUIVEL
Dir for Planning: LUIS BAÑUELOS FLORES
Dir for Research and Postgraduate Affairs: HULUE MIRIAM GARCÍA IGNACIO
Librarian: MARÍA DEL R. OREA GALICIA

Veracruz

In Veracruz, there are eight federal institutes, 13 state institutes, one research centre and 68 private institutions.

UNIVERSIDAD CRISTOBAL COLON
(Christopher Columbus University)

Universidad Cristóbal Colón, Veracruz
Telephone: (229) 923-2967
E-mail: informes@aix.ver.ucc.mx
Internet: www.ver.ucc.mx
Founded 1944
Private control
Rector: P. JUAN JAIME ESCOBAR VALENCIA
Vice-Rector for Academics: Dr ALICIA GARCIA DIAZ MIRON
Vice-Rector for Admin and Finance: FÉLIX ÁVILA GRAJALES
Vice-Rector for Logistics and Resources: MIGUEL UBIETA COBOS
Vice-Rector for Strategic Devt: Dr OSMAR ARANDIA PÉREZ

UNIVERSIDAD DE SOTAVENTO—VERACRUZ
(University of Sotavento)

Emiliano Zapata 175, El Espinal, Espinal, 94310 Orizaba, Veracruz-Llave
Telephone: (272) 726-3774
E-mail: informes@us.edu.mx
Internet: us.edu.mx
Founded 1994
Private control
1 Programme accredited by COPAES (*q.v.*)
Rector: Dr JUAN MANUEL RODRÍGUEZ GARCÍA
Dir of Academics: EDGAR ERNESTO PAXTIÁN ORTIZ
Dir of University Extension: JUAN MANUEL RODRÍGUEZ CAAMAÑO
Dir of Postgraduation and Research: Dra ROSA AURORA RODRÍGUEZ CAAMAÑO
Dir of Admin: ZOILA AMALIA VAUGHAN FERNÁNDEZ

UNIVERSIDAD PACCIOLI DE CÓRDOBA
(Paccioli University of Córdoba)

Avda 7203, Córdoba Centro, 94500 Córdoba, Veracruz-Llave
Telephone: (271) 712-1736
E-mail: paccioli@universidadpaccioli.edu.mx
Internet: www.universidadpaccioli.edu.mx
Founded 1990
Private control
3 Programmes accredited by COPAES (*q.v.*)

UNIVERSIDAD VERACRUZANA
(University of Veracruz)

Calle Veracruz No 46 Departmento 5, Fraccionamiento Pomona, 91040 Xalapa,
Telephone: (228) 841-5920
E-mail: accesoinformacion@uv.mx
Internet: www.uv.mx
Founded 1944
State control
Language of instruction: Spanish
Academic year: September to August
Rector: Dra SARA DEIFILIA LADRÓN DE GUEVARA GONZÁLEZ
Vice-Rector for Coatzacoalcos-Minatitlán Campus: Dr JORGE ALBERTO ANDAVERDE ARREDONDO
Vice-Rector for Orizaba-Córdoba Campus: Dra BEATRIZ EUGENIA RODRÍGUEZ VILLAFUERTE
Vice-Rector for Poza Rica-Tuxpan Campus: Dr JOSÉ LUIS ALANÍS MÉNDEZ
Vice-Rector for Veracruz Campus: ALFONSO GERARDO PÉREZ MORALES
Academic Sec.: LETICIA RODRÍGUEZ AUDIRAC
Sec. for Admin. and Finance: CLEMENTINA GUERRERO GARCÍA
Dir for Institutional Planning: LAURA ELENA MARTÍNEZ MÁRQUEZ
Dir-Gen. for Libraries: Dra DIANA EUGENIA GONZÁLEZ ORTEGA
Library of 476,070 vols
Number of teachers: 5,724
Number of students: 74,804
Publications: *La Ciencia y el Hombre*, *La Palabra y el Hombre*

UNIVERSIDAD VILLA RICA
(Villa Rica University)

Progreso Esq. Urano, Boca del Río, Veracruz 94299
Telephone: (229) 921-2001
E-mail: contacto@univillarica.mx
Internet: www.univillarica.mx
Founded 1972
Private control
Rector: Dr JAVIER CANTALPIEDRA MALPICA
Dir-Gen. for Academics: ROSA MATEU MORANDO
Dir for Graduate Studies: ARTURO CANTORS OREZA
Dir for Student Services: ANDRES ALBERTO VELA BACA

Yucatán

In Yucatán, there are four federal institutes, four state institutes, five research centres and 30 private institutions.

UNIVERSIDAD ANÁHUAC MAYAB
(Anáhuac Mayab University)

Carretera Mérida Progreso km 15.5, Cordemex, 97310 Mérida, YUC
Telephone: (999) 942-4800
E-mail: rectoria.anahuacmayab@anahuac.mx
Internet: www.anahuacmayab.mx
Founded 1984
Private control
16 Programmes accredited by COPAES (*q. v.*)
Rector: P. RAFAEL PARDO HERVÁS
Vice-Rector for Academics: Dr NARCISO A. ACUÑA GONZÁLEZ
Vice-Rector for Admin. and Finance: Ing. ALEJANDRO LARA TORRE
Vice-Rector for Integral Formation: Lic. SALVADOR CARRILLO CEPEDA

UNIVERSIDAD AUTÓNOMA DE YUCATÁN
(Autonomous University of Yucatán)

Calle 60 No 491-A por 57, Centro Histórico, 97000 Mérida, YUC
Telephone: (999) 930-0900
E-mail: uadyglobal@uady.mx
Internet: www.uady.mx
Founded 1922
State control
Language of instruction: Spanish
Academic year: September to July
Rector: ALFREDO JAVIER DÁJER ABIMERHI
Coordinator for Cooperation and Internationalization: ANDREAS GIAN ALUJA SCHUNEMANN
Coordinator for Institutional Planning and Devt: JUAN DE DIOS PÉREZ ALAYON
Dir-Gen. for Academic Devt: Dr JOSÉ DE JESÚS WILLIAMS
Dir-Gen. for Admin. and Personnel Devt: MANUEL ESCOFFIÉ AGUILAR
Sec.-Gen.: JOSÉ ANTONIO GONZÁLEZ FAJARDO
Librarian: J. ALBERTO ARELLANO RODRÍGUEZ
Library: 20 libraries with 242,575 vols, 5,318 periodical titles, 26,686 theses, 7,518 documents and folios, 739 maps
Number of teachers: 1,158 (775 full-time)
Number of students: 14,637
Publications: *Ingeniería: Revista Académica* (3 a year, www.revista.ingenieria.uady.mx), *Quimica'al* (2 a year, www.revista.quimica.uady.mx), *Revista Biomédica* (3 a year, www.revbiomed.uady.mx), *Revista de Economía* (2 a year, print and online, www.revista.economia.uady.mx), *Tropical and Subtropical Agroecosystems* (3 a year, in Spanish and English, print and online, www.veterinaria.uady.mx/ojs/index.php/TSA)

UNIVERSIDAD MARISTA DE MÉRIDA
(Marist University of Mérida)

Periférico Norte Tablaje Catastral 13941, 97300 Mérida, YUC
Telephone: (999) 942-9700
Internet: www.marista.edu.mx
Founded 1996
Private control
Accredited by FIMPES (*q.v.*)
Rector: MIGUEL BAQUEDANO PÉREZ
Publication: *Palabra Marista*

UNIVERSIDAD MODELO
(Model University)

Carretera antigua a Cholul, 200 m del periferico, Merida, YUC
Telephone: (999) 930-1900
E-mail: unimo@modelo.edu.mx
Internet: www.unimodelo.edu.mx
Founded 1910
Private control
1 Programme accredited by COPAES (*q.v.*); schools of architecture, business, design, engineering, health, humanities and law
Rector: Ing. CARLOS SAURI DUCH

Zacatecas

In Zacatecas, there is one federal institute, five state institutes and five private institutions.

UNIVERSIDAD AUTÓNOMA DE ZACATECAS
(Autonomous University of Zacatecas)

Jardin Juárez 147, Centro Histórico, 98000 Zacatecas, ZAC
Telephone: (492) 922-9109
E-mail: sii@uaz.edu.mx
Internet: www.uaz.edu.mx
Founded 1832
State control
Language of instruction: Spanish
Rector: FRANCISCO FLORES SANDOVAL
Sec.-Gen.: DELFINO GARCÍA HERNÁNDEZ
Academic Sec.: FRANCISCO VALERIO QUINTERO
Admin. Sec.: SALVADOR SANTILLÁN HERNÁNDEZ
Librarian: JUAN IGNACIO PIÑA MARQUINA
Library of 35,265 vols
Number of teachers: 1,100
Number of students: 14,800
Publications: *Azogue*, *Cuadernos de Investigación*, *Diálogo*, *Gaceta Universitaria*

DIRECTORS

School of Accounting and Administration: JESÚS LIMONES HERNÁNDEZ
School of Agronomy: Ing. PEDRO ZESATI DEL VILLAR
School of Animal Breeding and Veterinary Medicine: ANTONIO MEJÍA HARO
School of Chemistry: JUANA MARÍA VALADEZ CASTREJÓN
School of Dentistry: Dr RAÚL BERMEO PADILLA
School of Economics: Lic. RODOLFO GARCÍA ZAMORA
School of Education: SERGIO ESPINOSA PROA
School of Engineering: Ing. JUAN FRANCISCO ROCHÍN SALINAS
School of Humanities: Lic. VEREMUNDO CARRILLO TRUJILLO
School of Law: Lic. VIRGILIO RIVERA DELGADILLO
School of Mathematics: Lic. JUAN ANTONIO PÉREZ
School of Medicine: Dr GERARDO DE JESÚS FÉLIX DOMÍNGUEZ
School of Mines and Metallurgy: Ing. RUBEN DE JESÚS DEL POZO MENDOZA
School of Music: Lic. ESAUL ARTEAGA DOMÍNGUEZ
School of Nursing: MA ISABEL MEDINA HERNÁNDEZ
School of Physics: Lic. HUMBERTO VIDALES ROQUE
School of Psychology: Lic. RICARDO BERMEO PADILLA
School of Social Sciences: PEDRO GÓMEZ SÁNCHEZ

UNIVERSIDAD POLITÉCNICA DE ZACATECAS
(Polytechnic University of Zacatecas)

Plan del Pardillo s/n, Parque Industrial, Fresnillo, ZAC
Telephone: (493) 935-7106
E-mail: demsys@zac.sep.gob.mx
Internet: www.upz.edu.mx
Founded 2002
State control
Language of instruction: Spanish
Academic year: September to August
Rector: HÉCTOR ARTEMIO ROMO MORENO
Admin. Sec.: HILDA CÓRDOVA CASTILLO
Dir for Planning: MARÍA DEL CARMEN SALINAS FLORES

FEDERATED STATES OF MICRONESIA

The Higher Education System

The Federated States of Micronesia comprise the four named and autonomous states, namely Chuuk, Pohnpei, Yap and Kosrae. It is a small, developing nation made up of 87 islands and islets spread over four major island groups in 2.5m. sq. km of the Western Pacific. Its citizens speak 17 different languages and dialects. The College of Micronesia—FSM, which was founded in 1963 as the Micronesian Teacher Education Centre, offers two-year Associate degree courses as well as a number of short-term certificate programmes. The College has a state campus in each of the four states, with its national campus in the capital Palikir, Pohnpei. The College is administered by a Board of Regents and is accredited by the Accrediting Commission for Community and Junior Colleges of the Western Association of Schools and Colleges. Financial aid is provided to students at the College (in the form of grants or loans) by federal, state and institutional sources. In 2009/10 there were 2,360 students enrolled at the College. The Micronesia Fisheries and Maritime Institute, based on the island of Yap, is also part of the College and provides education and training in fisheries technology at secondary and tertiary levels. There is also an International Vocational Education Centre in Pohnpei, which was established in 2010. The Department of Education is the government ministry responsible for overseeing the education sector. Education is governed by Act PL 7-97, which was approved by Congress in 1992.

Regulatory Body

GOVERNMENT

Department of Education: POB PS-87, Palikir, Pohnpei 96941; tel. 320-2609; internet www.fsmed.fm; Sec. RUFINO MAURICIO.

Yap State Department of Education: POB 220, Colonia, Yap 96943; tel. 350-2151; e-mail doe@yapstategov.org; Dir VINCENT PARREN.

Learned Societies

GENERAL

Kosrae Island Resource Management Authority: POB DRC, Tofol, Kosrae 96944; tel. 370-2076; internet www.kosraecoast.com/aboutus.htm; f. 1992 as Devt Review Comm.; encourages sustainable economic and social devt; Dir ROBERT JACKSON.

NATURAL SCIENCES

Biological Sciences

Chuuk Conservation Society: Chuuk; f. 2005; protects and preserves local natural resources in order to sustain community livelihoods; Chair JOE KONNO; Sec. MARY ROSE NAKAYAMA.

Conservation Society of Pohnpei: POB 2461, Kolonia, Pohnpei 96941; tel. 320-5409; e-mail csp@mail.fm; internet www.serehd.org; f. 1998; aims to increase community involvement in the conservation and management of Pohnpei's natural resources; build local capacity through public and private partnerships; develop alternatives to unsustainable practices and promote laws and policies that support these objectives; current programmes: marine, terrestrial and educational awareness; Exec. Dir PATTERSON SHED.

Kosrae Conservation and Safety Organization: POB 1007, Tofol, Kosrae 96944; tel. 370-3673; e-mail info@kosraeconservation.org; internet www.kosraeconservation.org; protects marine biodiversity and ecosystems of Kosrae; Chair. MADISON NENA; Exec. Dir ANDY GEORGE; Sec. SONIA KEPHAS.

Micronesia Conservation Trust: POB 2177, Kolonia, Pohnpei 96941; tel. 320-5670; e-mail info@ourmicronesia.org; internet mctconservation.org; f. 2002; provides long-term, sustained funding to community-based orgs and other NGOs through grants programme; supports biodiversity conservation and related sustainable devt; Exec. Dir WILLIAM KOSTKA; Deputy Exec. Dir LISA RANAHAN ANDON.

Research Institutes

NATURAL SCIENCES

Biological Sciences

Yap Institute of Natural Science: POB 215, Colonia, Yap 96943; tel. 350-4630; e-mail mfalanruw@mail.fm; researches on sustainable devt, natural history and adaptive technology in Yap; focuses on fruit bat surveys, fishery studies and mariculture feasibility reports; Dir Dr MARJORIE C. FALANRUW.

Libraries and Archives

Kolonia

College of Micronesia Learning Resources Center: POB 159, Kolonia, Pohnpei 96941; tel. 320-2480; e-mail comfsmlib@comfsm.fm; internet www.comfsm.fm/?q=lrc; comprises an academic and research library, serials section, US Govt documents library; Micronesia-Pacific Research Center; depository for the Secretariat of the Pacific Community materials and a partial depository for UN documents; Nat. Archives contains materials from the Navy and Trust Territory eras; 67,071 vols; Dir JENNIFER HAINRICK.

Pohnpei Public Library: POB 284, Kolonia, Pohnpei 96941; tel. 320-2423; e-mail ppl@mail.fm; f. 1987; 1 mobile library; 30,000 vols; Head Librarian LESTER EZEKIAS.

Palikir

Congress Library: POB PS3, Palikir, Pohnpei 96941; tel. 320-2324; e-mail liwi@mail.fm; f. 1978; library of the legislative br. of nat. Govt; 15,000 vols, 30 periodicals; Librarian MARIETA J. PAIDEN.

Museums and Art Galleries

Kolonia

Lidorkini Museum: Kolonia, Pohnpei 96941; tel. 320-5299; artefacts from the Nan Madol site, pounding stones, handicrafts, items from the Japanese occupation of the islands (1914–44); Curator HENTER LAWRENCE.

Tofol

Kosrae State Museum: Tofol, Kosrae; artefacts, photographs of Kosrae history and culture.

College

College of Micronesia—FSM: National Campus, POB 159, Kolonia, Pohnpei 96941; tel. 320-2480; e-mail national@comfsm.fm; internet www.comfsm.fm; f. 1963 as Micronesian Teacher Education Center, present name 1975; campuses: Chuuk, Kosrae, Pohnpei and Yap; incl. Fisheries and Maritime Institute; library: see under Libraries and Archives; 2,360 students (incl. all campuses); Pres. JOSEPH M. DAISY; Vice-Pres. for Admin. Services JOE HABUCHMAI; Vice-Pres. for Cooperative Research and Extension W. JAMES CURRIE; Vice-Pres. for Student Services RINGLEN P. RINGLEN; Dir of Admissions JOEY ODUCADO.

MOLDOVA

The Higher Education System

The oldest institution of higher education is the Academia de Mizică, Teatru şi Arte Plastice (Academy of Music, Theatre and Fine Arts—founded 1919), which was established when the former Russian territory of Bessarabia was part of Romania. Other institutions dating from the period of Romanian control include Universitatea Agrară de Stat din Moldova (Moldovan State Agrarian University—founded 1933) and Universitatea Pedagogică de Stat 'Ion Creangă' (Ion Creangă Pedagogical State University—founded 1940). However, the USSR refused to recognize Romania's claims to the territory, and in October 1924 formed a Moldovan Autonomous Soviet Socialist Republic (ASSR) on the eastern side of the Dniester, in the Ukrainian Soviet Socialist Republic (SSR). The current institution of Universitatea de Stat din Tiraspol (Tiraspol State University), was founded in the Moldovan ASSR in 1930 (it was re-located to the capital Chişinău in 1992). In June 1940 Romania was forced to cede Bessarabia and northern Bucovina to the USSR, under the terms of the Treaty of Non-Aggression (the 'Molotov-Ribbentrop Pact'), concluded with Nazi Germany in August 1939. Northern Bucovina, southern Bessarabia and the Kotovsk-Balţa region of the Moldovan ASSR were incorporated into the Ukrainian SSR. The remaining parts of the Moldovan ASSR and of Bessarabia were merged to form the Moldovan SSR, which formally joined the USSR on 2 August 1940 and remained under Soviet rule until independence was declared in 1991. Following independence the self-styled 'Transnistrian Moldovan Republic' (formerly 'Transnistrian Moldovan SSR') was declared on the eastern side of the Dniester. The Law on Education of 1995 classified higher education as either long-term study programmes offered by universities, academies, and institutes or short-term study programmes offered by vocational colleges. In 2000 Moldova adopted the European Credit Transfer and Accumulation System (ECTS) in public universities and from 2005 the ECTS was introduced in all higher education institutions. Moldova has been a full member of the Bologna Process since 2005 and has adopted the three-tier Licence/Masters/Doctorate (LMD) degree system as well as drawing up a National Framework of Qualifications for Professional Formation. In 2010/11 there were 107,813 students enrolled in the country's 33 universities and 32,164 in the 48 colleges of higher education. In 2011/12 a total of 128,988 students were enrolled in both public and private tertiary education. Responsibility for higher education rests with the Ministry of Education, although a number of ministries also supervise specialized higher education institutions, for example the Ministry of Health oversees the State University of Medicine and the Ministry of Agriculture and the Food Industry oversees the Agrarian State University. In recent years the number of private institutions has been growing. Private higher education institutions are authorized by the Licensing Chamber, a central public authority that coordinates with the Ministry of Education.

Admission to higher education is determined by fixed quotas (numerus clausus/numerus fixus) drawn up by the Government. Consequently, students are usually required to sit a competitive entrance examination as well as holding the Diplomă de Bacalaureat, the main secondary school-leavers' certificate. Undergraduate degrees are divided into short- and long-term programmes of study. The Diploma of Short-Term Higher Education (Diplomă de Studii Superioare de Scurtă Durată) is the primary programme of short-term study and lasts two to three years. These are the only kinds of degrees offered by vocational colleges. The Diplomă de Licentă is a long-term programme of study lasting three to four years (180–240 ECTS credits); a number of professional courses (such as medicine and engineering) take four to five years to complete. The first postgraduate-level degree is the Diplomă de Magistru, awarded upon completion of one to two years of research (60–120 ECTS credits) following the Diplomă de Licentă. There are two doctoral degrees, Doctor of Sciences (Doctor în Stiinte) and Doctor Abilitat. The Doctor în Stiinte is awarded after three years of research and successful defence of a thesis. Doctor Abilitat is a post-doctoral scientific degree, awarded after two years following the Doctor în Stiinte.

Post-secondary technical and vocational education is available mainly through colleges and is regarded as short-term higher education. In 2009/10 there were 47 post-secondary colleges with a total enrolment of 32,249 students.

The National Council for Accreditation and Attestation (Consiliul Naţional pentru Acreditare şi Atestare) is the body responsible for the accreditation of institutions in the field of science and the attestation of scientific and scientific-pedagogical personnel of higher qualification. It gives out certificates of accreditation on the basis of which scientific institutes are financed from the state budget. It also approves the programmes of examinations for doctoral students and competitors, confers the scientific degrees, scientific and scientific-pedagogical ranks and gives out the diplomas of scientific degrees and certificates of scientific and scientific-pedagogical ranks.

Regulatory and Representative Bodies

GOVERNMENT

Ministry of Culture: 2033 Chişinău, Piaţa Marii Adunări Naţionale 1; tel. (22) 22-76-20; e-mail mc@mc.gov.md; internet www.mc.gov.md; Minister MONICA BABUC.

Ministry of Education: 2033 Chişinău, Piaţa Marii Adunări Naţionale 1; tel. (22) 23-33-48; e-mail viceministra@edu.md; internet www.edu.md; Minister MAIA SANDU.

ACCREDITATION

Consiliul Naţional pentru Acreditare şi Atestare (CNAA) (National Council for Accreditation and Attestation): 2004 Chişinău, Ştefan cel Mare bd 180; tel. (22) 29-62-71; e-mail cnaa@cnaa.md; internet www.cnaa.md; f. 2004; 17 mems; Pres. Acad. Dr hab. VALERIU CANTER; Vice-Pres. Acad. Dr hab. SIMION TOMA; Vice-Pres. Acad. Dr hab. VEACESLAV PERJU; Scientific Sec. Dr GHEORGHE GLADCHI.

Department of Higher Education Institution Accreditation: 2033 Chişinău, Piaţa Marii Adunări Naţionale 1; tel. (22) 21-03-79; e-mail mrotaru@inbox.ru; Dir MICHAEL EFIMOVICH ROTARU.

ENIC/NARIC Moldova: 2033 Chişinău, Information and Qualification Recognition Office, Min. of Education, Piaţa Marii Adunări Naţionale 1; tel. (22) 27-75-69; e-mail recognition@edu.md; internet www.edu.md; f. 2004; Head RODICA ISAC.

Learned Societies

GENERAL

Academy of Sciences of Moldova: 2001 Chişinău, 1 Ştefan cel Mare şi Sfînt Ave; tel. (22) 27-14-78; e-mail consiliu@asm.md; internet www.asm.md; f. 1946; scientific adviser to public authorities of the Republic of Moldova; attached research institutes: see under Research Institutes; 97 mems; library: see under Libraries and Archives; Pres. GHEORGHE DUCA; Scientific Sec.-Gen. AURELIA HANGANU; publs *Computer Science Journal of Moldova* (4 a year), *Economy and Sociology* (4 a year), *Elektronnaya Obrabotka Materialov* (6 a year), *Moldavian Journal of Physical Sciences* (4 a year), *Revistă de Filozofie şi Drept* (6 a year), *Revistă de Istorie a Moldovei* (4 a year), *Revistă de Lingvistică şi Ştiinţă Literară* (6 a year).

HISTORY, GEOGRAPHY AND ARCHAEOLOGY

Geographical Society of Moldova: 2028 Chişinău, str. Academiei 1; tel. (22) 73-96-18; e-mail geography_md@yahoo.com; Head of Laboratory Dr NICOLAE BOBOC.

LANGUAGE AND LITERATURE

Alliance Française: 2012 Chişinău, str. Sfatul Tarii 18; tel. (22) 23-45-10; e-mail alfr@alfr.md; internet www.alfr.md; f. 1993; offers courses and exams in French language and culture and promotes cultural exchange with France and French-speaking countries; has a media library; Dir EMMANUEL SKOULIOS; Deputy Dir ADRIAN CIBOTARU.

Goethe-Institut: see entry in Romania chapter.

PEN Centre of Moldova: 2012 Chişinău, bd. Ştefan cel Mare şi Sfînt 134, PO 12, POB 231; tel. (22) 23-24-79; e-mail contrafort@moldnet.md; f. 1991; 25 mems; Pres. VITALIE CIOBANU.

NATURAL SCIENCES

Biological Sciences

Entomological Society of Moldova: 2028 Chişinău, str. Academiei 1; tel. (22) 73-98-96; Chair B. V. VEREŞCIAGHIN.

Microbiological Society of Moldova: 2028 Chişinău, str. Academiei 1; tel. (22) 73-98-78; e-mail acadrudic@yahoo.com; Chair. Prof. VALERY RUDIC.

Ornithological Society of Moldova: 2028 Chişinău, str. Academiei 1; tel. (22) 73-75-09; Chair. (vacant).

Society of Botanists of Moldova: 2002 Chişinău, str. Pădurii 18; tel. (22) 52-38-96; Chair. A. G. NEGRU.

Society of Geneticists of Moldova: 2049 Chişinău, str. Mirceşti 44; tel. (22) 43-23-08; Chair. V. D. SIMINEL.

Society of Hydrobiologists and Ichthyologists: 2028 Chişinău, str. Academiei 1; tel. (22) 57-75-30; e-mail izoolasm@mail.md; f. 1968; 36 mems; Chair. Prof. ION TODERAŞ.

Society of Plant Physiology and Biochemistry of Moldova: 2002 Chişinău, str. Pădurii 26/1; tel. (22) 56-79-59; e-mail sbiochim@bio.asm.md; f. 1988; 40 mems; Pres. Prof. SIMION I. TOMA.

Teriological Society of Moldova: 2028 Chişinău, str. Academiei 1 (Room 220); tel. (22) 72-55-66; e-mail amunteanu@as.md; 19 mems; Chair. Dr ANDREI MUNTEANU.

Physical Sciences

Physical Society of Moldova: 2928 Chişinău, str. Academiei 5; tel. (22) 73-90-60; e-mail kantser@lises.asm.md; Chair. Acad. Prof. VALERIU KANTSER.

RELIGION, SOCIOLOGY AND ANTHROPOLOGY

Moldovan Sociological Association: 3121 Bălţi, str. Puşkin 38; tel. (231) 2-44-79; Chair. N. V. ŢURCANU.

Research Institutes

AGRICULTURE, FISHERIES AND VETERINARY SCIENCE

Crop Science Institute 'Porumbeni': 4834 Criuleni, R. Paşcani; tel. (22) 24-55-71; e-mail ifporumbeni@rambler.ru; internet www.porumbeni.md; f. 1973; research into breeding, seed production and cultivation of maize, sorghum and tobacco; improvement of seed strains; Dir Dr VASILE POJOGA.

National Institute for Viticulture and Vinification: 2070 Chişinău, s. Codru, str. Vierul 59; tel. (22) 28-54-31; e-mail invv@agriculture.md; internet www.agriculture.md/ispha; f. 1909; prepares nat. strategies for the devt of viticulture; creates new types of grapes, resistant to diseases and frost; elaboration of modern technologies for producing cuttings without viruses; devt of storage methods and use of grapes with nutritive and therapeutic purposes; creation of new wines, champagnes and liqueurs; design and sale of machines and equipment for viticulture.

Scientific and Practical Institute of Biotechnologies in Animal Husbandry and Veterinary Medicine: 6525 Anenii Noii, v. Maximovca; tel. (22) 35-93-50; e-mail shumanskii@mail.ru; f. 1958; devt of scientific base and preservation of genetic fund of agricultural animals; devt of technologies of breeding, reproduction and exploitation of animals; production and storage of animal feeds; prevention and treatment of animal diseases; library of 19,000 vols; Dir Dr Hab. ANDREI SHUMANSKII; publ. *Scientific Transactions* (1 a year).

Tobacco Research Institute: Chişinău, s. Gratieşti, str. Prieteniei 1; tel. (22) 46-06-86; e-mail tutunix@agriculture.md; internet www.agriculture.md/tutun; f. 1968; Dir Dr TUDOR ZAGORNEANU.

ECONOMICS, LAW AND POLITICS

Centre for the Study of Marketing Problems: 2001 Chişinău, bd. Ştefan cel Mare şi Sfînt; tel. (22) 26-23-91; attached to Acad. of Sciences of Moldova; Dir P. V. COJUCARI.

National Institute for Economic Research: 2064 Chişinău, Ion Creangă str. 45; tel. (22) 50-11-00; e-mail iefs@iefs.md; internet ince.md; attached to Acad. of Sciences of Moldova; Dir Dr Hab. ALEXANDRU STRATAN; Scientific Sec. Dr ANGELA TIMUŞ; publ. *Economie şi Sociologie* (Economy and Sociology, 4 a year, in Romanian and English, print and online).

FINE AND PERFORMING ARTS

Institute of the History and Theory of Art: 2001 Chişinău, bd. Ştefan cel Mare şi Sfînt 1; tel. (22) 26-06-02; f. 1991; attached to Acad. of Sciences of Moldova; fine art, architecture, music, performing arts; Dir LEONID M. CEMORTAN; publ. *Arta* (2 series: fine arts and architecture, 1 a year, music and the performing arts, 1 a year).

HISTORY, GEOGRAPHY AND ARCHAEOLOGY

Institute of Archaeology and Ancient History: 2712 Chişinău, str. Mitropolitul Banulescu-Bodoni 35; tel. (22) 22-22-42; attached to Acad. of Sciences of Moldova; Dir VALENTIN DERGACEV.

Institute of Ecology and Geography: 2028 Chişinău, str. Academiei 1; tel. (22) 73-98-38; e-mail ieg@asm.md; internet ieg.asm.md; f. 1992; attached to Acad. of Sciences of Moldova; scientific and applied research in the fields of geography and ecology; Dir Acad. TATIANA S. CONSTANTINOVA; publs *Buletinul Academiei de Stiinte a Moldovei. Stiintele vietii, Mediul Ambiant.*

Institute of History: 2012 Chişinău, str. 31 August 1989 82; tel. (22) 23-33-10; e-mail iist_asm@mtc.md; f. 1958; attached to Acad. of Sciences of Moldova; Dir DEMIR DRAGNEV.

LANGUAGE AND LITERATURE

Institute of Linguistics: 2012 Chişinău, str. 31 August 1989 82; tel. (22) 23-33-05; f. 1991; attached to Acad. of Sciences of Moldova; library of 10,000 vols; Dir Acad. SILVIU BEREJAN; publ. *Revistă de Lingvistică şi Ştiinţă Literară* (6 a year).

Institute of Literature and Folklore: 2001 Chişinău, bd. Ştefan cel Mare şi Sfînt; tel. (22) 27-27-19; e-mail ilfasm@yahoo.it; f. 1991; attached to Acad. of Sciences of Moldova; Dir Acad. HARALAMBIE CORBU; publ. *Revistă de Lingvistică şi Ştiinţă Literară* (6 a year).

MEDICINE

National Centre of Public Health: 2028 Chişinău, str. Gh. Asachi 67A; tel. (22) 57-47-01; e-mail msp_csd@yahoo.com; internet www.cnsp.md; library of 50,000 vols; Dir-Gen. MIHAIL PISLA.

NATURAL SCIENCES

Biological Sciences

Botanical Garden Institute of the Academy of Sciences of Moldova: 2002 Chişinău, str. Pădurii 18; tel. (22) 52-38-98; e-mail gradinabotanica@moldnet.md; internet www.gradinabotanica.asm.md; f. 1950; attached to Acad. of Sciences of Moldova; more than 10,000 species of plants; library of 43,000 vols; Dir Dr ALEXANDRU TELEUTA; publ. *Revistă Botanica*.

Centre for Pathology and Pathobiology: 2004 Chişinău, str. 31 August 1989 151; tel. (22) 22-75-19; attached to Acad. of Sciences of Moldova; Dir Acad. VASILE ANESTIADE.

Institute of Genetics and Plant Physiology: 2002 Chişinău, str. Pădurii 20; tel. (22) 77-04-47; e-mail dobynda@mail.md; f. 2005 by merger of the Institute of Genetics, the Institute of Plant Physiology, the aromatic and medicinal plant br. of the Research Institute for Maize and Sorghum, and the Centre of Plant Genetic Resources; attached to Acad. of Sciences of Moldova; Dir ANATOL JACOTĂ.

Institute of Microbiology and Biotechnology: 2028 Chişinău, str. Academiei 1; tel. (22) 72-55-24; e-mail microbiologie@mail.md; internet www.asm.md; f. 1992; attached to Acad. of Sciences of Moldova; Dir Acad. VALERIU RUDIC; publ. *Bulletin* (2 a year).

Institute of Physiology and Sanocreatology: 2028 Chişinău, str. Academiei 1; tel. (22) 72-51-55; attached to Acad. of Sciences of Moldova; specializes in study of the pancreas; Dir Acad. TEODOR FURDUI.

Institute of Zoology: 2028 Chişinău, str. Academiei 1; tel. (22) 73-98-09; e-mail izoolasm@mail.md; attached to Acad. of Sciences of Moldova; Dir ION TODERAŞ.

Research Institute for Plant Protection and Agricultural Ecology (Institutul de Protecţie a Plantelor şi Agricultură Ecologică): 2060 Chişinău, str. Pădurii, 26/1; tel. (22) 77-04-66; e-mail volosciuc@netscape.net; internet agriculture.md/icpp/index.shtml; attached to Acad. of Sciences of Moldova; Dir LEONID VOLOSCIUC.

Mathematical Sciences

Institute of Mathematics and Computer Science: 2028 Chişinău, str. Academiei 5; tel. (22) 72-59-82; e-mail imam@math.md; internet www.math.md; f. 1964; attached to Acad. of Sciences of Moldova; Dir Dr hab. COJOCARU SVETLANA; Scientific Sec. Dr NAVAL ELVIRA; publs *Buletinul Academiei de Ştiinţe a Republicii Moldova: Matematica* (3 a year), *Computer Science Journal of Moldova* (3 a year), *Quasigroups and Related Systems* (2 a year).

Physical Sciences

Centre of Experimental Seismology, Central Station: 2028 Chişinău, str. Academiei 3; tel. (22) 73-71-79; attached to Acad. of Sciences of Moldova; forms the central unit of the Institute of Geophysics and Geology's seismic network; operates in conjunction with 4 local stations and 4 strong-motion recorders; Dir I. ILIEŞ.

Institute of Applied Physics: 2028 Chişinău, Academiei str., 5; tel. (22) 73-81-50; e-mail director@phys.asm.md; internet www.phys.asm.md; f. 1964; attached to Acad. of Sciences of Moldova; Dir Prof. L. KULYUK; publ. *Surface Engineering and Applied Electrochemistry* (6 a year).

Institute of Chemistry: 2028 Chişinău, str. Academiei 3; tel. (22) 72-54-90; e-mail ichem@asm.md; f. 1959; attached to Acad. of Sciences of Moldova; Dir Dr hab. TUDOR LUPASCU.

Institute of Geology and Seismology: 2028 Chişinău, str. Academiei 3; tel. (22) 73-90-27; e-mail alcazv@gmail.com; internet www.igs.asm.md; f. 1968, current name adopted 2006; attached to Acad. of Sciences of Moldova; seismic regime study of Carpathian-Balkan region, seismic macrozoning of Moldova, research on regional geology, hydrodynamics, geochemical anthropogenic processes; Dir Prof. Dr VASILE ALCAZ; Scientific Sec. IGOR NICOARA.

RELIGION, SOCIOLOGY AND ANTHROPOLOGY

Institute of National Minorities Studies: 2001 Chişinău, bd. Ştefan cel Mare şi Sfint 1; tel. (22) 26-44-91; attached to Acad. of Sciences of Moldova; Dir C. F. POPOVICI.

Institute of Philosophy, Sociology and Political Sciences: 2001 Chişinău, bd. Ştefan cel Mare şi Sfint 1; tel. (22) 27-05-37; e-mail ifilos@cc.acad.md; internet www.asm.md; attached to Acad. of Sciences of Moldova; f. 2006; philosophy; sociology; political sciences; mythology; history of religion; social-demographic researches on families; 54 mems; Dir Dr ION RUSANDU; publs *Iconomie şi Sociologie* (Economy and Sociology), *Revistă de Filosofie şi Drept* (Philosophy and Law).

TECHNOLOGY

Institute of Power Engineering: 2028 Chişinău, str. Academiei 5; tel. (22) 72-70-40; e-mail mkiorsak@cc.asm.md; f. 1964; attached to Acad. of Sciences of Moldova; Dir Dr VLADIMIR P. BERZAN; Deputy Dir MIHAI TIRSU; publ. *Problems of the Regional Energetics* (online (www.ie.asm.md)).

Libraries and Archives

Bălţi

Bălţi Municipal Library: 3121 Bălţi, str. A. Puşkin 34; tel. (231) 2-34-59; f. 1880; Dir INGA COJOCARU.

Chişinău

Central Scientific Library 'Andrei Lupan' of the Academy of Sciences of Moldova: 2028 Chişinău, str. Academiei 5A; tel. (22) 72-74-01; e-mail library@asm.md; internet www.amlib.asm.md; f. 1947; 1,406,887 vols; Dir AURELIA HANGANU.

Centre for Scientific Information in the Social Sciences: 2001 Chişinău, bd. Ştefan cel Mare şi Sfint 1; tel. (22) 23-23-39; attached to Acad. of Sciences of Moldova; Dir V. I. MOCREAC.

Moldova State University Library: 2009 Chişinău, str. A. Mateevici 60; tel. (22) 57-75-05; e-mail library@usm.md; internet www.usm.md/bcu; f. 1946; 1,810,000 vols; Dir ECATERINA ZASMENCO.

National Library of the Republic of Moldova: 2012 Chişinău, str. 31 August 1989 78A; tel. (22) 22-14-75; e-mail bnrm@bnrm.md; internet www.bnrm.md; f. 1832; national library and principal depository of Moldova; national centre of inter-library loans; national centre for library automation and information; national centre for library science; 2,507,055 vols, 834 periodicals; Dir A. A. RĂU.

Scientific and Technical Library of Moldova: Chişinău, str. Creangă 45; tel. (22) 62-87-42; f. 1968; 560,000 vols, 11,000,000 patents, 750,000 standards; Dir P. T. RACU.

Tighina

Tighina County Public Library: Tighina; e-mail bpjt@fromru.com; internet ournet.md/~bpjt; f. 1943; 3 brs; 106,787 vols; Dir LARISA CAMENSCIC.

Museums

Chişinău

National Art Museum of Moldova: Chişinău, str. 31 August 1989 115; tel. (22) 24-17-30; internet www.mnam.md; f. 1939; Dir TUDOR ZBARNEA.

National Museum of Archaeology and History of Moldova: 2012 Chişinău, str. 31 August 1989 121A; tel. (22) 24-43-25; e-mail museum@starnet.md; internet www.nationalmuseum.md; f. 1983; preservation and protection of cultural and historic heritage; scientific exhibitions; museum pedagogy; cultural programs; scientific publs; library of 12,000 vols; Gen. Dir Dr hab. EUGEN SAVA; Deputy Dir AURELIA CORNETCHI; publ. *Tyragetia* (2 a year).

Universities

UNIVERSITATEA AGRARĂ DE STAT DIN MOLDOVA
(Moldovan State Agrarian University)

2049 Chişinău, str. Mirceşti 44
Telephone: (22) 31-22-58
E-mail: cimpoies@uasm.md
Internet: www.uasm.md
Founded 1933
State control
Languages of instruction: English, Romanian, Russian
Rector: Prof. Dr GHEORGHE P. CIMPOES
Library of 789,000 vols
Number of teachers: 400
Number of students: 6,400 (3,700 on campus, 2,700 distance)

DEANS

Faculty of Accountancy: Assoc. Prof. Dr VERONICA PRISACARU
Faculty of Agricultural Engineering and Transport: Assoc. Prof. Dr GRIGORE MARIAN
Faculty of Agronomy: Assoc. Prof. Dr MIHAI RURAC
Faculty of Animal Husbandry and Biotechnology: Prof. Dr NICOLAE EREMIA
Faculty of Economics: Assoc. Prof. Dr PETRU TOMITA
Faculty of Horticulture: Prof. Dr VALERIAN BALAN
Faculty of Land Surveying and Law: Prof. Dr TEODOR MORARU
Faculty of Veterinary Medicine: Assoc. Prof. Dr GHEORGHE DONICA

UNIVERSITATEA COOPERATIST COMERCIALĂ DIN MOLDOVEI
(Cooperative Trade University of Moldova)

2027 Chişinău, bd. Gagarin 8
Telephone: (22) 27-07-84
E-mail: webmaster@uccm.md
Internet: www.uccm.md
Founded 1993
State control
Languages of instruction: French, German, Russian, Spanish, Ukranian
Rector: Dr TUDOR MALECA
Pro-Rector: LARISA ŞAVGA
Library of 92,000 vols
Number of teachers: 200
Number of students: 1,200

DEANS

Faculty of Accountancy and Business Informatics: Dr SERGIU OPREA
Faculty of Management and Economics: Dr ELENA GRAUR
Faculty of Marketing and the Science of Commodities: Dr FEODOSIE PITUŞCAN
Faculty of Part-Time Studies: Dr SVETLANA MUŞTUC

UNIVERSITATEA DE STAT 'ALECU RUSSO' DIN BĂLŢI
(Alecu Russo Balti State University)

3100 Balti, str. Puskin 38
Telephone: (231) 5-23-40
E-mail: rectorat.usb@gmail.com
Internet: www.usb.md
Founded 1945
State control
Languages of instruction: English, French, German, Romanian, Russian, Spanish, Ukrainian
Academic year: September to June
Rector: Prof. GHEORGHE POPA
First Vice-Rector for Didactic Activity: Dr ALEXANDRU BALANICI
Vice-Rector for Int. Relations and European Integration: Dr VALENTINA PRITCAN
Vice-Rector for Part-Time Studies and Continuous Formation: Dr GHEORGHE NEAGU
Vice-Rector for Scientific Activity: Dr MARIA SLEAHTITCHI
Head of Univ. Scientific Library: ELENA HARCONIŢĂ
Library of 1,200,000 vols
Number of teachers: 315
Number of students: 7,210
Publications: *Art and Artistic Education*, *Biannual Journal of Applied Linguistics*, *Bulletin of Administration* (12 a year), *Scientific Papers* (every 2 years), *Speech and Context*

DEANS

Faculty of Economics: Dr ALA TRUSEVICI
Faculty of Educational Sciences and Arts: Prof. ION GAGIM
Faculty of Foreign Languages and Literatures: Dr LUDMILA CABAC
Faculty of Hard Sciences: Prof. PAVEL TOPALA
Faculty of Law: Dr VEACESLAV PINZARI
Faculty of Natural Science and Agro-Ecology: Dr STANISLAV STADNIC
Faculty of Philology: Dr NICOLAE LEAHU
Faculty of Psychology and Social Work: Dr GALINA PETCU

UNIVERSITATEA DE STAT 'BOGDAN PETRICEICU HASDEU' DIN CAHUL
(Bogdan Petriceicu Hasdeu State University of Cahul)

3901 Cahul, str. Piaţa Independenţei 1
Telephone: (299) 2-24-81

E-mail: rectorat@usch.md
Internet: www.usch.md
Founded 1999
State control
Rector: Dr ANDREI POPA

UNIVERSITATEA DE STAT DE MEDICINĂ ŞI FARMACIE 'NICOLAE TESTEMIŢANU' DIN REPUBLICA MOLDOVA
(Nicolae Testemiţanu State University of Medicine and Pharmacy)

2004 Chişinău, bd. Ştefan cel Mare şi Sfînt 165
Telephone: (22) 24-34-08
E-mail: rector@usmf.md
Internet: www.usmf.md
Founded 1945
State control
Languages of instruction: English, French, Romanian, Russian
Academic year: September to July
Rector: Prof. Dr ION ABABII
Vice-Rector for Education and Social Issues: Dr EMIL CEBAN
Vice-Rector for Int. Relations: Dr MIHAIL GAVRILIUC CHICU
Vice-Rector for Quality Assurance and Integration in Education: Prof. Dr OLGA CERNETCHI
Vice-Rector for Scientific Activity: Prof. Dr VIOREL PRISACARI
Dir of Univ. Library: LIUBOVI KARNAEVA
Library of 950,369 vols, 511 periodicals
Number of teachers: 1,062
Number of students: 5,059
Publication: *Curieurul medical* (6 a year)

DEANS
Faculty of Dentistry: Prof. Dr ION LUPAN
Faculty of Medicine I: Prof. Dr GHEORGHE PLĂCINTĂ
Faculty of Medicine II: Prof. Dr MIRCEA BETIU
Faculty of Pharmacy: Dr NICOLAE CIOBANU
Faculty of Postgraduate Continuous Education: Prof. Dr EUGEN BENDELIC
Faculty of Postgraduate Residency and Fellowship Training: Prof. Dr VALERIU REVENCO

UNIVERSITATEA DE STAT DIN MOLDOVA
(Moldova State University)

2009 Chişinău, str. A. Mateevici 60
Telephone: (22) 57-74-01
E-mail: rector@usm.md
Internet: www.usm.md
Founded 1946
Private control
Languages of instruction: Romanian, Russian
Academic year: September to June
Rector: Prof. GHEORGHE CIOCANU
Vice-Rector: Assoc. Prof. TUDOR ARNAUT
Vice-Rector: Assoc. Prof. OTILIA DANDARA
Vice-Rector: Prof. MIHAIL REVENCO
Registrar: Assoc. Prof. ANATOL TOPALA
Librarian: ECATERINA ZASMENCO
Library: see under Libraries and Archives
Number of teachers: 1,200
Number of students: 17,000
Publications: *Revistă Nationala de Drept (National Journal of Law)* (12 a year), *Scientific Annals* (1 a year), *Universitatea* (12 a year)

DEANS
Faculty of Biology and Soil Science: MIHAIL LESANU
Faculty of Chemistry and Chemical Technology: VIORICA GLADCHI
Faculty of Economic Sciences: GALINA ULIAN
Faculty of Foreign Languages and Literature: LUDMILA ZBANT
Faculty of History and Philosophy: IGOR SAROV
Faculty of International Relations, Political and Admin. Sciences: VASILE CUJBĂ
Faculty of Journalism and Communication: MIHAIL GUZUN
Faculty of Law: GHEORGHE AVORNIC
Faculty of Mathematics and Computer Science: ANDREI PERJAN
Faculty of Philology: CLAUDIA CEMARTAN
Faculty of Physics: FLORENTIN PALADI
Faculty of Psychology and Educational Sciences: VLADIMIR GUTU
Faculty of Sociology and Social Work: MARIA BULGARU

UNIVERSITATEA DE STAT DIN TIRASPOL
(Tiraspol State University)

2069 Chişinău, str. Ghenadie Iablocichin 5
Telephone: (22) 75-49-24
E-mail: scs_ust@moldova.cc
Founded 1930; moved from Tiraspol to present location in 1992, due to civil unrest
State control
Languages of instruction: Romanian, Russian
Rector: Prof. LAURENTIU CALMUTCHI
Vice-Rector: Prof. IGOR POSTOLACHI
Number of students: 3,140
Publication: *Light* (12 a year)

DEANS
Faculty of Biology and Chemistry: BORIS NEDBALIUC
Faculty of Geography: ION MIRONOV
Faculty of Pedagogy: VASILE PANICO
Faculty of Philology: LUDMILA SOLOVIOV
Faculty of Physics and Mathematics: BORIS KOROLEVSKI

UNIVERSITATEA PEDAGOGICĂ DE STAT 'ION CREANGĂ'
(Ion Creangă Pedagogical State University)

2069 Chişinău, str. I. Creangă 1
Telephone: (22) 35-84-15
E-mail: creangaups@yahoo.com
Internet: www.upsc.md
Founded 1940
State control
Languages of instruction: Romanian, Russian
Academic year: September to June
Rector: Dr NICOLAE CHICUŞ
Number of teachers: 353 (284 full-time, 69 part-time)
Number of students: 5,345 (3,437 full-time, 1,908 part-time)
Publication: *Annual Scientific Edition Psychology. Special Pedagogy. Social Assistance*

DEANS
Faculty of Continuing Education: Dr COJOCARU VASILE
Faculty of Fine Arts: Dr VATAVU ALEXANDRU
Faculty of Foreign Languages and Literatures: Dr GOGU TAMARA
Faculty of History and Ethno-Pedagogy: Dr MUSTEAŢĂ SERGIU
Faculty of Informatics and Information Technologies in Education: Dr DUMBRAVEANU ROZA
Faculty of Pedagogy: Dr SADOVEI LARISA
Faculty of Philology: Dr TOPOR GABRIELA
Faculty of Psychology and Special Psycho-Pedagogy: Dr PERJAN CAROLINA

UNIVERSITATEA TEHNICĂ A MOLDOVEI
(Technical University of Moldova)

2004 Chişinău, bd. Ştefan cel Mare şi Sfînt 168
Telephone: (22) 23-78-61
E-mail: extrel@adm.utm.md
Internet: www.utm.md
Founded 1964
State control
Languages of instruction: Romanian, Russian
Academic year: September to June
Rector: Acad. Prof. ION BOSTAN
First Vice-Rector for Education: Prof. Dr PETRU TODOS
Vice-Rector for Administration and Capital Construction: PAVEL SPÂNU
Vice-Rector for Continuing Education and International Relations: Assoc. Prof. Dr VALENTIN AMARIEI
Vice-Rector for Part-Time Studies and Distance Education: Assoc. Prof. Dr TIMOFEI ANDROS
Vice-Rector for Research: Prof. Dr hab. VALERIAN DOROGAN
Vice-Rector for Studies and Relations with Colleges: Prof. Dr DUMITRU UNGUREANU
Dean of Students: Dr CONSTANTIN STRATAN
Library of 1,080,000 vols
Number of teachers: 750
Number of students: 17,000
Publications: *Meridian Ingineresc* (4 a year), *Mesager* (newspaper, 12 a year)

DEANS
Faculty of Computers, Informatics and Microelectronics: Assoc. Prof. Dr ION BALMUS
Faculty of Economic Engineering and Business: Prof. Dr NICOLAE TURCANU
Faculty of Engineering and Management in Machine-Building: Assoc. Prof. Dr ALEXEI TOCA
Faculty of Engineering and Management in Mechanics: Assoc. Prof. Dr VASILE CARTOFEANU
Faculty of Power Engineering: Prof. Dr ION STRATAN
Faculty of Radioelectronics and Telecommunications: Assoc. Prof. Dr SERGIU ANDRONIC
Faculty of Surveying, Geodesy and Civil Engineering: Assoc. Prof. Dr VICTOR TOPOREŢ
Faculty of Technology and Management in the Food Industry: Assoc. Prof. Dr GRIGORE MUSTEATA
Faculty of the Textile Industry: Assoc. Prof. Dr CONSTANTIN SPINU
Faculty of Urban Planning and Architecture: Assoc. Prof. Dr NISTOR GROZAVU

Other Higher Educational Institutions

Academia de Mizică, Teatru şi Arte Plastice (Academy of Music, Theatre and Fine Arts): 2014 Chişinău, str. A. Mateevici 87; tel. (22) 22-19-49; e-mail usam@moldovacc.md; internet www.amtap.mdl.net; f. 1919; 1,500 students; Rector Dr AURELIAN DANILĂ.

Academia de Studii Economice (Academy of Economic Studies): 2005 Chişinău, str. Mitropolit Bănulescu-Bodoni 61; tel. (22) 22-41-28; e-mail r_gb@ase.md; internet www.ase.md; f. 1991; library: 317,000 vols; faculties of accountancy, business and administration, economics and law, finance, information technology and statistics and international economic relations; Rector Prof. Dr Hab. GRIGORII BELOSTECINIC.

Institutul de Stat de Relaţii Internaţionale din Moldova (State Institute of International Relations of Moldova): Chişinău, str. Puşkin 54; tel. (22) 21-09-62; e-mail irim@irim.md; internet www.irim.md; f. 2003; faculties of international relations and political science, languages, law, world economy and international economic relations; Rector Prof. Dr Hab. VALENTIN BENIUC; Chief Librarian IULIA MELNIC.

Institutul Naţional de Educaţie Fizică şi Sport (National Institute of Physical Education and Sport): 2024 Chişinău, str. A. Doga 28/2; tel. (22) 49-40-81; e-mail inefs@mdl.net; faculties of part-time studies, pedagogy, sports and teacher development; Rector VEACESLAV MANOLACHE.

MONACO

The Higher Education System

In 1861 Monaco became an independent state under the protection of France. The Académie de Musique et de Théâtre Foundation Prince Rainier III de Monaco, founded in 1933, is the oldest public institution of higher education and operates under French regulations and awards French qualifications. Two further public institutes awarding French qualifications are the Institut de Formation en Soins Infirmiers which offers nursing courses leading to the Diplôme d'État, and the École Supérieure d'Arts Plastiques which offers three-year courses leading to the Diplôme National d'Arts Plastiques and five-year courses leading to a Masters equivalent Diplôme National Supérieur d'Expression Plastique. There is also a private higher educational institution, the International University of Monaco (founded 1986), a business school where instruction is conducted in English and where US-style Bachelors, Masters and Doctoral degree courses are offered. The latter is recognized by the Directorate of National Education, Youth and Sports in Monaco and quality-assured by the Comité d'Evaluation et de Surveillance. Most Monégasque students undertake higher education in France. Post-secondary technical and vocational education is provided by the Sections de Technicien Supérieur. Programmes of study last for two years and lead to the award of the Higher Technician Certificate (Brevet de Technicien Supérieur—BTS). The admission requirement for BTS courses is the Baccalauréat or Brevet de Technicien.

Regulatory and Representative Bodies

GOVERNMENT

Directorate of National Education, Youth and Sports: ave de l'Annonciade, 98000 Monaco; tel. 98-98-83-05; e-mail denjs@gouv.mc; internet www.education.gouv.mc; attached to Department of the Interior; Dir ISABELLE BONNAL.

ACCREDITATION

ENIC/NARIC Monaco: Centre d'Information de l'Éducation Nationale, 18 ave des Castelans, 98000 Monaco; tel. 98-98-87-74; e-mail cien@monaco.mc; internet www.education.gouv.mc; Coordinator CÉCILE KAPPLER.

Learned Societies

HISTORY, GEOGRAPHY AND ARCHAEOLOGY

Association Monégasque de Préhistoire: Musée d'Anthropologie, 56 bis blvd du Jardin Exotique, 98000 Monte Carlo; tel. 98-98-80-06; internet www.monaco-prehistoire.com; f. 1984; 50 mems; Pres. Dr PATRICK SIMON.

LANGUAGE AND LITERATURE

Alliance Française: Maison de France, 42 rue Grimaldi, BP 300, 98006 Monte Carlo; tel. 93-50-08-24; offers courses and exams in French language and culture and promotes cultural exchange with France.

Research Institute

NATURAL SCIENCES

General

Centre Scientifique de Monaco: Villa les Pins, bloc C, 7 rue Honoré Labande, 98000 Monte Carlo; tel. 98-98-86-60; e-mail centre@centrescientifique.mc; internet www.centrescientifique.mc; f. 1960; pure and applied research in the fields of oceanography, marine biology and the protection and regeneration of the marine environment; laboratories in Musée Océanographique de Monaco (*q.v.*); Pres. of Admin. Council Prof. PATRICK RAMPAL; Sec.-Gen. CORINNE GAZIELLO; publ. *Bulletin* (1 a year, in English and French).

Libraries and Archives

Monte Carlo

Archives du Palais Princier de Monaco: BP 518, 98015 Monaco Cedex; tel. 93-25-18-31; e-mail archives@palais.mc; internet www.palais.mc; private archives of the Princes of Monaco; Dir THOMAS FOUILLERON; publ. *Annals Monegasque* (1 a year).

Bibliothèque Louis Notari: 8 rue Louis Notari, 98000 Monaco; tel. 93-15-29-40; f. 1909; 310,000 vols, 18,000 phonograms, 4,000 video cassettes; Librarian HERVÉ BARRAL; publ. *Bibliographie de Monaco* (database).

Princess Grace Irish Library: 9 rue Princesse Marie de Lorraine, 98000 Monaco; tel. 93-50-12-25; e-mail pglib@monaco.mc; internet www.pgil.mc; f. 1984; operates under the aegis of the Fondation Princesse Grace; Irish and Celtic studies library; 12,000 vols, 2,000 sheet items of Irish music and folk songs, 250 theses, 250 video cassettes and DVDs; reproduction of the Book of Kells; paintings, prints, sculptures; young readers' colln; English language activities for local school students; theatre, writing and poetry workshops; Administrator JUDITH GANTLEY; Admin. Asst GÉRALDINE LANCE.

Museums and Art Galleries

Monte Carlo

Musée d'Anthropologie Préhistorique de Monaco: 56 bis blvd du Jardin Exotique, 98000 Monte Carlo; tel. 98-98-80-06; e-mail map@map-mc.com; internet www.map-mc.com; f. 1902; prehistory, quaternary geology, palaeontology; library of 3,000 vols, 200 periodicals; Dir and Curator Dr PATRICK SIMON; publ. *Bulletin du Musée d'Anthropologie Préhistorique de Monaco* (1 a year).

Musée Naval de Monaco: Terrasses de Fontvieille, Niveau 2, 98000 Monte Carlo; tel. 92-05-28-48; e-mail claude_pallanca@libello.com; internet www.musee-naval.mc; more than 250 marine objects and models of famous ships, incl. several pieces from private colln of Prince Rainier III; Dir CLAUDE PALLANCA.

Musée Océanographique de Monaco: ave Saint-Martin, 98000 Monte Carlo; tel. 93-15-36-00; e-mail musee@oceano.mc; internet www.oceano.org; f. 1910 by Prince Albert I of Monaco; part of Institut Océanographique, Paris; museum of natural history and art collns; aquarium contains more than 6,000 fishes of 400 species, 200 species of invertebrates and 100 species of corals; mother-of-pearl holy art shells; library of 10,000 vols, 1,200 theses, 1,000 periodicals, 1,000 maps and charts; Dir ROBERT CALCAGNO; Dir of Heritage and Curator PATRICK PIGUET; publs *Anales* (1 a year), *Bulletin* (irregular), *Mémoires* (irregular).

Nouveau Musée National de Monaco Villa Sauber/Villa Paloma: Villa des Pins, bloc B, 8 rue Honoré Labande, 98000 Monaco; tel. 98-98-19-62; e-mail contact@nmnm.mc; internet www.nmnm.mc; f. 1972; Galéa colln: automatons, miniature furniture, antique dolls, nativity scenes; Dir MARIE-CLAUDE BEAUD.

University

INTERNATIONAL UNIVERSITY OF MONACO (IUM)

2 ave Albert III, 98000 Monte Carlo

Telephone: 97-98-69-86

E-mail: admissions@monaco.edu

Internet: www.monaco.edu/international-university-monaco.cfm

Founded 1986

Private control

Language of instruction: English

Bachelors, Masters and MBA courses in business administration, finance, international business; also offers courses in Paris, France, and London, UK

Prin.: Dr SANDRINE RICARD

Vice-Prin.: Dr ANTONELLA PATRAS

Registrar and Bursar: DAVID CRANMAN

Head of Library and Research Services: SUSAN WANGECI EKLÖW

Number of teachers: 61

College

Académie de Musique et de Théâtre Foundation Prince Rainier III de Monaco: 1 blvd Albert I, 98000 Monaco; tel. 93-15-28-91; f. 1933; 56 professors; 650 students; Dir MICHEL CROSSET.

MONGOLIA

The Higher Education System

Mongolia was formerly the Manchu province of Outer Mongolia. In 1911, following the republican revolution in China, Mongolian princes declared the province's independence. Russia (and, later, the USSR) competed with China for control of Mongolia and in November 1924 the Mongolian People's Republic was proclaimed. The oldest institutions of higher education date from this year, among them the Academy of Management, Higher School of Finance and Economics and Higher School of Trade and Industry. The oldest multi-faculty university-level institution is the National University of Mongolia (founded 1942 as Choybalsan University). Tertiary education consists of universities, institutes of higher education and colleges. In 2010/11 there were 16 state-owned higher education establishments with 104,400 students, and 92 private establishments with 65,300 students. For the 2011/12 academic year some 171,165 students were enrolled in tertiary education. Many Mongolian students continue their academic careers at universities and technical schools in Russia, Germany, the United Kingdom and the USA. Higher education is the responsibility of the Ministry of Education, Culture and Science, while the Consortium of Mongolian Universities and Colleges (founded 1995) is a non-governmental body representing some 31 public and private universities and colleges. During the 1990s major reforms were carried out in the higher education sector; institutions received a considerable degree of autonomy and the right to confer their own degrees (previously awarded centrally by the Government). Further changes included the introduction of compulsory tuition fees, although the Government continues to offer financial aid to students in the form of grants and bursaries known as the State Training Fund. New legislation also permitted the establishment of private higher education institutions, leading to rapid expansion in the private sector.

Admission to undergraduate education is based on a centralized entrance examination, which is organized and monitored by the Education Evaluation Centre. During the 1990s the structure of higher education was reformed to introduce a system consisting of three main cycles, and a credit system was implemented to monitor students' workload. The first stage of undergraduate higher education is the Bachelors degree, which generally lasts four years and for which students are required to accumulate a minimum of 120 'credit hours' and present a thesis or graduation project. Courses in professional fields such as medicine are normally longer and have a higher credit value. After the Bachelors has been awarded students are eligible to study for the Masters, which lasts one-and-a-half to two years and requires at least 35 credit hours and the submission of a dissertation. Finally, the Doctorate is the highest university-level degree; a doctoral course takes at least three years and requires a minimum of 60 credit hours as well as the public defence of a thesis.

In 2002 a new law on technical and vocational education and training (TVET) was implemented highlighting the importance of the sector for the establishment of a qualified workforce for Mongolia's developing economy. The Vocational and Technical Education Agency and the Council for Vocational Education and Training were subsequently set up to organize and monitor the TVET sector. The following types of institutions provide TVET courses: vocational education and training centres, technical colleges, vocational institutes and secondary schools. Programmes offered by vocational education and training centres lead to the award of the Certificate of Vocational Training, while those offered by technical colleges lead to the award of the Certificate of Technical Education. A number of TVET centres and colleges are affiliated to higher education institutions and the proportion of establishments in the private and public sectors is almost equal.

The Mongolian National Council for Education Accreditation (NCEA), which was established in 1998 and is an autonomous self-financing body, is responsible for the accreditation and quality assurance of higher education institutions (including TVET establishments) and programmes. Institutional and programme accreditation are both on a voluntary basis. The NCEA works in cooperation with the Ministry of Education and Science.

Regulatory and Representative Bodies

GOVERNMENT

Ministry of Culture, Sport and Tourism: Govt Bldg 10, Barilgachdyn talbai 1, Chingeltei District, Ulan Bator; tel. (11) 310986; e-mail info@mcst.gov.mn; internet mcst.gov.mn; Minister TSEDEVDAMBYN OYUUNGEREL.

Ministry of Education and Science: Govt Bldg 3, Baga Toiruu 44, Sükhbaatar District, Ulan Bator; tel. (11) 323589; e-mail info@mecs.gov.mn; internet www.meds.gov.mn; Minister LUVSANNYAMYN GANTÖMÖR.

ACCREDITATION

Mongolian National Council for Education Accreditation: Govt Bldg 10, Barilgachdyn talbai 2 38, Ulan Bator; tel. (11) 324507; e-mail accmon@mongolnet.mn; internet www.accmon.mn; f. 1998; accredits higher education instns, programmes and technical and vocational training centres; Officer of External Relations SARUUL BAT-ULZII.

NATIONAL BODY

Consortium of Mongolian Universities and Colleges: Box 672, POB 46, Ulan Bator; tel. (11) 318154; e-mail cmuc@mtu.edu.mn; internet www.cmuc.edu.mn; f. 1995; represents the common interests of public and private univs and colleges; supports scientific co-operation between the academic community and industry; promotes int. scientific co-operation; organizes biennial conferences on higher education reform; 18 mem. instns; Pres. Prof. Dr BADARCH DENDEV; publ. *Tavan Ukhaan* (12 a year).

Learned Societies

GENERAL

Mongolian Academy of Sciences: Sükhbaataryn talbai 3, Ulan Bator; tel. (11) 321638; e-mail mas@mas.ac.mn; f. 1921; Depts of agriculture, geology and geography, medicine and biology, chemistry, mathematics, physics and technology, social sciences; attached research institutes: see Research Institutes; Pres. BAATARYN CHADRAA; Scientific Sec. DÜGERIN REGDEL; publs *Proceedings of the Mongolian Academy of Sciences* (4 a year), *Studia Archaeologica, Studia Ethnographica, Studia Folclorica, Studia Historica, Studia Mongolica, Studia Museologica*.

AGRICULTURE, FISHERIES AND VETERINARY SCIENCE

Academy of Agricultural Sciences: Ulan Bator; f. 1998; Pres. N. ALTANSÜKH.

LANGUAGE AND LITERATURE

Union of Mongolian Writers: POB 896, PO 46, 12 Sukhbaatar Dist., Sixth Sub-Dist., Chingeltei Dist., Ulan Bator 210646; tel. (11) 327964; Exec. Dir KHAIDAVYN CHILAAJAV.

MEDICINE

Academy of Health Management: Ulan Bator; Pres. N. UDVAL.

Academy of Medical Sciences: Ulan Bator; e-mail info@mams.mn; f. 2005; Pres. PAGVAJAVYN NYAMDAVAA.

Society of Mongolian Surgeons: Ulan Bator; Pres. B. GOOSH.

RELIGION, SOCIOLOGY AND ANTHROPOLOGY

Academy of Astrology: Mongolian Youth Association Bldg, Baga Toiruu, Sükhbaatar district, Ulan Bator; tel. (11) 322982.

Academy of Nomadic Culture and Civilization: 'Ikh Zasag' University Bldg, 4th khoroo, B. Dorjiin St, Bayanzurkh dist., Ulan Bator; tel. (70) 157770; e-mail ikhzasag@ikhzasag.edu.mn; internet www.ikhzasag.edu.mn; f. 2002; research and scientific works in Mongolian studies; 80 mems; Pres. NAMSRAIN NYAM-OSOR; publ. *Ikh Zasag* (2 a year).

Genghis Khan World Academy: Bldg 6, 2nd sub-district, Bayanzürkh district, Ulan Bator (POB 21/174); internet www.chinggesacademy.mn.

Mongolian Muslims' Society: Ulan Bator; tel. (99) 110789; e-mail mail@mongolianislam.mn; internet www.mongolianislam.mn; f. 1990; Pres. KADYRYN SAIRAAN; Exec. Dir BAATARBEK KAHDES.

TECHNOLOGY

Mongolian Civil Engineers' Association: Baruun Dörvön Zam, Ikh Toiruu 1, Ulan Bator (POB 44/7); tel. (11) 328097; e-mail midiid@magicnet.mn.

Mongolian National Mining Association: 'Geosan' Company Bldg, Ikh surguuliin gudamj-8, Baga Toiruu, Sukhbaatar, Ulan Bator; tel. (11) 314877; internet www.miningmongolia.mn/minetech; f. 2003; Dir N. ALGAA.

Mongolian National Water Association: Govt Bldg 3, Baga Toiruu 44, Ulan Bator 11; tel. (11) 322828; e-mail baigyam@magicnet.mn; f. 2000; Pres. S. CHULUUNKHUYAG.

National Academy of Engineering: c/o Dr Badarch Dendevin, Mongolian Technical Univ., POB 46/672, Ulan Bator; tel. (1) 324121; e-mail badarch@magicnet.mn; f. 1998; Pres. P. OCHIRBAT.

Science and Technology Foundation: Ulan Bator; Dir KH. TSOOKHÜÜ.

Research Institutes

AGRICULTURE, FISHERIES AND VETERINARY SCIENCE

Agricultural Economics Research Institute: c/o Academy of Sciences, Sükhbaataryn talbai 3, Ulan Bator; attached to Mongolian Acad. of Sciences; Dir YU. ADYAA.

Agricultural Research Institute: Khovd; tel. (43) 3720; f. 1994; library of 10,000 vols; Dir P. BAATARBILEG.

Institute of Pasture and Fodder: Darkhan; Dir D. TSEDEV.

Institute of Veterinary Research: Zaisan, Ulan Bator; tel. (11) 341553; f. 1960; attached to Mongolian State Univ. of Agriculture; library of 4,000 vols; Dir B. BYAMBAA; publ. *Proceedings of the Institute of Veterinary Research and Training*.

Research Institute of Animal Husbandry 'J. Sambuu': Zaisan, Ulan Bator; tel. (11) 341572; e-mail riah@magicnet.mn; f. 1961; attached to Mongolian Acad. of Sciences; library of 800 vols; Dir DONDOVYN ALTANGEREL; publ. *Proceedings* (in Mongolian, with English summary).

Research Institute of Pastoral Animal Husbandry in the Gobi Region: Bulgan district, Ömnögobi province; f. 1959; attached to Mongolian Acad. of Sciences; camel and goat husbandry; Dir N. BIICHEE.

Research Institute of Plant Protection: c/o Academy of Sciences, Sükhbaataryn talbai 3, Ulan Bator; attached to Mongolian Acad. of Sciences; Dir D. TSEDEV.

Research Institute of Vegetable Growing and Land Cultivation Training: Darkhan-Uul province; tel. (37) 24132; attached to Mongolian State Univ. of Agriculture.

ARCHITECTURE AND TOWN PLANNING

Building Institute: c/o Academy of Sciences, Sükhbaataryn talbai 3, Ulan Bator; attached to Mongolian Acad. of Sciences; Dir D. LKHANAG.

Construction and Architecture Research, Experimental, Production and Business Corporation: c/o Academy of Sciences, Sükhbaataryn talbai 3, Ulan Bator; tel. (11) 341437; Exec. Dir D. KHAISAMBUU.

Institute of Architecture and Town Planning: c/o Academy of Sciences, Sükhbaataryn talbai 3, Ulan Bator; attached to Mongolian Acad. of Sciences; Dir (vacant).

Research Institute of Soils and Foundations Engineering: c/o Academy of Sciences, Sükhbaataryn talbai 3, Ulan Bator; attached to Mongolian Acad. of Sciences; Dir Dr A. ANAND.

ECONOMICS, LAW AND POLITICS

Centre for North-East Asian Studies: Mongolian Technical University Bldg (2nd Fl.), Ulan Bator (POB 51/4); tel. (11) 458317; f. 1990; attached to Mongolian Acad. of Sciences; library of 2,000 vols; Dir Prof. CH. DALAI; publ. *North-East Asian Studies* (2 a year).

Institute of Economics: Ulan Bator; tel. (11) 320802; f. 1962; attached to National University of Mongolia; fmrly attached to Mongolian Acad. of Sciences; library of 2,000 vols; Dir P. LUVSANDORJ.

Institute of International Studies: Room 806, Soyolyn töv örgöö, Sükhbaataryn talbai, Ulan Bator; tel. (11) 322613; attached to Mongolian Acad. of Sciences; Dir LUVSANGIIN KHAISANDAI; Scientific Sec. D. SHÜRKHÜÜ.

Institute of Mongol Studies: c/o Academy of Sciences, Sükhbaataryn talbai 3, Ulan Bator 11; attached to Mongolian Acad. of Sciences; Dir SH. BIRA.

Institute of National Development: Ulan Bator; attached to Mongolian Acad. of Sciences and the Presidential Secretariat; Dir RADNAASÜMBERELIIN RENCHINBAZAR; Scientific Sec. L. TSEDENDAMBA.

Institute of Oriental and International Studies: c/o Academy of Sciences, Sükhbaataryn talbai 3, Ulan Bator; attached to Mongolian Acad. of Sciences; Dir A. OCHIR.

Institute of Strategic Studies: Partizany gudamj, Ulan Bator (POB 870); tel. (11) 328188; attached to Min. of Defence; Dir Maj.-Gen. CHOYJAMTSYN ULAANKHÜÜ; Vice-Dir MASHBAT OTGONBAYAR.

Mongolian Development Research Centre: Room 50, Baga Toiruu 13, Chingeltei district, Ulan Bator (POB 20A/63); tel. (11) 315686; internet www.mdrc.mn.

'Prognoz' Institute of Socio-Political Studies: c/o Mongolian People's Party, Mongolian People's Party Headquarters, Zaluuchuudyn Ave, Ulan Bator 14191; e-mail contact@mprp.mn; internet www.mpp.mn; attached to Mongolian People's Party; Dir O. ERDENECHIMEG.

Research Institute for Land Policy: Chingünjavyn gudamj 2, Ulan Bator; tel. (11) 60506; f. 1975; library of 1,100 vols; Dir Dr G. PÜREVSÜREN.

FINE AND PERFORMING ARTS

Research Institute of Culture and Arts: c/o Academy of Sciences, Sükhbaataryn talbai 3, Ulan Bator 11; attached to Mongolian Acad. of Sciences; Dir S. TSERENDORJ.

HISTORY, GEOGRAPHY AND ARCHAEOLOGY

Institute of Archaeology: c/o Academy of Sciences, Sükhbaataryn talbai 3, Ulan Bator; attached to Mongolian Acad. of Sciences; Dir D. TSEVEENDORJ; Scientific Sec. B. TSOGTBAATAR.

Institute of Geography: c/o Academy of Sciences, Sükhbaataryn talbai 3, Ulan Bator; tel. (11) 350472; attached to Mongolian Acad. of Sciences; Dir Dr S. DORJGOTOV.

Institute of History: Jukovyn gudamj 77, Bayanzürkh district, Ulan Bator; tel. (11) 458305; internet www.mas.ac.mn; attached to Mongolian Acad. of Sciences; archaeology, ethnography, Mongolian history; Dir D. DASHDAVAA.

LANGUAGE AND LITERATURE

Folk Literature Research Institute: Ulan Bator; Dir B. KATUU.

Institute of Mongolian Language and Literature: c/o Academy of Sciences, Sükhbaataryn talbai 3, Ulan Bator; tel. (11) 451762; e-mail language@lang.mas.ac.mn; internet www.language.mas.ac.mn; f. 1921, present name and status 1961; attached to Mongolian Acad. of Sciences; organizes research and training to improve orthographical knowledge of the public; Dir TUMURTOGOO DOMII; publs *Folklore Studies* (1 a year), *Language and Literature Studies* (1 a year), *Mongolian Studies* (1 a year).

MEDICINE

Institute of Hygiene, Epidemiology and Microbiology: c/o Academy of Sciences, Sükhbaataryn talbai 3, Ulan Bator 13; tel. (1) 45-26-77; internet www.mas.ac.mn; attached to Mongolian Acad. of Sciences; Dir J. KUPUL.

Institute of Traditional Medicine: c/o Academy of Sciences, Sükhbaataryn talbai 3, Ulan Bator; attached to Mongolian Acad. of Sciences; Dir D. DAGVATSEREN.

Medical Research Institute: c/o Academy of Sciences, Sükhbaataryn talbai 3, Ulan Bator; attached to Mongolian Acad. of Sciences; Dir YO. BODIKHÜÜ.

National Center of Public Health: Peace Ave 17, Ulan Bator; tel. (11) 458645; e-mail info@ncph.gov.mn; internet www.ncph.gov.mn; f. 1933; attached to Min. of Health; Dir Dr GANCHIMEG ULZIIBAYAR.

National Centre for Communicable Diseases: Bayanzürkh district, Ulan Bator; tel. (11) 458699; f. 2001; Dir TOGOOGIIN ALTANTSETSEG.

National Forensic Research Centre: Ulan Bator; Dir CH. ALTANKHISHIG.

National Institute of Medicine: c/o Academy of Sciences, Sükhbaataryn talbai 3, Ulan Bator; attached to Mongolian Acad. of Sciences; Learned Sec. B. TSERENDASH.

Research and Production Centre of Biotechnology: Ulan Bator; attached to Min. of Health and Inst. of Public Health; Dir J. OYUUNBILEG.

Research and Production Institute of Biological Preparations and Blood: Ulan Bator; Dir A. DANDII.

State Research Centre for Maternal and Child Health: Amarsanaagiin gudamj, Bayangol district, Ulan Bator; tel. (11) 362633; f. 1930; attached to Mongolian

Acad. of Sciences; Dir G. CHOIJAMTS; publ. *Mother and Child* (2 a year).

NATURAL SCIENCES

Biological Sciences

Institute of Biology: Ulan Bator; tel. (11) 458851; f. 1965; attached to Mongolian Acad. of Sciences; Dir TS. JANCHIV.

Institute of Botany: Jukovyn gudamj 77, Ulan Bator; tel. (11) 451837; e-mail chdorj@yahoo.com; attached to Mongolian Acad. of Sciences; Learned Sec. D. MAGSAR.

Institute of Geoecology: c/o Academy of Sciences, Sükhbaataryn talbai 3, Ulan Bator; tel. (11) 321862; attached to Mongolian Acad. of Sciences; Dir J. TSOGTBAATAR.

Palaeontology Centre: Enkh Taivny gudamj 63, Ulan Bator; e-mail barsgeodin@magicnet.mn; attached to Mongolian Acad. of Sciences; Dir R. BARSBOLD.

Mathematical Sciences

Institute of Mathematics: Ulan Bator; attached to National University of Mongolia; fmrly attached to Mongolian Acad. of Sciences; Dir A. MEKEI.

Physical Sciences

Astronomical Observatory: Khürel-Togoot, Ulan Bator (POB 788); tel. (11) 52929; f. 1961; attached to Mongolian Acad. of Sciences; library of 1,500 vols; Dir G. NOONOI.

Centre of Seismology and Geomagnetism: c/o Academy of Sciences, Sükhbaataryn talbai 3, Ulan Bator; attached to Mongolian Acad. of Sciences; Dir U. SÜKHBAATAR.

Institute of Chemistry and Chemical Technology: Züün Dörvön Zam, Bayanzürkh district, Ulan Bator; tel. (11) 453133; attached to Mongolian Acad. of Sciences; Dir B. PÜREVSÜREN.

Institute of Geology and Mineral Enrichment: Peace Ave 63, POB 118, Ulan Bator; tel. (11) 457858; f. 1966; attached to Mongolian Acad. of Sciences; library of 1,000 vols; Dir O. TÖMÖRTOGOO; publ. *Khaiguulchin* (4 a year).

Institute of Meteorology and Hydrology: Khudaldaany gudamj 5, Ulan Bator; tel. (11) 326614; e-mail meteoins@magicnet.mn; f. 1966; library of 13,000 vols; Dir D. AZZAYAA; publ. *Environment*.

Institute of Physics and Technology: Enkh Taivny gudamj 54B, Ulan Bator; tel. (11) 458397; f. 1961; attached to Mongolian Acad. of Sciences; library of 50,000 vols; Dir TS. BAATAR.

Research Centre for Astronomy and Geophysics: c/o Academy of Sciences, Sükhbaataryn talbai 3, Ulan Bator; tel. (11) 458849; attached to Mongolian Acad. of Sciences; Dir B. BEKHTÖR.

RELIGION, SOCIOLOGY AND ANTHROPOLOGY

Institute of Philosophy, Sociology and Law: PO 38, POB 266, Chingeltei dist., Baruun Selbe St 15, Ulan Bator, 15141; tel. (11) 331512; e-mail info-mdg9@unet.mn; f. 1972; attached to Mongolian Acad. of Sciences; Dir G. CHULUUNBAATAR; Scientific Sec. Dr M. ZOLZAYA.

Social Sciences Institute: Ulan Bator; attached to National University of Mongolia (fmrly attached to Mongolian Acad. of Sciences); Dir O. MÖNKHBAT.

TECHNOLOGY

Agricultural Technology Science, Technology and Production Corporation: Ulan Bator; tel. (11) 341155; attached to Mongolian Academy of Sciences.

Communications Research and Production Corporation: c/o Academy of Sciences, Sükhbaataryn talbai 3, Ulan Bator; attached to Mongolian Acad. of Sciences; Dir D. LKHAGVAA.

Electronic Equipment and Machine Studies Science, Technology and Production Corporation: Ulan Bator; tel. (11) 328025; attached to Mongolian Acad. of Sciences.

Experimental and Research Centre for Leather: c/o Academy of Sciences, Sükhbaataryn talbai 3, Ulan Bator; attached to Mongolian Acad. of Sciences; Dir D. GANBOLD.

Experimental and Research Centre for Wool: c/o Academy of Sciences, Sükhbaataryn talbai 3, Ulan Bator; attached to Mongolian Acad. of Sciences; Dir G. YONDONSAMBUU.

Forestry and Wood Processing Industry Institute: c/o Academy of Sciences, Sükhbaataryn talbai 3, Ulan Bator; attached to Mongolian Acad. of Sciences; Dir SAINBAYAR.

Heat Technology and Industrial Ecology Institute: Ikh Surguuliin gudamj 2A, Sükhbaatar district, Ulan Bator; tel. 324959; attached to Mongolian Acad. of Sciences; Dir S. BATMÖNKH.

Informatics Institute: c/o Academy of Sciences, Sükhbaataryn talbai 3, Ulan Bator; tel. (11) 458090; attached to Mongolian Acad. of Sciences; Dir MAIDARJAVYN GANZORIG.

Information Technology Science, Technology and Production Corporation: Ulan Bator; tel. (11) 327133; attached to Mongolian Acad. of Sciences.

Light Industry Scientific, Technological and Production Corporation (ARMONO): Chingisiin örgön chölöö, Ulan Bator; tel. (11) 342536; e-mail armonocor@mongol.net; internet www.aeromongolia.co.kr; f. 1997; research into leather and timber industrial products; attached to Mongolian Acad. of Sciences.

Mining Institute: c/o Academy of Sciences, Sükhbaataryn talbai 3, Ulan Bator; attached to Mongolian Acad. of Sciences; Dir S. MANGAL.

Natural Freezing and Food Technology Institute: c/o Academy of Sciences, Sükhbaataryn talbai 3, Ulan Bator; attached to Mongolian Acad. of Sciences; Dir N. LONJID.

Petrochemical Technology Research Centre: Ulan Bator; tel. (11) 24779.

Power Institute: c/o Academy of Sciences, Sükhbaataryn talbai 3, Ulan Bator; attached to Mongolian Acad. of Sciences; Dir D. BUMAYUUSH.

Renewable Energy Science, Technology and Production Corporation: Chingisiin örgön chölöö, Khan-Uul district, Ulan Bator (POB 35/479); tel. (11) 342377; attached to Mongolian Acad. of Sciences; Dir B. CHADRAA.

Roads Research and Production Corporation: c/o Academy of Sciences, Sükhbaataryn talbai 3, Ulan Bator; attached to Mongolian Acad. of Sciences; Dir B. KHUNDGAA.

Standardization and Metrology National Centre: Enkh Taivny gudamj 46A, Ulan Bator (POB 51/48); tel. (11) 458349; f. 1953; attached to Min. of Industry and Trade; library of 130,000 vols; Dir NYAMJAVYN JANCHIVDORJ; publ. *Standards and Metrology* (12 a year).

Traditional Medicine Science, Technology and Production Corporation: Ulan Bator; tel. (11) 343103; attached to Mongolian Acad. of Sciences.

Transport Research and Production Corporation: c/o Academy of Sciences, Sükhbaataryn talbai 3, Ulan Bator; attached to Mongolian Acad. of Sciences; Dir L. TÜDEV.

Water Policy Research Institute: Baruun selbe 13, Ulan Bator 211238; tel. (11) 325425; f. 1965; library of 3,500 vols; Dir N. CHULUUNKHUYAG.

Libraries and Archives

Ulan Bator

Gandan Library: Gandantegchinlen Buddhist Monastery, Ulan Bator; tel. (11) 360023; f. 1838; Buddhist theology and philosophy, xylographs, secular works of science and literature.

National Archives of Mongolia: Ulan Bator 210646; tel. (11) 324533; e-mail national_archive@archives.gov.mn; f. 1996; history, art, literature, science, technology, film, sound recordings; Dir-Gen. DEMBERELIIN ÖLZIIBAATAR; publ. *Archives News* (2 a year).

State Central Library: Söüliin gudamj, Sükhbaatar district, Ulan Bator; tel. (11) 323100; f. 1921; 4m. vols, incl. rare and ancient editions; Dir GOTOVYN AKIM.

Ulaanbaatar Public Library named after D. Natsagdorj: 2nd sub-dist., Sükhbaatar dist., Ulan Bator; tel. (11) 70115705; e-mail info@pl.ub.gov.mn; internet pl.ub.gov.mn; f. 1980, centralized 1986; 4 br. libraries; Mongolian cyrillic, Mongolian scripts, Russian, English resource; 450,000 vols; Dir GANULZII U.; Deputy Dir ALTANTSETSEG CHOI.

Museums and Art Galleries

Arkhangai

Ethnographical Museum: Arkhangai; located in the Zayain Gegeenii Süm (temple founded in 1536).

Bayan-Ölgii

Town Museum: Bayan-Ölgii; Kazakh culture, especially costume and artefacts.

Dornogobi

Danzan Ravjaa Museum: Dornogobi; commemorates the life and works of the 19th-century writer and lama, Danzan Ravjaa.

Khentii

Ethnographical Museum: Khentii; located in the home of the former Tsetseg Khan.

Ulan Bator

Botanical Garden: Ulan Bator; attached to Mongolian Acad. of Sciences; Dir G. OCHIRBAT.

Memorial Museum of Victims of Political Persecution: Genden St 1, Ulan Bator; tel. (70) 110915; e-mail info@memorialmuseum.info; internet www.memorialmuseum.info; f. 1996; located in home of executed PM Genden; commemorates in documents and photographs the victims of the 1930s Stalinist purges; Dir BEKHBAT SODNOM.

Mongolian National Gallery of Modern Art: Ulan Bator; tel. (11) 327177; e-mail mnartgallery@mongolnet.mn; internet www.ulaanbaatar.net/artgallery; f. 1991; Dir D. ENKHTSETSEG.

Museum of Asian Art: Juulchny gudamj, Ulan Bator; private collection of religious art and artefacts in precious metals; Dir A. ALTANGEREL.

Museum of Military History: Enkh Taivny örgön chölöö, Ulan Bator; tel. (11) 454292; Dir Col P. BYAMBASÜREN.

Museum of Mongolian Costume: Enkh Taivny örgön chölöö, Ulan Bator; f. 2005; folk costume, felt tents and artefacts since the Genghis Khan period.

Museum of Mongolian Traditional Medicine: Next to Bogd Khan's Winter Palace (Museum of Religious History), Ulan Bator; f. 2005; Dir D. TSERENSODNOM.

Museum of Religious History: Chingis Khaany örgön chölöö, Ulan Bator; tel. (11) 324788; housed in Choyjin Lamyn Khüree, a former lamasery, and Bogd Khan's Winter Palace; Dir G. TÖVSAIKHAN.

National Museum of Mongolian History: Juulchmii gudamj 1, Ulan Bator 46, (POB 46/332); tel. (11) 326802; e-mail nmm@mongolnet.mn; internet www.nationalmuseum.mn; f. 1924 as Mongolian National Museum; present name 1990 by merger of State Central Museum and Museum of the Revolution; 46,000 historical and ethnographical objects from prehistory to present day; Dir Dr J. SARUULBUYAN; publ. *Museologia* (1 a year).

Natsagdorj Museum: Chingis Khaany örgön chölöö, Ulan Bator; tel. (11) 327879; life and works of the author and poet Dashdorjiin Natsagdorj.

Natural History Museum: Khuvisgalchdyn örgön chölöö, Ulan Bator; tel. (11) 321716; natural history, Gobi desert dinosaur eggs and skeletons; Dir P. ERDENEBAT.

Theatre Museum: Cultural Palace, Sükhbaatar Square, Ulan Bator; tel. (11) 326820.

Ulan Bator Museum: Enkh Taivny örgön chölöö, Ulan Bator; located in old Russian house; history of Ulan Bator.

Wildlife Museum: Öndör Gegeen Zanabazaryn gudamj, Ulan Bator; tel. (11) 360248.

Zanabazar Fine Arts Museum: Barilgachdyn talbai, Ulan Bator; sculptures by Mongolia's first Buddhist leader and *tankas* (religious paintings); Dir D. GUNGAA.

Zhukov, G. K., House Museum: Enkh Taivny örgön chölöö, 15th sub-district, Ulan Bator; tel. (11) 453781; career of Soviet Marshal Zhukov.

Universities

CHOI LUVSANJAV UNIVERSITY OF LANGUAGE AND CIVILIZATION

11th microraion, 7th sub-district, Sükhbaatar dist., Ulan Bator (POB 13/550)
Telephone: (11) 353524
Founded 1993
Mongolian and Chinese studies; training of English- and Japanese-speaking teachers and interpreters
Vice-Pres.: SOYOMBO LUVSANJAV
Number of teachers: 40 (22 full-time, 18 part-time)
Number of students: 380
Library of 10,000 vols

IKH ZASAG INTERNATIONAL UNIVERSITY

4 khoroo, B. Dorjiin St, Bayanzurkh dist., Ulan Bator (POB 349), 13381
Telephone: (976) 70157770
E-mail: ikhzasag@ikhzasag.edu.mn
Internet: www.ikhzasag.edu.mn
Private control; attached to Nat. Ccl on Higher Educational Accreditation
Languages of instruction: English, Mongolian
Academic year: September to July
Pres.: Prof. NAMSRAIN NYAM-OSOR
Vice-Pres.: Prof. JAMBAL TSETSEGMAA
Vice-Pres. for Marketing: NYAM-OSOR UCHRAL
Vice-Pres. for Social Matters: SUREN DAMCHAASUREN
Number of teachers: 250
Number of students: 7,000
Publication: *Ikh Zasag* (2 a year, journal, jtly with Acad. of Nomadic Civilization and Culture)

MONGOLIAN STATE EDUCATION UNIVERSITY

Baga toiruu 14, Sükhbaatar district, Ulan Bator
Telephone: (11) 326010
E-mail: togmid@mspu.edu.mn
Internet: www.mspu.edu.mn
Founded 1951
State control
Academic year: September to June
Rector: Prof. B. JADAMBAA
Vice-Rector for International Relations and Information: Prof. B. JADAMBAA
Vice-Rector for Research: Prof. D. TÖMÖRTOGOO
Vice-Rector for Teaching: Prof. TS. BATSUURI
Head of Academic Affairs: Prof. D. PÜREVDORJ
Head of Graduate Studies: Prof. N. JADAMBAA
Library of 300,000 vols
Number of teachers: 330
Number of students: 5,261
Publication: *Teacher Education* (2 a year)

DIRECTORS

School of Art and Technology: Prof. G. BATDORJ
School of Computer Science and Information Technology: Prof. L. CHOIJOOVAANCHIG
School of Education Studies: Prof. TS. SUMYAA
School of Foreign Languages: Prof. Z. GULIRAANZ
School of History and Social Sciences: Prof. D. NARANTSETSEG
School of Mathematics and Statistics: Prof. TS. BATKHÜÜ
School of Mongolian Studies: Prof. TS. ÖNÖRBAYAN
School of Natural Sciences: Prof. M. ÜINDEN
School of Physical Education: Prof. S. JAMTS
School of Physics and Technology: Prof. R. BAZARSÜREN
School of Pre-School Education: Prof. J. BATDELGER
School of Teacher Training: Prof. S. BATKHUYAG

MONGOLIAN STATE UNIVERSITY OF AGRICULTURE

Zaisan, 17024, Khan-Uul dist., 11th Khoroo, Ulan Bator
Telephone: (11) 341153
E-mail: infotech@magicnet.mn
Internet: www.msua.edu.mn
Founded 1942 as veterinary dept of Mongolian State Univ., became Institute of Agriculture 1958, univ. status 1991, current name adopted 1996
State control
Languages of instruction: Mongolian, Russian
Academic year: September to June
Pres.: Prof. Dr Acad. B. BYAMBAA
Vice-Pres. for Academic Affairs: BAASANSUKH BYAMBAA
Vice-Pres. for Int. Affairs: Assoc. Prof. Dr GOMBOJAV ALTANGEREL
Vice-Pres. for Social and Economic Affairs: Dr AMARSAIKHAN TS
Vice-Pres. for Scientific Affairs: Dr BAYARSUKH NOOV
Library of 200,000 vols
Number of teachers: 400
Number of students: 11,000

DEANS

School of Agrobiology: Dr D. NASANDULAM
School of Biological Resource and Management: Dr T. BALDAN
School of Ecology, Technology and Development: Dr E. TUMURTOGTOKH
School of Economics and Business: M. ERDENEBAYAR
School of Engineering: Dr G. ENKHBAYAR
School of Natural Sciences: Dr J. URANCHIMEG
School of Veterinary Medicine and Biotechnology: Dr P. .BOLORMAA

MONGOLIAN STATE UNIVERSITY OF ARTS AND CULTURE

Baga Toiruu 22, Chingeltei dist., Ulan Bator, 210646
Telephone: (11) 329137
E-mail: avrora2002@yahoo.com
Internet: www.msuac.edu.com
Founded 1990
State control
Academic year: September to June
Rector: ERDENETSOGT SONINTOGOS
Vice-Rector for Academic Affairs: GUNCHIN ALTANGEREL
Vice-Rector for Research: CHULUUN ALTANTSETSEG
Registrar: ALTANGERELIIN GANBAATAR
Librarian: BANZRAGCH TUNGALAG
Number of teachers: 237
Number of students: 3,117

DEANS

School of Culture: DASH BAT-ERDENE
School of Culture and Civilization: GURRINCHIN SUKHBAT
School of Fine Arts: LKHAGVAA BUMANDORJ
School of Music Arts: ADILBISH DASHPELJEE
School of Radio and Television: DORJ OYUNGEREL
School of Stage and Screen Arts: NAMSRAI SUVD

MONGOLIAN UNIVERSITY OF SCIENCE AND TECHNOLOGY

Baga Toiruu 34, Sükhbaatar dist., Ulan Bator (POB 46/520)
Telephone: (11) 325109
E-mail: info@must.edu.mn
Internet: www.must.edu.mn
Founded 1969
State control
Academic year: September to July
Rector: D. DASHJAMTS (acting)
Vice-Rector for Academic Affairs: Z. TSERENDORJ
Vice-Rector for Finance and Devt: L. BOLDBAATAR
Vice-Rector for Research and Technology: D. DASHJAMTS
Chief Admin. Officer: O. NASANBAT
Librarian: G. PÜREV
Library of 170,000 vols
Number of teachers: 781
Number of students: 17,000

Publications: *MUST News* (12 a year, in Mongolian), *Science and Technology* (4 a year, in Mongolian), *Scientific Transactions* (4 a year, in Mongolian)

DIRECTORS

School of Civil Engineering: Z. BINDERYAA
School of Computer Science and Management: S. BAIGALTUGS
School of Food and Biotechnology: D. NANSALMAA
School of Foreign Languages: T. BATBAYAR
School of Geology: D. CHULUUN
School of Humanities: A. ENKHBAATAR
School of Industrial Technology and Design: B. DAVAASÜREN
School of Materials Technology: P. MÖNKHBAATAR
School of Mathematics: J. BAASANDORJ
School of Mechanical Engineering: G. BATKHÜREL
School of Mining Engineering: B. PÜREVTOGTOKH
School of Power Engineering: H. ENKHJARGAL
School of Technology in Darkhan: S. TSEVEL
School of Technology in Erdenet: S. DAVAANYAM
School of Technology in Övörhangai Province: J. JANTSANDORJ
School of Technology in Sükhbaatar Province: MAJIGIIN KHÜRLEE
School of Telecommunications and Information Technology: B. DAMDINSÜREN
Graduate Study Centre: H. BUYANNEMEKH

NATIONAL UNIVERSITY OF MONGOLIA

Ikh Surguuliin gudamj 1, Sükhbaatar district, Ulan Bator (POB 46A/523)
Telephone: (11) 320892
E-mail: numelect@magicnet.mn
Internet: www.num.edu.mn

Founded 1942
State control
Language of instruction: Mongolian
Academic year: September to June

Pres.: S. TUMUR-OCHIR
Vice-Pres. for Academic Affairs: R. RINCHINBAZAR
Vice-Pres. for Research: CH. GANZORIG

Library of 450,000 vols
Number of teachers: 2,000
Number of students: 16,000

Publication: *Proceedings*

DEANS

Faculty of Chemistry: D. DORJ
Faculty of Earth Sciences: CH. GONCHIGSUMLAA
Graduate School: A. MEKEI
School of Mathematics and Computer Science: JAMTSYN BAATAR
School of Physics and Electronics: CHÜLTEMIIN BAYARKHÜÜ
School of Social Sciences: SH. SODNOM

ORKHON UNIVERSITY

Chinggis Khaany örgön chölöö, Khan-Uul dist., Ulan Bator (POB 36/176)
Telephone: (11) 342696
E-mail: info@orkhon.edu.mn
Internet: www.orkhon.edu.mn

Founded 1992
Private control

BA degree courses in languages (English, French, German, Japanese, Korean, Russian) and law; MA degree courses in linguistics

Dir: Prof. Dr NYAMAAGIIN KHAJIDSÜREN

Library of 25,000 vols
Number of teachers: 70
Number of students: 1,000

ULAANBAATAR UNIVERSITY

Bayanzürkh dist., Ulan Bator (POB 44/658)
Telephone: (11) 450179
E-mail: ubuniv@mongol.net
Internet: www.ulaanbaatar.edu.mn

Founded 1993 as Higher Technical School; received charter 1996
State control
Academic year: September to July

Faculties of language and literature, social sciences and technology

Rector: YONG SUNG JE
Vice-Rector: D. BOLD
Scientific Sec.: T. NAMJIL

Number of teachers: 78
Number of students: 800

Publication: *Proceedings of the Ulaanbaatar University* (1 a year)

UNIVERSITY OF HEALTH SCIENCES

POB 48/111, Ulan Bator 210648
Zorig St 3, Sükhbaatar Dist., Ulan Bator 210648
Telephone: (11) 328670
E-mail: int_rel@hsum.edu.mn
Internet: www.hsum-ac.mn

Founded 1942
State control
Academic year: September to July

Pres.: Prof. Dr TS. LKHAGVASÜREN
Vice-Pres. for Academic Affairs: Prof. Dr D. AMARSAIKHAN
Vice-Pres. for Clinical Affairs: Prof. Dr KH. ALTAISAIKHAN
Vice-Pres. for Research and Int. Relations: Prof. Dr N. SUMBERZUL
Centre for Medical Education: Dr D. OTGONBAYAR
Centre for Student Affairs: Dr A. GURBADAM
Graduate Training Centre: Dr G. ARIUNTUUL
Postgraduate Training Institute: Dr D. ZORIG
Librarian: N. TSAGAACH

Library of 300,000 vols, 100,000 periodicals
Number of teachers: 536
Number of students: 10,096

Publication: *Mongolian Journal of Health Sciences*

DEANS

Darkhan Medical College: Prof. Dr M. NYAMSUREN
Dornogobi Medical College: Prof. Dr B. NYAMKHUU
Gobi-Altai Medical College: Prof. Dr KH. OROSOO
School of Biomedicine: Prof. Dr G. BATBAATAR
School of Dentistry: B. AMARSAIKHAN
School of Medicine: Prof. Dr D. GONCHIGSUREN
School of Nursing: Prof. Dr D. TSERENDAGVA
School of Pharmacy: Prof. Dr D. ENKHJARGAL
School of Public Health: O. CHIMEDSUREN
School of Traditional Medicine: Prof. S. OLDOKH

UNIVERSITY OF THE HUMANITIES

POB 53, Ulan Bator 210646
Small Ring Rd, Sükhbaatar dist., Ulan Bator 20/4
Telephone: (11) 318524
E-mail: uh@humanities.mn
Internet: www.humanities.mn

Founded 1979 as Higher School of Russian Language Teachers, present name and status 1999
Private control
Language of instruction: Mongolian
Academic year: September to June

Schools of foreign languages, social sciences; Depts of business administration, culture and American and British studies, foreign languages, human resource management, information technology, journalism, literature

Dir: Dr CHULUUNDORJ BEGZ

Library of 130,051 vols
Number of teachers: 150
Number of students: 5,000

Publication: *Khumuun ukhaan*

Higher Schools

Academy of Management: Chingisiin örgön chölöö 7, Khan-Uul district, Ulan Bator; tel. (11) 343037; e-mail td@aom.edu.mn; f. 1924; govt agency; depts of computer science, economics; English language, management, public administration; 52 teachers; 739 students; Rector TOGOOCHIN LKHAGVAA; publs *Management* (4 a year, in Mongolian), *Public Administration* (4 a year, in Mongolian).

Darkhan Higher School: 4th Sub-Dist., Darkhan Dist., Darkhan-Uul Province (Darkhan POB 520); tel. (372) 35652; internet www.darkhandeed.mn; f. 1997; accounting, Chinese, English, hotel and restaurant management, Japanese, Korean, tourism; library: 25,000 vols; 90 teachers; 1,000 students.

Defence Academy: 16th sub-district, Bayanzükh district, Ulan Bator; tel. (11) 458673; accounting, communications, electronics, law, military history, military science, operation of motor vehicles, state administration, tracked vehicles and bridge-building machinery; Dir Col N. JALBAJAV.

Higher School of Arts and Crafts: Ulan Bator.

Higher School of Culture: Erkh Chölöönii talbai, Chingeltei district, Ulan Bator (POB 46/982); tel. (11) 326759; e-mail cclib@mongol.net; internet www.moncollege.150m.com; training of librarians, cultural managers, museum workers and archivists, printers, and music, song and dance teachers; Dir G. BAATAR.

Higher School of European Languages: located at: Ikh Surguuliin gudamj 9, Sükhbaatar district, Ulan Bator (POB 46/982); tel. (11) 320993; f. 1993; English, French, Russian and German interpreting; 52 teachers (11 full-time, 41 part-time); 632 students; Rector T. PELJID.

Higher School of Finance and Economics: Enkh Taivny gudamj 12A, Bayanzürkh district, Ulan Bator 49; tel. (11) 458378; internet www.ife.edu.mn; f. 1924; depts of accounting and audit, banking and finance, business and management, economics and econometrics, information technology, international studies; 65 teachers; 1,200 students; Dir JAMYANDORJIIN BATKHUYAG.

Higher School of Information Technology: Ulan Bator; Dir G. TSOGBADRAKH.

Higher School of International Economics and Business: 20th sub-district, Bayangol district, Ulan Bator; tel. (11) 681525; e-mail iieb_elselt@yahoo.com; internet www.iieb.edu.mn; banking and accounting, business management, international economics, taxation and audit.

Higher School of International Studies: Ikh Surguuliin gudamj 2A, Sükhbataar district, Ulan Bator, (POB 46/205); tel. (11) 329860; Dir NARANDULAM.

Higher School of Labour: Erkh Chölöönii talbai (bldg behing the Tengis cinema), Chingeltei district, Ulan Bator; tel. (11)

318176; e-mail mli_999@yahoo.com; attached to Mongolian Confederation of Trade Unions; accountancy and social work, business, finance, labour economics and management.

Higher School of Literature: Ulan Bator; Dir SHIRSEDIIN TSEND-AYUUSH.

Higher School of Mongolian Language and Literature: Chingisiin örgön chölöö 29, 3rd sub-district, Khan-Uul district, Ulan Bator; tel. (11) 342210; trains teachers and interpreters in French, German and Japanese; English-language journalism.

Higher School of Oriental Literature: Ulan Bator; Dir S. BATMÖNKH.

Higher School of Oriental Philosophy and Anthropology: 17th Sub-Dist., Bayangol Dist., Ulan Bator; tel. (11) 361461; e-mail ophsi@mongolnet.mn; Dir NANSALYN SARANTUYAA.

Higher School of Religion: Ulan Bator; tel. (11) 457454; Dir SH. SONINBAYAR.

Higher School of Social Studies: 2nd Sub-Dist., Bayanzürkh Dist., Ulan Bator (POB 23/277); tel. (11) 460356; e-mail uuds@magicnet.mn; f. 1993; library: 12,000 vols; Dir TS. ENKHEE.

Higher School of Technology: Darkhan, Darkhan-Uul province; tel. (372) 23368; e-mail technol@mongol.net; fmr polytechnic and technical college; electrical and heating engineering, geology, mining and ore concentration, power supply management.

Higher School of Trade and Industry: Oyuutny gudamj 14, Enkh Taivny örgön chölöö, Ulan Bator, (POB 48/404); tel. (11) 325724; e-mail icbm@magicnet.mn; f. 1924; accountancy, business management, international trade, marketing; library: 2 libraries, with 22,000 vols; 60 teachers; 1,200 students; Rector S. BUDNYAM; publ. *Mercury* (3 a year).

Khalkha Juram Higher School of Law: Tulga Co. Bldg, Ikh Toiruu 20, Sükhbaatar Dist., Ulan Bator, (POB 51/128); tel. (11) 350480; Dir T. DOOKHÜÜ.

Khan-Uul Higher School: Tulga Co. Bldg, Ikh Toiruu 20, Sükhbaatar Dist., Ulan Bator (POB 46/419); tel. (11) 351032; e-mail khan-uul@mongol.net; internet www.khan-uul.mn; f. 1994; applied mathematics, business economics, computer programming, computer technology; 25 teachers; 280 students; Dir TSERENGIIN DEMBEREL.

Mongol Higher School: Ulan Bator; Dir NAMJAAGIIN DASHZEVEG.

Mongolian Business Institute: Enkh Taivny örgön chölöö, Bayangol district, Ulan Bator, (POB 24/715); tel. (11) 361589; e-mail mbi_191@mol.mn; internet www.mbi.edu.mn; f. 1991; degree courses in economics, finance, management, marketing; 40 teachers; 500 students; Dir Dr B. ERDENESÜREN.

Mongolian National Higher School: Enigma Centre, 11th sub-district, Bayangol district, Ulan Bator; tel. (11) 300900; e-mail mni@mongolnet.mn; f. 1998; economics, economics of tourism, financial and business management, hotel and restaurant management, international trade, law, marketing; Dir TÖMÖRBAATARYN KHERÜÜGA.

Monos Higher School of Medicine: Songolongiin toiruu 5, 20th sub-district, Songinokhairkhan dist., Ulan Bator; tel. (11) 633235; medicine and pharmacy.

Otgontenger University: Jukovyn örgön chölöö, Bayanzürkh dist., Ulan Bator, (POB 51/35); tel. (11) 454560; e-mail oy_oyun@magicnet.mn; internet www.otgontenger.edu.mn; f. 1991; training of Russian- and English-language teachers and interpreters, Japanese-, German-, French-, Chinese- and Korean-language business and tourism managers, and Japanese-language int. tour guides, training in English-language journalism; 48 teachers; 650 students; Founder and Chair. DULAMSÜRENGIIN OYUUNKHOROL; Rector D. NARANCHIMEG.

Otoch Maramba Higher School of Medicine: 2nd sub-district, Bayanzürkh dist., Ulan Bator (POB 49/235); tel. (11) 457489; f. 1991; study of traditional medicine; 6 teachers; 68 students; Dir TSERENSODNOM.

Private Higher School of Oriental Philosophy and History: Enkh Taivny gudamj 35, Ulan Bator (POB 44/283); tel. (11) 322628; f. 1992; library: 5,000 vols; 150 students; Dir R. NANSAL.

Railway College: Enkh Taivny örgön chölöö 44, Bayangol district, Ulan Bator (POB 35/76); tel. (11) 322723; e-mail mtzcoll@mongolnet.mn; automation and telecommunications, construction, management, maintenance, railway transport organization, rolling-stock maintenance, passenger services; trains staff for Mongolian railways, the country's largest employer; Dir B. SERÜÜD.

Shikhikhutug Higher School of Law: Ikh Surguuliin gudamj 1, 6th sub-district, Ulan Bator (POB 46/1033); tel. (11) 323392; e-mail shihihutug@mongol.net; Dir D. OYUUNTSETSEG.

Shonkhor Higher School of Physical Culture: Baga Toiruu 55, 8th Sub-Dist., Sükhbaatar Dist., Ulan Bator (POB 960); tel. (11) 319858; Dir KH. BAYANMÖNKH.

Tenger Socio-Economic Higher School: Chinggissin örgön chölöö, 2nd sub-district, Khan-Uul dist., Ulan Bator; tel. (11) 342651; accounting, anthropology, business economics, social sciences, social work, state administration, tourism, trade economics; Chinese language jtly with Shandong Univ., China.

Zanabazar Buddhist University: Ulan Bator; attached to Gandantegchinlen monastery; Dir SH. SONINBAYAR.

Colleges

College of Agriculture: Darkhan; hydrology, land improvement, meteorology.

O. Tleikhan Building College: Baruun Dörvön Zam, Enkh Taivny örgön chölöö 35, Ulan Bator (POB 24/643); tel. (11) 322723; e-mail cwc@magicnet.mn; civil engineering, computer operations, electrical engineering, machine and vehicle repair, utilities; Dir B. CHIMIDDORJ.

Ulan Bator College: Construction College Bldg, West side of rd to Gandan monastery, Baruun Dörvön Zam, Bayangol district, Ulan Bator; depts of business management and computer programming, Korean-language teacher-training and interpreting; 10 teachers; 140 students; Rector YUM SUN JE.

MONTENEGRO

The Higher Education System

Following the dissolution of the Socialist Federal Republic of Yugoslavia in 1992, Montenegro became part of the Federal Republic of Yugoslavia, which was renamed the State Union of Serbia and Montenegro in 2003. In 2006 Montenegro declared independence from the State Union of Serbia and Montenegro. The Univerzitet Crne Gore Podgorica (University of Montenegro, Podgorica—founded 1974) is the main institution of higher education and was established while Montenegro was part of the Socialist Federal Republic of Yugoslavia. In 2006 the Univerzitet Mediteran (Mediterranean University), a private university, was founded. In 2003 the new Law on Higher Education introduced a range of reforms in accordance with the objectives of the Bologna Declaration. These included increased autonomy for institutions of higher education, the introduction in 2007/08 of a three-cycle system of degrees (Bachelors/Masters/Doctorate) and the adoption of the European Credit Transfer and Accumulation System (ECTS). In 2008/09 there were 38 institutions of higher education, including faculties, art academies and private institutions, and in 2010/11 a total of 22,163 students were enrolled in higher education. Responsibility for higher education rests with the Ministry of Education.

Admission to higher education is based on results obtained in the secondary school (school leaving examination/Matura) and—for entrance to certain institutions (e.g. faculties of arts and medicine)—results obtained in the entrance examination. The undergraduate Bachelors degree takes at least three years and requires the accumulation of a minimum of 180 ECTS credit units. The postgraduate Masters degree is a one- to two-year programme of study (60–120 ECTS credit units) following the Bachelors and requires the submission of a thesis. Finally, the Doctorate is the highest university-level degree and is awarded after a period of research culminating in defence of a thesis. In addition to the Bologna-style degrees, higher education institutions also provide a number of undergraduate and postgraduate Diploma programmes.

The Council for Vocational Education and Training and the Council for Adult Education are responsible for vocational and professional, and continuing education, respectively, while the Montenegro Council of Higher Education (MCHE), set up in 2003, is responsible for accreditation of higher educational institutions. Furthermore, all higher education establishments must also conduct self-evaluation in specified areas.

Regulatory and Representative Bodies

GOVERNMENT

Ministry of Culture: Cetinje, ul. Njegoševa, 81250 Podgorica; tel. (41) 232571; e-mail kabinet.kultura@mku.gov.me; internet www.ministarstvokulture.gov.me; Minister BRANISLAV MIĆUNOVIĆ.

Ministry of Education: Vaka Đurovića bb, 81000 Podgorica; tel. (20) 410100; e-mail mps@mps.gov.me; internet www.mpin.gov.me; Minister SLAVOLJUB STIJEPOVIĆ.

Ministry of Science: Rimski trg 46, 81000 Podgorica; tel. (20) 482145; e-mail kabinet@mna.gov.me; internet www.mna.gov.me; Minister SANJA VLAHOVIC.

ACCREDITATION

ENIC/NARIC Montenegro: ENIC Centre Montenegro, Rimski trg bb, 81000 Podgorica; tel. (20) 405301; internet www.enic-naric.net/index.aspx?c=montenegro.

Council for Higher Education: c/o Vaka Đurovića bb, 81000 Podgorica; f. 2003; responsible for assuring high quality higher education; advises Govt and assists the instns in improving and sustaining quality; evaluation and accreditation of instns and study programmes.

Learned Societies

GENERAL

Crnogorska akademija nauka i umjetnosti (Montenegrin Academy of Sciences and Arts): Rista Stijovića 5, 81000 Podgorica; tel. (20) 655450; e-mail canu@cg.ac.yu; internet www.canu.org.me; f. 1973 as Soc. of Sciences and Arts of Montenegro, present name and status 1976; organizes, initiates and implements scientific research, by itself or in cooperation with other scientific instns; 70 mems (32 full and 10 assoc. mems in the working body of the Academy, 28 foreign mems); library of 80,000 vols; Pres. MOMIR ĐUROVIĆ; Vice Pres. MIJAT ŠUKOVIĆ; Sec.-Gen. RANISLAV BULATOVIĆ; publs *Bibliografije* (Bibliographies), *Glasnik* (Review), *Godišnjak CANU* (1 a year), *Istorijski izvori* (Historical Issues), *Naučni skupovi* (Symposia), *Posebna izdanja* (Special Editions), *Posebni radovi* (Special Works), *Zbornici radova* (Works).

Udruženje Likovnih Umjetnika Crne Gore (Association of Fine Artists of Montenegro): Marka Miljanova br. 2, 81000 Podgorica; tel. (20) 622518; e-mail ulucg@t-com.me; internet www.ulucg.me; f. 1946; organizes collective and individual exhibitions; organizes, assists and conducts exhibition exchanges with other asscns and their mems, as well as foreign authors in the field of fine art; 400 mems (330 have completed Academy of Fine Arts, 70 have Masters degree); Pres. IGOR RAKČEVIĆ; Vice-Pres. ABAZ DIZDAREVIĆ.

EDUCATION

British Council: Ulcinjska 8, Gorica C, 81000 Podgorica; tel. (20) 618410; e-mail pginfo@britishcouncil.me; internet www.britishcouncil.org/montenegro.htm; f. 1934 as British Cttee for Relations with Other Countries; supports teachers and learners of English; works with Min. of Education and other partners on VET reforms; organizes recognized English language examinations; Dir VANJA MADZGALJ.

LANGUAGE AND LITERATURE

Montenegrin PEN Centre: St Gipos 1/3 postanski fah 117, Cetinje; tel. (41) 241733; internet www.montenegro.org/pen.html; f. 1990; promotes democratic values, friendship, cooperation and use of the Montenegrin language; defends freedom of expression; 53 mems; Pres. SRETEN PEROVIC; publ. *Doclea* (4 a year).

Research Institutes

BIBLIOGRAPHY, LIBRARY SCIENCE AND MUSEOLOGY

Republički zavod za zaštitu spomenika kulture (Republic Institute for the Protection of Cultural Monuments of Montenegro): Bajova 150, 81250 Cetinje; tel. (41) 231039; e-mail rzzsk@t-com.me; f. 1948 as Institute for Protection and Scientific Research of Cultural Monuments and Natural Rarities; attached to Min. of Culture; research, registration, conservation and protection of cultural property in Montenegro; library of 2,500 vols; Dir DJORDJIJE VUSUROVIC; publ. *Starine Crne Gore* (1 a year).

HISTORY, GEOGRAPHY AND ARCHAEOLOGY

Istorijski institut Crne Gore (Historical Institute of Montenegro): Blvr Revolucije 5, 81000 Podgorica; tel. (20) 241336; e-mail ii@ac.me; internet www.iicg.ac.me; f. 1948; attached to Univ. of Montenegro; educates experts; organizes professional devt of researchers; conducts research and publishing; library of 30,000 vols, 687 magazines; Dir Dr RADOSLAV RASPOPOVIC; publ. *Istorijski zapisi* (4 a year).

LANGUAGE AND LITERATURE

Institut za strane jezike (Institute of Foreign Languages): Jovana Tomaševića 37, 81000 Podgorica; tel. (20) 245334; e-mail isj@cg.ac.yu; internet www.isj.ac.me; f. 1978; attached to University of Montenegro; courses in English, Russian, Italian, French and German; promotes research in linguistics, literature and interdisciplinary fields (literary linguistics, sociolinguistics, psycholinguistics); library of 8,000 vols; Dean Dr IGOR LAKIC.

NATURAL SCIENCES

Centar za ekotoksikološka ispitivanja (Centre for Ecotoxicological Research): Put

Radomira Ivanovića br. 2, 81000 Podgorica; tel. (20) 658090; e-mail info@ceti.co.me; internet www.ceti.co.me; f. 1996; ecotoxicological studies of air, soil, water, noise and vibrations and ionizing and non-ionizing radiation; Dir NADA MEDENICA.

Hidrometeorološki zavod Crne Gore (Hydrometeorological Institute of Montenegro): IV proleterske 19, 81000 Podgorica; tel. (20) 655183; internet www.meteo.co.me; f. 1947; meteorological, hydrological, water quality and air quality stations; activities incl. automatic measuring of land temperature, agroclimatic research, agrometeorological service, quality control of surface and underground waters and air; scientific programmes, studies and projects related to environmental field; hydrographic, topographic surveys; data colln from hydrography, navigation, geology and geophysics; Dir LUKA MITROVIC.

Institut za biologiju mora (Institute of Marine Biology): Dobrota bb, POB 69, 85330 Kotor; tel. (32) 334569; e-mail biokotor@t-com.me; internet www.ibmk.org; f. 1961; attached to Univ. of Montenegro; scientific investigation, exploitation, control and protection of the sea; Dir Dr ALEKSANDAR JOKSIMOVIC; publ. *Studia Marina* (2 or 3 a year).

Institute of Biotechnology: Cetinjski put bb, 81000 Podgorica; tel. (20) 268437; e-mail bti@ac.me; internet www.ucg.ac.me/eng/biotehnicki_ins.htm; f. 1937 as Centre for Subtropical cultures in Bar; attached to Univ. of Montenegro; agriculture, veterinary medicine and forestry; Dir Dr LJUBOMIR PEJOVIĆ.

Institut za javno zdravlje (Institute of Public Health): Ljubljanska bb, 81000 Podgorica; tel. (20) 412888; e-mail ijzcg@ijzcg.me; internet www.ijzcg.me; f. 1922; conducts statistical research in the field of health; monitors and evaluates public health; monitors and conducts research through its 6 centres; Dir Dr BOBAN MUGOŠA; publ. *Statisticki godisnjak* (1 a year).

Libraries and Archives

Cetinje

Biblioteka Narodnog muzeja Crne Gore (Library of the National Museum of Montenegro): Novice Cerovica bb, 81250 Cetinje; tel. (41) 230310; e-mail nmcg@t-com.me; internet www.mnmuseum.org; f. 1926; 20,000 vols; Exec. Dept Prof. KRSTO MIJANOVIĆ.

Centralna narodna biblioteka Crne Gore 'Đurđe Crnojević' (Central National Library of Montenegro 'Đurđe Crnojević'): Blvr crnogorskih junaka br. 163, 81250 Cetinje; tel. (41) 231143; e-mail info@cnbct.vbcg.me; internet www.cnb.me; f. 1592, present name 1964, present bldg 1980; spec. colln of MSS, maps, picture postcards, photographs, records, exhibition catalogues; nat. copyright and deposit library; inter-library loan; 2,000,000 vols; Dir DJUROVIC JELENA; publ. *Bibliografski vjesnik* (3 a year).

Državni arhiv Crne Gore (State Archives of Montenegro): Novice Cerovica br. 2, 81250 Cetinje; tel. (41) 231045; e-mail dacg@t-com.me; internet www.dacg.me; f. 1951, inherited documents of the State Archive of Montenegro (f. 1895); explores and publishes archival heritage; official state documents of Montenegro since 1878; 3,760 m of documents; oldest document dates from 1539; Dir STEVAN RADUNOVIĆ; publ. *Arhivski zapisi* (Archive Records).

Herceg Novi

Herceg Novi Library: Herceg Stephan Sq. 6, 85340 Herceg Novi; tel. (31) 321900; e-mail biblhn@t-com.me; internet www.bibliotekaherceg-novi.org.rs; collns of Dušan Petkovic (5,500 books); Veljka Radojevic; Doklestic, Daljev, Lucic, Subotic; heritage colln; 55,000 vols; Dir NEVENKA MITROVIC.

Podgorica

Biblioteka istorijskog instituta Crne Gore (Library of the Historical Institute of Montenegro): Blvr Revolucije 5, 81000 Podgorica; tel. (20) 241336; e-mail ii@ac.me; internet www.iicg.ac.me/o_biblioteci.htm; f. 1948; 30,000 vols, 192 newspapers, 687 magazines.

Crnogorska Kinoteka (Film Archives of Montenegro): Wolves Miljana 59, Podgorica; tel. (20) 232016; internet www.cg-kinoteka.org; f. 2000; gathers and preserves films and supplementary film materials (documents, photographs, posters, publicity materials, old items related to film etc.); Dir BRANKO BALETIĆ.

Museums and Art Galleries

Cetinje

Narodni muzej Crne Gore (National Museum of Montenegro): Novice Cerovica bb, 81250 Cetinje; tel. (41) 230310; e-mail nmcg@t-com.me; internet www.mnmuseum.org; f. 1896; consists of 5 depts: Art Museum, Ethnographic Museum, Historical Museum, King Nikola's Palace and Njegoš's Museum Biljarda; contains archaeological sources, written and printed documents, war relics, furniture, ethnographic subject matter of present-day Montenegro; art works from medieval period to late 20th century; library of 30,000 vols; Dir PAVLE PEJOVIĆ; publs *Glasnik*, *Messenger* (online).

Herceg Novi

Josip Bepo Benković: Ul. Marka Vojnovića 4, 85340 Herceg Novi; tel. (31) 324051; e-mail galerijahn@cg.yu; internet www.rastko.rs/rastko-bo/muzej/gal_e.html; f. 1966, fmrly The Art School in Herceg-Novi; permanent exhibition of 200 paintings, sculptures and graphics; workshop for preservation and restoration; ateliers for painters and sculptors.

Zavicajni muzej Herceg-Novi (Regional Museum of Herceg-Novi): Ul. Mirka Komnenovica 9, 85340 Herceg Novi; tel. (31) 322485; e-mail muzej@cg.yu; internet www.rastko.rs/rastko-bo/muzej; f. 1949 as Nat. Museum of Herceg Novi, present bldg 2001; colln from Neolithic period to beginning of the Christian era; 30 icons; objects of traditional culture of the region, incl. tools for cattle breeding, agriculture, oil growing; nat. costumes, music instruments and household furniture; 100 Mediterranean and subtropical plants over 1,000 sq. m; Dir DJORDJE CAPIN; Curator VIKTOR VARGA; publs *Muzejske Sveske* (irregular), *Posebna Izdanja*.

Kotor

Pomorski muzej Crne Gore (Maritime Museum of Montenegro): Boka Marine Sq. 391, Kotor; tel. (32)304720; e-mail pom.muzej.dir@t-com.me; internet www.museummaritimum.com; f. 1880 by 'Boka Marine' Fraternity, present bldg 1984; models of ships, documents, paintings, weapons, Turkish guns, navigation instruments and compasses, folk costumes, jewellery, ornamental items and antique furniture; library of 16,000 vols; Dir MILEVA PEJAKOVIĆ-VUJOŠEVIĆ; publ. *Godišnjak Pomorskog Muzeja u Kotoru* (Yearbook).

Podgorica

Centar za arheološka istraživanja Crne Gore (Centre for Archaeological Research of Montenegro): Gojka Radonjica 33A, 20000 Podgorica; tel. (20) 620018; e-mail czaicg@t-com.me; f. 1961, fmrly Archaeological Colln of Montenegro, current name adopted 1997; colln, arrangement, maintenance, study and presentation of archaeological excavation sites in Montenegro.

Muzej grada Podgorice (Museum of the City of Podgorica): Marka Miljahova 4, 81000 Podgorica; tel. (20) 242-543; e-mail pgmuzej@t-com.me; f. 1950; 4 areas of study: archaeological, ethnographic, historical and cultural-historical; colln of displays from the classical period to the present; Roman fibula, Illyrian jewellery, old coins, metal objects and bones related to the settlements and influences of different civilizations and cultures in the area.

Prirodnjački muzej Crne Gore (Natural History Museum of Montenegro): Trg Vojvode Bećir Bega Osmanagića 16, POB 374, 81000 Podgorica; tel. (20) 633184; e-mail prmuzej@t-com.me; internet www.pmcg.co.me; f. 1961; research; exhibits on the fauna and palaeontology of Montenegro; museum collns; Dir ONDREJ VIZI; publ. *Natura Montenegrina* (online).

Universities

UNIVERZITET CRNE GORE
(University of Montenegro)

Cetinjska br.2, 81000 Podgorica
Telephone: (20) 414255
E-mail: rektor@ac.me
Internet: www.ucg.ac.me

Founded 1974, current name adopted 1992
State control
Academic year: September to June

Rector: Prof. Dr PREDRAG MIRANOVIĆ
Vice-Rector for Int. Cooperation: Prof. Dr MIRA VUKČEVIĆ
Vice-Rector for Field of Arts: Prof. NATAŠA ĐUROVIĆ
Vice-Rector for Finance: ZDRAVKO USKOKOVIĆ
Vice-Rector for Teaching Issues: Prof. Dr ANĐELKO LOJPUR
Sec.-Gen.: JELENA PAJKOVIĆ
Dir for Library: BOSILJKA CICMIL

Library of 1,030 vols, 9,992 library units of monographs (incl. a colln of 665 doctoral dissertations and Masters theses published at the Univ. of Montenegro)
Number of teachers: 764
Number of students: 20,475
Publication: *Bilten* (4 a year)

DEANS

Faculty of Applied Physiotherapy: Dr SOFIJA ŽITNIK-SIVAČKI
Faculty of Architecture: Prof. Dr GORAN RADOVIĆ
Faculty of Biotechnology: Prof. Dr NATALIJA PEROVIĆ
Faculty of Civil Engineering: Prof. Dr DUŠKO LUČIĆ
Faculty of Drama (Cetinje): SINIŠA JELUŠIĆ
Faculty of Economics: Prof. Dr MILORAD JOVOVIĆ
Faculty of Electrical Engineering: Prof. Dr SRDJAN STANKOVIC
Faculty of Fine Arts (Cetinje): NENAD ŠOŠKIĆ
Faculty of Law: Prof. Dr DRAGO RADULOVIĆ

Faculty of Maritime Studies (Kotor): Prof. Dr MILORAD RASKOVIC
Faculty of Mechanical Engineering: Prof. Dr GORAN ĆULAFIĆ
Faculty of Medicine: Prof. Dr BOGDAN AŠANIN
Faculty of Metallurgy and Technology: Prof. Dr KEMAL DELIJIĆ
Faculty of Natural Sciences and Mathematics: Prof. Dr PREDRAG STANISIC
Faculty of Philosophy: Prof. Dr BLAGOJE CEROVIĆ
Faculty of Political Sciences: Prof. Dr SRĐAN DARMANOVIĆ
Faculty of Sport and Physical Education: Doc. Dr DUŠKO BJELICA
Faculty of Tourism and Hotel Management: Prof. Dr TATJANA STANOVČIĆ
Independent Study Programme for Education of Teachers in Albanian Language: Prof. Dr DAVID KALAJ (acting)
Music Academy: Prof. Dr VLADIMIR BOČKARJOV

UNIVERZITET DONJA GORICA
(University of Donja Gorica)

Donja Gorica, 81000 Podgorica
Telephone: (20) 410777
E-mail: udg@udg.edu.me
Internet: www.udg.edu.me
Private control
Number of students: 1,500

UNIVERZITET MEDITERAN
(University Mediterranean)

Vaka Đurovića bb, 81000 Podgorica
Telephone: (20) 409204
E-mail: rektorat@unimediteran.net
Internet: www.unimediteran.net
Founded 2006
Private control
Academic year: September to July (2 semesters)

Rector: Dr SLOBODAN BACKOVIĆ
Vice-Rector for Int. Cooperation: Dr JANKO RADULOVIĆ
Gen. Sec.: DRAGICA ANDJELIC

DEANS
Faculty of Business Studies 'Montenegro Business School': Dr DRAGOLJUB JANKOVIC
Faculty of Foreign Languages: Prof. Dr JANKO RADULOVIĆ
Faculty of Information Technology: Dr RAMO ŠENDELJ
Faculty of Law: Prof. Dr MLADEN VUKCEVIC
Faculty of Tourism Bar—Montenegro Tourism School: Doc. Dr SANJA VLAHOVIC
Faculty of Visual Arts: Prof. Dr NENAD VUKOVIC

Colleges

Fakultet za državne i evropske studije (Faculty of Administrative and European Studies): Vaka Đurovića bb, 81000 Podgorica; tel. (20) 664262; e-mail info@fdes.me; internet www.fdes.me; f. 2005; Dean Dr ĐORĐIJE BLAŽIĆ.

Fakultet za menadžment u saobraćaju i komunikacijama (Faculty of Management, Transport and Communications): Donje Luge bb, 84300 Berane; tel. (51) 238100; e-mail fmsk-ba@t-com.me; internet www.fmsk.me; depts of traffic, e-communications, logistics; Dean Prof. Dr VUJADIN B. VEŠOVIĆ.

Fakultet za poslovni menadžment (Faculty of Business Management): Maršala Tita br 7, 85000 Bar; tel. (30) 312233; e-mail fpm@t-com.me; internet www.fpm.me; f. 2005; depts of social and economic science; engineering technology and computer science; managerial and marketing and finance institutes; 2,200 students; Dean Prof. Dr MILENKO RADOMAN.

MOROCCO

The Higher Education System

Université Quaraouyine Fès (founded 859), an institution for Koranic, Islamic and Arabic studies, is among the oldest universities in continuous existence in the world. From 1912 until 1958 Morocco was a French protectorate and, consequently, the higher education system displays strong French influences. The Université Mohammed V Agdal (founded 1957) is the oldest multi-disciplinary institution of secular studies. In 2009/10 there were 103 university-level institutions with a total enrolment in the 15 accredited universities of 308,005 students. According to government figures there were 192 private higher education institutions operating in 2009/10 with a total enrolment of 35,118.

The Ministry of Higher Education, Scientific Research and Management Training is the supreme authority of higher education, which is free to Moroccan students. The senior officers of universities, such as Presidents and Deans of Faculty, are state appointees, and are responsible for running universities in conjunction with University Councils, Faculty Councils and Faculty Scientific Councils. The main types of institutions of higher education are universities, higher schools (grandes écoles), teacher-training institutes and other specialist institutes. Technical and vocational training is overseen by the Ministry of National Education and Vocational Training and the public body, the Office de la Formation Professionnelle et de la Promotion du Travail (OFPPT), which has close links with industry, is responsible for coordinating specialist vocational courses and qualifications, and continuing education in the work-place. In 2009/10 OFPPT had at its disposal almost 300 establishments offering training in some 223 different professional areas.

Admission to higher education is often on the basis of the secondary school awards, Diplôme du Baccalauréat and Diplôme du Baccalauréat Technique, but additional two-year courses (classes préparatoires aux grandes écoles), culminating in an examination called the Concours National Commun, are required for entry to the grandes écoles. Most university degrees fall into one of three cycles, with some exceptions; these include degrees for disciplines that require longer periods of undergraduate study than the standard four years, such as engineering (five years), veterinary medicine and agronomy (six years) and medicine (seven years). The first cycle of higher education consists of certificates and diplomas awarded after two years of a broad-based programme of study in one of four subject groups (arts and humanities, science and economics, applied sciences, engineering and agriculture) appropriate to the intended area of specialization. Students in the arts and humanities are awarded the Certificat Universitaire d'Études Littéraires; students in science and economics receive the Certificat Universitaire d'Études Scientifiques; students in applied sciences are awarded Diplôme d'Études Universitaires Générales or Diplôme d'Études Universitaires de Technologie; while students in engineering and agriculture undertake a two-year preparatory programme of study. The second cycle of higher education is a period of specialist training and culminates in the award of either the Licence or the Maîtrise. Students who have the Certificat Universitaire d'Études Littéraires or Certificat Universitaire d'Études Scientifiques undertake a further two years of study for the Licence, while holders of the Diplôme d'Études Universitaires Générales or Diplôme d'Études Universitaires de Technologie are awarded the Maîtrise after the same period. Professional titles are awarded in some disciplines, like engineering (Diplôme d'Ingénieur d'État), veterinary medicine (Docteur Vétérinaire) and medicine (Doctorat en Médecine). The third cycle of higher education awards consists mainly of three degrees, Diplôme d'Études Supérieures Approfondies, Diplôme d'Études Supérieures Spécialisées and Doctorat d'État. Holders of the Licence are eligible for admission to the Diplôme d'Études Supérieures Approfondies, a two-year programme of study and research, culminating in submission of a dissertation, that allows admission to doctoral-level studies. The Diplôme d'Études Supérieures Spécialisées is also a two-year course, open to holders of either the Licence or Maîtrise, but does not normally qualify the student for doctoral-level studies. The Doctorat d'État is the highest university-level degree and comprises three to five years of research. Outside the university system, the grandes écoles offer specialist degrees such as Diplôme de Technicien Supérieur and Diplôme d'Ingénieur d'État.

Students with Diplôme du Baccalauréat and the Diplôme du Baccalauréat Technique may attend post-secondary vocational and technical education and study for the Brevet de Technicien Supérieur, which requires successful completion of a two-year programme of study.

In 2004 a number of faculties at Morocco's universities underwent reforms to bring them into line with European universities. As part of the new degree structure new curriculums and a system of transferable credits were introduced, allowing students to take courses from different departments and different institutions or to leave university and continue their studies later. Under the new structure the studies were reorganized into three years of first-cycle studies (Licence), two years of second-cycle studies (Masters) and three years of doctoral studies (Doctorat).

The national accreditation body for tertiary education is the National Accreditation and Evaluation Committee (Commission Nationale d'Accreditation et d'Evaluation).

In December 2009 the Moroccan Government launched a four-year US $1,700m. emergency plan to reform its education system. Particular emphasis was to be placed on improving university-level education in the fields of science and technology. In addition, universities were to be made financially independent from the Government to make them more responsive to research needs and better able to forge links with the private sector. Plans were announced in 2012 to bring to an end Morocco's system of free higher education. Also the 43 states of the Union of the Mediterranean were to set up the Euro-Mediterranean University of Morocco with a capacity to accommodate 3,000 students. The University was expected to be inaugurated in 2014 and to be fully operational by 2021.

Regulatory Bodies

GOVERNMENT

Ministry of Culture: 1 rue Ghandi, Rabat; tel. 37-20-94-94; internet www.minculture.gov.ma; Minister M. MOHAMED AMINE SBIHI.

Ministry of Higher Education, Scientific Research and Management Training: rue Idriss Al Akbar-Hassan, BP 4500, Rabat; tel. 37-21-75-01; e-mail enssup@enssup.gov.ma; internet www.enssup.gov.ma; Minister LAHCEN DAOUDI.

Ministry of National Education and Vocational Training: Bab Rouah, Rabat; tel. (53) 7771822; internet www.men.gov.ma; Minister RACHID BELMOKHTAR.

Learned Societies

GENERAL

Académie du Royaume du Maroc: Charia Mohammed VI, Km 11, BP 5062, 10100 Rabat,; tel. (5) 37-75-51-99; e-mail arm@alacademia.org.ma; f. 1980; promotes devt of research and reflection in principal fields of intellectual activity, publishes books on Moroccan and Islamic heritage; library of 20,000 vols; 60 mems; Permanent Sec. Dr ABDELLATIF BERBICH; publs *Academia* (1 a year), *Colloquiums* (2 a year), *Proceedings of Sessions* (2 a year).

UNESCO Office Rabat: BP 1777 RP, 10106 Rabat; 35 ave du 16 Novembre, Agdal, 10000 Rabat; tel. 37-67-03-72; e-mail rabat@unesco.org; f. 1991; designated Cluster Office for Algeria, Libya, Mauritania, Morocco and Tunisia; Dir ROSAMARIA DURAND.

AGRICULTURE, FISHERIES AND VETERINARY SCIENCE

Société d'Horticulture et d'Acclimatation du Maroc: BP 13.854, 20001 Casablanca; f. 1914; 260 mems; Pres. JOSETTE DUPLAT; Sec. RENÉ TRIPOTIN.

FINE AND PERFORMING ARTS

Association des Amateurs de la Musique Andalouse: c/o 133 blvd Ziraoui, 20000 Casablanca; f. 1956 to preserve and catalogue traditional Moroccan (Andalusian) music; maintains a School of Andalusian music at Casablanca, directed and subsidized by the Ministry of Culture; Dir Hadj DRISS BENJELLOUN.

HISTORY, GEOGRAPHY AND ARCHAEOLOGY

Association Nationale de Géographie Marocaine: Faculté des Lettres et des Sciences Humaines, Université Mohammed V Adgal, 10100 Rabat; tel. 37-77-18-93; f. 1916; Sec.-Gen. TAOUFIK AGOUMI; publ. *Revue de Géographie du Maroc* (2 a year).

LANGUAGE AND LITERATURE

Alliance Française: 22 ave de la Marche Verte, 24000 El Jadida; tel. 23-34-21-06; e-mail afm.eljadida@iam.net.ma; offers courses and examinations in French language and culture and promotes cultural exchange with France; attached teaching centre in Essaouira.

British Council: 11 rue Allal Ben Abdellah, BP 427, Rabat; tel. (5) 37-21-81-30; e-mail info@britishcouncil.org.ma; internet www.britishcouncil.org/morocco; teaching centre; offers courses and examinations in English language and British culture and promotes cultural exchange with the UK; attached teaching centre in Casablanca; library of 8,000 vols, 20 periodicals; Dir MARTIN ROSE; Teaching Centre Man. MARK BUCCIANTI.

Goethe-Institut: 7 rue Sana'a, 10001 Rabat; tel. 537-70-65-44 11, Place du 16 Novembre, 20000 Casablanca; tel. 522-20-04-45; e-mail progr@rabat.goethe.org; internet www.goethe.de/rabat; offers courses and examinations in German language and promotes cultural exchange; library of 10,850 vols; Dir FRIEDRICH DAHLHAUS.

Instituto Cervantes: 5 Zankat Madnine, 10000 Rabat; tel. 37-70-87-38; e-mail cenrabat@cervantes.org.ma; internet rabat.cervantes.es; offers courses and examinations in Spanish language and culture and promotes cultural exchange with Spain and Spanish-speaking Latin and Central America; attached centres in Casablanca, Fez, Tangier and Tétouan; library; Dir XABIER MARKIEGI CANDINA.

Research Institutes

GENERAL

Centre National pour la Recherche Scientifique et Technique: 52 Charii Omar Ibn Khattab, BP 8027, 10102 Agdal-Rabat; tel. 37-77-28-03; e-mail cnr@cnr.ac.ma; internet www.cnr.ac.ma; f. 1976; attached to Min. of Higher Education, Scientific Research and Management Training; research fields include food and agriculture, communication, environment, natural resources, astronomy, geophysics, biotechnology, geology, computer science, mathematics, social sciences, int. business, environmental science, energy and maintenance; library of 3,500 vols, 70 periodicals; Dir SAID BELCADI (acting); Sec.-Gen. (vacant); publ. *Lettre d'Information* (1 a year).

AGRICULTURE, FISHERIES AND VETERINARY SCIENCE

Institut National de la Recherche Agronomique: BP 415 RP, INRA Ave Ennasr, Rabat; tel. (5) 37-77-09-55; e-mail webmaster@inra.org.ma; internet www.inra.org.ma; f. 1930; library of 40,000 vols, 300 periodicals; Dir A. ARIFI; publs *Al Awamia* (4 a year), *Les Cahiers de la Recherche Agronomique* (irregular).

Institut National de Recherche Halieutique: Route Sidi Abderrahmane Club équestre Ould Jmel, Casablanca; tel. 522-94-07-73; internet www.inrh.ma; f. 1947; applied fisheries oceanography, marine biology, evaluation of resources, aquaculture, environmental studies, fishing gear technology, fish processing technology, fisheries management; library of 1,050 vols, 70 periodicals; Dir MOHAMED SEDRATI; publs *Bulletin*, *Notes d'Information*, *Travaux et Documents*.

ECONOMICS, LAW AND POLITICS

La Fondation du Roi Abdul Aziz pour les Études Islamiques et les Sciences Humaines (King Abdul-Aziz Al Saoud Foundation for Islamic Studies and Human Sciences): BP 12585, 20052 Casablanca; blvd de la Corniche, Ain Diab, Anfa, 20050 Casablanca; tel. (5) 22-39-10-27; e-mail secretariat@fondation.org.ma; internet www.fondation.org.ma; f. 1985; promotes study of social sciences and humanities in the Maghreb, by means of documentation and cultural activities; library of 310,000 vols, 1,289 periodicals; Dir PRINCE ABDULLAH IBN-ABD-AL-AZIZ-AL-SA'UD; publ. *Lettre d'Information* (2 a year).

HISTORY, GEOGRAPHY AND ARCHAEOLOGY

Comité National de Géographie du Maroc: Institut Universitaire de la Recherche Scientifique, BP 2122 Riad, Rabat; f. 1959; Pres. THE MIN. OF HIGHER EDUCATION, SCIENTIFIC RESEARCH AND MANAGEMENT TRAINING; Sec.-Gen. A. LAOUINA; publ. *Atlas du Maroc*.

MEDICINE

Direction de l'Epidémiologie et de Lutte Contre les Maladies: 71 ave Ibn Sina, Agdal, Rabat; tel. 37-67-12-71; e-mail delm@sante.gov.ma; internet www.sante.gov.ma/departements/delm/index-delm.htm; f. 1990; applied research in epidemiology and environmental health; Dir Dr NOUREDDINE CHAOUKI; publ. *Bulletin Epidémiologique* (3 a year).

Institut National d'Hygiène: POB 769, Rabat Agdal; tel. 37-77-19-02; e-mail relaouad@sante.gov.ma; internet www.sante.gov.ma/inh; f. 1930; depts of microbiology, parasitology, physics and chemistry, toxicology, serology, immunology, molecular biology, genetics, entomology; Nat. Poison Control Centre; 266 mems; library: Toxicological Documentation Centre of 400 vols; library of 3,000 vols; Dir Prof. RAJAE EL AOUAD.

Institut Pasteur du Maroc: 1 pl. Louis Pasteur, 20100 Casablanca; tel. 22-43-44-50; e-mail pasteur@pasteur.ma; internet www.pasteur.ma; f. 1911; research into infectious diseases, bacteriology, parasitology and virology, biochemistry and genetics, food and environmental safety; promotion of public health; Dir Prof. MOHAMMED HASSAR.

NATURAL SCIENCES

Physical Sciences

Direction de la Géologie: c/o Ministry of Energy, Mining, Water, and Environment, BP 6208, Rabat-Instituts; tel. 37-68-88-57; e-mail dsi@mem.gov.ma; f. 1921; Nat. Geological Survey; library of 25,000 vols; Pres ABDELHAQ SMIDI; publs *Mines, Géologie et Energie*, *Notes et Mémoires du Service Géologique du Maroc*.

TECHNOLOGY

Bureau de Recherches et de Participations Minières (BRPM): 5 Charia Moulay Hassan, BP 99, Rabat; tel. 37-76-30-35; e-mail benkhadra@brpm.org.ma; f. 1928; state agency to develop mining research and industry; Gen. Man. ASSOU LHA TOUTE.

Laboratoire Public d'Essais et d'Études: 25 rue d'Azilal, Casablanca; tel. 22-30-04-50; f. 1947; hydraulics, environment, roads, study of soil, materials and methods of construction; library of 7,000 vols; Dir-Gen. MOHAMED JELLALI; publs *LPEE-Magazine* (4 a year), *Revue Marocaine de Génie Civil* (4 a year).

Libraries and Archives

Fez

Bibliothèque de l'Université Quaraouyine Fès: BP 790, place des Seffarines, Fez; tel. (5) 46-17-75; 22,071 vols, 5,157 MSS, 38 archives.

Marrakesh

Bibliothèque Ben Youssef: ave 11 Janvier, Hay Mohamadi Daoudiat, Marrakesh; 21,223 vols, 586 periodicals, 1,840 MSS; Dir SEDDIK BELLARBI.

Rabat

Bibliothèque de l'Institut Scientifique: ave Ibn Battota, BP 703, Agdal, 10106 Rabat; tel. 537-77-45-48; f. 1920; zoology, botany, geomorphology, cartography, ecology, earth sciences, geophysics, remote detection; 15,700 vols, 1,728 periodicals; Librarian ABDELLATIF BAYED; publ. *Travaux de l'Institut Scientifique*.

Bibliothèque Générale et Archives: BP 1003, ave Ibn Battouta, Rabat; tel. (5) 37-77-18-90; e-mail bnrm@bnrm.ma; f. 1924; 600,000 vols, 31,000 MSS and 2,000 m of archives; Dir AHMED TOUFIQ; publ. *Bibliographie Nationale* (2 a year).

Centre National de Documentation: ave Hadj Ahmed Cherkaoui, Quartier des Ministères, 10100 Haut Agdal, BP 826, 10004 Rabat; tel. 37-77-49-44; internet www.abhatoo.net.ma; f. 1966; documentation on the economic, social, scientific and technical development of Morocco; library depository of World Bank publications; regional reps in Fez, Tangier, Casablanca, Agadir, Marrakesh, Meknès, Oujda; mem. of FID and IFLA; 9,000 vols, 120,000 microfiches, 350 periodicals; Dir ADNANE BENCHAKROUN; publ. *KATAB* (bibliography).

Tangier

Biblioteca Juan Goytisolo—Instituto Cervantes de Tánger: 99 ave Sidi

Mohamed Ben Abdellah, 90000 Tangier; tel. 39-93-23-99; e-mail bibtan@cervantes.es; internet tanger.cervantes.es/es/biblioteca_espanol/biblioteca_espanol.htm; f. 1941; attached to Instituto Cervantes; main colln in the Spanish language; antique Spanish publications from 18th and 19th centuries; periodical library incl. Spanish, Arab and African titles; Spanish sheet music from early 20th century; photographic archive from former Spanish tourist office in Tangier; 90,000 vols; Librarian SÍLVIA MONTERO GÓMEZ; publ. *Miscelanea de la Biblioteca Española*.

Tétouan

Bibliothèque Générale et Archives: 32 ave Mohammed V, BP 692, Tétouan; tel. 39-96-32-58; e-mail bgatetou@imam.net.ma; internet www.minculture.gov.ma; f. 1939; research and public library; 50,000 books, 3,500 periodicals, 2,400 MSS, 23,000 historical archive items, 1,200,000 admin. archive items, 45,000 photographs, 1,429 numismatic items; Dir Dr M. ZOUAK.

Museums and Art Galleries

Chefchaouen

Musée Ethnographique de Chefchaouen: Kasbah Outa Hammam, Chefchaouen; tel. (5) 99-98-67-61; f. 1985; musical instruments, arms, embroidery, carved boxes, local pottery.

Essaouira

Musée Sidi Mohamed ben Abdellah à Essaouira: Derb Laalouj, Essaouira; tel. (5) 44-47-23-00; f. 1981; musical instruments, jewellery, arms, carved wooden objects.

Fez

Musée Batha: Ksar el Batha, Fez; tel. 35-63-41-16; built as a royal residence in 19th century; converted into a museum in 1915; colln incl. sculpted wood and plaster objects, cast iron, local blue ceramics, embroidery, coins, carpets, jewellery, astrological instruments; Curator HNIA CHIKHAOUI.

Musée d'Armes du Borj-Nord: Borj-Nord, Fez; tel. 35-64-52-41; built as a military fort in the 16th century, converted into a museum in 1963; collection of 1,100 military artefacts; Curator MOHAMED ZAIM.

Larache

Musée Archéologique: 23 rue Brihi, Rabat; tel. (7) 70-19-19; f. 1932; remains found primarily at the Lixus archaeological site, from the Phoenician, Carthaginian, Mauritanian, Roman and Islamic ages.

Marrakesh

Musée Dar Si Saïd: Derb el Bahia, Riad El Zaitoun El Jadid, Marrakesh; tel. 24-44-24-64; internet www.minculture.gov.ma/fr/musee%20dar%20si%20said.htm; f. as a royal residence in 19th century, converted into a museum in 1932; artefacts from the Marrakesh region and southern Morocco, incl. wooden objects, jewellery, pottery and ceramics, arms, carpets and woven materials; archaeological remains; Dir HASSAN BEL ARBI.

Meknès

Musée Dar El Jamaï: pl. El Hedime, Meknès; tel. 35-53-08-63; e-mail margaa71@yahoo.fr; f. 1920; handicraft items from the region, incl. embroidery, wood carvings, leatherwork, carved chests, carpets, ceramics, ancient jewellery, wrought ironwork, copper and brass objects, painted woodwork, traditional costumes and ancient Korans; Chief Curator AHMED MARGAA.

Moulay Driss Zerhoun

Site Archéologique de Volubilis: Conservation du Site de Volubilis, Moulay Driss Zerhoun, Meknès; tel. 35-54-41-03; e-mail volubilisarcheosite@yahoo.fr; f. 1950; archaeological site; library of 250 vols; Archaeologist YOUSSEF BOKBOT.

Rabat

Musée Archéologique: 23 rue Al-Brihi, Rabat; tel. 37-70-19-19; f. 1931; history of Morocco from prehistory until the Islamic era; collns incl. stone tools, primitive furniture, Roman divinities, bronze and marble statues, early Islamic ceramics; Curator ABDELWAHED BEN-NCER.

Musée Ethnographique des Oudaïa: Kasba des Oudaïa, Rabat; tel. 37-72-64-61; f. 1915; clothing from various regions of Morocco, jewellery, astronomical tools, carpets, pottery, musical instruments; Curator HOUCEINE EL KASRI.

Safi

Musée National de la Céramique: Kachla, Safi; tel. 24-46-38-95; f. 1990; originally a military fort; Curator NOUREDDINE ESSAFSAFI.

Tangier

Musée d'Art Contemporain: 52 ave d'Angleterre, Tangier; tel. 39-94-99-72; f. 1990; constructed as British consulate; modern Moroccan art.

Musée de la Kasbah: Sahat El Kasba, Tangier; tel. 539-91-20-92; f. 1922; archaeology and folklore; Curator MOHAMMED HABIBI.

Tangier American Legation Institute for Moroccan Studies (TALIM): 8 Zankat America, Tangier; tel. 39-93-53-17; e-mail director.talim@gmail.com; internet www.legation.org; f. 1976; operated by the Tangier American Legation Museum Soc., Inc.; permanent colln paintings since 16th century, etchings, aquatints, prints and maps of Morocco; also documentation and artefacts concerning Moroccan-American relations; sponsors short-term exhibitions of contemporary artists; library: research library of 8,000 vols on N Africa and Morocco in Arabic, English, French, Portuguese, Spanish; Dir JOHN DAVISON.

Tétouan

Musée Archéologique: 2 rue Ben Hussain, Tétouan; tel. 39-96-73-03; f. 1939; prehistoric and pre-Islamic archaeological remains from northern Morocco; mosaics and coins.

Musée Ethnographique de Tétouan: Zankat Skala, 65 Bab El Okla, 93000 Tétouan; tel. 39-97-05-05; f. 1928; originally a fortress; carved wooden objects, copperware, pottery, embroidery.

Universities

UNIVERSITÉ ABDELMALEK ESSAÂDI TÉTOUAN

BP 2117, Quartier Haneche Me II, Palestine Avenue (near the Faculty of Science), Tétouan

Telephone: 539-97-93-16
E-mail: presidence@uae.ma
Internet: www.uae.ma

Founded 1989
State control
Languages of instruction: Arabic, French
Campus in Tangier; Faculties of arts and humanities, economics and social sciences, law, science and technology; schools of commerce and management, translation

Pres.: Prof. HOUDAIFA AMEZIANE

Number of teachers: 632
Number of students: 17,150

Publication: *Tourjouman* (Journal of the School of Translation)

UNIVERSITÉ AL AKHAWAYN IFRANE

POB 104, ave Hassan II, 53000 Ifrane
Telephone: 35-86-20-00
E-mail: info@aui.ma
Internet: www.aui.ma

Founded 1995
Private control
Language of instruction: English
Academic year: September to July

Pres.: Dr DRISS OUAOUICHA
Vice-Pres. for Academic Affairs: Dr AHMED LEGROURI
Vice-Pres. for Finance and Admin.: Dr ABDELILAH KAMAL
Vice-Pres. for Student Affairs: Dr CHERIF BEL FEKIH

Library of 84,000 vols
Number of teachers: 137
Number of students: 1,800

DEANS

School of Business Administration: Dr WAFA EL GARAH
School of Humanities and Social Sciences: Dr NIZAR MESSARI (acting)
School of Science and Engineering: Dr DAVID WYRICK

UNIVERSITÉ CADI AYYAD MARRAKECH

Blvd Prince Moulay Abdellah, POB 511, Marrakesh
Telephone: (524) 43-48-13
E-mail: presidence@ucam.ac.ma
Internet: www.ucam.ac.ma

Founded 1978
State control
Languages of instruction: Arabic, English, French
Academic year: September to July

Rector: Prof. MOHAMED MARZAK
Vice-Pres.: Prof. MOHAMED LARBI SIDMOU
Vice-Pres.: Prof. BOUMEDIEN TANOUTI
Sec.-Gen.: RACHID HILAL

Number of teachers: 1,868
Number of students: 33,359

Publications: *Revue de la Faculté de Droit*, *Revue de la Faculté des Lettres*, *Revue de la Faculté des Sciences*, *Manarat Al Jamiaa*

DEANS

Faculty of Law, Economics and Social Sciences: MRANI ZANTAR M'HAMMED
Faculty of Letters and Humanities: TEBBAA OUIDAD
Faculty of Medicine and Pharmacy: ALAOUI YAZIDI
Faculty of Science and Technics: ABBOUSSALAH MOHAMED
Faculty of Sciences (Semlalia): Prof. LOUIDIKI AHMED
Higher School of Technology (Essaouira): BELAID BOUGADIR
Higher School of Technology (Safi): MOHAMED EL ARBI EL ACHHAB
National School of Applied Sciences: AIT OUAHMAN ABDELLAH
National School of Applied Sciences (Safi): AHMED DERJA
National School of Business and Administration: RIGAR SIDI MOHAMED

Polydisciplinary Faculty: EL HASSANE BOUMAGGARD
University Centre (Kalaat Sraghna): HAMMADI BOUSLOUSS

UNIVERSITÉ CHOUAÏB DOUKKALI EL JADIDA

BP 299, ave Jabrane Khalil Jabrane, 24000 El Jadida
Telephone: 23-34-44-47
E-mail: contact@ucd.ac.ma
Internet: www.ucd.ac.ma
Founded 1989
State control
Languages of instruction: Arabic, English, French
Academic year: September to July
Faculties of arts and humanities, science
Pres.: BOUMEDIENE TANOUTI
Dean for Faculty of Letters and Human Sciences: ABDELOUAHED MABROUR
Library of 14,460 vols
Number of teachers: 483
Number of students: 14,662
Publications: *Magazine de la Faculté des Lettres Parallèles*, *Revue de la Faculté des Lettres*

UNIVERSITÉ HASSAN I SETTAT

Complexe Universitaire route de Casablanca Km 3,5, BP 539, 26000 Settat
Telephone: 23-72-12-75
E-mail: contact@uhp.ac.ma
Internet: www.uh1.ac.ma
State control
Languages of instruction: Arabic, French
Academic year: September to July
Faculties of economics and social sciences, law, science and technology; School of commerce and management; Engineering school
Pres.: AHMED NEJMEDDINE
Number of teachers: 344
Number of students: 19,724

UNIVERSITÉ HASSAN II — CASABLANCA

BP 9167, 19 rue Tarik Bnou Ziad, Mers Sultan, Casablanca
Telephone: 522-43-30-30
E-mail: presidence@uh2c.ac.ma
Internet: www.uh2c.ac.ma
Founded 1975
Languages of instruction: Arabic, French
Academic year: September to July
Pres.: MOHAMMED BARKAOUI
Vice-Pres. for Academic Affairs: IDRISS MANSOURI
Vice-Pres. for Research and Cooperation: JAAFAR KHALID NACIRI
Sec-Gen.: ABDELHADI MOSLIH
Librarian: (vacant)
Number of teachers: 1,027
Number of students: 26,000
Publication: faculty reviews

DEANS
Faculty of Arts and Human Sciences: SAID BENNANI
Faculty of Dentistry: AMAL OUAZZANI ECHCHAHDI
Faculty of Law: ESSALMI IDRISSI
Faculty of Medicine and Pharmacy: LHOUSSAINE LOUARDI
Faculty of Sciences: OUZZANI
National Higher School of Electronics and Mechanics: JANAH SAADI (Dir)
Teacher-Training College: OUBAHAMMO (Dir)
Technology High School: SARSOURI (Dir)

UNIVERSITÉ HASSAN II MOHAMMEDIA

BP 150, ave Hassan II, Mohammedia
Telephone: 23-31-46-35
Internet: www.uh2m.ac.ma
Founded 1992
State control
Languages of instruction: Arabic, English, French, Spanish
Academic year: September to June
Pres.: SAÂD CHARIF D'OUAZZANE
Number of teachers: 913
Number of students: 40,455

DEANS
Faculty of Arts and Humanities, Ben Msik Campus: ABD ELMAJID KADDOURI
Faculty of Arts and Humanities, Mohammedia Campus: RACHIDA NAFAA
Faculty of Economics, Law and Social Science, Ain Sebaa: JAMILA HOUFAIDI SETTAR
Faculty of Economics, Law and Social Science, Mohammedia Campus: JAMAL HATTABI
Faculty of Science, Ben Msik Campus: MOHAMED SAID EL KABBAJ
Faculty of Science and Technology, Mohammedia Campus: MUSTAPHA ALKHIDAR

UNIVERSITÉ IBN TOFAIL KÉNITRA

BP 242, 104 rue Ahmed Boughaba, Bir Rami Est, 14000 Kénitra
Telephone: 37-32-28-09
E-mail: ruitk@iam.net.ma
Internet: www.univ-ibntofail.ac.ma
Founded 1989
State control
Pres.: MOHAMMED ESSOUARI
Sec.-Gen.: ABDALLAH EL MALIKI
Library of 42,007 vols
Number of teachers: 405
Number of students: 11,884

DEANS
Faculty of Arts and Humanities: ABDELFETTAH BENKADDOUR
Faculty of Science: ALI BOUKHARI

UNIVERSITÉ IBNOU ZOHR AGADIR

BP 32/S, Agadir, 8000
Telephone: 528-22-71-25
Internet: www.uiz.ac.ma
Founded 1989
Faculties of letters and humanities, sciences
Pres.: Prof. OMAR HALLI
Number of students: 9,724

UNIVERSITÉ MOHAMMED I OUJDA

Présidence de l'Université Mohammed Premier, BV Mohammed VI, BP 524, 60000 Oujda
Telephone: 536-50-06-12
E-mail: presidence@ump.ma
Internet: www.univ-oujda.ac.ma
Founded 1978
State control
Languages of instruction: Arabic, French
Academic year: October to June
Rector: EL-MADANI BELKHADIR
Sec.-Gen.: ABDERRAHMAN HOUTECH
Librarian: ZOUBIDA CHAHI
Number of teachers: 593
Number of students: 19,872
Publications: *Al Mayadine*, *Cahiers du CEMM*, *Revue de la Faculté des Lettres*

DEANS
Faculty of Law and Economics: EL-LARBI M'RABET
Faculty of Letters and Human Sciences: MOHAMMED LAAMIRI
Faculty of Science: BENAÏSSA N'CIRI
Institute of Technology: MOHAMMED BARBOUCHA (Dir)

UNIVERSITÉ MOHAMMED V AGDAL

BP 554, ave des Nations Unies, Agdal, Rabat
Telephone: 37-27-27-50
E-mail: presidence@um5a.ac.ma
Internet: www.um5a.ac.ma
Founded 1957
State control
Languages of instruction: Arabic, French
Academic year: September to July
Pres.: WAIL BENJELLOUN
Vice-Pres. for Academic Affairs and Univ. Advancement: JAMAL EDDINE EL HANI
Vice-Pres. for Research, Cooperation and Partnership: DRISS ABOUTAJDINE
Sec.-Gen.: MOHAMED KHALFAOUI
Librarian: NAZIHA JABRI
Number of teachers: 1,122
Number of students: 28,012
Publications: *Annales du Centre des Études Stratégiques*, *Bulletin de l'Institut Scientifique*, *Bulletin Magnétique*, *Bulletin Séismologique*, *Documents de l'Institut Scientifique*, *Hespéris Tamuda* (1 a year, in English, French and Spanish), *Langues et Littératures* (1 a year, in European languages), *Revue de la Faculté des Lettres et des Sciences Humaines* (1 a year, in Arabic), *Revue des Sciences de la Terre*, *Revue Marocaine de l'Automatique, de l'Informatique et du Traitement du Signal*, *Revue Marocaine Juridique, Politique et Economique*, *Travaux de l'Institut Scientifique*

DEANS
Faculty of Law and Economics: LAHCEN OULHAJ
Faculty of Letters and Human Sciences: ABDERRAHIM BENHADDA
Faculty of Sciences: SAAID AMZAZI
Higher School of Technology (Salé): MOHAMMED RHACHI
Mohammadia School of Engineering: DRISS BOUAMI
Institute of Hispano-Lusophone Studies: FATIHA BENLABAH
Scientific Institute: AHMED EL HASSANI

UNIVERSITÉ MOHAMMED V SOUISSI RABAT

BP 8007, N.U. Agdal, Rabat
ave Med Benabdellah Regragui, Madinat al-Irfane, Rabat
Telephone: 37-68-11-60
E-mail: presidence@um5s.ac.ma
Internet: www.um5s.ac.ma
Founded 1993
Languages of instruction: Arabic, English, French
Academic year: September to July
Pres.: Prof. RADOUANE MRABET
Vice-Pres. for Academic Affairs: Prof. HASSAN ABOUABDELMAJID
Vice-Pres. for Research and Cooperation: Prof. RACHID BEZAD
Sec.-Gen.: RACHID AGADDOU
Number of teachers: 1,270
Number of students: 23,500
Publications: *Al Irfane* (information bulletin, 3 a year), *Reflexions* (science, 4 a year)

DEANS

ENSET (Electrical and Mechanical Engineering): LARBI BELARBI
Faculty of Dentistry: SANA RIDA
Faculty of Education: ABDESSALAM OUAZANI
Faculty of Law, Souissi: KHALID BERJAOUI
Faculty of Law, Salé: EL HOUSSINE SNOUSSI
Faculty of Medicine and Pharmacy: NAJIA HAJJAJ
National Higher School of Informatics and Systems Analysis: MOHAMED ESSAAIDI (Dir)
Research Institute for Africa (IEA): YAHYA ABOUALFARAH
Research Institute of Arabisation (IERA): MOHAMMED EL FERRANE
Research Institute of Science (IURS): AMINA AOUCHAR

UNIVERSITÉ MOULAY ISMAIL MEKNÈS

BP 298, Marjane I, Meknès
Telephone: (5) 35-46-73-06
Founded 1982; univ. status 1989
State control
Pres.: Dr AHMED LEBRIHI
Vice-Pres.: Dr EL MOSTAFA KHECHOUBI
Vice-Pres.: Dr MOHAMMED SABBANE
Number of teachers: 722
Number of students: 25,137
Publications: *Maksanat* (Journal of the Faculty of Arts and Human Sciences), *Minbar Al Mamiaa* (1 a year), *Zetouna* (Journal of the Faculty of Law, Economics and Social Studies)

DEANS

Faculty of Arts and Human Sciences: MAHMOUDI
Faculty of Law, Economics and Social Studies: MOHAMED BENJELOUN
Faculty of Sciences: MOHAMED SABBANE
Faculty of Sciences and Technology: ABDELLAH EL MANSSOUR
High Normal School: HAMMANI AKEFLI
High School of Technology: MOHAMED BENNASER
Polydisciplinary Faculty: MAJIDI LHOU

UNIVERSITÉ QUARAOUYINE FÈS

Dhar Mahraz, BP 2509, Fez
Telephone: 55-64-10-06
Founded founded in AD 859, enlarged in 11th century, reorganized 1963
State control
Language of instruction: Arabic
Academic year: September to July
Rector: Prof. ABDELOUAHHAB TAZI SAOUD
Sec.-Gen.: MOHAMMED BENNANI ZOUBIR
Number of teachers: 115
Number of students: 6,000.

CONSTITUENT INSTITUTES

Faculty of Arabic Studies: ave Allal Al-Fassi, BP 1483, Marrakesh; Dean Prof. HASSAN JELLAB.

Faculty of Shari'a: BP 52, Agadir; Dean Prof. MOHAMMED ATTAHIRI.

Faculty of Shari'a (Law): BP 60, Saïs, Fez; Dean Prof. MOHAMMED YESSEF.

Faculty of Theology: blvd Abdelkhalek Torres, BP 95, Tétouan; Dean Prof. DRISS KHALIFA

UNIVERSITÉ SIDI MOHAMED BEN ABDELLAH FÈS

BP 2626, ave des Almohades, 30000 Fez,
Telephone: 35-60-96-60
Founded 1975
State control
Languages of instruction: Arabic, French
Academic year: September to July
Pres.: ESSERRHINI FARISSI
Vice-Pres. for Academic Affairs: MOHAMED AÏT EL MEKKI
Vice-Pres. for Scientific Research and Cooperation: MOULHIME EL BEKKALI
Sec.-Gen.: ABDELKADER MAROUANE
Library of 225,000 vols
Number of teachers: 1,274
Number of students: 56,762

DEANS

Faculty of Law, Economics and Social Sciences (Agdal): ABDELAZIZ SQUALLI
Faculty of Letters and Human Sciences (Agdal): ABDELLILAH BENMLIH
Faculty of Letters and Human Sciences (Saiss): IBRAHIM AKDIM
Faculty of Medicine and Pharmacy (Saiss): MOULAY HASSAN FARIH
Faculty of Science (Agdal): MOHAMMED OUAZZANI JAMIL
Faculty of Science and Technology (Saiss): MOHCINE ZOUAK
High School of Technology (Saiss): ABDELLATI SAFOUANE
Higher Normal School (Saiss): ABDENABI RAJWANI
National Institute of Medicinal and Aromatic Plants (Taounate): ABDESLAM KHENCHOUFI
National School of Applied Sciences (Saiss): MOSTAFA MRABTI
National School of Business and Management (Saiss): MILOUD EL HAFIDI
Polydisciplinary Faculty of Taza: AHMED TALOUIZTE

Colleges

Conservatoire de Fès: rue Mustapha Lamaani, Dar Adaîl, Fez; tel. 35-62-39-93; f. 1960; 366 students; Dir MOHAMED BRIOUEL.

Conservatoire de Marrakech: Arçat al Hamed Bab Doukkala, 40000 Marrakech; tel. 24-38-70-66; f. 1948; teaches Western classical and modern music and classical Moroccan and Arab music; 320 students; Dir MOHAMED MAHASSIN.

Conservatoire National de Musique et de Danse, Rabat: 33 rue Tensift, Agdal, Rabat; tel. 37-77-37-94; trains students in Western and Arabic music and classical dance; the Conservatoire has an orchestra for modern Arab music, an orchestra for Andalusian and Moroccan music, 2 youth orchestras and a big-band orchestra; 1,685 students; Dir MOHAMMED EL BAHJA.

École Hassania des Travaux Publics: km 7, route d'El Jadida, BP 8108, Oasis, Casablanca; tel. 22-23-07-06; e-mail ehtpdg@menara.ma; internet www.ehtp.ac.ma; f. 1971; civil engineering, industrial engineering and telecommunication systems, meteorology, sciences of geographical information, computer engineering; MBA, Masters programmes, specialized courses, seminaries; 7 research and study centres; library: 15,000 vols; 73 full-time teachers, 180 visiting teachers; 480 students; Dir ABDESLAM MESSOUDI.

École Nationale d'Administration: BP 165, 2 ave de la Victoire, Rabat; tel. 37-72-44-00; internet www.ena.ac.ma; f. 1948; library: 18,000 vols; 36 teachers; 646 students; Dir AMINE MZOURI; publ. *Administration et Société* (3 a year).

École Nationale d'Architecture: BP 6372, Chariaa Allal El Fassi, Rabat; tel. 37-77-52-29; e-mail e.n.a@smartnet.net.ma; internet www.archi.ac.ma; f. 1980 under the Min. of Territorial Administration, Water Resources and the Environment; courses in architecture, regional town planning and housing; 60 teachers; 400 students; Dir ABDERRAHMANE CHORFI.

École Nationale Forestière d'Ingénieurs: BP 511, Salé; tel. 37-86-37-04; e-mail eauxetforets@iam.net.ma; internet www.enfi.ac.ma; f. 1968; library: 5,000 vols; 20 teachers; 160 students; Dir MY Y. ALAOUI.

École Nationale de l'Industrie Minérale: rue Hadj Ahmed Cherkaoui, BP 753, Agdal, Rabat; tel. 37-68-02-28; e-mail info@enim.ac.ma; internet www.enim.ac.ma; f. 1972; specializes in geology, material sciences, mining sciences, chemical process engineering, electro-mechanical engineering, energy sciences, computer science, industrial maintenance, production systems, energy systems; library: 11,000 vols; 86 teachers; 420 students; Dir OMAR DEBBAJ; publ. *Liaison Bulletin* (12 a year).

École des Sciences de l'Information: BP 6204, Rabat-Instituts; tel. 37-77-49-04; e-mail esi@esi.ac.ma; internet www.esi.ac.ma; f. 1974; 4-year undergraduate courses and 2-year postgraduate courses for archivists, librarians, documentalists; library: 18,000 vols, 50 current periodicals, 415 audiovisual documents; also UNESCO publs, research papers, courses, syllabuses, etc.; 64 teachers; 512 students; Dir MOHAMED BENJELLOUN.

École Supérieure de l'Agro-Alimentaire (Higher School of Food Science): 22 rue Catelet, Belvedère, Casablanca; tel. 522-24-54-05; e-mail supagro@casanet.net.ma; internet www.supagro.ma; f. 1997; 90 teachers; 70 students; Dir Prof. ABDELRHAFOUR TANTAOUI ELARAKI.

Institut Agronomique et Vétérinaire Hassan II: BP 6202, Madinat El-Irfane-Instituts, Rabat; tel. 37-77-17-58; e-mail dg@iav.ac.ma; internet www.iav.ac.ma; f. 1966; library: 45,000 documents, 1,200 periodicals; 327 teachers; 1,606 students; Dir Prof. FOUAD GUESSOUS; Sec.-Gen. Prof. MOSTAFA AGBANI; publs *Actes de l'Institut Agronomique et Vétérinaire Hassan II* (4 a year, in English and French), *AgroVet Magazine* (4 a year, in French), *IAVinfo* (6 a year).

Institut National des Sciences de l'Archéologie et du Patrimoine: ave Kennedy, route des Zaers, 10000 Rabat-Souissi; tel. 37-75-09-61; e-mail archeo@iam.net.ma; f. 1986; departments of anthropology, archaeology and cultural heritage, heritage studies, Islamic studies and archaeology and prehistory; 60 teachers; 50 students; Dir JOUDIA HASSAR-BENSLIMANE; publ. *Bulletin d'Archéologie Marocaine* (1 a year).

Institut National de Statistique et d'Economie Appliquée: BP 6217, Rabat; tel. 37-77-09-15; internet www.insea.ma; f. 1961; library: 15,000 vols; 398 students; Dir M. MOHAMED BENJELLOUN; publ. *Revue* (1 a year).

Institut Supérieur d'Art Dramatique et d'Animation Culturelle: Charia Allal Fassi Madinat Al Irfane, Rabat; tel. 37-77-28-46; f. 1985; provides practical and academic training in all areas of the dramatic arts; Dir SALAMA EL GHIAM.

Instituto Español de Enseñanza Secundaria 'Severo Ochoa' (Spanish Institute in Tangier): Plaza El Koweit 1, Tangier; tel. 39-93-63-38; e-mail luisbadosa@hotmail.com; internet arce.cnice.mecd.es/instituto.severo.ochoa; f. 1949; Dir LUIS BADOSA ORTUÑO; library: 8,000 vols; 38 teachers; 360 students; publs *Revista Babel* (1 a year, in several languages), *Revista Kasbah* (1 a year, in Spanish).

MOZAMBIQUE

The Higher Education System

From the 19th century until independence in 1975 Mozambique was a Portuguese colony. The oldest current institutions of higher education were founded during the period of Portuguese rule, most prominently the state-run Universidade Eduardo Mondlane (founded 1962; current name 1976). The other leading state institution is the Universidade Pedagógica (founded 1986); a third public university, the Universidade Lúrio, was founded in 2007. The main private institutions include the Catholic University and Higher Polytechnic Institute, both of which were established in 1996. The Ministry of Education is the agency responsible for state provision of higher education, which is publicly funded.

Students must be awarded the Certificado de Habilitações Literarias upon completion of secondary education and sit an entrance examination in order to be admitted to higher education. Currently, only undergraduate degrees are available. The Bacharelato is awarded after the first cycle of higher education, which lasts three years and is available in most subject areas. Depending on 'good' or 'very good' grades, students may be admitted to a Licenciatura programme of study, which lasts two years following the Bacharelato. Students of law, dentistry, medicine and veterinary medicine study for between five and seven years. The Faculty of Education of the Universidade Eduardo Mondlane offers one-year postgraduate programmes leading to the award of a Diploma or Maestrado in a number of different specialized areas. Since 1976, students have been required to spend as many years in state employment (usually teaching) as the length of the course, their degree being awarded once their public service has been completed. In 2011 a total of 107,465 students were enrolled in both public and private tertiary education.

Technical and vocational education is offered by technical schools and institutes controlled by the Secretary of State for Technical and Professional Education. In 2005 there were 41 technical institutes with 21,752 students. In 2002 there were 18 teacher training institutes with 9,314 students. Completion of medium-level technical and vocational education generally takes three years and results in the award of either the Engenheiro Técnico (technician engineer) or Técnico Medio (middle level technician).

The National Commission of Accreditation and Evaluation of Higher Education was established in 2003 and is responsible for all matters relating to quality assurance and accreditation in the higher education sector.

In 2010 the World Bank approved a loan of US $40m. for Mozambique for a five-year higher education reform project (2010–15); $27.7m. was earmarked for general higher education student support, with the remaining $12.3m. to be used to expand and improve the science and technology sector. The main aims of the project included an improvement in the number and quality of graduates, an increase in national research capacity, better student access and an improvement in the quality and relevance of teaching material.

Regulatory Body

GOVERNMENT

Ministry of Culture: Rua de Tchamba 86, Maputo; tel. 21492582; Minister ARMANDO ARTUR JOÃO.

Ministry of Education: Av. 24 de Julho, Nº 167, POB 34, Maputo; tel. 21490677; e-mail l_suporte@mined.gov.mz; internet www.mec.gov.mz; Minister AUGUSTO JONE.

Ministry of Science and Technology: Ave Patrice Lumumba 770, Maputo; tel. 21352800; e-mail secretariado@mct.gov.mz; internet www.mct.gov.mz; Minister LOUIS AUGUSTO PELEMBE.

Learned Societies

GENERAL

UNESCO Office Maputo: CP 1397, Maputo; Av. Frederick Engels 515, Maputo; tel. 21494450; e-mail maputo@unesco.org; Dir BENOÎT SOUSSOU.

LANGUAGE AND LITERATURE

British Council: Rua John Issa 226, POB 4178, Maputo; No 269, Av. Sociedade de Geografia 2nd Fl., Hollard Bldg, Maputo; tel. 21355000; e-mail info@britishcouncil.org.mz; internet www.britishcouncil.org/africa-mz-contact-us; offers courses and exams in English language and British culture and promotes cultural exchange with the UK; Dir ALAN RUTT.

Research Institutes

AGRICULTURE, FISHERIES AND VETERINARY SCIENCE

Instituto de Algodão de Moçambique (Mozambique Institute for Cotton): Av. Eduardo Mondlane 2221 (1° andar), CP 806, Maputo; tel. 21431015; e-mail iampab@zebra.uem.mz; f. 1991; depts of analysis and classing fibre, finance and administration, supporting the cotton associative sector, studies and projects; library of 2,500 vols, 260 journals and reviews; Dir NORBERTO MAHALAMBE; Deputy Dir GABRIEL PAPOSSECO; publs *Relatório Anual de Actividades* (1 a year), *Relatório Trimestral* (4 a year).

Instituto Nacional de Investigação Agronómica: CP 3658, Maputo 4; tel. 21460190; f. 1965; Dir Dr CALISTO BIAS; publ. *Comunicacões/INIA*.

MEDICINE

Instituto Nacional de Saúde (National Health Institute): Av. Eduardo Mondlane 296, CP 264, Maputo; f. 1980; study, research and training in ecology, epidemiology, immunology, malaria, microbiology, parasitology, trypanosomiasis; traditional medicine; documentation and information depts; 32 staff; library of 6,500 vols; Dir Dr RUI GAMA VAZ; publ. *Revista Médica de Moçambique*.

NATURAL SCIENCES

Physical Sciences

Direcção Nacional de Geologia: CP 217, Maputo; tel. 21427121; e-mail geologia@zebra.uem.mz; f. 1928; regional geology, geological mapping and mineral exploration; library of 30,000 vols, maps, technical material, etc.; Dir ELIAS XAVIER DAUDI; publs *Bibliografia Geológico-Mineira de Moçambique* (1 a year), *Boletim Geológico de Moçambique* (1 a year), *Boletim Informativo da DNG* (1 a year), *Notícias Explicativas da Geológico de Moçambique* (irregular), *Relatório Anual* (1 a year).

Instituto Nacional de Meteorologia: CP 256, Maputo; tel. (21) 491150; e-mail mozmet@inam.gov.mz; internet www.inam.gov.mz; f. 1907; library of 750 vols; Nat. Dir MOISES VICENTE BENESSENE; publs *Anuário de Observações* (in 2 vols: I *Observações Meteorológicas de Superficie*, II *Observações Meteorológicas de Altitude*), *Boletim Meteorológico para a Agricultura* (every 10 days), *Informações de Carácter Astronómico* (1 a year).

Libraries and Archives

Maputo

Arquivo Histórico de Moçambique: Av. Filipe Samuel Magaia 717, CP 2033, Maputo; tel. (1) 431296; e-mail rafaluga@hotmail.com; internet www.ahm.uem.mz; f. 1934; attached to Universidade Eduardo Mondlane; 25,000 vols, 11,600 periodicals; spec. collns: written reports of admin. or governmental offices and business; cartography; iconography; oral history; Dir Prof. Dr JOEL DAS NEVES TEMBE; publs *Arquivo*, *Documentos* (series), *Estudos* (series), *Instrumentos de Pesquisa* (series).

Biblioteca Nacional de Moçambique (National Library of Mozambique): Av. 25 de Setembro 1384, CP 141, Maputo; tel. 21311905; f. 1961; attached to Min. of Culture; 110,000 vols; Dir ANTÓNIO M. B. COSTA E SILVA.

Centro Nacional de Documentação e Informação de Moçambique: CP 4116, Maputo; tel. 21311246; e-mail cedimo@cedimo.gov.mz; internet www.cedimo.gov.mz; f. 1977; part of Council of Ministers Secretariat; 12,000 vols; Dir ARLANZA EDUARDO SABINO DIAS; publ. *Documento Informativo*.

Direcção Nacional de Geologia, Centro de Documentação: CP 217, Maputo; tel. 21420797; e-mail geologia@zebra.uem.mz; f. 1928; documentation centre for geology and mineral exploration; 10 spec. collns; Dir ELIAS XAVIER DAUDI; publs *Bibliografia Geológico-Mineira* (1 a year), *Boletim Geológico* (1 a year), *Boletim Informativo* (4 a year), *Notícias Explicativas da Geologia de Moçambique* (irregular), *Relatório Anual da DNG* (1 a year).

Museum

Maputo

Museu de História Natural: Praça da Travessia do Zambeze, CP 1780, Maputo; tel. 21485401; e-mail museologiasamp@uem.mz; internet www.mhn.museumoz.org; f. 1913; attached to Universidade Eduardo Mondlane; natural history museum and ethnographic gallery; Dir LUCILIA DA CONCEICAO CHUQUELA.

Universities

UNIVERSIDADE EDUARDO MONDLANE

CP 257, Maputo
Telephone: 21427851
Internet: www.uem.mz

Founded 1962
State control
Language of instruction: Portuguese
Academic year: February to December

Rector: Prof. Dr BRAZÃO MAZULA
Vice-Rector for Academic Affairs: (vacant)
Vice-Rector for Admin. and Resources: (vacant)
Dir of Documentation Services: POLICARPO MATIQUITE

Number of teachers: 1,069
Number of students: 9,712

DEANS

Faculty of Agriculture: Prof. Dr ANDRADE F. EGAS
Faculty of Architecture: Prof. JOSÉ FORJAZ
Faculty of Arts and Social Science: Prof. Dr ARMINDO NGUNGA
Faculty of Economics: Dr FERNANDO LICHUCHA (acting)
Faculty of Education: Prof. Dr MOUZINHO MÁRIO (acting)
Faculty of Engineering: Prof. Dr GABRIEL AMOS
Faculty of Law: Dr TAÍBO MUCOBORA (acting)
Faculty of Medicine: Prof. Dr EMILIA NOORMAHOMED
Faculty of Science: Dr FRANCISCO VIEIRA
Faculty of Veterinary Science: Dr LUÍS NEVES

UNIVERSIDADE LÚRIO

Av. Eduardo Mondlane 39, CP 364, Nampula
Internet: www.unilurio.ac.mz

Founded 2007
State control
Language of instruction: Portuguese

Library of 2,500 vols, 273 periodical titles
Number of students: 600

Faculty of health sciences—Nampula: courses in dentistry, pharmacology and medicine, nutrition and optometry; Faculty of engineering and natural sciences—Pemba (Cabo Delgado); Faculty of agrarian sciences—Lichinga (Niassa); Faculty of architecture

Rector: Prof. Dr JORGE FERRÃO

UNIVERSIDADE PEDAGÓGICA

Com. Augusto Cardoso 135, Maputo
Telephone: 21420860
E-mail: grupsede@zebra.uem.mz

Founded 1986
State control
Language of instruction: Portuguese
Academic year: August to June

Faculties of languages, natural sciences and mathematics, pedagogy, physical education and sports and social sciences

Rector: CARLOS MACHILI

Number of teachers: 215
Number of students: 1,400

MYANMAR

The Higher Education System

In the 19th century Burma (now Myanmar) was annexed to British India and remained under British rule until independence was achieved in 1948 (with a period under Japanese occupation in 1942–45). The oldest current institutions of higher education date from the 1920s, among them the University of Yangon (founded 1920), University of Forestry Yezin (founded 1923), Yangon Technological University and Yezin Agricultural University (both founded 1924). The Ministry of Education has overall responsibility for higher education, with the exception of specialized institutions attached to other ministries or the Public Services Selection and Training Board. The Universities' Central Council develops national higher education policies and the Council of University Academic Bodies ensures that new policies are adopted at institutional level. Over the last two decades or so there has been a rapid increase in the number of higher education institutions. Since 2001 the majority of government technological colleges and computer colleges have been redesignated as technological universities and computer universities. Most university degree programmes, which use a system of credit units, are taught in English. In 2004/05 there were 156 higher education institutions of which 64 were under the Ministry of Education, 56 under the Ministry of Science and Technology and 14 under the Ministry of Health. In 2011 the total student enrolment figure at tertiary-level institutions was 659,510. It has been reported that in recent years increasing numbers of Myanmar students are seeking university education abroad.

Admission to higher education is on the basis of results in the secondary school matriculation examination and, in the majority of instances, an entrance examination. Bachelors degrees are classified as either 'Pass' or 'Honours' depending on the length of study: three years for Bachelors (Pass) and four years for Bachelors (Honours). These courses generally entail the accumulation of 144 credit units and 192 credit units, respectively. Bachelors degrees in professional fields of study (engineering, forestry, medicine) take five to six years. Postgraduate degrees include the ordinary Masters, which takes two or three years (64–96 credit units) following the Bachelors, and Masters of Research, which is a one-year research-based programme following the Masters and qualifies successful candidates for direct entry to PhD study. The Doctorate degree takes at least a further four years of study and research after the Masters.

Admission to post-secondary technical and vocational education is also on the basis of secondary school matriculation examination and entrance examination. State-run technical institutes, technological colleges and universities, computer colleges and universities, and agricultural institutes specialize in three-year training programmes leading to the award of the Diploma or Associate title.

In 2012 a number of international partnerships were announced with France, the USA and the United Kingdom to improve higher education institutions, develop and promote research and teaching links between the countries and create a centre of excellence at the former Yangon University in collaboration with John Hopkins University of the United Kingdom. However, the 2012 Higher Education Bill was rejected by the Pyithu Hluutaw and calls were made for universities to be granted administrative independence. The Minister of Science and Technology also announced that of the country's 33 technological universities and 25 universities of computer studies, four—Yangon Technological University, Mandalay Technological University, Yangon Computer University and Mandalay Computer University—would be immediately upgraded to centres of excellence and that for the 2012/13 academic year a new system would be put in place leading to a Bachelors in engineering after six years of study and in computing after five years of specialization in a single subject (to replace what had been four-year multi-subject courses).

Regulatory Bodies

GOVERNMENT

Ministry of Culture: Office Number 35, Nay Pyi Taw; tel. (67) 408032; e-mail mocculture@gmail.com; Minister AYE MYINT KYU.

Ministry of Education: Bldg 13, Nay Pyi Taw; tel. (67) 407131; Minister Dr MYA AYE.

Ministry of Science and Technology: Bldg 21, Nay Pyi Taw; tel. (67) 404004; internet www.most.gov.mm; Minister Dr KO KO OO.

Learned Societies

LANGUAGE AND LITERATURE

British Council: 78 Kanna Rd, POB 638, Yangon; tel. (1) 254658; e-mail enquiries@mm.britishcouncil.org; internet www.britishcouncil.org/burma; offers courses and exams in English language and British culture; promotes cultural exchange with the UK; teaching centre; library of 30,000 books, video cassettes, DVDs and magazines; Dir Dr MARCUS MILTON; Teaching Centre Man. MICHAEL GORDON.

Research Institutes

AGRICULTURE, FISHERIES AND VETERINARY SCIENCE

Forest Research Institute: Yezin, Pyinmana, Nay Pyi Taw, Mandalay; tel. (67) 416521; e-mail friyezin@myanmar.com.mm; f. 1978; herbarium with limited colln of bamboo and rattan specimens; library of 9,207 vols; Dir OHN WINN.

MEDICINE

Department of Medical Research (Lower Myanmar): 5 Ziwaka Rd, Dagon PO, Yangon, 11191; tel. (1) 375457; internet www.moh.gov.mm; f. 1963, fmrly Burma Medical Research Institute; 24 divs and 7 clinical research units: animal services, bacteriology, biochemistry, computer diagnostics and vaccine research, epidemiology, experimental medicine, finance and budget, health systems research, clinical research, immunology, instrumentation, library, medical entomology, medical research statistics, nuclear medicine, nutrition, parasitology, pathology, pharmacology, physiology, publications, radioisotope and virology; clinical research units: malaria (DSGH), malaria (2MH), cerebral and complicated malaria (DMR), snakebites, traditional medicine, HIV/AIDS, research unit (IM II), oncology; WHO Collaborating Centre for Research and Training on Malaria; Dir-Gen. Dr MYO KHIN; publs *DMR Bulletin*, *Myanmar Health Sciences Research Journal*.

National Health Laboratories: Yangon; f. 1968 by amalgamating the Harcourt Butler Institute of Public Health, the Pasteur Institute, Office of the Chemical Examiner and Office of the Public Analyst; composed of five divs: Admin., Public Health, Chemical, Food and Drugs and Clinical; Dir Dr MEHM SOE MYINT.

RELIGION, SOCIOLOGY AND ANTHROPOLOGY

Department of Religious Affairs: Kaba-aye Pagoda compound, Yangon; internet www.mora.gov.mm; f. as a government supported centre for research and studies in Buddhist and allied subjects; reorganized 1972 as dept under the Min. of Religious Affairs; library of 17,000 vols, 7,000 periodicals, 7,650 palm-leaf MSS, etc.; Dir Gen. ANT MAUNG.

TECHNOLOGY

Department of Atomic Energy: Central Research Organization, 6 Kaba Aye Pagoda Rd, Yangon; f. 1955 as Union of Myanmar Atomic Energy, current name 1997; attached to Min. of Science and Technology; environmental radiation monitoring, nuclear instrumentation; Chair. ANG KOE.

Myanmar Scientific and Technological Research Department: No. 6 Kanbe, Pagoda Rd, Yankin PO, Yangon; tel. (1) 663024; e-mail most7@myanmar.com.mm; internet www.most.gov.mm; a dept of the Min. of Science and Technology; composed of the analysis dept, applied chemistry research dept, ceramics research dept, fine instruments dept and workshop, food technology research dept, metallurgy research dept, pharmaceutical research dept, physics and engineering research dept, polymer research dept, standards and specifications dept, technical information centre,; research in applied sciences; corresp. mem. of the International Organization for Standardization (ISO); library of 17,000 vols, 1,200 periodicals; Dir-Gen. Col TIN HTUT.

Libraries and Archives

Ayeyarwaddy

Bassein Degree College Library: Bassein, Ayeyarwaddy; f. 1958; 27,560 vols; Librarian NYAN HTUN.

State Library: Bassein, Ayeyarwaddy; f. 1963; 1,453 vols.

Kachin

Myitkyina Degree College Library: Myitkyina, Kachin; Librarian (vacant).

Magway

Magway University Library: Magway; tel. (62) 21522; f. 1958; 50,000 vols; Dir KHIN MYINT MYINT.

Mandalay

University of Mandalay Library: University Estate, Mandalay; 186,000 vols; Librarian U NYAN TUN.

University of Medicine Library: Seiktaramahi Quarters, Mandalay; f. 1964; 28,362 vols, 47 periodicals; Librarian KAUNG NYUNT.

University of Veterinary Science Library: Yezin, Pyinmana, Mandalay; tel. (67) 22449; e-mail drhsuvs@myanmar.com.mm; f. 1964; 4,500 vols; Librarian HTAY HTAY KHIN.

Yezin Agricultural University Library: Yezin, Pyinmana, Mandalay; tel. (67) 416516; f. 1924, autonomous 1964; 26,000 vols, 130 periodicals; Chief Librarian WYNN LEI LEI THAN.

Mon

Mawlamyine University Library: Mawlamyine, Mon; f. 2004; 106,920 books and periodicals; Librarian THEIN LWIN; Rector SAN TINT.

State Library: Mawlamyine, Mon; f. 1955; 13,265 vols; 1,262 MSS.

Rakhine

State Library: Kyaukpyu, Rakhine; f. 1955; 8,651 vols.

Shan

Taunggyi Degree College Library: Taunggyi, Shan; Librarian (vacant).

Yangon

Central Biomedical Library: Department of Medical Research (Lower Myanmar), 5 Ziwaka Rd, Dagon PO, Yangon, 11191; tel. (1) 251508; e-mail dmrlower@baganmail.net.mm; f. 1963, fmrly Burma Medical Research Institute Library; 27,000 vols, 250 periodicals on health and biomedical sciences; Chief Librarian NYUNT NYUNT SWE.

Institute of Education Library: University Estate, Yangon; f. 1964; 36,166 vols; Librarian DAW GILDA TWE.

Myanmar Education Research Bureau: 426 Pyay Rd, University PO, Yangon, 11041; tel. (1) 531468; f. 1966; dept of the Min. of Education; educational materials resource centre promoting and supporting research activities; 56,000 vols; Chair. MYINT HAN; publ. *The World of Education* (4 a year).

National Archives Department: 114 Pyidaungsu Yeiktha Rd, Dagon Township, Yangon; e-mail nad@mptmail.net.mm; internet www.mnped.gov.mm/nationalchives.asp; f. 1972; attached to Min. of National Planning and Economic Development; preserves national records and archives; retrieves records and archives that had migrated to a foreign land or are in the possession of any other organization or individual; 50,000 books and 15,000 microfilms, microfiches, tapes and photographs.

National Library: 85 Thirimingala Ave, Yankin, Yangon; tel. (1) 272058; e-mail nl.myanmar@gmail.com; f. 1952, incorporating the Bernard Free Library, present name 1967, present location 2008; 158,800 vols, 12,321 MSS, 411,426 periodicals; Chief Librarian SAN WIN.

Sarpay Beikman Public Library: 529 Merchant St, Yangon; f. 1956; 74,404 vols (56,729 Burmese, 17,675 English); Librarian NU NU.

Universities' Central Library: University PO, Yangon; f. 1929; central library for all higher education institutes; specializes in Burmese books, palm-leaf MSS (over 115,000), and books on Burma and Asia; 600,000 vols; Chief Librarian TIN WIN YEE.

University of Computer Studies Library: Yangon Hlaing Campus, Myanmar Thaming College PO, Yangon, 11052; tel. (1) 664709; e-mail ucsy1@most.gov.mm; internet www.ucsy.edu.mm; provides up-to-date computer books for students for their reference courses; Library Asst Daw YU YU TIN.

University of Medicine 1 Library: 245 Myoma Kyaung St, Lanmadaw Township, Yangon, 11131; tel. (1) 395560; e-mail khinmmtun07@googlemail.com; internet www.um1ygn.edu.mm; f. 1929; 50,000 vols; Librarian KHIN MAW MAW TUN.

University of Medicine 2 Library: N Okkalapa, Yangon, 11031; tel. (1) 699064; e-mail thelibrary@iomnoka.com.mm; internet www.um2ygn.edu.mm; f. 1964, fmrly Institute of Medicine II Library; participates in HELLIS; access to UN and WHO databases online (HINARI, AGORA, and OARE); 31,000 vols; Librarian THI TAR.

University of Yangon Library: Yangon, 11041; tel. (1) 530376; f. 1927; 200,000 vols; Head Librarian KHIN HNIN OO.

WHO Library: No. 2 Pyay Rd, 7 Mile, Mayangone Township, Yangon, 11061; tel. (1) 650-408; e-mail mlwin@searo.who.int; internet www.searo.who.int/myanmar; f. 1998; provision of WHO information material and global health literature; 3,000 vols; Librarian MARLA WIN.

Workers' College Library: Yangon; f. 1964; 19,500 vols; Librarian KHIN THIN KYU.

Yangon Institute of Economics Library: University Estate, POB 473, Yangon, 11041; tel. (1) 535847; e-mail ucl@dhelm-edu.gov.mm; f. 1964; 87,000 vols; Librarian DAW KHIN KYU.

Yangon Institute of Technology Library: Insein PO, Gyogone, Yangon, 11011; tel. (1) 665678; e-mail yit.yangon@pemail.net; internet welcome.to/yit; f. 1964; caters to the needs of postgraduate students and academic staff; 48,000 vols, 560 periodicals; Librarian TIN MAUNG LWIN.

Museums and Art Galleries

Mandalay

Bagan Archaeological Museum: opposite Gawdawpalin Temple, Bagan, Upper Myanmar, Mandalay; f. 1904, new bldg opened 1975, new Bagan Archaeological Museum opened 1998; site museum for ancient capital from 11th to 14th century; lithic inscriptions, Buddha's images, statuary and artefacts; administered by Dept of Archaeology; Curator KYAW NYEIN.

Mandalay Cultural Museum: 80th Rd and 24th Rd, Aung Myay Tha San Township, Mandalay; tel. (1) 239859; e-mail dcicoci@mptmail.net.mm.

State Museum: Cnr of 24th and 80th Sts, Mandalay; f. 1955; over 1,500 exhibits; br. museum in fmr Mandalay Palace grounds; Curator SOE THEIN.

Mon

Mon State Museum: Dawei Tada Rd, Mawlamyine, Mon; f. 1955; over 750 exhibits; Curator MIN KHIN MAUNG.

Rakhine

Mrauk U Archaeological Museum: Rakhine; displays artefacts from the Vesali, Launggret and Mrauk U periods, bronze Buddha icons of Rakhine, stone inscriptions in Sanskrit, Rakhine and Arabic, votive tablets, Krishna Vishnu, Bodhisattvas, dvarapala, stone htis, lintels coins, musical instruments and ceramic wares.

Rakhine State Cultural Museum: 70 Main Rd and Yetwin Rd, Sittwe, Rakhine; f. 1996; displays traditional dresses, traditional looms and arts of Rakhine people, models of stone inscriptions, musical instruments, coins, images and paintings of Buddha.

Rakhine State Museum: Chin Pyan Rd, Kyaung-gyi Quarter, Sitture, Rakhine; f. 1955; over 500 exhibits (silver coins, costumes, etc.); also site museum at Mrauk U, ancient capital; Curator DAW NU MYA ZAN.

Shan

Shan State Museum: Min Lan, Thittaw Quarter, Taunggyi, Shan; f. 1957; over 600 exhibits; Curator SAN MYA.

Yangon

Bogyoke Aung San Museum: 15 Bogyoke Aung San Lane, Bahan Township, Yangon; tel. (1) 250600; f. 1962; 571 exhibits related to the life and work of General Aung San.

Gems Museum: 66 Kaba Aye Pagoda Rd, Mayangon, Yangon; tel. (1) 660365; original clay votive tablets; cultural artefacts from the Bagan period; items from the Pinya, Innwa, Taungoo and Nyaung Yan periods.

National Museum: 66/74 Pyay Rd, Dagon Township, Yangon; tel. (1) 282563; f. 1952; displays ancient artefacts, works of art and historic memorabilia; exhibits on the evolution of the Myanmar script and alphabet, the Lion Throne Room and Yatanabon period pieces.

National Museum of Art and Archaeology: 26/42 Pansodan, Yangon; f. 1952; 1,652 antiquities; 354 paintings; replica of King Mindon's Mandalay Palace; Dir-Gen. Dr YE TUT; Chief Curator KYAW WIN.

Yangon Drugs Elimination Museum: cnr of Kyundaw Rd and Hanthawady Rd, Kamayut Township, Yangon; internet www

.myanmar-narcotic.net/heroin/drug_museum/museum.html; f. 2001; records and showcases national efforts to combat narcotics drugs trade in the country.

Universities

COMPUTER UNIVERSITY

Taungoo, Bago
Telephone: (54) 27173
Internet: www.ucsy.edu.mm/taungoocu/index.php
Founded 2000, fmrly the Government Computer College, university status 2007; attached to Min. of Science and Technology

DAGON UNIVERSITY

Min-Ye-Kyaw-Swar Rd, Dagon Myothit (E), Yangon, 11422
Telephone: (1) 585001
E-mail: dgnrector@mptmail.net.mm
Founded 1993
public control
Languages of instruction: English, Myanmar
Academic year: December to September
Faculties of arts and humanities, mathematics and computer science, natural sciences
Rector: HLA HTAY
Pro-Rector: AYE AYE TUN
Library of 45,011 vols, 500 ebooks
Number of teachers: 1,105
Number of students: 18,951
Publication: *Dagon University Research Journal* (1 a year)

HMAWBI TECHNOLOGICAL UNIVERSITY

Hmawbi Township, Yangon
Telephone: (1) 620072
Internet: www.most.gov.mm/hmawbitu
Founded 1989 as Technical High School, later Government Institute of Technology, university status 2007; attached to Min. of Science and Technology
Public
Rector: Dr AYE MYINT

INTERNATIONAL THERAVĀDA BUDDHIST MISSIONARY UNIVERSITY

Dhammapāla Hill, Mayanggone PO, Yangon
Telephone: (1) 650713
Internet: www.itbmu.org.mm
Founded 1998; attached to Min. of Religious Affairs
Public
Rector: Dr Sayadaw BHADDANTA NANDA
Library of 25,670 books, the *International Encyclopedia on Buddhism* 75 vols, *Encyclopedia of Religions and Ethics*

MAGWE UNIVERSITY

University Campus, Magwe, Magway
Telephone: (63) 21030
Founded 1958; attached to Min. of Education
Number of teachers: 130
Number of students: 3,550

MANDALAY TECHNOLOGICAL UNIVERSITY

Patheingyi, MTU, PO, Mandalay
Telephone: (2) 57006
E-mail: admin@mtu.edu.mm
Internet: www.most.gov.mm/mtu
Founded 1991; attached to Min. of Science and Technology
Bachelors, Masters and doctoral courses; Depts of architecture, chemical engineering, civil engineering, electrical power engineering, electronics engineering, mechanical engineering
Pro-Rector: Prof. Dr AUNG KYAW MYAT
Number of teachers: 144
Number of students: 2,418

MAWLAMYINE UNIVERSITY

Taung Waing Rd, Mawlamyine, Mon
Telephone: (32) 21180
Founded 1953, university status 1986; attached to Min. of Education
Languages of instruction: Myanmar, English
State control
Academic year: November to September
Rector: HLA TUN AUNG
Pro-Rector: HLA PE
Librarian: THEIN LWIN
Library of 106,000 books and periodicals
Number of teachers: 300
Number of students: 8,100

PROFESSORS

Chemistry: Prof. MAUNG MAUNG HTAY
Geography: Prof. THAN MYA
Geology: Prof. NYAN THIN
Physics: Prof. SEIN HTOON

AFFILIATED COLLEGES

Bago College: Prin. HLA MYINT.
Dawei College: Prin. THIN HLAING.
Hpa-an College: Prin. LAWRENCE THAW

MONYWA UNIVERSITY

Monywa, Sagaing
Founded 1996; attached to Min. of Education
Faculties of arts and humanities, mathematics and computer science, natural sciences
Rector: MAUNG HTOO

MYANMAR AEROSPACE ENGINEERING UNIVERSITY

Meiktila, Mandalay
Telephone: (64) 35-244
E-mail: aero.maeu001@gmail.com
Internet: www.most.gov.mm/maeu
Founded 2002; attached to Min. of Science and Technology
public control
Languages of instruction: English, Myanmar
Academic year: December to September
Rector: Prof. Dr KYI THWIN
Library of 2,500 vols
Number of teachers: 120
Number of students: 596

DEANS

Airport Management: Assoc. Prof. KYAW MOE KHINE
Fuel and Propellant: Assoc. Prof. MOE THANDAR KYI
Space System Engineering: Assoc. Prof. AUNG KO WIN

MYANMAR MARITIME UNIVERSITY

Thilawar, Thanhlyin, Yangon, 11293
E-mail: myanmarivarsity@mmu.gov.mm
Internet: www.mot.gov.mm/mmu/index.html
Founded 2004; attached to Min. of Transport
Public
Depts of marine electrical systems and electronics, marine engineering, nautical science, naval architecture and ocean engineering, port and harbours engineering, port management, river and coastal engineering, shipping management
Rector: CHARLES THAN
Number of students: 1,741

PATHEIN UNIVERSITY

Pathein, Ayeyarwaddy
Founded 1996; attached to Min. of Education
Faculties of arts and humanities, mathematics and computer science, natural sciences

PYAY TECHNOLOGICAL UNIVERSITY

Pyay, Bago
Telephone: (53) 25806
Internet: www.most.gov.mm/ptu
Founded 1999; attached to Min. of Science and Technology
Offers Dipl. in Engineering, Bachelor of Technology, BEng, MEng programmes
Rector: AUNG KYAW MYAT

SITTWE UNIVERSITY

Sittwe, Rakhine
Telephone: (1) 246704
E-mail: hivdig@indp.org
Founded 1996; attached to Min. of Education
Faculties of arts and humanities, mathematics and computer science, natural sciences
Rector: SEIN MOE MOE

TAUNGGYI UNIVERSITY

Taunggyi, Shan, 06011
Telephone: (81) 21160
Founded 1961; attached to Min. of Education
Faculties of arts and humanities, mathematics and computer science, natural sciences
Number of teachers: 125
Number of students: 3,500
Rector: Dr MAUNG KYAW

TAUNGOO TECHNOLOGICAL UNIVERSITY

Taungoo Township, Bago
Telephone: (54) 23734
Internet: www.most.gov.mm/taungootu
Founded 1982 as Technical High School, university status 2007; attached to Min. of Science and Technology
Offers BEng, Bachelor of Technology, Dipl. Civil Engineering, Dipl. Electronic Engineering, Dipl. Electrical Power Engineering, Dipl. Mechanical Engineering, Dipl. Mechatronic Engineering, Dipl. Architecture Engineering, Dipl. Chemical Engineering, Dipl. Information Technology Engineering, Dipl. Bio-technology

THANLYIN TECHNOLOGICAL UNIVERSITY

Thanlyin, Yangon
Telephone: (56) 25058
E-mail: dr.akmyat@gmail.com
Internet: www.most.gov.mm/thanlyintu
Founded 1993 as Industrial Training Centre, Govt Technological Institute 1995, univ. status 2007; attached to Min. of Science and Technology
Public
Academic year: December to September
Offers four-year Bachelor of Technology, five-year BEng and BArch and two-year MEng programmes
Rector: Prof. Dr AUNG KYAW MYAT
Number of teachers: 173

Number of students: 10,080

UNIVERSITY OF COMMUNITY HEALTH

Magway
Telephone: (9563) 23413
E-mail: prof.ssma@gmail.com

Founded 1951 as Health Assistant Training School, university status 1995; attached to Min. of Health
State Control
Language of instruction: English

Rector: Prof. Dr SAN SAN MYINT AUNG
Chief Admin. Officer: Prof. Dr MYO THAN
Registrar: KYI KYI MIN
Librarian: WAI MAUNG

Library of 4,997 vols, 1,000 periodicals
Number of teachers: 72
Number of students: 735

DEANS

Department of Biomedical Science: Dr SOE MIN NAING
Department of Botany: THEIN ZAN
Department of Chemistry: Dr CHO LWIN OO
Department of Community Health: Dr AYE AYE OO
Department of Educational Science: Dr THAN SOE LIN
Department of English: NANG KHAM SET
Department of Environmental Health: Dr MYA THANDAR
Department of Field Training: Prof. Dr MYO THAN
Department of Health Education: Dr MYAT OHNMAR WIN
Department of Physics: MU MU THET
Department of Zoology: SU SU THAN
Myanmar Subject: AYE MYINT

UNIVERSITY OF COMPUTER STUDIES

Hlaing Campus, Thaming College PO, Yangon, 11052
Telephone: (1) 664709
Hlawgar Campus, No. 4 Rd, ShwePyiThar Township, Yangon
Telephone: (1) 610633
E-mail: ucsy1@most.gov.mm
Internet: www.ucsy.edu.mm

Founded 1971 as Universities Computer Centre, autonomous Institute of Computer Science and Technology 1988, present name and status 1998; attached to Min. of Science and Technology
Public control
Language of instruction: English
Academic year: July to March

Rector: Dr NI LAR THEIN
Pro-Rector: Dr KYAW THEIN
Registrar: KYIN HTWE
Librarian: KHIN MAR AYE

Library of 11,000 vols
Number of teachers: 20
Number of students: 100

UNIVERSITY OF CULTURE, MANDALAY

Shwesayan Pagoda Rd, Patheingyi, Mandalay

Founded 2001; attached to Min. of Culture
State control
Language of instruction: English

Programmes in dramatic arts, music, painting and sculpture

Rector: NGWE TUN

UNIVERSITY OF CULTURE, YANGON

No. 26 Quarter, Aung Zeta Rd, S Dagon Myothit Township, Yangon, 11431
Telephone: (1) 590250

Founded 1993; attached to Min. of Culture
Language of instruction: English
Academic year: November to September

Depts of fine arts, dance, drama, music, painting, sculpture

Rector: TIN SOE

Number of teachers: 135
Number of students: 733

UNIVERSITY OF DENTAL MEDICINE, YANGON

Thanthumar Rd, Thingankyun POB, Yangon, 11071
Telephone: (1) 571270

Founded 1964, Institute of Dental Medicine 1974, present status 1998; attached to Min. of Health
Language of instruction: English
Academic year: November to September
Public control

Rector: PAING SOE

Publication: *Myanmar Dental Journal* (1 a year)

UNIVERSITY OF DISTANCE EDUCATION

Kamayut Yangon, 11041
E-mail: yuderector@mptmail.net.mm

Founded 1992; attached to Min. of Education
State control

32 Campuses across Myanmar

Rector: Dr TIN MAY TUN

Number of students: 560,000

UNIVERSITY OF EAST YANGON

Thanlyin, Yangon, 11292; attached to Min. of Education
State control

Offers 3-year and 4-year courses in BA, BSc and Bachelor of Law programmes

Rector: KYAW YE TUN

Number of students: 11,000

UNIVERSITY OF FOREIGN LANGUAGES, YANGON

119–131 University Ave, Kamayut, Yangon, 11041
Telephone: (1) 513193
E-mail: rectorufly@mptmail.net.mm

Founded 1964 as the Institute of Foreign Languages, current name and status 1996; attached to Min. of Education

Language courses in Chinese, English, French, German, Japanese, Korean, Russian and Thai; Myanmar language courses for foreign students

Rector: Dr MYO MYINT
Librarian: HLA HLA MYINT

Library of 26,000 vols
Number of teachers: 100
Number of students: 3,000

UNIVERSITY OF FORESTRY, YEZIN

Yezin, Pyinmana, Mandalay, 05282
Telephone: (67) 416-519
E-mail: uof.yezin@gmail.com

Founded 1923, present status 1992; attached to Min. of Environmental Conservation and Forestry
State control
Language of instruction: English

Rector: Dr MYINT OO
Librarian: WAH WAH MOE

Library of 3,672 vols
Number of teachers: 52
Number of students: 714

DEANS

Department of Forest Products: U. OHN LWIN
Department of Forestry: Dr SAN THWIN

UNIVERSITY OF MANDALAY

University Estate, Mandalay
Telephone: (2) 21211
Internet: www.mu.edu.mm

Founded 1925 as a college of the University of Rangoon, independent university status 1958; attached to Min. of Education
Language of instruction: Myanmar
Academic year: July to March

9 Affiliated colleges

Rector: Dr MYA AYE
Pro-Rector: LU NI
Registrar for Examination and Convocation: SEIN SEIN
Registrar for Student Affairs and Hostels: WIN MYINT
Librarian: NYAN TUN

Library of 175,000 vols
Number of teachers: 860
Number of students: 22,700

UNIVERSITY OF MEDICAL TECHNOLOGY

Patheingyi, Mandalay

Founded 2000; attached to Min. of Health
State control

Offers a 4-year Bachelor of Medical Technology degree programme in medical laboratory technology, physiotherapy, radiography and medical imaging technology

Rector: SOE TUN

UNIVERSITY OF MEDICINE 1

245 Myoma Kyaung St, Lanmadaw POB, Yangon, 11131
Telephone: (1) 251136
E-mail: rct.imy@mptmail.net.mm
Internet: www.um1ygn.edu.mm

Founded 1927 as first Dept of Medicine at Yangon Univ., Institute of Medicine 1964, present status 1973; attached to Min. of Health
State control

Offers a 6-year MBBS course

Rector: Prof. PE THET KHIN

Number of teachers: 685
Number of students: 3,500

UNIVERSITY OF MEDICINE 2

N Okkalapa, Yangon
Telephone: (1) 45507

Founded 1963 as Medical College 2 affiliated to Yangon Univ., Institute of Medicine 2 1964, present status 1973; attached to Min. of Health
Languages of instruction: Myanmar, English
Academic year: November to July

Rector: THA HLA SHWE

Library of 24,000 vols
Number of teachers: 320
Number of students: 1,500

Publication: *Medical Education Report* (4 a year)

UNIVERSITY OF MEDICINE, MAGWAY

Magway
Telephone: (9) 56323760
E-mail: r4-dms@moh.gov.mm
Internet: www.ummg.edu.mm

Founded 2001; attached to Min. of Health
Language of instruction: English
Academic year: January to November

Rector: Prof. Dr WIN MYAT AYE

Library of 5,713 vols
Number of teachers: 276
Number of students: 2,323

DEANS

Clinical subjects: ZAW LIN AUNG
Pre-clinical subjects I: THAN THAN AYE
Pre-clinical subjects II: KHIN THIDA

UNIVERSITY OF MEDICINE, MANDALAY

Between 73 and 74 Sts, 30-31 St, Chanayethazan, Mandalay

Telephone: (1) 236634
E-mail: ret.ummdy@dms.gov.mm

Founded 1954 as Branch Medical Faculty of Yangon Univ., Faculty of Medicine, Mandalay 1958, Institute of Medicine, Mandalay 1964, present status 1968

Dir: Prof. TIN MAUNG HAN

Library of 39,319 vols, 9,104 clinical and public health journals
Number of teachers: 727

UNIVERSITY OF PARAMEDICAL SCIENCE, YANGON

Insein, Yangon, 11011

Founded 1993, fmrly the Institute of Paramedical Sciences; attached to Min. of Health
State control

Offers a 4-year Bachelor of Paramedical Science degree programme

Rector: SAW KYAW AUNG

UNIVERSITY OF PHARMACY, YANGON

N Okkalapa, Yangon, 11031

Founded 1992; attached to Min. of Health
Public

Offers Bachelor of Pharmacy and Master of Pharmacy degree programmes

Rector: Dr AUNG MON

UNIVERSITY OF VETERINARY SCIENCE, YEZIN

Yezin, Pyinmanar Tsp., Mandalay

Telephone: (1) 22447
E-mail: tintinmyaing@mail4u.com.mm
Internet: www.myanmar.gov.mm/ministry/live&fish/university.htm

Founded 1957 as part of University of Yangon, Institute of Animal Husbandry and Veterinary Science, present status 1999; attached to Min. of Livestock and Fisheries

Languages of instruction: Myanmar, English

Faculties of animal husbandry, veterinary science; offers Bachelor of Veterinary Science, Master of Veterinary Science, MPhil and MSc programmes

Rector: Dr MYINT THEIN
Librarian: HTAY HTAY SAN

Library of 13,204 vols, 53 periodicals
Number of teachers: 65
Number of students: 620

UNIVERSITY OF YANGON

University Ave Rd, Kamayut, Yangon, 11041
Telephone: (1) 537250

Founded 1878 as Univ. College affiliated to Univ. of Calcutta, Univ. of Yangon (f. 1920) by merger of Univ. College and Judson College; attached to Min. of Education
Academic year: July to March
Language of instruction: Myanmar

Campuses in Hlaing Region, Kyimyindine Region, Botataung Region; 3 affiliated degree-granting colleges in Pathein, Sittwe and Yangon, and 2 colleges in Hinthada and Pyay

Rector: Dr TIN TUN
Registrar: NYUNT NYUNT WIN

Number of teachers: 2,060
Number of students: 47,131

WEST YANGON TECHNOLOGICAL UNIVERSITY

Hlaing Tha Yar Township, Yangon
Telephone: (1) 655266
Internet: www.most.gov.mm/wytu

Founded 2005; attached to Min. of Science and Technology
State control

Depts of architecture engineering, chemical engineering, civil engineering, electrical power engineering, electronic and communication engineering, engineering English, Myanmar, engineering mathematics, engineering physics, information technology, mechanical engineering, mechatronic engineering, metallurgy engineering, mining engineering, petroleum engineering, textile engineering

Rector: Dr WIN

YADANABON UNIVERSITY

Amarapura, Mandalay
Telephone: (2) 53894

Founded 2000 as Yadanabon College, university status 2003; attached to Min. of Education
Public

Bachelors and Masters programmes in Burmese, English, geography, history, philosophy, psychology, botany, chemistry, mathematics, physics and zoology

Rector: WIN MAUNG
Number of students: 22,000

YANGON TECHNOLOGICAL UNIVERSITY

Gyogon, Insein, Yangon, 11011
Telephone: (1) 651717
Internet: www.most.gov.mm/ytu

Founded 1924, independent status 1961; attached to Min. of Science and Technology
State control
Academic year: October to July

6-Year first degree courses, 1-year postgraduate diploma and 2- and 3-year postgraduate degree courses

Rector: Dr MYA MYA OO

Number of teachers: 204
Number of students: 8,000

YEZIN AGRICULTURAL UNIVERSITY

Yezin, Pyinmana, Mandalay
Telephone: (67) 416516
E-mail: rector-yau@cybertech.net.mm

Founded 1924, independent status 1964; present name 1998; attached to Min. of Agriculture

Depts of agriculture, agriculture botany, agriculture chemistry, agriculture engineering, agronomy, animal science, economics, English, entomology, horticulture, mathematics, Myanmar, physics

Rectors: Dr MYINT THAUNG
Pro-Rector for Academic Affairs: Dr CHO CHO MYINT
Pro-Rector for Admin.: HLA TUN
Registrars: TIN WAN, AUNG SAN

Number of teachers: 121
Number of students: 1,200

University-Level Institutions

Central Institute of Civil Service: near Phaunggyi Village, Hlegu Township, Yangon; tel. (1) 629501; e-mail rector@cics-phaunggyi.gov.mm; internet www.csstb.gov.mm; f. 1965 as Central People's Training School, upgraded as Central Institute of Civil Service 1977; attached to Min. of Home Affairs; Rector Col WIN MAUNG.

Defence Services Technological Academy: Pyin Oo Lwin, Mandalay; tel. (55) 532851; f. 1993; attached to Min. of Defence; offers 5-year BEng degree programmes; Rector Brig. Gen. WIN MYINT.

Institute of Education: Pyay Rd, University PO, Kamayut Township, Yangon, 11041; tel. (1) 504772; e-mail rectoryjoe@mptmail.net.mm; f. 1931, present status since 1964; attached to Min. of Education; languages of instruction: Myanmar, English; academic year June to March; a teachers training college; offers Bachelors and Masters and doctorate programmes in education; 126 teachers; 2,535 students; publ. *Magazine* (1 a year); Pro-Rector KHIN ZAW.

Institute of Marine Technology: Bayint Naung Rd, Kamayut Township, Yangon, 11041; tel. (1) 536166; e-mail principal.imt@mptmail.net.mm; internet www.mot.gov.mm/imt; f. 1972; attached to Min. of Transport; offers courses in both nautical and engineering fields; Prin. WIN THEIN.

Mandalay Institute of Nursing: 62nd–63rd Sts, Chanmyathazi, Mandalay; f. 1998; attached to Min. of Health; offers a four-year Bachelors degree in nursing; Rector KHIN NYUNT THAN.

Yangon Institute of Economics: University Estate, Kamayut Township, Yangon, 11041; tel. (1) 664684; f. 1964; attached to Min. of Education; city campus in Kamayut and satellite campuses in Hlaing and Ywathagi; library: 87,000 vols; 243 teachers; 7,000 students; Rector Dr KAN ZAW.

Yangon Institute of Nursing: 677–709 Bogyoke Aung San Rd, Lanmadaw, Yangon, 11131; f. 1986, as Nurse Training Center, university status 1991; attached to Min. of Health; offers a four-year Bachelors degree programme in nursing; Rector Dr WIN MAY.

Yangon Institute of Technology: Insein PO, Gyogon, Yangon, 11011; tel. (1) 665678; e-mail yit.yangon@pemail.net; internet welcome.to/yit; f. 1924, ind. status 1964; depts of aeronautical engineering, architecture, chemical engineering, civil engineering, electrical engineering, electronic engineering, mechanical engineering, metallurgical engineering, mining engineering, petroleum engineering, textile engineering; library: 48,000 vols, 560 journals; 250 teachers; 4,500 students.

Colleges

Defence Services Academy: Pyin Oo Lwin, Mandalay; f. 1954; attached to Min. of Defence; an independent degree college under the Min. of Defence; degree courses for cadets training for service as regular commissioned officers in the Myanmar Army, Navy and Air Force; 300 teachers; 6,500 students (5,000 undergraduates, 1,500 postgraduates); Rector Col ZAW WIN; Prin. Major Gen. ZAYAR AUNG.

Lacquerware Technological College: Maha Bawdi St, Bagan, Mandalay; f. 1924 as Government Lacquerware Training School, present status 2003; attached to Min. of Cooperatives; f. by the Cottage Industries Dept, Min. of Cooperatives; offers training in lacquerware production.

Magway Degree College: University Campus, Magway; tel. (63) 21030; attached to Min. of Education; 129 teachers; 3,555 students; Prin. SEIN WIN.

Meiktila Institute of Economics: Meiktila, Mandalay; f. 2006; attached to Min. of Education; programmes in commerce, economics and statistics; Rector Dr HSAN LWIN.

Myitkyina Degree College: University Campus, Myitkyina, Kachin; tel. (101) 21053; attached to Min. of Education; 90 teachers; 1,752 students; Prin. U SUM HLOT NAW.

Nationalities Youth Resource Development Degree College: c/o Ministry for Progress of Border Areas and National Races and Devt Affairs, Office No. 42, Nay Pyi Daw, Mandalay; e-mail edutd@mptmail.net.mm; 2 campuses: affiliated to Yangon and Mandalay Universities.

Pathein Degree College: University Campus, Pathein, Ayeyarwaddy; tel. (42) 21135; attached to Min. of Education; 178 teachers; 5,158 students; Prin. Dr MAUNG KYAW.

Sittwe Degree College: University Campus, Sittwe, Rakhine; tel. (43) 21236; attached to Min. of Education; 97 teachers; 1,730 students; Prin. KWAW MYA THEIN.

State School of Fine Arts: Ministry of Culture, Dept of Fine Arts, 66 Rd, between 20th and 22nd St, Nan Shae (in front of the Mandalay Nan Taw), Mandalay; tel. (85) 40296; f. 1953; attached to Min. of Culture; Prin. KAN NYUNT.

State School of Fine Arts: 131, Kanbawza Yeiktha, Kaba Aye Pagoda Rd, Bahan PO, Yangon; tel. (1) 52176; f. 1952; courses in commercial art, drawing, fine art, sculpture, wood-carving; Prin. SOE TINT; Dir MYAT THU YA.

State School of Music and Drama: East Moat Rd, Mandalay; tel. (2) 21176; f. 1953; offers courses in dancing, singing, Burmese harp and orchestra, xylophone, piano, oboe, stringed instruments and stave notation; Prin. KAN NYUNT; Dir MYAT THU YA.

State School of Music and Drama: 135 Kanbawza Yeiktha, Kaba Aye Pagoda Rd, Bahan PO, Yangon; tel. (1) 544151; f. 1952; offers courses in dancing, singing, Burmese harp and orchestra, piano, oboe, xylophone, stringed instruments, stave notation and Burmese verse; Prin. AUNG THWIN; Dir MYAT THU YA.

Taunggyi State College: Taunggyi, Shan, 06011; tel. (81) 21160; 125 teachers; 3,456 students; Prin. SAW HLINE.

Workers' College: 273–279 Konthe Lan, Botahtaung PO, Yangon, 11161; tel. (1) 292825; f. 1964 as the University for the Aged, renamed 1974; 47 teachers; 5,650 students; Prin. SAN MAUNG.

Zomi Theological College: Falam, Chin, 03031; tel. (70) 40081; e-mail ztc1953@gmail.com; internet www.ztccollege.com; f. 1959; attached to Myanmar Baptist Convention; undergraduate and graduate degrees in divinity, theology and religious education; library: 13,754 vols; Prin. DO SIAN THANG; Librarian HRANG PENG LING.